Dictionary of American Regional English

Volume V   Sl-Z

Joan Houston Hall

Chief Editor

The Belknap Press of Harvard University Press

Cambridge, Massachusetts, and London, England

2012

Sl-Z

Copyright © 2012 by the President and Fellows of Harvard College
All rights reserved
Printed in the United States of America

Design by Marianne Perlak

Library of Congress Cataloging in Publication Data

Dictionary of American regional English.

1. English language—Dialects—United States—Dictionaries.
2. English language—United States—Dictionaries.
3. Americanisms—Dictionaries.
I. Cassidy, Frederic Gomes, 1907–
II. Hall, Joan Houston.
PE2843.D52   1985   427′.973   84-29025
ISBN 0-674-20511-1 (v. 1 : alk. paper)
ISBN 0-674-20512-X (v. 2)
ISBN 0-674-20519-7 (v. 3)
ISBN 0-674-00884-7 (v. 4)
ISBN 978-0-674-04735-8 (v. 5)

DARE Staff, Volume V

CHIEF EDITOR
Joan Houston Hall

SENIOR EDITOR, PRODUCTION
Luanne von Schneidemesser

SENIOR SCIENCE EDITOR
Sheila Y. Kolstad

REVIEW EDITOR
George H. Goebel

GENERAL EDITOR, BIBLIOGRAPHER
Leonard Zwilling

GENERAL AND SCIENCE EDITOR
Roland L. Berns

ADJUNCT EDITOR
Audrey R. Duckert

BIBLIOGRAPHERS
Sally J. Jacobs
Janet L. Monk

PRODUCTION ASSISTANT,
TECHNICAL TYPIST
Catherine R. Attig

SENIOR PROOFREADER
Elizabeth R. Gardner

PROOFREADERS
Elizabeth Blake
Julie Schnebly

OFFICE MANAGERS
Virginia A. Bormann
Karen J. Krause
Barbara G. Wolfe

RESEARCH ASSISTANTS
Nathan E. J. Carlson
Scot LaFaive
Erin E. Meyer
David W. Nunnery
Jennifer Catherine (Kate) Peterson
Jill Priluck

DIRECTORS OF DEVELOPMENT
David H. Simon
Jon E. Sorenson

IN REMEMBRANCE
Audrey R. Duckert
1927–2007
Karen J. Krause
1945–2006

Contents

Preface

Readers of Volume V are reminded that the front matter to Volume I and the prefaces to Volumes II–IV provide detailed explanations of *DARE*'s history, maps, and editorial practices as well as providing useful information about American English pronunciation variation and folk speech. Volume I also includes the full text of the *DARE* Questionnaire (pp. lxii–lxxxv) and the list of Informants who answered all or part of a Questionnaire (pp. lxxxvi–cli). Specifics of age, sex, race, education level, and community type are included for each person, making it possible for readers to learn the backgrounds of Informants quoted in the text.

Because users of *DARE* have found them helpful, we reprint here several items from earlier volumes: from Volume I, the figure contrasting the *DARE* map with the conventional map of the United States; from Volume III, "The Anatomy of a *DARE* Entry"; from Volume IV, a brief Pronunciation Guide listing the phonetic symbols that appear in the head sections and the quotations in *DARE* entries. As in earlier volumes, a List of Abbreviations is included here, this one including a few new abbreviations specific to this volume or to the Bibliography.

Volume V also includes the Bibliography to the many thousands of published sources quoted in the five volumes of *DARE*. Its purpose is to provide all the information necessary for a reader to get to the original source of each quotation.

The preface to Volume IV explained that an innovation in that volume was the inclusion of quotations from digital libraries and the World Wide Web, reflecting "the staggering increase in the number of electronic sources available to lexicographers in the last few years." Little did we know then that the "staggering increase" was only a trickle compared with what would be available for Volume V. The explosion of digital resources during the last decade has meant that the job of the lexicographer has become much more challenging, while at the same time distinctly more rewarding. Large collections of digitized newspapers, both historical and contemporary, have been particularly valuable to *DARE* Editors, and the digitization of the contents of major university libraries has made millions of additional books open to our view. It has been a challenge to learn to discriminate among the myriad sources, trying to select the best quotations while understanding the limitations of the scope, production, and metadata of each collection. The vast body of unpublished writing on the Internet that reflects the casual, everyday speech of Americans has also provided much valuable material with which to document *DARE* entries. While it is not always possible to assign geographic locations to such quotations, the evidence of the use of a word "in the wild," so to speak, is welcome.

Although our use of these electronic resources inevitably delayed publication of this volume, *DARE* staff members are convinced that the resulting quality of the entries justifies the expense of time. Digital libraries have provided thousands of quotations that significantly antedate or postdate our other materials, or that expand the geographic range of our quotations. They have also allowed us to write more precise definitions based on a larger body of evidence. We have included the earliest available quotation for each entry or sense (recognizing that earlier ones will doubtless be discovered later), and we have included a contemporary example of use whenever possible. One qualification in our selection of recent examples is that if folk names for plants or animals seem simply to be taken from earlier lists of alternate names, we do not consider them examples of contemporary use.

Because electronic resources became available at different times, not all entries in this volume had the benefit of each one. And because digital collections are expanding at a very rapid rate, readers cannot assume that what is available to them when they read a *DARE* entry was necessarily available to staff members as they worked on the entry. As in the past, we have cited original texts whenever possible; if we have not been able to view the original, we attribute the quote to the source in which we found it. For example, if a digital newspaper collection assigns a date or page number, but the scanned image does not include that information, or it is unreadable, we include the quotation but attribute it to the collection.

In this final volume of text it is fitting to acknowledge, insofar as possible, the people who have contributed to the project. We therefore include, following the Acknowledgments, lists of staff, students, and volunteers; people who have provided information about words and phrases; and those who have made monetary contributions.

Acknowledgments

Any project the length and magnitude of *DARE* is hugely indebted to many people and organizations—those who helped to create the work, those who provided financial and administrative support, and those who provided words for the *Dictionary* as well as words of encouragement. Acknowledgments of those individuals and organizations are included on pp. xii–xxxix.

DARE has been blessed throughout its history with staff members who loved the idea of the project, worked hard in their various roles, and took pride in the accomplishments of the whole enterprise. Over a period of more than forty-five years, fieldworkers, computer programmers, editors, bibliographers, production staff, and office administrators all played their parts to make *DARE* a reality. Throughout the process, students and volunteers[1] provided essential services to move the project along.

Without a stable home in which the work could be done, the *DARE* staff could not have succeeded in bringing the project to fruition. The University of Wisconsin–Madison provided that home from the start. Chancellors, Deans, Department Chairs, and colleagues provided encouragement and support. Many of those individuals have been acknowledged in previous volumes, but in this volume it is a pleasure to express particular thanks to Chancellors John Wiley and Carolyn A. "Biddy" Martin; to Graduate School Dean Martin Cadwallader and Associate Dean Susan Cook; to College of Letters and Science Deans Phillip Certain and Gary Sandefur and Associate Dean Magdalena Hauner; to English Department Chairs Susan Stanford Friedman, Thomas Schaub, Michael Bernard-Donals, and Theresa Kelley; and to Information Processing Consultants Greg Putnam, Jim Kalupa, and their assistants, who have provided vital technical help, always with efficiency and good cheer. Through the College of Letters and Science Learning Support Services, Read Gilgen, Bruno Browning, and Sara Ziemendorf have also provided valuable technical assistance.

As has been true from the start, the librarians in the forty-nine UW–Madison libraries and the Wisconsin Historical Society have regularly provided invaluable assistance in finding obscure titles and obtaining necessary materials. They also provided access to the Online Computer Library Center, an essential resource. We thank Library Director Kenneth Frazier, and through him, all the generous and knowledgeable librarians across the UW–Madison campus.

DARE is also appreciative of the many people with whom we have worked at Harvard University Press since 1974. It has been a privilege to be associated with them, and we look forward to a productive collaboration on the electronic edition of *DARE*.

Throughout the history of the project, finding adequate financial support has been a major challenge. *DARE* is deeply grateful to the many organizations and individuals who have made it possible for the project not just to survive, but to thrive. They allowed us to forge an unusual collaboration among federal, university, foundation, corporation, and individual donors, whose common goal was to help *DARE* to a successful conclusion.

The National Endowment for the Humanities, an independent federal agency, has been the mainstay of our support since 1970.[2] Without its substantial assistance, through a combination of outright and matching grants, *DARE* would likely have faltered. The enthusiasm of Chairmen William Ferris, Bruce Cole, and Jim Leach has been gratifying, and *DARE* is honored to have been designated a *We the People* project. Senior Program Officer Helen Agüera has been unfailingly helpful over many years.

Support from the National Science Foundation has similarly been crucial to *DARE*'s success. We have been fortunate to work with Linguistics Program Directors Joan Maling, D. Terence Langendoen, Eric H. Potsdam, and William J. Badecker.

At the University of Wisconsin–Madison, *DARE* has been the beneficiary of many kinds of assistance. Through the Graduate School, funding for multiple awards has been provided by the Wisconsin Alumni Research Foundation; the Graduate School and College of Letters and Science have jointly supported many of *DARE*'s Project Assistants; the College has provided three years of development support; and the Brittingham Fund, Inc., the Evjue Foundation, Inc., and the Anonymous Fund have all contributed gifts essential to our support.

Among private foundations, the Andrew W. Mellon Foundation is unsurpassed in its advocacy for the humanities. *DARE* is extremely grateful for its long-term and substantial support. In particular, we express thanks to Presidents William G. Bowen and Don Randel, to former Secretary Richard Ekman, and to Program Officers Joseph Meisel and Donald Waters.

1. Two volunteers in particular deserve mention by name: Judith A. Taylor and Marjory McMickle have offered steadfast assistance for twenty-five and twenty-four years, respectively.

2. Any views, findings, conclusions, or recommendations expressed in this publication do not necessarily reflect those of the National Endowment for the Humanities.

The Franklin Philanthropic Foundation has been extraordinarily generous to *DARE* for a decade and a half. The foundation and its principals have not only contributed essential operating support, but have also provided major funding for technical development. In addition, they have offered valuable advice and guidance. All of these contributions have been critical to *DARE*'s success.

One very important group of contributors deserves special recognition: by virtue of their major contributions, eleven individuals or institutions have qualified to "Adopt a Letter" of *DARE*. Those donors and their chosen letters are John Sime (the letter A); Phillip Certain, representing the College of Letters and Science, (C); Sabrina Summers (D); the Franklin Philanthropic Foundation (F); the Gladys Krieble Delmas Foundation (G); John A. Shea (J); Martin Cadwallader and Susan Cook, representing the UW–Madison Graduate School, (M); Herrick Jackson (R); the Horace W. Goldsmith Foundation (S, in honor of William Safire); A. Richard Diebold (T); and multiple donors (Z, in honor of Frederic "On to Z!" Cassidy).

Other foundations without whose generous gifts we could not have continued include Carnegie Corporation of New York, the Salus Mundi Foundation, the John C. Sime Trust, the Pleasant T. Rowland Foundation, Vital Projects, Inc., the New York Times Company Foundation, Furthermore (a program of the J. M. Kaplan Fund), the Connemara Fund, and the Grace Jones Richardson Trust. Additional foundations, corporations, trusts, and individuals who have made financial contributions to *DARE* are listed on pp. xxxi–xxxix.

DARE's Board of Visitors, founded in 1999 to provide advice, visibility, and assistance, has been an extremely supportive organization. Its members have promoted the project through their syndicated columns and public lectures; they have provided scholarly, technical, and business guidance; and they have contributed financially, both by making personal donations and by finding like-minded colleagues. Current board members are Greg Alfus, Richard Ekman, Harlan Ellison, Morris F. Goodman, Robert D. King, David Maraniss, Erin McKean, Allan Metcalf (Executive Secretary, American Dialect Society, ex officio), Jacquelyn Mitchard, Mary Lu Mitchell, Cynthia L. Moore, Robert H. Moore, Donald Oresman, George L. Schueppert, Virginia Schwerin, John A. Shea, and Simon Winchester. Former members are John Bordie, Jane Appleby Flint, James J. Kilpatrick, Marianne Means, William Safire, and Bruce Walker.

Through the University of Wisconsin Foundation, *DARE* has been the beneficiary of research, advice, and service. We are particularly thankful for the Foundation's support of a Development Director and for the dedicated fulfillment of that role by David H. Simon and Jon E. Sorenson.

Since the beginning of the project, *DARE* has benefited from the knowledge and generosity of scholars who have shared their collections, their experience, and their guidance. For Volume V, Michael Montgomery has been particularly generous not only in sharing his materials on Appalachian English and citations from Civil War diaries, but also in reading drafts of the text and providing valuable suggestions. To him and to the many other scholars who have answered questions and pointed us in useful directions, we are grateful.

DARE Staff, Students, and Volunteers, 1965–2011

Catherine Abel
Kris Abelmann
George W. (Bill) Abernethy
Jurgen Adam
Johnnye Akin
Robert Alexander
Gerhard T. Alexis
John Algeo
Harold B. Allen
Jean W. Anderson
Kim Anderson
Leslie Anderson
Burr Angle
Frank Anshen
Lois Armstrong
Alice Arnett-Urban
John Ashbaugh
Catherine R. Attig
Quinn Bailey
Richard W. Bailey
Paul Baker
Alice Baldwin
Diane L. Balmer
Alice Banks
Dan Barber
Myra Barnes
Lillian Bart
Martha Bateson
Gwen L. Bauschka
B. Kathleen Beckett
Paul Beckett
Karen Beidel
John Bengtson
Larry Benson
Dick Berke
Roland L. Berns
John Berrington
Aaron Bibb
Suzanne Bible
Eric Biessman
Beth Binhammer
Sarah Lynne Bischel
Elizabeth Blake
Martha Blalock
David Bock
Matthias Bonjour
Lalia Boone
Enola Borgh
Virginia A. Bormann
Donald Boyd
Deena Brazy
Jean Ann Brehm
James Breuer
Karen Elizabeth Brindley
Sarah Broderick
Christopher Brooks

Jessica Brooks
Charlotte Brown
Peter Brunette
Clara Burke
Pamela Butkow
Joan Caberly
Owen Campbell
R. Milton Carleton
David Carlson
Sue Carlson
Helen S. Carlson
Nathan E. J. Carlson
Marvin Carmony
Craig M. Carver
Claire Cassidy
Frederic G. Cassidy
Kathryn Cassidy
Victor Cassidy
Pamela R. Catterson
Iven Chen
Clarence L. Cheshire
Susan Clapp
John F. Clark
Ruth Clark
Thomas L. Clark
Lurline Coltharp
Alan Cook
Stanley J. Cook
Jo Ann Cope
Betsy Corey
Robert L. Cowser
L. Benjamin Crane
Gladys F. Crawford
Helen L. Crickmay
Joyce Crim
James C. Crist
Toni Culjak
Jennifer Das
Monique Daviau
Carra Davies
Barbara G. Davis
Lawrence M. Davis
Dhruv Dawar
Jason Dawdy
Samir Dayal
Erin Decker
Barbara Dellinger
Gregory D'Eloia
Martha Dewees
Scott Dikkers
Steven C. Dittman
Peter Doane
Andrea Donner
Barbara Mary Dorn
Philomene Ducas
Laura Jean Ducker

Audrey R. Duckert
Warren L. P. Dwyer
Ginny Dymond
Jean Ehrenkranz
Jennifer K. Ellsworth
Jon Erickson
Gerald G. Esch
Allison Hales Espeseth
Carrie A. Estill
Susan Leslie Evangelista
Thomas G. Fairclough
Janet Faro
Marjorie Fenn
George Ferger
Charles Ferguson
Adria Fernandez
Candy Finkleston
Bruce W. Finnie
John Fisher
Kelly Flury
Joan Foeste
Lawrence Foley
Becky Forbes
Virginia Foscue
Charles W. Foster
David E. Foster
Melissa Fraebner
W. Nelson Francis
Timothy C. Frazer
Steve Frets
Dolores Fries
Nancy Gaines
Jacob Gamage
Elizabeth R. Gardner
Karen Gassman
Nina Gibson
Glenn G. Gilbert
Berit Givens
George H. Goebel
Nicholas Goetzfridt
Shanti Goetzfridt
Szabina Goger
David Goldberg
Leonard Goldberg
Susan Goldberg
Michelle Goodrich
Quinn Gorman
Bonnie Greatman
Feebee Greco
Iris Greenberg
Randy S. Gregory
Solveig Griebesland
Michael Grossinger
Diann Haggerty
Joan Houston Hall
Joseph S. Hall

Miriam Hall
Ralph Halpern
Steve Halpern
Eric Hamp
Eva C. Hanger
James W. Hartman
Jean M. Hartman
Abbie Hatton
Einar Haugen
E. Anne Hausmann
Robert Hausmann
Ajeenah Haynes
John M. Heasley
Mary Jo Heck
Kirk Hegbloom
Bob Henderson
Carol Henderson
Michael M. T. Henderson
Robert Henderson
Phillip Heyer
Edward C. Hill
Harold G. Hill
Tracy Hill
Jeffrey A. Hirshberg
Charles Arthur Hobbie
Wendy Hocking
Eileen Hodge
Barb Hoeger
Matt Hogan
Mary Louise Holmes
Jonathan Holz
Esther Hong
Lois Hood
Barbara Hornick
Tom Hove
Sharon Huizenga
Michele McKeegan Jacobs
Robert Jacobs
Sally J. Jacobs
Max W. Jacobson
Thelma G. James
Mary G. Jay
Cynthia Johnson
Thomas K. Johnson
Katie Jones
Mary Jay Jones
David Junker
Margaret E. Kailhofer
Frederic Kammann
William Katke
Robert Keenan
B. J. Keene
Kate Kemper
Jay H. Kendall
Annie Kenny
Frances Kerr

Thomas Knight Kerwin
Dolores Kester
Paulette Kilmer
Anne King
William Kirwin
Roger Klinkenborg
Robert J. Kloss
Sheila Knee Kolstad
Gabe Krambs
Stephen M. Kratky
Karen J. Krause
Helen Kreigh
Hans Krichels
Sherman M. Kuhn
Hans Kurath
Diane H. Kutzko
Philip C. Kutzko
Roger Ladd
Scot LaFaive
Denise Lamb
Michael Lampman
William H. Landram Jr.
Symington P. Landreth
Ronald A. Lanoue
C. M. Latta
Ann V. Lawler
Corey Leatherman
Mary Lee
Maurice Lee
Peter Lee
Winfred Lehmann
Suzanne E. Lehenertz
Roy Leslie
Gloria Levin
Wilson B. Lindauer
Francine Lindner
Alan J. Link
Kimberly Jo Liu
Matthew J. Livesey
Albert Logan
David Longfellow
Robert Lumiansky
Herbert Lust
Linda Alma Madaali
Reino Maki
Shirley Irene Maki
Albert Marckwardt
Jane Marek
Joseph D. Marek
Linda Marks
Lawrence Martin
Paula Martin
Mark Matson
Greg Matthews
Charles McCabe
Robert McCracken
Raven I. McDavid Jr.
John C. McGalliard
Lisa McGrane
Sheila McGrath
Michele M. McKeegan
Marsha McKeldin
Jane McMahon
Marjorie McMickle
James McMillan
Sheena McRae
Melissa Mendonsa
George S. Metes
Angela Meyer
Erin E. Meyer
Norbert Meyer-Wittmann

W. C. Middleton
Tamara Milbourn
Charlotte J. Miller
Leah M. Miller
Phillip J. Miller
Robert H. Miller
Cynthia Milne
Joseph Milosh
Jennifer R. Mitchell
Goldye Mohr
Janet L. Monk
Diana C. Moore
Robert H. Moore
Patricia A. Moriarty
Laura Murray
Barbara Myhre
Kristina Nailen
Gary T. Neal
Geoffrey Needler
Gordon Nelson
Mary Nelson
Melissa Ness
Gary Neuell
Claude Henry Neuffer
Georgine R. Neureiter
N. P. Neureiter
D. A. Nichols
Karen Nickels
Joan Niebauer
Lisa Nielsen
Alleen P. Nilsen
Don L. F. Nilsen
Evelyn Nimz
Edward C. Nolte
Helen Northup
David W. Nunnery
Kathleen O'Brien
Raymond O'Cain
Molly O'Connell
Mary O'Hare
Joy Parfitt
Jean Howell Patau
Betty Pearson
Irvin Wherry Peckham
Joyce Pederson
Mary Ann Pels
Robert Pender
Xavier Perez
Frances Perry
Robert A. Peters
Jennifer Catherine (Kate) Peterson
Beth Petroff-Beder
Boytcho Peytchev
Linda Pflager
Martha Phelps
Joe Pirri
John J. Pirri
Ruth Porter
Anna Potter
Susan Leslie Potter
Patrick Pranke
Jill Priluck
Thomas Pyles
Carol Radasky
Maureen Ramirez
Diana Rapp
Alysse S. Rasmussen
Allen W. Read
John Reddington
Rita Mae Reese
Brenda Regner

Paulette Reinke
Robin Reinke
Ellen Renecke
Sally J. Rentschler
Florence Rhodes
Judith Rich
Barbara A. Richmond
Sonja Ritchie
Kenneth A. Robb
Margaret Robertson
Fred Robinson
Rebecca V. Roeder
Orville F. Rogers
Susan Rouske
August Rubrecht
Dale Ruff
I. Willis Russell
Joe Russell
Geoffrey Russom
Barbara Rust
Phillip R. Rutherford
S. J. Sackett
Irene Sadowski
Gabriel Sanders
Jeff Sauer
Gladys Saunders
Janet Sawyer
Paul L. Schacht
Joann C. Scheu
Amy Schnapper
Julie Schnebly
Dan Schultz
Gretchen E. Schulz
Barbara Scott
John R. Searles
Charles V. Seastone Jr.
Marilyn Seastone
James F. Sefcik
Mindy Seidler
Alyssa Severn
Peter Shaheen
Ann Shannon
Paulette Sharkey
Esther K. Sheldon
Mo Shen
Heather Shimon
Francis X. Siciliano
Mohsin K. Siddiqui
Deborah Siegel
Wanda Sikes
Beth Lee Simon
David H. Simon
Richard Sims
Toby Sindt
Paul T. Siudzinski
Lindsay Skotterud
Timothy Sloan
Ann Smiley
Nevenah Smith
Thomas Smith
Beth Solomon
Jon E. Sorenson
Carle B. Spotts
James Sprowls
Betsy Stampe
Detlef Fritz Stark
Jim Staskowski
Chip Stearns
William J. Stevens
Robert Stevick
Joyce Steward

Jill Straub
Victor L. Strite
Rosemarie Strojny
L. C. Suddarth
William Howard Sullivan
Anne-Marie Svobodny
Jason Sweet
Fred A. Tarpley
Gary Tate
Judy Taylor
Sue Teigen
Joan Teller
Jenny Tetzlaff
Ednah S. Thomas
Sarah Thomas
Colleen Tierney
Martin Todaro
Mrs. Geoffrey Torney
Steve Toth
Conrad Treff
David G. Tucker
Gerald Udell
Francis Lee Utley
Ryan Van Cleave
David L. Vander Meulen
Patricia VanDyke
Elizabeth Van Guilder
James Van Sloun
Manu Varma
Richard Venezky
Luanne von Schneidemesser
Michael von Schneidemesser
Elisabeth Wagner
Lida Wagner
Judy Ward
Kathleen M. Ward
Mary L. Washington
Margaret Waterman
Erna Waters
Christoph Weisen
Julie Weiss
Timothy F. Weiss
C. Topf Wells
Joan M. Wendt
Aaron Wheeler
Earl J. Wilcox
Michael Williamson
Nancy Williamson
Amy Wilson
Carol Hunt Wilson
Carolyn Wilson
Michael Winnowski
Elizabeth Witherell
Sue Wittman
Barbara G. Wolfe
Rick Wolff
James Wood
Lois Wood
Christopher Woodard
Hensley C. Woodbridge
William Woodson
Brit Wortman
Min Xu
Lee (Emily) York
Su Yuen-Wei
Mary M. Zegers
Joan Zink
Vivian Zinkin
Terry Zwigoff
Leonard Zwilling

Contributors of Words and Wisdom, 1948–2011

Long before the *DARE* project was officially started, Frederic G. Cassidy began collecting interesting words wherever he could find them. In 1948 he hosted a weekly program called *Wisconsin Words,* as part of "The Wisconsin College of the Air" on WHA Radio. It was enthusiastically received and generated hundreds of postcards from listeners who wanted to ask or tell about their favorite regional terms. Those messages were the first entries in an extensive archive of letters (and later e-mail messages) from word-lovers across the country.

We try here to acknowledge all who have contributed words and expressions to the *DARE* files. The limitations of fifty-year-old penciled postcards and the idiosyncrasies of handwriting have doubtless resulted in some erroneous transcriptions of people's names; for those errors and any omissions, we apologize.

We also include here many individuals who have provided knowledge or advice along the way. We are grateful for their contributions.

Gemino Henson Abad
Frank Abate
Carl Abbott
Rona Abbott
Kris Abelman
Mrs. C. F. Abercrombie
F. E. Abernathy
Frances Smith Abernathy
George W. (Bill) Abernethy
Fred Abner
Julie Stevens Abner
Carolyn Hovick Abrahams
Helen Achtenberg
Laura Ackerman
Laurel Ackerman
Carol M. Adams
Cecil Adams
Fred C. Adams
Paul Adams
Raymond William Adams
Ruth K. Adams
Mrs. William D. Adams
Katherine Adamson
Jacob H. Adler
Jeff Agar
Hugh Agee
Michael Agnes
Jim Ague
Frederick J. Ahlfs
Lisa Ahlstedt
David G. Ainsworth
A. J. Aitken
James Akin
Johnnye Akin
Cyril N. Alberga
Timothy J. Albers
John L. Albert
Marian Peters Albrecht
Pat Alder
Ruth I. Aldrich
Rita Alevizon
Robert Alexander
Gerhard T. Alexis

Dan Alford
I. Alford
Katheryn S. Alfred
Greg Alfus
John Algeo
Jody Aliesan
Joan C. Alkula
Charles Allard Jr.
Marcia Allass
Mrs. F. W. Allbee
George Allen
Harold B. Allen
Irving Allen
Irving Lewis Allen
Mr. and Mrs. I. S. Allen
Lue Allen
M. S. Allen
Mrs. R. C. Allen
Sandra L. Allen
Mrs. A. M. Allison
R. Brooke Alloway
Donald Allyn
Colin Alteveer
Elsa E. Althen
Gloria Alvarado
Bil Alverson
Paul Alworth
Phil Ambrosino
Jay Ames
Joy Ames
Walter R. Amesburg Jr.
Maya T. Amis
Ashley C. Amos
O. L. Amsler
Barry Ancelet
Betsy S. Anderson
Dean Anderson
Don Anderson
John W. Anderson
Paul W. Anderson
Virginia K. Anderson
Mrs. W. A. Anderson
Russ Anderton

Peter Andreae
C. A. Andrews
E. William Andrews
Kelly Andrews
William L. Andrews
Denia Angevine
Erin Annis
Chuck Antony
Rose Antos
Ricardo Antunez
Helen Appel
Christopher Arata
B. L. Arenander
Emily Arkin
Iona Armstrong
Jack Armstrong
William H. Armstrong
Rob Arndt
Angela Arnold
Joy E. Arnold
Platt T. Arnold
Hariette Simpson Arnow
Audrey Arnst
Mark Aronoff
Ron Arruda
Carolyn M. Arteaga
Donald B. Arthur
Edward Artin
Rick Asam
Paul Asente
D. Wayne Ashby Jr.
Trina J. Asher
Judy Ashford
Leonard R. N. Ashley
Mrs. M. D. Ashman
George Ashworth
Mary Claire Aston
Jay Atherton
Gail Atkins
Ruth E. Atkins
Laura Atkinson
Lee Atkinson
Louie Attebery

Catherine R. Attig
John W. Attig
Nancy Attig
Richard Attix
Mrs. J. R. Atwater
Mrs. C. S. Atwood
Pam Ausman
C. Glenn Austin
Greg Austin
Beatrice Auty
Carolyn Auty
Walter S. Avis
Carol Avol
Richard Avol
Beth Ayers
James E. Ayres
Rosalind Ayres
Edgar Babcock
Jackie H. Baden
William B. Baer
Howard G. Baetzhold
John Bailar
Charles W. Bailey
Dudley Bailey
George Bailey
George F. Bailey
Guy H. Bailey
Karen Bailey
Lee Bailey
Merritt Bailey
Richard W. Bailey
Sallie Bailey
W. M. Bailey
W. E. Baily
C. A. Baird
Scott Baird
John Bakeless
Daniel Baker
John M. Baker
Ronald Baker
Ronald L. Baker
Walter E. Baker
Raivo Balciunas

Wanda Balducci
Alice Baldwin
Mrs. Ira Baldwin
Judy Baldwin
Sue Baldwin
Zelma Baldwin
James E. Bales
Sallie Ballew
Carroll Balmer
Gladys Balmer
David T. Bancroft
Mary K. Bandor
Willard T. Bangle
Alice Banks
Larry Banks
Portia Banks
Mrs. David Bannister
Jesse Bannister
Michael Baranelli
Mrs. Ted R. Barben
Fred Barber
Mary Barber
Warren Barclay
Shireen Barday
Marguerite Grossenbach Bariunn
Lenore Barkan
Bill Barker
Jo Ann Barker
William Wayne Barker
Martha Barkoff
Mrs. Samuel Barkoff
Greg Barnes
Mr. and Mrs. James E. Barnes
Myra Barnes
Teresa Barnes
Clarence L. Barnhart
David Barnhart
Kathryn S. Barnicle
Joel Barnitzky
Mrs. Charles Barnum
Dennis E. Baron
Hank Barrentine
Benjamin Barrett
Clyde Barrett
Dianne Barrett
Grant Barrett
James Barrett
Sheila Barrett
Mac E. Barrick
M. C. Barry
John Barsotti
Lillian Bart
David Bartholomew
Pearl H. Bartholomew
Robert Bartholomew
Deb Bartle
Alice J. Bartlett
Charles E. Bartlett
Eugene Bartley
Mrs. C. W. Barton
Mrs. Roland Bartz
Samuel Bassett
Jodey Bateman
E. F. Bates
H. L. Bates
Hugh Bates
Cornelius Bateson
William Bateson
Ivan Baugh
Sonya R. Baughman

Mrs. H. D. Bauman
Greg Baumgardner
George J. Baumgartner
William Baumrucker
Mrs. Walter Baurque
Gwen L. Bauschka
Victoria J. Bayerl
John Bayley
Mrs. W. M. Bazutto
Karen Beadling
C. Richard Beam
Theodore S. Beardsley Jr.
Cindy Beasley
W. G. Beasley
Debra Beck
Anthony D. Becker
Bart Becker
Mrs. George Becker
Janet H. Becker
Kathie Beckett
R. J. Beckham
W. M. Becks
William M. Becks
Josie Beckwith
David Bedell
Doyle V. Bedsole
Frederick J. Beharriell
Tim Behrend
Bruce Beicke
Mrs. Don Beig
Joyce Belanger
Elizabeth Belden
Pauline Belew
Carole R. Bell
Charles Bell
Mrs. Emerson L. Bell
K. Bell
John Bellamy
Mrs. Thomas E. Belshaw
Mrs. Ray Belter
Allen Belton
Jo Ellen Bence
John Bengtson
Carolyn Benischeck
Mrs. Howard Bennett
Jacob Bennett
Jean Bennett
Mike Bennett
Carole Cosine Benoit
Larry D. Benson
Mrs. Ralph Benson
Alan Berg
Lorie Berg
David Bergdahl
Mrs. Allen Berger
Don Berger
Howard Berger
Ruth Berkshire
E. Berman
Bobbi Bernard
Bonnie Bernard
Kurt E. Bernardo
Audrey Berns
Pam Berns
Robert Berns
Cynthia Bernstein
Mary S. Bernstein
John Berrington
Sister Marie Bertrand
Agnes Bertsch

Michael Berube
Lloyd Besant
Sandra Bessetti
Jess B. Bessinger Jr.
Joyce Bevus
Carryll Beyer
Suzanne Bible
Kara Bielli
Raymond G. Biggar
Gary Bijinsky
Mrs. R. Billings
Mrs. J. M. Billman
Mrs. A. E. Billquist
Garland D. Bills
Pam Bird
Mrs. Alfred Birdsell
Florence A. Bischel
Harry W. Bischel
Jane Bisco
J. M. Bishop
Melinda Bishop
Alex Bisset
Bryan T. Bitgood
Daniel W. Bix
Robert S. Black
Spencer Black
Mrs. W. F. Black Jr.
Minerva Blackburn
John Blackmer
Judy Blackmer
Carol Blackwood
Mrs. Robert Blair
Elmer P. Blake
Ruth D. Blake
Ruth E. Blake
Martha Lee Blalock
Benjamin Brookshire Blanchet
Peter Blankenheim
Jesse Blankenship
Katy Blantz
Josh Bleibtreu
Marty Bleyer
Stacey Bliss
Don Bloch
Morton M. Bloomfield
James Bluck
John Bluck
Emmett Boaz
Robert M. Bock
Carl Bode
John F. Bode
Lenore Bode
A. Bodenheimer
Carrie Bodensteiner
Brian Boeck
Rich Boehme
Susan Wallace Boehmer
Eleanor Bogan
Richard S. Bogart
Samuel N. Bogorad
Mrs. C. W. Bohmer Jr.
Eleanor S. Bohmer
Mary Bohn
Mrs. Howard H. Bolender
Bruce D. Boling
John K. Bollard
Anne Bolt
Barbara Bolt
Martha Anne Bolt
Elizabeth Bonar

Robert B. Bond
Ron Bonica
Larry Bonko
Pat Booker
John Bookout
Lalia Boone
Erik Bootsma
John G. Bordie
O. Borge
Iduna Borger
Enola Borgh
James Borland
Janet Borland
Susan Borowitz
Mary Patricia Borowski
Michael Borwell
Barbara Bossardt
Lloyd Bostian
Bruce O. Boston
Len E. Boswell
Paul Bothwills
Thomas W. Botsford
Karl Bottke
Julia Boulay
Mrs. H. D. Bourman
Charles S. Bouslog
Mrs. H. C. Boutton
Irene Boutton
Fredson Bowers
John Bowers
Bob Bowman
John L. Bowman
R. C. Bowman
Rosemary Bowman
Mrs. W. H. Bowman
Mrs. C. T. Boyd
Ann Boyer
Mr. and Mrs. Carl H. Boyer
Georgiana Boyington
Rose Josephine Boylan
J. A. Boyse
J. Bozic
Thomas Brackett
Haldeen Braddy
Mrs. Clinton Braden
Paul C. Brader
Margaret S. Bradford
Maria Bradford
Bert Bradley
Kyra Bradley
Nita L. Bradley
R. M. Bradley
Joel Bradshaw
Carol Braham
Caroline Bramley
A. Branach
Gertrude Brand
J. L. Brandenburg
Fred Branin
Cheryl Braswell
Kate Brauer
Mrs. Jessie Braun
Lee Braunschweig
Robert S. Bravard
Paul Braverman
Robert Brawer
James P. Brawner
Mrs. T. W. Brazeau
Erika Brazzle
Tony Breed

Jean Ann Brehm
Fred Brengelman
F. E. Brenin
Jeutonne Brewer
Paul G. Brewster
Angie Brey
William Brey
Bill Bridges
Bonnie Briggs
Mrs. Ellis O. Briggs
Hazel J. Briggs
John Briggs
Elizabeth A. Brinkman
Helen S. Brinsmade
F. M. Brisco
Patti Britt
Kelly Brittain
Robert Britton
Mrs. T. W. Brizeau
James Broaddus
Bonnie Broderick
Sarah Broderick
Howard O. Brogan
Mrs. W. S. Brogden
Ruth H. Bromley
Arthur Bronstein
Maxey Brooke
Carol S. Brookhyser
Bill Brooks
Mrs. Fred Broome
John Broughton
Agnes M. Brown
Mrs. Aron F. Brown
Calvin Brown
Charles R. Brown III
David P. Brown
Ernest Brown
Mrs. F. Brown
Geoffrey Brown
Gwen N. Brown
Howard W. Brown
Joyce Brown
Julia B. Brown
Marice Brown
Marion Brown
Morton Brown
Needa Brown
Mrs. P. M. Brown
Rhiannon N. Brown
Mrs. Robert Brown
Ross H. Brown
Ruth A. Brown
Ruth M. Brown
Samuel Brown
William J. Brown
Joseph D. Browne
Matthew Bruccoli
Marshall Brucer
Mollie Buckley
H. Brueckner
Joseph H. Bruening
Elizabeth P. Brush
Louise Bruton
David R. Bryan
Jeffrey Bryant
Margaret Bryant
Betty J. Brye
Catherine Bryer
Scott Bryson
Walter Bubbert

Timothy J. Buchanan
Joseph T. Buck
Lloyd Buck
Phyllis Buck
Susan Buck
Inez Buell
R. A. Buell
Elva Buenzli
A. Bugzavich
Joe C. Buice
Alice Bullen
Henrietta Bulthuis
Keith Bulthuis
Harold Bumpurs
Mrs. Hasse R. Bunnelle
Janet Bur
R. W. Burchfield
Russell Burck
C. Fred Burdett
Heather Burgess
Carolyn Burke
Becky Burket
Thomas G. Burket
Eva Mae Burkett
Joyce Burkhalter
Renee Burmester
Ollie Dee Burnett
Katherine W. Burnley
John F. Burnum
Dieter Burrell
Margaret M. Burrell
Lee A. Burress Jr.
Mark Burris
Abbie E. Burrows
Charles Burrows
Mrs. Jessie C. Burrows
Richard J. Burt
Yaakov Burton
Nell Bush
Sargent Bush Jr.
C. A. Butler
Charlotte Butler
Jennifer Butler
Lucile Butler
Melvin Butler
Paul Butler
Pierce Butler
Mrs. Richard Butler
Sally E. Butler
Kay Butler-Nalin
Ron Butters
Mrs. T. M. Buttimer
M. H. Buxbaum
Mrs. Edward Buxton
Rex C. Byle
Rose Byrd
Patricia Byrd
Tim Byrne
Jan Bzdyl
Patrick Cabe
Joan Caberly
Patricia Cadena
Maurice Cagnon
Patricia Caham
A. V. Cain
R. R. Cain
Robert Cain
Robert H. Cain
Scott S. Cairns
Stephen J. Caldas

H. Van Yorx Caldwell
Mrs. John Wesley Calhoun
Kenneth L. Calkins
Barbara Callahan
E. F. Callahan
Edward Callary
R. E. Callary
Stephen Calvert
Rebecca Calvo
Michael D. Cammisa
A. H. Campbell
Barbara Campbell
Darby Jo Campbell
Denise E. Campbell
Joan Campbell
John Campbell
John M. Campbell
Julian J. N. Campbell
Mrs. Leon J. Campbell
William T. Campbell
Wilma Campbell
Thomas J. Campbell
Charlotte Campion
Lisa Candelaria
Carol Caney
Lorraine J. Cann
Patricia R. Cannon
Marie Cansler
Ann T. Cantrell
Joe Cantrell
Michael Capek
Mrs. Michael Capek
Jerrold L. Caplin
Mabel S. Caporale
Candace Caraco
William Card
Al Cardinale
Ann Carey
Addis Carless Jr.
R. Milton Carleton
David Carlson
Helen S. Carlson
David C. Carmody
Marvin Carmony
Maureen Carolan
C. Leslie Carpenter
Tom Carpenter
Beau Carr
Elizabeth Carr
Gerald D. Carr
Warren P. Carrier
Joseph M. Carrière
Linda L. Carroll
Barbara Carrothers
B. S. Carswell
F. Carter
Gregg Carter
J. Hazel Carter
R. D. Carter
Ronnie Carter
Steven D. Carter
Tim Carter
Pat Caruthers
Maria Casali
Joseph Cascio Jr.
R. G. Case
Dave Casker
Genevieve Cass
Megan Cassat
Andy Cassell

Carol Cassell
Claire M. Cassidy
Frederic G. Cassidy
Kathleen E. Cassidy
Kathryn G. Cassidy
Margaret M. B. Cassidy
Michael M. Cassidy
Victor M. Cassidy
David Castell
Molly Castleberry
Laura Cates
Pafra Catledge
Scott Catledge
Vincent Catozella
Peggy Caudill
Alfred Cavanaugh
Mrs. E. J. Cayne
James Cerello
Phillip R. Certain
Mrs. Albert Cezar
Marjorie Chadwick
Jack Chambers
Janette Chambers
Kim Chambers
Glenn Chambliss
Ruth Chan
James L. Chandler
Margaret Chandler
Elsie Chaney
Joseph Chang
Paul Chapin
Joel Charles
Larry H. Charles
Addis Charless Jr.
Mr. and Mrs. Loyd J.
    Charlesworth Jr.
Jack Charlotte
Lucile Charlton
Jeffrey E. Chase
Martin Chase
Marie K. Chellman
Caroline Cheney
Frances M. Chenoweth
Judy Chermonte
Mrs. L. W. Cherry
Judy Chervenock
Iris Cheshire
Mrs. William W. Chichester
Leon Childress
Meredith Chiles
Marvin Ching
Bill Choisser
Peggy Choy
Jason Christian
Charlayne Christianson
Sheryl Christman
Debbie Christopher
Richard Chumley
M. Robbins Church
William Church
James Ciba
Bill Ciccone
Wladyslaw Cichocki
Susan Ciconte
Amelia Ciffone
Amy Ciffone
Peter M. Citi
Craig Claiborne
Marion Walker Clapp
Catherine T. Clark

Darra Clark
Donald B. Clark
Dorothy H. Clark
Erion J. Clark
George P. Clark
Jed A. Clark
John Williams Clark
Margaret Clark
Marion A. Clark
Morris Clark
Mrs. R. A. Clark
Thomas L. Clark
William H. Clark
Mrs. J. F. Clarke
Kenneth Clarke
Mary W. Clarke
Robert R. Claus
Lee Clayton
L. Cleary
La Verne W. Cleary
Phil Cleary
Caroline Cleaver
Margery L. Cleveland
Luella H. Clifton
Clarence L. Cline
D. H. Cline
Richard Clinger
Tom Clinger
Francis L. Clough
Jay Clough
Mrs. Ken Clover
Nellie Coats
Jessie L. Cobb
Joan Coberly
Helen Cockey
John Cocking
Stewart T. Coffin
Stuart Cogan
Gerald Cohen
Gloria L. Cohen
Howard R. Cohen
James Cohen
Chuck Coker
James H. Coker
Frank Colbourn
Bevra Cole
David Cole
George S. Cole
Joe Colella
Kate Coles
Alyce H. Collett
J. Reginald Collier
Roy Collier
Basil A. Collins
C. L. Collins
George Collins
Morris Colman
Lurline Coltharp
Henry D. Colton
Lela F. Common
Diana Comstock
Mrs. Jack Condra
Pat Condra
John Cone
Katie Conley
Richard Conniff
Patricia Connolly
Eleanor Connor
Ed Conrad
Charles M. Constantine

Nell Conway
Joan C. Cook
M. Thomas Cook
Manuel Cook
Jim Cooke
Mrs. L. O. Cooke
Liz Cooksey
Robert A. Cookson
Thomas Cooley
W. E. Cooney
Scott Cooper
Frederic H. Copp
Pearl Copp
P. Corby
Mick Corcoran
Jesse Core
Edith Cornell
Tim Cornett
Karen Cornwell
James Corrao
Becky Cors
R. G. Cortelyou
Frank Cosby
Mrs. Raymond J. Cothran
Michael Cotter
Steve Cotter
Judy Cotton
Mrs. J. Couliban
Kevin Coulson
Eleanor Coutts
Mrs. T. E. Cowan
Chris Cowap
Clay E. Cox
Ernest H. Cox
H. M. Cox
Dale Coye
Pat Crabtree
Roger Crabtree
Paul Cracroft
Donald Crafts
W. A. Craig
Morris C. Crandall
Mrs. S. D. Crandall
Susan E. Crandall
Robert Craven
Scott Craven
Lura Mae Craw
Borghilde Crawford
Ed R. Crawford
Gladys F. Crawford
Guy N. Crawford
Kathleen Crawford
Mrs. S. Crawford
Mrs. M. Creighton
Terry Cremers
Thomas Creswell
Helen L. Crickmay
Chris Crilly
Fleming Crim
Joyce Crim
David Crimmins
Edward Crist
E. H. Criswell
Sue Crockett
E. David Cronon
Stanley Cronquist
Marie Crooms
David Crosby
W. M. Crosby
Mary Cross

Stan Cross
Evelyn Crossman
Dennis Crosson
Mrs. Travis Crouch
Izora V. Crouse
Donald W. Crowe
Will Crowe
Daniel M. Crowl
Mr. and Mrs. Terence Crowley
Doris M. Crum
Mrs. Floyd C. Crumb
Mrs. J. W. Crumly
Katharine Culberson
Gary Culbert
Mrs. Gary Culbert
William M. Culin
Robert C. Cumming
John D. Cummings
Parke Cummings
Mrs. Ralph R. Cummings
Roxanne Cummings
Florence E. Cummins
Irma Cunningham
Joe Cunningham
Ernest J. Curcio
De'ah Curry
James M. Curry
N. M. Curry
John Curtin
Sarah Cushing
Mrs. Howard Custer
Cindy Cutler
Mary Cutler
Clara T. Cutshell
Agnes Cutts
Evelyn C. Cutts
J. Dahlborg
E. G. Dahlgren
Amy D'Aiuta
John Dalton
Laura Dalton
Susan Daly
Tom Dalzell
Frances Danely
Arthur G. Daniell
Peter T. Daniels
Darrell Danielson
Mrs. C. Dankelman
Jim Dankey
Martha Danner
Bob Darmody
Mrs. W. Darnell
Stephen Darst
Dallas Davenport
Charles Davidson
Mrs. R. K. Davidson
Richard F. Davidson
Leslie Paul Davies
Alva Davis
Boyd Davis
Christie Davis
Mrs. Douglas H. Davis
Jack A. Davis
Jacqueline Davis
Janice Davis
Katharine B. Davis
Mrs. M. W. Davis
Martha R. Davis
Rob Davis
Robert M. Davis

Beverly Davison
Amy Dawgert
Gordon Day
Nancy Day
Lisa Dean
Robert L. Dean
R. N. De Armond
David De Camp
Deborah De Church
Karl Decker
J. L. Decker
Mrs. J. L. Decker III
Liz De Coster
E. Degener
Mrs. Edens Degener
Francis Deignan
Joseph della Malva
Gregory M. D'Eloia
Gilles De Lorme
Marina Delrie
John Dendy
Marjorie Denney
Diane Dennigan
Leah Dennis
Ludwig Deringer
David E. Derk
August Derleth
Margaret De Rousie
Marie H. Derry
Dorothea M. Derwin
Bob de Smith
Joanne Despres
Antoinette Des Roches
Lorraine Desruisseaux
Jerry Detra
Randall A. Detro
Tom D'Evelyn
Marguerite Devers
Melvin E. Dick
Ron Dickey
Ruth Dickie
Gail Dickinson
Letha Farley Dickinson
Molly Dickmeyer
Emma Dickson
Jim Dickson
Naida Dickson
Paul Dickson
Walter Diefenderfer
Maude R. Diekman
Bernhard Diensberg
James Dierks
William Diesslin
Mrs. George Adams Dietrich
Pamela J. Diffee
Scott Dikkers
Mrs. Ray Dillard
Dayna Dimmen
E. J. Dimock
Mrs. F. D. Disdier
Albert E. Ditlow
Mrs. R. H. Dixon
Alger N. Doane
Susan H. S. Doane
Mrs. Robert Dobson
Mrs. John M. Dodds
Marshall Dodge
Jeff Dodson
John Doehner
Donald L. Doering

Ernest B. Doescher
Agnes Dogger
Angie Dogger
Marie Dogger
Stefan Dollinger
John Donahue
Aida Donald
Susan Donnelly
Thomas J. Donovan
Mrs. Richard Doorenbos
Carol Goedert Dopp
Robert Dopp
Robert B. Doremus
Donald Dorfman
Mr. and Mrs. Clyde H. Dornbusch
Lindsay C. Dorney
Barbara M. Doty
Edith Aultman Doty
Linda Dougherty
Patricia Dougherty
Mrs. Squires Doughman
Marjory Stoneman Douglas
C. G. Douglass
Jan Dowden
Alan S. Downer
Andrew F. Downey Jr.
Douglas V. Downey
Greg Downing
Helen Downing
Billy Downs
Debora Downs
George F. Downs III
Kathy Downs
Charles Clay Doyle
Mrs. H. T. Drake
Emanuel Drechsel
Mrs. John Dreger
Michael R. Dressman
Jeanne Drews
Mary Ann Driscoll
Sarah Kay B. DrowningBear
Barbara DuBois
Lois Duck
Audrey R. Duckert
Harold W. Duckert
Mabel Duckert
Luella Dudgeon
Edward L. Duesterhoeft
Cathy Duffy
Francis Duke
Mrs. J. H. Duke
Robert Duke
Bethany K. Dumas
Lucy Dunagen
A. R. Dunlap
D. Dunleavy
Dawn Dunleavy
Mildred Dunn
Narine Steele Dunn
George Dunsay
Mrs. L. Dunstan
Mary Jane Dunwiddie
Gerald Dupree
Diana Durden
Helen Durnen
Kenneth Durril
Mary A. Duryee
Lisa Dussault
Ottie Joe Dye
Jack Dyer

George G. Dykes
Robert D. Eagleson
Dorothy V. Earle
Addie Beall Early
J. Michael Early
Joyce Easley
Gordon Easson
Shirley Eastman
Robert Easton
Charles Eaton
Mr. and Mrs. Conan B. Eaton
Frances Eberhardy
Mrs. Leo Eberhardy
Herman J. Eberiel
Connie Eble
Kenneth E. Eble
Mark Eccles
Mary Eccles
Karyln R. Echols
Michael E. Eckstein
Eric Ederer
Linda Edmondson
Sylvia Edmunds
Ruth Edwards
Mrs. William W. Edwards
Dorothy C. Egan
Maryan Eger
Jodie Eggers
E. C. Ehrensperger
Pat Ehresmann
Todd Ehresmann
Jürgen Eichhoff
Fred Eikel Jr.
Richard Ekman
Ralph Ekwall
Janet Ela
Victor Elconin
Deborah Elgert
Lucille Elgin
Norman Eliason
Wayne Elliot
Brett Elliott
Ethel Elliott
Mrs. G. I. Elliott
Nancy Elliott
Elsie M. Ellis
Harry V. Ellis III
Jerry D. Ellis
Michael Ellis
Harlan Ellison
Paul M. Elvig
Cathy Ely
Kathleen Ely
Sheila Embleton
Mrs. John Emerick
Jessie Emerson
Marian R. Emerson
Mrs. C. Roy Emery Jr.
D. B. Emmert
Michael English
Werner Enninger
Steve Enniss
Donnie Eno
Lynn Entine
Susan Erdey
Jon Erickson
Louise W. Erickson
Mike Erskine
Sylvan Esh
Barbara J. Eshensen

Eden Force Eskin
Louise M. Espy
Jean Estill
Silas Estill
Paul Etzler
Susan Evangelista
Georgene Evans
Jim Evans
Michael Evans
Sue Evans
Thomas J. Evans
William Evans
Mrs. James O. Everett
Nesta Ewan
Eileen Ewing
Scott Ewing
Delbert Eyster
Edwin Ezor
Alice Faber
Linnea Pregler Faeth
Joe Fago
Jeanette E. Fairchild
Thomas G. Fairclough
Claire Faiver
Edward Fales Jr.
Lucile P. Falk
Paul S. Falla
Sandy Fanning
Frances D. Farber
Kirk Farber
David J. Farhi
Roberta N. Farmer
Joshua Farnum
Martin Farrell
Ted Farrell
Pete Farruggio
C. W. Faulkner
John C. Faulkner
Katherine Faydash
Mrs. Gust A. Federman
Dana M. Fee
Susan V. Feehan
Thomas P. Feeny
Ronald J. Fehrenbach
Ola V. Feighner
Julie Feit
Kenneth Felder
Mrs. Kenneth Felder
Bruce Feldt
Cynthia Felgar
Willard H. Fell Jr.
Larraine Felland
Mrs. P. Felser
Charles A. Ferguson
Donna Ferguson
Frederick Ferguson
Joseph Fernandez
Michael S. Fernandino
Sue Ferrara
Mrs. David S. Ferris
Guy Ferris
H. H. Ferris
David Fertig
Effie M. Fieldhouse
George Fieldman
Carolyn C. Finegar
Louis J. Finn
W. Bruce Finnie
Robert P. Fischelis
Mrs. E. E. Fischer

Hans M. F. Fischer
Henry G. Fischer
Martha Fish
Justin M. Fishbein
August D. Fisher
Doris Fisher
Helen Fisher
Jacob Fisher
John H. Fisher
William Fisher
Leon Fisk
Nancy Fitch
Connie Fitz
Bobby Fitzgerald
Will Fitzgerald
P. J. Flagg
Emily Flanagan
Gertrude Flanders
Beverly Flanigan
Allison Fleming
Charles Fleming
Mrs. S. F. Fleming
Kathy Flesch
Charles F. Fletcher
George B. Fletcher
Molly Fletcher
Stuart Flexner
J. Fliegel
John Fliegel
A. T. Flint
Jane Appleby Flint
Mrs. Nelson Flint
S. T. Flint
Margaret Flynn
Margaret Mannix Flynn
Mark Flynt
John Fobian
Mark Fockele
Marilyn Foit
Beulah Folkedahe
William D. Folland
Kate Follen
Brian Fone
Robert Forbes
Thelma Force
Kirkham Ford
Tammy Ford
Marguerite Forge
Guy Jean Forgue
Sandra Jo Forney
Maurice Forrester
Charles Forsmo
John E. Forss
Jerome S. Fortinsky
Ted C. Forziati
David Foss
Andy Foster
Elva M. Foster
Jerome Foster
John P. Foster
Joseph Foster
Mary Foster
Robert A. Foster
Roy Foster Jr.
Mrs. H. W. Fountain
Steve Fowle
Cynthia Fox
David Fox
W. Fox
Henry G. Francis

J. Dwight Francis	Jule Gardner	David Gold	Josephine A. Greer
W. Nelson Francis	Mrs. W. B. Gardner	Harris E. M. Goldberg	Bob J. Gregg
Carol Frank	Gerald Garfinkle	Meryl A. Goldberg	Adina Gregory
John Frank	Kathleen Garin	Mrs. Stephen Goldfarb	Douglas W. Gregory
Mabel Frank	Dave Garland	Rita Goldsberg	Elizabeth Gregory
Julia Frank-McNeil	Mrs. J. W. Garrard	Kathryn M. Goldsmith	O. Dean Gregory
S. M. Franz	Mrs. Carl Garrett	Albert Golloway	Andrea Grenadier
Charlene Fraser	Clifton N. Garrish	R. Gomoll	J. Ralph Gresham
S. W. Fratt	Dana Garrison	Dorothea R. Goodland	H. Grether
William J. Frawley	John Garrity	Mrs. Elmer Goodland	William Grey
Terry M. Fraze	Peggy Garties	Dan Goodman	Solveig Griebesland
Timothy C. Frazer	Joseph Gaskill	Morris F. Goodman	Deborah S. Griffin
Kenneth L. Frazier	J. Edward Gates	Ruth Goodpaster	Dorothy Park Griffin
Ann C. Fred	Judy C. Gates	Michelle Goodrich	Helen Griffin
Mr. and Mrs. E. B. Fred	Marion Gates	Mrs. William Goodridge	Joyce Griffin
Kathleen Fredricks	Tom Gatten	Mrs. C. T. Goolsby	Pamela J. Griffin
Susan V. Freehan	Tom Gebhart	Irene Gordon	Anna Griffith
Amanda W. Freeland	J. L. Gehrig	Junicha Gordon	Debi Griffith
Linda Freeman	John F. Geist	Matthew Gordon	Jim Griffith
Mrs. W. L. Freeman	Mrs. Paul Gelbert	Sarah Gordon	Kathy Griffith
Rudy Freench	Bruce Gelder	Ellen Cook Gore	Irwin Griggs
Helen Gugel Freidel	Mary Gelfan	Joseph F. Gore	Shirley Grindrod
Betsy Freitag	Victor Gell	Robert Gorkin	Jim Grinnell
Dale French	Howard Gelman	Virginia Gorman	Fox M. Grissette
Joe Frey	Elizabeth D. Gelvin	Sue T. Gornto	Eddie Griswold
Rosemary Frey	Bill Genda	Louis F. Gorr	Mrs. Theodore Grob
Gene Fried	Demetrius J. Georgacas	Suzanne Gose	Grant Groberg
Catherine L. Friedmann	Lillian D. George	Danusha Goska	Andrew Grogan
Franz Friedrich	Edith Ray Gerb	Eric Gossger	David Groos
Mrs. Charles C. Fries	Esther Ray Gerb	Mrs. L. J. Gosting	Lyle J. Gross
Charlotte Fries	John Gerber	Lee R. Goudee	Dana Grossman
Fred Fris	Phillip Gerber	B. Graaes	Maurice Grossman
Margie Fris	Barb Gerloff	Hugh Grady	Sidney S. Grotta
James Fritzhand	John Germaine	M. Grady	Deborah S. Grove
Carol Frome	Nancy Germaine	David L. Graham	Richard Grove
Helen S. Frothingham	Mark L. Gibbons	Rosemary Graham	Mrs. D. Russel Grover
R. L. Frothingham	Joyce Gibson	David L. Grambo	Dineen Grow
William Fry	Martha J. Gibson	Pat Watson Grande	Mrs. A. Gruel
Paul Fryxell	Nina G. Gibson	Cheri L. Grauer	Nina Grunseth
Paul Fuchs	Joy Gieseke	B. Graves	Stephen Guerra
John Fulco	Cindy Gilbert	Joni Graves	John Caldwell Guilds Jr.
Craig Fuller	Glenn G. Gilbert	Rick Graves	Mrs. J. E. Guilhaume
Dan Fuller	Hope Gilbert	Mrs. Andrew Gray	Chris Guinotte
F. Fuller	Nina Gilbert	F. Ruth Gray	Polly Gumpert
Mrs. M. Fuller	Mrs. Paul Gilbert	Mrs. Henry C. Gray	Alan M. F. Gunn
Stella Fuller	John Gildea	John Gray	Stephen Gunning
George Fullwood	Mrs. Billie Gile	Patrick Gray	Helen Guptil
Margaretta Fulton	Bernice Gilg	Wilson Gray	David B. Guralnik
Janice L. Funk	John Gilgun	Hugh P. Greeley	Meghan Gurley
F. J. Funke	Jack Gill	Edna W. Green	Gail Guzelian
Lawrence M. Furey	Isabel E. Gillespie	Eugene Green	John Robert Gwynn
S. R. Fussell	Nancy Gillespie	Georgia M. Green	Bob Haas
Al Futrell	Michele Anne Gillette	Gerald Allen Green	Mrs. Elmer Habeck
John Gabel	Mrs. John Lewis Gillin	Jerry Green	James D. Haber
Bruce Gaffney	E. Ward Gilman	John Green	Eve Marie Haberson
R. C. Gagen	Harry Gilmorado	Jonathon Green	Jane Hackney
John Gagnon	Janet Gilmore	Mrs. J. Paul Green	Lelia Hadley
Elliot N. Gale	Berit Givens	Michael Greenberg	Doris Proctor Haese
Sally M. Gall	H. R. Glascock	Joan Greenblatt	Bill Hagan
Jean Gallagher	Henry Gleason	Charles M. Greene	Mary Lou Hagan
Tracey Mulder Gallagher	Adam Glidden	David H. Greene	Marilyn Hagberg
Lisa Galvin	Gene Glock	Mrs. James Greene	Eva C. Hagen
Joan Gambill	Arthur W. Glowka	Mrs. Jim B. Greene	Otis Hager
Kenneth Gambone	Elisabeth E. Gmimler	Holly Greenfield	Phillip E. Hager
Mrs. Claude Games	James S. Gobble	Stanley B. Greenfield	Mrs. Daniel Hagge
David G. Gantt	Mrs. C. R. Gobrecht	Rebecca Greening	Joseph G. Hagloch
Robert E. Gard	Alan Godlewski	Daniel J. Greenwald III	Laura Hague
Elizabeth R. Gardner	Jane Crim Goforth	David Greenwald	Margaret Hahn
Gail I. Gardner	William J. Goggins Jr.	Ken Greenwald	Steve Hahn
Mrs. George A. Gardner	Walter Gojmerac	Mrs. W. C. Greenway	Wendy Hahn

L. Haibt
John T. Haight
Terrence Haines
Hap Hairston
Mary Hake
Susan Haldt
Rebecca Walker Hale
Wanda G. Hale
William C. Hale
Janice Haley
Mrs. A. William Hall
Anita Hall
Bethany Hall
Beverly W. Hall
Bunnie Hall
Edward B. Hall
George E. Hall
James V. Hall
Joan H. Hall
Joseph S. Hall
Mabelle Hall
Palmer Hall
Shirley M. Hall
W. Hansen Hall
James E. Hallen
David A. Haller Jr.
W. V. Halliday
Herbert Halpert
R. Halstead
Irene Nelson Halverson
John S. Hambrick
Paul Hamel
J. G. Hamilton
K. L. Hamilton
Marguerite Hamilton
George Hamlin
Willard B. Hamlin
Ken Hammel
Edward Hammond
Kerry Lin Hammond
Eric P. Hamp
Philip R. Hampe
Ian Hancock
Martha E. Hancock
David Hand
Wayland D. Hand
Louise W. Hanley
Lawton M. Hanna
James R. Hannay
Sallie Hannigan
Louise I. Hansell
Laura Hansen
Nan G. Hansen
Paul Hanson Jr.
William Hanway
J. Christopher Hapner
Leslie Happ
Kelsie Harder
Tim Hardin
John R. Harding
Nancy G. Harding
Clive Hardy
Orin Hargraves
Mrs. Richard Harlan
John Harllee
Charles Harmon
Tom Harmon
H. T. Harmsel
Marian Lee Harnach
Lynne Harnich

Blair E. Harper
Bruce Harper
Francis Harper
George G. Harper
Jocelyn Harrelson
Fred Harvey Harrington
Susanmarie Harrington
A. Harris
Barbara P. Harris
John S. Harris
Mary Harris
Roseanna Harris
Stephen P. Harris
Sue B. Harris
Cathy Harrison
Don Harrison
Helen A. Harrison
Lucy Harrison
Nigel K. Harrison
W. L. Harrison
Steve D. Harsin
J. D. Hart
Janet Hart
Norval K. Hart
Robert Hart
Betty Hartbank
Richard S. Hartenberg
Phillip Harth
Lori Hartman
Elizabeth Hartsfield
Larry Hartzke
Glynn Harvey
H. Harvey
Harriet A. Harvey
Harriet O. Harvey
Rebecca Harvey
Ray Harwood
Arthur H. Hasche
Floyd Hass
J. M. Hastings
James Hastings
Mrs. A. E. Hatch
W. D. Hathaway
Carl Hattery
Abbie I. Hatton
Libby Hatton
Robert B. Hatton Jr.
Robert B. Hatton Sr.
Einar Haugen
Eva C. Haugen
Anne Hausmann
Robert Hausmann
Bess Lomax Hawes
Kenneth Haxton
Sharyn Hay
Arthur J. Hayes Jr.
Gordon Hayes
Hannah Hayes
Susan M. Hayes
Teresa Hayes
Ajeenah Haynes
Kathryn Haynie
Ruth Chipman Hayward
Harry W. Hazard
Kristin Headley
Robert K. Headley
Mrs. Charles Heagle
Albert S. Heald
F. H. Healy
Norman A. Heap

Jean R. Heath
Sam Heaton
Linda Hebbe
Mrs. Milton P. Hebert
Mary Jo Heck
James Hedges
H. Robert Hedrick
Alice J. Hegmann
Lorraine Heidecker
Mrs. Herman Heiden
Mrs. R. C. Heidner
Mary S. Heidver
Mrs. Robert J. Heilbrunn
Edith Heilman
Matt Heilman
Robert Heilman
Mr. and Mrs. B. W. Heller
David S. Heller
Ruby Hemenway
Mr. and Mrs. R. L. Heminger
Peter A. Hemmy
Atcheson L. Hench
Bertha Hencke
Cherel Henderson
John Henderson
Robert Henderson
Mrs. E. T. Hendon
Mr. and Mrs. John E. Hendry
Isabelle Dodge Hendry
Marian Heneberg
Michael Heneghan
Simon Heninger
Stephanie Henkel
Patsy Hennessey
David M. Henry
David R. Henry
S. Henry
Sharon Henry
Terri Henry
William A. Henslee
Nancy Hepler
Anthony L. Herbert
Gretchen Herbkersman
M. J. Herman
Louise Herring
Frederick C. Hervey
Mrs. Theo Herwig
Alexander Hestoft
M. Sue Hetherington
Mrs. Hobart Hewett
Heather Hewitt
Phillip Heyer
Olga Heyn
Philip Hiche
Joe Hickerson
Matthew Hickman
Mrs. David T. Hicks
Kyle Hicks
Michael Hicks
Steve Hicks
Harrison E. Hierth
Scott Hiett
Beth Higby
Lucile Higginbotham
W. H. Higginbotham
Flora T. Higgins
Kathy Higgins
Worth J. Higgins
Ellesa C. High
Karin Highfield

Mrs. D. M. Highland
Charles Hikes
Paul Hilaire
Arthur Hildreth
Archibald Hill
Carolyn Hill
Dan Hill
Douglas D. Hill
Emily A. Hill
Mrs. Franklin J. Hill
Harold G. Hill
Mrs. I. Hill
John W. Hill
Roscoe W. Hilliker
Mrs. Ben Hill-Orr
Matthew Hills
Gary Hilton
Dorothy Himelhoch
James Hinkle
Herb Hinman
Norman Hinton
Dan H. Hinz
Betty Jean Hisle
Mrs. Carl Hittner
Adam Hixson
Lester Hochgraf
Charles F. Hockett
Eileen Hodge
Kenneth S. Hodge
Houston Hodges
Frank Hodgins
Peggy Hoehne
Al Hoekstra
Ryan Hoel
Armin Luis Hoempler
Charles S. Hoffman
Dean A. Hoffman
Frank A. Hoffman
Hilda Hoffman
Richard B. Hoffman
Kay Hoffmann
Mildred Hoffmann
Bill Hoffmeyer
Sandy Hofmann
Mrs. Roy Hogg
Frank Holan
Dan Holbrook
Nancy Holden
Ron Holder
Francis Hole
Claudia Holland
Pepper Holland
Prudence Holliger
Carolyn Hollingshed
Emily Holly
Jim Holloway
John Holm
Dorothy Holmes
Elizabeth B. Holmes
Mary Louise Holmes
Edith J. Hols
Ida Holt
Pat M. Holt
Thaddeus Holt
Cher Holt-Fortin
M. G. Holyoke
Greg Hom
Mrs. C. D. Homlerick
Bob Homme
Richard K. Hontz

Rodney T. Hood
Greg Hooker
Lydia K. Hooker
Angela Hoover
David Hopes
Mr. Hopkins
Felix Horaist Jr.
Edw. M. Horan
Gilligan Horgan
Lois Horlivy
Laurence Horn
Randolph Horn
Barbara Hornick
Mrs. Roger Hornig
Kathleen Horning
Richard Horstketter
Robert Horwitz
Mrs. Jerry J. Hosek
Heidi Crawford Hoskinson
Yvonne Hosler
John Houchens
Miriam Houchens
Charles L. Houck
Rebecca Houghton
Raynald Houghton
Doris Hounsell
R. C. House
Alston S. Householder
Hazel J. Housel
George P. Houser
Robert J. Houston
Carol R. Houston
Dorothy Houston
Maxine Houston
Milt Houston
Jane Houston
Richard K. Houtz
Mrs. Allen A. Hovda
G. Howard
Mrs. J. Reed Howard
Kathryn B. Howard
Martha C. Howard
William A. R. Howard
Katharine Howe
Mary Howe
Rosella Howe
Hulda Howell
Robert B. Howell
Florence Howe-Munat
Mrs. Warren Howland
C. R. Howlett
Mary Howley
Robert Howren
James Hoyt
Ron Hoyt
Michelle Hozer
Martha Hsu
Joe Hubbard
Richard A. Hubbard
Clarence Hubbuck
Charlie Huber
James C. Huber
Andrew Hudgins
Barbara Hill Hudson
H. Gary Hudson
Lucille Huestis
Emily Brasier Huffman
Mary E. Huffman
Scarlet Huffman
Brent Hugh

Marion Hughes
Leslie Huizenga
Chuck Hulin
Tracy Hulin
M. O. Hulsey
Edward Hume
Kerry Hummel
Philip C. Humphrey
Adria D. Humphreys
Crystal Humphreys
M. Humphreys
Edna Hunt
Gertrude Hunt
Kellogg W. Hunt
Margaret Hunt
John Hunter
Lore Hunter
Mike Huntington
Jeffrey Huntsman
Kathi Hurzeler
Mrs. John Huskey
Herman Hust Jr.
Mrs. William Hustedt
Lou Huston
William Hustrulid
Bettie Hutchinson
Geof Huth
Joel G. Hutsell
Randy Hutson
Rob Hutten
Jason A. Hutto
Clyde K. Hyder
Stephanie Hysmith
Nancy Iarossi
John S. Iavarone
Hugh Iltis
Merle Imes
John Ingham
Glen Ingle
Mark H. Ingrahan
Charlotte Ingram
Mark Ingram
M. K. Irish
Terry Irons
R. S. Irvine
Betty Irwin
Susan Isaacs
Edith Isele
Mabel Isenberger
Saul Isler
John Isom
Alfred W. Israelstam
Howard Jackson
James Jackson
Jamie Jackson
Mrs. N. S. Jackson
Prentiss W. Jackson
Elmer Jacobs
Mark S. Jacobs
Mrs. C. E. Jacobson
Harold W. Jacobson
Abigail N. James
Alfred O. James
L. C. James
Louis James
Thekla V. James
Thelma G. James
Lilias Jones Jarding
Mary Jay
Marie Jefferies

Charles M. Jenkins Jr.
Jane Jensen
Jean Jensen
Ken Jensen
Ronald Jensen
Bob Jerrolds
Stephen C. Jett
Elizabeth Jewell
Lisa Jillani
Doris Jimison
Ann Johes
Janet McCullough John
Claude Johns
Telise E. M. Johnsen
Don Johnsey
Abigail Johnson
Alice Johnson
Amanda Johnson
Ann Johnson
Barbara Y. Johnson
Betty Johnson
Mrs. C. H. Johnson
Mrs. Carl Johnson
Carol Johnson
Edith T. Johnson
Ellen Johnson
Mrs. Frank B. Johnson
Hazel Johnson
Herbert B. Johnson
Inez Lysle Johnson
John W. Johnson
M. T. Johnson
Maggie Johnson
Maggie L. Johnson
Marion T. Johnson
Miriam Johnson
Nan Johnson
Paul Johnson
Robert E. Johnson
Robert T. Johnson
Sallie Johnson
Scott Johnson
Mrs. C. T. Johnston
Mrs. Grant Johnston
Inez Johnston
Paul Johnston
Anne Johnstone
Virginia Carville Joki
Mrs. Jones
A. P. Jones
Alice R. Jones
Andrew Jones
Dennis Jones
Gwen M. Jones
Helen Jones
Howard Mumford Jones
J. H. Jones
Joseph Jones
Kirkland Jones
Morgan E. Jones
Mrs. Robert Jones
Sarah Jones
Timothy Jones
Tristan Jones
Mary Jordan
Mrs. Samuel Jordan
Peter Colt Josephs
Meredith Josey
David Jost
Betty Joyce

Fritz Juengling
Ellen Rhea Kai
Fred Kaiser
Jeffrey Kallen
Dorothy C. Kaminski
Naomi U. Kaminsky
Frederic Kammann
Sarah Kampman
Mrs. B. Kanatz
Alice Kane
M. Martin Kane
Monty Kane
Steve Kane
Chris Kantarjiev
Nathan Kantrowitz
Doris Kaplan
Mae Kaplan
Shane Karas
Elizabeth Karier
Esther Karolus
Karen Kassirer
Stanley Katz
Mrs. John A. Kay
Lorin L. Kay
Mrs. M. B. Keeley
Mrs. Leroy F. Keely
James E. Keenan
Don Keep
Edna Keep
Steve Hartman Keiser
Lisa Keith
Clay R. Kelleher
Rick Keller
Mrs. Ed Kelley
Esther Kellner
Carol Kelly
Kathleen Kelly
Robert Kelly
William H. Kelly
Susan Kelsey
John Conley Kelsh
Ann Kemler
Lorena E. Kemp
Robin Kemp
Theresa Kemp
Marshall Kemper
James G. Kennedy
Mrs. John A. Kennedy
Laura Kennelly
William B. Kenney
Amos Kent
Walter Keough
Audrey Kerber
Joy Kerby
Cinnamon Kern
Florence V. Kerr
Harry Kerr
Harry D. Kerr
William Kerwin
Tom Keslin
Mark Kessinich
June Kessler
David M. Key Jr.
Mary Ritchie Key
William E. Keys
Robert W. Keyser
S. Perry Keziah
James Kibler
Joyce Kiel
Evabeth M. Kienast

Nicholas Kiessling
James J. Kilpatrick
Amy Kinast
Beth Kiley Kinder
Bill King
Charles A. King
Christopher King
Howard King
Kitty King
Marge King
Robert D. King
Walter King
Warren J. King
Murray Kinloch
Willis Kinnear
Ruth Kinnersly
William Kinter
E. Kintgen
T. A. Kirby
Mary Chase Kirwin
William Kirwin Sr.
Kenneth Kister
Luke Kittell
Richard Kivi
Enno Klammer
Mark Klan
Catherine Klein
Ila Ware Klein
Jeff Klein
Philip E. Klein
Stephanie Klein
Thea S. Klein
Stephen Kleinedler
Emma F. Kleinhammer
Kay Klier
H. T. Kline
Helen T. Kline
Linda Kloss
Robert J. Kloss
Judith Klug
Thomas S. Knap
Russell W. Knapp
Sheila Y. Knee
Kenneth L. Knickerbocker
Betsy Knight
Carol Knight
G. M. Knight
Katharine E. Knight
Kevin Knight
Mrs. H. M. Knilans
Marguerite Knilans
Bruce Knoll
Joy Knoll
T. L. Knott
Richard Knowles
Judith Knowlton
James M. Knox
Bruce E. Knutson
Nicole Kobrowski
Julia A. Koenig
Miriam Koffler
Michael F. Kohl
James F. Kokolis
Gwin J. Kolb
Hal Kolb
Jean Kolb
Philip C. Kolin
Edward J. Kollar
Joseph Kolupke
Marsha Kong

Elsie Konkin
Bill Konther
Judith Kornblatt
Gregory Kornbluh
Nancy Korte
Art Kosatka
James Kotmair
Dave Kowal
Melinda Koyanis
Ralph Koziarski
Albert Krahn
Allan L. Kramer
Philip Krapp
Steve Kratzky
Lynn S. Kratz-Ryan
Beatrice Krauss
Steve Krauth
Mike Krejci
Charlotte Kretzoi
Robert Krieger
Lauren Kriz
Phil Kronenwetter
William E. Kruck
John R. Krueger
W. R. Krueger
Ken Krugh
Kevin Krugh
Virginia Moore Kruse
Mrs. W. Kube
Mai Kuha
Debbie Kuhlmann
Walter Kuhlmann
Sherman M. Kuhn
Ken Kuiper
Al Kulik
John Kulka
Max Kumerow
Theresa Kump
John Kunstadter Jr.
Hans Kurath
Charles Kurth
Tom Kysilko
William Labov
Eric La Cruze
Ken Ladwig
Rita Ladwig
Lois W. LaFord
Roland La France
Mrs. Beryl Lagerholm
Walter Lagerwey
Renee Lajcak
Valerie LaMay
Lois J. Lambie
Christian La Mont
Donald M. Lance
James A. Landau
Sidney I. Landau
Susan Landes
Mrs. L. Landfried
Symington P. Landreth
William Landrum
Nicholas Lane
William G. Lane
William T. Lane
Frank A. Lang
James Langdon
Kenneth I. Lange
Sue Lange
Mary Langenfeld
Elizabeth A. Langhorne

Virginia Langlois
Ron Langworthy
Joyce Lanoue
Carol Lapsley
Henry Lardy
Donald Larmouth
Kerri LaRoe
William L. Larsen
Christina Larson
Eleanor Larson
John Larson
Gerry Larvey
Jan Lathrop
Charles M. Latta
Mrs. H. W. Latton
Geraldine Laudati
Jeanne A. Lauge
Ann Lauinger
Perry Laukhuff
Greg Lauterbach
Hope J. La Vine
L. Lawcock
John Lawrence
L. Gillette Lawrence
R. Lawrence
William R. Lawrence
David Lawton
Jean Lawton
Margaret R. Lay
Jeri Laythe
Chuck Layton
Arnold Lazarus
Barbara Lazerson
Edna R. Leach
Jane Leake
James P. Leary
Warren D. Leary Jr.
Thomas A. Lechner
Nolan P. LeCompte
Ethel G. Lecount
Richard Lederer
Mrs. Fred C. Lee
Linda Lee
Margaret Lee
Matthew C. Lee
Rosa Lee
Sean Leenaerts
Mrs. John LeFeber
Mrs. C. M. Lefevre
Maxine LeGall
P. F. Legard
Mrs. L. I. Legrid
Larry Legus
Winfred P. Lehmann
Benjamin Lehr
Donald Lehr
Benjamin W. Leigh
H. P. Leighly Jr.
Edward P. Leight
Sara B. Leighton
Ray H. Leith
Mr. and Mrs. Lowell P. Leland
Rosie Lemanek
Walter Lemann
John Lemberger
Fannie LeMoine
William T. Lenehan
Jacob Lennon
Mrs. Clifford Leonard
Minita Bradford Leonard

Patrick Leonard
Girard Lepine
W. D. Lepping
Roy F. Leslie
Maryann Leuschner
Susan Leveille
Elizabeth D. Levers
Mrs. Louis H. Levi
Melissa B. Levi
Mimi K. Levin
Seymour R. Levine
Alfred Levinson
Hal Levy
Brian Lewis
Joy S. Lewis
Leon E. Lewis
Marjorie J. Lewis
Sammy Lee Lewis
Suzanne Lewis
Russell Libby
E. K. Liberatore
Ilse A. Liberto
Michael Licht
Warren Liddle
Edith K. Lieb
Herman W. Liebert
Dennis Lien
Susanna Lienhard
Richard A. Light
Bernice Lightbourn
George Lightbourn
Jonathan Lighter
Richard G. Lillard
Regina L. Linares
Ericka Lindemann
Dean Linder
John P. Linderman
Edith D. Lindsey
Clara L. Lindsley
Joe Lineberger
Brunetta Lingg
Kate Lingley
Mrs. R. L. Linkletter
Mike Linn
Larry W. Linnell
Jean G. Linton
Mrs. Thomas Linton
W. I. Linton
Daniel Lipkin
Billy Lipsey
Randal Livesay
Iva Livesey
Mrs. R. B. Livingston
Joan Livingston-Webber
Dave Lloyd
John B. Lloyd
Leah Lockett
Mrs. Arthur Loder
Dorothy Loder
Julie Loesch
Douglas A. Logan
Rita Logan
Marion Iverson Loges
Judith A. Lola
Barbara Long
Richard A. Long
Rob Long
David Longfellow
Robert Longley
Calvin Look

Battell Loomis
John Ward Wilson Loose
Anton P. Lorenzen
Ann G. Lorenzo
William L. Lorton
Mildred Burke Lothson
Brian Lotierzo
Charles Loucks
Mark Louden
Robert Louthan
Ed Lovelace
Louise Loveridge
Karen Lowe
Ernest H. Lowenthal
Mrs. Julius Lowin
Gail Lowry
Alex Lubertozzi
Hilda Lubui
Mavis C. Lueddecke
Mrs. Harold Lueder
Hans Luetscher
Henry S. Lufler
Miriam Luke
Robert M. Lumiansky
Kim Lundgren
Herbert Lust
Julie Luther
Orion W. Lutz
William Lutz
Rex Luxton
J. Lyle
Mrs. Frank Lyman
Cosima V. Lyttle
Mrs. Isenberger Mabel
Emmett W. MacCorkle
Michael MacDonald
Thelma MacDonald
Katherine MacFarlane
M. M. MacFarlane
Sandra Macias
Bentley MacKay
Stuart MacKenzie
Mrs. F. W. Mackie
Allan H. MacLaine
Vernon D. Mac Laren
Andrew MacLeish
William Connor MacLeod
Mr. and Mrs. John Maclin Jr.
William Mac Phuson
Linda Alma Madali
John P. Madison
Christine Madsen
Brooke L. Magnanti
Pat Maharg-Phila
Thomas Mahon
David E. Maier
Fred C. Maier
Natalie Mainland
Sara Mainquist
Helen R. Malin
Charles Malley
Laura Malley
Peter J. Malone
Loring Mandel
Mark Mandel
Gerry Mandell
Leon Mandell
David Mangan
Pat Manley
Herbert Mann

Mr. and Mrs. Morgan Mannchen
Margaret Mansfield
Mrs. C. L. Manson
Dorothy West Manson
Mike Manson
Rennie Custis Mapp
Elizabeth Marcheschi
Peter J. Marci
W. Marcin
Albert H. Marckwardt
Robert Marcom
Earl L. Marcoux
Barbara Hoch Marcus
George W. Marek Sr.
P. Marfilius
John Mariani
Avra Mark
Floyd Markham
Ingrid Swamberg Markhardt
Joan Markides
Sandra C. Markman
Brian Marrs
Mrs. J. W. Marsh
Kevin Marsh
Nadine Marsh
W. Marsh
Mrs. William Marsh
Elizabeth Marshall
Michele Marshall
Sandra Marshall
Sister M. André Marthaler
Ann Martin
Claude Martin
Delores Martin
Ellen Martin
Jack Martin
Jennifer Martin
Lauren Martin
Mrs. W. L. Martin
Carol Bird Martindale
Paul Marvel
Bill Marvin
Hal Marx
Robert L. Marx
Mrs. Henry Mashburn
Carrie L. Mason
Eileen Mason
Lou Mason
Mrs. N. P. Mason
Robert Mason
Stewart Mason
William L. Mason Jr.
Blanche Massey
H. E. Maston
George B. Mastovich
Myrl S. Mather
Mitford M. Mathews
Susan Mathews
Gerry Mathias
David Mathis
Lauren Mathis
John Mathison
Joy Hoffman Matkowski
Dan M. Matson
Mark Matson
David B. Mattern
Greg Matthews
Jean Matthews
Susan Benton Matthews
William Matthews

Ernest W. Mattison Sr.
Edward Mattson
David Maurer
Ellen Maurer
Richard D. Maxwell
Lisa May
Jo Harmon Mayer
Victoria Mayer
Greg Mayes
Mike Maynard
Natalie Maynor
D. B. McCallum
James L. McCamy
Julia B. McCamy
Michael McCauley
Devereaux McClatchey
Mark McClendon
Catherine McCloy
Scott McClure
Eleanor McClurkin
Sally McCluskey
Lynn McColl
June McCormack
Doug McCormick
Jane McCormick
Jackie McCowen
Jack M. McCreless
Jeff McCullers
Michael McCune
William H. McCurdy
Dorotha McDaniel
Susan McDaniel
Raven I. McDavid Jr.
Virginia Glenn McDavid
Douglas McDonald
W. U. McDonald Jr.
Tim McDonough
Sarah J. McDowell
Bonnie S. McElhinny
Allen McElwain
Mrs. Harry McEnerny Jr.
Kathryn A. McEuen
Mr. and Mrs. K. H. McFall
Anne McFarland
Mrs. Neal G. McFarland
Marjorie McFarlane
Christine McGeary
James C. McGhee
Jim McGill
Trish McGill
Barbara J. McGinness
Janet Fester McGlynn
Mrs. Robert L. McGlynn
Gladys H. McGowan
Joseph P. McGowan
Eric R. McGrail
Joyce McGrath
John McGraw
Peter McGraw
Sally McGraw
Dick McGwinn
Iris McHeurg
Pat McIlrath
Alexander H. McIntire Jr.
Mr. and Mrs. Dwight McIntosh
Robert B. McIntosh
Erin McKean
Alexander McKenzie
Rima McKinzey
Bill McLane

Jeff McLaughlin
Kathy McLaughlin
Patricia Mclean
Jim McLinden
Kate McLuskie
Jeffery L. McMahan
J. W. McMahon
Douglas R. McManis
Marjory McMickle
James B. McMillan
Charles McMorris
Mrs. F. J. McMurray
V. D. McMurray
Berenice McNett
Mrs. Elmer D. McNett
Jeff McQuain
Mrs. R. E. McQueen
Mary Anne McQuillan
Kevin McSweeney
Patrick McWhinter
J. W. McWilliams
Doug Meadows
Sandy Meadows
Marianne Means
Mary E. Mebane
Jeff Medaugh
Karen Medsker
Mrs. J. R. Meek
Robert Meek
Joseph W. Meeker
Mrs. Meidell
Tom Meier
Robert J. Meindl
George Melcher
Lewis B. Melson
Mrs. D. R. Melton
DeJean Melton
Joyce Melton
David Menich
Rick Mercado
Marilyn Mercer
Germaine Mercier
David Merciez
Mamie Meredith
Sally Meredith
Hortense Mergen
Gregory Merrick
Sue Merrick
Grant Merrill
O. E. Merrill
John Mertus
Linda Mertus
Mrs. E. E. Mescar
A'ndrea Elyse Messer
Jean Messersmith
Betty B. Messier
Allan Metcalf
Teri Metcalf
Conrad B. Metz
Julia Meuers
John W. Meyer
Lester Meyer
Martine Meyer
Terry Meyer
Timothy A. Meyer
Julia R. Meyers
Miriam Meyers
Bill Mican
Matthew M. Miceli
Katherine Michel

Pierre Michel
Ethelyn D. Michell
Mrs. Ed Middleton
William Middleton
Brad Midgette
George Mielke
Lee C. Milazzo Jr.
Joseph B. Milgram
Merrl T. Milks
Alan Miller
Anne Miller
Byron Miller
D. A. Miller
Elinor Miller
Ericka Miller
Gail Miller
Harvey Miller
Inez L. Miller
James L. Miller
Jerry Miller
Jess Miller
John W. Miller
Leah Miller
Mary Louise Miller
Michael I. Miller
Nancy E. Miller
Pat Searles Miller
Patricia Miller
Peggy Miller
Raymond A. Miller
Robert H. Miller
Roy E. Miller
Samuel J. Miller
Thomas H. Miller
Vern Miller
Roger E. Mills
David Millstone
Celia Millward
Roger Milnes
Joseph Milosh
Fred Milverstedt
Celia Milward
A. J. Mims
Mrs. Randolph Mincey
Karl A. Minch
Catherine Mintz
Frederick Mish
Margaret Mishoe
Jacquelyn Mitchard
Clint Mitchell
Eleanor R. Mitchell
Elinor Mitchell
Felicia Mitchell
John R. Mitchell
Mary Lu Mitchell
David Mladenoff
Esther Moak
Carol Mock
Sabine Mödersheim
Jacob W. Moelk
Bob Moers
Austin Moffat
Regan Moffat-Masti
Jennifer Mohr
Charles F. Moles
Bonnie Molina
Christine Molling
Kathleen Molling
Joseph B. Monda
Ruth Robbins Monteith

B. Elwood Montgomery
J. Anne Montgomery
Michael B. Montgomery
Marta Moody
Bill Moore
Bradley Moore
Caroline Moore
Cynthia L. Moore
Diana C. Moore
Douglas Moore
Mrs. H. S. Moore
Ive G. Moore
Mrs. J. F. Moore
Jane Moore
Mrs. L. A. Moore
Robert H. Moore
Rolland B. Moore
T. Allison Moore
Zerelda Moore
Aleta Moorhouse
Paul Mooring
Emily Morahito
Edmund Moran
Ethel Morey
Janina Morgalla
Bernard Morgan
Dorothy Morgan
Frances Morgan
Paul Morgan
Ruth Morgan
Tony Morgan
Mary Morginski
Eugene Moriarty
Michelle Morley
A. C. Morris
Acala Morris
George Morris
James Morris
John Morris
Martha Morris
Michelle Morris
Tom Morris
Mrs. V. E. Morris
William Morris
Chris Morrison
John W. Morrison
Steve Morrison
Walter Morrison III
Linda Morrison
Mrs. Matthew Morrow
Mildred Morrow
Carl M. Mortensen
Lynn Mortensen
Harvey W. Mortimer
Lynn Mortimer
Mary Mortimer
Colin Morton
Marian Morton
Ramon E. Mosteiro
William G. Moulton
Anna Moyer
Reid V. Mueller
Mrs. William A. Mueller
A. Lawrence Muir
Sharon Mulak
Bill Mullins
Mrs. H. F. Mullins
E. R. Mulvihill
Mrs. R. C. Munkwitz
Pam Munro

Alfred W. Munson
David Murdock
Alison Murie
Charles D. Murphy
Gertrude Murphy
Kathy Murphy
Lynne Murphy
Neil Murphy
R. Murphy
Richard Murphy
Thomas H. Murphy
Tom Murphy
Jean C. Murray
Ms. Ottilie M. Murray
Tammy Murray
Tom Murray
Mernice Murthy
Karin Murto
David Muschell
R. G. Musgrove
Warren Musgrove
Doris T. Myers
Mrs. Orvall Myers
Vera H. Myers
Younghee Na
Fred P. Naber
Eddie Lou Nachtrieb
Mrs. Thomas Nack
Virginia U. Nader
Franklyn G. Naffziger
Kristina Nailen
Michelle Napier
Vicki Nast
Simon Nathan
Bill Naughton
Julia Neal
L. E. Neal
Gay Neale
Barbara Need
Judy Chace Needham
Katherine Needham
Cheryl Cain Neelster
Priscilla Neil
Mrs. Belford Nelson
Burton R. Nelson
Cornelia Nelson
Ed Nelson
Gordon Nelson
Kari Bjorg Nelson
Linda Nelson
Mary Nelson
Marion Nereiw
Felix Nerod
Barbara Nesbit
R. D. Ness
Robert Ness
Harold R. Nestler
Stacy Nesvik
C. Netelkos
Claude Henry Neuffer
Gary T. Neul
Georgine R. Neureiter
N. P. Neureiter
Mark Nevelow
Bruce E. Nevin
Lee H. Newlon
Mrs. Carleton Newman
Colleen Newman
John B. Newman
Lelamae Newman

Cherry Underwood Newpher
P. M. Nibbelink
Spencer Nichol
Beverly Nichols
Mr. and Mrs. D. A. Nichols
Stanley A. Nichols
Wendalyn Nichols
Jane Nicholson
Joe Niedbala
Henry Niedzielski
Vic Nielsen
Mrs. Kio Nienow
Janis Vizier Nihart
Mrs. William Nikolai
Alleen P. Nilsen
Don L. F. Nilsen
Evelyn Nimz
John Nitti
Alma Nitz
Mrs. H. C. Nitz
Roberta H. Nixon
Dan Noland
Rutte C. Noland
Edward C. Nolte
Harriet Nordolm
Reinhold Nordsieck
Kim Norman
Dixie M. Normandy
Evan Norris
Katie Norris
Marie Norris
Dorotha Northrup
Helen Northup
Barbara Norton
Don Norton
Mrs. F. L. Norton III
Dwight Norwood
Tom Novak
Karen Nowac
Thomas D. Noyers III
Terry Noyes
W. Roger Nugent
Mark Nuhfer
Richard Nunley
Lisa Ann Nusynowitz
E. A. Nutt
Lisa Nygaard
Ann Oakes
L. Robert Oaks
David R. Obey
Dal O'Brien
Dave O'Brien
Greg O'Brien
Joan O'Brien
Kathy O'Brien
Vincent O'Brien
Ray O'Cain
Mrs. R. H. O'Callaghan
Barb O'Connell
Virginia Dayton O'Connell
Stephanie Oddleifson
Joan O'Donnell
Pat O'Donoghue
Marie R. Oesting
Mrs. C. W. Ofelt
Margaret Ogden
Guillermo Ogilvie
Mrs. P. J. O'Hanlon
Mary O'Hare
Ken Ohm

James Okkema
Rinkart E. Okorie
Robin Oldham
Edward Oleen
Mr. and Mrs. L. Oliver
Daphne Ollman
Robert Olmsted
Mrs. A. M. Olsen
Mrs. Jerome Olsen
W. Scott Olsen
Stella Lanna (Henderson) Olson
Storrs L. Olson
Travis Olson
Mike Olson
Frankie O'Neal
Libby O'Neal
Rex O'Neal
Steve O'Neal Jr.
Robert O'Neil
James C. O'Neill
Pat O'Neill
Linda H. O'Quinn
Pat Orcutt
Sarah Ord
Priscilla Ord
Naomi O'Reilly
Donald Oresman
Michael Orlowski
Donald Orth
Clifton Osbon
Chet Osborn
Allen Osborne
Volney R. Osha
S. H. Oslund
John Oughton
Mrs. C. L. Ouweneel
Marjorie Overacre
Mrs. Paul Overson
Scott Overton
Susan Ovington
Margaret Ovitt
Jerry W. Owen
Jim Owen
Mary Ozee
Yvonne Ozzello
George B. Pace
Daniel S. Padovano
Thomas Paikeday
Sylvia H. Paikowski
Shana Palm
Alice Palma
Allan Palmer
Roger Palmer
William Palmer
Vince Palumbo
Carrie Papa
Elizabeth Pape
Ray Pardue
Bob Parenteau
Mrs. E. W. Park
Jeanne R. Parker
John J. Parker
Michael P. Parker
Watson Parker
William R. Parker
Caryl Parks
Mary Celestia Parler
Ed Parolini
Cliff Parrett
Fred Parrow-Schuhle

Robert Parslow
Allyn Partin
Don Partridge
Monica Pataki
Linda Patch
Henry E. Patrick
Wilbur T. Patterson
Jean Patton
Raymond Paufil
James Paul
Edna W. Paulson
Wayne Pauly
Avis Payne
Dwight Payne
Mrs. H. A. Payne
Kevin J. Payne
Katy Elizabeth Pearce
Thomas M. Pearce
Betty Pearson
Stephanie Peck
Jim Peckosh
Rachel M. Peden
Joyce Pederson
Lee A. Pederson
David Peebles
Marion Peet
Debbie Peetz
Lisa Peinstein
Richard Peiser
Phillip Pellitteri
Ivan J. Pels
Liz Pelton
A. P. Pemrock
Arthur Pence
Robert Pender
Pam Pendergrass
Renee Pendleton
G. S. Penn
Karl L. Pennau
Lee C. Penry
Roi Penton
Robert F. Perkins
Sheila Perkins
Deborah Perkinson
Marianne Perlak
Vincent Perricelli
Aimee Perrin
Porter Perrin
Darby Perry
Frances Roberts Perry
Mrs. George Perry
Ginger Perry
M. Perry
Patricia Crotty Perry
Pauline Perry
Steve Perry
Ted Perry
Tom Perry
Frances B. Person
Philip H. Person
Dana Pertermann
Mrs. George Peschke
Alice Peters
Brenda Peters
Mrs. Gilbert E. Peters
Nancy L. Peters
Pearl H. Peters
Rise J. Peters
Robert A. Peters
Robert P. Peters

Kraig Petersen
Sabra Petersmann
Mrs. J. L. Peterson
Kristi Peterson
Robert Peterson
Herbert Petit
John Pettey
Lani Pettit
David Pfeiffer
Audrey I. Phelps
Beverly A. Phelps
Edward C. Phelps
George A. Phelps
George Phelps
Richard C. Phelps
Rita Phelps
Stephen E. Phelps Jr.
Betty S. Phillips
David Phillips
Terri Phillips
Frank G. Pickel
Joseph Pickett
Brian Pickrell
Erma Pieczonka
Jonathan Piel
Mrs. R. A. Piepenburg
Roy D. Pierce
William C. Pierce
Earl W. Pierson
Nancy A. Pietrafesa
Jill Pietrolewicz
Donna Pigeon
Wenceslaus J. Pilch
Jane Piliavin
Samantha Pillar
Sonya Pilley
Claude O. Pinkerton
Dave Piper
Mrs. H. B. Piper
Carmine J. Pisarro
Mrs. Philip Piton
Louis Pitschmann
Virginia Pitt
Frema T. Pittelman
Dan Pittillo
Sister Mary Dominic Pitts
Thomas Piturm
Lisa Pizzarello
Conrad Planas
Doris Platt
Mrs. H. W. Planeuf
Julie Plier
Mrs. E. W. Ploner
Jeff Plude
Ruth Pochmann
Charles D. Poe
Janet Poirrier
Herbert Pollan
Calvin E. Pollins
Geoffrey Polma
Marvin Polonsky
Joanne Pomar
Mrs. Alfred Pomerening
Joe Ponessa
Jason Poniatowski
John Popalis
Mike Pope
Barry Popik
Margaret Popovich
Jim V. L. Porter

K. W. Porter
Gregory E. Posey
Eric Potter
Brian Potter
Ted Potter
Sandra Pottieger
Mrs. Glenn Powell
Richard Powell
Mrs. T. R. Powell Jr.
William Powell
William S. Powell
Walter Pressey
Andrew Preston
Braxton Preston
Carol Preston
Dennis Preston
Antje Price
Robert P. Price
Walter V. Price
J. D. Prim
Mrs. Lewis Prosser
William Proxmire
Jeff Prucher
Denise Prutsman
Gordon R. Pscheidt
Gordon Pschudt
Rachel Psutka
Gregory Pulliam
Janice P. Pulsifer
William Pulte Jr.
Lenora Purcell
R. B. Purdum
Fritz Purnell
Thomas Purnell
Albert Purpura
Mrs. Albert Purpura
Jeff Putman
Allan Ray Putnam
Karen Putnam
Mrs. Willard Putney
Richard Pyle
Rex Pyles
Thomas Pyles
Avis Quackenbush
Jane Quell
H. W. Quick
Wilbert Quick
Elizabeth E. Quiemler
Madeline Quigley
Willard V. Quine
Thom Quinn
Randolph Quirk
Diane M. Rabson
John Race
B. C. Racine
Maureen Rada
Robert Rademacher
Bob Rader
Jim Rader
Lulu J. Radlund
Roger Radtke
Betsy Laucius Rafal
Sam Raff
Imogene Ragon
Marilyn Raia
John Raimo
Eric Raimy
Charles C. Raines
R. M. Rainwater
Margaret Rajkovich

Jan Ralston
William K. Ramage
Veronica Ramirez
James Waters Ramsey
Earle S. Randall
Mrs. Harry Randall Jr.
Phyllis R. Randall
William Randel
Mrs. Robert Randolph
S. John Rannazzisi
Kim Rapczak
Linda Rapp
Mrs. Donald L. Rasmussen
Fred W. Rasmussen
Walter E. Rasmusson
Mrs. E. H. Ratcliff
M. Ravenscraft
D. H. Rawlings
Frances P. Rawnsley
Barbara Ray
Lisa Ray
Richard Ray
Ethel S. Raymond
Loisjean Raymond
Allen Walker Read
Pettus Read
W. Charles Read
Norman Reamer
Jim Reddick
Mrs. Reddin
Daniel Reddin
John Reddington
Martha Redeker
Carroll Reed
David Reed
J. H. Reed
Monique Reed
Agnes Reese
Jane Reese
John Reesing
Pamela Reichmann
Karl-Eric Reif
George Reinecke
John E. Reinecke
Earl W. Reinhold
Dean Reinlein
Peter Reiser
Harriet DeMott Reiss
Mrs. W. A. Reitz
Cynthia Reitzi
Jeff Rembold
Mrs. Ralph Remeschatis
Owen J. Remington
David A. Remley
Kate Remlinger
Gemma Rendell
Maria M. Rerrich
Mrs. Edwin Respess
Mrs. M. G. Reuter
Cecil Reynolds
Ann Boon Rhea
Gerri Rhoades
Leila S. Rhodes
Sheryl Rhodes
Carlene Riccelli
Gladys Johnson Rice
John T. Rice
Michael Rice
Ruth Rice
T. E. Rice

Warner G. Rice
Mrs. William G. Rice
William Roy Rice
Robert Richamn
Frank Richards
Louise Richards
John C. Richardson
Judy Richardson
Lois Pestle Richardson
F. W. Richardson
Barbara A. Richmond
Laurence P. Richmond
Beverly Ricks
Walter B. Rideout
Robin Rider
Max Riedlsperger
Kris Ries
Bob Rihl
Deborah Riley
Kathryn Riley
Mark Riley
Grace G. Rinehart
Landon H. Risteen
Sylvia Ritz
Mrs. Frank Roach
Mr. and Mrs. Kenneth A. Robb
William Roberson
A. Hood Roberts
Dennis Roberts
Mrs. M. B. Roberts
Norman Roberts
Rachel Roberts
Randy Roberts
Robert R. Roberts
Mrs. W. R. Roberts
Marcia Graves Robertson
Margaret Robertson
Thomas Robertson Jr.
Thomas L. Robertson
Bill Robinson
Cathy Robinson
Mrs. Denis Robinson
Fred C. Robinson
Jennifer Robinson
Jodi Robinson
John Robinson
Kenneth Robinson
Michael H. Robinson
Myles Robinson
Barbara Robson
Will Roby
Lucian L. Rocke Jr.
Mr. and Mrs. Earl Rodeheffer
John Rodenbeck
B. Rodgers
Bruce Rodgers
Alyson Rodi
Charles Roe
Dawn Roe
Rose Rogalewski
Maxine Rogalski
Bruce Rogers
Catherine L. Rogers
Dennis Rogers
Don Rogers
Donald Rogers
H. L. Rogers
Orville F. Rogers
Rebecca Rogers
Mrs. T. Hunton Rogers

Tom Rogers
Joan H. Rohan
Dwayne Rohweder
Jeanne Romero
Ethel Grod-Zins Romm
Charlotte Rooda
Adrian Roop
Charlotte Roorda
Nick Roorda
Wilma Roorda
Rene Roper
Alvin R. Rose
Judy Rose
Mrs. R. A. Rose
Sarah Ryan Rose-Jensen
Tamara Rosemeyer
Regina A. Rosemire
Edward H. Rosenberry
Arthur J. Rosenthal
Charlotte A. Rosenthal
John Rosine
Susan Rosine
Charles Ross
Daniel Ross
Mrs. O. A. Ross
Peter B. Ross
Simeon Ross
Vanessa Rossi
Lynette Roth
Stephen Roth
Barbara Rouse
George F. Rovegno Jr.
Mrs. James Rowe
Norma H. Rowe
Bernice M. Rowell
Betty H. Rowell
Mrs. G. E. Rowell
Jeffery Craig Rowley
Sara Rozycki
Jerzy Rubach
Ann Elise Rubin
Linda Ruble
August Rubrecht
Susan Rucker
Tim Ruckle
Eric Rude
Robert S. Rudolph
Walter Rue
Grace S. Rueter
Charles J. Rufino
Catherine L. Rumbaugh
Lynda Rummel
Gwen Runkle
Jacob C. Ruppenthal
I. Willis Russell
Steven S. Russell
Marty Russo
C. Rutherford
Phillip R. Rutherford
Ann Rutledge
Jack Rutledge
Allan Ryan
Harry F. Ryan
Patricia Ryan
Mrs. A. N. Saalsaa
Lynn Sabin
Ellen Sachtjen
S. J. Sackett
Esther Safford
William Safire

Pat Sage
Andrea Sahlin
Mrs. E. N. Sainio
Linda Salazar
Paul Salazar
Joseph Salmons
Sarah Salmonson
Mike Salovesh
Peggy Salovesh
Mario G. Salvadori
Bill Salvatore
Barbara Sample
Barbara M. Samples
John Sanborn
Gary Sandefur
Toni Sandell
David Sanders
Frederick Sanders
Gabriel Sanders
Leon Sanders
Maria M. Sanders
Charles Harrison Sanderson
Donald Sands
H. G. Sandstrom
Mrs. H. R. Santa Cruz
Mrs. Albert Santos
G. Sanwick
H. Sanwick
Irv Saposnik
Mary Sargent
Alexander Sartwell
R. E. Sass
Patrick E. Saunders
Muriel R. Saville
Alice Sawell
Jacqueline J. Sawicki
Janet Sawyer
Mrs. D. F. Sayre
Lucia K. P. Sayre
Robert A. Scala
Kelly Purcell Scalzo
Alice Schacht
Paul L. Schacht
James M. Schaefer
Rosemary Schaefer
Paul Schaffner
Mrs. Oscar Schaubs
Hannah Schechter
Billie C. Scheel
Natalie Schenker
L. T. Schieffelin Jr.
J. T. Schiek
Mary E. Schiller
Barbara Schilling
Mrs. M. A. Schilling
Stephen Schilling
Lora Schlaefer
Walter Schlager
C. Schlei
Megan Schliesman
June Schmaal
Thomas W. Schmidlin
Eleanor Griswold Schmidt
Mrs. Ervin Schmidt
H. R. Schmidt
Ken Schmidt
N. Schmidt
Janet Schmoll
Amy Schnapper
C. G. Schneider

Gretchen Schneider
Marian M. Schneider
Steven C. Schoen
Roland L. Schoepf
Mrs. W. E. Schoepke
Ed Schten
Beth Schuett
Seth Schulberg
Monya Schulenberg
Dan Schultz
Dodi Schultz
Gloria Schultz
Sue Schultz
Karen Schumacher
W. Wilfried Schumacher
F. X. Schupper
Bill Schurk
Ardyth Schuster
Karen Schuster-Jones
Jay Schutawie
Mrs. Schveckert
Mrs. Walter Schwarz
V. Gerald Scordan
Barbara Scott
Charles T. Scott
Mrs. Ernest Lyman Scott
Garrett Scott
Helen Scott
Leona Scott
Paul R. Scott
Mrs. Robert D. Scott
Ruth F. Scott
Mr. and Mrs. Walter E. Scott
Bill Seal
Mr. and Mrs. Merton M. Sealts
John R. Searles
Linda Seebach
R. F. Seeburger
Alan K. Seeger
Lawrence Seeger
Rita Seeligson
Lester Seifert
Mrs. Thomas Seighman
Jennifer Selchow
Rosemary Selep
R. J. Selig Jr.
Jack Sell
Sheri Sell
Joe Selner
Mrs. R. M. Semrow
Alfred Senn
Mrs. S. Senseney
Mike Serafin
Mary C. Severinghaus
Keith Severns
Phil Sexton
Catherine Seybold
Richard K. Seymour
Deb Shafer
Richard J. Shaginaw
Irving Shain
Sharon Shaloo
Ron Shapella
Mrs. Albert Shapiro
Kevin A. Shapiro
Norman R. Shapiro
Aaron J. Sharp
Ann Sharp
Harry Sharp
William D. Sharpe

William A. Shauck
Paul Shawcross
John A. Shea
M. Sheaffer
Cindy Sheahan
Michael Sheehan
Fertelle P. Sheffield
Connie Shehan
Jesse Sheidlower
Esther K. Sheldon
Paul Sheldon
Harvey Shelton
Israel Shenker
Mrs. Robert O. Shephard
Mrs. R. C. Shepherd
Constance Sherman
Daniel J. Sherman
Laurence Sherman
Winthrop C. Sherman
Ann Sherman
Jane Sherwood
Mrs. H. R. Shimp
C. W. Shiner
Kent Shiner
Jillian Shingledecker
Charles W. Shinn
Norma Elaine Shinn
Sharyn Shipley
Marguerite Shonk
Zeb V. Shook
Charles D. Shopwin
David L. Shores
Charles Short
Mrs. John E. Short
Steven Short
Kathleen Shortridge
Homer T. Showalter
Antony Shugaar
Margave R. Shuping
Roger W. Shuy
Mrs. L. A. Sibley Jr.
Richard Sibley
Mohsin Siddiqui
Markus Siebler
Mrs. John Siegfried
Hank Sienzant
William J. Sier
Marie Sigler
Dwight C. Sigworth
Andrew Sihler
Bob Sikes
Wanda Sikes
Lee Sills
Benjamin Silverman
Stuart Silverman
Claire Silvers
Nancy Silverstone
Mr. and Mrs. Floyd R. Silvey
Albert W. Simmonds
Jason Simmons
David Simon
Gus Simon
Mrs. A. Simonson
Tucker C. Simpson
Elizabeth Sims
Max Sims
Saul Singer
Mack Singleton
Norman Sipowicz
William P. Sisler

Stanley Sivertson
Lynette Skiffington
Betty Skinner
Margaret Skinner
Gail Skipper
Seth Sklarey
Robert Skoglund
Ed Skoog
Mrs. H. E. Skott
Mrs. C. R. Skupski
William Slack
Betty Slaughter
Mrs. W. B. Slaughter
Donald Slavin
James Sledd
Mailande Cheney Sledge
Annabelle Sleezer
Helen Sleight
Jean Slesinger
A. C. Sloan
Mrs. A. C. Sloan
Alexander Sloan Jr.
David D. Slocum
Alan R. Slotkin
Catherine Sluett
Flora S. Small
Flore Small
Lyman Smart
Helen S. Smartl
Burton A. Smead
Jessica Smedley
Ruth Smelser
Geraldine C. Smies
Daniel Smiley
Nixon Smiley
Bernice Smith
Camille Smith
Carrie Smith
Chris Smith
Cindy Smith
Corrie E. Smith
Mrs. DeWitt H. Smith
E. V. Smith
G. R. Smith
Mrs. G. Reid Smith
Galen Smith
Mrs. Gayle Smith
Genevieve R. Smith
J. W. Smith Sr.
Jane S. Smith
Jeff Smith
Joseph T. Smith
Judy Smith
Julia Smith
Lee Smith
Linda McCollum Smith
Marion Smith
Mary C. H. Smith
Mary R. Smith
Nancie Smith
Philip H. Smith
Priscilla K. Smith
Valentine Smith
William H. Smith
André M. Smith
Una Smith
L. A. Smitherman
Kathleen Smokel
Diann Smothers
John Snell

Betty Sneller
Diane Snider
Steven Snider
Jennifer Snodgrass
Kathie Snodgrass
K. A. Snow
Gail Snowden
Grace Grant Snyder
Emily Soden
Tili Sokolov
Bob Soldner
William A. Solien
John Solon
Tim Somero
Timothy Somero
Holly Sommer
Vivian Sommerville
Christine Soner
L. G. Sorden
Leeann Sorenson
William C. Sorenson
E. Sorquist
Donald P. Soule
Bruce Southard
Mrs. C. F. Spangler
Tracy Spaulding
Richard A. Spears
Halbert Speer
Archer Speidel
Debra Spencer
Nancy Spencer
Paula Spencer
Caroline Spengler
Harold Spengler
Peter Spicer
Jean Spiroff
Mrs. I. H. Spoerri
Raymond A. Spong
Irv Sposnik
Carle B. Spotts
Kristine Spurgeon
Katherine Spurlock
Mr. and Mrs. E. H. Staats
Steve Stachowiak
John Stafford
Norman Stageberg
Theresa Stair
William S. Stalcup
James C. Stalker
Kenneth Stammerman
Leigh H. Standish
Wilmogene Stanfield
Christine M. Stanley
Helen Stanley
Mrs. Richard Stanley
Brenda Stansell
David Stansell
Jim Staskowski
Donald R. Statham
Henry J. Statkowski
Katherine St. Aubin
Mrs. Walter Stauffacher
F. Y. St. Clair
C. A. Steeby
Mr. and Mrs. Arthur Steele
Jeffrey Steele
P. Steen
Donald Steenburgh
Sharon Steffen
Margaret Steffenson

Barry N. Stein
Jess Stein
John Steiner
Sol Steinmetz
Rob Stelling
K. Stenger
Virginia L. Stenus
David Stephens
Jon Stephens
Margaret F. Stephens
Tom Stephens
Thomas M. Stephens
Lazeeta Stephenson
Michael Sterken
Joseph Sterlynne
Donald Sternbergh
Ann Stevens
Henry S. Stevens
Kevin Stevens
Mercedes Stevens
Paul R. Stevens
William J. Stevens
Robert D. Stevick
Joyce Steward
Al Stewart
Charles J. Stewart
Katherine Stewart
Eunice Stinchfield
Lisa Stivers
Zilla Stogner
Mrs. Kirk H. Stone
Sue Stone
Terry J. Stone
Vera E. Stone
Bessie Lloyd Storgan
Elizabeth H. Storm-Reif
G. M. Story
Elaine Stotko
Mrs. Claude D. Stout
Kathleen Stratton
Jean Strauble
Fred Strebeigh
Mrs. R. C. Stribling
Jim Strickland
Lana Strickland
Catharine P. Stringfellow
Rosemarie Strojny
Janet Strong
Margaret Strong
Harriett Stryker-Rodda
J. Stuart
James B. Stubbins
Kendon Stubbs
Irene H. Stuckey
B. Stucki
Ron Stultz
A. Brett Styles
Jack Sublette
Elmer F. Suderman
Catherine Sullivan
Debra Sullivan
Mary Rose Sullivan
Olga Sullivan
Mr. and Mrs. Roger Sullivan
Sara Sullivan
R. F. Sun
Carol A. Sundahl
Mrs. R. W. Sutton
Kester Svendsen
Mrs. Albert E. Swafford

Jena Swank
Scott Swanson
Linda M. Swearengen
Mrs. James R. Sweeny
Carol Sweenye
Michael Sweet
Michael J. Sweet
Jeff R. Sweinhart
Ray Swick
Thomas R. Swick
Kendall Swinford
Tom Swint
Bettie Swiontek
Russell Tabbert
Harriet Taber
Janice Taft
Dorothy Taishoff
Cyndy Talbot
Anne Marie Talbott
Erma A. Talbott
George E. Talmage
Peter Tamony
Mrs. Cary H. Tanner
Dazaifu Tara
Michael Tarabulsky
Olive Tardiff
Milton Tarlow
Arline V. Tarnoff
Fred A. Tarpley
Brent Tarter
Gary Tate
James H. Tate
Edith S. B. Tatel
Dorothea Tausinger
Cheryl Tausky-Hollscher
D. M. Tavsinger
Elmer E. Taylor
John W. Taylor
Judith A. Taylor
Judy Taylor
Kate Taylor
Rubye Taylor
Ruth Taylor
W. E. Taylor
William Taylor
Catharine C. Teague
Monroe Teague
Tom Teague
Mrs. A. E. Teeck
Tom Teegarden
Milford te Grotenhuis
Bethany Telle
Joan Teller
James Templeton
Harold Tendick
Arthur Tenenholtz
Henrietta Ten Harmsel
Waltraut Tepfenhardt
Beth Tepool
Reinold ter Kuile
K. Terwilliger
Mrs. John R. Tesser
Maria Testa
Gail D. Tewhey
Stan Thain
Sister Marie Therese
Anna Theriault
Bert Thomas
Mrs. Boyd Thomas
Carl Thomas

Charles Crabbe Thomas
Ednah Thomas
Eloise Thomas
Jean M. Thomas
Laura Thomas
Linda Thomas
Matt Thomas
Peter Thomas
Mrs. Ray Thomas
Roy Edwin Thomas
Sheree Renée Thomas
William A. Thomas
Charles Thompson
Donald F. Thompson
Emma L. Thompson
George A. Thompson
George W. Thompson
Gordon B. Thompson
Jodene Thompson
Joyce W. Thompson
M. Terry Thompson
Marion L. Thompson
Mrs. Olai B. Thompson
Valerie Thompson
J. Alexander Thorburn
Harvey Thorn Jr.
James Thornbery
Mary G. Thorstensen
Ellen Thro
William R. Thurman
Barbara A. Tibbetts
John Tibby
Mrs. A. E. Tiech
A. T. Tiedemann
Donna Tillem
James J. Tilton
F. Timmen
Richard Tinckhell
Jim Tingley
John Tinkler
Mary Tipton
Bill Tishler
Mary M. Tius
Wayne Tlusty
Mrs. D. G. Tobin
Martha Todd
Amanda Toering
Floyd C. Tolleson Jr.
Randy Tolleson
Joseph Tomasi
Estrella Tome
Mary Tompkins
Richard Tonachel
Leo C. Tonjes
Mary Torgoman
Amanda N. Torke
Mrs. Geoffrey Torney
Anne Torrans
Jens K. Touborg
John Toussaint
Harold Tower
Jane Towner
Sibley Towner
Frank P. Townsend
Roy Townsend
Russell Townsley
Sal Towse
Virginia F. Tozer
Phil Trautmann
Kathleen Trayte

D. W. Treadgold
Kathy Tredway
Robert F. Tredwell
Christine Tridente
Julie Tripp
Rudolph C. Troike
Robert Trombley
Mark Troy
Henry M. Truby
M. E. Trudeau
Mrs. Frank Trumpy
Grady Tucker
Linda Jordan Tucker
W. F. Tuhey
Dennis Tully
Al Tunis
Judith L. Tuohy
Mrs. A. E. Turek
Billie Turner
David Turner
Elizabeth C. Turner
G. W. Turner
Margaret Turner
Troy Turner
Mrs. W. C. Turner
Ralph Tuttila
Hope C. Tuttle
W. F. Twaddell
Mrs. H. G. Twitchell
Jane Tylus
Emily Tymus
Mrs. Francis B. Tyrell
Joe Tyson
Wayne Tyson
Fred Uhlman
Arley Uhrig
Priscilla Ulrichs
Dave Underhill
Gary Neal Underwood
Pat Underwood
Theda Upson
Laurence Urdang
Francis Lee Utley
Hedy Vahabzadeh
Jacob M. Valentine
Bob Vanarsdall
David Vancil
Vicki Lynn Van Cleary
Tom Van De Grift
Joyce Vanden Brink
Robert Vanderberg
Jim Vandergriff
Cassia van der Hoof Holstein
Bob Vander Meulen
David Vander Meulen
Sylvia Vander Meulen
Ruth Vandiver
Patricia VanDyke
Ed Van Gemert
E. W. Van Guilder
Jon Van Keuren
John F. Van Lieu
Ivy Vann
Mike Vanne
Robert Van Riper
L. C. Van Savage
A. B. Van Sciver
Dirck Van Sickle
Bill Varnedoe
Jerry Victor Vassalla II

Emma S. Vaughan
Deanne Vaughn
George Vaughn
Mrs. Harold Vaughn
Thelma Vaughn
Ann Marie Veca
Mrs. Juris Veidemanis
Mary Velinsky
Allison S. Veser
Phil Vettel
D. E. Vetter
Doris Vetter
George Vetter
J. R. Vickerman
Wolfgang Viereck
A. F. Vierheller
Don Vogel
Dorcas Rewey Volk
Chris von Rosenvinge
Erika von Schneidemesser
Luanne von Schneidemesser
Michael von Schneidemesser
Donald S. Voorhees
Paul Voorhis
Robert S. Wachal
Mrs. Paul Wachholz
Mrs. H. W. Wachtl
May Wachtl
Charles Wacouta
Steve Waddell
Denise Waddington
Franz R. Wagner
Louise Wagner
John G. Waidner
Violet Waisner
Mrs. Daye S. Wait
Rosemary Waitkus
Pat Wakefield
Matt Walcoff
Bruce Walker
Elsie H. Walker
Christopher Walker
Jana Walker
Mary Walker
Mary Beth Walker
Stephen Walker
Timothy D. Walker
Julie Walko
Bud Wall
Barbara Wallace
Margaret Wallace
Rex Wallace
Ira Wallach
Don Waller
Richard Walser
Birrell Walsh
John Walsh
Kathleen Walsh
Raymond Walston
Joe P. Walter
David Walton
Gerald W. Walton
Shana Walton
Babette Wampold
Charles H. Wampold Jr.
Harry Wandrus
Mr. and Mrs. F. W.
 Wandschneider
T. D. Wangemann
Zara Wanlass

David Ward
Doris Ward
Glen C. Ward
John A. Ward Jr.
Kathie Ward
Evelyn Warman
Elsie H. Warner
Madeline Warner
Kevin Warner
Mrs. James Warrack
Mrs. John Warrack
Nancy L. Warren
Mrs. C. R. Warrick
Joan Warriner
Mary L. Washington
Margaret Waterman
Barbara Waters
Erna Waters
Fred Waters
Raymond Waters
Tom Waters
W. A. Waters
Fred O. Watkins Jr.
J. O. Watkins
Pat Watkins
Tory Watkins
Merton M. Watnik
Mrs. James Watrous
Peg Watrous
Bill Watson
Mrs. C. L. Watson Jr.
Diane Watson
Mrs. John Watson
Lisa Watson
M. T. Watson
Stuart D. Watson
Deirdra Watts
Mrs. C. A. Weaver
H. Douglas Weaver
Jack W. Weaver
Jim Weaver
James W. Webb
Jane C. Webb
Margot S. Webb
Millie Webb
Norman D. Webb
R. Keith Webber
Carole Weber
Deb Weber
Robert William Weber
Charles R. Webster
Frank M. Webster
Sheila Webster
Diane Weddington
David M. Weeks
Horace Weeks
Ruth Weeks
Thelma E. Weeks
Mr. and Mrs. Lawrence Weighner
Jennifer Weimert
Lois Weinberg
David Weiner
Mrs. Roy Weir
Mrs. N. F. Weisensel
Miriam Weiss
Fred A. Weitzel
Evelyn Welch
R. E. Welch
Amy Weldon
Lucinda Welenc

Jewell S. Weller
Sam Weller
David M. Wells
Jack B. Wells
Mary E. Wells
Pam Wells
Topf Wells
Roger Welsch
Helen Welsh
Heather Weltin
Julia Wendemuth
Bernard Wentworth
Edward T. Wenzel
D. H Wernsing
Kathy Wesenberg
R. Wesner
Fred P. Wessells
Kay Wessner
Angela West
Mrs. Chas H. West
Constance E. West
Martha H. West
Richard G. West
Robert G. West
Robert H. West
Jim Westbrook
Bill Westerman
Relling Westfall
Frederick L. Westover
Tom Whalen
E. H. Whan
Chris Wheatley
Donna Lee Wheeler
Jean Wheeler
Mary B. Wheeler
Maurine Whipple
Edith I. Whitcomb
Alison White
Helen C. White
Mrs. Leo T. White
Mark White
Nellie R. White
Phil White
Rose P. White
Wanda White
John E. Whitehead Jr.
Larry A. Whitford
B. J. Whiting
Agnes Whitley
Edna I. Whitley
John Whitley
Mrs. Wade Hampton Whitley
Digby Butler Whitman
Phyllis Whitman
David Whorley
Howard Whyte
Mrs. Walter Wickliffe
Charles A. Wiel
Bronte Wieland
Stanley Wiersma
Jessie Wieseman
Joseph J. Wiesenfarth
B. Eliot Wigginton
Patricia Wigglesworth
Andrew A. Wilcox
Earl J. Wilcox
Maud Wilcox
Payson S. Wild
Mitchell A. Wilder
Belle Wildish

Treva Jewel Ferguson Wileman
John Wiley
Linda Wiley
Mary M. Wiley
Norbert F. Wiley
David A. Wilkie
George L. Wilkinson
Wayne Will
Rolland Willan
John Willard
Wesley Willard
Mary E. Willets
Arthur Dann Willett
Patsy Willhite
Andrew F. Williams
Cherry Williams
Cratis Williams
Donald V. Williams
G. Chambers Williams
Gary Williams
George Williams
John Williams
Joseph M. Williams
M. Leon Williams
Marijane Williams
Neal D. Williams
Ruth Williams
Mrs. Sanford Williams
Stephanie Williams
Anita Jean Williamson
Steven Williamson
Edmund P. Willis
Patricia C. Willis
Paul Wills
Michael Wilmeth
J. P. Wilmhurst
David B. Wilsey
Carol K. Wilson
Erik Hunt Wilson
Evan Wilson
Gordon Wilson
Mrs. H. H. Wilson
H. Rex Wilson
Helen D. Wilson
Jeffrey S. Wilson
John W. Wilson
Kenneth Wilson
Laurel Wilson
Ned Wilson
Rex Wilson
Robert H. Wilson
Ruth A. Wilt
Phyllis R. Winant
John N. Winburne
Simon Winchester
Etta Smith Winegarner
Lise Winer
Susan Wing
John Winner
K. M. Winrich
George Winship
Mrs. Danny Winskie
Danny P. Winskie
Ken Winter
Kathryn Wisdom
Claude Merton Wise
Doris Wise
Bridgett Wissinger
Cathryn Withers
Jim Withgott

Lillian Leith Witmer
Grace Witt
Jeanne M. Witte
Fred Woehr
Grace Wohlsen
Ted Wohlsen
Doris Wojta
Mrs. Ed Wolf
Jack Wolf
Ann Wolfe
Ann B. Wolfe
H. Wolfe
Melee Wolfe
Ralph H. Wolfe
Mrs. Willard Wolfe
Mrs. G. Louis Wolff
Andrea Wolford
Kate Wolicki
Ken Wolman
Francis C. Wolven
Harry Wonham
D. L. Wood

Jamie Wood
Marjorie Wood
Richard E. Wood
Willson Wood
Tracey Woodard
Hensley C. Woodbridge
Mrs. Murillo V. Woodruff
David Woodward
George Woodworth
Henry Bosley Woolf
Josephine M. Woolf
Clinton N. Woolsey
Sarah Worcester
Fred Wordell
George J. Worth
Mrs. Kenneth Worthing
Ruth S. Worthing
Tanner Wray
James J. Wrenn
Al Wright
Carol Wright
Diana Wright

Elizabeth H. Wright
Irene Wright
Lloyd Wright
Warren Keith Wright
Steve Wuerz
M. S. Wunderlich
Frank Wuttage Jr.
Eric Wyckoff
Faith Wyckoff
Lionel D. Wyld
Walker Wyman
Dudley Wynn
Joel S. Yaffa
Marie Yaras
Ardath Yehle
Mailyn Yensen
Bo Yerxa
A. Kenneth Yost
Gilbert Youmans
Carolyn Young
Harold F. Young
Jerry Young

Karen Young
Phyllis Young
Vicki New Yowan
David A. Yuenger
Mr. and Mrs. Zabel
Cheryl R. Zaret
Mr. and Mrs. Edmund Zawacki
Mary Brown Zeigler
Harold G. Zeitler
Wilbur Zelinsky
William Zelinsky
Linda Zerbee-Darrall
Mrs. J. A. Ziebarth
F. E. Zimmerman
Vivian Zinkin
Zea Zinn
Carla Zirk
Paula Zitzler
Elizabeth Clarkson Zwart
Marge Zwickel
Arnold M. Zwicky

Financial Contributors to *DARE*, 1965–2011

Ismail H. Abdalla
Patricia Otis Abel
Kris Ableman
Hilary L. Abraham
Allyn R. Adams
Flora Dickie Adams
Michael P. Adams
Susan S. Adams
Sandra A. Adell
Marjorie P. Adkisson
Barbara Agatstein
David G. Ainsworth
A. J. Aitken
Andrew B. Albert
Kathy Albert
Karl D. Aldinger
Ruth Aldrich
Alexander & Alexander Services Inc.
Elizabeth T. Alexander
Robert J. Alexander
Gregory P. and Carol Alfus
John and Adele Algeo
Barbara R. Alioto
Ashlea Allen
Jean E. Allen
Alliant Energy
R. Brooke Alloway
Jennifer L. Altman
Virginia A. Amann
William G. and Priscilla Ambrose
D. Wayne Ashby Jr.
American Automobile Association
American Dialect Society
American Heritage Publishing Company
American Map Company
American Trucking Association
Sally A. Anders
Brian A. Anderson
Don Anderson
Dorothy Anderson
Emmy L. Anderson
Floy Mae Anderson
Heidi R. Anderson
James E. and Patricia G. Anderson
Craig J. and Jean F. Anderson
Jean W. Anderson
Judith Petersen Anderson
Lari D. Anderson
Norman A. Anderson
Russ Anderton
Andrews McMeel Universal Foundation

Sonia R. Andrusier
Michael E. Anfang
Leisel Anne Angwin
Robert R. Antaramian
Jane B. Anthony
Appalachian Regional Commission
Jane E. Archer
Evan B. Arensberg
Jacqueline M. Armitage
Maureen E. Armstrong
Anne Arnesen
Barbara J. Arnold
Thomas J. Arthur
Edward Artin
Patricia M. Arvold
Raphael W. Asher
Martha K. Askins
Ann W. Astell
Joel C. Atkinson
Louie W. and Barbara Attebery
Emily K. Auerbach
Nina J. Auerbach
John J. and Barbara L. Augenstein
Ann H. Avery
Janice Ellen Axelrod
Fred Axley
Patricia L. Ayers
James E. Ayres
Anthony S. Azcona
Raffaella Baccolini
Judith S. Bach
Kaye Bache-Snyder
Sandra J. Bachrach
Leslie M. Bacig
Howard G. and Nancy Baetzhold
Dorothy D. Bailey
Nancy M. Bailey
Richard W. and Julia Huttar Bailey
Mr. and Mrs. Robert Bailey
John Bakeless
Daniel Baker
Laura J. Baker
Ronald L. Baker
Hannah R. Baker-Siroty
Gordon M. Bakken
Robert F. and Marlene M. Balas
Jeff and Karen D. Baldassari
Gordon B. Baldwin
Carl W. and Lisa A. Balge
Angelika M. Bammer
Lawrence J. Banchero

Edward M. and Penelope A. Bancker Jr.
Jacqueline M. Kuta Bangsberg
Donna S. Baranowski
Virginia S. Bare
John W. Barker
Grenville and Fiona R. Barnes
Dr. and Mrs. James E. Barnes
David Barnhart
Clyde Barrett
Sally E. Barnett
Sydona Baroff
Leslie Barratt
M. Rosabel Barroilhet
Charlene Barshefsky
Susan M. Barsness
Beverly Rae Bartels
Charles E. Bartlett
Abraham Z. and Elizabeth E. Bass
Elizabeth J. Bass
Jodey Bateman
H. L. Bates
Kathleen A. Bates
Jean M. Bathurst
Mrs. Keith A. Bauer
Clare L. Bauman
Arden C. and Barbara J. Baumgardt
David W. Baumgartner
Kurtis J. and Natalie M. Baumgartner
C. Richard and Dorothy P. Beam
Liza M. Bearman
Marvin T. and Ellouise W. Beatty
George E. and Mary D. Becker
Carl C. Beckwith
Paul D. and Lois L. Bednarowski
Laura G. Beenen
Stephen C. Behrendt
LeRoy J. and Shelly Behrens
Sara Tilda Behrman
Patrick R. Beirne
Ronna L. Belinky
Christopher Robert Bell
Todd K. and Patricia A. Bender
Karl N. Benghauser
Larry Benson
Charles R. and Mary B. Bentley
Lori M. Beranek
David Bergdahl
Jane L. Bergmann
Peggy A. Bergquist
Debra M. Bernardi
Jerry M. Bernhard
Joyce Berns

Roland L. Berns
Matthew H. and Natalie B. Bernstein
Robert A. and Cynthia Bernstein
Dennis A. Berthold
Peter J. and Mary L. Berthold
Marge Berube
Mary L. Berwanger
Lloyd Besant
Jess B. Bessinger
Judyth Beyerstedt
Vishwa and Indu B. Bhargava
Dale Raymond Bickley
Raymond G. and Cynthia Bland Biggar
James D. Biggs
Clair E. Bigler Jr.
Mary S. Bilder
Garland D. Bills
Richard E. Binkowski
Richard L. Birch
Mrs. Alfred Birdsell
Robert J. and Susie B. Birdsell
Lisa Birk
Harry W. Bischel
Michelle M. Bittle
James W. Bittner
Minerva Blackburn
Silas C. and Brenda K. Blackstock
Philip L. Blackwell
Heather A. Blahnik
Martha G. Blalock
Kathleen J. Blaser
Daniel S. Bleil
Don Bloch
Ryan T. Bloch
Stephen D. Blood
Kari A. Blowers
Elizabeth S. Bobrinskoy
Carl Bode
Laurie A. Boehme
Dwayne R. Boettcher
Pete and Jean Boettcher
Douglas R. and Emily W. Boettge
Eleanor Bogan
John A. Bogardus Jr.
Ann M. Bogle
Elizabeth Bogner
Becky J. Bohan
Leo L. Boiteux
Rosemary R. Bolas
Jean H. and Robert W. Bonar
Lynn A. Bonfield
Robert E. Boni
Larry Bonko

Robert S. and Susan H. Boone
Barbara W. Booth
Helen S. Booth
Russell H. Boothroyd
John G. Bordie
Carolyn L. Bormann
Virginia A. Bormann
Elizabeth Anne Borneman
Lloyd R. and Genevieve J.
  Bostian
Lowell Bouma
Brett A. Bowers
Frances M. Bowland
Bowling Green Motor Sales, Inc.
Mr. and Mrs. Carl H. Boyer
J. A. Boyse
Douglas Mahon Bradt
Mary M. Brady
Patricia A. Brady
Marguerite A. Branch
Dora A. Brand
Craig F. Brandhorst
Charles J. Braun
Helen L. Braun
Kent K. and Joyce S. Braunstein
Louise H. Bray
Jacqueline D. Bredar
Mitchell R. Breitwieser
Jude B. Brennan
Nicole A. Brennan
Charles A. Brien
Russell C. Brignano
Susan B. Brill-deRamirez
Elizabeth Abell Brinkman
Mary L. Briscoe
Bristol-Myers Squibb Foundation
Brittingham Fund, Inc.
Marcella R. Brockway
Richard C. and Diana Brodek
Mary P. Brody
David T. Brook
Jean P. Brookhart
Telise E. Broughton
Daniel J. Brown
Judith C. Brown
Marion F. Brown
Melanie Brown
Phillip S. Brown
Samuel Brown
Andrew R. Brumer
Brett L. Brunner
Malcolm P. Brunner
J. Steven and Barbara J. Brunsell
Lawrence D. Bryan
Margaret Bryant
Susan P. Bryant-Kimball
Jerome Buckley
Mark R. Buckley
Mollie E. Buckley
Scott H. Buechler
Richard R. and Sharon A. Buell
Laureen B. Buffo
Emily S. Bumble
Nancy L. Bunge
Nancy E. Burcham
Rita E. Burke
James W. Burkhead
R. Peter Burnham
Steven A. Burnham
Lee A. Burress Jr.

Fred L. Burwick
Susan K. Busenius
Cynthia B. G. and Sargent Bush Jr.
Evetta L. Bush
Amy C. Bushaw
Linda J. Busick
Martha G. Bustin
Butterick Company
Ronald R. Butters
Maurice Cagnon
Deborah Caise-Fitzpatrick
John Wesley Calhoun
Edward and Jean Callary
Susan J. Callaway
T. Cleve Callison III
Alan B. Cameron Jr.
Susan M. Camp
Christy Paige Cander
Beverly Ann Cannady
Michael J. Capek
William Card
Carl and Judith Carlson
Timothy J. Carlton
Marvin D. Carmony
Carnegie Corporation of New
  York
Elizabeth Carr
Benjamin B. Carroll
Robert A. Carroll
Barbara G. Caruso
Marjorie A. Cary
R. G. Case
Elizabeth P. Casey
Ellen M. Casey
Leonard R. Casper
Robert N. Casper
Charlotte Cassidy
Claire M. Cassidy
Frederic G. Cassidy
H. Alexander Cassidy
Helen G. Cassidy
Michael M. and Jacquelyn J.
  Cassidy
Nicholas M. Cassidy
Victor M. Cassidy
Jennifer Cassidy-Gilbert
Joseph A. Catania
Scott Catlett
Central Wisconsin Area
  Community Theatre
James Cerello
Genevieve Chaillou-Weber
Peter S. Chandler
Stephen J. Chandler
Alec Y. Chang
Ho Sheng Chang
Joanne H. Chapin
Michael J. Charles
Loyd J. and Rosalind
  Charlesworth Jr.
Ruth M. Chasek
Irene Check
Judith Cherington
Chevron Matching Gift Program
Emily S. Chesley
Randolph and Kathryn B. Chilton
Marvin K. L. Ching
Amy E. Christensen
Andrew T. and Kathleen M.
  Christenson

Donna M. Christian
Hannah A. Christian
Christian Science Monitor
Dane E. Christiansen
Edward B. and Dorothy
  Churchwell
Anthony L. and Catherine E.
  Ciaccio
Eileen M. Ciezki
Patricia M. Cinealis
Gary S. Cirilli
Cisco Systems, Inc. Matching
  Gift Program
Bernard Clair
Karen M. Clark
Virginia P. Clark
Lorraine Clayton
John L. Cleman
Kristine M. Clerkin
David W. Clewell
Mary A. Coan
Charyssa Ann Cobb
Daniel G. Cobb
John and Susan S. Cobb
Arthur B. Coffin
Gail H. Coffler
Abby D. Cohen
Edward B. Cohen
Jack S. Cohen
Theodore J. Cohen
Joyce S. Cohrs
Amber C. Coisman
Meredith L. Coleman
Roy Collier
Basil A. Collins
David Y. and Annabelle Collins
Mary Jo Trapani Collins
Luanne L. Coltman
Barbara J. Conder
Amy J. Conger
Connemara Fund
Peter H. Connor
Charles Constantine
William J. Conti
Judy and Dennis Cook
Marshall J. and Ellen Cook
Sue Katherine Cool
James E. Coomber
Robert L. and Nancy J. Cooper
Sandra J. Cooperman
Lark E. Copps
Michael W. Copps
Priscilla Lynn Copps
Thomas R. Copps
Copy Editor: Language News for
  the Publishing Profession
James D. Cornelius
Dan and Pat Cornwell
Karen Cornwell
Patricia E. Cosgrove
Howard P. and Susan T. Cosgrove
Martin J. Costello
Patrick J. and Susan C. Costello
Alfred C. and June C. Cottrell
Sandra E. Cowen
Dale Coye
H. M. Cox
William A. and Judith S. Craig
Christine M. Crawford
Joanne V. Creighton

F. Fleming Crim Jr.
Joyce W. Crim
E. H. Criswell
Thomas H. Crofts III
Daniel J. Cronin
James F. and Ann C. Crow
Maura A. Crowley
Terence and Jane Crowley
William R. Crozier
Kathleen Cruice
Edward and Margaret J. Cucci
Michaela Cudahy
Lee Cullen
Julie Cullman
Jean Eleanor Curnow
Mark J. and Sonia T. Curran
Joyce M. Curry
Robert L. Curry Jr.
William M. Curtin
Jane E. Curtis
Ellee L. D'Amore
Deborah L. Daberko
Giles A. Daeger
Alice Daer
Allison Mary Reak Dagel
E. G. "Ty" Dahlgren
Mary P. Dalles
Thomas C. and Mary M.
  Dallmann
John B. Dalsant
Susan S. Dalsimer
Kathleen F. Kiss Damon
The Charles A. Dana Foundation
Carroll B. Dana
Richard J. Dane
Barbara Daniels
Mary K. Darnieder
Bruce M. Davey
Virginia J. Davidson
Richard Davis Foundation
Barbara H. Davis
Richard Davis
Richard A. Davison
John Dawson
Robert L. Dean
R. N. De Armond
Mr. and Mrs. William DeBot
David D. and Mary G. Debruin
David De Camp
Lynn S. Decker
Kathleen R. DeGrave
Susan M. Deisinger
Nelson L. and Rosanne P.
  DeJesus
The Gladys Krieble Delmas
  Foundation
Richard B. and Marjorie W.
  DeMallie Jr.
Andrew J. DeMarco
Jeffrey R. DeMark
Robert H. Deming
Jerome A. Denis
Lynne C. Denis
Judith A. Dereszynski
August Derleth
John M. Desmond
Morgan J. Desmond
Sister Antoinette Des Roches,
  C.N.D.
Robert J. Detisch

Laurel I. DeVitt
Teague D. Devitt
Matthew J. and Annette S. Devlin
Barbara Groves Dewey
Michele DiBenedetto
Jerry G. and Elizabeth C. Dickason
Karen E. Dickerman
Richard M. Dickerman
Theodore J. Dickhudt
Lindsey M. Dickinson
Dictionary Society of North America
A. Richard Diebold Jr.
Gerald J. Diemer
Shirley W. Dieter
Elizabeth F. Dill
Vincent Dimarco
Mrs. F. D. Disdier
Stevan C. Dittman
Jill S. Dittrich
Nick Doane
Molly A. Doane
Rick Jay Dobson
Mrs. Robert Dobson
Marshall Dodge
William F. Dohmen
Norman R. Doll
Stefan Dollinger
Ellen R. Donovan
Donald Dorfman
Clyde H. and Joan Dornbusch
Rosemary M. Dorney
Jeremy M. Downes
Andrew F. Downey Jr.
Douglas W. and Anne Downey
David R. Draheim
Nancy L. Dray
D. Allan Drummond
Heather Dubrow
Audrey R. Duckert
Karen I. Dudley
Sarah A. Duffy
Zachary L. Duffy
David H. and Rebecca Dugger
Francis Duke
Katherine W. Dukehart
Gary S. Dunbar
Stephen Barnes Dunbar
A. R. Dunlap
John H. and Gwenn D. Dunn
Jonathan A. Dunn
Michelle Ascher Dunn
Robert P. Dunn
Jack A. Durra
Sylvia P. Duty
Kerry E. Dwyer
Timothy O. Dykstal
Robert Easton
Frank L. and Margery M. Eaton
Craig E. Eben
Eric K. Ebersberger
Connie C. Eble
Mary Eccles
Betty S. Eckberg
Robert W. Eckert
David J. and Mary L. Eckholm
Raymond E. Edelman
Kenneth V. Egan
David L. and Julie Egger

Russell Andrew Ehler
E. C. Ehrensperger
Susan E. and Henry Eichhorn
Daniel R. Einum
Ellen Beth Eisenberg
Karen L. Ekdahl
Richard H. and Caroline R. Ekman
Elisabeth S. Eldred
Sidney J. and Karen A. Ellenbecher
Wayne Elliot
Gary H. and Karen V. N. Ellis
William and Betty J. Ellis Jr.
Harlan Ellison
Catherine L. Ellsworth
Thomas R. Ellsworth
Lori J. Elmer
Anne I. Haberland Emerson
David A. Emerson
David E. and Pamela G. Emerson
Marian R. Emerson
Robert J. and Karen Engelhard
English Association of Northwestern Ohio
Sherman M. English
Leonard R. and Joan G. Epand
Matthew J. Epstein
Robert M. Esch
Nyles R. and Genevieve E. Eskritt
Robert A. Esposito
Carrie A. Estill
Russel C. Evans
Sharon R. Evans
Elizabeth M. and Jacob T. Evanson
Raymond M. Evers
Richard L. Eversole
The Evjue Foundation, Inc.
Marilyn R. Exler
Edwin Ezor
Kenneth O. Ezrow
Arnold S. Fabricant
Lucile P. Falk
James E. and Mary K. Farnum
Farrar, Straus and Giroux, Inc.
Bridget Dorothy Farrelly
Harold Frederick Farwell Jr.
Raymond P. Fassel
Linda S. Feirn
Joseph Fernández
Bonnie G. Fetzek
Michelle L. Finnegan
Murray D. Fintel
Robert P. Fischelis
Harold M. Fischer
Thomas J. Fischer
Betty J. Fisher-Bowers
B. Ellen Fisher
Kristin M. Fisher
Nancy K. Fishman
Mr. and Mrs. Theodore B. Fitz-Simons Jr.
Laurie A. Fitzgerald
Ross A. Flagg
Catherine J. Flaherty
Gertrude Flanders
Beverly J. Flanigan
Matthew D. Flannery
James E. and Evelyn J. Fleming

Katherine J. Fletcher
Diane F. Flinn
Sam H. and Jane Appleby Flint
Elizabeth A. Flynn
Joyce A. Foreman
Leslie L. Forester
Jane Z. Forman
Marian Forte
Elizabeth T. Forter
Virginia O. Foscue
James A. Fosdick
Jack F. and Helen M. Foster
Elspeth M. Fox
Betsy M. Foxwell
Franklin Philanthropic Foundation
Pleasant Rowland Frautschi
Ann C. Fred
Dr. and Mrs. E. B. Fred
Carol J. Freeman-Athey
Elizabeth J. Frensley
Susan Friedman
Mrs. Charles C. Fries
Polly J. Friess
Steven L. Frillmann
Peter W. Frutiger
Susan R. Fugate
F. Fuller
Toby E. and Laura Fulwiler
John Gabel
Allen Gabor
Marie D. Gadsden
Neil and Lorraine Gaiman
Donald F. and Nancy Gaines
Robert A. Gake
Gale Research, Inc.
Sheilah K. Plenke Gallagher
Kenneth F. Gambone
Cory Gann
Mitzi A. Gann
Robert E. Gard
Joan K. Gardiner
Gail I. Gardner
Suzanne M. Gardner
Dorothy R. Gariepy
Jane E. Garry
Marjorie A. Garthwaite
J. Edward and Marion Gates
Godfrey L. and M. Irene Gattiker
John P. and Christine L. Gauder
Cathy Gavin
Paul J. Gaynor
James B. and Karlene Gebhard
Jonathan S. Gelatt
Philip M. Gelatt
Victor Gell
Nancy R. Gellman
Elizabeth D. Gelvin
Eugenia C. and Paul G. Gengler
Demetrius J. Georgacas
Betty R. George
Douglas G. Gerth
Douglas L. and Jean K. Gessl
Tara Leigh Gibbs
Esmeralda T. Gibson
Martha J. Gibson
Timothy J. Gierke
James M. Giesen
James B. Gilbert
David B. and Susan M. R. Gill

Margaret S. Gillerman
Charlotte A. Gillespie
E. Ward and Jean B. Gilman
George Y. Gilpatrick
Maria Garcia-Bermejo Giner
Elizabeth Gladfelter
Kathleen Glaser
Jennifer R. Glatzer
Leonard M. and Lorraine Glodowski
George Glotzbach
Charles J. and Belle Goebel
James W. and Diane M. Goetz
William H. Gofen
Mrs. Stephen Goldfarb
Laurel Goldman
Horace W. Goldsmith Foundation
Robert W. Goldsmith
John F. Goodman
Leonard and Constance Goodman
Morris F. Goodman
BFGoodrich Company
Gary J. Gordon
Katie A. Gore
Anita G. Gorman
Deborah M. Gorman
Grant E. and Anne M. Gormley
Gary Goshgarian
Delorse V. Gospodar
Margaret A. Gother
Paul R. Gottinger
Harriet E. Gottlieb
Paula L. Gottlieb
Lynn M. Gould
Virginia A. Goulet-Gavrin
Margaret B. Grabowski
Tiffany J. Grade
Walter R. Graffin
James A. Graham
Gramercy Foundation
Eric Grant
Jan C. Grant
Marilyn Grant
Sarah B. Grant
David A. and Marcia E. Graves
Vicki Graves
Philip H. Gray
Susan M. Gray
Suzanne I. Gray
Hugh P. Greeley
Gerald A. Green
Judith A. Kent Green
Linda Greenberg
David R. Greene
Kevin M. Greene
Mary J. Greenewald
Joan Greenfield
Stanley B. Greenfield
Thelma C. Greenfield
Barbara J. Gregorich
Douglas W. Gregory
Martin L. Grenzebach
Noel N. Grey
Judith A. Griffey
Robert L. Grilley
Kris L. Grisa
Gail Coffin Grissom
Annette T. Griswold
Monica K. Gronert
David Groos

Jean Gross
Mimi D. Grossman
Mark A. Grote
Catherine E. Grothus
Robert D. Grotjohn
Shirley S. Gruen
William M. and Jennifer A. Guerriero
Kathleen P. Guinness
Karen E. Gulbrandsen
Alan M. F. Gunn
David B. Guralnik
Mark W. and Susan Gusho
Michael Guss
Howard E. Gustrowsky
David A. Guterman
Peter D. Haak
Robert A. and Jane B. Haas
Frederick W. and Sarah Bell Haberman
Robert E. Hable
Cynthia A. Hacker
Jane Hackney
Edwin T. Haefele
Joseph J. Haefner
Bezalel C. and Elizabeth Haimson
Shilo J. M. Halfen
Edward B. Hall
Joan Houston Hall
Reed Hall
Richard W. Halle
Haykaz Hambarssoomian
Gary D. and Donna Bechtel Hamilton
Kenneth Hammel
Sarah M. Hammes
L. Kenneth and Elizabeth D. Hammond
Eric Hamp
Lori A. Hanes
Mitch Haney
Louise W. Hanley
Anette B. Hansen
Forest W. Hansen
Marian R. Hansen
Donna Hapac
Earl N. Harbert
Kelsie B. Harder
Judy L. Harder-Dobson
Julia A. Harding
Heather K. Hardy
Orin K. Hargraves
Patricia A. Hario
HarperCollins Publishers, Inc.
Francis Harper
Kevin D. and Michaele Harried
Dolores R. Harris
Rodger S. and Kathryn Astrid Harris
Sarah E. Harrold
Zsolt Harsanyi
Janet H. Hart
Nathan W. Hart
Alan H. Hartley
James W. Hartman
Sally A. Hartman
Annette P. Hartung
Donald L. Hartzell
Harvard University

Matthea Harvey
Paula J. Harvey
Ronald W. Harris
Andrea L. Hasbrouck
Kathleen A. Hasse
Beverly Hasselberger
Jill Lineweber Hatleberg
John Hatton
Erin K. Hauber
Peter S. Hawkins
Carolyn M. Hayes
Jean P. Hayes
Margaret J. Hayes
James F. and Lynn S. Hazen
Alan G. Headbloom
William Hebal
Reva L. Heifetz
Erica M. Heisman
Elmer Helbach
Mr. and Mrs. B. W. Heller
Jane R. Heller
Janet R. Heller
R. L. and Golda Heminger
Mary Pat Henders
Michael M. T. and Carol Henderson
Robert Henderson
Elizabeth Mary Hendry
Solomon Henner
Standish and Jane N. Henning
Thomas G. and Judie L. Hermsen
Terry E. Herndon
Geraldine M. Herreid
Louise Herring
Phillip F. Herring
Walter J. Herrscher
Graham P. and Kristin Hershbell Charles
Hiram K. Hester
Matthew J. Hickel
Joseph C. Hickerson
James D. Hicks
Hidden Pond Foundation
Craig A. Higgason
The Henry Higgins of Hollywood Inc.
Cleo S. Higgins
F. Roger Higgins
Mary E. R. Higgins
Kit Hildebrand
Joyce B. Hile
George W. Hiles
Sara A. Hilgendorf
Douglas D. and Karen A. Hill
Roscoe W. Hilliker
Hillsdale Fund, Inc.
Gelston Hinds Jr.
Norman Hinton
Betty Jean Hisle
Christine B. Hoag
Charles J. Hodulik
Ann L. Hoegemeier
Rod and Laurel Hoeth
Lois J. Hofmeister
James Hogan
Betty D. Holcomb
Hope Holiner
Elizabeth B. Holmes
Ann Homstad
Harry J. and Margaret K. Hoole

Ellen M. Hooper
Thomas H. and Dorothy A. Hoover
Katherine L. Hope
Mary L. Horwarth
Houghton Mifflin Company
Robert J. and Carol R. Houston
Dorothy Houston
Thomas B. Hove
Barbara W. Howard
John E. Huber
Lynn H. Huber
Julia A. Huberty
Diane M. Hubler
H. Gary Hudson
Erin M. Hueffner
Lorrie Huff
Bradley T. Hughes
Erin P. Hughes
M. O. Hulsey
Margaret Banta Humleker
Kellogg W. Hunt
John P. and Merry Marx Hunter
Robert W. Huntington III
H. Robert Huntley
Willard J. and Frances W. Hurst
Paul O. and Sandra Huston
Gilda M. Hutchinson
Steven S. Hutkins
Gordon Hutner
Judith E. Huxhold-Hels
Virginia M. Hyde
Mary E. Hynes-Berry
Stephanie J. Hysmith
Gail K. Ibele
Richard J. and Mary A. Iglar
Elinor S. Ihlenfeldt
Julia A. Ihlenfeldt
The Louise H. and David S. Ingalls Foundation
Earl G. Ingersoll
Stanley L. and Shirley Inhorn
International Society of Anglo-Saxonists
James P. Irlbeck
Alice M. Irving
Betty J. Irwin
Nancy K. Italia
Herrick and Elaine N. Jackson
Jeffrey D. Jacobs
Robert S. and Gayle Jacobs
Ethel M. Jacobson
Veronica Jaeger
Jean D. Jagodzinski
Andrew C. Jakubczak
Dennis J. and Laurie L. Jalensky
John H. Jankoff
Linda Janoff
James G. Janssen
Irna M. Jay
Mildred G. Jaynes
Janet R. Jensen
Joan W. Jeruchim
Eric T. Jiobu
Thomas M. and Rose M. Jirous
Jane A. Johansen
Robert S. John
Telise E. Johnsen
Douglas N. and Mary K. Johnson
Edith Johnson

Ellen Johnson
Fern M. Johnson
The Johnson Foundation at Wingspread
Gregory M. Johnson
Nancy L. Johnson
Robert C. Johnson
Thomas J. and Barbara A. Johnson III
Richard Harry and Charlotte E. Johnston
Joyce D. Johnston
Barbara Johnstone
Mrs. Henry W. Johnstone Jr.
Charles Jonas
Ann M. Jones
Kirkland Jones
Petra Helen Jones
Susan C. Jones
Donald J. and Pamela J. Jonovic
Dorothy A. Jordan
Helene E. Jordan
Thomas C. Jorgensen
Andrea B. Joseph
David Jost
Randall J. and Colleen A. Kadlec
Gigi Kaeser
Sandra Kalscheur
Charles S. and Ellen W. Kaltman
Kari E. Kalve
John G. Kamps
Mary S. Kamps
Adrianne L. Kamsler
Joan M. Kane
M. Martin Kane
Nathan Kantrowitz
Alfred I. Kaplan
Furthermore, a program of The J. M. Kaplan Fund
Mae Kaplan
Susan B. Kaplan
Neil D. Karbank
Beth E. Kashner
Andrew C. Kasiske
Jane I. Katims
Ward A. Katz
Nicole E. Kavouris
Laura A. Kayacan
J. Kevin Keck
Paul L. Kegel
Mary Bridget Kehoe Coney
Carolyn C. Keith
Steven L. and Karen F. Keller
Stewart N. Kellerman
Charles Kelly Foundation
Elaine J. Kelly
Ellin M. Kelly
Maurine D. Kelly
Robert M. Kelly
Lorena E. Kemp
Coletta I. Kemper
Katherine E. Kemper
Dion Q. Kempthorne
Edward J. Kennedy Jr.
Gayle S. Kennedy
Sarajane M. Kennedy
Jesse L. Kercheval
Richard A. and Adrienne Kessler
Dolores A. Kester
Thomas J. and Ann M. Kiefer

Karen H. and Nicolas K. Kiessling
John L. Kijinski
Naomi S. Kilgore
James J. Kilpatrick
Phillip H. and Soyoung Kim
Rhonda S. Kimmel
Bruce Arthur and Melinda A. Kind
Robert D. King
Matthew J. Kingsley
A. Murray Kinloch
John M. and Joyce L. Kirsch
Marcy Kirsch
Lisa J. Kiser
Marilu S. Klasna
David H. Klein
Elaine M. Klein
Joyce Elaine Klein
Robert B. and Elaine C. Klein
Marcia R. Kleinerman
Christopher and Margaret Kleinhenz
James M. Knaack
Jeanette D. Knapp
Mrs. H. M. Knilans
Constance K. Knop
Elizabeth Knowles
Mary T. Knowles
Richard Knowles
James M. Knox
Gregory J. Koch
Julilly W. Kohler
Claire Kolbinger
Kosta Kolintzas
V. A. Kolve
Colleen M. Komarek
Nancy A. Kopp
Carol J. Kornheiser
Sally L. Koslow
Robert G. Kotewall
Lora M. Kovac
Kathleen A. Krahnke
Jan P. Krapel
Karen B. Krasnow
David C. Krause
Edith D. Kraus
Karen J. Krause
William A. and Claudia Kretzschmar Jr.
Lynn Frances Kreul
Stuart Krichevsky
Allen and Sharon Kriedeman
Mark W. Krivoruchka
Thomas J. and Deborah Krueger
Ellen J. Krupp
Sandra K. Kruse
John and Virginia Moore Kruse
John and Shirley E. Kurtilla
Dianne L. Kuehn
Jane Kugelman
Karen K. Kuhn
Diane M. Kujak
Ronald F. Kuka
Stanley J. and Diana T. Kulfan
Jason D. Kunesh
Norman Kunitz
Rita R. Kurzinski
William Labov
Janet M. LaBrie

Jonathan D. LaChance
Julie A. B. Lacy
Anne H. Lambert
Donald M. Lance
Sidney I. and Sarah Landau
Lenore E. Landorf
Arden and Jean Lange
Larry B. Langton
Jennifer M. LaRocco
Ralph C. LaRosa
Barbara J. Larson
Evelyn B. Larson
L. James and Jean L. Larson
Judy A. Larson
H. David Lasseter
Ronald R. Lassow
Phyllis K. Lathrope
Richard J. LaViolette
Deborah M. Lawson
Adam J. Lazewski
Jane Acomb Leake
Jane A. and Lowell Leake Jr.
Joan S. Lebow
Edmund Lechowicz Jr.
Nolan P. Le Compte Jr.
Jill S. Lederman
Lanning C. Lee
Maurice A. Lee
Karmen K. Leggett
Richard D. D. and Ann E. Lehan
Winfred P. Lehmann
Kristin M. Lehnert
Karen E. Leialoha
Charles Bronte Leicht
Mr. and Mrs. Lowell P. Leland
Shirley J. Lemke
Thomas G. Lemke
Roma E. Lenehan
Lester G. Lennon
Nancy Lennstrom
Judy M. Leonard
Jonathan Lepie
Alice R. Lev
Mrs. Louis H. Levi
Ephraim Y. and Ruth Levin
Alfred Levinson
Samuel M. Levy Family Foundation
Philip Goldiner Levy
Anthony J. Lewis
Nancy G. and Robert G. Lewis
Robert E. Lewis
Kimberley E. Li
Huei-Shiuan Liau
Herman W. Liebert
Betty B. Lies
Vincent J. Liesenfeld
Robert E. and Cathy A. Lieving
Ingrid Lind-Jahn
Henry J. Lindborg
Marilyn C. Lindsay
Ann S. Ling
Hubert and Mildred Ling
James G. Ling
Paul D. and Kay R. Ling
Ellen I. Linnihan
Gaylis M. Linville
Kathleen B. Lipkins
Susan C. Lisi
Florence M. Litzow

Judith H. Livingston
Susan L. Livingston
James B. Lockhart III
David Loewenstein
Lawrence S. Logue
Patricia B. Long
Richard A. Long
Frank A. Lorenz
Lindsay M. Lorenz
Barbara Lorman
Joan C. Loshek
Virginia A. Lott
Jason T. Loughrin
David Toay Lowell
Clinton Luckett
Cailin Lueders
Kara A. Luedtke
Patrick F. Luedtke
Louise Lueptow-Schwingel
John F. Luetscher
Juli A. Lund
S. Catharine Lutgen
Sandra J. Lyman
M. Juli Lynett
Charmaine B. and John O. Lyons
Melvin E. and Rosemary Lyon
Cosima V. Lyttle
Monica A. Macaulay
Ronald Macaulay
Frank Mack
Donald A. M. Mackay
Andrew and Barbara MacLeish
Genevieve MacLellan
Mr. and Mrs. John Maclin Jr.
Magdalen Madden
Pat Mages
Harmon D. Maher
Louis J. and Jane Maher Jr.
Susan N. Maher
Peter A. and Annette K. Mahler
Cassandra R. Mahoney
Fred C. Maier
Sara M. Mainster
William O. Makely
Phylis M. Makholm
John A. and Kristen A. Maki
Thomas J. and Judith A. Malueg
Beverly M. Mand
Christine A. Manesis
Joan D. Manning
Hadrian and Grace G. Manske
Gerald A. and Mary Manville
David A. Maraniss
Elliott and Mary C. Maraniss
Marathon Oil Company
Kate Marchewka
Joseph P. Marconi
Earl L. Marcoux
Kathryn H. Marczak
Stacy Schneider Marek
Joel P. Margolis
Bradley A. and Annette J. Markhardt
Elaine Marks
Jane Marshall
Jeanne A. Marshall
Kristina M. Marshall
Phyllis J. Marsteller
Todd K. Martens
Virginia L. Martens

Charles B. Martin
David G. Martin Jr.
Jack Martin
Lawrence T. and Claire E. Martin
Pamela S. Martin
Ruth W. Martin
Hal Marx
Cory A. Masiak
Bruce D. Mason
David H. and Judith F. Mason
Linda Mastalski
Evangeline Mastrogeannes
Jane M. Matsoff
Ella Mae Matsumura
Susan B. Matthews
William Matthews
Ernest W. Mattison, Sr.
John P. Mattke
Judith S. Mausner
Ann C. Maxwell
Richard D. Maxwell
Edwin G. and Phyllis I. May
Ruth H. May
Lori K. Mayer
Sandro Mayer
Mike Maynard
Natalie Maynor
Cheryl Ruth Mazer
Mary E. McAndrews
Dan McCammon
Norine McCarten
James E. McCauley
Catharine McClellan
Elizabeth D. McCutcheon
Glenn and Mia McDavid
Raven and Anne McDavid
Tom McDavid
Virginia G. McDavid
W. U. McDonald Jr.
K. H. and Dorothy E. McFall
John B. McFarland
James C. McGhee
Kathy McGinnis
Beverly A. McGraw
Carolyn A. McKee
Chandler L. and Beverly S. McKelvey
Andrew MacLeish
James B. McMillan
Geoffrey L. McNally
Bryan K. McNeely
Judy A. McQuade
Patricia I. Meagher
Grady Means
Marianne Means
Adam Jeffrey and Tamara A. Mehring
James E. and Lou Ann Meier
Mary G. Meikle
Robert J. Meindl
Amy K. Melchior
The Andrew W. Mellon Foundation
Robert G. and Helen E. Menefee
Richard J. Meng
Randal L. Merchen
Mamie Meredith
Bridget Sullivan Mermel
Stuart A. Merrill
Mark J. and Brigid Merriman

Michael R. and Jean A. Metcalf
Angela M. Meyer
John W. Meyer
Benjamin Meyers
Donald M. Michie
David L. Middleton
John C. and Judith A. Migas
Rodney H. Milbrandt
Sherwood J. Miles
Joseph B. Milgram
Alan Miller
Craig B. Miller
David R. and Marian M. Miller
Eric R. Miller
Harvey Miller
James D. and Bernadine Miller
John R. and Jan H. Miller
Lottie W. Miller
Mary G. Miller
S. R. Miller
Sylvia K. Miller
Martha Mills
David Milofsky
John H. Miner
William R. Miner
Andrew C. Mirer
Jacquelyn G. Mitchard
Doris J. Mitchell
Mary Lu and Wade T. Mitchell
Modernist Studies Association
Janet L. and Thomas C. Monk
Anthony P. and Susannah Brietz
    Monta
S. Martha Montevallo
Michael B. Montgomery
Robert E. Montgomery
Barbara M. Moore
Christopher R. Moore
Cynthia L. Moore
Edgar B. and Gracelouise Moore
J. B. Moore
Linda Moore
M. L. Moore
Mary Louise Moore
Randall L. Moore
Robert H. and Patricia M. Moore
Robert M. Moore
Rosemary Moore
William C. Moore
James T. Moran
Hal B. and Robin J. Morgan
Ruth Morgan
Stephen L. and Madeline B.
    Morgan
Arne A. Morgensen
Marilyn L. Morrill
Ellen Gibson Morris
Mrs. Matthew Morrow
Robert M. Morse
John and Karen Morser
Deborah Mortman
Herbert C. Morton
Pamela S. Morton
Nancy A. Muckenhirn
Kathryn J. Muehlhauser
Michael K. Mueller
Shirley I. Mueller
Stephanie Mueller
Willard F. Mueller
Anna Marie Mulvihill

Carol R. Munk
Emmanuel T. Munson-Regala
Sherrill J. Munson
Michaela J. Muntean
Elizabeth A. Murphy
M. Lynne Murphy
Martha K. Murphy
Mernice Murphy
Reed W. A. Murphy
Warren Musgrove
Peter A. Mutschler
Mark Muzi
Virginia U. Nader
Cristina Marie Nagel
Dennis B. and Linda Nash
National Endowment for the
    Humanities
National Science Foundation
Carolyn Pollard Neal
Julia Neal
Michael E. Neal Jr.
James W. and Lorrie Neale
Cheryl Cain Neelster
Stephanie C. Neils
Betty P. Nelson
Byron C. and Carolyn M. Nelson
Eric C. Nelson
James G. Nelson
Jenny K. Nelson
Nancy E. Nelson
Nicolas H. and Eveline D. B.
    Nelson
Maureen A. Nery
Victoria E. Neufeldt
The New York Times Company
    Foundation
Dorothy A. W. Newman
Frederick C. Newport
Mary S. Newton
Dennis K. C. and Marcella A. Ng
Kathleen B. Nigro
John D. Niles
Emily B. Nissley
Harold Q. Noack
Marcia J. Nolan
Francis G. Norder
J. Michael Norman
William C. Norsetter
Janna A. Northrup
Dorotha Northrup
Susan A. Notar
Joan E. Nucifora
Thomas Nunnally
Silvia G. Nussio-Rennie
Gerald M. and Mary J. O'Brien
James and Marjorie O'Connor
Christopher O'Malley Memorial
    Fund
Fred J. O'Malley
Kristine R. Oberg
Zachary F. Oberman
David R. Obey
Raymond K. O'Cain
Patricia T. O'Conner
Evelyn B. Odell
L. Terry Oggel
Ralph N. Olsen
David J. Olshanski
David A. and Karen L. Olson
Deborah H. Olson

Richard D. Olson
Steven Paul Olson
Nancy Oltman
William C. Oltman
David J. Onheiber
Donald and Patricia Oresman
Fred and Carole Orlosk
Henry D. Ormsby
Patricia D. Ostermick
Suzanne K. Ostfield
Alicia S. Ostriker
Douglas H. Ostrow
Maurice A. Ottinger
Peter J. Ouimet
Joanna A. Overn
John and Mary Owens
George B. Pace
Pacelli Athletic Association
Pacelli High School Band
    Association
David E. and Sandra J. Packard
Neil P. Pagano Jr.
Nancy J. Page
Sylvia H. Paikowski
Dorris V. Paille
Amalia C. D. Palaganas
Lalita D. Palekar
William Palmer
Peyton L. Palmore
Robert A. Papinchak
Elizabeth H. Parady
Angela J. Paratore
Elizabeth A. Parillo
James W. Parins
Ethel M. Parise
Mary Celestia Parler
Roger L. Parsons
Allyn Partin
James K. Pasell
Suzanne Patinkin
Joseph F. Patrouch Jr.
Jeffrey J. Patt
Arline E. Paul
Joan A. Paulson
Thomas C. Pavela
Frank D. Paynter
Thomas M. Pearce
Elizabeth A. Pearson
Lee A. Pederson
Gail A. Pederzoli-Dunn
Laura H. Peebles
Helen C. Peemoeller
Mary C. Pegg
Martin W. Penkwitz
Catherine S. Penner
Holly M. Pennington
Leslie W. Pennington
Penelope J. Perkins
Dennis R. Perry
Joan Perry
Kimberly A. Pesavento
Sarah Peter
Beth D. Petermann
John U. Peters
Lynn R. Peters
Erling W. Peterson
Harold F. Peterson
James B. Peterson
Jeffery L. and Barbara L. Peterson
Lynn A. Peterson

Richard V. and Ann Marie Pfeil
Jack O. and Beverly J. Pfister
Marianne R. Phelps
Betty S. Phillips
Faun M. Phillipson
Tom and Barb Phillis
David A. and Linda K. Pias
Frank G. Pickel
Marian J. Pickett
Jonathan Piel
Pieperpower Foundation
Judith M. Pier-Lybeck
Mary Connor Pierce
Joyce Pierro
Nancy L. Pinchar
Mary A. Pinkerton
Pitney Bowes Corporation
Margaret M. Pitts
Plaza Gynecology & Obstetrics
Julia B. Plier
Plover Family Practice SC
Sue O. Poethke
Nancy H. Pogel
William A. and Sue M. Pogue
John R. and Katherine H.
    Pompeii
Carole and John R. Pompeii Jr.
Cyrena N. Pondrom
Barry A. Popik
Philip L. Porte
Andrew J. Porter II
Patrick K. Porter
Frederick M. Poss
Eugene J. Potente
Mary J. Power
Don C. and Joan M. Prachthauser
John P. and Gail Prais
Terry Pratt
Heathre O. Prehoda
Braxton Preston
Dennis R. and Carol Preston
Mark J. and Susan Preston
Thomas R. Pribek
John K. Price
Robert P. Price
Carol A. Pringle
Mary Beth Protomastro
James T. Protsman
William Proxmire
Margo M. Ptacek
William Pulte Jr.
Richard M. and Barbara M.
    Purcell
Jane Pyle
Marian S. Quade
David E. Quady Jr.
The Quaker Oats Company
Susan C. Quatrini
Douglas Quine
Willard Van Orman Quine
Elizabeth E. Quinn
Richard H. and Bonnie B. Quinn
Randolph Quirk
Jean H. Radtke
Ryan R. Radtke
Barbara G. Raffel
Imogene Ragon
Peter S. and Beth Rahko
R. M. Rainwater
Richard D. and Krista M. Ralston

Richard N. Ramsey
Earle S. Randall
Mrs. Harry Randall Jr.
Carl J. and Catherine C. Rasmussen
Mrs. E. H. Ratcliff
Jean L. Rausch
Al Razner
Charlotte R. and Allen Walker Read
W. Charles Read
Fred M. and Sherry L. Reames
Daniel and Evelyn Reddin
Ruth Falk Redel
David Reed
William W. and Suzanne M. Reed
Don D. Reeder
Allen W. Reedy
Agnes Reese
Judith R. Reese
Delphina K. Reeve
John E. and Eva M. Regnier
Paul J. F. Regnier
Tom and Ann McDavid Reif
John E. Reilly Jr.
Arthur L. Reisman
John R. Remington
David A. Remley
Randall J. and Judy M. Rennicke
Gloria Resnick
Mary J. Resnik
Michael W. and Pamela S. Rewey
Marjorie Edna Rhine
Pauline C. Rhiner
Rice Clinic
Jennifer P. Rice
Mary Richards
Rhoda Richards
The Grace Jones Richardson Trust
Peter N. Richardson
Mary H. Richgels
Barbara A. Richmond
Ward I. and Ellen M. Richter
Rebecca K. Ricketts
Ruth C. Riddell
Philip M. Rideout
Eleanor M. Rifkin
Vivian J. Rightor
Richard N. and Karin E. Ringler
David L. Riordan
Linda J. Ripps
Landon H. Risteen
Robert Ritchie
Kenneth A. and Jane C. Robb
A. Hood Roberts
Catherine M. Roberts
Gloria B. Roberts
Rhys C. Roberts
Cindy Robinson
Fred C. Robinson
Sybil C. and John T. Robinson
Rockefeller Foundation
Mr. and Mrs. Earl Rodeheffer
Augusta D. Roddis
Elizabeth Rodman
Sara A. Rodriguez
James W. Roese
H. L. Rogers
Daniel R. Roos

Richard L. Rosen
Jennifer S. Rosenberg
Karen A. Rosenberg
Stephen M. Rosenberg
Shirley A. Rosenkranz
Rosenthal & Company
Barbara J. Rosenthal
Charlotte A. Rosenthal
Jerry and Bertha Roshak
John Rosine
Carol Rosofsky
Andrew A. Rossbach
James Roszak
Bonnie S. Roter
Marilyn L. Rothe
Rebecca A. Rothschild
Megan E. Rothstein
Laurie A. Rouleau
Lisa Rowe
Andrew M. Rubin
August Rubrecht
Robbie Ruby
Eric R. and Nancy Rude
Robert S. Rudolph
Bonnie B. Ruliffson
Maureen P. Runde
Marjorie D. Runser
Gene W. Ruoff
David C. Rupley
I. Willis Russell
William F. Russell Jr.
Margaret A. Ryan
Regina D. Sabbia
C. Ruth Sabol
Arthur B. Sacks
Mrs. E. N. Sainio
Peter J. Salber
William T. Salerno
Donna A. Salli
Joseph C. Salmons
Richard G. Salomon
Salus Mundi Foundation
Barbara J. Samuel
Olga Sanchez
Sarah M. Sanderson
James R. Sanger
Brandon J. Santos
Jane McCleary Saral
Hideki Sasaki
Mary H. Sasse
Mary E. Sasso
Muriel R. Saville
Julie K. Sazama
Marjorie Smith Scaletta
William David and Josephine Schaefer
Peter J. Schakel
Robert W. Schall
David L. Schanke
Robert H. and Glory A. Swoboda Schappe
Arlie W. Schardt
Thomas H. Schaub
Wilbert E. and Genevieve Schauer
Michael L. Scherf
Sherry A. Scheurell
Anne G. Schierl
Carl Schinasi
Patricia B. Schindhelm

Holly E. Schleicher
Elizabeth Schleyer
Sarah C. Schmelling
Becky M. Schmidt
Claude W. and Ila J. Schmidt
Gloria L. Schmidt
Jack G. Schmidt
Gretchen Schneider
Paul S. Schneider
Timothy S. Schneider
Caroline Schnog
William S. Schober
Miriam Schocken
Glenn Schoenenberger
Mary S. Schoenfeldt
Kristen R. Schoepke
Yvonne J. Schofer
Royal C. Schomp
Schönweitz
Frederick H. Schowalter
Susan Marie Schreier
William J. Schroeder
George L. and Kathleen K. Schueppert
Leslie M. Schultz
Ardeth Schulz
Gretchen E. Schulz
Robert M. and Kathleen Schuster
Natalie L. Schwab
Virginia Schwerin
Charla D. Scofield
Charles T. and Anne Mulgrew Scott
Judith Opatik Scott
Leslie J. Scott
Walter E. and Gertrude M. Scott
Ruth M. and Merton Sealts Jr.
Ryan C. and Melissa J. Sedevie
Steven K. and Alice J. Sedgwick
Rita Seeligson
Noel H. Seicol
Jean M. Seifert
Philip M. Seliger
Domenico Sella
Natalie R. Senecal
Frank E. Senk Jr.
George W. Setton
Joyce H. Sexton
Lawrence B. and Mary Steussy Shanahan
Fred Shapiro
Michael C. Shapiro
Ann W. Sharp
Hascall Sharp
William D. Sharpe
Dallis W. Shaver
Nancy J. Shaw
Dawn A. Shawkey
John A. Shea
John M. and Joan M. Sheehy
Pamela H. Sheff
Connie L. Shehan
Jesse Sheidlower
Stanley and Edith Sheidlower
Patricia R. Sheldrick
Samuel T. Shelton
Israel Shenker
Ruth Sherman
Bryan D. and Melanie T. Shirley
David L. Shores

Steven Short Living Trust
Homer T. Showalter
Roger W. Shuy
M. Ella Siddall
Matthew C. Siderits
Elizabeth Siedlecki
Paul J. and Janet E. Siedlecki
Frank L. and Margaret H. Siegel
Lewis A. Sierra
Laura Dee Silver
Joshua R. Silverman
Scott B. Silverman
Jennifer L. P. Simba
John C. Sime Trust
John H. Sime
William E. Simon Foundation, Inc.
David H. Simon
Terry J. Simon
John W. and Nancy P. Simons
Paul A. and Melanie J. Sims
Dorothy J. Sinclair
Rebecca L. Sinclair
Mary S. Siraki
Sister of the Sorrowful Mother Ministry Corporation
Jonathan M. Sitzer
Elizabeth P. Skerpan-Wheeler
Alexander N. and Margaret G. Skinner
Robert Skoglund
Mary L. Skutley
Claudia L. Slater
James Sledd
Alexander Sloan Jr.
Charles W. Sloan
Carroll G. and La Von Smith
Charles Smith
David L. and Alyce L. Smith
Jenna P. Smith
John M. Smith
Julia Smith
Rebecca A. Smith
Rose B. Smith
Geneva Smitherman
K. A. Snow
Sherwood Snyder III
Stephen M. and Angela M. Snyder
John D. Holm and Kelly J. Soley
Louis and Elsbeth Solomon
Nancy C. Sommers
L. G. Sorden
Scott A. Sorenson
Sara-Jane H. Sosa
Stephanie Ann Sommer
Stephen J. Spencer
Michael E. Spiegel
Joseph M. Spivey III
Claire Sprague
Walter V. Srebnick
Katherine St. Claire
St. Michael's Hospital, Stevens Point, Wisconsin
David W. St. Peter
John A. and Sally A. St. Peter
Bonnie L. Stack
David R. Stadelman
Joseph H. Stahl II
Ronald E. and Janet A. Standish

Blythe E. Stanfel
Jonathan C. Stapleton
Robert B. Starck
Frances Starkweather
Mary Louella Starling
Joshua P. and Emma R. Starr
Margaret L. Steckbauer
Arthur and Elizabeth S. Steele
Jeffrey A. Steele
Theresa A. Steele
Thomas J. Stefani
Margaret Steffensen
Jess Stein
Robin Moore Steinberg
Susan L. Steinfeldt
Julia L. Steinmetz
Elaine M. Stenzel
James W. Stephens
Robert W. Stephens
Thomas M. Stephens
Sidney Stern Memorial Trust
Edward Sternberg
Robert D. Stevick
June Stoddard
Linda L. Stolhanske
Ann M. Stone
Anne J. Stone
Anne Talbott Stone
Danica Stone
June Stone
Bessie Loyd Storgan
Christine E. Strand
Thomas N. Stratman
Peter F. and Susan P. Straub
Ann T. Straulman
Eric J. and Emily J. Strauss
Vicki A. Strauss
Katherine W. Streeper
Arthur W. Strelow Charitable
    Trust
David Strickon
Wylie C. Strout
Sharon L. Strover
Hariett Stryker-Rodda
Peter W. Sufka
Arthur G. Sullivan
Bonita Laper Sullivan
Katherine A. Sullivan
Sabrina A. Summers
Gary M. Sunada
SunTrust Bank Atlanta
    Foundation
Mildred M. Swanson
Sweet Adelines, Center Point
    Chapter
Shirley Swenson
Edwin Swillinger
Larry J. and Nikki Swingle
Tom Swint
Sean M. and Bridget M.
    McLernon Sykes
Keith R. and Mary L. Symon
Larry E. Syndergaard
Ingrid C. Sztukowski
Mr. and Mrs. William
    Szymkowiak
Berkley A. and Annemarie H.
    Tague
Patricia Takemoto
Molly M. Talcott

Merike Tamm
Peter Tamony
Carol H. Tarr
Kay Taube
Cary G. and Jeannie M. Tauchman
Agnes Taylor
Judith A. and Robert Taylor
Marilyn Taylor
Robert F. Taylor
Mr. and Mrs. Robert L. Taylor
Bradley B. Teague
Leslie M. Teague
Benjamin David Teitelbaum
Beatrice J. Temp
Temple Beth El Sisterhood,
    Madison, Wisconsin
Cynthia L. Terrill
K. Terwilliger
Joshua J. Teske
Jeffrey S. Theis
Darla S. Thomas
Ednah Thomas
Erik R. Thomas
Irene Thomas
Robert M. Thomas
Barbara J. Thompson
Peter J. Thompson
Mary G. Thorstensen
Paul J. Tilleman
Susan Tinkelman-Earl
John and Mary C. Tinkler
Karen S. Tipper
Mrs. D. G. Tobin
Joseph Tomasi
Kathleen M. Tomasovic
Leo C. Tonjes
Roger and Carol Sue Tonneman
Anne Torrans
Mary Totten
Elizabeth Trainer
Gerald J. Trecroci
James A. and Karen Trennepohl
Justin Trewartha
Renee R. Trilling
Robert S. Trimble
Joann E. Trimmer
R. C. and Muriel S. Troike
Philip R. Trosko
Henry M. Truby
Michele R. Tschopp
Kam-Wah Tsui
Bonnie H. Tucker
Linda Jordan Tucker
Michael J. Turano
Lea M. Turnbull
Thomas M. Turner
Sheila L. Tuttle
The Twice Ten Art Club
Sharon M. Twigg
Andrew John Twito
Gary L. Tyeryar
Charlane J. Tygum
Margaret Tysver
Gerald Udell
Mary Uecker-Hettinga
Fred Uhlman
United States Office of Education
University Book Store, Madison,
    Wisconsin

University of Wisconsin–Madison
    College of Letters and Science
University of Wisconsin–Madison
    Department of English
University of Wisconsin–Madison
    Graduate School
Linda Liden Urban
Michael K. Urban
Laurence Urdang
Francis Lee Utley
Richard P. Vacca
Steve J. VanDerWeele
Craig and Anne M. VanDyke
Patricia A. VanDyke
Cheryl S. Van Lear
Thomas M. Van Lieshout
David L. Vander Meulen
Glenn R. Vandergriff
Suzanne S. Vang
Silke Van Ness
Jozsef and Barbara J. Vass
Rosamond B. Veator
Richard G. Vega
Juriis Veidemanis
Jonathan A. Veitch
Laura Veltman
Nicole K. Vernon
Kent B. and Mary G. Verrill
Eugene B. Vest
George and Muriel Vetter
John B. Vickery
Wolfgang Viereck
Dana K. Vigna
Vital Projects Fund, Inc.
Lois Joanne Vitcenda
Paul D. Voelker
Bette L. Vogel
Luanne von Schneidemesser
Sandra C. Von Unwerth
Bonnie J. F. VonKrogh
Norine K. Voss
Richard A. Waack
Robert S. Wachal
Susan Lynn Wafer
Nelsen Robert Wahlstrom
Judith G. Waite
David P. Waldherr
Donald H. and Jacqueline M.
    Walker
Kevin C. Walker
Marla M. Wallace
Ronald W. and Margaret E.
    Wallace
Jack J. Walsdorf
Richard Walser
Jim S. Walter
Mr. and Mrs. F. W.
    Wandschneider
David F. Ward
Kathleen M. Ward
Dorothy M. Wartenberg
Harry E. Wastrack
Janet C. Waterhouse
Karen C. Watkins
Robert R. and Elizabeth Watson
Maynard J. Watson
David W. Watt Jr.
Joseph B. and Anne L. Way
Wayne State University
Joshua P. Weatherbee

Judith A. Weaver
Marguerite Dorothy Weaver
Thomas A. Weber
Alison M. Webster
John G. and Nancy E. Webster
Loudon C. Webster
Katherine J. Weese
Manfred Weidhorn
Etta Ruth Weigl
Marc S. and Leslie A.
    Weinberger
Howard D. Weinbrot
Andrew D. Weiner
James L. Weis
Susanne L. Wellford
David A. Welshhans
Ward P. Welty
Peter G. Wemeier
Mark J. Wendt
Suzanne May Weniger
Joy Werlink
Robert G. Westphal
Keith E. and April A. Wetherell
Christopher J. Wheatley
Jamie E. Wheeler
Jean Whitaker
Juanita J. Whitaker
Katharine Whitcomb
Trudy Whitman
Nancy Whitney-DeGoff
Norman E. and Joy R. Wideburg
Joseph J. and Louise H.
    Wiesenfarth
B. Eliot Wigginton
Douglas A. and Doris T. Wight
Cheri L. Wild
Mitchell A. Wilder
Ann Y. Wilkinson
John Willard
Margaret P. Willard
Mary E. Willets
Anna M. Williams
Charles H. Williams
James M. Willmore
H. W. Wilson Foundation
Carolyn F. Wilson
Michelle L. Wilson
Rex Wilson
Sharon R. Wilson
William H. Wilson
John N. Winburne
Lise Winer
Mark A. Winer
Kenneth Winkle
Halliman H. and Shirley
    Winsborough
Hyla J. Winston
Nancee M. Wipperfurth-Killoran
Shirley J. Wirth
Wisconsin Alumni Research
    Foundation
Rodney P. Wittwer
Robert A. Witz
Francis D. Wolfe Jr.
Walt Wolfram
Michael Wolkowitz
Willson Wood
David A. and Rosalind
    Woodward
Kristin M. Woodward

Henry Bosley Woolf
Christine M. Wootton
Marjorie L. Worth
Peter C. Wredling
Al Wright
C. Ben and Donna J. Wright
George T. Wright
Dennis W. Wurch
Lionel D. Wyld
Masayoshi Yamada

Joyce A. Yasner
Robert N. Yetter
Harry M. Yohalem
Gilbert Youmans
Julie A. Youmans
Steven W. and Susan I. G.
    Youngs
William and Ann Yudchitz
Arthur L. Zapel Jr.
Janice K. Zawacki

Rozanne M. Zeiger
Wilbur Zelinsky
Betty Zeps
Amy Lee Zern
Ilia Qiriako Zhulati
John M. Ziebell
Collene T. Ziegenfuss
Mary Brown Ziegler
Holly E. Zielinski
David T. Ziemann

Julia A. Ziercher
Bettie Zillman
Rachael Thiele Zimmermann
Judith Zinke
Mark B. Zirbel
Jerome S. Zuckerman
Ernest G. ZumBrunnen
Philip L. Zweifel
Arnold M. Zwicky

The Anatomy of a *DARE* Entry

headword.

part-of-speech abbreviation.

variant form. All variants are cross-referenced; a reader who looks up *drop egg* will find a reference to **dropped egg**.

etymology. *DARE* doesn't try to trace every word back to its ultimate origin, but only to explain how it got into American English. This etymology suggests that *dropped egg* is from Scots dialect, and refers the reader to the relevant entry in the *Scottish National Dictionary,* where the earliest citation is from 1824.

regional label. This generalization is based on all the available evidence, but especially, when possible, on evidence from the *DARE* survey.

social label. Like the regional label, this is based on all available evidence, but especially on evidence from the *DARE* survey.

definition.

map. The computer-generated map is deliberately distorted so that the area of each state is roughly proportional to its population. If every informant who was asked question H35 had answered *dropped egg,* the map would show 1,002 evenly spaced dots, each representing one of the communities selected for the *DARE* survey. This uniform spacing makes it much easier to interpret the map, since any "bunching" of dots is potentially significant, though it does take a little practice to recognize the states in their distorted forms.

quotation block. The quotations provide examples of the headword, beginning with the earliest known U.S. example. All quotations, unless explicitly attributed to a secondary source, have been verified in the original.

short-title. The bibliography, which appears in this volume, gives precise bibliographic details on every source cited in *DARE* (there are nearly 13,000), but the abbreviated titles allow the interested reader to identify the source.

regional label. Whenever possible, regional information is given for individual quotations. In this example, the reader finds that the story quoted was set in Massachusetts.

DARE question. This is the question to which *dropped egg* was a reply. The full questionnaire is printed in Volume I.

summary statement. This summarizes the regional distribution of the informants who gave this response.

informant code. Rarer responses are attributed to individual informants; a list in Volume I gives basic data on each one.

social statistics. In this entry, this is the main evidence for the social label *"somewhat old-fash."* When there are more informants, more elaborate statistics may be justified.

dropped egg n Also *drop egg* [Prob from Scots dial; cf *SND drap* v. 5. (2) (b) 1824 →] **chiefly NEng** See Map *somewhat old-fash*
A poached egg.

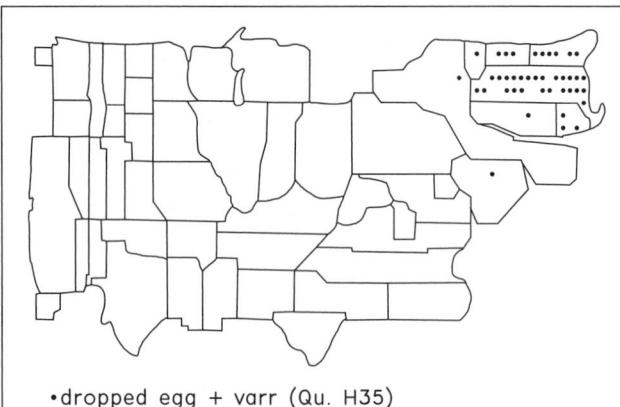

•dropped egg + varr (Qu. H35)

1884 *Harper's New Mth. Mag.* 69.306/1 **MA,** Martha was . . eating her toast and a dropped egg. **1896** (c1973) Farmer *Orig. Cook Book* 93, *Dropped Eggs* (Poached). **1933** *Hanley Disks* **neMA,** Dropped egg—take and put a pan of milk on the stove and boil and drop the egg in and let it cook. **1941** *LANE* Map 295 (Poached Eggs), **throughout NEng,** *Dropped eggs*. . . 1 inf, **ceVT,** Drop eggs. **1948** Peattie *Berkshires* 323 **wMA,** In Berkshire . . you could not get a poached egg, but you could get a "dropped" egg, which was the same thing. **1965** *PADS* 43.24 **seMA,** 6 [infs] poached eggs, 4 [infs] dropped eggs, 1 [inf] dropped egg on toast. **1965–70** *DARE* (Qu. H35, *When eggs are taken out of the shell and cooked in boiling water, you call them _____ eggs*) 40 Infs, **chiefly NEng,** Dropped; **NH**15, Dropped egg on toast. [33 of 41 Infs old] **1975** Gould *ME Lingo* 82, *Dropped egg*—Maine for poached egg, usually on toast. **1977** *Yankee* Jan 73 **Isleboro ME,** The people on Isleboro eat dropped eggs instead of poached.

The *DARE* Map and a Conventional Map of the United States

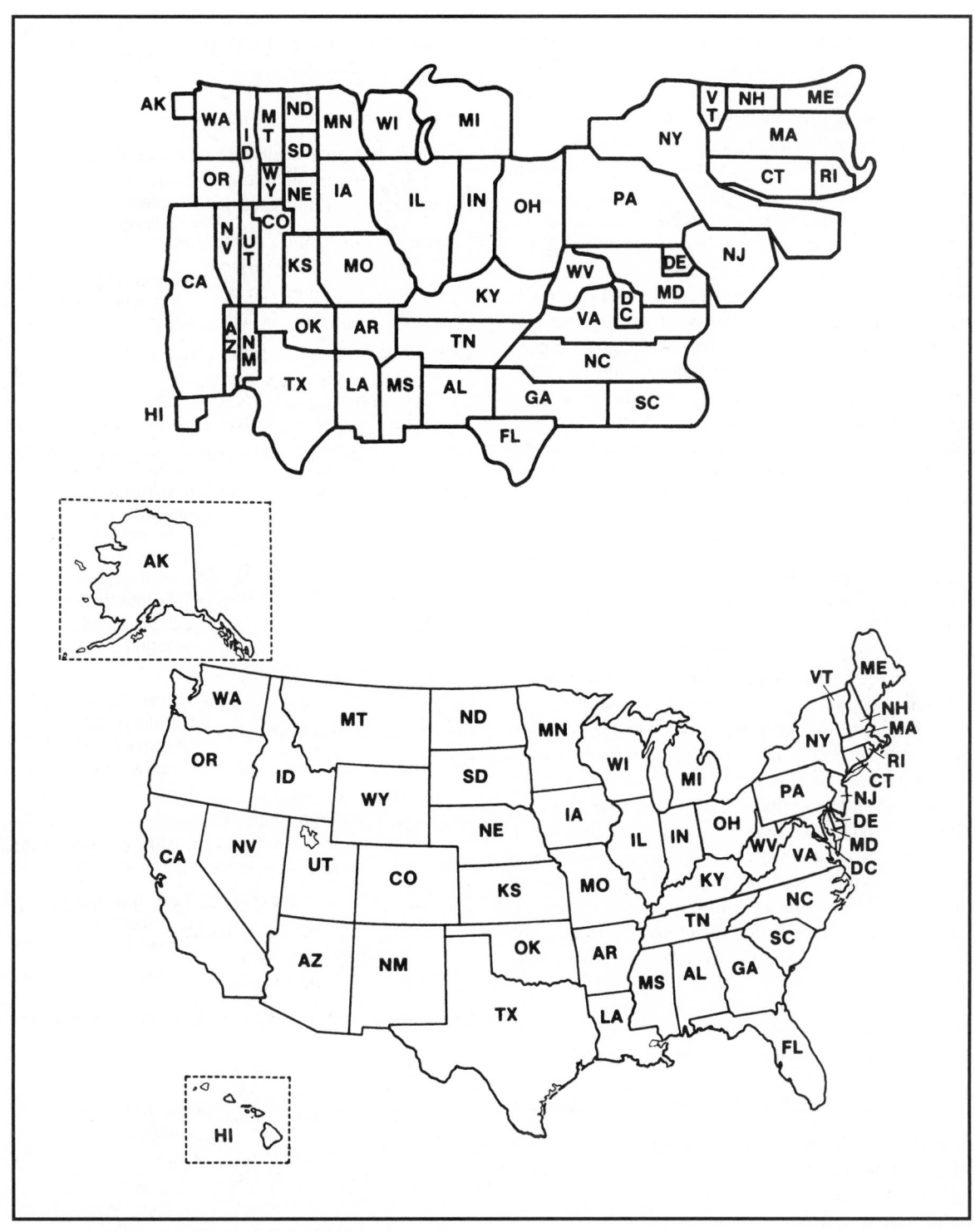

Pronunciation Guide

The following list of phonetic symbols and sample words is intended to provide a ready-reference guide to the system of transcription used in *DARE* entries. For an explanation of the criteria for inclusion of pronunciations and a more detailed discussion of the sounds and their regional distributions, readers are referred to the "Guide to Pronunciation" found on pp. xli–lxi of Volume I.

Pronunciations in the head sections of *DARE* entries are in "broadly phonetic" transcriptions using International Phonetic Alphabet (IPA) characters* enclosed in vertical lines. Those in quotations from *DARE* fieldwork are usually much more narrowly phonetic and are enclosed in square brackets. When quotations from sources other than *DARE* include pronunciations, the transcriptions are reproduced faithfully, with two exceptions: archaic or idiosyncratic systems are silently translated to *DARE*'s transcriptional system, and some of the minute details in sources such as the *Linguistic Atlas of the Gulf States* have not been preserved. Characters that are raised above the line of text are to be interpreted as weakly articulated; those enclosed in parentheses are variably present. Sequences of symbols not listed here should be interpreted as the sum of their parts. When two vowels in a transcription are contiguous but do not constitute a diphthong, they are separated by a hyphen.

In the list below, each symbol on the left is followed by a sample word containing the sound it represents. It must be remembered, however, that regional variation is complex, and one person's pronunciation of *father,* for instance, will not necessarily match another's. (In a few cases where readers are likely to recognize sounds characteristic of a particular region, notes regarding geographic distribution have been included.) Indented under the sample words are symbols for similar sounds that occur in the same phonetic environments. These include both those variants that occur frequently in *DARE* transcriptions and (in an effort to include symbols found in sources other than *DARE* materials) those that are less common. No attempt is made to determine an overall phonemic system.

*A few exceptions to the use of IPA characters are *DARE*'s use of |ɚ|, |š|, |ž|, |č|, and |ǰ|, which are traditional Linguistic Atlas symbols.

The Vowels

|i| *beat;* a higher-high-front unrounded vowel
- [ii] upgliding variant
- [iə] ingliding variant
- [ɨ] centralized variant
- [y] rounded variant

|ɪ| *bit;* a lower-high-front unrounded vowel
- [ɪə] ingliding variant
- [ɪ] centralized variant; usu unstressed
- [ʏ] rounded variant

|e| *bait;* a higher-mid-front unrounded vowel
- [eɪ] upgliding variant
- [eə] ingliding variant

|ɛ| *bet;* a lower-mid-front unrounded vowel
- [ɛɪ] upgliding variant
- [ɛə] ingliding variant
- [ɵ] rounded variant

|æ| *bat;* a higher-low-front unrounded vowel
- [æɪ] upgliding variant
- [æə] ingliding variant
- [a] lowered variant; used esp in parts of New England in such words as *ask, dance, path,* etc

|u| *boot;* a higher-high-back rounded vowel
- [uu], [ʌu] upgliding variants
- [uə] ingliding variant
- [ʉ] centralized variant
- [ɯ] unrounded variant; see also |l|

|ʊ| *book;* a lower-high-back rounded vowel
- [ʊə] ingliding variant
- [ʊɪ] front-gliding variant
- [ᵿ] centralized variant
- [ɤ] unrounded variant

|o| *boat;* a higher-mid-back rounded vowel
- [oʊ], [ɵʊ] upgliding variants
- [oə] ingliding variant
- [ɵ] slightly fronted variant (the "New England short *o*")

|ʌ| *cut;* a fronted, lower-mid-back unrounded vowel occurring in stressed syllables
- [ʌɪ] upgliding variant
- [ʌə] ingliding variant

|ɔ| *bought;* a higher-low-back rounded vowel; see also |ɔɪ| and Pronc Intro 3.II.9
- [ɔʊ] upgliding variant
- [ɔə] ingliding variant
- [ɒ] lowered variant

|ɑ| *cot;* a lower-low-central unrounded vowel; see also Pronc Intro 3.II.9, 10
- [a] fronted variant
- [ɑ] retracted variant

|ə| *sofa;* also *mother* (for speakers without postvocalic *r*); a mid-central unrounded, unconstricted vowel occur-

ring in unstressed syllables (except when the first element of a diphthong; see |aɪ|, |aʊ|)
  [ɐ]   lowered variant

|ɚ| *mother* (for speakers with postvocalic *r*); a mid-central unrounded, constricted vowel occurring in unstressed syllables

|ɜ| *bird* (for speakers without postvocalic *r*); a mid-central slightly rounded, unconstricted vowel occurring in stressed syllables
  [ɜɪ]   upgliding variant
  [ɞ]   fully rounded variant

|ɝ| *bird* (for speakers with postvocalic *r*); a mid-central slightly rounded, constricted vowel occurring in stressed syllables

|aɪ| *bite;* a front-upgliding diphthong
  [ɑɪ], [ɒɪ]   retracted variants
  [əɪ], [ʌɪ]   centralized variants (esp in Mid Atl and Canadian border regions)
  [aə], [ɑə]   ingliding variants
  [a:]   monophthongized variant (esp in parts of Sth and S Midl)

|aʊ| *about;* a back-upgliding diphthong
  [ɑʊ]   retracted variant
  [əʊ], [ʌʊ]   centralized variants (esp in Mid Atl and Canadian border regions)
  [a:]   monophthongized variant (esp in parts of Midl)

|ɔɪ| *boy;* a front-upgliding diphthong
  [oɪ]   raised variant
  [ɒɪ]   lowered variant
  [ɔə]   ingliding variant
  [ɔ:]   monophthongized variant (esp in parts of Sth and Midl)

The Consonants

|p| *pat;* a voiceless bilabial stop

|b| *bat;* a voiced bilabial stop
  [ƀ]   fricativized variant

|t| *tap;* a voiceless alveolar stop

|d| *dog;* a voiced alveolar stop

|k| *keep;* a voiceless velar stop
  [x]   fricativized variant

|g| *get;* a voiced velar stop

|ʔ| *bottle;* a glottal stop

|f| *fist;* a voiceless labiodental fricative

|v| *vice;* a voiced labiodental fricative

|θ| *thing;* a voiceless interdental fricative

|ð| *this;* a voiced interdental fricative

|s| *see;* a voiceless alveolar fricative

|z| *zoo;* a voiced alveolar fricative

|š| *shoe;* a voiceless palatal fricative (also represented as [ʃ])

|ž| *vision;* a voiced palatal fricative (also represented as [ʒ])

|č| *chin;* a voiceless palatal affricate (also represented as [tʃ])

|ǰ| *jump;* a voiced palatal affricate (also represented as [dʒ])

|m| *mad;* a voiced bilabial nasal
  [ɱ]   labiodental variant

|n| *new;* a voiced alveolar nasal
  [ɲ]   palatalized variant

|ŋ| *spring;* a voiced velar nasal

|h| *high;* a voiceless glottal fricative

|w| *witch;* a voiced velar frictionless continuant

|hw| *which;* a voiceless continuant, for those who distinguish it from *witch;* (also represented as [ʍ])

|j| *you;* a voiced palatal frictionless continuant

|r| *run;* a voiced alveolar frictionless continuant
  [ɾ]   flapped variant
  [ɹ]   fricativized variant

|l| *light;* a voiced alveolar lateral
  [ļ]   palatalized or "clear" variant
  [ł]   velarized or "dark" variant
  [ɯ]   fully vocalized variant; see also |u|

Diacritical Marks

ˈ   (raised, preceding a syllable) = having primary stress

ˌ   (lowered, preceding a syllable) = having secondary stress

~   (over a symbol) = nasalized

−   (through the middle of a symbol) = articulated toward the center of the mouth

·   (following a symbol) = slightly lengthened

:   (following a symbol) = significantly lengthened

< or �   (following a symbol) = forward in the mouth

> or ⊣   (following a symbol) = retracted in the mouth

^ or ⊤   (following a symbol) = higher in the mouth

ᵛ or ⊥   (following a symbol) = lower in the mouth

ʻ   (following a symbol) = aspirated

⁻   (following a symbol) = unreleased

̥   (beneath a symbol) = voiceless

̬   (beneath a symbol) = voiced

̮   (beneath a symbol) = labialized

̯   (beneath a consonant) = dentalized

̑   (beneath |ə|) = unsyllabic

̣   (beneath a consonant) = syllabic

̣   (beneath a vowel) = constricted

List of Abbreviations

Note: Periods are used for abbreviations in short-titles and bibliographic references, but are generally omitted elsewhere.

a	ante (before)
A	auxiliary informant
abbr(s)	abbreviated, abbreviation(s)
absol	absolute(ly)
abstr	abstract
acad	academy
acc	[date of] access; accusative
accd	according to
acct(s)	account(s)
ADD	Wentworth *American Dialect Dictionary*
addit	addition(al)
adj(s)	adjectival, adjective(s)
admin	administration
adv(s)	adverb(s), adverbial
advent	adventure(s)
advt	advertisement(s), advertiser
Afr	African
Afro-Amer	Afro-American
ag	agricultural, agriculture
agric	agricultur(al)ist
AHD	*American Heritage Dictionary of the English Language*
alt(s)	alternation(s), alternative
alter(s)	alteration(s)
Amer	America(n), Americana
AmFr	American French
AmInd	American Indian (language)
AmPort	American Portuguese (language)
AmSp	*American Speech*
AmSpan	American Spanish (language)
AND	Ramson *Australian National Dictionary*
anon	anonymous
AN&Q	*American Notes & Queries*
anthol	anthology
anthro	anthropological, anthropology
antiq	antiquarian, antiquity
aphet	aphetic
apoc	apocopated, apocopation
app	appendix
appar	apparent(ly)
approx	approximate(ly)
Apr	April
arch	archaic
archeol	archeological, archeology
art	article
assim	assimilated, assimilation
assoc	associate(d), association
asst	assistant
astron	astronomical, astronomy
Atl	Atlantic
attrib	attribution, attributive(ly)
Aug	August
Austr	Australia(n)
autobiog	autobiographical, autobiography
aux	auxiliary
BBC	British Broadcasting Corporation
bd	board
betw	between
bib	bibliographical, bibliography
biog	biographical, biography
biol	biological, biology
bot	botanical
Brit	Britain, Britannica, British
Bros	Brothers
bur	bureau
c	central; circa (about)
c.	copyright
Can	Canadian
CanEngl	Canadian English (language)
CanFr	Canadian French (language)
cap	capital
capt	captain
CB	citizens band
cent(s)	central; century (-ies)
Cent D	Whitney *Century Dictionary*
cf	confer (compare)
ch	chapter; church
chem	chemical, chemistry
Chr	Christian
chron	chronicle(s)
co	company; county
cogn	cognate
col	colonel
coll	collected, collection(s), collective; college
colloq	colloquial
comb(s)	combination(s), combine(s)
comm(s)	commission(ers); committee(s); community (-ies)
comp	compiled, compiler, composition
compar	comparative
concr	concrete(ly)
Cong	Congress
conj	conjunction
conjug	conjugation
cons	consonant
conserv	conservancy, conservation
constr(s)	construct(ed), construction(s); construed
contemp	contemporary
contr	contracted, contraction
contrib	contribution(s)
conv	conversation(al)
coop	cooperative
Corn	Cornish, Cornwall
corr(s)	correct, corrected, correction(s)

correl	correlated, correlation, correlative		eve	evening
corresp	correspondence		evid	evident(ly)
cpd	compound, compounded, compounding		ex(x)	example(s)
crit	critical		exag	exaggerated
cv	cultivar		exc	except
cyclop	cyclopedia		exclam	exclamation, exclamatory
			excr	excrescent
d	died		exped	expedition(s)
DA	Mathews *Dictionary of Americanisms*		exper	experiment(al)
DAE	Craigie-Hulbert *Dictionary of American English*		expl(s)	explain(ed), explanation(s)
Dan	Danish		explor	exploration(s), exploring
DARE	Cassidy-Hall *Dictionary of American Regional English*		expr(s)	expression(s)
DAS	Wentworth-Flexner *Dictionary of American Slang*		ext	extended, extension
dat	dative		eye-dial	eye-dialect
DBE	Holm-Shilling *Dictionary of Bahamian English*			
DCan	Avis et al. *Dictionary of Canadianisms*		f(f)	and following
DCEU	Allsopp *Dictionary of Caribbean English Usage*		famil	familiar(izing)
Dec	December		Feb	February
def art	definite article		fem	feminine
defin	defining, definition(s), definitive		fig	figurative(ly), figure
Delmarva	DE, eMD, eVA		Fin	Finnish
dem	demonstrative		folk-etym	folk-etymological, folk-etymology
dept	department		folkl	folklore
deriv	derivation, derivative, derived		foll	follow(s), followed, following
derog	derogatorily, derogatory		Fr	French
descr	description, descriptive		Franco-Amer	Franco-American
dial(s)	dialect(s), dialectal		FrCan	French Canadian (people)
dicc	diccionario		freq	frequent(ly)
dict	dictionary		Fri	Friday
dimin(s)	diminutive(s)		Fris	Frisian
diss	dissertation(s)		ft	foot (measures); fort
dissim	dissimilated, dissimilation		funct	function(al)
distrib	distribute(d), distribution, distributive		fut	future
div	division		*F&W*	Funk et al. *Funk and Wagnalls Standard Dictionary*
DJE	Cassidy-LePage *Dictionary of Jamaican English*		FW(s)	fieldworker(s)
DN	*Dialect Notes*		FWP	Federal Writers' Project
DNE	Story et al. *Dictionary of Newfoundland English*			
DNZE	Orsman *Dictionary of New Zealand English*		Gael	Gaelic
doc	document(ary)		gaz	gazette(er)
DOST	Craigie *Dictionary of the Older Scottish Tongue*		gen	general(ly); genitive
DPEIE	Pratt *Dictionary of Prince Edward Island English*		geneal	genealogical, genealogy
Dr	Doctor		genl	general
DS	Data Summary		geog	geography
DSL	Jamieson *Dictionary of the Scottish Language*		geogr(s)	geographer(s), geographic(al)
DSME	Montgomery-Hall *Dictionary of Smoky Mountain English*		geol	geological, geology
			Ger	German
DSNA	Dictionary Society of North America		Gk	Greek
Du	Dutch		gloss	glossary
			Gmc	Germanic
e	east(ern)		gov	governor
ed(s)	edited, edition, editor(s), editorial		govt	government
EDD	Wright *English Dialect Dictionary*		gram	grammar, grammatical
EDG	Wright *English Dialect Grammar*		gs	grade school
educ	educated, education(al)		gt	great
ellip	ellipsis, elliptical(ly)			
EModE	Early Modern English		Haw	Hawaiian
encycl	encyclopedia, encyclopedic		hdbk	handbook
engin	engineering		Heb	Hebrew
Engl	England, English		herb	herbaceous
entomol	entomologica, entomological, entomology (-ist)		hist	historic, historical(ly), history
epenth	epenthesis, epenthetic		hon	honorable
Episc	Episcopal		horticult	horticultural(ist), horticulture, horticulturist
equiv	equivalence, equivalent		hs	high school
erron	erroneous(ly)		Hung	Hungarian
esp	especially		hydrog	hydrographical, hydrography
est	established			
et al	et alii (and others)		*ibid*	ibidem (in the same place)
etc	et cetera (and so forth)		idiom	idiomatic
etym(s)	etymological, etymology (-ies)		ie	id est (that is)
euphem(s)	euphemism(s), euphemistic(ally)		illit	illiterate

illustr	illustrate(d), illustration	MHG	Middle High German
imit	imitation, imitative	mid	middle
imper	imperative(ly)	mid-aged	middle-aged (of Infs: 40–59)
imperf	imperfect(ly)	midl	midland
impers	impersonal(ly)	midwest	midwestern
in	inch	misc	miscellaneous, miscellany (-ies)
inc	incorporated	mispronc	mispronunciation
incl	include(d), including, inclusive	Missip	Mississippi
Ind	Indian	*MJLF*	*Midwestern Journal of Language and Folklore*
indef	indefinite(ly)	MLG	Middle Low German
indic	indicative(ly)	*MLJ*	*Modern Language Journal*
inf(s)	informant(s)	*MLN*	*Modern Language Notes*
infin	infinitive(ly)	mod	modern
infl	influence(d)	ModE	Modern English
info	information	Mon	Monday
infreq	infrequent(ly)	monogr	monograph(s)
init	initial(ly)	ms(s)	manuscript(s)
inst	institute, institution	mt(s)	mount, mountain(s)
internatl	international	mth(s)	month(s), monthly
interp	interpretation, interpreter	mw	midwest
interrog	interrogative(ly)		
intj	interjection	n	north(ern); noun
intr	intransitive(ly)	*NADS*	*Newsletter of the American Dialect Society*
intro	introduced, introducing, introduction	N Amer	North America(n)
Ir	Irish	narr(s)	narrative(s)
irreg	irregular(ly)	nat	natural
is	island(s)	natl	national
Ital	Italian	naut	nautical
iter	iteration, iterative	NB	New Brunswick
		nd	no date
Jan	January	ne	northeast(ern)
jct	junction	NEast	northeast
joc	jocular(ly)	neg	negative
jrl(s)	journal(s)	NEng	New England
		neut	neuter
l(l)	lake; line(s)	newsl	newsletter
lab	laboratory	newsp	newspaper(s)
LaFr	Louisiana French	Nfld	Newfoundland
LAGS	Pederson *Linguistic Atlas of the Gulf States*	no(s)	number(s)
LAMSAS	McDavid et al. *Linguistic Atlas of the Middle and South Atlantic States*	nom	nominative
		non-std	nonstandard
LANCS	*Linguistic Atlas of the North Central States*	Norw	Norwegian
LANE	Kurath *Linguistic Atlas of New England*	Nov	November
lang(s)	language(s)	np	no page
Lat	Latin	*N&Q*	*Notes & Queries*
LAUM	Allen *Linguistic Atlas of the Upper Midwest*	ns	new series
lect	lecture(s)	nth(n)	north(ern)
LGer	Low German	nw	northwest(ern)
lib	library	NYC	New York City
ling	linguistic(s)	*NYT*	*New York Times*
lit	literary, literature	NZ	New Zealand
Luth(s)	Lutheran(s)		
		obj	objective
m	meter(s)	obs	obsolete
M	Monsieur	occas	occasional(ly)
mag	magazine	Oct	October
malaprop	malapropism	OE	Old English
Mar	March	*OED*	Murray et al. *Oxford English Dictionary*
masc	masculine	*OED2*	Simpson-Weiner *Oxford English Dictionary,* 2nd ed
math	mathematical, mathematics	*OEDS*	Burchfield *Oxford English Dictionary Supplement*
ME	Middle English (in etymologies; elsewhere = Maine)	OF	Old French
med	medic(in)al, medicine	old-fash	old-fashioned
MED	Kurath *Middle English Dictionary*	ON	Old Norse
mem(s)	memorial(s)	orig	origin, original(ly)
metall	metallurgical, metallurgy	ornith	ornithological, ornithologist (-gist(')s), ornithology
metaph	metaphor, metaphorical(ly)	Oxfd	Oxford
metath	metathesis, metathetic(ally)		
Mex	Mexican, Mexico	p(p)	page(s); post (after)
MexSpan	Mexican Spanish	*PADS*	*Publication of the American Dialect Society*
mfg(r)(s)	manufacture, manufacturer(s), manufacturing	PaGer	Pennsylvania German

pejor	pejorative
perf	perfect
perh	perhaps
pers	person
pert	pertaining
petrol	petroleum
philol	philological, philology
philos	philosopher, philosophical, philosophy
phon	phonetic
phr(r)	phrase(s)
phys	physical
pl	plate; plural
PMLA	*Publications of the Modern Language Association of America*
poet	poetical
Pol	Polish
pop	popular(ly)
Port	Portuguese
poss	possessive; possible
ppl	participial
pple(s)	participle(s)
prec	preceded, preceding
pred	predicate, predication, predicative(ly)
pref	prefix(ation)
prehist	prehistoric, prehistory
prelim	preliminary
prep(s)	preposition(s)
pres	present
pret	preterite
prob	probable, probably
proc	proceedings
progr	progressive
pron	pronoun
pronc(s)	pronounced, pronouncing, pronunciation(s)
pronc-sp(p)	pronunciation-spelling(s)
Prot	Protestant
prov	proverb(ial); provincial
pseud	pseudonym
psych	psychological, psychology
pt(s)	part(s); port
pub	public; publication(s), published, publisher, publishing
punct	punctuation
qq	questions
QR	questionnaire
qrly	quarterly
qu	question
quot(s)	quotation(s)
r	recto; river
rec	record(s)
recoll	recollections
redund	redundant
redup	reduplicated, reduplication, reduplicative
ref(s)	refer, reference(s)
refl	reflexive
reg	register; regular(ly)
rel	related, relation, relative
relig	religion, religious
repet	repetition, repetitive
repr	represent(s), representative(s), represented, representing; reprint(ed), reprints
rept	report(s)
resp(s)	response(s)
rev(s)	review(s); revised, revision
revol	revolution(ary)
rr	railroad(s)
Russ	Russian
s	south(ern)

Sat	Saturday
Scan	Scandinavian
sci	science(s)
Scotl	Scotland
Scots	Scottish
se	southeast(ern)
sec(s)	section(s)
secy	secretary
Sept	September
ser	series
serv	service
sess	session
sg	singular
sig	signature
sl	sine loco (no place)
sn	sine nomine (no name)
SND	Grant *Scottish National Dictionary*
soc	society (-ies)
sociol	sociological, sociology
sp(p)	species; spelled, spelling(s)
Span	Spanish
SpanAm	Spanish American (people)
spec	specific(ally)
sp-pronc(s)	spelling-pronunciation(s)
st	saint; street
sta	station
statist	statistical(ly)
std	standard(ized)
StdE	Standard English
sth(n)	south(ern)
subj	subject
subjunc	subjunctive
subseq	subsequent(ly)
subsp(p)	subspecies
suff	suffix(ation)
sugg	suggest(ed), suggestion
Sun	Sunday
superl	superlative
suppl	supplement(ary)
surv	survey(s)
sw	southwest(ern)
Sw	Swedish
syll	syllable
syn	synonym(ous)
tech	technical, technological, technology
terr	territory (-ies)
Thu	Thursday
topog	topographic(al), topography
tr	transitive
trans	transaction(s)
transcr	transcribe(d), transcription
transf	transfer(red)
transl	translate(d), translating, translation, translator
treas	treasury
Tue	Tuesday
ult	ultimate(ly)
uncert	uncertain
uncom	uncommon
uncult	uncultivated
univ	university
unpub	unpublished
unstr	unstressed
US(A)	United States (of America)
usu	usual(ly)
v	verb; verso
var(r)	variant(s), variety (-ies), various, varying
vbl	verbal

vd	various dates	KS	Kansas
vet	veterinarian, veterinary	KY	Kentucky
viz	videlicet (namely)	LA	Louisiana
vocab(s)	vocabulary (-ies)	MA	Massachusetts
vol(s)	volume(s)	MD	Maryland
vs	versus	ME	Maine
		MI	Michigan
w	weekly; west(ern)	MN	Minnesota
W2	Neilson et al. *Webster's New International Dictionary,*	MO	Missouri
	2nd ed	MS	Mississippi
W3	Gove et al. *Webster's Third New International*	MT	Montana
	Dictionary	NC	North Carolina
wd	word	ND	North Dakota
Wed	Wednesday	NE	Nebraska
WELS	Cassidy-Duckert *Wisconsin English Language Survey*	NH	New Hampshire
wildfl	wildflower	NJ	New Jersey
wks	works	NM	New Mexico
WNID	Harris-Allen *Webster's New International Dictionary*	NV	Nevada
wrn	western	NY	New York
WWI	World War I	OH	Ohio
WWII	World War II	OK	Oklahoma
		OR	Oregon
x	hybrid	PA	Pennsylvania
		RI	Rhode Island
yd	yard	SC	South Carolina
yr(s)	year(s)	SD	South Dakota
		TN	Tennessee
zool	zoological, zoology	TX	Texas
		UT	Utah
		VA	Virginia
		VT	Vermont

State Abbreviations

AK	Alaska	WA	Washington
AL	Alabama	WI	Wisconsin
AR	Arkansas	WV	West Virginia
AZ	Arizona	WY	Wyoming
CA	California		
CO	Colorado		
CT	Connecticut		
DC	Washington DC		
DE	Delaware		
FL	Florida		
GA	Georgia		
HI	Hawaii		
IA	Iowa		
ID	Idaho		
IL	Illinois		
IN	Indiana		

Signs and Symbols

~   is used to avoid repetition of a previously spelled-out word or phrase

‡   is used to indicate a word or sense of questionable genuineness

*   is used to indicate unattested or hypothetical forms

+   is used for "and"

→   is used with dates to indicate first or last attestation

<   is used for "derived from"

>   is used for "from which is derived"

=   is used for "equals"

Dictionary of American Regional English

SL

slab n

1 also *slab highway,* ~ *road:* A road paved with concrete. **scattered, but esp IL, IN, MO** See Map Cf **hard road**

1921 *Decatur Daily Rev.* (IL) 2 Sept 20/5, The slab on the turns is no wider than on straight away road. **1923** *Ibid* 10 June 12/1, The slab is now well past the point where it was originally intended to leave off. **1930** *Durant* (Okla.) *D. Democrat* 4 Nov. 1/6 *(DA),* Efforts are being made to have the road opened for traffic Wednesday, but considerable dirt is to be removed from the concrete yet, and it is likely that the slab will not be opened before Thursday. **1937** *AmSp* 12.241, Around Fullerton, Missouri, and elsewhere in the state, the highway (paved) is called the *Slab.* **1941** *AmSp* 16.24 **sIN,** *Slab.* Concrete highway. **1948** Davis *Word Atlas Gt. Lakes* 246, *Road paved with concrete. . . slab* fairly common sInd & sILL. **1960** Criswell *Resp. to PADS 20* **Ozarks,** [Referring to paved roads:] Often it is called the *slab. . .* recent. **1961** Folk *Word Atlas N. LA* map 206, *Paved highway . . others . . slab* road. **1965–70** *DARE* (Qu. N23, *Other kinds of paved roads*) 13 Infs, **esp IL, IN, MO,** Slab; IL114, Slab—don't hear that much anymore; IL128, Slab—take the slab to Harrisburg; SD8, Concrete road [same as] slab road; [MO11, OK49, TX45, Concrete slab;] (Qu. N16a, *Names for a highway with two lanes on each side and a separation down the middle*) Inf IL135, Slab. **1966** Dakin *Dial. Vocab. Ohio R. Valley* 2.213, *Cement road. . .* Many speakers in Illinois regularly say *hard road* or *the slab, slab road* for a road paved with concrete. *(The) slab (road)* is also used in the Indiana pocket and nowhere else. **1969** *DARE* Tape IL78, [FW:] I don't even know what you mean by "hard road." [Inf:] I mean this slab here that you come from Carbondale up here today on. **1971** *Today Show Letters* **cIL,** They asked directions out in the country. I said "Go out to the *Slab* and go thus and so." I no longer use that word, but when the highway, pavement, hard road, concrete, or route first was built through here, slab was its name. **1973** Allen *LAUM* 1.238 (as of c1950), *Cement road. . .* The single instance of *hard road* in eastern Iowa reflects its popularity in Illinois. *Slab,* also found only in Iowa, likewise is probably an Illinois import. [*DARE* Ed: 1 inf, **ND,** reports that *slab highway* is "heard in the community."] **1982** *Smithsonian Letters* **IL, MO,** In rural western Illinois and rural northeastern Missouri, a concrete-surfaced highway is referred to as "the slab." **2003** *UrbanCyclez* Mar (Internet) **GA,** Touring bikes are. . . good for taking trips . . and rolling down the slab (highway) on a sunny day.

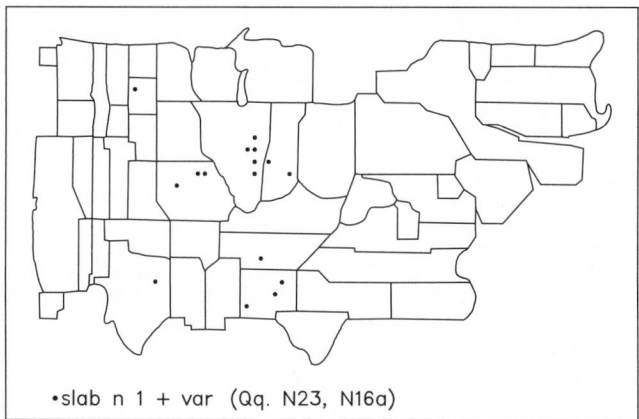

•slab n 1 + var (Qq. N23, N16a)

2 See **slab bacon.**
3 See **slab drag.**

4 A very large **soft-shell crab 1. chiefly Chesapeake Bay** Cf **whale crab**

1984 *DARE* File **Chesapeake Bay** [Watermen's vocab], Slabs. **2000** Shores *Tangier Is.* 223 **Chesapeake Bay,** With regard to mixture and meaning, there are many instances, of course, of words for the same thing: . . [as] *jumbo, whale,* and *slab* for the large softcrab. **2008** *DARE* File—Internet **Chesapeake Bay,** *Slabs*—very large soft crabs (also whales).

slab v

1 To traverse or cut into (a slope or mountain) obliquely or spirally; to ascend or descend in such a manner; hence vbl n *slabbing.*

1873 *Daily Rocky Mt. News* (Denver CO) 5 Aug 2/2, Over all this (Caribou) route there is not over 500 feet in length of rock cutting to be done, and that only as a kind of 'slabbing.' **1889** (1971) Farmer *Americanisms* 492, *To Slab. . .* To make roads round the sides of mountains. **1892** *Outing* 19.268 **NEng,** So we started blindly up the bank and into the forest, continuing for an hour and a half to "slab" the mountain, as the backwoodsmen say. **1917** *Guide Paths White Mts.* 267 **NH,** The path. . . rises by easy zigzags, slabbing the S.W. flank of Eagle Cliff. **1949** *PADS* 11.26 **CO,** *Slab. . .* To travel in diagonals. "He slabbed up the mountain." **1963** *Appalachian Trailway News* 24.3.43 *(Hench Coll.),* We zigzagged and slabbed mountains finally coming over Albert Mountain. **1964** *AmSp* 39.298 **MD,** 'Slabbing a mountain' is an old mountaineer expression meaning ascending or descending by going around it rather than up one side and down the other. **2002** *DARE* File **nwMA,** Instead of going straight up the hill, you slab the hill. In building a trail, I slab the hills all the time. I go around a contour and head for a saddle.

2 See **slab drag.**

slab bacon n Also *slab (belly),* ~ *meat,* ~ *side, slap bacon* **scattered, but more freq Sth** See Map Cf **side bacon** **=side meat.**

1848 *Brooklyn Daily Eagle* (NY) 23 May 1/1, Adventurers left Chicago in a large two horse wagon, loaded with sundry "fixins," such as hams, slab bacon, corn meal, . . and . . cooking utensils. **1943** *Sun* (Baltimore MD) 19 June 4/3, *Bellies Or Slab Bacon. . .* Fresh with rine. **1956** Ker *Vocab. W. TX* 270, Salt pork; home-cured bacon. . . *Slab, slab bacon . .* receive but one response each [from 67 infs]. **1961** Folk *Word Atlas N. LA* map 1015, Salt pork—home-cured bacon . . [less freq re-

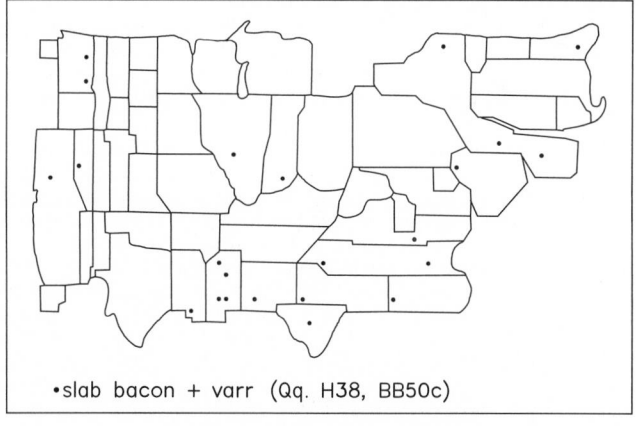

•slab bacon + varr (Qq. H38, BB50c)

sponses include] slab bacon. **1965–70** *DARE* (Qu. H38, . . *Words for bacon*) Infs **FL**33, **GA**88, **MS**85, **NV**7, **NY**20, **NC**1, **WA**1, Slab bacon; **ME**9A, Slab bacon—in one big uncut piece; **NY**39, Slab bacon—the whole piece before it's cut; **SC**38, Slab bacon—streak o' lean, streak o' fat; **IL**83, **MS**2, **NY**58, Slab; **AL**21, Slab and sliced; **NJ**3, Slab belly; **MS**79, **NC**55, Slab meat; **WA**6, Sliced or slab; **CA**170, Pork slab; **LA**24, Salt slab—pork salted down but not smoked; **MS**46, Slab side; **VA**39, Slap bacon; (Qu. BB50c, *Remedies for infections*) Inf **IN**35, Tie a piece of slab bacon on it. [19 of 23 Infs female] **1966** Dakin *Dial. Vocab. Ohio R. Valley* 2.336, The most common practice generally throughout the Ohio Valley is simply to refer to smoked (and possibly sugar-cured) side pork as *bacon.* In Illinois . . the terms *side* (sometimes *slab*) *bacon* . . are usual. **1989** Pederson *LAGS Tech. Index* 158 **Gulf Region** *(Salt pork)* 2 infs, Slab bacon. *Ibid* 159 **Gulf Region** *(Smoked meat)* 15 infs, Slab; 16 infs, Slab bacon. **2004** *DARE* File—Internet **VA,** You can taste the flavors of the old-fashioned south with our genuine Virginia slab bacon.

slabbing See **slab** v 1

Slab City See **Slab Town**

slab drag n Also *slab (harrow)* **scattered, but esp MD**
An improvised harrow made up of split logs; hence v *slab* to break up clods using such a harrow.
1866 *Amer. Agric.* 25.133 **cwMS,** The harrow is used by many for covering the seed, but a slab drag was thought to be the best. It is made of a piece of hard wood log, which is half round, or slab-shaped, about 30 inches long, 18 inches wide, and 8 thick, with handles, set in the bark side. **1907** Bailey *Cyclop. Amer. Ag.* 2.652, A revolving disk or harrow is run over the land in order to cut the sod to pieces, after which the field is smoothed over with a slab drag. **1912** *News* (Frederick MD) 2 Mar 2/6, [Advt:] 1 slab drag. **1968** *DARE* (Qu. L20, *The implement used in a field after it's been plowed to break up the lumps*) Inf **MD**31, Slab—made of split log [sic], round side down; **MD**26, Slab drag—long split logs dragged by horses in old days. **1973** Allen *LAUM* 1.409 (as of c1950) 1 inf, **SD,** Slab, *vb.* To drag over (the ground) a heavy structure of wood slabs, in order to break clods. **c1980** in **2004** *DARE* File—Internet **MD,** His farming equipment consisted of two horses, a plow, a cultivator, a home made spike and roller and of course that most important piece of equipment, a slab drag. **1986** Pederson *LAGS Concordance,* 1 inf, **nwTN,** Slab harrow.

slab highway See **slab** n 1

Slab Hollow See **Slab Town**

slab meat See **slab bacon**

slab road See **slab** n 1

slab shot n Cf **slab** v 1
Perh a glancing shot.
1926 (1992) McQueen–Mizell *Hist. Okefenokee* 184 **Okefenokee GA,** Being a quick shot he fired at the bear at close range, making a slab shot through the bear's shoulder.

slab side n See **slab bacon**

slab-side adj See **slab-sided**

slab-sided adj Also *slab-side, slap-sided*
Usu of an animal: having relatively flat sides; not filled out; of a person or animal: lanky, awkwardly-shaped, ungainly; also fig; hence n *slab-sides* a lanky person.
1817 Paulding *Letters from South* 2.122, He was what is usually called a tall slab-sided Virginian, . . with not enough fat about him to hold his ideas by the legs and wings. **1840** (1841) Dana *2 Yrs.* 263, Her captain was a slab-sided, shamble-legged Quaker. **1859** *N. Amer. Rev.* 89.359, It is only under the hand of such men as Robert Bakewell . . , that long-legged, slab-sided, ill-bred oxen are metamorphosed into small-boned, quick-fattening Devons and elephantine Durhams. **1862** *Continental Mth.* 2.29, They [=swine] were a long, lean, slab-sided race, with legs and shoulders like a deer. **1884** *Anglia* 7.274 **Sth, S Midl** [Black], *To be slab-sided* = to be awkward. **1893** Shands *MS Speech* 57, *Slab-sided.* . . [I]n Mississippi it is used by all classes to mean *crooked, cranky.* He is a *slab-sided* man, means that mentally, morally, or physically he is not as he should be, he is deficient in some way—he is not straight. This meaning may have come to this word from its having been confused with *crank-sided.* **1899** (1912) Green *VA Folk-Speech* 391, *Slab-sided.* . . Having flat sides like slabs; hence, tall and lank. **1910** *DN* 3.448 **cwNY,** Slab (slap)-sided. . . Long and lank; ungainly. **1936** Adams *Cowboy Lingo* 87, A broken-down

horse . . in poor condition . . was 'shad-bellied,' 'slab-sided.' **1941** *LANE* Map 463 *(Awkward, clumsy)* 1 inf, **swCT,** Slab-sided. **c1960** *Wilson Coll.* **csKY,** *Slab-sided.* . . Poorly proportioned. **1966–70** *DARE* (Qu. K15, *A thin, bony, or poor-looking cow*) Inf **TN**10, Slab-sided; (Qu. K44, *A bony or poor-looking horse*) Inf **VA**43, Just slab-side; (Qu. X49, *Expressions . . about a person who is very thin*) Inf **MI**20, Slab-sides. **1975** Gould *ME Lingo* 258, As applied to a person, let it be understood that a *slab-sided* woman will never become Miss America. **2004** *DARE* File—Internet, Sight hounds are slab sided or flat in the rib cage.

Slab Town n Also *Slab City, ~ Hollow* [See quot 1975] Cf **mill town, Sawmill Hollow**
Used as a derogatory nickname for a town or district, esp one having a mill, factory, or mine.
1833 *Niles' Weekly Reg.* 8.384 **SC,** The nullifiers, it seems, have resolved that *Slab-Town* shall eclipse Colleton, where they began their revolutionary movements. **1849** *S. Lit. Messenger* 15.44, Countless *"originals"* . . are met with in all our papers and periodicals, from the "Slab-town Genius of Liberty," up to the imposing pages of the established Reviews. **1881** *Atlantic Mth.* 47.53 **CO,** The little towns . . that had grown up while this gulch was yielding its millions of gold from the gravel washings, had rotted away, until the remnants were reduced to the name of Slab-town. **1935** *AmSp* 10.80 **seMO,** *Slabtown* suggests the small group of shacks which grows up around a sawmill. **1937** in 1976 *Weevils in the Wheat* 87 **VA** [Black], Most of them [=slaves] lived in slab houses in Slabtown. That was in Phoebus. **1941** *Vermonter* June 133 (as of 1880), It was the first time we ever saw a town except "Slab Holler" (that was what Plainfield Village was called at that time). **1965–70** *DARE* (Qu. C34, *Nicknames for nearby settlements, villages, or districts*) Infs **MA**23, 62, **NY**28, 103, 157, Slab City; **MA**1, Slab City—rural ex-slum; **NC**79, **VA**8, **WI**45, Slab Town; **MI**105, Slab Town—a lumber town; **MT**2, Slab Town—had sawmill; (Qu. C35, *Nicknames for the different parts of your town or city*) Inf **IN**17, Slab Town; **PA**176, Slab Town—area of company houses near the tannery; (Qu. II25, *Names or nicknames for the part of a town where the poorer people, special groups, or foreign groups live*) Inf **MA**1, Slab City—former hat factory area; **AR**3, Slab Town. **1975** Gould *ME Lingo* 258, *Slab city*—Term for the poorer section of town, and arising from the *slab*-sided houses that sprang up around new sawmills in the early days. The first cut off a log, with one rounded bark side, is a slab; and if a person is careful in selecting good slabs and takes the time to nail them properly, a comfortable rough dwelling can be turned out. Where actual *slab cities* existed in Maine towns, such rough homes were temporary, and today some of Maine's one-time *slab cities* are pretentious residential sections. The term is used more or less as "the other side of the tracks" for a less desirable section of town, without reference now to any sawmills. **2004** *DARE* File—Internet **nwMI,** 5 years ago he bought a house in town that was built in 1884 in an area called "Slab Town." . . [T]he reason it's called "slab town" is because it was located near all the lumber mills. . . They built their small homes using the free slab wood found around the mills.

slack adj
1 Disheveled, disordered, dirty—also in phr *slacker than dishwater.* **chiefly NEng**
1914 *DN* 4.80 **ME, nNH,** Slacker 'n dishwater. . . Untidy, dirty, slovenly. **1941** *LANE* Map 466 *(Slovenly)* **NEng,** [*Slack* occurs throughout the region; *slack looking* occurs less frequently.] **1966–69** *DARE* (Qu. W41, . . *Expressions . . for someone whose clothes never look right or who always dresses carelessly*) Infs **CT**15, **ME**11, **NY**96, Slack; **NH**16, Slack-looking. [All Infs old] **1975** Gould *ME Lingo* 258, In another sense, Mainers use *slack* as derived from the nautical meaning of not taut; the *slack* in a rope. This gives us *slack* for untidy and slipshod: "She's the slackest housekeeper in town." **2002** *DARE* File **nwMA,** Gramma and I . . have used "slack" in the sense of someone not doing their work properly or someone who is lazy or shiftless. As: "It looks a little slack around his place (house)." **2004** *DARE* File—Internet **NEast** (as of 1918), "Neatness"—There's another thing / For which the Colonel's strong,/ The slack untidy soldier / Sure as hell will get in wrong.

2 also *slack salt;* Of preserved fish: lightly or inadequately salted. Cf **slack-salt** v
1918 U.S. Congress House *Amer.-Can. Fisheries* 161 **neMA,** The first lot that he bought was a slack salt codfish. **1934** Pierce *Goin' Fishin'* 53 **NEng,** He must know how much salt the large fish require so that they will come out right and not be "slack" or "strong," if he uses too little. **1951** *Portland Sun. Telegram & Sun. Press Herald* (ME) 6 May

mag sec 2/3, [Caption:] Here's the makin's of a true New England fish dinner, the split, salt pollock being cured in Rockland. . . one of the remaining places where this old-fashioned slack salt pollock is still prepared. Takes only a few days of this sun-drying treatment before the fish is ready for marketing.

3 Of a cow or her udder: dry. **NEast** See Map

1966–69 *DARE* (Qu. K9, *If one quarter of a cow's udder does not give milk . . she's _____*) Infs **MA**25, **NY**160, Slack; **CT**36, **NY**72, Slack in one quarter; **ME**14, Has a slack quarter; **MA**74, Slack a quarter; **VT**2, Slack quarter. [6 of 7 Infs old]

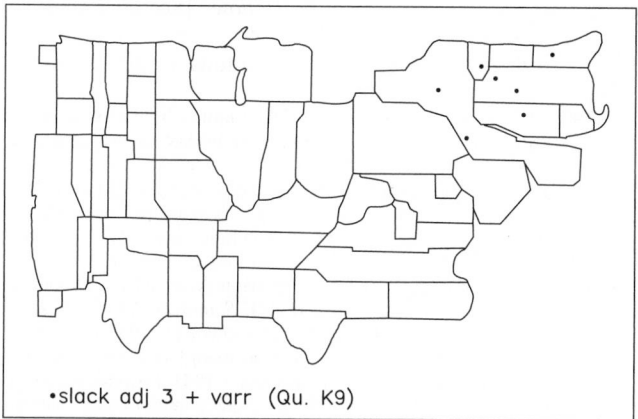

•slack adj 3 + varr (Qu. K9)

slack n   See **slack jaw**

slacker than dishwater   See **slack** adj 1

slack jaw n   Also *slack*   [Scots, Engl dial *slack jaw*] Impudence, impertinence.

1823 Doddridge *Logan* 46, At the peril of all of you . . none of your slack jaw. **1825** Neal *Brother Jonathan* 1.156 **CT**, None o' you slack, says I . . none o' your pokin' fun at me. **1903** *DN* 2.330 seMO, *Slackjaw. . .* Impudent language. 'Don't give me any of your slack-jaw!' **1909** *DN* 3.371 **eAL, wGA**, *Slack. . .* Impudence. **1930** in 1944 *ADD* **ceSC**, *Slack. . .* Impudence, impertinence.

slack-salt v   esp **NEng**   Cf **slack** adj 2

To salt (fish) lightly or inadequately; hence ppl adj *slack-salted.*

1808 *Repertory* (Boston MA) 6 May 1/2, An Act—To prevent fraud and deception in curing and packing smoked alewives and herrings. . . [T]he following shall be taken out as *Refuse:* all those which are belly broken, tainted, scorched or burnt, slack salted, or not sufficiently smoked. **1828** Webster *Amer. Dict.* (at *dunning*), At the Isles of Shoals . . the cod are taken in deep water, split and slack-salted. **1868** (1869) Kellogg *Charlie Bell* 320 **ME**, [We] have brought you some dry fish; . . Uncle Isaac slack-salted them, and told us how to cure them. **1890** *Century Dict.* 5681, *Slack-salted. . .* Cured with a small or deficient quantity of salt, as fish. **1896** *Scribner's Mag.* 19.83 **NEng**, Fresh fish, including frozen and slack-salted, was already free in our ports, competing sharply with our own catch. **1916** *Daily Kennebec Jrl.* (Augusta ME) 25 Oct 12/5, Slack salted or English cured Quoddy pollock are selling easily at $6.50 per qtl. [=**quintal**] retail. **1962** Morison *One Boy's Boston* 32 **MA**, My grandfather stoutly maintained that a scrod was, or should be, a small codfish that had been split and slack-salted the night before. **2004** *DARE* File—Internet **ME**, Mainers have been eating slack-salted hake (and pollock) for years.

slack salt adj   See **slack** adj 2

slack-salted   See **slack-salt** v

slack-twist n   [*EDD* (at *slack* adj.[1] 11.(15)) "an inactive, lazy, shiftless person"]   Cf **slack** adj 1, **slack-twisted**

1927 *AmSp* 3.134 **eME**, A poor housekeeper was commonly referred to as a "slack-twist."

slack-twisted adj   [*EDD* (at *slack* adj.[1] 11.(16))]   Cf **no-account**, **slack-twist**, **sorry** adj **B1**

Fig: lax, ineffectual, deficient in character or energy; hence n *slack-twistedness.*

1853 *Defiance Democrat* (OH) 19 Nov 1/4, A Slack Twisted Girl. . . Her dress generally has two or three grease spots upon the front breadths, her shoes are down at the heel, and she scuffs about rather than

walks. She is too lazy to open her windows to air her chamber [etc]. **1868** *De Bow's Rev.* 5.367 **MS**, The Bay St. Louis *Gazette* says that while the soil of Mississippi will produce everywhere cabbages, lettuces [etc] , . such is the slack-twistedness of the people that in many counties they live on hog and hominy the year round. **1876** *Scribner's Mth.* 11.632, The Great Story-teller palliates the "slack twisted" morals of . . Colonial society. **1883** *Overland Mth.* (2d ser) 1.124 **VT**, He isn't *lazy*—it isn't that; and he hasn't any bad habits. He means well and he works hard; but somehow there's no *succeed* to him. . . She's her father's daughter—good girl, but there's something slack-twisted about both of them. **1895** *DN* 1.394 **IN, KY, WV**, *Slack-twisted:* mentally weak, shiftless. **1899** (1912) Green *VA Folk-Speech* 391, *Slack-twisted. . .* Of little physical force or energy. **1941** Chase *Windswept* 60 **ME**, This dowser of ours is a kind o' slack-twisted fellow with a no-account wife and a parcel o' measley children. . . No one puts any stock in him at all except for his dowsin'. **1967** Williams *Greenbones* 42 **GA** (as of c1910), A fine tall figure of a man, but for all his size, Nin thought, he seemed without life, slack-twisted. **1972** *Atlanta Letters* cnGA, Slack Twisted—A person not specific in any thing they do. **1984** Wilder *You All Spoken Here* 16 **Sth**, *Slack-twisted:* Lacking in courage; said of someone who makes false excuses for failures; one who feigns excuses to escape military duty. **2003** *DARE* File—Internet **WA**, This will be a change from my occasional slack-twisted policy of voting only on issues that interest me.

slain   See **slay 1**

slained   See **slay 2**

slam adv   chiefly **Sth, S Midl**, esp **SE**   Cf **plumb** adv, **slap** adv

1 Directly, abruptly.

1843 (1916) Hall *New Purchase* 217 **IN**, Here's the silver cash money, right slam smack down. **1944** *PADS* 2.26 **cwNC**, *Slam. . .* Directly and violently. "He hit slam against that tree." **1965–70** *DARE* (Qu. KK53, *When one thing suddenly hits hard against something else: "He ran _____ into a car."*) 19 Infs, chiefly **Sth, S Midl**, esp **SE**, Slam. [16 of 19 Infs old]

2 All the way; completely.

1889 *Century Illustr. Mag.* 39.47 **NEng**, He set every inch of canvas there was a spar for, and drove her right slam across the Bay of Bengal. **1922** Gonzales *Black Border* 327 **sSC, GA coasts** [Gullah glossary], *Slam*—a synonym for "spang," expressing distance, all the way. **1949** Kurath *Word Geog.* 61 **VA, NC**, *Clear across. . .* Instead of, or by the side of, the common expression *clear across* (the bed), we encounter . . *slam across* from the lower James to the Cape Fear. **1952** Brown *NC Folkl.* 1.591, *Slam. . .* Entirely.—Central and east. **1966–70** *DARE* (Qu. LL26a, *. . 'All the way': "He drove _____ to the end of the road."*) Infs **SC**26, 31, 40, **VA**69, Slam. **1967** Faries *Word Geog. MO* 87, *Clear across. . .* A few instances of the Southern *slam* . . are scattered throughout the state. **1969** *DARE* FW Addit **cNC**, *Slam*—used for *all the way*—"Slam down to the axle." **1970** *DARE* Tape **TX**96, One old fella that was on there let his leg slip; got down in there, and this other beam . . cut that leg slam off. **1971** Mitchell *Blow My Blues Away* 67 **nwMS** [Black], Well, I played music slam on up till I was married. **1982** *DARE* File **NC**, "They were dried slam . . up" (speaking of her vegetable garden). **1986** Pederson *LAGS Concordance* chiefly **coastal Gulf Region**, [There are 20 exx of *slam*, in such phrr as "slam across," "slam out," "slam through," "slam full," "slam up."] **1994** *NC Lang. & Life Project Dial. Dict. Lumbee Engl.* 11 **seNC**, *Slam. . .* Very, extremely. *I ate so much I got slam full.* **2004** *York Daily Rec.* (PA) 30 May (Internet), We have two donated storage spaces slam full.

3 See **slam-bang 2.**

slam n

1 also *slam-down:* The act of throwing oneself onto a sled to coast face down; hence v *slam* to perform such an action.   esp **N Cent, Gt Lakes**   See Map on p. 4   Cf **belly-slam 1**

[**1924** *IA City Press-Citizen* (IA) 12 Jan 12/2, He slammed his sled down, as the others had done, and went flying down the hill. . . "Pick it up and slam it, like you saw me do," said the little man.] **1950** *WELS Suppl.* **csWI**, Slam—our word for belly-buster. *Ibid* **csWI**, Slam—child throws himself on top. **1965–70** *DARE* (Qu. EE25, *When a child picks up his sled . . runs with it, and then throws himself down on it, that's a _____*) Infs **IL**14, **NY**109, **OH**11, 42, **PA**206, 216, **UT**3, **WI**12, Slam; **MD**31, Slam-down; **MI**61, Slam; slamming—he is slamming downhill. **1973** Allen *LAUM* 1.391 **IA** (as of c1950), *Coast lying down. . .* slamming. . . Volunteered by inf.'s 19-year old son. **2003** *DARE* File **csWI** (as of 1930s), Boys and tomboys would *take a slam* (throw themselves face down onto a sled).

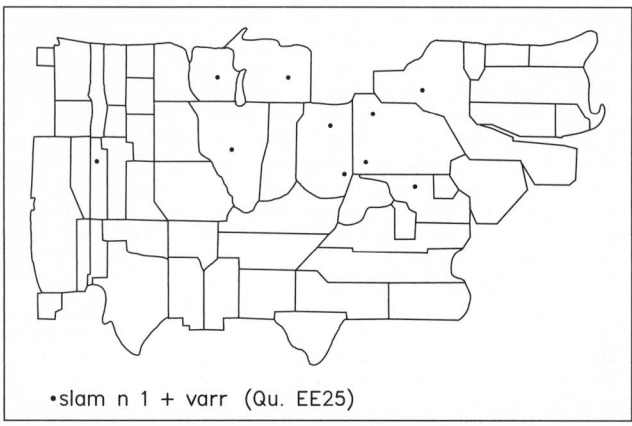

•slam n 1 + varr (Qu. EE25)

2 A multitude—in phr *a whole slam:* see quot. Cf *DS* LL8b, LL9a

1952 Brown *NC Folkl.* 1.591, *Slam, a whole.* . . A great many.—Central and east.

slam v   See **slam** n 1

slamakin   See **slommack**

slam-bang adv

1 As with a slam and a bang; violently, abruptly, directly. Cf **smack-dab**

1835 *Adams Sentinel* (Gettysburg PA) 30 Mar 1/5, Down I came slam bang. **1840** R.M. Bird *Robin Day* 25 *(OED2),* Five or six hundred field pieces blazing away slambang. **1879** *Scribner's Mth.* 18.545, I sent an arrow slam-bang into the lantern. **1905** *DN* 3.19 **cCT,** *Slam-bang.* . . Recklessly. 'He always goes at things slam-bang.' **1907** *DN* 3.217 **nwAR,** *Slam-bang.* . . Recklessly. **1909** *DN* 3.371 **eAL, wGA,** *Slambang.* . . "He ran slam-bang into a hornet's nest." **1910** *DN* 3.448 **cwNY,** *Slam-bang.* . . Recklessly. **1965–70** *DARE* (Qu. KK53, *When one thing suddenly hits hard against something else: "He ran _____ into a car."*) 39 Infs, **scattered, but somewhat more freq NEast, N Cent,** Slam-bang. [30 of 39 Infs old] **2002** *DARE* File—Internet, The plot heads slam-bang into thriller territory.

2 also *slam:* Exactly.

1887 (1967) Harris *Free Joe* 109 **GA,** I don't reckon he's right slam bang at home, but I lay he ain't fur off. **2004** *DARE* File—Internet, Knoxville date is right slam in the middle of the week.

slam-down   See **slam** n 1

slanch   See **slaunch**

slanchindicular   See **slantindicular**

slanchways, slanchwise   See **slaunchwise**

slang n

A Gram form.

Used as a count noun rather than a mass noun.

1864 *Athens Messenger* (OH) 3 Nov 2/6, [It was] a percussion shell, too, only it did not happen to "percuss,"—I use an army slang. **1871** *Overland Mth.* Feb 136, From the above [=the epitaph "R.I.P."] we derive one of our most expressive slangs. . . "Well, let her rip." **1918** in 1920 Tippett *Who Won?* 155 **OH,** "Zig-zag" is a French slang for "drunk." **1967** *DARE* (Qu. Y3, *To say uncomplimentary things about somebody*) Inf **MO38,** That's kind of a slang. **1968** *DARE* FW Addit **GA,** *Slang* has a plural; one slang expression is *a slang,* e.g., "that's a slang"; more than one is *slangs,* e.g., "they use so many slangs." Used by two college-educated Infs, one White, one Black. **1972** Carr *Da Kine Talk* 148 **HI,** "The reason this student was classified as a pidgin speaker was because of her phrases or slangs which the writer felt were characteristic of the local slangs." . . This sentence illustrates the use of the term *slangs* even by those whose speech is approaching standard American English. In a final examination, five of seventeen University of Hawaii sophomores used the form *slangs* meaning 'slang words.' **1986** Pederson *LAGS Concordance,* 1 inf, **seFL,** Slangs [=slang expressions]; 1 inf, **seFL,** Kids talk in little slangs; 1 inf, **seLA,** Hip slangs. **2004** *NY Daily News* (NY) 23 Apr 88 (Internet), Thomas blasted Martin for being a "fugazy", a slang for fake tough guy. **2004** [see **street card**].

B Sense.

Also attrib: An insult or insulting remark; insulting language. Cf **slang** v[1]

1822 *Adams Centinel* (Gettysburg PA) 28 Aug [3]/1 (newspaper-archive.com), Of General Hiesler, notwithstanding the rude, vulgar slang which his opposers constantly use towards him, we continue to entertain great respect. **1857** Long *Pictures Slavery* (2d ed) 272 **MD,** The man who . . insults the poor *slave girl* that has no protector but God, and *makes slang remarks* to her as she passes the street, is no gentleman. **1942** McAtee *Dial. Grant Co. IN* 79 (as of 1890s), *Slang* . . offensive language. **1965–70** *DARE* (Qu. Y4, . . *A very uncomplimentary remark*) Infs **NJ**56, 63, 67, **NY**209, **NC**45, 79, **OK**54, **SC**29, 34, Slang. [7 of 9 Infs old]

slang v[1], hence vbl n *slanging*

To insult or verbally abuse.

1848 *Amer. Whig Rev.* 8.428, We don't believe he would have dined with the Marquis of Hereford's mistress, as Croker *alias* Rigby used to do after slanging the immoral French novelists in that bulwark of orthodox principles, the London Quarterly. **1862** *Vanity Fair* 11 Jan 25, The Captain of an American merchant vessel writes to the Glasgow *Herald* complaining that he was slanged in good, set terms by the crew of H.B.M. ship *Hogue* . . on account of his flag. **1869** *Appletons' Jrl.* 5 June 310, The guest who hectors at him is guilty of an act analogous to that of a man who slangs a woman. **1879** *Ibid* Aug 112, No one . . when it comes to real slanging, can pitch in like a girl in a wax [=a fit of temper]. **1965** *DARE* (Qu. Y4, . . *A very uncomplimentary remark*) Inf **OK**15, Slang someone. [Inf old] **2004** *DARE* File—Internet, We can say, in the immortal words of GW "what's the difference?" and keep right on slanging him.

slang v[2]   See **sling** v

slang blade   See **sling blade**

slang-jang n   **chiefly TX**

See quots.

1894 Kute Kooking Klub *K.K.K. Cook Book* 35 **neTX,** *Slang Jang.* One can of oysters, one can of tomatoes, one bottle of pickles, one bottle of pepper sauce, three onions sliced; salt and pepper to taste. **1901** *Commerce Jrl.* (TX) 23 Aug [6]/2 (newspaperarchive.com), About fifteen couples enjoyed a "slang jang" party at Iceland Monday night, where dancing and music was had until a late hour. All report a most pleasant time with the "slang jang" as delicious. **1906** *DN* 3.156 **nwAR,** *Slang-jang.* . . A kind of salad containing raw oysters, onions, pickles, peppers, etc. Texarkana. **1915** *Clearfield Progress* (PA) 4 Nov 2/4 **ceTX,** Solicitor Cone Johnson . . recently admitted that he is the inventor of Texas . . "slang-jang." He went hunting with a party at home here 15 years ago and the cook struck. . . Cone got so hungry he heated a kettle of water, uncanned beans, pickles, tongue, tomatoes, peas, mustard, indiscriminately, cooked it and ate it. . . "Slang-jang" is on the menu of every cafe in the southwest today. **1974** *Dallas Times Herald* (TX) 12 July sec F 6/2, Everyone around Honey Grove has his own idea about what goes into Slang Jang, but Shirley's is about the best formula I've sat at a table with. **2000** *DARE* File—Internet **TX,** An original recipe was developed in Honey Grove during the 1920's or 1930's. It is called Slang Jang. . . It is a cold soup and served with crackers. People used to . . have Slang Jang suppers. . . There are several ways to make it with the main difference being the type of meat used. Some people prefer oysters and others like salmon or vienna sausage [plus tomatoes, pickles, onion, Tabasco sauce, salt, and pepper]. **2002** *Ibid,* Slang Jang. . . This is the southern equivalent of salsa. . . [Recipe includes tomato, celery ribs, bell pepper, onion, white vinegar, water, salt, sugar, whole dried chile.]

slank n   [Engl dial] **esp NJ** *obs* Cf **spung** =**slough** n[1].

1850 Herbert *Warwick Woodlands* 198 **NJ,** The grass was short . . with a rich close black mould . . under foot—with, at rare intervals, a slank, as it is termed in Jersey, or hollow winding course, in which the waters have lain longer than elsewhere, covered with a deep, rust-colored scum, floating upon stagnant pools. **1859** in 2002 *DARE* File—Internet **NJ,** In determining the extent of the injuries, you can take into consideration the actual damage done to the land by . . widening and deepening the slank, and thereby rendering it more difficult for the plaintiff to cross to his land [etc]. **1895** *DN* 1.383 **NJ,** *Slank:* low place at side of river, bay, or cove, filled with water at freshet. **1977** Talman *How Things Began* 266 **seNY** (as of c1850), On top of Scotland Hill near Spring Valley an area of wet ground was known as "Hopper's Slank." A slank is an upland swamp.

slank adj Also *slanky* [Scots, nEngl dial; *OED* 1668 →]
Thin, lank, scrawny.

   1899 (1912) Green *VA Folk-Speech* 392, *Slank*. . . Slim; slender; slanky. **1975** *DARE* File **Delmarva**, *Slanky*—slim, lanky, unattractive or unappetizing. "A slanky fish." **2001** in 2002 *DARE* File—Internet **AZ**, Thread the hook straight through the middle of a slanky bait such as a Senko or worm. *Ibid* **MA**, While doing a little night fishing offshore for stripers down in Falmouth . . I hooked up with a 32″ striper. This fish was remarkably low in weight (8lbs) long and slanky. **2004** *DARE* File—Internet, Long, slanky arms and legs, but still cut and buffed.

slank v, **slanked** See **slink**

slanky See **slank** adj

slant n
  1 In coal mining: see quots. Cf **fly** n² 3
   1881 Raymond *Gloss. Mining* 78, *Slant*. A heading driven diagonally between the dip and the strike of a coal seam. **1968** Thrush *Dict. of Mining* 1024, *Slant*. . . Any short inclined crosscut connecting the entry with its air course to facilitate the hauling of coal. **1973** *PADS* 59.53 [Bituminous coal mining vocab], *Slant* . . an *entry cut* off a *main entry* at more than a ninety degree angle.
  2 See **slant-eye.**

slant-eye n Also *slant, ~-eyes, slanty, ~-eye(s)* derog Cf **round eyes**
A person of Mongoloid ancestry, esp Chinese or Japanese.
   1899 *Daily IA State Press* (IA City) [23 Oct 6]/6 **AZ** (newspaperarchive.com), The slant-eye [=a Chinese man] knew how to shove good grub in front of his patrons. **1929** *AmSp* 4.344 [Vagabond lingo], *Slant eye*—An oriental. **1942** Berrey–Van den Bark *Amer. Slang* 385.19, *Oriental*. . . slant, slant-eye. **1957** Battaglia *Resp. to PADS* 20 **eMD**, Chinese: *slant-eyes*. **1964** *PADS* 42.31 **Chicago IL**, The . . other racial group to attract pejoratives . . was the Oriental. . . A few terms reflect stereotype racial characteristics . . *yellow belly* . . *slant eyes* . . *li'l eyes*. **1965–70** *DARE* (Qu. HH28, *Names and nicknames . . for people of foreign background: Japanese*) 12 Infs, **scattered**, Slant-eye(s); **PA**227, Slanty-eyes; (Qu. HH28, *Names and nicknames . . for people of foreign background: Chinese*) Infs **CA**8, **CT**21, **IN**14, **MN**10, **MO**18, **NY**209, Slant-eye(s); (Qu. HH28, *Names and nicknames . . for people of foreign background: Orientals*) Inf **TN**65, Slant-eye. **1976** M. Machlin *Pipeline* vii.79 (*OED2*), And the fuckin' Eskimo slants are tryin' to get the rest of it. **1986** Pederson *LAGS Concordance* **Gulf Region** (*Orientals; this question was asked chiefly in urban areas*) 11 infs, Slant-eyes; 1 inf, Slant-eyes—Japanese; 1 inf, Slant-eyes—Chinese, Japanese, Vietnamese; 1 inf, Slant-eyes—Chinese; 1 inf, Slant-eyes—chiefly Japanese; 1 inf, Slant-eye; 1 inf, Slant—any Oriental; 1 inf, Slants—any Orientals; 1 inf, Slanties. **2004** *DARE* File—Internet, Calling someone a "slant eye" . . is a response about Chinese, Koreans, and Asians in general.

slantie-gogglin adj Cf **antigoglin, si-antigodlin**
   1957 *Sat. Eve. Post Letters* (as of c1900) **ceIL**, Slantie-gogglin (diagonal).

slantindicular adj, adv Also *slanchindicular, slunchendikular;* for addit varr see quots [Blend of *slant* or *slanch* (at **slaunch**) + *perpendicular*]
Slanting, lopsided, sidelong; obliquely, at an angle.
   c1830 in Lib. of Congress *Amer. Memory: Amer. Singing* (Internet), [Song title:] *Jim Crow.* [Lyrics:] Den I grinn'd slantendicular, den wid one eye. **1832** in 1912 Thornton *Amer. Gloss.* 2.806, This is sorter a *slantindickelar* road, stranger. **1835** (1955) Crockett *Almanacks* 4 **wTN**, There was a fall in the river, which went slap-right straight down slantindicular with a descent of *sixty feet*. **1844** Stephens *High Life in NY* 2.204 **CT**, There the varmint stood a eyeing me kinder slantindiclar, whilst he whittled off a cud of tobacco. **1845** Kirkland *Western Clearings* 210 **MI**, I dug my trap plenty deep enough, and all the dirt I took out 'n was laid up o' one side, slantindicler, up hill like. **1848** in 1935 *AmSp* 10.42 **Nantucket MA**, *Slantingdicular.* Obliquely. **1865** Byrn *Advent. Fudge Fumble* 37 **TN**, They treated me with all the respect that I could have counted on, but still they eyed me in rather that slunchendikular manner that went to say, "my little rooster, you are trying to crow before you are feathered." **1873** (1969) Smith *Bill Arp's Peace Papers* 202 **nwGA**, If we could have slid into it quietly and slantendikular, if slavery could have sorter tapered out and freedom sorter tapered in, everybody could have got used to it. **a1883** (1911) Bagby *VA Gentleman* 79, I want to go whar I kin build my house cattycornered, lop-sided, slantingdicular, bottom-upward, any way I please. **1892** *DN* 1.232 **KY**, *Slanchindicular*. **1904** Day *Kin o' Ktaadn* 111

ME, The pole struck slantin'-dicular. **1953** Randolph–Wilson *Down in Holler* 285 **Ozarks**, *Slantendicular*. . . Not quite vertical, but nearly so. A *slantendicular* fence post is one that leans just a trifle. **c1960** Wilson *Coll.* **csKY**, *Slantindicular*. . . Humorous for slanting. **2004** *DARE* File—Internet [*Palm Beach Post*] (FL) 25 Apr], Shrady has done an amusing and literally slantendicular history of one of Italy's most famous landmarks, the Leaning Tower of Pisa.

slanty, slanty-eye(s) See **slant-eye**

slap adv [Engl dial] Cf **slam** adv
  1 Directly, abruptly.
   1830 *Anti-Masonic Star* (Gettysburg PA) [26 June 4]/3 **MA** (newspaperarchive.com), Down came the mysterious visitor slap into the fire place. **1835** [see **slantindicular**]. **1836** (1838) Haliburton *Clockmaker* (1st ser) 179 **NEng**, Down she fell slap off her seat on the floor. **1858** Hammett *Piney Woods Tavern* 178, Whang went an old musket slap at us. **1952** [see **2** below]. **1956** McAtee *Some Dialect NC* 40, *Slap* . . abruptly. "I was cool but did a few chores and was slap hot again"; directly: ["right slap on the nose." **2004** *DARE* File—Internet, [Interview with Uma Thurman:] I clocked him right slap in the face.
  2 All the way; completely. **chiefly Sth, S Midl** See Map
   1909 *DN* 3.371 **eAL, wGA**, *Slap*. . . Entirely. "We worked till slap dark." **a1930** in 1991 Hughes–Hurston *Mule Bone* 32 **cFL** [Black], Wese [=we is] gointer run him slap outa town sure as gun's iron. **1952** Brown *NC Folkl.* 1.591, *Slap*. . . Completely, directly. **1962** Fox *Southern Fried* 143 **SC**, [He] has gone slap out of his mind, living out there with all them dogs. **1965–70** *DARE* (Qu. LL26a, . . *'All the way':* "He drove _____ to the end of the road.") 12 Infs, **chiefly Sth**, Slap; **GA**, Plumb slap; (Qu. DD15, *A person who is thoroughly drunk*) Inf **TN**26, Slap drunk; (Qu. LL17, . . *There's no more of something:* "The potatoes are _____.") Inf **GA**23, Slap out. **1966** *DARE* Tape **NM**13, They worked hard, from daylight in the morning until slap dark. **1970** *DARE* File **neTX**, I slap forgot! **1972** *Atlanta Letters* **ceGA**, One of the many colloquialisms my mother-in-law translated for me . . Slap worn out. **1986** Pederson *LAGS Concordance*, 1 inf, **cwAL**, Slap across the barn; 1 inf, **cMS**, Reaches slap across the bed; 1 inf, **nwFL**, It went slap across; 1 inf, **ceTX**, Blew it slap away; 1 inf, **cwLA**, Just given slap out; 1 inf, **cAL**, Worn slap out; 1 inf, **cMS**, Slap through it; 1 inf, **neFL**, Slap to Palatka; 1 inf, **nwFL**, I come slap to the top; 1 inf, **swGA**, The weather may eat them slap up; 1 inf, **cnAL**, Burn slap up; 1 inf, **nwFL**, Slap up in Baltimore; 1 inf, **seLA**, Slap up the railroad track; 1 inf, **cnAL**, Their crop going burn slap up. **2004** *DARE* File—Internet **VA**, By then, it was slap dark.

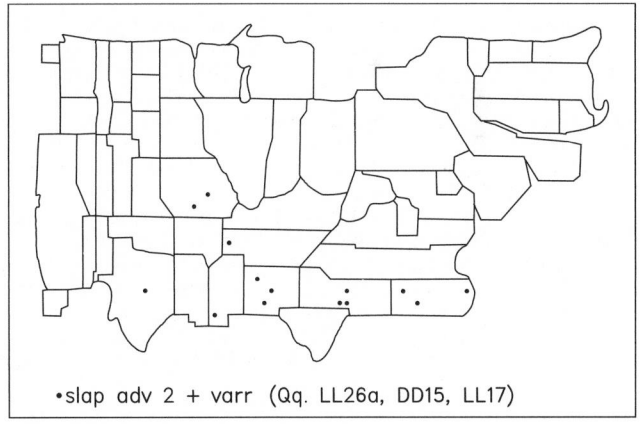

•slap adv 2 + varr (Qq. LL26a, DD15, LL17)

‡slap n Cf *DS* W13
=flip-flop 6.
   2001 *WI State Jrl.* (Madison) 16 July sec D 1/2, Flip-flops, slaps, thongs or zoris—whatever you choose to call them—are everywhere. . . It seems the sandals made for showering are out in the open.

slap bacon See **slab bacon**

slap ball n **NYC**
A variant of the game **punchball** in which the ball is hit with the open palm, rather than the closed fist.
   1935 Staley *Curriculum Sports* 128, [In a list of games:] 7. Sidewalk tennis. 8. Punch ball. 9. Hand baseball. 10. Slap ball. **1968** *DARE* (Qu. EE33, . . *Outdoor games . . that children play*) Inf **NY**119A, Slap ball. **1968** *DARE* Tape **NY**64, They [are] usually . . hitting it with a bat or running around playing slap ball with it. . . [FW:] What's slap ball?

[Inf:] You bounce the ball, and then you slap it, and then the child runs to first, or second, or third base. . . much the same as hitting it with a bat, only they slap it with their hand. **1975** Ferretti *Gt. Amer. Book Sidewalk Games* 195 **NYC,** *Slap Ball* . . is essentially Punchball except that the ball is hit with the open palm. **2002** *DARE* File—Internet **Brooklyn NYC,** I was raised in Greenpoint, Brooklyn, where . . I concentrated my energies upon mastering ball-based games of the streets (stoop ball, stick ball, slap ball, punch ball, and off-the point). *Ibid* **Brooklyn NYC,** *Which of the following games do you remember playing on the streets?* . . Slap Ball. *Ibid* **NYC,** Your friends were waiting to play stickball, softball, slap-ball.

slap-bang adv

1 also *bang-slap:* As with a slap and a bang; directly, abruptly. [*OED* 1785 →]

1836 (1838) Haliburton *Clockmaker* (1st ser) 199 **MA,** We let the British come right on till we see'd the whites of their eyes, and then we let them have it slap bang. **1852** Somerby *Hits & Dashes* 79 **ME,** Over went the huge volume from the desk, slap-bang! down upon the bald and reverend head of one of the deacons! **1889** *Overland Mth.* (2d ser) Sept 290, Them gents is busy taking a line that's going from the nor'-east corner right bang slap through my bar. **1899** (1912) Green *VA Folk-Speech* 392, *Slap-bang.* . . With a slap and a bang; hence, suddenly; violently; with a sudden, noisy dash; headlong; all at once. **1921** *DN* 5.117 **KY,** *Slap-bang,* "slap-dab" [=exactly, precisely]. **1930** Shoemaker *1300 Words* 55 **cPA Mts** (as of c1900), *Slap-bang*—Suddenly, or quickly. **1944** *PADS* 2.26 **cwNC,** *Slap-bang.* . . same as *slam* [=directly and violently]. **1960** Criswell *Resp. to PADS 20* **Ozarks,** *Slap-bang* [refers to something hitting hard]. **1968-70** *DARE* (Qu. KK53, *When one thing suddenly hits hard against something else: "He ran _____ into a car."*) Infs **KY92, MD30, MI102, MA73, NY146,** Slap-bang. [4 of 5 Infs old] **1998** in **2004** *DARE* File—Internet [*Software Magazine* 15 July], Those traits run slap-bang into a deadline that just doesn't budge.

2 All the way.

1935 *Coshocton Tribune* (OH) 1 Feb 9/4, [Syndicated sports column:] You get the impression the King must have covered it with mucilage and driven slap-bang thru an accessories store. **1937** in 1958 Brewer *Dog Ghosts* 97 **TX** [Black], Habs 'em a rail break-down ball what las' slap-bang up to de time de roosters staa't to crowin' for daytime Sunday mawnin'.

slapdab adv

1 Directly, abruptly; squarely. **scattered, but more freq Sth, S Midl** See Map

1864 *Centralia Sentinel* (IL) 24 Nov 1/3, [Reprinted from the *Rural New Yorker:*] [He] had a whole tun of butter and had lost $300 on it slap dab. **1886** *Turf Field & Farm* 42.174 **KY** [Black], He was goin' that fas' he run slap-dab agin me. **1895** *DN* 1.399 **c,swNY,** *Slap-dab* . . violently or awkwardly. "He rushed in slap-dab and broke things." **1905** *DN* 3.65 **eNE,** *Slap-dab.* . . "He ran slap-dab into a wall." **1912** *DN* 3.590 **wIN,** *Slap-dab.* . . "He ran slap-dab into a big fat woman." **1914** *DN* 4.113 **cKS,** *Slap-dab.* . . Plump. "He just went slap-dab into the pool." **1921** *DN* 5.117 **KY,** *Slap-dab,* exactly, precisely. "He hit him slap-dab in the eye." **1949** *PADS* 11.11 **wTX** (as of 1911-29), *Slap dab.* . . Squarely. "It jumped slap-dab in the middle." **1954** in 1958 Brewer *Dog Ghosts* 21 **TX** [Black], De Nigguh hauls off an' slaps de sheriff slap-dab in de face. **1965-70** *DARE* (Qu. KK53, *When one thing suddenly hits hard against something else: "He ran _____ into a car."*) 11 Infs, **scattered, but esp Sth, S Midl,** Slapdab. **1982** Slone

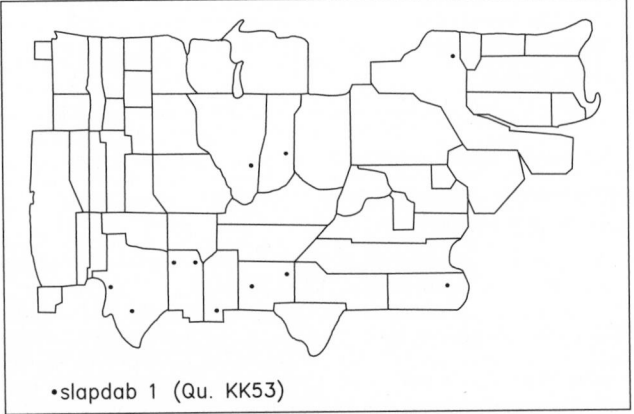

•slapdab 1 (Qu. KK53)

How We Talked 26 **eKY** (as of c1950), *Slap dab*—exactly. **2002** *DARE* File—Internet **TN,** We're slap-dab in the middle of "down town." *Ibid* **TN,** Stone Creek Cabins is located right slap dab in the middle of both rivers! *Ibid* **TX,** Shenandoah is "slap dab" in the middle of fun country.

2 All the way, completely. **esp Sth, S Midl**

1856 (1857) *Cincinnatus* 1.321 **CT** (as of 1813), Near abaout two hundred dollars gone slapdab for nothin'! **1946** Harder *Coll.* **cwTN,** *Slap-dab.* . . Completely, entirely. "I'm slap-dab done plowin'." **c1950** Halpert *Coll.* **wKY, wTN,** *Slap-dab.* . . Completely, absolutely, entirely, totally. . . "I'm slap-dab out of corn meal." "I worked yesterday till plumb, slap-dab dark." **1964** Wallace *Frontier Life* 97 **OK** (as of 1893-1906), If she was completely out of something, she was "slap dab out." **1966** *DARE* (Qu. LL26a, . . *'All the way': "He drove _____ to the end of the road."*) Inf **SC3,** Slapdab. **2004** *DARE* File—Internet **NC,** I ran slap-dab out of oil.

slapdash adv

Directly; abruptly.

1834 Davis *Letters Downing* 323, They thought the people would agree to it—slap-dash! **1899** (1912) Green *VA Folk-Speech* 392, *Slap-dash.* . . In a sudden, off hand, abrupt, random, or headlong manner; abruptly; suddenly; all at once. **1905** *DN* 3.65 **eNE,** *Slap-dash.* . . It fell slap-dash into the water. **1970** *DARE* (Qu. KK53, *When one thing suddenly hits hard against something else: "He ran _____ into a car."*) Inf **VA58,** Slapdash.

slaphazard adj [Blend of *slapdash* adj + *haphazard*]

Hasty, careless; flimsy.

1916 *Smart Set* Oct 249, At the slaphazard breakfast which Mrs. Rushton prepared, Bob swore at least twice. **1967** *DARE* (Qu. KK52, *To do something in an indirect and complicated way: "I don't know why he had to go _____ to do that."*) Inf **TN1,** In such a slaphazard way. **2001** *DARE* File—Internet, The counterterrorism drill doesn't admit such slaphazard case handling. **2004** *Ibid,* The characterless, slaphazard garbage the movie production lines are churning out . . sounding the death knell for the originality of cinema.

slap in, slap out See **clap in, clap out**

slap in the back n Also *slap to the right, swat* ~ Cf *slap the rabbit* (at **tap the rabbit**)

A chasing game played in a ring; see quot 2000.

1965-70 *DARE* (Qu. EE1, . . *Games . . children play . . in which they form a ring, and either sing or recite a rhyme*) Infs **AL3, IL113, OH87, PA28, WV3,** Slap in the back; **OK14,** Slap in the back—tag one in the ring on the back. **2000** *NADS Letters* **neTX** (as of c1940), Slap-in-the-back. . . It was a children's ring game. All the children got in a double circle. Then one child was "it" and chased another child around the circle. The chased child had to go around the circle at least one time without being caught. Then s/he could run in front of another pair of children, and the child at the back was the one being chased. If the child who was "it" caught up with the child who was being chased and gave her/him a "slap-on-the-back", then they reversed roles and the chased child became the chaser, or "it". After running around the circle at least once, the chased child could "cut the mustard" or cut across the circle to get away from the chaser. But s/he had to call out "cut the mustard" before running across the circle or be automatically "it". **2001** *Ibid* (as of 1950s), Slap in the back. . . I think this game is one that was played in Pittsburgh in the 50's called slap (or swat) to the right. A group of kids stood in a ring facing in. [One] kid was outside the ring with a rolled up towel, or some such thing. The kid on the outside walked around the ring and hit a kid on the back with the towel. The hitter then took off running counter clockwise around the ring and the kid who got hit chased him. If the hitter managed to get completely around the circle and back to the spot vacated by the kid who was hit, he got the spot, and the chaser became the new hitter. If the chaser managed to catch and tag the swatter, he resumed his place, and the swatter went again.

slapjack n

1 A pancake. **scattered, but chiefly Nth, N Midl** See Map Cf **flapjack 1**

1805 *New Amer. Cookery* 60, *Indian Slapjack.* One quart milk, 1 pint of Indian meal, 4 eggs, 4 spoons of flour. **1830** Martin *Narrative* 72 **NEng,** I procured a piece of a buckwheat slapjack. **1843** (1916) Hall *New Purchase* 303 **IN,** A snug breakfast of chicken fixins, eggs, ham-doins and corn slap-jacks. **1899** (1912) Green *VA Folk-Speech* 177, *Flap-jack.* . . A pancake. **1905** *DN* 3.19 **cCT,** *Slap-jack.* . . A pancake. **1941** *LANE* Map 289, *Flapjack, slapjack, flapover, flipper* . . are being replaced by *griddle cake, pan cake* or *fritter.* **1941** *Language*

17.335 **WI,** [*LANCS* fieldwork:] *Slapjacks*—8 [of 50 infs]. . . Scattered; not found west and north. . . [2 infs] remember it with amusement . . [another inf] says it was a lumber-camp word. . . Most current is *pancake,* but *flapjack* and *slapjack,* usually jocular, are widely known. **1941** Writers' Program *Guide UT* 437 (as of 1879), That Christmas dinner was "a slapjack of flour and water baked in a frying-pan." **1965–70** *DARE* (Qu. H20b, . . *Names . . for pancakes*) 23 Infs, **scattered, but chiefly Nth, N Midl,** Slapjacks; **CA**138, Slapjacks—especially menfolks would use this term; **PA**136, Called slapjacks if they don't taste good. **1986** Pederson *LAGS Concordance (Pancakes)* 9 infs, 5 **GA,** Slapjack(s); *(Other kinds of bread made of flour)* 1 inf, **ceMS,** Cornbread slapjack—made in skillet on the fire.

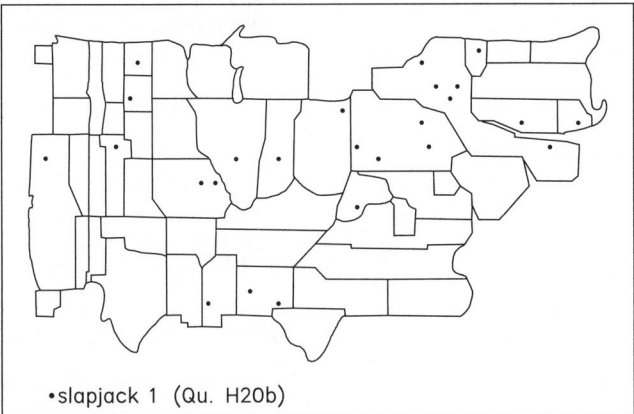

•slapjack 1 (Qu. H20b)

2 See quot.
1930 *AmSp* 5.393 [Language of N Atl fishermen], *Slapjacks*. . . Heavy rough shoes with wooden soles, used when fishermen are working on deck in fine weather.

slapper n Also *slapper cake* **esp DE, PA** Cf **corn slapper, fritter 2, Indian cake**
A fried cornmeal cake.
1844 Parkinson *Complete Confectioner* 123, *Indian Slappers.*—To a pint of Indian meal, add a handful of wheat flour and a little salt; beat three eggs very light and stir them, in turn with the meal, into a quart of milk. These cakes require no yeast, and should be baked . . on a griddle. **1852** Hale *Ladies' New Book Cookery* 390 **PA,** *Indian Slappers.* **1891** *AN&Q* 6.129 **Philadelphia PA,** Sometimes a further degradation occurs and the toothsome fritter becomes a *slapper.* . . You will frequently observe a placard bearing the words "Maryland slappers" in the window of some fourth-rate eating-house. **1952** Tracy *Coast Cookery* 106 **MA,** *Slappers* or Fried Indian Cakes. **1957** *DE Folkl. Bulletin* 1.28, Slapper cakes, or corn slappers (griddle cakes made of corn meal). **1968** *DARE* (Qu. F3, *When you're frying things—for example, eggs—you turn them over with a _____*) Inf **DE**3, Slapper turner.

slapping adj [Engl dial]
Outstanding; whopping. Note: *Slapping* "rapid" (in the phr *slapping pace*) is not treated here.
1930 Shoemaker *1300 Words* 58 **cPA Mts** (as of c1900), *Slapping*—A big, active horse, "A slapping team of horses." **1937** Gardner *Folkl. Schoharie* 103, "All right," agreed the farmer, and gave him a slapping pail of victuals.

slapping-high adj phr
See quot 1952.
1952 Brown *NC Folkl.* 1.591, *Slapping-high.* . . Of a child: high enough to be slapped.—Randolph county. **1958** Humphrey *Home from the Hill* 126 **neTX,** Right on her heels comes a little nigger boy just slapping high.

slap-sided See **slab-sided**

slap the fire out of someone See **fire B2b**

slap the rabbit See **tap the rabbit**

slap to the right See **slap in the back**

slash n[1] [Prob ult of imit origin; cf *plash, flash,* and Scots, nEngl dial *slashy* muddy, miry] Cf **slash pine**
1 also pl: A low, swampy area; a shallow, marshy pool, puddle, or stream. **chiefly Sth, S Midl**

1652 in 1940 *AmSp* 15.392 **VA,** Beginning neer a wett slash. **1658** *Ibid* 393 **VA,** The southern bounds runing [sic] by a Slash of Water which parts the County of York and the County of Denby. **1673** *Ibid* **VA,** To the Corner hicory by Piascum Swamp in the mouth of the small branch or slash. **c1738** (1929) Byrd *Histories* 96 **VA** (as of 1728), Within 3 or 4 Miles of Edenton, the Soil appears to be a little more fertile, tho' it is much cut with Slashes, which seem all to have a tendency towards the Dismal [=the Great Dismal Swamp]. **1808** (1892) Summer *Tour OH* 1.65 **VA,** The bottom is generally divided by three swamps or slashes running parallel to the river. **1883** Amer. Philol. Assoc. *Trans.* 14.52 **Sth,** *Slashes,* 'wet or swampy grounds overgrown with bushes.' The slashes of Hanover Co., Virginia, became famous as the birthplace of Henry Clay. **1894** *DN* 1.333 **seNJ,** *Slash:* swale filled with water. **1899** (1912) Green *VA Folk-Speech* 392, *Slashes.* . . A shallow pool of water left after a rain. Wet or swampy places overgrown with bushes. (2) Small places of standing water after a heavy rain, usually in roads. **1902** *DN* 2.245 **sIL,** *Slashes.* . . The spreading and separation of a stream over a large area into many labyrinthine channels. **1903** *DN* 2.331 **seMO,** *Slash.* . . Wet bottom land. A *slash* differs from a slough in having no perceptible channel. **1907** *DN* 3.237 **nwAR,** *Slash.* . . Wet bottom land. **1909** *DN* 3.405 **nwAR,** *Slash.* . . Swale filled with water. **1932** *DN* 6.233 **West,** *Slash* . . a wet, swampy bottom land. . . In the West . . [this] sense was brought in early by the first explorers who were in the main from the South. **1966–70** *DARE* (Qu. C6, . . *A piece of land that's often wet, and has grass and weeds growing on it)* Infs **IN**12, **KY**5, **NC**23, Slash; (Qu. C7, . . *Land that usually has some standing water with trees or bushes growing in it)* Infs **AR**32, **IL**117, Slash; [(Qu. C34, *Nicknames for nearby settlements, villages, or districts)* Inf **NC**15, Slashes]. **1966** *DARE* Tape **AR**32, A creek and a slough and a . . bayou and a slash. **1966** *DARE* FW Addit **seNC,** The wild geese used to have their nests down in the slashes. **1986** Pederson *LAGS Concordance (Swamp)* 1 inf, **neMS,** Slash or swamp; 1 inf, **ceLA,** Slash—water stands—grows hardwood trees; 1 inf, **ceAR,** Slash—low, swampy place; 1 inf, **cnMS,** A slash—wet all the time, too wet to plant; *(Marsh)* 1 inf, **neTX,** A slash; *(Ravine)* 1 inf, **ceAR,** A slash—larger than "draw"; things drain into it. **1995** *Brophy Coll.* 68 **swMO** (as of c1960), *Slash.* [A] low swampy open place in timber, surrounding a slough or old river course.

2 See **slash pine b.**

slash v, hence ppl adj *slashed,* vbl n *slashing* Also with *down* **Nth**
To clear (land) by cutting (and usu burning) the timber on it; to cut (trees) in order to clear land; to engage in clearing land in this way.
1822 *Port Folio* (Oldschool) 13.68, The act of hewing down the timber is called *slashing.* **1843** Amer. Agric. 2.354, Where these [=trees] are valueless . . , the *slashing* system of clearing is usually resorted to. **1843** *Yale Lit. Mag.* 8.332 **VT,** His eye wandered far away over acres of slashed timber. **1868** *Ladies' Repository* 2.7, Like most woodsmen they have a great predilection for slashing. . . If we can only protect our orchards and shade-trees from their ravages, it will perhaps be safe enough to let them slash in the "timber," remembering always that the land slashed must be burned over and sowed to grain, or a second growth worse than the first will spring up. **1883** Briggs *Hist. Concord* 110 **cwNY,** Another method of cutting timber for the purpose of clearing land, was "slashing it down." This consisted simply in cutting down the trees and letting them fall in any direction without trimming them out, or cutting up the bodies. **1885** *Century Illustr. Mag.* 29.836 **WA,** He would have plenty to do "slashing," *i.e.,* cutting down trees preparatory to burning them,—the usual process of clearing land where there is no market for timber. **1893** *Atlantic Mth.* 71.194 **WA,** All about the shanties the timber had been "slashed" for breathing and moving space, and lay tossed about in cyclonic confusion. **1912** U.S. Bur. Plant Industry *Bulletin* 239.10 **wWA,** All logged off land should be slashed. . . In slashing, the large second growth, old snags, and trees should be cut to a height of 3 or 3½ feet above the ground. . . The slashing can be burned at any time after the leaves upon the fallen trees become dry. **1919** *DN* 5.59 **WA,** *Slash.* . . ["]Purchased a five-acre tract and has commenced slashing the same.["] Island County Times, Coupeville, Wash. **1967** *DARE* (Qu. L36, . . *When you dig out roots and underbrush to make a new field)* Inf **WA**30, Slash; grubbing. **2004** *DARE* File—Internet, Farmers slash down trees and use the fertile soil for agricultural.

slash n[2] **chiefly Nth, nCA**
1 A **slashing** n 1; the operation of making a **slashing** n 1.
1854 Wetmore *Hermit's Dell* 258 **NY,** The approach to the cabin lay over burnt and fallen timber, heaped up in every imaginable form, the

débris of what is called in forest parlance, a "slash." **1860** Street *Woods & Waters* 336 **neNY,** You knows Bill Hoskin that made the slash last Spring jest t'other side o' Harrietstown. **1905** U.S. Forest Serv. *Bulletin* 61.47 [Logging terms], *Slash.* . . Forest land which has been logged off and upon which the limbs and tops remain, or which is deep in débris as the result of fire or wind. (Gen[eral]) **1966–69** *DARE* (Qu. C28, *A place where underbrush, weeds, vines and small trees grow together so that it's nearly impossible to get through*) Inf **MA**30, Slash; **NH**5, Slash—where larger trees have been cut and smaller bushes have grown up. **2001** Houston *Dead Water* 36 **nWI,** The landscape was grim: a stripped slash punctuated with scraggly, dying spires of trees that hadn't made the cut.

2 The debris left when a stand of trees has been cut down or destroyed by wind or fire.

1881 *Harper's New Mth. Mag.* Oct 688 **neNY,** They will follow the track with untiring vigor, crawling through the densest slash of burned and fallen timber. **1905** U.S. Forest Serv. *Bulletin* 61.47 [Logging terms], *Slash.* . . The débris left after logging, wind, or fire. (Gen[eral]) Syn.: slashing. **1914** *DN* 4.81 **ME, nNH,** *Slash.* . . Refuse tops and brush, in a clearing. **1923** *DN* 5.221 **swMO,** *Slash.* . . Refuse resulting from logging operations; a jungle. **1942** *AmSp* 17.224 **Nth** [Loggers' talk], *Slash.* Limbs and similar debris left by the fallers and buckers. **1949** Powers *Redwood Country* 123 **nCA,** Still without economic value, still left in the woods, is the slash, a vast litter and a great fire hazard—limbs, tops, decayed parts of aged trees, chunks, brush. **1956** *AmSp* 31.152 **nwCA** [Logger lingo], *Slash.* . . Branches, bark, tops, chunks, cull logs, uprooted stumps, and broken or uprooted trees left on the ground after logging. **1968** *Hungry Horse News* (Columbia Falls MT) 20 Dec 16/6, Appraised price for stumpage, slash disposal and stand improvement was $140,695.20. **1975** Gould *ME Lingo* 258, *Slash*—Limbs, tops, and unusable parts of trees left on the ground after logging off. It creates a fire hazard, and tourists will see State Forestry signs that read, "Slash Area—No Campfires Beyond This Point." A *slash* fire is a brush fire in a *slash* area. The state has laws requiring lumbering operations to reduce *slash* danger. **2004** CO State Univ. Coop. Ext. Tri R. Area *Dial-a-Garden Message* (Internet), If you do any thinning or removal of pinyons, it is important to remove the slash as it attracts the insects. . . Avoid chipping the slash and leaving it in the vicinity.

slash down, slashed See **slash** v

slasher n [**slash** n² 2]
1956 Sorden–Ebert *Logger's Words* 32 **Gt Lakes,** *Slasher.* . . Man who cleans up the slash after a logging operation.

slash fence n esp **nNEng** *hist*
A fence formed of felled trees.
1827 *Portland Advt.* (ME) 4 May 2/5, Wm Evans and his father were falling trees to make a slash fence. **1848** Eastman *Poems* 4 **VT,** Through the drifts by the old slash-fence they'd leap,/ And tumble each other in. **1883** Briggs *Hist. Concord* 118 **cwNH,** The fence that was constructed the easiest and cheapest by the pioneers . . was a brush fence, or a "slash fence." It was made by felling trees in together in a line in the desired direction. **1915** (1916) Johnson *Highways New Engl.* 62 **cwNH,** I found where he [=a bear] went out through what we call a slash or hedge fence. The fence is made by notching small trees at about the height of four feet so the tops will fall over but remain hanging on the stumps. **1956** *VT Hist.* 24.79 (as of 19th cent), "A slash fence" was the same as a brush fence, except it was made with trees.

slashing n
1 also pl: An area in a forest where trees have been felled and left lying or blown down. **Nth**
1840 *Jamestown* (N.Y.) *Jrnl.* 1 July 2/5 (*DAE*), On Monday, the body of Mr. Brown was found in a slashing. **1858** in 1859 Goodwin *Pioneer Hist.* 238 **NY** (as of c1805), Cattle, during the winter, for the want of 'fodder,' were turned out to 'browse' in the 'slashings.' **1876** Johnson *Centennial Hist. Erie NY* 488, The ground in front of the fortifications was cut up by numerous ravines, and for a thousand yards the trees had all been cut down, forming an almost impenetrable "slashing." **1894** *Outing* June 186 **neNY,** We got into a spruce thicket or an old "slashing"—the track of a hurricane. **1919** *DN* 5.58 **WA,** *Slashing.* . . August Schmitz has just finished burning his slashing which he is now seeding to various grass seeds. Kalama Bulletin. **1930** Shoemaker *1300 Words* 53 **cPA Mts** (as of c1900), *Slashing*—A region cut over by lumbermen. **1950** *Western Folkl.* 9.120 **nwOR** [Logger speech], *Slashing.* Logged-off land. **1956** Sorden–Ebert *Logger's Words* 32 **Gt Lakes,** *Slashings,* The area of recently cut timber. A land area full of slash. **1984** [see **2**

below]. **2003** *DARE* File—Internet **MI,** Slashings and clearcuts adjacent to roads where birds might move out to feed are good bets, too.

2 =**slash** n² **2.**
1891 *NY Times* (NY) 1 Nov 1/3, The fire caught from a pile of burning slashings, the heavy wind of yesterday blowing the flames into the woods. **1905** [see **slash** n² **2**]. **1950** *WELS Suppl.* **nWI,** *Slashings*—Trees, usually poplars (popple slashings) on cut-over land. Often they are without tops or dead and supported by their bark. **1984** *MJLF* 10.156, *Slashings.* Wisconsin: The same as shearings [=timberland that has been clean-cut]. Maine: The debris left after logging or pulping a timber lot. **2001** in **2004** *DARE* File—Internet **MI,** There was a time you wouldn't buy land up here at any price. It had all been lumbered over, and what topsoil there was got burned up in the fires that consumed the slashings the lumber companies left behind.

slashing vbl n See **slash** v

slash pine n
A **pine 1** which grows in a **slash** n¹ **1** or similar area, as:
a also *longleaf slash:* =**loblolly pine 1.**
1858 *Russell's Mag.* Nov 142 **NC, VA,** The only pines of the higher range of country . . is what is there called the "slash pine," common in the higher tide-water counties, and growing on high land, but only either in the narrow, oozy bottoms, or in the forest "slashes," or shallow depressions of the table or nearly level ridge-lands. **1882** Hough *Elements of Forestry* 328, Varieties [of *Pinus taeda*] are known in North Carolina as "Swamp Pine," "Slash Pine." **1897** Sudworth *Arborescent Flora* 25, *Pinus taeda.* . . Slash Pine (Va., N.C., in part). *Ibid* 26, *Pinus taeda.* . . Black Slash Pine (S.C.) *Ibid* 31, *Pinus heterophylla* [=*P. elliottii*]. . . Slash Pine (Ala., Miss., Ga., Fla.) **1966** *DARE* Tape **GA**7, This here slash pine—longleaf slash—the gum on it, when it runs out, it usually stays soft unlessen it's cold weather. **1981** Pederson *LAGS Basic Materials,* 1 inf, **neGA,** Slash pine—also called nigger pine. **2002** in **2004** *DARE* File—Internet **GA,** Examine your particular land to determine how well it is suited for loblolly or slash pines.

b also *slash:* A timber tree *(Pinus elliottii)* native mostly to low elevations from southern South Carolina to Louisiana. Also called **bastard pine 1b, Cuban ~, hard ~ 3, meadow ~ 1a, old-field ~, pitch ~ b(4), pond ~ 2, rock ~ c, she ~, shortleaf ~ 4, spruce ~ 2g, swamp ~ 1b, yellow ~ 9**
1884 Sargent *Forests of N. Amer.* 202, *P[inus] Elliottii.* . . Slash Pine. Swamp Pine. . . South Carolina . . , south near the coast to the southern keys of Florida, west along the Gulf coast to . . Louisiana. **1897** [see **a** above]. **1913** *Auk* 30.483 **Okefenokee GA,** The islands. . . The longleaf pine . . predominates in the drier areas, and the slash pine (*P. Elliottii*) in the more moist situations. **1922** U.S. Dept. Ag. *Farmers' Bulletin 1256* 14 **Sth,** Young or "sap trees" of slash pine are extensively cut for railroad ties. **1934** *Natl. Geogr. Mag.* 65.598, The Okefinokee prairies. . . are also dotted here and there with wooded islets—the so-called prairie "heads"—of cypress, slash pine, . . and other trees. **1965–70** *DARE* (Qu. T17, . . *Kinds of pine trees; not asked in early QRs*) 38 Infs, **SE, Gulf States,** Slash pine; (Qu. T16, . . *Kinds of trees* . . '*special*') Infs **FL**18, 22, Slash pine. [*DARE* Ed: Some of these Infs may refer instead to other senses.] **1966** *DARE* Tape **MS**14, We don't have as much longleaf now, because the loblolly and the slash will grow faster. **1979** *Sat. Review* 17 Feb 26 **FL,** It is warm enough on the barrier islands for camellias and then azaleas to brighten the trails of the mid-South, otherwise decorated with live oak and slash pine. **1997** in **2002** *DARE* File—Internet **FL,** *Pinus elliottii.* . . Slash pine has great economic value as a timber tree for lumber, pulp and paper, and formerly for the production of turpentine and naval stores.

c =**shortleaf pine 1.**
1896 Mohr–Roth *Timber Pines* 87 **NC, VA,** *Pinus echinata.* . . Slash Pine (N.C., Va.) in part. **1960** Vines *Trees SW* 25, *Pinus echinata.* . . Vernacular names are Yellow Pine, Rosemary Pine, . . Slash Pine, and Carolina Pine. **1981** Pederson *LAGS Basic Materials,* 1 inf, **seGA,** Slash—type of shortleaf pine.

slashways adv Cf *DS* MM14, 15
Diagonally.
1892 *Short Stories* 9.458 **Pacific NW,** Then he made a trumpet of his hands and shouted: *"Slashways—across—the—hill! Watch—out—be-l-o-o-w!"* Two peelers heard the warning, dropped their bars, and made off out of reach of the limbs. **1946** *PADS* 6.27 **ceNC** (as of 1900–10),

Slashways. . . Diagonally. . . Common. **1963** Hayden *Wanderer* 433, The rain came slashways down. **1986** Pederson *LAGS Concordance,* 1 inf, neTN, Slashways—cutting wood crooked, on an angle.

slat v

1 To hurl, dash down; usu with *off:* to knock off; spec, to throw (a fish) off the hook with a jerk. [Engl dial] **chiefly NEng**

1814 in 1947 *AmSp* 22.277 [Americanisms], *Slat.* To throw down violently: as, he slat the book upon the floor. **1833** in 1834 Smith *Life Jack Downing* 256 **ME,** I thought . . that he would stave his bench all to pieces, he slat things round so. **1857** *Harper's New Mth. Mag.* 15.540 **seMA,** Two pulls—then slat off your mackerel over the rim of the strike-barrel. **1859** Elwyn *Glossary* 103, He *slat* it on the floor, for dashing down violently, is the only application I know of the word. **1872** Schele de Vere *Americanisms* 544, *Slat.* . . "If you don't come into the house this minute, I'll slat your head off." The word was originally confined to the language of fishermen on the Eastern coast, who disengaged mackerel and other delicate-gilled fish by *slatting* them off the hook. **1897** Howells *Landlord* 95 **NEng,** She'll slat the letters down every which way. **1899** *Brooklyn Daily Eagle* (NY) 8 Nov 18/4, The current, running against the sea, slatted her [=a lightship] around most frightfully. **1941** in 1947 Botkin *Treas. New Engl. Folkl.* 335, The figures along the deck were still obviously tending their lines, still heaving over splashless leads and slatting airy shapes into the barrels. **1950** Moore *Candlemas Bay* 59 **ME,** The stern bounced upward with a jerk, slatting them against their handholds.

2 To strike, slap (something); to slap (at something). [Engl (esp swEngl) dial] Cf **slat** n

1900 *Atlantic Mth.* 86.241, "I'll mind him when the season opens!" cried Lewis, slatting the gunwale with a heavy hand. **1903** *Harper's Mth. Mag.* 108.12, She [=a dog] would . . leave that stranger looking profane and embarrassed, and the initiated slatting the floor with their tails in unison. **1975** Gould *ME Lingo* 259, A *slat* is a quick motion of the hand, as when one *slats* at a mosquito.

3 usu with *about, around:* To move around in an ostentatiously noisy way. **chiefly ME**

1834 Davis *Letters Downing* 200 **ME,** And with that I handed the Gineral my ax, and he slatted about the chamber with it for a spell. **1895** *New Engl. Mag.* 18.277, Her companion was "slattin'" round too vigorously to notice her. Miss Naomi slammed the last closet door, made a final onslaught upon one luckless fly, then . . seized upon the sewing which awaited her. [**1914** *DN* 4.80 **ME, nNH,** *Slat.* . . To go.] **1929** *AmSp* 5.121 **ME,** Children were told . . not to "slat around" if they slammed things too impatiently. **1975** Gould *ME Lingo* 259, A person who tears around in slapdash fashion is said to *slat about.* **2000** *NADS Letters* **ME,** As for slat, I heard it growing up, in the sense of "don't slat around," "she slatted across the kitchen," meaning more than a pronounced, lazy, maybe disrespectful or uncaring way of moving. An exaggerated "non-verbal behavior" conveying a "see if I care" message. *Ibid* **ME,** I grew up hearing my mother . . (age: 60) use the term "slat" to refer to the rough banging manner used by a child when doing a task that they have been told to do but do not want to do. Parents say: "Stop slatting." **2001** *Ibid* **cNH** (as of 1950s), Years ago, I heard the phrase "slat around" to mean bustle around overly noisily, generally out of annoyance. It would involve slamming cupboard doors and other doors, heavy-handedly slamming things down on a table, etc.

4 To flap, slap, bang repeatedly; rarely, to cause to flap; to move (something) by causing it to flap; hence vbl n *slatting.* **chiefly NEng**

1839 *Freeman & Messenger* (Lodi NY) 28 Mar 1/3, One of the crew who was on the yard, by the slatting of the sail, had the buntline thrown over his head. **1840** (1841) Dana *2 Yrs.* 38 **NEng,** The great jib flying off to leeward and *slatting* so as almost to throw us off of her head. **1871** *Galaxy* 12.798, We rarely spoke . . listened to the slatting of the wavelets under our bow. **1889** Twain *CT Yankee* 144, I couldn't seem to stand that shield slatting and banging, now about my breast, now around my back. **1897** *New Engl. Mag.* 22.475, All the windows were provided with pretty green blinds (rather the worse for many years of slatting in the wind). **1934** [see **slat** n]. **1940** White *Wild Geese* 193 **NW** (as of 1890s), Bob and slat around like a cork. **1957** Beck *Folkl. ME* 167, In everyday speech, clothes "slat" on the line. **1975** Gould *ME Lingo* 259, Wind will *slat* the laundry on the line, and a strong wind will *slat* it right off the line. A barn door will *slat* all night in the wind. **1998** in 2002 *DARE* File—Internet **CT,** Years ago sailors would have sat rolling in the swell, . . sails slatting and gear chafing relentlessly.

5 also with *along, around:* Of a sailboat: to drift with sails flapping.

1899 *Brooklyn Daily Eagle* (NY) 15 Oct 28/3, An' the floatin' ice delayed us twice, an' for goin' on a year / We slatted around the bloomin' sound. **1947** *Sun* (Baltimore MD) 18 Sept 14/6, Today's race . . sailed in a southerly that died out flat . . [and] left more than half the fleet slatting around in the middle of . . [the lake]. **1994** in 2002 *DARE* File—Internet **CA,** Many sailors were left behind . . slatting along with windseekers, going almost nowhere, very slowly. **1999** *Ibid* **swCT,** Significant holes appeared in the breeze and one yacht could be slatting while another boat nearby would be sailing at five knots.

slat n [swEngl dial] Cf **slat** v 2, 4

A slap, blow; a gust of wind.

1840 (1841) Dana *2 Yrs.* 276 **MA,** Our gang . . furled the sail, though it bellied out over our heads, and again, by a slat of the wind, blew in under the yard, with a fearful jerk. **1934** Pierce *Goin' Fishin'* 26 **ME,** Sumbudy cast off th' halyards an' she fetched er slat an' parted th' jib-sheet, an' that sail ripped open an' slat to pieces afore we could get it down. **1975** Gould *ME Lingo* 259, A *slat* is a quick motion of the hand. . . Mother will give a fractious child a *slat* behind the ear.

slat about   See **slat** v 3

slat along   See **slat** v 5

slat around   See **slat** v 3, 5

slat bonnet n   Also *slat sunbonnet, slatted bonnet*   **esp Mid Atl, S Midl**   See Map   Cf **poke bonnet, split bonnet**

A sunbonnet with stiffening inserts in the brim.

1876 *Golden Hours* 8.160, Her calico slat-bonnet hung from her shoulders. **1878** *St. Nicholas* Oct 797, As soon as they had thrown off their slat sun-bonnets . . Nimpo was seized with a bright idea. **1899** (1912) Green *VA Folk-Speech* 392, *Slat-bonnet.* . . A bonnet made of calico, long to come over the face, with *slats* of pasteboard to keep it extended. **1899** (1967) Chesnutt *Wife of Youth* 64 **NC,** Women in homespun frocks and slat-bonnets. **1913** (1980) Hardy *OH Schoolmistress* 85, They used to come sometimes . . , always wearing black lawn slat sun-bonnets and straight-skirted calico gowns. **1926** Eppes *Through Some Yrs.* 306 **FL** (as of 1865), Dressed in black calico, with a slatted bonnet of the same material, she went bright and early to camp. **1937** Sandoz *Slogum* 73 **NE,** Their women . . with their eyes turned curiously out the side of their slat sunbonnets as far as they could. **1939** *AmSp* 14.78, A *slat sun-bonnet* would seem to be almost as out-of-date as a 'sundown' although I have seen a few on the heads of Nebraska farm women. . . The bonnet is stiffened by strips or slats of cardboard about an inch wide pushed into the flat tubes formed by sticking together in parallel rows two thicknesses of calico or gingham. The cardboard is removed when the bonnet is laundered. **1944** *PADS* 2.60 **MO, NC, VA,** *Slat-bonnet.* **1966–70** *DARE* (Qu. W2, . . *A cloth bonnet worn by women for protection from the sun*) 23 Infs, **esp Mid Atl, S Midl,** Slat bonnet; **VA31,** Slat sunbonnet. [10 Infs specified that the slat bonnet is old-fashioned or no longer used; 17 of 24 Infs were old.] **1995** Heatwole *Shenandoah Voices* 14 **wVA,** He decided that it was best that he go in disguise, so he donned his mother's . . old slat bonnet.

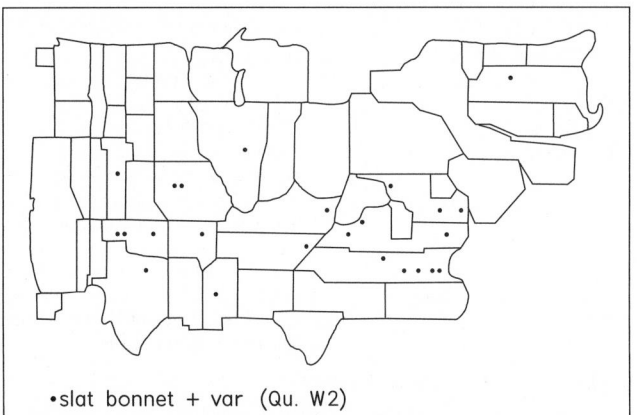

•slat bonnet + var (Qu. W2)

slatch n [*OED2* a1625–1769]   **esp Nantucket MA**

A short interval of good weather; an intermission, period of respite; hence adj *slatchy* of the sky: showing clear patches.

1848 in 1935 *AmSp* 10.41 **Nantucket MA**, *Slatch*. When it rains it is said, *I'll kitch a slatch & go there.* When the rain ceases or lessens. **1890** *DN* 1.9 **Nantucket MA**, A *slatchy* (pronounced [slætʃi]) sky (when blue sky appears through clouds). **1916** Macy–Hussey *Nantucket Scrap Basket* 165, *"Slatch"*—A word still in quite common use on the island among the older people. It means "a short gleam of fine weather, an interval in a storm." When caught away from home in a heavy rain, we plan, if possible, to "wait for a slatch" before starting to return. The term is also sometimes used in the sense of a respite from labor, as "I had a slatch in my work, and I thought I'd run over and see you."

slate-colored junco   See **junco** n[1]

slate-colored mockingbird n   Cf **mockingbird 3**
=**catbird 1.**

     1911 MI Pub. Instruction *Annual Rept. for 1910–11* 81, *Catbird; Slate-colored Mockingbird.* The slate-colored bird of the thickets which mews like a cat . . is the Catbird.

slat fence n   Also *slatted fence*
1 Any of var fences in which slats are nailed to stringers vertically, as a **paling fence** or picket fence, or nailed to posts horizontally; see quots.

     1790 (1905) Bentley *Diary* 1.180 **neMA**, The Principal Garden is in three parts divided by an open slat fence painted white. **1843** Emerson in 1892 *Atlantic Mth.* 69.592 **MA**, Ellery Channing works and writes as usual at his cottage, to which Captain Moore has added a neat slat fence and gate. **1933** Rawlings *South Moon* 16 **FL**, The slat fence about the yard went slowest. . . Post-holes were dug, posts driven deep, slats nailed between with square nails and at last, breast high to Lantry, a flat top was nailed on for finish. **1939** *LANE* Map 115 *(Picket fence)* **NEng**, [There are 16 instances of *slat fence* and 32 of *slatted fence* used as synonyms or near-synonyms of *picket fence*.] **c1960** *Wilson Coll.* **csKY**, *Slat fence.* . . A paling fence or picket fence. **1961** Folk *Word Atlas N. LA* map 602, Fence made of wooden rails . . [less freq responses include] slat fence. *Ibid* map 603, Fence made of slats standing upright . . [less freq responses include] slat fence. **1965–70** *DARE* (Qu. L64, *The kind of wooden fence that's built around a garden or near a house*) 18 Infs, **scattered**, Slat fence; **KY14**, Paling fence = slat fence; **KY68**, Slat fence—vertical; **LA44**, Slat fence—boards about a inch and three-quarters wide, square at top and bottom; **NH14**, Slat fence—boards are thinner than on a picket fence; **SC40**, Slat fence [FW illustr: slats nailed horizontally to two posts]; **NC52**, Slatted fence; (Qu. L65, . . *Kinds of fences*) Infs **AR51, LA22, NY84, RI4**, Slat. **1970** Tarpley *Blinky* 124 **neTX**, *Fence made of slats standing upright* . . slat fence [4 of 200 infs]. **1971** Wood *Vocab.* Change 104 **Sth**, *A kind of wooden fence.* . . slat fence [30 of approx 1000 infs]. **1973** Allen *LAUM* 1.192 (as of c1950), *Picket fence.* . . slat fence [4 infs, **MN, IA, NE**]. **1986** Pederson *LAGS Concordance* **Gulf Region** *(Picket fence)* 5 infs, (A) slat fence; 2 infs, Slat fence—paling fence; 1 inf, Slat fence—a board fence; 1 inf, Slat fence—pointed; nailed to railing or planted; 1 inf, Slat fence—vertical boards; 1 inf, Slat fence—horizontal slats; 1 inf, Slat fence—boards close together; 1 inf, Slat fence—rail fence; 1 inf, Wood slat fence—made of pine; nailed to posts; 1 inf, Slatted fence; [1 inf, Slat fencing—later type; pointed; 1″ apart].
2 A fence of vertical slats held together by horizontal wires.

     1929 *Edwardsville Intelligencer* (IL) 21 Mar 8/2, [Advt:] 4 foot red slat fence—painted and pointed—five wires. **1940** U.S. Dept. Ag. *Farmers' Bulletin* 1832.14, [Caption:] A movable slat or snow fence. [*DARE* Ed: Picture shows a fence of two eight-foot sections, each section comprising 31 1½″ x ½″ laths spaced 1½″ apart secured to each other with horizontal rows of wire that are attached to steel posts at each end.] **1966** Dakin *Dial. Vocab. Ohio R. Valley* 2.97, *Picket fence.* . . The name *slat(ted) fence,* scattered throughout Kentucky but rare north of the river, seems most often to be a synonym for *picket fence* = "woven in wire" in contrast to *paling fence* = "nailed." **1966** *DARE* (Qu. L64, *The kind of wooden fence that's built around a garden or near a house*) Inf **SD1**, Slat fence—slats wired together. **1986** Pederson *LAGS Concordance (Picket fence)* 1 inf, **cnTN**, Slat fence—with wires.

slather n   Cf **lashings, oceans**
Freq pl: A large number; a great quantity.

     1855 *Musical World* 40.190 **WI**, It contains "lots and slathers" of the choicest kind of music to please both old and young. **1893** in 1932 *AmSp* 7.260 **NE** [Hobo terms], *Slathers of gold*—abundance of money. **1905** *DN* 3.65 **eNE**, *Slathers.* . . Large quantities. . . "Slathers of

money." **1909** *DN* 3.415 **nME**, *Slathers and gobs.* . . A great quantity. **1927** *DN* 5.477 **Ozarks**, *Slathers.* . . A very large amount. "Them fellers has all got slathers o' money." **1940** Von Tempski *Paradise* 319 **HI**, We had slathers of friends. **1950** *WELS (A large amount or number, more than enough. . . "She has a whole _____ of cousins.")* 1 Inf, **seWI**, Slather. **1968** *DARE* (Qu. LL9a, *As much as you need or more . . "We've got _____ of apples.")* Inf **CA105**, Slathers. **1984** Wilder *You All Spoken Here* 71 **Sth**, *Slathers:* Plenty.

slat off   See **slat** v **1**

slat sunbonnet, slatted bonnet   See **slat bonnet**

slatted fence   See **slat fence**

slatter n   Similarly adj *slattery* [Varr of *slattern(ly)*] Cf Pronc Intro 3.I.22

     1927 *DN* 5.477 **Ozarks**, *Slattery.* . . Dirty, dilapidated. "Jim's pappy he lives in a ol' slattery shanty." **1954** *Harder Coll.* **cwTN**, *Slattery.* . . Dirty, dilapidated, in poor repair. **1967–68** *DARE* (Qu. HH36, *A careless, slovenly woman: "She's just an old _____.")* Inf **KS13**, Slatter ['slætɚ]; **MA71**, Slatter; (Qu. HH37, *An immoral woman*) Inf **TX33**, Slatter.

slatting   See **slat** v **4**

slaunch n, also attrib   Also *slanch*   Cf **slonching**
An angle, slant; hence adj *slaunch-eyed* walleyed.

     1899 Garland *Boy Life* 185 **nwIA** (as of c1870s), After a shock [of grain] has set for some time in the field, the ends of the outside bundles take on a "slanch" at the butt. **1933** *AmSp* 8.3.82, He [=a Southerner] responded by telling me of a carpenter who, making a miter joint, did not use a miter box but sawed the piece by guess and then sighted down it and said, "I guess that's about the right slaunch." **1966–68** *DARE* (Qu. X26b, *If a person's eyes look in different directions, looking outward, he's _____)* Inf **MI10**, Slaunch-eyed; [(Qu. MM15, *If a carpenter nails a board crossing another board at an angle . . "He nailed the board on _____.")* Inf **IL29**, Kitty-ki-slaunch]. **2004** *DARE* File—Internet, Two of the couples will likely be dancing at an angle to the center of the set they aren't used to and will need to maintain this "slaunch" position.

slaunchwise adj, adv   Also *slanchways, slanchwise, sl(a)unchways, slonchways, slonchwise, slunchwise* for addit varr see quots **scattered, but chiefly W Midl, West** See Map *somewhat old-fash* Cf **slunch**
Slanting, oblique, crooked; diagonally, obliquely, crookedly; also fig.

     1833 (1954) Paulding *Lion West* 54 **KY**, So he looked up at me "slantindickular," and I looked down on him "slanchwise." **1881** *Scribner's Mth.* 22.445 **GA** [Black], Den bimeby yer come trouble en snatch um slonchways. **1885** *Atlantic Mth.* 55.748 **sAppalachians**, He got up slanch-wise, an' in sech a hurry the cheer fell over ahint him. **1913** Kephart *Highlanders* 294 **sAppalachians**, Slaunchways denotes slanting. **1917** *DN* 4.417 **wNC**, *Slaunchways.* . . Slantingly. Also Ill., Kan. **1923** *DN* 5.236 **swWI**, *Slawnch-wise.* . . Slantwise, slanting, out of true. **1926** *DN* 5.403 **Ozarks**, *Slaunchways.* . . Slanting. **1930s** in 1944 *ADD* 566 **eWV**, Slanchways [slæ-], slaunchways [slɔ]-. **1933** *AmSp* 8.3.82 **TX**, He said he wanted a full-width bed so that he could lie *slaunchwise* part of the time. **1936** *Story* Nov 53 **NC**, Ben Edwards' carriage . . rolled . . till it ran slunchways into old man Hyman's store window and busted all to pieces. **1941** *Sat. Eve. Post* 5 Apr 23 **WA**, The tide race would slap him slanchways pronto. **1944** *PADS* 2.60 **MO, NC, VA**, *Slaunchways.* . . Diagonal, not level, not straight. "The road runs slaunchways across the field." "Don't hold your cup slaunchways; you'll spill your coffee." **1946** McAtee *Dial. Grant Co. IN Suppl. 3* (as of 1890s), *Kerslaunchways* . . obliquely. **c1950** Halpert Coll. **KY**, *Slonchwise.* . . crooked, not straight. "Those books are laid up there sort of slonchwise." **1965–70** *DARE* (Qu. MM15, *If a carpenter nails a board crossing another board at an angle . . "He nailed the board on _____.")* Infs **AR31, IL14, IN14, KY5, 11, MT5, SD8, WA24**, Slanchways; **OH92**, Slanchways [FW sugg; Inf has heard]; **CA102, 105, IN31, VT16**, Slaunchwise; **IN28, TX18**, Slanchwise; **IL72**, Schlaunchwise ['ʃlɑnšwɑrz] [FW: his grandfather's word]; (Qu. MM3, *When someone does something the wrong way round . . "This is the front, you've got the whole thing turned _____.")* Inf **WA3**, Slaunchwise; (Qu. MM13, *The table was nice and straight until he came along and knocked it _____)* Infs **CA30, IN70, OH38, 49, 61**, Slaunchwise; **IL25, IA23, KS13**, Slanchwise. [21 of 25 Infs old] **1970** *Mt. Democrat & Placerville Times* (CA) 26 Feb sec B 3/7, A world of Joshua trees bracing their queer, slick bodies, slunch-wise, against the wind. **1976** Garber *Mountain-ese* 83 **sAppalachians,** *Slaunchways* . . diagonal—I had to nail the board up sort of slaunchways to brace the fence. **1995** (1998) *Brophy Coll.* 69 **swMO** (as of c1960), *Slaunchwise, slaunchways.* [S]lantwise, crooked.

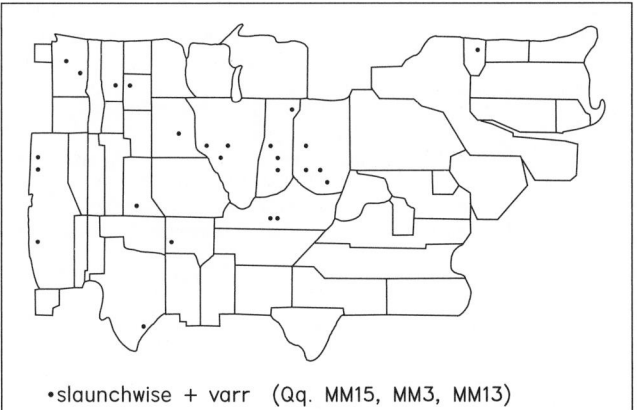

•slaunchwise + varr (Qq. MM15, MM3, MM13)

slave n   *among Black speakers*

A job.

1965 Little *Autobiog. Malcolm X* 45 [Black], "You mean you just want any slave you can find?" A "slave" meant work, a job. Shorty's slave in the poolroom, he said, was just to keep ends together. **1965** Brown *Manchild* 177 **Harlem NYC** [Black], A guy who worked in the garment center wouldn't say he had a job; he'd say, "Man, like, I got a slave." That was what it amounted to. It was a real drag. **1968** *Current Slang* 3.2.43 **swCA** [Watts slang; Black], *Slave.* . . A job.—Yeah, man! I found me a slave in L.A., but it was rough getting in. **1970** Major *Dict. Afro-Amer. Slang* 105, *Slave:* (1930's–40's) a job. **2004** *DARE* File—Internet [Black], Although I have a good slave that I enjoy, I hate slaving all the time. (For those of you who don't know, slave is a job.) I'm ready to be my own boss.

slay v

Std sense, var gram forms.

1 past: usu *slew;* also *slain, slayed, slewed.* **esp Sth, S Midl**

1845 Aaron *Light Truth Slavery* 26, They took the holy Lamb and slayed him. **1859** Taliaferro *Fisher's R.* 120 **nwNC** (as of 1820s), 'Twasn't long afore we cum to another fence, and thar I slayed 'Gius. **1884** *Anglia* 7.253 [Black], To the regular forms of the Irregular verbs as used by the whites, the Negro adds the following forms of his own. . . *Pres.* slay—*Past.* slayed, slewed, slain. **1906** *DN* 3.156 **nwAR,** *Slayed, pret. v., pp.* Slew, slain. **1916** *DN* 4.280 **NE,** *Slayed.* Frequent pret. of *slay.* **a1930** in 1991 Hughes–Hurston *Mule Bone* 38 **cFL** [Black], It says heah in Judges 15:16 dat Samson slewed a thousand Philistines wid the jaw-bone of a ass. **1941** Stuart *Men of Mts.* 307 **KY,** It [=an ax] slayed the saplins fer me. **1986** Pederson *LAGS Concordance,* 1 inf, **cAL,** It just nearly slayed me.

2 past pple: usu *slain;* also *slained, slayed, slew.*

1847 *De Bow's Rev.* 3.602, They have been slayed by hundreds. **1861** *S. Lit. Messenger* Aug 82, He told me when dat great beef was slayed. **1893** *DN* 1.278 **wCT,** *Slay*—[past and past pple:] slew. **1906** [see **1** above]. **1969** Wilson *Stars* 151 **Ozarks,** He wasn't in shape to do so; he was slayed dead. **1972** *Appalachian Oral Hist. Project* 355 *(Montgomery Coll.)* **eKY, C Appalachians,** You could just hear them being slained here and there. **1997** *WI State Jrl.* (Madison) 16 Nov sec C 1/2, The property tax dragon has not been slayed.

slayed   See slay 1, 2

sleazy adj   Usu |ˈslizɪ|; also *old-fash* |ˈslezɪ| Pronc-spp *slaz(e)y* [Cf *EDD sleeze* v., sb., "Also written *sleaze* . . and . . *slaze*"]

Std senses, var forms.

1827 *Norwalk Reporter & Huron Advt.* (OH) 20 Oct [4]/3 (newspaperarchive.com), Every one will recollect the slazy hum hums which we formerly imported from India at 2 and 3 shillings per yard. **1848** Bartlett *Americanisms* 306, *Slazy.* A corrupt pronunciation of *sleazy* or *sleezy;* i.e. weak, wanting substance; thin; flimsy. **1849** *De Bow's Rev.* 7.257, Where, then, are the profits of the New York and Philadelphia

jobbers? . . Why, on slazy calicoes, made in England. **1860** *Harper's New Mth. Mag.* 21.807, They're made of the cheapest kind of cotton stuff—old slazy velveteen. **a1883** (1911) Bagby *VA Gentleman* 70, It is . . built in that solid, honest way which was the rule everywhere in Virginia before the new-fangled, flimsy, slazy style of the Yankees was introduced. **1890** Holley *Samantha among Brethren* 100 **NY,** It [=a shawl] wuz kinder thin and slazy. **1899** (1912) Green *VA Folk-Speech* 392, *Slazy.* . . Badly woven. Of thin or flimsy substance, composed of poor or light material. . . Sleazy. **1904** *DN* 2.428 **Cape Cod MA** (as of a1857), *Slazy.* . . Thin, soft, and loosely woven. **1909** *DN* 3.404 **nwAR,** *Sleazy.* . . Thin and flimsy—said of cheap cloth. Rhymes with lazy. **1918** *DN* 5.16 **Martha's Vineyard MA,** *Slazey* [e]. . . Flimsy, poorly woven. Not durable. "That cloth is pretty slazy." **1965–70** *DARE* (Qu. KK6, *Something low-grade or of poor quality—for example, a piece of merchandise: "I wouldn't buy that, it's _____."*) 25 Infs, **scattered, but somewhat more freq Sth, S Midl, SW,** Slazy; (Qu. W29, . . *Expressions . . for things that are sewn carelessly . . "They're _____."*) Inf **CA**58, Slazy. [22 of 26 Infs old, 4 mid-aged, 17 coll educ, 22 female] **1981** *NY Times* (NY) 14 Jan (Internet), People in the [apparel] industry say an unshrunk fabric is "slazy," or limp.

sled n   [*OED* 1388 →]   widespread exc Nth   See Map and Map Section   Cf drag n 2, slide n 1, stoneboat

Freq in combs: A wheelless wooden vehicle for transporting heavy loads over dry ground.

1867 Harris *Sut Lovingood Yarns* 157 **TN,** They cum a-foot, on hoss's, on muels, on oxes, on bulls, on sleds, in carts, waggins an' buggys. **1913** Rothert *Hist. Muhlenberg Co.* 113 **KY,** Until comparatively recent times, some of the farmers used a ground-sled or a "landslide" for short hauls. It was built on the principle of a sled, and so used during all seasons. **1939** *LANE* Map 168 *(Stone boat)* 1 inf, **ceMA,** Stone sled; 1 inf, **neMA,** Sled, low, of wood; 1 inf, **csCT,** Ox sled—if drawn by oxen. 'Oxen used to draw on them at the fair', i.e. in contests; 1 inf, **seNY,** Stone sled, the old term, natural. **1949** Kurath *Word Geog.* 58, The wheelless horse-drawn vehicle made of heavy planks, which is used for dragging stones from the fields, is known as a *stone sled* or *drag sled* in the Midland and as a *stone boat* in the North, except for the coastal area of New England, which has *drag* or *stone drag.* **1965–70** *DARE* (Qu. L57, *A low wooden platform used for bringing stones or heavy things out of the fields*) 270 Infs, **widespread exc Nth,** Sled; **CA**211, **KY**49, **OR**1, **VA**10, 89, Rock sled; **OH**80, **PA**137, 147, Stone sled; **OR**2, Boulder sled; **TN**14, Half-sled; **PA**75, Plank sled; **PA**103, Wood-shod sled. [*DARE* Ed: The *sled* responses at Qu. N40a have not been included, since it is not possible in most cases to determine what type of vehicle the Infs were referring to.] **1966–69** *DARE* Tape **FL**26, Then it's put on what they call a tobacco sled and carried to the barn; **GA**7, Now most people have a wagon or a tractor or a sled, what we call a sled, to put that barrel [of turpentine] on; **KY**13, All those walls around this mill, it all come out of the same quarry, and was hauled in there with yokes and cattle and rock sled. **1967** *Hand Coll.* **NE** (as of 1905), *Stone sled*—Crude sled used for hauling water in Nebraska and hauling stones for fence lines. **1973** Allen *LAUM* 1.218 (as of c1950), *Stone boat* . . is common in the U[pper] M[idwest] except in strongly Midland-oriented territory, Nebraska, where Midland *sled* dominates. **1975** McDonough *Garden Sass* 206 **AR,** Today farmers still use these old sleds behind their tractors to haul apples, peaches, and other produce out of the orchards. They usually call them "sleds," although some people make the distinction that sleds were used only in winter and sledges

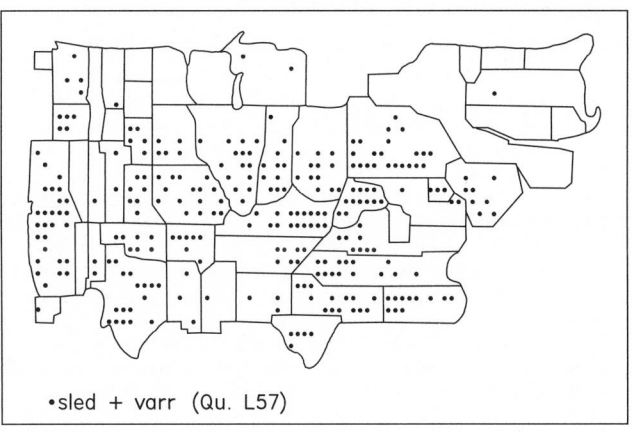

•sled + varr (Qu. L57)

were used the year around. **1983** *Greenfield Recorder* (MA) 22 Jan 6, Every farmer had a wood shod sled, with perhaps wider runners than a pung, but they were made of solid wood and could be used on bare or almost bare ground or in rough boggy places. **1986** Pederson *LAGS Concordance,* 1 inf, **neTN,** Sled—with runners made of sourwood; before wagons; 1 inf, **cnGA,** Sled—for hauling stones in a field; 1 inf, **csMS,** Sled—used in hauling wood; 1 inf, **cnAR,** Sled—a drag.

sledding n

Fig: circumstances or conditions regarded as favorable or unfavorable to the success of some enterprise—in combs *easy* (or *hard, rough, tough*) *sledding.*

1832 in 1835 Derby *Political Reminiscences* 116, This is hard sledding for the Nullies [=Nullifiers], but they will soon find it harder. **1838** *New-Yorker* (NY NY) 11 Aug 331/1, Hard sledding this; but 'the good times will come round again,' as the French proverb has it. **1903** *DN* 2.353 **MA, IA,** *Sledding (hard). . .* Used figuratively of hardship, as in 'pretty hard sledding.' **1908** Beach *Barrier* 127, Them kind of places [in the Yukon] is all right for married men but they're tough sleddin' for single ones. **1914** *DN* 4.74 **nNH, ME,** *Hard sleddin'. . .* Poverty, hardship, misery. **1923** *DN* 5.209 **swMO,** *Hard sleddin'. . .* Living or doing business under difficulties. **1959** *VT Hist.* 27.157, *Hard sledding. . .* Also, tough sledding. . . sickness or disaster or hard times for the family or community. Common. **1960** Criswell *Resp. to PADS 20* **Ozarks,** *Hard sledding*—Hard going with any job or task. Still common. **1965–70** *DARE* (Qu. CC12a, *. . Bad luck . . "Poor Joe. He's really been having _____."*) 42 Infs, **scattered,** Tough sledding; **IL4,** Hard sledding; **NY**152, Rough sledding; (Qu. KK41, *Something that is very difficult to do: "I managed to get through with it, but it was _____."*) 39 Infs, **scattered,** Tough sledding; **CO**29, **GA**31, **TX**5, Hard sledding; **CO**17, **GA**72, 84, **IN**7, Rough sledding; (Qu. KK42a, *Expressions about a person who does something very easily: "For him that would be _____."*) Inf **PA**150, Easy sledding; (Qu. KK44, *To continue doing something even though it is difficult: "For five winters we've _____.";* total Infs questioned, 75) Inf **OK**51, It's been hard sledding. **1979** *Arizona Daily Sun* 19 Apr. 4/2 *(OED2),* This part of the administration's plan likewise faces tough sledding on Capitol Hill.

sledge n

A Form.

Pronc-sp *sludge.* Cf **dredge** n¹, v

1982 *DARE* File **nwMS,** Sludge hammer. Town of Sludge, Mississippi. Yes, folks. That's how they say it [=Sledge]. No wonder no one can understand Delta people other than Delta people.

B Sense.

Freq in comb *old sledge:* =**seven-up 1.**

1830 *Corrector* (Sag Harbor, N.Y.) 26 June 1/1 *(DA),* Lieutenant Poole . . plays all cards from old sledge to ecarte. **1841** *Spirit of Times* 27 Mar 42 **AR,** Jim bears it better than Dan. I reckon he sorter waded out, on a soft snap at old sledge. **1870** Twain in *Galaxy* Oct 574 **KY,** About a dozen of the boys were detected playing "seven-up" or "old sledge" for money. **1887** (1892) Hinman *Corporal Si Klegg* 93, There were . . games of euchre and "old sledge." **1910** Porter *Strictly Business* 79 **NY,** I've heard of places in this here town where a fellow could have a good game or [sic] old sledge or peg a card at keno. **1922** (1926) Cady *Rhymes VT* 163, Both kinds of pasteboards, decks and packs,/ Was very dangerous, very;/ And "Sledge" and all the different "Jacks,"/ And "Pitch" and "Solitary." **1942** *CA Folkl. Qrly.* 1.286 **AZ, CA, NV,** *Sledge. . .* A card game popular with gamblers in the early days; seven-up; all-fours; old sledge.

sled length adj phr, also used absol **chiefly NEng**

Of firewood: cut in long pieces to fit lengthwise on a sled; hence adv phr *sled length* in pieces of this length; also fig.

1832 Mirick *Hist. Haverhill MA* 69, Their fire-places were of such enormous sizes, that they could burn their wood sled-length. **1867** *80 Yrs. Progress U.S.* 2.357 **MA,** Most of what [firewood] we used . . was cut and brought sled length by the farmers. **1876** Bagley *Old Times* 4 **MI,** Sled-length knotty wood that wouldn't make rails paid the minister. **1895** *Atlantic Mth.* 76.736 **NEng,** The woodpile grows at the farmhouse door in a huge windrow of sled-length wood or an even wall of cord wood. *Ibid* 737, The wood is cut "sled length," which is a saving of time and also of chips. **1975** Gould *ME Lingo* 259, *Sled length*—Random length; said of firewood which is brought out of the woods lengthwise of the sled instead of across it in four-foot cordwood. Gray birch and small growth are usually handled in *sled lengths* to save time

in the woods. . . When used to describe anything other than firewood *sled length* means random and unmeasured: "They got a whole bunch of sled-length kids."

sled ride v phr, hence vbl n *sled riding* **esp wPA, eIN, sAppalachians** See Map
=**coast** v **1.**

1845 *Lowell Offering* 5.268 **NH,** We assembled ourselves together, and hied for some favorite hill, where sled-riding could be performed. **1892** *DN* 1.215, *Coast. . .* In Western Pennsylvania is used . . *to sled-ride.* **1926** *AmSp* 2.80, In the winter the children . . "sled-ride," as they say in Pennsylvania. **1931** *AmSp* 7.20 **swPA,** *Sled-ride.* To coast or to slide. **1965–70** *DARE* (Qu. EE24b, *When children go down hill on a sled . . they say they're _____*) 36 Infs, **scattered, but esp wPA, eIN, sAppalachians,** Sled riding. **2001** *DARE* File **nwPA,** Here in Erie. . . They share P[ittsbur]gh's use of the term . . sled riding (sledding works for me).

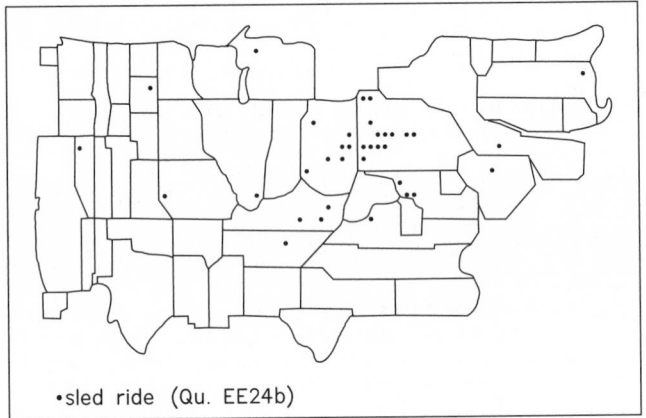

•sled ride (Qu. EE24b)

sleek See **slick** n **1**

sleep v

A Form.

Past and past pple: usu *slept;* also [slɛp], pronc-sp *slep.* Cf Pronc Intro 3.I.22, **creep** v **A, keep** v **A4**

1852 Eastman *Aunt Phillis's Cabin* 146 **VA** [Black], Aint slep none dese two, three nights. **1861** *Harper's New Mth. Mag.* 22.662 **CT,** He slep to Albany. **1871** Eggleston *Hoosier Schoolmaster* 40 **sIN,** Had-n been slep on more'n wunst or twicet. **1892** *DN* 1.238 **cwMO, NEng,** *Crept.* In *crept . . slept . . wept,* the *t* is generally left off. **1895** *DN* 1.376, **seKY, eTN, wNC,** *Slep* = slept. **1899** (1912) Green *VA Folk-Speech* 393, *Slep. . .* Slept. "I slep badly last night." **1909** *DN* 3.371 **eAL, wGA,** *Slep,* pret. and pp. of sleep. **1910** *DN* 3.455 **seVT,** *Slep. . .* "Yes, I slep well last night." **1916** Howells *Leatherwood God* 6 **OH** (as of 1830s), I reckon I overslep'. **1928** *AmSp* 3.405 **Ozarks** (as of 1916–27), In such words as *slept, crept, kept* and *wept* the *t* is invariably dropped. **1940** *AmSp* 15.47 **sAppalachians, Ozarks,** Final [t] is lost after [ɛp]: slep'. **1943** *LANE* Map 643, [The preterite of *sleep* as [slɛp] was incidentally noted in the conversation of 1 inf, **RI,** 2 infs, **VT.**] **1965–70** *DARE* (Qu. X43a, *If you sleep later than usual one day by accident . . "I _____."*) Infs **AK**1, **CO**47, **UT**3, 4, Slep in; **VA**54, Slep late; **VT**16, Slep over; (Qu. X43b, *If you sleep later than usual one day on purpose . . "I _____."*) Infs **AK**1, **IN**27, **KY**84, **UT**3, **VA**54, Slep in; **LA**40, **VA**39, Slep late; **VT**16, Slep all day; (Qu. OO19b, *Talking about stretching out to rest: "He'll feel better after he has _____ [down a while]."*) Infs **IN**41, **MN**20, Slep. **1975** Allen *LAUM* 2.79 (as of c1950), *Sleep. . .* the loss of *-t* has created a new strong preterite *slep* [2 infs, **MN,** 2 infs, **ND,** 1 inf, **SD,** 1 inf, **NE**].

B Sense.

To provide sleeping accommodations for (someone). Cf **eat** v **B2** Note: *Sleep* in the sense "to afford sleeping accommodations for (a specific number)" is regarded as standard.

1867 *Ladies' Repository* Mar 148, You had some company, I suppose. How did you contrive to 'sleep them?' **1877** Wright *Big Bonanza* 20 **NV,** The boys paid him fourteen dollars per week for board and "slept themselves"; that is, they were provided with blankets of their own, and rolling up in these, they just curled down in the sagebrush. **1892** *KS Univ. Qrly.* 1.99 **KS,** *Sleep:* to give lodgings. I have heard, We can eat and sleep him. **1911** *DN* 3.550 **WY,** *Sleep and eat,* provide with lodging and board. "Wages are $45 a month and you have to sleep and eat the man beside." **1916** *DN* 4.336 **Nantucket MA,** *Sleep.* . . To accommodate with sleeping quarters. "Yes, thee can come to us, but we shall be compelled to sleep thee in Coffins." Not local in hotels. **1927** *AmSp* 2.515 **GA,** Mr. Lowry Axley of Savannah, Georgia, writes that a tinner recently said to him: "I had to bring in men from the outside to do the work, and it was expensive, too, for I had to sleep them and eat them." **1977** Adams *Lang. Railroader* 140, *Sleep:* To give sleeping accommodations to someone.

sleep by v phr
=sleep in.

1965–67 *DARE* (Qu. X43a, *If you sleep later than usual one day by accident* . . "*I _____.*") Inf **MS59,** Slept by; (Qu. X43b, *If you sleep later than usual one day on purpose* . . "*I _____.*") Inf **TX35,** Slept by; [**TX26,** Slept by my regular time].

sleep dust n Also *sleeping dust* Cf *sleepy dust* (at **sleepy** n)
=sleeper n **4.**

1915 *Edwardsville Intelligencer* (IL) [29 Dec 2]/4 (newspaperarchive.com), On Christmas morning when I wake, and sleep-dust from my eyes I shake. **1983** *DARE* File **WY,** *(The stuff in the corner of your eyes when you wake up in the morning)* Sleeping dust. **1984** *Ibid* **UT,** Sleep dust.

sleeper n

1 An unmarked calf; a calf that has been **earmarked** v but not branded. [Prob a spec instance of the general sense "something whose quality or value proves to be greater than was generally expected; a 'dark horse'" (*OED2 sleeper* sb. 6 1892 →)] **West** Cf **maverick 1, sleeper** v, **slick ear 1**

1880 (1883) U.S. Census Office *Rept. Ag.* 3.1091, Many calves are necessarily missed, and when these leave their mothers, or are weaned naturally, they are called "slick-ears", "sleepers," or "mavericks", and belong to any cattleman who can get his brand on them. **1893** (1958) Wister *Out West* 198 **TX,** *Sleeper*—a cow with earmark and no brand. **1907** White *AZ Nights* 78, What's a sleeper? A sleeper is a calf that has been ear-marked, but not branded. **1916** *DN* 4.348 **TX** (as of 1896), *Sleeper.* . . A cow or steer found unbranded by a cattle thief and marked by him, but not with his own brand, though later he adds his own. **1920** Hunter *Trail Drivers TX* 313 (as of c1880), In those early days the earmark would not always be proof of ownership and an animal without brand was called a "sleeper." A sleeper was . . so called because some one had overlooked branding this animal in a previous round up—had slept on his rights. **1933** *AmSp* 8.1.30 **nwTX** [Ranch diction], *Sleeper.* A calf earmarked with owner's mark but not branded. *Making sleepers* was considered *a decent way to steal,* and was accomplished thus: A calf would be marked *in the mother's mark* but not branded. The owner, when looking over his cattle would notice that the calf was marked and assume that it was branded. Therefore it would go unbranded, and later the person who had made it a *sleeper,* would put his own brand on it, and thus add another to his growing herd. **1940** Writers' Program *Guide NV* 77, A *sleeper* is an animal earmarked but not branded.

2 **=dowitcher.** Cf **dormeur 2**

1911 *Forest & Stream* 77.174 **LA,** *Macrorhamphus griseus scolopaceus.* . . Sleeper, Gum Cove, La. **1916** *Times–Picayune* (New Orleans LA) 2 Apr mag sec 8, *Long-billed Dowitcher.* . . Sleeper.

3 **=ruddy duck.** [See quot 1924] **esp AL** Cf **sleepy-head 1**

1923 U.S. Dept. Ag. *Misc. Circular* 13.31 **AL,** *Ruddy Duck.* . . *Vernacular Names.* . . Sleeper. **1924** Howell *Birds AL* 65, *Ruddy Duck.* . . In Alabama this little duck is known to the local hunters as "sleeper," from its habit of sleeping on sandbars in the daytime. **1954** Sprunt *FL Bird Life* 85, *Ruddy Duck.* . . Sleeper. **1962** Imhof *AL Birds* 158, *Ruddy Duck.* . . Sleeper. . . A *small, grayish* duck with *white cheeks, dark wings.*

4 usu pl: A bit of gritty matter that sometimes forms in the eyes during sleep. Cf **sleepy** n

1942 Berrey–Van den Bark *Amer. Slang* 251.1, *Sleep.* . . *sleepers,* particles in the eyes after a sound sleep. **1950** *WELS Suppl.,* Granules either in the corners of the eyes or on eye-lashes: 2 Infs, **WI,** Sleepers. **1979** Wolfe *Right Stuff* 45, I 'spect they still got the *sleep*ers in their eyes. **1981** *AmSp* 56.80, *Sleep* seems to be the standard term for the 'ocular discharge.' . . a variant from Minnesota: *sleepers.* **1981** *NADS*

Letters **PA,** I have always used the word "sleeper" for the gunk that fills your eyes at night. I am originally from King of Prussia, PA, where I first heard the expression. In that area, most residents . . are familiar with the expression and use it frequently. **1983** *DARE* File **MN, UT,** *(The stuff in the corner of your eyes when you wake up in the morning)* Sleepers. **1984** *Ibid* **ID, IL, Boston MA, WY, UT,** Sleepers. **1985** *Ibid* **VA,** Sleeper. **1986** *Ibid* **VA, Sth,** Sleepers. **1987** *Ibid* **ceMA, neWV,** Sleepers.

sleeper v [**sleeper** n 1] West

1 also *sleeper-mark:* To **earmark** v (a calf) without branding it; to make a **sleeper** n **1;** hence vbl n *sleepering.*

1907 White *AZ Nights* 79, I took the chance to look at his ears, and saw that the marking had been done quite recent, so when we got in that night I reported to Buck Johnson that one of the punchers was gettin' lazy and sleeperin'. **1910** Mulford *Hopalong* 88 **West,** Either the H2 was sleepering Bar-20 calves for their irons later on, or rustlers were at work. **1936** Adams *Cowboy Lingo* 159 **West,** He [=a rustler] might make use of the 'picked brand' or the 'hair brand' . . or he might 'sleeper' the animal. **1943** Hamner *Short Grass* 97 **wTX,** Again cattle were "sleeper marked," that is, marked but left unbranded. **1944** Adams *Western Words* 146, *Sleepering*—The rustler's taking an unbranded calf, earmarking it with the mother's earmark, and turning it loose unbranded.

2 To apply a temporary (brand).

2003 *DARE* File—Internet **CO,** Competent theves [sic] can "sleeper" a brand on an animal with wet gunny sacks and a hot iron, scalding the hair off, and leaving the brand to fade at a later date, where the now unbranded (slick) animal can be branded as the far thinking thief wishes.

sleepering See **sleeper** v **1**
sleeper-inner See **sleep in**
sleeper-mark See **sleeper** v **1**

sleep in v phr [Scots dial; cf *EDD sleep* v. II.2] **widespread, but chiefly Inland Nth, N Midl, West** See Map Cf **lie in, sleep by, ~ over**

To remain asleep or in bed longer than one normally does, either by accident or, more commonly, by design; hence vbl n *sleeping in,* n *sleeper-inner.*

1910 *Gaz. & Bulletin* (Williamsport PA) 9 Apr 4/2, Manager Hugh Duffy excuses the White Sox from practice on Sunday mornings, that they may attend church. . . Most of them prefer to "sleep in." **1918** *DN* 5.28 **NW,** To sleep in. . . To oversleep. General. **1931** *AmSp* 7.20 **swPA,** *Sleep in.* To sleep late. "I'm going to sleep in to-morrow." **1946** *PADS* 6.27 **seVA,** *Sleep in.* . . To oversleep on the morning one is to work. . . Rare. **1953** *AmSp* 28.254 **csPA,** *Sleep in.* . . To sleep late. 'I think I'll sleep in tomorrow morning.' In general use. **1965–70** *DARE* (Qu. X43b, *If you sleep later than usual one day on purpose* . . "*I _____.*") 278 Infs, **widespread, but chiefly Inland Nth, N Midl, West,** Slept in; **AK1, IN27, KY84, UT3, VA54,** Slep in; **CO36,** Deliberately slept in; **CO47,** Sleeping in; **MO26,** Sleep in; **PA72,** Slept in late; (Qu. X43a, *If you sleep later than usual one day by accident* . . "*I _____.*") 40 Infs, **chiefly Inland Nth, N Midl, West,** Slept in; **FL39,** Sleep in; **AK1, CO47, UT3, 4,** Slep in; (Qu. CC7, . . *A person who goes to church very seldom or not at all*) Inf **WA22,** Sleeper-inner. **1971** *Today Show Letters* **cwCA,** Here are some of the strange sayings I hear out here. . . I'm going to sleep in tomorrow. **1982** *Grit* (Williams-

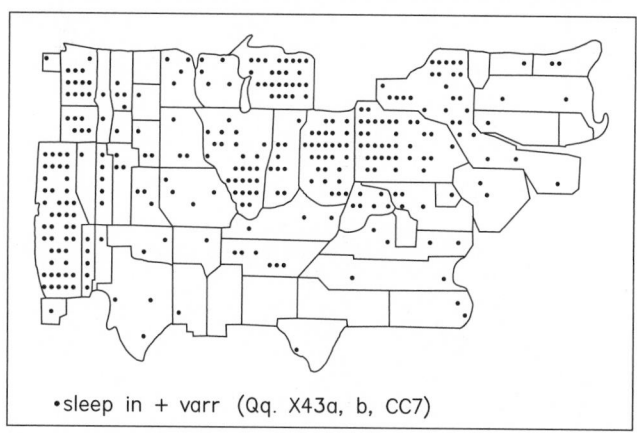

•sleep in + varr (Qq. X43a, b, CC7)

port PA) 4 July 17, Did you get any extra sleep this morning? You were "sleeping in" if you did. **1982** McCool *Sam McCool's Pittsburghese* 32 **PA,** *Sleep in:* to sleep late—"I like to sleep in Saturday." **1986** Pederson *LAGS Concordance (Skipped class)* 2 infs, **GA,** Slept in. **2007** *DARE* File ce**WI,** I'm taking the day off tomorrow so I can sleep in.

sleeping booby See **sleepyhead 1**

sleeping dust See **sleep dust**

sleeping hibiscus n

A **wax mallow** (here: *Malvaviscus arboreus* var *drummondii*).
1955 *S. Folkl. Qrly.* 19.233 **FL,** *Turks-Cup* (Malvaviscus drummondi), also called *Sleeping Hibiscus* though not hibiscus at all, bears single, scarlet, showy, half-opened blossoms that look like small tasselled fezzes. **1998** *Houston Chron.* (TX) 23 Aug (Internet) **FL,** Moss-covered trees and cane canopies shade narrow canals dotted with bougainvillea, sleeping hibiscus and wild poinsettias.

sleeping in See **sleep in**

sleeping Mollie n [Cf *EDD* sleeping Maggie for *Trifolium pratense* (at *sleeping* ppl. adj. (5))]

A **wood sorrel 1** (here: *Oxalis montana*).
1898 *Plant World* 2.1.14 s**PA,** Sleeping Mollie, for *Oxalis Acetosella* L. (a quaint name evidently suggested by the plant's habit of folding its leaflets at night.)

sleeping over See **sleep over**

sleeping plant n Cf **sleepyhead 2**

A **partridge pea** (here: *Chamaecrista fasciculata*).
1933 Small *Manual SE Flora* 663, C[*hamaecrista*] *fasciculata*. . . Partridge-pea. Sleeping-plant. **1949** Moldenke *Amer. Wild Flowers* 125, [*Partridgepeas*. . . Their pinnately compound leaflets are often very sensitive and will fold up tightly against the central rachis when touched.] *Ibid* 126, One of the largest flowered is *C[hamaecrista] fasciculata*, . . sometimes also called . . *sleepingplant*.

sleep over v phr **scattered, but esp NEng** See Map

=**sleep in;** hence vbl n *sleeping over;* n *sleep-over* see quot 1935.
1827 *Harvard Reg.* Sept 202 ce**MA,** They have indulged in the luxury of "sleeping over". **1831** (1940) Motte *Charleston to Harvard* 4 **MA,** I this morning indulged myself by *sleeping over*, a practice which is very frequently indulged in on Sunday mornings. **1871** Bagg *4 Yrs. at Yale* 47, *Sleep over*, to arise from bed too late for a college exercise. *Ibid* 570, On Sunday mornings, too, there is an unusual amount of "sleeping over,"—breakfast being often cut as well as chapel by the votaries of Morpheus. **1935** *AmSp* 10.236, In part of Pennsylvania, in college use, a *sleep-over* is a permission to stay away from church and remain in bed on Sunday morning. **1953** in 1965 *DARE* File cs**MA,** *Sleep over*—to oversleep; sleep later than usual—either intentionally or accidentally. [Appears to be the common term in these parts of New England. Confirmed for Vt. usage; not heard NY State.] **1965–70** *DARE* (Qu. X43a, *If you sleep later than usual one day by accident* . . "I _____.") 17 Infs, **scattered, but esp NEng,** Slept over; **VT**16, Sleep over; (Qu. X43b, *If you sleep later than usual one day on purpose* . . "I _____.") Infs **CT**34, **ME**21, **MA**59, **MN**2, **NY**217, **OH**48, **VA**9, 28, Slept over.

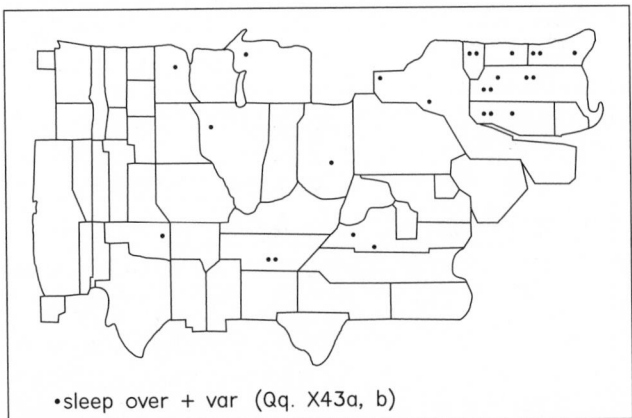

•sleep over + var (Qq. X43a, b)

sleep seed n Also *seed of sleep* Cf *sleepy seed* (at **sleepy** n)
Usu pl: =**sleeper** n **4.**
1929 *AmSp* 5.121 **ME,** It was often said that someone "had not been awake long enough to get the sleep seeds out of his eyes." **1979** *DARE* File cn**MA** (as of c1915), Sometimes people used to say when I was a child if a person had recently got out of bed, "Well, have you got the sleep seeds out of your eyes?" I think the reference was to the hardened mucus that sometimes gathers in the corners of the eyes. **1981** *NADS Letters,* Re *duck butter*, a friend of mine uses *sleep seeds* for this meaning. He spent the first half of his life in Minnesota but believes he may have picked this up from his wife, who was a resident of Dane county [WI]. . . Since 1946 my friend has lived in Iowa. *Ibid* **MI,** *Duck butter.* I don't know this expression. The term I use is 'seeds of sleep'.

sleepy adj
1941 *AmSp* 16.24 s**IN,** *Sleepy.* . . Used of matches which do not strike readily and of crackers and cookies which have lost their crispness. [Author: Still current in Missouri.]

sleepy n Also *sleepy bug,* ~ *dirt,* ~ *dust,* ~ *seed,* ~ *wink*
Freq pl: =**sleeper** n **4.**
1980 *AmSp* 55.160 **IN,** Paul Kennedy tells us that in Indiana what was washed out of the eyes was *sleepy.* Any more candidates as a term for 'ocular discharge'? **1981** *AmSp* 56.145 **IL,** In my family the stuff that accumulates in the eyes . . has always been *sleepy dust.* **1981** *DARE* File se**RI,** ["Sleep" in one's eyes is called] sleepy bugs; c**MA,** Sleepies; ne**MA,** Sleepy seeds; nw**NY,** Sleepy winks. **1982** *AmSp* 57.160, *On Ocular Discharge.* . . Both of us (Clark from a maternal background in the Boston and southern Maine area, Stanton from a maternal background in Mississippi) have, in mother-child talk, been accustomed to the term *sleepyseeds* for this phenomenon. And Clark's adult children unhesitatingly responded with *sleepyseeds* when asked "What do you call _____?" Does this family history suggest maternal, and hence very early, transmission? **1983** *DARE* File **UT,** (The stuff in the corner of your eyes when you wake up in the morning) Sleepy dirt, sleepy dust; **CO,** Sleepy. **1984** *Ibid* **UT, CO, AZ,** Sleepy; **CO,** Sleepies; **ID, UT,** Sleepy bug(s); **AZ, nCA,** Sleepy dirt. **1985** *Ibid* **VA,** 2 infs, Sleepies. **1986** *Ibid* **Sth,** Sleepy seeds. **1987** *Ibid* cs**WI** (as of 1930s), Sleepy seeds is what we used to call the matter you clean out of the corners of your eyes after sleeping; sw**CA,** Sleepy dust. **2004** *DARE* File—Internet **IL,** He [=a dog] has 'sleepies' in his eyes.

sleepy broadbill (or brother) See **sleepyhead 1**

sleepy bug See **sleepy**

sleepy catchfly n [See quot 1936]

A **catchfly 1** (here: *Silene antirrhina*). Also called **garter pink**
1822 Eaton *Botany* 459, *Silene.* . . *antirrhina* (sleepy catchfly). . . Flowers small. **1840** MA Zool. & Bot. Surv. *Herb. Plants & Quadrupeds* 88, *S. antirrhina.* . . Sleepy . . Catchfly. **1891** Jesup *Plants Hanover NH* 6, Sleepy Catchfly. . . Waste places. **1912** Blatchley *IN Weed Book* 78, Sleepy Catchfly. **1936** IL Nat. Hist. Surv. *Wildflowers* 85, *Sleepy Catchfly.* . . is called Sleepy because the flowers open only for a short time while the sun is shining and if they are picked and taken into the shade they quickly close. It is called Catchfly because a portion of the stem below each pair of leaves is sticky and insects which attempt to crawl up the stem are caught in this material and often perish there. **1973** Hitchcock–Cronquist *Flora Pacific NW* 117, Common weed throughout our area, often well up in mts., sleepy cat[chfly]. **1996** Arendt *Conserv. Design* 65 se**PA,** The wildflower meadow in the northwest corner of the property is noted for its wild strawberry, sleepy catchfly, tall anemone thimbleweed, and broomsedge.

sleepy coot See **sleepyhead 1**

sleepy daisy n [See quots] Cf **lazy daisy 1**

A yellow-flowered composite plant (*Xanthisma texanum*) native to much of the Southwest.
1936 Whitehouse *TX Flowers* 160, *Yellow Sleepy Daisy* (*Xanthisma texanum*) is a yellow daisy with lazy habits, for the heads do not open until noon. **1967** *DARE* Wildfl QR (Wills–Irwin) Pl.53D Inf **TX**44, Sleepy daisy. **2000** *DARE* File—Internet **TX,** *Sleepy daisy* (*Xanthisma texanum*) grows in open sandy areas, mainly in South and Central Texas. At night or on cloudy days, the ray flowers close up, and the daisy seems to "sleep".

sleepy dirt See **sleepy**

sleepy duck See **sleepyhead 1**

sleepy dust See **sleepy**

sleepy fern n   Cf **lazy daisy 1**

See quot.

1967 DARE (Qu. S6, . . *Queen Anne's lace: [Summertime roadside weed two feet high or so with a lacy white top]*) Inf **TX**32, Sleepy fern.

sleepy grass n   [See quots]

A **needlegrass 1** (here: *Achnatherum robustum*) native chiefly to the Southwest.

1890 *Century Dict.* 5951, S[*tipa*] *viridula*, var. *robusta*, of Mexico, New Mexico, etc., is reported to have a narcotic effect upon horses, and is called *sleepy-grass*. **1894** Coulter *Botany W. TX* 516, S[*tipa*] *viridula* . . var. *robusta*. . . *Sleepy grass*. . . Mountain valleys, western Texas and northward to Colorado. **1937** U.S. Forest Serv. *Range Plant Hdbk.* G120, Sleepygrass, so called because of its narcotic or sleep-producing effect upon livestock, . . is a coarse, leafy, bright green grass which grows in thick bunches. **1966** DARE (Qu. S9, . . *Kinds of grass that are hard to get rid of*) Inf **NM**6, Sleepy grass—might be called bunch grass—not hard to get rid of, but multiplies fast; makes horses sleepy—only turkeys do well with it. **1967** Green *Horse Tradin'* 304 **TX**, The Indians had herded those ponies down into the valley and had held them there on *sleepy grass*. I know now, though I didn't then, that the seeds of sleepy grass contain a dopey substance that acts on a horse much like today's modern tranquilizers. **2004** DARE File—Internet **AZ**, The low terrace . . has a dense stand of rabbitbrush with understory of dry grasses, including sleepy grass.

sleepyhead n

1 also *sleeping booby, sleepy broadbill,* ~ *brother,* ~ *coot,* ~ *duck,* ~ *jay:* =**ruddy duck. chiefly C Atl**   Cf **sleeper n 3**

1888 Trumbull *Names of Birds* 110, *Ruddy Duck.* . . in New Jersey at Barnegat, Tuckerton, and Atlantic City *sleepy broad-bill.* *Ibid* 111, At Cohasset, Mass., and Newberne, N.C., *sleepy-head;* in New Jersey at Pleasantville (Atlantic Co.), *sleepy-duck;* at Pleasantville, Atlantic City, and Somers Point, *sleepy coot;* at Crisfield, Md., *sleepy brother.* **1910** Eaton *Birds NY* 1.226, Its [=the ruddy duck's] colloquial names tell its natural history from the gunner's standpoint: Dumpling duck, Butter duck, . . Sleepy-head [etc]. **1917** *Wilson Bulletin* 29.2.77, *Erismatura jamaicensis.*—Sleeping booby, Wallops I[slan]d, Va., sleepy jay, . . Willapa Harbor, Wash. **1926** (1986) Phillips *Nat. Hist. Ducks* 4.159, *Ruddy Duck.* . . *Vernacular Names.* . . Sleepy Broadbill, . . Sleepy-head. *Ibid* 165, Some of the names, Booby, Sleepy-head, Fool Duck, Deaf Duck and many others that have been heaped on the innocent head of this confiding duck, give a good idea of its psychology. . . It would be hard to imagine a tamer duck. **1937** Natl. Geogr. Soc. *Book of Birds* 1.125, A *Ruddy Duck*, alias "fool duck," "sleepy duck," "blatherskite," and so on, proudly escorts his lady.

2 A **partridge pea** (here: *Chamaecrista nictitans*).   Cf **sleeping plant**

1967 DARE Wildfl QR (Wills–Irwin) Pl.105A Inf **TX**34, Sleepyhead.

sleepy jay See **sleepyhead 1**

sleepy John n   Cf **climber**

Prob a **blacksnake n 1.**

1923 Adams *Pioneer Hist. Ingham Co.* 615 **MI** (as of c1865), Great tree black snakes, known as 'sleepy johns,' very harmless but frightful to meet, were often seen hanging by their tails from the limbs of trees.

sleepy seed See **sleepy**

sleepy vine n

A **sensitive brier** such as *Mimosa microphylla* or *M. roemeriana.*

1951 PADS 15.34 **TX**, *Leptoglottis roemeriana* . . and *L. microphylla.* . . These are two of the sleepy vines; there are several more.

sleepy wink See **sleepy**

sleigh n

1 freq in combs; In logging: a heavy sled used for transporting logs. **chiefly Inland Nth, esp MI, WI, MN**   See Map   Cf **bobsleigh**

1859 *Grand Traverse Herald* (Traverse City MI) 18 Feb [2]/1 (newspaperarchive.com), After the logs have been measured by the 'marker,' and the chains are loosed which bound them to the sleigh, they go thun-

dering and crashing headlong down the steep. **1867** *Scientific Amer.* 16 Nov 311 **WI**, *Bunk for logging sleighs.*—James P. Davis, Stiles, Wis. **1876** McCracken *Michigan* 504, Near the western entrance to Agricultural Hall was an exhibition of Michigan pine logs. . . They were piled on a sleigh, just as they were hauled from the woods. **1893** *Scribner's Mag.* 13.706 **MI**, The log-sleighs have ten, twelve, and even fourteen-foot bunks, or cross beams, on which the load rests. **1925** *AmSp* 1.135, In the Northeast this is called "sled logging." Somewhere along the Great Lakes the sled is changed to "sleigh." **1938** (1939) Holbrook *Holy Mackinaw* 264, *Sleigh.* What a New England *sled* is, once it gets as far West as Michigan. **1965–70** DARE (Qu. N40c, *Other kinds of sleighs*) 39 Infs, **chiefly Inland Nth, esp MN, WI, MI,** Logging sleigh; **MI**2, 56, **NY**117, 220, **PA**218, Log sleigh; **MI**108, Logging sleigh—also called bunk sleigh; **WI**77, Sleigh or logging bunk; (Qu. N40a, . . *Sleighs . . for hauling loads*) Infs **MI**8, **MN**15, Logging sleigh; **NY**5, Bunk sleigh/sled—they had bunks for logs and things; **MT**4, Single-bunk sleigh, double-bunk sleigh—for logs; **MN**15, Double-bunk sleigh; **OH**42, Skid-row sleigh—for timber. [DARE Ed: Only compounds clearly referring to use in logging and other resps explicitly connected with logging are included here; it is likely that some other resps, esp at Qu. N40a, also referred to logging sleighs.] **1966–70** DARE Tape **MI**10, The workmen . . who had done more or less menial tasks in the woods, who worked on the sleigh roads, were called roadbunkies; **MI**20, They had about fifteen hundred acres of pineland to cut over, but all haulage was done in the winter by sleighs; **MI**125, Well, you'd skid that [=a log] out there somewheres and then you'd load it on. That was mostly done in the wintertime on a sleigh; **WI**59, They had the blacksmith, who could make sleighs for hauling the logs. **1984** *MJLF* 10.156 **cnWI**, *Sleigh.* Double sleds used for hauling logs.

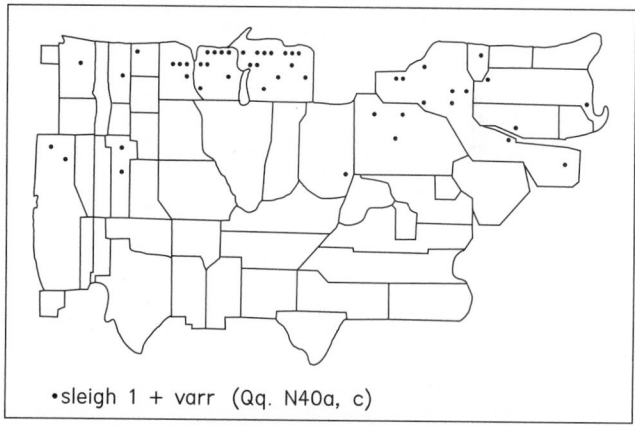

•sleigh 1 + varr (Qq. N40a, c)

2 A child's coasting sled; hence verbs *sleigh, sleigh-ride;* vbl nouns *sleighing, sleigh riding;* n *sleigh ride.* **scattered, but esp S Midl, C Atl, Inland Nth**   See Map on p. 16   Cf *handsleigh* (at **handsled n b**), DCan

1827 *Adams Sentinel* (Gettysburg PA) 28 Feb [2]/5 (newspaperarchive.com) **OH**, Two weeks since, it was . . covered with boys and men amusing themselves with skating and sleigh-riding on the ice, for want of snow. [**1855** Hammond–Mansfield *Country Margins* 184 **NY**, *Adam* never . . rode down hill on a hand-sleigh.] **1867** *Harper's New Mth. Mag.* 35.467 **NYC**, If one wants to skate or ride downhill on a sleigh, it is always practicable. **1892** *DN* 1.215 **DC**, In Georgetown, D.C., the word [for *coast*] is *sleigh-ride,* v. **1903** *Outing* 41.460, The word sled is used to designate the vehicle on which Young America coasts, in all sections of the country, except in Southern New York, New Jersey, and in parts of Connecticut, where it is called a "sleigh," and with them coasting is often called "sleigh riding." **1928** *Helena Independent* (MT) 24 Dec [10]/4 (newspaperarchive.com), The two boys, sleighing down Emmett street, ran broadside into a Henningsen ice truck. **1944** *AmSp* 19.38 **Philadelphia PA**, Idioms shared with metropolitan New York are: . . *sleigh,* 'sled,' i.e. a child's sled for coasting. **1948** WELS Suppl. **swWI**, In the area of Lone Rock where I grew up, and at Avoca . . , we refer to a sleigh ride on one's "tummie" as a "Belly Buster." **1950** WELS **WI** (*When there is snow, children _____ down the hill on a _____*) 1 Inf, Coast or sleigh-ride [on a] sleigh or sled; 2 Infs, [On a] sleigh or sled. **1965–70** DARE (Qu. EE24b, *When children go down hill on a sled . . they say they're _____*) 157 Infs, **scattered, but esp S Midl, C Atl, NYC,** Sleigh riding; **MS**1, Sleigh ride; 31 Infs, **scattered, but less freq NEast, N Cent,** Sleighing; **VA**27, Sleighing on snow; **NC**72, Snow sleighing; (Qu. EE24a, *When there's snow, children go down the hill on a _____*) 106 Infs **scattered, but esp S Midl, C Atl, NY, nMI,** Sleigh; [**ID**1, **NY**88, 199, Handsleigh] [Of all Infs responding to Qq. EE24b and EE24a, 28% were comm type 5, 25% gs educ or less; of those giving these responses, 39% were comm type 5, 33% gs educ or less.]; (Qu. EE26, *. . Games . . children play in the snow*) Infs **KY**11, 50, **NY**45, **NC**45, **OK**6, **VA**9, 24, 35, Sleigh riding (*or* ride); **NC**51, Pulling sleighs around; (Qu. EE25, *When a child picks up his sled . . runs with it, and then throws himself down on it, that's a _____*) Inf **MO**34, Sleigh ride; **NC**9, Sleighing. **1966–68** *DARE* Tape **MI**14, In the wintertime we made, out of barrel staves, we made some kind of sliding devices and we all had sleighs; **NY**61, It used to be a hill there, and we used to sleigh-ride down on that hill. **c1991** in 2002 *DARE* File—Internet **cKY** (as of c1935), They built a chain-link fence across the property line and that ruined Danville's best sleigh-riding hill. **1993** *DARE* File **nNJ**, Words & phrases particular to my area of northern New Jersey. We . . went "sleighing," not "sledding," in the winter. **2002** *DARE* File—Internet **Long Is. NY**, [First grade class writing project:] My favorite snow activity is sleigh riding. *Ibid* **cePA**, You'd be sledding along at mach 2 and hit wet road at Ohio Ave., that would usually stop the sleigh but not the rider. *Ibid* **ceNY**, A little further north was the old sleighing hill. **2008** *DARE* File **cePA**, The college girl guiding us around campus mentioned that in the winter when there is snow, students take the trays from the dining hall and go "sleighing" down the hill.

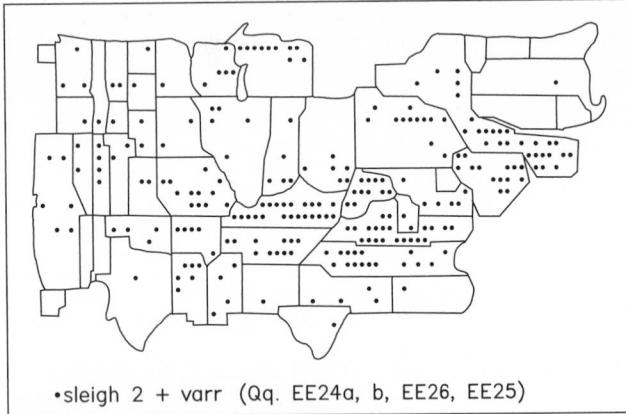

•sleigh 2 + varr (Qq. EE24a, b, EE26, EE25)

sleigh-bell duck n   [See quot 1955]

The American **scoter** *(Melanitta nigra).*

    1888 Trumbull *Names of Birds* 107 **ME**, I am credibly informed that in the vicinity of Rangely [sic] Lake, M[ain]e, this bird [=*Melanitta nigra*] is the *sleigh-bell duck.* **1955** MA Audubon Soc. *Bulletin* 39.377, *American Scoter. . .* Sleigh-bell Duck (Maine. From the ringing whistle made by the wings in flight.)

sleighing   See **sleigh 2**

sleigh-ride, sleigh riding   See **sleigh 2**

sleight n   Also sp *slight* [*OED2 sleight* sb.[1] 3 "Skill, skilfulness, . . Now *rare*"; 1390 →; 4 "The precise art or method . . *of* (doing) something. Now *dial*."; a1300 →] **chiefly sAppalachians, Ozarks**

A special skill or talent (at, rarely for, some activity); a knack or trick (to doing something).

    1896 *DN* 1.424 **swNC**, *Slight:* knack. "She had a good slight at hoein'." **1923** *DN* 5.221 **swMO**, *Sleight. . .* Deftness, expertness, a certain manner of manipulation. **1924** Raine *Land of Saddle-Bags* 98 **sAppalachians**, The Mountain mother refers to her daughter's skill as "Sally's sleight at buttermaking." **1927** *DN* 5.469 **Appalachians,** *Sleight. . .* Skill. **1931** *AmSp* 7.91 **eKY**, *Sleight,* a gift or knack for doing a specific thing. "Polly's sleight at biscuit-makin' made her the pattern helt up for the girls o' Coal Run." **1932** Randolph *Ozark Mt. Folks* 114, It warn't ever'body as knowed how t' handle 'em, even when I was a young-un. Thar's a kinder sleight to it. **1937** (1963) Hyatt *Riverlid* 47 **KY,** She is smart-turned to do good plain weavin' and she's got a sleight fer hit. **1949** Webber *Backwoods Teacher* 30 **Ozarks**, Wait'll I un-wahr [=unwire] that door. Kind of a sleight to it. **1952** in 1968 Haun *Hawk's Done Gone* 291 **TN**, Dorthea has a sleight at chicken raising. I let her tend to them. **c1960** *Wilson Coll.* **csKY**, *Sleight. . .* A knack at doing something. "He's got a sleight at setting tobacco."

sleighty adj |ˈslaɪtɪ| Cf **sleight**

Nimble, dexterous.

    1941 *LANE* Map 462 *(Handy at plowing)* 1 inf, **nwMA**, [slɑˆɪtɪˇ] = 'fast but careless at work'; 1 inf, **cwMA**, [slaˀɪtɪ æt]; 1 inf, **cwMA**, [slaˀɪtɪˆ]; 1 inf, **cwMA**, [slaɪtɪˆ] = 'able to perform a task well without effort.' **1992** *DARE* File **NEng**, Back in the days of running logs down the rivers they used to say that the men who were nimble on the logs were sleighty [ˈslaɪtɪ].

slender snakeroot   See **snakeroot b(11)**

slep   See **sleep A**

slew v   See **slay 2**

slew n   See **slough** n

slewed   See **slay 1**

slew-eyed adj

Squint-eyed.

    1807 Irving *Salmagundi* 1.63, Another Caliban!—Vernon *slew* eyed—people of Brunswick, of course, all squint. **1968** *DARE* (Qu. X26b, *If a person's eyes look in different directions, looking outward, he's _____*) Inf **GA**23, Slew-eyed. **2004** *NADS Letters* **IN**, Slew-eyed—"Squint-eyed." My grandmother used the term with above meaning; born Indiana 1880, of Irish parents. . . Lived in southern and central Indiana. **2010** *DARE* File **eTN**, *Slew-eyed. . .* I've heard this term used in reference to people of Asian descent . . here in East Tennessee.

slew-foot n   See **slue-foot** n

slew-foot(ed) adj   See **slue-footed** adj

slew-jawed adj   Cf **whopper-jawed 1**

See quot 1967.

    1921 *NY Times* (NY) 3 July 1/5, A slew-jawed functionary sowing powdered resin broadcast upon the canvas carpet of the ring amounts to a positive sensation. **1967** *DARE* (Qu. X6, *If a person's lower jaw sticks out prominently . . he's _____*) Inf **AR**55, Slew-jawed.

slice n, v   Usu |slaɪs|; also **chiefly Sth** |slaɪš| Pronc-spp *slish(e)*

A   Forms.

    1883 (1971) Harris *Nights with Remus* 300 **GA** [Black], Den Brer Rabbit built 'im a fier un cut 'im off a slishe er steak. **1889** *Century Illustr. Mag.* 39.319 **Sth**, Smell that aish-cake bakin' so / 'N eat a slish o' Sally Long. **1893** Shands *MS Speech* 57, *Slish* [slaɪš]. Quite a common pronunciation of *slice* by negroes and illiterate whites. **1909** *DN* 3.371 **eAL, wGA**, *Slice. . .* A wedge-shaped cut of watermelon. Sometimes *slish.* **1963** *Mt. Life* 39.2.51 **sAppalachians**, He'll git hisself slished in two on that old brute.

B   As noun.

In comb *clothes slice:* A paddle used to agitate clothes being washed.   Cf **battle** n[1], **battling stick**

    1885 NH Bd. Ag. *NH Ag.* 331, If the cow is in milk her ribs may show, and be flat, and as wide as a clothes slice. **1899** Brown *Tiverton Tales* 6 **NH**, With two russets for balls and the clothes-slice for a mallet . . , Della . . played her first game [of croquet].

slick adv   Cf **plumb** adv, *clean*

Completely, absolutely, simply.

    1818 Fearon *Sketches* 123 **ceMA**, Did she die slick right away? **1961** Seeman *In Arms of Mt.* 57 **eTN**, He slick forgot he'd left a picture of him and Rena Faye in the back of his billfold. **1966–69** *DARE* (Qu. JJ30a, *Other words or expressions for forgetting something: "I _____."*) Infs **AZ**1, **OK**18, Slick forgot it (*or* that); (Qu. LL25, *. . Entirely, completely: "He sold out the whole place, _____."*) Infs **MO**15, **MT**5, Slick (out). **1981** *Courier–Jrl.* (Louisville KY) 22 Mar mag sec 15/1, "But after that I settled down. I was highly motivated. I was just slick hungry." ("Slick" is a peculiar colloquialism used by Stumbo, apparently meaning anything from "simply," to "totally." For example, "I slick wasn't going to.") *Ibid* 43/1, We . . can spend weekends on end here and never spend a dime, and slick get off on it. In Frankfort you pay for recreation. *Ibid* 43/2, Maybe that's why the Lord just slick jerked me up and put me down here.

slick n

1 also *grayslick, sleek:* A smooth or oily-looking area on the surface of water.

    1872 Schele de Vere *Americanisms* 341 **ME**, *Grayslick. . .* belonging more properly to the fishermen of Maine, means a state of the sea when the wind has died away, and the water, unbroken by waves, assumes the familiar "glassy" appearance. The men will, hence, say: "We may just as well take to the oar, for we have gotten into a grayslick." While the first part of the word refers to the dim but beautiful color, *slick* (sleek) fully expresses the quiet, oleaginous condition of the sea in such places. **1942** McAtee *Notes Thornton's Gloss.* [4], *Slick.* This is applied to smooth areas on any waters (not necessarily the sea); a frequent cause is growths of plants reaching the surface in quantity sufficient to prevent rippling. **1945** Colcord *Sea Language* 89 **ME, Cape Cod, Long Island,** *Greyslick. Ibid* 170, *Slick.* An oily-looking streak on the water, caused by a calm patch amid flaws of wind. **1965–70** DARE (Qu. O17, *When the water is very smooth and still . . a* _____) Infs **CA**114, **FL**21, 24, **GA**76, **RI**6, Slick; **NC**27, Sleek.

2 also *slicker:* A horse or cow without a brand or other mark of ownership; hence adj *slick* unbranded; also fig. **West** Cf **maverick** n **1**, **slick-ear 1**

1890 *Stock Grower & Farmer* (Las Vegas NM) 12 July 6/3 *(DAE),* Seven of them were branded, the remainder were 'slicks,' or horses which had run wild from birth. **1920** *DN* 5.84 **NW,** *Slicker.* A wild range horse. **1920** Hunter *Trail Drivers TX* 28 (as of c1917), I hope to meet him over there in the Sweet Bye and Bye, where no mavericks or slicks will be tallied. **1937** Sandoz *Slogum* 49 **NE,** The stock was corraled, the slicks branded, and the ears cut off short in the Slogum crop. **1939** (1973) FWP *Guide MT* 416, *Slicker*—Unbranded animal. **1940** (1966) Writers' Program *Guide AZ* 66, They were . . branding the slicks (calves that had slipped through the roundup) on their part of the range. **1941** Writers' Program *Guide WY* 465, *Slick*—Unbranded. **1958** *AmSp* 33.272 **eWA** [Ranching terms], *Slick.* Unbranded. **1968** [see **slick-ear**].

3 A thicket, esp a rhododendron thicket. **wNC, eTN** Cf **bald** n, **hell 1**, **rough** n

1913 Kephart *Highlanders* 110 **sAppalachians,** I became enmeshed in a rhododendron "slick," and . . lost my bearings. **1939** *Hall Coll.* **wNC, eTN,** *Slick.* . . A laurel or rhododendron thicket; a rough. . . "The dogs then was a-goin' on in to head of the left hand fork of Deep Creek, into the slicks." **1939** FWP *Guide TN* 514 **ceTN,** Treeless areas or "balds"—called "slicks" by the natives because of their deceptive appearance of smoothness—are found on some of the ridge-tops. **1943** Peattie *Great Smokies* 40 **wNC, eTN,** Botanists speak of heath balds, meaning an area crowned with an intricate shrub tangle of the heath family, but mountain people call these slicks, and distinguish between laurel, rhododendron, and ivy (Kalmia or mountain laurel) slicks. **1956** (1964) Fink *That's Why* 4 **wNC, eTN,** A *slick* is never a smooth rock ledge or a cliff. While from a distance it might appear to be a grassy slope, in reality it is a tangle of low rhododendron or kalmia, through which a bear can scarcely push. **1967** DARE (Qu. C28, *A place where underbrush, weeds, vines and small trees grow together so that it's nearly impossible to get through*) Inf **TN**11, Laurel slick. **1982** Powers *Cataloochee* 444 **cwNC,** The heath balds. . . were called "yaller patches", "woolyheads" or "slicks."

4 also *country slick:* A rustic.

[**1919** Cormack *Aaron Slick from Punkin Crick* [title].] **1986** Pederson *LAGS Concordance* (A rustic) 1 inf, **ceTX,** Country slick; 1 inf, **ceAL,** Old country slick; 1 inf, **seAL,** Slicks.

5 also *slick dumpling, slicker:* A dumpling or large noodle. Cf **chicken slick, slip-go-down, slippery dumpling**

1934 Vines *Green Thicket* 49 **cnAL,** I learned to make slicks from Mother. . . Them Lispers always did like dumplings. **1937** *DN* 6.620 **swTX,** Chicken dumplings are *slickers.* **1937** *AmSp* 12.153 **SW** [Cowboy lingo], *Slickers.* Chicken dumplings. **1966** DARE (Qu. H45, *Dishes made with meat, fish, or poultry that everybody around here would know, but that people in other places might not*) Inf **OK**21, Chicken and slicks—same as dumplings. [**1995** in 2004 Montgomery–Hall *Dict. Smoky Mt. Engl.* 542 **eTN,** Dumplings were called slick and go down sometimes.] **2001** *NADS Letters* **AL,** "Slick" is the word my husband uses for slippery dumpling. . . He believes it is from Alabama. **2002** *Ibid* **eVA,** I grew up on the Eastern Shore of Virginia eating something called a "slick dumplin'." After she cooked a chicken for Sunday dinner, my mother would roll out a dough made of flour, Crisco, salt and water. . . Then she would cook them for about half an hour on top of the stove in the chicken broth in the same roasting pan that she cooked the chicken in. They turn out somewhere between noodles and pie crust that has cooked in the bottom of a pot pie, in that they absorb more broth than noodles would.

6 A baitfish such as a **stone roller 1** (here: *Campostoma*

anomalum); see quots. Cf **greased chub, slicker 2, tallow-mouth minnow**

1953 Randolph–Wilson *Down in Holler* 285 **Ozarks,** *Slick.* . . A certain kind of minnow *(Campostoma anomalum).* Boys around Protem, Mo., catch *slicks* in glass minnow traps, and sell them to city fishermen. **1967** DARE (Qu. P7, *Small fish used as bait for bigger fish*) Inf **TX**19, Slicks.

7 See quot. Cf **muley-head**

1967 DARE FW Addit **AR,** *Slick* or *muley-head*—doe shot illegally.

8 also *slick (and) go down:* See quots. **wNC, eTN** Cf **honey mushroom, oyster ~**

1955 Parris *Roaming the Mountains* 232 (2004 Montgomery–Hall *Dict. Smoky Mt. Engl.*) **wNC,** For a dish that belies its name, slick-go-downs is nothing more than mushrooms boiled and served with corn meal mush. **1995–98** in 2004 Montgomery–Hall *Dict. Smoky Mt. Engl.* 542 **wNC, eTN,** Slick go down. . . [1 inf] also called *slick* and *slick and go down;* . . [1 inf] *Slick go down.* . . Cherokee term for morel mushroom. . . ; [1 inf] *slick go down.* **2001** Bissell *In Forest* 201 **wNC,** "What did you call these?" "Slicks," replied Mary, her mouth full. "Oyster mushrooms. They're delicious." **2006** Ellison *Blue Ridge* 58 **wNC,** *Armillariella mella* is known to the Cherokees as "slicks" and to non-Indians as the honey mushroom. According to Cherokee native Amy Walker, . . her people call them slicks because they "just slide right down your throat." This is true. Once the cap of a slick is heated, it becomes viscous and does indeed slide down your throat, one after the other, just like oysters.

slick adj See **slick** n **2**

slick and a promise n [Var of *lick and a promise*] **chiefly NJ** See Map
A hasty or superficial performance (of a task).

1892 *Atlantic Mth.* 69.379 **sME** [Author from **Philadelphia PA**], Much sweepin' he 'll get out o' Eunice; it 's a slick 'n' a promise with her! **1965–70** DARE (Qu. A22, . . *'To start working hard':* "She had only ten minutes to clean the room, but she _____ [and had it done in time]."*) Inf **NJ**5, Did it with a slick and a promise; (Qu. W28, *When a woman is in a hurry and has to sew up a torn place quickly . . "I'll just _____."*) Inf **NJ**24, Slick and a promise; (Qu. KK49, *When you don't have the time or ambition to do something thoroughly:* "I'm not going to give the place a real cleaning, I'll just _____.") Infs **IN**16, **NJ**11, 18, 55, 57, Give it a slick and a promise; **PA**59, Give a slick and a promise; **NJ**4, Give it slick and a promise; **MA**5, Slick and a promise. [9 of 10 Infs old]

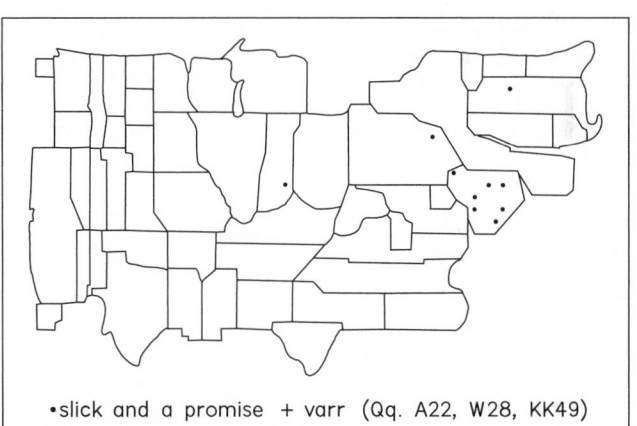

•slick and a promise + varr (Qq. A22, W28, KK49)

slick and go down See **slick** n **8**

slick as a smelt See **smelt 3**

slickbark See **slick elm**

slickbark oak See **slick oak**

slick-bark tree n
A **sycamore B** (here: *Platanus occidentalis*).
1969–70 DARE (Qu. T13, . . *Names . . sycamore*) Inf **VA**38, Slick-bark tree—some say.

slickbark yellow pine See **slick pine**

slick calm adj phr **chiefly Mid and S Atl, Gulf States** Cf **calm, slick** n **1**

Of a body of water: so calm that the surface appears perfectly smooth; hence n *slick calm* a complete absence of waves.

1914 *Fur News Mag.* Sept 231, Ten o'clock we left "Haunted Bayou" and headed for the Wolf River. The going was fine. It was a slick calm and the tide was in our favor most of the way, but it was after dark before we put down our pole about a mile up the river. **1966–70** *DARE* (Qu. O17, *When the water is very smooth and still . . a* _____) Infs **MD**45, **NC**12, **VA**47, Slick calm [kæm]; **TX**11, Slick calm. **1984** Wilder *You All Spoken Here* 143 **Sth**, *Slick ca'm:* A calm sea. **1994** NC Lang. & Life Project *Dial. Vocab.* Ocracoke 15 **eNC**, Slick cam. . . A very calm water, typically used with reference to the sound. *It was a slick cam out there today.* Also *slick calm.* [**1996** Horton *Island Out of Time* 159 **Chesapeake Bay MD**, The water is "slick, slatey c'am," waterman's jargon for smooth as glass.] **1999** in 2002 *DARE* File—Internet **swFL**, Again, when it's been slick calm, that's when they shine. *Ibid* **LA**, Just before sunup, we awoke to a slick calm. **2001** *Houston Chron.* (TX) 25 July (Internet), A powerful trolling motor can be a big asset. This especially is true on a "slick calm" day. **2002** *DARE* File—Internet **seGA**, Slick calm conditions will always be optimal for sighting Jacks.

slick dock n

A **dock** n[1]; see quot.

1932 *Sun* (Baltimore MD) 3 June 12/3, But I do think if someone would start canning the old-fashioned barnyard greens, composed of polk, slick dock, wild lettuce, etc., they would have something to talk about.

slick dumpling   See **slick** n 5

slick-ear n   West

1 A range animal that has not been earmarked or branded; hence adj *slick-eared* not earmarked; also fig.   Cf **full ear, longear 2, orejana, slick** n 2

1907 *Pacific Reporter* 90.641 **WA**, [The] appellant himself testified that the horse was not branded, but that he was a "slick-ear," an "outlaw," which, in effect, means that the real ownership was unknown. **1914** *World's Work* 27.447 **TX**, Any "slick-ear" (steer not marked on the ears or branded) found on the range about which inquiry was made was promptly assigned to his ownership, and "slick-ears" eventually became known as "mavericks." **1924** James *Cowboys N. & S.* 25 **AZ, MT, TX, WY**, A "remuda" changes to "caviada," "slick ear" to "Orejana," . . but it all goes to the same critter and the same things. **1926** Branch *Cowboy* 52 **TX**, They found in their herds "slick ears," as they called those yearlings that had been missed in the round-ups of the season before. **1933** *AmSp* 8.1.30 **nwTX** [Ranch diction], *Slick-ear.* An animal without earmarks. **1940** Writers' Program *Guide NV* 77, A maverick or *slick-ear* is an unbranded, unclaimed calf. **1952** FWP *Guide SD* 84, *Slick-ear:* an animal that has not had its ears notched or split. **1958** *AmSp* 33.272 **eWA** [Ranching terms], *Slick-eared.* 1. Without ear marks. 2. Metaphorically, stolen. **1964** O'Hare *Ling. Geog. E. MT* 147, An unbranded calf . . slick (ear) [3 of 18 infs].

2 Transf: a greenhorn.

1906 *Portsmouth Herald* (NH) 7 Aug 7/5, [In a syndicated Western story:] Black Jack is a bad man, . . but he don't dare run his brand on the little slick-ear that's standin' there in the middle of the room.

slick-eared   See **slick-ear 1**

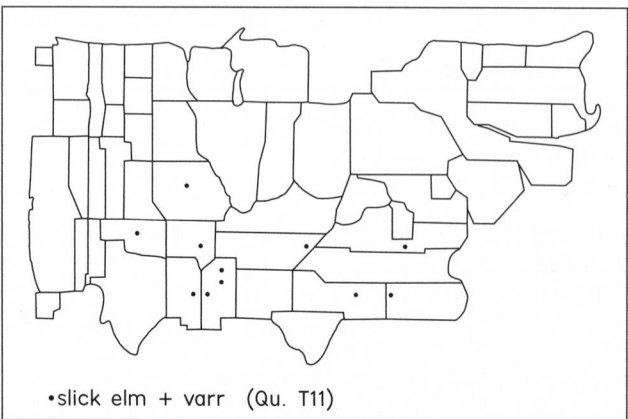

•slick elm + varr (Qu. T11)

slick elm n   Also *slickbark, slickery elm*   **chiefly Sth, S Midl** See Map

=**slippery elm 1.**

1912 *DN* 3.590 **wIN**, *Slickery-ellum.* . . Slippery-elm. "At recess let's go over to the thicket and get some slickery-ellum." **1965–70** *DARE* (Qu. T11, . . *Kinds of elm trees*) Infs **AR**32, **LA**7, **MS**16, 47, 60, **MO**8, **VA**38, Slick elm; **GA**9, Slickery elm—very few; **OK**11, Slickery elm—out in the county; **TN**11, Slickery elm; **SC**32, Slickbarks.

slickem   See **slickum**

slicker n

1 also *slick fish:* A silverfish (family Lepismatidae).

1896 Howard–Marlatt *Principal Household Insects* 8, Common species as the household centipede . . and the "silver fish" or "slicker" (*Lepisma* spp.) **1899** *Jrl. Amer. Folkl.* 12.291 **MA**, A common pest in dwelling-houses is the *Lepisma saccharina,* commonly known as *slick-fish* and *silver-fish.* **1901** Howard *Insect Book* 382, The little insects which are known to housekeepers, particularly in the Southern States, as the silver fish, or fishmoths, or slickers, belong to this family [= Lepismatidae]. **1928** Metcalf–Flint *Destructive & Useful Insects* 172, Order Thysanura. . . contains a few species known as silverfish, fish moths, slickers, or firebrats.

2 The blacknose **dace** *(Rhinichthys atratulus).*

1983 Becker *Fishes WI* 467, *Blacknose Dace.* . . Other common names . . slicker, "potbelly" or "pottbelly."

3 See **slick** n 2.

4 See **slick** n 5.

slickery adj   Cf **slicky**

Slick, slippery, also fig.

1856 Underhill–Thomson *Elephant Club* 159 **NY**, There was about twenty gentlemen, fixed off tu kill, and a table sot with bottles, and everything as slickery as could be. **1859** Taliaferro *Fisher's R.* 147 **nwNC** (as of 1820s), They [=eels] was so slickery. **1890** in 1950 *PADS* 13.9 **GA**, Yes, I'll be dadburned if I wouldn't have got him, but the dinged thing was so alfired slickery. **1897** *KS Univ. Qrly.* (ser B) 6.92 **neKS**, *Slickery:* slippery. **1911** *DN* 3.547 **NE**, *Slickery.* . . Contamination of *slick* and *slippery.* "That was a mighty slickery trick." Not common. **1912** [see **slick elm**]. **1965–67** *DARE* (Qu. N22, *When a road that is surfaced with smooth pavement gets wet so that cars slip or skid on it . . it's* _____) Inf **ID**4, Slickery; (Qu. T11, . . *Kinds of elm trees*) Infs **GA**9, **OK**11, **TN**11, Slickery elm. [All Infs old]

slickery elm   See **slick elm**

slick fish   See **slicker** n[1] 1

slick go down   See **slick** n 8

slick-headed scorpion   See **slick lizard**

slickhead jay n

Prob the **scrub jay.**

1968 *DARE* (Qu. Q16, . . *Kinds of jays*) Inf **CA**105, Jaybird—slickhead jay.

slick lizard n   Also *slick-headed scorpion*

A **skink:** either *Scincella lateralis* or a skink of the genus *Eumeces.*

1928 Baylor Univ. Museum *Contrib.* 16.13, *Leiolepisma laterale* [= *Scincella lateralis*]. . . This tiny species is sometimes called . . *Slick Lizard* on account of the smoothness of its scales. The . . name is also referred in a generic sense to all of the species of *Eumeces,* especially in those regions where the name Scorpion as applied to reptiles is unknown. **1986** Pederson *LAGS Concordance,* 1 inf, **cwAR**, Slick-headed scorpion = red-headed scorpion.

slick maple n   Cf **hard maple**

A **maple;** see quot.

1970 *DARE* (Qu. T14, . . *Kinds of maples*) Inf **VA**38, Slick maple—same as hard.

slick oak n   Also *slickbark oak*

A **black oak** (here: *Quercus velutina*).

1938 Van Dersal *Native Woody Plants* 354, Slick oak. . . Slickbark oak *(Quercus velutina).*

slick pine n   Also *slickbark yellow pine*   Cf **yellow pine**
A **pine 1**; see quots.
 1969 *DARE* (Qu. T17, . . *Kinds of pine trees;* not asked in early QRs) Inf **GA**77, Slickbark yellow pine.   **1986** Pederson *LAGS Concordance,* 1 inf, **swGA**, Great big slick pines—old.

slickrock n   **UT**
An expanse of naturally smooth, polished rock.
 1941 Writers' Program *Guide UT* 455, The slickrock is truly "slick," and when it catches the slanted rays of the sun in its wind-made whorls, it spatters the light almost as flint does.   **1968** Abbey *Desert Solitaire* 2 se**UT**, For myself I'll take Moab, Utah. I don't mean the town itself, of course, but the country which surrounds it—the canyonlands. The slickrock desert. The red dust and the burnt cliffs and the lonely sky.   **2000** *DARE* File s**UT**, "Slickrock" is commonly used in southern Utah to refer to an expanse of relatively smooth rock, usually the red sandstone in that area. Mountain bikers enjoy the challenge of riding over the slickrock found around Moab.

slick saddle n   **West**
See quot 1889.
 1889 in 2003 *DARE* File—Internet **CO** (as of 1869), [Horses at a rodeo should be ridden] with a slick saddle, free of the roll usually tied across the back.   **c1938** in Lib. of Congress *Amer. Memory: WPA Life Hist.* (Internet) c**TX** (as of c1900), Riding was my game. . . I soon got so I could bust the wildest of hosses using a slick saddle.   **1957** *Seattle Daily Times* (WA) 26 May np, [Caption:] Jumping through a flat loop while doing a slick saddle stand.

slickster n   *chiefly among Black speakers*
A crafty or untrustworthy person.
 [**1920** Penniman *Alley Rabbit* 9, We thought of calling him [=a cat] . . Slickster, because of his resourcefulness in attaining his object.]   **1924** Lloyd *Your Dollars* np, It is folly to engage in saving because there is always some slickster ready to take the savings away.   **1939** in Lib. of Congress *Amer. Memory: WPA Life Hist.* (Internet) **NYC** [Black], Fatso, the Slickster. . . He believed that a sucker was not only born every minute, but that he was born to be taken by Fatso, himself, in person.   **1965** Brown *Manchild* 332 **NYC** [Black], All the Muslims now felt as though 125th Street was theirs. It used to belong to the hustlers and the slicksters.   **1968–70** *DARE* (Qu. U17, *Names or nicknames for a person who doesn't pay his bills*) Inf **FL**51, Slickster; (Qu. V7, *A person who sets out to cheat others while pretending to be honest*) Infs **MD**29, **TN**50, Slickster; (Qu. HH2, *Names and nicknames for a citified person*) Infs **NY**241, **SC**68, (City) slickster. [4 of 5 Infs Black]   **1980** Folb *Runnin' Down* 117 cw**CA** [Black], There are many variations and permutations of the pimp front. Some, like the *slickster* or *con man,* rely more on verbal guile and deception than, say, on the display of possessions.   **1986** Pederson *LAGS Concordance,* 1 inf, ne**FL**, Slicksters—those able to gain political favors. [Inf Black]

slicktail n   Also *Mr. Slick*
=**opossum.**
 1966–68 *DARE* (Qu. P31, . . *Names or nicknames . . for the . . opossum*) Infs **DE**3, Mr. Slick; **MS**6, Slicktail.

slicktail rat n   Also *slick-tailed rat*
A **wood rat** (here: *Neotoma floridana*).
 1927 Boston Soc. Nat. Hist. *Proc.* 38.356 **Okefenokee GA**, *Neotoma floridana floridana. . .* Sam Mizell calls it 'Slick-tailed Rat,' perhaps in contradistinction to the 'File-tailed Rat' (*Rattus rattus rattus* and *R. r. alexandrinus*).   **1986** Pederson *LAGS Concordance* (Varmints) 1 inf, c**TX**, Slicktail rat.

slick tree n   Cf **lady legs, naked Indian**
A **madrone** (here: *Arbutus texana*).
 1926 *Torreya* 26.6 **TX**, *Arbutus texana. . .* Called Palo enquerado (naked tree) by the Mexicans, and slick tree by the Americans, Tough, Tex.

slickum n   Also sp *slickem*
1   Pomade; transf, any greasy or slimy substance; see quots.
 [**1901** *Post–Std.* (Syracuse NY) 12 May 11/4, Miss Wolf took some slickum slickum grease, which can cure almost anything, and rubbed it on Mr. Ram's horns.]   **1927** *Frederick Post* (MD) 2 May 4/2, There should be a maid-in-waiting whose duty it would be to supply the boys with lipsticks, powder and hair slickem between halves.   **1927** *Syracuse Herald* (NY) 3 Apr mag sec 3/1 **NE**, Not all sheiks, mark you, wear

slickum on their hair, baby burnsides, and bell-bottom pants.   **1930** *DN* 6.88 cw**WV**, *Slickem,* mess-shack term for butter.   **1942** Berrey–Van den Bark *Amer. Slang* 75.36, *Pomade; brilliantine. . .* slickum.   *Ibid* 685.1, *Football equipment. . .* slickum, grease or other slippery substance put on the clothes (forbidden).   **1950** *WELS* (He puts too much _____ on his hair) 3 Infs, **WI**, Slickum.   **1957** Battaglia *Resp. to PADS 20* e**MD**, *Slickum. . .* He puts too much slickum on his hair.   **c1960** *Wilson Coll.* cs**KY**, *Slickum. . .* Humorous name for what is put on hair to make it slick and smooth.   **1966** *DARE* FW Addit **OK**, *Slickum*—boiled okra.   **1969** *DARE* (Qu. KK38, *To put preparations on the hair to hold it close to the head and make it shiny:* "I wish he wouldn't _____ his hair down so!") Inf **CA**136, Put slickum on.   **1986** Pederson *LAGS Concordance,* 1 inf, c**AL**, Slickum.

2   See quot.
 1968 *DARE* (Qu. H27, . . *Joking names for doughnuts*) Inf **DE**4, Slickums.

slicky adj   *esp* **Sth, S Midl**   Cf **slickery, slicky slide, slippy**
Slick, slippery.
 1884 *Anglia* 7.278 **Sth, S Midl** [Black], *Mighty slicky* = very slippery.   **1939** in 1944 *ADD* w**WV**, *Slicky. . .* Slippery.   **1957** Combs *Lang. S. Highlanders* np s**Appalachians**, The ice is slicky.   **1966–69** *DARE* (Qu. N22, *When a road that is surfaced with smooth pavement gets wet so that cars slip or skid on it . . it's* _____) Infs **CT**7, **MS**8, 16, **NC**50, **TX**64, 74, **VA**27, Slicky; **GA**40, Slicky, slicky when wet.   **1972** *PADS* 58.24 cw**AL**, *The road is slippery.* Slippery (11 [of 27 infs]) and *slick* (9) are most frequent. . . *Slicky* and *wet* also occur.   **1986** Pederson *LAGS Concordance,* 1 inf, sw**GA**, Slicky and boggy—of roads in wet weather.   **2009** Hicks *Beech Mt. Man* 67 w**NC**, It was slicky, and we run off the road 'bout the time we run out of gas.

slicky slide n   *chiefly* **S Midl**, *esp* **WV**   Cf **slippery slide 2**
A playground slide.
 1919 *Jrl. Home Economics* 11.23 **WV**, Here on the giant stride, the swings, the slicky slide, the see saws, they develop their muscles while enjoying their play.   **1930** *Charleston Daily Mail* (WV) 29 Sept 2/3, A "slicky-slide" for the play grounds at Ward One school . . has been ordered.   **1976** *DARE* File s**IN**, *Slicky-slide*—children's playground slide.   **2000** *NADS Letters* **WV**, I always thought slicky-slide was unique to West Virginia.   **2002** in 2010 *DARE* File—Internet nw**TX**, On both sides of the stairs running from the top to the bottom was a long run of smooth concrete that the handrails were connected to, which made a perfect slicky slide.

slide v
Std sense, var forms.
1   past: usu *slid;* also *slide, sli(d)ded, slud.*   [*W3 slided "archaic"*]
 1838 *S. Lit. Messenger* 4.252, The old cow . . slided down the hill.   **1860** *Ibid* 31.94, He slided down it suddenly.   **1870** Van Tramp *Prairie & Rocky Mt. Advent.* 430, Occasionally one plunged outside of the trail, and slided along the field to the bottom.   **1926** Eppes *Through Some Yrs.* 273 **FL** (as of 1861–65), He slided down to the floor.   **1950** Fisher *Spitter* 23 **AR**, He slud.   **1952** Brown *NC Folkl.* 1.592, *Slud. . .* Past tense and past participle of *slide.*   **1959** Roberts *Up Cutshin* 134 e**KY**, That old horse slidded up and fell.   **1962** *Mt. Life* 38.1.17 s**Appalachians**, Verbs which retain either the strong preterites of Middle English or variant preterites of the English dialects . . *Present*—slide[,] *Past*—slid[,] slud[,] *Past Participle*— slid[,] slud.   **1971** *Foxfire* Spring–Summer 75 n**GA**, A big size tool box come a'slidin' down'n slide right up on th'hearth rock.   **1976** Garber *Mountain-ese* 84 s**Appalachians**, Hank slud into what he thought was third base.   **1981** Pederson *LAGS Basic Materials,* 2 infs, **AL**, **GA**, Slided—preterite of *slide.*   **1989** Dickson *Dickson Baseball Dict.* 125 (as of c1948), *Deanism. . .* Terms for any one of scores of words, phrases and statements coined by the late Dizzy Dean. . . In his own vernacular . . players always "slud" into base.   **1989** Nicholson *Field Guide S. Speech* 34, *Slud:* past tense of *slad.* "When I slipped and started to slad down the mountainsad, I just saddown and slud."

2   past pple: usu *slid;* also *slidden, slud.*
 1849 *Scientific Amer.* 29 Dec 116, Each leaden weight, which had slidden forward and downward upon its passing the vertical point, passes the opposite point below.   **1952** [see **1** above].   **1962** [see **1** above].

slide n
1   freq in combs: A sled or sleigh; a wheelless vehicle for

transporting loads over dry ground. [Engl dial] **chiefly Sth, S Midl, esp Gulf States, Lower Missip Valley, TX** See Map Cf **sled, sleigh** n **1, stoneboat**

1855 (1858) Bennett *Chronology of NC* 102, "Slides" or "sleds" . . [had been] the useful and ornamental vehicles in that rolling region. **1884** Murfree *TN Mts.* 156, Instead of a wagon, he had only a rude "slide." **1902** *DN* 2.245 **sIL,** *Slide.* . . Sleigh or sled. **1903** *DN* 2.330 **seMO,** *Slide.* . . Sled. **1907** *DN* 3.226 **nwAR,** *Slide.* . . Sleigh or sled. **1924** Raine *Land of Saddle-Bags* 3 **sAppalachians,** Some eight or ten grim-faced men were walking or riding beside a "slide" where on an armful of cornshucks lay the body, a gray blanket spread over it. **1954** *Harder Coll.* **cwTN,** *Slide.* . . A low wooden platform used for hauling stones or heavy things out of the fields. *Hay slide*—A sled on which hay is moved from one part of a field to another. **1965–70** *DARE* (Qu. L57, *A low wooden platform used for bringing stones or heavy things out of the fields*) 89 Infs, **chiefly Sth, S Midl, esp Gulf States, Lower Missip Valley, TX,** Slide; **VA**43, Ground slide; **KY**86, Ground slide—has runners; (Qu. EE24a, *When there's snow, children go down the hill on a _____*) 13 Infs, **chiefly Gulf States, Lower Missip Valley,** Slide; (Qu. N40a, *. . Sleighs . . for hauling loads*) Infs **AR**55, **KY**9, 74, **MO**8, **NC**50, **TN**24, Slide; **KY**84, Ground slide; **MD**20, Bob slide; (Qu. N41a, *. . Horse-drawn vehicles . . to carry people*) Inf **TX**32, Slide; (Qu. N41c, *Horse-drawn vehicles to carry light loads*) Infs **MS**47, **TX**32, Slide; (Qu. EE24b, *When children go down hill on a sled . . they say they're _____*) Inf **AR**51, Taking a slide ride. **1968** *KY Folkl. Rec.* 14.39 **KY,** The whole family, including the dog and perhaps a mule hitched to a *slide* or a wagon and team, went to the plant-bed and *pulled* [tobacco] plants. **1970** *DARE* Tape **VA**38, These leaf-slides . . you saw sittin' out here, they're just made out about two-by-sixes and got crocus sacks where fertilizer come in two-hundred-pound bag. **1972** *PADS* 58.16 **cwAL,** Tuscaloosa informants were not familiar with a wheeless vehicle used to drag stone, but a similar device, used most often to carry fertilizer into the fields, is called a *sled* (8 [of 27 infs]), a *ground slide* (6), a *slide* (3), and a *drag* (1). **1986** Pederson *LAGS Concordance,* 1 inf, **cwTN,** A slide—ground slide; a skid—put two mules to it; 1 inf, **cTN,** A slide—a skid for dragging; 1 inf, **cwMS,** A slide—pulled on ground; used to haul wood; 1 inf, **cnAR,** A slide—especially for hauling manure; 1 inf, **cnAR,** Ground slide—a skid; 8' long, crossbars, two mules.

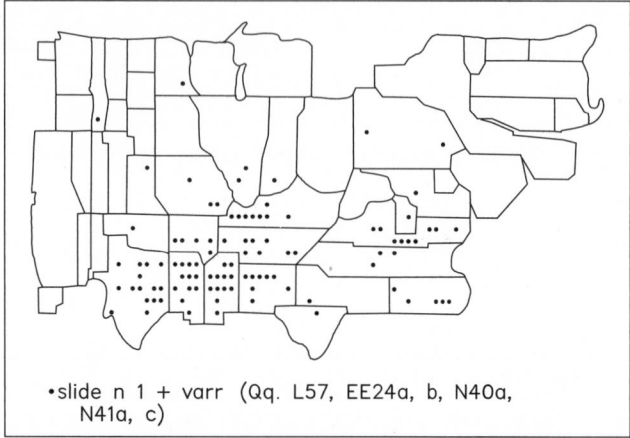

•slide n 1 + varr (Qq. L57, EE24a, b, N40a, N41a, c)

2 A slipper; a low or broken-down shoe. **esp Gulf States, Lower Missip Valley** See Map *esp freq among Black speakers*

1926 *AmSp* 1.652 [Hobo lingo], *Slides*—shoes. **1966–70** *DARE* (Qu. W8, *Names and nicknames for low canvas-top shoes with rubber soles*) Inf **TX**36, Slides; (Qu. W21, *Soft shoes that people wear only inside the house*) Infs **AL**42, **FL**28, **GA**59, **MO**29, **TN**53, **TX**9, 26, Slides. [2 Infs Black] **1967** *DARE* FW Addit **MI**72 [Black], *Slides*—raggedy shoes when you just slide your feet into them. **1970** Major *Dict. Afro-Amer. Slang* 105, *Slides:* (1930's–40's) shoes. **1981** Mebane *Mary* 182 **cnNC** [Black], Her mother had the odd habit of disciplining her children by taking off her "slides" (old shoes whose backs were bent under the feet, like slippers) and throwing them. **1986** Pederson *LAGS Concordance* (Shoes) 1 inf, **csTX,** Slide—heel and toe out. [Inf Black]

slided See **slide** v **1**

slider n

1 also *slider terrapin:* Usu a **red-bellied turtle,** but also any

of var other freshwater turtles such as a **map turtle.** [See quot 1928] **esp DE, MD; also Missip Valley** Cf **cooter** n **1**

1877 *Scribner's Mth.* 15.11 **Chesapeake Bay,** "Sliders," the common river turtles of almost all the rivers of the region, grow to a much larger size. **1883** *Science* 1.149, The heart of the 'slider' terrapin. **1884** Goode *Fisheries U.S.* 1.154, The "Red-bellied Terrapin," *Pseudemys rugosa* [=*P. rubriventris*]. . . is also known under the names "Potter," "Red-fender," and "Slider." **1916** *Copeia* 38.97, *Ptychemys rugosa.* . . These terrapins are known as "Sliders" and are assuming an important role in the localities where they are abundant, as a substitute for the more expensive "Diamond-back." The flesh is said to have an excellent flavor. **1928** Baylor Univ. Museum *Contrib.* 16.7, *Slider.* This name is applied to many species of turtles, especially those of the genus *Pseudemys.* These reptiles are in the habit on hot days of basking on river banks, and at the first alarm, slide into the water, frequently from a height of ten feet or more. Slider is the trade name, in the eastern markets, of the Cumberland, Texan, and Troost's Terrapins. **1934** *Sun* (Baltimore MD) 17 Nov 10 *(Hench Coll.),* The shocking revelation that North Carolina believes that beer goes well with terrapin begets suspicion that Tarheelers do not know the difference between diamond-back and slider, which is to say plain turtle. **1937** Cahn *Turtles IL* 105, *Graptemys geographica.* . . Map turtle; ridge-back; slider. *Ibid* 119, The turtles [=*G. pseudogeographica*] are more than ordinarily wary. . . At the least sign of disturbance every turtle slides into the water, and this characteristic action has given to them the local name of "sliders." **1948** in 1951 *DE Folkl. Bulletin* 1.6, The name skilpot was so familiar to me that I'd never given it a thought. Familiar, also, is the name "slider" in Delaware and Maryland and "cooter" from South Carolina to Florida, for the same little reptile. **1968** *DARE* (Qu. P24, *. . Kinds of turtles*) Inf **DE**3, Slider—terrapin; **MD**34, Slider—dark shell, lives in fresh water. **1984** Wilder *You All Spoken Here* 173 **Sth,** *Cooter, slider, red belly, yellow belly:* Terrapin; Pseudemys scripta.

2 also *slipper:* A fart, esp a noiseless one.

1942 McAtee *Dial. Grant Co. IN Suppl. 1* 8 (as of 1890s), *Slider* . . a breaking of wind without sound. There was a tale of a boy cautioned about farting at table and told to let them slide out. His first trial resulted

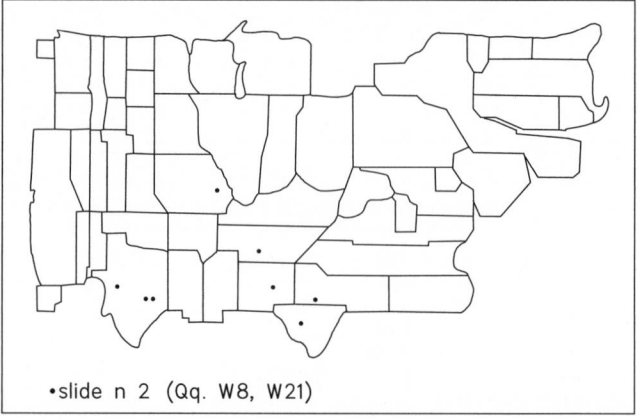

•slide n 2 (Qq. W8, W21)

in a turd, which he pulled out and exhibited, saying, "Here's one of your sliders". **1968–69** *DARE* (Qu. X55b, *Words for breaking wind from the bowels*) Inf **CT**6, Fart—two kinds: easy slider, noisy one; **PA**179, Sliders; **CA**106, Let a slipper.

3 A hamburger, esp a small one; also transf to var small, appetizing comestibles. Note: This term was orig assoc with the White Castle restaurant chain.

1986 Ries-Trout *Marketing Warfare* 166, Devotees call the White Castle Hamburger a "slider" for reasons you wouldn't want to know about. **1997** *Frederick Post* (MD) 22 Oct sec C 1/1 **Chicago IL,** We're at the local White Castle restaurant where, as a supplicant to the food gods . . I humbly give my order: Five "sliders" with cheese, fries and a shake. . . The slider defined: a 2 ½-inch-square beef patty with five evenly spaced holes, steam grilled on a bed of onions and served on a soft white-bread bun with a single dill pickle; also affectionately referred to as a "Whitey One-Bite"; known officially as the White Castle Hamburger. **2003** Turner *Men at War* 182 (as of c1970), One of the Navy pilots . . remarked that the sliders were especially good. The comment drew inquisitive looks from the Air Force pilots. "Hamburgers," he grinned. "I don't know exactly where the term came from, but that's what they're called in the Navy." **2005** *Boston Globe* (MA) 16 Nov sec

F 4 (Internet), There are no White Castles in Boston, but plenty of restaurants are serving some version of the diminutive bites. . . At 28 Degrees . . in the South End, the minis are called sliders, but between the
little buns is lobster salad, not hamburger. **2008** *DARE* File—Internet, I
grew up in the west, so I had no idea about Crystal/White Castle until I
was much older. When I was in the Navy, the term 'slider' refers [sic] to
all burgers, regardless of size/thickness/origin, mainly due to their tendency to 'slide' around the grill while the ship is rolling or pitching.
2008 *NY Times* (NY) 16 July sec D 1/1, In Manhattan, Sliders for All
Tastes. . . Are they greasy but lovable little staples of down-market fast
food? Or are they trendy, high-end bar food . . ? [S]liders are as likely
these days to be made with seafood, chicken or cheese as with beef.
Even White Castle, which began feeding the masses with their tiny burgers in 1921, now offers fish and chicken sliders. *Ibid* 5/1, I first
learned about sliders in Las Vegas. It's something that's served in fancy
places at the bar, not in fast food places. . . He had never heard of White
Castle, but chefs and others who went to high school . . especially in the
1960s, know it as the place where the slider was born. *Ibid,* Originally,
the term "slider" for the White Castle burger was derogatory, having to
do with the ease with which the greasy sandwiches went down. . . That
was, until 1993, when it [=White Castle] trademarked its sandwiches as
"slyders."

slider terrapin   See **slider 1**

slide stacker n   Cf *Mormon stacker* (at **Mormon derrick**)
An apparatus for stacking hay consisting of a ramp of smooth
poles or boards and a separate frame to which a team may be
hitched, which serves to push the hay up the ramp.

   1923 U.S. Dept. Ag. States Rel. Serv. *Exper. Sta. Rec.* 49.87 **CO,** The
slide stacker is cheap and has a high capacity, but has a limited applica-
bility. **1927** *Wellsboro Gazette* (PA) 16 June 7/5, A crew of eight men
in Colorado using a slide stacker and home-made sweep rakes will stack
about 65 tons of wild hay per day. **1929** U.S. Dept. Ag. *Farmers' Bulletin* 1615.2, A second type [of hay stacker] is represented by the homemade slide stacker and plunger. The entire stacker is constructed of long
poles, those forming the slide being placed at a 45° angle. A sweep rake
delivers its load at the bottom of the stacker and a plunger with a heavy
frame on the front, operated by a team pushes the hay up the slide and
onto the stack. **1967** *DARE* (Qu. L16, *Machines used . . in handling
hay*) Inf **WY**1, Slide stacker—used to use. [FW illustr] **2009** *DARE*
File—Internet **SD,** While working on my uncle's ranch in Todd county,
south Dakota, we only used the slide stacker to put up hay.

slide upon   See **sliding pond 2**

sliding board n
1 rarely *sliding plank:* A playground slide. Cf **sliding pond 2**
   1906 *PA School Jrl.* 73.182 **Philadelphia PA,** The affair was a great
sliding board. . . From the platform on top, the children precipitated
themselves down the shining polished surface of fine-grained wood.
c1935 in Lib. of Congress *Amer. Memory: FSA/OWI* (Internet), [Cap-
tion:] Glen Echo, Maryland. Climbing the ladder to the sliding board at
the swimming pool. **1950** *WELS Suppl.* **seWI,** *Sliding board*—for
slide, playground equipment; **eKS,** *Sliding board*—child's slide. **1966–
69** *DARE* (Qu. EE33, *. . Outdoor games . . that children play*) Infs **FL**2,
MO27, **OH**66, Sliding boards. **1977–78** Foster *Lexical Variation* 81
NJ, *Sliding board*—The common playground apparatus. . . *Sliding
board* is the standard term in Midland Jersey. . . Regardless of residence,
blacks show an overwhelming preference (13 of 15 responses) for *sliding board.* **1981** Pederson *LAGS Basic Materials* (in resp to qq designed to elicit *joggling board*) 2 infs, **AL, MS,** Sliding board; 1 inf,
swMS, Sliding plank—probably sliding board; seems unfamiliar with
joggling board idea. **1994** Bolton *Gal* 21 **seSC** [Black], He'd take us
for us to go on all the swings and the sliding board. **1995** Tyler *Ladder
of Yrs.* 193 **eMD,** See, I've always pictured life as one of those ladders
you find on playground sliding boards. **2000** *WI State Jrl.* (Madison) 1
July sec F 8/3, [*Jumpstart* comic strip:] They don't have swings, sliding
boards,—not even a sandbox. **2001** *DARE* File **nwPA,** Here in Erie. . .
They share P[ittsbur]gh's use of the term sliding board (I'd say slide, as
in playground).
2 A child's sled, esp a homemade one.
   1968 *DARE* (Qu. EE24a, *When there's snow, children go down the hill
on a _____*) Inf **PA**172, Sliding board. **1986** Pederson *LAGS Concordance,* 1 inf, **neTN,** [We] made sliding-boards to sled on pine straw.

sliding plank   See **sliding board 1**

sliding pond n   Also *sliding pon* [Engl *sliding + pond* prob

folk-etym var of Du *baan* path, spec (esp in more explicit compounds such as *glijbaan, sullebaan*) path for sliding on ice
or snow. Cf 1981 *AmSp* 56.18 and 1986 *Leuvense Bijdragen*
75.339] **chiefly NYC, nNJ** Cf **slippery slide**
1 A slippery surface, esp an icy patch on a street or sidewalk
adopted by children in winter for sliding on; also fig.
   1826 *NY Mirror* 4.87 **NYC,** The committee have wisely concluded to
fill up the "Hollow," . . which will be . . productive of no other harm
than to deprive little boys of an excellent sliding pond in winter. **1849**
(1853) Barrow *Aunt Fanny's Story Book* 8 **NYC,** It was a bright, frosty
day; . . and the little boys in the streets made sliding ponds of the gutters. **1871** *Harper's New Mth. Mag.* 43.649 **NYC** (as of 1825), On the
opposite side was . . a narrow two-story house, with . . a cellar in the
basement, protected from observation by doors, which, from their propi-
tious angle, formed the "summer sliding-pond" of Young New York.
1901 *Atlantic Mth.* 88.709 **NYC,** A dozen shrill voices could be heard
shrieking around on the avenue, where the gutter had been converted
into a sliding pond. **1901** *Brooklyn Daily Eagle* (NY) 6 Dec np,
[Advt:] Shoes that will stand the racket of Winter rough and tumble—
the "sliding ponds" that are all over the city now. **1914** *DN* 4.158 **PA,
Rutschi.* . . A sliding-pond [gloss provided by **NYC** author]. **1922** *IA
City Press–Citizen* (IA) 27 Mar 2/1, [Article by NYC Commissioner of
Health:] When I taught school in the country, teacher and pupils had a
gay time during the lunch hour. . . [W]e adjourned to the skating and
sliding pond and had a snow-ball fight or played "pum-pum-pull-away."
1922 *Stevens Point Daily Jrl.* (WI) 23 Dec 2/4, A skating rink and a
children's sliding pond, are two different characters. **1936** *NY Times*
(NY) 13 May 22, My mother . . believes that the seats of many of my
trousers played a part in at least polishing the grooves in that big rock
north of Sixtieth Street, which was the neighborhood's popular "sliding
pond." **1953** *Ibid* 16 June 29/6, Two husky 11-year-olds . . [objected]
that the new half-acre recreation site in Central Park had ruined a good
sliding pond. . . The hill has been a favorite take off spot for children
with sleds or ice skates. **1959** *Ibid* 9 Jan 30, Remember. . . sidewalk
sliding ponds? **1972** *NYT Article Letters* **NYC,** "Sliding Pond". (N.Y.
City) was not a children's playground slide, but a frozen sheet of ice on
the pavement which the kids, after a running start, would slide along.
1976 *NY Times* (NY) 3 Feb 20, Sal Ministero lives in Oradell, N.J., and
works in Manhattan. "To get here was like a sliding pond the whole
way," he said. **1981** *AmSp* 56.31 **NYC,** Growing up in the Bronx in the
1930s, I remember *sliding pon* as meaning anything one could slide
on—a wet pavement, a slick sidewalk, etc. I never thought of it as being
a children's slide. **1982** Safire *What's the Good Word* 187 **NYC,** In
Brooklyn, in winter, on our way to school we slid over all the sliding
ponds we were lucky enough to find in our course.
2 rarely, by folk-etym, *slide upon:* A playground slide.
   1943 *Pedagogical Seminary & Jrl. Psych.* 62.28, *Active, outdoor
play.* . . involve[s] gross, bodily movements such as . . the use of outdoor
equipment, e.g., jungle-gym, sliding pond, etc. **1945** *NY Times* (NY) 27
Aug 5, [Advt:] Browdy's cotton gabardine carefully tailored for long
and hard wear. Rugged enough to keep up with the sliding pond and
kindergarten crowd. **1950** *Ibid* 22 Apr 21, [Advt:] Playground For
Children Including Swings & Sliding Ponds. **1977–78** Foster *Lexical
Variation* 81 **nNJ,** *Sliding pond,* used by older informants throughout
North Jersey, is apparently a traditional Northern form, but among younger informants it is common only in Hudson, Bergen, and Passaic.
1979 *AmSp* 54.312 **NYC,** The term *sliding pond* is used in New York
City for the metal slide common in playgrounds. . . [I]t may hark back
to a time before playground slides, when a shallow pond that froze during the winter served much the same function. *Sliding pond.* . . is evidenced only in the New York metropolitan area. **1981** *AmSp* 56.17,
Sliding pond or *sliding pon* is the common term in and around New
York City for '(children's) slide.' . . I have recorded *sliding pon* for
Middlebush, New Jersey (1920s); Yonkers, New York . . 1920–30s . .
and Muncie [sic for *Monsey*], New York (1960s). **1981** *Seventeen Letters* **NJ,** Another word used in New Jersey is "sliding pond" for a slide
you find in a playground. **1992** in 2004 (acc) Lexis–Nexis *State Case
Law: NY* (Internet), Because the device was spiral, the child referred to it
as a twirly slide. In this case, the parties have termed it, variously, as a
slide, a slide upon, a sliding pon . . , and a sliding pond, which, although
perhaps the most curious, is most frequently cited in legal circles, at
least in New York. **2000** *DARE* File **NYC** (as of 1950s), Growing up in
Brooklyn during the '50s I knew only *sliding pon* for the playground
slide; I never heard *pond.*

sliding sled n   Cf **frame sled**
A child's coasting sled.

1943 *LANE* Map 573–74, A frame sled with post-supported seat and a device for steering . . *sliding sled* [2 infs, **ME**]. **1973** Allen *LAUM* 1.219 (as of c1950), *Sled.* . . Terms for a vehicle for travelling over snow. . . sliding sled [1 inf, **MN**].

slight See **sleight**

‡slight of hearing adj phr Cf *slight of stature*
1969 *DARE* (Qu. X19a, *When a person's hearing is not very good . . he's* _____) Inf **RI**4, Slight of hearing.

slighty adj [*OED2 slighty* a. 2 1642–74; *EDD slighty* adj. 2] Contemptuous, rude.
1880 *Scribner's Mth.* 19.681 **sAppalachians,** Was thar anybody thar . . as was slighty . . or onconsiderate? **1941** Justus *Cabin on Kettle Creek* 148 **eTN,** He was always saying something slighty about girls thinking too much of clothes. **1963** Edwards *Gravel* 25 **eTN** (as of 1920s), Now drat your greasy hide, Tom Barnhouse, . . just because I put on an apron to help fill yore big craw, don't think that calls for any slighty remarks.

slim adj **NEng**
Of a person: unwell, peaked, poorly; of health: poor.
1815 Humphreys *Yankee in England* 40, I guess I be [homesick] . . I feel pritty slim. **1867** in 1956 *VT Hist.* 24.79, Deacon Knight is slim[,] better than he was a few months ago. He has a very lame back. His wife is slim but works all the time. **1870** *Scribner's Mth.* 1.17 **NEng,** And go swift for the doctor. I've broken a limb,/ And I've taken a cold and I feel pretty slim. **1877** Jewett *Deephaven* 169 **ME,** She's had slim health of late years. **1914** *DN* 4.80 **ME, nNH,** *Slim.* . . In bad health; weak. **1927** *AmSp* 3.140 **eME,** When asked how they are, people still respond in these terms "Poorly," "not very rugged," "kind of slim," "first-rate," "nicely." **1941** *LANE* Map 459 (*Emaciated, peaked*) **NEng,** Thin, pale. . . *Slim* [20 infs; 1 defines *slim* as "unwell"]. **1969** *DARE* (Qu. X52, . . *A person . . who had been sick was looking* _____) Inf **NH**16, Mighty slim.

slime cat n
=**gaff-topsail catfish.**
1996 Hein et al. *Fisherman's Guide LA* 43, Gafftopsail Catfish (Sail Cat, . . Slime Cat) *Bagre marinus.* . . Presence of toxin in spines on dorsal and pectoral fins.

slime eel n Also *slime fish* [*OED2* 1860; cf Ger *Schleimaal,* Du *slijmaal,* Norw *slimål*]
A **hagfish 1** (here: *Myxine glutinosa*).
1873 in 1878 Smithsonian Inst. *Misc. Coll.* 14.2.36, *Myxine glutinosa.* . . Hag-fish; sucker; slime-fish. Polar regions to Cape Cod. **1890** *Century Dict.* 5696, *Slime-eel.* . . The glutinous hag, *Myxine glutinosa.* **1920** *Daily Kennebec Jrl.* (Augusta ME) 13 May 6/5, Did you ever hear tell of a slime eel? . . They are about 18 inches long, nearly always caught from clay bottoms in deep water. If you put them into a pail of water they will turn to slime, like a piece of soap if left in water too long. **1955** Zim–Shoemaker *Fishes* 19, Hagfishes, or Slime Eels, blind and slimy, are common marine pests and scavengers in water of 100 ft. deep. They eat dead fish and those trapped in nets.

slime fish See **slime eel**

slimer n [From the heavy slime that covers it]
A **toadfish b** (here: *Opsanus tau*).
1817 *Amer. Monthly Mag. & Crit. Rev.* 2.204 **Long Is. NY,** The fishermen . . call it by the name of *Yellow-Kusk, Sand Codling, Slimer,* &c. **1898** U.S. Natl. Museum *Bulletin* 47.2315, *Opsanus tau.* . . Slimer; Oyster-fish. . . Body robust, naked, . . mouth large, the very strong jaws closing with great force.

slime sole See **slippery sole**

slimp See **slimpsy 2, 3**

slimpsy adj [Prob blend of *slim* + *flimsy,* perh also infl by *limp;* cf *EDD slimp* "Slim, slender"; *slimsy* "Worthless, . . lazy, dawdling."]
1 also *slimpy, slimsy, slimzy:* Flimsy; thin; shoddy. **chiefly NEng**
1807 *Panoplist* 2.573 **MA,** Religion's gems can ne'er adorn / The slimsy robe by pleasure worn. **1845** Judd *Margaret* 329 **NEng** (as of 18th cent), Perhaps he would break out [of jail]. The building is old and slimsy, you know. **1858** *Atlantic Mth.* 2.419 **CT,** I see Miss Perrit comin' up the road, with her slimpsy old veil hanging off from her bumbazine bonnet. **1863** *Harper's New Mth. Mag.* 26.537 **RI,** You have slimsy muslins, I dare say. **1883** Buffalo Naturalists' Field Club

Bulletin 1.134 **NY,** The second and third broods hatched later in the season . . are put off with a slimzy makeshift of a nest, often so thin and sleezy that one can see the eggs and young through the bottom. **1892** *Atlantic Mth.* 70.786 **CA,** You feel so kind o' sheepish when you're barefooted and your dress is all slimpsy. **1898** (1899) Earle *Home Life* 238 **NEng,** Cradle sheets of this thin, closely woven, white worsted stuff are not slimsy like thin flannel, yet are softer than flannel. **1905** *DN* 3.19 **cCT,** Slimsy. . . Flimsy. **1970** *DARE* (Qu. KK23, *Weak or unsteady: "I think the footbridge will hold but it is a bit* _____.") Inf **NY**234, Slimpsy. **1979** Lewis *How to Talk Yankee* [31] **nNEng,** *Slimpsy.* . . [S]leazy, of poor quality, cheap. "She was braggin' up that bargain coat she got at the lawn sale, but *wan't* that slimpsy goods?" **1982** *DARE* File **coastal ME,** Slimpy: shoddy—goods or other products.

2 also *slimp:* Limp, droopy; feeble, weak.
1859 Victor *Miss Slimmens' Window* 10, There are usually two or three wrecks of Leghorn hanging, as slimp and melancholy as the prospects of Miss Slimmens herself. **1886** *Overland Mth.* (2d ser) 8.131, Truly, this was much wakefulness for the possible loss of one pupil in entomology, a slimpsy girl who was afraid of grass-hoppers. **1888** *Century Illustr. Mag.* 36.772 **csTN,** I feel ez slimpsy ez a dish-rag. **1891** *Arena* 3.107 **WI,** Monday mornin's they're sleepy and kind o' dreamy and slimpsy. **1932** *DN* 6.284 **swCT,** Slimpsy. Peaked, poorly, and the like. **1968** *DARE* (Qu. KK25, *Something that bends or yields easily: "That willow branch is very* _____.") Inf **NY**70, Slimpsy.

3 also *slimp:* Slim, slender.
1890 *Jrl. Amer. Folkl.* 3.311, *Slimpsy*—Slender. **1912** Green *VA Folk-Speech* 393, *Slimp.* . . Slim; slender.

slimpy See **slimpsy 1**

slim Solomon n esp **CA** Cf **fat Solomon**
A **false Solomon's seal** (here: *Maianthemum stellatum*).
1909 Jepson *Flora CA* 317, *S[milacina] sessilifolia.* . . Slim Solomon. . . rootstock slender; herbage bright green. . . Coast Ranges, mostly near the coast; Sierra Nevada. North to Washington. **1949** Moldenke *Amer. Wild Flowers* 335, The *slimsolomon, S. sessilifolia,* which does not extend north of the state of Washington, has its flowers in unbranched few-flowered clusters. **1961** Thomas *Flora Santa Cruz* 122 **cwCA,** Slim Solomon. Foothills and mountains, usually on wooded slopes in partial shade.

slimsy See **slimpsy 1**

slimwood n
=**ocotillo.**
1949 Curtin *By the Prophet* 89 **AZ,** *Fouquieria splendens.* . . Slimwood. . . Spiny shrub with wand-like stems which whip in the wind. Growing on dry mesas and slopes. **1960** Vines *Trees SW* 762, *Ocotillo.* . . Vernacular names for the plant are . . Slimwood, Jacob's Staff [etc]. . . The slender stems are used for walking sticks, and are planted close together to make fences and hut walls, often sprouting from the barren stem. **c1979** TX Dept. Highways *Flowers* 4, Ocotillo . . is also known as Slimwood. . . A native of West Texas. **1985** Dodge *Flowers SW Deserts* 42, Slimwood. . . with its long, unbranching stems is found on rocky hillsides . . from western Texas to southern California and south into Mexico.

slimzy See **slimpsy 1**

sling n
1 also *hay sling:* A contrivance for handling hay; see quot 1925. **esp MI, OH**
1872 U.S. Patent Office *Annual Rept. for 1871* 2.479, Sling for Hay-Elevator. . . George Smith, Rochester, N.Y., assignor to John C. DeLany, Detroit, Mich. . . A sectional hay-sling. **1895** (1969) Montgomery Ward *Catalogue* 587, *Hay Sling Trip Locks.* . . Which unite the two parts of the slings in the center. Pull the trip and the sling divides in the middle. If you wish to make your own slings order these trip locks. **1925** *Book of Rural Life* 4.2533, *Slings.* . . A sling consists of a basket made of wooden bars and ropes, with a suitable latch in the middle. When the hay is being unloaded, the ends of these slings are gathered and attached to the rope leading to the hay carrier. **1967–69** *DARE* [(Qu. L15, *When you are putting hay into a building for storage . . you are* _____) Inf **AK**4, Slinging;] (Qu. L16, *Machines used . . in handling hay*) Infs **IN**67, **MI**40, Hay sling; **MI**86, Picked it up loose on flat-top wagon, lifted it into mow on pulleys and slings—old-fashioned; **MI**65, **OH**22, Sling; **MI**47, Sling—is put on rack before you load the wagon; **MI**49, Sling—we always used to use. **1968** *DARE* Tape **OH**82, They'll put a sling in the bottom of the wagon and put a layer of hay on top, then put another

sling on top of that, usually . . three layers. . . A sling is a rope and . . wood device. . . and then this is attached to a rope in the barn that pulls the two ends of the sling together and squeezes the hay in between the two ends. Then they take this up into the mow.

2 also *sling-jing,* ~*-post,* ~*-tail:* The game of crack-the-whip.

[**1963** Allen *Legends & Lore S. IL* viii **csIL,** The boys played bull pen, move up, hat ball, old sow, sling dutch, whip cracker, wolf-on-the-ridge, stink base, and anti-over.] **1968–70** *DARE* (Qu. EE27, *Games played on the ice*) Inf **KY**74, Crack-the-whip—same as sling; **MD**34, Sling-post [FW: Inf's name for what most people call crack-the-whip]; **IN**14, Crack-the-whip—sling-tail; (Qu. EE33, *. . Outdoor games . . that children play*) Inf **DE**3, Sling-jing—get ahold of hands and start running, then all of a sudden stop and see if you could throw 'em down; a lot like crack-the-whip.

‡**3** See quot.

1947 McDavid *Coll.* **neFL,** *Sling*—dried beef.

‡**4** See quot.

1984 Wilder *You All Spoken Here* 133 **Sth,** Weeds often get a right good sling—a head start—if a farmer's hoe hands take sick or some other adversity develops.

5 See **sling blade.**

sling v

Std senses, var forms.

Past: usu *slung;* also *slang, slinged, slingt, slunged.*

1882 *WI Jrl. Educ.* 12.118, As the bell rings we hear some one say: . . "Jim slunged my ball over the fence." **1884** *Anglia* 7.253 [Black], To the regular forms of the Irregular verbs as used by the whites, the Negro adds the following forms of his own. . . *Pres.* sling—*Past.* slinged, slunged, slingt. **1968–70** *DARE* (Qu. Y10, *To throw something. . "The dog came at him, so he picked up a stone and _____ it at him."*) [23 Infs, **scattered,** Slung;] **MD**31, **TX**104, Slang; **KY**51, **PA**161, Slinged (it at him). **1986** Pederson *LAGS Concordance (Threw a stone)* 1 inf, **neTN,** Slinged.

sling blade n

Also *sling, slinger (blade), slinging blade* Pronc-sp *slang blade;* for addit varr see quots **chiefly Sth, S Midl** See Map Cf **swing blade, ~ sickle, weed sling, yo-yo**

A long-handled weed-cutting implement, usu a light one with the blade sharpened on both sides.

1939 *Cullman Democrat* (AL) 1 June [6]/4 (newspaperarchive.com), Any blooms that the mowing fails to get should be cut with a sling blade or hoe or pulled by hand. **1957** *Odessa American* (TX) 11 Sept (newspaperarchive.com), Reg. $1.89 Sling Blade—*Grass sythe* [sic]—$1.27. **1965–70** *DARE* (Qu. L37, *A hand tool used for cutting weeds and grass*) 53 Infs, **chiefly Sth, S Midl,** Sling blade; **LA**2, Sling blade [FW illustr]; **VA**40, Sling blade—blade sharp on each side [FW illustr shows a scythe.]; **VA**46, Sling blade—whip it back and forth [FW illustr]; 9 Infs, **Sth, S Midl,** Sling; **AL**15, Weed sling—2″, sharp on both sides; **AR**51, Weed sling [FW illustr]; **SC**12, Grass sling; **NC**3, **OK**14, 33, **VA**49, Slinger; **AR**52, **OK**33, **TX**54, Weed slinger; **TX**99, Hard slinger; **MS**21, Slinger blade; **AL**24, 29, **AR**55, **MS**53, **SC**63, **TN**66, Slinging blade; **TN**58, Slinging blade [FW illustr]; **VA**75, Slinging blade—whipped back and forth—double-edged blade [FW illustr]; **NC**12, Slinging bar; **TX**42, Slinging [slæŋɪn] hoe; **TX**45, Slinging knife; **AR**56, Sling [slæŋ] sickle; (Qu. L28, *Tools used in the past for cutting grain*) Inf **FL**50, Grass sling; **GA**52, Sling [slæŋ] blade; (Qu. L35, *Hand*

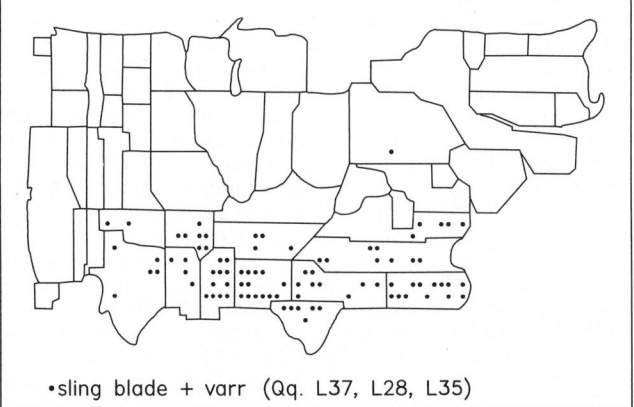

•sling blade + varr (Qq. L37, L28, L35)

tools used for cutting underbrush and digging out roots) Infs **FL**18, 22, 26, Sling; **OK**14, 33, Slinger (thing). **1996** Thornton *Sling Blade* 15 **AR,** I picked up a kaiser blade that was a layin' there by the screen door, some folks call it a sling blade, I call it a kaiser blade. It's just a long handle like a axe handle with a long blade on it that's shaped kind of like a banana. Sharp on one edge and dull on the other. It's what the highway boys use to cut down weeds and whatnot. **2006** *DARE* File—Internet **cwMO,** Vintage slang blade weed/crop cutter farm tool.

slinged See **sling** v

slinger (blade), slinging blade See **sling blade**

slinging pans See **sling pans**

slinging statues n

Also *sling statues* **scattered, but esp Inland Sth, PA** See Map Cf **swinging statues** =**statues 1.**

1965–70 *DARE* (Qu. EE33, *. . Outdoor games . . that children play*) 35 Infs, **scattered, but esp Inland Sth, PA,** Slinging statues; **AL**52, Called "sling statues"—"it" slings child, who must freeze in his position, then players judged for best position; **AL**19, Slinging statues—two players join hands and one slings the other off; the object is to guess what the fallen person represents; **AL**30, Slinging statues—sling one another; he froze when he landed and you had to guess what he was; **AL**46, Slinging statues—one child slings other; **AZ**1, Slinging statues—swing a kid around; he has to stay (when flung loose) as he lands; **KY**74, Slinging statues—player froze in the position the leader put him. **1968** Stem *Flagstone Walk* 10 **NC,** I sort of used myself in an extra slow game of "slinging statues". **2000** in 2002 *DARE* File—Internet **TX,** Summertime reminds me of things like: . . Playing "Red Light, Green Light", "Slinging Statues" and "Kick the Can" until dark.

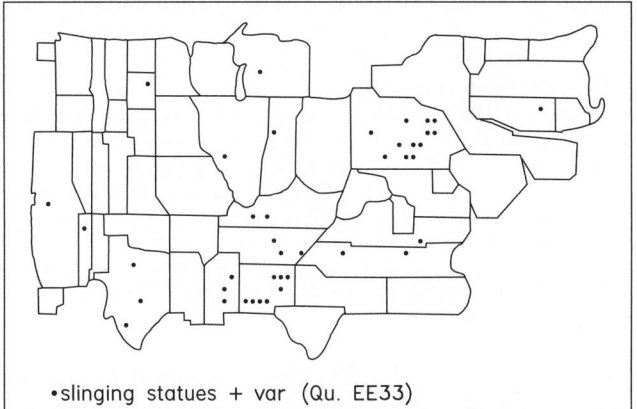

•slinging statues + var (Qu. EE33)

sling-jing See **sling** n 2

sling pans v phr, hence vbl n *slinging pans* Cf **tote** A8

To allow a household employee to take home leftover food; to take leftovers from one's place of employment.

2003 *DARE* File **New Orleans LA** (as of 1965), The phrase "slinging pans" [is used by maids] to let the employer know what the terms of payment will be. For example, a maid-to-be will say, "Does you do slingin' pans?" right up front, if she is honorable. . . In olden times when people cooked for you, it could be tricky because they would sling so many pans you had no leftovers. . . The employee says, "Does you sling pans?" and the employer either says yes or no. . . One way to deal with it is to say, "I will tell you what you can take home."

sling-post See **sling** n 2

‡slingshot gravy n Cf *DS* H37

1971 *Today Show Letters* **Sth,** Red-eyed gravy—Made by adding strong coffee to ham grease. Slingshot gravy—If flour is added.

sling statues See **slinging statues**

slingt See **sling** v

sling-tail See **sling** n 2

slink v

Std sense, var forms.

Past: usu *slunk;* also *slank(ed), slinked, slinkt, slunked.*

1870 *Harper's New Mth. Mag.* 41.334 **neNY,** The minute the varmint found I seed him, he slinked back down the log. **1884** *Anglia* 7.253 [Black], To the regular forms of the Irregular verbs as used by the

whites, the Negro adds the following forms of his own. . . *Pres.* slink—
Past. slinked, slunked, slinkt. **1890** *Century Illustr. Mag.* 40.917 **NEng,**
He slinked off pretty quick. **1942** in 1944 *ADD, Slank.* . . Slunk. . . You
were slinkin along, you slunk too much, so you slank. **1966–70** *DARE*
(Qu. Y26b, *To walk very quietly: "The children filled their pockets and
_____ out the back way."*) Inf **KY**94, Slanked; **ME**13, **NY**108,
Slinked; **KY**94, Slunked.

slinker n

A **pickerel 1.**

　　1927 Weed *Pike* 44, Northern Pike. . . Slinker; St. Lawrence River region. **1934** (1943) *W2, Slinker.* . . Local, U.S. A pickerel.

slinkt See slink

slinkweed n [*slink* to give birth to (an animal) prematurely]

Any of var plants that cause or are thought to cause abortion in
animals, as:

a =cardinal flower.

　　1858 in 1906 Thoreau *Writings* 17.134 **ceMA,** F. says they call the
cardinal-flower "slink-weed," and say that the eating it will cause cows
to miscarry. **1892** *Jrl. Amer. Folkl.* 5.99 **cMA,** *Lobelia cardinalis,*
slink-weed, Princeton, Mass.

b A swamp loosestrife 1 (here: *Decodon verticillatus*).

　　1876 Hobbs *Bot. Hdbk.* 189, Lythrum verticillatum [=*Decodon verticillatus*], Slink weed, Sw[am]p willow—H[er]b abo[rtifacient] to cattle.
1919 (1923) House *Wild Flowers NY* 1.184, [*Decodon verticillatus:*]
Maine to Florida, west to Minnesota, Tennessee and Louisiana. . . Also
known as peatweed or slink-weed, wild oleander and grass poly.

c A willow herb 1 (here: *Chamerion angustifolium*).

　　1889 *Chambers's Encycl.* IV.401/1 *(OED2),* This species *[Epilobium
angustifolium]* with several others is common in North America, where
it is sometimes called . . slink-weed, from a belief that it causes cows to
'slink' or miscarry.

d =creeping juniper.

　　1916 *Torreya* 16.236 **ME,** *Juniperus horizontalis.* . . Slink-weed.

e A snakeweed b(6) (here: *Gutierrezia microcephala*).

　　1961 Wills–Irwin *Flowers TX* 223, While . . annual Broom-weeds are
unpalatable to stock, ranchers believe the perennial species to be poisonous. G[utierrezia] microcephala . . , variously called . . Snake-weed,
Turpentine-weed, and Slink-weed, a clumped perennial . . , is perhaps
the most troublesome. **1964** Kingsbury *Poisonous Plants U.S.* 406,
Gutierrezia microcephala. . . Slinkweed. . . Texas to California, north to
Colorado and Idaho.

slip v

1 To steal, swipe. [Cf *EDD slipe* v. 6 "to steal; to seize, take
away suddenly"] **esp Sth, S Midl**

　　1933 *McDavid Coll.* **seGA,** Slipped—stole [2 infs]. **1967–70**
DARE (Qu. V5a, *To take something of small value that doesn't belong to
you—for example, a child taking cookies: "Who's been _____ the
cookies?"*) Infs **GA**28, **IN**3, **KY**76, **SC**34, **TX**35, Slipping.

2 To slide oneself, "scoot." **chiefly Sth, S Midl, esp S Atl**
See Map

　　1965–70 *DARE* (Qu. Y52, *To move over—for example on a long
bench: ". . . Can you _____ [a little]?"*) 44 Infs, **chiefly Sth, S
Midl, esp S Atl,** Slip over (*or* down); **NC**76, Slip; **NC**79, Slip a little
further.

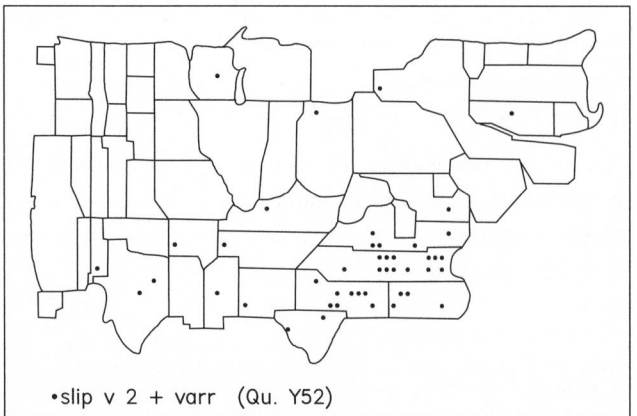

・slip v 2 + varr　(Qu. Y52)

---

slip n[1] [*OED2 slip* sb.[1] 2.a c1425 →]

Milk set to a jelly-like consistency, esp as prepared to be eaten
with cream and sugar.

　　1847 (1979) Rutledge *Carolina Housewife* 149, *Slip.* Put into a dish a
quart of cream and one of milk, and stir into it a table-spoonful and a
half of "Artichoke Extract." The length of time required to turn the milk
depends upon the weather. . . Grate nutmeg and cinnamon over the top,
and serve with sugar and cream. **1859** (1968) Bartlett *Americanisms*
416, *Slip.* . . Milk turned with rennet, etc., before the whey separates
from the curd. **1879** (1965) Tyree *Housekeeping in Old VA* 428, *Slip.*
One quart milk . . one tablespoonful wine of the rennet. After the milk is
turned, eat it with a dressing of cream, sugar and wine. **1906** Gregory
Woman's Cookbook 173, *Slip. Slip* is bonny-clabber, without its acidity,
and so delicate is its flavor that many like it as well as ice-cream.

slip n[2] [Cf *EDD slipe* sb. 29 "A sledge or sleigh used for agri-
cultural purposes."]

1 A wheelless conveyance such as a **stoneboat. esp West**
See Map

　　1939 *LANE* Map 168 *(Stone boat)* 1 inf, **seMA,** Stone slip; slip.
1966–68 *DARE* (Qu. L13, *The kind of wagon used for carrying hay*) Inf
OR1, Hay slip—no wheels, just slides along on hay; **UT**15, Hay slip—
that doesn't have wheels; it's two poles with boards nailed across them;
NM10, Slip—pulled by either horse or tractor; (Qu. L57, *A low wooden
platform used for bringing stones or heavy things out of the fields*) Infs
CO38, **ID**3, **OR**17, **UT**7, Slip. **1973** Allen *LAUM* 1.219 (as of c1950),
Stone boat. . . slip [1 inf, **NE**]. . . *slip:* Heard locally and in western Col-
orado.

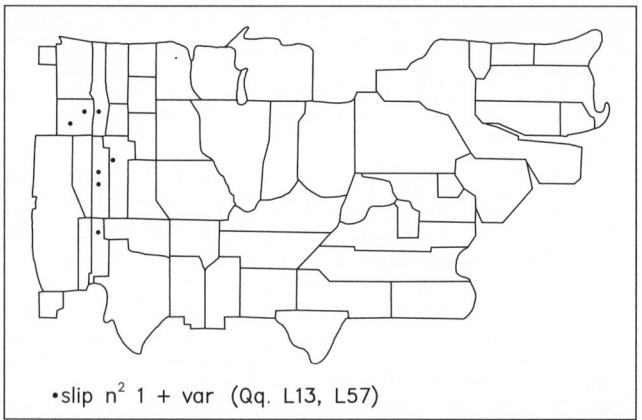

・slip n[2] 1 + var　(Qq. L13, L57)

2 also *slip scoop, ~ scrape(r), ~ shovel:* A horse- or mule-
drawn metal scoop for moving dirt. Cf **fresno 2, horse
scoop, scoop n 1, slusher**

　　1897 Cowgill *Irrigation Gt. Plains* 15, The land in the interior of the
reservoir is plowed and the loose earth is removed . . , usually with the
ordinary slip scraper. **1925** *Book of Rural Life* 8.4751, *Scrapers.* . . The
simplest form is the *slip,* or *scoop* scraper. This implement is simply a
large scoop arranged with a bail for drawing, and handles for dumping.
1934 *Sun* (Baltimore MD) 9 Nov 15/3 *(Hench Coll.),* While clearing
loose dirt with the aid of a horse and slip scraper, [he] lost his footing.
1942 Faulkner *Go Down* 155 **MS,** Grabs a shovel . . and starts throwing
dirt onto her faster than a slip scraper could have done it. **1958**
McCulloch *Woods Words* 170 **Pacific NW,** *Slip.* . . An old time dirt
scoop pulled by horse: killed off by the bulldozer. **1965–70** *DARE*
(Qu. L41, *A device for moving dirt and other loads*) Inf **LA**40, Road
slip [FW illustr]; **LA**3, Slip—dirt-moving device pulled by mules—no
wheels [FW illustr]; **LA**12, Slip—mule-drawn [FW illustr]; **LA**40, Slip
[FW illustr]; **MO**5, Slip—pulled by two horses; **CO**22, **IN**40, **OH**4,
Slip scraper; **WY**1, Slip scraper—no wheels, horse-drawn road-building
machinery. **1967** Jacobs *Rejoicing* 18 **cIN** (as of c1930), Farmers
brought their teams and slip scoops to excavate a basement. **1967**
Green *Horse Tradin'* 220 **TX,** He was going to need scrapes and plows
and slips and fresnos. **1967** *DARE* Tape **AR**55, They built a railroad. . .
In those days, it was just mules and what we call slips (or scrapers) and
hand-digging. **1978–79** *Midwest. Lang. & Folkl. Newsl.* 1–2.20, In
Maine the "fresno" is called a "horse scoop," in Indiana a "slip shovel."
1986 Pederson *LAGS Concordance,* 1 inf, **cMS,** A slip—digging implement, shovel-like, long [and] flat; 1 inf, **cwLA,** A fresno slip—device
for grading roads—3 mules; 1 inf, **cAR,** Road slip—picks up dirt,

pulled by mules; 1 inf, **cAL**, Slip scrape; 1 inf, **neLA**, Slips—road equipment, used for ditching roads; 1 inf, **cwLA**, Slips—mule-pulled rigs; earth moving apparatuses. **2002** *DARE* File **cnIN** (as of 1940s), The term we used in Indiana was slip scoop. They generally used a team of horses; they didn't think a single horse could pull it.

slip n³

1 also *slip-in:* A landslide. **esp KY, OH** See Map

1924 Raine *Land of Saddle-Bags* 29 **sAppalachians**, I noticed a great raw area where a large landslide had evidently just occurred, and as I mentioned it at the house where I stopped for dinner, a man recalled with a chuckle a similar "slip." **1967–69** *DARE* (Qu. C16, *When a mass of earth and rock comes loose from a high place and rushes down*) Infs **KY**28, 32, 46, 53, **OH**44, 65, Slip; **KY**21, Slip-in. **1968** *Athens Messenger* (OH) 28 May 2/3, Shepard said several slips have caused problems in the city.

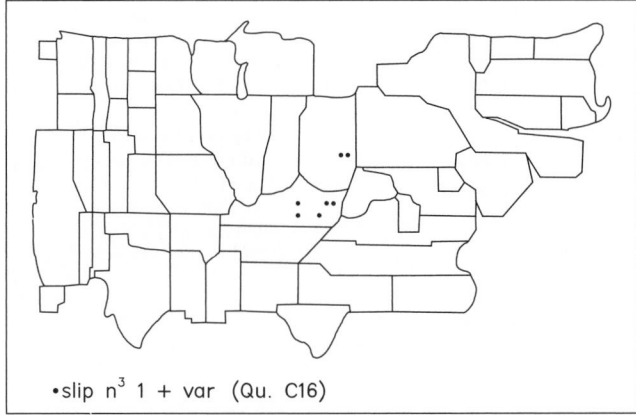

•slip n³ 1 + var (Qu. C16)

2 A children's game; see quots.

1957 *Sat. Eve. Post Letters* **WA**, A school ground game. . . It was a running game called 'Slip'. Usually anyone of us volunteered to be 'it'. The one so designated pointed out his quarry and took off after him to tag him 'out'. However anyone could 'slip' in between the pursuer and the pursued and immediately became the new quarry. **1968** *DARE* (Qu. EE12, *Games in which one captain hides his team and the other team tries to find it*) Inf **NY**86, Slip.

slip n⁴

1 A narrow channel of water. [Cf *OED2 slip* sb.² 7 "A strip, a narrow piece or stretch, *of* land, ground, etc."; 1591 →] Cf **gut** n **1**

[**1796** in 1940 *AmSp* 15.409 **VA**, To four Chesnuts in the head of a deep Wallow by a water slip.] **1967–70** *DARE* (Qu. C1, . . *A small stream of water not big enough to be a river*) Inf **VA**47, Slip—a small gut; (Qu. C14, *A stretch of still water going off to the side from a river or lake*) Inf **AL**20, Slip.

2 A church pew. **chiefly NEng**

1823 in 1889 East Hampton NY *Records* 4.427, That four slips be hired out . . and the money for which they are hired, be applied towards painting the meeting house. **1828** (1970) Webster *Amer. Dict., Slip.* . . A long seat or narrow pew in churches. [Webster: *U. States.*] **1848** Bartlett *Americanisms* 309 **NEng**, *Slip.* . . A pew. . . When there is a door, they are called pews; when without doors and free to all, *slips*. This, I believe, is the difference between them. **1878** (1977) Stowe *Poganuc People* 33 **wMA**, Why . . if there ain't the minister's boys down there in that front slip. **1906** Churchill *Coniston* 15 **NEng**, Jethro Bass . . sat in the rear slip. **1937** FWP *Guide VT* 181, Built in 1825, the church seats 300 people and remains unaltered; the interior has the old box pews, or 'slips,' each with an individual door. **1968** *DARE* (Qu. CC5, *Names for seats in a church, especially near the front*) Inf **CT**16, All the pews were called "slips"—old-fashioned.

slip-and-go-down See **slip-go-down**

slip-chuck See **slip-shuck** v **3**

slipe n [Engl dial; prob var of *slip*] **esp NC, VA**

A slice; a long strip (esp of land).

1628 in 1940 *AmSp* 15.393 **VA**, I . . ffarme let unto Thomas Dalmajor of James Citty Joyner a small slipe of land. **1710** *Ibid* **VA**, Take care . . that no small Slipes of Land be left between the Lotts. **1736** in 1975 N.

Castle NY *N. Castle Hist. Rec.* B100 **seNY**, The Ear Mark of *Mosses Quimby* is . . a Slipe on the off Ear. **1763** (1925) Washington *Diaries* 1.192 **VA**, A set of People which Inhabit a small slipe of Land between the said River Pequemen and the Dismal Swamp. **1886** *Atlantic Mth.* 57.30 **NC**, My neighborhood. . . consists of some half a dozen families . . crowded into as many little huts . . on a "slipe" of very poor, rocky ridge. **1890** *DN* 1.66 **KY**, *Slipe* . . a piece, or slice. "Cut me a slipe of bacon." **1899** (1912) Green *VA Folk-Speech* 393, *Slipe.* . . A long, narrow strip: as, a *slipe* of woods between the fence and the road; a *slipe* of bark from a tree. **1903** *DN* 2.330 **seMO**, *Slipe.* . . Slip or strip. 'I bought a slipe two rods wide off of the adjoining tract of land.' **1946** *PADS* 6.27 **eNC** (as of 1900–10), *Slipe.* . . A piece of arable land enclosed by ditches. Usually much longer than wide, say 20 by 250 yards. . . Common. **1952** Brown *NC Folkl.* 1.591, *Slipe.* . . A small piece of land.

slip gap n Cf **drawbar 1, gap** n¹ **2, pair of bars** **Sth, S Midl**

A temporary opening in a worm fence made by sliding one or more rails to the side; a fence opening that can be closed or opened by sliding rails to one side; the rails themselves.

1852 Morris *Lights & Shadows* 161 **KY**, People turned their attention to respectable labor, and then domestic improvements began. The big cracks were stopped, gates were substituted for slip-gaps, wells for wet-weather springs, coffee for buttermilk, and water for whisky. **1857** *S. Lit. Messenger* 24.123, He had not yet gone a mile, perhaps, when he came up to a fence through which his way had to be made by pulling down a slip-gap of heavy rails. **1859** (1968) Bartlett *Americanisms* 167, *Gap.* . . A *slip gap* is a place provided in a fence, where the bars may be slipped aside and let down. **1862** in 1897 U.S. War Dept. *War of Rebellion* 1st ser 50.2.163, The settlers have succeeded in destroying a large portion of the crops of small grain and the entire crop of corn. . . We have found as high as seven slip gaps of one morning, where they had raised up the corners of the fence, put in chunks, and slipped out the rails, until the largest hogs could walk in. **1872** U.S. Dept. Ag. *Rept. of Secy. for 1871* 507, In many counties in the South, few, if any, gates, are reported; while in others nearly all the openings are gates; in a few there are neither gates nor bars, but "slip-gaps." The correspondent in Henry County, Virginia, says that the fields there are entered by pulling down a corner of the fence. **1902** *DN* 2.245 **sIL**, *Slip-gap.* . . An opening made in a rail fence by turning out the end of one rail or more, and putting a bolster in its place, so that hogs may pass through, while larger animals are retained. Or all the rails of a corner may be turned on either hand, and rails for bars laid on the other projecting ends of the rails so laid out. This latter is for the passage of cattle and wagons. **1912** Green *VA Folk-Speech* 393, *Slip-gap.* . . A gap in a worm-fence, made so that two or three rails near the bottom might be slipped [to] one side to give passage without climbing over the top. **c1960** *Wilson Coll.* **csKY**, *Slip gap.* . . Poles or rails that can be drawn out of place to open a gap in a fence; drawbars. **1982** Powers *Cataloochee* 283 **cwNC** (as of a1940), The side of the pen had a 'slip gap'. . . two logs could be slid over and let hogs come outside. **1982** McDavid Coll. **cGA**, *Slip gap*—place in a rail fence where rails could be slid aside to let stock in and out. **1986** Pederson *LAGS Concordance,* 1 inf, **csTN**, Slip gap—pull one rail, let stock through.

slip-go-down n Also *slip-and-go-down, slip gut* [Cf *EDD slip-down* (at *slip* sb. 3.(7)) "old milk slightly curdled"; perh by folk-etym from **slip** n¹] **Nth, esp NEng** Cf **gap-and-swallow**

Cornmeal mush or other soft, pudding-like food.

1855 Hammond–Mansfield *Country Margins* 32 **NY**, We discussed *junkett* also, called in the vulgar, "slip and go down." **1909** *DN* 3.415 **nME**, *Slip-go-down.* . . A pudding made of buckwheat. **1915** York *Overlook Farm* 2.11 **MI**, The wheat and rye flour ground in the hand mill was coarse and unbolted, yet it made . . fine . . boiled slip-go-down pudding. **1941** *LANE* Map 288 (*Corn meal mush*) 1 inf, **cwMA**, Slip-and-go-down; 1 inf, **NH**, Slip gut. **1950** *WELS* (*Boiled corn meal*) 1 Inf, **cWI**, Slip-go-down. **1959** *VT Hist.* 27.158 **nwVT**, *Slip gut.* . . Cornstarch pudding. Rare. **1976** *Yankee* July 24, Sixty or more years ago, my grandmother used to make a delicious concoction she called "slip go down." It was pure white, custard like, and she used to make it in a milk pan used to set cream for butter. **1992** Nash–Scofield *Well-Traveled Casket* 31 **OR**, You asked me about recipes. I do remember two. The first one is a dessert, and I'm sure every pioneer woman made it. In our family it was called slip-go-down, and it was just simply berry juice that was strained through many thicknesses of cheesecloth until it was very clear, and then it was thickened with cornstarch. . . We would eat it with cream on top.

slip-in See **slip** n³ **1**

slip one's cable v phr   Also *slip one's lines*   [Naut; *OED2* 1751 →]   Cf *DS* BB56
Fig: to die.

1824 Cooper *Pilot* 2.59, My orders are to see it done . . or Mr. Griffith . . slips his cable from this here anchorage. **1869** *Overland Mth.* 2.454 **MA**, One night she slipped her cable and put to sea upon what parsons call the 'ocean of eternity.' **1919** Kyne *Capt. Scraggs* 179 **CA**, Mrs. Scraggs (to quote Captain Scraggs) "slipped her cable" in her forty-third year. **1948** McHenry–Myers *Home is the Sailor* 160, You're not going to slip your cable. . . You've just got a bad cold. **1985** Madson *Up River* 245 **Upper Missip Valley,** If he [=a riverman] dies he has "slipped his lines."

slip one's wind v phr
Fig: to die.

1762 in 1928 Watts *Letter Book* 101 **NYC**, I hope he'll slip his wind there yet & not enjoy the fruits of his underservd [*sic*], ill got wealth. **1824** *Tales Amer. Landlord* 1.15 **Sth,** Here I have come twenty miles . . , and because Charles Belton has slipped his wind, I am to be disappointed of the barbacue. **1838** in 1841 *U.S. Congress Serial Set* 378.189.46, Yesterday a man had slipped his wind, and was dragged into the hazel brush. **1869** *Overland Mth.* 2.354 **MA**, Our next trip was St. Jago de Cuba, where Captain Jones took the yaller fever and slipped his wind. **1907** *Atlantic Mth.* 99.221 **ME**, He took this 'ere kind of a bilious attact, and slipped his wind afore ever they knowed it. **1968** *DARE* (Qu. BB56, *Joking expressions for dying: "He _____."*) Inf **CT**16, Slipped his wind. **1991** *DARE* File **seNY**, Slipped his wind = died.

slippance exclam   Also *slippers, slipping, slippin's (over)*   **Sth, S Midl**   Cf **clearance(s), havance** n¹**, roundance 1, slips**
Used as a call in marble play to claim the right to shoot again, esp when the shooting marble accidentally slips from the shooter's fingers; hence n *slippance* the privilege so claimed.

1856 (1857) Wakeley *Heroes Methodism* 255 **VA**, Well, brethren, I askes the gentlemen to retire from those seats, and *they* did so. But it seems *that* man is determined not to move. We must, therefore, serve him as the little boys say, when a marble slips from their fingers—let him 'go for *slippance*.' **1891** *PMLA* 6.173 **TN**, He cries *slippance!* when his marble slips from his thumb, and this entitles him to another go. **1897** (1952) McGill *Narrative* 33 **SC**, Some boys would claim slippance and there was none, violating the orders "knuckle down and fire hard," no fudging, no clearance nor roundance nor extension of the span towards the ring or a man. **1909** *DN* 3.371 **eAL, wGA,** Slippance. . . Used especially in the game of marbles as a cry to get a second trial when the marble slips from the fingers. **1912** Green *VA Folk-Speech* 394, Slippance. . . When a boy's taw slips out of his fingers he says slippance and has a fair shoot. **1922** *DN* 5.188 **KY,** Slippin's. . . A case when the taw slips off one's finger accidentally. The player by calling "Slippin's," may take another shot unless his opponent first calls "Vence ye slippin's over." **1967** *DARE* Tape **LA**8, Sometimes a man could aim to shoot a marble and. . . it wouldn't go too far as he wanted, he could say "slipping" and he could take a shot over again. **1986** Pederson *LAGS Concordance*, 1 inf, **seFL,** Slippers—what you could call in marbles.

slipper n

1 with modifier: =**lady's slipper 1.** Cf **slipper root**
[**1743** Catesby *Nat. Hist. Carolina* 2.72, The Lady's Slipper of Pensilvania. . . The Flower . . resembles more a slipper than any other of this Tribe that I have seen. . . The Slipper is of a greenish Yellow, with a Tincture of Red.] **1933** Small *Manual SE Flora* 367, C[*ypripedium*] *reginae.* . . Queen's-slipper. . . *C. acaulis.* . . Purple slipper. **1949** Moldenke *Amer. Wild Flowers* 384, It [=*Cypripedium reginae*]. . . is sometimes called . . *queens-slipper.* **1950** Correll *Native Orchids* 20, *Cypripedium acaule.* . . Purple-slipper. *Ibid* 29, *Cypripedium candidum.* . . Violet-veined White Slipper. **1965** *Native Plants PA* 35, The Baby-slipper, *Cypripedium calceolus* v. *parviflorum* is a smaller plant with flowers up to 1 inch long.

2 See **slipperweed.**

3 See **slipper shell 1.**

4 A low-cut shoe; see quots.   Cf **low-quarter(ed) shoe**
1909 *DN* 3.371 **eAL, wGA,** Slipper. . . A low-cut shoe. Same as *oxford.* Slipper is the common term in the South. **1937** Hall Coll. **wNC, eTN,** Slippers. . . Men's low shoes or oxfords (a very common use which sounded quite strange to my ears at first!) **1941** *LANE* Map 366

(*Low shoes*) 4 infs, **MA, VT,** Slippers; 1 inf, **csCT,** Slippers, women's oxfords; 1 inf, **RI,** Slippers, applied to low shoes; 1 inf, **seNH,** Slippers, women's low shoes; 1 inf, **nME,** Slippers . . men's low shoes. **1942** *AmSp* 17.280 [Navy Yard talk], *Slipper.* Any low shoe. The word *shoe* is often restricted to footwear that covers the ankle. **1942** Warnick *Garrett Co. MD* 14 **nwMD** (as of 1900–18), Slippers . . low cut, as distinguished from high-topped shoes. **1942** McAtee *Dial. Grant Co. IN* 58 (as of 1890s), Slipper . . any low-cut shoe; such terms as oxford and pump were unknown. **1956** McAtee *Some Dialect NC* 41, Slipper . . any low-cut shoe. **c1960** Wilson Coll. **csKY,** Slipper. . . A low-cut or oxford shoe. **1965–70** *DARE* (Qu. W8, *Names and nicknames for low canvas-top shoes with rubber soles*) 21 Infs, **scattered,** (Tennis) slippers; **AR**47, **KY**44, **OK**1, Canvas (*or* cloth) slippers; (Qu. W11, *Men's low, rough work shoes*) Infs **IN**66, **MO**3, 39, **NC**35, **NY**219, Slippers; **NJ**28, 67, Low slippers; **MD**29, Slippers—oxfords, slippers—same thing; **NY**88, Slippers—these are laced; **MD**25, Work slippers; **NY**68, Work slippers—even with laces; **TN**27, Work slippers [FW illustr]; **WI**27, Everyday slipper. [28 of 36 total Infs old, 25 male, 24 gs educ or less, 22 comm type 5] **1968** *DARE* FW Addit **csOK,** Slipper—any shoe that did not cover the ankle; shoes covered the ankle. **1986** Pederson *LAGS Concordance,* 1 inf, **cnTX,** Slippers = low cut, oxford shoes.

5 also *slippery calf:* A very young calf sold for meat.   [Prob < *slip* to give premature birth to; cf *EDD* slip-calf (at *slip* v. 5)]   Cf **bob calf**
1969 *DARE* (Qu. K20, *A calf that is sold for meat*) Inf **NY**209, Slipper—an unfattened calf sold just after it's born. **1969** *DARE* FW Addit **ceCT,** Slippery calf—a "bob calf"—up to two weeks old—sold for early butchering (pre-veal).

6 =**slippery jim.**
1950 *WELS Suppl.* **seWI,** Here is another name for slippery Jack pickles—slippers.

7 See **slider 2.**

slipper elm See **slippery elm 1**

slipper flower See **slipper plant**

slipper horn n   Cf **slipper spoon**
A shoehorn.
1908 *Hamilton Eve. Jrl.* (OH) 11 Dec 3/6, [Advt:] Shoe buttoners and slipper horn. **1920** *San Antonio Light* (TX) 10 Dec 10/6, [Advt:] Hand made ribbon-covered slipper trees and slipper horn to match. **1962** *Frederick Post* (MD) 5 Apr 21/2, [Advt:] Leather Handle Slipper Horn—$1.00. **1962** [see **slipper spoon**].

slipper limpet See **slipper shell 1**

slipper plant n   Also *slipper flower*   [*OED2* (at *slipper* sb. 10) 1848]
=**jewbush.**
1890 *Century Dict.* 5699, *Slipper-flower.* . . The slipper-plant [= *Pedilanthus*]. **1900** Lyons *Plant Names* 279, *P[edilanthus] tithymaloides.* . . Jew-bush, Slipper-plant. **1953** Greene–Blomquist *Flowers South* 66, *Spurge Family.* . . includes . . the slipper-flower (*Pedilanthus*). *Ibid* 112, Slipper Plant (*Pedilanthus tithymaloides*). . . Its fleshy, zigzag stems bear sparingly pinkish, variegated leaves and small lopsided flowers like miniature red birds. **1982** Perry-Hay *Field Guide Plants* 70, *Pedilanthus tithymaloides* . . slipper plant; Jewbush.

slipper root n
A **lady's slipper 1:** usu *Cypripedium parviflorum,* but also *C. pubescens.*
1876 Hobbs *Bot. Hdbk.* 107, Slipper root, American valerian, Cypripedium pubescens and species. **1898** U.S. Dept. Ag. Div. Botany *Bulletin* 20.20, *Larger Yellow Lady's Slipper. Cypripedium hirsutum* Mill [= *C. pubescens*]. *Other names:* Lady's slipper . . yellow moccasin . . nerve root; Indian shoe; slipper root. **1924** *Amer. Botanist* 30.153, *Cypripedium parvulum* [=*C. parviflorum*] is the . . "downy yellow Lady's slipper," "yellow moccasin flower," . . "slipper root," . . all ringing the changes on the shope [*sic*] of the lower lip. **1940** Clute *Amer. Plant Names* 47, *C. parviflorum.* . . Slipper-root.

slippers n   See **slipperweed**

slippers exclam   See **slippance**

slipper shell n

1 also *slipper, slipper limpet, ~ snail:* A saltwater mollusk of the genus *Crepidula.* [*OED2* (at *slipper* sb. 10) 1858 →; see quot 1911] Also called **barnacle, boat shell, cup** n 2; for other names of *C. fornicata* see **half deck, quarterdeck**

1852 Essex Co. Nat. Hist. Soc. *Jrl.* 65 neMA, *Crepidula plana. . . Flat slipper Shell.* A very pretty, pearly vitreous species. . . Shell generally flat, but sometimes tortuous or reflexed. **1881** Ingersoll *Oyster-Industry* 248, *Slipper-limpet.*—Mollusks of the genus *Crepidula.* **1884** U.S. Natl. Museum *Bulletin* 27.197, *Crepidula plana. . . Crepidula fornicata. . .* The former is known as the "Slipper-Shell" and the latter as the "Boat-Shell." Both are found from Massachusetts to Florida, and on the northern shores of the Gulf of Mexico. **1911** Keep *West Coast Shells* 207, There is a large group of mollusks whose shells. . . when turned over . . somewhat resemble a Chinese slipper, with a place for the toes of the wearer's foot. So apparent is the resemblance that they are universally called Slipper-shells. *Crepidula adunca,* . . the Hooked Slipper-shell, . . is perhaps the commonest species. **1952** Morris *Field Guide Shells* 100, *Crepidula adunca.* . . Hooked Slipper. . . *Crepidula aculeata.* . . Prickly Slipper. . . Two species of slipper shells have been introduced in Pacific waters, presumably along with importations of the Atlantic oyster. One of them is a little fellow, . . *Crepidula convexa.* The other one is *Crepidula fornicata.* **1955** *Seattle Daily Times* (WA) 18 Sept mag sec 2, When we import sets from Japan or the East Coast we bring in barnacles, drills and slipper shells. **1978** Whipple *Vintage Nantucket* 243, The only shells that competed with the scallops in numbers, as we walked along the beach, were those of the slipper snail. **1981** Meinkoth *Audubon Field Guide Seashore* 487, *Common Slipper Snail* . . (*Crepidula fornicata*). . . Gulf of St. Lawrence to Florida and Texas; introduced into c. California. . . The Eastern White Slipper Snail (*C. plana*). . . ranges from Nova Scotia to Florida and Texas. The Hooked Slipper Snail (*C. adunca*) ranges from British Columbia to Baja California.

2 also *slippershell mussel:* A **freshwater clam:** usu *Alasmidonta viridis,* occas also *A. calceolus.*

1982 U.S. Fish & Wildlife Serv. *Fresh-Water Mussels* [Wall chart] **Upper Missip Valley,** *Slippershell.* . . *Alasmidonta viridis.* . . Shell yellow, green, or brown. **1991** IL Nat. Hist. Surv. *Biol. Notes* 137.21, *Alasmidonta viridis* . . slippershell mussel. **1992** Cummings–Mayer *Field Guide Freshwater Mussels MW* 86, *Slippershell mussel—Alasmidonta viridis.* . . Creeks and the headwaters of large rivers in sand, mud, or fine gravel. . . Endangered in Illinois and Iowa. Threatened in Wisconsin. **2000** *DARE* File—Internet sMI, Slippershell, *Alasmidonta calceolus.*

slipper slide n

1 A shoehorn.   Cf **slipper spoon**

1939 FWP *Guide NC* 98, Common phrases of the household may be quaint and humorous. . . a shoehorn is a "slipper-slide." **1952** Brown *NC Folkl.* 1.592, *Slipper-slide.* . . A shoe horn.—Central and east. **1996** in 2004 Montgomery–Hall *Dict. Smoky Mt. Engl.* 543 **eTN.**

2 =**slippery slide 2.**

1968 *Gt. Bend Daily Tribune* (KS) 31 Oct 9/2, [Advt:] 1 Slipper-slide, 10′ high, 20′ long, 2 Teeter-totters, 16′ and 20′. **1969** *Hamburg Reporter* (IA) 10 Apr 6/4, Patty . . happened to slide down the slipper slide and land bottom down in a very dirty mud puddle! **1973** *Walla Walla Union–Bulletin* (WA) 19 Aug 1/5, Peppie is a 5-year-old poodle who shares with her mistress, Tammy, a passion for the tall slipper-slide in Pioneer Park. **1994** Thomas Co. Hist. Soc. (KS) *Prairie Winds* Oct 8 nwKS, [Caption:] The donation of a slipper slide from the Halford School adds to the one room school experience.

slipper snail   See **slipper shell 1**

slipper spoon n   Cf **shoespoon, slipper horn, ~ slide 1**
A shoehorn.

1921 *Decatur Daily Rev.* (IL) 29 Nov 7/7, [Advt:] Toilet Sets In Lovely Cases. . . [contain] slipper spoon. **1962** *College English* 24.145, It was discovered that in the southern American English area *slipper spoon* was preferred by around 41.4% of the informants; *shoe slipper* by 13.1%; *shoe horn* by 37.6%; *shoe spoon* by 5.9%; and *slipper horn* by less than 1%. The reverse statistics obtained for the northern American speech area, where 76.4% preferred *shoe horn;* 8.5% used *slipper spoon;* 7.9% used *slipper horn;* and 7.1% used *shoe slipper* or *shoe spoon.* **1966** *Daily Times–News* (Burlington NC) 30 Sept sec B 1, [Advt:] *Boys' Shoes.* . . Free Slipper Spoon With Each Pair Shoes. **1968** *DARE* FW Addit csOK, *Slipper spoon*—a shoehorn. **1969** *Commerce Jrl.* (TX) 29 May 13, [Advt:] Clothes brush—Slipper spoon—Reg. $1.00—Now 59¢. **1986** *DARE* File csWI, [Speaker from **NY:**]

Do you have a shoehorn? [Speaker from **WI:**] You mean a slipper spoon, a shoespoon.

slipperweed n   Also *slipper(s)*   [See quot 1911]   Cf **lady's slipper 2**

A **jewelweed 1** (here: either *Impatiens capensis* or *I. pallida*).

1830 Rafinesque *Med. Flora* 2.231, *Impatiens. . . Slippers. . .* Two sp. *I. fulva* [=*I. capensis*] and *pallida,* both in common use for jaundice and asthma, as a tea. **1876** Hobbs *Bot. Hdbk.* 107, Slippers,—Celandine, Wild,—*Impatiens pallida.* **1892** *Jrl. Amer. Folkl.* 5.93 **OH,** *Impatiens fulva.* . . Slipper-weed. . . Mansfield, O[hio]. **1911** *Century Dict. Suppl., Slipper-weed.* . . The pale touch-me-not or jewel-weed, *Impatiens aurea* [=*I. pallida*]; also the spotted touch-me-not, *I. biflora* [=*I. capensis*]. . . Referring to the shape of the flowers. **1940** Clute *Amer. Plant Names* 130, *I[mpatiens] pallida.* . . Slipper.

slippery bass n   Also *slippery*
=**tautog.**

2000 *DARE* File—Internet [NJ Fishing], Tautog (blackfish, slippery bass). . . Off of bulkheads—out by the old fish factory in Great Bay. **2001** *Ibid* **NJ** [Somethin' Fishy Fishing Site], Tautog. . . Common Names: blackfish, slippery, slippery bass.

slippery calf   See **slipper** n **5**

slippery cap   See **slippery jack 2**

slippery dick n

1 A **wrasse** (here: *Halichoeres bivittatus*).

[**1884** Goode *Fisheries U.S.* 1.274, Several of the Parrot-fishes occur on the Florida coast, notably . . *P[latyglossus] bivittatus* [=*Halichoeres b.*], known in Bermuda as "Slippery Dick," recorded by Jordan from Charleston market.] **1898** U.S. Natl. Museum *Bulletin* 47.1595, *Iridio bivittatus.* . . *Slippery Dick.* . . Body very slender, compressed; head small and pointed. **1933** John G. Shedd Aquarium *Guide* 145, The Slippery Dick is the commonest member of the genus on our shore. . . It . . is considered a boy's fish. **1954** McAtee *Suppl. to Nomina Abitera* [6], Doncella (*Iridio bivittatus*) Slippery Dick. **1983** *Audubon Field Guide N. Amer. Fishes* 650, The Slippery Dick is perhaps the most common wrasse around shallow water reefs. It is less fastidious about its habitat and food selection than are other wrasses.

2 A **cusk eel** (here: *Rissola marginata*).

1933 John G. Shedd Aquarium *Guide* 153, *Rissola marginata—Cusk Eel; Slippery Dick.* . . A resident of the Atlantic coast from New York southward. **1954** McAtee *Suppl. to Nomina Abitera* [6], Cusk Eel, (*Rissola marginata*).—Slippery Dick (i.e. penis).

slippery dumpling n   PaGer settlement area   Cf **potpie 1, slick** n **5**

A large noodle or flat dumpling; hence n *slippery potpie* a stew containing such noodles or dumplings; also the dumpling itself.

1957 *Salisbury Times* (MD) 17 Sept 26/1, [Advt:] Luncheon special . . Chicken & Slippery Dumplings. **1968** *DARE* (Qu. H45, *Dishes made with . . poultry that everybody around here would know, but that people in other places might not*) Inf **DE4,** Slippery dumplings—chicken with dumplings made with flour, shortening, rolled paper-thin, cut into squares about one and a half inch square; these are dropped into hot broth. **1971** *Frederick Post* (MD) 15 Oct sec A 10/4, Mt. Moriah Church Luncheon. Slippery Pot Pie & Sandwiches. **1977** Anderson *Grass Roots Cookbook* 48 **sePA,** "Potpie" in Pennsylvania Dutch country means big squares of home-made egg noodles used to plump up chicken stew (Chicken Potpie). There are all kinds of potpie—fluffy ones leavened with baking powder, tender ones shortened with lard and "slippery" ones, which are plain egg noodles. **1987** *DARE* File nMD, *Slippery pot-pie* [on the menu of an inn in Pennsylvania Dutch country was] said by waitress to be a popular item in that area. Take rich stewed chicken with rich broth. Drop in dumplings made of biscuit dough, rolled out to half inch thickness and cut into 3″ triangles. **1997** in 2001 *DARE* File—Internet MD, Crafts/flea market, homemade goodies, famous slippery pot pie and more. **2001** *Ibid* **PA,** Stop long enough to enjoy a little bit of Pennsylvania with a PA Dutch Dinner. Will include Chicken corn Soup, Slippery Pot Pie & dessert. **2001** *NADS Letters* **DE,** A common dish . . is "chicken and dumplings" but the dumplings were not a fluffy, doughy biscuit. Rather, they were what is called a slippery dumpling. It is a flat noodle about 3 inches or so across, cooked in chicken broth and served in a bowl with the thickened broth and pieces of cooked chicken. *Ibid* **sePA,** Slippery potpie. . . PA Dutch potpie, made with noodles and sauce. *Ibid* **csPA,** Slippery pot-pie is a very common dish made with homemade noodles, ham, potatoes, carrots and peas. **2002** *Ibid* **eWV,** "Slippery potpie." . . [includes] thick homemade noodles in either a ham or chicken gravy. . . The broth thickens up from noodles, and is very gravy-ish. It was usually served on a plate, not in bowls.

slippery elm n

1 also *slipper elm, slippery-leaf ~:* An elm (here: *Ulmus rubra*) native to much of the eastern two-thirds of the US; also the bark or wood of this elm. [From the extremely mucilaginous inner bark] Also called **Indian elm, moose ~, mountain ~ 2, piss ~, red ~ 1, rock ~ 3, rough ~, slick ~, sweet ~, water ~ d** Cf **elm A, elm flour**

1780 in 1916 Mereness *Travels* 640 **Ohio Valley,** Bear fat is preserved sweet and pure by putting in a bunch of the Slippery Elem bark into it when rendering. **1810** Michaux *Histoire des Arbres* 1.37 **NY, NJ,** Ulmus fulva. . . *Slipery* [sic] *elm,* nom secondaire dans les Etats de New York et de New-Jersey. [=Ulmus fulva. . . *Slipery elm,* secondary name in the states of New York and New Jersey]. **1824** Bigelow *Florula Bostoniensis* 108, The slippery elm is well known for the mucilaginous qualities of its inner bark. **1848** in 1870 Drake *Pioneer Life* 73 **KY,** Of the whole forest the red or slippery elm was the best [for livestock fodder]. **1907** *DN* 3.199 **seNH,** *Slippery ellum.* **1909** *DN* 3.371 **eAL, wGA,** *Slippery ellum.* **1935** Wolfe *Of Time* 414 **NC,** He preached . . slippery-ellum for decaying gums. **1936** Stuart *Head* 81 **KY,** He'll need a good tonic of wild-cherry bark, may apple, slipper-elm, yellow root and sassafras boiled together. **1950** *WELS* **WI** *(Different kinds of elm trees)* 20 Infs, Slippery elm; 3 Infs, Slippery ellum; 1 Inf, Slippery elm—used in throwing spitballs; 1 Inf, Slippery-elm bark tea—a home remedy for children, diseases especially of the intestinal tract; *(Kitchen herbs . . used in your neighborhood)* 1 Inf, Slippery-elm bark—cough syrup; *(Remedies for constipation)* 1 Inf, Slippery-elm bark. **1965–70** *DARE* (Qu. T11, *. . Kinds of elm trees*) 160 Infs, **widespread exc West,** Slippery elm; **AR42, IN19, NY73, NY75, PA231,** Slippery ellum; **AR56, GA77, IN9,** Slipper elm; **WI72,** Slippery-leaf elm; (Qu. I35, *. . Kitchen herbs . . grown and used in cooking around here*) Inf **CT2,** Slippery elm; (Qu. T13) Infs **GA65, PA95,** Slippery elm; (Qu. BB22, *. . Home remedies . . for constipation*) Infs **KS5, KY41,** Slippery-elm bark; **OH87,** Slippery-elm tea; (Qu. BB50a, *. . Favorite remedies . . for a cough*) Inf **MA58,** Slippery elm; **SD8,** Slippery-elm bark poultice; **MD20,** Slippery-elm bark, wild cherry bark, and sweet annie root; (Qu. BB50c, *Remedies for infections*) Infs **AR55, IN13, KY21, 34,** (Boiled) slippery-elm bark; **MD17, SD8,** Slippery-elm (bark) poultice; **SC46,** Slippery-elm bark tea. **1967–68** *DARE* Tape **IN3,** There was slippery elm ['ɛləm]. That would get right slick—kind of like an egg white—and they would put something bitter in them, like quinine or something they didn't want you to have to taste, so they'd wrap it up in slippery elm; **TX1,** [FW:] What do you do for ulcers? . . [Inf:] Well, wherever you can find a slippery elm ['ɛləm] tree, just get the . . bark off the root of the slippery elm. Scrape that rough part off and cut it up in little pieces and pour boiling water on it. Then drink the water off that; **SC46,** They used . . slippery-elm ['ɛləm] bark to make a tea to mop a sore outside of an infection. **1986** Pederson *LAGS Concordance,* 1 inf, **neAL,** Slippery elm poultices; 1 inf, **cwAR,** Slippery elm; 1 inf, **cnTN,** Slippery elm—medicinal; 1 inf, **cwTN,** Slippery elm bark—make poultices for infection.

2 also *California(n) slippery elm:* A **flannel bush** (here: *Fremontodendron californicum*). [From the resemblance of the bark to that of **1** above; see quots] **CA**

1884 Sargent *Forests of N. Amer.* 26, *Fremontia Californica. . . Slippery Elm.* The mucilaginous inner bark used locally in poultices. **1897** Parsons *Wild Flowers CA* 158, *Californian Slippery-elm. . .* No more beautiful sight is often seen than a slope covered with the wild slippery-elm in blossom. **1923** Davidson–Moxley *Flora S. CA* 234, *California Slippery Elm. . .* Common at middle elevations in all our interior mountains. **1969** *DARE* (Qu. T11, *. . Kinds of elm trees*) Infs **CA107, 137,** Slippery elm. **1980** Little *Audubon Guide N. Amer. Trees W. Region* 555, This species is called "California Slippery-elm" because of the mucilaginous bark, which is sometimes used as a poultice.

3 A **globe mallow 1** (here: *Sphaeralcea coccinea*).

1966 Barnes–Jensen *Dict. UT Slang* 39, *Slippery Elm . .* a local name for the False Red Mallow (*Sphaeralcea coccinea*).

slippery-elm poultice See **slippery elm 1**

slippery jack n

1 See **slippery jim.**

2 also *slippery cap, ~ jill:* A **mushroom B1** of the genus *Suillus,* esp *S. luteus.*

1958 Smith *Mushroom Hunter's Field Guide* 96, *Suillus luteus (Slippery Jack). . .* The cap is very slimy and dull dark reddish brown at first. . . Edible and popular. Wipe the slime from the cap when you collect it. **1980** Marteka *Mushrooms* 155, *Suillus granulatus. . .* Slippery jack. **1981** Lincoff *Audubon Field Guide Mushrooms* 589, *Slippery Jill—Suillus subluteus. . .* Slippery Jill is a species complex of slimy-capped boletes with a slimy veil and dotted stalk that grows under pine. **1987** McKnight–McKnight *Mushrooms* 113, *Slipperycaps:* Genus *Suillus. . .* Upper surface of cap *often sticky. Ibid* 116, *Lake's Slipperycap—Suillus lakei. . . Slippery Jack—Suillus luteus. Ibid* 117, Numerous species of *Suillus* with a slimy cap and ringed stalk are frequently misidentified as Slippery Jack.

slippery jim n Also *slippery jack, ~ pickle* **chiefly WI** See Map Cf **flabberjack**
A soft sweet pickle made from ripe cucumbers; rarely, a watermelon pickle.

1941 *Racine Jrl.–Times* (WI) 12 Sept 17/5, [Advt:] Genuine Homemade *Slippery Jims*—Full Qt. 39c. **1943** in 2004 *DARE* File [unidentified newspaper clipping dated 15 Oct] **neIL,** Slippery Jacks—Pare and cut in half yellow cucumbers. . . boil in weak vinegar. . . Make a syrup. . . cook this mixture about 10 minutes, then add cucumbers and simmer until transparent. **1949** *Sheboygan Press* (WI) 8 Sept 2/1, [Advt:] Home-Grown Pickles. . . For dill, sweet sours, slippery Jims. **1950** *Portland Sun. Telegram & Sun. Press Herald* (ME) 5 Nov mag sec 6/2, John liked the sweet cucumber pickles that he called slippery pickles. These were made out of the big fat cucumbers that were golden yellow. When they were made into pickle they were transparent. **1950–54** *WELS Suppl.,* 8 Infs, **WI,** Slippery jim(s); 1 Inf, **seWI,** We've always called those long pieces of ripe cucumber pickles slippery jims; 1 Inf, **ceWI,** Around Neenah, the pickle is called "slippery jim." . . They are made from ripe (yellow) cucumbers. Tough skin . . is all peeled off. The slices or chunks of flesh are boiled slowly in a vinegar, sugar and water syrup until tender and transparent; 1 Inf, **cWI,** We use slippery Jacks or slippery Jims for pickles made from ripe cucumbers which have been peeled. My mother in South Dakota also used this term, but not everyone here knows what one means; 1 Inf, **csWI,** Slippery jack is a pickle made from ripe cucumbers. The pieces . . are soaked in salt water and then boiled in a vinegar, sugar, and spice mixture until they become translucent and slippery; 1 Inf, **seWI,** My mother used to make a kind of pickle called "Slippery Jims." It was made from the white inner rind of watermelon and was, as I recall, rather sweet; 1 Inf, **seWI,** The slippery Jacks are what our mothers called "sempf" . . pickles. The reason I suggest the association is the use of "slippery pickles" for the same and that has come to my attention within the last fifteen years. **1965–70** *DARE* (Qu. H56, *Names for . . pickles*) Infs **WI11, 20, 24, 47, 49,** Slippery jims; **WI13,** Slippery jims—old word; **WI71,** Slippery jims—used to be; **WI76,** Slippery jims—with seeds taken out; two-inch-square pieces, sweet and sour vinegar and spices; **MI108,** Slippery jacks—from ripe cucumbers. **1984** *MJLF* 10.156 **cnWI,** Slippery Jims. A sweet cucumber pickle, consisting of peeled, ripe cucumbers. **2002** *DARE* File **Milwaukee WI,** Slippery jims are made from watermelon rinds. The pickling solution has sugar and vinegar in it. My mom first heard this in the fifties.

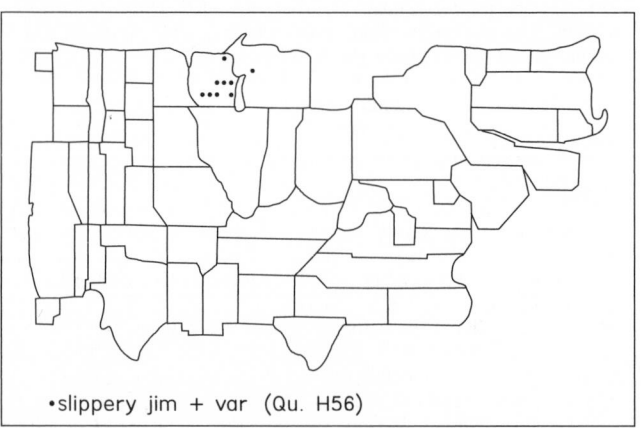

•slippery jim + var (Qu. H56)

slippery-leaf elm See **slippery elm 1**

slippery mullein n Cf **greasy bacon**
The moth **mullein** (*Verbascum blattaria*).

1897 *Jrl. Amer. Folkl.* 10.52 **seNY,** *Verbascum Blattaria,* . . slippery mullein (in distinction from fuzzy mullein, *V. Thapsus*), Southold, L[ong] I[sland].

slippery pickle   See **slippery jim**

slippery potpie   See **slippery dumpling**

slipperyroot n
=**comfrey.**
   1873 in 1976 Miller *Shaker Herbs* 160, *Comfrey.* . . Slippery Root. . . As an application to bruises, fresh wounds, sores and burns, and in nasal congestion and catarrh. **1940** Clute *Amer. Plant Names* 232, *Symphytum officinale.* Ass-ear, slippery-root.

slippery slide n   Cf **rutchie, sliding pond**
1 also *slippry glide, ~ jinny, ~ shute, ~ slide:* A slippery or precipitous surface, esp a muddy or icy surface adopted by children for sliding or sledding on.
   1874 *Scribner's Mth.* 8.199, It [=a brook] glassed along on the slippery slide,/ And shot away with an arrowy glide. **1888** *Overland Mth.* 11.19, Higher and higher we climbed, often . . winding along slippery slides above the torrent-bitten gorges. **1891** *Star & Sentinel* (Gettysburg PA) 17 Feb 4/3, Tobogganing down a slippery slide is the blissfullest kind of bliss. **1899** *Catholic World* 70.364, Have you ever experienced the hopeless, helpless sensation of walking on a slippery slide [=an icy, sloping sidewalk]? **1910** Burgess *Old Mother* 141, So Little Joe Otter found a nice smooth place on the bank, and Billy Mink and Jerry Muskrat brought mud and helped him pat it down smooth until they had the loveliest slippery slide in the world. **1916** Roosevelt *Book-Lover's Holidays* 48, The horse lost his footing on the slippery slide rock. **1926** *Athens Messenger* (OH) 26 Nov 3/1, The game was played on a slippery slide, a steady downpour of rain starting just before the end of the first half. **1950** *WELS Suppl.* **csWI,** Slippery slide—on ice; we usually wore them that way, sometimes carried water to make one. **1955** *Western Folkl.* 14.131, Is the term *"slippryjinny,"* for a mud slide, of occasional folk currency, or is it of local Lancaster County, Nebraska, creation? The institution it names is far from local. . . In addition to *mud slide* or *mud glide* may be heard *mud shute, slippry shute, mud glide, slippry glide, slippry slide* or the descriptive term may be *slide the slide.* [**1997** *Sports Illustr.* 8 Dec 118 **HI,** He didn't want the vonAppens or his teammates to leave the island without at least one trip down Slippery Slide, as locals call the falls.] **2000** *Hannibal Courier–Post* (MO) 5 Feb (Internet), *Slippery slide.* A lack of snow can't stop [them] . . from sledding. . . Pritchett kept snow on the hill by throwing water on it during the week.
2 A children's playground slide.
   1922 *Lincoln Sun. Star* (NE) 18 Jun 2/3, Not dangerously long nor too steep is the slippery slide. . . [T]wo or three are ever coming down, one is landing in a nice pile of sand, and a half a dozen others are ascending the ladder. **1940** *La Porte City Progress–Rev.* (IA) 20 June 1/6, Twenty Years Ago. . . A "slippery slide" which was placed on the school grounds . . was engaging the attention of the "youngest generation." **1950** *WELS Suppl.* **csWI,** Slide, also *slippery slide* (less frequent) (UW student, Madison native); **csWI,** *Slide* n.—24 H.S. pupils (Stoughton); *slippery slide* n.—1 H.S. boy (Stoughton); **csWI,** My children, who attend a school in Beaver Dam call what they slide down a slippery slide; **cwWI,** Slide—slipp'ry slide—used by all the school children here. **2000** *Contra Costa Times* (Walnut Creek CA) 5 Aug (Internet) **CA,** When I was 7, I was at the top of the slippery slide, waiting for Junior Swanson to take off. **2000** *DARE* File—Internet **FL,** Everytime they show little cuban alian [sic] they say he's out in the backyard playin' and then they show him on that yellow slippery slide!

slippery sole n   Also *slime sole*
A **flounder B** (here: *Microstomus pacificus*).   Also called **Dover sole**   Cf **sole** n[1] **2**
   1884 Goode *Fisheries U.S.* 1.188, The Slippery Sole—*Glyptocephalus pacificus* [=*Microstomus p.*] . . The whole body is excessively slimy when out of water, more so than in any other Flounder. **1898** U.S. Natl. Museum *Bulletin* 47.2655, *Microstomus pacificus.* . . Slippery Sole. . . This small flounder abounds in deep water about San Francisco. **1953** Roedel *Common Fishes CA* 64, *Microstomus pacificus.* . . Slippery sole, slime sole. **1973** Knight *Cook's Fish Guide* 391, Sole[5] . . slime—Dover [sole]; slippery [sole]—Dover [sole].

slippety-slop n   Also *slip-slop* [Echoic]   Cf **flip-flop 6**
A slipper or run-down shoe.

1859 (1968) Bartlett *Americanisms* 416, *Slip-slops.* Old shoes turned down at the heel. Southern. **1970** *DARE* (Qu. W21, *Soft shoes that people wear only inside the house*) Inf **SC**70, Slippety-slops—main kind.

slippey   See **slippy**

slipping, slippin's (over)   See **slippance**

slippry glide (or jinny, shute, slide)   See **slippery slide 2**

slippy adj   Also sp *slippey* [*EDD slippy* adj. 1 "In gen. dial. and colloq. use in Sc. Irel. Eng. and Aus."]   **chiefly PA; also Sth**   See Map   Cf **slicky**
Slippery.
   1868 *Blairsville Press* (PA) 17 July 2/2, The water was very deep and the bank slippy. **1875** McKeen *Theodora* 141 **VA,** It's tol'able slippey, is the worst on't. We had right smart o' rain yesterday. **1883** *Century Illustr. Mag.* 26.117 **Boston MA,** I don't believe in any thick'nin' myself; but if you *must* have it, let it be cracker crumbs: flour makes it so kind of slippy. **1900** *Atlantic Mth.* 86.814 **nNY,** The gravel was worn pretty thin raound that curve by the Pine Tree, an' 't wuz slippy as smooth glass. **1900** *Daily IA State Press* (IA City) 29 Sept [3]/1 (newspaperarchive.com), The slippy ground made playing hard. **1931** *AmSp* 7.20 **swPA,** Slippey. Slippery. "The walks are slippey to-day." **1964** *Ferhoodled Engl.* [6] [PaGer], This hands-in-the-pocket weather contraries me and it's slippy (icy) out there yet. **1965–70** *DARE* (Qu. N22, *When a road that is surfaced with smooth pavement gets wet so that cars slip or skid on it . . it's _____*) Infs **GA**92, **LA**8, **PA**7, 10, 29, 136, 154, 175, **SC**11, 26, 57, Slippy. **1972** *PADS* 58.24 **cwAL,** *The road is slippery. Slippery* . . and *slick* . . are most frequent. Three Negro informants gave *slippy.* . . *Slicky* and *wet* also occur. **1982** *Barrick Coll.* **csPA,** Slippy—slippery common. **1982** McCool *Sam McCool's Pittsburghese* 32 **PA,** *Slippy:* slippery. "Watch your step, the sidewalk's slippy." **1987** Dillard *Amer. Childhood* 111 **cwPA,** We ourselves used some pure Pittsburghisms. . . We said "slippy"—the sidewalks are "slippy." **1998** *DARE* File **cwPA,** I now live in Indiana, PA, . . where some native speakers . . describe some wet roads as "slippy." **2001** *Ibid* **sOH,** 'Slippy' . . [is] still used around here.

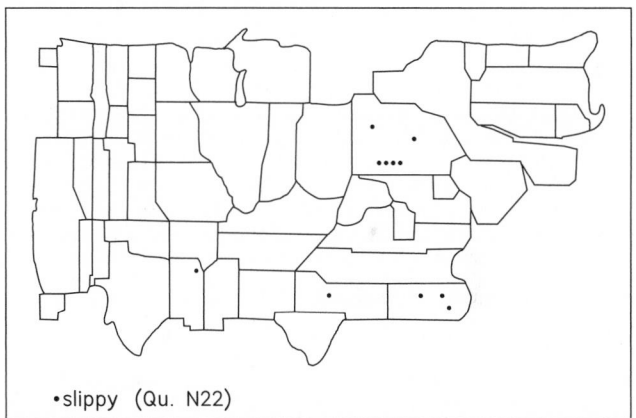

•slippy (Qu. N22)

slips exclam   Also *slips over* [*EDD* (at *slip* sb. 14) "pl. . . A cry which allows the player to shoot again, when the marble has slipped in his first attempt."]
=**slippance.**
   1934 *AmSp* 9.75 **ND,** *Slips.* Cried when one's marble slips in shooting. It permits him to shoot again. **1958** *Resp. to PADS 29,* Here are a few more marble terms: Slips over. Usually called by very small boys when the taw would slip out of hand when shooting. **1962** *PADS* 37.2 **cKS,** *Slips.* **c1970** Wiersma *Marbles Terms* **seMI** (as of c1940), *Slips*—you called slips on a miss [sic] thrown marble. If you called slips you got another chance to shoot.

slip scoop, slip scrape(r)   See **slip** n[2] **2**

slipseed   See **slipstone**

slip shovel   See **slip** n[2] **2**

slip-shuck v, hence vbl n *slip-shucking*   **chiefly Sth, S Midl**
1 To pick (an ear of corn) in such a way that the outer leaves of the husk remain on the stalk.   Cf **slip-shuck** n
   1850 U.S. Patent Office *Annual Rept. for 1849: Ag.* 155 **MS,** A barrel of corn must be closely slip-shucked to average . . a bushel of shelled

corn. **1854** Wailes *Rept. on Ag. & Geol. MS* 185, In gathering corn in the field, it is *slip-shucked . . ;* that is, the footstalk is broken off within the shuck, so as to leave the outer coarse and weathered folds attached to the stalk, the ear remaining enveloped in two-thirds of the inner sound and softer folds or layers. **1877** *Atlantic Mth.* 39.179 **SC,** Cotton was picked from the fields at night, and corn "slip-shucked." Gardens and orchards were stripped, and water-melons actually became a rarity on white men's tables. **1903** *DN* 2.330 **seMO,** *Slip-shuck. . .* To remove the outer husk only in husking corn. In gathering from the standing stalks (as is common in the West and South) it is usual to break off the ears with the inner husk, leaving the outer husk on the stalk. **1937** Heyward *Madagascar* 114 **sSC coast,** It would greatly please him to see the gang at work and the corn, slip-shucked, piling up between the rows. **1938** *AmSp* 13.237 **IA,** *Slip-shucking. . .* It is an expression frequently used by older farmers in Iowa, and it means to partly break and partly snap the ears of corn. **1970** *DARE* File **KY,** *Slip-shuck. . .* to pull the entire shuck off in a single motion instead of peeling it by bit. **1986** Pederson *LAGS Concordance (Tassel)* 1 inf, **ceTN,** Slip-shuck it—removing shuck by itself.

2 See quot.

1947 Croy *Corn Country* 223 **IA,** A man might bring in two hundred bushels of corn in a day but it would be slip-shucking. "Slip-shucking" means taking the big ears and letting the nubbins look after themselves; also not "cleaning" the corn. In other words, going into a field and grabbing the gravy.

3 also *slip-chuck;* Fig: to elude, deceive. [Cf quot 1877 at **1** above]

1970 *DARE* File **KY,** *Slip-shuck. . .* To cheat, trick, pull a fast one on somebody. **1979** Carpenter *Walton War* 173 **sAppalachians,** "We slip-shucked the crowd and he axed me to take the night with him." Meaning they slipped out of the crowd and one asked the other to spend the night with him. **1990** Merriman *Midnight Moonshine* 104 **TN** (as of c1930s–60s), How could Denny just disappear? I told him, "You were slipped [sic] chucked (given the slip)."

slip-shuck n [slip-shuck v]
The inner leaves of a corn husk—used esp in phrr *in (the) slip-shuck.*

1841 (1842) Holmes *S. Farmer & Market Gardener* 55 **SC,** If you intend keeping your corn any length of time, let it be harvested in the slip shuck. **1856** (1857) *Cincinnatus* 1.346, His corn is put up in the shuck, the whole shuck—no slip-shuck business with him. **1863** in 1887 U.S. War Dept. *War of Rebellion* 1st ser 17.2.830, We have . . a considerable quantity of corn in slip-shuck and on the ear. **1876** Dennett *Louisiana* 162, 8 bbls corn in slip-shuck. **1969** *DARE* Tape **GA**77, There was a corn with a slip-shuck and a husk shuck. The husk shuck generally stayed on the stalk and then the slip-shuck would come out of the husk. . . He'd save the best shucks of that type for our sausage.

slip-shucking See **slip-shuck** v

slip-slop See **slippety-slop**

slips over See **slips**

slipstone n Also *slipseed* **GA, SC**
=**freestone 2.**

1970 *DARE* (Qu. I51, *The kind of a peach where the hard center is loose*) Inf **SC**70, Slipstone. **c1970** Pederson *Dial. Surv. Rural GA* **seGA** (*A peach whose meat easily separates from the seed*) 1 inf, Slip seed; 1 inf, Slip stone. **1986** Pederson *LAGS Concordance,* 1 inf, **ceGA,** Slip seed.

slip the bridle v phr **esp Sth**
Fig: to put restraint aside; to go astray; to abscond.

1843 *Ladies' Repository* 3.150 **OH,** Amongst the guests was a young gentleman of Quaker parentage and training, who, having "slipped the bridle" of home discipline . . , had been recently converted among the Methodists. **1880** Hood *Advance & Retreat* 37, I was in conference . . when the Fifth Texas . . *slipped the bridle* and rushed forward, breaking loose from its brigade. **1912** Green *VA Folk-Speech* 393, *Slip. . .* A woman who has gone astray in her wifely duties, is said: "To have slipped the bridle." A horse tied by the briddle [sic] slips it off his head, and runs loose. **1966** *DARE* Tape **OK**29, He [=an oil worker] slipped the bridle . . he took off and quit, that's slippin' the bridle. **1984** Wilder *You All Spoken Here* 69 **Sth,** *Slipped the bridle:* Absconded.

slish(e) See **slice**

slithery adj [Cf *EDD slither* v. 3 "to do anything imperfectly or carelessly"]

1936 *AmSp* 11.191 **seWY,** *Slithery.* Sloppy, careless, as in spilling water on the floor. 'Don't be so slithery when you bring the water in.'

sliver n, v Pronc-spp *slive-er, slyver*

A Forms. Note: Brit pronouncing dictionaries listed only ['slaɪvə(r)] until late in the 19th cent.

1880 [see **B1** below]. **1909** [see **B1** below]. **1916** [see **B1** below]. **1936** *Hench Coll.* **VA,** Heard orally with the *i* pronounced as in *alive* or *drive.* Aug. 20, 1936, The Farm. Mr. Michie asked some one if he would have a sliver of ham. Immediately others said they'd never heard that pronunciation. They pronounced the *i* as in the verb *live* or *give.* **1951** [see **B2** below]. **1982** [see **B1** below].

B Senses.

1 A slice cut from the side of a fish for use at the table or as bait; to cut such a piece; hence vbl n *slivering;* ppl adj *slivered.* **coastal NEng**

1850 Beecher *Domestic Receipt Book* 56, Take thin slivers of codfish, lay them on hot coals, and when a yellowish brown, set them on the table. **1869** ME Laws Statutes *Acts & Resolves* 24 *(DAE),* Any person who shall cast or deposit . . any pumice, scraps or other offal arising from the making of oil or slivers for bait . . shall pay a fine. **1875** *Atlantic Mth.* 36.325 **coastal ME,** We soon found out what "slivering" meant, by seeing him take them [=porgies] by the head and cut a slice from first one side and then the other. **1880** Goode *Hist. Menhaden* 142 **coastal ME,** Fresh "slivers" are preferred to those which have been salted. *Ibid* 147, The slivers (pronounced *slyvers*) are salted and packed in barrels. **1893** *Harper's New Mth. Mag.* 87.443 **coastal NEng,** Now that he had tolled his hearers to him, as they toll up mackerel with slivered herring, he made ready to land them. **1916** Macy–Hussey *Nantucket Scrap Basket* 165, "Sliver"—(pronounced with a long "i")—Ask your city fish man to sliver a flounder, a plaice fish or a scup for you, and there's one chance in ten, if he's not an old fisherman himself, that he will know what you mean; yet the dictionary defines it exactly: "to cut each side of a fish away in one piece from the head to the tail,["] which is the only proper way to clean either of the fish mentioned, as every Nantucketer knows. **1982** *DARE* File **coastal ME,** "Slivers" is the universal term for fillet, pronounced *slyvers.* **1988** Nickerson *Days to Remember* 74 **Cape Cod MA** (as of c1915), There were various other methods used for the fresh fish market, such as "slivering" (filleting).

2 The sweet, pulpy inner bark usu of pine, esp as stripped off and eaten in the spring. [*EDD sliver* sb.¹, v.¹ 6 "To . . strip bark from a tree"] **NEng**

1868 Brackett *Farm Talk* 105 **ME,** You know the pine 'sliver' that boys like so well in the spring; well, that is the sap or wood-making substance just returning down the outside of the tree. *Ibid,* The sap passes up through the scion to the bud or leaf, and then back down, and if the sliver or bark is nicely joined to that of the stock, the sap continues its course. **1878** Shillaber *Ike Partington* 224 **MA,** This was the "sliver" season, when the sap in the pine-trees was running up from the roots, and the bark next the wood was a delicious sweet pulp, which the boys knew by instinct how to extract. This was done by cutting away an oblong section of the bark, and, stripping it up, the coveted delicacy was left exposed to the knife. The edge of the knife, slipped up the surface of the wood without cutting it, released a thin ribbon of the tender prize, and it was devoured with as much gusto as if it had been on the bill of fare at an alderman's feast,—perhaps more. **1912** *Boston Herald* (MA) 2 Sept 6 **ME,** "Sliver" in Maine. . . Seventy years ago in Maine, we boys used the word (with the long i) to describe the juicy inner bark of a pine tree. We used to climb the trees at the right time of the year with our jack-knives to get at the toothsome morsels. **1951** Graham *My Window* 46 **ME,** Ever eat slive-ers from the white pine? New bark jest formin' next to the wood. Git it in the springtime; good fer ye too.

sliver cat n **esp WI** Cf **splinter cat,** *DS* CC17
A large splinter on a stump that howls in the wind, or a contrivance that makes a similar sound, facetiously explained as the cry of an imaginary animal; the animal itself.

1950 *WELS* (Imaginary wild animals that people tell stories about) 1 Inf, **cWI,** Sliver cat. **1956** Sorden–Ebert *Logger's Words* 33 **Gt Lakes,** *Sliver-cat,* Splinters on stumps standing up two to four feet which whistle in the winter wind. **1969** Sorden *Lumberjack Lingo* 114 **cnWI,** *Sliver cat. . .* A splinter, usually about a yard long, attached to a pole by a piece of leather. The lumberjacks twirled this splinter by swinging the pole rapidly to make a howling, screaming sound that frightened the greenhorns. Often it was used while icing roads at night. Commonly used in camps around Rhinelander, Wisconsin.

slivered, slivering vbl n   See **sliver B1**

slobberchops n   [*OED2* 1667 →]
A messy eater.

· **1857** Holland *Bay-path* 192 **MA** (as of c1650), What do you mean, you little slobber-chops? **1903** *DN* 2.300 **Cape Cod MA** (as of a1857), *Slobber-chops.* . . A child that spills his food about his plate, used also of a calf or dog. **1911** *DN* 3.547 **NE**, *Slobberchops.* . . Epithet applied to a child, or an animal, that eats slobberingly. "What a slobberchops you are."

slobberhannes n   Also *slobberhan(te)s*   [Ger *Schlabberhannes* messy person or animal]   **esp WI**
1 A messy person or creature, esp a messy eater.

1989 *DARE* File **neWI** (as of c1960), A *slobberhannes,* when I was growing up, was a person who was a mess-maker, especially at the dinner table. If a child spilled milk or had an assortment of dribbles on his clothes, face or hands, he was called a *slobberhannes.* My father frequently called our spaniel a *slobberhannes,* either because she would play or roll in something and require a bath or because of the mess she made when she ate and drank. **2002** *Ibid* **seWI** (as of c1960), "Don't be such a slobberhannes," my German-American grandmother would say when we kids were messy. This usually came up around mealtimes. *Ibid* **nwWI,** My dad. . . [has] heard and used the phrase "slobber Hans" for as long as he remembers—so that would likely be as long ago as the late 1920s or thereabouts. . . He said yesterday that he'd used the phrase that very day to refer to how someone treated the space around their computer. **2003** *NADS Letters* **Chicago IL,** I heard my grandparents, who were of Danish descent, use slobberhans to refer to a sloppy person. Thay [sic] have been gone many years now, but my mother occasionally will use this term for a slob. They settled in Chicago when they immigrated here, and my family all continues to reside in the Chicago area. *Ibid* **nwMO,** Slobberhaunus [sic], as described on your website. . . my step father uses this word to describe a messy person or something soggy or slimy. He is of german descent. He also named his cat "Slobberhaunus". . . His family has resided in the Kansas City and St. Joeseph [sic], Missouri area for several generations and as far as I know, he's the only one in the family who really uses the term. **2003** [see **2** below]. **2004** *DARE* File **cKS,** My mother (second US generation and born in 1909) spoke no English until she entered school. All of my aunts and uncles spoke Low German fluently and carried on conversations in it during family gatherings, however, to my knowledge not one single cousin can speak a single word of it although we had all been called a slobberhannes and knew exactly what it meant. **2009** *Ibid* **MN** (as of c1970), My mother. . . would say "wash up for supper slobberhantes" or "your room needs cleaning slobberhantes". I grew up in Minnesota in the early '70's, but my mother was from Hoboken, NJ, and most certainly learned the term from her mother who was very Irish.

2 A bib.
2003 *DARE* File **csWI** (as of 1930s), *Slobberhans*—a child who doesn't always get the food from the spoon to his mouth. Also used for a bib. "You'll need a ['slɑbɚˌhəns] if you're going to eat all that soup."

slobgollion   See **slumgullion 1**

slocum-pokum   See **slowcome**

‡**slodgewise** adj   [Var of **slaunchwise**]
1967 *DARE* (Qu. KK70, *Something that has got out of proper shape: "That house is all _____."*) Inf **NE6,** Slodgewise ['slɑʤˌwaɪz].

sloe n
1 A **wild plum 1,** usu *Prunus alleghaniensis, P. americana,* or *P. umbellata;* also the fruit.   [*OED2* c725 → for *Prunus spinosa*]   **chiefly Sth**
1835 Irving *Crayon Misc.* 255, [From *A Tour on the Prairies:*] Among the thickets in the valleys, we met with sloes and persimmon. **1854** Wailes *Rept. on Ag. & Geol. MS* 355, Among the several species of our wild plums, . . I notice a small blue species, resembling in color the damson. It . . is sometimes called "the Sloe." **1884** Sargent *Forests of N. Amer.* 67, *Prunus umbellata.* . . Sloe. Black Sloe. South Carolina, south . . to . . Florida, and through central Alabama to eastern Mississippi. . . The black or red pleasantly acid fruit used as a preserve. **1897** Sudworth *Arborescent Flora* 237, *Prunus americana.* . . Sloe (Fla.) *Ibid* 238, *Prunus umbellata.* . . Black Sloe (S.C., Ga., Ala., Miss.) **1910** Graves *Flowering Plants* 244 **CT,** *Prunus alleghaniensis.* . . Alleghany

or Mountain Plum. Sloe. Rare. **1933** Small *Manual SE Flora* 648, *P[runus] umbellata.* . . Sloe. Black-sloe. Hog-plum. . . Fla. to La. and S.C. **1967–70** *DARE* (Qu. I46, . . *Kinds of fruits that grow wild around here*) Inf **AR52,** Sloes [slouz]; **LA12,** Sloes—people don't eat them; **VA35,** Sloes [slouz]—make good jelly; **VA48,** Sloes [slouz]—similar to grape; (Qu. T16, . . *Kinds of trees . . 'special'*) Inf **TX33,** Sloe. **1980** Little *Audubon Guide N. Amer. Trees E. Region* 492, "Alleghany Sloe"—"Sloe Plum"—*Prunus alleghaniensis.* . . An uncommon, thicket-forming shrub or small tree. *Ibid* 507, "Hog Plum"—"Black Sloe"—*Prunus umbellata.* **1987** Kindscher *Edible Wild Plants* 170, *Common Names*—Wild plum, . . hog plum, and sloe. . . *Prunus americana.*

2 also *sloe-leaved viburnum:* A **black haw 1** (here: *Viburnum prunifolium*).
1829 Eaton *Botany* 439, *Viburnum.* . . *prunifolium,* (black haw, sloe . .) leaves round-obovate and oval. **1847** Wood *Class-Book* 303, *V[iburnum] prunifolium.* . . Sloe. . . Flowers white, succeeded by oval, blackish berries which are sweet and eatable. **1897** Sudworth *Arborescent Flora* 339 **TN,** *Viburnum prunifolium.* . . Sloe. **1930** Sievers *Amer. Med. Plants* 12, *Viburnum prunifolium.* . . Sloe, sloe-leaved viburnum. . . Found in greatest abundance in the South. . . The fruit, which is sweet and edible, is about half an inch long, bluish black, covered with a bloom, and ripens in early autumn. **1971** Krochmal *Appalachia Med. Plants* 272, *Viburnum prunifolium.* . . Sloe, sloe-leaved viburnum. . . In Appalachia, a root tea is used as a tonic.

3 also *sloeberry:* A plant of the genus *Sideroxylon.*   Cf **black haw 2**
1926 *Torreya* 26.6 **GA,** *Bumelia* [=*Sideroxylon*] spp.—Sloe, black sloe, Sapelo I[slan]d, Ga. **1942** *Torreya* 42.164 **GA,** *Bumelia tenax* [=*Sideroxylon t.*] . . Sloe berry, coastal Georgia.

sloe-leaved viburnum   See **sloe 2**

slommack n   Also *slamakin, slummock*   [Cf *EDD* slammock, slammocking, slammocky in same senses]
A slovenly person; hence adjs *slommacky, sloomiky* untidy, slovenly; v phr *slommack around* to go about in a shambling way.
1834 *Life Andrew Jackson* 69, She was a rale slamakin, brawney, and look'd for all the world as if she cou'd swallow a nigger if his hed was butter'd and his ears pin'd back. **1848** Bartlett *Americanisms* 310, *Slommack.* A slattern. **1892** *KS Univ. Qrly.* 1.98 **KS,** *Sloomiky:* not neat. **1895** *DN* 1.383 **NJ,** *Slummock:* a dirty, untidy woman. **1930** Shoemaker *1300 Words* 55 **cPA Mts** (as of c1900), *Slommack*—A slatternly girl. **1951** West *Witch Diggers* 307 **IN,** And she herself a slommacky woman sitting here in mid-afternoon in her nightgown. **1986** Pederson *LAGS Concordance,* 1 inf, **cnAR,** Just slommack around—of clumsy teenage boys.

slomp(y)   See **slump 2**

slonching adj   Cf **slaunch, slaunchwise**
1936 *AmSp* 11.369 **nLA,** *Slonching.* . . Tapering; sloping; apparently a corruption of 'slanting;' as, 'Whittle me a stick slonching.'

slonchways, slonchwise   See **slaunchwise**

sloo   See **slough** n¹

sloodge   See **sloosh** n²

sloogie   See **saluggi**

sloomiky   See **slommack**

sloop n, v¹   Cf **dray** n 1, **dray** v
In logging: a sled used for hauling logs; to haul (logs) on a sled.
[**1890** *Century Dict.* **Canada,** *Sloop².* . . In *lumbering,* a strong crutch of hard wood, with a strong bar across the limbs, used for drawing timber out of a swamp or inaccessible place. . . To draw (logs of timber) on a sloop.] **1905** U.S. Forest Serv. *Bulletin* 61.48 **Nth,** *Sloop.* . . See Dray. *Sloop logs, to.* To haul logs down steep slopes on a dray or sloop equipped with a tongue. [*Ibid* 36, *Dray.* . . A single sled used in dragging logs. One end of the log rests upon the sled.]

sloop v²   [Perh echoic or var of *slurp,* but cf also *slup*]   Cf **sloosh** n²
To make a sucking noise when eating or drinking.
1966–67 *DARE* (Qu. H11b, *If he makes a noise with his food, he*

_____) Inf **NV**1, Sloop; **AL**1, Eats like a pig; slooping ['slupɪn] it down; **CA**32, Sloops.

sloosh n¹, v |sluš| [Engl, Scots dial; cf *SND sloosh* n. 2 "A dash of water, a splashing," v. "To splash or swill with water"] Cf **sloosh-hole**

See quots.

1913 *DN* 4.44, *Sloosh*, [sluʃ]. . . Same as *slish*. Perhaps from *sluice* and *slush, slosh*. [*Ibid, Slish*. . . To rinse by throwing water upon. "Slish the side of the sink."] **1969** *DARE* (Qu. DD17, *To drink a great deal, or too fast: "He doesn't just drink, he* _____") Inf **GA**77, Just slooshes it down. **1981** Pederson *LAGS Basic Materials (Heavy rain)* 1 inf, **cnAL**, [slʉuʃ]; 1 inf, **cnAR**, Come a [slʉuʃ] of rain.

sloosh n² Usu |sluš|; also |sluʃ| Pronc-spp *sloodge, slush* [Cf *EDD slush* sb. 5 "An indefinite quantity of anything."] An indefinitely large number.

1952 Brown *NC Folkl.* 1.592, *Sloosh* [sluʃ]. . . A great many. "I got a big sloosh of chickens this spring."—Central and east. **1964** Will *Hist. Okeechobee* 261 **FL**, Ritta Island . . had a plumb sloosh of snakes including moccasins of ample size. *Ibid* 288, A ceremony attended by a plumb slush of notables. **1968** *DARE* File **AL**, Sloodges ['sluǰɪz]—great numbers. People could descend upon one in sloodges.

sloosh-hole n [Cf *SND slush* n. 1 "A wet marshy place, a puddle, quagmire . . ; thin muddy liquid"] Cf **sloosh** n¹, v See quot.

1941 O'Donnell *Great Big Doorstep* 30 **sLA**, She found Paul and Gussie playing in a dome-shaped shelter some older boys had made of driftwood and willow branches. Her brothers had dug a sloosh-hole in the mud floor. *Ibid* 35, Evvie led her brothers along the riverbank, and for a long while they played in the shelter made of sticks and bushes. Evvie rolled up her skirt and put her legs into the sloosh-hole with theirs. The mud . . was the color of milk chocolate coating their legs.

slop n¹ [*OED2 slop* sb.¹ 2.a c1386 →; *EDD slop* sb.² 1 "A loose outer garment, *gen.* of linen, worn by workmen"] Cf **blickey** n², **rowdy**

A work jacket.

1936 *AmSp* 11.191 **seWY**, *Slop*. Any loose coat or jacket of coarse material worn while doing heavy work outside. 'Take your slop, because it is cold and may rain.'

slop n² *somewhat old-fash; derog*

A slovenly or disreputable person, esp a woman—often in comb *old slop.*

1930 Shoemaker *1300 Words* 43 **cPA Mts** (as of c1900), *Old slop*—A slatternly, dirty elderly woman. **1965–70** *DARE* (Qu. HH36, *A careless, slovenly woman: "She's just an old* _____.") 112 Infs, **widespread,** Slop [Of all Infs responding to the question, 63% were old; of those giving this response, 76% were old.]; (Qu. W41, . . *Expressions . . for someone whose clothes never look right or who always dresses carelessly*) 11 Infs, **scattered,** Slop; **CA**134, Old slop; **MI**70, Boy, is she a slop; (Qu. X50, *Names or nicknames for a person who is very fat*) Infs **GA**13, **KY**77, Slop; **MD**9, Fat slop; (Qu. DD12, . . *A person who drinks steadily or a great deal*) Inf **VT**12, Old slop; (Qu. DD17, *To drink a great deal, or too fast: "He doesn't just drink, he* _____.") Inf **CA**168, He's a slop—he don't know when to stop; (Qu. HH34, . . *A woman*) Inf **NC**82, Old slop. **1966** Goldstein-Byington *Two Penny Ballads* 154 **PA**, When you drop a dishrag a slop (sloppy person) is coming.

slop v [Prob infl by *slap together*] **esp Nth, N Midl** See Map Cf **slouch** v

Usu with adv, esp *together, up*: To assemble, fix, or clean (something) in a hasty, slipshod way; to do a poor job (over or through something); hence ppl adjs *slopped-together, ~-up* carelessly done.

1965–70 *DARE* (Qu. KK63, *To do a clumsy or hurried job of repairing something: "It will never last—he just* _____.") Infs **CT**42, **OH**31, Slopped it; **IN**45, Slopped it through; **NJ**10, Slopped it through; **GA**19, **IN**60, **MN**6, **NJ**19, **PA**29, 193, **SD**2, **WI**44, Slopped it together; **TX**35, Slopped through it; **NY**119, Did a slopped-up job; (Qu. W29, . . *Expressions . . for things that are sewn carelessly . . "They're* _____.") Infs **MN**6, **NE**11, **PA**105, 123, **WI**50, Slopped together; **OH**31, Slopped up; (Qu. KK49, *When you don't have the time or*

ambition to do something thoroughly: "I'm not going to give the place a real cleaning, I'll just _____.") Inf **NY**119, Do a slopped-up job; **WY**3, Slop it over; **UT**3, Slop over it. **2002** *DARE* File—Internet **Los Angeles CA**, [Book review:] He . . allowed his name to be put on something that reeks of a slopped together pastepot job.

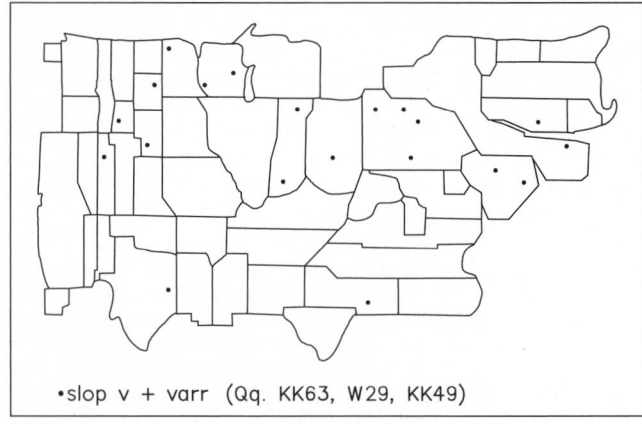

•slop v + varr (Qq. KK63, W29, KK49)

slop back v phr [*slop* spent mash]

In distilling: to make (mash) using the spent mash from a previous distilling; hence vbl n *slopping back* reusing mash in this way.

[**1942** Von Loesecke *Outlines Food Tech.* 411, A mash is made by adding water to molasses until it contains about 25 to 30 per cent sugar. A certain amount of . . spent mash (called "slopping back") is also added.] **1963** Carson *Social Hist. Bourbon* 46, The sour mash method prevails today. It involves scalding the meal with the thin, spent beer left over from a run. The procedure is called, somewhat inelegantly, "slopping back." **1974** Dabney *Mountain Spirits* xxv **sAppalachians**, *Slopping Back:* Using hot pot-tails from a run to "start" a new batch of mash, yielding sour mash whiskey. **1985** Wilkinson *Moonshine* 22 **neNC**, Bootleggers add more sugar and meal and malt and water (the original yeast is still active), and this is called slopping back. The initial run makes sweet-mash whiskey. Subsequent runs, slopped back, are sour mash. **2002** *DARE* File—Internet, First batch in will ferment 5–7 days and then form a cap. If you "slop-back" that mash it will work off in 3 days after the yeast is growing.

slop bucket n

1 also *slop barrel, ~ can, ~ pail;* for addit varr see quots: A container for food waste intended as animal feed; a garbage can. **widespread, but less freq NEast, Gt Lakes** See Map Cf **swill pail 1**

1831 Peck *Guide for Emigrants* 172 **IL**, With . . a dairy and slop barrel . . pork may be raised from the sow. **1834** *Man* (NY NY) 2.343/3 **NYC**, A deluge of—greasy and nauseous filth from the kitchen slop pail! **1835** *NY Mirror* 12.373, As for Cesar [=a dog] and Pompey [=a pig], they had so far forgotten old enmities and niceties, as to eat out of the same slop-bucket. **1864** *OH Med. & Surgical Jrl.* 16.109 **cOH**, Mary Freet had thrown the mush and milk into the slop bucket. **1899** *Freeborn Co. Std.* (Albert Lea MN) 12 July [4]/4 (newspaperarchive.com), *City Scavenger is Appointed. . . His* . . compensation per load, and for slop cans not to exceed a barrel, was established at 35 cents. **1946** *PADS* 5.38 **VA**, *Slop bucket:* Garbage pail; common everywhere. **1965–70** *DARE* (Qu. F24, *The container for kitchen parings and scraps—inside the kitchen*) 104 Infs, **widespread, but less freq NEast, Gt Lakes,** Slop pail; 28 Infs, **scattered,** Slop bucket; **FL**49, **GA**13, 88, **MT**5, **SC**11, **TN**44, Slop can; [**HI**1, Slop man—years ago;] **LA**12, Slop pot; (Qu. F25, *The container for kitchen parings and scraps—out of doors*) 40 Infs, **chiefly Sth, S Midl,** Slop bucket; **AR**26, **IL**76, **MD**14, **MN**23, **SC**9, Slop barrel; **CA**101, **FL**51, **GA**13, **HI**6, **KY**77, **LA**6, Slop can; **FL**6, **KY**74, **NC**50, **NV**2, Slop pail; (Qu. K59, *What do pigs eat out of?*) Inf **CA**117, Slop bucket; **LA**18, Slop cans; **NV**1, Slop jar; **NY**142, Slop pail; [**MD**24, Slop troft; **OH**31, Slop trough;] **SC**43, Slop tub. **1968** *AmSp* 43.269, In the eastern United States there are two regional terms for the container for garbage or for the liquid food given to pigs. The Northern term is *swill pail;* the term found in the Midland and Southern areas is *slop bucket.* **1983** *MJLF* 9.1.56 **ceKY** (as of 1956), *Slop bucket* . . a bucket for carrying scraps to the hogs. **1989** Pederson *LAGS Tech. Index* 67 **Gulf Region** (*Slop* *bucket*) 531 infs, Slop bucket; 34 infs, Slop can; 20 infs, Slop pail; 10 infs, Slop jar; 3 infs, Slop barrel; [1 inf, Slop cart;] 1 inf, Slop pan.

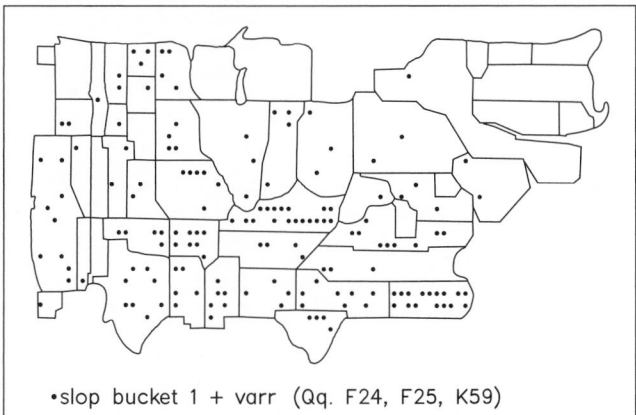

•slop bucket 1 + varr (Qq. F24, F25, K59)

2 See **slop jar 1.**
3 A **freshwater clam** (here: *Anodonta grandis*).

1982 U.S. Fish & Wildlife Serv. *Fresh-Water Mussels* [Wall chart], *Giant Floater*. Slop Bucket. Historically widespread, common to abundant; now somewhat less so. **1992** Cummings–Mayer *Field Guide Freshwater Mussels MW* 78, *Pyganodon (=Anodonta) grandis*. . . Floater, . . hogshell, slopbucket. . . Shell extremely variable but usually large, somewhat elliptical or elongate, and inflated. . . Widespread and common.

slop can See **slop bucket 1**

slope n

An **earmark** n made by cutting the tip of the ear off at an angle—often in combs *overslope, underslope*.   Cf **over C, under**

1662 in 1887 East Hampton NY *Records* 1.193, Joseph ffoster marked a horse coult of his owne haveinge . . a crop on the nere eare and a slope on the hinderpart of the same. **1751** in 1985 Lederer *Colonial Amer. Engl.* 214 **RI**, The Ear mark is two Slopes one on each Ear. **1774** in 2009 *DARE* File—Internet **SC**, Six Head to my Son Obadiah Osteen Marked with . . an under Slope on the Right Branded OO. **1792** in 1987 Fink *Barns* 346 **cwNY**, [Record of sheep earmarks:] John Salyer—Mark—A slope off the Under side of both ears. **1858** in 2009 *DARE* File—Internet **TX**, A red ox, points of his horns sawed off marked crop and underbit on the right ear, and upper slope off the left. **1875** *Atlanta Constitution* (GA) 8 June 3/6, White and yellow pided *cow*, with . . under slope in the right [ear]. **1906** *DN* 3.157 **nwAR**, *Slope*. . . A diagonal cut extending from the tip to about the middle of one side of an animal's ear. A *right slope* is taken from the right ear, a *left slope* from the left ear. An *upper* (*right* or *left*) *slope* is taken from the upper part of the ear, a *lower* (*right* or *left*) *slope* from the lower part. **1920** Hunter *Trail Drivers TX* 298, Some of the terms used in marking are . . "over slope," "under slope," etc. **1956** Gipson *Old Yeller* 94 **TX**, Then, from the under side of his [=a pig's] left ear, I slashed off a long strip that ran clear to the point. This is what we called an underslope. **1967** *DARE* (Qu. K18) Inf **TX**22, Overslope. [FW illustr: a slanted cut across the top of the ear]

slope v, hence vbl n *sloping* [Prob from Scots, nEngl, nIr dial *slope* to trick, cheat, evade (someone), also in phr *do a slope* to run off, abscond; of obscure origin]
Also with *along, off*: To leave suddenly or secretly, run away, abscond; to go; with *off*: to slack, shirk work.

[**1830** *Palladium of Brit. N. Amer.* (Toronto) 29 Aug. 224/1 *(DA)*, Bad climate indeed, wonder people dont all *slope*.] **1839** Marryat *Diary* 198, Here are two real American words:—"Sloping"—for slinking away. **1843** (1847) Field *Drama Pokerville* 78 **MO**, He finally *sloped* with a lively step for the theatre, and the screaming crowd took their way to the hotel. **1851** Hooper *Widow Rugby's Husband* 23 **AL**, Give me the mortgage and slope! **1855** (1940) Chambers *Jrl.* 135, Three Sioux charged on them they threw thier meat away & sloped. **1859** Taliaferro *Fisher's R.* 213 **nwNC** (as of 1820s), Sam Lundy always added a few items of his own . . when he "sloped" to market. **1866** Smith *Bill Arp* 19 **nwGA**, I'm afraid I'll get in a tight place . . and have

to slope out of it.   **1871** Eggleston *Hoosier Schoolmaster* 110 **sIN**, Set out for the village of Clifty a few miles away. No one knew what he went for, and some suggested that he had "sloped."   **1899** (1912) Green *VA Folk-Speech* 394, *Slope*. . . To run away; elope; decamp; disappear suddenly.   **1927** *DN* 5.463 [Underworld jargon], *Slope along*. . . To move on.   **1929** *AmSp* 4.344 [Vagabond lingo], *Slope*—To leave; to break jail.   **1983** *MJLF* 9.1.56 **ceKY** (as of 1956), *Slope off* . . to slink off.   **1995** *DARE* File **MT**, Forty years ago, Montana railroad workers were said to "slope" off, and "sloping off" was their version of sloughing. It meant both absenteeism and lateness, as well as slack performance.

slopehead n

A **grouper 1a** (here: *Dermatolepis inermis*).

1996 Hein et al. *Fisherman's Guide LA* 15, *Marbled Grouper* (Slopehead, John Paw) *Epinephelus inermis*. . . Forehead sloped sharply. . . Average 5–10 pounds.

slope off, sloping   See **slope** v

slop jar n

1 also *slop bucket,* ~ *pail,* ~ *pot*: A chamber pot. [Euphem use of *slop jar* large vessel used to collect household wastewater (including the contents of chamber pots)]   Cf **thunder mug**

1855 *Ballou's Pictorial* 8.194 **TN**, Each man [=convict] on going down to work takes his night slop bucket with him as he marches out, and at a certain part of the yard empties it and leaves it.   **1950** *PADS* 13.19 **cTX**, *Slop bucket*. . . A pail for liquid garbage. Distinct from *slop jar*, a large chamber pot.   **c1960** *Wilson Coll.* **csKY**, *Slop jar*. . . A very modern successor to the chamber pot.   **1965–70** *DARE* (Qu. F38, *Utensil kept under the bed for use at night*) 253 Infs, **widespread, but less freq NEast, NW,** Slop jar; **CA**134, **FL**8, **MD**24, **NC**25, 82, **SC**43, Slop bucket; **SC**70, **TX**38, Slop pail; **MO**5, Slop pot; (Qu. F37, . . *An indoor toilet*) Inf **MO**8, Slop jar.   **1976** Garber *Mountain-ese* 84 **sAppalachians,** *Slop jar* . . bedroom chamber.   **2000** Shores *Tangier Is.* 201 **Chesapeake Bay,** Like most villages today, Tangier has no use for the chamber pot. When they did, and they did longer than most, they usually called it a *slop jar* and upon more polite occasions, a *chamber pot*.   **2006** *DARE* File—Internet **Sth,** Heck, the chamber pot (slop jar in our slang) and outhouse was commonplace in my relatives homes in Florida, Alabama, and Tennessee.

2 See **slop bucket 1.**

slop pail n

1 See **slop bucket 1.**
2 See **slop jar 1.**

slopped-together, slopped-up   See **slop** v

slopping back   See **slop back**

slop pot   See **slop jar 1**

sloppy joe n

1 A dish consisting of crumbled ground beef in a sauce, often served on a bun.   Cf **spoonburger**   Note: Some of these quots may refer instead to **2** below.

1940 *Mansfield News–Jrl.* (OH) 27 Mar 14/4, [Advt:] Hamilton's New Sandwich Bar Featuring 5c Hot Dogs—Barbecues—Sloppy Joes.   **1953** *Salisbury Times* (MD) 13 Aug 16/5, To serve cut corn bread into squares. Toast until golden brown. Top with hot Sloppy Joe Mixture.   **1961** Church *Burger Cook Book* 42, *Sloppy Joes*—Also known as spoonburgers and scoopburgers, these are the popular "loose" kind. [Recipe includes ground beef, onions, celery, sweet pickle relish, brown sugar, Worcestershire sauce, chili sauce, vinegar, green pepper, hamburger buns.]   **1965–70** *DARE* (Qu. H41, . . *Kinds of roll or bun sandwiches . . in a round bun or roll*) 69 Infs, **scattered, but esp Gt Lakes, N Midl, KS,** Sloppy joe; (Qu. H42, . . *[A sandwich] . . in a much larger, longer bun, that's a meal in itself*) Infs **CA**59, **NJ**11, 64, Sloppy joe; (Qu. H45, *Dishes made with meat, fish, or poultry that everybody around here would know, but that people in other places might not*) Infs **IL**98, **NY**94, **OK**19, Sloppy joe.   **1966** *DARE* FW Addit **AL,** *Sloppy joes*—refers to a hamburger and tomato sauce dish.   **1967** *Ogdensburg Advance-News* (NY) 11 June 6/7, Sloppy Joe with Bun.   **1967** *Raymond Herald & Advt.* (WA) 9 Mar 5/5, [School menu:] Sloppy-joes, string beans, apple crisp, bread and butter sandwich, milk.   **2002** *DARE* File **seWI** (as of 1944–45), When I was a small child, and if my father were not going to be home, my mother frequently made "sloppy joes" for us at supper. This was a seasoned concoction of mostly ground beef and onion in a gravy-like sauce all served up on a round bun. Everyone called this a "sloppy joe". *Ibid* **neIL** (as of 1942–43), A 73 [year] old who attended high school in the Chicago suburb of Berwyn distinctly recalls that the "sloppy Joe" (under that name) was a staple of high school fare.

2 A sandwich of sliced meat and a variety of other ingredients, usu including Russian dressing and cole slaw.   **esp NJ**

1948 *Hopewell Herald* (NJ) 3 Nov 3/3 **NYC,** *Did You Know That: A Sloppy Joe* is the new name for a Dagwood Sandwich.   **1994** *NY Times* (NY) 31 July sec 13NJ 10/5 (Internet), To former residents of northern New Jersey . . the real sloppy Joe is a double-decker sandwich composed of three long, thin slices of specially baked rye bread layered with a combination of meats, coleslaw and . . Russian dressing. . . This tasty, overstuffed construction originated at the Town Hall Delicatessen . . in South Orange. . . The original sandwich came about in 1936. . . A customer . . asked the counterman to come up with a high-rise sandwich like those he had eaten in Havana at a bar called Sloppy Joe's.   **1997** *DARE* File **cNJ,** When I was growing up in South Jersey, a "Sloppy Joe" was a ground-beef sandwich. . . Once I moved to Central Jersey, I find out that Sloppy Joe's here are deli sandwiches made from turkey, cole slaw, and (Russian?) dressing.   **2001** *Ibid* **cNJ,** When I moved to central New Jersey [from sePA] I found that a Sloppy Joe was what I would call a "special" sandwich—deli meat (corned beef, turkey, roast beef) with russian dressing and cole slaw.   **2002** *Ibid* **NJ,** "Sloppy Joe" . . a sandwich made with cold cuts, russian dressing, and coleslaw. . . seems to be extremely common in north Jersey (Bergen and Passaic counties) and I've also heard it in central Jersey.

slop together (or up)   See **slop** v

slop worm n   **esp GA, AL**   Cf **red wiggler**
Any of var worms found in decaying vegetation, esp a **redworm 1;** a maggot.

c1970 Pederson *Dial. Surv. Rural GA* **seGA** (*Ordinary worms used for bait in fishing*) 1 inf, Slop worm—grown in worm beds; 1 inf, Slop worm[s], red worms, earthworms.   **1981** Pederson *LAGS Basic Materials (Earthworm)* 1 inf, **cAL,** Slop worm; 1 inf, **ceAL,** Slop worm—light or white in color, good for bait. Used to grow where people threw dishwater etc out into yard; 1 inf, **seAL,** Slop worm—develop around sink drainage, "they like greasy soil"; 2 infs, **GA,** Slop worms; 1 inf, **seGA,** Slop worms—small, in worm beds; 1 inf, **swGA,** Slop worms—are called red wigglers.   **2003** *NADS Letters* **neAL** (as of 1980s), "Slop Worm" I always understood to mean maggot, as in leaving food out long enough to get slop worms.   **2004** *DARE* File—Internet **nwFL,** Every Southerner knows that a person with a five gallon bucket, a can of slop worms, and a reed cane pole is going to the creek to give fish the sore mouth and a flying lesson.   **2005** *Atlanta Jrl.–Constitution* (GA) 10 July Northside sec 3 (Internet) **nwGA,** He said he uses slop worms, hot dogs and chicken livers as bait.

slorate v
To kill, slaughter.
1881 *Century Illustr. Mag.* 23.243 **GA** [Black], Brer Fox . . he say ter hisse'f dat he be dog his cats ef he don't slorate ole Brer Rabbit ef it take 'im a mont'.   **1909** *DN* 3.371 **eAL, wGA,** Slorate. . . To destroy, kill large numbers of. "We just simply slorated doves at the dove-shoot."   **1917** *DN* 4.417 **wNC,** Slorate. . . To slaughter.

slosh n   Also *slosh-marolly*   [Cf *EDD* slosh sb. 1 "Mud, mire . . dirty water . . a muddy wash."]   Cf **cush** n¹
A dish consisting of flour seasoned with drippings; a stew; see quots.
1858 Elliot *New England's Chattels* 83 **NEng,** "I dare say it is cheap," said Captain Bunce, "but I am rather afraid of tough beef, for the folks are a little lame in the jaws, you know, being oldish, and fond of slosh."   **1882** McCarthy *Soldier Life* 59 **nVA** (as of 1861–65), "Slosh" or "coosh". . . the bacon is fried out till the pan is half full of boiling grease. The flour is mixed with water until it flows like milk, poured into the grease and rapidly stirred till the whole is a dirty brown mixture.   **1957** *Sat. Eve. Post Letters* **TN,** Slosh-marolly: Combination of meats and vegetables cooked out of doors.

slouch n   [*OED2* 1515 →]   **widespread, but chiefly Sth, S Midl, SW**   See Map
A slovenly person, esp a woman; hence adj *slouchy* slovenly, shabby; untidy; rarely adv *slouchy* sloppily.
1838 Lieber *Pop. Essay* 65, It imparts an attention to the room, which

becomes the incipient stage of love of home, with those who have lived in slouchy disregard of it.   **1853** *Putnam's Mag.* 2.685, It is . . written in a style sometimes loose and slouchy, but often piquant and well turned.   **1863** *Atlantic Mth.* 11.414, A slouchy garb is both effect and cause of a slouchy mind.   **1887** Kirkland *Zury* 538 **IL,** Slouch. . . A poor, slovenly thing.   **1941** *LANE* Map 466 (*Slovenly*) **NEng,** [*Slouchy* is widespread throughout the region; *slouch* n was also offered in some cases.]   **1954** *Harder Coll.* **cwTN,** Slouch. . . A careless, slovenly woman. *Slouchy.* . . Of someone who always dresses carelessly. "She's jus' 'es slouchy's kin be."   **1965–70** *DARE* (Qu. HH36, *A careless, slovenly woman: "She's just an old _____."*) 133 Infs, **widespread, but chiefly Sth, S Midl, SW,** Slouch; **IA**15, **NC**16, **NM**9, Slouchy; **NM**9, Slouchy housekeeper; **GA**28, Slouchy woman; (Qu. W41, . . *Expressions . . for someone whose clothes never look right or who always dresses carelessly*) 130 Infs, **chiefly Sth, S Midl, SW,** Slouchy; 14 Infs, **scattered,** Slouch; **FL**26, Always looks slouchy; **FL**25, Looks slouchy; **MS**63, Mighty slouchy; **TX**106, Slouchy as he can be; **KY**63, **MS**23, **TX**1, Slouchy-looking; (Qu. U35, . . *Thrifty but not in a complimentary way: "She's not a bad housekeeper, but very _____."*) Inf **MO**6, **NC**55, Slouchy; (Qu. W24b, *Sayings to warn a man that his pants are torn or split*) Inf **OR**13, You're slouchy; (Qu. W29, . . *Expressions . . for things that are sewn carelessly . . "They're _____."*) Infs **AK**8, **CA**157, **KY**5, 37, **OR**13, **TX**42, Slouchy; **KY**5, Slouchy work; (Qu. W43, . . *Joking words . . for clothes in general*) Inf **GA**32, Slouchy clothes; (Qu. Y37, *To make a place untidy or disorderly: "I wish they wouldn't _____ the room so."*) Inf **OK**12, Be so slouchy in; (Qu. KK6, *Something low-grade or of poor quality—for example, a piece of merchandise: "I wouldn't buy that, it's _____."*) Inf **KY**47, Slouchy.   **1969** *DARE* Tape **GA**72, They'll come slouchy dressed, or very sloppily dressed.   **1986** Pederson *LAGS Concordance,* 1 inf, **neGA,** Slouchy—appearance, in ill-fitting clothes; 1 inf, **ceGA,** Slouchy—woman or man, badly dressed; 1 inf, **cwGA,** Slouchy—of funny-looking clothes; 1 inf, **cGA,** Slouchy—wearing funny clothes, woman or man; 1 inf, **ceGA,** Slouchy—baggy and unfitted clothing; 1 inf, **swGA,** Slouchy—the opposite of dressed up; 1 inf, **nwAL,** Slouchy—of a common girl, not pretty; 1 inf, **csMS,** Slouchy—appearance; 1 inf, **ceGA,** Dressed slouchy; 1 inf, **cwTN,** Kind of common or slouchy in dress; 1 inf, **seGA,** Looks slouchy—not clean or well groomed.   **2004** *Cleveland Plain Dealer* (OH) 21 Nov sec L 4 (Internet), Two T-shirts, a lightweight V-neck sweater, a zip-up sweater and a jean jacket hardly look slouchy for a day running around the East Village.

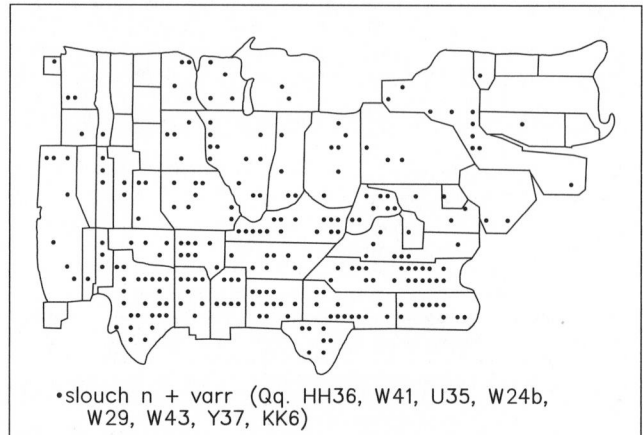

• slouch n + varr (Qq. HH36, W41, U35, W24b, W29, W43, Y37, KK6)

slouch v   With *up, over*   **esp S Midl**   Cf **slop** v
To make or repair (something) carelessly; to mess up; hence ppl adjs *slouched up, ~ over.*
1966–69 *DARE* (Qu. W29, . . *Expressions . . for things that are sewn carelessly . . "They're _____."*) Infs **NC**40, **OK**42, (Just) slouched over; **VA**2, Slouched up; (Qu. Y37, *To make a place untidy or disorderly: "I wish they wouldn't _____ the room so."*) Infs **LA**6, **OK**42, Slouch up; (Qu. KK63, *To do a clumsy or hurried job of repairing something: "It will never last—he just _____."*) Inf **KY**47, Slouched it up.

slouchways adv, adj   Cf **slaunchwise**
Crooked, sagging, out of square.
1876 *Athens Messenger* (OH) 9 Nov 3/1 [Black], Things is getting slouchways in dis country. . . Fust cum de cattypiller, den de chicken kollery, an' now here cum de grasshoppers; an' I hear talk de udder day

dat a nigger was pisened wid a mushmillion. Looks like hard times. **1919** *Washington Post* (DC) 24 Aug mag sec 9/2 **OH,** John wanted to lower the barn, so he chopped off the posts with an ax and didn't he darn thing fall over slouch-ways. **1960** Stuart *God's Oddling* 67 **neKY,** He [=a mule] would pull the express about two corn rows wide at a time coming up the bank slouchways. **1967** *Look* 26 Dec 43 **GA,** The bricks that propped the left-rear corner have crumbled, and the house twists slouchways and droops. **1969** *DARE* (Qu. MM13, *The table was nice and straight until he came along and knocked it* _____) Inf **KY**6, Slouchways.

slouchy See **slouch**

slough n[1] Usu |slu|; rarely |sə'lu, slau, slɔf| Also *slough-hole* Also sp *slew, sloo, slow, slu(e)* **widespread exc NEast, C Atl** See Map See also **slough grass, ~-pumper**

A marsh, pond, or backwater; a stream or channel, esp in a marsh or tidal flat; hence adj *sloughy* marshy.

1665 in *Springfield Rec.* II.216 *(DAE)* **MA,** There is grannted to Inhabitants of Skeepmuck a highway from ye Slow beyond the Swan pond. **1705** (1825) Knight *Jrls.* 68 **MA,** We . . had a pretty difficult passage the next day . . by reason of the sloughy ways then thawed by the Sunn. **1843** (1940) Ferris *Rocky Mts.* 203, We . . halted . . on a small *"slough",* west of Lewis river. This word is used in the mountains to designate that portion of a river separated from the main channel or current, by the intervention of an island. **1845** (1946) Moore *Diary* 22 **eIA,** We entered the slough (pronounced here sloo) which brought us out into the Mississippi. **1846** Farnham *Life in Prairie Land* 52 **sIL,** The road is so wet and the *slues* so full of water. **1899** (1912) Green *VA Folk-Speech* 395, *Slue.* . . A narrow channel or thoroughfare in water between shoals. Turn or new channel in a river. **1902** Wister *Virginian* 188, See them marshy sloos full of weeds. **1903** *DN* 2.330 **seMO,** *Slough.* . . Pronounced slew. **1909** *DN* 3.371 **eAL, wGA,** *Slew.* . . Slough. **1920** Lewis *Main Street* 57 **MN,** They ate their sandwiches by a prairie slew. **1932** *DN* 6.233 **West,** *Slough* or *slue*. A word pretty generally used in the West as elsewhere in the United States. On the Coast, in Washington, it would seem to be used as synonymous with *creek* or *stream,* whereas elsewhere it means generally the marshy land around a stream which meanders about a bottom. **1937** *AmSp* 12.239, In Colfax County, near Schuyler, Nebraska, there is a small stream called 'The Slough,' the vowels pronounced as in 'how.' Before the custom was established of marking creeks, rivers, etc., with signs (fixing the spelling), many persons in the locality referred to this stream as *'The Saloo.'* **1948** Pearson *Sea Flavor* 118 **NH,** There are, to be sure, lower spots in the marsh hay reaches—spots the farmers call sloughs. **1965–70** *DARE* (Qu. C14, *A stretch of still water going off to the side from a river or lake*) 138 Infs, **widespread exc NEast, C Atl,** Slough; **AL**14, [sə'lu]; **NJ**21, **NY**84, [slau]; **OH**4, [slɔf]; **OR**10, Man-made slough; **VT**16, Slough [slau]-hole; **WA**19, [sə'lu]; (Qu. C7, . . *Land that usually has some standing water with trees or bushes growing in it*) 69 Infs, **chiefly west of Missip R,** Slough; **VA**105, [slɔf]; **IL**32, Sloughy land; (Qu. C6, . . *A piece of land that's often wet, and has grass and weeds growing on it*) 42 Infs, **scattered,** Slough; **IL**45, [slau]; **VT**16, [slau]; (Qu. C9, *Water from a river that comes up and covers low land when the river is high*) 14 Infs, **scattered,** Slough; **OR**15, [slou]; (Qu. C1, . . *A small stream of water not big enough to be a river*) Infs **AR**17, **FL**29, 32, **ID**3, **IL**11, 53, **TX**9, 12, Slough; (Qu. C4a, . . *A fairly large body of fresh water*) Inf **OK**51, Slough; (Qu. C4b, . . *Would people go fishing or swimming in a pond?*) Inf **MN**34, Pond—a slough-hole; **ND**9, Slough; (Qu. C12, *A section of a river where the banks are much farther apart, and the water widens out for some distance;* total Infs questioned, 75) Inf **FL**6, Sloughs; (Qu. C19, . . *Low land running between hills [With and without water]*) Inf **OK**1, With water—a slough or spring; (Qu. C21, *A deep place cut in sloping ground by running water*) Inf **CA**111, Slough [slu]; (Qu. C28, *A place where underbrush, weeds, vines and small trees grow together so that it's nearly impossible to get through*) Infs **KY**86, **MN**6, Slough; (Qu. C34, *Nicknames for nearby . . districts*) Inf **IN**42, Pirogue Slough; (Qu. II24, . . *Where the well-off people live*) Inf **CA**119, Snob Slough. **1991** *Names* 39.343, *Slough.* . . *Slu, slue,* and *slew* are alternate spellings. **2002** *DARE* File **AL,** "Slough"—A regional topographical term for a small creek or stream. It seems more prevalent in the Alabama River drainage system and the Tennessee River Valley rather than in the rest of the State. Although I grew up with the term in Montgomery County [i.e. Baldwin Slough] I have had several people comment what an odd term when creek would have sufficed. **2005** *Telegraph–Herald* (Dubuque IA) 17 Aug sec A 1 (Internet), In backwater areas and sloughs, the main hazards are tree stumps and shallow areas where boats could drag on the bottom.

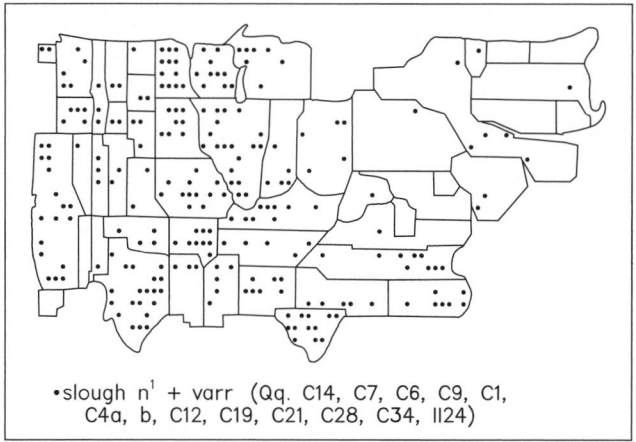

•slough n[1] + varr (Qq. C14, C7, C6, C9, C1, C4a, b, C12, C19, C21, C28, C34, II24)

slough v[1] |slʌf| Pronc-sp *sluff* **esp UT**

To play hooky; to absent oneself from (school); hence n *slough* a notice of truancy.

1922 *Ogden Std.-Examiner* (UT) 17 Sept 7/4, Now this arrangement . . causes people to think that students are not kept in check or controlled, that they are 'sluffing' classes. **1944** *Ibid* 1 Feb 7/2, The youth was arrested in company with two other lads for having sluffed school. **1953** *Soda Springs Sun* (ID) 24 Sept 2/1, It seemed a little thing, they sloughed school and went fishing out of season. **1965–68** *DARE* (Qu. JJ6, *To stay away from school without an excuse*) Infs **UT**3, 6, Slough. **1971** Bright *Word Geog. CA & NV* 200 **NV,** He . . skipped class . . sloughed school 1% [of 300 infs]. **1984** *DARE* File **UT, ID,** The boys decided to _____ school one day: sluff. *Ibid* **cnUT,** Kids "sluff" [slʌf] school here. **1988** *Ibid,* Utahisms. . . *Sluff, slough* class/school— Means to play hookey. . . Standard in Utah, Southern Idaho, and adjacent areas, and even heard in other western rural areas. **1994** *Ibid* **Salt Lake City UT,** Jan Brunvand . . tells me that in the public schools kids "sluff" school. And the school bulletins use this term in discussing school policy. *Ibid* **Provo UT,** "Sluff" is the usual term here. . . my wife says she used "sluff." She graduated from high school in 1966. *Ibid* **seID,** In the late '70s . . we used "sluff" to mean "ditch school." *Ibid,* In Washington State and Southern Nevada "sluff" is and has been used. In Washington State I went to a prep school, so we spelled it "slough." **1995** *Ibid* **UT,** In California (70's), we *cut* school. . . In Utah (then and now), students and administrators call it *sluffing.* A student may "get a sluff" if s/he is caught out of class. **2005** *Deseret Morning News* (Salt Lake City UT) 27 Sept (Internet), Other witnesses also put Olsen with Davis, "sluffing class" on the day she disappeared.

slough v[2] |slau| Also sp *slow*

To hit, attack, kill.

1911 *DN* 3.551 **WY,** *Slough* [slau], strike. "He sloughed him one," he struck him a blow. **1915** *DN* 4.235 **neOH** [College slang], *Slough, v.t.* To strike heavily. **1927** *DN* 5.477 **Ozarks,** *Slow.* . . To attack, to kill. The word is pronounced to rhyme with *plow,* and is perhaps a corruption of *slay.* **1934** Farrell *Young Manhood* 130 **neIL,** It had been just his luck to get sloughed in the eye. **1942** McAtee *Dial. Grant Co. IN* 58 (as of 1890s), *Slow* (rhyming with plow) . . to kill. **1968** *DARE* FW Addit **csIA,** *Slough* [slau]. "He would slough this fella with his cane every time." [Past, past pple:] *sloughed.* **1995** Brophy *Coll.* 69 **swMO** (as of c1960), *Slough.* [T]o plow into, strike, slam (rhymed with plow). **2006** *NADS Letters* **MT** (as of 1930s-40s), Slough. . . [M]y mother used it, not infrequently and always humorously with a thrust jaw and a fist, when, as a child, I teased her or minorly annoyed her. She pronounced it to rhyme with plow. "Oh, you little dickens, I'll slough you!"

slough n[2] See **sluff**

slough bass n

=**black bass 1,** usu **largemouth bass.**

1877 Hallock *Sportsman's Gaz.* 276, Locally they [=black bass] are termed perch, . . and are severally known as . . slough bass, etc. **1935** Caine *Game Fish* 10, Spotted Small-mouthed Black Bass. . . Slough Bass. **1956** Harlan–Speaker *IA Fish* 127, *Northern Largemouth Bass.* . . Slough bass. . . It is quite common in the river lakes, sloughs and ponds of the Mississippi River. **1983** Becker *Fishes WI* 809, *Micropterus salmoides.* . . Slough bass, lake bass. **2001** *Quad-City Times* (Davenport–Bettendorf IA) 13 May sec D 12/1, The largemouth bass, also called the slough bass or black bass, favors weedy, mud-bottom river areas, lakes and ponds.

slough buffalo n
=bigmouth buffalo.

1933 LA Dept. of Conserv. *Fishes* 440, The Common Buffalofish or Redmouth Buffalo. . . has come to be known under many popular names. . . They are . . Redmouth Buffalo, . . Slough Buffalo, Mud Buffalo and White Buffalo. **1983** Becker *Fishes WI* 615, *Ictiobus cyprinellus.* . . Slough buffalo. . . Widely distributed in the Mississippi River and its large tributaries.

slough-foot See slue-foot n

slough-footed See slue-footed adj

slough grass n

1 Any of var often coarse grasses, or occas other similar plants, that grow in a **slough** n¹ or similar area; often used for hay, hence n *slough hay.* **chiefly Upper MW, Upper Missip Valley, Plains States** See Map Cf **marsh hay, meadow ~, swale grass, swamp ~, swamp hay, wild ~** Note: Some of these quots may refer specifically to other senses below.

1844 *Alton Telegraph & Democratic Rev.* (IL) 23 Nov 1/5 **IA,** Why, I would as soon feed my horses on slough-grass cut in August. **1854** *Putnam's Mag.* 4.292 **IL,** There was fire in every form, from the small torch-light made by the tuft of slough-grass, to acres flaming from the long blue-joint on the river bottom. **1861** IL State Ag. Soc. *Trans. for 1859–60* 4.488, Then [I] make a band of whatever material I have at hand, (slough grass is preferable). **1867** *Scientific Amer.* 16.167 **IL,** Its business . . will be the manufacture of paper by the "Meech process," to reduce slough grass to pulp, without destroying the fiber. **1871** IL State Ag. Soc. *Trans. for 1869–70* 8.172 **neIL,** The entire bed should be covered with coarse prairie or slough hay. **1892** *Century Illustr. Mag.* 44.639, Wade in the cool and sparklin' crick,/ While cute spring bossies romp and play / With Ponto, in the tall slough hay. **1950** *WELS* **WI** (*Hay that grows naturally in damp places*) 2 Infs, Slew grass; 1 Inf, Slough grass; 1 Inf, Slough hay. **1965–70** *DARE* (Qu. L8, *Hay that grows naturally in damp places*) 26 Infs, **chiefly Upper MW, Upper Missip Valley, Plains States,** Slough grass; 16 Infs, **chiefly Upper MW, Upper Missip Valley, Plains States,** Slough hay; IL31, WY1, Slough; (Qu. L9a, . . *Kinds of grass . . grown for hay*) Inf IL31, Slough grass; (Qu. S9, . . *Kinds of grass that are hard to get rid of*) Inf CO20, Slough grass. **1978** Doig *This House* 35 **MT,** By late January [of 1920], . . the ranch families shipped in trainloads of slough grass which had been mowed from frozen marshes in Minnesota. **2002** *Bismarck Tribune* (ND) 13 Oct sec C 8 (Internet), Good alfalfa went for between $44 and $61 a bale. Lesser quality slough hay went for $30.

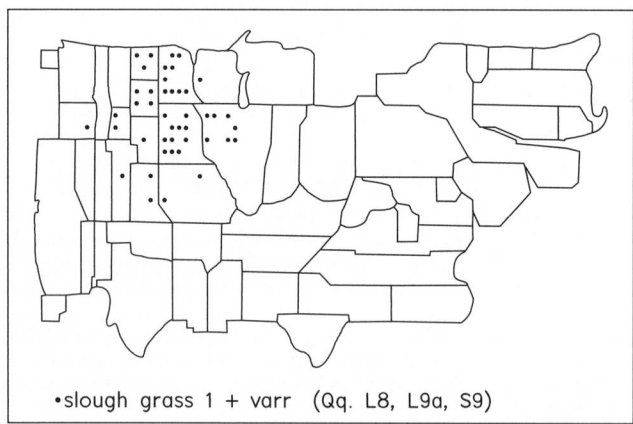

•slough grass 1 + varr (Qq. L8, L9a, S9)

2 Spec:

a A **muhly (grass)** (here: *Muhlenbergia mexicana* or *M. racemosa*).

1880 Bessey *Botany* 455, *Muhlenbergia glomerata* [=*M. racemosa*] and *M. Mexicana* constitute the "Fine Slough Grass" of the Mississippi valley prairies.

b also *slough sedge:* Any of several **sedges B1;** see quots.

1893 *Overland Mth.* (2d ser) 21.568, The kah hoóm is taken from the roots of a California variety of the well known slough grass, *carex Mendocinoensis,* so abominable to orchardists, and so defiant of his plow and hoe in efforts toward its eradication. **1923** Abrams *Flora*

Pacific States 1.339, *Carex obnupta.* . . Slough Sedge. . . In the coastal counties . . ; Monterey Bay, California, north to Vancouver and British Columbia. **1950** Stevens *ND Plants* 98, *Carex atherodes.* . . Slough Sedge. . . One of the commonest and most abundant of all slough sedges, frequently forming dense, pure stands 1–1.5 m. high in wet ground or shallow water. It is often used for hay where such areas become dry enough to mow late in summer. **1982** U.S. Fish & Wildlife Serv. *Resource Pub.* 144.3 **cND,** Emergent vegetation in seasonal wetlands included tall mannagrass . . slough grass . . slough sedge . . and marsh smartweed. *Ibid* 24, Slough sedge . . *Carex atheroedes.* **1986** Klinkenborg *Making Hay* 23 **wMT,** The soil carries . . some miscellaneous rushes and sedges (called sloughgrass locally) in the damp spots. **2003** *Seattle Times* (WA) 30 Apr sec H 12 (Internet), Hundreds of wetland species such as slough sedge and bulrushes also were planted as part of the wetland restoration.

c =**wheatgrass 4.**

1894 *Jrl. Amer. Folkl.* 7.103 **NE,** *Agropyrum glaucum* [=*Pascopyrum smithii*], . . slough-grass, . . S.W. Neb.

d A grass (*Beckmannia syzigachne*) found throughout much of the northern and western US, used for forage and for hay. Also called **rattlesnake grass 3**

1901 Jepson *Flora CA* 57, *Beckmannia erucæformis* [=*B. syzigachne*]. . . Slough-grass. . . Sloughs, borders of streams and wet bottom lands in mountain regions. **1912** Wooton–Standley *Grasses NM* 107, *Slough Grass.* . . occurs in very wet soil or beside running water at high levels: may be expected in mountains near the Colorado line. **1936** Winter *Plants NE* 25, *Spartina.* . . Marsh-grass. Slough-grass. . . *Beckmannia.* . . Western Slough-grass. . . Wet places in western Nebr. **1952** Davis *Flora ID* 92, *Beckmannia.* . . *Sloughgrass.* . . is a palatable and nutritive stock food, but not plentiful. **1968** Barkley *Plants KS* 38, *Beckmannia syzigachne.* . . American Sloughgrass. Wet ground. **1974** Welsh *Anderson's Flora AK* 557, *Sloughgrass.* . . Shallow ponds, streams, and muskegs; in much of continental Alaska and Yukon south of the arctic slope. **1982** U.S. Fish & Wildlife Serv. *Resource Pub.* 144.3 **cND,** Emergent vegetation in seasonal wetlands included tall mannagrass . . slough grass . . slough sedge . . and marsh smartweed. *Ibid* 24, Slough grass . . *Beckmannia syzigachne.* **2000** *DARE* File— Internet **IL,** In some cases, the plants could become extirpated without some immediate action, for example the American Sloughgrass (Beckmannia syzigachne) at Sauganash.

e A **cordgrass,** usu *Spartina pectinata.*

1899 KS Ag. Exper. Sta. Manhattan *Bulletin* 87.2, The commonest grass is usually called slough grass (*Spartina cynosuroides*). **1910** Johnson *Highways Rocky Mts.* 9 **NE,** Our early roofs were either of sods or of slue grass. This slue grass grew as tall as a man, and when cut early enough it made good fodder—fine! It made excellent roofs, too. **1936** [see **2d** above]. **1941** Ward *Holding Hills* 62 **IA** (as of early 20th cent), He never let up till the . . straw-pile was covered with slough-hay and weighted down with poles or rocks. **1948** *Annals IA* (3d ser) July 380 (as of c1880), On top of the banked-roof was a layer of long "slough grass", to keep out the rain. **1951** Porter *Ragged Roads* 75 **wOK,** This red clay [between the poles of the wall] had been sparsely reinforced with slough grass. **1967** Braun *Monocotyledoneae* 134, *Spartina pectinata.* . . Prairie Cord Grass. Slough Grass. . . Tall to very tall. . . Wet prairies, swamps, and coastal marshes, throughout much of the United States. **1991** Heat Moon *PrairyErth* 12 **ceKS,** Even today in moist vales protected from development and cattle, I've found big bluestem and sloughgrass, the grandest of the tallgrasses, eight feet high.

f =**quack grass 1.**

1945 Wodehouse *Hayfever Plants* 44, Quackgrass [=*Elymus repens*]. . . is known by many vernacular names . . , and locally by other names as . . slough . . grass.

slough gull n
=black tern.

1894 *Oölogist* 11.141 **IA,** We saw . . hundreds of Black Terns (commonly called "Slough Gull"). **1932** Bennitt *Check-list* 34 **MO,** *Black tern.* . . Slough gull; black gull. . . U[ncommon] T[ransient] V[isitant] throughout the state.

slough hay See slough grass 1

slough pickerel n Also *slough pike*
=grass pickerel 1.

1951 Harlan–Speaker *IA Fish* 52, *Esox vermiculatus* [=*E. americanus v.*] . . slough pike. . . Appears to have a strong preference for shallow, quiet or slow-moving water, and is often found in overflow ponds of the larger streams. **1983** Becker *Fishes WI* 393, *Esox americanus vermicu-latus.* . . Slough pickerel. . . Common in lakes and sluggish waters of extreme southeastern Wisconsin. . . This species prefers quiet water (lakes and sloughs), but it has occasionally been taken from fast currents in small streams.

slough-pumper n Also *slough-pump, slough-pup* [See quot 1950] **chiefly Upper Missip Valley, esp MN** Cf **thunder pumper 1**

A **bittern** (here: *Botaurus lentiginosus*).

1932 Roberts *Birds MN* 1.188, American Bittern: *Botaurus lentiginosus.* . . Other names . . Slough-pumper. **1938** FWP *Guide IA* 11, The American bittern, often called "shite poke" or "slough pump," was one of the most conspicuous of prairie birds to early settlers, but now is decreasing in numbers. **1950** WELS **WI** (*A small heron that makes a booming sound before rain, and often stands with its head pointed up*) 1 Inf, Slew pumper; 1 Inf, Slough-pump. **1950** WELS Suppl. **cwWI,** Slough-pump, slough-pumper—The bittern (large). So called because it lives in sloughs or marshes and makes a noise like an old wooden pump. **1955** MA Audubon Soc. *Bulletin* 39.313 **NEng,** American Bittern. . . Slough-pup (Maine, N.H., Mass. Corruption of slough-pump.) **1959** *Names* 7.119, Likening the bittern's vocalization to the sounds made by the operation of an old-fashioned suction-pump has also been a fruitful source of folk-names. Among these allusions are . . slough-pump (N. Dak., Man., Sask.), slough-pumper (Wis., Ill., Minn., N. Dak.) **1965–70** DARE (Qu. Q8, *A water bird that makes a booming sound before rain and often stands with its beak pointed almost straight up*) Infs **MN**36, 42, **WA**28, Slough-pumper; **MN**15, 33, 38, Slough-pump. **1985** Madson *Up River* 161 **Upper Missip Valley,** What the River lacks in duck production, though, it makes up for in herons. Night herons, both black-crowned and yellow-crowned, bitterns or "slough pumps," [etc]. **2004** *Star Tribune* (Minneapolis MN) 4 Feb sec H 4 (Internet), Dunk-a-doo: A folk name for the American bittern . . [which] approximates the bird's call. It also has another colorful common name: slough-pump.

slough sedge See **slough grass 2b**

sloughy See **slough** n¹

sloven n Also *sloven wagon* [Of eCanadian origin < Ir *sleamhnán* sledge]

A wagon with the bed beneath the level of the hubs.

1889 *AN&Q* 4.71, In parts of New England a rough one-horse farm wagon is called a sloven. [**1895** *DN* 1.381 **eCanada,** *Sloven:* a low truck wagon.] **1966** DARE (Qu. L13, *The kind of wagon used for carrying hay*) Inf **ME**1, Sloven wagon—a low wagon. [Inf old] **2004** DARE File—Internet **ME,** A sloven is a type of wagon with a freight bed lower than the wheel hubs. The freight beds of most wagons are above the straight axles that connect each pair of wheels. A drop-axle is "U" shaped and the freight bed rides on the lower part of the "U" . . below the wheel hubs.

slow n See **slough** n¹

slow v See **slough** v²

slow as pond water See **pond water 3**

slow as seven-year itch See **seven-year itch 2a**

slow bear See **slow elk**

slow brand n Cf **fast brand**

1929 Dobie *Vaquero* 121 **TX,** The law further required that every brand should be recorded in the county of its origin. A man who had blotted out a brand and put another in its place was naturally chary of putting this new brand on record. He simply ran it, trusting to get the cattle out of the country at the first opportunity. Such an unrecorded brand was called a "slow brand."

slow-bush n Also *slow-wood*

A **gum elastic** (here: *Sideroxylon lanuginosum*).

1913 *Torreya* 13.233 **LA,** *Bumelia lanuginosa* [=*Sideroxylon l.*] . . Slow-wood, slow-bush, . . Cameron, La.

slowcome n Also *slowcome-pokum, slocum-~* [*EDD* slow-come "Dev. Cor. Also in form *slocum*"]

A lazy, lethargic person.

1899 *Newark Daily Advocate* (OH) 8 Dec 2/3, "I knew a man in Salem, Mass., where my folks lived, who was always called Slowcome." "Well, wasn't that his name?" "No, it wasn't. He had a peculiar kind of a slow walk, and the Salem boys fixed that name on him." **1911** *DN* 3.540 **eKY,** Slowcome. . . A lazy, sluggish fellow. **1953** *AmSp* 28.254 **csPA,** Slowcome. . . A slow fellow, always late; a dawdler. In popular speech. Frequently heard in the composite, *slowcome-pokum* (*pokum,* from *to poke,* 'to potter,' 'to dawdle'), hence the variant spelling, *slocum.* 'Well if here isn't old slocum-pokum at last.'

slow consumption n Cf **galloping consumption**

A slow, wasting disease, esp tuberculosis.

1820 Irving *Giovanni Sbogarro* 1.11, That delusive flush . . that glows on the cheek of some lovely victim whom slow consumption is dragging to the tomb. **1850** Gilbert *Narr. Sojourner Truth* 83, He had a sick slavewoman, who was lingering with a slow consumption. **1856** *Ladies' Repository* 16.753, He fell into a slow consumption. **1900** *Atlantic Mth.* 85.190, No matter if a dull headache or the painful cough of slow consumption had delayed the absentee. **1939** in Lib. of Congress *Amer. Memory: WPA Life Hist.* (Internet) **FL,** My father's daddy . . lived with us when I was a little girl and for ten years before he died he was sick with slow consumption. **1967** DARE (Qu. BB10, . . *Names or nicknames . . for tuberculosis*) Infs **IA**3, **LA**2, **SC**31, Slow consumption. [All Infs old]

slow elk n **West**

A cow or calf, esp one that is stolen and butchered; the meat of such an animal; hence v *slow-elk* to steal and butcher (a cow); similarly n *slow bear* a hog that is stolen and butchered.

1869 *Overland Mth.* 3.129 **TX,** A hog clandestinely killed outside of camp and smuggled in under cover of darkness, was called a "slow bear." **1894** *CO Springs Gaz.* (CO) 14 Aug 1/4, They are devoting their leisure to hunting "slow elk." When marketed "slow elk" is choice range beef, and our cattlemen relish not this industry that has suddenly sprung up in the mountains near at home. **1910** Raine *Bucky O'Connor* 285 **West,** "Try this cut of slow elk, Miss Mackenzie. I think you'll like it." . . "Slow elk . . is veal that has been rustled. I expect Mr. Leroy has pressed a stray calf into our service." **1931** *AmSp* 7.120 **eID,** A *slow elk* is the cattle *rustler's* (cattle thief's) term for a calf. **1935** Sandoz *Jules* 37 **wNE** (as of 1880–1930), He would n't chaw slow elk, starving. But he's bit off a tough chunk—saving souls up there. **1936** Adams *Cowboy Lingo* 159 **West,** When a man killed an animal that belonged to someone else for food or for sale to butcher shops, he was said to 'slow-elk' it, and such an animal was called a 'slow elk' or 'big antelope.' **1939** (1973) FWP *Guide MT* 416, Slow elk—Beef butchered without the owner's knowledge. **1941** Writers' Program *Guide WY* 465, Slow elk—A cow that is stolen and butchered and the meat eaten or sold. **1958** McCulloch *Woods Words* 171 **Pacific NW,** Slow elk—A cow. **1979** *Oregonian Article Letters* **Pacific NW,** [Hunting terms:] Cow, or beef: is called a "slow-elk." **2004** in 2005 DARE File—Internet **CO,** I thought about everyone forgot about those slow elk. Been awhile since I thought of it myself. How come the neigbors [sic] beef always taste better than one's own?

slowful adj, rarely used absol [*OED2 slowful* a. 1 14 . . –1539] **esp Sth, S Midl** *esp freq among Black speakers* Note: *Slowful* had some currency in 19th cent literary contexts, perh as a conscious archaism; such exx are not included here.

Slow, slothful, lethargic; hence adv *slowfully;* n *slowfulness.*

1888 in 1991 *Jrl. S. Hist.* 57.75 **cnAL** [Black], A word to slowful members, we have some members that are very backward about attending meetings, be men of business, stay off the creeks and brooks fishing. **c1937** in 1976 *Weevils in the Wheat* 65 **VA** [Black], Den he sent some deacons around to collect the dues from de "slowful" members. **1967** DARE (Qu. A18, . . *A very slow person: "What's keeping him? He certainly is _____!"*) Inf **TX**26, Slowful; (Qu. Y21, *To move about slowly and without energy*) Inf **AL**20, Slowful; **MA**128, ['slaʊfəl]. [2 Infs old, 2 Black] **1981** Pederson *LAGS Basic Materials,* 1 inf, swGA, ['sloˇʊftʃ] [*LAGS* Ed:] "Slowful," strange, peculiar. [Inf Black] **1997** in 2002 DARE File—Internet **MN,** Are you slowful all the time or just when you have other things going on? . . [I]f it [=someone else's opinion] just so happen to differ from mine oh well. . . [T]he renter probably don't know that the neighborhood has these type of things in place. **2002** Ibid ceMO, Of course the slowful sounds of "Hanging Downtown" was a cut to be remembered. *Ibid* seKY, They say . . he understands that you are to [sic] lazy to pray and kill out your human feelings. . . theres no excuse for slowfulness. *Ibid* seKY, The slowful turns back over in his bed, and goes back to sleep. **2006** in 2007 Ibid **csNC** [Black], Let go of slowfulness . . step up to the plate . . all things come in there [sic] own time, however, they don't happen by themselves.

slow gravy n   Cf *DS* H37

See quots.

1935 *Kingston Daily Freeman* (NY) 25 Sept 16/7, [Advt:] *Regular Thursday Dinner. . . Prime Ribs of N.Y. Beef with Slow Gravy.* **1941** *AmSp* 16.16 **eTX** [Black], You skin that scoundrel [=a jackrabbit] and put him to soak all night, and in the morning you parboil him—nothing but water—and then you cook that scoundrel down to a slow gravy. **1956** McAtee *Some Dialect NC* 41, *Slow gravy . . thick gravy.* **1996** Livingston *Complete Fish & Game* 265 **coastal Carolina,** He killed some birds . . and put them in a big iron frying pan with water. He put some sides of hog meat in with the birds. . . he made some dumplings and cooked the stew down to a slow gravy.

slow hurry n

A purposeful but not rushed pace.

1849 *Knickerbocker* 34.17, We never sot down to an essay of his which was n't perfectly unique and readable-through, and dashed off with a concealed art and in a slow hurry. **1881** Nuttall Ornith. Club *Bulletin* 6.140, He hops along in a curious sidling manner just like a school girl in a slow hurry. **1933** Rawlings *South Moon* 216 **nFL,** He asked Kezzy to go to the river with him. "I'm in a slow hurry," she said. " 'Tain't right to leave my ol' man . . too long." They sat in silence while he paddled the rowboat through the swamp and down the river. **1934** Hurston *Jonah's Gourd Vine* 240 **AL** [Black], "You look lak you in uh kinda slow hurry." "Nope, jes' anxious tuh tell yuh uh thing uh two." **1945** *Morning News* (Florence SC) 16 Nov 1/8, "The machinery of the world is geared in high," he said, "and we Christians can't afford to be in a 'slow hurry.' " **1951** *Florence Morning News* (SC) 4 Mar sec A 4/2, *Slow Hurry*—An obvious fact about people is that those who are very slow are deterrents to progress. No less shameful are those who are speedy, but inaccurate. The suitably efficient media between the two, perhaps, is he who constantly keeps himself in a "slow hurry." **2004** *DARE* File—Internet **OR,** I decided to try downloading and installing updated USB drivers. Maybe that would help. Everything went to hell in a handbasket in a slow hurry.

slow John n   Also *slow Joe*   **sAppalachians**   Cf **lazy Tom**

A simple water-powered device for pounding corn.

1897 *St. Nicholas* 24.367 **eTN,** Lieutenant Coleman had once seen a rude hydraulic contrivance called a Slow-John which was sort of a lazy man's mill. **1939** FWP *Guide TN* 286 **neTN,** The gristmill, built . . in 1774, was one of the first water-powered mills in Tennessee and was an improvement over the hand-operated mill and the "hominy pounder" or "slow john," a crude but useful affair that operated by a process of hammering the corn with a wooden beam. **1952** Brown *NC Folkl.* 1.592, *Slow-joe. . . A water-run hominy beater.*—West. **1960** Williams *Walk Egypt* 270 **GA,** "What's folks doing for grinding?" "Store-bought meal or gone back to the Slow John."

slow on the draw   See **draw** n 7

slowpoke n

=**opossum.**

1966 *DARE* (Qu. P31, . . *Names or nicknames . . for the . . opossum*) Inf **FL7,** Slowpokes, possum. [**1970** *Daily Times–News* (Burlington NC) 1 Aug 1/1, Slow Poke became a famous possum recently when it was announced he would grace the dinner table of Gov. Bob Scott. But old Slow Poke has a new lease on life.]

slows n   Usu with *the*   Cf **milksick, trembles**

Milk sickness.

1851 (1856) Dunglison *Med. Lexicon* 792, *Slows,* Milk-sickness. **1860** Bell *Knowledge* 204, In parts of our western country a disease sometimes prevails among cattle, called *"milk-sickness,"* the *"tires,"* the *"slows,"* or *"stiff-joints"*—all these names are applied to the same disease. It is probably due to some species of *fungi* taken with their food. **1964** Kingsbury *Poisonous Plants U.S.* 402, Symptoms [of poisoning by *Eupatorium rugosum*] are comparable in various classes of livestock. The first symptom noticed is reluctance to move (one common name for trembles is "the slows") and sluggish behaviour.

slow time n   Cf **fast time**

1 Time reckoned according to the more westerly of two adjacent time zones.

1883 *Ft. Wayne Daily Gaz.* (IN) 12 Dec 4/2, To have their days a half hour late is a matter to which all Ohioans object. Had it been a half hour fast it would not have been so objectionable. But a slow time, like everything else slow, is not popular in this country. **1888** *Atlanta Constitu-*

tion (GA) 3 Apr 3/1, Since the railroads adopted the 75th and 90th meridians as standards, Augusta has been almost in the middle and has retained her old city time or sun time. This was 28 minutes slower than fast time and 32 minutes faster than slow time and created no little confusion. **1931** *AmSp* 6.466 **cnNE,** Central time is spoken of as "fast time," and mountain time as "slow time." Some sandhillers prefer to regulate their timepieces by "half time," meaning half an hour slower than "fast time" and half an hour faster than "slow time." **2001** *Bismarck Tribune* (ND) 27 Feb sec B 1 (Internet), Whether to be on fast or slow time—Central or Mountain—will be before the Morton County Commission. **2006** in 2007 *DARE* File—Internet **nwFL,** I looked at my watch. "It's seven, but we can't find anyplace open." She looked at her watch. " 'Pends on what time you running on. Fast time or slow time." I smiled. I had forgotten. Apalachicola is a very special place in America. . . [It] sits right near the official divider between the Eastern and Central time zones.

2 Standard time (as opposed to daylight saving time).

1921 *Trenton Eve. Times* (NJ) 21 May 6/2, Philadelphia's Common Council, by unanimous vote, has adopted a daylight saving ordinance. . . Camden Councilmen have been waiting on the action of Philadelphia and will follow suit. So will Atlantic City, which has been inconvenienced by the necessity of keeping "fast time" for New York and "slow time" for Philadelphia. **1942** *AmSp* 17.113 **SC,** The official terms (Eastern Standard and Daylight Saving) were, however, quite rare, especially in the country; they were frequently replaced . . most commonly by 'slow time' and 'fast time.' *Ibid* 281, 'Slow time' and 'fast time'. . . were commonly used by the Pennsylvania Dutch in eastern York County, Pennsylvania, as early as the summer of 1938. **1945** *Lima News* (OH) 21 June 1/5, Lima at present is on fast, or Eastern War Time, and councilmen will vote next Monday on whether to leave the clocks as they are until fall, or to turn them back to slow, or Eastern Standard Time, on July 1. **1950** *Woodford Sun* (Versailles KY) 7 Sept 1/4 (*Mathews Coll.*), Game time will be 7:30 p.m. (slow time). **c1960** *Wilson Coll.* **csKY,** *Slow time. . .* Standard time as opposed to daylight [savings time]. **1968** *DARE* FW Addit **MD20,** *Slow time*—ordinary standard time, unaffected by daylight savings time. **2001** *NY Times* (NY) 31 Jan sec A 18 (Internet) **IN,** Folks working in Kentucky factories or ordering supplies from Cincinnati find it easier to switch to daylight saving time, known here as "fast time." People whose schedules are Indiana-centric, like children going to school or employees at local bank branches, keep their clocks the same, on "slow time." **2001** in 2007 *DARE* File—Internet, If you are from out of the area, you better brush up on the concepts of "Slow Time" and "Fast Time." Just remember, the exemption to the law requiring states to use Daylight Saving Time is called the Indiana amendment. Fast Time is daylight time and Slow Time is standard time. All of the New Albany and Jeffersonville area does switch to Daylight time, Versailles stays on standard time as does most of Jefferson County.

slow-trail v phr, hence vbl n, ppl adj *slow-trailing*   Cf **slow-walk**

To track game with dogs trained not to run in pursuit; hence nouns *slow-trail dog, slow-trailer* a hunting dog trained not to run in pursuit of game.

1830 *Amer. Turf Reg.* 1.405 **VA,** We went out . . the first morning, on the slow trailing plan. . . He would occasionally call to his dogs when they seemed too eager . . and make them assume a slower pace. **1895** in 2007 *DARE* File—Internet **TX,** We took our Winchesters and old Red and tried slow trailing. **1904** *Indiana Eve. Gaz.* (PA) 15 Nov 2/4, [Advt:] *For Sale*—A thoroughly broken beagle hound; slow trailer. **1933** Rawlings *South Moon* 273 **nFL,** "What you think of my deer-dogs, Lant?" "They look all right. Kin they slow-trail?" **1975** Newell *If Nothin' Don't Happen* 184 **nwFL,** Fellers huntin' out in the sand hills and down in the prairie country and Everglades like to take a young hound and train him to be what they call a slow-trail dog. . . After while they get him so he'll trail a deer without barkin' or tryin' to run, just walkin' along a-waggin' his tail. *Ibid* 185 **nwFL,** Uncle Winton had the best slow-trailer I ever seen. **2006** *Joplin Globe* (MO) 31 Dec (Internet), The advantages of hunting with a good slow-trailing beagle are obvious: you'll see more rabbits.

slow-walk v   chiefly **S Atl**   Cf **slow-trail**

To pursue slowly but persistently; with *down:* to hunt (one) down in this way.

1948 *Delta Democrat–Times* (Greenville MS) 21 Oct 10/3 **GA,** Robert C. Ingram . . gave himself up to police today because, he said, "I'm tired of dodging you." . . "I wouldn't say they had me on the run," he said.

"You know how it is. They just slow walk you to death." **1962** in 2002 (acc) Lexis–Nexis Legal Research *State Case Law: NC* (Internet), Just a very brief time before he began hitting and stabbing his wife . . he said "I'll slow walk her." **1979** *DARE* File **cSC** [Black], Her mother used to say, "There's a dead cat on the line. I'm going to slow-walk you down." She told her daughters that when she was sure that they were lying about where they had been. *Slow walk* meant, I'm going to catch up with you. **1990** *Washington Post* (DC) 12 Mar sec B 1 (Internet) [Black], The single mother is saddened by the charges against Barry, but she is even more troubled that he was targeted by federal authorities who "slow-walked him down." **1997** Johnson-Coleman *Just Plain Folks* 114 **ceNC** [Black], But God don't like ugly. "Sin, my mama used to say, will sho 'nough slow walk you down." **2007** *DARE* File—Internet **cnGA,** Understand that men like a chase. . . I'm talking about allowing him to pursue you so that later on he can tell all his friends how he *'slow-walked you down.'*

slow-wood   See **slow-bush**

slubber v   Also with *up*   [*EDD* slubber v.¹ 5]   **esp S Atl**
To do (something) hastily, esp in a careless and slipshod manner; hence adj *slubbery* slipshod.

  1966–68 *DARE* (Qu. W29, . . *Expressions . . for things that are sewn carelessly . . "They're _____."*) Inf **NC3,** Slubbery work; (Qu. KK49, *When you don't have the time or ambition to do something thoroughly: "I'm not going to give the place a real cleaning, I'll just _____."*) Inf **NC79,** Slubber it; (Qu. KK63, *To do a clumsy or hurried job of repairing something: "It will never last—he just _____."*) Inf **GA7,** Slubbered it; **GA28,** Slubbered his work. **2002** *Virginian–Pilot* (Norfolk VA) 4 Feb sec B 1 (Internet), He wasn't one to slubber things up. He wanted a good product.

slubbern n   [Perh *sloven* infl by **slubber**]
  1968 *DARE* (Qu. W41, . . *Expressions . . for someone whose clothes never look right or who always dresses carelessly*) Inf **VA25,** Slubbern ['slʌbɚn].

slubber up, slubbery   See **slubber**

slud   See **slide** v **1, 2**

slue   See **slough** n¹

slue-foot n   Also sp *slew-foot, slough-foot*
1   One whose foot or feet turn out or are otherwise misshapen or awkward—freq used as a nickname for a person or animal.

  1845 *Ladies' Repository* Mar 80, To counteract this, our first lieutenant, who had been nicknamed "Old Sluefoot," passed up and down our lines, encouraging the men. **1926** *Oakland Tribune* (CA) 29 Sept 20/1 **OR,** He bagged "slewfoot," a monstrous deer. . . The leg wound had made the deer lame, causing it to limp badly, tracks indicated. **1938** Rawlings *Yearling* 14 **nFL,** He pictured old Slewfoot, the great black outlaw bear with one toe missing. **1947** *Trail Riders Bul.* Feb. 20/2 *(DA),* Jest like Sluefoot sez, there's them there rattlers holed up for the wintuh. **1960** Wentworth–Flexner *Slang* 486, *Slewfoot. . .* In baseball, an awkward player. . . Any clumsy person; a stumblebum. **1967–68** *DARE* (Qu. HH21, *A very awkward, clumsy person*) Inf **MO11,** Slue-foot; (Qu. CC8, . . *The devil*) Inf **MO9,** Slue-foot. **2005** *DARE* File—Internet **seFL,** My original CB handle was "slew foot"—I have very large feet (size 15)! Bigfoot was already taken and Saskwatch [sic] was too hard to say!

2   A foot that is turned out or otherwise misshapen or awkward; the condition of having the feet turned out.

  1893 *Atlanta Constitution* (GA) 11 Apr 7/2, Mims was called out and the tracks leading from the Dalrymple house compared to his big foot. They corresponded exactly, the foot being of the variety known as slew foot. **c1937** in 1976 *Weevils in the Wheat* 67 **VA,** Neatly pressed narrow grey trousers and large square toed shiny black shoes cover respectively his thick bow legs and large "slew" feet. **1954** *WELS Suppl.* **swWI,** Then a "slough foot" I have always heard was handed down from the many lumbermen in this vicinity, and was supposed to be a heavy step on one foot caused by stiffness or rheumatism from wet or damp feet, as the men's work with logs in the many sloughs emptying into Black River kept them wet with slough water most of the time. **c1960** *Wilson Coll.* **csKY,** Slew feet. . . clumsy ones, turning out or having no spring about them. Also *slue.* **1960** Bailey *Resp. to PADS 20* **KS,** *Slew-foot*—refers to big feet. **1965–70** *DARE* (Qu. X38, *Joking names for unusually big or clumsy feet*) 36 Infs, **scattered,** Slue-foot; (Qu. X37, . . *Words . . to describe people's legs if they're noticeably bent, or uneven, or not right*) Inf **SC32,** Slue-foot. **2003** in 2005 *DARE*

File—Internet **VA,** Stay away from serious conformation faults that may hurt the horse such as slew foot, pigeon toe.

3   A police officer, detective, or other person who enforces regulations.   Cf **flatfoot** n **2b**
  1931 *AmSp* 7.85 [Prohibition terms], Terms referring to representatives of the law. . . Slewfoot. **1932** *AmSp* 7.403 **WA** [Orphanage argot], *Sluefoot. . .* Same as *screw.* [*Ibid, Screw. . .* Night watchman, discipline officer, or proctor.] **1933** *AmSp* 8.3.31 [Prison terms], Slewfoot. Detective. [Corruption of *sleuthfoot.*] **1935** *AmSp* 10.52 [English of the comic cartoons], Epithets applied to detectives . . Slewfoot. **1960** Bailey *Resp. to PADS 20* **KS,** *Slew-foot*—refers to a sleuthing detective.

4   A **freshwater clam** (here: *Strophitus undulatus*).
  1992 Cummings–Mayer *Field Guide Freshwater Mussels MW* 82, *Strophitus undulatus . .* sloughfoot. . . Shell elliptical, moderately compressed, and thin when young. . . Widespread and common.

slue-footed adj   Also *slue-foot*   Also sp *slew-foot(ed), slough-footed*   **chiefly Sth, S Midl**   See Map   Cf **parrot-toed**
Having a foot or feet that turn out or are otherwise misshapen or awkward; shambling, clumsy; also fig.

  1876 in 2009 (acc) Lexis–Nexis Legal Research *State Case Law: AL* (Internet), [The witness] knew that said tracks were his tracks; that the defendant had very peculiar feet—he was 'slew-footed;' that his foot was remarkably broad just across the beginning of the big toe. **1899** (1912) Green *VA Folk-Speech* 395, *Slue-footed. . .* With the feet turned out. **1905** *DN* 3.94 **nwAR,** *Slough* [slu]-*footed. . .* Clumsy. 'He's terrible slough-footed.' Common. **1909** *DN* 3.371 **eAL, wGA,** *Slue-foot(ed). . .* Having big ugly feet; also having twisted or crooked feet. **1924** *Indianapolis Star* (IN) 27 Feb 6/4 **NYC,** Policemen and waiters here seem to be more slew-footed than others. Perhaps because they are on their feet more. **1934** Hurston *Jonah's Gourd Vine* 12 **AL** [Black], Dat's uh big ole resurrection lie, Ned. Uh slew-foot, drag-leg lie at dat. *Ibid* 308 **FL** [Black], Bet de wop-sided, holler-headed — thought Ah wuz gointer cry, but he's uh slew-footed liar! **1945** Saxon *Gumbo Ya-Ya* 496 **LA,** She is hoping that her galloping, slue-foot, light-brown, lazy husband . . will soon find a job. **1956** McAtee *Some Dialect NC* 58, *Slew-footed. . .* With the feet angling outward; the opposite of "pigeon-toed." **1960** Criswell *Resp. to PADS 20* **Ozarks,** *Slew-footed*—refers to big feet—often used, but not *slew-feet.* **1965–70** *DARE* (Qu. X37, . . *Words . . to describe people's legs if they're noticeably bent, or uneven, or not right*) 38 Infs, **chiefly Sth, S Midl,** Slue-footed [15 Infs reported that the feet (or toes) point out, 2 Infs that they point in.]; (Qu. X38, *Joking names for unusually big or clumsy feet*) Infs **DE3, FL30, LA12, MS59, 68, 73, OK20,** Slue-footed. **1967** *DARE* FW Addit **seOR,** Slew [slu]-foot—big-footed, clumsy-footed. **1986** Pederson *LAGS Concordance,* 1 inf, **cTX,** Slew-footed—lame. **2000** *Atlanta Jrl.–Constitution* (GA) 4 July sec A 1 (Internet), One suspect . . has jet black hair with long sideburns and walks slue-footed—his feet point outward. **2004** *NADS Letters* **IN,** My grandmother [was] born Indiana 1880, of Irish parents. . . Lived in southern and central Indiana. She . . used the term "slew-footed" which meant someone who walked with their feet turned out.

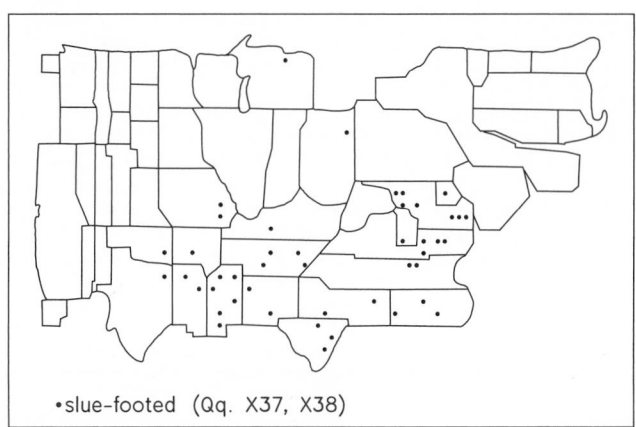

•slue-footed (Qq. X37, X38)

sluff n   Also sp *slough*   Cf **solo**
A card game related to **skat.**
  1901 *Anaconda Std.* (MT) 21 June 11/3, "I wouldn't play slough, and he pasted me wid a beer glass," said John. **1959** Robertson *Ram* 228 **ID** (as of c1875), Obe took pride in the neatness of his work and enjoyed

camp life. He liked to play sluff with the other men. **1968** *DARE* (Qu. DD35, . . *Card games*) Inf **UT4,** Sluff [slʌf]. **1974** Gibson *Hoyle* 320, *Slough:* Also termed *Sluff,* this is a form of *Frog.* [*Ibid* 125, *Frog:* A variant of *Solo. Ibid* 352, *Solo:* A name applied to various games related to *Skat.*]

sluff v   See **slough** v[1]

slug n

1 An irregularly shaped freshwater pearl.

1893 *Humeston New Era* (IA) 5 July [6]/5 (newspaperarchive.com) **sWI,** *Pearls from Wisconsin. . .* There are slugs in white, pink and fancy shades, slugs shaped like swans, shoes and dogs' heads. Of the pearls proper, there are rare whites [etc]. **1908** Kunz–Stevenson *Book of the Pearl* 352, Slugs: a name used for the very irregular, distorted pearls, frequently made up of masses or groups of small pearls; usually without luster or form, and of little value except for medicinal purposes. **1938** FWP *Guide IA* 328 **seIA,** The fisherman gambles on the chance that his haul will produce baroques or slugs, which bring good prices. **1955** *AmSp* 30.76 **cwTN** [Museseling terms], *Slug. . .* A formation within the mussel shells, not as perfectly formed as a pearl, but quite valuable and always searched for. **1979** *WI Week-End* 6 Apr 6, But clams in the Mississippi River produce only imperfect or baroque pearls, known as "blisters" or "slugs". **2001** AR Game & Fish Comm. *Life in the Rocks* July–Aug 1 (Internet), If the resulting shape happens to be a sphere, it is called a pearl; otherwise, it is known as a slug.

2 A large sport fish. **Pacific**

1961 *Independent* (Long Beach CA) 8 Aug sec C 3/1, Those fish out there [=albacore] are big slugs. We fished them Friday aboard Pierpoint's Hurricane, and took four of the 61 fish for the day—all above the 25-pound mark. **1964** *Oakland Tribune* (CA) 11 May sec E 37/1, The fish were big, too—real slugs. That's why we used 11.0 salmon hooks and whole Monterey sardines. **1968** *Argus* (Fremont–Newark CA) 13 Mar 19/1, The top bass are big slugs running to over the 6-pound mark and nearly all the fish are loaded with spawn. **1983** Neely *AK Calls* 91 **seAK,** We came in day after day [at Angoon] with a good catch of large kings. The natives called them "big slugs." **1986** Rustad *I Married a Fisherman* 5 **AK,** Fishing for the elusive king salmon and smaller cohos, or silvers, the trollers have learned the favorite hangouts of the big "soakers" or "slugs." **2005** *Marin Independent Jrl.* (Novato CA) 26 Aug (Internet), The slugs are on the move off Duxbury Buoy. Big salmon smacked anchovies as party boats loaded up yesterday.

3 One who hitches a ride with a driver who needs passengers in order to use a High Occupancy Vehicle Lane; hence v *slug* to travel, make (one's way) in this fashion, vbl n *slugging;* n *slugger* one who travels in this way; n *slug line* a line of people waiting for such rides. [See quot 1992 *Washington Post*] **chiefly Washington DC area**

1992 *Washington Times* (DC) 6 Feb sec G 2 (Internet), The average commuter tries to carpool or slug his or her way up Interstate 95. **1992** *Washington Post* (DC) 20 Sept sec B 1 (Internet), They call themselves slugs and are proud of it. . . Hanson said the symbiotic nature of slugging usually results in him getting a free lift within minutes. In return for picking up Hanson and at least one other rider, a driver gets to zip along in the less-congested HOV lanes of Shirley Highway, which can halve commuting time. Transportation officials politely call commuters such as Hanson "instant car poolers." They, in turn, use the moniker given them years ago, tradition has it, by bus drivers who compared them to counterfeit coins. **1998** *Ibid* 4 Aug sec B 1 (Internet), *D.C. Chief Won't Move Commuter 'Slug' Line; Pickup Site Stays South of Constitution. . .* Yesterday, slugs lined up on 14th Street said they were relieved that their meeting place would not be moved by D.C. police, at least for now. **2004** *Ibid* 10 Oct sec M 3 (Internet), Someone at work asked me, "Are you a slug?" I didn't know what she was talking about. . . I asked around, and co-workers knew people who have been slugging for twenty years. . . There are about 24 slug lines that form around the area. . . The first person in line hears the destination from the driver and shouts to the rest of the line. Only the first two available sluggers in line get in the car.

slugtoot n

A **bittern** (here: *Botaurus lentiginosus*).

[**1851** (1949) Thoreau *Jrl.* 3.69 **ceMA,** Minott calls the stake-driver "belcher-squelcher." Says he has seen them when making the noise. They go *slug-toot, slug-toot, slug-toot.*] **1959** *Names* 7.120 **MA,** The following list of onomats . . have been applied to the bittern as names. . . Slug-toot (Mass.)

sluice n   Also *sluice box*   **chiefly West, esp CA, AR**   Cf **long tom 2, riffle** n[1]

A long trough in which water washes over gold-bearing soil and gravel, allowing gold particles to settle to the bottom; hence n *sluice fork* an implement for removing stones from such a trough.

1851 in 1852 *NY Daily Times* (NY) 13 Jan 1/2 **CA,** The most of our gold in the market is derived from coyoting, drifting, and river sluice washings. **1854** *Mt. Democrat* (Placerville CA) [1 Apr 3]/5 (newspaperarchive.com), [Advt:] Also, a railroad in said Tunnel, one dirt car, one long tom, nine sluice boxes, one windlass and rope [etc]. **1856** *San Francisco Call* (CA) 16 Dec 4/2, As he went . . it commenced raining "sluice-forks." **1863** Hittell *Resources CA* 384, *Sluice,* a wooden trough about fourteen inches wide, and ten deep, and not less than thirty feet long, used for washing pay-dirt. . . *Sluice-Fork,* a fork similar to a manure fork, but with blunt prongs, as wide at the point as at the heel. The fork is used for throwing stones out of the sluices. **1879** *Harper's New Mth. Mag.* 59.508 **GA,** The methods adopted by the first white settlers . . were very rude, consisting merely of washing out the gravel of the beds of the streams by running it through sluice boxes and splint baskets into a "gum rocker." **1880** (1884) U.S. Census Office *Rept. Population Industries Resources AK* 48, Hydraulic monitors are tearing out a vast pit in the basin's floor, and the flood of débris leaves its gold dust in the sluice boxes as it rushes down through the tunnel. **1967–69** *DARE* Tape **AK10,** [FW:] Now, what do you call that arrangement with the boxes and the water and so forth? [Inf:] Well, that be, that be, sluice-box mining; **CA120,** They only let rocks a certain size go down in then . . turn and wash and go through a sluice box; **CA128,** You've heard of sluice boxes. . . That's just like a trough, only they put cleats across the bottom—that's your riffles— . . and let the water run through and they shovel it into there and the gold sticks behind these riffles; **CA137,** Then that dirt and water run through a box, a sluice box with the riffles in it, and the gold being heavier than the dirt and sand, it settled at the bottom; **OR3,** Well, they had sluice forks, too, don't you see, what they would take the big rocks out of the sluice boxes, don't you see. The sluice forks were a good deal like the spading fork. The tines were longer and they were crooked on the end. **1977** McPhee *Coming Country* 292 **AK,** In 1975 . . he set up a twenty-four-foot wooden sluice box that took in nearly a hundred and fifty dollars' worth of gold in every hour it ran. **2007** *DARE* File—Internet **CA,** This sluice box has been the standard in the industry for decades. . . Features a balanced handle for ease of carrying. . . Dimensions: 10″ x 51″ x 4.5″.

sluice v   [From *sluice* to send logs down a sluice or flume] **Nth, esp NEng**

In logging: to allow (a logging sled) to get out of control on a steep slope; to injure in such an accident; also fig; hence vbl n *sluicing* an instance of such an accident; ppl adj *sluiced* affected by such an accident.

1908 Day *King Spruce* [x] **ME,** When a load of logs is suddenly set free from the cable holding it back on a steep descent, . . it is said to be "sluiced." *Ibid* 5, "Hold on!" protested several of the men, in chorus, crowding close to this dangerous tale-teller. "You ain't goin' to sluice the rest of us, are you, just because you've gone to work and got your own load busted on the ramdown?" *Ibid* 247, The man that took my place got sluiced by the snub-line bustin', and about three thousand feet of spruce mellered the eternal daylights out of him. **1942** ME Univ. *Studies* 57.134, *Sluiced Horses.* Horses injured by loaded sleds gaining speed on hills where proper provision has not been made for braking the sleds. **1951** Reimann *Betw. Iron* 40 **nMI** (as of c1900), "Sluicing" a team meant letting a load of logs get away on the downhill haul. Should a sleigh runner strike an icy spot the sleigh would rush forward and get out of control, pushing the horses at breakneck speed down the hill, occasionally sending the animals and the load crashing off the road into the woods, crushing horses and drivers to death. . . If the teamsters survived one of these "sluicings", he was considered unfit to handle horses thereafter. **1964** Hargreaves–Foehl *Story of Logging* 61 **MI,** A common way to keep the heavily loaded sleigh from running over the horses (called "sluicing a team") and spilling the load, was for men to hook ropes to the sled, then loop the other ends . . around two or more stout trees or stumps to hold the sleigh in check. **1969** Sorden *Lumberjack Lingo* 114 **NEng, Gt Lakes,** *Sluiced. . .* Upset, said of a man who has accidentally gone off the road and piled up.

slum n   Cf **slumgullion 4**

A makeshift stew or hash.

1847 Mitchell *Reminiscences* 117 **CT,** That noted dish to which our predecessors . . gave the name of *slum,* which was our ordinary breakfast, consisting of the remains of yesterday's boiled salt beef and potatoes, hashed up, and indurated in a frying-pan. **1871** Bagg *4 Yrs. at Yale* 246 **CT,** An olla podrida, hashed up from the remnants of yesterday's dinner, and fried into a consistency which baffled digestion . . was known as 'slum,' and was served both dry and wet. **1909** Wason *Happy Hawkins* 246 **West,** He rolled up his sleeves an' started to peel spuds for the evenin' slum. **1926** *AmSp* 1.564, *Slum*—a term in universal usage to designate *slum-gullion* or beef-vegetable stew. No soldier ever uses the term "stew." *Ibid* 652 [Hobo lingo], *Slum*—a meat stew. **1927** *AmSp* 2.281 [Prison lingo], *Slum*—Prison food. **1936** *AmSp* 11.60 [Soldier speech], Meat stew is *slum* and the soldier a *slum driver.* **1939** [see **slumgullion 4**]. **1939** *AmSp* 14.77 [Naval Academy slang], For his meal, Joe Gish may have *sea gull* (supposedly chicken), or *slum* (stew). **1956** *AmSp* 31.192 [USMC slang], *Slum* is beef stew. **2007** *DARE* File **IN,** I encountered it [=slumgully] by way of an ex whose mother used to make it in Indiana. She called it Slum and it had hamburger, celery, onions, potatoes, and kidney beans and whatever else a person felt like adding.

slumgullion n

1 also *slobgollion:* Slimy or oily refuse from cutting up fish or whales; anything unpleasantly slimy or sticky. **NEng** Cf **gurry 1, 2**

1851 (1976) Melville *Moby-Dick* 412, It is called slobgollion; an appellation original with the whalemen. . . It is an ineffably oozy, stringy affair, most frequently found in the tubs of sperm, after a profound squeezing, and subsequent decanting. I hold it to be the wondrously thin, ruptured membranes of the case, coalescing. **1890** *Century Dict.* 5708, *Slumgullion.* . . Offal or refuse of fish of any kind; also, the watery refuse, mixed with blood and oil, which drains from blubber. [*Century* Ed: New Eng.] **1968** *DARE* (Qu. Y40b, . . *Words referring to sticky stuff: "I've got to wash my hands. They're all covered with _____."*) Inf **NH**14, Slumgullion—this could be anything: grease, etc. **1975** Gould *ME Lingo* 261, *Slumgullion*—In whaling and sometimes in other fishing, *slumgullion* is the oil, blood, salt water, and general crud that occurs in the flensing (Mainers and Massachusetts liked to call that flenchin' or flinchin'). Known, too, as lipperin's or dreenin's, *slumgullion* is considerable more than *gurry* (see *gurry*). *Slumgullion* is now used for anything that is an unpleasant mess, and particularly poor food.

2 A weak or disgusting beverage.

1872 Twain *Roughing It* 43 **West,** Then he poured for us a beverage which he called *"Slumgullion,"* and it is hard to think he was not inspired when he named it. It really pretended to be tea, but there was too much dish-rag, and sand, and old bacon-rind in it to deceive the intelligent traveler. **1876** (1877) Williams *Pacific Tourist* 44, Weary passengers . . were glad to regale themselves on pork and beans, corn bread, and "slumgullion"—the Far Western name for tea. **1897** *Ft. Wayne News* (IN) [8 Feb 3]/1 (newspaperarchive.com), Farmer Sutton claims that in disguising common goose livers as pate de foie gras, . . and slumgullion as cafe noir, the hotels are obtaining money under false pretenses. **1915** Muir *Travels AK* 88 **CA,** The meals are all alike—a potato, a slice of something like bacon, some gray stuff called bread, and a cup of muddy, semi-liquid coffee like that which the California miners call "slickens" or "slumgullion." **1924** Lincoln *Rugged Water* 10 **seMA,** But it takes about five of this slumgullion to make one of reg'lar coffee. **1967** *DARE* (Qu. H74b, . . *Coffee . . very weak*) Inf **PA**49, Slumgullion [ˌslʌmˈgɑliən].

3 A viscid mud deposited by sluicing operations.

1857 *Mt. Democrat* (Placerville CA) 3 Jan 2/5, Those who were . . compelled to shovel tailings and clean reservoirs half full of slumgullion. **1887** Harte *Millionaire* 146 **CA,** We preach at them for playing in the slumgullion, and gettin' themselves splashed, perhaps we mout ez well remember that that thar slumgullion comes from our own sluiceboxes, where we wash our gold. **1895** *McClure's Mag.* 5.235 **CA,** He [=a dog] certainly *was* yellow. . . His breast, legs, and feet, when not reddened by "slumgullin [sic]," in which he was fond of wading, were white. **1948** Weston *Mother Lode* 82 **CA,** The white miners . . insisted on calling it [=the place] "Slumgullion," because when it rained the knee-deep adobe mud was no small problem.

4 =slum.

1884 *Morning Oregonian* (Portland OR) 6 July [8]/5 (newspaperarchive.com), Along the highways where once the hopeful hundreds marched with long-handled pick and pan, cooking by the way thin salt pork and flapjacks and slumgullion now the road is lined with empty

beer bottles and peach cans. **1902** London *Daughter of Snows* 45 **AK,** [She] had poured the [rain-soaked] sea-biscuit into the frying-pan on top of the grease and bacon. To this she added a couple of cups of water. . . [and] sliced up the corned beef and mixed it in. . . "What do you happen to call it?" "Slumgullion," she responded curtly. **1924** in 1925 *New Castle News* (PA) [26 June 18]/2 (newspaperarchive.com), [Syndicated short story:] There was something vaguely familiar about the song: "Oh, don't you remember the typhoon we had,/ With the sea like a slum-gully pie." **c1929** Bowen *Sea Slang* 126, *Slum Gullion.* In American ships, a mixture of pea soup, powdered biscuits and fat, salt meat and scraps of all kinds. **1939** in Lib. of Congress *Amer. Memory: WPA Life Hist.* (Internet), On days we were in jungle, he would jumble up all the mixable portions of food . . into a big tin washboiler. . . He stewed up quite a palatable mess which he called 'slum' or 'slumgullion.' **1956** Ker *Vocab. W. TX* 292, Two old-timers . . report *slumgullion,* a stew of hashed meat and potatoes. **1958** McCulloch *Woods Words* 171 **Pacific NW,** *Slumgullion*—Like hash, only looser, but not as loose as soup. **1965–70** *DARE* (Qu. H45, *Dishes made with meat, fish, or poultry that everybody around here would know, but that people in other places might not*) Inf **AR**2, Slumgullion—chicken, ground meat, and vegetables cooked together; **FL**30, [sləmˈgʌljən]—made with corned beef, potatoes, tomatoes, spices, hog jowls, and black-eyed peas; always served on New Year's Day for good luck; **FL**37, [sləmˈgʌljn]—like a stew with everything in it; **GA**36, [sləmˈgʌljən]—a low grade of meat stew (that was in the army, way back yonder); old-fashioned—general usage; **IL**117, [sləmˈgʌjən]—old-fashioned; made of squirrel and whatever was available; during the Depression, this dish was popular; **IN**60, Slumgullion—everything goes in it; **OR**1, Slumgullion—like a goulash; (Qu. H49, *Dishes made by boiling potatoes with other foods*) Inf **CA**105, Slumgullion—logging-camp stew; **WA**30, Slumgullion—like stew; (Qu. H50, *Dishes made with beans, peas, or corn that everybody around here knows, but people in other places might not*) Inf **NC**10, [sləmˈgʌljən]—a mixture of vegetables. [8 of 10 Infs old] **1967** *DARE* FW Addit **ceNY,** *Slumgullion* [slʌmˈgʌliən]—a stew of all available leftovers. **2007** *DARE* File, My coworker and I were discussing a childhood dish our mothers made. My mom always called it goulash (sp?) and her mom called it slumgully. . . At first we thought the term had a geographical focus around Pennsylvania and Ohio, but we've found people who know it as slumgully from Boston.

slummock See **slommack**

slump n

1 A dessert of fruit cooked with biscuit dough; a cobbler. **chiefly NEng** Cf **grunt n 4**

1831 Finn *Amer. Comic Annual* 140, The pumpkin pies and apple slump . . were smoking on the table. **1848** Bartlett *Americanisms* 311, *Slump.* A favorite dish in New England, called an *apple slump,* is made by placing raised bread or dough around the edges of an iron pot, which is filled with apples and sweetened with molasses. **1903** *DN* 2.295 **Cape Cod MA** (as of 1850s), *Apple grunt* or *apple slump.* . . A kind of apple dumplings. **1905** *DN* 3.19 **cCT,** *Slump.* . . A dish of dough and fruit, as 'apple *slump.*' **1934** Harwich Port Lib. Assoc. *From Cape Cod* 119 **seMA,** *Huckleberry Slump.* **1939** Wolcott *Yankee Cook Book* 365, *Slump.* What State-of-Mainers call cooked fruit topped with dumplings or biscuit dough. **1947** Bowles–Towle *New Engl. Cooking* 178, Both the grunts and the slumps were transition desserts, halfway between the boiled and baked puddings but simpler to make. **1965** *PADS* 43.15 **seMA,** Other names for a deep-dish apple pie . . apple slump [5 of 9 infs]. **1989** *WI State Jrl.* (Madison) 9 Aug sec D 1/2, A slump is . . fruit and biscuit dough. Once baked, the dessert is turned upside-down onto a serving plate and the fruit is "slumped" into the biscuit by whacking it with a wooden spoon. Then cream is poured over the whole dessert. **2005** in 2007 *DARE* File—Internet **ceMA,** I . . decided to bake an apple slump . . —basically, its baked apples with a crust-ish topping. Very easy and yummy, and I had apples to either bake with or throw out.

2 also *slomp:* A sloven, slattern; hence adjs *slompy, slumpy* slovenly; slatternly. [Cf *EDD slump* sb.[3] "A careless workwoman"]

1905 Holland Soc. *Yr. Book* 174, It [=art] turned from . . weakling princes and slumpy mistresses, to men grown virile in their country's service. **1913** (1980) Hardy *OH Schoolmistress* 99, *Slompy* meant *slatternly.* **1926** *DN* 5.403 **Ozarks,** *Slump.* . . A large, fleshy, untidy, person. **1928** Ruppenthal Coll. **KS,** *Slomp.* . . A girl who is poor at housekeeping. **1968–70** *DARE* (Qu. W41, . . *Expressions . . for someone whose clothes never look right or who always dresses carelessly*) Inf **MD**19, Slump; **VA**73, Slumpy.

slump time n Cf **mud time, slumpy 1**

1970 *Yankee* Jan 138 **NEng,** When the snow did melt in earnest, for a few days or weeks the country thoroughfares must have presented the aspect of a sort of slushy quagmire, whence the poignant phrase "slump time" for this season.

slumpy adj

1 Marshy, muddy, slushy. [Engl dial] **chiefly NEast** Cf **slump time**

1843 *Ladies' Companion* 19.245 **CT,** The *January thaw* had set in, and it rained 'till the soft, slumpy snow . . had disappeared. **1848** Bartlett *Americanisms* 311, *Slumpy.* Marshy. **1850** *Daily Free Democrat* (Milwaukee WI) 27 Nov [2]/2 (newspaperarchive.com), We do not much admire this juicy, slumpy, drizzly, foggy weather, attended by muddy going, wet feet, tooth-ache, colds, coughs, and asthma. **1878** *Scribner's Mth.* 16.520 **NEng,** Roads grow "slumpy" and then so nearly bare that people begin to ponder whether they shall go forth on runners or wheels. **1900** *New Engl. Mag.* 22.694 **NEng,** When the snow was soft and slumpy there were frequent mishaps to heavy teams. **1920** in 2003 *DARE* File—Internet **ceNY,** It is a rainy day pretty soft & slumpy water everywhere now it is warm & thawing fast. **1971** *Daily Kennebec Jrl.* (Augusta ME) 19 Mar 11/2, Freezing weather would make it [= snowmobiling] great, thawing might bring slumpy going. **1993** *Daily Herald* (Arlington Heights IL) 5 Sept sec 5 3/1, Bettors studied racing forms . . as they tried to pick winners on a slumpy main track and soft turf. **2007** *NADS Letters* **NH,** *Slumpy:* . . in warm weather snow packs slump (fail abruptly from the bottom), hence the weather and/or snow is slumpy.

2 See **slump 2.**

slunch v Also with *back, over* [Blend of *slump* (or *slouch*) + *hunch*] Cf **slaunchwise**

To lean, slump, hunch; hence ppl adj (phrr) *slunched, ~ back, ~ over.*

1952 Brown *NC Folkl.* 1.592, *Slunch.* . . To slant. **1981** in 2007 (acc) Lexis–Nexis Legal Research *State Case Law: IL* (Internet), When he turned, he saw the defendant "in a slunched-over position." **1994** NC Lang. & Life Project *Harkers Is. Vocab.* 10 **eNC,** *Slunched.* . . Leaning to one side. *The baby was slunched in her car-seat.* **2003** in 2007 *DARE* File—Internet **seNY,** You couldn't even get to the beer. I had to slunch over cartons of this and that just to get a good look but I wasn't overly impressed. **2004** *Ibid* **OH,** It was a daily ritual that caused me to obliviously slunch over into a Neanderthal-like posture in front of the keyboard. **2006** in 2007 (acc) Lexis–Nexis Legal Research *State Case Law: WI* (Internet), Daugherty "was kind of slunched back," his head off to one side, his eyes closed, and one hand "kind of in a locked-up position on his torso."

slunchendikular See **slantindicular**

slunch over See **slunch**

slunchways, slunchwise See **slaunchwise**

slundger See **slunger**

slunged See **sling** v

slunger n |ˈslʌnǰɚ| Also sp *slundger* Cf **lunker**

An exceptional example of its kind; see quots.

1953 *AmSp* 28.254 **csPA,** *Slundger.* . . Anything exceptionally large for its class, a 'whopper.' 'Dave caught a slundger of a bass yesterday down at Burket's Bridge.' . . The medial consonant sounds are [nǰ]. **1968–70** *DARE* (Qu. Y11, *. . A very hard blow: "You should have seen Bill go down. Joe really hit him a _____."*) Inf **IN39,** Slunger [ˈslʌnǰɚ]; (Qu. LL5, *Something impressively big: "That cabbage is really a _____."*) Inf **IL115,** Slunger [ˈslʌnǰɚ]. **2005** in 2007 *DARE* File—Internet **TX,** A "Slunger" (real big boy [=a wild turkey cock]) walked out behind her. [*Ibid,* "Slunge" stopped in the farm road and blew up.] **2006** *Ibid* **NV,** A rainbow [trout] much larger than I expected . . took my #14 Royal Wulff and proceded [sic] to teach me a lesson. While trying to run up and down the slippery rocks in the stream, I fell down three times . . trying to stay with the Slunger.

slunk See **slunker**

slunked See **slink**

slunker n Also *slunk* [Varr of *slink*]

A spent fish; see quots.

1903 Goode–Gill *Amer. Fishes* 527, These spent females [=sturgeons] are called "slunkers," and are of little value. **1955** *Sun* (Baltimore MD) 16 June 14 (*Hench Coll.*) **Chesapeake Bay,** A special term for down-run shad is "slunk" or "slunker."

slunkweed n Cf **slinkweed**

A **boneset 1** (here: *Eupatorium purpureum*).

1898 Britton–Brown *Illustr. Flora* 3.582, Slunkweed f 3615. [*Ibid* 307, Eupatorium purpùreum L. . . (Fig. 3615.)]

slur v, hence vbl n *slurring*

1994 *DARE* File **ceMA,** When I was a kid, growing up in South Boston and Braintree, to slur meant that you had come alongside another "coaster", and pulled the steering bar, or lifted the runners (if he was small enough), and tipped his sled over. Slurring was the favorite pastime of bullies, but sometimes your own brothers would do it to you.

slurrup n, hence adj *slurrupy* [Cf *EDD slurrup* v. 2 "To walk in a slovenly, halting fashion."] Cf *DS* HH36

1916 Macy–Hussey *Nantucket Scrap Basket* 145 **seMA,** "Slurrup"— A shiftless, untidy woman; a slattern. The adjective "slurrupy" was also used to describe such a person.

slurt v Also with *out* [Cf *EDD slirt* v. "To squirt water"]

To squirt; to blurt.

1890 *Century Dict.* 5700, *Slirt.* . . [T]o eject quickly; squirt: as, a fish *slirts* her spawn. **1951** *DE Folkl. Bulletin* 1.7, *Slurt* (probably a combination of "slop" and "squirt"—as in "Don't slurt that water on me.") **1982** *Smithsonian Letters* **sIN,** Finally, she slurted out that she was "just in a faunch." **2002** *DARE* File—Internet **MI,** "You okay?" Lux slurted out as she laughed, looking at Corbin. *Ibid* **VA,** [Student reviews of simulated dissection software:] They should have blood slurt out at you when you do something wrong!

slush See **sloosh** n[2]

slush bucket See **slusher**

slushburger n **ND, SD**

=sloppy joe 1.

1960 *Bethany Cook Book* 248 **SD,** *Slushburgers* [Recipe includes chopped onion, catsup, chili powder, hamburger, prepared mustard, sugar, salt, vinegar.] . . Cook for 7 minutes, water, onion, catsup and chili powder. Add remaining ingredients, cook 30 minutes more. **2002** *DARE* File—Internet **ND,** Bison Slushburger Feed. Sponsored by City of Tioga & Tioga Schools. **2003** *Ibid* **ND,** Rickard Elementary Menu . . Lunch: Slushburger. **2009** *DARE* File **ND,** Williston, North Dakota is the only place I've heard a loose meat sandwich called a slushburger.

slush cook n Also *slush handler* Cf **cookee b**

A cook's assistant; see quots.

1887 *Current* 7.137, I had to work as slush-cook on a Mississippi steamer to get something to eat. **1930** Blair *Raft Pilot's Log* 108 **Upper Missip R** (as of 1880), The rest of the crew even to the 'slush cook' are interested and ready to 'trim ship' or do anything else to help their boat win. **1956** Sorden–Ebert *Logger's Words* 33 **Gt Lakes,** *Slush-handler,* A cookee. **1969** Sorden *Lumberjack Lingo* 114 **NEng, Gt Lakes,** *Slush cook*—An assistant cook. Same as cookee, taffle.

slusher n Also *slush bucket* **esp WI** Cf **fresno 2**

A horse- or mule-drawn scoop or scraper for moving dirt.

1969 Sorden *Lumberjack Lingo* 114 **NEng, Gt Lakes,** *Slusher*— Horse-pulled earth scoop with twin handles manipulated by the teamster on road and railroad right-of-way construction work. **1972** *Yesterday* 1.2.38, Others [=cellars] were added years after the house was built, either laboriously dug out by hand or scraped out by a horse or mule hitched to a "slush bucket." **1978–79** *Midwest. Lang. & Folkl. Newsl.* 1–2.20, In Maine the "fresno" is called a "horse scoop," in Indiana a "slip shovel," and in Wisconsin a "slusher." **2002** *DARE* File **nWI,** The term we used in Indiana was slip scoop. . . Here in northern Wisconsin they call it a slusher.

slush handler See **slush cook**

slush ice n

=mush ice.

1844 Hulett *Every Man Guide* 30, This ice . . is broken into small cakes, and forms what is termed slush ice; this ice passes down the current in a body, and partially congeals. **1894** *Overland Mth.* (2d ser) 24.347, There are the wild sky, the fantastic cliffs . . the river running thickly with slush ice. **1938** in Lib. of Congress *Amer. Memory: WPA Life Hist.* (Internet) **NE,** Here Mr. McCarthy cast his first ballot, and next day swum the river through slush ice to bring the results to Ogalalla. *Ibid* **ND,** I left Bismark [*sic*] the 9th of November on the steamer "Tompkins", there was slush ice in it [=the Missouri River] the time we left. **1966–68** *DARE* (Qu. B35, *Ice that will bend when you step on it, but not break*) Infs **NY93, SD5,** Slush ice. **1966** *DARE* Tape **OK30,** It was a regular blizzard, about ten below zero, and . . snowing and blowing, and I was riding on the creek, right side of our house, and it was filled up with snow, and it was just kind of slush ice in there. . . That calf jumped out in that slush ice and went under. **1971** Wood *Vocab. Change* 367 **Sth,** Other volunteered words [for a thin covering of ice included] *ice shell . . slush ice . . thin sheet ice.* **1994** *DARE* File **WI,** Slush ice is just like thick slush. Sometimes it will hold your weight if it is thick enough. Slush ice occurs when it snows just as ice is forming or on top of new, thin ice. The weight of the snow pushes the ice down and water comes up on top of the ice and turns it and the snow to slush. Sometimes it never really freezes solid all winter long. **2007** *DARE* File—Internet **AR,** There was only slush ice, and it was right down to the beach. . . Slush ice is usually the fall ice, but when it happens in January and February it's strange.

slush-up n Cf **break-up** n 1, **freeze-up**
    1910 *DN* 3.448 **cwNY,** *Slush up.* . . The slushy condition of country roads resulting from a sudden thaw. "The men are going to draw ice tomorrow, if a change of weather don't cause a slush up."

slut n

1 also *slut lamp:* An improvised candle or grease lamp, esp one consisting of a twisted rag set in a dish of grease. [Engl, nIr dial; *OED2* 1609 →] Cf **bitch** n 1, **grease lamp**
    1853 *Amer. Sun.-School Union Annual Rept.* 30, I asked the woman . . if she had any candles to take to the meeting. She said no, . . but she could make some *sluts,* i.e. cold tallow rolled in a rag in the shape of a candle. **1873** Holley *My Opinions* 50 **NY,** Bein' out of candles, I made for the first time what they call a "slut," which is a button tied up in a rag, and put in a saucer of lard; you set fire to the rag, and it makes a light that is better than no light at all, jest as a slut is better than no woman at all. **1875** (1876) Young *Hist. Chautauqua Co. NY* 79, A kind of substitute for candles was sometimes prepared by taking a wooden rod ten or twelve inches in length, wrapping around it a strip of cotton or linen cloth, and covering it with tallow, pressed on with the hand. These "sluts," as they were sometimes called, afforded light for several nights. **1914** *DN* 4.80 **ME, nNH,** *Slut-lamp.* . . Tin dish with rag wick, burning grease. **1921** *DN* 5.119 **IN,** *Slut.* . . A tallow light. **1922** (1926) Kephart *Highlanders* 319 **sAppalachians,** Kerosene, also, is hard to transport . . oftener the woman will pour hog's grease into a tin or saucer, twist up a bit of rag for the wick and so make a "slut" that, believe me, deserves the name. **1929** Ellis *Ordinary Woman* 103 **MO** (as of early 20th cent), Mama would fill a bowl with melted grease, then braid or twist pieces of rag, putting one end in the grease, lighting the other, and thus making a very good light. She called it a 'slut.' **1931** Randolph *Ozarks* 27, Not long ago, however, I visited a home in which the only artificial light was a "slut." **1949** McDavid Coll. **cnNY,** *Slut-lamp* improvised of a rag in a dish of grease. [Inf 94 years old] **1973** Allen *LAUM* 1.409 (as of c1950) 1 inf, **NE,** Slut lamp. . . grease light.

2 A female dog. *euphem*
    1821 (1898) Fowler *Jrl.* 42 **KY,** A large Slut Which belongs to the Party atacted the Bare. **1823** Cooper *Pioneers* 2.103 **NY,** The dogs came out at the well-known tones, and the slut jumped upon his person, whining and barking. **1845** in 1956 Eliason *Tarheel Talk* 295 **cn,cwNC,** Mr. Williams dog I have just bred from—having put him to my fine slut from Maryland. **1860** Hundley *Social Relations S. States* 36, This licensed rum-hole was full of . . dogs—old dogs and young dogs, puppies, sluts, and snarling curs. **1899** (1912) Green *VA Folk-Speech* 395, *Slut.* . . A female dog; a bitch. **1906** Casey *Parson's Boys* 138 **sIL** (as of c1860), Here they come; Ringwell, Tingwell, Towser, the old slut and nine pups. **1945** FWP *Lay My Burden Down* 122 **LA** (as of c1865) [Black], You could hear them old hounds and sluts a-baying. **1966–69** *DARE* (Qu. J2, *. . Joking or uncomplimentary words . . for dogs*) Infs **GA13, LA32, NV7,** Slut; **IA1,** Bitch, slut; **IN19,** Slut—for a female; **MI8,** Slut—female; **MA68,** Slut—a female dog; obsolete today. [6 of 7 Infs old] **1968** Haun *Hawk's Done Gone* 68 **TN,** That way he had of blurting, like he was scolding a slut dog.

slut fuzz See **slut's wool**

slut lamp See **slut 1**

slut pie n
    1983 *MJLF* 9.1.56 **ceKY** (as of 1956), *Slut pie* . . a pie made of alternate layers of dough and applesauce.

slut's wool n Also *slut fuzz* [*OED2* 1862 →]
A soft roll of dust found under furniture.
    1906 Gilliam *Uncle Sam & Negro* 279 **VA** [Black], "No slut's wool behin my broom, sah." "What do you mean precisely by slut's wool?" "Spider-webs and sich like stuff as what lazy ones leave or hide under de furditure." **1950** *WELS Suppl.* **seWI,** *Slut's wool.* . . Mother says this is a well known term for house moss. . . It was used more in her (she's 70) generation. . . "Common folk" used it. **1959** *VT Hist.* 27.167, *Slut's wool.* . . Dust under the bed. Occasional. **1967** Marshall *Christy* 40 **sAppalachians** (as of 1912), 'Course she ain't much of a hand to housekeep; slut's wool all over the place. **1968** Coatsworth *ME Memories* 155, The fluff under the bed is known as "slut's wool." **1968** *DARE* (Qu. E20, *Soft rolls of dust that collect on the floor under beds or other furniture*) Inf **NY105,** Slut fuzz; **WI58,** Slut's wool. **1975** Gould *ME Lingo* 262, *Slut's wool*—Those kitties of dust under beds and in neglected corners associated with indifferent housewives. **1982** *Smithsonian Letters* eMA (as of c1925), At the Theta Chi fraternity house in Boston. . . [it] was called "Slut's Wool." **2003** in 2006 *DARE* File—Internet **swVA,** What most people referred to as "dust bunnies," my mama called "slut's wool." **2004** in 2005 *Ibid* **cwMO,** How many maribou [*sic*]-bimbo birds does Victoria's Secret kill per year? Is it even a bird, or is it just recycled slut-fuzz swept from the floors of strip clubs?!

sly v [Scots, nEngl dial]
To move stealthily, sneak.
    1851 Thompson *Rangers* 2.120 **VT,** I noticed, . . some five or six scouts, slying along on the other bank of the river, over there. **1856** in 1862 Colt *Went to KS* 61 **NY,** We dare not leave them [=clothes] out . . for fear of the Indians, who come thieving round—slying about—taking everything they can lay their hands on. **1864** (1868) Trowbridge *3 Scouts* 123 **TN,** Whilst we was slying out o' the bushes, Crumlett . . undertook to run, and stumbled down the ravine. **1899** Garland *Boy Life* 167 **nwIA** (as of c1870s), Say, Owen, you sly along and peek in and see what they're up to. **1959** *VT Hist.* 27.158, *Sly around.* . . Sneak around. Rare.

slycoon n [By metath from *cyclone*]
    1883 *Eve. Observer* (Dunkirk NY) 9 July 2/1, I believe thar's one of them slycoons coming. **1885** *Landmark* (Statesville NC) 12 June [3]/7 (newspaperarchive.com), They [=mud turtles] . . have crawled to that spot thinking it was a "slycoon" coming. **1890** *Eve. Jrl.* (Waukesha WI) 22 July [16]/3 (newspaperarchive.com) **IL,** Maria, thet war the daggondest slycoon ever heern on. It hes blowed the well clean off the lot. **1912** *DN* 3.590 **wIN,** *Sly-coon.* . . Cyclone. **1920** *Charleston Daily Mail* (WV) 4 Feb 12/2, Kid Mitchell . . and Cyclone Jackson . . entered the ring in the second bout. . . [I]n the second [round] "Slycoon" Jackson suddenly thought of home and country, and thereupon set out for one or the other.

slyver See **sliver**

smack adv Cf **slam** adv, **slap** adv, **spang** adv
1 With a sudden blow; sharply, abruptly.
    1840 *S. Lit. Messenger* 6.524, I wish I may never die if he didn't hit me smack in the face. **1862** *Continental Mth.* 1.366 **Philadelphia PA,** On went the cow. Right smack into the office of the evening paper. **1870** *Atlantic Mth.* 26.526 **MA,** Primus he struck his spade smack on something that chinked like iron. **1893** Shands *MS Speech* 57, *Smack.* . . Used by all classes. . . "He knocked him smack down," "He hit me smack in the face," "I ran smack up against it." **1899** (1912) Green *VA Folk-Speech* 395, He hit him and knocked him smack over the chair. **1942** McAtee *Dial. Grant Co. IN* 59 (as of 1890s), *Smack on,* also *smack dab on* . . directly, accurately; "He busted Elmer _____ the nose". (Ark., western Indiana, Nebr., Va.) **1965–70** *DARE* (Qu. KK53, *When one thing suddenly hits hard against something else: "He ran _____ into a car."*) 397 Infs, **widespread,** Smack; 7 Infs, **scattered,** Right smack; **MI82, NJ55,** Smack on; **NY131,** Smack onto. **1984** Woods *WV Was Good* 222, *Smack*—in the sense of nearness, as in, "The rolling log lodged smack up against the barn."

2 Exactly, completely. **esp Sth, S Midl** Cf **smack smooth**
    1859 Taliaferro *Fisher's R.* 43 **nwNC** (as of 1820s), I want some hog's

gullicks and turnup greens right smack now. **1886** *Century Illustr. Mag.* 32.193 **VA** [Black], Mistis an' Meh Lady teoh up dee under-clo'es tell dee got smack nuf. **1938** Rawlings *Yearling* 59 **nFL,** Right smack at the edge o' Juniper Creek. **1952** Brown *NC Folkl.* 1.592, *Smack:* . . Completely.—Central and east. **1953** Randolph–Wilson *Down in Holler* 285 **Ozarks,** *Smack out of.* . . Completely out of. A stranger asked for sugar to put in his coffee. "We're just smack out of sweetenin'," said his hostess. **1966–68** *DARE* (Qu. LL26a, . . *'All the way': "He drove* _____ *to the end of the road."*) Infs **NY**39, **NC**14, Smack.

3 At once, immediately.

1892 *DN* 1.237 **cwMO,** *Smack.* "Go smack and do it," said to children, = go at once. Kansas City. **1944** *PADS* 2.61 **MO, VA, NC,** *Smack.* . . At once. "Go smack and do it." Foothills of Ozarks.

4 As far as.

1884 *Harper's New Mth. Mag.* 68.491 **VA** [Black], Dat was de bloodies' fight ob de war . . an' de folk hear de shootin' smack in Richmon' an' Petersbu'g.

smack n[1] Also *smackee* [*OED2* 1611 →] **scattered, but chiefly NEast**

A small fishing vessel, usu with a well for keeping fish alive; a vessel for transporting live fish, lobsters, etc, to market.

1811 Brown *Ormond* 1.20, He was master, it seems, of a fishing smack, and voyaged sometimes to New York. **1834** *New Engl. Mag.* 6.132, Some one must jump from the fishing smack to a rock. **1879** *Scribner's Mth.* 18.45 **NYC,** In the rear of the Fulton Fish Market I saw a smack unloading with a scoop-net live cod-fish from the well in her hold. **1888** *Outing* 11.513 **FL,** She proved to be one of those peculiar crafts called a "smack," which ply between Havana and the coast of Florida, and supply the markets of the "Ever-Faithful Isle" with fish and oysters. **1895** *U.S. Fish Comm. Bulletin for 1894* 209, Most of the fish . . are caught in the channels between the keys, the fleet of small smacks (known as "smackees") going out every morning and returning in the afternoon. The fish . . are brought to market alive in the wells of the smackees. **1901** *U.S. Fish Comm. Bulletin for 1899* 250 **ME,** *Transporting Vessels or Smacks.* . . In 1853 there were but 6 smacks [for lobsters]. . . In 1880 there were 58, of which 21 were dry smacks, while in 1898 there were 76, of which 17 were steamers and launches and 59 sailing vessels. These were all well-smacks. **1932** Wasson *Sailing Days* 112 **cME coast,** The term "smack" alone distinguished smaller schooners containing wells. . . Any craft not equipped with a well was no "smack," though in modern times landsmen wrongly apply the term "fishing smack" to all vessels engaged in fishing of any sort. **1948** Hedrick *Land Crooked Tree* 16 **MI,** Besides the sailing craft of commerce, there were fishing smacks pulled up alongside fish houses. **1966** *DARE* Tape **ME**25, Lobster smack is what they convey lobsters in—carry lobsters to market. . . It's practically the same as a little steamboat, only that they use crude oil engines in them now. Then there's a well built in the center that fills with water, and they put the lobsters in it. . . They don't freight them with lobster smacks very much more. **2007** *DARE* File—Internet **ME,** [Advt:] For Sale: . . 50′ Southern built Shrimper would make excelent [sic] inland cargo or lobster smack.

smack n[2] See **smacker 1**

smack n[3] [*smack* flavor, taste, infl by *snack*]

Food, esp when taken between regular meals; a snack.

1941 *LANE* Map 314 (*A bite [between meals]*) 1 inf, **seME,** Smack, sic (error for *snack*?). **1966–69** *DARE* (Qu. H5, . . *A small amount of food eaten between regular meals*) Inf **GA**79, Smack [laughter]; **NY**2, Smack, snack; (Qu. H6, *Words for food in general: "He certainly enjoys his* _____."*) Infs **GA**79, **MT**1, Smack(s). **1986** Pederson *LAGS Concordance* (*Food taken between regular meals*) 4 infs, **cTN, cwMS, csLA, csTX,** (A) smack; 1 inf, **cLA,** Smack—newer term.

‡**smack** n[4] Cf **black wax, gumbo 6a**

1968 *DARE* (Qu. C31, . . *Heavy, sticky soil*) Inf **OH**69, Blue smack, jack wax.

smack and smooth See **smack smooth**

smack-dab adv

1 also *smack-bang,* ~*-dab-dash,* ~*-jam:* =**smack adv 1.**

1852 Hannibal *Professor Hannibal's Discourses* 23, He put his hand true de broken pane ob glass and onbolted de dore, and in he went smack dab, as de Yankees say, into his bedroom, which so skared his wife dat she hollar fire. **1892** *DN* 1.232 **KY,** He hit him smack dab in the mouth. **1893** Shands *MS Speech* 75, *Smack-dab.* . . A term used by all classes, but more especially by the uneducated, to mean *exactly,* pre-

cisely; as, "I hit him smack-dab in the face." **1905** *DN* 3.65 **eNE,** *Smack-dab.* . . About the same as *slap-dab.* Ibid 94 **nwAR,** *Smack dab.* . . Squarely. 'He ran smack dab into him.'[*] . . Common. **1909** *DN* 3.372 **eAL, wGA,** *Smack-dab.* . . Same as *slam bang.* **1912** *DN* 3.590 **wIN,** *Smack-dab.* . . Same as *slap-dab.* **1942** [see **smack** adv 1]. **1965–70** *DARE* (Qu. KK53, *When one thing suddenly hits hard against something else: "He ran* _____ *into a car."*) 115 Infs, **scattered,** (Right) smack-dab; **CA**145, **NY**92, Smack-bang; **VA**11, Smack-dab-dash; **WA**3, Smack-jam. **2001** *Post–Std.* (Syracuse NY) 14 Oct sec C 8/4 (Internet), Scampering Nunes did a U-turn smack dab into pursuing Bryan Knight, fumbling at the 5.

2 =**smack adv 2.** **chiefly Sth, S Midl** Note: The phr *smack-dab in the middle* does not seem to be regional.

1902 Harben *Abner Daniel* 14 **GA,** It'll be started inside of the next yeer an' 'll run smack dab through my property. **c1950** Halpert Coll. 57 **wKY, nwTN,** He's run smack-dab (slap-dab) out of money. **1960** *Holiday* Mar 57 **AL,** I didn't say I come from smack dab up to the courthouse. **1967–70** *DARE* (Qu. LL26a, . . *'All the way': "He drove* _____ *to the end of the road."*) Infs **NV**9, **NC**52, **SC**45, **TN**46, Smack-dab. **1971** *Today Show Letters* **cLA,** There he was "smack dab" in front of me. **1972** Cooper *NC Mt. Folkl.* 96, *Smackdab*—exactly. **1976** Garber *Mountain-ese* 84 **sAppalachians,** I shot the deer right smack-dab between the eyes. **1985** *Columbia Missourian* (MO) 28 July sec B 6/1, Spring Hill sits smack-dab between the two larger towns of Franklin and Columbia. **2000** *Parade* 17 Dec 4 **seMI** [Black], "We all lived together right smack-dab on the edge of Black Bottom," Della Reese said, recalling her childhood in the inner-city of Detroit.

smack-dab-dash See **smack-dab 1**

smackee See **smack** n[1]

smacker n

1 also *smack, smackerino, smackeroo, smackola, smackum:* A dollar.

1918 *Chicago Tribune* (IL) 13 Jan sec 5 2/4, A thousan' smackers is a fancy hunk o' change, even for me. **1927** *AmSp* 3.254 [Carnival slang], *Smackers*—Dollars. **1929** *AmSp* 4.345 [Vocabulary of bums], *Smack*—One dollar. **1940** in 1942 *AmSp* 17.14, Charlie McCarthy: 'A hundred smackeroos, that's what I've got.' Radio, Mar. 10. **1945** O'Hara *Pipe Night* 33 **PA,** We're suing you for one million smackeroos. **1965–70** *DARE* (Qu. U20, . . *Dollars* . . *"It cost a hundred* _____."*) 82 Infs, **widespread,** Smackers; **AK**9, **ID**5, **MO**2, **NY**66, **VA**90, Smackeroos; **NY**66, Smackerinos; **VA**54, Smackolas; **TX**9, Smacks; **SC**3, Smackums; (Qu. U26, *Names or nicknames . . for a paper dollar*) Infs **LA**11, **MA**7, **VA**101, (One) smacker; **MN**28, Smackeroo; (Qu. U28a, . . *A five-dollar bill*) Infs **IL**114, **NJ**67, Five smackers; [**KY**28, Five-dollar smacker;] (Qu. U28b, . . *A ten-dollar bill*) Infs **KY**45, **NJ**67, **NY**146, Ten smackers; **WI**58, Ten smackeroos; [**KY**28, Ten-dollar smacker;] (Qu. U28c, . . *A twenty-dollar bill*) Inf **NJ**67, Twenty smackers; [**KY**28, Twenty-dollar smacker]. **2002** *DARE* File—Internet, These are funds that hold the stock of big, huge, monstrous corporations—companies that are typically worth more than $5 billion smackers.

2 =**belly-smacker 2.**

1966–67 *DARE* (Qu. EE29, *When swimmers are diving and one comes down flat onto the water, that's a* _____) Infs **ME**15A, **OH**31, Smacker.

smackerino, smackeroo See **smacker 1**

smack-jam See **smack-dab 1**

‡**smack-madam** n

1969 *DARE* (Qu. AA9, . . *A loud or vigorous kiss*) Inf **GA**77, Smackmadam.

smackola See **smacker 1**

smack smooth adv Also *smack and smooth* Cf **smack** adv 2, **smooth C**

1 also rarely *smick-smack and smooth:* So as to leave a smooth surface, so as to leave no trace; hence adj *smack smooth* completely smooth. [*OED2 smack-smooth* 1755 →]

1718 *Boston News–Letter* (MA) 24 Feb 2/2, A Man observing his Design, took out his Knife, before the Negro was aware, [and] cut off all his unruly parts smack and smooth. **1826** in 2006 *DARE* File—Internet **OH,** We . . cut and cleared off five acres, as the saying is "smack and smooth." **1833** in 1834 Smith *Life Jack Downing* 28 **ME,** He . . rolled [sic] them up in piles and sot fire to 'em and burnt 'em up smack smooth. **1834** [see **smooth A**]. **1855** Roe *Long Look Ahead* 74 **CT,**

Thinks I, that is too good a house to pull down. . . By jingo, if I don't ask the fellows what they 'll take, and have it moved right off smack and smooth. **1856** Simms *Eutaw* 110 **SC,** Cappin Travis ain't at his place, for its all burnt down, smack and smooth. **1890** *Centralia Enterprise & Tribune* (WI) 13 Dec 1/3, Waal, ef 'tis like a fire I sor ten year ago, 'twould, and lick up everything smack and smooth. **1957** *Daily Jrl.* (Commerce TX) 12 June 2/3 [Black], Instead of making the boards lap over, I set out to lay them smick-smack-and smooth. **2006** *DARE* File—Internet **UT,** The surface must be smooth and free of blemishes to produce a smack smooth finish.

2 Completely; directly, straight, all the way. **esp Sth, S Midl**

1871 [see **smooth A**]. **1890** *Herald & Torch-Light* (Hagerstown MD) 16 Jan 1/6 **Appalachians,** Now comes along a railroad an' wants to run smack, smooth over the spring house. *Ibid,* Fling the dirt smack smooth in the spring. **1897** *Atlanta Constitution* (GA) 12 Dec [30]/1 (newspaperarchive.com) **AL,** I'm smack and smooth outen snuff. **1945** in 2005 *DARE* File—Internet **OK** [Woody Guthrie *Ten Songs*], I know you're likeing [sic] it and it's tick-ling me smack smooth to death.

smackum See **smacker 1**

smaller states n pl **AK** Cf **lower** adj **2b**

With *the:* The states of the US other than Alaska, esp the contiguous states.

1958 *NY Times* (NY) 3 July 49/5, Robert Atwood, an Alaskan newspaper publisher. . . said: "The week-ends are spent just as they are throughout the smaller states of the Union." **1959** *Tri-City Herald* (Pasco WA) 9 Jan 3/6, The Fairbanks Daily News-Miner . . said that in the future it will refer to the other 48 states as "the smaller states." **1973** *River Times* Mar/Apr 5 (Tabbert *Dict. Alaskan Engl.*), The following article by Reggie Joseph tells about his experiences last fall while touring the smaller states. **1978** *Fairbanks Daily News–Miner* 9 Jan 4 (Tabbert *Dict. Alaskan Engl.*), A local beer connoisseur wasn't impressed with a six-pack of Billy Carter's 'Billy' beer a friend brought back from the smaller states recently. **2002** *DARE* File—Internet **AK,** They said someday it would attract mushers from all sections of Alaska the smaller states and even foreign countries.

small hominy See **little hominy**

small-leaf dahoon n Cf **dahoon**

A **holly** n[1] **1** (here: *Ilex myrtifolia*).

1960 Vines *Trees SW* 650, *Ilex myrtifolia.* . . Small, myrtle-like leaves. Common names are Small-leaf Dahoon [etc].

small magnolia n

A **sweet bay 2** (here: *Magnolia virginiana*).

1785 Marshall *Arbustrum* 83, Magnolia glauca [=*M. virginiana*]. *Small Magnolia, or Swamp Sassafras.* This grows naturally in low, moist, or swampy ground, often to the height of fifteen or twenty feet. **1850** Emerson *Rept. Trees & Shrubs* 529, The small magnolia may be propagated by layers, which require two years to root sufficiently, and by seed. **1900** (1927) Keeler *Our Native Trees* 3, *Small Magnolia.* . . A small tree, nearly evergreen, with slender trunk. **1950** Gray–Fernald *Manual of Botany* 676, *Small* or *Laurel-M[agnolia].* . . Swamps and low woods, Fla. to Miss., n. to Pa., N.J. and locally e. Mass. and Tenn.

small measure n

A quarter peck.

1854 Stephens *Fashion & Famine* 300 **NYC,** "Yes, they [=cranberries] are very fine," said the old lady; "do up a small measure neatly, they are for a sick person." **1875** Frothingham *Once More* 237 **NYC,** She purchased at the grocery . . a small measure (this term being commonly used for a quarter-peck, in which limited quantity a vast number of poor people in New York purchase most of their vegetables) of potatoes. **1890** *DN* 1.62 **swOH,** *Small-measure:* the fourth part of a peck. **1936** *AmSp* 11.141, The term *small measure,* meaning specifically two quarts dry measure or one fourth of a peck (as of apples, potatoes, etc.), I have heard commonly used in Cincinnati, Ohio, and Milwaukee, Wisconsin. In the latter city German-speaking market folk often say 'kleines Mass.' Some natives of Germany of whom I have inquired say they are not familiar with the term in native German speech.

smallmouth n

1 See **smallmouth bass.**

2 See **smallmouth buffalo.**

smallmouth bass n Also *smallmouth, smallmouth(ed) (black) bass*

Std: a **black bass 1** (here: *Micropterus dolomieu*). Also called **black perch 1a, bronzeback, brown bass, ~ trout 2, catoosa bass, gold ~ 1, grass ~ 2, green ~, green perch 1, ~ trout, hog bass, jumper 2, lake bass 1, linesides, marsh bass, mossback 2, moss bass, mountain trout 2, Oswego bass, perch** n[1] **B3, river bass, rock ~ 4, slough ~, speckled hen, spotted bass 1, swamp ~ 1, tiger ~, trout 2a, white bass 2, ~ trout 3, yellow bass 1, ~ perch 2, Welshman**

smallmouth buffalo n Also *smallmouth* Cf **bigmouth buffalo**

Std: a catostomid fish *(Ictiobus bubalus)* found throughout the Mississippi River system and Gulf Coast drainages. Also called **buffalo fish, ~ perch 2, humpback buffalo, quillback ~, razorback ~ (fish), roachback buffalo, white ~, white carp 2**

small-mouthed (black) bass See **smallmouth bass**

small mule n Cf **mule-eared rabbit**

=**jackrabbit 1.**

1917 Anthony *Mammals Amer.* 274, As long ago as 1851, Audubon and Bachman, writing of a species found along the Mexican border, said: "This species is called the jackass rabbit in Texas, owing to the length of its ears." For the same reason, in certain parts of California they have been called "narrow-gauge mules" and "small mules."

small on, from See **little C2**

small pewee n Cf **pewee** n **1**

A **flycatcher 1a** (here: *Empidonax virescens*).

1839 MA *Zool. & Bot. Surv. Fishes Reptiles* 295, The Small Pewee, *Muscicapa Acadia,* is a very common summer bird. **1844** DeKay *Zool. NY* 2.112, The *Small Green-crested Flycatcher,* or *Small Pewee* as he is sometimes called, in common with some others, from the sound of his usual note, . . appears in our State early in May, where it breeds. **1917** (1923) *Birds Amer.* 2.207, *Empidonax virescens.* . . Small Pewee.

small pokeberry See **pokeberry 2**

small pokeweed See **pokeweed 3**

smallpox plant n

A **pitcher plant 1,** usu *Sarracenia purpurea.*

[**1869** Porcher *Resources* 58, It is difficult to see how it [=*Sarracenia purpurea*] acquired any reputation in the cure of small-pox.] **1876** Hobbs *Bot. Hdbk.* 107, Small-pox plant, . . Sarracenia purpurea. **1900** Lyons *Plant Names* 335, *S[arracenia] purpurea.* . . Canada and eastern U.S. . . Small-pox plant. . . *Plant* tonic, anodyne, astringent. . . *S. variolaris* [=*S. minor*]. . . Southeastern U.S. Small-pox plant.

small tiger lily n Cf **tiger lily**

A **lily 1** (here: *Lilium parvum*).

1898 *Jrl. Amer. Folk.* 11.281 **CA,** *Lilium parvum,* . . small tiger lily. **1915** (1926) Armstrong–Thornber *Western Wild Flowers* 32, *Small Tiger Lily.* . . These little Lilies . . grow somewhat freely in the high Sierras . . and as far north as Oregon. **1949** Moldenke *Amer. Wild Flowers* 324, The *small tiger lily* . . has very numerous orange-yellow, purple-spotted flowers only 1 to 1¼ inches long. **1961** Peck *Manual OR* 220, Small Tiger Lily. . . Mountain bogs and stream banks.

small-tufted partridge See **tufted quail**

smart adj

1 Healthy; chipper, spry. **esp NEng** See Map on p. 46 *old-fash*

1788 in 1873 May *Jrl.* 116 **NEng,** Did n't feel smart enough to go to meeting. **1834** (1961) Strang *Diary* 45 **NY,** I am again smart for a sick person: that is I am able to walk about. **1836** in 1956 Eliason *Tarheel Talk* 295 **NC,** [After being ill] today I am pretty smart. **1864** in 1986 Messer *Civil War Letters* 29 **VT,** I will try and keep smart now. **1899** (1912) Green *VA Folk-Speech* 396, *Smart.* . . In good health; well; not sick. "I'm right smart." **1914** *DN* 4.80 **ME, nNH,** *Smart.* . . Healthy. "How's Luell? Oh, she's smart." **1941** *LANE* Map 461 *(Lively, spry),* [*Smart* occurs freq throughout **NEng, but slightly more freq in nNEng** than **sNEng.**] 1 inf, **ceRI,** She's smart for her age; 1 inf, **seMA,** She's a smart woman; 1 inf, **cnMA,** He's smart for his years; 1 inf, **swMA,** She's smart for a woman of her years; 1 inf, **nwMA,** He's a smart old man; 1 inf, **nVT,** He's smart of his age; 1 inf, **ceVT,** She was smart as lightning; 1 inf, **csNH,** Smart, older term; 1 inf, **nME,** Smart, of physical endurance. *Ibid* Map 497 *(Pretty well),* In answer to the casual greeting 'How are you?' or 'How are you feeling?' . . 1 inf, **cwMA,** All right, smart. **1965–70** *DARE* (Qu. KK27, *A very lively, active old person: "For his age, he's _____."*) Infs **CT**15, **ME**5, 19, 22, **MA**24, 29, 38, **MI**50, **VT**6, (Pretty *or* very) smart; **ME**1, Awful smart yet; (Qu. GG29, . . *"This morning he seems to be feeling _____."*) Inf **ID**2, Right smart. [10 of 11 Infs old] **1986** Pederson *LAGS Concordance (She's quite lively)* 1 inf, **cnGA,** Smart; 1 inf, **seMS,** Smart—always active, child or old person; 1 inf, **neLA,** Mighty smart = spry. [All infs old, Black]

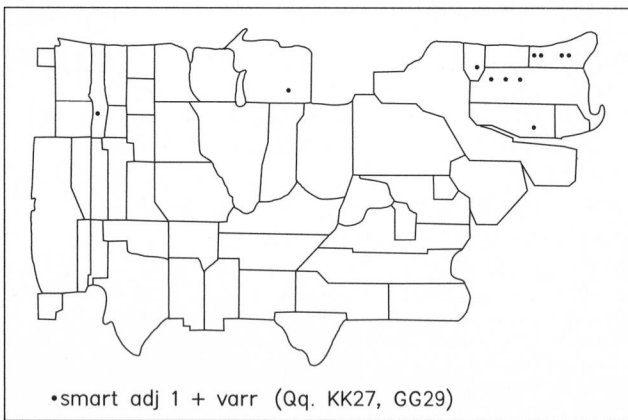

•smart adj 1 + varr (Qq. KK27, GG29)

2 Of a person: energetic and effective in working; industrious, diligent; hence n *smartness* competence, diligence. **chiefly Sth, S Midl** See Map *esp freq among Black speakers*
1859 Taliaferro *Fisher's R.* 118 **nwNC** (as of 1820s), It was corn-gathering time, and I tell you, I made things wake—wucked all day, wouldn't stop fur dinner—to show my smartness. **1866** in 1983 *PADS* 70.51 **ce,sePA,** Mary is very smart does all her own work milks a cow. **1886** *Amer. Philol. Assoc. Proc.* 17.xiii **ePA,** The word "smart" attributes to a young person the quality of moral regularity, conveying precisely the same idea that the word "steady" does in many localities. **1935** *AmSp* 10.157 **NC,** During a stay in North Carolina it was my good fortune to lodge in the house of a woman whose speech was strikingly rich in local idiom. . . 'Be smart now,' said my hostess, as I started off for Charleston one March morning. Although she had several times admonished me to 'be smart,' I did not fully understand her until she now added, 'and don't drive into the ditch.' **1965–70** *DARE* (Qu. KK28, *Feeling ambitious and eager to work*) Infs **KY**28, **NC**84, 88, (Real) smart; **GA**61, He's very smart; **LA**8, Smart—you know, ain't lazy; (Qu. KK29, *To start working very hard: "He was slow at first but now he's really _____."*) Infs **TN**52, **VA**69, Smart; **MS**61, Is a smart hand. [7 of 8 Infs Black] **1998** *Atlanta Jrl.–Constitution* (GA) 4 Oct sec M 1/1 **Sth,** When your son or grandson brings home a smart girl, we don't call her "industrious." "Smart" says it better.

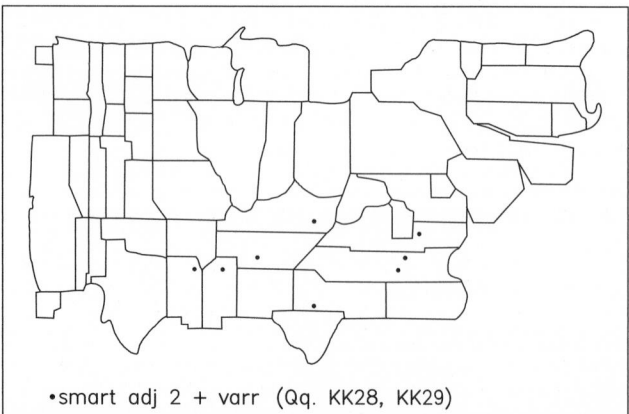

•smart adj 2 + varr (Qq. KK28, KK29)

3 Considerable, large. Cf **chance B1, right smart** adj phr
1823 *Natl. Intelligencer* (DC) 1 May (*DN* 4.47), *Western Dialect. . . smart. . . Large.* **1827** (1939) Sherwood *Gaz.* GA 139, *Smart chance,* for good deal, large quantity, large company, great number. **1850** McCallum *ME Letters* [2], I will stop after asking you what you want in

the hickory line for there is a smart chance of it here. **1859** (1968) Bartlett *Americanisms* 418, *Smart. . . In the South and West the word is frequently used (as it also is in the east of England) in the sense of considerable; and especially in such phrases as "right smart," "smart chance," "smart sprinkle," etc. Ibid* 419, *Smart piece.* A good bit; a considerable time. **1903** *DN* 2.330 **seMO,** *Smart chance. . .* A considerable quantity. 'There will be a smart chance of peaches this season.' **1937** *Hall Coll.* **wNC, eTN,** *Smart. . .* Large—"They was a pretty smart gang of 'em." **1967–69** *DARE* (Qu. MM25, . . *A long distance: "Texas is a _____ [from here]."*) Infs **KY**33, 41, 47, 60, Right smart piece; **NY**191, Smart piece. **1986** Pederson *LAGS Concordance,* 1 inf, **neAR,** A smart distance; 1 inf, **cwAL,** Smart amount of trouble.

smart n **esp Sth** Cf **right smart** n 1
A large amount.
1846 in 1956 Eliason *Tarheel Talk* 295 **cNC,** Put up smart of the eve spout. **1870** Duval *Advent. Big-Foot* 301 **cTX,** Crops have failed entirely, but there's pretty smart of good grass in that hollow yonder. **c1940** Eliason *Word Lists FL* 3 **nwFL,** *Quite smart: . .* Polite understatement for *a great deal.* "Yes, my pop knows quite smart." **1986** Pederson *LAGS Concordance,* 1 inf, **seMS,** There smart of them = much/many of them.

smart-ass weed n Also *smart-ash* Cf **ass-smart**
A smartweed.
1968 *DARE* (Qu. S21, . . *Weeds . . that are a trouble in gardens and fields*) Inf **NC**81, Smart-ass weed—maybe called pepperweed, grow in low places; **MD**26, Smart-ash [æš]—broad, pointed leaves, spreads over much ground.

smart grass See **smartweed**

smartness See **smart** adj 2

smartweed n Also *smart grass* [*OED2* "Chiefly *dial.* and *U.S.*"; 1787 →] **widespread, but chiefly Midl, N Cent, Cent** See Map Cf **pinktop smartweed**
Any of var plants of the genus *Polygonum.* Also called **gander grass 1, knotweed 1;** for other names of var of these see **ass-smart, birdweed 2, blackheart 4, chickweed 2, duckweed 3, heartsease 2, horse marsh, knotweed 1, jointweed 2, lady's thumb, mile-a-minute 2, pinkweed 2, smart-ass weed, tearthumb, turkey-troop, water pepper, ~ smartweed, wild bean 2**
1819 Schoolcraft *Lead Mines MO* 29, Plants from which colours have been extracted for dyeing . . [are] shumac, upland dock, and smartweed. **1845** Judd *Margaret* 105 **NEng,** Her little white and yellow chickens were peeping and dodging under . . the star-tipped hedge-mustard, and pink-tufted smart-weed. **1867** Harris *Sut Lovingood Yarns* 75 **TN,** A hollyhawk in a patch ove smartweed. **1884** Baldwin *Yankee School-Teacher* 37 **VA,** Smartweed tea is a dreadful stim'lant t' the intellect! **1891** *Jrl. Amer. Folkl.* 4.148 **NH,** P[olygonum] Hydropiper was *Smartweed.* **1911** CA Ag. Exper. Sta. Berkeley *Bulletin* 217.989, *Polygonum lapathifolium. . .* Smart Weed. . . *Polygonum punctatum.* . . (Dotted Smartweed). **1949** (1958) Stuart *Thread* 111 **KY,** I was careful as could be about touching the fringe of ragweed, Queen Anne's lace, smartweed, and sprouts that bordered my path. **1950** *WELS* **WI** (*Other kinds of plants that will cause itching and swelling*) 5 Infs, Smartweed; (*Other weeds common in your locality*) 3 Infs, Smartweed. **c1960** Wilson *Coll.* **csKY,** Smartweed—several varieties grow in the area and are known, generally, to the natives. **1965–70** *DARE* (Qu. S17, . . *Kinds of plants . . that . . cause itching and swelling*) 63 Infs, **widespread, but chiefly Midl, N Cent, Cent,** Smartweed(s); (Qu. S21, . . *Weeds . . that are a trouble in gardens and fields*) 48 Infs, **chiefly Midl, N Cent, Cent,** Smartweed(s); **VA**2, Smart grass; (Qu. L8, *Hay that grows naturally in damp places*) Inf **KY**80, Smartweed; (Qu. S15, . . *Weed seeds that cling to clothing*) Inf **IL**40, Smartweed; (Qu. S16, *A . . plant that . . makes people's skin itch and swell*) Inf **CO**22, Smartweed; (Qu. S26a, . . *Wildflowers. . . Roadside flowers*) Infs **KS**5, **MO**6, Smartweed; (Qu. S26b, *Wildflowers that grow in water or wet places*) Inf **NY**150, Smartweed; (Qu. S26e, *Other wildflowers not yet mentioned;* not asked in early QRs) Inf **MO**6, Smartweed; (Qu. BB50a, . . *Favorite remedies . . for a cough*) Inf **VT**8, Smartweed tea; (Qu. BB50b, *Remedies for chest colds*) Inf **WI**44, Smartweed tea. **1982** Slone *How We Talked* 47 **eKY** (as of c1950), Smart grass—used to get rid of fleas, also put in a hole of water to make the fish come to the top of the water and could then be caught. **1991** Heat Moon *PrairyErth* 595 **ceKS,** His people gathered grapes, gooseberries, blackberries, smartweed [etc].

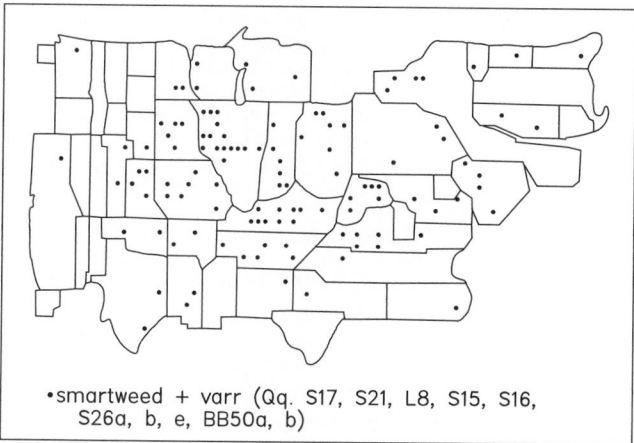

•smartweed + varr (Qq. S17, S21, L8, S15, S16, S26a, b, e, BB50a, b)

smash n

1 in phrr *play smash (with):* To cause confusion; to blunder; to wreak havoc with. **scattered, but esp S Midl**

1841 *Spirit of Times* 2 Jan 523 **AR**, Bill Spence got drunk and played smash with all the arrangements. **1884** Smith *Bill Arp's Scrap Book* 31 **nwGA**, Durn the staff and Joe Brown, too. He played smash amazingly, writing pages against conscription. **1887** *Courier–Jrl.* (Louisville KY) 17 Jan 1/7, [Headline:] Plays Smash With a Passenger Train on the Fitchburg [Massachusetts] Railroad. **1902** Harben *Abner Daniel* 11 **nGA**, Yore pa's as bull-headed as a young steer, an' he's already played smash anyway. **1912** in 1969 *PADS* 52.54 **seIL**, *Play smash.* . . Play havoc. " . . and it will play smash with my 30 subscribers." **1912** *DN* 3.585 **wIN**, *Play smash.* . . A euphemism for *play hell* or *play the devil.* **1915** *DN* 4.187 **swVA**, *Play smash.* . . To make a great blunder; do a thing wholly wrong. "Well, now you've played smash." **1948** *WELS Suppl.* **IL**, My grandfather used to jeer at us children by saying, "You'll play smash doing that," whenever we boasted about whatever we had in mind doing. **c1960** *Wilson Coll.* **csKY**, *Play smash with.* . . Tear up, disrupt. **2002** Proulx *That Old Ace* 129 **TX**, They turn them fans on, sucks out the ammonia and sulfide and if the wind is right, like it was this mornin, we almost die of it. It just plays smash with us.

2 in phrr *to have* (or *get*) *a smash on:* To be infatuated with, have a crush on. [Cf **smash v 1**, *have a mash on*]

1967–69 *DARE* (Qu. AA10, *A very special liking that a boy may have for a girl [or the other way round]* . . *"He _____ her." or "She _____ him."*) Infs **AL30, IN69**, Got a smash on. **1986** Pederson *LAGS Concordance,* 1 inf, **cGA**, He's got a smash on that girl—corrects: "mash."

3 Wine. *esp freq among Black speakers*

1972 *AmSp* 47.153 (as of 1970) [Black], Let's get in the wind and belt some smash. **1971** Roberts *Third Ear* np [Black], *Smash* . . wine. *syn. see* grapes. **1972** Claerbaut *Black Jargon* 80, *Smash* . . wine. See also *joy juice, juice.* **1980** Folb *Runnin' Down* 187 **cwCA** [Black], There are many vernacular names for wine—*the grapes, the berries, the vine, pluck, smash,* to name a few.

smash v

1 To kiss. Cf **smash n 2**

1986 Pederson *LAGS Concordance* (Kissing) 4 infs, **GA, cnFL, cwMS**, Smashing; 1 inf, **cnLA**, Been a-smashing.

2 =**mash v[1] 2.**

1994 NC Lang. & Life Project *Dial. Dict. Lumbee Engl.* 11 **seNC**, *Smash.* . . To press. This term is related to the General Southern term *mash* 'press'. *Jane smashed the wrong button on her computer.*

smash (all) to flinders See **flinders 1**

smather v [Ir dial < IrGael *smeadar* to smear, daub] **chiefly Sth, S Midl**

To smear, slather.

1960 *Max Hunter Folk Song Coll.* (Internet) **Ozarks**, I get my socks on wrong side out / I guess I will go smather / With tooth paste on my shavin' brush / An' fuss when it won't lather. **1996** *DARE* File **NC**, I seem to remember that grits could be ordered "plain," "covered," etc., and "smathered." That last is a word I've never heard elsewhere in America. *Ibid* **cTN**, I have heard "smathered" used quite frequently here in central Tennessee. It usually applies to a food that is covered with something such as butter. A typical usage would be, "Those bis-

cuits sure were good smathered in/with butter." **1999** in 2002 *DARE* File—Internet **Houston TX**, [Web diary:] I feel pretty and clean even though I've just smathered gunk all over my face. **2002** *Ibid* **ceIL**, [Restaurant menu:] We cook them until tender and smather them with our famous barbecue sauce. *Ibid* **VA**, It was a southern Baptist church, and for those of you who aren't sure what that means, well, it means they smather the guilt on extra thick. *Ibid,* Just kind a drizzled over with the grease and pan scrapins along with a fork full o good churned butter just smathered all over the top of them grits.

smather n See **smither**

smea See **smee**

smear n

1 Butter. [Prob infl by the cognates in other Germanic langs: Ger *Schmiere,* Du *smeer* grease; Norw, Dan *smør,* Sw *smör* butter]

1891 French *Otto* 330 **AR**, You an' Bulah Norman wud . . be projickin' roun' my kitchin for light bread an' smear. **1942** Berrey–Van den Bark *Amer. Slang* 91.18, *Butter.* . . Skid, smear, spread. **1958** McCulloch *Woods Words* 171 **Pacific NW**, *Smear*—Butter. **1966** Barnes–Jensen *Dict. UT Slang* 39, *Smear* . . butter. **1969** *DARE* (Qu. H37, . . *Words* . . *for gravy. Any joking ones?*) Inf **AZ10**, Smear—or is that butter? **1971** *NY Times* (NY) 5 Sept 7/2 [Diner cant], *Smear.* Butter.

2 often pronc |šmɪr|; pronc-spp *schmear, schmier:* A card game in which a card of value is played on one's partner's trick; such a play; also v *smear* to play such a card. [Ger *schmieren* to play a high card on one's partner's trick] **chiefly MI, WI, MN** See Map

1897 *KS Univ. Qrly.* (ser B) 6.92, *Smear:* . . to put in a valuable card under the protection of your partner's high card—General. **1904** *Daily Northwestern* (Oshkosh WI) 11 Jan 8/4, Such good old games as seven up, hearts, pedro, "smear" and others are played. **1909** *WI State Jrl.* (Madison) 27 Sept 2/2, [Headline:] Jail Term For Schmier Sharks—Three Flimflammers Trimmed For Gaming With Cards on Railroad Train. **1919** *LaCrosse Tribune & Leader–Press* (WI) 24 Jan 12/2 **neMN**, Between trips to the dining room and the "schmear" tables they cuss the weather man. **1942** Berrey–Van den Bark *Amer. Slang* 745.3, *Smear, the play of a counting card on one's partner's trick. Ibid* 745.6, *Smear, to play a counting card on one's partner's trick.* **1950** *WELS* (Card games played a good deal in your neighborhood) 12 Infs, **WI**, Smear. **1965–70** *DARE* (Qu. DD35) Infs **MI2, 19, 24, 105, MN10, 16, 29, 33, 35, ND1, WI40, 63**, Smear; **WI68**, Smear [smɪr]; **MI44, MN2**, Schmear [šmɪr]; **MN5**, Racehorse schmear [šmɪr]; **MI27**, The ladies go for bridge, the men go for smear; **WI77**, Smear—deal out six cards (or seven?) to each player, "shoot the moon"—try to win everything; very popular in Door County. [8 Infs old, 10 mid-aged] **1996** *DARE* File **ceWI** (as of 1921), I used to play "Schmier" with my cousin Myrtle in Appleton when I was nine years old. It was a common card game. We also played euchre, another card game, in which you "schmiered" on your partner's cards to make points. **1997** *DARE* File—Internet [Speak 'Scansin] **WI**, *Schmear and sheephead:* Two card games, probably of German origin. You can watch these games and have them explained for years, and you still won't know the rules. Actual names being smear and sheepshead. You can also schmear in sheephead.

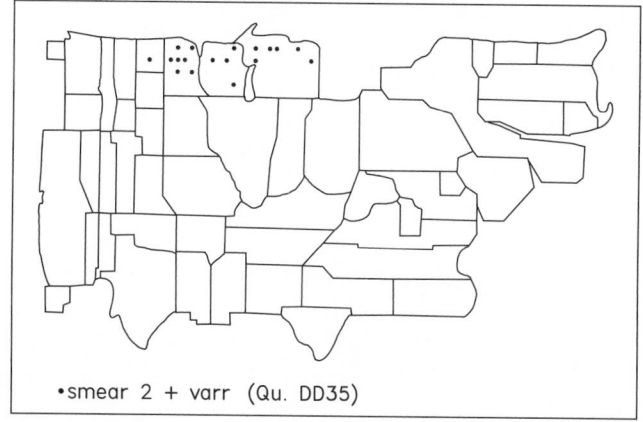

•smear 2 + varr (Qu. DD35)

smearcase n Usu |'smɪrˌkes| [PaGer *schmierkaes* (Ger *schmierkäse*), literally "spread-cheese"] Also *shmearcase,*

smear cheese, smiercase, smierkase **chiefly N Midl, esp PA, OH, MD, WV** See Map Cf **cook cheese, Dutch ~, pot ~**
A soft cheese made of curds of skimmed milk; cottage cheese.

1829 Royall *Pennsylvania* 1.471, A dish, common amongst the Germans, . . is curds and cream. It is very palatable, and called by the Germans *smearcase.* **1848** Bartlett *Americanisms* 314, *Smear-Case.* . . A preparation of milk made to be spread on bread, whence its name; otherwise called Cottage-Cheese. **1892** *KS Univ. Qrly.* 1.99 **KS**, *Smearcase:* a preparation of clabber, often called 'Dutch cheese.' **1906** *DN* 3.157 **nwAR**, *Smear-case.* . . Pot cheese, cottage cheese, clabber cheese, curd (Mississippi). **1909** *Daily Gaz. & Bulletin* (Williamsport PA) 22 Jan 6/5, [Advt:] Smear case, per ball. . . 5[¢]. **1915** Thomas *Mary at Farm* 277 **cePA**, From three quarts of sour milk you should obtain one good pound of smier-kase. **1930** *DN* 6.88 **cWV**, *Smearcheese,* cottage cheese. **1934** *AmSp* 9.319 **IN, Ohio Valley,** *Smearcase.* Cottage cheese, from German *Schmierkäse*—Pennsylvania Dutch. **1946** *PADS* 5.38 **VA**, *Smear case.* . . Cheese made of the drained curd of sour milk; west of the Blue Ridge. **1946** *PADS* 6.27 **swVA**, *Smearcase.* . . Cottage cheese. **1958** *PADS* 29.16 **TN**, *Smearcase:* Cheese made of curd and sour milk. **1965–70** *DARE* (Qu. H60, *The lumpy white cheese that is made from sour milk*) 102 Infs, **chiefly N Midl, esp PA, OH, MD, WV,** Smearcase; **CA**212, **IL**82, **PA**74, 95, 242, **TN**11, [ˈsmɪrke(ɪ)s]; **MD**8, [ˈsmɪrke(ɪ)s]; **MO**12, [ˈsmɪɹkæs]; **MO**36, Shmearcase; **OH**98, [ˈsmɪəkes]; **IL**113, [ˈsmerkeɪs]; **PA**29, **VA**26, [ˈsmirkes]; **CO**20, **MO**21, Smear cheese; **MO**13, [ˈsmɪrkeɪs] cheese. [36 of 119 Infs indicated that this term was old-fashioned or that they remembered it from the speech of a parent or grandparent.] **1969** *DARE* Tape IL66, The folks used to always make . . smearcase. . . They would take that milk and clabber it. **1976** Allen *LAUM* 3.292 **Upper MW** (as of c1950), *Cottage cheese.* . . *Smearcase* . . moved with the westward migration into southern Iowa and Nebraska, where more than one-third of infs. knowing the term consider it now old-fashioned. *Ibid* 293, 2 infs, **ceIA, ceNE,** Smear cheese. **1982** *Barrick Coll.* **csPA**, *Smear case*—cottage cheese. **1985** *AmSp* 60.234 **sePA**, Today in the Pennsylvania German area, *smear case* no longer means 'curds'. As a former student of mine who is employed as a salesperson in a farmers' market in Bird-in-Hand, Lancaster County, puts it: "Today *smear case* is never related to cottage cheese, but to a smooth, spreadable cheese." Indeed, the term is very much alive in the area—a fact clearly demonstrated by the availability of such "smooth, spreadable cheese" under this name at many local markets.

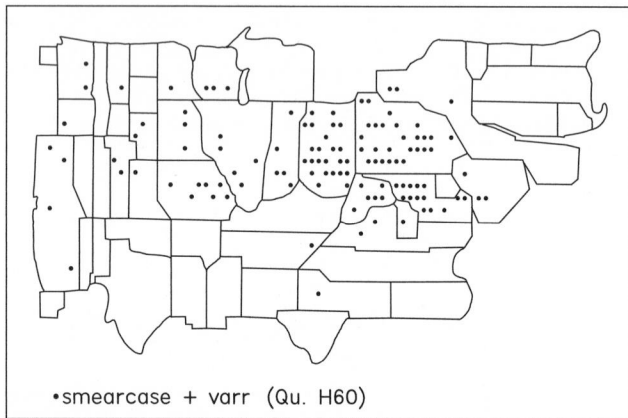

•smearcase + varr (Qu. H60)

smeared adj Cf **smear in**
Of the sky: overcast.

1950 *WELS Suppl.* **csWI**, My mother often used the word "smeared" in describing an overcast sky, when clouds were a grayish cover, hiding the blue sky. I think the word is taken from the German word "verschmiered" [sic]. In German an overcast sky is described thus. **1983** (2001) Rechy *Bodies & Souls* 71 **swCA**, He woke to a smeared sky.

smear in v phr [Perh folk-etym for **smur** v, but cf **smeared**]
Of the weather: to become overcast.

1975 Gould *ME Lingo* 262, *Smear*—To cloud in, but reserved mostly for the increasing evidence of the high cirrus clouds that make *mare's tails* and *mackerel sky:* "Been smearin' in so I doubt if I'll haul tomorrow."

smee n Also *smea, smees, smethe* [*OED2 smee* sb.[1] 1668; *smeath* 1622 →; both applied to var ducks] **esp eNJ**

=pintail 1.

1674 Josselyn *Two Voyages* 101 **NEng**, Of *Ducks* there may be many more sorts, as . . *Coots, Pochards,* a water-fowl like a *Duck, Plungeons,* a kind of water-fowl with a long reddish Bill, *Puets, Plovers, Smethes, Wilmotes,* [etc]. [*DARE* Ed: This may refer to some other duck.] **1846** *Spirit of Times* 16.50 **ceNJ**, I killed thirteen ducks before night, all Pin Tails or Smeas, as they are there termed. . . I scattered Widgeon, Smee, and Black-duck decoys. **1888** Trumbull *Names of Birds* 38, In New Jersey, at Manasquan . . [*Anas acuta*] *smee;* at Tuckerton, *smees;* while others at Tuckerton refer to it as *smethe.* . . The species has been so termed, it appears, for a very long time. "Most of us," said a venerable hunter, "call it Sprig-tail, but I suppose its real name is Smees." **1920** *Forest & Stream* 90.537 **ceNJ**, I saw it was a very large number of birds, nearly all "smees" and widgeons, strung out in a long thin line along the shore.

smell bug n Cf **stink bug**
1966–70 *DARE* (Qu. R30, . . *Kinds of beetles;* not asked in early QRs) Infs **DC**8, **KY**35, **MS**84, Smell bug.

smell-leaves n Also *smelling-leaves* **Pacific NW**
=vanilla leaf 1.
1919 *DN* 5.59 **Pacific NW**, *Smell-leaves.* Achlys triphylla. **1941** *Torreya* 41.48 **WA**, Angel-leaves, elkhorn, smell-leaves. **1949** Peattie *Cascades* 231 **Pacific NW**, The plant . . is vanilla-leaf, so named for its odor. When dried, the leaves are even more fragrant. . . The pioneers and settlers called them smelling-leaves. They used to dry them and hang them in bunches to perfume their cabins and log houses.

smell melon n **Sth**
A small melon (*Cucurbita melo* subsp *melo* Dudaim Group). Also called **pomegranate B2**
1806 Shecut *Flora Carolinæensis* 1.477, C[ucumis] *Orientalis* . . *Oriental Cucumber,* or *Smell Melon* . . the fruit is . . about the size of an orange, and of a most agreeable odour. **1888** *Chautauquan* 8.373 **swMS**, *Smell-melon* for species of dwarf cantelope, called in Tennessee and Georgia pomegranate. **1909** *DN* 3.372 **eAL, wGA**, *Smell-melon.* . . A small melon, curiously marked and having an agreeable odor; Queen Anne's pocket melon. **1941** O'Donnell *Great Big Doorstep* 78 **sLA**, There were no more smell-melon by our bay-gall. **1966–67** *DARE* (Qu. I26, . . *Kinds of melons*) Inf **MS**23, Smell melons—don't eat these; **TX**35, Smell melons. **1972** *Names SC* 19.31, *Smell Melon* (Lexington County) appears from the description to be the Ornamental Pomegranate or Queen's Pocket Melon, which is a gourd with a delightfully fragrant fruit. **1986** Pederson *LAGS Concordance (Melons)* 1 inf, **csAL**, Smell melons—very small cantaloupes, smell good; 1 inf, **ceTX**, Smell melons—small, yellow, sweet-smelling; 1 inf, **csTX**, Smell melon—like mushmelon, looks like cucumber. **1998** in 2000 *DARE* File—Internet **TX**, *Weeds controlled [in cotton].* . . Puncturevine, ragweed (common, giant), smell melon, spurge.

smell of v phr [*OED2* 1624 →] Cf **feel of, of** prep **Ba**
To smell (something).
1851 (1852) Stowe *Uncle Tom's Cabin* 1.224, She recommended to him to smell of hartshorn. **1852** Curtis *Lotus-Eating* 11 **seNY**, I have not yet done . . smelling of all the flowers. **1913–23** in 1944 *ADD* 421 **cNY**, 'Smell (or feel) of that.' Usual. **1919** O'Neill *Moon Caribbees* 30, His foot hits a bottle. He stoops down and picks it up and smells of it. **1936** in 1944 *ADD* 421 **eTX**, Almost universal. 'Taste of it.' 'Smell of it.'

smell one's piss v phr Also *smell one's pee, smell oneself*
To be aware of or feel the emotional effects of one's sexual maturity.
1934 Hurston *Jonah's Gourd Vine* 81 **AL** [Black], He must smell hisself—done got so mannish. *Ibid* 314, *Smell his self,* reaching puberty (girl or boy becoming conscious of). **1966** *DARE* Tape **MA**112, It's funny, a guy was using . . a vulgar expression: "Girls smell their pee at around thirteen years of age," he says. There's nothing more important in this world to them as themselves. . . When they walk down the street, boy, there's nobody else on this face of this earth that's . . as important as them. **1997** Johnson-Coleman *Just Plain Folks* 113 **ceNC** [Black], Soon as that boy started to smell hisself good, he was cuttin' up capers. **1998** Banks *Maid Shade* 8 **wTN**, Daddy said the only thing wrong with Buddy was he started "smelling himself too soon," and by the time (Auntie) Raylean met up with him, he was already worn out. **2002** *DARE* File—Internet, If you notice they *all* revert to personal insults when they have no answer for an intelligent comment. My guess is the

kid is about 12 years old, smelling his piss for the first time, and thinking he's 10ft tall and bulletproof.

smelt n   Cf **sea smelt**

1 Std: any of var fishes of the family Osmeridae such as *Osmerus mordax.* [*OED2* c725 → for *Osmerus eperlanus*] For other names of *O. mordax* see **frostfish 2, rainbow smelt, silver pike 1**; for other names of var fishes of this family see **capelin 1, day fish, eulachon, surf smelt, whitebait**

2 Any of var other small fishes, as:

a A **silversides 1**: *Atherinops affinis, Atherinopsis californiensis,* or *Leuresthes tenuis* of Pacific waters. [*OED2* at *smelt* sb.¹ 1.c 1776 for a related fish] **CA** Cf **green smelt, horse ~, jack ~, top ~**

1857 *U.S. War Dept. Rept. Explor. Railroad* 6.17 (Botany) **CA,** *Atherinopsis californiensis.* . . So called *Smelt* by the San Franciscans. **1863** Hittell *Resources CA* 412, *Smelts.*—We have four species of fish called smelts (*Atherinopsis californiensis, Atherinopsis affinis* [= *Atherinops affinis*], *Osmerus preciosus* [sic] [=*Hypomesus pretiosus*], and *Osmerus similis*). . . The *Atherinopsis californiensis* forms the great bulk of the smelts in our market. **1879** *U.S. Natl. Museum Bulletin* 14.53, *Chirostoma californiensis* [=*Atherinopsis c.*] . . "Smelt."—Coast of California. **1897** *Overland Mth.* (2d ser) 30.221 **CA,** I have added figures of a number of stages in the development of the California anchovy and smelt. **1911** *U.S. Bur. Census Fisheries 1908* 316, Some of the silversides (*Atherinidae*) are wrongly called "smelts;" this is especially true of *Atherinopsis californiensis,* which is widely known as "smelt." **1953** Roedel *Common Fishes CA* 76, *The Silverside Family, Atherinidae*[.] The species are known from California, the jacksmelt, topsmelt, and the grunion. These fishes are commonly called "smelt" which is a misnomer. . . *Jacksmelt—Atherinopsis californiensis.* . . The leading commercial "smelt" forming two-thirds to three-fourths of the State's "smelt" catch. *Ibid* 78, *California grunion—Leuresthes tenuis.* . . forms a very small portion of the statewide "smelt" catch. **1968** *DARE* Tape **CA**103, [FW:] What kind of surf fish do you catch? [Inf:] Well, there's smelt. I call 'em smelt. They're about that long, all the same size. . . They catch 'em with these dip nets, they come in on the beach. They've always been plentiful.

b A **cisco**: usu *Coregonus hoyi,* but also *C. artedi.* **NY**

1882 *U.S. Natl. Museum Proc.* 5.658, Description of a Species of Whitefish, *Coregonus hoyi.* . . called "Smelt" in some Parts of New York. **1903** *NY State Museum & Sci. Serv. Bulletin* 60.230, *Argyrosomus osmeriformis* . . Smelt of New York lakes. **1938** Schrenkeisen *Field Book Fishes* 60, *Leucichthys artedi* [=*Coregonus a.*] . . Common Names. . . Lake George Smelt. *Ibid* 61, The . . Seneca Lake Smelt, *Leucichthys osmeriformis* [=*C. hoyi*] . . , from lakes of central New York tributary to Lake Ontario, has a slender body and large eye.

c A freshwater cyprinid: either a **minnow B1** such as *Hybognathus nuchalis* or *H. regius* or a **shiner 1** such as *Notropis hudsonius.* Cf **silversides 2, smelt minnow, ~ shiner**

1884 *U.S. Natl. Museum Bulletin* 27.481, *Hybognathus regius.* . . Smelt. . . This species is abundant in the Potomac River, and is sometimes sold in the early spring as "smelt," to which it bears almost no resemblance except in size and color. The spawning season begins in March or April. **1903** *NY State Museum & Sci. Serv. Bulletin* 60.140, *Notropis hudsonius.* . . Spawn-eater; Smelt. *Ibid* 143, The gudgeon or smelt of Pennsylvania is a variety of N. hudsonius. . . It grows to a length of about 8 inches. . . This is a handsome silvery fish, and is as much used for food as its associate, the silvery minnow [=*Hybognathus nuchalis*]. **1938** Schrenkeisen *Field Book Fishes* 132, *Hybognathus hudsonius* [=*Notropis h.*] . . Spawn-eater; . . Smelt. *Ibid* 150, *Hybognathus nuchalis.* . . Smelt. . . West of the Alleghenies, from Georgia and Texas to the upper Missouri River. . . Represented from New Jersey to Virginia, east of the Alleghenies, by *Hybognathus nuchalis regius* [=*H. regius*].

d =**tomcod 1b(1)**.

1890 *Century Dict.* 5715, *Smelt.* . . A gadoid fish, *Microgadus proximus,* the tom-cod of the Pacific slope. [*Century* Ed: San Francisco.] **1916** *U.S. Dept. Commerce Bur. Fisheries Document* 830.10, The tom-cod, or wachna (*Microgadus proximus*), is found in abundance from Alaska to Monterey. In the more southern portions of its range it is often sold in the markets as "smelt."

3 in phrr *clean as a smelt, slick ~, smooth ~:* See quots. **chiefly ME**

1847 *Bangor Daily Whig & Courier* (ME) 6 May [2]/2 (newspaper-

archive.com), The New York Tattler has increased its size, looks slick as a smelt, and is as witty as ever. **1874** *Morning Oregonian* (Portland OR) 16 Dec 1/5 ceCA, Her planking and wales average from 75 to 80 feet in length without knots and smooth as a smelt. **1907** *DN* 3.249 eME, *Smooth as a smelt.* . . Of pleasing address. "He's smooth as a smelt." **1915** Lincoln *Thankful's Inheritance* 190 **Cape Cod MA,** She'll be smooth as a smelt. I'll bet you anything she'll say that, after all, she guesses the engagement's a good thing and that Imogene's a nice girl. **1921** *Sun. State Jrl.* (Lincoln NE) 25 Sept sec A 7/7, [Column by Edward G. Lowry, Washington DC correspondent:] Hays has come through as clean as a smelt. **1975** Gould *ME Lingo* 263, *Smooth as a smelt*—A simile to describe any pleasant situation; a batch of cider may be *smooth as a smelt.* **1976** *Daily Kennebec Jrl.* (Augusta ME) 20 July 22/1, [Advt:] '75 Chevrolet Chevelle Malibu Wagon—8 cyl., radio, power steering and brakes, clean as a smelt! **1997** *DARE* File—Internet **ME,** The file upload works smooth as a smelt with WN. **2002** in 2006 *Ibid* **ME,** Later that afternoon a canoe . . went down through the falls just "as slick as a smelt." **2003** *DARE* File **CT** (as of c1905), "The place cleaned up smooth as a smelt" meant that it looked really good. "He talks smooth as a smelt" and "He's smooth as a smelt" were distinctly uncomplimentary; the person was not to be trusted; nothing stuck to him.

smelt minnow n   Cf **smelt 2c**

A **minnow B1** (here: *Hybognathus nuchalis* or *H. regius*).

1884 *U.S. Natl. Museum Bulletin* 27.481, *Hybognathus regius.* . . Smelt; Smelt Minnow. . . This species is abundant in the Potomac River. . . The spawning season begins in March or April. **1938** Schrenkeisen *Field Book Fishes* 150, *Smelt Minnow—Hybognathus nuchalis.* . . A graceful, variable minnow, abundant in clear streams. **1966** *DARE* (Qu. P7, *Small fish used as bait for bigger fish*) Inf **NC**24, Smelt minnow. **1982** *Frederick Post* (MD) 5 Nov sec B 2/4, One Williamsport angler fishing the smelt minnows in the Cherry Run area . . landed three smallmouths.

smelt shanty   See **shanty 5**

smelt shiner n   Cf **smelt 2c**

A **shiner 1** (here: *Notropis hudsonius*).

1906 *NJ State Museum Annual Rept. for 1905* 141, *Notropis hudsonius amarus.* . . Gudgeon. Spawn Eater. Smelt Shiner. . . Sides silvery. . . Length 4 ¼ inches. Trenton.

smethe   See **smee**

smew n   [*OED2* 1674 → for *Mergus albellus*] =**hooded merganser**.

1888 Trumbull *Names of Birds* 74 **RI,** At Newport, R.I., [*Lophodytes cucullatus* is called] *smew.* The Hooded Merganser is about the size of the true Smew, *Mergus albellus,* and the drake of the latter species, when his crest is erected, looks considerably like our bird; very much as our bird might look in a state of partial albinism. **1899** Howe–Sturtevant *Birds RI* 35, *Lophodytes cucullatus.* . . Hooded Merganser. Hooded Sheldrake. Smew.

smidget n   [Var of *smidgen*]

A small amount; a small piece (of food).

1893 Shands *MS Speech* 57, *Smidget* [smɪʤɪt]. Used by negroes to mean a small part or portion of anything; as, "I just got a smidget of supper"; "I want a smidget of corn." [**1936** *AmSp* 11.82, *Molecules, smidgets* . . are quoted in the September 1935 issue of *State Government* . . as names for the new tax tokens which have been issued in some of the states.] **1966** *DARE* (Qu. LL6a, *A small, indefinite amount* . . "I'll take just a _____ of cream in my coffee."*) Inf **FL**4, Smidget; (Qu. LL6b, *A small, indefinite amount* . . "I'll put in just a _____ of butter."*) Inf **FL**4, Smidget. **1994** *NC Lang. & Life Project Dial. Vocab. Ocracoke* 15 eNC, Smidget. . . A small piece, sliver, usually referring to food. *Candy took a smidget of cake.* **2002** *South Bend Tribune* (IN) 16 Oct (Internet) **MI,** As soon as I see a smidget of something resembling a useful and truthful fact, an opponent's ad slams back with another meaningless, unsubstantiated claim. **2005** *DARE* File—Internet **DC,** Our 4-hour visit was too short to see but a smidget of the M[useum] o[f] S[cience]. *Ibid* **CA,** I'm having a smidget of trouble here.

smiercase, smierkase   See **smearcase**

smilax n   [*OED2* 1601 →] chiefly **Sth**

Any of var **greenbriers**. Note: *Smilax* is the name of the genus and hence std in technical use; only exx of non-technical use in ref to var spp of this genus are included here.

1791 Bartram *Travels* xxiii **Sth,** Some seeds, for instance, grapes, nuts, smilax, peas, and others, whose pulp or kernel is food for animals, such seed will remain several days without injuring in stomachs of pigeons and other birds of passage. **1807** in 1857 *S. Lit. Messenger* 24.308 **VA,** The church steeple [was] garlanded to its summit with irregular festoons of smilax and ivy. **1878** *Appletons' Jrl.* 5.424 **SC,** Beyond . . walking in quiet paths through the . . smilax thickets . . what she *did* was the same as usual. **1880** *Harper's New Mth. Mag.* 61.184 **VA, PA,** The woods at either side were edged with natural hedges of mammoth fern, laurel, and service-berries, . . webbed together with the waxed dark green vine of the smilax. **1907** *St. Nicholas* Oct 1120 **TX,** Long festoons of smilax were hung in graceful curves all around the top. **1930** Stoney–Shelby *Black Genesis* 187 **seSC,** Tis all tangle up wid jasmine an' cat briar, an' smilax, an' supplejack. **c1960** *Wilson Coll.* **csKY,** *Bamboo-vine* (or *brier*): Sawbrier, wild smilax, cat brier. **1968** *DARE* (Qu. S17, . . *Kinds of plants . . that . . cause itching and swelling*) Inf **GA**38, Cat's-paw, spylax [sic for *smilax*] are the same. **1969** *DARE* FW Addit **ceNC,** Catbrier—tree common on Hatteras Island. Also called "smilax." **1979** Bowden *Always Rivers Flow* 196 **nwFL** (as of 1930s–40s), Wild grapes and smilax provided fruits for the animals. **2003** *Washington Post* (DC) 14 Sept sec A 7 (Internet) **sePA,** "God's barbed wire," as park superintendent Bill DeCarme puts it. "If you have a desire to give blood and don't want to go to the Red Cross, you can walk through smilax," he said.

Smiley See **Smiling**

smilie n
In marble play: see quot.
c1970 Wiersma *Marbles Terms* **swMI** (as of 1973), *Smilies*—marbles w[ith] a blue outside [and] different color on inside.

Smiling n Also *Smiley, Smiling Indian* [From the family name *Smiling*] Cf **clapper 2, Goins, red bone 1**
A member of a mixed-race group living in Robeson County, North Carolina.

[**1897** *State* (Columbia SC) 27 May 3/1, The Redbone people with which [Jim] Smiling is identified, while they are colored, are really a distinct people from the "old time free negroes" proper.] [**1908** in 1993 Sider *Lumbee Ind.* 76 **SC,** The families of Smilings and Goinses of this [=Sumter] county have been known as "Red Bones" ever since I have been acquainted with the people. . . They are looked upon as a separate race, neither white nor negro.] **1957** *Daily Times–News* (Burlington NC) 18 Oct sec B 5/1, The Smiling Indians, one of four segregated groups in Robeson County, will soon have a new school. . . In 1911, the Smilings began moving into the county from an area near Sumter, S.C. They said they were Lumbee Indians. . . The Lumbees refused the Smilings entrance into their schools and the Smilings refused to attend school with Negroes. **1963** Berry *Almost White* 27, North Carolina, besides its thousands of Lumbees, also has its "Portuguese," Smilings, the Laster Tribe, and Person County Indians. **1968** *DARE* FW Addit **csNC,** Maxton has four "races." . . They are Whites, Blacks, Indians, and Smileys. From what I can gather, the Smileys or Smilings are probably a group of mixed-blooded people, possibly from South Carolina. They have their own little community outside of town and don't seem to be of much numerical or social significance.

smilo grass n
An introduced **mountain rice** (here: *Piptatherum miliaceum*).
1922 U.S. Bur. Plant Industry *Inventory* 58.61, *Smilo grass.* . . In California it has been called smilo grass, San Diego grass, mountain rice, and many-flowered millet. **1950** Hitchcock–Chase *Manual Grasses* 437, *Oryzopsis miliacea.* . . *Smilo grass.* . . Introduced in California; ballast, Camden, N.J., and Philadelphia, Pa.; Mediterranean region. **1961** Thomas *Flora Santa Cruz* 94 **cwCA,** *O[ryzopsis] miliacea.* . . Smilo Grass. . . Occasional as a weed in disturbed areas. . . April–November. **1999** *DARE* File—Internet **CA,** *Piptatherum miliaceum.* . . Smilo grass. . . Aggressive in SoCal creeks and canyons.

smirr n See **smur** n

smirr v See **smur** v

smith n
With *the:* =**carpenter frog.**
1938 Matschat *Suwannee R.* 67 **neFL, seGA,** There is one frog that

sounds like dozens of hammers striking against an empty barrel, and the natives call him the "smith."

smither n Also *smather* [*OED2* smithers 1847 →; cf *smithereens*]
A bit, fragment—freq in phrr *(all)* to smithers into small pieces.
1864 Barber *War Letters* 131, Won't thar be a dry-bones shakin,/ . . / When Yankee troops, for glory achin / Knock Smith to smithers in Fort Makin? **1899** (1912) Green *VA Folk-Speech* 396, *Smithers.* . . Fragments. "He broke it all to smithers." **1942** Berrey–Van den Bark *Amer. Slang* 21.2, *Small amount.* . . Smither, smithereen, *a small piece or fragment.* *Ibid* 25.2, *Part or fragment.* Flinder, flitter, smither, smithereen. . . Flinders, smithereens, smithers, *fragments.* **1950** *WELS* (*Broken to pieces, shattered completely:* "The jug fell out of the window and was _____.") 1 Inf, **cwWI,** Smashed or busted all to pieces or smithers or smithereens. **1966–69** *DARE* (Qu. KK22) Infs **MA**56, **WI**27, Broke(n) to smithers; **CO**4, **NJ**4, Smashed to smithers; **SC**11, Broken to smathers; (Qu. LL6a, *A small, indefinite amount . .* "I'll take just a _____ of cream in my coffee.") Inf **AZ**1, Smither. **2001** *Herald–Tribune* (Sarasota FL) 1 Dec sec A 19 (Internet), Would it be necessary . . to blow a village entirely to smithereens—or . . might mere smithers do just as well?

smoke n

1 A Black person. Cf **cloud** n[1], **smoked Irishman, smoke meat**
1902 *Bulletin* (San Francisco CA) 9 Dec 10 (*Zwilling Coll.*), A negro held that prize and he refused to quarrel with a "smoke." **1919** Kyne *Capt. Scraggs* 244 **CA,** "Over you go, you two smokes," rasped McGuffey, menacing the captives with his rifle. **1926** Van Vechten *Nigger Heaven* 286 **NYC** [Black], Smoke: Negro. **1932** Farrell *Young Lonigan* 162 **Chicago IL,** You got to keep these smokes in their place and not let 'em get gay. **1932** *AmSp* 7.336 [Johns Hopkins jargon], *Smoke*—a negro. **1940** Chandler *Farewell* 18 **CA,** There was five smokes carved Harlem sunsets on each other. **1965–70** *DARE* (Qu. HH28, *Names and nicknames . . for people of foreign background: Negro*) Infs **AL**50, **IL**138, **MS**35, **MA**71, **NY**36, **OK**55, **PA**98, **TN**43, 53, Smoke; [**NY**241, Smokestack; **GA**77, Smoky Joe].

2 rarely *smoke on the water:* Denatured alcohol used as a beverage; any inferior alcoholic beverage.
1926 *NY Times* (NY) 12 Sept 28/14, Three men died yesterday . . as a result of drinking denatured alcohol. . . The beverage . . is said by the police to be known as "smoke." According to the police it can be purchased . . in all shops where materials for paints are sold. **1929** *AmSp* 4.386 **KS** [Wet words], The term *smoke* is comparatively new in this part of Kansas, and means an inferior grade of whitish, cloudy alcohol, usually *re-run alky* at that. **1931** *AmSp* 7.87 [Prohibition terms], Terms used for intoxicating liquor. . . Smoke. **1940** *Sun* (Baltimore MD) 14 Nov 8/2 (*Hench Coll.*), Judge Eugene O'Dunne yesterday ruled that the sale of denatured alcohol diluted with water and known as "smoke"—comes within the effect of the liquor laws. **1949** *Harper's Mag.* Nov 55 **neOH,** Down here . . is a hobo campground—blackened embers, . . empty tin cans labeled "Do not take internally Will cause blindness" (but the hobos drink it anyway—"smoke," they call it, not torch fuel.) **1966–70** *DARE* (Qu. DD21b, *General words . . for bad liquor*) Inf **MA**80, Smoke—made out of swill and stuff; (Qu. DD21c, *Nicknames for whiskey, especially illegally made whiskey*) Inf **NC**30, Smoke. **c1970** Pederson *Dial. Surv. Rural GA* (What do you call homemade whiskey?) 1 inf, **seGA,** Smoke, moonshine. **1986** Pederson *LAGS Concordance* (Cheap whiskey) 1 inf, **ceTN,** Smoke on the water—paint thinner, rubbing alcohol.

3 in var phrr and combs: An imaginary object used as the basis of a practical joke. Cf **grind smoke, smoke-grinder 2**
1909 *Washington Post* (DC) 17 Sept [47]/5 (newspaperarchive.com), He has had his henchmen in his mystic castle busy for the past fortnight grinding all the smoke which issues from his mighty pipe. The smoke grinder is known as the royal whim a diddle. **1939** *Pt. Arthur News* (TX) 15 Sept 20/1 **OH,** [Headline:] Now Let's Go Look For The Smoke Shovel. **1942** Berrey–Van den Bark *Amer. Slang* 281.8, *Fictitious objects used in practical jokes.* . . Smoke curler (*machine shop*). **1966–69** *DARE* (Qu. HH14, *Ways of teasing a beginner or inexperienced person—for example, by sending him for a 'left-handed monkey wrench':* "Go get me _____.") Inf **MA**6, Bucket of smoke; **NY**211, Cup of smoke; **MI**108, Shovel smoke; **TX**18, **WI**22, Smoke-grinder; **CA**8, Smoke-shifter; **VA**15, Whimmy-diddle to a smoke-grinder. **1980** *DARE* File **sCA** (as of 1950s), In Boy Scouts we'd tease the youngest boys by

telling them to go get a smoke bender so the smoke from the campfire wouldn't get in our eyes. **2005** *DARE* File—Internet **FL**, PS: If that doesn't work, just touch it up with an adjustable angled smoke grinder.

4 in phr *like smoke:* Very quickly or vigorously. [*OED2* 1833 →]

1825 Neal *Brother Jonathan* 2.94 **CT,** If we didn't gallop 'um like smoke, . . the stage would run over 'um. **1839** *Madison Express* (WI) 28 Dec 1/6, If a man . . strike thee, thrash him like smoke. **1868** in 1949 Twain *Mark Twain to Mrs. Fairbanks* 55 **MO,** She . . lectures me like smoke, too. But I like it. **1894** *Scribner's Mag.* 15.556 **Sth,** You'd have to go into the thing hot, yourself. You'd have to push like smoke! **1899** (1912) Green *VA Folk-Speech* 396, *Smoke.* . . Like *smoke,* very rapidly. "He ran like smoke." **1909** Royall *Some Reminiscences* 12 **VA,** A comrade . . said he knew what I would have done—I would have turned around and run like smoke, and I suspect he was right.

5 in phr *cost like smoke:* To be very expensive.

1887 *Mt. Democrat* (Placerville CA) [5 Nov 4]/5 (newspaper-archive.com), [Attrib to *Brooklyn Eagle*:] Now they undress more than ever, but it costs more to do so; costs like smoke to put on nothing. **1897** in 2002 *DARE* File—Internet **TX,** I[t] cost like smoke to have them vaccinated but better that than to let them all die. **1909** Porter *Girl Limberlost* 349 **IN,** Hairdresser did that! . . It cost like smoke. **1942** Perry *Texas* 56, It costs like smoke but you've got it to do. **1976** Ryland *Richmond Co. VA* 377, *Smoke*—it costs like smoke. **2003** in 2006 *DARE* File—Internet **sePA,** Silicone rubber replicating kits that the pro's use cost like smoke.

smoke v   Usu with *over*   [Cf *OED2* smoke v. 10 "To observe, take note of, 'twig'. Now *arch.*"]

To look over, give the once-over to.

1928 Fisher *Walls Jericho* 305 **NYC** [Black], *Smoke over*—"Give the once over." Observe critically. **1935** Hurston *Mules & Men* 30 **FL** [Black], Get out de way there and let a real man smoke them toes over. **1942** Hurston in *Amer. Mercury* 55.223.96 **Harlem NYC** [Black], *Smoking,* or *smoking over*—looking someone over.

smoke ball n   Cf **oak apple 2**

A **puffball 1.**

1907 Richards–Elliott *Chem. Cooking* 75, The common puff-ball *(Lycoperdon),* the "smoke" ball of the country child, well illustrates both vegetative and spore stages. **1913** (1919) *WNID, Smoke ball.* . . A puffball. **1920** *WI Rapids Daily Tribune* (WI) 26 Dec [8]/2 (news-paperarchive.com) **IL,** Among these are species known as puffballs; to the uninitiated as 'smoke-balls'. . . As they mature, they turn to a yellowish or brownish color internally. . . Finally, the entire plant becomes filled with a brownish or purplish powder, and is then known as the 'smoke-ball' which the small boy delights to kick, in order to see the 'smoke' puff out. **1930** Shoemaker *1300 Words* 52 **cPA Mts** (as of c1900), *Smoke-ball*—The oak apple. **1968–69** *DARE* (Qu. S18, *A kind of mushroom that grows like a globe . . sometimes gets as big as a man's head)* Infs **CT**21, **VA**34, Smoke ball(s). **1974** (1977) Coon *Useful Plants* 274, *Lycoperdon cyathiforme*—Puffball and smoke balls; devil's snuffbox.

smoked bacon (or beef, ham)   See **smoke meat**

smoked Irishman n   [Cf **smoke meat** and obs *smoked Yank(ee)* applied to Black Union soldiers during the Civil War]

A Black or other "non-White" person; hence n *smoke Irish.*

1915 Gavin *Michael Freebern Gavin* 39 **MA,** Sometimes he would have to take the little colored boy, "the smoked Irishman." **1950** Goldin et al. *Dict. Amer. Underworld Lingo* 199, *Smoked Irishman.* . . A Negro. [Note: The expression is used to poke fun at Irish-American convicts.] **1966** *DARE* (Qu. HH28, *Names and nicknames . . for people of foreign background: Indian*) Inf **MI**10, Smoked Irishman; (Qu. HH29a, . . *People of mixed blood—part Indian*) Inf **MI**4, Smoked Irishman. [**1966** *DARE* FW Addit **OK**51, *Smoked Yankee*—a man who marries an Indian woman so he can trade with her tribe.] **1983** *NADS Letters, Smoke Irish.* Of course, refers to Negroes. Both terms are used between the Hudson and York Rivers along the East Coast. **2001** *La Prensa San Diego* (CA) 16 Mar (Internet), We [=Latinos] wear the Green and join our Irish friends . . for some mutual bonding. We take pride in being called their "smoke-Irish" friends.

smoke-grinder n   Cf **grind smoke**

1 See **smoke n 3.**

2 Either of two mechanical toys: a **bull-grinder** or one based on the principle of the pump drill.

1963 *Chr. Sci. Monitor* (Boston MA) 26 Apr 6/6 **nwNC,** The carvers' line of folk toys also includes: Cornstalk fiddle . . , the smoke grinder, and a fascinating cornstalk menagerie. **1980** *Foxfire 6* 162 **nGA,** Of course, bull grinders ain't the only name it had. I've heard them called do nothings and smoke grinders. *Ibid* 229, Another locally made toy Fred Potter stocks . . is this smoke grinder. The point of the toy is set in a slight depression, and as the horizontal bar is pumped with two fingers, the influence of the string twisting around the shaft and the weight of the wooden disk make the toy spin back and forth in the de-pression. **2002** *DARE* File—Internet [Mountain Craft Shop—Prod-ucts], Smoke Grinder—(Primitive drill)—Wholesale $2.25 each.

smoke hole n   Also called **steam hole**

The venthole in the top of a beaver lodge.

[**1869** Hardy *Forest Life* 185 **Canada,** The presence of the beaver in his snow-covered house is readily detected by the hunter in winter by the appearance . . of what is called the "smoke hole."] **1945** Hamlin *9 Mile Bridge* 226 **nME,** After trappers locate [beaver] houses, they can tell that they are occupied if the snow is soft and moist at the "smoke hole"—the top of the house where steam from the animal's body warmth escapes. **2000** *Wiscasset Newsp.* (ME) 28 Dec (Internet), Trap-pers often refer to this breather hole [in a beaver lodge] as the smoke hole or steam hole.

smokehouse greasy, keep one's   See **keep v B5d**

smoke Irish   See **smoked Irishman**

smoke like a freight train   See **train, smoke like a**

smoke like a tar kiln (or kettle, pot, wagon)   See **tar kiln b**

smoke meat n   Also *smoked bacon, ~ beef, ~ ham*   Cf **smoke n 1**

A Black or American Indian person or people.

1829 Brauns *Praktische Belehrungen* 18, Der Volksspott hat dem armen Afrikaner hier den Namen *Smoked-Beef* (geräuchertes Rind-fleisch) gegeben. [=The poor African is commonly taunted here [= America] with the name *smoked-beef.*] **1939** *AmSp* 14.92 **eTN,** Smoked Bacon. Negroes. 'There's no smoked bacon in these parts.' **1958** McCulloch *Woods Words* 172 **Pacific NW,** *Smoke meat*—An Indian. **1966** *DARE* FW Addit **neME,** *Smoked ham*—an Indian (somewhat de-rogatory). **1969** *DARE* (Qu. HH28, *Names and nicknames . . for people of foreign background: Negro*) Inf **GA**72, Smoke meat.

smoke on the water   See **smoke n 2**

smoke over   See **smoke v**

smoke pole n   Also *smoke stick, ~ stack*

1 A firearm.

1849 *WI Argus* (Madison) 20 Nov 1/4 **NC,** Some of old Lew's boys popped a cap on an old smoke pole at a partridge. **1905** *Washington Post* (DC) 23 July [20]/3 (newspaperarchive.com) **NV,** I stood for that all right, because I was framed up with a smoke pole as long as your leg. **1907** *AZ Republican* (Phoenix) 10 Feb 10/4, I yelled to my companion to 'light out' and climb the rocks, which he did, working that little auto-matic 'smoke stick' of his for all it was worth. **1920** *Syracuse Herald* (NY) 7 Apr sec 1 7/5 **ceIN,** It's a good thing you got me without my 'smoke pole' or you'd never have caught me alive. **1952** *Chillicothe Constitution-Tribune* (MO) 20 Nov 2/4, [Syndicated column by Warren Page:] The lending gun is that beat-up old smoke-pole on the end of the rack. **1955** *Sheboygan Press* (WI) 25 May 33/7, [Syndicated column by Warren Page:] He never had any trouble taking all the grouse and pheasants he had a right to . . with an old smoke-stick he'd shot for years. **1958** McCulloch *Woods Words* 172 **Pacific NW,** *Smoke pole*—A rifle. **1965–70** *DARE* (Qu. P37a, *Nicknames for a rifle*) Infs **AL**53, **CA**136, **KY**93, **TX**14, Smoke pole; **MT**4, **WY**1, Smoke stick; **GA**9, Smoke stack; (Qu. P37b, *Nicknames for a shotgun*) Infs **GA**1, 3, 12, **NC**35, **SC**69, **TX**78, Smoke pole; **GA**7, 9, Smoke stack; [**FL**7, Old smoke house]. **1980** *DARE* File **KS,** Other colloquial terms related to fire-arms. The only one I can think of is "smoke stick" for a revolver, which I learned from an old eighth-breed Cherokee ex-cowpuncher with whom I worked on a threshing machine in 1924. **2006** *DARE* File—Internet **OK,** In my experience in shotgun work, dealing with average customers who are looking for an improvement to their favorite old smoke pole, the screw-in choke tube is the most requested alteration.

2 also attrib; Spec: a muzzle-loader.

2003 in 2006 *DARE* File—Internet **MI,** I shot my new 50 caliber black powder rifle yesterday in preparation for the upcoming "smoke pole" season. **2004** *DARE* File—Internet **NH,** The either-sex season during the muzzle-loader season has been expanded . . for the 2004 season. Better get that smoke pole out for a pre-season tune-up. **2006** *Ibid* **MS,** I replaced the scope with the one from my muzzleloader and got it zeroed in and tested the open sights on the smoke stick. *Ibid,* Billy used the CVA Smoke Pole Shotgun to take several turkeys in his home state of VA.

smoker n

1 also *old smoker:* **=long-billed curlew.** [See quot 1888]

1888 Trumbull *Names of Birds* 198 **NJ,** *Long-billed curlew.* . . Known also at Pleasantville to some of the gunners as *smoker* or *old smoker* (the bill curving downward like the stem of a pipe, and the enlargement at the end answering for the bowl). **1946** Hausman *Eastern Birds* 267, *Numenius americanus.* . . Smoker.

2 **=pintail 1.**

1982 Elman *Hunter's Field Guide* 156, *Pintail.* . . *Common & Regional Names* . . smoker.

smoke stack (or stick) See **smoke pole**

smokethorn n Cf **smoke tree 2**

An **indigo bush 2:** either *Dalea lanata* or *Psorothamnus spinosus.*

1936 U.S. Dept. Ag. *Misc. Pub.* 217.31, Smokethorn (*Parosela spinosa* [=*Psorothamnus s.*]). Deserts of Arizona, California. Branches spiny. **1957** *Mt. Democrat* (Placerville CA) 7 Feb 3/4, The smoke tree or smoke thorn is a spiny, smoke-gray bush or small tree, native to desert washes. **1970** Kirk *Wild Edible Plants W. U.S.* 256, *Dalea terminalis* [=*D. lanata* var *t.*] . . Smokethorn. . . The roots of this plant are very sweet when eaten raw. **1971** Dodge *100 Desert Wildflowers* 35, *Smokethorn.* . . At a distance it resembles a plume of smoke rising from a campfire. . . *Dalea spinosa* [=*Psorothamnus s.*] **1985** Dodge *Flowers SW Deserts* 101, Smokethorn, indigobush. . . *Psorothamnus spinosus* . . Arizona and California deserts. **2004** in **2006** *DARE* File—Internet **TX** [Lady Bird Johnson Wildflower Center], Smokethorn or smoke tree is a spiny, intricately branched, nearly leafless shrub or small tree with an overall gray appearance except when covered with a profusion of violet or indigo-blue flower spikes. . . The smoky-gray twigs produce most of the food, by photosynthesis, since the plants have leaves for only a few weeks each year.

smoke tree n

1 A shrub or small tree of the genus *Cotinus:* either the introduced *C. coggygria* common esp in the northeastern US or the native *C. obovatus* found chiefly in the Inland South and Ozark regions. [See quot 1917] For other names of *C. obovatus* see **chittamwood 1, mist tree, yellowwood 8**

1850 Emerson *Rept. Trees & Shrubs* 500, The Venetian Sumach, *R[hus] cotinus* [=*Cotinus coggygria*], commonly called *Smoke-tree,* is much cultivated as a curious and beautiful plant. **1850** Judd *Richard Edney* 85 **NEng,** [Her hair] hung on her like the fringe of the smoketree. **1868** (1870) Gray *Field Botany* 84, *R[hus] Cotinus, Smoketree.* . . Usually most of the flowers are abortive, while their pedicels . . bear long plumy hairs, making large and light, feathery or cloud-like bunches. . . The same or one very like it is wild in Alabama. **1901** Mohr *Plant Life AL* 16, Passing over the detached spurs of the Cumberland Mountains in Madison County, . . he discovered the interesting American smoke tree (*Cotinus cotinoides* . .), before known only from a single locality in the Indian Territory near the borders of Arkansas. **1941** Writers' Program *Guide MO* 23 **Ozarks,** The smoke tree, one of the rarest of American trees, grows here, sometimes to the unusual height of 35 to 40 feet. **1980** Little *Audubon Guide N. Amer. Trees E. Region* 545, American Smoketree . . *Cotinus obovatus. Ibid* 546, The planted ornamentals are mainly the related Common Smoketree (*Cotinus coggygria* . .) of Eurasia. **2004** *Columbus Dispatch* (OH) 10 Oct sec I 21 (Internet), Do dogwoods need acidic fertilizer? . . Are they and smoke trees acid-loving plants?

2 An **indigo bush 2** (here: *Psorothamnus spinosus*). [See quot 1914] **Desert SW** Cf **smokethorn**

1910 Jepson *Silva CA* 260, *Dalea spinosa* [=*Psorothamnus s.*] . . The Smoke Tree is common in dry washes. . . It has been so named because of its appearance, being so truly deceptive as to cause the uninitiated to watch it with speculative wonder as to where "that column of smoke comes from." **1914** Saunders *With Flowers in CA* 75, My eyes had been caught by what seemed to be a cloudlet of smoke. . . [T]he supposititious smoke resolved itself into an airy tangle of grayish twigs and branches, and my cloudlet stood revealed as a small tree. . . "It is

Dalea spinosa," he said, "or smoke tree." **1944** (1967) McNichols *Crazy Weather* 24 **AZ,** On past was one smoke tree with a ghostly crown of innumerable gray, leafless twigs. **1966–67** *DARE* (Qu. S26e, *Other wildflowers not yet mentioned;* not asked in early QRs) Inf **CA4,** Smoke tree; (Qu. T16, . . *Kinds of trees . . 'special'*) Inf **CA2,** Smoke tree. **1973** *AZ Highways* Mar 4, A number of desert plants such as the Smoketree . . , like the cacti, function through their stems. **1997** in **2000** *DARE* File—Internet **Desert SW,** Because Smoke Trees require relatively abundant water, they are often found along sandy or gravelly flats, arroyos and washes.

3 **=tree of heaven.** [See quot]

1940 Steyermark *Flora MO* 321, *Tree of Heaven, Smoke Tree (Ailanthus altissima* . .*).* Scattered in southern and central Mo. Often planted as a street tree in cities on account of its ability to withstand smoke and poisonous gases, whence the name "Smoke Tree."

4 **=fringe tree.** [See quot 1972]

1972 *Names SC* 19.28, *Smoke Tree* (Charleston County) for Fringe Tree, *Chionanthus virginica.* In the early spring this choice little tree produces billowing clouds of small, shining white fragrant flowers. **1977** Kibler *Simms as Naturalist* 10 **SC,** The formal name of "old man's beard" is *Chionanthus virginica,* also called "Smoke Tree."

smoke vine n

1 A **virgin's bower** such as *Clematis ligusticifolia.* [Cf *OED2 smoke-wood* (at *smoke* sb. II.11)] Cf **old-man's-beard 3, pipestem b**

1901 *Mt. Democrat* (Placerville CA) 14 Sept 4/2, So many people . . miss the autumn season with . . the veiling of the trees with the delicate smokevine that spins itself lovingly over the branches like some beautiful bridal veil. **1913** London *Valley of Moon* 488 **CA,** On the stone slab above stood a huge Mexican jar, filled with autumn branches and trailing fluffy smoke-vine. [**1920** Rice–Rice *Pop. Studies CA Wild Flowers* 78, Long-tailed carpels [of wild clematis] become a silvery white as autumn advances, and clothe the vines with masses of feathery plumes. . . In some parts of England, Clematis is called . . "smoking-cane."]

2 **=cross vine 1.**

1960 Vines *Trees SW* 924, *Bignonia capreolata.* . . The sections of stems are smoked like cigars in some localities and given the name Smoke-vine. **1967** Harder Coll. **cwTN,** *Smoke vine.* . . A vine which boys use for smoking. The vine is cut, dried, and split into four sections. After smoking a few of these sections, the skin will be seared off the tongue. **1982** Slone *How We Talked* 90 **eKY** (as of c1950), Smoked pieces of the smoke vine for pretend cigarettes.

3 A **birthwort 1** (here: *Aristolochia macrophylla*). Cf **Dutchman's pipe 1, pipe vine 1**

1992 *News* (Frederick MD) 11 Feb sec B 6/5, A new area . . is The Pottery Shed, which includes "smoke vine" baskets from South Carolina. **2004** in **2006** *DARE* File—Internet **neTN,** You may have smoke vine. It looks almost like wild grape vine, but it's the one that is all twisty and gnarled looking. **2006** *Ibid* **Appalachians,** *Vines,* particularly grapevine (*Vitis* spp.) and smokevine (*Aristolochia macrophylla*) are used to make specialty wood based products. *Ibid* **cwNC,** I use Mountain Laurel, Rhododendron and Smoke Vine all of which are obtained from the Appalachian Mountains. . . Smoke Vine gets its name from its fireplace or campfire aromatic character.

smokeweed n

A **boneset 1.**

1933 Small *Manual SE Flora* 1327, *E[upatorium] maculatum.* . . Joe-Pye-weed. Smokeweed. **2002** in **2005** (acc) OH State Univ. *PlantFacts* (Internet), Other names for . . E[upatorium] fistulosum, E. maculatum, and E. purpureum include Boneset, Thoroughwort, and Smokeweed.

smokewood n

See quots.

1892 *KS Univ. Qrly.* 1.99 **KS,** *Smokewood:* dried water-soaked wood used by small boys as substitute for cigars. **1940** Stong *Hawkeyes* 249 **IA,** We smoked "smokewood"—twigs of driftwood so raddled by the river that they would hold fire like a cigaret. **2001** *Sou'wester* 36.1.5 (Internet) **swWA,** Sometimes we would hide under the approach to the dock and smoke something the twins called "smokewood"—porous bits of driftwood about the size of a cigar.

smokey so'wester See **smoky southwester**

smokie See **smoky** n 2

smoking bean n Also *smoking-bean tree* [See quots]

=**catalpa B1;** also its seed pod.

1867 Harte *Condensed Novels* 104, He has endeavored to break himself of the [tobacco] habit. He tells me that he has substituted . . the outer part of a leguminous plant called the smoking-bean. **1897** Sudworth *Arborescent Flora* 335 **RI,** *Catalpa catalpa* [=*C. bignonioides*]. . . Smoking Bean. **1933** Small *Manual SE Flora* 1241, *Catalpa.* . . *Smoking-beans.* . . *C[atalpa] catalpa.* . . The dried capsules are frequently smoked by children wherever the tree is found. **1952** Taylor *Plants Colonial Days* 27, *Catalpa bignonioides*—The common catalpa, native to the Gulf states, has long been naturalized as far north as New York. . . The catalpa is also called . . smoking-bean-tree, . . which reflect[s] the belief that the Indians smoked the foot-long, very thin, cylindrical pods and their papery winged seeds. **1968** *DARE* (Qu. T9, *The common shade tree with large heart-shaped leaves, clusters of white blossoms, and long thin seed pods or 'beans'*) Inf **NY79,** Smoking beans. **1978** in 1981 *NC Folkl. Jrl.* 29.60, I had discovered the joys of Indian cigars, those wondrous thin panatellas sometimes called smoking beans. Up to fifteen inches in length, these cigars cried out for an audience when the smoker lighted up. **2000** *DARE* File—Internet, *Catalpa bignonioides* is the Southern catalpa. Other common names for this species is . . smoking bean . . and fish bait tree.

smoking duck n
=**baldpate 1.**

1884 Baird et al. *Water Birds N. Amer.* 1.523 **AK, Canada** (as of 1861), Mr. Kennicott adds that the Bald-pate is generally known to the *voyageurs* throughout the Fur Countries by the name of 'Smoking Duck,' or by its Cree name of *Nimimipikhtwan*, which signifies a smoker.

smoky n

1 in comb *old smoky:* See quot. Cf **smoke pole**

1965–70 *DARE* (Qu. P37b, *Nicknames for a shotgun*) Infs **GA77, MS58, TX96,** Old smoky.

2 also sp *smokie:* A playing marble; see quots.

c**1970** Wiersma *Marbles Terms* **MI** (as of 1960), *Smokies*—opaque marbles. . . "A smokie is an opaque puree." **1973** Ferretti *Marble Book* 52, *Smokies.* Glassies with puffs of color inside.

3 The Nipigon **cisco** (*Coregonus nipigon*).

1976 *DARE* File **Isle Royale MI,** Smokies are a real dark fish, like a cisco; still found; spawned in the river mouth near Nipigon [Ontario] Island.

Smoky Hollow n   Also *Smoky Row*

Used as a nickname for a community or neighborhood.

1852 *Brooklyn Daily Eagle* (NY) 11 Sept 3/2, The following delightful retreats contain Pierce's constituents: Kelsey's Alley, Smoky Hollow, Darby's Patch and Young Dublin. These are the scourings of other countries, who are totally ignorant of the principles upon which this republic derives her support, and yet are entitled to vote. **1873** *Ibid* 31 May 2/4, The section of the city known as "Smoky Hollow". . . glories in the reputation of having produced more thieves and burglars, of accumulating more filth, of engendering more epidemics, and emptying more bottles of bad whisky than almost any other portion of our good and pious village. c**1903** Lib. of Congress *Amer. Memory: Prairie Settlement* (Internet) **NE,** [Caption:] Smoky Row. [Photo shows a row of employee houses on a ranch.] **1966–70** *DARE* (Qu. C34, *Nicknames for nearby settlements, villages, or districts*) Inf **NC5,** Smoky Holler; **GA77,** Smoky Row; (Qu. C35, *Nicknames for the different parts of your town or city*) Inf **IL11,** Smoky Hollow; **VA72,** Smoky Hollow ['hɑlə]—name no longer in use; **NC41,** Smoky Holler—old colored section; **AR39,** Smoky Row—same as Negro Town; **OH71,** Smoky Row—it was along the tracks; (Qu. II25, *Names or nicknames for the part of a town where the poorer people, special groups, or foreign groups live*) Inf **MN25,** Smoky Row—one in Monroe, Wisconsin, too. **2003** *Cleveland Plain Dealer* (OH) 5 July sec B 4 (Internet) **Youngstown OH,** In its heyday, the 63-acre enclave at the foot of campus was a vibrant place but a separate universe populated by working-class families. . . Then, as the city's steel industry crumbled in the 1970s, so did Smoky Hollow.

smoky Joe n

1966–70 *DARE* (Qu. N37, *Joking names for a branch railroad that is not very important or gives poor service*) Infs **FL33, SC69,** Smoky Joe.

smoky mulberry n   [See quot]

The paper mulberry (*Broussonetia papyrifera*).

1973 *DARE* File **sIN,** Smoky mulberry—paper mulberry (*Brousso-*

netia papyrifera). . . So called because catkins have touch-sensitive stamens which puff pollen out.

smoky oak n   [See quot 1980]
=**Lacey oak.**

1960 Vines *Trees SW* 160, *Quercus laceyi.* . . Vernacular names are Rock Oak, . . Smoky Oak, and Bastard Oak. The wood is occasionally used for fuel and posts. **1980** Little *Audubon Guide N. Amer. Trees E. Region* 390, *Lacey Oak* . . "Smoky Oak". . . Medium-sized tree with smoky gray-green foliage. . . Central Texas on Edwards Plateau.

Smoky Row   See **Smoky Hollow**

smoky southwester n   Also *smokey so'wester, smoky sou'-wester* [*smoky* misty, hazy + **southwester**] **chiefly NEng** Cf **DS B18**

See quots.

1855 *NY Daily Times* (NY) 12 Mar 8 (Internet), In a heavy northwest wind, like a smoky southwester of our coast, she passed in sight of a portion of Wellington Island. **1901** *Atlantic Mth.* 88.59 **ME,** We 'd got up 'long so's't to sight Isle o' Holt all good an' plain, an' we took one o' these here smoky sou'-westers right plumb in the teeth. **1929** Starbuck *My House* 261 **Nantucket MA** (as of c1860), I remember the sort of day it was, soft, moist, and gray in early spring, and as we walked . . the petulant gusts of a 'smoky sou'wester' blew gritty clouds of dust from the road. **1951** Hough *Singing in Morning* 116 **Martha's Vineyard MA,** But our own smoky sou'wester, which determines the taste, the feeling, and the look of summer, has no friendly colloquialism other than this; it remains the smoky sou'wester, nothing more, nothing less. **1996** in 2002 *DARE* File—Internet **ME,** It was one of those magic Maine afternoons at Popham. Sunlight glinting on granite, smoky southwester fading the distant edge. **2000** *Ibid* **RI,** A classic Newport smoky sou'wester provided 15–18 knots in the first race, accompanied by ocean swells and 2- to 3-foot seas. **2002** *DARE* File **Cape Cod MA,** Mom did confirm with her friends about a Smokey So'wester. The key is that it's a high wind, from the south west, it comes up late in the day on a hot summer day—no rain—but it's very hazy. If it matters, she relates to it from being on the water (sailing of course) and watching for the wind to come up late in the day.

smolick v   Usu with *around*   Also *smollick, smollok*   **Appalachians**

To romp, cavort; esp, to engage in sexual play.

1913 Johnson *Highways St. Lawrence to VA* 280 **MD,** Afterwards they kiss—yes, kiss right square in the mug and distribute their germs. . . They kiss and smollok too on Sunday when they meet at church. **1930s** in 1944 *ADD* 572 **eWV,** Smollick. . . To smear;—with *around*. . . 'These young girls & their lipstick, smearin' an' smollickin' around.' Rather common. [*DARE* Ed: The def is prob erron.] **1961** Seeman *In Arms of Mt.* 36 **eTN,** Old Brindle 'ud go to smolickin' around kickin' up her heels and actin' mighty quair. *Ibid* 61, An old sweet'art of his—she was his double cousin—come up and smolicked around with him. **1997** in 2004 Montgomery–Hall *Dict. Smoky Mt. Engl.* 545 **wNC, eTN,** *Smolick around.* . . =to carry on an illicit relationship with someone . . ; =to kiss and such . . ; =to date, go out together.

smooch n, v[1]   Also *smootch* [*OED2 smooch* v.[1] 1631 → "Latterly U.S."; *smooch* sb.[1] 1825 → "U.S."] **NEast, esp NEng**

A smudge, smear; to smudge, smear; with *up:* to become cloudy hence ppl adj *smooched;* vbl n *smooching.*

1825 Neal *Brother Jonathan* 2.46 **CT,** Cowhide shoes—newly greased . . which left a "smooch" upon whatever they came near. **1828** (1970) Webster *Amer. Dict., Smutch* v.t. . . We have a common word in New England, pronounced *smooch*, which I take to be *smutch*. It signifies to foul or blacken with something produced by combustion or other like substance. **1835** Willis *Pencillings* 1.237 **ME,** Attracting the attention and courtesies of every smooched petticoat far and near. **1870** (1871) Whitney *We Girls* 58 **seNY,** A smooch of stove-polish across her arm. **1895** *Youth's Companion* 27 June 319 **NH,** If you don't see it smoochin' up in th' east before long, it'll be—it'll be mos' likely because the storm has riz up in the middle o' the night, an' ketched ye nappin'! **1907** *DN* 3.200 **seNH,** Smooch. . . A smirch. "You've got a smooch on your face." . . To besmirch. "You've smooched your face all over." **1909** *DN* 3.416 **nME,** Smooch, n. Smirch. **1929** *AmSp* 5.129 **ME,** "You've got a smootch on your dress" referred to a spot resulting from spilling or contact. **1937** *DN* 6.595 **ceNY,** "Smooched," soiled. **1959** *VT Hist.* 27.158, Smooch. . . To foul or blacken with something produced by combustion or other like substance. . . Rare. **2005** *DARE*

File—Internet, Smooching is a technique artists use to smudge or smear an area of a drawing.

smooch v² Also *smootch*

1 =**smouch** v² **1.**

1905 *DN* 3.65 **eNE,** *Smootch, v.* "Swipe." "They smootched some turnips." **1941** in 1946 Cain *3 Novels* 3.156 **CA,** Then she . . went over to the cash box, and smooched four $10 bills. [**1946** Dadswell *Hey There Sucker* 98, *Smooch*—to borrow.] **2003** *NADS Letters* **OK,** I've lived in OK since '78 and have definitely heard the word *smooch* used in the definition you presented [=to cheat, finagle; to steal]. I have heard it quite often in fact. **2004** *Ibid* **nwWA,** Smooch . . to steal. . . I have used this word all my life, basically in the same way to mooch is used, but in a harsher context.

2 In marble play: =**fudge** v. Cf **smouch** v² **2**

1922 *DN* 5.188 **MN** [Marbles terms], *Smooch, v.i.* To extend one's hand beyond the proper limits.

smooched, smooching, smootch n, v¹ See **smooch** n, v¹

smootch v² See **smooch** v²

smooth adj, v, adv Usu |smuð|; also *chiefly among Black speakers* |smuv| Pronc-sp *smoove* See Pronc Intro 3.I.17

A Forms.

1834 *Star & Republican Banner* (Gettysburg PA) 15 Apr [3]/4 (newspaperarchive.com) [Black], Yes bless God cut he tail smack smoove off. **1868** (1869) Holt *What I Know* 327 **MS** [Black], He smoove enough now, ma'am. **1871** *Harper's New Mth. Mag.* 42.474 **VA** [Black], Massa Gibbon's mules got loose . . and run smack and smoove into Massa Linkum's lines. **1893** Shands *MS Speech* 58, *Smoove* [smuv]. Negro for *smoothe* [sic]. **1901** *DN* 2.183 **neKY** [Black], *Smooth*—smoove. **1936** Reese *Worleys* 17 **MD** (as of 1865) [Black], Smoove down dat hair. **2003** *DARE* File—Internet **NYC,** Girl we be smoove on the F [train] to Jay Street.

B As adj.

Of a horse: unshod.

1941 Writers' Program *Guide WY* 465, *Smooth*—Unshod.

C As adv.

Completely, entirely. [Perh abbr for **smack smooth 2**]

1984 Weaver *TX Crude* 126, *Smooth.* An infixed adverb. "My cousin took one look at his newborn baby and fainted smooth away." "That city boy fucked smooth up when he started makin' fun of Shorty." **2003** in 2006 *DARE* File—Internet **ceTX,** It will create too much back pressure and blow it smooth up. **2004** *Ibid,* They've gotten away with it, smooth away with it.

smooth as a smelt See **smelt 3**

smoothback n Cf **hackleback 1**

=**lake sturgeon.**

1974 WI Univ. *Fish Lake MI* 14, *Lake Sturgeon . . common names:* freshwater sturgeon, . . smoothback. **1983** Becker *Fishes WI* 221, *Acipenser fulvescens.* . . Smoothback. . . A typical inhabitant of large rivers and lakes.

smoothbark hickory n Also *smoothbark, smooth hickory* Cf **shagbark hickory**

A **pignut 1** (here: *Carya glabra*).

1908 Rogers *Tree Book* 134, For who would wish a "pignut" planted in his front yard? A "smooth hickory" will rather be chosen, every time—though it is the very same tree, *H[icoria] glabra. Ibid* 135, Its bark is close textured like that of a white ash. . . "Smooth hickory". . . is a literal translation of its scientific name. **1968** *DARE* (Qu. I43, *What kinds of nuts grow wild around here?*) Inf **CT**17, Hickory nuts . . shagbark . . pignut . . smoothbark. **1980** Little *Audubon Guide N. Amer. Trees E. Region* 347, *Pignut Hickory* . . "Smoothbark Hickory". . . Bark: light gray; smooth or becoming furrowed with forking ridges. **2004** in 2005 *DARE* File—Internet, I mostly use what is called Pignut here [=GA] (Carya Glabra) it is also called Smoothbark Hickory and has little bitty nuts.

smoothbark pine n **NJ**

=**shortleaf pine 1.**

1895 NJ Geol. Surv. *Annual Rept. for 1894* 251, The choicest timber on the upland was yellow pine *(Pinus echinata).* . . It is known to woodmen as the smooth-bark pine. **1903** *Ibid* 13, In many cases trees may be planted with considerable profit. This is particularly true of the cottonwood, . . smooth-bark pine, white pine, and . . the basket willow. **1968** *DARE* (Qu. T17, . . *Kinds of pine trees;* not asked in early QRs) Infs **NJ**31, 39, Smoothbark pine.

smooth blackfish See **blackfish 1**

smooth crop n **chiefly Sth**

See quot 1915.

1753 in 2002 *DARE* File—Internet **NC,** It is ordered that he have his mark Recorded to wit: a smooth Crop in the right ear. **1773** in 1929 Summers *Annals* 209 **swVA,** Ord. that Uriah Humphries's ear mark be admitted to record, towit: two smooth crops and a slit in the left ear. **1801** *NC Mercury & Salisbury Advt.* (Salisbury) 29 Jan 4/3, A gang of hogs . . having two smooth craps and a hole in the right ear. **1866** *Madison Co. Courier* (Edwardsville IL) 11 Jan 5/2, *Estrays.* . . [A] red heifer, smooth crop in right ear and swallow fork in left ear. **1915** *DN* 4.185 **swVA,** *Mark.* . . A cutting of the ear (of hogs, sheep, cattle) for identification,—of various kinds: *(smooth) crop,* the tip cut square off. **1967** *DARE* (Qu. K18, . . *Kind of mark . . to identify a cow)* Infs **LA**2, 7, **SC**43, Smooth crop.

smoothening harrow See **smoothing harrow**

smoothening iron See **smoothing iron**

smooth hickory See **smoothbark hickory**

smoothing harrow n Also *smoothening harrow, smoothing board,* ~ *drag* **scattered, but more freq Nth, esp wNEng** See Map

A harrow or **drag** n **1** used to level the ground and break up clods of earth.

1870 in 1872 *Rural Affairs* 6.25 **NY,** The Smoothing Harrow, an implement invented by the author of this work, consists essentially of teeth driven through pieces of plank hinged together, the teeth slanting backwards about forty degrees. **1873** *Daily Gaz.* (Davenport IA) 6 Apr 1/5, [Advt:] Thomas' Smoothing Harrow and *Broadcast Weeder.* . . J.J. Thomas & Co. . . Geneva N.Y. **1895** *Van Wert Times* (OH) 4 Oct [2]/7 (newspaperarchive.com), [Advt:] Disc harrow, smoothing harrow, large iron kettle [etc]. **1909** *Fitchburg Daily Sentinel* (MA) 27 Feb 6/5, Use a smoothing harrow with teeth set at an angle; work both ways of field. **1925** *Book of Rural Life* 4.2505, *Smoothing Harrow (peg tooth,* or *drag).* . . The most modern smoothing harrow has a lever for adjusting the angularity or pitch of the teeth. **1939** *LANE* Map 167, *Harrow.* . . The agricultural implement with which the ground is smoothed or the soil pulverized. . . 11 Infs, **scattered wNEng,** Smoothing harrow (or board, drag). **1965–70** *DARE* (Qu. L20, *The implement used in a field after it's been plowed to break up the lumps)* 9 Infs, **chiefly wNEng,** Smoothing harrow; **CT**2, Smoothing harrow—used afterwards to smooth ground; **MD**13, Smoothing harrow—last going-over, to smooth field very fine; **MA**16, Smoothing harrow—spring-tooth, a kind of smoothing harrow; **MA**31, Smoothing harrow—made of wood and shaped like an A; **NY**9, Smoothening harrow; **VA**40, Smoothing drag; **MD**42, Smoothing board—board to flatten out ground; **NJ**16, Smoothing harrer; **VT**2, Smoothing harrow—has peg teeth that be, can be set at any angle to leave a smooth surface after disk harrow has been over field; **VT**16, Smoothing harrow—has spikes. **1986** Pederson *LAGS Concordance,* 1 inf, **cnGA,** Smoothing harrow. **2002** *DARE* File—Internet **seGA,** *Farm Implements.* . . 12 Foot Smoothing Harrows. **2002** *OSU Ext. Facts F-6237* (Internet) **OK,** Just before planting [melon seeds], go over the soil with a smoothing harrow to prepare a seed bed.

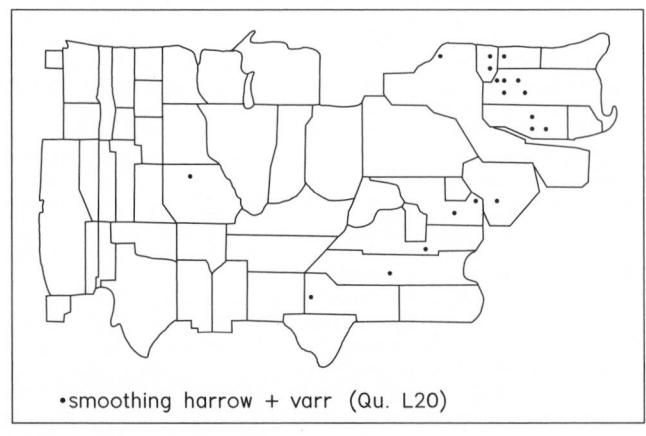

•smoothing harrow + varr (Qu. L20)

smoothing iron n Also *smoothening iron, smooth ~* [*OED2*
1627 →] **formerly widespread, now chiefly Sth, S Midl** See
Map *old-fash*
An iron for pressing cloth; now esp an old-fashioned non-elec-
tric iron.

    1638 in 1887 *Archives of MD* 4.48 **sMD,** 1. smoothing iron. **1671** in
1901 Portsmouth RI *Early Rec.* 423, I give the Saw to Mary and the
Smoth Iron. **1712** in 2006 *DARE* File—Internet **New Haven CT,** [In-
ventory:] Smoothing iron and heater. **1844** Thompson *Major Jones's
Courtship* 94 **GA,** I . . shaved my face as slick as a smoothin iron.
1853 *Bangor Daily Whig & Courier* (ME) 4 June 1/3, [Advt:] Housekeepers, look at this Admirable Invention! *Patent Self Heating
Smoothing Iron!* **1878** *NY Times* (NY) 26 Jan 8/6 **neNJ,** [He] yesterday
made an attack on his wife, and attempted to kill her with a smoothing-
iron. **1893** *Herald–Despatch* (Decatur IL) 3 June [4]/5 (newspaper-
archive.com), The last person to use this iron had neglected to discon-
nect the smoothing iron from the power wire. **1901** Harben *Westerfelt*
7 **nGA,** She stooped to put her smoothing-iron down on the hearth.
1906 *DN* 3.157 **nwAR,** Smoothin'-iron. . . Flat-iron. **1920** *Gettysburg
Comp.* (PA) 29 May [2]/5 (newspaperarchive.com), A gasoline smoothing iron . . exploded Monday afternoon. **1948** Hurston *Seraph* 124 **FL,**
That trifling woman's done shoved all the buttons off this shirt with the
smoothening-iron. **1953** *AmSp* 28.254 **csPA,** Smoothing iron. . . A
flatiron. In general use. **1964** Will *Hist. Okeechobee* 305 **FL,** In clothes
that never had seen a smoothing iron. **1965–70** *DARE* (Qu. F29, *Different kinds of irons—not electric—used . . for smoothing clothes after
they're washed*) 117 Infs, **chiefly Sth, S Midl,** Smoothing iron; **GA**19,
LA43, **MA**8, **TN**1, Smooth iron. **1966** *DARE* Tape **FL**6, She put her
smoothing irons, it was an iron that you iron clothes with, . . in the middle of that plate. **1986** Pederson *LAGS Concordance,* 26 infs, **Gulf Region,** Smoothing iron; 1 inf, **ceMS,** Smoothing iron—cast iron, 3–5
pounds, heated; 1 inf, **ceAR,** Smoothing iron—heated on stove in winter; 1 inf, **cAR,** Smoothing iron—heated on charcoal burner; 1 inf,
ceMS, Smoothing iron—heat in fireplace. **2003** *Commercial Appeal*
(Memphis TN) sec A 1 (Internet), In the summer we'd build a fire outside. We had the big, smoothing irons and we'd heat the irons and in the
winter we'd use a fireplace in the stove.

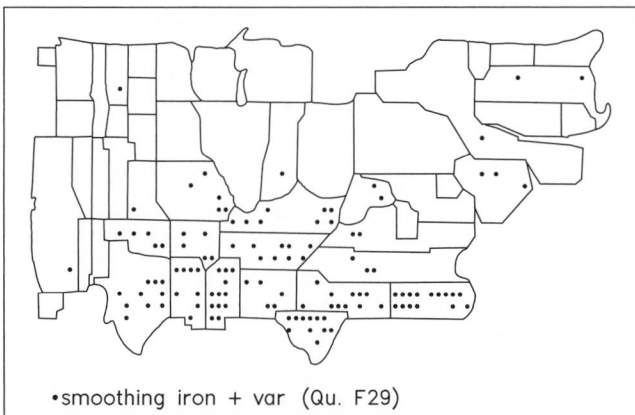

•smoothing iron + var (Qu. F29)

smooth mouth n **chiefly Missip-Ohio Valleys, West**

1 A horse's or mule's mouth in which all the incisors (or all
the lower incisors) are worn smooth, indicating that it is at
least about eleven (or nine) years old; a horse or mule in this
state; hence adj *smooth-mouth(ed).*

    1904 *Washington Post* (DC) 29 Aug 8/7, A ten-year-old is commonly
spoken of as a "smooth-mouthed"horse, i.e., no cups. **1910** *Daily Rev.*
(Decatur IL) 14 Dec 13/6, [Advt:] One full blood Clyde mare, smooth
mouth . . ; one smooth mouthed Clyde bred mare . . ; one 5-year-old
draft mare. **1937** *AmSp* 12.103 **eNE** [Farm terms], A horse that no
longer has *cups* in its teeth is said to be *smooth-mouthed* and is at least
eleven years old. **1941** *Sikeston Herald* (MO) 13 Mar 7/4, [Advt:] 20
Head Good Smooth Mouth Mules. **1958** *AmSp* 33.272 **eWA** [Ranching
terms], *Smooth mouth.* A horse five years old [sic] or better. The lower
front teeth are worn down smooth. **1977** *Times Recorder* (Zanesville
OH) 31 Mar sec B 8/4, [Advt:] Team of smooth mouthed sorrel mares.
2000 Loch–Bradley *Determining Horses Teeth* (Internet), In general, the
cups become smooth in the lower centers, intermediates, corners, upper
centers, intermediates, and corners at 6, 7, 8, 9, 10, and 11 years of age,
respectively. A "smooth mouth" theoretically appears at 11. A few horse

owners ignore cups in the upper teeth and consider a 9-year-old horse
smooth-mouthed. **2001** *DARE* File—Internet **MO,** I just recently purchased a "smooth mouthed" grade mare. . . So, how old is too old to
breed a mare?

2 A cow's or sheep's mouth in which the incisors are worn
down to the gums or missing; hence adjs *smooth-mouth(ed).*

    1942 *Van Wert Times–Bulletin* (OH) 11 Feb 3/5, [Advt:] 1 Jersey cow,
smooth mouth, due Feb. 18th. **1949** *Joplin Globe* (MO) 13 Mar sec D
5/1, [Advt:] 1 Spotted Jersey Cow, smooth mouthed milking good.
1992 *OSU Ext. Facts F-3860* (Internet), Broken and smooth mouth ewes
may be separated for additional feed or culled. **1998** in 2002 *DARE*
File—Internet **cwKS,** We sold 28 cows. . . These are the old cows that
have very few or no teeth. The cattleman's terms for these cows are,
"smooth mouth or broken mouth." When they can't eat, they can't produce enough milk to raise a calf without special feed. **2000** TX Farm
Bur. *TX Ag.* 20 Oct (Internet), You keep it up, you're gonna be worse 'n
some ol' smooth mouthed cow. **2007** FL Coop. Ext. Serv. *Fact Sheet
AN121,* By age 12, the row of teeth . . exhibits progressive wearing to
stubs. The animal may gradually become "smooth-mouthed," meaning
teeth are worn to the gums.

3 Transf or fig: see quots; hence adjs *smooth-mouth(ed).*

    1942 *AmSp* 17.104 [Truck driver lingo], *Museum piece.* Old truck.
Also *Smooth Mouth.* **1967** *DARE* Tape **IL**15, But I do want him [=a
man] without any teeth, because at my age he'd have to have his teeth all
pulled, and I'd be to the expense of pulling 'em and getting false teeth,
so I want him smooth-mouth. **1995** (1998) *Brophy Coll.* 69 **swMO** (as
of c1960), Smoothmouth. A toothless horse, occ. applied to a person.
1997 in 2006 *DARE* File—Internet **cnGA,** I remember a dog Alan
got, . . he was beautiful, he was small, but when he brought him over to
show me I noticed that all four of his canine Tushes were broken off. He
was smooth mouthed. *Ibid* **WA,** I have always been told a bit is only as
cruel as the hands that hold the reins. Being of a smooth-mouthed age
myself, that included the old spade and halfbreed bits.

smooth sumac n

1 Std: a **sumac B** (here: *Rhus glabra*) native throughout the
US. Also called **bright sumac, kinnikinnick 1, red sumac,
scarlet ~, senhalenac, upland sumac, vinegar tree, white
sumac 2**

2 =**dwarf sumac.**

    1897 Sudworth *Arborescent Flora* 275, *Rhus copallina.* . . *Common
Names.* . . Smooth Sumach. **1960** Vines *Trees SW* 633, *Rhus copal-
lina.* . . Vernacular names for this plant are Mountain Sumac, Smooth
Sumac [etc]. . . The bark and leaves contain tannin. **1979** Erichsen-
Brown *Med. N. Amer. Plants* 115, *Rhus copallina.* . . *Range.* s. Ont., s.
Maine, N.H. and Mo., s. to Fla. and Tex. . . *Common names.*
Smooth or common sumac.

smoove See **smooth**

smother v

1 To cook slowly in a covered pan; hence ppl adj *smothered.*
[*OED2 smother* v. 4.b 1706–7 →, *smothered* ppl. a. 3 1748 →]
chiefly Gulf States See Map on p. 56 Cf **smother** n 1

    1839 Bryan *KY Housewife* 118, To Smother Young Chickens. . . Split
them open . . season them with salt, pepper, nutmeg and lemon, dredge
them with flour, and put them in a pan, with four ounces of butter, and
enough water to cover them; cover the pan, and stew them slowly. **1847**
(1979) Rutledge *Carolina Housewife* 73, Smothered Veal. Cover your
veal (generally the knuckle) with three or four thin slices of the fat of
bacon, and cover that with roasted chestnuts, potatoes, carrots, turnips,
onions, roots of celery, a sprig of thyme, one of parsley. . . Moisten well
with broth . . ; cook by a slow fire, and in a Dutch oven.—*Madame de
Genlis.* **1871** *Appletons' Jrl.* 5.743 **GA,** My breakfast is generally a
smothered chicken and a stewed catfish or two or three trout [etc].
1905 Chesnutt *Col.'s Dream* 45, The supper was typically Southern. . .
There was smothered chicken, light biscuit, . . and tea. **1965–70** *DARE*
(Qu. H45, *Dishes made with meat, fish, or poultry that everybody
around here would know, but that people in other places might not*) Inf
MO20, Smothered chicken—prepared with milk; **TX**91, Smothered
chicken; **AL**25, Smothered steak—onion and gravy; (Qu. H47, *Kinds of
fried potatoes*) Inf **LA**20, Smothered potatoes—these are the same as
what they call hash browns in restaurants; (Qu. H51, *Dishes made with
cooked cabbage;* total Infs questioned, 75) Infs **MS**60, 72, Smothered
cabbage. **1968** *DARE* FW Addit **New Orleans LA,** Smothered cabbage—leftover cabbage put in a frying pan with potatoes; **neLA,**
Smothered potatoes—cooked on top of stove with a little grease and

some water in a covered skillet. **1986** Pederson *LAGS Concordance,* 1 inf, **cnLA,** Smother it—the liver; 1 inf, **neFL,** Smother the chicken with grease and water; 1 inf, **seLA,** Smothered cabbage, smothered squash, smothered string beans with salt meat; 1 inf, **cTX,** Smothered rabbit. **2006** *DARE* File—Internet **csLA,** My Favorite food is Rice and Gravy, smothered chicken with smothered potatoes.

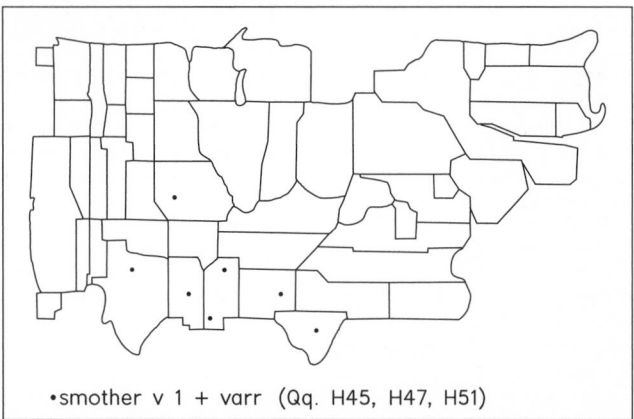

•smother v 1 + varr (Qq. H45, H47, H51)

2 To experience shortness of breath; hence vbl n *smothering* experiencing shortness of breath—freq in comb *smothering spell.* **formerly widespread, now chiefly Sth, S Midl** See Map   Cf **smother** n **3**

1837 *S. Lit. Messenger* 3.444, Fain would I have learned something of Isadore; but a smothering sensation overwhelmed me, and I mounted my horse and fled for home. **1878** *Chester Daily Times* (PA) 30 Jan [3]/4 (newspaperarchive.com), A lady who came from Philadelphia by rail, was taken suddenly sick with a smothering spell, as she alighted at the depot. **1902** *DN* 2.245 **sIL,** Smother . . to be short-winded. *smotherin' spell.* . . Congestion, or palpitation of the heart, where there is difficulty in breathing. **1903** *DN* 2.330 **seMO,** Smothering spell. . . Difficult respiration. **1907** *DN* 3.226 **nwAR,** Smother . . to be short-winded. *Smotherin' spell.* . . Congestion or palpitation of the heart where there is difficulty in breathing. **1912** *Gazette* (Stevens Point WI) [10 July 8]/3 (newspaperarchive.com), Her illness first appeared with smothering spells and the best physicians were called in and her trouble diagnosed as fat of the heart. **1945** Saxon *Gumbo Ya-Ya* 392 **LA,** I had me a smotherin' spell this mornin' and I don't feel no good yet. **1965–70** *DARE* (Qu. BB7, *A feeling that lasts for a short while, with difficult breathing and heart beating fast*) 33 Infs, **chiefly Sth, S Midl,** Smothering spell(s); **AL**19, **AZ**11, **CT**42, **KY**28, **MA**122, **SC**34, Smothering; [**OR**13, Smothered; **IL**143, Smothery]. **1990** Cavender *Folk Med. Lexicon* 31 **sAppalachians,** *Smothering*—difficulty with breathing. **1993** Gibbons *Charms* 44 **NC** (as of c1930), One of the children began to cough. She had what we called smothering sickness, and there with the room so stifling-thick with oil smoke and camphor, she struggled to breathe. **2005** *DARE* File—Internet **wTX,** The new publisher of the Fort Stockton Pioneer . . surely had a smothering spell when the latest edition arrived and the page one headline seemed to be, well, lacking.

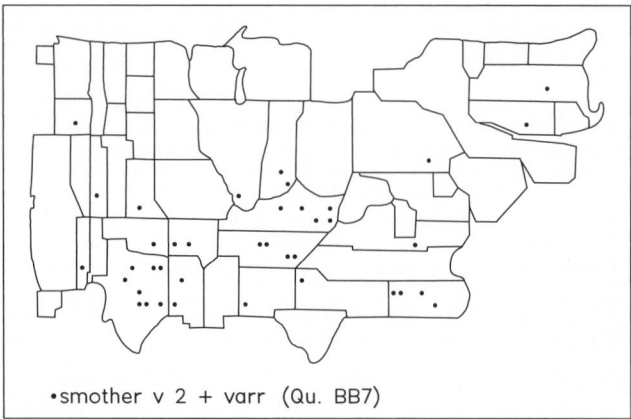

•smother v 2 + varr (Qu. BB7)

smother n

1 also *smotheration:* A dish of stewed or braised meat; a potpie. **chiefly NEng** Cf **smother** v **1, stifle** n

[**1850** Herbert *Warwick Woodlands* 135 [Brit speaker in **seNY**], The old woman's got some beautiful fresh onions—she'll make a stew of them—a smother, as you call it.] [**1852** U.S. Congress *Serial Set* 676.23.260 **New Brunswick Canada,** The visiter [sic] . . is treated to *fresh smother, duff,* and *jo-floggers.* [Note:] Potpie of sea-birds, pudding, and pancakes.] **1869** (1870) Kellogg *Ark* 27 **ME,** Many a smother was made, and many a chicken roasted, in that galley. **1890** *Century Dict.* 5721 **NEng,** *Smotheration.* . . A sailors' dish of beef and pork smothered with potatoes. **1907** *DN* 3.249 **eME,** *Smother.* . . Pot roast. "This beef will make a beautiful smother." **1977** *Yankee* Jan 73 **ME,** Smother is another name for pot pie. **1998** *Los Angeles Times* (CA) 4 Nov sec H 5 (Internet), I have absolutely no idea what to call the bird I made the other night. . . I suppose I'd call it a modern kind of dark fricassee. . . But I prefer to think of it as that prototypically American dish, the smother.

2 A smudge fire built to repel insects.

1938 FWP *Guide DE* 399, This was one of the worst mosquito-ridden spots in Delaware . . ; even "smothers" of damp seaweed could not make enough acrid smoke to protect picnickers. *Ibid* 405, Farm families no longer huddle around "smothers" of smoldering green leaves, and farm animals are no longer driven to bellowing madness by swarms of stinging insects.

3 also pl; also with *the:* See quots.   Cf **smother** v **2**

1968 *DARE* (Qu. BB7, *A feeling that lasts for a short while, with difficult breathing and heart beating fast*) Inf **NJ**53, A smother. **1976** *Urban Health* June 54 **Sth,** Terms used by patients may be . . vague, as when inability to breathe easily is referred to as "smothering," or "the smothers."

smotheration   See **smother** n **1**

smothered   See **smother** v **1**

smother fry v phr   **chiefly Sth, S Midl**

=**smother** v **1**; hence ppl adj *smother fried;* n pl *smother fries* potatoes cooked in this manner.

1942 Rawlings *Cross Creek Cookery* 107 **FL,** Smother Fried Quail, Dove, Rabbit, Squirrel—I use this method when the game is of uncertain age. . . Brown on all sides. Almost cover with boiling water. Cover tightly and let simmer . . until meat is meltingly tender. **1954** *Panama City News* (FL) [19 Mar 4] (newspaperarchive.com), [Advt:] *Young, Tender Beef Liver.* . . Try this smother fried with onions. **1966** *DARE* (Qu. H47, *Kinds of fried potatoes*) Inf **FL**31, Smother fries—smother fry them; cut round pieces of potatoes, put in pan and cover. **2000** *Sun. Star-News* (Wilmington NC) 26 Mar sec C 9 (Internet), It was a smorgasbord with bear stew, deer ham, fried quail, shrimp, smother-fried duck and more. **2002** in 2006 *DARE* File—Internet **AL,** How many people out there like smother fried fox squirrel? **2004** *Ibid* **nwSC,** [Product review:] This pan is the one you want for smother frying and braising things (like frying cubed steak then simmering in gravy, making smother fried pork chops, or making a pot roast.) **2006** *Ibid* **cCO,** [Restaurant menu:] *Smother Fries* with green chili & cheese.

smothering (spell)   See **smother** v **2**

smotherly adj

Suffocating, oppressive.   Note: The metaphorical sense "overprotective" (with allusion to *motherly*) is not treated here.

1928 *Bee* (Danville VA) 27 Dec 10/1, [Advt:] Relieves that stuffy, smotherly feeling. It's bringing relief to thousands who have been slaves to constipation. **1968** Haun *Hawk's Done Gone* 63 **eTN,** I noticed that it was a smotherly evening. **2002** in 2006 *DARE* File—Internet **NV,** The pain stabs in my heart for hours and radiates down my arm, along with a smotherly feeling.

smothersome adj   Cf **-some** suff

Oppressively hot or humid.

1864 in 2006 *DARE* File—Internet **cnOH,** 17th All quiet. Wether being hot. . . Sept 19th The wether very smothersome. **1946** *AmSp* 21.271 **neKY,** *Smothersome.* . . Hot and humid; suffocating. 'Kind of a smothersome day.' **2006** *DARE* File—Internet **SC,** The heat is on and my electric blanket is starting to be a little smothersome.

smouch n, v[1]   Also sp *smoutch*

=**smooch** n, v[1].

1844 Beecher *7 Lect.* 124 **NEng,** Around a broken table, sitting upon boxes, kegs, or rickety chairs, see a filthy crew dealing cards smoutched with tobacco, grease and liquor. **1865** *Harper's New Mth. Mag.* 31.141, I poked over fires which would not burn, scorched my fingers, or smouched my only shirt. **1882** *Ibid* 65.379, They keep carefully away from the smouch of the cigarette trays. **1896** *Ibid* 93.618, A baby . . smiling and cooing, but with a great crimson smouch on its tiny shoulder. **1915** Abbott *Indiscreet Letter* 40 **MA,** The Young Electrician reached up . . and smouched one more streak of black across his forehead in a desperate effort to reduce his tousled yellow hair to . . smoothness.

smouch v² Also *smouge, smoutch*
1 To steal, pilfer; to appropriate to one's own use or benefit. [*OED2* 1826 →] Cf **smooch** v² **1**
 1851 Hall *College Words* 286 **cNY,** *Smouge.* At Hamilton College, to obtain without leave. **1871** Twain in *Galaxy* 11.158, Old Mann used to . . steal along the coast of the dangerous Kill von Kull . . to smouch oysters from unguarded beds. **1893** *KS Univ. Qrly.* 1.142 **MO,** *Smouge:* to steal. **1893** Twain in *Century Illustr. Mag.* 47.237, They would smouch provisions from the pantry whenever they got a chance. **1902** *DN* 2.245 **sIL,** *Smouge* [smauʒ]. . . To take secretly more than one's rightful share. To make false returns, and *smouge* the difference. **1905** *DN* 3.65 **eNE,** *Smouge.* . . (1) Filch, or wring out of; (2) sneak in, or through, dishonorably; encroach on. "I smouged a piece of goods"; "He smouged the chairmanship." **1919** Mencken *Prejudices* 33 **MD,** In "The Research Magnificent" he smouches an idea from Nietzsche, and then mauls it so badly that one begins to wonder whether he is in favor of it or against it. **1943** *LANE* Map 566 *(Swiped)* 1 inf, **ceMA,** *Smouched* [sma‹otʃt], the regular term in the informant's family. **1998** in 2004 *DARE* File—Internet **AZ,** My scooter was stolen! . . it was smouched on saturday . . from tucson arizona. **2004** *NADS Letters* **seMI,** "Smoudge" . . meaning "pilfer" was used routinely by (among others) my father (born 1918) as late as the 1970's (in Detroit). . . It would rhyme with "gouge."
2 To cheat (one); intr: to engage in devious or underhanded activities, cheat, crib, finagle; hence vbl n *smouging*; ppl adj *smouched.*
 1840 *WI Enquirer* (Madison) 7 Nov 1/3, The map of the city of Chicago, was a curiosity, and we opine that by this time, many "smouch'd" (cheated) individuals think it also a "caution." **1848** Bartlett *Americanisms* 314, *To smouch.* To gouge; to take unfair advantage. Colloquial in New York. **1855** *WI Patriot* (Madison) 16 June 2/4, The modesty of the "speculators" here would not allow them to attempt to *smouge* Hamilton county more than $5,000 or $6,000. **1868** *New Englander & Yale Rev.* 28.92, Twenty or thirty loved classical studies . . ; but these were held back by, perhaps, seventy, who dreamed, or lounged, or 'ponied,' or 'smouged,' through. **1873** *OH Constitutional Convention Official Rept.* 1.218, He said that looked very suspicious to make it so particular—the cents at the end of the bill of a lawyer or doctor. It looked as though there was a little "smouging" likely to be going on, to use the expression of my friend from Richland. **1883** (1890) Peck *Peck's Bad Boy No. 2* 104 **WI,** I am going to leave my burnt cork on, cause if I washed it off Pa would know there had been some smouging somewhere. **1900** *DN* 2.61 **cwNY** [College slang], *Smouge, v. i.* To crib. **1903** *DN* 2.330 **seMO,** *Smouge, v. i.* To overreach; to cheat. 'He tried to smouge on me.' **1921** Kelland *Scattergood Baines* 231 **NEng,** I'm a-goin' cautious. I might git smouged. . . What I aim to do is to go careful till I git on to the ropes and know who to trust. **1922** *NE State Jrl.* (Lincoln) 13 Feb 4/3, For many years the profiteers / Were after me like thunder;/ They trimmed and smouged and robbed and gouged / Until I plumb went under.

smouge See **smouch** v²

smouging See **smouch** v² **2**

smoul v Also with *around*
To slobber (over something).
 1961 *Mt. Life* 37.2.9 **sAppalachians,** Ye can see the lowdown thang [=a dog] a-layin' on the hathrock a-snappin' at its fleas and a-smoulin' over hisself. **1962** *Ibid* 38.1.18 **sAppalachians,** The farmer scolds the child for taking out more "grub" than he can eat and "a-smoulin' around over it and a-mommickin' it up till nobody else can stommick it."

smoutch v¹ See **smouch** n, v¹

smoutch v² See **smouch** v²

smuch o'britches See **much o'britches**

smudder v, n Also *smutter* [Varr of *smother; smudder* represents the expected pronc in dialects where [ð] is regularly replaced by [d] (see Pronc Intro 3.I.17), but in NEng and Upstate NY it is presumably inherited from Brit dial (see *EDD* [at *smother*] and *SND*).]

1839 Thompson *Green Mt. Boys* 2.258 **VT,** Hurra! ye poor half smuddered divils . . do you hear? **1876** Harte *Gabriel Conroy* 347 **CA** [Black], Fore God, Mars Jack—you's smuddering dat chile. **1927** *AmSp* 3.138 **eME,** When sweeping one was told not to make such a "smutter" or "smudder," and dust in the road was spoken of in the same way. Perhaps these terms, meaning smoke from fire, or dust, are derived from "smother"? **1939** (1962) Thompson *Body & Britches* 189 **NY,** We thought by the cracking and the snapping the boat was in pieces. When the smudder cleared away, they found the boat all right. **1985** Rattray *Advent. Dimon* 166 **Long Is. NY,** There was a great smudder of foam and blood. **2002** *DARE* File—Internet **cIL,** The last 3 minutes of cooking time smudder *with your favorite Pappy LeDeaux's B.B.Q. & Dipping Sauce.*

smur n Also sp *smirr, smurr* [Brit dial *smirr, smurr* a drizzle]
A drizzle or wet mist.
 1914 [see **smur** v]. **1944** *PADS* 2.49 **NC, VA,** *Smur* [smɝ]. . . A fog almost as heavy as a rain. Caldwell and Avery cos., N.C. Reported.

smur v Also sp *smirr, smurr* [Cf **smur** n and Brit dial *smirr, smurr* to drizzle] **chiefly eNEng**
Usu with *up:* To become foggy or cloudy.
 1914 *DN* 4.112 **cKS,** *Smirr,* n. and v. Variant of *smurr.* *Ibid* 156 **Cape Cod MA,** *Smurr up.* . . Gradually to become a bit hazy. [*Smurr* is so used in Kansas.—*[DN]* Ed.] "When it's smurrin' up like that to west'ard, you know it's goin' to be squally." **1916** *DN* 4.264 **Cape Cod MA,** A similarly interesting term is employed by the weather-wise when a light haze begins to dull a clear sky or dim a bright sun: "Guess we're in for a spell o' rain; it's smurrin' up to the east'ard; and when it gets smurry with the wind this way, it's sure to rain." **1939** *LANE* Map 90 *(Clouding up)* 13 infs, **chiefly coastal ME,** Smurring up; 1 inf, Smurring; 1 inf, Smurring up for a storm. **1942** *ME Univ. Studies* 56.60, When the sky clouded over it was said to *smur* up.

smurr n See **smur** n

smurr v See **smur** v

smurry adj **chiefly eNEng** Cf *lowery* (at **lower** v¹)
Hazy, overcast, cloudy.
 1887 Goode *Fisheries U.S.* 4.63 **NEng,** If in the southwest you see a smurry sky,/ Douse your flying kites, for a storm is nigh. [Footnote to *smurry:*] . . If the sky assumes a hazy, greasy look—called "smurry" by the fishermen—with small patches of leaden or inky clouds, a storm is imminent. **1914** *DN* 4.156 **Cape Cod MA,** *Smurry.* . . Hazy. "It's all smurry to west'ard.["] **1924** *DN* 5.287 **Cape Cod MA,** A smurry i.e., hazy breeze from the southwest is commonly called a 'yellow eyed sou'-wester', perhaps owing to the dirty colored atmosphere. **1939** *LANE* Map 88 *(A cloudy day)* 18 infs, **chiefly coastal ME,** Smurry. **1988** Nickerson *Days to Remember* 140 **Cape Cod MA** (as of c1915), *Smurry*—When unformed clouds start to obscure the bright sunshine, the sky was "smurry".

smur up See **smur** v

smut n Cf **sleeper** n **4**
 1981 *DARE* File **Brooklyn NYC,** ["Sleep" in one's eyes is called] smut.

smut ball n Also *smut mushroom* [*EDD* at *smut* sb. 2.(1) 1854 for *Lycoperdon bovista* [=*Calvatia gigantea*]]
A **puffball 1.**
 1900 Lyons *Plant Names* 232, *L[ycoperdon] Bovista* [=*Calvatia gigantea*]. . . Giant Puffball, . . Smut-ball. **1970** *DARE* (Qu. S18, *A kind of mushroom that grows like a globe . . sometimes gets as big as a man's head*) Inf **KY**74, Smut balls. **1986** Pederson *LAGS Concordance* *(Mushrooms)* 1 inf, **cwGA,** Smut mushrooms—wild ones.

smut grass n [See quots]
A **dropseed 3** (here: *Sporobolus indicus*) common esp in the southern US.
 1879 U.S. Dept. Ag. *Rept. of Secy. for 1878* 173, *Sporobolus Indicus*—Smut grass. . . It occurs more or less abundantly in all the Southern States, and is called smut-grass, from the fact that after flowering the heads become affected with a blackish smut. **1939** Tharp *Vegetation TX* 46, Smut-grass . . is a tough perennial. **1944** *AL Geol. Surv. Bulletin* 53.68, "Smut grass". . . alludes to the fact that its seeds are often covered with black powdery fungus spores. **1966–68** *DARE* (Qu. S9, . . *Kinds of grass that are hard to get rid of*) Inf **AL**15, Smut grass—grows straight, in clusters, ragged leaf; **FL**31, Smut grass; (Qu. S21, . . *Weeds . . that are a trouble in gardens and fields*) Inf **LA**4, Smut

grass—you walk through and get black stuff on your leg; **LA**31, Smut grass. **1970** Correll *Plants TX* 222, *Sporobolus indicus. . . Smutgrass. . .* Grain often sticking persistently instead of falling readily as in many dropseeds. **2002** *St. Petersburg Times* (FL) 29 June sec 3 (Internet), This very minute, your garden is probably in the grip of rampant weed growth. . . They have ancient, formidable names: . . smutgrass, cupid's shaving brush, henbit.

smut mushroom See **smut ball**

smutter See **smudder**

smutty n See **smutty coot**

smutty v

To soil, dirty.

1933 Rawlings *South Moon* 19 **nFL**, No use lettin' them dirty men smutty it.

smutty-breast n

=**red-backed sandpiper.**

1917 *Wilson Bulletin* 29.2.79 **VA**, *Pelinda* [sic] *alpina sakhalina* [= *Calidris alpina*].—Smutty-breast, Wallops and Revels I[slan]ds., Va.

smutty coot n Also *smutty* Cf **brown coot**

The immature or female American **scoter** (*Melanitta nigra*).

1888 Trumbull *Names of Birds* 107 **MA**, The female (and young) [of the American scoter] . . [are] known at Salem as *smutty.* **1917** (1923) *Birds Amer.* 1.148, *Oidemia americana* [=*Melanitta nigra*]. . . Smutty Coot. . . *Adult Female:* Sooty-brown, paler below. **1925** (1928) Forbush *Birds MA* 1.271, *Oidemia americana. . . Other names* . . (for female and immature) . . *smutty coot; smutty. . . Young in juvenal plumage:* Similar to adult female; dark brown above with dark cap. . . *Downy young:* Above dark sooty-brown.

smutz See **schmutz**

snab v [Perh blend of *nab* and *snag,* but cf **snabble**]

Also with *onto:* To seize, grab.

1889 Munroe *Golden Days* 316 **CA**, We have evidence to prove that you and your pal . . are the galoots that snabbed onto our pile . . and lit out with it. **1967** *Mt. Life* 43.1.14 **sAppalachians**, He snuck up right easy and rech aout and snabbed it [=a bumblebee] and popped it into a poke he had with 'im. **2003** in 2006 *DARE* File—Internet **neIL**, The cop who snabbed me turned around and then snabbed a co-worker of mine. **2004** *Ibid* **cwFL**, I snabbed a pair of "minor cosmetic shipping damage" sub frame connectors . . for $65. **2005** *Ibid* **swCA**, Glad you snabbed a copy!

snabble v Also *snable* [Cf *OED2* snabble "slang. *Obs.*"; 1725 *New Cant. Dict.* "to rifle, to strip, or plunder. . . *Snabbled* . . apprehended, seized, or taken."]

See quots.

1930 Shoemaker *1300 Words* 56 **cPA Mts** (as of c1900), *Snable*—To steal, to take away by stealth. **1935** *AmSp* 10.172 **PA** [Engl of PA Germans], Other terms more rarely used include the following: . . *Snable* or *snabble* for intrude stealthily, often with intent to steal.

snab onto See **snab**

snack n

1 pl, in phr *go snacks:* To share equally. [*OED2* (at *snack* sb.² 3.c) 1693 →] **chiefly Sth, NEng** Cf **snook** n², **snuck** n

1769 in 1953 Woodmason *Carolina Backcountry* 234 **SC**, They . . whipped the Magistrates Who went Snacks with them in their Plunder. **1808** in 1892 *S. Hist. Mag.* 1.56 **VA**, I am just going to breakfast myself, and you are welcome to go snacks with me. **1872** in 1952 *AmSp* 27.77 **CA**, Orville Grant . . proposed to Jussen . . to go snacks on a fraudulent "divy" with the runner of a distillery there. **1883** Amer. Philol. Assoc. *Trans.* 14.53, The expression *to go snacks,* i.e. 'to go shares,' is the common one in the South, while *to go snucks* is the usual form in the North and West; though the former is still used in Massachusetts. **1884** *Anglia* 7.272 **Sth, S Midl** [Black], *To sorter go snacks* = to go into partnership. **1899** (1912) Green *VA Folk-Speech* 398, *Snacks, n. pl.* Partnership; shares; halves. "We go snacks." **1922** (1926) Cady *Rhymes VT* 16, They've fixed it so you'll all go snacks / On mother's put-up cooking. **1947** Ballowe *The Lawd* 36 **LA**, When the hearers had gone, Unc' Simba and the Duppy went snacks, which was scarcely a diet for a rabbit. **1975** Gould *ME Lingo* 263, In cooperative ventures like fishing, men "went snacks," or share-and-share-alike.

2 A small amount of food; a light meal. [*OED2* 1757 →] **formerly esp Sth, S Midl, now widespread** Cf **piece** n 8

1775 (1971) Calk *Jrl.* 36 **VA**, Peopel makes out a little snack and agree to go on till Night. **1827** (1936) Bolling *Diary* 44.324 **VA**, Mrs. Harrison, Senr., called and took a snack on her way to Dover. **1841** *S. Lit. Messenger* 7.168 **wVA**, Having discussed a "snack" of eggs and bacon . . we scale the heights on the eastern side. **1860** Street *Woods & Waters* 50 **neNY**, There's somebody taking a snack on Bark Canoe Island to the right there. **1871** Eggleston *Hoosier Schoolmaster* 111 **sIN**, A "snack" was eaten. **1899** (1912) Green *VA Folk-Speech* 398, *Snack. . .* A portion of food that can be eaten hastily; a slight hasty repast; a luncheon; a bite. **1909** *DN* 3.372 **eAL, wGA**, *Snack. . .* A slight or insufficient lunch. *Ibid* 405 **nwAR**, *Snack. . .* Bite, bit. **1911** *DN* 3.540 **eKY**. **1912** *DN* 3.590 **wIN**. **1915** *DN* 4.190 **swVA**. **1921** *DN* 5.117 **KY**, *Snack,* a light, cold repast. **1927** *AmSp* 2.364 **cwWV**, *Snack* . . a cold lunch. **1929** *AmSp* 5.129 **ME**, A "snack of vittles" meant a hasty meal, a bite of food between meals. **1930** Williams *Logger-Talk* 29 **Pacific NW**, *Snack:* A bite to eat. **1940** Faulkner *Hamlet* 48 **MS**, You want to eat a snack of dinner until they get back? **1949** Kurath *Word Geog.* 71, *Snack* is not confined to the South and the South Midland but is used also in Philadelphia and enjoys great popularity in Greater New York City and the Hudson Valley. **1965–70** *DARE* (Qu. H5, . . *A small amount of food eaten between regular meals*) 850 Infs, **widespread**, Snack(s); AR47, FL17, MO20, Between-meal snack; LA11, Short snack; PA77, Little snack; (Qu. D39) 25 Infs, **scattered**, Snack bar (*or* house, joint, place, shop); (Qu. G6) Inf WA27, Snack tray; (Qu. H2) Infs IL94, MI88, NV7, NY96, Snack; NC55, Evening snack; (Qu. H3) Infs CA10, 200, NJ69, OH52, PA60, Snack; (Qu. H6) Infs GA29, HI9, NE8, NY173, TX58, Snack(s); (Qu. O21) Infs CT6, MI68, Snack; (Qu. JJ5) Inf NJ2, Snack time; (Qu. LL13) Infs AR51, MN26, MS1, NY92, VA2, 39, Snack; KY25, Snack and a bite. **2005** *Chicago Tribune* (IL) 21 Aug (Internet), America's love affair with snacks has grown along with the obesity crisis.

snacking n

=**snack 2.**

1856 (1857) Hall *Old Whitey* 56 **NYC**, The old boy [=a horse] . . munched away with his stubby, ground-down teeth like an alderman at a corporation-snacking in the mystical labyrinths of the tea-room. **1927** *DN* 5.477 **Ozarks**, *Snackin'. . .* A lunch. "I aint et nothin' only a leetle snackin' out'n thet 'ar poke." **1968–69** *DARE* (Qu. H2, *The meal that people eat around the middle of the day*) Inf KY44, Snacking; dinner—old-fashioned; (Qu. H5, . . *A small amount of food eaten between regular meals*) Infs KY40, 44, Snacking; VA1, Snacking [VA2, who was also present, responded *snack*].

‡snack picker n [Perh folk-etym for *snag picker*]

1998 *DARE* File **OK**, *Snack picker* for "toothpick"—from a white woman born around 1964 who grew up on a farm near Clinton, Oklahoma.

snade See **snead**

snaffles n

A **lousewort 1** (here: *Pedicularis canadensis*).

1876 Hobbs *Bot. Hdbk.* 107, Snaffles . . Lousewort . . Pedicularis Canadensis.

snag n

1 An indefinite but usu large quantity or amount; a lot, bunch. **chiefly NEast, N Cent** Cf **jag** n² **1b,c**

1895 *DN* 1.400 **cNY**, *Snag* . . a great quantity, common in sing. and plur. "A snag of hooks," "snags of fun." [**1900** *DN* 2.61 [College slang] **cNY**, *Snag. . .* A large amount of work. Cor[nell University].] **1913** Johnson *Highways St. Lawrence to VA* 32 **seNY**, I'm turning this sod under on account of the hawkweed. There's a snag of it on this lot. **1950** *WELS* (*A large amount or number, more than enough: . . "She has a whole _____ of cousins."*) 1 Inf, **seWI**, Raft or snag; (*"He caught a _____ of fish."*) 1 Inf, **seWI**, Lot, snag, pile. **1950** *WELS Suppl.* **cwWI**, *Snag* . . a large number. Oftenest used with *whole.* "I have a whole snag of stockings to mend." **1969** in 2006 *DARE* File—Internet **neSD**, I got the letter ready . . Then took it to the box. Washed a big snag of dishes first. **2003** *DARE* File **nIL, sWI**, Do you have any information on the use of the word "snag" to indicate a small amount? My father farmed in northern Illinois and southern Wisconsin all his life and one way he might have used the term would be when he wanted me to go out to a cornfield and pick just enough ears to feed our cows and/or pigs for that day and perhaps the next morning. "Snag" would have been used to distinguish such interim corn picking from the overall total harvest. **2004** in 2006 *DARE* File—Internet **cWI**, Rich, I'll bring the engine and a whole snag of other stuff too.

2 See quot.

1966 *DARE* FW Addit **neWA**, A bony or poor-looking horse—old snag.

snag tree n

A **black gum 1** (here: *Nyssa sylvatica*).

1846 Emerson *Rept. Trees & Shrubs* 313 **seMA**, The Tupelo Tree. . . In Bristol County and the other south-eastern counties, this is called the Snag Tree, and sometimes Horn Pine. **1960** Vines *Trees SW* 802, Vernacular names [of black tupelo] are Swamp-hornbeam, Yellow Gum, Snag-tree [etc.].

snail n Also *snail bun*, ~ *roll* **esp CA** See Map Cf **schnecke**

A cinnamon roll or similar pastry.

1909 *Chillicothe Constitution* (MO) 25 Nov 3/5, These are a few of the rolls we make: . . London Hot-Cross buns, Cinnamon buns and Snails. **1925** Mullin *Advent. Tramp* 167 **VA**, At a little restaurant I had a hasty breakfast of coffee and "snails" (cinnamon rolls). **1927** *AmSp* 2.278 **CA** [Stanford expressions], *Snail*—a large sweet-spiced cruller of baked dough in a flat spiral. **1946** *AmSp* 21.89 **nCA**, *Snail* . . refers to a western sweet bread baked with raisins in it. . . The dough is coiled in a spiral. **1950** *WELS* (Names for different kinds of biscuits) 1 Inf, **cnWI**, Soda, baking powder, bread, snails. **1965–70** *DARE* (Qu. H32, . . *Fancy rolls and pastries*) Infs **CA**4, 112, 126, 196, **OR**1, Snails; **CA**70, Plain snails, raisin snails; **PA**40, Snail buns; **CA**15, Snails—coffee cakes, round, raisins, white icing; **CA**32, Snails—a dinner roll, has cinnamon, raisins, frosting; [(Qu. H19, *What do you mean by a biscuit? How are they made?*) Inf **MN**1, Snail rolls.] **1971** Bright *Word Geog. CA & NV* 177, Sweet roll—snail 58% [of 300 infs]. **1986** Pederson *LAGS Concordance*, 1 inf, **cwFL**, Snails—California term for Danish rolls. **2004** in 2006 *DARE* File—Internet **IA**, Our apple fritters are a U[niversity] N[orthern] I[owa] tradition. New items we are making are *cinnamon snails, big texas donut holes* and *tiger tails*.

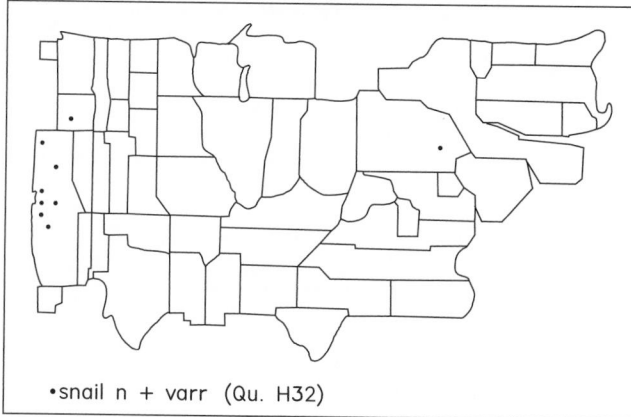

•snail n + varr (Qu. H32)

snail v **West** Cf **snake** v 1

To drag or haul with a rope; also fig.

1878 Hart *Sazerac Lying Club* 43 **NV**, We'd row the skift up to the ground-hog and grab the piece of line, and snail him inter the boat. **1899** Garland *Trail Goldseekers* 153 **West**, Occasionally a horse went down into a hole and had to be "snailed out," and we were wet and covered with mud all day. **1907** White *AZ Nights* 13, "That's all right!" thinks I, "they're back in their camp, and haven't discovered Johnny yet. I'll snail him out of there." **1944** Adams *Western Words* 148, *Snail*—To drag with a rope.

snail bird See **snail hawk**

snail bun See **snail** n

snail cat n

A **bullhead 1b** : see quots.

1955 Carr–Goin *Guide Reptiles* 63 **FL**, *Ameiurus platycephalus* . . Snail Cat; Flat Bullhead. . . A medium-sized (10 inches or less), slender catfish with pattern of rounded gray or golden spots. . . North Carolina to the Chattahoochee River, Florida. **2005** in 2006 *DARE* File—Internet, *Ameiurus serracanthus*. . . The spotted bullhead is. . . mainly found in the Apalochicola, Ochlockonee, and Suwannee river systems in Florida, Alabama and Georgia. . . Snails have been found to be the domi-

nant food type by volume, and another common name for this fish is "snail cat".

snail flower n

1 A **burr clover** (here: *Medicago sativa*).

1922 *Amer. Botanist* 28.71, "Snail flower" probably refers to the coiled seed-pod [of *Medicago sativa*], though by rights *Medicago scutellata*, a species often cultivated in gardens, is entitled to this name.

2 A **scorpionweed 2** (here: *Phacelia congesta*).

1936 Whitehouse *TX Flowers* 112, Fiddle-Neck (*Phacelia congesta*) is also known as spider-flower, caterpillars, snail-flower, and wild heliotrope. It has curled flower clusters.

snail hawk n Also *snail bird*, ~ *kite*

=**everglade kite.**

1881 Nuttall *Ornith. Club Bulletin* 6.16, The Everglade Kite. . . Their food . . consists of a kind of large fresh-water snail . . and the local name of "Snail Hawk" is particularly applicable. **1898** (1900) Davie *Nests N. Amer. Birds* 201, Everglade Kite. . . abundant at Panasofkee Lake . . where it was feeding on a kind of fresh-water snail, which was very abundant, and the local name given the bird is "Snail Hawk." **1942** U.S. Natl. Park Serv. *Fading Trails* 167 **FL**, One victim of the sudden recession of 'Glades water was the Everglade kite or snail bird. **1977** Bull–Farrand *Audubon Field Guide Birds* 482, Everglade Kite. . . Also called the "Snail Kite." **2000** *DARE* File—Internet, Everglade Kite. . . The beak of this Kite enables it to quickly remove the snail from its shell, giving it the name "Snail Hawk."

snail roll See **snail** n

snail-seed n Also *snail-seed vine* [From the spiral form of the seed]

1 also *Carolina snail-seed (vine)*: =**moonseed 2.**

1933 Small *Manual SE Flora* 537, E[pibaterium] *carolinum* [=*Cocculus carolinus*]. . . Snailseed. . . Fla. to Tex., Kans., and Va. **1948** Stevens *KS Wild Flowers* 72, Cocculus carolinus—Carolina Snailseed. **1960** Vines *Trees SW* 275, Carolina Snailseed-vine. . . Stone solitary, flattened, curled into a spiral. **1968** Barkley *Plants KS* 153, Cocculus carolinus. . . Carolina Snailseed. . . In rocky woods and thickets. **2000** in 2006 *DARE* File—Internet **cTX**, We have one specimen of snailseed vine (*Cocculus carolinus*), near a large oak tree in our neighbor's yard.

2 A closely related plant (*Cocculus diversifolius*).

1960 Vines *Trees SW* 276, Diverse-leaf Snailseed-vine—*Cocculus diversifolius*. **2002** (acc) U.S. Dept. Ag. *Plants Database* (Internet), *Cocculus diversifolius* . . snailseed.

snake n

1 In var compar phrr:

a *poor as a snake* and varr:

(1) also *skinny* (or *thin*) *as a snake* and varr: Very thin. **chiefly Sth, S Midl, West** See Map Cf **poor** adj B

1787 *Amer. Museum* 1.56, I'm as thin as a snake. **1828** in 1899 *New Engl. Mag.* 20.25 **seNY**, He [=a horse] is as poor as a snake and his spirits have entirely failed him. **1860** *Vanity Fair* 2.135, She came here used up like an old umbrella; thin as a whip-snake. **1869** *Harper's New Mth. Mag.* 39.851 **OH**, I give more'n the danged thing [=a cow] was wuth, any how; she's poor as a black-snake. **1940** Stuart *Trees of Heaven* 239 **eKY**, If you let 'em run out and kick up their heels they git poor as snakes. They git so poor you can count their ribs. **1965–70**

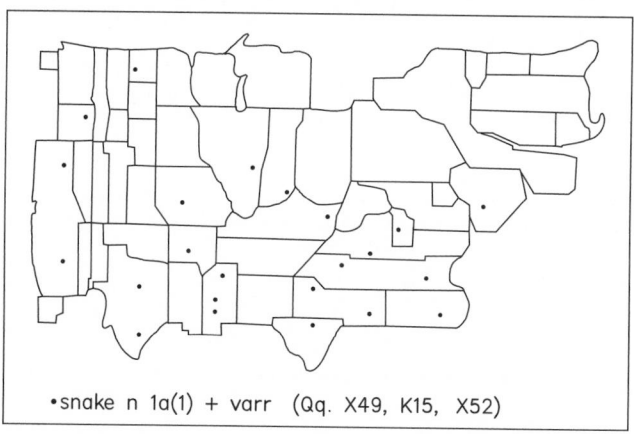

•snake n 1a(1) + varr (Qq. X49, K15, X52)

DARE (Qu. X49, *Expressions . . about a person who is very thin*) 19 Infs, **chiefly Sth, S Midl, West,** Poor (*or* skinny) as a snake; **VA**9, Poor as a black snake; (Qu. K15, *A thin, bony, or poor-looking cow*) Infs **MO**37, **TX**78, Poor as a snake; (Qu. X52, *. . A person . . who had been sick was looking* _____) Inf **GA**12, Poor as a snake. **2005** *Knoxville News–Sentinel* (TN) 3 July sec D 18 (Internet), It had a big head, a long body and was poor as a snake. . . All the other guys did was make fun of my fish.

(2) Very impoverished; hence adj *snake-poor*. **chiefly Sth, S Midl** See Map

1797 (1907) Freneau *Poems* 3.162, Poor as a snake, and ever vile / Shall his condition be. **1942** McAtee *Dial. Grant Co. IN* 59 (as of 1890s), *Snake-poor . .* poverty-stricken. **1965–70** *DARE* (Qu. U41b, *Somebody who has lost everything and is very poor: "He's poor as* _____.*") 16 Infs, **chiefly Sth, S Midl,** Snake; **MD**36, Poorer than a snake. **2005** *Palm Beach Post* (W. Palm Beach FL) 17 Apr sec E 1 (Internet), No alien in his right mind would have tried to take us over in the 1930s. We were poor as snakes.

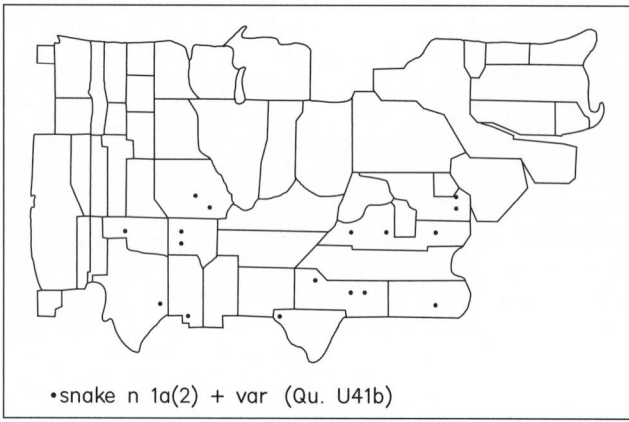

•snake n 1a(2) + var (Qu. U41b)

b *meaner than a snake* and varr: Very vicious or contemptible. **chiefly Sth, S Midl, esp sAppalachians** See Map

1880 *Decatur Daily Rev.* (IL) 17 Mar [4]/4 (newspaperarchive.com), It may be a satisfaction to see a thing meaner than a snake sent out of this country. **1895** *Living Age* 206.816 **NM**, "Now don't forget what I told you last night," said my partner. . . "Though Mexicans are meaner than snakes on the ranches, . . they take a different line on their own ground." **1940** Stuart *Trees of Heaven* 176 **eKY**, They was a triflin lot and mean as striped-tailed snakes. **1952** Brown *NC Folkl.* 1.477, As mean as a snake. As mean as a striped snake. **1953** Randolph–Wilson *Down in Holler* 174 **Ozarks**, A schoolmarm from Blue Eye, Missouri, told me that her pupils were all *meaner than snakes,* and I believe they were, at that. **1965–70** *DARE* (Qu. HH22b, *. . A very mean person . . "He's meaner than* _____.*") 47 Infs, **chiefly Sth, S Midl,** A snake; 13 Infs, **chiefly Sth, S Midl,** A rattlesnake; **SC**2, 40, Mean as a snake; **CA**66, A low-down snake; **VT**12, Snake shit; **KY**59, **NC**72, **TX**72, Snakes; **GA**72, 77, **IL**96, **NC**36, 37, **VA**15, A striped snake. **1986** Pederson *LAGS Concordance,* 1 inf, **nwTN**, Mean as a snake. **2000** *St. Louis Post–Dispatch* (MO) 11 Nov 14 (Internet) **IL,** He shares his modest cottage with . . a cat that Hand says is "meaner than a snake."

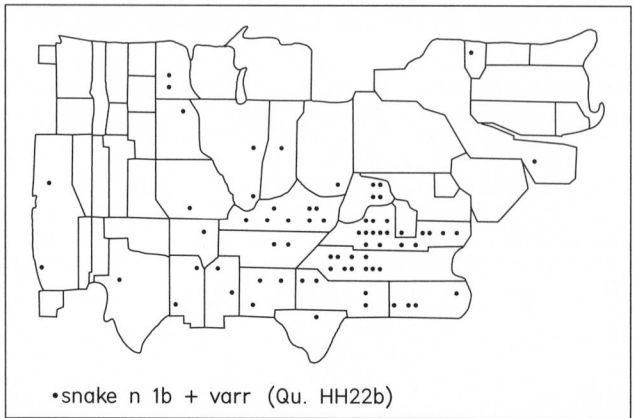

•snake n 1b + varr (Qu. HH22b)

2 pl; also in combs: Used as an exclamation, usu of surprise or indignation.

1839 *Spirit of Times* 17 Aug 283 **NY,** Snakes! such a row! **1847** *Scientific Amer.* 2.233, Snakes alive! Then you want to put down the old man, I s'pose—don't you? **1862** *Harper's New Mth. Mag.* 25.568 **KY,** Why, great snakes and alligators! Tom's a whole team on Muddy Creek and a hoss to let. And do you think he'd sneak off with a miserable hank o' cotting yarn? **1878** Hart *Sazerac Lying Club* 151 **NV,** "Great snakes!" exclaimed Robinson, "you're a nice pill to be talking about the corruptions of the Administration, ain't you?" **1894** Wister in *Harper's New Mth. Mag.* 89.509 **West,** Snakes! but it feels good. **1927** *DN* 5.277 [Exclams], *Snakes:* holy snakes, suffering snakes. **1932** Tooné *Yankee Slang* 33, *Snakes alive:* Why, snakes alive, ain't that too bad! **1965–70** *DARE* (Qu. NN29a, *Exclamations beginning with* '*great': "Great* _____!*") Infs **CA**3, 39, **FL**18, **MN**1, **PA**161, **WV**10, Snakes; [**CA**209, Snake [FW sugg];] (Qu. NN29c, *Exclamations beginning with* '*holy': "Holy* _____!*") Inf **NJ**2, Snakes. **2005** *Seattle Times* (WA) 22 Sept sec E 2 (Internet), Snakes alive! Some of the deadliest kinds known to man got loose when their transport van overturned in Germany.

3a pl; also with *the:* Delirium tremens. **scattered, but more freq Inland Nth, N Midl, West** See Map

[**1854** Lynn *Durham Village* 59 **NEng,** What if he should have delirium tremens? It 's a probable thing—hooting and hissing, and haunted with snakes.] [**1865** *Harper's New Mth. Mag.* 31.701 **swNV,** He is only taking a parting smile at the snakes.] **1892** *Courier-Jrl.* (Louisville KY) 3 Oct 3/4, A crazy man, with "snakes," jumped overboard. **1929** Ellis *Ordinary Woman* 34 **CO** (as of early 20th cent), No matter if he had just made a winning, or if hungry, down and out, or getting over a bad case of snakes. **1942** Berrey–Van den Bark *Amer. Slang* 130.9, *Delirium tremens. . .* Snakes. **1950** *WELS* (*Delirium tremens*) 37 Infs, **WI,** Snakes. **1965–70** *DARE* (Qu. DD22, *. . Delirium tremens*) 179 Infs, **chiefly Inland Nth, N Midl, West,** (The) snakes; **CA**97, He's got the snakes; **VA**27, That man had the snakes; **FL**22, Monkeys and snakes; **MI**65, Pink elephants and snakes; (Qu. DD24, *. . Diseases that come from continual drinking*) Infs **MI**2, **OH**80, Snakes; **FL**22, Monkeys and snakes.

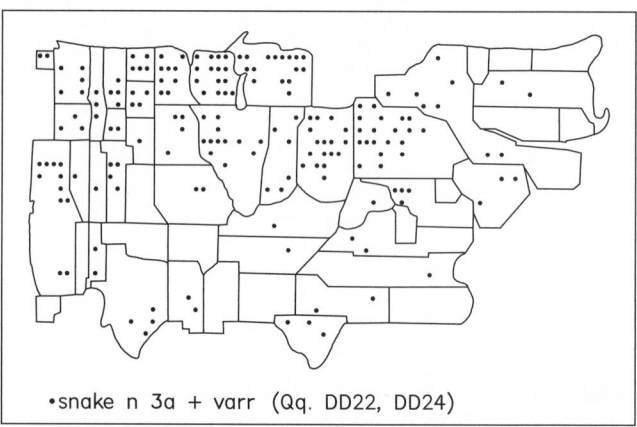

•snake n 3a + varr (Qq. DD22, DD24)

b in phrr *snakes in one's boots:* =**3a** above. **chiefly Missip-Ohio Valleys, KS, OK** See Map

1854 *Alton Weekly Courier* (IL) 19 Jan [3]/7 (newspaperarchive.com), A young man, very industrious, and steady as a general thing, had been to a ball, and came home with a large "brick in his hat," or rather one would have thought he had snakes in his boots. He took off his coat, hat and boots, threw out his money and watch, breaking the latter considerably. **1876** (1877) Habberton *Barton Exper.* 97 **KY,** He's been pretty high on whiskey for two or three days, . . and they say he's got snakes in his boots now. **1883** in 2006 *DARE* File—Internet **neOH,** James Callehan . . received into the infirmary disease Snakes in his Boots Age 25 Years. **1906** *DN* 3.157 **nwAR,** *Snakes in one's boots. . .* Delirium tremens. "I had to help hold that man when he had snakes in his boots." **1941** Stuart *Men of Mts.* 132 **eKY,** I've had snakes in my boots many a time. **1942** McAtee *Dial. Grant Co. IN* 32 (as of 1890s), *Have snakes in the boots . .* be deliriously drunk. **1965–70** *DARE* (Qu. DD22, *. . Delirium tremens*) 61 Infs, **chiefly Missip-Ohio Valleys, KS, OK,** Snakes in the (*or* his, your) boots. [Of all Infs responding to the question, 65% were old, 26% gs educ or less, 30% comm type 5; of those giving this

response, 82% were old, 49% gs educ or less, 56% comm type 5.]
1988 *DARE* File **wOH** (as of c1950), *To die with snakes in one's boots*—To die of alcoholism. Inf claims to have heard the same expression in Indiana. **2004** *Albuquerque Jrl.* (NM) 17 Sept sec B 8 (Internet), The centerpiece of the exhibition . . are the adjacent paintings . . "Dying With Snakes in Your Boots" and "Bottles & Boots & Snakes."

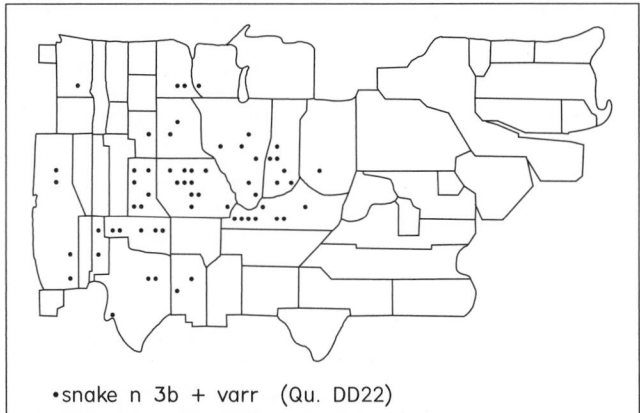

•snake n 3b + varr (Qu. DD22)

c in phrr *see* (or *have*) *snakes:* To suffer from delirium tremens; hence vbl n *seeing snakes.*
[**1854** *Alton Weekly Courier* (IL) [22 June 2]/4 (newspaper-archive.com), He drank too much, and was taken very sick. . . It was a horrible time to see the little fellow screaming at and jumping from the snakes that he thought he saw.] **1865** Sedley *Marian Rooke* 225 **eMO, wIL,** There's them down our way that case-hardened they don't see snakes under a week! **1897** *Chicago Tribune* (IL) 22 Jan 1 (Internet), *Boys Sees Snakes On an "L" Train.* Fifteen-Year-Old William Harris Tries to Jump Off While Suffering from Delirium Tremens. **1942** Berrey–Van den Bark *Amer. Slang* 130.27, *Have delirium tremens.* . . *Have or* see snakes. **1965–70** *DARE* (Qu. DD22, . . *Delirium tremens*) 17 Infs, **scattered,** (Spell of) seeing snakes; **AL**4, **CA**15, **MN**16, **MS**30, **MO**21, **OH**23, Sees (*or* to see, saw) snakes. **1967** *DARE* FW Addit **LA**11, He's seeing snakes now. **1982** Barrick *Coll.* **csPA,** Snakes—delirium tremens (i.e., to see snakes). **2005** in 2006 *DARE* File—Internet **AZ,** It was a great run and I'm proud to have been a part of it. . . I'll probably see snakes as I detox from the routine [of playing house concerts].

4 In railroading: see quots. [From the letter *S;* see quot 1945]
1929 *Soda Springs Chieftain* (ID) 14 Nov [2]/5 (newspaper-archive.com), A "snake" is a yard switchman and a "stinger" is a brakeman. **1945** Hubbard *Railroad Ave.* 361, *Snake*—Switchman, so named from the large serpentine letter S on membership pins of the Switchman's Union of North America. Sometimes called *reptile* or *serpent.* **1967** *DARE* Tape **ID**6, [FW:] You said that the switchmen were called snakes and you mentioned you didn't know why. Was that not a good job to have? [Inf:] Oh, the switchmen thought it was a good job. They were a rather drunken, rough crew, but they could certainly switch boxcars, drunk or sober. But I don't know where the term originated. **1975** McDonough *Garden Sass* 261 **AR,** These were names that the railroad men had for each other: . . a switchman was a "snake."

5 =**snake-killer 3.**
1937 [see **snake-killer 3**].

6 in phr *snake in the bag:* Something one buys or trades sight unseen. Cf **cat in a bag, pig in a bag**
1970 *DARE* (Qu. U13, *When buying or exchanging something that you have not seen . . you're getting it* _____) Inf **VA**35, Snake in the bag; (Qu. U14, . . *Exchanging with somebody when neither one has seen what the other has*) Inf **VA**35, Snake in the bag.

7 also *snake pickerel:* A thin **northern pike 1.** [See quots] **esp WI**
1913 *Daily Northwestern* (Oshkosh WI) 15 May 7/1, A great deal of spawn of "snake pickerel" is brought into this lake [=Winnebago] by the bog, and he does not regard this brand of fish as very desirable. **1927** Weed *Pike* 27 **nMI, WI,** Pickerel, Pike, Jack, etc. . . Young specimens are very slender and are frequently called "Snakes" in Wisconsin and northern Michigan. **1936** *WI Rapids Daily Tribune* (WI) 18 Aug 5/1,

Limits for three of us, including several 16-inchers, with two fair-sized wall-eyes and a snake (pickerel) for good measure, were easy. **1950** *WELS Suppl.* **csWI,** *Snake pickerel.* . . A northern pike that is rather thin. "There's mostly snake pickerel in Mendota now." **1956** Harlan–Speaker *IA Fish* 64, Northern Pike. . . Other Names—Common pike, . . snake [etc]. **1958** *Mansfield News–Jrl.* (OH) 18 May 25/1, Not long ago any angler who hooked into a pike was considered unfortunate. This fish was called a snake or a snake pickerel and it was said that he never fought until after he had been boated. **1983** Becker *Fishes WI* 398, Northern Pike. . . Other common names . . snake, snake pickerel.

8 also *snake pickerel:* =**chain pickerel.**
1935 Caine *Game Fish* 22, Pickerel—*Esox reticulatus.* . . *Synonyms.* . . *Snake.* **1975** Evanoff *Catch More Fish* 86, The chain pickerel (*Esox niger*) . . [is] also called the banded pickerel, . . jack, jackfish, and snake. **2003** *Morning Call* (Allentown PA) 19 Jan sec F 5 (Internet), Shiners in the 2–4 inch range are tops for these slender "snakes," another nickname for the toothy, chain-sided fish. **2006** *DARE* File—Internet **ePA,** Promised Land State Park is off Route 390. . . The park's upper lake has lots of "snake" pickerel.

snake v
1 To drag (esp a log) along the ground; to drag or tow with a rope or chain; hence vbl n *snaking;* n *snaker* one who drags logs.
1829 Flint *George Mason* 21, Logs . . could be drawn, or, as it is technically phrased, *snaked* into church and placed parallel to the mud-daubed wall, and a fire kindled along the whole length. **1859** in 1942 Hafen *Overland Routes* 11.111 **VA,** By doubling teams we snaked both wagons through. **1870** *Punchinello* 1.302, We had to Fork over twenty dollars to the Captain of a tug boat which came and Snaked us off with a Coil of Rope when the tide rose. **1878** *Lumberman's Gaz.* 26 Jan 66/3 **MI,** Where the haul is very short, and so close to the streams that the logs are "snaked" in without being skidded. **1903** (1965) Adams *Log Cowboy* 219 **West,** Our four mules were pressed into service as an extra team in snaking logs. **1903** *DN* 2.301 **Cape Cod MA** (as of a1857), *Snake.* . . To drag. **1905** U.S. Forest Serv. *Bulletin* 61.39, The path followed in skidding logs. . . snaking trail. **1915** Hall *Claib Jones* 10 **KY,** We would . . tie the bear to a single-tree by their heads and snake them in home. **1921** *DN* 5.111 **CA,** *Snaking-team.* . . The six or eight horses used to haul logs out from the woods. Lumbermen. **1931** *AmSp* 7.119 **eID,** There is a growth of stunted and twisted red cedars, highly valued in this desert land, for posts and fuel. It is *snaked* or *skinned* into camp or settlement. **1958** McCulloch *Woods Words* 172 **Pacific NW,** *Snaking machine*—A donkey used in ground lead yarding. **1965–70** *DARE* (Qu. OO46a, *Talking about dragging something heavy: "We hitched the log on and* _____ *it out [of the woods]."*) 95 Infs, **widespread,** Snake(d); **MA**47, **MO**4, **VA**95, 70, Snaking (logs); (Qu. OO46b, *Talking about dragging something heavy: "Half a mile or so we must have* _____ *[it]!"*) 19 Infs, **scattered,** Snaked; (Qu. L54, *If someone was transporting firewood [or dirt] in a wagon . . he was* _____ *firewood*) Inf **AK**8, Snaking. **1966** *DARE* Tape **GA**1, It [=timber] was hauled in by mules and oxens. It was drug in, snaked in, we called it; **MA**5C, We could pick 'em right up from where they was chopped and put 'em on our drag sleds without snaking only just one log out of the four hundred thousand; **SC**9, I mean snaking log. I'm a snaker, a snaker. I was a snaker. **2004** in 2006 *DARE* File—Internet **WI,** My question is has anyone used a Rule chainsaw winch? . . I . . thought it would be handy for loading logs to a trailer and snaking logs out of tight spots etc.

2 To extract forcefully or abruptly, snatch, haul; also fig.
1833 in 1834 Davis *Letters Downing* 14, We snaked him out of that scrape as slick as a whistle. *Ibid* 273, In come Kindle and Blair, lookin as though they had jest ben snaked through a gimblet hole. **1848** Lowell *Biglow* 146 **'Upcountry' MA,** *To snake a thing out* is to snatch it out. **1867** Twain *Jumping Frog* 15, He'd spring straight up and snake a fly off'n the counter. **1885** Twain *Huck. Finn* 164 **MO,** You ain't the only person that's ben snaked down wrongfully out'n a high place. *Ibid* 254, The lawyer . . says: "Well, it beats *me*"—and snaked a lot of old letters out of his pocket, and examined them. **1905** Lincoln *Partners* 200 **MA,** If you've got a loose tooth a string and a door'll snake it out as quick as the dentist will.

3 To remove or obtain by stealth or deceit; to filch, steal. [*EDD snake* v. "To sneak. . . To snatch surreptitiously"; appar ult unrelated to sense **1** above]
1867 Lowell *Biglow* 90 **'Upcountry' MA,** The cusses an' the promerses make, one gret chain, an' ef / You snake one link out here, one

there, how much on 't ud be lef'? **1885** Twain *Huck. Finn* 322 **MO,** We snaked her [=a brass warming pan] out, private, and took her down there. **1892** *KS Univ. Qrly.* 1.99 **KS,** *Snake:* to snatch stealthily. **1897** *Ibid* (ser B) 6.92, *Snake:* to remove anything stealthily.—General. **1906** *DN* 3.157 **nwAR,** *Snake.* . . To appropriate, to filch. "I just snaked it." **1913** *DN* 4.5 **ME,** *Snake.* . . To take slyly or stealthily. **1921** in 1959 Dreiser *Letters* 1.333 **IN,** Start the ball and if I snake the forty thousand . . you get five thousand. **1975** *AmSp* 50.66 **AR** (as of c1970), *Snake.* . . Steal (one's date)—"Carol tried to snake my date last night." **2000** in 2006 *DARE* File—Internet **NC,** I still think my "best friend" snaked it from me . . he seemed to like it *a lot* just before it vanished.

4 To search for snakes in (a place); to rid (a place) of snakes.

1941 Stuart *Men of Mts.* 50 **eKY,** "Looks like it ought to be snaked." . . "What do you mean by snaking corn?" . . "W'y, Pap used to tell us . . that when weeds got knee high in a corn patch, we ought to go through with a stick and shake the weeds and run the vipers, copperheads, rattlesnakes, and blacksnakes out." **1953** *PADS* 19.14 **sAppalachians,** *Snake the bed.* . . To search the bed before retiring to see if any snakes have crawled under the covers. Snakes often enter cabins that are not screened or have a hole in the floor, and sometimes crawl into beds for warmth. **1984** Wilder *You All Spoken Here* 28 **Sth,** *Snake the kivvers:* Before retiring, give the bedclothes a smart flirt to dislodge snakes that might've sneaked in.

snake-back road n

See quots.

1967 *DARE* (Qu. N27a, *Names . . for different kinds of unpaved roads*) Inf **MI**49, Snake-back road—years ago, one track, wound in and out. **2006** Curran et al. *Murrieta* 127 **CA,** The snake-back road, once the route from Murrieta to the Parker Dear picnics at Rancho Santa Rosa . . was closed to traffic . . in 1978.

snake bean n

1 =**bagpod.**

1926 *Torreya* 26.5 **GA,** *Glottidium vesicarium.* . . Snake bean, Sapelo I[slan]d.

2 A kind of cultivated bean (*Phaseolus vulgaris* cv); see quots.

1869 *Daily Gaz.* (Davenport IA) 19 Aug [4]/2 (newspaper-archive.com), Yesterday, Mr. Tank . . brought two pods of the Snake Bean to the *Gazette* office. Each pod was eighteen inches in length. . . As for culinary purposes, the Snake Bean said is [sic] to be superior to any other. Mr. T. expects to have some seed for sale next spring. **1915** *Fitchburg Daily Sentinel* (MA) 7 Sept 16/4, Alex Ruflange—First for tomatoes, . . first for snake beans. **1932** *Ibid* 3 Aug 9/1, [Advt:] Kentucky Wonder Snake Beans, 3 lbs. 25¢. **1966** *DARE* (Qu. I20, . . *Kinds of beans*) Inf **NH**12, Snake bean—a shell bean—long, green.

snake-belly v

To creep or crawl.

1933 Williamson *Woods Colt* 111 **Ozarks,** Clint is snake-bellyin' back'ards, keepin' out of sight. **1944** *Natl. Geogr. Mag.* July 8, Then they "snake-bellied," or crawled on hands and knees, through the jungle.

snakeberry n

1 also *snake plum:* =**partridgeberry 1.**

1892 *Jrl. Amer. Folkl.* 5.98 **NY,** *Mitchella repens.* . . snake-berry. **1898** *Ibid* 11.228 **ME,** *Mitchella repens* . . snake plum, Turner, Me. **1911** Henkel *Amer. Med. Leaves* 34, Squaw Vine. . . *Other common names* . . oneberry, pigeonberry, snakeberry [etc]. **1967** *DARE* (Qu. I44, *What kinds of berries grow wild around here?*) Inf **NY**28, Snakeberries. [*DARE* Ed: This Inf may refer instead to other senses below.]

2 =**red baneberry.**

1900 Lyons *Plant Names* 14, [*Actaea*] *rubra.* . . Red Cohosh, Snakeroot, Snakeberry [etc]. **1933** Small *Manual SE Flora* 513, [*Actaea*] *rubra.* . . Coralberry. Poisonberry. Snakeberry. **1955** U.S. Arctic Info. Center *Gloss.* 74, *Snakeberry.* . . The baneberry. **1979** Erichsen-Brown *Med. N. Amer. Plants* 348, Red Baneberry. . . Common names: Red cohosh, . . snake berry.

3 A **bittersweet** (here: *Solanum dulcamara*).

1900 Lyons *Plant Names* 349, [*Solanum*] *Dulcamara.* . . Bittersweet, . . Snake-berry [etc].

4 =**Indian strawberry 1. SE**

1933 Small *Manual SE Flora* 612, [*Duchesnea*] *indica.* . . Yellow-strawberry. Indian-strawberry. Snake-berry. **1944** AL Geol. Surv. *Bulle-*

tin 53.116, [*Duchesnea*] *Indica.* . . Sometimes called "snake berry." . . The fruit looks much like a strawberry, but is tasteless, and we do not know what animal eats it to scatter the seeds. **1986** Pederson *LAGS Concordance,* 1 inf, **cnGA,** Snakeberries—look like strawberries; 1 inf, **cwGA,** Snakeberries—not edible; 1 inf, **ceAL,** Snakeberries—small, like strawberries, not edible; 1 inf, **cAL,** Snakeberries—wild strawberries—tasteless. **2000** *News & Rec.* (Greensboro NC) 19 July 7 (Internet), Among these are day lilies, . . seedling grape vines and a wild strawberry, often called snake berry.

5 An **inkberry 1** (here: *Ilex glabra*).

1974 Morton *Folk Remedies* 77 **SC,** Gallberry; Bitter Gallberry; "Snakeberry". . . *Ilex glabra.*

snakebird n

1 =**anhinga.** [From its long, flexible neck]

1791 Bartram *Travels* 132 **FL,** Here is in this river and in the waters all over Florida, a very curious and handsome bird, the people call them Snake Birds. [*Ibid* 133, When we approach them, they drop off the limbs into the water as if dead, and for a minute or two are not to be seen; when on a sudden at a vast distance, their long slender head and neck only appear, and have very much the appearance of a snake.] **1814** Wilson *Amer. Ornith.* 9.80, The Snake-bird is an inhabitant of the Carolinas, Georgia, and the Floridas. . . It seems to have derived its name from the singular form of its head and neck. **1853** *Harper's New Mth. Mag.* 7.769 **sLA,** Here you may see . . the snake-bird, the pelican, and the ibis. **1885** Thompson *By-Ways* 31 **Sth,** The snake-bird, too, that veritable water-dragon of the South, was there, wriggling and squirming in the amber-brown pools amongst the lily-pads and lettuce. **1955** [see **2** below]. **1968** *DARE* (Qu. Q10, . . *Water birds and marsh birds*) Inf **GA**18, Snakebird—same as anhinga. **2005** *Facts* (Clute TX) 29 Sept (Internet), A similar bird [to the double-crested cormorant] is the anhinga that is seen more often in south and east Texas. The bird is usually called a "snake bird" because of its long neck.

2 also *little snakebird:* Either of two **crested flycatchers:** *Myiarchus crinitus* or *M. cinerascens.* [See quots] Cf **snake-skin bird**

1913 Bailey *Birds VA* 180, The local name of "Snake Bird" was probably given them on account of seeing birds, when building their nests, carrying snake skins in their beaks. **1955** *AmSp* 30.183 **TX, NY, PA, VA, LA, FL,** The habit of working shed snakeskins into their nests has suggested folk names for two of our flycatchers. The ash-throated is called *snakebird* in Texas and the great-crested by the same designation in New York, Pennsylvania, Virginia, and Louisiana. Additionally, the latter is . . *little snakebird* (Fla.), the *big snakebird* there probably being the anhinga.

3 =**lark sparrow** or **vesper sparrow.**

1955 *AmSp* 30.183 **KS, TX, UT, PA,** Sparrows whose racing through the grass 'like a streak,' has earned for them the name *snakebird* are the lark sparrow (Kans., Texas, Utah) and the vesper sparrow (Pa.)

4 =**swallow-tailed kite.** Cf **snake hawk 1**

1955 *AmSp* 30.183 **FL,** The most frequent reason for folk-conferring of a *snake* name is that the bird eats snakes. So, we have plain *snake-bird* for the swallow-tailed kite in Florida and for the road runner in California.

5 =**double-crested cormorant.**

1955 *AmSp* 30.183 **WI, UT,** Birds with that part of their anatomy [= the neck] long and sinuous enough to suggest the name *snakebird* include the double-crested cormorant. **1992** *Orlando Sentinel* (FL) 20 Feb 1 (Internet), [Caption:] A cormorant, commonly known as a snake bird, stretches its wings as it dries its feathers.

6 =**roadrunner 1.** Cf **snake-eater 3, snake-killer 1**

1955 [see **4** above].

snake-bit adj

1 See **-bit.**

2 also *snake-bitten;* Fig: unlucky, doomed. **chiefly Sth**

1871 (1872) Whittlesey *Bertha* 157 **VA,** What a world of inconsistencies there is on the outside of this beautiful but snake-bitten earth! **1942** Faulkner *Go Down* 152 **MS,** "Make room, gamblers," he said. "Make room. Ah'm snakebit and de pizen cant hawm me." **1957** *Daily Progress* (Charlottesville, Va.) 18 Nov. 14/1 (*OED2*), Commenting on the game last Saturday afternoon Martin said: 'We're just snake-bit that's all there is to it.' Snake-bit is a term used by coaches when referring to a team which never seems to have a break in its favor. **1967–69** *DARE*

(Qu. CC12b, . . *If a person has a lot of bad luck . . "He's been* ———*."*) Infs **GA**82, **PA**185, 209, **TX**37, 73, Snake-bit; **LA**46, Snake-bit—the most common expression for bad luck. **1968** *State* (Columbia SC) 23 May sec D 5, And it [*sic*] that isn't enough to make one believe Lee Roy is snakebitten, his Columbia home was hit by lightening [*sic*]. **1976** Garber *Mountain-ese* 84 **sAppalachians,** *Snake-bit . .* jinxed, unlucky—Mark cain't seem to win atall . . he must be snake-bit. **1986** Pederson *LAGS Concordance,* 9 infs, **AL, TX,** Snake-bit—bad luck. **2006** *WI State Jrl.* (Madison) 9 Mar sec F 1 (Internet), Monroe was trying to shed its skin as the snake-bit program that couldn't carry regular-season perfection into the postseason.

snakebite n Cf rattlesnake root

1 also *snakebite plant:* =**nodding trillium.**

1876 Hobbs *Bot. Hdbk.* 107, Snake bite, Beth root, Trillium pendulum. **1949** Moldenke *Amer. Wild Flowers* 339, The nodding wakerobin, *T. cernuum. . .* also called groundlily, coughroot, white-benjamin, and snakebite. **1959** Carleton *Index Herb. Plants* 108, *Snake-bite plant:* Trillium cernuum.

2 =**bloodroot 1.**

1892 *Jrl. Amer. Folkl.* 5.92 **NH,** *Sanguinaria Canadensis,* snake-bite. **1903** *Outlook* 7 Nov 580 **SC,** He pointed out a white flower he called snake-bite which he said he would rub on if one of the creatures bit him, and that would take out the poison. **1930** Sievers *Amer. Med. Plants* 14, Bloodroot. . . Other common names.—Redroot . . snakebite [etc]. **1979** Erichsen-Brown *Med. N. Amer. Plants* 318, Bloodroot. . . Common names. Puccoon root, . . snake-bite.

3 See **snake poison.**

4 =**Indian burn.**

1988 *DARE* File, [He] grabbed my wrist with two hands and began rubbing it by turning his hands in opposite directions. . . Two others yelled "Indian burn! Indian burn!" Someone else said, "That's not an Indian burn, that's a snake bite." **2007** *DARE* File—Internet, [Friends say] an Indian burn is like pinching and a snake bite is twisting the arm. **2008** *Ibid,* When I was a teenager (way back in the 70s) I knew a little boy who liked to do "snake bites" on peoples' arms. **2010** *Ibid, How to give a snakebite as in a Indian burn. . .* You simply use both hands to wring the arm like a wet towel.

snakebite medicine See snakebite remedy

snakebite plant See snakebite 1

snakebite remedy n Also *snake(bite) medicine, snake remedy* Cf anti-snakebite, snake oil, ~ piss, ~ poison

Liquor, whiskey; rarely, wine.

1865 *Harper's New Mth. Mag.* 31.276 **NV,** A fine spring of water, aided by a little snake-medicine, set us all right. **1909** *DN* 3.372 **eAL, wGA,** *Snake-medicine. . .* Whisky. **1950** *WELS* (Names and nicknames *for liquor in general)* 1 Inf, **csWI,** Snakebite remedy. **1950** *WELS Suppl.* nwWI, Snakebite remedy—liquor or wine. **1954** *Julian Apple Day* [4] **csCA,** A group of city slickers from San Diego arrived . . the night before election day with . . money enough to freely purchase the local snake-remedy. **1958** Blasingame *Dakota Cowboy* 246 **SD,** By the time we reached camp, rollicky Jim Kennedy had swallowed a lot of "snake medicine." **1965–70** *DARE* (Qu. DD21a, *General words . . for any kind of liquor)* 10 Infs, **scattered,** Snakebite remedy; **VA**12, Snakebite medicine; **GA**72, Snake medicine; (Qu. DD21c, *Nicknames for whiskey, especially illegally made whiskey)* Infs **CA**158, **GA**72, Snake medicine; **VA**75, Snakebite medicine; (Qu. DD27, . . *Nicknames . . for wine)* Inf **NM**3, Snakebite medicine [Inf queries]. **1976** Garber *Mountain-ese* 84 **sAppalachians,** *Snake-bite-medicine* whiskey—I allers take along a bottle uv snake-bite medicine, jist in case. **1977** *New Yorker* 2 May 65 **AK,** "Arctic snakebite medicine." There are no snakes in Alaska. But what if a snake should unexpectedly appear? The serum in my pack is from Lynchburg, Tennessee. **2006** *DARE* File—Internet **WV,** We passed the snake bite medicine and after everyone was properly medicated we turned into bed.

snake-bitten See snake-bit 2

snake bug See snake fly

snake bush n Cf ground hemlock

A **yew 1** (here: *Taxus canadensis*).

1913 *Harper's Mth. Mag.* 126.61 **MA,** In the center are the remnants

of a ground-hemlock (or "snake bush," as we call it in Massachusetts)—the *Taxus Canadensis.*

snake charmer n

1 also *snake caller:* =**catbird 1.** [See quot 1863]

1863 Hopley *Life South* 1.93 **VA,** Another sweet songster is the catbird, or "snake-charmer," thus named from its cry of alarm, as the popular belief is, when a snake is near. **1970** *DARE* FW Addit **MD,** Catbird—snake caller, snake charmer.

2 =**dragonfly.** Cf **snake doctor 2**

1950 *WELS Suppl.,* 1 Inf, **WI,** Snake charmer—dragonfly. **1966–68** *DARE* (Qu. R2, . . *The dragonfly)* Infs **MT**5, **PA**143, Snake charmer. **1973** Allen *LAUM* 1.319 (as of c1950), *Dragonfly. . .* snake charmer [1 inf, **NE**].

snake cotton n [From the cottony flowers and wandlike stems] chiefly TX

A plant of the genus *Froelichia.* Also called **bird's nest weed, cottonweed 5**

1946 Reeves–Bain *Flora TX* 110, [*Froelichia] drummondii. . .* (Snake Cotton.) **1961** Wills–Irwin *Flowers TX* 104, Snake-cotton or Cotton-weed, a plant of the eastern half of Texas . . often grows in dense masses along highway shoulders and in abandoned cultivations. **1967** *DARE* Wildfl QR (Wills–Irwin) Pl.7B [=*Froelichiana floridana*] Inf **TX**44, Snake cotton. **1970** Correll *Plants TX* 568, *Froelichia* [spp]. . . Snake-cotton. Cotton-weed.

snake doctor n

1 A **hellgrammite 1** or similar creature.

1863 *S. Lit. Messenger* 37.598 **VA,** The water under the bridge is . . full of all manner of nasty and confounded "mud-kittens," "snap'n-turkles" and snake-doctors. **1889** in 1901 Howard *Insect Book* 212 **RI,** Professor W.W. Bailey, of Brown University, collected the names in use in Rhode Island alone for [the dobsonfly]. . . They are: Dobsons, . . flip-flaps, alligators, Ho Jack, snake-doctor, dragon and hell-diver. **1958** *Lima News* (OH) 24 Aug sec A 6/5, All is not lost—the horse flies, sweat bees, leeches, mosquitoes, "snake doctors," and crabs still wait to greet the swimmers.

2 =**dragonfly.** [See quots 1893, 1926, 2001] **chiefly Midl, Sth** See Map on p. 64 and Map Section Cf **doctor n 5, horse doctor, mosquito ~, snake charmer 2, ~-eater 4, ~ feeder 1, ~ fly, ~ guarder, ~ heeder, ~ servant, ~ waiter**

1860 *Gardener's Mth. & Horticult. Advt.* 2.327 **ePA,** In the order Neuroptera, we have the various species of "dragon-flies," variously denominated "snake doctors," "devil's needle," &c. **1877** Bartlett *Americanisms* 617, *Snake-Doctors.* Dragon flies. South-western. **1893** Shands *MS Speech* 58, *Snake-doctor.* The ordinary Mississippi name for the dragon-fly. . . The two bumps sometimes seen on the snake-doctor, just behind his wings, are called his saddlebags, and in them he is reputed to carry medicine for the snakes. **1899** (1912) Green *VA Folk-Speech* 398, *Snake-doctor. . .* Mosquito hawk; dragon-fly. **1909** *DN* 3.372 **eAL, wGA,** *Snake-doctor. . .* The dragonfly. **1926** *TX Folkl. Soc. Pub.* 5.58 **AR, LA, TX,** Any thorough-going old-time swamp negro knows that he [=a snake] has not been disposed of. A moment after you leave . . , a beautiful insect—the "snake doctor"—alights on the head of the still squirming serpent. It gently and soothingly raises and lowers its transparent wings, accompanying this action by a peculiar movement of the head. In the course of a few minutes, the stump-tail shows signs of life, the wounds made by your bludgeon quickly heal, and soon he squirms to the edge of the water and disappears. **1929** *KY Folkl. & Poetry Mag.* 4.1.11, I have found very few school or college boys who know what is a dragon fly. But, the Kentucky boy always responds to "snake doctor." And it is supposed to render professional services to the snakes in its vicinity. **1946** *PADS* 5.38 **VA,** *Snake doctor. . .* A dragonfly; common everywhere except on Chesapeake Bay and west of the New River. **1949** Kurath *Word Geog.* 30, In large parts of West Virginia the Virginia Piedmont term *snake doctor* is now more common than *snake feeder. . .* The common occurrence of *snake doctor* on either side of Delaware Bay as well as on the lower Susquehanna makes it probable that both *snake feeder* and *snake doctor* have been current in the Philadelphia area since Colonial times. *Ibid* fig 141 **Mid and S Atl,** 615 of 1162 infs, Snake doctor. **1956** Ker *Vocab. W. TX* 231, Snake doctor [36 of 67 infs]. . . [snake duster [1 inf]]. **1958** *PADS* 29.9 **TN,** Snake doctor was general 25 years ago [but] dragon fly seems universal now. **c1960** *Wilson Coll.* **csKY,** Dragon fly. . . A literary name for a snake doctor. **1965–70** *DARE* (Qu. R2, . . *The dragonfly)* 194 Infs, chiefly **Midl, Sth,** Snake doctor; **DC**2, Snake doctor—the darkies always said during my childhood; [**IN**35, Schlangedoktor—my father's expression]. **1967** Faries *Word Geog. MO* 112, The most frequently used [regional expression] is the Southern *snake doctor.* **1970** Tarpley *Blinky* 173 **neTX,** For the majority of Northeast Texans, this insect [= the dragonfly] is a *snake doctor.* **1985** *AmSp* 60.235 **sePA,** Of the eighteen occurrences of *snake doctor* [among sixty informants], thirteen are to be ascribed to speakers over age fifty. Only two persons under forty indicated that they regularly employ this expression. **1986** Pederson *LAGS Concordance* **Gulf Region,** 352 infs, Snake doctor; 1 inf, Snake doctor—it doctors snakes; 1 inf, Snake doctor—near water; supposed to cure snakes; 1 inf, Snake doctors—"doctored" injured snakes; 1 inf, Snake doctors—can cure snakebite; old term. **2001** *DARE* File **AL,** I asked him why they [=dragonflies] were called "snake doctors" and he replied that they picked off the gnats that would gather in a small cloud around a sunning snake.

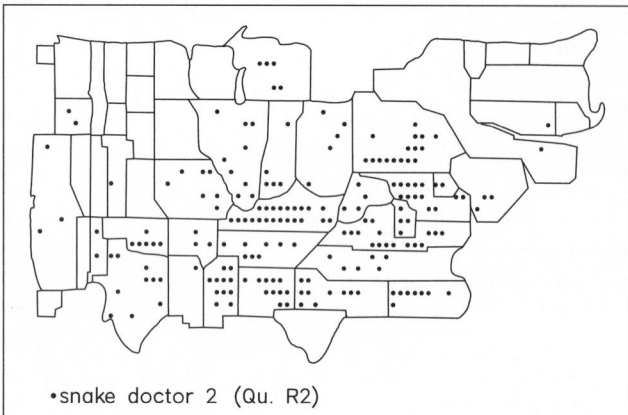

•snake doctor 2 (Qu. R2)

3 =praying mantis B.

1968 *AmSp* 43.56 **KS,** The various names commonly cited for the dragonfly are also used by some people to refer to the praying mantis. In fact . . one informant used only *snake doctor* for both insects. *Ibid* 52, Other answers include . . *snake doctor* (praying mantis), 5 [of 1,518 infs]. **1986** Pederson *LAGS Concordance,* 1 inf, **neAR,** Snake doctor = praying mantis; not dragonfly.

4 Either copperhead snake 1 or kingsnake 1.

1973 *AmSp* 48.74 **Ozarks,** There is a species of snake in the Ozarks called the *snake doctor,* which, like the darning needle, also cares for injured snakes. This snake is more generally called a *snake pilot,* but, like the dragonfly, the snake pilot is always nearby, ready to warn the rattlesnake of the approach of danger.

snake-eater n

1 =bittern.

1916 *Times–Picayune* (New Orleans LA) 2 Apr 5/2, American Bittern. . . Garde-Soleil; Sun-Gazer; Biorque; Snake Eater.

2 =northern pike 1. Cf snake n 7

1927 Weed *Pike* 44 **neMI,** [In a list of names for *Esox lucius:*] Snake Eater; Cheboygan, Michigan. **2005** *Traverse City Rec.–Eagle* (MI) 21 Aug (Internet), In the waters of the Great Lakes State one might hook a . . "snake eater" (northern pike).

3 =roadrunner 1.

1955 *AmSp* 30.183 **TX,** Besides *snakebird,* . . the road runner has won three other names denoting its prowess in snake-despatching: *snake-eater* (Texas), *snake-killer* (Kans., Texas, N. Mex., Calif.), and *rattlesnake-killer* (Texas). **2002** *AR Democrat–Gaz.* (Little Rock) 31 Jan sec G 1 (Internet), One of the more fantastic legends is associated with one of the roadrunner's other common names, "snake killer," or in some cases "snake eater."

4 =dragonfly. [Perh var of **snake heeder**]

1966 Dakin *Dial. Vocab. Ohio R. Valley* 2.402, *Dragon fly.* . . snake eater [3 infs, **OH,** 1 inf, **KY**]. **1969** *DARE* (Qu. R2, . . *The dragonfly*) Inf **KY**35, Snake-eater. **1973** Allen *LAUM* 1.319 **Upper MW** (as of c1950), *Snake eater:* Two boys, not infs., added that this term is common here among young boys. **1978** *AmSp* 53.204 **KS,** The two instances of *snake eater,* occurring as they do in German settlement areas, may be variations of the Pennsylvania-Germanism *snake heeder.*

snake-eye See **snake's eye**

snake feeder n Cf **fish feeder**

1 =dragonfly. [See quot 1986] **chiefly Midl, Plains States** See Map and Map Section

1821 *Sat. Eve. Post* 18 Aug 2 **PA,** On the 7th of June last, about 5 o'clock in the afternoon, there passed over Willistown and Goshen, a swarm of the animal denominated the 'Devil's darning Needle,' or the 'Snake feeder,' or the 'Snake servant.' **1861** *IL State Ag. Soc. Trans. for 1859–60* 4.341, A particular species of *dragon-fly,* or *snake-feeder,* as it is absurdly called in this country. **1889** *N. Amer. Rev.* 149.367 **OH,** Again, I well remember, when a small boy upon the hill of eastern Ohio, gazing with open-eyed wonder upon the beautiful forms of these insects . . , and heard my older companions speak of them as "snake-feeders." "Look out! There's a snake somewhere near! Here's a snake-feeder!" **1897** *Harper's New Mth. Mag.* 94.934 **VA,** "There's a snake-feeder, Lizzy, just back of your ear!" Lizzy screamed and beat wildly at the darting insect. **1929** Bell *Some Contrib. KS Vocab.* 190, Snake-feeder. . . The common name in Kansas for the dragon-fly called the *devil's darning needle.* **1948** Davis *Word Atlas Gt. Lakes* 80, *Snake feeder* [common in central and southern IL, IN, OH]. **1949** Kurath *Word Geog.* 30, The distinctive Midland term for the dragon fly is *snake feeder* . . , which is found in the Delaware Valley above Trenton and westward. It is in regular use in central and western Pennsylvania and in the Ohio Valley, as well as in the Blue Ridge province of North Carolina and the westernmost part of Virginia. *Ibid* fig 141 **esp PA, WV, nMD, wNJ, wVA, wNC,** 448 of 1162 infs, Snake feeder. **1950** WELS (*Dragonfly*) 1 Inf, **csWI,** Snake feeder. **1955** Potter *Dial. NW OH* 87, *Dragon fly.* . . Of the seventy responses on this item, there were twenty-nine for *snake feeder* and twenty for *dragon fly.* **1965–70** *DARE* (Qu. R2, . . *The dragonfly*) 97 Infs, **chiefly Midl, Plains States,** Snake feeder; **CA**40, Snake feeder [FW: Inf admits that she probably brought term from Kansas.]; **MD**32, Snake feeder [FW: Inf didn't recognize *dragonfly.*]; **MO**1, Snake feeder—I didn't know we even had a dragon-fly; [(Qu. R4, *A large winged insect that hatches in summer in great numbers around lakes or rivers, crowds around lights, lives only a day or so, and is good fish bait*) Inf **MO**37, Snake feeders]. **1966** Dakin *Dial. Vocab. Ohio R. Valley* 2.403 **OH, IN, IL,** The usual Midland expression in the East, *snake feeder,* is regular throughout Ohio and Indiana (except in the extreme southwest . .), and in Illinois north of a line from Edwards to Fayette Counties. **1967** Faries *Word Geog. MO* 112, The usual Midland expression, *snake feeder* (174 occurrences) . . appears to be, in Missouri, concentrated in two distinctly separate areas—the western part of the Ozark Highland and along the Iowa border. **1973** Allen *LAUM* 1.318 **Upper MW** (as of c1950), Most Midland equivalents [of *dragonfly*] include *snake* as the first component. Most common is *snakefeeder,* the Iowa and Nebraska incidence of which correlates closely with its eastern popularity in central and western Pennsylvania and the upper Ohio valley. **1986** Pederson *LAGS Concordance* 59 infs, **chiefly eTN,** Snake feeder(s); 1 inf, **eTN,** Snake feeder—they feed the snakes, they say.

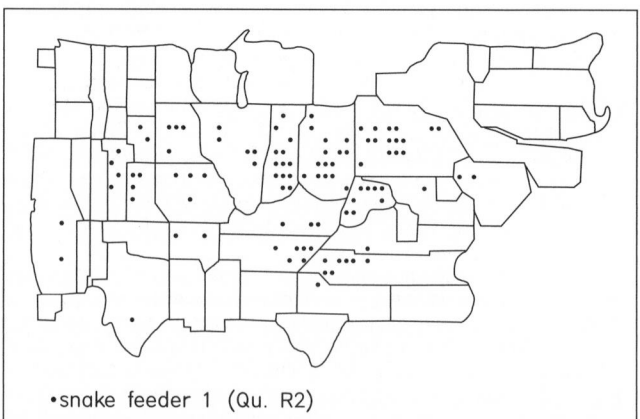

•snake feeder 1 (Qu. R2)

2 =hellgrammite 1.

1890 *Century Dict.* 5725 **OH,** Snake-feeder. . . Same as *snake-doctor,* 1. [*Ibid, Snake-doctor.* . . 1. The dobson or hellgrammite.]

3 =praying mantis B.

1968 *AmSp* 43.52 **KS,** *Snake feeder*—praying mantis—2 [of 1518 infs].

snake fence n Also *snake-rail fence*
=worm fence.

1805 Parkinson *Tour* 48 **VA,** Snake-fences; which are rails laid with the ends of one upon another, from eight to sixteen in number in one length. **1841** Combe *Notes* 1.35 **NY,** The timber lies horizontally, one portion obliquely advancing, and the rest obliquely receding from the road, and constitutes what is called a snake-rail or worm-fence. **1853** in 1855 Willis *Out-Doors at Idlewild* 199 **NY,** I dismounted, and tied my mare to the snake-fence. **1874** Coues *Birds NW* 174, As we walk along the weedy old "snake" fences and thick hedges. **1886** *Century Illustr. Mag.* 32.385 **GA,** He . . crawled behind snake fences to abstract . . watermelons. **1926** *AmSp* 2.81 **ME,** When I was a boy I used to see a good many so-called "snake-fences," zig-zag piles of quartered small-logs, spaced and supported by crossed uprights at the overlapping corners. **1933** White *Dog Days* 37 **CA,** Stubble fields bounded by stump or "snake" fences of rails. **1936** (1951) Faulkner *Absalom* 214 **MS,** You came to the old rotting snake fence and crossed it. **1949** *Boston Daily Globe* (MA) 14 Aug fiction mag 10/3 **WI,** The waxing moon's light lay green-white upon the new grass with the barred shadows of the snake-rail fence across it. **1950** *WELS (Fences made of split logs)* 1 Inf, **csWI,** Snake or worm fence is made of rails crossed at the end, and so named because of crookedness; 1 Inf, **seWI,** Snake fence—becoming rare. **1965–70** *DARE* (Qu. L62, *A fence made of split logs*) 12 Infs, **NEast, N Midl,** Snake fence; **AR**52, Wormwood fence, old untreated zigzag fence or snake fence; **DC**2, Snake fence—zigzag, very few left; **NJ**20, Snake fence—when it zigzags; **PA**204, Snake fence—woven and ambles about; **VA**33, Snake fence, worm fence; (Qu. L61, *Fences made of solid logs, now or in the past*) Inf **CO**44, Snake fence—solid poles, notched, set at such an angle, they divide. **1979** Jordan *Yesterday in TX Hill Country* 27, At first these pens were enclosed with zigzag or snake-rail fences. **1986** Pederson *LAGS Concordance,* 1 inf, **cwMS,** Snake fence—zigzag; 1 inf, **ceGA,** Snake fence—worm fence; 1 inf, **swGA,** Heard them called snake fences; 1 inf, **cAL,** Snake fences—rail fences; 1 inf, **ceTX,** Snake fence. **1995** *Brophy Coll.* 69 **swMO** (as of c1960), *Snake rail fence.* [A] worm fence, a stake and rider fence, a zigzag fence.

snake fern n
=**hart's tongue 1,** or similar fern.

1899 Parsons *How to Know Ferns* 184, Common Polypody. Snake Fern—*Polypodium vulgare.* **1900** Lyons *Plant Names* 338, *[Scolopendrium] scolopendrium. . .* Snake Fern, Snake-leaves [etc]. **1961** *Press-Gaz.* (Hillsboro OH) 9 June 5/7, Along the first part of the trail members saw . . snake fern and some tiny wild strawberries.

snake flower n
1 An **iris B1.** Cf **snake lily 1**

1965–70 *DARE* (Qu. S24, *A wild flower that grows in swamps and marshes and looks like a small blue iris*) Infs **FL**51, **IL**10, 40, **IA**34, 41, **MO**2, 37, **OK**3, **SC**10, **VA**69, **WI**17, Snake flower; (Qu. S26a, . . *Wildflowers. . . Roadside flowers*) Inf **NE**7, Snake flowers; (Qu. S26b, *Wildflowers that grow in water or wet places*) Inf **IA**29, Snake flower—like a snapdragon—purple.

2 =**tiger lily.**
1999 *Washington Post* (DC) 22 Aug sec E 1 (Internet) **sLA,** On one small island covered with orange snake flowers, I count 15 roseate spoonbills. **2006** *DARE* File—Internet **cnNC,** One of my fondest childhood memories is playing in the creek and discovering a bed of orange tiger lilies growing wild . . we called them snake flowers.

snake fly n Also *snake bug*
=**dragonfly.**

1948 MacDowell *W. Trout* 133, Dragonflies and damsel flies, familiarly known as dragonfly, snake fly, or devil's darning needle. **1949** *AmSp* 24.113 **SC,** *Snake fly. . .* Dragonfly. **1950** *WELS Suppl.* **WI,** Snake fly—dragonfly. **1966** Dakin *Dial. Vocab. Ohio R. Valley* 2.405 **eKY, OH, IN,** *Snake fly* (once ~ *bug*) appears a few times in eastern Kentucky and once each in Ohio and Indiana. **1968–70** *DARE* (Qu. R2, . . *The dragonfly*) Infs **CA**181, **IN**58, **IA**41, **MO**32, Snake fly. **1973** Allen *LAUM* 1.319 (as of c1950) 1 inf, **SD,** Snake fly. **1986** Pederson *LAGS Concordance,* 3 infs, **AL, MS,** Snake flies.

snake frog n
A **gopher frog** (here: *Rana areolata aesopus*).

1894 U.S. Natl. Museum *Proc.* 17.339 **cwFL,** *Rana Aesopus. . .* Of this species I have collected one specimen at Ozona, Hillsboro County. It . . was called "snake frog" by the population there.

snake gentian n
A **rattlesnake root 2b** (here: *Prenanthes serpentaria*).

1900 Lyons *Plant Names* 257, *[Nabalus] serpentarius. . .* Snake Gentian. **1901** Lounsberry *S. Wild Flowers* 493, *Nabalus serpentarius. . .* Our present species . . not infrequently passes under the name of snake gentian.

snake-grass n

1 Any of var coarse grasses, but esp a **love grass** (here: *Eragrostis cilianensis*). Cf **rattlesnake grass**

1868 Williams *Steel Safe* 55, "I don't know how it strikes the bulk o' you, my friends," said the leader, rubbing his horse's legs with a bunch of wet snake-grass. **1870** (1871) Warner *My Summer* 21 **CT,** It is the bunch, or joint, or snake-grass—whatever it is called. . . This grass has a slender, beautiful stalk: and when you cut it down, or pull up a long root of it, you fancy it is got rid of; but, in a day or two, it will come up in the same spot in half a dozen vigorous blades. . . If you follow a slender white root, it will be found to run under the ground until it meets another slender white root; and you will soon unearth a network of them, with a knot somewhere, sending out dozens of sharp-shoots, healthy shoots. *Ibid* 28, Snake-grass, or quack-grass as some call it. **1898** *Jrl. Amer. Folkl.* 11.283 **KS,** *Eragrostis major. . .* snake grass. **1912** Baker *Book of Grasses* 180, Strong-scented Eragrostis. Snake Grass. . . Throughout nearly the entire United States. **1923** in 1925 Jepson *Manual Plants CA* 93, *[Eragrostis] cilianensis. . .* Stink Grass. Snake Grass. **1935** (1943) Muenscher *Weeds* 155, *Eragrostis cilianensis. . .* Stink-grass, Meadow snake-grass [etc]. **1950** Gray–Fernald *Manual of Botany* 124, *[Eragrostis] megastachya. . .* Stink-, Snake- or Skunk-Grass. **1967–68** *DARE* (Qu. S8, *A common kind of wild grass that grows in fields: it spreads by sending out long underground roots, and it's hard to get rid of*) Infs **GA**38, **IL**10, Snake-grass; (Qu. S9, . . *Kinds of grass that are hard to get rid of*) Inf **GA**38, Snake-grass; **CA**40, Snake-grass—a tall, coarse grass. [*DARE* Ed: Some of these Infs may refer instead to other senses below.] **1986** Pederson *LAGS Concordance,* 1 inf, **cwAL,** Snake grass—skunk grass? **2002** *Lowell Sun* (MA) 13 Feb (Internet) **AZ,** [Serialized short story:] There on the steep slope were four horses and two young colts grazing in the snake grass.

2 also *snake-rush:* A **horsetail 1** (here: *Equisetum arvense* or *E. hyemale*).

1914 Georgia *Manual Weeds* 20, Field Horsetail—*Equisetum arvense. . . Other English Names:* Meadow Pine, . . Snake Grass. **1937** FWP *Guide ID* 63, More widely distributed in Idaho is the scouring-brush [=*Equisetum hyemale*]. . . Known variously as scrub-grass, snake-rush, gun-bright, snake-grass [etc]. **1975** Zwinger *Run River* 165 **UT,** Walking back through the woods I can still hear the rapids boom, sound trespassing into this gentle, subdued land world: pale gray-blue berries on the junipers, a stalk of snake grass with one pure coral segment as if strung with an Indian bead. **1992** Martone *Townships* 119 **IA,** There was milkweed. There was what we called snakegrass, which pulled apart in sections. **2002** *DARE* File—Internet **WA,** [Caption:] Fallen Log and Snake Grass.

3 A **spiderwort** (here: *Tradescantia virginiana*).
1940 Clute *Amer. Plant Names* 150, *[Tradescantia] Virginiana. . .* Snake-grass [etc]. **1967** *DARE* Wildfl QR Pl.7 Inf **AR**46, Snake-grass.

snake guarder n [Calque of PaGer *schlangehieter*] **sePA** Cf **snake doctor 2, snake heeder**
=**dragonfly.**

1949 Kurath *Word Geog.* 75, We find a number of local expressions [for *dragonfly*]: . . *snake servant, snake guarder,* and *snake heeder* in the Pennsylvania German area. **1985** *AmSp* 60.235 **sePA,** Large winged insect seen around water . . *snake guarder* 2% [of all responses]. . . Kurath . . found that *snake servant, snake guarder,* and *snake heeder* were "local expressions. . . [of] the Pennsylvania German area"; today only one informant [out of 60], a thirty-five-year-old female, admitted to using any of these three terms. **1997** *Sun. News* (Lancaster PA) 2 Mar sec A 4/2, When Norman Gerhart was young . . a dragonfly was a "snake guarder."

snake handling n Also *serpent handling* chiefly S Midl
The practice of handling venomous snakes as a religious rite; see quot 1982; similarly nouns *snake handler, serpent* ~ one who belongs to a group that practices this rite; adjs *snake-handling, serpent-handling.*

1934 *Galveston Daily News* (TX) 14 Oct 13/8 **TN,** Permanent Waves and Snake Handling Given Disapproval of Church. **1938** *Jefferson City Post–Tribune* (MO) 2 Nov 4/7 **KY,** No More 'Snake Handlers' For Judge's Court. . . One 'pastor' is reported to have been conducting the snake handling rite for 28 years in the Kentucky and Tennessee hills. **1940** *NE State Jrl.* (Lincoln) 6 Aug 3/2, *Adel,* Ga. . . Two members of a snake handling religious cult remained in jail here. **1945** *Reno Eve. Gaz.* (NV) 30 July 6/4, *St. Charles,* Va. . . A cry that their religious freedom had been violated went up from a hill-country cult of snake handlers today. **1947** *Ibid* 3 Oct 9/2, *Harlan,* Ky. . . Twelve-year-old Faye Nolan was reported recovering today from a snake bite suffered during recent serpent-handling rites of a religious sect. **1962** Fox *Southern Fried* 120 **SC,** He looked down on all of the "Snake Handlers." **1982** *Foxfire 7* 393 **sAppalachians,** I believe in serpent handlin' a hun'erd percent. My wife never did believe in it. *Ibid* 481, The snake handlers read the verses located in the final portion of the Gospel of Mark [= 16:17–18 "In my name . . they shall speak with new tongues; They shall take up serpents"] and insist that those words must be taken literally. Indeed they declare that if those prophecies are not true, none of the Bible is true. **2001** *Charleston Daily Mail* (WV) 17 Aug sec A 1 (Internet), Alfred "Pooch" Preast came from a family of snake handlers. . . Preast's daughter . . said, "I don't go to no snake handling churches." **2002** *DARE* File—Internet **seKY,** I have a lot of serpent handling friends that I love with my heart and I want God to open their eyes to the scriptures. *Ibid* **seKY,** My x-husband's brother, use to treat me like trash. He called me snake handler. *Ibid* **seKY,** Angels Webpage—Ex-lady serpent handler speaks out!

snake hawk n

1 =**swallow-tailed kite. chiefly SE**

1731 Catesby *Nat. Hist. Carolina* 1.4, *The Swallow-Tail Hawk.* . . They are said to prey upon Lizards and other Serpents; which has given them (by some) the name of *Snake-Hawk.* **1781** Latham *Genl. Synopsis Birds* 1.1.61 **NC, SC,** *Swallow-tailed F[alcon]* inhabits *Carolina* in the summer months; where it is called *Snake-hawk.* **1863** Russell *My Diary* 149 **csSC,** The young gentleman was good enough to bring over a snake-hawk he had shot for me. **1870** *Harper's New Mth. Mag.* 41.665 **FL,** It was at Pilatka also we first saw that rare and most beautiful of birds, the swallow-tailed hawk. . . The natives will tell you he is the "snake-hawk," because he makes war upon those creatures. **1873** *Amer. Naturalist* 7.202 **sIL,** Numbers of exquisitely graceful swallow-tailed kites or "snake hawks" . . were seen. **1919** Pearson et al. *Birds NC* 162, Swallow-tailed Kite. . . While not of common occurrence, it is evidently a regular summer visitor in Craven County, where it has acquired the name of "Snake Hawk" from its habit of eating such reptiles. **1924** Howell *Birds AL* 129, Its fondness for snakes has given it in some sections the name of "snake hawk." **1955** *AmSp* 30.183, Catesby in 1731 called the swallow-tail *snake hawk* and this name is reported in popular use from North Carolina, Florida, Alabama, and Texas. **1962** Imhof *AL Birds* 167, Swallow-tailed Kite. . . Other Names: Snake Hawk, Fish Hawk [etc.].

2 =**marsh hawk 1.**

1927 Forbush *Birds MA* 2.99, *Circus hudsonius.* . . *Other names:* bog hawk; mouse hawk; frog hawk; snake hawk. **1932** Bennitt *Check-list* 24 **MO,** *Marsh hawk.* . . snake hawk. **1953** Jewett *Birds WA* 178, American Marsh Hawk. . . Other Names: Mouse Hawk; Snake Hawk [etc.]. **1955** [see **3** below].

3 =**broad-wing.**

1955 *AmSp* 30.183, Other *snake hawks* are the broad-wing in Wisconsin and the marsh hawk in Connecticut.

snakehead n

1 also *snakehead bitter herb, snake's-head:* A **turtlehead** (here: usu *Chelone glabra*). Cf **snakemouth 2**

1784 in 1785 *Amer. Acad. Arts & Sci. Memoirs* 1.464, *Chelone* . . Chelone. Fish-head. Snake-head. Blossoms in spikes; white. **1834** Audubon *Ornith. Biog.* 2.150, *The Snake's Head.* . . grows on the banks of rivers and swamps, in the Middle and Southern States. **1859** Colton *Mt. Scenery* 96 **wNC,** I was much struck with a flower called, by the inhabitants, snake's head. **1864** *Catalogue of Herbs* **swME,** Snakehead bitt'r herb—Chelone glabra. **1911** NJ State Museum *Annual Rept. for 1910* 678, Chelone. . . Snakehead, Turtlehead. . . common in the Northern and Middle districts and occasional on the Cape May peninsula. **1966** *DARE* FW Addit **NY**16, Snake's-head—*Chelone glabra*—whitish-pink, little, waxy-like, pointed like snake's head; July, August. **1975** Hamel–Chiltoskey *Cherokee Plants* 168, Turtlehead; Snakehead—*Chelone glabra. Ibid,* Snakehead—*Chelone obliqua.*

2 also *snakehead morel:* A **morel** n²: usu *Morchella semilibera,* but also *M. elata* or *Verpa bohemica.* Cf **dog pecker**

1999 in 2006 *DARE* File—Internet **cIN,** Found beautious [sic] fresh grays . . in Clinton County Indiana. . . Plus 2 snakeheads and one yellow. *Ibid* **swOH,** We also found 3 "Snakeheads" (half free morels).

2000 *Ibid* **cVA,** Mushrooms found in Woods Creek . . Morchella hybrida [=*M. semilibera*]—Snakehead morels. . . Verpa bohemica—Snakehead morels. **2003** Roody *Mushrooms WV* 484, *Morchella elata.* . . Black Morel; Snakehead. . . consisting of a conical to elongated, bluntly triangular pitted head on a cylindrical, hollow stalk.

snakehead bitter herb See **snakehead 1**

snake heeder n [Partial calque of PaGer *schlangehieter,* literally "snake guarder"] Cf **snake guarder, snake doctor 2** =**dragonfly.**

[**1924** Lambert *PA Ger. Dict.* 134, *Schlangehieter* . . dragon-fly.] **1949** [see **snake guarder**].

snake herb n

A perennial southern plant of the genus *Dyschoriste* (here: esp *D. linearis*). For other names of var spp see **twinflower 2**

1961 Wills–Irwin *Flowers TX* 204, *Dyschoriste linearis.* . . Snakeherb, an attractive, low, branched perennial. **1999** *DARE* File—Internet **TX,** Snake herb is a low growing perennial that makes a good groundcover in partly sunny places.

snake hip(s) n *orig esp freq among Black speakers* Cf **buzzard lope 1**

A dance or dance step characterized by sinuous gyrations, esp of the hips; hence vbl n *snake-hipping* performing such a dance step.

1928 in 2005 *DARE* File—Internet [Catalog of jazz recordings], A Snake Hip Dance. **1932** *Daily Progress* (Charlottesville VA) 20 Apr 4/3, There is a distinct class clash between the Harlem intelligentsia and snake-hip dancers and chanters of hot-cha-cha and skiddle-de-scow in the black and tan auberges. **1944** *Hammond Times* (IN) 3 Dec 22/1 **Los Angeles CA,** The defense attorney asked: "In the part of the hula you did do, did you do the snake hips?" "No," Hall said. . . "Was Mrs. Dorsey dancing the snake hips?" "Yes, the snake hips, the hula, or whatever you call it." **1968–70** *DARE* (Qu. FF5a, . . *Different steps and figures in dancing—in past years*) Inf **CA**81, Snake hip; **MO**23, Snake-hipping. [Both Infs Black, mid-aged] **1969** (1970) Angelou *Caged Bird* 200 [Black], She sang and did the Time Step and the Snake Hips and the Suzy Q. **1970** Major *Dict. Afro-Amer. Slang* 106, *Snake Hips:* (1900's–30's) a Baltimore- and New York-oriented jazz dance. **1972** Jones–Hawes *Step it Down* 45 **eGA** [Black], *Snake Hips.* . . The movement is the same [as in **ball the Jack 2**], but the knees are not kept together [as they are rotated] and move forward and back, first one knee, then the other. **2003** *DARE* File—Internet [StreetSwing.com Dance History Archive], The Eccentric dance style called the Snake Hips dance was made popular by Earl "Snake Hips" Tucker. Basically the dance was just a contortion, twisting, shaking kind of dance done around the stomach area.

snake horse n [**snake** v 1]

A horse used to **snake** logs.

1985 Wilkinson *Moonshine* 85 **neNC,** We got to using him a lot as a snake horse. A snake horse is one that you hook up to a log, and he drags it to the truck.

snake in the bag See **snake** n 6

snake-in-the-grass n

1 A guessing game similar to **hull-gull.** Cf **Jack-in-the-bush 2**

1952 Brown *NC Folkl.* 1.60 **nwNC** (as of c1927), Snake in the grass. . . This is the same as *A* [=Jack-in-the-bush] except for the questions and answers, which run: "Snake in the grass." "Bust his head." "How many licks?" **1953** Brewster *Amer. Nonsinging Games* 9, Jack in the Bush. . . A common name in the South is Snake in the Grass. The guesser says, "Mash his head!" and the holder of the counters challenges with "How many licks?"

2 See quot. Cf **snake-in-the-gully**

2001 *DARE* File **swCA** (as of 1970s), When I was a kid . . , we played a game of tag called "snake in the grass." Whoever was "it" had to crawl on hands and knees. When he or she tagged someone, then they would both be "it" and try to crawl around and tag the rest of us. Continue this way til only one person is standing. Usually we played on the front lawn, and if you stepped off the grass onto sidewalk or driveway, you were penalized somehow.

snake-in-the-gully n

A children's game; see quot 1969–70.

1906 [see **stealing steps**]. **1939** Harris *Purslane* 103 **cNC,** She led the gay games around the cane-mill and invented new ones after "red statue," "pretty girls' house," and "snake-in-the-gully" were stale. **1969–70** *DARE* (Qu. EE33, . . *Outdoor games . . that children play*) Inf **VA**35, Snake-in-the-gully—find a gully in the woods, one goes in the middle, he was the boogerbear, the others run across the gully without being caught; if caught, then you're the boogerbear; **VA**42, Snake-in-the-gully—cross gully without getting caught.

snake iris   See **snake lily 1**

snake-jabber   See **snake-kicker (boot)**

snake juice   See **snake piss**

snake-kicker (boot) n   Also *snake-jabber*   Cf **shit-kicker 1**, **toad stabber**

    1966–68 *DARE* (Qu. W42a, . . *Nicknames . . for men's sharp-pointed shoes*) Infs **MI**2, 78, **NY**10, Snake-kickers; **CA**101, Snake-jabbers. **2004** *DARE* File—Internet **WY**, It is my gut level hope . . that the American people . . give Geeeeedubya and TOHA Cheney . . the toe of their snake kicker (how's that for cleaning up the rhetoric?) boots.

snake-killer n

1 =**roadrunner 1.**

    1872 Coues *Key to N. Amer. Birds* 189, *Geococcyx*. . . Road Runner. Snake Killer. **1897** *Oölogist* 14.79 **TX**, In Texas this bird [=the roadrunner] is almost universally known as the Chaparal [sic] Bird or Mexican Peafowl; sometimes it is called the Ground Cuckoo, Snake Killer and Paisano. **1955** *AmSp* 30.183 **KS, TX, NM, CA**, Besides *snakebird*, . . the road runner has won three other names denoting its prowess in snake-despatching: *snake-eater* (Texas), *snake-killer* (Kans., Texas, N. Mex., Calif.), and *rattlesnake-killer* (Texas). **1969** *DARE* FW Addit **NM**, Ground cuckoo . . also called roadrunner, chaparral cock, chaparral hen, and snake-killer.

2 =**swallow-tailed kite.**

    1955 [see **snake-killer hawk**].

3   A cultivator for listed corn.   **esp Plains States**

    1899 in 2005 *DARE* File—Internet **NE**, The Grand Detour plows . . are among the specialties, also the "Snake Killer" two row cultivators for listed corn. **1937** *AmSp* 12.106 **eNE** [Farm terms], The listed-corn cultivator . . has caused a problem in farm nomenclature. Among its names are *gopher, badger, snake, snake-killer, cracker-jack, go-devil, go-digger, go-dig, two-row monitor,* and *two-row eli.* **1967** *DARE* FW Addit **cnCO**, Snake-killer—said to be the Missouri name for a listed-row corn cultivator; in Loveland CO, called a *go-dig.* **1969** *Hamburg Reporter* (IA) 9 Oct 2/1, [Advt:] Single-row Snake-killer. **1991** Heat Moon *PrairyErth* 377 **ceKS**, We'd cultivate the weeds out, pulled a curler—called it a snake killer—behind our lister and turned dirt up over little weeds.

4   See **snake poison.**

snake-killer hawk n

=**Mississippi kite.**

    1955 *AmSp* 30.183 **TX**, The swallow-tailed kite is known as *snake killer* in Texas, and the Mississippi kite gets the fuller designation of *snake-killer hawk* in the same state.

snakeleaf n

A **dogtooth violet** (here: *Erythronium americanum*).

    1848 *Independent Amer. & Genl. Advt.* (Platteville WI) 8 July 1/3, Beauty looks down from the showery cloud,/ Beauty springs up in the snake-leaf's shroud. **1876** Hobbs *Bot. Hdbk.* 107, Snake leaf, Adders' tongue, Erythronium Americanum. **1910** Graves *Flowering Plants* 121 **CT**, Dog's-tooth violet. . . Snake-leaf [etc].

snake lily n

1   also *snake iris:* An **iris B1** (here: *Iris missouriensis* or *I. versicolor*).

    1833 Eaton *Botany* 189, [*Iris*] *versicolor* . . snake lily, blue flag. **1963** Craighead *Rocky Mt. Wildflowers* 34, Rocky Mountain Iris. . . Flag, Fleur-de-lis, Snake-lily. **1967–70** *DARE* (Qu. S24, *A wild flower that grows in swamps and marshes and looks like a small blue iris*) Infs **MA**3, **OH**12, 25, **OK**54, **SC**41, Snake lily; **NY**92, Snake iris.

2   A **fritillary** (here: *Fritillaria lanceolata*).

    1934 Haskin *Wild Flowers Pacific Coast* 23, Rice Root. . . This graceful flower bears so many common names that each person may call it differently and still be right. The name[s] . . chocolate and brown lily, as well as speckled-hen and snake lily come from its peculiar color and markings.

3   A **brodiaea** (here: *Dichelostemma volubile*).

1959 Carleton *Index Herb. Plants* 108, Snake-lily: Brodiaea volubilis. **2003** Munz *Intro. CA Mt. Wildflowers* 143, Twining brodiaea, or snake-lily, (*D[ichelostemma] volubile*) is another striking member of this genus and is often encountered in the northern mountains.

4   A **dogtooth violet.**   Cf **snakeleaf**

    1970 *DARE* (Qu. S11, . . *Dog-tooth violet*) Inf **VA**38, Snake lily.

snake mackerel n

A fish of the family Gempylidae, esp *Gempylus serpens.*

    1896 U.S. Natl. Museum *Bulletin* 47.883, Gempylus [spp] . . Snake Mackerels. **1926** Pan-Pacific Research Inst. *Jrl.* 1.1.8, Gempylidae, the Snake-Mackerels. **1999** in 2001 *DARE* File—Internet, [Title:] Opening a whole new can of worms: parasites and biology of the snake mackerel (*Gempylus serpens*).

snake medicine   See **snakebite remedy**

snake milk   See **snake's milk 1**

snakemouth n

1   also *snakemouth arethusa, ~ orchid:* =**rose pogonia.**

    1822 Eaton *Botany* 397, [*Pogonia*] *ophioglossoides* (snake-mouth arethusa). **1832** MA Hist. Soc. *Coll.* 2d ser 9.152 **cwVT**, [*Malaxis*] ophioglossoides, Snake-mouth. **1902** (1909) Mathews *Field Book Amer. Wild Flowers* 80, Snake Mouth. . . In wet meadows and swamps, Me., south, and west to Kan. **1961** House *Wild Flowers* 1.76, Snake-mouth. . . In swamps, low meadows and boggy depressions, epecially in sandy regions, . . Florida, Kansas and Texas. **2001** (acc) U.S. Dept. Ag. *Plants Database* (Internet), *Pogonia ophioglossoides*. . . snakemouth orchid.

2   A **turtlehead.**   Cf **snakehead 1**

    1894 *Jrl. Amer. Folkl.* 7.96 **NC**, Chelone, sp., snake-mouths, Banner Elk, N.C. **1971** Krochmal *Appalachia Med. Plants* 84, *Chelone glabra*. . . Common Names . . snakehead, snakemouth [etc].

snakemouth arethusa (or orchid)   See **snakemouth 1**

Snakenavel n   Also *Snake's Navel*   Cf *DS* C33

Used as a name for an imaginary, extremely remote town.

    1976 *Lima News* (OH) 11 Apr sec D 2/1 **swCA**, The difference would be money gained if we could sell it, take the money and move to some place like Snake Navel, Wyo. **1984** Weaver *TX Crude* 126, Snakenavel. A fictitious city, usually said to be in Idaho. Used to give someone an idea of where you live—the wrong idea. "I've been from Bumfuck, Egypt, to Snakenavel, Idaho." **1997** in 2002 *DARE* File—Internet, Snakenavel, MO: Researchers here have recently discovered a new disorder affecting thousands of rural communities nationwide. The disorder now named *Wegonnagetagrant* also seems to be somewhat prevalent among some water and sewer districts. **2002** *Ibid* **PA**, The author would like to personalize your copy with . . a typed label such as "John and Mary Smith are pleased to present this book to The Public Library of Snake's Navel, Montana."

snake oil n   Cf **rattlesnake oil**

=**snake poison.**

    1950 *WELS* (Names and nicknames for liquor in general) 1 Inf, **csWI**, Snake oil. **1958** McCulloch *Woods Words* 172 **Pacific NW**, Snake oil—A drink of any unknown stuff in prohibition days. **1966–69** *DARE* (Qu. DD21a, *General words . . for any kind of liquor*) Infs **GA**72, **SC**19, Snake oil; (Qu. DD21b, *General words . . for bad liquor*) Inf **KY**6, Snake oil; (Qu. DD21c, *Nicknames for whiskey, especially illegally made whiskey*) Inf **GA**72, Snake oil. **1969** *DARE* Tape **GA**72, We have a variety of names for this homemade whiskey in this county. . . snake oil, rattlesnake juice.

snake owl n

1 =**burrowing owl.** [See quots 1923, 1925]

    1923 Dawson *Birds CA* 3.1120, Burrowing Owl. . . Synonyms. . . Snake Owl [etc]. [*Ibid* 1124, One need not kill these Owls to learn what else they feed upon, for half-eaten mice, dismembered frogs and headless snakes litter the floor.] **1925** Bailey *Birds FL* 77, Florida Burrowing Owl. . . (*Ground owl, Snake owl*). . . Many people still believe that the owls live in harmony with the rattler, . . owing to the rattling like noise made by the birds. **1953** Jewett *Birds WA* 361, Western Burrowing Owl. . . Other Names: Ground Owl; Snake Owl [etc].

2 =**barn owl 1.**

    1925 Bailey *Birds FL* 75, Barn Owl. . . The name of snake owl no doubt was derived from their habit of hissing, and when given with the side to side swaying motion of their body,—is a most grewsome and terrifying moment to the young observer.

snake peter n   Also *peter snake*   Cf **snake feeder 1**
=dragonfly.

1950 *WELS* (*Dragonfly*) 1 Inf, **cwWI,** Devil's darning needle, darning needle, also snake peter. Rare.   **1977–78** Foster *Lexical Variation* 53 **neNJ,** The sole *peter snake* response [as a folk name for the dragonfly] is from Union.

snake pickerel   See **snake** n **7, 8**

snake piss n   Also *snake juice, ~ water*   **chiefly West**
=snake poison.

1890 *Union Pacific Employes' Mag.* 5.223 **WY,** A large party . . has gone to the hills, loaded down with guns, provisions and lots of Snake Juice.   **1898** *ID Daily Statesman* (Boise) 20 Oct 2/1, The gentleman who narrates the story declares that he had not been drinking snake water either when he saw the phenomenon.   **1910** London *Burning Daylight* 21 **AK,** Name your snake-juice, you-all—the winner pays.   **1936** Adams *Cowboy Lingo* 228 **West,** The Westerner's names for whiskey were legion . . 'snake water.'   **1940** White *Wild Geese* 215 **AK** (as of 1890s), That's the best of it. I got, besides this, Nitric Acid and Chain Lightning and Snake Juice and Battle Ax.   **1941** Writers' Program *Guide WY* 465, Snake juice—Liquor.   **1950** *WELS* (*Names and nicknames for liquor in general*) 1 Inf, **cWI,** Snake juice.   **1986** Pederson *LAGS Concordance* (*Cheap whiskey*) 1 inf, **seFL,** Snake piss.   **1986** Friedman *Greenwich* 145 **TX,** I bought a shot of snake piss and I looked around through the smoke.

snake plantain n   [See quots]
A **hawkweed** (here: *Hieracium venosum*).

1830 Rafinesque *Med. Flora* 2.228, Hieracium venosum. . . *Hawkweed, Bloodwort, Snake plantain*. . . long used bruised or chewed and applied for bites of rattle and pilot snakes.   **1901** Lounsberry *S. Wild Flowers* 491, Snake Plantain. . . The country people group it with those plants of supposed virtue in curing the bites of rattlesnakes, and they apply the flat leaf quickly to such wounds. It seems that this superstition appeals mostly to their credence whenever some colouring of a plant is suggestive of the reptile's skin.

snake plum   See **snakeberry 1**

snake poison n   Also *snakebite, snake killer*   Cf **snakebite remedy, snake oil, ~ piss**
Liquor, whiskey.

1889 *Cornhill Mag.* 59.1.51 **CA,** It was variously called for as tanglefoot, snake-poison, . . chain-lightning, or other fancy name, but it was *never* called for as *whisky*.   **1907** *Sun. Rev.* (Decatur IL) 9 June 20/1, The place became popular with those who desired to metamorphose the dull verities of life with the enlivening "snake killer."   **1930** Shoemaker *1300 Words* 59 **cPA Mts** (as of c1900), *Snake-bite*—Moonshine whiskey; originally name of a strong drink made from Elder blossoms.   **1965** *WV Folkl.* 16.30, In his little shack he distilled his own brand of "snake poison", as the residents of Carolina labeled it.   **1967–70** *DARE* (Qu. DD21a, *General words . . for any kind of liquor*) Inf **AL10,** Snakebite—snakebite store = liquor store; (Qu. DD21b, *General words . . for bad liquor*) Infs **CA208, MA5,** Snakebite; **WA3,** Snake poison; (Qu. DD21c, *Nicknames for whiskey, especially illegally made whiskey*) Inf **SC43,** Snakebite.   **2006** *DARE* File—Internet **CA,** The trip back was a little rough, but with my handy bottle of snake bite, I made it out just fine.

snake-poor   See **snake** n **1a(2)**

snaker   See **snake** v **1**

snake-rail fence   See **snake fence**

snake remedy   See **snakebite remedy**

snake room n   [Cf **snake** n **3**]   **esp Gt Lakes**   Cf *DCan*
Esp among loggers: see quot 1956.

1908 Whittles *Lumberjack Sky Pilot* 163 **MN,** During the days and nights of debauchery he had not changed his clothes or even washed his hands. This was his condition when Mr. Higgins found him senseless with drink in the "snake room."   **1911** *Stevens Point Daily Jrl.* (WI) [9 Feb 2]/7 (newspaperarchive.com) **Pacific NW,** He packed his turkey and went out to blow his stake. Where did he land? You know. He ended in the snake room. And there the old man found him and took him home and sobered him up.   **1938** FWP *Guide MN* 322 **neMN** (as of c1895), Saloons [in Hibbing MN] outnumbered the stores. In the "snake rooms" adjoining the bars, many of the patrons slept off their drunkenness on the floors, pillowed on their baggage.   **1956** Sorden–Ebert *Logger's*

Words 33 **Gt Lakes,** *Snake-room,* A room off a saloon, usually two or three steps down, into which a bar-keeper or the bouncer could slide drunk lumber-jacks head first through swinging doors from the barroom.   **1962** *Appleton Post–Crescent* (WI) 8 Apr sec B 5/1 **neWI,** The old hotel . . was once a bustling place. . . Its 14 sleeping rooms (plus a "snake room" for drunks in the basement) were almost always occupied by lumbermen, 'jacks and salesmen.

snakeroot n   Cf **rattlesnake root, snakebite**
A plant or its root thought at one time to be effective against snakebite:

a   Used generically, or in ref to specific plants not identifiable from the context.

1635 (1976) *Relation MD* 17, They have a roote which is an excellent preservative against Poyson, called by the *English,* the *Snake roote.*   **1697** in 1870 Perry *Hist. Coll.* 1.30 **VA,** I make bold to send a small quantity of snake root, the best sudorific . . and counter poison that nature . . can afford.   **1709** (1967) Lawson *New Voyage* 78, Asarum wild in the Woods, reckon'd one of the Snake-Roots.   **1712** Pomet *Compleat Hist. Druggs* 1.26, Of Virginia Snake-Root. This *Snake-Root* . . is call'd by some *Dittany,* by others *Contrayerva* of *Virginia.*   **1796** Morse *Amer. Universal Geog.* 1.681 **SC,** Snakeroot, pinkroot, and a variety of medicinal herbs grow spontaneously.   **1872** Schele de Vere *Americanisms* 212, The backwoodsman. . . has . . countless *snakeroots,* reputed to cure snake-bites, and mostly inherited from the Indians.   **1882** *Harper's New Mth. Mag.* Nov 855, He is no New-Englander, certainly, who has never heard of "snakeroot tea."   **1938** Rawlings *Yearling* 87 **nFL,** If she guessed that his trouble had been the colic, the medicine she held would be either snake-root tonic or a blood purifier.   **1965–70** *DARE* (Qu. S26b, *Wildflowers that grow in water or wet places*) Infs **RI1, WI64,** Snakeroot; (Qu. S26c, *Wildflowers that grow in woods*) Infs **IL78, KY68, VA24, 26,** Snakeroot; **NY233,** Snakeroot—in damp soil—used medicinally; (Qu. S26e, *Other wildflowers not yet mentioned;* not asked in early QRs) Inf **SC46,** Snakeroot—give babies for colic; **VA11,** Mountain people call it snakeroot because of its medicinal properties.   **1986** Pederson *LAGS Concordance* **Gulf Region,** 5 infs, Snakeroot; 1 inf, Snakeroot—recently people are digging it here; 1 inf, Snakeroot—tuberous root, used for tranquilizer.

b   Used specifically, often with qualification:

(1) also *Red River snakeroot, snakeroot aristolochia, Texan snakeroot, Texas ~:* A **birthwort 1.**   Cf **snakeweed b(1), Virginia snakeroot**

1753 Chambers *Cyclopaedia Suppl.* app, *Snake-root, aristolochia,* in botany, the name of a genus of plants, otherwise called *birthwort.*   **1859** (1880) Darlington *Amer. Weeds* 268, [*Aristolochia*] *Serpentaria.* . . Snake-root Aristolochia.   **1887** *Encycl. Brit.* (9th ed) 22.189, The root of *Aristolochia reticulata,* . . which is known in the United States as Red River or Texan Snake-root.   **1933** Small *Manual SE Flora* 1282, *A[ristolochia] hastata.* . . *Snakeroot.* . . Damp woods, various provinces, Fla. to La. and S Va.   **2001** *DARE* File—Internet, *Aristolochia reticulata.* . . Snakeroot, Texas Snakeroot. *Ibid, Aristolochia rotunda.* . . Snakeroot.

(2) also *dwarf snakeroot, evergreen ~:* A **milkwort:** usu either the **Seneca snakeroot** or the **fringed polygala.**

1792 Belknap *Hist. NH* 3.125, Snake Root (*polygala senega*).   **1822** Eaton *Botany* 399, [*Polygala*] *verticillata* (dwarf snake-root).   **1830** Rafinesque *Med. Flora* 2.63, Polygala paucifolia. . . *Vulgar.* Little Pollom, Evergreen Snakeroot.   **1866** Lindley–Moore *Treas. Botany* 2.1067, Snake-root. The root of *Polygala Senega.*

(3) also *Canada snakeroot, southern ~, Vermont ~:* A **wild ginger 1** (here: *Asarum canadense*).   Cf **black snakeroot 3, coltsfoot ~, heart ~**

1828 Rafinesque *Med. Flora* 1.70, *Asarum Canadense.* . . Vulgar Names—Wild Ginger, Indian Ginger, Canada Snakeroot, Heart Snakeroot, Coltsfoot &c.   **1868** (1870) Gray *Field Botany* 282, Canada Wild Ginger, sometimes called Snakeroot.   **1876** Hobbs *Bot. Hdbk.* 108, Snakeroot, Vermont, Canada snakeroot, Asarum Canadense.   **1891** *Jrl. Amer. Folkl.* 4.148 **swNH,** Asarum Canadense was *Snakeroot.*   **1930** Sievers *Amer. Med. Plants* 19, Canada Wildginger. . . Other common names. . . Canada snakeroot, Vermont snakeroot, heart snakeroot, southern snakeroot, black snakeroot, coltsfoot snakeroot [etc].   **2001** *DARE* File—Internet, Canada Snakeroot—1.50 per oz. . . Uses—Chest complaints, dropsy, and spasms in the bowels.

(4) also *big snakeroot, heart-leaved ~, tall ~:* A **bugbane 1** (here: *Cimicifuga racemosa*).   Cf **black snakeroot 1**

1859 (1880) Darlington *Amer. Weeds* 34, [*Cimicifuga*] *racemosa.* . .

Tall Snake-root. Black Snake-root. **1902** Bailey *Cyclop. Horticult.* 4.1673, Snakeroot. Black S. *Cimicifuga racemosa* and *Sanicula Marilandica.* **1931** Harned *Wild Flowers Alleghanies* 171, *Black Cohosh (Cimicifuga racemosa).* . . The name Snake Root has also been applied to the plant. The Indians regarded the thick knotty root as a certain cure for venomous snake bites. **1937** *Torreya* 37.97 **MD,** *Cimicifuga racemosa.* . . Big snake-root. **1967** *DARE* FW Addit **AR**44, Snake-root—*Cimicifuga racemosa.* **1967** *DARE* Wildfl QR Pl.64 [=*C. racemosa*] Inf **OH**37, Snakeroot. **1971** Krochmal *Appalachia Med. Plants* 96, Black snakeroot, . . heart-leaved snakeroot [etc]. **2005** *Milwaukee Jrl. Sentinel* (WI) 13 Mar (Internet), Snakeroot, also known as bugbane (Cimicifuga), is a tall plant with summer or fall blooming varieties.

(5) A **boneset 1** (here: *Ageratina altissima*). Cf **white snakeroot**

1960 *NY Times* (NY) 21 Aug sec E 10/2, In the edge of the woodland is the snow-white froth of snakeroot, still another cousin [of Joe-Pye weed]. **1967** *DARE* FW Addit **AR**44, Snakeroot—*Eupatorium urticaefolium* [=*Ageratina altissima*]. **1967** *DARE* Wildfl QR Pl.231 [= *Eupatorium urticaefolium*] Infs **OH**14, **SC**41, Snakeroot. **1997** *Pittsburgh Post–Gaz.* (PA) 28 Sept sec D 19 (Internet), My first question concerned the abundant white flower that occurs throughout the woods. Snakeroot, I was told (genus Eupatorium).

(6) =**Indian pink 1.**

1892 (1974) Millspaugh *Amer. Med. Plants* 131-1, *Pink Root.* . . Indian Pink, . . Snake Root [etc]. **1958** Jacobs–Burlage *Index Plants NC* 140, *Spigelia Marylandica.* . . Carolina pink . . Indian pink . . snake root. **1971** Krochmal *Appalachia Med. Plants* 240, *Spigelia marilandica.* . . pinkroot, snakeroot [etc]. . . The root is used as a vermifuge, anthelmintic, and cathartic.

(7) A **golden ragwort** (here: *Senecio aureus*).

1894 *Jrl. Amer. Folkl.* 7.92 **MA,** *Senecio aureus* . . snake-root, Concord, Mass. [Footnote to *snake-root:*] From the aromatic and bitterish flavor of the roots, like that of *Polygala Senega.*

(8) A **Jacob's ladder 1** (here: *Polemonium reptans*).

1897 *Jrl. Amer. Folkl.* 10.50 **IN,** *Polemonium reptans* . . snake root, blue valerian, Parke County.

(9) also *adobe snakeroot, long-fruited ~, purple ~, short-styled ~:* =**sanicle 1.** Cf **black snakeroot 2**

1898 Davidson *CA Plants* 259, *Sanicula* [spp]. Snake-root. **1901** Lounsberry *S. Wild Flowers* 369, Short-styled Snake-root. *Sanicula Canadensis.* . . For a long time the genus has been renowned for its powers of healing, especially in the matter of snake bites. **1903** Porter *Flora PA* 228, *Sanicula trifoliata.* . . Long-fruited Snake-root. **1936** Winter *Plants NE* 84, *Sanicula* [spp]. . . Snake-root. **1961** Peck *Manual OR* 554, [*Sanicula*] *bipinnatifida.* . . Purple Snake-root. **1961** Thomas *Flora Santa Cruz* 256 **cwCA,** [*Sanicula*] *arctopoides.* . . Yellow Mats, Footsteps-of-Spring, Snake Root [etc]. **1968** Barkley *Plants KS* 263, *Sanicula marilandica.* . . Snakeroot. . . Rocky open woods and thickets. **2001** (acc) U.S. Dept. Ag. *Plants Database* (Internet), *Sanicula maritima.* . . adobe snakeroot.

(10) =**white baneberry.**

1900 Lyons *Plant Names* 14, [*Actaea*] *alba.* . . Snakeroot. **1979** Erichsen-Brown *Med. N. Amer. Plants* 348, White Baneberry. . . Common names. White cohosh, . . snake root.

(11) also *slender snakeroot:* A **blazing star 3** (here: *Liatris punctata, L. scariosa,* or *L. acidota*). Cf **button snakeroot 1**

1936 Winter *Plants NE* 142, [*Lacinaria*] *punctata.* . . Snake-root. Ibid, [*Lacinaria*] *acidota.* . . Slender Snake-root. **1941** *Amer. Midland Naturalist* 26.564, The low blueberry . . , the snakeroot (*Liatris scariosa* . .) [etc] . . are characteristic members of the shale-barren flora.

(12) =**red baneberry.**

1940 Clute *Amer. Plant Names* 1, [*Actaea*] *rubra.* . . snake-root.

(13) as *Kansas snakeroot, Missouri ~:* A **purple coneflower** (here: usu *Echinacea angustifolia*). Cf **rattlesnake weed 1c**

1941 *Torreya* 41.53, *Brauneria angustifolia.* . . Snake-root, Kansas. **2001** *DARE* File—Internet, *Echinacea* root, most often as the species Echinacea angustifolium (Kansas snakeroot) has been a popular medicine with American herbalists for more than a century. *Ibid,* *Echinacea purpurea.* . . Kansas Snakeroot, Missouri Snakeroot.

(14) A **dogtooth violet.**

1949 Moldenke *Amer. Wild Flowers* 328, Universally loved throughout our land are the fawnlilies or troutlilies, *Erythronium,* . . most of which are commonly known under the far less euphonious and ever [sic] inac-

curate names of adderstongue and dogtoothviolets, as well as starstrikers, rattlesnakeviolets, snakeroots, and scrofularoots.

snakeroot aristolochia See **snakeroot b(1)**

snake-rush See **snake-grass 2**

snake servant n PA Cf **snake doctor 2**
=**dragonfly.**

1821 [see **snake feeder 1**]. **1892** *Jrl. Amer. Folkl.* 5.181 **PA,** The only name by which I knew the dragon-fly in my boyhood was "snake-servant." I was told that these flies warned the snakes of approaching danger, and aided them in the acquisition of food. **1949** Kurath *Word Geog.* 75, In addition to these regional terms we find . . *snake servant, snake guarder,* and *snake heeder* in the Pennsylvania German area.

snake's eye n, also attrib Also *snake-eye* Cf **cat's-eye 1**
A playing marble; see quots.

1941 *NY Times* (NY) 27 Apr mag sec 8/2, Kids stare at you if you ask about "clay miggleousers." They've never heard of them. . . They don't appreciate a "snake's eye" special. **c1970** Wiersma *Marbles Terms Pacific NW* (as of 1931), *Snake's Eye* . . large marble, usually blue, used for shooting. **2002** *Press-Enterprise* (Riverside CA) 1 Mar sec B 1 (Internet), Lindquist loved the competition, especially when he won with his treasured snake-eye marbles.

snake's-head n

1 See **snakehead 1.**

2 A **desert dandelion** (here: *Malacothrix coulteri*).

1907 Hall *Compositae S. CA* 263, M. Coulteri. . . Snake's Head. . . Occurs sparingly from S. Diego Co. and Santa Cruz Island to the San Joaquin Valley and extends to the borders of the desert . . but not found in the mountains. **1957** Jaeger *N. Amer. Deserts* 274, Snake's-Head. . . A handsome annual of sandy areas. Appears in March and April, southwestern Utah to southern Arizona and southern California. **1971** Dodge *100 Desert Wildflowers* 98, There are many species of malacothryx native to the western and southwestern United States. Some are locally called "desert dandelion," "snake's head," "yellow saucer," and "cliff aster." **2001** in 2005 *DARE* File—Internet **CA,** Coming down from Hell's Gate we noted *Malacothrix coulteri* (snake's head).

snakes in one's boots See **snake n 3b**

snakeskin bird n [See quots] Cf **snakebird 2**

A **crested flycatcher** (here: *Myiarchus crinitus*).

1899 Weir *Dawn of Reason* 128 **KY,** The snakeskin bird gets its name from its habit of using the cast-off skins of snakes for decorative purposes. **1917** (1923) *Birds Amer.* 2.196, Crested Flycatcher. . . Snakeskin Bird. . . This bird is famous for its curious habit of almost always including in the material of which it builds its nest part or all of a cast snake-skin. **1955** *AmSp* 30.183, The habit of working shed snakeskins into their nests has suggested folk names for two of our flycatchers. . . The great-crested [flycatcher]. . . is *snakeskin bird* (Mich., Ill., La.) and *little snakebird* (Fla.)

snake's milk n

1 also *snake milk:* =**flowering spurge.**

1828 Rafinesque *Med. Flora* 1.181, *Euphorbia corollata.* . . Vulgar Names—Milkweed, . . Snake's milk [etc]. **1876** Hobbs *Bot. Hdbk.* 107, Snake milk, Blooming spurge. **1892** (1974) Millspaugh *Amer. Med. Plants* 148-1, Flowering spurge, . . wandering milkweed, Snake's-milk [etc].

2 =**spreading dogbane.**

1959 Carleton *Index Herb. Plants* 108, *Snake's-milk:* Apocynum cannabinum. **2000** OH State Univ. *Ohioline: Horse Nutrition Bulletin 762* (Internet), Hemp dogbane, Indian hemp, choctaw root, rheumatism weed, and snake's milk are names for this native perennial weed that is common in all counties of Ohio.

Snake's Navel See **Snakenavel**

snake soup n

1968 *DARE* (Qu. H67, *Food that was not finished at one meal but saved for another*) Inf **PA**126, Snake soup—a pot of soup made with meat base, put on back of stove; next day something else is added and so forth—it is snake soup because it is endless.

snake spit n [Cf *OED2* (at *snake* sb. 12.a) 1823; *EDD* (at *snake* sb.[1] 1.(4)) 1879] **NEast**
=**frog spit 3.**

1891 *Pop. Sci. Mth.* 39.379 **NEng,** Occurring in great abundance in summer upon the young shoots of many plants . . [are] little flecks of froth . . supposed to be the spittle of some animal. . . In Reading, Mass., [it] . . is called either toad-spit or snake-spit. . . Snake-spit is the name applied to [it] . . in many other localities in New England. **1914** *DN* 4.156 **Cape Cod MA,** *Snake-spit.* . . A white foam often seen on grass and weeds, supposedly caused by an insect. **1979** *DARE* File **cnMA** (as of c1915), I never saw a spitting snake but there used to be something on the grass (not dew—I still don't know what it was) early in the morning that looked like spit. *Snake spit* is the only word I know for it. **1999** *Ibid* **NEng,** "Rabbit dew" might be similar to what we called "snake spit"—in New England—damp morning dew or wet cobwebby material seen in grass. **2000** in 2002 *DARE* File—Internet **seNY,** Remember snake spit? That's the small white bubbly mass you see stuck to a blade of wild grass in a field. **2003** *DARE* File **neMA** (as of 1960s), "Snake spit" is what it was called in my area of growing up . . North Shore Massachusetts.

snake spruce n

Either of two similar cultivars of the Norway **spruce** or the **red spruce;** see quots.

1950 Gray–Fernald *Manual of Botany* 54, *P[icea] rubens.* . . Forma *virgata* . . (wand-like), Snake-S[pruce], has long, slender branches almost without branchlets. **1976** Bailey–Bailey *Hortus Third* 871, *[Picea] rubens.* . . Cv. *'Virgata'.* Snake s[pruce]. **2002** *DARE* File—Internet **IL,** One of the most unusual trees is a conifer, *Picea abies* 'Cranstonii', often referred to as the snake spruce for its convoluted branches.

snake strawberry n [The Chinese and Japanese names for this plant also mean literally "snake strawberry," but this may be coincidence; cf **snakeberry 4**]

=**Indian strawberry 1.**

1969 *DARE* (Qu. I44, *What kinds of berries grow wild around here?*) Inf **GA85,** Snake strawberries—not edible, look like wild strawberries. **2004** (acc) Tallapoosa Co. Ext. *Weed Control* (Internet) **AL,** *Mock Strawberry.* . . Also commonly referred to as "snake strawberry." **2004** *DARE* File—Internet **seVA** (as of c1933), In our younger days most of us were curious about that little red strawberry covered with pimples. This was the Indian Strawberry (Duchesnea indica). . . At the time the local scoop was, "Don't taste them snake strawberries."

snake terrapin See **snake turtle**

snake time n Cf **flytime 1**

The part of the year when snakes are active.

1888 in 2002 *DARE* File—Internet **cnAR,** Someone entered Dr. Wilson's drug store one night recently and appropriated some alcohol. Snake time is nearly at hand, and it is supposed the thief wasted [sic] the alcohol for snake bites. **1928** *AmSp* 4.156 **NE** [Black], "Snake time" is a term used to indicate warm spring weather. "I'll be all right, if you'll jes' help me pull through till snake time," said an old ill colored woman to a Nebraska social welfare worker visiting her. She did not mean, as might be supposed, that she would eat the snakes, but that when warm weather came she could get dandelion "greens" and other "doctor stuff" (medicinal plants).

snake turtle n Also snake terrapin

A **red-bellied turtle** (here: *Chrysemis picta*).

1916 *Copeia* 38.98 **MA,** I . . recognized the carapace as . . suggestive of a huge "snake" turtle (the local name for the Painted Terrapin). **1970** *DARE* (Qu. P24, . . *Kinds of turtles*) Inf **MA80,** Snake turtle; **MD36,** Snake terrapin. **1986** Pederson *LAGS Concordance,* 1 inf, **cLA,** Snake turtle—striped.

snake violet n

=**bird's-foot violet 1.**

1893 *Jrl. Amer. Folkl.* 6.138 **MA,** *Viola pedata* . . snake violet; horseshoe violet. Swansea, Mass.; Boston, Mass.

snake waiter n esp MD

=**dragonfly.**

c**1940** *LAMSAS Materials (Dragonfly)* 10 infs, 9 **MD,** Snake waiter(s). **1967** Faries *Word Geog. MO* 112, Two local expressions, *spindle* . . and *snake waiter* . . , occur three and two times respectively [from 700 infs]. **1984** Moelleken *Dialectology* 138 **nwSC,** A lone occurrence of "snake waiter" 'dragon fly' in northwestern South Carolina suggests analogous forms in central Pennsylvania.

snake water See **snake piss**

snakeweed n

Any of var plants thought at one time to be effective against snakebite, or otherwise associated with snakes:

a Used in ref to specific plants not identifiable from the context.

1630 in 1836 Force *Tracts* 1.12.12 **NEng,** There are some Serpents called Rattle Snakes, that . . will flye vpon him and sting him so mortally, that he will dye within a quarter of an houre after, except the partie stinged haue about him some of the root of an Hearbe called Snake weed to bite on, and then he shall receiue no harme. **1631** (1908) Winthrop *Jrl.* 1.68 **MA,** He always carried about him match and a compass, and in summer time snake-weed. **1642** Lechford *Plain Dealing* 47 **MA,** He that is stung with any of them [=rattlesnakes] . . dyes, unless he timely get some Snake-weed. **1795** Winterbotham *Amer. U.S.* 3.395, Other poisonous plants, are . . the Stinking Snakeweed [etc]. **1886** Ebbutt *Emigrant Life* 73 **KS,** Another plant was known as "snakeweed." One was popularly supposed to find a snake under it, but this rule did not always hold good, though we certainly found snakes near the weeds sometimes. It was rather a peculiar weed, something like a broad bean, with flowers of the lupin kind. **1967–69** *DARE* (Qu. S9, . . *Kinds of grass that are hard to get rid of*) Inf **GA35,** Snakeweed; (Qu. S20, *A common weed that grows on open hillsides: It has velvety green leaves close to the ground, and a tall stalk with small yellow flowers on a spike at the top*) Inf **IL40A,** Snakeweed; (Qu. S24, *A wild flower that grows in swamps and marshes and looks like a small blue iris*) Inf **IA13,** Sandflower or snakeweed—a member of iris family, blue, grows by itself in sand. **1982** Slone *How We Talked* 111 **eKY** (as of c1950), Cure for snake bite: Snake Weed. It was believed that man was as poison to the snake as the snake was to man. If, after biting a man, the snake did not get some of this snake weed to eat, it would die.

b Used specifically, often with qualification:

(1) also *Virginia snakeweed:* A **birthwort 1** (here: *Aristolochia serpentaria*).

1633 Gerarde *Herball* 848, The much admired Snakeweed of Virginia seems no otherwise to differ from it [=*Pistolochia Cretica*]. **1698** Royal Soc. London *Philos. Trans.* 20.402, *Mr.* Ray's *Virginia* Snakeweed, *Pulegium* Virginianum *nonnulis, aliis* Serpentaria *aut* Colubrina Virginiana *Raii.* [=*Virginia* fleaweed to many, to others serpentweed or snakeweed of Virginia (Ray)]. **1890** *Century Dict.* 5726, *Snakeweed.* . . 2. The Virginia snakeroot. **1971** Krochmal *Appalachia Med. Plants* 64, *Aristolochia serpentaria.* . . Common Names: Virginia snakeroot, snakeweed [etc].

(2) also *poison snakeweed:* =**spotted cowbane 1.**

1814 Bigelow *Florula Bostoniensis* 70 **MA,** Cicuta maculata. . . Water Hemlock. Snakeweed. . . In wet meadows. **1828** Rafinesque *Med. Flora* 1.107, Cicuta maculata. . . Vulgar Names—Snakeweed, Death of Man, Water Parsley, Poison root, Wild hemlock, Children's bane. **1876** Hobbs *Bot. Hdbk.* 108, Snakeweed, Poison, Poison hemlock. **1898** U.S. Dept. Ag. Div. Botany *Bulletin* 20.40, Water Hemlock. . . Other names: American water hemlock, . . snakeweed [etc]. **1970** *DARE* (Qu. K28, . . *Chief diseases that cows have*) Inf **IL134,** Snakeweed poisoning. [*DARE* Ed: This Inf may refer instead to **b(4)** below.]

(3) A **horsetail 1** (here: *Equisetum hyemale*). Cf **snakegrass 2**

1897 *Jrl. Amer. Folkl.* 10.147 **IA,** *Equisetum hyemale.* . . snake weed, Jones and Delaware counties. **1923** *IA City Press–Citizen* (IA) 25 Sept 4/3, The ancient Chinese method is to use a fish skin or a rush similar to the American snakeweed. **2000** *Assoc. Press State & Local Wire* 17 Aug (Internet) **sIL,** Then he planted a variety of aquatic plants, mostly such native species as horsetail or snakeweed, cattails and swamp lilies.

(4) also *poison snakeweed:* =**poison hemlock 1.**

1898 U.S. Dept. Ag. Div. Botany *Bulletin* 20.43, *Poison Hemlock.* . . *Other names:* Hemlock; . . poison root; poison snakeweed [etc]. **1930** Sievers *Amer. Med. Plants* 46, Poison Hemlock. . . Other common names.—Spotted parsley, . . poison snakeweed.

(5) A **fern;** see quot.

1899 Bergen *Animal Lore* 118 **TN,** Ferns are popularly known as "snake-weeds," because snakes are supposed to harbor among them.

(6) also *broom snakeweed:* A chiefly western plant of the genus *Gutierrezia.* Also called **broomweed, fireweed i, horseweed 6, lightning brush, matchweed, resinweed 3, torch-**

weed 1, turpentine bush d, ~ weed 4, yellowtop 2.   For other names of var spp see **kindling weed, rabbit brush 1f, rabbitweed 1f, sheepweed 4, slinkweed e, yellow broom 6, yellowweed 4**

1913 (1979) Barnes *Western Grazing* 236, In the southwest and on some of the ranges in the northern regions there is a little green weed (Gutierrezia) known locally as snakeweed. **1931** U.S. Dept. Ag. *Misc. Pub.* 101.163, Broom snakeweed . . ranges from Manitoba to western Nebraska, Kansas, and Texas, southern California, and Idaho. **1951** *PADS* 15.42 **TX**, *Gutierrezia texana. . .* snake weed. Rattlesnakes are alleged to be one of the reptile forms fond of lurking under the dense masses of fine little flowering twigs that top the broom-weed patches. This may well be true as insects swarm over the plants, and lizards, birds, and small rodents are after the insects; the snakes have a good shady hiding place from which they may seize unwary birds, smaller snakes, and four-footed reptiles. **1971** Dodge *100 Desert Wildflowers* 81, Snake-weed—Common throughout the Southwest, particularly on overgrazed rangelands and deserted clearings. **1989** Mayes–Lacy *Nanise* 115, Broom snakeweed may cover more acres than any other perennial plant in Navajoland.

(7) A **burr sage** (here: *Ambrosia deltoidea*).

1931 U.S. Dept. Ag. *Misc. Pub.* 101.154 **AZ**, Triangle bur-sage . . , sometimes called snakeweed, is a low shrub or undershrub. . . common in dry foothills and mesas of low elevation in central and southern Arizona.

(8) =**coral tree.**

1933 Small *Manual SE Flora* 716, *Erythrina* [spp]. . . Coral-beans. Cherokee-beans. Dragon's-teeth. Snakeweeds.

(9) =**self-heal.**

1933 Small *Manual SE Flora* 1155, *P[runella] vulgaris. . .* Also called Snakeweed from the belief that a snake hole is hidden under the plant.

(10) A **boneset 1** (here: *Ageratina altissima,* formerly *Eupatorium urticaefolium*).   Cf **snakeroot b(5)**

1966 *DARE* Wildfl QR Pl.231 Inf **MI**31, Snakeweed.

snake with legs n

=**congo snake 1.**

1925 TX Folkl. Soc. *Pub.* 4.50 **nwLA**, The *Amphiuma means . . ,* a long slender amphibian with four diminutive limbs, has a habit of coiling in deep holes or under water-soaked logs in marshy places. This attitude is very snake-like and many of the bottom negroes call the animal the "snake with legs."

snakewood n

=**nakedwood 1.**

[**1903** U.S. Natl. Museum *Contrib. Herbarium* 8.123 **Puerto Rico,** *Colubrina ferruginosa.* Snake wood.] **1970** Correll *Plants TX* 1009, *Colubrina* [spp]. . . Snakewood. **2000** in 2006 *DARE* File—Internet **TX**, On a recent trip . . , I collected some Texas snakewood (Colubrina texensis) seed. **2001** *DARE* File—Internet **AZ**, *Colubrina californica. . .* Las Animas snakewood.

snakeworm   See **worm snake 2**

snaking   See **snake v 1**

snaky adj

1 Of an animal, esp a horse or cow: unpredictable, wild; hence adv *snaky* in comb *snaky wild.*   **West**

1902 *Perry Daily Chief* (IA) [7 Aug 3]/1 (newspaperarchive.com) **West,** [Short story:] He'll be a sight more of a freak when he gets through with them snaky horses of old Doby's. **1929** Dobie *Vaquero* 126 **West,** Our cattle were as "snaky" as so many jack rabbits. If they got a chance to scatter into that brush they would certainly get away from us. **1933** (1950) Allen *Cowboy Lore* 100 **West,** If you reckon your mounts are some snakey [sic] and raw / Just try ridin' herd on a stove that won't draw. **1956** Gipson *Old Yeller* 75 **TX**, The only trouble was, this heifer Spot . . had been snaky wild from the day she was born. **1966** *DARE* (Qu. K42, *A horse that is rough, wild, or dangerous*) Inf **ND**5, Such a horse is said to be snaky or raunchy. **1980** *Blair & Ketchum's Country Jrl.* Oct 43 **SW**, That last practice started in the mines, where a "shavetail" was a snaky mule, not to be trusted. **2001** *Assoc. Press State & Local Wire* 1 Sept (Internet) **NM**, He's a snaky, spooky kind of horse, but he seems to know he's done something pretty special.

2 Jittery, shaky, esp as the result of delirium tremens.   Cf **snake n 3**

1884 *Eve. Observer* (Dunkirk NY) 23 May 4/3, His eyes are gray, with a yellowish tinge, and move about in a snaky, restless way. **1914** *Chicago Tribune* (IL) 22 May 8, There once was a man . . who, being given tremors and snaky fidgets by the touch of the fuzzy outside of a peach skin, put himself to the torture of rubbing his cheeks with it daily. **1930** Williams *Logger-Talk* 29 **Pacific NW,** *Snaky:* Harassed by delirium tremens; nervous. **1966** *DARE* (Qu. DD22, *. . Delirium tremens*) Inf **MI**24, D.T.'s, gone snaky. **1995** Brophy *Coll.* 69 **swMO** (as of c1960), *Snaky. . .* [V]ery drunk, i.e. imagining snakes.

snaky wild   See **snaky 1**

snallygaster   See **snollygoster 1**

snap v

1 Esp of a dog: to bite.   [*OED2* 1687 →]

1851 *Tioga Eagle* (Wellsborough PA) 28 Sept [2]/4 (newspaperarchive.com), [From *Lowell News:*] The proprietor, with the same lugubrious expression that an unbreeched urchin wears when he drops his dumpling and the dog snaps it, was measuring out . . the distance from one end of the shop to the other. **1877** *Chester Daily Times* (PA) 15 Jan [3]/1 (newspaperarchive.com), On Saturday afternoon a rabbit came to town and was snapped by a dog at 4th and Welsh Sts. **1967** *DARE* (Qu. OO12a, *Talking about dogs biting: "Some dogs will bite—last week the mailman was _____."*) Inf **NC**41, Snapped. **1986** Pederson *LAGS Concordance (Bite)* 1 inf, **ceAL,** Snap you; 1 inf, **seMS,** Most dogs, however, snap you; 1 inf, **nwGA,** Snapped. **2002** *DARE* File—Internet, We see a bit of blood where a lobster snapped him.

2 In farming:

a To break off (an ear of corn), usu along with the husk; hence vbl n *snapping;* comb *snapped corn* ears of corn in the husk.   **esp Upper MW, Cent**   Cf **break v B7**

1868 IA State Ag. Soc. *Rept. for 1867* 126, Feed in open lots from seventy-five to one hundred bushels of corn in the ear, snapped or pulled. **1874** McCoy *Cattle Trade* 246 **KS**, In Central Kansas by far the larger portion of the corn crops are harvested by husking, or snapping the corn from the stalk, leaving the immatured ears and nubbins on the stalks with the fodder. **1925** Snapp *Beef Cattle* 353, The term 'snapped corn' is applied to corn that has been gathered with the inner layers of the husks remaining on the ears. **1937** *AmSp* 12.106 **eNE** [Farm terms], When corn is gathered with shucks left on the ears it is being *snapped. Snapped* corn is not shelled but fed in the ear. **1938** *AmSp* 13.19 **wNE, SD** [Cornhusking terms], Pulling the ripe ear from its covering of dried shucks on the stalk, in western Nebraska and South Dakota is sometimes called *snapping* or *picking* as well as husking. **1948** Wolfe *Farm Gloss.* 299, *Snapped corn*—Ear corn with some husks adhering. **1948** Jacobs *We Chose Country* 136 **csWI,** The whole family went out, on a cold and sparkling Sunday morning, to "snap corn," which means husking it off the stalk. **1952** FWP *Guide SD* 83, *Snapping:* picking corn without removing the husks. **1984** *NebGuide* G74-100-A (Internet) **NE**, Ground snapped corn (cob and shuck, included) will have 6 to 8 percent more roughage equivalent than ground ear corn.

b To harvest (cotton) by breaking off the entire boll; hence vbl n *snapping;* comb *snap(ped) cotton* cotton harvested in this way.

1925 *Commerce Jrl.* (TX) [30 Oct] 2/4 (newspaperarchive.com), Texas cotton farmers are facing heavy losses . . if they continue to snap the cotton instead of picking it. . . It is a well-known fact that only a few mills can use snap cotton. **1948** Wolfe *Farm Gloss.* 299, *Snapping Cotton*— Practice of harvesting cotton by snapping off the entire boll without removing the locks of cotton from the burs. Such cotton is called snapped cotton. **1997** *DARE* File **nwMS** [Black], To snap—to break off a whole boll in picking cotton (instead of pulling out the fiber). **1999** *OSU Current Rept.* 2119 (Internet) **OK**, Picked lint percent is the percent lint in a sample of seed cotton while pulled lint percent is the percent lint in a sample of snapped cotton. Producers . . who harvest with strippers should examine pulled lint percents.

3 To blink (the eye).   **esp Mid and S Atl, nNEng**   See Map on p. 72   Cf **bat v² 1**

1824 *Republican Compiler* (Gettysburg PA) 15 Dec 4/4 **MD**, Runaway . . a Mulatto man named *Charles,* About 5 feet 10 inches high, stout made, about 32 years old, quick when spoken to, and snaps his eyes. **1854** (1855) Parton *Ruth Hall* 71 **NEng,** "Doctor," said the old lady, snapping her eyes, "I never can argue with you but you are sure to get off the track, sooner or later." **1873** *Galaxy* 15.141, You snap your eyes hard, and try to assume animation; the lids droop like lead. **1900** *New Engl. Mag.* new ser 21.700, He would swallow a little and then snap his eyes and smack his lips smartly. **1965–70** *DARE* (Qu. X24, *When a person opens and closes his eyes quickly, he* _____) 14 Infs, **esp Mid and S Atl, nNEng,** Snaps (his eyes, them); **GA**28, **NC**79, Snapping his eyes; **VA**13, Snaps his eyes like a frog in a hailstorm; [**NC**49, Snappin'-eyed].

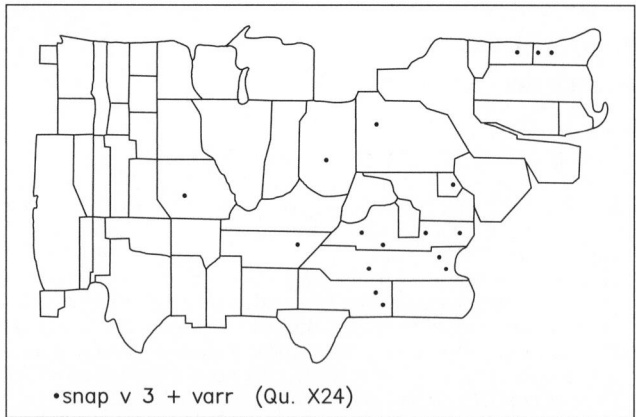

•snap v 3 + varr (Qu. X24)

4 also with *from:* To absent oneself from without permission; to skip a class.

1831 in 2005 NC Univ.–Chapel Hill *True Compositions* (Internet), I should not have had time to write this, but our tutor snapped this evening, some say he had forgotten to jump out of his tub of water untill the bell had rang. **1842** in 1956 Eliason *Tarheel Talk* 296 **NC,** [College student's diary entry:] I snapped from church today and McNary answered for me. **1900** *DN* 2.61 **IL, LA, MN, MO, NJ, NY, NC, PA** [College slang], Snap, v.i. To skip recitation. **1967** *State* (Raleigh, N.C.) 15 Sep. 19/3 (*Mathews Coll.*), But my generation "snapped school." "Cut" was unheard of, and "hookey" was an affectation. "Snap" was the word, used by students, teachers and parents alike. But I haven't heard it in 40 years.

snap n

1 See **snap bean.**

2 also *snap and catch ('em):* A party game; see quots; hence nouns *snap party,* ~ *social* a social gathering where the game is played. **chiefly Sth, S Midl**

1857 *Quinland* 1.192 **NY,** Then began the fun. Some danced, some played snap and catch. **1865** in 1906 Ridley *Battles* 481 **TN,** Games [in Georgia] soon began—"Thimble," "Snap," and kissing songs. **1914** *DN* 4.112 **cKS,** Snap and catch 'em. . . A children's game. **1945** Wilson *Passing Institutions* 93 **KY,** Our liveliest game was Snap, a game that used to seem very exciting but now somewhat resembles Drop the Handkerchief. **1949** Hedgecock *Gone Are the Days* 119 **swMO,** Some of our favorite games were . . "Skip to my Lou," and "Snap." There were two kinds of Snap, Arkansas and Missouri. In Arkansas Snap you kissed the girl when you caught her. In Missouri Snap you just caught her. **1964** Wallace *Frontier Life* 122 **OK** (as of 1890s), No party was complete in this era without a few rough games of "snap," so named because the person "snapped" his fingers at the one chosen to catch him. They would then race around a couple standing in the middle of the floor holding both hands together, so that they would not be pulled apart as the chaser steadied himself by holding onto one of the persons as he made the sharp turns around the couple. After the person succeeded in catching the one who "snapped" him, he then chose one of his favorite friends of the opposite sex to chase him around the couple, one of whom would always be the person who had just been caught in the race. **1966–70** *DARE* Tape **AL**3, I have had the most fun playing snap of any game I've ever played. . . A boy and a girl holds hands . . and then . . this boy snaps at a girl, and she must catch him, going round these people, these two holding hands; **KY**77, We always played snap, too. . . [T]wo stand up, and then . . you snap this one to come be your partner; **TX**36, Oh, they'd . . play snap, and cross questions, and dance the josie; **TX**89, At those play parties, we played snap. . . Snap is a game where you choose your partner and go out and two hold hands and the other couple chase you around. **1967–70** *DARE* (Qu. EE33, *. . Outdoor games . . that children play*) Inf **AR**52, Snap—for courting couples; a

whole roomful of people, one was "it"; boy and girl would hold hands and stand; "it" (either boy or girl) started chasing one he chose; when he caught her, he changed places with the one standing up, and the boy who had been standing chooses one to chase; [**LA**12, Snap [FW: seems to be same as crack-the-whip];] (Qu. FF2, *. . Kinds of parties*) Inf **TX**91, Snap party: "snap" is played—a boy and a girl stand and hold both hands; another girl snaps her fingers at another boy and he chases her until he catches her (around the two holding hands); the boy who caught the girl then sits and someone else joins in. It wasn't much of a game; the purpose was to get to hold hands. **1986** Pederson *LAGS Concordance,* 1 inf, **swAL,** Snap = tag/game; (*Parties*) 1 inf, **ceTN,** Snap socials—mixer, boys snapped fingers at girl.

3 A gingersnap. [*OED2* 1818 →; "*Sc.* and *north. dial.*"]

1850 *Brooklyn Daily Eagle* (NY) 31 Aug 3/1, The humor of "Bones" was as dry and acute as the music of his own lively, rattling instruments, and "Ginger" was as spicy as . . a well baked "snap." **1899** (1912) Green *VA Folk-Speech* 398, Snaps. . . Thin, round and brittle ginger-cakes. [**1944** *AmSp* 19.120 **NEng,** The *DAE* gives several meanings for *snap,* but fails to give it as short for *gingersnap.* This use is not only familiar in conversation and in the literary reproduction of conversation, but may be found in cookbooks, some of which print 'ginger snaps' with a space. . . A recent newspaper prints a receipt for 'chocolate snaps.'] **2001** *Star–Herald* (Scottsbluff NE) 7 June sec A 4/5, [Syndicated column:] Today, cumin is among the top 10 selling spices in America. So is ginger—a spice hitherto confined to snaps.

4 =eelsnap.

1913 *DN* 4.57 **seMA,** Snap. . . An "eel-snap."

snap adv Cf **smack adv 2**

All the way.

1965 *DARE* (Qu. LL26a, *. . 'All the way': "He drove* _____ *to the end of the road.")* Inf **MS**56, Clean, snap, plumb.

snap and catch ('em) See **snap n 2**

snap and wink 'em See **wink**

snap bean n Also *snap (pea)* **scattered, but chiefly Sth, S Midl** See Map Cf **break bean, green ~, string ~**

A cultivated bean (*Phaseolus vulgaris*) that is grown for its edible pod; the edible pod of such a bean.

1770 in 1937 *VA Mag. Hist. & Biog.* 45.156, A Breast of Veal for Dinner Snap Beans & gooseberry tart. **1826** (1924) Randolph *Treatise Gardening* 6 **VA,** French Beans and snaps are the same. **1841** *Daily Picayune* (New Orleans LA) 4 May 2/1, What Kentuckian would believe that *porc fumé aux haricôts verts à la Kentucky* in French, was plain *bacon and snaps* in English? **1842** Kirkland *Forest Life* 2.165 **MI,** I must tell my reader what I did not always know myself, that "snaps" are young green beans. **1899** (1912) Green *VA Folk-Speech* 398, Snaps. . . String-beans. **1906** *DN* 3.157 **nwAR,** Snap-bean. . . String-bean; a green beanpod which is broken into short lengths before being boiled for eating. **1909** *DN* 3.372 **eAL, wGA,** Snap-bean. **1949** Kurath *Word Geog.* 73, Three terms for string beans are current over large areas: *string beans* north of the Potomac, *snap beans* south of it, and *green-beans* in the West Midland. . . *Snap beans* is the regular term in most of Virginia and in the adjoining parts of North Carolina east of the Blue Ridge. It competes with the Midland *green-beans* in westernmost Virginia and in western North Carolina and South Carolina, and with *string beans* on the Northern Neck of Virginia and on the Carolina coast. **1962** Atwood *Vocab. TX* 59, The usual terms for fresh beans in the pod are *snap beans* (or *snaps*) (52[% of 273 infs]), *green beans* (36), and *string beans* (30). *Snap beans,* a Coastal Southern usage, is strongly favored in Louisiana, and it extends to all parts of Texas. . . It is becoming less common. **1965–70** *DARE* (Qu. I14, *Kinds of beans that you eat in the pod before they're dry*) 205 Infs, **scattered, but chiefly Sth, S Midl,** Snap beans; 16 Infs, **VA, SC, NC,** Snaps; **IA**30, **LA**12, Snap beans—old-fashioned; **KY**17, Green snap beans; **MI**68, Snap beans—alternate form for string beans; you don't often hear that term; **SC**4, Snap beans, string beans—snap beans is more common; **VA**42, Snap beans—older term; move-in-ers say string beans; **GA**11, **MS**72, **SC**62, Snap peas; (Qu. I15, *Some of the beans that you eat in the pod have yellow pods; you call these* _____) 10 Infs, **scattered,** Yellow snap bean(s); **LA**9, **MO**13, **NM**2, **TX**89, Snap beans; **FL**15, **VA**46, Yellow snaps; **MS**87, Bunch snap beans; **LA**20, Dry snap beans; (Qu. I20, *. . Kinds of beans*) 13 Infs, **scattered,** Snap beans; **PA**210, Green snap beans; **TN**52, Foot-long snap beans; **VA**35, Cornfield snaps; (Qu. H49, *Dishes made by boiling potatoes with other foods*) Inf **GA**17, White potatoes in snap beans and garden peas and add soup; **LA**16, Some people put 'em on top of their snap beans; **VA**35, Potatoes and snap beans; (Qu. H50, *Dishes made with beans, peas, or corn*) Inf **NC**31, Snap beans; **LA**11, Cook snap beans with dry salt meat; (Qu. I16, *The large flat beans that are not eaten in the pod*) Inf **GA**17, Snap beans; (Qu. I18, *The smaller beans that are white when they are dry*) Inf **GA**46, Snap beans; (Qu. L34, . . *Most important crops grown around here*) Infs **NJ**20, **NC**80, Snap bean. **1986** Pederson *LAGS Concordance* **Gulf Region,** 472 infs, Snap bean(s); 17 infs, Snap(s); 1 inf, Snap bean—green bean eaten in pod, general name; 1 inf, Snap beans—because you snap them; 1 inf, We say snap beans, but they're pole beans; 1 inf, Green beans and snap beans—green are shelled; 1 inf, Snap beans about the onliest thing we eat and don't shell them, ain't it? **2006** *DARE* File—Internet **GA,** Mountaineer ½ Runner Bush Bean—An early half runner used by home gardeners for snap beans when young and shell beans at late maturity.

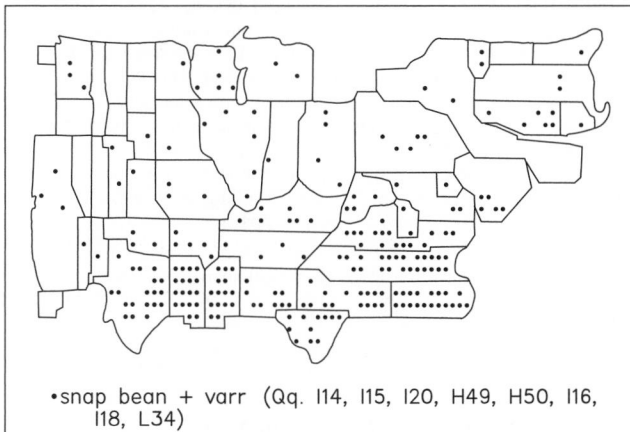

•snap bean + varr (Qq. I14, I15, I20, H49, H50, I16, I18, L34)

snap beetle   See **snap bug**

snapberry n

A **coralberry 1** (here: *Symphoricarpos orbiculatus*).

1900 Lyons *Plant Names* 361, *S[ymphoricarpos] Symphoricarpos*. . . New Jersey to Texas and Dakota. . . Snap-berry [etc]. **1960** Vines *Trees SW* 948, Indian-currant Snowberry. . . It is also known under the vernacular names of Coralberry, Snapberry [etc.].

snap bone n   Cf **breakbone**

The wishbone.

1966 *DARE* (Qu. K74, *A bone from the breast of a chicken, shaped like a horseshoe*) Inf **GA**16, Snap bone.

snap bug n   Also *snap beetle, snapjack bug, snapping beetle,* ~ *bug,* ~ *jack*   [See quot c1930]   Cf **jack snapper**

A **click beetle** of the family Elateridae.

1702 Petiver *Gazophylacii Naturae* 16, The Velvet-eyed Virginia Snap-Beetle. **1832** Cuvier *Animal Kingdom* (transl. McMurtrie) 373, North America is extremely rich in this genus. The Insect is usually called a *Snap-bug.* [*DARE* Ed: This appears to be an addition by the translator.] **1843** (1973) Porter *Big Bear AR* 91 **NC,** You have seed one of them Snapjack bugs. **1865** IL State Ag. Soc. *Trans. for 1861–64* 5.416, There is scarcely an individual, child or adult, to be found who is unacquainted with the "Spring-beetles," or as they are often termed, "Jumping-Jacks," "Snapping-Jacks," "Click-beetles," etc. **1869** U.S. Dept. Ag. *Rept. of Secy. for 1868* 93, These insects [=Elateridae] are known . . in America as "snapping beetles," and erroneously "snapping bugs." **1905** Kellogg *Amer. Insects* 267, Click-beetle—snapping-bugs and skipjacks are other common names for them. **1913** (1980) Hardy *OH Schoolmistress* 73, Another insect playfellow was a large spring-beetle "snapping bug" (afterwards known as the Eyed Elater). **c1930** Brown *Amer. Folkl. Insect Lore* 5, Snap or spring beetles (also called click-beetles) were insect acrobats. Children held them between the thumb and forefingers to hear them "click," or placed them on their backs to see them exert their power of leaping. **1965–70** *DARE* (Qu. R30, . . *Kinds of beetles;* not asked in early QRs) Inf **IA**6, Snap beetle; **CT**37, **IN**17, **OH**22, Snapping beetle; **SC**46, Snapping beetle—put your finger on him and he snaps a joint; **AR**56, **MA**15, **VA**79, Snapping bug; **LA**15, Snapping bug—grayish, about a inch long; **VA**15, Snapping bug—click beetle; (Qu. R5) Inf **CA**136, Snap bug; (Qu. R8, . . *Kinds of creatures that make a clicking or shrilling or chirping kind of sound*) Inf **VA**2, Snap bug.

snap cotton   See **snap** v **2b**

snapdragon n

1 Std: a plant of the genus *Antirrhinum,* usu the cultivated *A. majus.* For other names of *A. majus* see **bulldog 4, dog's mouth, dragon's-mouth 2, lion's-mouth 1, rabbit B3, rabbit's-mouth**

2 A **toadflax 1,** usu **butter-and-eggs 1.**   [*OED2* 1753 →]

1814 Bigelow *Florula Bostoniensis* 151 **MA,** Toad flax. . . The mouth . . gapes open upon lateral pressure, a character which has given the genus the name of *Snap dragon.* **1843** Torrey *Flora NY* 2.32, Common *Toad-flax.* . . It is sometimes called *Snapdragon,* and *Continental-weed.* **1895** U.S. Dept. Ag. *Farmers' Bulletin* 28.29, Snapdragon. . . *Linaria vulgaris* . . New England to Wisconsin. **1936** Winter *Plants NE* 128, [*Linaria*] *linaria.* . . Butter-and-eggs. Wild Flax. Snap-dragon. . . Common locally in eastern Nebr. **2003** *Anchorage Daily News* (AK) 10 July sec D 2 (Internet), Almost every garden in this area has butter-and-eggs . . on display in early August. It is hard not to like these yellow snapdragon wildflowers. As you may have noticed in last week's cover story, they are an introduced and noxious weed.

3 =**jewelweed 1.**   esp **NEng**

1857 Parton *Fresh Leaves* 189 **ME,** Mrs. Quip, with her snap-dragon, touch-me-not-manners, . . was such a contrast to her dear grandmother, with her . . gentle ways. **1892** *Jrl. Amer. Folkl.* 5.93 **NH,** *Impatiens fulva,* snap-dragon. **1898** *Ibid* 11.224 **ME,** *Impatiens fulva* . . snap-weed, snap-dragon, South Berwick. **1940** Clute *Amer. Plant Names* 130, [*Impatiens*] *biflora.* . . snapweed, snapdragon [etc.].

snapdragon vine n

A chiefly Southwestern perennial plant *(Maurandella antirrhiniflora)* that resembles the **snapdragon 1.**   Also called **twist-leaf vine**

1915 (1926) Armstrong–Thornber *Western Wild Flowers* 466 **AZ,** Snap-dragon Vine . . may be found growing in the bottom of the Grand Canyon, near the river. **1951** *PADS* 15.40 **TX,** *Antirrhinum maurandioides* [=*Maurandella antirrhiniflora*]. . . climbing snapdragon; snapdragon vine. **2003** *DARE* File—Internet, Snapdragon Vine. . . native mixed in with shrubs in the southern deserts.

snap-eye n   [**snap** v **3**]

See quot 1929.

1855 Howe *Life & Death* 494 **ME** (as of 1799), I . . helped myself to bread, cheese, and other eatables, not forgetting a glass of *'snap-eye.'* **1929** *AmSp* 5.129 **ME,** "Snap-eye" was either a condiment as strong "pepper-sauce" or something alcoholic.

snapjack bug   See **snap bug**

snap mackerel n   See **snapping mackerel**

snap mackerel v phr   [**mackerel snapper**]

To observe the Catholic tradition of eating fish on Friday.

1968 Bradford *Red Sky* 95 **AL,** Lacey is still snapping mackerel and she's going to be the biggest thing in the Church maybe Pope. **1997** *Washington Post* (DC) 7 Dec sec C 3 (Internet) **NY,** A Catholic snapping mackerel on Friday may be ready to answer such tough questions as, "Why are you doing this? What do you believe?" **2005** in 2006 *DARE* File—Internet **CO,** I'll continue regarding Padre Pio as my spiritual father, that is, when I'm not busy snapping mackerel and worshipping the pope.

snap out   See **clap in, clap out**

snap party   See **snap** n **2**

snap pea   See **snap bean**

snapped corn   See **snap** v **2a**

snapped cotton   See **snap** v **2b**

snapper n

1 Std: a fish of the family Lutjanidae. For other names of var spp see **black snapper 1, dog** ~**, gray** ~**, gunmouth** ~**, kalikali, mahogany snapper, mangrove** ~**, muttonfish 1, opakapaka, red snapper 1, red-tailed** ~**, schoolmaster, spot snapper, uku, ula-ula, yellowtail 8**

2 also *snapper turtle, snappy* ~: =**snapping turtle 1.** See also **snapper soup**

1792 (1849) Darlington *Mem. John Bartram* 474, Of these [=tortoises] I have gathered the shells, and would be exceeding glad to get some more. I have the Snapper, Land Turtle or *Carolina*, L., . . dotted, musk [etc]. **1807** (1935) Janson *Stranger in Amer.* 318 **NC, SC,** The swamps produce a variety of what may be denominated land turtle. The natives call them loggerheads, tarapins, snappers, and haw[k]sbills. **1858** *Atlantic Mth.* Jan 328, "Chelydra Serpentina,"—"snapper" or "snappin' turtle," in the vernacular. **1892** IN Dept. Geol. & Nat. Resources *Rept. for 1891* 557, Chelydra serpentina. . . *Snapper; Snapping Turtle.* **1928** Pope–Dickinson *Amphibians* 74, *Macrochelys temminckii.* . . Other common names are Mississippi or Loggerhead Snapper. **1938** FWP *Ocean Highway* xxiv **NJ,** Lowlands of south Jersey abound with snapping turtles, popularly known as snappers. **1965–70** *DARE* (Qu. P24, . . *Kinds of turtles*) 107 Infs, **chiefly Gt Lakes, N Midl, NEast,** Snapper; 12 Infs, **scattered,** Snapper turtle; (Qu. H36, *Kinds of soup*) Infs **NJ**15, 21, 32, 40, Snapper soup; (Qu. H45, *Dishes made with meat, fish, or poultry that everybody around here would know, but that people in other places might not*) Inf **NJ**15, Snapper (snapping turtle) soup; **NJ**32, Snapper soup; (Qu. Y21, *To move about slowly and without energy*) Inf **NJ**52, Slow as a snapper. **1967** *DARE* Tape **LA**5, A loggerhead gets a whole lot bigger than a snapper. **1968** McPhee *Pine Barrens* 133 **NJ,** The snappers grabs the ducks by the feet and pulls them right under there. **1986** Pederson *LAGS Concordance* **Gulf Region,** 2 infs, Snapper turtle(s); 1 inf, Common snapper—one type of snapping turtle; 1 inf, Snappy turtle; 1 inf, Snapper turtle = loggerhead turtle.

3 =**rosefish.**

1839 MA Zool. & Bot. Surv. *Fishes Reptiles* 26, *S[ebastes] Norvegicus.* . . *The Norway Haddock.* . . By our fishermen it is known by the names of *"Rosefish," "Hemdurgan,"* and *"Snapper."* **1911** U.S. Bur. Census *Fisheries 1908* 314, Rosefish. . . It is also called "red perch," "redfish," "Norway haddock," "snapper" [etc].

4 also *blue snapper, snapper blue:* A young **bluefish 1.** Cf **snapping mackerel**

1884 Goode *Fisheries U.S.* 1.433 **NEng,** Young Bluefish are in some parts of New England called "Snapping Mackerel" or "Snappers"; about New Bedford "Blue Snappers." **1939** Natl. Geogr. Soc. *Fishes* 84 **NEng,** Bluefish furnish good sport when trolled for from sailboats and the young fishes, known as snappers, are plentiful around the wharfs and piers in New England during the summer where they snap greedily at most any kind of bait. **1965–70** *DARE* (Qu. P2, . . *Kinds of saltwater fish caught around here* . . *good to eat*) Inf **NY**36, Snapper—young bluefish; **NY**40, Snapper—snapper blues; **RI**4, Snapper blues—baby bluefish, about six inches long. **1972** Sparano *Outdoors Encycl.* 378, Bluefish—Common Names . . tailor, snapper, jumbo. **2002** *SouthCoastToday* (New Bedford MA) 16 Aug sec C 5 (Internet), Snapper blues are running along the coast from Wareham to Westport.

5 pl: =**bladder campion.**

1892 *Jrl. Amer. Folkl.* 5.93 **MA,** Silene cucubalus, snappers. Salem, Mass.

6 =**wiggler 1.**

1968 *DARE* (Qu. R14, *Small worm-like things [seen in rain barrels or standing water] that hatch into mosquitoes*) Inf **NY**71, Snappers—because of the twitch they make to move.

7 pl: Teeth; false teeth. *joc*

1923 *Indianapolis Star* (IN) 26 June sec 2 8/4, The friction of constantly brushing wears / The gloss from one's snappers too soon. **1950** *WELS* (Joking names for . . false teeth) 1 Inf, **cWI,** Choppers, snappers. **1951** in 1960 Wentworth–Flexner *Slang* 494, People who think they can tell the age of anything by its teeth are kind of up against it when it comes to fish. Not that some fish are not well stocked with snappers. But teeth don't help. **1965–70** *DARE* (Qu. X13b, *Joking names for false teeth*) 9 Infs, **scattered,** Snappers; (Qu. X13a, . . *Joking names* . . *for teeth*) Infs **IA**30, **IN**13, Snappers; **TN**23, Punkin-snappers. **2001** in 2005 *DARE* File—Internet **NY,** How to get your snappers movie star white.

8 In marble play: =**shooter n 1.**

1916 *Stevens Point Jrl.* (WI) [29 Apr 2]/2 (newspaperarchive.com), When Miss Emily took your pennies for an "aggie" or a "snapper" or a big glass "popper," she did so sternly. **1950** *WELS Suppl.* **neWI,** Snapper—the marble used to knock the others out of the ring. **1967** *DARE* (Qu. EE6a, . . *Different kinds of marbles—the big one that's used to knock others out of the ring*) Infs **MA**27, 52, Snapper(s); (Qu. EE6b, *Small marbles or marbles in general*) Inf **MA**33, Aggies, snappers—a more recent term.

9 See quots.

1936 *AmSp* 11.45 [Soda jerker jargon], *Snappers.* Plate of baked beans. **1975** Gould *ME Lingo* 263, *Snapper*—The magic ingredient in baked beans which causes flatulency. Maine hostesses have been known to assure timid guests that, " . . the snappers have been removed."

snapper blue See **snapper 4**

snapper soup n   *chiefly* NJ, ePA

A soup made with **snapper 2.**

1859 *Compiler* (Gettysburg PA) 20 June 1/6, He had heard of snappers, snapper soup, and other kind of "snaps," but he had never seen more than the shell of an original inhabitant of the marshy fens of the silvery Delaware. **1938** FWP *U.S. One* xxii **NJ,** *Snapper Soup:* ground snapper, boiled slowly in salt water; crab meat, green peppers, thyme, parsley, small cubes of Jersey red-skin potatoes, garlic, salt, and red pepper. . . Lowlands of south Jersey abound with snapping turtles, popularly known as snappers. **1968** *DARE* (Qu. H36, *Kinds of soup*) Infs **NJ**21, 32, 40, Snapper soup; **NJ**15, Snapper soup—thinner than stew; (Qu. H45, *Dishes made with meat, fish, or poultry that everybody around here would know, but that people in other places might not*) Infs **NJ**15, Snapper (snapping turtle) soup; **NJ**32, Snapper soup. **1968** *Burlington Co. Herald* (Mount Holly NJ) 8 Aug sec A 5/5, Mr. and Mrs. Earl Braddock entertained members of the family and friends for their annual snapper soup dinner on July 28. **1987** *Daily Intelligencer* (Doylestown PA) 13 Feb 66/3, Ask anyone from Philadelphia to name four different foods the city is famous for, and they might [sic] answer with snapper soup, soft pretzels, cheese steak sandwiches and scrapple. **2006** *DARE* File—Internet **Philadelphia PA,** [Restaurant review:] Other top sellers: jumbo crab cake, old-fashioned snapper soup.

snapper turtle See **snapper 2**

snapping See **snap** v 2a, b

snapping beetle (or bug) See **snap bug**

snapping hazel n   Also *snapping hazelnut, snappy hazel* [Because the seed capsule snaps open and forcefully ejects the seeds]

A **witch hazel** (here: *Hamamelis virginiana*).

1828 Rafinesque *Med. Flora* 1.227, Hamamelis virginica. . . Vulgar Names—Witch hazel, Snapping hazelnut [etc]. **1876** Hobbs *Bot. Hdbk.* 108, Snapping hazel, Witch hazel, Hamamelis Virginica. **1897** Sudworth *Arborescent Flora* 205, Witch Hazel. . . Snapping Hazel . . Lit[erature] of domestic medicine. **1933** Small *Manual SE Flora* 600, *H[amamelis] virginiana.* . . Snappy-hazel. **1979** Erichsen-Brown *Med. N. Amer. Plants* 177, Witch Hazel. . . Common names. Spotted-alder, snapping hazel [etc].

snapping jack See **snap bug**

snapping mackerel n   Also *snap mackerel*   Cf **snapper 4**

A young **bluefish 1.**

1842 DeKay *Zool. NY* 4.131, From the avidity with which they seize even an unbaited hook, they [=young bluefish] have received at that age the name of *Snapping Mackerel.* **1873** in 1878 Smithsonian Inst. *Misc. Coll.* 14.2.29, Blue-fish. . . white-fish and snap-mackerel (young). **1884** [see **snapper 4**]. **1903** NY State Museum & Sci. Serv. *Bulletin* 60.446, Some of the many names applied to this widely distributed fish are . . snapping mackerel (New England and New Jersey) [etc]. **1968** *DARE* FW Addit **DE,** Snapping mackerel—old-fashioned for bluefish. **1975** Evanoff *Catch More Fish* 204, The bluefish is also called the skipjack, fat back, snapping mackerel [etc].

snapping turtle n

1 Std: either a freshwater turtle (*Chelydra serpentina* and subspp) common throughout the US east of the Rockies or a large, voracious freshwater turtle *(Macroclemys temminckii)* of the Gulf States and Mississippi Valley.   For other names see **alligator cooter, ~ snapper, ~ terrapin, ~ turtle 1, 2, caouane, hardnose turtle, land ~, loggerhead 5b, mossback 1, mud turtle 2a, snapper 2, snap turtle, swamp turtle 1, torup**

2 A **witch hazel** (here: *Hamamelis virginiana*).   Cf **snapping hazel**

1940 Clute *Amer. Plant Names* 260, Hamamelis virginiana. Spotted alder, striped alder, tobacco-weed, snapping-turtle.

3 See quots.   Cf **squeezer**

1920 Hunter *Trail Drivers TX* 297, An arrangement for holding the cattle while they are being branded is called a "squeezer" or "snappin' turtle." **1941** Writers' Program *Guide WY* 465, *Snappin' turtle*—A chute for branding.

snapping up   See **snap up**

snappy hazel   See **snapping hazel**

snappy turtle   See **snapper 2**

snaps n

An **owl's clover** (here: *Orthocarpus erianthus*).

1898 *Jrl. Amer. Folkl.* 11.276 **CA,** *Orthocarpus versicolor* [=*O. erianthus*] . . snaps, San Francisco.

snap social   See **snap** n **2**

snap-the-whip n   **chiefly NEast**   See Map   Cf **pop-the-whip**

The game of crack-the-whip; hence v phr *snap the whip* to play the game.

1845 Judd *Margaret* 199 **NEng,** The boys betaking themselves to their several diversions, snapping-the-whip, skinning-the-cat, racing round the Meeting-house, or what not, she found herself engaged with a group of girls. **1852** (1908) Richards *Diary* 14 **NY,** We played snap the whip at recess to-day and I was on the end and was snapped off against the fence. **1890** Howells *Boy's Town* 70 **OH,** You had been beguiled, as a little boy, into being the last in the game of snap-the-whip. **1896** *DN* 1.424 **CT, MA, NY, OH,** *Snap the whip:* a boys' game in which a line of boys with hands joined run sharply and one end of the line suddenly stops, the other going round it in a circle. **1899** Garland *Boy Life* 28 **nwIA** (as of c1870s), They were forced to be content with "dare-gool," "snap the whip," and "pom-pom pull away." **1910** *DN* 3.449 **cwNY,** *Snap the whip.* . . The name of a game. **1944** Holton *Yankees Were Like This* 115 **Cape Cod MA** (as of c1890), Sometimes the big girls drove them off and played snap-the-whip. **1946** *PADS* 6.27 **eNC,** *Snap the whip.* . . To rotate a line of children horizontally and "snap off" (loose the hands of) the child on the end. ((In s. Va.: *to crack the whip.*)) Pamlico. Common among boys. **1947** *PADS* 8.23 **cKY,** *Snap the whip:* Usually *crack the whip.* **1957** *Sat. Eve. Post Letters* **cCT, nwCT, swMA,** Snap the whip. **1965–70** *DARE* (Qu. EE27, *Games played on the ice*) 39 Infs, **chiefly NEast,** Snap-the-whip; **IA**32, Snap-the-whip—all kids in line holding hands; first skater goes fast, tries to get skater on end to fall down; **MA**14, Crack-the-whip or snap-the-whip—everyone skates around in a big circle, then the last person would stop suddenly and snap the others; **MA**29, Snap-the-whip—children hold hands and skate quickly, the one on the end stops quickly, snapping the others; **MA**52, Snap-the-whip—line of skaters, then you get going, stop short, and snap them; **NH**11, Snap-the-whip—make long line, skating, and go around sharp corner, snapping off end; **NY**42, Snap-the-whip—a line of kids, they try to snap the last one off; **NY**78, Snap-the-whip—line of people whipping around; person on end might break loose; (Qu. EE1, . . *Games . . children play . . in which they form a ring, and either sing or recite a rhyme*) Inf **ME**5, Snap-the-whip; (Qu. EE33, . . *Outdoor games . . that children play*) Infs **CA**212, **CT**5, **MA**14, 42, 205, **WA**20, Snap-the-whip; **NY**68, Snap-the-whip—take hold of hands and then run; then the one in front, he'd stop and swing the others around. **2001** in 2006 *DARE* File—Internet **Philadelphia PA,** [Skating rink rules:] Games such as Snap the Whip or any form of tag cannot be played.

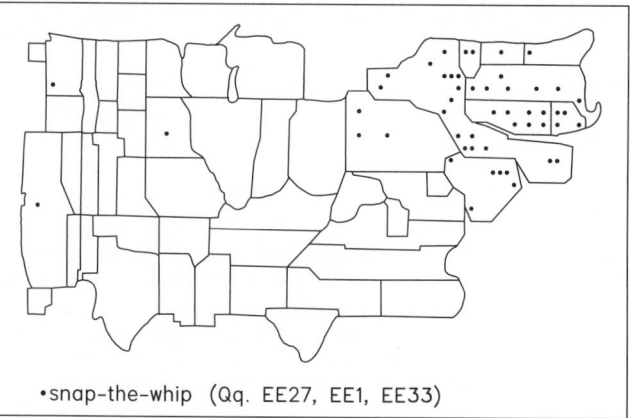

•snap-the-whip (Qq. EE27, EE1, EE33)

snap turtle n

=**snapping turtle 1**; also fig.

1817 Ferguson *Abaddon's Steam Engine* 41, One of your keen-tongued great men . . would have . . shut their snap turtle eyes and lips upon him. **1857** Hopkins *Ella Lincoln* 168 **IL,** I may not always have modified the truth sufficiently to suit all the crabs and snap-turtles living in those western sloughs. **1901** Lounsberry *S. Wild Flowers* 272, Turtle-heads are single flowers which grow at the ends of the stems. . . They look like snap turtles. **1967–69** *DARE* (Qu. P24, . . *Kinds of turtles*) Infs **MI**93, **NY**24, **RI**1, Snap turtle. **2003** *South Bend Tribune* (IN) 1 May sec D 1 (Internet), At the wildlife station, students were shown a snap turtle and frog.

snap up v phr

To respond sharply or critically to (one); hence n *snapping up* a scolding.

1850 (1852) Warner *Wide World* 2.85 **NY,** They with one accord sat longer at meals; more talking and laughing went on; nobody felt afraid of being snapped up. **1862** *Atlantic Mth.* 9.553 **MA,** "My Indian corn, though," began Halicarnassus; but I snapped him up before he was fairly under way. I had no idea of travelling in that direction. **1876** *Harper's New Mth. Mag.* 52.580 **MA,** Temper enough, the Lord knows, but I *couldn't* have snapped him up, my dear, as he did me. **1883** *Atlantic Mth.* 51.483 **ME,** "I do' know 's I 'm going to be good for anything this winter," he whined dolefully; and Miss Dunn snapped him up with exceeding promptness:—"Folks would be astonished if you was!" [**1950** *WELS* (Somebody who talks back or gives rude answers: "She is certainly _____." "Did you ever see such a _____.") 1 Inf, **cnWI,** A snap-up.] **1966–70** *DARE* (Qu. II27, *If somebody gives you a very sharp scolding* . . "I certainly got a _____ for that.") Inf **TX**98, I got snapped up; **GA**7, Blessing out, snapping up.

snapweed n   [See quot 1848; *OED2* 1823 →]

=**jewelweed 1.**

1826 Darlington *Florula Cestrica* 29 **sePA,** *I[mpatiens] pallida.* . . *Vulgò*—Snap-weed. Touch-me-not. **1848** Gray *Manual of Botany* 76, *Impatiens* [spp]. . . Name from the sudden bursting of the pods when touched, whence also the popular appellations *Touch-me-not*, or *Snap-weed.* **1898** *Jrl. Amer. Folkl.* 11.224 **ME,** *Impatiens fulva* . . snap-weed, snap-dragon, South Berwick. **1948** Stevens *KS Wild Flowers* 94, Pale Snapweed (Touch-me-not). **1953** Greene–Blomquist *Flowers South* 63, Two native species [of *Impatiens*] are found in the South: spotted-snapweed (*I. capensis*) . . and pale touch-me-not (*I. pallida*). **1961** Douglas *My Wilderness* 184 **MD,** There were occasional bushes of the pale snapweed still showing yellow flowers. **1970** Campbell et al. *Gt. Smoky Wildflowers* 54, *Impatiens pallida.* . . Known also as *pale jewel weed* and *snapweed.* . . When the mature pods are touched, the fruits "explode," hence "touch-me-not." **1977** in 1981 *NC Folkl. Jrl.* 29.55, I became a firm believer in jewelweed [as a remedy for poison oak], or snapweed, as I occasionally hear it called in the Appalachians.

snarl n   Also sp *snarle*   Cf **snurl** n

A knot or area of irregular grain in wood; hence adj *snarly.*

a1890 *Tribune Book of Sports* 12 (*Century Dict.*), Let Italian or Spanish yew be the wood, clear of knots, snarls, and cracks. **1899** (1912) Green *VA Folk-Speech* 398, *Snarl.* . . Snarle. A knot in wood. . . *Snarly.* . . Knotty. **2006** *DARE* File—Internet **cNY,** Oh I hate splitting maple! That snarly ole stuff takes the steam right out of ya.

snat   See **snath**

snatch v

=**snap** v **3.**

1968 *DARE* (Qu. X24, *When a person opens and closes his eyes quickly, he _____*) Inf **MO**4, Snatches 'em.

snatch-and-grab n   Also *snatch grabs*

A game played as a practical joke; see quots.

1957 *Sat. Eve. Post Letters*, *Snatch grabs* or *snatch and grab:* Boys play it on new members of neighborhood. Everyone donates an article to a sack under pretense that everyone will grab for one of the items in exchange. Bag is hidden, and under paper is placed a pan of mud. All but new boys know that mud and not treasures are under the paper. At signal to grab, new boy gets hands dirty. **1967** *DARE* (Qu. EE3, *Games in which you hide an object and then look for it*) Inf **AR**47, Snatch-and-grab—hide stuff under a hat; everybody keeps what they grab, then put the hat over soft shit.

snatch burr n **KY** Cf **snatchweed**

A burr that clings to clothing.

1919 *DN* 5.35 **KY**, *Snatch-burr.* . . A bothersome, flat, triangular shaped little burr. Knott Co. "Beggar lice" in Oklahoma. **1940** (1978) Still *River of Earth* 43 **KY**, "I put a handful of snatchburs behind the saddle," she said. **1967–69** *DARE* (Qu. S15, . . *Weed seeds that cling to clothing*) Inf **KY**34, Snatch burrs [FW illustr: drawing of **beggar ticks 1**]; **KY**40, Snatch burrs—round, sticky all over; **KY**43, Snatch burrs—small and flat [FW illustr: triangular seed]; **KY**47, Snatch burrs. **1982** Slone *How We Talked* 116 **eKY** (as of c1950), Snatch burrs.

snatched adj **esp S Midl**

In a hurry.

1903 *DN* 2.330 **seMO**, *Snatched.* . . Hurried. 'Don't be snatched!' Meaning 'do not hurry away.' **1916** *DN* 4.343 **cnMD**, *Snatched, to be.* . . To be in a hurry. "Don't be snatched." **1927** *AmSp* 2.364 **cwWV**, *Snatched* . . in a hurry. "Don't get snatched. There's plenty of time." **1968** *DARE* (Qu. A21, *When someone is in too much of a hurry* . . *"Now just slow down! Don't _____."*) Inf **IN**30, Get snatched. **1984** Woods *WV Was Good* 226, You hadn't oughta be so snatched. (You shouldn't get in a hurry.)

snatch grabs See **snatch-and-grab**

snatching adj Cf *fetching*

Attractive; charming.

1909 *DN* 3.372 **eAL, wGA**, *Snatchin(g).* . . Fine, charming. **1930** *DN* 6.85 **eSC**, Expressions based on more or less buried figures of speech. . . *snatching*, charming.

snatch row n **esp Gulf States**

See quots.

1988 McKenzie *Avinger TX* 26 **neTX**, A method referred to as "snatch row picking" was used by the real pros, from time to time. The two expert pickers would designate an extra row between their already assigned ones. **1998** *DARE* File **MS** [Black], I learned another word I had not heard before from a black woman—also from Marks, Mississippi—born in 1929, dropped out of high school but got a GED. *Snatch row*—in picking cotton when two people have a row of cotton between them from which they both pick, they call it a *snatch row*. **2003** in 2006 *DARE* File—Internet **neAR** (as of 1947), Polly and I were picking a row each and a "snatch row" between us. That is, the two of us picked three rows as we went along. The one having her row ahead would pick the snatch row to keep all three rows even. **2005** *News-Star* (Monroe LA) 10 July (Internet) **neLA** [Black], I'd get one row and Ben would get another one row over. The row in the middle was what we called the 'snatch row', where we'd both pick from.

snatch team n

A team of draft animals used to move loads for short distances or to supplement a regular team temporarily.

1888 *Sioux Valley News* (Correctionville IA) [26 Apr 2]/3 (newspaperarchive.com), [Advt:] Wanted! Four men and teams to work on Cornell's dam. . . Five teams with the snatch team. **1893** *Democratic Std.* (Coshocton OH) 4 Aug 1/3, A number of excavators, requiring two horses and a snatch-team of three more while being filled are in readiness. **1902** *Galveston Daily News* (TX) 11 Oct 12/5, A snatch team, consisting of a couple of mules hitched to an iron chain and a hook to clasp the logs, could clean up the beach in a week's time. **1931** *AmSp* 6.336 [Circus and carnival slang], *Snatch-team.* . . "They took a snatch-team down and hauled the cage out." **1948** *Traverse City Rec.-Eagle* (MI) 25 May 1/5, All the kids and oldsters will again have an opportunity to watch the "snatch" teams load and unload the [circus] wagons and then hang around the lot while the canvas goes up. **1966** *DARE* FW Addit **SC**, Snatch team for heavy loads in rough places, logging, etc. **1967** *DARE* (Qu. K32b) Inf **AL**33, Snatch team—an extra team. **1986** Pederson *LAGS Concordance*, 1 inf, **ceAL**, Snatch team—as many as six animals; on hills.

snatch-trap n

A type of deadfall; see quot.

1968 *DARE* FW Addit **DE**, *Snatch-trap*—heavy board supported by a stick about 6–8 inches long. You put feed under the board and when birds come, snatch the stick out with a string.

snatch up v phr Cf **drag up 1, jerk** v[1] **C5**

To rear (a child) with little attention to manners or civility.

1966–68 *DARE* (Qu. Z17, *To take care of or bring up a child: "All her children were _____ [on the farm]."*) Inf **AL**6A, Snatched up—half

brought up, fetched up; old, Negro; (Qu. II21, *When somebody behaves unpleasantly or without manners: "The way he behaves, you'd think he was _____."*) Infs **MD**2, **SC**24, 39, Snatched up. **1970** *Thompson Coll.* **cnAL** (as of 1920s), [Excuse for children's bad manners:] The reason ain't they been raised wrong, cause they jus been snatched up.

snatchweed n

A **cleavers** (here: *Galium aparine*).

1900 Lyons *Plant Names* 167, *G[alium] Aparine.* . . Cleavers . . Snatch-weed [etc].

snath n Also **chiefly NEast** *snathe, sne(a)th, sneathe;* rarely *snat, snythe* Note: The plural *snathes* sometimes corresponds to the singular *snath;* see quot 1851. [*snathe* and *sneath* (as well as *snath,* which is std in the US) are Engl dial varr of **snead;** cf *OED2* (at *snath*), *EDD* (at *snead*), and 1994 Upton et al. *Surv. Engl. Dial.*] Std sense, var forms.

1645 in 1916 MA (Colony) Probate Court (Essex Co.) *Records* 1.45, A sieth & a sneath. **1698** in 1936 *DN* 6.525 **RI**, A stubb sithe with sneaths, nebbs & Rings. **1817** Webster *Letter* 15, [They] never have had occasion to mention . . the *snathe* of a scythe. **1848** in 2002 *DARE* File—Internet **ceMO**, 1 Scyth & Sneath. **1850** *Scientific Amer.* 6.46 **ceNY**, Each [rod of a grain cradle] may be turned . . in the direction desired, and when separated from the sneath, each wire is placed in the position as represented. **1851** Norton *Notes* 52 **CT**, The scythes and snathes that are used in this country by far excel anything that I have ever seen in England or Scotland. [*Ibid* 62, Our curved snath is so adapted to its work, that the cradler can stand almost upright.] **1856** MA Secy. of State *Statist. Info.* 193, Scythe Snathe Manufactories, 1; Scythe Snathes m'd., 8,000. **1874** Washburn *Notes Livermore ME* 50, Henry Aldrich . . was engaged in the manufacture of scythe sneaths. **1894** *DN* 1.333 **NJ**, *Sneathe:* snath of a scythe. **1899** (1912) Green *VA Folk-Speech* 399, *Snathe.* . . The curved handle of a scythe. **1924** in 2002 *DARE* File—Internet **cwIL**, 1 Scythe and Snathe. **1966–67** *DARE* (Qu. L28, *Tools used in the past for cutting grain*) Inf **ME**5, Scythe—often called scythe and sneth [sneθ]; [**MA**6, **MI**47, **NY**92, (Scythe and) snath [snæθ];] (Qu. L35, *Hand tools used for cutting underbrush*) Inf **TN**7, Briar snythe [sna:ð]; (Qu. L37, *A hand tool used for cutting weeds and grass*) Inf **ME**5, Clipping out—to cut corners around fences and stumps with a scythe and sneth after mowing machine has passed by; [**NY**32, 219, Scythe and snath]. **a1975** in 2002 *DARE* File—Internet **ME** (as of 1890s), Father would always buy a new pitchfork, a scythe and sneth and a hand rake. **1984** *MJLF* 10.157 **cnWI**, *Snat.* Snathe.

snawfus n

An imaginary creature; see quots.

1936 *Arcadian Life* Oct 6 **nwAR**, This fabulous creature, the invention of a small boy in Arkansas, was to me the epitome of mystery and adventure. Members of my family habitually dismissed unexplainable circumstances by the remark: "I don't know what it was. It must have been a Snawfus." **1950** *AR Hist. Qrly.* 9.70, The snawfus, according to some backwoods folk, is just an albino deer with certain supernatural powers, puzzling to human beings but not dangerous. Some hillmen say that it can make tremendous leaps into the treetops; others endow it with great feathery wings, claiming that it can "fly through the timber, quiet as a hoot-owl." **2003** *DARE* File—Internet **TX**, You may have heard of a snipe, or a snawfus, a whing-whang or a hoopajuba, but have you heard of the side hill gougers?

snead n Also *sne(e)d;* rarely *snade* [Engl and (esp in form *sned*) Scots dial, ult < OE *snǣd;* cf *OED2, EDD, SND,* 1994 Upton et al. *Surv. Engl. Dial.*] **chiefly Midl** Cf **snath**

The shaft of a scythe.

1821 in 2002 *DARE* File—Internet **csPA**, A sythe & sned—1.25. **1824** *Ibid* **cwNC**, Jacob Burns—a sise & snead—.27½. **c1840** *Ibid* **ceIN**, 1 fire shovel and 1 scythe & snead—.37½. **1852** *Ibid* **ceIN**, Mowing scythe & sned—.60. **1899** (1912) Green *VA Folk-Speech* 399, *Snead.* . . The long, bent handle of a scythe. **1903** *DN* 2.330 **seMO**, *Snead.* . . Snath; the handle of a scythe. **1917** *DN* 4.417 **wNC, KY**, *Sneed.* . . The snath of a scythe. **1927** *AmSp* 2.364 **cwWV**, *Sneed* . . stick for a scythe. "The sneeds are all broken." **1962** Dykeman *Tall Woman* 172 **NC** (as of 1860), In one corner she saw . . a nub for a sneed. **1966** *DARE* Tape **MI**23, He had a cradle . . that was attached to the sy, and that attached right at the end of the snade where the blade, the sy blade, attached. [**1969** *DARE* (Qu. L38, *What do you use* . . *to sharpen* *tools in the field?*) Inf **PA**204, Snead [snid].] **1976** *PA Folklife* Spring 29 **cPA,** A rapid examination of some three hundred salebills in the author's collection issued between 1968 and 1975 provides numerous examples of archaisms, dialectal forms and neologisms. The word *sned* . . is used consistently instead of *snath.* **1986** Pederson *LAGS Concordance,* 1 inf, **neTN,** Sneed = snath. **2001** *DARE* File **eTN,** "Sneed," . . a curved wooden handle which held a cutter blade used to cut high weeds. Often called a scythe or more commonly, a "mowing blade."

sneak v

Std senses, var forms.

1 pres: usu *sneak;* also rarely *snink, snuck.*

1895 *Hamilton Daily Republican* (OH) 8 Apr 1/4 **NYC,** Just keep them dukes up an' snuck back down the street, d' ye hear? **1930** in 1944 *ADD* **CA,** Snuck. Snunk. Reported. Present tense *snink.* **1944** Howard *Walkin' Preacher* 256 **Ozarks,** They seemed oblivious of property rights, believing that "if ye kin snuck hit, ye kin have hit." **1982** *Barrick Coll.* **csPA,** Sneak—[pron. snĭnk]. **2000** in 2002 *DARE* File— Internet **neMA,** The show was sold out. So a friend of ours snucks us in the back. . . I feel bad cuz i missed one of my favorite bands . . and that i also snuck in. **2002** *Times–News* (Burlington NC) 30 Mar (Internet) (as of 1940s), "If I come snucking back,/ Would you still be my darlin'/ Or have I been gone too long?" . . I didn't know Daddy even knew any of the songs we listened to on the radio, but here he was singing one of them, with a little change in the words.

2 past, past pple, ppl adj: usu *sneaked;* also:

a *snu(c)k;* rarely *snook, snunk.* [The origin of these strong forms is obscure. It is possible that they arose from confusion of *sneak* with the Brit dial (weak) verb *snoke* (with many varr, incl *snook*) to sniff, smell; to snoop, sneak. Cf *OED2, SND snoke; EDD snook, snowk, snuck.*] *esp freq among younger speakers*

1879 *Bucks Co. Gaz.* (Bristol PA) 2 Oct [4]/1 (newspaperarchive.com), [From *Cincinnati Inquirer:*] Your boy Aleck got a straw, snuck up behin' a sorrel mule, tickled him on the heels, an'—. **1887** in 1950 *AmSp* 25.38 **New Orleans LA,** Snuck. Sneaked . . 'an' den snuck home.' **1898** *Century Illustr. Mag.* 57.230 **LA** [Black], I war n't gwine to have my fine net snook away no mo' by a passel o' no-'count boys. **1906** *DN* 3.157 **nwAR,** Snuck. . . Did sneak. **1912** *DN* 3.590 **wIN,** Snuck, *pret.* and *pp.* of *sneak.* "When he saw them coming, he snuck up through the thicket." **1916** *DN* 4.281 **NE,** Snuk. . . Occasional preterite of *sneak.* "He got the shivers and snuk out." Usually jocular; sometimes serious. [DN Ed: Also Phila.] **1923** *DN* 5.221 **swMO,** Snuk. . . Sneaked. **1930** [see **1** above]. **1939** Aurand *Quaint Idioms* 27 [PaGer], I *snuck* up to her, and gave her a big hug and kiss. **1940** Faulkner *Hamlet* 35 **MS,** Ab . . had snuck the wagon out the back way. **1942** McAtee *Dial. Grant Co. IN* 59 (as of 1890s), *Snuck* . . past part. of *sneak.* . . (Md., Nebr., Ohio, Pa.) **1944** *PADS* 2.12 **AL, LA, SC, TN,** *Snuck* . . pret. and p p. of *sneak.* . . Low popular. . . Obsolescent in Va., N.C.; often used jocosely by the educated. **1959** *VT Hist.* 27.158 **neVT,** Snuck . . p.p. and past tense of *sneak.* Common. Caledonia. **1965–70** *DARE* (Qu. Y26b, *To walk very quietly: "The children filled their pockets and _____ out the back way."*) [365 Infs, **widespread,** Sneaked;] 171 Infs, **widespread,** Snuck; **AK**1, Snuck off; **CT**8, Snook; (Qu. Y26a, *To walk very quietly)* [Infs **MA**58, **NJ**2, **NY**84, **OH**16, **WI**13, Sneaked]; **AK**1, **OH**89, **WI**33, Snuck (in); (Qu. Y47, *To hide something away for future use: "I know he's got it _____ somewhere."*) Infs **MS**1, **NM**9, Snuck away; **NH**14, [Sneaked it out of sight;] snuck it out of sight. [Of all Infs responding to Qu. Y26b, 11% were young, 25% mid-aged, 64% old; of those giving the response *sneaked,* 7% were young, 23% mid-aged, 70% old; of those giving the response *snuck,* 25% were young, 33% mid-aged, 42% old.] **1973** *DARE* File **swPA** (as of 1920s), No one ever said "sneaked." The word they used was "snuck." **1982** *Barrick Coll.* **csPA,** Snuck—[pron. snŭnk] p.t. of *sneak.* **1986** Pederson *LAGS Concordance,* 3 infs, **cnGA, seTN, ceTX,** Snuck (off). **1998** *Jrl. Engl. Ling.* 26.216 **MW,** Some of the negative responses I collected . . came from teachers of English, though the vast majority of the teachers . . accepted *snuck* with no qualms whatsoever. On the other hand, *sneaked* elicited no negative comments at all; . . even . . my informants who did not accept it as a legitimate preterite could find nothing worse to say than "it sounds awkward" or "it just doesn't sound smooth." *Snuck* may indeed be "well-established, fully standard, and widely used in speech and writing in the U.S.," . . but clearly not in all the same circles as *sneaked.* **2001** *DARE* File **AZ,** One student, who grew up in Phoenix, astonished me by saying that she also has the form [snʊk] . . and that she uses it only in the plural: I [snʌk] but we [snʊk]. I surveyed the class to see if anyone else had heard or used this form, and a student from St. Louis confirmed it, that she heard it in the speech of her teenage son and his friends. *Ibid* **nCA,** I've definitely heard and used "we snook" (rhymes with "look"). . . For some reason, I associate this with my teenage years in the 70's. *Ibid* **MN,** I just remembered that my mother (b. 1906) used "snook" [snʊk] all the time, in Minnesota. . . But my siblings and I only used "snuck." *Ibid* **cwNY,** Growing up in Buffalo in the 1970s and '80s, "I snuck/we snook" was current usage in my cohort, (say, those born 65-75).

b *snooked, snucked.*

1885 *Ft. Wayne Daily Gaz.* (IN) 31 Dec 7/3, [From *Youth's Companion:*] "I don't care," sobbed the owner of the sneaking dog. "I guess your dog snooked first." **1890** *DN* 1.62 **swOH,** Snuck . . trans. and intrans.: to sneak. "He snucked that," "he snucked up to it." **1901** *Century Illustr. Mag.* 61.784 **NY,** Rest on 'em snooked off when the gun hollered. **1967** *DARE* (Qu. Y26b, *To walk very quietly: "The children filled their pockets and _____ out the back way."*) Inf **HI**9, Snucked. **1967** *DARE* Tape **TN**6, Everything gets snucked up there in that old room. **1986** *DARE* File **OK,** Snucked—past tense of sneak. **1986** Pederson *LAGS Concordance,* 1 inf, **nwFL,** Snooked—a child might say [for *swiped*]. **1996** in 2002 *DARE* File—Internet **LA,** Children who had sustained serious injuries at the hands of other children reported being "snooked" or "snuck" (being assaulted by surprise by other offenders whom they did not know well). **2002** *Ibid* **ceMA,** [Sixth-grader's online diary:] She could've snucked it back in when I was done searching and wasn't looking. *Ibid* **FL,** The winner . . quietly snucked in and answered without giggles or what not.

sneak n Rarely *sneak-up* [*OED2* 1862 →] **chiefly NEast** See Map Cf **sneaker 1** **=tennis shoe.**

[**1888** *Brooklyn Daily Eagle* (NY) 16 Sept 6/3, I [=a prison guard] was in the habit of walking through the corridors with sneak (felt) shoes on to see if everything was all right.] **1901** *DN* 2.148 **cNY,** Sneak. . . Shoe with rubber sole and cloth top. **1915–23** in 1944 *ADD* **cNY,** *Sneaks* usual. *Sneakers* not observed. **1965–70** *DARE* (Qu. W8, *Names and nicknames for low canvas-top shoes with rubber soles*) 28 Infs, **chiefly NEast,** Sneaks; **NJ**33, Sneak-ups. **1967** *AmSp* 42.53 **OH** [College slang], Sneaks. Rubber-soled canvas shoes, tennis shoes. **1969** *DARE* Tape **NY**175, We got caught last year out in a storm and we were wet. . . and our sneaks were wet, and it was a mess. **1995** *DARE* File **NJ,** In New Jersey I had to remember to say sneakers or sneaks.

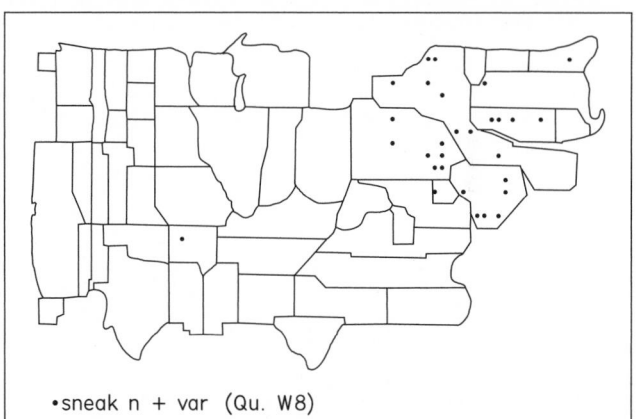

•sneak n + var (Qu. W8)

sneak boat n Also *sneak box (boat)* **chiefly C Atl** Cf **sink boat**

A small, shallow-draft boat designed for stealthily approaching floating waterfowl.

1853 *MD Laws Laws Genl. Assembly* 220, Any person or persons [who] shall use any sink boats, sneak boats or floats . . shall be subject to a fine. **1875** *Fur Fin & Feather* 120, On the Jersey coast no batteries are allowed, but each gunner hiding his little sneak-box boat in the point of meadows, or covering it with sea-weed, and setting out his decoys, awaits the coming of the broad-bill flocks. **1923** *U.S. Dept. Ag. Farmers' Bulletin* 1375.21 **MD,** Sinkbox, sneak boat, blind, pusher. **1940** *Writers' Program Guide MD* 119 **cn,neMD,** The name of Susquehanna Flats is synonymous with good duck hunting. To old-timers it brings to mind sink boats, sneakboxes, swivel guns, 'long tom' and pump guns. **1952** *DE Folkl. Bulletin* 1.10, So I seen 'em comin': the sheriff, an' deputy sheriff, an' ol' man Pete, all three in this lil' sneak boat. **1968–70** *DARE* (Qu. O1, . . *A small rowboat, not big enough to hold more than two people*) Infs **VA**47, **NJ**55, Sneak box; (Qu. O9, . . *Kinds of sailboats*) Inf **NJ**55, Perrine sneak box; (Qu. O10, . . *Kinds of boats*) Inf **PA**155, Sneak boats—9 inches deep. **1968–70** *DARE* Tape **NJ**39, There are boat builders. . They build these gunning boats called sneak boxes; **VA**55, He had a battery and he had that mounted on a sneak boat. **2003** *DARE* File **ceNY** (as of 1960s), We used to call them sneak boxes. It was a low boat that you could lie down in, and it usually had a battery board on the front that you could put brush on. It was for floating or paddling up to a raft of ducks.

sneaker n

1 =**tennis shoe. widespread, but somewhat more freq NEast, N Cent** See Map Cf **sneak** n

1887 *NY Times* (NY) 2 Sept 4/5, It is only the harassed schoolmaster who can fully appreciate the pertinency of the name boys give to tennis shoes—sneakers.—*Boston Journal of Education.* **1889** *Fitchburg Daily Sentinel* (MA) 21 May 2/7, [Advt:] Sneakers—Men's Best Quality Rubber Sole Tennis Shoes . . Only 45 cts. **1909** *Baseball Mag.* Aug 23, He dressed his feet in a pair of rubber-soled, canvas shoes—call 'em "sneakers" now,—and journeyed to Fall River. **1916** Kephart *Camping & Woodcraft* 1.159, Canvas "sneakers" may be used. But beware the rubber soled variety. They are very hot, and will make your feet more tender than ever. **1965–70** *DARE* (Qu. W8, *Names and nicknames for low canvas-top shoes with rubber soles*) 650 Infs, **widespread, but somewhat more freq NEast, N Cent,** Sneakers; [(Qu. W11, *Men's low, rough work shoes*) Infs **CA**112, **MO**37, Sneakers; **PA**244, Eagle Hill sneakers; (Qu. W21, *Soft shoes that people wear only inside the house*) Infs **AR**52, **CO**45, **ME**6, **MN**10, **MO**4, Sneakers;] (Qu. Y26a, *To walk very quietly: "She came _____ to the baby's bed."*) Inf **MN**18, In on her sneakers. **1981** *New Yorker* 19 Jan 53 **swOH** (as of 1941), My suitcases contained . . three pairs of plimsolls (which I was soon to learn to call sneakers). **1986** *AmSp* 61.366, The *Sneaker/Tennis Shoe Boundary*. . . At eastern schools, where every local knows their correct name is *sneakers,* people from the West often find themselves kidded when they talk about putting on their *tennis shoes.* . . I conducted a survey of Princeton University students from different parts of the United States. The result indicates the existence of a heterogloss running from Cleveland east into central Pennsylvania, then, roughly, south to Washington, D.C. The Northeast, including Washington, uses *sneakers;* the rest of the country uses *tennis shoes.* . . In the Northeast. . *tennis shoes* was never considered a synonym. . . Where *tennis shoes* was the first response . . nine informants indicated . . *sneakers* as a synonym, but the remaining fifty-four said they would rarely if ever use the word. When asked if they knew what it meant, their response was either that they didn't know, that it was an eastern word for *tennis shoes,* or that it was a kind of "little kid's *tennis shoe.*" **2004** *NY Times* (NY) 5 Dec sec 6 69 (Internet) **MI,** The day I met her, [she] was wearing a really cool pair of sneakers.

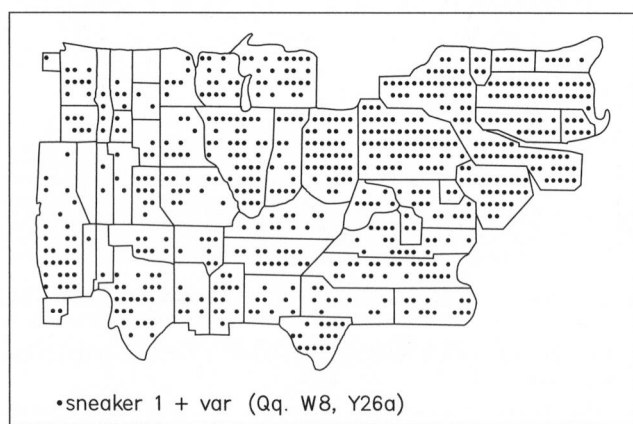

•sneaker 1 + var (Qq. W8, Y26a)

2 =**cheater 1b.**

1967 *DARE* (Qu. X23, . . *Joking words . . for eyeglasses*) Inf **AZ**1, Sneakers.

sneaking See **sneaky**

sneak-up See **sneak** n

sneaky adj Also *sneaking* [PaGer *schnieki(s)ch*] **PaGer area**
Fastidious, particular (about food).
1914 *DN* 4.158 **PA,** *Sneaky.* . . Fussy or finnicky (about eating). **1935**

AmSp 10.171 **PA** [Engl of PA Germans], *Sneaky.* Fastidious, persnickety. 'He is sneaky in his eating.' **1968** *Helen Adolf Festschrift* 38, *Sneaky* (Pennsylvania German *schniekich*) for 'persnickety or dainty in eating.' **1982** *Barrick Coll.* **csPA,** *Sneakin'*—finicky. "He's so sneakin' he ought a have his tongue scraped." **1984** Moelleken *Dialectology* 98 **c,cePA** [English of PA Germans], A number of vocabulary items peculiar to the English of the Pennsylvania Germans occur spontaneously without specific elicitation. Items such as "sneaky" (finicky about food) . . occur across age groups.

sneaky Pete n

1 Any of var inexpensive intoxicating beverages of poor quality, esp cheap wine. **chiefly Atlantic** See Map

1943 *NY Times* (NY) 5 Sept 22, Charles A. Crowley . . of 25 The Bowery . . blamed "sneaky Pete," a potent wine concoction. **1949** *Collier's* 3 Sept 40 **NYC,** A group . . was . . discussing the effects of "sneaky-pete," a generic term for fortified wines. **1952** *Commonwealth* 12 Dec 253 *(DAS),* A pint of forty-cent wine known under the generic title of 'Sneaky Pete.' **1955** *AmSp* 30.88 **SW** [Narcotic argot], *Sneaky Pete.* . . Marijuana mixed in wine. **1958** *Life* 28 Apr 75, All the gang piled into the Ritz Bar and polished off a whole row of 'sneaky pete wine.' **1965–70** *DARE* (Qu. DD27, . . *Nicknames . . for wine*) 18 Infs, **Atlantic,** Sneaky Pete; (Qu. DD21a, *General words . . for any kind of liquor*) Inf **NY**80, Sneaky Pete; (Qu. DD21b, *General words . . for bad liquor*) Inf **DE**1, Sneaky Pete. [15 of 18 total Infs old] **1968** *DARE* Tape **NJ**53, People will only work long enough to get a pint of the sneaky Pete wine. . . That's this poison wine what you buy. Well, it'll make you drunk, so drunk that you'll fall down. **1982** *Barrick Coll.* **csPA,** *Sneaky pete*—cheap wine or other liquor [sic].

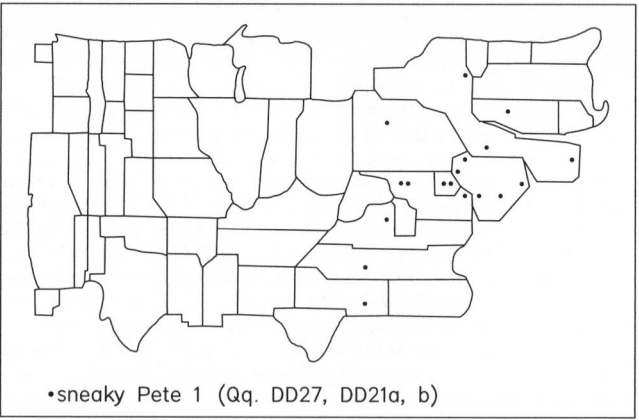

•sneaky Pete 1 (Qq. DD27, DD21a, b)

2 A furtive, underhanded person.

1968 *DARE* (Qu. II33, *To get an advantage over somebody by tricky means: "I don't trust him, he's always trying to _____."*) Inf **PA**74, Do a sneaky Pete. **2005** *DARE* File **Detroit MI** (as of 1950s–60s), "He's a real sneaky Pete." He's always snooping around. I've used this since I was a kid. *Ibid* **cwCA** (as of c1960), He's really a sneaky Pete. Don't trust him for a minute.

sneap v, hence ppl adj *sneaping*
To prowl, sneak.
1854 Riley *Puddleford People* 92 **MI,** She walks out arm-in-arm in broad daylight with her cousin that's been sneaping around here on a visit. **1934** (1943) *W2, Sneap.* . . Local, U.S. To spy; sneak. **1942** (1971) Campbell *Cloud-Walking* 40 **seKY,** "Me, I ain't no sneaping carry-tale," Ishmael said.

sneart See **snert**

sneath(e) See **snath**

sneck n, v [Scots, nEngl dial]
A latch; to latch.
1851 *Scientific Amer.* 6.392, The lock is composed of a vibrating latch or sneck . . to catch on the outside of the wall to retain the blind when it is open. This sneck passes through the blind . . and is retained in its place by metal pieces. **1950** *WELS Suppl.* **seWI,** *Sneck.* . . Close, lock, latch. . . Sneck the door. **1954** *PADS* 21.38 **SC,** *Sneck.* . . A latch or fastening.

sne(e)d See **snead**

sneeder See **schneider**

sneetered ppl adj [Cf *EDD snite* sb. 3 (also *sniter*) "A mean, treacherous person"]

2005 *DARE* File **Louisville KY** (as of c1950), "Sneetered" was common in my speech and those around me for "tricked," "deceived," "done in" (usually by subterfuge).

sneeze n Cf **snort** n

A short interval of time or space.

1938 *Appleton Post-Crescent* (WI) 6 Apr 6/3, Knickerbocker Village . . is located . . just a sneeze from Chinatown. **1967–70** *DARE* (Qu. A14, *. . A very short period of time: "I'll be ready in _____."*) Inf **HI1**, A sneeze; (Qu. MM24, . . *'A short distance': "The river is just a _____ from the house."*) Inf **VA42**, Sneeze. **2001** *St. Louis Post-Dispatch* (MO) 29 Apr sec D 12 (Internet) **NC**, The massive packs of 30 to 35 cars were a sneeze away from mayhem.

sneezeweed n

1 A plant of the genus *Helenium*, esp *H. autumnale*. [Because the powdered plant causes sneezing] For other names of var spp see **bitterweed, dog fennel 2, false sunflower 1, fennel, fever grass, oxeye 2c, sneezewort 2, staggerweed 2, staggerwort, swamp flower, ~ sunflower 1**

1828 Rafinesque *Med. Flora* 1.235, *Helenium autumnale*. . . Vulgar Names—Sneezeweed, Sneezewort [etc]. **1837** Darlington *Flora Cestrica* 487 **sePA**, *H[elenium] autumnale*. . . *Vulgò*—False Sun-Flower. Sneeze-weed. **1901** Lounsberry *S. Wild Flowers* 530, The little sneezeweeds, or false sunflowers . . are readily known because they have their disk flowers raised in rounded heads. . . In a powdered form these plants are used in medicine for the purpose of producing sneezing, a practice of which their common name is an outcome. **1931** Goodrich *Mt. Homespun* 68 **sAppalachians**, She made a note of the fact that "sneezeweed" makes a pretty yellow, but not fast color. **1945** Saxon *Gumbo Ya-Ya* 248 **LA**, When a person couldn't stop hiccoughing, all you had to do was to make him smell sneezeweed. He sure start sneezing then and not hiccough no more. **1960** Williams *Walk Egypt* 215 **GA**, Sneezeweed blew down the highway and clung to car radiators. **1967** *DARE* (Qu. S7, *A kind of daisy, bright yellow with a dark center, that grows along roadsides in late summer*) Inf **OH37**, Sneezeweed. **1967** *DARE* Wildfl QR Pl.261A [=*Helenium autumnale*] Infs **OH37**, **TX44**, Sneezeweed. **1976** Bruce *How to Grow Wildflowers* 240, And there were the clear yellow daisylike flowers of Sneezeweed, *Helenium autumnale*. . . Incidentally, the rather unpleasant common name Sneezeweed (which nurserymen avoid, using "Helen's Flower" instead) is supposedly a reference to the fact that the dried leaves of the plants may be used as a substitute for snuff.

2 A **yarrow** (here: *Achillea ptarmica*). Cf **sneezewort 1**

1830 Rafinesque *Med. Flora* 2.185, The *A[chillea] ptarmica*, or Sneezeweed, is said also to grow in New York; few botanists have seen it. **1914** Georgia *Manual Weeds* 487, *Achillea Ptarmica*. . . *Other English names:* White Sneezeweed [etc]. **1950** Gray–Fernald *Manual of Botany* 1515, Sneezeweed. . . Damp fields, roadsides. **1966** WI Acad. *Trans.* 55.196, Sneezeweed. . . occasionally escaped from old gardens along roadsides, railroads, vacant lots, and near abandoned homes.

3 =**orange sneezeweed.**

1964 Kingsbury *Poisonous Plants U.S.* 411, Sneezeweed [=*Hymenoxys hoopesii*] is a major economic problem for sheep raisers on the summer ranges of the central Rocky Mountains.

sneezewort n

1 also *sneezewort tansy, ~ yarrow:* A **yarrow**, usu *Achillea ptarmica*. [*OED2* 1597 →] Cf **sneezeweed 2**

1822 Eaton *Botany* 154, [*Achillea*] *ptarmica* (sneeze-wort). **1854** King *Amer. Eclectic Dispensatory* 155, *Achillea Ptarmica*, or Sneezewort, grows in hedges and thickets. . . The powder of the dried leaves when snuffed into the nostrils, produces sneezing, which is supposed to be owing to their small, sharp, and marginal teeth. **1891** Jesup *Plants Hanover NH* 23, *A[chillea] ptarmica*. . . (Sneezewort.) In old gardens; both single and double. **1940** Clute *Amer. Plant Names* 73, *A[chillea] ptarmica*. . . sneezewort, sneezewort-yarrow, . . sneezewort-tansy [etc]. **2002** *Boston Globe* (MA) 19 May mag sec 58 (Internet) **NH**, Further on, there's a dramatic stand of old-fashioned sneezewort, Achillea ptarmica.

2 =**sneezeweed 1.**

1828 [see **sneezeweed 1**]. **1840** MA Zool. & Bot. Surv. *Herb. Plants & Quadrupeds* 132, *H[elenium] autumnale*. . . Sneezewort. False Sun Flower. **1914** Georgia *Manual Weeds* 481, Sneezeweed. . . *Other English names:* Sneezewort, Staggerweed [etc]. **1987** *Chicago Tribune* (IL)

25 Oct 9 (Internet), The last item on this "golden" shopping list is autumn sneezewort—also known as "Helen's flower."

sneezewort tansy (or yarrow) See **sneezewort 1**

snerl See **snurl** n

snert n Also sp *sneart* [Du] **Du settlement areas** =**erwten soup.**

1936 *Hammond Times* (IN) 30 Jan 13/8, The weekly quilting bee was held today, at the home of Mrs. Peter Schoon. . . The ladies enjoyed the old Dutch treat "snert" (pea soup to you) at noon. **1940** *AmSp* 15.83 **swMI, Cleveland OH**, Snert [sneːrt]. Pea soup. **1951** *Sun* (Baltimore MD) 13 Jan 8/6, Snert (Dutch Pea Soup). **c1965** Randle *Cookbooks* (Ask Neighbor) 4.13 **eGt Lakes**, *Sneart* [Recipe includes green dry peas, pork hocks, salt, pepper, potatoes, onions.] . . Let simmer . . until soup becomes thick. **1970** *DARE* (Qu. H36, *Kinds of soup*) Inf **MI122**, Snert [snɛrt]—Dutch slang name [for] pea soup. **1989** *Hist. Pella IA* 2.215 **csIA**, Pea soup, erwtensoep or snert was a second favorite memory [of old-timers]. Split, whole, or a mixture of split and whole peas, frankfurters, bacon or ham hock, potatoes, onions (no carrots or celery in older recipes) were the ingredients cited. **2000** *Daily Herald* (Arlington Heights IL) 9 Apr Travel sec 5 (Internet), During the Dutch Days Festival just about everyone goes Dutch, . . including about 15,000 visitors who head to Fulton [IL] for the festivities. You'll not only find them trying on klompen (wooden shoes), but also tasting the likes of snert and hutspot.

sneth See **snath**

snib n, v [Scots dial]
=**sneck.**

1897 *Brooklyn Daily Eagle* (NY) 25 May 2/7, Ray came in through a window. He had a long knife in his hands with which to throw up the door snibs, but he did not use it on the officers. **1973** *DARE* File swPA (as of 1920s), To set the snib on a door lock to lock it. . . So you either 'snibbed' or 'unsnibbed' the lock. **1993** Thomas Co. Hist. Soc. (KS) *Prairie Winds* Mar 5 (as of c1890), The screen door would be snibbed on the inside to keep the flies out. *Ibid*, He was terrified and my brother and I ran and grabbed him and. . . fell into the house and snibbed the screen door behind us.

snibble, snibblin See **schnibble**

snibbling adj

1927 *DN* 5.477 **Ozarks**, *Snibbling*. . . Dark, cloudy, rainy. "I caint go nowhar on sich a bad, snibblin' day as this hyar, nohow."

snibel, snibill See **snipe-bill**

snickadoodle See **snickerdoodle**

snickeltyfritz See **schnickelfritz**

snicker n, v [*OED2 snicker* v. 2 1824 →] Cf **laugh B2, nicker** n[1], v

A sound made by a horse, esp a soft, low sound; to make that sound.

1900 *Chicago Tribune* (IL) 23 Dec 40/4, The young horse snickered with joy, and said "Merry Christmas" to No. 7,643. **1939** *LANE* Map 198 (*Whinny*) 2 infs, **VT**, Snicker; 1 inf, **seMA**, It [=a horse] snickers when it wants an apple. **1956** Ker *Vocab. W. TX* 211, *Gentle noise made by horse (at feeding time)*. . . snicker. [1 of 67 infs] **1966** Dakin *Dial. Vocab. Ohio R. Valley* 2.255, *Whinny*. . . An interesting variant, *snicker* appears in widely separated locations—Tuscawaras County, Ohio, and Madison County, Illinois. Both sections had many German-speaking settlers. **1968** *DARE* (Qu. K40, *The sound that a horse makes*) Inf **OH80**, Snicker. **1973** Allen *LAUM* 1.253 **Upper MW** (as of c1950), *Whinny*. . . *Snicker* is used by a Minnesota Iron Range inf. and by another in southwestern Nebraska. **1981** *PADS* 67.30 **Mesabi Iron Range MN**, *Whinny*. . . Snicker (1 occ. [from 17 infs]). **1986** Pederson *LAGS Concordance* (*Whinny*) 1 inf, **cAL**, Snicker; 1 inf, **csGA**, Snickering—not sure; 2 infs, **TN, TX**, (He) snickers. **1989** Lesley *River Song* 259 **cnOR**, When his horse snickered, he gave it a handful of corn from the saddlebag. **2005** *Chicago Sun-Times* (IL) 13 Feb Showcase sec 13 (Internet), Writers who do not read their copy critically are asking . . for the kind of embarrassment suffered by the author of a brochure for a children's camp in Florida. There the "sun flashes through the trees, and horses snicker from the barn." **2006** *DARE* File—Internet **CO**, I can't imagine a world without . . the snicker of a horse outside a mountain camp.

snickerdoodle n Also *snickadoodle, snickerdroodle, snippie* *doodle* [Varr, perh partly by folk-etym, of Ger (Swabian dial) *Schneckennudel* a pastry of sweet yeast dough coiled up, usu with a filling of raisins and cinnamon; cf **schnecke**]

Any of var cinnamon-flavored cookies or small cakes; see quots.

1898 in 2006 *Popik Coll.* [*Boston Daily Globe* 14 June 8], Snickerdoodles. . . Three quarters of a cup of butter, 2 cups of sugar, 1 cup of milk, 3 cups of flour, 2 eggs, 2 teaspoons of cream of tartar, 1 teaspoon of soda. Mix; drop on a tin in spoonfuls, sprinkle with sugar and cinnamon. **1915** *DN* 4.240 **MA,** *Snickerdoodles.* Rich cakes made with raisins and currants. **1924** in 2000 *Popik Coll.* **PA,** *Snickadoodles* [Recipe includes sugar, eggs, flour, raisins, butter, milk, baking powder.] . . Drop spoonfuls on buttered tins; sprinkle thickly with mixed sugar and cinnamon. . . A very good plain cooky. **1929** *Ibid* ce**MA,** *Snippie Doodles.* [Spices include cinnamon and nutmeg.] *Ibid* se**ME,** *Snickerdoodles.* **1930** Splint *Art of Cooking* 158, *Snicker Doodles* . . 1½ teaspoons cinnamon. . . Cream Crisco, sugar and egg yolks. . . Add raisins, currants and nuts. . . Mix . . flour, salt and spices. . . Pour into well-greased muffin pans. . . This recipe makes 18 medium-sized cup cakes. **1939** Wolcott *Yankee Cook Book* 272 **MA,** *Snickerdoodles* [Recipe includes sugar, salt, eggs, raisins, butter, milk, flour, vanilla, baking powder, sugar, cinnamon.] . . Sprinkle cookies generously with sugar and cinnamon mixed together. **1959** *VT Hist.* 27.158, *Snickerdoodle* . . a crisp cookie. **1972** Beard *Amer. Cookery* 705, In the middle to late nineteenth century regional cookbooks these appear under many names. The earliest church society cookbooks from the Hudson River region call them Schnecken Noodles, Schneckenoodles, or Snecke Noodles. Lower Midwest cookbooks, especially those of Kentucky and Missouri, list them as Snickerdoodles. **c1980** *DARE* File **NEng** (as of c1915), *Snickerdoodle*—A cookie . . made by my grandmother around WWI in central MA. She was from Keene, NH. **1996** Huth *Famil. Words* 111 cs**PA,** *Snickerdroodle.* . . a simple type of cinnamon-spiced butter cookie. **2003** *NY Times* (NY) 25 Aug sec B 2/2 **NYC,** *Me:* "Do you ever bake snickerdoodles?" *Baker:* "No, but my mom does." *Me:* "Just thought I'd ask." *Baker:* "You're the first one. From around here?" *Me:* "Ohio." *Baker:* "I'm from Idaho. Must be a Midwest thing."

snicketyfritz See **schnickelfritz**

snickle v, hence vbl n *snickling* [Prob var of *sniggle*] *esp freq among Black speakers* Cf Intro "Language Changes" IV.4

To snicker.

1881 *Scribner's Mth.* 22.449 **GA** [Black], Hit's dish yer ev'lastin' snickle en giggle, giggle en snickle. **1979** *DARE* File ce**TX,** [Said in the Nacogdoches area:] "snickling" for giggling. **2003** in 2006 *DARE* File—Internet sw**CA** [Black], Me and him both were just snickling and smiling the whole time because we were major underdogs in this situation. **2006** *Ibid* **LA** [Black], There was a hush around the site for what seemed like forever and then slowly I heard snickling as my father, uncles, and cousins rushed forward to get this drunk, 250 pound woman out of the grave.

snicklefritz See **schnickelfritz**

sniddydid n

=**katydid B1.**

1970 *DARE* (Qu. R8, . . *Kinds of creatures that make a clicking or shrilling or chirping kind of sound*) Inf **VA**75, Sniddydids.

snidge See **snudge 2**

snifter n [From Brit dial *snifter* (in var senses) < *snift* to sniff]

1 A nose.

1893 *Brooklyn Daily Eagle* (NY) 15 Jan 16/5, You don't raise yer snifter in the air when de boys pass yer as if ye smelt onions. **1937** *Writer* 50.239 ne**OH** [Black], *Snifters*—cooked pigs' snouts. **1967** *DARE* (Qu. X14, *Joking words for the nose*) Inf **MA**33, Snifter; [5 Infs, Sniffer; (Qu. K61, . . *The pig's nose*) Inf **TX**54, Sniffer, snoot].

2 also *snuff-snifter:* One who takes snuff by sniffing it up the nose. Cf **snufter**

1950 *WELS* (*A person who uses snuff*) 1 Inf, cw**WI,** Snifter. **1967–70** *DARE* (Qu. DD3a) Infs **IL**5, 64, 81, 128, **MA**27, **PA**110, Snifter; **PA**71, Snuff-snifter.

snigglefritz See **schnickelfritz**

snink See **sneak** v **1**

snip v, hence vbl n *snipping*

To propel with a flick of the finger or thumb; hence n *snip* a flick of the finger or thumb; n *snip in the hole* a marble game; see quot 1976.

1899 Hughes *Dozen Lakerim* 1 **IA,** Some people think it great fun to build a house of cards . . and then knock it to pieces with one little snip of the finger. **1901** *Davenport Daily Republican* (IA) 10 May 6/5, The point is to send the marble by a snip of the thumb into a series of holes. **1940** Marran *Games Outdoors* 69, The players kneel around the game and snip their marker from tee to hole with their fingers. Checkermen may be used for snipping, but if marbles are used they may be rolled. *Ibid* 70, Every snip or roll counts 1 point. **1976** *WI Acad. Rev.* Mar 10 (as of 1920s), *Snip in the Hole* was played by two to five players. . . The thumb, index or middle finger was the snipping equipment. If a player missed, the next person tried. The person who snipped the last marble in the hole claimed the pot.

snipe n

1 also rarely *sniper;* often with modifier: Any of var upland game birds characterized by a long bill, as **Wilson's snipe** or **woodcock 1.**

1698 (1848) Thomas *Hist. & Geog. Acct.* 13, There are an Infinite Number of Sea and Land Fowl, of most sorts. *viz* . . Geese, Divers, Brands [sic], Snipe. [*DARE* Ed: This quot may refer instead to **2** below.] **1709** (1967) Lawson *New Voyage* 144, The Snipes here frequent the same Places, as they do in *England,* and differ nothing from them. They are the only wild Bird that is nothing different from the Species of *Europe,* and keeps with us all the Year. **1799** Barton *Fragments Nat. Hist.* PA np, Scolopax gallinago. Common snipe. (Wood-cock.) **1812** Wilson *Amer. Ornith.* 6.18 **PA, KY, Sth,** Snipe: *Scolopax gallinago* . . is usually known by the name of the *English Snipe,* to distinguish it from the Woodcock. **1830** *Cabinet Nat. Hist.* 1.97, This bird [=*Philohela minor*] is known throughout the United States, under different names, as the snipe, big snipe, red-breasted snipe, and mud snipe. **1844** DeKay *Zool. NY* 2.256, *The Common American Snipe. Scolopax wilsoni.* . . The *Common Snipe,* or *English Snipe* as it is ignorantly called from its resemblance to the *S. gallinago* or *Common Snipe* of Europe. **1888** Trumbull *Names of Birds* 151, Many old people will tell you that as children they knew this bird [=*Philohela minor*] by the name of *snipe.* Not merely as *a* snipe, be it understood, but as *the* snipe, and our woodcock is the "snipe" still, in rural districts far too numerous to mention, the species being commonly referred to collectively as "snipes" in these localities. **1898** (1900) Davie *Nests N. Amer. Birds* 134, Although known to the majority of people by its name of Woodcock, it nevertheless has many aliases in different parts of the country which it visits, and is called Big, Mud, Big-headed, Blind and Wood and Whistling Snipe. **1955** *Oriole* 20.1.7, American Woodcock. . . *Snipe* (in early days this was the general name of the bird.) *Ibid,* Wilson's Snipe. . . Snipe (universal). **1965–70** *DARE* (Qu. Q7, *Names and nicknames for . . game birds*) 35 Infs, **scattered,** Snipe; **IL**32, Snipe—jacksnipe—same as Wilson snipe; **IA**3, Snipe—used by many people for any long-billed bird; **MI**65, Snipe or woodcock were getting scarce when I quit hunting 25 years ago; **NY**10, Snipe or woodcock; **NY**103, Snipe—real bird—a type of plover; **VA**105, Woodcock/snipe; (Qu. Q3, . . *Birds that come out only after dark*) Infs **GA**91, **NY**92, Snipe; **LA**2, Snipe—feed at night [FW: Snipe is the common name for woodcock.]; **NJ**45, Snipe and woodcock come out at dusk; (Qu. Q10, . . *Water birds and marsh birds*) Inf **AL**56, Snipe—wood hen—long beak, size of quail; **CA**87, Snipe—a long-legged water bird also called jacksnipes; **GA**76, Snipe—same as woodcock; **IL**9, Snipe—Wilson snipe; **NJ**45, Woodcock or snipe; **OK**52, Snipe—jacksnipe; **MD**22, Sniper—long bill, speckled brown, stays near water, small. [*DARE* Ed: Some of these Infs may refer instead to other senses below.]

2 Any of var shore or marsh birds; see quots. Cf **red-bellied snipe, redbill ~**

1806 (1905) Lewis *Orig. Jrls. Lewis & Clark Exped.* 4.135, The common snipe of the marshes and the small sand snipe are the same of those common to the Atlantic Coast tho' the former are by no means so abundant here. **1841** *S. Lit. Messenger* 7.77, Innumerable species of the snipe are every where to be met with, from the little Bobtail of the sandbar, up to the Beccasse of the plain. **1955** *Oriole* 20.1.7 **GA,** Any shore bird may be called a snipe. **1965–70** *DARE* (Qu. Q10, . . *Water birds and marsh birds*) 76 Infs, **widespread,** Snipe; **CA**191, Snipe—curlew; **NJ**1, Snipe—teeter-ass snipe; **NJ**8, Snipe—robin-sized—teeter-ass snipe; **OH**67, Tip-up and snipe are the same; **PA**104, Snipe or sandpiper—called tip-ups; (Qu. Q7, *Names and nicknames for . . game birds*) Inf **AK**1, Snipe—sandpipers are called so, too; (Qu. Q9, *The bird* *that looks like a small, dull-colored duck and is commonly found on ponds and lakes*) Infs **ME**3, **MI**107, **MN**10, **MS**21, **NY**177, **WA**20, Snipe; **OK**42, Snipe—long-legged; found around shallow water; **WI**32, Snipe—called teeter-ass. [*DARE* Ed: Some of these Infs may refer instead to other senses.]

3 =**cutthroat trout.** [From the red mark near the gills]

1902 Jordan–Evermann *Amer. Fishes* 180, Lake Tahoe Trout. . . "Snipe"—*Salmo henshawi* [=*Oncorhynchus clarkii*]. **1904** *Salmon & Trout* 234, There is another form of the Lake Tahoe cut-throat, known technically as *Salmo clarkii henshawi*, and locally as the "pogy" when mature, and as the "snipe" when young. **1911** *Century Dict. Suppl.*, Snipe. . . The Lake Tahoe trout, *Salmo clarkii henshawi*, found in western Nevada and neighboring parts of California.

4 *also rarely sniper:* =**killdeer 1.**

1950 *WELS* (Killdeer) 5 Infs, **WI**, Snipe. **1965–70** *DARE* (Qu. Q14, . . *Names . . for . . killdeer*) 10 Infs, 7 **Inland Nth**, Snipe; **LA**40, Killdee—sometimes called snipe; **MI**42, Snipe, some people call them; **NY**52, Snipe or teeter-ass—killdeer is the proper name; **WI**54, Sniper; **TX**62, Killdee or snipes. [*DARE* Ed: Some of these Infs may refer instead to other senses.]

5 A **mosquito** n[1] **B1.** *joc*

[**1872** *Brooklyn Daily Eagle* (NY) 16 Sept 1/9, The story that Philadelphia sportsmen were caught firing at New Jersey mosquitoes, mistaking them for snipe, is . . [an] invention. . . The Philadelphians knew what the insects were, but despaired of killing them in any other way.] **1916** *DN* 4.338 **PA,** Snipe. . . A mosquito.

6 A **tree frog 1;** see quots.

1966 Dakin *Dial. Vocab. Ohio R. Valley* 2.388 **OH,** These [names for spring frog] are recorded in Ohio: *kwee-quacks, snipes, whistlers . .* and *pipers.* **c1970** McDavid *Coll.* **seOH,** Snipes—black spring frogs—Athens Co.

7 Used as a term of abuse; see quots. [*OED2* 1604 →]

1852 Cobb *Yankee Champion* 35 **MA,** I'll wager a pipe of brandy against a barrel of your ale that it was him, come. The little snipe's been over to the port more'n once when you didn't know. **1900** *N&Q* 15 Sept 215 **sePA,** The word *snipe,* as expressive of contempt with an intimation of priggishness or pettiness, especially impertinence, was very common in Philadelphia as far back as 1835, as I can well recall my indignation when called by it. **1904** *Newark Advocate* (OH) 2 Feb 6/2, [Short story:] Maybe he intends to . . have some young snipe of a clerk ask us to swear that we are the person named on the check. **1919** *DN* 5.70 **NM** [Among hs students], Snipe, a term of disparagement. "You little snipe, where did you get that money?" **1942** Warnick *Garrett Co. MD* 14 **nwMD** (as of 1900–18), *Snipe* . . applied in reproving a child. "You little snipe." **1967** *DARE* (Qu. II36a, *Somebody who talks back or gives rude answers: "Did you ever see such a _____?"*) Inf **CO**15, Snipe. **2002** in 2006 *DARE* File—Internet **neIL,** When you're 20, you're aware—or you should be, you little snipe—of the intimidating volume of things you haven't read yet.

8 *also rarely sniper:* A cigar or cigarette butt, esp one scavenged from the street—often in phr *shoot a snipe* to scavenge a butt; hence nouns *snipe-shooter* (or *-hunter*) one who picks up butts; vbl n *snipe-shooting.* [**snipe** v 3] **chiefly Inland Nth, N Midl, West** See Map *somewhat old-fash*

1882 *Chicago Tribune* (IL) 17 July 3/5 **cwCA** [Thieves' jargon], The end of an unfinished cigar is a 'snipe.' Small boys who gather cigar stumps in the streets are called 'snipe-hunters,' a term applied also to an objectionable person to indicated that he is very low or degraded. **1889** *NY Herald* (NY) 2 Jan 4/4, Farewell, old year; adieu, dear pipe;/ Goodby, cigar; goodby, old 'snipe'. **1891** (1893) Campbell *Darkness & Daylight* 124 **NYC,** The "Snipe-Shooter" was guilty of smoking cigar-stubs picked out of the gutter, a habit known among the boys as "snipe-shooting". **1897** *KS Univ. Qrly.* (ser B) 6.57 **KS,** *Shoot a snipe:* to pick up a thrown-away cigar stump. **1900** Willard *Tramping* 397, Snipe: cigar-butts—the favorite tobacco among hoboes. **1905** *DN* 3.94 **nwAR,** *Shoot a snipe.* . . Pick up a cigar (or cigarette) stub. 'Where'd you shoot that snipe?' Used by boys. *Ibid* 95, Snipe-shooter. . . A boy who picks up and smokes cigar-stubs and cigarette-stubs. . . Used by Fayetteville boys. **c1939** in 1984 Lambert–Franks *Voices* 183 **OK,** A tankie dropped a cigarette snipe on a tank floor and set it on fire. **1940** *AmSp* 15.335 **NE** [Smokers' slang], A cigaret partly smoked by another person is a *snipe,* a butt, a short, a stub or *stoopin' tobacco.* **1942** McAtee *Dial. Grant Co. IN* 73 (as of 1890s), *Shoot a snipe* . . pick up a cigar or cigarette butt. **1950** *WELS* **WI** (*The end of a smoked cigar or cigarette, thrown away and picked up by somebody else*) 23 Infs, Snipe; 1 Inf,

Shooting snipes—circa 1890–1900; (*Expressions meaning to pick up cigarette ends that have been thrown away*) 3 Infs, Snipe hunting. **1965–70** *DARE* (Qu. DD8, *The part left over when a cigar or cigarette is smoked*) 30 Infs, **esp Inland Nth, N Midl, West,** Snipe; **CA**65, Shooting snipes; **MA**27, Sniper—when it's long enough to smoke again; (Qu. DD6b, *Nicknames for cigarettes*) 20 Infs, **esp Inland Nth, N Midl,** Snipe; (Qu. DD6a, *Other names or nicknames for cigars*) Infs **IL**81, **IN**35, **NY**10, **OK**1, Snipe; **IL**126, Sniper. [41 of 50 total Infs old] **1966** *DARE* FW Addit **ID,** *Snipe*—a cigarette butt. **2005** *DARE* File—Internet **TX,** I would take a Zig-Zag paper, and roll what little tobacco I could extract from the snipes (cigarette butts that aren't smoked all the way) in the ash tray.

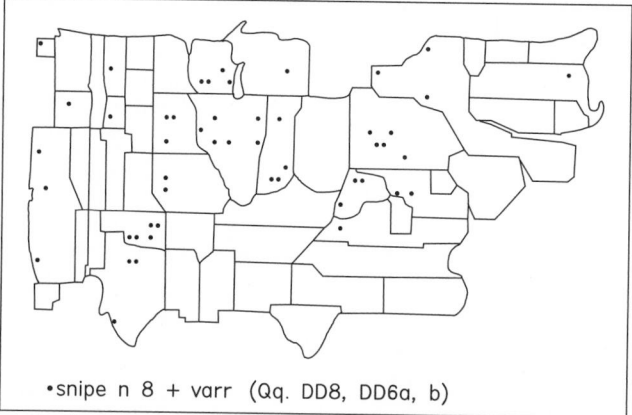

•snipe n 8 + varr (Qq. DD8, DD6a, b)

9 In logging and railroading: a section hand; hence n *king snipe* the foreman of a section crew; n *queen snipe* the wife of a foreman. Cf **jerry**

1891 *San Antonio Daily Light* (TX) 18 Nov [8]/3 (newspaperarchive.com), Let me here give a brief illustration of the duties required of a section foreman which often cause him many perplexities and often makes him weary of his position as king snipe without a crown. . . No class of men in the employ of a railway company are poorer paid for their services . . than a section foreman and the snipes. **1906** *NY Eve. Post* (NY) 21 Feb (*DA*) **SW,** 'Snipes,' in the vernacular of the Panhandle and the Santa Fe, are . . section men. **1916** *DN* 4.357 [Railroad terms], Snipe. . . A track laborer: used in the west. "The section foreman is King Snipe, and his wife Queen Snipe." **1926** *AmSp* 1.250 **PA,** Here is some of the railroad man's patois . . track laborer, "jerry" or "snipe." **1931** *AmSp* 7.52 **Sth, SW** [Lumberjack lingo], Section men are known as "snipes" and their boss is the "King Snipe." **1938** (1939) Holbrook *Holy Mackinaw* 262, King snipe. Boss of a track-laying crew. **1940** Cottrell *Railroader* 131, *King snipe*—Foreman of a track gang. *Ibid* 136, Snipe—Track laborer. **1941** *AmSp* 16.233 [Lumberjack jargon], *King snipe*—The boss of a railroad track laying crew. **1962** *AmSp* 37.134 **nwCA,** *King snipe.* . . The foreman in charge of logging-railroad maintenance. **c1974** Jones *Ozark Hill Boy* 15, [It] was a thriving mill town being made up of loggers, . . timber cutters (flat heads) . . , section hands (snipes) who were responsible for the upkeep of the many miles of railroad tracks.

10 See **snipe hunt.**

11 See **snipe** v 1.

snipe v

1 In logging: to round or bevel (the end of a log); hence vbl n *sniping* rounding or beveling (a log); n *snipe* a beveled end on a log; n *sniper,* also *log snipe,* a logger who bevels the end of a log. Cf **nose** v

1870 *Overland Mth.* 5.56 **WA,** The fourth man is the "hook tender," whose duties are to wait on the team and "snipe the logs." [Footnote:] Rounding off the sharp corners of that end of the log to which the chain is hooked. **1905** U.S. Forest Serv. *Bulletin* 61.48 [Logging terms], Snipe. . . See Nose. Sniper. . . One who noses logs before they are skidded. (Gen[eral]) **1909** *DN* 3.416 **nME,** Snipe. . . To trim off the end of a log; to round it. **1920** *DN* 5.84 **NW,** Sniper. One who snipes logs. Logging Industry. *Snipe, to.* . . To chop off the angle of the end of a log, so that the log may be pulled out of the forest more easily. Western Washington Logging. **1950** *Western Folkl.* 9.123 **nwOR** [Team-logging terms], *Snipe, To.* To trim the end of a log to keep it from hooking the skids of a skid road. **1956** Sorden–Ebert *Logger's Words* 33,

Sniping. **1958** McCulloch *Woods Words* 110 **Pacific NW,** *Log snipe*—The logger who rounded off the head ends of logs. *Ibid* 173, *Sniper*—The logger who shaped the nose of a log for skidding in ground lead operations. **1959** *AmSp* 34.79 **nwCA** [Logger lingo], *Snipe.* . . To round off the end of a log in order to facilitate skidding. **1961** Labbe–Goe *Railroads* 260 **Pacific NW,** *Snipe:* A beveled edge chopped around the end of a log to prevent its catching as it was skidded. **1966** *DARE* Tape **ME5,** They didn't have 'em sniped off at the end so the logs would roll on easy.

2 To search diligently, forage about; esp to prospect for gold on a small scale, usu on unclaimed or already worked-over areas; to work (ground) in such a way; hence vbl n *sniping;* n *sniper.* [This and the following senses are prob from the snipe's habit of probing the mud with its beak in search of food.] **chiefly AK, CA**

1886 *Olean Democrat* (NY) 21 Jan 1/4, I often see the track of the coyote in the forests below here, as he goes sniping around after the frisky jack rabbit. **1899** in 1900 U.S. Congress *Serial Set* 3896 Doc 1023 727, We saw a number of men at work with sluice boxes, although water for sluicing was very scarce. The miners were "sniping" on deserted claims, simply trying to make a stake. **1902** U.S. Geol. Surv. *Professional Paper No. 10* 51 **AK,** Some unsystematic work was done during the fall of 1901 by snipers, usually working with rockers. **1922** *Anchorage Daily Times* (AK) 13 Oct 5/3 **AK,** For some years an old man from San Francisco has been taking out an annual stake in the region by sniping the ground, indicating that there are places sufficiently rich to justify shoveling in. **1936** *Helena Independent* (MT) 13 July 9/4, Micky Gage went to Belt . . after spending his summer vacation in Benton gulch sniping around the placer diggings. **1939** FWP *Guide CA* 474, Along State 49, near the ruins of crude cabins built by the men who first panned the creeks are the shacks and tents of "snipers," who work the river gravels for what little gold they can find, which is rarely more than enough to keep them in coffee and beans. **1969** *DARE* FW Addit **cnCA,** *Sniping*—dig holes here and there, pan dirt.

3 also with *off:* To take surreptitiously something unattended or discarded (esp a cigar or cigarette butt); to swipe, steal; hence vbl n *sniping;* nouns *sniper(-shooter).* Cf **snipe n 8**

1926 *AmSp* 1.653 [Hobo lingo], *Sniping*—stealing. . . *Sniping a gooseberry*—stealing off a clothes line. **1932** Farrell *Young Lonigan* 106 **Chicago IL,** When the coast was clear he sniped a butt from the street. **1943** *LANE* Map 565 *(Swiped)* 1 inf, **seCT,** Sniped. **1950** WELS **WI** *(The end of a smoked cigar or cigarette, thrown away and picked up by somebody else)* 1 Inf, A person who picks up cigarette or cigar butts is called a sniper or sniper-shooter; *(Expressions meaning to pick up cigarette ends that have been thrown away)* 3 Infs, Snipers; 3 Infs, Sniping (butts); 1 Inf, A cigarette sniper. **1966–68** *DARE* (Qu. V5a, *To take something of small value that doesn't belong to you—for example, a child taking cookies: "Who's been _____ the cookies?"*) Infs **CA210, IN32, LA13, OH73, OR16,** Sniping; (Qu. V4, . . *Words for stealing something valuable . . "Yesterday somebody _____ my watch."*) Infs **IN26, LA13, 40, OH25,** Sniped; (Qu. V5b, *If you take something that nobody seems to own . . "Before anybody else gets it, I'm going to _____ this."*) Inf **SC10,** Snipe; snipe it off. **1977** *New Yorker* 20 June 81 **AK** (as of late 1890s), He "sniped" a lot of his gold—just took it from likely spots without settling down to the formalities of a claim. [*DARE* Ed: Cf sense **2** above] **1986** Pederson *LAGS Concordance (Swiped)* 1 inf, **cnLA,** Sniped it. **2005** in 2006 *DARE* File—Internet **neOH,** Okay, so I didn't take that picture—I sniped it from the Eating Well website.

4 To snoop.
1933 *AmSp* 8.1.52 **Ozarks,** *Snipe.* . . To pry into another's affairs.

snipe-bill n Pronc-spp *snibel, snibill* **chiefly NEng** *obs*
A pin with a loop or hook at one end used to form a flexible coupling.

1704 in 1891 *Dedham Hist. Reg.* 2.52 **MA,** To Comfort Starr . . seven shillings for making a doore to the Schoole house, and cupboard, lock, and snips [sic] bills. **1723** in 1901 Providence RI Rec. Comm. *Early Rec.* 16.266, To a paier of snipe bills and an Jron Cart pin 00–05–00. **1774** in 1977 Jones *Amer. Colonial* 358 **DE,** A Cart Snibels and Stancher. **1831** in 1912 Jenks *St. Clair Co. MI* 1.122, A floating bridge . . confined to the main bridge with iron hooks or snibills. **1835** *Jrl. Franklin Inst.* 15.251 **RI,** The slats of blinds . . are usually turned by a rod on their inside, each slat being fastened to the rod by a snipe bill. **1849** *MA Ploughman* 9.2.1, The fault lies in the hinges, or snipe bills,

that are usually placed on the hind corner of a wide axle. **1877** Bartlett *Americanisms* 619 **RI,** *Snipe-Bill.* (Pron. *snibill.*) The iron bolt which connects the body of a cart or other two-wheeled vehicle with the axle. **1900** *Machinery* 6.194, We hear a blacksmith speak of a "snibel," meaning a hook and short piece of rod not unlike a snipe bill in shape. **1901** *N&Q* 9th ser 8.183 **NEng,** One of them is still in use in the farming sections of New England: it is *snibel,* meaning the pin that fastens the tongue of a cart to the body.

snipefish n [*OED2* 1668 →]
Also with modifier: A fish of the family Centriscidae (here: usu *Macroramphosus scolopax,* but also *M. gracilis*). For other names of the former see **bellows fish 1**

1873 in 1878 Smithsonian Inst. *Misc. Coll.* 14.2.15, Centriscus scolopax Linn.—Snipe-fish. . . accidental in American waters. **1936** Barnhart *Marine Fishes S. CA* 35, *Macrorhamphosus hawaiiensis* [=*M. gracilis*]. . . Snipefish. . . A fish of the Hawaiian Islands . . a small specimen reported from Catalina Island. **2001** *FishBase* (Internet), *Macroramphosus scolopax*—Longspine snipefish. *Ibid, Macroramphosus gracilis*—Slender snipefish.

snipe-gutted adj
Of a horse: having a barrel that tapers to the rear.

1946 Mora *Trail Dust* 104 **West,** This allows the space between the cinches to be regulated, and also keeps the flank cinch from crawling back on a horse that's inclined to be "snipe-gutted."

snipe hunt n Also *jacksnipe hunt* **widespread exc NEast** See Map Cf **elbedritsch**
A practical joke in which the victim is left in a remote place holding a bag for the quarry to run into; also vbl nouns *snipe(r) hunting* playing such a joke; hence nouns *(jack)snipe, sniper, whooper-snipe* the (sometimes imaginary) quarry in such a hunt.

[**1854** Riley *Puddleford People* 151 **MI,** Preparations were immediately made for the sniping expedition. . . Ike procured a large bag. . . 'You jest take this ere bag, creep softly down to the log, slip the bag over the end on't, and wait there until we drive in the snipe.'] **1893** *Pacific Med. Jrl.* 36.251, [They] have grappled with this subject with all the admirable and trusting confidence . . that characterizes the bag holder in the midnight snipe hunt. **1896** *Harper's New Mth. Mag.* 92.352 **TX,** [Title of short story:] A Snipe-Hunt. *Ibid* 354, "It ain't every man that gets a chance to go on a snipe-hunt." . . "Now, Bud," Mr. Collum said, when the bag was set on the edge of the gully, with its mouth toward the prairie, "you just scrooch down behind this here sack an' hold the candle. . . An you whistle as hard an' as continual as you can, whilst the balance of us beats aroun' an' drives in the snipe." *Ibid* 356, They rode away, leaving the snipe-hunting gear. **1909** *DN* 3.372 **eAL, wGA,** *Snipe-hunting.* . . A practical joke in which the victim is led to some distant swamp and left to hold the bag for the snipe to run into. **1942** McAtee *Dial. Grant Co. IN* 80 (as of 1890s), *Snipe hunt* . . time-honored practical joke. **1946** *PADS* 6.27, *Snipe hunting.* . . This sport was once widely practiced in the colleges and private schools of Va. . . and N.C. **1958** Humphrey *Home from the Hill* 40 **neTX,** Any you fellows be interested in going on a snipe hunt? **1965–70** *DARE* (Qu. CC17, *Imaginary animals or monsters that people . . tell tales about—especially to tease greenhorns*) 34 Infs, **scattered exc NEast, Atlantic,** Snipe hunting; 30 Infs, **scattered exc NEast, Atlantic,** Snipe hunt(s); 19 Infs, **scattered exc NEast, Atlantic,** Snipe(s); **AL49,** Snipe—a small animal with possum-like shape and poked-out eyes. . . Greenhorn is taken on snipe hunt; **IL71,** Hunting snipe at night with a bag; **IN30,** Snipe—for hunting; **KY72,** They take them snipe hunting; **LA31,** They send boys on snipe hunts; **OH44,** Snipes—but they're not monsters; **TX26,** Snipes—greenhorn stays out all night "hunting snipes"; **WV2,** Snipe—furry like a mink; **WV3,** Snipe—small furry animal; snipe hunt—go out with a burlap bag at night; **WA9,** Fish for snipes—[Inf corrects herself:] snipe is a bird; **MN3,** Whooper-snipe; (Qu. HH14, *Ways of teasing a beginner or inexperienced person—for example, by sending him for a 'left-handed monkey wrench': "Go get me _____."*) 56 Infs, **scattered exc NEast,** Snipe hunt(ing); **LA17, MD49, MI101, MS30, UT5,** Send him on a snipe hunt; **IL5, MN28, OH52,** Snipe; **MI13, NY75,** Go (*or* take him) on a snipe hunt; **LA32,** Snipe—on a snipe hunt; **MO19, PA180, VA103,** Go snipe hunting; **CA137, 158,** Send him on a jacksnipe hunt (with a flour sack); **FL1, NM12,** Send someone (*or* them) snipe hunting; **LA35, NC23,** Take him (out) snipe hunting; **IL40,** Bag of snipe; **IA3,** Catch a snipe; **TN37,** Get him to take part in a snipe hunt and leave him holding the bag; **CA**165, Hunting snipers; **CA**136, Jacksnipe hunt; **OH**84, Sent him on snipe hunts; **WA**30, Snipe bag; **MI**113, Snipe hunting for new hunters; **MN**3, Whooper-snipe; (Qu. EE33, . . *Outdoor games . . that children play*) 55 Infs, **scattered exc NEast, Upper MW, Cent,** Snipe hunt; **VA**5, Sniper hunting; (Qu. EE3) Inf **NC**72, Snipe hunt; (Qu. EE16, *Hiding games that start with a special, elaborate method of sending the players out to hide*) Inf **MO**18, Snipe hunt. **1986** Pederson *LAGS Concordance (Initiation rites)* 2 infs, **AL, TN,** Snipe hunt(s); 1 inf, **swAL,** Snipe hunting.

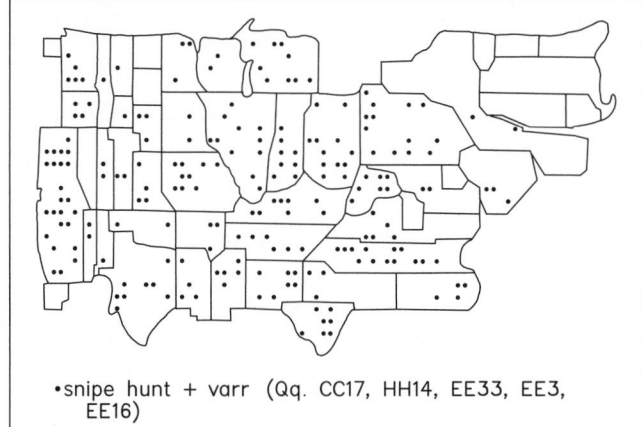

•snipe hunt + varr (Qq. CC17, HH14, EE33, EE3, EE16)

snipe-hunter   See **snipe** n 8

snipe hunting   See **snipe hunt**

snipe off   See **snipe** v 3

sniper n¹
1   See **snipe** n 1, 4, 8.
2   See **snipe hunt.**

sniper n²   See **snipe** v 1, 2, 3

sniper hunting   See **snipe hunt**

sniper-shooter   See **snipe** v 3

snipe-shooter, snipe-shooting   See **snipe** n 8

sniping   See **snipe** v 1, 2, 3

snip in the hole   See **snip**

snipper n   Cf **snook** n²
Pl, in phr *go snippers:* =**snack 1.**
    1966 *DARE* (Qu. II9, *If several people have to contribute in order to pay for something . . "Let's all _____."*) Inf **ME**5, Go snippers in it.

snippick   See **skippick**

snippie doodle   See **snickerdoodle**

snipping   See **snip**

snipple   See **schnibble**

snipshus(h)   See **sniptious**

snipsle   See **schnibble**

sniptious adj   Also sp *snipshus(h)*   **scattered, but esp Sth, S Midl**
Spruce, attractive; fastidious; lively, pert.
    1827 *MA Spy & Worcester Co. Advt.* (Worcester MA) 24 Oct *(DAE),* We mought paddle our canoes together pretty snipshush like. **1830** *VA Lit. Museum* 1.479, *Sniptious. . .* Smart, spruce. **1830** *City Gaz. & Commercial Daily Advt.* (Charleston SC) 13 May 2/4, *Cracker Dictionary—* . . Sniptious, Finically nice. **1834** *Life Andrew Jackson* 43, They seed that he was the rale grit, independent of law, and not very sniptious about going at work when he found his inemies. **1892** Harper *Iola Leroy* 156 **NC** [Black], Couldn't yer come an' stop wid me, or isn't my house sniptious 'nuff? **1895** *DN* 1.394 **wNY,** *Sniptious:* smart, "perky," forward. **1899** (1912) Green *VA Folk-Speech* 399, *Sniptious. . .* Smart and finical. **1905** *DN* 3.95 **nwAR,** *Sniptious. . .* Active, lively. **1911** *DN* 3.547 **NE,** *Sniptious. . .* Fine or attractive. "She looked sniptious in her new dress." "That pudding was sniptious." **1912** *DN*

3.590 **wIN,** *Sniptious. . .* Attractive; neat. **1916** *DN* 4.343 **NE, Sth,** *Sniptious. . .* Fine; grand. **1927** *AmSp* 2.364 **cwWV,** *Sniptious . .* fine. **1954** *Harder Coll.* **cwTN,** *Snipshus. . .* Smart; spruce. **c1960** *Wilson Coll.* **csKY,** *Snipshus. . .* Great, smart, spruced-up. **1966** *DARE* (Qu. BB47, *Feeling in the best of health and spirits: "I'm feeling _____!"*) Inf **NC**33, Sniptious.

snirl n   See **snurl** n

snirl v   See **snurl** v¹

snirly adj   See **snurl** n

snirt n   [Blend of *snow + dirt*]   **esp Upper MW**
A mix of windblown snow and dirt; hence v *snirt* to precipitate as a mixture of snow and dirt; adj *snirty.*
    1957 *Hammond Times* (IN) 7 Apr sec A 8/2 **ND,** Soil conservationist R.M. Davis used the word "snirt" to describe the mixture of snow and dirt whipped into the air by winter gales in these parts. **1975** *DARE* File **ceND,** *Snirt*—Combination of snow and windblown dirt picked up off the fallow fields. **1989** Frazier *Gt. Plains* 197 (as of c1934), In the winter, snow mingled with the blowing dusters. These were called "snirt" storms. **1996** in **2002** *DARE* File—Internet **IA,** That will prevent a lot of wind erosion this winter and what we Iowans fondly refer to as "snirt." **2000** *Bismarck Tribune* (ND) 17 Dec sec C 6 (Internet), All through the strange, dry blizzard Saturday, as the wind howled, . . and started turning the election day snowfall into what we North Dakotans call—snirt—snow and dirt, I kept trying to figure out what Nature was trying to tell me. **2002** *DARE* File—Internet **cMN,** Winter winds take dust and dirt, depositing them on the snow. Usually, more snow falls and the surface is sparking [sic] white again. But the dirt is still there. More than three decades ago, people started calling this combination of snow and dirt "snirt." *Ibid* **nMI,** It finally snowed in the UP of Michigan and we got to ride a variety of [snowmobile] trails, ice, snow covered ice, hard pack and loose snirt. **2005** *DARE* File **NE,** When I looked out in the morning I could see that it snirted last night. **2006** Doig *Whistling* 187 **MT** (as of c1910), What scrunched under our overshoes as we trudged through the stubble of the grainfield was the nasty mix of moistureless snow and windblown dirt that we called "snirt". . . The snirty field was heavy going.

snit n   Also *schnit(z)*   [Ger *Schnitt* a piece, slice; a small glass of beer]   **chiefly wGt Lakes, esp WI**   Cf **shell** n¹ 1
A small amount, esp a small beer.
    1867 Bowman *You & Me* 187 **IL,** I had started with a quart bottle full of powder [=snuff] . . , but that was all gone except a "snit." **1949** *Post–Std.* (Syracuse NY) 1 June 6/2 **WI,** Many readers in and around Milwaukee have written in [to] say that a snit is a small beer. **1950** *WELS* **WI** *(A little drink)* 2 Infs, Snit; 1 Inf, Schnit. **1950** *WELS Suppl.* **ceWI,** Schnitz—short beer. **1968** *DARE* (Qu. LL1, *Something very small:* "I only took a _____ one.") Inf **PA**161, Schnitz; (Qu. LL6a, *A small, indefinite amount . . "I'll take just a _____ of cream in my coffee.")* Inf **MN**12, Snit. **2002** *NADS Letters* **MI** (as of c1999), I have heard "schnitz" used in place of "beer back" to refer to a small portion of beer served with a bloody mary or other drink. **2002** *Badger Herald* (Madison WI) 8 Nov (Internet), Made with a secret recipe, the Bloody Mary is served with a snit of beer for $4.50. **2003** *NADS Letters* **cWI** (as of c1960), I often accompanied my father to his favorite local tavern. . . If I was good, he would instruct the bartender to give me a schnitz. What I received was a glass of draught beer approx 5 oz. . . Occasionally I would hear other patrons order a shot and a schnitz. **2005** in **2006** *DARE* File—Internet **ID,** Without a more balanced line-up all the pitching in the world won't make a snit of difference. **2006** *DARE* File **csWI,** [Bartender:] Hey, you want a snit with that Bloody Mary? [Second bartender:] Schnit.

snitch n¹   Cf *DS* U36a, b
A mean or stingy person; hence adj *snitchy* mean, stingy.
    1905 *DN* 3.65 **eNE,** *Snitchy. . .* Petty, mean. "A snitchy trick." **1911** *DN* 3.547 **NE,** *Snitch. . .* Some one who is *snitchy,* i.e., petty, mean, or stingy. "You are a snitch, not to let me have that." **1933** *Lincoln Star* (NE) 5 Dec 10/2, Coach Bible's boys have been the victims of a snitchy deal!

snitch n²   Also *snitchel, snitchen, snitchet, snitchit*   [Varr of *smitch, smidgen*]   Cf **snit**
A little bit; a small amount; something small.
    1912 *Syracuse Herald* (NY) 31 July 5/1, This buzz thing has blew ev-

ery snitch o' curl out o' my crowning glory. **1920** *Collier's* 7 Aug 15, We do not care a snitchet. **1950** *WELS* (*A very small, indefinite amount: "I'll take just a _____ of cream in my coffee."*) 1 Inf, **seWI,** Snitch; (*Could I borrow just a _____ of cinnamon from you?*) 1 Inf, **cwWI,** Snitch. **1965–70** *DARE* (Qu. LL1, *Something very small: "I only took a _____ one."*) Infs **MN**6, **OH**8, 88, **VT**8, Snitch; (Qu. LL2, . . *Too small to be worth much: "I don't want that little _____ potato."*) Inf **CA**138, Snitch of a; (Qu. LL6a, *A small, indefinite amount . . "I'll take just a _____ of cream in my coffee."*) Infs **IL**119, **MN**6, **UT**4, **WI**61, Snitch; **NC**38, Snitchen; (Qu. LL6b, *A small, indefinite amount . . "I'll put in just a _____ of butter."*) Infs **MD**38, **MI**66, **MN**6, Snitch; (Qu. LL6c, *A small, indefinite amount . . "It still needs just a _____ of cinnamon."*) Inf **CA**133, Snitch. **1967** *DARE* File **neMN** (as of c1945), A short distance: "Just a frump and a snitchel from here." **1993** *Coast Watch* Sept/Oct 15 **Outer Banks NC,** [Caption:] Snitchit—just a pinch.

snitchy See **snitch** n[1]

snits See **schnitz** n[1]

snitsle See **schnitzel** n

snitz n See **schnitz** n[1]

snitz v See **schnitz** v

snitzen(s) See **schnitz** n[1]

sniv(v)er prep
Immediately after.
1860 *Atlantic Mth.* 6.672 **Nantucket MA,** "Where be you a-cruising to?" asks one Nantucket matron of her gossip. "Sniver-dinner, I'm going to Egypt." . . The good woman was dressed up, intending, "as soon as ever dinner was over," to go . . to the negro-quarter of the town. **1916** Macy–Hussey *Nantucket Scrap Basket* 145 **seMA,** "Snivver"—Here's a queer word, still used occasionally. One says "I'll be over to your house snivver dinner." The presumption is that the speaker means "as soon as ever I have had my dinner."

snivy n Cf **hookem-snivey**
1911 *DN* 3.547 **NE,** Snivy [ɪ]. . . Term of disparagement. (1) Some one who is contrary, or unreasonable. "You are a snivy, and you are acting snitchy." (2) Having about the same meaning as *floozy,* the noun. "That fellow has another little snivy on his string."

snob v [Prob by folk-etym from *snub*]
To snub (someone).
1856 Olcott *Torchlight* 26 **NEast,** What are you but a shadow, following these Castlemans, who have, every one, root and branch, snobbed you since my father's death. **1908** *Indianapolis Sun. Star* (IN) 20 Sept [18]/2 (newspaperarchive.com), Snobbing a Snob. . . There are many stories of the rebukes that snobs have suffered at his hands. **1967–70** *DARE* (Qu. II6, *If you meet somebody who used to be a friend, and he pretends not to know you: "When I met him on the street he _____."*) Infs **GA**86, **LA**25, **MD**16, **MI**55, 111, **NY**35, **VA**2, Snobbed me. **1998** *Post-Std.* (Syracuse NY) 17 Aug sec F 2/1, At our next civic club meeting the mother of the bride gave me the cold shoulder. . . — Snobbed in Schenectady.

snoball See **snowball** 7

Snob Hill n Also *Snob Alley, ~ Knob, ~ Row, ~ Slough;* for addit varr see quots
=**Nob Hill.**
1873 *Dixon Sun* (IL) 24 Dec [7]/1 (newspaperarchive.com), Two handsome, well-dressed ladies stepped from their carriage, . . and disappeared within the aristocratic Snob's Hill mansion. **1925** *Star* (Kansas City MO) 14 Jan E/7, F.G., a K.U. alumnus, feels safe in surmising that the present controversy will ultimately bring forth a new college song entitled, "When I was a Degenerate on Snob Hill." **1952** Callahan *Smoky Mt.* 199, The first residential dwellings [at the Oak Ridge atom bomb project] were three hundred units for the scientists, each of them having a woodburning fireplace. These were located on an elevated section which later became known as "Snob Hill." **1957** Battaglia *Resp. to PADS 20* **eMD** (*Names or nicknames for the part of a town where the well-off people live*) Snob Hill. **1965–70** *DARE* (Qu. II24, *Names or nicknames for the part of a town where the well-off people live*) 44 Infs, **scattered,** Snob('s) Hill; **VA**31, Snob Alley; **CA**81, **OH**63, **VA**5, 26, Snob('s) Knob; **SC**40, Snob Row; **CA**119, Snob Slough; **MI**24, Snob's Point; (Qu. C35, *Nicknames for the different parts of your town or city*) Infs **CA**105, **KS**1, **OR**1, **WV**1, Snob Hill; (Qu. II23, *Joking names for*

the people who are, or think they are, the best society of a community: The _____) Inf **NM**9, From Snob Hill. **2002** *Anchorage Press* (AK) 3 Jan (Internet), We drive through an area in South Anchorage that he calls "snob hill." He points to $600,000 houses.

sno-go n, v Also sp *snow-go* **chiefly AK** Cf **snowmachine**
A snowmobile; to travel or transport by snowmobile.
1950 *Post–Reg.* (Idaho Falls ID) 22 Feb 8/2, *Jackson, Wyo.* . . A Jackson Hole native . . won national recognition in a snow machine demonstration. . . Nearly three hundred persons observed and kept points on the performance of cats, sno-goes, snowbugs, mavericks[.] In fact every type of snow machine known in the U.S. **1961** *AK Sportsman* Apr 23, Tommy Heckman has a sno-go and all the little ones call it car. **1968** *Fairbanks Daily News–Miner* (AK) 23 Dec 19/2, [Advt:] Mittens—Sno Go Suits—Shoe Pacs—Insulated Underwear. **1976** *Ibid* 7 Feb sec A 15/5, Mr. Martinoff graciously snogoed us to some of the distant homes. **1977** *Ibid* 14 Mar sec A 14/3, Quite a few people can be seen in the woods skiing, walking, or sno-going and taking in the great air. **1983** *Cama-i Book* 358 **AK,** These sleds are called freight sleds and are mostly used by hitching to a sno-go. **1991** Tabbert *Dict. Alaskan Engl.* 230, Another frequent Alaskan name for this vehicle is *sno-go,* especially in rural Alaska. **2008** Kantner *Shopping* 182 **AK,** At eighteen months she snowgoed with us more than a hundred miles. *Ibid* 203, They had left Cape Krusenstern on snowgos.

snollygoster n [Perh fanciful expansion of **gauster;** the often-repeated suggestion that this is from an assumed Ger *schnelle Geister,* literally "swift spirits," appears to be unsupported by any positive evidence.]
1 also *snallygaster, snollegoster, snol(l)igoster:* =**ring-tailed roarer. esp MD, KY** Cf **half horse, half alligator**
1846 in 1953 *AmSp* 28.142 **KY,** Now here I am a rale propelling, double revolving locomotive Snolly Goster, ready to attack anything but a combination of Thunder-lightning-smoke-railroad, iron and hot water. **1864** in Lib. of Congress *Amer. Memory: We'll Sing to Abe Our Song* (Internet), [Minstrel song:] I come from Lousiana [sic] down below;/ I'm a reg'lar Snolly goster, Contraband and darky teazer. **1884** Henshall *Camping in FL* 27 **KY,** "Ge-whillikens! What a snolligoster!" shouted Ed. And so it was—the largest we caught in Florida. **1910** Cox *Fearsome Creatures* 15, In form the snoligoster resembles a huge crocodile, but it is covered with long, glossy fur and has no legs or fins, except one long spike on its back. . . When a snoligoster catches [a black human victim] . . , upon which it delights to feed, it tosses the victim up and backward so as to impale him upon the spike fin. **1918** *Amer. Angler* 3.60 **nwMS** [Black], Dem big trout's jus' natcherly bad and verashus, and dat ole snollegoster 'ud snash [sic] yo' lil' pole lak a bullrush! **1940** Writers' Program *Guide MD* 348, Residents of a Negro settlement near the distillery are firm in their belief that the neighborhood has a 'Snallygaster'—a fabulous reptilian bird of vast size that preys on poultry and Negro children after nightfall. **1949** *Sun* (Baltimore MD) 28 July 14/1 (Hench Coll.), Then, for several weeks, a snallygaster terrorized the Middletown Valley. This was the famous Bovalopus snallygaster, with the form of a great bird. It was said to have a wingspread of from twelve to fourteen feet. As it whipped across the sky it threw out streamers like an octopus. **1954** *Sun* (Baltimore MD) 31 Oct mag sec [front cover], Is this, at last, the snallygaster that has been said to terrorize Western Maryland but that most persons have considered legendary? **1995** *Frederick Post* (MD) 7 Dec mag sec 7/1, The name The Snallygaster came from a local legend. The Snallygaster was half reptile, half bird and was supposed to be seen flying across the valley and roosting in a home in Braddock Heights. **2005** *DARE* File—Internet **KY,** The Snallygaster has the same description [as the Jersey Devil], except some say it has only one eye, and it was reported to have killed one man.

2 A shameless, unscrupulous, self-promoting person, esp a politician. **esp Sth, S Midl**
1892 *Chicago Tribune* (IL) 6 Dec 12, They have a thing down in Georgia called a "snollygoster," which is described as a picayune fellow who goes sneaking around for a little office that he can't get, and that he couldn't fill with ability if he should get it. **1895** *Columbus Dispatch* (OH) 28 Oct 4/3 **GA,** A Georgia editor kindly explains that "a snollygoster is a fellow who wants office, regardless of party, platform or principles, and who, whenever he wins, gets there by the sheer force of monumental talknophical assummacy." **1903** in Lib. of Congress *Amer. Memory: Traveling Culture* (Internet) **GA,** The subject of the lecture [by Col. H.W.J. Ham] was, "The American Snollygoster in Politics." The speaker told how the word "snollygoster" was coined, many years ago,

in a heated political debate between two Georgia crackers, both desirous of representing the state in the legislature. Gradually the pretentious, swaggering, prattling fellow had grown and multiplied his kind. **1912** *DN* 3.590 **wIN,** *Snolly-goster.* . . A shyster. **1916** *DN* 4.280 **NE, NC,** *Snollygoster.* . . Exact meaning unknown, but plainly a term of disparagement. "We once knew a miserly old snollygoster who used to look in a mirror to see the reflection of a saint." **1952** *NY Times* (NY) 3 Sept 20/2 *(Hench Coll.)* **MO,** I [=President Harry S Truman] wish some of these snollygosters would read this New Testament and perform accordingly. **1952** Brown *NC Folkl.* 1.592, *Snollygoster.* **2002** *DARE* File—Internet **MO,** I felt like coming back at him with, "now you listen to me one G—d— minute you ill-informed snollygoster!"

snoo(d)ge See **snoose** n[2]

snook n[1] Also *snooks* [*OED2* 1697 →]
1 =cobia.
1882 *U.S. Natl. Museum Bulletin* 16.909, *Elacate canada* is known in Florida as "Sergeant-fish," from its lateral stripes; also, as "Snooks" and "Ling." **1884** Henshall *Camping in FL* 34, The sergeant-fish *(Elacate canada),* called "snooks" in East Florida, belongs to the *Elacatidæ,* or crab-eaters. **1933** LA Dept. of Conserv. *Fishes* 197, The Cobia, *Rachycentron canadus.* . . is invariably known in Louisiana as the Ling or Lemon Fish, in Florida as the Crabeater or Sergeant Fish, and on the Atlantic Coast as the Black Bonito, while it also occasionally receives the name of Snook.
2 A fish of the genus *Centropomus,* esp *C. undecimalis.* For other names of this species see **pike** n[1] **4, robalo, saltwater pike 2, sea ~ 2, sergeantfish 2**
1889 *Newark Daily Advocate* (OH) 15 Aug [2]/5, Charlotte Harbor, Fla., is said to be so full of fish that it is actually running over. One day recently fully thirty pounds of fish jumped out on shore. . . There was one fifteen pound redfish, three five pound snooks and five jackfish. **1896** U.S. Bur. Fisheries *Rept. for 1895* 176 **seFL,** [In a list of fishes observed at Key Biscayne:] Snooks *(Centropomus undecimalis).* **1902** Jordan–Evermann *Amer. Fishes* 369, We have never taken the snook with the fly or on the hook, but it is said to take the hook readily and even to rise to the fly. **1933** LA Dept. of Conserv. *Fishes* 69, The Snook is one of the sea fishes that seem to like to wander into fresh water. **1966** *DARE* (Qu. P2, . . *Kinds of saltwater fish caught around here* . . *good to eat)* Inf **FL**29, Snook or sergeantfish. **1975** Evanoff *Catch More Fish* 218, The snook *(Centropomus undecimalis)* is also called the sargeant fish, salt-water pike, and robalo. . . Snook are most plentiful in Florida, especially in the southern part of the state. **1983** *Audubon Field Guide N. Amer. Fishes* 532, The Snook should be handled carefully, as the sharp gill covers can cause deep cuts.

snook n[2] esp **SE, NEast** Cf **snuck** n
Pl, in phr *go snooks:* =**snack 1.**
1853 (1854) Baldwin *Flush Times* 301 **AL,** Well done, Tommy, here's a V.; go, buck it off on a horse-race next Sunday, and we'll go snooks. **1893** Shands *MS Speech* 58, *Snooks* [snuks]. This word is used by all classes to mean *equal shares.* Men *go snooks* with a certain amount of valuables when they divide them equally. **1896** [see **snuck** n]. **1898** Lloyd *Country Life* 44 **AL,** If you will go snooks with me and we play the game close and steady the pot will be ours. **1950** *PADS* 13.7 **AL, GA,** They had went snooks to buy the dog, and each man owned an undivided one-third interest in him. **1968–70** *DARE* (Qu. II8, *When one person wants to share or divide something with another person* . . *"Let's _____ [on that]."*) Infs **CT**35, **NY**75, 219, 231, Go snooks; **NY**131, Go snooks—years ago they used this.

snook v See **sneak** v **2a**

snooked See **sneak** v **2b**

snooks See **snook** n[1]

snooksies exclam Cf **snook** n[2]
Used as a call to claim first choice.
1956 *AmSp* 31.37, *I hosie*—or . . *honie* . . or *whackie—that.* All these assert 'This is mine.' Then there is the negative form . . the claimant fends off all other claims, down to the smallest: . . *no dibs.* . . Finally, there is the *I've got* . . *wholsies* . . or *benches—on your seat* pattern. And there are its shortened forms, . . *First bores on the apple! Snooksies,* or *licksies, on the lollypop!* . . for "First choice!"

snool n [Scots, Ir, nEngl dial]
1979 *Today Show Letters* (as of early 20th cent), My mother . . and her mother . . used a number of words which I never heard elsewhere. . . A

few which stick in my mind are . . "snool"—a worthless disregarded person.

snooled down adj phr [Scots dial *snool* to bully; to keep in subjection]
1959 *VT Hist.* 27.158 **cn,neVT,** *Snooled down.* . . Beaten down; henpecked. Occasional. Orleans.

snoopy adj [Prob PaGer *schnuppich*] esp **PA, OH, MD**
Finicky, particular (about one's food).
1936 *Mansfield News-Jrl.* (OH) [10] Jan 21/1 (newspaper-archive.com), The celery-cabbage, cut in inch slices and served with salad dressing, will make the "snoopiest" members of the family sit up and take notice. **1942** Warnick *Garrett Co. MD* 14 **nwMD** (as of 1900–18), *Snoopy* . . finicky about one's food. **1965–69** *DARE* (Qu. H12, *If somebody eating a meal takes little bits of food and leaves most of it on his plate, you say he _____*) Infs **OH**88, **PA**41, Snoopy; **OH**70, Is a snoopy eater; **OK**1, Is snoopy or finicky. **2002** in 2005 *DARE* File—Internet **cPA,** In my family, we have always called someone who is a fussy or picky eater "snoopy."

snoose n[1] Usu |snus|; rarely |snuz, snʊs, snʊz| Also *snooss, snuss* [Dan, Sw, Norw *snus*] chiefly **Pacific NW, Rocky Mts, Upper MW, WI** See Map on p. 86 Also called **Swedish condition(er) powder**
Snuff for chewing; also fig, strength; power; hence v *snoose* to use snuff; nouns *snooser, snoosy* one who uses snuff; transf, *snoose burner, ~ chewer, snooser* a Scandinavian.
1921 *ID Forester* 22, They say he smokes a big, strong pipe / And carries matches, too,/ Chews black snoose / And spits the juice;/ Of course it can't be true. **1925** *AmSp* 1.137 **Pacific NW,** "Come on, boy; ride the old cross-cut, but don't drag your feet. Give 'er snoose." . . When he leaves the cookhouse he . . takes a "rear of snoose." "Snoose" is a certain brand of Swedish snuff; it is moist and hot with pepper, and the man who is not used to it will find his gums burning and his head swimming when he tries his first "rear." **1930** Williams *Logger-Talk* 16 **Pacific NW,** *Snooser:* A Scandinavian. **1946** Peattie *Pacific Coast* 235, The commissary . . sold all the items needed by the well-dressed logger and much for his insides as well. "Snoose," or chewing snuff, was a major item. **1948** Manfred *Chokecherry* 41 **nwIA,** Me, I chew snoose. Heifer dust. **1950** *Western Folkl.* 9.120 **nwOR** [Logger speech], *Snooseburner.* One who chews snuff; one of Scandinavian extraction, so called because of their addiction to snuff. **1950** *WELS Suppl.* **nwWI,** Snoose n [snus]/[snuz]. **1965–70** *DARE* (Qu. DD3a, . . *A person who uses snuff*) 55 Infs, chiefly **Pacific NW, Rocky Mts, Upper MW, WI,** Snoose (bug, chewer, eater, hound, taker, *or* user); 23 Infs, chiefly **Pacific NW, Rocky Mts, Upper MW, WI,** Snooser; **IA**8, **MN**28, **PA**223, **WA**9, Chews (snuff or) snoose; **AK**8, [snus]; **CA**15, [snuz]— Swedes put it in their lips; **WI**77, He snooses [snus]; **IL**11, Snoosy; **VT**12, [snuz] chewer; **NM**11, Snoose hound—used by Scandinavian loggers [FW: heard by Inf in Pacific Northwest]; [**MI**101, Snouser ['snɑuzɚ];] (Qu. DD1, . . *Forms* . . *[of]* chewing tobacco) 32 Infs, chiefly **Pacific NW, Rocky Mts, Upper MW, WI,** Snoose; **WA**16, Loose snoose; **SD**5, Snoose box; (Qu. C35, *Nicknames for the different parts of your town or city)* Inf **WA**11, Snoose Junction—Scandinavian neighborhood; (Qu. DD2, *The portion or quantity of tobacco chewed at one time:* "He's always got a big _____ *in his cheek."*) Inf **IA**5, Pinch of snoose; **CA**59, Snoose; (Qu. DD3b, *How* . . *people take snuff*) Infs **CA**137, 163, Snoose; (Qu. DD4, *Moisture in the mouth, colored brown by snuff or chewing tobacco)* Inf **MN**21, Snoose juice; (Qu. HH27b, *Of a very able and energetic person who gets things done* . . "He's got lots of _____.") Inf **MN**16, Snoose. **1966** *DARE* Tape **MI**10, The snuff was snoose [snus]. **1968** *Hungry Horse News* (Columbia Falls MT) 20 Dec 2/1, Someone is going to get killed on this old bridge if the commissioner doesn't shift his cud of snoose over to the other side of his mouth and do something about it! **1978** Kalibabky *Hawdaw* 1.[12] **neMN,** *Snooss:* Chewing tobacco, snuff. . . "Good snooss chewers buy Copenhagen by da roll." **1978** Doig *This House* 73 **MT** (as of c1950), Hold on, I'm gonna give her [=a pickup truck] snoose to get up this sidehill. **1998** Leary *WI Folkl.* 62 **nwWI** (as of 1950s), Swedes and Norwegians alike might be teased as "herring chokers," "Scandihoovians," "snoose chewers," and "squareheads." **2001** in 2002 *DARE* File—Internet **seIL,** J.W. looked at me, cocked an eye-brow, looked back at the calves . ., picked up his coffee (You've got to learn to wait a while for J.W. to answer.), reached for his can of snoose, tapped it, looked back at me and asked, "How come?"

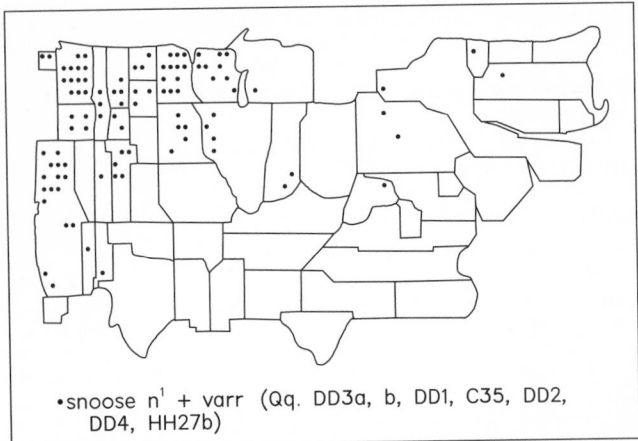

•snoose n¹ + varr (Qq. DD3a, b, DD1, C35, DD2, DD4, HH27b)

snoose n² Also *snoo(d)ge* [Prob varr of Engl dial *snooze noose, snare*]

A snare for catching rabbits.

1943 Weslager *DE Forgotten Folk* 182, A third trapping device for catching game is locally known as a "snoose" or "snooge." Its name is a result of combining snare and noose. It consists of a slip noose arranged in the animal track and concealed by brush. The loose end of the noose is fastened securely to a tree or fence post. The unsuspecting rabbit enters the noose, which is larger than his head but not large enough to permit the entrance of his body. **1955** *DE Folkl. Bulletin* 1.18, He told us how to make and use a "snoose"—which he called a "snoodge"—to catch rabbits.

snoose burner (or chewer), snooser, snooss, snoosy See **snoose** n¹

snooter n scattered, but esp Sth

The nose.

1903 *Iola Daily Reg.* (KS) 15 Sept 3/3, If any of the boys . . have a hankering to swat the festive Turk on the end of his snooter, they . . may get into the army and do things. **1952** *Paris News* (TX) 2 Nov 4/4, I don't believe in just waiting on the guy to hit me in the snooter either. **1965–68** *DARE* (Qu. X14, *Joking words for the nose*) Infs **FL**27, **MS**16, **MO**9, **OK**47, **VA**13, Snooter. **1994** Moon *Untold Tales* 397 **Detroit MI** [Black], It's quinine and heroin mixed. . . Used to call it "tooter for the snooter."

snoot, make a v phr Also *make a snout, make snoots* [Though not recorded in the *OED2*, *make a snout* is found in 19th cent Engl; US use may in some cases reflect the equivalent Ger phr *eine Schnauze* (or *Schnute*) *machen*, PaGer *en schnut mache*]

To grimace, to make faces (at someone); also fig.

1844 *Brooklyn Eagle & Kings Co. Democrat* (NY) 20 June 2/4, The Albany Atlas says, "This reminds us of the language of the little fellow to the chap that had him down . . : 'If I can't lick you, I can *make snoots* at your sister!'" **1884** *Daily News* (Frederick MD) 27 Aug 1/4, She made a snoot at me and told me to scat. **1908** *German Amer. Annals* 10.32 **sePA**, *Make a snout* (snoot). Grimace. "Teacher, he's making snouts at me." . . fr. Pa. Ger. *schnoot mŏchă*; Ger. *schnauze machen*. **1910** *Orange Co. Times–Press* (Middletown NY) 18 Oct 8/7, On leaving the stand, Mr. Rogers made a snout at Mr. Thompson. **1911** *DN* 3.547 **NE**, *Snoots* . . Grimaces, made by wrinkling the nose. "Teacher, Willy's making snoots at me." **1935** *Oakland Tribune* (CA) 20 Apr [20]/1 (newspaperarchive.com), The dictator of Louisiana has defied Uncle Sam. A Kingfish has made snoots at the Eagle! **1942** McAtee *Dial. Grant Co. IN* 59 (as of 1890s), *Snoots, make* . . grimace, "make faces." **1982** Barrick Coll. **csPA**, *Snoot, make a*—pucker one's lips and wrinkle the nose; an insulting gesture. **2006** *DARE* File—Internet **cwCA**, If I push my finger against the tip of my nose and make a snout, I can breathe better and look like a pig at the same time.

snoozer n West

A sheep rancher or herder.

1893 James *Cow-Boy Life in TX* 105, The snoozer was not allowed to herd or turn his sheep loose on the range that he didn't own. **1907** Porter *Heart of West* 67 **TX**, I never had believed in harming sheep men. . I never thought it was worth while to be hostile with a snoozer. **1915**

DN 4.229 **wTX**, *Snoozer*. . . The cowboy's name for a sheep-herder. **1936** Adams *Cowboy Lingo* 198, Held in greater contempt by the cowboy was the 'snoozer,' or sheepman, a man who 'favored mutton instead of beef.'

snort v Also with *up* [Perh back-formation < **snorting pen, ~ post 1**]

See quots.

1879 [see **snorting post**]. **1958** *AmSp* 33.268 **eWA** [Ranching terms], *Snort* . . may . . be used in the more general senses of *tie*. Thus, an animal on a picket rope may be said to be *snorted up* . . an animal may be *snorted*, meaning trussed up tightly.

snort n Cf **sneeze**, *DS* MM24

See quots.

1938 *AmSp* 13.236 **MS**, I was in northern Mississippi for a short time and noted the colloquialisms "a snort" and "a pinch" meaning "a short way" used by people who specified short distances of travel. **1998** in 2005 *DARE* File—Internet **OK**, He's just a snort up the road from Denton.

snorter n

=**ripsnorter**.

1824 *MO Intelligencer* (Franklin MO) 29 May 1/3, Their *sink*, too you'd guess was a snorter, With cross-legs, some like a table. **1842** *Knickerbocker* 19.66 **NYC**, He's a snorter when he's riz. **1855** Wise *Tales Marines* 54, "We shall have a snorter this afternoon," muttered old Jack, rubbing his paws joyfully; "the trade wind always blows fresh for three days, just like three heavy rollers on a beach." **1859** Taliaferro *Fisher's R.* 86 **nwNC** (as of 1820s), I'm a snorter in that line, sartin. **1899** (1912) Green *VA Folk-Speech* 399, *Snorter*. . . Something fierce or furious, especially a gale; something large of its kind. **1905** *DN* 3.20 **cCT**, *Snorter*. . . An unusually good one. **1907** *DN* 3.217 **nwAR**, *Snorter*. . . Something unusually good. **1939** FWP *Guide TN* 135, Backcountry folk are prone to use parts of speech in strange ways. . . An extravagant lie is a "ripper," a "snorter," a "screamer." **1956** Ker *Vocab. W. TX* 60, Storm with rain and thunder and lightning . . snorter. [1 of 67 infs] *Ibid* 61, The West Texan of earlier days called anything unusual a *snorter*. . . Ker. **1968** *DARE* (Qu. B25, . . *Joking names* . . *for a very heavy rain*. . . "*It's a regular _____.*") Inf **MD**24, Snorter. **1998** *Sailing* June 63 **nMI**, I expected to be swallowed up in a monumental Cape Horn tempest, a "snorter" like the one that drove Drake's sistership *Marigold* to the bottom of the sea.

snorting pen n Cf **snorting pole 1**

See quot.

1958 *AmSp* 33.272 **eWA** [Ranching terms], *Snorting pen*. . . A small, circular corral placed inside a larger corral, usually having a post firmly planted in its middle. . . A particular type of snorting pen is used in breeding mules: a mare is put in a rather narrow chute; a stallion is driven in from the front of the chute to excite her; then a jackass is turned in the opposite end to cover her.

snorting pole n

1 A horizontal rail over which a mare and stallion are allowed to make contact as a preliminary to mating; also fig.

1887 *Atchison Daily Globe* (KS) 7 July [4]/2 (newspaperarchive.com), Atchison is, or rather was until the editor of the *Champion* made out of her prosperity a kind of political snorting pole over which to court the favor of the prohibitionists of Kansas, as a stepping stone to gubernatorial honors, a prosperous city. **1928** *Troy Call* (IL) 13 July 4/3, What Edwardsville people should do is to segregate the petters; give some unused portion of the city limits over entirely to that purpose, in fact establish a kind of municipal snorting pole. [**1991** Still *Wolfpen Notebooks* 104 **eKY**, There have been two 'jenny barns' I've visited in my life. . . There was the Stiff Curve over in Knott County. . . And there was The Snorting Pole on the Colson Road in Letcher County. Both stocked with good-looking women.] **1997** Ringholz *On Belay* 15 **ID** (as of c1915), Paul often watched as a horse was unloaded, tied under a tree, and protected from the stallion's flailing hooves by a "snorting pole" placed beside her.

2 In logging: see quots.

1931 *Outdoor Amer.* Mar 35, Kawin slept on the outer side . . his place beside the "snorting pole" which divided the double bunk. **1956** Sorden–Ebert *Logger's Words* 34 **Gt Lakes**, *Snorting-pole*, A sapling or cant-hook-handle which was laid under the hay in a muzzle-loading-bunk to keep the sleepers apart. **1958** McCulloch *Woods Words* 173

Pacific NW, *Snorting pole*—A pole across the foot of loggers' bunks, to shove against in order to get the cramps out of legs.

3 A whipping post or pillory.

1928 in 1970 Gaddis–Long *Killer* 59 **TX** (as of 1911), The next day I ran away, got caught, brought back and whipped at the Snorting Pole. **1980** Malsch *Capt. Lone Wolf* 78 **TX** (as of 1929), "Some of them tried to get smart with us," the "Lone Wolf" recalled, "but we just smacked 'em around and hitched a few to the snortin' pole at the jail." . . The snorting pole was a large, twelve-inch-diameter pole . . to which those arrested could be fastened by means of chains locked around their ankles or necks.

4 See **snorting post 2.**

snorting post n

1 A hitching or snubbing post.

1879 *GA Weekly Telegraph & GA Jrl.* (Macon) 13 May 6/5, It shall be their duty to erect a snorting post, and to direct the sheriff to take all lawyers under 30 years of age before the assembling of court each day, and to snort them; lawyers under fifty years to be snorted once a week, and those under one hundred, once a month, and if this does not shorten their speeches, it shall then be the duty of the grand jury to sew up their mouths. **1905** *Out West Mag.* 22.63, The now hilarious punchers swaggered out to their ponies standing quietly at the "snorting Post," in front. **1936** Adams *Cowboy Lingo* 15, The hitching-post, or rack, in front of the ranch-house was called a . . 'snortin'-post.' **1958** *AmSp* 33.272 **eWA** [Ranching terms], *Snorting post.* . . A stout post used to dally the rope on a caught animal. Most corrals have several planted at strategic spots.

2 also *snorting pole;* Fig: =**snubbing post.**

1884 Royal Arch Masons CA *Proc.* 401, In trying to bring up some of our recalcitrant brethren 'to the snorting pole,' this very question was brought up. **1890** *Landmark* (Statesville NC) 6 Feb [2]/5 (newspaperarchive.com), It may be that said Commissioner can be led up to the snorting pole to do service for grand moguls, but we doubt it. **2004** in 2005 *DARE* File—Internet **TN,** We are now at the snorting post—where we must summarize our findings.

snort up See **snort** v

snot n

1 also *snot crab:* =**fat crab.** esp **MD** Cf **shedder**

1905 U.S. Bur. Fisheries *Rept. for 1904* 411, As the crab approaches the shedding period it begins to show its condition by various external "signs." . . The first indication is a narrow white line which appears just within the thin margin of the last two joints of the posterior pair of legs. . . and the individual bearing it is classed as a "fat crab," or more vulgarly as a "snot." *Ibid* 420, It was formerly customary to break a crab's claw to ascertain whether it had begun to shed, the term "snot" no doubt having arisen from the watery substance which issued from the break. **1976** Warner *Beautiful Swimmers* 27 **eMD,** Mike reads these crabs by examining the translucent next-to-last segment of their swimming legs. Some will be "white sign" crabs, also known as "snots" or "greens." **1984** *DARE* File **Chesapeake Bay** [Watermen's vocab], White sign crab / snot / fat crab. **2001** *DARE* File—Internet **DE, MD,** [Blue Crab Glossary:] Snot Crab—White sign crab, so named because of the watery substance which issues from the "nicking" of the claws. *Ibid,* Fat Crab (also Green Crab, Snot Crab)—Refers to a crab approaching the molting stage and showing a white-rim color sign within the margins of 2 outer segments of the swimming legs. Also describes any crab, between the Buckram and Peeler stages, with firm meat.

2 usu pl; with *the:* Excessive secretion of nasal mucus.

1967 *DARE* (Qu. K47, . . *Diseases* . . *horses or mules commonly get*) Inf **PA23,** Cold, or the snot. **1997** *DARE* File—Internet **WA,** Faculty from the College of Veterinary Medicine . . will make presentations on the following topics. . . Has my foal got pneumonia or just the snots [etc]. **2004** *DARE* File—Internet **FL,** Opened my package and found a green bottle inside. Can't wait for the remains of my case of the snots to wear off so it can be properly savored. **2006** *Ibid* **WA,** Got sick twice. . . The first was the sore throat/flu and the second was the snots.

snot agate n Also *snot marble, snottie, snotty*

A glass playing marble, usu either one that is clear with cloudy inclusions or one that is pale green.

1935 *AmSp* 10.159 **seNE,** *Snot-agate.* . . A glass agate of any color streaked with white. **1957** *Sat. Eve. Post Letters* **NE,** The full name for "snotties" was snot-agates. They were very superior marbles. One with a nicely clouded center was worth a whole handful of "commies." *Ibid*

MI, Snotties—the veined and clouded ones, occasionally quite lovely. *Ibid* **Chicago IL,** Our "mibs" included . . snotties. **1966–69** *DARE* (Qu. EE6a, . . *Different kinds of marbles*—the big one that's used to knock others out of the ring) Inf **MI14,** Snotty—a clear marble with a coloring in it; (Qu. EE6d, *Special marbles*) Infs **IL96, MI103, MT5,** Snotties; **DE2,** Snotties—had all colors—no particular pattern. **1969** O'Connor *Horse & Buggy West* 84 **AZ,** Daring and reckless lads, the cream of the marble elite, gambled with precious agates, glassies, and snot agates. **1969** *DARE* Tape **MI**103, We would have the set-ups, which were onyx, agates, snotties, steelies. **c1970** Wiersma *Marbles Terms* **swMI** (as of c1918), *Snotty* . . a clear marble with a filmy colored swirl through the center. *Ibid* **swMI,** *Snot marble.* . . A catseye. *Ibid* (as of c1920), *Snotty.* . . A regular-sized playing marble; pale green in color. *Ibid, Greeny.* . . In some marble-playing circles it is referred to as a "snotty." *Ibid, Snottie.* . . opaque, with colors foggy and mixed. (Old term). **1974** *DARE* File **KS** (as of 1890), *Snot agate*—All boys used the term. **1983** *MJLF* 9.1.56 **ceKY** (as of 1956), *Snot agate* . . a glass marble with a cloudy, folded interior, like a glob of mucus.

snot crab See **snot 1**

snot-flower n

See quot.

1968 *DARE* FW Addit **neIL,** *Snot-flower*—a flower which exudes a clear, slimy juice when picked. (Children throw them at each other.)

snot horn See **horn** n 4

snot marble, snottie, snotty See **snot agate**

snotweed n

A **four-o'-clock 1** (here: *Mirabilis nyctaginea*).

1942 *Torreya* 42.159 **KS,** *Allionia nyctaginea* Michaux.—Snotweed, Allen County.

snouse v Also with *around* [PaGer *schnausse,* Ger dial *schnäuzen* to stick one's nose into things]

To snoop, rummage; to scout.

1954 *PADS* 21.38 **SC,** *Snouse.* . . To rummage around in another's belongings without permission, on the sly. . . Dutch Fork. **1982** *Barrick Coll.* **csPA,** *Snouse*—nose into something without permission. *Snouse around*—poke curiously through. **2003** in 2005 *DARE* File—Internet **cnVA,** "Snouse" is something my father and his brothers . . and sometimes even one or both of my grandfathers and I did every year in the first several weekends leading up to the opening of deer hunting season. . . Simply put, "snouse" is to visually sniff around. To "snouse" for signs of deer or turkey. **2004** in 2005 *Ibid* **OH,** I did learn however not to let Maud the horse, snouse around in the wagon.

snout v, hence vbl n *snouting*

See quots.

1912 *Gazette* (Stevens Point WI) 30 Oct [3]/2 (newspaperarchive.com), This is the device I use in ringing and snouting hogs. **1937** *AmSp* 12.104 **eNE** [Farm terms], Most farmers *snout* their hogs; that is, they cut slits in the gristle of the hog's nose to prevent rooting. If they do not snout them they sometimes *ring* them, or clamp metal rings in the gristle.

snoutbean n

A plant of the genus *Rhynchosia.* For other names of var spp see **dollar weed 1, wild bean 1e**

1972 Brown *Wildflowers* LA 87, Snout Bean—*Rhynchosia minima.* . . Widespread and common, fields and pinelands. Also Texas, Arkansas, and Mississippi. **2000** *Capital* (Annapolis MD) 14 July sec B 1/5, The proposed changes would affect . . obscure plants, including the seven-angled pipewort and hairy snoutbean.

snouting See **snout**

snow n See **snow goose 1**

snow v[1], hence vbl n *snowing*

To spread snow on (a thoroughfare) to facilitate travel.

1905 U.S. Forest Serv. *Bulletin* 61.48 [Logging terms], *Snow a road, to.* To cover bare spots in a logging road with snow, to facilitate the passage of sleds. (N[orthern] F[orest]) **1959** *VT Hist.* 27.158, *Snow a bridge.* . . To spread snow in a covered bridge so that sleds or cars can pass through. Rare. **1983** *Greenfield Recorder* (MA) 22 Jan 6, There might be good sledding in some places on a road, then an almost bare stretch where the wind had blown the snow off, or the sun shone in hot, so horses could not draw the sled load on that partly bare ground, and the teamsters had to cart or shovel snow onto all that stretch of road, which made the trip long, and a late chore time when they got home. It was called "snowing the road."

snow v[2] |snau| [Prob blend of **snum** v + **swow**]

Used in exclam phr *I snow:* see quot.

1951 *PADS* 15.67 **cwNH,** *Snow!, I:* [snau] exclamation of amazement.

snow angel n   **chiefly Nth, N Midl**   See Map   Cf **angel 4, fairy 3**

The figure of an angel made by lying on one's back in the snow and moving one's extended arms and legs back and forth.

1931 *Chicago Tribune* (IL) 18 Dec 8, [Advt:] You can make snow angels or skim the highest jumps . . for they take to snow like an eskimo. **1945** *Middletown Times Herald* (NY) 12 Oct 4/3, Can you imagine me down on my back in the middle of the sidewalk down in Chelsea Village where I live, flapping my arms to make a snow angel. **1965–70** *DARE* (Qu. EE26, . . *Games . . children play in the snow*) 87 Infs, **chiefly Nth, N Midl,** Snow angels. **2002** *DARE* File—Internet **ND,** North Dakotans of all ages and sizes are invited to . . join the fun in setting a world record for making the most number of snow angels at any one time.

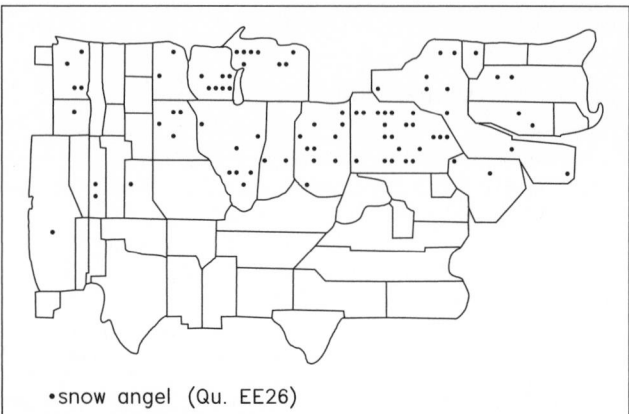

•snow angel (Qu. EE26)

snowball n   [*OED2* 1760 →]

1 also pl; also *snowball bush,* ~ *tree:* A shrub of the eastern US, usu **hydrangea 1** or **viburnum,** having showy white flowers in globular clusters; the flower itself.   Cf **wild snowball 2**

1773 *NY Gaz. & Weekly Mercury* (NY) 18 Oct 2/4, [Advt:] Timber Trees and flowering Shrubs . . Snow-ball tree, 2s. **1832** Hale *Flora's Interp.* 165, Snow ball. *Viburnum. opulus.* . . A genus found in Europe, America and Japan. **1834** Audubon *Ornith. Biog.* 2.121, The swamp snowball. *Hydrangea quercifolia.* . . found on the broken sandy banks bordering small water-courses, and is abundant in such situations in the uplands of Louisiana. **1899** (1912) Green *VA Folk-Speech* 399, *Snowball.* . . A shrub bearing large white balls of flowers. *Viburnum opulus.* (2) The flower itself. **1907** in 1953 *PA Dutchman* Apr 5, If it were spring, you went back with a shining quarter to exchange for tightly bunched narcissus . . or lilac and snowballs, enough to fill the house when released from their string bondage. **1938** Stuart *Dark Hills* 209 **eKY,** That smell of crab-apple blossoms was sure sweeter than the smell of the snowballs in the back yard. **1966–70** *DARE* (Qu. S26e, *Other wildflowers not yet mentioned;* not asked in early QRs) Inf **MD**13, Snowball—white, many tiny flowers cluster together in ball the size of orange; **PA**235, Snowball—spreads in yard (may not be wild)—roundish leaves coming to point, large bunches of white flowers in a ball; grows up to 5 feet high; **VA**43, Snowball bush. **1967** *DARE* FW Addit **cePA,** *Snowball bush*—a white hydrangea. **1978** *Yankee* Oct 56 **NH,** The knot is from a cranberry tree, sometimes called a snowball tree. **1986** Pederson *LAGS Concordance,* 3 infs, **TN,** Snowball; 1 inf, **GA,** Snowball—tall bush, large white blooms; in hills. **1996** Horton *Island Out of Time* 19 **Chesapeake Bay MD,** Note with approval that the "snowball bush," a prominent hydrangea behind Miss Virginia Evans's house, is about to bloom. **2001** House *Clay's Quilt* 146 **eKY,** The yard was wide and flat, with a huge snowball bush to one side.

2 A **snowberry 1** (here: *Symphoricarpos albus*).

1898 *Jrl. Amer. Folkl.* 11.228 **NY,** *Symphoricarpos racemosus* [=*S. albus*] . . snowball, Alcove N.Y. **1910** Graves *Flowering Plants* 367

CT, *Symphoricarpos racemosus.* . . Snowberry. Snowball. Rare. Roadsides and about old house sites as an escape from cultivation. **1957** *NY Times* (NY) 8 Dec sec D 33/6, The berries of the snowball bush (symphoricarpos) look for all the world like snowballs.

3 also pl; also *snowball bush:* A white-flowered plant of the western US such as **butterball 4, buttonbush 1,** or **sand verbena 1.**   Cf **little snowball**

1915 (1926) Armstrong–Thornber *Western Wild Flowers* 92, Butter Balls, Snow Balls—*Eriogonum orthocaulon.* . . These are attractive plants, with pretty odd little balls of flowers. *Ibid* 104, Sand Puffs—*Abronia salsa.* . . This is sometimes called Snow-ball. **1945** Benson–Darrow *Manual SW Trees* 301, *Cephalanthus occidentalis.* . . The distinctive balls of flowers have given rise to application of a variety of vernacular names, including button willow, globe flower, honeyballs, and snowball. **1966** Barnes–Jensen *Dict. UT Slang* 39, *Snow Ball* . . a name often given to Sand Puffs *(Abronia salsa).* **1966–68** *DARE* (Qu. S6) Inf **NM**9, Could be a snowball bush—has a large number of tiny daisy-like flowers in clusters; (Qu. S26e, *Other wildflowers not yet mentioned;* not asked in early QRs) Inf **CA**60, Butterballs or snowballs—desert—white, round flower, grows on 18-inch stalk if enough moisture. **1990** *Plants SW* (Catalog) 17, *Abronia fragrans.* . . Snowball, Sweet Sand Verbena—Large, round, snowball-like clusters of white, fragrant flowers on long trailing stems.

4 also *snow-belly:* A recently molted crab.   **Chesapeake Bay** Cf **buckram, buster 5, comer 2, green** adj **1, papershell 1, peeler crab, rank** adj **4, whitebelly 3, whitey 4**

1976 Warner *Beautiful Swimmers* 161 **Chesapeake Bay,** The crabs in the Number Three basket showed the telltale grayish cast on their topsides and the lustrous white on their abdomens that are the marks of a recently moulted adult crab. Post-buckrams, you might say. Lester calls them "whiteys." In other parts of the Bay they are known as "snowballs" or "white bellies" and not taken by crabbers. **2000** Shores *Tangier Is.* 220 **Chesapeake Bay,** When the crab first becomes hard, it is not of great market value because it is not *fat,* meaning, if cooked, its body cavity would not be solidly packed. *White-belly, snowball,* and *snow-belly* are names for this crab.

5 also *snow cone:* A Black person—usu used as a nickname for a Black man.   [*OED2* 1795 →]   *usu derog*

1821 *New-York Spectator* (NY) 4 Sept 1/2, You insulted Jacky Snowball, by peeping into do window, ven he vas charming de bon and lubly Missa Dinah. **1832** *NY Mirror* 20 Oct 123 **NY,** His negro wench, "poor old Snow Ball," . . "slipped her bridle, and went out like a flash in the pan." **1834** *Sun* (NY NY) 20 Mar 1/2, A huge looking 'yaller gall' was 'hammering away at the eyes of a small white man . . because he had called her a *snow ball.*' **1843** *S. Lit. Messenger* Nov 650 **Sth,** "Well done fur the nigger!" ejaculated my betting friend—"here's a *dime* for you, snowball." **1850** *Proc. U.S. Senate on the Fugitive Slave Bill* 6, Well, General Snowball comes back to South Carolina, and he goes to his master, and tells him, "Sir, I am a citizen, and I demand to be put in the enjoyment of all the rights to which the white citizen is entitled. . ." The idea is preposterous, not to say revolting. **1905** *DN* 3.20 **cCT,** *Snowball.* . . A jeering appellation for a negro. **1907** *DN* 3.218 **nwAR,** *Snowball.* . . A jeering appellation for a negro. **1909** *DN* 3.372 **eAL, wGA,** *Snowball.* . . A common appellation for a very black negro. **1968** *DARE* File **Madison WI,** [Postcard caption:] Snowball—Nicknamed affectionately by students at the University of Wisconsin—a window washer and a reader of books. Madison, 1967. **1970** Tarpley *Blinky* 265 **neTX,** Teasing and derogatory names for Negroes . . snow balls, snow cones [rare]. **2005** *DARE* File—Internet **ME** (as of a1819), It is said that this man [who died in 1819] followed James Fowler home from the Rev. War. . . His nickname was "Snowball." He was a Negro.

6 A poor White person.

1986 Pederson *LAGS Concordance (The poor whites)* 1 inf, **ceAL,** Snowballs—blacks called whites when they were young.

7 also sp *snoball:* Shaved or crushed ice molded into a ball over which a flavored syrup is poured.   Cf **hokey-pokey** n[1], **shave ice,** *DJE* **snowball**

1895 *Newark Daily Advocate* (OH) 10 June 3/3, **NYC,** The street fakirs have something new. It is a delusive arrangement of ice and gingery—or rather peppery—sirups. The products are called "snowballs." **1911** *Washington Post* (DC) 11 July 14/3, Alarmed by the return to Washington of venders [sic] of cheap candy, scraped ice snowballs, hokey-pokey ice cream, and other forms of low quality confectionery, . . the government's pure food expert . . announced his intention . . to stop . . the sale of these articles. **1941** Writers' Program *Guide LA* 229, Today, in hot

weather children enjoy "snowballs," a confection made of crushed ice and brightly colored syrups. **1948** *AN&Q* 8.77 **NYC,** Homemade "snowballs," a concoction made of shaved ice and flavoring, which must have borne a marked similarity to the old-time "hoky-poky," were sold in New York City during the 1948 heat wave. **1950** *AmSp* 25.306, In Pittsburgh around 1900 we boys bought from the itinerant 'hokeypokey ice-cream man' a one-cent confection called a *snowball.* . . The vendor made a snowball by shaving a handful of ice, molding it into a ball, laying it on a piece of paper, and squirting into it two or three shots of brightly colored fruit juice. . . During the summer of 1949 . . signs in little stores [in Maryland] said 'Snowballs for Sale.' **1984** Stall *Proud New Orleans* 179, New Orleans is the undisputed world capital for snoballs. And we don't mean snow cones, those miserable cone-shaped chunks of ice doused with thin spearmint, strawberry or grape syrup. . . New Orleans snoballs, with shaved ice and rich-flavored syrups, are enjoyed by Orleanians with the same intensity as a good bowl of gumbo. **2004** *Times–Picayune* (New Orleans LA) 8 July Food sec 2 (Internet), Snowball ice is much finer and fluffier, never crunchy like a snow cone's pellets. . . There are also other pockets in the United States where snowballs are popular. Utah is one, as well as Baltimore.
8 See quot.
  1939 FWP *ID Lore* 244, The following is reported as the talk of a southwest Idaho cowboy: . . the cowboys fall in line to grab their shoe soles (pancakes) and snowballs (biscuits) and sheepdip (coffee).

snowball bush See **snowball 1, 3**

snowball cactus n
1 also *snowball pincushion:* A **pincushion cactus 3** (here: *Coryphantha vivipara*).
  1942 Hylander *Plant Life* 322, Our representatives [of pincushion cacti] include . . the Snowball Cactus and the Finger Cactus. *Ibid,* The Snowball Pincushion . . is a spherical low-growing plant thickly covered with white spines; it is a cactus of the prairies from Colorado to Kansas, ranging south into Texas and north into Canada. **2005** *DARE* File—Internet **AZ,** Coryphantha vivipara var. rosea—Rose Beehive Snowball Cacti.
2 A **pincushion cactus 5** (here: *Pediocactus simpsonii*).
  1976 Bailey–Bailey *Hortus Third* 832, [Pediocactus] Simpsonii. . . Snowball cactus. . . to 6 in. high and 5 in. thick. . . W. Kans., w. to New Mex., Mont., Idaho. **2001** *DARE* File—Internet **Rocky Mts,** Snowball cactus (Pediocactus simpsonii var. minor).
3 also *snowball cushion cactus:* A **pincushion cactus 1** (here: *Mammillaria candida* or *M. bocasana*).
  2001 *DARE* File—Internet, [Mammillaria] bocasana—Snowball Cactus, Powder Puff. [M.] candida—Snowball Cushion Cactus. *Ibid,* The Snowball Cactus is spherical with snow-white short spines, appearing through a quantity of fine white hair.

snowball pincushion See **snowball cactus 1**

snowball rain n Also *snowball winter* [Perh in allusion to **snowball 1**] **esp S Midl** Cf **blackberry winter**
A period of inclement weather in the spring; see quots.
  1894 *News* (Frederick MD) 5 May [5]/2 (newspaperarchive.com), May . . dawned warm as the days of July. Its first two days brought out the summer dresses, but . . it turned cool again and brought the snowball rain. **1932** *AmSp* 7.233 **MO,** In Missouri we have *blackberry winter,* referring . . to a belated spell of winter weather at the time that wild blackberries are in bloom. We have also *snow-ball winter,* a similar recurrence at the time of the first whitening of the bloom of the common snow-ball (*viburnum,* var. sterile). **1955** *Sun* (Baltimore MD) 28 Apr 38/2 *(Hench Coll.),* The Weather Bureau delved into some ancient lore . . and announced that the period of rainy, cloudy weather from which Baltimore should emerge today was the period of "sheep rains" or "snowball rains." . . During this season of the year the snow ball bush comes into full bloom and possibly because of this and the fact that snow indicates rather cold conditions, the term "snowball rains" came into being. **2002** *News & Rec.* (Greensboro NC) 8 May People sec 4 (Internet), Unfortunately . . our usual "blackberry winter," also called "snowball winter," moved in during the night.

snowball saxifrage n [See quot 1953]
A **saxifrage 1** (here: *Saxifraga rhomboidea*).
  1913 *Bedford Gaz.* (PA) 17 Oct 2/3 **CO,** Beautiful snowball saxifrage, . . and arctic gentian seem to bloom in vain. **1953** Nelson *Plants Rocky Mt. Park* 87, Snowball, or diamondleaf saxifrage. . . a stout stem

is sent up from the center . . bearing a dense headlike cluster of small white flowers. **2005** *Aspen Times* (CO) 12 Aug (Internet), Snowball saxifrage and alpine spring beauty are examples you'll see here.

snowball shoe n esp **NEng** Cf **mud shoe**
A horseshoe designed for use on snow.
  1866 *Bangor Daily Whig & Courier* (ME) 8 Dec [3]/6 (newspaperarchive.com), [Advt:] It will be remembered that Mr. Bither is the inventor of the famous *snow-ball shoe.* **1898** *Portsmouth Herald* (NH) 20 Aug 1/7, Bay horse, nine years old, . . has snowball shoes on well worn down. **1942** ME Univ. *Studies* 57.46 **nwME** (as of 1935–40) [Pulpwood terms], In the winter, for work in snow, a so-called "snow-ball" shoe is used. This shoe is considerably lighter than the mud shoe, having a convex edge on the inside that will not hold dirt or snow as readily as the square edge of the mud shoe.

snowball tree See **snowball 1**

snowball winter See **snowball rain**

snowbell n
1 Std: a plant of the genus *Styrax.* For other names of var spp see **mock orange 1d, spring ~**
2 A **silverbell 1** (here: *Halesia diptera*).
  1960 Vines *Trees SW* 842, Vernacular names [of *Halesia diptera*] are Snowdrop-tree, Snow-bell, and Cowlicks. . . Silver-bell flowers are attractive but unfortunately the tree is generally irregular in shape.

snow-belly See **snowball 4**

snowberry n [Because the berries are white]
1 A plant of the genus *Symphoricarpos;* the fruit of such a plant. **esp West** For other names of var spp see **buckbrush 3a, buckbush, coralberry 1, deerberry e, honeysuckle 5b, partridgeberry 4, snowball 2, snowdrop 1, waxberry 2, wolfberry 1**
  1813 in 1905 Lewis *Orig. Jrls. Lewis & Clark Exped.* 7.393, I have growing . . a very handsome little shrub of the size of a currant bush. Its beauty consists in a great produce of berries of the size of currants, and literally as white as snow. . . We call it the snow-berry bush, no botanical name being yet given to it. **1844** Lapham *Geogr. Descr. WI* 80, Symphoricarpus racemosus . . snow berry. **1870** MO State Entomol. *Annual Rept.* 113, The White-berry or Snow-berry (*Symphoricarpus racemosus*). **1937** U.S. Forest Serv. *Range Plant Hdbk.* B151-2 **West,** Common snowberry and mountain snowberry are the two most common and widely distributed western snowberries. **1941** Jaeger *Wildflowers* 256, Long-flowered snowberry. . . This handsome, exceedingly sweet-scented shrub, 1–4 ft. high, is common in the piñon-juniper belt of the Inyo and other mountains of the Death Valley region [of seCA]; east to Nev. and Utah. **1953** [see **2** below]. **1957** Barnes *Nat. Hist. Wasatch Summer* 51 **UT,** The dogwood . . and the partridge berry (*Symphoricarpos rotundifolius*), sometimes called the "snowberry" or "waxberry" have harmless white berries. **1961** Douglas *My Wilderness* 17 **CO,** Snowberry that shows white pulpy fruit by September is common. **1966–67** *DARE* FW Addit **WA10,** Symphoricarpos—snowberry—white berry all over Washington in late fall; shrubs in honeysuckle family; **WA**12, 30, Snowberry. **1967** *DARE* (Qu. I44, *What kinds of berries grow wild around here?*) Inf **OR1,** Snowberries. **2005** *Milwaukee Jrl. Sentinel* (WI) 10 Apr sec N 8 (Internet), Before conifers became the best-loved foundation plantings . . , a variety of bushes including forsythia, spirea and snowberries graced front yards across the land.
2 A tropical plant of the genus *Chiococca.* [*OED2* 1815 →] Also called **milkberry, rat-root**
  1876 Hobbs *Bot. Hdbk.* 108, Snowberry, . . Chiococca racemosa. **1933** Small *Manual SE Flora* 1259, Chiococca [spp]. . . Snowberries. **1953** Greene–Blomquist *Flowers South* 121, Snow-berry (*Chiococca alba*)—This attractive shrub should perhaps be called the "southern snow-berry" since another "snow-berry" (*Symphoricarpos albus*) occurs in the North. . . Fruit is a white, berry-like drupe. **1970** Correll *Plants TX* 1492, Chiococca alba. . . David's milkberry, snow-berry, perlilla, canica. . . In palm groves and brushlands. **2003** in 2005 *DARE* File—Internet **FL,** Chiococca parvifolia, pineland snowberry, is a low ground cover with small white flowers and showy white fruits.
3 A **wintergreen 2** (here: *Gaultheria hispidula*). Cf **creeping snowberry**
  1916 *Torreya* 16.239 **ME,** Chiogenes hispidula. . . Sugar plum, snowberry, moxie vine, Matinicus I[slan]d. **2006** *DARE* File—Internet **WI,** Snowberry—Gaultheria hispidula—Shrub.

snowbird n

1 Either the snow bunting *(Plectrophenax nivalis)* or a **junco** n[1] (here: usu *Junco hyemalis).*

1674 Josselyn *Two Voyages* 100 **NEng,** The *Snow*-bird is like a *Chaf-Finch,* go in flocks and are good meat. **1709** (1967) Lawson *New Voyage* 150, The Snow-Birds are most numerous in the North Parts of *America,* where there are great Snows. They visit us sometimes in *Carolina,* when the Weather is harder than ordinary. They are like the Stones Smach [=the stonechat], or Wheat-Ears, and are delicate Meat. **1792** Belknap *Hist. NH* 3.172, *Snow bird,—Emberiza hyemalis?* The *snow bird* is smaller than a sparrow, and appears in little flocks, in the winter, enlivening the gloom of that dreary season. **1839** Audubon *Synopsis Birds* 106, Niphæa hyemalis. . . Common Snow-Bird. . . Distributed, in winter, over the Southern, Western, and Middle Districts, as far as the base of the Rocky Mountains, and in the Fur Countries. **1869** *Atlantic Mth.* June 707 **NY,** In a certain locality in the interior of New York, I know, every season, where I am sure to find a nest or two of the slate-colored snowbird. **1939** FWP *Guide TN* 17, Among the winter visitors from the North are the horned lark, and the junco, or "snowbird." **1966–70** DARE (Qu. Q14) Inf **KY**76, Snowbird—junco; (Qu. Q21, . . *Kinds of sparrows)* Inf **MI**23, Snowbird—whiter than the regular sparrow; always stays in a flock. **1973** Nelson *Hunters Nthn. Forest* 82, One man said that despite their [=snow buntings'] small size "snow birds" were used in the recent past to make a tasty stew. **1982** Ginns *Snowbird Gravy* 22 **nwNC,** Back when we growed up, . . we'd catch snowbirds. . . Makes as nice a pot of gravy as you've ever seen if you get enough of 'em. **1991** Tabbert *Dict. Alaskan Engl.* 167, In Canada and Alaska *snowbird* is especially used for the snow bunting *(Plectrophenax nivalis),* a sparrow-like ground bird of white and black summer plumage and one of the first to return in the spring. **1995** *Brophy Coll.* 70 **swMO** (as of c1960), Snowbird. [T]he slate-colored junco, conspicuous in winter.

2 A **redpoll 1** (here: *Carduelis flammea).*

1811 Wilson *Amer. Ornith.* 4.42, *Lesser Red-poll.* . . They appear . . with the first deep snow, and on that account are usually called by the title of Snow-birds. **1890** Warren *Birds PA* 229, Acanthis linaria. . . Redpoll; Little Snow-bird.

3 A sparrow; see quots.

1909 *DN* 3.373 **eAL, wGA,** Snowbird. . . Applied to the common field-sparrow. Called also *grass-sparrow.* **1956** MA Audubon Soc. *Bulletin* 40.254 **MA,** Tree Sparrow. Snowbird. . . As being seen in the snowy, or wintry, season. **1965–70** DARE (Qu. Q21, . . *Kinds of sparrows)* 10 Infs, **scattered,** Snowbird; **KS**5, Snowbird—that's a form of a sparrow; **MD**18, Snowbird—smaller than English sparrow, brown spot on top of head, darker brown than the rest of his feathers; **SD**8, Grass sparrow—called snowbirds in winter; (Qu. Q11) Inf **TX**73, Snowbird—comes in when cold; (Qu. Q14) Infs **CA**101, **KY**56, **NC**35, **WI**78, Snowbird; (Qu. Q20, . . *Kinds of swallows and birds like them)* Infs **CA**137, **DC**13, Snowbird. [DARE Ed: Some of these Infs may refer instead to other senses.] **1986** Pederson *LAGS Concordance,* 1 inf, **neMS,** Snowbirds—smaller than sparrows, brown or gray.

4 =**white-tailed ptarmigan.**

1928 Bailey *Birds NM* 205, A local hunter whom Mr. Bailey met on Costilla Peak said that he usually found the "Snowbirds," as he called them [=southern white-tailed ptarmigan], very tame and sitting around on the little benches near a snow-bank at about 13,300 feet.

5 =**chickadee** n[1] **1.**

1928 *Athens Messenger* (OH) 20 Feb 8/6, The junco shares the name snowbird with the chickadee. **1966–67** DARE (Qu. Q14) Inf **NY**6, Snowbird—very small winter bird, same as chickadee; (Qu. Q23) Inf **NM**13, Chickadee—also called a snowbird. **1982** Slone *How We Talked* 99 **eKY** (as of c1950), If the chickie-dee birds (snow birds) gather together under trees, it's going to snow that night.

6 =**horned lark.** Cf **snow lark**

1921 in 2005 DARE File—Internet [*Omaha Sunday World–Herald* 30 Jan sec E 6] **NE,** Often described as a "Snowbird," which it isn't, the horned lark commences its affairs of the heart even as early as this date, and nests while the snow is yet upon the ground. **1967** DARE (Qu. Q15, . . *Kinds of larks)* Inf **MI**53, Horned lark—often called the snowbird.

snowboys n

1 A **wood anemone** (here: *Anemone quinquefolia).*

1933 Small *Manual SE Flora* 517, A[nemone] *quinquefolia* . . Nightcaps. Snowboys. Wood-anemone.

2 =**Dutchman's breeches 1.**

1951 Voss–Eifert *IL Wild Flowers* 5, Dutchman's Breeches (Boys and Girls. Snowboys).

snow bread n

Corn bread made with snow as a leavening agent; similarly nouns *snow fritter,* ~ *griddle cake,* ~ *pancake.*

1832 in 2005 DARE File—Internet **IN,** Told Gen. McLane how to make snow bread and he told me how to make snow soap. **1836** in 1959 AmSp 34.31, Both this and the snow bread bake very well in a stove. **1846** Cornelius *Young Housekeeper's Friend* 35 **NEng,** Snow Fritters. Stir together salt, milk, and flour, to make rather a thick batter. Add new-fallen snow in the proportion of a teacup full to a pint of milk. Have the fat ready hot, at the time you stir in the snow, and drop the batter into it with a spoon. **1880** (1881) Parloa *Miss Parloa's Cook Book* 367 **NEng,** Snow Pancakes. . . Beat the egg light, and add the milk to it. Pour gradually on the flower, and beat until smooth and light. Add the apple and salt, and at the last moment the snow. Drop by spoonfuls into boiling fat. **1913** (1980) Hardy *OH Schoolmistress* 61, It [=snow bread] was a bread of corn meal made with snow. **1940** Brown *Amer. Cooks* 437 **MN,** *Minnesota snow pancakes.* . . Speed is essential with Snow Pancakes, since the air in the snow is the only leaven. **1986** Pederson *LAGS Concordance,* 1 inf, **ceTN,** Snow bread—corn bread with snow put on [sic] it. **1996** Goldstein *Vegetarian Hearth* 203 **NEng,** Lucia Gray Swett . . [in] her *New England Breakfast Breads,* published in Boston in 1891, also includes. . . instructions for "Snow Griddle Cakes." [**2003** DARE File **nwMA** (as of early 20th cent), Yes, my mother used snow in her doughnuts. No, I have no idea why she did it.]

snowbrush n

1 A **buckbrush 3c,** esp *Ceanothus velutinus.* For other names of the latter see **greasewood 2j, mountain balm 3,** ~ **laurel 4, snowbush, sticky laurel, tobacco brush, varnish-leaf ceanothus**

1898 Coville *Forest Growth OR* 19, The yellow-pine forests are denser . . with an undergrowth of snow brush *(Ceanothus velutinus).* **1915** (1926) Armstrong–Thornber *Western Wild Flowers* 282, Snow Brush, Mountain Lilac—*Ceanothus velutinus.* . . The small, sweet-scented flowers are crowded in compact, creamy clusters, sometimes four or five inches long, very handsome, but not so delicate as Deer-brush. **1937** U.S. Forest Serv. *Range Plant Hdbk.* B47, Snowbrush—*Ceanothus velutinus.* . . Snowbrush refers to the abundant fluffy masses of white flowers. **1942** Hylander *Plant Life* 369, The Snow Brush of the prairie states [=*Ceanothus sanguineus*], (known as Oregon Tea farther west) is a taller shrub. **1951** *PADS* 15.16 **sCA,** *Ceanothus prostratus.* . . Snow-brush. **1969** DARE (Qu. T5, . . *Kinds of evergreens, other than pine)* Inf **CA**136, Snowbrush. **1973** Stephens *Woody Plants* 370, *Ceanothus fendleri.* . . Snow brush, deer brush, deer brier. **2002** *Washington Post* (DC) 16 Sept sec A 9 (Internet), The most studied surprise plant is shiny leaf ceanothus, commonly known as snowbrush for its masses of small white flowers.

2 A **rhododendron** (here: *Rhododendron albiflorum).*

1910 *Mountaineer* (Seattle WA) 3.20 **nwWA,** On all sides of camp were clump after clump of the white rhododendron *(Rhododendron albiflorum).* . . The packers said that this bush is always called by them "Snowbrush." **1937** U.S. Forest Serv. *Range Plant Hdbk.* B30, False-azalea [=*Rhododendron albiflorum*]. . . is also variously known as small azalea, white-flowered rhododendron, Rocky Mountain rhododendron, and snowbrush; the latter name, in use by stockmen of the Northwest, is more correctly applied to *Ceanothus velutinus.*

snowbush n

Any of var western spp of **ceanothus** with profuse white flowers, esp a **snowbrush 1** (here: *Ceanothus velutinus)* or *C. cordulatus.*

1890 *Century Dict.* 5735, *Snowbush.* . . One of several shrubs bearing profuse white flowers. Such are *Ceanothus cordulatus* of Californian mountains [etc]. **1920** Rice–Rice *Pop. Studies CA Wild Flowers* 13, A variety [of ceanothus] known to botanists as *C. cordulatus* . . , bordering higher altitudes, is popularly called "Snow Bush"; for when in full bloom it resembles fields of newly fallen snow. **1924** Hawkins *Trees & Shrubs* 97, Mountain laurel, snow bush, chaparral, and New Jersey tea are other common names [of *Ceanothus velutinus*]. **1940** Writers' Program *Guide NV* 12, Also in . . [the belt converging into the subalpine] are the glossy-leafed snow bush or tobacco bush *(Ceanothus velutinus)* and its prostrate relative, the squaw mat *(Ceanothus prostratus).* **1946**

Peattie *Pacific Coast* 55, The most characteristic chaparral plants are the gnarled tree-shrubs, numberless in species and variously called wild or California lilac or blue blossom when their flowers are blue or lavender, and whitethorn or snowbush when they are white. **1957** Barnes *Nat. Hist. Wasatch Summer* 12 **UT**, As we rest we can smell the rich fragrance of the mountain lilac whose white flowers inspired the name "snowbush." **1961** Douglas *My Wilderness* 14 **CO**, Snowbush, the fragrant shrub that is abundant in the Pacific Northwest, is only sparingly present. **1967** *DARE* FW Addit **OR**12, Snowbush—shiny evergreen shrub *(Ceanothus velutinus)*. **2003** *Mt. Democrat* (Placerville CA) 20 June sec C 2/5, C. cordulatus, "Snowbush" has white flowers.

snow cone   See **snowball 5**

snow cream n   Also *snow ice-cream, snow mush*
A confection of snow, sugar, and cream or milk.
  1849 *Cultivator* 6.97 **NJ**, Snow Cream. . . Take any quantity of cream. . . Add pure snow, . . stir in . . sugar. . . Apply a few drops of essence of lemon, vanilla or rose water. **1898** *Harper's New Mth. Mag.* 97.527 **sePA**, Theophilus had made acquaintance with Katy by offering her . . a tumbler of snow ice-cream. Katy, as silently, ate the slushy mixture of sugar and milk and snow. **1939** Wolcott *Yankee Cook Book* 190, *Uncooked snow cream [A child's delight; some children call it "Snow Mush"]*—Fill a tall glass with light new clean snow. Pour in rich milk. Add a tablespoon of sugar, a few drops of red (vegetable) coloring, 2 or 3 drops of vanilla to taste. Beat mixture . . and serve immediately. **1942** McAtee *Dial. Grant Co. IN* 59 (as of 1890s), *Snow-ice-cream* . . children's mixture of snow, sugar, and milk or cream. **1956** McAtee *Some Dialect NC* 41, *Snow cream*. . . Snow mixed with milk and sugar. **c1960** *Wilson Coll.* **csKY**, *Snow-cream*. . . Sugar and milk added to snow, to form a back-country ice-cream. **c1965** Randle *Cookbooks* (Ask Neighbor) 80 **neOH**, *Snow Ice Cream.* [Recipe includes milk, sugar, eggs, flavoring, salt.] **1968** *DARE* FW Addit **Sth**, First we would get a big pan of snow. . . Then, rushing to keep it from melting, Mama would mix a bit of real cow cream seasoned with vanilla into the snow, and the result was snow cream. **2004** *Pantagraph* (Bloomington IL) 7 Feb sec A 12 (Internet), What about taking advantage of those drifts with a little old-fashioned snow ice cream.

snow cup n
A **mallow B** (here: *Anoda cristata*).
  1959 Carleton *Index Herb. Plants* 109, *Snow cup:* Anoda lavateroides [=A. cristata]. **2005** *DARE* File—Internet **CT** [Select Seeds catalog], "*Anoda* 'Snow Cup'"—Satiny white cup-shaped flowers bloom in summer.

snowdrop n, also pl
1 also *snowdrop berry:* A **snowberry 1** (here: *Symphoricarpos albus*).
  1892 *Jrl. Amer. Folkl.* 5.97 **OH**, Symphoricarpus racemosus, snowdrop. Mansfield, O. **1900** Lyons *Plant Names* 361, *S[ymphoricarpos] racemosus.* . . Snow-berry, Snow-drop . . , Snow-drop-berry. **1968** *DARE* (Qu. S26e) Inf **CA**79, Snowdrops—a tiny white flower, grows in clusters on hillsides.
2 A **wood anemone** (here: *Anemone quinquefolia*) or the closely related **rue anemone.** Cf **snowflower 2**
  1884 *Olean Democrat* (NY) [15 July 2]/3 (newspaperarchive.com) **NYC**, Among them was a large quantity of bulbs of the anemone, commonly called the snowdrop, which is white, has five petals, and comes up and flowers as soon as the violets do. **1896** *Jrl. Amer. Folkl.* 9.179 **MA**, Anemone nemorosa [=A. quinquefolia] . . snow-drops, Lynn, Mass. **1940** Clute *Amer. Plant Names* 1, *A[nemone] quinquefolia.* Wood Anemone. Windflower, nightcaps, snowdrops. **1968** *DARE* FW Addit **DE**, [Photograph of rue anemone:] Snowdrops. **1969–70** *DARE* (Qu. S2, . . *The flower that comes up in the woods early in spring, with three white petals that turn pink as the flower grows older*) Inf **CT**42, Snowdrops—white flower, early spring; (Qu. S11) Inf **MI**93, Snowdrop—early spring flower, shaped like a lily; (Qu. S26c, *Wildflowers that grow in woods*) Infs **IL**99, **KY**9, 71, 82, Snowdrops. **1989** *Chron.-Telegram* (Elyria OH) 28 Apr 35/5, Spring Hill Nurseries . . has a new Snowdrop anemone whose white flowers on 1-foot stems add a decorative touch beneath trees.
3 A **fritillary** (here: *Fritillaria pudica*). **UT**
  1915 (1926) Armstrong–Thornber *Western Wild Flowers* 38 **UT**, Yellow fritillary. . . the local Utah names, Crocus, Snowdrop, and Buttercup are absurd. **1966** Barnes–Jensen *Dict. UT Slang* 11, *Crocus* . . the orange fritillaria *(Fritillaria pudica),* snowdrop or yellow bells is some-

times called crocus. **2005** *DARE* File—Internet **OH** [Hirt's Gardens], Golden Snowdrop. . . *Fritillaria pudica.*
4 A **wintergreen 1** (here: *Moneses uniflora*).
  1916 *Torreya* 16.239 **ME**, Moneses uniflora. . . Snowdrop, Matinicus I[slan]d.
5 A **mariposa lily** (here: *Calochortus albus*).
  1923 in 1925 Jepson *Manual Plants CA* 238, White Globe Lily. . . Also called Snow-drops, Indian Bells, and Satin Bells. **1969** *DARE* (Qu. S26a, . . *Wildflowers.* . . *Roadside flowers*) Inf **CA**127, Tiger lilies, mariposa lilies, snowdrops. [*DARE* Ed: It is impossible to determine whether the Inf was equating or differentiating the second and third responses.]
6 A **turkey pea 2c,** usu *Orogenia linearifolia.*
  1963 Craighead *Rocky Mt. Wildflowers* 129, Orogenia linearifolia. . . This is one of the first spring flowers to appear in the high mt. valleys. It frequently emerges through the melting snowbanks, thus earning the local name of Snowdrops. **1966** Barnes–Jensen *Dict. UT Slang* 39, *Snow Drops* . . local name for Turkey Peas *(Orogenia linearifolia).* **1970** Kirk *Wild Edible Plants W. U.S.* 122, *Orogenia fusiformis* and *linearifolia.* . . Indian Potato, Snowdrops. **1974** (1977) Coon *Useful Plants* 261, *Orogenia linearifolia*—Turkey pea, Indian potato, snowdrops.

snowdrop berry   See **snowdrop 1**

snowdrop tree n   [See quot 1846]
=**silver bell 1.**
  1797 Smith *Nat. Hist. GA* 91, Halesia Tetraptera [=Halesia carolina]. . . Snow-drop Tree. **1846** Browne *Trees* 366, Halesia tetraptera, The Common Snowdrop-Tree. . . Its flowers are produced in great abundance; and, from their shape, colour, and pendulous appearance, they are considered as resembling those of the snowdrop (Galanthus nivalis). **1857** Gray *Manual of Botany* 266, Halesia. . . Snowdrop or Silver-bell-tree. **1897** Sudworth *Arborescent Flora* 323, *Mohrodendron dipterum* [=Halesia diptera]. . . Snowdrop-tree. **1953** Greene–Blomquist *Flowers South* 95, *H[alesia] diptera* . . called locally "snowdrop-tree" or "cow-licks," has been reported from the Coastal Plain and lower Piedmont from N. Fla. to Tex., Ark., and S.C. **1980** Little *Audubon Guide N. Amer. Trees E. Region* 637, Carolina Silverbell—"Snowdrop-tree." **2005** *St. Louis Post–Dispatch* (MO) 10 Mar (Internet), The plants sought include the Carolina silver bell tree, also called the snowdrop tree.

snowflake n
=**dead nettle 1.**
  1950 Gray–Fernald *Manual of Botany* 1230, *L[amium] album* . . Snowflake. . . Waste places, roadsides and old lawns.

snow flea n
Any of var springtails (order Collembola) that are typically seen on snow in early spring; occas an insect, such as *Boreus coloradensis,* of similar habit.
  1792 Belknap *Hist. NH* 3.183, Snow Flea, Podura nivalis. **1849** *Scientific Amer.* 4.182, We find a communication from Mr. Josiah F. Polk giving a description of what he calls the Snow Flea, seen by him in the Winter of 1826, in the State of Michigan. . . "They would spring up to the height of 18 inches or more. . . The body was slender, and more than a quarter of an inch long. The wings were longer." **1850** in 1906 Thoreau *Writings* 8.125 **MA**, The snow everywhere was covered with snow-fleas like pepper. **1896** Robinson *In New Engl. Fields* 247, The snow-fleas, harbingers and attendants of thaws, are making the snow in the woods gray with their restless myriads. **1960** *VT Hist.* 28.222, When the snow-fleas start flying, it is time to tap the maple trees. **1967** *DARE* (Qu. R14) Inf **WY**1, Snow fleas—come out in spring; blacken snow. **2000** in 2011 (acc) ME Dept. Conserv. Forest Health Div. *Insect & Disease Fact Sheets* (Internet), The two [snowflea] that we encounter most often are the typical and more common snowflea, *Hypogastrura nivicola* . . , which is sooty or gunpowder (dull) black. . . The other less common species we have called the snowmelt snowflea, *Hypogastrura armata* . . , which is rusty or bloodmeal (dull) red. **2006** *DARE* File—Internet **CO**, Though not as common as the springtail, Boreus coloradensis is also referred to as a "snow flea" because it has also adapted [sic] a hopping mode of transportation. . . The similarity between the two snow fleas makes discerning whether your speck of jumping soot is a scorpion-fly or springtail, nearly impossible to tell in the field.

snowflower n
1   See **snowflower tree.**

2 A **wood anemone.** Cf **snowdrop 2**

1936 *Helena Independent* (MT) 17 Oct 6/8, Mrs. Welton discovered a large bed of wild anemone or snow flowers in bloom at the top of the divide. **1967** *DARE* FW Addit **csOR,** Snowflower—five petals, come up through last thin crust of snow in very early spring. **1968** *DARE* (Qu. S2) Inf **NY54,** Snowflower—same as anemone.

3 See **snow plant.**

snowflower tree n   Also *snowflower(s)* [*OED2* 1862 →]
=**fringe tree.**
  1876 Hobbs *Bot. Hdbk.* 108, Snowflower—*Chionanthus Virginica.*
1897 Sudworth *Arborescent Flora* 332 **TN,** *Chionanthus virginica.* . . Snowflower-tree.   **1974** (1977) Coon *Useful Plants* 194, *Chionanthus virginica*—Fringe tree, flowering ash, graybeard tree, snow-flowers.

snowfoot See **snowshoe rabbit**

snow fritter See **snow bread**

snow-go See **sno-go**

snow goose n   Also *blue snow goose, greater ~, lesser ~;* abbr *snow*
The white color phase of a northern goose (*Chen caerulescens*).   Also called **blue goose, fish brant, Mexican goose 1a, swan ~, Texas ~ 1** Note: The **blue goose,** formerly considered a separate species, is now recognized as a color phase of *C. caerulescens.*
  1785 Pennant *Arctic Zool.* 2.549, Snow Goose. *Anser Grandinis* . . : head, neck, and body, of a snowy whiteness. **1814** Wilson *Amer. Ornith.* 8.76 **eDE, NJ,** Snow Goose. *Anas hyperborea.* **1879** *Scribner's Mth.* Oct 839 **MN,** Our party bagged . . twenty-one Canada, four white-fronted, and three snow geese. **1888** Trumbull *Names of Birds* 8, Two varieties are recognized by ornithologists, viz.: Lesser Snow Goose, *Chen hyperborea,* and Greater, *Chen hyperborea nivalis,* these being practically alike in form and coloration. *Ibid* 9, Names of the *whiter* birds, as follows: Snow Goose: White Brant [etc]. *Ibid,* Names of *Chen caerulescens,* as follows: Blue Goose: Blue Snow Goose [etc]. **1949** Kitchin *Birds Olympic Peninsula* 34 **nwWA,** When a flock of snow geese passes there is no doubt about their identification. **1950** *WELS Suppl.* **csWI,** Snow goose—large white migratory goose. Snow brant. **1965–70** *DARE* (Qu. Q6, . . Kinds of wild geese) 109 Infs, **scattered, but chiefly Nth, West,** Snow geese; **MA30,** Arctic snow geese; **IA29, PA163,** Canadian snow geese; **NY207,** White snow geese. **1967** *PA Game News* Nov 51 **PA,** This week . . several hundred real, honest-to-goodness snow geese did pay us a visit. Even a tyro bird watcher could recognize them from their white plumage with black wing tips, pink bills and feet, and typical gooselike proportions. **1982** Elman *Hunter's Field Guide* 287, Lesser snow geese are far more abundant than greater snows and far more likely to pass over the gun in massive formations or waves. **2005** *South Bend Tribune* (IN) 7 Jan sec C 3 (Internet), Lesser snow geese have two color phases, a dark phase called a blue goose and a white phase called snow goose.

snow griddle cake See **snow bread**

snow grouse n   Cf **snow partridge**
=**ptarmigan.**
  1859 *New Amer. Cyclop.* 8.518, Grouse. . . the toes usually naked . . but feathered to the claws in the snow grouse or ptarmigan. **1888** Roosevelt in *Century Illustr. Mag.* 36.210 **nID,** Up above the timber line were snow-grouse and huge, hoary-white woodchucks. **1898** (1900) Davie *Nests N. Amer. Birds* 175, White-tailed Ptarmigan. . . The Rocky Mountain Snow-Grouse inhabits the Alpine regions of Western North America from British America south to New Mexico. **1928** Bailey *Birds NM* 205, The furry-footed, White or Snow Grouse, named locally from its snow white winter plumage. **1961** Ligon *NM Birds* 87, The former range of this Ptarmigan [=*Lagopus leucurus*], or "Snow Grouse," included all of the ridges and peaks of the Sangre de Cristo Range above timber line. . . Today it is restricted in the state to a few peaks in the northern extremity of its former habitat. **1982** Elman *Hunter's Field Guide* 79, Common & regional names: For willow ptarmigan—*snow grouse* [etc]. . . For rock ptarmigan—*snow grouse* [etc]. . . For white-tailed ptarmigan—*snow grouse, snow partridge, Rocky Mountain snow grouse* [etc].

snow gull n
A **kittiwake** (here: *Rissa tridactyla*).
  1850 *WI Democrat* (Madison) [6 July 4]/1 (newspaperarchive.com),

[Poem by W.H.C. Hosmer:] Is it the snow-gull glancing,/ A rover wild and free—/ Far off the white caps dancing;/ Or phantoms that I see? **1925** (1928) Forbush *Birds MA* 1.62, *Rissa tridactyla tridactyla.* . . Other names: Frost-bird; Snow gull [etc]. **1956** MA Audubon Soc. *Bulletin* 40.22 **MA,** Common Kittiwake. . . Snow Gull, Squaretail, Winter Bird, Winter Gull.

snow ice-cream See **snow cream**

snowing See **snow** v[1]

snowing down South, it's phr   Also *there's snow down South, ~ on the ground, ~ on the mountain;* for addit varr see quots
widespread, but less freq Sth, Cent See Map Cf **cotton 4**
Used to indicate that a woman's slip is showing.
  1942 Davis *Quicksilver* 295, "Hey, Tizzy," piped Nicky. "It's snowing down South." Thelma glanced at her hem-line. **1950** *WELS* (*Expressions or sly words of warning for: . . A woman's slip showing*) 7 Infs, **WI,** It's snowing down South; 1 Inf, **ceWI,** It's snowing in Florida; 1 Inf, **seWI,** Snow down South. **1957** Battaglia *Resp. to PADS 20* **eMD** (*Expressions . . of warning for . . A woman's slip showing*) Snowing down South. **c1960** Wilson *Coll.* **csKY,** It's snowing down South—signal to girl that her slip is showing. **1965–70** *DARE* (Qu. W24a, . . *Expressions . . to warn a woman slyly that her slip is showing*) 171 Infs, **widespread, but less freq Sth, Cent,** It's snowing down South; 11 Infs, **scattered,** It's (a-)snowing; **MI78,** I see snow; **OR10,** It snowed last night; **OH16,** It's snow down South; **CT12, 23, NY224, VA42,** It's snowing behind (*or* a little bit, in Florida, in the South); **NY219,** Snow down South; **PA42, TX55,** Snow is falling (*or* showing); **IL19,** Snow's blowing down South; **CO27, KY33, NJ3, NY22, NC76, OH48,** Snowing down South (*or* in Florida, in the South); **GA81, IA27, NY145, PA194, 224,** There's snow down South (*or* on the ground, on the mountain). [Of all Infs responding to the question, 62% were old; of those giving these responses, 42% were old.] **1995** Brophy *Coll.* 70 **swMO** (as of c1960), Snowing down south. [T]he petticoat exposed.

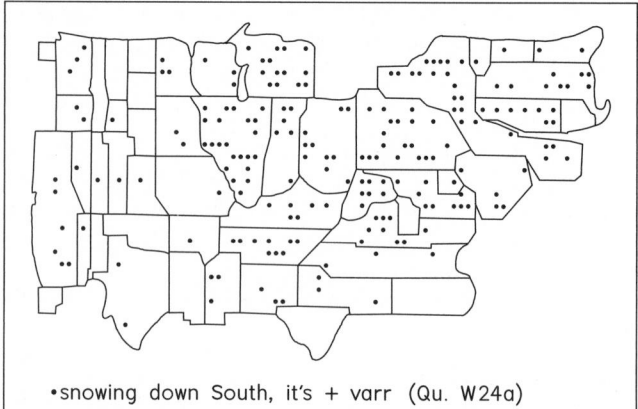

•snowing down South, it's + varr (Qu. W24a)

snow-in-summer n
A **chickweed 1b** (here: *Cerastium tomentosum* or *C. biebersteinii*).
  1913 Adams *Flower Gardening* 179, Perennials. . . *Cerastium tomentosum* . . Snow-in-summer. **1926** *NY Times* (NY) 20 June sec E 7, "Snow in Summer" appears in two varieties, Cerastrium [sic] tomentosum, a woolly-leaved type, and Cerastrium Bieberesteni [sic] with a lighter green leaf. **1950** Gray–Fernald *Manual of Botany* 627, *C[erastium] tomentosum* . . Snow-in-Summer, a depressed and matted perennial with stems, leaves and calyx densely white-woolly. **1951** Graham *My Window* 192 **ME,** Johnny-jump-ups and snow-in-summer were everywhere. **2003** *Pantagraph* (Bloomington IL) 6 June sec D 2 (Internet), It would be prudent to start selecting your landscape plants to include their drought resistance. . . Ground covers: . . snow-in-summer (Cerastium).

snowl n
=**hooded merganser.**
  1888 Trumbull *Names of Birds* 74 **MD,** At Crisfield, Md. (east shore of Chesapeake), [the hooded merganser is called] *snowl;* a name as weird as some of those in *Alice's Wonderland,* and the only one by which the bird is known, so far, at least, as I could discover in 1885.

snow lark n   Cf **snowbird 6**
=**horned lark.**

1847 in 1848 *U.S. Congress Serial Set* 517.41.544 **West,** Flocks of the pretty snow lark were continually taking wing as we advanced. **1927** Forbush *Birds MA* 2.362, Horned Lark. *Other names:* Shore Lark; Snow Lark. **1932** Bennitt *Check-list* 44 **MO,** Northern horned lark. . . Shore lark; snow lark. **1956** MA Audubon Soc. *Bulletin* 40.84 **MA,** Horned Lark. . . Snow Lark (Mass. From being seen in winter.)

snow lily n   [See quot 1953]   **esp Rocky Mts**

A **dogtooth violet** (here: *Erythronium grandiflorum*) of western North America.

1906 Henshaw *Mt. Flowers Amer.* 318, Yellow Adder's Tongue— *Erythronium gigantum.* . . A lovely yellow flower, frequently called "Snow Lily," from the fact that it grows in such close proximity to the great alpine *névés.* **1953** Nelson *Plants Rocky Mt. Park* 46, *Snowlily* or *yellow fawnlily, Erythronium grandiflorum* ssp *chrysandrum.* . . A striking plant with bright yellow flowers, blooming as the snow melts in the subalpine zone. . . It follows the snow up the slopes, and all stages, from ripened seed to pointed shoots just breaking the ground, may be found in a climb of from 9,000 to 11,000 feet. **1963** Craighead *Rocky Mt. Wildflowers* 23, Dogtooth Violet. . . Other names: Fawnlily, Glacier Lily, Snow Lily, Adders-tongue. **2001** *DARE* File—Internet **cnCO,** June flowers include . . alpine forget-me-not, snow lily, and kittentails above the timberline.

snowmachine n, v   **formerly widespread, now esp AK**   Cf **sno-go**

A snowmobile; to travel by snowmobile; hence vbl n *snow-machining,* noun *snowmachiner.*

1918 *Pop. Mechanics* 30.587, More and more motorcycle sleds appear on snow-covered roads of the North each winter. . . [Caption:] Three Hand Sleds and a Few Pieces of Lumber Made This a Good Snow Machine. **1947** *Walla Walla Union–Bulletin* (WA) 5 Mar 1/4, *Norden, Calif.* . . Four army planes, a snow machine and 20 skiers searched without success. **1965** *Fairbanks Daily News–Miner* (AK) 4 Dec 6/4, Skiland, Inc., is sponsoring a snow machine meet Sunday. **1968** *Pinedale Roundup* (WY) 4 Jan [5]/1 (newspaperarchive.com), Several avid snow machiners welcomed in the New Year at the Flying A Ranch. **1970** *Daily Kennebec Jrl.* (Augusta ME) 29 Dec 17/2, Found guilty of a charge of operating a snowmachine on a public way. **1970** *Fairbanks Daily News–Miner* (AK) 11 Nov 4/6, The only time I go snowmachining is on weekends. **1975** *New Mexican* (Santa Fe NM) 18 Mar sec B 8/4, [Advt:] *Trailer for* motorcycle or snowmachine. **1991** Tabbert *Dict. Alaskan Engl.* 230, The most common . . , perh even exceeding *snowmobile* in frequency, is *snowmachine.* . . Most people here tell me that they are familiar with the term *snowmachine* only from its Alaskan use. **1993** *Daily Sentinel* (Sitka AK) 7 Dec 3/1, Snowmachiners and cross-country skiers here are squaring off over the opening of a proposed snowmachine trail. **2001** *Ibid* 26 Dec 3/2, She said her husband . . has never snowmachined. **2002** in 2010 *DARE* File—Internet **AK,** This is a disappointment to the snowmachiners (they're not called "snowmobilers" up here. They ride *snowmachines.* Say "snowmobile" and they look at you like you're a tourist). **2009** *Anchorage Daily News* (AK) 6 Apr (Internet), The event has never had any trouble attracting snowmachine racers. . . It is an event hard for dedicated snowmachiners to ignore.

snow mallard n

A **mallard 1;** see quot 1947.

1923 McAtee in *U.S. Dept. Ag. Misc. Circular* 13.8 **IL,** Mallard *(Anas platyrhyncha).* . . Vernacular names. . . *In local use.* . . Snow mallard. **1947** McAtee in *Auk* 64.147 **IL,** Four of the names cited: "frostybeak," "icebreaker," "snow mallard," and "twister," were collected at Browning, Illinois, by Frederick C. Lincoln, who makes the following interesting remark: "These names used to designate a small mallard that arrives late in the season. Hunters insist they are a different species, and I must admit that they are readily distinguishable, principally by size and erratic, cork-screw flight."

snow morel   See **snow mushroom**

snow mosquito n

A large, early-season **mosquito** n[1] **B1.**

1923 Herms *Med. & Vet. Entomol.* 171, *A. cataphylla* Dyar, a Rocky Mountain snow mosquito. **1950** *Pan-Pacific Entomol.* 26.111 **CA,** The snow *Aedes* are mainly in the subgenus *Ochlerotatus.* . . *Aedes increpitus.* . . This species is the most widespread snow mosquito in California. **1962** Salisbury *Quoth the Raven* 256 **AK,** Some of the big bass-singing snow mosquitos were around early, but they are clumsy, heavy fliers and their droning hum, like that of an airplane, gives ample warning of their

presence and makes an offensive against them easy. **1967–68** *DARE* (Qu. R15b, . . *An extra-big mosquito*) Inf **CA**53, Snow mosquito—in the mountains, come out from under the snow; **WY**1, Snow mosquito— only for first two or three weeks in the spring. **2002** *Assoc. Press State & Local Wire* 5 May (Internet) **AK,** The birds begin nesting in mid-May, about the same time the largest of the Alaska mosquitoes—the slow-moving snow mosquito—begins biting.

snow mush   See **snow cream**

snow mushroom n   Also *snow morel*

A **false morel,** usu *Gyromitra gigas.*

1958 Smith *Mushroom Hunter's Field Guide* 51, *Gyromitra gigas* & *G. korfii (Snow Mushroom, Bull Nose).* . . Both species are edible and choice in our experience. . . However, at least one recent European guide lists *G. gigas* as poisonous unless parboiled. **1967** *DARE* FW Addit **neOR,** *Snow mushroom*—mushroom appearing right after melting of last snow. **1972** Miller *Mushrooms* 216, *Gyromitra gigas.* . . "Snow Morel". . . Several to numerous near melting snowbanks in P[acific] N[orth]W[est] and R[ocky] M[ountains] in early Sp[ring]. **1975** Smith *Field Guide W. Mushrooms* 41, *Gyromitra gigas* and *G. fastigiata* (Snow mushrooms). . . Fruiting in mountain conifer forests usually near melting snow banks. **1985** Ammirati et al. *Poisonous Mushrooms* 125, *Gyromitra gigas.* . . Common names. Snow mushroom, snow morel, giant helvella.

snow-on-the-mountain n

1 also *mountain snow, snow-on-the-mountains:* A **spurge,** usu *Euphorbia marginata,* but also *E. bicolor.*   Cf **fire-on-the-mountain, snow-on-the-prairie**

1873 *KS Mag.* 502 **seKS,** Their miller's-plant, or snow-on-the-mountain, is nothing but our spurge. **1889** Murfree *Despot* 159 **eTN,** He mechanically noted . . how the blooming "mountain snow" brushed his mare's fine coat. **1891** *Jrl. Amer. Folkl.* 4.149 **MA,** *Euphorbia marginata,* cultivated in flower gardens is called *Snow on the Mountain*—not a local name, I think. **1892** *Ibid* 5.102 **NH, NE,** *Euphorbia marginata,* Snow-on-the-mountains. **1897** *Ibid* 10.143 **ND, OH, TX,** *Euphorbia marginata* . . snow-on-the-mountain, Sulphur Grove, Ohio; N. Dak. . . Waco, Tex. **1914** *DN* 4.113 **cKS,** *Snow on the mountain.* . . A milkweed having white flowers and leaves with white edges. **1933** Small *Manual SE Flora* 797, Snow-on-the-mountain. . . Extensively cultivated for the showy effect of the massed foliage which suggested the popular name. **1961** Wills–Irwin *Flowers TX* 147, *Euphorbia bicolor.* . . This is one of two common plants called Snow-on-the-mountain, the other being the closely related *E. marginata.* . . Both are attractive annuals with milky juice, brightening late summer fields and roadsides with their white-bordered upper leaves. **1965–70** *DARE* (Qu. S26e, *Other wildflowers not yet mentioned;* not asked in early QRs) 111 Infs, **widespread, but chiefly east of Missip R,** Snow-on-the-mountain; (Qu. S17, . . *Kinds of plants . . that . . cause itching and swelling*) 9 Infs, **scattered,** Snow-on-the-mountain; (Qu. S6) Inf **MS**82, Snow-on-the-mountain; (Qu. S25) Inf **MS**47, Snow-on-the-mountain; (Qu. S26d, *Wildflowers that grow in meadows;* not asked in early QRs) Infs **KS**7, **PA**176, Snow-on-the-mountain. **2002** *Post–Std.* (Syracuse NY) 17 Mar 26/1, [Question:] I planted "snow on the mountain," and it is taking over my flower bed. . . [Response:] "Snow on the mountain" is Euphorbia marginata. It's a beautiful plant, with bright white variegation on the leaves. . . I suspect, however, that what you are growing is not "snow on the mountain" but the variegated form of Bishop's weed, or goutweed, Aegopodium podagraria.

2 =**jewbush.**

1955 *S. Folkl. Qrly.* 19.234, All varieties [of *Pedilanthus*] are commonly called *Devil's Backbone* or *Jacob's Ladder.* . . The variegated, white-flowering variety is called *Joseph's Coat* and *Snow on the mountain.*

3 as *snow-on-the-mountains:* =**goutweed.**

1967 *DARE* Tape **NY**30, [FW:] Those leaves that you mentioned out front. . . [Inf:] Snow-on-the-mountains. [FW:] And what was the other name for that? [Inf:] Bishop's weed. **2002** [see **1** above]. **2002** *Star Tribune* (Minneapolis MN) 13 June (Internet), One ground cover that seems to grow in anything short of asphalt is snow on the mountain, also known as variegated goutweed.

snow-on-the-prairie n   Cf **snow-on-the-mountain 1**

A **spurge** (here: *Euphorbia bicolor*).

1970 Correll *Plants TX* 966 **OK, TX,** *Euphorbia bicolor.* . . Snow-on-the-prairie. . . Locally abundant, usually in tight clay soil. . . also Okla. **2005** *Austin Amer.–Statesman* (TX) 27 Nov sec F 14 (Internet), The rather large task of providing a visual celebration of the native plants . . comes together under the capable supervision of Lancaster. . . Among them: . . snow-on-the-prairie, small clusters of white flowers that signal the beginning of fall when they spread across fields in Central Texas.

snow orchid n
=**phantom orchid.**

1950 Correll *Native Orchids* 134, *Cephalanthera Austinae.* . . Common names: Phantom Orchid, Snow Orchid. **1973** Hitchcock–Cronquist *Flora Pacific NW* 701, *Eburophyton.* . . Phantom-orchid; Snow-orchid. **2005** *DARE* File—Internet **Seattle WA,** Heller Phantom or Snow Orchid. . . Perennial orchid; extant; collected in Seattle in 1937; still here in 2005 and on Cougar Mountain.

snow owl See **snowy owl**

snow pancake See **snow bread**

snow partridge n Cf **partridge B4, snow grouse**
=**white-tailed ptarmigan.**

1982 Elman *Hunter's Field Guide* 79, White-tailed Ptarmigan. . . Common & Regional Names. . . snow grouse, snow partridge [etc].

snow plant n

A bright red saprophyte (*Sarcodes sanguinea*) of the Sierra Nevada that appears in early spring; hence n *snowflower* the flower of this plant.

1863 CA Acad. Nat. Sci. *Proc.* 2.343, California Snow Plant, (*Sarcodes sanguinea*). **1890** *New Engl. Mag.* Dec 462 **Yosemite Valley CA,** Some of these pilgrims had with them a beautiful and curious plant, the like of which we have never seen, and upon inquiry we find it is called the snow-flower, a strange, bright, scarlet-crimson blossom like a fleshy hyacinth. **1897** *Jrl. Amer. Folkl.* 10.49 **CA,** *Sarcodes sanguinea* . . snow plant, Sierra Nevada. **1940** Writers' Program *Guide NV* 13, In the early spring, as the snow begins to melt, the blood-red snowplant pushes its way through snow banks in clumps of from one to twenty plants. . . The snowplant is found only in the Sierra Nevada and dies if transplanted. **1967–69** *DARE* (Qu. S26a, . . *Wildflowers. . . Roadside flowers*) Inf **CA**7, Wild snowflower—in mountains; (Qu. S26c, *Wildflowers that grow in woods*) Inf **CA**53, Snowflowers—the big red ones that come through the snow; **CA**126, Snow plant—in mountains; **CA**167, Snowflowers; (Qu. S26e, *Other wildflowers not yet mentioned; not asked in early QRs*) Inf **CA**117, Snowflower—high in mountains; **CA**167, Snowflower is like a hyacinth; **CA**170, Snowflower. **1979** Spellenberg *Audubon Guide N. Amer. Wildflowers W. Region* 699, Snow Plant. . . Once seen, never forgotten. **2005** *DARE* File—Internet **CA,** *Snowflower* is the red flower of the Snow-plant "Sarcodes sanguinea."

snow queen n

A **kittentails** of the Pacific coast (here: *Synthyris reniformis*).

1951 Abrams *Flora Pacific States* 3.798, *Synthyris reniformis.* . . Snow-Queen. . . Pacific Slope in Washington and Oregon. Type locality: Columbia River. March-May. **1961** Peck *Manual OR* 716, Snow-queen. . . Woods, west slope of the Cascades and westward, to Wash. and Calif. **1979** Spellenberg *Audubon Guide N. Amer. Wildflowers W. Region* 780, Snow Queen. . . One of the humbler, early-flowering *Synthyris* species; in the dim light of the early-spring woods its low, dark flowers are easily overlooked. **2001** *Oregonian* (Portland OR) 2 Aug (Internet), Favorite native and basically disease-free plants for borders. . . Synthyris reniformis . . (grouseflower, queen of spring, snow queen).

snow roller n **formerly chiefly NEng, now more widespread**

A horse-drawn or motor-driven device made of one or more heavy cylinders and used to pack down snow on a road or trail.

1901 ME Bd. Ag. *Annual Rept. for 1900* 15, In 1888 we built our first snow roller. . . They roll the snow down solid enough so that two heavily loaded teams can pass each other without any trouble. **1947** *NY Times* (NY) 27 Jan 13, He said the seaman had been crushed beneath a snow roller just as a tractor had started to tow the machine. **1950** *Ibid* 15 Dec 46 **NH,** Jutting rocks . . have been eliminated and with . . the "magic carpet" snow rollers all trails will be kept in the best possible condition. **1969** Sorden *Lumberjack Lingo* 116 **NEng, Gt Lakes,** Snow roller—Huge, heavy roller used to pack down snow on roads. **1965** *Yankee* Dec 150 **swNH,** [Caption:] Four teams pulling a snow roller. **1992** Phelps *Famous Last Words* 10 **NEng** (as of c1910), He was raised in Ludlow Vermont and used to drive a six horse team on the big snow roller that flattened the snow for good sledding, before the days of the automobile. **2003** *DARE* File **nwMA** (as of c1915), A snow roller. . . They're essen-

tially cylinders, six or seven feet in diameter, and a traffic lane wide and they're rolled over the roads to pack down the snow so that horse-drawn sleds and sleighs can travel without making the horses wallow through soft snow. The ones I'm familiar with were horse-drawn. . . The rollers I've seen were wooden, the staves made from heavy planking. . . [Two friends remember that] the roller came in sections instead of being just one long piece. The reason . . was that when turning, a single section roller would have scuffed the ground (or snow) since on a corner the inside wheel always has to turn fewer revolutions than the outside wheel. **2003** *DARE* File—Internet, Snow Grooming Equipment for Cross Country Skiing. . . The Snow Roller is the perfect tool for pre-packing deep snow or working early season base. The deep ribs will leave a grooved pattern that catches blowing and drifting snow and adds to the snow base.

snow saucer See **saucer B2**

snowshed n **West**

A structure built over a section of railway or roadway as protection against snow, esp snowslides.

1870 *Overland Mth.* 4.513 **ceCA,** I could go around by the trail . . or ride up to the railroad-track, tie my horse, and walk through the snowsheds. **1898** (1899) Warman *Story RR* 206 **West,** During the summer of 1886 showsheds were built, with troughs at the tops, through which ran water from adjacent springs, to be used in case of fire, and with "splits" to protect the open breathing spaces between the sheds. **1956** Almirall *From College* 79 **CO,** At the top of Corona were huge snowsheds through which the trains passed. In winter the trains were sometimes stalled for hours because of the heavy snows which had to be cleared by whirling plows attached to snorting engines. **1977** Adams *Lang. Railroader* 142, *Snow shed:* A shelter built over the track to protect against snow slides. **1998** *Denver Post* (CO) 2 Mar sec A 1 (Internet), People who know about the highway are scared of it. . . An initial 184-foot section of snowshed, containing 300 tons of reinforced steel, was opened in 1985. **2003** *DARE* File—Internet, [Caption:] Snowshed Number 12—The whine of the dynamic brakes echoes out of the snowshed as the Through Train continues down from the pass. Soon the train will glide through . . Essex, MT. *Ibid,* [Caption:] Snowshed Ruins at Pacific Portal [CO]. *Ibid,* [Caption:] Lake Keechelus Snowshed. . . Built 1951—This structure is the only concrete snowshed in Washington. *Ibid* **CA,** [Caption:] Southern Pacific Snowshed—Donner Summit 1950.

snowshoe n

1 A ski. *old-fash*

1868 (1869) Browne *Resources Pacific Slope* 142, The abundance of the snow and its long duration renders it necessary for the people to accustom themselves to snow-shoes, and snow-shoe races are the chief amusement in the winter. . . The shoes are thin pine boards 12 or 16 feet long, 4 inches wide, turned up at the toe. **1886** *Calif. Maverick* (S.F.) 13 Feb. 6/6 *(DA),* The snow shoes. . . consist of long, narrow boards turned up at one end, which are laced to the feet. **1890** *Century Dict.* 5736, *Snow-shoe* . . n. . . . There are two principal kinds—the web or Canadian, and the long or Norwegian. . . The Norwegian is merely a thin board, . . slightly curved upward in front. See *skee.* **1950** *WELS Suppl.* **cwWI,** Snowshoes used for *skis* by our community as late as 1905. **1969–70** *DARE* Tape **CA**144, We didn't have skis then; we called 'em snowshoes. . . They were built just like the skis are now; they were not built like snowshoes. . . I think he made them out of one-by-fours and then sawed cracks across one end . . to make the point tip up, and then they'd soak that in hot water, and then I guess they tied it to fix it someway; **CA**196, Well, if they wanted to go anywhere, they'd . . go on snowshoes or they didn't get there. We called 'em snowshoes, but they're really skis. The skis they have nowadays are short compared to what they used to make 'em; **CA**198, Over there now, but they haven't put them on display yet, is a pair of snowshoes, the long boards.

2 A large foot; hence n *snowshoe tracker* a man with large feet. **Nth**

1958 McCulloch *Woods Words* 173 **Pacific NW,** *Snowshoe tracker*—A man with very big feet makes a very big track. **1965–70** *DARE* (Qu. X38, *Joking names for unusually big or clumsy feet*) Infs **MI**42, **MN**33, **MA**72, **NY**23, **PA**184, **VT**16, **WI**19, 27, 57, Snowshoes.

3 See **snowshoe rabbit.**

snowshoe flounder n **esp Long Is. NY, NEng**

A large **flounder** n **B.**

1955 *Bridgeport Telegram* (CT) 14 Apr 55/3, [Advt:] *Charter Fishing Boat.* . . Starting May 15 Pollack Cod and snow shoe flounder at Block Island, Montauck Point. **1975** Evanoff *Catch More Fish* 105, The bigger "snowshoe" flounders are caught around Block Island, Rhode Island. **1997** in 2001 *DARE* File—Internet **Long Is. NY,** Snowshoe flounder—big, sea flatties that often weigh between 2 and 4 pounds—are also available at Montauk and their numbers seem to peak sometime in May or early June. **2001** Ibid **NY, RI,** In Search of Snowshoe Flounder—We have all heard stories of monster winter flounder reaching sizes of 4–5 pounds off the East End of Long Island.

snowshoe rabbit n Also *snowshoe (hare); rarely snowfoot*
[From the size of the hind feet]
=varying hare.
    1878 *Mt. Democrat* (Placerville CA) 30 Nov 1/5, A snow-shoe rabbit is at the Smithsonian Institute. It was caught . . at the head of the Yellowstone river. It differs from the other rabbits in the feet, which are as broad as a man's hand. **1890** *Century Dict.* 4924, *Snow-shoe rabbit,* that variety of the American varying hare which is found in the Rocky Mountains. It turns white in winter, and at that season the fur of the feet is very heavy. **1899** *Century Illustr. Mag.* June 227 **WY,** Bat . . shot a snow-shoe rabbit. . . The feet are webbed like those of a duck, a provision of nature to enable the animal to make his way over the snows that are almost perpetual where he makes his home. **1938** *AK Sportsman* Feb 21, Before reaching Friday Creek cabin we obtained several "low-bush moose," commonly known as snowshoe rabbits. **1956** Almirall *From College* 89 **CO,** We might get a shot at a coyote or snowshoe. **1961** Jackson *Mammals WI* 108, *Lepus americanus phaeonotus.* . . In Wisconsin commonly called snowshoe hare, snowshoe rabbit, or simply snowshoe. **1965–70** *DARE* (Qu. P30, . . *Wild rabbits*) 58 Infs, **chiefly Nth, Rocky Mts,** Snowshoe; 16 Infs, **chiefly Nth, Rocky Mts,** Snowshoe rabbit; 10 Infs, **chiefly Nth,** Snowshoe hare; **CT29,** Snowshoe or white hare; **ME8,** Snowshoe hare—generally called jackrabbit; **MI10,** Snowshoe—technically he's a snowshoe hare, but we call him a snowshoe rabbit; **NV8,** Mountain hare—a big rabbit, also called snowshoe rabbit; **NY68,** Snowshoe rabbit—I think them and jackrabbits is the same—used to be jackrabbits years ago; **VA27,** Snowfoot. **1966** *DARE* Tape **MI23,** And then the small game, of course. The partridge or grouse and rabbits, snowshoe rabbits; **MI32,** My favorite sport is hunting snowshoe rabbit, or some states call it a varying hare; **MI36,** Same thing with the snowshoe rabbits. I've always got tame rabbits that are around the house. **1977** *UpCountry* Dec 12 **VT,** The snowshoe hare is a notable example, for the splayed hind feet from which it gets its name provide support in even the deepest and softest snow. **1982** Elman *Hunter's Field Guide* 389 **NY,** It can be startling if not downright unnerving for a New York hunter to kick out a big, white, slab-footed hare. . . The snowshoe rabbit, as most of us call the animal, is supposedly long gone from there. **2005** *Cleveland Plain Dealer* (OH) 27 Jan sec D 5 (Internet), The snowshoe hare should have a leg up on survival in the snow belt of Lake and Ashtabula counties.

snowshoe tracker See **snowshoe 2**

snow snake n
1 An imaginary animal; see quots. Cf **hoop snake**
    1900 *CO Springs Gaz.* (CO) 30 Aug [5]/4 (newspaperarchive.com), *Snow Snake Joke Again Perpetrated*—A once popular Pikes Peak hoax has been sprung again. **1939** Tryon *Fearsome Critters* 45, The venom is deadly. . . Its pure white color makes it wholly invisible to its prey. One strike is sufficient. . . "I was treed by a Snow Snake" is still a much-used explanation of a late home-coming. **2005** *DARE* File—Internet **csWI,** I don't mind the cold weather or snow when I go shooting. The problem we have is with those pesky snow snakes. . . The problem I have found with these is you don't know when you have been bit. The first indication is you start to get the shakes which get progressivly [sic] worse the more you shoot. The only thing to do is . . hunker down in front of the fire place and take liberal amounts of anti-venom. The only problem or side effect with the anti-venom is it will give you a head ache the next day.
2 In logging: see quots. Cf **crazy dray**
    1969 Sorden *Lumberjack Lingo* 116 **NEng, Gt Lakes,** *Snow snake*—A travois. Sometimes used in reference to steam hauler. **2005** *DARE* File—Internet **WI,** The invention of the steam log hauler or "snow snake" before World War 1, delivered more hardwood logs to railroads and mills. This was the forerunner of the caterpillar tractor which took over the skidding and hauling of logs to mills and/or railroad landings after World War 1.
3 A thin ribbon of drifting snow.
    1983 *DARE* File **MN,** Snow snakes are thin ribbons of drifting snow on the highway. They move quickly and can be very disconcerting to drivers. **1999** Proulx *Close Range* 31 **WY,** The snow snakes writhing

across the asphalt straightened into rods. He was driving in a rushing river of cold whiteout foam. **2000** in 2005 *DARE* File—Internet, In the U[pper] P[eninsula] mother nature shows her bueaty [sic] in so many ways and yes, some are harsh. Those howling winds and the swirling snows make those ever so intransing [sic] "snow snakes" that glid [sic] across the road ways.

snow sparrow n Cf **snowbird 1**
Usu a **junco** n[1], but see quots.
    1855 *IL State Ag. Soc. Trans. for 1853–54* 604, Snow sparrow, Niphaea Hyemalis [=*Junco h.*]. **1884** Coues *Key to N. Amer. Birds* 377, *Junco.* . . Snow Sparrows. **1966–70** *DARE* (Qu. Q21, . . *Kinds of sparrows*) Infs **IN19, NY58, OH72, PA245,** Snow sparrow; **CA210,** Snow sparrows or chickadees; **SC19,** Snow sparrow—shows up when snow comes; already here, but he seems more plentiful when it snows; **SC43,** Snow sparrow—comes every winter, very dark. **2005** *DARE* File—Internet **nCA,** I buy the costco bird feed, cheap and no filler and the finches and snow sparrows and titmice feed from a suspended feeder next to the window.

snow squall n chiefly **NEast** See Map
A snow shower; a sudden snowstorm of short duration.
    1775 in 1886 *MA Hist. Soc. Proc.* 2d ser 2.287, The weather is attended with Snow Squalls. **1832** *N. Amer. Rev.* 35.249, It had the signs of a fierce snow-squall, such as sometimes happens in a New England winter, the vehemence of which seldom admits of a long duration. **1871** in 1983 *PADS* 70.52 **ce,sePA,** Cloudy some snow squalls. **1911** *Natl. Geogr. Mag.* June 521 **NY,** At Lake O'Hara . . snow squalls were not infrequent on the higher summits. **1965–70** *DARE* (Qu. B39, *A very light fall of snow*) 15 Infs, **chiefly NEast,** Snow squall; [**NH5, OH79, PA126,** Squall]. **1998** *DARE* File—Internet **Gt Lakes,** *Lake-Effect Snowfalls*—Lake-generated snow squalls form when cold air, passing for long distances over the relatively warm waters of a large lake, picks up moisture and heat and is then forced to drop the moisture in the form of snow upon reaching the downwind shore. [**2002** *DARE* File—Internet **Portland ME,** The Snow Squall Restaurant & Lounge.]

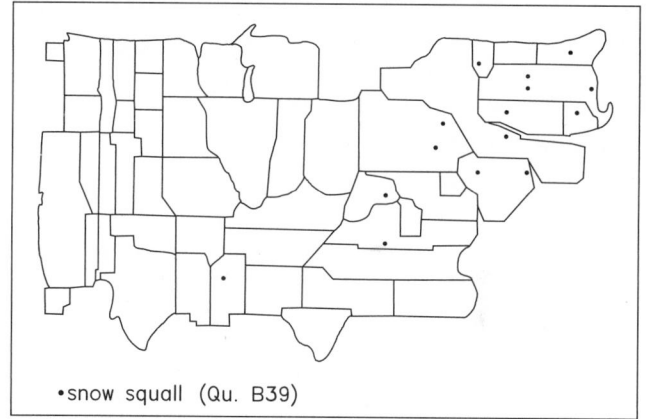

•snow squall (Qu. B39)

snow water n
Fig, in phr *not to give snow water to* and varr: to regard with contempt or disdain.
    1904 in 2003 *Pittsburgh Post-Gaz.* (PA) 23 Apr (Internet), Those darned fool North Versailles supervisors wouldn't give us snow water, so we decided to hike for ourself. **1931** Hannum *Thursday April* 110 **wNC,** I wouldn't give the gal snow water, myself, but efn Squar' is dead sot on sparkin' her, why, we got to keep him from lookin' like a . . fool. **1942** (1971) Campbell *Cloud-Walking* 152 **seKY,** Draxie and Mort were a sight to humor Lexie so they give in to be at the singing though they wouldn't give snow water to Shy Isaacs. *Ibid* 234, They weren't nary girl amongst them I'd give snow water to, say nothing of setting up to spark 'em.

snowy egret n Also *snowy*
A small white **egret** (*Egretta thula*), once hunted nearly to extinction for its breeding plumage. Also called **crazy crane, golden slipper bird, heron blanc, little snowy, little white crane 1, little white egret, plume bird, poor Job, snowy heron, white crane 2, ~ egret, ~ heron, ~ poke, ~ squawk**
    1854 Boston Soc. Nat. Hist. *Proc.* 4.326, *Egretta candidissima.* Snowy Egret. American; accidental in Europe. **1869** *Amer. Naturalist* 3.231

NEng, The Snowy Egret, and the larger White Egret . . are occasionally tempted to visit our coast. **1899** in 1900 *LA Soc. Naturalists Proc.* 92, *Ardea candidissima. . . Snowy Egret.* Once exceedingly common, . . this species has been nearly exterminated of late years. **1928** Bailey *Birds NM* 90, While the persecuted Snowys are now rarely seen, the protection afforded them in recent years by the game wardens of the Audubon Society has enabled them to increase in numbers in a few localities. **1932** Howell *FL Bird Life* 101, The Snowy Egret was formerly an abundant breeder over the greater part of Florida. **1949** Sprunt–Chamberlain *SC Bird Life* 83, The Snowy Egret is one of the most active of the herons. **1961** Ligon *NM Birds* 31, In recent years the Snowy Egret has become a regular nesting bird, in both the Pecos and Rio Grande Valleys. **1967–68** *DARE* (Qu. Q10, . . *Water birds and marsh birds*) Infs **GA**18, 20, 25, **SC**62, Snowy egret. **1968** *DARE* Tape **GA**30, You got the snowy egret and the cow egret. . . The snowy egret's got a yellow foot. **1969** Longstreet *Birds FL* 24, The snowy egrets make their homes in swamps and marshes and add beauty to these wide flat stretches of land. **1977** Bull–Farrand *Audubon Field Guide Birds* 380, Snowies are agile, often seen sprinting about in shallow water, or even hovering as they seek small shrimps and minnows. **2005** *NY Times* (NY) 23 May sec F 3/2, Penikese Island is a small grass-covered island . . that juts westward into Buzzard's Bay. . . There are large numbers of nesting herring gulls and . . a few snowy egrets.

snowy heron n
=**snowy egret.**
 1785 Latham *Genl. Synopsis Birds* 3.1.92, *Snowy H[eron].* Ardea nivea. **1839** Audubon *Synopsis Birds* 267, Ardea candidissima. . . Snowy Heron. . . Resident from Texas to Florida. Migrates in spring as far as Massachusetts. **1858** U.S. War Dept. *Rept. Explor. Railroad* 9.665, *Garzetta candidissima.* . . Snowy Heron. . . Coast of Middle and Gulf States, and across to California. **1884** Coues *Key to N. Amer. Birds* 267, *Little White Egret. Snowy Heron.* . . Plumage always entirely white. **1898** Grinnell *Birds Pacific Slope* 14, Snowy Heron. Formerly a common visitant like the American Egret, but now only seldom seen. **1964** Phillips *Birds AZ* 6, Snowy Egret; Snowy Heron. . . Found year-long in Colorado Valley, especially common as a transient and in recent years as a winter resident. **1999** *FL Times–Union* (Jacksonville) 12 June (Internet), Fiddler crabs scramble on the muck exposed by low tide as a snowy heron tiptoes by.

snowy medlar See **medlar bush**

snowy orchid n   Also *snowy orchis*
 A **fringed orchid:** usu *Platanthera nivea,* but also *P. blephariglottis.*   Note: Both of these were formerly included in the genus *Habenaria.*
 1893 *Cosmopolitan* 15.173, In moss-deep woods the snowy orchid blows. **1929** *Acad. Nat. Sci. Philadelphia Yr. Book for 1928* 24 **sNJ,** The most conspicuous member of this group is the Snowy Orchis (*Gymnadeniopsis* [=*Platanthera*] *nivea*). **1946** Tatnall *Flora DE* 89, *H[abenaria] nivea.* . . Snowy Orchis. Rare, in wet places of the Coastal Plain. . . Here reaching its northern limit. **1950** Correll *Native Orchids* 57, *Habenaria blephariglottis.* . . Common names: White Fringed-orchid, Snowy-orchid [etc]. *Ibid* 89, *Habenaria nivea.* . . The Snowy Orchid. **1972** Brown *Wildflowers LA* 38, Snowy Orchid—*Habenaria nivea.* . . Widely distributed in moist pinelands and bogs. **2006** *DARE* File—Internet **TN,** May Prairie. . . supports disjunct plants known from the Atlantic and Gulf Coastal Plains including the only state location for . . the snowy orchid (*Platanthera nivea*).

snowy owl n   Also *great snowy, snow owl*
 1 A large white or mostly white northern owl (*Nyctea scandiaca*).   Also called **Arctic owl, ermine ~, ghost bird 2, hawk owl 3, white ~ 1**
 1781 Latham *Genl. Synopsis Birds* 1.1.132, *Snowy O[wl]* . . the whole plumage is white as snow. **1811** Wilson *Amer. Ornith.* 4.53, *Snow Owl. Strix Nyctea.* . . Inhabits the coldest and most dreary regions of the northern hemisphere. **1838** Geol. Surv. OH *Second Annual Rept.* 179, *S. nyctea.* Snow owl. The large white owl sometimes visits this State during severe and long continued cold weather. **1844** Giraud *Birds Long Is.* 22 **seNY,** Surnia Nyctea. . . Snowy Owl. . . A few are seen every winter on the south side of Long Island. **1903** Dawson *Birds OH* 1.386, During January and February of 1902 there occurred a remarkable invasion of Snowy Owls, which was reported from localities as diverse as Southern Michigan and Long Island. **1939** *LANE* Map 230, 2 infs, **MA, NH,** Snowy owl; 1 inf, **ME,** Snow owl—large, white, spotted. **1963** Murie *Birds Mt. McKinley* 57 **AK,** The snowy owl is a winter visi-

tor. . . They nest on hummocks in the open tundra, especially near Bering Sea and the Arctic coast. **1965–70** *DARE* (Qu. Q2, . . *Kinds of owls*) 27 Infs, **chiefly Nth,** Snowy owl; 17 Infs, **chiefly Nth,** Snow owl; **MI**36, Arctic owl—called the snow owl here; **MA**58, Great snowy—occasionally from north; (Qu. Q1, . . *Kind of owl that makes a shrill, trembling cry*) Inf **PA**1, Snowy owl. **1998** *Syracuse Herald–Jrl.* (NY) 3 Mar sec B 3/6, The snowy owl spotted last week was still in Fairfield, Herkimer County.

 2 =**barn owl 1.**
 1890 Warren *Birds PA* 143, Some persons, not versed in ornithological matters, name both the Snowy Owl (*N. nyctea*) and Barn Owl (*S. pratincola*) "White" or "Snowy" Owls. Such local names, used to designate the Barn Owl, are confusing and should be discarded.

snowy plover n   Also *snowy ring plover*
 A small **plover** (here: *Charadrius alexandrinus*) of the western US.
 1868 Cronise *Nat. Wealth CA* 470, There are two other little species found along the sea shore. . . The first is called Ring Plover, the second Snowy Plover. **1876** NY Acad. Sci. *Annals Lyceum Nat. Hist.* 11.11 **UT,** Snowy Plover. Very abundant on shores of Salt Lake in May. **1898** (1900) Davie *Nests N. Amer. Birds* 157, The Snowy Ring Plover inhabits the United States chiefly west of the Rocky Mountains. **1923** Dawson *Birds CA* 3.1314, The Snowy Plover is part and parcel of the sand. His clothes assimilate its hue so perfectly that a crouching bird may be invisible. **1940** Gabrielson *Birds OR* 238, Western Snowy Plover. . . a silent little bird, running ahead of the observer on swift feet. **1961** Ligon *NM Birds* 112, The Snowy Plover is a summer resident about the barren alkali-bordered lakes of the Rio Grande, Estancia and Pecos Valleys. **2005** *Salt Lake Tribune* (UT) 11 Aug sec D 2 (Internet), The best place to see snowy plovers now is along the north side of the Antelope Island State Park Causeway.

snozzle n   Also *snozz(ler)*   [Varr of **schnozzle**]
 The nose.
 1860 *Harvard Mag.* 7.8, Good! there's a snozzle-splitter! First claret for Killey. **1929** Baer in *San Antonio Light* (TX) 27 Oct sec 4 7/1, I have one of those large, red snozzles with a bulbous annex on the end that makes it look like a fireman's boot. **1930** *Collier's* 20 Dec 13 **NYC,** He no sooner pokes his snozzle into the joint than a guy by the name of Louie the Lug . . jumps up. **1965–70** *DARE* (Qu. X14, *Joking words for the nose*) 176 Infs, **widespread,** Snozzle; 19 Infs, **scattered,** Snozz; **MD**25, **WI**27, Snozzler; (Qu. X15, . . *Kinds of noses, according to shape or size*) Infs **KY**60, **WA**11, Snozzle (nose); (Qu. K61, . . *The pig's nose*) Inf **CA**111, Snozzle. **2002** in 2005 *DARE* File—Internet **NJ,** There's something about an oversized snozzle that inspires universal mirth, particularly among boys, and I've endured years of mostly good-natured abuse on its account.

snub v[1], hence vbl n *snubbing*   **chiefly ME**
 To guide (a canoe down a stretch of rapid water) using a pole; with *down:* to guide (a canoe) downstream or descend in a canoe in this manner.
 1915 (1916) Johnson *Highways New Engl.* 18 **ME,** We started promptly right after breakfast, and Pete went off alone to "snub" down the quick water of Webster Stream, standing in the stern of the canoe, pick-pole in hand, ready for all emergencies. **1931** *Appalachia* 18.456 **NEng,** Let him not be loath to stand up and use the pole for snubbing the canoe down every rapid where the channel is intricate. Held back by the pole, and guided by its thrust made with small pressure but at just the right moment and in the right direction, the canoe slips slowly down the channel. **1937** FWP *Guide ME* 421, The *Allagash River* . . is swift and full of rapids. The trip here becomes strenuous and exciting, as the canoe is poled through roaring swash past banks dark with evergreen. In a tight bad place in short rapids the canoes are sometimes 'roped down,' but the guide more often resorts to the pole and the art of 'snubbing her down.' Old-timers say that skill at snubbing down is fast vanishing from the Maine woods. [**1979** *Bittersweet* 7.2.51 **Ozarks** (as of 1919), The snubber's job was mostly to snub, or brake, the raft by dragging his pole against the bottom.] **2003** *DARE* File **ME** (as of 1960s), Snubbing the canoe down the river. I've heard that in Maine. That's where they do most of the poling. **2003** *DARE* File—Internet **ME,** At one point it was like looking down a staircase. We put away our paddles and broke out our poles and began snubbing down the river. . . Snubbing down we followed the channel.

snub v[2], hence vbl n *snubbing*   [Engl dial *snob* to sob; cf *EDD snob* v.[1]]   **chiefly sAppalachians, Ozarks**

To sob, whimper; hence n pl *snubs* fits of sobbing.

1852 Southworth *Discarded Daughter* 2.57 **MD,** "I have been a housekeeper—this—fifty-odd *year*," said Miss Joe, snubbing and sobbing . . "*year,* and never, *never* did I sit down to supper on New Year's Eve without . . cake and *sweetmeats*." **1880** *Scribner's Mth.* 20.300 **VA,** I heerd her a-cryin' an' a-snubbin', all night. **1903** *DN* 2.330 *seMO, Snub*. . . To sob. 'She sat in a corner snubbing for half an hour.' **1907** *DN* 3.236 *nwAR, Snub*. . . To sob. **1915** *DN* 4.243 *eTN, Snub*. . . To sob. "She was crying and snubbing." **1933** *AmSp* 8.1.52 **Ozarks,** *Snub*. . . To cry, to snivel. Usually refers to children. *Them kids has been a-snubbin' round all day, on account somebody went an' run over th' pup.* **1940** Harris *Folk Plays* 5 **eNC,** Last night I heard her a-snubbin' way sometime in the night. **1954** *PADS* 21.38 **SC,** *Snub*. . . To sob involuntarily after a fit of crying. Usually of children. **1955** Ritchie *Singing Family* 24 *seKY,* 'Listen to her a-snubbin. What you crying about? . . Never could stand to hear a young un snub.' . . We churned. I snubbed once in a while but Mommy kept talking to the time of the churning and my heart began to ease. **1957** Combs *Lang. S. Highlanders* **sAppalachians,** *Snob*—to sob, whimper. . . *Snub*—to sob, whimper. **c1960** Wilson *Coll.* **csKY,** *Snub*. . . To sob. **1982** *Smithsonian Letters* **cnKY** (as of 1930s), A baby "snubbed" himself to sleep. **1983** *MJLF* 9.1.56 *ceKY* (as of 1956), *Snubbing* . . sniveling. **2004** Adams *My Old Love* 2 **wNC** (as of 1848), Mommie was holding Emily who had cried so long she had the snubs. **2005** *Chattanooga Times Free Press* (TN) 10 June sec E 1 (Internet), Look at each one until you cry or at least snub and sniffle.

snubbing vbl n¹ See **snub** v¹

snubbing vbl n² See **snub** v²

snubbing post n Cf **snorting post 2**

Fig: a situation in which one must submit to discipline, face unpleasant facts, "bite the bullet."

1878 *Atlantic Mth.* 41.645 *neNY,* Tom's a nice kind of a boy, but he's got to come up against a snubbin'-post one of these days. **1889** *Standard* (Ogden UT) 5 Oct 1/1, [Headline:] *Mrs Burns Brings Brown to the Snubbing Post.* **1997** *St. Petersburg Times* (FL) 31 Dec (Internet), *Jeer to Pasco County Commissioner Pat Mulieri for bungling an opportunity to bring her fellow commissioners to the snubbing post. Mulieri created the perfect opportunity to force a meaningful discussion about conflicts of interest.* **2001** *Congressional Record* 31 Oct 147.15.21195/1 **WY,** I know it is a difficult thing to do. . . But I think collectively we ought to come to the snubbing post and say we have these things to do and here is what we have to do to them.

snub down See **snub** v¹

snubnose darter n

A **darter 1** of the genus *Etheostoma;* see quots.

1955 Carr–Goin *Guide Reptiles* 101, *Etheostoma stigmaeum*. . . Snubnose Darter. . . A slender trim little fish with two dorsal fins. **1957** Blair et al. *Vertebrates U.S.* 192, *Etheostoma simoterum*. . . Tennessee snubnose darter. *Ibid, Etheostoma duryi*. . . Blackside snubnose darter. *Ibid, Etheostoma atripinne*. . . Cumberland snubnose darter. **1983** Becker *Fishes WI* 926, Bluntnose Darter—*Etheostoma chlorosomum*. . . snubnose darter. **1995** *Knoxville News–Sentinel* (TN) 11 June (Internet), The net contained several darter species. . . One . . , a snubnose darter about 3 inches long, was still showing its spawning colors.

snuck n **chiefly Nth, esp NEast** Cf **snook** n²

Pl, in phrr *go (in) snucks:* =**snack 1.**

1850 in Lib. of Congress *Amer. Memory: CA Narrs.* (Internet) **IL,** If you want business you may go snucks with my Indians in catching salmon or crickets. **1870** *Punchinello* 1.267 **NYC,** Banks were robbed, and Judges went snucks with the robbers. **1883** [see **snack 1**]. **1887** (1895) Robinson *Uncle Lisha* 87 **wVT,** Tu go snucks along wi' he a-ownin' of a haouse. **1895** *DN* 1.400 **NEng, cNY,** *Snucks* [snʌks]. . . "They went snucks and bought candy." **1896** *DN* 1.425 **nNY,** *Snucks:* pron. [snʌks] sometimes heard. *Ibid* **cNY,** *Snucks:* "To go in snucks" is common in Otsego Co., N.Y. **1898** Westcott *Harum* 364 **nNY,** After that's paid we'll go snucks on anythin' that's left. **1914** *DN* 4.154 **NH,** *To go snucks,* to share work and profit evenly. **1917** *DN* 4.400 **neOH,** *Snucks* [snʌks]. . . Shares; in the phrase to go snucks. Snacks may exist here, but I do not recall it. Also Vt., Ky., N.Y. **1927** *AmSp* 2.365 **cwWV,** We will go snucks on the game we get. **1950** *WELS Suppl.* (For dividing up apples, candy, etc) 1 Inf, **cwWI,** Go snucks on it. **1967–69** *DARE* (Qu. II8, *When one person wants to share or divide something with another person* . . "*Let's _____ [on that].*") Inf

MI55, Go snucks [snʌks]—that was quite common, but I haven't heard it now in quite a while; **VT**12, Go snucks [snʌks]; (Qu. L5, *When a farmer gets help on a job from his neighbors in return for his help on their farms later on*) Inf **CT**32, Snucks [snʌks]—each one does half. **1969** *DARE* FW Addit **cCT,** Snucks—[snʌks]. Two guys buy an apple tree and "go snucks on it"—each take half of the apples.

snuck v See **sneak** v **1, 2a**

snucked See **sneak** v **2b**

snudge v

1 To wander about; see quots. [*OED2* 1677 →; "Now *dial.*"]

1904 Day *Kin o' Ktaadn* 198 **ME,** Don't go snudgin' round a stage, nor sing "Come play wiz me!" **1981** Pederson *LAGS Basic Materials,* 1 inf, **nwFL,** A-snudging [ə'snʌ·dʒɪn] around (looking for firewood).

2 also *snidge;* In marble play: to cheat; hence vbl n *snudging;* see quots. Cf **fudge** v

1905 *DN* 3.65 **eNE,** *Snidge, snudge*. . . Term used in playing marbles. Same as *fudge*. **1962** *PADS* 37.3 **KS,** *Snudge.* To move the hand up and forward while shooting. **c1970** Wiersma *Marbles Terms* **UT** (as of 1965), *Snudging* . . illegally stepping over line while shooting . . to snudge. **1993** *Orange Co. Reg.* (Santa Ana CA) 23 Apr Metro sec 1 (Internet), Snudging: a violation of the knuckles-down position, usually a forward movement of the shooting hand.

snuff v, hence vbl n *snuffing* Cf **quill** v **2**

To hasten labor in (a woman) by using snuff to provoke sneezing.

1926 Ferber *Show Boat* 19, The fat midwife, busy with ministrations, had said to the perspiring young doctor, "D'you think it's time to snuff her?" . . To his horror and amazement, before he could stop her, she had stuffed a great pinch of strong snuff up either nostril of Magnolia Ravenal's delicate nose. And thus Kim Ravenel was born into the world on the gust of a series of convulsive a-*choos*! **1970** *NC Folkl.* 18.6, To induce sneezing and earlier delivery of baby, "snuff" the pregnant woman by holding finely powdered tobacco under her nostrils. **1984** Wilder *You All Spoken Here* 36, *Snuffing:* Putting pinches of snuff into the nostrils of an overdue woman to cause violent sneezing, thus inducing delivery.

snuffball See **snuffbox 1**

snuffbox n

1 also *snuffball, snuff mushroom:* A **puffball 1.** [Engl dial] **esp S Midl, Lower Missip Valley** See Map Cf **devil's snuffbox 1, Indian ~**

1890 *Century Dict.* 5738, *Snuff-box*. . . 2. A puffball: same as *devil's snuff-box*. **1965–70** *DARE* (Qu. S18, *A kind of mushroom that grows like a globe . . sometimes gets as big as a man's head*) 10 Infs, **esp VA, Lower Missip Valley,** Snuffbox(es); **KY**83, Snuffballs; **OK**20, Devil's snuffbox or snuffball—it makes a kind of a brown dust if you step on it; **TX**43, Snuffball—pulverizes into snuff if you kick it; **WV**7, Snuffball—same as a puffball; **VA**38, Snuff mushrooms—old people put the snuff on sores. **1992** *Atlanta Jrl.–Constitution* (GA) 30 Oct sec P 5 (Internet), Shun the Satanic snuff balls.

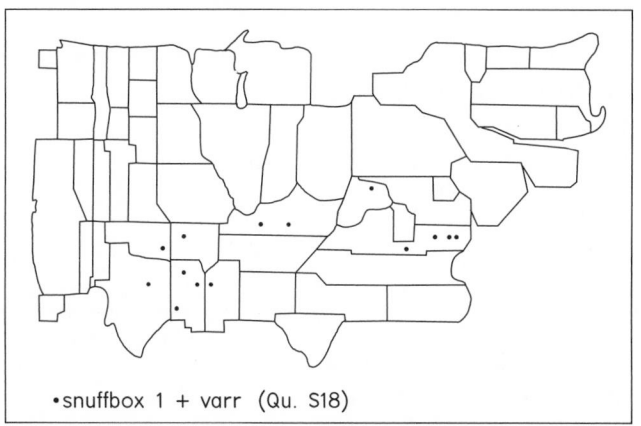

•snuffbox 1 + varr (Qu. S18)

2 A **freshwater clam** (here: *Epioblasma triquetra*).

1982 U.S. Fish & Wildlife Serv. *Fresh-Water Mussels* 36, Snuffbox. . . *Plagiola . . triquetra*. . . Shell yellow, green, or brown . . elongate . . or box-like. **1992** *Nature Conserv. Mag.* 42.6.22, [Caption:] Snuffbox, *Epioblasma triquetra.*

snuffbox fern n
=**marsh fern.**

1822 Eaton *Botany* 197, *[Athyrium] thelipteris* [=*Thelypteris thelypteroides*] (snuff-box fern . .). **1950** Gray–Fernald *Manual of Botany* 33, *D[ryopteris] Thelypteris* . . var. *pubescens* . . Snuffbox-Fern. **1976** Bailey–Bailey *Hortus Third* 1106, *[Thelypteris] palustris.* . . The more hairy American plants *(snuffbox fern, meadow f.)* . . are distinguished by some authors as var. *pubescens.*

snuff brush See **snuff stick**

snuff eater n   Also *snuff chewer*   Cf **dipper 6**
One who uses snuff; by ext, a rustic.

1845 Green *Jrl. Texian Exped.* 138 **TN,** While he found in me no apologist for the "snuff-dippers" and snuff-eaters of my own country, he failed to convince me that it was right for a pretty girl to smoke. **1950** *WELS (A person who uses snuff)* 2 Infs, **WI,** Snuff eater; 1 Inf, **cnWI,** Snuff chewer. **1965–70** *DARE* (Qu. DD3a) 28 Infs, **scattered, but esp W Midl,** Snuff eater; 22 Infs, **scattered, but esp Nth,** Snuff chewer. **1986** Pederson *LAGS Concordance (A rustic)* 1 inf, **cTX,** Snuff chewer.

snuffer n[1]   **chiefly Nth, N Midl**   See Map   Cf **dipper 6, snifter 2,** *snooser* (at **snoose** n[1])
One who uses snuff, esp by inhaling it.

1833 *Republican Compiler* (Gettysburg PA) [1 Oct 4]/5 (newspaper-archive.com), These old snuffers when ruffled from any cause, consume a much larger quantity than usual of their powder, and suffer accordingly. **1835** *New Engl. Mag.* 9.134, The snuffer and chewer is made, but the smoker is born. **1870** (1871) Crane *Arts Intoxication* 79, The snuffer is as little liable to molest his neighbors; but even he may scatter his powder about, while his nasal exercises are anything but harmonious to the ear or pleasant to the eye. **1950** *WELS (A person who uses snuff)* 2 Infs, **WI,** Snuffer. **1965–70** *DARE* (Qu. DD3a) 90 Infs, **chiefly Nth, N Midl,** Snuffer. **1976** *Bucks Co. Courier Times* (Levittown PA) 18 July sec A 12/1, Dry snuff is a powder which snuffers put between their lips and gums and work into a wad. . . Local chewers, pluggers and snuffers say smokeless tobacco not only tastes good but is good for its users.

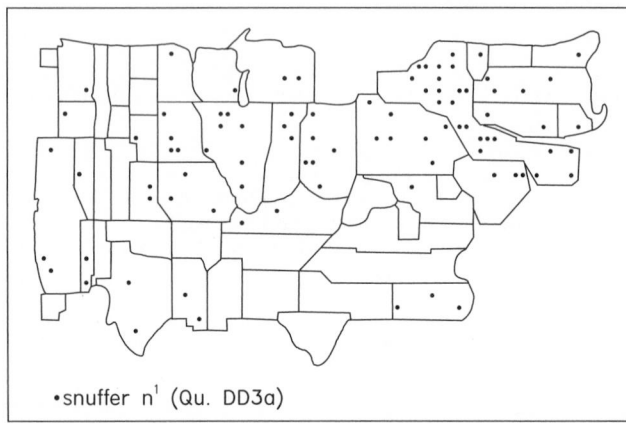

•snuffer n[1] (Qu. DD3a)

snuffer n[2]   See **snuffing pig**

snuffing See **snuff**

snuffing pig n   Also *snuffer*   Cf **puffing pig**
=**harbor porpoise.**

[**1829** Haliburton *Hist. & Statist. Acct. Nova-Scotia* 2.404, *Fish—Whale Species.* . . Snuffer.] **1879** U.S. Natl. Museum *Bulletin* 14.11, *Phocæna brachycion.* . . The *Snuffing Pig* or *Herring Hog.*—Atlantic Coast. **1911** U.S. Bur. Census *Fisheries 1908* 314, Porpoise *(Phocæna communis).*—A cetacean found on the north Atlantic and north Pacific coasts, ascending rivers. It is known as "harbor porpoise," "herring-hog," "puffer," "snuffer," "snuffing pig," etc.

snuff juice See **snuff spit**

snuff mop See **snuff stick**

snuff mushroom See **snuffbox 1**

snuff rubber n   Also *rubber*   **esp DE, MD, PA, WV**   See Map
One who takes snuff by rubbing it on the gums.

1857 Long *Pictures Slavery* (2d ed) 192 **MD,** I would rather that a wife or daughter of mine should drink wine than be a snuff-rubber. **1880** *Scribner's Mth.* 20.139 **SC,** There it is, with German houses and German customs, dropped down right into the middle of Carolina snuff-rubbers, and Georgian clay-eaters. **1914** *Amer. Flint* 5.4.53 **WV,** We are still living in the land of Snakes and Snuff rubbers. **1953** *Charleston Daily Mail* (WV) 6 Jan 4/3, Ever been over to Jackson County? . . Now there's a place plumb full of snuff rubbers. Ain't ashamed to admit it, either. **1965–70** *DARE* (Qu. DD3a, . . *A person who uses snuff*) Infs **DE**1, 3, **MD**15, 22, 40, 42, **NE**3, **PA**93, 134, Snuff rubber; **WV**2, Rubber. **1998** Dyer *Bloodroot* 161 **WV,** We were fox chasers, sheep herders, turtle hunters, snuff rubbers, tale tellers, and whiskered wizards and witches in the eyes of little kids.

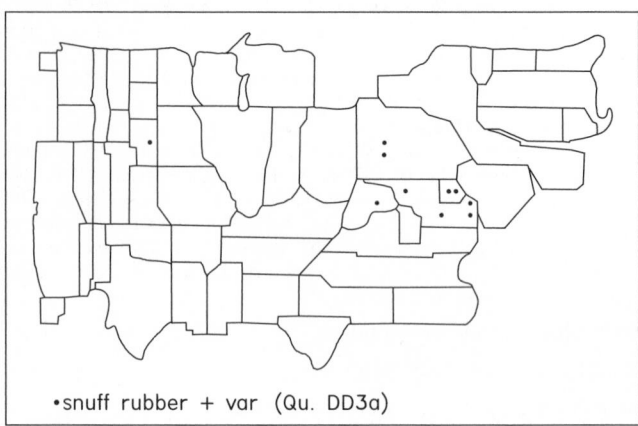

•snuff rubber + var (Qu. DD3a)

snuff-snifter See **snifter 2**

snuff spit n   Also *snuff juice,* ~ *spittle*
Saliva darkened by snuff.

1859 Whittlesey *Stranger's Stratagem* 110 **NC,** Aunt Dinah baptized the back-log with an enormous mouthful of snuff-spittle. **1870** *Overland Mth.* 5.37 **Sth,** Clad in a dirty cotton dress, hair uncombed, face unwashed, feet bare, a snuff-stick in her mouth, and the snuff-juice running down her chin, she presented a picture for "hirelings" to gaze upon. **1941** Writers' Program *Guide AL* 123, Some hold that snuffspit does as well as tobacco juice [for flavoring bait], but your real fish will leave it in disdain to the cats and bony white suckers. **1944** Wellman *Bowl* 165 **KS,** "Jesus," said Dilly with awe, spitting a brown stream of snuff juice. **1950** *WELS (Saliva colored brown by snuff)* 1 Inf, **seWI,** Snuff spit. **1966–70** *DARE* (Qu. DD4, *Moisture in the mouth, colored brown by snuff or chewing tobacco*) Inf **ME**9, Snuff juice; **FL**52, **GA**3, **LA**8, **NC**49, 63, **OH**40, Snuff spit; **NC**7, 82, Snuff spittle. **2006** *DARE* File—Internet **TN,** I get the biggest thrill from going to visit my stepdad's mom. . . You go in, she is sitting there in her dress with her legs sprawled out . . , snuff juice dribbling down her mouth and she still manages to be just the cutest and funniest person.

snuff stick n   Also *snuff brush,* ~ *mop,* ~ *swab*   **chiefly Sth, S Midl, SW, TX**   See Map   Cf **dipping stick 1, toothbrush 1**
A twig chewed on one end until frayed and used for applying snuff to the inside of the mouth.

1845 Green *Jrl. Texian Exped.* 137 **TN,** In the morning this lady showed all the languor of previous excess, and she was as uninteresting until she spent an hour with her snuff-mop as if she had just awaked form the excessive use of ardent spirits. **1863** *Janesville Daily Gaz.* (WI) 17 Feb [2]/2 (newspaperarchive.com), I would like to have some of the northern friends of the "wayward sisters" encounter the tongue of a secession termagant, a real nymph of the cane-brake, with her snuff stick in the corner of her mouth. **1868** *Harper's New Mth. Mag.* 37.493 **Sth,** Love her, and that snuff-stick 'tween her lips? Faugh! **1869** in 1881 Tourgée *Royal Gentleman & Zouri* 74, The well-laden snuff-brush, with its burden of "Carolina Belle," found its way into her mouth. **1870** *Overland Mth.* 5.36 **VA,** In the door-way of the house stood a dirty-looking female with a snuff-stick in her mouth. **1872** Schele de Vere *Americanisms* 63 **Sth,** The *dipping-stick* is also called *snuff-swab.* **1880** *Harper's New Mth. Mag.* 61.20 **MS,** "What's dat, 'Onymous?" she would say, pointing at random with her snuff brush to a letter. [**1889** Edwards *Runaways* 221 **GA,** Cis'ly looked about her as she took her seat, and got out her snuff-cup and mop.] **1909** *DN* 3.372 **eAL, wGA,** *Snuff-swab.* . . A wooden swab for rubbing snuff. **1950** *WELS (A little stick used to rub snuff on the gums)* 2 Infs, **WI,** Snuff stick. **1953** Randolph–Wilson *Down in Holler* 286 **Ozarks,** *Snuff-mop.* . . The chewed peach or black-gum twig used in dipping snuff. The term *snuff stick* is also heard occasionally.   **1954** *Harder Coll.* **cwTN,** *Snuff-mop.* **c1960** *Wilson Coll.* **csKY,** *Snuff-mop* (or *brush*). . . A toothbrush made of a black gum twig, or of hickory bark, or of sycamore stick.   **1965–70** *DARE* (Qu. DD3b, *How . . people take snuff*) 31 Infs, **chiefly Sth, S Midl, TX,** Rub it on (the) gums with a snuff stick; **IL96,** Rub it in with a snuff stick; **MO4,** Rub it on the gums with a snuff stick or toothbrush; **AL26, AR56,** Snuff stick; **NM11,** Use a snuff stick and stick it in corner of mouth; **NC13, OK20, TN42,** (Put it on) snuff brush. [31 of 38 total Infs old]

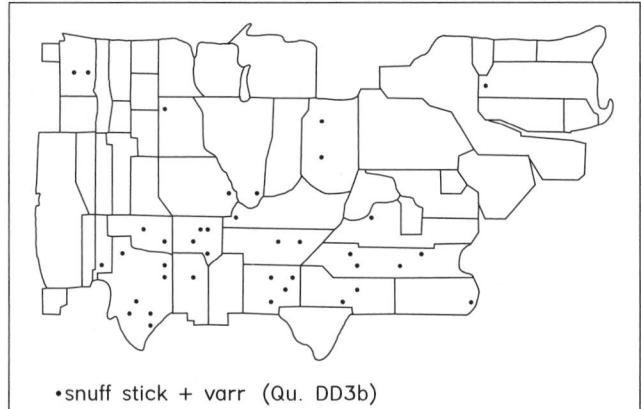

•snuff stick + varr (Qu. DD3b)

snuff-taker n [See quots]
Usu the **surf scoter,** but also the **white-winged scoter.**
1852 in 1876 *Forest & Stream* 7.212 **eMA,** The adult male of the so-called coot or white-wing *Melanetta velvetina* [=*Melanitta fusca*] is on the Connecticut coast called "snuff-taker," another striking name, given no doubt in allusion to the bright red of the bill near the nostril.   **1888** Trumbull *Names of Birds* 103 **CT,** At Stony Creek and Milford, [the surf scoter is called] *snuff-taker* (the drake's variegated beak reminding duckers of a careless snuff-taker's nose).

snuffy adj **West**
Of a horse or cow: short-tempered, nervous.
1927 Sandburg *Amer. Songbag* 13 **SW,** Ride around, little dogies,/ Ride around them slow,/ For the fiery and snuffy are a-rarin' to go.   **1952** *Kerrville Times* (TX) 26 Nov 3/5, He [=a photographer] caught . . cowboys scooting for the fence for safety from the horns of a snuffy cow in a picket corral.   **1961** Adams *Old-Time Cowhand* 292 **West,** The best cowhands could ride the snuffy ones. . . The ordinary cowhand didn't claim to be a bronc rider.   **1967** *DARE* (Qu. K16, *A cow with a bad temper*) Inf **TX22,** Snuffy.   **1971** Green *Last Trail Drive* 18 **TX,** They were pretty snuffy and tried to buck and did most of the layin' down and gettin' up that wild horses do when you are saddlin' them.   **2001** *Birdscapes* Spring/Summer 21 **seTX,** It reminds me of some of the cowboys that work for me— . . let one of them get on some subject like how their good young horse go on getting that ole snuffy longhorn cow out of the brush with her displaying her "hookers" with such a nasty attitude—well, I excuse them for talking so much about something close to their heart.

snufter n [Prob **snuffer** n[1] + excrescent *t,* but cf *EDD snufter* v. "To sniff, snort"]   Cf **snifter 2**
1967 *DARE* (Qu. DD3a, *. . A person who uses snuff*) Inf **MO12,** Snufter.

snug adj
1 Of winter weather: very cold.   **chiefly Nth**   *old-fash*
1845 *WI Argus* (Madison) 9 Dec [2]/6 (newspaperarchive.com), With us it is as cold as charity and as dry as a contribution box. . . We have had snug winter weather for the last eighteen or twenty days with very delicate sprinklings of snow.   **1864** in 2006 *DARE* File—Internet **OH,** [Letter:] Our weat weather has sat in now for cirtain fur the next 4 months to come. We have had pirty snug winter weather fur the past 2 weeks fur this country, but it was dry and cold, now weat and cold.   **1888** *Reno Eve. Gaz.* (NV) 17 Mar [2]/1 (newspaperarchive.com), Even here we had the unusual phenomenon of three weeks of real snug weather. It would only have been moderate winter weather anywhere in the East, but it seemed particularly severe to people accustomed to this climate.   **1897** *NE State Jrl.* (Lincoln) 17 Dec 5/5, Snug winter weather has prevailed here all the week. Yesterday morning a more severe cold wave was wafted from the northward, accompanied by flurries of snow.

1917 in 2006 *DARE* File—Internet **MI,** [Letter:] Weather here has been bitter cold for last week or two. Snug winter weather and no mistake.   **1932** *Dunkirk Eve. Observer* (NY) 1 Feb 4/3, A continuance of the snug weather which started Saturday may bring ice of sufficient thickness to afford skating.   **1987** *DARE* File **cwMA** (as of c1900), Sunshine this morning but still below zero. Ruby Hemenway, who turns 103 tomorrow, said the old folks used to speak of this kind of day as "a snug winter day."

2 Stingy, tight.   [Cf *EDD snug* adj. 5]   **NEng**
1900 Day *Up in ME* 14, They never tackled his pocket-book./ 'Twould a-broke his heart, for he's dretful snug.   **1914** *DN* 4.80 **ME, nNH,** *Snug.* . . Stingy, "near."   **1941** *LANE* Map 484 (*Miser, tightwad*) 1 inf, **seMA,** Pretty snug.

snuggy n   Also *snuggie(s)*
=**Melvin.**
1986 *DARE* File **OH, IA,** Snuggy—Among school children, to hoist someone by the back of their underwear elastic is to give him a snuggy.   **1989–91** *DARE* File, [From a survey at Brigham Young University:] (*The act of lifting a person from behind by the belt, belt buckle, top of the underwear, the seat of the pants*) 95 resps, **chiefly West,** Snuggy; snuggies.   **1992** *DARE* File **csWI,** I . . recalled that trick the bigger kids used to play in school, where they would reach down the back of my pants, grab my shorts, and pull hard. . . I couldn't remember the word we used to describe it . . , but I did a poll of people I work with and came up with. . . Binder . . Creeper . . Grundie (that was also apparently slang for undershorts) . . Hinder-binder . . Snuggie . . Wedgie.

snuk See **sneak** v 2a

snum v [Etym unknown]   **esp NEng**   Cf **i** prep, **swan**
Used in exclam or parenthetic phr *I snum* to express surprise, indignation, or emphasis.
[**1825** Neal *Brother Jonathan* 2.315 **CT,** By snum; but you're a precious fellow.]   **1831** *Huron Reflector* (Norwalk OH) 12 Sept [4]/1 (newspaperarchive.com), *Jonathan's Visit to New York.* . . There's plenty of fokes too, I snum—/ Thicker'n bees in a hive altogether.   **1867** *Atlantic Mth.* 20.425 **NEng,** Why, I snum, you might marry a man o' twenty-five any day, if you had a mind.   **1892** *KS Univ. Qrly.* 1.99 **KS,** *Snum:* to vow, as in, Well, I snum. Reported as common among girls.   **1904** Day *Kin o' Ktaadn* 102 **ME,** We worked it foxy-like, I snum, a-waitin' so's to each take turn.   **1905** *DN* 3.20 **cCT,** *Snum.* . . 'I snum' for I swear; I declare.   **1907** *DN* 3.218 **nwAR,** *Snum.* . . "I snum," I vow, I declare.   **1907** Lincoln *Cape Cod* 57 **MA,** They didn't have anything to do but to look "picturesque" and say "I snum!" and "I swan to man!"   **1914** *DN* 4.80 **ME, nNH,** *Snum! I.* Exclamation. Probably a euphemism for "I swear!" Same as I swow! I swanny!   **1922** (1926) Cady *Rhymes VT* 191, Such piles of four-foot wood! I snum!   **1943** *LANE* Map 601–602 (*For goodness sake*) 1 inf, **seNY,** I snum.   **1947** Botkin *Treas. New Engl. Folkl.* 849, I snum I am a Yankee lad. [Footnote:] Cf. George Stuyvesant Jackson, *Early Songs of Uncle Sam* (Boston, 1933), p. 46: Any character who said "tarnal," "snum," and "plaguey" was a true blue Yankee.   **1951** *PADS* 15.67 **cwNH,** *Snum!, I:* exclamation of amazement.

‡**snum** adv   Cf **plumb** adv 2
Completely, entirely.
1969 *DARE* (Qu. JJ30a, *Other words or expressions for forgetting something: "I _____."*) Inf **MI103,** Snum [snʌm] forgot.

snummy v [Var of **snum** v]   **esp NEng**   Cf **swanny**
Used in var exclam phrr; see quots.
1858 *Ballou's Dollar Mth. Mag.* 7.431 **MA,** The money wasn't much to brag on, I snummy!   **1906** *New Engl. Mag.* 34.95, I snummy, I never see sich a fast runnin' tongue, nor sich a thin man, in my life!   **1921** *Sun. State Jrl.* (Lincoln NE) 11 Dec sec B 6/4, I snummy, if this isn't my old friend Silas Burnham.   **1959** *VT Hist.* 27.138, *Gosh Snummy!: interj.* Rare. Essex. *Ibid* 158, *I Snum!: interj.* Var. I Snummy! . . Common. Caledonia; Orange. *Snummy to Gracious!: interj.* Rare. Rutland.

snunk See **sneak** v 2a

snurl n   Also sp *snerl, snirl* [*EDD snirl* sb.[2] 5. "A knot, tangle," 6. "A gnarl or knot in wood"]   **S Midl, esp sAppalachians**   Cf **knurl**
A tangle, knot, area of irregular grain or surface; hence adjs *snurly, snirly* knotty, gnarly, twisted.
1851 Byrn *Life AR Dr.* 125, I was a poor climber, and it was a bad tree, a little snurly oak.   **1903** *DN* 2.330 **seMO,** *Snurl.* . . Gnarl. 'The wood is full of snurls and hard to split.'   **1914** *KY Geol. Surv.* (4th ser)

2.3.27, In all these localities the typical concretionary or bouldery bedding is conspicuous—"snurly," as a farmer living in the vicinity of one of its outcrops very aptly designated it. **1925** Dargan *Highland Annals* 21 **wNC,** It had lost so many limbs when it was young and pushin' up, that it was jest the snirliest tree I ever saw. **1941** *Hall Coll.* **eTN,** *Snurl. . .* A knot in wood. "Here's a damn snurl that busted out on it," of a piece of wood on which a knot has busted out of the grain. *Ibid,* "I hit a snurly place in the wood," i.e., "wood that's just as wavy as hell, with the grain running in four or five different directions." **1946** *AmSp* 21.191 **seKY,** *Snirl* or *snurl . .* a gnarl. 'I pulled up the plant to see if hit was a-growin', and thar was a big-old white snurl on the root.' **1952** Brown *NC Folkl.* 1.592, *Snurly. . .* Twisted, knotty. **1961** Seeman *In Arms of Mt.* 234 **eTN,** "Do you know what a 'snerl' is?" Edwin will ask. "Burr Guthrie says a snerl is the lowest part of a tree trunk, at its base, where its roots are 'crankled in.'" **2006** *DARE* File—Internet **nwGA,** I was learning to appreciate intelligence in a man. Steve, with that snurly little smile, was just the perfect model of what was to be the type of husband I would have someday.

snurl v¹ Also sp *snirl* **chiefly S Midl**

1 also with *up:* To wrinkle up (the nose), curl (the lip). [*EDD snirl* v.² 4]

1893 Owen *Voodoo Tales* 198 **MO** [Black], Ole Rabbit, he sniff, he snurl up de nose, he wuhk de whiskehs. **1932** (1933) Poole *Nurses* 151 **seKY,** Many women nowadays sent their wool to mills outside of the hills. . . But Nancy "snurled up her nose" at that. **1941** in 2004 Montgomery–Hall *Dict. Smoky Mt. Engl.* 549 **wNC,** She snurled her nose up when she passed me. **1946** *AmSp* 21.191 **seKY,** *Snirl* or *snurl . .* to wrinkle (the nose) in contempt. 'He snurled up his nose.' **1969** *Max Hunter Folk Song Coll.* (Internet) **cnAR,** Th cow she kicked, th cow she jumped / Th cow she snurled her nose. **1972** Cooper *NC Mt. Folkl.* 96, *Snurl*—to curl the lips. **1972** *Daily Times–News* (Burlington NC) 4 May sec A 6/1, The Colonel would snurl up his lip and give us a sly glance and reply: "They ain't made the pitcher that could get the Colonel out." **1984** *NY Times* (NY) 26 July sec A 22/6, [Letter:] Far be it from me to snurl my nose at the new game that two letter writers . . have, perhaps inadvertently, concocted. **2005** *DARE* File—Internet **ceOK,** In every picture I take I am making a face!! snirling nose or talking. **2005** in 2006 *Ibid* **neAL,** The foxdog snurled up his nose and stated "Help you with what *stupid,* That tree aint gonna *run!!!!*' **2006** *Ibid* **swCA,** He snurled up his nose and commented that it stunk. He said it smelled like cows.

2 To sneer (at).

1937 in 2006 *DARE* File—Internet **OK,** I hadn't much time to visit my neighbors, but when I did go to church, we were not snurled at because we were not dressed in silks and satins.

3 with *up:* To become tangled. [*EDD snirl* v.² 1; cf **snurl** n]

1999 WV Humanities Council *People & Mts.* Sept (Internet), Folk Weather Predictions. . . If the wool "snurls" up when you spin, it is a sign of rain.

snurl v², hence vbl n *snurling* [*EDD snirl* v.¹ 2]

To grumble, growl; hence ppl adj *snurling.*

1948 Hurston *Seraph* 9 **wFL,** Brock Henson snurled behind his back that Middleton ought to be mortally ashamed of himself. *Ibid* 97, Kenny gave the outraged matron a snurling look. **1969** *Max Hunter Folk Song Coll.* (Internet) **cnAR,** Th rich man closed his door an' snurled / No room nor bread for th poor. **2004** *AR Democrat–Gaz.* (Little Rock) 16 June (Internet), The first taste [of margarine] sent him into a snurling fit—if he couldn't have butter, he would have nothing.

snurl up See **snurl** v¹ 1, 3

snurly See **snurl** n

snuss See **snoose** n¹

snyder See **schneider**

Snyder's pup n Also *Snyder's hound,* ~ *house cat* **sAppalachians**

Used in var comparisons; see quots.

1937 *Hall Coll.* **wNC, eTN,** *Snyder . .* used in proverbial comparisons. "That plane went over here as fast as Snyder's pup." **1939** *Ibid* **wNC, eTN,** As fast as Snyder's house cat. **1960** Hall *Smoky Mt. Folks* 63, To take off like a scalded dog or like Snyder's pup. **1976** Garber *Mountain-ese* 85 **sAppalachians,** *Snyder's-house-cat*—He's so hard up he haint no better off than snyder's house-cat. **1998** in 2004 Montgomery–Hall *Dict. Smoky Mt. Engl.* 549 **wNC, eTN,** Peart as Snyder's pup . .

quick as Snyder's pup . . smart as Snyder's pup. **2000** in 2003 *DARE* File—Internet **nwGA,** It was only a matter of time until our small town [=Dalton] took off like "Snyder's pup." Large chenille plants appeared here and there and everyone who wanted to work had their pick of a job. **2001** in 2004 Montgomery–Hall *Dict. Smoky Mt. Engl.* 549 **wNC,** As fast as Snyder's hound.

snythe See **snath**

so adv **chiefly NEng**

Foll by neg aux + subj to make a positive addition to or express agreement with a preceding positive statement—freq in phr *so don't I* so do I.

1912 McKinney *Nora* 316 **NY,** "Say, I know a secret 'bout to-morrow," said Rob. "So don't I, dozens of 'em, and some that aren't about to-morrow." **1962** *NYT Book Rev.* 28 Jan 16/1, This expression [= "Don't be surprised if he doesn't visit you one of these days"] is akin to the old jocular negative in the following piece of dialogue: "I wish I had an orange." "So don't I." **1980** *Daily Hampshire Gaz.* (Northampton MA) 9 Sept 16/2, And just as the mood of the once-solemn convocation has changed over the past few years, so hasn't the opening address by President Jill Ker Conway. **1980** *DARE* File **MA,** *So* (+ neg = agreement)—Heard in New England at least since 1959, esp. among younger people. E.g. "I really like blueberries!"—"So don't I!" . . "We're going to the movies tonight."—"So aren't we! Let's go together." **1982** Chaika *Speaking RI* [8], *So don't I* = I shaw do (also used in past tense, e.g. *so didn't I*). **1998** *NADS Letters* **nwPA** (as of c1980), The standard response indicating agreement was "so don't I" (. . Also "so didn't I," "so doesn't she," etc.) . . While it had more currency among the harder-core locals, it seemed to be pretty much standard fare for everyone, barring those who moved in from outside. **1999** *DARE* File—Internet [Boston Online *Wicked Good Guide to Boston English*], *So don't I*—An example of the Massachusetts negative positive. Used like this: "I just love the food at Kelly's." "Oh, so don't I!" **2000** *NADS Letters* **VT,** In Vermont we often hear "natives" use the term "so don't I" which actually means "so *do* I." **2000** *DARE* File **nwMA** (as of 1960s), "I have a new bike." "Well, so don't I." *Ibid* **nwMA,** "So don't I" . . is so ingrained a speech pattern that I've always taken it for granted. Grandma . . said . . "I was born in '09 and my folks were using it before I was born." **2001** in 2002 *DARE* File—Internet **ceMA,** While he/she may have some quirks, so don't we all. **2005** in 2010 *Ibid* **cNY,** I thought "so don't I" was from the hillbillies of central NY. . . they use it in all forms: "so wouldn't I" "so didn't I" "so can't I." *Ibid* **NH,** I also sent them the link for my site for my bio. They seem quite happy, and so aren't I! **2010** *Ibid* **MA,** They have always been there for me and always will and so won't I for them. . . The city is my home but so isn't my small town—I have a little bit of both going for me. *Ibid* **seNH,** Have you ever found yourself wishful thinking? . . Sure you have. So haven't I.

so conj [*OED2 so* adv. and conj. c1000 →]

=so as 2. Note: The comb *just so* in this sense is common and is not treated here.

1905 *DN* 3.95 **nwAR,** *So, conj.* Provided that. 'So you come, it's all right.' 'Just so' is more common than '*so'* in this sense. **1909** *DN* 3.372 **eAL, wGA,** *So, conj.* Provided that.

so adj Cf **barefooted 1, dry so** adj phr

Of food or drink: plain, without addition.

[**1887** (1888) Smedes *Mems. S. Planter* 56 **Sth** [Black], Dey had two gre't harmper-baskets full o' bottles o' whiskey. . . An' dey used to larf an' say to de young gals, 'You young gals ought not to drink whiskey so; you ought to put water in it.' . . Miss Mary . . always put mine an' Sis Patsy's in a pail, an' put water an' sugar in it, an' gib it to us so.] **1903** *DN* 2.330 **seMO,** *So. . .* Without change. 'I drink my coffee just so,' that is without sugar or cream. 'I always take my whisky so,' or 'straight.' The *so* is accented. **1907** *DN* 3.237 **nwAR,** *So. . .* Without addition, without change. (Accented.) **1909** *DN* 3.372 **eAL, wGA,** *So. . .* Straight, without adulteration or addition. "I always take my coffee so." **1968** *Helen Adolf Festschrift* 38 **cePA,** *So* (Pennsylvania German *so*) for 'unchanged,' 'unaltered,' or 'plain'; for example, "I don't want no milk on mine, I'll eat it so."

so exclam, often repeated |so(ʊ), so:|; for addit varr see quots [Cf *EDD so* int. 2] Cf **saw** exclam

Freq in combs *so-boss(ie):* Used as a command to a farm animal, spec:

a Stand still!—used to a cow during milking. **chiefly Nth, N Midl, West; also S Atl** See Map

1855 Philleo *Twice Married* 86 **CT**, "So, so boss!" said John soothingly. "Stand still, now." **1899** (1912) Green *VA Folk-Speech* 404, *Sowench.* . . Word to make a cow stand still when milking. **1933** Miller *Lamb in His Bosom* 145 **GA**, She beat a cow unmercifully that would not so for her to milk it. **1949** Kurath *Word Geog.* 64, Calls to Cows during Milking. . . The call *so!* is current nearly everywhere in the Eastern States from Maine to Georgia and westward to the Ohio. However, it is not used in Virginia, except in the southwestern part. It is uncommon in adjoining parts of North Carolina, in Maryland west of the Bay, and in south-central Pennsylvania. **c1955** Reed–Person *Ling. Atlas Pacific NW (Call to cows to get them to stand still during milking)* 24 infs, So-boss(ie); 5 infs, So; 1 inf, So now. **1965–70** DARE (Qu. K81, *To make a cow stand still—for example, when milking her—you say, "_____."*) 180 Infs, **chiefly Nth, N Midl, West,** So-boss (so-boss); **CA**3, **IN**63, **KS**1, **NJ**3, 8, **PA**106, 129, **UT**3, So-bossie; 147 Infs, **widespread,** So; **FL**6, **IL**142, **SC**19, 26, **VA**46, So-cow; **CA**163, **NM**6, **OK**1, So-now; **CA**23, **FL**7, So-gal; **CA**136, So-boy; **FL**27, So-baby; **GA**19, So! Back your foot; **GA**33, So-Bessie so; **MD**48, So-sookie; **MI**113, So-there; **NV**8, So-so-Bess; **PA**10, So-wench; **PA**51, So-sookie-so. **1991** Pederson *LAGS Social Matrix* 103 **esp coastal Gulf Region** *(Calls to cows)* 36 infs, So (cow).

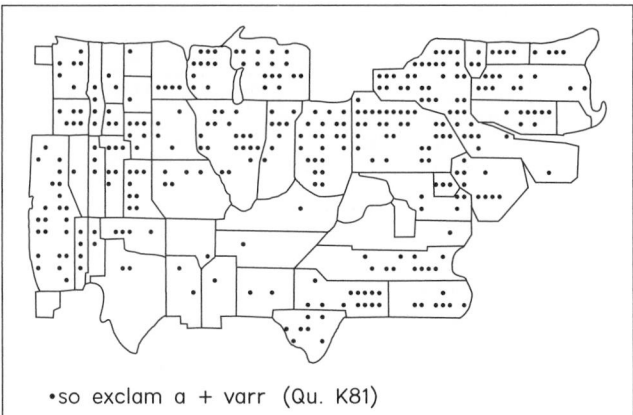

•so exclam a + varr (Qu. K81)

b Come!—see quots. Cf **co** v

1901 *Chicago Tribune* (IL) 27 Jan 39, Words used in this country in addressing cows and calves: (1.) Cows—To come: . . so boss. **1924** DN 5.277 [Exclams], *So* or *so so* (to call cows). **1949** Turner *Africanisms* 201 **sSC, GA coasts** [Gullah], [Words used in conversation:] So! so! 'a call to horses.' **c1955** Reed–Person *Ling. Atlas Pacific NW (Call to cows to get them in from the pasture)* 1 inf, So bossie; 1 inf, So. **1965–70** DARE (Qu. K80, *The call that's used . . to get the cows in from the pasture)* 12 Infs, **scattered,** So-boss(ie); **CA**199, **PA**1, So-o-o; **PA**23, So-so-so; **NJ**8, So-boy; **SC**26, So-cow; (Qu. K82, *The call used . . to get horses in from the pasture)* Inf **IN**82, So; (Qu. K83, *To call a calf to you at feeding time)* Infs **IL**5, 116, **KS**15, 18, So-boss (so-boss); **OK**53, So-bossie; **GA**7, **MS**63, **WI**44, So-calf; (Qu. K84, *The call used . . to get the pigs in at feeding time)* Inf **MA**72, So-so-so; **NC**36, So-pig.

soak v, hence ppl adj *soaked* [OED2 1686 →]
To bake or roast thoroughly.

1848 Bartlett *Americanisms* 319 **NEng**, To soak. . . To bake thoroughly. It is particularly applied to bread. **1896** DN 1.425, Soak (v.t. and i.). To roast. "Let it soak." [DN Ed: Cf. *soak*, to bake.] **1899** (1912) Green *VA Folk-Speech* 400, *Soak.* . . To receive a prolonged baking; bake thoroughly: said of bread. **1958** Hench Coll. **cVA**, Mrs. Adele Hall . . Charlottesville raised woman . . was talking today about her home-made bread. She used these sentences: 1. The bread hasn't soaked yet. 2. I'll leave the bread in the oven a few more minutes to soak. **1971** DARE File **cNC**, *Soaked*—of a cake: cooked, done.

soak n[1] Also with *old* [Engl dial] **chiefly Nth, N Midl, West** See Map Cf **soaked**

A heavy drinker; an alcoholic—also in combs *booze-soak, whiskey-soak.*

1852 *Janesville Gaz.* (WI) 15 May 1/8, An "old soak" that you never saw before approaches you in a patronizing way, and calls you by your name. **1873** Wheeler *Shells* 25, Just then an old toper dropped in from the street,/ A jolly old soak, with a nose like a beet. **1899** (1912) Green

VA Folk-Speech 400, *Soak.* . . A tippler; a hard drinker. **1900** DN 2.61 [College slang], *Soak.* . . A drunken fellow. **1919** DN 5.67 **CA, NM** [Among hs students], *Soak,* a drunkard. "Billy Sunday preaches to the old soaks." **1965–70** DARE (Qu. DD12, . . *A person who drinks steadily or a great deal)* 75 Infs, **chiefly Nth, N Midl, West,** (Old) soak; **WA**3, Booze-soak; **AR**3, **AK**8, **IN**18, **MD**31, Whiskey-soak; (Qu. X53b) Inf **VA**5, Soak; (Qu. DD15, *A person who is thoroughly drunk)* Inf **MO**36, A soak; **MA**6, Old soak; (Qu. DD34, *A party at which there is considerable drinking)* Inf **MO**38, Bunch of soaks; (Qu. HH40, *Uncomplimentary words for an old man)* Inf **PA**197, Soak—if he's a drinker; **WA**11, Soak; (Qu. NN10a) Inf **MN**15, Hello, you old soak. **2004** in 2005 DARE File—Internet **MN**, I can be pretty sure they aren't all at the water cooler today saying what a soak I am.

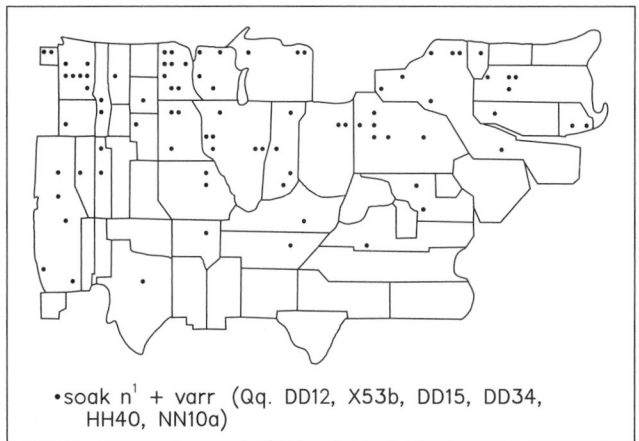

•soak n[1] + varr (Qq. DD12, X53b, DD15, DD34, HH40, NN10a)

soak n[2] Also *old soak, soak-about, soak(e)y* [*soak* to strike, to hit; a blow]

Any of var games in which players are hit with a ball; hence n *soaker* a hard throw of the ball; see quots.

1887 Eggleston *Graysons* 78 **IL**, At school, when the young master saw the boys playing at the boisterous and promiscuous "soak about," he would . . rush out of the door to mix in the confusion, throwing the yarn ball at one and another with a vigor and an accuracy of aim that doubled the respect of his pupils for him. **1890** Howells *Boy's Town* 70 **OH**, [It was] as if, when the fellows were playing soak-about, and he got hit in the pit of the stomach with a hard ball, he had complained of the fellow who threw it. **1890** DN 1.66 **KY**, *Soaky* . . a free-for-all scramble for the ball, and the privilege to hit whomsoever one will. "Soak him!" they all cry. When one is hit hard, they say, "That was a soaker!" **1940** Harbin *Fun Encycl.* 182, *Soakey.* . . All players stand ready beside their caps while one of the end players tosses or rolls a tennis ball or soft rag ball, trying to get it into one of the caps. If he succeeds the player in whose cap the ball lands immediately picks it up and throws, trying to hit one of the other players. . . If the thrower misses [etc] . . [t]hat player must stand bent over against a wall or tree while each of the other players throws the ball at him. **1942** McAtee *Dial. Grant Co. IN* 60 (as of 1890s), *Soak,* or *"ole-soak"* . . a game of town-ball or old-cat in which players were put "out" when off base by being hit by a thrown ball.

soaked adj Also with *up* *old-fash*
Drunk; under the influence of alcohol.

1737 PA Gaz. (Philadelphia) 6–13 Jan 2/2, He carries too much Sail, Stew'd, Stubb'd, Soak'd, Soft. **1900** DN 2.62 [College slang], *Soaked* . . in phrase 'to get soaked.' . . To get drunk. **1912** DN 3.590 **wIN**, *Soaked.* . . Very drunk. **c1960** Wilson Coll. **csKY**, *Soaked.* . . Full of liquor. **1965–70** DARE (Qu. DD15, *A person who is thoroughly drunk)* 21 Infs, **scattered,** Soaked; **PA**71, Soaked to the gills; **SC**11, **WA**20, Well soaked; (Qu. DD14, *When a person is partly drunk, "He's _____."*) Infs **CT**10, **GA**84, **IL**126, **MO**10, **WY**2, Half-soaked; **MT**2, Soaked; **ID**2, Soaked up. [27 of 31 Infs old]

soaked ppl adj See **soak** v

soaked up See **soaked**

soaker n[1] [OED2 1789 →] **chiefly Nth, N Cent** See Map on p. 102 Cf **root-soaker, sod-soaker**

A soaking rain.

1853 *Bangor Daily Whig & Courier* (ME) 25 June [2]/2 (newspaperarchive.com), There was a nice little rain yesterday forenoon. . .

We hope soon to have a regular soaker. **1864** *Janesville Daily Gaz.* (WI) 18 June 1/3, The great clouds assemble, and look as if they intended to marshal themselves for . . a real soaker such as would make the fields laugh and the hills rejoice. **1935** Sandoz *Jules* 40 **wNE** (as of 1880–1930), Unless another hard soaker came soon there would be no sod cutting for building. **1948** Manfred *Chokecherry* 234 **nwIA,** The thirsty land wasn't going to get a soaker after all. **1965–70** *DARE* (Qu. B25, . . *Joking names . . for a very heavy rain. . . "It's a regular _____."*) 17 Infs, **esp Nth, N Cent,** Soaker; **ME5,** Old soaker; (Qu. B24, . . *A sudden, very heavy rain*) Infs **AL24, ID1, IL42, OH87, VT16,** Soaker. **2005** *Telegraph–Herald* (Dubuque IA) 13 Aug (Internet), "This was the best soaker we've had all summer," said Tom McMullen, a . . farmer outside Cascade, Iowa.

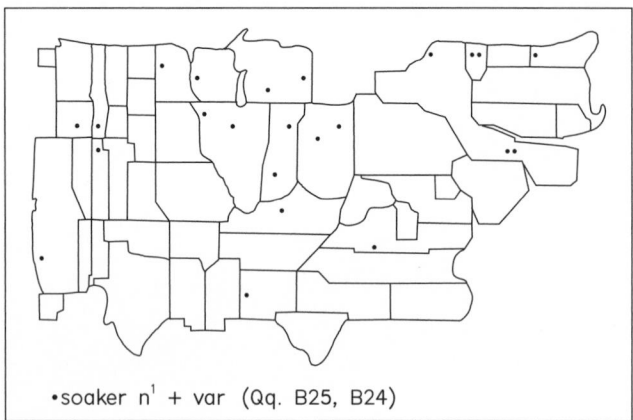

•soaker n¹ + var (Qq. B25, B24)

soaker n² See **soak** n²

soakey See **soak** n²

‡**soakus** n
=**second cutting.**
1968 *DARE* File **KY,** *Soakus*—the second growth of hay or clover.

soaky See **soak** n²

soap n
A game for two players in which the object is to fill the squares in a paper grid with letters spelling the word "soap"; see quot.
1966–70 *DARE* (Qu. EE39, . . *Games played on paper by two people*) Inf **MO23,** Soap; **AR18,** Soap—guessing to fill in the blanks; **GA6,** Soap—each person has this chart [FW illustr: a grid four squares across and five squares down]; "A" writes down a letter, "B" guesses it; if he is right, he gets to add it to the chart; if wrong, "A" adds it to his chart; object is to complete chart; **IL116,** Soap—squares made and players try to guess letter written in *soap;* if they do, they get letter, and the idea is to get the word "soap" written in the squares; **NC53,** Soap—guess letters and fill in squares.

soapball n Cf **soapweed 2**
The flower head of a **yucca.**
1907 Cook *Border & Buffalo* 280 **TX,** "Soap-balls," said Squirrel-eye, who had been raised in Texas. And so they were. There was a soap-root growing profusely in all this region, with which the Mexicans washed their clothes. From the top of its stalk grew a round, fuzzy ball about four inches in diameter, which would ignite at the touch of a burning match.

soapberry n
1 Std: a tree of the genus *Sapindus,* esp *S. saponaria;* the fruit of such a tree. For other names of var spp see **China tree 2, Chinaberry 2, false dogwood 2, Indian soap plant, palo blanco 4** Cf **Chinawood**
2 A **buffalo berry** (here: *Shepherdia canadensis*). **chiefly AK**
1868 *Sheboygan Co. Herald* (Sheboygan Falls WI) 22 July [2]/4 (newspaperarchive.com) **AK,** Soap a-lalley berries, or soap berries are to be found in immense quantities throughout Alaska. **1950** Gray–Fernald *Manual of Botany* 1045, *S[hepherdia] canadensis.* . . Soapberry. . . Calcareous rocks and banks and on sandy shores. **1959** Anderson *Flora*

AK 348, *S[hepherdia] canadensis.* . . Soapberry, Soopolallie. . . Native Indians mix the berries with sugar and water and beat it into a froth much relished by them. . . Noatak—Mackenzie delta . . N.Y.—Utah—Ore. **1962** Salisbury *Quoth the Raven* 135 **seAK,** We have been told that the natives have a dish of their own which they call "sopally" or Indian ice cream, which is made by beating up with the hands crushed soap berries in warm water in a big bowl or dishpan. Sugar is added and the whole is beaten . . until the proper stiffness has been secured. All then gather around the dish and eat it with spoons. **2006** *DARE* File—Internet **AK,** As I walked along the edge of the gravel bar looking for a place to camp [in Denali National Park] in the trees, I noticed lots of ripe soapberries. . . I also noticed many grizzly tracks.
3 A **nightshade 1** (here: *Solanum asperum*).
1897 *Jrl. Amer. Folkl.* 10.52 **FL,** *Solanum radula,* Vahl, soap berry, Florida keys.
4 A **bearberry 2** (here: *Arctostaphylos uva-ursi*).
2002 *AK Mag.* Sept 50, Highbush cranberries and kinnikinnick berries (also called soap berries) are favorite foods in the fall.

soapbloom n [See quot 1974]
=**Oregon tea tree** or a related *Ceanothus.*
1931 U.S. Dept. Ag. *Misc. Pub.* 101.110, *Red soapbloom (C[eanothus] sanguineus),* sometimes called Oregon tea-tree, a red-stemmed, white-flowered species of the Northwest, ranging from British Columbia to western Montana, and northern California, is one of the largest-leaved species of the genus and is of fair to fairly good palatability. **1974** (1977) Coon *Useful Plants* 235, Throughout the West there are a number of other species [of *Ceanothus*] commonly called wild lilac, buckbrush, and soapbloom. This latter name comes from the fact that the fresh flowers of some species make an excellent lather when crushed and rubbed in water, making the skin soft and faintly fragrant.

soap box See **soaper**

soapbush n
1 A **deer brush 1** (here: usu *Ceanothus integerrimus*). **West**
1898 *Jrl. Amer. Folkl.* 11.225 **CA,** *Ceanothus integerrimus* . . mountain birch, soap bush, white tea-tree. **1915** (1926) Armstrong–Thornber *Western Wild Flowers* 282, There are many kinds of Ceanothus, largely western. . . The flowers make a soapy lather when rubbed in water, hence the name Soap-bush.
2 =**sweet pepperbush.** Cf **poor man's soap c**
1911 NJ State Museum *Annual Rept. for 1910* 608, *Clethra alnifolia.* . . At Manahawkin it is called Soap Bush, from the idea that the flowers when rubbed together in water make a sort of soapy lather. Our results have not been very startling, however. **1968** *DARE* (Qu. T13) Inf **GA28,** Soapbush. **1968** *DARE* Tape **GA30,** [Inf:] You had the soapbush. . . [FW:] Do you know how to make soap out of 'em? [Inf:] Oh, yeah. . . You just pull the leaf from 'em, you know, and use it just like you use a soap. **1974** Morton *Folk Remedies* 49 **SC,** Sweet Pepperbush; White Alder; Puppytail; Soapbush—*Clethra alnifolia.* . . Flowers rubbed in water make suds for washing.
3 =**Texas porlieria.**
1938 Van Dersal *Native Woody Plants* 198, *Porlieria angustifolia.* . . Soap-bush. . . A large shrub to small tree; evergreen. . . wood very durable, used locally for fence posts. **1960** Vines *Trees SW* 575, Vernacular names for the plant are Soap-bush, Guayacán, and Guayacum. . . The bark of the roots is sold on the Mexican markets as a soap for washing woolens. **1970** Correll *Plants TX* 902, *Porlieria angustifolia.* . . Soap-bush. . . The bark of the root is used as a source of soap. **2005** in 2006 *DARE* File—Internet [*Del Rio News–Herald* 11 Apr] **TX,** Lee's trail work is surrounded by clumps of vermilion caret cup cactus, . . and rangy mounts of violet guayacán or soapbush.

soaper n Also *soap box, ~ horse* Cf **fox farm, ready for the**
A worthless, worn out horse.
1966–70 *DARE* (Qu. K44, *A bony or poor-looking horse*) Inf **OK27,** Soap box—ready for the soap factory; **TX78,** Soap horse; **TX16, 22,** Soaper. **2001** *Livestock Weekly* 22 Feb (Internet) **TX,** Every time I pass the crowded pet food aisle . . , I yearn for more of the action than shipping an occasional old soaper horse.

soap gentian See **soapwort gentian**

soap gourd n **Sth, S Midl** Cf **gourd 1a**
A container for soft soap.
1835 Crockett *Account* 192 **TN,** I'd give my head for a soap-gourd,

that Andrew Jackson never made the proposition for letters of marque and reprisal. **1862** *S. Lit. Messenger* 34.569, Benjamin dipped his paint brush into the soap-gourd, lathered me anew, and kept on shaving. **1884** *Atlantic Mth.* 53.365 **eTN,** Ye ain't wantin ter gin Vander the soap-gourd ter drink out'n. **1909** *DN* 3.372 **eAL, wGA,** *Soap-gourd.* . . A gourd or other receptacle for holding soft homemade soap. **1939** FWP *Guide TN* 502, Large families often make a barrel of this soap, and at intervals the soap gourd is filled from the barrel. . . Soap gourds are often handed down in families for several generations. **1967** DARE Tape **AL**33, You'd let it boil till it'd get thick. . . And we had a great big soap barrel and we'd put that soap in that barrel. . . We had . . an old gourd we called a soap gourd. **a1975** Lunsford *It Used to Be* 43 **wNC,** A soap gourd. . . was a gourd with all of the seeds taken out, dried, . . and with a piece cut out about one-quarter of the way in. . . You'd hang the gourd up by that crooked neck on a long nail.

soap grass n
=squaw grass 1.
1934 Haskin *Wild Flowers Pacific Coast* 43, I have been reliably informed that in early spring bears seek the open hillsides where these plants grow and dig up the roots for food. The same informant said that the roots boiled in water make a very good substitute for soap, and that he had often used them for that purpose. These two items explain two vernacular names for the plant, those of bear grass, and soap grass. **1950** FWP *Guide ID* 71, Stonecrop. . . Called variously soap grass, squaw grass, and elk grass.

soap horse See **soaper**

soap lily See **soap plant 1**

soap or eats exclam phr Also *soap or grub*
Used by children on Halloween to request treats.
1947 *Fresno Bee* (CA) 30 Oct 15/3, [Advt for a national chain:] When the "spooks" arrive on the porch saying "soap or eats" they can help themselves to apple treats. **1956** *Lima News* (OH) 31 Oct 28/7, There are sections where the children say "soap or grub," instead of "trick or treat." **1966** DARE File **MN** (as of 1940), *Soap or eats*—what was said on Halloween by the children in Minnesota. (Nowadays it is "trick or treat"). **1976** *Ibid* **csWI** (as of 1945), *Soap or grub*—said by children asking door-to-door for a handout of goodies—and threatening to soap windows if it is refused. (Later superseded by "trick or treat.")

soap plant n
1 also *soap lily:* A western plant of the genus *Chlorogalum,* esp *C. pomeridianum.* **esp CA** Also called **amole 1a, Indian soap root, soap root 1.** For other names of *C. pomeridianum* see **wild potato 4c**
1848 Bryant *What I Saw in CA* 452, The "soap-plant" *(amóle)* is one which appears to be among the most serviceable. The root, which is the saponaceous portion of the plant, resembles the onion, but possesses the quality of cleansing linen equal to any "oleic soap." **1859** (1968) Bartlett *Americanisms* 425, Soap-Plant. *Chlorogalum pomeridianum.* A plant common in California and New Mexico, where it is called *ammole,* and which, when pounded and broken, answers the purposes of soap. **1897** Parsons *Wild Flowers CA* 82, Soap-Plant. . . This the early Spanish-Californians used extensively in lieu of soap, and esteemed greatly as a hair tonic. **1921** *DN* 5.114 **CA,** *Soap-lily, soap-plant.* . . Chloragalum [sic] pomridianum [sic]. **1959** Munz–Keck *CA Flora* 1329, *Chlorogalum* [spp]. . . Soap Plant. Amole. . . The bulbs were roasted and eaten by the Indians. **2001** *Assoc. Press State & Local Wire* 8 Nov (Internet) **CA,** Purple amoles, commonly called "soap plants" because of the soapy lather that can be produced from their bulbs, were listed as threatened under the Federal Endangered Species Act in March 2000.

2 A **yucca** such as **banana yucca** or **soapweed 2.**
[**1844** (1954) Gregg *Commerce* 113, Among the wild productions of New Mexico is the *palmilla*—a species of palmetto, which might be termed the soap-plant—whose roots . . when bruised, form a saponaceous pulp called *amole,* much used by the natives for washing clothes, and is said to be even superior to soap for scouring woollens.] **1845** Frémont *Rept. Rocky Mts.* 249 **CA,** Great quantities of *ammole,* (soap plant) the leaves of which are used in California for making . . mats for saddle cloths. **1850** Garrard *Wah-to-yah* 46 **NM,** The soap plant (Amole or Yucca augustifolia [sic]) dotted the prairie, here and there, in the strange-looking garb of green. Its root is much used by the New Mexicans in washing clothes. **1898** *Jrl. Amer. Folkl.* 11.282 **CO,** *Yucca angustifolia* [=*Y. glauca*], Pursh, soap plant [etc]. **1900** Lyons

Plant Names 401, *Y[ucca] baccata.* . . Soap-plant. *Fruit* edible. *Leaves* yield Tambigo fiber. **1970** DARE (Qu. S26e) Inf **VA**77, Adam-and-Eve thread—a soap plant. **2003** Eastman *Book Field & Roadside* 321, The soap-plant *(Y[ucca] glauca)* is the only other *Yucca* that occurs eastward to the midwestern states.

3 =**death camas.**
1890 *Century Dict.* 5741, *Zigadenus Fremontii,* also Californian, is another soap-plant. **1897** Parsons *Wild Flowers CA* 6, *Zygadenus Fremonti.* . . It has sometimes been called "soap-plant," but this name more appropriately belongs to *Chlorogalum.* **1935** (1943) Muenscher *Weeds* 185, *Zygadenus venenosus.* . . Meadow death camas, Soap plant, Alkali-grass, "Lobelia."

4 A **goosefoot** (here: *Chenopodium californicum).* **CA**
1898 Davidson *CA Plants* 117, *C[henopodium] californicum.* . . Soap Plant. Frequent on open foothill slopes throughout our region. **1920** Saunders *Useful Wild Plants* 174 **CA,** Another well-known California soap plant is a species of Pig-weed *(Chenopodium Californicum . .),* abundant throughout much of the State in arroyos and on moist hillsides. **1923** in 1925 Jepson *Manual Plants CA* 322, Soap Plant. . . Stream beds and moist slopes or swales in open foothills: Coast Ranges; Sierra Nevada foothills. . . The root is grated on a rock by the native tribes and used as a soap.

soaproot n
1 =**soap plant 1.** esp **CA** Cf **Indian soap root**
1874 *Overland Mth.* Dec 544 **CA,** When wild clover came into blossom they [=the Suisun Indians] frequently ate it so greedily as to become distressingly inflated with gas . . and amusing scenes ensued. One remedy was a decoction of soap-root administered internally. [DARE Ed: This quot may refer instead to another sense below.] **1876** (1877) Williams *Pacific Tourist* 233, At one time soap-root, a bulb, growing like the stub of a coarse, brown mohair switch, just emerging from the ground, was gathered by the Chinamen. **1897** Parsons *Wild Flowers CA* 84, The Indians of the Sierra foothills have a curious use for the bulb [=*Chlorogalum pomeridianum*]. After the June freshets have subsided, many fish are usually left in small pools in the streams. The squaws go to these pools with an abundance of soap-root, and kneeling upon the banks, rub up a great suds with it. The fish soon rise to the surface, stupefied, and are easily taken. **2003** *Sacramento Bee* (CA) 8 Mar (Internet), Other Pine Hill Preserve rare plants. . . Red Hills soaproot (Chlorogalum grandiflorum).

2 A **yucca;** see quots.
1866 in 1955 Lee *Mormon Chron.* 2.31 **UT,** I went up comances Kanyon with a Horse Team . . for oose or soap root. **1876** *Galaxy* Apr 21.514 **NM,** In Holy Week the members of a lodge meet together, and after prayers and chanting form a procession, some carrying whips made of fibres of Spanish bayonet and soap-root, with which they beat themselves and each other. **1943** Elmore *Ethnobotany Navajo* 33 **NM,** On the sixth day of the Mountain Chant Ceremony, before the couriers are sent on their way, a basin of water containing soap root [=*Yucca baccata*] is brought in, and after the medicine man has daubed the couriers with a little of the suds, they wash themselves from head to foot, and clean their hair as well. **2001** *DARE* File—Internet, The Yucca . . commonly known as *Amole,* Soaproot, Spanish Bayonet, or Dagger, has an extensive accounting of uses by Native Americans.

3 =**sand lily 2.**
1890 *Century Dict.* 5742, Soaproot. . . A Californian bulbous plant, *Leucocrinum montanum,* of the lily family. . . Soaproot is used by the Digger Indians to take trout. **1900** Lyons *Plant Names* 222, *Leucocrinum.* . . Soaproot. . . One species, Nebraska to California.

4 =**bouncing Bet 1.**
1900 King et al. *King's Amer. Dispensatory* 1723, The root and leaves of *Saponaria officinalis.* . . *Common names:* Soapwort, Soaproot, Bouncing Bet, Fuller's-herb. **1958** Jacobs–Burlage *Index Plants NC* 35, *Saponaria officinalis.* . . Soapwort; bouncing bet; sapanory; common soapwort; soaproot [etc].

5 A **death camas** (here: *Zigadenus venenosus).* Cf **poison soaproot**
1934 Haskin *Wild Flowers Pacific Coast* 35, As a stock poisoning plant death camas is one of the worst. . . Other names locally applied to this plant are lobelia, poison sego, poison grass, alkali grass, water lily, and soap-root.

soaproot plant n
A **camas 1** (here: *Camassia quamash).*

1898 *Jrl. Amer. Folkl.* 11.281 **CA**, *Camassia esculenta . . camass, amole,* soap-root plant.

soap shaker n

A wire mesh container with a handle used to dissolve scraps of soap for washing.

1875 (1876) *Home Cook Book* 41, The soap-shaker (a little tin box with soap in it, and perforated with holes having a long handle like a dipper). 1884 *Chicago Tribune* 24 Feb 3/1, [Advt:] 10 *cents* For . . Soap Shakers. 1887 Parloa *Miss Parloa's Kitchen Companion* 57, A soap-shaker is a convenient and economical utensil to have in both the kitchen and china-closet. All the small pieces of soap can be saved and used in this shaker. 1894 *Harper's New Mth. Mag.* 89.4, A dish-strainer, dish-cloths and mops, a soap shaker . . are necessary . . although he may be forced to confess that he would not have thought of a soap-shaker. 1988 Nickerson *Days to Remember* 89 **Cape Cod MA** (as of c1900), Bits of soap left when the cake had become worn down were saved and put into a "soap shaker". This was a wire mesh container with a metal handle which hung in the sink. It was swished about in the dishpan containing warm water for dishwashing to create suds. 2004 *Union Leader* (Manchester NH) 4 Oct (Internet), Customers who cling to tradition will find wooden wash boards and metal soap shakers those small wire container [sic] that holds slivers of soap.

soap stick n

1 A stirring stick used in making homemade soap.

[1835 Longstreet *GA Scenes* 219, Wait till you see him lift the old Soap-stick [=a rifle], and draw a bead upon the bull's-eye.] 1889 Habberton *All He Knew* 854, I wish she'd 'a' broke a soap-stick, or a axe-helve, 'cross his head. 1899 (1912) Green *VA Folk-Speech* 400, *Soap-stick. . .* A long paddle-shaped stick used for stirring the soap in country soap-making where the ingredients are boiled together in a large forty gallon iron pot. 1937 NE Univ. *Univ. Studies* 37.113 [Terms from play-party songs], *Soapstick. . .* (Satiric.) "Next old soapstick in the wilderness." . . "We're marching round the soapstick." 1982 Slone *How We Talked* 66 **eKY** (as of c1950), *Homemade lye soap. . .* Stir with a long-handled paddle or "soap stick."

2 Used as a derog term for a man.

1858 *OH Repository* (Canton) 26 May [2]/2 (newspaperarchiv.com), The poor miserable *soapsticks*—gulled and deceived, or bribed and per-jured fools or rascals—whichever they may prefer to call themselves—voted for the English bill. 1885 (1887) Harmon *Ptocowa* 227 **nwMS**, The populace know him [=an old bachelor] as old 'Soap-stick' or 'Bone-cart.' If rich, he is a miser; if poor, a vagabond. 1897 Allison *Dropped Stitches TN Hist.* 106 (as of 1788), [Andrew] Jackson de-nounced the Loves as a "band of land pirates". . . Love retorted by call-ing Jackson "a damned long, gangling, sorrel-topped soap-stick." 1913 *Daily Independent* (Monessen PA) [13 Jan 2]/2 (newspaperarchive.com), [Sermon:] A man and his wife went to a hall. She was quite a dancer. He was not much for it, but went along and sat there and watched other old soap sticks hug his wife all over the floor. 1939 *AmSp* 14.92 **eTN**, *Soap-stick.* Husband. 'Mary's soap-stick is bedfast.'

soaptree yucca n Also *soap tree*

A **soapweed 2** (here: *Yucca elata*).

1937 U.S. Forest Serv. *Range Plant Hdbk.* B157, The roots of soaptree yucca are used locally (under the name amole) as soap by both Indians and white men. 1970 Correll *Plants TX* 400, *Yucca elata. . .* soap-tree. 1971 Dodge *100 Desert Wildflowers* 8, *Soaptree yucca. . .* Called "soaptree" because of its height . . and the fact that its roots contain saponin. 1973 *AZ Highways* Mar 29, A handsome and familiar speci-men is the Soap Tree Yucca, New Mexico's state flower. . . The Soap Tree gets its name from the substance of its root and trunk which the early settlers and Indians used as a substitute for soap. 2003 *Albuquer-que Jrl.* (NM) 4 Apr sec B 1 (Internet), Other xeric plants in the arbore-tum are . . soap tree yucca, red yucca [etc].

soapweed n

1 An **agave.**

1847 Edwards *Campaign NM* 77, We first met, on this part of the road, with the species of palm called by us Soap-weed, from the fact that the Mexicans use its root as a substitute for soap, for which it answers very well. . . I believe it is rightly named the Lechuguilla. 1890 *Century Dict.* 5742, *Soapweed. . .* A plant, *Agave heteracantha,* or some other species of the same genus. 1995 *Brophy Coll.* 70 **swMO** (as of c1960), *Soapweed.* [T]he yucca or agave.

2 also *soapweed yucca:* A **yucca:** usu *Yucca elata* or *Y.*

glauca. Also called **amole 1b, soap plant 2.** For other names of *Y. elata* see **God's candle, palmilla 1, soaptree yucca;** for other names of *Y. glauca* see **Indian cabbage 1, oose, soapwell** [*DARE* Ed: Some of these quots may refer in-stead to **1** above.]

1848 (1932) Robinson *Jrl. Santa Fe* 65 **NM,** Here the soap-weed be-comes almost a tree. 1854 in 1932 *SW Hist. Qrly.* 35.305, I picked up a soap weed instead of the Poker. 1894 *Jrl. Amer. Folkl.* 7.102 **IA,** *Yucca angustifolia . .* soap-weed. 1908 Johnson *Highways Pacific Coast* 9 **AZ,** You dry the roots of that soap-weed, . . and then put them in water and they make a foam right off. 1937 U.S. Forest Serv. *Range Plant Hdbk.* B157, Small soapweed *(Y. glauca)* [is] also called soapweed yucca. 1967–69 *DARE* (Qu. S20, *A common weed that grows on open hillsides: It has velvety green leaves close to the ground, and a tall stalk with small yellow flowers on a spike at the top*) Inf **MO2,** Soapweed; **CO20,** Soapweed—flowers more white; (Qu. S21, . . *Weeds . . that are a trouble in gardens and fields*) Infs **KS15, KY49,** Soapweed; (Qu. S26d, *Wildflowers that grow in meadows;* not asked in early QRs) Inf **KS1,** Soapweed—it's a type of yucca; (Qu. S26e, *Other wildflowers* not yet *mentioned;* not asked in early QRs) Inf **CO15,** Soapweed; **KS19,** Milkweed—another name for this is soapweed. [*DARE* Ed: Some of these Infs may refer instead to **1** above.] 1969 *DARE* FW Addit **KY5,** *Soapweed*—also called thread-and-needle. Old-fashioned. 1981 Benson–Darrow *Trees SW Deserts* 48, *Yucca elata. . .* Palmilla, Soap-weed. *Ibid* 49, The name "soapweed" may be traced to the large quan-tity of soapy material in the roots and stems. A slice of the trunk or root cut straight across is not only soapy, but also with the ends of the fibers forms an effective soft brush. 2001 *Rocky Mt. News* (Denver CO) 3 Mar sec D 4 (Internet), Yucca glauca is the native "soapweed" with sharp, blue-green leaves.

soapwell n

A **soapweed 2** (here: *Yucca glauca*).

1973 Hitchcock–Cronquist *Flora Pacific NW* 696, *Y[ucca] glauca. . .* Soapwell, beargrass. . . prairies and light woodl[ands] into the lower mts. 1987 Kindscher *Edible Wild Plants* 225, *Yucca glauca. . .* Common names—Small soapweed, soapweed, soapwell (these three names refer to the fact that the root is used as a soap substitute).

soapwort n

1 Std: a plant of the genus *Saponaria,* usu *S. officinalis,* the leaves and roots of which contain saponin and may be used as soap. [*OED2* 1548 →] Also called **bouncing Bet 1, devil-in-the-bush 2, sheepweed 2** Cf **latherwort**

2 also *field soapwort:* =**cowherb.**

1822 Eaton *Botany* 447 **MA,** *[Saponaria] vaccaria* (field soapwort). . . Probably introduced; but it now grows wild along the Hosick, near Wil-liams College. 1901 U.S. Dept. Ag. Div. Botany *Bulletin* 26.113 **MT,** Cow Cockle. *(Vaccaria vaccaria . .)* Other names: Cow herb, soapwort [etc]. 1910 Graves *Flowering Plants* 180 **CT,** *Saponaria Vaccaria. . .* Cow-herb. Field Soapwort. . . Cultivated ground and waste places.

soapwort gentian n Also *soap gentian* [*OED2* 1578 →; see quot 1840]

A **gentian** (here: *Gentiana saponaria*). Also called **creeping wintergreen 2, harvestbells, Sampson's snakeroot 1, swamp gentian 3**

1814 Bigelow *Florula Bostoniensis* 64 **MA,** Soapwort Gentian. . . A very fine plant, distinguished by its large purple flowers. 1837 Darling-ton *Flora Cestrica* 165 **sePA,** *G[entiana] Saponaria. . .* Gentian. Soap-wort Gentian. 1840 MA Zool. & Bot. Surv. *Herb. Plants & Quadru-peds* 147, Soap Gentian. The leaves resemble those of Saponaria, or soapwort. 1901 Lounsberry *S. Wild Flowers* 430, *G[entiana] Sapo-naria,* soapwort gentian, which occurs in wet soil from Louisiana and Florida to Canada, shows often its bright blue and large corolla as late as November. 1972 Brown *Wildflowers LA* 137, Soapwort Gentian. . . Moist depressions and gullies in pinelands of southeastern Louisiana. Also Texas and Mississippi. 2005 *DARE* File—Internet, The flowers of the closed gentian are sealed shut . . , while those of the soapwort gen-tian are somewhat paler in color and open slightly.

so as conj phr Pronc-spp *so ez, sois, so's, soz(e)* Cf **as B1, so 's 't**

1 With the purpose or result that, so that. [*OED2* so adv. and conj. 29.a 1523 →; "Now *dial.*"]

[1624 Smith *Genl. Hist. VA* 35, All these they tie by their tailes, so as all their tailes meete in the toppe of their head like a great Tassel.] **1846** (2001) Meachum *Address to All* 19 (Internet) **MO** [Black], I would recommend manual labor schools to be established in the different states, so as the children could have free access to them. **1848** Lowell *Biglow* 137 **'Upcountry' MA,** An' Pomp poked out the leg a piece, jest so ez I could see. **1871** Eggleston *Hoosier Schoolmaster* 32 **sIN,** He's . . pulled back the board so as you can't help a-tippin' it up, and a-sowsin' right in ef you step there. **1876** Clark *Elbow Room* 214, Well, sir, when she [=a balloon] was up so's she looked as small as a pinhead something or other burst. **1889** *Harper's New Mth. Mag.* 80.147 **ME,** She starches his shirt bosoms so's you can hear 'em creak 'way across the meeting-house. **1911** *DN* 3.540 **eKY,** I came soze I can help you. **1928** in 1952 Mathes *Tall Tales* 44 **sAppalachians,** Then I put up that monument stone an' gravened it thataway so's ye couldn't never fergit! **1935** Sandoz *Jules* 18 **wNE,** [He] snubs it to a tree on top of the bluffs so's them riders what's coming in can see where the ranch is. **c1937** in 1976 *Weevils in the Wheat* 228 **VA** [Black], Stay here en work hard sois us can feed de men at war, en sois us can look af'er de women folks en de young. **1944** *PADS* 2.49 **NC, VA,** *So as: conj.* So that. . . Rather general in the South. **1952** Brown *NC Folkl.* 1.592, *So as: conj* . . So that. **1965–70** *DARE* (Qu. X49, *Expressions . . about a person who is very thin*) Inf **PA**237, Drinks muddy water so's you won't see through him; (Qu. KK55c, . . *Expressions of strong denial*) Inf **OK**9, Not so's you can tell; (Qu. NN4, . . *Ways of answering 'no': "Would you lend him ten dollars?"* "_____.") Infs **CT**19, **WA**1, Not so's you'd notice (it). **1970** *Thompson Coll.* **Birmingham AL** (as of c1920), You gotta do it enough soz you don't be afraid any more. **2006** *DARE* File—Internet **TX,** I have to go find a comp[uter] that has CS2 on it just so's I can save out a CS version.

2 Provided that, if only. [*OED2 so* adv. and conj. 1585 →]
   1870 Twain in *Galaxy* 10.731, Lord bless you, so's he got planted before he sp'iled, he was perfectly satisfied. **1886** *Century Illustr. Mag.* 31.569 **CO,** It makes no odds to me what you say, so's you don't name us to no one. **1920** (2003) Fitzhugh *Roy Blakeley's Advent.* (Internet), You were glad enough to see his poor little skinny legs kicking in the water, just so as you could get something out of it. **1977** Miles *Ozark Dict.* 9 **nwAR, swMO,** *Sose*—So. "Just sose you git home before dark." **2004** Randall *Pushkin & Queen* 99 **Detroit MI** [Black], When you really needed a basket, just so as it wasn't the last throw of the night, he would get you one.

so as 't See **so 's 't**

so as to be about *adj phr* For addit varr see quots
Tolerably well—used in response to a question about one's health.
   1857 Riley *Puddleford Papers* 119, 'How is your old man, Mrs. Brown?' 'Well, he's gruntin' some—but so's to be about.' **1910** *DN* 3.449 **cwNY,** So's to be round. . . Able to get about. "Father's better; he's so's to be round." **1957** *Sat. Eve. Post Letters* **AR** (as of c1900), Asked how one feels he may say . . "So as to be about." *Ibid* **OK** (as of c1890), "How you come on?" . . The answers were . . "Just tolable", or "So's to be about." **1959** *VT Hist.* 27.158, *So's to be around.* . . Answer to the question, "How are you?" Generally meaning well. Occasional. **1965** *PADS* 43.27 **seMA,** *Pretty well* in answer to 'How are you' or 'How are you feeling?' . . 1 [of 9 infs] *so's to be up and have the bed made.* **1984** Wilder *You All Spoken Here* 202 **Sth,** So as to be about.

sob *v* [*OED2 sob* v.[2], *sobby* a. "Now *dial.* and *U.S.*"] **chiefly Sth, S Midl** See Map   Cf **sog** *v* 1
To soak or become soaked with water; hence ppl adjs *sobbed*, *sobbing*, *water-sob(bed)*, adjs *sobby* (also rarely *subby*), *sob(bing) wet* soaked, soggy, sodden.
   1814 in 1956 Eliason *Tarheel Talk* 296 **NC,** She [was] kept too hot especially while asleep, her skin looked water-sobbed and her flesh parboiled. **1847** *N. Amer. Rev.* 64.191, [Quoted from unnamed newspaper:] They were sent in their wet and sobby condition to New York. **1851** *De Bow's Rev.* 11.45 **LA,** The sweet gum . . logs soon sob when on the ground, and thereby are nearly indestructible by fire. **1883** *Amer. Philol. Assoc. Trans.* 14.53 **Sth,** *Sobbed* or *sobby*, 'soaked *or* wet,' commonly applied to land, though also to other things, is the Southern word for *soggy*. **1899** (1912) Green *VA Folk-Speech* 401, *Sob.* . . To sop; soak with a liquid. *Sobby.* . . Sobbed; soaked with a liquid. *Sobbing-wet. Ibid* 475, *Water-sobbed.* . . Soaked with water. **1903** *DN* 2.336 **seMO,** *Water-sobbed.* . . Watersoaked. **1917** *DN* 4.417 **wNC,** *Sob.* . . To become soggy. "If you let a pine pole stay out and sob, the bark will rot off." **1924** Raine *Land of Saddle-Bags* 81 **sAppalachians,** Ye sob 'em and rensh 'em and rub 'em in the trough.

1944 *PADS* 2.12 **AL,** *Sobby.* . . Soggy, heavy, underdone. Said of biscuit, bread, pie-crust, cake. . . "I do want a biscuit cooked quick; if there's anything I can't stand, it's an old sobby biscuit." **1946** *PADS* 6.32 **eNC** (as of 1900–10), *Water-sobbed.* . . Heavy with water, soaked with water. Said of potatoes dug after a rainy season. ((Also applies to wood.)) Pamlico. Common. **1952** Brown *NC Folkl.* 1.592, *Sob.* . . To be thoroughly wet, soaked. "Your shoes are sobbing." *Ibid, Sobbing.* . . "Your clothes are sobbing wet." **1953** Randolph–Wilson *Down in Holler* 286 **Ozarks,** *Sobby.* . . Wet, soggy, mouldy. When stovewood is heavy or water-soaked, it is said to be *sobby*. The word applies also to dressed lumber that turns dark or mouldy. **1965–70** *DARE* (Qu. KK56, *Wood that is heavy from being in water a long time: It's* _____) Infs **LA**6, **MO**8, **SC**26, **TN**23, **TX**36, **VA**29, Sobby; **SC**26, Sobby wet; **DE**7, **LA**14, **NC**1, 26, 76, **VA**15, Water-sobbed; **SC**19, Sobbed; (Qu. C6, . . *A piece of land that's often wet, and has grass and weeds growing on it*) Inf **FL**51, Sobby area; **TX**96, Sobby; (Qu. C7, . . *Land that usually has some standing water with trees or bushes growing in it*) Inf **ID**3, Subby ['sʌbi] ground; (Qu. C31, . . *Heavy, sticky soil*) Inf **VA**38, Sobby soil. **1986** Pederson *LAGS Concordance (Swamp)* 1 inf, **cwMS,** Water-sob place; 1 inf, **swMS,** Sobby land; *(Dishcloth)* 1 inf, **cnAR,** Sobbing wet; *(Loam)* 1 inf, **swMS,** Sobby—wet; 1 inf, **cwLA,** Sobby—low; *(Bottomland)* 1 inf, **neMS,** Sobby land—wet bottomland, not necessarily good. **1996** Horton *Island Out of Time* 146 **Chesapeake Bay MD,** I watched a ball of snow gathering in the hollow of his neck under his chin, and he never moved, and the ball growin' bigger and bigger, and him sob wet [Horton: drenched] all down his front when we landed.

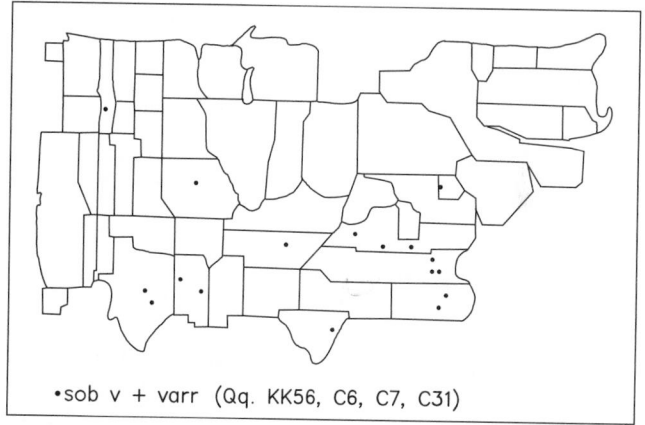

•sob v + varr (Qq. KK56, C6, C7, C31)

‡sob *n*   Cf **sob** *v*
   1970 *DARE* (Qu. C6, . . *A piece of land that's often wet, and has grass and weeds growing on it*) Inf **FL**51, Sobby area, or just sob.

sobbed, sobbing (wet), sobby See **sob** *v*

so be *conj* [Abbr for **if so be**]
If.
   1931 *PMLA* 46.1321 **Appalachians,** I'm a-goin', so be he's there. **1931** Rathborne *Lend-a-Hand Boys' Sanitary Squad* 52, Here's a good place to eat so be we mean to stop, and have a bite.

so-boss(ie) See **so** *exclam*

sob wet See **sob** *v*

socdolager, socdoliger See **sockdolager**

sochan *n* Also *cochan, coach-ann, coachie-ann* [Cherokee *sochani*] **chiefly wNC** Cf **cullowhee**
=golden glow.
   1966 *DARE* (Qu. I28b, *Kinds of greens that are cooked*) Inf **NC**44, [souǎxn]. **1973** *Foxfire 2* 90, Tall coneflower (*Rudbeckia laciniata*) . . (cochan, coach-ann). . . Mrs. Hershel Keener said, "There's a plant that grows along this branch called coachie-ann; now I don't know how you spell it, and it's got such an odor when it's cooking." [**1975** Hamel–Chiltoskey *Cherokee Plants* 30, Coneflower, green-headed; so-cha-ni—*Rudbeckia laciniata*—Used as cooked spring salad to keep well.] **1995** Williams *Gt. Smoky Mts. Folklife* 100 **wNC,** Most of the wild plants commonly consumed by the North Carolina Cherokee today, such as ramps, sochan, poke, creases, and wild berries, are also eaten by non-Indians in the region. **2001** *Smoky Mt. News* (Waynesville NC) 28 Mar (Internet), "Before there were many cars the old folks used to walk all over the mountains gathering greens," Cherokee Lucinda Reed told me

before her death several years ago. . . "You can eat off the land all year round if you want to. I find sochan mainly along streams."

sociable n　*somewhat old-fash*　Cf **socializing**

A party; a social gathering, esp one held under the auspices of a church.

1750 in 1867 *Hours at Home* 5.420 **MA**, Within doors, it appears in quilting-parties, apple-paring bees . . and other evening sociables. **1826** in 1886 Longfellow *Life of H.W. Longfellow* 1.74 **ME**, [I] went with them to a little "sociable" in the evening, where we had dancing. **1868** *Ladies' Repository* 2.438, In the evening there was a Church sociable at my father's house. **1909** *DN* 3.404 **nwAR**, Sociable. . . A social gathering : a party : an entertainment provided by some charitable organization at which food is sold. **1912** *DN* 3.590 **wIN**, Social. . . A sociable, which is rarely used. **1915** *DN* 4.229 **wTX**, Social. . . An entertainment, a "sociable." **1941** *LANE* Map 414 (*Social gathering*) **NEng**, [*Sociable* is widespread throughout the region.] **1951** West *Witch Diggers* 25 **IN**, Christie, I was supposed to have a sociable this Saturday evening. **c1960** *Wilson Coll.* **csKY**, Social (sociable). . . A social gathering or party. **1965–70** *DARE* (Qu. FF1, . . *A kind of group meeting called a 'social' or 'sociable'. . . [What goes on?]*) 62 Infs, **scattered**, Sociable; 23 Infs, **scattered**, Church (or Sunday School) sociable; 9 Infs, **esp Nth**, Box (*or basket*) sociable; 8 Infs, **scattered**, Ice cream (*or grange, poker, school, strawberry*) sociable; [**PA**148, **SC**10, Sociable club (*or meeting*);] (Qu. H70, *When people bring baked dishes, salads, and so forth to a meeting-place and share them together, that's a _____ meal*) Inf **NY**52, Sociable; [(Qu. DD34, *A party at which there is considerable drinking*) Infs **MO**20, **NC**80, Sociable party;] (Qu. FF4, *Names and joking names for different kinds of dancing parties*) [Inf **NY**75, Sociable dance;] **NY**94, Sociables; (Qu. FF9, *A Christmas gathering, at church or at someone's home, where there are songs and presents: "Are you going to the _____?"*) Inf **NM**12, Christmas sociable; **NJ**48, Sociable. [73 of 88 total Infs old] **1973** *DARE* File **MA**, In the old days when we used to have church sociables . . some would be asked to bring apple or mince . . pies. **1984** Wilder *You All Spoken Here* 188 **Sth**, Sociable: A party in a rural household.

socializing n
=**sociable.**

1969 Wilson *Stars* 15 **Ozarks**, Uncle Zeb Hatfield, who hadn't been at a socializing for a month of Sundays, got nervous and chanced to pour buttermilk instead of cream into his coffee.

'sociate v　[Aphet form of *associate*]　**Sth**　Cf **association**

1835 Ingraham *South-West* 2.189 **MS** [Black], I neber 'sociate wid you 'gain. **1852** Hannigan *Swamp Steed* 6 **SC**, "No," replied the woodsman; "I make it a pint not to 'sociate with people any more'n I kin help." **1860** *Harper's New Mth. Mag.* 20.216 **FL**, Folks seem to be havin' purty fair time up stairs. They 'sociate a good 'eal here. **1890** *Overland Mth.* (2d ser) 15.194 **Sth** [Black], Dem ez comes atter won't nebber 'sociate wid Miss Chev. **1922** Gonzales *Black Border* 275 **sSC, GA coasts** [Black], All kind'uh low-down buckruh, w'at couldn' 'sociate wid we w'ite people' fambly. **1927** Adams *Congaree* 20 **cSC** [Black], Her hide is thick as a ox hide, an' she don't belongs to 'sociate wid no other kind er mind. **c1937** in 1972 *Amer. Slave* 2.1.250 **SC**, They frets and fumes 'cause they can't 'sociate wid big folks. **1946** McCullers *Member* 14 **AL**, I sociate the two of them together. **1968** *DARE* (Qu. Y51, . . *Ways of saying 'to avoid' things or people . . "He's not your kind—you'd better _____ him."*) Inf **GA**30, Not 'sociate ['soˌset] with.

sock　See **white sock(s)**

sock ball n　Cf **soak** n[2]

1884 *Denton Jrl.* (MD) 2 Aug [2]/4 (newspaperarchive.com), When dinner was announced one of the half-grown boys of the family sidled up to Mr Daniel with the invitation, "Let's you and me go out an' play sock ball while the grown folks eat dinner." **1901** *DN* 2.148 **neOH**, Sock ball. . . A game in which ball is thrown at player, =patch scrub. **1963** *Lima News* (OH) 18 Aug sec D 2/5, "You are going to play ball with Billy Swank, Lady Bird, Dick Casebeer and me down on the Academy grounds." . . We played sock ball all afternoon and the sun was low in the west when we quit.

sockdolager n　Also sp *sockdollager, sockdol(l)oger;* for addit varr see quots　[A fanciful formation; the first element is prob from *sock* to strike hard; cf also **sollaker**]

1　A decisive blow; fig, a conclusive argument, decisive attack.

1830 *VA Lit. Museum* 1.479, Sockdolager. "A decisive blow"—one, in the slang language "capable of setting a man thinking." **1851** Burke *Polly Peablossom* 61 **GA**, "I'm kin to a rattlesnake on the mother's side!" shouted the earth's ancestor. This seemed to be a *"socdoliger;"* (which translated into Latin, means a *ne plus ultra*). **1899** (1912) Green *VA Folk-Speech* 401, Sockdologer. . . A conclusive argument; a settler. . A knock-down or decisive blow. **1905** *DN* 3.65 **eNE**, Sockdollger. . . Knockout argument, or blow. "He gave him a sockdollger." **1909** *DN* 3.372 **eAL, wGA**, Sock-dollager. . . A knockout blow, argument, etc. **1951** West *Witch Diggers* 146 **IN**, If Lib handed him a sockdologer let him hand her one back. **1960** Criswell *Resp. to PADS 20* **Ozarks**, Sockdolager—To hit him a sockdolager (old term). **1967–69** *DARE* (Qu. Y4, . . *A very uncomplimentary remark*) Inf **KY**63, Sockdolager; (Qu. Y11, . . *A very hard blow: "You should have seen Bill go down. Joe really hit him a _____."*) Infs **CA**15, **NY**34, Sockdolager. **2001** *Houston Chron.* (TX) 26 Oct (Internet), I recently came across a brief reference to a speech . . that must have been a genuine sockdolager, based upon the results it achieved.

2　also attrib: A large or impressive specimen of its kind; a "whopper." Cf **gollsocker**

1838 Cooper *Home as Found* 1.221 **NY**, A sogdollager, young lady, is the perfection of a thing. I know Mr. Grant used to say there was no such word in the dictionary; but then there are many words that ought to be in the dictionaries that have been forgotten by the printers. In the way of salmon trout, the sogdollager is their commodore. **1841** *Spirit of the Times* 30 Jan 571 (*AmSp* 40.23), Sockdollager [=a horse of unusual size and stamina]. **1854** *Knickerbocker* 43.536 **TN**, The successful fisherman, staggering under the weight of a regular "sockdolager." **1868** *Living Age* 99.654, And, in the evening waters of Horicon, the Sogdollager fish, the solitary lord of the lake, still shows his monstrous head above water. **1892** Smith *Farm & Fireside* 311 **GA**, Yes, . . and it seemed to me that every time a big old sockdolager [=a hailstone] struck me I could hear somebody say, 'Oh, you old sinner, . . I'll maul the grace into your unbelieving soul.' **1899** (1912) Green *VA Folk-Speech* 401, Sockdologer. . . Something very big; a whopper. **1905** *DN* 3.20 **cCT**, Socdolager. . . 'That was a sockdolager of a hymn.' Something impressive or conclusive. **1910** *DN* 3.458 **Chicago IL**, Sockdolager. . . A very tremendous person or thing. "Wasn't that a sockdolager of a man?" **1940** White *Wild Geese* 341 **AK** (as of 1890s), His deep-seated hunter instinct died slowly. "But he's such a sock-dolager!" It took him some time to get over the idea of that bear. Critter that size down in the States would be famous, make history. **1953** Randolph–Wilson *Down in Holler* 286 **Ozarks**, Sockdolager. . . Something surprising in size or quality. "Ain't he a sockdolager?" cried a boy who had just caught a very large catfish. **1966** *DARE* (Qu. B25, . . *Joking names . . for a very heavy rain. . . "It's a regular _____."*) Inf **GA**15, Sockdolager. **1975** Gould *ME Lingo* 266, Sockdollager—This is a whopper in any category. **1979** *NYT Article Letters* **cnKS**, Sockdollager. . . It means something forceful, such as a heavy rainstorm, or windstorm. **2002** *DARE* File—Internet **FL**, Don't be the only person in the whole teleproduction industry to miss the *awesome* 2002 ***Technology Retreat***. . . It's definitely going to be a sockdolager of a retreat!

sockeye salmon n　Also *sockeye;* for pronc-spp and obs varr see quots　[Folk-etym for Salish *suk-kegh* red fish]　**esp AK**

A Pacific **salmon** **B1b** (here: *Oncorhynchus nerka*).　Also called **blueback salmon, kokanee (salmon), landlocked salmon 2, little redfish, redfish c, red salmon, silver ~, yank** n[2]

[**1869** *Mainland Guardian* (New Westminster, B.C.) 25 Sep. 2/1 (*DCan*), The most important from the latter point of view, is the Sockeye.] **1882** U.S. Natl. Museum *Bulletin* 16.308, O[ncorhynchus] nerka. . . *Blue-back Salmon; Red-fish; Frazer's River Salmon; Sugk-eye Salmon* [etc]. **1896** U.S. Bur. Fisheries *Rept. for 1895* 290, Oncorhynchus nerka. . . *Saw-qui, Sockeye,* or *Sauk-eye Salmon*. **1962** Salisbury *Quoth the Raven* 121 **seAK**, The commercial species used by the canneries, the sockeye, humpback, dog and coho, enter the Alaskan streams usually in the order named and then is when the really hard work of the natives occurs. **1966–69** *DARE* (Qu. P1, . . *Kinds of freshwater fish . . caught around here . . good to eat*) Inf **AK**1, Sockeye—a "red"—spawn only in lakes; **CA**130, Kokanee salmon—a landlocked salmon, they plant them; actually, they're a sockeye; **MT**4, Sockeye salmon. **1976** Tryckare et al. *Lore of Sportfishing* 76, Sockeye Salmon. . . Other common names: Kokanee, redfish, sawkeye, Sau-qui salmon, Sukkegh salmon [etc]. **1978** *AK Fishing Guide* 55, Sockeye that become landlocked are commonly found in various lakes from Oregon into Alaska.

1991 Tabbert *Dict. Alaskan Engl.* 132, In Alaska, although *sockeye* is used, the more frequent name is *red salmon.* **2000** Metcalf *How We Talk* 132 **cwWA,** "You might be from Seattle," says one columnist, "if you know the difference between Chinook, Coho, and Sockeye Salmon."

socks on, with adj phr   Also *with one's socks on*   Cf **barefooted 1**

Of coffee or tea: with milk or cream.

1940 in 1944 *ADD* **WV,** *Barefooted.* . . One mountaineer said he drank his coffee 'barefooted.' Further investigation revealed that the people in that section drank their coffee 'barefooted' or 'with socks on,' meaning with or without cream. **1984** Wilder *You All Spoken Here* 91 **Sth,** *With socks on:* Coffee with cream. **1986** Pederson *LAGS Concordance (With milk)* 1 inf, **cnAL,** With your socks on.

socks, throw up one's v phr   For addit varr see quot 1965–70
scattered, but esp Cent, TX   See Map

To vomit copiously or violently.

1902 *DN* 1.233 **KY,** *Throw up.* "To throw up one's socks" = to vomit vehemently and copiously. **1965–70** *DARE* (Qu. BB18, *To vomit a great deal at once*) Infs **AR39, CO20, IL143, KS6, MO2, TX3,** Threw up his (*or* my, your) socks; **IL118, KY84, TX6,** Throw up his (*or* your) socks; **CA59,** Heave up your socks; **TX40,** Lose one's socks; **WA33,** Puked his socks; **TX4,** Threw their socks; **GA72, SC34,** Throwed up his socks; **TX45,** Urp up your socks; **MO19, TX39,** Vomit up his (*or* your) socks. **1986** Pederson *LAGS Concordance (Vomit)* 1 inf, **nwTN,** Throwing up his socks. **2002** *Wilderness & Environmental Med.* 13.182 **MO,** I was on my knees trying to throw up my socks when I started salivating like a rabid dog.

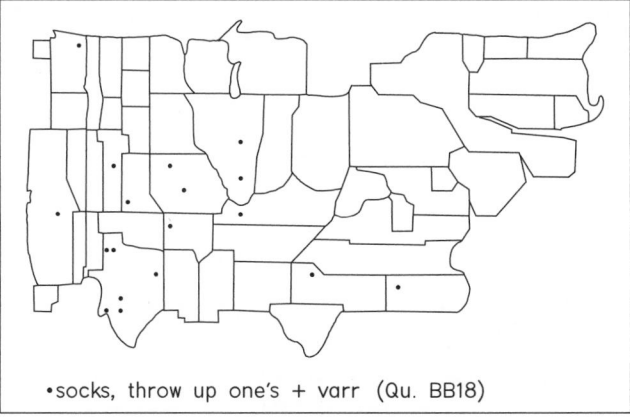

•socks, throw up one's + varr (Qu. BB18)

sod n attrib   **chiefly Plains States, IL, IN**

Of a crop: grown in newly broken sod; hence n *sod-corn (whiskey)* whiskey made from corn grown in this way.

1832 *Home Missionary* 4.85 **IL,** Our main dependance for grain the next year is "sod corn." **1835** Shirreff *Tour N. Amer.* 248 **IL,** Indian corn is dropped into every third furrow . . and covered with the next cut turf. This crop receives no farther cultivation of any kind, [and] is termed sod corn. **1841** *Cultivator* 8.147 **nIL, nIN,** "Sod wheat" is the term given to the first crop on the prairie. **1846** Farnham *Life in Prairie Land* 214 **IL,** A very respectable crop of corn, called by the farmers "sod corn," may be raised on the broken turf. **1848** U.S. Patent Office *Annual Rept. for 1847* 539 **IN,** This gave a sod crop without tending of thirty to forty bushels per acre. **1857** (1923) Beadle *To Nebraska* 197, Found the family enjoying themselves over their "Sod corn whiskey." **1879** *Scribner's Mth.* Nov 133 **KS,** It is not uncommon for sod-wheat in Kansas to make fifteen bushels to the acre . . , and sod-corn often reaches forty bushels per acre. **1896** U.S. Dept. Ag. *Yearbook for 1895* 357 **Plains States,** Sometimes, on early breaking, a crop of sod corn or flax is grown the same year. **1927** Eubank *Horse & Buggy Days* 94 **KY,** They . . ate their dinners, . . munching cheese, or oysters or sardines, which was helped along in its onward course by a tumbler or so of sod corn, made in a moonshine still especially for the occasion. **1941** Smith *Going to God's Country* 70 **MO,** We had ten acers of old land coton that made one bale per acer but the sod coton did not make so much. **1950** Reeves *Man from SD* 28, But the sod wheat was a thinner stand and still hung on, and the sod corn was a healthy green. **1967** *DARE* Tape **CO1,** He broke out ten acres and planted it to sod corn.

sod adj   See **sod widow 1**

soda n   Usu |ˈsodə|; also **chiefly Sth, S Midl, NEast** |ˈsodɪ, -i|
Pronc-spp *sod(e)y, sodie*   Cf Intro "Language Changes" IV.1.b,
sofa

A Forms.

1834 *Atl. Club-Book* 2.281 **NEng,** There was a lot o' cheeses, and sody-water. **1846** *Adams Sentinel* (Gettysburg PA) 24 Aug 1/5, "I don't want no syrup," ses I, "I want sody water." "Ah!" ses he, "you want extra sody." **1867** Harris *Sut Lovingood Yarns* 79 **TN,** Well, wun day a cussed, palaverin, inyun-eatin Yankee pedlar . . cum tu ole man Burns wif a carryall full ove . . calliker, ribbons, sody-powder, an' uther durn'd truck. **1876** *Appletons' Jrl.* 1.540 **Sth,** Some kind ob washin'-sody or horse powder. **1892** *DN* 1.241 **Kansas City MO,** Soda. Always [sodɪ]. . . [*DN* Ed: Common in New England.] **1893** Shands *MS Speech* 6, [sodɪ] for soda. **1904** Day *Kin o' Ktaadn* 96 **ME,** An' ice-cream sodys ev'ry night. **1906** *DN* 3.157 **nwAR,** Soda [sodɪ] *pop.* **1907** *DN* 3.210 **seNH,** Sody. **1918** *DN* 5.22 **NW,** Sodysquirt. **1928** *AmSp* 3.402 **Ozarks** (as of 1916–27), Soda is invariably turned into *sody.* **1933** *AmSp* 8.44 **neNY,** Soda [sodɪ]. **1936** *AmSp* 11.160 **eTX,** Among older or less well educated people in rural districts . . *soda* . . [is] pronounced with [ɪ] in the final syllable. **1942** Hall *Smoky Mt. Speech* 76 **wNC, eTN,** Words in which [ɪ] was heard . . soda. **1959** *VT Hist.* 27.158, *Soda* [sōˈdē] . . pronc. Occasional. Rural areas. **1965–70** *DARE* (Qu. H78, *Ordinary soft drinks, usually carbonated*) 18 Infs, **scattered, but esp eMO, TX,** Sody (pop, water); (Qu. H16, *What do people use to raise the bread before it's baked?*) Inf **KY28,** Sody; (Qu. H19, *What do you mean by a biscuit? How are they made?*) Inf **KY28,** Sody biscuits; (Qu. L17, . . *Names . . for manure used in the fields: [Also joking names]*) Inf **NC49,** Sody. **1968** Moody *Horse* 52 **nwKS** (as of c1920), He bought Scotty plumb out of sody-pop and near-beer and ceegars. **1970** *DARE* Tape **CA205,** There used to be mines, and then there was the soda [ˈsodɪ] plant down here. **1975** Gould *ME Lingo* 266, *Sody*—Soda. Either bicarbonate of or for a *tonic.* **1991** *DARE* File **cwIL,** The word is "sodie" to refer to soda pop. **1995** [see **soda dope**]. **2000** *DARE* File **sIL,** My elderly cousins . . [say] 'sody pop.'

B Senses.

1 =**soda water.** **widespread, but esp freq NEast, eMO, sIL**   See Map on p. 108   Cf **pop** n[1], **soda dope, ~ pop**

1834 *Huron Reflector* (Norwalk OH) 26 Aug [4]/5 (newspaper-archive.com), *Temperance Tavern.* . . N.B. Instead of ardent spirits, his Bar will be furnished with Small Beer and Soda. **1844** *Uncle Sam Peculiarities* 1.43 **NYC,** On the outside . . is printed the following thirsty announcement: . . Congress Water, Sarsaparilla Soda, Ginger Champaign [sic]. **1846** [see **A** above]. **1860** *Vanity Fair* 1.156, Could they get their . . lemon-soda and cinnamon cigars, by working as men? **1933** O'Neill *Ah Wilderness* 58 **CT** (as of 1906), Ever drink anything besides sodas? **1956** Algren *Walk on the Wild Side* 105 **New Orleans LA,** Last night I bought a sody . . 'n it were only five cents. . . All I know is this coke tastus right fine. **1965** *PADS* 43.15 **seMA,** A soft drink, usually carbonated: soda [8 of 9 infs]. **1965–70** *DARE* (Qu. H78, *Ordinary soft drinks, usually carbonated*) 286 Infs, **widespread, but esp freq NEast, eMO, sIL,** Soda(s); **SC43, 62,** Soda—Negro; **VA78,** Soda—Negro usage; **MI68,** Lemon sodas; **LA9,** Orange sodas; **CA32,** Soda drink; **IL143, MO4, 29, 38, MA57, OK1, PA136, TX35,** Sody; (Qu. X49, *Expressions . . about a person who is very thin*) Inf **NJ2,** Soda straw; **WI49,** So skinny she drinks a cherry soda and looks like a thermometer. **1970** Tarpley *Blinky* 194 **neTX,** *Carbonated beverage in a bottle* . . cold drink [62 of 200 infs] . . soda pop [56 of 200 infs] . . soda [rare]. [*DARE* Ed: *Soda* is the least frequent of the "other responses."] **1971** Bright *Word Geog. CA & NV* 181, *Soft drink* . . soft drink 56% [of 300 infs] . . *soda* 13%. **1974** Rubrecht *Regional Dial.* WI 18, *Pop* occurs state-wide except in the southeastern portion of the state where *soda* occurs in the Milwaukee area with a transition zone extending north to Green Bay and south and west to Janesville. **1993** *DARE* File, There was a difference between sodas and root beers. *Soda* was cola or lemon-lime; *root beer* was a root beer; *orange* was an orange; etc. *Ibid* **cwOR,** At a restaurant or fast food joint, if I don't ask for 7Up, RootBeer, or Dr. Pepper, I'll say "I want a soda . . what have you got?" When I go to the grocery store, I buy pop. Very young fast food clerks often ask me to repeat my question if I ask for soda instead of pop. *Ibid* **Boston MA,** Growing up outside Boston, I used *tonic* not *soda.* My mother, from St. Louis said she grew up with *pop,* but my father who grew up in a very rural farm town north of Hartford CT, grew up with *tonic.* By the mid-seventies, everyone around Boston was using *soda.* **2000** *Ibid* **AZ,** I just checked with my undergrad American English class this morning, and found solid support for "soda" in Arizona. Several related stories of being regarded peculiarly after moving from the midwest using "pop". None had ever heard "soda pop". **2002** *Ibid* **MN,** Saturday the 13th, an ice cream social's refreshments included "soda"—in what once was solid "pop" territory. **2002** [see **soda water**].

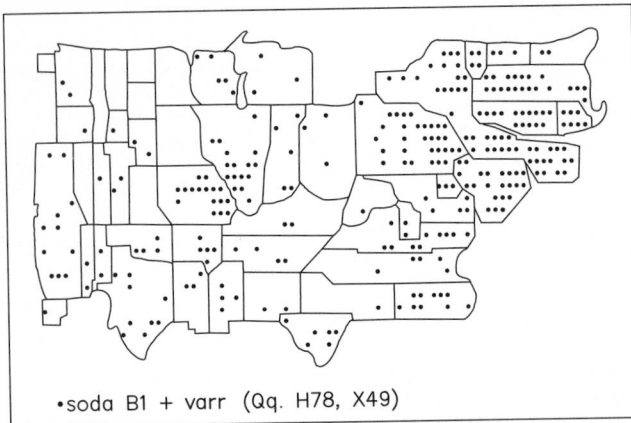

•soda B1 + varr (Qq. H78, X49)

2 An ice-cream soda.

1904 *Lima Times–Democrat* (OH) 19 July 3/6, [Advt:] Come and learn where the *good* soda, the *best* soda ever served, is to be had this season. We use Bower's Jersey Ice Cream only. **1917** Norris *Martie* 3 **CA,** Five o'clock was the hour for "sodas." **1973** Hunter *Hail Chief* 94, Toy . . put the straws between her lips, and busied herself with the soda. **1974** Rubrecht *Regional Dial. WI* 18, *Float* (drink made with ice cream and carbonated beverage) . . soda 7 [of 58 infs] . . ice cream soda 4 [infs]. **2000** *DARE* File **seIA, csWI** (as of c1968), When my cousins and I talked about "a soda," we meant an ice-cream soda. A carbonated beverage (such as Coke or root beer) with nothing added to it was "pop." *Ibid* **cwCA** (as of c1958), A real treat was to go out for an ice-cream soda, or a "soda" for short.

soda-apple n Also *soda-apple nightshade*

A **nightshade 1** (here: *Solanum capsicoides*).

1858 NC State Geologist *Rept. NC Geol. Surv.* 43, [*Solanum*] *aculeatissimum* . . Soda Apple. **1933** Small *Manual SE Flora* 1114, *S[olanum] aculeatissimum.* . . Soda-apple. . . Sandy soil, fields, thickets, and roadsides, Coastal Plain, Fla. to Tex., and N.C. **1953** Greene-Blomquist *Flowers South* 106, Soda-Apple, Love-Apple. . . A perennial, partly woody plant, it bears relatively large, orange to red, papery berries which make up the ornamental dried bouquets often seen in florists' shops in the fall. **1970** Correll *Plants TX* 1398, *Solanum aculeatissimum.* . . Cockroach berry, soda apple nightshade. . . In open woodlands along rivers and in waste grounds in s.e. Tex. **2004** *DARE* File—Internet **FL,** The cockroach berry or soda apple (*Solanum capsicoides* Allioni) is a subshrub native to the states bordering the Gulf of Mexico and has been found in the Carolinas.

soda cracker n *esp freq among Black speakers; derog* Cf **cracker 2, 3**

A White person.

1966 *DARE* FW Addit **SC,** *Soda* [ˈsoʊdɪ] *cracker*—what Negroes here call Whites. **1986** Pederson *LAGS Concordance (Caucasian)* 1 inf, **swAL,** Soda cracker [inf White]; 1 inf, **cnAL,** Soda cracker—derogatory [inf Black]; 1 inf, **cGA,** Soda cracker—blacks' derogatory term; 1 inf, **cnGA,** Soda crackers—joking—used by black children. **2004** Williams *My Soul* 118 **ceNC** (as of c1940), We would go and have rock fights with these kids. They would call us "soda crackers" and we would call them "niggers." That's just the way the world was.

soda dope n *esp NC* Cf **dope** n 4, **soda B1**

A carbonated soft drink.

1995 Williams *Gt. Smoky Mts. Folklife* 103 **wNC, eTN,** Inhabitants also resemble other southerners in their passion for soft drinks (still called "dope" or "sodey dope" by some old-timers). **1995** Adams *Come Go Home* 95 **wNC** (as of c1970), There must've been thirty women and men standing around eating southern fried chicken and drinking "sodey-dopes." **2003** Davis *NC Gt. Depression* 211 **wNC** (as of 1930s), Price's General Store was a favorite gathering place for residents near the Rutherford County–Cleveland County line. "Pop," as we all called the owner, allowed no profanity from his friends and neighbors who gathered regularly at the end of the day and enjoyed a "Three Center" or a "sody dope" as they talked. **2005** in 2006 *DARE* File—Internet **AL,** When I was a kid in Alabama, "Coke" was sort of a generic

term for soft drink. . . But the oldtimey country folks still called Cokes "dopes." Or occasionally, "soda dopes."

soda pop n **widespread, but less freq Nth** See Map Cf **pop** n[1], **soda B1**

A carbonated soft drink.

1851 *Elyria Courier* (OH) [14 Oct 2]/5 (newspaperarchive.com), [Advt:] Lewis's Sarsaparilla & Soda Pop. **1863** in 1978 Whitman *Daybooks & Notebooks* 3.655, The continual soda-pop-like burstings of members calling "Mr. Speaker! Mr. Speaker!" **1872** *Ft. Wayne Daily Sentinel* (IN) 4 Jan 4/2, The crowd would take lemonade, or a cheap quality of soda-pop. **1896** *Harper's New Mth. Mag.* 93.776 **TN,** There is a bucket of lemonade at one end, some jugs of summer cider, and half a dozen mysterious bottles labelled "Soda pop." **1916** *Ft. Wayne News* (IN) 12 Feb 13/6, Right there is where John Wes' ten dollar a bottle sody-pop stuff we was soppin' up must a foolished me plumb silly. **1922** *Coshocton Tribune & Times–Age* (OH) 27 Apr 6/1 **Kansas City MO,** "Soda pop" was originally a home-made drink. . . "It's [sic] principal ingredients were water, vinegar and baking soda, with a fruit flavoring. When the cork was pulled it made a loud 'pop' not unlike the explosion of certain 'home brews,' and from that it got its name." **1941** *LANE* Map 312 *(Soft drink)* 16 infs, **scattered NEng,** Soda pop. **1953** in 1958 Brewer *Dog Ghosts* 40 **TX** [Black], Dey stopped by de sto' to buy 'em a soda-pop, o' some cheese an' crackers. **1965–70** *DARE* (Qu. H78, *Ordinary soft drinks, usually carbonated*) 109 Infs, **widespread, but less freq Nth,** Soda pop; **GA1, MS25,** Soda pops; **TX32,** Sody pop. **1976** Garber *Mountain-ese* 85 **sAppalachians,** Jodie got strangled while swiggin' on a bottle uv orange sodie-pop. **1989** *Gettysburg Times* (PA) 6 Sept sec B 5/1 **Baltimore MD,** In Ballmer [=Baltimore], people drink 'melk' and 'sody pop.' **1998** Hillerman *First Eagle* 54 **AZ,** You don't drink hard liquor. If I'm wrong about that, . . I'll get you something better than soda pop. **2004** *Sun* (Baltimore MD) 14 July Business sec 1 (Internet), Everything really is going up—gas prices, corporate profits, soda pop prices . . except your salary.

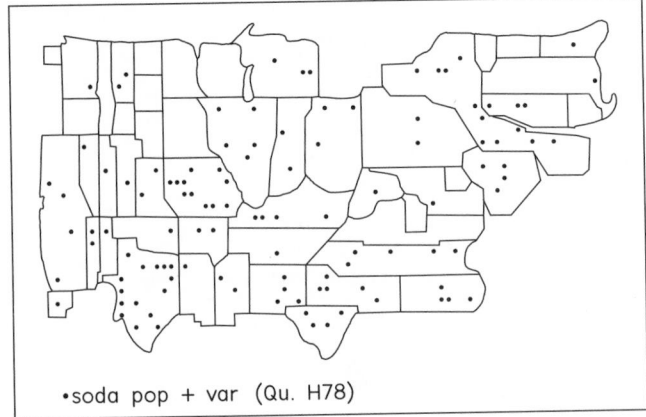

•soda pop + var (Qu. H78)

soda water n **scattered, but esp TX, Lower Missip Valley** See Map

Carbonated water, often sweetened and flavored; a carbonated soft drink.

1813 (1927) Gerry *Diary* 168 **OH,** We had not gone far, before the girls ordered the charioteer to stop at the soda water room. **1834** [see **soda A**]. **1860** *Vanity Fair* 2.29, At the corner of Ann-street the procession will halt for ten minutes, when a glass of soda water, sarsaparilla syrup, will be presented to the illustrious guest. **1877** *Harper's New Mth. Mag.* 54.253 **NYC,** He took another, and another, until he had drunk *six* glasses of soda-water, and had tried as many kinds of syrup. **1890** *Century Dict.* 5747, *Soda-water.* . . A drink generally consisting of ordinary water into which carbonic acid has been forced under pressure. . . It is generally sweetened and flavored with syrups. **1929** (1951) Faulkner *Sartoris* 122 **MS,** A number of customers stood about . . with sandwiches and bottles of soda-water. **1958** Humphrey *Home from the Hill* 97 **neTX,** Underneath the table, with their rims touching, were tubs packed with ice, . . some filled with bottled beer, some with colored sodawater. **1961** Folk *Word Atlas N. LA* map 1102, Soft drink . . cold drink 60% [of 275 infs] . . [less freq responses include] soda water. **1965–70** *DARE* (Qu. H78, *Ordinary soft drinks, usually carbonated*) 31 Infs, **scattered, but esp TX, Lower Missip Valley,** Soda water; **CA132, NY37, TX85, 94, 99, WI13,** Soda water—old-fashioned; **ME23,** Soda water—any flavor; **GA46,** Soda water—colored people; **LA17,** Soda water—especially colored; **ME**23, Soda water—"sody water" heard; **CA**77, **KY**90, **MO**16, **TX**26, 32, 36, 37, Sody water; (Qu. H74b, . . *Coffee . . very weak*) Inf **CA**105, Weak as soda water; (Qu. X49, *Expressions . . about a person who is very thin*) Inf **TX**98, You could drink a red soda water and look like a thermometer. **1970** Tarpley *Blinky* 194 **neTX**, *Carbonated beverage in a bottle . .* soda water [18 of 200 infs]. . . *Soda water* is not found in the city. **1975** *Austin Amer.–Statesman* (TX) 19 June 25, [Advt:] Regular or Sugar Free Dr. Pepper Soda Water. **1986** *DARE* File **cTX**, [Advt:] Pleasure Time is Austin's only soda water maker. . . We've made our 19 flavors, diets, and mixers, here in Austin for several years now. **1986** Pederson *LAGS Concordance (Soft drinks)* 7 infs, **AL, TX**, Soda water(s); 1 inf, **ceTX**, Soda water—of cola, generic term; 1 inf, **ceTX**, Soda water—usual term; 1 inf, **ceTX**, Soda water—blacks say; 3 infs, **GA, TX**, Soda water—soft drink; 1 inf, **swGA**, Soda water—old name for pop; 1 inf, **nwFL**, A soda water—a soft drink. [9 of 15 infs Black] **2002** *DARE* File **cnKY**, For me, "soda" is "seltzer" or "soda water." *Ibid*, In the west, 'soda water', or just plain 'soda', is what you'd call 'seltzer' in the east. 7-Up is a type of 'pop.' *Ibid* **NJ**, While I was back visiting the folks in NJ (Point Pleasant) last week, my sister-in-law ordered "soda water" in a restaurant. The waitress, about 20 years of age and who by her accent and usage of "youse guys" was clearly a native, was thoroughly confused by this. My sister-in-law explained that she meant "club soda" and all was fine.

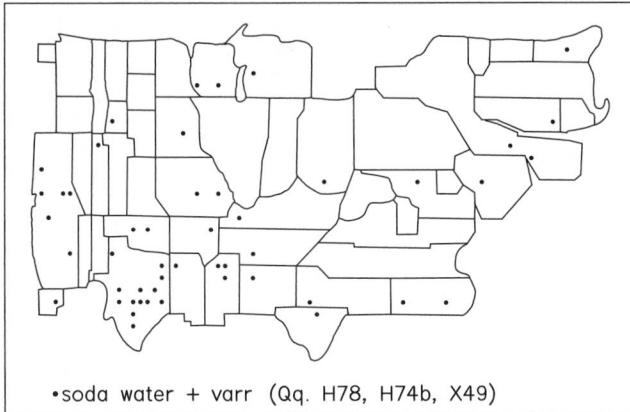

•soda water + varr (Qq. H78, H74b, X49)

sod breaker   See **sodbuster 1, 2**

sodbuster n

1 also *sod breaker:* =**breaking plow.**

1857 *Cultivator* 5.np, Index To Illustrations. . . Two-Horse Sod Breaker . . 280. **1884** *Overland Mth.* (2d ser) 4.173 **CA**, After it [=the period 1848–55] comes sod-breaker and reaper, wheat field and garden. **1937** *AmSp* 12.105 **eNE** [Farm terms], A *breaking plow* or *sod buster* is a special plow with a long moldboard and is used in *turning over* native sod. **1966–68** *DARE* (Qu. L18, *Kinds of plows*) Infs **AR**9, **CO**2, 19, **KS**20, **MN**23, Sodbuster; **IL**9, Sod breaker. **1967** *DARE* Tape **CO**2, I can remember my father plowing sod with a sod breaker and a mule and a milk cow hitched to the plow. **1986** Pederson *LAGS Concordance (Plow)* 1 inf, **seMS**, Sodbuster.

2 also *sod breaker:* A homesteader, farmer, or rustic. **orig chiefly West, now more widespread**   Cf **soddy 2**

1897 *KS Univ. Qrly.* (ser B) 6.92, *Sod buster:* farmer.—General. **1918** *DN* 5.28 **NW**, *Sodbuster. . .* A farmer. General. **1936** McCarthy *Lang. Mosshorn* np **West** [Range terms], *Sodbuster. . .* A farmer or homesteader. **1937** Sandoz *Slogum* 348 **NE**, No weaning these old sod-busters away from the places they broke out. **1939** (1973) FWP *Guide MT* 416, *Sodbuster*—Homesteader. **1940** Stong *Hawkeyes* 73 **IA**, A good deal of liquor must have gone over the palates of the God-fearing sod-breaker. **1958** McCulloch *Woods Words* 174 **Pacific NW**, *Sod-buster*—A part time logger who farms the rest of the year. **1966–70** *DARE* (Qu. U6, *Someone who sells vegetables or other articles from a wagon or truck, going from house to house*) Inf **MN**38, Sodbuster; (Qu. HH1, *Names and nicknames for a rustic or countrified person*) Infs **MN**38, **NC**35, **NY**66, 219, 234, **PA**219, Sodbuster. **1970** *DARE* FW Addit **cNY**, Going from sodbuster up to the sow's ear—rags to riches. **1973** Allen *LAUM* 1.350 (as of c1950), A rustic. . . sodbuster [7 infs, **ND, NE**]. *Ibid* 351, 1 inf, **SD**, *Sodbuster:* Cattlemen's term for farmers. **1986** Pederson *LAGS Concordance (A rustic)* 2 infs, **GA, LA**, Sodbuster.

3 also *sod-crusher:* =**clod-crusher 1.**

1918 *Tractor & Gas Engine Rev.* Jan 34 **WI**, Our outfit . . included . . one sod crusher and a tool wagon. **1966–69** *DARE* (Qu. L20, *The implement used in a field after it's been plowed to break up the lumps*) Infs **IN**63, **KY**34, **NC**12, Sodbuster; **MI**40, Sod-crusher—series of wheels of heavy steel, serrated, close together.

4 also *sodbuster boot:* A heavy shoe or boot.

1916 *Edwardsville Intelligencer* (IL) [13 July 5]/5 (newspaper-archive.com), The quartermaster at Camp Dodge started to issue heavy farm shoes to the 4500 guardsmen preparing for border service instead of the regulation army shoes. . . Department officials could not supply the regulation shoe and guardsmen say the "sod busters" are not proper for marching. **1950** *WELS* (*Men's low, rough work shoes*) 1 Inf, **cnWI**, Sodbusters. **1975** (1996) Henry *I Tom Horn* 14, I don't think she ever got more than that about his going to the emigrant wagon grounds outside the county seat of Memphis, Scotland County, Missouri, and whipping five grown men with nothing but his bare knuckles and sodbuster boots.

5 also *sodbuster foot:* A large foot.

1950 *WELS* (*Humorous or uncomplimentary words for big feet*) 1 Inf, **seWI**, Sodbusters. **1968** *DARE* (Qu. X38) Inf **KS**12, Sodbuster feet.

6 =**soaker.**   Cf **sod-soaker**

1941 *Chillicothe Constitution–Tribune* (MO) 9 June 1/7, This morning's rain was termed by many farmers a "sod buster." **1954** *NY Times* (NY) 4 Aug 23/8, In Westchester County, George S. Haight, superintendent of parks, said the rain was neither a "sod buster" nor a "gully washer" but had done a lot of good to the parched lawns. **1967** *DARE* (Qu. B25, . . *Joking names . . for a very heavy rain. . .* "It's a regular _____.") Infs **CO**41, **MI**47, Sodbuster.

sodbuster boot   See **sodbuster 4**

sodbuster foot   See **sodbuster 5**

sod-corn (whiskey)   See **sod** n attrib

sod-crusher   See **sodbuster 3**

sodda, sodder   See **solder**

soddy n

1 A sod dwelling. **chiefly Cent, esp KS, NE**

1887 *Athens Messenger* (OH) 28 July 5/4 **SD**, Arbor days have to take the place of log-rollings and wood-choppings of early times back east. The "Shack" and the "Soddy" are seen instead of the little log hut. **1894** *Overland Mth.* 24.149 **MT**, The fiercest rain will not penetrate, nor the hardest wind blow down your little "soddy." **1914** *DN* 4.113 **cKS**, *Soddy. . .* A house with walls of sods. "Only in the western counties are there any soddies standing now." **1933** *AmSp* 8.4.48 **NE** [Pioneer vocabulary], Probably no *sod house* ever boasted a *punch-room,* for the majority of *soddies* had at the most two rooms neither of which was likely to be large. **1935** Sandoz *Jules* 16 **wNE** (as of 1880–1930), Finally he saw a little half soddy, half dugout, beside the trail. No horse, no cow, no strip of breaking, only the little door and half window with a crooked, rusty stovepipe pushing up through the sod-covered roof. **1937** Ruede *Sod-House* 57 **KS** (as of 1877), Many of the young bachelors . . were building their own "soddies." **1944** Wellman *Bowl* 171 **KS**, Simeon had seen the soddy just once—a hint of earth-gray wall glimpsed through tree trunks. **1963** Ottoson *Land Use Policy* 49 **nwNE** (as of c1910), A few stayed . . to live in the covered wagon until a dugout or a soddy could be prepared on the new homestead. **c1965** *DARE* File **swOK**, *Soddy*—another name for a sod hut. **1967** *DARE* Tape **IA**8, They had an old soddy, and that's where we lived was in this old soddy. **1995** *Brophy Coll.* 70 **swMO** (as of c1960), *Soddy.* [A] sod house.

2 Transf: one who lives in a sod dwelling; a rustic.

1968 Adams *Western Words* 292, *Soddy*—A cowboy's name for a nester, because the early ones usually lived in sod houses. **1973** Allen *LAUM* 1.351 (as of c1950) 1 inf, **SD**, *Soddy:* Cattlemen's term for farmers.

sodey   See **soda**

sodger   See **soldier**

sodie   See **soda**

sodjuh   See **soldier**

sodle v   [Cf *EDD* *sowdle* "To creep"]   Cf **sog** v 2

1944 *PADS* 2.49 **NC, VA**, Sodle ['sodl]: vb. To make no progress. "My fire jes' sets and sodles—won't catch up." Randolph Co., N.C. Rare. Reported.

so-dl-whirr See **so till**

Sodom berry n

The berry of the **apple of Sodom.**

1960 Williams *Walk Egypt* 55 **GA,** Apple of Sodom thrust up prickly leaves and hung orange fruit everywhere between the rows of turnips, yams, and catnip. Sodom berries dried on the screen frames on the porch. There was nothing better for making a woman "come 'round."

so don't I See **so** adv

sod relation n Cf **grass relation, sod widow 1**

A person related to another through remarriage of a widow or widower.

1942 (1960) Robertson *Red Hills* 51 **SC,** Our step-mother and our step-step-grandmother were sod relations of ours—not grass relations. We do not believe in divorce in South Carolina; it is against the law in South Carolina to seek divorce, so even until now we have never had a grass widower among our kinfolks.

sod runner n

A **ground squirrel b** (here: *Spermophilus tridecemlineatus*).

1929 Seton *Lives of Game Animals* 4.228, Chippie, Grass-runner, Sod-runner, Prairie Striper *Citellus tridecemlineatus.*

sods n pl, but sometimes sg in constr **Appalachians** Cf **slick** n **3** =**bald** n.

[**1939** *Charleston Daily Mail* (WV) 4 Aug 5/5, The [beacon] lights were placed at Wardensville, Dolly Sods, Bickle Knob and Helmick Rocks.] **1942** Thomas *Blue Ridge Country* 105 **sAppalachians,** The bald is sometimes called the sods—where the trees can't grow because of high winds. **1969** *Sun. Gaz.–Mail* (Charleston WV) 11 May sec E 6/4, Elleber Knob is the summit of an area known as Elleber Sods, high-country pastureland in the Monongahela National Forest. . . The mountains around the sods are known for their good turkey hunting. **2003** in 2005 *DARE* File—Internet **WV,** Dolly Sods. . . In this part of the Appalachians, an open grassy area at high elevation is called a "sods". The name "Dolly" is a corruption of "Dahle", the name of the German immigrants who first owned this land.

sod-soaker n Also *land-soaker, (new)ground-~* **chiefly Sth, S Midl** Cf **root-soaker**

=**soaker.**

1879 *Daily Constitution* (Atlanta GA) 19 July [5]/2 (newspaperarchive.com), Atlanta and the section roundabout has been visited by a heavy fall of rain, of several hours' duration, and the indications are that it extended over a very wide area. It was what the farmers call a . . ground-"soaker." **1903** Fox *Little Shepherd* 59 **seKY,** Send us not a gentle sizzle-sozzle, but a sod-soaker, O Lord, a gully washer. **1923** *Star* (Kansas City MO) 23 Apr *(DA),* That part of the state known as the short grass country needs a sod-soaker. **1932** Hench Coll. **VA,** The gentle rain . . I've heard called a "sod-soaker." **1944** *Clarke Co. Democrat* (Grove Hill AL) 20 July 2/2, A real rain is a gully washer. A little less rainfall may be a sod-soaker. **1965–70** *DARE* (Qu. B24, . . *A sudden, very heavy rain)* Inf **AL**52, Newground-soaker; (Qu. B25, . . *Joking names . . for a very heavy rain. . . "It's a regular _____.")* Infs **IN**30, **KY**31, **NJ**39, **NM**11, **VA**8, Sod-soaker; **GA**73, Ground-soaker; **VA**13, Land-soaker. **1968** Haun *Hawk's Done Gone* 106 **TN,** These here sod soakers make pine trees and cedars easy to blow up by the roots. **1970** Tarpley *Blinky* 54 **neTX,** *Very heavy rain that doesn't last long . .* ground-soaker [rare]. **1978** *DARE* File **Kansas City MO,** In describing a heavy rainstorm we say it is a "sod soaker" or a "gully washer." **1986** Pederson *LAGS Concordance (A steady drizzle)* 1 inf, **ceAL,** Ground soaker. **2002** *Daily News Los Angeles* (CA) 9 Nov sec N 1 (Internet) **swCA,** "It was a ground-soaker," said Stuart Seto with the National Weather Service. "This one came in kind of slow at first, so it got soaked into the ground. . . It did help reduce the possibility of fire danger."

sod widow n *old-fash* Cf **grass widow**

1 A woman who has lost her husband through death; similarly n *sod widower* a man who has lost his wife through death; hence adj *sod* of a woman no longer married: widowed (as opposed to divorced).

1901 *N&Q* (London) 6 Apr 268 **Philadelphia,** The term "sod widow"—a woman whose husband is dead—is also in use in the United States. **1905** *Decatur Daily Rev.* (IL) 4 Aug 5/5, Galesburg [MI] has 700 population and fifty three of the residents are widows and not one of

the fifty-three is listed among the 'grassers.[?] Every one is a sod widow. **1927** *AmSp* 2.278 **CA** [Stanford Univ expressions], *Sod (widow)*—husband dead. **1936** *Chicago Tribune* (IL) 23 Apr 14/6, He is a sod widower, and a lonely one. **1946** Stimpson *Book about Things* 349, A grass widow's husband was alive while a sod widow's husband was under the sod. **c1955** Reed–Person *Ling. Atlas Pacific NW,* 1 inf, Sod widow [=widow]. **1956** Ker *Vocab. W. TX* 363, *Woman whose husband is dead. . .* sod widow. [8 of 67 infs] **1965–70** *DARE* (Qu. AA25, *A woman whose husband is dead)* 31 Infs, **scattered,** Sod widow; (Qu. AA24, *A man whose wife is dead)* Infs **IA**3, **OH**28, **PA**177, Sod widower; (Qu. AA26) Inf **GA**81, Is she grass or sod?—i.e., "[Is she] a divorcee or is her husband dead?" [27 of 32 total Infs old] **1970** Tarpley *Blinky* 249 **neTX,** *A woman whose husband is dead . .* grass widow[?] sod widow [rare]. **1973** Allen *LAUM* 1.337 (as of c1950), *Widow. . .* [2 infs, **IA, MN**] volunteer also . . *sod widow* for one whose husband has died. **1973** *News & Observer* (Raleigh NC) 12 Mar 34/2, Last but not least is our large number of widows (sod). There are 70. **1984** Wilder *You All Spoken Here* 41 **Sth,** Sod widow: One widowed by death. **1986** Pederson *LAGS Concordance* **Gulf Region** *(Widow)* 10 infs, Sod widow(s); 1 inf, Sod—widow, husband has died. **2006** *DARE* File—Internet **MT,** A sod widow for over a year, after be[i]ng a straw widow for 22 years, I am eager for a good holy happy Catholic marriage.

2 Transf: a divorced woman.

1966 Dakin *Dial. Vocab. Ohio R. Valley* 2.418, Folk term for a divorcee. . . A few instances of a jocular *sod widow* are also attested, always in addition to *grass widow.* **1966–68** *DARE* (Qu. AA26, *A divorced woman)* Infs **AR**3, **MA**72, **NY**105, Sod widow; [**TX**3, Widowed by sod or by God]. [All Infs old] **1970** Tarpley *Blinky* 249 **neTX,** Sod widow and *grass widow . .* usually refer to divorcees.

sod widower See **sod widow 1**

sody See **soda**

so ez See **so as**

sofa n Usu |'sofə|; also |'sofɪ, -i|; occas |'sofɚ| Pronc-spp *soffie, sofy* Cf Intro "Language Changes" IV.1.b
Std senses, var forms.

1848 Lowell *Biglow* 146 'Upcountry' **MA,** *Soffies,* sofas. **1871** (1882) Stowe *Fireside Stories* 30 **MA,** Then there was gret wide rooms, and sofys, and curtains. **1893** Shands *MS Speech* 6, [sofɪ] for *sofa.* **1894** Riley *Armazindy* 163 **IN,** He mocks the music-box an' clock,/ An' roller-sofy an' the chairs. **1907** Lincoln *Cape Cod* 50 **MA,** My face ain't no plush sofy. **1911** Porter *Harvester* 338 **IN,** Marthy's old blue coverlid also carefully spread on a splinter new sofy. **1923** (1946) Greer-Petrie *Angeline Steppin'* 29 **csKY,** We drapt down on a big leather sofy. **1936** *AmSp* 11.160 **eTX,** Among older or less well educated people in rural districts . . *sofa . .* [is] pronounced with [ɪ] in the final syllable. **1960** Criswell *Resp. to PADS 20* **Ozarks,** Sofa [sofɪ]. **1961** Kurath–McDavid *Pronc. Engl.* 168, *Sofa, china. . .* These words usually end in /ə/. But in folk speech [ɨ ~ ɪ] occur with some frequency in northern New England, in West Virginia, and in the Upper South, and relics of it appear elsewhere. **1989** Pederson *LAGS Tech. Index* 36 **Gulf Region,** *Sofa.* [Of 914 primary infs, 604 offered proncs of the type [sofə]; 36, proncs of the type [sofɚ]; 27, proncs of the type [sofɪ]; and 1, pronc of the type [sofi].] **2000** Shores *Tangier Is.* 181 **Chesapeake Bay,** "Sofy" and "chiny" for *sofa* and *china,* respectively, are still found . . in regions of the South, particularly in the Appalachians. Although I have never heard these forms on Tangier, they were recorded in the thirties, but from two elderly people, which may mean that they were relics of the distant past.

so fanciful See **suffancified**

so far as See **as far as**

so-fashion adv phr *esp NEng*

Thus, in this or that manner; like so.

1843 *U.S. Mag. & Democratic Rev.* 13.93 **Philadelphia PA,** To be cutting up, so fashion, all in a jam, why people go on t'other side of the way, and retailing's done for. **1846** in 1854 Lowrie *Memoirs* 309 **PA** [Author a missionary to China], *Chay-yang* which is colloquial Mandarin, meaning "so-fashion," or "in this way," in one dialect is *sz'-ka-go,* which cannot be written at all, i.e., has no characters to express it. **1864** *Atlantic Mth.* 14.176 **NEast,** Put your hands over across my breast. Could n't manage to hold the umbrella over us, could you? So fashion. Now steady, while I rise with you. [**1865** Bowles *Across the Continent* 250 **CA,** [Illustrating Chinese pidgin in San Francisco:] My no likee takee care that sheep, so fashion my hear you got fightee this side.]

1874 McCabe *Hist. Grange Movement* 119 **NY,** I jes' went up to th' man, reached one arm 'round his neck, so fashion. **1890** *DN* 1.23, *So fashion,* meaning so, in that way. Is this known all over New England? *Ibid* 79 **ME, NH, MA, wPA,** *So fashion.* **1892** *DN* 1.218 (as of c1845) **ceMA,** *So fashion.* . . Common in Boston in my youth. **1892** *KS Univ. Qrly.* 1.99 **KS,** *So fashion:* thus, as, Do it so fashion. **1899** (1912) Green *VA Folk-Speech* 401, *So fashion.* . . So; in that way; in this manner. "You ought not to put on your hat that way, but so fashion." **1903** Wasson *Cap'n Simeon's Store* 115 **ME,** Wal, o' course I was nach'ally kind of pleased like to git aboard the ole packet ag'in so fashion, being's how I see her built and launched. **1945** Colcord *Sea Language* 26 **ME, Cape Cod, Long Island,** This piece wants to go right 'thwartships of the crate, *so-fashion!* **1975** Gould *ME Lingo* 266, *So fashion*—In this manner: a man to a boy, "No, Sonny, not like that; hold it this way and swing it so fashion."

soffie See **sofa**

sofkee n Also *sofkey, sofki, sophky* [Muskogee *safki*] **FL, OK** Cf **skinned corn**
A soup or gruel consisting principally of boiled corn; hence n *sofkee dog* a dog of mixed breed.

1796 in 1916 Hawkins *Letters* 28 **nGA,** She [=a young Creek Indian] . . gave me . . some sofkey (hommony) and ground peas. **1845** Hooper *Advent. Simon Suggs* 75 **AL,** She had scarcely time to cook the sophky for her children, or drink a spoonful herself. **1898** (1910) Willoughby *Across Everglades* 130 **sFL,** Their [=Seminole Indians'] great dependence is "sofkee," which is made in the pot and helped out with a large carved wooden spoon. . . The best description I can give of "sofkee" is to say that it is the analogue of the Spanish "olla podrida." **1911** *S. Workman* 40.158 **FL,** Before you is a bucket of "sofkee" (a general term for any kind of soup or stew). **c1937** in 1970 Yetman *Voices* 83 **OK** [Black slave of Creek Indian], When you make de sofki you pound up de corn real fine, den pour in de water and drain it off to get all de little skin from offen de grain. Den you let de grits soak and den boil it and let it stand. Sometime you put in some pounded hickory nuts meats. **1939** FWP *Guide FL* 44, Turkeys, curlews, herons, gophers, and venison find their way into the Seminole kettle, but the staple food is *sofkee,* a mush made of ground corn meal. . . There are no fixed meal hours; the sofkee pot is on the fire all day, to be dipped into whenever a member of the family is hungry. **1965** *DARE* (Qu. H45, *Dishes made with meat, fish, or poultry that everybody around here would know, but that people in other places might not*) Inf **OK**9, Only local dishes like that would be Indian dishes; they make sofkee—hominy with venison added; (Qu. J1, *. . A dog of mixed breed*) Inf **OK**10, Indians call them ['sɔfki] dogs . . [from] name of a food made with corn. **2001** *DARE* File **OK,** For the second time I have heard from an Oklahoma black person that their family made *sofkee*—the puffy corn that most Americans call *hominy* (to old-fashioned people in eastern Oklahoma, *hominy* is ground-up). I have heard of *sofkee* now from two black women who are *Creek freedwomen*—descendants of slaves of Creek Indians.

soft See **soft-shell crab**

soft-back turtle See **soft-shell turtle**

soft beer n Cf *pop beer* (at **pop** n¹) **esp ME** *old-fash*
A soft drink.

1887 *NY Times* (NY) 7 Oct 4/5 **ME,** We have ginger ale and soft beer. . . I will advise you not to take any strong drink. I will make you a present of a bottle of ginger ale or soda water if you will try to get along without the other. **1899** *Daily Kennebec Jrl.* (Augusta ME) 24 Mar 4/3, The sap of the maple tree can be put up in bottles and charged as are the soft beers and mineral waters. **1901** *Post-Std.* (Syracuse NY) 2 May 6/5, The representatives of the Soft Beer Bottlers' Union announced that a new scale of wages . . had been signed by nearly all of the bottling establishments. **1914** *Syracuse Herald* (NY) 7 Sept 3/3, Eugene Reilly headed the fourth division, made up of . . brewery workmen,[;] beer drivers, coopers, soft beer bottlers, maltsters, barbers [etc]. **1925** *Candy and Ice Cream Retailer* July 36 *(Popik Coll.)* **ME,** Even today in the remote northern part of Maine, carbonated beverages are referred to as "soft beer." **1926** *Daily Kennebec Jrl.* (Augusta ME) 16 May 6/2, A country barnyard golf tournament and soft beer drinking contest will feature the annual exhibition of the Hancock County Fair Association. **1941** *LANE* Map 312 *(Soft drink)* 5 infs, **ME,** Soft beer. **1971** *Today Show Letters* **ME,** I would like to add to your collection of words, "soft beer" which we, in Maine, called what other people call "soda, tonic, pop," etc.

soft clam See **soft-shell clam**

soft corn n

1 Indian corn 1 that is high in moisture, either because it has not yet matured or because frost damage has kept it from maturing. Cf **flour corn, hard ~**

1743 (1751) Bartram *Observations* 60, Last of all was served a great bowl, full of *Indian* dumplings, of new soft corn, cut or scraped off the ear. **1770** in 1918 *MD Hist. Mag.* 13.72, I Have a great deal of soft Corn at all the Plantations. **1817** in 1918 IN Hist. Soc. *Pub.* 6.2.320, We obtained some soft corn from them to boil. **1868** MI State Bd. Ag. *Annual Rept.* 7.160, Early frosts made considerable "soft corn." **1868** *NY Times* (NY) 31 Oct 1/3, Considerable injury, from frost, to the corn crop, is reported in northern Indiana, Illinois, Iowa and the more northern latitudes. In some portions of Iowa an estimate of two-fifths of soft corn is made. **1945** *Chicago Daily News* (IL) 19 Apr 27/2, Today she [=Nebraska] has an estimated 50,000,000 bushels of "soft" (high moisture) corn which has little market value but is relished by livestock. **1968** *DARE* (Qu. I33, *. . Ears of corn that are just right for eating*) Inf **IN**16, Soft corn. **2004** MN Univ. Ext. Serv. *MN Crop eNews* (Internet), The term "soft corn" has been used to describe grain of frosted corn plants and implies that very little drying occurs after the killing frost.

2 A variety of **Indian corn 1** (*Zea mays* var *amylacea*) with kernels high in soft starch.

1884 Sturtevant *Maize* 1 **NY,** Soft corn seems first to have been described as Tuscarora. *Ibid* 2, *Soft corn*—the chit and visible starch constituting the whole structure, no corneous matter being present. **1902** Bailey *Cyclop. Horticult.* 4.2004, Brazilian Flour Corn sold by seedsmen is a type of the Soft Corn. **2001** *DARE* File—Internet **NEng** (as of 17th cent), There was also grown in the northeast [of New England] another type of corn called flour or soft corn. This variety has a softer inner starch which makes it easier for grinding into meal.

soft crab See **soft-shell crab**

soft-crab gull n Also *soft-shell gull* [See quots]
=**laughing gull.**

1968 *DARE* (Qu. Q10, *. . Water birds and marsh birds*) Inf **MD**36, Soft-crab gull—small, black, eats soft crabs. **1970** *DARE* FW Addit **seVA,** Soft-shell gull: laughing gull—because it eats soft-shell crabs. **2001** MD Ornith. Soc. *MD Yellowthroat* Mar–Apr 6 (Internet) **eVA, eMD,** In the old days there's [sic] was but one gull in summer and that was the Cacklin' Gull, called Soft Crab Gull, too.

soft flag n
=**cattail 1.**

1959 Munz–Keck *CA Flora* 1367, *T[ypha] latifolia.* . . Soft-Flag. . . Freshwater Marsh; throughout Calif. below 5000 ft; to Alaska, Atlantic Coast. **2001** *DARE* File—Internet **eCA,** Cat Tail/Soft Flag—*Typha latifolia*—Rhizomes can be dried and ground into flour.

soft maple n Also *soft-leaf(ed) maple* **chiefly wNEng, Upstate NY, nPA, N Cent, Upper Missip Valley** See Map on p. 112 Cf **hard maple**
Any of several maples with soft wood, usu **red maple** or **silver maple.**

[**1778** Carver *Travels N. Amer.* 496, The Maple. Of this tree there are two sorts, the hard and the soft, both of which yield a luscious juice, from which the Indians by boiling make very good sugar.] **1812** Michaux *Histoire des Arbres* 2.210, *Red Flowring Maple.* . . On donne à cet arbre différens noms dans les États-Unis: à l'est des monts Alléghanys, on le nomme *Red flowring maple,* . . *Swamp maple,* . . *Soft maple,* . . et à l'ouest des montagnes, *Maple tree.* [=*Red Flowering Maple.* . . This tree is given different names in the United States: east of the Alleghany mountains, it is called *Red flowering maple,* . . *Swamp maple,* . . *Soft maple,* . . and west of the mountains, *Maple tree.*] **1822** Eaton *Botany* 153, [*Acer*] *rubrum* . . red maple, soft maple. . . Large tree. **1832** MA Hist. Soc. *Coll.* 2d ser 9.146 **cwVT,** *Acer rubrum,* Red maple; soft maple. **1897** Sudworth *Arborescent Flora* 284 **UT,** *Acer glabrum.* . . Soft Maple. *Ibid* 287, *Acer saccharinum.* . . Soft Maple. *Ibid* 290, *Acer rubrum.* . . Soft Maple. **1898** *Jrl. Amer. Folkl.* 11.225 **WA,** *Acer macrophyllum.* . . soft maple, Pierce Co[unty]. **1941** *LANE* Map 247 **NEng,** Terms denoting other varieties of maples [than sugar maple]. . . *Soft maple* [7 infs, one of whom identifies it with sugar maple]. **1965–70** *DARE* (Qu. T14, *. . Kinds of maples*) 287 Infs, **chiefly wNEng, Upstate NY, nPA, N Cent, Upper Missip Valley,** Soft maple; **CO**9, Soft-leafed maple; **NY**75, Cut-leaf soft maple—weed tree; **WA**3, Soft-leaf maple; (Qu. T3, *The tree that produces syrup and sugar*) 20 Infs, **chiefly N Cent,** Soft maple; (Qu. T15, *. . Kinds of swamp trees*)

Infs **CT**4, 13, 17, **MA**42, **NY**84, 150, 233, Soft maple; (Qu. T16, . . *Kinds of trees . . 'special'*) Infs **IN**26, **MI**26, Soft maple. **1968** *DARE* Tape **IN**36, I've got a few soft maples scattered through the woods, . . and I always tap 'em. They run just as much water and taste just sweet as the other. **1973** Allen *LAUM* 1.335 (as of c1950), 7 infs, 6 **IA, MN,** Soft maple; 1 inf, **MN,** Soft maple: Not tapped. **1989** Mosher *Stranger* 65 **nVT** (as of 1952), He overturned a dead limb that had dropped off the soft maple tree behind us. **2003** *St. Louis Post–Dispatch* (MO) 12 Oct Travel sec 7 (Internet), In central Illinois, the soft maples are just starting to turn a pale green.

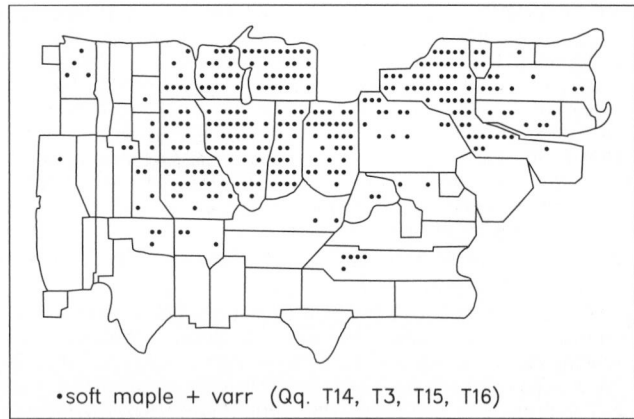

•soft maple + varr (Qq. T14, T3, T15, T16)

soft oyster n Cf **hard oyster**

An **oyster B1** (here: *Dendrostrea frons*).

1881 Ingersoll *Oyster-Industry* 248, Soft Oyster.—The "Virginia plant," or southern oyster (Staten Island sound), as distinguished from the "hard" native oyster.

soft peach n chiefly **S Midl,** esp **sAppalachians**
=**freestone 2.**

1823 *Republican Compiler* (Gettysburg PA) [22 Oct 3]/4 (newspaperarchive.com) **VA,** A soft peach has ripened its fruit twice this year in a garden near this city. **1903** *DN* 2.331 **seMO,** *Soft-peach.* . . Freestone peach. **1907** *DN* 3.236 **nwAR,** *Soft-peach.* . . Freestone peach. **1909** *DN* 3.372 **eAL, wGA,** *Sof(t)-peach.* . . Freestone peach. See *clear-seed.* **1915** *DN* 4.190 **swVA,** *Soft peach.* . . The freestone peach. **1949** Kurath *Word Geog.* fig 130 *(Freestone peach),* [There are 103 instances of *soft peach,* 67 in **VA,** 27 in **NC,** 4 in **GA,** 2 in **MD,** 2 in **SC,** and 1 in **WV.**] [*DARE* Ed: This information was compiled before 9 addit interviews were done in SC and 40 in GA.] **c1960** *Wilson Coll.* **csKY,** *Freestone peach* . . also open or soft peach. **1967–70** *DARE* (Qu. I51, *The kind of a peach where the hard center is loose*) Infs **MO**8, **OH**67, **VA**42, 56, Soft (peach). **1972** *PADS* 58.21 **cwAL,** *Freestone peach.* . . *Mellow peach* (1 [inf]), Virginia Piedmont *soft peach* (1), and Coastal Southern *open-seed* (1) also occur. **1973** Allen *LAUM* 1.306 **NE** (as of c1950), One Nebraskan has the Virginia Piedmont *soft peach.* **1986** Pederson *LAGS Concordance* *(Freestone peach)* 13 infs, **Gulf Region,** Soft peach(es).

soft pie n esp **NEng**

A pie with a soft filling and no top crust.

1874 *Oneida Circular* 11.208, I . . made one mental resolution—either to eat my pie at the table, especially custard, or ask for it at other times like a man, . . and above all things never to put soft pie into pantaloons' pockets! **1893** *Daily Rev.* (Decatur IL) [5 Feb 3]/3 (newspaperarchive.com), No genuine soft pies, such as cocoanut or lemon, are being made by the bakers now on account of that variety requiring eggs in their make-up. **1959** *VT Hist.* 27.158, *Soft pie.* . . A pie with a smooth, creamy filling, such as lemon or chocolate. Occasional. **1967** *DARE* (Qu. H63, *Kinds of desserts*) Inf **CO**11, Soft pies—lemon, etc. **1973** *DARE* File **cnMA,** In the old days when we used to have church sociables . . some would be asked to bring apple or mince and others to bring *soft pies*—that would be an *open pie,* custard or lemon or squash usually, and with a meringue on top. **1986** *Ibid* **cwMA,** Soft pie—A pie without top crust—e.g., cream pies. **2003** *Ibid* **nwMA,** Grandma . . said "a soft pie is something like a custard pie, one without a top crust."

soft pine n Cf **hard pine**

Any of var **pines 1** such as *Pinus strobus* or *P. monticola* with soft, easily worked wood.

1876 *U.S. Dept. Ag. Rept. of Secy. for 1875* 180 **CA,** *Pinus monticola.* . . Soft Pine. **1897** Sudworth *Arborescent Flora* 13 **PA,** *Pinus strobus.* . . Soft Pine. *Ibid* 15 **CA,** *Pinus monticola.* . . Soft Pine. **1908** Rogers *Tree Book* 22, The "soft pines" have soft, light wood, with little resin, easy to work—the carpenter's delight. The principal ones are *P[inus] Strobus,* in the North and East, *P. Lambertiana,* of the Pacific coast, and two Rocky Mountain species, *P. monticola* and *P. flexilis.* **1950** Moore *Trees AR* 16, Shortleaf Pine. . . Local Names . . Arkansas Soft Pine [etc]. *Ibid* 17, Loblolly Pine. . . Arkansas Soft, Longleaf Pine. **1965–70** *DARE* (Qu. T17, . . *Kinds of pine trees;* not asked in early QRs) 13 Infs, **chiefly N Cent, NEng,** Soft pine; **MA**40, Pitch pine—same as soft pine; [**TN**65, Soft southern pine;] (Qu. T8, *Joints of pine wood that burn easily and make good fuel*) Inf **IL**16, Soft pine. **1974** (1977) Coon *Useful Plants* 208, *Pinus strobus* . . soft pine. . . It was a tree important in the development of the thirteen colonies, when the giant trees were cut for masts for the British navy, and always since, it has been a source of an easily worked, soft, white wood. **2004** *Austin Amer.–Statesman* (TX) 15 May sec F 1 (Internet), Central Texas builders, who mostly use southern soft pine plywood, pay slightly cheaper prices.

soft-shell n

1 See **soft-shell turtle.**
2 See **soft-shell Baptist.**
3 See **soft-shell crawfish.**
4 See **soft-shell crab.**
5 See **soft-shell clam.**

soft-shell Baptist n Also *soft-shell* Cf *hard-shell Baptist* (at **hard-shell** adj 2), **Primitive Baptist**

See quots 1872, 1983.

1845 *Knickerbocker* 26.285, They have singular denominational distinctions in the west, among which the '*Hard and Soft Shell Baptists*' are most remarkable. . . A 'Hard-Shell' recently turned a 'Soft-Shell' out of church [because he had joined a temperance society]. **1867** *Harper's New Mth. Mag.* 36.54, You didn't mention . . whether he was a hard or soft shell Baptist. **1871** Eggleston *Hoosier Schoolmaster* 121 **sIN,** I don't know whether you're a Hardshell or a Softshell . . or a Millerite. **1872** Schele de Vere *Americanisms* 241, Such are the *Soft Shell* Baptists, so called on account of their less stern manners and less rigid principles, which allow them to be indulgent to certain worldly usages, and to educate their ministers carefully for the pulpit. **1893** Frederic *Copperhead* 65 **nNY,** The travelling preachers who came to us represented these great sects, with lots of minute shadings off into Hard-shell, Soft-shell, Freewill, and other subdivided mysteries which I never understood. **1945** *Chicago Tribune* (IL) 10 Aug sec 1 9/3 **KY,** The Rev. Scott Hall, 94, 'Soft-shell' Baptist minister . . died last night. **1983** *MJLF* 9.1.56 **ceKY** (as of 1956), Softshell Baptists . . all Baptists not Primitive Baptists. . . Softshells . . Softshell Baptists. **1986** Pederson *LAGS Concordance,* 1 inf, **cAR,** Soft-Shell (Baptists); 1 inf, **cTN,** Soft-Shell Baptist. **2006** *DARE* File—Internet, You should try the P[rimitive] B[aptist] church. If it is hard-shell, there will be no musical instruments, only voices, and the preaching will be unscripted. I know of hardly any PB churches that allow instruments, but that's not to say there aren't a few soft-shell out there that have incorporated them into worship services.

soft-shell clam n Also *soft clam, soft-shell(ed clam)* **chiefly N and C Atl** See Map Cf **gosling clam, hinge ~**

A clam of the genus *Mya,* usu the orig Atlantic *M. arenaria.* For other names of this sp see **butterfish 4, long clam 1, maninose, mud clam 1, piss ~, sand ~ 1, squirt ~, steamer ~ 1, stem ~;** for other names of *M. truncata* see **sea clam b**

1782 Crèvecoeur *Letters* 135 **Nantucket MA,** The shores of this island abound with the soft-shelled, the hard-shelled, and the great sea clams. **1806** (1904) Roe *Diary* 25 **NY,** I . . got Sum Soft Clams. **1855** *Knickerbocker* 46.222 **NJ,** Along the strand, . . those great delicacies, 'soft clams' and sand-crabs may be found. **1902** *Jrl. Amer. Folkl.* 15.247 **MD,** *Mananosay.* . . A name given in Maryland, etc., to the soft-shelled clam *(Mya arenaria).* **1939** *LANE* Map 235 *(Round clam)* 5 infs, **CT, MA, RI,** Softshell clam. **1954** Abbott *Amer. Seashells* 455, *Mya truncata.* . . Truncate Soft-shell Clam. **1965–70** *DARE* (Qu. P18, . . *Kinds of shellfish*) Infs **MD**15, 36, 40, 42, **VA**79, **RI**4, Soft-shell clam(s); **MA**55, A lot of people call a quahog a hard-shell clam and the regular clam that they steam a soft-shell clam; **NJ**22, **NY**47, **VA**47, Soft clams. **1966–70** *DARE* Tape **ME**24, [FW:] What kind of clams they get around here? [Inf:] I think they call 'em soft-shell clams. . . The

Maryland clams are sort of a harder shell than what we have around here; **VA**55, They ain't but two kinds . . a clam, and a butterfish we dig out the bottom. . . Some calls 'em mannoses, but what they're generally called is soft-shell. **1975** Gould *ME Lingo* 168, *Long neck*—The true Maine clam, also called the soft shell. **1976** Warner *Beautiful Swimmers* 174 **Chesapeake Bay,** For many years the soft or steamer clam was neglected and even despised in the Chesapeake. **1989** Mickelson *Nat. Hist.* 26 **AK,** Common clams (based on a sampling in Montague Straits) include: butter, softshell and little-neck clams [etc]. **2004** *NY Times* (NY) 21 July sec F 1/2 (Internet), Soft-shells are more elongated, and you can easily crack them open with your fingers; they are steamed whole or shucked and deep-fried.

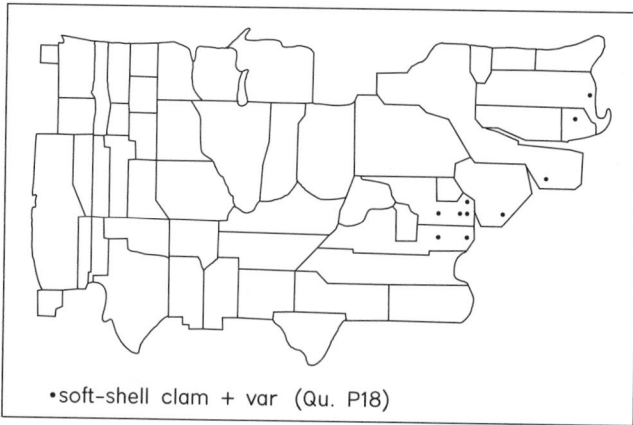

•soft-shell clam + var (Qu. P18)

soft-shell cockle n

A **littleneck 2** (here: *Protothaca tenerrima*).

1920 CA Fish & Game Comm. *Fish Bulletin* 4.38, In the Los Angeles markets they [=hard-shell cockles of the genus *Chione*] rank next after the Pismo and rock cockle (*Paphia* [=*Protothaca*]) in importance and there are known as hard-shell cockles in contrast to the more brittle *Paphia* which is called a soft-shell or paper-shell cockle.

soft-shell cooter n   Also *soft-shelled cooter*

=**soft-shell turtle.**

1915 *Brooklyn Museum Qrly.* 2.237 **seGA,** Deer, raccoons, opossums, rabbits, squirrels, fish, soft-shelled 'cooters' (turtles), . . and many of the larger water birds are secured for the table. **1942** Rawlings *Cross Creek* 227 **nFL,** The soft-shell cooter is a flat fellow, like a flounder, an enormous brown pancake. The outer rim of his shell is a soft gristle, and when prepared like the meat itself, cooks to the texture of gum drops, and is of a flavor to make you eat until you are weak and faint from surfeit. **1986** Pederson *LAGS Concordance* **Gulf Region,** 4 infs, Soft-shell cooter(s); 1 inf, Soft-shelled cooter. **2005** *DARE* File—Internet **swGA,** Henry, I'm gonna double-check, but I'm purty sure softshell cooters are legal to take.

soft-shell crab n   Also *soft (crab), soft-shell(ed crab), softy* **chiefly Delmarva, N Atl**   See Map   Cf **hard-shell crab**

A newly molted crab (here: usu the blue crab, *Callinectes sapidus*) whose shell has not yet begun to harden.

1772 in 1906 *William & Mary Qrly.* 1st ser 14.38, Like the shell of a soft crab, the body of the crab after the shell is off seems by much too large for the shell. **1817** Acad. Nat. Sci. Philadelphia *Jrl.* 1.5.66, The shell is cast annually, generally in the spring, and they are then known by the name of soft-shell crab, are very delicate, and in particular request for the table. **1879** U.S. Natl. Museum *Bulletin* 14.261 **MA,** "Soft-shelled" (in certain stages only) crab (*Callinectes hastatus* [=*C. sapidus*] Say). Vineyard Sound. **1884** Goode *Fisheries U.S.* 1.776, The terms "Soft Crab," "Paper-shell," and "Buckler" denote the different stages of consistency of the shell, from the time of shedding until it has become nearly hard again. For instance, immediately after shedding it is a "Soft Crab." **1899** (1912) Green *VA Folk-Speech* 401, *Soft-crab.* **1904** *DN* 2.396 **MA,** *Fat.* . . The crabber's name for a soft-shell crab, or one which has shed its shell and is covered only with a thin, tender skin. **1933** Hench Coll. **seVA,** The closer to the actual act of "busting" a crab can be caught, the better he is as a soft-shell crab. **1965–70** *DARE* (Qu. H45, *Dishes made with meat, fish, or poultry that everybody around here would know, but that people in other places might not*) Inf **VA**48, Fried soft-shell crabs; **MD**37, Soft-shelled crabs; **NY**43, Fried

soft crabs; **MD**8, Soft crabs—without hard shell after animals slough; **MD**50, Soft crabs, broiled or fried; (Qu. P18, . . *Kinds of shellfish*) Infs **MD**15, **NJ**67, 69, **NY**1, 132, 151, Soft-shell crab(s). **1966–70** *DARE* Tape **DE**2, Paperbacks are just a stage in between a soft-shell and a hard-shell; **MD**15, You take a hard crab. Every two-three months he'll shed, during the summer season. But he goes from a hard crab to a peeler. Then a peeler is when he's first began to make a new crab within his shell. Then he becomes a buster. That's about the time he's supposed to crack out of his old shell as a soft crab; **MD**43, And then we have what we call the rank peeler. . . That's the last stage before it's a soft crab; **NC**1, The soft crab, they just fry them; **VA**47, The soft crabs . . you can find anytime in different places; **VA**112, They . . have a crab trap . . that catches these little peelers that sheds out to become soft-shell crabs. **1984** *DARE* File **Chesapeake Bay** [Watermen's vocab], Soft crabs / softs / softies. **1994** *Ibid* **DE,** Crabs molt about once a month— that's where soft crabs come from.

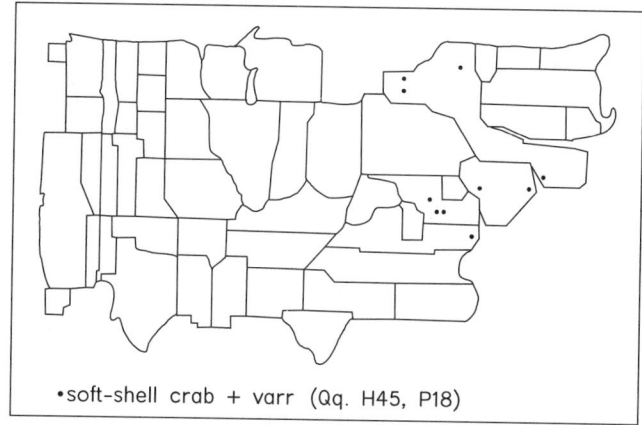

•soft-shell crab + varr (Qq. H45, P18)

soft-shell crawfish n   Also *soft-shell(ed crab)*   Cf **crab n 1**

A newly molted **crawfish n B1.**

1917 Katz *Kinks* 120, Black bass strike at different baits . . helgramites, soft shell crawfish, angleworms, minnows [etc]. **1926** *News* (Frederick MD) 30 July 8/1, Here's a list of the food these fish like best. . . Catfish—angleworms, liver, tail of a soft-shell crawfish. **1956** Harlan–Speaker *IA Fish* 175, It is immediately after shedding its armor that the helpless animal [=a crawfish] is known as a "soft-shell", and at this time it is at its best for bait. **1968** *DARE* (Qu. P18, . . *Kinds of shellfish*) Inf **WI**61, Soft-shelled crabs; (Qu. P19, . . *Small, freshwater crayfish*) Inf **PA**168, Crab—soft-shell, hard-shell. **1985** Madson *Up River* 103 **Upper Missip Valley,** Each of the other two lines was armed with a single hook that was baited with live "softshell" crawfish that Tar and I had captured the day before in a clear, rockstrewn feeder creek. **2001** *DARE* File—Internet **cnOH,** Softshell crawfish are only available from May until they go under in the first half of October.

soft-shelled clam   See **soft-shell clam**

soft-shelled cooter   See **soft-shell cooter**

soft-shelled crab n

1   See **soft-shell crab.**

2   See **soft-shell crawfish.**

soft-shelled hickory   See **soft-shell hickory**

soft-shelled tortoise (or turtle)   See **soft-shell turtle**

soft-shell gull   See **soft-crab gull**

soft-shell hickory n   Also *soft-shelled hickory*   Cf **hard-shell hickory, iron ball (hickory nut)**

A **hickory n B1** such as the **pecan B1.**

1865 *Horticulturist & Jrl. Rural Art* 20.390 **OH,** The profit of growing chestnuts and soft-shell hickory nuts . . is equal to that of peaches or apples. **1883** *Hist. Marion Co. OH* 278 **cOH** (as of 1820s), When the soft-shelled hickory-nuts were plenty, the deer would chiefly subsist on them. **1900** Lyons *Plant Names* 191, *H[icoria] Pecan* [=*Carya illinoensis*]. . . Soft-shell Hickory. **1969** *DARE* (Qu. T16, . . *Kinds of trees . . 'special'*) Inf **KY**47, Soft-shelled hickory. **2002** *DARE* File— Internet **seNY,** I have a question regarding a soft shelled hickory nut tree. . . It has never produced nuts and my father believes it was due to the lightening strike.

soft-shell turtle n Also *soft-back turtle, soft-shell (terrapin), soft-shelled tortoise, ~ turtle, soft turtle* Cf **hard-shell turtle**
Std: a freshwater turtle of the genus *Trionyx*. For other names of var spp see **king turtle, leatherback 2, mud turtle 2d, queen turtle, soft-shell cooter**

softy See **soft-shell crab**

sofy See **sofa**

sog v [Engl dial]
1 To soak with water, make sodden; to remain sodden; hence ppl adjs *sogged, sogging, water-sog(ged); adj phr sogging wet* soaked, sodden. **scattered, but esp Sth, S Midl** See Map Cf **sob** v
  1837 *ME Mth. Mag.* 1.158, His corn was cut off in the milk; his potatoes sogged in the boiling, for the frost nipped them yet unripe. **1851** *Horticulturist & Jrl. Rural Art* 6.502 **NEast,** Great care should be taken not to over-water. . . If given, the roots become sogged or rotten. **1864** in 1894 U.S. War Dept. *War of Rebellion* 1st ser 45.2.296 **VA,** Pursuing an enemy . . over mud roads, completely sogged with heavy rains, is no child's play. **1896** *Overland Mth.* (2d ser) 27.66 **NE,** He had seen it parched by drought, and sogged by rain. **1909** *DN* 3.373 **eAL, wGA,** *Sog. . .* To saturate with water, etc. Used especially in the *pp.* "We were all completely sogged by the rain." *Sogging. . .* Saturated. "Our clothes were sogging." As *adv.* often in the phrase 'sogging wet.' *Ibid* 387 **eAL, wGA,** *Water-sogged. . .* Water-soaked. **1965–70** *DARE* Qu. KK56, *Wood that is heavy from being in water a long time: It's _____*) 37 Infs, **scattered, but esp Sth, S Midl,** Water-sogged; **SC**10, Water-sog; **CA**117, Water-sogged log; **KY**83, **TX**51, **VA**69, Sogged. **2003** *DARE* File nwMA (as of c1960), His rubber boots had holes in them so his socks were sogging wet. This was a common term in our house when I was growing up. I can remember my mother saying, "Don't leave that wet bathing suit on the floor to sog all day, hang it on the line." I still use the word today. **2004** *St. Petersburg Times* (FL) 16 Sept 1 (Internet), Water sogged the sands off Eldorado Avenue but stopped just short of waterfront houses. **2006** *Pittsburgh Tribune–Rev.* (PA) 9 Nov (Internet), The turkey, stuffing and potatoes were swimming in gravy. . . [T]he liquified salt lick sogged everything.

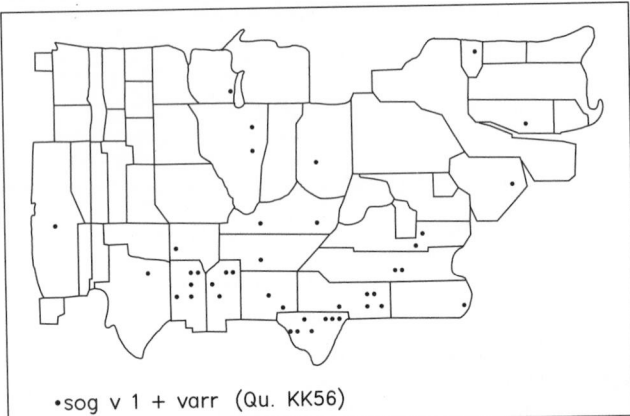

•sog v 1 + varr (Qu. KK56)

2 To smolder. Cf **sodle**
  1857 Duganne *Tenant-House* 154 **NEast,** These rags, in a vile accumulation, had sogged and burned, with smothered fire. **1858** (1859) Beecher *Notes Plymouth Pulpit* xxxii **seNY,** What wonder that he who is so vivid there [=in the pulpit] *should* sometimes sog and smolder, when the excitement of his work is over. **1933** *AmSp* 8.1.52 **Ozarks,** *Sog. . .* When a stick of wood doesn't burn properly, but just turns black and smoulders, it is said to *sog. That 'ar ellum wood aint no good—hit'll jest kinder sog on ye.* **1954** *Harder Coll.* **cwTN,** *Sog. . .* of wood; to smoulder from being green or wet.

sog n [swEngl dial] **ME** *arch*
A state of lethargy or stupor.
  1810 *Trial David Lynn* 75 **ME,** *Q.* How was his mind? . . *A.* . . He would lie in a sog, and then rouse up. **1870** Kellogg *Young Ship-Builders* 302 **ME,** When Ben was first taken sick, he had a high fever; then he was out of his head; after that he went into a sog. **1881** *Atlantic Mth.* 48.21 **ME,** "How does he seem to be?" "Laying in a sog. . . The doctor says there ain't much he can do." **1885** *Lippincott's Mag.* new

ser 10.101 **ME,** "Good-evenin', gentlemen," said the captain, rising quickly as we entered. "I was settin' here in a sog like, and didn't hear ye." [**1892** *DN* 1.211 **seMA,** *Soggy:* comatose (of a dying person).] **1908** Day *King Spruce* 269 **ME,** "He was in a sog when I put him to bed," said the cook. "Didn't know what, who, or where. They say lunatics want to be woke up careful."

sogdollager See **sockdolager**

soger See **soldier**

sogged, sogging (wet) See **sog** v **1**

soggum See **sorghum**

sogin See **sugan**

sogrum, sogum See **sorghum**

so-gun See **sugan**

soil n[1], v Pronc-sp *sile* Similarly adj *sily* Cf Pronc Intro 3.I.11, **hoist, join, joist 1**
Std senses, var forms.
  1818 Fessenden *Ladies Monitor* 172 **NEng,** Provincial words . . to be avoided. . . *sile* for soil. **1841** *Spirit of Times* 27 Mar 42 **AR,** He beat up some eggs into Sam Walker's Sunday hat, and brought them out fine pan-cakes, and never siled her. **1851** Burke *Polly Peablossom* 117 **KY,** There ain't no rock down in them rich sily bottoms in our parts. **1858** Hammett *Piney Woods Tavern* 44, Ef thar hadn't been sile enough *in* his fat chops to hev raised the crap [=crop], thar wer a plenty outside. **1867** Lowell *Biglow* 21 **'Upcountry' MA,** Quallerties o' heart an' intellec'/ Peculiar to Columby's sile, an' not to one one else's. **1893** Shands *MS Speech* 11, Negroes and illiterate whites. . . [saɪl] for *soil.* **1899** (1912) Green *VA Folk-Speech* 387, *Sile. . .* A variant of *soil.* **1923** *DN* 5.221 **swMO,** *Sile. . .* Soil. **1928** *AmSp* 3.404 **Ozarks** (as of 1916–27), In such words as *spoil, soil, hoist, . . .* and *join* the *oi* takes the sound of long *i—spile, sile, hist, . . .* and *jine.* **1991** *Macoupin Co. Enquirer* (Carlinville IL) 3 Jan 6/3, [From a 1961 issue quoting "oldsters":] Farmers harred ground until the sile was meller.

soil n[2] [Pronc-sp for *sorrel*]
  1965–70 *DARE* (Qu. K37, . . *A horse of mixed colors*) Inf **MD**18, Checky soil [ˈčɛki ˌsɔɪl]—gray mixed with sorrel [ˈsɔrl] [*DARE* Ed: Note std pronc in stressed position.]; **TN**53, Chestnut soil; (Qu. K39, . . *Names . . for horses according to their colors*) Inf **TN**53, Chestnut soil; **DE**1, Soil [ˈsɔɪəl]; **MS**60, Soil horse.

sois See **so as**

soitain See **certain**

soitainly See **certainly**

sojer See **soldier**

sol n Also *old sol* [Abbr for *solitaire*]
A game, esp a card game, that requires only a single player; the game personified.
  1909 *Chicago Tribune* (IL) 11 Apr sec F 8/6, The game of solitaire, where the player or "Old Sol" wins or loses, is fascinating. **1966–68** *DARE* (Qu. DD35, . . *Card games*) Infs **TX**42, **VA**3, Sol; **SC**40, Double sol, single sol; **OK**25, Old sol; (Qu. DD37, . . *Table games played a lot by adults*) Inf **OK**25, Sol—domino game for one player. **1977** Taylor *Miro District* 22 **TN,** He . . wasn't on the wicker settee in the sun parlor, with a game of old sol going on the cushion beside him. **1996** *DARE* File csWI (as of c1970), My mother always called the game of solitaire "sol"; double solitaire was "double sol." If she failed to win a game of solitaire, she would complain that "the cat got it" or "Old Sol got it." **2005** *DARE* File—Internet, Oh well, I guess it's time to get back to beating old Sol.

sold See **soul**

solder n, v Usu |ˈsadə(r), ˈsɔdə(r)|; sp-pronc |ˈsaldə|; rarely |ˈsɔrdə| Pronc-spp *sawder, sodda, sodder*
Std senses, var forms.
  1806 (1970) Webster *Compendious Dict.* 283, Sod'der or Sol'der, *n.* . . Sod'der, *v.t.* to unite by sodder. **1836** (1838) Haliburton *Clockmaker* (1st ser) 78, The *'soft sawder'* of the Clockmaker had operated effectually on the beauty of Amherst, our lovely hostess. **1847** *Scientific Amer.* 3.45, There will be no difficulty in causing the adhesion of tin or soft sodder. **1852** in 1956 Eliason *Tarheel Talk* 296 **NC,** I speak a little of their [Eliason: Irish laborers] brogue . . and can by a little soft sodda get

them make [sic] the dust fly. **1871** Eggleston *Hoosier Schoolmaster* 118 **sIN,** You don't come no gum games over me with your saft sodder. **1875** *Scribner's Mth.* 10.441 **NEng,** I'd git some tin things, an' have 'em soddered on. **1903** *DN* 2.328 **seMO,** *Sawder. . . Solder.* **1907** *DN* 3.235 **nwAR,** *Sawder. . . Solder.* **1942** Hall *Smoky Mt. Speech* 88 **wNC, eTN,** *Solder* varies ['sɔdɚ], ['sɔɚdɚ], ['sɑldɚ]. **c1960** *Wilson Coll.* **csKY,** *Solder* /'sɔdɚ, 'sɔrdɚ/. **1969** *DARE* Tape **GA**72, Quite often we use a condenser, which is two sections of copper welded or soldered ['sɑldɚd] together. **2005** *DARE* File—Internet **cFL,** I can sodder a wire, that's about it.

soldier *n, v* Pronc-spp *sodger, sodjuh, soger, sojer*

A Forms.

1825 [see **C** below]. **1834** Caruthers *Kentuckian* 1.12 **MD** [Black], I smokes the old sodgers what the gentlemen throws on the bar-room floor. **1840** [see **B**1 below]. **1847** Hurd *Grammatical Corrector* 89, *Soldier* ["incorrect" pronc = ['soʲɚ]; "correct" pronc = ['soljɚ]]. **1862** (1864) Browne *Artemus Ward Book* 95, At Camp Scott there was a lot of U.S. sojers. **1890** [see **B**1 below]. **1890** [see **C** below]. **1892** [see **C** below]. **1922** Gonzales *Black Border* 327 **sSC, GA coasts** [Gullah glossary], *Sodjuh . . soldier, soldiers; soldiering, etc.* **1929** (1951) Faulkner *Sartoris* 5 **MS,** He never even had on no sojer-clothes. **1937** NE Univ. *Univ. Studies* 37.113 [Terms from play-party songs], *Sojer. . .* (Negroism.) Soldier. "A bull frog dressed in sojer's clo'es." **1968** **B**7 below]. **2004** *Frontline* (Television Program), There's a term in the Army that's not always used as a form of praise, calling somebody a "muddy boots sojer."

B As noun.

1 also *old soldier:* A malingerer; a shirker; a loafer; hence v phr *play soldier* to sham illness.

1840 (1841) Dana *2 Yrs.* 154, The captain called him a "soger," and promised to "ride him down as he would the main tack." [Footnote:] *Soger* (soldier) is the worst term of reproach that can be applied to a sailor. It signifies a *skulk,* a *sherk,*—one who is always trying to get clear of work, and is out of the way, or hanging back, when duty is to be done. **1890** *DN* 1.79 **neMA,** *Sojer. . . An old soldier* = a person that shirks work, is common in Salem and Beverly. **1898** [see **C** below]. **1967** *DARE* (Qu. BB27, *When somebody pretends to be sick . . he's* _____) Inf **AL**26, Playing soldier.

2 pl; also *Virginia soldiers:* A **stickseed 1a** (here: *Hackelia virginiana*).

1892 *Jrl. Amer. Folkl.* 5.101 **eMA,** *Echinospermum Virginicum* [= *Hackelia virginiana*], soldiers. **1940** Clute *Amer. Plant Names* 67, *L[appula] Virginiana* [=*Hackelia virginiana*] . . Virginia mouse-ear, — soldiers.

3 pl: =**buckhorn plantain.**

1897 *Jrl. Amer. Folkl.* 10.53 **MA,** *Plantago lanceolata. . .* soldiers, Cambridge, Mass.

4 An unidentified woodpecker.

1904 Fountain *Gt. North-West* 224 **OH,** A bird known locally [in Ohio] as "the marshal", and sometimes "the soldier". . . It is a very gaudy woodpecker with a great deal of scarlet in the colour of its plumage.

5 =**mayfly 1.** Cf **Canadian soldier 1**

1929 *Chron.–Telegram* (Elyria OH) 10 July 1/3, *Lake Cities Are Invaded By "Soldiers" . .* Riding a brisk wind off the lake, millions upon millions of "Canadian soldiers" or may flies today invaded lake shore cities. **1968** *DARE* (Qu. R4, *A large winged insect that hatches in summer in great numbers around lakes or rivers, crowds around lights, lives only a day or so, and is good fish bait*) Inf **OH**87, Soldiers.

6 A **black-eyed Susan.**

1968 *DARE* (Qu. S7, *A kind of daisy, bright yellow with a dark center, that grows along roadsides in late summer*) Inf **MD**36, Soldiers—same as black-eyed Susan.

7 A **raspberry B.**

1968 *DARE* Tape **IN**36, Then up north the house here I had a good big patch of purple—called soldiers [souʲɚz]—raspberries. That's a cross between the red and the black.

C As verb.

To malinger; to shirk; to loaf; hence vbl n *soldiering*—in phr *go soldiering* to sham illness. **chiefly Nth, N Midl, West** See Map *somewhat old-fash* Cf **soldier B1**

1825 Neal *Brother Jonathan* 2.39 **CT,** Is he sick—or is he gwyin' a

sojerin'? **1830** Ames *Mariner's Sketches* 193 **MA,** The number of officers on the Doctor's list amounted to more than one third of their original number, while the men were less favored, though many of them as well as officers 'shammed Abraham' or 'sogered' as it was called, to get out of the weather. **1840** (1841) Dana *2 Yrs.* 32, There is no time to be lost—no "sogering," or hanging back. **1872** Twain *Roughing It* 529, He used to . . keep an eye on his subjects at work for him and see that there was no "soldiering" done. **1890** *DN* 1.19 **seNH,** *Sojer:* loiter, lounge, shirk work, waste time. Common throughout New England. Even a horse that lags in the traces and throws an undue share of the work on his mate, is said to 'sojer' (or even to 'soldier'). **1892** *DN* 1.218 **seMA,** *Sojer. . . Soldiering* = shirking, used of a horse that makes his mate do more than a fair share of work. Plymouth, Mass. **1898** (1899) Warman *Story RR* 96 **West,** If a man is caught soldiering, he is jacked up. . . As a parting shot to the discharged man, he advises him to buy a drum if he wants to be a soldier. **1903** *Boston Herald* (MA) 17 May 4/1, These physicians were appointed . . for the ostensible purpose of preventing 'soldiering' among employes. **1905** *DN* 3.95 **nwAR,** *Soldier. . .* To neglect work. 'We soldiered on him to-day.' **1935** *AmSp* 10.79 [Sailor slang], *Soldier.* Same as *to swing the lead* [="To avoid work, to loaf"]. **1943** *LANE* Map 568 *(Loafing)* **NEng,** [*Soldiering* is widespread throughout the region, as are proncs of the types [souʤɚɪn, souʤɚɪŋ]]. **1965–70** *DARE* (Qu. A9, *. . Wasting time by not working on the job*) 23 Infs, **scattered, but esp Nth, N Midl, West,** Soldiering; **CT**7, Soldiering on the job; (Qu. BB27, *When somebody pretends to be sick . . he's* _____) 15 Infs, **scattered, but esp Nth, N Midl, West,** Soldiering; **MO**6, Soldiering on them; (Qu. A11, *When somebody takes too long about coming to a decision . . "I wish he'd quit* _____.") Inf **CA**113, Soldiering; (Qu. Y21, *To move about slowly and without energy*) Inf **SD**8, Soldier along; (Qu. JJ7, *. . Cheating in school examinations*) Inf **MD**16, Soldiering on the job—not doing his work; (Qu. JJ26, *If somebody has been doing poor work or not enough, the boss might say, "If he wants to keep his job he'd better* _____.") Infs **MI**4, **NJ**20, Quit (*or* stop) soldiering. [33 of 39 total Infs old]

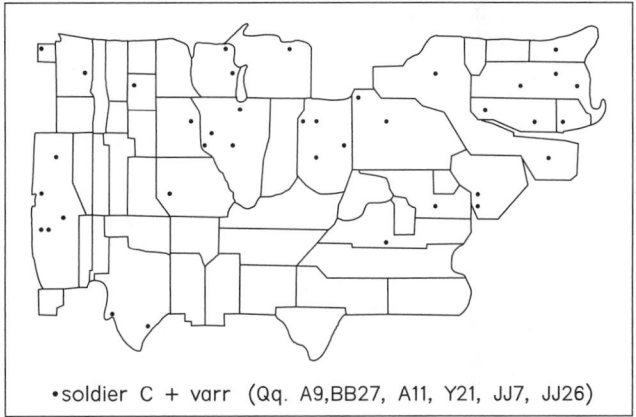

•soldier C + varr (Qq. A9, BB27, A11, Y21, JJ7, JJ26)

soldier bean *n* **chiefly NEng** See Map on p. 116 Cf **pinkeye soldier**

A cultivated bean (*Phaseolus vulgaris* var).

1915 *Bedford Gaz.* (PA) 29 Oct 2/1, Mrs. Sarah J. Bagley, Brittle beans, 38c, Soldier beans. 38c; Yellow Kidney beans, 38c. **1941** O'Donnell *Great Big Doorstep* 62 **sLA** [Black], If Ah evva make greens / Ah'll seddle em down / Wid soldier-beans. **1947** Bowles-Towle *New Engl. Cooking* 77, North Country Baked Soldier Beans. **1965–70** *DARE* (Qu. I17, *Beans . . that are dark red when they are dry*) Infs **MA**58, 72, Soldier bean; **VT**2, Soldier beans—kind of mixed color; (Qu. I18, *The smaller beans that are white when they are dry*) Infs **FL**36, **NC**12, **NH**3, Soldier beans; **RI**1, Soldier beans—from New Hampshire—cook like baked beans; (Qu. I19, *Small white beans with a black spot where they were joined to the pod*) Inf **MA**6, Soldier beans—have red eye; **RI**16, Soldier bean—it's brown where joined, brown spot looks like soldier; (Qu. I20, *. . Kinds of beans*) Infs **ME**20, **NH**16, **VT**16, Soldier beans; **VT**13, Soldier beans—a little larger than pea bean, white with blue spot—for baked beans. **1977** *Yankee* June 68 **ME,** I wanted some Jacob's cattle beans, but I couldn't find any in the market here [=Lynnfield MA]. It was even hard to find a soldier bean. **2001** *DARE* File—Internet, Soldier Bean (a.k.a. European Soldier Bean). . . Well known in early New England, this heirloom bean is great as a baking or soup bean. The name is from the markings near the eye that resembles [sic] an 18th Century European soldier. White with reddish brown markings.

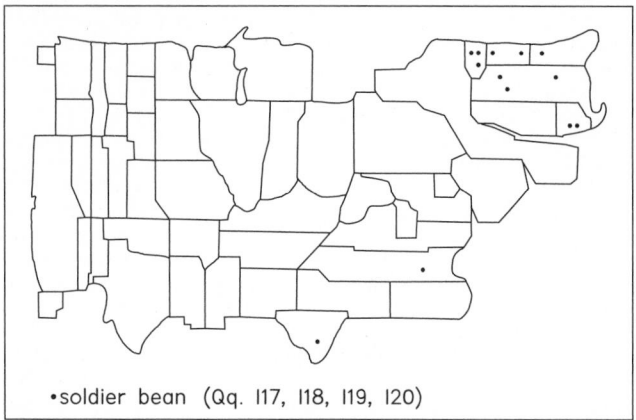

•soldier bean (Qq. I17, I18, I19, I20)

soldier berry n

A **currant B1** (here: *Ribes cereum*).

1927 Garrett *Spring Flora Wasatch* 74 **UT,** *R[ibes] cereum.* . . Locally called Wolf-berry and Soldier berry.

soldier blackbird n   [Because the male has red epaulets]

A **red-winged blackbird** (here: *Agelaius phoeniceus*).

1891 U.S. Natl. Museum *Proc.* 13.572, *Agelaius phoeniceus.* Red-winged Blackbird. Soldier Blackbird. **1901** *Brooklyn Daily Eagle* (NY) 27 Jan 22/6, I saw a soldier blackbird, too, with red epaulets, and I heard a field lark sing. **1917** Bailey *Sand Dunes IN* 134, My coming frightened a whole army of soldier blackbirds into flight. **1938** Rawlings *Yearling* 312 **nFL,** Soldier blackbirds shrilled from the rushes.

soldier crab n

=**fiddler crab.**

1814 in 1815 *Lit. & Philos. Soc. NY Trans.* 1.401, The soldier crab or fiddler, (ocypoda,) will frequently tempt him when he refuses to taste the other [bait]. **1844** DeKay *Zool. NY* 6.14, This species [=*Gelasmius vocans* (=*Uca pugilator*)], occupying oblique holes in marshes near the sea, occurs along our whole Atlantic coast as far as Cape Cod. In its movements . . it carries its enlarged hand raised from the ground, and, upon the slightest alarm, elevates it, and extends the fingers in a menacing attitude. This bold demeanor has doubtless given rise to the name of *Soldier Crab.* **1871** *Harper's New Mth. Mag.* 42.525 **FL,** Upon a long wide beach at low-water we met one of those curious armies of soldier-crabs, or *fiddlers.* A space of several rods was wholly occupied by them, and so closely did they march that their various movements seemed simultaneous, like sardines. **1891** *Century Illustr. Mag.* 42.4 **FL,** The soldier-crabs . . had recovered from their alarm and were crawling over the prostrate fisherman. **1947** *NY Times* (NY) 5 Feb 28/6 **csFL,** He even had a few soldier crabs which, according to Harry Snow, the veteran guide, can be smelled by a bonefish for a dozen yards.

soldier darter   See **soldierfish**

soldier duck n

=**ruddy duck.**

1923 U.S. Dept. Ag. *Misc. Circular* 13.31 **MT,** Ruddy Duck. . . Vernacular names. . . *In local use.* . . little soldier. . . soldier duck.

soldierfish n   Also *soldier darter*   [Perh from the brightly colored bands of the breeding male]

=**rainbow darter.**

1882 U.S. Natl. Museum *Bulletin* 16.517 **Missip Valley,** P[oecilichthys] caeruleus. . . *Blue Darter; Rainbow Darter; Soldier-fish.* **1908** Forbes–Richardson *Fishes of IL* 309, *Etheostoma caeruleum.* . . Rainbow Darter; Soldier-fish. **1943** Eddy–Surber *N. Fishes* 201, Northern Rainbow Darter (Blue Darter, Soldier Fish).

soldiering   See **soldier C**

soldier's cap n

=**Dutchman's breeches 1.**

1897 Britton–Brown *Illustr. Flora* 2.104, *Bicuculla Cucullària.* . . Dutchman's Breeches, Soldier's Cap. **1910** Graves *Flowering Plants* 198 **CT,** *Dicentra Cucullaria.* . . Soldier's Cap [etc]. **1933** Small *Manual SE Flora* 550, Soldier's-cap. . . Rich woods, Blue Ridge and Appala-

chian provinces in the S[outh], various provinces in the N[orth], Ga. to Nebr., Minn., and Ont.

soldiers' feathers   See **feather** n **B4**

soldier's plume n

A **fringed orchid** (here: *Platanthera psycodes*).

1848 in 1850 Cooper *Rural Hours* 168 **ceNY,** The handsome, large purple-fringed orchis is also found here. . . The country people call it soldier's plume. **1894** *Jrl. Amer. Folkl.* 7.100 **NY,** *Habenaria psycodes,* . . soldier's plume. **1949** Moldenke *Amer. Wild Flowers* 386, *B[lephariglottis] psycodes,* . . often known as *flaming orchis* or *soldiers-plume.*

soldier weed n   [See quot 1896]

An **amaranth** (here: *Amaranthus spinosus* or *A. hybridus*).

1896 *OH Farmer* 90.273, *Spiny Amaranth.* . . The weed is a native of the South, originally from tropical America; it is well distributed over southern Ohio where it appeared with the returning soldiers, and hence is called war weed or soldier weed. **1902** *Ibid* 102.225, This is spiny amaranth, . . known many years ago as "soldier weed" in southern Ohio.

soldier wood n

A **nakedwood 1** (here: *Colubrina elliptica*).

1897 Sudworth *Arborescent Flora* 300 **FL,** *Colubrina reclinata.* . . Naked-wood. . . Soldierwood. **1946** West–Arnold *Native Trees FL* 136, The soldierwood is local and rare in Florida, occurring only in the Everglade Keys and on the Florida Keys. **1979** Little *Checklist U.S. Trees* 94 **sFL,** *Colubrina elliptica.* . . soldierwood. . . Range—Upper Fla. Keys . . , absent from Fla. mainland. **2010** *DARE* File—Internet **sFL,** Bring nature to your own yard—plant a soldierwood and keep your binoculars handy!

sole n[1]   [*OED2* 1347 →]

1 Std: a fish of the family Soleidae.   Cf **hogchoker**

2 Any of var **flounders** n **B.**   Cf **English sole, French ~, gray ~, petrale ~, sand ~, slippery ~**

1873 in 1878 Smithsonian Inst. *Misc. Coll.* 14.2.16 **NY,** *Pseudopleuronectes americanus* [=*Pleuronectes americanus*]. . . sole. **1884** Goode *Fisheries U.S.* 1.182 **CA,** The Bastard Halibut. . . South of San Francisco, . . the young [are] rarely distinguished from the other "Soles." *Ibid* 185, *Lepidopsetta bilineata* [=*Pleuronectes bilineatus*]. . . This species has no other distinctive name than "Sole." *Ibid, Parophrys vetulus* [=*Pleuronectes vetulus*]. . . This species is always called Sole by the fishermen. *Ibid* 186, *Citharichthys sordidus.* . . About San Francisco it becomes, like the others, a "Sole." **1902** Jordan–Evermann *Amer. Fishes* 525 **Pacific,** The single species of *Psettichthys* is *P. melanostictus.* This is one of the most common flounders on the Pacific Coast from Monterey Bay to Sitka, and is everywhere known as "sole." **1906** NJ State Museum *Annual Rept. for 1905* 390, *Lophopsetta maculata* [=*Scophthalmus aquosus*]. . . Window Light. . . Sole. **1935** Caine *Game Fish* 67, *Paralichthys lethostigmus.* . . Sole. **1953** Roedel *Common Fishes CA* 51, All the important commercial species known on the West Coast as "sole" belong to family Pleuronectidae. The two minor species, the fantail and bigmouth soles, belong to family Bothidae. **1966–68** *DARE* (Qu. P2, . . *Kinds of saltwater fish caught around here . . good to eat*) Infs **CA**72, **WA**17, Sole; **AL**22, Flounder—same as sole; **OR**4, Flounder and sole are bottom fish; (Qu. P14, . . *Commercial fishing . . what do the fishermen go out after?*) Infs **CA**31, **OR**4, **WA**11, Sole; **CA**168, Halibut—same as filet of sole. [*DARE* Ed: Some of these Infs may refer instead to **1** above.] **2000** Dobbs *Gt. Gulf* 55, Thus, the American plaice is also a dab, though not a mud dab, which is another name for a winter flounder, which is also called a sole, not to be confused with a gray sole, however, which is a witch flounder, which is also a Craig fluke but not a plain fluke, which is a summer flounder.

sole n[2]   See **shoe sole**

sole leather   See **side of sole leather**

solemncholy adj   Also *solemcoly, solemncholly, solumcolly* [Blend of *solemn* + *melancholy*]

Very solemn or melancholy; rarely n *the solemncholies* a state of depression.

1772 (1900) Fithian *Jrl.* 1.27 **PA,** Being very *Solemncholly* and somewhat tired, I concluded to stay there all night. **a1824** (1937) Guild *Jrl.* 3.283 **VT,** Then I returned to a tavern and sat down on a seat with a solumcolly look. **1834** Caruthers *Kentuckian* 1.23 **KY,** It [=chewing tobacco] drives away the solemncholies, and makes a fellow feel so good-natured, and so comfortable. **1867** Harris *Sut Lovingood Yarns* 184 **TN,** He cudn't hev look'd more solemncoly, ef his mam hed died that mornin a-owin him two dullars an' a 'alf. **1887** (1892) Hinman *Corporal Si Klegg* 567, Tain't only nat'ral ter feel sort o' solemncholy when . . ther' ain't nobody on earth 't keers a picayune whether I'm dead er 'live. **1891** Johnston *Primes & Neighbors* 185 **GA,** She knows how to manage Lihu with his solemncholy ways. **1898** Lloyd *Country Life* 86 **AL,** If religion made me as solemncholy and sorry lookin as some folks I know, I reckon I would have to take my chances with the great unwashed. **1909** *DN* 3.373 **eAL, wGA,** *Solemncholy.* . . Solemn. Facetious. **1911** *DN* 3.547 **NE,** *Solemncholy.* . . A crossing of *solemn* and *melancholy.* Facetious. **1931** *Oakland Tribune* (CA) 24 Sept [26]/4 (newspaperarchive.com), It never costs a cent to josh and grin: no use to be a solemncholy owl.

solid adj **chiefly Sth, S Midl** Cf **case** n² 2, **hard dollar**
Used with the name of a coin to indicate that it is the coin itself (not the equivalent in some other form) that is meant; also in comb *solid dollar* a dollar bill.

1931 Patterson *Road to Canaan* 167 **Sth** [Black], I spec' you'd a give a solid quarter 'fo'e you'd a let it lef' yo' han'. **1975** *AmSp* 50.66 **AR** [Black], *Solid dime.* . . Ten-cent coin in contrast to ten cents in nickels and pennies—"Will you give me two nickels for a solid dime?" **1983** *DARE* File *se*WI [Black], When people come into my dry cleaning store to get coins for the laundromat next door they ask for "a solid quarter" or "a solid dime". **2000** *Ibid* **nMS,** I'm not sure I've ever heard "case quarter," but I've heard "solid quarter" with the same meaning—or "solid dime." **2002** *Ibid* **AL,** "Paper box"—A box-like container which dispenses newspapers for two "solid quarters". **2003** *DARE* File—Internet, Can I have a solid dime? **2005** in 2006 *DARE* File—Internet **New Orleans LA,** *Solid Qwahta* [sic]. . . What you get when you cash in your dimes and nickles [sic] for a "solid quarter" in order to play video games. . . I only heard this expression used by local black kids. **2006** *Ibid* **cwCA,** *A solid dollar* is a dollar bill. . . A guy had a need for specifically a dollar bill but had four quarters. He might ask if you had *a solid dollar. Ibid* **cwMD,** Student Assessment Services. . . Don't forget when you come to the testing center: Bring a solid quarter—No dimes, nickels, dollars or pennies.

solid adv **chiefly S Midl**
Really, certainly.

1937 *AmSp* 12.232 [Black], Negroes use *solid* as an adverb meaning 'surely, definitely': 'Are you taking Amelia to the Charcoal Dance?' 'I solid am.' **c1940** in 1944 *ADD* **swWV,** *Solid.* . . Surely, definitely. . . 'He solid threw the ball, didn't he?' 'He solid whipped him, didn't he?' Reported. **1946** *PADS* 6.28 **seNC,** *Solid.* . . Certainly. "I solid did do it." . . Semi-illiterate. **1979** in 1981 *NC Folkl. Jrl.* 29.69 **wNC,** If you ain't back with it in a half hour I'll solid skin your hide. **1992** (1993) Gabbard *Return to Thunder Road* 39 **wNC,** I paid $600 for a brand-new Cadillac engine. . . They would solid fly. **1996** Horton *Island Out of Time* 286 **Chesapeake Bay MD,** Mary Ada, one of the best pickers, announced the other day that even after a long, hot summer's immersion in crabs, "I get solid excited" at the big jimmies her husband is bringing her to pick now from pots he has set over by the Potomac. **2003** *DARE* File—Internet, I felt the piano beneath my fingers and it felt good to be back at that machine and I solid did not worship this finger folded over.

solid n Cf *DS* EE6b, c, d
Any of var homogeneous translucent or opaque playing marbles.

c1970 Wiersma *Marbles Terms* **swMI,** *Solid* . . an opaque, single-colored marble. . . an aggy. *Ibid, Solid(s).* . . Another name for "steelies." *Ibid, Solid* . . an opaque or translucent marble of one and only one color. *Ibid* **swMI** (as of c1960), *Solids* . . monotone milky colored marbles, not to be confused with "clearies" which were translucent to light. Solids were opaque. **2002** *Antiques & Collecting Mag.* July 32, "If you like my new shooter, you can have it for a peewee steely. Throw in a clear and a solid for a gold cat's eye." So goes the jargon of pint-sized marble junkies—and future collectors.

solid dollar See **solid** adj

solid rent n
1985 Wilkinson *Moonshine* 82 **neNC,** He paid solid rent, which means that he gave a flat fee for the farm and kept the yield.

‡solitare v
1953 *PADS* 19.14 **sAppalachians,** *Solitare.* . . To live alone; to avoid

companionship. "Old Miz' Adams likes to solitare by herself." "Tim, he don't want no company. He solitares by himself."

solitary n [Folk-etym for *solitaire* a card game played by one person]
1882 *Marion Daily Star* (OH) 1 Apr [4]/1 (newspaperarchive.com), *Eli Bennet*, the main brick layer of this city, is again on deck. . . Korsey can now play solitary. **1923** *Syracuse Herald* (NY) 4 Apr 3/2, His father sits all day playing solitary at cards with himself and drinking milk punches. **1966–70** *DARE* (Qu. DD35, . . *Card games*) Infs **GA**72, 77, **KY**84, **MD**31, **ME**19, **NY**234, Solitary. **2000** *DARE* File **WI,** "I sat up all night and played solitary." In my eighteen years at the VA Hospital in Madison rarely have I heard any of the elderly Wisconsin vets I've seen say *solitaire* for a card game played alone; for these folks the standard word is *solitary.*

solitary sandpiper n [See quot 1977]
A **sandpiper** (here: *Tringa solitaria*). Also called **blacksnipe 1, bullhead 2d, grass-bird 2f, green sandpiper, hermit ~, jacksnipe 2, peetweet 2, sand peep, solitary tattler, steelyard bird, swee-sweet, tattler, teeter** n **2, tilter 3, tip-up 1, wood snipe 1**
1813 (1824) Wilson *Amer. Ornith.* 7.58 **PA,** The Solitary Sandpiper is eight inches and a half long. **1858** U.S. War Dept. *Rept. Explor. Railroad* 9.733, *Rhyacophilus solitarius.* . . Solitary Sandpiper. **1898** (1900) Davie *Nests N. Amer. Birds* 145, The Solitary Sandpiper is well named, when its personal habits or the localities which it frequents are considered. **1923** Dawson *Birds CA* 3.1271, Our Solitary Sandpiper deposits its eggs in the deserted nests of Passerine birds. **1977** Bull–Farrand *Audubon Field Guide Birds* 428, Solitary Sandpiper (*Tringa solitaria*). . . As its name suggests, this bird is most often seen by itself—a single migrant foraging along the margin of a wooded pond or stream. **2005** *Yakima Herald–Republic* (WA) 9 July 1 (Internet), In the past week nine species of shorebirds have been seen . . , including . . Solitary Sandpiper.

solitary tattler n
=**solitary sandpiper**.
1839 MA Zool. & Bot. Surv. *Fishes Reptiles* 370, The *Solitary Tattler, Totanus chloropygius,* . . is very unsuspicious. **1844** Giraud *Birds Long Is.* 257, Not being considered game by sportsmen, the Solitary Tatler [sic] becomes quite familiar. **1861** (1949) Thoreau *Jrl.* 14.336 **MA,** Saw in a roadside gutter at Simon Brown's barn a bird like the solitary tattler, with a long bill, which at length flew off to the river. **1898** (1900) Davie *Nests N. Amer. Birds* 145, The Solitary Tattler, or the American Green Sandpiper, is found throughout . . North America. **1907** Anderson *Birds IA* 222, The Solitary Sandpiper, or Solitary Tattler, is a common migrant in most parts of the state. **1953** Jewett *Birds WA* 261, Western Solitary Sandpiper. . . Other name: Solitary Tattler.

sollaker n [Also in Austr slang (*AND* **sollicker** 1898 →); cf *EDD* **sollock** "Impetus, force"] **VT** Cf **sockdolager**
An unusually impressive example of its kind; a whopper.
1887 (1895) Robinson *Uncle Lisha* 35 **wVT,** 'Killed tew hawgs terday,' says 'e, 'both on 'em good ones, but one on 'em was a sollaker, I tell ye—weighed ninety!' **1937** Crane *Let Me Show You VT* 35 **VT,** Who among us knows what a 'sollaker' is? **1959** *VT Hist.* 27.159, *Sollaker.* . . A big fish; anything large. Common.

‡sollybuster n Cf **gollybuster, sollaker**
1942 Warnick *Garrett Co. MD* 14 **nwMD** (as of 1900–18), *Sollybuster* . . an unusual or extraordinary thing, usually of large size.

solo n esp **NW, NV** See Map on p. 118 Cf **skat**
Any of var card games; see quot 1974.
1890 *Daily NV State Jrl.* (Reno) 21 Feb [3]/2 (newspaperarchive.com), A great many men who could not get to their own places of business assembled and played "solo" all day. **1895** *Century Illustr. Mag.* 50.678 **nwID,** It doesn't seem the nearest way to a fortune, going twice a week on snow-shoes to play solo at the Mule Deer mine. **1913** *Official Rules of Card Games* 5, Solo. **1959** Martin *Gunbarrel* 73 **WY,** On Jack's visits, we played solo far into the night. **1966–68** *DARE* (Qu. DD35, . . *Card games*) Infs **AK**1, **MO**25, **MT**2, **NV**1, **OR**10, **WY**2, 4, Solo; **NV**9, Solo—a German card game that makes you think. **1968** *Hungry Horse News* (Columbia Falls MT) 20 Dec 14/1, The veteran of two wars likes to play pinochle, cribbage and solo, and he's right in with the boys. He's achieved status. **1974** Gibson *Hoyle* 352, Solo: A name applied to various games related to *Skat* . . and the name has been applied to *Ombre. Ibid* 127, *German solo:* A modern development of *Ombre.*

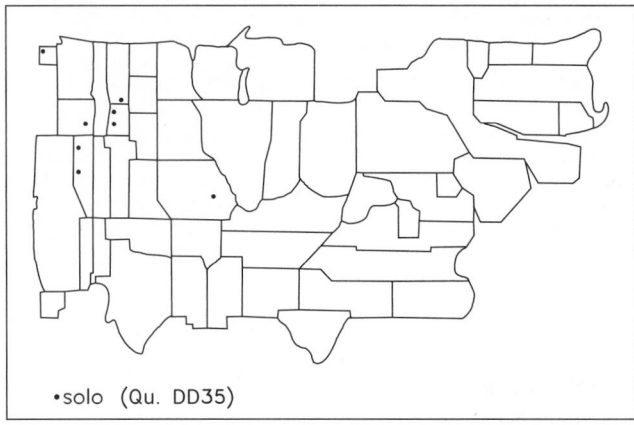

•solo (Qu. DD35)

Solomon feather (or plume)   See **Solomon's feather**

Solomon seal   See **Solomon's seal 1, 2**

Solomon's feather n   Also *Solomon feather, Solomon('s) plume*
=false Solomon's seal.
   1933 Small *Manual SE Flora* 297, *Vagnera* [=*Maianthemum*] [spp]. . . Solomon's Feathers. Solomon's-Plume.   **1949** Moldenke *Amer. Wild Flowers* 334, Many folks confuse the solomonseals *(Polygonatum)* with the falsesolomonseals or solomonsplumes *(Smilacina).   Ibid* 335, The solomonfeather, *S[milacina] australis.* . . lives in Georgia and Alabama.   **1963** Craighead *Rocky Mt. Wildflowers* 27, False Solomonseal—*Smilacina racemosa.* . . Other names: Solomonplume [etc].   *Ibid* 28, Wild Lily-of-the-Valley—*Smilacina stellata.* . . Other names: Wild Spikenard, Solomonplume [etc].   **1969** *DARE* (Qu. S26e, *Other wildflowers not yet mentioned;* not asked in early QRs) Inf IL37, Solomon's plumes—genus *Smilacina.*   **2001** *DARE* File—Internet, There is also a native plant look-a-like [sic], *Smilacina racemosa* sometimes referred to as *False Solomon's Seal,* Solomon's Feather or Solomon's Plume.

Solomon's seal n   [*OED2* 1543 →]   Cf **little John the conqueror, ruler's root**
1 also *Solomon seal:* A plant of the genus *Polygonatum,* usu *P. biflorum.*   Also called **conquer John, fairy bell 4, lily of the valley vine, sealwort, sweet salad**   [*DARE* Ed: Some of these quots may refer instead to other senses below.]
   1672 Josselyn *New-Englands Rarities* 45, *Salomons-Seal,* of which there is three kinds; . . . the second, *Virginia Salomons-Seal.*   **1778** Carver *Travels N. Amer.* 514, *Solomon's Seal.* . . grows on the sides of rivers, and in rich meadow land.   **1805** (1905) Lewis *Orig. Jrls. Lewis & Clark Exped.* 3.220 **Pacific NW,** I Saw in my ramble to day a red berry resembling Solomons Seal berry.   **1837** Darlington *Flora Cestrica* 220 **sePA,** *P[olygonatum] multiflorum* [=*P. biflorum*]. . . Solomon's Seal.   **1911** Porter *Harvester* 475 **IN,** She drew lady's slipper and Solomon's seal.   **1941** Justus *Cabin on Kettle Creek* 147 **eTN,** Star root in the hollow, sang, too, and Solomon's seal.   **1965–70** *DARE* (Qu. S26c, *Wildflowers that grow in woods*) Infs CT37, ID5, MI42, 100, MA49, 71, NY30, 155, Solomon's seal; NJ29, PA99, 169, Solomon seal; (Qu. S26a, . . *Wildflowers.* . . *Roadside flowers*) Infs KY60, NJ45, Solomon's seal; RI15, True Solomon's seal; (Qu. S26b, *Wildflowers that grow in water or wet places*) Inf MI67, Solomon's seal; MI31, Solomon seals; (Qu. S26d, *Wildflowers that grow in meadows;* not asked in early QRs) Inf CT23, Solomon's seal; CT30, IL113, Solomon seal; (Qu. S26e, *Other wildflowers not yet mentioned;* not asked in early QRs) Infs PA49, VA21, Solomon's seal; IN19, MA6, Real Solomon's seal; IA13, MA78, Solomon seal.   [*DARE* Ed: Some of these Infs may refer instead to other senses below.]   **1965–70** *DARE* Wildfl QR Pl.21 [=*Polygonatum biflorum*] 10 Infs, **scattered,** Solomon's seal; OH14, MI31, SC41, True Solomon's seal.   **1971** Krochmal *Appalachia Med. Plants* 202, *Polygonatum biflorum.* . . Common names: Small solomonseal, . . dwarf solomon's seal, hairy solomon's seal, . . solomon's seal.   **2003** *Cleveland Plain Dealer* (OH) 17 July sec E 13 (Internet), Don't overlook plants that have showy berries. Jack-in-the-pulpit (Arisaema triphyllum), . . and Solomon's seal (Polygonatum biflorum) are just a few of the wildflowers with attractive fruit.
2 also *Solomon seal:* A **false lily-of-the-valley** or **false Solo-**

mon's seal (here: *Maianthemum* spp).   Cf **fat Solomon, slim ~, two-leaved Solomon's seal**
   1672 Josselyn *New-Englands Rarities* 45, *Salomons-Seal,* of which there is three kinds . . the third . . is called *Treacle Berries.*   **1814** Bigelow *Florula Bostoniensis* 80 **MA,** Convallaria racemosa [= *Maianthemum racemosum*]. . . *Clustered Solomon's seal.*   **1822** Eaton *Botany* 247, *[Convallaria] multiflora* (giant solomon seal).   *Ibid* 248, *[Convallaria] racemosa* . . (spiked solomon seal).   **1869** Porcher *Resources* 613 **Sth,** Solomon's Seal, *(Convallaria multiflora . .*).   *Ibid,* Species of the genus *Smilacina* [=*Maianthemum*], (Solomon's seal), growing in the Southern States, yield starch from their roots.   **1920** Rice–Rice *Pop. Studies CA Wild Flowers* 97, The Star Flowered Solomon's Seal *(Smilacina sessilifolia)* . . is found in the shady woods of the Coast Range mountains.   **1954** CA Div. Beaches & Parks *Pt. Lobos Wild Flowers* 36, *Smilacina amplexicaulis*—Western Solomon's Seal.   **1965–70** *DARE* Wildfl QR Pl.18 [=*Vagnera racemosa*] Infs AR44, 46, MI7, NH4, OR9, WA12, WI80, Solomon's seal; OR12, Star-flowered Solomon's seal; Pl.19 [=*Unifolium canadense*] Infs NH4, WA15, WI80, Solomon's seal; ND4, Solomon seal; Pl.32A [=*Vagnera trifolia*] Inf OH37, Solomon seal.   **1998** *Birmingham News* (AL) 10 May sec E 9 (Internet), I will not even bother to get more confused by looking up the references to the mayflower of English literature (a hawthorn, Crataegus oxycanthus), or the mayflower we also call spring-beauties (Claytonia virginica), or the mayflower of the northern states (Maianthemum canadense) which the Yankees also call "wild lily-of-the-valley" and Solomon's seal which is no relation to what we call Solomon's seal.
3 A **fringed orchid** (here: *Platanthera orbiculata*).
   1892 *Jrl. Amer. Folkl.* 5.103 **VT,** *Habenaria orbiculata,* Solomon's seal. Barre, Vt.
4 A **twisted stalk 1** (here: *Streptopus lanceolatus*).
   1897 *Jrl. Amer. Folkl.* 10.145 **West,** *Streptopus roseus.* . . Solomon's seal.   **1966** *DARE* (Qu. S26c, *Wildflowers that grow in woods*) Inf ME8, Solomon's seal (twisted stalk—real name).

Solomon's zigzag n   Also *zigzag Solomon's seal*
A **false Solomon's seal** (here: *Maianthemum racemosum*).
   1900 MI State Horticult. Soc. *Annual Rept. for 1899* 251, Vagnera racemosa . . (Smilacina racemosa . .). Wild spikenard. False solomon's seal. . . Zigzag solomon's seal. Solomon's zig-zag.   **1936** Winter *Plants NE* 9, Called . . Golden-seal or Zig-zag Solomon's Seal. *Smilacina racemosa.*   **1943** Fernald–Kinsey *Edible Wild Plants E. N. Amer.* 135, False Spikenard, False Solomon's Seal, Solomon's-zig-zag, scurvy-berries, *Smilacina* (or *Vagnera*) *racemosa.*   **1961** Smith *MI Wildflowers* 49, Solomon's Zigzag. . . *Smilacina racemosa.*

solph(a)more   See **sophomore**

solumcolly   See **solemncholy**

sombrerillo n   [Span "little hat"]
A **marsh pennywort** (here: *Hydrocotyle bonariensis*).
   1970 Correll *Plants TX* 1169, *Hydrocotyle bonariensis.* . . Sombrerillo.   **2001** (acc) TX A&M Univ. *Vascular Plant Image Lib.* (Internet), *Hydrocotyle bonariensis*—native, from Bolivar Peninsula, Texas. Known as Sombrerillo.

some adj   [By ext from the emphatic attrib use of *some,* as in "That was some meal!"]   *arch*
As pred adj: remarkable, extraordinary.
   c1845 in 1981 *AmSp* 56.156 **swIL,** [The singing master could hold a note for forty seconds] which was *some.*   **1848** (1855) Ruxton *Life Far West* 54 **Rocky Mts,** When a boy, our trapper was "some," he said, with the rifle, and always had a hankering for the west.   **1851** Hooper *Widow Rugby's Husband* 88 **AL,** That bonnet o' hern, too, hit's some.   **1867** Lowell *Biglow* lxxix **'Upcountry' MA,** Thet night, I tell ye, she looked *some!*   **1890** *DN* 1.70 **LA,** Some. To say of a woman that "she looks *some,*" with emphasis on the *some* . . is equivalent to saying that she looks remarkably well.   **1947** Guthrie *Big Sky* 107 **MT** (as of 1830), Painter meat, now, that's some. Painter meat, that's top, now.   **1965** *AmSp* 40.22 (as of 1844), Exceptional feats were expected of any horse called a perfect *rasper,* for he would be *some* in any race.

some adv
1 also *some old:* Very, quite.   Note: Some of these quots may illustrate the sense "somewhat."
   1817 in 1918 IN Hist. Soc. *Pub.* 6.285 **NY,** We got some wet, there being a very heavy shower.   **1839** Walker in 1940 Drury *Pioneers*

Spokanes 136 **ME,** I am getting some lazy. **1913** (1941) Burgess *Mother West Wind's Neighbors* 135 **MA,** Mr. and Mrs. Skunk were having a little family talk, and Mr. Skunk was speaking some loud. **1960** Carpenter *Tales Manchaca* 132 **cTX,** Since I was afflicted with incipient malaria, as I afterward discovered, my baby's skin bore a jaundiced tinge. He was some ugly. **1968–70** DARE (Qu. B26, *When it's raining very heavily. . "It's raining _____.")* Inf **NC87,** Some hard out there; (Qu. H11a, *If somebody eats rapidly and noisily, you say he _____)* Inf **LA20,** He's some noisy when he eats; (Qu. LL35, *Words used to make a statement stronger: "This cake tastes _____ good.")* Inf **NJ40,** Some. **1968** Moody *Coming of Age MS* 4 [Black], I was some scared. Mama had never left us at home alone before. **1968** DARE FW Addit **NJ,** *Some* used as "very": It was some cold. I was some homesick. **1971** in 1993 Major *Calling the Wind* 320 **LA** [Black], Juanita's some pretty. I hope [=wish] I was big so I could love her. **1972** Carr *Da Kine Talk* 149 **HI,** "Da party was *some* good, boy!" *Some good,* uttered with an especially wide 2-3-1 falling intonation pattern, is said to be characteristic of the island of Maui, but the phrase is heard on the other islands also. . . "[S]ome neat," "some nice." **1975** Gould *ME Lingo* 267, *Some.* . . The Mainer's use of *some* in sentences where he could properly insert somewhat ("I was somewhat wet!") does not mean that *some* and somewhat convey the same thing. Somewhat wet could never convey the thought in, "We were *some* wet by the time we got home." The nuance of "very" is clear in *some* pretty for a young lady or *some* foggy for low vision. **1979** Lewis *How to Talk Yankee* [31] **nNEng,** *Some.* . . Often "some old." Peculiarly, this word . . serves as an adverb in Yankeeland: "some old homely," "some pretty." "Joe was some ugly when he found out he had to register his twelve foot canoe if he wanted to put his little electric outboard on it." **1989** (1990) Baden *Maryland's E. Shore* 112, The gals who mind the store are some proud of their little, tiny town. **2000** DARE File **coastal ME,** She's some funny.

2 To an extraordinary degree; in an extraordinary manner— freq used in v phr *go some* to go fast or well, be successful; to make a strong claim, "say a lot."

1848 (1855) Ruxton *Life Far West* 18, Them English are darned fools; they can't fix a rifle any ways; but that one did shoot 'some;' leastwise he made it throw plum-center. **1851** Hooper *Widow Rugby's Husband* 37 **AL,** That's Jim Ed'ards; he loves cat fish, some! Well, he does! Don't do nothin' but ketch 'em. **1907** London *Road* 212 **cwCA,** He told me I was risking my life, that it was a fast freight and that she went some. I told him I was used to going some myself, but it was no go. **1908** McGaffey *Sorrows* 19 *(DA),* I still retain my pure English, even when I lose my temper, which is going some for a lady. **1909** DN 3.404 **nwAR,** *Some.* . . Well. Emphasis on *some.* General term of approval. "Well, I reckon that is goin' some." **1914** DN 4.107 **KS,** *Going some. . .* Making rapid progress. **1923** DN 5.208 **swMO,** *Gorn some. . .* Proceeding rapidly, making great progress. **1924** Lardner *How to Write* 98 **MI,** Well, her sister's about twict as good-lookin' as her, and that's goin' some. **1932** Stong *State Fair* 36 **IA,** They'll have to go some if they get the sweepstakes away from him this time. **1945** Thorp *Pardner* 280 **SW,** That horse is running *some!* **1956** McAtee *Some Dialect NC* 41, *Some:* . . in a high degree, superlatively. "That's goin' some." **1968** DARE (Qu. Y20, *To run fast: "You should have seen him _____!")* Inf **NY96,** Traveling some. **2006** DARE File—Internet **KY,** I figger Texas is the only place in the country where the politics are weirder than they are here in Kentucky—and that's going some! *Ibid* **neIL,** I think you are just hoping a player is injured, which shows even less class than people thought you had, and that's going some.

-some suff **chiefly Sth, S Midl; also NEng** Cf **curioussome, longsome, mannersome**

Added to nouns and verbs to form adjectives, also freq pleonastically to adjectives themselves; see quots.

1843 (1916) Hall *New Purchase* 136 **IN,** There's a speretil [=spiritual] and bettersome idee. **1891** Page *Elsket* 137 **VA,** You mus'n' say you ain' do it, 'cuz dat's dangersomer 'n allowing you *is* do it. **1895** DN 1.374 **seKY, eTN, wNC,** *Sweltersome:* sweltering. **1898** Lloyd *Country Life* 128 **AL,** I know that will seem marvelsome strange to the general public. **1899** (1912) Green *VA Folk-Speech* 100, *Bungersome. . .* Clumsy. *Ibid* 222, *Hendersome. . .* obstructive. *Ibid* 441, *Tediousome. . .* Tedious. *Ibid* 491, *Wranglesome. . .* Contentious; quarrelsome. *Ibid* 495, *Youthsome. . .* youthful. **1906** DN 3.150 **nwAR,** *Pestersome. . .* Bothersome. **1908** Wasson *Home from Sea* 37 **ME** *(AmSp* 37.251), Ef it didn't sound some beautysome to hear them old chanties acrosst the river. **1910** in 1919 Hale *Letters* 463 **MA,** He was surrounded by two females, . . a cook, a sort of marmsome house-

keeper, . . and his typewriter amanuensis. **1913** Porter *Laddie* 386, He can be awful ragesome when he's excited. **1914** DN 4.78 **ME, nNH,** *Queeresome. . .* Queer. **1916** DN 4.347 **cTX** (as of 1896), *Realsome. . .* Antonym to *ideal.* Rare. **1958** Babcock *I Don't Want* 19 **eSC,** In what other kind of hunting are the relations between man and dog so intimate, so constant, and oftentimes so humorsome? **1986** Pederson *LAGS Concordance,* 1 inf, **cnAL,** An idlesome man. **1997** AmSp 72.19 **MD, NC,** In Smith Island [MD], *-some* is used to lessen the intensity of the adjective to which it is attached; however, in Ocracoke [NC] it serves to heighten intensity. Thus, to a Smith Islander, the phrase *he's tallsome* means 'he is somewhat tall', whereas to an Ocracoker the phrase means 'he is very tall'.

somebody n esp **Sth, S Midl** *old-fash* Cf **something B**

A person.

1836 *Yale Lit. Mag.* 1.72, We can only conceive of him as a love-sick somebody. **1852** Webber *Prairie Scout* 81 **KY,** The lieutenant, as they called him, impressed me as a greasy, easy, good-for-nothing sort of a somebody. **1884** *Anglia* 7.262 [Black], Er mighty keerless somebody—a very careless person. **1888** Jones *Negro Myths* 67 **GA coast** [Gullah], Eh see one tall somebody all wrop up head en yez een white. **1928** Peterkin *Scarlet Sister Mary* 117 **SC** [Gullah], She thought some poor sick somebody had sent for her. **1931** AmSp 7.159 **Sth,** "She is a funny old somebody," "He's a cute somebody" are sentences heard from Southerners. **1965–70** DARE (Qu. Y28, *A person who loiters about with nothing to do)* Inf **GA28,** Lazy somebody; (Qu. GG36a, *The kind of person who is always poking into other people's affairs: "She's an awful _____.")* Infs **DC8, GA67, MO36, NY73,** Nosy (old) somebody; (Qu. HH4, *Someone who has odd or peculiar ideas or notions)* Inf **GA28,** Peculiar somebody; (Qu. HH7a, *Someone who talks too much, or too loud: "He's an awful _____.")* Inf **MD35,** Loud somebody; (Qu. HH13, *Expressions meaning that a person is not very alert or not aware of things: "He's certainly _____.")* Inf **SC59,** Sleepiest somebody I ever saw; (Qu. HH20a, *An idle, worthless person: "He's a _____.")* Inf **GA36,** No-good somebody; (Qu. HH23, *A person who gets along well with everybody: "Now there's a _____.";* total Infs questioned, 75) Inf **MS6,** Good-natured somebody; (Qu. II36a, *Somebody who talks back or gives rude answers: "Did you ever see such a _____?")* Infs **GA28, TX102,** Sassy somebody; (Qu. KK37, *Words to describe a very sly person: "He's _____.")* Inf **GA28,** Sneakin' somebody. [All Infs old, White] **1975** Newell *If Nothin' Don't Happen* 47 **nwFL,** I'll be derned if he didn't come down with the mumps. And he was a sick somebody, I mean! **2001** (2004) Rodowsky *Clay* 125 **MD,** And I stepped inside somebody else's world. It was the world of a somebody with about a million stuffed animals and Barbies and picture books.

some'er(e)s See **somewheres**

somehow another See **another B**

somehows adv [Engl dial (though not in *OED2, EDD*)] Cf **-s suff¹**

Somehow.

1851 Lewis *Across Atl.* 207 **VA,** Well, suspicion did, somehows, fix on Hiram. **1870** *Our Boys & Girls* 7.844 **NEng,** What did I tell you? . . I knew the doings would be spiled somehows. **1878** in 1884 Hughes *Gone to TX* 10, He says, "Oh, never mind, guess I'll fix it somehows." **1885** Murfree *Prophet of Smoky Mts.* 7 **eTN,** But they hed crost him somehows, an' he war ailin' in his temper when I got home. **1888** *Century Illustr. Mag.* 36.559 **GA,** But somehows, or somehows else, I don't know as I may never know how sech things comes about. **1931** PMLA 46.1320 **sAppalachians,** These forms are common: "somehows" . . "nohows," due to fondness for the *s.* **1947** Tyre *Red Wine* 144 **Sth,** Doris was down there near the sewer and somehows or other fell in.

some kind of adv phr Pronc-sp *some kinda* [Prob from widespread *some kind of* "a remarkable instance of" through reanalysis of contexts in which the following noun is modified by an adj; see quot 1969] **chiefly VA, S Atl**

Extremely, extraordinarily.

c1937 in 1976 *Weevils in the Wheat* 27 **VA** [Black], Don't know why, ah guess he was little bit skeered to whip dat big man. . . But old Marser was some kind of mad. *Ibid* 32 **VA** [Black], Do you know, I slept all night an' didn't catch cold? Oh, I wuz some kinda tough! **1944** PADS 2.9 **AL, SC, VA,** *Some kind of. . .* Remarkably, extraordinarily. "She's some kind of smart." **1968** DARE FW Addit **VA,** *Some kind of*—used same way I use *very:* of food: "some kind of good"; of a difficult task: "some kind of hard," etc. Common. **1969** *Ibid* **NC,** *Some kinda*—for

real, right, particularly, etc. "Some kinda hot weather." **1970** *DARE*
(Qu. KK37, *Words to describe a very sly person: "He's* _____.") Inf
VA75, Some kind of slick; (Qu. LL35, *Words used to make a statement
stronger: "This cake tastes* _____ *good."*) Inf **VA**75, Some kind of.
1975 Newell *If Nothin' Don't Happen* 177 **nwFL**, He sure must have
been some kind of hungry! **1976** Ryland *Richmond Co. VA* 377, *Some
kind of*—emphasis, ". . . some kind of pretty. . . " **1988** Naylor *Mama
Day* 135 **GA, SC coast** [Black], It may be taking forever, but it's gonna
be some kind of beautiful. **1994** Berendt *Midnight* 110 **eGA**, That
abortion was some kinda good. **1996** Wells *Divine Secrets* 309 **LA**,
You are some kind of gorgeous.

some of these odd-come-shorts　See **odd-come-short 1**

some old　See **some** adv **1**

somepin'　See **something A3**

somepin n'er　See **something or other**

somep'n　See **something A3**

some pumpkins　See **pumpkin** n¹ **B2**

somerce, some'r(e)s　See **somewheres**

somersault n　Usu |ˈsʌmɚˌsɔlt, -salt|; also occas |ˈsʌməˌsɔt|; for
addit varr see quots　Pronc-sp *somersot*　Cf **somerset, sumblesault, sumbleset**
Std sense, var forms.
　1943 *LANE* Map 578 *(Somersault)*, [11 infs, chiefly **MA** and **CT**,
offered proncs of the type |ˈsʌməˌsɔt|.] **1966–68** *DARE* (Qu. EE9a,
*The children's trick of turning over rapidly straight forward close to
the ground*) Inf **GA**28, Somersot [ˈsʌmɚˌsat]; **ME**5, Somersot [-sɔt];
OK42, Somersot [sʌmɚˈsɔt]; (Qu. EE9b, *If children jump forward, land
on the hands, and turn over*) Inf **ME**5, Turning somersots. **2000** Shores
Tangier Is. 183 **Chesapeake Bay**, *Call, gall, Baltimore, somersault,
squall, gulf, wolf, golf,* and *salt* are all pronounced with the vowel of
"bull." **2009** in 2010 *DARE* File—Internet **swOH**, My daughter, Faith,
is doing *fantastic* in her kindergarten work. Charity did several somersots by herself today.

somerset n　Also *summerset* [*OED* 1596 →]　**widespread,
but esp Sth, S Midl**　See Map　Cf **tumbleset**
A **somersault**; also fig.
　1829 *Adams Sentinel* (Gettysburg PA) [9 Sept 4]/5 (newspaper-
archive.com), Wonderful somerset from a horse at full speed, by Mr.
Downie. **1831** *Biblical Repertory & Theological Rev.* 3.29, To use the
saw, the plane, the axe, or the hoe, will excite perspiration . . as effectually as to . . turn a somerset. **1841** *Ladies' Repository* 1.44, He cocked
his eye up to the mizen-peak, where the national flags were taking a
summerset extraordinary. **1864** (1868) Trowbridge *3 Scouts* 173, All I
have to say, is that you'll see me turn summersets to the moon before I
ever set on a court-martial again! **1903** Murrie *White Castle LA* 95
[Black], De ghost would be turnen summersets. **1909** *DN* 3.373 **eAL,
wGA**, *Somersets.* **1910** *DN* 3.449 **cwNY**, *Somerset.* **1943** *LANE* Map
578 *(Somersault)* **NEng**, [Both *somerset* and *somersault* are found
throughout the region.] *Somerset* is described as the usual or more common term by [6 infs]; as natural by [6 infs]; as less common or less natural by [3 infs]; and as older or old-fashioned though still in use by [20
infs]. Eight informants report that they used this term in their childhood
but have since given it up. **1946** *PADS* 5.39 **VA**, *Somerset:* A somersault; common everywhere. **1947** *PADS* 8.24 **wNY**, *Somerset: Somersault* equally common. **1955** Ritchie *Singing Family* 49 **seKY**, Us
young uns turned summersets, and stood on our heads. **c1955** Reed–
Person *Ling. Atlas Pacific NW,* 4 infs, Somerset. **1965–70** *DARE* (Qu.
EE9a, *The children's trick of turning over rapidly straight forward close
to the ground*) 149 Infs, **widespread, but esp Sth, S Midl**, Somerset;
AR28, Turning somersets; **TN**27, Turning somersetses; (Qu. EE9b, *If
children jump forward, land on the hands, and turn over*) Infs **CO**21,
FL33, **GA**33, **MO**15, Somerset; (Qu. EE9c, *. . If children spread their
arms and turn over sideways*) Infs **MI**44, **TN**27, Somerset. **1989**
Pederson *LAGS Tech. Index* 349 **Gulf Region** *(Somersault)* 200 [of 914]
infs, Somerset; 1 inf, Cut a somerset; 3 infs, Double somerset. **1996**
Houston Chron. (TX) 27 Aug 13 (Internet), Back when they were trying
to teach me to spell in school, we were spelling it summerset, which is
just the way we pronounced it.

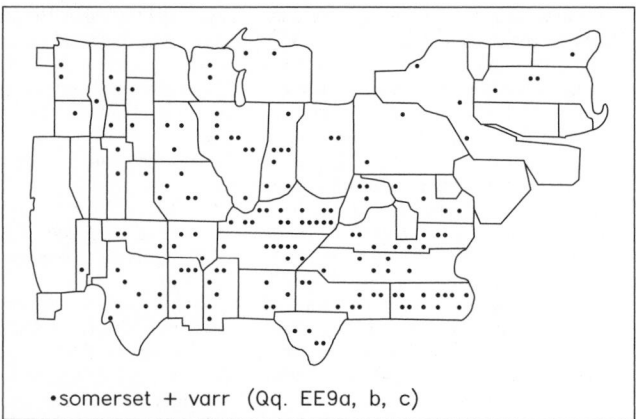

•somerset + varr (Qq. EE9a, b, c)

somersot　See **somersault**

some several pron phr, adj phr　Cf **several C**
Quite a few, many.　Note: The sense "a few, some" is std and
is not illustrated here.
　1895 *DN* 1.374 **seKY, eTN, wNC**, *Some several.* "Are there many
squirrels this season?" "Yes, there's some several." **1974** Fink *Mountain Speech* 24 **wNC, eTN**, *Some several . .* goodly number. "They was
some several folks there."

some shuckins　See **shuckins** n

something n, adj, adv
A Forms.
1 |ˈsʌmθɪn, ˈsʌmθən, ˈsʌntn̩|; pronc-sp *sunthin.*
　1838 (1843) Haliburton *Clockmaker* (2d ser) 41 **NEng**, I guess he'll
do sun'thin for the country. **1846** *Madison Express* (WI) 15 Dec 1/1,
He was afeered sunthin' would split afo' day. **1853** *Putnam's Mag.*
2.459 **MA**, 'Pears to me's though I smelt sunthin. **1867** Lowell *Biglow*
151 'Upcountry' **MA**, [Title:] Sunthin' In The Pastoral Line. **1895** *DN*
1.375 **seKY, eTN, wNC**, *Sunthin.* **1943** *LANE* Map 632 *(Something)*
NEng, The word *something* was recorded in many different contexts, often from the informants' conversation. The pronunciation varies greatly
with relative stress and speed of utterance. Since the field workers noted
only such forms as were used in response to their inquiry or as they happened to observe in conversation, our material does not present a complete record of the variations used by each speaker. [Variant proncs of
the types [sʌn(t)θɪn, sʌθɪn, sʌmpn, sʌmpm] are about equally common
throughout the region.] **1968–69** *DARE* FW Addit **MA**40, Something
[ˈsʌθɪn, ˈsʌnθɪn]; **NY**75, Something [ˈsʌnθən, ˈsʌntn̩]. **1989** Pederson
LAGS Tech. Index 364 **Gulf Region**, 1 inf, [ˈsʌnθn̩]; 1 inf, [ˈsʌntn̩].
1991 *Macoupin Co. Enquirer* (Carlinville IL) 3 Jan 6 **cwIL**, [From a
1961 issue quoting "oldsters":] A man under the weather and not working. . . might even have sunthin that was ketchin'.
2 |ˈsʌθɪn|; pronc-spp *suthin(g), sutthin.*
　1835 (1841) Cooper *Monikins* 3.42 **CT**, Look out for suthin' to pay
port charges with. **1840** in 1944 *ADD*, Something. . . A leetle suthin'.
1848 Lowell *Biglow* 17 'Upcountry' **MA**, There 's sutthin' gits into my
throat thet makes it hard to swaller. **1851** Burke *Polly Peablossom* 59
IN, So, I . . rolls up my sleeves, when all at once suthing struck me— . .
as I was sayin', suthin struck me—. **1858** Hammett *Piney Woods Tavern* 20 **CT**, We'd best be a pushin' on, wet legs or dry ones, or we'll
catch suthing a nation sight worse. **1887** *Amer. Field* 27.30 **MS**, That
ole cuss is onto suthin. **1907** Mulford *Bar-20* 27 **West**, Why didn't he
say suthin' about it? **1914** *DN* 4.71 **ME, nNH**, *Suthin'.* **1923** *DN*
5.222 **swMO**, Hit graveled me suthin' tur'ble. **1943** [see **A1** above].
1968–69 [see **A1** above]. **1989** Pederson *LAGS Tech. Index* 364 **Gulf
Region**, 1 inf, [ˈsʌθn̩]. **1989** Flynt *Poor But Proud* 228 **neAL** (as of
1920s), It's about the only chance I git tuh say suthin.
3 |ˈsʌmpn̩, ˈsʌmpm̩|; pronc-spp *sompen, somep(i)n', sumpen,
sump(i)n, sump'm.* **chiefly Sth, S Midl**
　1852 Haliburton *Traits* 1.259 [Black], Gor a mity, Massa, don't hit
yet—dar's sumpen else. **1856** Cutler *Household Mysteries* 157 **Sth**, He
pour somep'n down her throat. **1881** *Scribner's Mth.* 22.242 **GA**
[Black], De minnit he say dat, Brer Rabbit, he know sump'n 'uz up.
1893 Shands *MS Speech* 61, *Sumpen* [sʌmpn̩]. Used by all classes, to a
very large extent, for *something.* **1894** Riley *Armazindy* 69 **IN**, And
somepin' else she *laughed* to hear. **1899** Chesnutt *Conjure Woman* 14
csNC [Black], Dey wuz sump'n good ter eat. **1909** *DN* 3.377 **eAL,**

wGA, *Sump-m.* . . Something. **1916** in 1953 Botkin–Harlow *Treas. Railroad Folkl.* 428, Yeah, but jist wait, and ye'll see somep'n wuss. **1927** Adams *Congaree* 19 **cSC** [Black], Ole Sister got a kind er mind dat don't dwell long on sompen she can't hurt. **1943** [see **A1** above]. **1965–70** *DARE* (Qu. V1) Inf **IL**126, Somebody puttin' sumpin' over on me; (Qu. HH4) Inf **AR**47, Comical-looking sump'm; (Qu. HH37) Inf **MI**120, Sumpin' else; (Qu. KK1a) Inf **TN**46, Sumpin' else; (Qu. KK35) Inf **MO**16, Sump'm t' talk about; (Qu. NN12b) Infs **FL**18, **IL**130, **TX**88, **WA**1, (Just a-making) sumpin'. **1975** [see **B** below]. **1976** Garber *Mountain-ese* 89 **sAppalachians**, You kaint git sumpin' fer nothin'. **1984** Burns *Cold Sassy* 104 **nGA** (as of 1906), You need to understand that in Cold Sassy . . [w]e . . say . . *sump'm* for something. **1989** Pederson *LAGS Tech. Index* 364 **Gulf Region**, [Of 914 infs, 376 offered proncs of the type ['sʌmpm̩] and 39, proncs of the type ['sʌmpn̩].]

4 Pronc-spp *suppen, suppin', supm.*

1893 *Frank Leslie's Pop. Mth.* 36.266 **NYC** [Black], See me er comin'—suppin' else comin'. **1899** (1912) Green *VA Folk-Speech* 429, *Supm.* . . Something. "Tell me sup'm." *Suppen.* . . Something. **1906** Brady *Patriots* 181, She grab Miss 'Adny in her arms an' she say suppin' an' kiss an' kiss her. **c1937** in 1976 *Weevils in the Wheat* 252 **VA** [Black], God knows he was so mean, God had to do suppin' to him. **1996** *Ledger* (Lakeland FL) 23 May sec C 1 (Internet), At the risk of sounding Chicagoan ("Ay, lemme taya supm, okee?"), I'll go even further.

5 Pronc-spp *sometin(g), sumptin(g), sumtin(g).*

1838 Gilman *S. Matron* 95 **SC** [Black], Someting bad gwine for happen, marmy, sure. **1852** *Democratic Rev.* 30.150 **TX** [Black], Whafor you no shoot yuself, and do sometin good? **1888** *Century Illustr. Mag.* 35.353 **sLA**, Him and you . . be takin' some cawntrac' for . . raise somet'in' what been sunk. **a1938** [see **B** below]. **1938** *Pointer* (Riverdale IL) 20 Oct 1/2, Here is someting dat maybe you can print. **1968** Moody *Coming of Age MS* 52 [Black], Why should I . . give 'em sumptin' to talk about? **1976** *Bucks Co. Courier Times* (Levittown PA) 30 Nov sec A 17/5 **NYC**, It's . . sometin' in my life what makes me feel good. **1993** *Anchorage Daily News* (AK) 28 June sec B 1 (Internet), The sentence, "The first time I Reid a Book it was sumting had for me to Do," was part of a one-paragraph essay by a sixth-grader. **2001** *Times–Picayune* (New Orleans LA) 25 Feb 1 (Internet), A parade-goer . . will have earlier yelled, "Trow me sumtin mistuh!"

B As noun.

With preceding modifier: A thing; a subject of interest; a person; also as mass noun: material, "stuff." **chiefly Sth, S Midl**

1853 Simms *Sword & Distaff* 116 **SC** [Black], So long as . . dere's pattridge and dub (dove) . . Tom will always hab 'nough somet'ing to cook. **1935** Hurston *Mules & Men* 270 **LA** [Black], Write his name on a slip of paper and put it in a sugar bowl or some other deep something like that. **a1938** in 1977 *Amer. Slave Suppl. 1* 11.197 **SC** [Gullah], Don't want to see no more sumpting like dat! **1943** Chase *Jack Tales* 163 **wNC** (as of 1880s), The old woman got out all kinds of good somethin' to eat and set it on the table. **1967** *DARE* (Qu. HH4, *Someone who has odd or peculiar ideas or notions*) Inf **AR**47, Comical-looking sump'm. **1971** Roberts *Third Ear* np [Black], *That's another something*—an expression denoting a complete change of subject or orientation. **1975** Newell *If Nothin' Don't Happen* 201 **nwFL**, They was one of them great big old hammer-nose sharks. . . He were a vygrus-lookin' sump'n.

something another   See **something or other**

something dead up the creek *n* Also *something dead up the branch;* for addit varr see quots   **Sth, S Midl**   Cf **dead cat on the line, nigger in the woodpile 1a**

Something suspicious.

1899 (1900) Harris *On the Wing* 143 **GA**, As sure as you're born there's something dead up the creek. **1903** *DN* 2.330 **seMO**, *Something dead up the branch.* . . An expression of suspicion; equivalent to 'something rotten in Denmark.' **1965–70** *DARE* (Qu. V1, *When you suspect that somebody is trying to deceive you, or that something is going on behind your back* . . "There's _____.") Infs **AL**10, **SC**34, **TN**24, **TX**26, Something dead up the branch (*or* creek); **AR**55, **SC**11, 34, 56, Something (lost) up the creek; **AL**6, Something fishy about that, dead up the creek; **GA**3, Something rotten up the branch. **1978** *AP Letters* **neGA** (as of c1900), Expressions . . of the pioneers . . from . . mountain and rural areas: . . A mystery was "something dead up the creek." **1998** *Chattanooga Free Press* (TN) 20 Oct sec B 4 (Internet), Mr. Hardin said

he feels the whole deal "smells—there is something dead up the creek. One thousand people are going to be affected by this."

something nother   See **something or other**

something on a stick *n* [Euphem for **shit on a stick**] **chiefly S Midl**

1934 *Story* June 37, He just kept looking at the chief with an expression as if he thought the cop was something on a stick, as if he were a man he figured was worth about that much, I mean. **1938** *Star* (Kansas City MO) 21 Aug sec C 7/2 **Ozarks**, A hillman will say of a braggart, "he thinks he's something on a stick." **1940** (1968) Haun *Hawk's Done Gone* 44 **eTN**, She told me how Barshia's ma had raised him up to think he was something on a stick, and how she had learnt him to think he was too pretty to work. **1953** Randolph–Wilson *Down in Holler* 286 **Ozarks**, *Something on a stick.* . . Something unusually fine or valuable. "Jim treats that old woman like she was somethin' on a stick." **1954** *Harder Coll.* **cwTN**, *Something on a stick.* . . Derogatory, of someone who thinks that [s/he] is great, or of a pompous person. **c1960** *Wilson Coll.* **csKY**, *Something on a stick.* . . Something special. **1966–69** *DARE* (Qu. Y22, *To move around in a way to make people take notice of you:* "Look at him _____.") Inf **VA**11, Look at him—he thinks he's something on a stick; (Qu. GG19a, *When you can see from the way a person acts that he's feeling important or independent:* "He surely is _____ these days.") Inf **OK**31, Thinks he's something on a stick; (Qu. GG19b, *When you can see from the way a person acts that he's feeling important or independent:* "He seems to think he's _____.") Infs **GA**1, **IL**96, **OK**31, **TN**23, **TX**18, 104, Something on a stick; (Qu. HH41, *Someone who has a very high opinion of himself;* total Infs questioned, 75) Inf **OK**31, Thinks he's something on a stick; (Qu. II23, *Joking names for the people who are, or think they are, the best society of a community: The* _____) Infs **IL**96, **NV**9, Something on a stick; **OK**31, They think they're something on a stick. [7 of 8 total Infs comm type 4 or 5, 6 old, 5 women] **1979** *DARE* File **cwNY**, I have heard a friend of mine—born in 1888—say of a person who was impressed with herself, especially her elegant clothes, "Well, doesn't she think she's something on a stick!" **2005** in 2006 *DARE* File—Internet **AR**, I'm not one of those people that gets a new car and thinks that they are 'something on a stick that can't be shook off', if you know what I mean.

something on one's hip, have   See **hip** n¹ 1

something or other *phr* Pronc-spp *somepin n'er, something (a)nother, sumpener;* for addit varr see quots   **chiefly Sth, S Midl**

Std sense, var forms.

1843 (1916) Hall *New Purchase* 145 **IN**, Jist then I hears somethin a nuther in the beech above. **1848** Lowell *Biglow 2* 'Upcountry' **MA**, Our Hosee's gut the chollery or suthin anuther ses she. **1887** (1967) Harris *Free Joe* 190 **ceGA** [Black], Miss 'Ria say she wish ter goodness ole Miss 'ud sen' word ef she gwine stay ter dinner so she kin fix up somepin er nice. **1893** Shands *MS Speech* 61, *Sumpener* [sʌmp-nʌ]. Negro and illiterate white for *something or other.* **1894** in 1941 Warfel–Orians *Local-Color Stories* 737 **sAR** [Black], Won't you please . . gimme a little drop o' some'h'n 'nother? **1914** *DN* 4.113 **cKS**, *Something another.* . . Something or other. **1922** Gonzales *Black Border* 330 **sSC**, **GA coasts** [Gullah glossary], *Sump'n'nurruh*—something or other. **c1938** in 1970 Hyatt *Hoodoo* 1.139 **seGA** [Black], Dey went up de chimley an' got somepin othah. **1940** (1941) Bell *Swamp Water* 101 **Okefenokee GA**, He's got a something-another on his tail to make him travel. **1955** Roberts *S. from Hell-fer-Sartin* 149 **seKY**, And he heared something nother on the outside. And it was this old bear. **1972** Thomas *Pop. Dict. Ozarks Talk* 83, Under the brush arbors, they'd have church or a revival, or sump'n a-nother. **2008** *DARE* File **eTX**, Used by the voiceover-guy for "sumpnother," as my Texas granddaddy used to say.

sometime *adv* [*W3* "archaic"] **chiefly Sth**

Sometimes, at times.

1820 *Republican Compiler* (Gettysburg PA) [26 Apr 4]/2 (newspaperarchive.com) **MD**, It would some time happen, that fruit was neglected until it became hard. **1856** Adams *Lost Hunter* 77 **NEng** [Black], When I was in de army in de glorious war ob de Resolution, we say prayers sometime as well as you folks who stay at home. **1895** Burwell *Girl's Life VA* 18 **VA** (as of 1850s) [Black], Sometime he . . dance an' jump an' howl tell we skeer we chillun to deaf. **1934** *AmSp* 9.130 [Engl dial of HI], Often final *-s* is lost, as in *sometime* for 'sometimes' and *United State* for 'United States.' **1934** Hurston *Jonah's Gourd Vine* 75 **AL** [Black], Ah laks it over here where dey talks about biscuit-bread some time. **1940** (1941) Bell *Swamp Water* 93 **Okefenokee GA,** D'ruther had the buck, but they horns gits in the way sometime. **1966–69** *DARE* (Qu. A15, *Something that happens only occasionally: "He comes around _____."*) Infs **GA**84, **KS**4, **SC**9, **VA**1, Sometime. **1966** *DARE* Tape **MI**3, Sometime we end up with more people than we start out with. **c1970** Pederson *Dial. Surv. Rural GA,* 1 inf, **seGA,** Sometime we call it downpour. **1986** Pederson *LAGS Concordance,* 1 inf, **ceAL,** Gather them in sometime by the bushel; 1 inf, **csGA,** Everybody have the devil in them sometime; 1 inf, **swGA,** Sometime it don't take twenty-four hours; 1 inf, **neLA,** Sometime the mother be dark, and the father bright; 1 inf, **swGA,** Sometime they be run a long way; 1 inf, **nwLA,** They'd do that sometime; 1 inf, **cnGA,** Sometime you sleep good at night. **2003** (2004) Price–Thompson *Proverbs* 428 **MS** [Black], Sometime I'm scared, Willie B. Sometime I think they gonna hang me like they done Tim Tidmore.

sometime adj Also rarely *sometimes* esp **S Atl** *esp freq among Gullah speakers*

=**sometimey.** Note: the phr *sometime thing* (often in weakened sense) is now widespread, presumably popularized by the song in *Porgy and Bess* (see quot 1935). These derivative uses, as well as other exx of *sometime* in the sense "occasional," are not illustrated here.

1909 *S. Atl. Qrly.* 8.46 **seSC** [Gullah], Dem nyoung gal is a sometime t'ing; that is . . *inconstant, enigmatic* [sic], *and unsure.* **1928** Peterkin *Scarlet Sister Mary* 260 **SC** [Gullah], "But July left Cinder de same way." Mary laughed carelessly. "No 'oman livin couldn' keep a sometime man like July." **1930** Stoney–Shelby *Black Genesis* 30 **seSC** [Gullah], Well, eberybody know, 'oman is a *sometime t'ing.* **1935** Heyward–Gershwin *A Woman Is a Sometime Thing* [title of song from *Porgy and Bess*]. **1952** Brown *NC Folkl.* 1.593, *Some-time.* . . Undependable; acting only at such time as would seem favorable to oneself; opportunistic. "She's a some-time friend; I don't want to have anything to do with her."

sometimey adj Also *sometimesy* esp **S Atl** *esp freq among Black speakers*

Fickle, moody, inconsistent.

1905 Chesnutt *Col.'s Dream* 79 **GA,** White gentlemen, in their intercourse with coloured people, were apt to be, in the local phrase, "sometimey," or uncertain in their moods. **1946** (1972) Mezzrow–Wolfe *Really Blues* 338, Sometimey: *unstable, unpredictable, neurotic.* **1952** Brown *NC Folkl.* 1.593, *Sometimey.* . . Same as *some-time.* **1966** *DARE* (Qu. LL13, *Not full or sufficient: "She gave us a _____ meal."*) Inf **SC**21, Sometimey. **1969** in 1972 Chapman *New Black Voices* 62 **Harlem NYC,** She's the evilest and sometime-iest woman I ever shacked up with. **1972** Claerbaut *Black Jargon* 80, *Sometimesy* . . inconsistent in one's personality; moody: *She's sometimesy.* **1975** Newell *If Nothin' Don't Happen* 199 **nwFL** [Black], Them black folks has got a way of puttin' things now and then that just tells the whole story. Like Aunt Effie's washwoman sayin' to Ma, "You know, Mrs. Epps sho' is sometimesy." Nothin' could describe Aunt Effie better'n that. **1987** Kytle *Voices* 49 **NC,** He was sometimesy. He used to be thick as thieves with Bubba Blankenship in the second grade. . . Then, all in a minute, he wouldn't have prayed for rain if Bubba's clothes were on fire. **1992** *DARE* File **FL** [Black], Women are sometimey. They's moody, you know. Sometimes they talk to you and sometimes they don't. **2002** O'Neal *Shaq Talks* 181 **NJ** [Black], I like Van Horn, but he don't play mean enough for me. He's sometimey.

sometin(g) See **something A5**

someuns pron [Pl of *someun,* pronc-sp for *someone*] Cf **we-uns** pron, **you-uns**

An indefinite number of people; some people (as contrasted with others).

1888 Roe *Miss Lou* 243 **Sth,** Beyond, ez ef some uns had hidden in the bushes . . air two little woman-like tracks en two men tracks. **1959** (1965) Ruark *Poor No More* 374 **Sth,** I never taken off sick, not like someuns.

someways adv [*OED2* a1225 →] Cf **-s** suff[1]

Somehow, in some manner.

1852 Warner *Dollars & Cents* 2.345 **NEast,** There ain't much of anything to day Mrs. Howard—a place gets cleared out once in a while someways. **1860** in 2005 Nation *At Home Hoosier Hills* 91 **IN,** Wey live harder now then wey ever lived someways but thire may bee something for us again. **1863** *Atlantic Mth.* 11.17 **wVA,** Someways she's

been beside me all day, as if she was grippin' me by the sleeve. **1898** *New Engl. Mag.* 24.31 **NEng,** He got into the machinery someways. **1938** Burman *Blow for a Landing* 4 **MS,** I ain't had no kind of luck with this guitar. . . Never can get it to acting right someways. **1955** Ritchie *Singing Family* 121 **seKY,** Hit's a common-like little fooling tune, keeps dodging about in my head, but I'll get it out in a minute. Someways like this: [music]. **1979** *AmSp* 54.95 **sME** (as of 1899–1910), Adverbs formed with *-way* always end in *-s,* such as . . *someways.* **2000** Kingsolver *Prodigal Summer* 156 **sAppalachians,** Everybody within sixteen miles of here is uncles or cousins to you someways. **2006** *DARE* File—Internet **WA,** The farmers, when interviewed, sort of chuckl[e] and say, . . "Don't seem ra'ht someways, but it is free money!"

somewheres adv Pronc-spp *some'er(e)s, somerce, some'r(e)s, somewhars, sommers, summerce, summers, sumwheres* Cf **anywheres, nowheres, -s** suff[1]

Somewhere.

1815 Humphreys *Yankey in England* 108, *Sumwheres,* somewhere. **1848** Lowell *Biglow* 146 '**Upcountry' MA,** *Som'ers,* somewhere. **1894** Riley *Armazindy* 73 **IN,** That man's allus *somers else!* **1899** (1977) Norris *McTeague* 79 **San Francisco CA,** Well, you'd 'a' had to sleep *somewheres,* wouldn't you? **1899** (1912) Green *VA Folk-Speech* 402, *Som'ers.* . . Somewheres, somewhere. **1905** *DN* 3.20 **cCT,** *Somewheres.* . . Somewhere. **1907** *DN* 3.250 **eME,** *Somewheres.* . . Somewhere. **1909** *DN* 3.373 **eAL, wGA,** *Somewheres.* . . Somewhere. Often abbreviated to *somers. Ibid* 404 **nwAR,** *Som'ers.* . . Somewhere. **1923** (1946) Greer-Petrie *Angeline Steppin'* 31 **csKY,** He could put him up a pen summers back of the Hotel. **1938** Rawlings *Yearling* 10 **nFL,** Oh, I reckon he's around here some'eres. **1946** (1972) Mezzrow–Wolfe *Really Blues* 74, We got hold of a piano somewheres. **1949** Webber *Backwoods Teacher* 30 **Ozarks,** Some'res. **1953** Brewer *Word Brazos* 50 **eTX** [Black], De Yankee soldiers done come . . from way somewhars down de Gulf. **1955** Roberts *S. from Hell-fer-Sartin* 193 **seKY,** She went on and maybe got some blackberries sommers else. **1965–70** *DARE* (Qu. MM11, *When you're trying to find something—you don't know where it is . . "I must have left it _____."*) 112 Infs, **widespread,** Somewheres; **GA**73, **ME**9, Somewheres around here; **CA**74, **IA**46, **MD**38, **NH**14, **OK**1, Somewheres else; **NJ**3, Somewheres in the house; (Qu. B5, *When the weather looks as if it will become bad . . it's _____*) Inf **MN**23, Storm brewing somewheres; (Qu. Y47, *To hide something away for future use: "I know he's got it _____ somewhere."*) Inf **OH**89, Hid somewheres; (Qu. NN26b, *Weakened substitutes for 'hell': "Go to _____!"*) Inf **MO**16, Go lay down somewheres. **1969** *DARE* FW Addit **NC,** *Somewheres*—['sʌmɚz]. **1983** *MJLF* 9.1.56 **ceKY** (as of 1956), *Somers* . . somewhere. **2000** Berry *Jayber Crow* 59 **KY,** Are you from around here somewheres, or are you from somewheres else? **2000** Shores *Tangier Is.* 187 **Chesapeake Bay,** Sometimes, one hears . . "some'ers" for *somewhere.* **2005** Williams *Gratitude* 525 **wNC** (as of 1940s), *Somerce, summerce:* somewhere(s).

some you-all See **you-all A1c**

somp See **swamp**

sompen See **something A3**

son n esp **NC** Cf **chap** n 2, **fellow** 3, **man** n C2

Used as a term of address to a female as well as a male; see quots; also used as an intensifier without reference to gender.

1946 *PADS* 6.28 **eNC** (as of c1906), *Son.* . . An affectionate term applied to a small boy and sometimes a small girl, usually in times of crisis. . . Once common, now obsolete. **1947** *PADS* 8.23 **KY,** [In ref to quot 1946:] *Son:* Obsolescent perhaps but not obsolete. **1968** *DARE* (Qu. A19, *Other ways of saying "I'll have to hurry": "I'm late, I'll have to _____."*) Inf **NC**81, Get a move on, son. **1994** NC Lang. & Life Project *Harkers Is. Vocab.* 10 **eNC,** *Son.* . . Referring to either sex, this is often used as a general address to a person, an intensifier, or an exclamation. *You better believe that, son.*

song-ballad n **sAppalachians, Ozarks** Cf Intro "Language Changes" I.4, **ballad B**

A song; the words or written text of a song.

1864 in 1866 Powers *Hospital Pencillings* 151 **AL,** You spoak of not gittin the letter that I sent the song ballet in I was very sorry in deed fer I wanted you to have the balet. **1896** *DN* 1.425 **swNC,** *Song-valet:* words of a song. **1908** Fox *Lonesome Pine* 100 **KY,** She knew lots more "song-ballets," she said. **1915** *DN* 4.190 **swVA,** *Song-ballad.* . . A song or ballad. **1927** *DN* 5.472 **Ozarks,** *Ballot.* . . The written words of a song. . . The combination *song-ballot* is also common. **1931** Goodrich *Mt. Homespun* 51 **sAppalachians,** The talk and the old tales and the singing of "song-ballets" lessened the tedium and made the workers forget their fatigue. **1931** *AmSp* 7.94 **eKY,** *Song-ballet,* the long-hand copy of the words of a ballad. "Illa sent me a good song-ballet, 'Barbara Ellen.'" **1939** *Hall Coll.* **wNC, eTN,** Her mother kept notebooks and had a collection of song ballits. **1946** *PADS* 5.39 **VA,** *Song ballad, song ballet:* Used with various meanings: a folk-song or ballad, or the actual manuscript copy of it; not common. **1952** Brown *NC Folkl.* 1.593, *Song ballit.* . . A ballad, a folk song. **c1960** *Wilson Coll.* **csKY,** *Song ballad (ballet).* . . The words to a song, sometimes written down in a composition book. **1982** Slone *How We Talked* 76 **eKY** (as of c1950), *A song ballet*—Song ballad. The written form of a song, usually handwritten.

song bow n
=**mouth bow.**

1889 *OH Hist.* 2.498 **MS** (as of 1858) [Black], Paul [=a slave] . . could play upon various musical instruments. The most curious of these was one which he called a "song-bow," a simple contrivance, consisting of a string stretched tight from one end to the other of a long, flexible, narrow board or bow, and which the performer breathed upon in such a way as to cause a musical vibration, while at the same time, he sang. **1980** *Foxfire 6* 84 **cwNC,** Momma helped me and I made one and I played 'Chickens Crowing on Sourwood Mountain.' . . It's kinda hard to play 'cause you have to keep your finger moving and you have to work your mouth, too. . . But anyway I love my songbow. **1998** Olson *Blue Ridge Folklife* 150, Toys that served to help children develop their musical aptitude included . . songbows. **2006** *DARE* File—Internet, As a solo artist Curley, [Ennis] accompanies himself on guitar, banjo, mountain dulcimer, song-bow, and harmonica.

song sparrow n chiefly Nth, N Midl See Map

An eastern sparrow *(Melospiza melodia)* and its western races; rarely other sparrows, as **field sparrow a** and **vesper sparrow.** For other names of *Melospiza melodia* see **bull sparrow, bush ~, everybody's darling, ground bird b, ~ chippy 1, ~ sparrow c, hedge sparrow, marsh ~ 1, red grass-bird, spring bird 1, swamp finch**

1810 Wilson *Amer. Ornith.* 2.125, [The] *Song Sparrow, Fringilla melodia,* . . is fond of frequenting the borders of rivers, meadows, swamps. **1832** Nuttall *Manual Ornith.* 1.486, Common Song-Sparrow. . . This familiar and almost domestic bird is one of the most common and numerous Sparrows in the United States. **1896** *Harper's New Mth. Mag.* 93.66, Everywhere the song-sparrow was filling the volume of tumult with his cheerful, homely singing. **1928** Beston *Outermost House* 164 **Cape Cod MA,** The road to the bay leads off at the town hall, passing an old windmill. . . Song sparrows perch on the arms that have not turned for years. **1938** Oberholser *Bird Life LA* 677, Mississippi Song Sparrow—*Melospiza melodia beata. Ibid* 678, Dakota Song Sparrow—*Melospiza melodia juddi.* **1953** Jewett *Birds WA* 661, Mountain Song Sparrow. *Melospiza melodia montana. Ibid* 662, Modoc Song Sparrow. *Melospiza melodia fisherella.* **1965–70** *DARE* (Qu. Q21, . . *Kinds of sparrows*) 168 Infs, **chiefly Nth, N Midl,** Song sparrow; **CA78,** San Diego song sparrow; **NC36,** Song sparrow = vesper sparrow; **OH33,** Song sparrow—same as wood sparrow. **2004** *Chron.-Telegram* (Elyria OH) 13 Aug sec B 7/2, Mel is a Song Sparrow *(Melospiza melodia).* This is the sparrow to learn, and compare all others to.

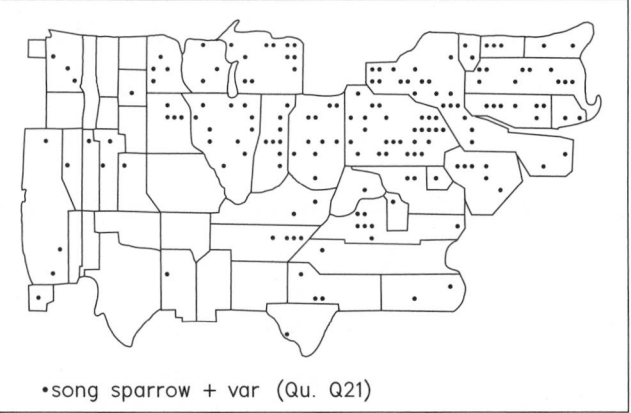

•song sparrow + var (Qu. Q21)

song thrush n
=**brown thrasher.**

1876 (1877) Minot *Land-Birds New Engl.* 48, Harporhynchus . . Rufus. Brown Thrush. "Song Thrush." "Thrasher." "Mavis." **1895** (1907) Wright *Birdcraft* 80, Song Thrush, Red Thrush, Brown Mockingbird, Mavis, are four of the local names for this most exultant and . . dashing of our song-birds. **1956** MA Audubon Soc. *Bulletin* 40.128 **ME,** Brown Thrasher. . . Song Thrush.

sonker n [Etym unknown] esp sAppalachians Cf sinker 2a
A deep-dish fruit pie.

1936 Morehouse *Rain on Just* 261 **NC,** Dolly had bribed Hector and Lector with fried pies and blackberry sonkers. **1944** *PADS* 2.30 **eKY,** *Sonker* ['saŋkɚ]: . . A fruit cobbler. Perhaps related to an old Manx word meaning "heavy." . . [R]are. **1984** Wilder *You All Spoken Here* 82 **Sth,** *Sonker.* . . A deep-dish fruit pie sweetened with molasses. The name comes from the advice, on being handed a ladle or dipper: "Sonker down to the bottom of the pan." **1986** Pederson *LAGS Concordance,* 1 inf, **neTN,** Apple sonker—thick bread with apples mixed in. **1987** *Gettysburg Times* (PA) 1 Sept sec A 4 **cnNC,** A local expert informs me that sonker is pronounced as it's spelled and not, as I'd erroneously assumed, "zonker." Apparently there is nothing very distinctive about the sonker itself—it may be made with either flour or breadcrumbs—except for this: The filling is whatever's handy at the time. . . My source was first introduced to the sonker at a meeting of the Beulah Extension Homemakers, and the filling on that occasion was sweet potato. Usually, however, sonkers are made with apples, peaches, or berries. **2005** *News & Observer* (Raleigh NC) 23 Oct sec D 10 (Internet), After living and eating in North Carolina since the age of 3, I thought I knew about what people in this state liked to cook. But there are always surprises, and one is sonker. . . The name, so far as I can tell, is unique to the Surry County area.

son of a birch See birch

son of a biscuit-eater See biscuit-eater 2

son-of-a-bitch See son-of-a-bitch stew

son-of-a-bitch in a sack n West
A bag pudding.

1941 Rollinson *Hoofprints* 151 **WY,** He made a real steamed pudding. It must have taken plenty of patience and plenty of cussing to make it, for it had to be hung in the twenty-gallon hot-water bucket over the pot rack to steam, wrapped in a clean white flour sack. . . I must agree with a lot of other cowmen that the cook gave it a befitting name when he affectionately branded it "son-of-a-bitch in a sack." **1958** *AmSp* 33.272 **eWA** [Ranching terms], *Son-of-a-bitch-in-a-sack.* A kind of pudding made of dried fruit, etc. **1973** Allen *LAUM* 1.409 (as of c1950) 1 inf, **nwSD,** Sonofabitch in a sack. A sweet pudding. *A cowhands' term.*

son-of-a-bitch stew n Also son-of-a-bitch, son-of-a-gun (stew) West, esp TX See Map on p. 124 Also called county attorney, cowboy stew, cow-camp ~, district attorney

A stew made of whatever is available, esp the internal organs of a freshly-killed beef.

1864 in 1946 Holmes *Touched with Fire* 139 **MA,** The soldiers . . have a sort of mush of hard tack wh[ich] they call "Son of a b_____h." **1915** *DN* 4.229 **wTX,** *Son-of-a-bitch.* . . A kind of stew, composed of a conglomeration of vegetables and meats, of which Texas cowmen are very fond. It has no other name. **1933** *AmSp* 8.1.27 **nwTX** [Ranch diction], *Son-of-a-gun.* A dish made of the liver, heart, sweetbreads, marrow-gut, brains, kidneys, and choicest tender meats from a young calf, together with salt, chili peppers, black pepper, and red pepper. **1937** *DN* 6.621 **swTX,** A hash or goulash composed of tripe, kidneys, haslets, etc. is happily called *son of a gun.* **1941** Vestal *Short Grass Country* 91, When all else failed, the Plainsman relied upon whatever was available, throwing it into an iron pot kept boiling on the fire—a pot which was constantly replenished with whatever came to hand. Such a hodgepodge or pot pourri or hunter's stew is known on the Short Grass as Son-of-a-Gun Stew. Sometimes it deserves—and receives—a stronger name. **1942** Perry *Texas* 125, In the western part of the state there is a favorite stew known . . by the name of "son of a bitch." Like most stews it is composed chiefly of the kitchen residuum, but usually the basic ingredients are corn, beans, onions, and the late genitals of an ex-bull. **1946** Mora *Trail Dust* 163 **West,** We're having a son-of-a-bitch for supper. . . "What in hell is a son-of-a-bitch?" . . "It's a marrow gut stew." **1956** Almirall *From College* 118 **NM,** I knew a "son-of-a-gun stew," made of brains, sweetbreads, and nice pieces of a freshly killed calf, such as we had eaten in New Mexico, would meet a big welcome sign within me. **1965–70** *DARE* (Qu. H36, *Kinds of soup*) Inf **TX**39, Son-of-a-gun; (Qu. H43, *Foods made from parts of the head and inner organs of an animal*) Infs **NM**12, **TX**65, 71, Son-of-a-gun; **TX**29, Son-of-a-gun stew; **AZ**8, Son-of-a-bitch; (Qu. H45, *Dishes made with meat, fish, or poultry that everybody around here would know, but that people in other places might not*) Infs **NM**12, **TX**3, 43, Son-of-a-gun; (Qu. H49, *Dishes made by boiling potatoes with other foods*) Inf **TX**11, Son-of-a-gun stew. **1986** Burgess *Homage* 77 **MT,** There is, I see too late, an *estofado de toro* on the menu, and I wonder if this is at all like the son-of-a-bitch stew (pizzle, testes and all, washed down by Bloody Marys) that I met in Montana. **1999** Proulx *Close Range* 92 **WY** (as of 1886), Pull up a chair and have some a this son-of-a-bitch stew.

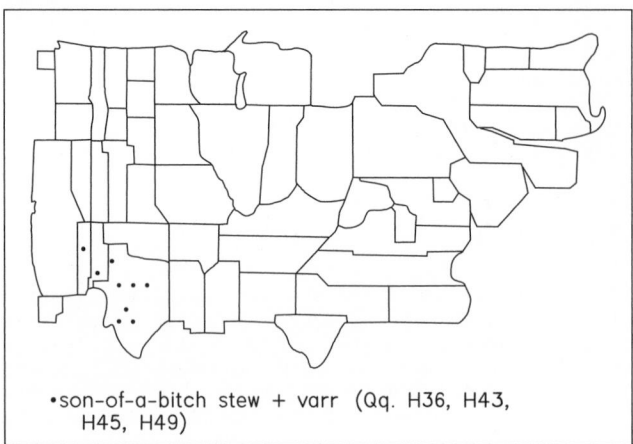

•son-of-a-bitch stew + varr (Qq. H36, H43, H45, H49)

son of a blood See **blood** n 4

son-of-a-gun (stew) See **son-of-a-bitch stew**

son of a sea biscuit See **sea biscuit**

son of ebony See **ebony** 1

son of Ethiopia See **Ethiopian** 1

sonsy adj Also *sonsi(e)* [Scots, nEngl dial] *old-fash*
Cute, charming; lively, healthy.
1852 Warner *Queechy* 2.44 **NYC,** A comfortable Liverpool-coal fire in a state of repletion burned away indolently and gave everything else in the room somewhat of its own look of sonsy independence. **1857** Parton *Fresh Leaves* 279, None of your poor-house hearses . . ; but a smart, sonsie, gay-looking New York turn-out. **1865** *Atlantic Mth.* 16.130, And although this burly rover is not our little bee of the hive, but his saucy, sonsy country-cousin, the song of the one is scarcely sweeter than that of the other. **1915** *Lincoln Daily News* (NE) 19 Feb sec A 2/1 **NYC,** The Fifth avenue shop windows all dolled up in their sonsy spring models look like . . the dashing windows of those funny little costume shops that hire out the making of a dashing cavalier. **1959** *VT Hist.* 27.159 **cn,neVT,** Sonsi [sǒn'sĭ]. . . Healthy. Occasional. Scotch. **1963** *New Yorker* 30 Nov 55 **eMA** (as of c1915), "She's a sonsy little snip," my father said. It was a favorite word of his, Scots, and meant, roughly, "cute." **1986** *DARE* File **IL** (as of c1930s), I grew up on Chicago's North Shore—where I heard the word [=*sonsie*] from my Dad. . . describing my sister and me as "sonsie lassies". His heritage was largely Scottish. His grandfather . . came to America in 1833.

sont See **send** 2

soo exclam, often repeated |su(:)| Cf **saw** exclam, **so** exclam, **sook** exclam, **suboy, swoo**
Used as any of var commands to an animal, spec:
a Come!—see quots. **widely scattered, but rare NEast, C Atl, West** See Map
1885 *Atlantic Mth.* 55.194 **wNC, eTN,** Dorinda, hunting for the vagrant "crumply cow," . . called with long, vague vowels, "Soo—cow! Soo!" **1886** in 1932 *AmSp* 7.454, It is amusing to notice the different ways people call their pigs. . . Our Buckeye [Ohio] neighbor coaxingly cries, in a soothing voice, Soo, soo, soo, soo. **1948** Davis *Word Atlas Gt. Lakes* 234, Call to hogs at feeding time . . soo-boy! [*DARE* Ed: This was the majority response in 8 of 63 communities, all in eastern Ohio.] *Ibid rapp qu* 70, 5 [*of* 233] *infs,* **IN, MI, OH,** Soo-pig! **1955** *DE Folkl. Bulletin* 1.292, Soo cow, soo cow, soo, soo (calling cows). **1965–70**

DARE (Qu. K80, *The call that's used . . to get the cows in from the pasture*) 35 Infs, **scattered, but esp Midl, Sth,** Soo-cow (also repeated); **IN**30, **MS**21, 46, **NM**3, **OH**47, **OK**1, 14, **PA**1, Soo (also repeated); **IA**8, 12, **IL**65, **IN**59, **OH**81, **WI**24, Soo-boss (also repeated); **IN**67, **OH**43, **OK**53, Soo-bossie; **GA**12, Soo soo-cow; **MO**18, Soo-calf; **TN**37, Soo-o-o; (Qu. K83, *To call a calf to you at feeding time*) 19 Infs, **chiefly Sth, S Midl,** Soo-calf (also repeated); **AR**4, **GA**5, 46, **NM**3, **OK**20, **SC**34, **TX**35, Soo-calfy (also repeated); **AL**2, **GA**14, **PA**1, Soo (soo); **OH**43, 75, Soo-boss; **FL**20, Soo-Bess, soo-bossie; **MS**39, Soo-cow; (Qu. K84, *The call used . . to get the pigs in at feeding time*) Infs **KY**29, **MS**39, **OH**43, **OK**27, **SC**23, **TX**69, **WA**23, Soo-pig(s); **NM**13, Soo-pig, soo-pig pig; **IL**59, **KS**11, **MA**58, **OH**77, **SC**4, **WI**30, Soo (also repeated); **MT**3, Come piggy, soo soo soo; **TX**57, Soo-calf [sic]; (Qu. K85, *The call to sheep to come in from the pasture*) Inf **AL**11, Soo. **1966** Dakin *Dial. Vocab. Ohio R. Valley* 2.266, *Calls to cows (in pasture). . .* Throughout the entire Valley, . . the Midland calls *sook!, sookie!, sook cow!* predominate. . . Less frequent forms are those which might best be represented in conventional spelling as: *soo!, soo-cow!, ~-kefer!, ~-boss!, ~-bossie!* *Ibid* 269, *Soo boss!, soo bossie!* are scattered. *Ibid* 274, The usual calls [to calves] are *sook calf(ie)!* or *soo-calf(ie)!* *Ibid* 284, The Ohio counties along the river from the Hanging Rock region to above the National Road all have the commonly used call [for pigs] *soo-boy!* **1972** *PADS* 58.18 **cwAL,** Calls to calves. Variants of Midland *sookie* were most frequently given: *soo-calf(ie)* (8 [of 27 infs]), *sook-calf(ie)* (4), and *soo* (1). **1973** *AmSp* 48.63, The common Midland call to cattle is *Soo, cow!* or *Sook, cow!* . . But the dialect contacts have yielded the compounds *Soo, boss!* and *Sook, boss!* within and around the Midland *Sook, cow!* region of southern and southeastern Iowa as well as in eastern Nebraska, together with one instance in eastern South Dakota. . . Two occurrences of . . *Soo, bossy!* also occur in Iowa and another in South Dakota. **1986** Pederson *LAGS Concordance (Calls to cows)* 153 infs, **Gulf Region,** Soo-cow (*or* soo baby, boss, bossy, calf, cow sook, etc). [*DARE* Ed: Although the fieldworkers were guided to contextualize the responses either as A, getting cows in from the pasture, or B, making them stand still for milking, contexts are provided for only 26 of the above responses, 25 for A, and 1 for B.]

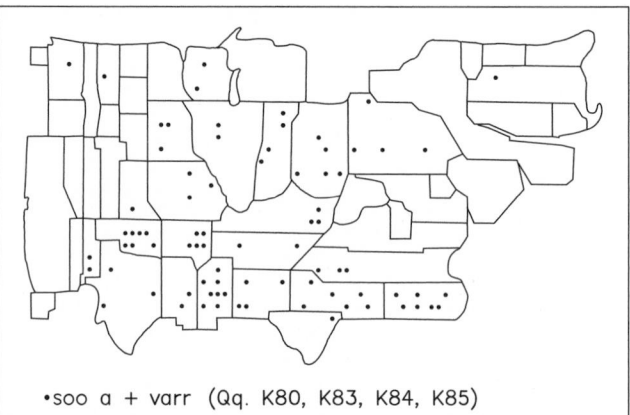

•soo a + varr (Qq. K80, K83, K84, K85)

b also *sough:* Stand still!—used to a cow during milking. [Cf *EDD so* int. 2]
1899 (1912) Green *VA Folk-Speech* 402, Soo wench. . . To make a cow stand still. **c1955** Reed–Person *Ling. Atlas Pacific NW,* 1 inf, Soo boss. **1965–70** *DARE* (Qu. K81, *To make a cow stand still—for example, when milking her—you say, "_____."*) 20 Infs, **scattered,** Soo (Bess, boss, Molly, sooky). **1972** Dakin *Dial. Vocab. Ohio R. Valley* 2.272, *Calls to cows (while milking). . .* In southeastern Indiana some speakers use . . *soo.* **1986** [see **a** above]. **2007** *DARE* File **sGA,** "Sough"—term used to tell a milk cow to be still while being milked.

c also *su:* Go on!—see quots. Cf **sooey** exclam, **suboy**
1903 [see **suboy**]. **1915** *DN* 4.190 **swVA,** Soo-y. . . Used in urging on hogs. **1967–68** *DARE* (Qu. NN22d, . . *Expressions used to drive away people or animals*) Infs **CO**4, 17, **LA**17, **NE**11, **OH**44, **OR**4, Soo (bossie, boy, cat, sow).

sooboy See **suboy**

soo cat n Also *seccat, siccat, succat* [Etym unknown] **SC** Cf **cat** n **6, polecat 5**
A home-brewed beer, esp **cane beer;** a distilled liquor made from this.

1955 *AmSp* 30.158 **SC,** [Names for sugar-cane beer:] *Soocat* . . was heard by Mrs. Flora Rush in Bamberg County, South Carolina, forty years ago. . . F.W. Bradley writes me that the name here discussed assumes the form *siccat,* as well as that already given, in the region of Columbia, South Carolina. **1966–67** *DARE* (Qu. DD28b, . . *Fermented drinks . . made at home*) Infs **SC**26, 43, Soo cat; **SC**19, Soo cat—made from sugar cane; **SC**40, Soo cat—cane skimmings fermented when cooking sugar. **1966** *DARE* Tape **SC**26, I have seen 'em drunk . . drunk off of soo cat. And now if you want to make a beer . . soo cat, you take grits and meal and sugar . . put it in a barrel and put a top over, then put a hole in it and let it set about six days. **1966** *DARE* FW Addit **SC,** *Soo cat*—fermented drink; boil the squeezings from sugar cane, skim off the foam that comes up, save them and let it ferment—old-fashioned. **1967** *Ibid* **SC,** *Soo cat*—dip the slut (scum) off cooking sugar cane and let it set up. **1973** *News & Courier* (Charleston SC) 25 Nov sec E 4/1, A potent white lightning, as much as 150 proof, called succat or seccat (probably derived from the word *succade* meaning sweet, candied fruit) was made by barreling the skimmings, letting them ferment and distilling the spirits.

soock See **sook** exclam

sooey exclam Usu |ˈsu-i|; also |ˈsu-ɪ, ˈsʊ-ɪ| Also sp *sooi(e), sooy, souy, s(o)uwee* **chiefly Sth, S Midl, Cent, TX** See Map Cf **soo**

Get along! Move! Shoo!—usu used as a command to an animal; see quots. Note: As the call to get pigs to come in at feeding time, *sooey* is not regional.

1886 Amer. Philol. Assoc. *Trans.* 17.46 **Sth,** List of common Southern expressions—many of them vulgarisms—that have not, so far as I know, either old English or provincial English authority. . . *Sooi* (call to frighten hogs). **1892** *DN* 1.237 **cwMO,** *Steboy* . . used in driving pigs. [suɪ], pronounced very rapidly, is also used. The same word with its [u] much prolonged is often used in calling pigs. **1893** Shands *MS Speech* 58, *Sooey* [su-ɪ]—The sound used to drive hogs out of one's way. **1899** (1912) Green *VA Folk-Speech* 402, *Sooy.* . . Words used to drive away hogs. **1903** *DN* 2.331 **seMO,** *Souy* or *souwee!* . . Used in driving hogs. In the North 'whee!' **1909** *DN* 3.373 **eAL, wGA,** *Souy, suwee.* . . Used in driving pigs. **1912** *DN* 3.590 **wIN,** *Sooey.* . . Go on. Used in driving hogs. **1915** *DN* 4.190 **swVA,** *Soo-y* [ˈsu-i]. . . Used in urging on hogs. **1941** Faulkner *Men Working* 21 **MS,** "Sooey out of here," he said. . The shoat gave a grunt of startled surprise and scrambled out of the spring. **1946** *PADS* 6.28 **ceNC** (as of 1900–10), *Sooy* [ˈsuɪ]. . . A command used to drive hogs away. . . Common. **1947** *PADS* 8.15 **IN,** *Sooy:* To drive away hogs; never to call them. **1950** *PADS* 14.62 **SC,** *Sooey.* . . Used to frighten hogs out of one's way. In some sections of lower S.C., used to call hogs to the trough for slops. **1954** *Harder Coll.* **cwTN,** *Sooey.* . . Command to force pigs to leave. . "Sooey 'way from here,' and kick at 'em." **1956** McAtee *Some Dialect NC* 42, *Sooey* . . a command used in driving hogs, meaning "git along" or "git out o' here." **c1960** *Wilson Coll.* **csKY,** *Soo-ey*—to make a hog go away. **1965–70** *DARE* (Qu. NN22d, . . *Expressions used to drive away people or animals*) 148 Infs, **chiefly Sth, S Midl, Cent, TX,** Sooey; 29 Infs, **scattered, but esp Sth, S Midl, Cent, TX,** Sooey (for a hog *or* pig *or* cow); **AR**51, 52, **LA**2, 11, [suɪ]; **GA**3, 9, **SD**3, [suɪ]; **OK**6, [su:wɨ]; **MO**19, Sooey, get out of here; (Qu. J8, *To tell a dog to attack*) Inf **LA**10, Sooey; (Qu. K84, *The call . . to get the pigs in at feeding time*) Inf **AL**2, Sooey—when you want to scare them; **AL**15, Sooey—to chase them; **OK**10, Sooey—when you run them away; **OR**2, Sooey—to drive them

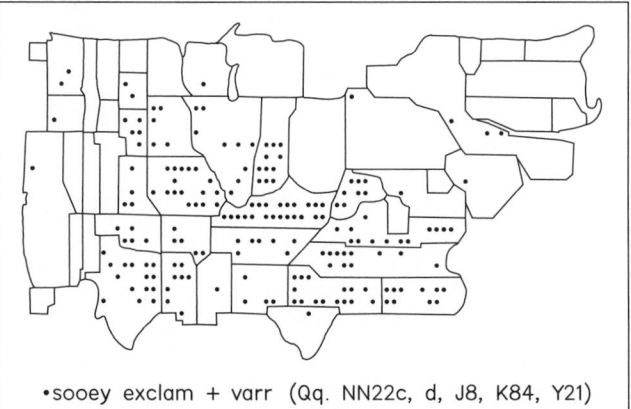

•sooey exclam + varr (Qq. NN22c, d, J8, K84, Y21)

away; **WA**12, Sooey—to make them move; (Qu. Y21, *To move about slowly and without energy*) Inf **TN**38, So lazy he wouldn't holler "sooey" if the hogs were eating him up; (Qu. NN22c, *Expressions used to drive away a dog*) Inf **GA**1, Sooey. **1968** *DARE* FW Addit **GA**35, *Sooey* [ˈsuɪ]—to make a hog leave. Inf criticized ex-President Eisenhower's use of *sooey* to call a hog to him. Said "that's to make a hog leave." **1983** *MJLF* 9.1.56 **ceKY** (as of 1956), *Sooie!* . . a sound made to drive pigs away. **2003** *Augusta Chron.* (GA) 30 Nov sec B 1 (Internet), Mr. Campbell is a serious student of porcine vocalizations. . . He also knows what "Sooey" really means—go away, hogs.

sooey n
=**sow and pigs.**
   1953 Brewster *Amer. Nonsinging Games* 159 **IN,** *Sooey.* . . The object of the game is for the player who is "It" to knock the can into the hole in the center of the circle despite the efforts of the others to prevent it. When the can is knocked into the center hole, all yell "Sooey!" run to a previously designated spot . . , and then run back and stick the ends of their bats into any of the holes in the circle. Since there are fewer holes than players, the player who is a slow runner fails to find a hole for his stick and automatically becomes "It" for the next game.

soofling See **suffling**

soogan, soogum See **sugan**

sooi(e) See **sooey** v

soojet n Also *sujjit* [Etym unknown] Cf **budget 1, sugan 3** See quot 1913.
   1913 Kephart *Highlanders* 75 **sAppalachians,** "Sujjit" (the *u* pronounced like *oo* in look) is true mountain dialect for a pouch, valise, or carryall, its etymology being something to puzzle over. **1944** *PADS* 2.21 **sAppalachians,** *Soojet* [ˈsuədʒɛt]. . . A sack, pouch.

sook exclam, often repeated Usu |sʊk|; also |suk|; in phrr *sook cow, ~ calf* usu assim to |ˈsʊˌkau, sʊˈkæf|; for addit varr see quots Also sp *soock, soolk, suk(e)* [Scots, nIr, nEngl dial as a call to calves, lambs, or pigs; var of *suck*] **chiefly Midl, Sth, TX** See Map on p. 126 Cf **soo, sookie**

Used as a call to a farm animal, esp a cow; hence n *sook* used as a nickname for an animal; see quots.

   1850 Garrard *Wah-to-yah* 178, The cows . . looked quite differently from the patient, chewing "Suke" of the American farmer. **1867** Harris *Sut Lovingood Yarns* 24 **TN,** Yu mout jis' es well say . . Suke cow to a gal. **1872** Haldeman *PA Dutch* 17, Cows are called . . when close at hand with 'suk suk suk' (as in for*sook*)—used also in the English of the locality. **1883** Sweet-Knox *Mexican Mustang* 597, 'Here, suke, suke!' And he . . threw some of the grains on the ground, to inspire the hogs with confidence. **1892** *DN* 1.237 **cwMO,** *Suke.* Cows are often called by the word [suk] or [sukɪ]. **1893** Shands *MS Speech* 76, *Suke* [suk]. The commonly used word for calling cows. The word *cow* is sometimes added to it, so as to make *sukow* [sukau], the *u* being long drawn out in the pronunciation. **1902** *DN* 2.245 **sIL,** *Sook, cafe* [sʊk kef]. A jodel; never 'co-bos.' **1903** *DN* 2.330 **seMO,** *Sook cafe, sook, sook.* Used in calling cows. **1906** *DN* 3.123 **sIN,** *Sook.* . . The call to cattle. **1907** *DN* 3.226 **nwAR,** *Sook, cafe* [suk kef]. **1909** *DN* 3.373 **eAL, wGA,** *Sook.* . . Used in calling calves. "Sook, sook, sook, sook-calf!" . . Also used in driving cows or calves. "Sook out of here, madam!" *Ibid* 404 **nwAR,** *Sook.* . . Call to cattle. Vowel both long and short. . . The usual call is 'So, cow, sook, sook, cow, sook!' The first rhymes with coke; the second with cook. **1915** *DN* 4.190 **swVA,** *Sook.* . . Call to cattle at feeding time. Sometimes *sook-calf(y).* **1929** Gordon *Born to Be* 54 [Black], I also held honors for calling stock, when salting cattle. Not having any occasion to make the soock call, I used this call for warning the travellers on the road. **1940** (1968) Haun *Hawk's Done Gone* 63 **eTN,** I got my bucket and called Old Heif. "Soolk, Heif, soolk, soolk." **1961** *AmSp* 36.266 **CO,** The expressions *sook boss!* and *salt side* appear to be blends from a Northern-Midland dialect mixture somewhere. . . *Sook boss!* is common in parts of the Great Lakes region. **1965–70** *DARE* (Qu. K80, *The call that's used . . to get the cows in from the pasture*) 91 Infs, **chiefly Midl, Sth, TX,** Sook-cow; **IN**44, [sʊˈkæu]; **LA**12, 29, [ˈsʊkˌːau]; **LA**15, [ˈsʊkˌau]; **MO**4, [sʊkaˈoː]; **MO**11, [ˈsʌ·kau:]; **SC**32, [ˈsʊˌkjæu]; **TN**26, [ˈsʊˌkau]; 74 Infs, **chiefly Midl, TX,** Sook (often repeated); **AR**4, 29, **IN**49, **MS**1, 53, **PA**163, **TX**69, [suk]; **AR**55, **IL**69, **LA**15, **MD**32, **MS**72, **OK**52, [su(:)k]; 16 Infs, **esp Midl, Cent,** Sook-boss (*or* bossie, calf, calves, heifer, jersey, Molly); **IN**32, [sʊˈkæf]; **PA**6, Come sook; **PA**211, Come sookie sook sook; **KY**35, 62, Hoo sook sook sook; **MO**5, Sook-boss co-boss wo; **MO**37, Sook-cow sook-cow come on; **VA**7, Sook jers sook sook; **KY**64, **TN**10, Sook sook sook sook (sook)-cow; **MO**3, Sook sook woo; **LA**29, Sook sook-cow sook; **KY**16, 43, 46, Sook (plus name); (Qu. K83, *To call a calf to you at feeding time*) 83 Infs, **chiefly Midl, Sth, TX,** Sook-calf (or -calfy); **AR**47, 51, **KY**29, **LA**7, **MS**63, **OH**31, ['suˌkæf]; **IN**44, **SC**32, [ˌsuˈkæɪf]; **IN**32, ['su'kæəf]; **IA**14, **MI**91, **WI**44, ['sʌˌkæf]; **IL**4, **TX**105, [ˌsəˈkæf]; 32 Infs, **chiefly Midl, TX,** Sook (also repeated); 14 Infs, **esp Midl,** Here sook (here sook); 10 Infs, **Midl, esp KY,** Sook-calf sook-calf; **TX**78, Sook here; **NM**10, Sook (plus name); **GA**68, Sook sook sook sook calf; **IN**54, Sook sook sookie; **PA**71, Sook-abbie; **GA**77, Sook-calfy come here calfy; **TN**1, 2, Sook-calve(s); **TN**14, Sook-calvy; **MO**24, **NC**37, **TN**2, Sook-cow; (Qu. K81, *To make a cow stand still—for example, when milking her—you say, "_____."*) Inf **DC**8, Saw sook saw sook; **IN**19, **KY**64, Sook; **LA**14, Sook sook sook; **IL**19, Sook-cow; **VA**7, Sook-jer; (Qu. K84, *The call used . . to get the pigs in at feeding time*) Infs **DC**5, **ID**4, **KS**1, **PA**103, **TX**11, 82, Sook (sook sook); (Qu. NN22d, . . *Expressions used to drive away people or animals*) Inf **GA**45, Sook—for a cow. **1989** Pederson *LAGS Tech. Index* 139 **Gulf Region** *(Calls to cows)* 194 infs, Sook (boss/cow); *(Calls to calves)* 17 infs, Sook; 1 inf, Sook, baby; 65 infs, Sook, calf(y); 1 inf, Sooky sook, calf. *Ibid* 142 *(Calls to pigs)* 1 inf, Sook; 3 infs, Sooky (sook sooky). **1999** Mason *Clear Springs* 38 **wKY,** My first word was "sook-cow"—the cry my family used to call the cows at milking time.

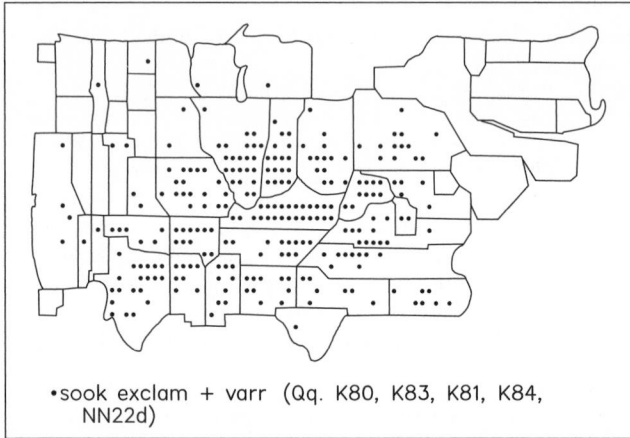

•sook exclam + varr (Qq. K80, K83, K81, K84, NN22d)

sook n   **chiefly Chesapeake Bay**   Cf **silk (crab), sow crab**
A mature female blue crab *(Callinectes sapidus).*

1942 Chesapeake Biol. Lab. *Pub.* 52.9 **Chesapeake Bay,** It is at this final molt that the female acquires the broad semi-circular apron and becomes a "sook," "silk" or "sow" crab. **1955** *Sun* (Baltimore MD) 16 June 14/7, The latter [=a female crab] is a "sook" if she has reached her last stage of growth and is ready to become a mother. **1970** *DARE* (Qu. P18, . . *Kinds of shellfish*) Inf **VA**55, Peeler—about to become a sook. **1970** *DARE* FW Addit **VA**47, Sook [suk]—a female crab. **1976** Warner *Beautiful Swimmers* 16 **Chesapeake Bay,** A sook, easy to recognize, is a sexually mature female. **1996** Horton *Island Out of Time* 20 **Chesapeake Bay,** It is only on the final shed that the maiden crab becomes a "sook," capable of reproducing once before she dies. **2010** *NYT Mag.* 13 June 28 **Chesapeake Bay,** Crabs, blue-clawed and olive-backed. . . a picnic table is sheathed in old newspaper and a bounty of jimmies and sooks piled high atop it.

sook calf (or cow)   See **sook** exclam

sookie exclam   Also sp *sooky, sukee, sukey*   [Dimin of **sook** exclam; cf *EDD sucky* sb. 6 "A call-word for a calf, occas. also for a sheep or pig; hence a pet name for a calf."]   **scattered, but rare NEast**   See Map   Cf **sook** exclam
Used as a call to a farm animal, esp a cow or calf; hence n *sookie* used as a nickname for an animal; see quots.

1838 Drake *Tales & Sketches* 154 **OH,** With a bellicose bellow, forwards and downwards went the old sukey. **1870** *Overland Mth.* 5.432 **CA,** John's evening experience was worse than mine of the morning, for Sukey seemed aware that she had fallen into green hands. . . If John went one side, she turned sheer round 'tother. If he got his little stool camped down, and bucket ready, the merest touch sent her whirling round again. . . [H]e attempted conciliation by "So now, Sukey! whoa, Sukey!" **1892** [see **sook** exclam]. **1899** (1912) Green *VA Folk-Speech*

402, *Sooky.* . . Name given to a female hog. **1918** *DN* 5.19 **NC,** *Sookie,* a cow. **1944** *PADS* 2.61 **MO, SC,** *Sukee, suk* ['su:ki; suk]. . . A term (repeated) used in calling cows. . . Common. **1951** *AmSp* 26.253 **nNY,** Terms typical of the Midland . . are also found as sporadic examples. . . *sookie!* (call to calves). **c1955** Reed–Person *Ling. Atlas Pacific NW (Call to cows to get them in from the pasture)* 1 inf, Sookie. **1960** Bailey *Resp. to PADS 20* **KS,** I've heard "here sukey" but our calves never had to be called at feeding time. **1965–70** *DARE* (Qu. K83, *To call a calf to you at feeding time*) 27 Infs, **scattered, but more freq Mid and S Atl, OH,** (Here,) sookie; **MD**24, **PA**67, ['su(:)ki]; **MD**29, **NC**41, **VA**27, ['suki]; **MD**22, [su'ki:]; **VA**97, [suk'i]; **GA**28, Come on, sookie; **IN**54, Sook sook sookie; **MD**48, **OH**72, 86, Sookie sookie (sookie); (Qu. K80, *The call that's used . . to get the cows in from the pasture*) 23 Infs, **scattered, but esp Appalachians,** Sookie (also repeated); **VA**32, Come on, sookie; **PA**211, Come, sookie sook sook; **MO**12, Here, sookie sookie; (Qu. K8, *Joking terms for milking a cow: A farmer might say, "Well, it's time to go out and _____."*) Infs **KY**16, **VA**24, Milk (old) sookie; **AR**52, Juice old sookie; **WA**30, Sap the sookies; (Qu. K81, *To make a cow stand still—for example, when milking her—you say, "_____."*) Infs **NJ**56, **PA**51, So-sookie (so); **MD**48, **PA**6, Soo sookie; (Qu. K82, *The call used . . to get horses in from the pasture*) Inf **MD**48, Sookie sookie sookie; (Qu. K84, *The call used . . to get the pigs in at feeding time*) Infs **LA**33, **NJ**29, **WY**1, Sookie (sookie). **1989** Pederson *LAGS Tech. Index* 139 **Gulf Region** *(Calls to cows)* 14 infs, Sooky (cow); 1 inf, Hoo-oke sooky; 1 inf, Sooky kwo aa. *Ibid* 140 *(Calls to calves)* 6 infs, Sooky; 1 inf, Co sooky; 1 inf, Sooky sook, calf. *Ibid* 142 *(Calls to pigs)* 3 infs, Sooky (sook sooky).

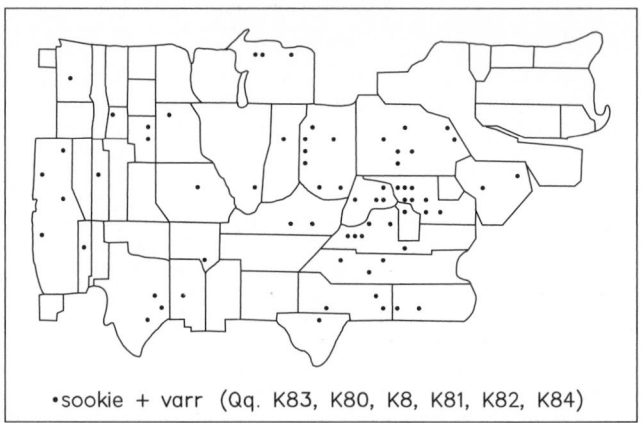

•sookie + varr (Qq. K83, K80, K8, K81, K82, K84)

soolk   See **sook** exclam

soon adv

1 Early—usu in phr *soon in the morning.*   [*OED2 soon* adv. 3.a a1300 →]   **chiefly Sth, S Midl**

1805 Rush *Med. Inquiries* 2.138 **PA,** Avoid travelling too soon in the morning. **1831** (2001) Earlham College Libraries *Josiah Parker Papers* 34 (Internet) **NC,** It commenced snowing soon in the morning snowed all day or nearly so. **1854** *Harper's New Mth. Mag.* 10.130, You'll never have health, you'll never have wealth,/ Unless you're up soon in the morning! **1886** *Amer. Philol. Assoc. Trans.* 17.43 **Sth,** Soon, for 'early,' . . is a misuse common in the South and perhaps West. I should have supposed that the above was well-nigh universal, if all my Northern correspondents, except two from the West, had not disclaimed knowledge of it. . . An example sent me from East Tennessee is, "You must get up soon, or the corn won't grow." "Soon in the morning" is very common all over the South. **1898** Lloyd *Country Life* 13 **AL,** Soon in the mornin or along in the shank of the evenin. **1899** (1912) Green *VA Folk-Speech* 402, *Soon.* . . Early; before the time specified is much advanced; when the time, event, or like has but just arrived. **1902** *DN* 2.245 **sIL,** Soon [sun]. . . Early, as 'Right soon in the morning.' **1903** *DN* 2.331 **seMO,** We'll get up soon in the morning. **1907** *DN* 3.227 **nwAR,** Soon. . . Early. *Ibid* 236 **nwAR,** I'll start soon in the morning. **1908** *S. Atl. Qrly.* 7.342 **SC** [Gullah], Soon is used as . . a substitute for *early.* **1909** *DN* 3.373 **eAL, wGA,** Soon. . . Early. The latter is seldom heard. **1910** *DN* 3.457 **KY,** I shall get up soon to-morrow morning. **1926** *AmSp* 1.412 **Okefenokee GA,** It wuz soon in the mornin', an' I didn't find no Deer. **1927** Adams *Congaree* 76 **cSC** [Black], You up soon, Bubber. **1937** (1977) Hurston *Their Eyes* 66 **FL** [Black], They could carpenter, so Jody hired them to go to work on his store bright and soon the next morning. **1987** Kytle *Voices* 163 **NC** [Black], She got to work soon in the morning, and some days he'd already be there.

2 Tightly—usu in phr *fit too soon* and varr: to fit too tightly; to be too small. Cf **quick** adv **3**

1879 Bland *Oh Dem Golden Slippers* 4, [Song lyrics:] And my long, white robe dat I bought last June, I'm gwine to git changed Kase it fits too soon. **1928** Nason *Sergeant Eadie* 76, "If I sit down quick, I'm liable to sit right out of this blouse." "Man," agreed Jake, "It does fit you kind of soon. Be careful when you open your mouth you don't get your jaw caught under the collar." **1942** McAtee *Dial. Grant Co. IN* 26 (as of 1890s), *Fit too soon* . . said of a garment, which upon trial is manifestly too small. **1947** Ballowe *The Lawd* 82 **sLA,** Ma grave clo'es. . . They fits soon in some places an' late in 'tothers, but the quality there. **1959** *VT Hist.* 27.136, *Fit too soon.* . . To be too small. Common. **1969** *DARE* (Qu. OO38a, *About shoes fitting just right: "When I tried these shoes on, they _____.")* Inf **IL**96, They fit too soon. **2003** in 2006 *DARE* File—Internet **NYC,** Everything fits too soon one way, too late the other. **2004** *DARE* File **csWI** (as of c1975), Tight pants were in fashion during my high school years. "Don't you think those jeans fit just a little too soon?" my mother would ask pointedly.

soon adj —freq in phr *a soon start.* **Sth, S Midl**

1 Early—freq in phr *a soon start.* **Sth, S Midl**

1869 *Overland Mth.* 3.131 **Sth,** *Soon* is used adjectively all over the South; as, "If I get a soon start in the morning, I'll be thar before sunup." **1889** *MLN* 4.207 **TN,** *Soon.* . . is still heard among the uneducated . . in the sense of 'early.' **1895** *DN* 1.374 **seKY, eTN, wNC,** *Soon* . . early. "We'll have a soon supper." **1908** *S. Atl. Qrly.* 7.342 **seSC,** A *soon brukwuss* is an *early breakfast; a soon sta't* is an *early start.* **1913** Kephart *Highlanders* 84 **sAppalachians,** Rustle out, boys; we've got to git a soon start if you want bear brains an' liver for supper. **1924** Raine *Land of Saddle-Bags* 100 **sAppalachians,** They "git up afore day to git a soon start." **1929** Sale *Tree Named John* 10 **MS,** She wanted a "soon budder." **1930** Stoney-Shelby *Black Genesis* 47 **seSC,** Git here firs' t'ing in de mornin' an' we'll mek a soon start. **1931** Randolph *Ozarks* 77, The Ozarker very often says *soon* when he means early, as in the sentence: "You-all better git a right soon start in th' mornin'." **1952** Brown *NC Folkl.* 1.593, *Soon.* . . Early. . . General. **c1960** *Wilson Coll.* **csKY,** *Soon.* . . Early . . a soon start. **1968** *DARE* FW Addit **swMD,** "I went to soon church"—meaning the early service. Remembered by . . old people as said by their parents and grandparents. **1975** Chalmers *Better* 65 **Smoky Mts,** One should rise early and get a soon start if the way is long.

2 Enterprising, smart, clever—esp in comb *soon man.* **chiefly Sth, S Midl** *esp freq among Black speakers* Cf *DJE* **suun-man**

1866 *Ballou's Mth. Mag.* 23.51 **NEng,** The Owl was still in sight, . . gaining on us as if we were tied to a post. 'That's a "soon" brig, and a "soon" man commands her,' said one of our fellows. **1883** (1971) Harris *Nights with Remus* 62 **GA** [Black], Co'se Mr. Ram mighty smart man. I aint 'spute dat; but needer Mr. Ram ner yet Mr. Lam is soon creeturs lak Brer Rabbit. **1884** *Anglia* 7.262 **Sth, S Midl** [Black], De soones' nigger on de plantashun = the cleverest, &c. *Ibid* 268, Er soon beas' = a clever creature. **1886** *Current* 6.166 **TX,** Ned were a soon boy, you bet. Well, sir, in a month Ned en Jack hed a load er hides, en right-smart cattle marked. **1888** Jones *Negro Myths* 102 **GA coast,** Buh Rabbit es er soon man. You haffer git up befo day fuh head um. **1892** *DN* 1.232 **KY,** *Soon* . . shrewd. "He is a soon man." **1922** Gonzales *Black Border* 327 **sSC, GA coasts** [Gullah glossary], *Soon-man*—a smart, alert, wide-awake man. **1930** Stoney-Shelby *Black Genesis* 101 **seSC,** Time an' agin Br' Wolf lay for him, but Br' Rabbit is a *soon* man.

soonah See **sooner** n[1]

soon dog See **sooner** n[2] **2**

sooner n[1] Pronc-sp *soonah*

1 also *sooner man, ~ nigger:* A quick, clever, or enterprising person. [**soon** adj **2**]

1883 *Janesville Daily Gaz.* (WI) 24 Oct [4]/3 (newspaperarchive.com), Mr. Free Press, you need a "sooner" man when you come to riding on wheels. You ought not put out your "bantams" in a bevy of thoroughbreds. **1892** *DN* 1.232 **KY,** *Soon* . . shrewd. "He is a soon man." "He is a sooner." [*DN* Ed: Is the word *sooner* here a comparative, or does the second example (also heard at Saginaw, Mich. . .) mean the same thing as the first one, and is the ending *-er* added somewhat as in *goner?*] **1892** *TX School Jrl.* 10.492, Well, if Mr. Contractor is a "sooner" he *will* allow for a wide margin, and the state will pay a large per centage addi-

tional for school books. **1909** *S. Atl. Qrly.* 8.46 **seSC,** A *soonah niggah,* for one under whose swift feet no grass grows; . . a fast negro is a *soonah,* . . a phrase which I believe is now wide-spread. **1939** Aurand *Quaint Idioms* 31 [PaGer], He's a *sooner* (quick, fast, shrewd).

2 also *sooner babe, ~ child, ~ kid:* A child conceived or born out of wedlock. Cf **come-too-soon**

1953 Randolph-Wilson *Down in Holler* 286 **Ozarks,** *Sooner.* . . A child born less than nine months after its parents' wedding. **1960** Criswell *Resp. to PADS 20* **Ozarks,** Bastard; once in a while the word *sooner* was used. **1965–68** *DARE* (Qu. Z11b, . . *[A child whose parents were not married])* Infs **NY**113, **OK**1, **SC**7, **SD**8, **WI**60, Sooner. **1972** Clauser *Girl Named Sooner* 55 **sIN** (as of c1935), She done *said* the babe was my boy Jason's—a sooner babe cause they wasn't married yet for the full term. **1973** Allen *LAUM* 1.344 (as of c1950), *Illegitimate child.* . . sooner kid [3 infs, **IA**]. **1973** *DARE* File **Ozarks** (as of c1910), An illegitimate child was a woods colt, a sooner, or love child. **1995** Brophy *Coll.* 70 **swMO** (as of c1960), *Sooner.* [A] bastard, a child born less than nine months after its parents' marriage. **2005** *DARE* File—Internet, Are you dubba and noel's illegitimate sooner child?

3 See quot.

1968 *DARE* (Qu. K43, *A horse that was not intentionally bred, or bred by accident)* Inf **NY**80, Sooner.

sooner n[2] [Ironic reinterpretation of **sooner** n[1] **1** on the basis of *sooner* rather]

1 also *sooner man:* A lazy, good-for-nothing person.

1871 *Janesville Gaz.* (WI) 6 Dec [4]/1 (newspaperarchive.com), There is a sooner man at the Myers house. He had sooner be loafing around the dining room, fooling with the waiter girls, than any other place in town. **1956** in 1972 Hall *Sayings Old Smoky* 128 **wNC,** We're sooners here. We'd just as soon lay in bed as get up.

2 also *soon(er) dog, sooner hound:* An inferior or mongrel dog. **scattered, but esp Sth, S Midl** See Map

1873 *Daily Republican* (Decatur IL) 8 May [3]/3 (newspaper-archive.com), A gentleman . . said it was half hunter and half setter—that he hunted until he found a bone, and then sat down to eat it. This wonderful "purp" must be some relation to the "sooner dog" of which we have heard so much. **1897** *KS Univ. Qrly.* (ser B) 6.92 **neKS,** *Sooner:* a mongrel cur. **1940** Smiley *Gloss. New Paltz* **seNY,** A rather mangy-looking hound dog wandered past. Oscar Coddington remarked that it looked like a 'soon' dog. I asked them what they meant. They said: "He would as soon sit as hunt." **1956** in 1972 Hall *Sayings Old Smoky* 128 **eTN,** I've got a sooner dog. He'd rather lay in the house as out in the yard. **1957** Battaglia *Resp. to PADS 20* **eMD,** A dog of mixed breed: sooner—slang—recent usage. **c1960** *Wilson Coll.* **csKY,** *Sooner.* . . A cur or mongrel dog. **1965–70** *DARE* (Qu. J2, . . *Joking or uncomplimentary words . . for dogs)* 30 Infs, **scattered, but esp Sth, S Midl,** Sooner; **AR**55, Half sooner and half setter; **MS**47, Old sooner; **TN**26, Sooner dog; (Qu. J1, . . *A dog of mixed breed)* 16 Infs, **scattered, but esp Sth, S Midl,** Sooner; **OH**76, Sooner dog. **1984** *MJLF* 10.157 **cnWI,** *Sooner hound.* A poor hunting dog. "Sooner lie down than hunt." **1986** Pederson *LAGS Concordance* **Gulf Region** (Mongrel) 42 infs, (A) sooner [or] sooners; 2 infs, Sooner dog(s); 1 inf, Sooner hound. **2000** in 2002 *DARE* File—Internet **neFL,** I felt like a "Sooner" at a Schnauzer dog show.

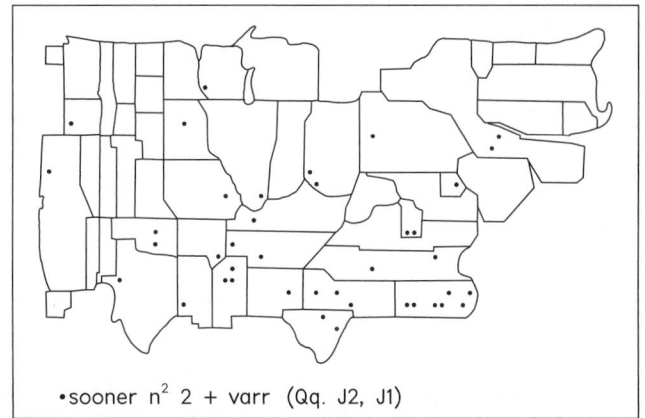

•sooner n[2] 2 + varr (Qq. J2, J1)

sooner babe (or child) See **sooner** n[1] **2**

sooner dog (or hound) See **sooner** n[2] **2**

sooner kid See **sooner** n¹ 2

sooner man n
1 See **sooner** n¹ **1.**
2 See **sooner** n² **1.**

sooner nigger See **sooner** n¹ 1

soon in the morning See **soon** adv 1

soon man See **soon** adj 2

soop See **soup**

soopeeny See **subpoena**

soople adj, v |'supəl, 'supḷ| Also sp *soopl, souple* [Brit dial varr of *supple*]

1825 Neal *Brother Jonathan* 1.268 **CT,** Walter was very graceful; quick, sharp, and "soople, as a great snek." 1845 *Living Age* 4.156 **NEng,** If I hadn't a been as soople as moose wood, I couldn't have gotten the ins and outs of high life as I have. 1887 (1967) Harris *Free Joe* 111 **GA,** He wuz a mighty nice-lookin' young feller, peart an' soople. 1890 *DN* 1.72 **LA,** *Soople:* supple. 1892 *DN* 1.218 **seMA, NEng,** *Soople.* . . The pronunciation [supḷ] is . . common in . . New England generally. 1899 Chesnutt *Conjure Woman* 24 **csNC** [Black], He got young ag'in, en so soopl en libely. 1899 (1912) Green *VA Folk-Speech* 403, *Souple.* . . Soople. Plaint [sic]; flexible; easily bent. 1902 *DN* 2.246 **sIL,** *Supple* [supḷ]. 1903 *DN* 2.332 **seMO,** *Supple.* . . Pronounced souple. 1907 *DN* 3.237 **nwAR,** *Supple.* . . Pronounced [supḷ]. 1909 *DN* 3.377 **eAL, wGA,** *Supple.* . . [supḷ]. 1916 *DN* 4.281 **NE,** *Soople.* . . Frequent for *supple.* 1923 (1946) Greer-Petrie *Angeline Steppin'* 35 **csKY,** All them solemn-lookin' folks . . would feel better if they'd . . soople up a little. 1927 *AmSp* 2.365 **cwWV,** *Soople* . . supple. "He is a very soople man." 1941 *LANE* Map 461 *(Lively, spry)* 1 inf, **cwVT,** [suupḷ]. 1946 *PADS* 6.28 **eNC,** *Souple* ['supḷ]: . . *Supple.* . . Common. 1965–70 *DARE* (Qu. KK25, *Something that bends or yields easily: "That willow branch is very _____."*) 34 Infs, **scattered, but chiefly east of Missip R,** Soople; (Qu. KK27, *A very lively, active old person: "For his age, he's _____."*) Inf **IL4,** Quite soople; **TN26,** Really soople ['supəl]; **IN45,** Very souple. [32 of 35 total Infs comm type 4 or 5] 1976 Ryland *Richmond Co. VA* 377, *Soople*—supple. 1982 *Barrick Coll.* **csPA,** *Supple*—pron. ['supḷ].

sooplejack See **supplejack** 2

soopolallie n Also *soopoo-lalia, sopalally* [Chinook Jargon] Cf **Eskimo ice cream**

A **buffalo berry** (here: *Shepherdia canadensis*); a dish made with this berry.

1913 Britton–Brown *Illustr. Flora* 2.576, Lepargyraea canadénsis. . . Canadian Buffalo-berry. . . On banks, especially along streams, Newfoundland to Alaska, British Columbia, Maine, New York, Wisconsin and New Mexico. . . Soopoo-lalia (Indian). 1959 Anderson *Flora AK* 348, S[hepherdia] canadensis. . . Soapberry, Soopolallie. . . Native Indians mix the berries with sugar and water and beat it into a froth much relished by them. 1962 Salisbury *Quoth the Raven* 135 **seAK,** We have been told that the natives have a dish of their own which they call "sopally" or Indian ice cream, which is made by beating up with the hands crushed soap berries in warm water in a big bowl or dishpan. Sugar is added and the whole is beaten . . until the proper stiffness has been secured.

soot n Usu |sut|; also **chiefly Sth, S Midl, less freq NEast** |sʌt|; occas |sut| Similarly adj *sooty* |'sʌdɪ| Pronc-spp *sut(ty)* [All three proncs are old; [sʌt] was given as std by several late 18th-cent English dictionaries, but appar went out of fashion soon after 1800.]
Std sense, var forms.

1806 (1970) Webster *Compendious Dict.* 284, *Soot, Sut,* . . a substance formed by combustion. [*DARE* Ed: The sp *sut* does not appear in Webster's English model.] *Ibid* 301, *Sutty.* 1862 *S. Lit. Messenger* 34.569 **Sth** [Black], He would make it all right "by plarsterin de beard-holes with a little sut." 1890 *DN* 1.59 **seSC,** *Soot* is commonly pronounced [sʌt]. 1890 Holley *Samantha among Brethren* 54 **NY,** There wuz sut all over the floor. 1893 Shands *MS Speech* 61, *Sut* [sʌt]. The ordinary pronunciation of *soot.* This is heard also in South Carolina and Tennessee. 1896 *DN* 1.425 **NY,** *Soot:* pron. [sʌt], common in Ontario, Seneca, Chenango, Otsego, and Albany Cos., N.Y. 1899 (1912) Green *VA Folk-Speech* 430, *Sut.* . . A black substance formed by combustion. Soot. . .

Sutty. . . Covered with sut. 1909 *DN* 3.377 **eAL, wGA,** *Sut* [sʌt]. . . Soot. 1915 *DN* 4.190 **swVA,** *Soot* [sʌt]. 1959 *VT Hist.* 27.159, *Soot* [sʌt]. . . Common. Rural areas. 1961 Kurath–McDavid *Pronc. Engl.* 155, *Soot.* . . /sut/ is the predominant pronunciation in the North and in large parts of Pennsylvania, but /sʌt/ and/or /sut/ are used by a considerable minority, the former especially in folk speech. This diversity is found even in the cities. . . In the South and the South Midland *soot* has the vowel /ʌ/ of *flood* quite regularly in the speech of the folk. . . /sʌt/ also predominates in some of the southern counties of Pennsylvania and adjoining parts of West Virginia and Maryland, in southern New Jersey, and . . in northeastern Pennsylvania. . . In the remainder of the North Midland and in the North it is strictly a folk pronunciation. *Soot* with the vowel /u/ of *food* . . occurs most frequently in the New England settlement area, but scattered instances make their appearance in all parts of the Eastern States, especially in cultivated speech. 1963 Watkins-Watkins *Yesterday Hills* 131 **cnGA,** Smut or soot (the former said "sut") mixed with sugar would stop the flow of blood. 1965–70 *DARE* (Qu. H74a) Inf **SC21,** Black as soot [sʌt]; (Qu. K38) Inf **GA3,** Sooty [sʌdɪ]; (Qu. BB50c) Inf **MS29,** Soot [sʌt]; **TN12,** Soot [sut]. 1970 *DARE* Tape **VA112,** Blacker'n [sʌt]. c1970 Pederson *Dial. Surv. Rural GA* **seGA** *(The soft thick black stuff that collects in a chimney is _____)* [30 [of 64] infs, proncs of the type [sʌt]; 14 infs, proncs of the type [su(ə)t]; 5 infs, proncs of the type [suut].] 1984 Burns *Cold Sassy* 104 **nGA** (as of 1906), You need to understand that in Cold Sassy . . [w]e . . say . . *sut* for soot. 1989 Pederson *LAGS Tech. Index* 35 **Gulf Region,** *Soot.* . [Of 914 infs, 390 offered proncs of the type [sut]; 380 infs, proncs of the type [sʌt]; 37 infs, proncs of the type [sut].] 2003 *DARE* File—Internet **AZ,** I would say they [=spark plugs] are black and sutty, almost oily looking.

soothsayer n [Transl of Gk *mantis*]
=**praying mantis B.**

1841 Harris *Rept. Insects MA* 116, The Mantes or soothsayers are predacious and carnivorous. 1909 Smith *Insect Friends* 95, The Mantids or soothsayers are voracious feeders. 1954 Borror–DeLong *Intro. Insects* 137, They usually lie in wait for their prey with the front legs in an upraised position; this position has given rise to the common names "praying mantid" and "soothsayer" that are often applied to these insects.

sooty adj See **soot**

sooty n See **sooty shearwater**

sooty grouse n
=**dusky grouse.**

1881 U.S. Natl. Museum *Bulletin* 24.196, Canace Obscura Fuliginosa. . . Sooty grouse. 1898 (1900) Davie *Nests N. Amer. Birds* 168, Sooty Grouse. . . abundant in Washington county, in the northern part of Oregon. 1918 Grinnell et al. *Game Birds CA* 544, Sierra Grouse—Dendragapus obscurus sierrae. . . Other names . . Sooty Grouse. 1923 Dawson *Birds CA* 4.1595, A northern observer claims that Sooty Grouse will hiss like a gander, especially when treed by a dog. 1953 Jewett *Birds WA* 196, Oregon Blue Grouse. . . Other names: Sooty Grouse [etc]. 2006 *DARE* File—Internet **cwWA,** We have the Sooty Grouse in our area, the Dusky Grouse living exclusively east of the Cascades.

sooty shearwater n Also *sooty*
A **shearwater 1** (here: *Puffinus griseus*). Also called **dark petrel, hagdon, moaning bird, whale ~ 2**

1858 U.S. War Dept. *Rept. Explor. Railroad* 9.834, Puffinus Fuliginosus. . . The Sooty Shearwater. . . The entire upper plumage is sooty brown. 1923 Dawson *Birds CA* 4.1999, Dark-bodied Shearwater. . . Synonyms.—Sooty Shearwater. Whale-bird. 1977 Udvardy *Audubon Field Guide Birds* 344, Sooty Shearwater. . . Millions of these birds migrate or summer off the coast from Alaska to California. 1986 Rustad *I Married a Fisherman* 59 **AK,** "Get up! The sooties are here," called Norman to me asleep. . . For five crisp, invigorating mornings, . . I had crawled out of my bunk at dawn to witness the spectacular migration of thousands, even millions of sooty shearwaters, or "whale birds," as the fishermen call them. 2004 *Oregonian* (Portland OR) 23 Sept 28 (Internet), My heart soars when I see sooty shearwaters, and not just because it means good fishing.

sooy See **sooey** v

sop n

1 also *sopping(s), sopping sauce, sopple, soppy, sops:* A liquid in which food is dipped or soaked before being eaten;

gravy, meat drippings. **chiefly W Midl, SE, West exc TX**
See Map Cf **black sop, dip-sop, white sop**

1845 Hooper *Advent. Simon Suggs* 33 **AL,** He travelled away down
into the low country "whar they call sop, *gravy.*" **1874** *Harper's New
Mth. Mag.* 49.175, Handfuls of coals keep hot the flesh soups . . while
on the ground sit groups of eaters, dipping their bread in the sop. **1893**
Shands *MS Speech* 59, *Sop.* . . Illiterate white for *molasses, gravy,* or
anything in which bread is *sopped.* This class of people in Mississippi
have changed the meaning of *sop* from the piece of bread to that in
which the bread is dipped. **1899** (1912) Green *VA Folk-Speech* 402,
Sop. . . The gravy of meat in which bread is *sopped* or moistened. **1905**
DN 3.95 **nwAR,** *Sop.* . . Gravy. 'That sop's good on bread.' **1916** *DN*
4.281 **NE,** *Soppins.* . . Gravy, rather thin or liquid, made from meat.
"Here is some soppins from the meat." **1923** *DN* 5.221 **swMO,** *Sop.* . .
A mixture of butter or grease and molasses. The word sometimes refers
to gravy. **1925** *AmSp* 1.137 **Pacific NW,** Gravy is "goozlum" or "sop."
1926 *AmSp* 1.653 [Hobo lingo], *Soppings*—gravy. **1927** *DN* 5.477
Ozarks, *Sop.* . . Gravy, usually made from pork. The upper transparent
grease is called *top-sop,* while the heavier, opaque part is known as *bot-
tom-sop.* **1937** *AmSp* 12.102 **eNE** [Farm terms], *Sop* is used by some
for meat gravy made by dashing water into the fryings in a hot skillet.
1944 *PADS* 2.61 **MO,** *Sop.* . . A vulgar term for *gravy.* . . Uneducated.
1955 Ritchie *Singing Family* 98 **seKY,** Mom took up a long dish of bacon with plenty of sop to put on the lettuce, with salt. **1965–70** *DARE*
(Qu. H37, . . *Gravy*) 105 Infs, **chiefly W Midl, SE, West exc TX,** Sop;
9 Infs, **scattered,** Sops; **KY**8, Soppy; **KY**41, Big sop; **MO**19,
Biscuit soppin'; **VA**42, Julie sop; **MO**37, Logan sop; **FL**36, Soppin';
CA64, Soppin's; **SC**32, Soppings; **NY**107, Sopple. **1973** *DARE* File
Ozarks (as of c1910), *Soppy.* . . Gravy made with flour and milk. **1978**
AP Letters **swPA,** *Sop* is gravy, . . thin, for mopping with bread or bis-
cuit. **1986** Pederson *LAGS Concordance (Maple syrup)* 1 inf, **csGA,**
You used to call syrup sopping. **1996** Wilson *Threadgill's Cookbook* 22
TX, I . . pan-fry my steaks. Then . . I make a gravy or sopping sauce of
some sort with the juices and the butter left in the pan. **2008** Wiegand
Outer Banks Cookbook 308 **eNC,** Peggy remembers her mother serving
the chocolate frosting many mornings as a "sopping" sauce over hot
homemade biscuits.

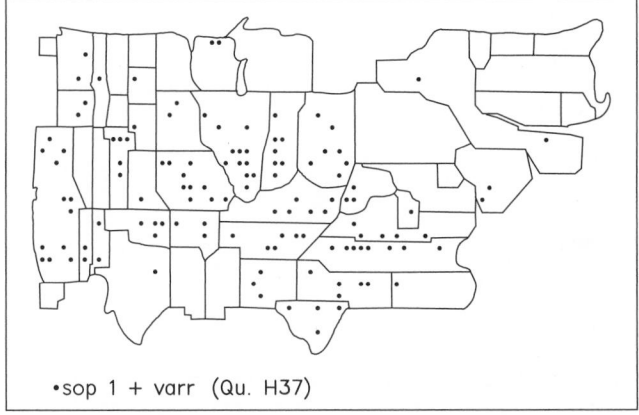

•sop 1 + varr (Qu. H37)

2   also *sop(ping) sauce, soption:* Barbecue sauce; basting
sauce. **esp SW**

1940 Brown *Amer. Cooks* 632 **NC,** The "soption," as the basting sauce
is called . . consisting of a couple of quarts of hot vinegar, well seasoned
with salt and red pepper pods, floating with melted butter. **1942** Perry
Texas 116, There is usually a barbecue in conjunction, a few slaughtered
beeves and sheep and pigs roasting on an open fire, being mopped with
"sop" by a colored man. **1970** Longstreet *War Cries* 28 **seNM,** Steers
were roasted, on great beds of charcoal with hot sop sauce and *socorro*
mush in pots. **1972** *Vidette–Messenger* (Valparaiso IN) 8 July 3/1, *Ro-
tisserie Beef* With Soppin' Sauce. . . Brush with sauce as meat cooks.
1986 Pederson *LAGS Concordance (Sauce)* 1 inf, **ceTX,** Sop—barbecue
sauce. **1987** *TX Mth.* Mar 96, Higgins' moments in the limelight [as
winner of a barbecue contest] have been as sweet as his sopping sauce.
2001 Dewitt–Gerlach *Barbecue* 28 **NM,** A sop, sometimes called mop,
is a thin basting sauce that is applied during the smoking process. It
keeps the meat moist and adds flavor.

3   also *beer sop, sop-head, sopper:* A drunkard. [Cf **sot** n]
esp Inland Nth, W Midl   See Map

1942 Berrey–Van den Bark *Amer. Slang* 97.9, *Drunkard.* . . sop.
1965–70 *DARE* (Qu. DD12, . . *A person who drinks steadily or a great
deal*) Infs **CO**17, **DC**3, **KY**72, **MI**64, **MO**9, **NY**12, **WI**68, Sop; **MI**64,
Drunken sop; **MO**37, Old beer sop; **PA**94, Sop-head; **NY**68, Sopper.
2002 *Chicago Daily Herald* (IL) 30 Apr 1 (Internet), He invites the gang
to a farewell get-together where Rhea Perlman's bar-maid Carla and
George Wendt's beer-sop Norm figure to turn up.

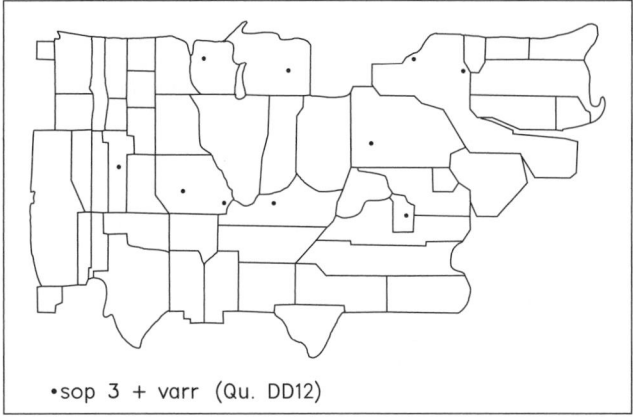

•sop 3 + varr (Qu. DD12)

4   also *barley sop:* Beer.
1968 *DARE* (Qu. DD25, . . *Nicknames . . for beer*) Inf **MO**21, Barley
sop; **IN**45, Sop.

5   An easy task.
1966–70 *DARE* (Qu. KK42a, *Expressions about a person who does
something very easily: "For him that would be _____."*) Infs **LA**11,
MS49, A sop; **FL**48, It's a sop, man, ain't nothing to it. **2005** *DARE*
File—Internet **CA,** I had been assured by my friends that the class was a
sop, an easy "A". . . I was willing to take a sop course if one fell in my
lap.

sopaipilla n |ˌsopəˈpijə| Also *sopapilla* [AmSpan] **esp NM**
A kind of deep-fried pastry; see quots.

1927 Fergusson *Wolf Song* 47 **NM,** She was also thinking of *sopapillas* and how they collapse under the teeth into tender crumbling sweetness. **1940** Writers' Program *Guide NM* 118, *Sopapillas* . . Squares of
short biscuit dough fried in deep fat until puffed up. **1951** Fergusson
New Mexico 407, *Sopaipilla*—a sort of fritter made of tortilla dough
fried in deep fat. **1952** Tracy *Coast Cookery* 139 **NM,** *Sopaipillas
(Sweet Fried Cakes).* . . flour . . salt . . baking powder . . eggs . . sugar. . .
Roll out [dough] . . , cut into 1½-inch squares, and fry in hot deep fat
until brown. . . While the sopaipillas are still hot, roll them in a mixture
of . . cinnamon . . sugar, or serve with butter, jam, or honey. **2003**
DARE File **NM** (as of 1968), When my husband went to graduate school
in New Mexico he discovered sopaipillas [ˌsopəˈpijəz]. They were very
delicate deep-fried pastries that had puffed up in the frying so that if a
corner were bitten off, honey could be poured inside.

sopalally   See **soopolallie**

sopamore   See **sophomore**

sopapilla   See **sopaipilla**

sop-head   See **sop 3**

sophky   See **sofkee**

sophomore n   Pronc-spp *solph(a)more, sophromore, sop-
(a)more, soth(o)more, souphmo(re), southmore;* for addit varr
see quots Note: The sp *sophmore,* which reflects a widely used
pronc, is not treated here.

Std sense, var forms.

1821 *Amer. Masonic Reg. & Ladies' & Gentlemen's Mag.* 1.63, The
students of this academy have . . generally entered in the sophromore,
or junior classes. **1903** in 2010 *DARE* File—Internet **NH,** Tuesday
the School team . . played the Harvard Southmores. . . Yesterday . .
[they played] the Harvard Freshmen. **1916** *DN* 4.281 **NE, PA,** *Sotho-
more, sothmore.* Occasional for *sophomore.* **1930** *AmSp* 4.270 **NE,** The
word *sophomore* seems peculiarly unable to get itself properly pronounced by high school and college students. . . The colloquial variants
of *sophomore* are as follows: sophmore, sothamore, sothmore, southa-
more, southmore, solphamore, solphmore, sopamore, sopmore. **1930s**

in 1944 *ADD* **cNY,** *Sophomore. . . Southmore.* Reported used by football coaches. **1934** *AmSp* 9.319 **NE,** *Sophomore.* **1950** *WELS Suppl., Southmore* for sophomore—I have heard this expression used by people from northern & southern Wisconsin as well as the Chicago area of Illinois. **1995** *Providence Jrl.* (RI) 21 Jan sec B 5 (Internet), Southmore Matt Noury finally got the job done. **2000** *DARE* File **OH,** *Sophomore*—My wife, who grew up around Toledo and has an M.Div., also says, or used to say, southmore. *Ibid* **cIL,** I heard an educated . . alumnus of a small liberal arts college in central Illinois . . speak of second-year college students as "southmores." There's a colleague in the history department of my small college who has the same pronunciation. **2007** in 2010 *DARE* File—Internet **nwWA,** It would be really cool if all the freshman and southmores get involved. **2008** *DARE* File, "Souphmore," ['saʊf,moɚ] "souphmo'," etc. are pretty much "standard" in B[lack] E[nglish].

sop(hro)more   See **sophomore**

sopper   See **sop 3**

sopping(s)   See **sop 1**

sopping sauce   See **sop 1, 2**

sopple, soppy, sops   See **sop 1**

sop sauce   See **sop 2**

soption   See **sop 2**

sor   See **sorry** adj

sora n [Etym unknown]
1 also *sora rail;* formerly *saurer, soree (bird), soris, sorus:* A **rail 2** (here: *Porzana carolina*); hence vbl n *sorising* hunting this bird. **formerly chiefly VA, NC; now more widespread** Also called **chickenbill 1, coot** n[1]**, English rail 1, marsh hen 1a, meadow chicken, ~ hen 1, mud hen 1a, ortolan 1, peep** n **1, rail** n[2]**, railbird, reedbird 3, rice hen 3, ~ rail, sedge hen 1, water ~ 1b**
1705 Beverley *Hist. VA* 2.37, The Shores . . are also stor'd with . . Snipes, Woodcocks, Saurers [etc]. **1731** Catesby *Nat. Hist. Carolina* 1.70, The Soree. . . These Birds become so very fat in Autumn, by feeding on Wild Oats, that they can't escape the *Indians,* who catch Abundance by running them down. In *Virginia* . . they are as much in Request, for the Delicacy of their Flesh, as the Rice-Bird is in *Carolina.* **1759** in 1775 Burnaby *Travels* 25 **VA,** The sorus is not known to be in Virginia, except for about six weeks from the latter end of September: at that time they are found in the marshes in prodigious numbers, feeding upon the wild oats. **1791** Bartram *Travels* 296, Rallus Virginianus, the soree bird or little brown rail, also called widgeon in Pennsyl. **1840** (1970) Wilson *Amer. Ornith.* 419 **VA,** The natural history of the Rail, or as it is called in Virginia, the Sora, . . is . . involved in profound and inexplicable mystery. **1888** Trumbull *Names of Birds* 132, [*Porzana carolina* is] generally known in Virginia and southward to southern part of North Carolina as *sora* and *soree.* **1899** *New Engl. Mag.* 20.561 **CT,** The Sora rail finds feeding grounds, offering sport to the gunner from New York. **1912** Green *VA Folk-Speech* 402, *Sora.* . . Also *soris.* "I'm going sorising to-morrow." *Sora.* . . A bird found in numbers in the marshes in the fall. **1936** Roberts *MN Birds* 1.446, The Sora is the most abundant and generally distributed of the Rails in Minnesota. **1955** Richardson *House on Nauset Marsh* 198 **Cape Cod MA,** Many times, while tramping swampy, fresh-water meadows, I have jumped rails, usually soras or Virginias. **1968–70** *DARE* (Qu. Q10, . . *Water birds and marsh birds*) Infs **VA**57, 75, Sora; **MN**18, Sora rail. **1977** Bull–Farrand *Audubon Field Guide Birds* 432, Sora (*Porzana carolina*). . . These birds are especially numerous in fall and winter in southern marshes and rice fields. **2002** *Star Tribune* (Minneapolis MN) 7 Mar 6 (Internet), The marshy edges of the lake are home to red-winged blackbirds, the sora rail, herons and more sparrows.
2 See **sora wind.**

sora rail   See **sora 1**

sora wind n   Also *sora*
A northwest wind occurring in September; hence n *sora tide* an exceptionally high tide believed to be caused by this wind.
1948 *AN&Q* 8.63 **VA,** South of the James River—where since colonial days colloquialisms have often differed from those of the section north of the River—"sora wind" was at one time the common name for the September northeast wind, more commonly known as the "equinoctial,"

from its supposed occurrence at the time of the autumnal equinox. . . The sora piles high tides over the marshes—"sora tide"—and creates conditions most favorable to sora shooting. Superstitious people used to believe that the wind brought sora to the region. I myself have not heard the term used, however, in fifteen years or more.

sore-back n [Etym unknown] Cf **hit-your-back**
Used as a nickname for a Virginian.
1906 Casler *Four Yrs.* 164 (as of 1863), We would ask the North Carolinians if they had any "tar." . . They would reply that . . they had let us Virginians have all they had to make us stick in the last fight, and call us "sore-backs," as they had knocked all the skin off our backs running over us to get into battle. **1918** *DN* 5.19 **NC,** *Sore-back,* a Virginian. The word has been explained to me as follows: "The North Carolinians say that they had to climb over the backs of the Virginians to get at the enemy during the Civil War and that the tar on their heels gave the Virginians sore backs." [**1920** *DN* 5.86 **NC,** *Sore-back* was originally applied to the indentured servant class, the victims of the whipping-post, and later came to be used as a general term of contempt.] **1937** Shankle *Nicknames* 555, The nickname *Sorebacks,* applied to Virginians. . . [T]he Virginians are so hospitable that they slap one another on the backs until their backs become sore. **1938** *Cullman Democrat* (AL) 27 Oct [7]/3 (newspaperarchive.com), You will go a long ways, before you will find a person who comes closer to having both feet on the ground . . than this here old Soreback down there in Virginia—Mr. Carter Glass. **1970** *DARE* FW Addit **VA**41, *Sore-back* ['sɔɪbæk], *hit-your-back*—nicknames for Virginian—terms originated from slave days. Old-fashioned. **2005** *DARE* File—Internet **VA,** I just noticed . . TXRoadTrip asked . . "why is your back sore?" I'm a fugitive from the State of Virginia . . hiding out in Ohio.

soreback adj, also used absol   **esp Pacific NW**
Of a salmon: having lesions on the back typical of spawning fish.
1910 *Hunter-Trader-Trapper* May 87 **CA,** They had seen a few [= salmon], but did not get any good ones; one had caught a sore-back but let him lay, as they take only the good ones that are fresh up and without blemish. **1925** *Science* new ser 61.341 **OR,** A number of dogs developed typical symptoms and died after eating "sore-back" salmon. **1967** *DARE* (Qu. P14, . . *Commercial fishing . . what do the fishermen go out after?*) Inf **WA**20, [In a list of kinds of salmon:] Soreback—in process of dying from spawning. **2003** in 2006 *DARE* File—Internet **WA,** By then they were worn and tired. Their backs were sore with large red spots. We called the salmon "sorebacks." They came to my stream . . to lay eggs and die. **2006** *Ibid* **WA,** [Caption:] One lone soreback spawned out female left. [*Ibid,* Picture was taken Jan 4th, with most all the fish spawned out & dead, with this one lone female left. She has a lot of whitish sores on her back & fins.]

soree (bird)   See **sora 1**

sore-eye (poppy) n [See quots]
=**globe mallow 1.**
1939 *AZ Highways* 19.28, The "sore-eye poppy" . . will indeed be painful to children's eyes if they play with it. **1941** Jaeger *Wildflowers* 143 **AZ,** The sphaeralceas are locally known in Arizona as "sore-eye poppies" because the hairs on the plants are irritating to the eyes. **1969** *DARE* (Qu. S26a, . . *Wildflowers. . . Roadside flowers*) Inf **AZ**15, Desert mallow—Anglos use "sore-eye"; Mexicans use "mal ojo." **1985** Dodge *Flowers SW Deserts* 44, A local belief that the hairs of the plant are irritating to the eyes has given the name "sore-eye poppies," an appellation carried out in the Mexican name *mal de ojos.*

sorensified   See **suffancified**

sorghum n   Usu |'sɔrgəm, 'sɔrgəm|, less freq |'sɑrgəm|; also |'sɔ(r)grəm|; for addit varr see quots   Pronc-spp *soggum, sog(r)um, sorg(h)rum, soughum*
A   Pronc varr.
1905 [see **B** below]. **1923** *DN* 5.221 **swMO,** *Sogrums. . .* Sorghum. Always used as if plural in form. **1942** Hall *Smoky Mt. Speech* 98 **wNC, eTN,** *Sorghum* ['sɔgrəmz] (once). **1949** Webber *Backwoods Teacher* 132 **Ozarks,** My reasons for going . . were several. One was to get me a bucket of "sogrum." Uncle Johnny was "give up to be" the best molasses maker . . and the making of sorghum is an art as well as a science. **1965–70** *DARE* (Qu. H21) 14 Infs, 8 **AR, OK,** ['sɑr,gəm]; 10 Infs, **scattered,** [sɔrgəm]; **AL**41, **KY**25, **NY**12, **TN**11, 57, **WI**24, 49, [sɔrgəm]; **GA**70, ['sɔrgm̩]; **AL**52, ['sɔgəm]; **KY**44, ['sɔɚgəm]; **GA**85,

MO3, [ˈsɔrgɪm]; **MO**6, 11, 38, [ˈsorgɪm]; **IN**7, [ˈsourˌgəm]; **IL**117, **KY**37, [ˈsoɚˌgəm]; **TN**37, [ˈsarˈgʌm]; **AR**52, **GA**81, **KY**5, [ˈsagrəm]; **AL**24, [ˈsagm̩]; **TN**24, 44, 57, [ˈsagəm]; **GA**81, **KY**44, [ˈsɔəgrəm]; **AL**1, [sɔgi-əm]; **AL**52, **GA**81, **SC**38, [sɔg(r)əm]; **WI**41, [ˈsurˌgəm]; (Qu. A18) Inf **LA**12, [ˈsagəm]; (Qu. L9a) Inf **HI**12, [sorgəm]; **IA**6, [ˈsorgəm]; **NY**209, [ˈsɚˌgəm]; (Qu. L9b) Inf **AL**26, [sɔgrəm]; **LA**29, **NC**81, [ˈsargəm(z)]; **TX**11, [sargɪm]; (Qu. L21) Inf **FL**6, [ˈsɔəˌgrəm]; **FL**26, [ˈsaurgəm]; **OK**10, [sargəm]; (Qu. L34) Inf **KS**5, [ˈsorgəm]; (Qu. Y40b) Inf **KY**21, [ˈsoɚ-grəm]; (Qu. BB50d) Inf **KS**5, [ˈsorgəm]. **1978** *DARE* File **nAL** (as of c1900), *Soughum.* . . The spelling *sogum* also was used. **1996** *Ibid* neTX (as of 1920s–30s), We also had sorghum syrup—*dark* brown—thick—strong—but good. In Pinehill, it was pronounced *soggum syrup.* **2003** [see **B** below]. **2006** *DARE* File—Internet **GA**, There are many variety [sic] of sorgrums out there. Many of the commodity Sorgrums are high in Tannic Acid. . . This greatly limits the amounts of the sorgrum that wildlife can ingest.

B   Gram form.

Used as pl with ref to syrup; see quots.   [Prob by analogy with **molasses B**]   **chiefly S Midl**

1905 *DN* 3.95 nwAR, *Sorghum,* pl. *sorghums* (also pronounced with metathesis [sogrəm(z)]). . . Molasses. 'I would like some of those sorghrums.' **1923** *DN* 5.208 swMO, I've b'iled sogrums till I'm all gaumed up. *Ibid* 221, [see **A** above]. [**1939** FWP *Guide TN* 458 nwTN, After the "making" is over, there is a big "get-together" and a candy pulling. "They" (sorghum is never referred to as "it") are "larrupin good truck" for the table.] **1942** [see **A** above]. **1953** Brewer *Word Brazos* 77 **eTX** [Black], So she go out to her smokehouse an' fetch Revun Wheeler a whole gallon jug of good ole thick homemade sorghums. **1974** Fink *Mountain Speech* 24 **wNC, eTN**, *Sorgrums* . . sorghrum. Molasses made from locally grown cane. Always plural. **1976** Garber *Mountain-ese* 85 **sAppalachians**, We raised a big patch uv cane this year to make sorgums. **2003** in 2006 *DARE* File—Internet swNC, [In list of recipe ingredients:] Molasses (sogrums).

C   Sense.

Std: a plant of the genus *Sorghum,* esp *S. bicolor* or *S. halapense.* For other names of var spp see **chicken corn 1, Egyptian ~ 2, guinea ~ 1, high-gear, Indian millet 1, Jerusalem corn, Johnson grass 1, kafir corn, low-gear, milo maize, pearl millet 2, redtop cane**

sorilla   See **zorillo**

soris(ing)   See **sora 1**

sor'r   See **sorrow** n, v

sorrel n
Std: =**dock** n¹.

sorrel dock n
A **dock** n¹ (here: *Rumex acetosa* or *R. acetosella*).
1849 Amer. Med. Assoc. *Trans.* 2.891 **MA**, *Rumex acetosella.* Sorrel; sorrel dock. The leaves have an agreeable acid taste, and are refrigerant, antiscorbutic, and diuretic. **1895** U.S. Dept. Ag. *Farmers' Bulletin* 28.28, Sorrel dock, sour dock—Rumex acetosa—South Carolina to Georgia. **1910** Graves *Flowering Plants* 159 **CT**, Rumex Acetosa. . . Sorrel or Belleville Dock. . . Sometimes cultivated for spring greens. **1950** Stevens *ND Plants* 121, *Rumex acetosella.* . . Sorrel Dock. . . a well known weed in acid, sandy soils in eastern U.S.

sorrel tree n   [Because the leaves have the sour taste of sorrel] =**sourwood 1.**
1687 in 1739 Royal Soc. London *Philos. Trans.* 41.152, The *Sorrel-tree.* . . grows plentifully on the South-side of *James* River in *Virginia.* **1731** Catesby *Nat. Hist. Carolina* 1.71, The Sorrel-Tree. The Trunc of this Tree is usually five or six inches thick, and rises to the Height of about twenty Feet. **1733** (1876) Byrd *Journey to Eden* 27 **VA**, The Sorrel Tree is frequent there, whose leaves, brew'd in Beer, are good in Dropsyes, Green-Sickness, and Cachexys. **1813** Michaux *Histoire des Arbres* 3.222, *Andromeda arborea.* The Sorel Tree. *Ibid* 224, C'est de l'acidité très-marquée des feuilles de cet arbre, que lui est venu le nom très-approprié du *Sorel tree.* [=From the pronounced acidity of this tree's leaves derives the very appropriate name of *Sorel tree.*] **1942** Hylander *Plant Life* 414, Sour Wood or Sorrel Tree. . . This deciduous tree is found from Georgia to Alabama. **1980** Little *Audubon Guide N. Amer. Trees E. Region* 625, Sourwood—"Sorrel-tree."

sorrel vine n   [*OED2* 1864 →]

A **possum grape 2** (here: *Cissus trifoliata*) with acid leaves.
1890 *Century Dict.* 5777, *Sorrel-vine.* . . A shrub, *Cissus (Vitis) acida,* found in tropical America, reaching into Florida. It is a low tendril-bearing climber, with acid juice. **1933** Small *Manual SE Flora* 839, *C[issus] trifoliata.* . . Sorrel-vine. . . Hammocks, mostly near the coast, S pen. Fla. and the Keys. **2006** (acc) U.S. Natl. Park Serv. *Canaveral Natl. Seashore* (Internet), In the early 1970's a botanical survey of Turtle Mound . . revealed that the mound was the northernmost location for eight species of subtropical plants. These included . . marine vine/sorrel vine *(Cissus trifoliata)* [etc.].

sorrer   See **sorrow** n, v

sorriness   See **sorry** adj B1

sorrow n, v   Pronc-spp **chiefly Sth, S Midl** *sorrer, sor'r, sorry;* similarly adj *sorryful*   Cf Pronc Intro 3.I.12, **borrow** v, **sorry** adj, **-y** suff² b
Std senses, var forms.
1837 *Philadelphia Visiter & Parlour Companion* 3.71 **NEng**, When sorrer on sorrer comes on yer foe . . call his mis'ry and horrer a judgment o' the Lurd. **1851** *Godey's Lady's Book* 43.264, Miss Sloman had the knack of makin' a little go a good ways, as I larnt to my sorrer. **1883** (1971) Harris *Nights with Remus* 188 **GA** [Black], 'T is full me up wit' sorry wun you do lak dis. **1888** Jones *Negro Myths* 126 **GA coast**, All de sorry wuh Buh Alligator bin sorry fuh Buh Wolf yent bin done um no good. **1889** Edwards *Runaways* 210 **GA**, Ef't had n' be'n fur sorryin' fur ther critter, I'd er busted wide open. **1906** Casey *Parson's Boys* 31 **sIL** (as of c1860), By the grace of God I shall yet triumph over sin, sorrer and Satan. **1929** Sale *Tree Named John* 30 **MS** [Black], Nothin' but sin on sor'r. **1932** Strong *Behind Gt. Smokies* 113, No one hain't layin' hands on me the way ye did yesterday without sorryin' fer hit. **1942** (1971) Campbell *Cloud-Walking* 215 **seKY**, He never said nothing but he just eased around real sorryful-like. **1969** (1970) Angelou *Caged Bird* 5 **AR** [Black], The minister's wife leaned toward me, her long yellow face full of sorry. **1972** Clauser *Girl Named Sooner* 94 **sIN** (as of c1935), Maybe your tame critters ain't sorried by it [=being put in cages] none. **2005** *DARE* File—Internet **AZ**, I Say a Sorryful goodbye to his family.

sorrow adj   See **sorry** adj

sorry adj   Usu |ˈsari, ˈsɔri|; also esp **MN, WI** |ˈsori| Pronc-spp *sarry, sor;* arch spp *sorrow, surrow*

A   Forms.   Cf **sorrow** n, v
c1675 in 1888 Goodwin *Pilgrim Republic* 550 **MA**, I am sorrow that I have done so much wrong to you. **1810** in 1956 Eliason *Tarheel Talk* 318 nw,cwNC, Sorry [was written] sorrow. **1853** *Ibid*, Sorry . . [was written] surrow. **1857** *Ibid*, Sorry . . [was written] sarry. **1892** *Amer. Missionary* 46.84 **TX**, I am Sorrow to say that i Am not able to come. **1910** *DN* 3.457 **KY**, *Sorrow.* . . Sorry. . . This use is common among our students. "Stevenson had the power to make a person feel very sorrow." "I am sorrow I haven't worked harder." **1923** *DN* 5.221 swMO, *Sorrow.* . . The written form of *Sorry.* **1926** *DN* 5.403 **Ozarks**, *Sorrow.* . . Sorry. "I'm right sorrow I caint holler no louder." . . A native who came to play my victrola at Pineville, Missouri, always referred to a certain ancient foxtrot as "Who's Sorrow Now," although he was quite able to read the s-o-r-r-y on the record. **1968** *Current Slang* 2.4.9, *Sor.* . . To be sorry (ironic). . . College students, both sexes, Kansas. . . *Sor* about that. **1972** Davis *Studies McDavid* 51 **wPA, OH**, This subsystematic central (unrounded) versus back (rounded) variation has a peripherally linguistic, and therefore relevant, place in such matters of phonemic incidence as the occurrence of, and disputes about /sari/ vs. /sori/ for *sorry.* . . While the pronunciation /sari/ seems primarily to exhibit prestige-dialect borrowing, it also satisfies the [a] + /r/ allophonic selection of Pattern A illustrated above. From a different point of view, /sori/ treats *sorry* as a transparent derivation from *sore.* Both motivations for phonemic incidence have a clear place in any W[estern] P[ennsylvania] O[hio] idiom. [**1994** *Time* 7 Nov 76, All that is left to distinguish Canadian fare is the telltale northern accent—"about" for *about,* "sore-y" for *sorry.*] **2000** *DARE* File **MN** (as of c1950), What about 'sorry'? It used to rhyme with 'sore' for me. *Ibid* **Upstate NY** (as of c1960), I became self-conscious enough to adapt to the indigenous [ɔr] (as in *sore* . .) in such words as "forest", "moral", . . "corridor". . . but I don't think I ever switched over on "sorry". *Ibid* seWI (as of c1955), Sorry [ˈsoɚi]. This was the usual pronunciation for this word in a community of many Danish and German immigrants. **2003** *Ibid* csWI (as of 1975), When I moved to Wisconsin I was surprised to hear that *sorry* is often pronounced [ˈsoɚi].

Ibid **seWI,** I decided that it would take only one skunk to make me sorry ['soɚi]. **2006** *Ibid* **Milwaukee WI,** *Sorry* rhymes with *glory,* of course. **2007** *Ibid* **MN,** I'm sorry ['soɚi], but I don't have time to wait.

B Senses.

1 Exhibiting a contemptible or exasperating failure to meet reasonable expectations; useless, shoddy, wretched; hence n *sorriness.* [*OED2* c1250 →] Note: In reference to abstractions ("a sorry excuse," "a sorry state of affairs," etc) this appears to be widespread. **scattered, but esp SE, Lower Missip Valley, TX, OK** See Map

1804 *Lit. Mag. & Amer. Reg.* 2.192, Then food he sought, and found enough,/ But found it very sorry stuff. **1820** *N. Amer. Rev.* 11.92, Some of the richest lands . . would afford the richest returns, instead of a sorry crop of salt hay. **1899** (1912) Green *VA Folk-Speech* 402, *Sorry, adj.* Vile; wretched; worthless; mean: as, a *sorry* horse. Of a poor quality. "As the corn crop is sorry this year." **1906** *DN* 3.157 **nwAR,** *Sorry.* . . Inferior, despicable, of poor quality. "He's a mighty sorry fellow." "The crops are sorry this year." **1910** *DN* 3.457 **KY,** *Sorry.* . . Bad. "This flour is such sorry stuff that I can't make good bread out of it." **1916** *DN* 4.281 **NE,** *Sorry.* . . Inferior. "The cotton crop is sorry this year." Reported from Oklahoma. [*DN* Ed: Also Ill., W. Va., N. Car.] **1923** *DN* 5.221 **swMO,** *Sorry.* . . Of a poor grade. "He's a sorry farmer." "That's a sorry calf." **1933** Rawlings *South Moon* 297 **nFL,** Jim said, "If it's who I figger 'tis, I reckon you're not like to be bothered. The sorriest kind of a feller don't gin'rally steal from his own kin." **1940** *AmSp* 15.214 **TX,** Frequently non-Southern Americans do not conceal their amusement upon hearing Southerners refer to *a sorry fellow, a sorry tire,* or *a sorry book.* **1944** *PADS* 2.12 **Sth,** *Sorry.* . . Inferior, of low quality or standard; squalid. A *sorry crop,* or *mule,* or *carpenter,* etc.; a *sorry sight.* Frequently combined with *looking:* a *sorry-looking nag.* Ala., sections of Mo. ((very common in the South)). Colloquial. General. **1965–70** *DARE* (Qu. KK6, *Something low-grade or of poor quality—for example, a piece of merchandise: "I wouldn't buy that, it's _____."*) 27 Infs, **chiefly SE,** Sorry; **GA**36, **MS**61, **NC**72, **TN**62, Sorry stuff; **SC**34, Sorry-looking; (Qu. K15, *A thin, bony, or poor-looking cow*) 24 Infs, **scattered,** Sorry-looking (cow); **AL**34, **NC**21, Sorry cow; (Qu. HH18, *Very insignificant or low-grade people*) 20 Infs, **scattered, but esp S Midl, S Atl,** Sorry; **TX**5, Sorry folk; **AL**6, **OH**72, Sorry bastards; **VA**42, Sorry trash; [**PA**247, Sorry-ass person;] (Qu. D21, *A small, poorly-built house, or one in rundown condition*) Inf **FL**37, Sorry place; (Qu. H74b, . . *Coffee . . very weak*) Inf **SC**67, Sorry; (Qu. J2, . . *Joking or uncomplimentary words . . for dogs*) Inf **FL**48, Old sorry dog; (Qu. K44, *A bony or poor-looking horse*) Inf **NC**53, Sorry plug horse; **OK**53, Sorry-looking horse; (Qu. K55, *A pig that doesn't grow well and is not worth keeping*) Inf **FL**36, Sorry pig; (Qu. N12, . . *Somebody who drives carelessly or not well*) Infs **AR**47, **MD**13, Sorry driver; (Qu. W29, . . *Expressions . . for things that are sewn carelessly . . "They're _____."*) Inf **AL**33, Sorry; **FL**6, Sorry job; (Qu. W41, . . *Expressions . . for someone whose clothes never look right or who always dresses carelessly*) Inf **LA**32, Sorry; (Qu. W43, . . *Joking words . . for clothes in general*) Inf **NY**165, Sorry rags; (Qu. AA23, *Joking names that a woman may use to refer to her husband*) Inf **MS**63, Sorry husband; (Qu. BB53b, . . *A doctor who is not very capable or doesn't have a very good reputation*) Infs **AL**30, **FL**26, He's sorry; **AL**20, **FL**36, **SC**7, Sorry doctor; **NC**79, Sorry person; (Qu. HH16, *Uncomplimentary words with no definite meaning—just used when you want to show that you don't think much of a person: "Don't invite him. He's a _____."*) Inf **AR**55, Sorry fellow; **GA**19, Sorry, no-good so-and-so; (Qu. HH19, *Other words or nicknames for a tramp*) Inf **PA**247, Sorry cat; (Qu. HH20a, *An idle, worthless person: "He's a _____."*) Infs **GA**17, 30, **NC**61, Sorry; **NC**55, Sorry good-for-nothing; (Qu. HH20c, *Of an idle, worthless person . . "He isn't worth _____."*) Inf **GA**77, Sorry as gully dirt; (Qu. KK64, *Speaking of the part of a city that was once very fine, but isn't any more: "The neighborhood is sort of _____."*) Infs **AL**33, **IL**11, **OK**13, Sorry; (Qu. LL2, . . *Too small to be worth much: "I don't want that little _____ potato."*) Infs **KY**47, **VA**21, Sorry; (Qu. LL13, *Not full or sufficient: "She gave us a _____ meal."*) Infs **NC**79, **SC**67, **TX**104, Sorry. **1999** *Cattle Today* Feb (Internet) **TX,** I've seen grand champions at some of the most prestigious shows mature into animals so sorry they were never allowed to breed a cow. **2002** *Atlanta Jrl.–Constitution* (GA) 24 May sec C 7, Georgia's chief medical examiner told a group that he believed the Tri-State Crematory scandal was caused by "pure sorriness." **2006** *DARE* File—Internet **seWI,** But one sorry fellow was a little too anxious to try to keep pace. *Ibid* **OR,** We transformed a sorry-looking community garden plot into Buckman's first learning garden.

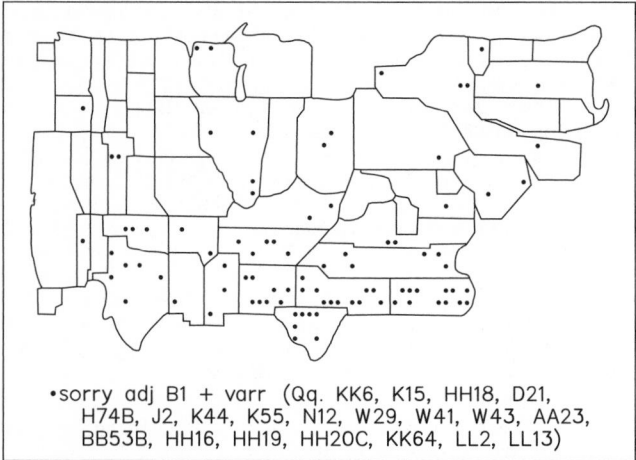

•sorry adj B1 + varr (Qq. KK6, K15, HH18, D21, H74B, J2, K44, K55, N12, W29, W41, W43, AA23, BB53B, HH16, HH19, HH20C, KK64, LL2, LL13)

2 Sickly, ill; lacking in energy. [Engl dial; cf *EDD sorry* adj. 3] **esp Sth, S Midl**

1966–69 *DARE* (Qu. X43b, *If you sleep later than usual one day on purpose . . "I _____."*) Inf **NC**49, Felt sorry; (Qu. BB5, *A general feeling of discomfort or illness that isn't any one place in particular*) Inf **KY**35, Feel sorry; (Qu. BB39, *On a day when you don't feel just right, though not actually sick . . "I'll be all right tomorrow—I'm just feeling _____ today."*) Inf **KY**24, Plumb trifling and sorry; **MS**51, Sorry; (Qu. KK30, *Feeling slowed up or without energy: "I certainly feel _____."*) Infs **GA**84, **LA**20, **MO**15, **NC**30, Sorry. **1985** Ladwig *How to Talk Dirty* 25 **Ozarks,** I'm pretty sorry this morning. (sort of sickly).

sorry adv

Badly, shabbily.

1967–70 *DARE* (Qu. X37, . . *Words . . to describe people's legs if they're noticeably bent, or uneven, or not right*) Inf **VA**42, Sorry-built; (Qu. HH36, *A careless, slovenly woman: "She's just an old _____."*) Inf **TN**14, Right sorry dressed.

sorry n See **sorrow** n, v

sorryful See **sorrow** n, v

sorus See **sora** 1

so's See **so as**

sosation See **association**

so 's 't conj Also *so as 't, sost* [Prob **so as 1** pronc [soz] infl by metanalysis of *so as to* ['sostə] in the parallel infin constr] **chiefly NEng** *old-fash*

1 =**so as 1.**

1848 Lowell *Biglow* 138 'Upcountry' **MA,** He made me larn him readin', tu . . / . . So 'st he could read a Bible he 'd gut. *Ibid* 146, So 'st, so as that. **1860** *Harper's New Mth. Mag.* 20.620 **Cape Cod MA,** 'Taint a good sign when a young feller gits so's't he kin stand it to be tail o' the heap. **1877** *Atlantic Mth.* 40.78 **CT,** I put in my finger that time so 's 't she should n't quarrel with you. **1892** *Ibid* 70.629 **CA,** The rains was late and lodged yer maw's barley, so as 't she did n't have half a crop. **1897** *Ibid* 80.209 **VT,** I guess suthin' 'll happen so 's 't you won't go tu no tavern tu-night. **1913** Johnson *Highways St. Lawrence to VA* 12 **neNY,** Father had inflammatory rheumatism and wa'n't sost he could do anything. **1968** Moody *Horse* 22 **wKS** (as of c1920), It used to be, back before the war commenced, a valley farmer could do right good with a mixed herd of cattle; one with some Jersey and Guernsey blood mixed in with his beef stock, so's't he'd have milkers enough that the butter'd square the grocery bill.

2 =**so as 2.**

1881 *Atlantic Mth.* 48.152 **NEng,** It don't make any difference how you git the balsam into your system, so 's 't you *git* it there.

sot n Also *sot-drinker, ~-drunk(ard), ~-head, ~-pot* [*OED2* 1592 →] **widespread, but esp Sth, S Midl** See Map A drunkard, alcoholic.

1798 Munford *Plays* 33 **VA,** You drunken sot! **1806** (1970) Webster *Compendious Dict.* 285, *Sot* . . a drunkard, toper. [*DARE* Ed: This entry was carried over from Webster's English model.] **1831** *Biblical Reper-*

tory & Theological Rev. 3.49, The debased and squalid sot . . even now, flatters himself that he is not detected. **1908** Randall *Maryland, My Maryland* 129, Upon reflection, I will *not* / Become an interesting sot,/ And sprout a nasal apricot! **1945** *Harder Coll.* **cwTN,** Sot. . . I don't think I could stand it if you turn out to be a sot drunkard. **1965–70** *DARE* (Qu. DD12, . . *A person who drinks steadily or a great deal*) 206 Infs, **widespread, but esp Sth, S Midl,** Sot; **GA**16, **IA**8, **KS**15, **MI**72, **NY**163, **TN**16, Drunken sot; **GA**3, 72, 74, 77, **OK**52, **TX**100, (Old) sot-drunkard; **FL**32, **IN**58, **NC**13, 41, 61, Old sot; **TX**1, Regular sot; **SC**58, Regular sot(-drinker); liquor-sot; **KY**11, Sot-head; **MN**2, Sot-pot; (Qu. DD15, *A person who is thoroughly drunk*) Infs **CO**9, **FL**20, **MS**71, **PA**110, **VA**26, **WA**9, **WI**51, Sot; **FL**30, **MD**32, **OK**48, Drunken sot; **NC**82, **PA**4, Old sot; **GA**74, **VA**43, Sot-drunk; (Qu. X53b) Inf **VA**5, Sot; (Qu. DD13, *When a drinker is just beginning to show the effects of the liquor . . he's _____*) Inf **NC**41, Old sot; (Qu. DD17, *To drink a great deal, or too fast: "He doesn't just drink, he _____."*) Inf **MO**9, Is a sot; (Qu. HH16, *Uncomplimentary words with no definite meaning—just used when you want to show that you don't think much of a person: "Don't invite him. He's a _____."*) Inf **IN**70, Old sot; (Qu. HH28, *Names and nicknames . . for people of foreign background*) Inf **MA**30, Whiskey-sot—Irish; (Qu. HH40, *Uncomplimentary words for an old man*) Infs **IN**70, **NJ**45, Old sot; **OH**13, **PA**214, Sot. **1986** Pederson *LAGS Concordance (Drunk)* 8 infs, **Gulf Region,** Sot.

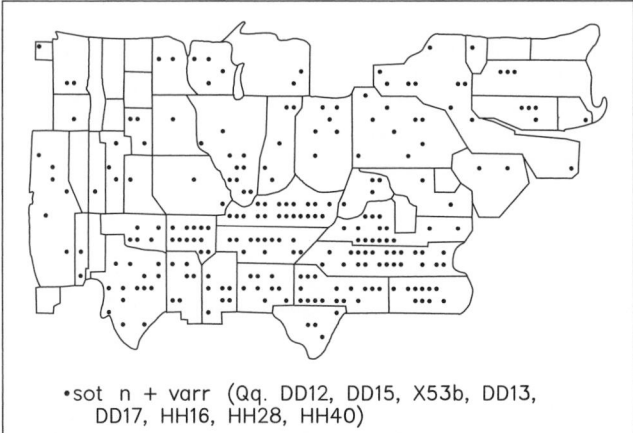

•sot n + varr (Qq. DD12, DD15, X53b, DD13, DD17, HH16, HH28, HH40)

sot v[1]   See **set** v[1] **A1a, 2a, 3, 4**

sot v[2]   See **sit** v[1] **1b, 2c, 3c**

sot-drinker (or -drunk, -drunkard)   See **sot** n

so tell   See **so till**

sot-head   See **sot** n

s'o'ther   See **south-southerly**

soth(o)more   See **sophomore**

so till conj   Also *so till where*   Pronc-spp *so tell, so-dl-whirr* [Creole Engl; cf *DCEU so* adv 7.10]   *esp freq among Black speakers* Cf **till C1a**
So that, to the point that.

1888 Jones *Negro Myths* 40 **GA coast,** Eh skade [=scared] so tell eh scacely kin keep eh seat. **1893** Shands *MS Speech* 64, *Til* or *till* has another peculiar use in negro dialect in sentences like the following, where it is used in the place of *that:* "It hurt me so till I cried." **1930** Stoney– Shelby *Black Genesis* 8 **seSC,** God holler at Br' Dog so till he is shut up he mout'. **1935** Hurston *Mules & Men* 164 **FL** [Black], De old lady tried to milk de cow but she was buckin' and rearin' so till de ole man felt he couldn't stand it no mo'. **1970** Thompson *Coll.* **AL** (as of 1930s), *So till where.* . . Until. "It hurt me so-dl-whirr it might nigh kilt me." White Alabaman, 1930's; also used by Blacks.

sot in one's ways   See **set** v[1] **A4**

sotol n   [AmSpan < Nahuatl]   **TX, NM, AZ**

1 also *sotole:* A yucca-like southwestern plant of the genus *Dasylirion,* esp *D. texanum* or *D. wheeleri.*   Also called **bear grass 1c;** for other names of var spp see **desert candle 3, ~ spoon, saw yucca**

1881 *Amer. Naturalist* 15.874, The home of the sotol is Western Texas, Southeastern New Mexico and Northern Chihuahua. **1883** in 1958

AmSp 33.140 **swTX,** Plants of special value to stock are found, as the "juahia," the "sotal [sic]," the "nopal" cactus [etc]. **1892** *DN* 1.194 **TX,** *Sótole:* a species of cactus not identified. *Ibid* 252, *Sótole* (p. 194). Add: The same name is applied also to a species of yucca, undetermined, from which a vile liquor is distilled. In Arizona the name applies to soap weed. **1905** Bray *Vegetation* 3 **TX,** In Texas, the main body of the sotol country is embraced in the rough limestone region lying between the breaks of the Devil's River and the front ranges of the Cordilleras near Marathon over 150 miles west. **1931** U.S. Dept. Ag. *Misc. Pub.* 101.15, Plants of the related genera, sotol . . and sacahuista . . are also sometimes machine-cut or shredded, like soapweed, as emergency feed or silage, especially for cattle. **1940** Writers' Program *Guide TX* 613 **sw,csTX,** This marks the eastern edge of the sotol region. Sotol, a low-growing plant with stiff leaves having sawtooth edges, was once roasted by the Apaches and the trunks used for food. Mexicans make a fiery liquor from its roots, and soap from the same source. **1967–69** *DARE* (Qu. S21, . . *Weeds . . that are a trouble in gardens and fields*) Inf **TX**3, Sotol—variety of cactus; livestock could eat underground root; (Qu. I29, *Names or nicknames for asparagus*) Inf **TX**67, Sotol stalks. **1987** Bowers *100 Roadside Wildflowers* 2, Sotol grows in desert grassland and oak woodland from southern Arizona to western Texas and northern Mexico. **2001** *St. Louis Post–Dispatch* (MO) 22 July 1 (Internet) **TX,** The sotols looked like a stick forest.

2 An alcoholic beverage made from **sotol 1.**
[**1885** U.S. Natl. Museum *Proc.* 8.471, Surrounding the City of Chihuahua. . . we found a flourishing Sotol-mescal factory, the favorite alcoholic beverage of frontier Mexicans, made from the Sotol or Bear-Grass.] [**1892** see **1** above.] **1909** *Mt. Democrat* (Placerville CA) 28 Jan [7]/5, The sotol liquor still is a favorite beverage among the Mexicans of the border. The American cowboy of this region has an intimate knowledge of the "fighting" qualities of this liquor. **1923** *Deming Headlight* (NM) 27 July 1/3, 23 pints of tequilla and three qaurts [sic] of sotol was found in the various pockets of her specially constructed dress. **1961** Wills–Irwin *Flowers TX* 96, The alcoholic drink "sotol" is prepared from roasted, fermented stems. **2004** *San Antonio Express–News* (TX) 22 Oct sec A 2 (Internet), The liquor sotol, a cousin of tequila, is emerging as a popular spirit in San Antonio.

sotole   See **sotol 1**

sot-pot   See **sot** n

sots n   Also *sotts*   [PaGer < MHG *saz* sediment]   **esp PA**
A type of homemade yeast.

1796 in 1799 Weld *Travels* 65, They [=farmers] raise it with what they call *sots;* hops and water boiled together. **1817** *Niles' Weekly Reg.* 12.10.165, The result was . . that kind of rising called here "sotts," a Dutch term, I presume. **1872** Haldeman *PA Dutch* 59 [English influenced by German], Sots . . home-made 'yeast' as distinguished from 'brewer's-east.' **c1902** Clapin *New Dict. Amer.* 377, Sots. Yeast is so called, in Virginia and Pennsylvania. **1908** *German Amer. Annals* 10.43 **sePA,** Sots (sŏts). Yeast. "I must borrow some sots for my baking." **1953** *AmSp* 28.245 **csPA,** The older residents in the area still refer to *sots.* . . It is actually a yeast culture, a cup of which could usually be borrowed from a neighbor to start one's own batch. Commercial mixes, and bakeries, have just about banished the dishpan full of bread or buckwheat cake dough redolent of sots. **1969** *DARE* (Qu. H16, *What do people use to raise the bread before it's baked?*) Inf **PA**203, Sots.

sot suppe n   [Norw *søtsuppe*]   **Norw settlement areas** =fruit soup.

1951 Tufford *Scandinavian Recipes* 20, Søt Suppe (Sweet Soup) . . tapioca . . water . . salt . . vinegar . . sugar . . grape juice . . cinnamon . . currants . . raisins . . prunes . . chopped apples. . . Serve hot with rusks. May be served cold as dessert. **1983** *Capital Times* (Madison WI) 11 May PM sec 19/2, On the menu for the smorgasbord will be . . sot-suppe (sweet soup). **1999** *WI State Jrl.* (Madison) 31 Oct sec C 1/6, For the first time since 1980, Christ Lutheran Church will serve up a full-fledged lutefisk dinner, complete with lefse, meatballs, sot-suppe, egg coffee, and the lye-preserved cod.

sott   See **set** v[1] **A2a**

sotts   See **sots**

sot work n   Cf **set** v[1] **A4, sit** v[1] **3c**
1953 Randolph–Wilson *Down in Holler* 287 **Ozarks,** Sot-work. . . Knitting, mending, needlework, and so on. One woman says to another, "Come over to our place. Bring your sot-work an' stay all day."

souce See **souse** v¹, n¹

sou'east See **southeast**

sou'easter See **southeaster**

souf(f) See **south**

sougan See **sugan**

souge See **souse** v¹, n¹

sough See **soo** b

soughum See **sorghum**

soul n Pronc-spp *sold, sould* Cf **mile**, Intro "Language Changes" I.8

A Forms.

    1898 Lloyd *Country Life* 33 **AL,** The onlyest livin sould I could see was a yearlin boy. **1914** *DN* 4.77 **ME, nNH,** *My soul an' senses!* "Soul" usually pronounced "sold." *Ibid* 80, *Sould an' deliv'rance!* Ejaculation (women).

B Sense.

See quot. [Engl dial; cf also *OED2 soul* sb. IV.16] Cf **lights 1**

    1899 (1912) Green *VA Folk-Speech* 403, *Soul*. . . The shrivelled lungs of a dead duck, or chicken, or any fowl.

soul-case n [Engl dial] Cf *DCEU, AND*

1 The supposed seat of the intellect and emotions; one's heart, life. **chiefly Sth** *esp freq among Black speakers*

    1805 *Balance* (Hudson NY) 4.176, So, as a comfort to his soul-case,/ To smooth the wrinkles on his old face,/ He sits him down, and feels right glad,/ That he can make poor prose run mad. **1833** *Mail* (Hagers-Town MD) [22 Nov 3]/1 (newspaperarchive.com) [Black,] Yes I see you scull so long-gated, I speck you soul case be very obsquassious. **1835** Longstreet *GA Scenes* 169, When you come to the last half mile of each heat, run his [=a horse's] heart, liver, lights, and soul-case out of him. **1845** *Amer. Whig Rev.* 2.656, The angel . . that hired the least of the many cuddies, and corners, and closets, (all unfurnished,) in the soul-case of a Hero that we wot of, would certainly find the place a little less quiet than paradise. **1884** Harris *Mingo* 23 **GA,** I was a Christun 'nuff to thank the Lord that they was a tender place in that pore mizerbul creetur's soul-case. **1896** Harris *Sister Jane* 277 **GA,** The way that hoss flung around wi' you was enough to jolt your soul-case loose. **1898** Dunbar *Folks from Dixie* 117 **Sth** [Black], I ain't a-gwine to waih my soul-case out a-tryin' to pinch along an' sta've to def at las'. **1956** (1986) Childress *Like One Family* 46 **NYC** [Black], O yes, Marge, I know there are people who do these things, but their soul case is worn thin. **2000** Marshall *Fisher King* 137 **NYC** [Black], [He heard] a new kind of music: splintered, atonal, profane, and possessing a wonderful dissonance that spoke to him, to his soul case.

2 The body.

    1841 *Knickerbocker* 17.495, The Angel sped like lightning into the deserted soul-case, reänimating the corpse. **1848** *Rock R. Pilot* (Watertown WI) 15 Mar [2]/3 (newspaperarchive.com), Every time my feet was put on shore, my soul case was pierced with many an arrow. **1848** in 1975 Foster *Down East Diary* 115 **ME,** Shouts . . urged them through the sloughs and quagmire and over the soul-case-racking causeway. **1856** Deming *Speech* 14 **CT,** She [=ancient philosophy] . . thought that hunger, thirst, pain, the loss of friends, and all the other ills that assail this worthless and contemptible *soul-case,* could be baffled by some superlative . . state of the soul itself. **1869** Stowe *Oldtown Folks* 292 **MA,** Lady Widgery had always been rushed for and contended for by the other sex . . and after all the beautiful little hoax [=pretender] had nothing for it but her attractive soul-case. **1885** *Galveston Daily News* (TX) 3 May 8/3, Blowser called Brimble . . a "desiccated coyote." Brimble . . went to a lawyer. . . The disciple of Blackstone . . ran his legal eye over the old parchment cover of Brimble's "soul case." **1963** *Mt. Life* 39.2.51 **sAppalachians,** Elz'd better watch aout er he'll git hisself slished in two on that old brute—hif it don't fall daown with 'im ra't in the middle o' the big road and plumb sqush his soul-case.

sould See **soul**

sound v, hence vbl n *sounding* Also with *down, on* *esp freq among Black speakers; esp in urban areas* Cf **the dozens** (at **dozen** n B1), **joan, rank** v 3, **signify 1**

To taunt or insult (someone), esp in a ritualized exchange of insults; hence n *sound* an insult; n *sounding* a ritualized exchange of such insults.

    1958 Salisbury *Shook-Up* 63 **NYC,** He had heart. He would do things no other boy would dare. He would sound a cop on the beat and run away laughing. **1962** *Jrl. Amer. Folkl.* 75.209 **sPhiladelphia PA** [Black], The dozens are commonly called "playing", or "sounding". *Ibid* 215, When men do "sound" . . it provides a very different kind of release than when adolescents do. **1971** Malamud *Tenants* 73 **NYC** [Black], I'm not soundin on you, Lesser, but how can you be so whiteass sure of what you sayin if my book turns out to be two different things than you thought? **1972** Labov *Lang. Inner City* xxii **NYC** [Black], Johnny . . had a curious bald spot on the top of his head several months ago . . and is still sounded on regularly by reference to this bald spot. *Ibid* 297, The system of ritual insults known variously as *sounding, signifying, woofing, cutting,* etc. **1972** Kochman *Rappin'* 275 [Black], To initiate sounding . . we used such primitive sequences as: What would you say if someone said to you, "Your momma drink pee?" The answer is well known to most peer-group members: "Your father eat shit." This standard reply allows the exchange to begin along conventional lines, with room for elaboration and invention. . . The simplest of all sounds is the . . identification of the mother with something old, ugly, or bizarre. **1974** Foster *Ribbin'* 183 **NYC, PA** [Black], In Pottsville, Pennsylvania, the term is sounding. . . In a Brooklyn, New York, secondary school the terms ranking and sounding are still used. **2006** *DARE* File—Internet **ceMO** (as of 1950s) [Black], When I was a kid in St. Louis, "playing the dozens" didn't necessarily apply to the classic form of the game. The usual terms . . were: Front [someone] off—Square [someone] off—Jone with [someone]—Play with [someone]—Sound on [someone]—Sound [someone] down.

sounding the horn n

    1936 McCarthy *Lang. Mosshorn* np **West** [Range terms], *Soundin' the Horn*. Taking a hold on the saddle horn when a horse starts to buck or rear into the air.

sound on See **sound**

soup v Also sp *soop* [Engl dial varr of *sup* to sip] *esp freq among Black speakers*

To slurp, sip.

    1903 *DN* 2.331 **seMO,** *Soup*. . . To sip. 'He souped his coffee.' **1908** Day *King Spruce* 131 **ME,** There they . . devoured huge chunks of brown bread deluged with molasses, and "sooped" hot coffee. **1965–70** *DARE* (Qu. H11b, *If he makes a noise with his food, he* _____) Inf **AL**14, Soupin'; **MS**85, **NJ**67, Souping; **SC**70, Souping up like a Jew; **NC**84, **NY**5, **SC**67, 70, **VA**69, Soups; **WI**24, Soups her; **NY**218, Soups his food; **CT**24, **PA**245, Soups it; **CA**101, Soups it up. [7 of 13 total Infs Black]

soup bunch n **chiefly Sth, esp LA, MS**

A variety of vegetables sold in a bundle for making soup.

    1875 *Amer. Agric.* 34.186, A soup-bunch is variable. . . It is essentially celery tops, parsley, leeks and thyme: . . so far as we have noticed those sent to the New York market, there are rarely any other than these in the bunch. **1878** *Sedalia Daily Democrat* (MO) 7 Apr 1/5, [Advt:] New green peas, lettuce, soup bunches, oyster plants, . . etc. at S. Gerye's. **1923** *DN* 5.244 **GA, LA,** *Soup bunch*. A small bundle of vegetables for soup. **1937** *Natl. Geogr. Mag.* Sept 317 **MS,** Venders [sic] call colorful "soup bunches"—carrots, beans, tomatoes, and various greens—all made up in proper proportion for a favorite Provençal vegetable soup. **1938** FWP *Guide MS* 286, Along the coast. . . The grocery stores and the fruit and vegetable stands sell "soup bunches" which provide the base for home-cooked vegetable soup. **1940** Brown *Amer. Cooks* 277 **New Orleans LA,** One of the features of the old Creole Market is the "soup bunch" composed of a section of cabbage, carrot, celery, turnip, leeks, parsley, a red chili pepper, etc., correctly proportioned for the consommé or *pot-au-feu,* and tied together with a string. **1950** *PADS* 14.634 **SC,** *Soup bunch*. . . A variety of vegetables tied up in a bunch to be used for making soup. **1966** *DARE* (Qu. I36, . . *A bunch of kitchen herbs—for example, used in soup;* total Infs questioned, 75) Inf **MS**34, Soup bunch. **1986** Pederson *LAGS Concordance,* 1 inf, **seMS,** A soup bunch—all soup vegetables sold together. **2005** *Commercial Appeal* (Memphis TN) 31 Aug sec M 6 (Internet), Not many of us are old enough to remember seeing a "soup bunch" in the produce department of the grocery store in this country.

soup-crock cut See **crock cut**

souphmo(re) See **sophomore**

soup hound n Cf **pot-licker** n[1] **2**

A cur; a dog of mixed breed.

1922 *Oakland Tribune* (CA) 20 Oct 12/4, Now Bill is cussing the man who sold him the animal and his own efforts to make a good hunting dog out of a "Soup hound." **1950** *WELS* (A dog of mixed breed) 1 Inf, **cwWI**, Soup hound; *(Joking or uncomplimentary words for dogs)* 3 Infs, **WI**, Soup hound. **1956** Ker *Vocab. W. TX* 227, Worthless dog. . . soup houn'. [2 of 67 infs] **1965–70** *DARE* (Qu. J2, . . *Joking or uncomplimentary words . . for dogs*) 22 Infs, **scattered,** Soup hound. **1970** Tarpley *Blinky* 168 **neTX,** A worthless dog . . soup hound [rare]. **1971** Wood *Vocab. Change* 369 **Sth,** Volunteered [for *worthless dog*]: . . soup hound. **1986** Pederson *LAGS Concordance* (Mongrel) 1 inf, **neMS,** Soup hound; 1 inf, **ceTN,** Soup hound—mixed breed; 1 inf, **cwMS,** Soup hound—does nothing; eats; 1 inf, **cnAL,** Soup hound—worthless—all he's fit to do is eat; 1 inf, **cAR,** Soup hound—a straggler, a stray. [4 of 5 infs Black] **2006** *Spokesman-Rev.* (Spokane WA) 30 Jan sec A 1 (Internet), All dogs, big, small, Shar-Pei or soup hound, are better off with a job.

souple See **soople**

soupon See **supawn**

sour n

A lime; see quots.

1942 Kennedy *Palmetto Country* 246, Besides wrecking, they fished, cut mahogany, and cultivated pineapples and their favorite fruits "sours and dillies" (limes and sapodillas). **1946** *FL Dept. Ag. Qrly. Bulletin* new ser 77.11, The Conch liked his . . "sour and dillies," the common name for limes and sapodillas.

sour bait n

=**stink bait 1.**

1905 *New Engl. Mag.* 32.544, A backwoodsman who has neither honey, nor syrup, nor sugar, with which to prepare bee bait, will steep corn-cobs for a couple of days in what, by way of euphemism, he calls "sour-bait." **2003** *DARE* File—Internet **WI,** What is sour bait you say? Well, it sure isn't any magic potion. Put simply, it is just cut catfish bait from suckers, carp, baitfish etc. that turns very rotten with a little time.

sourball bush n

=**dwarf sumac.**

1926 *Torreya* 26.5 **GA,** *Rhus copallina.* . . Sourball bush, Jekyl I[slan]d.

sour beef n

=**sauerbraten.**

[**1863** *Harper's New Mth. Mag.* 27.164, [An American family in Germany:] At *Mittag* . . we dine on . . sour beef, spiced and sweetened.] **1906** *News* (Frederick MD) [16 June 4]/3 (newspaperarchive.com), *Sour beef.* The round is the best cut for sour beef. . . This is a German dish, and potato dumplings are always served with it. **1917** WI *Farmers' Inst. Women's Bulletin No. 10* 36, *Sour beef.* Take a pound and a half of beef, using the tough or cheaper cuts. . . then add two onions, salt and pepper to taste. **1935** *Sun* (Baltimore MD) 2 Mar 18/3, Mrs. Haberkorn was "a world champion" sour beef cooker. **1947** *Ibid* 3 Nov 11/8, Baum's Sour Beef and Potato Dumplings $1.35. **1968** *DARE* (Qu. H65, *Foreign foods favored by people around here*) Inf **MD8,** Sour beef—beef cooked in vinegar and spices—German. **2002** *DARE* File—Internet, Sour Beef and Dumplings. **2003** *Ibid,* Serve French fries and add a spoonful of sour beef.

sour belly n Also *sour bosom,* abbr *s.b.* [Varr, perh *joc,* of **sowbelly, sow bosom**]

Bacon; salt pork.

1862 in 2003 *DARE* File—Internet **WV,** We . . now and then get a little beef but I tell you the sour belly is played out. **1915** *DN* 4.229 **wTX,** *Sour bosom.* . . Bacon. Very common. A less elegant variant is *sour belly.* Frequently one hears at the dinner-table, "Pass me the S.B." **1962** Atwood *Vocab. TX* 62, *Salt pork.* . . Two informants [of approx 270] convert *sowbelly* into *sourbelly,* by a kind of folk etymology. **1967** *DARE* (Qu. H38, . . *Words for bacon [including joking ones]*) Inf **WY3,** Sour belly. **1970** Green *Ely* 22 **TN,** Lets have dinner. We have sour belly, black eyed peas, and apple pie, which I cook special for you.

sourberry n

1 =**French mulberry.** *obs*

1788 Schöpf *Reise Staaten* 2.127 **VA,** Laubholz ist seltener; doch sahe man hie und da einige Stechpalmen . . , nebst . . der Sauerbeere. (*Sower-*

berry, Callicarpa americana L.) [=Broadleaf trees are less common, but one sees here and there some hollies . . , along with . . the sourberry (*Callicarpa americana* L.)]

2 also *sourberry bush:* A **sumac** (here: *Rhus integrifolia*).

1845 (1847) Palmer *Jrl.* 36 **OR,** Occasionally there is a grove of quaking aspen, and a few sour-berry bushes. **1910** Jepson *Silva CA* 28, Sour Berry (*Rhus integrifolia*), [and] Sugar Bush (*Rhus ovata*) are southern shrubs sometimes arborescent. **1938** Van Dersal *Native Woody Plants* 355, Sour berry (*Rhus integrifolia*). **2002** *DARE* File—Internet **CA,** J. Littledeer is Midwestern Osage. She weaves baskets from natural materials collected in the Sierras, including willow, wild grape, alder, sourberry, . . and many others. **2002** *DARE* File—Internet **NM,** Some species, like the brown thrasher, can consume as many as 6,000 insects a day, so planting sour berry and protective bushes to feed and house these winged helpers is a great idea.

sour bosom See **sour belly**

sourbush n

=**French mulberry.**

1869 Cook *Physio-Med. Dispensatory* 300, *Callicarpa Americana*—Sourbush, French mulberry. **1900** Lyons *Plant Names* 75, [*Callicarpa*] *Americana*. . . Virginia to Florida and Texas. French Mulberry, . . Sourbush. **1936** Whitehouse *TX Flowers* 118, French Mulberry . . also known as the Bermuda mulberry or sour-bush.

sour cherry n

An introduced cultivated cherry (here: *Prunus cerasus*). Also called **pie cherry, red ~ 2**

1835 *Star & Republican Banner* (Gettysburg PA) [24 Aug 2]/6 (newspaperarchive.com), [Advt:] *Fruit:* about 200 Apple trees, 20 Sweet Cherry trees, besides Peach, Sour Cherry, Plum trees, &c. **1837** Darlington *Flora Cestrica* 288 **sePA,** Common Cerasus. Vulgò—*Red or Sour Cherry. Morello Cherry.* **1903** Porter *Flora PA* 178, Prunus Cerasus. . . Sour Cherry. . . In woods and thickets, N.Y. and Pa., to the Gulf States. **1939** Medsger *Edible Wild Plants* 48, The Sour Cherry, Prunus Cerasus, introduced from Europe, has also escaped from cultivation from New England to Georgia and farther west. **1969** *DARE* (Qu. H63, *Kinds of desserts*) Inf **PA**213, Sour cherry pie. **2002** *Capital* (Annapolis MD) 19 June sec C 1/2, We had four sweet and one sour cherry tree.

sour clover n [Because it exudes an acid juice]

Either of two chiefly Pacific clovers: *Trifolium fucatum* or *T. obtusiflorum.* For other names of the former see **puff clover, sweet ~ 2,** for other names of the latter see **salt clover, spring ~**

1902 U.S. Natl. Museum *Contrib. Herbarium* 7.361, *Trifolium obtusiflorum.* . . very distinctly characterized by the peculiar sticky exudation. . . This exudation has a strong acid taste and on this account the clover is variously known as "sour" or "salt" clover. **1915** (1926) Armstrong–Thornber *Western Wild Flowers* 262, Sour Clover—*Trifolium fucatum* . . Wash., Oreg., Cal. **1920** Saunders *Useful Wild Plants* 140 **CA,** Next to this [=*Trifolium virescens*] in favor [with the Indians of Mendocino County] is the "sour" or "salt clover" (*T. obtusiflorum* . .) with narrow, saw-toothed leaflets, whitish blossoms with purple centers, and a clammy, acidulous exudation that covers the leaves and flowers. **1949** Moldenke *Amer. Wild Flowers* 143, The sour clover, *T[rifolium] fucatum* . . is common along railroad tracks, along roads, and in low alkaline and brackish places in Oregon and California. **1977** *New Yorker* 17 Oct 44 **Sth,** First down the step, then out onto the sour-clover ridges that man had harrowed by mistake. **1979** Spellenberg *Audubon Guide N. Amer. Wildflowers W. Region* 512, Sour Clover; Bull Clover; Puff Clover (*Trifolium fucatum*) . . Southern Oregon and most of California. **1998** in 2007 *DARE* File—Internet **ceCA,** Three-quarters of the way up the mountain. . . I saw a different mix of flowers: [including] . . sour clover (*Trifolium fucatum*).

sour coon See **sow coon 2**

sour crab See **sow crab**

sour craw n

Sour crop, thrush (in chickens).

1960 Williams *Walk Egypt* 211 **GA,** A dozen chickens had died of sour craw. **1966–67** *DARE* (Qu. K78, . . *Diseases . . chickens commonly get*) Infs **SC**26, 43, Sour craw. **2006** *DARE* File—Internet, The importance of checking the craw before feeding, to make sure it is empty, is because birds can get sour craw if new food is feed [sic] while it has old food left.

sourcrout See **sauerkraut**

sour dock n Also *sour dick* [*OED2* c1325 →] Cf **speckled dick**

A **dock** n[1] with sour juice, as **canaigre, curled dock,** or **sheep sorrel.**

1831 (1832) Flint *Hist & Geog. Missip. Valley* 61, Rumex *acetosella . . sour dock . .* is recommended against inveterate ring-worms. **1837** Darlington *Flora Cestrica* 236 **sePA,** Curled Rumex. *Vulgò*—Sour Dock. Curled Dock. **1895** U.S. Dept. Ag. *Farmers' Bulletin* 28.28, Sorrel dock, sour dock—Rumex acetosa—South Carolina to Georgia. **1897** *Jrl. Amer. Folkl.* 10.54 **OH,** Rumex obtusifolius . . sour dock, poison dock, Sulphur Grove, Ohio. **1923** in 1925 Jepson *Manual Plants CA* 292, R[umex] hymenosepalus . . Canaigre. . . The stem is used as a substitute for rhubarb, whence the names Wild Rhubarb, Pie Dock, and Sour Dock. **1935** (1943) Muenscher *Weeds* 197, Rumex Acetosa. . . Sour dock. *Ibid* 198, Rumex crispus. . . Sour dock. **1965–70** *DARE* (Qu. S26d, *Wildflowers that grow in meadows;* not asked in early QRs) 68 Infs, **scattered,** Sour dock; (Qu. I28a, . . *Kinds of things . . you call 'greens' . . [Those that are eaten raw]*) Infs **CA**205, **IL**142, **MO**11, 19, Sour dock; **OH**89, Sour dock—you wilt it and flavor it with pork; (Qu. I28b, *Kinds of greens that are cooked*) Infs **KY**37, **MO**18, **OH**22, **TX**89, Sour dock; (Qu. S15, . . *Weed seeds that cling to clothing*) Inf **OH**69, Sour dock; (Qu. S20, *A common weed that grows on open hillsides: It has velvety green leaves close to the ground, and a tall stalk with small yellow flowers on a spike at the top*) Inf **CO**4, Sour dock—same as Indian tobacco—gets in hay meadows; **OR**1, Indian tobacco or sour dock; (Qu. S21, . . *Weeds . . that are a trouble in gardens and fields*) Infs **CA**200, 208, **ID**5, **MS**16, Sour dock; **IA**29, Sour dock—called Indian tobacco when it dried—could be smoked; (Qu. S26e, *Other wildflowers not yet mentioned;* not asked in early QRs) Infs **OH**64, **OK**1, 52, Sour dock. **1968** *DARE* Tape **IN**32, One thing that I've always done is to be able to hunt my own greens in the spring. . . I get mountain sprouts, sour dock, wild beets, Shawnee, crow foot, deer tongue, hen pepper, and oh so many others. **1977** McPhee *Coming Country* 32 **AK,** They eat what they call "white-man food," mainly from cans, but they also eat owl soup, sour dock, wild rhubarb, [etc.]. **1991** Still *Wolfpen Notebooks* 77 **sAppalachians,** What you want to look for is plantain, bird's-toe, fiddleheads, speckled dick and sour dick [etc.]. **2002** *Star Tribune* (Minneapolis MN) sec G 8 (Internet) **SD,** Ten colors of specially bred corn are used [in the Corn Palace], along with rye, sour dock, wheat, wild grasses and other natural material.

sourdough n

1 freq attrib: Fermenting dough, esp from a continuously replenished supply, used as leavening; a bread made with such dough. **orig chiefly West; now widely known** See Map

1837 Hazen *Panorama* 28, Methods of baking bread. . . adding . . a small quantity of sour dough, or leaven, to serve as a fermenting agent. **1854** *Harper's New Mth. Mag.* 8.535, The beer is merely a kind of fermented toast and water, made by steeping cakes, baked from sour dough, for a few hours in water. **1885** *Century Illustr. Mag.* 31.30 **CA,** The most of the folks we ever see wouldn't know sour-dough bread from salt-risin'. **1889** *Overland Mth.* (2d ser) 14.267 **West,** One can still make as good bread with a lump of sour dough as can any woman that breathes. **1900** *Atlantic Mth.* 85.86 **AK,** Prince bared his womanly arms and kneaded sour-dough bread. **1900** *Outing* 36.153 **CO,** Preparations are made that result in light 'sour-dough' rolls . . and steaming coffee. **1907** *DN* 3.250 **eME,** Sour dough biscuit. . . Biscuit mixed with fermented dough. The bread provided woodsmen in the logging camps. **1933** *AmSp* 8.1.27 **nwTX** [Ranch diction], Sourdough. Biscuits made with fermented dough as the leavening agent, by adding water and flour. **1939** (1973) FWP *Guide MT* 416, Sourdough—Bread leavened with sponge from a previous baking. **1965–70** *DARE* (Qu. H18, . . *Special kinds of bread*) 44 Infs, **esp West,** Sourdough bread; **IN**48, Sourdough biscuits; **CA**32, 91, 118, Sourdough french bread; **NC**11, Sourdough rolls; (Qu. H17, . . *Kinds [of] yeast*) Infs **IN**7, **LA**31, **MN**23, **MT**2, **NM**9, **OR**1, **TX**42, 43, 45, Sourdough; **CO**7, Sourdough riser; **CO**7, 27, **OR**15, Sourdough starter; **IL**5, **MO**5, **OR**4, Sourdough yeast; (Qu. H15, *Bread made with wheat flour*) Inf **TX**3, Sourdough bread; (Qu. H16, *What do people use to raise the bread before it's baked?*) Infs **AK**8, **CA**136, **IN**60, Sourdough; (Qu. H19, *What do you mean by a biscuit? How are they made?*) Infs **IA**13, **IN**48, **ME**2, **SC**51, **SD**8, Sourdough biscuit(s); (Qu. H20b, . . *Names . . for pancakes*) Inf **AK**8, Sourdough hotcakes; (Qu. H65, *Foreign foods favored by people around*

here) Inf **WA**6, Sourdough bread. **1968** Adams *Western Words* 294, *Sourdough keg*—A small wooden keg, usually holding about 5 gallons, in which the cook kept his sourdough. **1986** Pederson *LAGS Concordance* 22 infs, **Gulf Region,** Sourdough (bread). **2000** *DARE* File—Internet, Baldwin Hill Organic Sourdough Breads—Phillipston, Massachusetts, bakery makes organic sourdough bread for delivery around the country.

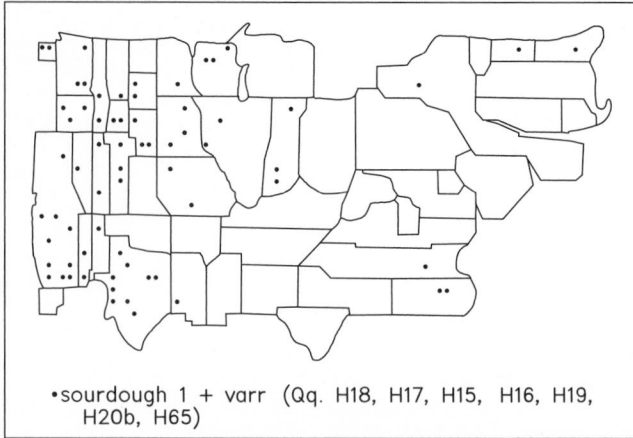

•sourdough 1 + varr (Qq. H18, H17, H15, H16, H19, H20b, H65)

2 A veteran dweller in the wilds, esp a prospector for gold; an old-timer, esp a long-term resident of Alaska. [See quot 1966] **chiefly NW, AK** Cf **cheechako**

[**1898** *Klondike Nugget* (Dawson, Yukon Terr) 20 July 1/4 *(OED2),* Mr. Chee Chaco was not looking for information from his old friend Mr. Sour Dough.] **1899** *Overland Mth.* (2d ser) 34.117 **AK,** Grizzled "sourdough boys," . . patronized the spruce-looking tenderfeet and lied eloquently. **1913** *DN* 4.28 **NW,** Sour dough. . . A man of the hills and open. Usually a prospector for minerals. Used also in Alaska. **1929** *AmSp* 5.76 **NE** [Cattle country talk], An "old timer," "old time cowhand," or a pioneer is sometimes called a "sour-dough." **1939** FWP *ID Lore* 242, Sourdough—old-timer. **1944** Williamson *Far North* 46 **AK,** In gold mining, as in war, experience comes fast. At Cook Inlet you might be on Monday morning a mere cheechakho, as a tenderfoot was called; by Saturday night you might well have gone through enough, learned so much and unlearned so much more, that the fellows would refer to you as a regular old sourdough, meaning an old-timer. **1958** McCulloch *Woods Words* 174 **Pacific NW,** Sourdough. . . A mountain man or prospector. **1966** Barnes-Jensen *Dict. UT Slang* 39, Sourdough: . . one who spends much time in the open, especially as a prospector. The term originated from the lump of sour dough that a prospector saves from his last batch of dough to start fermentation of a new. **1968** *DARE* Tape **AK**13, There's an old sourdough and he has ceramics up in here. **1969** *DARE* (Qu. CC13b, . . *The person who knows how to use a forked stick to find water*) Inf **MA**40, Sourdough—to find metal. **1989** *Fairbanks Daily News-Miner* (AK) 26 Jan 1/3, In the attempt to keep from freezing to death, even sourdoughs have been known to set themselves or their houses on fire.

3 See quot.

[**1929** *Syracuse Herald* (NY) 18 Aug mag sec 4/1, But Paul's chief cook, Sourdough Sam, who married Paul's oldest daughter, knew more about Paul [Bunyan] than anyone. Sourdough was the most intelligent of any of Paul's crew.] **1936** Adams *Cowboy Lingo* 150 **West,** The cook also had his slang titles, such as . . 'sour-dough.'

sourdough lily n

A **fritillary** (here: *Fritillaria affinis*).

1934 Haskin *Wild Flowers Pacific Coast* 23 **CA,** [The name] sourdough lily [comes] from its peculiar odor, and from the fact that it grows in the land of the "sour-doughs."

sour fly n Cf **sour gnat**

A fruit fly or similar small, irritating insect.

1907 *School Sci. & Math.* 7.672 **NY,** The fruit fly—known as "sour fly," "vinegar fly," and "pomace fly"—can be found at almost any time in any fruit store or about vinegar or pickle barrels. **1918** Lutz *Field Book* 276, Drosophila melanogaster—The little red-eyed Pomace-fly . . —also called Sour Fly and Vinegar-fly. **1957** *DE Folkl. Bulletin* 1.28, Sour fly (fruit fly). **1966–68** *DARE* (Qu. R10, *Very small flies that don't sting, often seen hovering in large groups or bunches outdoors in* *summer*) Infs **NJ**10, 21, Sour fly; (Qu. R13, *Flies that come to meat or fruit*) Infs **KS**8, **NJ**10, 31, **WA**1, Sour fly; **VA**15, Sour fly—comes to spoiled fruits. **1982** *Barrick Coll.* **csPA,** *Sour fly*—fruit fly, gnat. **1998** in 2002 *DARE* File—Internet **ME,** Fresh squeezed lemonade stands are always popular with happy hippies and sour flies.

sour gnat n **chiefly W Midl** See Map Cf **drunkard 1, sour fly, vinegar ~**

A fruit fly or similar small, irritating insect.

1938 Miller–Blaydes *Methods & Materials* 399, Drosophila, the common fruit fly or vinegar fly (also called "sour gnat"). **1946** Stuart *Tales Plum Grove* 174 **eKY,** I was as wet as sweat could make me and my eyes were smartin' with sweat like I had a dozen sour-gnats in my eyes. **1953** Randolph–Wilson *Down in Holler* 287 **Ozarks,** Sour gnat. . . Any sort of small insect that gets into one's eye, causing severe pain. An ordinary gnat is bad enough, but a *sour gnat* or *p'izen gnat* is much more painful. **c1960** *Wilson Coll.* **csKY,** Fruit flies. . . also called sour gnats, drunkards. **1965–70** *DARE* (Qu. R13, *Flies that come to meat or fruit*) 13 Infs, 6 **IN,** Sour gnat; **OK**42, Gnats or sour gnats—hang around bananas and other fruit; **VA**34, Sour gnat—same as fruit fly. **1983** *MJLF* 9.1.57 **ceKY** [as of 1956], *Sour gnat* . . a type of gnat that hurts worse than ordinary gnats when one gets in your eye. **2002** Marion *Hollow Ground* 24 **TN,** He tried to clean off the front bench for her. He was afraid there could be black flakes of flesh or sour gnats, and he wished the hull of the boat wasn't full of rotten leaves.

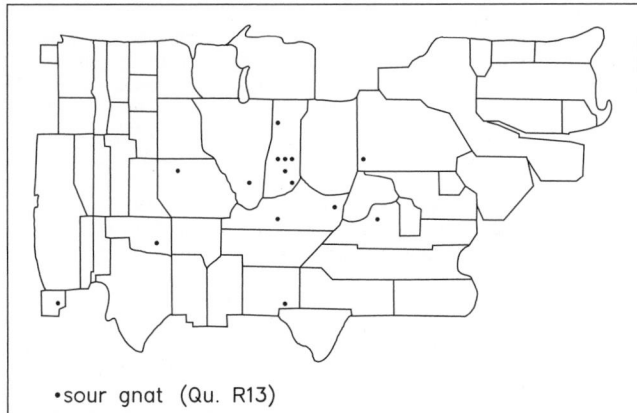

•sour gnat (Qu. R13)

‡**sour grape** n Cf **sweet grape**

An enemy; an adversary.

1939 *AmSp* 14.92 **eTN,** *Sour-grape.* An enemy. 'He's been my sour-grape since the 'lection two years ago.'

sour grass n

Any of var grasses or other plants with a sour taste or odor, as:

a =**rush** n¹ **B.**

1878 Killebrew *Grasses TN* 14, The large, coarse grasses that border our ponds and mat in our swamps . . are looked upon as *sour grasses.* **1894** *Jrl. Amer. Folkl.* 7.103 **NE,** *Juncus,* sp., sour-grass.

b A **sedge B1.**

1878 [see **a** above]. **1899** *Plant World* 2.198 **swPA,** *Sourgrass* for species of *Carex;* doubtless because cattle's distaste for it suggests sourness in the plant.

c A **dock** n¹: usu **sheep sorrel,** but also *Rumex acetosa.*

1889 Britton *Catalogue Plants NJ* 211, R[umex] Acetosella. . . Sour Grass. Sheep sorrel. **1894** *Jrl. Amer. Folkl.* 7.97 **cCT,** *Rumex aceto-sella.* . . sour grass, Hartford. **1900** Lyons *Plant Names* 327, *R[umex] Acetosa.* . . Sour-grass, Sour-sauce [etc]. **1951** Martin *Amer. Wildlife & Plants* 386, Sheepsorrel, or sourgrass (R[umex] acetosella), is by far the most important member of this group in so far as wildlife is concerned. **1965–70** *DARE* (Qu. L8, *Hay that grows naturally in damp places*) 11 Infs, **scattered,** Sour grass; (Qu. S9, . . *Kinds of grass that are hard to get rid of*) Infs **MA**1, **MI**15, **NJ**1, **PA**70, 181, 204, **RI**1, Sour grass; (Qu. S21, . . *Weeds . . that are a trouble in gardens and fields*) Infs **FL**48, **OH**72, 78, **PA**70, **SC**7, 63, 70, **VA**2, Sour grass; (Qu. S26d, *Wildflowers that grow in meadows;* not asked in early QRs) Infs **KY**77, **MI**9, Sour grass; **OH**16, Sour grass—that's dock; (Qu. S26e, *Other wildflowers not yet mentioned;* not asked in early QRs) Infs **OH**66, **SC**46, Sour grass; **NY**88, Sour grass [FW: Sheep sorrel]; **SC**11, Sour grass—red top and it's chewed for a peculiar sour-sweet taste. [*DARE*

Ed: Some of these Infs may refer instead to other senses.] **1977** Churchill *Don't Call* 140 **nwOR** (as of c1918), I was familiar with sour grass and watercress because we kids used to eat them. . . Sour grass was found along stream banks as well as back in the heavily wooded areas. **c1980** *DARE* File **cnMA** (as of c1915), We called the little arrow-shaped leaves of dock *sour grass* and pretended to enjoy eating them when I was a child.

d A **wood sorrel 1** (here: *Oxalis* spp). [*OED2* 1866 →]

1885 *Gardener's Mth. & Horticulturist* 27.43, Oxalis lutea is but an old synonym of Oxalis corniculata, the well-known "sour-grass" of children. **1896** *Jrl. Amer. Folkl.* 9.184 **IN,** *Oxalis corniculata,* var. *stricta.* . . sour grass. **1909** *DN* 3.373 **eAL, wGA,** *Sour-grass.* . . Wood-sorrel. **1953** Greene–Blomquist *Flowers South* 62, Wood Sorrels, Sour-Grasses *(Oxalis).* **1956** McAtee *Some Dialect NC* 42, Sour grass: . . any species of *Oxalis.* **1964** Campbell et al. *Gt. Smoky Wildflowers* 52, Wood Sorrel—*Oxalis montana.* . . There are five other species of sorrel in the park, all of which are also called *sour grass.* **1966** *DARE* (Qu. S26e, *Other wildflowers not yet mentioned;* not asked in early QRs) Inf **SC**27, Sorrel—best known as sour grass. **1966–67** *DARE* Wildfl QR Pl.121A [=*Oxalis violacea*] Inf **TX**44, Sour grass; Pl.121B [=*Oxalis stricta*] Infs **NY**16, **TX**44, Sour grass. **2001** *Topeka Capital–Jrl.* (KS) 17 Mar (Internet), Called "sour grass" by some people because of the pleasantly sour taste the leaves have when chewed, yellow wood sorrel is considered to be an indicator for moist, fertile sites.

e =**squaw grass 1.**

1897 Parsons *Wild Flowers CA* 52, In the north, where it [=*Xerophyllum tenax*] is sometimes very abundant, and occupies extensive meadows, it is known as "sour-grass." **1898** *Jrl. Amer. Folkl.* 11.282 **CA,** *Xerophyllum tenax* . . sour grass, deer grass [etc].

f A **wild buckwheat 2** (here: *Eriogonum latifolium*).

1902 U.S. Natl. Museum *Contrib. Herbarium* 7.345, *Eriogonum latifolium.* . . The white woolly plant called "sour grass," which grows about 2 feet high. . . The young stems have a very agreeable acid taste, and are eagerly sought after by children in May or June.

g An arrow grass (here: *Triglochin maritima*).

1901 Carpenter *Forests & Snow* 7 **CO,** Arrow Grass . . Other Common Names. . . Sour grass, goose grass. **1963** Craighead *Rocky Mt. Wildflowers* 4, Arrowgrass. . . Other names: Podgrass, Goosegrass, Sourgrass. **1966** Barnes–Jensen *Dict. UT Slang* 39, *Sour grass* . . a local name for the Arrowgrass *(Triglochin maritima).* **1970** Kirk *Wild Edible Plants W. U.S.* 159, Sourgrass. . . The plants, especially in times of drought, often contain toxic quantities of hydrocyanic acid. **1996** Barnard *Reptile Hdbk.* 180, Sourgrass *(Triglochin maritima);* leaves; plant is cyanogenetic.

h A **panic grass** (here: *Panicum dichotomiflorum*).

1942 *Torreya* 42.157 **seKS,** *Panicum dichotomiflorum.* . . Sour grass, Allen County. **1957** (1974) Spencer *All About Weeds* 31, *Fall Panic Grass*—[*Panicum dichotomiflorum* Michx.]. . . Farmers often call this weed, along with several other grass species, "sour grass" and "swamp grass."

i *Digitaria insularis,* a grass of the southeastern and Gulf states. [See quots]

[**1950** Hitchcock–Chase *Manual Grasses* 570, *Trichachne insularis* [= *Digitaria insularis*] is not relished by cattle, hence the name sourgrass by which it is called in the West Indies.] **1970** Correll *Plants TX* 148, *Trichachne nutans* [=*Digitaria insularis*]. . . The name sourgrass alludes to the unpleasant odor of the bases of the plants when bruised, reminiscent of rotting lemons. **1998** Mueller-Dombois *Vegetation* 492 **HI,** Sourgrass, a medium-tall grass, often forms rings around invading shrubs, such as *Acacia farnesiana.* Unpalatable to cattle, *Digitaria* (syn. *Tricachne* [sic]) *insularis* was accidentially [sic] introduced from tropical America in 1906.

sour greens n

A western **dock** n¹ (here: *Rumex venosus*).

1917 Rydberg *Flora Rocky Mts.* 231, R[umex] *venosus.* . . Sour Greens. **1950** Gray–Fernald *Manual of Botany* 568 **WI,** R[umex] *venosus.* . . Sour Greens. . . local, Wisc. **1976** Bailey–Bailey *Hortus Third* 988, [*Rumex*] *venosus.* . . sour greens.

sour gum n

1 also *sour-gum tree:* Any of several **tupelos,** but esp **black gum 1** (here: *Nyssa sylvatica*).

1785 Marshall *Arbustrum* 97, Nyssa sylvatica. *Upland Tupelo-Tree, or Sour Gum.* This grows naturally in Pennsylvania and perhaps elsewhere, rising with a strong upright trunk to the height of thirty or forty feet.

1812 Michaux *Histoire des Arbres* 2.261, Nyssa *Sylvatica. . . Dans ces diverses parties des États-Unis, il est désigné sous le nom de *Black gum . . ;* de *Yellow gum . . ;* et de *Sour gum . . ;* dénominations qui ne se rattachent à aucune de ses propriétés particulières, et par conséquent sont assez mauvaises, mais qui sont consacrées par l'usage. [=Nyssa *Sylvatica. . .* In these various parts of the United States, it is called by the name of *Black gum . . ; Yellow gum . . ;* and *Sour gum . . ;* designations not tied to any of its specific properties, and consequently rather ill suited, but hallowed by usage.] *Ibid* 265, Nyssa *Aquatica. . .* Il y est désigné assez indistinctement sous les différens noms de *Tupelo;* de *Gum tree, . .* de *Sour Gum, . .* et de *Peperidge.* [=Nyssa *Aquatica. . .* It is there rather haphazardly called by the different names of *Tupelo; Gum tree, . . Sour Gum, . .* and *Peperidge.*] **1830** Rafinesque *Med. Flora* 2.247, Nyssa. . . *Tupelo, Peperidge, Sourgum, Blackgum.* Six sp[ecies] of trees. . . Fruits bitter and acid. **1867** De Voe *Market Asst.* 373, *Black gumberries, sour gumberries, tupelo,* or *pepperidgeberries.*—These small, blue, oval berries, with large pits, are found growing on large trees. **1898** *NY Times* (NY) 16 Oct 8 **NYC,** The nyssa, or sour gum tree, greets the Autumn with a yellowish tinge. **1908** Rogers *Tree Book* 408, Tupelo, Pepperidge, Sour or Black Gum. *Ibid* 409, The name, "sour gum," refers to the fruit. **1943** Weslager *DE Forgotten Folk* 160, Sour Gum Sap—*Nyssa sylvatica . .* used as chewing gum. **1968–70** *DARE* (Qu. T13) Inf **MA**78, Sour gum; (Qu. T15, . . *Kinds of swamp trees*) Infs **NJ**21, 31, Sour gum. **1974** Morton *Folk Remedies* 105 **SC,** Sour gum. . . *Nyssa sylvatica. . .* Because the branchlets "chew up well into a little brush at the end," Carolina people have always used them as toothbrushes. **2000** *Frederick Post* (MD) 5 Oct sec B 7/2, If you are looking for fall color the sour gum (Nyssa sylvatica), also known as black tupelo (30 to 50 feet), is one of the prettiest native trees.

2 also *sour-gum bush* = **sourwood 1.**

1897 Sudworth *Arborescent Flora* 314, *Oxydendrum arboreum. . .* Sour Gum Bush (Ohio). Sour Gum (W. Va.). **1950** Peattie *Nat. Hist. Trees* 529, Sourwood. . . Other Names: Sorreltree. Sour Gum [etc]. [*Ibid* 531, Once on a time in the days of home medicine, the leaves were brewed as a tonic, and they still, with their pleasant acid taste, quench the thirst of the hot, perspiring mountain climber.] **1960** Vines *Trees SW* 812, Vernacular names are Sorrel-tree, Sour-gum, Elk-tree, and Titi. **2002** *Seattle Post–Intelligencer* (WA) sec D 8 (Internet), Sourgum (Oxydendrum arboreum)—Deciduous tree to about 30 feet high and 20 feet wide; bright orange fall foliage.

sour-gum tree See **sour gum 1**

sour hen n [Sw *sur höna* sour (i.e. ill-tempered) hen] **in Swedish settlement areas** Cf **cluck** n **1**

A setting hen.

1910 Kiner *Hist. Henry Co. IL* 1.169, My face fell as long as a horse collar. It wore an expression such as man might wear just after tasting a sour hen's nest. **1931** *AmSp* 6.216 **IL, MN, WI** [Infl of Swedish on English], The *sour hen* pecked me. . . The setting hen pecked me. . . Expression in Swedish. . . Den sura höna hackade på mig. **1937** *AmSp* 12.104 **eNE** [Farm terms], A setting hen may be a *cluck,* . . a *clucking hen,* a *settin' hen,* a *sour hen* (Scandinavian from *sur hona*) or a *skrock hen* (German). **1966–67** *DARE* (Qu. K72, *When the hen stops laying and begins to sit on the eggs to hatch them, she's a _____*) Inf **MN**4A, Sour hen—the old standby; **SD**3, Sour hen. **1973** Allen *LAUM* 1.255 (as of c1950), *Setting hen. . . Sour hen,* the form used by a Swedish inf. in n. Minnesota, and reported by a North Dakota inf. as heard in the community, is a direct translation from Swedish. **1981** *PADS* 67.30 **neMN,** Ten of 13 Iron Range respondents offered one of the general terms *setting hen, sitting hen,* or *setter hen. . . sour hen. . .* a Swedish translation, is the response of the Finland Swedish informant . . ; another Swedish-speaking informant . . offered it as a heard form.

sourings n pl Cf **emptins 1, sourdough 1**

A homemade leavening agent.

1909 in 2006 *DARE* File—Internet **KS** (as of 1870s), Our mid-afternoon meal was buffalo meat stewed with dumplings made out of biscuit dough, which was made up with what the hunters called sourings [f]lour, water and yeast mixed together and let stand still [sic] sour. **1935** Davis *Honey* 110 **OR,** Old Simmons could never feel right about dumping his bread-sourings into the wrong-size bottle. *Ibid* 111, In the meantime his sourings would have gone flat and he would have to make up a new batch. **1973** *Oakland Tribune* (CA) 17 Mar sec E 14/3, He also mentioned that some old-timers found it handy to add a tablespoon

of vinegar to the original batch or to any aged sourings that needed reviving.

‡sour john gate n

1969 *DARE* FW Addit **swNC,** Sour john gate—I'm not sure but I think it's a gate in the old rail fences which has no door, but because it's zigzagged, the animals can't get out.

sourkraut, sourkrout See **sauerkraut**

sour milk n [nEngl, Scots, Ir dial; cf *EDD sour* adj. 1.(18), *SND sour* I.1.(13)]

Buttermilk.

1866 Peterson *Natl. Cook Book* 287 **sePA,** *To Make Butter. . .* Strain your milk. . . Let the milk stand about three days, then skim off the cream with a skimmer made for the purpose, and take care to get as little of the sour milk with it as possible. Then churn it. . . Then salt it and work it well, to get out all the remaining buttermilk. **1886** *S. Bivouac* 4.349 **sAppalachians,** Sour milk (butter-milk). **1976** Garber *Mountainese* 86 **sAppalachians,** *Sour-milk . .* buttermilk—We jist churned a whole batch uv sour milk and it's real good. **1982** Slone *How We Talked* 55 **eKY** (as of c1950), Buttermilk can be substituted for the sweet milk, making sourmilk gravy.

sour-milk cheese n Cf *DS* H60

Cottage cheese.

[**1810** *Cries of New York* 25 (OED2), The good housewife, by hanging it [*sc.* buttermilk], mixed with other sour milk, over a slow fire, turns it to a curd; and with the addition of a little butter, salt, and sometimes sage, makes what is called pot-cheese.] **1883** (1884) Lincoln *Mrs. Lincoln's Boston Cook Book* 283, Sour Milk Cheese (sometimes called Dutch, Curd, or Cottage Cheese). **1939** Wolcott *Yankee Cook Book* 215, Sour Milk Cheese [Called also Dutch, Curd, Cottage Cheese and Connecticut Pot Cheese]. **1941** *Language* 17.332 **WI,** [*LANCS* fieldwork:] *Sour-milk cheese* [for *cottage cheese*]—5 [of 50 infs] . . an old term to all. Eastern and central parts of the state. **1949** Kurath *Word Geog.* 71, *Cottage cheese* is the trade name for curds in all the Eastern States. . . The earlier regional terms, however, are still in rather general use, even in the cities. . . In coastal New England, from the mouth of the Connecticut River to Cape Cod and northward to the Kennebec River, *sour-milk cheese* predominates. **1956** Ker *Vocab. W. TX* 265, Homemade cheese made of curds. . . *Sour milk cheese.* [1 of 67 infs]. **1962** Atwood *Vocab. TX* 81, Of words characteristic of Eastern New England. . . *sour milk cheese* (3.7[% of approx 270 infs]). **1967** Faries *Word Geog. MO* 105, *Sour-milk cheese* [for *cottage cheese*] (15 occurrences [in 700 infs]). **1986** Pederson *LAGS Concordance* (Cottage cheese) 2 infs, **AL, MS,** Sour-milk cheese.

soursap n [Var of *soursop*]

A **custard apple 1.**

1872 U.S. Navy Dept. *Rept. Explor. & Surv.* 72, Guanabana. . . the sour-sap. **1898** *Century Illustr. Mag.* 56.672, There were also custard apples. . . The most astonishing and the best of all was a fruit called *pulmo*—in our language, sour-sap. **1966** *DARE* Tape **FL**23, [FW:] How about that soursap you were talking about? [Inf:] That is a tropical fruit. It has a very rough skin. In fact it looks almost thorny on the outside. But on the inside . . the meat is white, cottony white, and has black seeds. The meat is removed and the seeds are removed. And then put through a colander to obtain the pulp . . which is the basis for the ice cream, the tropical soursap ice cream. . . It's tart. **1967** *DARE* (Qu. I53, . . *Fruits grown around here . . special varieties*) Inf **HI**11, Soursap.

sour sop n Cf **sop 1**

1991 Still *Wolfpen Notebooks* 77 **sAppalachians,** During Depression Days the mines were closed and we lived on sour sop. That's buttermilk poured into hot grease and with cornbread crumbled in.

sour spinach n

=**dock** n[1].

1968 *DARE* (Qu. I28b, *Kinds of greens that are cooked*) Inf **CT**9, Sour spinach—same as sorrel.

sour stick n

A **rhubarb B** (here: *Rheum rhabarbarum*).

1968 *DARE* (Qu. I30, *Other names for rhubarb*) Inf **IL**27, Sour sticks—when we were kids we called them this.

sour top (blueberry) n

A **blueberry 1** (here: *Vaccinium myrtilloides*).

1897 ME Ag. Exper. Sta. *Annual Rept. for 1896* 241, Sour top blueberry . . 166. *Ibid* 166, Velvet Leaf or "Sour Top." . . Vaccinium canadense. **1910** Graves *Flowering Plants* 313 **CT,** *Vaccinium canadense.* . . Sour-top or Velvet-leaf Blueberry. **1989** Whealy *Fruit Inventory* 216, *Vaccinium myrtilloides* (Sourtop Blueberry, Velvet-Leaf Blueberry). . . Native from Labrador to Virginia and west to British Columbia. **2003** *Portland Press Herald* (ME) 18 May sec B 1 (Internet), The sour top blueberry grows up to 24 inches tall with smaller and less sweet berries.

sour tupelo n
=**Ogeechee lime.**

    1810 Michaux *Histoire des Arbres* 1.30 **GA,** N[yssa] candicans. . . *Sour tupelo* . . dans l'Etat de Géorgie. [=N[yssa] candicans. . . *Sour tupelo* . . in the state of Georgia.] **1898** Sudworth *Forest Trees* 101 **FL, SC,** *Nyssa ogeche.* . . Names in use.—Sour Tupelo [etc]. **1980** Little *Audubon Guide N. Amer. Trees E. Region* 619, "Sour Tupelo". . . Extreme S. South Carolina, S. Georgia, and N. Florida.

sour vine n
An unidentified vine; see quots.

    1938 Stuart *Dark Hills* 46 **KY,** The smell of sourvines, smartweeds, ragweeds and cockleburrs. [**1949** Arnow *Hunter's Horn* 2 **eKY,** Lister Tucker—he's got a pretty good hound name a Sourvine.] **1982** Slone *How We Talked* 47 **eKY** (as of c1950), *Sour vine*—resembles the poison vine, except it has five leaves in a cluster; the poison variety has only three.

sourweed n
=**sheep sorrel.**

    1895 U.S. Dept. Ag. *Farmers' Bulletin* 28.28, Sorrel, . . sheep sorrel, sourweed—Rumex acetosella. **1912** Blatchley *IN Weed Book* 63, Red Sorrel. Sheep Sorrel. Sour-weed. **1960** Williams *Walk Egypt* 133 **GA,** Sourweed bloomed nearby. Bite the red stem, and bitterness filled your mouth. **1966** *DARE* FW Addit Inf **WA**10, Rumex acetosella—sheep sorrel, sourweed. **1973** *Foxfire 2* 63, Sheep sorrel. . . sour grass, sour dock, redtop, sourweed. **2004** in 2007 *DARE* File—Internet **GA,** I grin at the face Dal makes . . as I introduce him to the joys of chewing sourweed.

sourwood n

1 A small tree *(Oxydendrum arboreum)* common in the mountains of the eastern US. [Because the leaves have a sour taste] **chiefly sAppalachians** Also called **arrowwood d, elk tree, lily-of-the-valley ~, sorrel ~, sour gum 2, titi 2c**

    1709 (1967) Lawson *New Voyage* 104 **NC, SC,** The Sorrel, or Sowr-Wood-Tree, is so call'd, because the Leaves taste like Sorrel. **1828** Rafinesque *Med. Flora* 1.41, Andromeda arborea. . . Vulgar Names—Sour Tree, Sour Wood [etc]. **1863** Porcher *Resources* 379 **SC,** Sourwood, sorrel tree. . . I collected it in St. John's, and Spartanburg district, S.C. **1937** Thornburgh *Gt. Smoky Mts.* 30, You know sourwood; hit's the fust of all the trees to turn red in the fall and ye want to git it while hit's red. **1953** Stuart *Beatinest Boy* 50 **KY,** Orphan was standing with his front paws upon the side of a little sourwood. **1966–69** *DARE* (Qu. S26e, *Other wildflowers not yet mentioned;* not asked in early QRs) Inf **SC**32, Sourwood; (Qu. T9) Inf **GA**70, Sourwood; (Qu. T15, . . *Kinds of swamp trees*) Inf **FL**16, Sourwood; (Qu. T16, . . *Kinds of trees* . . *'special'*) Infs **KY**16, 34, 47, **VA**43, Sourwood; (Qu. CC13a, . . *A forked stick that's used to show where there's water underground.* . . *[What kind of wood?]*) Inf **VA**1, Sourwood stick four feet long, forked. **1966** *DARE* Tape **NC**36, The maples are the first trees that turn, and the sourwoods and the dogwoods which are in shades of red, and then the maples are shades of yellow on up into deep red and russets. **1969** *DARE* FW Addit **seKY,** *Sourwood*—bees make superb honey from the blossoms of this tree (Oxydendrum arboreum). **1972** in 1983 Johnson *I Declare* 145 **nwFL,** Take the taste: There's the sourwood tree (bite a leaf, it's sharp enough to flavor a salad). **1996** in 2004 Montgomery-Hall *Dict. Smoky Mt. Engl.* 355 **wNC, eTN,** They call them leprechaun hats. That's sourwood blooms. **1999** Morgan *Gap Creek* 22 **NC,** The sourwood runners appeared to sink down in the ice a little.

    ‡**2** See quot.

    1940 *AmSp* 15.447 [TN mountain speech], *Sour-wood.* An unexpected male caller.

souse v[1], n[1] Usu |saʊs|; also **esp Sth, S Midl** (chiefly for the verb) |sauz| Also sp *souce, souge, souze, sows*

    A Forms.

    c1700 [see **B1** below]. **1824** [see **B2** below]. **1871** [see **B4** below]. **1892** [see **B6** below]. **1905** [see **B2** below]. **1909** *DN* 3.373 **eAL,**

---

wGA, *Souse, v.* Pronounced [saʊz]. *Ibid* 404 **nwAR,** *Souse* [sauz], *n.* **c1937** [see **B2** below]. **1966** [see **B2** below]. **1970** [see **B2** below]. **2003** *DARE* File—Internet **IN,** Most of the crowd was good and "souzed." Intertwining Igloo daiquiris and plastic cups of Coors Lite had invaded the pavilion and the lawn. **2005** Williams *Gratitude* 526 **wNC** (as of 1940s), *Souse* (rhyme with house) is a gelatin-like meat dish made from the parts of a hog's head. . . [S]ouse (souze), said with a *z* instead of an *s,* means to plunge something out of sight.

    B As verb.

1 To pickle (a food item); hence ppl adj *soused;* vbl n *sousing* (sp *sowsing*). [*OED2 souse* v.[1] 1.a 1387 →; *soused* 1 a1550 →] Cf **C1** below

    c1700 in 2004 Harbury *Colonial Virginia's Cooking* 270, Boyl it when tis cold keep it in sowsing drink. **1837** *Sandwich Is. Gaz. & Jrl. of Commerce* (Honolulu HI) 12 Aug 1/4, For sale at the store of Benja. Pitman. . . Generally on hand Fresh Pork, Sausages, and Soused Pork. **1847** (1852) Crowen *Amer. Cookery* 106, Pigs' Feet Soused.—Scald and scrape clean the feet. . . wash them and put them in a pot of hot (not boiling) water, with a little salt and let them boil gently. . . When done, take them from the hot water into cold vinegar, . . add whole pepper and alspice. . . Soused feet may be eaten cold from the vinegar . . or . . dip them in wheat flour and fry in hot lard. **1859** (1860) Edgeworth *S. Gardener* 109, Souse. Clean pig's feet and ears thoroughly, and soak them a day in salt and water; boil them tender and split them. To souse them cold, pour boiling vinegar, spiced with mace and pepper-corns, over them. **1895** *DN* 1.394, Souse. . . Pigs' feet pickled or soused in brine. **1938** FWP *U.S. One* xix **ME,** Soused Clams: freshly shucked clams stewed in vinegar. Served either hot or cold. **1968** *DARE* (Qu. H43) Inf **DE**3, Souse [*DARE* Ed: Prob assimilated pronc of *soused*] pig feet—pig feet in vinegar. **1975** Gould *ME Lingo* 267, *Soused.* . . Soused clams . . steamed clams shucked and pickled lightly with spices.

2 To immerse abruptly; to slosh (something) about; hence n *sousing* a ducking. [*OED2 souse* v.[1] 2 1470–85 →] **scattered, but esp freq Sth, S Midl**

    1807 Irving *Salmagundi* 362 **NY,** A sagacious old matron . . proposed to ascertain the fact by sousing him into a kettle of hot water. **1824** *Old Colony Mem.* (Plymouth MA) 6 Mar 180/1, I'll be souzed in a butter tub, if ever I seed such curiosity thingums in all my born days! **1838** *S. Lit. Messenger* 4.405 **GA,** So I fims [=puts] on a fresh long-worm, and soused in my hook. **1850** *Zanesville Courier* (OH) 31 Dec [2]/2 **LA,** I began a race . . after a piece of a shattered plank. I finally reached it, and putting one hand rather rudely upon it got a sousing for my pains—the piece was too small to render me any material service. **1886** Alcott *Jo's Boys* 159 **MA,** Of course after sousing the poor girl I had to be attentive to her, hadn't I? **1889** *Harper's New Mth. Mag.* 79.569, The curling short ends of Joe's hair were wet . . , as if his head had lately been soused in a pail of water. **1893** *Manufacturer & Builder* 25.285, The scourer . . plunges the garment into it, souses it up and down, rubs the dirty places. **1899** (1912) Green *VA Folk-Speech* 403, Souse. . . To plunge into water or other liquid. **1905** *DN* 3.65 **eNE,** Souce. . . Souse. "She souced it in the rench water." **1906** (1907) London *Before Adam* 130 **nCA,** He . . shifted his weight rashly on the log. It turned over, sousing him under. Three times again it soused him under as he tried to climb out upon it. **1930** Shoemaker *1300 Words* 57 **cPA Mts** (as of c1900), *Souse*—To immerse, to duck. **1932** (1974) Caldwell *Tobacco Road* 105 **GA,** Sometimes he could manage to make it [=his hair] lie down for a few minutes by sousing his head in a pan of water. **c1937** in 1976 *Weevils in the Wheat* 278 **VA** [Black], They had to be very good and serious before they could make up their minds to go under the deep dark waters that the Baptist "Souge" you in. **1966** *DARE* Tape **AL**3, We'd fill up a barrel full of that hot water and take that old hog and souse [sauz] him down in there, turn him about. **1970** *DARE* (Qu. EE28, *Games played in the water*) Inf **KY**84, Pushing each other under the water—souse [sæʊz] one another. **1975** Gould *ME Lingo* 267, *Soused.* . . Souse is interchangeable with *douse* and *rense* for the action of washing clams in a clam *hod.* **1986** Pederson *LAGS Concordance* 1 inf, **neFL,** Souse him [=a hog] in hot water; 1 inf, **neTN,** Soused him [=a hog] into that [=boiling water].

3 To drench, splash, wash vigorously; hence adj phr *sousing wet.* [*OED2 souse* v.[1] a1542 →]

    1896 *New Engl. Mag.* 21.302, There was a dreary little frame tavern . . and a half-dozen farm hands sousing their heads at the tavern pump, preparatory to dinner. **1899** (1912) Green *VA Folk-Speech* 403, Souse. . . cover or drench with a liquid. **1925** *AmSp* 1.137 **Pacific NW,** In the bunkhouse they hang up their "louse cages"—hats—and "souse themselves." **1935** in 1953 Botkin–Harlow *Treas. Railroad Folkl.* 77 **NEng** (as of 1848), The fireman . . clung precariously to the cow-catcher while sousing the running parts with liquid paraffin. **1968** Haun *Hawk's Done Gone* 209 **eTN,** She tries to make her hair pretty by sousing it in sap from wild grape vines. **1969** Wilson *Stars* 147 **Ozarks,** That'll flood all the valley underneath. Not drowndin' deep, but it'll be sousin' wet. **1993** *Coast Watch* Sept/Oct 12 **Outer Banks NC,** [Caption:] Souse—wet down. **2001** *Power & Motoryacht* May (Internet) **FL,** Although the 5370 ultimately described a tight, high-speed corkscrew under deplorable sea conditions, not a soul on board got soused. **2002** *NY Daily News* (NY) 25 July (Internet) **NYC,** Le Pape places one lonely scallop on a poof of whipped potatoes . . and souses it with heavy-handed bacon jus. **2002** *MetroActive* 30 May (Internet) **CA,** It's like a waiter sousing a platter of duck al'orange with ketchup in the hope a kid will eat it.

4 intr: To plunge (into water). [*OED2* (at *souse* v.[1] 6.a) 1584–7 →] **esp Sth, S Midl**

1851 *U.S. Mag. & Democratic Rev.* 28.329 **S Midl,** Both soused heels over head into the water. **1864** in 2002 *DARE* File—Internet **KY,** Lathered well & then soused in good & took a swim. **1868** *Harper's New Mth. Mag.* 36.390 **sOH,** He says . . the bridge whisht away afore he got tow it, and he soused in head fust. **1871** Eggleston *Hoosier Schoolmaster* 32 **sIN,** He's . . pulled back the board so as you can't help a-tippin' it up, and a-sowsin' right in ef you step there. **1902** White *Blazed Trail* 334 **MI,** A vast roar of Homeric laughter went up as some unfortunate slipped and soused into the water. **1926** *AmSp* 1.410 **Okefenokee GA,** The water erbout up ter hyere . . on me. . . I could hear that Bear come a-sousin' right in behind me.

5 To dash (a liquid).

1859 Taliaferro *Fisher's R.* 197 **nwNC** (as of 1820s), He broke his holt as quick as when you souse a bucket uv cold water on two bull-dogs a-fightin'. **1893** *Century Illustr. Mag.* 46.824, In the mean time the captain went below alone, and soused dilute carbolic acid over every place and thing which had been associated with the sick man.

6 To fire (a shot), plunge (a sharp instrument) into. [Perh infl by *OED2 souse* v.[2] 1 "To strike, smite, or beat severely or heavily"]

1855 Adams *Our World* 305, It would make the longest-faced deacon in the district laugh to see the fire flash out o' the nigger's big black eyes, when he sees the *cur* drop, knowin' how he'll get the next plugs souced into him. **1865** Byrn *Advent. Fudge Fumble* 68 **TN,** I . . took hold of the carving utensils, and soused the fork into one of the chickens. **1892** *DN* 1.232 **KY,** Souse [saʊz]: to plunge, to stick in. "Souse a pin into him." **1936** Green *Hymn Rising Sun* 26 **Sth,** I reckon the man you killed was sick too, when you soused that knife in him.

7 To wash oneself.

1895 *DN* 1.400 **nwIL, seMN, cNY,** Souse . . a bath, to bathe. "I'll go and souse," or, "take a souse." **1898** in Lib. of Congress *Amer. Memory: Film Coll.* (Internet), Imagine forty or fifty soldier boys each with a pail of water on the ground before him, sousing and splattering and scrubbing away for dear life.

8 also *souse it up:* To drink heavily, carouse; to drink (an alcoholic beverage). [Appar back-form from *soused* drunk]

1892 *Herald & Torch-Light* (Hagerstown MD) 27 Oct 1/8, When he was sousing beer in the saloons of Buffalo the armies were marching past the front door. **1921** O'Neill in *Theatre Arts Mag.* 5.32, Ain't you sousin' with 'em most every day? **1923** Watts *Luther Nichols* 43 **OH,** Just so they're middling honest and don't souse. **2001** *Sun* (Baltimore MD) 23 May sec F 1 (Internet), Shrek is a Rat Packer (and a rat eater, as you'll see later) when it comes to sousing it up.

C As noun.

1 Var parts of a hog, esp the feet and all or parts of the head, intended or prepared as food; spec:

a Some or all of these parts, boiled in large pieces, usu seasoned with vinegar and eaten hot or cold; less freq, the uncooked parts from which this dish is made.

1824 (1984) Randolph *VA House-Wife* 20, *To Make Souse.* . . Boil the feet in one pot, the ears and noses in another, and the heads in a third; these should be boiled till you can take all the bones out; . . season the insides . . make it in a tight roll, sew it up close in a cloth, and press it lightly. **1841** *S. Lit. Messenger* 7.39 **Sth,** There is not much diffidence observed in introducing the *hog family* upon the table. Beside the animal figuring in part and in whole . . it may be traced in the stewed chine and souse, the head-cheese and sausages. **1853** (1982) Lea *Domestic Cook-*

ery 171, To make Souse. Boil the [pigs'] feet till the bones come out easily, and pick out all the large bones; pack them [=the feet] in a stone pan with pepper and salt, and cover it with vinegar; they may be eaten cold or dipped in flour and fried. **1879** (1965) Tyree *Housekeeping in Old VA* 123, *To Make Souse from Hog's Feet.* As soon as the hog is cleaned, cut off the feet and throw them in a tub of cold water with a handful of salt; let them remain covered in water until you are ready to clean them. . . When you have scraped and changed the water for a week, then wash them clean and put them on to boil. . . take them up and throw them into a firkin of clean salt and water. . . They are now ready to fry, which should be done by splitting the foot in half and fried in egg batter. **1889** Cooke *Steadfast* 242 **CT,** Sausages, head-cheese, and souse, were the matters in hand. **1899** (1912) Green *VA Folk-Speech* 403, *Souse.* . . Something kept or steeped in pickle; especially, the head, ears, and feet of swine pickled. **1938** FWP *U.S. One* xxiii **PA,** *Souse:* pig's feet; eaten cold or hot with vinegar. **1941** *LANE* Map 305 *(Head cheese; souse)* 1 inf, **swCT,** Souse is put down in a pot. It is more of a stew; 1 inf, **swCT,** Souse is boiled and served hot; 1 inf, **nwCT,** For head cheese the meat is ground; for souse, 'the ears and hocks are cut into chunks'; 1 inf, **nwCT,** Souse is left in large pieces, bone and all; 1 inf, **csCT,** Souse, made of pig's feet and ears which are boiled with potatoes and served hot; 1 inf, **swCT,** Souse, made of parts of the head (snout, ears, jowls), the feet; 1 inf, **cnCT,** The souse are the feet, the hock joints and the jowls; 1 inf, **cwCT,** We spoke of souse: the ears and snout, and even the tail. But I never heard a cooked food called souse; 1 inf, **cwCT,** Souse is cut up and made into head cheese; 1 inf, **nwCT,** Souse is sometimes made into head cheese; 1 inf, **swMA,** Head cheese is made from souse; 2 infs, **NH,** Souse is used in making hogs-head cheese. **2002** *Washington Post* (DC) 16 Oct sec F 1 (Internet) **PA,** They bring, in their words, "wonderful good" meats, poultry, produce, canned and baked goods, which include Pennsylvania Dutch specialties—whoopie pies . . souse (pickled pig's feet) [etc].

b also attrib; also *pig's-foot souse* = **headcheese 1;** see quots. **chiefly Midl, Sth, TX** See Map Cf **cheese n B2, souse meat**

1875 (2001) Mason *Young Housewife's Counsellor* 155 (Internet), The skins should all be saved for the souse; boiled with the feet, and a head or two, they will make excellent souse-cheese. **1895** *DN* 1.394, *Souse.* . . otherwise known as "head cheese." **1909** *DN* 3.404 **nwAR,** *Souse.* . . A jellied compound made of hog's ears, feet, and most usually taken from the head of the hog; head cheese; served in slices usually pressed and highly spiced with pepper, considered a great delicacy. **1938** *Amer.–German Rev.* 5.1.41 [PaGer], Souse or pig's foot jelly with diced meat. **1942** Warnick *Garrett Co. MD* 14 **nwMD** (as of 1900–18), *Souse* . . pigs knuckles cooked well done, then chopped and jelled in their broth, not pickled. **1956** McAtee *Some Dialect NC* 42, *Souse:* . . the same as hog-head cheese. **1961** *PADS* 36.14 **LA, sAR, TX,** Still more widespread is *hog('s)-head cheese* (pork loaf), which extends into central Texas, partially displacing the older term *souse.* **1965–70** *DARE* (Qu. H43, *Foods made from parts of the head and inner organs of an animal*) 214 Infs, **Midl, Sth, TX,** Souse; **CT24, IN82, KY44,** Souse— [same as] headcheese; **FL1,** Souse—hog-head cheese; **FL33,** Souse— hog cheese or headcheese; **GA12,** Souse—hog's head cheese; **IL55,** Souse—like headcheese; **MD12,** Souse—made of hog feet—no corn-meal—plus seasonings and vinegar. Some people put vinegar in mixture, some soak the loaf in vinegar; **MD19,** Souse—hog foot meat, cooked and thickened—no cornmeal; **MO7,** Souse—the organs are cooked and ground up; it's jellied; **NC5,** Souse—boil up head, mash meat, let it congeal, put in vinegar; **NC20,** Souse—feet, ears, head; boil it; it congeals;

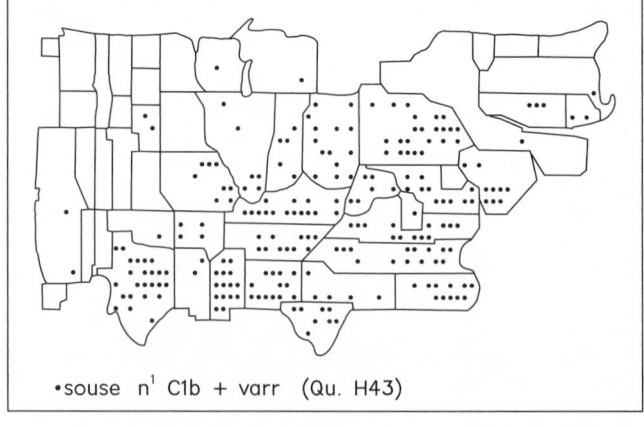

•souse n[1] C1b + varr (Qu. H43)

slice it; **NC**82, Souse—from a hog's head and parts of feet; boil and add sage, and it congeals; **SC**7, Souse—hog-head cheese, called souse now; **SC**29, Souse—head-meat is cooked and pressed and flavored with vinegar and spices; **VA**78, Souse—has vinegar, nose, ears, feet, head-meat; **MO**8, Pig's-foot souse; **AL**52, Pressed souse; **MI**72, Souse loaf—I remember years ago we used to eat headcheese and we also called it souse. [*DARE* Ed: Some of these Infs may refer instead to **C1a** above.] **2001** *NC State Univ. Ext. Newsletters* (Internet), *Chitlings and Souse. . .* [I]n the same pot, you're boiling pigs' feet, snouts, a few ears, and usually a whole hogs head or two. These, when the meat boiled off the bone and was seasoned with salt, pepper, and vinegar made what we called souse. (I think grocery stores call it headcheese.)

2 A person's ears. [*OED2* a1658 →]

1811 *Port Folio* (Oldschool) 5.287 **VA,** His progenitors had been *spoon-stealers* . . and invariably lost their ears in consequence. It was a family fatality, and since his own *souse* must sooner or later be put in the same pickle, he wished the business over, without delay. **1839** Lester *Chains & Freedom* 121 (Internet) **NJ,** I flew and *on* to him, and clinched hold on his souse, and planted my knees in his belly, and jammed his old head up and down on the floor. **1895** *DN* 1.383 **NJ,** *Souse:* slangy for ears. "Bounder your souse well" = wash your ears well. **1969** *DARE* (Qu. OO15b, *About freezing your ears: "If he had been out last night he would have _____ [his ears]."*) Inf **MA**30, Chilled his souse.

3 A ducking, drenching, immersion.

1844 (1863) Cooper *Miles Wallingford* 212 **NY,** He let go his hold, and went into the ocean. The souse did him good, I make no doubt. **1885** *Atlantic Mth.* 55.436 **eTN,** He washed his face in a tin pan which stood on a bench . . , treated his head to a refreshing souse, and then . . came lounging across the clearing. **c1938** in Lib. of Congress *Amer. Memory: WPA Life Hist.* (Internet) **TX,** There anyone broke a rule he got the leggin's or a souse in the river. **1996** *Providence Jrl.–Bulletin* (RI) 5 Feb sec B 1 (Internet), During heat waves, the purebred runners get plenty of cold drinks and a souse with the garden hose.

4 also *souse-pot, souser:* A habitual drunkard. [**souse** v¹ **B8**] **chiefly Nth, N Midl, West** See Map

1914 (1917) London *Star Rover* 210, I remember you mentioned playing chess with that royal souse of an emperor's brother. **1950** *WELS (A person who drinks steadily or a great deal)* 8 Infs, **WI,** Souse; 1 Inf, **csWI,** Souse. **1951** Johnson *Resp. to PADS 20* **DE** *(A person who drinks steadily or a great deal)* Souse. **1953** (1954) Chandler *Long Goodbye* 24 **CA,** Sylvia is not a souse. When she does get over the edge it's pretty drastic. **1957** Battaglia *Resp. to PADS 20* **eMD** *(A person who is very drunk)* Souse. **1965–70** *DARE* (Qu. DD12, . . *A person who drinks steadily or a great deal)* 46 Infs, **chiefly Nth, N Midl, West,** Souse; **FL**5, **MA**62, Old souse; **NY**42, Souse-pot; **IN**31, Souser. **2006** Millersville Univ. Center for PA Ger. Studies *Jrl.* Winter 12 **sePA,** His lack of self discipline with alcohol would ultimately defeat him. An olympic class souse.

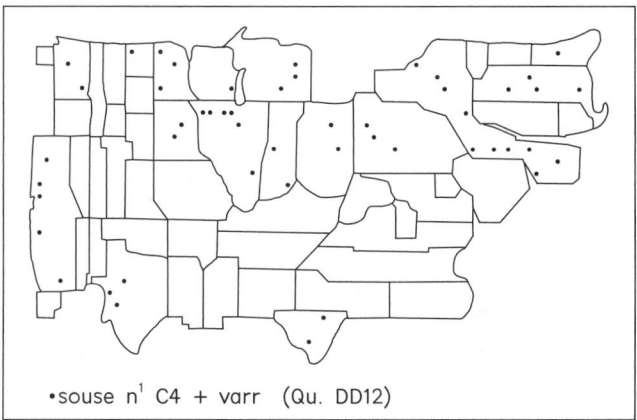

•souse n¹ C4 + varr (Qu. DD12)

5 A bout of drinking; a spree.

1903 Ade *People* 13, [Title:] The Periodical Souse, the Never-Again Feeling and the Ride On the Sprinkling Cart. **1913** London *Valley of Moon* 173 **cwCA,** You must a-had a souse last night. **1946** O'Neill *Iceman Cometh* 199 **NYC,** Bejees, We'll go on a grand old souse together!

‡**souse** v² [Cf *OED2* souse v.² 3 "To fall heavily" and *souse* adv.¹ 3 "With strong or violent impact"] To dash (against).

1943 Chase *Jack Tales* 124 **wNC** (as of 1880s), The head jerked back down. Come up again directly, soused against the window, Wham!

souse v³, n² Also sp *sowse* [*OED2* souse v.³ 1 "Of a hawk, etc.: To swoop down; to descend with speed and force"; *souse* n.³ 2 "The act, on the part of a hawk, of swooping down upon a bird."]

1899 (1912) Green *VA Folk-Speech* 403, *Souse. . .* A pouncing down; a swift or precipitate descent, especially for attack. A dip or plunge into the water. [*"*]The fish-hawk made a *souse* down and picked up a fish from the river." Also *souse v. Sowse.*

souse n³ See **south**

souse cheese See **cheese** n B2

soused See **souse** v¹ **B1**

souse it up See **souse** v¹ **B8**

souse meat n Also, perh by folk-etym, *sauce meat, south meat, sows meat* **chiefly Sth, S Midl** See Map Cf **press meat** =**souse** n¹ **C1.**

1854 *Ladies' Repository* 22.299, Her lard was beautifully white, . . her souse-meat all soused. **1899** (1912) Green *VA Folk-Speech* 403, *Souse-meat. . .* Meat used for sousing; the feet, ears, and noses of hogs. **1938** FWP *U.S. One* xxvi **GA,** Souse Meat: hog's head, ears, and feet stewed, mashed, seasoned, pressed, and sliced when cold. **1939** Wolcott *Yankee Cook Book* 78, Hog's Head Cheese [Also Called Souse Meat]. **1941** Justus *Cabin on Kettle Creek* 56 **eTN,** The talk went on about other good things being made ready for the feast, come Thanksgiving; sausage and souse meat from the week's hog killing. **1941** Writers' Program *Guide SC* 429, Nothing is allowed to go to waste—head cheese, liver mush, liver pudding, sausage, and souse meat account for the various odds and ends. **1952** Callahan *Smoky Mt.* 97 **wNC, eTN,** Head cheese, known as "souse meat," is made from the head, jowls, and brains. **1965–70** *DARE* (Qu. H43, *Foods made from parts of the head and inner organs of an animal)* 52 Infs, **chiefly Sth, S Midl,** Souse meat; **AL**34, Souse meat—cook pig's head until all bones are loose and fall free; mash head up; put it in pan with weight on it; cooks into a cake-like substance; **AR**47, Souse meat—headcheese; **FL**6, Souse meat—hog-head cheese; **GA**13, Souse meat—hog head congealed, ground up with sage, salt, and pepper; **KY**28, Souse meat—hog's head cheese; **NC**52, Souse meat—ears, hoof, and snout chopped; jells itself; **SC**42, Souse meat— press meat; (Qu. H45, *Dishes made with meat, fish, or poultry that everybody around here would know, but that people in other places might not)* Inf **TN**5, Souse meat. **1966** Dakin *Dial. Vocab. Ohio R. Valley* 2.339, *Head cheese. . .* In Kentucky, where *meat* unless qualified frequently means "pork," the expression *souse meat* is common; north of the Ohio this expanded expression is rare. **1972** *Foxfire Book* 20 **nGA,** Souse meat. Boy, that's the best stuff I ever eat. I love it better'n sausage. **1972** *Atlanta Letters* **cnGA,** Here are some "Southern-isms" I have heard: . . Sousmeat [sic] (Sowsmeat)—Hogshead Cheese. **1972** *PADS* 58.20 **cwAL,** Souse meat. . . and the variant *south meat* (given by three Negro informants) are most common. **1982** Slone *How We Talked* 64 **eKY** (as of c1950), *Souse meat*—Sauce meat. Remove the bones from a cooked hog's head and feet. Cook the ears, liver, kidneys and melt. Mix with the head and feet and chop real fine. **1989** Pederson *LAGS Tech. Index* 161 **Gulf Region,** *(Headcheese)* 201 infs, Souse meat; 4 infs, South meat. **2002** *Atlanta Jrl.–Constitution* (GA) 19 Dec sec K 9 (Internet), Hogshead cheese . . is made only from the lean meat of the head. Souse meat is made mostly from the feet and contains gelatinous substance.

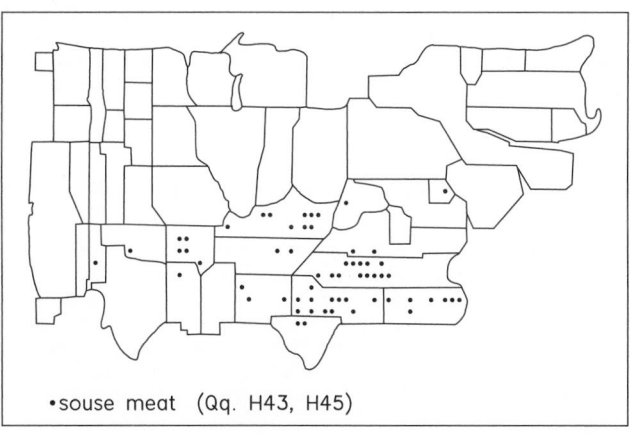

•souse meat (Qq. H43, H45)

souse-pot See **souse** n¹ **C4**

souser n
1 See **souse** n¹ **C4.**
2 also *souzer:* See quot.
   1968 *DARE* (Qu. B25, . . *Joking names . . for a very heavy rain.* . . *"It's a regular _____."*) Inf **NY**116, Souser; **IA**17, Souzer.

sousing See **souse** v¹ **B1, 2**

sousing wet See **souse** v¹ **B3**

sousle See **sozzle 1**

sou-sou-sally duck, sou'-sou'-southerly, sou'-southerland (or -southerly) See **south-southerly**

south n, adj, adv Usu |saʊθ|; also |sæʊθ, saʊθ|; also **esp eVA,** |səʊθ, sɛʊθ|; *esp among Black speakers* |saʊf|; occas |saʊs, saʊt|; for addit varr see quots Pronc-spp *saath, sahth, saouth, souf(f), souse*
Std senses, var forms.
   1852 Hannibal *Professor Hannibal's Discourses* 29 [Black], De milkey way . . runs doo nort, west, and souf, clar from away down below de Battery, clar up to Orange county. **1862** *Vanity Fair* 5.64, On top o' that air highest peak o' snow,/ Eternally a viewin' things below,/ Sets aöur great Bird, his awful eyes a flashin'—/ Waitin' to see us gin the Saöuth a thrashin'! [*DARE* Ed: The speaker is presumably a New Englander.] **1862** *Continental Mth.* 1.772 **SC** [Black], De paper say dat lots ob sogers hab cum from Gorgia and Al'bama and 'way down Souf. **1877** *Galaxy* 24.519, You uns are from the Nawth and we uns from the Saouth. **1890** *PMLA* 5.198 **ceVA,** [ɛʊ] in . . *house, out, about, south.* **1899** (1967) Chesnutt *Wife of Youth* 143 [Black], Dat kinder weavin' come f'om down to'ds Souf Ca'lina. **1901** *DN* 2.183 **neKY** [Black], *South* . . souff. **1916** [see **southeast**]. **1927** Shewmake *Engl. Pronc. VA* 24, In typical Eastern Virginia speech, diphthongal ou or ow is given the dialectal sound represented by (uh-oo) when the diphthong is immediately followed in the same syllable by the sound of a voiceless consonant. . . Examples . . [include] *south.* **1930** *AmSp* 6.96 **seVA** [Speech of older inhabitants of Guinea Neck], *South* [suθ]. **1937** in 1976 *Weevils in the Wheat* 153 **VA** [Black], Dey had been carrin' 'em souf from Lynchburg to dat terrible prisun in Andersunville. **1939** *AmSp* 14.125 **neTN,** [sæʊθ]. **1940** *AmSp* 15.85 **neTN,** [We were driving] [sæʊθ]. **1942** *AmSp* 17.150 **seNY,** *South* . . [æʊ] 19 [infs]—[aʊ] 73 [infs]—[ɑʊ] 27 [infs]. **1964** *Ferhoodled Engl.* [21] [PaGer], You know Pop when I first vent to school—I couldn't say norse or souse—now I can say bose of em. **1966** *DARE* Tape **DC**3, They had a little more freedom than they had in the various states [sɛʊθ] of Washington [Inf Black]; **DC**8, They're trucked in from down [sɛʊˇθ] [Inf Black]. **1989** Pederson *LAGS Tech. Index* 318, [In the phrase *South Carolina* the predominant pronunciation of *South* was [saʊθ] with 662 infs; other proncs were [saʊf] 6 infs; [saʊ] 5 infs; [saʊs] 5 infs; [saʊt] 5 infs.] **2000** *DARE* File **Pittsburgh PA,** The most distinctive pronunciation oddity is /aʊ/ > /a/, the usual Pittsburgh examples being . . "South Side" /saθsaid/ ('Saath Side' or 'Sahth Side') (a district of Pittsburgh). **2003** *DARE* File **csWI,** A television weather forecaster routinely says [sɛoθ].

southard See **southward**

South Carolina poplar See **Carolina poplar**

southeast n, adj, adv Usu |'saʊθ,ist; ,saʊθ'ist|; also |,saʊ'ist| Pronc-sp *sou'east* Cf **southeaster, southwest, southwester**
Std senses, var forms.
   1851 (1976) Melville *Moby-Dick* 504, "East-sou-east, sir," said the frightened steersman. **1866** *Atlantic Mth.* 17.711 **coastal NEng,** But the devil and all is in that puff from the sou'east. **1889** *Century Illustr. Mag.* 39.229 **Long Is. Sound,** We talked of the . . cussed sou'east wind. **1904** Day *Kin o' Ktaadn* 172 **ME,** With a sou'east wind she thrashed her way. **1916** *DN* 4.336 **Nantucket MA,** *Southeast* [saʊ ist]. . . Southsoutheast [saʊ-saʊθist], south-southwest [saʊ-saʊwɛst].

southeaster n Pronc-sp *sou'easter* [*OED2* 1797 →] Cf **southwester**
A strong or stormy southeasterly wind.
   1836 Irving *Astoria* 1.261, They were wafted steadily up the stream by a strong southeaster. **1850** (1852) Lossing *Pictorial Field-Book* 2.64 **RI,** The wind was piping with all the zeal of a sudden "sou'easter." **1866** *Atlantic Mth.* 17.711 **NEng,** If that sou'easter turns out the gale it promises, the best anchor aboard won't be so good as a gridiron. **1891** Cooke *Huckleberries* 234 **RI,** I'd ruther sail a pinky round Pint Judy pint

in a sou'easter. **1965–70** *DARE* (Qu. B18, . . *Special kinds of wind*) 10 Infs, **scattered,** Southeaster; **CA**21, **GA**11, **NJ**55, Sou'easter; (Qu. O19, . . *Kinds or degrees of wind that are important when you're in a boat*) Infs **MA**35, **NJ**27, Southeaster; (Qu. O20, *Winds from particular directions;* total Infs questioned, 75) Infs **FL**16, 21, Southeaster. **1986** Pederson *LAGS Concordance (Southeast wind)* 17 Infs, **Gulf States,** Southeaster. **1990** *Boston Globe* (MA) 8 Dec Metro sec 1 (Internet) **Cape Cod MA,** Tuesday's sou'easter, coinciding with extraordinarily high tides, battered the site. **2000** Shores *Tangier Is.* 187 **Chesapeake Bay,** In reference to direction or winds . . Tangiermen speak of "sou'westers," "sou'easter," and "nor'easter."

south end (of a chicken going north) See **north end of a chicken flying south**

south end of a horse going north n Also *south end of a northbound horse* Cf **north end of a chicken flying south**
A horse's rump; fig, an unattractive or contemptible person.
   1908 Westover *Scientific Steel Worker* 192 **WV,** The man that knocks is a sore head, a block head, a chronic kicker and the south end of a horse going north. **1941** *AmSp* 16.23 **sIN,** Like the south end of a horse going north. **1942** Berrey–Van den Bark *Amer. Slang* 397, *Contemptible person.* . . south end of a north-bound horse. **1943** *AmSp* 18.67 **LA, SC** [IN sayings used elsewhere], Like the south end of a horse goin' north, of a north-bound horse. **1999** *DARE* File **cKY,** I could eat the south end of a northbound horse. **2004** *Sacramento Bee* (CA) 1 May sec B 6 (Internet), To watch . . the Band of Brothers . . is to see these WW II vets make Kerry look like the south end of a horse going north.

southerland, southerly See **south-southerly**

southern buckthorn n
Std: a plant of the genus *Sideroxylon* (formerly *Bumelia*), usu *S. lycioides.* For other names of this plant see **Carolina buckthorn 2, mock orange 1f;** for other names of var spp see **chittamwood 2, gum elastic, ironwood b(2)**

southern engineering See **southern gentleman's engineering**

southerner See **south-southerly**

southern fir n
=**Fraser fir.**
   1884 U.S. Dept. Ag. *Rept. Forestry* 4.379, The Southern fir (*Abies Fraseri*) grows upon the highest points of the Alleghanies, and is more abundant to the south, in Tennessee. **1950** Gray–Fernald *Manual of Botany* 53, *A[bies] Fraseri.* . . Southern F[ir]. **1979** Little *Checklist U.S. Trees* 35, Fraser balsam fir, . . southern fir [etc]. **2004** *Roanoke Times & World-News* (VA) 24 Dec 6 (Internet), Try . . "Prostata" cultivated variety of Southern Fir (Abies fraseri "Prostata").

southern fox n
=**gray fox.**
   1961 Jackson *Mammals WI* 306, Wisconsin Gray Fox. . . *Vernacular names.*—Gray fox, maned fox, southern fox [etc].

southern gentleman's engineering n Also *southern engineering*
A process resulting in something that is poorly made or repaired.
   1966 *DARE* FW Addit **OK,** Southern gentleman's engineering—Rigging etc., Put together or repaired quickly and poorly. Inf says term *Nigger-rigged* is not used anymore. "Now it has to be called 'Southern Gentleman's Engineering.'" **1984** Weaver *TX Crude* 93, *Southern engineering.* . . sloppily assembled. **2004** in 2007 *DARE* File—Internet **neOK,** Aren't we politically correct. . . I thought it was "Southern Engineering".

southern goose n
A **Hutchins's goose** or similar goose.
   1843 *Amer. Jrl. Sci. & Arts* 44.269 **CT,** It [=*Anser Hutchinsii*] is not unfrequently taken here [=in Connecticut] in the spring, and is called the southern goose, because it does not winter here. **1888** Trumbull *Names of Birds* 4 **CT,** Though this name "Southern Goose" is still remembered in Connecticut, at Stratford, . . and at Milford as well, the descriptions of the goose to which it belongs, as given by different gunners, vary very materially.

southern leatherwood See **leatherwood 3**

southern magnolia n

Std: a **magnolia 1** (here: *Magnolia grandiflora*). Also called **bat tree, big laurel 1, big-leaved magnolia, bull bay, evergreen magnolia, laurel ~, loblolly bay 2, swamp magnolia**

southern oak n

=**Durand oak.**

   1908 Britton *N. Amer. Trees* 325, Southern Oak—*Quercus austrina. . .* A rough barked tree of river borders in Georgia and Alabama. . . It is also called Pin oak and Bastard oak.

southern pine n Cf **northern pine**

=**longleaf pine 1.** Note: *Southern pine* is a std commercial name for the wood of var Southern pine trees, including the longleaf pine; this sense is not illustrated here.

   1810 Michaux *Histoire des Arbres* 1.64, *The Long Leaved Pine. . .* Dans les Etats du Nord, où il est importé par la voie du commerce, [il est connu] sous ceux [=noms] de *Southern pine, . .* et quelquefois encore de *Red pine.* [=*The Long Leaved Pine. . .* In the Northern States, where it is imported commercially, [it is known] by those [names] of *Southern pine, . .* and sometimes also *Red pine.*] **1842** Buckingham *Slave States* 1.177, The Georgia pitch-pine is abundant, and it is a highly valuable tree. This is called by a great variety of names, such as the southern, the red, the brown, the yellow, and the long-leaved pine; but they all indicate the same kind of tree. **1896** Mohr–Roth *Timber Pines* 28, The Longleaf Pine. . . Local or Common Names. . . Southern Pine (N.C., Ala., Miss., La.) **1966** *DARE* Tape **MA**5, There used to be . . a tree that they called the southern pine. . . that didn't have a limb on them till they got up way up awful tall. **1969** *DARE* (Qu. T17, . . Kinds of pine trees; *not asked in early QRs*) Inf **IN**83, Southern pine. **1971** Krochmal *Appalachia Med. Plants* 192, *Pinus palustris. . .* Common Names: Longleaf pine, . . southern pine, southern yellow pine [etc].

southern red lily See **red lily b**

southern red oak See **red oak 2b**

southern rock elm See **rock elm 4**

southern shrike n Cf **northern shrike**

A **loggerhead shrike,** usu *Lanius ludovicianus.*

   1857 U.S. Patent Office *Annual Rept. for 1856: Ag.* 86 **IL,** The Southern shrike, *(Lanius ludovicianus,) . .* breeds largely in the prairie districts. **1956** MA Audubon Soc. *Bulletin* 40.129, Southern Shrike. . . Butcher Bird . . ; Cricket Hawk . . ; Grasshopper Hawk . . ; Joree . . ; Kite . . ; Mouse Hawk. **1957** *Lima News* (OH) 9 July 6/2, Southern butcher birds (also called southern shrikes or loggerhead shrikes) nest and live chiefly south of the Mason and Dixon Line.

southern snakeroot See **snakeroot b(3)**

Southern War n Also *Southern War for Independence*

The American Civil War.

   1861 Faulkner *Faulkner's Hist. Revol.* app 1, Diary of the Southern War. [*DARE* Ed: Covers the period from Jan–Oct 1861] **1863** Pollard *2d Yr. of War* iii, In presenting a second volume of a popular History of the Southern War for Independence, the author gratefully acknowledges the kind reception by the Southern public of his first volume. **1865** (1867) Moore *Anecdotes* 169, Ah me! alas! we saw / The name of our noble brother,/ Who went to the Southern War. **1869** *Appletons' Jrl.* 2.530, Soon after the outbreak of the Southern War the historian of the Dutch Republic was appointed American minister at Vienna. **1877** *Galaxy* 23.486, But luckily the Southern war came, and it made places for a good many men. **1879** *Atlantic Mth.* 43.86 **NEng,** A forlorn descendant . . figures in the annual Blue Book, down to the close of the Southern war, as a state pensioner. **1969** *S. Speech Jrl.* 34.200, *Southern War* appears [in the *Linguistic Atlas of US and Canada*] three times in New Hampshire, three times in New York State, twice in Virginia, and twice in South Carolina. **1986** Pederson *LAGS Concordance (Civil War)* 1 inf, **ceAR,** The Southern War. **2001** *Virginian–Pilot* (Norfolk VA) 30 Sept sec B 3 (Internet), Col. Walter Herron Taylor . . grew up to serve as Gen. Robert E. Lee's aide-de-camp for the four years of what some diehard Rebels still like to refer to as The Southern War for Independence.

southern wild rice See **wild rice 2**

southernwood n [*OED2* c1000 →]

Std: a plant of the genus *Artemisia,* usu *A. abrotanum* which is also called **boy's-love, old man 1a, sweet benjamin.**

Southland n Usu with *the* **sCA**

Southern California.

   1884 Truesdell *CA Pilgrimage* 35 **swCA,** Sierra Madre. . . Nestling 'twist [sic] this Mount and Valley,/ Smiles an Infant City fair,/ Basking in the Southland sunshine,/ Bathed in balmy scented air. **1896** *Oakland Tribune* (CA) 22 Aug 6/2, Afterward, the bride and groom ran away to the Southland. **1926** *Los Angeles and the Wonderful Southland of CA* [title]. **1943** Rodd *Souvenir-Album, Los Angeles, Hollywood and the Southland at a Glance* [title]. **1970** *NY Times* (NY) 27 Sept 30/2, Most experts expect that at least two of the new [Congressional] seats will go into San Diego and Orange counties . . and that two others will be somewhere in the "southland." **1988** Ellroy *Big Nowhere* 399, Buzz took Pacific Coast Highway down to LA. . . Dark clouds were brewing, threatening a deluge to soak the Southland. **1991** Koontz *Cold Fire* 85, She restrained herself . . trying to think of another way to locate Jim Ironheart down there in the part of California that locals called "the Southland." **2003** *DARE* File—Internet, Welcome to the Southern California Beer Guide, the beer enthusiast's guide to what's brewing in the Southland. *Ibid,* Welcome to the Southland Ski Server, serving Southern California ski resorts plus the Eastern Sierra. *Ibid,* Southland Sheltie Rescue. . . is located in Southern California. *Ibid,* Southland WX . . Complete weather information for Southern California.

south meat See **souse meat**

south-moon-under n Cf **underground moon**

The lower transit or culmination of the moon; similarly n *south-moon-over* the upper transit or culmination of the moon.

   1933 Rawlings *South Moon* 109 **nFL,** The deer and the rabbits, the fish and the owls, stirred at moon-rise and at moon-down; at south-moon-over and at south-moon-under. . . The moon rose in the east. . . Six hours later it hung at its zenith . . , and that was south-moon-over. It set in the west. . . Then it passed from sight and swung under the earth. . . And when it was directly under the earth that was south-moon-under. **1997** in 2002 *DARE* File—Internet **FL,** [Lyrics to the song "South Moon Under" by John Anderson:] South moon under, it's a natural wonder / It makes lovers fall in love / It can make you wanna laugh or cry / South moon under, it hits you like thunder / And girl I've got a feeling / There's a south moon under tonight. **2007** *DARE* File **nwFL,** Although [he] . . had been to college . . I am not sure that he graduated and he was not what I would call a bookish person. He was an avid fisherman and firmly believed that the moon was a factor in fishing success. I several times heard [him] . . use the term "south moon under", which caught my attention as I had heard of the Rawlings title. Although I never found out what it meant, "south moon under" was a real term for a real phenomenon for [him] . . and doubtless for the backwoodsmen he associated with in the Tallahassee area where he spent his whole life.

southmore See **sophomore**

south-southerly n Also *s'o'ther, sou-sou-sally duck, (sou'-) sou'-southerly, (sou'-)southerland, southerner, south-south-southerly, (old sou')southerly, sudley* [Echoic] **Atlantic, esp Mid Atl**

=**old-squaw.**

   1814 Wilson *Amer. Ornith.* 8.93, This Duck is very generally known along the shores of the Chesapeake Bay by the name of *South Southerly,* from the singularity of its cry, something imitative of the sound of those words. **1870** *Fur Fin & Feather* 119, For instance, the long-tailed duck (Fuligula Glaciates) has its own specific name at different points of the [Atlantic] coast. Along the coast of New England it is generally called the quondy; at other New England points and on Long Island and Jersey it is known as the old wife or old squaw; while at the South it is called the South Southerly. **1888** Trumbull *Names of Birds* 88, On Chesapeake Bay, it [=the old-squaw] is the *South Southerly,* frequently pronounced Sou' Southerly, and a corruption of this, viz., *Sou' Southerland,* is also common. . . At Crisfield, Md. (east shore of Chesapeake), *Southerly,* and at Eastville, Va., *Southerland. . .* I remember that while learning to shoot, at Stonington, Conn., some thirty-five years ago, I was more familiar with the name South Southerly and its elongated form, *South-South Southerly,* than with any other. **1890** *Century Dict.* 5787, *South-southerly. . .* [An imitative name; also *south-south-southerly, sou'-southerly, sou'-sou'-southerly, southerly, southerland* [etc]]. The name, in all its variations, seems to be suggested by the limpid piping notes of the bird, almost to be called a song. **1906** *Forest & Stream* 8 Dec 898 **Chesapeake Bay,** Across the silence came the yelping of great flocks of sou'southerlys from just inside the point. **1923** U.S. Dept. Ag. *Misc. Circular* 13.24, Old-squaw. . . Vernacular Names. . . *In local* *use.* . . sou-sou-sally duck (Alaska); south-southerly (a name much varied as s'o'ther, southerland, southerly, south-south-southerly, etc.) (R.I. to Va.) **1955** MA Audubon Soc. *Bulletin* 39.375, Old-Squaw. . . Old Sou'southerly (Mass. In imitation of its notes.) **1970** *DARE* (Qu. Q5, . . *Kinds of wild ducks*) Inf **VA**52A, [ˌsɑʊˈsʌdlɪn]; **VA**79, Southerner (oldsquaw)—same as whistler. **1970** *DARE* Tape **VA**112, The southerly is white and black with wings, and it's got a black spot right here round his eyes, side of his head. That's a southerly. He's a fishy duck. **1996** Horton *Island Out of Time* 241 **Chesapeake Bay MD,** We warn't hungry none—we ate pheasant and sudleys one whole week. [Footnote:] *pheasant* and *sudleys:* merganser and old squaw, both poor-eating, fishy-tasting waterfowl.

southward adv, adj, n Usu |ˈsaʊθwə(r)d|; also **chiefly N Atl** |ˈsʌðə(r)d| Pronc-spp *s(o)uthard* Cf **east'ard, northward**
Std senses, var forms.

   1823 Cooper *Pioneers* 1.266 **cNY,** The wind was here at the south'ard and east'ard. **1903** *DN* 2.291 **Cape Cod MA** (as of a1857), The *w*-sound frequently assimilated or disappeared after a consonant: . . *sŭðard* [*DARE* Ed: =[ˈsʌðəˑd]] . . southward. **1912** Green *VA Folk-Speech* 430, Suthard. . . For southward. **1916** Macy–Hussey *Nantucket Scrap Basket* 8 **Nantucket MA,** Replying that you are "bound to the south'ard" or to the "east'ard," as the case may be, you are urged to "heave to" or to "come alongside." **1937** in 1983 Beyle *How Talk Cape Cod* 12 **seMA,** A wind blows from the 'no'thard,' the 's'uthard,' from the 'east'ard' or from the 'west'ard.' **1945** Colcord *Sea Language* 173 **ME, Cape Cod, Long Island,** *Southward* (Pronounced suth'ard, to rhyme with mothered). Toward the south. **1948** Beston *N. Farm* 93 **cME coast,** The warm day closes with a thunderstorm to the "suth'ard." **1985** Rattray *Advent. Dimon* 78 **Long Island NY** (as of c1890), Diving for small clams and mussels and whatever else they might find on the bottom, before flying on to the southard. **2005** Seavey *Working Sea* 34 **ME,** If she keeps on her present course, she will not go two miles south'ard of us.

southwest n, adj, adv Pronc-sp *sou'west*
Std senses, var forms.

   1847 *Bangor Daily Whig & Courier* (ME) 6 Dec 1/6, [Advt:] Rubber . . Sou west Hats. **1851** *Ladies' Repository* 14.441, The vessels were struck by a violent "sou'-west" gale. **1878** *Appletons' Jrl.* 5.415 **NEng,** "Day before yesterday," he [=a New Englander living alongshore] will tell you, "the wind was blowing *nōthe*-east, while yesterday it had hauled to *sou*-west." **1897** *Overland Mth.* (2d ser) 30.516, The first day out from the Golden Gate was . . fine . . with every dancin' wave tippin' a plumed crest to a sou'west wind. **1916** *DN* 4.336 **Nantucket MA,** *South.* . . southwest [saʊ wɛst] . . south-southwest [saʊ saʊwɛst]. **1927** *NY Times* (NY) 11 Sept mag sec 6/5, The passengers are indebted to Captain Sou'west for his permit and patronage. **1966–70** *DARE* (Qu. B18, . . *Special kinds of wind*) Infs **ME**16, **OR**4, **WI**75, Sou'west wind; (Qu. O19, . . *Kinds or degrees of wind that are important when you're in a boat*) Inf **MA**97, Sou'west. **1998** *Boston Globe* (MA) 12 Apr sec D 5 (Internet), Nor'west and sou'west do drop the th . . but sailors who needed to talk about where they were headed, even in a howling gale, meant to keep the pronunciations distinct.

southwester n Pronc-sp *sou'wester* See also **smoky southwester** Cf **southeaster**
A strong or stormy southwesterly wind.

   1845 *New Englander & Yale Rev.* 3.489, All your preaching . . will have little more effect on his mind than the blast of a "stiff sou'wester." **1854** *Scientific Amer.* 9.240, Such storms . . may be called "southwesters" from the fact that they always approach us from that point. **1872** *Atlantic Mth.* 29.604, Till the rains came, and far-breaking, on the fierce southwester tost. **1927** *DN* 5.287 **Cape Cod MA,** [A] hazy breeze from the southwest is commonly called a 'yellow eyed sou'wester', perhaps owing to the dirty colored atmosphere accompanying a sou-wester. **1947** (1962) Henry *Misty* 93 **eVA,** Reckon we're in fer a blow. A sou'-wester come up this afternoon, and I never seed a nor'easter take no back talk from a sou'wester. **1965–70** *DARE* (Qu. B18, . . *Special kinds of wind*) 17 Infs, **esp Atlantic, Gulf States, Pacific Coast,** Sou'-wester; **CA**105, 189, **DE**4, **IN**33, **MD**43, **MI**110, **MN**15, **OH**36, Southwester; **CA**145, Heavy southwester; (Qu. O19, . . *Kinds or degrees of wind that are important when you're in a boat*) Infs **NC**18, **WA**20, Sou'wester; (Qu. O20, *Winds from particular directions;* total Infs questioned, 75) Inf **FL**16, Southwester. **1986** Pederson *LAGS Concordance* (Southwest wind) 13 infs, **Gulf Region,** Southwester; (The wind's . .) 3 infs, **FL,** Southwester.

southwestern buffalo grass n
A **galleta** (here: *Hilaria belangeri*).

   1911 HI Ag. Exper. Sta. *Press Bulletin* 23.37, Grasses introduced for range improvement but not yet established. . . Curly mesquite or southwestern buffalo grass. **1937** U.S. Forest Serv. *Range Plant Hdbk.* G69, Curly-mesquite, sometimes called southwestern buffalo grass because of its similarity in growth to the true buffalo grass . . is identifiable at some distance because it forms light green patches.

southwestern white pine See **white pine 9**

souvian n [Aphet for *varsouviana* var of *varsoviana* a mazurka-like traditional dance < Span *varsoviano* of Warsaw]

   1966–67 *DARE* (Qu. FF5a, . . *Different steps and figures in dancing—in past years*) Inf **ID**1, Souvian [ˈsuvɪˈæn]; **OR**13, Souvian [ˌsuviˈæn]. [Both Infs old]

souwee See **sooey** v

Souwegian See **Sowegian**

sou'west See **southwest**

sou'wester See **southwester**

souy See **sooey** v

souze See **souse** v[1], n[1]

souzer See **souser 2**

souzle See **sozzle 1**

sow n[1] See **sow and pigs**

sow n[2] [Scots, nEngl dial] Cf *DS* L30a, b

   1967 Borland *Hill Country* 270 **nwCT,** The other day I was talking to Albert . . about his corn crop, and he said, "When I was a boy we used to put corn into sows and husk it out later in the fall." I said, "Put it into sows? What do you mean by that?" Surprised, he said, "Why, just put it into sows. Bundles. Shocks."

sow and pigs n Often *old sow (and pigs)* Also *old Sal, sowball, sow in the hole;* for addit varr see quots. [Cf Scots *sow in the kirk; sowball* is a calque of Ger *Sauball* for the same game] **chiefly Missip-Ohio Valleys** See Map Cf **sooey**
A game in which players use sticks to try to hit a ball or puck-like object into holes dug in the ground; hence *sow* the ball or puck.

   1896 Horne *PA Ger. Manual* 77, The Old Games—In school they were corner ball, bat ball, chase ball, shooting, old sow, and . . deer. **1904** *Decatur Daily Rev.* (IL) 13 June 3/5, The All Stars were defeated in what the natives of that heath call baseball, but in reality it resembles more a game the boys call 'old sow.' In the latter game you put the ball in a hole in the ground; and there is where the ball goes when you hit it in the Ivesdale diamond. **1940** Kennedy–Harlow *Schoolmaster* 225 **IN,** In my boyhood we were still playing the games of my father's and grandfather's time—Anty-over, Bull Pen, Old Sow Out. . . A circle of basemen . . guarding the pen. . . The bases also consisted of little depressions . . and the basemen were armed with sticks. . . There was a herder, anywhere outside the circle, with another club and an object as nearly spherical as possible. . . This was the "sow," and his object was to put it into the pen, past the opposition of the basemen. **1942** McAtee *Dial. Grant Co. IN* 60 (as of 1890s), Sow-and-pigs, or 'ole _____". . . A game played with a ball or substitute and shinny sticks; a central hole was the goal into which the player who was "it," attempted to drive the "sow" or ball; the other players kept the striking end of their sticks in holes surrounding the "sow hole", but quickly removing them when opportunity presented, endeavored to knock the "sow" away; if the driver could get his stick into any unoccupied hole while a player was attempting to hit the "sow", the player thus dispossessed became "it." **1957** *Sat. Eve. Post Letters* **neIL,** "Old Sow"—a non-team game was commoner. The puck was never anything but a beat-up tin can, and the object of the game was to keep from being "it." *Ibid* **neWA,** "Old Sow" and "Chuck the Wicket" called only for some sticks or clubs that could be quickly had at the nearest thicket of brush. *Ibid* **NE,** Old sow: . . Each player has club. One boy is picked to herd the old sow into the sow hole. The boys around the sow hole try to keep it out of the hole with their clubs. The boys can sally out to keep the sow herder away from the sow hole. When this happens if the sow herder thinks he can beat the other boys back to the holes he runs for them and each boy must have his club in a hole. The one who is left becomes the next sow herder. *Ibid* **IA,** We had another game we called "Sow ball." . . The center hole was defended by the one called 'it.' He tried to drive a wooden block inside the center hole. If he succeeded, every one . . had to run to a base . . , then run back to the holes. . . If . . 'it' could steal a hole while the others were trying to keep the block out of the hole, the hole he stole was his. **c1960** *Wilson Coll.* **csKY,** *Old sow* or *old sow and pigs. . .* A rough game somewhat like shinny. **1963** Allen *Legends & Lore S. IL* viii **csIL,** The boys played bull pen, move up, hat ball, old sow, [etc]. **1965–70** *DARE* (Qu. EE18, *Games in which the players set up a stone, a tin can, or something similar, and then try to knock it down*) Inf **IL**130, Old Sal ['old 'sæl]—played with a stick, resembles hockey, uses can for puck; **IL**143, Old Sal ['ol 'sæl]—kick it, the can, around; **KS**13, Old sow—tin can and a stick are used; **NJ**3, Old sow and pigs—throw sticks at a tin can; **SD**1, Sow in the hole—had to knock something out of a hole with a shinny club; (Qu. EE33, . . *Outdoor games . . that children play*) Inf **IA**29, Old sow—made holes in the ground, used sticks and a can, if he got it in your hole (he was keeper) you were the old sow; **MO**38, Old sow—make four holes, that was the shed for the sow; the sow was a ball, anything you could get; and these four outside holes was supposed to be the fence; four players put sticks in those holes; you'd stand and hold this hole; then whoever tried to put this old sow in the pig pen, you'd knock her away; **OH**70, Old sow—hole in the ground, one fellow was it, others would try to kick a can into his hole; if he gets his club into their hole, that person is it; **TX**42, Old sow—kick-the-can; **KY**5, Old sow wants a corner; **MO**13, Sally in the hole.

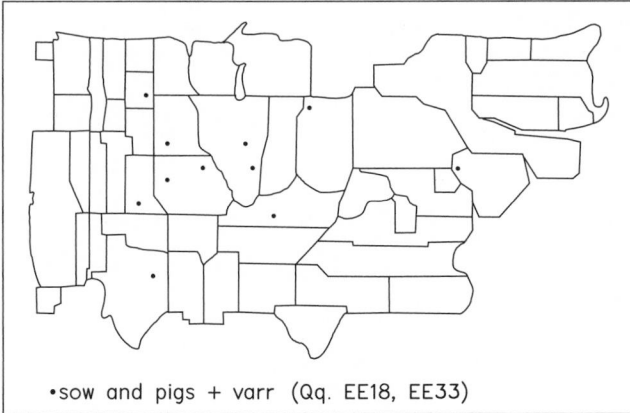

•sow and pigs + varr (Qq. EE18, EE33)

sowbane n [*OED2* 1657 →] Cf **pigweed 1**

A **Jerusalem oak 1** (here: *Chenopodium ambrosioides*) or other **goosefoot.**

[**1875** *Amer. Cyclop.* 13.508, *Pigweed,* the popular name in this country for several species of *chenopodium. . .* In England the term pigweed (also sowbane) is confined to one species, *C. rubrum,* which was supposed to be fatal to swine.] **1900** Lyons *Plant Names* 95, *C*[*henopodium*] *hybridum. . .* Sowbane. **1914** Georgia *Manual Weeds* 114, *Chenopodium murale. . . Other English names:* Sowbane.

sowbelly n Also *sowbelly meat, sow's belly* **widespread, but less freq N and Mid Atl, PA, c,sCA** See Map Cf **sow bosom**
Bacon; fatty meat from the underside of a hog.

1862 in 2002 *DARE* File—Internet **KY,** I have ed so menny hard crackers and fat sowbelly that my teeth is all wore out. **1865** *Harper's New Mth. Mag.* 31.300 **NY,** He used to laugh and say . . that providing "hard tack and sow-belly" wasn't in his line. **1904** *DN* 2.421 **nwAR,** Sow-belly. . . Pork. 'They can live all summer and raise a crop on cornbread and sow-belly.' **1912** *DN* 3.590 **wIN,** Sow-belly. . . Side-meat. **1915** *DN* 4.190 **swVA,** Sow-belly. . . Side-bacon. **1923** *DN* 5.221 **swMO,** Sow belly. . . Bacon. **1940** Stong *Hawkeyes* 94 **IA,** Thanksgiving celebration where we had duck, turkey, . . a joint of lamb, squirrel pie, guinea fowl, wild goose, sowbelly strippings. **1941** Writers' Program *Guide WY* 465, Sow belly—Salt pork. **1944** *PADS* 2.13 **Sth,** *Sow belly. . .* Pork from the belly or sides of the animal, fried or used to cook with vegetables. Negro, vulgar white. **1959** *AmSp* 34.79 **nwCA** [Logger lingo], Sow belly. . . Bacon in the cookhouse. **1965–70** *DARE* (Qu. H38, . . *Words for bacon [including joking ones]*) 237 Infs, **widespread but less freq N and Mid Atl, PA, c,sCA,** Sowbelly; **NY**9, Fried sowbelly; **DE**2, **LA**16, 40, **OH**4, Sow's belly; (Qu. H50, *Dishes made with beans, peas, or corn that everybody around here knows, but people in other places might not*) Inf **IN**35, Beans with sowbelly; **TX**104, Peas boiled with sowbelly; **KY**84, Sowbelly and beans; (Qu. BB51b, . . *'Magical' cures for corns or warts*) Inf **NC**36, Sowbelly. **1966** *DARE*

Tape **AL**1, We had plenty o' hams and sowbelly meat. . . The belly of the hog. **1989** Pederson *LAGS Tech. Index* 158 **Gulf Region,** *Salt pork* [127 infs [of 914 primary infs], Sowbelly; 2 infs, Sow bellies; 1 inf, Sow's belly; 1 inf, Sowbelly meat; 1 inf, Sowbelly with the buttons [*DARE* Ed: =teats] on it.]

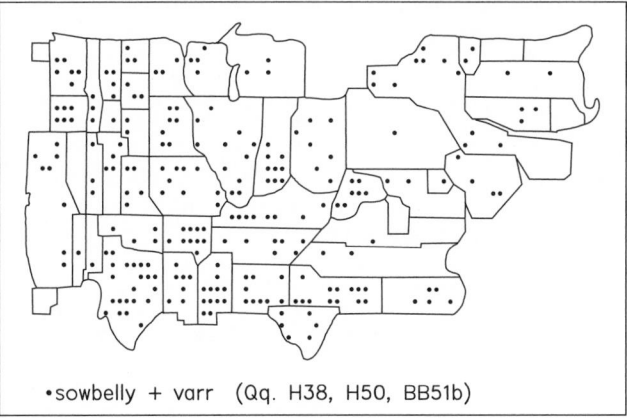

•sowbelly + varr (Qq. H38, H50, BB51b)

sow berry n

1 See **sow-tit.**
2 =**French mulberry.** [Prob var of **sourberry 1**]
1960 Vines *Trees SW* 892, American Beauty-berry. . . Other local names in use are Spanish-mulberry, . . and Sow-berry.

sow bindweed n
=**black bindweed.**
1910 Graves *Flowering Plants* 163 **CT,** *Polygonum Convolvulus. . .* Black, Corn, Sow or Blackbird Bindweed. . . Cultivated or waste grounds.

sow bosom n Also *sow's bosom* **chiefly Sth, S Midl, SW**
=**sowbelly.**
1874 in 1971 *SW Hist. Qrly.* 75.211, Lunch on hard tack and sow's bosom, coffee being out of the question. **1883** *IA State Reporter* (Waterloo) 29 Nov [5]/3 (newspaperarchive.com), We have a soldier's supper of hard tack, coffee, beans, and our Q.M. ransacked every meat market in the city . . , but could not find any what we used to call sow bosom, so we have had to substitute pork. **1927** *AmSp* 3.25 **eTX** [Sawmill talk], The saw mill commissary. . . sells bacon—"sow bosom." **1931** *AmSp* 7.51 **Sth, SW** [Lumberjack lingo], "Sow-bosom" is another name for bacon. **1933** *AmSp* 8.1.27 **nwTX** [Ranch diction], Sow-bosom. Bacon. **1934** Hurston *Jonah's Gourd Vine* 316 **AL,** Sow-bosom, salt pork, a very important item in the diet of both negroes and poor whites in the South. **1936** *AmSp* 11.276 **eTN,** *Sow's bosom.* Bacon, variant of *sowbelly* or *sow's belly.* 'I eat sow's bosom for breakfast.' **1958** Blasingame *Dakota Cowboy* 248 **SD,** This is corn. . . Cowboys like it now and then, in place of so much sow bosom. **1966–70** *DARE* (Qu. H38, . . *Words for bacon [including joking ones]*) Infs **AR**38, **MS**1, **SC**8, **TN**52, Sow bosom; **VT**8, Sow bosom [FW sugg]. **1969** Lyons *My Florida* 29, It was depression and the cheapest grade of salt pork, called "sow bosom with the buttons," retailed for a nickle a pound. **1973** Allen *LAUM* 1.290 (as of c1950), *Salt pork. . .* A . . western Nebraska "old-timer" offered the synonymous *sow bosom.* **1986** Pederson *LAGS Concordance (Salt pork)* 1 inf, **swGA,** Sow bosom—facetious; 1 inf, **csAL,** Sow bosom—with the teats on it; 1 inf, **cwAR,** Sow bosom—better than fatback.

sow brier n

A **greenbrier** (here: either *Smilax glauca* or *S. rotundifolia*).
1960 Vines *Trees SW* 75, Vernacular names for the plant [=*Smilax rotundifolia*] are Biscuit-leaves, . . Cat-brier, Horse-brier, and Sow-brier. *Ibid* 78, Vernacular names in use [for *Smilax glauca*] are . . Sow-brier, and Sarsaparilla-vine.

sow bug n Cf **damp bug**
Std: a small insect-like crustacean of the family Oniscidae often noted for rolling itself into a ball. Also called **ball bug, chinch** n[1] **4, doodlebug 3, pill bug, potato ~ 5, roll-bug, roll-'em-up, roly-poly 6, stone bug, tabernacle B**

sow cat n [*OED2* 1676 →] **esp S Midl** Cf *boar cat* (at **boar a), ramcat, sow coon 1**

A female cat; also fig.

1859 *NY Atlas* (NY) 20 Feb 3/6 **TN,** Well—I've seed cats—hearn ove cats—all sorts ove cats, wild cats, sow cats and stink cats, but—oh my soul! *sich a cat!* **1899** (1912) Green *VA Folk-Speech* 404, *Sow-cat.* . . A female cat. **1915** *DN* 4.190 **swVA,** *Sow-cat.* . . A she cat. **1967** *DARE* (Qu. AA22, *Joking names that a man may use to refer to his wife:* "*I have to go down and pick up my _____.*") Inf **TN**15, Sow cat. **1994** NC Lang. & Life Project *Dial. Dict. Lumbee Engl.* 11 **seNC,** *Sow cat.* . . Also cooter cat. Term of endearment for a child. *Come to grandpa, you little sow cat!*

sow coon n

1 A female raccoon. **esp Lower Missip Valley** Cf *boar coon* (at **boar c), sow cat**

1890 in 2002 *DARE* File—Internet **swMS,** Wed. 30th. . . Pa, Dick and rest of us killed an old sow coon at dusk NW of new ground. **1953** Randolph–Wilson *Down in Holler* 287 **Ozarks,** *Sowcoon.* . . The word means female raccoon. **1954** *Harder Coll.* **cwTN,** *Sowcoon.* . . A female raccoon. **1995** *OzarksWatch* 8.3.3, He had even showed me the differences between the spoors of boar and sow coon. **2002** *DARE* File—Internet **sIL,** A sow coon has raised a family of three in an old corn crib . . and as far as I am concerned is not hurting anything or anyone.

2 also *sour coon:* A cyclone. **esp S Midl** *joc*

1949 *Macon Co. Times* (Lafayette TN) 14 July supp [2]/4 **cnTN,** He never did call the word, "cyclone," correctly, always calling it "sow coon." This might have been done by him on purpose, but this is what he called the word. **1949** *PADS* 11.11 **wTX** (as of 1911–29), *Sow coon.* . . Cyclone. Humorous. An old joke tells of a colored man seeing the damage done by a cyclone and asking, "If a sow coon done dat, what'd a boah coon do?" **1953** Randolph–Wilson *Down in Holler* 287 **Ozarks,** *Sowcoon.* . . A jocular name for cyclone. **c1960** *Wilson Coll.* **csKY,** *Sowcoon.* . . Facetious name for a cyclone, which always means tornado. **1968** *DARE* (Qu. B16, *A destructive wind that comes with a funnel-shaped cloud*) Inf **VA**13, Sour coon ['saʊə kun]: Old-fashioned pronunciation in the past said seriously but now referred as a joking word; probably once misheard.

sow crab n Also *sour crab* Cf **silk crab, sook** n

A mature female blue crab *(Callinectes sapidus)*.

1942 [see **sook** n]. **1970** *DARE* FW Addit **Chincoteague VA,** Sour crab . . a sook or female crab. **2002** *DARE* File—Internet **MD,** Town Dock Restaurant. . . Steamed Sow Crab Legs.

Sowegian n Also *Souwegian, Sow-wegian* Cf **Scowegian** =**Scandihoovian.**

1897 *Newark Daily Advocate* (OH) 26 Jan 7/3, Then the Irishman cut it short. 'Ye ould Sowegian, Oi said thot the Betts was watherlogged. Can yez understand thot?' **1906** *News* (Frederick MD) [3 Oct 6]/5 (newspaperarchive.com), [Serial novel:] "Shut the door," he snarled. "Them Souwegians ain't none too full." **1923** *DN* 5.237 **swWI,** *Sow-wegian.* . . A Norwegian immigrant; a term of derogation. (Perhaps, it is suggested by jocular association of *sow* with *sou'*, for south.) "A darn Sow-wegian!" **1950** *WELS* (*Names and nicknames for people of foreign background: Norwegian*) 1 inf, **cwWI,** Souwegian. **1967** Will Dredgeman 28 **FL,** One of them wood choppers was with us, some kind of Rooshian or Sowegian or somethin', can't hardly talk English. **2001** in 2003 *DARE* File—Internet, One Paw, you old sowegian! How ya been?

sowel n Also *suwel, suel* [Engl dial; cf *EDD sowl(e)* sb.]

Anything eaten with bread; a relish.

1912 Green *VA Folk-Speech* 404, *Sowel.* . . Anything eaten with bread. **1930** *Hench Coll., Sowel* (or *suwel, suel*) = relish. Told me in April 1930 by [a] graduate student . . as being still in usage.

sow in the hole See **sow and pigs**

sows See **souse** v¹, n¹

sow's belly See **sowbelly**

sow's bosom See **sow bosom**

sow's bread n [Cf *OED2 sowbread* "A plant of the genus *Cyclamen*, esp. *C. europæum*"; c1550 →]

A **shooting star 1.**

1920 Rice–Rice *Pop. Studies CA Wild Flowers* 87, A rather unlovely

name by which the plant was known to old settlers was that of "Sow's Bread." This may be due to the fact that swine were fond of digging and eating the tender roots.

sowse See **souse** v³, n²

sow's ear n

1 =**self-heal.** [See quot]

1968 *DARE* FW Addit **VA**15, Sow's ear = heal all. . . the upper part of each flowerlet resembles a sow's ear.

2 See quot. Cf **pig's ear 2**

1966 *DARE* (Qu. H20b, . . *Names . . for pancakes*) Inf **MS**1, Sow's ears—when tough.

3 See quot.

1998 *DARE* File **OK,** Here are some words. . . from a college-educated male from Purcell, Oklahoma, who was born in 1958: . . *sow's ear* . . the bunch of leaves around the ear of corn—not the corn itself.

sow side n Cf *hog side* (at **hogback 1), sowbelly**

1967 *DARE* (Qu. H38, . . *Words for bacon [including joking ones]*) Inf **MO**18, Sow side.

sowsing See **souse** v¹ B1

sows meat See **souse meat**

sow-teat blackberry (or strawberry) See **sow-tit**

sow thistle n Cf **cow thistle, hog ~**

Std: a plant of the genus *Sonchus*. For other names of var spp see **hare's lettuce**

sow-tit n Also *sow berry, sow-teat blackberry, ~ strawberry* Cf **sheeptit (berry)**

Either a strawberry *(Fragaria vesca)* or a blackberry *(Rubus* spp).

1788 in 1888 Cutler *Life* 1.410, A white oak . . [has a] cavity in the middle covered with sow-tits. **1795** Winterbotham *Amer. U.S.* 3.395, Sawteat [sic] blackberry or bumblekites, Rubus fruticosus. **1893** *Jrl. Amer. Folkl.* 6.141 **NH, CT,** *Rubus villosus*, "sow-tit" (teat). N.H.; Farrington, Conn.; Goshen, Conn. **1898** *Ibid* 11.226 **ME,** *Fragaria vesca* . . sow berry, Oxford and Piscataquis Co[unties]. **1950** Gray–Fernald *Manual of Botany* 802, *F[ragaria] vesca* . . Sow-teat S[traw-berry]. *Ibid* 854, *R[ubus] allegheniensis* . . Sow-teat B[lackberry]. **2000** *Post-Std.* (Syracuse NY) 13 Feb garden sec 29 (Internet), Some of the species are upright, like our native R. allegheniensis, the Allegheny or sow teat blackberry.

Sow-wegian See **Sowegian**

sow-your-wheat bird n Also *sow-wheat* [Echoic] =**white-throated sparrow.**

1951 [see **wheat bird 4**]. **1956** MA Audubon Soc. *Bulletin* 40.255 **ME,** *White-throated sparrow.* . . Sow-your-wheat Bird. [*Ibid,* One rendering of the song is "Sow wheat, Peabody, Peabody, Peabody."]

soz(e) See **so as**

sozzle v chiefly **NEng**

1 also *sousle, souzle:* To splash, drench; to agitate (something) in water; hence vbl n *sozzling*, ppl adj *sozzled.* Cf **sizzle-sozzle, souse** v¹ B3

1845 Judd *Margaret* 8 **NEng,** She sat down and sozzled her feet in the foam. **1892** *Century Illustr. Mag.* 42.914 **Upper MW,** Rolling up his sleeves preparatory to sozzling his face at the sink. **1903** McFaul *Ike Glidden* 9 **VT,** Ef yer call it thoughtlessness for a grown young man like him . . ter sozzle my broody hen . . with a pail o' water. **1905** *DN* 3.20 **cCT,** *Sozzle.* . . To splash, to mess with liquids. **1911** *DN* 3.547 **NE,** *Souzle.* . . Shake up and down in a dish. "Souzle it in the rinse water." **1927** *AmSp* 3.140 **eME,** "Sozzle" is to soak, "all wet and sozzled in the rain." **1938** Rawlings *Yearling* 23 **nFL,** He soused his hands and face in the water. **1959** *VT Hist.* 27.159, *Sozzle.* . . To rinse; to wash by splashing; to souse or douse. . . Occasional. **2002** *DARE* File **nwMA,** *Sozzle*—commonly used as in rinsing something out: "Sozzle it up and down in the bucket."

2 To idle, laze about; with *up:* to perform (a task) in a negligent manner; hence ppl adj *sozzling* lazy; shiftless.

1848 Bartlett *Americanisms* 321 **CT,** To sozzle. To loll; to lounge; to go lazily or sluttishly about the house. A term used by housekeepers in certain parts of Connecticut. 'This woman sozzles up her work.' **1878** (1887) Cooke *Happy Dodd* 368 **CT,** 'Tain't natur that a great lazy sozzlin' girl is one a woman will fellowship. **1911** *DN* 3.547 **NE,** *Sozzling.* . . Shiftless, or sloppy. "Don't be so sozzling."

sozzled   See **sozzle 1**

sozzle up   See **sozzle 2**

sozzling   See **sozzle 1, 2**

spa n [Prob orig applied to a soda fountain, in allusion to the Belgian resort *Spa* noted for its mineral waters; cf *artificial spa* in quot 1866] **NEast, esp MA**

Any of var usu small establishments where food and drink are sold; a restaurant, tavern, soda fountain, or, esp recently, convenience store.

   [**1866** *Atlantic Mth.* 18.719 **NYC,** At the artificial Spa he may recuperate with Vichy or Kissingen.] **1895** *Eve. Democrat* (Warren PA) 12 July [2]/4 (newspaperarchive.com) **Boston MA,** In Boston Thompson's Spa, the greatest soda resort at the Hub, easily clears for its owner $50,000 a year. **1909** *Chr. Sci. Monitor* (Boston MA) 4 Sept 18 *(Popik Coll.), Retaurants.* . . *Students' Spa / 228 Huntington Ave., Boston.* 12 ¹⁄₂% discount meal ticket $3.50. **1918** *Boston Post* 24 Feb *(W3* File) **neMA** (as of 1882), His idea was that a restaurant selling first-class food . . would "go big" at that particular spot. . . [H]e decided to use the name of a relative who had helped him, and call the shop "Thompson's Spa." **1925** Krapp *Engl. Lang.* 1.143, In Boston and New England a restaurant is often called a *spa.* **1940** in Lib. of Congress *Amer. Memory: WPA Life Hist.* (Internet) **cVT,** You can tell from all the drinking places you see along Main Street. . . Pirpo's, Silver Top, Luigi's, Mario's, Barre Restaurant, and Andy's Spa, Cellar Grill, so many you can't remember them. **1945** in 2002 (acc) Lexis–Nexis Legal Research *State Case Law: MA* (Internet), The plaintiff went downstairs and found his wife in the spa seated at a counter. *Ibid: RI,* In this store there were booths, shelving and a soda fountain, and defendant conducted therein a business described in the testimony as a spa. **1978** *DARE* File **csMA,** Soon after I came to Springfield in 1955 I discovered a variety store called Bay Path Spa on Chestnut St. For the next 15 or 20 years I patronized it now and then: it was open on holidays and sold newspapers, and it was open at night and sold milk. . . The Springfield spas are not soda fountains. **1979** in 2002 (acc) Lexis–Nexis Legal Research *State Case Law: ME* (Internet), Richard Thompson was shooting pool at Wally's Spa, Bangor. *Ibid: MA,* The central issue on appeal is whether the part owner and manager of Sam's Spa, a neighborhood variety store in Everett, was properly convicted of knowingly disseminating obscene matter. **1979** *Today Show Letters* **ceMA** (as of c1927), A little corner store, with a soda fountain and selling confectionary, fruits, maybe some groceries, was called a spa! **1986** *NADS Letters* **NYC,** *Spa*—The Gem Spa, on the corner of Second Avenue and St. Mark's Place in . . *The East Village,* has for most of this century been a local landmark. **1999** *DARE* File—Internet [Boston Online *Wicked Good Guide to Boston English*], *Spa*—A luncheonette or ma-and-pop convenience store. **2000** *DARE* File—Internet **cnMA,** The Pepperell Spa near the north end of the Business District features an old fashioned soda fountain.

spaats   See **spatzie**

spachel, spachle   See **spatula**

spack   See **speck** n²

spaddle n [Var of *spattle,* perh infl by *paddle*]

A flat wooden blade for stirring or scraping.

   1839 Bryan *KY Housewife* 275, Weigh your butter, wash it in one or two cold waters, and work it with a wooden spaddle till firm. **1849** *Godey's Lady's Book* 38.155, Put half a pound of powdered white sugar into a *deep* pan, and cut up in it a half a pound of the best fresh butter. Stir them together with a wooden spaddle, till perfectly light. **1865** *Mrs. Goodfellow's Cookery* 162, For creaming butter and sugar a wooden spaddle or flat mush stick is the best, two inches wide and two feet long, of cedar or hickory. **1898** *New Engl. Mag.* 24.380 **NEng,** "Called twict—and me spattin' butter here in the back cellar!" . . and she went upstairs with her butter tray and spaddle. **1969** *DARE* (Qu. F3, *When you're frying things—for example, eggs—you turn them over with a* _____) Inf **KY20,** Spaddle—some form of spatula and paddle? **2002** *DARE* File—Internet **TX,** The Old Texas Woodcarvers Shop—Spreaders, Spaddles, Scrapers & Love Spoons.

spade n

1 A Black person. [In allusion to the suit at cards; cf the simile *black as the ace of spades*]

   1910 *NY Eve. Jrl.* (NY) 16 July 6 *(Zwilling Coll.),* Herman Fliffer the

Sausalito spade who is as black as the inside of a cow has no yellow streak visible. **1929** Gordon *Born to Be* 236 [Black], *Spade* . . *;* Nicknames for Ethiopians. **1934** *AmSp* 9.27 [Prison terms], *Spade.* A very dark Negro. **1954** Armstrong *Satchmo* 146 **LA,** With something like that happening and only a few Spades (colored folks) around, it wasn't so good. **1956** Algren *Walk on the Wild Side* 84 **Chicago IL,** I found a friend. . . A little deaf-and-dumb Spade chick. **1965** Little *Autobiog. Malcolm X* 95, He had asked her, "Why is a white girl like you throwing yourself away with a spade?" **1967–70** *DARE* (Qu. HH28, *Names and nicknames . . for people of foreign background: Negro*) Infs **AL50, CA**15, 177, **PA**202, 208, **RI**6, 11, Spade. [All Infs White] **1970** Bullins *Electronic* 69 **sCA** [Black], Is it because . . I am different? Is it because I talk like a spade? **1989** Pederson *LAGS Tech. Index* 250 **Gulf Region,** *Negro* [32 (of 914 primary) infs, Spade].

2 See **spade toe.**

spade v, hence vbl n *spading,* ppl adj *spaded;* also sp *spaydded, spayted* [*OED2* spade v.² 1611 →; *spaded* ppl. a.² 1648 →] **formerly esp NEast, now widespread** Cf Intro "Language Changes" II.5 Note: The frequent use of the sp *spade* for *spayed* is not treated here.

To spay (or rarely to castrate) a domestic animal.

   1892 *DN* 1.211 **seMA,** *Spade.* . . to spay. **1907** *DN* 3.250 **eME,** *Spaydded.* . . Spayed. **1914** *DN* 4.80 **ME, nNH,** *Spade.* . . To spay. *Spaded.* . . spayed. "He had his old sow spaded." **1930** Shoemaker *1300 Words* 54 **cPA Mts** (as of c1900), *Spayted*—An unsexed female dog. **1959** *VT Hist.* 27.159, *Spayed* ['spedɪd] . . pp. of *to spay.* Common. Rural areas. **1965–70** *DARE* (Qu. J3a, *To make a female dog so that she can't breed, she must be* _____) 225 Infs, **widespread,** Spaded; (Qu. J3b, *To make a female cat so that she can't breed, she must be* _____) 184 Infs, **widespread,** Spaded; (Qu. K70, *Words used . . for castrating an animal*) Infs **CT**7, **KY**62, **MO**21, **NH**14, Spaded; **KS**4, Spading. **1967** *DARE* File **neMA,** 'Spaded'—I have never heard the word 'spayed' (referring to dogs, cats, etc) pronounced other than 'spaded.' **1979** Lewis *How to Talk Yankee* [31] **nNEng,** *Spaded.* . . spayed. "I had to get my Judy spaded before she got knocked up by that Pekinese next door." **1982** *Barrick Coll.* **csPA,** *Spaded*—spayed. **1986** Pederson *LAGS Concordance* **Gulf Region** *(Castrate)* 12 infs, Spade; 10 infs, Spaded; 3 infs, Spading. [*DARE* Ed: Some of these infs specified that this was used of female animals, or of both sexes indifferently.]

spadefish n

1 =**paddlefish.** Cf **shovelfish 2**

   1803 (1805) Harris *Jrl. Alleghany Mts.* 116 **OH,** A curious fish called the *Spade-Fish.* . . is furnished with a bony weapon projecting from the nose . . ; thin and like a narrow shovel. This appears designed to enable its possessor to dig up its prey from the mud. **1818** *Amer. Monthly Mag. & Crit. Rev.* 3.354, P[olyodon] pristis [=*Polyodon spathula*], Raf.—Spade-fish. **1877** U.S. Natl. Museum *Bulletin* 9.45, Western Spade-Fish, Polyodon folium [=*Polyodon spathula*]. **1908** Forbes–Richardson *Fishes of IL* 18, Various names . . have been applied to this fish, the commonest of which are spoonbill, shovel-fish or shovel-cat, duck-bill cat, and spade-fish. **1933** LA Dept. of Conserv. *Fishes* 374, Spoonbill, Duckbill Cat, Shovelfish and Spadefish, all these popular names refer to the Paddlefish's most striking characteristic, the long, thin, expanded, blade-like snout.

2 A disk-shaped fish *(Chaetodipterus faber)* of Atlantic and Gulf waters, much esteemed as food. Also called **angelfish 2, moonfish 1, pogy 3, porgy** n¹ **3, tripletail 2**

   1884 Goode *Fisheries U.S.* 1.445, In the northern parts of the Gulf of Mexico it [=the moonfish] is called the "Spade-fish." **1946** Kopman *Wild Acres* 56 **LA,** The fishermen . . spend their time matching strategy . . with wily, nimble spadefish and sheephead feeding . . about the pilings. **1966** WI Acad. *Trans.* 55.127 **LA,** Chaetodipterus faber. . . Atlantic spadefish. **1966–68** *DARE* (Qu. P2, . . *Kinds of saltwater fish caught around here . . good to eat*) Infs **LA**26, 37, **MS**73, **TX**19, Spadefish; (Qu. P4, *Saltwater fish that are not good to eat*) Inf **LA**44, Spadefish. **2002** *DARE* File—Internet **MD,** Bill Jacobs of New York City established the first Atlantic spadefish State record.

spadefoot n

Std: a toad of the genus *Scaphiopus.* For other names of var spp see **rainfrog 2**

spade grass n

A **horned rush** (here: *Rhynchospora corniculata*).

1920 *Torreya* 20.19 **GA**, *Rhynochspora* [sic] *corniculata*. . . Spade grass, Savannah, Ga.

spade toe n   Also *spade*

A shoe with a broad square toe; the toe itself; hence adj phr *spade-toed;* see quots.

1922 *Lima News & Times–Democrat* (OH) 26 May 17/6, [Advt:] Dark Tan, Toney Red, Black Calf, English, Medium Spade Toe or Broad Toe Styles. **1950** *WELS Suppl.* **csWI**, *Spade toe*—is similar to the French toe of today. It tapers gradually and the toe itself is more square, like that of a spade. **1967–70** *DARE* (Qu. W42a, . . *Nicknames . . for men's sharp-pointed shoes*) Infs **MA**44, **PA**94, **WI**47, Spades; (Qu. W42b, . . *Nicknames for men's square-toed shoes*) Infs **IL**140, **NC**87, **VA**69, 73, Spade-toed.

spading   See **spade** v

spads   See **spods**

spaghetti n   Also *spaget, spaghetti-bender, ~-eater*

An Italian; hence *spaghetti people* Italians.

1918 Hunt *Blown in Draft* 226, "You kick me again like that, you darn spaghetti eater, and I'll knock yer darn block off!" . . Phil . . admonished Bologna, known on the company payrolls as Tony Perrone, that kicking was against all the articles of war. **1928** *Charleroi Mail* (PA) 10 Nov [5]/7 (newspaperarchive.com), The South Brownsville Sons of Italy football team. . . is an outfit comprising eleven honest-to-Jack, real, live spaghetti eaters. **1930** (1931) Anderson *Milk & Honey Route* 38, Italian hobos are . . rare. They are the "wops" or "spaghettis." **1941** *LANE* Map 453 *(Italian)* 1 inf, **swNH**, Spaget; 1 inf, **cnMA**, Spaghetti. **1942** Berrey–Van den Bark *Amer. Slang* 385.25, *Italian*. . . spaghette [sic], spaghetti bender. **1964** *PADS* 42.40 **Chicago**, Italian. . . other terms were unique within the survey . . *spaghetti-eater, spaghetti-bender.* **1965–70** *DARE* (Qu. HH28, *Names and nicknames . . for people of foreign background: Italian*) Infs **NM**9, **PA**193, Spaghetti; **MA**68, **PA**94, 227, 230, Spaghetti-bender; **CO**34, **CT**23, **SD**5, **TX**11, 95, Spaghetti-eater. **1970** Tarpley *Blinky* 250 **neTX**, *Nicknames for Italian people* . . other responses . . spaghetti eaters. **1970** *DARE* FW Addit **nwPA**, *Spaghetti-bender*—an Italian. **1986** Pederson *LAGS Concordance (Italians)* 1 inf, **nwLA**, Spaghetti eaters; 1 inf, **cMS**, Spaghetti people. **2001** *Dallas Observer* (TX) 16 Apr (Internet), But first, the fun-loving spaghetti-benders come to call.

spaghetti and meatballs n   Cf *DS* P35a

1982 *DARE* File **coastal ME**, Another euphemism for illegal lobsters, this time "shots" or undersized specimens is "We're having spaghetti and meatballs."

spaghetti-bender (or -eater, people)   See **spaghetti**

spagnum   See **sphagnum**

spaldeen n   Also *spauldeen*   [Pronc-sp for the trademark *Spalding*]   **chiefly NYC**

A smooth, hollow, pink rubber ball.

1960 *NY Folkl. Qrly.* 16.301 **NYC** (as of 1940s), With a pink, five-cent Spalding rubber ball (known as a "spal*deen*") the boys played fifteen varieties of ball games. **1968** *DARE* Tape **NY**118, We used to play this game called hoop ball in which you take a spaldeen [spɔl'din]. **1975** Ferretti *Gt. Amer. Book Sidewalk Games* 43, The spaldeen is basic to many, many sidewalk games. . . A tennis ball, no matter how new . . is no substitute for the spaldeen. **1977–78** Foster *Lexical Variation* 83 **NJ**, Red Rubber Ball—Street games such as stickball and Hit the Penny are best played with a hollow rubber ball, usually pink in color. The best of these, manufactured by Spalding and imprinted with the company logo, is invariably called a /spɔl'di:n/ in New York City. In New Jersey, *spaldeen* is well-attested only in Hudson County and Trenton. . . In part the failure of *spaldeen* . . to become established in New Jersey may result from the fact that hollow rubber balls are most useful in games played on pavement. **1999** *NY Times* (NY) 5 May Metro sec 1/4, *The Spaldeen, Stickball's Bouncy Foundation Makes a Comeback.* . . Spaldeens were first sold in the 1950's by the Spalding Company, a leading producer of tennis balls. **1999** *WI State Jrl.* (Madison) 25 July sec C 1/4, Middle-aged guys [from the Northeast, Detroit, and Chicago] tend to get teary-eyed talking about their "Spauldeens"—pink rubber balls that were about the only equipment you needed for the game. **2001** *DARE* File **wNY**, Spaldeen. . . a tennis ball with the cover removed.

spalt adj   Also *spaulted*   [Engl dial *spalt* (*OED2* 1567 →)] **NEng**

Of wood: easily broken; decayed.   Note: In the form *spalted* this word has recently (*OED2* 1977 →) become widely known

in the specialized sense "showing a decorative figure caused by incipient decay"; this sense is not illustrated below.

1858 *New Englander & Yale Rev.* 16.177, There is not a stick of smart, hard timber in all California . . ; every hardest, soundest tree, even the oak, being always brittle to such a degree ("*brash*" they say in California, and in New England "*spalt*") that the trunk will commonly break asunder five or six times when it is felled. **1959** *VT Hist.* 27.159 **VT**, Spaulted. . . Rotting, as of wood. Rare. Washington; Windsor [counties]. **1969** *DARE* (Qu. KK7, *When wood . . is starting to decay inside . .* "It's _____ inside.") Inf **MA**58, Gone spalt [spɑlt]—when just starting to go rotten; old-fashioned.

span n   Also *spannies*

In marble play: the distance from the tip of the thumb to the tip of one of the other fingers of the same hand; the right to move one's marble this distance; also nouns *spangy, spanners, spanning* any of various marbles games; hence v *span* to measure a distance or describe an arc by means of the outstretched fingers; to bring two marbles together with the outstretched fingers; vbl n *spanning.*

1885 *Daily Miner* (Butte MT) 24 Jan [3]/3 (newspaperarchive.com), The game depends . . upon the breadth of the span covered by the thumb and second finger of the player. **1899** (1912) Green *VA Folk-Speech* 404, Span. . . The extent between the tips of the thumb and little finger when outstretched. A measure used by boys when playing marbles. **1901** *DN* 2.148, Span. . . A term used in slab. [*Ibid* 147 **ME**, Slab. . . Name of a game at marbles.] **1942** McAtee *Dial. Grant Co. IN* 61 (as of 1890s), Span . . a marble game in which the taws were bounced from a wall; if a player's marble came to rest within a distance he could span of that of an opponent, he was entitled to it. **1955** *PADS* 23.34 **seKY**, Span. . . Before shooting from a hole in the game of knucks, to describe a semicircle with one's thumb at the edge of the hole and fingers outstretched. **1957** *Sat. Eve. Post Letters* **eKY** (as of c1930), The first player shot for the first hole; if he made it he was allowed to move his marble a span. **1966** *DARE* Tape **AL**3, If he rolled in the hole . . he was allowed to span so far with it. Put his finger down at the edge of the hole . . and if he had big hands, he could span bigger than the fellow that had small hands; **NC**22, And we would take a span, which was put your thumb in the side of the . . hole and . . just span your hand out. And if you could call "double span" before the other people . . said "no spans," why, you could get double; **OK**42, And I can say "span" and I get . . then to take my hand like that, and as far out as I can reach like that, I can shoot from this line up here. **1969–70** *DARE* (Qu. EE7, . . *Kinds of marble games*) Inf **CT**23, Spanning—#1 throws marble—#2 throws marble at #1's—if it comes within spanning (handspan) distance, #2 wins marble; **VA**69, Span—The arcs are the "spans." A span is reached by each player holding his thumb against his extended forefinger, holding thumbnail at some point on the circle, and, holding the thumb steady, tracing the natural arc or span of the forefinger. A player had to shoot from the highest point of the span. **c1970** Wiersma *Marbles Terms* **neIL** (as of 1928), Span. . . If in playing the Chicago version of Pot, you succeeded in moving a date out of the square, you would be allowed to move your shooting marble the span of your hand in order to line it up for another shot. **1973** Ferretti *Marble Book* 52, Spannies. A shooting distance. The measurement between the tip of the thumb to the tip of the middle finger when stretched apart. *Ibid* 66, In the United States it [= **boss-out**] is also known as . . Span. **1998** Levine–Scudamore *Marbles* 25, Spanning. . . If you are allowed to span and a marble lands within a handspan of your target marble, open your hand wide. Place your thumb next to the shooter and another finger, usually your pinkie or third finger, next to the target marble. Close your hand in such a manner that the marbles knock together. If you can do this, both marbles belong to you. *Ibid* 83, Spangy. . . Draw a 1-foot . . square. . . Place a marble in each corner and one in the center of the square. . . Draw a circle of diameter 10 feet . . around the square. . . Each player takes a turn trying to knock a target marble out of the square, shooting from outside the circle. . . If a player hits the marble from the square, the marble belongs to him and he continues shooting. . . If your shooter lands within a handspan of any target marble, you may "span" the marbles. *Ibid* 84, Spanners. . . Any player who can hit a target marble or get within a handspan of it gets back her shooter. . . Any player not within a handspan loses her marble to Player 1.

span adv   [Cf *OED2* span-new c1300 →]   **chiefly Nth**

Perfectly (new); spotlessly (clean).

1838 Rask *Compendious Gram. Icelandic* (transl. Marsh) 103 **NEng**, Span-new. . . is still in frequent use in New England. **1844** Stephens

High Life in NY 2.100, The men folks had on span white gloves. **1848** Bartlett *Americanisms* 322, *Span-clean*. . . Very clean; perfectly clean. **1851** *Democratic Rev.* 28.328, [It] had a quaint air of old times about it, which contrasted strikingly to me with the . . span-new white houses . . of the more southern towns I had just left. **1899** (1912) Green *VA Folk-Speech* 404, *Span new*. . . Quite new; brand-new; fire-new. **1905** *DN* 3.20 **cCT**, *Span clean*. . . Perfectly clean. **1914** *DN* 4.80 **ME, nNH**, *Span clean*. . . Perfectly clean. **1958** Carrighar *Moonlight* 150 **AK**, A bevy of teen-age girls would stand around talking to him . . each looking her sweetest and prettiest, shiny black hair braided sleekly, parki cover span-clean, and little wool tassels bouncing at the top of her boots. **1968** *DARE* Tape **NJ**42, It was a beautiful room, span-clean and all spick and new, you know. **2003** in 2006 *DARE* File—Internet **CA**, It did not have a scratch that I could see, and even the alloy wheels where [sic] span clean!

span v¹   See **spin 1**

span v²   See **span n**

‡**spancel onto** v phr
To appropriate; to take.
   1968 *DARE* (Qu. V5b, *If you take something that nobody seems to own* . . *"Before anybody else gets it, I'm going to _____ this."*) Inf **MD**43, Spancel [spænsl] onto.

spandy adv   [Perh var of Engl dial *spandal* or *spander;* cf *EDD spandal, spander-new*]   **chiefly NEng**
=**span** adv.
   1838 Kettell *Yankee Notions* 116 **NEng**, I have heard of a ghost that always came in a new coat, smartly buttoned up, and a spandy clean dickey. **1869** Alcott *Little Women* 2.11 **MA**, I am morally certain that the spandy-new kitchen never *could* have looked so cosy and neat. **1890** [see **spandy** adj]. **1891** *Century Illustr. Mag.* 41.462 **RI**, Look a' them pantalets, now, . . put on spandy clean this mornin', I vow and declare! **1903** Wiggin *Rebecca* 14, These [shoes] are spandy new. **1968** Updike *Couples* 227 **MA**, Comically new topsiders, cup-soled, spandy-bright. **2000** in 2007 *DARE* File—Internet **cwCA**, The school sure was spandy clean that first day. **2007** *Ibid* **cnKY**, I have a spandy-new, limited-release blog up now. *Ibid* **eMA**, The recording quality isn't fantastic, and my spandy new speakers are proving that to me.

spandy adj
Fine; elegant.
   1868 (1871) Alcott *Little Women* 1.126 **MA**, My silk stockings and two pairs of spandy gloves are my comfort. **1890** *DN* 1.19 **seNH**, *Spandy:* clean, spick-span, of linen. 'Spandy' alone is used; elsewhere 'spandy-clean,' or 'spandy-dandy.' **1893** *Harper's New Mth. Mag.* 87.113 **Nantucket MA**, And that day she felt specially spandy in a whole suit of *receding* green. **1937** Sandoz *Slogum* 305 **NE**, By God, drivin' around in a slick and spandy buggy, tony as the devil.

spanferkel n   [Ger]   **in German settlement areas, esp WI**
A suckling pig, esp when roasted for food; a gathering at which roast suckling pig is eaten.
   1909 *Sheboygan Daily Press* (WI) 6 Feb 1/6, Spanferkel lunch at Guenther & Kistner tonight. **1935** Frederick *PA Dutch* 139, *Spanferkel or Roast Little Pig* . . 1 suckling pig . . butter . . pepper . . salt . . water. **1950** *WELS (A young pig)* 2 Infs, **WI**, Spanferkel. **1968** *DARE* (Qu. K51) Inf **WI**14, Spanferkel; **WI**71, Spanferkel—a small pig that you roast. **1977** *Capital Times* (Madison WI) 16 Sept 2 **csWI**, The Badger Shrine Club and the Beaver Dam Knights of Columbus Council will co-sponsor a spanferkel Sunday. **1983** *DARE* File **seWI**, [Sign in tavern:] Spanferkel—All you can eat—March 27th. $5.00. **2001** *Milwaukee Jrl. Sentinel* (WI) 27 July sec B 1 (Internet), Go ahead and keep serving spanferkel, but don't make us look at the impaled porkers.

spanfired adv   Also *spangfired, spankfire*   [*EDD spangfire new*]   Cf **brand-fire-new**
=**span** adv.
   1844 Stephens *High Life in NY* 2.82, Jase was a going to send down his span fired new carriage to the Astor House. **1909** *DN* 3.416 **nME**, *Spankfire new*. . . Brand new. **1914** *DN* 4.80 **ME, nNH**, *Spanfired new*. . . Brand new. (Also *spangfired*.) **1974** Fink *Mountain Speech* 24 **wNC, eTN**, Spanfired new. **2001** *Modesto Bee* (CA) 28 Feb sec B 1 (Internet), Ramsay returned to Modesto on Monday to fly a spank-fire new red biplane he bought last week.

spang adv   Also *spank*
1 also *spango:* =**smack** adv **1.**

1798 (2004) Munford *Coll.* 100 (Internet) **VA**, The words were hardly out of my mouth, before spang he took me with his foot. **1851** *S. Lit. Messenger* 17.761, If some folks . . were to come spang up to two such lines, they'd grow a little pale. **1862** *Continental Mth.* 2.120 **NEng**, We give the most all-firedest shove—and over we went, . . head-fo'most, spang into them crows and dead kaow! **1884** *Anglia* 7.258 **Sth, S Midl** [Black], There are many peculiar intensives in the Negro dialect designed to give emphasis to an assertion: . . *Spang: he done come spang down! Ibid* 269, *To drap spang* = to let fall suddenly. *Ibid* 276, *To walk right spang inter* = to walk blindly. **1908** Wasson *Home from Sea* 288 **sME coast**, She would n't hesitate a secont to up and tell anybody so, right out spango. **1912** Green *VA Folk-Speech* 404, *Spang*. . . Implying force: "As it went spang out of the window." **1950** *WELS (When one thing suddenly hits against something else. . . "The iron tipped over and fell _____ on the floor.")* 1 Inf, **seWI**, Spang. **1966–70** *DARE* (Qu. KK53, *When one thing suddenly hits hard against something else: "He ran _____ into a car."*) Infs **MA**98, **NJ**4, **SC**5, **VA**33, Spang; **AK**5, **TN**12, Spank.

2 also *spank dab:* =**smack** adv **2.**   **chiefly Sth, S Midl**
   1843 (1916) Hall *New Purchase* 147 **IN**, She'd stay alone a readin Scott's Family Bible: so that she got three times right spang through it. **1888** Johnston *Mr. Absalom Billingslea* 384 **GA**, The main, straight-forrards public road a-leadin' spang up to the very gate. **1901** Harben *Westerfelt* 277 **nGA**, I seed 'im lay hold of 'er wrists an' look 'er spank, dab in the eyes. **1909** *DN* 3.373 **eAL, wGA**, *Spang, spank*. . . Exactly, squarely, completely. **1917** *DN* 4.417 **wNC**, *Spang*. . . Exactly; directly. "He was right spang on the spot." "Spang fraish." Also Ky. In Ill., *bang-spang*. **1922** Gonzales *Black Border* 327 **sSC, GA coasts** [Gullah glossary], *Spang*—all the way, expressive of distance. **1929** *AmSp* 5.129 **ME**, A competition might be "nip and tuck" and something might lie or hit just "spang in the middle." **1933** Williamson *Woods Colt* 66 **Ozarks**, Still farther off is the federal pen, spang in the middle of nothin' but flat country. **1951** Porter *Ragged Roads* 26 **OK**, He was certain, too, that everything would be under my control "spank up" to the Texas State Line. **1965** Will *Okeechobee Boats* 8 **FL**, From the custard apple woods along the lake shore, spang down to Ft. Lauderdale. **1966** *DARE* (Qu. LL26a, . . *'All the way': "He drove _____ to the end of the road."*) Inf **SC**5, Spang. **1966** *DARE* FW Addit **SC**, "Right spang in front of our door"—exactly in front, right on a point. **1968** *DARE* Tape **NJ**20, Where they're moving, they'll be right spang on the . . public road and the house not too far back. **1995** MacLeod *Odd Job* 33 **Boston MA**, It was typical of her to invite herself, set her own time, and arrive spang on the dot. **1995** Brophy *Coll.* 70 **swMO** (as of c1960), *Spang*. "[S]mack-dab," as "spang in the middle."

spang n   Cf *DS* H37
   1953 Randolph–Wilson *Down in Holler* 287 **Ozarks**, *Spang*. . . Gravy. Louise Platt Hauck, of St. Joseph, Mo., tells me that this word was in common use at Blue Eye, Mo., in the late nineteen twenties. I have heard *spang* used to mean a mixture of gravy and butter.

spang-cubes n   Also *spanquittin'*
   1957 Combs *Lang. S. Highlanders* **sAppalachians**, Spanquittin'—a mythical disease in horses. Heard in the expression "He's got the spanquittin', he can't fart for shittin'." **1967** *DARE* (Qu. BB28, *Joking names . . for imaginary diseases: "He must have the _____."*) Inf **TN**16, Spang-cubes ['spæŋ‚kjubz].

spangfired   See **spanfired**

spanging adv   [Var of *spanking*]
Very, exceptionally.
   1907 *Atlantic Mth.* 99.218 **sME coast**, In room of letting all them brand, spanging new sails slat a year's wear out of 'em that way, Cap'n allowed he'd better . . furl the most of 'em. **2003** in 2007 *DARE* File—Internet **CA**, The eyepiece came back about a couple of weeks later . . and it looked brand spanging new!

spangle out v phr, hence ppl adj phr *spangled out*   Cf *sprangle*
To branch or spread out in different directions.
   1863 *Janesville Daily Gaz.* (WI) 24 Jan [2]/3 (newspaperarchive.com), Has raised Cuba tobacco. Can't cure it. Spangles out from bottom. Cures green. **1954** Harder *Coll.* **cwTN**, *Spangled out*. . . Ey spangled out, split plumb apart. **1969** *DARE* FW Addit **KY**42, *Spangled out*—the top of the sissel [*DARE* Ed: =sweet cicely?] is "all spangled out" in late Aug. and early Sept.; that is, it blossoms and the small flowers are spread out in different directions. **2005** *Lively Arts* Jan/Feb (Internet) **AZ**, She would then pull it into a ponytail and secure it with red elastics.

It spangled out of the back of my head in all directions like a spewing fountain.

spangles n   Also *sprangles*

A **New Jersey tea** (here: *Ceanothus americanus*).

1900 Lyons *Plant Names* 88, *C[eanothus] Americanus*. . . Red root, New Jersey Tea, . . Sprangles.   **1960** Vines *Trees SW* 689, It [=Jersey-tea Ceanothus] is also known under the names of Wild Snowball, Spangles [etc].

spango   See **spang** adv **1**

spangy   See **span** n

Spaniard n   Cf **Spanish** adj

A Spanish-speaking person not of Spanish birth or immediate ancestry, as:

a A Mexican or Mexican-American.   **esp TX, NM**

1842 *Brooklyn Eagle & Kings Co. Democrat* (NY) 23 May 2/5, A company consisting of about eighty men arrived in Independence [MO] . . from Chihuahua and Santa Fe. . . These men are Americans and Spaniards, . . the latter under Seignors Amigo (nephew of the Governor of Santa Fe,) and Basan.   **1848** (1932) Robinson *Jrl. Santa Fe* 40 **NM,** The Spaniards who were to accompany us and drive the pack mules, were rather late.   **1848** (1855) Ruxton *Life Far West* 15 **NM,** The Mexicans are called "Spaniards" or "Greasers" (from their greasy appearance) by the Western people.   **1956** Ker *Vocab. W. TX* 374, *Mexican (nicknames)*. . . More formal and even respectful terms . . *Spaniard*. [1 of 67 infs]   **1970** Tarpley *Blinky* 258 **neTX,** *Nicknames for Mexican people* . . Spaniards [rare].   **1986** Pederson *LAGS Concordance,* 1 inf, **cAR,** Spaniards—Mexicans; 1 inf, **ceTX,** Spaniards—Mexicans in US.

b A Puerto Rican.

1898 *Fitchburg Daily Sentinel* (MA) 10 Aug 6/1, If you tell the Porto Ricans they are Spaniards they will jump about two feet and then get excited and talk to beat the band.   **1968** *DARE* (Qu. HH28) Inf **NY**68, Spaniard—Puerto Ricans, occasionally.

spaniel n   Usu |ˈspænjəl|; also |ˈspænəl| Pronc-sp *spannel* [Cf *OED2 spannel(l*, "obs. forms of *spaniel*"]   Cf **Daniel**

Std sense, var pronc.

1846 Goodrich *Third School Reader* 29, Faults of Pronunciation. . . *Span-nel*, for span-iel.   **1850** Herbert *Warwick Woodlands* 80 **seNY,** I wish I were a spannel, and he'd try it on with me!   **1873** Soule–Campbell *Pronc. Hdbk.* 85, *Spaniel,* span'yel, *not* span'el.   **1936** *AmSp* 11.311 **Upstate NY,** Except for its variations as part of the 'long *u*' glide, [j] is relatively stable. It occasionally drops out of *spaniel* in the speech of older people.   **1942** *AmSp* 17.41 **seNY,** *Spaniel* . . [j] included . . 127 [infs] . . [j] omitted . . 3 [infs].   **1959** *VT Hist.* 27.159, *Spaniel* ['spænl].   **2002** in 2007 *DARE* File—Internet **ceMA,** I guess that I'm just a sucker for spaniels (we call 'em "spannels" in the [sic] parts).   **2004** *Ibid* **nCA,** From a lady in northern california . . who loves springer spannels.   **2007** *Ibid* **AZ,** I do have a cocker spannel dog that is very friendly!

Spaniola   See **Spanish fly**

Spanish adj

1 Spanish-speaking, though not a native of Spain or of immediate Spanish descent, as:

a Mexican or Mexican-American.   **esp TX, NM**

1956 Ker *Vocab. W. TX* 373, *Mexican (nicknames)*. . . Spanish. [1 of 67 infs]   **1966** *DARE* (Qu. HH28) Inf **NM**4, Around here they call the Mexicans Spanish; **NM**6, Mexicans [are] always referred to as Spanish.   **1970** Tarpley *Blinky* 259 **neTX,** Few informants would call a Mexican *a Mexican* in his presence, even if he were a citizen of Mexico; instead, they would address him as *a Spanish person*. . . The reason for this . . is that *Mexican* often has a derogatory connotation to Northeast Texans and is applied to farm workers from Mexico or the Rio Grande Valley brought into the region annually for cotton and onion harvests.   **1986** Pederson *LAGS Concordance,* 1 inf, **ceTX,** Spanish—Mexican; 1 inf, **ceTX,** Spanish—same as Mexican-American; 1 inf, **csTX,** Spanish—often used for Mexican—polite.   **2001** *DARE* File **cnTX** (as of 1950), When I was eight years old in 1950 and went to visit in Knox County, Texas my grandparents told me I should never use the word "Mexican" around the Mexican-American couple who worked on the land my grandfather owned. . . I was told that all Mexican-Americans I met should be called *Spanish* to their face, that Mexican was an offensive word to them.

b Puerto Rican; hence n *Spanish* Puerto Rican people.

1968 *DARE* (Qu. HH28) Inf **NY**40, Spanish—Puerto Ricans.   **2001** *DARE* File **NYC,** In the early 1950s, Puerto Ricans (who at that time were the only significant Spanish-speaking ethnic group in New York) were routinely called "Spanish." For example, the "super" of our building and his family were "Spanish," even though everyone knew they were actually Puerto Rican, and when people would say of someone that "He (or she) is Spanish," everyone understood that to mean Puerto Rican.   *Ibid* **NYC,** When I was growing up in Brooklyn in the 1950s, Puerto Ricans were referred to as Spanish; for example, "They hired a Spanish guy at work," or "There are a lot of Spanish moving into that neighborhood."

2 in var ironic combs: See quots.   Cf **Mexican B1**

1912 Alpha Chi Sigma *Hexagon* 3.84, Our Spanish athlete Edwards then read a satirical paper, supposedly a resumé of recent achievements in chemical research.   **1929** Dobie *Vaquero* 158 **TX,** The water was good and I took a "Spanish supper"—tightened my belt up a notch.   **1932** *AmSp* 7.337 [Johns Hopkins jargon], *Spanish athlete*—one who talks nonsense (one who "throws the bull").   **c1938** in Lib. of Congress *Amer. Memory: WPA Life Hist.* (Internet) **TX** (as of c1900), Five of us never stopped for chuck and my tape worm was howling plenty but we took what was called a Spanish supper, just tightened our belts.   **1953** *AmSp* 28.144, *Bird bath, Dutch bath, Spanish bath, spit bath, thimble bath,* and *wipe-off* are baths requiring a minimum of water.   **1975** Gould *ME Lingo* 281, *Struck with the Spanish mildew*—Anybody feigning or imagining some kind of illness, when his perfect health is evident to the world, is said to be *struck with the Spanish mildew;* an ailment not otherwise diagnosed by competent authority. Gold-bricking.   **1995** *Brophy Coll.* 70 **swMO** (as of c1960), *Spanish sore throat.* [D]ysentery; venereal disease.

Spanish n   See **Spanish** adj **1b**

Spanish bayonet n

1 Any of var **yuccas** such as *Yucca aloifolia* or *Y. baccata.* [See quot 1968]   Cf **Spanish dagger(s), ~ needle 2**

[**1823** Faux *Memorable Days* 82 **eSC,** Hedges of *bagonet* plants and myrtles.]   **1843** *Knickerbocker* 22.566 **FL,** A few large flowers of the Spanish-bayonet . . [looked] like sentries with white feathers.   **1884** (1885) McCook *Tenants* 246 **TX,** Then there are . . thorn trees of many sorts, the soap plant [and] the splendid Spanish bayonet, certainly well named.   **1888** Lindley–Widney *CA of South* 170, The leaves [of the yucca are] narrower than those of the Spanish bayonet proper.   **1898** *Jrl. Amer. Folkl.* 11.282 **CO,** *Yucca angustifolia* . . soap plant, Spanish dagger, Spanish bayonet.   **1951** Teale *North with Spring* 19 **FL,** Our road from Royal Palm Hammock, south of Naples, had carried us past gumbo-limbo trees, . . Spanish bayonets and orange dodder vines.   **1968** Abbey *Desert Solitaire* 25 **seUT,** This one is formed of a cluster of bayonetlike leaves pointing up and outward, each stiff green blade tipped with a point as intense and penetrating as a needle. . . This plant, not a cactus but a member of the lily family, is a type of yucca called Spanish bayonet.   **1969** *DARE* (Qu. S26a, . . *Wildflowers. . . Roadside flowers*) Inf **NC**76, Spanish bayonets—white flower; (Qu. S26e, *Other wildflowers not yet mentioned;* not asked in early QRs) Inf **GA**89, Yucca—called Spanish bayonet here—a cactus with a white bloom.   **1991** Hiaasen *Native Tongue* 135 **FL,** "They got those Spanish bayonets under the windows," he reported. "God, I hate them things." Wicked needles on the end of every stalk—absolute murder, even with gloves.

2 =**beggar ticks 1.**   Cf **Spanish needle 1**

1949 *WELS Suppl.* **csWI,** Up in Sauk County where I lived as a girl . . stick-tights were "Spanish bayonets."   **1968** *DARE* (Qu. S14, . . *Prickly seeds, small and flat, with two prongs at one end, that cling to clothing*) Inf **NY**103, Spanish bayonet.

Spanish buckeye n

=**Mexican buckeye.**

1850 Lindley–Paxton *Paxton's Garden* 1.153, Ungnadia Speciosa. . . A hardy deciduous shrub, with rose-colored flowers. Native of Texas. . . Its popular name is *Spanish Buckeye.*   **1884** Sargent *Forests of N. Amer.* 44, Spanish Buckeye. Valley of the Trinity River . . through western Texas to the cañons of the Organ mountains, New Mexico.   **1931** U.S. Dept. Ag. *Misc. Pub.* 101.104, *Mexican-buckeye* . . known also as monillo, Spanish buckeye, and New Mexican buckeye.   **1980** Little *Audubon Guide N. Amer. Trees W. Region* 543, Spanish-buckeye. . . Shrub or small tree with irregular crown of upright branches and showy pink flowers.

Spanish buttons n

A **knapweed** (here: *Centaurea nigra*).

1910 Graves *Flowering Plants* 407 **CT,** *Centaurea nigra.* . . Spanish Buttons. **1914** Georgia *Manual Weeds* 521, Black Knapweed. . . *Other English names:* Horse-knobs, . . Spanish Buttons [etc]. **1976** Bailey-Bailey *Hortus Third* 243, [*Centaurea*] *nigra.* . . Black k[napweed], hardheads, Spanish-buttons.

Spanish clover n

1 =**Mexican clover.**

1881 Phares *Farmer's Book of Grasses* 14, *Richardsonia scabra.* . . It is called Mexican Clover, Spanish Clover, Florida Clover [etc]. **1889** Vasey *Ag. Grasses* 103, *Richardsonia scabra* (Mexican Clover; Spanish Clover [etc]). . . naturalized in the United States, especially along the Gulf coast.

2 A **deervetch** (here: *Lotus purshianus*).

1901 Jepson *Flora CA* 302, L[otus] *Americanus.* . . Spanish Clover. . . (Hosackia Purshiana Benth.) . . very common and widely distributed. **1937** U.S. Forest Serv. *Range Plant Hdbk.* W110, Birdsfoot deervetch, or "Spanish clover" (*L[otus] americanus*) [=*L. purshianus*]. **1973** Hitchcock-Cronquist *Flora Pacific NW* 264, Spanish-clover. . . *L. purshiana.* **2005** in 2007 *DARE* File—Internet **CA,** Beyond the southern junction of the North Los Santos trail . . I also noticed a lot of Spanish clover (*Lotus purshianus*).

Spanish curlew n

1 =**white ibis.**

1791 Bartram *Travels* 148 **FL,** The first of these [birds] I shall mention is a perfect white . . ; the bill and legs of a beautiful clear red, as also a space clear of feathers about the eyes. The other species is black on the upper side, the breast and belly white. . . [B]oth species are called Spanish curlews. [*DARE* Ed: The latter species is the immature bird.] **1814** Wilson *Amer. Ornith.* 8.43 **FL, LA,** White Ibis. . . are usually called Spanish Curlews. **1898** (1900) Davie *Nests N. Amer. Birds* 107, The White Ibis or Spanish Curlew is distributed in summer throughout the South Atlantic and Gulf States from the Carolinas southward. **1917** (1923) *Birds Amer.* 1.177, The young birds before they assume the adult plumage are called "Stone Curlews" by the fishermen, and the old birds, which are popularly supposed to be of a different species, are usually referred to as "Spanish Curlews" or "White Curlews." **1955** *Oriole* 20.1.3 **GA,** White Ibis. . . *Spanish Curlew* (various birds with decurved beaks are miscalled curlews); "Spanish" to distinguish it from the true curlews. **1957** *AmSp* 32.184 **FL, GA, LA,** Spanish curlew—White ibis. **1969** Longstreet *Birds FL* 29, White Ibis—*Other names:* Spanish Curlew, White Curlew [etc].

2 =**long-billed curlew.**

1845 in 1943 Carleton *Prairie Logbooks* 231, It was quite as large as the Spanish curlew, or sickle-bill, but had a brown head—white body—black wings, and blue legs. **1854** Wailes *Rept. on Ag. & Geol. MS* 322, Numenius longirostris. Spanish curlew. **1888** Trumbull *Names of Birds* 198, Sickle-bill Curlew. . . To many gunners along the shores of South Carolina and Georgia, and at St. Augustine, Fla., it is the *Spanish Curlew*—this name being given in books to the White Ibis. **1910** Wayne *Birds SC* 55, The "Spanish Curlew," as this species is locally known, is now almost extinct on the South Carolina coast, where it once swarmed in countless multitudes. **1934** *Wilson Bulletin* 46.174 **SC,** In 1867 Long-billed Curlew, locally known as Spanish Curlew, were plentiful on Lady's Island, S.C. **1957** *AmSp* 32.184 **FL, GA, MS, SC,** Spanish curlew—Long-billed curlew.

3 =**willet.**

1946 Hausman *Eastern Birds* 272, *Eastern Willet.* . . Other Names . . Spanish Curlew, Pied-winged Curlew, White-winged Curlew. . . The extended wings are strikingly black and white.

4 =**Hudsonian curlew.**

1957 *AmSp* 32.184 **SC, TX,** Spanish curlew—Hudsonian curlew.

Spanish dagger(s) n Also *Spanish dagger tree* [See quot 1861] Cf **Spanish bayonet 1,** ~ **needle 2**

Any of var **yuccas** such as *Yucca aloifolia* or *Y. gloriosa*.

1837 (1962) Williams *Territory FL* 68, It [=pomegranate] certainly would be very ornamental, and if interspersed with . . Spanish dagger (*yucca draconis,*) the hedge would be also formidable. **1853** Bremer *Homes* (transl. Howitt) 2.375 **GA,** One of those plants, called *Yucca gloriosa,* as well as the Spanish dagger, sends forth its pointed dagger-like leaves in all directions from the stem, and has a cluster of splen-

did white bell-shaped flowers. **1861** Wood *Class-Book* 709, Yucca [spp]. . . Bear's-grass. Spanish Daggers. *Ibid,* Y. aloefolia. . . Spanish Daggers. . . Leaves a foot or more long, sharp and rigid like daggers. **1867** *Harper's New Mth. Mag.* 34.776 **TX,** I would have a Spanish dagger-tree in full bloom, with the motto, 'Joy after Sorrow'. **1894** *Jrl. Amer. Folkl.* 7.102 **AL,** Yucca aloifolia . . Spanish daggers. **1898** [see **Spanish bayonet 1**]. **1929** Dobie *Vaquero* 203 **West,** The proud Spanish dagger, which affords a poison effective in antidoting rattlesnake bite. **1939** Pickwell *Deserts* 25 **CA,** The Spanish Daggers (Yucca mohavensis [=Y. schidigera]) were blooming, in March, in the famous San Gorgonio Pass. **1953** Greene–Blomquist *Flowers South* 10, Spanish-dagger (Y. gloriosa). . . grows naturally further inland. **1967** *DARE* (Qu. T5, . . *Kinds of evergreens, other than pine*) Inf **TX22,** Spanish dagger—yucca. **1967** *DARE* Tape **TX24,** [FW:] Now, dagger string is stripped off of—? [Inf:] These Spanish daggers. You see, you can take and roast that just a little bit and it's pliable; **TX29,** We have Spanish dagger around here. . . The Spanish dagger grows tall and has the great white bloom. **2002** (acc) U.S. Dept. Ag. *Plants Database* (Internet), *Yucca baccata* Torr. var. *brevifolia.* . . Spanish dagger.

Spanish drake n

=**red-breasted merganser.**

1916 *Times–Picayune* (New Orleans LA) 26 Mar 2/2, Red-breasted Merganser. . . The variety of local names possessed by this bird (Becscie de mer, saw-bill, fish-duck, Spanish drake) show that it is a well known winter visitor. **1931** Read *LA French* 8, It [=the red-breasted merganser] is known in English as the "Spanish drake" or "fish duck."

Spanish flag n [See quot 1887]

A California **rockfish 3** (here: *Sebastes rubrivinctus*).

1880 U.S. Natl. Museum *Proc.* 3.292 **sCA,** The "Spanish Flag" . . is the most brilliantly colored large fish on the Pacific coast. **1887** Goode *Amer. Fishes* 266 **CA,** At Monterey, the Spanish-Flag, *Sebastichthys rubricinctus* [=*Sebastes rubrivinctus*], is known by the very appropriate name of "Spanish Flag," from its broad bands of red, white, and red. **1928** Pan-Pacific Research Inst. *Jrl.* 3.13, *Sebastodes rubrivinctus.* . . Spanish flag. Recorded for California and Queen Charlotte Islands.

Spanish fly n Also *Spanish leapfrog, Spaniola*

Any of var leapfrog games played by children; see quots.

1864 *Amer. Boy's Book* 18, Spanish Fly. The first boy out, by counting, sets a back as in playing "Leap-Frog." . . Then they all leap back; and then over him in the second position of leap-frog. In the last leap, the leader leaves his cap on the boy's back, and the others must jump over without displacing the cap, until the last, who must take it with him as he leaps. If either fail to do this, the failing boy sets a back for the rest. **1891** *Jrl. Amer. Folkl.* 4.228 **Brooklyn NYC,** *Spanish fly.* This game is similar to "Head and Footer" and "Par," except that the one who is "it" remains stationary, and the "leader," who vaults first, practises or suggests various feats or tricks, in which the others must follow him. **1901** *DN* 2.148 **csNH,** *Spanish fly.* . . A kind of leap-frog. **1909** *DN* 3.373 **eAL, wGA,** Spanish leap-frog. . . A game in which three players are down, as in leap-frog, two with buttocks together with hands clasped underneath, the third putting his head underneath and grasping a leg of the other two. The other players must turn somersault over these. **1940** Harbin *Fun Encycl.* 185, *"Hat's on Davy!"* (Spanish fly).—This is still another variation of leapfrog. . . The leader calls "Spanish Fly!" as he leaps over the "bender." As he goes over he must hot hand the "bender" on the thigh. . . Finally, "Hats on Davy!" is the call. Each player leaps over depositing his cap on the "bender's" back as he leaps over. If a player fails or if he knocks a hat off he is "It." **1957** *Sat. Eve. Post Letters* **CA,** *Spaniola*—A leap-frog game. Must do stunt over boy who is down (who squats with side to contestants with hands braced on knees). If you do not do same stunt as leader you are down—such as 1 or 2 hand knucks—swats—licks, etc. **1963** Allen *Legends & Lore S. IL* 392 **csIL,** Among the almost forgotten games were hat ball, bull pen, old sow, . . Spanish leap frog [etc].

Spanish grunt n

A **grunt n 1** (here: *Haemulon macrostomum*).

1941 Longley *Systematic Catalogue Fishes* 123, Haemulon macrostomum. . . Spanish Grunt; Gray Grunt. **2002** *DARE* File—Internet **FL,** The Spanish grunt is identified by bold black stripes on the upper body, a yellowish-green tint on the dorsal hump and a yellow saddle spot on the base of the tail.

Spanish gull n

Either the Caspian **tern** or the **royal tern.**

1921 LA Dept. of Conserv. *Bulletin* 10.137, The Caspian tern is found on the coast throughout the year. It is known sometimes, like the next species [=the royal tern], as "Spanish gull" and "red-billed gull."

Spanish hamburger n

=**sloppy joe 1.**

1916 *Ogden Std.* (UT) 28 Oct 9/1, [Advt:] Lunch Specials . . *10c* . . Hamburger Sandwich, Spanish. **1926** *Van Nuys News* (CA) [5 Feb] 8/5 (newspaperarchive.com), The menu consisted of Spanish Hamburger with spaghetti, carrot and orange salad [etc]. **1936** *WI Rapids Daily Tribune* (WI) 3 Jan 7/8, [Advt:] Introducing Something New—"Spanish Hamburger Sandwich." **1957** Showalter *Mennonite Cookbook* 59 **OR,** Spanish Hamburger. . . Fry onion and hamburger . . until browned. Add chopped celery, green pepper and seasoning. Add tomato soup and simmer 30 minutes. **1974** *Lancaster Eagle–Gaz.* (OH) 9 July 4/4, [Advt:] Spanish Hamburger Plate *99¢.* **2002** in 2009 *DARE* File—Internet ne**WI,** Booyah- Bratwurst & Spanish Hamburger Festival August 10 At The Brown County Sportsmen's Club. *Ibid* **IN** (as of 1950s), They served a great Spanish Hamburger (similar to today's Sloppy Joes). **2009** *Ibid* ne**WI,** Spanish Hamburger . . [recipe includes hamburger, onions, green pepper, ketchup, vinegar, sugar, salt, pepper, mustard, Worcestershire sauce, lemon juice]. . . Eat on buns. *Ibid* **Milwaukee WI,** Spanish hamburger—sloppy Joe to everyone else.

Spanish jack n

=**rainbow runner.**

1973 Knight *Cook's Fish Guide* 383, Jack . . spanish see Runner, Rainbow.

Spanish ladyfish n   Also *Spanish lady*   Cf **ladyfish 2**

A **hogfish a** (here: *Bodianus rufus*).

1862 *NY Times* (NY) 17 Aug 7/6, [Advt:] *Barnum's American Museum.* . . [T]he Aquaria is now swarming with *fifty beautiful angel fish,* . . *Spanish lady fish,* and other rare and splendid specimens, all of brilliant colors. **1876** U.S. Natl. Museum *Bulletin* 5.37, *Harpe rufus* [= *Bodianus rufus*]. . . Spanish Lady-fish. [*Ibid* 38, The name is not inappropriate, for the species is remarkable for the grace of its form and the beauty and elegance of its colors.] **1887** Goode *Amer. Fishes* 205, In this limpid pool were many gorgeously-colored species, . . the rainbowfish, the Spanish-lady [etc]. **2002** U.S. Food & Drug Admin. *Seafood List* (Internet), Scientific Name: *Bodianus rufus.* . . Vernacular: Spanish ladyfish.

Spanish leapfrog   See **Spanish fly**

Spanish lettuce n

A **miner's lettuce** (here: *Claytonia perfoliata*).

1888 *West Amer. Scientist* 5.126, C[laytonia] Perfoliata. . . A succulent annual, with small white or rose-colored flowers. . . in California it is known as Spanish Lettuce. **1895** Torrey Bot. Club *Bulletin* 22.107, C[laytonia] perfoliata . . , of the Pacific States, where it is known as "Spanish Lettuce," is eaten as salad and cooked as greens. **1939** Medsger *Edible Wild Plants* 145, Indian Lettuce, or Spanish Lettuce, or Miners' Lettuce.

Spanish lily n

A **blue dicks** (here: *Dichelostemma capitatum,* formerly *Brodiaea pulchella*).

1894 *Jrl. Amer. Folkl.* 7.101 **CA,** *Brodiæa capitata* . . hog onion, Spanish lily. Santa Barbara Co. **1897** Parsons *Wild Flowers CA* 262, *Brodiæa capitata.* . . They have a number of other common names, such as "Spanish-lily" [etc]. **1905** *Out West Mag.* 22.312 s**CA,** Here and there are colonies of the drooping Brodiaea or "Spanish Lily," that [are] tall, violet-colored and most gracious.

Spanish mackerel n

1 Std: a fish of the genus *Scomberomorus,* usu *S. maculatus.* For other names of this fish see **houndfish 4;** for other names of var spp see **cavalla 1, kingfish 2, king mackerel, Monterey Spanish ~, painted ~, pintado, sierra**

2 A **greenling** (here: *Pleurogrammus monopterygius*).

1886 Turner *Contribs. AK* 96, *Pleurogrammus monopterygius.* . . Several persons referred to these fish as "Spanish Mackerel". . . and all who ate of them . . spoke of their great resemblance in taste to the Atlantic Mackerel.

3 =**bonito 1.**

1887 Goode *Amer. Fishes* 208 **CT, NY, RI,** Great quantities of them [=bonito] are taken to New York, and there, as well as in Rhode Island and Connecticut, they are sold exclusively under the name of "Spanish Mackerel," at prices ranging from thirty-five to fifty cents a pound. **1939** Natl. Geogr. Soc. *Fishes* 338, There are complications even among mackerel. Spanish mackerel serves as the better-known New England and vice versa. King mackerel serves as Spanish, and bonito may be served as either Spanish or King mackerel.

4 =**jack mackerel 2.**

1946 La Monte *N. Amer. Game Fishes* 40, California Horse mackerel. . . Names: Spanish Mackerel, Saurel. **1953** Roedel *Common Fishes CA* 83, Pacific Jack Mackerel. . . Unauthorized Names: Horse mackerel, Spanish mackerel. **2005** *Los Angeles Times* (CA) 22 June sec F 1 (Internet), There is aji, Trachurus japonicus, usually labeled Spanish mackerel, though it is more accurately a jack mackerel.

Spanish man-of-war n

=**man-o'-war bird.**

1955 *Oriole* 20.1.2, Man-o'-war-bird.—Spanish Man-of-war (elaboration of the name comparing this bird to a great ship, like which it has superior navigating, i.e., flying, ability.)

Spanish mockingbird n

Either a **loggerhead shrike** (here: *Lanius ludovicianus ludovicianus*), **phainopepla,** or a **scissortail 1** (here: *Tyrannus forficatus*).

1900 *Auk* 17.345 cs**TX,** *Milvulus forficatus.* . . Abundant summer resident. . . Local name, 'Spanish Mockingbird.' **1926** Kyne *Understanding Heart* 243 **CA,** He came out whistling, the soft, mellow, warbling notes of a Spanish mockingbird. **1946** *Condor* 48.50 sw**CA** (as of c1890), It took me some time to discover that our 'Spanish Mockingbird' was the Phainopepla. **1957** *AmSp* 32.184, Spanish mockingbird[:] Phainopepla—Calif. Scissor-tailed flycatcher—Texas[.] Southern shrike—La., Texas.

Spanish moss n   Cf **cypress moss 1, gum ~**

Std: a pendant epiphytic bromeliad, *Tillandsia usneoides,* common in the southern US.   Also called **barbe espagnole, black moss, cattle ~, chinking ~, crepe ~, deer ~ 1, Dole's beard, Florida moss, gray ~, hanging ~, hinahina 1, long moss, moss n 2a, old-man's-beard 1, ~-whiskers 2, swamp moss 2, tree ~ 2a**   Cf **ball moss, gum ~, pine 2, wild pine**

Spanish mulberry n   TX

=**French mulberry.**

1818 Darby *Emigrant's Guide* 63 **LA,** The underwood, spice wood, Spanish mulberry . . and other vines . . [are] indicative of a productive soil. **1920** *Torreya* 20.24 **TX,** *Callicarpa americana.* . . Spanish mulberry. **1951** *PADS* 15.40 **TX,** *Callicarpa americana.* . . French mulberry in eastern Texas; Spanish or Mexican mulberry in central and southern parts of the state. **1970** Correll *Plants TX* 1339, American beautyberry . . Spanish-mulberry [etc]. **2002** (acc) TX Parks & Wildlife—State Parks *Rusk & Palestine State Parks* (Internet), Some species found in both parks include loblolly pine, . . Spanish mulberry [etc].

Spanish needle n

1 also *Spanish nettle;* freq pl: =**beggar ticks 1** or its seed. **chiefly Midl, Sth**   See Map   Cf **needle 2, Spanish bayonet 2**

1739 (1946) Gronovius *Flora Virginica* 94, Bidens Americana. . . semine bidentato tenui nigro, vestibus tenaciter adhærente. *Spanish-needle.* [=The American bidens. . . with a thin, black, two-pronged seed that clings tenaciously to clothing. *Spanish-needle.*] **1819** (1821) Nuttall *Jrl.* 29, The corn-fields . . are so overrun with . . seeds of different species of Bidens or Spanish-needles, as to prove extremely troublesome to woollen clothes. **1873** *Winfield Courier* (KS) 17 July 1/4, Sensations of exquisite joy . . thrill through it like Spanish needles through a pair of tow linen trowsers. **1892** *Jrl. Amer. Folkl.* 5.98, Bidens (all species), Spanish needles. Ill. and Central States generally. **1930** OK Univ. Biol. Surv. *Pub.* 2.83, Bidens bipinnata. . . Spanish Needles. Bidens cernua. . . Water Spanish Needles. **1934** *Torreya* 34.132 **FL,** We call similar fruits in the north, Beggar-ticks, but these are named Spanish or Shepherd's needles, Bidens pilosa. **1949** *WELS Suppl.* sw**WI,** I . . was especially interested in the names of the little brown stick-tights. . . We always called them "Spanish needles." *Ibid* sw**WI,** We called those little pests, "Spanish needles." *Ibid* se**WI,** Spanish needles—seems to me they were under pine trees, at any rate long and sharp, and we pinned leaves with them. *Ibid* **eNC,** Spanish needle. *Ibid* **cIL,** In central Illinois we called the thing you described *Spanish needles.* **1950** *WELS* (*Small, flat weed seeds with two prongs that cling to clothing*) 1 Inf, **WI,** Stick-tight—Spanish needle. **1965–70** *DARE* (Qu. S14, . . *Prickly seeds, small and flat, with two prongs at one end, that cling to clothing*) 203 Infs, **chiefly Midl, Sth,** Spanish needles; **FL27, HI4, OH69,** Spanish needle; **DC8,** Spanish needles—long like toothpick, flared at one end, 1–1½″ long, stick to dogs; **GA70,** Spanish needles—2 kinds: long and short; long ones called darning needles; **IL126,** Spanish nettles; **MD32,** Spanish needles—proper name for darning needles; **MD42,** Spanish needles—needle-like shape; **NJ2,** Spanish needles—in Delaware; **VA24,** Spanish needles—like a little needle, black; 2 types, one in fields, another in woods; (Qu. S15, . . *Weed seeds that cling to clothing*) 14 Infs, **chiefly Midl, Sth,** Spanish needles; **KY56, MO39, SC31,** Spanish needle; **KY68,** Spanish needles—long, thin; **MD49,** Spanish needles—long, needle-like shape; **SC34,** Spanish needle—1–1½″—like a needle; (Qu. S13) Infs **IL78, MO1, OH59,** 65, 72, **PA70,** Spanish needles; (Qu. S21, . . *Weeds . . that are a trouble in gardens and fields*) Infs **FL27, NC33,** Spanish needle; **FL4, KY40,** Spanish needles; (Qu. S25) Inf **IA29,** Spanish needle. **1976** Bruce *How to Grow Wildflowers* 229, Spanish Needles (*B. bipinnata*) is a plain relative whose two long teeth are barbed, making its seeds an adhesive nuisance to anyone unlucky enough to blunder into a patch of it. **1981** Pederson *LAGS Basic Materials,* 1 inf, **csMS,** Spanish needle leaves—used to make a poultice to cure shingles; 1 inf, **cnAR,** Spanish needles. **2007** *DARE* File—Internet **FL,** My neighbors with the dog are not gardeners. . . They do grow a lot of spanish needles.

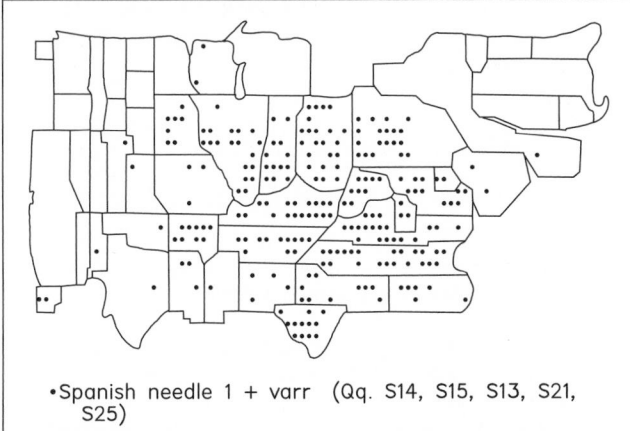

•Spanish needle 1 + varr (Qq. S14, S15, S13, S21, S25)

2 also pl: A **yucca.** Cf **Spanish bayonet 1, ~ dagger(s)**
  1966 *DARE* (Qu. S15) Inf **WA6,** Spanish needles—yucca. **2002** *DARE* File—Internet, These adults [=skipper butterflies] lay eggs upon the leaves of the Spanish needle or yucca.

3 A **dragonfly.**
  1973 Allen *LAUM* 1.319 (as of c1950) 1 inf, **NE,** Spanish needle.

4 A plant (*Palafoxia arida*) of the Desert Southwest.
  1942 Kearney *Flowering Plants* 978 **CA,** *Palafoxia lincaris*. . . This plant known in California as Spanish-needles apparently is rapidly spreading eastward along highways in Arizona. **2002** *DARE* File—Internet **CA,** Giant Spanish needle (Palafoxia var. gigantea) is an attractive pink-flowered member of the sunflower, or aster family. *Ibid,* The common Spanish needle [=*Palafoxia arida* var *arida*] generally grows to be only two feet tall, or less, and is found throughout much of the Sonoran and Mojave deserts.

Spanish nettle n
1 =**buffalo burr.**
  1940 Steyermark *Flora MO* 468, Buffalo Bur, Spanish Nettle (*Solanum rostratum*). . . A weed introduced from the Southwest and spreading north over the state.

2 See **Spanish needle 1.**

Spanish oak n
Any of var **oaks** native chiefly to the southern and eastern US:
a Used generically or in ref to specific trees not identifiable from the context.
  1671 in 1897 SC Hist. Soc. *Coll.* 5.333, This Land bears very good . . Spanish, & liue oak. **1716** Petiver *Petiveriana* 11, *Spanish Oak.* Splits very well. **1775** *Amer. Husbandry* 1.376 **SC,** *Red oak* grows sometimes

very large and lofty. . . *Spanish oak,* more durable, is used sometimes in ship-building. **1965–70** *DARE* (Qu. T10, . . *Kinds of oak trees*) 20 Infs, **chiefly Sth, S Midl,** Spanish oak.
b Used specifically:
(1) =**red oak 2b. esp Delmarva**
  1681 in 1904 New Castle DE Court *Records* 503, Beginning att a Corner marked spannish oake. [*DARE* Ed: Cf quot 1837.] **1785** Marshall *Arbustrum* 123, *Upland Red Oak*. . . The timber is generally worm eaten, or rotten at heart, therefore of little esteem. It is likewise commonly known by the name of Spanish Oak. **1812** Michaux *Histoire des Arbres* 2.104, Quercus falcata. . . Dans le Maryland, le Delaware et la Virginie, cette espèce de Chêne est connue sous le seul nom de *Spanish oak* . . , tandis que, dans les deux Carolines et la Géorgie, elle est désignée sous celui de *Red Oak*. [=Quercus falcata. . . In Maryland, Delaware and Virginia, this species of oak is known only as *Spanish oak* . . , while in the two Carolinas and Georgia, it is called *Red oak*.] **1837** Darlington *Flora Cestrica* 532 sePA, Q[uercus] rubra. . . I think both this and the preceding [=Q. coccinea] are often called *Spanish Oak;* but that name seems properly to belong to another species (viz. Q. *falcata* . .), which . . is abundant in the Counties of New Castle [DE], and Cecil [MD], on the South of us. **1859** *Scientific Amer.* 1.302, There are four species of oak barks chiefly used in tanning. The first is the Spanish oak, which thrives in Maryland, Delaware, and Virginia, and in all the States south of 41°N. . . In Georgia and the Carolinas it is known by the name of "red oak." **1860** Curtis *Cat. Plants NC* 39, Spanish Oak. (Q. falcata, Michx.)—This is generally known in this State, I think, by the name of *Red Oak,* though sometimes called as above. **1950** Peattie *Nat. Hist. Trees* 222, On many a campus of Virginia's old colleges, the ancient boles of Spanish Oak are marbled with a growth of pale lichens till they look like columns. **1980** Little *Audubon Guide N. Amer. Trees E. Region* 389, [Quercus falcata is] often called Spanish Oak, possibly because it commonly occurs in areas of the early Spanish colonies. It is unlike any oaks native to Spain.
(2) =**scarlet oak 1.**
  [**1812** Michaux *Histoire des Arbres* 2.116, Partout où je viens d'indiquer que le *Quercus coccinea* se trouve dans les Etats-Unis, il est confondu soit avec le vrai Chêne rouge, ou avec le vrai Chêne d'Espagne, *Quercus falcata;* . . dans les Etats du Nord, il est connu des habitans sous le nom de Chêne rouge; et dans ceux du milieu et du Sud, à partir de Philadelphie, sous celui de Chêne d'Espagne. [=In all the places I have just shown that *Quercus coccinea* is found in the United States, it is confused with either the true Red oak or the true Spanish oak, *Quercus falcata;* . . inhabitants of the Northern States know it by the name of Red oak; and in the middle and Southern [states], south of Philadelphia, by that of Spanish oak.]] **1837** [see **b(1)** above]. **1860** Curtis *Cat. Plants NC* 40, Scarlet Oak. . . This is generally confounded with the preceding species [=*Quercus tinctoria*], and called *Spanish* and *Red Oak* in this State. **1908** Britton *N. Amer. Trees* 293, Scarlet Oak. . . A tree preferring sandy, dry soil, from Maine to Minnesota, North Carolina and Missouri. . . It is also called Red oak, Black oak, and Spanish oak. **1947** Collingwood–Brush *Knowing Trees* 190, Known widely as scarlet oak, it is also called red oak and Spanish oak. **1979** Little *Checklist U.S. Trees* 228, Scarlet oak. . . Other common names—black oak, Spanish oak.
(3) =**red oak 2a.**
  1837 [see **b(1)** above]. **1860** Curtis *Cat. Plants NC* 41, Red Oak (Q. rubra, Linn.)—This, like the preceding species [=the scarlet oak], is sometimes called *Spanish Oak,* though it is as strongly marked a tree as can be found in our forests. **1882** U.S. Natl. Museum *Proc.* 5.83, *Quercus rubra*. Red Oak; "Spanish Oak"; "Turkey Oak." **1898** *Bot. Gaz.* 26.254 swMO, *Quercus rubra* . . red oak, Spanish oak (lowland variety). **1960** Vines *Trees SW* 186, Northern Red Oak. . . Vernacular names are Leopard Oak, . . Champion Oak, Black Oak and Spanish Oak.
(4) =**Texas oak.**
  1897 Sudworth *Arborescent Flora* 167 **TX,** Texan Oak. . . Spanish Oak. **1939** Tharp *Vegetation TX* 52, Spanish oak (Q. texana). **1970** Correll *Plants TX* 489, Texas red oak, Spanish oak. . . On rocky limestone slopes of the cen[tral] Tex[as] uplands; endemic. **1979** Little *Checklist U.S. Trees* 241, Texas oak. . . Other common names—Texas red oak, Spanish oak, spotted oak. **2001** in 2006 *DARE* File—Internet **TX,** Spanish Oak (Quercus Shumardii var. texana) is also known as Texas Oak (Quercus texana or Quercus buckleyi).
(5) =**cherrybark oak. Cf swamp Spanish oak 2**
  1899 NC Ag. Exper. Sta. *Bulletin* 164.340, Quercus . . falcata pagodaefolia. . . Spanish Oak. **1903** Small *Flora SE U.S.* 352, *Quercus*

pagodaefolia. . . In river swamps or low grounds, Virginia and Indiana to Missouri and Georgia. *Spanish Oak.* **1960** Vines *Trees SW* 189, Cherry-bark Red Oak. . . Vernacular names are Spanish Oak, Turkey Oak [etc].

(6) =Shumard oak.

1903 Small *Flora SE U.S.* 351, *Quercus Schneckii* [=*Q. shumardii*]. . . On plains and prairies, Iowa to Florida and Texas. Spanish Oak. **1913** TX Acad. Sci. *Trans. for 1910–12* 12.73, *Quercus Schneckii.* . . Spanish Oak. Also called Scarlet Oak. **1939** Tharp *Vegetation TX* 52, Spanish oak *(Q. shumardii).* **1960** Vines *Trees SW* 192, Shumard Oak. . . Vernacular names are Spotted Oak, Leopard Oak, and Spanish Oak.

(7) =pin oak 1a. Cf **swamp Spanish oak 1**

1874 Geol. Surv. OH *Report* 2.1.637, The chestnut . . and the Spanish oak *(Quercus palustris)* are everywhere characteristic trees. **1908** *Jrl. Economic Entomology* 8.202, Spanish oak. Pin oak. (*Quercus palustris* Durni.) West to San Antonio. A good honey and pollen plant. **1945** Wodehouse *Hayfever Plants* 78, Spanish oak *(Q. palustris).* **1960** Vines *Trees SW* 185, Pin Oak. . . Vernacular names are Swamp Spanish Oak, Swamp Oak, and Spanish Oak. **1973** Stephens *Woody Plants* 120, Pin oak, swamp oak, Spanish oak, water oak. **1980** Little *Audubon Guide N. Amer. Trees E. Region* 403, Pin Oak . . "Spanish Oak."

(8) Any of var other **oaks** such as **canyon oak 1, oracle oak,** or **overcup oak 1.**

1910 Jepson *Silva CA* 47, *Quercus Morehus* [=*Quercus* x *moreha*]. . . In El Dorado County it is termed Spanish Oak by the settlers, who value its wood above that of either parent. *Ibid* 223, Maul Oak [=*Quercus chrysolepis*]. . . Woodsmen frequently know it as Spanish Oak. **1913** *Torreya* 13.229 **AR**, *Quercus lyrata.* . . Spanish oak, Big Lake, Ark.

Spanish pincushion n Cf **pincushion flower 3**
=buttonbush 1.

1923 FL Dept. Ag. *Qrly. Bulletin* 33.24, Button-Bush, or Spanish pincushion as it is known in Florida. **1960** Vines *Trees SW* 938, Vernacular names for the shrub are Spanish Pincushion, River-brush, Swampwood [etc].

Spanish stopper n

A **stopper 1a** (here: *Eugenia foetida*).

1884 Sargent *Forests of N. Amer.* 88, *Eugenia buxifolia* [=*E. foetida*]. . . Gurgeon Stopper. Spanish Stopper. Semi-tropical Florida, cape Canaveral to the southern keys, west coast. **1962** Harrar–Harrar *Guide S. Trees* 544, Spanish Stopper. . . This is a West Indian tree that extends northward to southern Florida, where it seldom becomes more than a large shrub. **1982** *Miami Herald* (FL) 24 Oct sec H 11, *E. foetida*, Spanish stopper, grows its fruit all along its branches, and has lots of tightly packed little leaves.

Spanish tea n

A **Jerusalem oak 1** (here: *Chenopodium ambrosioides*).

1851 Dunglison *Med. Lexicon* 196, Chenopo′dium Ambrosioï′des. . . *Mexico Tea, Spanish Tea.* **1935** (1943) Muenscher *Weeds* 206, Spanish-tea, Strong-scented pigweed. **1974** Morton *Folk Remedies* 43 **SC**, Spanish tea. . . Plant juice or infusion valued as a vermifuge for children.

Spanish thistle n

1 A **cockleburr 1** (here: *Xanthium spinosum*).

1837 Elliot *Washington Guide* 309 **DC**, Xanthium spinosum. Spanish thistle. **1935** (1943) Muenscher *Weeds* 527, *Xanthium spinosum.* . . Spiny cocklebur, Spiny clotbur, Clotweed, Spanish thistle, Dagger cocklebur. **1959** Munz–Keck *CA Flora* 1105, *X[anthium] spinosum.* . . Spiny Clotbur. Spanish-Thistle. . . Common weed of old pastures and waste places. **1970** *DARE* (Qu. S21, . . *Weeds . . that are a trouble in gardens and fields*) Inf **CA**189, Spanish thistles. [*DARE* Ed: Inf may refer instead to **2** below.] **2003** Beidleman–Kozloff *Plants San Francisco Bay* 110, *Xanthium spinosum.* . . Spanish Thistle.

2 =buffalo burr.

1896 KS Ag. Exper. Sta. Manhattan *Bulletin* 57.23, *Solanum rostratum.* . . (Texas-nettle, Buffalo Bur, Bull-nettle, Spanish Thistle, Mexican Thistle, Texas Thistle, Colorado Bur, Bull Thistle, Beaked Horse-nettle, Spiny Nightshade.) Annual, very prickly. Leaves lobed. Flowers yellow. Fruit prickly. A common and troublesome weed found throughout Kansas. Native. **1898** *Jrl. Amer. Folkl.* 11.276 **KS**, *Solanum rostratum.* . . Spanish thistle, Texas thistle, bull thistle [etc]. **1957** *Chillicothe Constitution–Tribune* (MO) 18 Sept 7/7, The clear, intense yellow of the sunflower, the goldenrod, the squareweed and the Spanish thistle all combine . . to lend the mellow glow that is September's greatest charm.

Spanish, walk v phr

To walk or proceed under physical compulsion, esp partially suspended; to obey, "toe the line"—often in phr *make one walk Spanish.*

1815 *Amer. Republican* (Downington, Pa.) Feb. *(DA)*, The vet'ran troops who conquer'd Spain, Thought they our folks would banish; But Jackson settled half their men, And made the rest *walk Spanish!* **1865** *Harper's New Mth. Mag.* 32.64 **NEng**, Jenkins married agin, and his wife's got a pianny, and her and the girls they keep hot water in the house all the time. She makes Jenkins walk Spanish, I can tell you. **1884** Baldwin *Yankee School-Teacher* 31 **NY**, I ain't 'fraid o' you nor any other man; wa'n't a man in old Onta' I [=a woman] couldn't make walk Spanish. **1890** *DN* 1.63, *Wheelbarrow.* . . Cf. the New England phrase to "walk Spanish." A boy is said to walk Spanish when he is lifted from behind by the seat of his trousers, so that he has to walk on his toes. **1906** Lincoln *Mr. Pratt* 257 **NY**, He moved then, "walking Spanish," like the boy in the school-yard. **1912** *DN* 3.582 **wIN**, Make one walk Spanish. . . To make one walk hurriedly by lifting him up a little by the hair on the back of the head.

Spanish water oak See **water oak 2f**

Spanish whippoorwill n
=chuck-will's-widow.

1854 Wailes *Rept. on Ag. & Geol. MS* 322, The *variety* [of whippoorwill] found in the southern part of the State . . is known familiarly as the *Spanish* whippoorwill, or Chuckwill's widow. **1932** Howell *FL Bird Life* 297, Chuck-will's-widow. . . Other Names: Dutch Whip-poor-will; Spanish Whip-poor-will. **1957** *AmSp* 32.184 **FL, MS**, Spanish whippoorwill—Chuck-will's-widow.

Spanish wild cherry n
=islay 1.

1893 *Jrl. Amer. Folkl.* 6.140 **CA**, *Prunus ilicifolia*, Spanish wild cherry. **1908** Britton *N. Amer. Trees* 512, Islay. . . Among Californian common names for it are Holly-leaf cherry, Evergreen cherry, Spanish wild cherry.

spank See **spang** adv

spank-brand new adj phr [Var of *spanking-brand new*] **esp Sth** Cf **brand-spanking-new, spanfired**

Completely new.

1937 in 1958 Brewer *Dog Ghosts* 94 **TX** [Black], She looks on top of de chifferobe an' tecks down a spank-brand new breeches quilt what Mirandy, Jim's fuss wife, done quilted. **1971** Killens *Cotillion* 36 **NYC** [Black], If I could hit the numbers for ten thousand dollars just one time, I'd buy me a spank brand-new long white Caddy. **2002** in 2007 *DARE* File—Internet **eTX**, I heard this term used by folks that live in East Texas. I got me a spank brand new truck. **2004** *Ibid* **swGA**, I have a friend who sells industrial motors and just gave me a spank brand new 1 hp GE "farm" motor. **2007** *Ibid* **seTN**, Box Chevy 4 door, Spank Brand New paint (white).

spank dab See **spang** adv 2

spankfire See **spanfired**

spannel See **spaniel**

spanners, spannies, spanning See **span** n

spanquittin' See **spang-cubes**

‡**span together** v phr Cf *DS* II3

Fig: to get on well, be compatible.

[**1828** Webster *Amer. Dict.*, Span, . . To agree in color, or in color and size; as, the horses span well. *[New England.]*] **1951** West *Witch Diggers* 251 **IN**, Dandie and me speak the same language. Yes, sir, we span together pretty near perfect.

spanworm n [See quot 1842]
=looper.

1820 *Amer. Farmer* 1.375 **MD**, What can our obliging correspondents tell us about the . . best method of destroying that dreadful plague of our orchards, the *span worm*. **1842** Harris *Treatise Insects* 330 **NEng**, The caterpillars of the *Geometrae* of Linnaeus, earth-measurers, as the term implies, or geometers, span-worms, and loopers, have received these several names from their peculiar manner of moving. **1864** *Scientific Amer.* 11.293 **NYC**, It [=the reed bird] eats the canker worm and it eats your span worm that gets on the trees in this city. **1884** (1885) McCook *Tenants* 107 **PA**, If . . the cocoons [were] . . burned in winter, there would be a scant crop of span-worms in summer. **1892** Kellogg *Common Insects KS* 395, Familiar to all observers . . are the inchworms, spanworms, or loopers as they are variously called. **c1930** Brown *Amer. Folkl. Insect Lore* 4, If a measuring worm or span-worm crawled over one's clothes he was thought to be measuring one "for a new suit." **1972** Swan–Papp *Insects* 293, The Bruce spanworm is a major defoliator of aspen in the prairie regions. **2003** *Patriot Ledger* (Quincy MA) 17 May 1 (Internet), Cankerworms and spanworms are the usual culprits, although new species have been popping up in recent years.

spar See **sparrow**

sparagrass See **sparrowgrass** n[1]

sparagus n Also *sparegu(t)s, spargus* [Aphet forms of **asparagus;** *OED2 sparagus* 1542 →; "*Obs.*"]
1672 Josselyn *New-Englands Rarities* 90, *Sparagus* thrives exceedingly. **1867** Beecher *Norwood* 77 **NEng,** Some children are like poke weed. When it first comes up it's just as good to bile as 'sparagus. **1950** *WELS* (Names or nicknames for asparagus) 4 Infs, **WI,** Sparagus; 1 Inf, **cwWI,** Sparegus; 1 Inf, **csWI,** Spareguts, spargus. **1966** *Wilson Coll.* **csKY,** ['spɑrɡəs]. **1966–68** *DARE* (Qu. I29, *Names or nicknames for asparagus*) Infs **CT**17, **NY**70, **SC**26, ['spæɾɡəs]; **MO**11, ['spɛɾəɡəs]; **NY**94, ['spɛɾɡəs]; **LA**11, ['spæɾɡəs] tips; **MD**37, ['spɑrɡəs]; **MD**39, ['spɑrɡɪs]. **1997** in 2004 *Dict. Smoky Mt. Engl.* 27 **wNC, eTN,** The old timers said, "Spargus." **2007** *DARE* File—Internet **FL,** We ordered sparagus au gratin. We got sparagus with balsamic vinegar!

spare grass See **sparrowgrass** n[1]

sparegu(t)s See **sparagus**

spargassing vbl n [Cf *spargus* (at **sparagus**)]
1996 Horton *Island Out of Time* 70 **Chesapeake Bay MD,** You might go mudlarkin'—that's picking up oysters in the shallows—or spargassin', hunting wild asparagus.

spar grass See **sparrowgrass** n[1]

spargus See **sparagus**

spark v, hence vbl n *sparking* Formerly also with *it* old-fash
To court (someone); to engage in courtship; to go together as sweethearts; hence nouns *spark(er)* a beau, lover; *sparking* a courting.
1790 Tyler *Contrast* 31 **NEast,** She promised not to spark it with Solomon Dyer while I am gone. **1815** Humphreys *Yankey in England* 108, *Sparked it* (young men keeping company with young women and sitting by the fire after the family has gone to bed), courting. **1838** Kettell *Yankee Notions* 102, And jovial gallants gaily sparking / In wild excursion. **1843** (1916) Hall *New Purchase* 119 **IN,** Then is the grand sparking time, and young men go expressly as they say, to find "a most powerful heap of gals!" **1859** Taliaferro *Fisher's R.* 115 **nwNC** (as of 1820s), The young misses loved to see the young "sparkers" exercise their ingenuity in the game of "catch and keep." **1892** *DN* 1.232 **KY,** *Sparkin':* courting. "To go sparkin'." "What girl were you sparkin' last Sunday?" . . It is common in New England and Michigan. **1899** (1912) Green *VA Folk-Speech* 405, *Spark.* . . A lover; a gallant; a beau. **1905** *DN* 3.20 **cCT,** *Sparking, n.* A courting. **1911** *DN* 3.540 **eKY,** "He's out sparking every night." "He sparks every girl he sees." **1915** *DN* 4.229 **wTX,** *Sparking, pp.* or *n.* Courting, wooing. **1916** Lincoln *Mary-'Gusta* 108 **MA,** There's liable to be a good-lookin' young feller sparkin' 'round here and he'll want to marry her. **1937** Sandoz *Slogum* 54 **NE,** The old bachelor up in Dakota came sparking. **1949** (1958) Stuart *Thread* 28 **KY,** "You didn't tell me she dated anybody else!" "Yep, she's sparked Bill for a couple of years now." **1965–70** *DARE* (Qu. AA1, *When a man goes to see a girl often and seems to want to marry her, he's _____ her*) 71 Infs, **scattered,** Sparking; **KY**42, A-sparking, going a-sparking; **NC**40, **WI**27, Sparking with; **FL**36, They're sparking [Of all Infs responding to the question, 64% were old; of those giving these responses, 81% were old.]; (Qu. AA7a, . . *A woman who is very fond of men and is always trying to know more—if she's nice about it*) Inf **CA**15, Sparking; (Qu. AA8, *When people make too much of a show of affection in a public place* . . "*There they were at the church supper _____ [with each other].*") Inf **NC**22, Sparking. **1991** Still *Wolfpen Notebooks* 163 **sAppalachians,** *Spark* . . court.

spark n [Norw, Sw] **Nth**
A sled on runners with raised handles and usu a seat in front, propelled by a person standing with one foot on a runner and

using the other to push; hence v *spark* to use such a sled; vbl n *sparking*.
2004 *DARE* File **nVT** (as of early 1970s), Every winter my family would go up to Northeast Kingdom, Vermont, to visit friends. One of our favorite pastimes was to use their spark on the packed snow roads. One person would sit on the seat and the other would stand on the iron runners behind, holding on to the back of the seat, and we'd go whizzing down the hills. **2006** *Reg.–Guard* (Eugene OR) 7 Feb (Internet), The forecast was tight for some sweet sparking. . . Wasn't long after we hit the rails that Gunderson started hearing the usual buzz. "Yo, where your dogs?"[?] they hounded us, over and over again, everywhere we went. . . "Yo, where your dogs?" is generally the first response folks make when they see someone sparking by. On a spark. . . The hackneyed phrase popped forth simply because a spark looks like a dog sled, minus the dogs. **2007** *DARE* File—Internet **nMN,** One of our favorite modes of winter transportation/entertainment . . is through the use of our Sparks. *Ibid* **csWI,** Our sparks are handsomely crafted from solid oak, assembled with hot rolled steel runners and finished with multiple coats of spar varnish.

sparked-back n [*sparked* spotted, streaked]
=ruddy turnstone.
1888 Trumbull *Names of Birds* 186 **MA,** At Falmouth [the turnstone is called] *sparked-back, streaked-back,* and *bishop plover.* **1955** MA Audubon Soc. *Bulletin* 39.446 **MA,** Sparked-back, Streaked-back. . . From the bold cinnamon, black and white markings of the back wings of adult birds.

sparker, sparking vbl n[1] See **spark** v

sparking vbl n[2] See **spark** n

spark it See **spark** v

sparkle n
A **sandwort** (here: prob *Minuartia caroliniana*).
1967 *New Yorker* 25 Nov 128 **NJ,** An *Arenaria* [=*Minuartia*] . . is small and beautiful, and on its white flowers there is always a shining fluid. The plant's common name is sandwort. The pineys call it sparkle.

sparkleberry n Also *tree sparkleberry* **chiefly S Atl** Cf **parkerberry**
=farkleberry.
1837 *Boston Jrl. Nat. Hist.* 1.100 **NC,** Vaccínium arbòreum, *Sparkleberry.* **1855** (1856) Story *Caste* 93 **NEng speaker in SC,** See there is a sparkle-berry bush, all covered with jasmine. **1873** Stowe *Palmetto-Leaves* 104 **FL,** In this same hammock are certain tall, gracefull shrubs, belonging, as we fancy, to the high-huckleberry tribe, but which the Floridians call sparkleberry. **1901** Mohr *Plant Life AL* 657, Vaccinium arboreum. . . Farkleberry. Sparkleberry. **1904** (1913) Johnson *Highways South* 41 **seGA, nFL** [Black], Yo' c'n make wine out of sparkle berries. **1926** *Torreya* 26.6 **seGA,** Batodendron arboreum [=*Vaccinium a.*] . . Parker berry, "only the negroes call it sparkle berry," said my informant. **1941** Writers' Program *Guide LA* 447, Along the creeks and river grow dogwood, wild honeysuckle, bright sparkleberries, and laurel. **1946** West–Arnold *Native Trees FL* 166, The tree sparkleberry, common in hammocks and open woods, is found as far south as Manatee County. **1966–70** *DARE* (Qu. I44, *What kinds of berries grow wild around here?*) Infs **FL**49, **GA**12, **SC**62, Sparkleberries; **LA**6, Sparkleberry—a lot like huckleberries, same color as blackberries, one seed in the center; **SC**11, Sparkleberries—almost like huckleberry, but not as sweet and not as juicy, smaller. **1968** *DARE* FW Addit **GA**46, The sparkleberry doesn't make a big tree. **1974** in 1983 Johnson *I Declare* 190 **nwFL,** If you want to go in for fall color planting in greater detail, consider the . . sparkleberry, . . abundant in our North Florida woods. **2003** *Atlanta Jrl.–Constitution* (GA) 9 Jan (Internet), Sparkleberry, Vaccinium arboreum, is in the blueberry family, but the fruit is very bitter.

spar pole See **spar tree**

sparrer See **sparrow**

sparrer grass See **sparrowgrass**

sparrow n Usu |'spɛro, 'spæro|; also **Sth, S Midl** |'spar(ə)|; for addit varr see quots Pronc-spp *spar(rer), sparruh, sparry, sporrer, sporrow, sporry* See also **sparrowgrass** n[1] Cf **bar** n[4], **farrow** adj, **harrow, marrow, narrow, -y** suff[2] b
Std sense, var forms.
1849 *Knickerbocker* 34.188 **Sth** [Black], De Scripture say dat two sparrer-hawks am sold for a farden. **1860** *Atlantic Mth.* 6.557 **Sth**

[Black], Twarn't de sparrer-house. **1899** (1912) Green *VA Folk-Speech* 405, *Sparrer.* . . For *sparrow. Sporrer.* **1909** *DN* 3.373 **eAL, wGA**, *Sparrow.* . . Pronounced [spɑrə]. **1915** *DN* 4.190 **swVA**, *Spar* [spɑr]. Clipped form of *sparrow.* **1917** in 1944 *ADD* **cWV**, *Sparrow.* . . Sporrow. **1922** Gonzales *Black Border* 327 **sSC, GA coasts** [Gullah glossary], *Sparruh*—sparrow, sparrows. **1931** *PMLA* 46.1317 **sAppalachians**, *Ow* final becomes *er*, or *y*, or else is dropped entirely. . . "sparr(ow)." **1933** Miller *Lamb in His Bosom* 77 **GA**, Thee dost note the sporrer's fall. **1934** Vines *Green Thicket* 60 **cnAL**, He had a little old trunk nearly full of feathers and down . . from tiny birds like the . . English spar (sparrow). **1936** *AmSp* 11.161 **eTX**, Another group of words . . lose their final vowel sound entirely in illiterate speech. In all these words *rr* precedes the final vowel in spelling. They are: *borrow* . . *sparrow* . . *wheelbarrow.* **1938** FWP *Guide DE* 500, A sparrow is a *sporry* in some spots. **1940** Stuart *Trees of Heaven* 14 **KY**, They won't nest on the ground like a ground spar. **1942** Hall *Smoky Mt. Speech* 80 **wNC, eTN**, Words of the type *arrow.* When *-r-* precedes *-ow* . . the treatment is . . usually with [ə]. . . Examples: arrow . . sparrow . . wheelbarrow. . . Often the unstressed vowel is lost, as in . . [spɒɚ:] *sparrow*, usually with lengthening either of the vowel of the preceding syllable or of [r]. **1946** *PADS* 6.28 **ceNC** (as of 1900–10), *Spar-bird* [spɑr]. . . The sparrow. . . Common. **1967–70** *DARE* (Qu. Q4, . . *Kinds of hawks*) Inf **KY**88, Spar hawk; **KY**43, 75, **NC**67, [spɑ(ə)r] hawk; **AR**51, [spær] hawk; (Qu. Q21, . . *Kinds of sparrows*) Inf **KY**39, Spar [spɑɚ] bird; (Qu. Q22, *Joking names or nicknames for the common sparrow*) Inf **VA**47, City spar; **KY**31, Spar bird; **TN**6, Sparrers ['spærɚz]; **IL**126, Sparry ['spɛɛri]; **KY**39, Yard spar. **1983** *MJLF* 9.1.57 **ceKY** (as of 1956), *Spar bird* . . a sparrow. **2000** Shores *Tangier Is.* 180 **Chesapeake Bay**, *Arrow, sparrow*, and *narrow* usually occur with "a" for "ow," but at times one may think that he hears a weakly-colored "r" sound for the final syllable, which results in "arrer," "sparrer," and "narrer." **2004** *NADS Letters* **KY**, Spar: More Kentucky verification on this one.

sparrowgrass n¹ Also *sparagrass, spar(e) grass, sparrer grass, sparrow's grass* [*OED2* 1649 →; folk-etyms for **sparagus**] **chiefly east of Missip R** See Map Cf **spear grass** n², **spire ~**

1795 Dearborn *Columbian Grammar* 138, *List of Improprieties.* . . Sparrowgrass for Asparagus. **1837** Sherwood *Gaz. GA* 71, *Provincialisms.* . . *Sparrow-Grass*, for asparagus. **1883** (1971) Harris *Nights with Remus* 13 **GA** [Black], W'en Brer Rabbit . . see de . . sparrer-grass, . . hit make he mouf water. **1893** Shands *MS Speech* 59, *Sparrow-grass* [spærə-græs]. Negro for *asparagus.* **1894** *DN* 1.328 **NJ**, *Asparagus:* pron. [spærəgrəs]. **1899** (1912) Green *VA Folk-Speech* 405, *Sparrer-grass.* . . Asparagus. **1905** *DN* 3.20 **cCT**, *Sparrow-grass.* . . Asparagus. **1911** *DN* 3.540 **cKY**, *Sparrow-grass.* . . "asparagus." **1913** (1980) Hardy *OH Schoolmistress* 81, Next it toward the fence was a bunch of asparagus, pardon me, spare-grass, used only as an ornament when full grown. **1926** *DN* 5.389 **ME**, *Sparrow-grass* (sparrer-grass). . . Asparagus. Obsol[ete]. **1946** *AmSp* 21.99 **sIL**, Asparagus is called *spargrass.* **1965–70** *DARE* (Qu. I29, *Names or nicknames for asparagus*) 63 Infs, **chiefly east of Missip R**, Sparrowgrass; 21 Infs, **scattered**, Spare grass; **GA**46, **IL**13, 78, 134, **KY**17, 40, 42, **MD**41, **OH**41, Spar grass; **CA**107, **MA**3, **NY**65, **PA**200, Sparagrass; [**AL**15, Sparrow;] **IL**44, Sparrow's grass; (Qu. I4, . . *Vegetables . . less commonly grown around here*) Inf **MS**87, Spare grass. **1968** Pochmann *Triple Ridge* 41 **cWI**, "September's the time to move sparrowgrass," said this octogenarian. **1976** Garber *Mountain-ese* 86 **sAppalachians**, Ma cut a bunch uv

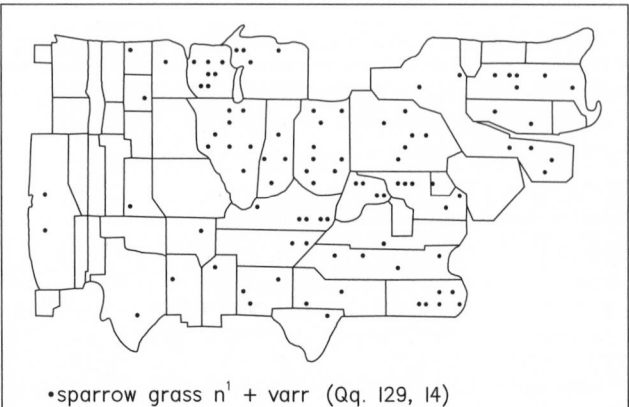

•sparrow grass n¹ + varr (Qq. I29, I4)

spargrass frum the garden. **1983** *MJLF* 9.1.57 **ceKY** (as of 1956), *Spargrass* . . asparagus. **2004** *Boston Globe* (MA) 19 May sec E 1 (Internet) **cMA**, Nancy Merritt of Hatfield has been waiting for what she calls "sparrow grass" or simply "grass" since the weather began to turn warm.

sparrow grass n² [From its providing forage and cover to sparrows]

A **beardgrass** (here: prob *Andropogon virginicus*).

1911 *DN* 3.540 **eKY**, *Sparrow-grass.* . . Fox-grass, a small variety growing in fields of maize. This meaning is confined to Eastern Kentucky.

sparrow hawk n [Because they prey on small birds]

1 Std: the American kestrel *(Falco sparverius)*. Also called **bird hawk 1, chilly ~, cleek cleek, desert hawk, grasshopper ~ 1, killy ~, mangeur poulette, mouse hawk 1c, pigeon ~ 2, swallow ~, tilly ~** Cf **billy hawk, chippy ~, ringtail ~**

2 =**sharp-shinned hawk.**

1917 (1923) *Birds Amer.* 2.66, Sharp-shinned Hawk. . . Other Names,—Pigeon Hawk; Sparrow Hawk [etc]. **1953** Jewett *Birds WA* 163, Northern Sharp-shinned Hawk. . . Other names: Bird Hawk; Sparrow Hawk; Little Blue Darter. **1966–69** *DARE* (Qu. Q4, . . *Kinds of hawks*) Inf **KY**68, Sparrow hawk—same as blue-tail hawk; **OK**42, Sparrow hawk—same as blue darter.

3 Perh =**peregrine falcon.**

1968 *DARE* (Qu. Q4, . . *Kinds of hawks*) Inf **LA**31, Sparrow hawk—duck ain't got a chance with him. [FW: Inf is not referring to what the books call sparrow hawk, though I saw these around Cameron [LA]. He apparently applies the term to one of the larger falcons, perhaps the duck hawk.]

sparrow owl n [From their brown and white coloring and small size]

1 =**saw-whet owl.**

1831 Richardson *Fauna Boreali-Amer.* 2.97, Strix Acadica. . . American Sparrow Owl, the size of the Common Thrush, primaries crossed by three or four bands of white spots; outer webs of the secondaries unspotted; two interrupted bands on the tail. **1917** (1923) *Birds Amer.* 2.107, Saw-whet Owl. . . Sparrow Owl. **1963** Gromme *Birds WI* 216, Owl, . . Sparrow (Saw-whet Owl).

2 Richardson's owl *(Aegolius funereus)*.

1858 U.S. War Dept. *Rept. Explor. Railroad* 9.xxvii, *Nyctale richardsoni.* . . Sparrow Owl. Northern North America; Canada. **1899** Howe-Sturtevant *Birds RI* 62, Richardson's Owl. *Sparrow Owl.*—A very rare and irregular winter visitant. **1917** (1923) *Birds Amer.* 2.106, Richardson's Owl. . . American Sparrow Owl; Sparrow Owl. **1946** Hausman *Eastern Birds* 364, Richardson's Owl. . . Sparrow Owl. . . Upper parts chocolate brown spotted with white.

3 A **screech owl 1** (here: *Otus asio*).

1919 Burns *Ornith. Chester Co. PA* 58, *Otus asio asio* Screech Owl, . . "sparrow owl." Common resident.

4 =**pygmy owl.** [*OED2* 1831 →]

1857 U.S. War Dept. *Rept. Explor. Railroad* (Birds) 6.77, *Glaucidium Infuscatum.* The Sparrow Owl. I procured specimens of this diminutive owl on the Cascade mountains, in Oregon, where it is not very uncommon. It occurs also in California. **1890** *Century Dict.* 5799, *Sparrow-owl.* . . Any one of many small owls of the genus *Glaucidium*. Two occur in western parts of the United States, *G. gnoma*, the gnome-owl, and *G. ferrugineum.* **1955** *AmSp* 30.181 **CA, OR**, Of bird names given for size, consider . . *Sparrow owl* (pygmy owl).

sparrow's grass See **sparrow grass**

sparruh, sparry See **sparrow**

spar tree n Also *spar pole* **chiefly Pacific NW** Cf **home tree, tail tree**

In logging: a tall tree, limbed and topped, to which rigging is attached, used esp in **high-lead** logging.

1905 *Logging by Steam* 92, The snaking or pulling lines lead from the drums on the engine through skidding blocks rigged on the spar tree. **1921** *Sandusky Star–Jrl.* (OH) 31 Jan 10/1 **NW**, The first thing they do . . is to establish their electric yarding and loading engines. These are at the foot of the spar tree, whose top has been chopped off at 250 feet. **1933** *Natl. Geogr. Mag.* Feb 152 **WA**, A straight Douglas fir makes an ideal spar tree for high-lead logging. **1940** Writers' Program *Oregon*

357, At certain locations are towering spar-trees from which "high lead" lines swing huge logs across hills and canyons for miles, and drop them beside the road. **1958** McCulloch *Woods Words* 175 **Pacific NW,** *Spar pole. . . Spar tree*—The key to cable logging. The tree in which rigging is hung for one of the many cable hauling systems. The use of spar trees is still recent enough that the first tree ever topped by the Coos Bay Lumber Company still stood in 1953. **1959** *AmSp* 34.79 **nwCA** [Logger lingo], *Spar tree. . .* The tree at the landing to which one end of the skyline is attached in cableway logging. *High lead tree* is also heard. **1961** Labbe-Goe *Railroads* 260 **Pacific NW,** *Spar Tree:* A tree from which the top and limbs have been trimmed, used to hang rigging for logging. Usually a tree was chosen where it grew, but if none was available, one might be brought in and raised for the purpose. **1967** *DARE* Tape **WA**20, Ground logging, they called it ground lead, because everything was on the ground. And then as they advanced, they finally put up a spar tree. Usually a tree would be eight feet through with the ground and two hundred feet high with a high lead block and necessary guy lines and everything.

spasm band n esp New Orleans LA

An impromptu musical group playing makeshift instruments, sometimes accompanied by dancers.

1906 *Everybody's Mag.* 15.76, In New Orleans the Spasm Band was famous, or, rather infamous—a group of boys who sold papers by day, and spent half the night making "spasms" in front of saloons upon instruments constructed from some part of a barrel. **1926** (1974) Whiteman–McBride *Jazz* 266 **New Orleans LA,** [His instruments were a cheese box for a banjo, a soap box guitar, a cigar box violin and a half barrel bass fiddle. He had also an old tambourine, a zither and a harmonica. The leader trained his gang until the noise they made was adequate even to their small-boy ears.] *Ibid* 267, When the last fearful note died, he turned to the leader. "Stale Bread," said he, "you may be a band, but you're a spasm band. Discharged." The name stuck and the spasm band went on playing. **1941** Writers' Program *Guide LA* 692, *Spasm band*—A soap-box orchestra and accompanying tap dancers, usually, young Negroes, who perform on street corners in the French Quarter of New Orleans. **1945** Saxon *Gumbo Ya-Ya* 48 **New Orleans LA,** Spasm bands, composed of small Negro boys using makeshift instruments, who tap-dance and 'put it on' for pedestrians . . go into violent twistings and contortions, accompanied by pleas of 'Gimme a penny, Mister!' **1987** Rose *I Remember Jazz* 240, We had this little spasm band—you know—most all homemade instruments. We were really lousy but we had good rhythm—just kids, you know. **2000** *Post & Courier* (Charleston SC) 7 Sept sec D 18 (Internet) **VT,** Chorney calls viperHouse a "modern day spasm band," a reference to street bands in turn-of-the-century New Orleans that gave rise to the genre of collectively improvised music.

spat v Cf spatter n³

To smack, slap; to clap (the hands), pat (the feet) on the ground; intran: to pat with the hand; to move with light slapping footfalls.

a1824 (1937) Guild *Jrl.* 3.263 **VT,** I told her that I thought she was smarter than Yanke Girls. She would spat her feet and say, Oh Dutch Girls ant afraid of cold weather. **1845** Judd *Margaret* 156 **NEng,** The little Isabel leaped up and down spatting her hands. **1868** Alcott *Little Women* 231 **MA,** Amy spatted away energetically. **1872** Edmonds *Trials on Impeachment* 2.1226 **MI,** We shall show you . . that he spatted his knees and danced what they call the juba. *Ibid* 1262, Some of them were spatting and others dancing, and having various kinds of sport. **1887** (1967) Harris *Free Joe* 113 **GA,** Down in these parts you can't spat a man harder betwixt the eyes than to set back an' not break bread wi' 'im. **1924** (1946) Greer-Petrie *Angeline Gits an Eyeful* 22 **csKY,** The fust dance wuz called . . and them gals spatted around thar in thar bar' feet. **1928** Ruppenthal *Coll.* **KS,** Fly spatter . . a device to kill house flies. . . A person strikes at a fly to 'spat' or 'swat' the fly, and disable or kill it. **1939** Steinbeck *Grapes* 19 **OK,** He spatted the metal door with the palm of his hand. **1939** Aldrich *Song of Yrs.* 420 **eIA,** "Hark! What's that?" Sarah said, spatting her hands together to quiet the crowd so she could hear. **1951** Giles *Harbin's Ridge* 25 **KY,** We spatted our feet in the hot dust and squiggled it up between our toes. **1957** [see **spat** n¹ 2].

spat n¹

1 A sharp blow, esp with the flat of the hand; a pat, slap, smack.

1837 in 1892 Thoreau *Autumn* 334 **ceMA,** But, alas! how often when thoughts choke me, do I resort to a spat on the back, . . or do anything but expectorate them. **1854** *S. Lit. Messenger* 20.121, William [=a billy goat] . . hit him such a spat between the eyes as made him think another set of falling stars had come down. **1889** *Scribner's Mag.* 5.489, Then she . . administered a corrective slap to his cheek so that the spat of her little palm on it rang through the room. **1892** *Atlantic Mth.* 69.349, The owner of bare feet . . delighted in making the drenched sand "lighten" . . by quick, forcible spats of the bare feet upon the wet ground. **1905** *DN* 3.20 **cCT,** *Spat. . .* A slap. **1907** *DN* 3.218 **nwAR,** *Spat. . .* A slap. **1960** Carpenter *Tales Manchaca* 137 **cTX,** He then picked Buck up in his arms, gave him a hard spat on his bottom, and said firmly, "Son, don't you *ever* build a fire in the barn again."

2 in combs *spat and kick, spat or a kick;* also *spats:* A game of leapfrog; see quot. Cf **Spanish fly**

1957 *Sat. Eve. Post Letters* **NE** (as of c1890), *Spat and kick,* or *Spat or a kick.* Any number can play. A boy is picked out to start. The game is played much the same as leap-frog except the one picked to stand bends over, facing at right angles to the players. Each player must leap over him with-out touching him. If any of the players touches the boy bent over he has the choice to either spat or kick him and that boy has to stand bent over and the process [is] repeated. *Ibid* **Seattle WA** (as of c1900), 'Knucks.' You dug your knuckles into the 'down' man's spine as you vaulted over. Or 'Spats' whereupon you whacked him on the rump.

spat n² See spatterer

spat n³ [Abbr for *spatula;* cf *OED2* spat sb.² 1 "*Obs.*"] Cf spatter n², spatule

1967–68 *DARE* FW Addit **CA,** A spat [spæt]—nickname for spatula; **seOR,** *Spat* [spæt]—a spatula. **1968** *DARE* (Qu. F3, *When you're frying things—for example, eggs—you turn them over with a _____*) Inf **NY**90, Spat. **2002** in 2006 *DARE* File—Internet **ceMA,** These terms have migrated across industries, and into regular life, but I first began using them and others as a teenage line cook at a busy restaurant. . . *Spat: Spatula.* As in, "I once saw him spit on his spat, man." **2004** *DARE* File **csWI,** My mother commonly refers to a spatula (either the rubber variety used to scrape a bowl or the metal one used to turn a pancake or serve cake) as a "spat."

spat and kick See spat n¹ 2

spatchy See spatzie

spat or a kick, spats See spat n¹ 2

spatter n¹ See spatterer

spatter n² [Alter of *spatula,* but cf *OED2* spatter sb.¹ "*Obs.*"]

1968–70 *DARE* (Qu. F3, *When you're frying things—for example, eggs—you turn them over with a _____*) Inf **MO**35, Spatter; **SC**70, Spatter ['spædə].

spatter n³ [spat v]

=flyspatter.

1968 *DARE* (Qu. F47, *. . Wire or rubber device with a handle, that is used to kill flies; not asked in early QRs*) Inf **NJ**9, Spatter.

spatterdock n Also *splatterdock* [*OED2* 1832 →]

A **water lily 1** (here: *Nuphar lutea* and subspp). For other names see **alligator bonnet(s) 2, beaver lily, ~ root, bonnet B1a, brandy bottle, bullhead lily, buttercup waterlily, candock, cow lily 1, dog ~, ducks n¹ 1, frog lily, gold watch, hog lily, Holy Trinity ~, horse ~, Indian pond ~, lily pad 1, mud lily, mulefoot n², toad lily 1, tuckahoe 1, tule lily, wokas**

1807 in 1942 *Torreya* 42.160 **sePA,** *Nymphaea advena* [=*Nuphar luteum*]. . . Can-dock, splatter-dock, Philadelphia. **1814** Wilson *Amer. Ornith.* 8.30, [The Great Heron] also eats the seeds of that species of nymphae usually called splatter docks. **1837** *Farmers' Reg.* 4.678 **NJ,** From thence up the river, (the water being fresh,) grow the bull rush, . . spatter dock, and the water lily. **1881** *Harper's New Mth. Mag.* 63.684, The broad dark leaves and coarse yellow flowers of the splatterdock mingle with the lighter and more delicate leaves and shining white blossoms of the pond-lily. **1901** Lounsberry *S. Wild Flowers* 163, *Nymphæa advena,* large yellow pond lily, or spatter dock, is common in the stagnant waters of ponds and the lower courses of streams. **1940** Steyermark *Flora MO* 187, Ozark Spatter Dock, Yellow Pond-lily (*Nuphar ozarkana*). **1966–68** *DARE* Wildfl QR Pl.56 Infs **MI**31, **OH**14, 82, **OR**12, **WI**80, Spatterdock. **1968** *DARE* (Qu. S26b, *Wildflowers that grow in water or wet places*) Infs **OH**82, **PA**99, Spatterdock. **1976** Bruce *How to Grow Wildflowers* 277, *Nuphar*—Spatterdocks or Cow-lilies. These have leaves like their relatives the true waterlilies, but these usually stand above the water rather than float upon it. **2003** *Tampa Tribune* (FL) 19 Oct (Internet), It's fun to watch a big mamma bass come through a field of spatterdocks.

spatterer n   Also *spat, spatter (duck)*   [See quot 1923] **=ruddy duck.**

1918 Grinnell et al. *Game Birds CA* 205, Ruddy duck. . . Other names—Wiretail; . . Spatterer; Spatter. **1923** Dawson *Birds CA* 4.1840, Ruddy Duck. . . Spatterer. Spatter Duck. Spat. *Ibid,* Another nickname applied to the birds by California sportsmen is "Spat," or "Spatterer." This is said to have been applied because of the noisy strokes made by the duck's feet upon the surface of the water as it is getting under way; but, somehow, I fancy that it is rather the combination of dandified gentility and squattiness which makes the name "Spat" stick.

spatule n   Pronc-spp *spachel, spachle*   [*OED2 spatule* sb. a1425 →]
A spatula.

1914 *Lincoln Daily News* (NE) 11 May [16]/3 (newspaper-archive.com), A complete kitchen set—carvers, spatchel, parers, fruit knives, vegetable knives and cleaver. **1924** *Bradford Era* (PA) [25 Dec 13]/5 (newspaperarchive.com), The sets include a spatule, two basting spoons . . and other convenient combinations. **1938** *Charleston Gaz.* (WV) 17 June 15/2, *Kitchen Accessories.* . . Cake Turner—Knife Sharpener—Spatchel. **1943** *AmSp* 18.308 wLA, eTX [Cafe terms], *Spachel* [spatula]. A flat, shovel-like instrument used to turn eggs, hamburgers, and the like. **1969** *DARE* (Qu. F3, *When you're frying things—for example, eggs—you turn them over with a _____*) Inf **NY68**, Spatule ['spæčəl]. **2007** *DARE* File—Internet **KY,** There are plenty of spoons and spachles and cooking utensils etc.

spatzie n   Usu |'spætsɪ, 'spɑtsɪ|; for addit varr see quots 1965–70, 1990   Also *spatchy, spatz(en), spatzer, spatzy, sputzie;* for addit varr see quots   [Ger *Spatz(en)* sparrow(s)]
1 =English sparrow. chiefly Missip-Ohio Valleys, PA See Map   Cf **kitsie**

1950 *WELS* WI (*Different kinds of sparrows:* [Include nicknames]) 2 Infs, Spatz; 2 Infs, Spatzer; 2 Infs, Spotsy(s); 1 Inf, Spatzie; 1 Inf, Spatzen; 1 Inf, Spaats—English sparrow; 1 Inf, Spatzes—English sparrow. **1950** *WELS* Suppl. **seWI,** English sparrows = spotsies. (Milw[aukee].) **1965–70** *DARE* (Qu. Q22, *Joking names or nicknames for the common sparrow*) 23 Infs, **chiefly Missip-Ohio Valleys,** [Proncs of the type ['spætsɪ]; 14 Infs, **chiefly Missip-Ohio Valleys,** [Proncs of the type ['spɑtsɪ]]; **PA76, WI**12, 17, 48, [Proncs of the type ['spʌtsɪ]]; **AL22,** [spæts]; **IN**19, ['spɪtsi]; **IN**35, 58, ['spæti]; **IA**8, 34, ['spæčiz]; **IA**32, ['špɑtsə]; **IL**4, ['spɑtsə]; **MI**93, ['špɑtsɛn]; **MO**36, [spɑts, 'spɑtsɪn]; **NY**227, ['špɑtsi]; **OH**82, [špɑts]; **PA**6, [spɑt]; **PA**92, ['spɑtsɚz]; [**MN**36, Dreckspatz;] (Qu. Q21, . . *Kinds of sparrows*) Inf **PA**75, Spatzie. **1978** *MJLF* 4.1.37 c**KS** (as of 1910–20), Spatchie. . . English sparrow. (We knew, of course, the correct name . . but to use it would then have been regarded as pretentious.) **1986** *DARE* File c**wIA,** c**sIL,** *Spatzie/spatzy,* apparently a Midwestern word for the house sparrow, *Passer domesticus.* It was the term my grandfather used in Sioux City, Iowa, and one informant from southern Illinois recently confirmed the word is used near Carbondale. **1990** *Ibid* c**eWI,** *Sputzie* ['spʌtzi]—used by my aunt for "sparrow." **1991** Heat Moon *PrairyErth* 489 c**eKS,** When a sparrow (he called them *spatsies*) would squirt on him, he'd open fire. **2000** *DARE* File c**eIL** (as of c1940), "Spatchy" [was] commonly used for "sparrow" in East Central Illinois. **2003** *NADS Let-*

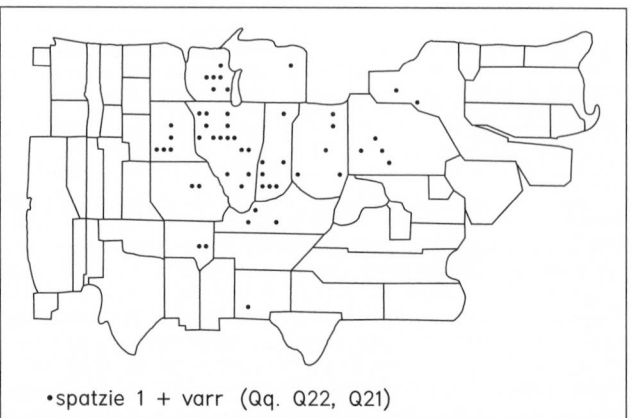

•spatzie 1 + varr (Qq. Q22, Q21)

ters c**sIA,** It occurred to me that in my own family we use the word "spatch" for sparrow, or spatchies for sparrow. My dad and uncle have used this word since we were children, and I believe it was commonly used in the area where they grew up, around Knoxville, Iowa. **2004** *Ibid* sw**PA,** John[s]town is my birthplace. . . my mom and dad often called sparrow sputzies. **2004** Ohm *Spatzies* 185 **KS** (as of c1944), "Spatzie" meant "little sparrow," and was one of the few German words that we all used on a daily basis.

2 By ext: a small, dull-colored bird.

2003 *DARE* File—Internet w**PA,** "That's what we call nondescript birds—that's just a sputzie." There were three "sputzies" at the feeder, all females: house finch, purple finch, and rose-breasted grosbeak. **2004** *Nat. Resources Jrl.* 44.1073 **IA** (as of 1960s), When I was an undergraduate in a fish and wildlife biology program, many students and faculty marginalized species not harvested by sportsmen. . . Small non-game, passerine birds, for example, were referred to with the implicitly derogatory phrase "spatzies." **2004** *DARE* File—Internet **NY,** The little "sputzies," whatever we like to call the small birds that are too swift to identify, remain numerous.

spauldeen   See **spaldeen**

spaulted   See **spalt**

spawl   See **spoil A3**

spawn   See **supawn**

spawneater n   Also *spawn-eater minnow*   [See quot 1842]
A **shiner 1** (here: *Notropis hudsonius*).

1824 NY Acad. Sci. *Annals Lyceum Nat. Hist.* 1.1.50, Clupea *hudsonia.* . . Frequent at Albany, and other places on the Hudson River. . . This delicate and beautiful fish is familiarly known under the name of *Spawn-eater,* in allusion to its supposed food. **1882** U.S. Natl. Museum *Bulletin* 16.171, C[liola] hudsonia. . . *Spawn-eater.* . . Streams coastwise, New York to Virginia. **1938** Schrenkeisen *Field Book Fishes* 132, Spawn-eater Minnow—*Hybopsis hudsonius.* **1983** Becker *Fishes WI* 543, It has also been reported that larger spottails eat both their own eggs and their young; it is this habit that has led to the name "spawneater" for this fish.

spayded, spayted   See **spade v**

speak v

A Forms.

1 pres 3rd pers pl: usu *speak;* also *speaks.*

1854 in 1917 Holmes *Letters* 50, [Humorous letter in the persona of Goliath Tittle, a sailor from Kennebunk ME:] I . . find it exseding hard for to spel alsoe having been so much in forren parts where they speaks so defferint. **1856** in 1978 Miller *Dear Master* 209 **AL** [Black], They speaks of going to Arkansas this fall. **1921** Lardner in *Indianapolis Sun. Star* (IN) 14 Aug 6/4, Now days some of the best people speaks of the devil and their underclothing without a quaver. **1965** Belfrage *Freedom Summer* 75 **MS** [Black], They speaks different over there. **1986** Pederson *LAGS Concordance,* 1 inf, c**GA,** Lots of people speaks (like that).

2 past: usu *spoke;* also *speaked, spoked, spoken(ed).*

1852 Byrn *Rattlehead's Chron.* 133 **TN,** Tha all seated themselves kumfortable, an up I jumped on the log, an what you reckin I spoked about—ef I didn't speak 'bout the price of meal, you may roar me up salt river. **1859** Pollard *Black Diamonds* xii **Sth** [Black], I trust he remember as how I spoked of him perlitely. **1879** *Scribner's Mth.* 17.694, She hardly ever speaked above her breath. **1884** *Anglia* 7.253 [Black], To the regular forms of the Irregular verbs as used by the whites, the Negro adds the following forms of his own. . . *Pres.* speak—*Past.* speaked, spoked, spoken, -ed—*Pass. Part.*—. c**1938** in Lib. of Congress *Amer. Memory: WPA Life Hist.* (Internet) **TX,** One of the officials . . turned to Kerchain, who spoked English brokenly. **2006** *DARE* File—Internet, [Her] dad speaked out about asthma attack.

3 past pple: usu *spoken;* also *spoke.*

1781 *PA Jrl. & Weekly Advt.* (Philadelphia) 16 May, Common vulgarisms . . [include] I had spoke. **1828** Webster *Amer. Dict., Speak* . . pret *spoke,* [*spake,* nearly obs.;] pp spoke, spoken. **1846** Worcester *Universal Dict.* 682, *Speak.* . . *spoke* is little used as a *participle,* except colloquially. **1871** Eggleston *Hoosier Schoolmaster* 66 **sIN,** When they're spoke to. **1872** Holmes *Poet* 342 ce**MA,** I beg your pardon, ma'am,—says I,—I thought you had spoke of changing your condition. **1893** *DN* 1.278 w**CT,** *Speak*—[pret and past pple:] spoke. **1909** *DN* 3.374 e**AL,** w**GA,** *Spoke,* pp. of *speak.* **1969** *DARE* Tape **IL**77, Used to be a lot of

German spoke around here.   **1986** Pederson *LAGS Concordance,* 1 inf, **neMS,** Since you've spoke about that; 1 inf, **swGA,** Next one ain't spoke of; 1 inf, **cwGA,** They're spoke of; 1 inf, **csTN,** We've done spoke (of that already).   **2007** *DARE* File—Internet **CA,** You've spoke about problems with body image/bulimia before.   *Ibid* **MN,** It's looking like ~ $50K is reasonable, at least that's the number some of the recruiters I've spoke with have said.

B Senses.

1 also with *out:* To admonish, denounce.

1942 Hurston *Dust Tracks* 25 **FL** [Black], My mother rode herd on one woman with a horse-whip about Papa, and "spoke out" another one. . . The woman who got "spoken out" threatened to whip my mother.   **1956** McAtee *Some Dialect NC* 58, *Speak.* . . Publicly admonish in church. "That boy is so bad that the preacher spoke him last Sunday." Knott's Island, Upper Currituck Sound.

2 in phrr *I('d) speak:* See quot.   Cf **declare**

1903 *DN* 2.317 **seMO,** *I speak* or *I'd speak.* . . An exclamation of surprise. Equivalent to 'Indeed.'

3 in phr *speak howdy:* To offer greetings, say hello.   **esp S Midl**

1911 U.S. Congress House *Contested Election Kinney vs. Dyer* 569 **MO,** I saw him at Chattaroy . . and I just spoke "Howdy" like.   **1934** (1970) Wilson *Backwoods Amer.* 18 **AR, MO,** I seed him all right— . . passed him and spoke howdy to him.   **1963** Edwards *Gravel* 123 **eTN** (as of 1920s), The cap'm come over and spoke howdy to Pap and me thar at the shop.   **1969** Wilson *Stars* 115 **Ozarks,** They spoke howdy, both of 'em shy.   **1973** in 2004 Montgomery–Hall *Dict. Smoky Mt. Engl.* 312 **eTN, wNC,** Is these girls crazy? Every time they would pass a man have to speak howdy to him?   **2005** *KentuckyLiving.com* Mar (Internet), Recently I picked up the phone and spoke howdy over there to Blevin's Grocery alongside the old Chesapeake and Ohio track.

speakeasy n   Also *speak, speakeasily, speakie* [See quot 1932] **widespread, but chiefly Nth, N Midl, West** See Map Cf **blind tiger 1**

A place where liquor is sold illegally.

1889 *Pittsburgh Commercial Gaz.* 17 Apr 2/1 *(Popik Coll.),* [Headline:] Novel and Palace. The Gilded 'Speak-Easy' Found on Water Street.   **1901** *DN* 2.148 **nwPA,** *Speak-easy.* . . A saloon. The same as blind-pig.   **1903** *DN* 2.331 **seMO,** *Speak-easy.* . . An illicit dram-shop; a 'blind tiger.'   **1932** Tooné *Yankee Slang* 34, *Speak easy:* Speak low, softly. "Speak easies" or speakies are so-called clubs, or licensed parlours for the sale of soft drinks, but where illicit liquors are obtainable "under the rose"—hence speak easy (low); also known as "Hush! Hush!!["] joints.   **1965–70** *DARE* (Qu. DD30, *Joking names for a place where liquor is [or was] sold and consumed illegally*) 397 Infs, **widespread, but chiefly Nth, N Midl, West,** Speakeasy; **FL39, MD4, NY131, 249, PA199, 241,** Speak; **IN58,** Speakeasily.

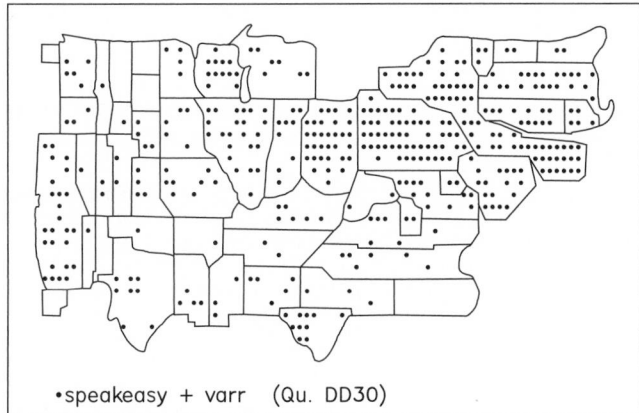

•speakeasy + varr   (Qu. DD30)

speaked   See **speak A2**

speak howdy   See **speak B3**

speakie   See **speakeasy**

speaking n   **Sth, S Midl**

1 A meeting at which speeches are made or public issues discussed; a political gathering.   Cf **singing n 1**

1816 in 2005 NC Univ.–Chapel Hill *True Compositions* (Internet), At

the conclusion of Wm. Shepard's speech, in defiance of authority, was a very general plaudit in the Hall in token of approbation. That at the end of the speakin[g,] as the students went to the College, there were noisy shoutings for Wm. Shepard, and great noise and riot in the buildings during a great part of the night.   **1840** *Ibid,* After dinner I attended the Senior Speaking.   **1842** Buckingham *Slave States* 2.245 **TN,** The farmers of the neighbourhood . . had come in to attend "the speaking" . . the rival candidates for the governorship being both here.   **1903** *DN* 2.331 **seMO,** *Speaking.* . . A political meeting. 'There will be a speakin at the cross roads to-morrow and all the candidates will be there.'   **1907** *DN* 3.236 **nwAR,** *Speakin'.* . . A political meeting.   **1909** *DN* 3.373 **eAL, wGA,** *Speakin(g).* . . Political meeting where candidates 'orate.'   **1924** Raine *Land of Saddle-Bags* 212 **sAppalachians,** [Caption:] A "meeting" is always a religious gathering; discussion of politics, good roads, or community betterment is a "speaking."   **1931** (1957) Justus *Other Side of Mt.* 108 **TN,** In the afternoon came the speaking. . . There were short speeches, long speeches, sad speeches, and funny speeches. [*Ibid* 109, Thus ended school for that year.]   **1942** Thomas *Blue Ridge Country* 155 **VA,** Men . . will travel miles to a speaking—which may be a political gathering or one for the purpose of discussing road building.   **1946** *AmSp* 21.192 **seKY,** Thar's a-goin' to be a speakin' at the schoolhouse.   **a1975** Lunsford *It Used to Be* 12 **wNC,** If there was something to go to the next day—a speaking or a singing or a funeral—that would have to be provided for.   **1978** in 2004 Montgomery–Hall *Dict. Smoky Mt. Engl.* 556 **wNC, eTN,** They will travel miles to a speakin', religious or political, and [take] unusual delight in being swayed by oratory.

2 A speech, sermon.

1863 Hopley *Life South* 1.57, Then came the "speaking," as the sermon was called.   **1924** Raine *Land of Saddle-Bags* 184 **sAppalachians,** After a hospitable supper, he addresses a little group who have gathered to hear the "speakin'."   **1962** Dykeman *Tall Woman* 189 **NC** (as of 1860), Never crossed your mind, did it, that we'd let Robert Moore give a speaking out here and us not come to hear it?   **1967** Green *Horse Tradin'* 41 **TX,** That weekend there was fall fair and Old Settlers reunion coming up. . . They were going to have a big program—speakin's, dinner on the grounds, games, something for everybody.

speaking meeting n

A meeting, esp a religious gathering, at which all are free to express their opinions or share their experiences.

1840 *W. Chr. Advocate* (Cincinnati OH) 13 Mar 186/3 **cwOH,** They have a speaking meeting, with prayers and exhortation, at ten o'clock, and preaching, with a prayer meeting after it, at night.   **1851** OH Constitutional Convention *Report* 1.94, This Convention seems to have resolved itself into a general "speaking meeting."   **1882** *Atlantic Mth.* 49.758 **ceOH,** [She raised] her voice to the tone she used in speaking-meeting when exhorting sinners.   **1888** *Century Illustr. Mag.* 35.564 **IL,** She told him . . of the woman she had heard relate in a morning "speaking-meeting" that, when convinced of the sin of wearing jewelry, she had immediately taken off her ear-rings and given them to her sister.   **1953** Brewer *Word Brazos* 41 **eTX** [Black], De speakin' meetin's de one what meet de favuh of mos'. . . Sistuh Carrie . . wait till attuh all de res' of de brothuhs an' sistuhs gits thoo tellin' dey 'speriunce 'fo' she riz to tell her 'speriunce.

speak out   See **speak B1**

spean v   Also *speen* [Cf *EDD spean* sb.[1] "The teat of any female animal, esp. used of a cow."]

See quots.

1954 *PADS* 21.38 **SC,** *Spean.* . . 1. To milk as a cow. . . 2. To spurt out in a fine stream, especially said of the teats of a milk cow. "The cow's bag was so full the milk was speaning out."   **1993** *DARE* File **neMS,** I was at a party last night with a writer who said he used the expression "tobacco juice speening down his chin." His agent, or editor, told him there is no such word as *speen,* and none of the 15 or so people at the party had ever heard of it.

spear n   Also called **spud** n **1**

A sharp, metal point fitted to the end of a **tobacco stick;** hence v (phr) *spear (up)* to pierce through (tobacco plants) with the spear-shod stick, stringing the plants together; to perform such a task; also vbl n *spearing.*

1850 U.S. Patent Office *Annual Rept. for 1849: Ag.* 321 **MD,** It [=tobacco] may be put away in three different modes, by *"pegging," "spearing,"* and *"splitting."*   **1869** Porcher *Resources* 533 **Sth,** Spearing is the plan I pursue. . . A spear on the other end of the stick, is all the apparatus required; the plant is then . . run over the spear and thus strung upon the sticks, which, when full, are taken to the house and hung up at once. **1939** in Lib. of Congress *Amer. Memory: FSA/OWI* (Internet) **WI,** [Caption:] Daughters of tobacco farmer spearing tobacco leaves. **1944** *PADS* 2.71 **S Midl,** *Spear.* . . A round sharp-pointed instrument for piercing a hole in the stalk in preparation for curing; to make a hole with such an instrument. **1965–69** *DARE* Tape **DC**5, You take your tobacco and spear it up; **KY**9, There's a spear . . on a stick. Slip it off and on the stick, each stick, and you put so many plants on that stick; **WI**1, Another man comes along and spears it, puts it on lath. They have a sharp spear, call it tobacco spear, put on a regular lath. **1966** *PADS* 45.23 **KY,** *Spear.* . . A sharp steel point that is fitted to one end of a tobacco stick. . . "You take the spear off when the stick gets full." . . To string stalks of tobacco on a stick shod with a spear. . . "It takes less time to spear than to split." **1967** Key *Tobacco Vocab.* 206 **CT, KY, MD, MO, TN,** *Spear* [*DARE* Ed: Author gives no indication as to whether *spear* is n or v.]; **PA,** *Spear* n., *spear up* string. **2007** *DARE* File—Internet **KY,** We use a spear which is a very sharp cone shaped steel piece placed on the upper end of the wooden stick which has been driven far enough into the ground to stay upright. The stem of the tobacco plant is pressed onto this about a foot from the larger (bottom) end.

spear-chucker n Also *spear-carrier, ~-thrower* derog
A Black person.

1967 Johnson *Ebony Brass* 51, You got to be recommended to get promoted, and no Dixiecrat commander is going to recommend a spear-chucker. **1968** *DARE* (Qu. HH28, *Names and nicknames . . for people of foreign background: Negro*) Inf **PA**94, Spear-chucker. **1969** *Current Slang* 3.3.10 **OH,** *Spearchucker.* . . Negro.—General young adults, both sexes. **1986** Pederson *LAGS Concordance,* 1 inf, **ceTX,** Spear carriers, spear throwers—derogatory for Negroes. **2000** *DARE* File—Internet, Spearchucker get your white ass cold at the morgue.

spearfish n

1 Std: a fish of the genus *Tetrapterus,* esp *T. albidus.* For other names of the latter see **billfish 1, skillygoelle, spike-fish 2**

2 A carpsucker, usu *Carpiodes velifer.*

1878 IL State Lab. Nat. Hist. *Bulletin* 1.2.65, *Carpiodes velifer.* . . Spear-fish, Sail-fish, Skim-back, Quill-back. **1902** Jordan-Evermann *Amer. Fishes* 43, *C[arpiodes] velifer,* the quillback, spearfish, sailfish, or skimfish, is a small species found pretty well throughout the Mississippi Valley.

3 =**sailfish 1.**

1926 Pan-Pacific Research Inst. *Jrl.* 1.1.8, *Istiophoridæ.* The Spear Fishes. **1975** Evanoff *Catch More Fish* 209, The Atlantic sailfish (*Istiophorus americanus*) is also called the spearfish, spindlebeak, and sail. *Ibid* 210, The Pacific sailfish (*Istiophorus greyi*) is also called the spearfish and pez-vela.

spear grass n[1]

Any of var grasses or grasslike plants having a pointed leaf or inflorescence, as:

a A **bluegrass 1,** usu **Kentucky bluegrass.**

[**a1747** Franklin in 1822 *Amer. Jrl. Science* 4.359, The grass which comes in first, after ditching, is spear grass and white clover.] **1822** Eaton *Botany* 394, [*Poa*] *pratensis* (common meadow grass, spear grass). **1837** Darlington *Flora Cestrica* 75 **sePA,** *P[oa] pratensis.* . . Meadow Poa. *Vulgò*—Spear grass. **1849** Emmons *Agriculture NY* 2.68, An earlier kind of grass than timothy, is the Spear grass, Meadow grass, or Kentucky blue grass. **1892** IN Dept. Geol. & Nat. Resources *Rept. for 1891* 158, *Poa annua.* . . Low Spear-Grass. *Ibid, P. pratensis.* . . June Grass. Spear Grass. **1910** Graves *Flowering Plants* 72 **CT,** *Poa annua.* . . Low Spear Grass. . . Cultivated ground and waste places. **1937** U.S. Forest Serv. *Range Plant Hdbk.* G103-1, Kentucky bluegrass. . . is known by numerous common or local names, including lawn grass, spear-grass, junegrass, and greensward. **2004** *Houston Chron.* (TX) 10 Apr 1 (Internet), He points to . . Poa annua seed, a grassy weed also known as wintergrass or speargrass.

b A **love grass** such as *Eragrostis pectinacea, E. pilosa,* or *E. trichodes.*

1859 (1860) Flint *Grasses & Forage* 19, Branching Spear Grass . . Eragrostis tenuis [=*E. trichodes*]. . . Sterile plains. **1881** Phares *Farmer's Book of Grasses* 59, *E[ragrostis] purshii* [=*E. pectinacea*], Southern Spear Grass. . . is found in cultivated grounds and waste lands. *Ibid, E. tenuis,* Branching Spear Grass . . found on river banks and rich sandy soils. **1901** Mohr *Plant Life AL* 380, *Eragrostis purshii.* . .

Southern Spear Grass. . . Alabama: Over the State. **1935** (1943) Muenscher *Weeds* 156, *Eragrostis pilosa.* . . Tufted spear-grass.

c =**needlegrass 1.**

1878 Havard *Bot. Outlines* 1681, The prairies are generally covered with grass. . . It consists mostly of Buffalo Grass . . ; Porcupine or Spear Grass (*Stipa comata,* the prevalent species, *S. spartea, S. viridula*); Quick Grass [etc]. **1890** *Oölogist* 7.201 **SD,** A hollow measuring four inches in diameter and two in depth was . . lined with "spear grass." (*Stipa comata*). **1923** in 1925 Jepson *Manual Plants CA* 124, Stipa [spp]. . . Porcupine Grass. Spear Grass. **1970** Correll *Plants TX* 121, *Stipa leucotricha.* . . Texas speargrass. . . The calluses of the "fruits," when the latter are properly thrown, easily penetrate clothing and stick into skin. The plants, therefore, are of considerable recreational value to boys. **1996** in 2007 *DARE* File—Internet **TX,** Cover in the ground layer is variable depending perhaps on degree of shading; cedar sedge (*Carex planostachys*) and spear grass (*Stipa leucotricha*) are the most common species.

d An **alkali grass 2.**

1889 (1890) Gray *Manual of Botany* 668, *P[uccinéllia] marítima.* . . Sea Spear-Grass. . . Marshes along the coast. **1912** Baker *Book of Grasses* 217, Spreading Spear Grass (*Puccinellia distans*). . . opens wide panicles of small, crowded spikelets. *Ibid,* Sea Spear-grass. *Puccinellia maritima.* . . Salt marshes and sea beaches. **1948** Pearson *Sea Flavor* 118 **NH,** Above the thatch-grass area is the zone of . . the salt grass. . . Here . . one can find three grasses—fox grass [=*Spartina patens*], spear grass [=*Puccinellia maritima*], and spike grass [=*Distichlis spicata*]. They grow from 10 to 15 inches tall. **2006** in 2007 *DARE* File—Internet, From Spreading Spear-grass (Puccinellia distans) Goose-grass differs in that it rise [sic] spikelets.

e A **glasswort.**

1916 *Torreya* 16.237 **VA,** *Salicornia* spp. Pickle-grass, spear grass, Revels I[slan]d.

f A **horned rush** (here: *Rhynchospora corniculata*).

1916 *Torreya* 16.237 **SC,** *Rhynchospora corniculata.* . . Spear grass, Santee Club, S.C.

spear grass n[2] [Var of asparagus, infl by the shape] Cf sparrowgrass n[1]

1887 *Good Housekeeping* 5.56 **MA,** Asparagus is quite plentyful. . . The kind called "spear grass" and cullings may be bought for 10 and 15 cents a bunch. **1947** Humphreys *Of Me* 40 **seWV** (as of 1870s), Spear-grass—meant for asparagus. **1965–70** *DARE* (Qu. I29, *Names or nicknames for asparagus*) Infs **AL**11, **AZ**8, **CA**87, **NY**39, 109, Spear grass; **MD**17, **MA**74, **NY**30, Spear grass [FW sugg]; **WI**68, Spear grass—have heard, but it's used very seldom. **2000** *Tech* (Cambridge MA) 11 Feb (Internet), This week's recipe is for Asparagus Quiche. I am a big fan of "spear grass" as my family calls it.

spear hog n
=**porcupine.**

1969 *DARE* (Qu. P31, . . *Names or nicknames . . for the . . porcupine*) Inf **GA**80, Spear hog.

spearing n Also *ground spearing, spearling* chiefly NEast
A young **silversides 1** (here: *Menidia* spp) or other small fish, often used as bait.

1875 Scott *Fishing Amer. Waters* 104, The Spearing, or Silversides.— *Genus Atherina.* **1884** Goode *Fisheries U.S.* 1.612, Our Anchovy has recently been sold in considerable numbers in New York under the name "Whitebait," although the fishermen distinguish it from the true "Whitebait," the young of the herring, calling it "Spearing." **1896** U.S. Natl. Museum *Bulletin* 47.533, Trachinocephalus myops. . . Ground Spearing; Lagarto. Tropical parts of the Western Atlantic . . and ranging on our Atlantic Coast to South Carolina. **1903** NY State Museum & Sci. Serv. *Bulletin* 60.359, The common silversides, or spearing, lives in Gravesend bay almost all the year. **1911** U.S. Bur. Census *Fisheries 1908* 307, The silver anchovy (*Anchovia browni*) [=*Anchoa hepsetus*]. . . is also known as "sardine" and "spearing." **1939** *LANE* Map 234 (*Minnow*) 1 inf, **swCT,** Spearing—a shiner; 1 inf, **swCT,** Spearing = minnow, very small; 1 inf, **ceMA,** Spearling—a young herring. **1968** *DARE* (Qu. P7, *Small fish used as bait for bigger fish*) Inf **NJ**39, Spearing, silversides; **NY**44, 47, Spearing. **1975** Evanoff *Catch More Fish* 102, Baitfish such as spearing or silversides, [etc] . . are used. **1999** in 2007 *DARE* File—Internet **NJ,** Use the minnows and spearing on a #12 fish hook supported 18″ below the surface. **2007** *Ibid* **RI,** You can find all the bait that you need including . . clams, spearing, live killies and more.

spearing vbl n

‡**1** In marble play: see quot.

c1970 Wiersma *Marbles Terms, Spearing*. . . Guiding marble toward target with the hand.

2 See **spear.**

spearling See **spearing** n

spear-thrower See **spear-chucker**

spear up See **spear**

spearweed n

Any of var weeds, as a **marsh elder 1** (here: *Iva xanthifolia*) or **mullein** (here: *Verbascum thapsus*); see quots.

1922 *Amer. Botanist* 28.131, We youngsters called it [=*Iva xanthifolia*] "spear-weed" because its shining leafless trunks made such light, straight, shooting darts after frost shrivelled the leaves. **2006** in 2007 *DARE* File—Internet **sTX,** The previous replies were wonderful! Seeing the photo [=of common mullein], my immediate thought was "spearweed"! As a child growing up in south Texas, a slow day during summer vacation would eventually bring one to thoughts of mayhem. And of course, in late summer the "spearweed" had died and dried. They can be pulled up quite easily when dead and dry, and even have a spear point (the root). You strip the dried leaves off and you have a spear with a very stiff shaft, perfect for "chunkin" at the 'Bad Guys'. **2007** *Ibid* **cwCA,** Ugh, found lots of spearweed and thistles, but no cache. *Ibid* **cTX,** We saw a big snake and later had a spear-weed fight with what got caught on our socks and shoes.

'spec v[1] See **expect**

'spec' v[2] See **suspect**

special n **chiefly NEast** See Map *old-fash* Cf **ethyl, extra C2, high-test**

High-octane gasoline.

1965–70 *DARE* (Qu. N15b, . . *Gasoline* . . *expensive kind*) 20 Infs, **chiefly NEast,** Special. [18 of 20 Infs old]

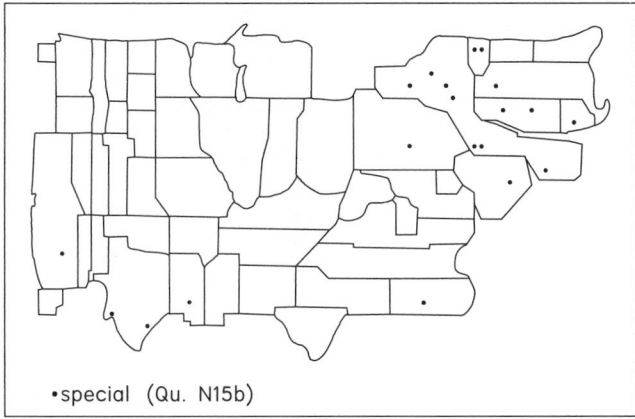

•special (Qu. N15b)

specie n [Back-formation from *species;* cf *OED2 specie* II.7.b "*Obs. exc.* as erron. sing."] Cf **Chinee, Maltee,** *Portagee* (at **Portuguese**)

1837 *NY Farmer & Amer. Gardener's Mag.* 10.226, Campeachy Teak—a specie of Piscidia. **1851** *Internatl. Mag.* 3.291, There are . . natural histories, containing . . digested accounts of every specie of game, beast, bird, and fish. **1872** Twain *Roughing It* 327, I used to have a cat here. . . He was a large gray one of the Tom specie. **1905** *DN* 3.95 **nwAR,** Specie. . . Species. 'The lynx is a specie of cat, you know.' **1907** *DN* 3.250 **eME,** Specie. . . Species. "It's a different specie of animal." **1914** *DN* 4.81 **ME, nNH,** Specie. . . Species. **1922** Gonzales *Black Border* 327 **sSC, GA coasts** [Gullah glossary], Specie'—species. **1966–69** *DARE* Tape **CA**103, That's a specie of fish; **MI**21, They're a different specie altogether; **WI**75, Every really useful specie of fish is gone from this bay. **1980** *Pan Am Clipper* Oct. 48/1 *(OED2),* Is he descended directly from apes, or is he a specie that evolved from an entirely new . . branch of the primate tree? **2005** *CT Post* (Bridgeport) 3 Apr (Internet), Such a ruling would end all commercial fishing on the specie. **2007** *Palm Beach Post* (W. Palm Beach FL) 15 June sec C 1 (Internet), A Hyacinth Macaw, also an endangered specie for sale, can go for about $70,000.

specify v **esp S Atl** *esp freq among Black speakers*

1 usu in neg constrs: To prove adequate; to come up to the mark.

1922 Gonzales *Black Border* 234 **sSC, GA coasts** [Gullah], You smaa't 'nuf fuh know w'en man got gun een 'e han', but yo' eddycashun cyan' specify w'en 'e come fuh tell w'en shell' cawn got pizen een um. *Ibid* 257, W'en 'e *graff* at de rokkoon . . de limb couldn' specify, en' de limb bruk. *Ibid* 327 [Gullah glossary], *Specify*—from specify, but greatly extended to include almost all meanings of "specifications"— proving inadequate, not coming up to expectations, etc. **1930** *DN* 6.83 **cSC,** Specify. . . To make good. "He loss that good job he got, 'cause he just couldn't specify." Frequent. **1986** Pederson *LAGS Concordance,* 1 inf, **seFL,** That doesn't specify. [Inf White] **1992** Geraty *Bittle* 40 **Charleston SC** [Gullah], Steemuh specify berrywell fuh cook en' fuh clean, alltwo.

2 To give an account of someone's shortcomings or inadequacies. Cf **signify 1**

1927 Kennedy *Gritny* 11 **sLA** [Black], If any de members hyuh tonight raise de queshton concernin' Bell, you ain' goin' leave 'um specify, is you? **1942** Hurston *Dust Tracks* 194 **FL** [Black], I heard somebody, a woman's voice "specifying" up this line of houses from where I lived and asked who it was. "Dat's Big Sweet" my landlady told me. "She got her foot up on somebody. Ain't she specifying?" She was really giving the particulars. She was giving a "reading." . . She was giving her opponent lurid data and bringing him up to date on his ancestry, his looks, smell, gait, clothes, and his route through Hell in the hereafter.

speciation See **speculate**

speciment n [Var of *specimen*] Cf Intro "Language Changes" I.8

1855 Brougham *Basket* 386, Judgin' from a fiery speciment I saw this morning. **1887** *Overland Mth.* (2d ser) 9.644 **Ozarks,** I reckon 't would crowd her putty tight to find another sich a speciment. **1912** Rankin *Story* 16 **TX,** He was gawky and angular and a grotesque speciment of humanity. **1940** in Lib. of Congress *Amer. Memory: WPA Life Hist.* (Internet), [From a work of fiction:] The night he came to us I had to go get a speciment, so I brought him the urinal. **1944** *PADS* 2.49 **NC, VA,** *Speciment* ['spɛsaɪˌmɪnt]. . . Specimen.

speck n[1]

1 A **darter 1** (here: *Etheostoma stigmaeum*).

1878 *NY Acad. Sci. Annals* 1.95, Speck. . . *Boleosoma stigmaeum.* **1890** *Century Dict.* 5808, Speck. . . A percoid fish, *Ulocentra stigmaea* of Jordan, common in ponds of the hill-country from Georgia to Louisiana.

2 A **sand darter 1** (here: *Ammocrypta pellucida*).

1877 *Amer. Naturalist* 11.86, We have often brought home with us a "Johnny," "Speck," or "Crawl-a-bottom." . . After much searching through the scattered . . descriptions which eastern naturalists have given us . . , we decided that our little friend was the "pellucid darter," or better, the "sand darter."

3 See **specklebelly 1.**

4 See **speckled bass.**

5 A **weakfish** (here: *Cynoscion nebulosus*). **esp TX** Cf **speckled trout 2**

1967 *DARE* FW Addit **TX,** Specks—kind of fish caught in surf in Texas. **1968** *Beaumont Enterprise* (TX) 2 Mar 15/5, Salt Water Report. . . Offatt's Bayou is calm and clear. Some specks are working near the deep holes. **1975** Evanoff *Catch More Fish* 172, Also in southern waters a boat caster can have a ball with southern weakfish or sea trout, often called "specks." **2002** *Houston Chron.* (TX) 14 Apr (Internet), Our first speck was caught last week when we had a spell of calm, green surf. **2002** *DARE* File—Internet **GA,** The most prevalent, one of the best eating and easiest to catch of the available species is the spotted sea trout or "speck" as it is often referred to by locals along the Georgia coast. **2005** [see **speckled trout 2**].

6 =**brook trout.** Cf **speckled trout 1**

1955 *Traverse City Rec.-Eagle* (MI) 13 Oct [20]/6 (newspaper-archive.com), Mostly they caught brook trout and Arctic char. The specks weighed over five pounds and the char ran up to 15. **1972** Sparano *Outdoors Encycl.* 355, Brook Trout—Common Names . . speckled trout, speck, squaretail. **2005** *Post–Std.* (Syracuse NY) 3 July sec D 13 (Internet), DEC biologists invited anglers to submit subsequent catches of brookies weighing 4 pounds or more. . . Three new records were recognized . . including a 5-pound, 14-ounce speck caught in Clear Pond in Franklin County in April, 2000.

speck n[2]   Also *spack, spex*   [Orig < Du *spek;* later reborrowed < PaGer, Ger *speck*]   **chiefly in Ger, esp PaGer, settlement areas**

Fat meat, esp bacon or pork; fat; hence adjs *specki, specky* fatty.

1691 in 1850 Munsell *Annals Albany* 2.116 **NY,** The plaintiff demands 180 lb. *speck.*   **1848** Bartlett *Americanisms* 321, *Spack and applejees. . .* Pork and apples cooked together. An ancient dish made in New York. **1872** Haldeman *PA Dutch* 58 [English influenced by German], *Speck,* the flitch of salt bacon, particularly when boiled with sourcrout, hence, 'speck and sourcrout.'   **1886** *Amer. Philol. Assoc. Proc.* 17.xii **ePA,** "Speck" is the hybrid offspring of English pronunciation and German *Speck* (pronounced schpeck), the generic term applied to all kinds of fat meat.   **1895** *DN* 1.383 **NY,** *Spack:* pork.   **1908** *German Amer. Annals* 10.46 **sePA,** I like sourkrout and speck.   **1935** *AmSp* 10.169 **PA** [Engl of PA Germans], *Speck* has the primary meaning of 'fat,' as when a neighbor said of our baby, 'Ei, ei, he has much *speck* on him, ain't not?' but it is also generally used for 'bacon.'   **1940** Writers' Program *Guide OH* 78, Succotash . . is cooked in many a Hocking Valley kitchen, as well as spex, a concoction of kraut and pork.   **1950** *WELS (Words for bacon)* 1 Inf, **seWI,** Speck.   **1954** *AmSp* 29.52, *Speck. . .* is a household word in many German-American families. . . The loan word in PaG [=Pennsylvania German] English nearly always designates pork fat or other meat fat. The loan adjective *specky* (from *speckig*) is almost as common as the noun. Children who refuse to eat meat which is too 'specky' are told that this will put 'speck' on their bones. The expression *speck and beans* can mean pork and beans but usually refers to string beans cooked with ham. In *sauerkraut and speck,* however, *speck* usually means pork. In the combination *speck and eggs* this loan word can mean either bacon or ham.   **1967–69** *DARE* (Qu. H38, . . *Words for bacon [including joking ones]*) Infs **MI**102, **MO**25, 36, **NY**34, Speck; (Qu. BB50c, *Remedies for infections*) Inf **PA**29, Piece of speck; **PA**150, Speck.   **1967** *DARE* FW Addit **csPA,** I had a splinter, and the *doctor* said, "Tie a piece of speck [spek] on it and it will be out by morning."   **1968** *Helen Adolf Festschrift* 36 **cePA,** *Speck* and *specki. . .* The noun *Speck* is still a common designation for 'fat'; for example, "The meat has too much speck on it." "This will put speck on your ribs." The adjective *specki* is frequently used as the equivalent of 'fatty'; for example, "That meat is too specki."   **1982** *Barrick Coll.* **csPA,** *Speck—fat—*"You need to put on some speck." [++]"Fry it in a low pan with some speck."   **1987** *Jrl. Engl. Ling.* 20.2.175 **ePA,** *Speck* 'fat'. . . *Speck* is used by a variety of age, regional, and educational groups.   **2006** Wolfram–Ward *Amer. Voices* 261 **sePA,** Many Pennsylvania German words have made their way into the English language of the area. These words include . . *speck* 'fat, bacon.'

'speck v[1]   See **expect**

speck v[2]   See **suspect**

speck n[3]   See **spik**

speck-back (tick) n   [See quot 2002]   **AL, AR, LA, TX**   Cf **spotted tick**

=lone star tick.

1943 *Mexia Weekly Herald* (TX) 3 Sept 4/7, Listed as "multiple-legged leaders of sabotage" were the ordinary house-fly, . . the "speck-back" tick which hunters sometimes encounter [etc].   **1967–70** *DARE* (Qu. R23a, *Insects or other creatures that fasten themselves to the skin and suck blood—on land*) Infs **AL**35, **AR**56, **TX**37, 96, Speck-back ticks; **LA**6, Speck-back tick—a large tick with a speck on his back; **LA**18, Speck-back ticks—red with one white dot.   **1970** *DARE* Tape **TX**96, But those old speck-back ticks'd just crawl up your britches legs and bite you every time you'd come out. . . They were plenty of them still around.   **2002** *DARE* File—Internet **TX,** Female specimens are easily recognized by the conspicuous silvery-white spot at the tip of the scutum, hence the name "speck-back" in the Ozark Mountains and the common name "lone star tick".

specked-back turtle   See **speckle-back turtle**

specki   See **speck** n[2]

speckle   See **speckled trout**

speckle-back turtle n   Also *speck turtle, specked-back turtle, speckled-back terrapin*   **esp NJ, DE**   Cf **speckled turtle**

=spotted turtle.

1926 *Ft. Wayne Jrl.–Gaz.* (IN) 24 Sept 1/8, She was almost as secure

in her privacy as a speckled-back terrapin in his shell.   **1966–69** *DARE* (Qu. P24, . . *Kinds of turtles*) Infs **NJ**39, 56, Speckle-back turtle; **DE**3, Speckle-back turtle—black with gold dots; **GA**7, Speckled-back terrapin; **NJ**53, Specked-back turtle; **NJ**55, Speck turtle.

speckle-bellied summer duck   See **specklebelly 4**

specklebelly n

1   also *speck, specklebelly brant* (or *goose*), *specklebreast* (*goose*), *speckle-breasted brant, speckled-bellied goose, speckled belly, ~ brant:* **=white-fronted goose.**   [See quot 1886]

1874 Coues *Birds NW* 546, *Anser albifrons* var. *Gambeli. . .* White-fronted Goose; Speckle-belly.   **1886** *Forest & Stream* 26.349 **IL,** American White-Fronted Goose (*Anser albifrons gambeli*). . . occasionally it is called speckle-belly, on account of the black patchy feathers on the breast.   **1898** Elliot *Wild Fowl* 47, Although the name by which this species is generally known to the gunners of the west is Brant, it has also various others in differing parts of its dispersion. Some of these are Laughing Goose, . . Speckled Belly, Speckled Brant [etc].   **1918** Grinnell et al. *Game Birds CA* 219, *Anser albifrons gambeli. . .* Other names—Speckle-breast; Speckle-belly; Checker-breast; Checker-belly. **1923** U.S. Dept. Ag. *Misc. Circular* 13.35, White-fronted Goose. . . Vernacular Names. . . *In local use.* . . specklebreast (Calif.); speckle-breasted brant (Ariz.); speckle-breast goose (Oreg.)   **1940** Gabrielson *Birds OR* 131, The Speckle Breast, or Gray Goose, is ardently sought by hunters of wild fowl, many of whom will let a shot at Snow or Cackling Geese pass if there is a possibility of a flock of "Specks" approaching their shooting blinds.   **1967–70** *DARE* (Qu. Q6, . . *Kinds of wild geese*) Inf **LA**31, Specklebelly—white-fronted goose; **LA**33B, Blue geese, also called specklebellies; **TX**33A, Specklebelly geese; **VA**84, Speckled-bellied geese.   **1982** Elman *Hunter's Field Guide* 295, White-fronted Goose. . . Common & Regional Names: whitefront, specklebelly, specklebelly brant, speckled brant, . . speckled goose, specklebreast [etc].   **2002** (acc) Topeka Zoo *Waterbird Ponds* (Internet), Pacific White-fronted Goose. . . Sometimes called a "Specklebelly."

2   **=gadwall.**

1888 Trumbull *Names of Birds* 24 **Long Is. NY,** Gadwall. . . Though rather a rare visitant on Long Island, it is known (when it does appear) at Moriches as *speckle-belly.*   **1955** *MA Audubon Soc. Bulletin* 39.314 **MA,** Gadwall. . . Speckle-belly. . . The speckling is rather on the breast and sides.   **1982** Elman *Hunter's Field Guide* 147, Gadwall. . . Common & Regional Names: gadwell, . . specklebelly.

3   also *speckled belly:* **=sharp-tailed grouse.**

1904 Doubleday *Birds* 281, Prairie Sharp-tailed Grouse. . . *Called also:* Pin-tailed Grouse; Speckled or White Belly.   **1936** Roberts *MN Birds* 1.395, Prairie Sharp-tailed Grouse. . . *Other names:* Pintail Grouse, . . Speckle-belly [etc].

4   also *speckle-bellied summer duck:* **=baldpate 1.**

1955 *MA Audubon Soc. Bulletin* 39.314, Baldpate. . . speckle-bellied summer duck, speckle-belly.

5   An immature **black-bellied plover.**

1955 *MA Audubon Soc. Bulletin* 39.446, Black-bellied Plover. . . Speckle-belly. . . Subadult birds with the black coloration underneath not fully developed.

specklebelly brant (or goose)   See **specklebelly 1**

specklebill, speckle-billed coot   See **speckled-billed coot**

specklebreast, speckle-breasted brant, specklebreast goose   See **specklebelly 1**

speckle britches   See **speckled britches**

speckle-check n

=ladder-backed woodpecker 1.

1900 *Auk* 17.344 **csTX,** *Dryobates scalaris bairdi.* Texan Woodpecker.—Much the commonest of the Picidae. . . Local name, 'speckle-check.'   **1941** Jaeger *Wildflowers* 19, The red-shafted flicker and the little speckle-check or cactus woodpecker dig holes in the fibrous trunks and branches [of the tree yucca].   **1944** Hausman *Amer. Birds* 453, Texas Woodpecker. . . The little Speckle-check, as this bird is often called, is an inhabitant of junipers, oaks [etc].

speckled-back terrapin   See **speckle-back turtle**

speckled bass n   Also *speck*

=crappie.

1867 De Voe *Market Asst.* 293 **NY,** Calico bass, speckled bass, or partridge-tailed bass.   **1938** Schrenkeisen *Field Book Fishes* 260, The calico bass is also known as Grass Bass, . . Speckled Bass [etc]. **1967–70** *DARE* (Qu. P1, . . *Kinds of freshwater fish . . caught around here . . good to eat*) Infs **MI**112, 123, **TX**9, Speckled bass; **FL**35, Specks—crappies; (Qu. P3, *Freshwater fish that are not good to eat*) Inf **MI**123, Speckled bass or specks (i.e., crappies). **2002** *DARE* File—Internet **WI**, White Crappie. . . Other Names: crappie, speckled perch, speckled bass.

speckled-bellied goose See **specklebelly 1**

speckled belly See **specklebelly 1, 3**

speckled-bill coot n Also *specklebill, speckle-billed coot*
=**surf scoter.**
  1888 Trumbull *Names of Birds* 103 **CT**, At Stratford [the surf scoter is called] *speckled-bill coot.* **1917** (1923) *Birds Amer.* 1.151, Surf Scoter. . . Other Names.—Surf Duck; Surf Coot; Surfer; . . Speckle-billed Coot [etc]. **1955** MA Audubon Soc. *Bulletin* 39.377 **CT**, Surf Scoter. . . Speckled-bill Coot. . . The bill is parti-colored. **1982** Elman *Hunter's Field Guide* 240, Surf Scoter. . . Common & Regional Names. . . surf coot, specklebill, . . surfer [etc].

speckled brant See **specklebelly 1**

speckled britches n Also *speckle britches* Cf **speckled John 1**
=**evening primrose a.**
  1969 *DARE* (Qu. I28b, *Kinds of greens that are cooked*) Inf **KY**42, Speckle britches. **2001** *Appalachian Alternatives* Spring (Internet), We return to the potherbs which our forbearers [sic] knew could break the effects of cabin fever. . . Evening primrose or "speckled britches" (early in cold frames and tasty as dandelions).

speckled brook trout See **speckled trout 1**

speckled bullhead n
=**brown bullhead 1.**
  1908 Forbes–Richardson *Fishes of IL* 188, We have found both the mottled and the brown forms [of the brown bullhead], with occasional specimens of the black bullhead . . indiscriminately referred to as "bullpouts" or "speckled bullheads" by the fishermen who were dressing them. **1951** Harlan–Speaker *IA Fish* 92, Northern Brown Bullhead. . . Other Names—Bullhead, . . speckled bullhead. **1983** Becker *Fishes WI* 702, Brown Bullhead. . . Other common names: northern brown bullhead, . . speckled bullhead, speckled cat [etc]. **2005** *Ledger* (Lakeland FL) 11 Aug sec C 2 (Internet), Catfish might be most consistent catch, with plenty of speckled bullheads 1–2 pounds at Saddle Creek Park, reports Phillips Bait and Tackle.

speckled caille n Cf **half caille, little ~, red ~, yellow ~**
=**wood thrush 1.**
  1900 Rightor *Std. Hist. New Orleans* 357, Speckled Caille (Creole). Wood Thrush. (Turdus mustelinus.) Clear brown upper parts, black-streaked, satiny-white under parts; great musical powers. **1916** *Times-Picayune* (New Orleans LA) 30 Apr mag sec 5/7, Wood Thrush. . . Big Caille; Speckled Caille [etc].

speckled cat n
1 =**bowfin.**
  1933 LA Dept. of Conserv. *Fishes* 383, Louisianians also know the Grindle as the Cottonfish, the Speckled Cat and the Cypress Trout.
2 also *speckled catfish:* =**brown bullhead 1** or the closely related *Ameiurus serracanthus.* Cf **speckled bullhead**
  1883 *Athens Messenger* (OH) 27 Dec 2/3 **cwGA**, Mr. Jones is also experimenting with another variety of fish, which he feels sure will prove profitable. . . This is the speckled catfish. . . No fish increase faster than the speckled cat. **1906** Amer. Fisheries Soc. *Trans.* 180, Have you ever tried the speckled cat? A. No, we have tried the channel cat, but cannot keep them. **1955** Carr–Goin *Guide Reptiles* 62, *Ameiurus nebulosus marmoratus.* . . Southern Brown Bullhead; Speckled Cat. **1983** [see **speckled bullhead**]. **2004** *DARE* File—Internet **GA**, Muddy water can come from a variety of sources so careful investigation of the problem is the only way to get a long-term fix. Is it from runoff, from speckled catfish, common carp, or maybe just too many channel catfish? . . Speckled cat and common carp are notorious for muddying up ponds. **2005** in 2007 *Ibid* **NC**, Within its hallowed depths can be caught over 19 species of fish, the most popular being . . channel catfish, flathead catfish, speckled catfish, crappie, and sauger. **2006** *Ibid*, If I am not mistaken, that is a Spotted Bullhead (Ameiurus serracanthus) ARA—"Speckled Cat" locally down in Georgia and Florida. **2007** *Ibid*, Catfish (Ameiurus serracanthus)—*Other names:* Speckled Cat—*Range:* Re-

stricted to a few watersheds in North Florida, from the Suwannee west to the Aplachicola [sic].

3 also *speckled catfish:* A **channel catfish** (here: *Ictalurus punctatus*).
  1850 in 1974 OK Ornith. Soc. *Bulletin* 7.45, The rest [of the fish] are what they call trout & speckled Cat fish. Kerls caught a tremendous Cat Fish and it was as much as he could do to get him into Camp. **1913** Geogr. Soc. Chicago *Bulletin* 5.126 **IL**, There are many first-class food fishes . . [that] breed in these shallows. There are the large-mouthed black bass . . , the bluegill, the pumpkinseed, the green sunfish, the perch . . , the speckled catfish, and the crappie. **1918** St. John *Practical Bait* 137 **IL**, The channel or speckled catfish *(Ictalurus punctatus),* unlike other catfish, prefers running water. **1943** Eddy–Surber *N. Fishes* 152, Channel Catfish (Speckled Catfish, Fiddler). **1967–69** *DARE* (Qu. P1, . . *Kinds of freshwater fish . . caught around here . . good to eat*) Infs **AL**17, **GA**25, 65, 84, **SC**40, Speckled cat; **LA**40, Speckled cat, [corr to] spotted cat; **SC**45, Speckled catfish. [*DARE* Ed: Some of these Infs may refer instead to **1** or **2** above.] **1975** Evanoff *Catch More Fish* 94, The channel catfish *(Ictalurus punctatus)* is one of the gamest and is also called the speckled catfish, fiddler, and silver catfish. **1986** Pederson *LAGS Concordance,* 2 infs, **cnGA, nwFL**, Speckled cat; 1 inf, **seAL**, Speckled catfish. [*DARE* Ed: Some of these Infs may refer instead to **1** or **2** above.] **2006** in 2007 *DARE* File—Internet **cnKY**, Speckled cats here are usually young channels also called fiddlers.

speckled catfish See **speckled cat 2, 3**

speckled chub n
A **minnow B1** (here: *Macrhybopsis aestivalis*).
  1951 Harlan–Speaker *IA Fish* 76, The speckled chub is largely confined to the major rivers of Iowa. **1957** Trautman *Fishes* 311 **OH**, It is quite possible that previous to 1925 the Speckled Chub was more abundant and widespread than it has been since. **1966** WI Acad. *Trans.* 55.100, The speckled chub is locally abundant in large rivers. **1983** *Audubon Field Guide N. Amer. Fishes* 420, The Speckled Chub lives on or near the bottom. **2004** *Assoc. Press State & Local Wire* 6 May (Internet) **KS**, The river quality has improved enough that the state is considering removing a fish called the speckled chub from the endangered species list, Johnson said.

speckled crappie n
The black **crappie** *(Pomoxis nigromaculatus).*
  1951 Harlan–Speaker *IA Fish* 123, Black Crappie. . . Other Names—Calico Bass, crappie, speckled crappie. **1966** *Lima News* (OH) 24 Apr sec D 7/3, The speckled crappie or whatever name he is known as, and he will have several, depending upon the location, produces a great deal of excitement. **2002** *DARE* File—Internet, Painting a Black Crappie. . . Perhaps the greatest challenge in the painting process is the task of re-creating the black markings and patterns that dominate the overall appearance and give the fish that "speckled crappie" look.

speckled dace n
A **dace** of the western US (here: *Rhinichthys osculus*).
  1949 *Jrl. Wildlife Management* 13.246, Large populations of speckled dace *(Rhinichthys oscula carringtoni),* and redside shiner . . also appeared unaffected by the poison. **1957** Blair et al. *Vertebrates U.S.* 113, *Rhinichthys osculus.* . . Speckled dace. . . Widely distributed from western slopes of the Rocky Mountains to the West Coast. **1963** Sigler–Miller *Fishes UT* 84, The speckled dace occurs in all the major streams and in many of the desert springs of Utah. **1983** *Audubon Field Guide N. Amer. Fishes* 454, The Speckled Dace is one of the most widespread minnows in western waters. **2005** *Assoc. Press State & Local Wire* 29 Nov (Internet) **AZ**, Biologists say the numbers of trout are dropping while the number of natives [sic] species the program is designed to help—speckled dace, bluehead and flannelmouth suckers and chub—are up.

speckled dick n Also *speckled dock, speckle dick* Cf **speckled John 1**
A **dock** (here: *Rumex obtusifolius*) or similar plant used for greens.
  1921 *Amer. Child* 3.248 **Sth**, There was wild mustard . . wild lettuce, "mouse's ear," speckled dock . . and other "sallet greens" growing everywhere. **1969** *DARE* (Qu. I28b, *Kinds of greens that are cooked*) Inf **KY**37, Speckled dick—like pussley, but speckled. **1973** *Foxfire 2* 62 **nGA**, Patience dock *(R[umex] patientia)* and the speckled dock *(R. obtusifolius)* are common in waste places. **1973** Kluger *Wild Flavor* 72 **sIN**, To . . a fellow greens-hunter from another town nearby . . "speckled

Dick" is "wild beet." **1982** [see **tongue grass 1**]. **1991** [see **sour dock**]. **2002** *DARE* File—Internet **ceKY,** Right about this time of year, I start remembering going "green picking" with mommy and friends. . . Now I can tell you the difference in "sour dock" and "speckled dick" in a heartbeat. *Ibid* **neTN,** Nobody in our family said greens or landcress, it was Sallet. I especially like the homey names of plants Granny taught me to recognize, Narrow dock, speckled Dick, woolly britches. **2006** in 2007 *Ibid* **eTN,** We had lots of it [=poke] in east Tennessee. And we were pretty poor. So we were eating lots of wild greens, pinto beans, corn bread, eggs. We used to eat sour dock and speckled dock and something called "seven tops", too.

speckled gravy n Also *spotted gravy* **chiefly S Midl**
=red-eye gravy.

1906 *DN* 3.157 **nwAR,** Speckled gravy. . . Ham gravy. **1928** in 2002 *DARE* File—Internet **KY,** We bought the nicest country ham and boiled off half of it and will have the other with nice spotted gravy. **1954** *Harder Coll.* **cwTN,** Spotted gravy. **1967** *DARE* (Qu. H37, . . *Words* . . *for gravy. Any joking ones?*) Inf **TX32,** Speckled gravy—made from hog meat. **1975** McDonough *Garden Sass* 73 **AR,** Redeye gravy . . also called speckled gravy. **1984** Wilder *You All Spoken Here* 87 **Sth,** *Red-eye gravy, speckled gravy, calico gravy:* A gravy made of grease from fried country ham—add a couple of sloshes of black coffee and boiling water and stir. **1997** in 2004 Montgomery–Hall *Dict. Smoky Mt. Engl.* 556 **wNC, eTN,** *Speckled gravy.* . . Same as *red-eye gravy.* **2001** *DARE* File—Internet **AR,** Biscuits and speckled gravy (made by pouring some coffee in bacon grease) is one of my favorite meals. *Ibid* **sTX,** We were there for a breakfast that included fresh made biscuits and speckled gravy.

speckled ground snake n Cf **ground snake**
=speckled racer.

1937 Pope *Snakes Alive* 200 **TX,** Speckled ground snake (*D[rymobius] margaritiferus* [sic]). Extreme southern Texas. **1953** Schmidt *N. Amer. Amphibians* 192, *Drymobius margaritiferus.* . . *Common name.—* Speckled ground snake.

speckled hen n
=black bass 1.

1871 *Fur Fin & Feather* 88, The Spotted Bass or Speckled Hen. . . a common fish in the fresh waters of the Western States. **1887** Goode *Amer. Fishes* 56, "Black Perch" and "Speckled Hen" are other names applied to one or both species [=largemouth and smallmouth bass]. **1933** LA Dept. of Conserv. *Fishes* 313, Large-mouthed Black Bass . . Speckled Hen; Spotted Bass [etc]. **1935** Caine *Game Fish* 4, Large-mouthed Black Bass. . . *Synonyms:* Bass . . Speckled Hen [etc]. *Ibid* 7, Small-mouthed Black Bass. . . Speckled Hen. *Ibid* 10, Spotted Small-mouthed Black Bass. . . Speckled Hen. **1976** Tryckare et al. *Lore of Sportfishing* 101, Smallmouth Black Bass. . . Other common names . . speckled hen [etc].

speckled-hen lily n
A **fritillary** (here: *Fritillaria lanceolata*).

1934 Haskin *Wild Flowers Pacific Coast* 23, This graceful flower [= *Fritillaria lanceolata*] bears so many common names that each person may call it differently and still be right. . . [S]peckled-hen and snake lily come from its peculiar color and markings.

speckle dick See **speckled dick**

speckled Jack n Cf **speckled britches**
Prob =**evening primrose a.**

1911 *DN* 3.540 **eKY,** *Speckled jack.* . . An (unidentified) plant cooked as "greens." **1940** (1978) Still *River of Earth* 14 **KY,** Before the garden was ready, Mother and Euly gathered a mess of plantain and speckled jack and we had salet greens cooked with meat rind.

speckled jewels n
A **jewelweed 1** (here: *Impatiens capensis*).

1822 Eaton *Botany* 318, *[Impatiens] biflora* [=*I. capensis*] . . speckled jewels. **1854** King *Amer. Eclectic Dispensatory* 557, *Impatiens Fulva* [=*I. capensis*], or *Speckled Jewels* is the most common variety. **1900** Lyons *Plant Names* 201, *I[mpatiens] biflora.* . . Speckeled [sic] Jewels or Jewel-weed.

speckled John n

1 =evening primrose a. Cf speckled britches, ~ dick, ~ Jack, spotted John

1896 KS Ag. Exper. Sta. Manhattan *Bulletin* 57.13, *Oenothera biennis,*

L. (Evening Primrose, Golden Candlestick, Speckled John.) **1898** *Jrl. Amer. Folkl.* 11.227 **KS,** *Oenothera biennis* . . golden candlestick, speckled John.

2 A **Saint-John's-wort** (here: *Hypericum perforatum*).

1914 Georgia *Manual Weeds* 284, Common St. John's-wort. . . *Other English names* . . Speckled John. . . Leaves opposite, . . more or less black-dotted and specked all over with pellucid dots.

3 A **milkweed 1** (here: *Asclepias* spp).

1957 *KY Folkl. Rec.* 3.45, Milkweed (called "speckled John" by the colored folks).

speckled mountain trout See **speckled trout 1**

speckled perch n Also *speckle perch, specks* **chiefly Sth** See Map
=crappie.

1856 *Harper's New Mth. Mag.* Sept 448 **neNC, seVA,** The waters also abound in fine fresh-water fish, the most esteemed of which are the speckled perch. **1877** Hallock *Sportsman's Gaz.* 378, Silver Perch, or Speckled Perch; called also Strawberry Bass and Calico Bass. **1933** LA Dept. of Conserv. *Fishes* 333, More northern anglers know this fish better under the name of White Crappie. This species' popularity is very well attested by the variety of names it has been given. . . [including] Speckled Perch. **1965–70** *DARE* (Qu. P1, . . *Kinds of freshwater fish* . . *caught around here* . . *good to eat*) 11 Infs, **chiefly Sth,** Speckled perch; (Qu. FF16, . . *Local contests or celebrations*) Inf **FL36,** Speckled perch festival—early spring. **1966** *DARE* Tape **FL16,** The big specialty in this area is speckled perch fishing; . . further north they call 'em croppie or crappie fish. **1968** *DARE* FW Addit **LA,** Speckled perch—occasional. Alternate term for "crappie" . . general or southern Louisiana; the man who gave [this name] was well-traveled in the Cajun country. **1986** Pederson *LAGS Concordance* **Gulf Region,** 16 infs, Speckle perch(es); 1 inf, Speckle perch—some call crappie; 1 inf, Crappie—we call them speckle perch; 1 inf, Speckled perch. **2001** *DARE* File—Internet **IN,** Black Crappie. . . *Other Common Names:* Bream, . . speckled perch, specks [etc].

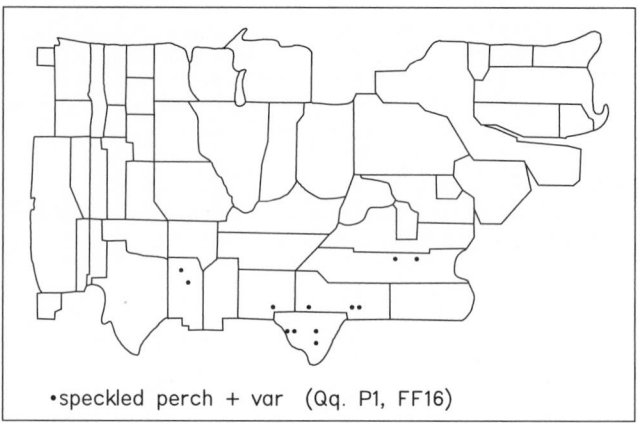

•speckled perch + var (Qq. P1, FF16)

speckled racer n

A colubrid snake of southernmost Texas *(Drymobius margaritiferus).* Also called **speckled ground snake**

1957 Blair et al. *Vertebrates U.S.* 342, *Drymobius margaritiferus.* . . Speckled racer. . . The Brownsville region of Texas. **1979** Behler–King *Audubon Field Guide Reptiles* 603, Speckled racer. . . Fast-moving and difficult to capture.

speckled rattlesnake n Also *speckled rattler*

A **rattlesnake 1** (here: *Crotalus mitchelli* and subspp) of the Mohave and Sonoran Deserts. Also called **prairie rattlesnake 1, white ~**

1937 Pope *Snakes Alive* 225, Speckled rattlesnake *(C[rotalus] mitchellii).* Two subspecies of this snake are recognized, a southern one *(pyrrhus)* found in central and southwestern Arizona and extreme southern California, and a northern one *(stephensi)* confined to southwestern Nevada and adjacent southern California. **1957** Jaeger *N. Amer. Deserts* 102, On the Colorado Desert the most commonly seen reptiles include the . . speckled rattler *(Crotalus mitchelli)* [etc]. **1974** Shaw–Campbell *Snakes West* 222, The speckled rattlesnake ranges from southern Nevada, where it is called the Panamint rattlesnake . . to the tip of Baja California and from southern California into central Arizona. In the southern part of its range it is called the southwestern speckled rattlesnake. **2002** (acc) San Diego Nat. Hist. Museum *Checklist Reptiles* (Internet), Speckled Rattlesnake. . . Black speckles form indistinct cross bars or dorsal blotches across the back. Some desert specimens are colored like decomposed granite.

speckled sapsucker See **speckled woodpecker**

speckled snake n

A **king snake 1** (here: *Lampropeltis getulus*).

1778 Carver *Travels N. Amer.* 487, The *Speckled Snake* is an aqueous reptile about two feet and a half in length, but without venom. Its skin . . is used by the Americans as a cover for the handles of whips, and it renders them very pleasing to the sight. **1789** Morse *Amer. Geog.* 61, Of the Snakes which infest the United States, are the following viz. . . Speckled. **1908** Biol. Soc. DC *Proc.* 21.75 **TX**, *Lampropeltis getula sayi* Holbrook. . . The king or "speckled" snake is rather common. In Waco examples the markings are seldom in the form of bands, but the whole upper surface is minutely speckled with small yellow dots.

speckled terrapin (or tortoise) See **speckled turtle**

speckled trout n Also *speckle (trout)*

1 also *speckled brook* (or *mountain*) *trout, spreckle, spreckle(d) trout:* Usu =**brook trout,** but also **Dolly Varden 1** and **rainbow trout.** Cf **speck** n[1] **6**

1805 (1904) Lewis *Orig. Jrls. Lewis & Clark Exped.* 2.151, These trout . . resemble our mountain or speckled trout [=*Salvelinus fontinalis*]. **1838** Geol. Surv. OH *Second Annual Rept.* 195, *S[almo] fontinalis.* The speckled trout are to be found in Ohio in only two streams. **1859** Taliaferro *Fisher's R.* 109 **nwNC** (as of 1820s), We had nothing but chubs, . . eels, speckled trout, and a few other small varieties of the finny tribes. **1869** U.S. Dept. Ag. *Rept. of Secy. for 1868* 322, [It is] rank folly to allow so great a delicacy as the speckled brook trout *(Salmo fontinalis)* to become extinct. **1884** Goode *Fisheries U.S.* 1.475, The Rainbow Trout. . . generally known as the "Brook Trout," "Mountain Trout," "Speckled Trout" [etc]. *Ibid* 504, This species [=*Salvelinus malma*] is known in the mountains [of the western US] as "Lake Trout," "Bull Trout," "Speckled Trout," and "Red-spotted Trout." **1887** Smull's *Hand Book* 120 **PA**, It is made illegal to catch spreckled trout, save only by rod, hook and line, at any time. **1904** *Salmon & Trout* 295, These four subspecies may be distinguished from *[Salvelinus] fontinalis* on sight by the absence of the dark mottlings or wormlike markings on the back which are always present on the "speckled trout." **1931** *Appleton Post–Crescent* (WI) 30 May 4/4, They caught the limit of spreckle trout. **1937** *Frederick Post* (MD) 23 Jan 3/4, The worm fishermen . . gives 'Spreckles' plenty of time to swallow the hook. **1937** Thornburgh *Gt. Smoky Mts.* 41, Native mountain speckled trout, a variety of eastern brook trout, is now confined to the headwaters, usually up above 3,800 feet. **1965–70** *DARE* (Qu. P1, . . *Kinds of freshwater fish . . caught around here . . good to eat*) 30 Infs, **scattered,** Speckled trout; **GA**72, Speckled trout—same as brook trout; **NY**6, Brook trout or speckled trout; **KY**43, **TX**101, Speckle trout; **CO**12, Speckled mountain trout; **VA**46, Speckle. **1966** *DARE* Tape **MI**32, Quite a few inland lakes have been stocked with [what] . . they call a splake . . a cross between a speckled trout and a lake trout. **1974** WI Univ. *Fish Lake MI* 24, Brook Trout. . . Common names: Eastern brook trout, speckled trout [etc]. **1986** Pederson *LAGS Concordance,* 1 inf, **ceTX,** Speckled trout—freshwater fish. **2002** in 2008 *DARE* File—Internet, Pretty good morning fishing backwaters of Naples Fl . . 17 spreckled trout 15–19″. **2007** *Ibid* **NC**, Brook Trout is the only species of trout native to Western North Carolina. Known as "spec" or "speckled trout" by mountain folk, the brook is not a true trout, but a "char."

2 A **weakfish** (here: *Cynoscion nebulosus*). **chiefly Sth** See Map Cf **speck** n[1] **5**

1896 NC State Bd. Ag. *NC Resources* 299 (Internet), Still fishing for Gray and Speckled Trout (cynoscion regalis and c. nebulosus) known further north as Weakfish, is a fascinating sport. **1931** *Copeia* 2.49 **TX**, *Cynoscion nebulosus.* . . A "speckled trout," . . from Shamrock Cove, Corpus Christi Bay. **1965–70** *DARE* (Qu. P2, . . *Kinds of saltwater fish caught around here . . good to eat*) 18 Infs, **chiefly Sth,** Speckled trout; **GA**11, Speckled trout = weakfish; **LA**26, Speckled trout [FW: =spotted weakfish]; **LA**22, 43, **NC**49, 80, 82, Speckle trout; (Qu. P14, . . *Commercial fishing . . what do the fishermen go out after?*) Infs **FL**16, **LA**43, **TX**88, Speckled trout; **LA**40, Speckled trout = weakfish; **NC**80, Speckle trout. **1967** *DARE* Tape **TX**18, We catch the trout, or weakfish, better known as weakfish, except in this area we call 'em speckled trout. **1967** *DARE* FW Addit **TX**, *Speckled trout*—kind of fish caught in surf

in Texas. **1986** Pederson *LAGS Concordance* **Gulf Region,** 23 infs, Speckle trout; 17 infs, Speckled trout(s); 1 inf, Speckled trout—weakfish—in Gulf. [*DARE* Ed: 8 of these infs specify a saltwater fish; others may refer to **1** above.] **2005** *News & Observer* (Raleigh NC) 22 Dec sec C 10 (Internet), Called the speckled trout by Tar Heel anglers, the "speck" is one of the more popular winter fish on our coast, along with the gray trout. **2007** *Ibid* **seLA,** Captain *Rory Rorison* will take you and your guests to the scenic marshes and coastal islands of South Loiuisiana in search of Speckled Trout and Redfish.

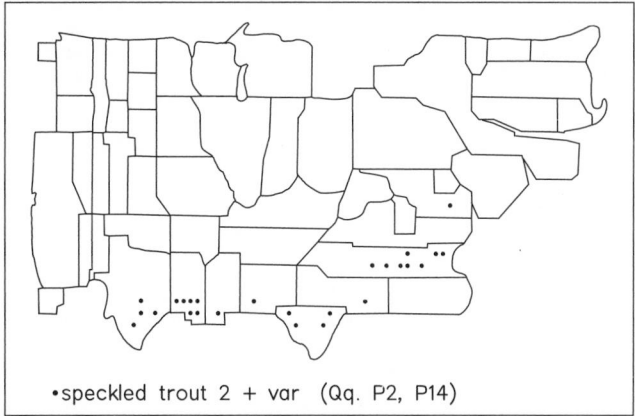

•speckled trout 2 + var (Qq. P2, P14)

speckled turtle n Also *speckled terrapin, ~ tortoise* =**spotted turtle.**

1792 Belknap *Hist. NH* 3.174, Speckled Turtle, *Testudo carolina?* **1839** *N. Amer. Rev.* 49.152, *Emys guttata* (our common and beautiful speckled tortoise). **1842** DeKay *Zool. NY* 3.14, Under the name of *Speckled Turtle,* this little animal [=the spotted tortoise] is found throughout the Union. **1891** *Century Dict.* 6246, Speckled terrapin, the spotted turtle, *Chelopus guttatus,* a small fresh-water tortoise of the United States, whose black carapace has round yellow spots. **1891** Jesup *Plants Hanover NH* 64, C[helopus] guttatus. . . Speckled Tortoise. **1928** Pope–Dickinson *Amphibians* 76 **WI**, Spotted Turtle. . . Also called Pond Turtle and Speckled Tortoise in some localities. **1986** Pederson *LAGS Concordance (Turtle)* 1 inf, **ceGA,** Old speckle [sic] turtle. **1994** Mitchell *Reptiles VA* 87, Spotted Turtle. . . A vernacular name used in Virginia is 'speckled tortoise.'

speckled woodpecker n Also *speckled sapsucker, speckle woodpecker, ~ peckerwood, spreckled woodpecker* Either a **flicker** n[2] **1** (here: *Colaptes auratus*) or the **hairy woodpecker.** Cf **little speckled woodpecker**

1791 Bartram *Travels* 182, P[icus] villosus, the hairy, speckled and crested woodpecker. **1792** Belknap *Hist. NH* 3.166, Speckled Woodpecker—*Picus maculosus.* **1806** (1905) Lewis *Orig. Jrls. Lewis & Clark Exped.* 5.136, Saw the speckled woodpecker, bee martin and log cock or large woodpecker. **1855** Larrabee *Rosabower* 149, A speckled woodpecker is seen working away on the body of an apple-tree. **1930** OK Univ. Biol. Surv. *Pub.* 2.118, Dryobates villosus villosus. . . Local names: Speckled woodpecker, . . speckled "sapsucker." **1965–69** *DARE* (Qu. Q17, . . *Kinds of woodpeckers*) Infs **AR**28, **IL**67, **ME**3, **MS**63, **TX**37, Speckled woodpecker; **IL**14, Speckled woodpecker—like a sapsucker; **OH**67, Speckled woodpecker—same as sapsucker; **GA**16, Spreckled woodpecker. **1986** Pederson *LAGS Concordance (Woodpecker)* 1 inf, **seAR,** Speckle peckerwood; 1 inf, **csGA,** Speckle woodpecker.

speckle perch See **speckled perch**

speckle trout See **speckled trout**

speckle woodpecker See **speckled woodpecker**

specks See **speckled perch**

speck turtle See **speckle-back turtle**

specky See **speck** n[2]

speckylate, speckylation See **speculate**

'spect v[1] See **expect**

spect v[2] See **suspect**

spectacle case n

Either of two formerly widespread **freshwater clams:** *Cumberlandia monodonta* or *Villosa lienosa*.

1905 *Acad. Sci. St. Louis Trans.* 15.249 **nwIA,** *Margaritana monodonta.* . . Only two specimens were obtained from the gigantic quantity of shells held by the fishermen, who call this species the spectacle case. **1914** *U.S. Bur. Fisheries Rept. for 1912* 30 **KY, TN,** The spectacle case *(M. monodonta)* was once common here, but has been nearly exterminated by being used for fish bait. **1915** *Amer. Midland Naturalist* 4.98, *Cumberlandia monodonta.* . . "Spectacle Case." **1916** *Ibid* 432, *Eurynia (Micromya)* [=*Villosa*] *lienosa.* . . "Little Spectacle Case." **1941** *AmSp* 16.156 **Missip Valley,** There are many varieties of fresh-water mussels. . . The following list gives the common names as applied by the cutter and fisher of shells. . . Spectacle-case [etc]. **1985** Madson *Up River* 59 **Upper Missip Valley,** Spectacle case. **1992** Cummings–Mayer *Field Guide Freshwater Mussels MW* 22, Spectaclecase. . . Elongate shell, usually pinched in the middle, dark brown to black.

spectacle coot n   Also *spectacled coot, spectacle duck*   [See quot 1888]

=**surf scoter.**

1844 Giraud *Birds Long Is.* 330, The Surf, or "Spectacle Duck," as it is by some called, associates with [the velvet duck]. **1875** *Fur Fin & Feather* 119, Of the various fowl called vulgarly coot, are the pied-duck (the skunk head), the velvet-duck (white-winged coot), the surf-duck (spectacle duck), and the American scoter. **1888** Trumbull *Names of Birds* 103 **CT,** At Stratford, [the surf scoter is called] *speckled-bill coot* and *spectacle coot* (this latter name like Goggle-nose, the patches of black, one at either side of the bill, being likened to colored spectacles). **1895** Elliot *N. Amer. Shore Birds* 203, The Surf Scoter has many trivial names, and is known as the Hollow-billed Coot, Skunk Head Coot, Spectacle Coot, Spectacle Duck [etc]. **1903** Huntington *Our Feathered Game* 200, The Surf-Scoter . . is often called "spectacled coot," "bay coot," and has other local names by which it may possibly deceive the unwary.

spectacles plant n   Cf **grandpa's specs**

An **honesty** (here: *Lunaria annua*).

1940 Clute *Amer. Plant Names* 263, *Lunaria annua.* . . spectacles plant, silver dollar [etc].

speculate v   Usu |ˈspɛkjəˌlet|; also |ˈspɛkəˌlet| Pronc-spp *speckylate, spekalate*   Similarly nouns *speciation, speckylation, spekilater*

Std senses, var forms.

1854 Stimson *Easy Nat* 176 **MA,** I'm offered a hundred dollars to bring ye in, and I'm good for the speckylation! **1858** Hammett *Piney Woods Tavern* 287, Sam went to England on some curus kind of specilations. **1891** *DN* 1.163 **cNY,** [ˈspɛkəˈleʃn̩]. **1899** Chesnutt *Conjure Woman* 42 **csNC** [Black], A spekilater come erlong. **1929** Sale *Specialist* 6, Then he speckylates on who / God made *first,* us fokes or you. **1937** Crane *Let Me Show You VT* 29 **VT,** There are words which some persons perpetuate in mispronunciation. . . F'r instance, *spekalate* for speculate. **1944** *PADS* 2.30 **eKY, wNC,** Speculate [ˈspɛkəleɪt]. . . Somewhat rare. **1959** *VT Hist.* 27.159, Speculate [ˈspɛkələt]. . . Common. Rural areas.

speed breaker n   Also *speed blocker,* ~ *break*   **Sth, S Midl**

A speed bump.

1925 TN *Private Acts 1925* 1.603, It shall be unlawful for anyone to construct across the road a ridge, embankment, speed breaker, or other obstruction . . which endangers the lives of the users of the road. **1965** *Charleston Daily Mail* (WV) 28 July 24/6, Speed breakers installed on some streets a few months ago have been removed. **1967–70** *DARE* (Qu. N30, . . *A sudden short dip in a road*) Infs **AL**31, **MO**29, Speed breaker. **1979** in 2001 (acc) Lexis–Nexis Legal Research *State Case Law: GA* (Internet), Plaintiff tripped and fell over a "speed breaker." **1986** Pederson *LAGS Concordance,* 53 infs, **Gulf Region,** Speed breaker(s); 1 inf, **cnTN,** Speed breaks; 1 inf, **cwFL,** Speed blocker. **2000** *Amarillo Globe–News* (TX) 19 Jan (Internet), No telling how long the bump would have stayed there had it not been for an incident which took place after the newfangled speed breaker was installed. . . He changed his route and drove down Purnell Street where the speed bump was located.

speeder n   Also *speeder car*   **scattered, but esp freq NW**   Cf **crummy** n 2, **galloping goose** 1

In logging and railroading: a small motorized track car for transporting people or supplies.

1901 *Ft. Wayne Jrl.–Gaz.* (IN) 22 Aug 4/3, The robbers were coming toward Huntington on a hand car. "Officers Ross and Riley took a Wabash "speeder" and went to the bridges." **1934** *Sun* (Baltimore MD) 6 Aug 2/1, Section men went over the President's route in gasoline "speeders." **1940** *RR Mag.* Apr 50, *Pop car*—Gasoline car, or *speeder,* used by section men, linemen, etc. **1958** McCulloch *Woods Words* 175 **Pacific NW,** *Speeder*—A rail motor car, often used to bring mail and small supplies to camp, as well as to haul men to work; known as a crummy when hauling men. **1961** Labbe-Goe *Railroads* 260 **Pacific NW,** *Speeder:* Gasoline or diesel cars ranging in use from those of the section gang to those used for transporting the crew back and forth from the woods. The latter were usually called crew speeders. **1962** *AmSp* 37.135 **nwCA** [Logging railroad language], *Speeder.* . . A rail motor car employed to repair the railroad, to bring supplies to camp, or to haul men. **1967** *DARE* (Qu. N37) Inf **WA**30, Speeder—jalopy that runs on railroad track with car engine—to haul men to work in woods. **1967** *DARE* Tape **WA**30, A speeder is a four-wheeled thing like a galloping goose. . . Maybe it's twelve, fourteen feet long, or maybe longer. Isn't a hand car. It's got an engine, a car engine, in it, sides on it, windows in it. Transports men back and forth to work. **1977** Churchill *Don't Call* 183 **nwOR** (as of c1918), The engine of a speeder is small and noisy but it can send the little four-wheel car scooting along the rails like a jack rabbit. **2002** *DARE* File—Internet **seMA,** Speeders is the nickname given to all kinds of motorized inspection cars that railroads use. *Ibid* **csWI,** The Wisconsin Heritage Rail Corporation will offer Speeder car rides on the former Illinois Central Railroad. *Ibid* **neMN,** They're called speeders; self propelled rail cars intended to carry maybe half a dozen iron miners.

speedie   See **spiedi(e)**

speedpod n

A **milk vetch** (here: *Astragalus missouriensis*).

1940 Gates *Flora KS* 204, Astragalus missouriensis. . . Speedpod. . . Plains and prairie hills. **1968** Barkley *Plants KS* 199, Speedpod. Missouri Milk Vetch.

speedwell n

Std: a plant of the genus *Veronica*.   For other names of var spp see **bluebell 1e, corn speedwell, creeping Veronica, eyebright 9, forget-me-not 5, gypsyweed 2, henbit 2, lady-at-the-gate, mouse-ear 7, necklaceweed 3, neckweed, rattlesnake master f, skullcap 2, wallink 1**

speedy n[1]

In railroading: =**callboy;** see quot 1976.

1932 *RR Mag.* Oct 370, Speedy—Call boy. **1940** Cottrell *Railroader* 136, Speedy—Call boy. **1976** Gould *Blackie's RR Hdbk.* 2, Clerk (who summons train, engine and yard crews for duty): Call Boy—Caller—Speedy. **2003** *DARE* File—Internet [Railroad glossary], Speedy—slang term for a *callboy.*

speedy n[2]   See **spiedi(e)**

speejink n   Cf *pee-jink* (at **pee-jib**)

1970 *Thompson Coll.* **cnAL** (as of 1920s), Speejink—A small clay marble, usually out of round, sometimes cracked when new.

speen   See **spean**

'spe'ence   See **experience**

speerit   See **spirit**

speeritual   See **spiritual** adj

spegnet   See **spignet**

spekalate, spekilater   See **speculate**

‡**spelling baker** n   [*baker* US military code word for the letter B, with pun on *bee*]   Cf quot 1894 at **A-B-ab**

A spelling bee.

1906 *DN* 3.157 **nwAR,** Spellin' baker. . . Spelling match. "We used to have a spellin' baker at the Lead Hill school every once in a while."

spend v   Pronc-spp *'pend, spind*

A Forms.

1909 *S. Atl. Qrly.* 8.52 **seSC,** The elimination of initial *s* in . . *sp* . . as . . *'pend* [etc] . . are all characteristics of *Gullah.* **1933** *AmSp* 8.1.32 **wTX,** The West Texan. . . has also a tendency to front and raise vowels;

e.g., *spind* for spend.   **2006** in 2008 *DARE* File—Internet **DC** [Black], They go be spindin alot of money on baby stuff.

B Senses.

1 Of consumables: to last, stretch.   [*OED2 spend* v.¹ 16.a 1673 →; "Now *dial*."]   **NEng**

1841 *Farmers' Reg.* 9.592 **neMA**, The hay cut on this land is . . swail hay, which is very good and spends well.   **1849** (1863) Allen *Amer. Farm Book* 299, Wood designed for fuel, will spend much better when cut within the same periods, and immediately housed.   **1857** Flint *Practical Treatise* 138 **eMA**, The grass this year . . was well set in the spring and grew very quick when the warm weather came on, but still we had much good, warm sun to bring it to maturity, and I think it will spend pretty well.   **1868** Brackett *Farm Talk* 21 **ME**, Perhaps it will spend better if cut then; but the question is, when to cut it so that the hay will make the best quality of food.   **1908** Day *King Spruce* 242 **ME**, No more too liberal dosing of bread dough with soap to make the flour "spend" in lighter loaves.   **1913** *DN* 4.6 **ME**, *Spend*. . . To last; to hold out. "Some butter spends better than others."   **1963** Adamson *Household Hints* 112 **NEng** (as of late 19th cent), The olive soap is a great improvement on the common yellow soap. If it is several months old, it spends economically, cleanses quickly, and is not sharp to the hands.

2 To state or express (an opinion).   [*OED2 spend* v.¹ 3.d "Now *dial*."]   **sAppalachians, Ozarks**

1782 Harrison in 1978 Morris *Papers* 4.465 **VA**, The doctrine that an American has no right to spend his opinion on public measures is so totally new to me I shall pass it over.   **1864** Longstreet *Master William* 230 **GA**, At length William began to spend his opinion upon the play of one and another, demonstrating by the doctrine of chances that they were injudicious.   **1924** Raine *Land of Saddle-Bags* 100 **sAppalachians**, He carries a *budget* on his back, and *spends* his opinions as Othello did.   **1930** *VA Qrly. Rev.* 6.244 **AR**, An up-country Arkansawyer . . tarries now and then to spend an opinion.   **1937** *Hall Coll.* **wNC, eTN**, I would rather not spend my opinion.   **1942** (1971) Campbell *Cloud-Walking* 81 **seKY**, Because he favored learning so strong Nelt learned to spend his opinions before the teacher women and not be shamed.   **c1960** *Wilson Coll.* **csKY**, *Spend an opinion*. . . Express an opinion, esp a pronounced one.   **1976** Garber *Mountain-ese* 86 **sAppalachians**, I'm not well enough informed on this to spend an opinion on it.   **2010** *DARE* File **eTN**, My mother was pretty uninhibited and generous in spending her opinion.

spender   See **suspender**

spendie   See **spendy**

spendrift, spendswift   See **spendthrift**

spend-the-night (party) n   **chiefly Sth**
A slumber party.

1914 Greene *One Call* 52 **Sth**, I had just shipped the boys off to the plantation with Mammy, and was getting ready to have a good old 'girl' spend-the-night party.   **1951** *Cullman Democrat* (AL) 22 Feb [92]/4 (newspaperarchive.com), At a spend-the-night party at Chris and Helen Huffstutler's Monday night were Sharon Howard [etc].   **1969** *DARE* (Qu. FF2, . . *Kinds of parties*) Inf **GA**89, Spend-the-night parties—girls have.   **1986** Pederson *LAGS Concordance (Parties)* 2 infs, **AL, GA**, Spend-the-night (parties); 1 inf, **swGA**, Spend-the-night parties—up all night, eat, talk.   **1987** Flagg *Fried Green Tomatoes* 8 **AL**, Three of the girls . . were more or less my own age, so I was always over there playing and having spend-the-night parties.   **1992** Kincaid *Crossing Blood* 178 **nwFL** (as of 1950s), Karol had a spend-the-night on her thirteenth birthday.   **2005** *DARE* File **seTN** (as of 1984), In elementary school, I would ask my mother for permission to invite one or two girls over for a spend-the-night.

spendthrift n, adj   Also *spendrift, spendswift*
Std senses, var forms.

1914 *Sat. Eve. Post* 12 Sept 16/3, It hurts his feelings to have somebody else buy the drinks. Then Levy says Oh he is one of these here spendrifts, is he?   **1969** *DARE* (Qu. W40, . . *A woman who overdresses or . . spends too much on clothes*) Inf **NY**219, Spendrift.   **1983** *MJLF* 9.1.57 **ceKY** (as of 1956), *Spendswift* . . a spendthrift.   **2005** in 2006 *DARE* File—Internet **UT**, Where we spent time, in precious minutes and cherished moments, our only fortunes, today we are wasteful and spendswift with that inheritance.   **2007** in 2008 *Ibid* **neIL**, I also keep telling him to be careful with money because had we been spendrift, we would never ever could afford this apartment for him.

spendy adj   Also sp *spendie*   **chiefly Nth, esp NW**
Expensive.

1980 *Oregonian Article Letters* **OR**, It's an everyday usage word here in Corvallis when one says, "My, that's *spendie!*"   **1986** *San Diego Union* (CA) 3 Apr sec C 1 (Internet), It's a bit spendy, about $200, but well worth the cost.   **1992** *DARE* File **OR**, The first item is found in my Oregonian variety. . . It's the word "spendy". It means "expensive" and would be used in such a conversation: "Well, John, are you gonna buy that new car you've been lookin' at?" "No, I don't think so, it's pretty spendy."   **1995** *Boston Herald* (MA) 19 Nov 2d ed sec S 14 (Internet), A couple of Allston bar owners are out on assignment . . inspecting the scene at Cafe Mojo, the spendy, trendy new bistro.   **1997** Hassler *Dean's List* 237 **nMN**, Bats are better, they ain't so spendy to house.   **1999** *DARE* File, People in Washington State, and Oregon, and Idaho, and Montana, and maybe Minnesota know what "spendy" means: expensive. . . Seattle: "Ferry Ramp Proves Spendy Folly." Portland, Oregon: "Parking Overtime in Portland Gets Spendy."   **2000** *NADS Letters*, "Spendy"—means "expensive" in eastern South Dakota.   **2001** *DARE* File **CA** (as of 1969), There's this big musical number at the end where they . . sing a song about status, and within it, they rhyme trendy and spendy, and they use spendy in the sense ["expensive"].   **2002** *Oregonian* (Portland OR) 19 Apr sec C 6/1, The race for this Senate seat is one of the state's spendiest, with the two candidates having raised nearly $200,000 so far.   **2004** *Isthmus* (Madison WI) 26 Mar 36/4 **csWI**, The mayor's staff has been hanging out here, but leather couches and spendy martinis?

speret   See **spirit**

speretil   See **spiritual** adj

'sperience, 'speriunce   See **experience**

sperit   See **spirit**

speritual   See **spiritual** adj

sperl   See **spoil A2**

sperlt   See **spoil B**

sperret, sperrit   See **spirit**

sperritual   See **spiritual** adj

spert   See **expert**

spesh(ual)ly   See **especially**

speunce   See **experience**

spew v

1 intr; rarely *spewl;* also with *up:* To vomit.   **chiefly Mid Atl**
See Map on p. 168

1849 *Ft. Wayne Times* (IN) 4 Jan 1/1 **OH**, There are some who tobacco chew,/ And though it often made them spew /. . . The practice they did still pursue.   **1864** in 1986 Messer *Civil War Letters* 40 **VT**, I will give you a little idea of how we were tossed on the boat. . . its [sic] was splendid & I like to ride in that way but my internal aparatus did not like it so well so I had to *spew* every little while.   **1899** (1912) Green *VA Folk-Speech* 406, *Spew*. . . To discharge the contents of the stomach; vomit; puke.   **1940** Harris *Folk Plays* 90 **NC**, I eat so many cracklin's last week I spewed all night long.   **1943** *LANE* Map 504 (*Vomit*) 97 infs, **chiefly nNEng**, Spew.   **1965–70** *DARE* (Qu. BB17, . . *Vomiting*) 31 Infs, **chiefly Mid Atl**, Spew; (Qu. BB18, *To vomit a great deal at once*) Infs **MD**37, **NE**3, **NC**72, Spewed (up *or* up a sight); [**NJ**39, Spewed his insides out;] **NJ**54, Spewing; **PA**162, Spewl.   **1966** Dakin *Dial. Vocab. Ohio R. Valley* 2.484, *Vomit*. . . Other . . terms are attested only once or twice. These include *retch* . . and *spew*.   **1973** Allen *LAUM* 1.369 (as of c1950), *Vomit*. . . Historic *spew*, oldest of all the expressions . . clearly suffers from a rapid decline as a viable term. Only four . . infs [1 each from **IA, MN, NE, ND**] use it, and three of them are in Type I [=old, with little educ].   **1986** Pederson *LAGS Concordance (Vomit—neutral terms)* 1 inf, **cnGA**, Spew; (*Vomit—crude and jocular terms*) 1 inf, **seGA**, Spew—old people say; 1 inf, **ceLA**, Spewed; 1 inf, **ceAL**, Spewed—sounds too "boogery"; 1 inf, **cwFL**, Spewed up.

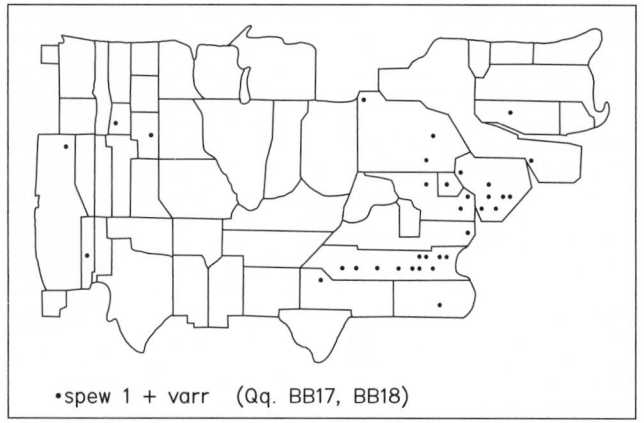

•spew 1 + varr   (Qq. BB17, BB18)

2 pronc-sp *spoo;* Chiefly of a liquid: to spray; to gush out. [Cf *OED2 spew* v. 6 1670–1892; "Now chiefly *dial.*"] **formerly chiefly Sth, S Midl, West; now more widespread** See Map   Cf **spewer, spritz**

1865 Gesner *Practical Treatise Coal* 52 **NY,** The charge in the still spewed out and took fire. **1935** *Centralia Daily Chron.* (WA) 28 Feb 1/3, At first I thought of an oil leak, but I found later the spewing oil was coming from the breather pipes due to overheating. **1965–70** *DARE* (Qu. Y45, *Talking of a liquid—to scatter in all directions: "When he opened the can, the beer _____ [all over the kitchen]."*) 172 Infs, **chiefly Sth, S Midl, SW,** Spewed (out); **SC**58, Spewed everywhere; **TX**4, Spewed up; **MA**123, Spooed [spu·d]; (Qu. Y36, *To spill something over the sides of a container: "See if you can carry that water without _____ [it all over]."*) Inf **CA**17, Spewing; **OK**31, Spewed over. **1986** Pederson *LAGS Concordance,* 1 inf, **ceTX,** The juice will spew out. **1998** in 2008 *DARE* File—Internet **swCA,** One of the smaller freeze plugs had popped out, and all the coolant had spewed all over the engine. **2000** *Telegram & Gaz.* (Worcester MA) 1 Sept sec B 2 (Internet), The accident ripped the hydrant from the ground, and thousands of gallons of water spewed out. **2007** in 2008 *DARE* File—Internet **NYC,** The reason all the fluid spewed out was because the first Pep Boys improperly installed the transmission cooling line.

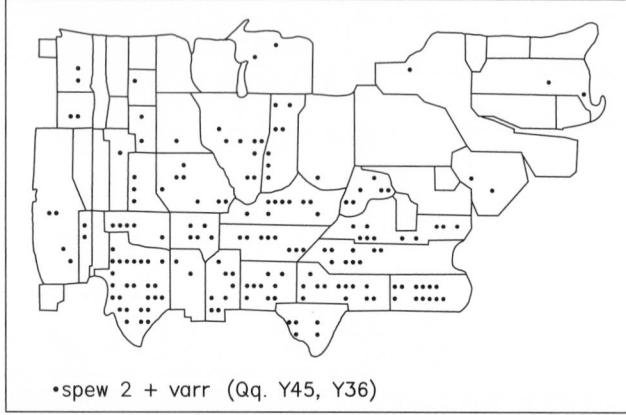

•spew 2 + varr   (Qq. Y45, Y36)

3 also with *out, up;* Of frost: to heave up (the ground or plants); of the ground: to be heaved up so that plants or ice crystals are extruded; of a plant: to be so extruded; hence ppl adjs *spewed up, spewing;* vbl n *spewing.* [Cf *OED2 spew* v. 4.a quot 1707 ("The Frosts are apt to spew them out of the Ground"), 4.b quot 1664, and 6.b "Of the ground: To swell through excess of moisture; to slip or run when unsupported" (the Brit exx at this sense, however, do not appear to involve frost).] **chiefly Sth, S Midl**

1769 (1976) Washington *Diaries* 2.125 **VA,** A Very spewing frost among Wheat particularly in the little field at Doeg run. *Ibid* 126, Another Spewing frost. **1838** KY Genl. Assembly Senate *Jrl.* app 171, The frost penetrates deep, and the earth spews up, or is much opened or thrown up by its action. **1860** Worcester *Dict., Spew.* . . To swell, as wet land affected by frost, so as to throw seed out of the ground, as "The ground spews." **1886** *Spirit L. Beacon* (IA) [27 Aug 7]/5 (newspaperarchive.com), No crop is benefited more than wheat by under-

draining. Wheat is "spewed out" by the freezing of the water in the ground. **1913** Kephart *Highlanders* 86 **sAppalachians,** The ground, to use a mountaineer's expression, was "all spewed up with frost." *Ibid* 219, They would say: "La! many's the night I've been out when the frost was spewed up so high . . and that right around the fire, too." **1945** *Richmond Times–Dispatch* (VA) 10 Feb 12/1 *(Hench Coll.),* What Eastern and Central Virginia need is a good snow. . . A snow, they pointed out, would help these crops immeasurably by preventing the "spewing" of soft soil as a result of repeated freezes and thaws. Without the snow . . the ground cracks and bulges and pushes the tender young [plants] upward, causing many of them to die. **1948** *Ibid* 31 Mar 7/1 *(Hench Coll.),* Agriculture officials explained that no damage to grain crops was anticipated except in scattered spots where the thawing process after the freeze might cause plants to "spew" from the soil. **1975** *Appalachian Jrl.* 2.158 **wNC,** The ground is said to be *spewin' up* when there comes a hard frost—perhaps a bitter-cold *blue frost* and the ground freezes and buckles. **1986** Pederson *LAGS Concordance,* 1 inf, **cnGA,** The ground just freezes and spews up with icicles. **1997** *News Herald* (Panama City FL) 14 Dec (Internet), But I had to go over these big humps where the frost spews the ground up. **2002** *DARE* File—Internet **NC,** The accumulation of soil moisture during the winter is conducive to frost heaving. Frost heaving refers to the spewing, or movement of the seedling upward along with the soil when the soil freezes and the failure of the seedling to settle back in place when the soil thaws. **2003** *NADS Letters* **nwSC,** Look how that ground (ice) spewed up last night. **2007** *DARE* File **GA,** [Spew] is used in South Georgia when the top of the ground is frozen and ice can be seen between the soil particles. The ground is said to be "spewed-up"!

spewer n   [*EDD* "A kind of firework; a squib"] **Sth, S Midl** See Map

A firecracker that is broken in the middle and then ignited.

1954 *Harder Coll.* **cwTN,** *Spewer.* . . a firecracker that is broken in the middle and lit. **c1960** *Wilson Coll.* **csKY,** *Spewer.* . . A firecracker that fails to explode. **1965–70** *DARE* (Qu. FF15, *When a firecracker doesn't go off, and you break it in the middle and light the powder, you call it a _____*) 19 Infs, **Sth, S Midl,** Spewer.

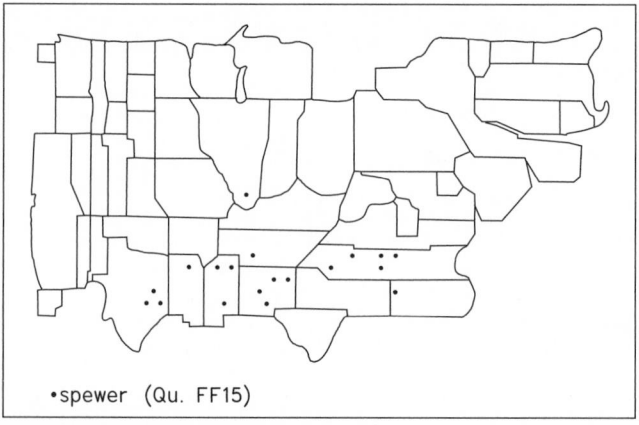

•spewer   (Qu. FF15)

spewing ppl adj, vbl n   See **spew 3**

spewl   See **spew 1**

spew out   See **spew 3**

spew up   See **spew 1, 3**

spex   See **speck** n[2]

sphagnum n   Pronc-spp *spagnum, spragnum* Std sense, var forms.

1918 *Kingston Daily Freeman* (NY) 28 Aug 10/6, The following materials or ingredients are declared to be adulterants: . . Spagnum moss. **1933** *Sun* (Baltimore MD) 23 Feb 6/8, The spagnum moss and the sparrow grass / And the partridge berries—Ho! **1968** McPhee *Pine Barrens* 60 **cNJ,** Fred says "spragnum" for "sphagnum." **2004** *DARE* File—Internet **ND,** Obtain a 12 x 15′ piece of plastic and two handfuls of moist spagnum moss. Wrap the cut on the stem with moist spagnum moss to form a ball. *Ibid,* I guess I had best get the large bag of spagnum. I will never again get the blocks of compressed spagnum that you must rehydrate. *Ibid* **WI,** A variety of Fungi: Indian Pipe, Lichen, Reindeer Moss, Peat Moss, Spragnum Moss. *Ibid* **FL,** These are shipped bare root and packed in damp spragnum moss. *Ibid,* A hide box . . containing moistened vermiculite or spragnum moss, should be provided. **2004** *DARE* File **cwCA** (as of c1960), I recall hearing people talk about [ˈspægnəm] moss.

sphinx moth n
Std: a moth of the family Sphingidae. For other names of var spp or their larvae see **horn-blower, hornworm, hornworm fly, hummingbird moth, joe bucks, miller 1, tobacco buzzer, ~ fly 1, ~ hawkmoth**

spic See spik

spiceberry n
1 A **wintergreen 2** (here: *Gaultheria procumbens*).

1792 Imlay *Western Terr.* 216 **KY,** There is a variety of shrubs in every part of the country, the principal of which are the myrtle and spice berry. [*DARE* Ed: This quot may refer instead to another sense below.] **1828** Rafinesque *Med. Flora* 1.202, *Gautiera repens.* . . *Vulgar Names*—Partridge-berry, Grouse-berry, Deerberry, Spiceberry [etc.]. **1872** Schele de Vere *Americanisms* 404, Others give the prize to the *spice-berry,* the "little, creeping *wintergreen,* with its scarlet berries." **1924** *Amer. Botanist* 30.13, The pungent oil that permeates all parts of the plant give[s] reason for names like "spice wintergreen," "ginger-berry," "spice-berry" [etc.]. **1971** Krochmal *Appalachia Med. Plants* 128, *Gaultheria procumbens.* . . Common names: Checkerberry wintergreen, . . spiceberry, spicy wintergreen [etc.].

2 A **stopper 1a** (here: *Eugenia rhombea*).

1897 Sudworth *Arborescent Flora* 306 **FL,** *Eugenia procera* [=*E. rhombea*]. . . Common Names. . . Spiceberry. **1908** Britton *N. Amer. Trees* 726, Red stopper. . . It is also called Spiceberry. **1994** Nelson *Trees FL* 240, *Spiceberry Eugenia or Red Stopper.* . . Rare species found in its natural habitat only in one or two locations in the Florida Keys.

3 A **spicebush 1** (here: *Lindera benzoin*) or its berry.

1892 (1974) Millspaugh *Amer. Med. Plants* 145-1, Benzoin. . . Com[mon] Names . . Spice-berry [etc.]. **1971** Krochmal *Appalachia Med. Plants* 160, Lindera benzoin. . . spiceberry, spicebush [etc.]. **2005** in 2006 *DARE* File—Internet **cIN,** The DH (dear husband) and I are trying a new tisane (herbal tea) called Spiceberry Tea. . . The lovely red berry is ground and steeped to make the tea.

spice birch n Also spicy birch
=sweet birch 1.

1822 Eaton *Botany* 204, *[Betula] lenta.* . . spicy birch. . . very sweet-scented. **1830** Rafinesque *Med. Flora* 2.200, *Birch Tree.* . . The best is *B. lenta;* many vulgar names, *Sweet Birch,* . . *Spice B[irch]* [etc.]. **1876** Hobbs *Bot. Hdbk.* 11, [Birch], Spicy, . . [Betula] lenta. **1930** Sievers *Amer. Med. Plants* 54, Sweet Birch. . . Other common names.—Black birch, cherry birch, spice birch [etc.]. **1971** Krochmal *Appalachia Med. Plants* 76, *Betula lenta.* . . Spice birch. . . The bark of this plant . . has a pleasant aromatic flavor similar to wintergreen.

spicebush n
1 A shrub of the genus *Lindera,* usu *L. benzoin,* but also *L. melissifolia.* For other names of *Lindera* spp see **pond spice 2, spicewood 1;** for other names of var spp see **feverbush 1, Jove's fruit 1, pondberry, pondbush 1, spiceberry 3, spice tree 2, wild allspice, wild pimento** [*DARE* Ed: Some of these quots may refer instead to other senses below.]

1770 (1925) Washington *Diaries* 1.409 **swPA,** The Growth, [is] Walnut, Cherry, Spice Bushes, etca. **1822** Eaton *Botany* 328, *[Laurus] benzoin* . . spice-bush, fever-bush. . . A shrub from 4 to 8 feet high, spicy tasted. **a1843** (1958) Barker *Recoll. First Settlement OH* 65, Discusing over the Collapsing times over a Cup of spice bush Tea & a piece of dry Johnny Cake. **1860** Curtis *Cat. Plants NC* 91, Spice Bush. . . Known also as *Spice Wood, Wild Allspice,* and *Fever Bush.* **1863** Porcher *Resources* 355 **SC,** The soldiers of the upper country of South Carolina . . came into camp fully supplied with the spice bush for making a fragrant, aromatic, diaphoretic tea. **1864** *Catalogue of Herbs* **swME,** *Spice, or fever bush*—Benzoin odoriferum. **1894** Coulter *Botany W. TX* 383 **cTX,** *B[enzoin] aestivale.* . . Spice bush. **1948** Stevens *KS Wild Flowers* 75, Common Spicebush. . . A fragrant tea is made from the young twigs, leaves, and fruits. **1953** Greene–Blomquist *Flowers South* 78, *Spice-Bush, Benjamin-Bush.* . . The bark and twigs are used medicinally and the fruits as a condiment. The "hairy spice-bush" or "Jove's-fruit" (*L. melissaefolium*) is more showy with larger flowers. **1970** *DARE* FW Addit **OH,** In Van West Co., Ohio, there is a bush known as a spicebush, from which the tender tips of branches are taken in spring;

a tea is made and drunk as a spring tonic. **2005** *Buffalo News* (NY) 1 July sec C 3 (Internet), Larval food plants include Lindera benzoin (Spicebush), [etc.].

2 =**California laurel.**

1866 Lindley–Moore *Treas. Botany* 821, *O[reodaphne] californica* [= *Umbellularia c.*] is a common tree in the mountainous parts of California, where it goes by a variety of names, such as . . Spice-bush [etc.]. . . When bruised it emits a strong spicy odour which is apt to excite sneezing, and the Spanish–Americans use the leaves as a condiment. **1897** Parsons *Wild Flowers CA* 373, California Laurel. . . This tree is known in different localities by a variety of names, such as "spice-bush" [etc.].

3 A **spikenard** (here: *Aralia racemosa*).

1894 *Jrl. Amer. Folkl.* 7.89 **CT,** *Aralia racemosa* . . spice-bush, Hartford.

4 A **sweet shrub** (here: usu **Carolina allspice** or *Calycanthus occidentalis*). Cf **spicewood 3**

1896 *Jrl. Amer. Folkl.* 9.180 **seMA,** *Calycanthus floridus* . . spice-bush, Middleborough. **1897** Parsons *Wild Flowers CA* 352, Western Spice-bush. *Calycanthus occidentalis.* . . There is a pleasant fragrance about the whole shrub, and the leaves, when crushed, are agreeably bitter. **1911** Jepson *Flora CA* 172, *C[alycanthus] occidentalis.* . . Called . . "Spice Bush" in Napa Valley. **1974** (1977) Coon *Useful Plants* 85, *Calycanthus floridus*—Sweet shrub, strawberry-bush, spice bush, Carolina allspice. . . Its purple-brown flowers are not beautiful, but are most delightfully fragrant. The aromatic bark has been noted as a substitute for cinnamon. **2001** *Washington Times* (DC) 12 Dec sec B 4 (Internet), Calycanthus floridus (sweetshrub or spicebush). I chose one of these for my garden because it flowers in shade and the scents of both its foliage and its flowers repel deer.

5 A **false indigo 1** (here: either *Amorpha canescens* or *A. fruticosa*). Cf **sachet bush**

1931 U.S. Dept. Ag. *Misc. Pub.* 101.83, Desert indigobush (*A[morpha] occidentalis* . .), locally known as Arizona spicebush . . , is a fragrant-flowered shrub. **1960** Vines *Trees SW* 519, Lead-plant Amorpha. . . Also known under the vernacular names of Shoe-strings and Spice-bush.

6 A **wax myrtle** (here: *Morella cerifera*).

1933 Small *Manual SE Flora* 409, *C[erothamnus] ceriferus.* . . Waxberry. Wax-myrtle. Spice-bush. **1960** Vines *Trees SW* 118, Southern Wax-myrtle. . . Vernacular names are Wax-berry, Spice-bush, Candle-berry [etc.].

7 A **sumac B** (here: *Rhus trilobata*).

1947 (1976) Curtin *Healing Herbs* 112, Lemita. . . spice bush. . . The leaves of the *lemita* . . release a pungent scent when bruised.

8 A **sweet pepperbush** (here: *Clethra alnifolia*).

1960 Vines *Trees SW* 803, Summersweet Clethra. . . Some vernacular names are White-alder, White-bush, Spice-bush, and Sweet Pepper-bush.

spice pink n Cf clove pink
A **pink n² 1** (here: *Dianthus caryophyllus*).

1868 Davis *Dallas Galbraith* 133 **Sth,** Gerty, as fresh and sweet as a spice-pink, always was the first of the household to break in on him in the library. **1883** *Overland Mth.* (2d ser) 1.508 **West,** She . . stood to watch him as he placed spice-pinks tenderly check to cheek. **1891** *New Engl. Mag.* 10.223, The air was full of the perfume of the mignonette and spice-pinks. **1967** *DARE* (Qu. S26e, *Other wildflowers not yet mentioned;* not asked in early QRs) Inf **MA5,** Spice pinks = cemetery pinks (small carnations).

spice tree n
1 =**California laurel.** Cf **spicebush 2**

1856 U.S. War Dept. *Rept. Explor. Railroad* 4.5.133, *Oreodaphne Californica.* . . The inhabitants of California call it Mountain Laurel and Spice-tree. **1884** Sargent *Forests of N. Amer.* 120, *Umbellularia Californica.* . . California Spice Tree. . . Rogue River valley, Oregon, south through the California coast ranges to San Diego county. **1889** *Harper's New Mth. Mag.* 79.654 **CA,** Often in mid-day, in the close and sultry cross cañons, one will be driven almost insane by the heavy perfume of the mountain laurel or spice tree. **1897** Sudworth *Arborescent Flora* 203 **OR,** California Laurel. . . Spice Tree. **1979** Little *Checklist U.S. Trees* 292, *Umbellularia californica.* . . Other common names—California-bay, . . spice-tree.

2 =**spicebush 1.**

c1738 (1929) Byrd *Histories* 168 **VA,** Near this Creek we discovered likewise Several Spice-Trees, the Leaves of which are fragrant, and the

Berries they bear are black when dry, and of a hot taste, not much unlike Pepper. **1997** Nelson *Country Folkl.* 40 **wNC,** To help measles, use sassafras or spice tree tea.

spicewood n

1   =spicebush 1. now chiefly Appalachians See Map
  1748 in 1970 Kalm *Resejournal* 2.204 **Philadelphia PA,** Laurus . . Spice-wood. **1792** Belknap *Hist. NH* 3.97, *Spice-wood (laurus benzoin)* or as it is commonly called *Fever-bush,* is another species of the *laurus,* common in New-Hampshire. It is more aromatic than the sassafras. **1796** in 1904 Thwaites *Early W. Travels* 3.91 **KY,** I had supped the previous evening on Tea made from the shrub called Spice-wood. **1824** Bigelow *Florula Bostoniensis* 160 **MA,** Laurus Benzoin. . . *Fever Bush. Spice Wood.* . . An aromatic shrub with a flavour resembling Benzoin. **1860** [see **spicebush 1**]. **1893** *Atlantic Mth.* 72.373 **OH, WV,** My grandfather, himself an old pioneer, told me . . that in his childhood the pioneers in West Virginia and eastern Ohio said that when the spicewood began to put forth leaves a sharp lookout must be kept for the Indians, . . whose approach could from that time on be partly hidden by the increasing foliage. **1967–70** *DARE* (Qu. T16, . . *Kinds of trees . . 'special'*) Infs **TN**6, **VA**12, Spicewood; (Qu. BB22, . . *Home remedies . . for constipation*) Inf **KY**24, Spicewood tea; (Qu. BB50d, *Favorite spring tonics*) Inf **MD**17, Spicewood and sarsaparilla tea; **KY**24, **VA**26, 42, Spicewood tea; (Qu. DD3b, *How . . people take snuff*) Inf **VA**12, Take a spicewood twig and chew the end. **1968** *DARE* FW Addit **VA**15, Spicewood . . common . . made tea from it. **1975** in 1981 *NC Folkl. Jrl.* 29.32, Gather spice wood when the sap first comes up, store away to dry. It makes good tea, but if you have any kind of wild meats, just break up some of the spice wood and wash clean, power boil [parboil] with your wild meat. **1982** Slone *How We Talked* 102 **eKY** (as of c1950), Another cure [for a cold] was . . spicewood tea. **1986** Pederson *LAGS Concordance,* 1 inf, **swMS,** Spicewood; 1 inf, **neTN,** Spicewood tea.

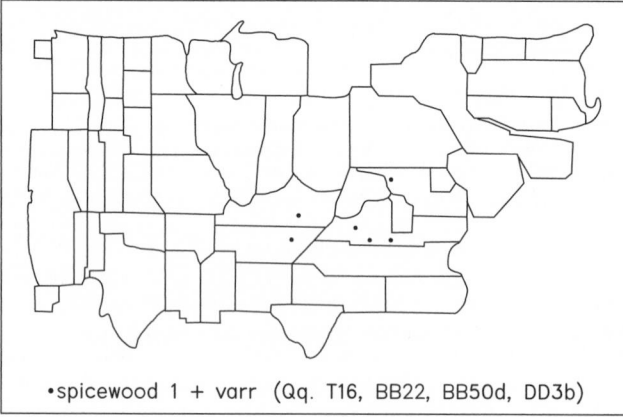

•spicewood 1 + varr (Qq. T16, BB22, BB50d, DD3b)

2   A Florida tree of the genus *Calyptranthes.*   For other names of *C. zuzygium* see **myrtle-of-the-river, stopper 1c**
  1908 Britton *N. Amer. Trees* 730, Spicewood—Genus *Calyptranthes.* . . [Plants of this genus] are permeated by aromatic and astringent principles, on account of which the flowers, buds or fruits of some are used as spices, similar to Cloves and Pimento. **1933** Small *Manual SE Flora* 938, *C[alyptranthes] pallens.* . . Spicewood . . Hammocks, coast of S. pen[insular] Fla., Everglade Keys, and Florida Keys. **1979** Little *Checklist U.S. Trees* 69, *Calyptranthes zuzygium.* . . Other common name—spicewood. **2006** *DARE* File—Internet **FL,** Spicewood—*Calyptranthes pallens*—Spicewood is a card-carrying member of the prestigious Myrtle family of flowering trees and shrubs, and has all of the best characteristics that made the family famous in the first place.

3   A **sweet shrub** (here: *Calycanthus occidentalis*) of California.   Cf **mountain spicewood, spicebush 4**
  1888 *Forest Leaves* 1.85 **ceCA,** When we climb the rugged heights, by the bridle path to Glacier Point, . . we meet with Spicewood (*Calycanthus occidentalis*), [etc.]. **1911** Jepson *Flora CA* 172, *C[alycanthus] occidentalis.* . . Along cañon streams in the North Coast Ranges and Sierra Nevada. Called "Spice-wood" on Howell Mt.

spicion   See **suspicion**

spick n[1]   See **spigot**

spick n[2]   See **spik**

spicket   See **spigot**

spickety   See **spiggoty**

spickle   See **spigot**

spicknard   See **spikenard**

spicy birch   See **spice birch**

spider n

1   Orig a large, bowl-shaped iron pan with legs and a long handle; now usu a cast-iron frying pan.   **chiefly Nth; also Mid and S Atl**   See Map   *old-fash*   Cf **skillet 1**
  1780 in 1947 *AmSp* 22.1.2.50 **nwCT,** Spidor. **1790** *PA Packet & Daily Advt.* (Philadelphia) 1 Mar 3/3, For Sale . . bake pans, spiders, skillets. **1844** (1940) Arnold *Diaries* 167 **VT,** Went to Walpole with Mary Ann to select cook stove—one was 30 dols. with furniture . . 1 spider—cast iron pot and dish kettle with tin covers. **1853** (1982) Lea *Domestic Cookery* 48, *To Fricassee Tomatoes.* . . do not peel them or they go too much to pieces; have a broad speeder or stove-pan. **1899** (1912) Green *VA Folk-Speech* 406, *Spider.* . . A cooking utensil with a long handle, having three or four legs or feet to keep it from contact with the coals; made of cast-iron, with a top of the same metal. For baking or frying. **1903** *DN* 2.301 **Cape Cod MA** (as of a1857), *Spider.* . . A frying pan with high sides. **1905** *DN* 3.20 **cCT,** *Spider.* . . A cast-iron frying-pan without legs. **1909** *DN* 3.416 **nME,** *Spider.* . . A cast iron frying pan with short handle. **1910** *DN* 3.449 **cwNY,** *Spider.* . . Frying-pan. **1912** *DN* 3.569 **cNY,** *Spider.* . . Frying-pan or skillet. **1914** *DN* 4.156 **Cape Cod MA,** *Spider-stifle.* . . A species of food composed of sliced potatoes, sliced onions, pork-fat, and water, salted, sometimes peppered, and cooked slowly in a frying-pan or 'spider.' **1917** *DN* 4.421 **CA,** *Spider.* . . A large, deep skillet or oven, with three legs. **1934** *Hanley Disks* **swCT,** What we used to use was an iron spider. . . Legs? Yes . . three legs . . a small handle . . and usually . . they were round, round-bottomed . . from nine to twelve inches. . . They've never used 'em much since I can remember. **1934** Hurston *Jonah's Gourd Vine* 13 **AL** [Black], Ned sat down by the crude fireplace where the skillets and spiders (long-legged bread pans with iron cover) sprawled in the ashes. **1939** *LANE* Map 132 (*Frying pan*) **throughout NEng,** Spider. . . *Spider* is often felt as old-fashioned or reported as obsolete. . . The cast iron spider with three short legs, used for cooking in the fireplace, is recalled by . . [10] informants. **1949** Kurath *Word Geog.* 56, *Frying pan* (of cast iron). . . *Spider* occurs in two large separate areas: (1) in the New England settlement area (all the way to the Western Reserve of Ohio), and (2) in the tidewater area from the Potomac southward to the Peedee in South Carolina. It appears also on the Jersey coast from Sandy Hook to Cape May. **1958** McCulloch *Woods Words* 175 **Pacific NW,** *Spider.* . . Thick iron frying pan for use over an open fire. **1965–70** *DARE* (Qu. F1, . . *A heavy metal pan that's used to fry foods*) 182 Infs, **chiefly Nth, also Mid and S Atl,** Spider; **MA**57, Iron spider; (Qu. H14, *Bread that's made with cornmeal*) Inf **PA**66, Spider bread; **MA**98, Spider cake; (Qu. H18, . . *Special kinds of bread*) Infs **CO**20, 27, Spider bread. [Of all Infs responding to the question, 70% were old; of those giving these responses, 82% were old.] **1989** Pederson *LAGS Tech. Index* 68 **Gulf Region** (*Frying pan*) 79 infs, Spider; 1 inf, Iron spider. **2000** Shores *Tangier Is.* 200 **Chesapeake Bay,** *Spider* was used for the heavy pan for tops of stoves well into the forties and perhaps beyond. . . On Tangier, *spider* is more than a remnant even in the memories of the not-so-old and not just for the heavy iron pan but for the lighter ones as well.

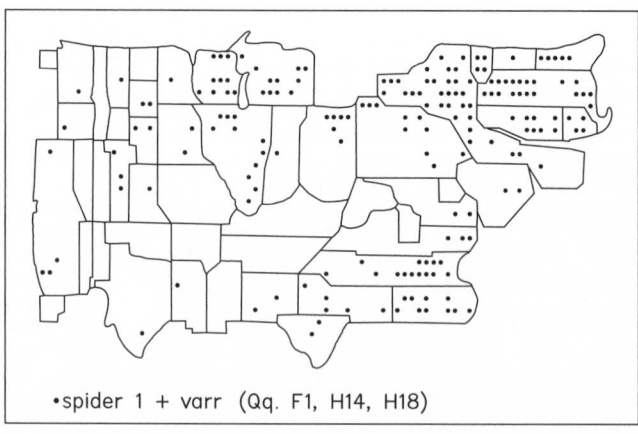

•spider 1 + varr (Qq. F1, H14, H18)

2 A trivet. Cf **cricket** n[3]

1876 Knight *Amer. Mech. Dict.* 3.2266, *Spider.* . . A three-legged iron stool for supporting a pan or pot upon the hearth. A trivet. **1930** Shoemaker *1300 Words* 56 **cPA Mts** (as of c1900), *Spider*—A stand for a copper kettle. **1986** Pederson *LAGS Concordance,* 1 inf, **csAL,** Spider—trivet; 1 inf, **swAL,** Spider—like a trivet; to put hot plates on; 1 inf, **neMS,** Spider—a type of trivet.

3 also *bungee spider web* (or *net*) and varr: A net or radiating set of elastic cords for securing cargo on a vehicle. Cf **octopus**

1984 Safire *I Stand Corrected* 330, In ski country where they are in constant use—these bungees (that was new to me) are called *spiders.* **2004** *DARE* File—Internet **GA,** I'm trying to find a Bungee Spider Web or Cargo net that's about 1.5′ x 2′ or something close. I use this to strap my laptop bag to my motorcycle. **2006** *Ibid* **ID,** I absolutely love this [motorcycle] trailer. . . The spider bungie [sic] that came with is very handy as well. **2007** *Ibid* **OK,** At one garage sale I found a "spider web bungee net" like Johnny's. It's basically a bunch of bungee cords woven together to look like a big spider's web, with plastic hooks around the perimeter. *Ibid* **CO,** We stored all our camping gear that wouldn't be affected by rain or snow in the roof top basket. . . Then used the bungee spider net . . to hold every thing in place.

4 also *mangrove spider:* A mangrove thicket.

1971 Craighead *Trees S. FL* 123, Farther inland, the white [mangrove] drops out and the red forms low red mangrove clumps, or "spiders," 3 to 6 feet tall, rooted in the numerous solution holes of the bedrock. These clumps are widely scattered inland. *Ibid* 125, At places these [=bromeliads and orchids] festoon the hosts, giving a distinctive character to the "spider." The glade marl between the scattered mangrove spiders is occupied by a number of plants.

5 A lobster.

1979 Lewis *How to Talk Yankee* [18] **nNEng,** He may have caught enough *spiders* that month to pay for his new Chrysler Marine. **1982** *DARE* File **coastal ME,** Spiders: Away from the coast, a cast iron skillet. On the coast, lobsters.

spider bird n

1 =cedar waxwing.

1850 Conn. *Public Acts* 5 *(DAE),* It shall not be lawful in this State for any person to shoot . . [any] spider-bird or wax-bird. **1956** MA Audubon Soc. *Bulletin* 40.129 **CT,** Cedar Waxwing. . . Spider Bird. . . From feeding on those creatures.

2 A phoebe (here: *Sayornis phoebe*).

1916 in 1917 *Wilson Bulletin* 29.82 **KY,** *Sayornis phœbe.* . . spider bird.

spider bread n   Also *spider cake;* for addit varr see quots **chiefly NEng**

Bread or cake that has been baked in a **spider 1;** see quots.

1845 *Universalist Union* 8.14 **NY,** The roasted potatoes and hot, nice spider cakes were smoking most invitingly, on the table. **1850** Abbott *Mary Erskine* 131 **NEng,** Mary Bell liked to *bake* a spider cake. . . carrying the cake in her two hands to the fireplace, and laying it carefully in the spider, and then setting it up before the fire to bake. **1870** (1871) Whitney *We Girls* 80 **NEng,** The flaky spider-cake, turned just as it blushed golden-tawny over the coals. **1879** *Scribner's Mth.* 18.567 **VA** [Black], Is y' all niggers gwine set up all night foolin' long o' dat dar ole bull beef an' spider-bread? **1902** (1904) Rowe *Maid of Bar Harbor* 185 **ME,** A hot spider cake or, as Mandy called it, a "fresh smother." **1932** (1946) Hibben *Amer. Regional Cookery* 18 **ME,** *Spider Corn Cake.* . . Turn into well-greased, sizzling-hot iron skillet. **1939** Wolcott *Yankee Cook Book* 166 **MA,** *Spider Corn Bread.* . . Mix and sift dry ingredients. . . Turn into an iron spider (about 8 inches in diameter). . . Spider bread should have a line of creamy custard through the center. It is sliced as a pie . . and it is eaten with a fork. **1941** *LANE* Map 284 (*Doughnut*), *Fried bread, etc.* . . 1 inf, **ceMA,** Spider bread; 1 inf, **cMA,** Spider cake—bread dough fried in spider. **1967–70** *DARE* (Qu. H14, *Bread that's made with cornmeal*) Inf **PA66,** Hoecake—also spider bread—fried on stove; **MA98,** Spider cake; (Qu. H18, . . *Special kinds of bread*) Inf **CO20,** Spider bread—let it raise partially—fried in a little grease in the spider; **CO27,** Pan bread is spider bread. **1975** Gould *ME Lingo* 269, *Spider*-cake is a hot bread cooked in a *spider.* **1989** *DARE* File **RI** (as of c1900), *Spider bread* = Corn muffins [cooked] in a frying pan. **2008** *DARE* File—Internet **NEng,** *Martha's Spider Bread.* . . In New England, these [=three-legged frypans] were called "spiders" and that name was continued for black iron frypans used on the wood cook

stove. . . This bread is for special diets and lacks yeast, wheat, dairy and is sweetened with raisins.

spider bungee   See **spider 3**

spider cake   See **spider bread**

‡**spider cradle** n   Cf *DS* R29a, b

A spider's web.

1942 (1971) Campbell *Cloud-Walking* 38 **seKY,** As they come along through the woods Squire brushed the spider cradles off as they caught on his clothes.

spider flower n

1 Std: a plant of the genus *Cleome.* Also called **Indian pink 9.** For other names of var spp see **electric light plant, pink queen, Rocky Mountain bee plant, spider plant 2**

2 A **scorpionweed 2** (here: *Phacelia congesta*).

1936 Whitehouse *TX Flowers* 112, Fiddle-Neck (*Phacelia congesta*) is also known as spider-flower. . . The 5 spreading stamens extending from the flowers are responsible for the name of "spider-flower."

spider grass n

A **needlegrass 2** (here: *Aristida ternipes*).

1951 Kearney–Peebles *AZ Flora* 119, *Aristida ternipes.* . . The name spider grass is sometimes applied to this species. **1970** Correll *Plants TX* 261, Aristida ternipes. . . Spider grass. . . Tex. and N.M. to Ariz. **2000** Phillips–Comus *Nat. Hist. Sonoran Desert* 274, Spider grass (*A. t. var. ternipes*). . . is very responsive to rainfall.

spider hawk n   Cf **mud dauber 1, tarantula hawk**

A wasp, usu of the family Sphecidae or Pompilidae, that preys on spiders.

1892 *Bucks Co. Gaz.* (Bristol PA) 28 July 1/7 **CO,** Nature furnished us a remedy and a friend when she gave us the spider hawk. The name is given by miners to a small, steel blue wasp about three-fourths of an inch in length. **1905** U.S. Bur. Entomol. *Bulletin* 54.89 **TX,** *Arachnophroctonus ferrugineus* . . , the "red spider hawk;" kills spiders and buries them. **1958** in 1980 Silverberg–Greenberg *Arbor House Treas. Sci. Fiction* 267, I had set my net with all the audacity of a spider waiting for a fly, yet I knew that when my anticipated victim arrived he would more likely resemble a spider hawk. **1998** *DARE* File **TX,** *Spider hawk* meaning a wasp who makes nests of mud. I heard spider hawk from a white male born 1954 who grew up on the edge of Dallas. He also calls the insect a *dirt dauber.* **2002** *Argus Leader* (Sioux Falls SD) 3 Aug Sioux Empire sec B 1 (Internet), The *spider hawk* is another digging wasp. It is metallic blue or metallic black in color and preys on spiders. **2003** *NADS Letters* **OK,** My husband and all of his family still use the term *spider hawk,* but not for a mud dauber. Instead they use it for those formidable looking yellow jacket wasps that live underground and are the size of a grown man's thumb. No kidding. **2004** *Ibid* **sIL,** When I was a boy, in the 1960s, older people . . would occasionally say "spider hawk" [for "dirt dauber"], which my younger brother and I found curious. **2008** *DARE* File—Internet **AZ,** [Caption:] Spider Hawk drags the paralyzed tarantula back to its lair for dinner.

spider lily n

1 A southern wetlands plant of the genus *Hymenocallis.* [See quot 1936] For other names of var spp see **alligator lily, raggedy Ann 1**

1887 *Harper's New Mth. Mag.* 74.351 **csLA,** All the marsh was gay with flowers, vast patches of the blue *fleur-de-lis* intermingled with the exquisite white spider-lily, nodding in clusters on long stalks. **1901** Lounsberry *S. Wild Flowers* 67, Spider Lily. *Hymenocallis occidentalis.* . . As a genus these plants are known . . by the graceful crown which unites their filaments, and which gives to many of them a curious, although enchanting appearance. **1936** Whitehouse *TX Flowers* 12, Texas Spider Lily (*Hymenocallis galvestoniensis*). . . The 3 linear petals and the three similar sepals are about 6 in. long, united at their lower half into a slender tube. The upper half spreads, giving rise to the common name of spider lily. **1961** Wills–Irwin *Flowers TX* 98, Spider-lily—*Hymenocallis liriosme.* . . low places in East Texas. **1968** *DARE* (Qu. S26b, *Wildflowers that grow in water or wet places*) Inf **LA40,** Spider lily. **c1979** TX Dept. Highways *Flowers* 33, Spider Lily is a fragrant flower with dramatic white petals. **2002** *DARE* File—Internet **LA,** Spider Lily. . . A genus of about 40 species of bulbous perennials. . . In spring, summer, or winter, they bear terminal umbels of fragrant flowers resembling spidery daffodils, each with 6 narrow petals and a large cup.

2 A **spiderwort**, usu *Tradescantia virginiana*.

1849 *Buffalo Med. Jrl. & Mth. Rev.* 4.723, The wiseacres of Wisconsin pretend to cure the bite of the rattle snake by the root of the tradescantia or spider lily. **1894** *Jrl. Amer. Folkl.* 7.103 **NY, LA,** *Tradescantia Virginica* . . spider lily. **1898** *Ibid* 11.282 **MA, WI,** *Tradescantia Virginica* . . spider lily, Middleboro, Mass., Monroe, Wis. **1951** Voss-Eifert *IL Wild Flowers* 114, Spiderwort (Spider Lily. Trinity Flower)—*Tradescantia ohiensis.* **1970** Correll *Plants TX* 360, *Tradescantia* [spp]. . . Spider Lily. **1970** *DARE* (Qu. S3, *A flower like a large violet with a yellow center and small ragged leaves—it comes up early in spring on open, stony hilltops*) Inf **MS**82, Spider lily; (Qu. S26c, *Wildflowers that grow in woods*) Inf **KY**74, Spider lily. **2002** in 2008 *DARE* File—Internet **OR,** *Spiderwort, Spider lily.* The bases of the dark green leaves are pink at first, maturing to white. Pale pink flowers.

3 A **swamp lily g** (here: *Crinum americanum*).

1901 Lounsberry *S. Wild Flowers* 67 **FL,** American crinum—*Crinum americanum.* . . So spreading and slender are the segments of the perianth that the greater number of the natives call the plant, and not inappropriately, the "spider lily." **1933** Rawlings *South Moon* 166 **nFL,** The spider lilies were ivory washed with thin gold. **1961** Douglas *My Wilderness* 151 *Everglades* **FL,** Here were white lilies, the delicate spider lily, and the swamp lily. **2002** *DARE* File—Internet **FL,** Florida has a native crinum called bog lily and/or spider lily that grows wild in all the waterways here. . . It is smallish, maybe up to 12–18 inches, and has the thin, spider like white flower.

4 A liliaceous plant of the genus *Lycoris*. [See quot 2002] Cf **British soldier**

1900 Bailey *Cyclop. Horticult.* 2.959, [*Lycoris*] *aurea.* . . Golden Spider Lily. **1941** (1942) Seymour *New Garden Encycl.* 1157 **Sth,** In the S[outh], Spider-lily is *Lycoris radiata*, and Yellow Spider-lily is *L. aurea.* **1951** *PADS* 15.9 **NC,** *Lycoris radiata.* . . Spider lily, Chapel Hill. **1953** Greene–Blomquist *Flowers South* 152, Red Spider-Lily (*Lycoris radiata*). . . The spidery blossoms with long, protruding stamens come before the linear leaves. **2002** *DARE* File—Internet, Spider lilies sport gorgeous bright red flowers adorned with long, curling filaments (the source of the "spider" moniker).

5 A **fritillary** (here: *Fritillaria lanceolata*).

1967 Gilkey–Dennis *Hdbk. NW Plants* 55, Fritillaria lanceolata. . . *Riceroot lily. Spider lily.* . . Shaded spots in clearings and shady moist roadsides.

6 An **agave** (here: *Agave americana*).

1967 *DARE* Wildfl QR (Wills–Irwin) Pl.5A Inf **TX**34, Spider lily. [FW: Inf knows a great deal about flowers.]

spiderling n

Std: a plant of the southern and southwestern genus *Boerhavia*. For other names of var spp see **jiggerweed**

spider milkweed n

A **milkweed 1** (here: *Asclepias asperula* or *A. viridis*). For other names of *A. asperula* see **antelope horn(s), inmortal** Note: These spp were formerly included in the genus *Asclepiodora*.

1915 (1926) Armstrong–Thornber *Western Wild Flowers* 378, Spider Milkweed—*Asclepiodora decumbens* [=*Asclepias asperula*]. . . grows on dry hillsides. **1957** Barnes *Nat. Hist. Wasatch Summer* 64 **UT,** The Indians hereabout sought the spider milkweed or antelope horns (*Ascelpiodora* [sic] *decumbens*), which grows on these dry hillsides and has green flowers with paler margins. **1972** Brown *Wildflowers LA* 145, Spider Milkweed—*Asclepias viridis.* . . Common in prairie, fresh marshes, and mixed woods, pinelands. **1993** *Ecology* 74.1281, Only four species of forbs were recorded, . . [including] spider milkweed (*Asclepias viridis*).

spider plant n

1 A northern **saxifrage** n^2 (here: *Saxifraga flagellaris*). [See quot 1852]

[**1855** Murray *Encycl. Geog.* 3.354 **Canada,** Many [plants of Melville Island] are found upon the Rocky Mountains, as is the case with that very singular vegetable, the Saxifraga flagellaris . . , whose long runners, radiating from a central plant, like the legs from the body of a spider, induced the sailors to call it the Spider Plant.] **1966** Heller *Wild Flowers AK* 15, Spider Plant. . . basal leaves in a rosette from which radiate long naked runners. **1968** Hultén *Flora AK* 569, *Saxifraga flagellaris.* . . Spiderplant.

2 A **spider flower 1** such as *Cleome hassleriana*.

1839 Buist *Amer. Flower Garden* 25, *Flowering annuals adapted for sowing on a hot-bed.* . . Cleome-grandiflora, large lilac flowering spider plant. **1925** Jepson *Manual Plants CA* 407, *Cleome* [spp]. . . Spider Plant. **1970** Correll *Plants TX* 710, *Cleome Hassleriana.* . . *Spider plant, spider flower, pink queen.* . . Petals large, showy, pink to purple (rarely white). **2005** *State Jrl.–Reg.* (Springfield IL) 23 Apr 17 (Internet), They may have planted things the previous year, like cleome (also known as spider plant or spider flower).

spider web bungee   See **spider 3**

spiderwort n

Std: a plant of the genus *Tradescantia*, esp *T. virginiana*. For other names of this sp see **bluegrass 3, cat-bells, four-o'-clock 3, Job's tears 4, meet-me-early, snake-grass 3, true blue;** for other names of var spp see **blue jacket 3, cindy-in-the-meadow, corn lily 1, Indian paint 5, Jacob's ladder 11, joint plant, Joseph's coat, Moses-in-the-bulrushes 1, nine o'clocks, spider lily 2, twelve-o'clock 2, widow's tears 1, wild crocus 2** Cf **bog lily**

spiedi(e) n   Pronc-spp *speedie, speedy*   [Ital *spiedo* a spit] chiefly **csNY**

A dish consisting of cubes of marinated meat cooked on a skewer and served with a slice of bread; see quot 1979.

1942 Popik Coll. **csNY,** *SDS Grill*—Spiedi Lamb Barbecue. . . Bngtn 4-9692. [*DARE* Ed: Apparently taken from a city directory for Binghamton NY.] **1979** *AmSp* 54.312 **cNY,** *Spiedi* is the name for a meat dish barbequed with a special marinade and served on skewers. . . [T]he diner wraps a slice of bread around the meat and so removes it from the skewer. **1991** *NY Times* (NY) 16 Jan sec C 3/1 **csNY,** Buffalo has its chicken wings. . . Binghamton has the spiedie. This local delicacy (pronounced "speedy") is sold in dozens of restaurants and supermarkets in this city. . . A spiedie consists of marinated chunks of meat—lamb, pork, chicken or beef—skewered, grilled and served on a slice of Italian bread. . . The word spiedie derives from the Italian word "spiedo," meaning "spit." **1991** *DARE* File, [Postcard caption:] *The Spiedie Fest & Balloon Rally*, Binghamton, NY. **2001** *Ibid* **csNY,** I lived for a dozen years in Binghamton NY. Dom Salameda puts out a Speedie Survival Kit, which includes skewers and a couple of bottles of his special speedie sauce, which he sends to afficionados around the country. **2005** *NY Sun* (NY) 20 July 15/1 **csNY,** Spiedies remain positively ubiquitous in Broome County but virtually unheard of elsewhere.

spifflicated adj   Also *spiffed, spiflocated, spiffocated* =**pifflicated.**

1902 (1906) Porter *4 Million* 114, He uses Nature's Own Remedy. He gets spifflicated. **1918** *DN* 5.28 **NW,** *Spiffed.* . . Intoxicated. General. **1927** *New Republic* 9 Mar 71, Words denoting drunkenness now in common use in the United States . . spifflicated. **1928** *AmSp* 4.102 [Slang synonyms for "drunk"], Spifflicated. **1931** *Sun* (Baltimore MD) 6 Jan 6/7, Almost every name you could think of to describe the state of being drunk was given, but one splendid one that I know was omitted—"spiffilicated." **1950** *WELS* (A person who is very drunk) 1 Inf, **cWI,** Spifflicated. **1960** Bailey *Resp. to PADS* 20 **KS,** Spiflocated. . . Dead drunk. **1967–68** *DARE* (Qu. DD13, *When a drinker is just beginning to show the effects of the liquor . . he's _____*) Inf **MI**67, Spifflicated; **CT**16, Spiffocated. [Both Infs old]

spig   See **spik**

spiggoty n, also attrib   Also *spickety, spigotti, spigoty, spikity* [See quots 1908, 1913] =**spik;** hence adj *spiggoty*.

1899 *Daily IA State Press* (IA City) [24 Aug 7]/1 (newspaper-archive.com), [American soldier in Puerto Rico:] You're not the first Spickety that has been here to-day. **1904** in 2002 *DARE* File **wNY,** [Letter from U.S. Marine in Panama:] Some one goes down the hill to buy fruit if it is bananas . . , they cost 10¢ spickety (Columbian) which equals 5¢ American. *Ibid*, Jest to show you what kind of police these spicketies are I will tell you some thing that happened here a few weeks ago. **1908** *Sat. Eve. Post* 14 Mar 3, The Panamanians presented themselves . . with the statement . . "Spik d'English." . . [or] "No spik d'English." . . and those early Americans soon classed the whole race of men who could or could not "Spik d'Eng." as "Spikities," and from that grew the harmonious and descriptive Spigotty. **1908** *NY Eve. Jrl.* (NY) 26

Mar 16 (*Zwilling Coll.*), [Cartoon caption:] Prince Bunkie De Jagon Admits His Identity. [Text:] How is it that a "spiggoty" can come over here and cop out a live one while us good Americans get nothing but the left overs? **1913** *NY Times* (NY) 9 Aug 6/5, The Zone Americans make too free use of the ugly word "Spigoty" in referring to their new neighbors—a word that is not the less trying to native tempers because it is merely a humorous approximation to their attempt to announce the ability to speak English. One hears down there not only of "Spigoties," but of "Spigoty money" and "Spigoty ways." **1913** [see **spik**]. **1914** *DN* 4.151 [Navy slang], *Spiggoty.* . . A Latin-American. **1914** in 1950 O'Neill *Lost Plays* 37, Say, you're getting to be a regular talker of spigoty! Slip me the answer to that word 'basta,' will you? **1918** in 1972 *AmSp* 47.106, We . . had a white man's dinner with some spigotti liquor. **1919** Kyne *Capt. Scraggs* 219 **CA**, McGuffey whipped a bartender. He was ordered arrested, and six spiggoty little policemen, sent to arrest him, were also thrashed. **1949** *Newark Advocate* (OH) 28 June 4/6 [Headline:] Helped Plan Panama Revolt Which Flopped; He's in Spiggoty Clink.

spignard   See **spikenard**

spignet n   Also *spegnet, spignot, spinit*   **scattered, but esp sAppalachians**

A **spikenard**; see quots.

    1833 (1835) Whitney *Family Physician* 195, Spikenard, spignard, or spignet. [Aralia Racemosa.] **1867** Rockwell *Catskill Mts.* 97 **NY** (as of 1782), They were now nearly out of provisions, and began to suffer, living four days almost entirely upon spignet, until they reached the Connecticut River. **1876** Hobbs *Bot. Hdbk.* 110, Spignet, Spikenard, American, Aralia racemosa. **1894** *Jrl. Amer. Folkl.* 7.90 **NC**, *Aralia racemosa,* . . spignet, Banner Elk. **1917** *DN* 4.417 **wNC, KY,** *Spignet.* . . Wild spikenard. **1925** Dargan *Highland Annals* 46 **cwNC,** There's . . pokeweed for rheumatiz, an' spignet for consumption. **1937** Thornburgh *Gt. Smoky Mts.* 29, Spignot was used as a remedy for felons. **1967** Hall *Coll.* **eTN,** My mother used spignet a few times. She used spignet medicine for kidney trouble. **1969** *DARE* FW Addit **nwCA,** *Spignet root*—For a spring tonic take Oregon grape fruit, mountain balm, and spignet root (plant growing along streams and gulches) and brew them all together. **1970** *NC Folkl.* 18.17, Spignet was prescribed for consumption. **1982** Slone *How We Talked* 48 **eKY** (as of c1950), Spegnet. *Ibid* 102, Pneumonia. . . Cure: given spinit tea to bring down the fever. **1982** Powers *Cataloochee* 257 **cwNC** (as of a1940), Spignet, like Indian turnips, said Mark, was good for the back. **2002** *DARE* File—Internet, Spikenard (Spignet)—Root, Cut—Aralia racemosa—$1.75/oz.

spignet tree   See **spikenard tree**

spigot n   Usu |ˈspɪgɪt, -ət|; also **widespread, but more freq east of Missip R** (See Map) |ˈspɪkɪt, -ət| Pronc-spp *spicket, spikit*; rarely *spick(le)* [Cf *OED2* spicket sb.¹ 14 . . →] Cf **spit** n²

A   Forms.

    1836 (1838) Haliburton *Clockmaker* (1st ser) 301 **NEng,** I'll whip out of the bung while he's a lookin arter the spicket. **1856** *Scientific Amer.* 11.362 **PA,** *Lard Lamps.* . . Nor do I claim, simply, the use of a spicket for regulating a flow of the material to the lamp. **1877** *Atlantic Mth.* Jan 32, Pouring fierce oaths like an open spicket,/ Stood a rival there. **1956** McAtee *Some Dialect NC* 42, Spicket: pronunc., spigot. **1965–70** *DARE* (Qu. F15, *What you turn to let the vinegar or cider run out of a barrel*) 290 Infs, **widespread, but more freq east of Missip R,** Spicket; **NC**50, Sink spicket; **GA**19, Spick; (Qu. F27a, *What you turn on and off inside the house to get running water*) 186 Infs, **chiefly Appalachians, C and Mid Atl,** Spicket; **GA**19, Spick; (Qu. F27b, *What you turn on and off outside the house to get running water*) 180 Infs, **chiefly Appalachians, C and Mid Atl,** Spicket; **GA**72, **NC**16, **NJ**55, **OH**90, **PA**22, 66, **TN**11, **WV**3, Outside spicket; **GA**19, Spick; **NY**210, Spickle; **GA**88, Water spicket; (Qu. C34, *Nicknames for nearby settlements, villages, or districts*) Inf **PA**202, Spicket Valley; (Qu. BB20, *Joking names or expressions for overactive kidneys*) Inf **VA**13, Unruly spicket. **c1970** Pederson *Dial. Surv. Rural GA* **seGA** (*That thing at the kitchen sink that the water comes out of, that thing where you can turn the water off and on*) 24 [of 64] infs, Proncs of the types [ˈspɪkɪt, -ɪt, -ət]; 5 infs, [ˈspɪgɪt]; (*This same thing that you turn on a barrel*) 15 infs, [ˈspɪkɪt, -ɪt]; 3 infs, [ˈspɪgɪt, -ət]; (*The same kind of thing out in the yard that water comes out of*) 38 infs, [ˈspɪkɪt, -ɪt]; 5 infs, [ˈspɪgɪt, -ət]. **1982** Barrick *Coll.* **csPA,** Spigot—pron. spikit. **2005** in 2008 *DARE* File—Internet **IA, I**

---

plan to add a spicket in our garage and use it, mainly, for washing our cars. **2007** *Ibid* **sME,** We hooked up direct to an outside frostless water spicket. **2008** *Ibid* **TX,** [Advt:] Pottery Keg with spicket.

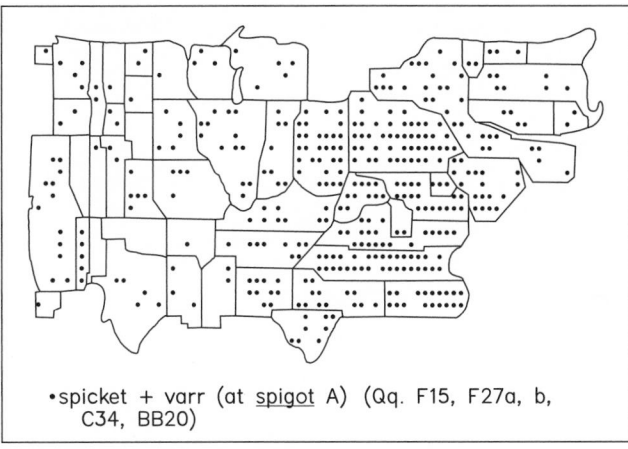

    •spicket + varr (at <u>spigot</u> A) (Qq. F15, F27a, b, C34, BB20)

B   Senses.

1   =faucet B2.

    1826 *Amer. Farmer* 7.406, It is to be drawn off by a spigot placed two or three inches from the bottom [of the barrel]. **1846** *Scientific Amer.* 10 Oct 24, Straw must be placed to prevent the pumice from filling up the spigot. . . Draw it [=peach wine] off, from the spigot. **1897** (1968) Sears *Catalogue* 784, Spigots. . . 141. [*DARE* Ed: On the page referred to, they are called *faucets*.] **1934** Carmer *Stars Fell on AL* 74, Five-gallon keg from which a small spigot projected. **1965–70** *DARE* (Qu. F15, *What you turn to let the vinegar or cider run out of a barrel*) 372 Infs, **widespread, but less freq S Atl,** Spigot; 290 Infs, **widespread, but more freq east of Missip R,** Spicket; **GA**19, Spick. **1967** *DARE* Tape **TX**1, Put a hole in there [=in the keg] with a little spicket on that, that's to drain the dregs off of it if you can. **2008** [see **A** above].

2   =faucet B1.   **widespread, but chiefly Appalachians, Mid and C Atl, eOH**   See Map

    1852 Cox *Buckeye Abroad* 234 **OH,** Spigots turned the water out, which fell into white marble shells, or bath-basins. **1869** *Harper's New Mth. Mag.* 39.419 **sePA,** She thought she would just rub them off a little, if that was hot water in one of those spigots over there in the corner. **1890** *Scribner's Mag.* 8.689 **NYC,** He dipped a wash rag in the water from the spigot in the hall. **1944** *AmSp* 19.38 **sePA,** *Spigot,* pronounced *spicket* and commonly used for 'faucet.' **1949** Kurath *Word Geog.* 56, *Faucet.* . . The water *faucet* is known by that name only in the Northern area. The entire Midland and the South have *spicket* (occasionally *spigot*). **1955** Stong *Blizzard* 72 **IA,** He took the bedside water bottle and put it under the spigot—icy water gushed from the tap. **1965–70** *DARE* (Qu. F27b, *What you turn on and off outside the house to get running water*) 180 Infs, **chiefly Appalachians, Mid and C Atl, eOH,** Spicket; **GA**74, **NC**16, **NJ**55, **OH**90, **PA**22, 66, **TN**11, **WV**3, Outside spicket; **NY**210, Spickle; **GA**88, Water spicket; **GA**19, Spick; 74 Infs, **scattered,** Spigot; **PA**126, 176, 200, Outside spigot; (Qu. F27a, *What you turn on and off inside the house to get running water*) 186 Infs, **chiefly Appalachians, eOH, C and Mid Atl,** Spicket; **GA**19, Spick; 58

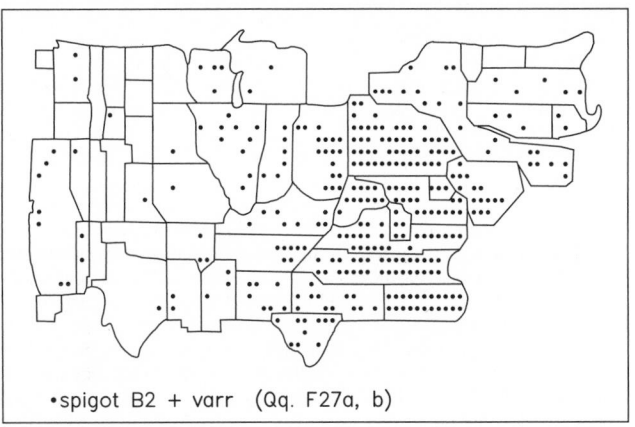

    •spigot B2 + varr (Qq. F27a, b)

Infs, **scattered,** Spigot. **1968** *Star Leader* (Clinton MD) 26 July 6/4, The clear water that comes from the spigot in the Suburban Maryland Area is the product of the Washington Suburban Sanitary Commission. **1982** McCool *Sam McCool's Pittsburghese* 32 **PA,** When are you going to fix the hot water spicket? **1989** Pederson *LAGS Tech. Index* 71 **Gulf Region,** *Faucet . . at sink . .* Spicket (125 [of 914 primary infs]) . . Spigot (38) . . *outside . .* Spicket (157) . . Spigot (33). **2005** [see **A** above]. **2007** [see **A** above].

spigotti, spigoty See **spiggoty**

spik n Also *speck, spic(k), spig* *derog* Cf **Spaniard, Spanish** adj, **spiggoty**

A Latin American or other Spanish speaker, now usu a Puerto Rican or Mexican; by ext, an Italian, Greek, or Pacific Islander; the Spanish language.

1913 Franck *Zone Policeman 88* 10 **Panama Canal Zone,** It was my first entrance into the land of the *panameños,* technically known on the Zone as "Spigoties," and familiarly, with a tinge of despite, as "Spigs"; because the first Americans to arrive in the land found a few natives and cabmen who claimed to "Speaga dee Eng-leesh." **1914** *Ft. Wayne Sentinel* (IN) 25 May 12/1, "What is a 'spik'?" I asked. "All Cubans, Filipinos and Mexicans are 'spiks,'" the sentry said. **1917** in 1972 *AmSp* 47.106 [Slang of Amer Forces in Europe], We had mostly 'Spigs' on board which is navy slang for Spaniards. **1921** *DN* 5.111 **CA,** *Spick, spig. . .* A Philippino, Hawaiian, or native of other Pacific Islands. Navy; Marine Corps. **1930** *AmSp* 5.393 [Language of N Atl fishermen], *Spk* [sic] or *Spick. . .* A Spaniard. **1933** Hemingway *Winner Take Nothing* 194, I wish I could talk spik. **1933** *AmSp* 8.3.31 [Prison terms], *Spic.* Mexican. [From *spaghetti.* [A]pplied to Italians and, loosely, to other Latins and Latin Americans.] **1944** Adams *Western Words* 151, *Spic—* A common name for the Mexican. **1954** *Restaurant Man* Dec 12/2 *(Popik Coll.)* **NYC,** Where there has been a large influx of Puerto Ricans the taverns have been hit very hard as the so-called "Spics" are a low income group and with large families can't afford to patronize bars. **1964** *PADS* 42.36 **Chicago IL,** *Terms for Nationality Groups. . . Mexican . .* spick [10 of 31 infs] *. . Puerto Rican . .* spick [12 infs] *. .* speck [1 inf]. **1965–70** *DARE* (Qu. HH28, *Names and nicknames . . for people of foreign background)* 69 Infs, **esp NEast,** Spik—Puerto Rican; 33 Infs, **scattered,** Spik—Mexican; 10 Infs, **scattered,** Spik—Puerto Ricans, Mexican; **CA**74, 169, **CT**19, **FL**28, **NY**42, 67, Spik—Spanish; **CO**34, **MO**12, **WI**47, Spik—Italian; **CO**7, **TX**33, Spik—Italian, Mexican; **GA**11, Spik—Cubans; **IN**68, Spik—Greek; **CO**39, Spik—Mexican, Spanish-Americans; **CA**5, Spik—Puerto Ricans, Spanish; **NY**1, Spig—Puerto Rican; (Qu. W42a, *. . Nicknames . . for men's sharp-pointed shoes)* Inf **MA**1, Spik boots—above ankle length, with elastic on cuff, especially favored by Puerto Ricans; **NY**10, Spik shoes—Puerto Rican shoes. **1975** *AmSp* 50.67 **AR** (as of c1970), *Spic . .* 1: Spanish language. 2: Course in the Spanish language—"I've had two years of Spic." **1989** Pederson *LAGS Tech. Index* 406, *Italians . .* spik (9 [of c160 chiefly urban infs]). *Ibid* 407, *Cubans . .* spiks (17). *Ibid* 408, *Puerto Ricans . .* spiks (23). *. . . (Mexicans) . .* spiks (26). **2000** Launspach *ID Dial. Project* 6 **seID,** *(Terms for Mexicans)* 42 [of 99] infs, Spics. **2001** *DARE* File **wNY,** Spic . . a Puerto Rican; broadly, anyone of Hispanic descent (disparaging).

spike n

1 freq attrib: An immature specimen of any of var fish, as **mackerel 1** (here: *Scomber scombrus*), **walleye,** or **weakfish** (here: *Cynoscion nebulosus*).

1884 Goode *Fisheries U.S.* 1.298 **MA,** Fish of this size [=six and a half or seven inches in length] are sometimes called 'Spikes,' but I do not know their proper name. **1911** U.S. Bur. Census *Fisheries 1908* 312, Small mackerel are known as "spikes" (5 to 6 inches long), "blinkers" (7 to 8 inches long), and "tinkers" (9 inches long). **1930** U.S. Bur. Fisheries *Rept. for 1928* 282 **nOH,** *Stizostedion vitreum. . .* [Other names include:] *Spike* (small specimens about 8 inches long, at Maumee Bay, Sandusky Bay, Port Clinton, etc.) **1932** Wasson *Sailing Days* 115 **cME coast,** One season they [=mackerel] might be so plentiful as to glut the market and the next, not even a small tinker, or still smaller "spike," would show itself. **2002** *Cleveland Plain Dealer* (OH) 11 Aug sec D 15 (Internet), Perch fishermen around Western Lake Erie are somehow confusing small "spike" walleye with yellow perch and keeping them, killing the 7- to 9-inch fish that have little in the way of a fillet just yet. **2002** *DARE* File—Internet **ME,** The mackerel have moved back in. They are either huge, over two pounds or the little spike or tinker size. **2008** *Ibid* **seNC,** There's no truth to the belief that if you start

catching spikes (small trout) in one area, then that's all you'll catch there.

2 Either the common **merganser** *(Mergus merganser)* or the **hooded merganser.** Cf **spikebill 2, spiky**

1923 U.S. Dept. Ag. *Misc. Circular* 13.5 **NY,** American Merganser. . . Vernacular Names. . . *In local use. . .* spike. *Ibid* 7 **MI,** Hooded Merganser. . . spike. **1968** *DARE* (Qu. Q5, *. . Kinds of wild ducks)* Inf **KS**16, Spike. [*DARE* Ed: This Inf may refer instead to **3** below.]

3 =**pintail 1.** Cf **spiketail 2**

1923 U.S. Dept. Ag. *Misc. Circular* 13.15 **NE,** Pintail. . . Vernacular Names. . . *In local use. . .* Spike (Nebr.); spike-tail (Ill.) **1932** Bennitt *Check-list* 19 **MO,** American pintail. . . Sprig; sprigtail; spike; spiketail.

4 also *spike clam:* A **freshwater clam** (here: *Elliptio dilatata).*

1941 *AmSp* 16.156, [In a list of button-cutters' names for freshwater mussels:] Spike. **1982** *WI State Jrl.* (Madison) 22 Aug sec 7 3, Indians once ate spike clams, which can still be found in smaller Wisconsin streams. **1991** IL Nat. Hist. Surv. *Biol. Notes* 137.11, The spike appears to be declining statewide. **1992** *Nature Conserv. Mag.* 42.6.22 **VA,** A mussel sampler from the remarkable Clinch Valley. . . spike, *Elliptio dilatata.*

5 =**needle 1.**

1970 *DARE* (Qu. T6, *The pointed leaves that fall from pine trees)* Inf **TN**52, Spikes.

6 The larva of a blowfly (family Calliphoridae), commonly used as bait in ice fishing.

1982 Sternberg *Fishing* 88, Silver wigglers, or *spikes,* are the larvae of flies such as the housefly and blowfly. **1992** *Capital Times* (Madison WI) 11 Jan sec A 2, Now what blue gills like are these little things that I'm sure you'll find thoroughly disgusting: spikes—they're the larvae of a fly. **2002** *DARE* File—Internet **MI,** I like spikes (maggots) myself. . . A guy I fish with uses moussies, and we can't see much difference in our catches. **2004** *Ibid* **ND,** Hanger rigs tipped with spikes, wax worms, minnows, or perch eyes have been the better baits.

7 An arrow or arrowhead. **chiefly S Midl**

1897 *Galveston Daily News* (TX) 5 Dec 11/2, Davis was badly wounded with an arrow which went through the left shoulder, the spike coming through on the opposite side. **1945** *SW Rev.* 30.340 **Ozarks,** Skaggs hands . . took to a knife as an Indian boy's took to a bow-and-spike. **1946** in 1980 Still *Run for Elbertas* 89 **KY** (as of 1920s), Tomorry I'm bringing my bow and spike. **1953** Randolph–Wilson *Down in Holler* 287 **Ozarks,** *Spike. . .* An arrow. One hears little boys talking of "a bow an' spike" just as children elsewhere would say "a bow and arrow." The flint arrowheads found in the fields are known as "Injun spikes" and occasionally as "Injun darts." **1954** *Harder Coll.* **cwTN,** *Spike. . .* An arrow. **1991** *OzarksWatch* 4.3 (Internet), Many of yesterday's fishermen were as skilled as Osage braves with the bow-and-arrow. Fishing with "Bow-and-spike," they called it. . . The spikes were two-barbed, slim, steel arrowheads made by blacksmiths. The spike shafts were usually of native cane.

8 See **spikenose.**

spikebill n

1 =**red-throated loon.**

1875 *Fur Fin & Feather* 119 **N Atl,** The smaller species of loon I have heard variously called the spike-bill, the cape-race [etc]. **1955** MA Audubon Soc. *Bulletin* 39.309 **MA,** Red-throated Loon. . . Spike-bill (Mass. The bill is long and pointed.) **2001** *Richmond Times–Dispatch* (VA) 6 May sec K 2 (Internet) **NC,** I once witnessed the rescue of a dying loon from the surf and . . told a woman . . about how the bird was . . treated and released back into the wild. "That's one more of those durn spike bills that can go through my tire again," she said.

2 =**hooded merganser.** Cf **little spikebill, spike 2, spiky**

1888 Trumbull *Names of Birds* 74 **MI,** At Detroit, [the hooded merganser is known as] Spike-Bill. **1923** U.S. Dept. Ag. *Misc. Circular* 13.7, Hooded Merganser. . . spikebill (N.Y., Del., Mich., Tex., Ariz., . . Wash.)

3 See **spike-billed curlew.**

spike-billed curlew n Also *spikebill* =**marbled godwit.**

1888 Trumbull *Names of Birds* 207 **NJ,** In New Jersey at Pleasantville . . and Cape May City, [the marbled godwit is called] *Spike-Bill,* and less frequently, *Spike-Billed Curlew.* **1918** Grinnell et al. *Game Birds CA* 396, Marbled Godwit. . . Other names . . Straight-billed

Curlew; . . Spike-bill. **1946** Hausman *Eastern Birds* 289, Marbled Godwit. . . Spike-billed Curlew.

spike camp n Also called **stub camp**
A remote camp used as a temporary base for logging, conservation work, firefighting, hunting, or other wilderness activities.

1915 *Portsmouth Daily Times* (OH) 7 Sept 12/7, The elevation of our spike camp at timber line was about 8500 feet. Unfortunately for our goat hunting, the snow never went off the peaks. **1958** McCulloch *Woods Words* 176 **Pacific NW,** *Spike camp*—A temporary camp for a short time, away from the main camp. **1984** Doig *English Creek* 170 **nMT,** Some CCC guys had taken all the spare ones [=horses] in a big packstring to set up a spike camp for a tree-planting crew. **2003** *DARE* File—Internet **MN,** As a MCC residential corpsmember, you'll spend several weeks on "spike camp." *Ibid* **AK** [Deltana Outfitters], Our sheep camp . . features a comfortable base camp, but much of your time will be in mountain wilderness hiking after Dall sheep based out of spike camps. *Ibid* **AR,** In October 1935 it [sic] spike camp at Blue Springs was closed and moved to the main [CCC] camp in Hermitage. *Ibid* **nME,** For those looking for more adventure than hunting out of our lodge, we offer our remote spike camp bear hunt. **2003** *AK Mag.* Dec/Jan 54 **AK,** Ted's jet boat can make the 30-mile run down Lake Iliamna almost two hours before the most bold pilot can fly, guaranteeing the [fishing] rock for his clients unless, as sometimes happens, another lodge has set up a spike camp.

spike clam See **spike 4**

spiked rush See **spike rush**

spiked team See **spike team**

spikefish n
1 =**sailfish 1.**
1884 U.S. Fish Comm. *Bulletin for 1884* 4.77 **FL,** With these are occasionally found the Spike-fish (Histiophorus). **1896** U.S. Natl. Museum *Bulletin* 47.891, *Istiophorus nigricans* [=*I. platypterus*]. . . Sailfish; Spikefish; Boohoo [etc]. **2002** *Redbone Jrl.* Summer (Internet) **sFL,** Around the turn of the century, offshore anglers and skippers in the Keys were often troubled by a pesky fish they considered to be a "damned nuisance". . . This piscatorial plague was called a "spikefish," but was actually a sailfish.

2 A **spearfish 1:** in the Atlantic, the white marlin *(Tetrapturus albidus);* in the Pacific, the striped marlin *(Tetrapturus audax).*
1879 U.S. Natl. Museum *Bulletin* 14.39, *Tetrapturus albidus.* . . Spikefish.—Cape Cod to West Indies. **1976** Tryckare et al. *Lore of Sportfishing* 125, White Marlin. . . Other common names: skiligollee . . , Spikefish. **2002** *DARE* File—Internet, *Spikefish*—A name given to the marlins or spearfish in the family *Istiophridae* [sic]. Spikefish is usually applied to the striped marlin in the Pacific off the west coast of the United States.

spike-grass n
1 A grass of the central Atlantic and southern US *(Uniola paniculata).* Also called **oat grass d, sea oat(s)** Note: Some species formerly included in *Uniola* have been reassigned to *Chasmanthium;* cf **3** below.
1771 Forster *Flora* 4 **NC, SC,** *Uniola* paniculata—Spike grass, paniculated. **1790** in 1793 *Amer. Philos. Soc. Trans.* 3.161, *Uniola,* Spike-grass. **1843** Torrey *Flora NY* 2.473, Uniola [spp]. . . Spike-grass. **1881** Phares *Farmer's Book of Grasses* 68 **Sth,** U[niola] paniculata, Spike Grass, growing from two to eight feet high among the sands along the coast. **1933** Small *Manual SE Flora* 127, Uniola [spp]. . . Spikegrasses. **1976** Bailey–Bailey *Hortus Third* 1139, Uniola. . . *paniculata* . . Sea oats, spike-grass.

2 =**salt grass a(2).**
1814 Bigelow *Florula Bostoniensis* 23, Uniola spicata [=*Distichlis* s.] . . *Spike grass.* . . A common grass of the salt marshes. **1840** MA Zool. & Bot. Surv. *Herb. Plants & Quadrupeds* 242, U[niola] spicata. . . Spike Grass. **1886** Havard *Flora W. & S. TX for 1885* 530, *Brizopyrum spicatum* [=*Distichlis spicata*] (Spike-Grass); another salt grass, common on low, marshy places, sometimes affords fair pasturage. **1898** Davidson *CA Plants* 57, Distichlis. Spike-grass. **1946** Tatnall *Flora DE* 24, Spike Grass. Salt meadows. . . One of the chief constituents of "marsh hay." **2002** *DARE* File—Internet **FL,** *Distichlis*

spicata—Salt grass, Spike grass. The medium-tall salt grass is found in salt and brackish coastal marshes and can grow into large monocultures.

3 A grass of the genus *Chasmanthium.* For other names of *C. latifolium* see **oat grass d, wild oats 2d, ~ rice 3** Note: Some plants now in *Chasmanthium* were formerly included in *Uniola;* cf **1** above.
1822 Eaton *Botany* 497, [*Uniola*] *gracilis* [=*Chasmanthium laxum*]. . . spike-grass. **1843** Torrey *Flora NY* 2.473, Uniola gracilis. . . *Slender Spike-grass.* **1881** Phares *Farmer's Book of Grasses* 68, U[niola] gracilis, Slender Spike Grass, found in rich, damp soils. *Ibid,* U[niola] nitida [=*Chasmanthium nitidum*], Shining Spike Grass, found in swamps. **1941** Walker *Lookout* 50 **TN,** [Here] also is met large beds of spike grass along creeks. This . . makes attractive cuttings to fill vases. **1969** U.S. Dept. Ag. *Ag. Hdbk. No. 356* 69, Uniola latifolia [=*Chasmanthium latifolium*]. . . Spikegrass.

spike muhly n
A **muhly (grass)** (here: *Muhlenbergia wrightii*).
1937 U.S. Forest Serv. *Range Plant Hdbk.* G85, The common names spike muhly, timothy-like muhly, black-timothy, and wild-timothy have originated from the characteristic flower head. **1950** Hitchcock–Chase *Manual Grasses* 387, *Muhlenbergia wrightii.* . . Spike muhly. **1970** Humphrey *AZ Range Grasses* 113, Spike muhly occurs at moderately high to high altitudes in Arizona. **2004** Phillips *NM Gardener's Guide* 75, Junegrass and spike muhly are a beautiful combination of cool-season grasses.

spikenard n Also *spi(c)knard, spignard*
A plant of the genus *Aralia,* esp *A. racemosa.* For other names of the latter see **false sarsaparilla 1, hungryroot, Indian root 1, king of the woods, life-of-man 1, old-man's-root, petty morel, pigeonweed 1, spicebush 3, spignet, whiteroot 4;** for other names of var spp see **elk clover, ginseng B2, Hercules'-club 1, sarsaparilla B2, shotbush, wild elder, wild sarsaparilla 1**
[**1640** Parkinson *Theatrum Botanicum* 1744, Virginia Spikenard.] **1778** Carver *Travels N. Amer.* 511, *Spikenard,* vulgarly called in the colonies Petty-Morrell. . . appears to be exactly the same as the Asiatick spikenard. **1810** in 1923 Hand *Letters Hand Family* 37 **VT,** My cough is extremely bad yet. If you could bring me down some Spignard I should be very glad. **1817** (1890) Long *Jrl.* 34 **MN,** There were also various kinds of herbage and flowers, among which were the wild parsely [sic], rue, spikenard, etc. **1828** Rafinesque *Med. Flora* 1.53, *Aralia nudicaulis.* English Name—Small Spikenard. . . Vulgar Names—Spiknard [sic] [etc]. **1840** MA Zool. & Bot. Surv. *Herb. Plants & Quadrupeds* 13, Spikenard. . . A[ralia] racemosa. . . Spikenard. . . The root is highly aromatic, and formerly was used in a bruised state upon wounds. **1891** *Jrl. Amer. Folkl.* 4.148 **swNH,** A[ralia] racemosa we generally called by the correct name, *Spikenard,* but we pronounced it with short *i,* as if Spicknard. **1893** *Amer. Bee Jrl.* 31.816 **CA,** Among the late honey-plants that flourish here, may be mentioned the spignard. **1896** *Ibid* 9.189 **ME,** Aralia racemosa . . spikenard, Oxford County. **1897** Parsons *Wild Flowers CA* 76, Californian Spikenard. *Aralia Californica.* **1974** (1977) Coon *Useful Plants* 68, *Aralia nudicaulis* . . American spikenard. . . *Aralia racemosa* . . American spikenard. **2002** [see **spignet**].

spikenard tree n Also *spignet tree*
=**Hercules'-club 1.**
1828 Rafinesque *Med. Flora* 1.56, A[ralia] *spinosa* or Spikenard Tree. . . From New-York to Georgia, and west to Missouri, &c. **1876** Hobbs *Bot. Hdbk.* 110, Spikenard tree, Prickly elder, [Aralia] spinosa. **1898** Bacon *Lyddy* 54 **GA** (as of 1830s), Cuddled in a warm nest, between the limbs of a spikenard tree, were four bare-bodied birds. **1941** Writers' Program *Guide SC* 224, Shading the Sims monument an overhanging spikenard tree is heavy with lavender blossoms. **1950** Peattie *Nat. Hist. Trees* 493, Hercules'-club. . . Other Names: Angelica-tree. Spikenardtree [etc]. **1953** Stuart *Good Spirit* 212 **neKY,** "There's a cure fer every ill right here on Laurel Ridge!" . . Op was staring at a small tree with little red berries on its boughs beside him. "Here's a spignet tree." . . Op started digging. "It'll put pounds on ye."

spikenose n Also *spike*
A **walleye.**
1884 Goode *Fisheries U.S.* 1.421 **cnNY,** At Cape Vincent Pike [here: =*Stizostedion vitreum*] are abundant. The fish of one variety, with a longer and more pointed head than the Upper Lake fish, are called

"Spike-noses". . . They are common everywhere. **1935** Caine *Game Fish* 31, Wall-Eyed Pike. . . Spike.

spike pitcher n [See quot 1958; cf *DCan*] **Plains States, Upper MW, NW** Cf **spiker 1**

A member of a threshing crew who tosses sheaves into the machine; broadly, one who helps unload, or less freq load, a farm wagon; hence, by back-formation, v phr *spike pitch,* vbl n *spike pitching.*

[**1907** *Manitoba Morning Free Press* (Winnipeg) 28 Oct 14/3, There remains about two weeks of threshing in this district. Men are scarce and wages are: Teamsters, $2.50; spike pitchers, $3.00 [etc].] **1909** *Austin Daily Herald* (MN) [30 Oct 2]/2 (newspaperarchive.com), I helped hauled [sic] over 2,500 bushels of oats and bin them. . . There were six teams hauling the grain away. . . They have twelve bundle teams with two spike pitchers, "whose business it is to stay at the machine" and help pitch the loads in. **1913** [see **spiker 1**]. **1914** *IA Homestead* 17 Sept 5/3, Each man pitches his own load in the field. One spike pitcher at the [silage] cutter, one feeder and three men in the silo. **1920** *DN* 5.84 **NW,** Spike pitcher. One who helps unload hay. Employment Agency. **1928** *Ruppenthal Coll.* **KS,** Spike pitcher. . . In farm work, one who helped unload hay or grain etc. from wagon, using a pitch fork. **1937** *AmSp* 12.106 **eNE** [Farm terms], Among the threshing crew are . . the *spike pitchers* (who help the *bundle haulers*). **1944** in 2008 *DARE* File—Internet **SD,** Spike pitched yesterday and today [at German P.O.W. camp]. **1954** Scholl *Arnewood* 78 **IA** (as of c1940), I managed to get by with four racks to haul bundles from the field to the machine, and two spike pitchers in the field to help load the wagons. **1958** Goff *Nobles Co. Hist.* 55 **MN,** The pitchers would toss the bundles into the feeder, heads first as they threshed better that way. When the stacks were lowered a bit a second man would get on each stack and by-pitch to the spike pitcher. The slats in the feeder had spikes in them to carry the bundles into the cylinder, hence the name "spike pitcher." **1963** in 2008 (acc) *Steam Traction Archive* (Internet) **ND,** I threshed in North Dakota four years. First year, 1911, I spike pitched bundles and drove bundle wagon. *Ibid* **MT,** The crew consisted of 14 on bundle wagons, 7 field pitchers, 2 spike pitchers, a man to haul water for the engine and horses, a separator man and myself as the engineer. One spiker helped the separator man and the other was available to me. **1966** *Ibid* **SD,** I went farther west and went to spike pitching on another job. . . On finishing this job, the other spiker and I rode the separator the several miles home. **1975** *Ibid* **ND,** Spike pitching, or spiking as it was called, was a form of slavery which had not been abolished by the Civil War. **1982** in 2001 *DARE* File—Internet **ND** (as of 1930s), About twenty men were needed to thrash the bundles. It took from six to eight teams. One man called the Spike Pitcher was out on the field helping load all teams. **1989** Whipple *Cox Family Hist.* 240 **KS** (as of c1919), Two men were spike pitchers. The spike pitchers . . pitched the bundles head-first into the feeder on the separator.

spiker n

1 =**spike pitcher;** hence vbl n *spiking.*

1913 *IA Homestead* 11 Sept 4/1 **NE,** We use one man besides the hauler as spike pitcher to the [silage] cutter, also two men as spikers in the field. . . About every six or eight loads the spiker at the cutter changes with the tramper in the silo, and generally the field spikers of the forenoon are the trampers of the afternoon. **1963** [see **spike pitcher**]. **1966** [see **spike pitcher**]. **1975** [see **spike pitcher**]. **1994** in 2000 Dregni *100 Yrs. Tractors* 80 **IA** (as of 1940s), The intermediate step of spike pitcher was an apprenticeship in learning how to load bundles properly. The "spiker" would help a farmer load his rack. . . Spiking was actually harder work than having one's own rack because there were no rest periods while waiting to unload.

2 See quots.

1956 Sorden–Ebert *Logger's Words* 18 **Gt Lakes,** *Hiker.* A lumberjack who has quit the job. Same as spiker. **2004** Forester *Forest Trees* 59 **MN,** Skid row spikers—retired lumberjacks who lived in shanties along the skid trails.

spike rush n Also *spiked rush* [*OED2* 1829 →]

A **sedge B1** of the genus *Eleocharis.* For other names of var spp see **cunt-hair grass, dog hair** n **1, hairgrass 2, kill cow, poverty grass 2b, spike sedge, wire grass 2i**

1843 Torrey *Flora NY* 2.346, Eleocharis palustris. . . *Common Spike-rush.* . . Swamps and low grounds. **1861** Wood *Class-Book* 736, Eleocharis [spp]. . . Spiked Rush. **1903** Porter *Flora PA* 49, Eleocharis palustris. . . Creeping Spike-rush. **1923** in 1925 Jepson *Manual Plants*

CA 148, E[leocharis] acicularis. . . Slender Spike-rush. **1930** OK Univ. Biol. Surv. *Pub.* 2.54, Eleocharis rostellata. . . Walking Spike-rush. **1959** Anderson *Flora AK* 108, E[leocharis] nitida. . . Slender Spike-rush. **2002** (acc) U.S. Dept. Ag. *Plants Database* (Internet), Eleocharis austrotexana. . . Rio Grande spikerush.

spike sedge n

A **spike rush;** see quots.

1915 *Plant World* 18.118 **AZ,** Eleocharis palustris. . . Spike sedge. **1953** Nelson *Plants Rocky Mt. Park* 44, The few-flowered spikerush or few-flowered spikesedge, Eleocharis pauciflora . . , also occurs here. **1954** Harrington *Manual Plants CO* 142, Eleocharis [spp] . . Spikesedge; Spike-rush. **1968** Barkley *Plants KS* 82, Eleocharis compressa. . . Flatstem Spikesedge. **2002** (acc) U.S. Dept. Ag. *Plants Database* (Internet), Eleocharis equisetoides . . jointed spikesedge.

spiketail n

1 also *spike-tailed grouse:* =**sharp-tailed grouse.**

1878 *Forest & Stream* 11 Apr 175, Pedioecetes phasianellus columbianus . . in other words, the southern sharp- or spike-tailed grouse. **1904** Doubleday *Birds* 281, Prairie Sharp-tailed Grouse. . . *Called also* . . spike-tail.

2 =**pintail 1.** Cf **spike 3**

1877 Hallock *Sportsman's Gaz.* 177 **WI,** Red-heads, mallards, black-heads and spike-tails, . . make up the attractive list of the shooting. **1888** Trumbull *Names of Birds* 38 **IL,** Dafila acuta. . . At Chicago, *Spike-tail,* and less commonly *Pike-tail.* **1900** Ball *NW IN* 449, Birds named are. . . ducks, especially "the mallard, blue wing teal, widgeon, wood-duck, spoonbill, and spike-tail."

3 =**ruddy duck.**

1923 U.S. Dept. Ag. *Misc. Circular* 13.31 **NY, MI,** Ruddy Duck. . . Vernacular Names. . . *In local use.* . . spiketail [etc]. **1938** Oberholser *Bird Life LA* 140, Probably no duck has so many different names as this well-known bird. Some of those commonly heard are . . 'spiketail' [etc]. **1949** Sprunt–Chamberlain *SC Bird Life* 144, Ruddy Duck. . . Local Names: Spiketail [etc].

4 =**porcupine.**

1969 *DARE* (Qu. P31, . . *Names or nicknames . . for the . . porcupine*) Inf **CA**130, Spiketail.

spike-tailed grouse See **spiketail 1**

spike team n Also sp *spiked team*

A team of three draft animals with two harnessed abreast and one in front; similarly n *spike yoke* such a configuration consisting of oxen.

1848 Bartlett *Americanisms* 324, Spike team. A waggon drawn by three horses, or by two oxen and a horse, the latter leading the oxen or span of horses. **1890** *Atlantic Mth.* 66.111 **Boston MA,** From December to April every engine house contains an equine guest, as an extra horse for making up a "spike team," in case the streets are blocked with snow. . . The new-comer does not serve as a leader: one of the regular team is put in that post, the extra horse taking the other's place at the pole. **1892** *Lippincott's Mth. Mag.* July 28 **sAppalachians,** A heavy farm-wagon, drawn by a "spiked team,"—that is, two mules and a lead-horse,—came round a bend and pulled up near the mill. **1905** *DN* 3.95 **nwAR,** Spike team. . . A team of three horses or three mules. Universal. **1939** *LANE* Map 174, 1 inf, **swCT,** Spike team, three horses. [**1967** *DARE* (Qu. K26, *If six oxen are hitched together two and two, you have three _____*) Inf **TN**2, Spike team—horses or mules; spike yoke—oxen.] **1986** Pederson *LAGS Concordance (Pair of mules)* 1 inf, **cTN,** Spike team—with three; [1 inf, **nwAL,** Spike team—four-horse team;] *(The lead horse)* 1 inf, **swAL,** Spike team—three horses hitched to a wagon; 1 inf, **cnFL,** Spike team—three horses, 2 abreast, one in lead. **1989** Flynt *Poor But Proud* 129 **ceAL,** In small mines, a three-mule team or "spike team" carried the cars [which carried the coal] up inclines. Sometimes miners used teams of as many as seven or eight mules.

spikeweed n esp **CA**

A **tarweed 1b(3);** see quots.

1901 Jepson *Flora CA* 532, C[entromadia] pungens [=Hemizonia p.] . . Common Spikeweed. **1960** Abrams *Flora Pacific States* 4.180, Hemizonia laevis. . . Smooth Spikeweed. . . Dry fields. *Ibid,* Hemizonia australis. . . Southern Spikeweed. . . Low alkaline fields near the coast. **2002** (acc) CA Univ. Digital Lib. Project *CalFlora* (Internet), Hemizonia fitchii. . . Fitch spikeweed, . . spikeweed. *Ibid,* Hemizonia parryi ssp. australis. . . Spikeweed.

spike yoke See **spike team**

spiking See **spiker 1**

spikit See **spigot**

spikity See **spiggoty**

spiknard See **spikenard**

spiky n
=**hooded merganser.** Cf **spike 2**
   1923 U.S. Dept. Ag. *Misc. Circular* 13.7 **NY,** Hooded Merganser. . .
spiky.

spil See **spoil A1**

spile n¹
1 A tap for a barrel or similar container.
   1814 in 1947 *AmSp* 22.275 **NH,** [Americanisms:] Spile for a spigot.
1828 Webster *Amer. Dict., Tap, n.* . . A spile or pipe for drawing liquor
from a cask. **1830** *VA Lit. Museum* 1.479, Spile, "A spigot." **1939**
LANE Map 143, Wooden faucet in a barrel. . . [T]erms . . were not systematically asked for. . . 1 inf, c**ME,** Spile; 1 inf, c**sNH,** *Spile,* old-fashioned term; 1 inf, sw**NH,** *Spile,* on a beer or cider barrel. **1966–68**
DARE (Qu. F15, *What you turn to let the vinegar or cider run out of a
barrel*) Inf **ME5,** Spile; **PA136,** Some used to call them spiles. [Both
Infs old]
2 also rarely *spill:* A spout or tube inserted into a sugar maple tree for conducting the sap into a pail or other receptacle.
   1829 *Amer. Farmer* 11.107 c**sPA,** The trees are tapt with an auger. . .
In the hole is placed a spile or spout 18 [sic] inches long, made of sumach. **1844** *Knickerbocker* 23.444 **NEast,** The clean white-pine buckets . . into which the sap drips from the spiles, are made expressly for
this use. **1859** MI State Ag. Soc. *Trans. for 1857* 314, I tap with an
inch augur; my spills are made of basswood and pine. **1911** *Porter
Harvester* 34 **IN,** When the Harvester hitched Betsy, loaded his spiles
and sap buckets into the wagon . . almost his entire family came to see
him. **1923** *DN* 5.221 sw**MO,** *Spile.* . . A small tube made by removing
the pith of elder or sumac or similar woods. *Ibid* 236 sw**WI,** *Spill.* . . A
split piece of alder used to lead "sugar water" from the tree to the receptacle which is to catch it. **1947** *AmSp* 22.152 w**PA** [Maple syrup production vocab], *Spile.* The spout through which the sap flows from the
tree. This may be of metal or of elder branches from which the pith is
removed. **1966** *DARE* Tape **NH5,** We have what they call plastic tubing. It's fastened to the spile, or the spout, and the sap drips through
that . . until it comes to a tank. **1967** *DARE* (Qu. F15) Inf **MA5,**
Spile—used for running sap out of the tree. **1968** *DARE* FW Addit
VA27, *Spiles*—small tubes made out of shoemake and inserted into
holes bored in the *water* (sap). **2001**
DARE File c**wIL,** In response to my dad's insistence that the thing you
drive into a tree to collect sap for making maple syrup is a spile, my
mom insisted it's a spigot. She collected sap in the 1940's and 1950's
and they're from the same fairly small town.

spile n² [*OED2* 1513 →] **chiefly NEast, MI** See Map
A heavy timber driven into soft ground as a support for a superstructure, esp a dock or pier; hence n *spiling* a series of
such timbers.
   1655 in 1883 Suffolk Co. MA *Deeds* 2.158, The westerly side of the
land & wharfe of Rich. Nortons and so along up to the stake or spile
standing on the west end of the sajd wharfe. **1814** in 1947 *AmSp*
22.275, [Americanisms:] *Spile* . . vulgarly for a pile. **1857** in 1923 *Jrl.
Amer. Hist.* [New Haven] 17.228 **RI,** The only objection to this place, by
some, is the Michigan Railroad which is built on spiles, immediately in
front, about 200 or 300 feet from the shore. **1893** in 1956 Ritchie *Block
Is. Lore & Legends* 59 **RI,** A straight line of oak spiles, 25 feet apart, is
run from the shore at right angles to the beach for perhaps a 1000 feet or
more. These are driven down firmly with a spile driver. **1931–33** *LANE
Worksheets* se**MA,** *Spile.* . . Posts of a wharf. **1942** ME Univ. *Studies*
57.134, *Spiling.* A series of *spiles* driven in front of a dam. **1965–70**
DARE (Qu. O5, *The posts standing in the water which these platforms
rest on*) 24 Infs, **chiefly NEast, MI,** Spiles; **MI20, OH67,** Spiling.
1969 Sorden *Lumberjack Lingo* 118 **NEng, Gt Lakes,** *Spile*—A small
log used as a pile in dam construction. *Spiling*—A series of spiles driven
in front of a dam. **1975** Gould *ME Lingo* 269, *Spile*—A pile for piers.
1985 Rattray *Advent. Dimon* 175 **Long Is. NY,** Father maintained that if
you didn't wear something to protect the top of your head, you'd go soft
on top, like a rotting spile. **2005** *WI State Jrl.* (Madison) 20 Mar sec I

10 (Internet) **Gt Lakes,** Pound nets, strung between spiles sunk in shallow water, herded fish into a central point.

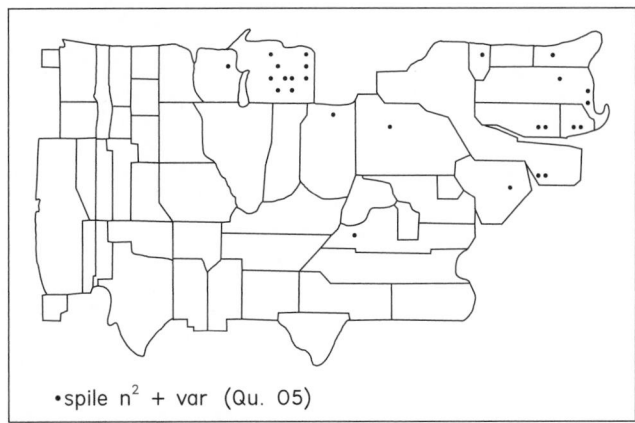

•spile n² + var (Qu. O5)

spile v See **spoil A1**
spile-market See **spoil-market**
spiling See **spile** n²

spill n¹ Also *pine-spill* [From *spill* splinter; cf *OED2* spill sb.¹
1.a, 2.a] **now chiefly ME** See Map
=**needle** n **1.**
   1874 *Overland Mth.* 13.527 **CA,** I was tryin' to git the bark and pine-
spills out o' my eyes. **1887** *Atlantic Mth.* May 580 **NEng,** 'T was allowed to be difficult for folks to git about in old times, or to git word
across the country, and they stood in their lot an' place, and were n't all
just alike, either, same as pine-spills. **1888** *Oölogist* 5.12 **ME,** Took
two sets of Bobolink eggs . . ; nests composed of pine spills. **1909** *DN*
3.416 n**ME,** *Spill.* . . The leaf of a softwood evergreen tree. **1941** *Nature Mag.* 34.139 n**ME,** In northern Maine, spills is the indigenous term
for the leaves of pine. **1959** Martin *Gunbarrel* 274, Mimicking the lady
from Boston, [she] referred to the pine needles falling on the roof of her
cabin as "spills." **1966** *DARE* (Qu. T6, *The pointed leaves that fall from
pine trees*) Infs **ME3, 8, 12, 14, 21,** Spills; **ME5,** Spills, pine spills; (Qu.
T17) Inf **ME14,** California pine—long spill. **2002** *DARE* File—Internet s**ME coast,** Discussed volunteers at Camp Laughing Loon bringing
in things into the Transfer Station from their spring clean up. Motion . .
to allow them to bring in pine spills, brush and leaves. **2004** *Down East*
July 88 n**ME,** Jack climbed up onto the roof of his house and swept off
the accumulated pine spiles [sic].

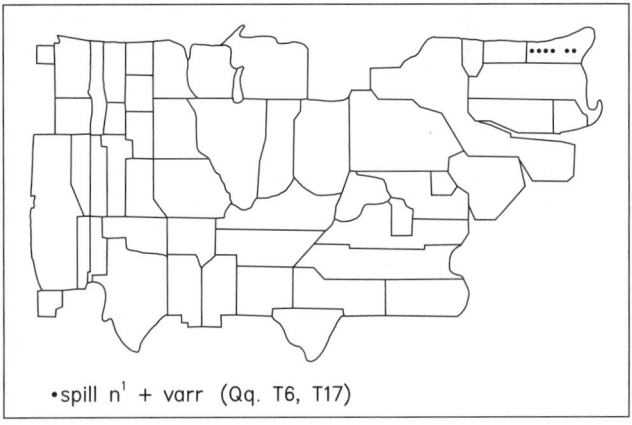

•spill n¹ + varr (Qq. T6, T17)

spill n² See **spile** n¹ **2**
spill one's cookies See **cookie** n¹ **3**
spill-quirley See **quirley**
spilt See **spoil B**

spin v
Std sense, var forms.
1 past: usu *spun;* also *span, spinned, spint, spunt.*
   1851 *De Bow's Rev.* 11.77, They neither toiled nor spinned. **1884**
Anglia 7.253 [Black], To the regular forms of the Irregular verbs as used

by the whites, the Negro adds the following forms of his own. . . *Pres. spin—Past.* spinned, spint, spunt. **1906** *DN* 3.158 **nwAR,** *Spinned.* . . Spun. "Then I spinned my top." **1947** *McDavid Coll.* **nwGA,** *Spinned* (pret) = spun. **1962** *Mt. Life* 38.1.17 **sAppalachians,** The *-d* and *-ed* endings of past forms of verbs are frequently pronounced *-t,* particularly when the ending is preceded by *l, m, n,* or *r.* A few such verbs are . . spun, spunt [etc]. **1968** *DARE* Tape **VA25,** She spinned the thread herself, you know, made it . . so it'd be usable. . . I seen they took and. . . spun it . . and they'd spin this thread and put so much, so many threads together, you know, made it in for weaving. **1982** *DARE* File **csWI,** I span the ball back. **2006** in 2008 (acc) Lexis–Nexis Legal Research *State Case Law: OH* (Internet), Appellant then "opened [the firearm] up and spinned it."

2 past pple: usu *spun;* also *spinned.*

1817 *Amer. Monthly Mag. & Crit. Rev.* 1.391 **ME,** Miss Lavinia Weeks . . has spinned in one day . . 20 skeins of woollen filling. **1920** in 2008 (acc) Lexis–Nexis Legal Research *State Case Law: TX* (Internet), He heard the visiting girl friend ask his daughter if she had ever "spinned" and she replied that she had "spinned" three times. **1939** in Lib. of Congress *Amer. Memory: WPA Life Hist.* (Internet) **NC,** It ain't much I can't do in the mill. I have spooled, spinned, run the winders and worked in the knitting rooms. **1986** *Decatur Daily* (AL) 14 Nov sec B 1/3, A bale will eventually reach a cotton mill where it is opened, cleaned, spinned into thread and then used to produce cloth. **2001** *Pantagraph* (Bloomington IL) 3 Mar 5 (Internet), The blood was spinned and red blood cells were separated from platelet-rich plasma.

spinach dock n   Cf sour spinach

A **dock** n[1] (here: *Rumex patientia*).

1902 Bailey *Cyclop. Horticult.* 4.1690, The Spinach Dock *(Rumex Patientia)* is one of the best and earliest. **1942** Hylander *Plant Life* 202, The leaves of one species [of *Rumex*], the Spinach Dock, are eaten as greens. **2002** *DARE* File—Internet, Spinach Dock is a strong growing perennial, reaching 5 feet when in flower. . . Leaves are used as greens, especially leaves which develop in early spring.

spind   See spend

spinder   See suspender

spindle n   Usu |'spɪndl|; also |'spɪnl| Pronc-spp *spin'le, spinnel* Similarly adj *spinly*   Cf Pronc Intro 3.I.22

A Forms.

1912 Rice *Romance Billy-Goat Hill* 89 **KY,** The third one is a boy, . . sick and spin'ly. **1930s** in 1944 *ADD* **eWV,** *Spindle.* . . spin'le [spɪnl]. **1937** in 1969 Stuart *Come Gentle Spring* 266 **neKY,** We couldn't get a stand of corn. It just wormed up spiny stuff through the swamp grass. **1955** Roberts *S. from Hell-fer-Sartin* 59 **seKY,** When you are eighteen years old you shall prick your finger on a spinnel and shall die. **2001** in 2008 *DARE* File—Internet **nwGA,** It was a tall spinly weed with lota tiny purple flowers on them.

B Senses.

1 A **dragonfly.** scattered, but esp NJ

1810 (2001) Brinch *Blind African Slave* 51 (Internet), Why, said my father, they [=white people] . . float along on high shells like the Slough Barrow, only the shell contains hundreds of them, and it has wings like the Ethelry. [Footnote to *Ethelry:*] *Ethelry, is Needle or Spindle, which have wings and hover or light upon the water at pleasure.* **1845** *Amer. Penny Mag.* 1.376, They are called spindles, darning-needles, and other names which convey ideas of their being able and disposed to inflict injury. **1895** Comstock–Comstock *Manual Insects* 90, Darning-needles, Devil's-needles, Snake-doctors, Spindles, and Dragon-flies are some of the names given to those insects which dart back and forth over streams and wet places. **1949** Kurath *Word Geog.* 75 **NJ,** In addition to these regional terms [for *dragonfly*] we find a number of local expressions: *spindle* in New Jersey. **c1955** Reed–Person *Ling. Atlas Pacific NW,* 1 inf, Spindles. **1967** Faries *Word Geog. MO* 112, Two local expressions, *spindle* . . and *snake waiter* . . , occur three and two times respectively. **1968–69** *DARE* (Qu. R2, . . *The dragonfly*) Infs **NJ39, 52,** Spindle; (Qu. R4) Inf **MA15,** Spindle—wings about three inches long. **1973** Allen *LAUM* 1.319 (as of c1950), *Spindle* . . is the term used by one southern Minnesotan of Ohio parentage and by one North Dakotan of New York parentage. **1977–78** Foster *Lexical Variation* 30 **NJ,** Middlesex and Ocean [counties] together supply all four responses of *spindle* 'dragonfly,' . . one of the three distinctly New Jersey words.

2 The tassel of **Indian corn 1;** hence v *spindle,* v phr *spindle*

out to mature into tassels, ppl adj phr *spindled out.*   **esp NEng** Cf **topgallant** n

1816 in 1824 Knight *Letters* 82 **NEng,** They [=Virginians] also call, what we [=New Englanders] call the spindle, the tassel. **1843** *S. Planter* 3.218 **MA,** It was all spindled out, and beginning to silk. **1847** *Knickerbocker* 30.239, The tall corn, whose spindles were high above your head. **1871** *Amer. Naturalist* 5.245, The corn . . sent forth a new tassel or spindle. **1949** Kurath *Word Geog.* 22 **NEng,** *Spindle* . . for the top of the corn stalk, and *to spindle (out),* meaning 'top out,' occur from Narragansett Bay to Cape Cod, and again from Essex County, Massachusetts, to eastern Maine. **1966–69** *DARE* (Qu. I31, *When a corn stalk is well grown, what comes out at the top?*) Inf **MA55,** Spindle; **ME20,** Spindle—at top of stalk.

spindle-assed adj   Also *spindly-ass(ed)*

Having narrow hips or buttocks; by ext, puny, weak, good-for-nothing.

1947 (1964) Randolph *Ozark Superstitions* 262 **nwAR,** It's in the Book all right, an' any o' these here spindle-assed preachers can tell you all 'bout it. **1949** *PADS* 11.26 **CO,** *Spindle-assed.* . . 1. Said of a cow, narrow rumped and therefore a poor beef animal. 2. Of a man: worthless. **1951** Wilson *Dark & Damp* 233 **IN,** I'm runnin' that pot-licker in the state trials next week and he's lettin' a spindly-assed pup out-run him! **1995** *Brophy Coll.* 70 **swMO** (as of c1960), *Spindle-assed.* [S]lim-hipped, especially in the sense of "no-account, puny." **2004** in 2008 *DARE* File—Internet **CO,** I see spindly-assed flames all over the hood and front fenders. . . with light to medium blue metallic blue faded flames with a heavy-ass silver metallic outline. **2006** *Ibid* **NJ,** In any event it's probably much better than my spindly ass radius rods.

spindlebeak n

A **sailfish 1** (here: *Istiophorus platypterus*).

1975 Evanoff *Catch More Fish* 209, The Atlantic sailfish (*Istiophorus americanus* [=*I. platypterus*]) is also called the spearfish, spindlebeak, and sail. **2002** *DARE* File—Internet [Fly Fishing World], The mullet was danced on the edge of the boats [sic] wake and the dark shape materialized into a very large Atlantic sailfish. The big "spindlebeak" sped up and pursued the mullet teaser.

spindle buoy n   esp NEng

A conical buoy that floats vertically.

1877 Kellogg *Forest Glen* 118 **ME,** The bladders held them perpendicularly in the water, like a spindle buoy on a ledge. **1918** Riesenberg *Under Sail* 63, We also harpooned our first bonita, a very active, virile fish, shaped like a short double ended spindle buoy. **1968–70** *DARE* (Qu. O14b, . . *Kinds of buoys*) Infs **CT4, 39, MA80, NY47, RI17,** Spindle buoy. **2001** *DARE* File—Internet **ceMA,** [In Nahant Dory Club's list of racing marks:] Portable Mark near Spindle Buoy.

spindle bush   See spindle tree

spindle(d) out   See spindle B2

spindle root n

A **false loosestrife** (here: *Ludwigia hirtella*).

1970 Correll *Plants TX* 1134, *Ludwigia hirtella.* . . Spindle-root. . . Erect hirsute herb with fascicled spindle-shaped roots. . . Rare along wet places in pine woods, e. Tex., June–Sept.; e. along Coastal Plain to Fla. and N.J. **2002** *DARE* File—Internet **AL,** Hairy Seedbox (also known as Spindle-Root), *L[udwigia] hirtella.*

spindletail n

=**pintail 1.**

1859 (1949) Thoreau *Jrl.* 12.149 **eMA,** Once shot an eider duck here. Has often shot the pintail (he calls it spindle-tail) duck here. **1884** Baird et al. *Water Birds N. Amer.* 1.514 **Long Is. NY,** In Long Island it [=*Dafila acuta*] is well known to hunters as the "Sprig-tail" and the "Spindle-tail."

spindle tree n   Also *spindle bush* [*OED2* 1548 → for *Euonymus europaea;* see quot 1908]

=**burning bush 1.**   For other names of *Euonymus europaea* see **bitchwood, death alder, dogwood 7, pegwood, prickwood**

1713 Royal Soc. London *Philos. Trans.* 28.64 **VA,** Virginia *Spindle-tree* with rough Fruit. **a1782** (1788) Jefferson *Notes VA* 38, Spindle-tree. Euonymus Europæus. Evergreen spindle-tree. Euonymus Americanus. **1822** Eaton *Botany* 276, [*Euonymus*] *atropurpureus* . . spindle-tree. **1852** Beach *Amer. Practice Med.* 3.71, Spindle bush.

Common Names.—Spindle-Tree, Indian Arrow-wood, &c. *E. atropurpureus.* **1901** *Plant World* 4.159, The American spindle-bush *(Euonymus Americanus).* **1903** Porter *Flora PA* 204, *Euonymus Europaeus* L. Spindle-tree. **1908** Rogers *Tree Book* 365, The European Evonymus [sic] is called spindle tree, for its wood has long been used in making spindles, knitting needles, and other small articles requiring hard, close-textured wood. **1937** Thornburgh *Gt. Smoky Mts.* 25 **wNC, eTN,** One of the showiest shrubs in the Great Smokies [is] the evonymous [sic], wahoo or spindlebush. **1960** Vines *Trees SW* 661, Vernacular names [of *Euonymus atropurpureus*] are Spindle-tree, Burning-bush [etc]. **1964** Campbell et al. *Gt. Smoky Wildflowers* 78 **wNC, eTN,** Hearts-a-bustin'. . . Common names include strawberry bush, swamp dogwood, spindle bush [etc]. **1972** GA Dept. Ag. *Farmers Market Bulletin* 11 Oct 8/1, Hearts-a-Bustin is only one of many common names for Euonymus americanus. Others include "Puppy Toes", "Strawberry Bush", "Swamp Dogwood", "Spindle Bush", "Arrowwood", "Wahoo", and "Burning Bush".

spine n [*OED2* 1859 →]
=**needle** n **1.**
   1968–69 *DARE* (Qu. T6, *The pointed leaves that fall from pine trees*) Infs **AZ**10, **IN**83, **MD**29, Spines.

spine-flower n
   A plant of the western genus *Chorizanthe* or another genus formerly included therein. For other names of var spp see **horned-toad buckwheat, Turkish rugging**
   1941 Jaeger *Wildflowers* 40, Brittle spine-flower. *Chorizanthe brevicornu.* . . The dry stems are exceedingly fragile and readily break into many pieces when handled. **1944** Abrams *Flora Pacific States* 2.6, *Chorizanthe cuspidata.* . . San Francisco Chorizanthe or Spine-flower. *Ibid* 15, *Chorizanthe californica* [=*Mucronea c.*] . . California Chorizanthe or Spine-flower. **1961** Thomas *Flora Santa Cruz* 141 **cwCA,** Chorizanthe [spp]. . . Spine-flower. **2002** (acc) U.S. Dept. Ag. *Plants Database* (Internet), *Dodecahema leptoceras.* . . slenderhorn spineflower. *Ibid, Systenotheca vortriedei.* . . Vortriede's spineflower.

spinemound n
   A **hedgehog cactus 3** (here: either *Echinocereus stramineus* or *E. triglochidiatus*).
   1967 Dodge *Roadside Wildflowers* 45, Crimson hedgehog—Mound cactus. . . Some species of this group are called claretcup while others are known as spinemound. **1970** Correll *Plants TX* 1098, *Echinocereus enneacanthus.* . . Var. *stramineus* [=*E. s.*] . . Strawberry cactus, spinemound. **2002** *DARE* File—Internet **CO,** Claret Cup Cactus. . . *Echinocereus triglochidiatus var. melanacanthus.* . . spinemound.

spine of one's back n [Engl dial; cf *EDD* spine sb. 4.(6)]
   The spine, backbone.
   1825 NY Acad. Sci. *Annals Lyceum Nat. Hist.* 1.238, This covering is loose throughout, except along the spine of the back. **1867** Holmes *Guardian Angel* 410 **NEng,** [From a fictional village newspaper:] Sad to relate, he received such a violent blow upon the spine of the back, that palsy of the lower extremities is like to ensue. **1874** *Overland Mth.* 12.168 **West,** The doctor advised her to take brandy. . . At first she rubbed it on the spine of her back. **1878** Hart *Sazerac Lying Club* 198 **NV,** He swears, by all the gods above, that stooping and lifting give him a crick in the "spine of his back." **1899** (1912) Green *VA Folk-Speech* 407, Spine of the back. . . The spine, not mentioned alone. **1912** *DN* 3.591 **wIN,** Spine of one's back. . . The spine. **2007** in 2008 *DARE* File—Internet **CA,** It all depends on where you have your tattoo. I have mine on the spine of my back. **2008** *Ibid* **TX,** She [=a dog] . . had no hair other than on her head and a little down the spine of her back due to sarcoptic mange.

spinetail n Also *spine-tailed duck*
=**ruddy duck.**
   1862 Smith *Hist. Delaware Co. PA* 439, Ruddy Duck. Spine-tail. Occasionally on the Delaware. **1869** Turnbull *Birds E. PA* 37, Ruddy Duck. . . Spine-tail. . . Rare. **1874** NY Acad. Sci. *Annals Lyceum Nat. Hist.* 10.390 **IL,** Ruddy Duck; Spine-tailed Duck. **1890** Warren *Birds PA* 49, Although the Spine-tailed Ducks are found here in winter, they are much more numerous during the spring and fall migrations. **1923** Dawson *Birds CA* 4.1841, These saucy tails [of ruddy ducks] are composed of stiff, spiny feathers, having shafts denuded toward the tips, more or less, according to season, so that the birds are popularly known as Pintails, Sprig-tails, Quill-tails, Spine-tails, etc. **1932** Bennitt *Checklist* 20 **MO,** Butter-ball; bristle-tail; spine-tail [etc].

spinit See **spignet**

spin jenny See **spinning jenny**

spink-and-span adj phr, adv phr Also *spink and spandy* [Varr of *spick-and-span*]
   1913 *DN* 4.5 **ME,** *Spandy.* . . Used in . . spink and spandy. **1920** *Lancaster Daily Eagle* (OH) 7 June 6/4, Mr. H.E. Crumley has run out a spink and span new Dodge touring car. **1968** *DARE* (Qu. KK34, . . *Very neat and clean: "Her house always looks _____."*) Inf **NC**55, Spink-and-span.

spinking spanking bran new See **brand-spanking-new**

spin'le, spinly See **spindle**

spinned See **spin 1, 2**

spinnel See **spindle**

spinner n
1 =**mayfly 1.** [*OED2* 1787 →]
   [**1972** Swan–Papp *Insects* 167, Mayflies are important in the food chain. . . Anglers imitate the adults in dry flies—they refer to them as "duns" or "spinners."] **1982** Sternberg *Fishing* 83, After a day or two, the dun molts into a mature insect called an *imago* or *spinner.* **1985** Madson *Up River* 176 **Upper Missip Valley,** Vast numbers of burrowing mayfly nymphs occur in the silts and oozes of impounded portions of the Upper River where slackening currents have dropped sediment loads. There the nymphs live for one, two, or even three years depending on their species, developing into adult "spinners" that come up out of the River in clouds. **1989** Mosher *Stranger* 64 **nVT** (as of 1952), Over the long pool hovered the largest hatch I'd ever seen: thousands upon thousands of the gigantic pale yellow mayflies I called spinners because of the way they twisted down onto the water. **2002** *DARE* File—Internet, The spinner is . . bright and shiny, with long tails (twice as long as the body), and clear transparent wings. **2004** *DARE* File **ceNY, ME** (as of 1960s–70s), The standard term for an emerging mayfly, among fly fishermen, is *spinner.*

2 A horse or rodeo bull that bucks and whirls about at the same time. Cf **spiral twister**
   1936 Adams *Cowboy Lingo* 99, A 'spinner' was a horse which went up and whirled forward instead of up and forward. **1938** *Western Horseman* 3.10 **West,** The type of horse known as a "spinner". . . will buck in a tight circle, spinning either to the right or left. **2008** *DARE* File—Internet, *Spinner:* a [rodeo] bull that spins or turns as if chasing its tail. Scores high, especially if it spins both left and right.

3 A simple device consisting of a wooden paddle with a handle near the smaller end, used to make twisted cords, esp of horsehair. Also called **hair twister, tarabilla**
   1949 *S. Folkl. Qrly.* 13.192 **LA,** An Indian girl . . rotating the spinner in a clockwise direction, backed away just rapidly enough to maintain tension on a growing length of Spanish-moss cord or yarn. **1953** *Western Folkl.* 12.180, An appeal directed to "old timers" through the columns of the *American Cattle Producer* brought prompt and conclusive information. The results appear on the accompanying map . . , which professes to show the areas where the spinner was used and the names by which it was locally known. [Map shows *spinner* in use in AZ.]

spinning jenny n Also *spin-jenny, spinning board* **Sth, S Midl**
=**flying jenny 1a.**
   1916 *DN* 4.270 **New Orleans LA,** *Spinning-jinny.* . . Flying-jinny. **1961** Deal *It's Always 3* 232 **nAL** (as of 1939), They told about play-parties and weddings and spinning jennies and foot-logs, and buggies and snakes, and singings and storms. **1966–67** *DARE* (Qu. EE32, *A homemade merry-go-round*) Inf **SC**40, Spin-jenny; **NC**7, Spinning jenny. **1986** Pederson *LAGS Concordance (Flying jenny)* 9 infs, **scattered Gulf Region,** Spinning jenny; 1 inf, **seMS,** Spinning jennies; 1 inf, **seAL,** Spinning board. **2003** Jai *Confessions* 14 **Sth** [Black], A group of children are playing on a spinning board.

spinning shark See **spinner 3**

spinning street yarn See **street yarn**

spinning wheel n **Sth, S Midl**
=**flying jenny 1a.**
   1966 *DARE* (Qu. EE32, *A homemade merry-go-round*) Inf **DC**8, Spinning wheel. **1986** Pederson *LAGS Concordance (Flying jenny)* 9 infs, **scattered Gulf Region,** Spinning wheel.

spin street yarn See **street yarn**

spint See **spin 1**

spiny mouse n

A **pocket mouse** (here: *Liomys irroratus*).

1928 Anthony *N. Amer. Mammals* 297, Texas Spiny Mouse.—*Liomys irroratus texensis.* . . A large Mouse or small Rat with fur-lined cheek-pockets and pelage composed of normal hairs mingled with stiff bristles or spines. **1947** Cahalane *Mammals* 434, The spiny mouse . . is bristling all over with flattened "spines." Spreading thickly through the soft fur, especially over the back and flanks, these coarse, stiff guard-hairs are conspicuous by their darker shade.

spiral twister n Cf **spinner 2**

1929 *AmSp* 5.67 **NE** [Cattle country talk], On the smaller ranches, a "bronc" might be a "kept up," "broom tail," "pinto" that "can't be beat for cutting and wrangling" and a "swell sun fisher" besides, (or, as the young, up-to-date cow-poke might say, "A keen nose-diver" or "spiral twister").

spirchal, spirchully See **spiritual** adj

spirea n

Std: a plant of the genus *Spiraea.* Also called **meadowsweet 1** For other names of var spp see **bridal-wreath 1, buckbrush 3p, hackmatack 2, hardhack 1, horseweed 4, iron bush, pipestem c, poor man's soap b, Quaker lady 2, queen of the meadow 2, Saint-Peter's-wreath, steeplebush, tea weed 1**

spire grass n [Perh folk-etym for **asparagus,** infl by the shape] Cf **spear grass** n[2]

1912 *DN* 3.590 **wIN,** Sparrow-grass or spire-grass. . . Asparagus. **1975** *Appalachian Jrl.* 2.150 **wNC,** With oral transmission primary in the community. . . *Spire grass* is not a grass at all but rather the vegetable that is known to most as *asparagus.*

spirit n Usu |'spɪrɪt|; also **chiefly Sth, S Midl** |'spɛrɪt|; rarely |'spɪrɪt| Pronc-spp *speerit, sper(r)et, spe(r)rit, spirt, sprit* Cf **spiritual** adj

Std senses, var forms.

1785 in 1956 Eliason *Tarheel Talk* 318 **cnNC,** Spirt. **1795** Dearborn *Columbian Grammar* 139, *List of Improprieties.* . . Sperrit for Spirit. **1815** Humphreys *Yankey in England* 108, *Sperit,* spirit. **1825** in 1956 Eliason *Tarheel Talk* 318 **nw,cwNC,** Speret. **1827** *Ibid* 317 **cnNC,** Sprits. **1858** Hammett *Piney Woods Tavern* 126, The cabin was all still 's a quaker meetin' when the speret don't move. **1867** Harris *Sut Lovingood Yarns* 139 **TN,** Thar am a fur-seein wisdum in quiltins, ef they hes proper trimmins: 'vittils, fiddils, an' sperrits in 'bundunce.' **1890** *DN* 1.72 **LA, NEng,** *Sperrit:* spirit. **1891** *PMLA* 6.165 **WV,** (Sperit) for *spirit.* **1893** Shands *MS Speech* 59, Sperrit [spɛrɪt]. Negro for *spirit.* Negroes rarely ever say *speerit,* although illiterate whites use both *sperrit* and *speerit.* **1896** Harris *Sister Jane* 136 **GA** [Black], Do she do like her sperret done broke? **1909** *DN* 3.405 **nwAR,** Sperrit. **1916** *DN* 4.281 **NE,** *Spirt.* . . Spirit. **1928** *AmSp* 3.403 **Ozarks** (as of 1916–27), The Ozarker always says *sperrit* and *peth.* **1952** Brown *NC Folkl.* 1.593, *Sperit* ['spɛrɪt]. **1955** Ritchie *Singing Family* 90 **seKY,** Just one more truth afore the Sperrit leaves me. **2008** *DARE* File—Internet **seNC,** The boys got out of the hospital yesterday and seam to be in good sperits and i think thay will be ok. *Ibid* **PA,** I clean the spring with a rag soaked in mineral sperits.

spirit duck n

Any of var waterfowl that dive out of sight quickly when alarmed, as:

a =**bufflehead 2.** Cf **ghost duck 1**

[**1747** Edwards *Nat. Hist. Uncommon Birds* 2.100, *The little black and white duck.* . . was brought from *Newfoundland* in *America,* where the Seamen call it a *Spirit.*] **1831** Richardson *Fauna Boreali-Amer.* 2.437, *Clangula vulgaris* [=*Bucephala clangula*] and *albeola* [=*B. a.*] . . are by no means shy, allowing the sportsman to approach sufficiently near; but dive so dexterously at the flash of the gun or the twanging of a bow, and are consequently so difficult to kill, that the natives say they are endowed with some supernatural power. Hence their appellation of "Conjuring" or "Spirit Ducks." **1838** Audubon *Ornith. Biog.* 4.217, Buffel-headed Duck. . . The secluded creeks of the Middle States are equally favoured by it as the stagnant bayous and lakes of Lower Louisiana; in the Carolinas and on the Ohio, it is not less frequent; it being known in these different districts by the names of Spirit Duck, Butter Box,

Marrionette, Dipper, and Die-dipper. **1855** (1949) Thoreau *Jrl.* 7.323 **neMA,** I think it was the smallest duck I ever saw. Floating buoyantly asleep on the middle of Walden Pond. Was it not a female of the buffle-headed or spirit duck? **1923** Dawson *Birds CA* 4.1819, Buffle-head. . . Spirit Duck. **1955** MA Audubon Soc. *Bulletin* 39.316 **MA,** Buffle-head. . . Spirit Duck.

b A **goldeneye 1** (here: *Bucephala clangula*).

1831 [see **a** above].

c =**pied-bill(ed) grebe.**

1893 *Oölogist* 10.226, This bird is properly known as the . . Pied-billed Grebe, . . Spirit Duck, and by at least a dozen other names. . . It will dive at the flash and escape when less than thirty feet away from the hunter, as I have repeatedly proven.

d =**horned grebe.**

1904 Doubleday *Birds* 9, Horned Grebe. . . *Called also* . . Spirit duck. [*Ibid* 10, The maddening cleverness of their disappearance, which can be indefinitely prolonged owing to their habit of swimming with only the nostrils exposed above the surface, makes it simply impossible to locate them again on the lake.] **1955** MA Audubon Soc. *Bulletin* 39.310 **MA,** Horned Grebe. . . Spirit Duck. . . Any small water bird may be called a duck; "spirit" refers to the bird's "supernatural" ability in getting under the water quickly.

e =**ruddy duck.**

1943 Musgrove–Musgrove *Waterfowl IA* 71, Ruddy Duck. . . Other names: bullneck, . . spirit duck [etc].

spiritual adj Pronc-spp *speeritual, speretil, sper(r)itual, spirchal, spirchully* Cf **spirit**

Std sense, var forms.

1843 (1916) Hall *New Purchase* 136 **IN,** He took occasion to illuminate us as to its "Speretil meaning." **1893** Shands *MS Speech* 59, They [=illiterate White people] say also *speeritual* for *spiritual.* **1909** *DN* 3.374 **eAL, wGA,** *Sperit, speritual,* etc. Spirit, spiritual, etc. **1922** Gonzales *Black Border* 328 **sSC, GA coasts** [Gullah glossary], *Sperritual*—spiritual, spirituals, the Negro religious songs. **c1938** in 1970 Hyatt *Hoodoo* 2.1182 **seGA** [Black], Yo' know de bottles . . wit dese candles in—yo' know, yo' call dem *spirchal* candles. *Ibid* 1210, Whut ah'm speakin' about, where dey doin' about crystal or doin' about *spirchully* work. **1985** Benes *Amer. Speech* 74 **cME coast** (as of a1847), *T* and *d* do not become *ch* and *j* sounds in the words . . *spiritual, education,* and *gradual.*

spiritual n See **spiritual wife**

spiritual doctor n Also *spiritual (person), spiritualist person* =**hoodoo** n **1b.**

c1938 in 1970 Hyatt *Hoodoo* 1.280 **Memphis TN** [Black], An' den a lotta dese peoples, dey read cards—an' some of 'em are *spiritualist peoples. Ibid* 690 **New Orleans LA** [Black], Like if I want a job, I go to one of them *spiritual people. Ibid* 772 **New Orleans LA** [Black], Some people call 'em the *hoodoos*—some call 'em *spirituals. Ibid* 2.994 **Memphis TN** [Black], A medical doctor couldn't tell yo' but a *spiritual doctor* could tell yo'.

spiritual wife n Also *spiritual* **chiefly West, esp UT** Cf **seal** v

Among Mormons: a woman who is "sealed" to a Mormon man for eternity, according to the rites of the faith; broadly, esp among non-Mormons, such a woman living with a man outside the legal bonds of marriage; a plural wife; hence n *spiritual wifery.*

1842 Bennett *Hist. Saints* 287, On the 17th day of May, A.D. 1842, Joe [=Joseph] Smith requested to see me *alone.* . . [H]e locked the door, *put the key in his pocket, drew a pistol on me,* and said, 'The peace of my family requires that you should sign an affidavit . . exonerating me from all participation whatever . . in the *spiritual wife doctrine,* or private intercourse with females in general; and if you do not do it *with apparent cheerfulness,* I will make *cat-fish bait* of you. **1843** *Quincy Herald* (IL) 15 Dec 3/1 **wIL,** Hyram Smith has had a revelation confirming the spiritual wife system. **1852** in 1855 *Putnam's Mag.* 6.147 **UT,** These extra wives are known by sundry designations—some call them *"spirituals,"* others, *"sealed ones."* **1853** *Ibid* 5.648, And so, according to the advice and best judgement of the Saints, Elizabeth Colton will be sealed to me . . as my spiritual wife. **1861** Burton *City Saints* 359 **UT,** This . . the Mormons deny, declaring the existence of . . spiritual wives, to be, and ever to have been, literally and in substance totally and entirely untrue. **1871** (1872) Kneeland *Wonders Yosemite* 20 **CA,** The "spiritual wife" system, which now seems tottering to its fall, was not an original tenet of the Mormon creed. **1925** *Ladies' Home Jrl.* Apr 38 **UT,** It was considered by the elderly women of Utah a great and sacred privilege to be the spiritual wife of Brigham Young or the Prophet Joseph Smith in the world to come. **2003** *DARE* File **ID,** If someone were to ask me what a spiritual wife is I would say she is the object of some saint's desire, irrespective of whether she is already married and irrespective of whether the saint already has a wife, to whom he can be married in the afterlife, provided the proper ceremony (ies) be undertaken. The object of the desire need not be Mormon, need not know of the desire, is powerless to forfend the action which is efficacious regardless of all other considerations. I believe the object of the desire need not be alive. **2003** Krakauer *Under Heaven* 12 **UT, AZ,** Polygamy is illegal in both Utah and Arizona. To avoid prosecution, typically men in Colorado City will legally marry only the first of their wives; subsequent wives, although "spiritually married" to their husband by Uncle Rulon [=a Mormon Fundamentalist leader], thus remain single mothers in the eyes of the state. *Ibid* 91 **UT,** Dan also announced that he intended to engage in spiritual wifery at the earliest opportunity. And the first woman he proposed taking as a plural wife was . . his own stepdaughter. *Ibid* 123, By 1844 several members of the prophet's [=Joseph Smith's] inner circle had been told the truth about his spiritual wifery, and . . a few were even practicing polygamy themselves. *Ibid* 166 **UT,** Ron had brought to that meeting a woman named Becky, whom he'd recently taken as a spiritual wife without benefit of a license or civil ceremony.

spirit weed n

=**redroot c.**

1876 Hobbs *Bot. Hdbk.* 184, Lacnanthes tinctoria, Spirit weed, (Red root).

spirt See **spirit**

spishun See **suspicion**

spit v Cf **spit** n[1] **1**

In phrr indicating that a person has a close resemblance to another; see quots. [*OED2* 1602→]

1970 *DARE* (Qu. Z10, *If a child looks very much like his father . . "He _____ his father."*) Inf **NY241,** His father spit him out; just spit that boy out. **1986** Pederson *LAGS Concordance (The boy resembles his father)* 1 inf, **cLA,** He looks like he spit him out; 1 inf, **nwFL,** Looks like his daddy just spit him out—has heard. **2005** Griggs *Wings* 1, They were twins, born December 4, 1935, while I was away on business. A boy and a girl: the boy looking as though I had spit him out.

spit n[1]

1 =**spitting image.** [*OED2* 1825 →] *old-fash* Cf **spit image**

1858 *Harper's New Mth. Mag.* 16.177 **wNC,** Well, the child *is* handsome, but too proud and fierce-like—the very spit of her father. **1886** *S. Bivouac* 4.350 **sAppalachians,** Spit (image, counterpart). **1899** (1912) Green *VA Folk-Speech* 407, Spit. . . Image; likeness: as, "He is the very spit of his father." **1916** *DN* 4.336 **Nantucket MA,** "Dead spit of his father." North Irish immigrants. **1919** *DN* 5.35 **seKY,** Spit. . . Exact likeness, replica. "That chap's the very spit of his daddy." **1927** *AmSp* 2.365 **cwWV,** Spit . . likeness. **1928** Peterkin *Scarlet Sister Mary* 83 **SC** [Gullah], De finest lil boy-chile ever was. De pure spit o July [=his father] too. **1931–33** *LANE Worksheets* **CT,** He's the spit of his father. **1936** *AmSp* 11.191 **seWY,** Spit. Image, likeness. 'He's the spit of his father.' **1940** Von Tempski *Paradise* 290 **HI,** You're the spit of me, First Born. **1966–69** *DARE* (Qu. Z10, *If a child looks very much like his father . . "He _____ his father."*) Inf **NY14, CT23,** (Is the) dead spit of; **AR27, NY14, TX26, WY4,** Is the spit of. [All Infs old] **1986** Pederson *LAGS Concordance (The boy resembles his father)* 2 infs, **GA,** The very spit of his daddy (*or* father); 2 infs, **GA, TN,** (Is) the spit of his father; 1 inf, **cnAR,** That boy's just the spit of him; 1 inf, **cLA,** He's just the spit of him; 1 inf, **csTN,** Just the very spit of his father; 1 inf, **cnGA,** The very spit of him; 1 inf, **cwFL,** Is the very spit of the old man. [8 of 9 infs 63 years of age or older] **2002** Weaver *These Hands* 60, Mama taps another picture of Dorothy, this time as a young girl wearing long, lace-edged bloomers and camisole. "Ain't Sisi the spit of her?"

2 In tobacco cultivation: see quots.

1940 *AmSp* 15.135 [Tobacco market language], *Spit.* The body or consistency of a leaf. **1966** *PADS* 45.23 **cnKY** [Tobacco word list], *Spit.* . . Heavy body in a leaf, thought to induce profuse salivation. . . "They used to look at a heavy leaf and say, 'That's got spit in it.'"

spit n[2]

=**spigot B1.**

1968 *DARE* (Qu. F15, *What you turn to let the vinegar or cider run*

out of a barrel) Infs **KS7, MI89,** Spit. **1986** Pederson *LAGS Concordance,* 1 inf, **ceTX,** Spit—on water barrel.

spit an(d) image See **spitting image**

spit and whittle club n For varr see quots

A group of men gathered for informal talk or recreation.

1932 *Charleroi Mail* (PA) 28 Sept 4/2, In the pool rooms and cigar stores the Spit and Argue clubs have already elected a president. **1942** Whipple *Joshua* 444 **UT** (as of c1860), Alongside the Social Hall, where the usual spit-'n'-whittle gang and some Indians squatted in the shade. **1950** *NY Folkl. Qrly.* 6.138, [Title:] The Spit and Whittle Club at Dryden. **1966** *DARE* FW Addit **OK,** Spit and argue club—a group of old-timers who meet in a clubhouse (erected by the city) to play dominoes, etc. **1967–70** *DARE* (Qu. FF23, . . *Joking names . . for . . clubs or lodges*) Inf **MA55,** Spit and gab society; **MO11,** Spit and whittle club—joking name for the loafers around town; **TX104,** Spit and whittle club—courthouse sitters. **1998** *DARE* File—Internet **AR,** I am referring to the Magnolia, Arkansas, Nod, Spit & Whittle Club. Ever since I can remember . . the N. S. & W. Club convened every Saturday on the town square. . . And there the world's problems were sorted out, and discussed, and turned every whutch-a-ways [sic]. . . until every body . . had a chance to be heard. **2001** *Ibid* **OK** (as of c1940), It cleared the bench of the National Order of the Reed, Oklahoma "Spit and Whittle" Club.

spit bath n

1 A hurried or partial washing of the body. Cf **cat bath, jaybird ~, spot ~**

1922 *Los Angeles Times* (CA) 27 Aug sec 3 31/1, Yes, I think it is being overdone, these picture romances of the land of the Arabian steed, the sand-storm, the moonlit desert, the flea hunt and the spit bath. **1939** *Chron. OK* 17.185 (as of c1889), We got only a "spit bath," that is those who were too long to get into a wash tub. **c1950** Halpert Coll. **wKY,** To take a jaybird bath = confined to parts that show, usually the face and hands. Vars. Spit bath[.] Sponge bath. **1953** *AmSp* 28.144, *Bird bath, Dutch bath, Spanish bath, spit bath, thimble bath,* and *wipe-off* are baths requiring a minimum of water. **1968** *DARE* Tape **NY78,** [Inf:] I know Saturday used to be bath day. We only got that one bath a week. In between times, I mean, we'd just get what they call a spit bath. . . [T]hat was just more or less with a little washcloth, you know. [FW:] I guess what would be now called a sponge bath. [Inf:] Right, right. **1986** Pederson *LAGS Concordance,* 1 inf, **nwAL,** Spit bath—at the sink; 1 inf, **ceLA,** Spit bath—pan of warm water, soap, rag. **1989** Gibbons *Virtuous Woman* 64 **NC,** I'd change and take a little spit-bath, the kind mama would've only allowed if I was sick. **2001** *DARE* File—Internet [CNN.com], There's no locker room on Alpha. Crewmembers basically have to settle for the orbital equivalent of a spit bath. "We had wet towels and dry towels. . . Maybe only 50–60 grams (about 2 ounces) of water. It was enough."

2 See quots.

1980 *DARE* File **cnMA** (as of c1915), A mother . . notices that her young charge has a dirty spot—say on his cheek. She takes out her handkerchief and either touches her tongue to a corner of it or allows him to provide the spit. And she "gives him a spit bath," i.e., wipes off the spot. **2003** *Ibid* **cwCA** (as of c1960), If a child had smudges of food on his mouth, his mother might give him a spit bath by wetting her handkerchief with her tongue and dabbing at the dirty spots.

spitberry n [Because the bark is salivant]

A **prickly ash 1** (here: *Zanthoxylum americanum*).

1950 Peattie *Nat. Hist. Trees* 427, Zanthoxylum americanum. . . Other Names: Prickly Ash. Wait-a-bit. Sting-tongue. . . Spitberry.

spit bug See **spittlebug 1**

spit-devil (bug) See **spitting devil**

spite v [*OED2* spite v. 3 c1563 →] *esp* **PA**

To anger, irritate, offend; hence ppl adj *spited.*

1842 Caruthers *Sketch David Caldwell* 206 **NC,** The one who had taken the mare, . . and who, of course, felt much spited at the trick wich [sic] had been played, accosted him. **1859** Rice *Mabel* 291, Here on one corner [of a Chinese shawl] is a little dot of a greasy finger mark. I am that spited I could cry every time I think of it. **1904** Martin *Tillie* 34 **sePA,** Then she was some spited that I would n't buy a box of complexion lotion off of her. **1911** *PA Dept. Ag. Annual Rept. for 1910* 134 **cPA,** All that spites me was that there was not another man along. We would have gotten over more of the orchard, but I am satisfied with the amount we did do. **1930** Shoemaker *1300 Words* 60 **cPA Mts** (as of c1900), *Spited*—Angry at oneself. **1935** *AmSp* 10.167 **PA** [Engl of PA Germans], It spites him wonderful (he was greatly irritated). **1953** *PA*

Dutchman 15 Jan 15, "It spites me so" that people forget to sign their names when sending in their receipts. . . It doesn't seem right when I can't come back to say "Hello" and "Thank you." **1997** in 1999 Millersville Univ. Center for PA Ger. Studies *Jrl.* Fall 22, *It spites me._____that they didn't come. . .* The feature *it spites me* was originally pointed out to me by a former Mennonite schoolteacher, during preliminary research, as a common "mistake" of Pennsylvania German English. Also in preliminary interviewing, most respondents used it with the knowledge that it is a nonstandard form. **2003** *Montgomery Coll.* **eTN,** That story spites him.

spit en image   See **spitting image**

spitfire n   Cf **spitting devil**

Prob the bombardier beetle (*Brachinus* spp).

    1967 *DARE* FW Addit **cnLA,** *Spitfire*—an insect that lives under bark and fogs out some kind of stuff that burns your eyes. **2004** Johnson *25 Milk Runs* 14, I finally named them "Spitfires," because the mist burned my finger. I later learned that they were called "Bombardier" beetles.

spitfire new adj   Also *spitfire brand new, splitfire new*
=**brand-fire-new.**

    1915 *DN* 4.191 **swVA,** *Spit* (or *split*) *fire new . .* =*bran fire new* [= "Absolutely new"]. **1950** *PADS* 13.22 **sKY,** *Fire-new, brand-new, brand-fire-new, spit-fire-new* are all fairly common. "Jim driv in his spit-fire-brand-new car this evenin'." **2006** *DARE* File—Internet, Lynn Richards, . . the spitfire new Talk Show DJ on KBST in Los Angeles.

‡**spit gravy** n
=**red-eye gravy.**

    1967 *DARE* FW Addit **swWA,** *Spit gravy*—after ham is fried, just add water to the pot liquor. Inf says "from South."

spit harp n   Cf **harp** n **1,** *juice harp* (at **Jew's harp B3**)

A harmonica.

    1965 *DARE* (Qu. FF7, *A small musical instrument that you blow on, and move from side to side in your mouth*) Inf **UT3,** Spit harp. **1986** Pederson *LAGS Concordance (Harmonica)* 1 inf, **ceAL,** Spit harp. **2001** *DARE* File—Internet **San Francisco CA,** I . . bought a harmonica. . . He told me to concentrate on learning to blow/pull one note at a time, so I sat there sucking on the spit harp. **2007** in 2008 *DARE* File—Internet **WV,** I guess that is what being raised in the hills of West Virginia will do!! Banjos, Spit Harps and all of that.

spit image n   chiefly **Sth, S Midl**   See Map   *old-fash*
=**spitting image.**

    1893 Shands *MS Speech* 75, *Spit and image . .* an exact likeness. . . The expression sometimes appears as the *spit image.* **1941** *Herald-Advt.* (Huntington WV) 14 Sep 8/7 *(ADD),* A sweet potato which is the spit image of Franklin D. Roosevelt. **1941** in 1980 Welty *Coll. Stories* 46 **MS,** Whoever Shirley-T. was, she was the spit-image of Papa-Daddy if he'd cut off his beard. **1965–70** *DARE* (Qu. Z10, *If a child looks very much like his father . . "He _____ his father."*) 15 Infs, **chiefly Sth, S Midl,** Is the spit image (of); **FL22, NC79,** Spit image (of). [16 of 17 Infs old] **1972** *Atlanta Letters* **nwGA,** Spit-image of his Dad. Perfect likeness. **1986** Pederson *LAGS Concordance (The boy resembles his father)* 3 infs, **AR, GA, MS,** The spit image (of his daddy); 1 inf, **ceAL,** He's a spit image of his father; 1 inf, **neAR,** Very spit image of his father; 1 inf, **cTN,** The spit image of the old man. [5 of 6 infs 65 years of age or older] **1993** Kingsolver *Pigs in Heaven* 223 **MS,** I swear he's the spit image of Roscoe, when I first met him.

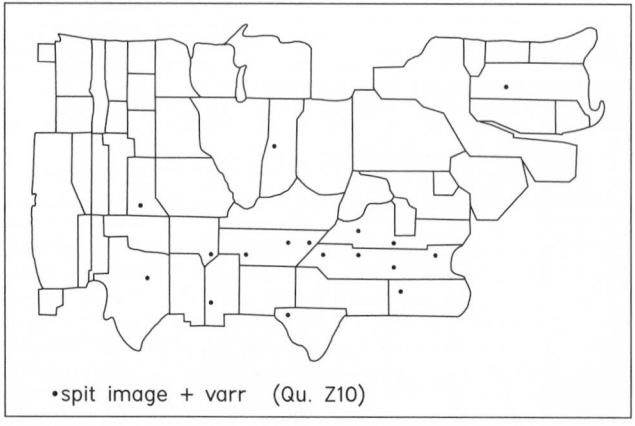

•spit image + varr   (Qu. Z10)

spit 'n' image   See **spitting image**

spit (quick) or puke n   Also *spit or drown tobacco*

Chewing tobacco.

    1929 Dobie *Vaquero* 181 **West,** Some man . . drove into the "colony" with a wagon loaded principally with bandanas, a case of sardines, a box of soda crackers, and a caddy of "spit-or-drown" tobacco. **1930** Williams *Logger-Talk* 29 **Pacific NW,** *Spit-quick-or-puke:* Chewing tobacco. **1958** McCulloch *Woods Words* 176 **Pacific NW,** *Spit-or-puke*—Snoose. **a1966** in 2006 *DARE* File—Internet **ceIN** (as of c1910), Enzie Parker . . supplied me with my first chew of tobacco when a carton of Scrapple cut plug fell off the back of a dray. Spit quick or puke, we called it. **a1979** in 2006 *DARE* File—Internet **MO** (as of 1917), The boys looked at each other, and one of them ask me what I was shooing [sic] and I said Spit Quick or puke. **1996** Harrison *Trails* 116 **TX** (as of 1940s), He called "Brown Mule", and other such brands, "spit or drown tobaccos" because he couldn't hold the "chaw" very long without spitting.

spitten image   See **spitting image**

spitter   See **tobacco spitter**

spitting-ass n

A **gull;** see quot.

    1945 McAtee *Nomina Abitera* 38 **Pacific,** Gulls *(Larus),* not further identified. . . spitting-ass, west coast (because of its defecating in the air, sometimes on ferry-boat passengers).

spitting devil n   Also *spit-devil (bug), spitting Charlie, ~ Jenny* esp **Gulf States**

A **walkingstick 1** (here: *Anisomorpha buprestoides*) that emits a blinding chemical spray when disturbed, or any of var other insects popularly confused with this species.

    1966–69 *DARE* (Qu. R6, *. . Names . . for grasshoppers*) Inf **AL20,** Spitting devil—hadn't thought of that in years; (Qu. R9a, *An insect from two to four inches long that lives in bushes and looks like a dead twig*) Inf **FL4,** Praying mantis or spit-devils—they'd blind you; **FL34,** Spitting Jenny—in corn fields—supposedly could spit in your eye and blind you; (Qu. R9b, *An insect that holds up its front feet as if saying a prayer;* not asked in early QRs) Inf **GA77,** Spittin' Charlie [laughter]. **2001** *DARE* File—Internet **ceTX coast,** We hurried past the scary spit-devil bugs that always seemed to be waiting on the wall near the back door. **2002** *Ibid* **sAL,** *Spit Devil:* This is the South Alabama title for the praying mantis, which is reputed to have the ability of spitting poison into your eyes and blinding you. **2003** *Ibid,* Some stick insects, such as the Florida spitting devil *(Anisomorpha buprestoides),* are marathon maters and literally copulate for days on end!

spitting image n   Usu |ˈspɪtn̩ ˈɪmɪʤ| Also *spit an(d) image, spit en ~, spit 'n' ~, spitten ~* [Prob orig *spitten image* (cf *EDD spitten picter* 1859, *spitten image* nd), but also interpreted early as redund **spit** n¹ **1** + *image* (cf *OED2 spit and fetch* 1859, *EDD spit an' pictor* 1869, *spit an' image* 1892). The current prevailing form, *spitting image,* is doubtless a folk-etym. For a full discussion of the possibilities, see 2004 *AmSp* 79.33–58.]   Cf **spit** v, **spit** n¹ **1, spit image**

A person (or rarely thing) that closely resembles another.

    1880 (1881) Harris *Uncle Remus Songs* 82 **GA** [Black], He had a wife en th'ee chilluns . . en dey wuz all de ve'y spit en image er de ole man. **1887** *Atlantic Mth.* 60.333 **VA** [Black], As purty as Mis' Agnes, an' de spittin' image of her. **1892** *DN* 1.232 **KY,** Spit. "The ve'y spit an' image o' him" = the exact image of him. **1893** Shands *MS Speech* 75, *Spit and image* [spɪt æn ɪmɛʤ]. A negro expression for an exact likeness. **1909** *DN* 3.374 **eAL, wGA,** *Spit. . .* Image, likeness. The common expression 'spit and image' is pronounced *spittin image,* and in the popular mind the word is related to the verb *spit,* to expectorate. **1926** *DN* 5.403 **Ozarks,** He's th' spit 'n' image o' his ol' pappy. **1930** Shoemaker *1300 Words* 59 **cPA Mts** (as of c1900), *Spitting-image*—i.e., "Spit and image", an exact resemblance. **1941** Faulkner *Men Working* 105 **MS,** Ifen it ain't the spitten image of that church acrost the street. **1958** Humphrey *Home from the Hill* 285 **neTX,** "Did you-all *see* that baby?" "Why, it was him to the life." "The spitting image." **1965–70** *DARE* (Qu. Z10, *If a child looks very much like his father . . "He _____ his father."*) 253 Infs, **widespread,** Is the spitting image (of); **CT12, PA200,** Is the spittin' image of; **AL42,** Is the spittin' [spɪtn̩] image of; **AK1, IL113,** Is the spittin' [spɪtn̩] image of; **MA69,** Is the spittin' [spɪʔn̩] image of; **CO7, GA3, MA123, MI72, MO7, 17,** Spitting image (of); (Qu. KK65, . . *'The same sort': "If you like Bob, I'm sure you'll like his brother—they're _____."*) Inf **NE**3, Spittin' images of each other; **NC**79, Spitting image of each other.   **1981** Pederson *LAGS Basic Materials* **Gulf Region,** [64 infs gave the resp *spitting image*. Most used proncs of the type [ˈspɪtɪŋ] for the first element; 7 gave proncs of the type [ˈspɪtɪŋ] and 2 [ˈspɪtɪ̩].]   **2006** *Cleveland Scene Online* (OH) 12 April (Internet), Rafferty was slender, pale, and the spitting image of Pee Wee Herman.

spitting Jenny   See **spitting devil**

spitting rattlesnake n

A **diamondback rattlesnake** (here: *Crotalus atrox*).

1928 Baylor Univ. Museum *Contrib.* 16.20 **TX,** Several years ago I heard ranchmen speak of a *Spitting Rattlesnake.* They admitted that this snake was probably the same as the Diamond Rattlesnake, but that when it was angered, it had the habit of spitting saliva or venom at its annoyer. . . I now have a genuine spitting specimen of *Crotalus atrox* and am willing to grant the use of the vernacular name as applied to certain specimens.

‡spitting time n   Cf *DS* AA27

1954 *AmSp* 29.298 [Vernacular of menstruation], The following are additional terms which have been reported. . . *Periodicity. . . spittin' time (W[omen]).*

spittlebug n

1 also *spit bug, spittle fly, ~ insect:* A small jumping insect of the family Cercopidae.   [Because the nymph covers itself in white froth]   Also called **froghopper 1**

1882 VT State Bd. Ag. *Rept. for 1881–82* 7.77, Dr. Cutting spoke of the frog hopper, usually known as the spittle bug on grass.   **1890** *Century Dict.* 5845, Spittle-insect. . . a spit-bug or froghopper. *Ibid,* Spittle-fly. . . A spittle-insect.   **1948** *Sun* (Baltimore MD) 9 June 26/8 **MD,** Spittle-bug infection has damaged alfalfa fields in Allegany county.   **1959** *Wall St. Jrl.* (NY NY) 21 Apr 1/5, A weaker threat is also posed by grain-eating chinch bugs, hay-damaging spittlebugs.   **1965** Teale *Wandering Through Winter* 46 **CA,** As a kind of dessert, these Indians also ate the froth of the spittlebugs, or froghoppers, which is slightly sweet when made on certain plants.   **1967–68** *DARE* (Qu. R30, . . *Kinds of beetles; not asked in early QRs*) Inf **IA**1, Spittlebug; **VA**21, Spittlebugs—same as spit bugs.   **1968** *WI Conserv. Bulletin* Mar–Apr 30, They are called spittle insects because the frothy white masses resemble spittle.   **1980** Milne–Milne *Audubon Field Guide Insects* 495, Spittlebug nymphs cover themselves with masses of bubbly, wet spittle, which accounts for their common name.   **2002** *DARE* File **TX** (as of 1950s), My father showed me what he called a spitbug. He pointed out the little ball of spit on a plant stem and said, "There's a bug in there."

2 A **grasshopper 1.**

1969 *DARE* (Qu. R6, . . *Names . . for grasshoppers*) Inf **MA**73, Spittlebug.

spittle fly (or insect)   See **spittlebug 1**

spit-tobacco n   Also *spit-tobacco-and-I'll-let-you-go*   Cf **tobacco spitter**

A **grasshopper 1.**

1967–68 *DARE* (Qu. R6, . . *Names . . for grasshoppers*) Inf **IL**26, Spit-tobacco; **MD**9, Spit-tobacco-and-I'll-let-you-go.

spittum n   Also *sputtum*   [Varr of *sputum,* prob infl by *spit*]

1915 Rose *W. Reserve* OH 2.472, They . . have sought to prevent the foul disease-bearing spittum on the pavement.   **1931** Hawes *Talks on Tuberculosis* 24, Associated with the cough there may or may not be sputum or phlegm, and I beg of you to pronounce it correctly and not as if it were spelled 'spittum' or 'sputtum.'   **1968–69** *DARE* (Qu. DD4, *Moisture in the mouth, colored brown by snuff or chewing tobacco*) Infs **CT**7, **MO**32, 34, Spittum.   **1998** in **2006** *DARE* File—Internet **SC,** Chewing tobacco spittum or soda leaks into a wall cavity after partially filled bottles left [in] the wall break from freezing.   **2004** in **2008** *Ibid* **swCA,** [Headline:] The Spittum of my Subconsciousnessisess [sic].

spizzerinctum n   Also *spiz, spizzeranctum, spizzerinktum* [*spizzerinctum,* obs in the 20th cent in its orig sense "money," was perh revived through the infl of *pizzazz* (*OED2* 1937).]   Cf **moxie 2, sugarinctum, tizzyrinctum**

Get-up-and-go, nerve, ambition.

[**1914** *Lincoln Daily Star* (NE) 8 July 7/5, Be a spizzerinktum—It's a Brand New Word, But It Means a Lot—Here Is Its Meaning. . .

"A spizzerinktum is a person who possesses initiative, vim, vigor, efficiency, intelligent persistency and an overmastering will to succeed," comes the explanation.]   **1924** Wingfield *Hist. Caroline Co.* VA 406 (as of 1869), I was young and full of spizzerinktum, hence soon found myself deep in politics.   **1942** Berrey–Van den Bark *Amer. Slang* 273, Ambition. . . spizzerinctum.   **1947** *Newsweek* 24 Feb 28, Tirelessly he promised "to put spizzerinctum into the Republican party." Explaining that "spizzerinctum" means the "old get-up-and-go," Sigler was nonplussed.   **1949** *PADS* 11.11 **wTX** (as of 1911–29), Spizzerinktum. . . Energy; nerve. "He certainly has the old spizzerinktum."   **1955** Roberts *S. from Hell-fer-Sartin* 180 **seKY,** Well, when I was a good deal younger than I am now and had more spizzeranctum in me I loooved [sic] to travel over the land and country.   **c1960** *Wilson Coll.* **csKY,** Spizzerinktum. . . Spirit, zeal, "pep."   **1965–70** *DARE* (Qu. HH27b, *Of a very able and energetic person who gets things done . . "He's got lots of _____."*) Infs **IL**128, **IN**14, 39, **OH**37, Spizzerinctum; (Qu. A22, . . *'To start working hard': "She had only ten minutes to clean the room, but she _____ [and had it done in time]."*) Inf **OK**1, Was full of spizzerinctum; (Qu. KK28, *Feeling ambitious and eager to work*) Infs **OK**1, **WI**21, Full of spizzerinctum.   **1968** *DARE* File **nOH** (as of 1930s), *Full of (the old) spiz—full of (the old) spizzerinctum* = full of get-up-and-get, zip, zing, etc.   **1998** *Ibid* **nAL,** From the hills of North Alabama, where I was born in 1935: . . How about "spizzerinctum"? [My] uncle used it frequently, meaning "energy" or "get-up-and-go".   **2004** *DARE* File **csWI,** My eighty-year-old mother told me she had just phoned a family friend who was recovering from surgery, "How did she sound?" I asked. "Great—full of spizzerinctum," Mom answered.

splake n   Also *splake trout*   [Blend of *speckled* + *lake*]

A hybrid of the male **brook trout** and female **lake trout 1.**

[**1954** *Chicago Tribune* (IL) 18 Apr sec 2 7/5, [Canadian] biologists who developed the fish . . had named it Splake.]   **1955** *Bennington Eve. Banner* (VT) 29 Sept 5/5, Don't be surprised if you're fishing in New Hampshire and hook a trout that you can't identify. It's probably a "splake" trout. . . Recent plantings in this pond will provide the initial test of how the new hybrid—a cross between lake trout and brook trout alleged to retain the best fishing qualities of both—will actually respond to the lures of Waltonians.   **1966–68** *DARE* (Qu. P1, . . *Kinds of freshwater fish . . caught around here . . good to eat*) Infs **MI**26, 32, **NY**6, 92, Splake; **NY**93, Splake is a cross of speckled and lake trout.   **1966** *DARE* Tape **MI**32, Quite a few inland lakes have been stocked with [what] . . they call a splake . . a cross between a speckled trout and a lake trout.   **1983** Becker *Fishes WI* 329, The splake is a hybrid developed by fertilizing the eggs of a lake trout with the milt of a brook trout.   **2005** *Post-Std.* (Syracuse NY) 16 Sept sec D 14/5, About 2,600 splake are stocked annually in Meacham Lake.

splanify v   [Aphet var of **explanify**]

To explain.

1852 Hannibal *Professor Hannibal's Discourses* 14 **NY** [Black], But I muss 'splanify to you dat dere am seberil kinds ob rats.   **1887** *Overland Mth.* (2d ser) 10.69 **AL,** Mebbe hit dew splanify the reason Cherrykee don't git married.   **1972** *Atlanta Letters* **cGA,** Southernisms. . . If you'll wait, I'll splanify everything to you.

splash n

1 also *splash flood;* In logging: the sudden release of water from a dam in order to move logs down a stream that would otherwise not float them; hence nouns *splash logging, splash dam.*   Cf **flood dam, splash** v

1866 in **2008** (acc) Lexis–Nexis Legal Research *State Case Law: PA* (Internet), On this stream different persons . . had erected dams, called "bracket-dams," for the purpose of collecting the water and letting it off, to assist them in floating their rafts, when the natural rise of the stream was not sufficient. These lettings-off were called "splash floods."   **1870** [see **splash** v].   **1876** Maury–Fontaine *Resources WV* 156, It would certainly seem that . . the vast amount of timber . . would induce capitalists to open it up by tram railroads, booms and splash dams.   **1879** *Lumberman's Gaz.* 27 Aug 6, The river was rising rapidly and the prospect was that the splash would result advantageously to the lumberman at Eau Claire [WI].   **1894** *Overland Mth.* (2d ser) 24.380 **nwCA,** We were informed of a "splash dam," on the main stream, . . about twenty miles from Ukiah.   *Ibid,* I have used the term "splash dam" as I heard it used in the lumbering districts of Pennsylvania. It applies to a dam for the storage of water, and when the quantity desired has collected, it is suddenly allowed to pass through the floodgates in such force as to float the timber placed in the bed of the stream below it.   **1896** [see **splash** v].   **1897** *Garden and Forest* 10.262, Clearing the creeks for a splash means doing away with any obstacles or obstructions to the watercourse. **1905** U.S. Forest Serv. *Bulletin* 61.49 [Logging terms], *Splash dam.* A dam built to store a head of water for driving logs. (Gen[eral]). **1924** Raine *Land of Saddle-Bags* 24 **sAppalachians,** A creek is usually too shallow to float logs down to the river where they can be assembled into rafts. At some suitable place, between high banks, a splash dam is built. **1991** Weals *Last Train* 11 **eTN** (as of early 20th cent), Walker did tolerate splash logging from upriver property that adjoined his, and is believed to have sold limited amounts of yellow poplar and valuable ash timber from his land late in the 19th century.

‡**2** also *splashing:* Bird excrement.

2002 *NY Times* (NY) 18 Apr sec F 1/1 **KY,** [He was] pointing to what looked like white paint spilled on brown leaves. . . "This is what they call owl splash, which is a nice word for, you know," said Mr. Offutt. **2004** *DARE* File **NEng** (as of 1970s), The seagulls leave splashings on the park picnic tables. *Ibid,* We'd look for splashings in the woods as woodcock sign. **2004** *Post & Courier* (Charleston SC) 18 Jan sec C 11 (Internet), While some keen-eyed hunters might notice probe holes left by woodcock, the more visible sign is the white splash deposited by defecating birds. If you notice a quarter-sized splash on the ground then you're in the right place.

splash v, hence vbl n *splashing*   Also with *out*   Cf **flood, splash** n **1**

In logging: to float (logs) down a small stream by suddenly releasing water from a dam.

1870 in 2008 (acc) Lexis–Nexis Legal Research *State Case Law: PA* (Internet), The dam was built, and during the season of floating logs was kept up and managed for raising "splashes" for the purpose of driving logs down the stream. . . Vincent, the other defendant, attended to the splashing under Woodward who had the contract for doing it. **1875** *Ibid* **PA** (Internet), If, by the use of it in splashing out logs, they did not seriously interfere with the plaintiff's reasonable use of it below, . . then their use of it could not be said to be unreasonable. **1896** NC State Bd. Ag. *NC Resources* 53, Splash dams will be built on the creeks in Pisgah Forest, and the logs will be splashed into the French Broad river and carried on down to the mill. **1905** U.S. Forest Serv. *Bulletin* 61.49 [Logging terms], *Splash.* . . To drive logs by releasing a head of water confined by a splash dam. (Gen[eral]). **1924** Raine *Land of Saddle-Bags* 24 **sAppalachians,** As I travelled up one creek, a man told me he had "splashed out" thirteen thousand logs that season. **1958** McCulloch *Woods Words* 176 **Pacific NW,** *Splash.* . . To move logs down river by use of a splash dam. Water is held back while logs are yarded into the river, then when the dam gate is kicked loose the flood of water will wash logs for miles down stream when ordinarily the current would not move them. This was used on Coos River, Oregon, and other coastal streams as late as 1952, now outlawed.

splashboard n   [**splash** n **1**]

In logging: see quot 1905.

1905 U.S. Forest Serv. *Bulletin* 61.49 [Logging terms], *Splash boards.* Boards placed temporarily on top of a rolling dam to heighten the dam, and thus to increase the head of water available for river driving. (N[orthern] F[orest]). **1958** McCulloch *Woods Words* 176 **Pacific NW,** *Splash boards*—Planks added to the top of a splash dam to hold back an extra head of water.

splash dam (or flood)   See **splash** n **1**

splashing n   See **splash** n **2**

splashing vbl n   See **splash** v

splash logging   See **splash** n **1**

splash out   See **splash** v

splatter n   [See quot]

=**coot** n[1] **1.**

1917 (1923) *Birds Amer.* 1.214, *Coot.* . . *Other Names.* . . Splatter; Shuffler. . . Not that it is exactly a feathered Pavlowa, but with marked ability it can run, walk, swim, and "skitter." In the "Mud Hen Skitter," which might well be made a new dance for society, it can beat even the celebrated dancer, for it is practiced on a peculiar floor, the surface of the water—as the flock flutter away, pattering with their feet as they go.

splatter-ass n   [See quot 1955] **CA, NV, OR**

=**bufflehead** **2** or **ruddy duck.**

1945 McAtee *Nomina Abitera* 32 **CA,** Bufflehead. . . Splatter-ass, Gilroy, California. *Ibid* **CA, OR,** Ruddy Duck. . . splatter-ass, Ore-

gon . . , Suisun Marshes, California . . , and Alturas and Cedarville, Calif. [**1955** Forbush–May *Birds* 89, In rising from the water the Ruddy Duck flutters and splatters along the surface.] **1968** *DARE* FW Addit **cwNV,** *Splatter-ass, butterball*—joking names for the ruddy duck.

splatterdab n   Cf *DS* H20b

A pancake.

1910 *DN* 3.458 **FL, GA,** *Splatterdabs.* . . Pancakes. **1941** *Jefferson City Post–Tribune* (MO) 19 Sept 8/3 **NYC,** A list of nicknames for foods . . compiled by the head chef at the Hotel New Yorker. . . "splatter dabs," pancakes. **1944** Adams *Western Words* 151, *Splatter dabs*— slang name for hot cakes.

splatterdock   See **spatterdock**

splay v   [Var of *spay*]

A Gram form.

Past pple: usu *splayed;* also rarely *splayded.*   Cf Intro "Language Changes" II.5

1968 *DARE* (Qu. J3a, *To make a female dog so that she can't breed, she must be _____*) Inf **GA**54, Splayded; (Qu. J3b, *To make a female cat so that she can't breed, she must be _____*) Inf **GA**54, Splayded.

B Sense.

To spay.   [*OED2* 1601 →]   **chiefly NJ, PA, OH, MI**   See Map   *old-fash*   Cf **spray**

1899 *Ft. Wayne Sentinel* (IN) 16 Nov [9]/7 (newspaperarchive.com), [Advt:] For Sale—A Llwellyn [sic] splayed bitch, 2 years old. **1965–70** *DARE* (Qu. J3a, *To make a female dog so that she can't breed, she must be _____*) 20 Infs, **chiefly NJ, PA, OH, MI,** Splayed; **NJ**56, Splay; **GA**54, Splayded; (Qu. J3b, *To make a female cat so that she can't breed, she must be _____*) 14 Infs, **chiefly NJ, PA, OH, MI,** Splayed; **NJ**53, 56, **NY**209, Splay; **GA**54, Splayded. [21 of 23 total Infs old] **1999** *Columbus Dispatch* (OH) 18 Apr sec D 1 (Internet), My mother also contributes 'splayed,' as in, 'They have to get their female dog splayed.'

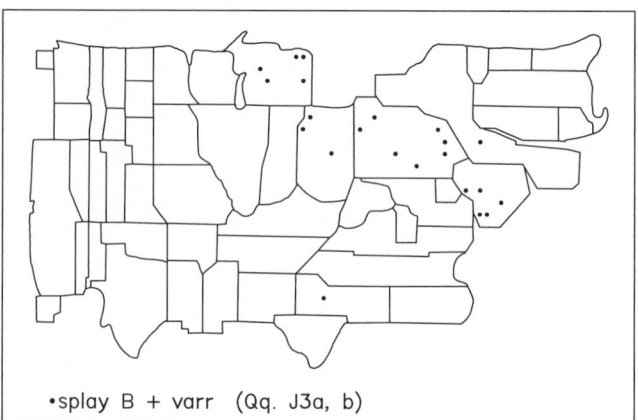

•splay B + varr (Qq. J3a, b)

splayded   See **splay A**

spleen n

1 usu with *against:* A rooted hostility or prejudice.   [*OED2* *spleen* sb. 7.b *"Obs."*]

1789 in 1988 Maclay *Diary* 77 **PA,** I . . said no former transaction was so likely to throw light on this Subject, as a Short History of the British Navigation Act. Cromwell originated it, in Spleen against the Dutch. **1851** *Internatl. Mag.* 4.128, Johnston's *Notes on North America* is treated with a spleen excited by the author's refusal to recognize the greatness assumed for certain persons connected with Harvard College. **1872** U.S. Congress *Rept. Joint Select Comm. Insurrectionary States* 9.1026 **AL,** There was no purpose avowed at all, but it was done; I understand that it was a spleen against the freedmen—more against the republican party than anything else. **1891** *Catholic World* 53.813 **NY,** Do you think I'm goin' to . . put the deacon to shame just to favor a spleen against him? **1966** *DARE* (Qu. II28, *An unexplainable dislike that you feel from the first moment you meet a person: "I took a _____ to him."*) Inf **MA**6, Spleen against him.

2 with *for:* A liking, tolerance.

1940 in 1944 *ADD* **nWV,** *Spleen.* . . Liking, taste, 'stomach.' . . 'Have no spleen for' = have no stomach for. Reported. **1959** *VT Hist.* 27.159, *Spleen.* . . Liking for. Rare.

3 also with *the:* A condition characterized by enlargement of the spleen.   Cf **ague cake**

1899 (1912) Green *VA Folk-Speech* 407, *Spleen. . . The spleen,* ague-cake, enlargement of the organ under malarial poisoning.   **1903** *DN* 2.331 **seMO,** *Spleen. . .* An enlarged spleen. 'My little boy is not well; I'm afraid he has a touch of the spleen.'   **1907** *DN* 3.236 **nwAR,** *Spleen. . .* An enlarged spleen.

spleen v

Often with *at* or *against:* To feel disgust or anger.

1883 Flower *Life Matthew Hale Carpenter* 292 **WI,** Cameron's name. . . was satisfactory to a majority of the bolters, but most of the democrats spleened against him.   **1885** Cooke in *Congregationalist (Cent.) (DAE),* I spleen at it.   **1889** Cooke *Steadfast* 198 **CT,** [It] makes me spleen to think on't!   **c1901** in 2002 *DARE* File—Internet **NY,** Grandmother spleened against wild meat of every sort, unless possibly venison, thinking it had a wild taste.   **1902** Wilson *Spenders* 31 **West,** I spleened against it and let him know it.   **1922** *Century Illustr. Mag.* 103.855 **nME,** Every night he brought in all that would have been too spoiled to sell the next day, and I had to cook it. . . But mebbe I wouldn't 'a' spleened against it so if I hadn't 'a' been in a family way.   **1959** *VT Hist.* 27.159, *Spleen. . .* 2. To revolt against. . . She is always spleening against something. Common.

spleen for   See **spleen n 2**

spleenwort n

Std: a fern of the genus *Asplenium.*   For other names of var spp see **backache root 3, bird's-nest fern, hart's tongue 1, Indian-hair fern, wallink 2**

spleeny adj   **chiefly NEng**

Hypochondriacal; overly sensitive to feelings of fear, discomfort, or distaste.

1812 Rush *Med. Inquiries* 14, For many years it [=hypochondriasis] was known in England by no other name than the spleen, and even to this day, persons who are affected with it are said to be spleeny, in some parts of the New England states.   **1854** Milne *Uncle Sam's Fence* 102 **NY,** Tell him the house is on fire; that will rouse him, he's spleeny about fire.   **1859** *Ladies' Repository* 19.725, You call the nervous friend, who always sees the sword of Damocles suspended over her head, "spleeny."   **1897** *Century Illustr. Mag.* 54.727 **NEng coast,** Eli's spleeny, 'n' he's notional. . . The way his mother cosseted him wuz enough to spoil any man.   **1902** (1904) Rowe *Maid of Bar Harbor* 141 **ME,** You've no idea how good company kind o' chirks a body up when they get spleeny and down sperited.   **1914** *DN* 4.80 **ME, nNH,** *Spleeny. . .* Hypochondriacal, complaining, fussing over health: lacking in stamina and courage.   **1926** *AmSp* 2.80 **ME,** Persons who are ill but still able to be about regard themselves as "poorly," but their skeptical neighbors may unfeelingly call them "spleeny."   **1926** *DN* 5.389 **ME,** "There hain't nothin' the matter with her; she's just spleeny." Common.   **1941** *LANE* Map 459 *(Emaciated, peaked)* 3 infs, **MA,** Spleeny; 1 inf, **ceMA,** Spleeny—of a hypochondriac = complaining; 1 inf, **ceMA,** Spleeny—'always complaining.'   **1966** *DARE* (Qu. HH10, *A very timid or cowardly person: "He's _____."*) Inf **ME9,** Spleeny.   **1968** *DARE* (Qu. H12, *If somebody eating a meal takes little bits of food and leaves most of it on his plate, you say he _____*) Inf **NY96,** Spleeny eater.   **1975** Gould *ME Lingo* 270, If a child whimpers at having a splinter removed from his finger, Mother will say, "Now, don't be so spleeny, this isn't going to hurt!"   **1977** *Yankee* Jan 73 **Isleboro ME,** Anybody who can't stand the cold is spleeny.   **2005** *Bangor Daily News* (ME) 24 Nov sec B 1 (Internet), The consensus seemed to be that real men regard umbrellas as vain accessories for urban folks, as silly props for spleeny fops who fear the bedraggling effects of rain on their expensive business attire.

splendiferous adj   Cf **angeliferous, eujifferous**

Splendid; wonderful.

1837 Bird *Nick of Woods* 1.226, At a close hug, a squeeze on the small ribs, or a kick-up of heels, he's all splendiferous.   **1875** *Harper's New Mth. Mag.* 50.854, There is no end to our superlative language. . . [S]plendiferous is only tolerable.   **1905** *DN* 3.20 **cCT,** *Splendiferous. . .* Splendid.   **1913** *DN* 4.20 **NE,** *Splendiferous.* Splendid, fine, brilliant, gorgeous.   **1967–68** *DARE* (Qu. FF17, *. . . A very good or enjoyable time: "We all had a _____ last night."*) Infs **NY23, 68,** Splendiferous time.   **2001** *DARE* File—Internet, [Advt:] A Splendiferous Sweepstakes! Enter to Win a Winnie the Pooh Collector's Limited Edition Sericel!

splib n   [Etym unknown]   *chiefly among Black speakers*

1 A Black person.

1964 *NYT Mag.* 23 Aug 62, *Soul brother*—Negro; also referred to as . . *splib.*   **1967–68** *DARE* (Qu. HH28, *Names and nicknames . . for people of foreign background: Negro*) Infs **MI**69, 72, **PA**66, Splib. [2 of 3 Infs Black]   **1967** *DARE* FW Addit **TN** [Black], *Splib* [splɪb]—used by Negroes to refer to themselves (as a race)—a neutral term—this instance recorded from a college grad (Negro) from Mt. Pleasant, Tenn.   **1968** *Current Slang* 3.2.45 [Watts slang; Black], *Splib. . .* Negro (used by Mexicans).   **1969** (1973) Young *Dancing* 5 [Black], Dont nobody want no nice nigger no more. . . [T]hey want an angry splib.   **1971** Roberts *Third Ear* np [Black], *Splib. . .* a black person.   **1972** Claerbaut *Black Jargon* 81, *Splib . .* a black child.   **1974** *AmSp* 49.184, *Splib . .* [*spade* 'black person' + *lib*eral]—Liberal black who looks angry but will not upset the status quo.   **1994** Smitherman *Black Talk* 213, *Splib. . .* A generic reference to any Black person; a fairly neutral term.   **2004** *DARE* File—Internet, When I was in the Marine Corps in the late Sixties a very common term we used for a black Marine was a splib. It wasn't a derogatory term and was freely used by both blacks and whites. I have never heard the term used outside of the Corps. *Ibid* [Black], Nobody ever referred to a chick as a "splib." Well, back in the day, nobody did. . . I've never, from 1949 to the present, known splib to be a term other than neutral. . . The term is quite antiquated. Its heyday was the 'Fifties.

‡2 See quot.

1970 *DARE* (Qu. U26, *Names or nicknames . . for a paper dollar*) Inf **MO29,** Splib.

splint n

=**splinter.**

1855 Squier *Waikna* 174, The Poyer boy was dispatched to the camp for fire and pine splints, which . . answered for torches.   *Ibid* 239, Meanwhile a fire had been kindled of pine splints and branches.   **1866** *Atlantic Mth.* 17.461 **ceMA,** As to crackers, they are of course no more available than pine splints.   **1874** *Overland Mth.* 12.49 **CA,** She reached out her hand to throw upon them some fresh pine splints, but withheld it.   **1967** *DARE* Tape **PA**14, My dad would get pine and then we'd have to splint, make pine for splints to start the fire.   **1968** *DARE* (Qu. D34, *. . The small pieces of wood and other stuff that are used to start a fire*) Inf **PA**164, Splints.   **1972** *DARE* File **nwFL,** *Splints* = Kindling wood. (Woman, 53, 8th-grade educ, no travel.)   **1986** Pederson *LAGS Concordance (Lightwood)* 2 infs, **neFL, csTX,** Splints.   **2001** *Buffalo News* (NY) 25 Mar sec B 4 (Internet), Kathleen has brought along some kindling from the basement, and we wad some newspaper and light it, leaving the splints of wood to catch while we scout for larger stuff.

splint broom n   **esp NEast**

=**split broom.**

1837 Darlington *Flora Cestrica* 547 **sePA,** Pig-nut Hickory. Broom Hickory. . . The young saplings, of this species, were formerly much used for making splint brooms.   **1848** *Amer. Phrenological Jrl. & Misc.* 10.364 **NEast,** He made half a dozen *splint brooms,* and with these upon his shoulder, as a stock in trade, . . started through the snows.   **1849** *Scientific Amer.* 7 Apr 230 **NY,** To Jno. Crum and A. Larwill, of Ramapo, N.Y., for improvement in Splint Broom machines.   **1869** Brewster *Rambles* 266 **NH,** A round splint broom . . was enveloped in a dress, with a mask for the face.   **1883** Briggs *Hist. Concord* 143 **cwNY,** The big barn floor would be made perfectly clean by a free use of the splint broom.   **1968** *DARE* (Qu. F36, *. . Kinds of brooms*) Inf **NY72,** Splint broom—take a green stick and shave it down and turn the shavings over and bind them with wire.

splinter n   [*OED2 splinter* 3.b [Of a strip of wood:] "Used as a torch, or dipped in tallow and used as a candle"; 1751 →]   **chiefly Sth, S Midl**   See Map on p. 186 and Map Section   Cf **chip n¹ 4, splint**

A split piece of wood used for kindling or to give light.

1791 Bartram *Travels* 470 **PA,** Some take with them little fascines of fat Pine splinters for torches.   **1845** Thompson *Pineville* 165 **GA,** He had gone to the kitchen and lit a few light-wood splinters.   **1852** *S. Lit. Messenger* 18.358 **VA,** A large negro, then engaged in setting some pine splinters in a blaze in the fireplace, opened his eyes to an immoderate width.   **1873** (1876) Cozzens *Marvellous Country* 139, Bethinking himself of some pitch-pine which he had in his luggage, he proceeded to light a splinter, that he might see its effect upon the rocks and cliffs and fissures, which towered far above.   **1939** Harris *Purslane* 110 **cNC,** Uncle Hen . . went to the wood-pile to cut an armful of lightwood splinters to start morning fires. **1965–70** *DARE* (Qu. D34, . . *The small pieces of wood and other stuff that are used to start a fire*) 31 Infs, **chiefly Sth,** Splinters; **MS**73, Lightered splinters; **TX**94, Pine splinters; **SC**56, Split splinters; (Qu. T8) Infs **GA**18, **PA**214, Splinters. **1966** *DARE* Tape **FL**41, [FW:] What do you use to start your fire in your wood stove? [Inf:] We use. . . a little pine along with the oak; . . old pine is old standard, we call it "Get the splinters in, don't forget the splinters." **1972** *PADS* 58.11 cwAL, *Kindling.* The term *kindling* (23 [of 27 infs]) predominates over Midland *pine* . . ; *splinters* occurs as the primary response of one informant . . and as the alternate response of five informants. **1989** Pederson *LAGS Tech. Index* 34 **Gulf Region** (*Lightwood*) 106 infs, Splinters; 29 infs, Lighterd splinters, fat splinters, cedar splinters [etc]. **2001** *Charleston Gaz.* (WV) 14 Dec sec D 2 (Internet), After the splinters of kindling began to burn, I added several sticks of stove wood.

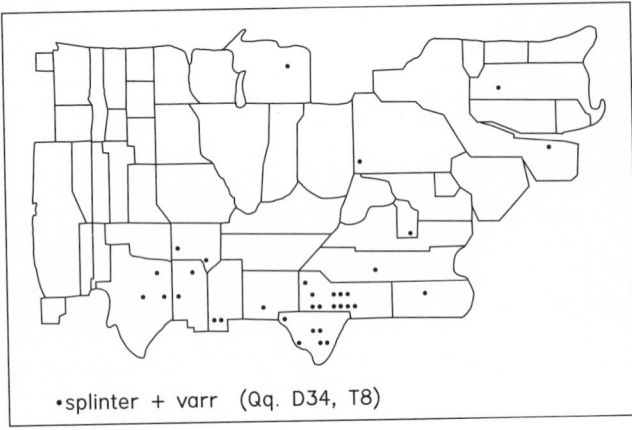

•splinter + varr (Qq. D34, T8)

splinter cat n Cf **sliver cat,** *DS* CC17

An imaginary creature; see quots.

1910 Cox *Fearsome Creatures* 37, Striking squarely with its hard face, the splinter cat passes right on, leaving the tree broken and shattered as though struck by lightning or snapped off by the wind. **1918** *DN* 5.25 NW, *High-behind, splinter-cat.* . . Fabulous creatures, capable of amazing feats, that infest the sage brush when the cowpunchers hump about their fires. **1939** Tryon *Fearsome Critters* 47, The Splinter Cat . . climbs a tree, guns himself at the desired bole, and projects himself at it with terrific force. If the Cat finds food in the ruptured trunk, he is temporarily appeased. If not, he goes immediately for another tree. **2000** *DARE* File—Internet MN, A display of chainsaw-carved "Northwoods Creatures"—the Mall's concession to Minnesota folklore—lines the walls, and includes a Hodag . . and something called a Splinter Cat.

splintereens n pl

Smithereens, bits.

1914 Peterson–Hanson *Pilot Knob* 152 **MO,** A shot from one of the 32-pounders knocked one piece of their artillery into splintereens. **1920** (2002) Cory *Billy Bunny & Uncle Bull Frog* (Internet), A big stone hit one of the lamps on the automobile and broke it to splintereens. **1965–66** *DARE* (Qu. KK22, . . *Completely shattered: "The jug fell out of the window and was _____."*) Inf **NC**4, Broken to splintereens; **OK**9, Busted all to splintereens. **1999** *Kalamazoo Express Weekly* (MI) 16 Dec (Internet), One wrong move would result in the plastic light assembly shattering into splintereens. **2005** *Palm Beach Post* (W. Palm Beach FL) 11 May 6 (Internet), I was still under the ridiculous illusion that I could win . . when one, then two, wheels fell off the car, which careened from the track and broke into splintereens.

splinter-new adj

=**brand-fire-new.**

1838 Rask *Compendious Gram. Icelandic* (transl. Marsh) 103, *Splinter-new* is not unfrequently heard in New-England. **1862** in 1922 Hayes *Diary & Letters* 2.366 **OH,** Colonel Scammon dressed up in a splinter-new uniform. **1875** *Athens Messenger* (OH) 8 Apr 5/4, The prize . . proved to be a splinter new penholder and point. **1911** Porter *Harvester* 338 **IN,** Marthy's old blue coverlid also carefully spread on a splinter new sofy. **1928** *Warren Morning Mirror* (PA) 16 Apr 7/2, [Headline:] Second Hand Car Just As Good As A Splinter New One. **1970** *Sun. News & Tribune* (Jefferson City MO) 15 Nov 23/5, [Advt:] Splinter new three bedroom brick rancher with country Kitchen.

split v

1 =**bust** v **1.** esp **Sth, S Midl**

1785 in 1891 Washington *Writings* 12.225 **VA,** Before the seed was sown, these ridges were split again by running twice in the middle of them, both times in the same furrow. **1851** in 1927 Jones *FL Plantation Rec.* 361 nwFL, 14 Ploughs Splitting middles and Bedding cotton land. **1902** *DN* 2.239 sIL, *Middles.* . . Hence to *bust out* or *split* the middles is to plow the balks, throwing earth back to the row. **1946** *PADS* 6.28 eNC (as of 1900–10), *Split.* . . To plow out middles or balks with a cotton plow, throwing one furrow to the left and the other to the right. . Common. **1959** Lomax *Rainbow Sign* 28 **AL** [Black], Papa . . made a plow hand outa Sukie. . . He used to side cotton and she'd split middles behind him. **c1960** *Wilson Coll.* csKY, *Split the middles.* . . Plow out the space left between rows of corn that has been laid by. **1998** *News & Rec.* (Greensboro NC) 16 June sec A 7 (Internet), Cotton is plowed in two stages: first with a one-sweep 'siding' plow to throw dirt up around the plants sitting on top of the row; then with a two-sweep plow to 'split the middle.'

2 To run; to go with great speed. Note: The recent colloquial sense "to depart, depart from" is not treated here. Cf **split the wind**

1790 Tyler *Contrast* 29 **NEast,** I was glad to take to my heels and split home. **1845** Thompson *Pineville* 174 **GA,** I jest drapt [=dropped] old Betsey [=a shotgun] and put out for the camp as hard as I could split. **1848** Bartlett *Americanisms* 324, *To split.* To go at a rapid pace; to drive along. **1899** (1912) Green *VA Folk-Speech* 408, *Split.* . . To run or walk with long strides. "Go as hard as you can split." **1902** *DN* 2.245 sIL, *Split.* . . To go with speed, as 'He jes went a splittin thro the timber.' **1907** *DN* 3.226 nwAR, *Split.* . . To go with speed. **1909** *DN* 3.374 eAL, wGA, *Split.* . . To run away hurriedly.

split n

1 An **earmark** n made by cutting partway into the ear of an animal. chiefly **Sth, S Midl** See Map Cf **over** C, **under**

1790 in 1961 Nash *Hist. Augusta* 586 **ME,** Benjamin Pettingil's mark . . is an L in the under side of the left ear, and a split in the under side of the right ear. **1854** in 2001 *DARE* File—Internet **AL** [Mark and Brand Book of Washington County, Alabama], Margaret Grimes No. 60—records hi [sic] mark a crop and split in each ear. . . Elijah Williford No. 61 . . records his mark a crop and underbit in the left ear and undersquare and split in the right ear. **1908** *DN* 3.303 eAL, wGA, Other marks [include] . . the *split* (of which there are several kinds, the simple split being a straight downward slit). **1920** Hunter *Trail Drivers TX* 298, Some of the terms used in marking are "crop," . . "split," . . "underslope," etc. **1965–68** *DARE* (Qu. K18, . . *Kind of mark . . to identify a cow*) Infs **FL**17, **LA**20, **NV**8, Split; **FL**7, Split, two splits; **FL**20, Split and upper cut; **LA**14, Splits and cuts in the ears; **LA**18, Crop and split; **GA**77, **SC**9, Ear split(s); **TN**37, Split in ear. **1968** Adams *Western Words* 71, *Comet split*—An earmark similar to the *key split* . . except that the tail end is curved. Also called *tail split. Ibid* 169, *Key split*—One of several earmarks resembling cotter keys of different shapes. **1975** *Foxfire 3* 112 nwGA, You'd know your hog by your mark. . . Me and my daddy had the same mark—crop and split in the left ear, and a split in the right. **1986** Pederson *LAGS Concordance,* 1 inf, cnTN, Crop and a split on top and underbit.

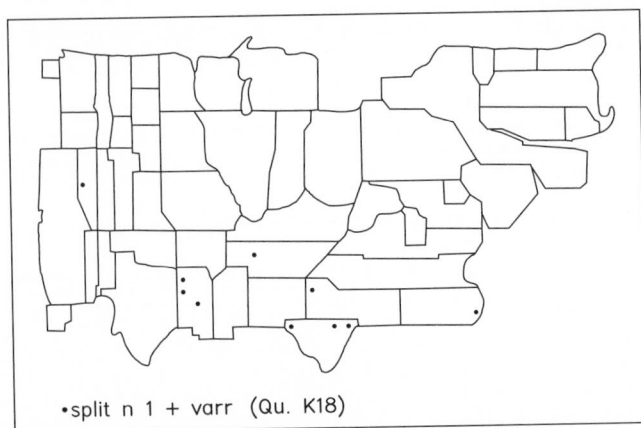

•split n 1 + varr (Qu. K18)

2 A knife game; see quots. esp **Sth, S Midl**

1966–68 *DARE* (Qu. EE5, *Games where you try to make a jackknife stick in the ground*) Infs **IN**35, **ME**15, **OH**46, Split; **LA**37, Split—you throw a knife beside someone's foot and he has to move his foot where the knife hit; **MO**26, Split—two players. One starts by trying to make a knife stick in the ground, thrown from an upright position. If it failed to stick, it was the other player's turn. If it stuck, the other player put his foot on the spot where the knife stuck. The thrower then tried again to make the knife stick. If it stuck again, the other player had to place his other foot on that spot. If he couldn't without falling, he lost the game; **NC**53, Split—throw at another person and make him split his legs; (Qu. EE33, . . *Outdoor games . . that children play*) Inf **LA**34, Split—start with legs together; opponent sticks knife in ground beside one foot; you put your foot there; process repeated. **1967** *DARE* File **OH** (as of c1950), *Splits*—We played this as kids. Two boys face one another. The one with a jackknife sticks it in the ground a couple of feet to the left or right of his opponent. Opponent puts his foot on that spot, then throws the knife in turn. The game progresses, with the legs getting farther and farther apart until one player either does the splits or falls down. **1986** Pederson *LAGS Concordance,* 1 inf, **swAL**, Split—throw knife; person must stretch to reach; 1 inf, **ceTX**, Split—knife game; put foot where it hit last.

3 also pl: A drink composed chiefly of raw alcohol and water. **NEng**

1892 *Nation* 28 July 66 **ME**, One of the principal of the illicit beverages is a deadly compound called "split," composed of alcohol and water. **1907** *DN* 3.250 **eME**, *Split. . .* A beverage consisting of alcohol and water. **1914** *DN* 4.80 **ME, nNH**, *Splits. . .* A native drink composed of alcohol, sugar and water. **1924** in 1931 McCorrison *Letters Fraternity* 61 **NEng**, Sarah and I have had a slight cold, but a few doses of split knocked it "sky high." **1932** in 2008 (acc) Lexis–Nexis Legal Research *State Case Law: ME* (Internet), One man testified that before noon on that day Remi Michaud drank "split" with him. **1938** *Ibid: NH*, In the McGinley case the insured voluntarily drank "splits," a mixture of alcohol and ginger ale, in such quantities as to cause acute alcoholism and death.

split a gusset   See **gusset, bust a 2**

split basket n   esp Sth, S Midl

A basket made from flexible wooden strips; a splint basket.

1835 Kenrick *New Amer. Orchardist* 241 **MA**, They should be formed of canes or rattans, or light split basket stuff. **1876** *Scribner's Mth.* 12.306 **VA**, Here the huge fire-place blazing welcome, and the brass andirons and split basket of pine knots upon the hearth-side. **1887** *Atlantic Mth.* 60.331 **cVA** [Black], Dey ain't got no ledger minutes for ter stop for an ole nigger, wid nothin' but split baskets. **1902** in 1993 *White R. Valley Hist. Qrly.* 32.4.15 **Ozarks**, Made a split basket and tinkered around. **1904** Glasgow *Deliverance* 503 **VA**, The split basket of plants was on his arm. **1968** *DARE* (Qu. F17, *What peaches come in—different kinds*) Inf **SC**56, Split basket; (Qu. P13) Inf **SC**57, Split basket—made of white oak splits. **1995** Williams *Gt. Smoky Mts. Folklife* 83 **wNC**, While the rib basket was the most distinctive of the Appalachian baskets, the simpler split basket was more widespread. **2002** *DARE* File—Internet **AL**, Originally from Alabama, I grew up with traditional white oak split basket and chairmakers. *Ibid* **OH**, We Have A Split Basket Size That's Right For You.

split beans from coffee, not to know v phr   chiefly S Midl, TX   See Map   Cf **beans, not to know**

To be very ignorant or stupid.

1905 *DN* 3.85 **nwAR**, *Know split beans from coffee. . .* Negatively, to be stupid. 'They don't know split beans from coffee.' Common. **1950**

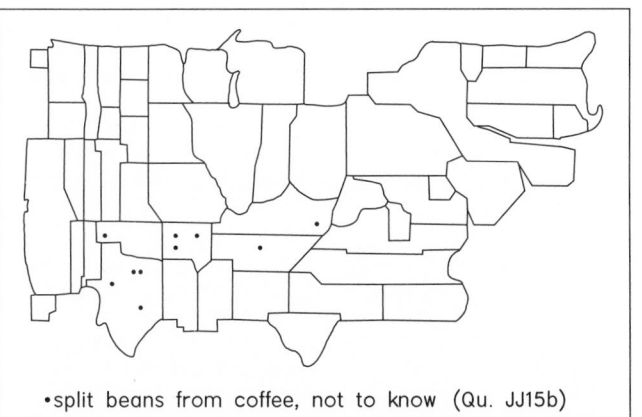

•split beans from coffee, not to know (Qu. JJ15b)

in 2001 *DARE* File—Internet **sIN**, [Sermon:] I'd rather have a man that didn't know split beans from coffee, and knowed God in His heart to deal with my people, than I would some man with enough education to choke a mule. **1965–70** *DARE* (Qu. JJ15b, *Sayings about a person who seems to you very stupid: "He doesn't know _____."*) 10 Infs, **chiefly S Midl, TX**, Split beans from coffee. **2005** *Austin Amer.-Statesman* (TX) 3 Dec sec A 1 (Internet), Former Rep. Barry Telford of DeKalb [TX], a Democratic leader under Laney, said: "Bush didn't know split beans from coffee about the Legislature when he was first elected."

split blankets   See **split the blanket(s)**

split bonnet n   Also *split(-board) sunbonnet*   **chiefly S Midl, TX**   See Map   *old-fash*   Cf **poke bonnet**
=**slat bonnet.**

1863 Burnett *Incidents* 24 **OH**, Riding up to the bevy of women in lathed and split bonnets, he inquired, . . "What in _____ are all you women doing here?" **1909** (1910) Bushnell *John Arrowsmith* 379, All wore split sun-bonnets, which came well over their faces. **1917** Baldwin *Making of a Township* 436 **ceIN**, We could almost see the split-board sun-bonnets of the pioneer women as they gathered cranberries in the marshes. **1937** (1963) Hyatt *Kiverlid* 12 **KY**, She took the split bonnet from the toil-browned hands and hung it on the top shutter of the half-door. [*Ibid* 61, Here, Mammy, is yer bonnet-splits you've been pesterin' me fer.] **c1938** in Lib. of Congress *Amer. Memory: WPA Life Hist.* (Internet) **TX** (as of 1868), I can remember how the soldiers came to his home and fired into the house and hit Mrs. Steward . . but the bullet struck the splits in the old split bonnet she had on and it grazed off and did not hurt her. **1956** McAtee *Some Dialect NC* 42, *Split bonnet. . .* A sun-bonnet, the hood of which was stiffened with thin slips of wood (splits); later, cardboard strips were substituted; and finally quilting or starch alone was used for stiffening. **c1960** *Wilson Coll.* **csKY**, *Split bonnet. . .* A sunbonnet with pasteboard "splits" to make it stand out. **1965–70** *DARE* (Qu. W2, . . *A cloth bonnet worn by women for protection from the sun*) 13 Infs, **S Midl, TX**, Split bonnet. [11 Infs old]

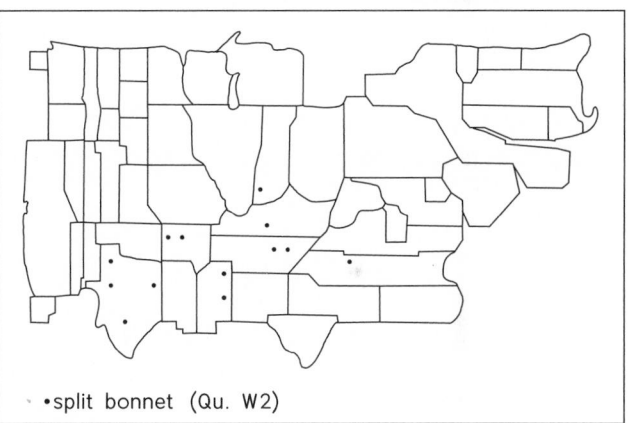

•split bonnet (Qu. W2)

split broom n

A broom whose head is made of finely split strands of wood and which is typically made from a single length of green sapling.

1846 (1847) Judson *Probe* 256 **wPA**, Some men use their wives, as farmer's girls do split brooms. **1848** in 1870 Drake *Pioneer Life* 94 **KY**, We always used a split broom. . . A small hickory sapling was the raw material. **1860** (1863) Mayhew *Mayhew's Practical Book-Keeping* 35 **MI**, H.M. Roberts has purchased of me . . one Split Broom worth 25 cents. **1865** Brainerd *Life* 420 **cNY**, The Delawares . . soon were around amongst the white inhabitants selling their commodities, split brooms and baskets. **1899** (1912) Green *VA Folk-Speech* 408, *Split-broom. . .* A broom made of young white-oak by splitting thin pieces back several inches from the point until all the stick is split, then splitting from several inches above this leaving a stick big enough for a handle, the whole tied together and trimmed even. **1917** Baldwin *Making of a Township* 89 **ceIN**, For scrubbing, sweeping the yard and barn floor they made a split broom by taking a pole of hickory wood and shaving it down within three or four inches of one end and then turn the splits over that stub, tie it and trim off even. It made a stout, serviceable broom. **1927** *AmSp* 2.365 **cwWV**, *Split broom . .* a broom made from shaving down a pole and wrapping the shavings.

splitfire new   See **spitfire new**

Splitfoot n   Cf **old 1**

The devil—freq in comb *Old Splitfoot.*

   1830 in 1957 Old Farmer's Almanac *Sampler* 52 **NEng,** It is said that Old Splitfoot has always hated asses since the affair of Balaam. **1863** Howitt *Hist. Supernatural* 2.190 **NY** (as of 1848), 'Here, old Split-foot, do as I do!' The child had evidently heard it suggested that it was the devil who had made the noises. **1867** Lowell *Biglow* lviii **'Upcountry' MA,** I subjoin a few phrases not in Mr. Bartlett's book which I have heard. . . *Old Splitfoot;* the Devil. **1954** Forbes *Rainbow* 20 **NEng,** Old Split Foot . . is a country word for the devil. **1966** Dakin *Dial. Vocab. Ohio R. Valley* 2.520, *The Devil. . .* Other terms seem to be local or individual. Kentuckians say . . *split foot* (Owsley County). **1966** *DARE* (Qu. CC8, . . *The devil*) Inf **FL**14, Splitfoot. **2001** *Patriot–News* (Harrisburg PA) 13 Jan sec A 13 (Internet), One can almost see ol' Splitfoot in there poking at the hapless islanders with his long-handled fork.

split image   See **splitting image**

split-leaf maple n   Also *split maple*   esp **NEast**

A **silver maple** or similar tree; see quots. Note: This is std in the sense "Japanese maple."

   1969 *DARE* (Qu. T14, . . *Kinds of maples*) Inf **PA**210, Split-leaf maple [*DARE* Ed: This Inf may be referring to the Japanese maple.]; **NH**16, Silverleaf [maple]—"Split maple." **2001** in 2008 *DARE* File—Internet **swVT,** In front of our house we had 3 gigantic (80–90′) split leaf maple trees. **2002** *DARE* File—Internet **NH,** I was at the kitchen sink, when I noticed something fluttering on the trunk of the big split-leaf maple at the edge of my shady garden. *Ibid* **NH,** Under the mammoth split leaf maple tree, this little one room cabin has offered cozy accommodations for summer guests since 1927.

split-mouth sucker n

=**harelip sucker.**

   1876 Jordan *Manual Vertebrates N. U.S.* 311, *Q[assilabia] lacera* [= *Lagochila l.*] . . Hare Lip Sucker, Split Mouth Sucker.

split one's blankets   See **split the blanket(s)**

split pea soup n   Also *split peas soup*   **chiefly Nth, Pacific** See Map

=**pea soup 1.**

   1847 (1852) Crowen *Amer. Cookery* 21 **NY,** Split Peas Soup.—Put a quart of split peas in water to cover them. *Ibid* 441, [Index:] Pea soup, split . . 21. **1896** (c1973) Farmer *Orig. Cook Book* 124, *Split Pea Soup.*—1 cup dried split peas [etc]. **1950** *WELS Suppl.* **ceWI,** Split pea soup and johnny cake / Make a Dutchman's belly ache. **1965–70** *DARE* (Qu. H36, *Kinds of soup*) 33 Infs, **chiefly Nth, Pacific,** Split pea soup; **MI**69, Ham and split pea soup; **NY**144, Homemade split pea soup; **KS**7, Split pea and ham soup; **WI**13, Split pea with ham soup; (Qu. H50, *Dishes made with . . peas . . that everybody around here knows, but people in other places might not*) Infs **CO**27, **CT**5, **IL**98, Split pea soup. **2006** *Albuquerque Tribune* (NM) 13 Jan sec C 2 (Internet), I have been known to make an enormous pot of split pea soup . . on a Sunday and dine on it for the rest of the week.

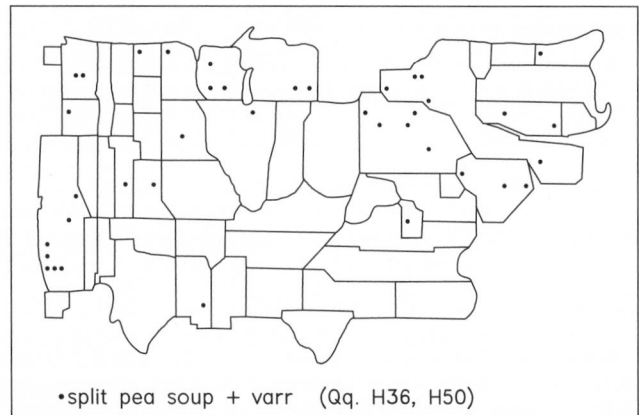

•split pea soup + varr   (Qq. H36, H50)

split-rock n

An **alumroot 1.**

   1828 Rafinesque *Med. Flora* 1.241, *Heuchera acerifolia. . .* Vulgar Names—Alumroot, Sanicle, Ground Maple, Cliffweed, Split-rock, &c. **1876** Hobbs *Bot. Hdbk.* 110, Split rock, Mapleleaf alum root, Heuchera

acerifolia. **1900** Lyons *Plant Names* 189, *H[euchera] Americana. . .* Split-rock, Cliff-weed. **1976** Miller *Shaker Herbs* 127, Alumroot. . . Cranesbill. Splitrock.

split silk, (as) fine as adj phr, adv phr   [*split silk* very fine silk thread made by dividing a thicker thread]   Cf *DS* BB47

Very thin or fine; transf: excellent, superior; very well.

   1889 U.S. Dept. Ag. *Rept. of Secy. for 1888* 648, Sumatra excels as cigar-wrappers, being described as "fine as split silk, tough as whalebone." **1893** James *Cow-Boy Life in TX* 168, If an animal was good blood, it was as "fine as split silk." **1902** Harben *Abner Daniel* 279 **nGA,** You worked 'im to a queen's taste—as fine as split silk. **1905** *DN* 3.79 **nwAR,** *Fine as split silk. . .* Extremely fine. **c1938** in Lib. of Congress *Amer. Memory: WPA Life Hist.* (Internet) **TX** (as of c1870), We had another fine horse we called Silk Stockings, because of his nice stocking legs. The owner of his mother once said, "She's as fine as split silk." **1950** *PADS* 14.78 **FL,** *Fine as split silk.* Hernando County simile in answer to "How are you?"

split sunbonnet   See **split bonnet**

splittail n   [See quot 1882]

1   A cyprinid fish of the genus Pogonichthys, native to California.

   1868 Cronise *Nat. Wealth CA* 496, They inhabit the interior rivers, growing about a foot long, and are probably the fish called "split-tail" in some places. **1882** U.S. Natl. Museum *Bulletin* 16.223, [Pogonichthys] macrolepidotus. . . *Split-tail. . .* Singularly distinguished from our other *Cyprinidae* by the great development of the upper lobe of the caudal [fin]. **1983** *Audubon Field Guide N. Amer. Fishes* 451, Splittail *(Pogonichthys macrolepidotus).* **2004** *Sacramento Bee* (CA) 25 Apr sec E 3 (Internet), Juvenile Chinook salmon move in from the river to fatten up on abundant invertebrates while Sacramento splittail move up from the estuary to spawn on submerged weeds and rice stems. **2007** *Bay Nature* Oct–Dec (Internet) **CA,** The Clear Lake splittail *(Pogonichthys ciscoides),* the lake-bound cousin of the Sacramento splittail, is said to have schooled in great numbers in Clear Lake. . . [I]t wasn't until 1973 that the fish was belatedly recognized as a species. At about the same time splittail vanished from the lake.

2   =**pintail 1.**

   1888 Trumbull *Names of Birds* 38 **MA,** In Massachusetts . . at Salem and West Barnstable [the pintail is known] as *split-tail.*

splitten image   See **splitting image**

split the blanket(s) v phr   Also *split (one's) blankets, split the quilt,* ~ *sheets*   **Sth, S Midl, West**

To divorce, separate; to part company.

   1882 in 1883 *Jrl. of Discourses* 23.297 **UT,** I believe the only Christian church in America that did not, over the slavery question, split the blanket, divide its property, its franchises and ecclesiastical organization, was the Roman Catholic church. **1903** *DN* 2.331 **seMO,** Split the blanket. . . Parted (man and wife). 'They split the blanket after living together ten years.' (Facetious.) **1907** *DN* 3.237 **nwAR,** Split the blanket. . . Of a married pair, to part, to separate. **1942** *AmSp* 17.73 [Westernisms], *Split our blankets*—Osborne Russell's expression for parting company from a partner. **1944** *PADS* 2.40 **wNC,** Blanket, to split the. . . To separate, to get a divorce (and divide the property?) **1953** Randolph–Wilson *Down in Holler* 117 **Ozarks,** Mr. and Mrs. Jones . . have separated. . . *split the quilt.* **1954** *Harder Coll.* **cwTN,** Split the blanket. . . separate, get a divorce. **1954** *PADS* 21.34 **SC,** Part the bedclothes. . . Of a married couple: to separate. . . The phrase *split blankets . .* is used in the same way. These expressions are not common, but are still used. **1958** McCulloch *Woods Words* 177 **Pacific NW,** Split the blankets—To get a divorce. **1966–69** *DARE* (Qu. AA13, *When two people who have been 'going steady' or were engaged, stop going together . . . "I guess they _____."*) Infs **AL**4, **AK**1, **AR**18, **ND**5, **SD**8, Split the blanket; **OR**1, 10, Split the sheets. **1976** Hobbs–Specht *Tisha* 80 **AK,** "Don't let that worry you. We split the blanket a while back." . . They were like man and wife for a long time until they finally broke up about a year ago. **1978** Massey *Bittersweet Country* 207 **Ozarks,** Split the blanket (dissolve a marriage): I heard Sam and Alice split the blanket. **1986** Pederson *LAGS Concordance,* 1 inf, **cnAR,** Splitting the blanket—parting, separating; 1 inf, **cwAR,** Split their blanket—couple decides to split up. **2004** *Houston Chron.* (TX) 17 Oct 3 (Internet), The Texans are young and hungry, and only a handful of them know about the divorce that saw the Oilers and Houston split the blanket in the 1990s.

split the breeze See **split the wind**

split the quilt (or sheets) See **split the blanket(s)**

split the wind v phr Also *split the breeze* **esp freq Nth, West**
Cf **hit the breeze**
To go very fast.
    1856 *Porter's Spirit of Times* 27 Sept 55 **VT**, The veteran "Columbus
[=a horse]," . . was there, and split the wind, showing the crowd that age
had not crept into his heels. **1883** (1971) Harris *Nights with Remus* 123
GA [Black], W'en dem creeturs got dey lim's tergedder dey split de
win', dey did dat. **1915** *DN* 4.245 **MT**, *Split the wind.* . . To go fast.
"We'll split the wind some if we get there on time." **1922** (1926) Cady
Rhymes **VT** 79, To break a colt and make him know / Jest how to back
and whoa and go,/. . . / And so he'll pull in snow or sand,/ And so he'll
"split the wind" or stand. **1936** Moore *Wind Over the Range* 197 **West**,
Then I split the wind for the Cross Slash. **1940** Cunningham *Spiderweb
Trail* 44 **West**, You can split the breeze down to Vado and tomorrow
come back. **1942** McAtee *Dial. Grant Co. IN* 61 (as of 1890s), *Split
the wind* . . go fast. **1966–70** *DARE* (Qu. Y20, *To run fast: "You should
have seen him _____!"*) Infs **CA**181, **SD**8, Split the breeze; **WA**6,
Split the wind. [All Infs old] **2000** *Modesto Bee* (CA) 10 May sec C 1
(Internet), Lamont Matthews followed with a drive to right that split the
wind and carried over the fence for a 4–3 San Bernardino lead.

splitting image n Also *split(ten) image* [*OED2* (at *splitting*
ppl. a. 5) 1880 →, (at *split* ppl. a. 3.a) 1981; varr, prob by folk-
etym, of **spit image, spitting image**]
=**spitting image.**
    c1920 in 1944 *ADD* nw**WV**, He's a split image of his father. **c1930s**
Ibid e**WV**, Splittin' image. **1946** *Hench Coll.* **VA**, [A] U. Va. instructor
in English . . says that he never says any form of "spittin' image" than
"splittin' image." He never heard of "spittin' image" till he got away
from his home in Woodstock, Va. **1967–70** *DARE* (Qu. Z10, *If a child
looks very much like his father . . "He _____ his father."*) Infs **DC**13,
MA33, 52, **PA**7, (Is the) splitting image; **MI**61, Is the split image of.
1986 Pederson *LAGS Concordance,* 1 inf, cw**TN**, Splitting image—in
looks. **2000** in 2008 *DARE* File—Internet **AZ**, Biological father now
wants to be a part of my son's life since he has seen him and is the
splitting image of his father. **2006** *Ibid* **OH**, We had a son in January
who is a splitten image of his dad, I would say he is also a splitten image
of his grandfather.

splo n Also rarely *Jo splo, splo whiskey* [See quot 1974] **Sth,
S Midl, esp KY, TN**
Liquor, esp when illegally made and of poor quality; hence n
splo house an establishment where liquor is sold.
    1940 Rice *Inky Way* 237 **KY** (as of 1920s), Most of the owners were
bootleggers, manufacturing their elixir from the refuse fruit and vegetables collected from the garbage heaps, and selling it under the name of
"Splo." **1952** Rowan *South of Freedom* 183 **TN**, "This ain't nothin' but
rotgut liquor—just plain old Jo Splo," said this taller Negro. . . [H]is
chatter about the liquor, using the terminology for bootleg booze that I
had not heard for years, turned something over inside me. **1957** *Jet* 28
Nov 50 ne**MS**, One theory . . was that Jesse . . unwittingly discovered a
cache of "splo" (Mississippi corn whisky) and was spirited out of town
by bootleggers. **1970** *DARE* (Qu. DD21b, *General words . . for bad liquor*) Inf **KY**72, Splo; (Qu. DD27, *. . Nicknames . . for wine*) Inf **DC**11,
Splo—not sure. **1972** *NYT Article Letters* **KY**, Splo; moonshine, bootleg booze. **1974** Dabney *Mountain Spirits* 26 **Sth**, The ghetto blacks of
southern cities, moonshine's greatest consumers, . . have coined such
nicknames as . . "splo'" (because of the " 'splosion" it causes in your innards). **1977** *AmSp* 52.117 **Sth**, These terms . . , particularly *splo,* mark
the Knoxville [TN] focal area. . . Although *splo* has not yet been observed in Atlanta, D.W. Maurer tells me that it is a commonplace expression among the less fortunate alcoholics in most Southern metropolitan areas. **1985** Wilkinson *Moonshine* 28 ne**NC**, "After that they'd
serve you North Carolina Corn." It is called . . 'splo. **1986** Pederson
LAGS Concordance (*Terms for cheap whiskey and for home-brewed
beer or whiskey*) 11 infs, **scattered Gulf Region, but esp TN**, Splo; 1
inf, e**TN**, Splo—old moonshine liquor; 1 inf, e**TN**, Splo—a newer term
for cheap, poor whiskey; 1 inf, e**TN**, Splo—a little worse than white
lightning; splo drinker—a bum; 1 inf, e**FL**, Splo—moonshine; 1 inf, c**TN**,
Splo whiskey. [8 of 17 infs Black] **1991** *Durham Morning Herald*
(NC) 14 July (as of 1960s–70s) [Black], Minnie Hester's was a liquor
house, or splo house as we called them then. . . Almost anything you

might want could be had at Minnie's, from a chitterling sandwich to a
soul-rousing whitz game.

spludge v Also *spludge (it) around*
To have a lavish or showy good time, "live it up," show off;
hence vbl n *spludging.*
    1835 in 2008 *DARE* File—Internet **KY**, Edward L Royall . . has been
spludging for the last six weeks in New York. He stays at the American
Hotel goes to bed late rises at 11 a.m. puts on a Wheeler suit brushes his
hair looks three times in the glass gets a smile walks out. **1859** Potter
Hairdresser's Experience 245 **NY**, She may be spludging it around in
New York, and boasting of her family and wealth, but I know of one
transaction . . that does not add much to her credit. **1906** *DN* 3.158
nw**AR**, *Spludge around.* . . To make a display. **1914** *DN* 4.113 c**KS**,
Spludge, n. and *v.* Splurge. **1954** Daugherty *Out of Red Brush* 116 s**OH**
(as of c1900), All the young folks a ridin tried to show off when they got
in sight of the church an crowd. That's what cuttin a rusty or spludgin
meant.

spludge n [Var of *splurge*]
A lavish or showy good time—often in phrr *cut* (or *make,
take*) *a spludge* to make a lavish display.
    1831 *Essayist* II.80/2 (*OED2*) **TN**, I was naturally anxious to see a lit-
tle more of Tennessee life, and inasmuch as it was said there was to be a
great *spludge* at the shooting, I went with him. **1856** Whitcher *Bedott
Papers* 89 **NY**, She tries to cut a spludge and make folks think she s a
lady. [**1859** (1968) Bartlett *Americanisms* 112, *To cut a splurge.* . . to
make a show or display.] **1864** in 1998 Winters *Musick* 104 **IN**, We
will have to endure it the best way we can for a while longer and take a
bigger spludge when we do get home. **1892** *DN* 1.232 **KY**, *Spludge.*
"To cut a spludge." **1905** *DN* 3.95 nw**AR**, *Spludge.* . . Splurge. 'They
cut a spludge.' **1914** [see **spludge** v]. **1915** *IA City Daily Press* (IA) 2
Oct [5]/3 (newspaperarchive.com), My wife says she wants some pin
money. I'm wealthy and would like to make a spludge. How much
should I give her? **2001** in 2008 *DARE* File—Internet **NJ**, Wasn't exactly a "spludge" meal, but our most enjoyable meals were at Bon-
familles in PO. Its now closed. With the little one now, a spludge meal
for us is a food court.

spludge (it) around, spludging See **spludge** v

splunge v, n, hence ppl adj, vbl n *splunging* [Var of *plunge* v,
n, prob infl by *splash*] **Sth, S Midl, esp sAppalachians**
    1839 Marryat *Diary* 1.198, Here are two real American words:—
"Sloping"—for slinking away; "Splunging," like a porpoise. **1843**
(1916) Hall *New Purchase* 228 **IN**, There's somethin about river in it,
and it was talkin of the young doctur's splunge, made me think of the
toone. **1883** (1971) Harris *Nights with Remus* 107 **GA** [Black], Brer
B'ar he make a splunge en duck hisse'f. **1895** *Century Illustr. Mag.*
50.146 **GA**, I had no more ideas of getting married again than I had of
splunging head foremost into the very bottom o' Rudisill's mill-pond.
1904 (1913) Johnson *Highways South* 71 n**FL**, se**GA**, I know a young
lady whose parents are Baptists, but who say she'll never jine the chu'ch
if she got to be splunged or soused. **1923** in 1952 Mathes *Tall Tales* 18
s**Appalachians**, I seed that angel splunge right into the tide an' swim
like no man on earth ever swum afore. **1941** *Hall Coll.* w**NC**, e**TN**,
Splunge. . . Let's take a splunge from the divin' board. **1968** Haun
Hawk's Done Gone 223 e**TN**, She would fill the kittel to the crack with
muddy water and splunge chips and leaves down deep into it with her
hands. **1975** Chalmers *Better* 66 w**NC**, e**TN**, His woman-person . .
rinsed the clothes by splunging them in the creek. [**1986** Pederson
LAGS Concordance (*Names of streams in the neighborhood*) 1 inf,
cn**AL**, Splunge Creek.]

‡**splut** n [Cf *EDD splutter* sb. 7 "A hurry, bustle"] Cf **splutterment**
A hurry.
    1940 in 1968 Haun *Hawk's Done Gone* 187 **TN**, I noticed how big a
splut he was always in to get ready every night. But I didn't think about
who he was in such a hurry to see. **1968** *Ibid* 247, He just looked like
he was in such a splut to get away.

splutteration See **splutterment**

splutter-headed adj [Cf *EDD splutter* v. 3 "To . . talk quickly
and incoherently"]
    1970 *DARE* (Qu. HH7a, *Someone who talks too much, or too loud*) Inf
KY91, Splutter-headed.

splutterment n Also *splutteration, spluttermint* [*EDD splutter sb.* 8 "A fuss, disturbance" + **-ment**]

A commotion; a disturbance.

1859 Taliaferro *Fisher's R.* 57 **nwNC** (as of 1820s), He kep' . . sich a splutteration that I couldn't git a bead at his head. **1961** *Mt. Life* 37.1.15 **sAppalachians,** They's the biggest spluttermint in that house ever I hearn tell of, I reckon. **1967** *Ibid* 43.1.16 **sAppalachians,** This hyar old preacher he was jist a-tryin to raise his failin voice up above the uproar and spluttermint so's he could be hyared.

spodge n[1] Cf **spodge** v, **spudge** n, **spudge iron**

1 also *spodge hook:* A stick with a hook at the end used for catching catfish.

1892 [see **spodge** v 2]. **2008** *NADS Letters* **eMD,** Spodge. . . I have heard my grandfather use this as meaning a long stick with a hook used for catching carp fish during mating season. He is from the wetlands of the Eastern Shore of Maryland.

2 See quot.

1970 *DARE* (Qu. L40, *A long iron bar used to move rocks and other heavy things*) Inf **KY**72, Spodge [spaɟ].

spodge v Cf **spodge** n[1], **spudge** v

1 To stab; to thrust (something).

1907 *Life Mag. Chr. Metaphysics* 12.27 **MO,** He told her that the bee had a sharp sword . . and that he would draw it out . . and spodge it into any one he happened to meet at that time. *Ibid* 232, The frenzied doctors did go around one whole session to spodge the little ones [=vaccinate schoolchildren].

2 as vbl n *spodging:* Fishing for catfish with a spear or a stick with a hook at one end; hence n *spodger* one who does this. **KY**

1892 *Forest & Stream* 38.450 **KY,** The Kentuckians have a method of taking the big catfish . . , which they call "spodging." . . The instrument used is called a "spodge hook"—say a broom handle to which a big hook is attached. . . When the "spodger" has tracked the fish to his den he probes carefully with the butt end of his rod. If he feels the fish he thrusts the hooked end under it and with a vigorous "yank" hauls the fellow out. **1918** KY Genl. Assembly Senate *Jrl.* 2.1811, It shall be lawful for any person to catch any specie of catfish in any stream by spodging. **1954** McDowell *Iron Baby* 79 **cKY** (as of 1909), We are going right in under the rocks after them [=catfish] with our spodging hooks. . . We'll get a tubful of them. [*Ibid* 80, The spears had sharp points and inverted gaff hooks sprouting off them.] *Ibid* 81, Up by the big rocks Mr. Baptist let Harold try his hand at spodging. Mr. Baptist hooked a big one and let Harold pull him out. . . He turned loose the handle of the spodging spear and wriggled loose from Mr. Baptist. *Ibid* 82, By the time Harold had gotten dry . . the spodgers were coming back.

spodge n[2] See **spods**

spodge hook See **spodge** n[1] 1

spodger, spodging See **spodge** v 2

spods n pl |spɑdz| Also *spads, spodge*

In tobacco cultivation: =**flyings 2.**

1926 U.S. Congress House *Tobacco Statistics* 17 **KY,** The character of each leaf is known by a grade. The one closest to the ground is the lightest . . ; the one next in line is called the flyings or spods; coming on up, you have the lugs or cutters [etc]. **1944** *PADS* 2.71 **S Midl** [Tobacco words], Spads [spɑdz]. . . The lower leaves (marketable). **1959** *KY Folkl. Rec.* 5.148, *Spodge:* High grade of burley consisting of lowest leaves. **1966** *PADS* 45.23 **cnKY** [Tobacco word list], Spods [spɑdz] . . = flyings. . . "Years ago, farmers used to throw away the spods." **1967** Key *Tobacco Vocab.* 138 **MO,** Spods—Name for flyings.

spoil v Usu |spɔɪ(ə)l|; for varr see **A** below

A Pronc forms.

1 |spaɪl|; pronc-spp *spil(e).* **chiefly Sth, S Midl; formerly also NEng** *somewhat old-fash* Cf Pronc Intro 3.I.11, **boil** n[1], v

1833 *Sketches D. Crockett* 144 **KY,** I . . thought I would spile if I wasn't kivured up in salt. **1838** Gilman *S. Matron* 76 **Sth** [Black], My ole missis spile eberyting! *Ibid* 326 **MA** [White], If you will spile the puddin, you must bake it yourself. **1845** *Living Age* 4.158 **NEng,** A good story is never spiled in the tellin'. **1855** Wise *Tales Marines* 21 **VT,** I'd spile his face in no time! **1884** Jewett *Country Dr.* 91 **ME,** If

ever you set a mug of flowers into one o' the spare-rooms again and leave it there a week or ten days to spile, I'll speak about it to the doctor. **1884** *Anglia* 7.274 **Sth, S Midl** [Black], To be jes' spilin' fer = to be very anxious to. **1909** *DN* 3.374 **eAL, wGA,** Spile. . . To spoil. **1923** *DN* 5.221 **swMO,** Sp'il. . . To spoil. Past tense, Spi'lt. **1927** Adams *Congaree* 22 **cSC** [Black], Rain was comin' so fast it was spilin' de carpet. **1928** *AmSp* 3.404 **Ozarks** (as of 1916–27), In such words as *spoil* . . the *oi* takes the sound of long *i*—*spile.* **c1937** in 1976 *Weevils in the Wheat* 148 **VA** [Black], If dey bruised dey spile. **c1940** Eliason *Word Lists FL* 14 **wFL,** Spoil [spaɪl]: In rural areas. **1941** *LANE* Map 306 *(Spoiled)* **NEng,** Pronunciations of the type of [spaɪld, spaɪlt] are regarded as older though still in use by [30 infs]. [*DARE* Ed: Many others simply label it as old, out of date, or obsolete; others offer it without comment.] **1941** Writers' Program *Guide IN* 122 **csIN,** As one old-timer said, 'a music-box would spile the gals.' **1969** *DARE* (Qu. Y35, *To spoil something so that it can't be used* . . "*My new coffee pot—it's completely _____.*") Inf **IL**34, Spiled. **1975** *Appalachian Jrl.* 2.151 **wNC,** Diphthongs yield considerable variety of pronunciation. . . *Oi* becomes long *i,* as in . . *spile.* **1989** Pederson *LAGS Tech. Index* 161 **Gulf Region** *(Spoiled)* 3 infs, [spaɪl]; 2 infs, [spaɪld].

2 |spɝˑl|; pronc-sp *sperl.* **esp NYC**

1925 [see **B** below]. **1930s** in 1944 *ADD* **NYC,** Spoil. . . [spəˑl] sperl. Freq. attributed. **1938** Liebling *Back Where* 72 **NYC,** What did he do only sperl a lot of t'ings dat gave people what to eat? **2006** in 2008 *DARE* File—Internet **NYC,** A lackluster offensive outing on Friday night sperled Mike Mussina's decent outing.

3 |spɔ(ə)l| and varr; pronc-sp *spawl.* **esp NEng, Sth, S Midl**

1941 in 1944 *ADD* **MD,** Spoil. . . Spawled fruit. **1941** *LANE* Map 306 *(Spoiled),* [Proncs of the types [spɔəl, spɔɛl] are **scattered, but esp freq sNEng and wNEng.**] **1989** Pederson *LAGS Tech. Index* 161 *(Spoiled)* 14 infs, **Gulf Region,** [spɔld]. **2003** *DARE* File—Internet **MD,** Baltimore's speech shows a distinctly Southern character. The diphthong *oi* is flattened to *aw: bawl* (boil), *spawled* (spoiled).

4 Addit varr; see quots.

1941 *LANE* Map 306 *(Spoiled)* 5 infs, **CT,** [spo(ə)ld]; 5 infs, **scattered NEng,** [Proncs of the types [spaɛlt, spɛld]]; 1 inf, **cnCT,** [spʌˑɪl]; 1 inf, **ceRI,** [spoʳld]. **1989** Pederson *LAGS Tech. Index* 161 **Gulf Region** *(Spoiled)* 5 infs, [spɔɪ(d)]; 4 infs, [spɔɪj(d)]; 1 inf, [spoʊlt]; 1 inf, [spoʊld]; 1 inf, [spo]; 1 inf, [spoʊɪd]; 1 inf, ['spɔlɪd]; 1 inf, [spɔrld]; 1 inf, [spɔrld̥].

B Gram forms.

Past, past pple, ppl adj: usu *spoiled;* also, esp for ppl adj, var forms with devoiced final consonant; see quots; pronc-spp *sperlt, spilt, spoilt.* Note: The form *spoilt* seems to have been std well into the 20th cent. *now esp freq among rural speakers and among speakers with little formal educ; somewhat old-fash*

1815 *N. Amer. Rev.* 1.27, 'Twas built by some journeyman mason of Nature's;/ And spoilt by its master's continued neglect. **1867** Harris *Sut Lovingood Yarns* 265 **TN,** The ole cuss wer pow'fly 'stonish'd hisself, . . fur hit spilt Wat's title tu choke him tu deth. **1893** *DN* 1.278 **nwCT,** Spile . . [past and past pple:] spilt. **1899** (1912) Green *VA Folk-Speech* 406, Spilt. . . A form of *spoilt.* **1909** in 2003 *DARE* File **wMA,** Sledding is spoilt. **1923** [see **A1** above]. **1925** in 1944 *ADD* **NYC,** Spoil. . . sperlt. **1926** *AmSp* 1.419 **Okefenokee GA,** We 'uz in there too long, an' 'e sp'ilt before we got out er there. **1941** *LANE* Map 306 *(Spoiled)* **NEng,** [Proncs of the type [spaɪlt] are **esp freq nNEng;** those of the type [spɔɪlt] occur **throughout NEng.**]; 1 inf, **ceCT,** '[spɔɪlt], or is it [spɔɪld]?'; 1 inf, **neMA,** [spaʒɪʔt], reported as heard, but used when off-guard; 1 inf, **neMA,** [spaɪl̥t], when off-guard; 1 inf, **cnMA,** [spɔɪlt], older pron.; 1 inf, **swNH,** [spɔɪlt], modern, natural pron.; 1 inf, **cwNH,** [spɔɪlt], usual pron.; 1 inf, **sME,** [spoˬɪlt], older than [spoˬɪld̥]; 1 inf, **sME,** [spaˤɪlt], very old, 'countrified.' **1953** Atwood *Survey of Verb Forms* 21, Spoil. . . The past participle (adjective) form is recorded in the context "The meat is (spoiled)." The only two forms in use in the East are *spoiled* /spɔild/ and *spoilt* /spɔilt/ (with the variants /spaild/ and /spailt/). In N. Eng. and N.Y. the form with /d/ predominates strongly . . with the /t/ form characteristic of (but not confined to) old-fashioned speech. In most other areas of the East the /t/ form is more common. **1965–70** *DARE* (Qu. Z14b, . . "*That child is _____.*") 81 Infs, **scattered,** (Really) spoilt; **AR**40, **GA**37, **MN**15, **MO**3, **NY**70, **OK**18, **VA**102, Spoilt brat; **CA**59, 202, **KY**19, **OK**28, **TX**45, **VA**42, Spoilt rotten; **FL**10, Spoilt to death; **VT**8, Been spoilt [Of all Infs responding to the question, 65% were old, 29% comm type 5, 27% gs educ or less; of those giving these responses, 75% were old, 52% comm type 5, 47% gs educ or less.]; (Qu. K9, *If one quarter of a cow's udder does not give* *milk . . she's* _____) 11 Infs, **scattered Sth, S Midl,** (One) quarter spoilt; **CO**4, **KY**32, **MO**1, **WY**4, Spoilt; **CA**124, **KY**35, **OK**20, Has (*or got*) a spoilt bag; **IN**27, One tit spoilt; **NM**3, One part spoilt; **MO**4, Spoilt tit; **TX**42, Spoilt bag; (Qu. Y35, . . "*My new coffee pot—it's completely* _____.") 9 Infs, **scattered,** Spoilt; (Qu. H46, *When meat begins to go bad*) Infs **AR**47, **KS**18, **MD**19, **MA**69, **VA**1, Spoilt; (Qu. H58, *Milk that's just beginning to become sour*) Inf **KY**12, Spoilt; (Qu. I8, *When root vegetables get old*) Infs **MN**6, **NY**68, Spoilt; (Qu. K7, *What sickness can a cow get in her udder*) Inf **KY**39, Spoilt bag; (Qu. K41, *A horse with its tail cut short*) Inf **LA**29, Spoilt horse; (Qu. K42, *A horse that is rough, wild, or dangerous*) Inf **LA**29, Spoilt horse; (Qu. K43, *A horse that was not intentionally bred, or bred by accident*) Inf **LA**29, Spoilt; (Qu. Z14a, . . "*Everyone* _____ *that child.*") Inf **OK**42, Get him spoilt; (Qu. Z16, *A small child who is rough, misbehaves, and doesn't obey, you'd call him a* _____) Inf **WA**13, Spoilt; **TX**35, Spoilt chicken; **NY**68, Spoilt kid; (Qu. KK7, *When wood . . is starting to decay inside*) Inf **MA**58, Gone spoilt; (Qu. KK21, . . "*They ran the wagon over the coffee pot and* _____.") Inf **NH**14, Spoilt it. **1975** Allen *LAUM* 2.27 **Upper MW** (as of c1950), In the eastern and North Central states *spoilt* is most frequent in Midland speech territory. Consistently, in the U[pper] M[idwest] it is most frequent in Iowa. Again, in the eastern and North Central states, *spoilt* is more likely to be used by old-fashioned and less-educated speakers. Consistently, in the UM one-fourth of Type I infs. [=old, with little educ] have *spoilt* but only one-tenth of the Type II's [=mid-aged, with approx hs educ] have it. It barely survives among educated speakers. **1989** Pederson *LAGS Tech. Index* 161 **Gulf Region,** 47 infs, [spɔɪəlt]; 16 infs, [spɔɪlt]. **2000** Shores *Tangier Is.* 248 **Chesapeake Bay,** Nonstandard forms showing past times are common: . . *boilt . . spoilt.*

C Senses.

1 To render (livestock) unmanageable; hence ppl adj *spoiled* rendered unmanageable; hard to control. **chiefly West**

1929 Dobie *Vaquero* 105 **West,** After the great stampedes on Solomon River we pointed our herd north by west for the River Platte. The cattle were "spoiled" now and they gave us lots of trouble. **1929** *AmSp* 5.63 **NE** [Cattle country talk], An intelligent "bronco buster" will "break" a good horse to saddle without "spoiling" him, i.e., making him furiously fear and resist saddles and mounters. **c1938** in Lib. of Congress *Amer. Memory: WPA Life Hist.* (Internet) **TX** (as of c1898), I remember the N U Bar outfit had a spoiled horse that nobody could ride. He'd pitch awhile and if he didn't throw the rider he would fall down and then turn over on him. *Ibid* **TX** (as of c1880), Every time I got on him he would rear up and fall over backward. I went to the house and told Mrs. Boone I had a horse that had been spoiled. She called her son . . [who] told her there had been two men tried to break him and couldn't do anything with him. **1944** Adams *Western Words* 151, *Spoiled herd*—One that has acquired the habit of stampeding at every opportunity. *Spoiled horse*—One abused at the breaking period until he has had his character ruined—a man-made outlaw. **1954** *True* June 66 **TX,** There were outlaw, or "spoiled" cattle—tame cattle gone wild or the maverick offspring of tame cattle gone wild. **1968** *DARE* (Qu. K42, *A horse that is rough, wild, or dangerous*) Inf **LA**29, Spoilt horse—one that gets out of control after he gets broke.

2 with *out, off:* To erase; to make an erasure. **chiefly Sth** *esp freq among Black speakers*

1867 Bonnell *Manual Prose Comp.* 52, *Spoil out*—for *rub out* or *erase.* **1894** *Amer. Missionary* 48.262 **cAL** [Black], The words of our pupils sometimes need translating, and they continually interest even a teacher of long-standing among them. Only recently the writer has come upon . . "I've done spoiled it out," the excuse of one who had erased his examples before the teacher could correct the same. **1898** Lloyd *Country Life* 132 **AL,** We agreed to spit on the slate and spile out and start over. **1917** Rudd–Bond *From Slavery* 21 **AR** [Black], The overseer had some of the slaves make brooms of brush and spoil out the mule and wagon tracks to keep the Yankees from following. **1926** Puckett *Folk Beliefs S. Negro* 284, The woman quickly paid him in order to get him to "spoil out the conjure" which he did by simply erasing it [=a double crossmark in the dirt] with the toe of his shoe. **1967** *DARE* File **Chicago IL** [Black], *Spoil it out* (or *off*)—erase it. **a1979** in 2004 Fagaly *Tools* 79 **eAL** [Black], Dont you know its / written and you /cant spoil it out.

spoiled adj

1 Of a female animal's udder or teat: unable to produce milk. **chiefly W Midl, Lower Missip Valley, West** See Map Cf **three-titter**

1851 MI State Ag. Soc. *Trans. for 1850* 127, The heifer calf has

sucked a cow that was not worth milking, on account of a spoiled bag. **1868** MO State Bd. Ag. *Annual Rept. for 1868* 135, A man should spot . . ewes with spoilt, or partially spoilt bags. **1907** IN State Bd. Ag. *Annual Rept. for 1905–06* 241, She [=a sow] may be returned to suckle them . . till there may be no danger of . . spoiled teats. **1941** Dobie *Longhorns* 169, Nobody ever saw a Longhorn cow on the range with a spoiled bag. **1960** Criswell *Resp. to PADS 20* **Ozarks,** Spoiled (or *spoilt*) *udder.* . . Udder of a cow which has usually become useless because of failure to extract the milk. May happen to a cow who stays out in the wilds. Not so common now. **1965–70** *DARE* (Qu. K9, *If one quarter of a cow's udder does not give milk . . she's* _____) 13 Infs, **esp W Midl, Lower Missip Valley, TX,** One quarter spoiled (or spoilt); 9 Infs, **esp W Midl, Lower Missip Valley, TX,** Spoiled (or spoilt); **AR**55, **CO**33, **GA**7, **TX**54, 69, (Got a) spoiled tit; **IN**32, **KS**11, **TX**39, Quarter spoiled (or spoilt); **CA**124, **KY**35, **TX**42, (Has a) spoilt bag; **CA**87, **LA**10, Got a spoiled bag; **CA**210, **MO**1, Spoiled bag (or udder); **AR**21, **TN**17, Has a spoiled tit (or sack); **KS**5, **KY**64, It's (or her bag was) spoiled; **MD**24, **TX**66, Partly (or part of her bag is) spoiled; **CA**87, Got one spoiled side; **FL**36, That tit's spoiled; **IN**27, One tit spoilt; **KY**86, One side spoiled; **MD**24, One tit was spoiled; **MO**4, Spoilt tit; **MO**10, Bag is spoiled; **NM**3, One part spoiled; **OK**20, Got a spoilt bag; **TX**43, Spoiled-tit cow; [**CA**136, Spoil bag; **MO**9, Spoil sack;] (Qu. K7, *What sickness can a cow get in her udder—for example, if she's left unmilked too long?*) Infs **CA**139, **GA**7, Spoiled bag; **KY**39, Spoilt bag; [**MS**46, Spoil; **TX**66, Spoilbag cow.] **2007** in 2008 *DARE* File—Internet, Ewes with spoiled udders have decreased or no future production value.

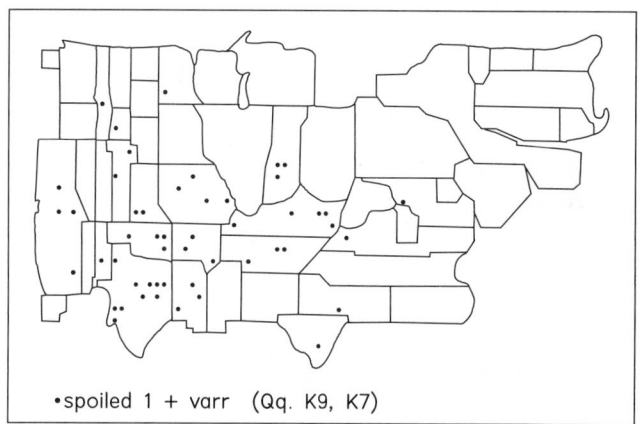

•spoiled 1 + varr　(Qq. K9, K7)

2 See **spoil C1.**

spoil-market n Pronc-sp *spile-market* [See quot]

A **horned rush** (here: *Rhynchospora corniculata*).

1937 *Torreya* 37.96 **csSC,** *Rhynchospora corniculata.* . . Spile- [*Torreya:* spoil-] market, . . from the effect of the presence of its akenes in reducing the grade of rice; a name persisting from the now rather remote days of rice farming.

spoil off (or out) See **spoil C2**

spoilt See **spoil B**

spoke See **speak** v A3

spoked, spoken(ed) See **speak** v A2

spon n [Abbr for **spondulicks 1**]

1900 *DN* 2.63 [College slang], *Spon.* . . Money. **1967** *DARE* (Qu. U19a, . . *Money in general: "He's certainly got the* _____.") Inf **NC**38, Spon. [Inf old]

spondulicks n Also *spondoolix, spondulics(es), spondulix, spondulux, sponjewlicks*

1 used as mass noun or pl: Money, dollars; also rarely *spondulic(k)* money.

1847 *Tioga Eagle* (Wellsborough PA) [22 Dec 4]/3 (newspaperarchive.com), [Advt:] Bill has got the *rocks, tin, spoons, spondulix,* or *John Davis,* to pay for any quantity of *green hides.* **1856** Thomson *Pluri-bus-tah* 113, Spondulicks, or ye Tin. **1860** *Vanity Fair* 17 Nov 247, My friend the Senior got out of spondulix, and borrowed it to spout for the purpose of bucking the Tiger. **1872** *Harper's New Mth. Mag.* 46.156, You will never get any spondulick from Ebenezer Weatherby. **1885** Cable *Dr. Sevier* 341 **LA,** As she laughingly and confidentially informed Dr. Sevier, "raked in the sponjewlicks." **1887** (1892) Hinman

Corporal Si Klegg 113, "I'll jest give ye five dollars. . . " "Hand over yer spondulix." **1905** *DN* 3.65 **eNE,** *Spondulicks. . .* Money. "They have the spondulicks." **1909** *DN* 3.374 **eAL, wGA,** *Spondulix. . .* Money. **1915** (1916) Johnson *Highways New Engl.* 290, 'That's a good idee,' I told him, 'but supposin' a feller ain't got the spondulux to pay for't?' **1948** Sandburg *Remembrance* 821 **IL** (as of c1850), He's retail and wholesale, spondoolix to burn, stuck on me and jealous as a catfish in spring. **1953** Macfadden–Gauvreau *Dumbbells* 220 **MO,** If they made a "showing" they walked out with the "spondulic," as it was called in Missouri. *Ibid* 228, We got the million spondulics from the banker. (In the case of that amount of spondulics, I am informed that Missouri borrowers use the plural: spondulicses.—Collaborator's note.) **1965–70** *DARE* (Qu. U19a, . . *Money in general: "He's certainly got the _____."*) 44 Infs, **scattered,** Spondulicks; (Qu. U20, . . *Dollars . . "It cost a hundred _____."*) Inf **NY**205, Spondulicks. [40 of 45 Infs old] **1966** Barnes–Jensen *Dict. UT Slang* 40, *Spondulics . .* cash, money. **1976** Hobbs–Specht *Tisha* 299 **AK,** "You got a hundred dollars, Fred?" he called back. "A hundred spondulicks says I make it to Cross Creek before ya!" **2003** *Chicago Tribune* (IL) 7 Nov Friday sec 20, For a little spondulix, fans' dreams of performing in the musical can come true with a high bid in the . . annual Casting Auction.
2 Transf: see quots. Cf **cadulix**

1906 Casey *Parson's Boys* 84 **sIL** (as of c1860), William asked Dick if it [=a Roman candle] couldn't be made to shoot some more, but that expert said no, the "spondulicks" were all out of it. **1952** Brown *NC Folkl.* 1.593, *Spondulix. . .* The usual meaning is money, but in some sections the term refers to sexual desire.—Central and east.

spong See **spung**

sponge n
1 Std: any of var porifers; the absorbent skeleton of such an animal. For other names of var spp see **dead-man's-fingers 2, glove sponge, grass ~, hardhead 4, loggerhead 7, redbeard, sheepswool**
2 See **sponge mushroom.**

sponge crab n [See quot 1953] **Chesapeake Bay**
An egg-bearing female blue crab.
[**1890** *Century Dict.* 5852 **Chesapeake Bay,** *Sponge. . .* The coral, or mass of eggs, under the abdomen of a crab.] **1928** *Galveston Daily News* (TX) 16 Sept 1/7, Evidence that the supply of hard shell crab is being rapidly depleted in the coastal waters of Texas, due to no protection being afforded the female or sponge crab during the spawning season, is indicated in comparative catch figures for that state and the neighboring state of Louisiana and Mississippi. **1933** *Sun* (Baltimore MD) 23 May 20/2 **Chesapeake Bay,** The repeal of the law . . has allowed the crabbers a year to catch the egg-bearing, or sponge crab. **1935** *Ibid* 15 Jan 3/2 **Chesapeake Bay,** The Virginians asked that the prohibition against catching sponge crabs—females during the breeding season—be taken out of the code. **1940** *Panama City News–Herald* (FL) 19 July 6/2, The State Board of Conservation again has adopted a closed season . . on all female sponge crabs in all waters of the State. **1953** MD Dept. Educ. *Our Underwater Farm* 26 **Chesapeake Bay,** The eggs are attached to the underside of the female and resemble a sponge, almost one-half as large as the crab itself. In this stage crabs are called sponge crabs. **1968** *DARE* Tape **MD**45, They call 'em a sponge crab. . . They call 'em sponge crab, but they're a mother crab. **1984** *DARE* File **Chesapeake Bay** [Watermen's vocab], Sponge crab, brood crab, cushion crab, . . busted sook [etc]. **1988** *Brazosport Facts* (Clute TX) 27 Apr [521]/4 (newspaperarchive.com), If you catch a "sponge" crab . . throw her back. It's illegal to keep them. **2005** *FL Times–Union* (Jacksonville) 22 Mar sec B 1 (Internet) **GA,** *Atlanta*—A bill extending an existing ban on harvesting egg-bearing blue crabs along the Georgia coast won House approval Monday. . . Egg-bearing blue crabs—or "sponge" crabs—are female crabs that carry eggs on their bodies.

sponge hummer n
A **hummingbird 1** (here: *Archilochus alexandri*).
1953 Jewett *Birds WA* 384, *Black-chinned Hummingbird. Archilochus alexandri. . .* Other names: . . Sponge Hummer [etc].

sponge mushroom n Also *sponge(-type mushroom)* [See quot 2002] **chiefly N Cent, IA** See Map
Usu a **morel** n[2], but also a bolete; see quots.
1905 *Star* (Kansas City MO) 21 Apr 8/1, A variety of sponge mushrooms will be offered at 20 cents a quart. **1908** Hard *Mushroom Edible*

486, *Morchella esculenta. . .* The Common Morel. . . It grows from two to four inches high and is known by most people as the Sponge mushroom. **1925** *Book of Rural Life* 6.3722, There are numerous wild mushrooms that offer delicious food and are easy to identify with certainty. Prominent among these are the *morels,* or *sponge mushrooms.* **1965–70** *DARE* (Qu. S18, *A kind of mushroom that grows like a globe . . sometimes gets as big as a man's head*) Infs **IL**7, **IN**54, **OH**64, **WI**37, Sponge mushroom(s); **IA**38, **OH**66, Sponge; **IN**26, Sponge musheroon; (Qu. I37, *Small plants shaped like an umbrella that grow in woods and fields—which are safe to eat*) Inf **IL**27, Sponges; **IN**7, Sponge-type mushrooms—morels; **IA**22, Sponge mushrooms, the northern Illinois morel; **IA**30, Sponge mushroom [FW:=the morel]; **OH**95, Sponge mushrooms; (Qu. S19) Inf **OH**56, Sponge mushrooms; (Qu. S26e) Inf **MD**23, Sponge mushrooms—grow under apple or oak trees, stem thick as finger, football-shaped mushrooms. Good to eat. **1973** *Foxfire 2* 53 **sAppalachians,** [Caption:] Morel *(Morchella esculenta, M. crassipes, M. angusticeps)* (sponge mushroom, markel, merkel). **2002** *DARE* File—Internet **IL,** The bolete is fairly common and several members of the family are edible and choice. In some circles it is called the sponge mushroom because its underside resembles a bath sponge. Here's the problem with regional names again, the morel is also called the sponge mushroom because it resembles a scrap of sea sponge.

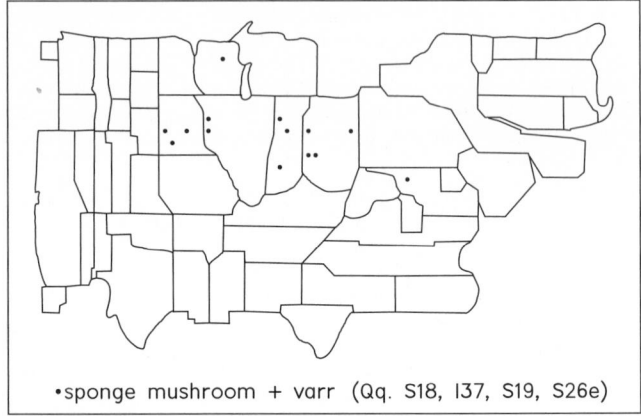

• sponge mushroom + varr (Qq. S18, I37, S19, S26e)

sponge starter See **sponge yeast**

sponge tree n [*OED2* 1829 →]
A **huisache** (here: *Acacia farnesiana*).
1861 Wood *Class-Book* 299 **Gulf States,** *Vachellia. . . Sponge Tree. . .* Fl[ower]s in globular heads, yellow. *V. Farnesiana. . .* Grows about N. Orleans . . and along the Gulf to St. Marks, Fla. **1890** *Century Dict.* 5853, *Sponge-tree. . .* An evergreen shrub or small tree, *Acacia Farnesiana . .* found in the United States along the Gulf of Mexico. **1976** Bailey–Bailey *Hortus Third* 5, *[Acacia] Farnesiana. . .* Sponge tree.

sponge-type mushroom See **sponge mushroom**

sponge yeast n Also *sponge starter*
Leavening maintained or prepared in the form of a fermenting batter or sponge.
1966–69 *DARE* (Qu. H17, . . *Kinds [of yeast]*) Inf **OK**19, Everlasting yeast—same as sponge yeast—made at home by adding a starter to potato water and sugar; **PA**9, Cake, powdered, sponge; **SD**8, Sponge yeast—carried over—use [yeast] cakes and potato water; **TX**58, Sponge yeast. **1973** Allen *LAUM* 1.284 (as of c1950), Terms for the kinds of homemade liquid or sponge yeast used before the advent of the commercial cake variety. . . *sponge yeast* [1 inf, **NE**]. **2002** *DARE* File—Internet, A dough with an added sourdough starter also takes longer to rise, than when using packaged or sponge yeast. *Ibid,* Start a sourdough or sponge starter from scratch. . . The "sponge method" is when a regular pancake-like batter is made from the part of the flour . . and . . water, plus a third one being packaged yeast or a piece of an active sourdough starter.

sponjewlicks See **spondulicks**

spoo See **spew 2**

spoofed up adj phr [Var of *spiffed up*]
Smartly dressed; prettied up; hence adj *spoofy* smart, elegant.
1964 in 1982 *Barrick Coll.* **csPA,** *Spoofy*—fancy, elegant, elaborate. "The squirrels with the spoofy tails is the young ones." **1967** *DARE*

(Qu. W37, *When a woman puts on her good clothes and tries to look her best . . she's* _____) Inf **NY**20, Spoofed up. **1982** *Barrick Coll.* **csPA,** *Spoofed up*—fancy, elegantly dressed. **2001** in 2003 *DARE* File—Internet **seMA,** My new nephew is being christened on Sunday and Shawn and I are the godparents. So I have to get spoofed up a little.

spook n [Du *spook,* Ger *Spuk*]
1 A ghost, spirit, or apparition. **scattered exc Inland Sth** See Map and Map Section Cf **haunt B**
  1737 *NY Weekly Jrl.* (NY) 16 May 1/2, Read thou the Books,/ That frighten Spooks,/ When I am gone to lay them. **1794** *Greenleaf's NY Jrl.* (NY) 29 Oct 3/5, [Advt:] *Greenleaf's . . Almanack. . .* Containing . . The cracking of the crockery, a poetic Dialogue, designed to ridicule the old-wives notions of spooks, signs, wonders, and tokens. **1815** Humphreys *Yankee in England* 108, *Spook* (a word used by the Low Dutch in some parts of America), apparition, ghost, hobgoblin. **1886** Amer. Philol. Assoc. Proc. 17.xii e**PA,** "Spook," from Spūk, a 'ghost' or 'hobgoblin,' . . is, in this region, confined for the most part to the descendants of the Pennsylvania Germans. **1905** *DN* 3.20 c**CT,** Spook. . . A ghost. **1907** *DN* 3.218 nw**AR,** Spook. . . A ghost. **1930** Shoemaker *1300 Words* 58 c**PA Mts** (as of c1900), *Spook*—A ghost, or apparition. **1937** Gardner *Folkl. Schoharie* 95 ce**NY,** We have lots of spook houses near Jefferson, and here is a story about one of them. **1965–70** *DARE* (Qu. EE41, *A hobgoblin that is used to threaten children and make them behave*) 37 Infs, **scattered, but less freq S Atl, Inland Sth, Upper MW, Rocky Mts,** Spook(s); (Qu. CC17, *Imaginary animals or monsters that people . . tell tales about—especially to tease greenhorns*) 16 Infs, 13 **east of Missip R,** Spooks; **NJ**41, Spook bridge; **MN**35, Spook stories; (Qu. C35, *Nicknames for the different parts of your town or city*) Inf **CA**79, Spook Canyon; (Qu. D21, *A small, poorly-built house, or one in rundown condition*) Inf **WI**35, Spook house; (Qu. X52, *. . A person . . who had been sick was looking* _____) Inf **PA**244, Like a spook; (Qu. BB61b, *. . Joking names for a cemetery*) Infs **MT**4, **WA**22, Spook place; **NC**88, Spook town; **CT**11, Where the spooks are; (Qu. CC14, *. . Where one person supposedly casts a spell over another*) Inf **LA**15, Put the spooks on; (Qu. CC15, *When people say there are ghosts in a certain place, or when it gives you a creepy feeling to go near it: "They say that the old house is* _____*"*) Infs **MI**76, **NM**5, Full of spooks; **MA**1, Got spooks in it; (Qu. CC16, *A small light that seems to dance or flicker over a marsh or swamp at night*) Inf **WI**30, Spooks. **1979** Jordan *Yesterday in TX Hill Country* 134, Spooks and ghosts did not bother us, but there were several families that had frequent encounters. **1989** Pederson *LAGS Tech. Index* 337 **Gulf Region** *(Spooks)* 623 infs, Ghosts; 250 infs, Haunts; 134 infs, Spooks.

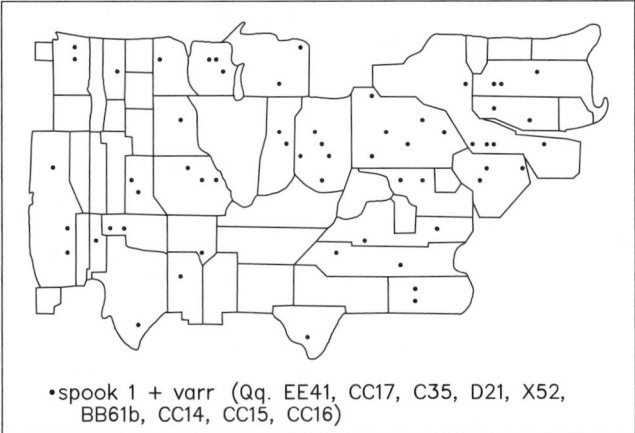

•spook 1 + varr (Qq. EE41, CC17, C35, D21, X52, BB61b, CC14, CC15, CC16)

2 A Black person. Cf **smoke n 1**
  [**1937** *AmSp* 12.181 [Jazz slang], In general a black musician is a 'boog' and a white, a 'spook.'] **1945** L. Shelly *Hepcats Jive Talk Dict.* 17/2 (*OED2*), Spook. . . frightened negro. **1964** *PADS* 42.29 **Chicago IL,** Negro. . . *Spook, spade,* and *jazzbo* were . . elicited only from Negroes in this survey, but these three, especially the first two, are common in the speech of Caucasian Chicagoans. **1965** Little *Autobiog. Malcolm X* 48 [Black], You wait until you see a spooks' dance! Man, our own people carry on! **1965–70** *DARE* (Qu. HH28, *Names and nicknames . . for people of foreign background: Negro*) 11 Infs, **esp Atlantic,** Spook; **CA**81, Spook—a Negro's word for his race [Inf Black]; **PA**236, Nigger[,] black[,] spook. [7 of 13 Infs Black] **1969** *Current Slang* 3.3.10 **OH,** Spook. . . Negro male.—College students, both sexes.

1989 Pederson *LAGS Tech. Index* 250 **Gulf Region** (Negro) 11 infs, Spook; 1 inf, Black spook.

spook light n
=will-o'-the-wisp 1.
  1907 *Washington Post* (DC) 12 Feb 6/7, [Headline:] Spook Light Saved Train. **1908** Megargel–Mason *Car & Lady* 72, You can put it down it's one of those spook lights you read about in books. Say—I walked four miles or more and that light never got any nearer than it is now. **1946** *Star* (Kansas City MO) 19 May sec C 1/4 **Ozarks,** In The Star office we have received reports of these "spook" lights for many years. **1965–70** *DARE* (Qu. CC16, *A small light that seems to dance or flicker over a marsh or swamp at night*) 11 Infs, **scattered,** Spook light. [9 Infs old] **2002** *DARE* File—Internet, The Hornet Spook Light located 11 miles southwest of Joplin, Missouri has been appearing since at least the late 1800's. *Ibid,* Vander, NC is a spot in the road, 3.5 miles SE of Fayetteville. . . The town's claim to fame is a spook light seen along the railroad tracks near Old Vander Road.

spooky See **spucky**

spook yeast n **chiefly N Cent** Cf **hex yeast, old witch 2, witch yeast**
=emptins 1.
  1911 (1927) *Inglenook Cook Book* 119 **IL,** *To Make Bread with Spook Yeast*—Spook yeast is a liquid. . . After the yeast is started some should be saved from one baking, to bake with the next time, by sealing it up in a fruit jar. . . 1 cake of yeast foam . . 1 cup of warm, unsalted potato beer . . one tablespoonful of sugar. **1950** *WELS* (*What is used to raise bread before baking? Describe different kinds*) 3 Infs, **WI,** Spook yeast; 1 Inf, cs**WI,** Spook yeast—a little kept on hand to start yeast next time baking; 1 Inf, ce**WI,** Spook yeast—made with potato water, sugar, and yeast foam, and saved from baking to baking; 1 Inf, cs**WI,** Spook yeast—kept from one baking to another; *(Special kinds of bread made now or in past years in your neighborhood)* 1 Inf, se**WI,** Spook yeast bread. **1968–70** *DARE* (Qu. H17, *. . Kinds [of yeast]*) Infs **IL**117, **WI**29, Spook yeast [FW sugg]; **IL**134, Spook yeast—use a sponge—keep in a sponge, save up a while; **WI**5, Spook yeast—old term. **1968** *DARE* Tape **IN**3, There was spook yeast, jug yeast, and witch yeast. . . There's not really much difference between 'em, but different people had different names for 'em. . . And then if it was good . . it begin to ooze and come up and come down over your can. And that was the spooks in your yeast. **1973** Allen *LAUM* 1.284 **Upper MW** (as of c1950), Terms for the kinds of homemade liquid or sponge yeast used before the advent of the commercial cake variety. . . *Spook yeast . .* is the term of a Crow Wing, Minnesota, housewife who describes the variety as sweetened and salted potato water into which a cake of yeast has been put. Others in the community, she said, know the term. **1995** *DARE* File cs**WI** (as of 1930s), Spook yeast—the liquid mixture. Known in Cottage Grove, 1930's—old-fashioned then.

spool bush n Cf **spindle tree**
See quot.
  1975 Gould *ME Lingo* 270, *Spool bush*—The term applies to several dooryard shrubs and small trees with botanical names Maine housewives never knew. The *spool bush* is a pith-wood, and when the pith was pushed from the center of a branch, the hollow piece left made a useful spool or bobbin that could sit over a peg. Almost all early Maine homes had *spool bushes* as well as lilacs, *Balm o' Gileads,* and other traditional flora; and while about everything had its own name, the *spool bush* remained the *spool bush.* Anybody of timid nature, unwilling to assert himself, may be called a *spool bush*—no backbone, no guts, a spineless jellyfish.

spool of plaid (sewing) silk n Also *spool of plaid thread*
A nonexistent item used as the basis of a practical joke.
  1967–69 *DARE* (Qu. HH14, *Ways of teasing a beginner or inexperienced person—for example, by sending him for a 'left-handed monkey wrench': "Go get me* _____.*"*) Infs **CT**16, **MA**20, Spool of plaid (sewing) silk; **NY**34, Spool of plaid thread.

spoolwood n esp **ME**
Wood, usu that of a **paper birch** (here: *Betula papyrifera*), of a quality suitable for making spools or other small items.
  1879 in 2003 (acc) Lexis–Nexis Legal Research *State Case Law: ME* (Internet), Hathorn cut about 400 cords of spool wood from said lot. **1881** in 2003 *DARE* File—Internet ce**CT,** Wanted.—300 cords of White Birch Spool Wood in the month of November, for which we will pay

cash on delivery. The National Thread Co. Mansfield Centre. **1888** *Garden and Forest* 1.506 **ME,** The wood used in the manufacture of spools is an item of no small importance already in the forest-crop of some of the Northern States. . . The wood of the Canoe Birch is used almost exclusively for this purpose, although the Gray Birch is used also in small quantities. Maine, and especially Piscataquis County, is now the headquarters of the spool-wood industry. . . The wood for this purpose must be clear and entirely free of knots and other imperfections. **1894** *Jrl. Amer. Folkl.* 7.98 **NH,** *Betula papyrifera* . . spool-wood. **1897** *New Engl. Mag.* 22.237 **ME,** In addition to the usual shipments of fruit box shooks to the Mediterranean and spoolwood to Scotland, there have gone abroad two cargoes of deals. **2002** *DARE* File—Internet **ME,** White Birch. . . Spoolwood. . . $156.48/cord.

spoon n, v Usu |spun|; also *esp* NEast |spʊn|; also |spʌn, sprun|; for addit varr see quots Pronc-spp *spoom, spun* Cf **food**

A Pronc varr.

1795 Dearborn *Columbian Grammar* 139, *List of Improprieties.* . . Spunful for Spoonful. **1890** *DN* 1.6 **cNY,** The sound [ʊ] instead of [u] in . . spoon. **1896** *DN* 1.425 **NEng, c,s,wNY,** *Spoon:* pron. spun, common. **1905** *DN* 3.57 **eNE,** In *spoon* [u] sometimes becomes [ʌ]. Words like *spoon* . . generally shorten the vowel to [ʊ]. **1909** *DN* 3.416 **nME,** *Spoon.* . . Pronounced [spʊn]. **1941** *LANE* Map 249 *(Mountain laurel)* 14 infs, **sNH, c,neMA,** [All infs who offered the terms *spoon bush, spoonhunch, spoonhunt,* and *spoonwood* used proncs of the types [spʊn-, spʊᵊn-].] **1950** *WELS Suppl.* **cswI,** Spoon [spuˣn]. . . [used by] 80+ Yankee . . farmwife. **1959** *VT Hist.* 27.159, *Spoon* [spʌn] . . pronc. Common. Rural areas. **1982** Slone *How We Talked* 32 **eKY** (as of c1950), *Spoom*—spoon. **1989** Pederson *LAGS Tech. Index* 69 **Gulf Region,** *Spoon.* [714 infs offered proncs of the type [spun(z)]; 42 infs, proncs of the type [sprun(z)]; 5 infs, proncs of the type [spʊn].] **2002** *DARE* File **NYC** (as of 1950s–60s), *Spoon* was commonly pronounced [ˈspuˌən] among White, working-class ethnics.

‡B As noun.

The hollow (of a footprint). [Cf *OED2 spoon* sb. 5.a, b "*Obs.*"]

c1938 in 1970 Hyatt *Hoodoo* 2.1834 [Black], Take dat [=a splinter from the footboard of a grave] an' stick dat down in de simple thing as makin' dey track. Dey'll make a track dataway. Don't put it in de *spoon* [Hyatt: hollow] of de track.

C As verb.

To court; to show amorous affection; hence vbl n *spooning;* n *spooner.* [*OED2* 1831 →] *old-fash*

1869 *Overland Mth.* 3.568 **West,** Instead of my triumphs reciting / I'm spooning on Joseph—heigh-ho! **1870** *Scribner's Mth.* 1.224, *Spooning!* Well, I tried it once—/ Acted like an awful calf—/ Said I *really* loved her; then / You should just have heard her laugh. **1905** *DN* 3.20 **cCT,** *Spoon.* . . To show foolish fondness, even in public. **1907** *DN* 3.218 **nwAR,** *Spoon.* . . To show foolish fondness, even in public. **1927** *AmSp* 2.365 **cwWV,** *Spoon* . . to court. "They spooned all night." **1932** Randolph *Ozark Mt. Folks* 124, Sometimes there is a chance to sit on the grass beside the spring branch and "spoon" a bit—they still call it spooning in the Ozark country. **1933** Williamson *Woods Colt* 118 **Ozarks,** "You been a-spoonin'. Come on, let's see your knees, if thar's dirt on 'em!" Windy and Jee Darby guffaw at that. **1951** West *Witch Diggers* 36 **IN,** If she come over with Bert she's had her fill of spooning for one night. **1965–70** *DARE* (Qu. AA8, *When people make too much of a show of affection in a public place* . . "*There they were at the church supper _____ [with each other].*") 28 Infs, **scattered,** Spooning; **KY24,** Spooning in public; **MO17,** Spooners; (Qu. D40, *Names and nicknames . . for the upper balcony in a theater)* Inf **NE7,** Spoonin' joint; (Qu. AA1, *When a man goes to see a girl often and seems to want to marry her, he's _____ her)* Inf **NC41,** Spooning. [28 of 32 total Infs old, 22 female] **1968** *DARE* Tape **CA100,** You spoon with your lady and you didn't have to watch the road. **1982** Barrick *Coll.* **csPA,** *Spoon—neck.* . . *Spooners—neckers—*A car sitting along a dark road is said to have "spooners" in it. **1989** Pederson *LAGS Tech. Index* 297 **Gulf Region** *(Kissing)* 23 infs, Spooning. [*DARE* Ed: A check of the *LAGS Concordance* shows that approx half of these infs characterized the response as "old fashioned," "from an older generation," "mother or grandmother's term," and the like.]

spoonbill n

1 Std: =**roseate spoonbill.**
2 See **spoonbill duck.**
3 See **spoonbill cat.**

4 =**ruddy duck.**

1888 Trumbull *Names of Birds* 110 **MA,** *Ruddy Duck.* . . To some in the vicinity of Plymouth, Mass., *Spoon-bill.*

5 also attrib: =**duckbill 2.**

1940 *AmSp* 15.134 **KY,** *Duckbill or Spoonbill.* Small hand truck used to move baskets of tobacco around the warehouse floor. **1966** *PADS* 45.12 **KY** [Tobacco word list], *Duckbill.* . . A small hand truck used to move baskets to the floor of the warehouse. (Also *spoonbill*). **1967** Key *Tobacco Vocab.* **MD,** *Truckers*—the workers who push the spoonbill trucks.

spoonbill cat n Also *spoonbill, ~ (cat)fish, spoon-billed cat, spooney, spoonfish* Cf **spoonbill sturgeon**
=**paddlefish.**

1847 *Knickerbocker* 29.332 **AL,** The shovel or spoon-bill fish is only found in the Alabama and its tributaries. **1854** [see **spoonbill sturgeon**]. **1858** Redfield *Zoöl. Sci.* 548, Some of the species of this order seem, however, to make an approach to the osseous divisions. This is especially true, (1) of the *Spoonbill, Polydon* [sic for *Polyodon*] *reticulatus,* an extraordinary fish, two feet or more long, found in the Mississippi, known at once by its snout, which is excessively prolonged, very flat and lanceolate, and in length nearly equal to the whole body. **1882** U.S. Natl. Museum *Bulletin* 16.83, *P[olyodon] spathula.* . . Paddle-fish; Spoon-bill Cat. **1908** *Century Illustr. Mag.* 54.457, In Mississippi, [the paddlefish is known as] spoon-billed-cat or spooney; and in Arkansas as the spoonbill or spoon-billed-sturgeon. **1931** *Sat. Eve. Post* 12 Sept 135 **MS,** Buffaloes and spoonbills are depressed, like stocks and cotton. Catfish that formerly sold for ten cents now go begging at six. **1965–70** *DARE* (Qu. P1, . . *Kinds of freshwater fish* . . *caught around here* . . *good to eat)* Infs **AR**52, 55, **IN**18, **KY**60, 75, 86, **LA**40, **MO**3, Spoonbill cat; **IN**13, **LA**10, **MS**16, 21, Spoonbill; **IA**29, **OK**11, Spoonbill catfish; **PA**92, Spoonfish; (Qu. P3, *Freshwater fish that are not good to eat)* Inf **IL**119, Spoonbill; **MS**21, Spoonbill cat; **AL**14, Spoonfish. **1967–68** *DARE* Tape **LA**5, [FW:] How about paddlefish or spoonbill cat? Which do you call them here? [Inf:] Well, we call them spoonbill; **OH**58, Well, they have different kinds of catfish. . . They have spoonbill cats; we don't catch many of those round here anymore. **1968** *DARE* FW Addit **sLA,** *Spoonbill cat* = paddlefish. (Though it resembles a catfish only in the absence of scales, the paddlefish is always classed with the catfish in South Louisiana by ordinary fishermen.) **1986** Pederson *LAGS Concordance* **AL, LA, MS** *(Freshwater fish)* 2 infs, Spoonbill cat; 2 infs, Spoonbill catfish; 1 inf, Spoonbill cat—snout like a duck—valuable oil; 1 inf, Spoonbills. **2000** *DARE* File **cLA,** The spoonbill catfish. . . It's a skinfish similar in color and size to most catfish, but I don't believe it's a true catfish.

spoonbill duck n Also *spoonbill, spoon-billed duck, ~ teal, ~ widgeon, spoon(e)y, spoonie*
=**shoveler.**

a1782 (1788) Jefferson *Notes VA* 77, Spoon billed duck. **1789** Morse *Amer. Geog.* 59, American Birds [include] . . Ilathera Duck . . Spoon bill [duck]. **1844** DeKay *Zool. NY* 2.342, The *Shoveller,* or *Spoonbill,* is . . more frequently obtained along the rivers and lakes than on the coast. **1888** Trumbull *Names of Birds* 43, It [=the shoveler] is known at Lake St. Clair; the Detroit River; Chicago; Long Island; in New Jersey . . ; in Maryland at Havre de Grace and Baltimore; in Virginia at Alexandria and Norfolk; at Morehead, N.C., and Savannah, Ga., as *spoon-bill. Ibid,* I have heard it oftener referred to there [at Savannah, GA], and at St. Augustine [FL], as *spoon-billed widgeon;* and it is commonly called in the markets, and by the market-gunners of Savannah, the *spoon-billed teal.* **1918** Grinnell et al. *Game Birds CA* 129, Shoveller. . . Other names: Spoonbill; Spoonie. **1926** (1949) McQueen–Mizell *Hist. Okefenokee* 136 **seGA,** Other migratory ducks include the . . spoonbill. **1961** Ligon *NM Birds* 50, The Shoveler, or Spoonbill, is one of the most common of the puddle- or surface-feeding ducks in the state. **1965** Guthrie *Blue Hen's Chick* 16 **MT,** But now we were laden, now we had spoonbills or mallards or widgeons or teals or butterballs or grouse or more likely a variety. **1965–70** *DARE* (Qu. Q5, . . *Kinds of wild ducks)* 41 Infs, **widespread,** Spoonbill; **CA**87, Spoonbill duck; **CA**168, Spoony. **2005** *San Diego Union–Tribune* (CA) 4 Dec sec E 2 (Internet), "We were in a section called 'Looney Spooney.'" "Looney" because it's crazy? "Because there are a lot of spoonbill ducks that migrate to that area."

spoon-billed butterball n
=**ruddy duck.**

1888 Trumbull *Names of Birds* 110 **NY,** *Ruddy Duck.* . . in the neighborhood of Niagara Falls, [called] *spoon-billed butter-ball.*

spoon-billed cat See **spoonbill cat**

spoon-billed duck See **spoonbill duck**

spoon-billed sturgeon See **spoonbill sturgeon**

spoon-billed teal (or widgeon) See **spoonbill duck**

spoonbill fish See **spoonbill cat**

spoonbill sturgeon n Also *spoon-billed sturgeon* Cf **spoonbill cat**
=**paddlefish.**

1854 Wailes *Rept. on Ag. & Geol. MS* 336, The Spoon-bill Sturgeon, *Polyodon folium,* more familiarly known in Mississippi as the *Spoon-bill Cat,* is abundant in our bayous and lakes. **1884** U.S. Natl. Museum *Bulletin* 27.493, *Polyodon spathula.* . . Spoon-billed Sturgeon. Ohio and Mississippi Valleys, generally abundant. **1903** NY State Museum & Sci. Serv. *Bulletin* 60.61, This [=*Polyodon spathula*] is known as the paddlefish, spoonbill or spoon-billed sturgeon, shovel fish, billfish, and duck-billed cat. Called "salmon" in western hotels. **1908** [see **spoonbill cat**]. **1951** Harlan–Speaker *IA Fish* 34, Paddlefish. . . Other Names—Spoonbill cat, . . and incorrectly, spoonbill sturgeon. **2003** *DARE* File—Internet **IN,** One of the most spectacular sites [sic] seen by SCUBA divers at France Park is the Spoonbill Sturgeon, also known as the paddlefish. . . The Spoonbill is distinguished by its elongated, paddle-shaped snout.

spoon biscuit n   esp S Midl   Cf **drop biscuit 2**
A soft biscuit made by dropping the dough from a spoon onto a pan or baking sheet.

1883 Wilcox *Practical Housekeeping* 395, *Supper*—Spoon biscuit, cold beef, jelly and cake. **1950** *Charleston Gaz.* (WV) 8 Dec 18/4, For Spoon Biscuit, mix thinner, drop on hot greased pan with spoon. **1966–69** *DARE* (Qu. H19, *What do you mean by a biscuit? How are they made?*) Inf **NC20,** Spoon biscuits—drop them in a pan and they rise up; **TN30,** Spoon biscuits—my father . . made spoon biscuits. He made the batter softer with more milk and dropped the batter by spoonfuls onto the baking sheet. **1986** Pederson *LAGS Concordance,* 1 inf, **csAR,** Spoon biscuits. **2006** in 2008 *DARE* File—Internet **WV,** I prefer cookie cutter biscuits to spoon biscuits.

spoon bread n   Also *spoon cake*
1 also *corn spoon bread, spoon corn bread:* Any of var kinds of corn bread, but esp one made with eggs and having a soft texture. **chiefly Sth, S Midl, TX** See Map Cf **batter bread 1**

1847 (1979) Rutledge *Carolina Housewife* 27, *Corn Spoon Bread.* One pint of corn flour; boil to a mush; add . . two eggs . . butter . . milk. . . Bake on a griddle, or grease a pan and drop in spoonfuls. **1906** *DN* 3.158 **nwAR,** Spoon corn-bread. . . Soft corn-bread served with a spoon. **1929** *Mod. Priscilla Cookbook* 39, *Spoon Bread* . . milk . . corn meal . . salt . . baking powder . . eggs . . shortening . . cook in a double boiler until thickened like mush. . . Turn into a greased baking dish and bake. **1949** Kurath *Word Geog.* 68, *Batter bread.* . . A soft cake of corn meal and eggs, baked in a pan, is served in the Carolinas, in Virginia, and southern Maryland. . . Another term, *spoon bread,* is current in scattered communities on Chesapeake Bay . . on the lower Shenandoah, and on the Cape Fear in North Carolina. **1950** *WELS (Names for bread made with corn meal)* 5 Infs, **WI,** Spoon bread. **1952** *NY Folkl. Qrly.* 8.187 **cwNY,** Soups and breads were ever-present foods at meals. . . "Spoon bread" was wet corn-meal bread baked in a "spider." **1965–70** *DARE* (Qu. H14, *Bread that's made with cornmeal*) 72 Infs, **chiefly Sth, S Midl, TX,** Spoon bread; **KY**37, Spoon cake; (Qu. H18) 16 Infs, **Sth, S Midl, TX,** Spoon bread; (Qu. H20b, . . *Names . . for pancakes*) Inf **SC**26, Spoon bread; **KY**37, Spoon cakes—made of corn bread; (Qu. H24, . . *Names or nicknames . . for boiled cornmeal*) Inf **AR**35, Southern spoon corn bread—not quite like boiled cornmeal; **TX**69, Spoon bread; (Qu. H25, . . *Names or nicknames . . for fried cornmeal*) Inf **SC**21, Spoon bread—spoon the dough out into the hot oil; (Qu. H50, *Dishes made with beans, peas, or corn that everybody around here knows, but people in other places might not*) Inf **IN**37, Spoon bread. **1968** *DARE* Tape **MD**1, [FW:] What is spoon bread? [Inf:] Spoon bread is Virginia. . . It's cornmeal; cornmeal pudding. That's what I would call it. . . [FW:] Does it come in rolls, or does it come in a dish? [Inf:] No, it's a pan. **1977** Anderson *Grass Roots Cookbook* 133 **cwAL,** Spoon bread is actually a sort of corn-meal soufflé—certainly this one is because it comes from the oven puffy, moist and fragile. This recipe *must* be made with stone-ground meal . . which has a floury texture. The more granular meal is too heavy to make a good spoon bread and the mixture will sink to the bottom of the baking dish. **1983** *MJLF* 9.1.57

ceKY (as of 1956), *Spoon bread* . . a soft cake of cornmeal and egg. **1986** Pederson *LAGS Concordance (Corn bread)* 95 infs, **Gulf Region,** Spoon bread; 1 inf, **swGA,** Southern spoon bread. [Recorded comments point mostly toward the soft, pudding-like type of spoon bread, but note the following comments: "Fry by spoonful, like flitter cakes"; "Now called 'pancakes'"; "Spooned from bowl into hot grease"; "Hot water-fried in hot fat."]

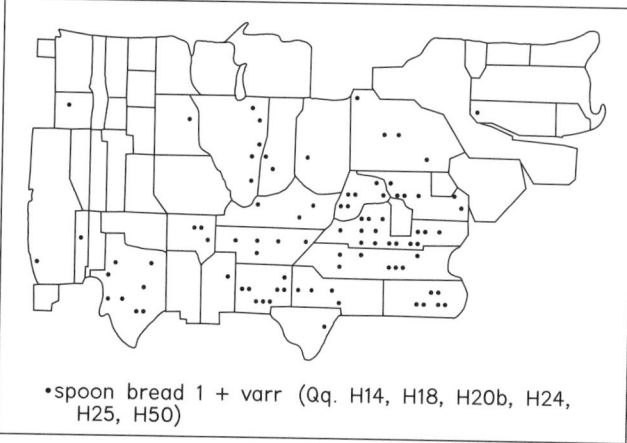

•spoon bread 1 + varr (Qq. H14, H18, H20b, H24, H25, H50)

2 Any of var baked or fried quick breads made from a soft dough or batter.   Cf **spoon biscuit**

1939 Wolcott *Yankee Cook Book* 137, *Connecticut Spoon Cakes* . . soda . . milk . . egg . . salt . . flour. . . Combine . . so that batter will "drop off" teaspoon into hot fat. **1986** Pederson *LAGS Concordance,* 1 inf, **seFL,** Spoon bread—made in frying pan with wheat flour; 1 inf, **neGA,** Spoon bread—doughnut dough, without hole; 1 inf, **neMS,** Spoon bread—thin, made in skillet, not cornmeal. **2002** *DARE* File—Internet **VA,** A traditional bread in the Blue Ridge is spoon bread. . . Spoon bread is essentially the same batter as biscuit, except that it is more moist. Use self-rising flour, solid shortening and buttermilk. They are the only ingredients necessary. . . You can grease . . a cast iron skillet and cook it on top of a stove. . . You can also grease a baking pan and bake it in a 400 degree oven. . . When done, turn it out onto a plate. No need to slice it, just break off the size hunk you want.

spoonburger n   Cf **loose-meat sandwich, sloppy joe a, tavern**
A dish of crumbled ground beef in a sauce, freq served on a bun.

1952 *Walla Walla Union–Bulletin* (WA) 23 Oct 20/7, *Coulee Spoonburger Casserole.* . . To serve: place a biscuit on dinner plate and spoon "burger" mixture over top. **1953** *Oshkosh Daily Northwestern* (WI) 21 July 10/6, *Supper Spoonburgers.* . . Toast buns and pile meat mixture on one half of each bun. **1960** *Bethany Cook Book* 248 **SD,** *Spoonburgers* . . ground beef . . chopped onion . . fat . . chicken gumbo soup . . catsup, optional . . prepared mustard, optional . . salt . . pepper[.] Brown meat in hot fat. Add onion and cook until golden brown. Add remaining ingredients. Simmer over low heat about 30 minutes. Serve on hamburger buns. **2003** *DARE* File—Internet [LDS Recipe File], *Spoonburgers* . . double *No-Rise Crust* recipe. . . Roll half of dough into bottom of cake pan. Cook . . hamburger. . . Put over crust. Sprinkle grated cheese over hamburger, topping with the top crust. After cooking at 400 for about 20 minutes, each person can open up their piece and put ketchup, mustard, pickles, etc. *Ibid* **NV,** [School menu:] [April] 14 . . Sloppy Joe on Bun . . [April] 22 Spoonburger. *Ibid* **WY,** [School menu:] [May] 6th . . Spoonburgers . . [May] 28th . . Sloppy Joes. *Ibid* **MN,** [Church menu:] March 5, we will begin our Lenten menu. . . Friday, the 7th, you can choose a spoonburger or a tuna bumstead. **2008** *DARE* File—Internet, Spoonburger casserole. . . This is like having you[r] burger and bun all in one dish—a very different kind of hamburger dish.

spoon bush See **spoonwood 1**

spoon, by the great horn See **horn spoon 2**

spoon cake See **spoon bread**

spoon corn bread See **spoon bread 1**

spooner n   See **spoon C**

spooney adj   See **spoony** adj

spooney n
1 See **spoonbill cat.**
2 See **spoonbill duck.**

spoonfish See **spoonbill cat**

spoonflower n [See quots]
An **arrow arum** (here: *Peltandra virginica*).
1886 *Vick's Mag.* 9.111 **eNC,** In the brooks and pools we find abundance of . . the elegant, glossy-leaved Spoon-Flower. **1890** *Century Dict.* 5855, *Spoonflower.* . . A plant, *Xanthosoma sagittifolium* [= *Peltandra virginica*], more specifically *arrow-leafed spoonflower,* considerably resembling a calla-lily. . . Local, U.S. **1955** *S. Folkl. Qrly.* 19.232, *Spoonflower* (Peltandra sagittaefolia [=*P. virginica*]) . . bears crowds of minute blossoms on a fleshly stalk and surrounds them with a flower-like envelope shaped very much like a big spoon. **2002** *DARE File*—Internet **NC,** Peltandra sagittaefolia (also known as White arrow arum or sometimes Spoonflower) is found only along the coastal areas of NC down to Florida and west to Mississippi. . . Its flower has a white, rounded sheath around the spathe, hence the name Spoonflower.

spoonhaunch See **spoonhunt**

spoonhead n Also *spoonhead muddler,* ~ *sculpin*
A **sculpin 1:** usu *Cottus ricei,* but also **mottled sculpin.**
1943 Eddy–Surber *N. Fishes* 229, The spoonhead muddler has a stout body with a large, flat head. **1965** *IL Nat. Hist. Surv. Biol. Notes* 54.11, *Cottus ricei* . . spoonhead sculpin. Sporadic in deep water of Lake Michigan. **1983** Becker *Fishes WI* 969, Mottled Sculpin. . . Other common names . . spoonhead [etc]. *Ibid* 979, In Wisconsin, the spoonhead sculpin [=*Cottus ricei*] occurs in Lakes Michigan and Superior. **2001** *Star Tribune* (Minneapolis MN) 1 June sec B 1 (Internet), Its cousins—the mottled, slimy and spoonhead sculpins—live in shallower water. . . Lundell came away with one slimy and two spoonhead sculpins.

spoonhunt n Also *spoonhaunch, spoonhu(t)ch, spoonhunch* [Prob folk-etym for some AmInd term] **chiefly sNH, neMA** Cf **spoonwood 1**
1 =**calico bush 1.**
1784 in 1785 *Amer. Acad. Arts & Sci. Memoirs* 1.422, *Great laurel. Wintergreen. Spoonhaunch.* . . The Indians are said to have made small dishes, spoons, and other utensils, out of the roots. They are sometimes employed by people in the country for similar purposes. **1826** Jewett *New-Engl. Farrier* 56 **neMA,** There is a bush that is ever green, called spoonhunt; this poisons sheep. **1840** in 1911 Emerson *Jrls.* 5.143 **MA,** It is droll that the Laurel in our woods is called Lamb-kill, and even the larger laurel Spoon-hunt. **c1846** (1949) Thoreau *Jrl.* 1.435 **MA,** I have watered . . the cornel and spoonhunt and yellow violet, which might have withered else in dry seasons. **1852** *Farmer's Mth. Visitor* 12.81 **csNH,** In Goffstown and Bedford . . is found in abundance, the beautiful species of laurel, known as *Kalmia latifolia,* but here known by the name of *spoonhunch,* a corruption doubtless of an Indian word. **1856** Potter *Hist. Manchester NH* 634 **csNH,** Upon the hill sides is found in abundance the splendid spoonhuch (*Kalmia latifolia*). **1892** *New Engl. Mag.* 12.305 **NH,** Mr. Atkinson . . had brought home that noon a great mass of delicate pink flowers and glossy leaves. "Here's some spoonhunch I found up in the pastur'." **1892** *Jrl. Amer. Folkl.* 5.100 **NH,** Kalmia latifolia, spoon-hunt. Mason, N.H. **1941** *LANE* Map 249 *(Mountain laurel)* 2 infs, **ne,cnMA,** Spoonhunt, usually; 1 inf, **neMA,** Spoonhunt; 1 inf, **cnMA,** Spoonhunt, thought to be a smaller variety, with pinker blossoms; 1 inf, **csNH,** Spoonhunt, older term; 1 inf, **swNH,** Spoonhunt, thought to be a kind of twisted tree; 4 infs, **csNH,** [Proncs of the type [spuᵊn haᵊntʃ]].
2 as *spoonhutch:* A **rosebay** (here: *Rhododendron maximum*).
1897 Sudworth *Arborescent Flora* 315 **NH,** Rhododendron maximum. . . Spoon Hutch.

spoonhutch See **spoonhunt**

spoonie See **spoonbill duck**

spooning See **spoon C**

spoon meat n [Specialized use of *OED2* spoon-meat "Soft or liquid food for taking with a spoon"; 1555 →] **HI**
The meat of an immature coconut.
1967 *DARE* (Qu. H63, *Kinds of desserts*) Inf **HI6,** Spoon meat—jelly of immature coconut. **1969** *DARE File* **HI,** Spoon meat—soft, unripened coconut. **1999** *Waikiki News* (Honolulu HI) Oct (Internet) **HI** (as of 1940s), I . . [u]sed to climb the highest coconut trees to get spoon

meat. **2000** *DARE File*—Internet **HI,** A drinking coconut, a green immature nut. . . After the water is out the coconut may be split open letting you enjoy the soft meat inside. This soft meat is usually called spoon-meat or pudding. It can be scooped out with a spoon.

spoon victuals n pl **esp NEast** Cf **victual**
Liquid or soft food.
1777 *PA Eve. Post* (Philadelphia) 11 Feb 73/2, *Philip Clark* . . has a remarkable way of throwing his head back when he eats spoon victuals. **1842** Kirkland *Forest Life* 1.89 **MI,** [Addressed to horses in a rainstorm:] Think of your own swimming oats, and as ye love not "spoon-vittles," hasten. **1909** *DN* 3.416 **nME,** Spoon victuals. . . Same as *spoonfeed.* **1910** *DN* 3.449 **wNY,** Spoon victuals. . . Food which is usually eaten with a spoon. **1914** *DN* 4.80 **ME, nNH,** Spoon victuals. . . Invalid diet. **1923** *DN* 5.222 **swMO,** Spoon victuals. . . Soft foods, as for a young child or for an invalid. **1958** *VT Hist.* 26.291, So sick he can eat only spoon victuals.

spoonwood n [Cf **spoonhunt**]
1 rarely *spoon bush:* =**calico bush 1.** **NEast, esp MA, NH** Cf **spoonwood ivy**
[**1748** in 1970 Kalm *Resejournal* 2.243 **NJ,** Som nyss nämdes, så kalla de svenska laurel . . skedträd, emedan indianerna, som i fordna tider mycket vistades här, brukade at giöra skedar af det samma. [=As just mentioned, the Swedes call the laurel "spoon-tree," because the Indians who formerly lived here in large numbers used to make spoons out of it.]] **1778** Carver *Travels N. Amer.* 234, They fashion their spoons . . from a wood that is termed in America Spoon Wood, and which greatly resembles Box Wood. *Ibid* 507, The *Spoon Wood* is a species of the laurel. **1832** Williamson *Hist. ME* 1.116, It has been called *mountain Laurel, Spoonwood, Ivy* and *Calico Bush.* Its wood is dense and hard, and is used as a material in constructing musical instruments, and by mechanics for handles to their tools. **1898** (1899) Earle *Home Life* 88 **NY, PA,** In Pennsylvania and New York laurel was called spoonwood, because the Indians made pretty white spoons from that wood to sell to the colonists. **1941** *LANE* Map 249 *(Mountain laurel)* 5 infs, **cMA,** Spoonwood; 1 inf, **swNH,** Spoon bush. **1967** *DARE* (Qu. T16, . . *Kinds of trees . . 'special')* Inf **MA5,** Mountain laurel—spoonwood. **1969** *DARE* Tape MA58, Another name for laurel, common laurel, [is] spoonwood—I suppose 'cause they grow so darn crooked they used to make wooden spoons out of it. . . It's very hard. **1982** *Greenfield Recorder* (MA) 28 Aug 4/2, I found a woman in Leverett Center . . who knew mountain laurel only by that name, while up over the hills in North Leverett it was known as "spoon wood." They actually used to make spoons of it when in Colonial days.
2 Either a **linden** (here: *Tilia americana*) or the **sweet bay 2.**
1814 Pursh *Flora Americae* 2.362, Tilia. . . glabra [=*T. americana*]. . . This tree is known by the name of *Lime-* or *Line-tree; Basswood; Spoonwood.* **1830** Rafinesque *Med. Flora* 2.268, Tilia, L. Linden, Basswood, Whitewood, Spoonwood [etc]. . . Wood very white and soft, used for canoes, models, spoons, turning, &c. **1857** *NJ Geol. Surv. Geol. Cape May* 76, In the *timber swamps* . . there is a heavy growth of . . Spoonwood . . *Magnolia glauca* [=*M. virginiana*].

spoonwood ivy n Cf **spoonhunt 1, spoonwood 1**
A **sheep laurel** (here: *Kalmia angustifolia*).
1892 *Jrl. Amer. Folkl.* 5.100 **CT,** Kalmia angustifolia, spoon-wood ivy.

spoony adj Also *spooney* [**spoon C**]
Romantically sentimental; foolishly fond; affectionate.
1851 Kip *Volcano Diggings* 83, He said nothing about her, but looked very spoony and sentimental. **1855** Wise *Tales Marines* 41, I was charged also with a small packet of letters, which are always kept ready by the spooney chaps of a ship, for a chance to send to their sweethearts. **1890** Holley *Samantha among Brethren* 87 **NY,** In two hours' time he would be jest as good as the very best kind of pie, affectionate and even spoony. **1899** (1912) Green *VA Folk-Speech* 409, Spoony. . . Weakly or foolishly fond; sentimental. **1905** *DN* 3.20 **cCT,** Spoony. . . Demonstratively fond. 'She is spoony over him.' **1907** *DN* 3.218 **nwAR,** Spoony. . . Demonstratively fond. **1930** Shoemaker *1300 Words* 56 **cPA Mts** (as of c1900), Spoony—A girl easily loved or petted. **1941** *LANE* Map 404 *(Courting her)* 1 inf, **csRI,** They are spoony. **1968** *DARE* (Qu. AA6a, . . *A man who is fond of being with women and tries to attract their attention—if he's nice about it)* Inf **MO36,** Spoony.

spoony n See **spoonbill duck**

sporrer, sporrow, sporry See **sparrow**

sport n **NEng, esp ME**

One on a hunting or fishing vacation, esp as the client of a guide; a vacationer.

1905 Stanton *Where the Sportsman* 74 **ME,** A guide always breathes easier when the "sports" inform him that they are going to take the Allagash trip. **1907** *DN* 3.250 **eME,** *Sport.* . . A sportsman who hunts or fishes in the Maine woods. **1941** *LANE* Map 449 *(Tourist)* 2 infs, **VT,** Sport. **1975** Gould *ME Lingo* 271, *Sport*—The Maine term for a paying guest at a hunting or fishing camp, and usually one who has hired a registered guide. The word is now something of an inland synonym for the coastal *summer complaint,* when seasonal visitors are discussed in the aggregate: "We've seen more sports this year than ever before." **1979** McPhee *Giving Good Weight* 143 **ME,** The guides of old did all the cooking and, often, all the paddling. Their customers were known as "sports." **1979** Lewis *How to Talk Yankee* [32] **nNEng,** *Sport* . . hunting or fishing client. **1995** Dobbs–Ober *N. Forest* 137 **ME,** As the guests finish their breakfasts and return to the cabins for fishing rods and windbreakers and caps, Dale gives each guide a few details about the client, or "sport," that Dale has assigned him. **2004** *Down East* Dec 27 **ME,** Sports are going to want to spend at least a few days [at a remote camp], because they'll have to work hard even to get there.

sport pepper n Also *Louisiana sport pepper, sport* [*sport* a plant that varies from the parent stock, often as a result of mutation; a new variety produced from such a variant] **chiefly Chicago IL, but becoming more widely known**

A small, moderately hot, chili pepper that is freq served pickled as a condiment, esp on Chicago-style hot dogs.

1937 LA Ag. Exper. Sta. *LA Bulletin* 287.13, The Sport pepper was badly mixed. **1944** *Pt. Arthur News* (TX) 5 July 7/5, [Advt:] Fancy Green Sport Peppers 8 Oz. Jar 27¢. **1954** *Chicago Tribune* (IL) 29 July sec 5 8/4, [Advt:] Jane Addams 8 oz. Jar *Sport Peppers*—21¢. **1982** in 2004 *DARE* File—Internet, Someone wanted to know what a sport pepper was. (RE: Hotdogs ala Chicago)—Well, I don't know what to tell you if you cannot find some at your local grocery store except that they are hot, green, and about 1 inch long. Only 2 or 3 of these little fellows can really "light up" a hot dog. **1986** *Chicago Tribune* (IL) 10 Apr food sec 10/1 (Internet), The half-hour program focuses on the Chicago-style frankfurter, a steamed hot dog traditionally topped with mustard, pickle relish and chopped onions as well as fresh sliced tomato, wedges of dill pickles, hot sport peppers, shredded lettuce, cucumber slices and celery salt. **1996** *Times–Picayune* (New Orleans LA) 25 July food sec 3 (Internet) **sLA,** Stewed greens were enhanced with vinegar steeped with tiny sport peppers. **2000** in 2004 *DARE* File—Internet [American Botanical Council], *Capsicum annuum* var. *longum* . . Louisiana long pepper or hybridized to the Louisiana sport pepper. **2001** *Milwaukee Jrl. Sentinel* (WI) 4 Feb 4 (Internet), A full Chicago hot dog. . . begins with an all-beef, hickory-smoked hot dog. . . [and always includes] two midget sport peppers. . . The Italians get credit for those little green sport peppers, which are from the same family as pepperoncini. (The little green pepper, just about the size of a golf tee, is grown in Louisiana. Today, 80% to 90% of the sport pepper crop is shipped to Chicago specifically for use on hot dogs.) **2004** *DARE* File—Internet, *Sport.* . . This *Capsicum annum* type. . . is especially well known as an essential condiment in a Chicago-style hot dog. Peppers resemble Tabasco peppers, but the Sport pepper is larger, about 1-½ inches long and ½ inch wide. They are medium hot. **2004** *NY Times* (NY) 14 Apr (Internet) **Chicago IL,** A proper Chicago hot dog must be. . . dressed with a crisp pickle spear, a sweetish fluorescent green relish, a slice or wedge of raw tomato, some chopped onions . . and two or three hot little green chilies, which Chicagoans for some reason always call sport peppers.

sposh n **chiefly NEng**

Mud; slush; hence adj *sposhy* muddy; slushy; mushy.

1836 *Peter Parley's Almanac for 1836* 32 **MA,** Wo to those . . who are journeying through the mud and *sposh* with their sleighs! **1842** *Yale Lit. Mag.* 8.96, I can't always decipher *quail tracks*—'specially in *sposhy* weather. **1845** in 1848 Bartlett *Americanisms* 325, The morning was blue and streaked, and the streets were one shining level of black sposh. **1878** *Scribner's Mth.* 15.305 **NEng,** A calm day is always best, and if warm enough for the snow to pack without being at all "sposhy," so much the better. **1884** Jewett *Country Dr.* 22 **ME,** There's a sight o' difference between good upland fruit and the sposhy apples that grows in wet ground. **1895** *DN* 1.394 **MO,** *Sposh:* slush; soft snow mixed with water in thawing weather. **1905** *DN* 3.20 **cCT,** *Sposh.* . . A mixture of mud or snow and water. **a1945** in 1967 Hough *Vineyard Gaz. Reader* 69 **MA,** The refreshments. . . consisted of cookies & crackers &

salted nuts & coffee & a congealed sposh that I believe is called frozen salad.

spot n

1 also *Norfolk spot:* A **croaker** n[1] **1a(1)** (here: *Leiostomus xanthurus*). [See quot 1865] **chiefly Mid Atl** See Map Also called **Cape May goody 1, goody 3, Lafayette 1, old-wife 1d, porgy** n[1] **2, post croaker, roach** n[1] **3, yellowtail 2**

1865 Norris *Amer. Angler's Book* 290 **DE,** It [=*Leiostomus obliquus* [=*L. xanthurus*]] is known at Lewes, Delaware, where it sometimes appears in great numbers, as the "Spot," from the mark near the gill-cover. **1882** Eggleston *Wreck Red Bird* 23 **VA,** They call croakers "spot" in Virginia. **1884** Goode *Fisheries U.S.* 1.370, The Lafayette . . is known in New York and elsewhere as the "Spot". . . in the Chesapeake region also as the "Spot". . . and at Pensacola as the "Spot" and *"Chopa blanca."* **1933** LA Dept. of Conserv. *Fishes* 180, A common fish of the Louisiana Gulf Coast, the Spot, is a fine pan-fish, though small. **1953** MD Dept. Educ. *Our Underwater Farm* 13 **Chesapeake Bay,** Like the croaker, the spot comes to the Bay only in the summer to feed and grow and leaves with the arrival of winter. **1965–70** *DARE* (Qu. P2, . . *Kinds of saltwater fish caught around here* . . *good to eat*) 23 Infs, **chiefly Mid Atl,** Spot(s); (Qu. P1) Inf **DC8,** Spot—run by hundreds when biting; (Qu. P7, *Small fish used as bait for bigger fish*) Infs **DE4, MD45, VA55,** Spot(s); **VA47,** Cut spot; (Qu. P14, . . *Commercial fishing* . . *what do the fishermen go out after?*) Infs **MD10, NC78, VA55,** 79, Spot; **MD10,** Norfolk spot. **1968–70** *DARE* Tape **MD3,** And then we have spots, and they're delicious. They compare to the pompano in Florida, and it's a little, moist fish; **NC60,** Then he caught spots . . in his nets; **VA112,** Nothing but good fish: trout, spot, flounder. **2002** *Virginian–Pilot* (Norfolk VA) 19 Sept sec C 8 (Internet), They might not be the biggest fish in the sea, but around these parts, spots are huge. . . Drive by any seafood restaurant in the fall and look at the sign outside for the day's special. It often reads: "Norfolk spot."

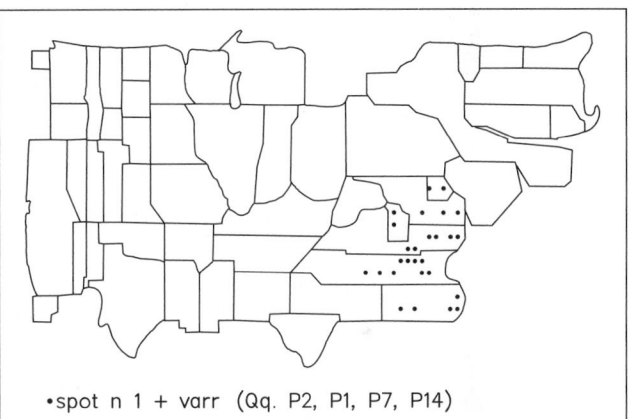

•spot n 1 + varr (Qq. P2, P1, P7, P14)

2 =**red drum.**

1879 (1972) Kilbourne *Game Fishes* 37, "Spot" is another name erroneously applied to this fish [=the red drum], and which is the property of a much smaller species of the same family, otherwise known as "Lafayette," or "Cape May Goody."

3 A **pinfish 1;** see quots.

1902 Jordan–Evermann *Amer. Fishes* 444, The pinfish or spot, *Diplodus holbrooki*. . . is found on our South Atlantic and Gulf coasts from Cape Hatteras to Cedar Keys. **1935** Caine *Game Fish* 55, Salt-water Bream or Sailor's Choice. . . *Synonyms* . . Spot. **1969** *DARE* FW Addit **ceNC,** *Spot*—A type of fish. Also called bream and pinfish. **2003** *St. Petersburg Times* (FL) 13 Dec 6 (Internet), It was caught on what most anglers refer to as a "spot" or spot-tailed pinfish, which is considered to be a last-resort live bait.

4 See **spotted bass 1.**

spot v, hence vbl n *spotting* **scattered, but esp PA, VA** =**spotlight** v.

1933 *McKean Co. Democrat* (Smethport PA) 30 Nov 1/2, Local people have followed the popular pastime of spotting deer with flashlights from motor cars. **1936** *Ibid* 8 Oct 8/2, Spotlighting the deer is a popular pastime. Game authorities do not object, but warn all motorists not to carry firearms in their cars while spotting deer. **1951** *Warren Times–Mirror* (PA) 29 Nov [14]/2 (newspaperarchive.com), [Advt:] *Like To Spot Deer?* Try the new 100,000 candle power lite on sale at Schaeffer Elect. Co. **1965–70** *DARE* (Qu. P35b, *Illegal methods of shooting deer;*

not asked in early QRs) Inf **VA**20, Spot 'em at night with a spotlight on the car; **NC**35, Spot at night—spotlight; **NV**5, **NY**92, **PA**157, 166, **VA**79, Spotting; **CA**25, 31, **PA**50, 176, Spotting deer; **NC**53, Spotting them at night; **WA**20, Spotting with a flashlight. **1990** in 2008 (acc) Lexis–Nexis Legal Research *State Case Law: PA* (Internet), No effort was made to sight upon or fire the guns. They were not taken out of the car at any time and were not used at any time in spotting the deer. **1993** *DARE* File **sPA, swVA**, Spotting or spot-lighting deer is the term I am familiar with. **2004** in 2008 (acc) Lexis–Nexis Legal Research *State Case Law: VT* (Internet), The game wardens responded to a complaint that someone was spotting deer in a field.

spot back(s) exclam **Pacific**
=place back(s).

2000 *NADS Letters* **cnCA**, The elementary school children at my daughter's bus stop yell, "Spot back," when they leave the line for a moment. This formulation seems very similar to "Place backs!" to me. **2004** in 2008 *DARE* File—Internet **CA**, Things I have learned today:— don't say "spot backs" and expect to actually get your spot back. **2006** *Ibid* **nwWA**, This ain't elementry [sic] school there are no spot backs at the club.

spot-back tick See **spotted tick**

spot bath n Cf **spit bath 1**
See quots.

1953 *AmSp* 28.144, Baths involving only a portion of the body are variously called *cat bath, spot bath, French dry clean.* **2002** *DARE* File— Internet, The only time I bathe my dogs is if they get into or roll in something that smells disgusting. Then it's only a spot bath on the parts that smell.

spot dance n esp **NEng** Cf **spotlight dance**
A dance in which the dancers dance until the music suddenly stops, at which time the couple standing on or nearest a prearranged mark on the floor is awarded a prize.

1915 *Fitchburg Daily Sentinel* (MA) 6 Aug 5/6, Weather did not permit the prize spot dance being held last night. **1966** *St. John Valley Times* (Madawaska ME) 23 June 4/3, Spot dances were won by Stephen Miller and Ramona Lehr and Jeffrey Dunn and Sandra Street. **1973** *DARE* File **cnMA** (as of c1927), *Spot dance*—These dances were a regular feature at our high school dances. . . The dance committee made tiny marks for spot dances on floors and kept track of the general area where they were. Then when a spot dance had been announced, the orchestra (they weren't called bands then) stopped suddenly and everyone stood still until the committee member found *the spot* and awarded a small box of candy to the couple standing on or nearest the spot. **1993** *Capital* (Annapolis MD) 16 Dec sec C 9/6, The evening will include . . spot dance contests.

spot hunting See **spotlight hunting**

spotlight n Cf **flashlight tag**
See quot 1970.

1970 *DARE* (Qu. EE13a, *Games in which every player hides except one, and that one must try to find the others*) Inf **TX**90, Spotlight—"it" carries a flashlight. **2006** *DARE* File—Internet **IN**, At night I play spotlight with my friends. . . In the field we have a good spot to hide but I can't tell you where it is because it is a secret.

spotlight v **scattered, but chiefly West, Mid Atl** See Map
Cf **jacklight** v, **shine** v, **spot** v
To locate and immobilize (a deer or other animal) with a bright light at night, esp in order to shoot it; to engage in this activity; hence vbl n *spotlighting;* n *spotlighter.*

1934 (1943) *W2*, Spotlight. . . Hunting, to jack. **1936** [see **spot** v]. **1949** Arnow *Hunter's Horn* 45 **KY**, Give me that carbide an a rifle an I'll kill him [=a fox], spotlight an bust him right between th eyes. **1954** *SD Conserv. Digest* Apr 2, Spotlighting or "jacklighting" as it is sometimes called, has been a favored method used by many generations of poachers during their nocturnal forays for wild game. **1961** *Daily Progress* (Charlottesville VA) 27 Jan 3/7, Deer 'Spotlighting' Convictions Hit 14. . . The report . . said that the deer "spotlighters" were ordered to pay . . fines and costs. **1965–70** *DARE* (Qu. P35b, *Illegal methods of shooting deer;* not asked in early QRs) 89 Infs, **scattered, but chiefly West, Mid Atl**, Spotlighting. **1968** *Daily Progress* (Charlottesville VA) 26 Jan 3/4, LeSueuer . . and a juvenile had been fined for spotlighting and killing the deer. **1995** Lesley *Sky Fisherman* 238 **OR**, "The winners always went out at night and spotlighted". . . "When

Meeks was in here after slaughtering those rabbits, he bragged about freezing them with the spotlight. In fact, he hit it with a big chunk of ice." **2006** *Belleville News–Democrat* (IL) 6 Apr (Internet), The sting resulted in the arrest Tuesday of 14 people, including two Madison County men who were charged with, among other things, spotlighting deer at night from vehicles.

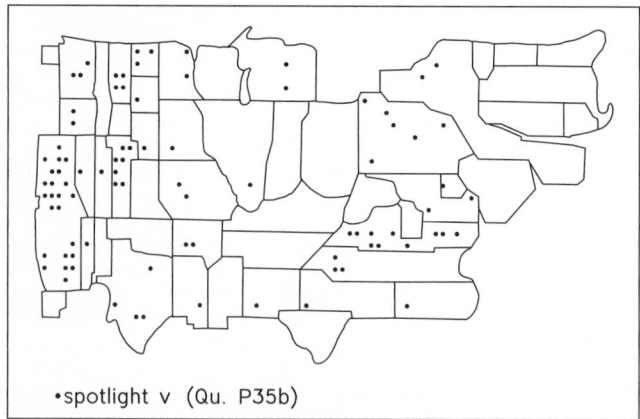

•spotlight v (Qu. P35b)

spotlight dance n Cf **spot dance**
See quot 1967.

1920 *Grand Rapids Daily Tribune* (WI) 5 June 1/5, A "spotlight" dance was one of the features of the evening. **1922** *Galveston Daily News* (TX) 28 July 2/2, Nine imported prizes direct from the Orient . . will be given on spotlight dances. **1967** *DARE* (Qu. FF5a) Inf **PA**7, Spotlight dance—spot turned on and cake given to persons in it. **2001** *Intelligencer Jrl.* (Lancaster PA) 28 Apr sec A 7 (Internet), The two generations came together on the dance floor as they danced to polkas, formed conga lines, took part in spotlight dances, and the all-important dollar dances.

spotlighter See **spotlight** v

spotlight hunting n Also *spot hunting* **scattered, but esp PA**
See Map
=spotlighting (at **spotlight** v).

1916 *Richwood Gaz.* (OH) 16 Nov [21]/3 (newspaperarchive.com), Spotlight hunting was condemned vigorously at a meeting of four Farmers Protective Associations. . . Resolutions were adopted to the effect that hunting of rabbits at night by autoists, who drive slowly along a road and shoot "cotton-tails" that loom ahead in the path of the spotlight, is "unsportsmanlike, dangerous and extremely annoying to farmers." **1933** *Mt. Democrat* (Placerville CA) 29 Sept 3/2, We understand some of the hunters are resorting to spotlight hunting, which will be just too bad for them if caught. **1965–70** *DARE* (Qu. P35b, *Illegal methods of shooting deer;* not asked in early QRs) Infs **CO**41, **PA**182, 192, 198, Spot hunting; **NY**185, **PA**188, 209, Spotlight hunting; **MD**22, Spotlight hunting—at night, blind deer with a spotlight; **PA**180, Spotlight hunting—spot hunting more common term. **2006** in 2008 *DARE* File— Internet **NC**, It gets rural with a quickness north of Greensboro and I mean that in the spotlight-hunting-'coon-in-your-yard sense.

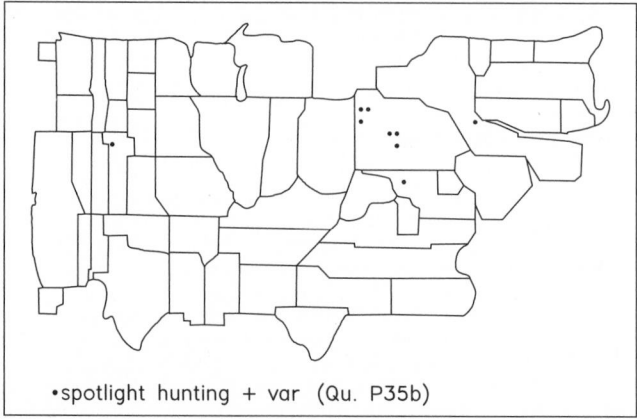

•spotlight hunting + var (Qu. P35b)

spotlighting See **spotlight** v

spot-necked snake n Also *spotted-neck snake* [See quot 1839]
=red-bellied snake.
   1839 MA Zool. & Bot. Surv. *Fishes Reptiles* 230, *The spotted-neck Snake. . .* black or fuliginous markings . . appearing upon the anterior plates like black dots. **1974** Shaw–Campbell *Snakes West* 132, The red-bellied snake . . is also called Storer's snake, . . spot-necked snake [etc].

spotrump n
=Hudsonian godwit.
   1881 *Forest & Stream* 17.226 **NEng,** The other godwit (*Limosa Hudsonica . .),* better known here as "spot rump," is very rare in spring. **1888** Trumbull *Names of Birds* 209 **MA,** At North Scituate, Province-town, and Chatham [the Hudsonian godwit is called] *spot-rump.* **1946** Hausman *Eastern Birds* 290, Hudsonian Godwit. . . Spotrump, White-rump, Blacktail.

spot snapper n [*OED2* 1876 →]
A **snapper 1:** usu the lane snapper *(Lutjanus synagris),* but also the **gray snapper.**
   [**1876** Goode *Fishes Bermudas* 55 (*OED2*), The Spot snapper and the Yellow-tail correspond doubtless to *Mesoprion uninotatus* [=*Lutjanus synagris*] and to *Ocyurus chrysurus*.] **1946** La Monte *N. Amer. Game Fishes* 59, Lane Snapper. . . Names: Red-tail Snapper, Biajaiba, Spot Snapper. **2001** U.S. Food & Drug Admin. *Seafood List* (Internet), Common Name: Lane Snapper—Vernacular: Spot Snapper—Redtail Snapper—Silk Snapper.

spotsy See **spatzie**

spot tag n Also *sore spot tag*
A game of tag; see quots.
   1912 *LaCrosse Tribune* (WI) 31 Dec 2/6, Games, spot tag and beater goes round, Junior As and Bs. **1932** (1953) Smith *Games* 135, *Sore Spot Tag . .* (Japanese Tag, Spot Tag). . . is played like simple tag, with the exception that "It," when tagging a player, must hold his hand on the "sore spot" where he was tagged. **1968** *DARE* (Qu. EE33, . . *Outdoor games . . that children play*) Inf **NJ**8, Spot tag—could only touch person in certain spot. **1995** Heatwole *Shenandoah Voices* 26 **wVA** (as of 19th cent), Spot Tag must have been hilarious to watch as it progressed from one child to another. It was played like traditional tag for the most part, but what made it different was that when a person was tagged, he had to hold a hand to the place where he was touched. He was then "it" and had to pursue the next victim, holding his "spot" as he ran. **2006** in 2008 *DARE* File—Internet **CT,** Voted on what broadway show to go see . . and played spot tag and vampire.

spottail n
1 also *spot-tail(ed) minnow, spotted-tail ~, spottail shiner:* A **shiner 1** (here: *Notropis hudsonius*).
   1876 NY Acad. Sci. *Annals Lyceum Nat. Hist.* 11.337, *Photogenis stigmaturus* [=*Notropis hudsonius*]. . . It is everywhere known as the Spotted Tail Minnow, or Spot Tail. **1896** U.S. Natl. Museum *Bulletin* 47.269, *Notropis hudsonius.* . . Spawn-eater; Spot-tailed Minnow; Shiner. **1902** Jordan–Evermann *Amer. Fishes* xli, For bass fishing the following additional species are superior live-bait . . shiner or spottail minnow *(N. hudsonius).* **1943** Eddy–Surber *N. Fishes* 142, The spottail shiner is apparently distributed through the Great Lakes basin except for Lake Superior. **1968** *DARE* (Qu. P7, *Small fish used as bait for bigger fish*) Inf **MN**42, Lake shiner—hard to keep alive—also called spottails. **1983** Becker *Fishes WI* 540, Spottail Shiner. . . Other common names: spawneater, spottail minnow, spottail. **2006** *Post–Std.* (Syracuse NY) 24 May 47 (Internet), The trick is to use a lure matching the lake's pinky finger-size perch fry and spot-tail shiners and find the fishes' favorite depth.
2 also *spot-tail(ed) bass:* **=red drum.**
   1935 Caine *Game Fish* 39, Channel Bass. . . A black spot about as large as the eye, at the base of the tail. . . *Synonyms:* . . Spottail [etc]. **1967–70** *DARE* (Qu. P2, . . *Kinds of saltwater fish caught around here . . good to eat)* Inf **SC**63, Spottail bass; **SC**69, Spot-tailed bass. **2002** *DARE* File—Internet **Savannah GA,** I have had a lot calls [sic] . . about spottail bass. . . During the fifties we called them "Stag Bass." . . As time went on they became known as "channel bass." We started catching them in the channels, rivers, and creeks. The smaller ones became known as "spottail bass," because of the spot on the tail. When the commercial fishing industry got the so-called "money making vision" they became known as redfish.

3 **=bowfin.**
   1951 Harlan–Speaker *IA Fish* 38, Bowfin. . . Other Names—Dogfish, grindle, spot-tail, and mudfish. **1983** Becker *Fishes WI* 251, Bowfin. . . Other common names: dogfish, . . spot-tail.

spot-tail(ed) bass See **spottail 2**

spot-tailed minnow See **spottail 1**

spot-tailed pinfish See **pinfish 1b**

spottail minnow See **spottail 1**

spot-tail pinfish See **pinfish 1b**

spottail shiner See **spottail 1**

spotted adder n
1 Either the **fox snake** or a **milk snake 1** (here: *Lampropeltis triangulum*). **chiefly NEast, Gt Lakes** See Map
   1848 Lanman *Tour R. Saguenay* 60 **ceNY,** But what was my sur-prise . . when re-seated in the same place, to find another snake, and that a large spotted adder, passing along the same track. **1876** Jordan *Man-ual Vertebrates N. U.S.* 180, [*Ophibolus doliatus*] Var. *triangulum.* . . Milk Snake. House Snake. Spotted Adder. **1892** *New Englander & Yale Rev.* 56.146, Something makes me aware of the movements of a spotted adder that is crawling stealthily towards me from behind. . . Measuring him with my eye, I take him to be nearly three feet long. **1928** Ruthven et al. *Herpetology MI* 97, Milk-snake, Spotted Adder. . . Neither name has anything to recommend it. The snake is not addicted to milk, nor is it an adder. **1949** Dickinson *Lizards & Snakes WI* 9, Another belief has to do with the milk snake or spotted adder. **1953** Schmidt *N. Amer. Am-phibians* 197 **IL,** *Elaphe vulpina vulpina.* . . *Common name.*—Spotted adder (Illinois), pine snake (Wisconsin). **1965–70** *DARE* (Qu. P25, . . *Kinds of snakes*) 26 Infs, **chiefly N Cent, Gt Lakes,** Spotted adder; **NY**71, Spotted adder—book name is milk snake; **MI**99, Spotted adder snake. **1981** Vogt *Nat. Hist. WI* 143, Milk snakes, along with fox snakes, are most often mistaken for copperheads and killed. Some peo-ple call them spotted adders. **2005** in 2008 *DARE* File—Internet **NY,** My friend from upstate N.Y. said her grandfather killed what he called a Spotted Adder.

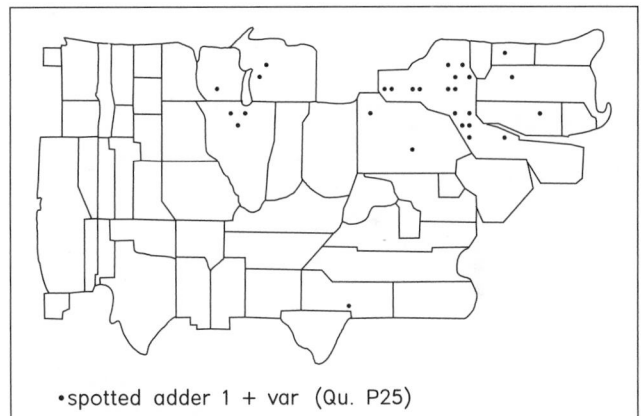
•spotted adder 1 + var (Qu. P25)

2 See **adder's tongue 1.**

spotted alder n
A **witch hazel** (here: *Hamamelis virginiana*).
   1854 King *Amer. Eclectic Dispensatory* 521, *Hamamelis Virginica.* Witch Hazel. . . An indigenous shrub, sometimes called *Winter-bloom, Snapping-hazlenut, Spotted Alder.* . . This plant grows in almost all sections of the United States. **1860** *Harper's New Mth. Mag.* Oct 594, We drove through and among the clumps of white poplar and spotted al-der. **1897** Sudworth *Arborescent Flora* 205, *Hamamelis virginiana.* . . Spotted Alder. . . of domestic medicine. **1911** Henkel *Amer. Med. Leaves* 12, Witch-hazel. . . *Other common names.*—Snapping hazel, . . striped alder, spotted alder [etc]. **1974** Morton *Folk Remedies* 69 **SC,** Spotted Alder. . . Fresh leaves stuffed up nose to clear passages.

spotted bass n
1 also *spotted black bass, spot:* A **black bass 1,** esp *Micropt-erus punctulatus.* For other names of the latter see **lake bass 1, linesides, mossback 2, moss bass, Oswego ~, painted tail, redeye 1e, red-eyed bass 1, river ~, swamp bass 1, tiger ~, Welshman, yellow bass 1, ~ perch 2**

1817 Rafinesque in *Amer. Monthly Mag. & Crit. Rev.* 2.120, *Bodianus Achigan* [=*Micropterus dolomieu*]. . . vulgar names in the United States Black-bass, Lake-bass, Big-bass, Oswego bass, Spotted-bass, &c. **1875** Scott *Fishing Amer. Waters* 285, The Spotted Bass or Speckled Hen. . . This is one of the numerous small pan-fishes of the Western waters which naturalists have not yet classified. **1883** *Century Illustr. Mag.* July 376, Much of the confusion attending the common names of the black bass arises from the coloration of the species, which varies greatly, even in the same waters; thus they are known as black, green, yellow, and spotted bass. **1887** Goode *Amer. Fishes* 56, "Spotted Bass," "Green Perch," [etc] . . are other names applied to one or both species [= largemouth and smallmouth bass]. **1957** Trautman *Fishes* 491 **OH**, Lower sides yellowish-white, most of the scales with dusky bases, resulting in the formation of horizontal lines; it is from these distinctive spots that the species derives its name of Spotted Blackbass. **1965–69** *DARE* (Qu. P1, . . *Kinds of freshwater fish . . caught around here . . good to eat*) Infs **GA**76, **MS**25, Spotted bass. **1966** *Victoria Advocate* (TX) 19 Jan 8/1, I haven't seen this many spots (he means spotted bass) in the river in several years. **1976** Tryckare et al. *Lore of Sportfishing* 101, Spotted Bass. . . Other common names . . Kentucky spotted bass, spotted black bass, northern spotted bass, Alabama spotted bass, Wichita spotted bass [etc]. **2004** *Marysville Jrl.–Tribune* (OH) 19 June sec B 2/3, Spotted bass are being caught by anglers floating between the villages of McDermott and Arian. Most "spots" are running in the 10- to 12-inch range.

2　=red drum.

1857 Emory *Rept. U.S. Mex. Boundary* 14, Johnius ocellatus [= *Sciaenops o.*] . . Spotted Bass. **1877** Holder et al. *Hist. Amer. Fauna* 3.ccxli **NC, SC**, Bass; Red Bass; Sea Bass *(Sciænops ocellatus* . .).— Called, also, Spotted Bass in Carolinas. **1884** Goode *Fisheries U.S.* 1.372, This fish [=the red drum] is very much in need of a characteristic name of its own. . . In the Carolinas, Florida, and the Gulf, we meet with the names 'Bass' and its variations, 'Spotted Bass,' 'Red Bass,' 'Sea Bass' [etc]. **1935** Caine *Game Fish* 39, Channel Bass. . . Synonyms . . Spotted Bass [etc].

spotted bat n

Std: a large bat *(Euderma maculatum)* of the Southwest. Also called **death's-head bat, jackass** ~

spotted black bass　See **spotted bass 1**

spotted black rockfish　See **black rockfish 1**

spotted cat n　Also *spotted catfish*

Usu a **channel catfish** (here: *Ictalurus punctatus*), but also **flathead catfish 1.**

1820 Rafinesque *Ohio R. Fishes* 62, *Silurus maculatus* [=*Ictalurus punctatus*]. . . Vulgar names—Spotted, White, and Channel Catfish. **1856** *De Bow's Rev.* 20.23 **FL**, Spotted catfish, *(silurus maculosus).* **1903** *Ft. Wayne Jrl.–Gaz.* (IN) 20 July 7/2, Mr. Pearce said that he had 10,000 black bass and spotted cat fish when he started on the trip . . , and all were distributed in the rivers of Ohio and Indiana. **1939** Natl. Geogr. Soc. *Fishes* 104, The Spotted Catfish belongs in the Mississippi Valley and the Great Lakes, but is also in the Potomac River. **1957** Trautman *Fishes* 415, Young less than 14″ long . . colloquially called squealers, ladycats, spotted and silver cats. **1967–69** *DARE* (Qu. P1, . . *Kinds of freshwater fish . . caught around here . . good to eat*) Infs **KY**65, **LA**7, 15, Spotted cat; **AR**51, Spotted cat or appaloosa; **LA**29, Opelousas cat or spotted cat; **LA**40, Speckled cat, [corr to] spotted cat; (Qu. P14, . . *Commercial fishing . . what do the fishermen go out after?*) Inf **LA**15, Spotted cat. **1986** Pederson *LAGS Concordance,* 2 infs, **nwAR, cnLA**, Spotted cat; 1 inf, **cwLA**, Spotted catfish.

spotted cowbane n　[Because the stem is spotted]

1 A **water hemlock** (here: *Cicuta maculata*).　Also called **beaver poison, children's bane, cowbane 1, death-of-man, muskrat weed 1, musquash root, poison hemlock 2, snakeweed b(2), spotted hemlock, ~ parsley, wild hemlock 1, ~ parsnip 2a**

1837 Darlington *Flora Cestrica* 185 **sePA**, C[icuta] maculata. . . Spotted Cicuta. *Vulgò*—Spotted Cowbane. Water hemlock. **1891** *Garden and Forest* 16 Sept 443 **WI**, In every case where fatal effects occurred it was found that the root eaten was not the Parsnip but *Cicuta maculata,* a plant which belongs to the same family, and is known under the common names of Spotted Cowbane, Musquash Root, and Water Hemlock. **1931** Harned *Wild Flowers Alleghanies* 351, Water Hemlock. . . It also goes by the name of Spotted Cowbane and Beaverpoison. **1975** Hamel–Chiltoskey *Cherokee Plants* 31, Cowbane, spot-

ted. . . *Suicide to eat large quantities.* **2002** Hemmerly *Ozark Wildflowers* 52, Spotted Cowbane—*Cicuta maculata.*

2　=poison hemlock 1.

1900 Lyons *Plant Names* 113, [Conium] maculatum. . . Spotted Cowbane (often confounded with Cicuta maculata). **1914** *Georgia Manual Weeds* 300, Poison Hemlock. . . Spotted Cowbane, Spotted Parsley [etc]. **1930** Sievers *Amer. Med. Plants* 46, Poison Hemlock. . . Other common names.—Spotted parsley, spotted cowbane [etc].

spotted crane n

The immature **little blue heron;** see quot.

1955 Lowery *LA Birds* 139, The so-called "calico bird" or "spotted crane" is the immature Little Blue Heron in the process of losing its white plumage and acquiring the blue.

spotted dog　See **spotted pup**

spotted dove n

A large dove *(Streptopelia chinensis)* introduced to California and Hawaii and distinguished by a white-spotted black band about the neck.　Also called **lace-necked dove, ringneck** ~

1960 Booth *Birds* 354 **HI**, Spotted Dove. . . common everywhere throughout the state, in open country especially. **1972** Berger *Hawaiian Birdlife* 199, The Spotted, Lace-necked, or Chinese Dove was introduced at an early date, the exact year being unknown. This is a large (12 inches), grayish-brown dove with . . a band of black with discrete white spots on the back and sides of the neck. **1977** Udvardy *Audubon Field Guide Birds* 585 **CA**, Spotted Dove. . . Introduced from southeastern Asia to Los Angeles, some have spread to neighboring southern California towns. **1994** Stone–Pratt *Hawai'i's Plants* 116, Spotted or lace-necked doves . . somewhat resemble, and are the same size . . as, the mourning dove of the U.S. Mainland.

spotted frog n

1　=leopard frog.

1867 *Amer. Naturalist* 1.109 **MA,** The other species of Frogs found in Massachusetts. . . are the Spotted Frog, Marsh Frog, or Pickerel Frog *(Rana palustris . .*). **1906** (1907) Dickerson *Frog Book* 197, This species of frog. . . is apparently much nearer the . . spotted frogs *Rana pipiens.* **1919** *Copeia* 74.82 **NY,** *Rana pipiens.* . . Leopard-frog. "Spotted Frog." Abundant. **1932** Wright *Life-Hist. Frogs* 419 **Okefenokee GA,** *Rana sphenocephala.* . . *Common Names*—Southern Leopard Frog. . . Spotted Frog [etc]. **1992** Elliott *Calls Frogs & Toads* 12 **Sth,** *Southern leopard frog (Rana utricularia).* . . The common "spotted frog" of southern swamps and marshes. Found throughout the southern states.

2　Either of two closely related western frogs: *Rana pretiosa* or *R. luteiventris.*

1947 Pickwell *Amphibians* 23, *Rana pretiosa pretiosa,* the Western Spotted Frog. . . ranges from Alberta and Montana west to the Pacific Ocean and southward west of the Cascade-Sierra Mountains through Oregon and into northern California. *Ibid, Rana pretiosa luteiventris* [=*R. l.*], the Nevada Spotted Frog, is a desert subspecies. **1953** Schmidt *N. Amer. Amphibians* 85, *Rana pretiosa.* . . Common name: Western spotted frog, red-bellied frog. *Ibid, Rana pretiosa luteiventris.* . . *Common name:* Great Basin spotted frog. **1979** Behler–King *Audubon Field Guide Reptiles* 378, Spotted Frog (*Rana pretiosa*). . . Large and brown, with *ill-defined dark spots, sometimes with light centers.* **2002** (acc) N. Prairie Wildlife Research Center *Biol. Resources* (Internet), The Columbia Spotted Frog and the Oregon Spotted Frog were long regarded as the same species (the Spotted Frog, *Rana pretiosa*).

spotted geranium n

A **cranesbill 1** (here: *Geranium maculatum*).

1814 Bigelow *Florula Bostoniensis* 161 **MA,** *Geranium maculatum.* . . *Spotted geranium or Cranesbill.* . . The root is perennial, very astringent, and useful for its medicinal properties. **1837** Darlington *Flora Cestrica* 392 **sePA,** Spotted Geranium. **1930** Sievers *Amer. Med. Plants* 62, Wild Geranium. . . Other common names.—Crane's-bill, spotted crane's-bill, wild crane's-bill, spotted geranium [etc]. **2006** *DARE* File—Internet **SC,** Other than Carolina and Spotted geraniums, nearly all wild geraniums of the United States originated elsewhere.

spotted gravy　See **speckled gravy**

spotted ground squirrel n

A **ground squirrel** n **b** (here: *Spermophilus spilosoma*).

1928 Anthony *N. Amer. Mammals* 208, Large Spotted Ground Squirrel.—*Citellus spilosoma major.* . . from eastern New Mexico north into Colorado as far as the valley of the Arkansas River. **1947** Cahalane

Mammals 348, Spotted ground squirrel. . . Upper parts are various shades of brownish or grayish, marked with squarish white spots. **1980** Whitaker *Audubon Field Guide Mammals* 401, Spotted Ground Squirrel. . . Grayish or brownish above, with small, squarish, *indistinct light spots scattered on back;* whitish below. **2003** in **2008** *DARE* File—Internet **cwCA**, [Caption:] These Spotted Ground Squirrels are pretty common around here.

spotted grouper n

1 Any of var **groupers 1a;** see quots.

1876 U.S. Natl. Museum *Bulletin* 6.62, Spotted grouper, *(Epinephelus guttatus.)* **1935** Caine *Game Fish* 74, Red Grouper—*Epinephelus morio. . . Synonyms:* Brown Snapper . . Spotted Grouper. **1972** Sparano *Outdoors Encycl.* 382, Giant Sea Bass—Common Names . . spotted jewfish, . . spotted grouper. . . *Epinephelus itajara.* **2006** *DARE* File—Internet, The well-known jewfish, or spotted grouper, found from Florida to Brazil, is among the largest.

2 A **grouper 1b** (here: *Mycteroperca venenosa*).

1935 Caine *Game Fish* 77, Yellow-fin Grouper—*Mycteroperca venenosa. . . Synonyms* . . Spotted Grouper. *Ibid* 76, Rock Grouper—*Mycteroperca apua* [=*M. venenosa*]. . . *Synonyms* . . Spotted Grouper.

spotted hemlock n [Because the stem is spotted]

Usu =**poison hemlock 1,** but also **spotted cowbane 1.**

1895 Gray–Bailey *Field Botany* 202, Poison Hemlock. . . Spotted H[emlock]. . . a virulent poison, used in medicine. **1898** U.S. Dept. Ag. Div. Botany *Bulletin* 20.40, Water Hemlock. *Cicuta maculata* L. Other names . . spotted hemlock [etc]. **1930** Sievers *Amer. Med. Plants* 46, Poison Hemlock. . . Spotted parsley, spotted cowbane, . . spotted hemlock [etc]. **1964** Kingsbury *Poisonous Plants U.S.* 379, *Conium maculatum* L. Poison hemlock, hemlock, spotted hemlock [etc]. . . This genus is often confused, especially in common name, with its relative *Cicuta maculata.* **2004** *Roanoke Times & World-News* (VA) 25 July 18 (Internet), Water hemlock or spotted hemlock grows mostly in marshy areas and along streams and ditches. It is considered to be one of the most poisonous plants in the United States.

spotted ink See spotted paint

spotted jewfish See jewfish 1a

spotted John n Cf speckled Jack, ~ John 1

See quot.

1969 *DARE* (Qu. I28b, *Kinds of greens that are cooked*) Inf **KY**66, [In a list of wild greens:] Spotted John.

spotted lily n

=**dogtooth violet.**

1967 *DARE* (Qu. S11, . . *Dog-tooth violet*) Inf **IA**3, Spotted lily; (Qu. S26c, *Wildflowers that grow in woods*) Inf **IA**3, Spotted lily.

spotted-neck snake See spot-necked snake

spotted oak n Cf pinto oak

Any of several mostly southern and eastern **oaks,** as a **black oak** (here: *Quercus velutina*), **laurel oak 2, scarlet oak 1, Shumard oak, Texas oak,** or **water oak 2b.**

1859 in **1940** *AmSp* 15.386 **VA,** Beginning at a beech and two spotted oaks, on the top of the Locust rough. **1897** Sudworth *Arborescent Flora* 167 **TX,** *Quercus texana.* . . *Ibid* 169 **MO,** *Quercus velutina.* . . Spotted Oak. *Ibid* 175 **TX, AL,** *Quercus nigra.* . . Spotted Oak. **1938** Van Dersal *Native Woody Plants* 347, Spotted [Oak] *(Quercus coccinea).* **1947** Collingwood–Brush *Knowing Trees* 194, Southern Red Oak—*Quercus falcata.* . . Locally called Spanish oak, Spanish water oak, spotted oak [etc]. **1950** Moore *Trees AR* 54, Shumard Oak. . . Local Names: Texas Oak, Spotted Oak. . . Bark on old stems . . characterized by pale or light colored plate-like ridges between which are rough, dark furrows. **1960** Vines *Trees SW* 181, Water Oak. . . Vernacular names are Bluejack Oak, Duck Oak, Pin Oak, Spotted Oak [etc]. *Ibid* 182, Diamond-leaf Oak. . . It is also known as . . Spotted Oak, and Laurel-leaved Oak. *Ibid* 192, Shumard Oak. . . Vernacular names are Spotted Oak, Leopard Oak [etc]. **1967** *DARE* (Qu. T10, . . *Kinds of oak trees*) Inf **TX**35, Spotted oak—maple bark. **2008** *DARE* File—Internet **AR,** [Advt:] Beautiful ranch in the Ozarks! Mostly woods. . . Red and white oak, spotted oak, hickory.

spotted paint n Also spotted ink Cf checkered paint, striped ~

A nonexistent item used as the basis of a practical joke.

1968–69 *DARE* (Qu. HH14, *Ways of teasing a beginner or inexperienced person—for example, by sending him for a 'left-handed monkey*

wrench': "Go get me _____.") Infs **MA**35, **OH**47, (Can of) spotted paint; **CT**4, Spotted ink.

spotted parsley n [Because the stem is spotted]

Either of two closely related plants: **poison hemlock 1** or **spotted cowbane 1.**

1828 Rafinesque *Med. Flora* 1.118, *Conium Maculatum.* . . Vulgar Names—Poison Parsley, Spotted Parsley. **1898** U.S. Dept. Ag. Div. Botany *Bulletin* 20.40, Water Hemlock. . . Other names . . spotted hemlock; spotted parsley [etc]. **1914** Georgia *Manual Weeds* 300, Poison Hemlock—*Conium maculatum.* . . Deadly Hemlock, Spotted Cowbane, Spotted Parsley [etc]. . . [T]he close resemblance of its leaves to those of parsley sometimes is the cause of fatal poisoning.

spotted plover n obs

=**golden plover.**

[**1750** Edwards *Nat. Hist. Uncommon Birds* 3.140, *Spotted-Plover.* . . This Bird was brought from *Hudson's-Bay* by Mr. *Isham.* I suppose when it is living it has a bright shining Eye, because I find by my Friend Mr. *Isham's* Account, that the *English* settled in *Hudson's-Bay* call it the *Hawk's-Eye.*] **1792** Belknap *Hist. NH* 3.169, Large Spotted Plover, *Charadrius maculatus.* **1837** (1962) Williams *Territory FL* 75, Plover. . . Of these there is the kildear, spotted plover and ring-neck. **1872** Flagg *Woods New Engl.* 181, The youthful angler . . watches with delight the little spotted plover, as it runs nimbly upon the lily-pads.

spotted pup n Also spotted dog [OED2 spotted dog (at spotted a.) 1854 →] esp West

A pudding containing raisins.

1944 Adams *Western Words* 151, *Spotted pup*—Rice and raisins cooked together. **1958** McCulloch *Woods Words* 177 **Pacific NW,** *Spotted dog*—A steamed pudding containing raisins. **1978** *Greenfield Recorder* (MA) 19 Aug [Hemenway column], In my mother's old cookbook under "Pudding recipes," is this note in her handwriting. "Rice pudding with raisins is called "spotted pup." [*n*] **1998** *Sunset* Jan 108 **MT,** *Spotted Dog.* . . [Recipe includes rice, milk, cinnamon stick, sugar, salt, raisins.] . . Spoon into bowls and serve warm. **2002** *DARE* File—Internet **cwTX** (as of c1900), [Reminiscences of ranch life:] Roxie's specialty was "Spotted Pup"—a rice and raisin steamed pudding which he made in a flour sack suspended from a stick which was laid across a big kettle of boiling water.

spotted sandpiper n

Std: a robin-sized **sandpiper** (*Actitis macularia*) common to most of the US. Also called **bobtail 4, chevalier de batture, dab-ass, dodge-ass, grayback 1e, guttersnipe 2, jerk-bird, maggot-eater, oxeye 1a, pant-ass, peetweet 1, pewit 2, pin snipe, river ~, sand bird 1, ~ lark, ~ peep, ~ snipe, sea chicken, seesaw 2, steelyard bird, swee-swee, tattler, teeter n 1, tilt 2, tilter 3, tilt-up 1, tiptail, tip-up 1, twitchet 2**

spotted sapsucker n

=**hairy woodpecker.**

1930 OK Univ. Biol. Surv. *Pub.* 2.118, Hairy Woodpecker. . . Local names: Speckled woodpecker, . . spotted "sapsucker" [etc].

spotted seatrout n Also spotted trout

A **weakfish** (here: *Cynoscion nebulosus*).

1873 Smithsonian Inst. *Misc. Coll.* 14.2.26, *Cynoscion carolinensis* [= *C. nebulosus*]. . . Salmon-trout; spotted sea-trout *(south coast);* spotted silver-sides. . . Cape Hatteras to Florida. **1882** U.S. Natl. Museum *Proc.* 5.285, Cynoscion maculatum. . . *Speckled Trout; Spotted Trout.* . . One of the most abundant and valuable of the food fishes of the Gulf coast. **1955** Zim–Shoemaker *Fishes* 119, The Spotted Seatrout or "speckle trout" . . has dark spots on fins and body. **1967–69** *DARE* (Qu. P2, . . *Kinds of saltwater fish caught around here . . good to eat*) Infs **NC**60, **SC**43, Spotted trout. **2001** *Palm Beach Post* (W. Palm Beach FL) 21 June sec C 7 (Internet), Many anglers think of spotted seatrout as a winter or spring fish. But the handsome speckled trout can be caught over sea grass beds throughout the summer by those ready to cast at first light.

spotted skunk n

Std: a **skunk n 1** of the genus *Spilogale.* Also called **four-lined skunk, hydrophobia ~, polecat 1, striped skunk** Note: Some taxonomists consider *S. putorius* and *S. gracilis,* the eastern and western spotted skunks, to be one species, *S. putorius;* others consider them to be separate on the basis of reproductive habits.

spotted squeteague n

A **weakfish** (here: *Cynoscion nebulosus*).

1814 in 1815 *Lit. & Philos. Soc. NY Trans.* 1.398, *Spotted Squeteague. . .* There are black, well-defined *spots* among the *specks* over the back and sides, and chequering the caudal and second dorsal fins. **1884** Goode *Fisheries U.S.* 1.365, *The Spotted Squeteague. . .* It becomes more abundant as we proceed southward, until off the coast of North Carolina and Georgia, where it is one of the most abundant food-fishes. **1933** John G. Shedd Aquarium *Guide* 118, Slightly smaller than the common Squeteague, which it replaces on the more southerly shores, the Spotted Squeteague is an equally important food and game fish. **1951** Taylor *Surv. Marine Fisheries NC* 127, Also known as spotted or speckled weakfish or squeteague, the speckled trout . . is found from New York to Texas.

spotted sucker n

Std: a **sucker** (here: *Minytrema melanops*). Also called **black sucker 1**.

spotted-tail minnow See **spottail 1**

spotted tick n Also *spot-back tick* Cf **speck-back (tick)**
=**lone star tick.**

1967–70 *DARE* (Qu. R23a, *Insects or other creatures that fasten themselves to the skin and suck blood—on land*) Infs **CO**22, **VA**38, Spotted ticks; **LA**12, Spotted tick—one white spot on his back; **LA**14, Spotted ticks—with one spot. **1986** Pederson *LAGS Concordance*, 1 inf, **cwAR**, Spot-back tick. **1988** *DARE* File **ceTX**, A woman about 50 who hauls cattle told me about—*spotted ticks* ("about ten times as big as a seed tick" a man said—"with a white spot on their back" the woman said). **2002** *DARE* File—Internet **SC**, Ticks are a common parasite in the Beaufort, Hilton Head Island and SC Lowcountry areas. The most common tick in this area is the spotted tick, also called the "Lone Star" tick. It is reddish-brown in color and has a white spot on its back.

spotted tortoise See **spotted turtle**

spotted trout n

1 See **spotted seatrout.**

2 =**cutthroat trout.**

1884 Goode *Fisheries U.S.* 1.475, The Black spotted Trout—*Salmo purpuratus* [=*Oncorhynchus clarkii*]. This fish is known as the "Trout," "Mountain Trout," "Spotted Trout," "Black Trout," "Silver Trout," etc., in the mountains, but when in the ocean, full grown, as "Salmon Trout" or "Steel-head." **1904** *Salmon & Trout* 239 **WA**, The other cut-throat, popularly called "the spotted trout" (*Salmo clarkii jordana*), is also found in Lake Sutherland. **1938** Schrenkeisen *Field Book Fishes* 43, Cut-throat Trout. . . Common names.—Cut-throat; . . Spotted Trout [etc.]. **1976** Tryckare et al. *Lore of Sportfishing* 73, Cutthroat Trout. . . Other common names . . black-spotted trout, . . spotted trout [etc.]. . . Native to mountainous areas ranging from California north to Alaska.

spotted turtle n Also *spotted tortoise*

Std: a freshwater tortoise (*Clemmys guttata*) with yellow spots on the carapace as well as on the head, neck, and limbs. Also called **hicatee, mud turtle 2c(4), polka-dot ~, pond ~ 2, scorpion B3, speckle-back turtle, speckled ~, sun ~**

spotted weakfish n Cf **squeteague**

A **weakfish** (here: *Cynoscion nebulosus*).

1875 Scott *Fishing Amer. Waters* 82, Anglers along the coast of New Jersey term it [=the southern sea trout] the spotted weakfish, to distinguish it from the other [=the squeteague], which they call the mottled weakfish. **1902** Jordan-Evermann *Amer. Fishes* 457, Spotted Weakfish; Spotted Sea-trout. . . This species is associated on the coasts of New Jersey and Virginia with the squeteague, from which it may readily be distinguished by the presence of numerous black spots on the body posteriorly. **1951** [see **spotted squeteague**]. **1975** Evanoff *Catch More Fish* 205, The spotted weakfish (*Cynoscion nebulosus*) is best known as the sea trout or speckled trout. **2000** *Intelligencer* (Doylestown PA) 13 Nov sec B 4/3 **C Atl**, There are spotted weakfish in the sounds and around the inlets.

spotted wintergreen n

A **pipsissewa** (here: *Chimaphila maculata*). Also called **dragon's tongue, king's cure, ratsbane 1, rheumatism root c, ~ weed a, wild arsenic**

1822 Eaton *Botany* 236, [*Chimaphila*] *maculata. . .* spotted wintergreen. . . Woods. **1890** *Harper's New Mth. Mag.* Sept 628, The two pipsissewas, known as princess-pine and spotted-wintergreen . . are perhaps the most beautiful. **1902** *Jrl. Amer. Folkl.* 15.253, The "spotted *pipsissewa*" . . [is] also known as "spotted wintergreen." **1924** *Amer. Botanist* 30.56, Our only other species of *Chimaphila* is *C. maculata* almost universally called "spotted wintergreen." **1976** Bruce *How to Grow Wildflowers* 23, I might . . discover a clump of Spotted Wintergreen, its pointed, variegated leaves as garish as any popular houseplant, nestling among the fallen pine needles. **2003** *Knoxville News–Sentinel* (TN) 21 Apr sec B 1 (Internet) **ceTN**, Carman pointed out spotted wintergreen and shrub yellowroot.

spotted woodpecker n Cf **little spotted woodpecker**

Either the **downy woodpecker** or the **hairy woodpecker**; see quots.

1730 Royal Soc. London *Philos. Trans.* 36.427, *Picus varius minimus,* the small spotted Woodpecker. **1731** Catesby *Nat. Hist. Carolina* 1.21, *The smallest spotted Wood-pecker. . .* so nearly resembles the Hairy Wood-pecker . . in its marks and colour, that were it not for disparity of size, they might be thought to be the same. **1865** *IL State Ag. Soc. Trans. for 1861–64* 5.731, All of our spotted *Woodpeckers,* and even the *Nuthatchers,* are, by many, indiscriminately called Sap-Suckers . . . [I]n anatomy, habits, and voice, it [=the sap-sucker] is widely distinct from the so-called Spotted Woodpeckers. **1930** OK Univ. Biol. Surv. *Pub.* 2.118, Hairy Woodpecker. . . Local names: Speckled woodpecker, spotted woodpecker [etc.]. **1968–70** *DARE* (Qu. Q17, . . *Kinds of woodpeckers*) Inf **CA**137, Small spotted woodpecker; **LA**33, Spotted woodpecker = downy woodpecker; **NJ**15, Spotted or downy woodpecker; **VA**61, Spotted woodpecker.

spottedy adj Cf Intro "Language Changes" III.1, **flowerdy**

Spotted.

[**1925** *DN* 5.343 **Nfld**, *Spottedy. . .* Spotted.] **1949** Webber *Backwoods Teacher* 198 **Ozarks**, You can get spots . . by hangin' a spottedy cloth in front of the cow's feed box. Then she has spottedy calves. **1974** *NC Folkl. Jrl.* 22.105, Here come something big and spottedy floating down out of the air.

spotting See **spot** v

spout n Also *spout pipe, waterspout* [*OED2 spout* sb. I.1.a 1392 →] *somewhat old-fash* Cf **spouting**

A downspout or, less freq., gutter.

1806 (1970) Webster *Compendious Dict.* 137, *Gutter . .* a passage for water, . . spout. *Ibid* 288, *Spout . .* a wooden gutter, pipe, mouth, waterfall. **1821** Knapp *Biog. Sketches* 108 **NEng**, The window of the room . . was open, and near a spout which extended from the roof of the building to the ground. **1835** (1906) Bradley *Jrl.* 218 **NH**, They [= buildings in Cincinnati] are very generally *dated,* the year of their erection being placed close to the waterspouts, near the roof. **1941** *Language* 17.333 **WI**, [*LANCS* fieldwork:] Spout(s)—6 [of 50 infs]. . . used by [1 inf] . . for the pipe bringing the water down to the ground, more often called the *downspout* or *conductor.* . . waterspouts [1 inf]. **1949** [see **spouting**]. **c1960** Wilson *Coll.* **csKY**, Spout pipe. . . The pipe that takes the water from the eaves to the ground, a downspout. **1965–70** *DARE* (Qu. D29, *The pipe that takes the collected rain-water down to the ground or to a storage tank*) 39 Infs, **scattered,** Spout; 9 Infs, **scattered,** Waterspout; 1 Inf, **MO**15, Spout pipe; (Qu. D28, *What hangs below the edge of the roof to carry off rain-water?*) 10 Infs, **scattered,** Spout(s); **MI**81, **PA**165, Waterspout; [45 of 58 total Infs old] **1986** Pederson *LAGS Concordance* (Eaves trough) 6 infs, **scattered Gulf Region,** Spout(s); 1 inf, **neTN,** Spout = downspout; 2 infs, **GA,** Spout—from gutter to ground.

spouting n [Cf *Concise Ulster Dict.,* "Spouting . . a drainpipe . . a gutter along the edge of a roof"] **chiefly PA, OH, Gt Lakes** See Map Cf *eave(s) spouting* (at **eaves spout**), **rainspouting, spout**

A roof gutter or downspout; the material of which it is made.

1869 *Scientific Amer.* 21.110 **OH**, [In an official list of patents issued by the U.S. Patent Office:] Rain-Water Spouting. [*DARE* Ed: The residence of the patent holder is given as West Middleburg, Ohio.] **1876** Knight *Amer. Mech. Dict.* 3.2288, *Spout-plane . .* A round-soled plane used in hollowing out stuff for spouting and troughs. **1949** Kurath *Word Geog.* 29, The gutters on the roof are known as the *spouting* or the *spouts . .* in the Midland, except for West Jersey and the Blue Ridge. **1965–70** *DARE* (Qu. D28, *What hangs below the edge of the roof to carry off rain-water?*) 37 Infs, **chiefly PA, OH,** Spouting; (Qu. D29, *The pipe that takes the collected rain-water down to the ground or to a stor-*

age tank) 18 Infs, **chiefly PA, OH, Gt Lakes,** Spouting. [42 of 48 total Infs old] **1966** Dakin *Dial. Vocab. Ohio R. Valley* 2.61, *Spouting. . .* is clearly a newer term. Some Ohio speakers indicate that for them *spouting* is a name for the later galvanized metal troughs which replaced the earlier wooden *eave(s) trough(s).* **1973** Allen *LAUM* 1.178 (as of c1950), *Eave(s) troughs. . .* spouting [8 infs, IA]. **1977** *WI State Jrl.* (Madison) 2 Oct sec 5 7/1, My street used to wake up lazily to chirping birds, an occasional clatter of milk bottles, and the gentle thud of newspaper as it lodged in the spouting. **1984** *AmSp* 59.326, *Spouting. . . Gutter. . .* One of these [words], *spouting,* is restricted to western Pennsylvania, Maryland, West Virginia, and the Shenandoah Valley, and might therefore be ascribed to the Scotch-Irish presence in this area. **1986** Pederson *LAGS Concordance (Eaves troughs)* 1 inf, **neTN,** Spouting. **2008** *DARE* File—Internet **sePA,** [Advt:] Spouting is installed with "hidden hangers." . . Downspouts also come in all matching colors. *Ibid* **neOH,** We offer a combination of hidden hanger applications and standard spouting fasteners in an attempt to optimize the beauty of your spouting system.

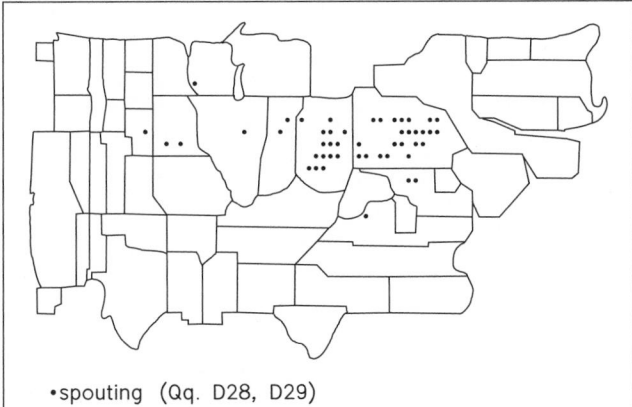

•spouting (Qq. D28, D29)

spout pipe See **spout**

spouty adj [*OED2* 1705 →] *old-fash*
Of ground: soggy, spongy; given to oozing water.

1811 *Ag. Museum* 1.308 **MD,** The soil for Hemp should be rich, light, deep and moist; but not spouty, or wet. **1843** (1916) Hall *New Purchase* 49 **IN,** They had been . . fortunate as to get a taste of "buttermilk land,"—"spouty land,"—and . . "mash land." **1859** in 1942 Hafen *Overland Routes* 11.85 **VA,** Several buildings . . add to the lonesome and dreary appearance of a vast wet, spongy, spouty prairie. **1859** (1968) Bartlett *Americanisms* 437, *Spouty.* Wet clay land is called in the West "spouty" land," possibly because, when trodden upon, the water *spouts* up through any holes or depressions in the surface. **1892** in 2002 (acc) Lexis–Nexis Legal Research *State Case Law: PA* (Internet), If the jury believe that the lands . . are wet or spouty or swampy lands . . the plaintiff . . is not entitled to recover in this action. **1903** *DN* 2.331 **seMO,** *Spouty* (land). . . Saturated with water. Also 'springy.' **1930** in 2002 (acc) Lexis–Nexis Legal Research *State Case Law: MO* (Internet), There is no showing that the lavatory floor was wet because of some permanent condition such as a leaking pipe or a spouty place in the ground.

spraddle-horn n
A **longhorn 1.**

1944 Sykes *Westerly Trend* 68 **TX** (as of 1880s), Our 500 "spraddle-horns" kept the herd restless and were ready to lead it into mischief at a moment's notice. **1961** Adams *Old-Time Cowhand* 155 **TX,** Because of the many twists and turns of the horns of the old longhorns they were sometimes called "twist-horns" or "spraddle-horns."

spradling bug n Cf **straddlebug 1**
A **dung beetle;** see quot.

1955 Roberts *S. from Hell-fer-Sartin* 120 **eKY,** *Irishman Eating Dung-beetles. . .* And those old tumblebugs was all over the ground, you know. And so Pat he's just a-catchin' 'em and eatin' 'em just as hard as he could. . . He says, "Fat-to-my-jassum, if I ain't eat my belly full of spradlin' bugs."

sprag n[1] [Cf *EDD sprag* sb.[1] 1 "A spray; a branch or bough"]
A dead tree limb; hence adj *spraggly.*

1927 *AmSp* 2.365 **cwWV,** *Sprags . .* dry limbs on trees. "Hemlocks

have lots of sprags." *Spraggly . .* covered with sprags. "Those trees are all spraggly."

sprag n[2] [*sprag* a stout bar thrust between the spokes of a wheel (esp of a mine car) to prevent its moving]
In fig phr *put a sprag in one's wheel* and varr: To bring one's activities to an abrupt halt, bring one up short. Cf **scotch** v[1] **2**

1917 *Warren Eve. Times* (PA) 16 Mar 9/3, A sprag was thrown into the wheels of progress. **1922** *Clearfield Progress* (PA) 28 Dec 1/6, William Collins . . had a "sprag" put in his business. **1966** *DARE* FW Addit, [My] father, northern Minn., would say, "I'll put a sprag in his wheel." **1968** *DARE* (Qu. JJ27, *To give somebody a hint for his own good: "He had no idea that she was up to anything, but I put _____."*) Inf **MD22,** [A] sprag in the wheel. **1997** *Chattanooga Times* (TN) 14 July sec D 1 (Internet), Bully for John Schuerholz, Bobby Cox and anyone else in the Atlanta Braves' hier archy [sic] who played a role in putting a sprag in the wheels of the Braves' runaway bullpen gravy train Saturday. **2004** in 2006 *DARE* File—Internet **AL,** The decision . . to increase from two to three the number of big public meetings a month has really put a sprag in the wheels.

sprag v [Prob < *sprag* to slow (a mine car) by thrusting a stout bar between the spokes of one of its wheels; cf **sprag** n[2]]
chiefly PA
To drag one's foot or feet, usu to slow or steer a coasting sled; to slow by dragging; to drag (one's foot).

1936 in 2008 (acc) Lexis–Nexis Legal Research *State Case Law: PA* (Internet) **swPA,** He "spragged" his sled with his foot, as he expressed it, in an effort to turn to his left and pass behind the truck, but the sled turned all the way around and continued down the hill backwards. **1956** *AmSp* 31.39 **ceMA,** When I hear a boy from a near-by town say 'Don't sprag till you're halfway down the hill,' I prick up my ears at a verb I have never heard. **1980** *NYT Article Letters* **nePA** (as of 1920s), When I was a child in Scranton, Pennsylvania in the 1920's. . . we *spragged* with our feet to make the sled go slower. **1986** *DSNA Letters* **nePA** (as of 1930s), In sleigh-riding we used the word sprag in two senses, one to slow down by spragging with the foot and also to indicate a change in direction, that is, to "sprag to the right" or "sprag to the left." Although I grew up in Kingston, PA across the river from Wilkes-Barre in the heart of the anthracite coal region, I do not think that the origin of "sprag" from the mining industry occurred to me at that time. **1996** *DARE* File—Internet **Scranton PA,** When I was a child the word "spragging," indicating an action like dragging your feet to slow down a wagon, was a standard part of the local vocabulary. I have never heard it used in the Philadelphia area. **1997** in 2003 *Ibid* **Scranton PA,** Roger himself often felt impelled to run. It was steep. He'd be galloping by the time he got home, spragging and burning shoe leather. **1999** *Pottsville Republican* (PA) 29 Apr (Internet), Sattizahn also spragged his shoes and pointed the imager to the floor; friction was detected. **2003** *DARE* File—Internet **nePA** [CoalSpeak], I got goin' down the hill so fast on my bike I had to sprag my feet to slow down. **2004** *NADS Letters* **swPA,** My husband . . has always used the word "sprag" to refer to stopping any vehicle without brakes. Usually, it's in the form of "you'll have to sprag your feet." He grew up in and around Pittsburgh. **2005** *Ibid* **cnIL,** "Sprag" (meaning to slow down by dragging one's feet). . . I'm quite certain that I learned this usage from my mother. . . I have a distinct memory of her telling me or my brother either to "sprag" or stop "spragging." She spent her entire life in Spring Valley, Illinois.

spraggly See **sprag** n[1]

spragnum See **sphagnum**

spraguetail See **sprigtail 1**

sprang n See **spring B1**

‡**sprang** adv
=**spang** adv **2.**

1957 *Julian Apple Day* [2] **csCA,** Jake has been observing scenery with the rear exposure of a donkey sprang in the middle of the picture for umpteen years.

sprangle(-grass) See **sprangletop 1**

sprangles See **spangles**

sprangletop n
1 also *sprangle(-grass), sprangletop grass:* A plant of the genus *Leptochloa.* **esp West** For other names of var spp see **red sprangletop, salt grass a(5), salt-meadow grass b**

1901 *Racine Daily Jrl.* (WI) 26 Feb 7/4, Sprangle, a native of Texas and regions west of that state, promises to be one of the most productive and finest bay grasses grown on the trial grounds. **1912** Wooton–Standley *Grasses NM* 111, *Leptochloa dubia.* . . Sprangle. In the lower mountains and rocky hills of the southern part of the State. **1950** Hitchcock–Chase *Manual Grasses* 491, *Leptochloa* [spp]. . . Sprangletop. **1961** Thomas *Flora Santa Cruz* 98 **cwCA,** [*Leptochloa*] *fascicularis* [=*L. fusca* subsp *fascicularis*]. . . Sprangletop Grass. **2002** *DARE* File—Internet **TX,** Post Oak Parks/Woods. . . Commonly Associated Plants. . . sprangle-grass [etc].

2 A **whitetop 5** (here: *Scolochloa festucacea*).
   1902 U.S. Bur. Plant Industry *Bulletin* 15.34, The most valuable forage plants . . [include] sprangle top (*Scolochloa festucacea*). **1932** Rydberg *Flora Prairies* 121, *Fluminia* [=*Scolochloa* spp]. . . Spangle-top [sic]. **1950** Stevens *ND Plants* 58, Fluminea festucacea. . . Hollowstem. Sprangletop. **1989** *Jrl. Range Management* 42.323 **ND,** Species selected . . [include] whitetop or sprangletop (*Scolochloa festucacea*).

sprangletop grass   See **sprangletop 1**

‡spratch n [Cf *SND spret* n.[2] 1 "A sudden spring or leap, jump, bound"]
   1908 *S. Atl. Qrly.* 7.345 **cSC,** [Footnote:] A rider in broken country will put his horse at a bank, crying, while he spurs, "Now, boy! make a spratch!"

sprawl n[1] [*EDD sprawl* (at *sproil*)] **NEng**
Energy, initiative, spunk; hence adj *sprawlless* lazy.
   1833 Neal *Down-Easters* 2.175 **NEng,** He may be one of our native New-Englanders who value themselves on their *sprawl,* as they term it. **1890** *DN* 1.19 **neMA,** Sprawl: life, animation, vigor. 'He has no sprawl.' **1892** *DN* 1.218 **neMA,** Sprawl. . energy; as, "I haven't any sprawl today." **1904** Day *Kin o' Ktaadn* 77 **ME,** The boys he left had sprawl an' pride. **1914** *DN* 4.80 **ME, nNH,** Sprawl. . . Energy, vigor. "He's got lots o' sprawl." *Ibid* 156 **Cape Cod MA,** Sprawl. . . Initiative, energy. . . "He ain't got no more sprawl to him 'n day-old kitten!" **1927** *AmSp* 3.134 **eME,** A man who lacked energy or was downright lazy was said not to have "sprawl" enough to dig his potatoes, or whatever he neglected. **1966** *DARE* (Qu. A9, . . *Wasting time by not working on the job*) Inf **ME16,** They're sprawlless. **1966** *DARE* FW Addit **cME coast,** Sprawl—get-up-and-go.

sprawl n[2] [Folk-etym for *spall;* cf *EDD sprawl* sb.[2] "A chip of a stone or brick"]
   1858 *Bibliotheca Sacra & Biblical Repository* 15.472 **NY,** We walked over heaps of chips and sprawls, such as fill every stonecutter's yard. **1873** (1877) *Annual Rec. Sci. & Industry for 1872* 330, Between these [=stone implements] and the stone sprawls, of . . natural origin, there occurs every variety of form. **1900** in 2008 (acc) Lexis-Nexis Legal Research *State Case Law: TN* (Internet), None of the projecting stones had been removed to make a level surface for that course, but broken stones and sprawls had been used to level the same. **1935** *Ibid: VA,* Petitioner took a sprawl fork, which he was using to load the stone on the truck. **1953** (1977) Hubbard *Shantyboat* 204 **Missip-Ohio Valleys,** Then came the bare face of the quarry. From the water's edge rose a steep bank of loose stone which Uncle Jim called the "sprawl" bank, which I suppose should be spall bank, where the broken stones too small to use were dumped. **2006** in 2008 *DARE* File—Internet **cCT,** [Cemetery regulations:] The lower base of all monuments must be dressed to a true level on the bottom so as to bear evenly at all points upon the foundation without the use of chips, sprawls or underpinnings.

sprawlless   See **sprawl** n[1]

spray v [Malaprop for *spay*] Cf **splay B**
   1968 *DARE* (Qu. J3a, *To make a female dog so that she can't breed, she must be _____*) Inf **NJ35,** Sprayed; (Qu. J3b, *To make a female cat so that she can't breed, she must be _____*) Inf **NJ35,** Sprayed; (Qu. K70, *Words used . . for castrating an animal*) Inf **NJ35,** Sprayed. **1986** Pederson *LAGS Concordance* (Castrate) 2 infs, **AL, MS,** Spray.

spray gun n   Also *spraying machine* Cf **scatter-barrel (shotgun)**
   1967–68 *DARE* (Qu. P37b, *Nicknames for a shotgun*) Infs **MN2, WI48,** Spray gun; **OH56,** Spraying machine.

spread v
   A Gram form.
   Past, ppl adj: usu *spread;* also *esp freq among Black speakers,* spreaded.   Cf **-ed 1**
   1909 *DN* 3.374 **eAL, wGA,** Spreaded, pret. and pp. of spread. **c1938**

in 1970 Hyatt *Hoodoo* 1.231 **seVA** [Black], So the whole town—it was [a] small town—so it [=a story] just spreaded all at once. **1947** *True* 32.104 **New Orleans LA** [Black], After Storyville closed down—the people of that section spreaded out all over the city. **1968** *DARE* (Qu. X15, . . *Kinds of noses, according to shape or size*) Inf **PA66,** Spreaded nose. [Inf Black] **1986** Pederson *LAGS Concordance,* 1 inf, **neGA,** 1 inf, spreaded; 1 inf, **ceMS,** See everybody spreaded out like that; 1 inf, **neLA,** They done spreaded out. [2 of 3 infs Black] **2003** *Houston Chron.* (TX) 12 Jan 10 (Internet), He spreaded the ball around to Todd Pinkston and . . to anybody who wanted it.

   B Senses.

   1 also with *up:* To arrange the coverings on (a bed), make (a bed).   **chiefly Sth, S Midl**
   1859 Rice *Mabel* 332 **OH,** She spread up the bed quickly and neatly. **1886** (1888) Wiggin *Birds' Christmas Carol* 33, Now, Susan, you an' Kitty wash up the dishes; an' Peter, can't yer spread up the beds? **1940** Hench Coll. **cVA,** Alonzo, colored janitor of Colonnade Club said this morning "I'm going to spread up Mr. Sirich's bed." I asked Virginia what the phrase meant & she said " 'Make up'. Everybody around here knows that *to spread up* means *to make up*." **1951** Giles *Harbin's Ridge* 43 **eKY,** It troubled me a heap the way the woman had spread up her bed. Careless like. **1959** *VT Hist.* 27.160, Spread the bed. . . Also, spread up the bed. To make the bed. Occasional. **1977** Morrison *Song of Solomon* 215 [Black], You have yet to wash your own underwear, spread a bed, wipe the ring from your tub, or move a fleck of your dirt from one place to another. **1984** Wilder *You All Spoken Here* 28 **Sth,** Spread: Arrange; make, as in "Spread the bed." **1997** in 2002 *DARE* File—Internet **MD,** I . . turned on the dishwasher; feather dusted a couple of tables; spread the bed. **2001** *Ibid* **TX,** We spread up the bed as soon as we get up. **2003** *NADS Letters* **swMO,** To spread up the bed is to make it a little hastily. . . [I]f you are in a hurry in the morning, you just spread up the bed, or pull up the bedspread, and let it go. **2004** *Ibid* **cFL,** I grew up in central Florida (I'm 48 now) with Scots-Irish parents and grandparents. We say "to spread up the bed."

   2 To set (a table).   **esp Sth, S Midl** Cf **fix v B1c**
   1842 *Ladies' Repository* 2.208, If you have help to dress the food and spread the table for your family, there will still be many calls for patience. **1864** *Atlantic Mth.* 13.162 **eKY,** I well knew that there was nobody but myself to mix the corn-cake, spread the table, or run the dozen errands that would be needed. **1906** *DN* 3.158 **nwAR,** Spread the table, v. phr. To set the table. **1968–70** *DARE* (Qu. G9, *When you have to get the table ready for a meal . . "It's time to _____."*) Infs **AL46, 61, OK53, VT16,** Spread the table; **NC84,** Spread the table—corr to "set the table." [3 of 5 Infs Black] **2003** *NADS Letters* **SC,** "Spread the table" is somewhat familiar to me as well. **2004** *Ibid* **KY,** Spread the bed/table: very common among both sides of my family. Usually in "One of you young'uns get in here and spread this table for supper!" *Ibid* **LA** (as of c1960), Growing up, we were asked (told) to *spread the table* for supper. *Ibid* **NYC** (as of c1970), My mother or maternal grandmother used to tell me to "spread the table" when they wanted me to set out silverware, plates, glasses, napkins, etc. for a semi-formal type of dinner (e.g., a holiday meal). *Ibid* **VA,** I grew up in Virginia and heard "spread the table" there.

spread n
   1 See **spread chain.**
   2 An expanse of land, esp a ranch or farm and its appurtenances.   **chiefly West**
   1927 James *Cow Country* 67, He'd paid a big price for the said spread, and he was lord and master there sure enough. **1936** in Lib. of Congress *Amer. Memory: WPA Life Hist.* (Internet) **cnTX** (as of 1870s), You see, my dad's spread wasn't much shakes, and he couldn't hire much help because he didn't have so much money. . . They branded 10,000 dogies a year when the spread was going. **1945** *Greeley* (Colo.) *D. Tribune* 13 March 1/6 (*DA*), Loss of trained men for several types of semi-skilled jobs on a sheep spread is a major cause for the drop. **1956** Almirall *From College* 57 **CO,** My sister was really the one financially responsible for the upkeep and success of their spread or layout, as her thirty thousand fenced acres were called. **1963** *AmSp* 38.302, In the midwest cattle country, the terms *spread* and *ranch* are used interchangeably to refer to an owner's land holdings. The owner, or operator, is called a rancher in either case. **1966** *Julian Apple Day* 13 **csCA,** [She] is well acquainted with the wilds of northern Montana, because her son was a wheat spread up there. **1968** *Post–Reg.* (Idaho Falls ID) 25 Jan 32/2, 6,400 Acres combination dry farm and cattle spread East of Idaho Falls. **1986** Pederson *LAGS Concordance* (He owns a _____) 4 infs, **AL, AR, GA, TX,** Big (or large) spread; 1 inf, **ceTX,** Big

spread—Western term for a lot of land; 1 inf, **seAL**, Nice little spread; 1 inf, **csTX**, A pretty good spread. **2002** *Denver Post* (CO) 20 Jan sec T 3 (Internet), The 4 Eagle Ranch is the West as it was—a working cattle spread north of Wolcott.

3 pl: An area where a river broadens out into a shallow lake or maze of narrow channels. **esp Upper Missip Valley, MI**

1903 *DN* 2.331 **seMO**, *Spreads.* . . Shallows formed by the filling up of the channel of a river by sediment. The 'spreads' of the St. Francis river cover many square miles. **1911** in 2008 (acc) Lexis–Nexis Legal Research *State Case Law: WI* (Internet), The spreads of the river within the district are not separate bodies of water constituting inland navigable lakes or ponds. **1916** U.S. Congress House *St. Frances R. Hearings* 13, It is impenetrable. It is what they call the "spreads" of the [St. Francis] river. It has above there a defined channel, and when it gets down to a certain part of the river it spreads. **1944** WI Acad. *Trans.* 36.64, There are also large stretches, particularly at the spreads called Big and Lucius Lakes in which the river is dropping muck, largely of organic nature. **1985** Hendrickson *Angler's Guide MI* 169, Do not try to float it from Main River Bridge to Clark Bridge. The river divides into several narrow channels too small to float a canoe at the "spreads" on the Black River property. **2008** *DARE* File—Internet **cnMI**, This scenic 5-mile stratch features the "spreads" of the Indian River as it enters Mullett Lake to the north of town, then suddenly bursts out onto the lake a mile or so below Topinabee.

spread adder See **spreading adder**

spread chain n Also *spread* Cf **spreader**

A pair of chains united at one end by a ring and held apart at the other by a bar, used to transmit the draft from two **single-trees** to a vehicle.

1780 in 1837 Lafayette *Memoirs* 1.483, The man . . adds that they wanted their double trees and spread chains. **a1849** Ibid, [Will cited from Willbook 3, Westmoreland County, Pennsylvania, p. 3:] I give and bequeath unto my beloved wife Eliza Martin . . my plough harrow double trees and spread Chain. **1874** *Stevens Point Jrl.* (WI) 29 Aug [3]/1 (newspaperarchive.com), [Advt:] It . . is supplied with whiffletrees and spread chain. **1935** *Indiana Progress* (PA) 10 Apr 8/1, [Advt:] Lumber and Log Chains, Spread Chains, Double and Singletrees [etc]. **1939** *LANE* Map 173, Several informants . . offered terms denoting not a solid wooden cross bar but an arrangement of chains used for the same purpose consisting of two chains running from the whiffletrees to the center of the front axle and presumably spread into a V-formation by a rigid cross piece. . . 2 infs, **neME**, *Crotch chain,* a spread chain on a plow; 1 inf, **ceNH**, *Spreader,* a spread chain; 1 inf, **swNH**, *Spread chain;* 1 inf, **swME**, *Spreader* = spread chain; 1 inf, **swME**, *Spread,* a spread chain.

spreaded See **spread** v A

spreader n [Cf *EDD spreader* "The stick or stretcher used to keep apart the chain traces worn by cart-horses"] **scattered, but chiefly NEast, Gt Lakes** Cf **evener 1, stretcher 1**

The bar that holds apart the two ends of a **spread chain;** a **spread chain;** a **doubletree;** hence n *spreader chain* a **spread chain.**

1833 *OH Repository* (Canton) [22 Nov 3]/5 (newspaperarchive.com), [Advt:] One Spreader and Fifth Chain. **1863** in 1890 U.S. War Dept. *War of Rebellion* 1st ser 30.1.268, *Report of quartermaster's stores captured and destroyed by the enemy at the battle of Chickamauga, September 19 and 20, 1863.* . . Means of transportation: . . Fifth chains. . . Bearing chains. . . Spreaders. . . Halter chains. **1876** Knight *Amer. Mech. Dict.* 3.2289, *Spreader.* . . A stick which stretches apart the ends of a chain to which the single-trees are attached. It is a substitute for a double-tree. **1909** *DN* 3.416 **nME**, *Spreader.* . . A wooden bar hooked to the roller of a bob to each end of which a whiffletree is fastened. **1939** *LANE* Map 173 (*Evener*), Five informants use *evener* and *spreader* as synonyms. . . One . . uses *evener* of a straight cross bar, *spreader* of a forked . . piece serving the same purpose. . . [O]ne . . says that an evener is bolted to the wagon tongue by a clevis in the center, while a spreader is attached to the vehicle by two chains . . ; another . . exactly reverses this distinction. . . Occasionally a special term is used for the cross bar on a plow[;] . . the term *spreader* is [thus restricted] by three. . . The term *spreader* is twice defined specifically as the cross bar on a stone drag. . . 16 infs, 14 **ME**, Spreader. **1942** ME Univ. *Studies* 54.146, [Caption:] Double Tree or Spreader Chain. **1965–70** *DARE* (Qu. L47, *The two movable bars behind a team of horses are fastened to a longer piece; this is a* _____) Infs **DC**8, **HI**12, **ME**5, 9, **MA**16, **NH**14, **NY**82, 87, **OH**95, Spreader; **MN**2, **OH**86, **WI**58, Spreader [FW sugg]; (Qu. L46, *Behind each horse there's a movable bar [the leathers or*

ropes from the collar are fastened to it]) Inf **CA**211, Spreader. **1969** Sorden *Lumberjack Lingo* 118 **NEng, Gt Lakes**, *Spreader*—A wooden hitching device that held apart a crotched chain used in skidding in place of doubletrees. **1973** Allen *LAUM* 1.216 **Upper MW** (as of c1950), *Evener*. . . *Spreader,* rare in the field records, is reported in 15 checklists, 12 of which are from Minnesota. **1983** *MJLF* 9.1.57 **ceKY** (as of 1956), *Spreader* . . a doubletree. **1986** Pederson *LAGS Concordance (Doubletree)* 1 inf, **neMS**, Spreader; 1 inf, **nwFL**, Spreader (guessing); 1 inf, **cwLA**, Spreader—same as evener—had "stay chains."

spreader dam n **chiefly West**

An earthen dam that interrupts the flow of runoff in order to reduce erosion and promote infiltration.

1935 *Woodland Daily Democrat* (CA) [11 Jan 8]/2 (newspaperarchive.com), "Spreader dams" . . cause the water to spread over the entire stream bed. . . The purpose of this is to allow the water plenty of opportunity to percolate into the soil. **1937** *Ada Weekly News* (OK) 18 Feb 1/7, Practices for which payments will be made include . . construction of spreader dams, terraces or reservoirs. **1950** in 2002 (acc) Lexis–Nexis Legal Research *State Case Law: TX* (Internet), Defendant was . . building spreader dams for the Taylors on their ranch. **1951** Fergusson *New Mexico* 408, [Glossary:] *Spreader dam*—an earth dam, thrown up on the surface of the land to spread surface water and prevent its cutting a gully. **1974** in 2002 (acc) Lexis–Nexis Legal Research *State Case Law: WY* (Internet), The court ordered that Scott be enjoined . . from continuing the use and operation of . . spreader dams . . and that he restore the natural channel . . of Wild Cat Creek. **1986** Ibid: SD, The type of irrigation system available, be it . . spreader dams or subsoil irrigation, appears relevant to some extent. **1998** in 2002 *DARE* File—Internet **cwCA**, [Minutes of the Board of Directors Meeting of the Santa Clara CA Water District:] He referenced the spreader dam sites and suggested that the District review replacing them with injection well technology. **2002** Ibid **seWA**, The barrier dam is a spreader dam right at the salmon hatchery. **2005** *DARE* File **TX**, Spreader-dam . . something I've heard about all my life in central and west Texas.

spreadhead n Also *spread-headed viper, spreadhead moccasin, ~ snake* [Because it flattens out its head and neck when threatened] **chiefly S Midl** See Map Cf **spreading adder, ~ viper**

A **hognose snake** (here: *Heterodon platirhinos*).

1844 (1855) Lewis *New Hope* 83 **WV**, 'Twas like the mixin' of a blacksmith's bellows and the hissing of a thousand spreadhead snakes. **1891** *Decatur Daily Republican* (IL) [3 Sept 2]/4 (newspaperarchive.com) **MO**, Howard Davis Jr. . . declares he plowed up and killed . . 38 spread-head snakes. **1915** *Copeia* 18.6 **VA**, *Heterodon platirhinos*. . . Spread-head moccasin. **1918** Ibid 53.25 **VA**, "Spreadhead". *Heterodon contortrix* [=*H. platirhinchos*]. **1940** Hall Coll. **wNC**, Spread-head, . . "A plain old adder." **1958** Randolph *Sticks* 108 **nwAR**, He seen a big old spread-head, the worst poison snake there is. **1965–70** *DARE* (Qu. P25, . . *Kinds of snakes*) 10 Infs, **KY, MO, VA, WV**, Spreadhead; **KS**1, Hog snake or spreadhead; **KY**68, Spreadhead—when you disturb them, they'll spread their heads and hiss; **TN**7, Blowing vipers . . , spreadhead—same snake; **VA**38, 75, Spreadhead moccasin; **VA**105, Spreadhead snake; **KY**72, Spread-headed viper. **1995** *Brophy Coll.* 71 **swMO** (as of c1960), *Spreadhead.* [A] spreading viper or hog-nosed snake, a small snake which hisses and flattens its head, and finally "sulls" or plays dead. **2002** *DARE* File—Internet **seNJ**, Eastern hognose snakes are commonly referred to as "spreadhead," "puff adder," or "hissing viper."

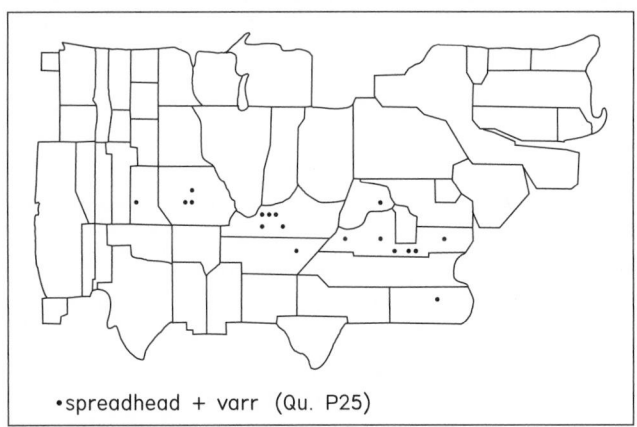

•spreadhead + varr (Qu. P25)

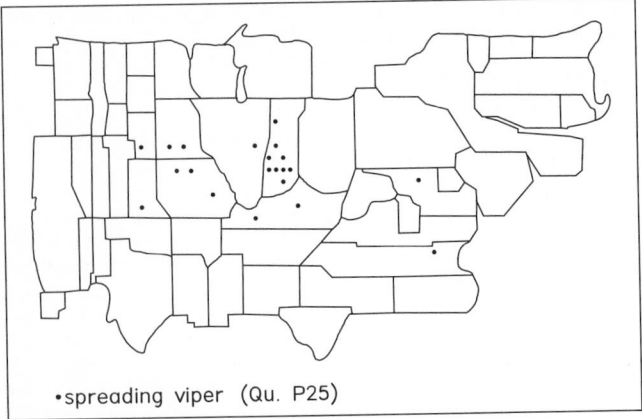

•spreading viper (Qu. P25)

spreading adder n   Also *spread(in) adder, spread(in) nadder*
chiefly Sth, TX, Lower Missip Valley   See Map   Cf **spreadhead, spreading outer, ~ viper**
A **hognose snake** (here: *Heterodon platirhinos*).
    1842 DeKay *Zool. NY* 3.52, Hog-nosed snake. . . It is also called *Deaf
Adder, Spreading Adder, Hog-nose* and *Buckwheat-nose.* **1852** in 1854
U.S. War Dept. *Explor. Red River* 193 **LA,** Though perfectly harmless,
they exhibit a threatening appearance, when approached, in the flattening
of their head and violent hissings; hence the names of blowing-viper,
spreading-adder, &c. **1906** *DN* 3.124 **nwAR,** Spreadin' nadder. . .
Blowing viper. "Spreadin' nadders won't hurt you." **1909** *DN* 3.374
eAL, wGA, *Spread-nadder.* . . A snake, otherwise called *spreading-adder.* **1929** Sale *Tree Named John* 109 **MS** [Black], All de folkses got
out'n de way . . cep'm' Brer Addersnake, en Brer Elefunt step on 'is
haid en . . mash hit out so flat he spread all over de groun', en ever since
den, eve'body been call 'im "Spreadin' Adder." **1931** Faulkner in *Amer.
Mercury* 22.261 **MS,** Her mouth pursed out like a spreading adder's, like
a rubber mouth. **1944** *PADS* 2.50 **sVA,** *Spread-nadder.* . . Spreading-
adder. **1965–70** *DARE* (Qu. P25, . . *Kinds of snakes*) 72 Infs, **chiefly
Sth, TX, Lower Missip Valley,** Spreading adder; NC53, SC34, TX35,
Spread adder. **1986** Pederson *LAGS Concordance* 18 infs, **Gulf Region,** Spreading adder. **1996** in 2006 *DARE* File—Internet **sAppalachians,** Then again don't know how old mama was when she figured out
there was no such snake as a spread nadder. **2003** in 2008 *Ibid* **nTX,**
We had some adders in North Texas. . . Supposedly, though, the "spreading adder" can't bite.

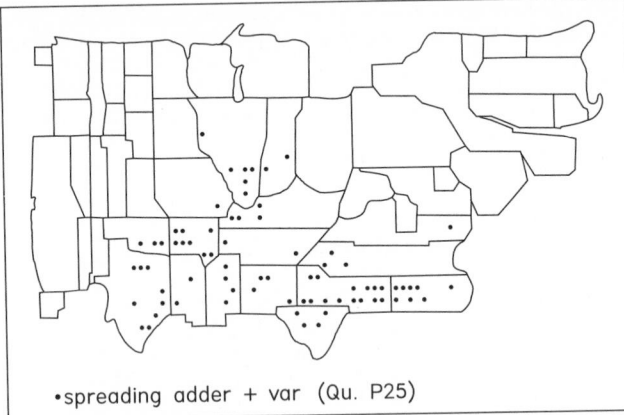

•spreading adder + var (Qu. P25)

spreading dogbane n
Std: a **dogbane a** (here: *Apocynum androsaemifolium*). Also
called **angel's turnip, bitter dogbane, bitterroot 1, Chickasaw 3, colicroot 7, cruel plant, flytrap n 1, honeybloom,
milk ipecac 1, milkweed 3, rheumatism root d, ~ weed b,
sarsaparilla B7, snake's milk 2, staggers, wild ipecac 3**

spreading outer n   [Folk-etym for **spreading adder**]
    1921 *DN* 5.113 **CA,** *Spreadin'-outer, spreading-outer.* . . The spread-
ing adder or hognose snake. From southern negro usage. Rare in California.

spreading viper n   **chiefly Missip-Ohio Valleys, esp IN**   See
Map   Cf **spreadhead, spreading adder**
A **hognose snake** (here: *Heterodon platirhinos*).
    1872 *Daily Eve. Bulletin* (San Francisco CA) 13 Sept 1/5, [He] was re-
cently bitten by a spreading viper, and engulfed a square gallon of
whisky as an antidote. **1885** *Daily Gaz.* (Ft. Wayne IN) 27 Oct 8/4,
Mrs. Runkle . . killed the snake, which proved to be a spreading viper a
little over three foot in length and one of the most venomous reptiles
known. **1887** *Courier–Jrl.* (Louisville KY) 15 Feb 6/6, Early in the fall
the girl was playing in a field and was bitten on the arm by a spreading
viper. **1892** IN Dept. Geol. & Nat. Resources *Rept. for 1891* 510, Hog-
nosed Snake; Spreading Viper. **1965–70** *DARE* (Qu. P25, . . *Kinds of
snakes*) 19 Infs, **chiefly Missip-Ohio Valleys, esp IN,** Spreading viper;
IA28, Spreading viper—one that spreads its head; **KS**12, Spreading viper—when I was a kid. **1995** [see **spreadhead**]. **2002** *DARE* File—
Internet **IL** (as of early 20th cent), He encountered in the narrow foot
path which he was following, a spreading viper.

spread(in') nadder   See **spreading adder**

spread oneself v phr   *somewhat old-fash*
To exert oneself; to show off, make a display of oneself.
    1832 in 1868 McCall *Letters Frontiers* 433, Champion [=a horse]
brought me safely out of the flat, and *spread himself,* or bounded forward on the broad level plain. **1857** *Harper's New Mth. Mag.* 16.139
PA, Now that he had the responsibilities of a new office on his shoulders
he felt the importance of it, and was quite willing to spread himself generally. **1879** *Atlantic Mth.* 43.356, It's almost impossible to get a bit of
good honest bounce out of an American, nowadays,—to get him to
spread himself, as you say. **1904** *DN* 2.421 **nwAR,** *Spread one's
self.* . . To make a display of one's self; to attract attention. 'He just
wanted to spread himself.' **1905** *DN* 3.21 **cCT,** *Spread oneself.* . . To
make an unusual effort. **1907** Lincoln *Cape Cod* 252 **MA,** He begun to
tell her the story of his life. 'Twas a fine chance for him to spread himself, and I cal'late he done it to the skipper's taste. **1909** *DN* 3.374
eAL, wGA, *Spread oneself.* . . To make an unusual effort, go to considerable expense in entertainment. **1942** McAtee *Dial. Grant Co. IN* 61
(as of 1890s), *Spread one's self* . . assume airs, act ostentatiously.

spread up   See **spread** v **B1**

spreadwater n
    1914 *DN* 4.113 **cKS,** *Spreadwater.* . . The overflow along the banks of
a stream.

spreckle n   [Brit dial]
1   A speckle, spot, freckle; hence adjs *spreckled* (pronc-sp
spreckle), *spreckly,* speckled, spotted, freckled.
    1841 *Adams Sentinel* (Gettysburg PA) 13 Dec [3]/6 (newspaper-
archive.com), [Advt:] One spreckled Heifer, one brindled Heifer. **1886**
Century Illustr. Mag. 32.190 **eVA** [Black], A spreckle-face feller run
up an' ketch Remus' head. **1928** Ruppenthal *Coll.* **KS,** Spreckles. . .
freckles—used by some of German extraction. **1930** Shoemaker *1300
Words* 54 **cPA Mts** (as of c1900), *Spreckled*—A spotted, or more latterly
a dominique fowl. **1966** *DARE* (Qu. Q17, . . *Kinds of woodpeckers*) Inf
GA16, Spreckled woodpecker. **1991** *DARE* File **csPA,** The nest . . had
four small blue eggs with brown speckles, or "spreckles," as most people
around here pronounce it. **2001** *DARE* File—Internet **VA,** Fortissima
Colori sock yarn in spreckly colors. 231 yds/50g ball. **2002** *Ibid* **cCA**
[Catalog], Brown Gold Spreckled Bangle—Wide. . . A wood looking
brown bangle with gold flake speckles all over.
2   See **speckled trout 1.**

spreckled   See **spreckle 1**

spreckle(d) trout   See **speckled trout**

spreckled woodpecker, spreckle peckerwood   See **speckled
woodpecker**

spreckly   See **spreckle 1**

spree n, v
A display of sexual excitement; to display sexual excitement;
see quots.
    1902 *DN* 2.246 **sIL,** *Spreein.* . . Rutting. **1916** *DN* 4.329 **KS,** *Spree,
n.* and *v.* Display (of) sexual desire: of a female animal.

spreet n   [Pronc var of *sprit*]   **esp Mid Atl**
    [**1844** see **sprittail.**] **1856** Kane *Arctic Explor.* 1.316, She carried . . a
stouter mainsail . . with a spreet eighteen feet long. **1899** (1912) Green

VA Folk-Speech 410, *Spreet.* . . A sprit, a small pole, spar, or boom which crosses a sail diagonally from the mast to the upper aftmost corner, which it is used to stretch and hoist. **1956** McAtee *Some Dialect NC* 58, *Spreet:* pronunc., sprit. *Dial.* Church's Island, Upper Currituck Sound. **1966–69** *DARE* (Qu. O9, . . *Kinds of sailboats*) Inf **NC**21, Spreet—named for the sails; **NC**78, Spreet [sprit] sail. **1976** Warner *Beautiful Swimmers* 253 **eMD**, Thing to do was head for the shallers . . unstep the mast and right your boat. Then step her up, set your spreet pole and off you go again. **2000** (acc) NC Maritime Museum *Self-Guided Tour* (Internet), The basic rig consists of a mainsail, which is supported by the sprit (pronounced "spreet").

spreettail See **sprittail**

sprew v   [Perh blend of *spray* + *spew*]   Cf **skeet** v **4**
See quots.

    1966–69 *DARE* (Qu. Y45, *Talking of a liquid—to scatter in all directions:* "When he opened the can, the beer _____ [all over the kitchen]."*) Inf **SC**26, Sprew; **KY**51, Sprewed [sprud]. **2000** *DARE* File—Internet, All grundle_James-WoG has done is sprew Repubaboobie propaganda. **2002** *Ibid* **MD**, If you fly off the handle and start sprewing forth a torrent of offensive ranting, all will not be well.

sprig n
1 =**pintail 1.** [Abbr for **sprigtail 1**]
    1844 Giraud *Birds Long Is.* 311 **NY**, Pintail Duck. . . This beautiful species is well known to our gunners by the name of "Sprig," or "Spreettail." **1888** Trumbull *Names of Birds* 38, At Baltimore, Washington, Alexandria, Norfolk, and at Morehead, N.C., [the pintail duck is called] *sprigtail,* this being sometimes shortened to *sprig.* **1910** Hart *Vigilante Girl* 113 **nCA**, As for the varieties up here, I have myself shot . . sprig. **1938** Oberholser *Bird Life LA* 109, The Pintail, commonly known also as 'sprig' or 'sprigtail', is one of the most abundant and best known ducks of North America. **1965–70** *DARE* (Qu. Q5, . . *Kinds of wild ducks*) 15 Infs, **scattered**, Sprig; **CA**130, 145, **IA**22, **IL**32, **OR**5, Sprig—same as pintail; **DE**3, Sprig—a gray duck with a sharp tail. **1968** *DARE* Tape **DE**7, I like mallards and blacks and teals. Sprigs is not a bad duck. **1975** [see **sprigtail 1**]. **2001** MD Ornith. Soc. *MD Yellowthroat* March–Apr 6 **eVA, eMD**, Other places got more ponds and freshwater than here, they got more ducks like Sprigs, Spoonbills and teal. **2002** *DARE* File—Internet, Here in the Atlantic Flyway, our early season sprigs *never* have the long pintails.
2 A bit; a small amount or portion. [By ext from *sprig* a small shoot or twig] **esp sAppalachians** Cf **scrid**
    1937 Hall Coll. **wNC, eTN**, *Sprig.* . . A bit, a small amount. I have heard this word only in the following use, "Dad gone it, there weren't even a sprig of fire in his place." **1954** *Harder Coll.* **cwTN**, *Sprig.* . . A small amount; as a *sprig o' salt.* **1963** Edwards *Gravel* 18 **eTN** (as of 1920s), A twist for a sprig of your sweet. **1969** *DARE* (Qu. LL6c, *A small, indefinite amount . .* "It still needs just a _____ of cinnamon.") Inf **GA**84, Sprig. **1976** Garber *Mountain-ese* 87 **sAppalachians**, *Sprig* . . tiny particle—There was jist barely a sprig uv life in the animal when we found it.

sprig of Jerusalem n
=**bugleweed.**
    1898 *Bot. Gaz.* 26.251 **ME**, *Lycopus Virginicus.* . . sprig-of-Jerusalem, South Berwick.

sprigtail n
1 also *spraguetail, sprig-tailed widgeon:* =**pintail 1.**
    1768 (1925) Washington *Diaries* 1.254, Killd 2 Ducks, viz. a sprig tail and Teal. **a1782** (1788) Jefferson *Notes VA* 77, Ballcoot. Sprigtail. Didapper, or Dopchick. **1814** Wilson *Amer. Ornith.* 8.72 **PA**, The Pintail, or . . the Sprigtail, is a common . . duck in our markets, much esteemed for the excellence of its flesh. **1835** Audubon *Ornith. Biog.* 3.214, The Pintail, which, in the United States, is better known by the name of Sprigtail, arrives on the western waters early in October. **1873** *Appletons' Jrl.* 10.467 **Chesapeake Bay**, The pin-tail, or sprig-tail, is also choice eating when fat. **1876** *Scribner's Mth.* 13.152 **Long Is. NY**, In both autumn and spring, vast numbers of canvas-backs, red-heads, widgeon, teal, dippers, and sprig-tail are killed. **1888** Trumbull *Names of Birds* 39 **SC, GA**, At Charleston and Savannah [the pintail is called] *sprig-tailed widgeon.* **1965–70** *DARE* (Qu. Q5, . . *Kinds of wild ducks*) Infs **FL**22, **IL**6, **MD**45, **NC**78, 80, **SC**9, **TX**23, **VA**8, Sprigtail; **VA**47, 75, Sprigtail or pintail; **IL**6, Sprigtail—tail sharply pointed and is smaller than a mallard; **IA**29, Spraguetail—looks like a hen mallard. **1975** Newell *If Nothin' Don't Happen* 137 **nwFL**, We jumped several

good bunches of canvasbacks and one real big bunch of sprigtails off the mouth of Salt Creek. It sure was pretty to see them old sprigs climb up into that nor'west wind, hang up there for a little piece and then drop off and go barrelin' downwind.
2 also *sprigtail grouse, ~ prairie chicken:* =**sharp-tailed grouse.**
    1859 in 1890 Hall *Hist. CO* 2.522, Phil killed two sprigtail grouse. **1877** Hallock *Sportsman's Gaz.* 117, *Pedioecetes phasianellus.* . . Sharp-tailed Grouse, Sprig Tail [etc]. **1895** Ridgway *Ornith. IL* 2.13, Prairie Sharp-tailed Grouse. . . Popular synonyms. Spike-tail, Pin-tail, or Sprig-tail Prairie Chicken.
3 also *little frost sprigtail:* =**ruddy duck.**
    1917 (1923) *Birds Amer.* 1.152, Ruddy Duck. . . Other Names. . . Stifftail; Pin-tail; Bristle-tail; Sprig-tail; Stick-tail; Spine-tail [etc]. **1923** Dawson *Birds CA* 4.1841, These saucy tails are composed of stiff, spiny feathers, having shafts denuded toward the tips . . so that the birds [= ruddy ducks] are popularly known as Pintails, Sprig-tails, Quill-tails, Spine-tails, etc., in confusion with *Dafila acuta* . . which owes its common name not to the stiffness but to the graceful length of its caudal appendage. **1940** Trautman *Birds Buckeye Lake* 202 **OH**, [Footnote:] Because of the habit of appearing on mornings following frosty nights the bird was called the "little frost duck" or "little frost sprig-tail" by many sportsmen.

sprig-tailed widgeon See **sprigtail 1**

sprigtail grouse (or prairie chicken) See **sprigtail 2**

sprill n   Also *pine-sprill*   [Var of **spill** n[1] **1**, perh infl by *sprig*] **ME**
=**needle** n **B1.**
    1973 Graham *Where Morning Lies* 98 **ME**, You wonder how the sprills even get upstairs, but you find them in your bed and all over. **1989** *NY Times* (NY) 23 Nov sec C 10/5 **ME**, "Working at home you've got sprills everywhere—in your hair, in your clothes. It's awful." Sprills are the little odds and ends of fir that break off as wreaths are tied. **2004** in 2008 *DARE* File—Internet **ME**, The cold forces the tree to set a waxy coating on the sprills. . . Once the waxy coating is set the sprills shouldn't dry out and drop until well after Christmas. **2006** *Ibid* **ME**, Nothing deadly mind you, just a mild wallop should curious feline touch so much as one little pine sprill. **2008** *Ibid* **ME**, [Advt:] This 3″ square pillow is packed with balsam "sprills" as the old-timers call them.

sprills n pl   **esp NEast**
=**jimmies** n pl[2].
    1934 *Modesto Bee & News–Herald* (CA) [10 Oct 35]/5 (newspaperarchive.com), [Caption to cartoon by Gluyas Williams, of **eMA:**] Taking orders for cones . . one with chocolate sprills on it and one without. **1977–78** Foster *Lexical Variation* 25 **NJ**, *Jimmies* and *sprinkles* 'little candy bits put on a sundae'. . . *Sprills,* used by two Middlesex informants, is probably a variant of *sprinkles.* **2002** *DARE* File—Internet **ceMA** [Russo's Candy and Ice Cream House], Brazil Truffle—creamy fudge, dipped in milk chocolate, rolled in sprills. *Ibid* **Boston MA** [Local Lingo], *Sprills*—same as jimmies or sprinkles!

sprinch n
    1968 *DARE* (Qu. LL6b, *A small, indefinite amount . .* "I'll put in just a _____ of butter.") Inf **MO**4, Sprinch. **1995** in 2006 *DARE* File—Internet, Sprinkle with a dash of cayenne and a sprinch (between a sprinkle and a pinch) of salt and pepper.

spring n, v   Usu |sprɪŋ|; also **esp S Midl** |spræŋ, sprɛŋ, sprɛŋ| Pronc-sp *sprang*   Cf Pronc Intro 3.I.6.d
A Forms.
    1915 in 1944 *ADD* **eTN**, Spring. . . (Season.) . . sprang. **1934** *AmSp* 9.210 **Sth**, A few words having standard [ɪ] before [ŋ] change [ɪ] to [e] or [eɪ]. . . The number of words is small, but the sound is rather general and decidedly noticeable. *Bring . . spring . . thing.* **1941** *AmSp* 16.4 **eTX** [Black], Before *ng* . . [ɪ] becomes [ẽ], [eĩ]: *bring . . spring . . wing.* **1942** Hall *Smoky Mt. Speech* 16 **wNC, eTN**, [ɛɹ] or [ɛ] often occurs in *drink . . spring . . wing.* **1949** Webber *Backwoods Teacher* 16 **Ozarks**, I'll have the younguns lug up some fresh water from the sprang. **1954** *Harder Coll.* **cwTN**, I ain't no sprang chicken. **c1960** Wilson Coll. **csKY**, *Spring* is often /spræŋ/. **1966** *DARE* FW Addit **swNC**, [spræŋ]. **1976** Garber *Mountain-ese* 86 **sAppalachians**, *Sprang* . . spring—We got a cool drink at the sprang. **1982** Slone *How We Talked* 8 **eKY** (as of c1950), Others had a "spring," a natural spring of underground water. . . A "sprang house" was built over it.

B As verb.

1 To sprain, strain; hence ppl adjs *sprang, sprung* sprained. **esp Sth, S Midl**

1869 *Newport Jrl.* (RI) 31 July 1/1, The "pitcher" two [sic] has sprung his wrist / The Umpire's brain is in a mist. **1933** Rice *Mr. Pete* 86 **KY**, One of the Miss Clarks had stumbled over a loose board in the hall and "sprung a' ankle." **1938** in 2008 (acc) Lexis–Nexis Legal Research *State Case Law: KY* (Internet), He also had a sprung wrist and thumb. **1945** Hench Coll. **VA**, [Quoting a student's theme:] They [=leaves] conceal things as . . holes to spring my ankle. **1946** *AmSp* 21.98 **sIL**, *Sprung his back,* sprained his back. **1958** *Progress–Index* (Petersburg VA) 10 Aug [15]/1 (newspaperarchive.com), In an effort . . to catch the motorcycle he sprung his wrist. **c1960** *Wilson Coll.* **csKY**, *Spring*. . . To sprain. "He sprung his ankle." **1970** *Thompson Coll.* **AL** (as of 1920s), He's done went and sprung his back again. **1998** in 2003 *DARE* File—Internet **TX**, Jordan played 4 square today after lunch and sprang her ankle. **1999** *Morning News* (Springdale AR) 5 Dec sec B 8/6, Our point guard sprang her ankle and hit her head. **2003** *DARE* File—Internet **NC**, The pilot, when the plane snapped in two he was slung and hit pretty hard and sprung his back. **2007** in 2008 *DARE* File—Internet **AR**, I took my son in the ER last year, I was told he had a sprang wrist.

2 Usu of a cow or heifer: to show any of var signs of advanced pregnancy or imminent parturition; to be close to parturition; hence ppl adj, vbl n *springing.* [*EDD spring* v. 1; cf *OED2 spring* v. 5] Cf **come fresh, come in 1, freshen 2**

1765 *NY Gaz.* (NY) 18 Feb 3/2, [Advt:] *William Gilliland* . . wants . . Twenty Milch, or Springing Cows, . . and one Bull. **1838** *Sun* (Baltimore MD) 23 June 2/4, [Advt:] *An Estray.*—Came to the subscriber's . . a *brown springing cow;* she now has a calf. **1896** *Gettysburg Comp.* (PA) 17 Mar [2]/6 (newspaperarchive.com), [Advt:] 1 Springing Heifer. **1914** *DN* 4.113 **cKS**, *Spring*. . . To expand greatly near the end of pregnancy—Said of animals. **1923** *DN* 5.222 **swMO**, *Spring*. . . To increase in girth as the end of pregnancy approaches. **1937** *AmSp* 12.103 **eNE** [Farm terms], A cow that is about to calve is called a *springer;* she is *springin'.* **1958** *AmSp* 33.272 **eWA** [Ranching terms], *Springing*. Due to calve; *springing heavy* means nearing the time of delivery. A cow which has been bred is called a *springer.* A *springing heifer* is a heifer carrying her first calf. **1965–70** *DARE* (Qu. K10, *Words used about a cow that is going to have a calf*) 69 Infs, **scattered,** (She's) springing; **DC**5, Springing real heavy; **IN**63, Starting to spring; (Qu. AA28, . . *Joking or sly expressions . . women use to say that another is going to have a baby . . "She['s] _____."*) Infs **MS**1, **WV**3, **WI**47, Springing. **1965** *Bee* (Phillips WI) 19 Aug [6/3], For sale: Springing Holstein Heifers. **1982** Powers *Cataloochee* 280 **cwNC**, Aunt Polly raised cain with her menfolk for carrying their 'springing' milk cow along with the others to the mountains. As a result, at the time of her calving, without attention, she died. **1986** Pederson *LAGS Concordance* (Daisy [=a cow] *is going to _____*) 11 infs, **scattered Gulf Region,** (She's) springing; 2 infs, **AL, AR**, She's a-springing; 1 inf, **ceTX**, A springing cow; 2 infs, **AL, AR**, A cow (*or* that one) is springing; 1 inf, **cwTN**, This cow's springing; *(Pregnant)* 1 inf, **ceTX**, She's springing—men say of women. **2002** *Beef* (St. Paul MN) June 11 **sFL**, Friends and family tell me I might "calve" any day since I've really started springing heavy. **2002** in 2003 *DARE* File—Internet [Cattle Pages Discussion Boards], Most premature calves that I have seen the cow was not springing at all and then she just had it. **2003** *Ibid* **WI**, [Auction notice:] (12) cows springing or due within the next 30–60 days. Balance of herd is bred back and due for year-round freshening. *Ibid* **WI**, [Auction notice:] 2 close springing Holstein heifers (1—due sale day).

3 Usu of a cow: to give birth; to bear (offspring)—freq in phr *spring a calf.*

1948 Davis *Word Atlas Gt. Lakes* 228, *To calve* . . [4 infs, **IN, OH**] spring a calf. *Ibid* app qu 64, 2 [of 233] infs, **IL, MI**, Spring. **1966–68** *DARE* (Qu. K11, *When a cow has a calf . . she _____*) Inf **OH**43, Sprang; **GA**12, Springs a calf; **AL**43, **MN**34, **NC**33, **NY**45, **WV**4, Sprung a calf. **1986** Pederson *LAGS Concordance* (Daisy [=a cow] *is going to _____*) 5 infs, **GA, LA, TN**, Spring; 1 inf, **cnAL**, Spring—a calf. **2000** Kingsolver *Prodigal Summer* 165 **sAppalachians**, If it gets real cold, you'll need to get the mothers [=goats] in your barn when they're ready to spring.

spring beauty n

1 A plant of the genus *Claytonia,* esp *C. virginica.* **chiefly Nth, esp N Cent, PA, Upstate NY** For other names of var spp see **daisy 3, Eskimo potato, fairy spuds, good-morning-spring, grassflower 2, groundnut B7, mayflower 4, May**

pink 3, miner's lettuce, pigeon root, tangle-gut 2, turkey pea 3b, wild potato 4b Note: Some of these quots may refer instead to other senses below.

1832 *MA Hist. Soc. Coll.* 2d ser 9.148 **cwVT**, Claytonia virginica, . . Spring beauty. **1844** Lapham *Geogr. Descr. WI* 78, Claytonia Virginica, . . spring beauty. **1849** Howitt *Our Cousins in OH* 58, Among them were the spring-beauty. . . It has five petals veined with pink; the anthers, also, of its five stamens, are pink; the flowers grow in a cluster, and it has long grass-like leaves. **1862** *Atlantic Mth.* 10.650, Our next wild-flower . . is the Claytonia, or Spring-Beauty, which is common in the Middle States. **1913** (1980) Hardy *OH Schoolmistress* 76, The clumps of spring-beauties and bunches of Johnny-jump-ups. **1941** Walker *Lookout* 45 **TN**, Lusty plants from the advent of spring beauties and hepaticas, until the dwarflike frost aster, last to wither in the freezing breath of autumn. **1961** Douglas *My Wilderness* 20 **CO**, Wet spots show monkey-flowers and spring beauties. **1965–70** *DARE* (Qu. S2, . . *The flower that comes up in the woods early in spring, with three white petals that turn pink as the flower grows older*) 28 Infs, **chiefly Nth, esp N Cent**, Spring beauty; (Qu. S26c, *Wildflowers that grow in woods*) 17 Infs, **esp N Cent**, Spring beauty (*or* beauties); (Qu. S11) Infs **MS**38, **OH**72, Spring beauty; (Qu. S23) Infs **DC**2, **OH**6, **TN**31, Spring beauty; (Qu. S26a, . . *Wildflowers. . . Roadside flowers*) Infs **IN**30, **NY**232, **OH**37, 95, **WA**12, Spring beauty (*or* beauties); (Qu. S26b, *Wildflowers that grow in water or wet places*) Infs **IL**113, **MA**67, **PA**242, Spring beauty; (Qu. S26d, *Wildflowers that grow in meadows;* not asked in early QRs) Infs **MN**14, **OH**21, Spring beauties; (Qu. S26e, *Other wildflowers not yet mentioned;* not asked in early QRs) Infs **IN**19, **MI**96, **NY**106, **OH**2, 94, Spring beauty. [*DARE* Ed: Some of these Infs may refer instead to other senses below.] **1965–70** *DARE* Wildfl QR Pl.69A [=*Claytonia caroliniana*] 13 Infs, 9 **IA, MI, OH, WI**, Spring beauty; Pl.51A [=*C. virginica*] Infs **CO**7, **MI**7, 57, **MN**37, **OH**14, **SC**41, **WA**12, 30, **WI**80, Spring beauty. **2002** *NY Times* (NY) 7 Apr sec 14CN 13/1 **NJ** (Internet), Spring beauties [=*Claytonia virginica*] are scattered throughout my gardens, both in sunny and in shady areas.

2 A **hepatica** (here: *Hepatica nobilis* subsp *acuta* or *obtusa*).

1893 *Jrl. Amer. Folkl.* 6.136 **NY**, Hepatica triloba [=*H. nobilis acuta* or *H. n. obtusa*]. . . Spring beauty. **1896** *Ibid* 9.180 **WI**, *Hepatica acutiloba* [=*H. nobilis acuta*] . . spring beauty, Brodhead. **1966** *DARE* Wildfl QR Pl.69B [=*Hepatica acutiloba*] Inf **WI**79, Spring beauty. **1974** (1977) Coon *Useful Plants* 220, *Hepatica acutiloba*. . . spring beauty.

3 An anemone or similar plant; see quots.

1896 *Jrl. Amer. Folkl.* 9.179 **ME**, *Anemone trifolium,* spring beauty, Oxford County. **1966** *DARE* FW Addit **NY**16, Spring beauties—anemone—first thing up in May. **1998** *News & Rec.* (Greensboro NC) 8 Apr 12 (Internet), Spring beauties, Anemone nemrosa [sic]; [etc] . . are all in bloom.

4 A **toothwort** (here: *Cardamine nuttallii* var *nuttallii*).

1934 Haskin *Wild Flowers Pacific Coast* 125, Spring Beauty—*Dentaria tenella* [=*Cardamine nuttallii* var *n.*] . . This is not the spring beauty of the East, which is a different plant. **1967** Gilkey–Dennis *Hdbk. NW Plants* 167, Dentaria tenella. . . *Spring beauty.* . . Open woods, or fields and hillsides without trees.

5 A **phlox** (here: *P. subulata*).

1967 *DARE* Wildfl QR Pl.178 Inf **SC**41, Pink phlox—spring beauty—a misnomer hereabouts.

spring bird n

1 A **song sparrow** (here: *Melospiza melodia*). **NEng**

1760 (1849) Smith *Jrls.* 273 **seME**, The robin and spring birds came a week or ten days sooner than usual. **1792** Belknap *Hist. NH* 3.173, Spring Bird, *Fringilla.* **1824** Z. Thompson *Gazetteer Vt.* 18 (DAE), The singing birds are the robin, thrush, . . springbird, goldfinch, and hangbird. **1832** Williamson *Hist. ME* 1.143, The *Spring Bird* is larger than a chipping bird, and is one of the very first to sing the vernal song. **1873** Whittier in *Atlantic Mth.* 32.64, Sing softly, spring-bird, for her sake. **1956** *MA Audubon Soc. Bulletin* 40.255 **NH**, Song Sparrow. . . Spring Bird. . . as a notable singer in springtime.

2 =**Carolina wren.**

1991 *DARE* File **csPA**, The same informant identified the Carolina wren as a bird called locally *spring bird,* because of its early appearance.

spring black duck n

A **black duck 1** (here: *Anas rubripes*).

1917 (1923) *Birds Amer.* 1.116, Black Duck. . . Other Names.—Dusky Duck; . . Summer Black Duck; Spring Black Duck. **1923** U.S. Dept.

Ag. *Misc. Circular* 13.9 **NEng,** The brown-legged black duck. . . is locally known as . . spring black duck.

springboard n chiefly Pacific NW
In logging: a plank inserted in a notch in a tree trunk to provide a surface for the faller to stand on.
1883 *Harper's New Mth. Mag.* 66.200 **cwCA,** [He] began chopping out some mortise-holes in the trunk about four feet above the ground. These were intended for the insertion of their iron shod "springboards"—pieces of flexible planking . . upon which they were to stand while chopping at a height too great to reach from the ground. **1905** U.S. Forest Serv. *Bulletin* 61.49 [Logging terms], *Spring board. . .* (P[acific] C[oast] F[orest], S[outhern] F[orest]). **1949** Peattie *Cascades* 147 **Pacific NW,** The first thing for them in squaring off at a Douglas fir was to notch for springboards, their working footrests. **1956** *AmSp* 31.152 **nwCA** [Logger lingo], *Springboard.* **1958** McCulloch *Woods Words* 178 **Pacific NW,** *Springboard. . .* Springboards are disappearing with the wide use of power saws. **1967** *DARE* Tape **WA29,** The object of using a springboard was to work on the level. You'd work on side of a mountain and you'd be one foot down here like this and the other up here like this. **1982** *Smithsonian Letters* **swWA, nwOR,** I was raised in the lower Columbia River logging country . . (Early 1900). . . The axe head was about 12 inches long and 3 inches wide. Made especially for cutting "springboard holes" in the tree.

‡spring bone n Cf DS K74
A wishbone.
c1970 Pederson *Dial. Surv. Rural GA,* 1 inf, **seGA,** Pully bone, spring bone.

spring branch n chiefly Sth, S Midl Cf branch 1
A small stream fed by a spring or springs.
1650 in 1940 *AmSp* 15.396 **VA,** Bounded on the North East with a Spring branch or cove. **1814** (1922) Tatum *Jrl.* 7.27 **NC,** A fine spring branch, or creek, on the left at the end of this distance. **1819** (1915) Mason *Pioneer West* 67 **MO,** It is more than probable not even near a spring branch that would float a cornstalk boat. **1853** in 1928 OR Pioneer Assoc. *Trans.* 53 **MA,** Crossed Sandy (or Zig-zag) River once and have encamped close to a spring branch. **1867** Harris *Sut Lovingood Yarns* 201 **TN,** He . . sot intu flingin the bes' kine ove show actor summersets amung the roun rocks in the spring branch. **1883** (1971) Harris *Nights with Remus* 177 **GA** [Black], I monst'us glad dey aint no bad chilluns on dis place fer ter be wadin' in de spring-branch. **1923** *DN* 5.222 **swMO,** *Spring branch. . .* The stream flowing from a spring. **1942** (1960) Robertson *Red Hills* 59 **SC,** The colored women at the wash place at the spring branch. **1965–70** *DARE* (Qu. C1, *. . A small stream of water not big enough to be a river*) Infs **AR14, FL18, KY84, LA15, MO37, NC46, TN7, 11,** Spring branch; (Qu. C4b) Inf **MO15,** Spring branch. **1989** Pederson *LAGS Tech. Index* 110 **Gulf Region** (Creek) 35 infs, Spring branch. **2008** *DARE* File—Internet **cwTX,** [Advt:] Water on the property includes . . a spring branch running between the bluff and the river.

‡spring buck n Cf Mississippi buck
=red-breasted merganser.
1923 U.S. Dept. Ag. *Misc. Circular* 13.6 **IL,** Red-breasted Merganser. . . Vernacular Names. . . *In local use. . .* spring-buck.

spring cellar See springhouse

spring cheeper See cheeper

spring chirper See chirper n 1

spring clover n [See quot]
A sour clover (here: *Trifolium obtusiflorum*).
1902 U.S. Natl. Museum *Contrib. Herbarium* 7.361 **West,** *Trifolium obtusiflorum. . .* The name "spring clover," which is sometimes applied to it, was given because it so often grows near springs in the mountains.

spring dace n
A dace (here: *Rhinichthys osculus*).
1937 MI Univ. Museum Zool. *Occas. Papers* 343.3 **WY,** The total present population of the spring dace was estimated to be between 200,000 and 500,000. **1948** Blackwelder *Gt. Basin* 57 **UT,** The other fish taken is a spring dace, very much like the highly distinctive types that also occur in Steptoe, Butte, and Ruby valleys. **1963** Sigler–Miller *Fishes UT* 84, Speckled Dace. . . Common Names . . western dace, spring dace, dusky dace.

spring dock n
A dock n[1] (here: *Rumex patientia*).
1910 Graves *Flowering Plants* 157 **CT,** *Rumex Patientia. . .* Patience or Spring Dock.

spring fern n [See quot]
A lady fern 1 (here: *Athyrium filix-femina*).
1951 *PADS* 15.26 **TX,** *Athyrium filix-foemina. . .* Spring fern, because common about springs.

springfish n [Appar coined by Rafinesque]
=mottled sculpin.
1820 Rafinesque *Ohio R. Fishes* 85, Springfish. Pegedictis. . . The name means Fountain-fish. *Ibid,* Catseye Springfish. *Pegedictis ictalops* [=*Cottus bairdii*]. . . I have discovered this species in the summer of 1820 near Lexington. It has no vulgar name. **1898** U.S. Natl. Museum *Bulletin* 47.1950, *Cottus ictalops. . .* Miller's Thumb; Blob . . Springfish.

spring frog n
1 =tree frog 1. [Because they are often heard early in the spring]
1803 in 1913 *Auk* 30.337 **sePA,** March 11. Wood Cock . . arrived. Spring Frog whistles. **1939** *Copeia* 129 **neKY,** *Pseudacris brachyphona. . .* —A very common spring frog. Breeding begins as early as February 12, when the marshes ring with the songs of this species and of *Hyla crucifer.* **1942** *Amer. Midland Naturalist* 28.297 **Ocracoke Is. NC,** The small, green "spring-frog" (*Hyla?* sp.) described to me by the islanders may also have disappeared in the past few years. **1950** *WELS* **WI** (Small frogs that sing or chirp loudly in the spring) 1 Inf, Spring frogs; 1 Inf, Could be tree frogs or just spring frogs. **1955** *Herpetologica* 11.30 **seVA,** A frog . . resided in his mailbox. It proved to be a [*Hyla*] *squirella,* which species was known to our informant by the name "Spring Frog." **1965–70** *DARE* (Qu. P21) 85 Infs, **chiefly Sth, S Midl,** Spring frogs. **1973** Allen *LAUM* 1.325 **MN, NE** (as of c1950), Infs were asked to name the small tree frog (*Hyla crucifer*) to be heard making shrill peeping sounds in the bushes near lakes or marshes in the spring. . . Three infs. . . have *spring frog.* **1986** Pederson *LAGS Concordance* **Gulf Region,** 138 infs, Spring frogs; 1 inf, Spring frog—little green frog, tiny, long legs; 1 inf, Spring frogs—fall from sky in a rain, locals say; 1 inf, Spring frogs—rainfrogs. **2006** *News & Observer* (Raleigh NC) 15 Jan sec A 26 (Internet), Deep in the swamps the peeping of early spring frogs can be heard.

2 Any of var frogs of the genus *Rana,* esp *R. clamitans* or a leopard frog. [From their occurrence in springs]
1825 NY Acad. Sci. *Annals Lyceum Nat. Hist.* 1.282, I present indications of six new species. . . *Rana fontinalis,* or common spring frog. **1842** Thompson *Hist. VT* 1.120, The Spring Frog. *Rana fontinalis* [= *Rana clamitans*]. . . It is common in most of the small streams, and especially about springs, and hence its name, Spring Frog. **1842** DeKay *Zool. NY* 3.62, The Spring Frog is one of our commonest species, and is that usually eaten as a delicacy. . . It is one of the earliest that appears in spring. **1861** *Atlantic Mth.* June 752 **MD,** Each of these young gentry is armed with a dead spring frog, perhaps by way of tribute. **1894** U.S. Natl. Museum *Proc.* 17.339 **FL,** *Rana Pipiens. . .* It is called "spring frog." **1928** Baylor Univ. Museum *Contrib.* 16.10 **LA, TX,** Spring Frog is a name frequently applied to the Green Frog on account of its being frequently found in the vicinity of springs. (Texarkana, Texas, and Gayle, Louisiana.) **1932** Wright *Life-Hist. Frogs* 423 **Okefenokee GA,** Some of the residents of the swamp maintain its [=the southern leopard frog's] common name of "Spring Frog" is from its ability to leap or *spring.* Others hold it likes *springy* places but usually it is called "spring frog" from its time of breeding and croaking in the *spring* months. **c1938** in 1970 Hyatt *Hoodoo* 2.1472 **seGA,** Yo' gets yo' a frog. Yo' hunt fo' an' get chew a *toadfrog* [Hyatt: land frog]—a *spring frog* [Hyatt: water frog] won't do. **1967–69** *DARE* (Qu. P21, *Small frogs that sing or chirp loudly in spring*) Inf **IL74,** Spring frog—different from a tree frog, spotted; **LA2,** Spring frog—he's a fairly large frog, spotted; **LA22,** Spring frog—you eat him—he's spotted and larger than a rain frog; (Qu. P22, *Names or nicknames for a very large frog that makes a deep, loud sound*) Inf **GA19,** Spring frog. **1969** *DARE* FW Addit **seGA,** *Spring frog*—frog which stays around springs and springy water. **1986** Pederson *LAGS Concordance* **Gulf Region,** 8 infs, Spring frogs; 1 inf, Spring frog—long-legged, long jumper; 1 inf, Spring frog—bullfrog—because he can jump so far; 1 inf, Spring frog—green frog or branch frog; 1 inf, Spring frog—it jump for 6 foot; 1 inf, Spring frog—a young bullfrog; 1 inf, Spring frogs—long, green, slim-bodied, around water; 1

inf, Spring frog—slender, looks like bullfrog; 1 inf, Spring frog—long and slender, large.

spring gold n

1 Std: a yellow-flowered Pacific plant of the aster family (*Crocidium multicaule*). Also called **gold fields 2, ~ star**

2 A **biscuit root 1** (here: *Lomatium utriculatum*).

1967 Gilkey–Dennis *Hdbk. NW Plants* 289, *Lomatium utriculatum*—Spring gold. . . Among our earliest spring flowers. **2002** DARE File—Internet **OR**, Spring gold will begin its show on the rock faces along the North Umpqua Highway shortly.

spring goldenglow n

A **forestiera** (here: *Forestiera pubescens*).

1960 Vines *Trees SW* 850, *Forestiera pubescens*. . . Also known under the vernacular names of Devil's-elbow, . . Spring-herald, Spring-goldenglow, and Tanglewood.

springhalt See **stringhalt** n

springhaltered See **stringhalted**

spring herald n

A **forestiera** (here: *Forestiera acuminata* or *F. pubescens*).

1960 [see **spring goldenglow**]. **1961** Wills–Irwin *Flowers TX* 170, Spring-herald, or Devil's-elbow, *Forestiera acuminata*, . . is a native shrub of this [=the olive] family. **1970** Correll *Plants TX* 1200, *Forestiera pubescens*. . . Elbow-bush, spring herald, stretch-berry.

spring herring n Cf fall herring

An **alewife** (here: *Alosa pseudoharengus*).

1814 in 1815 *Lit. & Philos. Soc. NY Trans.* 1.454, *Spring Herring, or Alewife. (Clupea vernalis).* Comes with the shad to New-York, in the latter part of March and the first of April, annually. Is about twelve inches long, and three deep. **1839** MA *Zool. & Bot. Surv. Fishes Reptiles* 114, *Spring Herring.* . . are still taken in some places in immense numbers. **1873** in 1878 Smithsonian Inst. *Misc. Coll.* 14.2.33 **NEng**, *Pomolobus pseudoharengus* [=*Alosa p.*] . . spring-herring. **1884** Goode *Fisheries U.S.* 1.579, Two species which we recognize at the present time under the names now accepted by us, the "Spring" and "Summer" Herrings, respectively *C[lupea] vernalis* and *C. aestivalis*. **1950** *Chicago Tribune* (IL) 17 Jan sec 1 14/3 **MA**, The spring herring is known as "Taunton turkey." **1976** Tryckare et al. *Lore of Sportfishing* 70, Alewife. . . Other common names: . . spring herring [etc]. **2000** DARE File—Internet **Chesapeake Bay**, I started at Parkers River to the west trying to capitalize on the spring herring-hunting keeper bass but to no avail.

spring hole n, also attrib

A pit or hollow in the ground or in the bed of a stream or lake formed by a spring.

1835 *Hagerstown Mail* (MD) 12 June [2]/1 (newspaperarchive.com) **NJ**, One of the gentlemen, observing a muddy spring hole at a short distance, thrust his hand in. **1845** Kirkland *Western Clearings* 69 **MI**, If we hadn't sich bad luck this summer . . losing that heifer, and the pony, and them three hogs,—all in that plaguey spring-hole, too. **1869** Murray *Adventures* 49 **NY**, No better fishing can be found than spring-hole fishing. **1897** *Century Illustr. Mag.* 55.236, It was a spring-hole at the mouth of the Rivière du Milieu—an open space, about a hundred feet long and fifteen feet wide, in the midst of the lily-pads, and surrounded on every side by clear, shallow water. **1902** White *Blazed Trail* 63 **seMI**, Muddy swamp and spring-holes caused endless difficulty and necessitated a great deal of "corduroying." **1915** (1916) Johnson *Highways New Engl.* 274, The turtles crawl into spring holes and spend the winter 'bout a foot down in the mud. **1955** *Moosehead Gazette* (Dexter ME) Feb 2/2 *(Hench Coll.)*, A deep cove of boulders, bars and spring holes, it is one of the best and for the not very best trout fishing [sites]. **1967** DARE (Qu. C6, . . *A piece of land that's often wet, and has grass and weeds growing on it*) Inf **AL**14, Spring hole. **1973** Allen *LAUM* 1.233 (as of c1950), *Swamp*. . . spring hole [1 inf, **MN**]. **2002** in 2006 DARE File—Internet **ME**, A spring hole would be an underwater inlet where the ambient temp would be much cooler than the surrounding water. It need not be deep.

springhouse n Also *spring cellar*, *spring shed* **formerly widespread, now chiefly Midl, Sth, esp Appalachians** See Map Cf **dairy 1a, milk house**

A structure built over or near a spring and used as a storage place for keeping perishable food cool.

1784 (1978) Washington *Diaries* 4.27 **VA**, A good single Barn, dwell-

ing House Spring House & several other Houses. **1817** *Adams Centinel* (Gettysburg PA) 15 Oct 1/1, [Advt:] A stone Spring House. **1837** (1924) Higbee *Diary* 27 **NJ**, The rain . . has again interfered with our plans for . . visiting the farmer's dwelling, springhouse, canal bank, etc. **1859** *Atlantic Mth.* 3.100 **NEng**, I was a-settin' in the spring-house, this mornin', a-workin' my butter. **1883** (1971) Harris *Nights with Remus* 320 **GA** [Black], Dey put it [=butter] in de spring-house. **1885** *Harper's New Mth. Mag.* 71.12 **KS**, The small spring house was built into a hill. **1899** (1912) Green *VA Folk-Speech* 410, *Spring-house*. . . A small house generally of stone or brick, built over a spring or brook, where milk, fresh meat, etc., is put, in order to be kept cool in or near the running water. **1903** DN 2.331 **seMO**, *Spring-house*. . . A small house built over a spring of water, in which milk, butter, etc., are kept cool. **1906** DN 3.158 **nwAR**, *Spring-'ous.* . . A shed built over a spring. **1942** (1960) Robertson *Red Hills* 135 **SC**, I remember . . the springhouse and the coolness of the interior and the clearness of the spring. **1965–70** DARE (Qu. M18, *The separate building where milk is kept cool*) 103 Infs, **chiefly Midl, Sth, esp Appalachians**, Springhouse; **WV**13, Spring cellar; **OR**1, Spring shed; (Qu. M22, . . *Kinds of buildings . . on farms*) 22 Infs, 14 Infs **PA**, Springhouse; (Qu. D10a, *The place to keep food cool, usually with ice, so that it won't spoil*) 18 Infs, **scattered**, Springhouse; (Qu. D22, . . *Place to go to in case of a violent windstorm*) Infs **IL**113, **OH**65, Springhouse; (Qu. M19, *A place for keeping carrots, turnips, potatoes, and so on over the winter*) Inf **KY**43, Springhouse. **1966–68** DARE Tape **IN**36, By golly, they took a knife and run around them there gallon crocks they's setting in a milk trough in the springhouse; **NC**36, The vine can be pulled up with the green tomatoes and hung in the smokehouse, springhouse, and they will ripen gradually during the winter; **TX**47, You had this spring, beautiful spring, that came—flowed—through a rock springhouse where they kept milk and so forth. **1988** Pederson *LAGS Genl. Index* 360 **Gulf Region**, [Of 1121 primary and secondary infs, 85 responded with *springhouse(s)* to Qu. 15.5 *Dairy*/place for milk and butter.]

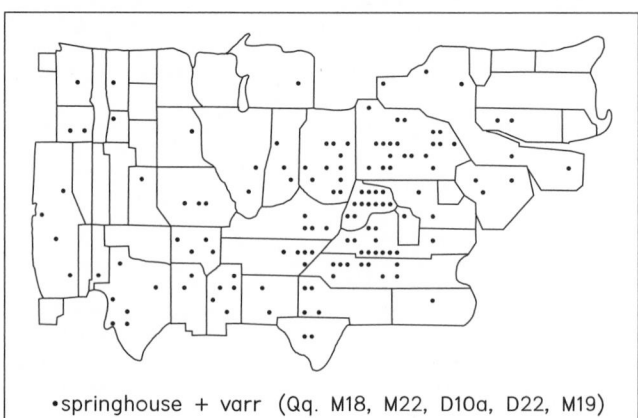

•springhouse + varr (Qq. M18, M22, D10a, D22, M19)

springing See **spring B2**

spring-keeper n [Appar of Engl dial origin; used in 1790 by Gilbert White for *"squilla aquatica,"* prob a water beetle larva.]

1 =**salamander 1. esp VA** Cf **spring lizard**

1859 (1968) Bartlett *Americanisms* 502 **PA, Atlantic**, Water-Dogs. . . In Pennsylvania and the Eastern States they are called Spring-keepers and Man-eaters. **1893** *Forest & Stream* 41.80 **VA**, This little salamander (*Spelerpes* [=*Pseudotriton*] *ruber*) is known as the "spring-keeper" in Virginia, is protected by farmers as of good to their springs, freeing them from insects, etc., and is generally common from Maine to Nebraska, east of the Alleghanies south to the Carolinas. **1899** (1912) Green *VA Folk-Speech* 410, *Spring-keeper*. . . A water newt living in a spring and thought to keep the water flowing and good. A *water-puppy*. . . If you kill the spring-keeper the spring runs dry. **1921** [see **2** below]. **1926** [see **2** below]. **1938** Hench Coll. **VA**, Up Sugar Hollow we had cleaned out a spring and found true lizards in the water. . . Those are spring-keepers, and whenever you find them, you know you've got good water. **1940** Ibid **VA**, The folklore about a spring-keeper is that if you drink water from a spring where there are spring-keepers, you will swallow their eggs and they will hatch inside you. **1945** *AmSp* 20.230 **VA**, While collecting salamanders near Munson Hill, Virginia, years ago, I was informed by a colored woman that the red salamander (*Pseudotriton ruber*) which I caught in her presence was called a *spring-keeper*.

2 Any of var small crustaceans or insect larvae that live in springs; see quots.

1902 *Mansfield News* (OH) 1 Oct 7/6 **LA,** No doubt the chameleon is a degenerate alligator, just as the snail is a degenerate conch, the spring keeper a degenerate shrimp, and so on. **1921** in 1949 Abbott *Life William T. Davis* 196 **VA** [Black], Colored folks call salamanders and crayfish that live in the springs "spring-keepers," and believe that they keep the springs open by burrowing in the soil. **1926** Puckett *Folk Beliefs S. Negro* 434 **MS,** In Mississippi and elsewhere there is the idea that you may drink up the "spring-keeper" (described as much like a crawfish or a water lizard . .) and cause the spring to go dry. **1940** *Amer. Midland Naturalist* 23.191 **Ozarks,** *Gammarus limnaeus.* . . This and other species of amphipods were called "spring-keepers" by one resident of the Ozarks, who believed water from a spring to be impure and unfit for drinking unless the spring contained them. **1979** in 1982 *Barrick Coll.* **sePA** [Black], *Spring keeper . .* insect found on running streams.

3 A cave fish; see quot.

1995 *Buffalo News* (NY) 28 May sec F 12 (Internet) **MO,** "Historically, people called it 'well keeper' or 'spring keeper' because they'd pump it up or pull it up in buckets from their wells," said Brian Canaday, a fisheries management specialist with the Missouri Department of Conservation. "The cavefish was kind of a good luck charm."

spring larkspur n

A **delphinium,** usu *D. tricorne.*

1937 U.S. Forest Serv. *Range Plant Hdbk.* W60, Low larkspur, which resembles spring larkspur *(D. menziesii)* is a small, perennial, poisonous larkspur. **1968** *DARE* (Qu. S26c, *Wildflowers that grow in woods)* Inf **PA**99, Spring larkspur. **2003** *DARE* File—Internet **MO,** The dark blue-purple flower stalk of Spring Larkspur, also called Dwarf Larkspur, catches the eye.

springle out v phr   esp S Midl   [Cf *sprangle* and *SND springly* "?Twiggy, having many small shoots or branches"]

To sprout out in twigs; hence adj *springly* twiggy, straggly.

1934 *Charleston Daily Mail* (WV) 16 Dec 7/1, Balsam fir is usually preferred in the east on account of its long, horizontal, spreading, springly branches and deep green, fragrant foliage. **1936** Morehouse *Rain on Just* 239 **NC,** [They] let their home place go clear to ground with fire. . . Only a chimney, mantel rock, and some springly cherry trees last time I was by. **1967** *DARE* FW Addit **AR**55, *Springle out*—to sprout out in various directions in a bunch. "Them little old button willows will just springle out, a whole bunch in one wad." **1980** Rinzler–Sayers *Meaders Family* 81 **neGA,** The flames . . began to "feather, to springle out, more or less like a branch on a tree, and it's more or less free-floating."

spring lily n

A **dogtooth violet;** see quots.

1900 Lyons *Plant Names* 151, *E[rythronium] albidum.* . . White Adder's-tongue, Spring Lily. **1934** Haskin *Wild Flowers Pacific Coast* 25, Giant dog-tooth violet [=*Erythronium grandiflorum*]. . . Other local names are spring lily, Easter lily [etc]. **1959** Carleton *Index Herb. Plants* 111, *Spring-lily:* Erythronium americanum.

spring lizard n   chiefly Sth, S Midl   Cf lizard 2, spring-keeper 1

=**salamander 1.**

1848 Tuomey *Rept. Geol. SC* app x, Triton . . dorsalis . . [Triton] niger . . Spring Lizard. **1892** Smith *Farm & Fireside* 323 **GA,** The water is still running, and though the frog and the craw-fish and the spring-lizzard that used to excite her youthful fears, have departed this life intestate, they left children to inherit and enjoy that peaceful, shady spring. **1892** Harris *Uncle Remus & Friends* 313 **GA** [Black], I want you ter ketch me sev'n spring lizzuds. **1915** *Copeia* 18.5 **VA,** *Diemictylus viridescens* [=*Notophthalmus v.*] . . Land form "ground puppy," water from [sic] "spring lizard." **1965** Davis *Summer Land* 10 **cnNC,** I . . drank from the spring with my face in the water and saw the salamander, that we called the spring lizard; we all believed that you couldn't have a sweet spring without a lizard to keep it. **1967–69** *DARE* (Qu. P6x, . . *Kinds of worms . . used for bait;* not asked in early QRs) Infs **NC**72, **WV**2, Spring lizard(s); (Qu. P13, . . *Ways of fishing . . besides the ordinary hook and line)* Inf **SC**40, Spring lizards; **KY**6, Spring lizards—for catfish. **1968** *DARE* Tape **NC**53, [FW:] What are spring lizards? [Inf:] They're a salamander that lives in a branch. . . They're black and they get about six inches long—the biggest ones. **1969** *DARE* FW Addit

Okefenokee **GA,** *Spring lizard* = a salamander (because it stays in or near a spring or spring water). **1982** Sternberg *Fishing* 108, *Lungless salamanders.* Often called *spring lizards,* these salamanders live along the edges of cold springs, brooks or streams. **1986** Pederson *LAGS Concordance,* 3 infs, **GA,** Spring lizard(s) [used as bait]; 1 inf, **TN,** Spring lizards. **2003** *NY Times* (NY) 8 June sec 1 35/1 (Internet) **NC,** "I was thinking of him scrambling under rocks for spring lizards and how hungry he must have been," said the cook, Elizabeth Swanson.

springly   See springle out

spring mackerel n   Cf fall mackerel

A **mackerel 1** (here: *Scomber scombrus*).

1814 in 1815 *Lit. & Philos. Soc. NY Trans.* 1.423, *Spring Mackerel (Scomber vernalis).* . . Is caught off Sandy-Hook in great numbers with the hook, and brought in abundance to the New-York market. **1842** DeKay *Zool. NY* 4.101, The Spring Mackerel . . appear on our coast in the months of May and June. **1897** *Harper's New Mth. Mag.* Mar 616, Connecticut sloops of moderate tonnage were often seen, forty or fifty years ago, on the spring mackerel-grounds from off Sandy Hook to Block Island. **1919** *Stevens Point Daily Jrl.* (WI) 16 Oct 3/1, In the case of the spring mackerel fishery it is believed that the use of aircraft would save much time in locating the fish. **1997** *DARE* File—Internet **NJ,** Over the years, I have noticed that a strong run of spring mackerel has left coastal waters in New Jersey with a significant amount of "tinker" or juvenile mackerel. **2001** *Ibid* **DE,** Year 2001 Charter Rates. . . Spring Mackerel (8 hours)—March & April. . . \$450.00.

spring mole n

A **mole cricket.**

1969 *DARE* FW Addit **KY,** *Spring mole*—an insect-like creature ¾ to 1 inch long and ¼ or so inches wide. Mostly head and eyes—they crawl out of their holes along creek banks and marshes in springtime and holler. People think they're frogs hollering, but the sound's not from frogs but the spring mole. He hollers in spring only. Since he is a secretive creature, he is rarely seen.

spring mosquito n

A **mosquito n¹ B1** (here: *Culiseta* spp).

1955 U.S. Arctic Info. Center *Gloss.* 77 **AK,** *Spring mosquito.* Any slow-flying insect of the genus *Culiseta,* family Culicidae, unusually large mosquitoes that appear in early spring, and are particularly abundant in Alaska. Spring mosquitoes are bloodsuckers and may be annoying, but their season is short. **2000** Smith *Sierra E.* 221 **eCA, wNV,** Another common species is the Giant Spring Mosquito, *Culiseta inornata.*

spring mushroom n

A **morel n²** (here: *Morchella esculenta*).

1911 *Newark Advocate* (OH) 29 Apr 6/3, Joseph Kuster, Jr., served the first spring mushrooms of the season to his patrons Saturday. **1924** *Torreya* 24.18 **NY,** The spring mushroom *(Morchella esculenta)* or "honeycomb" mushroom as it is sometimes called makes its appearance in this section almost exclusively in the month of May. **1967** *DARE* Tape **MI**65, The morel or spring mushroom—it's conical-shaped and looks like a sponge; it's a great delicacy. **1968** *DARE* (Qu. I37, *Small plants shaped like an umbrella that grow in woods and fields—which are safe to eat)* Inf **IA**30, Spring mushroom or sponge mushroom. [FW: the morel] **1995** in 2002 *DARE* File—Internet **VA,** I would soon be searching in trusted areas for the delicate, pocked, conical spring mushrooms. **2002** *Ibid* **OH,** To the outdoors person, the appearance of the dogwood flowers tell [sic] one that the spring mushroom (morel) is here.

spring nettle(s) n   Pronc-sp spring neddles

A skin rash; see quots.

1858 in 2006 *DARE* File—Internet **GA,** He says that little Jimmy is sick something like spring nettle. **1873** *Health Reformer* 8.133, My little girl . . broke out with something like spring nettle. First appearance was a smooth, white whelk, itching, forming scabs, till it spread over the face, neck, and part of the body. **1954** *Harder Coll.* **cwTN,** *Spring nettles.* . . A sudden rash. **1968** *DARE* (Qu. BB25, . . *Common skin diseases around here)* Inf **LA**28, Spring nettle—break out in whelps—the symptom. **1982** Slone *How We Talked* 112 **eKY** (as of c1950), *Spring neddles*—Whelps and bumps that came in the spring. Probably from an allergy to weeds.

spring onion n   [*OED2* 1882]   scattered, but chiefly Sth, Midl   See Map on p. 212   Cf bunch onion, green ~ 1, salad ~ 1, seed ~, shallot B, summer onion

A **scallion,** usu *Allium cepa* var *cepa;* see quots.

1881 *Herald & Torch-Light* (Hagerstown MD) [22 June 4]/1 (newspaperarchive.com), To make sweet salad lettuce, take six or eight heads of lettuce, twelve small spring onions, one cup of vinegar, a half cup of sugar, two sprigs of garden mint. **1896** *Garden and Forest* 11 Mar 110, New leeks and spring onions are shown, and full-grown onions, in all sizes. **1939** in Lib. of Congress *Amer. Memory: WPA Life Hist.* (Internet) **AL,** She says folks in the alley take her flowers and her vegetables, especially the tender Spring onions. **1940–41** Cassidy *WI Atlas* **seWI,** Greenings . . the green tops of spring onions. **1941** *LANE* Map 258 *(Scallion)* 4 infs, **MA, NH,** Spring onions. **1965–70** *DARE* (Qu. I6, *The kind of onions that come up fresh early in the year, and you eat them raw)* 166 Infs, **scattered, but chiefly Sth, Midl,** Spring onions; **NC37,** Spring onions—used in area; (Qu. H57, *Tasty or spicy side-dishes served with meats)* Inf **DC7,** Spring onions; (Qu. I5, . . *Kind of onions that keep coming up without replanting year after year)* Inf **DC12,** Spring onions; (Qu. I7, *The small plants like onions with hollow green leaves that are cut up in a salad)* Infs **GA90, NC39,** Spring onions; **MS25,** Tops off spring onions; (Qu. I28a, . . *Kinds of things . . you call 'greens' . . [Those that are eaten raw])* Inf **AL6,** Top of spring onions; (Qu. I35, . . *Kitchen herbs . . grown and used in cooking around here)* Inf **DC12,** Spring onions. **1966** Dakin *Dial. Vocab. Ohio R. Valley* 2.367, *Green onion, spring onion,* and *young onion* seem most often to mean the onions which are planted in the spring and grow singly. **1975** Purkey *Home in Madison Co.* 106 **cwNC** (as of 1915), I will never forget the endless bundles of crisp spring onions with their long white heads and their tender green blades. **1986** Pederson *LAGS Concordance* **Gulf Region,** 102 infs, Spring onion(s); 3 infs, Spring onion = shallot; 2 infs, Spring onions—green onions; 1 inf, Spring onion—fewer in cluster than nest onion; 1 inf, Spring onion—the one that multiplies; 1 inf, Spring onion = a young onion; 1 inf, Spring onion—an "uncured" onion. **2000** *NADS Letters* **wNC, eTN,** "Sallet peas" are the first garden items next to spring onions to come in season.

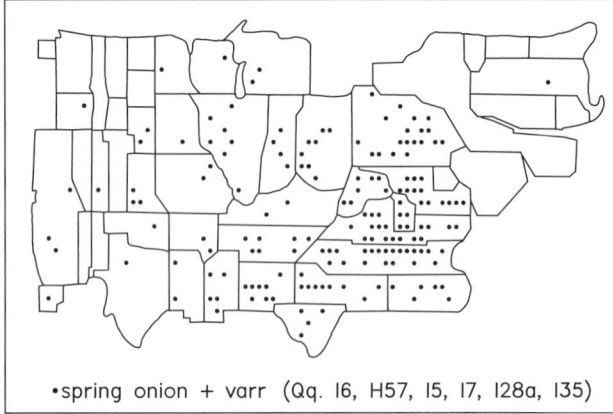

•spring onion + varr (Qq. I6, H57, I5, I7, I28a, I35)

spring orange n

A **snowbell 1** (here: *Styrax americanus*).

1830 Rafinesque *Med. Flora* 2.266, Styrax . . *Spring Orange.* Blossoms fragrant like orange. **1876** Hobbs *Bot. Hdbk.* 111, Spring orange, Styrax Americana.

spring peeper n scattered, but esp PA, OH, nNJ See Map Cf **March peeper**

A **tree frog 1** of the family *Hylidae,* esp *Pseudacris crucifer.* Also called **cheeper, chirper 1, grasshopper frog, March bird, peewink, pinkletink, pinkwink, tinky**

1855 *Putnam's Mag.* 6.38 **cNY,** The deep bass of the bull-frog, the sharp whistle of the "spring-peepers," and the cheerful, bird-like twitters of the tree-frog, are among the sounds most intimately associated with our spring and early summer. **1892** Gibson *Sharp Eyes* 6 **CT,** Almost any bright, genial day now we may listen for the first note of the spring peepers, the tiny piping frogs that wet their whistles in the lowlands. **1914** *Copeia* 4.1 **Long Is. NY,** I heard two Spring Peepers *(Hyla pickeringii)* singing at noon in a swamp. **1919** *Ibid* 74.81 **NY,** *Pseudacris feriarum* [=*P. triseriata* f.] . . Spring Peeper. Common. **1965–70** *DARE* (Qu. P21, *Small frogs that sing or chirp loudly in spring)* 16 Infs, **scattered, but esp PA, OH, nNJ,** Spring peepers; (Qu. P23, *Names for the animal similar to the frog that lives away from water)* Inf **OH16,** Spring peeper. **1966** Dakin *Dial. Vocab. Ohio R. Valley*

2.388, Only *(spring) peeper* which appears in scattered records from Ohio (8 [of 207 infs]), Indiana (3), and north-central Kentucky (2), and *green frog . .* approach being regional terms. **1967** Borland *Hill Country* 105 **nwCT,** The scientific name of the spring peeper is *Hyla crucifer. . .* The peeper yelps or peeps in a high, shrill call. **1981** Vogt *Nat. Hist. WI* 67, Spring peepers are especially abundant in moist woodland communities in Wisconsin. **1986** Pederson *LAGS Concordance,* 2 infs, **seAL, cnAR,** Spring peeper. **2003** *DARE* File—Internet **NY,** Now that Spring is returning to our island, you can hear the glorious sounds of part of Staten Island's native frog population—especially the mellifluous Spring Peepers.

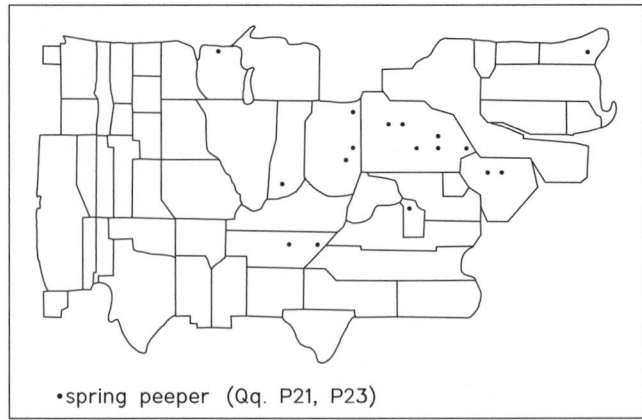

•spring peeper (Qq. P21, P23)

spring poor adj phr Cf **poor** adj **Ba**

Usu of a domestic animal: emaciated as a result of an inadequate winter diet; also fig.

1820 *Plough Boy* 30 Sept 141 **NY,** The horns become hollow in proportion to the poverty of the creature that wears them, those of a very spring-poor kine are almost as deficient as a powder horn. **1857** Chase *Life-Line* 97 **WI,** They survived the frosts and sufferings of the winter, and came out, as usual, "spring poor." **1868** IA State Ag. Soc. *Rept. for 1867* 128, I do not believe in turning them out on watery grass to shift for themselves 'spring poor.' **1877** VT State Bd. Ag. *Report* 4.93, Under such treatment the stock literally came to grass in the spring, 'spring poor.' **1905** Wood *Back Home* 229 **OH,** Nowadays we hardly know what is meant by the expression, "Spring poor." **1914** *DN* 4.80 **ME, nNH,** Spring poor. . . Said of animals, when lean in the spring. **1941** *Daily Kennebec Jrl.* (Augusta ME) 15 Oct 6/1, All indications are the Nazis will come out of the Russian winter "spring poor" and in no condition for any such campaigning as they have been doing this year.

spring queen n Cf **snow queen**

A **kittentails** (here: *Synthyris reniformis*).

1920 *DN* 5.84 **NW,** *Spring queen.* Synthyris rotundifolia. **1934** Haskin *Wild Flowers Pacific Coast* 323, Synthyris rotundifolia [=*S. reniformis*]. . . Children sometimes call them blue-bells; some people call them spring queen, though there is nothing queenly in their low growth and modest, retiring habit. **1997** Native Plant Soc. OR *Bulletin* Mar (Internet), Perhaps the secretive spring queen *(Synthyris reniformis)* will be discovered.

spring rabbit brush See **rabbit brush 1d**

spring sagebrush n

=**bud sagebrush.**

1973 Hitchcock–Cronquist *Flora Pacific NW* 487, Bud s[agebrush], spring s[agebrush] . . *A[rtemisia] spinescens* [=*Picrothamnus desertorum*].

spring salmon n esp Pacific NW

=**chinook salmon.**

1850 Hines *Voyage Round World* 331, In this country [=the Oregon Territory] they are generally distinguished by the names of spring-salmon and fall-salmon. **1882** U.S. Natl. Museum *Bulletin* 16.306, Quinnat Salmon; King Salmon; Columbia Salmon . . spring salmon. **1910** in 1981 Tabbert *Alaskan Engl.* 206, Oncorhynchus tschawytscha. . . tyee salmon, or spring salmon. **1940** Smith *Puyallup-Nisqually* 235 **WA,** Since the tyee is generally the earliest to arrive, the term "spring salmon" is occasionally used as referring only to this species. **1968** *DARE* (Qu. P1, . . *Kinds of freshwater fish . . caught around* *here . . good to eat*) Inf **AK**1, Chinook = spring salmon (Puget Sound). **2000** *DARE* File—Internet **MI,** These fishermen never encountered Salmon before and were amazed at the brute strength of Spring Salmon, they now know why they're called Kings.

spring shed   See **springhouse**

spring sheldrake n
=red-breasted merganser.

1869 *Amer. Naturalist* 2.661 **ME,** They are among the birds which form the rear of the great migratory flight in late spring, as well as among the first to appear early in the spring; and "spring ducks" and "spring sheldrake" are common terms at the shore. **1888** Trumbull *Names of Birds* 68 **ME,** At Bath, Me., [the red-breasted merganser is called] spring-sheldrake. **1955** MA Audubon Soc. *Bulletin* 39.379 **ME, MA,** Red-breasted Merganser. . . Spring Sheldrake.

springtail n   Cf **sprigtail 1**
=pintail 1.

1870 *Amer. Naturalist* 4.49 **MA,** Pintail Duck. . . By some it is called Spring-tail. **1911** *Forest & Stream* 77.173 **LA,** *Pintail. . .* Spring-Tail is used about Venice, La. **1982** Elman *Hunter's Field Guide* 156, Pintail. . . Common & Regional Names: *pinnie, sprig, sprigtail, springtail.*

spring teal n

1   **=green-winged teal.**   Cf **winter teal**

1923 U.S. Dept. Ag. *Misc. Circular* 13.13 **MS,** *Green-winged Teal. . . Vernacular Names. . . In local use. . .* spring teal.

2   The blue-winged teal (*Anas discors*).   Cf **fall teal, summer teal**

[**1916** *Times–Picayune* (New Orleans LA) 26 Mar mag sec 2/4, Blue-winged Teal. . . *Sarcelle Autonniere; Sarcelle Printanniere. . .* It is about the first of the visitors to arrive in the fall and the last to leave in the spring, hence the local Creole designations.] **1931** LA Dept. of Conserv. *Bulletin* 20.151, Sarcelle d'éte; Blue-wing; Spring Teal; Fall Teal; Summer Teal; Necktie Teal. **1951** *AmSp* 26.271, For an entirely different reason—time of migration— . . the blue-winged teal is the *spring teal* in Alabama, Louisiana, and Texas.

spring titi n   Cf **titi 1a**
=buckwheat tree.

1926 (1949) McQueen–Mizell *Hist. Okefenokee* 144 **seGA,** Spring Ty Ty. **1968** *DARE* (Qu. T5, . . *Kinds of evergreens, other than pine*) Inf **GA**25, Spring titi; summer titi. **2002** *DARE* File—Internet **FL,** Spring Titi is almost a sure thing, blooming in late January, February, and March.

sprinkler n

1   In logging: a device for sprinkling water over a logging road during freezing weather in order to make and maintain an **ice road.   chiefly Gt Lakes, esp MI**

1878 *Davenport Daily Gaz.* (IA) 11 Feb [4]/1 (newspaperarchive.com) **MI,** Some of the more energetic and determined loggers prolong the hauling by the use of sprinklers. **1893** *Scribner's Mag.* 13.708 **MI,** In freezing weather the sprinkler is run. **1902** White *Blazed Trail* 68 **MI,** They [=camp cooks] are supposed to serve a . . variety of lunches up to midnight for the sprinkler men. **1905** U.S. Forest Serv. *Bulletin* 61.49 [Logging terms], *Sprinkler. . .* A large wooden tank from which water is sprinkled over logging roads during freezing weather in order to ice the surface. (N[orth] W[oods], L[ake] S[tate Forest]) **1952** *Badger Folkl.* 1.17 **WI** [Logging language], *Sprinkler—*Large wooden box mounted on two-way sleigh used to haul water in making ice roads. **1964** Hargreaves–Foehl *Story of Logging* 62 **MI,** [Glossary:] *Sprinkler—*A device used to ice the sleigh roads. **1966** *DARE* Tape **MI**27, In the wintertime I was on the sprinklers, making ice roads. . . We used to load the sprinkler with a barrel. . . on a sleigh. . . on bobsleds. **2001** *MI Hist.* 85.46 (as of c1919), After regular hauling started, the snowplow and sprinkler worked to keep the road in first-class condition for heavy sled loads used during the day hauling.

2   A member of a religious group that practices baptism by sprinkling rather than immersion.   **esp Sth, S Midl**   Cf **deepwater Baptist**

1844 Fowler *Religion* 19, The Baptist draws his doctrine of immersion from the same Bible from which sprinklers draw their opposite doctrine. [**1865** Davis *Morning Lect.* 338, Whether God be a Quaker, or a Sprinkler, or a Plunger, it is of little consequence in the great future of true religion.] **1954** *Harder Coll.* **cwTN,** *Sprinklers . .* nickname for members

of Methodist Church. **1966–69** *DARE* (Qu. CC4, . . *Nicknames . . for various religions or religious groups*) Infs **GA**74, 89, **SC**26, Sprinklers—Methodists. **2002** *DARE* File—Internet **TX,** While the Methodists were first to establish a congregation in Midland [TX], the Baptists were first to build a structure. They kindly let the sprinklers meet in their Church building until 1889.

sprinkles n pl   [Trademark]   **scattered, but esp freq NYC, nNJ**   Cf **sprills**
=jimmies n pl[2].

1921 *Western Confectioner* June 63/2 *(Popik Coll.),* Chocolate Sprinkles for Sundaes—A new product is being put on the market by the Stollwerck Chocolate Company in the form of "Chocolate Sprinkles." They are made of chocolate compressed in highly finished particles and have a bright reddish brown color. **1928** *Vidette–Messenger* (Valparaiso IN) 24 Feb 2/4, [Advt:] Oh, for an ice cream cone with sprinkles on it. **1938** *Amarillo Globe* (TX) 8 Mar 2/8, [Advt:] Our sundaes are topped with . . plenty of chocolate sprinkles or chopped nuts. **1957** *Salina Jrl.* (KS) 9 Sept 6/1, Decorate cookies with frosting and candy sprinkles or nuts if desired. . . Mrs. Rhoda Pinkall—Lindsborg, Kansas. **1968** *DARE* (Qu. H82b, *Kinds of cheap candy that used to be sold years ago*) Inf **NY**119, Ice cream with sprinkles. **1973** *DARE* File **NY,** Sprinkles. . . The small bits of chocolate on an ice cream cone—so in NY; called jimmies in Boston. **1977–78** Foster *Lexical Variation* 25 **NJ,** Mercer County is divided, with Trenton and its near suburbs using the Midland *jimmies . .* and northern Mercer preferring the Northern *sprinkles.* The fact that far more informants in the pure *sprinkles* areas of North and Northwest Jersey deny *jimmies* than *jimmies* users in South Jersey deny *sprinkles . .* suggests that *sprinkles* is the older or more general term. **1982** *NY Times* (NY) 25 Nov sec A 22, What do you call the tiny multicolored flecks of candy that are . . scattered on . . cakes, or into which ice cream cones are dipped? . . "They're sprinkles," New Yorkers insist. **1993** *DARE* File **nNJ,** Words & phrases particular to my area of northern New Jersey. We . . put "sprinkles," not "jimmies," on our ice cream. **2001** *NADS Letters* **Brooklyn NYC,** The 86th St. variety offers sprinkles [on ice-cream cones]. *Ibid* **NYC,** Growing up in NYC it was sprinkles, and I didn't hear jimmies till I got to California. **2008** *DARE* File **MA,** I differentiate between jimmies, which are chocolate, and sprinkles, which are multi-colored.

sprit   See **spirit**

sprittail n   Also *spreettail*
=pintail 1.

1844 Giraud *Birds Long Is.* 311, This beautiful species [=*Anas acuta*] is well known to our gunners by the name of "Sprig," or "Spreet-tail." **1923** U.S. Dept. Ag. *Misc. Circular* 13.15 **Long Is. NY,** *Pintail. . .* sprittail.

spritz v   [PaGer *spritze* < Ger *spritzen*]   **chiefly PA**   See Map on p. 214

To splash, spray, sprinkle, or squirt; hence n *spritz* a squirt; vbl n *spritzing* squirting.

1886 Amer. Philol. Assoc. *Proc.* 17.xii **ePA,** "Spritz," from *spritzen,* to 'spatter' or 'squirt,' was bodily incorporated by the Pennsylvania schoolboy into his English vocabulary. **1908** *German Amer. Annals* 10.46 **sePA,** *Spritz.* Splash; sprinkle. "Look out or I'll spritz you!" **1935** *AmSp* 10.169 **PA** [Engl of PA Germans], *Spritz* is in common use for 'sprinkle.' The man with the garden hose is *spritzing* his lawn. **1939** Aurand *Quaint Idioms* 20 [PaGer], The boy didn't want to *spritz* water on the old man but he got mad anyhow. **1965–70** *DARE* (Qu. Y45, *Talking of a liquid—to scatter in all directions: "When he opened the can, the beer _____ [all over the kitchen]."*) 10 Infs, 8 **PA,** Spritzed; **PA**29, Spritzed [sprĭčt]; **PA**243, Spritzed—[s] or [š]; **PA**40, Use spritz when it's getting on someone. **1976** *Natl. Observer* 21 Aug 12/3, I found myself inexplicably caught up by the . . inevitable spritzing of the seltzer bottle. **1987** *Milwaukee Jrl.* (WI) 19 May Xtra sec 10, Those were the days when Clarabell the Clown would spritz Buffalo Bob smack in the puss with seltzer. **1987** *Jrl. Engl. Ling.* 20.2.175 **ePA,** *Spritz* 'to squirt, to sprinkle'. . . Obviously, *spritz* "is still in common use" . . without limitation to particular subgroups of speakers. **1997** in 1999 Millersville Univ. Center for PA Ger. Studies *Jrl.* Fall 22, To spritz. *If there is just little rain coming down, it's _____.* 27.5% [of 40 infs], *spritzing.* **2002** *Boston Globe* (MA) 30 Mar sec A 1 (Internet), Forsyth scientists expect next month to meet with three companies interested in sponsoring tests of a cavity vaccine that would be given to toddlers with a spritz up the nose.

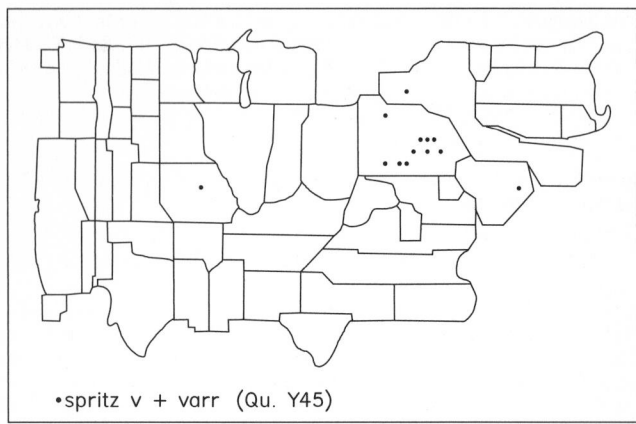

• spritz v + varr (Qu. Y45)

spritz n

1 See **spritz** v.

2 also *spritzer:* A light rain shower. **chiefly PA**

1935 *AmSp* 10.168 **PA** [Engl of PA Germans], The local weather prophet looks at the clouds and thinks it's going *to make down,* and later the comment is, 'It's making rain down.' (At other times the expression is *gives,* as 'It gives spritzers' (showers) . .). **1937** *AmSp* 12.204 [Engl of PaGer area], The doctor, lawyer or professor in a Pennsylvania German community. . . will speak of a 'spritz' (light rainfall). **1967** *DARE* FW Addit **sePA,** We had a little spritz [sprɪts]—a small shower. **1979** *NYT Article Letters* **PA,** A light rain . . was called "spritz" in Pennsylvania. **2003** *NY Post* (NY) 27 May 3 (Internet) **NYC,** And on three more [days], "we had spritzers," said Manhattan weather historian Steve Fybish.

spritzer See **spritz** n **2**

spritzing See **spritz** v

sprout v¹

1 To remove sprouts from potatoes. [Scots, nEngl dial]

[**1852** *Scientific Amer.* 7.259, To separate the potatoes from the sprouts is generally the work of women and boys; and the writer, when a boy, well remembers "sprouting potatoes," in old England.] **1854** (1969) Thoreau *Walden* 278 **ceMA,** [I have] an uncle who goes to sleep shaving himself, and is obliged to sprout potatoes in a cellar Sundays, in order to keep awake. **1890** *Century Dict.* 5867, *Sprout.* . . To remove sprouts from: as, to *sprout* potatoes. [*Century* Ed: Prov. Eng. and U.S.] **1899** (1912) Green *VA Folk-Speech* 411, *Sprout.* . . To remove sprouts from: as, to *sprout* potatoes. **1915–23** in 1944 *ADD* **cNY,** *Sprout.* . . To remove sprouts from, as potatoes. Usual term. Common. **1942** McAtee *Dial. Grant Co. IN* 61 (as of 1890s), *Sprout* . . to remove sprouts as from potatoes. Dial. **1942** Warnick *Garrett Co. MD* 14 **nwMD** (as of 1900–18), *Sprout* . . to remove sprouts from (as potatoes) (Dial.) **2008** *DARE* File—Internet **NE** (as of 1940s), During the winter months we would sprout the potatoes that was stored in the old storm cellar.

2 To chop or grub out suckers; also with *off:* to clear (land) of suckers; by ext, to dig up (a plant); hence vbl n *sprouting.* **chiefly S Midl** See also **sprouting hoe**

1902 *DN* 2.246 **sIL,** *Sproutin.* . . 1. Grubbing. 2. Cutting young sprouts out of a new ground crop with a hoe. **1905** *DN* 3.95 **nwAR,** *Sprout.* . . To dig up, to take up. 'After the first frost is the time to sprout bulbs.' Universal. **1906** Johnson *Highways Missip. Valley* 146 **Ozarks,** The women do the milking, and they go out sprouting with axe and mattock in the fields and pastures, and they pick up loose stones off the grassland, and do all sorts of jobs. **1907** *DN* 3.226 **nwAR,** *Sproutin.* . . 1. Grubbing. 2. Cutting young sprouts out of a new ground crop with a hoe. **1938** Stuart *Dark Hills* 342 **KY,** We have to make the fences this month and get the pastures sprouted off in August. You can be sprouting the pastures while I paint the house and fix the roof. **c1960** *Wilson Coll.* **csKY,** *Sprout.* . . To remove sprouts from a growing plant or to cut sprouts, such as the ubiquitous persimmon and sassafras sprouts of the area. **1966–69** *DARE* (Qu. L36, . . *When you dig out roots and underbrush to make a new field*) Infs **KY46, MS46,** Sprouting. **1978** Massey *Bittersweet Country* 381 **Ozarks,** I've been out a-sprouting all this morning. I'm not in very good shape. **1986** Pederson *LAGS Concordance (Cleared [the land])* 1 inf, **cwAR,** Sprouting it—cutting sprouts.

sprout n Cf **sprout** v²

A faucet or spigot.

1966 *DARE* Tape **AL**14, Then they had a sprout to the end of this barrel. . . They had these great big old hundred-gallon barrels of syrup with a top on it and then it had a sprout. . . You'd turn it off and on for the syrup to run out. **1968** *DARE* (Qu. F15, *What you turn to let the vinegar or cider run out of a barrel*) Inf **GA**17, Sprout; **MI**89, Sprout, [corr to] spout; (Qu. F27a, *What you turn on and off inside the house to get running water*) Inf **GA**17, Sprout [FW: also used in conv]. **1986** Pederson *LAGS Concordance,* 1 inf, **seLA,** Sprout [=spout]—on kettle. **2002** in 2006 *DARE* File—Internet **Sth,** Do both the hot and cold water come out the same faucet sprout? . . [Y]ou might have the same thing stuck in the faucet where the hot and cold mix into the one faucet sprout?

sprout v² [Cf *OED2* sprout v.² "*Obs.* exc. *dial.*" and **sprout** n]

Of a liquid: to gush forth; to spout; also fig in v phr *sprout off* to declaim at length in a pompous manner.

1942 *Capital Times* (Madison WI) 12 July [18]/5 (newspaper-archive.com), These same firms are out in front sprouting off about "our way of life." **1968** *DARE* (Qu. Y45, *Talking of a liquid—to scatter in all directions: "When he opened the can, the beer _____ [all over the kitchen]."*) Inf **WI**57, Sprouted; (Qu. HH7b, *Someone who talks too much, or too loud: "He's always _____."*) Inf **WI**57, Sprouting off. **2000** in 2003 *DARE* File—Internet **CA,** I was sprouting off at a cop. I don't sprout off unless I'm right. **2003** *Ibid* **NV,** I for one am getting sick and tired of other people, non-golfers, sprouting off about how golfers . . are not paying our fair share.

sprout flow n **Sth** *hist* Cf **flow** n¹ **1, harvest flow**

In rice cultivation: the first flooding of the field after sowing, which causes the seed to sprout.

1828 *S. Agriculturist* 1.217 **SC,** I do not point flow on land infested with salt spots, and on land of this kind I keep on the sprout flow for a shorter term than on any other land. **1850** *De Bow's Rev.* 9.422 **Sth,** This first watering is called the 'sprout flow,' and is continued until the seeds 'pip,' or the sprouts burst the envelope of chaff. **1859** *Harper's New Mth. Mag.* 19.727 **Sth,** The first flow which immediately follows the sowing is called the sprout flow. **1922** Gonzales *Black Border* 263 **sSC, GA coasts** [Gullah], I yerry dat Mistuh FitzSimmun done tek de sprout flow off 'e rice. **1984** Joyner *Down by Riverside* 46 **SC coast** (as of a1866), The first flooding, known as the sprout flow, remained on the [rice] fields only until the grain sprouted.

sprouting See **sprout** v¹ **2**

sprouting hoe n [**sprout** v¹ **2**] **chiefly S Midl, esp KY**

A hoe or **mattock** used for removing sprouts and roots from a field.

1776 in 2003 *DARE* File—Internet **MD,** 2 mattocks, 1 sprouting hoe, 1 garden hoe, 2 weeding hoes. **1800** in 1969 Herndon *Wm. Tatham Tobacco* 12 **VA,** There are three kinds of the hoe . . the first is what is termed the sprouting hoe, which is a smaller species of mattock that serves to break up any particular hard part of the ground. **1827** in 2003 *DARE* File—Internet **cNC,** 1 Seythe . . 1 Sprouting hoe. **1831** *Ibid* **neTN,** Two mattocks, one sprouting hoe, one foot adze, one pick axe. **1864** *Maine Agric. Soc. Returns 1863* 159 *(DA),* After the beds are thus burnt, . . they are dug up with a common sprouting hoe. **1906** *DN* 3.158 **nwAR,** *Sprouting hoe.* . . A hoe used in digging up sprouts, roots, etc. **1935** *Yale Rev.* new ser 25.176 **KY,** Dig all the loose roots out with one-eyed sproutin' hoes. **1941** Stuart *Men of Mts.* 65 **neKY,** Pa bends over and pecks with his sprouting hoe. He cuts the soft tender sprouts from the stumps. **1983** *MJLF* 9.1.57 **ceKY** (as of 1956), *Sprouting hoe* . . a grubbing hoe. **2006** *Evansville Courier & Press* (IN) 21 Aug sec A 1 (Internet), It's what used to be called a sprouting hoe. That's kind of a lighter version of a grubbing hoe and was meant for whacking off bush sprouts that haven't yet advanced to the size that require the larger, heavier grubbing hoe.

sproutland n **chiefly NEng, esp CT, MA**

Land covered with saplings or young trees, esp ones grown from suckers.

1842 in 2003 *DARE* File—Internet **sePA,** John W Gault . . doth grant . . unto the said Samuel B Kerst . . all the certain messuage and tract of sprout and woodland situate in Union township Berks County and state aforesaid. . . to have and to hold the said messuage and tract of sprout land. **1851** in 1906 Thoreau *Writings* 8.156 **MA,** It is refreshing to walk over sprout-lands, where oak and chestnut sprouts are mounting swiftly up again into the sky. **1874** *VT State Bd. Ag. Report* 2.493, In Massachusetts the 'sprout lands,' . . are those which have once been cultivated, but which have since been covered with trees in a natural way from roots remaining in the soil and from seed sown by the winds. **1896** *New Engl. Mag.* 20.721 **MA,** The reservation is 'sprout land' covered with stumps. **1900** Shelton *Salt-Box House* 40 **CT,** Daniel grew tall and straight and slim like the young saplings in the sprout-land. **1944** *Fitchburg Sentinel* (MA) 15 Jan 7/6, [Advt:] Sprout Land, 19 acres more or less. **1967** Borland *Hill Country* 26 **nwCT,** It was what is listed on the tax books as "sprout land," a mixed stand of trees that had been cut over a number of times. **1969** *DARE* (Qu. T2a, *. . A piece of land covered with trees . . only a few acres*) Inf **MA68,** Sproutland—trees not full grown. **1973** *Nashua Telegraph* (NH) 20 Jan 23/1, [Advt:] Acreage consists of approx. 20A open-rolling fields, 35A "sprout" land & balance heavily wooded. **2001** Sargent *Yr. in the Notch* 93 **NH,** It is a tangle of skinny, straight saplings. . . In former times, farmers would have called this area a sproutland and cut it every ten years for fence rails.

sprout off v phr[1]   See **sprout** v[1] **2**

sprout off v phr[2]   See **sprout** v[2]

sprouts n pl   [Cf *OED2 sprout* sb.[1] 1.c "*pl.* Young or tender shoots or side-growths of various vegetables, esp of the cabbage kind."]   **esp C Atl**
Kale, esp young shoots sold for greens.
  [**1840** *Mag. Horticult.* 6.228 **seNY,** 1 bushel Kale sprouts.] **1850** *Amer. Farmer* 6.103 **MD,** *Siberian Kale.*—For many years we grew this fine variety of spring sprouts under the name of *"Brussels sprouts;"* but . . we find it has found another name, and we will have to conform to it. **1890** Greiner *How to Make Garden* 204, Kale or Borecole. . . This vegetable of the cabbage family is grown and used in various ways, most usually as "sprouts" for winter greens, similar to spinach or collards. *Ibid* 255, Various plants are now used as substitutes for spinach, among them . . : *Sprouts.*—Much grown at the south for home and northern markets. See Kale. **1909** Rorer *Mrs. Rorer's Cookery* 117 **sePA,** There are two varieties of kale. . . Both varieties are sold . . under the name of sprouts. **2006** *DARE* File **Baltimore MD,** Something reminded me recently that when I was growing up my mother called kale "sprouts." . . After I set up housekeeping it took quite some time before I realized I couldn't find "sprouts" liked [sic] my mother served because it was really kale. **2008** *Ibid* **Baltimore MD,** My parents (and theirs) referred to the vegetable that most people call kale as "sprouts". . . My sister will occasionally still use "sprouts", but I have never heard it outside of East Baltimore.

spruce n
1 Std: a tree of the genus *Picea.*   For other names of var spp see **black spruce 1, blue ~, mountain ~, red ~, silver ~, Sitka ~, weeping ~ 2, white pine 5, white spruce, yellow ~ 2**   =**Douglas fir.**
  1894 *Jrl. Amer. Folkl.* 7.99, *Abies Douglasii.* . . Called spruce in some regions. **1897** Sudworth *Arborescent Flora* 47 **MT,** *Pseudotsuga taxifolia* [=*P. menziesii*]. . . Spruce. **1908** Britton *N. Amer. Trees* 70, The Douglas spruce, also called . . Spruce [etc] . . is the most abundant as well as the most widely distributed tree of western North America.
3 A **hemlock 2:** usu *Tsuga canadensis,* but also *T. caroliniana.*
  1897 Sudworth *Arborescent Flora* 42 **PA, WV,** *Tsuga canadensis.* . . Spruce. **1969** *DARE* Tape **KY16,** But the herb remedy for a cough was she'd take . . a hemlock, we call it spruce here, and she'd boil it down and add sugar to it and use that for a cough. **1983** in 2004 Montgomery–Hall *Dict. Smoky Mt. Engl.* 294 **wNC, eTN,** Some call 'em [= *Tsuga canadensis*] hem pines an' some calls 'em spruce.

spruce beer n   [*OED2* 1500 →]   Cf **birch beer,** DS H78
A spruce-flavored alcoholic beverage; a similar nonalcoholic beverage.
  1766 Stork *Acct. East-FL* 44, The spruce fir here is quite a different tree from that to the northward, but answers the same end for making spruce beer. **1839** Randolph *VA Housewife* 175, *Spruce Beer.* [A mixture of] hops . . sassafras root . . molasses, two spoonsful of the essence of spruce . . powdered ginger, and . . allspice . . [and] yeast. **1852** *Yankee Notions* 1.354, I went into a shawp to get a drink of . . spruce beer. **1871** (1892) Johnston *Dukesborough Tales* 107 **GA,** Susan made gingercakes and spruce beer. **1880** *Scribner's Mth.* 19.508 **NEng,** The boys had the noise and smoke and excitement of a Fourth-of-July celebration without a penny's expense, but alas! with no gingerbread nor spruce beer. **1939** Wolcott *Yankee Cook Book* 324 **NH,** Spruce Beer. [Recipe

includes boiling water, oil of spruce, oil of sassafras, oil of wintergreen, cold water, molasses, yeast.] **1940** Brown *Amer. Cooks* 677 **OH,** Spruce beer. [Recipe includes hops, water, molasses, essence of spruce, yeast.] **1941** *LANE* Map 312, Soft drink. . . carbonated water containing flavoring or plant extracts . . spruce beer [2 infs, **MA, NH**]. **1986** Pederson *LAGS Concordance* (Home-brewed beer) 1 inf, **cwLA,** Spruce beer.

spruce chewing gum   See **spruce gum**

spruce chicken n   [Because it lives principally on evergreen buds and needles; cf **prairie chicken**]   **AK**
=**spruce grouse.**
  1906 *Annual Rept. Reindeer AK for 1905* 93, Mr. Bahr went out with his gun and brought back six spruce chickens, which we enjoyed for supper. **a1933** in 1967 Heller *Sourdough Sagas* 43 **AK,** Next day we went moose hunting and separated for the hunt, but had no luck as we got only five spruce chickens. **1951** *AK Sportsman* Oct 26, Most widely distributed [of the grouse in Alaska] is the "spruce chicken," . . said to be swifter and cleverer than any of the others and a match for the best hunters. **1981** Billy McCarty, Sr. *Ruby* 59 **AK** (Tabbert *Alaskan Engl.*), Or if I'm in the hills I kill a spruce chicken and eat the guts. **2003** *DARE* File—Internet **AK,** I like to play football and sometimes I go spruce chicken hunting with Victor.

spruce grouse n
Std: a grouse (*Dendragapus canadensis*) of northern coniferous forests.   Also called **blue grouse 2, ~ hooter, chicken B1, democrat 1, fool bird 1, ~ hen 2, heath hen 2, mountain grouse 2, spruce chicken, ~ hen, ~ partridge 1, swamp partridge, timber grouse, tyee ~, wood ~**

spruce gum n   Also *spruce chewing gum*   **chiefly NEng**
Spruce resin used as chewing gum.
  1836 *Spirit of Times* 6.112 **ME,** The down East girls . . have a droll way of amusing themselves, viz.—by *chewing* spruce gum, mingled as it frequently is, with dirt, dead mosquitoes, and swamp flies. **1887** *San Antonio Daily Express* (TX) 22 Feb [8]/3 (newspaperarchive.com), Boston chews more spruce gum than any other place in the country, and dealers say that Chicago consumes the next largest quantity. **1907** *St. Nicholas* June 678 **NH,** The little knickknack shop around the corner . . [sells] picture papers, spruce gum, needles and Malaga raisins. **1908** Day *King Spruce* 247 **ME,** Do you call that a ha'nt—a man walkin' 'longside the road in daylight—some hump-backed old spruce-gum picker? **1946** Jones *Skinny Angel* 141, From then on we had only the spruce chewing gum to which Vivian was addicted. **1957** *Sat. Eve. Post Letters* **NH,** A class-mate of mine of 65 years ago has given me his recollections of some candies. . . There were also lumps of natural spruce gum, sticks of natural slippery elm and sticks of licorice wood. **1966–69** *DARE* (Qu. H82b, *Kinds of cheap candy that used to be sold years ago*) Infs **MI106, NH15,** Spruce gum; (Qu. T7, *The sticky stuff that comes out of pine trees*) Inf **NY10,** Spruce gum; **RI4,** Spruce gum—to chew. **1968** *DARE* FW Addit **Upstate NY,** Spruce gum—"It's pitch first, and then when it hardens it's gum." **1979** *DARE* File **cnMA** (as of c1915), Some children used to chew spruce gum but I didn't. Some of the gum may have been picked off spruce trees, but I think it was available commercially too. It was pink—the shade of cheap dentures, stiff; and it tasted awful. **2004** in 2006 *DARE* File—Internet, Have you tried the spruce gum sold by the Durgan [sic] Park restaurant in Boston?

spruce hen n   [See **spruce chicken**]   **esp MI, AK**   See Map on p. 216
=**spruce grouse.**
  1878 in 1880 Pioneer Soc. MI *Pioneer Coll.* 2.466 (as of 1839), Occasionally a spruce hen or grouse was killed, which was invariably made into broth for a sick man of the party. **1900** U.S. Copper R. Explor. Exped. *AK 1899* 137, *Birds found in the Copper River Valley.* . . grouse or spruce hen, which are smaller than the Pacific coast grouse of lower latitudes. **1936** Roberts *MN Birds* 1.369, The typical haunt of the Spruce Hen is in dense, dark, wet, spruce-tamarack-white-cedar swamps. **1959** McKennan *Upper Tanana Indians* 21 **AK,** Of the native birds the ptarmigan is the most numerous and important. Next comes the spruce hen or grouse. **1961** *AK Sportsman* Nov 17 **AK,** Adult male spruce grouse (also, incongruously, called spruce hens) are heavily barred with black on the breast. **1962** Salisbury *Quoth the Raven* 128 **seAK,** The spruce hen takes on the flavor of the spruce buds on which it feeds. **1965–70** *DARE* (Qu. Q7, *Names and nicknames for . . game birds*) 11 Infs, **Nth, esp MI,** Spruce hen; **MI10,** Spruce hen—takes care

of both male and female—the spruce grouse.   **1966** *DARE* Tape **MI**2, We have the spruce hen; **MI**14, There are a few spruce hens. They're, well, you can kill 'em with a club. . . They seem to be awfully dumb. Up in Canada they call 'em fool hens.   **2002** *DARE* File—Internet **AK**, I have this teacher. She loves spruce hens out of her mind. That is, she loves to eat them.

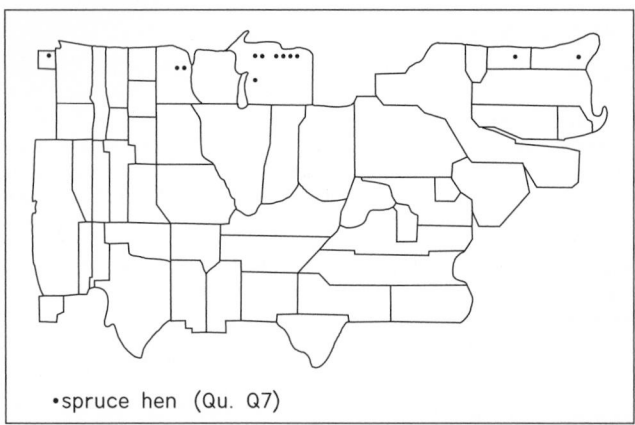

•spruce hen (Qu. Q7)

spruce owl n

=great gray owl.

1936 Roberts *MN Birds* 1.624, *Great Gray Owl. . . Other names:* Cinereous Owl, Spruce Owl.   **1946** Hausman *Eastern Birds* 361, Spruce Owl. . . In winter it descends irregularly . . as far south as New Jersey . . , New England, and westward to Wisconsin and Indiana.   **1955** Forbush–May *Birds* 273, Spruce Owl. . . In appearance our largest owl.

spruce partridge n   [*DCan* 1771 →]   esp **ME**

=spruce grouse.

1832 Williamson *Hist. ME* 1.144, *Quails* are not with us so plenty as in the other States of New-England. . . [M]any think the spruce Partridges are the same.   **1857** U.S. Patent Office *Annual Rept. for 1856: Ag.* 154, The spruce partridge or Canada grouse breeds in the States of Maine, New Hampshire, and Vermont about the middle of May.   **1888** Trumbull *Names of Birds* 141 **ME**, At Eastport, Me. . . the name Spruce-partridge is used to designate this bird [=the Canada grouse].   **1917** (1923) *Birds Amer.* 2.15, There is no such bird as the Spruce Partridge. It is the Spruce Grouse (*Canachites canadensis* [=*Dendragapus c.*]); but it is called Spruce Partridge in common parlance to distinguish it from the Birch Partridge (Ruffed Grouse).   **1935** *AK Sportsman* Dec 8, Similar in appearance to the Hooter, but much smaller in size, is the common Spruce Partridge or Chicken (Canachites canadensis).   **1945** Hamlin *9 Mile Bridge* 73 **nME**, Spruce partridge, a darker variety of ruffed grouse, is mistakenly shunned by some hunters, but preferred by those who know how tasty they are when baked with beans.   **2000** *DARE* File—Internet **ME**, Paul saw nothing except for four spruce partridges being spooked by something unseen.

spruce pine n

1 A hemlock   **2.** chiefly **Sth, S Midl**

1743 Catesby *Nat. Hist. Carolina* 2 [app] xxii, There is also in *Carolina* a fir which is there called *Spruce-Pine.* [*DARE* Ed: This quot may refer instead to another sense below.]   **1794** in 1971 Denny *Military Jrl.* 210 **PA**, The timber, [is] hemlock or spruce pine, and beech.   **1860** *De Bow's Rev.* 28.608 **SC**, The extreme mountain growth is met with in Pickens and Greenville Districts. This belt is characterized by . . Hemlock, or spruce pine [etc].   **1913** Kephart *Highlanders* 295 **sAppalachians**, The hemlock tree is named spruce-pine, while spruce is hebalsam.   **1931** Goodrich *Mt. Homespun* 86 **sAppalachians**, Hemlock. (Called in North Carolina mountains, *Spruce Pine.*) Dyes wool a reddish brown.   **1940** *Hall Coll.* **wNC, eTN**, Spruce-pine—Same as hemlock or hem-pine. Spruce and balsam and hemlock are the same thing, I reckon.   **1952** Strausbaugh–Core *Flora WV* 46, Hemlock. . . Often called "spruce-pine" in West Virginia; note names of certain topographic features, as Spruce-Pine Hollow, Kanawha County.   **1965–70** *DARE* (Qu. T17, . . *Kinds of pine trees;* not asked in early QRs) 22 Infs, **chiefly Sth, S Midl**, Spruce pine; **GA**70, Spruce pine—sometimes called a hemlock; **KY**16, Spruce pine—here called hemlock; (Qu. T5, . . *Kinds of evergreens, other than pine*) Inf **MD**30, Spruce pine, hemlock spruce—same thing; **VA**26, Spruce pine; **TN**14, Hemlock—also called spruce pine; (Qu. T16, . . *Kinds of trees . . 'special'*) Inf **NC**67, Spruce

pine. [*DARE* Ed: Some of these Infs may refer instead to other senses below.]   **1986** Pederson *LAGS Concordance* **Gulf Region,** 5 infs, Spruce pine(s); 1 inf, Spruce pine tree.   [**1999** see **spruce** n 3.]

2 Any of var **pines 1,** as:

a **=shortleaf pine 1.**

1739 (1946) Gronovius *Flora Virginica* 119 **VA**, Pinus conis agminatim nascentibus, foliis longis ternis ex eadem theca. [=A pine with cones borne in bundles [and] long triple leaves [growing] from each sheath.] Pinus setis brevioribus viridioribus, conis minoribus in congerie pauciores. [=A pine with shorter, greener needles, [and] smaller cones in thinner bundles.] *Spruce-Pine. Clayt.*   **1810** Michaux *Histoire des Arbres* 1.54, La cime de cet arbre n'embrasse pas un espace aussi considérable que sembleroit l'annoncer sa hauteur et son diamètre, et c'est probablement de cette disposition . . que lui est venu le nom de *Spruce pine,* Pin sapin. [=The top of this tree is not so broad as its height and diameter would seem to promise, and it is probably from this configuration . . that the name *Spruce pine . .* derives.]   **1824** Elliott *Sketch* 2.634 **NC, SC, GA,** *[Pinus] Variabilis* [=*P. echinata*]. . . This species is, I believe, universally known along the sea-coast of Carolina and Georgia as the spruce or short-leaved pine.   **1860** Curtis *Cat. Plants NC* 19, Yellow Pine. . . This, with us, is called *Short-leaved Pine* and *Spruce Pine.*   **1897** Sudworth *Arborescent Flora* 29 **AR, DE, MS,** *Pinus echinata*. . . Common Names. . . Spruce Pine.   **1968** *DARE* (Qu. T17, . . *Kinds of pine trees;* not asked in early QRs) Inf **MD**13, Spruce pine—another name for shortleaf.

b A long-needled pine *(Pinus glabra)* of the southeastern coastal states. Also called **cedar pine 1, old-field ~, pitch ~ b(5), poor ~, white ~ 7**

1765 (1942) Bartram *Diary of a Journey* 30, Ye 2 leaved or spruce pine grows very large in swamps; ye bark very smooth & hath very little appearance of A pine but ye leaves & cones very like ye Jersey Pine but not so tough as it.   **1863** Porcher *Resources* 506, Pinus glabra, Walter's pine. . . common spruce pine of our swamps.   **1884** Sargent *Forests of N. Amer.* 201, Spruce Pine. . . South Carolina, south to the Chattahoochee region of western Florida, generally near the coast, and through the Gulf states . . to the valley of the Pearl river, Louisiana.   **1901** Lounsberry *S. Wild Flowers* 2, Walter's pine, or spruce pine, is very local in its habit and seldom found growing over fifty miles away from salt water.   **1962** Harrar–Harrar *Guide S. Trees* 70, Spruce pine is easily distinguished by its slender, dark-green, twisted needles . . which are borne in fascicles of 2.   **2002** *Auk* 119.73, Conifers [were] predominantly represented by loblolly pine . . , spruce pine (*P. glabra*), and a few plots of longleaf pine.

c **=Jersey pine.** [See quot 2003]

1785 Marshall *Arbustrum* 102, Pinus virginiana. *Two-leaved Virginian, or Jersey Pine.* . . This is called, in some places, Spruce Pine.   **1860** Curtis *Cat. Plants NC* 20, Jersey Pine. . . This tree is . . also called *Short-leaved Pine* and *Spruce Pine.*   **1897** Sudworth *Arborescent Flora* 27 **NJ, NC,** *Pinus virginiana.* . . Spruce Pine.   **1950** Gray–Fernald *Manual of Botany* 57, *P[inus] virginiana* . . Jersey, Spruce-, Poverty-, or Scrub-P[ine].   **2003** OH Dept. Nat. Resources Div. Forestry *More Trees* (Internet) **OH**, Needles generally remain on the twigs from three to four years, and their stiff, short appearance gives this tree [=the Jersey pine] yet another common name, Spruce Pine.

d **=loblolly pine 1.**

1859 Perry *Turpentine Farming* 26, Among the various qualities of pines, we may distinguish four in particular, viz., common short-straw pine; rosemary, or what some call spruce pine; pitch, or long-straw pine; and the white pine of Mississippi.   **1896** Mohr–Roth *Timber Pines* 107 **VA**, The Loblolly Pine. . . Common or Local Names. . . Spruce Pine (Va.), in part.   **1913** *Auk* 30.485 **Okefenokee GA**, The tree growth here consists of such species as 'spruce pine' *(Pinus Taeda)* [etc].   **1970** *DARE* (Qu. T17, . . *Kinds of pine trees;* not asked in early QRs) Inf **VA**46, Rose pine—same as spruce pine—cones rose-shaped. [*DARE* Ed: This Inf may refer instead to another sense.]

e **=lodgepole pine.**

1884 Sargent *Forests of N. Amer.* 195, Pinus Murrayana [=*P. contorta*]. . . Lodge-pole pine. Spruce Pine.   **1897** Sudworth *Arborescent Flora* 23 **CO, ID, MT,** *Pinus murrayana*. . . Spruce Pine.   **1908** Britton *N. Amer. Trees* 29, Lodge Pole Pine. . . also called Prickly pine, . . Spruce pine [etc].   **1966** Barnes–Jensen *Dict. UT Slang* 40, *Spruce Pine . .* a name sometimes given to the Lodge-pole or Black pine.

f **=sand pine 1.**

1884 Sargent *Forests of N. Amer.* 199 **FL**, Pinus clausa . . Spruce Pine. Florida, shores of Pensacola bay, south, generally within 30 miles of the coast. **1908** Britton *N. Amer. Trees* 46, Sand Pine. . . also known as Old field pine, Spruce pine, Scrub pine, and Florida spruce pine. **1919** *Copeia* 70.49 **sFL,** The sterile areas of fine white "ridge sand" where the Spruce Pine *(Pinus clausa)* grows. **1934** *Torreya* 34.133 **FL,** The Spruce Pine has needles only two to three inches long and only two in a bunch so that it may be easily identified as one rides along the road. **1980** Little *Audubon Guide N. Amer. Trees E. Region* 287, Spruce Pine. . . Florida's small to medium-sized pine, a tree with rounded or flattened crown.

g =slash pine b.
1896 Mohr–Roth *Timber Pines* 74 **sAL,** The Cuban Pine. *(Pinus heterophylla* [=*P. elliottii*]). . . Spruce Pine. **1908** Britton *N. Amer. Trees* 37, Slash pine—*Pinus caribaea* [=*P. elliottii*]. . . It is also called the Swamp pine, . . and Spruce pine.

h =white pine 1.
1897 Sudworth *Arborescent Flora* 13 **TN,** White Pine. . . Spruce Pine. **1930** Sievers *Amer. Med. Plants* 61, White Pine—*Pinus strobus.* . . Northern pine, . . spruce pine. **1971** Krochmal *Appalachia Med. Plants* 194, Spruce pine. . . An evergreen tree that sometimes grows to 200 feet in height.

i =foxtail pine 1.
1897 Sudworth *Arborescent Flora* 18 **CA,** Foxtail Pine. . . Common Names. Spruce Pine [etc].

j =pond pine 1.
1908 Britton *N. Amer. Trees* 32, Pond pine. . . It is also known as Loblolly pine, Marsh pine, Bull pine, Black pine, Bastard pine, Meadow pine, and Spruce pine.

3 =black spruce 1.
1894 *Jrl. Amer. Folkl.* 7.100 **WV,** *Picea nigra,* Link. . . spruce-pine. **1897** Sudworth *Arborescent Flora* 34 **WV, PA,** *Picea mariana.* . . Spruce Pine. **1938** Van Dersal *Native Woody Plants* 356. **1968** *DARE* (Qu. T5, . . *Kinds of evergreens, other than pine)* Inf **MD**43, Spruce pine, spruce—same thing.

spruce squirrel n
A **red squirrel 1** (here: *Tamiasciurus hudsonicus).*
1909 (1910) Powell *Trailing & Camping AK* 244, A little spruce squirrel will descend from a tree near you, chatter "clinket" and then run up the tree a few feet. **1952** Burt *Field Guide Mammals* 77, Spruce Squirrel. *Tamiasciurus fremonti* [=*T. hudsonicus*]. . . In the *spruce forests* of the southern Rocky Mountain states, this small squirrel adds life and beauty. **1967** *DARE* (Qu. P27, . . *Kinds of squirrels)* Inf **CO**12, Spruce squirrel—about like gray ground squirrel—bushy tail. **2002** in 2006 *DARE* File—Internet **MI,** They [=chipmunks] drove off the little red or spruce squirrels, which I like (they don't bury nuts all over).

sprucy adj [Cf *OED2 spruce* a. 1 "Brisk, smart, lively. *Obs.*"] **chiefly Sth, S Midl**
Lively, spry, chipper.
1858 *Tyrone Star* (Tyrone City PA) [7 Dec 3]/2 (newspaper-archive.com), The lady and those of her "train" "what *could* help themselves," made a *hurried* exit, forgetting, in their haste a fine sprucy little youngster of about *five or six months old!* **1880** (1881) Harris *Uncle Remus Songs* 61 **GA** [Black], "You don't look sprucy like you did, Brer Tarrypin," sez Brer Fox, sezee. . . "W'at ail you, Brer Tarrypin? Yo' eye look mighty red." **1918** Linebarger *Bugle Rhymes* 86, There is something that will set you up, as sprucy as can be,/ And make a hero out of mud—and that's a pint of tea. **1966** Dakin *Dial. Vocab. Ohio R. Valley* 2.464, *Quite lively.* . . Miscellaneous terms of single occurrence include . . *sprucy.* **1966–70** *DARE* (Qu. GG29, *To be in a good or pleasant mood: "This morning he seems to be feeling _____."*) Inf **GA**77, Sprucy; (Qu. KK27, *A very lively, active old person: "For his age, he's _____."*) Infs **GA**13, **KY**85, Sprucy. **1986** Pederson *LAGS Concordance* (Quite lively) 2 infs, **FL, TN,** Sprucy; 1 inf, **cTN,** Sprucy—old person; gets around like young person; 1 inf, **ceTX,** Sprucy—old person; young sometimes.

sprung adj
1 See **spring B1.**
2 Tipsy; drunk. Cf *DS* DD13, 14, 15
1833 Greene *Life Dr. Dodimus* 2.176, He was seldom downright drunk; but was often . . all-firedly sprung. **1851** Hall *College Words* 291, *Sprung.* The positive, of which *tight* is the comparative, and *drunk* the superlative. [Verse:] "One swallow makes not spring," the poet sung,/ But many swallows make the student sprung. **1899** (1912) Green *VA Folk-Speech* 411, *Sprung.* . . Tipsy; drunk. **1927** *New Republic* 9

Mar 71, Words denoting drunkenness now in common use in the United States. . . lit . . sprung . . saturated.

spucky n Also *spooky, spu(c)kie* [Etym uncert] **chiefly Boston MA area**
A type of sandwich roll; by ext, the sandwich made with such a roll; a **submarine sandwich.**
1968–70 *DARE* (Qu. H41, . . *Kinds of roll or bun sandwiches . . in a round bun or roll)* Inf **MA**122, Spooky [spu·ki]; (Qu. H42, . . *[A sandwich] . . in a much larger, longer bun, that's a meal in itself*) Inf **MA**7, Spucky [spʌki]. **1972** *DARE* File **eMA,** *Spucky* ['spʌki] = grinder, submarine sandwich. So in Somerville, Lynn, Dorchester, Boston area—Mass. **1990** *NY Times* (NY) 11 Sept sec A 12/6 **Boston MA,** It has always been an accepted practice that we could just go in a place, grab a spuckie and a beer, and leave. **1993** in 2002 *DARE* File—Internet **Boston MA** [*Middlesex News* (Framingham MA) 13 Oct], In the old neighborhood, Mission Hill in Boston, an elongated roll stuffed with meat and stuff was known by people of a certain age not as a sub but as a "spucky." . . Go anywhere in the North End and ask for a "sausage and pepper roll on a spucky" or even just "a sausage on a spucky" and they'll whip one up for you quick as a flash. **1997** *DARE* File **sBoston MA,** We called submarine sandwiches "spuckies" in the '50s and '60s. **1999** *DARE* File—Internet **ceMA** [*Boston Online Wicked Good Guide to Boston English*], *Spuckie*—Sometimes, spukie. What some Bostonians still call a sub or hero. . . From spucadella, a type of Italian sandwich roll you can still buy at some of the bakeries in the North End and Somerville. David Keene reports: " 'Spuckie' is indeed a Boston word. It is not used much anymore, the older Italians used it. Growing up in Chelsea we alway [sic] bought 'spuckies' at Gallo's market. My wife bought spuckies at the Italian stores in Eastie when she was a kid". **2001** *DARE* File **Boston MA,** Spukie. . . My South Boston and Dorchester students use it all the time instead of "sub" or "hero". **2002** *DARE* File—Internet **Boston MA** [Local Lingo], Spucky—submarine sandwich. . . "Spuckie" dates you as an old Italian. **2003** *Verbatim* 28.3.5 **eMA,** Boston has its own local name for the sandwich, *spuckie* (also *spukie, spooky,* and *spucky*). . . This local Southie name appears to be dying, being replaced by the generic *sub.*

spud n
1 also *tobacco spud:* **=spear;** hence v *spud;* vbl n *spudding.*
1880 *Janesville Gaz.* (WI) 9 Aug [4]/6 (newspaperarchive.com), [Advt:] All kinds of Tobacco Shed goods. . . Only good Tobacco Spud in town. **1898** *Lima Daily News* (OH) 6 Sept 1/4, Martin Ridenour, while spudding tobacco; . . struck his jugular vein . . against a spud. **1901** *Columbus Med. Jrl.* 25.264, [He] was stringing tobacco, and by accident he fell on the tobacco spud. **1916** WV Ag. Exper. Sta. *Bulletin* 152.18, In the second method the tobacco . . is first cut and then forced on the stick by the use of a sharp spear called a "spud." The "spud" is about eight inches long and is made to slip down over the end of the stick. . . This method is spoken of as "spudding." . . [A] plant that has been split will cure more rapidly than one that has been spudded. **1946** *Janesville Daily Gaz.* (WI) 23 Sept 11/3, [Advt:] Wire stretcher; tobacco spuds; grain sacks. **1960** *Jrl. Natl. Med. Assoc.* 52.69 **sePA,** Judge Millen was born in 1892. . . As a boy he "spudded" tobacco on the farms near his home. **1963** North *Rascal* 112 **WI,** This is heavy work—chopping the tobacco stalks, spudding these plants on laths, and hanging the tobacco in the sheds to dry. **1975** *Piqua Daily Call* (OH) 3 Apr 22/1, [Advt:] *Antiques & Collectors Items . .* brass tobacco spud. **1998** Leary *WI Folkl.* 480 **swWI,** The old method uses a spearing horse (or spearing jack, or spudding horse or jack), which holds the lath in a horizontal position as the [tobacco] plants are slipped onto it over a steel spear point. **2008** in 2010 *DARE* File—Internet **wNC,** I used to work burly in WNC . . spudding, hanging, setting . . hardest work I have ever done!
2 also *spuds:* A children's game in which the player who is "it" tries to hit other players with a rubber ball; an unsuccessful attempt to hit a player with the ball; a call in the game. Cf **baby-in-the-air, nigger baby 2b**
1909 (1923) Bancroft *Games* 404, *Spud.* . . The players stand in a group, with one in the center holding the ball. The center player drops the ball, at the same time calling the name of one of the other players. All but the one called immediately scatter, as they are liable to be tagged with the ball. The player called secures the ball . . and tries to hit one of the other players with it. He may not run to do this. . . If he misses, he secures the ball, stands where he gets it, and tries again. . . If he hits a player, that one . . secures the ball, tries to hit some one else with it . . and so on. Whenever a player misses hitting another . . it is called a

"spud," and counts one against him. When any player has three spuds against him, he must stand twenty feet from the other players, with his back to them, and they each have one shot at him with the ball. **1968–70** *DARE* (Qu. EE33, . . *Outdoor games . . that children play*) Infs **GA**58, **IL**100, Spud; **IL**97, Spud—everyone has a number; the ball is thrown up and a number called; the number catches the ball and yells "spud," throws ball at nearest runner (after three giant steps); if he hits, that player gets a letter S-P-U-D; **LA**23, Nigger baby is called spud now; **PA**126, Baby-in-the-air or spud—ball in the air—try to hit; **VA**83, Spud—ball game in which each player is assigned a number; the player whose number is called has to catch the ball and try to hit one of the other players with it; **WI**47, Spud—everybody has a number; "it" throws up a ball, calls number; person must catch ball and hit someone. **1975** Ferretti *Gt. Amer. Book Sidewalk Games* 57, In Manhattan, Baby in the Air becomes *Spuds*. It is essentially the same game, but the person hit with the ball receives an S and then the other letters spelling out *spuds*. **1986** Pederson *LAGS Concordance (Games)* 1 inf, **cwFL**, Spud—assign numbers, throw ball, call number; 1 inf, **csTX**, Spud—person in middle throws ball into air.

3 A person of Irish descent. **Cf Mick 1, 3**
1942 Berrey–Van den Bark *Amer. Slang* 385.11, *Irishman. . . spud.* **1968** *DARE* (Qu. HH28, *Names and nicknames . . for people of foreign background: Irish*) Inf **IN**10, Spud.

4 See quot. [*OED2* 1960 →; cf *OED2 potato* sb. 5.d]
1966 *DARE* File **neMN** (as of 1940s), *Spud*—hole in stocking.

5 A dollar; in pl, money. [Cf *OED2 potato* sb. 5.e]
1923 *DN* 5.237 **swWI**, *Spuds. . . Money. . .* "He's got the spuds." **1942** Berrey–Van den Bark *Amer. Slang* 559.1, *Money . . spuds.* **1968–69** *DARE* (Qu. U26, *Names or nicknames . . for a paper dollar*) Inf **NC**79, Spud; (Qu. U27, . . *A silver dollar*) Inf **KY**37, Spud.

6 A playing card of the suit of spades.
1896 *DN* 1.425 **cNY**, *Spud:* a spade in cards. Sometimes heard. **1900** *DN* 2.64 [College slang], *Spud. . .* Spade, in cards. **1942** Berrey–Van den Bark *Amer. Slang* 744.6, *Spades. . . spuds.*

‡7 A cigar. [Cf *EDD spud* sb.¹ 6 "Any person or thing very short or stumpy"; cf also *Spud* a now defunct brand of cigarettes]
1967–70 *DARE* (Qu. DD6a, *Other names or nicknames for cigars*) Infs **MA**127, **PA**19, Spud.

8 =red drum.
1887 Goode *Amer. Fishes* 102, "Spot" sometimes corrupted to "Spud" is another name erroneously applied to this fish [=the red drum], and which is the property of a much smaller species of the same family, otherwise known as "Lafayette" or "Cape May Goody."

9 =English sparrow. **Cf spug**
1968 *DARE* (Qu. Q22, *Joking names or nicknames for the common sparrow*) Infs **UT**4, 5, Spud.

spud v

1 usu with *around* (or *along*): To loiter, idle; to amble, wander about; hence vbl n *spudding*. [Cf *EDD spuddle* v.¹ 3 "to be uselessly busy; to fuss about doing little or nothing"] **chiefly sAppalachians**
1913 Kephart *Highlanders* 203 **sAppalachians**, "No, I ain't workin' none—jest spuddin' around." . . "Spuddin' around" means toddling or jolting along. **1928** Chapman *Happy Mt.* 313 **seTN**, *Spudding around*—ambling about, loitering here and there. **1929** in 1952 Mathes *Tall Tales* 149 **sAppalachians**, Reckon I'll have to be spuddin' along if I'm goin' to sell the balance of this here white mule! **1936** *AmSp* 11.276 **eTN**, *Spudding around.* Loitering, doing nothing worthwhile. 'John is just spudding around.' **1937** (1977) Hurston *Their Eyes* 188 **csFL** [Black], Ah wants tuh git in de game whilst de big money is in it. Ah ain't fuh no spuddin' tuhday. Ah'll come home wid de money an' Ah'll come back on a stretcher. **1938** Matschat *Suwannee R.* 62 **neFL**, **seGA**, He decided to hitch up to . . the big pine and climb high enough to spot a familiar landmark. "Mayhap," he thought, "we-uns kin git our bearin' without need for spuddin' aroun'."

‡2 See quot.
1903 *DN* 2.353 **neOH**, *Spud. . .* To punish, as a child.

‡3 also with *in:* See quot.
1916 *DN* 4.341 **seOH**, *Spud. . .* To evade a question. Also *spud in.*

4 See **spud** n 1.

spud along (or around), spudding vbl n¹ See **spud** v 1

spudding vbl n² See **spud** n 1

spudge v [Appar var of *spud* v in generalized sense "poke, prod"] **chiefly NEng** Cf **spodge** v, **spudge** n

1 To stab (something) with a pointed instrument.
1892 *DN* 1.211 **seMA**, *Spudge:* to stick (as with a knife). Plymouth (or Salem?). **1937** [see **4a** below]. [**1988** Poteet *S. Shore Phr. Book* 107 **Nova Scotia Canada**, *Spudge the fire*—poke the fire, make it burn up, or blaze up.]

2 with *in:* To make a stabbing motion.
1896 (1897) Newhall *Gt. & Genl. Courte* 402 **eMA**, The boys told old Crosscudgell that a snake run into the wall; and so he spudged in with his kane, where they told him.

3 with *up:*

a To stir up. **Cf spudger**
1995 U.S. Congress Senate *Federal Regulations Balancing* 38 **ME**, On the third day we go back in the hold tank area . . and they're spudged up again, the salt is pressed down into the fish.

b To come up with (a sum of money).
1856 Kelly *Humors* 386, The clerk explained it, clear as mud; the trio "spudged up" the amount, looked very sober, and walked out. **1868** *Flag of Our Union* (Boston MA) 23.783, Forest has had to spudge up $65,000 to his divorced wife. **1885** *Sun. Oregonian* (Portland OR) 20 Dec 6/3 **NEng**, I shall have to make my blue Scotland shawl do, and a prayer-book, and Harry just *must* spudge up a little money besides for them!

c To rouse (one) to action.
1903 in 1967 Peabody *To Be Young* 347 **MA**, Went to Emmanuel Guild to try to spudge them up to do something for the Sailors Haven. **1958** Brooks *Gramercy Park* 52 **NYC** (as of c1900), Wish your mother would spudge him up a little more.

d To rouse oneself, begin to show energy and initiative.
1881 *Atlantic Mth.* 48.25 **ME**, I've wondered . . he did n't spudge up and be somebody. **1896** *Harper's New Mth. Mag.* 93.896 **NEng**, You see you've got to spudge up in your mills, get a move on, don't you see. **1917** *Syracuse Herald* (NY) 20 Aug [20]/6 (newspaperarchive.com) **NEng**, "I think she's inclined to be rather spleeny. . . I think she'd be better off if she'd 'spudge up' a bit and not think so much about herself." So I heard one woman characterize another the other day.

4 with *(a)round:*

a To poke about (with a pointed instrument).
1937 Brooks *Small Business* 76, The experienced eeler . . will in the winter time chop a hole two or three feet in diameter in the ice above the mud, and spudge around with a spear. . . When he strikes an eel he can recognize it by the vigorous movements of the spudged eel.

b To act energetically, bustle or potter about.
[**1864** *Knickerbocker* 64.150 **Nova Scotia Canada**, I felt my courage all oozin' out . . ; but as there wa n't no sech thing as backin' out, I had to spudge round an' go ahead, feelin' my way along by the headstones.] **1920** *Scribner's Mag.* 68.247 **NEng**, "I'd like to see *him* trying to get three dawdling children ready for school," I can hear her say. "I guess he'd soon be trying to make them spudge round a little." **1948** Moore *Fire Balloon* 31 **ME**, He'd get mixed up with some slimpsy woman who never got her housework done—that Emly'd spudge around all day in a two-quart dish.

5 with *along:* To mosey along. **Cf spud v 1**
1906 *Amer. Mag.* 62.550, And there came that fat devil [=an elephant], spudging along, his feet padding the deck, and his little eyes gleaming. **1951** Mayo *Oct. Fire* 110 **ME**, Yesterday afternoon, he'd been spudging along, minding his own business, whacking the bushes alongside the road for the rewarding sound of glass, when he'd heard the voice.

6 with *on:* To secure (bait) in a lobster trap using a **spudge iron.**
2008 *DARE* File—Internet **ME**, [Caption:] Baiting a lobster trap in maine—Spudging on some pogies getting ready for the big Summer Lobster shed.

spudge n [Appar var of *spud* n; cf *OED2 spud* sb. 1 "A short and poor knife or dagger," 4 "A short or stumpy person or thing"; *EDD spud* sb.¹ 4 "A worn-out tool"] Cf **spodge** n¹, **spudge** v
See quot.
1954 Roberts *I Bought Dog* 14 **seKY**, He took out his spudge of a knife and cut the line.

spudge along See **spudge** v 5

spudge around See **spudge** v 4

spudge hole n [Prob var of *spud* any of several digging or drilling tools + *hole*; cf **spudge** n, v]
See quot.

1937 *Daily Kennebec Jrl.* (Augusta ME) [12 Apr 7]/6 (newspaper-archive.com), The strike started May 2 [1892], when the quarrymen laid down their drills and demanded . . 3 cents a hole for drilling "spudge holes" (to split the rock).

spudge in See **spudge** v 1

spudge iron n Cf **spodge** n¹, **spudge** v 6
=**bait iron.**

1974 *Salt* 1.1.28 **ME,** While Dan is hauling traps, I have already baited the spudge iron (pronounced "spudgin"). The spudge iron looks like an ice pick that has a hole near the end of the point. First I put the bait bag on the spudge iron, then poke the point of the spudge iron through the eyes of the redfish. After Dan finishes measuring the lobster, I hand him the spudge iron. He threads the bait line attached to the trap through the hole in the spudge iron, transferring the fish to the line. The bait line keeps the fish from floating outside the trap. **1993** ME Dept. Marine Resources Educ. Div. *Teacher's Guide* np, Tools of the lobster industry. . . What is the function of the . . spudge iron.

spudge on See **spudge** v 6

spudger n [**spudge** v] chiefly **NEng**
Any of var tools for poking, stirring, or manipulating something; see quots. Note: The recent use of this term in the electronics industry appears to be widespread and is not illustrated here.

1880 U.S. Supreme Court *Rec. & Briefs* 258.15 **neMA,** They used a stick made round at one end, for a handle to hold on to, and sharp at the other end . . ; with that they would dig the accumulated matter from the rolls. The above stick was . . called by isinglas manufacturers a "spudger." **1899** U.S. Fish Comm. *Bulletin for 1898* 438 **NEng,** In some localities, the masses [of fish] are separated by stirring them with a spudger, consisting of a thick board 10 inches long and 2 or 3 inches wide, nailed in the center to a wooden handle. **1922** *Jrl. New Engl. Water Wks.* 36.83 **MA,** When we get to the corporation cock and find that stopped up so that we can't push in a reaming tool there, we use an instrument which we call a spudger, which is a section of brass pipe which we secure to the end of the service pipe in the cellar. **1944** Coffin *Mainstays ME* 101, Better take the smelts out with a spudger—you know, the perforated shovel you turn the morning's flapjacks over with. **1995** U.S. Congress Senate *Federal Regulations Balancing* 37 **ME,** We put two bags [of salt] on, and take a spudger, which is a long stick, or another stick attached to the small stick at the bottom, and the salt is pushed down into the fish. **2006** in 2008 *DARE* File—Internet **TX,** Looking for a source for *stainless steel spudgers*—the greenhouse propagation tool for lifting plants from cells during transplanting.

spudge round See **spudge** v 4

spudge up See **spudge** v 6

spud in See **spud** v 3

‡**spudnut** n
=**peanut 1.**

1966 *DARE* (Qu. I42, . . *Names or nicknames . . for peanuts*) Inf **MI**19, Spudnuts.

spuds See **spud** n 2, 5

spug n [Scots, Engl dial "house sparrow"; cf *EDD, SND*] Cf **spud** n 9
=**English sparrow.**

1966 *DARE* (Qu. Q22, *Joking names or nicknames for the common sparrow*) Inf **ID**1, Spug.

‡**spug-hole** n [Prob < **spung**] Cf **spring hole**

1891 *AN&Q* 7.249 **sNJ,** I heard a new word lately, down among the pines of Southern New Jersey. A man, in speaking of a wet and muddy spot in a field, called it a *spug-hole*.

spukie See **spucky**

spun See **spoon**

spung n |spʌŋ| Also sp *spong* [Cf *EDD spong* sb. 3 "A low bog, a morass"] chiefly **sNJ** Cf **cripple** n¹, **pocosin 1, slank** n
An area of low, swampy ground.

[**1890** *DN* 1.76 **seNJ, MD,** *Spungy:* the land between swamp and hard ground. [*DARE* Ed: This may be a var of *spongy.*]] **1894** *DN* 1.334 **NJ,** *Spung:* piece of low ground at the head of a stream in the tide-water district. **1940** Weygandt *Down Jersey* 50 **sNJ,** Most Jerseymen lay emphasis on a spong being a long and narrow strip of swampy land with a stream seeping through it. It is a word far from obsolete in South Jersey. **1942** *Sat. Eve. Post* 5 Sept 9 **sNJ,** The site [of the dwelling] was protected from intrusion by two spungs and a cripple on the west and north, and by a . . throwback from Stow Creek on its remaining flanks. **1954** *DE Folkl. Bulletin* 1.16, *Spung* (low ground at the head of a stream). **1968** McPhee *Pine Barrens* 61 **cNJ,** If no cedars grow there, the wet area is called a spong, which is pronounced to rhyme with "sung." Some people define spongs and cripples a little differently, saying that water always flows in a cripple but there is water in a spong only after a rain. Others say that any lowland area where highbush blueberries grow is a spong. **1968–69** *DARE* (Qu. C6, . . *A piece of land that's often wet, and has grass and weeds growing on it*) Inf **NJ**55, Spung [spʌŋ]; [(Qu. L8, *Hay that grows naturally in damp places*) Inf **NJ**20, Sour grass—grows in spony [sic] ['spʌŋgi] places—this is a boggy or wet place]. **1985** *DARE* File **sNJ,** Spong—pronounced along the lines of "wrung," is a South Jersey Pine Barrens regionalism for a low, wet place in the woods, more or less a hollow, with just about enough water except in the dry time to make it over one's bootsoles. **2000** *Ibid* **sNJ,** *Spung* . . refers to a swampy area but not as wet. A lowland but not a tidal lowland. **2003** *DARE* File—Internet **cNJ,** [Caption:] A seasonal spung on the North Branch of the Forked River. **2003** Geol. Assoc. S. NJ *Periglacial Features* 51 **sNJ,** Spungs are enclosed wetland basins, created by deflation under periglacial conditions. They served as oasis-like watering places for wildlife and ambulant peoples over a period of 12,000 years.

spunk n [*OED2 spunk* sb. 2 1582 →] **scattered, but esp S Midl**
Decayed wood or a woody substance used as tinder; punk; hence adj *spunky,* punky.

1815 in 1947 *AmSp* 22.281 [Americanisms], *Spunk*—punk. **1841** Catlin *Letters Indians* 1.147, It contained also his flint and steel, and spunk for lighting. *Ibid* 189, A spark of fire is seen and caught in a piece of spunk. **1853** Finley *Autobiog.* 83 **KY,** The hunter takes a long, slim pole, attaches some spunk or rotten wood to it, . . and, igniting the end, sets fire to the hole, which is filled with rotten wood. **1875** (1876) Young *Hist. Chautauqua Co. NY* 316, With the aid of a gun and spunk, they struck up a fire. **1892** *DN* 1.232 **KY,** *Spunk:* punk. **1923** *DN* 5.222 **swMO,** *Spunk.* . . Rotten wood. *Spunky.* . . Also decayed or rotten, as wood. **1953** Randolph–Wilson *Down in Holler* 287 **Ozarks,** *Spunk.* . . Dry, partially decayed wood. The pioneers used *spunk* to catch the sparks from the flint-and-steel gadgets which they carried in lieu of matches. **1954** *Harder Coll.* **cwTN,** *Spunk.* . . "Dry, partially decayed wood." [**1967** *DARE* (Qu. KK7, *When wood . . is starting to decay inside . . "It's _____ inside."*) Inf **CA**15A, Spunky, [corr to] punky.] **2001** *DARE* File—Internet, Campfire in the southern woods starts with a layer of spunk, covered with a layer of lightard knots.

spunk knot n esp **Delmarva**
=**pumpknot.**

1917 Stanton *Fata Morgana* 153 **Sth** [Black] (as of 1807), Dat sho' am dis nigger's big foot track. Dat sho' am de mark uv my spunk-knot (bunion) on my big toe. **1968** *DARE* (Qu. X60, . . *A lump that comes up on your head when you get a sharp blow or knock;* not asked in early QRs) Infs **DE**3, **MD**12, Spunk knot. **2000** *DARE* File—Internet, *Ryan Stevens* was noted to have a large spunk knot on the back of his head, the result of being smashed in the head with a pipe. . . Testing revealed no concussion, only minor bruising and the aforementioned spunk knot. **2004** McCleaf *For They Know Not* 185 **MD,** After several minutes and some serious scrubbing, Sean had removed most of the blood and had placed a bandage over the spunk knot on his head. **2007** in 2008 *DARE* File—Internet **sMD,** I got pegged in the forhead [sic] with an 8 ball and met his parents with a big spunk knot.

spunk up v phr **orig chiefly NEast, now more widespread**
To gather one's strength or courage; to assert oneself; to demonstrate (courage, determination).

1828 *DE Patriot & Amer. Watchman* (Wilmington) 2 May [2]/2 (newspaperarchive.com) **VT,** Now thinks I heer,s [sic] the divvle tu pay, but i,le [sic] spunk up tu him—so sis I yew Darnashun Black sun ov a turnup. **1853** Jerdan *Yankee Humor* 109, Just spunk up to the old codger—let him know you are not afraid of him. **1867** Higginson *Harvard Mem. Biog.* 7 **MA,** I am not at all well . . and sometimes I feel as if I must lie down . . but I 'spunk up,' and have thus far held out. **1890** Holley *Samantha among Brethren* 109 **NY,** "I guess I have got a few rights left, and a little spunk." "Yes," sez I, sadly, "you have got the spunk." "Wall," sez he, "I guess I can spunk up, and do somethin' for one of my own relations." **1907** Lincoln *Cape Cod* 72 **MA,** Eben hadn't spunked up anywhere nigh enough courage to propose. **1909** *DN* 3.374 **eAL, wGA,** *Spunk. . .* To show courage: with *up.* **1919** Gale *Peace* 169 **WI,** Mis' Postmaster Sykes, she invited her real cordial to be married in her sitting-room, but Hannah spunked up and wouldn't. **1929** *AmSp* 4.292 (as of 1874) [Yankee terms], An old fashioned Yankee. . . talks of 'spunkin' up to an all-fired, tarnation slick gall.' **1940** Yoder *Rosanna* 140 **PA,** Spunk up, Cristly, show Isaac that you can give him all he wants to do. **1947** Botkin *Treas. New Engl. Folkl.* 409, But on the night of his dance, having been to a husking-bee where he had "kept his spirits up by pouring spirits down," . . for he had kissed his pretty partner twenty times, he spunked up and chanced it straight across the hill. **1997** Cutler *Spaceman* 3, "Stay with us, now, Gary," Mr. Rudolph said, when Gary looked confused. "Spunk up, Gary," Mr. Rudolph said, when Gary drooped. **2008** *DARE* File—Internet **OR,** He [=a horse] "spunked up," I could see a change in his eyes. In ten days there was a definite difference in the way he walked, a little smoother. By the end of the month he was quite obviously feeling a lot better than ever before.

spunk-water n   Sth, S Midl   Cf **stump water 1a**

Rainwater that has collected in the hollow of a rotten stump and is used as a home remedy, esp for removing warts.

1875 (1876) Twain *Tom Sawyer* 65 **MO,** He took and dipped his hand in a rotten stump where the rain water was. . . trying to cure warts with spunk-water. . . Spunk-water, spunk-water, swaller these warts. **1931** Randolph *Ozarks* 96, One of my neighbors tells me that he rid himself of forty-two warts in a fortnight, simply by washing his hands in "spunk-water"—rainwater which falls into the hollow of a rotten stump. **1933** *AmSp* 8.1.52 **Ozarks,** *Spunk water.* Rain water which remains in cavities of trees or stumps, used in removing warts, etc. **1949** *Time* 29 Aug 7, Spunk-water, spunk-water, wash away my warts! **1960** Bailey *Resp. to PADS 20* **KS,** *Spunkwater. . .* Barley-corn, barley-corn / Injun meal shorts—/ Spunkwater, spunkwater / Swallow these warts. **1970** *NC Folkl.* 18.20, Eczema and tetter are treated by use of rain water ("spunk water") caught in a stump. **1970** Anderson *TX Folk Med.* 4 **neTX,** Arthritis—Take a dead cat into the woods to a hollow tree stump that has spunk water in it.

spunky adj

1 Irritable, angry.

1809 in 1853 U.S. Congress *Debates & Proc.* 10th Cong 2d Sess 31 Jan 1259, It may be a spunky spiteful child, but will have no strength. **1838** (1843) Haliburton *Clockmaker* (2d ser) 249 **NEng,** Well, says she, you make me feel quite spunky, and if you don't stop this minit, I'll go right out of the room; it ain't fair to make game of me so. **1887** (1892) Hinman *Corporal Si Klegg* 7, Ye don't need ter git spunky 'bout it. . . Ye know I didn't mean nothin'. **1892** *KS Univ. Qrly.* 1.99 **KS,** *Spunky:* pouting, incensed. **1894** *DN* 1.343 **wCT,** *Spunky:* angry, irritated. **1910** *DN* 3.449 **wNY,** *Spunky. . .* Irritable. **1912** *DN* 3.569 **cNY,** *Spunk. . .* Pluck or courage, but also ill-humor as in "a spunky child." **1915** *DN* 4.216 **wCT,** *Spunky,* irritable. "If I had a kid as spunky as that I'd whip him." **1917** *DN* 4.400 **neOH,** *Spunky* is not exactly "irritable," . . but rather "angry" as a result of being irritated, with a suggestion of triviality. "Now, don't get spunky over this." Also Vt., Ill., Ia., Ky. **1923** *DN* 5.222 **swMO,** *Spunky. . .* Belligerent. **1941** *LANE* Map 472 (*Angry*) 1 inf, **seVT,** Spunky = angry, of children. **1973** Allen *LAUM* 1.360 (as of c1950), *angry. . .* spunky [1 inf, **IA**]. **1982** Brooks *Quicksand* 31 **swUT** (as of c1902), To me, struggling with a spunky baby, the thing seemed endless.

2 See **spunk.**

spunt v   See **spin 1**

‡**spunt** n

1916 *DN* 4.281 **NE,** *Spunt. . .* Old lame horse. "What does he want with that spunt on the premises?"

spurge n

Std: a plant of the family Euphorbiaceae, esp of the genus *Euphorbia* or *Chamaesyce.* For other names of var spp see **bowman's root 1, creeper milkweed, cypress spurge, eyebright 5, fire-on-the-mountain, flowering spurge, French pursley, ghostweed, golondrina, gopher plant 1, Japanese poinsettia 1, milk ipecac 2, ~ purslane 1, milkweed 2, mole plant 1, mountain spurge 2, painted leaf, poinsettia B1, rat-**

tlesnake weed 1h, sassy jack, seven sisters 2, snow-on-the-mountain 1, snow-on-the-prairie, summer poinsettia 2, wax plant 3, wild ipecac 1, ~ poinsettia**

spurge nettle n   Cf **cow nettle**

Std: a plant of the genus *Cnidoscolus,* esp *C. stimulosus.* For other names of var spp see **bull nettle, finger-rot, fly-fly, nettle n 3, stinging ~ 4, tread-soft(ly) 1**

spurrer n   Also sp *spurrow*   Cf **-er affix 1**

A rider's spur.

1870 *Our Young Folks* 6.676 **Sth** [Black], So Mr. Har' put his bridle and martingale on Mr. Fox and buckle on his spurrers. **1880** (1881) Harris *Uncle Remus Songs* 38 **GA** [Black], Brer Rabbit slap de spurrers inter Brer Fox flanks, en you better b'leeve he got over groun'. **1899** Chesnutt *Conjure Woman* 180 **csNC** [Black], Yo' thighs is des [=just] raw whar de spurrers has be'n driv' in you. **1909** *DN* 3.374 **eAL, wGA,** *Spurrer. . .* A horseman's spur. **1928** *Ruppenthal Coll.* **KS,** *Spurrows*—spurs.

spurt grass n

=**salt-marsh bulrush.**

1876 Hobbs *Bot. Hdbk.* 211, Scirpus maritimus, Spurt grass. **1933** Small *Manual SE Flora* 171, *S[cirpus] robustus. . .* Spurt grass. . . Brackish marshes, Coastal Plain and New England Coast, Fla. to Tex.

'spute v, hence vbl n *'sputing*   [Aphet form of *dispute; OED2 spute* v.[1] "*Obs.* or *dial*"; a1225 →]   **chiefly Sth**   *among Black speakers*

1852 *Republican Compiler* (Gettysburg PA) 19 Jan 1/5 [Black], "I tell you wat, Sam, I hab a monstrous 'spute wid massa dis morning." . . "Wa, wa, wat you 'spute about?" **1870** Redford *Hist. Methodism KY* 3.520, An illiterate negro joined the Campbellite Church, and immediately after his immersion . . met a person whom he knew, and accosted him by saying, *"Don't you want to 'spute?"* **1880** *Scribner's Mth.* 22.242 **GA** [Black], Brer Fox b'leeve dat Brer Rabbit wuz de 'casion er Mr. Dog bein' in de neighberhoods at dat time er night, en Brer Rabbit ain't 'spute it. **1884** *Anglia* 7.272 **Sth, S Midl** [Black], To 'spute over = to have a dispute about. **1888** Jones *Negro Myths* 59 **GA coast,** Day bin a big yaller Rooster een de gang wuh try fuh spute Buh Chanticleer, and mek eh brag say eh kin lick um. **1927** Adams *Congaree* 68 **cSC** [Black], An' I ain't 'sputin' nobody when dey says it b'longs to em. **1930** Stoney–Shelby *Black Genesis* 5 **seSC,** All de argifyin', an' 'sputin', an' cussin', an' fussin', wouldn't hab a chance for tek place. **1959** Lomax *Rainbow Sign* 152 **LA** [Black], I never 'sputed my mother's word, I never 'sputed my father's word in my life. **2003** Campbell *Robert G. Clark's Journey* 46 **MS** [Black], I don't mean to 'spute your word, Boss, but I got to go vote.

sputterbudget n   Also *sputterbridget*   Cf **budget n 3, flutterbudget**

A finicky, fussy, or fretful person.

1915 *DN* 4.210, *Sputter-budget, -bridget,* fuss-budget. "Don't be such a sputterbudget! Come and put it on." **1967** *DARE* (Qu. GG14, *Names and nicknames for someone who fusses or worries a lot, especially about little things*) Inf **IA3,** Sputterbudget; (Qu. HH11a, *Someone who is too particular or fussy—if it's a man*) Inf **NY27,** Sputterbudget; (Qu. HH11b, *Someone who is too particular or fussy—if it's a woman*) Infs **IA3, NY27,** Sputterbudget. **1994** O'Rourke *All the Trouble* 4, A colossus that stood astride the earth now lies on the floor pounding its fists and kicking its feet, transformed into a fussy-pants and a sputter-budget.

sputtum See **spittum**

sputzie See **spatzie**

‡**spy on** exclam

=**I spy** exclam.

1967 *DARE* (Qu. EE15, *When he has caught the first of those that were hiding what does the player who is 'it' call out to the others?*) Inf **NY2,** Spy on (name), the rest come in free.

sqoz See **squeeze** v Bb

squab n   [*OED2 squab* sb. 3 a1700 →, *squabby* a. 1754 →] **scattered, but esp Sth, S Midl**   See Map

A fat person; hence adjs *squab(by)* fat; stocky.

1806 Fessenden *Mod. Philos.* 109 **NH,** Thus Darwin's squabby fiend . . /Evanishes before a *stink.* **1826** in 1827 Carter *Letters Europe* 2.45 **NH,** I have seen . . the King himself, a squab of a monarch, who battens upon anchovies and sugar-plums. **1851** Hooper *Widow Rugby's Husband* 148 **AL,** Granny Mitchum is short, fleshy, squab. **1874** (1875) Warren *30 Years' Battle* 117 **NYC,** Huge-limbed and squabby, they show in their make-up the low breed of the human animal from which they spring. **1899** (1912) Green *VA Folk-Speech* 411, *Squabby.* . . Thick; squat; short; fat. **1965–70** *DARE* (Qu. X50, *Names or nicknames for a person who is very fat*) Infs **IN**82, **TN**3, **TX**98, Squab; **MO**19, **OK**18, (Big) old fat squab; **IN**32, **LA**18, **MI**2, **NC**9, 79, **VA**39, 42, Squabby. [9 of 12 Infs comm type 5, 3 comm type 4] **1995** *Brophy Coll.* 71 **swMO** (as of c1960), *Squabby.* [S]quat, squatty. "[F]at and squabby." **2003** in 2008 *DARE* File—Internet **GA,** The bottle is sort of short and squabby to accommodate a wider than normal silicon [sic] nipple.

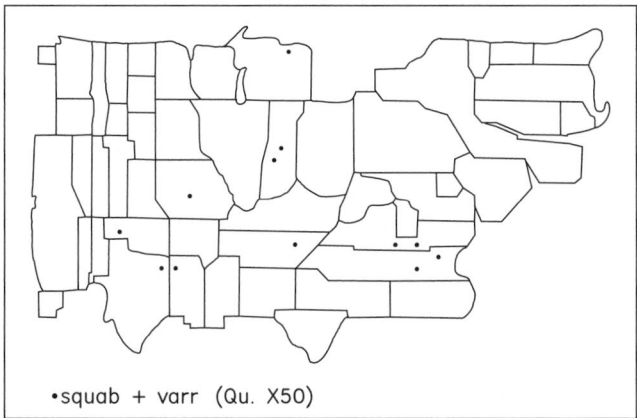

•squab + varr (Qu. X50)

‡squabbed over adj phr Cf **squawed**
    1966 *DARE* (Qu. KK70, *Something that has got out of proper shape: "That house is all _____."*) Inf **NC**2, Squabbed over.

squabby See **squab**

squack n
=gray squirrel 1.
    1911 *DN* 3.540 **eKY,** *Squăck.* . . The ordinary gray squirrel. **1957** Combs *Lang. S. Highlanders* **sAppalachians,** Squack—noise made by the squirrel; also, the squirrel, itself. [**1979** in 2003 *DARE* File—Internet **WV,** Squirrel season is in, and "Squacky" is out there somewhere waiting to teach some unskilled stalker the principles of invisibility.] **2003** *Ibid* **KY,** I ask him if he could walk a ways without any trouble and he replied, "I reckon I can for good squack hunting." *Ibid* **cNY,** It fires up the squacks and they chatter back revealing there [sic] position. *Ibid* **neIL,** [Bulletin-board posting:] How far can you go and still kill a squak [sic] with a 22LR? *Ibid* **nwAR,** [Response to preceding:] Whatever distance that is for you, you can kill a squack at that range. [*Ibid* **cMN,** [Response to preceding:] Forgive my ignorance, but what's a squak?]

squad car n Also *squad* **scattered, but esp IL, WI** See Map Cf **cruiser 3**
A police car; hence n *squad-car man* a policeman.
    1924 in 2008 (acc) Lexis–Nexis Legal Research *State Case Law: MO* (Internet), Stroud, Gartland, and the defendant Pauly, patrolmen, were riding in a squad car. **1926** in 2002 *Ibid: IL* (Internet), Detectives in

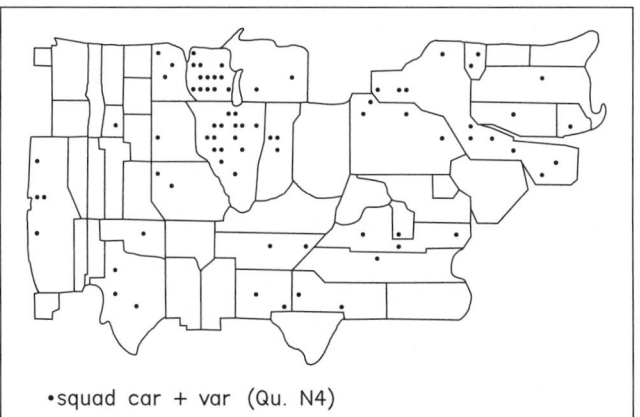

•squad car + var (Qu. N4)

two squad cars took him to the undertaker's. **1938** in Lib. of Congress *Amer. Memory: WPA Life Hist.* (Internet) **CT,** Pretty soon we see a squad car come tearin' up the street. **1965–70** *DARE* (Qu. N4, *A police vehicle with a red, blue, or yellow flashing light on top*) 77 Infs, **scattered, but esp IL, WI,** Squad car; **WI**57, Squad. **1986** Pederson *LAGS Concordance (Police sedan)* 43 infs, **scattered Gulf Region,** Squad car; *(Policeman)* 1 inf, **swTN,** Squad-car man. **2008** *WI State Jrl.* (Madison) 2 Apr sec B 5/4, A Madison man was arrested Monday after he allegedly . . punched a police officer in the face several times after running into a squad car.

squadrol n [Blend of *squad car* + *patrol*] **IL, esp Chicago**
A police van.
    1948 *Garfieldian* (Chicago IL) 19 Aug 3/3, She was pronounced dead at Loretto hospital . . , Squadrol Patrolman John Kennelly said. **1949** Algren *Man with Golden Arm* 86 **Chicago IL,** He had to take a short cut through an alley toward the florist's when the squadrol slid up beside him. **1954** in 2003 *DARE* File [*Chicago Tiny Sun–Times* (IL) 5 Apr 1/3], Assistant City Editor Joe Fay. . . thought up and put into circulation the word squadrol. He reasoned that this type of police vehicle combines the functions of a squad car and a patrol wagon, so he combined the two terms into one. **1970** *DARE* (Qu. N4, *A police vehicle with a red, blue, or yellow flashing light on top*) Inf **IL**144, Squadrol. **1972** in 2003 (acc) Lexis–Nexis Legal Research *Federal Case Law: Court of Appeals: Seventh Circuit* (Internet) **Chicago IL,** He witnessed petitioner's two co-defendants exiting from a squadrol. **1993** *St. Louis Post–Dispatch* (MO) 24 May 1 (Internet) **swIL,** East St. Louis police will get a new van next month. . . called a Squadrol. **1999** Paretsky *Hard Times* 367 **Chicago IL,** The remaining two men . . had been carried off by a squadrol that the firemen had summoned. **2002** *Chicago Sun–Times* (IL) 2 Oct 41 (Internet), It was paid as part of a pre-trial settlement to the family of a man who died of asphyxiation in a squadrol two years ago.

squael See **squail**

squagin See **scoggin 2**

squail v Also sp *squael, squale* [Engl dial] **esp NEng** arch Cf **scale** v[2] **2**
To throw a stick, stone, or other object; to throw such an object at (a target); to pelt (one); also fig.
    1816 Pickering *Vocab.* 179 **NEng,** *To Squale.* To throw a stick, or other thing, with violence and in such a manner, that it skims along near the ground. **1820** in 1944 *ADD, Squale, squail.* . . Nothing loth to squale loose jaw, & slam an angry oath. **1890** *Century Dict.* 5873, *Squail, squale . . intr.* To throw a stick, loaded stick, disk, flat stone, or other object at a mark. . . [*Century* Ed: Prov. Eng. and New Eng.] **1891** *Jrl. Amer. Folkl.* 4.159 **MA,** *Squael.*—To throw stones, to pelt. "Squael him," that is, throw stones at him. **1895** *DN* 1.394 **neMA,** *Squail* (v.t.) to throw stones at. Marblehead, Mass. **1921** Morison *Maritime Hist. MA* 140, 'Squaeling,' in Marblehead dialect, meant hurling a stone, or other hard object. "I don't remember any one being squaeled," said an old lady of Marblehead to a friend of mine not many years ago—"unless 't were a Lynn man!" she added, thoughtfully.

squair See **square** n[1], adj, adv

squak See **squawk**

squale See **squail**

squalker n Cf **squawk**
=black-crowned night heron.
    1955 MA Audubon Soc. *Bulletin* 39.312 **CT,** Black-crowned Night Heron. . . Squalker.

squall v
1 usu with *out:* To shout, call loudly. **chiefly S Midl**
    1881 *Scribner's Mth.* 22.445 **GA** [Black], Den Brer Rabbit, he squall out: "Dis de way a big man spit." **1884** *Anglia* 7.267 **Sth, S Midl** [Black], *To squall out* = to cry out. **1892** *Century Illustr. Mag.* 44.461 **nGA** [Black], An' de coon say: 'I knows w'at I 'll do,'/ . . / An' he wife she squall out, 'I does too!' **a1902** in 2003 *DARE* File—Internet **AR** (as of 1860s), I did not know anyone was in the tent and Paul ran out. Squalled out, "Who shot that gun?" Says I, "I did it Litenant, see I killed a crow." **1953** Brewer *Word Brazos* 18 **eTX** [Black], He ain't gone ver' far though 'fo' he wheel 'roun' rail quick an' squall out to de white man to wait a minnit, he wanna tell 'im sump'n. **1966** *DARE* File **PA,** "I squalled for my daughter, but there was no answer." (Daughter was 17 years old). Heard on radio—speaker was a "Pennsylvania mountaineer."

2001 House *Clay's Quilt* 171 **eKY,** "He ain't hurt!" Geneva squalled out.

2 In hunting: to imitate any of var harsh animal cries in order to attract game; to lure (an animal) in this way; hence vbl n *squalling.* Cf **squaller**

1953 *Star* (Kansas City MO) 13 Dec sec B 6/1, The veteran also is a professional at standing on the ground and squalling at a coon in a tree and making the animal walk down or jump out of it. **1961** *McDavid Coll.* **csOK,** *Squall that coon down*—bring down with the aid of a coon call. **2000** in 2003 *DARE* File—Internet, We try to get him back on the tree but he won't go after everything. i have squalled like their was a coon and he still won't go back on to the tree. **2002** *Ibid* **CO,** I've never found any rhyme or reason as to what calls in bears except that you want to squall as loudly as you can. *Ibid* [Prohound Online] **KY,** We squalled about another two minutes and guess what ran out? A real live coon. *Ibid,* He would make a den tree and I could squall them out of there. **2003** *Ibid* **TX,** I had a Haydell's Hog Squaller . . and started squalling loudly. I saw the hogs react at once, they started trotting—getting the heck out of there! So much for hog squalling.

squaller n [**squall** 2]
A noisemaker, esp one used as a call for attracting prey.

1923 *DN* 5.222 **swMO,** *Squaller.* . . A whistle made from a straw or from the stem of a pumpkin or squash. **2002** *DARE* File—Internet, *Primos Coon Squaller* . . Attracts raccoons, foxes and predators. Reproduces the high pitched squall of a raccoon. *Ibid, Jack Rabbit Squaller* . . Simple to use, reproduces deeper squalls and screams of a wounded jack rabbit. A Coyote special. **2003** [see **squall** 2].

squalling See **squall** 2

squall out See **squall** 1

squalmish See **squamish**

‡squalmy adj   Cf **squamish**
   1950 *WELS* (If somebody's food did not agree with him, he might . . feel _____) 1 Inf, **cwWI,** Squalmy.

squam duck n [*Squam* common place-name in New England] =**eider duck.**
   1844 Giraud *Birds Long Is.* 332 **ME,** Eider Duck. . . With us, its breeding range extends from Maine, where it is called 'Squam Duck,' to the higher northern latitudes.

squamish adj   Also *squalmish, squawmish* [Var of **qualmish,** perh infl by *squeamish*] **scattered, but esp NEast, Mid Atl**
Nauseated, queasy; squeamish.

   1833 Greene *Life Dr. Dodimus* 1.221 **NEast,** The squamish portion, I dare say, is what makes people squamish. **1866** (1867) Gross *Compar. Materia Medica* 254, Apoplexy . . red, puffed face . . squamish . . trembling. **1867** in 1935 Twain *Notebook* 59, I am . . very tired of being seasick. . . All I take an interest in is being squalmish and getting to shore again. **1891** *Century Illustr. Mag.* 42.538 **Nantucket MA,** The South Shoal Lightship so pitched and rolled that even an old whaleman . . felt "squamish." **1892** *DN* 1.211 **seMA,** *Squawmish* [skwɔ-]: queasy. **1923** *DN* 5.222 **swMO,** *Squamish.* . . Entertaining vague doubts about the propriety of doing a certain thing. **1929** *AmSp* 5.126 **ME,** "Squ'amish" (for squeamish). **1943** *LANE* Map 503 (*Sick at his stomach*) 3 infs, **MA, ME,** Squamish. **1948** *Daily Progress* (Charlottesville VA) 24 Jan 4/4, I am not only not interested in food but maybe a little squalmish at the very thought of it. **1966–69** *DARE* (Qu. BB16b, *If something a person ate didn't agree with him, he might just feel a bit* _____) Infs **CA**160, **IN**79, **ME**22, **NC**79, **NJ**16, 18, 22, **OH**4, Squamish. [7 of 8 Infs old] **1975** Gould *ME Lingo* 272, *Squamish*—Squeamish, and pronounced halfway between squammish and squawmish. . . It is reserved mostly for that god-awful moment that precedes *mal de mer:* "Never been seasick in my life, but I was squamish once in a Fundy cross-chop." **1994** NC Lang. & Life Project *Harkers Is. Vocab.* 10 **eNC,** Squamish. . . Sick to the stomach. . . *I felt squamish on the ferry.* [**2000** Shores *Tangier Is.* 197 **Chesapeake Bay,** The younger sort do not use . . *squamish* . . ; instead, they say . . queasy.] **2002** *Herald* (Rock Hill SC) 1 Aug sec A 6 (Internet), U.S. District Judge Joe Anderson said he is "a little squamish" about delving into this dispute.

squanch See **squinch** v²

squanch-eyed See **squinch** adj 1

squander v [Arch or dial in Brit Engl; cf *OED2, EDD*]
1 also with *off:* To cause to scatter or disperse; hence ppl adj *squandered* scattered, dispersed. **VA**
   1830 in 2003 *DARE* File—Internet **VA,** Capt. Jones and his wife are dead & the land sold and the children Squandered off. **1899** (1912) Green *VA Folk-Speech* 411, *Squander.* . . To scatter; disperse; go at random. "His family are squandered about the country." **1916** *DN* 4.302 **csVA,** *Squander.* . . To scatter; disperse. "He saw a lot of quail and squandered them." **1937** Hench *Coll.* **cVA,** Heard orally: "Quit squandering those chickens." [Said to a little boy who was chasing chickens.]
2 also with *about, around, off:* To go off in all directions, scatter; to wander. **chiefly S Midl**
   1823 in 1830 Jefferson *Memoir* 4.367 **VA,** Each shifted for himself, and left his brethren to squander and do the same as they could. **1835** (1927) Evans *Exped. Rocky Mts.* 14.213 **IN,** Our horses had squandered off some of which we did not find until next day. **1872** U.S. Congress *Rept. Joint Select Comm. Insurrectionary States* 10.2002 **AL,** They have come to Mississippi squandering about. **1912** James *Allen Outlaws* 126 **VA,** Why, when they commenced to pop [=fire their guns], we-all jes' squandered! **1937** Hench *Coll.* **cVA,** Heard orally: "When I turned the chickens loose from the pen they squandered all over the barn-yard." **1942** *Ibid* **cVA,** Susie [our cook] having heard all this greeted me with a smile when I finally came back after having hunted the last group: "Well, I hear the children squandered, didn't they?" **1953** Randolph–Wilson *Down in Holler* 287 **Ozarks,** *Squander.* . . To scatter; disperse. "That gun don't shoot true no more; the bullets just goes a-squanderin' round every which way." **1967** *DARE* FW Addit **cNC,** *Squander.* . . to scatter: The geese squandered in all directions. **1974** Fink *Mountain Speech* 24 **wNC, eTN,** *Squander* . . scatter or wander idly. . . *"Them little turkeys jest squandered around every which way." . . "I jest squandered around all day."* **2001** in 2003 *DARE* File—Internet **VA,** We kinda squandered around the mall. **2006** in 2008 *Ibid* **cwCA,** Where do you want to eventually be? Many of us are just squandering around and haven't found a calling. **2008** *Ibid* **cwNY,** Four adolescent chums were squandering around, wondering what to do with all their musical talents.

squandered See **squander** 1

squander off See **squander** 1, 2

squantum n, occas cap [From an annual event held in the early decades of the 19th cent at *Squantum,* a promontory in Quincy Massachusetts, which involved the consumption of chowder and other seafood and the imitation of supposed Pilgrim or American Indian customs]
1 A picnic or clambake; in phr *Nantucket squantum:* a chowder eaten on such occasions. **chiefly eMA** Cf **tuckeruck**
   [**1812** *Weekly Messenger* (Boston MA) 28 Aug [3]/5, The Feast of Squantum was celebrated, on Monday last, with its accustomed hilarity.] [**1827** Whitney *Some Acct. Quincy MA* 29 **ceMA,** *Squantum* is a large tract of land, on the northerly part of the town. . . Here, for many years, was celebrated a Pilgrim Feast, to which people, from all parts of the State, resorted, and spent the day in social glee, partaking of the produce of sea and shore, in memory of the Pilgrim Fathers. . . It has, however, been discontinued for some years past.] **1850** (1852) Jerauld *Poetry & Prose* 380 **eMA,** Now and then, in country towns, where there are only fresh-water fish . . a subscription is got up among the lovers . . of the finny tribe, a quantity of fish procured from the nearest seaport town or city, and with what can be procured from their own ponds . . the party proceed to some convenient spot. . . The dinner consists of fish chowder, fried, boiled and broiled fish,—literally a fish-feast, bread and cheese being extras. . . and this is a Squantum! **1855** Wise *Tales Marines* 21 **NEng,** I wish . . I was . . hazin' round with Charity Bunker and the rest o' the gals at a squantum. **1856** Davis *Hist. Sketch Sturbridge* 140 **csMA,** It was formerly a custom of the inhabitants, on certain days in the Autumn, to gather about these ponds [near Sturbridge] to enjoy a season of festivity and amusement. Pork, fish, green corn, crackers and cider, composed the bill of fare. . . This gathering was called, a *Squantum.* **1881** *Lippincott's Mag.* Sept 309 **Nantucket Is. MA,** The amusements are boating, bathing, shark- and blue-fishing, and going on squantums, or clam-bakes. **1883** in 1902 *Jrl. Amer. Folkl.* 15.259, The Squantum is a peculiar institution of this island (Nantucket), being an informal picnic on the beach-sands, where the dinner is made of fish and other spoils of the sea. **1916** Macy–Hussey *Nantucket Scrap Basket* 146, "*Squantum*"—Doubtless of Indian origin; the Nantucketer's name

for a party outing or picnic—differing from a "rantum scoot" . . in that a squantum usually implies some definite destination for the cruise. **1940** Brown *Amer. Cooks* 358 **MA,** Squantum is the name taken from an old Indian chief and applied to a picnic in the woods, where a chowder, gone grand with chicken in it, called Nantucket Squantum, is prepared and eaten on the spot, much in the spirit of a Cape Cod clambake.

2 See quot.

1940 Brown *Amer. Cooks* 740 **RI,** This is a scrumptious brown bread, but why it's called Squantum we can't imagine, for in neighboring Massachusetts, Squantum is not mere bread but any picnic or chowder party worthy of the name of that old Indian chief.

square n¹, adj, adv Usu |skwɛə(r)|; also **esp NEast, Sth, S Midl** |skwæə(r)|, less freq |skweə(r)|; **esp S Midl** |skwɑr| Pronc-spp *squair, squar, squay(re)*

A Forms.

1842 [see **B2** below]. **1864** *Harper's New Mth. Mag.* 29.118 **Sth,** I squatted down right squar. **1877** *Scribner's Mth.* 14.543 **MS** [Black], De Yankee soldiers . . formed a hollow squar. **1884** *Anglia* 7.264 **Sth, S Midl** [Black], *To stan' up mighty squar'* = to be open about, not to be afraid. **1889** *Harper's New Mth. Mag.* 80.120 **sAppalachians,** He's mighty fa'r an' squar'. **1891** *PMLA* 6.163 **WV,** We find words like . . *pair, there, where, fair, . . square, . .* in all of which the mid-back-wide [vowel] is heard (. . paar, dhaar, whaar, etc.); we seldom hear the low-front-narrow (dhæær, etc.) as in Charleston, S.C., but more usually the low-front-wide (=a in man). **1913** Kephart *Highlanders* 347 **sAppalachians,** You can't fight a man fa'r and squar who'll shoot you in the back. **1922** Gonzales *Black Border* 328 **sSC, GA coasts** [Gullah glossary], Squayre—(also squay) square. **1926** *DN* 5.402 **Ozarks,** We done swapped fa'r an' squa'r. **1936** *AmSp* 11.19 **eTX,** Share, spare, square, stair, . . , etc. In educated speech, the vowel in all these words is usually [æ]. **1942** Hall *Smoky Mt. Speech* 24 **wNC, eTN,** [æ] occurs in: . . square. . . It is often a decidedly open sound, verging somewhat toward [ɑ]. . . It may, in a given utterance, suggest both [æ] and [ɑ], and it is no doubt often misinterpreted as [ɑ]. **1942** in 1944 *ADD,* Pseudo-Western. [fɑr ən skwɑr]. Radio. **1943** *LANE* Map 546 *(Park, common)* **chiefly ME, NH, VT,** Proncs of the type [skwɛə] are common; **chiefly MA, RI, CT,** Proncs of the type [skwɛə] are common; 7 infs, **wCT,** Proncs of the type [skwær]; 3 infs, **MA, RI,** Proncs of the type [skweə]. **1976** Garber *Mountain-ese* 87 **sAppalachians,** Squar . . square—Johnnie built a squar block house.

B As noun.

1 A city block, often used as a measure of distance. **scattered, but esp Philadelphia PA area** Cf **diamond B1**

1787 *Gentleman's Mag.* 57.266 **Richmond VA,** After . . destroying a square of the principal houses and stores, [the fire] abated. **1833** Coke *Subaltern's Furlough* 1.64 **Philadelphia PA,** The city is consequently chequered, as it were, like a chess-board. . . the squares (as the inhabitants term them) being solid, or blocks of buildings. **1860** *S. Lit. Messenger* 30.56 **VA,** So Battlewick determined to go home, (it was only a square and a half off,) wind or no wind. **1910** Rinehart *Window at the White Cat* 74 **PA,** Does it always take you an hour and a quarter to walk the three squares to the house? **1911** Porter *Harvester* 77 **IN,** He crossed the sidewalk, ran down the gutter for a block. . . He tried one more square. Still he could not see her. **1912** *DN* 3.566 **cNY,** Block. . . Distance between intersecting streets. In Philadelphia, *squares* is used. **1944** *AmSp* 19.37 **PA,** One lexicographical peculiarity of this dialect which is rather widely known is the use of the word *square,* '(city) block.' This term, it should be noted, has spread throughout eastern and central Pennsylvania, and is supposed to be derived from William Penn's innovation in city planning: he laid out his city with straight, parallel streets, forming rectangles which the inhabitants then called *squares.* Apparently the early German settlers were impressed and carried this English term with them as they moved inland. **1945** Street *Gauntlet* 106 **NJ** (as of 1920s), The shortest route . . was six blocks, or squares as they were called in Linden. **1949** in 1986 *DARE* File **Cincinnati OH,** Square . . = block. "I'm going around the square." **1954** *DE Folkl. Bulletin* 1.16, Square (city block). **1968** *DARE* (Qu. MM24, . . *'A short distance'*: *"The river is just a _____ from the house."*) Inf **IN19,** Square. **1968–69** *DARE* FW Addit **cwNJ,** Turn at the next square—the next block; **seOH,** Square for "block"—"The post office is three squares over from the courthouse"; **PA91,** *Square*—". . a city block. "Go three squares down and to your left." **2000** Metcalf *How We Talk* 87 **PA,** Pennsylvania cities are likely to have at their center a *diamond* instead of a square. A *square,* in Pennsylvania, more often refers to a city block.

2 also *cotton square:* The bud of the cotton plant together with the three bracts that enclose it. **Sth, S Midl**

1842 in 1925 Bassett *Southern Overseer* 163 **Sth,** I have cotton squairs too and three on a stalk. **1854** Davis *Farm Bk.* 83 *(DA)* **AL,** Cotton shedding squares and young bolls—wants rain. **1903** *DN* 2.331 **seMO,** Square. . . The flower-bud of the cotton plant. (These buds are triangular, not quadrangular.) 'My cotton is dropping its squares.' **1907** *DN* 3.236 **nwAR,** Square. . . The triangular flower-bud of the cotton plant. **1909** *DN* 3.375 **eAL, wGA,** Square. . . The triangular flower bud of the cotton plant. **1927** Sandburg *Amer. Songbag* 253 **TX** [Black], De farmer say to de weevil: "What you doin' on de square?" **1941** Writers' Program *Guide LA* 657 **nwLA,** Cotton is planted in Louisiana in March. The flower buds, called "squares," begin to develop about six weeks after planting. **1966** *DARE* Tape **NC15,** The square will come, then the bloom will come in the square. And then the boll, the cotton boll, forms from that, and you open that up and there's your cotton. **1986** Pederson *LAGS Concordance,* 1 inf, **cnGA,** Cotton squares—where bloom was "fixing to come"; 1 inf, **cnMS,** Cotton squares—part boll weevil attacks. **1986** *DARE* File **cnAL,** When the pink of opening cotton blossoms begins to show, people say, "We have squares," referring to the appearance of the blossoms. They never say the cotton is "starting to blossom." **2003** *Facts* (Clute TX) 14 Oct sec A 2/6, After the deadline, cotton stalks must not be allowed to develop squares.

3 A cigarette. *chiefly among Black speakers* Cf **straight 2**

1970 *DARE* (Qu. DD6b, *Nicknames for cigarettes*) Infs **MO30, TN50, TX86,** Square. [All Infs Black] **1971** *Black Scholar* Sept 36, Why, why, he kept asking himself, as he lit a square. **1972** Claerbaut *Black Jargon* 81, *Squares* . . cigarettes. **1974** *Black World* Nov 57, Light me up a square, baby. **1986** Pederson *LAGS Concordance (Cigarettes)* 2 infs, **LA, TX,** Squares; 1 inf, **seMS,** "Do you have a square?"—used by blacks [and] whites. [All infs Black] **1988** *AmSp* 63.135 **TN** [Prison talk], Square. . . Tobacco cigarette. **1994** Smitherman *Black Talk* 214, Square. . . A cigarette. This meaning has not crossed over. **2004** *Boston Globe* (MA) 31 Jan sec B 1 (Internet), "It was like, you got a square? Let's go outside and smoke a square," recalled Ed, 18, a Latino, using the slang term for cigarette.

4 in combs referring to var types of **earmarks:** See quots.

1793 in 2003 *DARE* File—Internet **CT,** Strayed . . about the last of June, a light red Steer, two years old last spring, ear mark if any, a square crop off the right ear. **1854** in 2002 *Ibid* **cwFL,** Swallowfork, upper & underbit in one, upperssquare on the other, brand 89. **1908** *DN* 3.303 **eAL, wGA,** Other marks are the *over-square* and *under-square.* **1968** *DARE* (Qu. K18, . . *Kind of mark . . to identify a cow*) Inf **WV8,** Carpenter's square—cut carpenter's square in top of both ears.

square n² See **squire**

square around v phr Also *square round* [nIr dial; see *EDD* at *square* v. 10.(5)]

Of people in a group: to arrange themselves in a circle; to make room (for someone) in a circle of people.

1852 *SW Mth.* 1.142 **TN,** All *squared* round, as the saying is, to give Brummige elbow room. **1875** *Overland Mth.* 14.377 **CA,** Talkin' about vigilantes, boys, jest square round, an' I'll tell you how we did it on Scott's Bar once. **1952** Brown *NC Folkl.* 1.593, Square (a)round. . . To make room for one. "Square around for John and let him have a seat."— Central and east. **1956** McAtee *Some Dialect NC* 42, Square around. . . Make room for one to sit. **c1960** Wilson *Coll.* **csKY,** Square around. . . Make room for another "cheer" around the "farplace."

square change n Cf **case n² 2**

1969 *DARE* FW Addit **NC** [Black], "Give me some square change" = $1.00 bills. Occasional.

square-dab adv **chiefly Sth, esp TX** Cf **smack-dab**

Exactly, squarely.

1912 *Lincoln Daily News* (NE) 23 Sept sec B 8/2 [Black], Ah went right square dab ovah to the city office an' looked it up. **1938** in 1979 *Amer. Slave Suppl. 2* 10.8.3614 **TX** [Inf born **LA**], An' 'bout dat time de Yanks jes' tore loose a-shootin' right square dab at us. **1956** Ker *Vocab. W. TX* 195, Square dab—exactly on the nose. **1962** Atwood *Vocab. TX* 77, Square-dab. Exactly in the middle, as "square-dab on the nose." **1970** *DARE* (Qu. KK53, *When one thing suddenly hits hard against something else: "He ran _____ into a car."*) Inf **IL116,** Square-dab. **1997** *DARE* File—Internet **Gulf coast TX,** I was going to sink that thing square dab on top of Formosa's discharge point. **2003** *Ibid* **TX,** I was . .

born . . right square-dab in the middle of cattle country. *Ibid* **LA**, Kincaid Lake. . . Located square dab in the middle of Louisiana. *Ibid* **NC**, The Abbey is right square dab in the middle of anything you want to do that the Pinehurst area has.

squarehead n

1 A Scandinavian or German; a person of Scandinavian, Germanic, or similar northern European heritage. **scattered, but esp NEast, TX** See Map Note: In the Northeast the reference is chiefly to Scandinavians, while in Texas it is esp to Germans. Cf **roundhead 1, Scandihoovian**

[**1903** Farmer–Henley *Slang* 6.333, *Squarehead*. . . a German or Scandinavian.] **1904** *NY Times* (NY) 19 May 8/5, All North Europeans are known [by English and American sailors] as "square heads" or "Dutchmen," whether they be Swedes, Norwegians, Danes, Russians, Germans, or real Dutchmen. **1918** *Stars & Stripes* (Paris France) 16 Aug 7/1, Suppose one of those squareheads back in Germany had cheated a little in making up his next charge of powder and spilled some of it on the floor. **1930** Williams *Logger-Talk* 16 **Pacific NW**, *Square-head:* A Teuton. **1950** *PADS* 14.77 **FL**, *Square-head*. . . A Swede. **1950** *WELS* (*Names and nicknames for people of foreign background*) 5 Infs, **WI**, Squarehead—German; 1 Inf, **seWI**, Squarehead—Norwegian; 1 Inf, **cwWI**, Squarehead—Swedish. **1958** McCulloch *Woods Words* 179 **Pacific NW**, *Square head*—A term applied to a Scandinavian, German or other man new to the woods. **1960** [see **2** below]. **1965–70** *DARE* (Qu. HH28, *Names and nicknames . . for people of foreign background*) 31 Infs, **scattered**, Squarehead—Swedish; 17 Infs, 10 **TX, LA**, Squarehead—German; **MA**35, 71, **NY**36, 80, Squarehead—Norwegian and Swedish; **AK**8, **CT**21, **ME**16, Squarehead—Norwegian; **MI**110, **TX**95, Squarehead—Hollander(s); **MA**11, Squarehead—Swedish, Norwegian, and Danes; **NH**1, Squarehead—Scandinavian; **NY**96, Squarehead—Danish and Swedish; **LA**46, Squarehead Dutchman—German. **1966** Barnes–Jensen *Dict. UT Slang* 40, *Square head* . . a name pinned on the Germans, meaning blockhead. **1968** *DARE* FW Addit **LA**, *Squarehead* = nickname for Germans. **1986** Pederson *LAGS Concordance*, 1 inf, **seFL**, Squareheads—Norwegians and Swedes; 1 inf, **csTX**, Squareheads—Germans—derogatory. **1995** [see **2** below]. **1998** Leary *WI Folkl.* 62 **nwWI** (as of 1950s), We knew that Swedes and Norwegians alike might be teased as "herring chokers," "Scandihoovians," "snoose chewers," and "squareheads."

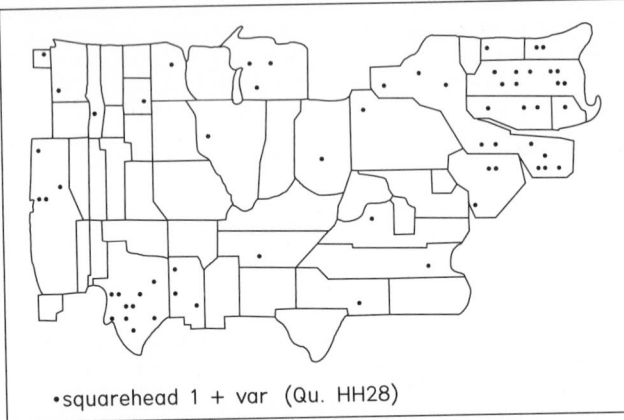

• squarehead 1 + var (Qu. HH28)

2 A blockhead; a dullard.

1912 *Oakland Tribune* (CA) 2 Apr 2/5, Minnie Dahl Gilmore Tyson called her husband Mitchell a "square head" according to his complaint for divorce. **1919** *DN* 5.62 **NM** [Among hs students], *Square-head,* a dull, stupid person. "He is a big square-head, he can't get his algebra." **1960** Criswell *Resp. to PADS 20* **Ozarks**, *Squarehead*. . . A person of slow comprehension. Often used of a German interloper into the hill country. . . Once common, prob. not now. **1967–68** *DARE* (Qu. HH3, *A dull and stupid person*) Infs **NJ**2, **WI**27, Squarehead. **1995** Brophy *Coll.* 71 **swMO** (as of c1960), Squarehead. [A] thickheaded person; a German or Scandinavian. **2006** *DARE* File—Internet, Hahaha—go back to school squarehead.

square-mouth n

=**chiselmouth.**

1896 U.S. Natl. Museum *Bulletin* 47.208 **WA**, *Acrocheilus aluta-ceus*. . . Chisel-mouth; Square-mouth. . . Lower Columbia River and tributaries, as far up as Spokane and Shoshone Falls; locally abundant.

square nut n Also *square-nut hickory, square walnut* **esp NEng**

=**mockernut hickory.**

1850 Emerson *Rept. Trees & Shrubs* 194, The Mockernut Hickory. . . also known by the name of the square-nut hickory. **1941** *LANE* Map 277 **neMA**, 1 inf, Square walnut; 1 inf, Square nut = walnut; 1 inf, Square nut, the usual name for walnut. **1967–69** *DARE* (Qu. I43, *What kinds of nuts grow wild around here?*) Inf **NH**16, Square nut; **MA**72, Square nut—it may be the shagbark—hard shell, very little meat in it.

square out v phr, hence vbl n *squaring out* Cf **come down on 2**

1972 Claerbaut *Black Jargon* 81, *Squaring out* . . ridiculing or satirizing a person in his presence; verbally embarrassing another.

square round See **square around**

square stalk n

A **figwort 1** (here: *Scrophularia marilandica*).

1813 Smith *Ind. Doctor's Dispensatory* 31 **OH**, The Square-stalk root, and its leaves, are both medicinal. The stalk is square, nearly the size and shape of the catnip stalk. . . The root when pulled up, appears tender and white like a white radish. . . This root has frequently been used to make poultices for sores, but its chief use by the Indians is for women's complaints. **1847** in 1976 Miller *Shaker Herbs* 148, Carpenter's Square. . . Heal-All. Square Stalk. Figwort. **1947** (1964) Randolph *Ozark Superstitions* 101, A weed called square stalk, apparently a kind of figwort, is used in making poultices to reduce swelling.

squaretail n

1 The black-legged **kittiwake** (*Rissa tridactyla*).

1852 in 1876 *Forest & Stream* 7.212 **eMA**, *Rissa tridactylus*. Square-tail.

2 A **prairie chicken 1** (here: *Tympanuchus cupido pinnatus*).

1905 *Illustr. Outdoor News* 18 Nov 2, Looking at the Square-tail he is an extremely handsome bird. **1942** U.S. Natl. Park Serv. *Fading Trails* 153 **seTX, sLA**, They called them "chickens," "prairie chickens," or "square-tails," the last name being used to distinguish them from sharp-tailed grouse. **1982** Elman *Hunter's Field Guide* 26, Pinnated Grouse. . . squaretail, broadtail [etc]. [*Ibid* 27, At first light they see loose prairie-chicken flocks coming in low—big, blocky grouse with square tails.]

3 See **square-tailed trout.**

squaretail catfish n

=**brown bullhead 1.**

[**1875** *Waukesha Co. Democrat* (WI) 6 Feb [3]/7 (newspaperarchive.com), If I were asked for a list of fishes to be kept in waters not suitable for trout or grayling it would comprise white fish, ciscoes, smelts, the large carp of Europe and the square-tailed variety of catfish that is known in the Eastern States as a bull-head, hornpout, etc.] **1936** *Oakland Tribune* (CA) 23 Sept 22/8, Catfish are not native to California. . . The first introduction was in 1874 and consisted of . . 70 squaretail catfish from Lake Champlain, Vermont. **1946** La Monte *N. Amer. Game Fishes* 164, Brown Bullhead. . . Names: Speckled Bullhead, . . Squaretail Catfish [etc].

square-tailed trout n Also *squaretail (trout)* **chiefly ME, VT** Usu =**brook trout,** but also **rainbow trout.**

1887 *Bangor Daily Whig & Courier* (ME) 17 June 1/3, The largest brook trout exhibited this season, was seen in Houlton, Monday. . . It was a square tail trout. [**1900** *New Engl. Mag.* July 567 **ME**, In no other region of the world are such large, spotted, square-tailed trout to be found.] **1904** Day *Kin o' Ktaadn* 131 **ME**, Makes a fellow . . think of reels / Whirring, purring with the outrush of a whopping squaretail's bite. **1904** *Salmon & Trout* 165 **Pacific**, The steelhead (*Salmo gairdneri*), while in reality a trout, is popularly regarded as a salmon, and on the west coast is known as winter salmon, hardhead, salmon-trout, and square-tailed trout. **1945** Hamlin *9 Mile Bridge* 125 **nME**, To me, trout meant the colorful, flashy brook trout, or squaretail. Curly assured me that the fishermen were right. Togue are trout, even though they are grayish and silvery and not as colorful and "fighting" a fish as the squaretail. **1961** Douglas *My Wilderness* 241 **nME**, A bogan is a slack-water cove in a bend of the river. . . Squaretail trout often congregate there. **1966** *DARE* (Qu. P1, . . *Kinds of freshwater fish . . caught around here . . good to eat*) Inf **ME**8, Squaretails. . . All natives eat are trout and salmon. **1975** Gould *ME Lingo* 272, *Squaretail*—Mainers like this term for their beloved eastern brook trout, *Salvelinus fontinalis*.

1989 Mosher *Stranger* 252 **nVT,** [The brook] was jumbled with big pink granite boulders breaking up the current into ideal feeding spots for the colorful wild squaretails my father so prized. **2003** *DARE* File—Internet **VT,** Seyon Ranch State Park is a natural habitat for squaretail trout.

squaretail gull n
=**Bonaparte's gull.**
1852 in 1876 *Forest & Stream* 7.212 **eMA,** *Chroicocephalus philadelphia.* Square-tail gull.

squaretail trout See **square-tailed trout**

square walnut See **square nut**

square-weed n [See quot 1973]
=**self-heal.**
1834 in 1972 Andrews *Community Industries Shakers* 95 **NY,** [List of herbs:] Summer savory, saffron, "squareweed," stoneroot [etc]. **1945** *Prairie Schooner* 19.32 **Ozarks,** She . . took a hickory basket and a knife / to gether greens for supper:/ Deer tongue, fresh poke, sheep-sorrel, thick / square-weed [etc]. **1969** *DARE* (Qu. I28a, . . *Kinds of things . . you call 'greens'*) Inf **MO**19, Square-weed. [FW: He said they ate none of these raw.] **1973** *Foxfire 2* 84, Ground Hog Plantain. . . selfheal, square-weed, heal-all. . . Stems are square with green leaves, and spikes of purplish flowers. **1977** *Alton Telegraph* (IL) 1 June sec A 3/4, The children also . . gathered wild greens, such as poke and square weed, which they cooked and ate one evening.

squaring out See **square out**

squark See **squawk**

squash n[1] Usu |skwɑš, skwɔš|; occas |skwɑrš, skwɔrš| Pronc-spp *squarsh, squoish, squorsh, sqush* Cf **wash**
A Pronc varr.
1920s in 1944 *ADD* **cNY,** [skwɑʃ], not -[ɔ]-.· **1930s** *Ibid* **eWV,** Squorsh. -[ɔr]-. **1981** Pederson *LAGS Basic Materials,* 1 inf, **cnLA,** [skwɔˑɚʃ]. **2003** *DARE* File—Internet **Sth,** His favorite things to grow are beans and squarsh. *Ibid,* Acorn Squash Microwave. . . Pierce the squarsh several times with a fork. *Ibid,* [Menu:] *Vegetarian Fajitas*—Grilled zucchini, red peppers, yellow squarsh. **2004** *DARE* File **cwCA** (as of c1960), A neighbor would "do the [wɑɚʃ]" and "pick the [skwɑɚʃ]." I don't know where she was from originally. **2005** Williams *Gratitude* 527 **wNC** (as of 1940s), Sqush, squoish: . . squash that you eat.
B Senses.
1 Std: the fruit of a plant of the genus *Cucurbita;* the plant itself. For other names of var spp see **banana squash, blue hubbard ~, bunch ~, butterball ~, buttercup ~, butterneck ~, button ~, calabacilla, candy roaster, chilacayote, cinnamon squash, cowhorn ~, coyote melon, crown squash, cushaw, cymling 1, Des Moines squash, dish ~, dry-land fish 2, flathead 6, gooseneck squash, hard-shell ~, harlequin ~, hat ~, highland potato 2, honeydew squash, honey-melon ~, hookneck ~, hooknose ~, hubbard ~, Indian ~, Italian ~, long-neck ~, marblehead 2, marrow squash, Mexican gourd, Missouri ~, mock orange 2b, Mother Hubbard squash, pancake ~, pattypan ~, peanut ~, pie ~, pie-crust ~, potato ~, ringneck ~, round ~, saucer ~, scallop ~, Seminole pumpkin, summer squash, vegetable marrow, winter squash**
2 The head. *joc* Cf **gourd 2**
1967–70 *DARE* (Qu. X28, *Joking words . . for a person's head*) Infs **MA**1, 3, 4, 72, 75, 122, **PA**184, Squash.

squash n[2] See **musquash**

squashberry n
The fruit of the **highbush cranberry** or **dockmackie.**
[**1898** *Jrl. Amer. Folkl.* 11.228, *Viburnum pauciflorum* [=V. edule] . . squash berry, Labrador and Newfoundland.] **1928** Rosendahl-Butters *Trees MN* 345, *Viburnum pauciflorum.* . . Squashberry. **1938** Van Dersal *Native Woody Plants* 356, Squashberry *(Viburnum acerifolium, Viburnum pauciflorum).* **1976** Bruce *How to Grow Wildflowers* 134, A variety [of viburnum] . . equally valuable for edible fruits but not so ornamental, . . is *edule:* Mooseberry, Squashberry, or Pimbina.

squat v [*OED2* a1300 →; "Now *dial.*"] **ME, NH** *arch* Cf *DNE*
To pinch, crush, squeeze; also fig.
1814 in 1947 *AmSp* 22.275 **seNH** [Americanisms noted by an Englishman], Squat for squeeze or press, the boy has squat his finger. **1890** *DN* 1.19 **seNH,** *Squat:* pinch. 'I've squat my finger.' *Ibid* 79 **cME, sME coast** (as of 1864–68), *Squat.* . . Common among unlettered people in Bangor, Me. . . *Squat,* meaning "rather *squeeze, crush,* than *pinch,* as 'I squat (pret.) my finger in the door.'" **1904** Day *Kin o' Ktaadn* 199 **ME,** Some folks can us'ly squat a little good out of even the wust misfortunes. [**1925** *DN* 5.343 **Nfld,** *Squat,* v.t. Crush.]

squat n[1] See **squato**

squat n[2] Also *jack squat*
=**doodl(e)y squat.**
1967 Wentworth-Flexner *Slang Suppl.* 705, *Squat.* . . *zot.* [*Ibid* 712, *Zot.* . . A grade or a score of zero.] **1970** *DARE* (Qu. HH20c, *Of an idle, worthless person . . "He isn't worth _____."*) Inf **PA**236, Squat. **1975** Higgins *City on Hill* 18, A lot of people . . didn't care squat about the war. **1993** *San Diego Union-Tribune* (CA) 23 June sec B 4/4, On some counts, they have lots of evidence. On some counts, they have squat. **1994** in 2003 *DARE* File—Internet, [Student newspaper headline:] Fogerson doesn't know jack squat. **1995** Lesley *Sky Fisherman* 206 **OR,** But [football] linemen never get any credit. . . You could drive dump trucks through the holes we opened up, but the paper never said jack squat about us. **2003** *DARE* File—Internet, The Hog's not gonna lie to you. He doesn't know squat about baccarat. *Ibid,* Only one of those guys really knows anything about cars, and the other guy doesn't know squat. *Ibid,* The *LA Daily News* was even tougher, calling the proposal "a union protection bill that doesn't care squat about children." *Ibid,* Okay, know jack squat about music, but will try anyway.

squat doodle See **doodl(e)y squat**

squato n Also *squat* **CA**
An **angel shark** (here: *Squatina californica*).
1884 Goode *Fisheries U.S.* 1.675, Sharks of the Pacific Coast. . . *Squatina angelus* . . Angel-fish, Angelo or Squat. **1911** *Century Dict. Suppl.* **CA,** Squato. . . A California fishermen's name for *Squatina squatina,* a shark of the family Squatinidae.

squat poison n *esp* S Midl Cf **guinea squat, poison B1a, squat tag**
A children's game; see quot 1966.
1966–69 *DARE* (Qu. EE1, . . *Games . . children play . . in which they form a ring, and either sing or recite a rhyme*) Infs **AL**3, **MS**46, **WV**8, 18, Squat poison. **1966** *DARE* Tape **MS**76, [FW:] What was this game, squat poison, that you mentioned? [Inf:] Squat poison . . when we were found where we couldn't stand on wood, we had to squat, and after he'd come around, running around, you squat, and if you didn't squat, you'd be poison. If he put his hand on you afore you squat, you poison. You had to get out of the ring. Just like all the time there be one, there be two sides. You'd have to get all them that's poison, then the next one have to lead out.

squat quail n [See quot 1961]
=**harlequin quail.**
1961 Ligon *NM Birds* 98, When in danger, the Harlequin Quail rely for protection on inaction and on simulating surroundings by "freezing" to the ground rather than by seeking cover as do other quail. . . Their conduct probably accounts for their numerous aliases, some disparaging, as Crazy Quail, Fool Quail, and Squat Quail. **1991** *Birder's World* Oct 20 **SW,** It's [=the Massena quail is] also known as . . Painted, Crazy, and Squat quail, among others.

squat snipe n Also *squatter*
=**pectoral sandpiper.**
1888 Trumbull *Names of Birds* 176 **CT,** In Connecticut at Milford, [the pectoral sandpiper is known as] Squat-snipe; at Stratford, Squatter.

squat tag n *esp* NEast See Map on p. 226 Cf **scooch tag, squat poison, stoop tag** n[1]
A game of tag in which the players squat to avoid being tagged.
1883 Newell *Games & Songs* 159, In *squat tag,* the fugitive is safe while in that position, or is allowed a given number of "squats," during which he cannot be touched. **1891** *Jrl. Amer. Folkl.* 4.222 **Brooklyn NYC,** *Squat tag.* This game is played within boundaries, and the one

who is "it" may chase any of the other players. When closely pursued, they may escape being tagged by squatting down. This immunity is only granted to each individual a certain number of times, usually ten, as may be agreed upon, and after his "squats" are exhausted he may be tagged as in the ordinary game. **1960** Williams *Walk Egypt* 95 **GA,** Half a dozen children played Squat Tag around a wagon. **1965–70** DARE (Qu. EE1, . . *Games . . children play . . in which they form a ring, and either sing or recite a rhyme*) Inf **WA**1, Squat tag; (Qu. EE17) Inf **NJ**8, Squat tag; (Qu. EE33, . . *Outdoor games . . that children play*) Infs **CT**37, **MA**14, **MI**106, **NY**28, 98, **RI**17, **VT**16, **VA**18, Squat tag. **1986** DARE File **NYC** (as of c1925), *Squat tag* . . anyone squatting could not be tagged for "it." **2004** DARE File—Internet, Does their marketing department over there play squat tag all day long?

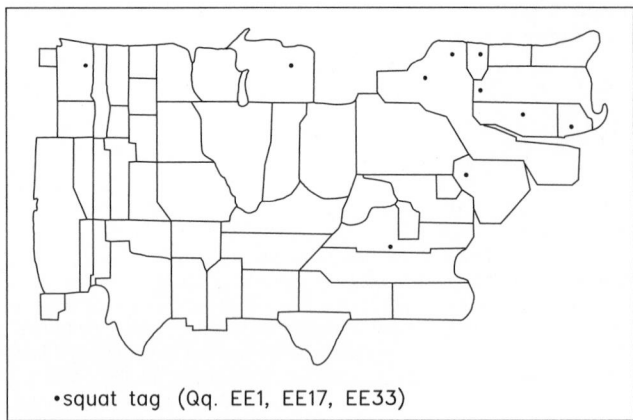

•squat tag (Qq. EE1, EE17, EE33)

squatter See **squat snipe**

‡**squatters** n [Cf *OED2* squatter v. 2 *"Obs."*] Cf **squitters** =**skitters.**

1970 DARE (Qu. BB19, *Joking names for looseness of the bowels*) Inf **NC**83, Squatters.

squatting snipe n [See quot 1932] **Sth** =**Wilson's snipe.**

a1782 (1788) Jefferson *Notes VA* 77, Besides these, we have The Royston Crow. . . Squatting snipe [etc]. **1923** U.S. Dept. Ag. *Misc. Circular* 13.50 **AL,** Common snipe (*Gallinago gallinago*). . . squatting snipe. **1931** LA Dept. of Conserv. *Bulletin* 20.266, *Jack snipe—Capella Gallinago delicata. . . Other Names.—Cache cache, beccassine,* Wilson snipe, English snipe, Squatting snipe. **1932** Howell *FL Bird Life* 226, Wilson's snipe. . . Other Names. . . Squatting Snipe. [*Ibid* 227, They crouch close to the ground, apparently depending for protection on their concealing coloration, and often do not fly until nearly trodden upon.] **1962** Imhof *AL Birds* 234, Common Snipe. . . Squatting Snipe.

squat where you be n Cf **squat tag, statues 1**
A children's game; see quot 1968.

1892 in 2006 DARE File—Internet **cIN,** Siddie and me played Lotto this after noon and we played squat where you be and hide and get home. **1968** DARE (Qu. EE33, . . *Outdoor games . . that children play*) Inf **IN**39, Squat where you be—similar to [the game] statues.

squaw n See **squaw duck 1**

squaw v See **squawed**

squaw apple n
A western shrub (*Peraphyllum ramosissimum*) that bears a small, bitter fruit resembling an apple. Also called **buckbrush 3j, Oregon apple, wild ~**

1891 *Zoe* 2.102 **CO,** *Peraphyllum ramosisimum* [sic] is one of the earliest. Its beautiful clusters of pinkish flowers are followed by the queerest little bitter apples, commonly called "squaw apples." **1931** U.S. Dept. Ag. *Misc. Pub.* 101.66, Squaw-apple . . is a monotypic genus, consisting only of this much-branched, rigid-twigged shrub. **1938** Van Dersal *Native Woody Plants* 180, Squaw-apple. . . Apparently of some value as sheep and cattle browse. **1975** Lamb *Woody Plants SW* 124, Squawapple. . . The small apple-like fruits are yellow with pink or reddish cheeks and bitter to the taste. **2003** *Jrl. Range Management* 56.603 **CO,** The Gardner Canyon site had few vegetation differences af-

ter over 50 years. Squaw apple cover was greater inside . . than outside [areas protected from grazing].

squawberry n

1 A **partridgeberry 1** (here: *Mitchella repens*). Cf **squaw plum 1**

1829 *Hist. Co. Berkshire MA* 63, *Mitchella . . repens.* Squaw-berry. June. Moist woods. **1856** Hill *Treatise* 146 **NY,** Bittersweet, blackberries, and squawberries, form a remarkable compound. Equal parts of their juices mixed, and imparted to paper previously soaked in dilute muriate of tin, have given me very brilliant colors. **1869** *Putnam's Mag.* Jan 35 **NY,** There was a large, oblong boulder, at least twenty feet about, covered with oak-moss . . with squawberry and wintergreen running through. **1881** *Scribner's Mth.* Mar 839, The prettiest sweet-scented flowering-vine our woods hold, is the common mitchela vine, called squaw-berry and partridge-berry. **1920** *Torreya* 20.25 **MI,** *Mitchella repens. . .* Squawberry, Traverse Ciy [sic]. **1967** DARE Wildfl QR Pl.211B [=*Mitchella repens*] Inf **CO**11, Squawberry—in a tree around here; **SC**41, Twinberry, partridgeberry, squawberry—edible. **1968** DARE (Qu. I44, *What kinds of berries grow wild around here?*) Inf **NY**72, Squawberry—little red berry runs and grows in the woods on a vine down on the ground. **1969** DARE Tape **NY**223, There were wintergreen berries and squawberries, and the squawberries were mushy. They were not good to eat.

2 =**bearberry 2.**

1863 in 2003 (acc) Buffalo Museum of Sci. *Bot. Jrl. G.W. Clinton* (Internet) **NY,** The true bearberry, *Arctostaphylos,* Steve [=an Upstate NY guide] calls squawberry. [**1872** (1873) Grant *Ocean to Ocean* 156 (*DCan*), The sasketoon are simply what are known in Nova Scotia as Indian pears, and the kinni-kinnick creeper is our squaw-berry plant.] **2003** DARE File—Internet **eOR,** We found out that the plentiful berries around the campground were (large) blue mountain huckleberries and (small) red squawberries, or kinick-kinick.

3 A **deerberry a** (here: *Vaccinium stamineum*).

1876 Hobbs *Bot. Hdbk.* 111, Squaw berry, Dangle berry, Vaccinium stamineum. **1930** OK Univ. Biol. Surv. *Pub.* 2.75, *Vaccinium stamineum. . .* Deerberry. Squawberry. **1973** Wharton–Barbour *Trees KY* 558, Deerberry, Squawberry. . . Common in most regions of the state. **2003** DARE File—Internet **OH,** Vaccinium stamineum: deerberry or squawberry. Large shrub. Occasional on dry hillsides.

4 A **sumac B:** in the western US usu *Rhus trilobata,* and in the eastern US **fragrant sumac.** Cf **squawbush 3**

1878 *Amer. Naturalist* 12.597 **SW,** *Rhus aromatica* var. *triloba* (Squaw berry), so named because the Indian women gather large quantities of the berries which are used as food. **1931** U.S. Dept. Ag. *Misc. Pub.* 101.96, The most valuable sumacs from a forage viewpoint are the lemonade sumacs. . . Their slender twigs are very important in basketry work among the Indians, which is probably the reason that many people call them squawbush or squawberry. **1944** *UT Hist. Qrly.* July–Oct 120, Among the native fruits gathered in season were the wild grapes and sour squawberries of the stream banks. **1966–68** DARE (Qu. I44, *What kinds of berries grow wild around here?*) Infs **AZ**8, **CA**2, **UT**6, 8, Squawberries; **NM**8, Squawberries—tart, made into julep—small, round, red; (Qu. T16, . . *Kinds of trees . . 'special'*) Inf **NM**9, Squawbush—grows twelve feet high, has red squawberries; (Qu. DD28b, . . *Fermented drinks . . made at home*) Inf **NM**10, Squawberry julep. [DARE Ed: Some of these Infs may refer instead to other senses.] **1981** Benson–Darrow *Trees SW Deserts* 141, Squaw Berry, Squaw Bush. . . Oregon to the Great Plains States and southward to Mexico.

5 =**osoberry.** Cf **squaw plum 2**

1885 Onderdonk *Idaho* 30, *Nuttallia cerasiformis, . .* Squawberry. **1920** *DN* 5.84 **OR,** *Squaw berry.* Osmarina cerasiformis.

6 A **mountain cranberry 1** (here: *Vaccinium vitis-idaea*).

1955 U.S. Arctic Info. Center *Gloss.* 53, Mountain cranberry. A low creeping shrub, *Vaccinium vitis-idaea. . .* Also called . . 'squawberry.'

7 A **wolfberry 2** of the southwestern US. Cf **squawbush 4**

1909 *Condor* 11.49 **AZ,** In places not cleared and cultivated by the Indians, is a dense growth of mesquite . . , screw-bean . . , and arrowwood . . , besides a number of scattered plants of squaw-berry (*Lycium berlandieri*) and jujube. **1937** U.S. Bur. Ind. Affairs *Indians Work* 5.3.15 **AZ,** Squaw berries ripen in the spring and the desert is alive with women and children securing this succulent orange berry, eaten both raw and stewed. **1942** San Diego Soc. Nat. Hist. *Trans.* 9.372 **AZ,** All were feeding on squaw berries (*Lycium*). **2003** DARE File—Internet, Squawberries—Red-orange berries from thorny desert bushes.

8 A **currant B1** (here: *Ribes cereum*).

2003 *DARE* File—Internet **ID,** The Squawberry (Squaw Currant, Wax Currant), *Ribes cereum,* is the most common species of *Ribes* found in our area. . . Indians used them [=the berries] for pemmican, explaining the name "squaw-berry."

squaw bird n [Echoic] Cf quabird
=black-crowned night heron.

1955 *Oriole* 20.1.2, Squaw bird, variant of qua bird.

squaw boot n

A soft, knee-length, flat-soled boot with a fringed cuff at the top and often other decoration.

1952 Howard *Strange Empire* 336 **ND** (as of 1879), All the women had beaded ornaments and lavishly embroidered "squaw boots". **1968** Stegner *Edge* 34 **NM,** Ryan . . shuffles along . . , his squaw boots detonating little explosions of red dust. **1975** Calasibetta *Fairchild's Dict. Fashion* 50, *Squaw b[oot].* Below-the-knee boot made of buckskin with fringed turned down cuff at top, soft sole, no heel, worn by American Indian women and popular with young people in the 1960's. **2000** in 2003 *DARE* File—Internet **CA,** If I see one more idiot in Squaw Boots and a kilt I'm going to have Tony tie him to a stake and light a fire!

squaw bread n

Any of var simple, usu quick, breads that are fried, deep fried, or baked in a thin cake over a campfire. Cf **fried bread**

1879 in 1905 *Friend* 406 **NY,** As for bread they did not have their corn ground by grist mills but the women pounded them with a mortar and pestle and made *squaw* bread. They did not season them with salt or saleratus but simply mixed it up with boiling water. **1891** *New North* (Rhinelander WI) 13 Aug 1/4, Our cook prepared us a good meal of fat pork and baking powder biscuits, coffee and boiled rice which was a gratifying change from rare fish, canned beans and squaw bread. **1928** *Appleton Post–Crescent* (WI) 23 July 9/4 **OK,** "Squaw bread," explains Chief Lucy Tayiah-Eads, "is made just like biscuit dough but without shortening. It is cut into strips and squares and cooked in kettles of boiling lard or grease. . . All Indians consider it the staff of life, and all Indian women have it at home frequently." **1928** *Syracuse Herald* (NY) 26 July 19/2, *Squaw Bread*—These are huge biscuits mixed with a spoon out of white flour, a little lard or bacon grease, salt, baking powder and milk or water. . . Bake in a frying pan. When the bottom has browned, tip the pan up and hold with a stick to brown the tops. This is the kind of bread which old lumbermen mix in the top of the flour sack which requires great proficiency. **1935** Sandoz *Jules* 18 **wNE** (as of 1880–1930), The cook . . lifted the pan of squaw bread off the stove and spit his tobacco into the fire. **1940** Brown *Amer. Cooks* 678 **OK,** *Squaw Bread* (Osage Indian) [Recipe includes flour, lard, salt, water, baking powder.] . . Roll out thin, cut into squares, punch holes with knife in the squares of dough, and drop them into hot fat. **1966** *DARE* (Qu. H18, . . *Special kinds of bread*) Inf **NM5,** Tortillas—Indians make a similar squaw bread. **1966** *DARE* Tape **OK**19, She used to fry some of that light bread and they called it squaw bread. **1986** Pederson *LAGS Concordance* (Other kinds of bread and cakes made of cornmeal) 1 inf, **swGA,** Indians made squaw bread in grease, milk added.

‡squaw buggy n

1954 Jordan *Hell's Canyon* 237 **ID,** They would have to use a travois or "squaw buggy," Len decided.

squawbush n

1 A **red osier** (here: *Cornus sericea*) or **bunchberry 1.**

1832 Williamson *Hist. ME* 1.125, But *Indian Tobacco,* called by the Natives '*Squaw-bush,*' is a perennial herb, or shrub; the bark of which they scrape off, mix with their tobacco, and smoke it. **1894** *Jrl. Amer. Folkl.* 7.90 **ME,** *Cornus stolonifera* . . squaw-bush, Penobscot Co. **1902** *Ibid* 15.111, *Squaw bush.* 1. A name for the *Cornus stolonifera* [= *C. sericea* var *stolonifera*] and *C. sericea* in Maine and the West respectively. 2. A California name for the *[Cornus] Canadensis.* **1940** Clute *Amer. Plant Names* 98, *C[ornus] stolonifera.* . . squaw-bush, gutter-tree. **1979** Little *Checklist U.S. Trees* 99, *Cornus stolonifera* [=*C. sericea*]. . . American dogwood, . . squawbush.

2 =**highbush cranberry.**

1876 Hobbs *Bot. Hdbk.* 111, Squaw bush, High cranberry, *Viburnum opulus.* **1960** Teale *Journey into Summer* 10, A cranberry tree spread its broad, three-pointed leaves. This north-country viburnum, *Viburnum opulus,* is variously known as the squaw bush, the water elder, the highbush cranberry and the pincushion tree. **2003** *DARE* File—Internet, A

traditional Native American folk remedy, known as "Squawbush," has been used as a menstrual regulating tonic.

3 A **sumac B:** in the western US usu *Rhus trilobata,* and in the eastern US **fragrant sumac.**

1891 Wickson *CA Fruits* 59, The fruit of the "squaw bush" *(R. trilobata)* is pleasantly acid and very refreshing. It is eaten by the Indians, who also use the slender twigs in their choicest basket work. **1898** *Jrl. Amer. Folkl.* 11.225 **CA,** *Rhus Canadensis* . . var. *trilobata* . . squaw bush, Indian lemonade. **1914** Saunders *With Flowers in CA* 150, This wrapping [of coils used in basket-weaving] . . is made of one of two plants. . . One is a species of sumac *(Rhus trilobata),* abundant throughout California, and so well known for its use in this way as to be popularly called "squawbush." **1931** [see **squawberry 4**]. **1942** Whipple *Joshua* 58 **UT** (as of c1860), Shadrach Gaunt, who had sacrificed his tobacco for the Word of Wisdom, went on chewing his squawbush gum. **1957** Barnes *Nat. Hist. Wasatch Summer* 85 **UT,** A sumac *(Rhus trilobata),* locally known as squawbush. **1966** *DARE* (Qu. T16, . . *Kinds of trees . . 'special'*) Inf **NM9,** Squawbush—grows twelve feet high, has red squawberries. **1981** [see **squawberry 4**]. **1982** Brooks *Quicksand* 301 **swUT** (as of 1928), You know, of course, that young squaws gather and chew it as a mating bait. Big medicine for them—squawbush gum! **2003** *DARE* File—Internet **SW,** Squawbush has been used for centuries in the Four Corners region for food and basketmaking.

4 A **wolfberry 2** (here: *Lycium* spp). Cf **squawberry 7**

1903 *Torrey Bot. Club Bulletin* 30.306 **AZ,** *Lycium Fremontii,* or squawbush of the prospectors, is quite an ornamental shrub of the outskirts of our cactus desert. **1931** U.S. Dept. Ag. *Misc. Pub.* 101.142, Wolfberries. . . A wealth of vernacular names has been bestowed upon them, including . . squawbush, squawthorn [etc]. **1949** Curtin *By the Prophet* 87 **AZ,** Squawbush bears an abundance of juicy berries.

5 A shrub or small tree *(Condalia globosa)* of the Desert Southwest. Also called **abrojo, chamise 2, crucillo 1**

1931 U.S. Dept. Ag. *Misc. Pub.* 101.111, Condalia, a genus of shrubs and small trees, includes three species of the southwestern United States, *Condalia spathulata,* locally known as squawbush [etc]. **1938** Van Dersal *Native Woody Plants* 107, Condalia spathulata. . . Squawbush. . . A large, more or less evergreen shrub. **1970** Correll *Plants TX* 1014, Condalia spathulata. . . Squaw-bush. . . Locally abundant in dry open brushy areas.

squaw cabbage n Also *squaw's cabbage*

1 See **squaw lettuce 1.**

2 A **wild cabbage 1,** usu *Caulanthus inflatus.*

1933 Jaeger *CA Deserts* 131, In the desert's interior we see . . fields stippled lemon and green with countless stalks of caulanthus *(C. inflatus),* the squaw's cabbage of the Indians and pioneers. **1939** Pickwell *Deserts* 47, When the desert rains have fallen properly, the swollen stems of Squaw Cabbage grow in circles about the Creosote Bushes in the Mohave. **1966–68** *DARE* (Qu. I28b, *Kinds of greens that are cooked*) Inf **CA**62, Squaw cabbage; (Qu. S26e, *Other wildflowers not yet mentioned;* not asked in early QRs) Inf **CA**2, Squaw cabbage or desert candle; **CA**4, Squaw cabbage—purple flower with bulging stem. **1970** Kirk *Wild Edible Plants W. U.S.* 35, *Caulanthus crassicaulis.* . . Squaw Cabbage is found in open woodlands, particularly pinon-juniper, in California, Arizona, Nevada, southern Idaho, Colorado and Wyoming. **2003** *DARE* File—Internet **CA,** [Caption:] The Desert Candle . . commonly known as Squaw Cabbage.

squaw candy n Also *Indian squaw candy* chiefly AK Cf Eskimo ice cream

Strips of salmon smoked until hard; a piece of such salmon.

1943 *NY Times* (NY) 29 July 15 **AK,** "Smokehouses are getting the G.I. brush treatment this week," says the Alaskan fishing editor, "in preparation for the main run of salmon, which will then be cured into what the Aleuts call 'squaw candy.'" **1948** *AK Sportsman* Jan 31, Long strips of smoked king salmon are called squaw candy. **1954** *Ibid* Aug 28, Indian squaw candy—hard-smoked salmon—has long been marketed in small quantities in the Interior. **1965** Bowen *Alaskan Dict.* 31, *Squaw candy.* Dried or smoked salmon. A popular finger food at Alaska gatherings and for generations a staple winter diet for men and dogs. **1991** Tabbert *Dict. Alaskan Engl.* 79, *Squaw candy, siwash candy, Eskimo candy, Alaska candy, Yukon candy*—A delicacy especially popular among Natives of Interior and Western Alaska. Narrow strips of salmon are cut lengthwise, salted, and then smoked. The *candy* terms are used primarily by whites. **1995** *DARE* File **cAK,** [In a list of seafood gift packs offered by an Anchorage vendor:] King Crab . . Squaw Candy . .

Lox. *Ibid* **cAK,** Squaw candy is a strip of hard-smoked salmon, smoked harder than regular smoked salmon. It's traditionally done with king salmon in long strips an inch thick with skin on one edge. **2003** Rex–Johnson *Pike Place Market Cookbook* 3 **WA,** Native Americans. . . often left their salmon in the smokehouse for two weeks, which resulted in a dark brown, very smoky salmon. The Indians then took the smoked salmon, dried and seasoned it, and cut it into thin strips to make "squaw candy"—something similar to beef jerky that was eaten between meals as a snack.

squaw carpet n   Also *squaw's carpet* Cf **squaw mat**
A **ceanothus,** usu **mahala mats.**

1897 Parsons *Wild Flowers CA* 326, Squaw's Carpet. Mahala Mats. . . Upon half-shaded slopes in the Sierras . . this little trailing shrub makes a clean, delightfully springy carpet underfoot. **1926** *Torreya* 26.5 **CA,** *Ceanothus prostratus.* . . Squaw-carpet, Sequoia National Park. **1931** U.S. Dept. Ag. *Misc. Pub.* 101.107, Trailing bluebrush *(C. diversifolius),* known also as dwarf, or lac ceanothus, and squaw-carpet. *Ibid* 111, Squaw-carpet *(Ceanothus prostratus),* or mahala-mats, of Washington to western Idaho and California. **1961** Peck *Manual OR* 514, *C[eanothus] prostratus* . . Mahala Mat. Squaw Carpet.

squaw corn n

1 Any of var types of **Indian corn 1** associated with American Indians, esp those types producing starchy grains in dark or variegated colors.

1824 Doddridge *Notes Indian Wars* 90 **WV, wPA,** How widely different is the large squaw corn, in its size, and the period of its growth from the Mandan corn. **1873** Beadle *Undeveloped West* 582 **cwIN,** It rarely grows more than two feet high, and the ear is short and thick, with dark, round, very hard grains, much like that variety we used to call "squaw corn" on the Wabash. **1874** in 1932 *AmSp* 7.420 **NE,** Holt county . . has sent us an ear of 'squaw' corn raised in the sod this year. . . It is about fifteen inches long and the kernels are as smooth and firm as ivory. **1912** in 1914 Stewart *Letters* 151 **WY,** They had a small patch of land . . on which was raised the squaw corn that hung in bunches from the rafters. Down where we live we can't get sweet corn to mature, but here, so much higher up, they have a sheltered little nook where they are able to raise many things. **1932** *AmSp* 7.421 **NE,** "Squaw" corn is a "flour" corn, the kernel is starchy inside, relatively soft—the sort of corn used by the Indians; hence its name. **1938** in 2003 *DARE* File—Internet **OK,** The only crops raised by the Indians of early territorial days were small patches of Squaw corn, called Tom Fuller corn and later named Squaw corn because the Squaws or women, did all the raising of this particular crop. **1939** *Ibid* **OK,** We raised 4 kinds of corn. . . After my fathers death, we . . still raised stock & the wonderful garden & Potatoes, Irish & Sweet, & Rostin ear Patch. Always a Squaw Corn patch. Flour corn for meal & a Flint Corn for hominey. **1948** *Milwaukee Jrl.* (WI) 18 July sec 5 2/7, There's pop corn, sweet corn, squaw corn, flint corn, hybrid corn and then there is just plain corn, the kind we get on the radio. **1965** Guthrie *Blue Hen's Chick* 8 **MT,** When the garden offered, she picked squaw corn, which grew, particolored, on a small and tortured cob and was the only fresh corn that our short season could supply. **1966** *DARE* (Qu. I34, *If you don't have sweet corn, you can always eat young* _____) Inf **MT**5, Squaw corn—colored. **1973** Allen *LAUM* 1.312 (as of c1950), *Squaw corn* . . having variegated kernels, mostly purplish, and cultivated especially by Indians, is used also in Manitoba and recalled by one northern Iowan housewife of Maine parentage. **2003** *DARE* File—Internet [Heirloom Seeds], *Squaw corn* 105 days—Ornamental flint corn with kernels in shades of yellow, red, orange and blue. Large ears with strong stalks. May also be ground for corn meal.

2 A dish made with corn and bacon or ground beef; see quots.

1924 *Olean Eve. Times* (NY) 20 Sept 6/4, Squaw Corn—½ c. diced bacon. 1 can sweet corn. Salt and pepper. Method: Cook bacon until crisp, and pour contents of a can of corn into skillet, cook for a few minutes. **1950** *WELS* **WI** *(Dishes made with corn)* 7 Infs, Squaw corn; 1 Inf, Squaw corn—1 pint corn, 4 eggs, ½ c. fried diced bacon with its fat, ¼ c. milk mixed together and cooked thick in frying pan. **1952** Tracy *Coast Cookery* 29 **CO,** *Rocky Mountain Squaw Corn.* . . Cut bacon into small pieces. . . Then add onion and brown. Pour off about half the bacon grease. Add tomatoes, corn, salt, and pepper. Cook until fairly thick. **1967** *DARE* (Qu. H50, *Dishes made with beans, peas, or corn that everybody around here knows, but people in other places might not)* Infs **IL**9, **MN**1, Squaw corn. **1994** in 2003 *DARE* File—Internet, As a girl scout . . our favorite part of day camp was Squaw Corn. [Recipe includes hamburger, onion, canned corn, cheese, canned tomato soup.]

1999 *Sun Newspapers* (Cleveland OH) 16 Sept (Internet), Squaw corn is an old-time favorite, once served from camp kitchens to hungry lumberjacks in the Minnesota and Wisconsin wilderness.

3 =**squawroot 1.**

1970 Campbell et al. *Gt. Smoky Wildflowers* 12, Squaw-root. . . This parasite, growing on oak roots, is also known as *cancer-root* and *squaw-corn.* Ranging in height from 4 to 9 inches, the brown-colored plant, without chlorophyll, resembles a slender pine cone or a small ear of corn.

squaw currant n

A **currant B1** (here: *Ribes cereum*).

1909 CO College *Sci. Ser.* 12.6.146 **cCO,** The squaw currant *(Ribes cereum)* occurs in the gullies. **1931** U.S. Dept. Ag. *Misc. Pub.* 101.41, Wax currant *(Ribes cereum)* . . and squaw currant *(R. inebrians* [=*R. cereum*]) . . are two of the commonest and most widely distributed species of this genus. **1952** Davis *Flora ID* 376, *R[ibes] cereum.* . . Squaw Currant. . . fruit insipid. **1975** Lamb *Woody Plants SW* 139, Squaw currant—*Ribes inebrians.* **2003** [see **squawberry 8**].

squaw duck n

1 also *squaw:* =**old-squaw.**

1853 NY State Museum *Catalogue Cabinet Nat. Hist.* 28, Fuligula glacialis, *Oldwife,* or *Squaw Duck.* **1902** *Everybody's Mag.* Feb 179, I think that there is no swifter flier among birds than this garrulous "Squaw." **1923** U.S. Dept. Ag. *Misc. Circular* 13.24 **NY, WI,** Old-squaw. . . vernacular names. . . squaw. **1967–69** *DARE* (Qu. Q5, . . *Kinds of wild ducks)* Infs **CO**7, **IA**3, **NY**58, 183, Squaw duck; **MI**53, Squaw duck—barred gray and white; many call them old-squaw; **MN**15, Squaw duck—in Superior—come up first thing when the ice goes out; **WI**12, Squaw—similar to bufflehead.

2 =**scoter. WA**

1923 U.S. Dept. Ag. *Misc. Circular* 13.27 **WA,** Scoters. . . squaw ducks. **1949** Kitchin *Birds Olympic Peninsula* 53 **WA,** White-winged Scoter. . . Squaw-duck. *Ibid* 55, American Scoter. . . Squaw-duck. **1953** Jewett *Birds WA* 148, Surf Scoter. . . Other names: Surf Duck . . Squaw Duck [etc.].

squawed adj   [Prob var of *skewed*] esp **S Midl**
Lopsided, askew, aslant; also rarely, by back-formation, v *squaw* to make crooked or out of shape.

1952 *Florence Morning News* (SC) 13 Feb 3/1, He also confirms for us the use in his neighborhood of . . squawed, meaning out of plumb. **1954** *PADS* 21.38 **SC,** Squawed. . . Out of plumb, said of a door or window frame, house, or other construction when warped or careened out of the rectangular shape or vertical position. Used mostly by builders. **c1960** Wilson *Coll.* **csKY,** Squawed. . . Out of shape. **1965–70** *DARE* (Qu. KK70, *Something that has got out of proper shape: "That house is all* _____.") Infs **AR**31, **KY**5, 28, **OK**6, Squawed; **GA**23, Squawed out of shape; **KY**91, Squawed to one side; (Qu. MM13, *The table was nice and straight until he came along and knocked it* _____) Inf **AR**31, Squawed it over.

squawfeather n

An **Indian paintbrush 1** (here: either *Castilleja integra* or *C. sulphurea*).

1949 Moldenke *Amer. Wild Flowers* 274, In the squawfeather, *C[astilleja] integra,* found in dry ground from Colorado to Arizona and Texas, the bracts are red or rose-colored. **2003** *DARE* File—Internet **UT,** Castilleja sulphurea (Yellow Paintbrush, Squawfeather, Sulphur Paintbrush).

squaw fire n   Cf **squaw wood, white man's fire**
A small fire made with fuel that can be gathered without tools.

1968 Abbey *Desert Solitaire* 12 **seUT,** I range around the trailer, pick up some dead sticks from under the junipers and build a little fire, for company. **2002** Stehno *Hard Rock Trilogy: Book I* 30 (Internet) **NE,** "You got a nice little fire goin' for you here." "Squaw fire," the fellow replied. "Just enough for a little light and a little warmth, and we don't burn down the whole forest." **2003** *DARE* File—Internet **WA,** I also had to start a "squaw" fire a few times. *Ibid* **NH,** Wife and kids in NH, me here in Florida. . . Maybe later I'll walk to the beach and build a little squaw fire to ward off the city and warm my soul. *Ibid,* I think fires are *bad* in the popular areas—if you have to have one try a squaw fire and keep it small.

squawfish n

1 A Pacific **surfperch** (here: *Embiotoca lateralis*).

1882 Nash *2 Yrs. OR* 85, Now for a sea-perch. . . The fishermen on this coast call this the "squaw-fish" from this sheltering, maternal instinct [=the reputed swallowing of the young by the parent]. **1928** Pan-Pacific Research Inst. *Jrl.* 3.3.13 **OR, WA,** *Taeniotoca lateralis.* . . Squawfish.

2 A western cyprinid fish of the genus *Ptychocheilus.* For other names of var spp see **bigmouth 2, boxhead, minnow B1, pike** n[1] **3, roundtail 1b, Sacramento pike, ~ squawfish, salmon B2a(3), whitefish 5, white salmon 5, yellowbelly 4**

1892 *Overland Mth.* (2d ser) Mar 255 **UT,** There were but two kinds of these [=fish] in the river. . . These are white salmon and squaw-fish, both very fine eating. **1902** Jordan–Evermann *Amer. Fishes* 69, The squawfish is one of the largest of the minnows. . . This fish is highly esteemed by the Indians, hence its most popular name. **1939** Natl. Geogr. Soc. *Fishes* 279, The squawfishes . . in the Colorado River . . are said to reach a weight of 80 pounds. **1965–70** DARE (Qu. P3, *Freshwater fish that are not good to eat*) 9 Infs, **NW, CA,** Squawfish. **1967** DARE Tape **OR**15, Squawfish—it's a trash fish, like suckers. **2003** DARE File—Internet **CA,** The Eel River Squawfish Derby was begun as a way to remove the non-native Sacramanto [sic] Squawfish from the Eel River.

squawflower n

1 A **trillium** (here: *Trillium erectum*).

1892 (1893) Spear *Leaves & Flowers* 94, There are other kinds of trilliums. . . One kind is called a Benjamin flower and a squaw-flower. **1894** *Jrl. Amer. Folkl.* 7.102 **VT,** *Trillium erectum,* squaw-flower, Ferrisburgh. **1910** Hodge *Hdbk. Amer. Indians* 2.630, After the squaw have been named . . squaw flower (*Trillium erectum,* called also squaw root) [etc]. **1930** Sievers *Amer. Med. Plants* 48, Purple trillium. . . squaw-flower, squawroot [etc]. . . Many of these names are applied also to other species of trillium. **1971** Krochmal *Appalachia Med. Plants* 256, Squaw flower, squaw root. . . The Indians of Appalachia cooked pieces of the root in food as an aphrodisiac.

2 =**squaw grass 1.**

1938 Farrington *Gardener's Travel Book* viii **MT,** Bear grass (also called squaw flowers) in Glacier National Park, Montana. **2008** DARE File—Internet **OR,** [Comment on photo:] I love the white Squaw Flowers in the forground [sic]! seen in Beautiful Oregon pool. . . [Response:] My mother told me it was Bear Grass. Have I been wrong all these years?

3 An **Indian paintbrush 1** (here: *Castilleja coccinea*).

1906 Campbell *WI in Three Cents.* 2.238, The . . painted cup or "squaw flower" two feet high, the large yellow ladyslipper, . . roses, violets, lilies and asters . . ; all these and hundreds others grew rank everywhere. **1940** Clute *Amer. Plant Names* 254, *Castilleja coccinea.* Squaw flower. **1967** DARE (Qu. S26a, . . *Wildflowers. . . Roadside flowers*) Inf **NE**4, Squawflower.

squawfoot n

A **freshwater clam:** usu *Strophitus undulatus,* but also *Lasmigona costata.*

1916 U.S. Bur. Fisheries *Bulletin 1914* 34.402, It was found that some glochidia of the squaw-foot mussel (*Strophitus edentulus*) developed into young mussels without becoming parasitic. **1941** *AmSp* 16.156 **Missip Valley,** The following list gives the names [of freshwater clams] as applied by the cutter and fisher of shells. . . Squawfoot [etc]. **1979** *WI Week-End* 6 Apr 6, Such shellfish as the elephant's ear, . . squawfoot [etc] . . , go right on living their private lives in the quiet waterways of the Mississippi. **1991** IL Nat. Hist. Surv. *Biol. Notes* 137.14, *Strophitus undulatus.* . . A relatively common and widespread species in Illinois, the squawfoot. **1992** Cummings–Mayer *Field Guide Freshwater Mussels MW* 94, Fluted-shell—*Lasmigona costata.* . . Other common names—Sand mussel, squawfoot.

squaw grass n

1 also *Indian squaw grass:* A **turkey beard 1** (here: *Xerophyllum tenax*). Also called **basket grass 1, bear ~ 2a, bear lily, deer grass 2, elk ~, fire lily 2, Indian basket grass, Indian bear ~, moose ~, mountain lily 3, pine grass 3, ~ lily 1, soap grass, sour grass e, squawflower 2, Turk's beard**

1897 Parsons *Wild Flowers CA* 51 **nCA,** The name "squaw-grass" is also applied there, because the leaves, which are long, wiry, and tough, are used by the Indians in the weaving of some of their finest baskets. **1901** James *Indian Basketry* 89 **OR,** The squaw grass—Zerophyllum Lenex [sic]—of the Klickitats' basketry in its natural color is white. **1917** Eaton *Green Trails* 85 **nwMT,** I discovered . . the so-called Indian

basket grass, or squaw grass (*Xerophyllum tenax*). **1945** Atwood *Rocky Mts.* 132, [Caption:] Indian squaw grass, or bear grass, in bloom in Glacier National Park. **2003** DARE File—Internet **WA,** It is a large, flexible basket made of cattail, with an overlay of squaw grass in yellow and black.

2 A **wild rye** (here: *Elymus triticoides*).

1902 U.S. Natl. Museum *Contrib. Herbarium* 7.312 **CA,** *Elymus triticoides.* . . The seed is abundant, and it is so well known to be used for pinole that the plant has been called "squaw grass" by the whites. **1939** Medsger *Edible Wild Plants* 128, Wild Wheat, or Squaw Grass. **1970** Kirk *Wild Edible Plants W. U.S.* 179, Squaw Grass. . . The hairs on the grain must be singed off before it is used as food.

squaw hitch n

1 A pattern of knots used in securing a pack to an animal; see quot 1964. [*DCan* 1887 →] **West**

1887 (1888) Thayer *Marvels New West* 571, The tarpaulin . . and the blankets, comprising his bed, are wrapped around the gentlest of his horses and made fast with a lariat in a good 'squaw hitch'. **1903** (1965) Adams *Log Cowboy* 32 **West,** He showed me what he called a squaw hitch, with which you can lash a pack single-handed. **1907** White *AZ Nights* 18, There were plenty of horses, so our bedding we bound flat about their naked barrels by means of the squaw hitch. **1913** (1979) Barnes *Western Grazing* 368, There are an endless number of hitches used by western men, as the squaw, the stirrup, the bed and the basco. **1914** in 2002 DARE File—Internet [Camp Fire Girls Handbook], Packing: Pack a horse and tie a squaw hitch. **1964** Jackman–Long *OR Desert* 267, The squaw hitch was designed by the Indians, who used it originally with no packsaddle at all. It was designed for wrapping a pack right around the horse, fastening at the top with a half hitch drawn tight, then running the loose ends around the horse and tying them again, giving two chances to pull the rope tight. **1968** Adams *Western Words* 298, Squaw hitch. . . This hitch was first used by the trappers of the Hudson's Bay Company among the Indians of the Northwest.

2 In logging: see quots. **Pacific NW** Cf **squaw link**

1958 McCulloch *Woods Words* 179 **Pacific NW,** *Squaw hitch*—a. One way of choking a log. b. A poor method of making a coupling of any kind. **1959** *AmSp* 34.80 **nwCA** [Logger lingo], *Squaw hitch.* . . The bite of the choker . . about the corner or corners of the log for the purpose of turning or changing the position of the log. **2000** in 2003 DARE File—Internet **Pacific NW,** A squaw hitch is a way of choking a log when you can't get under it in order to move it so that you can. You may know it by another name.

squaw huckleberry n

=**deerberry a.**

1837 Darlington *Flora Cestrica* 255 **sePA,** *V[accinium] stamineum.* . . *Vulgò*—Squaw Huckleberry. Deerberry. . . *Berries* large . . of a mawkish bitterish taste. **1843** (1844) Johnson *Farmer's Encycl.* 1141, The species first named by Mr. Nuttall, is what is commonly called in the Middle States squaw huckleberry and deerberry, the stems of which are low. **1871** U.S. Dept. Ag. *Rept. of Secy. for 1870* 415 **MI, WI,** *Squaw huckleberry, (Vaccinium stamineum.)*—This is an agreeable fruit, growing in Wisconsin and Michigan, of which the Indians make extensive use. **1901** Lounsberry *S. Wild Flowers* 400, Deerberry or squaw huckleberry. . . The berry is mostly green, or yellow, and even when fully ripe is hardly fit to eat. **1981** Howell *Surv. Folklife* 68 **neTN, seKY,** *Vaccinium stamineum*—Deerberry; squaw huckleberry—Fruit inedible raw but can be made into pies with heavy sweetening. **2006** Mohlenbrock *This Land* 28, Beneath the hardwoods is a layer of shrubs that consists of two gnarled members of the heath family, farkleberry and squaw huckleberry [etc].

squawk n Also *night squawk, squawk heron* Pronc-spp *squa(r)k* Cf **white squawk**

Usu the **black-crowned night heron,** but also the **yellow-crowned night heron.**

1867 Essex Inst. *Proc.* 5.290 **NEng,** Night Heron. "Qua-bird." "Squawk." Very abundant summer resident. **1903** Dawson *Birds OH* 2.477, Black-crowned Night Heron. . . Night Squawk. **1913** Bailey *Birds VA* 50, Night Crane. Night Squawk. . . Residents of the country bordering water are familiar with them by their loud "squawk," as they pass overhead about twilight. **1914** *Condor* 16.246 **cnUT,** They had no text book to guide them, but named each in their own vernacular—the Great Blue Heron they called the Blue Crane; the Black-crowned Night Heron, the Squawk. **1925** Bailey *Birds FL* 38, Yellow-crowned night heron. . . *Nyctanassa violacea (Squak, Gallding)*. **1955** *Oriole* 20.1.2 **GA,** Yellow-crowned night heron. . . *Qua Bird, Squark* (names from a common call). **1966–69** *DARE* (Qu. Q3, . . *Birds that come out only after dark*) Inf **NC**12, Squawk; **PA**192, Squawk heron; (Qu. Q8, *A water bird that makes a booming sound before rain and often stands with its beak pointed almost straight up*) Inf **CT**2, [skwɑks]. **1967** Will *Dredgeman* 85 **Everglades FL,** Sometimes one of those night herons, appropriately called a "squawk" might wing overhead uttering his raucous cry.

squawker n
=**bullfrog 1.**

　　1967 *DARE* (Qu. P22, *Names or nicknames for a very large frog that makes a deep, loud sound*) Inf **PA**35, Bullfrogs—also called squawkers.

squawk heron　See **squawk**

squaw lettuce n

1　also *squaw('s) cabbage:* A **miner's lettuce,** usu *Claytonia perfoliata.*

　　1902 U.S. Bur. Plant Industry *Bulletin* 12.63 **nwCA,** Squaw lettuce *(Claytonia perfoliata)* is said to be the favorite food of cattle and hogs. **1911** Jepson *Flora CA* 160, *M[ontia] perfoliata*. . . Also called Indian Lettuce and Squaw Cabbage. **1917** Rydberg *Flora Rocky Mts.* 263, *Limnia* [here =*Claytonia*]. . . Spanish Lettuce, Squaw Lettuce, Squaw Cabbage, Miner's Lettuce. **1920** Rice–Rice *Pop. Studies CA Wild Flowers* 88, One of the plants which the miners in the days of "Forty-nine" learned to regard with favor is the one now known as "Miner's Lettuce" *(Montia perfoliata).* It was known as Squaw's Cabbage or Indian's Lettuce.

2　A **waterleaf** (here: *Hydrophyllum occidentale*).

　　1925 Jepson *Manual Plants CA* 810, *H[ydrophyllum] occidentale*. . . Squaw Lettuce. . . open pine woods or brushy slopes. **1937** U.S. Forest Serv. *Range Plant Hdbk.* W98, Western waterleaf . . , also known as squawlettuce, because of its use for food by the Indians, ranges from Oregon to California and Western Nevada. **1949** Moldenke *Amer. Wild Flowers* 252, The squawlettuce, *H. occidentale*. **1984** Venning *Wildflowers N. Amer.* 204 **West,** Squaw-lettuce, *H[ydrophyllum] occidentale* . . Oreg. to Calif., e to Ida. and Ariz. [**2003** *DARE* File—Internet **Yukon Terr. Canada,** I especially remember the meadows filled with a special high country plant, Squaw's Lettuce.]

squaw lily n

A **fritillary** (here: *Fritillaria camschatcensis*).

　　1938 (1958) Sharples *AK Wild Flowers* 57, *F[ritillaria] camschatcensis*. . . "Squaw Lily," "Rice Root," and "Indian Rice" are some of its many vernacular names, suggested by the fact that where it grows in abundance it is a common article of food among the Indians. **1951** Jaques *As Far Yukon* 98 **seAK,** This was *F[ritillaria] camschatcensis*—the squaw lily or rice root.

squaw link n　Cf **squaw hitch 2**

　　1952 *Badger Folkl.* 1.17 **WI** [Logging language], *Squawlink*—A double ended grablink used to connect the loose ends of a broken chain as temporary or emergency repair.

squaw man n　esp NW, AK　usu derog

A non-Indian married to, or cohabiting with, an American Indian (or rarely Eskimo) woman.

　　1856 *Harper's New Mth. Mag.* 13.525 **OR,** The white women were awfully severe upon the five poor squaws who had come to the fort with their mining protectors, who were contemptuously styled "squaw-men." **1883** Harte *In Carquinez Woods* 156 **CA,** There are men, sir, who violate the laws of the Most High by living with Indian women—squaw men, sir, as they are called. **1894** *Outing* 24.87 **MT,** A negro squaw-man (that is, one having an Indian wife) who went by the name of 'Smoky'. **1900** Spurr *Through Yukon Diggings* 26, There was another Alaskan—one of those who settle down and take native women as mates and are therefore somewhat scornfully called 'squaw-men'. **1905** [see **squaw patch**]. **1914** *DN* 4.164 **NW,** *Squaw-man*. . Any white that has lived with an Indian woman. **1931** *AmSp* 7.121 **eID,** *Squaw man* is a white man married to an Indian wife. **1962** Salisbury *Quoth the Raven* 4 **seAK,** Several "Squaw men"—whites who have married Indian women. **1967** *DARE* FW Addit **neOR,** *Squaw man*—a White man married to an Indian woman.

squaw mat n　Also *squaw's mat* [Cf **mahala**]　Cf **squaw carpet**
=**mahala mats.**

　　1891 *Zoe* 2.155 **CA,** *C. decumbens,* slender and trailing with small heads of pale blue flowers, and *C. prostratus* covering its "squaw mats"

with a profusion of purple flowers, are found at higher altitudes. **1940** Writers' Program *Guide NV* 12, Also in . . [the belt converging into the sub-alpine] and its glossy-leafed snow bush or tobacco bush *(Ceanothus velutinus)* and its prostrate relative, the squaw mat *(Ceanothus prostratus),* whose beautiful blue flowers form a delicate carpet for the forest floor. **1940** Writers' Program OR *Mt. Hood* 17, Mahala mat, or squaw mat, is a dwarf creeper bearing dainty balls of lavender that blooms in May and June. **1947** Peattie *Sierra Nevada* 99 **CA,** Mountain-misery is on excellent terms with a creeping lilac called squaw's-mat. **1971** Bakker *Is. Called CA* 187, Underbrush is usually scarce, and the litter is a springy layer of golden-brown needles broken by occasional carpets of mountain misery, squaw mat, bracken, grasses, and flowering forbs.

squaw mint n

A **pennyroyal B1** (here: *Hedeoma pulegioides*).

　　1828 Rafinesque *Med. Flora* 1.231, American Pennyroyal. . . Vulgar Names—Pennyroyal, . . Squaw-mint, &c. **1901** Lounsberry *S. Wild Flowers* 455, American Pennyroyal. Squaw Mint. **1970** GA Dept. Ag. *Farmers Market Bulletin* 9 Sept 8/1 **GA,** American pennyroyal or squaw mint—Hedioma pulegioides, is a sweet-smelling herb that makes one of the best teas of any wild plant. . . It gets one of its common names, "squaw mint", because of the many ways the Indians used it in their medicines. **2000** *Palm Beach Post* (W. Palm Beach FL) 3 Aug sec E 6 (Internet), Pennyroyal oil—derived from the pennyroyal, squaw mint or mosquito plant—hasn't clearly demonstrated effectiveness against fleas.

squawmish　See **squamish**

squaw oak n
=**tanbark oak c.**

　　1910 Jepson *Silva CA* 238, Acorns are produced in great abundance and in Mendocino and Humboldt counties were used in former days in bread-making by the native tribes, and this oak [=the tan oak] is therefore locally known as "Squaw Oak."

squaw patch n　esp OK, Plains States　Cf **Indian field**

A small, often irregular, field or garden area, orig one used by American Indians; also fig.

　　1873 *St. Louis Med. & Surgical Jrl.* 10.662 **MO,** An uncultivated mind thrust in professional science is like a "squaw patch" in a dense forest. **1898** *Decatur Daily Rev.* (IL) 11 Oct 4/5 **OK,** All work that is to be done . . in the woods or in the fields or "squaw patch," as their little field of perhaps an acre of clearing is called. **1905** *Oelwein Reg.* (IA) 17 May 4/2 **OK,** You will find the Indian with a squaw patch and a few ponies. . . The white or squaw man's arrangements and situation is covered with about the same description, except he possibly cultivates more land and has a bunch of cattle. **1910** (1980) Morton *Hist. Pendleton Co. WV* 189 (as of 1768), It is said that when Jacob Sr. came to the South Branch, he found on his land a "squaw patch" of about one acre, which formed the nucleus of his cleared land. **1932** *AmSp* 7.420 **NE,** "Squaw patch" is the charmingly descriptive name used by Nebraska farmers to designate the favored, fertile plots of ground often found near rivers, especially within the bends. **1937** Sandoz *Slogum* 283 **NE,** Sometimes they did have a squaw patch fenced out to farm, with enough pasture for a cow and a team. **1939** *LANE* Map 121 **Block Is. RI,** Squaw patch . . a small flower garden in a vegetable garden. **1945** *ND Hist.* 12.79 **seKS** (as of c1870), Our first garden plot was the "squaw patch" in the woods along Cow Creek which had been the garden of the Indian women who had just moved out.

squaw pine n

1　Either the **digger pine** or the **lodgepole pine.**

　　1886 CA State Bd. Forestry *Biennial Rept. for 1885–86* 184, The Tamarack Pine (Pinus contorta). . . Locally known as Bull Pine, and not generally distinguished from *Pinus muricata;* if so distinguished, then often—as in the vicinity of Eureka—known as Squaw Pine. **1910** Jepson *Silva CA* 90, Digger Pine is the familiar white man's name for the species [=*Pinus sabiniana*]. . . The name Squaw Pine is less commonly used and has a similar origin, but pays tribute to the women who harvested the winter's store of nuts. **1915** *Auk* 32.295 **AR,** Forrester Island is of volcanic origin. . . It is heavily timbered with spruce, hemlock, and squaw pine from the water's edge up to the top of the island. **1926** *Camera Craft* 33.159 **ceCA,** Ahead lay the foothills of the Sierras . . on which the silver-gray squaw-pines grow.

2　See **squaw wood.**

squaw plum n

1　A **partridgeberry 1** (here: *Mitchella repens*).　Cf **squawberry 1**

　　1886 Dudley *Cayuga Flora* 44, *M[itchella] repens*. . . Partridge-berry.

Squaw-plum. One-berry. **1900** Lyons *Plant Names* 250, *M[itchella] repens*. . . Squaw-vine, . . Squaw Plum. **1911** Henkel *Amer. Med. Leaves* 34, Squaw Vine. *Mitchella repens* L. *Other common names* . . squawberry, . . squaw plum.

2 =**osoberry.** Cf **Indian plum 2, squawberry 5**

1927 Gunther *Klallam Ethnography* 1.304 **nwWA,** At childbirth the inner bark of the squaw plum is scraped into water and given to the mother "to drive the blood out." **1973** Gunther *Ethnobotany W. WA* 37, *Osmaronia cerasiformis* [=*Oemleria c.*] . . Squaw Plum, Indian Plum.

squawroot n

1 A leafless parasitic plant *(Conopholis americana)* of the eastern US. Also called **bear corn 3, beechdrops 2, clap-wort, earth club, squaw corn 3**

1818 Eaton *Botany* 336, *Orobanche*. . . *uniflora* (squaw-root . .). **1848** Gray *Manual of Botany* 290, Squaw-root. . . *C[onopholis] Americana*. . . A singular plant . . covered with scales, which are at first fleshy, then dry and hard. **1872** Schele de Vere *Americanisms* 62, *Squaw* Root (Conopholis americana), and *Squaw* Weed (Senecis [sic] aureus) hold their places among the medicinal plants of the country, but owe their names to modern, not to Indian, usage. **1902** *Jrl. Amer. Folkl.* 15.260, *Squaw root,* in various parts of the country the *Trillium erectum,* the black and the blue cohosh, the *Caulophyllum thalictroides* (also called "pappoose root"), the *Conapholis* [sic] *Americana.* **1931** Harned *Wild Flowers Alleghanies* 455, Among the parasitic plants found in moist, rich woods, none are more curiously constructed or less attractive at first sight than the Squaw Root. **1975** Duncan–Foote *Wildflowers SE* 180, Squaw-root. . . Parasitic on the roots of several kinds of trees, mostly oaks and beeches. **2008** *DARE* File—Internet **wNC,** [Caption:] Squaw Root, a favorite spring food of bears in the Smoky Mountains.

2 A **bugbane 1** (here: *Cimicifuga racemosa*).

1813 (1901) Smith *Ind. Doctor's Dispensatory* 39 **OH,** The Squaw root, is also called Rattle weed and Black Snake root. . . [A]dhering to the stool is a great bunch of small black roots: these roots are purgative, make a good bitter when put in spirits, famous for curing the chronic rheumatism, and strengthening the system when moderately used. **1815** Drake *Natural View Cincinnati* 85 **OH,** *Plants Useful in Medicine and the Arts*. . . Actaea racemosa—squaw root. **1828** Rafinesque *Med. Flora* 1.88, It [=*Cimicifuga racemosa*] is an article of the materia medica of the Indians, much used by them in rheumatism, and also in facilitating parturition, whence its name of Squaw-root. **1848** Bartlett *Americanisms* 328, Squaw-root. (Lat. *macrotys racemosa*.) A medicinal plant put up by the Shakers. It is recommended for correcting the secretions, and possesses narcotic properties. **1876** [see **3** below]. **1930** Sievers *Amer. Med. Plants* 23, Cohosh bugbane. . . Other common names . . squawroot [etc]. **1971** Krochmal *Appalachia Med. Plants* 96, *Cimicifuga racemosa*. . . papoose root, . . squaw root. **2004** *Albuquerque Jrl.* (NM) 16 May 13 (Internet), Black cohosh, also known as black snakeroot, bugbane, squaw root and rattle weed, is a North American forest plant that has been fairly well studied in Germany, where it is used to treat hot flashes.

3 =**blue cohosh 1.**

1828 Rafinesque *Med. Flora* 1.97, *Caulophyllum thalictroides*. . . Vulgar Names—Cohosh, . . Squaw root [etc]. [*Ibid* 99, It is used by the Indians and their imitators. . . [and] it promotes delivery, menstruation, and dropsical discharges.] **1876** Hobbs *Bot. Hdbk.* 112, Squaw root, Blue cohosh, . . Black cohosh. **1902** [see **1** above]. **1951** Voss–Eifert *IL Wild Flowers* 67, Blue Cohosh. . . The medicinal root was used by the Indians as an antispasmodic in infant convulsions—papoose root—and as an aid in quick childbirth—squawroot. **1971** Krochmal *Appalachia Med. Plants* 78.

4 A **trillium** (here: *Trillium erectum*).

1891 *Jrl. Amer. Folkl.* 4.149 **NH,** *Trillium erectum* we called *Squaw Root.* **1902** [see **1** above]. **1930** Sievers *Amer. Med. Plants* 48, Purple trillium. . . Other common names. . . squawflower, squawroot [etc]. . . Many of these names are applied also to other species of trillium. **1971** Krochmal *Appalachia Med. Plants* 256, Squaw root. . . The plant has been used as an antispasmodic, emmenagogue, emetic, expectorant, and uterine astringent.

5 An **Indian hemp 1** (here: *Apocynum cannabinum*).

1901 Mohr *Plant Life AL* 674, *Apocynum cannabinum*. . . The root is . . the "squaw root" of the Choctaw Indians.

6 A **yampah,** usu *Perideridia gairdneri*.

1906 Rydberg *Flora CO* 445, Squaw root (*Carum* [=*Perideridia*] [spp]). **1937** U.S. Forest Serv. *Range Plant Hdbk.* W48, Yampa . . is also known as squawroot. . . The roots were cleaned by placing them in

baskets in running water where squaws trod them with bare feet to remove the dark outer skin and make them smooth and clean. **1964** Jackman–Long *OR Desert* 299, *Food from Roots and Tubers*. . . Ipo (squawroot). **2003** *DARE* File—Internet **CA,** *Carum* [=*Perideridia*] *gairdneri*—Squaw Root. . . Like Small Potatoes.

squaw's cabbage   See **squaw cabbage**

squaw's carpet   See **squaw carpet**

squaw side n   Cf **Indian side**

In ref to mounting or handling a domestic animal: the right-hand side.

1938 FWP *Guide SD* 88, *Squaw side of a horse:* right side, due to squaw's preference for mounting from that side. **1942** *NV State Jrl.* (Reno) 10 Oct 5/2, Properly, the picture should be entitled "Squawside Cow" since these range animals, broken to milk by Piaute [sic] Indians, are milked "squaw-side."

squaw's mat   See **squaw mat**

squaw summer n   Cf **Indian summer, squaw wind, ~ winter**

A period of unseasonably warm weather in late autumn or early spring.

1878 *Observer* (Richland Center WI) 7 Feb 8/1, "Squaw summer" still continues. Let not the farmers "forget to remember" it is still mid winter, and not maple sugar time. **1884** *Eve. Observer* (Dunkirk NY) 28 Nov 4/2, Last week we had a squaw summer. This week we have a buck winter. **1900** *Newport Mercury* (RI) 28 Apr [4]/4 (newspaperarchive.com), The hot wave or squaw summer occurs about the time the whippoorwill begins his well known serenades. **1950** *NV State Jrl.* (Reno) 7 Nov 16/6, Wells [=a community] basked in "squaw summer" last week (Indian summer passed this way in October). **1950** *WELS (A period of warm weather late in the fall)* 1 Inf, **seWI,** Squaw summer—old-fashioned. **1969** *DARE* (Qu. B32) Inf **PA**197, Squaw summer. **2002** *DARE* File—Internet **CO,** The potted ones [=plants] are getting a sunbreak now that we are into Papoose summer (the summer that follows Squaw summer, that follows Indian summer).

squaw tea n

=**Mormon tea 1.**

1897 *Dubuque Sun. Herald* (IA) 24 Oct 11/2 **West,** It was accepted as a matter of course . . that Sam should take entire charge of him and dose him with wild sage and "squaw" tea. **1918** CA State Comm. Horticult. *Mth. Bulletin* 7.671, Stems of the squaw-tea *(Ephedra)* and leaves of the mesquite form an important element of the diet [of ground squirrels]. **1957** Jaeger *N. Amer. Deserts* 252, Desert Tea or Squaw Tea. *Ephedra viridis. Ibid,* Nevada Squaw Tea. *Ephedra nevadensis.* **1962** Balls *Early Uses CA Plants* 39, Mexican Tea, Squaw Tea *(Ephedra)*. . . The Indians, Mexicans, and Spanish settlers all brewed a pleasant refreshing drink by steeping the stems, either green or dried, in boiling water. **2008** *DARE* File—Internet **NV,** Growing up we knew Mormon tea by the name squaw tea. It is also referred to as Indian tea, Brigham tea, Joint Fir, and its Generic name, ephedra.

squaw thorn n

A **wolfberry 2** (here: *Lycium* spp).

1925 Jepson *Manual Plants CA* 890, *L[ycium] torreyi* . . Squaw Thorn. . . Roughish but often sparingly thorny erect shrub 4 to 8 ft. high. **1931** U.S. Dept. Ag. *Misc. Pub.* 101.142 **West,** Wolfberries. . . These bushes are common and characteristic and a wealth of vernacular names has been bestowed upon them, including . . squawbush, squawthorn, and tomatilla (-o). **1941** Jaeger *Wildflowers* 227 **CA, NV,** Squaw-thorn. *Lycium Torreyi*. . . The juicy, many-seeded berries are bright, shining red and though rather insipid were eaten by native peoples. **1985** Dodge *Flowers SW Deserts* 110, Squaw-Thorn. . . These plants have contributed much to the subsistence of the Indians, their insipid, slightly bitter, juicy berries being eaten raw or prepared as a sauce.

squaw vine n

A **partridgeberry 1** (here: *Mitchella repens*).

1832 (1833) Beach *Amer. Practice Med.* 3.53, Partridge-berry. Common names.—Squaw-Vine, Checkerberry, One-berry, Winter Clover, &c. *M[itchella] repens.* **1848** in 1850 Cooper *Rural Hours* 32 **NY,** It was a perfect bed of the squaw-vine and partridge berry. **1892** *Jrl. Amer. Folkl.* 5.98 **NEng,** *Mitchella repens,* Squaw-vine. **1911** Henkel *Amer. Med. Leaves* 34, The squaw vine is common in woods from Nova Scotia to Minnesota and south to Florida and Arkansas, where it is generally found creeping about the bases of trees. **1970** Anderson *TX Folk Med.* 75, A general tonic is made from the roots of sarsparilla [sic], squaw vine [Anderson: partridge berry], and queen's-delight [queenroot] mixed in whiskey. **1975** Hamel–Chiltoskey *Cherokee Plants* 47, Squaw vine. . . to facilitate childbirth; . . for baby before it takes the breast; for monthly period pains; for pregnant cat; for her kittens. **1986** Pederson *LAGS Concordance,* 1 inf, **neTN,** Squaw vine—medicinal—harvested locally.

squaw waterweed n

A **groundsel tree** (here: *Baccharis sergiloides*).

1925 Jepson *Manual Plants CA* 1059, B[accharis] sergiloides . . Squaw Waterweed. . . Moist places in desert cañons. **1959** Munz–Keck *CA Flora* 1227, Squaw Waterweed. . . Washes and canyon-bottoms. **1981** Benson–Darrow *Trees SW Deserts* 337, Squaw Waterweed. . . Sandy washes and canyons in the Mohavean, Colorado, and Arizona deserts.

squaw-weed n

1 =**fleabane.**

1828 Rafinesque *Med. Flora* 1.167, They [=plants of the genus *Erigeron*] were known to the Northern Indians by the name of Cocash or Squaw-weed as menagogue and diuretics.

2 Any of var **ragworts,** but esp **golden ragwort.** Note: Some ragworts formerly included in the genus *Senecio* are now assigned to *Packera.*

1837 Darlington *Flora Cestrica* 497 **NY,** S[enecio] obovatus [= *Packera obovata*]. . . An agricultural writer, in New York, denounces the plant—under the name of "Squaw-weed"—as poisonous to sheep; but I have no knowledge of its properties. **1848** Bartlett *Americanisms* 328, Squaw-weed. (Lat. *senecio obovatus.*) A medicinal plant used for diseases of the skin. **1930** OK Univ. Biol. Surv. *Pub.* 2.86, *Senecio tridenticulatus* [=*Packera tridenticulata*]. . . Western squaw-weed. **1936** Whitehouse *TX Flowers* 187, Texas Squaw-weed. . . *Senecio ampullaceus* . . forms a carpet of gold for miles and miles. **1938** Madison *Wild Flowers OH* 162, Balsam Squaw-weed. *Senecio balsamitae* [= *Packera paupercula*]. **1963** Craighead *Rocky Mt. Wildflowers* 225, Groundsel—*Senecio integerrimus.* . . Squaw-weed. **1975** Hamel–Chiltoskey *Cherokee Plants* 52, Squaw weed—*Senecio aureus* [= *Packera aurea*]—Tea for heart trouble; tea to prevent pregnancy. **1976** Elmore *Shrubs & Trees SW* 74, Threadleaf Groundsel [=*Senecio flaccidus*]. . . squawweed. . . The Navajo used the fuzzy tops as whisks to brush the spines from cactus fruit. **1978** in 2003 (acc) KY Univ. Oral Hist. Program *Frontier Nursing Serv. Oral Hist. Project* (Internet), Well, I'll tell you what you can do with that [=bleeding during delivery of a child]. Go up there in the hills and get you some squaw weed. . . Squaw weed, sarsaparilla, and rattleweed, and boil that & let her drink it.

3 =**cocash 2.**

1854 King *Amer. Eclectic Dispensatory* 265, *Aster puniceus.* Red-stalked Aster. . . This plant is variously known by the names of *Cocash, Meadow Scabish, Squaw-weed,* etc. **1876** Hobbs *Bot. Hdbk.* 112, Squaw weed, Red stalked aster, Aster puniceus.

4 A **boneset 1** (here: *Ageratina altissima*).

1900 Lyons *Plant Names* 155, E[upatorium] ageratoides [=*Ageratina altissima*]. . . White Snake-root, . . Squaw-weed. **1935** (1943) Muenscher *Weeds* 487, Eupatorium urticaefolium [=*Ageratina altissima*]. . . Indian sanicle, Deerwort, Squaw-weed. **1958** Jacobs–Burlage *Index Plants NC* 53, Eupatorium urticaefolium. . . squaw-weed. . . grows on mountain sides and in rich woodlands.

5 A **sumac B** used in basket-weaving. Cf **squawbush 3**

1901 James *Indian Basketry* 73, The Hopi use yucca and fine grass; . . the Southern California Indians, tule root and squaw weed. **1923** Saunders *S. Sierras* 172 **sCA,** Add . . squaw-weed *(Rhus trilobata)* and grass for fire, and you have the physical basis of that remote urban life on a desert mountain slope.

6 A **pennyroyal B1** (here: *Hedeoma pulegioides*). Cf **squaw mint**

1940 Clute *Amer. Plant Names* 24, H[edeoma] pulegioides. . . squaw-weed.

7 A **bugbane 1** (here: *Cimicifuga racemosa*).

1811 Titford *Sketches* 74, *Black Snake Root, Acta Racemosa* . . called also Squaw Weed [etc]. **1940** Clute *Amer. Plant Names* 220, Bug-wort, fairy candles, . . squaw-weed. **2003** *DARE* File—Internet, The root of Black cohosh . . , native to deciduous forests of North America, has a long tradition of use by Native Americans for rheumatism and as a women's herb. It's more commonly known as . . "squaw-weed", or "black snakeroot".

squaw whortleberry n obs

A **deerberry a** (here: *Vaccinium stamineum*).

1822 Eaton *Botany* 503, [Vaccinium] stamineum (squaw whortleberry). . . Berries of this species are large and light green, when ripe. **1845** (1849) Phelps *Lectures on Botany* 181, [Vaccinium] stamineum . . squaw whortleberry. . . Car[olina] to Fl[orida].

squaw wind n Cf chinook n 2, squaw summer

A warm wind, esp one associated with winter; see quots.

1935 Davis *Honey* 214 **OR,** A warm squaw-wind eased in from the direction of China. **1997** in 2002 *DARE* File—Internet, [American mountain men terms:] *Squaw wind*—An unexpected warm wind in the middle of a very cold spell. Like a chinook, but in the dead of winter. **2002** *Ibid* **cnCA,** *Squaw Wind:* Light wind from the Yolly Bolly [=Yolla Bolly Wilderness area].

squaw winter n Cf Indian winter, squaw summer

An early period of wintry weather, esp one preceding **Indian summer;** see quots.

1849 Howitt *Our Cousins in OH* 218, The first approaches of winter, often bitterly severe, and which were called *Squaw-winter,* had been felt and were over; and now Indian summer was come. **1886** *Athens Messenger* (OH) 18 Nov 5/1, An installment of squaw winter . . has been followed by very delightful weather. **1903** (1965) Adams *Log Cowboy* 361 **West,** We found a wet, slushy snow some two inches in depth on the ground. . . This was but the squaw winter which always preceded Indian summer. **1904** *DN* 2.402 **cNY,** *Squaw winter.* . . An early cold snap accompanied by flurries of snow. **1912** Woodrow *Sally Salt* 297 **NEng,** Indian Summer . . had been succeeded by the gusts and snowflakes of Squaw Winter. **1916** *DN* 4.329 **KS,** *Squaw-winter.* . . A sudden cold snap following Indian summer. **1950** *WELS (Name for the cold weather that usually comes right after the first frost)* 12 Infs, **WI,** Squaw winter. **1966–69** *DARE* (Qu. B31, *A period of cold weather that comes early in the fall, after the first frost;* total Infs questioned, 75) Inf **MS24,** Squaw winter; (Qu. B32, *A period of warm weather late in the fall)* Inf **IL47,** Squaw winter—the period of cold weather just preceding Indian summer; **OH59,** Squaw winter [Inf uncertain]; (Qu. B39, *A very light fall of snow)* Inf **NY106,** Squaw winter; **MA30,** Squaw-winter snow. **1982** *Chron.–Telegram* (Elyria OH) 14 Nov sec B 3/4, Since we had Squaw Winter last week, our warm weather of this week can be properly designated as Indian Summer. **2007** in 2008 *DARE* File—Internet **AL,** Indian Summer and Squaw Winter continue to battle it out, but the cool or cold will eventually win, with the first average frost being on November 11.

squaw wood n

1 Firewood consisting of easily gathered dead branches, driftwood, etc; hence n *squaw pine.* Also called **women's wood**

1914 *Outing* 64.191 **TN,** The cooking fire is only the beginning of the possibilities of 'squaw wood.' **1944** [see **2** below]. **1949** Peattie *Cascades* 219 **Pacific NW,** We built a small fire with the help of squaw-wood and pitch strips and warmed our cold fingers. **1953** Randolph–Wilson *Down in Holler* 287 **Ozarks,** *Squaw-wood.* . . Small or badly cut firewood. Often used in a jocular fashion with a negative, as when a man selling stovewood says: "An' that ain't no squaw-wood neither." **1958** Carrighar *Moonlight* 61 **AK,** For quick fires they were burning driftwood, called "squaw wood" since women and children collected it. **1984** Doig *English Creek* 55 **nMT,** My father sat up enough to put his boot against a pine piece of squaw wood and shove it farther into the fire. **2002** *DARE* File—Internet, Have lots of "squaw" wood on hand before lighting the fire. That is any wood you can make into fire sized pieces. **2003** *DARE* File **NH,** My fishing buddies and I have always thought of squaw pine as . . those dead limbs on pine trees that were always seemingly dry and readily available for the morning fire, or the quick start of a later fire.

2 See quot.

1944 Adams *Western Words* 153, *Squaw wood*—A slang name for dried cow chips; also used in speaking of small, dry, easily broken sticks when used for fuel.

squay(re) See **square** n[1], adj, adv

squdders See **squtters**

squeachy See **skewgee** adj[1]

squeak bean n [See quot]

The seed of the **honey locust 1.**

1909 Fultz *Fly-Aways* 106 **IA,** The seeds of the honey locust are. . .

dark brown and almost as hard as bone. Boys call them "squeak beans." **1931** Clute *Common Plants* 60, The hard ripe seeds of the honey-locust *(Gleditsia triacanthus)* emit the most delightful squeaks when twisted under foot on a hard surface, as any mischievous schoolboy is aware, and in his vocabulary are known as squeak-beans.

squeaker n

1 also *squeak rabbit:* =**pika.** Cf **piping hare**

1946 Dufresne *AK's Animals* 124, The pika, little chief hare, or "squeaker," is commonly found among the rock slides of the Alaska Range. **1956** *Pinedale Roundup* (WY) 21 June 1/3, The pike or co-ney. . . is known by nearly a dozen names . . [including] rock rabbit[,] calling hare[,] whistling hare, little chief hare[,] tailless hare, starved rat, slide rat, mouse hare and squeak rabbit.

2 =**harlequin duck.** Cf **squealer 2**

1955 MA Audubon Soc. *Bulletin* 39.376 **ME,** Harlequin Duck. . . Squeaker, Squealer. [**1985** Benes *Amer. Speech* 43 **ME,** There are numerous ones that once were lexical items and that now few people, local or otherwise, know anything about—for example . . that *squeaker* in the names of various offshore features refers to the harlequin duck.]

3 =**northern phalarope.**

1956 MA Audubon Soc. *Bulletin* 40.21 **ME,** Northern Phalarope. . . Squeaker.

‡squeak-eyed adj phr Cf squeech, squinch adj 1

1968 *DARE* (Qu. X21b, *If the eyes are very sharp or piercing*) Inf **LA35,** Squeak-eyed.

squeak heel n

Esp among loggers: see quots.

1956 Sorden-Ebert *Logger's Words* 35 **Gt Lakes,** *Squeak-heel.* . . Sore heel from getting feet wet and chilled. **1958** McCulloch *Woods Words* 179 **Pacific NW,** *Squeak heel*—A very painful tightening of the cords in the heel, due to continuous cold, or working in snow or water. **1984** Petzoldt-Ringholz *New Wilderness Hdbk.* 84 **ID,** Many boots have scree collars, tight padded rings at the top intended to prevent stones ("scree") or debris from entering the boot. Most scree collars cause "squeak heel," or tendonitis, which is an inflammation of the sheath of the Achilles' tendon, or soreness above the heel, caused by continuous slight pressure over long periods of time.

squeaking duck n

=**old-squaw.**

1917 (1923) *Birds Amer.* 1.141, Old-Squaw. . . Other Names. . . Scolder; . . Squeaking Duck.

squeak owl n

A **screech owl 1** (here: *Otus asio*).

1939 *LANE* Map 230 *(Screech owl)* 1 inf, **neMA,** Squeak owl. **c1940** *LAMSAS Materials,* 2 infs, **PA, VA,** Squeak owl. **1986** Pederson *LAGS Concordance* **Gulf Region,** 2 infs, Squeak owl(s); 1 inf, Squeak owl— "hollers" occasionally while flying; 1 inf, Squeak owls—sign of death if you heard them.

squeak rabbit See squeaker 1

squeaky cheese n Also *squeaky cheese curds* [See quot 1950] chiefly Nth, esp WI

Fresh cheese curd(s); see quot 2007.

1950 *Capital Times* (Madison WI) 14 July [18]/2 (newspaper-archive.com), Many people like cheese when it is still young and squeaky. . . If there are not enough customers for all the squeaky cheese, it will get older as time goes on, and should decay enough to suit somebody. **1978** *NY Times* (NY) 26 Mar (Internet) **VT,** After we've poured out the whey . . we transfer the curd cubes over to this sink. . . We mound them all up and then break up the mound with our hands, crumbling the stuff into bits of what's known as 'squeaky cheese.' **1994** *Post–Std.* (Syracuse NY) 31 Jan sec B 1/2 **WI,** Cheese was like candy to kids when I grew up in Wisconsin. We'd hang out at the cheese factory . . snitching samples of . . squeaky cheese curds. **2002** *DARE* File, If you live in the upper Midwest . . you probably know all about squeaky cheese. But it's an oddity to much of the nation, where cheese only comes from supermarkets. . . people from Wisconsin seem to take particular pride in their squeaky cheese. **2006** *DARE* File—Internet, Squeaky Cheese curds. . . you may have been a Wisconsinite in a past life! *Ibid,* Squeaky cheese curds!! I learned of those wonderful things from my wisconsin and western new york friends. *Ibid* **swVA,** Hey, we even have squeaky cheese down here! *Ibid,* Squeaky cheese curds. . . I just had some for the first time in Wisconsin. *Ibid,* Come visit us in

Minnesota, and I promise to bring you plenty of squeaky cheese curds. *Ibid,* You can get squeaky cheese at the Tillamook Cheese plant in Tillamook, Oregon. *Ibid,* Squeaky cheese. . . I love the ones [=curds] made by the Amish in Iowa. **2007** *Ibid* **ID,** These pop-in-your-mouth mild morsels of cheddar are so fresh that they squeak! That's why they are called "squeaky cheese."

squeal v

Std sense, var form.

Past: usu *squealed;* also *squole.*

1874 *Sedalia Daily Democrat* (MO) 19 Feb [2]/2 (newspaper-archive.com), You could have heard them more than a mile, they squole so loud. **1878** *Kinsley Graphic* (KS) 22 June 3/2 **KS,** He was promised entire immunity from punishment if he would 'squeal,' therefore he squole. **1923** *DN* 5.222 **swMO,** *Squole.* . . Squealed. **1931** Randolph *Ozarks* 127, An acquaintance once told me very seriously that he thought his hogs were bewitched; it seems that they did not come as usual when he called them, but "jest sot on their tails an' squole!" **1995** *Brophy Coll.* 71 **swMO** (as of c1960), *Squole* . . squealed.

squeal n Also *Indian squeal* Cf Indian B1b, Indian pudding

A dish of boiled cornmeal, molasses, and sometimes pork.

1903 *DN* 2.294 **Cape Cod MA** (as of a1857), *Squeal.* . . A dish of boiled meal served with molasses. **1941** *LANE* Map 288 *(Corn meal mush)* 1 inf, **seNH,** Indian squeal, cooked with pork and molasses; 1 inf, **neMA,** Squeal; 1 inf, **seNH,** Squeal, made of corn meal, sweetened, served with pork fat ('a whole meal').

squeal-cat n Cf cat n 1f

A tattletale.

1943 *LANE* Map 587 *(Tell-tale)* 1 inf, **csCT,** Squeal-cat; 1 inf, **csCT,** Squeal-cat—grandson's term. **1966** *DARE* (Qu. JJ4, *A child who is always telling on other children*) Inf **MI32,** Squeal-cat. **2002** in 2003 *DARE* File—Internet **NY,** What do I spy? Is this another convention thread that has lost its way? Man, I'm sta[r]ting to feel like a squealcat for pointing these things out.

squealer n

1 =**golden plover.**

1852 in 1876 *Forest & Stream* 7.212 **eMA,** *Charadrius virginicus.* Squealer. **1876** *Ibid* 245 **MA,** The loud, rather startling note of the golden plover gives him his title of "squealer." **1925** (1928) Forbush *Birds MA* 1.462, Golden Plover. *Other names:* Black-breast, . . Squealer [etc].

2 =**harlequin duck.** Cf **squeaker 2**

1888 Trumbull *Names of Birds* 91 **ME,** *Harlequin Duck.* . . Known also as *Squealer* at Machias Port. **1925** (1928) Forbush *Birds MA* 1.261, *Voice.* . . males have a "low piping whistle"—probably the note that gives bird name of Squealer or Sea Mouse by which it is often known on Maine coast where gunners say they "squeak like mice."

3 also *squealing sapsucker:* =**yellow-bellied woodpecker.**

1889 Ridgway *Ornith. IL* 1.380, Yellow-bellied Sapsucker—Popular synonyms. . . Squealing or Whining Sapsucker. **1936** Roberts *MN Birds* 1.679, The whining utterance [of the sapsucker] . . is very like a squeal and has given rise to one of the colloquial names of the bird, "the Squealer."

4 A **wood duck 1** (here: *Aix sponsa*). chiefly Sth, S Midl

1897 *Auk* 14.286 **LA,** *Aix sponsa.* . . —Known as *Branchier;* also as Squealer. **1911** *Forest & Stream* 77.173 **AR, LA,** Woodduck. . . Squealer is used at Lake Wapanoca, Ark., and in Louisiana also. **1932** Bennitt *Check-list* 19 **MO,** Wood Duck. . . Squealer; black; plumer. **1966–68** *DARE* (Qu. Q5, . . *Kinds of wild ducks*) Infs **MS6, NC24, TX33,** Squealer; **LA15,** Squealer = wood duck. [*DARE* Ed: Some of these Infs may refer instead to **5** below.] **1967** *DARE* Tape **LA1,** [FW:] What kind of ducks do you have when they're coming in? [Inf:] Mostly squealers. [*DARE* Ed: This Inf may refer instead to **5** below.] **1982** Elman *Hunter's Field Guide* 186, Wood Duck. . . *squealer.* [*Ibid,* When startled, they [=drakes] let loose a high, hooting squeal, while females are likely to intersperse squeals with chirping quacks.] **2003** *DARE* File—Internet **IN,** The best hunting for this species—known to farm boys as the little black squealer—is nigh. *Ibid* **VA,** The wood duck or "squealer" as he is affectionately called in rural areas is well known the entire year. *Ibid* **MS,** The wood duck was once endangered, yet now it is Mississippi's most plentiful duck. How did we bring back the squealer?

5 A **tree duck 1** (here: *Dendrocygna bicolor*). Cf **Mexican squealer**

1918 Grinnell et al. *Game Birds CA* 246, Fulvous Tree-duck. . . Other Names—Mexican Duck; Squealer [etc]. . . Voice—A long-drawn squealing whistle. **1954** Sprunt *FL Bird Life* 58 **LA, TX,** The characteristic notes, which cause this duck to be known as "Squealer" in Louisiana and Texas, were noted by Reed and his guide. **1962** Imhof *AL Birds* 122, Fulvous Tree Duck. . . Other Name: Squealer. **2003** *Sun. Advocate* (Baton Rouge LA) 9 Nov Outdoors sec (Internet) **swLA,** Their take included . . the seldom seen Fulvus tree duck, a bird most southwest Louisiana hunters call "squealers."

6 =cackling goose.

1940 Gabrielson *Birds OR* 127, Cackling Goose: *Branta canadensis minima.* . . This species has a distinctive high-pitched call . . recognized by many hunters who, in various localities, call it "China Goose," "Cackler," "Cack," or "Squealer."

7 =red phalarope.

1956 MA Audubon Soc. *Bulletin* 40.21 **ME,** Red Phalarope. . . Squealer . . Sonic.

8 A tree frog 1.

1967 *DARE* (Qu. P21, *Small frogs that sing or chirp loudly in spring*) Inf **TN**14, Squealers.

9 also *squealer cat:* A young **channel catfish** (here: *Ictalurus punctatus*).

1915 *Coshocton Morning Tribune* (OH) 27 June 3/5, The catch consisted of over 200 pounds of catfish ranging from the squealer size to some weighing four pounds. **1953** Randolph–Wilson *Down in Holler* 287 **Ozarks,** *Squealer.* . . A small catfish which produces a squeaking noise when taken from the water. **1957** Trautman *Fishes* 415 **OH,** Channel Catfish—*Ictalurus punctatus.* . . Young less than 14.0″ long (colloquially called squealers, ladycats, spotted and silver cats, and fiddlers). **1968** *DARE* (Qu. P1, . . *Kinds of freshwater fish . . caught around here . . good to eat*) Inf **OH**42, Squealers—those are catfish. **2003** *DARE* File—Internet **SC,** A buddy of mine swears by small squealer cats, lip hooked and fished live for his big boys.

10 =shiner 1.

1969 *DARE* (Qu. P7, *Small fish used as bait for bigger fish*) Inf **GA**72, Squealers—same as shiners.

squealer cat See **squealer 9**

squealing hawk n   Also *squealer hawk*   Cf **squirrel hawk 2**
A **red-tailed hawk** or similar hawk.

1884 *Harper's New Mth. Mag.* 68.622, While flying it [=the red-tailed hawk] utters a very harsh, peculiar, and disagreeable scream, and by some is called the squealing hawk. **1935** May *Hawks N. Amer.* 33, *Buteo borealis* . . *Other Names.* Red-tail, Red-tailed Buzzard, Red Hawk, Hen Hawk, Big Hen Hawk, Chicken Hawk, White-breasted Chicken Hawk, Squealing Hawk, Buzzard Hawk. . . Its common call is a shrill long-drawn-out whistle or wheezy scream or squeal . . which suggests escaping steam. **1968** *DARE* (Qu. Q4, . . *Kinds of hawks*) Inf **GA**25, Squealer hawk.

squealing sapsucker See **squealer 3**

squeasy adj   [Prob blend of *squeamish* + *queasy; OED2* → 1655]   Cf **squamish**
Nauseated; also fig.

1871 Jones *Life Batkins* 230 **MA,** I did feel some squeasy about selling my seat. [**1890** *DN* 1.19 seNH, *Squeezy:* fretful.] **1959** *NV State Jrl.* (Reno) 9 Sept 2/1, "Sick" jokes are the kind which make you cringe and feel a little squeasy about the stomach. **1967–68** *DARE* (Qu. BB16a, *If something a person ate didn't agree with him, he might be sick _____ his stomach*) Inf **IL**5, Squeasy; (Qu. BB16b, *If something a person ate didn't agree with him, he might just feel a bit _____*) Infs **CT**19, **IL**5, **KS**7, **MI**68, **NE**11, **OH**80, Squeasy. **2006** in 2008 *DARE* File—Internet **CA,** Snausages [sic] on the other hand still have me feeling squeasy.

sque-ball See **skewbald**

Squedunk See **Squeedunk**

squee- See **skew-**

squeech v   Also with *up*   esp **Sth, S Midl**   Cf **screech, squinch** v[2] **2**
To narrow the eyes; hence ppl adj *squeeched up,* adj *squeechy* narrowed (of the eyes).

1897 *Century Illustr. Mag.* 54.282, His head was 'bout as big as the biggest watermillon you ever saw, like it is now, an' his eyes was just as

squeeched up. **1967–68** *DARE* (Qu. X25, *To close your eyes part way—for example, when looking at the sun*) Infs **AR**55, **LA**37, **TX**13, Squeech; (Qu. X21b, *If the eyes are very sharp or piercing*) Inf **LA**20, Squeechy eyes. **1986** Pederson *LAGS Concordance (Orientals)* 1 inf, **neMS,** Anybody with squeechy eyes. **2002** in 2003 *DARE* File—Internet **cIN,** Is it possible that they [=stray cats] also sense that if they rub around my legs and squeech their eyes up that I'll melt?

squeech owl n   Also *squeeching owl*
A **screech owl 1** (here: *Otus asio*).

1888 Bellamy *Old Man* 25 **FL** [Black] (as of 1857), Well, tubbe sho, . . put off yo' lef' shoe when the squeech owl hollers, en' you'll ward off dezaster. **1906** *DN* 3.158 **nwAR,** Squeech owl. . . Screech-owl. Hot Springs. **1912** *DN* 3.591 **wIN,** Squeech-owl. **1915** *DN* 4.229 **wTX,** Squeech-owl, squinch-owl. . . Variants of *screech-owl.* **1939** *LANE* Map 230 (*Screech owl*) 4 infs, **wCT,** Squeech owl; 1 inf, **wCT,** Squeech owls—little fellows who rob birds' nests. c**1940** *LAMSAS Materials,* 69 infs, **chiefly PA, WV, VA, SC,** Squeech owl. **1966** Dakin *Dial. Vocab. Ohio R. Valley* 2.386, The *screech owl* ranges throughout the Ohio Valley and is commonly known by this name everywhere except in the Mountains and in westernmost Kentucky. The occasional Midland variant of this name, *squeech owl,* is used in the northern Bluegrass, along the National Road in Indiana, and occasionally in Ohio and Illinois. **1968** *DARE* (Qu. Q1, . . *Kind of owl that makes a shrill, trembling cry*) Inf **IN**35, Squeech owl. **1973** Allen *LAUM* 1.316 **Upper MW** (as of c1950), Midland *squeech owl* survives feebly in the speech of three southeastern Iowans and of one South Dakotan of Ohio parentage. **1986** Pederson *LAGS Concordance* **Gulf Region,** 6 infs, Squeech owl(s); 2 infs, Squeeching owl. **2006** *DARE* File—Internet **cPA,** I could certainly borrow a smaller version of one to catch two squeech owls who presently prey on the frightened squirrels in my Alexandria backyard.

squeech up, squeechy See **squeech**

Squeedunk n   Also *Ske(w)dunk, Sque(w)dunk*
=Podunk 1.

c**1865** in Lib. of Congress *Amer. Memory: Amer. Singing* (Internet), There was Henry Beecher, and Barnum's What-is-it;/ The Mayor of Squedunk, with an Albany gal. **1870** *Punchinello* 1.247, Way down in Skewdunk they held prayer-meetings when they heard that news. **1872** *Harper's New Mth. Mag.* 45.794, Brother Kalb was a famous exhorter in the "Squedunk meetin'-house." **1894** *Overland Mth.* (2d ser) 24.227, When a Congressman is anxious to get a bill through for a five hundred thousand dollar post-office for Squedunk, he looks around for some appropriation he can attack and cut down. **1942** Berrey–Van den Bark *Amer. Slang* 45.4, *Imaginary "Hick" Town.* . . Squewdunk. **1945** Stewart *Names on Land* 338, In 1846 a series of humorous magazine articles used the title *Letters from Podunk,* and the name became established as the joking equivalent of an insignificant, backward village. In time it sprouted a variant, Squeedunk. **1966–69** *DARE* (Qu. C33, . . *Joking names . . for an out-of-the-way place, or a very small or unimportant place*) Inf **TX**40, Skedunk; **AL**6, **GA**15, Squeedunk; **NY**130, Squeedunk—father's word. **2002** in 2003 *DARE* File—Internet, Many years ago while working at a Squedunk newspaper, I suggested [etc].

squeege v, hence ppl adj *squeeged*   [Var of *squeeze; OED2* 1782 →]

1849 *Knickerbocker* 34.334, His hand is every where squeeged by hands that have waxed strong by the fulness of bread. **1886** *Atlantic Mth.* 58.526 **eTN,** I hed n't been engaged in a unlawful act, preferrin' ter squeege the juice out'n my apples. **1893** *Century Illustr. Mag.* 45.608 **NYC,** Der wuz er dude wunst give me haffer-doller jest fer runnin' fer er keb when he'd squeeged his ankil er somethin' gettin' off er car. **1916** Tarkington *Seventeen* 61 **IN,** I just waited kind of squeeged up against the wall, an' he never saw me. **1961** *Lima News* (OH) 19 Aug 1/1 **seWI,** A buxom housekeeper confessed Friday she "squeeged" two small brothers to death against her bosom.

squeegee adj   See **skewgee** adj[1]

squeegee v   Also *skewgee, skweejee*   [Cf **squeege**]   Cf **skew- a**
To push or squeeze oneself through a crowd; to force (something) into a tight-fitting space.

1911 *DN* 3.547 **NE,** Skweejee. . . To thrust or push one's way zigzag through a crowd. "We skweejeed through the crowd." **1949** in 1986 *DARE* File **MI,** Squeegee in there and get me that rope. **1968** *DARE* Tape **CT**5, On the other side of the track were two elms and they were so close together that the house wouldn't go straight between them. And so there they [=the movers] were, sitting on the track, figuring out how to get the house skewgeed ['skjuǰid] between these two elm trees.

squeegee n Cf **pounder**
Among loggers: see quots.

1956 Sorden–Ebert *Logger's Words* 35 **Gt Lakes,** *Squeegee,* A plunger made out of a large tin can and a stick. Used when washing clothes in a tub or a large can of water. **1958** McCulloch *Woods Words* 179 **Pacific NW,** *Squeegee*—A logger's homemade washing machine, a tin can nailed to the end of a stout stick, open side of the can downward, to make a vacuum.

squee-gee(d) See **skew- a**

squee-haw(ed) See **skew- b**

squee-jaw(ed) See **skew- c**

squeeril, squeerrel See **squirrel** n

squee-wampus See **skew- d**

squee-wobbled See **skew- g**

squeeze v Rarely aphet *queeze*
A Pronc var.

1922 Gonzales *Black Border* 322 **sSC, GA coasts** [Gullah glossary], *'Queeze*—squeeze, squeezes, squeezed, squeezing. **1966** *DARE* Tape **SC15,** We queeze 'em, queeze 'em so tight.
B Gram forms.
Past, past pple, ppl adj: usu *squeezed;* also:
a *squoze.*
1844 [see **squinch** v² 1]. **1883** (1971) Harris *Nights with Remus* 277 **GA** [Black], He squoze 'im so hard dat Brer Rabbit wuz fear'd he 'uz gwine ter cut off his breff. **1899** (1912) Green *VA Folk-Speech* 413, *Squoze. . .* Past tense, *squeezed.* **1906** *DN* 3.158 **nwAR,** *Squoz* [sic] [skwoz]. . . Squeezed. **1907** White *AZ Nights* 230, I squoze the bulb and jumped twenty foot over the remark she made. **1923** *DN* 5.222 **swMO,** *Squoze. . .* Squeezed. **1931** *Sun* (Baltimore MD) 1 Sept 8/7, "Orange?" repeated Waitress No. 1. "Do you want it squoze?" **1968** *DARE* (Qu. Y33, *. . Squeezing or crushing something . . "I _____ my finger in the door."*) Inf **NY109,** Squoze. **1974** *DARE* File **cwMA** (as of 1957), *Squoze. . .* Squeezed. . . Middle aged woman, Polish bkgrd. **1985** *NY Times* (NY) 6 Aug 11, Mr. Reagan said he had had a "pimple" on his nose. . . ". . I picked at it and I squoze it and so forth and messed myself up a little bit." **2004** *DARE* File—Internet **AZ,** An assay furnace and shelves of chemicals squoze in beside a neat shelf of books . . occupied the west wall. **2005** [see **b** below].
b *squez; less freq sq(u)oz, squz.* **Sth, S Midl**
1873 *Indiana Progress* (PA) [11 Dec 6]/6 (newspaperarchive.com), When he . . ketcht holt of my hand, and squez it . . he began breathin' hard. **1884** *Century Illustr. Mag.* 28.959 **Sth** [Black], He squez hisself up. **1895** *DN* 1.376 **seKY, wNC,** *Squez* = squeezed. **1899** (1912) Green *VA Folk-Speech* 412, *Squez. . .* Past tense; *squeezed.* **1909** *DN* 3.375 **eAL, wGA,** *Squez, sqoz—prets.* of *squeeze.* **1954** *Harder Coll.* **cwTN,** The nesties is long, squez in two in the middle. **1955** Roberts *S. from Hell-fer-Sartin* 138 **seKY,** He just helt it up and squez till the water just poured out of this piece of cheese. **1970** *Foxfire* 4.80 **nGA,** Th' big bear just wheeled around an' grabbed th'cub an' squz it t'death. **1976** Garber *Mountain-ese* 87 **sAppalachians,** She squz the juice outen the orange. **1997** in 2004 Montgomery–Hall *Dict. Smoky Mt. Engl.* 563 **wNC, eTN,** *Squez* [1 inf]; *squoz* [4 infs]. **2002** *DARE* File **eKY,** As a past-tense form of the verb "squeeze," this person said "squz" [skwʌz]. **2005** Williams *Gratitude* 527 **wNC** (as of 1940s), *Squoze, squz:* squeezed.
C Sense.
In phrr *squeeze a dollar* (or *nickel, penny, eagle,* etc) and varr: To be very stingy. Cf *pinch pennies,* **skin a flea for its hide (and tallow)**

1885 *Daily Northwestern* (Oshkosh WI) 9 Oct 1/3, When I see a man attending a missionary meeting praying half an hour for God to send the Holy Spirit abroad . . and then squeeze a dime until the Goddess of Liberty yells like a Modoc Indian on the war path, I call him a man with a 100-yard theory and a half-inch practice. **1911** Saunders *Col. Todhunter* 44, He squeezes ev'y dollar o' his'n till the eagle screams and flies back into his own pocket, and you know it. **1928** *Ruppenthal Coll.* **KS,** *To squeeze a dollar till you hear the eagle scream . . to be thrifty;* close with money. **c1950** *Halpert Coll.* **wKY,** So tight they'd squeeze

the eagle on a quarter till it hollers. **1965–70** *DARE* (Qu. U33, *Names or nicknames for a stingy person*) Inf **WI64,** So tight he can squeeze a nickel until the Indian is riding the buffalo; **WA6,** Squeezes his pennies; **MI24,** Squeezes the dough, squeezes it till the eagle cries; **NY199,** Squeezes the eagle until the buffalo screams; **FL26,** Will squeeze a nickel till the eagle hollers; (Qu. U36b, *. . A person who saves in a mean way or is greedy in money matters: "She certainly is _____."*) Inf **AR52,** Does squeeze the eagle; **VA51,** Squeeze a dollar till the eagle hollers; **WA28,** Squeezes a nickel so hard the buffalo farts; **NH6,** Will squeeze a penny till it squeals. **1978** Gould *Greenleaf* 16 **ME,** He could squeeze a nickel so hard that the buffalo on the back would be wrung dry. **2008** *DARE* File—Internet **PA,** You are already getting your wine for pennies on the dollar, don't "squeeze the nickel till the buffalo screams".

squeeze n
=**main squeeze 2.**
1970 *DARE* (Qu. HH34, *General words . . for a woman, not necessarily uncomplimentary*) Inf **DC11,** Squeeze—more slang; relatively new. **1971** Roberts *Third Ear* np [Black], *Squeeze . .* 1. a girl friend. 2. a boy friend. 3. an intimate acquaintance. **2005** in 2008 *DARE* File—Internet **NH,** I just bought my squeeze a new 30gb Photo iPod and he will format to a PC.

squeeze Lizzie See **squeeze the apple**

squeezer n **West** Cf **snapping turtle 3**
A section at the end of a narrow chute with a movable side panel that can be clamped against an animal to immobilize it for branding, dehorning, etc.

1901 U.S. Bur. Animal Industry *Annual Rept. for 1900* 38, [Caption:] A chute used in vaccinating against blackleg, showing squeezer. **1909** U.S. Dept. Ag. *Farmers' Bulletin* 350.12 **West,** After the animal enters the squeezer the squeeze gate is pressed close against its side to prevent lateral movement, the stanchion is closed on the neck, and the head is turned and secured to the post . . as required for the removal of the horns. **1910** *McClure's Mag.* 36.28 **West,** With a yell, Big John sprang to the lever of the squeezer and threw all his strength on it, gripping the plunging steer about the middle. **c1910** in 2002 *DARE* File—Internet **MT,** [Caption on picture postcard postmarked 1910, Helena, MT:] No. 170 Branding Cattle In A Squeezer. **1920** Hunter *Trail Drivers TX* 297, Some cattlemen now employ a branding chute where an arrangement for holding the cattle while they are being branded is called a "squeezer" or "snappin' turtle." **1941** Writers' Program *Guide WY* 465, *Squeezer*—A chute for branding.

squeeze the apple v phr Also *squeeze Lizzie,* ~ *the biscuit,* ~ *the safety grip* **West** Cf **apple** n 1, **biscuit B3, Lizzy 1**
=*pull leather* (at **leather 1a**).
1929 *AmSp* 5.64 **NE** [Cattle country talk], A skilled horseman can . . generally "grave yard" well, ride a wild horse without the use of either saddle or bridle. The less skilled rider might "hunt leather," "take leather," "touch leather," "pull leather," or "choke" or "squeeze the safety grip (the horn)." **1937** *DN* 6.619 **swTX,** The cowboy violates the rules of the game if he catches hold of the pommel or any part of the saddle in order to stay on the pitching horse; and if he does so the spectators say he is *squeezing the biscuit.* **1942** Berrey–Van den Bark *Amer. Slang* 921.7, *"Pull leather." . .* squeeze Lizzie, squeeze the apple *or* biscuit.

squeeze the eagle See **squeeze** v C

squeeze the safety grip See **squeeze the apple**

squeezings n
=**corn squeezings.**
1969 *DARE* (Qu. DD21c, *Nicknames for whiskey, especially illegally made whiskey*) Inf **IL67,** Squeezin's. **1986** Pederson *LAGS Concordance,* 1 inf, **csTX,** Squeezings—not distilled; not as powerful. **2003** *DARE* File—Internet, If you sneak a bottle of Grandpa's Best Squeezings up to your own room and a six-pack of YooHoo for a chaser, that's up to you.

sque-lopper-jawed adj phr Cf **skew- c**
=**lopper-jawed.**
1916 *DN* 4.281 **NE,** *Sque-lopper-jawed. . .* Askew, crooked, etc. "This whole room is sque-lopper-jawed."

squench v¹ Also *squinch* [Varr of *quench; OED2 squench* 1535 →] **scattered, but chiefly Sth, S Midl** Cf Intro "Language Changes" I.8, *squestion* (at **question**), **squinch** v²

1795 Dearborn *Columbian Grammar* 139, *List of Improprieties.* . . Squinch for Quench. **1834** in 1925 *Chron. OK* 3.190 **IN,** Through this valley run a beautiful clear christol stream . . prehaps never before squench the thirst of civilized man. **1834** *Life Andrew Jackson* 8, He will jist squinch his glory in a puddle. **1871** *Overland Mth.* 6.558 **TX,** The formations are igneous, or, in the words of honest Dave, "It looks like all these mountains had been afire sometime, and then, all on a sudden, been squinched." **1883** (1971) Harris *Nights with Remus* 145 **GA** [Black], 'E do run un dife in da' crik fer squinch da' fier 'pon 'e bahk. **1892** *DN* 1.232 **KY, MI,** *Squinch* [skwĕnč]: quench. [*DN* Ed: Also in Michigan.] **1893** Shands *MS Speech* 76, *Squench* [skwĕnč]. A negro word for *quench.* . . The word is sometimes pronounced [skwĭnč], which form is also used by negroes for *squint.* **1899** (1912) Green *VA Folk-Speech* 412, *Squench.* . . To quench. . . *Squinch.* **1901** *Atlantic Mth.* 87.102 **ME** (as of c1776), I could ha' squinched him so all the friends he'd ever needed 'd be clargy an' saxon. **1923** *DN* 5.222 **swMO,** *Squench.* . . To quench. Also, *Squinch.* **1934** Hurston *Jonah's Gourd Vine* 130 **AL** [Black], Ah sho ain't gwine squench mah feelin's fuh Lucy. **1935** Hurston *Mules & Men* 167 **FL** [Black], Them chillun went to squinch they thirst. **1966–68** *DARE* (Qu. Y43b, . . *To put out a fire*) Inf **GA**44, **SD**2, Squench; **CA**196, Squinch. **1969** Wilson *Stars* 52 **Ozarks,** Brethern now is the hour for every true and transformed and purified spirit amongst us to jine hands in squenching the carnal flames that is seering the underpinnings of our younger generation. **1979** Carpenter *Walton War* 180 **sAppalachians,** When I find my feelins air aimin' to burst forth, I jest grit my teeth and squinch 'em. **2004** in 2008 *DARE* File—Internet **OH,** [Caption:] Abby squenches her thirst with some fresh coconut water.

squench v[2] Cf **squeech owl, squinch** ~
To screech.
   1937 in 1976 *Weevils in the Wheat* 247 **VA** [Black], Ef you wonna stop a screech owl from squenching, jes' tro a bit o' salt on de fire an' let it burn. It sho' stops 'em; I done it many times.

squench v[3] See **squinch** v[2]

squenched in See **squinch** v[2] 4

squenge See **squinch** v[2] 3

squer'l, squerrel, squerril See **squirrel** n

squeschun, squestion See **question**

squeteague n Also *scuteeg, skwiteague, squetauge, squeterg, squet(t)ee, squit(eeg), squitie, squitteag, squit(t)ee, succoteague* [See quot 1910] **chiefly NEng**
A **weakfish** (here: usu *Cynoscion regalis*).
   1803 in 1804 *MA Hist. Soc. Coll.* 1st ser 9.202 **RI,** The fishes . . are called the sheepshead, . . mackerel, squeterg, grunters [etc]. **1807** in 1846 *Ibid* 2d ser 3.57 **Martha's Vineyard MA,** The squittee, or drummer, is taken in the Sound, but principally in the harbours and lagunes. **1815** *Ibid* 4.289, The fish, common to this bay, are found at Wareham, such as . . squitteag, scuppeag, . . and alewives. **1848** Bartlett *Americanisms* 328, *Squeteague,* or *Squetee.* . . A very common fish in the waters of Long Island Sound and adjacent bays. **1887** Goode *Amer. Fishes* 111, The name "Squeteague" is of Indian origin, and "Squit," "Succoteague," "Squitee" and "Chickwit" are doubtless variations. **1892** *Outing* Apr 54/1 **MA,** The squetauge or weak-fish [is] . . known about Cape Cod as the 'drummer,' 'silver fish,' and 'spotted boy.' **1895** *Sun* (NY NY) 30 July 9/2, Squeteague, a name of the weakfish, variously corrupted to squettee, squitie, squit, scuteeg [etc]. **1902** *Jrl. Amer. Folkl.* 15.260, Squeteague. A sea-fish (*Labrus squeteague*) of the waters of Long Island, etc., known also as "weak-fish." The forms *squeeetee* and *squit* are also found. **1910** Hodge *Hdbk. Amer. Indians* 2.631, Squeteague. . . The Narraganset . . used the "sounds" [=swim bladders] of the fish for making a glutinous substance . . hence the name *pĕsäkweteauaq,* 'they make glue' . . contracted to *p's'kwĕteauaq, s'kwĕteauaq,* and *skweteague.* Among other spellings of the name are squettee, squiteeg, squitie, succoteague, skwiteague, scuteeg, and squit. **1969** *DARE* (Qu. P2, . . *Kinds of saltwater fish caught around here . . good to eat*) Inf **MA**55, Squeteague. **1984** *DARE* File **Chesapeake Bay** [Watermen's vocab], Squeteague.

Squewdunk See **Squeedunk**

squez See **squeeze** v **Bb**

squib n [*EDD* squib sb.[3]]
A squirrel.
   1935 *Atlantic Mth.* July 44 **nAL,** I seed some young squirrels. . . I took

a red flint rock about the size of a Dommer hen egg from my pocket and throwed it at the bunch of squibs. **1998** in 2003 *DARE* File—Internet, [In answer to a question about freezing squirrels for taxidermy:] You can put the whole squib in the freezer but then you will have to thaw before skinning.

squich owl See **squitch owl**

squid See **scrid**

‡**squidged** adj
   1917 *DN* 4.417 **wNC,** *Squidged.* . . Subsided. "His hand was all swoll up, but now its [sic] all squidged down."

squid-hound (bass) n [Because it eagerly pursues squid]
A **striped bass 1** (here: *Morone saxatilis*).
   1883 Rich *Truro–Cape Cod* 255, With almost superhuman effort, he recovered the line, and landed upon the sand an immense squid-hound bass of sixty pounds. **1884** Goode *Fisheries U.S.* 1.425 **NEng,** Large sea-going individuals [=striped bass] are sometimes known in New England by the names "Green-head" and "Squid-hound." **2006** *DARE* File—Internet **Martha's Vineyard MA,** [Caption:] A nice "squid hound."

squin n Also *skwin, squn* [Etym unknown] **esp RI**
Some or all of the edible viscera of an animal, esp a swine.
   1890 *AN&Q* 4.221 **CT,** A school-teacher, asking if he would be expected to "board around," was answered "yes," and replied "that then he would be obliged to live upon *squn* all winter." I learn that *squn* is that part of the hog which is usually fried on the day of butchering, or the day after; and is supposed to be composed of the liver, sweetbread, round robin, and perhaps parts of the diaphragm. By extensive inquiry, I have found a very few persons who have heard of the word. What was its origin? **c1930** in 1944 *ADD, Skwin.* . . The edible viscera of various animals. . . Reported. **1939** *LANE* Map 209 (*Pluck, haslet*) **RI,** The *squin* may include the heart, liver and lights (. . [2 infs]) or denote the liver only (. . [1 inf]). [Map records four instances of *squin,* all in RI. All four infs specified that the term is applied to pigs or hogs only. Another inf reported hearing the term from an elderly woman in Newport RI.]

squinch v[1] See **squench** v[1]

squinch v[2] Pronc-spp *squanch, squench*
1 freq with *up:* To contract (oneself or a part of one's body); esp, to contract, contort (one's face or eyes). **scattered, but chiefly S Midl** Cf **squinched up 1**
   1835 Longstreet *GA Scenes* 202, If I did'nt [sic] see that fellow wink, and that woman *squinch* her face, then hell's a dancing room. **1840** Haliburton *Clockmaker* (3d ser) 153, Lord! how she'll kick and squeell when I spread her out on the close-horse. How it will make her squinch her face. **1844** Stephens *High Life in NY* 2.195, Harnsome gals, that squoze close together and squinched themselves up to make room for me. **1884** *Anglia* 7.272 **Sth, S Midl** [Black], To squinch yo' eyeballs = to close the eyes. **1888** Jones *Negro Myths* 4 **GA coast,** Wen de rain duh po down, eh set on de fench an eh squinch up isself. Eh draw in eh neck, an eh try fur hide eh head. **1892** *DN* 1.232 **KY,** He squinches his eyes. **1899** *Century Illustr. Mag.* 58.644 **Sth** [Black], Bimeby, de toad he squinch up he eye. **1905** *DN* 3.95 **nwAR,** He squinched up his eyes. **1909** *DN* 3.375 **eAL, wGA,** Squinch, v. tr. To squint. **1950** *PADS* 13.23 **sKY,** *Squinch (up).* . . Variant of *squint.* Fairly common among uneducated. "Kin you look at the sun without squinchin' up your eyes?" *Squinch-eyed.* . . Variant of *squint-eyed.* . . "Sally wouldn't be so bad lookin' is [sic] she wasn't so squinch-eyed." **1954** *Harder Coll.* **cwTN,** *Squanch* . . to close the eyes part way. "Squanch ye eyes at tis [sic] 'ere pitcher." *Squanch-eyed.* **1960** Rockwell *Adventures* 253 **NY,** He wouldn't change his expression until I'd finished [painting] the left side of his face. Then he'd work his mouth around a few times and squinch up the right side. **1966–69** *DARE* (Qu. X25, *To close your eyes part way—for example, when looking at the sun*) Inf **TN**30, Squinch my eyes up; (Qu. Y32, *To squeeze yourself into a small space: "If you're going to fit in there you'll have to _____."*) Inf **WI**34, Squinch yourself up; (Qu. NN21a, *Exclamations caused by sudden pain—a pinched finger*) Inf **NC**33, Squinch up the face. **2003** *DARE* File—Internet **ceTX,** I feel a slight nauseous sensation and promptly squench my eyes shut. *Ibid* **cnGA,** Tense your neck then let it go limp. Squench your face muscles and let them go limp. **2008** *Ibid* **WI,** Drawing, talking in mini-sentences, climbing on furniture, squinching her face up when she thinks somethings funny.

2 To draw up one's face; esp, to narrow one's eyes, squint; hence ppl adj *squinching* narrowed; n *squinching* a squint. **chiefly Sth, S Midl, TX** See Map Cf **squeech**

1864 *Daily Dispatch* (Richmond VA) 11 May 2/4, Said negro is square built, dark but not black, slightly squinching about the right eye, and is very muscular. **1885** (1886) Murfree *Down the Ravine* 173 **TN,** Them eyes jes' set up sech a outdacious winkin' an' wallin', an' squinchin', ez I knowed he war makin' faces at me. **1890** *Century Illustr. Mag.* 40.892 **Sth** [Black], Bimeby er man he come f'om town, an' fotch er leetle bar'l an' he squinch through it, at dis cornder er de fence. **1897** *KS Univ. Qrly.* (ser B) 6.92 **NEng,** *Squinch:* to smirk. **1921** *DN* 5.117 **eKY,** *Squinch,* squint. **1923** *DN* 5.222 **swMO,** *Squinch. . .* To squint, as the eyes. **1965** Davis *Summer Land* 63 **cnNC,** Grandpa squinched at him and made the walking stick hiss in the air over his head. **1965–70** *DARE* (Qu. X25, *To close your eyes part way—for example, when looking at the sun*) 128 Infs, **chiefly Sth, S Midl, TX,** Squinch; (Qu. X24, *When a person opens and closes his eyes quickly, he* _____) Inf **NC40,** Squinches.

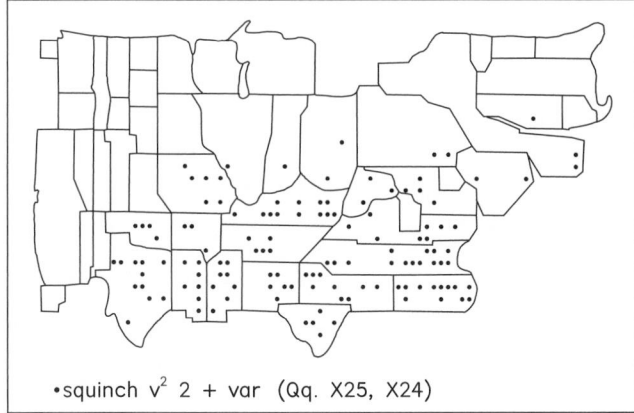

•squinch v² 2 + var (Qq. X25, X24)

3 also *squenge:* To flinch, cringe; to cause to cringe.

1854 Stephens *High Life in NY* 291, I felt streaked about makin any more touse about a leetle cider, and poured the glass down without squinchin. **1886** *Century Illustr. Mag.* 32.196 **eVA** [Black], When he say dat, she sort o' squinch 'way from him like she mos' done hit her. **a1978** (1983) Carpenter *Aunt Arie* 190 **swNC,** I can't walk in th'snow t'save my life. I just squenge. It squenges me all over. **1998** *Honolulu Star–Bulletin* (HI) 3 Dec (Internet), Growing up in a "glass fishbowl" . . has caused him "to kind of squinch" at the mere thought of politics. **1999** in 2003 *DARE* File—Internet, With older people, you can actually see them squinching from the music. . . When older people lose the high frequencies, they hear a distortion. **2006** *DARE* File—Internet, There are a lot of people out there who squinch at the idea of any speculation about the Custers' private lives.

4 with *up, down, over, in:* To hunch, huddle, squeeze one's way; hence ppl adjs *squinch(ed) up, squenched in* huddled up, squeezed. **scattered, but esp Sth, S Midl** See Map

1869 Stephens *Wives & Widows* 211 **NEng,** I've been two hull hours squinched up in that big rosewood book-case with the green silk lining. **1890** *Harper's New Mth. Mag.* 82.115 **VA** [Black], I jes stoop down, an' peep on der de bed, an' sho 'nough, dyah wuz P'laski squinch up under dyah. **1937** (1977) Hurston *Their Eyes* 224 **FL** [Black], She ran out in the back somewhere and got her husband to put a stop to things. He came in, took a look and squinched down into a chair in an off corner and didn't open his mouth. **1937** Thornburgh *Gt. Smoky Mts.* 14, Here's a little tree to *squinch up by* to shelter from a shower. **1941** O'Donnell *Great Big Doorstep* 73 **sLA,** A crawling rhinostrich always squinching through the canes like Evvie Crochet on nothing to eat. **1942** [see **squinched up 1**]. **1965–70** *DARE* (Qu. Y32, *To squeeze yourself into a small space: "If you're going to fit in there you'll have to _____."*) 19 Infs, **chiefly Sth, S Midl,** Squinch up; 10 Infs, **esp Sth, West,** Squinch; 9 Infs, **Atlantic, Gt Lakes,** Squinch down; **SC40,** Squinch in; (Qu. Y52, *To move over—for example on a long bench: ". . . Can you _____ [a little]?"*) Inf **PA167,** Squinch over. **1990** in 2003 *DARE* File—Internet, [Transcript of an interview with Sarah McClendon:] I had to squinch down . . to try to even see the desk where [Franklin Delano] Roosevelt was. **1996** Wells *Divine Secrets* 66 **LA,** She's squenched in between Caro and me with her head at my end. **2001** in 2003 *DARE* File—Internet **TX,** I decide that Burger King seems

more appealing than squinching onto the crowded bus. *Ibid* **cTX,** There is no room in this bedroom but I will squench in somehow. **2003** *Ibid* **cOH,** A dad and pre-pubescent son arrived during the readings . . , and the usher made me squinch in.

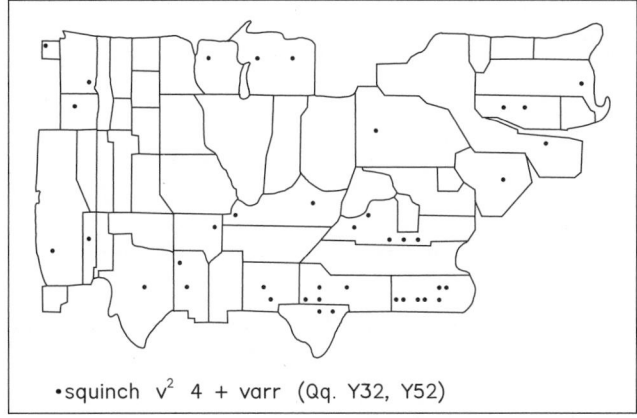

•squinch v² 4 + varr (Qq. Y32, Y52)

5 also with *up:* To squeeze, crush (something).

1890 *Newark Daily Advocate* (OH) 17 Dec [3]/8 (newspaper-archive.com), How do you stone them [=raisins] anyhow? . . Why, you just squinch 'em up like this. **1901** *DN* 2.148 **cNY,** *Squinch. . .* Pinch. Northern Seneca Co., N.Y. **1968** *DARE* (Qu. KK21, *When something hollow is crushed by a heavy weight, or by a fall: "They ran the wagon over the coffee pot and _____."*) Inf **VA15,** Squinched it. **2003** *DARE* File—Internet **seVA,** I did not bother to move any of the crap on my desk, I just squinched it a little closer together. *Ibid* **MI,** I squinched up jackets and snow pants and tried not to think of my pillows, blissfully warm and only a short distance away.

squinch adj

1 Usu of the eyes: narrowed, contracted; transf: having the elongated shape typical of people of Asian ancestry; rarely, of the face: contorted—usu in adj combs *squinch-eye(d)* (pronc-sp *squanch-eyed*), n combs *squinch-eye(s).* **chiefly S Atl, Gulf States, TX** See Map Cf **squinch v² 1, 2, squinchy 2, squint-eye 2**

1884 Harris *Mingo* 177 **GA,** Mrs. Hendrick's brother . . was on his way home from China, where he had been engaged in converting (to use a neighborhood phrase) the 'squinch-eyed heathen.' **1907** White *AZ Nights* 221, I was sittin' on the beach . . , when a little squinch-eye round-face with big bow spectacles came up and plumped down beside me. **1921** *DN* 5.117 **eKY,** *Squinch-eyed,* squint-eyed. **1950** [see **squinch v² 1**]. **1954** [see **squinch v² 1**]. **1965–70** *DARE* (Qu. X21b, *If the eyes are very sharp or piercing*) 17 Infs, **esp S Atl, Gulf States, TX,** Squinch-eyed; **SC34, VA2,** Squinch-eyes; **SC11,** Squinch-eye; (Qu. X25, *To close your eyes part way—for example, when looking at the sun*) Inf **LA18,** Look squinch-eyed; **FL22,** Squinch-eye; **GA72, LA6, TX103,** Squinch-eyed; (Qu. HH28, *Names and nicknames . . for people of foreign background: Japanese*) Inf **TX26,** Squinch-eyes. **1986** Pederson *LAGS Concordance* (Orientals) 1 inf, **ceTX,** Squinch eye—Oriental; in general. **2002** *Las Vegas Mercury* (NV) 8 Aug (Internet), But don't get all squinch-faced over that.

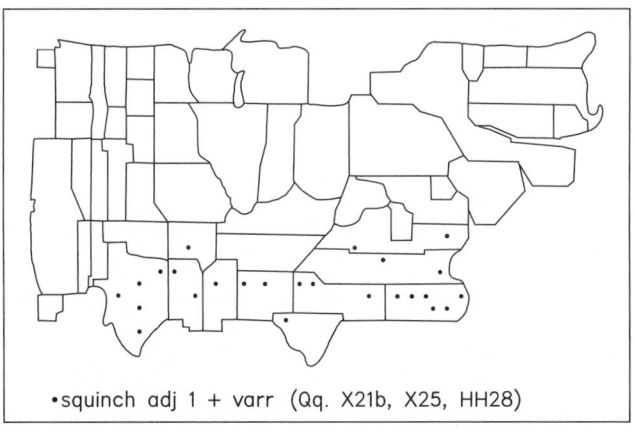

•squinch adj 1 + varr (Qq. X21b, X25, HH28)

2 in comb *squinch-eyed:* Cross-eyed.

1966–67 *DARE* (Qu. X26a, *If a person's eyes look in different directions, looking inward, he's _____*) Infs **LA**14, **NC**1, Squinch-eyed.

squinch n   Also *squinch-apple* [*EDD* 1837 → "A dial. form of 'quince'"]

=quince.

1832 *Godey's Lady's Book* 5.174 **sePA,** Drusa appeared at the door, and called out, "Miss Albinar, the presarved squinches are all working." **1856** *IL State Chron.* (Decatur) 27 Nov 1/6 **Mid Atl,** An if so be you dem wants any plums, or pears, or squinches, for serves, we'd 'sply you in like manner. **1863** *Continental Mth.* 4.635 **NEast,** I . . tried what Mr. Bull denominated 'presarved squinches'—which might have passed for fragments of granite, and were a trifle sour in addition. **1874** *Overland Mth.* 12.169, Where will he get his Sunday dinner of fried chickens, squab pie, squinch jelly, and butter-biscuit now? **1899** (1912) Green *VA Folk-Speech* 412, *Squinch.* . . A variant of *quince.* **1903** *DN* 2.326 **seMO,** *Quince-apple.* . . Quince. Sometimes 'squinch-apple.' **1912** *DN* 3.591 **wIN,** *Squinch.* . . The quince. Much used by children. **1953** *AmSp* 28.255 **csPA,** *Squinch.* . . A folk-speech variant of *quince.*

squinch down   See **squinch** v² 4

squinched up ppl adj phr

1 Shrunken, shriveled up, contracted.   **esp Sth**   Cf **squinch** v² 1, **squinch** adj 1

1869 *Harper's New Mth. Mag.* 38.218, You had such a squinched-up look when you first came home from the Seminary, I almost despaired of you. **1895** *Scribner's Mag.* 18.752, "How about the dilation of her pupils?" "There isn't none," said Uncle Beamish, "they are rather squinched up if anything." **1899** (1912) Green *VA Folk-Speech* 413, *Squinched up.* . . To have a squinched-up look, to be thin and shrivelled; a lean and shrunken look. **1927** Kennedy *Gritny* 52 **sLA** [Black], Play on yo' comb till you make dese squinched-up niggers 'maginashun change. **1942** McAtee *Dial. Grant Co. IN* 61 (as of 1890s), *Squinched up* (usually preceded by "all") . . descriptive of a lean or shrunken look, also of the posture induced by chilliness. **1969** Lyons *My Florida* 203, They were wind bitten and toil gnarled, with pale eyes squinched up from too much sun and neck skin as wrinkled as a turkey gobbler's. **1976** Ryland *Richmond Co. VA* 377, *Squinched up*—shrivelled or pursed up. **1986** Pederson *LAGS Concordance (Shrivel)* 1 inf, **neLA,** All squinched up. **2003** *Pittsburgh Post–Gaz.* (PA) 27 Dec sec A 15 (Internet), But he had smiley kind of squinched-up eyes, looked like someone who laughed a lot.

2   See **squinch** v² 4.

squinch-eye n, adj   See **squinch** adj 1

squinch-eyed   See **squinch** adj 1, 2

squinch in   See **squinch** v² 4

squinching   See **squinch** v² 2

squinching owl   See **squinch owl**

squinchity adj

=squinchy 2.

1930 Stoney–Shelby *Black Genesis* 126 **seSC,** Br' Rabbit look 'bout de bes' he kin wid he little eye—he eye been real little an' squinchity den.

squinch over   See **squinch** v² 4

squinch owl n   Also *quinch owl, squinching ~, squink(y) ~, squint ~, swinch ~, swink ~*   **chiefly Sth, S Midl**   See Map Cf **scrinch owl**

A **screech owl** (here: *Otus asio*); also fig.

1845 Thompson *Pineville* 115 **GA,** He ought to go to the penitentiary this very minit—the old squinch owl—so he ought. **1880** (1881) Harris *Uncle Remus Songs* 89 **GA** [Black], Word went roun' dat ole man Squinch Owl done kotch nudder watzizname. **1892** *DN* 1.232 **KY,** *Squinch-owl.* Sometimes for *screech-owl.* **1893** Shands *MS Speech* 59, *Squinch-owl.* . . Negro for *screech-owl.* **1905** *DN* 3.95 **nwAR,** *Squinch-owl.* . . Screech-owl. The former is in general use. **1909** *DN* 3.375 **eAL, wGA,** *Squinch-owl.* **1917** *DN* 4.417 **wNC,** *Squinch-owl.* **1922** *DN* 5.184 **GA,** *Squinch-owl.* **1927** *DN* 5.477 **Ozarks,** *Squinch owl.* **1929** (1954) Faulkner *Sound & Fury* 45 **MS** [Black], Here, les finish drinking this here sassprilluh. It make me feel just like a squinch owl inside. *Ibid,* I heard a squinch owl that night. **1935** Hurston *Mules & Men* 17 **FL** [Black], From the earliest rocking of my cradle, I had

known . . what the Squinch Owl says from the house top. **1939** *LANE* Map 230 *(Screech owl)* 1 inf, **cCT,** Squinch owl. **c1940** *LAMSAS Materials,* 33 infs, **esp Mid Atl,** Squinch owl; 1 inf, Squint owl. **1955** *PADS* 23.47 **e,cSC, eNC, seGA,** Squinch owl, skrinch owl—'screech owl'. **1965–70** *DARE* (Qu. Q1, . . *Kind of owl that makes a shrill, trembling cry*) Infs **FL**51, **KY**82, **LA**20, **MO**38, **SC**19, **TX**26, Squinch owl; **TN**11, Squinch owl—Negro speech; **SC**69, Quinch owl; (Qu. Q2, . . *Kinds of owls*) Infs **TN**53, **VA**70, Squinch owl. [7 of 10 Infs old, 6 Black] **1974** Fink *Mountain Speech* 24 **wNC, eTN,** Squinch owl . . screech owl. **1986** Pederson *LAGS Concordance* **Gulf Region** *(Screech owl)* 41 Infs, Squinch owl(s); 2 infs, Squinching owls; 1 inf, Squink owl; 1 inf, Squinky owl; 1 inf, Squint owl; 1 inf, Swinch owl; 1 inf, Swink owl—small, old term, prophesies death. **2006** *DARE* File—Internet **NC,** I hear the high-pitched, wavery voice of a little screech owl—"squinch" owl, an acquaintance used to call it.

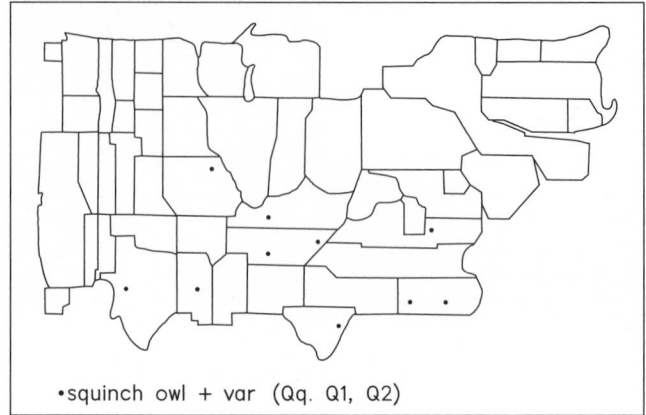

•squinch owl + var (Qq. Q1, Q2)

squinch up   See **squinch** v² 1, 4, 5

squinchy adj

1 Tiny, undersized; wizened.

1898 (1899) Bates *Puritans* 132 **MA,** "I see Dr. Strong . . and the other doctors was all after him; even to that little squinchy electrical image that's round the corner on Front Street." . . "She means the eclectic physician." **1906** *Harper's Mth. Mag.* 113.887, Land! Look at all those tiny squinchy little seams! **1930** *Folk-Say* 4.253 **Sth** [Black], John Bias was a squinchy runt,/ Four foot two. **1952** *Argosy* (NY) June 100, They came back with a drove of a dozen, led by a squinchy and fretful little black sow. **1968** *DARE* (Qu. LL2, . . *Too small to be worth much:* "*I don't want that little _____ potato.*") Inf **NC**82, Squinchy. **1989** Gurganus *Oldest Confederate Widow* 441 **Sth,** One was walking a squinchy little dog no bigger than a dinner roll. **2003** *Houston Chron.* (TX) 13 Feb (Internet), A tomato-sauced shellfish stew . . was less than thrilling and stocked with some squinchy little shrimp of the sort you see in cheap Chinese restaurants. **2003** *DARE* File **csWI,** *Squinchy*—I think this has always been part of my vocabulary, meaning "small and insignificant," with no implications of "shriveled" or the like. Usually, I think, linked with *little.*

2 Of the eyes or face: narrowed, contracted; puckery.

1898 (1899) Bates *Puritans* 272 **MA,** Did n't she send for old Burnham, with the squinchy eyes and the wife that had a wart on her nose, and have it all writ over. **1918** *Oakland Tribune* (CA) [9 June 2]/5 (newspaperarchive.com), She had a sharp, squinchy face and a tart method of response. **1952** *Amer. Mercury* Apr 55 **KY,** We weren't a-fightin' no dang squinchy-eyed heathen set. **1967** *DARE* (Qu. X21b, *If the eyes are very sharp or piercing*) Inf **AR**47, Squinchy-eyed. **1998** *Hollywood Reporter* 21 May 18, In close ups, Lovett does delightful tiny takes with only the squinchy muscles around his eyes. **2000** *Baltimore City Paper Online* (MD) 12–18 July (Internet), She reminds me of one of the *Facts of Life* girls, the one who was kind of chunky and squinchy-eyed but got treated like a bombshell because she was tall and blond. **2002** *DARE* File—Internet **NYC,** He's just a guy . . who's way past his prime and makes squinchy faces when he sings.

‡squinge n¹   [Cf *EDD squinge-grub* "A small, shrivelled pippin"]   Cf **squinchy** 1

1967 *DARE* (Qu. LL1, *Something very small*) Inf **TX**10, Squinge.

squinge n²   [Cf *EDD squinges* sb. pl. 2 "Shooting pains"]   Cf **scrinch** 1, **squinch** v² 3

A twinge, a feeling of unease.

1923 *Bee* (Danville VA) 10 Apr 3/1, Would you laugh at such a foolish superstition or would you begin to get little mental squinges that maybe there might be something in this curse-of-the Pharaohs stuff after all? **1948** Hurston *Seraph* 105 **wFL,** It might give Jim a chance to comment on the state of things, and the very thought of that put a squinge in her. **2002** in 2006 *DARE* File—Internet **KS,** The bright gaudiness of the lab-created ruby and emerald also give me squinges.

squink v [Pronc var of *squint* perh infl by *wink;* cf Intro "Language Changes" IV.4, *EDD swink*]

To narrow (the eyes); to squint; hence ppl adjs *squinked (up).*

1970 *DARE* (Qu. X25, *To close your eyes part way—for example, when looking at the sun*) Inf **TX86,** Squink [skwɪŋk]. **2004** in 2008 *DARE* File—Internet **NJ,** They both have kind of squinked up eyes. **2006** *Ibid* **swCA,** That's skeptical with one eyebrow raised and both eyes squinked in suspicion. *Ibid* **nAZ,** I wear a flip up black eye cover. . . Easier on the eyes as opposed to squinking one shut. **2007** *Ibid* **MO,** [Caption:] Me squinking at the fishermen. **2008** *Ibid* **nwGA,** You are always on the computer and you could be squinking your eyes to see.

squink(y) owl See **squinch owl**

squinny v, n[1] [*OED2 squinny* v. 2 a1825 →; *squinny* sb.[2] 1881 →; *squinny-eyed* a1825 →]

Also with *up:* To narrow or contract (the eyes or face); a squint, narrow glance; hence ppl adj (phr) *squinnied (up);* adj *squinny-eyed.*

1839 *W. Messenger* 7.136, The horses started; the crowd shouted; . . near-sighted gentlemen squinnied up their eyes. **1868** *Overland Mth.* 1.381 **NV,** Harry, he declared, "favored his father mightily; . . his eyes had the same queer kind of a squinny that Hank's did." **1869** Whitney *Hitherto* 465 **NEng,** I alwers knew it never'd do, after I put them two names together in my own mind, and took just one single squinny at 'em. **1870** Dodge *Battle of Books* 89, Now do squinny up your eyes and try to see it, there's a dear. **1893** Richards *When I Was* 142 **ceMA,** Fichte had a sneezing sort of face, with the nose all "squinnied up," as we used to say. **1956** Moody *Home Ranch* 119 **CO** (as of 1911), Hazel sat there with her eyes squinnied up. *Ibid* 140, Her eyes were squinnied half shut. **1995** White *Sleeping* 105 **VT,** Other children are getting their educations in . . modern school buildings . . with squinny-eyed chinks of windows.

squinny n[2] **IA** Cf **grinnie 1, 2**

A **ground squirrel b** (here: *Spermophilus* spp).

1973 Allen *LAUM* 1.323 **IA** (as of c1950), Ground squirrel. . . squinny [4 infs, 3 Des Moines]. **2003** *DARE* File **IA,** My girlfriend is from Iowa and she and her parents use "squinny" in just this way [=for a ground squirrel]. *Ibid* (as of c1990), I do use the word 'squinny', but it's for a different animal other than a squirrel. It's more gopher-like, has stripes, and is much smaller than a squirrel, not as furry and without a fluffy tail. I see them a lot on the golf course; they run around the ground and dig holes to escape into. *Ibid* **IA,** My father in law also uses the word [=*squinny*] in the same way. He said it's smaller than a squirrel. He grew up in Miami, Florida, but insists he never heard it used until he got to Des Moines. **2003** *DARE* File—Internet **cIA,** I probably spent about as much time there as the residents playing ball . . and catching squinnies etc.

squinny-eyed, squinny up See **squinny** v, n[1]

squint-eye n

1 also *old squint-eye;* Among loggers: see quot 1931.

1931 *AmSp* 7.47 **Sth, SW** [Lumberjack lingo], "Old Hard Eye" or "Old Squint Eye," the filer, so named because he closes one eye while filing the fine edge to the saw-teeth, is popular with all because at his work he has time to invent good stories for later telling. He is the clearing house for "woods gossip." **1958** McCulloch *Woods Words* 179 **Pacific NW,** Squinteye—A saw filer.

2 A person of Asian descent; see quots. *usu derog* Cf **squinch** adj **1**

1942 *Edwardsville Intelligencer* (IL) 21 Jan 4/1, The Japs will undoubtedly lose many more vessels of all types. The little "squint-eye" will learn that the Americans are much better marksmen. **1967–69** *DARE* (Qu. HH28, *Names and nicknames . . for people of foreign background*) Inf **GA72,** Squint-eyes—Chinese, Japanese; **IL7,** Squint-eyes—Japanese; **PA230,** Squint-eyes—Chinese. **1986** Pederson *LAGS Concordance* (Orientals) 1 inf, **cTN,** Squint eyes. **2004** in 2006 *DARE*

File—Internet **TX,** Try out TokyoHana over on Greenville if you like the squint eye food.

3 =**wink.**

1966 *Good Old Days* 2.10.7 **seWI,** "Squint Eye" or "Winkum" was a good game to play at young people's meetings or parties. The girls would sit on chairs placed in a circle, with a boy [s]tanding behind each chair. One chair was vacant and the boy standing behind this chair would wink at one of the girls, who would attempt to get to his chair. The boy behind her chair would try to keep her from leaving.

squint owl See **squinch owl**

squiogling See **skew- g**

squire n Usu |skwaɪr|; also |skwɑ(r), skwɑr|; for addit varr see quots Pronc-sp *square*

A Forms.

1844 *Lowell Offering* 4.52 **MA,** When you get back . . , the *square* will make you suffer for it. **1871** Eggleston *Hoosier Schoolmaster* 41 **sIN,** Wot is all this ere spoutin' about the Square fer? **1906** *DN* 3.158 **nwAR,** 'Squire. . . Esquire. Sometimes pronounced [skwæə] and [skwɑ]. **1907** *DN* 3.200 **seNH,** Square. . . Esquire. "Square Ordway was the leading man in West Hampstead." Thus pronounced. **1909** *DN* 3.416 **nME,** Square. . . Esquire. **1910** *DN* 3.449 **cwNY,** Square. . . Esquire. "How's Square Brown to-day?" **1914** *DN* 4.113 **cKS,** Square. . . Squire. Rare. **1915** *DN* 4.191 **swVA,** Square (sometimes [skwɑr]). Felicitous variant of *esquire,* as a title given to a justice of the peace. "Square Moore tried the case." **1939** [see **B1** below]. **1940** in 1944 *ADD* **AR,** Square. . . [skwɒr]. **1976** Garber *Mountain-ese* 87 **sAppalachians,** Square . . squire, magistrate—We went to the square to git a warrant issued fer them crooks.

B Senses.

1 A magistrate, lawyer, judge, or other local official; a prominent person—freq used as a title or term of address for a person of authority. *occas joc*

1802 *Adams Centinel* (Gettysburg PA) [6 Jan 6]/3 (newspaperarchive.com), To the late Brigade-Inspector we would present the muzzle, being the mouth or organ of utterance; the fractured scull to 'Squire H_____, as an emblem of his justice. **1811** (1817) Bradbury *Travels* 320 **Ohio Valley,** He is not in the least danger of receiving a rude or an uncivil answer, even if he should address himself to a *squire,* (so justices are called.) **1828** (1970) Webster *Amer. Dict.,* Square. . . In the *United States,* the title of magistrates and lawyers. In New-England, it is particularly given to justices of the peace and judges. **1851** Hooper *Widow Rugby's Husband* 67 **AL,** "No, you don't, 'squire," he replied. **1859** Taliaferro *Fisher's R.* 45 **nwNC** (as of 1820s), He was highly respected by all who knew him, . . and bore two titles which were quite honorable then and there. . . He was always addressed very respectfully as "'Squire Charles Taliaferro" and "Cap'en Taliaferro." **1915** [see **A** above]. **1927** *DN* 5.477 **Ozarks,** Square. . . This word is in very common use, meaning justice of the peace. "Th' squire has went a-fishin', but he'll git back afore night." **1938** (1964) Korson *Minstrels Mine Patch* 319 **nePA,** Squire: An unofficial title given Justices of the Peace in townships, and aldermen in boroughs and cities, who act as magistrates in Pennsylvania's antiquated petty court system. **1939** Hall *Coll.* **wNC, eTN,** Squire. . . Justice of the peace. . . Politics has gone too far. . . We've got two squires [skwɑrz] to every district; one's a plenty. **1966–68** *DARE* (Qu. V10a, *. . Joking names . . for a sheriff*) Inf **DC7,** Squire; (Qu. V10c, *. . A constable*) Inf **PA94,** Squire; (Qu. Z1, *. . 'Father'*) Inf **MI81,** Squire; (Qu. HH44, *Joking . . names for lawyers*) Inf **ME13,** Squire. **1967** Fetterman *Stinking Creek* 89 **seKY,** The county did come and rake a little dirt over the rocks in the road. . . Hobert Mills was only one ever did nothin' when he was a squire. He brought in a bulldozer. **1968** McPhee *Pine Barrens* 47 **cNJ,** For lawful weddings, people had to travel beyond the woods, to a place like Mt. Holly. Many went to native "squires," who performed weddings for a fee of one dollar. **1976** [see **A** above]. **1986** Pederson *LAGS Concordance,* 1 inf, **neTN,** Squire—member of quarterly county court; 1 inf, **nwTN,** Squire—local designation of authority; 1 inf, **ceTN,** A good squire— a political office; 1 inf, **swTN,** Squires—on county court in Shelby County.

2 See quot. Cf **gentleman** n **B2**

1967 *DARE* (Qu. K23, *Words used by women or in mixed company for a bull*) Inf **MN2,** Squire.

squirl See **squirrel** n

squirmish adj   [Var of *squeamish* infl by *squirm*]   Cf **squamish**

1857 Denslow *Owned* 287, But some of the spectators [at a slave auction] were merciful, and cried out—"Set her up—we're ready to bid—never mind the speech if the gal's squirmish!"   **1881** *Century Illustr. Mag.* 23.140 **NEng,** There's always got to be some give to a jury, just as in everything else, and you ought to lay right down on the rest of us. It isn't as if we were at all squirmish.   **1921** Thorp *Songs Cowboys* 85 **TX,** When we reached the Reservation how squirmish we did feel.   **1966–68** *DARE* (Qu. BB16b, *If something a person ate didn't agree with him, he might just feel a bit* _____) Infs **ME**15, **MO**1, **VT**8, Squirmish.   **2001** in 2003 *DARE* File—Internet **cwCA,** What makes you squirmish in a relationship? is there anything that in a relationship, once something happens[?] you really start to get squeamish? . . i get squirmish when I feel that they aren't really responding to me.   **2003** *Ibid* **GA,** Warning—this post is not for the squirmish.

squirrel n   Usu |'skwɜ˞(ə)l|; also |'skwɛɚ(ə)l, 'skwɪɚ(ə)l|; less freq |'skwɔɚ(ə)l|; for addit varr see quots   Pronc-spp *squeeril, squeerrel, squer'l, squerrel, squerril, squirl, squrl*

A Forms.

1825 Neal *Brother Jonathan* 2.7 **NEng,** He clumb, like a squirl—and jumped like a cattermount.   [**1831** see **squirreling 1.**]   **1843** (1916) Hall *New Purchase* 412 **IN,** Here, I've brung a dozen squirl for your ole-woman.   **1853** Simms *Sword & Distaff* 116 **SC** [Black], So long as dere's . . squerril and rabbit in de wood . . Tom will always hab 'nough somet'ing to cook!   **1883** *Century Illustr. Mag.* 26.780 **GA** [Black], Dar sets a squer'l in dat tree.   **a1883** (1911) Bagby *VA Gentleman* 264, I'd a had you some squrls.   **1886** Jewett *White Heron* 8 **ME,** I never wanted for pa'tridges or gray squer'ls.   **1890** Howells *Boy's Town* 47 **Sth,** Tell ye 'twa'n't a squeerrel; 'twas a maouse.   **1891** *Century Illustr. Mag.* 41.799 **Sth** [Black], De squeeril an' de pattridge bofe, dey laughs at my gun.   **1893** Shands *MS Speech* 57, Skwel [skwɛl]. Negro pronunciation of *squirrel*. I have known one or two very well educated immigrants from Virginia who used exactly this pronunciation.   **1903** *DN* 2.290 **Cape Cod MA** (as of a1857), You needn't chuck chuck (=tut tut) like a squerrel, Josey.   **1909** *DN* 3.375 **eAL, wGA,** Squirrel. . . Pronounced [skwɜ˞l].   **1915** *DN* 4.191 **swVA,** Squirrel [skwɜ˞l].   **1936** *AmSp* 11.161 **eTX,** Squirrel . . ['skwɜ˞l].   **1940** Faulkner *Hamlet* 267 **MS,** Borrowing Mr Snopes' gun last fall to go squirl hunting.   **1941** *AmSp* 16.7 **eTX** [Black], Squirrel . . [skwʌ:l], [skwʌɪᵛl].   **1961** Kurath–McDavid *Pronc. Engl.* 127, Squirrel rather generally appears as disyllabic /skwɜəl ~ skwɜrəl ~ skwʌrəl/, exhibiting the same three regional types as *furrow*; but monosyllabic /skwɜl/, riming with the regional variants of *girl* /gɜl/, is not uncommon. Only scattered instances of /skwɛrəl ~ skwɛrɪl/ and /skwɪrəl ~ skwɪrɪl/ survive, notably in Eastern New England, in the Middle Neck of Virginia, and in the Low Country of South Carolina. All American variants of *squirrel* have their counterparts in the folk speech of England.   [*Ibid* 126, *Furrow.* . . (1) Disyllabic [fɜ˞ə ~ fɜɚə]. . . phonemically . . /fɜə/. . . is current throughout the Midland except Metropolitan New York and vicinity, in Upstate New York and western New England, on the Delmarva Peninsula, and along the coast of North Carolina. . . (2) Disyllabic [fɜrə . . fərə]. . . predominate in eastern New England and in the South (except for Delmarva and the coast of North Carolina), and have some currency in the German settlements of eastern Pennsylvania and in the southern part of the South Midland. . . (3) Disyllabic [fʌrə . .]. . . is in regular use in Metropolitan New York and vicinity and occurs by the side of /fɜrə/ in eastern New England and the South.]   **1965–70** *DARE* (Qu. P27) 386 Infs, **widespread,** [Proncs of the type [skwɜ˞(ə)l]]; 29 Infs, **scattered,** [Proncs of the type [skwɪr(ə)l]]; 27 Infs, **chiefly Atl,** [Proncs of the types [skʌl, skɜ˞(ə)l, skɜ(ə)l, skɪrəl]]; 24 Infs, **scattered,** [Proncs of the type [skwɜ(ə)l]]; 17 Infs, **scattered,** [Proncs of the type [skwʌr(ə)l]]; **IL**97, **IN**68, 69, **PA**132, 166, [Proncs of the type [skwɔrl]].   **1967** *DARE* FW Addit **seAR,** Squirrel [skwɔl].

B Senses.

1 in adj phr *with squirrel:* Pregnant.   Cf *DS* AA28

1933 *AmSp* 8.1.53 **Ozarks,** With squirrel. . . Pregnant.

2 See **squirrel whiskey.**

squirrel v, hence vbl n *squirreling*

1 also with *up:* to climb nimbly; to **shinny.** esp **GA**

1929 *Bookman* 69.527 [Railroad lingo], *Squirrel a car:* Climbing to the top of a train to set hand brakes.   **1940** Cottrell *Railroader* 137, *Squirrel*—To climb nimbly up the side of a car is to "squirrel up."   **1942** *Farm Jrl. & Farmer's Wife* Apr 57 **MT,** I squirreled up the corral fence and from there tossed a half hitch over his nose.   **1945** Hubbard *Rail-*

road *Ave.* 362, *Squirreling*—Climbing a car.   **1952** *Panama City News–Herald* (FL) 22 Apr 4/1, There must be people who never. . . squirreled up a vine-hung sweet gum tree to pluck the tempting muscadine.   **1966–70** *DARE* (Qu. EE36, *To climb the trunk of a tree by holding on with your legs while you pull yourself up with your hands*) Infs **GA**3, 19, Squirrel up; **GA**1, 33, Squirreling; **GA**9, **KY**66, Squirrel up; [**KY**89, Squirrel climbing].   **1997** Jones *Mark Twain* 88 **wNE,** While his beam swung wildly around the yard, I squirreled up my favorite linden tree.   **2003** *DARE* File—Internet **Sth,** Bartolomew took a fleet step, leapt, and squirreled up the great tree trunk.

2 with *up:* To make a muddle of; hence ppl adj phr *squirrel(l)ed up* muddled, confused.

1918 *Eve. State Jrl.* (Lincoln NE) 10 Sept 8/5, This fall's harvest is certainly going to look all squirrelled up by the time that the stylish farmerettes are thru with it.   **1967–68** *DARE* (Qu. GG2, . . 'Confused, mixed up': "So many things were going on at the same time that he got completely _____.") Inf **NY**10, Squirreled up; (Qu. JJ42, *To make an error in judgment and get something quite wrong: "He usually handles things well, but this time he certainly* _____.") Inf **PA**74, Squirreled it up.   **1997** in 2003 *DARE* File—Internet **cwMA,** His phones have been squirreled up for weeks, so don't get discouraged if you get the FAX sound when you dial his number.   **1999** *Ibid* **swCA,** It looks like our [software] installation got squirreled up but we are not sure what's wrong.   **2004** in 2006 *Ibid* **MN,** The car is an all numbers matching Red X55 4speed car that's never seen salt. Right now it's squirreled up a little from the previous owner.

squirrel brier n
=greenbrier.

1899 *Outlook* 61.539, I come to a ravine on the leeward side of a hill, where a grove of cedars is overgrown and tied together with squirrel-brier.   **1910** Graves *Flowering Plants* 125 **CT,** Smilax rotundifolia. . . Horse, Cat, Bull or Squirrel Brier. *Ibid,* Smilax glauca. . . Saw, Cat or Squirrel Brier.   **1924** *Youth's Companion* 98.647, The ridge proved to be a huge entanglement of barbed squirrel briers and similar thorny creepers.   **1977** *Salina Jrl.* (KS) 6 May 20/2, On 3 nature trails . . can be seen the cottonwood, the black walnut, squirrel briar, mulberry.

squirrel can n

1933 *AmSp* 8.1.27 **nwTX** [Ranch diction], Squirrel can. A large can holding five to ten gallons used for a general cooking utensil when the boys were fed from the *chuck wagon.* Some of the boys declare that this vessel was never emptied and washed during a trip, and that the cook merely added to the contents from day to day.

squirrel corn n   Also *squirrel's corn*   [From the small yellow tubers on the roots]

A bleeding heart 1: usu *Dicentra canadensis,* but also **steershead.**   For other names of the former see **colicweed 2b, girls-and-boys, Indian potato f, turkey corn, ~ pea 3a**

1843 Torrey *Flora NY* 1.46, Dicentra canadensis. *Squirrel Corn. Turkey Corn.*   **1887** *Century Illustr. Mag.* 34.325, The more northern species [=*Dicentra canadensis,* called "squirrel corn" from the small golden tubers at its root, blooms in May.   **1901** Lounsberry *S. Wild Flowers* 196, *B[icuculla] Canadensis,* squirrel corn.   **1915** (1926) Armstrong–Thornber *Western Wild Flowers* 170, *B[icuculla] uniflora.* . . is called Squirrel Corn and Steer's Head.   **1932** *Country Life* 62.67 **sAppalachians,** Close of kin is the Squirrelcorn.   **1961** Douglas *My Wilderness* 193 **MD,** Most of our spring flowers along the Potomac are more durable, such as the squirrel corn, kin to Dutchman's-breeches, that arrives with the bloodroot.   **1966–68** *DARE* (Qu. S26c, *Wildflowers that grow in woods*) Infs **IA**8, **NY**92, Squirrel corn or Dutchman's britches; (Qu. S26e, *Other wildflowers not yet mentioned;* not asked in early QRs) Inf **MA**6, Squirrel's corn . . small blossom, also called Dutchman's britches.   **1967–68** *DARE* Wildfl QR Pl.78 Inf **MI**57, Squirrel corn. . . Dutchman's britches; **NY**91, Squirrel corn.   **1975** Duncan–Foote *Wildflowers SE* 50, Squirrel-corn. . . Stems and leaves arising from a rhizome bearing yellow round pea- or corn-like structures.   **2004** *Pittsburgh Post–Gaz.* (PA) 21 Feb sec B 2 (Internet), Squirrel corn (Dicentra canadensis), a close relative of Dutchman's-breeches, has similar foliage.

squirrel cups n   Also *squirrel cup*   esp **NEast**
=hepatica.

1848 in 1850 Cooper *Rural Hours* 48 **NY,** Perhaps it is this position [at the foot of trees], which, added to their downy, furred leaves and stems, has given them the name of squirrel-cups.   **1859** *Harper's New Mth. Mag.* 19.200 **NEng,** Under the next tree, right at its foot, basking in a gleam of sunshine, stood a tiny cluster of blue squirrel-cups—"liverworts," as the country people call them. **1893** *Jrl. Amer. Folkl.* 6.136 **NY, VT,** *Hepatica triloba* [=*H. nobilis* var *acuta*], squirrel cups. N.Y.; Ferrisburgh, Vt. **1893** *Niagara Book* 179 **wNY,** Our two Liverworts or Squirrel-cups (*Hepatica acutiloba* [=*H. nobilis* var *acuta*] and *H. triloba* [=*H.n.* var *obtusa*]), scarcely distinguishable from each other except by the leaf. **1896** Robinson *In New Engl. Fields* 10, The flat-pressed purple lobes of squirrelcup with a downy heart of buds full of the promise of spring. **1922** (1926) Cady *Rhymes VT* 132, About six weeks from squirrel cup,/ Along in May, when things warm up,/ It's time to plant your "Early Rose" [potatoes]. **1959** Carleton *Index Herb. Plants* 111, *Squirrel cups:* Hepatica triloba.

squirrel ear n   Also *squirrel's ear*

A **rattlesnake plantain 1** (here: *Goodyera repens*).

   [**1823** Hunter *Manners & Customs* 393, Se-in-ja-shu.—*A little squirrel's ear. White plantain.*—This is a small ever-green plant. . . The Indians have great confidence in it for the cure of coughs, colds, and fevers.] **1876** Hobbs *Bot. Hdbk.* 112, Squirrel ear, White plantain, Goodyera repens. **1910** Graves *Flowering Plants* 134 **CT,** *Epipactis repens* [= *Goodyera r.*] . . Lesser Rattlesnake Plantain. Squirrel-ear. **1924** *Amer. Botanist* 30.151, *Epipactis repens* is the "lesser rattlesnake plantain," "white plantain" and "squirrel's ear," all of which are suggested by the leaves. **1950** Correll *Native Orchids* 238, *Goodyera repens* var *ophioides*. . . Common names: Net-leaf, Squirrel-ear [etc].

squirreled up   See **squirrel** v 2

squirrelfish n   [Because when taken from the water they make a noise like the bark of a squirrel]

1 A **grunt 1,** usu *Haemulon plumieri*.

   1787 Gesellschaft Naturforschender Freunde *Schriften* 8.167, P[erca] formosa. . . Squirralfish. **1803** Shaw *Genl. Zool.* 4.2.439, *Squirrel Sparus. Sparus sciurus*. . . Size of a common Perch: native of the American seas, where it is known by the name of the Grunt, or Squirrel-fish. **1842** DeKay *Zool. NY* 4.86, The Squirrel-fish. . . The specimen from which I drew the preceding description, was caught in the harbor of New-York in July. **1884** Goode *Fisheries U.S.* 1.398, From their habit of uttering a loud, rather melodious sound when taken from the water they [=*Diabasis* spp] have acquired the name of "Grunt" and "Pig-fish." In some localities they are also called "Squirrel-fish," in allusion to the same habit. **1946** La Monte *N. Amer. Game Fishes* 66, White Grunt. . . Names: Boca Colorado, . . Squirrelfish [etc].

2 A **sand perch 2b** (here: *Diplectrum formosum*).

   1867 Latham *Black & White* 122 **SC,** The fisherman . . ladled strange bright fish out of the well, to show me bastard snappers and squirrel-fish. **1884** Goode *Fisheries U.S.* 1.410 **SC,** The Squirrel-fish is usually to be seen in the markets of Charleston, north of which it has never been discovered. **1966–70** *DARE* (Qu. P7, *Small fish used as bait for bigger fish*) Inf **FL**13, We use squirrelfish and crabs for tarpon; (Qu. P3, *Freshwater fish that are not good to eat*) Inf **GA**91, Squirrelfish. [*DARE* Ed: These Infs may refer instead to other senses.] **2003** *DARE* File—Internet **FL,** Squirrelfish live on sand bottoms, so if you started to catch them it meant the boat had drifted off of the good grouper bottom.

3 =**pinfish 1a.**

   1884 Goode *Fisheries U.S.* 1.393 **GA,** The "Sailor's Choice" . . [is known] at Brunswick, Georgia, as the "Squirrel-fish" and "Sailor's Choice." **1935** Caine *Game Fish* 55, Salt-water Bream or Sailor's Choice. . . Squirrelfish. **2003** Marine Recreational Fisheries Statistics Surv. *Atlantic & Gulf Coast Local Fish Names* (Internet), Squirrelfish (Miscalled). . . *Lagodon rhomboides*.

squirrel grass   See **squirreltail (grass) 1**

squirrel hake n   chiefly **NEast**

A **hake 2,** usu *Urophycis chuss*.   For other names of the latter see **ling 1b, old English hake, red ~, thimble-eyed ling**

   1863 ME Scientific Surv. *Annual Rept. for 1862* 31, Phycis filamentosus, *Squirrel Hake*. **1873** in 1878 Smithsonian Inst. *Misc. Coll.* 14.2.17 **MA,** Phycis chuss. . squirrel hake. **1903** NY State Museum & Sci. Serv. *Bulletin* 60.707, *Squirrel Hake*. . . It inhabits the Atlantic coast from the Gulf of St. Lawrence to Virginia, being very common northward. **1914** *Copeia* 3.2 **NY,** Squirrel Hake, *Urophycis chuss,* . . abundant. **1933** John G. Shedd Aquarium *Guide* 66, The Squirrel Hake closely resembles the White Hake and is usually mistaken for it. **2003** *DARE* File—Internet **ME,** And when did so many squirrel hake start living on the hard bottom?

squirrel hawk n

1 also *California squirrel hawk:* A large western hawk *(Buteo regalis)* notably fond of ground squirrels and related rodents.   **esp CA**

   1858 U.S. War Dept. *Rept. Explor. Railroad* 9.34 **CA,** *Archibuteo Ferrugineus*. . . California Squirrel Hawk. . . This is one of the most handsome of the American Falconidae. **1869** *Amer. Naturalist* 3.183 **CA,** Ground Squirrels (*Spermophilus Beecheyi*) abound. . . But occasionally a Squirrel Hawk . . is seen sitting on the ground devouring one of these audacious burrowers. **1874** Coues *Birds NW* 366 **CA,** This bird is known as the "California Squirrel Hawk" in some localities. . . The name is gained from their feeding extensively, in California, upon the "ground squirrels" (*Spermophilus beecheyi*), which abound in many parts of that State. **1923** Dawson *Birds CA* 1699, As destroyers of those hated rodents *Citella beecheyi* and their allies, the Squirrel Hawks were *worth their weight in gold* to the young State of California. **1969–70** *DARE* (Qu. Q4, . . *Kinds of hawks*) Infs **CA**191, 199, Squirrel hawk; **CA**137, Squirrel hawks—big red ones. [*DARE* Ed: Some of these Infs may refer instead to **2** below.]

2 A **red-tailed hawk** or similar hawk.   **chiefly S Midl**

   1891 *Auk* 8.327 **SC,** *Buteo borealis.* Red-tailed hawk.—Tolerably common. The Duck Hawk, or 'Squirrel Hawk' as locally called, is reported to breed commonly, a pair at one time having a nest in the cliff at the Head. **a1925** in 2003 *DARE* File—Internet **MO,** The object proved to be . . a squirrel hawk with a large coachwhip snake wrapped around the neck and body of the hawk. **1934** Vines *Green Thicket* 60 **cnAL,** He had enough feathers from wild things to make a feather bed. . . He had a little old trunk nearly full of feathers and down from . . squirrel hawks. **1953** Randolph–Wilson *Down in Holler* 288 **Ozarks,** *Squirrel-hawk.* . . Any large slow-flying hawk, usually the redtail *(Buteo jamaicensis).* **c1960** *Wilson Coll.* **csKY,** Squirrel hawk. . . Any large hawk, esp. the red-tailed. **1966–69** *DARE* (Qu. Q4, . . *Kinds of hawks*) Infs **KY**17, **MO**19, **NC**44, **TN**13, **VA**1, Squirrel hawk; **GA**72, Squirrel hawk—same as redtail hawk; **KY**39, Squirrel hawk—big hawk.

squirrel-headed adj   [*OED2* 1637 →]   **esp S Midl**

Foolish, stupid.

   1892 in 2010 (acc) Lexis–Nexis Legal Research *State Case Law: MO* (Internet), Neither was it proper for the prosecuting attorney to call the defendant "a sugar-loaved, squirrel-headed Dutchman." **1905** *DN* 3.95 **nwAR,** *Squirrel-headed.* . . Narrow-minded. 'They're a squirrel-headed lot.' **1907** *Van Wert Daily Bulletin* (OH) 28 Dec 8/4 **AR,** The candidate usually referred to the newspaper men as "those squirrel headed editors." In the rural districts the description "squirrel headed" always made a hit. **1928** *Kokomo Daily Tribune* (IN) 24 Jan 10/3 **AL,** [They] roared with laughter as the Alabama senator charged "squirrel headed and cowardly pen pushers" in the press gallery had exaggerated his warning. **1956** *Sun* (Baltimore MD) 24 May sec B 1/6 **MO,** He [=former president Harry S. Truman] had been quoted as saying the Salerno and Anzio landings were unnecessary "and planned by some squirrel-headed general." **2006** *DARE* File—Internet **ceCA,** Show me a wheel in a corner and I'll glad[l]y move over and apologise for being a squirrel headed bastard.

squirreling vbl n

1 Squirrel hunting.   [Cf *OED2 squirreling* vbl. sb. "*Obs.*"]   **esp S Midl**

   1831 *Maysville* (Ky.) *Eagle* 5 July (*DAE*), Suppose we make a squirriling tour to the country today. **1843** (1916) Hall *New Purchase* 412 **IN,** Come boys, let's be off. . . Who's goin' squirrilin'. **1913** Kephart *Highlanders* 282 **sAppalachians,** Are ye fixin to go squirrelin'? **1943** Peattie *Great Smokies* 147 **wNC, eTN,** Are you a-fixin to go squirrelin'? **1968** *DARE* FW Addit **DE**2, *To go out squirreling* . . to hunt squirrels. **1986** Pederson *LAGS Concordance,* 1 inf, ceTX, (To go) squirreling (=to hunt squirrels). **2002** in 2006 *DARE* File—Internet **RI,** He was always enthusiastic about my tales of squirreling and encouraged me to push the envelope.

2   See **squirrel** v.

squirrel juice (or liquor)   See **squirrel whiskey**

squirrelled up   See **squirrel** v 2

squirrel load n   [From *squirrel load* a small charge of powder suitable for use in shooting squirrels or other small game]   Cf **buck load**

A small drink of liquor.

   1871 (1892) Johnston *Dukesborough Tales* 263 **GA,** Sperrits . . is a thing I sildom teches—that is, I don't tech it reglar; but I'll try a squirrel-load with you—jes' a moderate size squirrel-load. **1899** (1912) Green *VA Folk-Speech* 413, *Squirrel load.* . . A small drink of liquor.

squirrel nut n Cf **square nut**

Perh =**mockernut hickory.**

1968 *DARE* (Qu. I43, *What kinds of nuts grow wild around here?*) Inf **DE**4, Squirrel nuts—look like an English walnut but hard as the dickens.

squirrel poison See **squirrel whiskey**

squirrel's corn See **squirrel corn**

squirrel's ear See **squirrel ear**

squirrel's grandfather n

=**ground cone.**

1880 Rattan *Pop. CA Flora* 137, Squirrel's Grandfather (Boschniakia). **1899** *Overland Mth.* (2d ser) 33.429 **CA,** Another still more odd leafless plant is the "squirrel's grandfather," which sends up its scaly stem from deep-seated tubers till it reaches the open air, where it resembles a Norway pine cone. **1900** Lyons *Plant Names* 66, *B[oschniakia] strobilacea.* . . California. Squirrel's-grandfather.

squirrel shoes n Also *squirrels' shoes*

=**lady's slipper 1.**

1894 *Jrl. Amer. Folkl.* 7.100 **CT,** *Cypripedium acaule.* . . whip-poor-will's shoes, squirrels' shoes. **1900** Lyons *Plant Names* 129, Names applied indiscriminately to our native species [of *Cypripedium*] . . are Moccasin-flower, . . Squirrel-shoes [etc]. **1950** Correll *Native Orchids* 20, *Cypripedium acaule.* . . Common names: Pink Moccasin-flower, . . Squirrel-shoes. **2003** *DARE* File—Internet, *Cypripedium candidum*—Small White Lady's Slipper, . . Squirrel Shoes.

squirrel-shooter n Cf *DS* HH1, **squirrel turner**

1906 *DN* 3.158 **nwAR,** *Squirrel-shooter.* . . An uncouth rustic. **1985** Yeager *Yeager Autobiog.* 272 **WV,** I ran up against officers who looked down their noses at my ways and accent and pegged me as a dumb, down-home squirrel-shooter.

squirrel's jump n esp Sth Cf **frog hop**

A short distance.

1809 in 1976 Merrill *Jefferson's Nephews* 165 **VA,** He has his Ague at this time. I am within a squirrel's jump of one today for I feel very unwell. **1818** in 1830 Royall *Letters AL* 49, They won't let such an old fellow come within a squirrel's jump of 'em. **1838** *Knickerbocker* 12.506 **GA,** I've never been a squirrel's jump from it. **1856** *Harper's New Mth. Mag.* 12.570 **GA,** I've walked it, man and boy, these sixty years, and I've never been a squirrel's jump *from* it. **1891** *Scribner's Mag.* 10.317, Standing at the back of one of the fields . . and almost within a squirrel's jump of the great forest . . is an odd home worthy of imitation. **1968** *DARE* (Qu. MM6, . . *'Very close' or 'only a short distance away':* "The house is _____ the park.") Inf **IN**38, Just a squirrel's jump from; (Qu. MM24, . . *'A short distance':* "The river is just a _____ from the house.") Inf **IN**38, Squirrel's jump. **2006** *DARE* File—Internet, Hersey lives in the hired help quarters, a ramshackle building just a squirrel's jump from the [Mexican] border.

squirrels' shoes See **squirrel shoes**

squirrel tail n

1 =**blazing star 2.**

1933 Small *Manual SE Flora* 276, *Chamaelirium* [spp]. . . Blazing-stars. Devil's-bits. Squirrel-tails.

2 See quot. Cf **pigtail n 6,** *DS* JJ12

1906 *DN* 3.158 **nwAR,** *Squirrel-tail.* . . A flourish in writing. [**1998** *Washington Post* (DC) 9 Aug (Internet), He wrote in fountain pen, in elegant strokes that squirreled up a little when he was touched by despair or drink.]

squirreltail (grass) n

1 also *squirrel grass, squirreltail barley:* =**wild barley.**

1814 Bigelow *Florula Bostoniensis* 28, *Squirrel tail grass.* . . is remarkable for the length and fineness of its awns. **1844** Lapham *Geogr. Descr. WI* 84, *Hordeum jubatum,* squirrel tail grass. **1894** *Jrl. Amer. Folkl.* 7.104 **NE,** *Hordeum jubatum,* . . squirrel-tail-grass. **1912** NM Ag. Exper. Station *Bulletin* 81.153, *Hordeum jubatum* . . Squirrel-tail Grass. Sometimes incorrectly called Fox-tail. **1914** Georgia *Manual Weeds* 64, Wild Barley. . Squirrel-tail, Flicker-tail, Skunk-tail. **1937** U.S. Forest Serv. *Range Plant Hdbk.* G74, Foxtail barley, commonly known as foxtail or squirreltail barley and squirreltail grass, is a pestiferous perennial. **1941** Writers' Program *Guide CO* 306 **seCO,** In spring

and early summer, stretches of prairie land here are carpeted with squirrel-tail grass (or wild barley), porcupine grass, and several kinds of bunch and brome grasses. **1968** *DARE* FW Addit **CA**101, Squirrel grass—"when it heads up, it has seeds that get into dogs' eyes and ears—has barbs." **1986** Klinkenborg *Making Hay* 45 **MN,** The ground stays too moist for alfalfa and produces instead . . foxtail barley, also called squirreltail grass.

2 A **wild rye** (here: *Elymus elymoides*) of the western US. Also called **bristlegrass 2**

1937 U.S. Forest Serv. *Range Plant Hdbk.* G107, Bottlebrush squirreltail, sometimes called bristle grass, bushtail, and foxtail is a bright green, bristly headed, perennial bunch grass. **1950** Hitchcock–Chase *Manual Grasses* 263, *Sitanion hystrix* [=*Elymus elymoides*]. . . Squirreltail. . . Dry hills, plains, open woods, and rocky slopes, South Dakota to British Columbia, south to Missouri, Texas, California, and Mexico. **1991** in 2003 *DARE* File—Internet **CA,** Grasses included Reed Grass . . , Squirrel Tail grass *Sitanion hystrix* [etc].

squirrel turner n chiefly S Midl Cf **squirrel-shooter, turn v B3**

In squirrel hunting: one who drives squirrels from one side of a tree so that another hunter can shoot them; by ext, a yokel, rustic.

1906 *DN* 3.158 **nwAR,** *Squirrel-turner.* . . 1. A man who aids a squirrel-hunter by driving the game around the branches of a tree within range of the hunter's rifle. 2. Uncouth rustic. **1909** in 1947 Lomax *Advent. Ballad Hunter* 52 **CO,** He also said they were going to have a squirrel-turner's reunion [dance] over a cross the river next week. **1909** *Railway Carmen's Jrl.* 14.369 **TX,** This stealing . . is being done by squirrel turners who were in the bushes about a year ago. **1926** *Printer's Ink* 137.17 **TX,** There is little in common between the aggressive and successful farmer and the shiftless squirrel-turner who scratches a precarious livelihood out of a rugged field. **1945** (1999) Huie *From Omaha to Okinawa* 133 **TN,** When you're huntin' squirrels alone, the squirrel'll always try to keep the tree between you and him. So you take a 'squirrel-turner' with you—another guy who can ease around the tree and make the squirrel expose hisself to one or t'other of you. **1950** *Joplin Globe* (MO) 12 Jan sec A 7/3, The Old Squirrel Turner—that's what he often calls himself—is Senator H.R. (Ray) Williams, Cassville republican. . . A squirrel turner is a fellow who walks around the tree to get the squirrel on the side where his hunting partner can shoot. **1999** *AR Times* (Little Rock) 10 Sept (Internet), So what is your specialty. . . Is it the bootlegging or the dynamiting of fish? . . [W]e've heard you was a whiz as a squirrel turner back when they was in high demand.

squirrel up See **squirrel v 1, 2**

squirrel whiskey n Also *squirrel (juice), ~ liquor, ~ poison* chiefly Nth

Liquor, esp when illegally distilled or of poor quality.

1891 *Railway Conductor* 8.191, He slept of[f] his load of squirrel whiskey and went home forgetting a duty for which he was discharged. **1892** *Cedar Rapids Eve. Gaz.* (IA) 30 Dec 5/2, The constable loaded up on squirrel whisky and took the manacles from the prisoner. **1919** in 2002 *DARE* File—Internet **ND** [*Hansboro News* (ND) 29 Aug], Minot—A cache of 1,000 bottles of squirrel whiskey was recently unearthed. **1920** Munson *Broken Shackles* 25 **NY,** A man emerged, a man so drunk with the squirrel liquor of the place that he half-fell down the steps. **1929** *AmSp* 4.385 **KS,** Common names for whiskey—*moonshine . . shine . . squirrel.* **1935** Davis *Honey* 350 **OR,** People who lead such lives can scarcely be reproached for oiling themselves up with squirrel whisky. **1946** Peattie *Pacific Coast* 272, In Ferry's Tavern, Squirrel Whiskey was the favorite drink of Indians and whites. **1948** McDavid Coll. **cnNY,** Squirrel whiskey—low grade, cheap—bought for lumber camp. **1950** *WELS (Names for any kind of bad liquor)* 1 Inf, **nwWI,** Squirrel juice; 1 Inf, **cWI,** Squirrel liquor; 1 Inf, **csWI,** Squirrel whiskey. **1960** Criswell *Resp. to PADS 20* **Ozarks,** *Squirrel whiskey.* . . Whiskey of low grade which, I suppose, makes a man a nut. Common once. **1966–69** *DARE* (Qu. DD21a, *General words . . for any kind of liquor*) Inf **NY**220, Squirrel whiskey—makes you climb trees; (Qu. DD21b, *General words . . for bad liquor*) Infs **MI**19, **NY**75, Squirrel whiskey; **CA**36, Squirrel poison; (Qu. DD21c, *Nicknames for whiskey, especially illegally made whiskey*) Inf **MI**19, Squirrel whiskey; (Qu. DD28b, . . *Fermented drinks . . made at home*) Inf **IN**13, Squirrel whiskey—made from rye; (Qu. DD31, *Joking names for homemade hard liquor;* total Infs questioned, 75) Inf **MS**1, Squirrel liquor. **1974** Dabney *Mountain Spirits* 24 **sAppalachians,** *Squirrel likker:* This is a hill country expression. After three or four drinks of "squirrel likker," imbibers would throw down their guns and climb the trees to get their squirrels.

1986 Pederson *LAGS Concordance (Terms for cheap whiskey and for home-brewed beer or whiskey)* 1 inf, **nwGA,** Squirrel whiskey.

squirt clam n

A **soft-shell clam** (here: *Mya arenaria*).

1885 *Acad. Nat. Sci. Philadelphia Proc. for 1884* 12 **seNJ,** Certain common mollusks were conspicuously absent, as the Oyster, *Ostrea virginiana,* the Clam, *Venus mercenaria,* the Squirt-clam, *Mya arenaria,* and the Horse mussel, *Modiola plicatula.* **1887** Goode *Fisheries U.S.* 5.2.581 **NY,** *Mya arenaria.* . . In Long Island Sound and at New York it is most spoken of as the 'long clam' and 'squirt clam.' **1969** Lyons *My Florida* 21, My Florida is . . squirt clams from those few places where some are left around the inlet. **2000** *Wine Spectator* 31 Aug 33, There is basically only one soft-shell clam, but it has more nicknames than God: steamer, piss clam, maninose, nannynose, Ipswich, squirt clam and longneck, to name a few.

squirt dam n Cf *splash dam* (at **splash** n 1)

See quots.

1885 (1888) Farrar *Androscoggin Lakes* 75 **nNH,** They are called "squirt dams" from the fact that they only hold a small amount of water which is let out all at once, and this squirts or pushes the logs along. **1967** Pike *Tall Trees* 208 **VT** (as of 1908), The steepness of the valley was such that the amount of water that could be held by each of the squirt dams was limited.

squirt plum n

A **crowberry 1** (here: *Empetrum nigrum*).

1897 *Jrl. Amer. Folkl.* 10.144 **cME,** *Empetrum nigrum.* . . squirt plum, Rumford.

squirts n pl Also with *the* [Engl dial] **chiefly Sth, S Midl**

See Map Cf **runs**

Diarrhea.

1777 in 1864 *New Engl. Hist. & Geneal. Reg.* 18.31, I immediately sent off to collect all the regular surgeons . . , but the devil a bit of one was there to be found, except three mates, one of whom had the squirts; the other two I took with me. **1899** (1912) Green *VA Folk-Speech* 413, Squirts. . . Diarrhoea. **1942** McAtee *Dial. Grant Co. IN Suppl. 1* 9 (as of 1890s), Squirts . . diarrhoea. **1952** Brown *NC Folkl.* 1.594, Squirts. . . Diarrhea. **1954** *Harder Coll.* **cwTN,** Squirts. . . Diarrhea. **1960** Criswell *Resp. to PADS 20* **Ozarks,** Squirts, the. . . Dysentary [sic]. Very common once. **1965–70** *DARE* (Qu. BB19, *Joking names for looseness of the bowels*) 33 Infs, **chiefly Sth, S Midl,** Squirts. **1984** *MJLF* 10.157 **cnWI,** Squirts. Severe diarrhea in calves. **1990** Cavender *Folk Med. Lexicon* 31 **sAppalachians,** (The) *squirts*—diarrhea. **2006** *DARE* File—Internet **LA,** Otherwise . . beans and rice wouldn't give me the squirts. **2008** *Ibid* **CT,** Bodie's got the squirts again, and I'm thinking maybe because the big bag [of dog food] lasts longer, it may go bad or something.

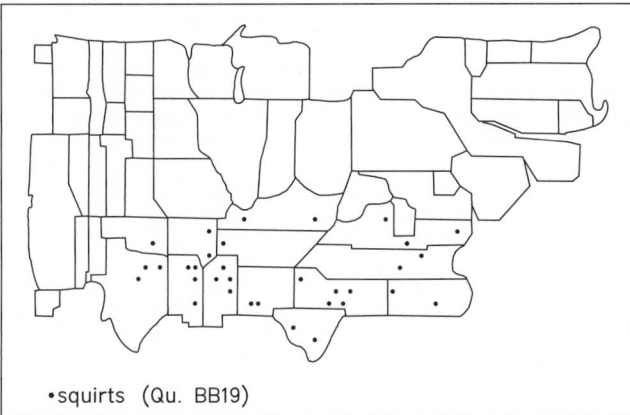

•squirts (Qu. BB19)

squit See **squeteague**

squitch v, n [*EDD squitch* sb.², v.¹ "A dial. form of 'switch.'"] **NEast**

To hit or whip (one) with a switch; a switch, a switching.

1856 Starbuck *Hampton Heights* 106 **seNY,** She had n't better let me lay hands on her either, for I sartinly shall try the vertue of a good squitch. **1901** *DN* 2.148 **cNY,** Squitch, v. tr. Switch. **1911** in 2008 *DARE* File—Internet **IA** (as of 1855), To avoid a "squitch" he sought protection in the hazel brush by road side. His truancy caused no end of

anxiety. [*DARE* Ed: Author was born in **NY** and grew up in **VT.**] **1941** *LANE* Map 398 *(Switch)* 1 inf, **nwVT,** Squitch [skwɪtʃ], small limb from a tree; *whip,* larger and more painful. **1968** *DARE* Tape **CT**10, When he came down the street with the oxen, he might be a quarter-, half-mile ahead of 'em, reaching his whip out and squitching the oxen a little.

squitch grass n [*OED2* 1785 → for *squitch*]

=**quack grass 1.**

1819 in 1944 *Thomas Jefferson's Garden Book* 583 **VA,** Lentils— squitch spots. [Editor's note: It evidently means here that lentils were planted in spots where couchgrass formerly grew.] **1826** *New Engl. Farmer* (Fessenden) 5.9/3, Remarks by the editor. . . Couch grass is known by many different names, among which are *twitch-grass, squitch-grass, quitch-grass, knot-grass,* &c. **1851** Colman *European Ag.* 2.521 **MA,** An old country . . is liable always to be much infested with weeds, and especially with the squitch grass, *(triticum repens,)* which is their chief trouble. **1887** Beal *Grasses N. Amer.* 1.167, Quack, Quitch, Quick, Twitch, Couch, Scutch, Rye, Durfee, Chandler, Witch, Quake, Squitch, or Fin's Grass.

squitch owl n Also *squich owl, switch ~* esp **VA**

A **screech owl 1** (here: *Otus asio*).

1899 (1912) Green *VA Folk-Speech* 23, A squitch-owl hollering near the house is a sign of death. **1919** Glasgow *Builders* 172 **VA** [Black], Dat's one er dem old squitch-owls out dar now. Ain't he hollerin' jes like he knows sump'n? **c1938** in 1970 Hyatt *Hoodoo* 1.136 **seMD** [Black], They say when they catch dem [Hyatt: witches] it's nothing but a bunch of rags. Dey turn into snakes and turn into a squich [Hyatt: screech] owl. . . My uncle, he was laying in bed and de witch pitched right on de foot of de bed. And when he drawed his foot up to kick her, den she left. The witch looked just lak a little squich owl. Dat was in slavery time here. **c1940** *LAMSAS Materials,* 19 infs, 10 **VA,** Squitch owl; 2 infs, **VA,** Switch owl.

squitee, squiteeg, squitie, squitteag, squittee See **squeteague**

squitters n Also *squitter;* also with *the* [*OED2* 1664 →] Cf **squtters**

=**skitters.**

1877 Bartlett *Americanisms* 651, Squitters. The diarrhea. **1968** *DARE* (Qu. BB19, *Joking names for looseness of the bowels*) Inf **OH**72, Squitters. **2002** *DARE* File—Internet (as of 1944), To add to the woes of the troops, dysentery struck at the same time—the "squitters" it was called. **2002** Proulx *That Old Ace* 79 **TX,** That's squitter water. It'll make you want a die, make you think your guts is bein pulled out a your asshole. **2002** in 2004 Latham *Storyteller's Guide* 2 **MT,** That was the last time she ever went to the outhouse without her .45-caliber Army-issue pistol. "Where's my forty-five? I've got the squitters," she would announce loudly. **2007** in 2008 *DARE* File—Internet **NH,** Under attack I take Colchecine until the hot squitters come; oh what fun it is!

squiveled up adj phr [Var of *shriveled up*]

1966 *DARE* FW Addit **ME**23, All squiveled ['skwɪvl̩d] up—shrunken and wrinkled. **2006** *DARE* File—Internet **NYC,** U look like a fucking squiveled up boy on crack.

squiwinikie See **skew- g**

squizzit See **quizzit**

squizzle v

1 also with *up*: To wrinkle, contort, shrivel; hence ppl adj *squizzled up* wrinkled, shriveled. **chiefly ME**

1865 *Janesville Gaz.* (WI) 7 Oct [4]/3 (newspaperarchive.com), Don't muss her hair, scratch down her collar, bite her cheek, squizzle her rich ribbons, and leave her mussed, rumpled and flummuxed. **1868** *Cedar Valley Times* (Cedar Rapids IA) 26 Mar 1/7 **NH,** The baby began to squizzle up its face, and flourish its heels and fists. **1904** Day *Kin o' Ktaadn* 93 **ME,** She'd squizzle all to nubbin's a speech an hour long. *Ibid* 196 **ME,** Along comes one o' them rustly, starchy, crispy, pinky summer sojourners an' makes the wimmin folks squizzle all up. **1927** *AmSp* 3.137 **eME,** "Squizzle" is used in speaking of the wrinkling of the face in crying or frowning, also of a badly wrinkled person, or apple. "Her face was all squizzled up." **1966** *DARE* (Qu. I8, *When root vegetables get old and tough and are not good to eat*) Inf **ME**5, Squizzled up. **2003** *DARE* File—Internet, Her lean red face was all squizzled up. **2007** in 2008 *Ibid* **ME,** There was a troup of women (old, squizzled up women) that scrubbed us down like we haven't been scrubbed down since we were small enough to be bathed in a sink. . . So, here I was, face squizzled up to the screen, glasses low on my nose, trying to read documents such as scanned W-2 forms. *Ibid* **ME,** He is the most greedy squizzled up little troll of a man that I have ever met.

2 also with *out:* To fizzle, fail; hence ppl adj (phr) *squizzled (out)* worn out.

1904 Holley *Samantha at St. Louis* 291 **neNY,** It all squizzled out, nothin' done about it, only jest talk. **1945** Coffman *Studies Lang. & Lit.* 327 **NY** (as of a1904), Squizzled out = 'failed.' **1969** *DARE* (Qu. KK10, . . *Words for something failing* . . *"He didn't work it out carefully enough, and his plan _____."*) Inf **VT**12, Squizzled; (Qu. KK20b, *Something that looks as if it might collapse any minute: "Our old washing machine is _____."*) Inf **VT**12, Squizzled.

squizzle(d) up See **squizzle 1**

squn See **squin**

squnch See **squunch**

squnched out See **squunch 1**

squnched up See **squunch 2**

squoish See **squash** n¹

squole See **squeal** v

squonk n   Cf *DS* CC17

An imaginary creature; see quots.

1910 Cox *Fearsome Creatures* 31 **PA,** The squonk is of a very retiring disposition. . . Because of its misfitting skin, which is covered with warts and moles, it is always unhappy. . . [T]he animal weeps constantly. When cornered . . or when surprised and frightened, it may even dissolve itself in tears. **1939** Tryon *Fearsome Critters* 49 **PA,** Moonlight nights are best for Squonk hunts, for then the animal prefers to lie quiet in its hemlock home. **2006** *Deseret Morning News* (Salt Lake City UT) 7 Nov (Internet), Caricatures of a phoenix, squonk and demon strutted, rolled and stomped across the stage.

squoosh See **squush**

squooshed See **squush 1**

squorsh See **squash** n¹

squoz See **squeeze** v **Bb**

squoze See **squeeze** v **Ba**

squrl See **squirrel** n

sqush v See **squush**

sqush n See **squash** n¹

squtters n pl   Also *squdders*   Cf **scutters**
=**skitters.**

1899 (1912) Green *VA Folk-Speech* 413, Squtters. . . Diarrhoea. **1996** Horton *Island Out of Time* 103 **Chesapeake Bay MD,** How she wouldn't even want that crabmeat if she knew how much bacteria might be in it. And Ma's hollerin—look, you; I don't care if it give me the squdders [Horton: trots] three weeks runnin', I want my crabmeat!

squunch v   Also sp *squnch*   [Varr of **scrunch**]

1 also with *down:* =**scrunch 1;** hence ppl adj phr *squnched out.*

1833 *NY Mirror* 11.21 **NJ,** Well, I swon, If I wurn't purty near squnched to death. **1879** *Puck* 6.421, He caught him with a rapid wrench / And squunched him underneath a bench. **1914** *Syracuse Herald* (NY) 21 Sept 8/3, My first thought was to fall over on him and squnch him, but my second thought was that it wouldn't be dignified. **1933** *Fresno Bee the Republican* (CA) 24 Dec [58]/2 (newspaperarchive.com), In its center lay a squnched-out cigarette, the end carminesplotched. **1950** *WELS Suppl.* **nwWI,** Squunch = squash . . by Superiorites. **2001** in 2003 *DARE* File—Internet **WA,** I turned a new filter on by hand, but caught the old gasket, squunched it and it leaked. **2003** *Ibid* **Sth,** You may have to squunch down your scarf a bit to show this off.

2 usu with *up, over, down:* =**scrunch 2.**

1877 Bartlett *Americanisms* 797, Squnch. To stoop or lie down; to squeeze one's self within the smallest compass; hence ppl adj phr *squ(u)nched up.* **1895** *Youth's Companion* 27 June 319 **NH,** But when I ketch a holt of her [=a bell rope] . . an' she's all squnched up together jest as dry as an old bone . . why, I know what to expect. **1967–68** *DARE* (Qu. Y32, *To squeeze yourself into a small space: "If you're going to fit in there you'll have to _____."*) Inf **TX**28, Squunch [skwʌnč] up; (Qu. Y52, *To move over—for example on a long bench: ". . . Can you _____ [a little]?"*) Inf **OR**6, Squunch [skwʌnč] over.

2003 *DARE* File—Internet **TX,** She [=a cat] started squunching down and wiggling her butt like she was going to jump me. *Ibid* **TX,** Grace (5 weeks old) looks quite squunched up in the sling.

squunch down   See **squunch 1, 2**

squunched up   See **squunch 2**

squunch over, squunch up   See **squunch 2**

squush v   Usu |skwʌš, skwuš|; infreq |skwʌ̄š, skwɜ·š| Also *skwush, squoosh, sqush*

1 To squash, crush, squeeze; to squeeze oneself; hence ppl adjs *squushed, squooshed* squashed, crushed. **scattered, but esp Sth, S Midl, NEast**   See Map

1838 Neal *Charcoal Sketches* 45, The next time I meet that chap . . I'll sqush it with my foot. **1883** (1971) Harris *Nights with Remus* 53 **GA** [Black], Ef I fling um [=peaches] down dar whar you is, Brer Fox, en you misses um, dey'll git squshed. **1884** *Anglia* 7.268 **Sth, S Midl** [Black], *To sqush* = to crush. **1897** *KS Univ. Qrly.* (ser B) 6.92 **neKS,** Sqush: to squeeze. **1899** (1912) Green *VA Folk-Speech* 413, Sqush. . . To crush. Mash. *Squush.* **1905** Wasson *Green Shay* 134 **NEng,** He like to have squshed my hand into porgy-chum. **1905** *DN* 3.21 **cCT,** *Sqush.* . . To mash. 'Sqush the bug.' **1907** *DN* 3.218 **nwAR,** *Sqush.* . . To crush. **1909** *DN* 3.375 **eAL, wGA,** *Squush.* . . To mash. **1911** *DN* 3.548 **NE,** *Squush* [ʊ, ʌ]. . . Squeeze, crush. "I stepped on the worm and squushed it." **1915** *DN* 4.191 **swVA,** *Squush.* Variant of *squash, v. t.* and *i.* **1926** *AmSp* 1.411 **Okefenokee GA,** Jest squushed 'em down ter earth an' killed 'em right there. **1934** *AmSp* 9.212 **Sth,** Standard [ʌ] before [ʃ] or [tʃ] sometimes becomes [ʌ̄]. . . *sqush* (vulgar variant of *squash* 'to mash,' 'to make soft') **1947** Ballowe *The Lawd* **LA,** She fell to the marble floor below her and was squshed like a June bug. **1959** *VT Hist.* 27.160, *Sqush.* . . A blend, combining *squash* and *crush,* meaning to crush or mash. Common. **1965–70** *DARE* (Qu. KK21, *When something hollow is crushed by a heavy weight, or by a fall: "They ran the wagon over the coffee pot and _____."*) 41 Infs, **scattered, but esp Sth, Midl,** Squushed it; **MS**6, Squushed it in; **AL**6, **AR**52, 55, **LA**23, **NC**13, 15, **SC**8, [skwʌšt]; **NY**18, Squushed; also [skwɜ·št]; **SC**39, [skwʌ̄št]; (Qu. Y32, *To squeeze yourself into a small space: "If you're going to fit in there you'll have to _____."*) Inf **LA**37, Sqush [skwʌš]; (Qu. Y33, . . *Squeezing or crushing something* . . *"I _____ my finger in the door."*) Inf **WA**1, Squooshed; (Qu. Y35, *To spoil something so that it can't be used . . "My new coffee pot— it's completely _____."*) Inf **FL**35, Squooshed; (Qu. KK22, . . *Completely shattered: "The jug fell out of the window and was _____."*) Inf **MS**6, Squushed. **1968–69** *DARE* Tape **CA**138, Sometimes an ordinary footprint in the snow will melt and expand, and sometimes in the mud it will squush [skwʌš] out, too; **GA**30, His head was all squushed [skwʌ̄št] in up there and busted through. **1972** Thomas *Pop. Dict. Ozarks Talk* 80, Squash, skwush: v.t. To crush. **1980** *DARE* File **cnMA** (as of c1915), I don't think I was ever faced with spelling the word we children pronounced /skwʌš/ in such sentences as, "Step on that bug and /skwʌš/ it" and "The car was pretty crowded but we managed to /skwʌš/ in." **1994** in 2003 *DARE* File—Internet **MA,** The tires at the bottom of the stack would tend to get squooshed by the weight of the tires on top. **2002** *Ibid* **TN,** Leave a penny on a train rail for it to be squushed. **2002** in 2003 *Ibid* **TX,** I didn't mind the window seat too much except for the fact the plane was narrow and I was squooshed.

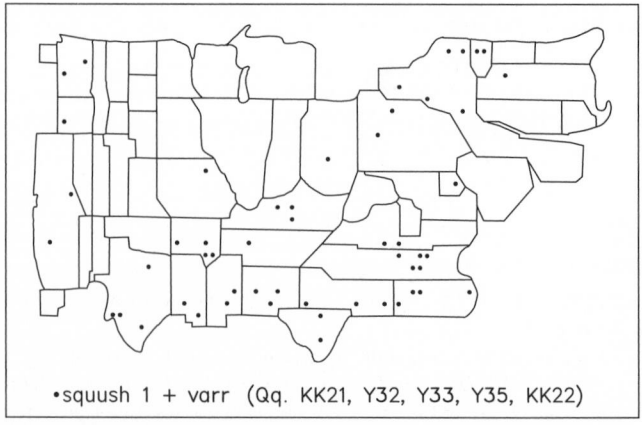

•squush 1 + varr (Qq. KK21, Y32, Y33, Y35, KK22)

2 To gush, spurt; to cause to gush.

[**1863** *Continental Mth.* 3.57 **NEast,** 'Sqush' went the juicy rhubarb, completely saturating Gregory's new garments.] **1870** *Catholic World* 11.589 **ceMA,** It means water dripping over gutters, . . and squshing from shoes of poor folks at every step they take. **1922** Brown *Old Crow* 312 **neMA,** There were plenty [of peaches] to be . . gobbled in the garden with the juice squshing over your white frock. **1965** *DARE* (Qu. Y45, *Talking of a liquid—to scatter in all directions: "When he opened the can, the beer* _____ *[all over the kitchen]."*) Inf **FL**22, Squushed all over everything. **2002** in 2003 *DARE* File—Internet **WA,** When the airpot was full, I squooshed out my first mugful.

squushed See **squush 1**

squz See **squeeze** v Bb

sriek See **shriek**

srimp(y) See **shrimp**

srink See **shrink**

srub n¹ See **shrub** n¹

srub n² See **shrub** n²

S.T. See **sugar tit**

sta'ar See **stair** n¹

staa't-nakid See **start-naked**

stable n

1 in combs *hog stable, pig ~:* A building in which pigs are kept. [Perh simply survival of the earlier broad sense of *stable* (cf **cow stable**), but the regional distribution suggests this is primarily a calque of Ger *Schweinestall < Stall,* the generic term for a building in which domestic animals are kept.] **esp PA, Upper Missip Valley**

1793 in 2003 *DARE* File—Internet **sePA,** [Will:] [She] shall have a hog stable absented for her use. **1827** *Republican Compiler* (Gettysburg PA) 18 July [3]/5 (newspaperarchive.com), [Advt:] One-story stone Dwelling-house, double log Barn, log Smith-shop, log Hog-stable, and an Orchard. **1879** *DARE* File—Internet **sePA,** [Diary:] Started white-washing and till evening had done fence, pig stable, and privy. **1903** *Ibid* **MN,** [Diary:] While it rained we manured in the pig-stable, then we spread manure the rest of the day. **1950** *WELS (Building where pigs are kept)* 1 Inf, **seWI,** Pig stable. **1967–69** *DARE* (Qu. M15, *The place outdoors where pigs are kept*) Inf **OH**89, Hog stable; **PA**51, 158, Pig stable. **1971** *AmSp* 46.170 **Chicago IL,** 'Shelter and enclosure for hogs and pigs' . . *hog stable* 1 [of 37 infs]. **1973** Allen *LAUM* 1.188 (as of c1950), Shelter and enclosure for hogs and pigs. . . hog stable [1 inf, **IA**]. . . pig stable [1 inf, **IA**]. **2003** *DARE* File—Internet **IL,** I am planning to built [sic] a pig stable for 10 females and one male. *Ibid* **PA,** [Real estate advertisement:] Outbuildings include . . a pig stable.

2 in phrr *(your) stable door is open* and varr: See quot. **esp C and S Atl** See Map Cf *your barn door is open* (at **barn door 2b**), **X-Y-Z**

1945 Karig *Lower Angels* 9 **NYC,** "When can I have pants that button down the front like Father's?" "Hi-yi, Marvin's stable door is open!" **1965–70** *DARE* (Qu. W24c, . . *To warn a man that his trouser-fly is open*) Infs **AR**23, **GA**70, **MD**21, **NJ**3, 8, **PA**244, **TX**26, Stable door (is) open; **DE**2, **FL**31, **NC**22, 24, 30, 55, (Your) stable door's open; **GA**77, Left your mule stable open; **NJ**53, Your horse'll be out of the stable if you don't watch it; **SC**68, Horse 'bout to come out the stable; **VA**9, Button up your pants, your horse will get out of the stable; **VA**69, Your stable is open.

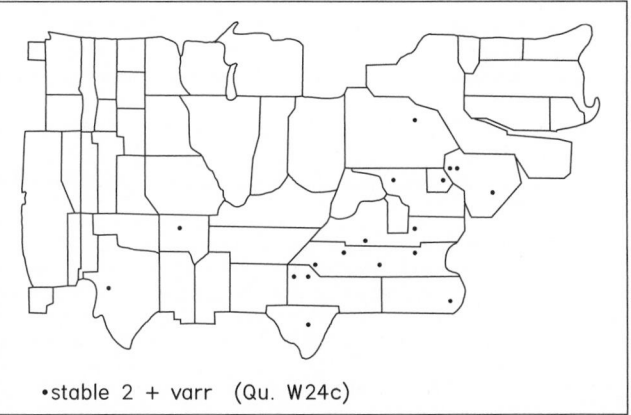

•stable 2 + varr (Qu. W24c)

stable fly n [Because it is a pest of horses]
A biting fly, usu *Stomoxys calcitrans.* Also called **barn fly 1**

1842 *N. Amer. Rev.* 54.98, Toward the close of summer, the stable-flies, which resemble them [=house flies] in every thing but their sharp proboscis, enter our dwellings at the approach of rain, and bite us through our stockings. **1890** *Chillicothe Constitution* (MO) 24 Aug [7]/2 (newspaperarchive.com), A handful of tansy leaves rubbed over the cow's legs before milking will drive away the annoying stable flies. **1909** Smith *Insect Friends* 171, The term "stable flies" is rather an indefinite one, but applies chiefly to one species, *Stomoxys calcitrans.* **1949** Swain *Insect Guide* 207, Stable fly. . . The bloodsucking adults are commoner about barns than houses, but they do attack humans. **1966–69** *DARE* (Qu. R12, . . *Other kinds of flies*) Infs **FL**7, **IL**62, **NJ**45, **TX**62, **WI**77, Stable fly; **MI**37, Some call them beach flies, others call them fish flies, and one person I know calls them stable flies—size of a house fly, stings terribly. **2000** MI State Univ. *Landscape Crop Advisory Team Alert* 15.15 (Internet), [Title:] Stable Flies: No Beach Blanket Bingo When They Are Around.

stable horse n **chiefly Sth, S Midl** *euphem*
A stallion.

1843 in 2010 (acc) Lexis–Nexis Legal Research *State Case Law: IL* (Internet), Doyle said he had a stud horse he wished to put in. . . Teas said he wanted a stable horse if it suited him. **1849** *WI Tribune* (Mineral Point) 16 Feb [3]/3 (newspaperarchive.com), [Advt:] He also offers for sale a good Stable Horse and Breeding Mare. **1872** U.S. Congress *Rept. Joint Select Comm. Insurrectionary States* 6.387 **GA** [Black], They had us all stripped there, and laughed and made great sport. Some of them just squealed the same as if they were stable horses just brought out. **1902** *DN* 2.246 **sIL,** Stable-horse. . . A stallion. **1906** *DN* 3.123 **sIN,** Stable-horse. . . A stallion. **1914** *DN* 4.113 **cKS,** Stable-horse. . . Stallion. **1915** *DN* 4.191 **swVA,** Stable-horse. . . Stallion. **1923** *DN* 5.222 **swMO,** Stable horse. . . A stallion kept for breeding purposes. **1931** Randolph *Ozarks* 79, The names of male animals must not be mentioned when women are present. . . A stallion is sometimes called a *stable-horse.* **1983** *MJLF* 9.1.57 **ceKY** (as of 1956), *Stable horse* . . a stud horse. **1986** Pederson *LAGS Concordance (Stallion)* 2 infs, **LA, MS,** Stable horse; 2 infs, **LA, TN,** Stable horse—euphemism; 1 inf, **cMS,** I prefer saying stable horse to women; 1 inf, **neTN,** Stable horse—term used around women; 1 inf, **neTN,** Stable horse—used years ago in presence of women; 1 inf, **nwTN,** Stable horse—would use this term around women; 1 inf, **cnLA,** Stable horse—has to be kept in stable separate; [1 inf, **cTX,** Stable horse—doesn't know what this is].

stable lot n **chiefly Sth, S Midl** Cf **lot** n **1a, b** =**barn lot.**

1809 in 2010 (acc) Lexis–Nexis Legal Research *State Case Law: VA* (Internet), His wife should receive . . full use of the mansion-house and other houses . . together with the ground on which they stand, and the garden, stable, and stable-lot. **1841** *Adams Sentinel* (Gettysburg PA) 9 Aug [4]/1 (newspaperarchive.com) **IL,** It [=stolen money] was buried in three places:—A part of it in the Diamond Grove; part of it north of town on the barrens; and the gold in the stable lot. **1869** in 1884 Lanier *Poems* 172 **GA,** And he riz and he walked to the stable lot. **1887** *Century Illustr. Mag.* 34.858 **KY,** With them he went clandestinely to the fatal duck-pond in the stable lot, to learn the art of swimming. **1899** *Atlantic Mth.* 84.202 **NC,** I was by that time slippin' easy inside th' stable lot an' catchin' the pony. **1902** *DN* 2.246 **sIL,** Stable-lot. . . The yard about the stable; never barnyard. **1907** *DN* 3.227 **nwAR,** Stable-lot. . . Barnyard. **1936** Smith–Sass *Carolina Rice* 61 **SC coast** (as of 1850s), Beyond the circle was the fence with a wild-orange screen or hedge which separated the garden from the "stable-lot." **1946** *PADS* 5.10 **VA,** *Barn lot, stable lot, lot:* Barnyard; common everywhere except in the Shenandoah Valley and on the Eastern Shore. **1949** Kurath *Word Geog.* 55, *Barn yard.* . . The yard adjoining or surrounding the barn is regularly called *barn yard* north of the Potomac, *lot* (or *stable lot, barn lot, farm lot*) to the south of it. **1970** *DARE* (Qu. M13, *The space near the barn with a fence around it where you keep the livestock*) Inf **VA**43, Stable lot. **1986** Pederson *LAGS Concordance (Barnyard)* 1 inf, **cGA,** Stable lot.

staboy See **stuboy**

stacey salad n [Folk-etym for Cherokee *ustesgi* + *salad*]
A **scorpionweed 2** (here: *Phacelia dubia*).

2001 *DARE* File—Internet **wNC,** Stacey salad (small-flowered phacelia, "Phacelia dubia"), sweet salad (Solomon's-seal, "Polygonatum biflorum") . . are collected as young plants, cleaned, and then parboiled or fried or both.

stack cake n   Also *stack fruit cake*   **chiefly S Midl, esp sAppalachians**   Cf **stack pie**

A layer cake typically made with alternating layers of cake (often gingerbread) and fruit filling.

1848 Clay *Writings* 402 **KY,** The procession was headed by two tall, gaunt fellows, in women's clothes, with caps, and most *capacious pockets.* Without ceremony the stack cakes were thrust into these; then followed pyramids of candles, wreaths of flowers, . . and the untold paraphernalia of a wedding supper.   **1866** in 2002 Culpepper *All Things Altered* 250 **swMS,** Stack cake & 2 Jelly cakes.   **1907** *Daily Advocate* (Victoria TX) [8 Mar 3]/4 (newspaperarchive.com), One of the nicest little ladies in the settlement sent him a nice snow-white stack cake.   **1940** Brown *Amer. Cooks* 768 **TN,** Stack cake for brides is said to have originated in the Smoky Mountains. The height of the cake shows the popularity of the bride, since each guest brings one layer to add to it.   **1941** Justus *Cabin on Kettle Creek* 137 **eTN,** The big stack-cake stood all by itself on a shelf in the corner cupboard. . . ten layers high and as big around as a water bucket!   **1955** Ritchie *Singing Family* 181 **seKY,** Edna . . mashed up dried apples and spiced them with cloves and sticks of cinnamon to go between the seven layers of Mom's ginger-bread stack-cake.   **1970** *DARE* File **seKY,** Stack cake—a type of cake made in Barbourville, Ky., and environs: alternate layers of molasses-bread, thin as pancakes, and cooked, sliced apples.   **1986** Pederson *LAGS Concordance,* 2 infs, **TN,** Stack cakes; 1 inf, **neTN,** Stack cake—large layer cake; 1 inf, **ceTN,** Stack cake—a baked layer pie; 1 inf, **cTN,** Stack cake—layers of fruit; 1 inf, **cnTN,** Stack cake—not a pie.   **1987** in 2004 Montgomery–Hall *Dict. Smoky Mt. Engl.* 564 **wNC, eTN,** Her mother would make gingerbread and stack fruit cake all the time.   **1993** Mason *Feather Crowns* 165 **KY** (as of c1900), She had come into the kitchen to help Lena make dried-apple stack-cake.   **2004** in 2008 *DARE* File—Internet **wKY,** Stack cakes were very popular at church socials where I grew up in western Kentucky. . . The layers, about ½ inch thick, were baked individually, usually in the same old black skillet as regular cornbread and turned out and the top "leveled" or trimmed. . . Dried apples or dried peaches or pears were chopped up and cooked with just enough water and sugar for them to plump and develop a thick sticky syrup, then the hot mixture was ladled over the first layer then the second layer was added and so on.   **2006** *Herald* (Rock Hill SC) 26 Nov sec D 7 (Internet) **NC,** My favorite among all of her baked goods was the old-fashioned stack cake at Thanksgiving. Hers always ran to six layers, and each layer was quite thin. Between the layers was a liberal amount of a spiced apple mixture.

stack chimney n

1 also *stacked chimney:* A chimney with more than one flue, esp one that serves two back-to-back fireplaces.   **esp Sth, S Midl, but also NEng**

1843 *New Englander & Yale Rev.* 1.211, None of these objections obtain, when we consider the . . stacked chimneys of the cottage style. . . [T]he carriage of the chimneys separately to the top, while it favors their picturesque union above the ridge, ensures a constant draft.   **1846** in 1973 Assoc. Preservation Tech. *Bulletin* 5.75 **MO,** There shall be a good stack chimney in the middle of the partition wall with a fire place in each room, of good Bricks.   **1892** *New Engl. Mag.* 13.212 **NC,** There were two chimneys in our room, and both were stack chimneys—that is to say, there were two flues in the chimney, one for the fireplace in our casemate, and one for the fireplace of the adjoining one.   **1916** Shackleton *Book of Boston* 272, Near the waterside . . is an ancient, nestled, low-set house, with ancient stack-chimney of brick.   [*Ibid* 273, And a wonderful roof-line the house has, with its clustered gables and that old central chimney, "stacked" like those of Tudor days.]   [*DARE* Ed: This house is supposed to have been Hawthorne's model for *The House of the Seven Gables.*]   **1936** in Lib. of Congress *Amer. Memory: WPA Life Hist.* (Internet) **TX,** The heating arrangements were a "stacked chimney" built of rock and this was located between two rooms, with a grate or fire place on either side.   *Ibid* **AL,** The house has two stack chimneys making it very comfortable.   **1948** Forbes *Running Tide* 222 **MA,** They gazed upward at the tiny figure close by the stacked chimney.   **1953** *Hall Coll.* **wNC, eTN,** Stack chimney—That was a big chimley built in the middle of the house with two fireplaces to it, and it was built up right through the center of the house and out the top of it.   **1956** Ker *Vocab. W. TX* 195, Stack chimney—fireplace in two rooms with one flue.   **1989** Pederson *LAGS Tech. Index* 32 **Gulf Region,** Chimney . . stack chimley (19 [of 914 primary infs]) . . stack chimney (8 [of 914 primary infs]).   **2006** *Kilgore News Herald* (TX) 24 Feb (Internet), I wax nostalgic for the fireplace of my 30s. It was a huge, stone structure, dividing the living room from the kitchen, with a stacked chimney and openings on both sides.

2   =**stick-and-clay chimney.**   **chiefly Sth, S Midl**

1843 (1916) Hall *New Purchase* 92 **IN,** As to the cabin it was as yet unchinked, undaubed, and without its stack chimney.   **1854** Prime *Later Yrs.* 100 **NY,** We have a new chimney, broader and deeper than the old one: that was a stack chimney, made of pine-wood strips carefully covered with mud; this is well made of stone, and covers the whole end of the cabin.   **1888** *Century Illustr. Mag.* 35.468 **GA,** A log hut with a stack chimney . . disappears under a great spreading black-gum.   **1888** Venable *Footprints Pioneers* 126 **Ohio Valley,** They are not built on the earliest model, but they are essentially the cabin of the back-woods. Even the stack chimney, plastered with mud, is seen now and then.   **1968** Booker *Hist. Tar Heel Stories* 64 **NC,** The cabin was heated by an open fireplace in a big stack chimney. This chimney was formed of stacked sticks daubed with clay.

stacked chimney   See **stack chimney 1**

stack fruit cake   See **stack cake**

stack of bones n   **chiefly Sth, S Midl**   See Map
=**rack of bones.**

1881 *Californian* 4.349, For God's sake, look at me! A woman living and dying an old maid for a stack of bones overgrown with wild hair.   **1896** *Newark Daily Advocate* (OH) 12 Aug 2/4, They said "get out you stack of bones, we want the fat, sleek cream colored horse."   **1902** Dixon *Leopard's Spots* 20 **NC,** Tom was . . seated proudly on a stack of bones that had once been a horse.   **1902** OH State Bd. Ag. *Annual Rept. for 1901* 642, Born an unsightly stack of bones he [=a lamb] is destined ever so to remain.   **1905** *DN* 3.95 **nwAR,** Stack of bones. . . An emaciated horse. 'Why doesn't he feed that stack of bones?' The most usual expression in this sense.   **1909** *DN* 3.375 **eAL, wGA,** Stack of bones. . . An emaciated horse.   **1920** *Jrl. Amer. Osteopathic Assoc.* 20.665 **AL,** In October 1897, after having been an invalid for seven years, I went to Kirksville—a stack of bones covered with some yellow skin.   **c1960** Wilson *Coll.* **csKY,** Stack of bones. . . A skinny old horse.   **1965–70** *DARE* (Qu. K44, *A bony or poor-looking horse*) 18 Infs, **chiefly Sth, S Midl,** Stack of bones; [**KS**11, Bone stack;] (Qu. K15, *A thin, bony, or poor-looking cow*) Infs **FL**21, **GA**74, 87, **IN**35, **NC**37, **VA**26, 43, Stack of bones; (Qu. K16, *A cow with a bad temper*) Inf **FL**26, Stack of bones; (Qu. X49, *Expressions . . about a person who is very thin*) Infs **FL**17, **IL**114, **MS**59, **MO**9, 23, **NC**68, 72, Stack of bones.

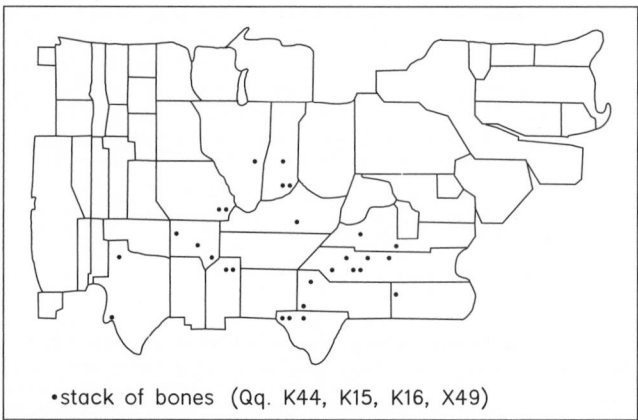

•stack of bones (Qq. K44, K15, K16, X49)

stack of wheats   See **wheat cake**

stack pie n   Also *stacked pie*   **chiefly S Midl**   Cf **stack cake**
A dessert made of alternating layers of pie crust and filling.

1903 *OH Farmer* 103.594 **ceIL,** Stack Pie.—Make a rich biscuit crust, slightly sweetened. . . Bake in a moderate oven until done but not hard. Divide the layers, place a crust, then a thick layer of ripe, crushed, well-sweetened fruit, then another layer of crust and fruit. . . Serve with good sweet cream.   **1922** *Star* (Kansas City MO) 6 Nov 20/7, From the Ohio State Journal. Another pathetic little feature of everyday life is a conscientious stylish stout ordering spinach and tea . . while her very soul hungers after chicken salad and cream stack pie.   **1935** Sheppard *Cabins* 218 **wNC,** There was much inviting of relatives . . to help themselves to . . stacked pies.   **1940** Brown *Amer. Cooks* 640 **NC,** Stack pies—Pile thinnish apple pies one on top of the other, like a layer cake, then cut down in narrow triangles. At social occasions in the Blue Ridge, guests bring their own pies to make stacks 10 high, like the wedding stack cakes of the Great Smokies in near-by Tennessee.   **1949** *Long Beach Independent* (CA) 27 Nov sec B 11/4 **TN,** *Vinegar Stack Pie.* . . Make 5 or 6 layers. Put in separate pans and bake in oven as for any other pie crust.

Cook filling on top of stove. . . Then spread between pie crust layers just as if you were icing a layer cake. **1962** Dykeman *Tall Woman* 87 **NC** (as of 1860), I'm making ready to fix corn pudding and bake a batch of stack pies. **1976** *Baytown Sun* (TX) 23 Nov 4/1, Baytown grandmothers shared some of their very favorites with us. . . *Lemon Stack Pie.* **1986** Pederson *LAGS Concordance,* 4 infs, **cnAL, neGA, ne,ceTN,** Stack pie(s); 1 inf, **cnGA,** Stack pie—several layers; 1 inf, **cnTN,** Stack pie—layers of fruit. **1997** in 2004 Montgomery–Hall *Dict. Smoky Mt. Engl.* 565 **eTN,** *Stack pie.* . . made from dried fruit baked into pies and stacked about 4–6 [layers] high. **2004** in 2008 *DARE* File—Internet **WV,** He got one of his favorite aunts to talk about traditional dishes, and she, being a great baker, mentioned lots of pies and cakes—including "stacked pies". I think one of the traditional fillings is usually dried apples.

stack pole n   Cf gin pole 2

1 A pole fixed in the ground to support a pile of hay, straw, or another crop.

1712 (1901) Hempstead *Diary* 12 **CT,** I got Stack Poles & Stackt hay. **1816** in 1854 U.S. Congress *Debates & Proc.* 15th Cong 1st Sess 2.2456 **NEast,** I began by erecting . . a signal . . in form of a tripod, made of a ladder and two stack-poles. **1868** *Prairie Farmer* 5 Sept 74 **nwIL,** *Stacking Navy Beans.* . . I select the most branching saplings I can find, and cut off the branches about a foot from the body of the tree, for a stack pole. **1888** *Scribner's Mag.* 3.691 **MA,** Poorer hay is stacked out-of-doors about a skewer for a stack-pole. **1909** *Atlanta Constitution* (GA) 26 July 10/2, The blades [of corn] must be . . tied into bundles, hauled to the stack pole and stacked. **1914** *DN* 4.81 **ME, nNH,** *Taller'n a stackpole.* . . Very tall. **1931** *Morning News* (Florence SC) 10 Apr 1/2, The stack poles should be put up only as needed and be sure to get them set firmly in the ground, and by all means but [sic] two cross pieces 18 inches from the ground to start the stack [of peanut vines] on. **1968** Towler *Genealogy* 171 **sVA** (as of a1920), A perfect stack of straw placed around a stack pole was supposed to be in proportionate ratio to an egg set up on its blunt end with the tip of the stack pole just sticking through the top end. [**1969** *DARE* (Qu. L14, *A large pile of hay stored outdoors*) Inf **GA**77, Pole stack—stacked around a pole.] **1986** Pederson *LAGS Concordance (Haystack)* 1 inf, **cwGA,** Haystack around a stack pole; 1 inf, **neGA,** In field, hay stacked around a stack pole; 1 inf, **cwTN,** Stack poles used in building haystacks; 1 inf, **cTN,** Gin pole—stack pole. **2006** *Charleston Gaz.* (WV) 3 June sec B 2 (Internet), With the modern tractors that we have now, it is a much simpler task than in days gone by. We pitched the hay around a stack pole, and tromped it down until we had a tall haystack.

2 A pole forming part of a hay-stacking derrick. Cf **gin pole 1**

1907 *Monroe Weekly Times* (WI) [5 Aug 3]/1 (newspaperarchive.com), Mr. Thorp was caught under falling stack poles and was struck on the head by one of the heavy poles. . . A cable was strung for a 40-foot stack and Mr. Thorp was working at the fork when the timber in the ground which served as an anchor for the guy rope was pulled out and the two poles went over on the stack under the weight of a loaded fork. **1913** in 2008 (acc) Lexis–Nexis Legal Research *State Case Law: WA* (Internet), Hay is usually stacked in the Yakima valley by means of a derrick. . . Large timbers were set on the ground, and upon these a stack pole forty-five feet high was reared. On the top of the stack pole there was an arm eighteen feet long. The whole superstructure was so arranged that it would swing or revolve freely. **1929** *Ironwood Daily-Globe* (MI) 11 Sept 7/5, When helping his son . . stack hay . . , Joseph Bourque . . was struck by a falling stack pole and suffered a fractured skull.

staddle n   [*OED2 staddle* sb. 3.b 1729 →]   chiefly NEng

A platform of stakes and poles used to support a haystack; also transf.

1774 in 1880 Brookhaven NY *Records* 1.194, Every person that owned Staddles on said Beach should have Liberty to take them away by the first of December next. **1809** Kendall *Travels* 2.177 **MA,** To protect the stacks, they are either built upon high ground, or, if in the marshes, upon stadles [sic] or piles. **1848** Lowell *Biglow* 146 '**Upcountry' MA,** Staddles, stout stakes driven into the salt marshes, on which the hayricks are set, and thus raised out of the reach of high tides. **1911** Essex Inst. *Coll.* 47.14 **MA,** The 'staddles' were about three feet above the marsh. **1941** Williams *Strange Woman* 430 **NEng,** John set them to work putting up hay, stacking it on staddles made by driving poles into the ground and laying other poles across them to keep the hay clear of possible flood waters. **1948** Coatsworth *South Shore* 89 **MA,** The last hay was out there so long ago that not a rotting staddle remains where a domed beehive of a mow might rest. **1975** Gould *ME Lingo* 273, *Stad-*

dles—The arrangement of short stakes driven in the mud to support a cock of *salt hay* . . and hence any small platform on poles. A man may rig a *staddle* as an aid to getting in and out of a canoe. **2003** *DARE* File—Internet **ceMA,** Today remains of the wooded [sic] staddles—structures used to store the hay above the marsh—still dot Rumney Marsh.

staff n   Also *pen staff;* for addit varr see quots   Pronc-sp *staft*   chiefly Sth, S Midl, TX   See Map   Cf stock n C5

The shaft into which a pen point is inserted; the barrel of a pen; hence n *staff pen* a **dip pen.**

1862 Boston Soc. Med. Improvement *Extracts from Rec.* 4.165 **MA,** Touched them with a mixture of muriatic acid and honey . . applied with a small camels-hair brush on the end of a pen-staff. **1868** *Radical Rule GA* 41, I saw Dr. Kirksey probe the wound on his head with a pencil or pen staff. **1901** *DN* 2.145 **AR,** *Pen-staff.* . . A pen-holder. **1904** *DN* 2.420 **nwAR,** *Pen-staff.* . . Penholder. 'Do you want a pen-staff with the pen-points?' **1909** *DN* 3.356 **eAL, wGA,** *Penstaff.* . . A penholder. *Pen-stock* is rarely heard. **1950** *WELS* (Parts of a pen. . . *The long wooden part*) 1 Inf, **cWI,** Staff. **1965–70** *DARE* (Qu. JJ10b, *Parts of an ink pen*) 123 Infs, **chiefly Sth, S Midl, TX,** Staff; 24 Infs, **esp Sth, S Midl, TX,** Pen staff; **KY**75, Ink staff; **MN**15, Scribbling staff; **MS**65, Staff and pen; **VA**42, Staff pen; **TN**4, Staft; (Qu. JJ10a, *Different kinds of pens*) 9 Infs, **esp Sth, S Midl, TX,** Staff pen; **FL**28, 29, **NC**52, **TX**40, Pen staff; [**NC**61, Pen staffers]. **1986** Pederson *LAGS Concordance,* 1 inf, **seMS,** Pen staff—pen; 1 inf, **neAR,** Pen staff—pen holder, shaft where point inserted.

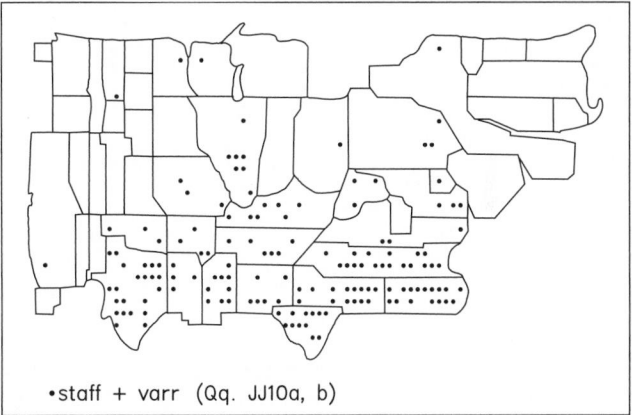

•staff + varr (Qq. JJ10a, b)

staff tree n   [*OED2* 1633 →]

A **bittersweet** (here: *Celastrus scandens*).

1771 Forster *Flora* 11 **VA,** *Celastrus bullatus* [=*C. scandens*]—Staff tree, elegant. **1785** Marshall *Arbustrum* 28, Celastrus. The Staff-Tree. . . The *Corolla* has five petals. **1832** MA Hist. Soc. *Coll.* 2d ser 9.148 **cwVT,** Celastrus scandens, Staff-tree. **1876** Hobbs *Bot. Hdbk.* 112, Staff tree, Climbing, False bittersweet. **1936** [see **staff vine**]. **1940** Clute *Amer. Plant Names* 127, Bittersweet. Staff-tree, staff-vine.

staff vine n

A **bittersweet** (here: *Celastrus scandens*).

1830 Rafinesque *Med. Flora* 2.206, *Celastrus scandens* . . Fevertwig, Staff vine, Bittersweet. **1892** (1974) Millspaugh *Amer. Med. Plants* 42–2, The common Bittersweet, or, better, Staff Vine (*Celastrus scandens*), so often confounded, by the laity, with Dulcamara, has orange-colored fruit. **1936** IL Nat. Hist. Surv. *Wildflowers* 188, The Climbing Bittersweet is called by various names in different places, such as Shrubby or False Bittersweet, Staff Tree, Staff Vine and Fever Twig. **1976** Bailey–Bailey *Hortus Third* 240. **2006** *DARE* File—Internet **MA,** Leaves, acorns, pine cones, nuts or sprigs of Staff Vine or Winterberry are beautiful, natural accents that can be found in wooded areas.

staft   See staff

stag v

1 Among loggers: to shorten (an article of clothing, esp trousers) by cutting; fig, to reduce (a paycheck); hence ppl adj (phr) *stagged (off)* shortened.   chiefly Inland Nth   Cf **stag pants, ~ shirt, ~ shoe**

1902 White *Blazed Trail* 190 **MI,** A gigantic young riverman in the conventional stagged (*i.e.,* chopped off) trousers. **1905** U.S. Forest Serv. *Bulletin* 61.49 [Logging terms], *Stag.* . . To cut off trousers at the knee, or boots at the ankle. **1914** *Outing* 63.556 **Gt Lakes,** He [=a riverman] found the tails were heavy and clinging when it rained, so he again used his jackknife and "stagged" his shirt. **1930** *DN* 6.88 **cWV,** *Stagged-off trousers,* trousers the legs of which have been cut off crudely with a knife, slightly below the knee, as worn by lumbermen. **1940** Writers' Program *Oregon* 371, Loggers . . are identified . . by their . . "tin pants" (water-proofed canvas trousers cut short or "stagged"). **1941** Writers' Program *Guide WA* 345 **cnWA,** The loggers are colorful in their woods garb: mackinaws and waist overalls, "stagged," at the boot tops. **1958** McCulloch *Woods Words* 180 **Pacific NW,** *Stag.* . . To cut pants legs off short; a logger always has to be ready to jump. . . To cut a large piece off a pay check for various deductions. **1977** Churchill *Don't Call* 198 **nwOR** (as of c1918), But I wore calk shoes, stagged pants, and a hickory shirt and worked on the rigging. **2003** Guterson *Our Lady* 105 **swWA,** Schein's stagged jeans would be stagged so high he might be wearing knickers on the Disney Channel.

‡**2** **=chink** v.

c1904 in 1942 Beck *Songs MI Lumberjacks* 23, M is for moss we stag our camp with.

stag n

1 See **stag pants.**
2 See **stag shoe.**

stag bass n chiefly ceGA

=red drum.

1963 *Florence Morning News* (SC) 20 Sept sec B 4/1, The big stag bass should be roaming into the beaches in greater numbers during the next few weeks. **1966** *DARE* (Qu. P2, . . *Kinds of saltwater fish caught around here . . good to eat*) Inf **GA**3, Stag bass. **1966** *DARE* Tape **GA**3, If you're bottom fishing. . . you don't catch any freshwater bass, . . but you do catch a lot of rockfish and stag bass, and whities also. **1998** in 2003 *DARE* File—Internet **Savannah GA,** Also this week Doug saw one boat catch, weigh and release a 57-pound stag bass at the Broad River Bridge. **2002** *Ibid* **Savannah GA,** Large stag bass have been reported in the surf. **2002** *DARE* File—Internet **Savannah GA,** I have had a lot calls [sic] with regards to information about spottail bass. . . During the fifties we called them "Stag Bass." . . As time went on they became known as "channel bass." . . The smaller ones became known as "spottail bass," because of the spot on the tail. When the commercial fishing industry got the so-called "money making vision" they became known as redfish.

stag beetle n

Std: a beetle of the family Lucanidae with branched mandibles suggesting a stag's antlers. Also called **horn bug 2, imp-of-the-devil, pinch bug**

stagbush n

A **black haw 1** (here: *Viburnum prunifolium*).

1884 Sargent *Forests of N. Amer.* 94, *Viburnum prunifolium.* . . Black Haw. Stag Bush. . . A small tree, sometimes 6 to 9 meters in height. **1900** (1927) Keeler *Our Native Trees* 184, Stag Bush. . . Ranges from Connecticut to Georgia westward to Kansas and Indian Territory. **1950** Peattie *Nat. Hist. Trees* 513, Stagbush. Sheepberry. Nannyberry. Sweet Haw. . . bushy understory tree with its short, crooked, spindling, bandy-legged trunk and its graceless rigid branches.

stage n Also *auto-stage, motor stage* [Transf from *stage* abbr for *stagecoach*] **esp Nth, West**

A bus or other motorized vehicle carrying passengers usu with a fixed route and schedule.

1896 *Hawaiian Gaz.* (Honolulu) 17 July 4/4, Wall street capital is being invested in lines of motor stages to be run in Cleveland and in various parts of the South notably in South Carolina. **1912** Milne *John Jonathan* 92, A fleet of motor-buses, which the New Yorkers call "stages," short for stage-coaches, meanders up and down [Fifth Avenue]. **1925** *AmSp* 1.149 **NV,** A girl traveling from a mining camp into a larger town explains to the stage driver, "I want out at the bank because this sack of silver is too heavy to pack around with me." She is dressed in up-to-date garb and the "stage" is a late-model Ford. It is only in her speech that she is Western. **1939** *Natl. Geogr. Mag.* Feb 133 **CA,** Mammoth sleeper buses (which they still call 'stages'). **1943** *CA Folkl. Qrly.* 2.41, An hour out of Truckee every Easterner notices the use of *stage* for *bus.* [**1959** *VT Hist.* 27.160 **neVT,** *Stage.* . . The automobile driven by the mailman. Rare.] **1965** Rice *Ambassador* 187 **UT,** Our good friend, Warren Cox, had established an auto-stage between the two towns and this was one of his first runs in his new Studebaker touring car. **1975** Gould *ME Lingo* 273, Today a good many older Maine peo-

ple will speak of "taking the *stage*" when they refer to an autobus. **2004** *DARE* File **ID, NV** (as of 1950s), When my family drove through Nevada to Idaho in the 1950s (and perhaps into the 1960s as well), we frequently saw buses from a company called the Boise–Winnemucca Stage. My Dad remembered that in the early days in the West a touring car used to be called a stage. *Ibid* **wWA,** He reminded me that the Whidby Island bus was called the Oak Harbor Stage. He had ridden it in the late fifties and sixties when it was chartered by his school for skiing trips. **2008** *DARE* File—Internet **IA,** *Welcome to Hawkeye Stages.* . . Motorcoach travel has never been more fun, more comfortable or more affordable!

stagecoach n Also *stagecoach upset*

A game in which players scramble for seats; also used as a call in the game; see quot 1899.

1855 *Putnam's Mag.* 5.300 **NEng,** On the particular evening which comes before me, we have finished one good old game of "stage coach." **1872** (1895) Woolsey *What Katy Did* 89, They all fell to playing "Stage-coach" . . in spite of close quarters and an occasional bump. **1892** *Nation* 24 Nov 397, What happened on the demise of the Grand Prince resembled a game of 'stage-coach,' with swords thrown in. **1899** Champlin–Bostwick *Young Folks' Games* 679, *Stage-Coach,* a game in which all the players sit in a circle except one, who stands in the middle. Each of those sitting takes the name of some part of a stage-coach . . or of something else connected with a stage ride. The one in the middle of the room tells a story. . . Whenever he speaks the name a player has taken, that player must rise and turn around. . . When the word "stage-coach" is spoken, all must rise and turn. The story ends with the words "the stage turned over," at which all change seats. **1968–70** *DARE* (Qu. EE2, *Games that have one extra player—when a signal is given, the players change places, and the extra one tries to get a place*) Inf **MA**73, Stagecoach—played at parties; each had a chair somewhere in the room, not in a line; when someone called "stagecoach," everyone tried to get a seat; **NY**60, Stagecoach—child in middle of circle told stories and called out things you take on a journey; then someone called "stage-coach upset" and everyone changed places; **OH**98, Stagecoach upset. [All Infs old]

stage plank n Also *stave plank* chiefly Gulf States, esp LA

A gingerbread cake or cookie; see quots.

1882 *Ft. Wayne Daily Gaz.* (IN) 9 Sept 5/3, [Advt:] Fresh cocoa drops. Fresh stage plank. Fresh B.B. crackers. **1890** *Outing* 15.474 **MS,** There were crackers, cheese and a large flat cake of gingerbread, called, perhaps from its wooden toughness, "stage plank" by the shop's proprietor. **1916** *DN* 4.270 **New Orleans LA,** Stage planks. . . A kind of gingerbread, flat, rectangular, with scalloped edges. **1946** Tallant *Voodoo* 157 **New Orleans LA,** Another plate, containing the flat hard cakes called "stage planks," was put in front of the dried basile. **1947** Ballowe *The Lawd* 187 **LA,** He and Anderson went snacks at the store on crackerjack, or stage plank [Footnote: A brown gingercake] with pop to wash it down. **1966–70** *DARE* (Qu. H30, *An oblong cake, cooked in deep fat*) Inf **TX**32, Stage plank; **MS**46, Stave plank; [**SC**70, Plank [Inf uncertain];] (Qu. H32, . . *Fancy rolls and pastries*) Inf **LA**23, Stage planks—big gingerbread cookie. **1986** Pederson *LAGS Concordance,* 1 inf, **seMS,** Stage planks—plank-like tea cakes; hard icing; looked just like a plank with icing. **1996** McDowell *Leaving Pipe Shop* 54 **AL** (as of 1950s) [Black], Stage planks, the large gingerbread squares with pink frosting scalloped on the edges. **2007** in 2008 *DARE* File—Internet **GA,** I pulled in to a little gas station in north Georgia to fill up my tank and get a Coke, and instead wound up making quite a find: Uncle Al's Stage Planks. . . They're pink-frosted gingerbread-y cookies, big and flat. I remember getting them from the convenience store in Warrenton where I used to work.

stagged (off) See **stag** v **1**

stagger n

1 An attempt, try, "stab." [Also attested from nIr, though US evidence is earlier]

1859 *Harper's New Mth. Mag.* 19.137, Considering how most of our singers mouth their words, my little friend made a pretty good stagger at it. **1886** *Century Illustr. Mag.* 32.888, Bellingham arranged for Lemuel to go with him that afternoon . . and make, as he phrased it, a stagger at the job. **1966** *DARE* FW Addit **NM**2A, "I can make a stagger at it" = "I can make a try" (speaking of a tape recording). **1984** Wilder *You All Spoken Here* 154 **Sth,** *A good stagger at it:* A good try.

2 See **staggerweed 1.**

staggerbush n [Cf **staggerweed**] Cf **highland ti-ti**

A shrub of the genus *Lyonia* (formerly *Andromeda*), esp *L. mariana.* For other names of var spp see **fetterbush 1, hardhead 6c, hurrah bush, kill-lamb 2, maleberry, pipestem a, pipewood 2, poor grub, summer huckleberry, tetterbush, titi 2b, wicky.**

1837 Darlington *Flora Cestrica* 260 se**PA**, *A[ndromeda] mariana. . .* Maryland Andromeda. *Vulgò*—Stagger-bush. . . It is very abundant in New-Jersey;—where the farmers are of opinion it is destructive to sheep, when eaten by them,—producing a disease called the *staggers.* **1860** Curtis *Cat. Plants NC* 95, Stagger Bush (*A. Mariana*, Linn.)—Grows in the Lower and Middle Districts, on the margin of low grounds. **1924** *Amer. Botanist* 30.61, *Lyonia Mariana . .* is familiarly and appropriately known as "stagger-bush". Like so many other members of the Ericaceae, its foliage is poisonous to stock. **1939** FWP *Guide NJ* 18, The staggerbush, with delicate, pinkish-white, nodding flower clusters, blossoms from April to June. **1964** Batson *Wild Flowers SC* 87, Stagger-bush. . . Dry or wet woods and borders. Lower Piedmont and Coastal Plain. . . Rhode Island to Florida. **2005** in 2008 *DARE* File—Internet, *Staggerbush*—*Lyonia mariana*—Staggerbush is believed to be extinct in Connecticut. These photos were taken in New Jersey, where the plant is still common.

stagger grass n [Cf **staggerweed**]

1 A **zephyr lily** (here: *Zephyranthes atamasco*).

1821 Elliott *Sketch* 1.384 **SC, GA**, *Atamasco lilly. Stagger-grass.* Generally supposed to be poisonous to cattle, and to produce the disease in calves called "staggers." **1830** Rafinesque *Med. Flora* 2.190, Amaryllis atamasco. . . Ground lily, Stagger grass. Said to poison horses and cattle. **1901** Lounsberry *S. Wild Flowers* 66, Atamasco Lily. Stagger-grass.

2 =**copper lily.**

1936 Whitehouse *TX Flowers* 11, Stagger Grass (*Zephyranthes texana*) is a copper-colored lily blooming in August and September in Central Texas. **1951** *PADS* 15.29 **TX**, *Atamosco texana.* . . Copper-lily; stagger-grass.

3 =**fly poison 1.**

1913 U.S. Dept. Ag. *Bulletin* 536.4, In the Carolinas, cattle are poisoned by "stagger grass" (*Amianthium muscaetoxicum*) only in the spring. This lily then grows luxuriantly, at a time when there is little or no grass, and the cattle eat it in default of something better. **1964** Kingsbury *Poisonous Plants U.S.* 448, *Amianthium muscaetoxicum.* . . Staggergrass. . . Instances of loss of cattle have been reported in North Carolina. **2007** in 2008 *DARE* File—Internet, Here's a list of some known plants that could be dangerous to horses. . . Stagger grass (Amianthium muscaetoxicum; Chrosperma muscaetoxicum).

stagger juice n Also *stagger soup, ~ water* Cf *DS* DD21a, b, c

Liquor.

1862 *Weekly Oregonian* (Portland OR) 27 Sept [3]/2 (newspaperarchive.com), The poor fellow was so full of stagger-juice that he mistook the wooden image for a real live klootchman. **1886** *Ft. Wayne Weekly Gaz.* (IN) 12 Aug [2]/2 (newspaperarchive.com), An inebriated individual, who labored along under an overload of stagger juice, ambled wearily along. **1941** *AmSp* 16.70, *Liquor . .* stagger soup. **1942** Berrey–Van den Bark *Amer. Slang* 99.1, *Liquor.* . . stagger juice, -soup or water. **1951** West *Witch Diggers* 183 **IN**, Maybe not champagne. But I reckon there'll be stagger juice of some kind. **1968** Adams *Western Words* 300, *Stagger soup*—A logger's name for whisky.

staggers n [Cf **staggerweed**]

=**spreading dogbane.**

1968 *DARE* FW Addit **VA**15, Staggers = spreading dogbane. It is said to be poisonous to sheep and cattle.

stagger soup (or water) See **stagger juice**

staggerweed n [Because they cause (or are believed to cause) staggers in livestock]

1 also *stagger*: A **delphinium** or a **monkshood 1**; see quots. **chiefly sAppalachians, esp wVA**

1761 in 1926 *William & Mary Qrly.* Oct 320 **VA**, You say you never found any real species of the true *Aconite,* except that tall one, near our South Mountains. Now I should be glad to know what you take our Stagger-weed to be. **1802** in 1938 *Castanea* 3.98, I observed a single specimen of the American Wolfs Bane, Aconitum uncinatum? . . I take this to be the plant which in some parts of the United-States, is called

Stagger-weed. **1851** (1856) Dunglison *Med. Lexicon* 812, Staggerweed, Delphinium. **1898** U.S. Dept. Ag. Div. Botany *Bulletin* 20.24 **OH**, Dwarf Larkspur—*Delphinium tricorne.* . . Other name: Stagger-weed. **1901** Lounsberry *S. Wild Flowers* 175, The dwarf larkspur. . . is generally called stagger-weed . . because it is poisonous to stock which in April eat of its young shoots. **1941** in 1992 Perdue *Pigsfoot Jelly* 29 sw**VA**, *Stagger Weed:* Not many people use stagger weed for salit, but some prefer it to any others. . . Cattle are fond of the herb and in feeding on it they sometimes pull up the root and it is said that one small root will kill a cow. . . Crowsfoot grows in the same locations and it is difficult for the average person to tell one from the other. **1956** McAtee *Some Dialect NC* 58, *Stagger* . . the larkspur (*Delphinium tricorne*), because it poisons livestock that eat it, causing them to stagger. Mitchell County. **1968** *DARE* (Qu. S23, *Pale blue flowers with downy leaves and cups that come up on open, stony hillsides in March or early April*) Inf **IN**14, Staggerweed; (Qu. S26c, *Wildflowers that grow in woods*) Inf **VA**24, Staggerweed—same as larkspur; (Qu. S26e, *Other wildflowers not yet mentioned;* not asked in early QRs) Inf **VA**7, Staggers—blue bloom—will kill cattle. **1980** *Castanea* 45.244 sw**VA**, The slopes. . . are protected from grazing during the spring growing season because of the presence of *Delphinium tricorne . . ,* locally known as stagger-weed because of its toxic effect on livestock. **1987** Young *Latchpins* 28 **TN**, The pieded cow and the heifer that was not yet with calf had wandered off. . . It was a wonder they hadn't been poisoned on staggerweed.

2 A **sneezeweed 1** (here: *Helenium autumnale*).

1890 SC Exper. Stations *Annual Rept. for 1890* 107, Specimens of this plant [=*Helenium autumnale*] were submitted by Mr. Thos. W. Holloway, who wrote as follows: "I send you a bundle of weeds, called by our old people Sneeze, or Stagger Weed." **1914** Georgia *Manual Weeds* 481, Sneezeweed. . . Sneezewort, Staggerweed [etc].

3 A **bleeding heart 1** such as **Dutchman's breeches 1.**

1858 Coe *Concentrated Organic Medicines* 334, Common Names.—*Turkey Corn, Turkey Pea, Staggerweed, etc.* Part Used.—*The Root.* . . This plant is the . . *Diecentra Eximia* of Gray's botany. **1925** *Logansport Morning Press* (IN) 1 Apr 8/3 s**IN**, Early spring losses [of cattle] . . have been attributed to eating Dutchmans' breeches. . . Mild cases are characterized by a staggering gait, which accounts for the common name staggerweed. **1942** *Torreya* 42.160 **VA**, *Bicuculla cucullaria.* . . Staggerweed. **1976** Lindsay *Hist. Grassy Balds* 74 w**NC**, e**TN**, Of course, the *Dicentra* never killed any cattle, but it would give them the staggers. A common name for it was staggerweed.

4 A **boneset 1.**

1981 *Knoxville Jrl.* (TN) 22 Oct sec D 3/2 e**TN**, The plant that caused [milk sickness] . . was and is *white snakeroot,* a species of *eupatorium.* In Glenn's Smoky Mountain neighborhood it was commonly called *staggerweed,* because of the behavior of livestock after they ate the leaves.

staggerwort n [Cf **staggerweed 2**]

A **sneezeweed 1** (here: *Helenium autumnale*).

1910 Graves *Flowering Plants* 398 **CT**, *Helenium autumnale.* . . Sneezeweed. Staggerwort. . . The flowers are poisonous and cattle and horses are sometimes killed by eating freely of them. **1958** Jacobs–Burlage *Index Plants NC* 54, Staggerwort. . . probably has some narcotic properties.

staggle v chiefly **Sth** *esp freq among Black speakers*

See quot 1947; hence comb *staggle-legged.*

1947 *AmSp* 22.73 **Sth**, Another unreported dialecticism is the frequentative *staggle,* which appears to indicate a pose commonly assumed by belligerent inebriates. Hence, both *stagger* and *swagger* are required to describe accurately the characteristic manner referred to in the following declaration from Columbus, Georgia: 'When a drunk comes *staggling* toward you, get out of his way.' **1950** Hughes *Simple Speaks* 223 **NYC** [Black], You can't even get drunk and walk staggle-legged down the street without somebody accusing you of disgracing the race. **1961** *Mt. Life* 37.1.7 s**Appalachians**, [In some words] *l* is substituted for *r*: . . *flitter* (fritter), *swaggle* (swagger), staggle (stagger). **1965** in 1974 Jackson *Get in the Water* 195 **TX** [Black], When Shine reached New York people was on the panic,/ they talkin' about the great *Titanic./* Shine staggled [Jackson: sic] through the crowd just about drunk. **1966** Ibid 215 **TX** [Black], When you staggle out the door you wobble in your knees,/ and you wanna knock hell out a everybody you sees:/ boy, you high. **1991** Abbott *MS Writers* 4.41 [Black], You should've seen the look on his face when his butt hit the ground. . . He looked like a klansman who just staggled into [a] NAACP rally.

staggon See **staging**

staghorn cholla n Also *staghorn (cactus)* Cf **buckhorn cholla, deerhorn cactus**

A **prickly pear 1,** esp *Opuntia versicolor.*

1924 Austin *Land of Journeys' Ending* 130 **AZ,** Inside the choyital . . there will be islands of needlegrass, preferred by the reddish-stemmed *Opuntia* which is called, from the manner of its branching, "stag-horn," and dense, globose clumps of *Opuntia arbuscula.* **1929** in 1949 Denton *Pages from a Diary* 263 **cCO,** About us were low pines and cedar, oaks, greasewood, stag horn cactus, . . and desert flowers. **1947** Carr *Desert Parade* 83, Staghorn or tree cholla. . . a conspicuous treelike plant with upright greenish purple trunk and rounded crown of branches that are sometimes reddish in color and may suggest the branching formation of a stag's antlers. **1967** DARE (Qu. S26e, *Other wildflowers not yet mentioned; not asked in early QRs*) Inf **CA4,** Staghorn cholla. **1973** *AZ Highways* 49.3.29, The . . Staghorn Cholla *(Opuntia acanthocarpa),* also known as the Buckhorn Cholla. **2008** DARE File—Internet, Fruits are the most distinctive indicator: Staghorn cholla fruit is fleshy when mature, usually spineless, and stays on the plant for more than a year.

staghorn moss n Also *staghorn evergreen, stag's horn* [OED2 1741 →]

A **club moss** (here: usu *Lycopodium clavatum*).

1882 *Amer. Homoeopathic* 309, *Common Names,* Club-Moss. Stag's Horn. Witch Meal. Wolf's Claw. The sporules of Lycopodium Clavatum, *Linn.* **1897** *Jrl. Amer. Folkl.* 10.147 **MA,** *Lycopodium clavatum.* . . stag-horn evergreen, Concord. **1938** Small *Ferns SE States* 415, *L[ycopodium] clavatum.* . . Staghorn-moss. **1954** Bodenberg *Mosses* 2, One Lycopodium is known as "stag-horn moss" because the candelabra-like fruiting structures (strobili) resemble the antlers of the stag. **1974** (1977) Coon *Useful Plants* 181, Lycopodium clavatum—Club moss . . plus such other interesting names as . . hog's bed, snake moss, and stag's horn.

staghorn sculpin n [From the preopercular spine]

A **cabezon** (here: *Leptocottus armatus*).

1948 *Jrl. Marine Research* 7.461 **sCA,** Morro Bay has. . . the southern California subspecies of the staghorn sculpin, *Leptocottus armatus,* and the northernmost population of the pipefish. **1953** Roedel *Common Fishes CA* 140, Staghorn Sculpin. . . a large antlerlike spine on the preopercle. **2001** in 2003 DARE File—Internet **CA,** Unfortunately, small speckled sanddab and staghorn sculpin (bullheads) will often fight to get on to your hook first.

staghorn sumac n

Std: a chiefly eastern **sumac B** *(Rhus hirta).* Also called **buckhorn 1, drupe, hoghorn sumac, velvet ~, vinegar tree, Virginia sumac, white sumac 2**

staging n Also *stag(g)on* esp **Missip-Ohio Valleys**

A length of twine used to connect a hook to a **trotline** n[1] or float; also *staging twine:* a kind of twine suitable for this purpose; hence v *staging* to attach (a hook) to such a length of line.

1863 *Portsmouth Times* (OH) 20 June [2]/6 (newspaperarchive.com), [Advt:] Trot Lines, Staging, and Small Lines, at Wholesale and Retail. **1886** *Daily Rev.* (Decatur IL) 5 May [2]/2 (newspaperarchive.com), [Advt:] Seine twine, trout lines, staging and a complete line of fishing tackle. **1902** *Shop Talk* 2.11.7 **Missip Valley,** To each of the gas pipes is attached twenty-four-foot stagons, similar to those used on an ordinary trout line, and each stagon has four hooks with four hooks. **1914** *Indianapolis Star* (IN) 18 Feb 4/6, [Advt:] Chalk Lines, Staging Twine, Seine and Trout Line [etc]. **1953** (1977) Hubbard *Shantyboat* 69 **Missip-Ohio Valleys,** We put out a trot line. . . Andy "stagin'd" about fifty hooks, showing us the clever way in which he tied each hook to a short piece of light twine he called a staging. **1957** Clark *Song of the River* 49 **KY,** He figured that he had about enough money for a good line, a few extra hooks, and maybe a ball of staggon for nibs. **1960** Criswell *Resp. to PADS 20* **Ozarks,** Staging. . . Heavy line used to tie hooks to a trot line. **1968–69** DARE Tape KY5, I've got the needle here that I've sewed my broom through with, with staging ['stejɪŋ] twine; **OH58,** A hand line was just a piece of staging ['stejŋ] with a rock tied on one end. . . The hooks would have probably a eighteen-inch piece of staging tied to it. **2003** DARE File—Internet **NC,** The jugger's gear consists of a gallon jug or oil can rigged with a two- to three-foot staging and a large hook. Ibid **TX,** The only thing left to do is to place your hooks and staging on the trotline. **2008** Ibid **cnKY** (as of 1950s), Sometimes

the catch was . . slimy eels that wrapped themselves in a tangle too taut to unwind in the relatively thin cotton cord we called "staggon".

stag pants n Also *stags* [**stag** v **1**]

Among loggers: trousers cut off at mid-calf or manufactured in this length.

1907 *Tech. World Mag.* 8.311 **nMI,** There is a full stock of Mackinaw jackets, stag-pants, heavy underwear, socks, hurons, shoe-pacs, mittens and caps. [**1914** see **stag shirt**.] **1931** *WI Rapids Daily Tribune* (WI) 21 Oct 4/2, Around nearly every small railroad depot in Wisconsin's lumbering regions today there is a small band of weather beaten men, with wool shirts, abbreviated stag pants, leather boots, and pack sacks on their backs. They are the remnants of Wisconsin's colorful lumberjacks. **1956** Sorden–Ebert *Logger's Words* 35 **Gt Lakes,** Stags, Pants cut off at the bottom of the legs about at boot tops. **1958** McCulloch *Woods Words* 180 **Pacific NW,** Stag pants—Work pants cut off short to get rid of dangerous cuffs which can catch and trip a man. Also cut off to give greater leg action; and to dry out faster when working in the water. **1984** [see **stag shoe**].

stag shirt n [By analogy with **stag pants**]

Orig among loggers: a heavy shirt with the tails cut off, or manufactured without tails, and worn as a jacket.

1914 *Outing* 63.556 **Gt Lakes,** When manufacturers of woodsmen's clothing learned of the lumberjack's waste of perfectly good cloth, they began making short-length trousers and heavy shirts that reached to the middle of the hips. The lumberjack has been wearing such clothing for years, but . . I have never seen a stag shirt on sale except in small towns in the North Woods. Last year a firm in Duluth, Minn., placed them on the market for hunters and canoeists. **1944** Binns *Timber Beast* 32 **WA** (as of c1940), You should have seen me in my Paul Bunyan days! I wore a stag shirt and tin pants sagged [sic] off at the top of my logging boots. **1979** Keith *Hell* 31 **MT** (as of c1920), Half a dozen of us would take a blanket or stag shirt and fold up our share of grub in it. **2008** DARE File—Internet, [Advt:] Woolrich Classic Wool Stag Shirt—Long Sleeve—Men's.

stag shoe n Also *stag* [By analogy with **stag pants**]

Esp among loggers: a boot or shoe with the uppers cut down to form a slipper.

1956 Sorden–Ebert *Logger's Words* 35 **Gt Lakes,** Stag-shoes, Shoes with tops cut off to form slippers. **1969** Patty *N. Country* 101 **AK** (as of 1940s), He was wearing . . heavy wool socks tucked into "stags"— shoe-pacs with the tops cut off to form homemade slippers. **1984** *MJLF* 10.157 **ME, WI,** Stags. Boots with the tops cut off, or shortened trousers.

stag's horn See **staghorn moss**

stahb See **stob** n

stair n[1] Usu |stɛr|; also |stær|; also **Sth, S Midl** |star, stɑr|; for addit varr see quot 1989 Pronc-spp *sta'ar, star(r)* Cf Pronc Intro 3.I.1.b, **star** n[1]

Std sense, var forms.

1827 (1939) Sherwood *Gaz. GA* 139, Starrs, for Stairs. **1850** Garrard *Wah-to-yah* 255 **NM,** He went first, cautioning me not to slip on the dark sta'ars. **1863** *Continental Mth.* 3.292 **Sth** [Black], Dey'm upstars in a room. **1881** *Scribner's Mth.* 22.444 **GA** [Black], She had 'er upsta'rs en down-sta'rs. **1899** (1912) Green *VA Folk-Speech* 415, Stars. . . Stairs. "He went up stars to bed." **1942** Hall *Smoky Mt. Speech* 24 **wNC, eTN,** [æ] occurs in . . stair. **1961** *Language* 37.560 **Pacific NW,** [ɛ] ten, egg, . . stairs, care. **1961** Kurath–McDavid *Pronc. Engl.* 119, The vowels in *stairs*. . . [T]he folk speech of the piedmont of Virginia and adjoining parts of North Carolina have a low vowel [a ~ ɑ] in *stairs, theirs.* **1989** Pederson *LAGS Tech. Index* 42 **Gulf Region,** Stairs. [Of 914 infs, 505 infs responded with proncs of the type [stær]; 158 infs, [stɝ]; 16 infs, [stɑr]; 15 infs, [ster]; 3 infs, [stɪr]; 1 inf, [stʌr].] **1990** Amory *Cat & Curmudgeon* 192 **eTX,** On the way to our first pasture I kept thinking about that East Texas accent. . . "stars" for stairs.

stair n[2] See **star** n[1]

stairsteps n pl **chiefly Sth, Midl** See Map *old-fash*

A stairway, flight of stairs.

1794 (1936) Parry *Jrl.* 34.386 **PA,** Ky. hill on the south shore is exceeding bad, being long, steep, & broken with Limestone, somewhat resembling stair-steps. **1860** *Weekly Std.* (Raleigh NC) 18 July [3]/4 (newspaperarchive.com), The fire, which had been kindled under the stairsteps inside the building, was extinguished. **a1883** (1911) Bagby *VA Gentleman* 77 **VA,** One summer night, years ago, . . a young lady tripped noiselessly down these old stair steps. **1896** *DN* 1.425 **seNY,** *Stair-steps:* for stairs. **1909** *DN* 3.375 **eAL, wGA,** *Stairsteps.* . . Stairway. Universal. **1910** *DN* 3.458 **FL, GA,** *Stair-steps.* . . Stairs. **1912** Green *VA Folk-Speech* 413, *Stairsteps.* . . The steps for going up stairs. **1943** Chase *Jack Tales* 163 **wNC** (as of 1880s), So Jack went on up the stair steps. **1956** McAtee *Some Dialect NC* 43, *Stairsteps:* . . a flight of steps. **1965–70** *DARE* (Qu. D6, *To get to the second floor, you walk up the* _____) 34 Infs, **chiefly Sth, S Midl,** Stairsteps. [31 Infs old, 30 comm type 4 or 5] **1974** *Charleston Daily Mail* (WV) 24 Sept sec B 10/2, [Advt:] Follow me up the spiral stair steps to 4 bedrooms. **1983** *MJLF* 9.1.57 **ceKY** (as of 1956), *Stairsteps* . . a flight of stairs. **1986** *Barrick Coll.* **csPA** (as of 1940s), *Stair-steps*—stairs. . . He fell down the stair-steps and broke his leg. **1986** Pederson *LAGS Concordance (Stairway)* 67 infs, **Gulf Region,** Stairstep(s). **2006** in 2008 *DARE* File—Internet **OH,** I always walk up the stair steps at Treasure Island to the garage.

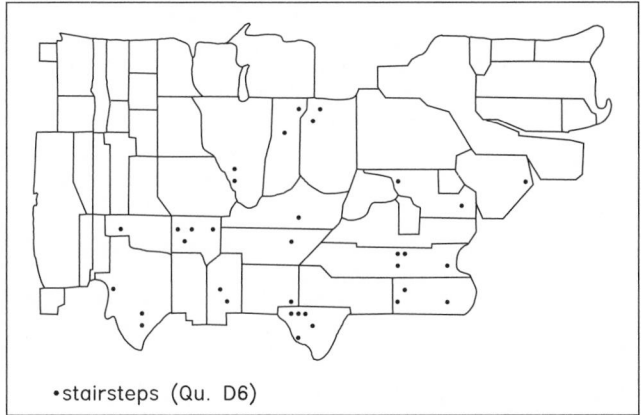

•stairsteps (Qu. D6)

stake n, often attrib   Also *stake of Zion*   **Mormon settlement areas**

In the Mormon Church: a territorial division composed of a number of **wards;** hence n *stake house* the building housing the offices of the divisional administrators and other church facilities.

[**1833** J. Smith in Linn *Story of Mormons* 120 *(DAE),* It is expedient in me that this Stake that I have set for the strength of Zion be made strong. **1839** *Ibid,* I have other places which I will appoint unto them, and they shall be called Stakes for the curtains, or the strength of Zion.] **1842** Kidder *Mormonism* 121, The church that was to be established in Jackson county was called Zion, . . and those established by revelation, in other places, were called stakes of Zion, or stakes; hence the stake at Kirtland, the stake at Far West, the stake at Adamondiamon, &c. **1852** Stansbury *Expedition* 142 **UT,** The settlement at San Pete was begun, sixty families leaving in a body, under one of the high officers of the church, . . to establish another "stake" in the wilderness. **1931** Foster *Larry* 131 **AZ,** Then we all paraded down to the Stake House (Mormon Districts are called 'Stakes'), where there was a pioneer's meeting. **1966** Barnes–Jensen *Dict. UT Slang* 40, *Stake.* . . In the Mormon Church a stake comprises several wards . . and presiding over it is a President and Counsellors. **1966** *DARE* Tape **ID**1, There are thirteen of these wards that comprise about four thousand people. That is known as the stake in the Mormon Church. **1968** *DARE* (Qu. FF2, . . *Kinds of parties*) Inf **UT**5, Stake dances—through the LDS Church. **1969** *DARE* FW Addit **seID,** *Stake house*—in Mormon church, the church building that serves as the center of the stake. "There will be a dance at the Pocatello stake house." Heard on radio. **1969** O'Connor *Horse & Buggy West* 244 **AZ,** Mesa, a town only seven miles away, was heavily Mormon, had a temple, and there were Mormon "stake houses" scattered around. **1983** *Salt Lake Tribune* (UT) 29 May sec B 19/5, [He] was chorister and organist in both stake and ward organizations. **1996** *Verbatim* Autumn 8 [Mormon English], The towns were organized politically in a way previous Mormon colonies in the eastern states (Kirtland, Ohio, and Nauvoo, Illinois) were, into *stakes* and *wards.*

stake v   Cf **rider** n 1, **stake-and-rider fence**

To reinforce a fence with stakes—in v phr *stake-and-rider (in)* to build or reinforce a fence with stakes and **riders;** hence ppl adj phr *staked-and-ridered* provided with a **stake-and-rider fence** or, of a fence: reinforced with stakes and **riders.**

1787 (1925) Washington *Diaries* 3.208 **VA,** Women [were] staking and ridering fence of the said field. **1816** *OH Repository* (Canton) 6

June [3]/4 (newspaperarchive.com), [Advt:] About 22 acres enclosed with good fence, staked and ridered. **1844** (1930) W. Sewall *Diary* 265 **ME,** I staked and ridered in about half of the cross fence. **1852** MI State Ag. Soc. *Trans. for 1851* 3.333, The staked and ridered domicil, lopped over like some old lame hen. **1872** U.S. Dept. Ag. *Rept. of Secy. for 1871* 501 **NY,** A part of the worm-fence is staked and ridered, and some is wired, and varies from 4 to 5 ½ feet high, the latter only in Livingston. **1885** *Atlantic Mth.* 55.757 **eTN, wNC,** The corn . . waved above the staked and ridered fence. **1984** Wilder *You All Spoken Here* 53 **Sth,** Ugly as a mud fence staked and ridered with tadpoles.

stake-and-bunk fence   See **bunk-and-toggle fence**

stake-and-cap fence n   Cf **cap-and-stake fence,** *DS* L61, 62

Usu a rail fence reinforced by pairs of vertical stakes connected at the top by a **cap** n[1] **12,** but see quot 1853.

1843 *Farmers' Reg.* 1.65 **cwVA,** The common rail, with 4½ feet worm, is in most general use, but occasionally you see the "Jefferson," or stake and cap fence. **1853** WI State Ag. Soc. *Trans.* 2.191, We concluded . . to make what we call a "stake and cap fence." This kind of fence is made by splitting stakes from logs cut five and a half feet long, somewhat smaller than ordinary rails, sharpening the end . . , then setting them in the ground. . . The stakes should be set in a line and drove evenly upon the top to receive the cap board, which should be of white oak, sawed one by three inches, and nailed to the top end of the stakes. **1860** Todd *Young Farmer's Manual* 76, *Stake and Cap Fence.* . . Fig. 18 represents two different modes of staking a zigzag fence. . . Let the stakes all be sharpened for driving, and the top ends dressed off, so that the caps will go on readily before they are brought on to the ground. **1890** *Century Illustr. Mag.* 40.937 **NY,** She had built the stake-and-cap fences that divided the fields. **1931–33** *LANE Worksheets* **VT,** *Stake and cap fence.* . . A zigzag fence, with the intersections of the rails capped.

stake-and-rail fence n   esp **NEast**   Cf *DS* L61, 62

Usu a rail fence reinforced by pairs of vertical stakes, but see quot 1939.

1844 NY Ag. Soc. *Trans. for 1843* 499, There are 250 rods of good board fence, the rest good stake and rail fence. **1858** (1859) Buck *Hist. Montgomery Co.* 91 **PA,** In the vicinity of the present prison, was the old jail lane, with a stake and rail fence on each side. **1860** Todd *Young Farmer's Manual* 86, This kind of fence [=a rod fence] is made like the zigzag stake and rail fence, with an iron rod passing through all the rails at the joints. **1871** ME Dept. Ag. *Annual Rept. for 1870* 315, If you want to build a stake and rail fence, you must have, for every length of fence, two stakes, a cap, a bunk, and four rails of ordinary size, to satisfy the fence viewers. **1890** NJ State Bd. Ag. *Annual Rept. 1889–90* 463, Farmers consider the best all-purpose farm fence cedar and chestnut stake and rail worm fence. **1903** *Post-Std.* (Syracuse NY) 27 Nov 5/6, He has, unaided, built thirty rods of stake and rail fence, which stands as straight as any a man of 50 could build. **1939** *LANE* Map 117, *Rail fence.* . . The *stake-and-rail fence,* [is one] in which the rails rest in crotches formed by crossed stakes driven into the ground. The rails may slant from these crotches to the ground or may be placed horizontally. . . 2 infs, **CT,** Stake-and-rail.

stake-and-rider   See **stake** v

stake-and-rider fence n   Also *stake-and-rider, stake-and-ridered fence*   old-fash

A fence reinforced with, or consisting of, crossed stakes supporting a top bar; broadly, a rail fence; see quots.

1829 *MA Spy & Worcester Co. Advt.* (Worcester MA) 11 Feb 2/5, Meeting a man in a lane with a *stake and rider* fence on each side he inquired of him if he knew Peter Francisco. **1846** *Knickerbocker* 27.208, Already the 'stake and ridered' fence was beginning to enclose the cleared land. **1885** Cable *Dr. Sevier* 402 **LA,** They followed him, along a line of stake-and-rider fence, with the woods on one side. **1895** *Century Illustr. Mag.* 50.625 **KY,** The stake-and-ridered fences everywhere, and the barbed wire in the Blue Grass, would make following [the fox] impossible. **1899** (1912) Green *VA Folk-Speech* 414, *Stake and rider.* . . A fence made higher by another rail being put on the locks. **1909** *DN* 3.416 **nME,** *Stake and rider fence.* . . A fence made in the following manner: heavy logs called bunks about two and a half feet long are laid at right angles to the line of the fence, nearly the length of a rail apart. Two large holes are bored in each bunk into which are set upright stakes. Rails, usually split, are laid from bunk to bunk between the stakes. Short blocks called toggles are laid on top of the rails between the stakes and other rails are laid on these. Thus the fence is built as high as desired. The stakes are held in place at the top by riders resembling bunks, but lighter. **1917** *DN* 4.389 **neOH,** *Cap, fence-cap.* . . A rectangular piece of wood . . with a large hole near each end. It is placed over the upper ends of two stakes in making a stake-and-rider fence. **1928** Aldrich *Lantern* 37 **NE,** She slipped out of the clearing, climbed the stake-and-rider fence, and saw Mary coming. **1931** Webb *Gt. Plains* 281, Another fault of the worm fence was that stock could push the top rails off. . . This was prevented by setting up across the interlocking corners two rails which served to hold the other rails in place and afforded a crotch in which the top rail could be laid. This was called a stake-and-rider fence. **1941** Justus *Cabin on Kettle Creek* 112 **eTN,** They burned their garden palings and rails from the stake-and-rider fence. **1965–70** *DARE* (Qu. L61, *Fences made of solid logs, now or in the past*) 34 Infs, **scattered,** Stake-and-rider fence; **CA**187, Stake-and-rider fence—a zig-zag fence; **IA**31, Stake-and-rider fence—poles laid together like your fingers interlaced, zigzagged back and forth; had a corner stake; **IL**31, Stake-and-rider fence—type of rail fence; stake goes upward and holds the corner, a zigzag fence; **PA**75, Stake-and-rider fence—same as a worm fence; (Qu. L62, *A fence made of split logs*) Infs **AR**4, **CA**136, Stake-and-rider fence; (Qu. L65, . . *Kinds of fences*) Infs **CO**7, **MA**5, **OH**53, **PA**141, 204, **WA**11, Stake-and-rider fence. [38 of 46 Infs old] **1965** Needham–Mussey *Country Things* 16 **sVT,** The stake-and-rider took more poles [than a pole fence] but it was harder to break through. You drove your two stakes to make an X, the same as for a pole fence. Then you laid a pole in the X, but let the far end rest on the ground. You drove another X over this pole about halfway along, and laid another pole on that, with its far end on the ground; and so on all around the pasture. **1983** *MJLF* 9.1.57 **ceKY** (as of 1956), *Stake and rider fence* . . a rail fence in which the top rail is laid on crossed stakes driven into the ground. . . *Stake and ridered fence* . . a stake and rider fence.

stake-bound See **stakey**

staked-and-ridered See **stake** v

staked-and-ridered fence See **stake-and-rider fence**

stake driver n [See quot 1853] **chiefly NEng** See Map Cf **pile driver 1**
=**bittern.**

1814 in 1815 MA Hist. Soc. *Coll.* 2d ser 3.101 **NH,** Among the birds that are found here [=in Lancaster] are . . stake-driver or bittern [etc]. **1851** (1949) Thoreau *Jrl.* 3.69 **ceMA,** Minott calls the stake-driver "belcher-squelcher." **1853** Thompson *App. to Hist. VT* 27, This bird is called by a great variety of names, but is most generally known in Vermont by the name of *Stake Driver.* This name is given it, on account of the resemblance of the sound, it makes in the breeding season, to that made by a smart blow and its echo, in driving a stake into the ground, resembling somewhat the uncouth syllables of *'pump-au-gah.* **c1870** in 1950 *AmSp* 25.183 **CT,** Stake-driver. A species of heron. **1897** *Oölogist* 14.81 **IL,** When an amateur is told that the sound is produced by a bird [=the great bittern], the Stake-driver, he is not surprised by the name. **1950** *WELS* (*A small heron that makes a booming sound before rain, and often stands with its head pointed up*) 2 Infs, **WI,** Stake driver. **1965–70** *DARE* (Qu. Q7, *Names and nicknames for . . game birds*) Inf **MA**42, Stake driver; (Qu. Q8, *A water bird that makes a booming sound before rain and often stands with its beak pointed almost straight up*) Infs **MA**30, 78, **MI**2, 65, **NH**14, **NY**92, Stake driver; **MA**42, Stake driver—generally hear it in afternoon or early morning; (Qu. Q10, . . *Water birds and marsh birds*) Infs **MA**15, **MI**2, Stake driver. **1975** Gould *ME Lingo* 273.

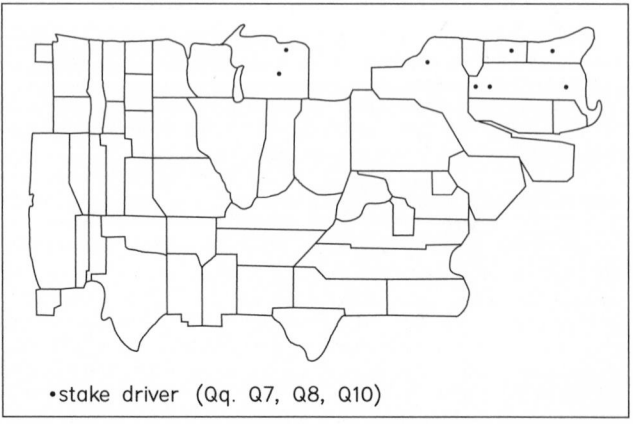

•stake driver (Qq. Q7, Q8, Q10)

stake house, stake of Zion See **stake** n

stakey adj Also sp *staky;* also *stake-bound* [*OED2* stakey 1919 →; "chiefly *Canad.*"] **chiefly Inland Nth**
Esp among loggers: having money to spend, flush.

1927 *AmSp* 2.392 [Vagabond argot], *Weed* and *pay-off* are expressions used by stiffs who clutter up the skidroad. When a *staky* worker comes to town, his giving money to his impecunious acquaintances is called the *pay-off.* **1930** Williams *Logger-Talk* 29 **Pacific NW,** Staky: Having a sum of money and apt to quit the job any time; also *stake-bound.* **1956** Sorden–Ebert *Logger's Words* 35 **Gt Lakes,** Stake-bound, See stakey-logger. *Stakey,* With lots of money. *Stakey-logger,* One who has wages enough due him to make him restless to get to town. Same as stake-bound. **1958** McCulloch *Woods Words* 180 **Pacific NW,** *Stakebound.* . . A logger with too much money; won't go back to work until he is broke. **1961** in 1990 Brehm *Sweetwater* 65 **nWI,** "He must be hard up as hell." . . "Alky," Petersen said. "Looking to get stakebound." **1965** Bowen *Alaskan Dict.* 31, *Stakey.* Twitchy. A term describing a man who has made his stake and doesn't want to stay on the job any longer. **1966** *DARE* Tape **MI**10, If you were headed out of the woods for Newberry or Eckerman or Trout Lake. . . and if you were thirsty, which you were apt to be, and loaded for bear, everybody conceded that you were stake-bound.

stalded See **stall**

stale n

1 also sp *steal:* A long handle for a tool, esp a rake. [*OED2* stale sb.² 2 a1200 →] **NEast**

1816 Pickering *Vocab.* 181 **NEng,** Steal (pron. *stail*). The handle of various implements; as a *rake-steal,* a *fork-steal,* &c. Used by the farmers in some parts of New England. **1850** *Scientific Amer.* 6.71 **NY,** Price of Lathe for turning broom and hoe handles, rake stales, scythe snaths, windsor and cottage chair legs and pillars, $100. **1894** *DN* 1.342 **wCT,** *Stale:* handle of a tool. . . In regular use in *rake-stale,* less common in *fork-stale. Pipe-stale* is rare. **1924** U.S. Golf Assoc. *Bulletin Green Sec.* 217 **MA,** A rake, the teeth of which are so blunt that a considerable pressure upon the rake stale is required to make them bite, is a labor-wasting tool. **1965** Needham–Mussey *Country Things* 85 **VT,** Ash was another wood that Gramp used quite a lot. Rake handles (stales, he called them) and pitchfork handles was nearly always ash. **2008** *DARE* File—Internet **RI,** The quahogs are scooped into the curved basket by the tines, conventionally twenty teeth. The aluminum poles, or stales, that attach to the rake can be obtained in various lengths and are made to be interchangeable.

2 in comb *poke-stale:* See quot.

1917 *DN* 4.398 **neOH,** *Poke-stale.* . . The pole, or swinging part of a poke for domestic animals, extending down and forward from the yoke.

stalk See **stock** n

stalk field n Also *cornstalk field*
A cornfield in which the stalks are left standing for livestock fodder after the ears have been picked.

1841 (1930) W. Sewall *Diary* 223 **IL,** Turned cattle into stalk field. **1845** *Cultivator* 2.125 **NY,** The stalk fields are the main dependance of half the farmers in the country for wintering the stock. **1871** Eggleston *Hoosier Schoolmaster* 188 **sIN,** The forests, the stalk-fields, the dark hollows through which he passed, seemed to be peopled with terrors. **1885** U.S. Bur. Indian Affairs *Report* 93 **AR,** 750 tons [of hay] . . with the stalk-fields and other forage will be fair provision for the stock on hand. **1887** *Living Age* 172.693 **VA,** Amid a crashing and scattering of rotten chestnut-rails, the doctor . . lands safely in the corn-stalk field upon the other side. **1966** *DARE* (Qu. L27, *When you turn the pigs into a cornfield to finish it off, you _____;* total Infs questioned, 75) Inf **OK**52, Got the hogs and cattle in the stalk field. **2007** in 2008 *DARE* File—Internet **KS,** The next morning I set up with the outfitter on an open knoll between the roost and a cut cornfield or a "stalk field" as them Jayhawks call it. **2008** *Ibid* **nwIL,** It wasn't very fun running around in a muddy corn-stalk field chasing goats in an expensive pair of tennis shoes.

stall v Cf Intro "Language Changes" II.5, **-ed** suff **1**
Std senses, var forms.

Past, past pple: usu *stalled;* also **chiefly Sth, S Midl** *stal(l)ded, stalted.*

1855 *Harper's New Mth. Mag.* 11.289 **VA,** May I be stalded in a mud-hole. **1889** *Ibid* 78.908 **GA,** They tryin' to prize out one o' their waggins that's been stallded in a mud-hole. **1903** *DN* 2.331 **seMO,** *Stall.* . . To stick fast in the mud. 'My team stalded three times on the way to town.' **1907** *DN* 3.236 **nwAR,** *Stallded, pret.* of stall. Stuck fast in the mud. **1909** *DN* 3.375 **eAL, wGA,** *Stalded, pret.* and *pp.* of *stall,* to mire or be brought to a standstill. "My horses stalded, and I couldn't go no further." **1914** *DN* 4.113 **cKS,** *Stalted.* . . Stalled; unable to move. **1919** *DN* 5.35 **seKY,** *Stalded,* p. and p. p. of *stall.* . . "Our car stalded." **1968** *DARE* Tape **VA25,** They would always take and get stallded going up. **1986** Pederson *LAGS Concordance,* 1 inf, **cTN,** I'm stallded up on that. **2002** in 2006 *DARE* File—Internet **PA,** When my brother came to get us from school in his car we went to get gas and stalded in the drive way.

stallion n

1 An attractive woman. *among Black speakers* Cf **fox** n **1**

1970 Major *Dict. Afro-Amer. Slang* 108, *Stallion:* a good-looking black woman. **1971** Roberts *Third Ear* np [Black], *Stallion* . . a nice looking girl. **1972** *AmSp* 47.152 (as of 1970) [Black], Hey man, did you see that stallion? **1972** Claerbaut *Black Jargon* 81, *Stallion* . . a physically appealing female; beautiful girl. **1986** Pederson *LAGS Concordance (A very attractive girl or woman)* 1 inf, **swAL,** Stallion; 1 inf, **cnTN,** Stallion—woman with "outstanding" proportions. [Both infs Black] **1994** Smitherman *Black Talk* 214, *Stallion*—See Fox. [*Ibid* 115, *Fox*—A good-looking female.] **2007** *DARE* File—Internet [Black], A stallion has to be *plus-sized.* Think Chaka Khan or Queen Latifah. E.g., Halle Berry is a fox, but she ain't no stallion. It's not necessary that the woman be black. Any "fine" or "fine and healthy" . . B[ig]B[eauti-ful]W[oman] is a stallion.

2 also *sawstallion:* See quots. [By analogy with *sawhorse*]

1975 Gould *ME Lingo* 273, *Stallion*—A sawhorse, but one with the crossed legs on one end only. A long pole extends in the other direction, so the *stallion* is an elongated tripod. It is meant for *sled-length* firewood, which runs too long to balance on the ordinary four-legged sawhorse. Usually called a sawstallion. **2006** *DARE* File—Internet **CT,** I need the ability to hoist log ends up so that I can place a set of saw stallions appropriately. My initial thoughts center on a taller saw horse design.

stalted See **stall**

stammerwort n

1 A **ragweed 2** (here: *Ambrosia artemisiifolia*). [Because it was prescribed for speech impediments]

1876 Hobbs *Bot. Hdbk.* 112, Stammerwort, Roman wormwood, Ambrosia artemisiifolia.

2 A **ragwort** (here: *Senecio jacobaea*).

1940 Clute *Amer. Plant Names* 272, *Senecio Jacobaea.* Stinking nanny, . . stammerwort [etc.].

stamp v [Engl folkl; cf 1959 (1967) Opie–Opie *Lore Schoolchildren* 206–8]

To strike the palm of the left hand with the right fist upon seeing (something deemed a good omen)—freq in phr *stamp a white horse;* hence vbl n *stamping* a performance of this ritual; see quots.

1913 *Anaconda Std.* (MT) 10 Oct 6/4, What has become of the old-fashioned boy who used to "stamp" white horses? **1939** FWP *Guide KS* 104, Beliefs prevalent among Kansas children include "stamping a white horse." **1940** in 1966 Goldstein–Byington *Two Penny Ballads* 160 **PA,** If you stamp a white horse by licking the right index finger, placing it in your left palm, and then striking the spot with the right fist—at a certain number of such "stampings" you will be granted your wish. **1958** *Resp. to PADS 29,* My own two sons had a custom which I have never heard explained. We called it "stamping white horses." No matter where they were or what they might be carrying, they stopped dead still and stamped their fists, or one fist upon the palm of the other hand, whenever or wherever they saw a white horse. [**1967** *DARE* (Qu. BB51b, . . *'Magical' cures for corns or warts*) Inf **MI65,** See a white horse, wet fingers on mouth and slap hands.] **1970** *NC Folkl.* 18.58, If you see a white horse or mule, spit on your hands and stamp him for good luck. **c1970** *DARE* File **csKY,** Stamp the white horses—Lick thumb on right hand, place it in palm of left, double right fist, hit left palm. After you have 100 objects (or if a mule, 10 times) good luck would follow. **2002** *DARE* File—Internet, Each time you stamp a white horse you add a year to your life. . . If a red automobile is seen, stamp it and make a wish. . . If you see a gray horse, stamp it and you will have good luck. . . Stamp a white horse for luck. Stamp one hundred and fifty

gray mules for luck. . . When you see a horse, stamp him for good luck. **2004** *DARE* File **cwCA** (as of 1950s), On seeing a white horse, we would "make a wish and stamp it." After making the wish we would lick the tip of the right index finger, put it in the left palm, strike the left palm with the right fist, and the wish would presumably come true.

stamp brand See **stamp iron**

stampies exclam

See quots.

1976 *Philadelphia Mag.* Mar 125, Whenever somebody got a new pair of shoes, you said, "stampies" and stepped on their feet. If you had shoes and said, "No stampies!" *before* the other person said "stampies," then they couldn't step on you. **2006** *DARE* File—Internet **NJ,** *Tagggg.* . . No stampies—no earsiesz—no touch baq—ur still it. *Ibid* **WI,** I tricked you into being my girlfriend, and I officially call no take backs, no stampies.

stamping See **stamp**

stamp iron n Also *stamping iron* **West** Cf **running iron**

A branding iron that burns a fixed brand in a single application; hence n *stamp brand* a brand so applied.

1919 *Mt. Democrat* (Placerville CA) [11 Aug 6]/6 (newspaperarchive.com), The easiest brands to read are those made with the stamp iron, that is, an iron forged into the figure or character desired. **1944** Adams *Western Words* 153, *Stamp brand*—One made with a set branding iron which burns the complete brand with one impression. **1946** Mora *Trail Dust* 181 **West,** There are two different types of branding irons: the stamp iron and the running iron. *Ibid* 184, The stamping iron, as the name indicates, is a mechanically made die that stamps its design at one quick pressing.

stan' See **stand** v **1**

stance n [Cf *EDD stance* sb. 3 "A stall; a separate place for each animal in a stable"] Cf **staunch**

A stanchion.

1967 *DARE* (Qu. M11, *What do you put the cow's head through when she stands in the barn?*) Inf **NJ3,** Stances [stænsɛz].

stanch See **staunch**

stanchel n Also sp *stanchil(l), stantial* [Scots and chiefly nEngl dial; *OED2* 1586 →; "now only *Sc.*"] **scattered, but esp NEast** See Map *old-fash* Cf **staunch**

A stanchion.

1852 Allen *Rural Architecture* 295 **NY,** The wooden stanchion, or *stanchel,* as it is called, to open and shut, enclosing the animal by the neck, we do not like. **1890** Holley *Samantha among Brethren* 193 **NY,** She wanted dretfully to see some new stanchils that Josiah had been a makin'. **1913** *DN* 4.6 **ME,** *Stantial.* . . Stanchion in a cow stall. **1914** *DN* 4.80 **ME, nNH,** *Stanchel.* . . A pole to which cattle are tied. **1924** *DN* 5.295 **csNH,** *Stanchel.* . . A stanchion for holding cows' heads. **1931–33** *LANE Worksheets* **VT,** *Stanchel*—stanchion; old-fashioned. **1950** *WELS (What do you put the cow's head through when she stands in the barn?)* 2 Infs, **WI,** Stanchel—old-fashioned; 1 Inf, **seWI,** Stanchel—occasional. **1954** *WELS Suppl.* **csWI,** Most farmers . . call a stantion [sic] for cows a "stanchill." **1959** *VT Hist.* 27.160, *Stanchion* ['stæn,ʃɪl] . . pronc. Also ['stæn,ʃɛl]. Occasional. Rural areas. **1965–70** *DARE* (Qu. M11, *What do you put the cow's head through when she*

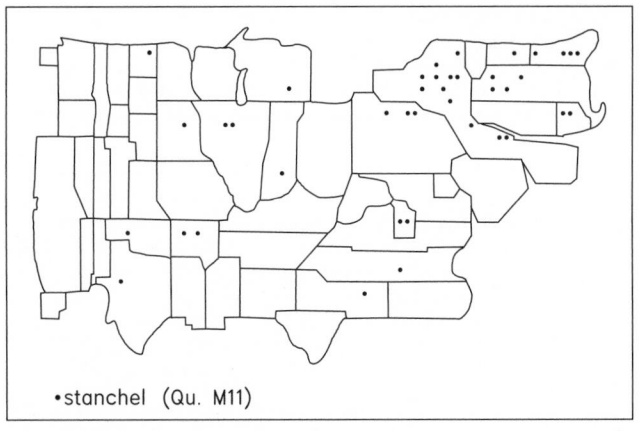

•stanchel (Qu. M11)

stands in the barn?) 40 Infs, **scattered, but esp NEast,** Stanchel. [33 Infs old] **1967** *DARE* Tape **IA**10, Then they's a little thing on top with a notch in it that you drop it down and shets their head in there—stanchels, they call 'em. **1977** *Chron.-Telegram* (Elyria OH) 19 Dec sec D 3/3, [Advt:] 3 Jamesway cow stanchels complete.

stancheous adj Also sp *stanchious* [Abbrs for arch Scots dial *substantious*]
Substantial.

1844 Thompson *Major Jones's Courtship* 33 **GA,** It's a mighty stancheous lookin bildin, and looks far off at a distance when you're gwine up to it. **1909** *DN* 3.375 **eAL, wGA,** Stanchious. . . Substantial.

stanchil(l) See **stanchel**

stanchious See **stancheous**

stand v

1 pronc-spp *stan', 'tan':* To be; to appear to be. **seSC** *Gullah* Cf 1996 Allsopp *Dict. Caribbean Engl. Usage*

1867 Allen et al. *Slave Songs* xxvii **seSC,** *Stan'* is a very common word, in the sense of *look.* "My black stan' like white man," was a boast which meant that it was not scarred with the lash. "Him stan' splendid, ma'am," of the sitting of a dress. I asked a group of boys one day the color of the sky. . . "Tom, how sky stan'?" "Blue," promptly shouted Tom. **1883** (1971) Harris *Nights with Remus* 135 **GA** [Black], I no lakky dem gal wut tie 'e wool up wit' string; mekky him stan' ugly fer true. **1892** (1969) Christensen *Afro-Amer. Folk Lore* 89 **seSC,** When Wolf come up de sun was settin' in de wes', so red stan' like fire. **1908** *S. Atl. Qrly.* 7.344 **seSC,** "How does the weather stand?" I asked my man, one morning. . . " 'E 'tan' cleah." . . "See how dem orange stan' ma'am!" said the housemaid, pinching the fruit in the basket. . . "How you stan', ol' man?" is the greeting of courtesy to old Daddy Jack. . . "Me 'tan' not berry wut; bress Go'd!" . . "Dat bu'd two foots 'tan' red," was the way a negro boy described a strange bird he had seen in the woods. **1922** Gonzales *Black Border* 300 **sSC, GA coasts** [Gullah glossary], *'E stan' so*—it, he or she, stands so, it is so, it looks so, etc. **1930** Stoney–Shelby *Black Genesis* 70 **seSC,** He pay him a heap o' compliment on how fine dat bushy head look, an' how nice dat back stan', wid de yaller marks on it. **1971** Cunningham *Syntactic Analysis Gullah* 51, C[reole:] The sky stand pretty. E[nglish:] The sky looks pretty. *Ibid* 117, Stand 'look, is'. **1992** Geraty *Bittle* 10 **Charleston SC** [Gullah], Dey [=old roosters] stan' so oagly de hen nebbuh pay'um no min'.

2 To stay, remain. [Prob calque of var foreign idioms; see quot 1962]

1937 *Times Recorder* (Zanesville OH) 19 Jan 10/4, Joe Jacobs . . guessed that boycott of the Schmeling-Jimmy Braddock fight "should have stood in bed." **1941** O'Donnell *Great Big Doorstep* 252 **sLA,** 'Listen, what do you expeck *me* to do for you?' Elna asked. 'I say you oughta stood home, any damn how.' **1943** *New Yorker* 6 Mar 13/2 **NYC,** "They should of stood in the city," Frank the Crank put in, plainly concerned over the plight of the pioneers. **1962** *AmSp* 37.202 [Yiddishisms], The clowning 'I shoulda (should have, should of) stood in bed'—rhyming the first-generation Jews' confusion of *stood* and *stayed* (the Yiddish word *shtey* means both 'stand' and 'stay'). . . [O]n radio . . a Pennsylvania announcer, after making several slips of the tongue, commented, 'Better I should have stood in bed.' **1978** Kalibabky *Hawdaw* 2.[11] **neMN,** Stood over: To have spent the night at another's home. "Yah, we stood over da last night." **1979** *DARE* File **New Orleans LA,** *Stand on the phone* . . to monopolize it or stay on too long. **1989** Nicholson *Field Guide S. Speech* 7, Stood: laid down. "We could have stood in bed and caught as many fish as we did today." **1990** in 1998 Wojcicka Sharff *King Kong* 190 **NYC,** I tried, I tried and I stopped [using crack] for three days and I stood at home. **2008** *DARE* File **LA,** When I was stationed at Fort Polk, (Louisiana), man, I *stood* in New Orleans.

3 To be said (in the newspaper, magazine, etc). [Calque of an idiom found in most Germanic languages other than English] **esp Gt Lakes**

1911 *Sun. Mercury & Herald* (San Jose CA) 3 Dec 29/1 **Gt Lakes,** [Short story:] "Yes," added Sophie, "You read so often how it stands in the paper—'a quiet wedding'—quiet is always stylish." **1932** (1969) Stephenson *Relig. Aspects* 430 **MN,** Very few of them [=children of Swedish background] now say that "it stood in the paper." **1958** *WELS Suppl.* **Milwaukee WI** (as of c1920), It stands in the paper. **1968** *DARE* (Qu. FF21b, . . *About old jokes people say: "The first time I heard that one _____."*) Inf **MN**36, It stands in the German paper

already. **1981** De Vries *Sauce* 98 **IN,** It stood in the paper the other day . . —Incidentally, Dirk says that that, you know, location, gauche as it is in English, derives from a perfectly correct Dutch, and I suppose German, construction. **2002** *DARE* File **csWI** (as of c1980), "It stood in the paper this morning," said my mother's friend Chirpie, a woman of German ancestry who had lived her entire life in Watertown, "that there are more fat people here than anywhere else in Wisconsin!"

stand n

1 A tub, barrel, or large can used to store foodstuffs—often in comb *lard stand.* [*OED2 stand* sb.² "*Obs.* exc. *dial.* . . An open tub; a barrel set on end"; c1250 →] **Sth, S Midl** Cf **stenner**

1775 Adair *Amer. Indians* 395, All his war store of provisions consisted in three stands of barbicued venison. **1782** in 2003 *DARE* File—Internet **seVA,** [Inventory:] 1 meal stand. **1811** *Ibid* **seNC,** I give and bequeath to my wife Rachel . . one oak barrel my flour stand and what flour I have [etc]. **1826** *Ibid* **eSC,** [Inventory:] Lard stand and tray—.75. **1827** *Ibid* **seNC,** Item. I give and bequeath unto my beloved wife Elizabeth Rhodes . . One large Hogshead, Ten empty Barrels, One meal stand, two Jugs [etc]. **1899** (1912) Green *VA Folk-Speech* 414, Stand. . . A tub, vat, or cask: as, a *lye-stand.* **1927** *DN* 5.470 **Appalachians,** Stand. . . A tub, churn or the like, filled, as with honey or beer. **1929** *AmSp* 5.19 **Ozarks,** Lard-stand. . . A large vessel in which lard or meat is stored. **1936** *AmSp* 11.317 **Ozarks,** Stand. . . A large can, such as is used to ship lard. 'A stand of lard,' according to the Pineville (Mo.) *Democrat,* was stolen from a house in Goodman, May 29, 1931. **1939** Hench *Coll.* **eNC,** H.P. Johnson saw a sign in Clifton, N.C. I read: "Lard 3.57 a stand." **1946** *PADS* 6.19 **eNC,** Lard stand. . . A large (twelve to sixteen quarts) tin can used to hold lard derived from hog killings. . . Common. **1952** Giles *40 Acres* 112 **KY,** I now buy it [=lard] by the stand, a stand being a fifty-pound can. **1953** *PADS* 19.14 **ceKY,** Stand. . . Vessel for lard or molasses, etc. **1966** Dakin *Dial. Vocab. Ohio R. Valley* 2.144, A related term also commonly used by those who say *(bee) gum* is *stand.* This word—usually used in compounds a *stand of lard,* a *stand of honey* . . or *lard stand, fat stand, molasses stand* is not a synonym for *barrel* or *gum.* . . Comments indicate that a *lard stand* . . might be a *barrel* or a *gum*—but that in more recent years it might also be a five gallon tin container. This old substantive use . . is attested only in Kentucky and here only rarely except in the Mountains south of the headwaters of the Kentucky River. **2003** *DARE* File—Internet **csTN,** Soak the ham overnight in a large pot or lard stand.

2 Any of var small vessels used to hold salt, sugar, syrup, or other condiments for table use. **chiefly Sth, S Midl**

1778 in 1907 *PA Archives* 6th ser 12.602, 4 salt stands. . . 18 pr. salt stands. **1813** in 2008 *DARE* File—Internet **VA,** [Inventory:] 1 Waiter cruet & salt stand. **1821** in 2003 *DARE* File—Internet **ceNC,** [Estate sale record:] 1 salt stand & salt 26 cents. **1842** (1854) Beecher *Treatise Domestic Economy* 307 **NEast,** Casters and salt-stands should be put in order, every morning. **1853** in 2002 *DARE* File—Internet **TX,** [Divorce record:] 1 molasses stand / 1 caster stand. **1860** *Ibid* **KY,** [Estate sale record:] Molasses stand .50 . . water stand $1.50. **1863** in 2003 *Ibid* **neTX,** [Estate inventory:] 1 preserve stand—2.00. . . salt stand & pepper box—1.00. **1881** *Allen Co. Democrat* (Lima OH) 6 Jan [5]/5 (newspaperarchive.com), [List of wedding gifts:] Silver syrup stand. **1903** *DN* 2.333 **seMO,** Syrup-stand. . . Syrup-cup or pitcher. **1906** *DN* 3.161 **nwAR,** Syrup . . stand. . . Syrup pitcher. **1954** *Harder Coll.* **cwTN,** Molassey stand. . . A container for molasses which is set on the table. **1965–70** *DARE* (Qu. G3, *A container for salt that's put on the table—if it's open [without a cover]*) Infs **KY**81, **VA**36, Salt stand; (Qu. G4, *A container for salt that has a cover with holes in it*) Inf **GA**4, Salt stand; (Qu. G6, . . *Dishes that you might have on the table for a big dinner or special occasion*) Inf **AR**20, Honey stand; **NC**14, Celery stands; **NC**55, Jelly stands; **NM**2, **VA**36, Preserve stand. **1986** Pederson *LAGS Concordance* **Gulf Region,** 18 infs, Molasses stand; 1 inf, A molasses stand—6″ tall, faucet, used on table; 6 infs, Stand [*DARE* Ed: described by infs as a container or pitcher for table use]; 1 inf, Stand—for sugar; 1 inf, Stand—glass jugs to keep molasses; 1 inf, Stand—glass or crockery, 5″ tall with lid; 1 inf, Stand of molasses—small, on table; 1 inf, Stand of molasses—a little-old bottle concern; 2 infs, Syrup stand; 1 inf, Syrup stand—container on table; 1 inf, Syrup stand—for molasses and syrup, used on table; 1 inf, Syrup stand—little vessel [with] lid, now called pitcher.

3 A beehive. **Sth, S Midl** Cf Intro "Language Changes" II.7, **bee stand**

[**1825** in 2003 *DARE* File—Internet **swOH,** [Estate inventory:] Four bee stands—4.00.] **1845** *Ibid* **nVA,** [Estate sale record:] 1 stand of bees—1.11. **1902** *DN* 2.246 **sIL,** *Stand.* . . A hive of bees. **1903** *DN* 2.331 **seMO,** *Stand.* . . Hive of bees, including the bees. 'He sold four stand of bees.' **1906** *DN* 3.158 **nwAR,** *Stand.* . . Hive. "I'd like to sell you a fine stand of bees." **1926** Roberts *Time of Man* 168 **KY,** My grandpap was a master hand for honey bees. . . Twenty stands he had if he had one. **c1960** *Wilson Coll.* **csKY,** *Stand.* . . A hive of bees. **1969** *DARE* (Qu. R19a, *The place where bees live and store their honey— tame bees*) Inf **TN30,** Stand. **1974** Fink *Mountain Speech* 24 **wNC, eTN,** *Stand* . . hive of bees. "Davis had nigh onto a hundred stand o' bees." **1999** *SC Market Bulletin* 4 Nov 6/2, [Advt:] *1 stand of bees,* or 1 super treated in August, requeened July.

4 The speaker's platform or pulpit at a camp meeting or in a church. **esp Sth, S Midl**

1820 in 1858 Dewees *Letters TX* 17, On the third day there was considerable excitement at the stand; some persons professed conversion, and there was a good deal of shouting. **1852** Regan *Emigrant's Guide* 175, Immediately in front of the pulpit or *stand,* as it is called, was a square of about four hundred superficial feet. **1860** Hundley *Social Relations S. States* 93, We have ourself seen an intelligent audience convulsed with laughter, while a weak brother occupied the "stand" and labored . . (sobbing convulsively all the time himself) to produce a different result. **1891** Sloan *Fogy Days* 159, We were invited down to the stand, as it was about time for the morning services. **1954** *Harder Coll.* **cwTN,** *Stand.* . . Pulpit in a church. **1963** Edwards *Gravel* 79 **eTN,** So he was capable of filling the stand (i.e., pulpit) when the pastor failed to appear at the regular monthly meeting. **1966–70** *DARE* (Qu. CC6, *The place where the preacher stands to give the sermon*) Infs **GA74, KY19, OK55,** Preacher's stand; **UT10,** Speaker's stand; **AR27, KY40, VA13,** Stand.

5 See quot. Cf **I spy** n **1**

1901 *DN* 2.149 **swMA,** *Stand.* . . A variety of I-spy.

6 A group (of buildings). [Prob by analogy with *stand* (of wheat, trees, etc)] **scattered, but esp ME**

1888 *Daily Kennebec Jrl.* (Augusta ME) 6 Jan [2]/4 (newspaperarchive.com), Edwin Sprague contemplates building a fine stand of buildings the coming season. **1914** *DN* 4.80 **ME, nNH,** *Stand o' buildin's.* . . Set of buildings. **1947** *Portland Sun. Telegram & Sun. Press Herald* (ME) 7 Dec sec A 7/1, [They] are now in their new home just a little over a month after their stand of buildings was burned to the ground. **1999** *Chr. Sci. Monitor* (Boston MA) 27 Aug (Internet) **ME,** After a mile or so we came upon a clearing and a stand of buildings. The ample barn suggested a dairy farm. **2003** *DARE* File—Internet **ME,** His whole stand of buildings was burned to the ground July 1, 1884. *Ibid* **UT,** It's an elevated, verdant section of town; the last stand of buildings as you pass east from downtown. *Ibid* **swCA,** San Diego's Loma Portal neighborhood is not the city's oldest stand of houses; nor indeed, is it rich old hardwood growth.

7 A team (of mules).

1971 *Max Hunter Folk Song Coll.* (Internet) **Ozarks,** He didn't think his title / Was so very clear / So he sold it to his Brother / For a saddle n' stand of mules. **1986** Pederson *LAGS Concordance,* 1 inf, **neTN,** A stand of mules—a team.

stand-alone child n Cf **set-along**

A child old enough to stand unaided.

1951 Craig *Singing Hills* 120 **sAppalachians,** When she was a standalone child, her uncle had her sitting on the saddle in front of him.

stander n **formerly chiefly Sth, S Midl** Cf **driver** n **3**

A hunter who waits at a particular place for the game to be driven within shooting range.

1834 *Amer. Turf Reg.* 5.299 **LA,** The major had remained in the drive the whole chase, . . but the buck eluded him as well as the standers. **1838** Gilman *S. Matron* 210, They were to scream behind them, and force the deer out to the standers. **1851** *S. Lit. Messenger* 17.46 **LA,** When the deer is certainly coming, the stander experiences a degree of excitement which would scarcely be credited. **1900** *Outing* 35.371 **seGA,** After Charles had placed all the standers, he blew several short blasts on his horn, which was a signal to Dick and Daddy Bob to put in the dogs. **1939** *Hall Coll.* **wNC, eTN,** So our drivers driv the Easy Ridge . . and the standers stood on Bear Waller Ridge. **1966** *DARE* Tape **AR15,** We've already had the standers out on stand about where we think the deer might run. **2003** *Capital Times* (Madison WI) 10 Dec sec D 6 (Internet) **swWI,** One of the standers in their deer drive saw a huge buck walk out of a wooded area that members of the group already

had driven. **2008** *DARE* File—Internet **sePA,** Our drivers make as much noise as possible in attempt to direct the game [=foxes] toward the standers.

standing cypress n Cf **fox fire 4**

Std: a **gilia** *(Ipomopsis rubra).* Also called **flaming cypress, Indian plume 4, Texas ~, Texas star f**

standing rent n [*OED2 standing* ppl. a. 14.a "Of employment, income, prices, etc.: Fixed, settled"; 1473 →] **chiefly Sth** Cf **half-hand 2, sharecropper, third and fourth**

A fixed rent paid for agricultural land (as opposed to a share of the produce); often esp a rent paid as a fixed amount of produce, esp cotton (as opposed to cash rent).

1872 U.S. Congress *Rept. Joint Select Comm. Insurrectionary States* 9.1006 **AL** [Black], I rented his land, standing rent. I had to give him eleven hundred pounds of lint cotton for twenty-eight acres. **1877** *S. Cultivator* 35.138 **GA,** My rates of renting land for standing rent are from $3 to $3.50 for upland, and $4 for bottom. . . [I]t is better, less trouble, and more agreeable to rent on reasonable terms for so many dollars or so many pounds lint cotton per acre. **1904** *S. Atl. Qrly.* 3.112 **GA,** In the last decade there has been a marked increase in the number of "standing rent" and cash tenants—the former far outnumbering the latter. According to the "standing rent" plan the land owner furnishes the land and house and gets in return a stipulated amount of cotton. **1907** *Amer. Mag.* 64.305 **Sth,** The better class of tenants rent the land for cash, a "standing rent" of some $3 an acre, though in many places in Mississippi it ranges as high as $6 and $8 an acre. **1920** U.S. Dept. Ag. *Farmers' Bulletin* 1164.4, Standing rent. . . The tenant agrees to pay so many bushels of grain or so many bales of ginned cotton for the use of the farm. **1972** Thomas *Pop. Dict. Ozarks Talk* 81, *Standin' rent.* . . Cash rental paid for use of another's land. The alternative was to pay "thirds and fourths" in kind, on cotton and corn raised.

stand in with v phr [Prob by ext from *stand in with* to be in economic or political collusion with; cf *OED2 stand* v. 95.d] **formerly more widespread, now chiefly Sth, S Midl** See Map

To side or be in league with; to be on the good side of; to ingratiate oneself with.

1873 O'Connor *Wanderings* 333, It was necessary that a magistrate should "stand in" with them, in their plans. **1884** *Century Illustr. Mag.* 27.794 **KS,** The saloon men who "stand in" with the dominant local party are protected. **1887** in 1950 *AmSp* 25.38 **New Orleans LA,** I stan' in wid de roughs. **1893** *KS Univ. Qrly.* 1.142 **KS,** *Stand in with:* to get, or keep on the right side of. **1896** *Harper's New Mth. Mag.* 92.578 **WY,** Us boys 'll stand in with him on this. **1905** (1906) Sinclair *Jungle* 111 **Chicago IL,** Mike Scully was a good man to stand in with. **1913** Wharton *Custom of Country* 258 **NY,** How far he "stood in" with the parties he left it to Ralph to conjecture. **1934** Hurston *Jonah's Gourd Vine* 230 **AL** [Black], De majority of 'em [=the congregation] don't keer what he do, some uh dese people stands in wid it. **c1960** *Wilson Coll.* **csKY.** Stand in with. . . Be on the side of, have influence with. **1963** Owens *Look to River* 53 **TX,** I hoped you'd stand in with me. Me and you make good hands together. **1965–70** *DARE* (Qu. II20b, *A person who tries too hard to gain somebody else's favor: "He's always trying to _____ the boss."*) 17 Infs, **esp Sth, S Midl,** Stand in with; (Qu. JJ3a, *When a school child makes a special effort to 'get in good' with the teacher in hopes of getting a better grade: "He's trying to _____*

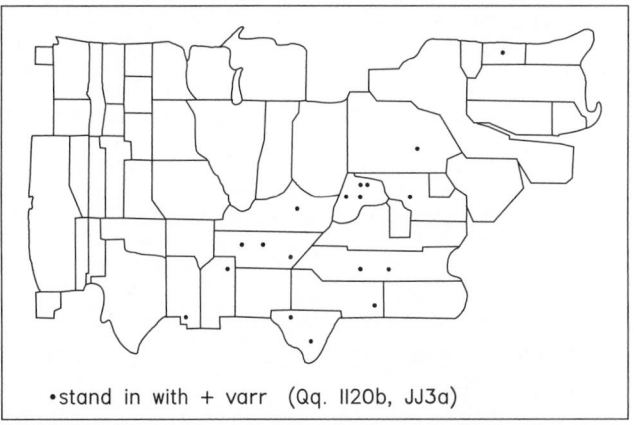

•stand in with + varr   (Qq. II20b, JJ3a)

again.") Infs **GA**28, **TN**56, Stand in with her (*or* the teacher). [17 of 19 Infs old, 18 comm type 4 or 5, 7 gs educ, 7 coll educ] **1967** Bourne *Woman in Levi's* 180 **sAZ**, Ole Pussyfoot was a newcomer who strained openly to stand in with the boss. **c1995** in 2003 *DARE* File—Internet **MS**, If you accept Christ's atonement on the cross for your sins, then you "stand in" with God the same as Billy Graham does.

stand one down v phr

1 To maintain one's opinion against, contradict stubbornly.

1905 *McClure's Mag.* 25.180 **OH**, I . . explained to him how it simply could not be, but no sir! he stood me down. Finally . . I took the almanac . . and—I bedog my riggin's if the old skidamalink wasn't right after all. **1942** Hough *All Things* 150 **MA**, Of course I called him a liar, but he stood me down. At the end of it he told me to look in my pocket, and I did, and sure enough, there was the money. **1945** U.S. Congress House *Conserv. Wildlife Hearings* 16 **MD**, They stood me down; they did not breed south of New Jersey. **1978** U.S. Congress House *Dept. Defense Appropriations* 6.147 **AL**, I was on one of those confounded call-in radio programs the other day and some guy just stood me down; he said that we have American-flag tankers sitting in ports doing nothing. **2007** in 2008 *DARE* File—Internet **SC**, I've had people stand me down about this and some of them don't get it until I take them on the grand tour of every antilock system in the lot. **2008** *Ibid*, And the Brownies leader mommy was like: "That was very good dear, except that. . . Egypt isn't in Africa!" . . I stood her down. She stood her ground. I insisted that we get out a map or a globe.

2 also *stand one up and down:* To insist to one. **Sth, S Midl**

1868 (1869) Holt *What I Know* 301 **NC**, He would have stood me down that it was false if you hadn't come with those letters. **1892** *DN* 1.232 **KY**, *Stand*. "To stand one up and down" = to contend vehemently. "She stood me up and down that I was mistaken." **1892** Harris *Uncle Remus & Friends* 290 **GA** [Black], She sot in de hall dar en stood me down dat dey wan't no ha'nts. **1905** *DN* 3.97 **nwAR**, *Stand up and down*. . . To insist. 'He stood me up and down that it was so.' **1935** Hurston *Mules & Men* 156 **FL** [Black], Devil stood Him down dat dat was a turtle. **1941** Percy *Lanterns* 327 **MS**, She walks slowly and observantly, insulting me every step. . . None of my flowers floriferous as hers. . . On leaving, after standing me down my prize Mrs. Krelages are paper-whites, she proves her case by musing wearily. **1974** *Sheboygan Press* (WI) 6 Mar 35/1 **AL**, A friend stands me down the Hagers on Hee Haw are not twins. **2006** in 2007 *DARE* File—Internet **Sth**, I was right! I had 3 people stand me down that it was "all of the sudden".

‡**3** To dress one down.

1967 *DARE* (Qu. II27, *If somebody gives you a very sharp scolding . . "I certainly got a _____ for that."*) Inf **CO**27, He stood me down.

stand one in hand v phr [*OED2 stand* v. 47.b c1400 →; "Now *dial.*"]

To be advantageous to one; to behoove one.

1816 Whelpley *Triangle* 58, But as ministers now are not inspired, . . it stands them in hand to be cautious how they drive away their hearers by pressing upon their consciences. **1835** (1841) Cooper *Monikins* 2.135 **NY**, The seamanship of Captain Poke, however, stood us in hand. **1848** Bartlett *Americanisms* 331 **NEng**, *To stand in hand*. To concern; to behoove. . . This phrase is a colloquial one in New England. Ex. 'It stands you in hand to attend to your business.' **1870** Beadle *Life in UT* 421, Governor, it stands you in hand to be careful. **1881** *Century Illustr. Mag.* 23.162 **IN**, His good penmanship stood him in hand, and he was, for a while, a copyist of deeds. **1882** *Ibid* 25.299 **NY**, It stands them in hand to know, and they do know. **1890** *DN* 1.19 **seNH**, *Stand in hand:* behoove, beseem. 'It stands you in hand to be careful.' Widely used. **1892** *DN* 1.218 **NC, TN**, *Stand in hand*. **1892** in 2003 *DARE* File—Internet **MO**, But his ingenuity, his quick perceptions, and his ardour in whatever cause he espoused, stood him in hand. **1909** *DN* 3.375 **eAL, wGA**, *Stand one in hand*. . . To be to one's advantage, behoove. **1910** (1913) White *Book Daniel Drew* 163 **NYC**, Tweed had in turn seen that it stood him in hand to be on intimate terms with me. **1945** in 2003 *DARE* File—Internet **MO**, It stood us in hand to watch for the rattlers as we had used up all the good apple brandy that we had brought with us for snake bites. **1969** *Post-Crescent* (Appleton WI) 23 Oct [4]/3 (newspaperarchive.com), It stands us in hand to do our own thinking, when we enter the voting booth.

stand one up and down See **stand one down 1**

stand-table n **chiefly S Midl** Cf Intro "Language Changes" I.4

A table; see quots.

1853 *Milwaukee Daily Sentinel* (WI) [15 Feb 3]/5 (newspaper-archive.com), [Advt:] 3 Mahogany Card Tables, . . 4 mahogany Stand Tables. **1863** *Harper's New Mth. Mag.* 26.569 **MO**, "Don't run!" exclaimed the elder. . . coming down out of the pulpit and taking his seat by the stand-table in front. **1902** *DN* 2.246 **sIL**, *Stand-table*. . . Always for stand, article of furniture. **1906** *DN* 3.123 **sIN**, *Stand-table*. . . A stand, or piece of furniture. Stand always added. **1907** *DN* 3.226 **nwAR**, *Stand-table*. . . Stand (article of furniture). **1944** *PADS* 2.61 **MO**, *Stand-table*. . . A small decorative table used in a living-room or bed-room to place books, pictures, or trinkets on. **1950** Stuart *Hie Hunters* 21 **eKY**, There was one big bed in the room, a homemade stand table and an unpainted dresser with a broken mirror. **1955** Roberts *S. from Hell-fer-Sartin* 194 **seKY**, Those two men which was there at his place had a big stand table out in the floor. **1964** Wallace *Frontier Life* 11 **OK** (as of 1893–1906), On the walnut "standtable," handcarved and notched around the edges of the side boards, lay two heartshaped, beaded pincushions. **1966** *Cynthiana Democrat* (KY) 9 June 8/1, [Advt:] *Public Auction*. . . roll-a-way bed; stand table; library table; utility table. **1986** Pederson *LAGS Concordance*, 1 inf, **swAR**, Stand table; 1 inf, **nwAR**, Stand table—a big, square table in the corner; 1 inf, **cwAR**, Stand table—bedroom furniture. **2000** Berry *Jayber Crow* 36 **KY**, I would go through the house . . looking at everything: . . Aunt Cordie's chair in the living room, her little stand table, her Bible lying on the table by the good Aladdin lamp [etc].

stand up v phr [Calque of Ger *aufstehen*, PaGer *uffschteh*, Yiddish *oyfshteyn*] **Ger settlement areas** Cf **get awake**

To get up from bed.

1904 *NY Teachers' Monogr.* ser B 6.1.32 **NYC**, A common excuse for lateness is: "I *stood up* too late," "*stood up*" meaning "rose." **1935** *AmSp* 10.167 **PA** [Engl of PA Germans], I stood up late this morning, though I usually get awake about five o'clock. **1950** *WELS Suppl.* **seWI**, Stand up in the morning. **1997** in 1999 Millersville Univ. Center for PA Ger. Studies *Jrl.* Fall 23, *To stand up. . . This morning, I _____ at 6:00 AM.* . . 10% [of 40 infs], stood up.

stantial See **stanchel**

staple n[1] Usu |'stepl|; also **chiefly Sth, S Midl** |'stipl| Pronc-sp *steeple* [Scots dial] Cf **drain** v, n[1] A, **steeple** n[2]

Std senses, var forms.

1819 *Adams Centinel* (Gettysburg PA) 29 Dec [4]/4 (newspaper-archive.com), [He] observed a flaw in the point of his bolt, which he forced into the steeple that fastened him to the floor. **1825** in 1956 Eliason *Tarheel Talk* 318 **nw,cwNC**, Steeples. **1893** Shands *MS Speech* 76, *Steeple* [stipl]. *Staple*, the bent wire for holding in place the barbed wire on fences, is so pronounced by the illiterate. **1903** *DN* 2.331 **seMO**, *Staple*. . . Pronounced steeple. 'The gate was held by a hook and steeple.' **1907** *DN* 3.236 **nwAR**, *Staple*. . . Pronounced steeple [stipl]. **1914** *DN* 4.113 **cKS**, *Steeple*. . . =staple. **1915** *DN* 4.191 **swVA**, *Steeple*. Variant of *staple*. **1923** *DN* 5.222 **swMO**, *Steeple*. . . Staple. **1937** *AmSp* 12.103 **eNE** [Farm terms], The staple he drives into the fence post is sometimes called a *steeple*. **1942** Hall *Smoky Mt. Speech* 18 **wNC, eTN**, *Staple* (a kind of nail) is ['stipəl]. **1942** Warnick *Garrett Co. MD* 2 **nwMD** (as of 1900–18), *Steeple* (staple). **1957** *Sat. Eve. Post Letters* **cIN**, My community has yielded up such . . expressions as . . fence "steeples". **1967** *DARE* FW Addit **csPA**, [stipl] = staple. **1968** *DARE* (Qu. L39, *An iron bar with a bent end, used for pulling nails, opening boxes, and so on*) Inf **MO**34, Steeple-puller. **1986** Pederson *LAGS Concordance*, 1 inf, **cTX**, Steeples = staples—used to attach wire to posts; 1 inf, **csTX**, Steeples = staples—has heard; 1 inf, **cwAR**, Fasten wire to posts with steeples. **2006** in 2007 *DARE* File—Internet **OK**, That is the reason that the kid at Home Depot thought I was nutso when I asked where their fence steeples were.

staple n[2] See **steeple** n[2]

star n[1] Usu |star|; also |stæ(r)| Pronc-spp *stair, stare* Cf **stair** n[1]

Std sense, var forms.

1815 in 1947 *AmSp* 22.281 [Americanisms], *Stairs*—stars. **1827** (1939) Sherwood *Gaz. GA* 139, *Stare*, for Star. **1893** Shands *MS Speech* 59, *Stairs* [stæəz]. Illiterate whites frequently thus pronounce *stars*. **c1960** *Wilson Coll.* **csKY**, *Star* is often [stær] among older people.

star n[2] See **stair** n[1]

star anemone n Cf **starflower 1**

A **chickweed wintergreen** (here: *Trientalis borealis*).

1872 *Old and New* 532 **MA**, Let us touch our hat to the jolly buttercups, the yellow and bird-foot violet, the golden ragwort, and the star anemone. **1892** *Jrl. Amer. Folkl.* 5.100 **MA,** *Trientalis Americana* [=*T. borealis*], Star-of-Bethlehem. N.H. star anemone. Cambridge. **1894** *Ibid* 7.94 **MA,** *Trientalis Americana.* . . star-anemone, Concord.

star anise n   [See quot 1830]   Cf **star bush**
=**Florida anise-tree.**

1830 Rafinesque *Med. Flora* 2.9, Illicium Floridanum. *Names* . . *Vulgar.* Staranise. . . Capsules ranged like a star around a central receptacle. **1901** Mohr *Plant Life AL* 506, *Illicium floridanum.* . . Florida Star Anise. **1979** Little *Checklist U.S. Trees* 151, *Illicium floridanum.* . . star-anise, starbush. **2005** *Ledger* (Lakeland FL) 14 Oct sec D 3 (Internet), Native to moist, shady areas from Louisiana to north Florida, star anise bears small, spidery, deep-red flowers in spring.

starbloom n   [See quot 1830]
=**Indian pink 1.**

1830 Rafinesque *Med. Flora* 2.89, Spigelia marilandica. *Names* . . *Vulgar.* Carolina Pink, Starbloom [etc]. . . Corolla very handsome . . with five acute spreading segments, like a golden star. **1892** (1974) Millspaugh *Amer. Med. Plants* 131–1, *Spigelia marilandica.* . . Com[mon] Names. . . Star bloom [etc]. **1971** Krochmal *Appalachia Med. Plants* 240, Pinkroot, snakeroot, star bloom.

star bush n   Cf **star anise**
=**Florida anise-tree.**

1979 Little *Checklist U.S. Trees* 151, *Illicium floridanum.* . . Other common names—polecat-tree, . . starbush [etc]. **2006** *Advocate* (Baton Rouge LA) 23 Jan sec C 1 (Internet), "I think we oversell the 'bug-free' part," he said. "My starbush is full of holes from those shiny beetles." . . Illicium floridanum (Florida anise).

starchwort n   [*OED2* (at *starch* sb. 5.b) 1597 → for *Arum maculatum*]
A **jack-in-the-pulpit 1** (here: *Arisaema triphyllum*).

1876 Hobbs *Bot. Hdbk.* 112, Starchwort, Dragon root, Arum [= *Arisaema*] maculatum and triphyllum.

star duckweed n
A **duckweed 1** (here: *Lemna trisulca*).

1853 NY State Museum *Catalogue Cabinet Nat. Hist.* 40, *Lemna trisulca,* Star Duckweed. **1925** *Ecology* 6.289 **seWI,** The bulk of this sample was made up of thousands of plants of star duckweed *Lemna trisulca* and hundreds of thousands of those of water meal, *Wolffia brasilensis.* **1951** Martin *Amer. Wildlife & Plants* 448, Star duckweed *(L[emna] trisulca)* . . is encountered in many places in the northern states. **1982** *Jrl. Wildlife Management* 46.67, Star duckweed *(Lemna trisulca).*

stardust n   Cf **starflower 8**
A **gilia** (here: *Linanthus androsaceus*).

1959 Carleton *Index Herb. Plants* 112, *Star Dust:* Linanthus parviflorus (Gilia micrantha). **2006** in 2007 *DARE* File—Internet **CA,** What did I get? Little California natives to tuck in here and there. *Isomeris arborea,* and a *bonus* freebie: Linanthus 'Stardust'.

stare   See **star** n[1]

star-eye(d) grass n   [Appar a blend of **star grass 3** + **blue-eyed grass 1**]
A **blue-eyed grass 1** (here: *Sisyrinchium angustifolium*).

1894 *Jrl. Amer. Folkl.* 7.101 **MA,** *Sisyrinchium angustifolium.* . . star-eyed grass, Concord . . (children). **1936** Winter *Plants NE* 15, *S[isyrinchium] angustifolium.* . . Called also Blue-eyed Mary or Star-eye Grass. **2003** *DARE* File—Internet **CA,** I am growing . . star-eyed grass, hair-cap moss and coontail.

starflower n
1 =**chickweed wintergreen.**   Cf **star anemone, star-of-Bethlehem 1**

1848 Gray *Manual of Botany* 282, *T[rientalis] Americana* [=*T. borealis*] . . Star-flower. . . Damp cold woods, through the Northern States. **a1862** (1864) Thoreau *ME Woods* 318, *Trientalis Americana* (star-flower), [seen at] Pine Stream, 1853. **1897** Parsons *Wild Flowers CA* 202, Star-flower. Chickweed-wintergreen. *Trientalis Europaea, var. latifolia.* . . pink, starry flowers. **1928** in 1931 McCorrison *Letters Fraternity* 177 **NEng,** There were two kinds of trilliums . . ladies slipper, . . star flowers, . . and numerous other kinds. **1961** Douglas *My Wilderness* 230, The starflower seems ever-present. It is a bright forest sprite.

We have its cousin in the Cascades. The White Mountain species is *Trientalis borealis.* **1966** *DARE* FW Addit **WA**12, Starflower—four inches high, starlike pink blossom. **1966–68** *DARE* Wildfl QR Pl.165B Infs **MI**7, 31, 57, **MN**14, **WI**79, Starflower. **1967–69** *DARE* (Qu. S26c, *Wildflowers that grow in woods*) Infs **MA**67, **NY**205, Starflower; (Qu. S26e, *Other wildflowers not yet mentioned; not asked in early QRs*) Infs **MA**42, **VT**16, **WI**78, Starflower. [*DARE* Ed: Some of these Infs may refer instead to other senses below.] **1982** *AK Geographic* 9.3.26, The starflower *(Trientalis europaea)* springs forth from beds of moss.
2 =**cinquefoil.**

1896 *Jrl. Amer. Folkl.* 9.187 **MA,** *Potentilla,* sp., star-flower, Waverly, Mass. **1967** *DARE* (Qu. S26c, *Wildflowers that grow in woods*) Inf **MO**2, Starflower—they look like buttercups, except they're white.
3 A **rain lily 2** (here: *Cooperia drummondii*).

1897 *Jrl. Amer. Folkl.* 10.145 **TX,** *Cooperia Drummondii* . . rain lilies, star flowers, Waco, Tex.
4 =**rue anemone.**

1898 *Jrl. Amer. Folkl.* 11.221 **MA,** *Anemonella* [=*Thalictrum*] *thalictroides,* Spach, starflower, Newton, Mass.
5 A **bluet 2** (here: *Houstonia caerulea*).

1898 *Jrl. Amer. Folkl.* 11.228 **MA,** *Houstonia caerulea* . . star flower, Medford, Mass.
6 A **woodland star.**

1917 Rydberg *Flora Rocky Mts.* 377, *Lithophrágma* [spp]. . . Starflower, Prairie Star, Woodland Star. **1957** Barnes *Nat. Hist. Wasatch Spring* 45 **UT,** A tiny star flower *(Tellima parviflora* [=*Lithophragma parviflorum*]) with quarter inch petals like paper shreds. **1963** Craighead *Rocky Mt. Wildflowers* 72, Starflower—*Lithophragma parviflora.* . . Slender stems invisible from a distance make the "little white stars" appear suspended in a sky of green. **1975** Zwinger *Run River* 178 **UT,** A short walk upstream still leads . . through thickets of waist-high rustling horsetails, through garlands of butterflies, yellow violets and wallflowers, . . starflowers and opulent drifts of pale blue chiming bells. **1994** *Wildflowers Kootenai Natl. Forest* np **MT,** Other names for the Starflower are Woodland Star, Prairie Star and Fringe Cup.
7 Prob a **colicroot 2.**   Cf **star grass 1**

1968 *DARE* (Qu. S26c, *Wildflowers that grow in woods*) Inf **VA**24, Starflower [FW: =star grass].
8 A **gilia** or its flower.

1971 Dodge *100 Desert Wildflowers* 65, Starflower—More commonly known as "gilia". . . the flowers are usually small and range in color from white to lavender, pink, and yellow. **1972** *New Mexican* (Santa Fe NM) 16 July 30/2, Everywhere . . were the flowers of lavendar [sic] gilia, their long corollas seeming to shoot the starflowers away from the plant.

stargazer n
1 Std: a fish of the family Uranoscopidae, with eyes on the top of its head.   For other names see **dogfish 5**
2 A **sculpin 1.**

1842 DeKay *Zool. NY* 4.61, The Little Star-gazer. *Uranidea quiescens* [=*Cottus bairdii*]. . . Eyes large, and nearly vertical. **1906** NJ State Museum *Annual Rept. for 1905* 372, *Uranidea gracilis viscosa* [=*Cottus bairdii*]. . . Blob. Star Gazer.
3 =**bittern.**   Cf **sungazer**

1955 *Oriole* 20.1.2 **GA,** American Bittern. . . *Sky-gazer, Star-gazer.*

star gentian n
Either of two closely related plants: **marsh felwort** or *Swertia perennis.*

1926 (1955) Clements *Flowers* 23, The starry blue-purple or white flowers of the Star Gentian . . grow along brook-banks and in wet meadows. **1953** Nelson *Plants Rocky Mt. Park* 124, *Star-gentian, Swertia perennis.* . . Slender plants of subalpine and alpine marshes with dark bluish or purplish flowers. **1968** Hultén *Flora AK* 761, *Lomatogonium rotatum* . . Star Gentian. . . Wet meadows, along streams. **1975** Zwinger *Run River* 21 **UT,** Star gentian *(Swertia perennis).* **2004** *DARE* File—Internet **AK,** *Lomatogonium rotatum* . . star gentian—marsh felwort.

star grass n
1 =**colicroot 2.**

1687 Clayton in 1739 Royal Soc. London *Philos. Trans.* 41.158 **VA,** There is another Root of the Species of *Hyacinths,* the Leaves whereof are grasslike, but smooth and stiff, of a willow-green Colour, and spread like a Star upon the Ground; from the Middle shoots a tall long rush-like Stem, without Leaves, near two Feet high; on one Side grow little white Bell-flowers one above another: The Root is black outwardly, but brown within. It is bitter, and I take it to have much the same Virtues as *Little Centaury.* Some call it *Ague-grass,* . . others *Star-grass.* **c1738** (1929) Byrd *Histories* 152 **VA,** I found near our Camp some Plants of that kind of Rattle-Snake Root, called Star-grass. The Leaves shoot out circularly, and grow Horizontally and near the Ground. **1824** Bigelow *Florula Bostoniensis* 131 **MA,** Aletris farinosa. *Star Grass.* **1837** Darlington *Flora Cestrica* 218 **sePA,** Mealy Aletris. *Vulgò*—Star Grass. Colic root. **1901** Lounsberry *S. Wild Flowers* 54, *A[letris] farinosa,* colic-root, star-grass. **1953** Greene–Blomquist *Flowers South* 12, Colic-Roots, Star-Grasses *(Aletris). Ibid,* White star-grass *(A. farinosa)* is the most common and widespread species but is most abundant in the Coastal Plain. **1976** Bruce *How to Grow Wildflowers* 167, I . . found my first Star-grass or Colic-root, *Aletris farinosa.* **2003** Boughman–Oxendine *Herbal Remedies* 88, *Star Grass (Aletris Farinosa).* . . Star Grass is a native, spreading, perennial grass that grows in large clumps from three to six feet in height.

2 also *yellow star grass:* A plant of the genus *Hypoxis,* esp *H. hirsuta.* For other names of the latter see **gold-eyed grass, star-of-Bethlehem 1, yellow-eyed grass 2**

1817 Eaton *Botany* 37, *Hypoxis. . . erecta* [=*hirsuta*], (star grass). **1869** Fuller *Uncle John* 127 **NEng,** The yellow flower is called the *Hypoxis,* or star-grass. **1931** Harned *Wild Flowers Alleghanies* 129, Yellow star-grass. . . It is easily recognized by its long grass-like leaves and . . bright yellow, star-shaped flowers. **1951** *PADS* 15.29 **TX,** *Hypoxis hirsuta* . . Piney woods star grass. **1966–67** *DARE* Wildfl QR Pl.25 [=*Hypoxis hirsuta*], Infs **AR**44, 46, **NC**28, Star grass; **MI**31, **SC**41, Yellow star grass. **1969–70** *DARE* (Qu. S26c, *Wildflowers that grow in woods*) Inf **MA**78, Yellow star grass—same as amaryllis; (Qu. S26d, *Wildflowers that grow in meadows;* not asked in early QRs) Inf **GA**70, Star grass—looks like grass, but has little yellow flowers. **2000** *News & Rec.* (Greensboro NC) 12 July 9 (Internet), A nice planting of yellow star-grass, Hypoxis hirsuta, found in woodlands and meadows throughout North Carolina, flourished for years.

3 often with modifier: =**blue-eyed grass 1.**

1836 *Scientific Tracts* 103, Of the same family is the *Sisyrinchium anceps,* or blue Star-grass of the meadows, and its lustrous blue flowers often make them appear azure at a considerable distance. It is a very delicate grass-like plant. **1898** *Jrl. Amer. Folkl.* 11.281 **MA,** *Sisyrinchium angustifolium* . . star grass, Auburndale. **1951** *PADS* 15.30 **TX,** *Sisyrinchium* spp.—Blue or yellow star grass; prairie stars; Texas stars. **1967** *DARE* Wildfl QR Pl.28A [=*Sisyrinchium angustifolium*] Inf **AR**46, Star grass; **SC**41, Blue star grass. **1970** *DARE* (Qu. S26d, *Wildflowers that grow in meadows;* not asked in early QRs) Inf **MA**78, Blue star grass. **2008** *DARE* File—Internet **KY,** The list of "blooming things" is quite long this week! Columbine, goldenseal, . . blue star grass [etc].

4 A **yellow-eyed grass 1** (here: *Xyris caroliniana*).

1966 *DARE* Wildfl QR Pl.2B [=*Xyris caroliniana*] Inf **AR**44, Star grass. **1988** Crum *Focus on Peatlands* 99 **Gt Lakes,** *Xyris montana,* yellow star grass, is a small plant of poor fens in the upper Great Lakes region.

5 =**chickweed wintergreen.**

1967 *DARE* Wildfl QR Pl.165B [=*Trientalis borealis*] Inf **SC**41, Star grass.

starhead topminnow n Also *starhead, star-headed minnow* A **killifish 1** (here: usu *Fundulus notti*).

1890 U.S. Fish Comm. *Bulletin for 1888* 227, *Zygonectes notti* Agassiz. *"Star-headed minnow."* **1947** Hubbs–Lagler *Fishes Gt. Lakes* 78, Northern starhead minnow . . usually near the surface of clear, weedy backwaters. **1966** *WI Acad. Trans.* 55.108, Starhead topminnow—*Fundulus notti.* . . from a lagoon of the Wisconsin River. **1977** N. Amer. Native Fishes Assoc. *Amer. Currents* 5.3.7 **seGA,** Starhead topminnows, *Fundulus notti.* . . the females have bright lipstick like red streaks scattered about the facial mask. *Ibid,* At my approach starheads . . scurry from bankside toward open water. **1998** *Ibid* 24.4.13 **FL,** I first encountered the Eastern starhead topminnow *(Fundulus escambiae)* in the Florida panhandle, while searching the backroads of Bay and Washington counties in November of 1995.

star jasmine n
Std: a shrubby vine of the genus *Trachelospermum,* esp *T. jasminoides.* For other names of var spp see **Confederate jasmine, dogbane b, doublepod, jasmine 2f, maile haole**

stark buck naked See **buck naked**
stark naked See **naked B1**
star lance n
A **black snakeroot 1** (here: *Cimicifuga racemosa*).

1903 Small *Flora SE U.S.* 432, *Cimicifuga racemòsa.* . . Black Snakeroot. Black Cohosh. Star-lance.

starleaf n
=**Mexican orange.**

1931 U.S. Dept. Ag. *Misc. Pub.* 101.91, Starleaf *(Choisya dumosa)* . . known also as Mexican-orange, and, to Mexicans, as sorilla and zorillo, is a low, rather bizarre-looking shrub, with thickish stems and rather slender twigs. **1934** NM Ag. Exper. Station *Bulletin* 714.2, A very attractive and unusual plant found in the southern part of the State in the mountainous sections is the starleaf or Mexican orange *(Astrophyllum).* **1981** Benson–Darrow *Trees SW Deserts* 131, *Choisya dumosa.* . . Star Leaf, Mexican Orange. . . New Mexico on the Rio Grande drainage; TransPecos Texas.

star-leaved gum n
=**sweet gum.**

1884 Sargent *Forests of N. Amer.* 86, Star-leaved gum. . . A large tree . . reaching its greatest development in the bottom lands of the Mississippi basin. **1908** Rogers *Tree Book* 276, In summer time the leaves of the sweet gum are our sure guide to its identity. "Star-leaved gum," it is often called. There is no other tree whose leaf so closely resembles a regular six-pointed star with one point missing where the petiole is fastened on. **1974** Morton *Folk Remedies* 91 **SC,** *Star-leaved gum* . . *Liquidambar styraciflua.* . . Leaves or only the bases of the petioles are chewed and the juice swallowed to relieve sorethroat and also to overcome "loose stomach" (diarrhea).

starlight, moonlight n Also *starlight; ~, starbright; ~, moonlight, hope to see a ghost tonight* (and varr) **Upper MW, WI**
A variety of the game of tag played at night; see quots.

[**1939** in 1947 Derleth *Village Daybook* 120 **WI,** The children played in the evening tonight, their voices rising joyously into the windy summer air. . . Starlight, moonbright,/ I hope I see a ghost tonight.] **1950** *WELS Suppl.* **csWI,** *Starlight, starbright.* We sing-songed: "Starlight, starbright,/ I wish I may, I wish I might,/ Have the wish I wish tonight./ Starlight, starbright,/ I hope I see a ghost tonight." The ghost, who was "it," would try to jump out from his hiding place and tag as many people as possible. I have also heard "Starlight, moonlight" followed by the same words. We never played this game if the stars weren't out. *Ibid* **cwWI,** *(Hiding games that start with some special, elaborate way of sending the players out to hide)* Starlight, moonlight. **1968** *DARE* (Qu. EE13a, *Games in which every player hides except one, and that one must try to find the others)* Inf **IA**46, Starlight—when only one person hides. **2000** *Cincinnati Enquirer* (OH) 15 Sept (Internet) **neSD,** We went outside and played "Starlight, moonlight, hope to see a ghost tonight," a game we played by yard light so we could scream and scare the beejeebers out of each other. **2003** *DARE* File—Internet **seMN,** I grew up in South Minneapolis, and we played all the games that both Chicago and Wisconsin played. How about Captain May I, King of the Hill, Pom Pom Poll-away, Starlight, Starbright. **2004** in 2008 *Ibid* **nwIA,** Star light, Star bright was . . an exclusively after-dark activity. . . It was your basic game of tag, only played under the stars with a ghostly theme. He who was "it" was the ghost and he had to capture those who dared stray from base in search of him. **2008** *Ibid,* Starlight, Starbright. . . Choose one player to be the "ghost". This player goes and hides somewhere while the remainder of the group counts to a certain number. . . When the group have finished counting then they *must* stay together and walk around the area being played in and chant: "Starlight, starbright, I hope I see a ghost tonight"—When the group gets near the place where the ghost is hiding, the ghost jumps out and tries to tag someone. Everyone runs back to base . . before being tagged by the ghost. If a player is tagged they become the ghost for the next round. *Ibid* **MN,** We also played "Star-light, Moon-light, I hope to see the Ghost tonight" on those dark chilly fall evenings. **2008** *DARE* File **nwMA** (as of late 1960s), A family from Minnesota moved into my neighborhood . . and the children taught us a new game. . . It was a hide and seek game played at night, called "Starlight, starbright". The person who was "it" covered their eyes and counted while all the rest of the children hid. Then "it" had to chant "Starlight, starbright, hope to see a ghost tonight, and if I do I'll take my shoe and beat him 'til he's black and blue" while roaming around the yard looking for the hidden children. Meanwhile, the hiders . . would try to run to the "safe" or "home" spot without being caught.

starlights n

A **bluet 2** (here: *Houstonia caerulea*).

1894 *Jrl. Amer. Folkl.* 7.90 **MA,** *Houstonia caerulea* . . starlights, Cambridge.

star lily n

1 =**sand lily 2.**

1898 *Jrl. Amer. Folkl.* 11.281 **WY,** *Leucocrinum montanum* . . star lily. **1953** Nelson *Plants Rocky Mt. Park* 47, Sand-lily or starlily, *Leucocrinum montanum*. . . A snow-white lily blooming close to the ground in early spring. **1979** Spellenberg *Audubon Guide N. Amer. Wildflowers W. Region* 584, Star Lily. . . A low plant with several *star-like, white flowers.* **2008** *DARE* File—Internet **SD,** [Caption:] Star Lily—Leucocrinum montanum.

2 A **death camas,** usu *Zigadenus fremontii.*

1954 CA Div. Beaches & Parks *Pt. Lobos Wild Flowers* 28, In January, notably in the warmer open areas, yellow-green lily leaves of the Star Zygadene, or star lily, thrust through the earth. **1957** Barnes *Nat. Hist. Wasatch Spring* 64 **UT,** That dangerous star lily, death camas or poison sego (*Zigadenus paniculatus*). **1974** Munz *Flora S. CA* 931, *Z[igadenus] fremontii* . . Star-Lily. **2006** Quinn–Keeley *Intro. CA Chaparral* 147, Star lilies (*Zigadenus* spp.) . . are common in chaparral burns. Fremont's star lily (*Z. fremontii*) and smallflower death camas (*Z. micranthus*) are the species most likely to be encountered.

3 =**rain lily 2** or **zephyr lily.**

1961 Wills–Irwin *Flowers TX* 98, Bulbs of nearly all the Rain-lilies and Atamascos are marketed by seedsmen under such names as Star-lilies, Zephyr-lilies, Fairy-lilies, and Copper-lilies.

starling n

1 Std: a European bird (*Sturnus vulgaris*) with dark iridescent white-spotted plumage, introduced to the US in 1890. Also called **English lark, German sparrow, Jacob bird, mule ~** Cf **German blackbird**

2 A bird of the family Icteridae such as the **red-winged blackbird.** Cf **meadow starling, red-winged ~**

1674 Josselyn *Two Voyages* 100 **NEng,** *Starlings,* black as *Ravens,* with scarlet pinions. **a1676** Royal Soc. London *Philos. Trans.* 12.1065 **NEng,** The Ear [of maize] is cloathed and armed with several strong thick Husks. Not only defending it from the Cold of the Night . . and from unseasonable Rains: but also from the Crows, Starlings and other Birds. **1811** Wilson *Amer. Ornith.* 4.37, [Red-winged starlings] are known by various names . . such as the *Swamp Blackbird,* . . Starling, &c. **1869** *Atlantic Mth.* 23.586 **DC,** The kingbird and orchard starling remain the whole season, and breed in the tree-tops. The rich, copious song of the starling may be heard there all the forenoon. **1872** *Galaxy* 13.43 **West,** In most localities where these flies are found in troublesome numbers, there are also found flocks of starlings, a species of blackbird. **1885** Cable *Dr. Sevier* 442 **sLA,** So Mary would look again and see, out in the prairie, in the morning . . the starlings, with their red and yellow epaulets. **1890** *Century Dict.* 5908, The name *starling* is extended . . , erroneously, to the American birds of the family *Icteridæ,* sometimes known collectively as *American starlings.* . . The bird with which the name is specially connected in this sense is *Agelæus phœniceus,* . . often called *red-winged starling.* The name *meadow-starling* is often applied to *Sturnella magna.* **1956** MA Audubon Soc. *Bulletin* 40.130 **MA,** Red-winged Blackbird. . . Starling.

‡**starlit** n Cf **beazlestone, eyestone 2, jewelhead, lucky stone, madstone**

A small white stone said to be found in the head of a snail.

c1938 in 1970 Hyatt *Hoodoo* 2.1474 **seGA** [Black], Ketch a snail an' yo' put him up in salt, . . airtight him an' let him stay dere. . . when yo' go back de biggest majority of dat snail is turnt to water. An' yo' po' dat water out in a strainer an' yo'll see a *starlit,* a little white clear stone dat be's in his head. Yo' git dat *starlit* an' yo' rub dat *starlit* until it gets hot—hit's a little stone like a little rock—till it gets hot in yore hand.

star lotus n

=**white water lily.**

1953 Greene–Blomquist *Flowers South* 38, One of the most widely distributed of these [=water lilies] is the white to pinkish "alligator bonnet" or "star-lotus" (*N[ymphaea] odorata*) which ranges from Fla. to La. **1974** Morton *Folk Remedies* 103 **SC,** Star lotus; alligator bonnet. . . for itch of private parts, people bathe with and also drink decoction.

star moss n

A **reindeer moss** (here: *Cladonia cristatella*).

1968 Pochmann *Triple Ridge* 106 **cWI,** Star moss invites close inspection . . the male plants send up tiny brown spires, and the females sport a globular bloom of bright red about the size of a pinhead.

starn See **stern**

‡**star-naked** adj [Prob folk-etym for *stark-naked*]

1966 in 1982 *Barrick Coll.* **csPA,** Star-naked—stark naked.

star-nose(d) mole n Also *star-nose* [Because it has tactile processes radiating from its nose; see quot 1948]

A long-tailed mole (*Condylura cristata*).

1811 Philadelphia Soc. for Promoting Ag. *Memoirs* 2.138, We have, at least, two species of moles near Philadelphia . . ; I mean the *Sorex aquaticus* . . , and the species called by our farmers, the "star-nose-mole," or *Sorex cristatus.* **1842** DeKay *Zool. NY* 1.12, The Common Star-nose. *Condylura cristata.* **1884** *Science* 3.540, The meadow-haunting, star-nosed mole (*Condylura cristata*). **1927** Boston Soc. Nat. Hist. *Proc.* 38.268 **seGA,** Sam Mizell discovered some live young Star-nosed Moles in a nest above the water inside the stump of a bay tree. **1948** *Time* 14 June 1, This underground dweller is identified by a 22-point star that he wears on his nose. He's a *star-nosed mole.* **1969** *DARE* (Qu. P32, . . *Other kinds of wild animals*) Inf **NY196,** Star-nosed mole. **2006** *Cleveland Plain Dealer* (OH) 10 Oct sec B 1 (Internet), A new preserve will offer Northeast Ohio wildlife fans a chance to spot a variety of rarely seen creatures, including star-nosed moles and state-protected northern harriers.

star-of-Bethlehem n

1 also *Bethlehem star:* A **star grass 2** (here: *Hypoxis hirsuta*). obs

1793 Amer. Philos. Soc. *Trans.* 3.114 **sePA,** [In a list of plants used to treat rattlesnake bites:] Hypoxis *erecta* . . *Star of Bethlehem.* **1851** (1949) Thoreau *Jrl.* 2.266 **MA,** *Hypoxis erecta,* yellow Bethlehem-star, . . is a thick, wiry grass. **1901** Lounsberry *S. Wild Flowers* 68, *H[ypoxis] hirsuta,* yellow star-grass. . . Formerly the little plant was called the "Star of Bethlehem."

2 A **chickweed wintergreen** (here: *Trientalis borealis*). Cf **starflower 1**

1892 *Jrl. Amer. Folkl.* 5.100 **NH,** *Trientalis Americana* [=*T. borealis*], Star-of-Bethlehem. **1894** *Ibid* 7.94 **eMA,** *Trientalis Americana* . . Star-of-Bethlehem. **1897** *Ibid* 10.50 **MA, VT,** *Trientalis Americana* . . Star of Bethlehem, Fairhaven, Mass., and Vermont. **1966** *DARE* Wildfl QR Pl.165B [=*Trientalis borealis*] Inf **NC28,** Star-of-Bethlehem.

3 A **bluet 2** (here: *Houstonia caerulea*).

1872 *Old & New* 531 **MA,** While the botanists have at different times flung upon it the names Hedyotis, Oldenlandia, and Houstonia, . . the less initiated have known it as bluets, innocence, and Star of Bethlehem. **1892** *Jrl. Amer. Folkl.* 5.97 **MS,** *Houstonia caerulea.* . . star of Bethlehem.

4 A **woodland star** (here: *Lithophragma affine*).

1897 Parsons *Wild Flowers CA* 24, Woodland Star of Bethlehem. *Tellima affinis* [=*Lithophragma affine*]. . . "Star of Bethlehem" is the common name by which many of our children know this fragile flower. **1915** (1926) Armstrong–Thornber *Western Wild Flowers* 199, Woodland Star—*Lithophragma heterophylla.* . . This is sometimes called Star of Bethlehem, but that name belongs to an Ornithogalum, grown in gardens. **1967** *DARE* (Qu. S26e, *Other wildflowers not yet mentioned;* not asked in early QRs) Inf **CA20,** Star-of-Bethlehem—early, white, feather-edged flower.

5 =**sand lily 2.**

1906 Rydberg *Flora CO* 445, Star of Bethlehem (*Leucocrinum*). **1979** Spellenberg *Audubon Guide N. Amer. Wildflowers W. Region* 584, Star-of-Bethlehem (*Leucocrinum montanum*). . . A low plant with several *star-like, white flowers blooming in a basal rosette of narrow, grass-like leaves.*

star of Texas See **Texas star a**

starr See **stair** n¹

star root n

1 A **colicroot 2** (here: *Aletris farinosa*); the root of this plant. **esp sAppalachians** Cf **star grass 1** Note: Some of these quots may refer instead to **2** below.

c1738 (1929) Byrd *Histories* 145 **VA,** We pursued our Journey, & in

the way Richard Smith Shew'd me the Star-Root, which infallibly cures the Bite of the Rattlesnake. **1789** in 1793 *Amer. Philos. Soc. Trans.* 3.xx, The root of Aletris *farinosa* is taken in powder, or bruised and steeped in liquor: this root is called star-root, blazing star, devil's bit. **1813** (1901) Smith *Ind. Doctor's Dispensatory* 41 **OH,** The Devil's bit. . . is, in some places, known by the name of Star root. It has a small round stalk, about nine inches or a foot high, scattered round with leaves, resembling corn leaves, and has a white tasselled bloom on the top; the root is conical. **1892** (1974) Millspaugh *Amer. Med. Plants* 172-1, Aletris *farinosa*. . . Com[mon] Names.—Star wort, Star root [etc]. **1937** Thornburgh *Gt. Smoky Mts.* 29, Other herbs and roots used by the old folks in various ways are . . star root, . . butterfly root, . . galax, wild indigo, yellow fringed orchid or rattlesnake master. *Ibid* 30, Git ye some star root. Hit grows in the glades. **1941** Justus *Cabin on Kettle Creek* 147 **eTN,** Star root in the hollow, sang, too, and Solomon's seal. **1967** DARE (Qu. S26c, *Wildflowers that grow in woods*) Inf **TN13,** Star root. **1975** Hamel–Chiltoskey *Cherokee Plants* 57, Star-grass, star-root—Aletris *farinosa*. . . root prevents abortion. **2003** in 2006 DARE File—Internet **swNC,** Aletris farinosa, most people call it unicorn plant or star root.
2 =**blazing star 2.**
   1832 Howard *Improved Botanic Med.* 2.285, Aletris *alba*. Common Names—*Unicorn, Star Root, Blazing Star*. Leaves . . in the winter lying flat on the ground, in rays resembling a star. **1867** Hale *Homoeopathic Materia Medica* 55, The Aletris far[inosa] is designated by many common names, as Blazing star, . . Star-root, Devils-bit, etc. But all these names are also applied to the Helonias dioica, (Chamaelirium luteum. *Gray.*) and other plants, so that there is no reliance to be placed upon the collections of uneducated plant-gatherers, or the preparations of the druggists.

starry campion n
Std: a **catchfly 1** (here: *Silene stellata*).   Also called **king's cure-all 2, rattlesnake master e, widow's frill**

star-strikers n pl
A **dogtooth violet.**
   1917 Rydberg *Flora Rocky Mts.* 164, Erythrònium. . . Dog-tooth Violet, Adder-tongue, Star-strikers.

start v
1 in phr *start to school:* To begin to attend school.
   1836 (1930) W. Sewall *Diary* 172 **IL,** Henry and Catherine started to school. **1868** Keckley *Behind the Scenes* 216 **KY,** You are getting to be a big boy now, and must start to school next fall. **1883** *Century Illustr. Mag.* 26.140 **nGA,** I wuz thes a-thinkin' ef maybe you oughtn't to bresh up and start to school down in Gullettsville. **1899** (1912) Green *VA Folk-Speech* 415, *Start*. . . "They will start to school on Monday." **1931** *AmSp* 7.20 **swPA,** *Start*. Begin to go. Used mainly in the one expression, start to school. "I started to school when I was five." (Widespread.) **1938** in Lib. of Congress *Amer. Memory: WPA Life Hist.* (Internet) **cwIL,** I didn't start to school until I was fifteen. **1986** Pederson *LAGS Concordance,* 2 infs, **AR,** 1 inf, **cnGA,** Start to school. **2000** in 2008 DARE File—Internet **GA,** It's been a busy year. We had a new daughter, my son started to school, and my company has gone through two mergers. **2008** DARE File **csWI,** "Has your granddaughter started to school yet?" "Oh, yes—she's in second grade already!"
2 in phr *start with me last:* See quots.   **WI**
   1977 DARE File—Internet **WI** [Speak 'Scansin], *Start wit me last:* This is used to tell a waitress to go on to someone else before taking your order. **1999** *Ibid* **WI** [Central Florida Green Bay Packer Backers], *Start wit me last:* to forfeit your turn. **2004** DARE File **csWI,** "Start with me last"? Yes, I've heard that. I may even have said it. It didn't sound strange to me until someone queried it. It just means "Go ahead and start taking people's orders. I'll be ready by the time everyone else has ordered."
3 To send or mail (a letter). [Cf *EDD start* v. 2 "To dispatch, send off"]   **chiefly sAppalachians**
   1859 Atson *Heart Whispers* 223 **TN,** I wrote you to start a letter for me to Raleigh, N.C. **1861** (1943) McDowell–Blankenship *Fiddles* 41 **cTN,** They have had several letters started to them, but we do not know whether they got them or not. *Ibid* 83, White started a letter to me by Fayette, but he said he either lost it or left it at Jack's office. **1909** *Baptist Home Mission Mth.* 31.177 **WV,** After baptism he started a letter home, stating that mother's prayers were answered. . . Since that time he has been holding [revival] meetings. **1918** *OR Countryman* 10.337, [He] started a letter [from Brazil] on February 13, which has just

reached Corvallis. **1952** Giles *40 Acres* 4 **csKY,** Here there is a pocket of pure Appalachianism and our older people still speak the tongue. . . The envelope for a letter is not addressed, it is "backed." It is not mailed or posted, it is "started."

start-bod(il)y-naked See **start-naked**

start dog n   Cf **catch dog, find ~**
A hunting dog trained to pick up a trail.
   1886 *Galveston Daily News* (TX) 28 June 5/4, We soon enter a hunting-trail, and the old start-dogs trot on ahead. **1941** Writers' Program *Guide AR* 79, The "start dog" is released in fox territory to pick up a trail, and the pack rallies at his long-drawn notes. **1984** Wilder *You All Spoken Here* 57 **Sth,** *Start dog:* An experienced brag dog depended on to pick up a fox trail at the start of a night hunt. **2002** DARE File—Internet **KY,** They broke up camp and had gone a short distance when their old start dog jumped a bear. *Ibid* **sTX,** I guess I have hunted hogs almost every way possible. Ranging from either two bay dogs and a 22 pistol, or four or five dogs and a 30-30, or one start dog and one catch dog and a piece of string. *Ibid* **MO,** Finally, we had a start dog that we called Rube. He was getting old, and he couldn't go very fast, but you'd turn him loose and he'd . . pick up the scent.

star thistle n   [*OED2* 1578 →]
Std: a weedy plant of the genus *Centaurea*.   For other names of var spp see **basket flower, cornflower 1, dusty miller 3, horse knobs, knapweed, mother-in-law's button, pasture weed, powder puff 5, pink** n² **2, Texas thistle 1, tocalote, wild bachelor's button 3**

star tick n
Prob =**lone star tick.**
   1863 *Ladies' Repository* Oct 605 **eOK,** These ticks [=seed ticks] reappear, much larger in size and with a lustrous circle on their backs and are then called "star-ticks," or "yearling-ticks." **1966** DARE (Qu. R23a, *Insects or other creatures that fasten themselves to the skin and suck blood—on land*) Inf **MS6,** Star tick. **1986** Pederson *LAGS Concordance,* 1 inf, **csTX,** Star tick.

start-naked adj phr   Also **start-bod(il)y-naked, start-mother-~** Pronc-sp *staa't-nakid* [The earlier form of which *stark-naked* is appar a folk-etym; *OED2* a1225 →; "*Obs. exc. dial.*"]   **Sth, S Midl**
Entirely naked.
   1764 Wigwagg *The Author of Quaker Unmask'd, Strip'd Start Naked* [title] **sePA.** **1858** *S. Lit. Messenger* 27.200, This heer Cockrun's galry gits his naim from a white marvel gal, rite start bodily nakid, standin on a velvet stump. **1863** *Ibid* 37.173 **VA,** Thar's a man thar that'll make catfish bait out of you in a minute, if you go to fooling 'bout him, stripped start naked, certain. **1892** *DN* 1.234 **KY,** *Start-naked:* stark naked. "He is a start-naked villain." . . Mr. A.W. Long, of North Carolina, reports that he never heard any other form than *start-naked* used in conversation in that state; and that two of his friends—one from Virginia, the other from South Carolina—make the same statement for those two states. **1899** (1912) Green *VA Folk-Speech* 415, *Start-naked*. . . Entirely naked; *start*-body-naked; *start*-mother-naked. **1909** *DN* 3.375 **eAL, wGA,** He was plum start naked. **1915** *DN* 4.191 **swVA,** *Start*. . . Stark, as *start* naked. **1922** Gonzales *Black Border* 328 **sSC, GA coasts** [Gullah glossary], *Staa't nakid*—stark naked. **1944** *PADS* 2.21 **sAppalachians,** *Start*. . . "Look yander, that youngun is start necked!" **1946** Hench *Coll.* **cVA,** Her mammie used to say "start-naked" too and also "start-mother-naked" and explained the word as meaning that you were naked as when you started your life directly from your mother. **1952** Brown *NC Folkl.* 1.594, *Start-naked*. . . Stark-naked. **1976** Garber *Mountainese* 87 **sAppalachians,** The boys were swimmin' in the old mill pond start naked. **2000** Shores *Tangier Is.* 203 **Chesapeake Bay,** A person without clothes on would have been described as *startnaked*.

start to See **to** prep **B8**

start to school See **start 1**

star tulip n   esp **CA**
Any of var **mariposa lilies** with upright, star-shaped flowers; see quots.
   1897 Parsons *Wild Flowers CA* 278, This plant [=cat's-ears] belongs to the section of *Calochortus* whose species are known as "star-tulips." **1902** U.S. Natl. Museum *Contrib. Herbarium* 7.323 **nwCA,** *Calochortus maweanus*. . . It is one of several species that have the same

common name [=cat's-ears] and are also called "star tulips." **1915** (1926) Armstrong–Thornber *Western Wild Flowers* 56, They [=*Calochortus* spp] are allied to true Tulips, so the popular name is suitable, and they fall into three groups . . Star Tulips, with erect, star-like flowers [etc]. **1932** *Ecological Monogr.* 2.22 **CA,** The following plants are commonly eaten: . . *Calochortus nudus,* Sierra star tulip [etc]. **1967** Dodge *Roadside Wildflowers* 1, Sego lily—star tulip. **2006** *Los Angeles Times* (CA) 27 Apr sec F 3 (Internet), It's fairly easy to distinguish the various types [of calochortus]. The tallest ones, called tall mariposas, bear large, upright, chalice-shaped flowers. . . Globe lilies and fairy lanterns have round, nodding flowers. . . Star tulips grow low and have cupped blossoms.

start with me last See **start 2**

starve v, hence ppl adj *starved*

1 To perish or suffer from cold—often in phr *starve with cold.* [*OED2 starve* v. 2.c, 5.a; *starved* ppl. adj. 4 "Perished with cold. Now chiefly *dial.* and *poet.*"] *arch*

1820 Irving *Sketch Book Crayon* 2.267 **NY,** Either exhausted by swimming, or starved with cold and hunger, she was found dead and naked near the water side. **1862** *Continental Mth.* 2.593, The Roman shopkeepers . . don't know enough to shut their shop doors when they are starved with cold. **1862** in 1887 U.S. War Dept. *War of Rebellion* 1st ser 18.451, The Government owes it . . to the people of Norfolk, who are starving with hunger and cold, to do something. **1870** *Nation* 28 July 56 **sePA,** "My feet are starved," the best fed of them would say if his feet were very cold. [**1899** (1912) Green *VA Folk-Speech* 415, *Starve.* . . To die or perish of or with *hunger;* and not in consequence of *cold.*] **1908** *S. Atl. Qrly.* 7.334 **sSC coast** [Gullah], 'Im berry f'osty; me sta'be wud col.

2 in phr *starve for water:* To perish or suffer from thirst. Note: The extended use of this phr of plants, regions, and the like is widespread and not illustrated here.

1862 in 2000 Lee–Chepesiuk *SC Civil War* 123, [We] were treated as dogs[,] half fed and half-starved for water. **1863** in 1994 Matthews *149th PA Volunteer* 68, The sun was awful hot and dust so mouth deep we nearly starved for water. **1872** Powers *Afoot* 225, Deceived, . . and thinking it was the faintness of hunger—there is not a little truthfulness in that Western phrase, "starving for water"— . . I ate half a biscuit. **1889** *NY Times* (NY) 21 Jul 12/4, The poor creature [=a horse] has been starving for water, and takes at one time more than is good for him. **1930** Dobie *Coronado* 220 **West,** Three days later some soldiers . . found his horse entangled in a picket rope and almost starved for water. **1937** *Hall Coll.* **wNC, eTN,** I was starved to death for water. *Ibid,* The poor thing's a-starvin' for water. **1961** Borland *Dog Who Came to Stay* 94 **CT,** They found John Nowell dead in his house, several days dead, and the oxen were starving for water. **1979** *Foxfire 5* 486 **nGA,** See, what had happened, he was starving for water. **1985** in 2008 *DARE* File—Internet **TX,** [Transcript of L.B. Johnson tape:] Fellas at the shelter were saying they was thirsty and their [sic] starving for water. **1995** in 2004 Montgomery–Hall *Dict. Smoky Mt. Engl.* 567 **wNC, eTN,** *Starve.* . . To be very thirsty (esp in phr *starve for water*). **2004** *DARE* File—Internet **swTN,** I drink drink drink all day long too. It is as if I am starving for water.

starved rat n [See quot 1917]
=**pika.**
1884 Kingsley *Std. Nat. Hist.* 5.81, The miners and hunters in the West know these oddities as "conies" and "starved rats."

starve for water See **starve 2**

starve with cold See **starve 1**

star violet n

1 =**bluet 2.**
1896 *Jrl. Amer. Folk.* 4.190 **TX,** *Houstonia,* sp., Venus' pride, wild forget-me-not, star violet, Waco, Tex. **1898** *Ibid* 7.228 **TX,** *Houstonia caerulea*. . . star violet. **1953** Greene–Blomquist *Flowers South* 120, The first [flower] to appear is the small, winter-annual *H[oustonia] patens* with a deep-purple corolla and dark center. Sometimes called "small-bluets" or "star-violets."

2 =**dewdrop.**
1933 Small *Manual SE Flora* 619, Dewdrops. Star-violet. . . Woods, often in acid soil, . . N.C. to Minn. and N[ew] B[runswick]. **1948** Wherry *Wild Flower Guide* 80, Star-violet (*Dalibarda repens*). . . The common name refers to the fact that, although the leaves look like those of a Violet, the flowers are starry.

starwort n

1 A **colicroot 2** (here: *Aletris farinosa*).
1828 Rafinesque *Med. Flora* 1.37, Mealy Starwort. . . Vulgar Names . . Star-root [etc]. **1907** Henkel *Amer. Root Drugs* 17, Chamaelirium and Aletris (*Aletris farinosa*) have long been confused by drug collectors and others, owing undoubtedly to the transposition of some of their similar common names, such as "starwort" and "stargrass." **1971** Krochmal *Appalachia Med. Plants* 40, *Aletris farinosa*. . . Common Names . . stargrass, starwort [etc].

2 =**chickweed 1a.**
1836 (1840) Phelps *Lectures on Botany* 142, [*Stellaria*] *longifolia* (long-leafed starwort). **1910** Graves *Flowering Plants* 176 **CT,** *Stellaria graminea*. . . Lesser Stitchwort or Starwort. **1937** U.S. Forest Serv. *Range Plant Hdbk.* W13, Starworts and Chickweeds. . . *Stellaria* spp. *Ibid,* Tuber starwort, known also as starweed and mountain chickweed, is a sticky-hairy herb. **1973** *Foxfire 2* 70, Chickweed. . . starweed, starwort [etc].

3 also *drooping starwort:* =**blazing star 2.**
1892 (1974) Millspaugh *Amer. Med. Plants* 177-1, Devil's Bit, . . Drooping Starwort, . . Starwort [etc]. **1901** Lounsberry *S. Wild Flowers* 46, Drooping Starwort. . . The natives . . make a tincture out of it with whiskey which they then drink in rather astonishing quantities. **1907** [see **1** above]. **1949** Moldenke *Amer. Wild Flowers* 317, Other names for this attractive plant [=*Chamaelirium luteum*] are devilsbit, unicornroot, droopingstarwort [etc].

state Colored See **state Negro**

statehouse n Cf **federal building,** *DS* M21a, b
1909 *DN* 3.375 **eAL, wGA,** State-house. . . Privy, water-closet.

state Negro n Also *state Colored* **OK** *hist*
A Black person who came to the Indian Territory, now in Oklahoma, after the Civil War (rather than being a former slave of a member of the Five Civilized Tribes).

2000 *DARE* File—Internet **OK** (as of c1900), The "free" African-Creek Indians . . called the southern blacks "Watchina" or "State Negroes." **2001** *DARE* File **OK,** I have heard of *sofkee* now from two black women who are *Creek freedwomen*—descendants of slaves of Creek Indians. . . [T]he *Creek freedmen* called blacks who came after Oklahoma became a state in 1907 *State Colored* or *State Negroes.* These words were in use, at least by older people, as late as 1940. (A *Creek freedman* born in 1947 said he never heard them.) **2003** *DARE* File—Internet **OK,** These troops mostly consisted of what were called by the five nations Citizens, "State Negroes", i.e. Black citizens of the United States as opposed to the black Indians who were citizens of the 5 nations.

States, the n [From the general colloquial use of "the States" as an abbr for "the United States of America," but reflecting the situation that obtained before 1959, when Alaska and Hawaii were admitted to the Union] **AK** Cf **lower** adj **2, outside** n **1**
The contiguous, continental United States; hence adj, adv *stateside* of, in, or to the contiguous states.

[**1889** *NY Times* (NY) 5 Aug 3/6, The American people are vitally interested in the work [of education in Alaska], not only to the extent of $50,000 spent in it, and raised by taxation in the States each year, but from the large and noble principle of duty to elevate these men and women.] **1959** *AK Sportsman* Apr 18, Here workmen of Nikolski push off a scow-load of Umnak wool which the waiting *Expansion* will transship at Seward to the "States." **1965** *Fairbanks Daily News–Miner* (AK) 8 July 11/2, [Advt:] Small payments. Part trade for home in Alaska or Stateside. **1968** *DARE* (Qu. HH31, *Somebody who is not from your community, and doesn't belong*) Inf **AK5,** From the States. **1974** *Fairbanks Daily News–Miner* (AK) 10 Dec 11/3, [Advt:] Going *stateside.* Need a good home for two lovely cats. **1989** *Fairbanks Daily News–Miner* (AK) 27 Jan 5 (Tabbert *Dict. Alaskan Engl.*), I have shipped large bulk samples to the states in special containers. **2000** *Daily Sentinel* (Sitka AK) 18 Feb weekend sec 1/2, Students . . frequently ask Rioux . . what stateside Native dances are like.

state trunk See **trunk 2**

statie n Also sp *statey* **chiefly NEast, esp MA**
A state police officer.

1934 (1947) O'Hara *Appointment* 186 **PA,** Ride out to the state police barracks and watch the staties drill and shoot.   **1989** *Boston Globe* (MA) 1 Jan mag sec 73 (Internet) **ceMA,** [Headline:] Political Journal; Flynn inflames the Staties.   **1994** *Boston Herald* (MA) 17 June 4 (Internet) **ceMA,** Here's a State Police report of an arrest of a 28-year old Providence man. . . Under the section of the report labelled 'Peculiarities,' the Statie notes, 'Tattoos all over body.'   **1997** *DARE* File—Internet **cePA** [CoalSpeak], *Statey:* State Trooper: "Hide your kortz, there's a statey!"   **1999** in 2003 *DARE* File—Internet **MD,** I've been pulled over by a Maryland Statie for "not speeding."   **2000** Higgins *At End of Day* 100 **Boston MA,** One of them was gonna get himself grabbed by some kid Statie two weeks outta the academy.   **2000** in 2003 *DARE* File—Internet **WA,** When I realize the car is a statey, I slow way down.   **2001** *DARE* File—Internet **MA,** I remember "statie" from quite a while back—probably at least the 70s—in good old eastern MA. Haven't heard it used in western MA, though, at least during the time I've lived here (i.e. since 1991).   *Ibid* **RI,** The term 'staties' has been commonplace in my dialect (Rhode Island) and even in my parents[']. **2001** in 2003 *Ibid* **NYC,** If a statey saw you doing that shit . . you'd be so dead. **2002** *Boston Globe* (MA) 9 Feb sec D 1 (Internet) **ceMA,** I hit the ramp and reach the top. I'm feeling mighty high / I see the Statie miss the turn and I just wave bye-bye.

statue See **statues 1**

statue maker n

A var of **statues 1;** a player in the game; see quots.

1967 Cook Co. IL Forest Preserve *Nature Bulletin* 287–A (Internet), Old Schoolyard Games. . . Boys and girls still play Pom-pom-pullaway or . . Statue Maker.   **1968** *DARE* (Qu. EE33, . . *Outdoor games . . that children play*) Inf **CA**80, Statue maker.   **1972** *Yesterday* 1.3.32, Statues were played with any number of kids. The statue-maker swung the other kids around until they got dizzy and then let them go. Whatever position you wound up in when the statue-maker hollered "Stop!" you had to hold as though you were a statue.   **2002** *DARE* File—Internet, *Statues.* . . The person in the middle is the statue maker. He has each one come to him in turn to be swung around . . and then released.   *Ibid, Statue Maker Game.* . . One [player] becomes the Statue Maker, another is the Buyer, and the rest are the statues. The buyer hides his eyes or goes out of sight while the statue maker takes each remaining child by the hand and turns in a circle, letting go after a few seconds. The spun child falls or remains standing in whatever position they stop in, becoming a "statue". When all the statues have been made, the buyer comes back and decideds [*sic*] which statue to buy. The chosen statue becomes the buyer and the buyer becomes the statue maker, with the original maker becoming a statue.

statues n pl, but sg in constr

1 also *living statues, statue:* A children's game with many variations in which the players assume, or are put into, usu awkward postures, which they must hold.   **chiefly Nth, N Midl, West**   See Map   Cf **falling statues, red light 1, slinging statues, squat where you be, statue maker, swinging statues**

1871 *Scribner's Mth.* 1.678, Or there is the "Game of Statues." Everybody is a statue, excepting two who enact a showman and a would-be purchaser. The showman must be the "funny one" of the family. He describes the statues, turns them round, gives the prices . . regrets that this one's nose was a little injured in packing, and that one got dirty on the voyage and hasn't had its face washed yet; the statues meantime standing perfectly still, with immovable faces. Any one who moves or laughs is punished by a forfeit.   **1906** *DN* 3.158 **nwAR,** *Statues.* . . The name of a game in which children pose.   **1935** Mason–Mitchell *Active Games* 249, *Statues.*—Line up the players in a single rank. "It" stands about twenty feet in front. The players demonstrate the statue or pose they will assume. "It" turns his back to the players, counts ten, and turns to observe the players. Any player whom he sees moving or whose pose is not like that demonstrated, exchanges places with "it."   **1957** *Sat. Eve. Post Letters* **ceIL,** What you termed "Red light, green light", we called "Statue".   **1965–70** *DARE* (Qu. EE33, . . *Outdoor games . . that children play*) 118 Infs, **chiefly Nth, N Midl, West,** Statues; **CA**82, Statues—a bigger kid grabbed the other kids by the arm and slung them around; they kept whatever position they fell in; **MA**14, Statues—not swung around—just made a statue; **MA**21, Statues—when the leader yelled, the others would get into a pose; if the leader guessed what they were, that person would become the leader; **NY**40, Statues—one person turns his back, everyone else does crazy things; the one person calls "freeze," everybody freezes; if you move, you're "it"; 10 Infs, **scattered,** Statue; **CA**51, Living statues—a big kid threw the little kids into goofy positions; (Qu.

EE1) Inf **PA**68, Statues; (Qu. EE4) Inf **NH**11, Statue; (Qu. EE16) Infs **PA**26, 115, Statue(s); **AL**6, Statue—another freeze game.   **1966** *DARE* Tape **AL**3, I'm sure you've played the game of statues. . . The leader throws the person. . . He has to freeze in the position in which he's thrown.

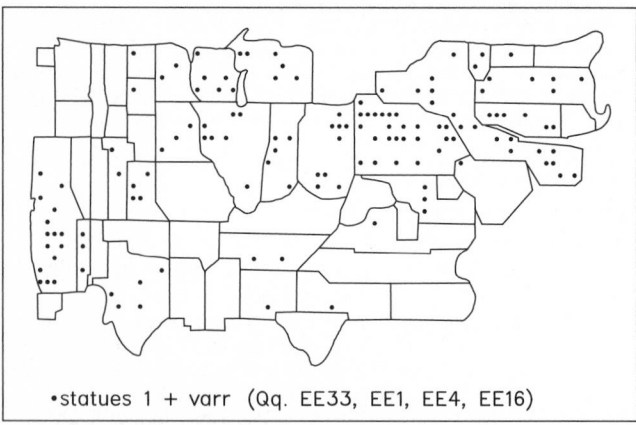

•statues 1 + varr (Qq. EE33, EE1, EE4, EE16)

2 The activity of making **snow angels.**

1966–68 *DARE* (Qu. EE33, . . *Outdoor games . . that children play*) Inf **IN**19, Statues—snow angels; **MN**6, Statues—fall down in snow and make an impression.

staub n   See **stob** n

staub v See **stob** v **B1**

St. Augustine grass   See **Saint Augustine grass**

staunch n   Also *stanch*   [Prob back-formation from *sta(u)ncheons* heard as *sta(u)nches*]   Cf **stance, stanchel**

A stanchion.

1843 in 2006 *DARE* File—Internet **KY,** 1 Rifle Gun and Shot Pouch—10.00. . . 1 Waggon, Feed trough and staunches—60.00.   **1929** *Chron.-Telegram* (Elyria OH) 28 Jan 10/4, [Advt:] Barn . . 64x40 stanches for 17 cows; stalls for four horses.   **1948** *Charleston Gaz.* (WV) 21 Aug 11/6, [Advt:] Big dairy barn, has 30 stanches.   **1949** *Indiana Eve. Gaz.* (PA) 27 Jan 27/1, [Advt:] School Bus and milk route pass the buildings. Staunches in barn.   **1965** *Independent Press–Telegram* (Long Beach CA) 31 Aug 11/3, [Advt:] 64 cow barn. . . holding pen, steel stanches. **1965–70** *DARE* (Qu. M11, *What do you put the cow's head through when she stands in the barn?*) Infs **AR**15, 33, **CA**199, **MD**13, **NJ**31, **NC**21, **VA**57, Staunch(es); **MO**36, Stanches; **NV**1, Stanch [stæntʃ]. [All Infs old]   **1973** *Salt Lake Tribune* (UT) 7 Oct sec C 14/4, [Advt:] Modern Grade A dairy, . . 8 elevated HB Staunches.   **1981** in 2008 *DARE* File—Internet **UT,** We never had stanches to put the cows in, we would just have to train the cows.   **2008** *Ibid* **swOH,** Elmer and his family were dairy farmers, the barn has cow staunches where the cows were milked.   *Ibid* **TX,** She needs stanches to be milked by hand or by machine.

stave n   esp Sth, S Midl   Cf *shaves* (at **shaft 2**)

One of the shafts between which an animal is hitched to a vehicle.

1913 in 1996 Witkay *Brooke Family* 143 **nIL,** Vere smashed the buggy staves by running into a stump when going a 3-minute pace. **1967–68** *DARE* (Qu. L44, *On a buggy, two long pieces of wood stick out in front and the horse goes between them. You call them the* _____) Infs **AL**26, **VA**7, Staves.   **1986** Pederson *LAGS Concordance (Shafts of a buggy)* 1 inf, **cnTN,** Buggy staves; 1 inf, **cnTN,** Staves = shafts; 1 inf, **seTX,** Staves = buggy shafts.   **2006** in 2008 *DARE* File—Internet **sAppalachians,** The line up of vehicles for the auction looked like Yoder's Used Buggy Lot. As point of reference, there was no vehicle so ponderous that one stout man could not pull it by the tongue or staves into the ring when it was auctioned.   **2008** *Ibid* **KS** (as of 1934), The newlyweds were put into an old buggy, the staves of which were tied up so they would not catch the ground, and so that the buggy would go only straight ahead.

stave v, hence ppl adjs *staved, stove(n)*

1 To break to pieces, crush.   **chiefly NEast**

1716 (1865) Church *King Philip's War* 1.24 **MA,** There *Philip* had staved all his Drums, and conveyed all his Canoo's to the East-side of *Metapoiset*-River.   **1719** in 1897 Hedges *Hist. East-Hampton* NY 11,

Feb. 24, 1719.—This day a whale-boat being alone the men struck a whale and she coming under ye boat in part staved it. **1831** in 2003 *DARE* File—Internet **eMA,** The Whale . . stove the boat and broke Mr Briggs Legg. **1846** *Amer. Whig Rev.* 4.235, The Bon Homme Richard . . lay a perfect wreck on the sea, riddled through, and literally stove to pieces. **1849** Cheever *Whale & Captors* 151 **NEng,** We pulled around and around the spot where the boat was stoven. **1862** in 1898 U.S. Navy Dept. *Official Records Union & Confederate Navies* 1st ser 7.360, The launch and first cutter are badly stoven, and the gig slightly hurt by a piece of shell. **1872** in 2003 *DARE* File—Internet **NJ,** Of fifty cans of milk in the stoven [railroad] car, which is almost completely wrecked, but two were spilled. **1881** *Ft. Wayne Daily Gaz.* (IN) [4 May] 5/2 (newspaperarchive.com), The hack was very badly stoven to pieces, but happily the horses were not injured. **1920** in 2003 *DARE* File—Internet **eMA** (as of c1855), We struck a Whale and he stove us so that the boat rolled over and We were all in the water. . . John Green left the stoven boat and got hold of me and they hailed me to the boat. **1939** Coffin *Capt. Abby* 91 **ME** (as of 1860s), His vessel had been stove to pieces. **1966** *DARE* (Qu. KK22, . . *Completely shattered: "The jug fell out of the window and was _____."*) Inf **ME16,** Stove all to pieces; **ME19,** Stove all to hell. **1968** Moody *Horse* 136 **nwKS** (as of c1920), The water come up so fast it was knee-high to a mounted man before we could get out of the dooryard, and when the bridge went out it stove the feed lot fence all to kindlin'. **1975** Gould *ME Lingo* 280, *Stove*—Past participle of stave. A barrel which has had its staves smashed is *stove.*

2 with *in:* To crush or smash inwards; to smash (a hole). **chiefly NEast** Cf **stove** v² **1**

1815 *N. Amer. Rev.* 1.255, One of the prisoners . . exclaimed, that the ship's broadside was stove in. **1834** *New Engl. Mag.* 7.448, The boat was staved in at the side. **1868** *Putnam's Mag.* 11.631 **NY,** A terrific sea landed on the hurricane deck; stove it in, and precipitated tons of water on the heads of the poor Chinamen. **1939** (1962) Thompson *Body & Britches* 244 **NY,** About three days out, we struck a rock / . . / It gave the boat quite a shock,/ And stove in quite a hole. **1965–70** *DARE* (Qu. KK21, . . *"They ran the wagon over the coffee pot and _____."*) 10 Infs, **esp Nth,** Stove it in; **MA98,** Stove in. **1975** Gould *ME Lingo* 280, Inland, Maine speech often uses *staved,* as when a cart rolled ahead and staved in a barn door, but coastal people always use the *stove* . . "his dory was stove in." **1982** *Smithsonian Letters* **ME,** The burglar stove the door in. **1986** Pederson *LAGS Concordance,* 1 inf, **neAL,** Stove in = caved in. **1990** Simpson *Gt. Dismal* 20 **nNC, sVA,** Nat Midgette and two other men were working on the top of the *Jungle Queen,* for last night's big wind had stove in its roof. **1998** in 2003 *DARE* File—Internet **MA** [MIT Sailing Newsletter], Each winter the staff rebuilds staved in bows. **2003** *Ibid* **PA,** See what she did to the back stall wall? Stove it in with kicks. *Ibid* **NYC,** I've seen the sides of a HP Netserver staved in by a poorly aimed forklift. **2003** *DARE* File **seME,** I heard my brother use this [=*stove in*] the other day referring to his sail boat that suffered some injury when it was being taken out of the water for the season.

3a with *up:* To damage by crushing; to wreck, ruin (a tool, machine, etc); to injure or incapacitate (a person or animal). **chiefly NEast** Cf **stove** v² **2a**

1852 Vose *Fresh Leaves* 29 **NYC,** I have not only run away from home; but I have stove up this and that—such as dashing carriages, costly sleighs, rich mirrors, . . and gentlemen's eyes. **1857** *Putnam's Mag.* 10.4 **NH,** The boat was badly stove up. **1860** Todd *Young Farmer's Manual* 120 **NY,** Otherwise the posts will be split, or the staples "stove up" before they are half driven in. **1870** *Manufacturer & Builder* 2.213, Tools and implements are collapsed, "stove up," smashed carelessly, or damaged by improper usage. **1956** Moody *Home Ranch* 125 **CO** (as of 1911), A man owes it to his horse to think about them things 'fore he staves 'em up. **1966** *DARE* (Qu. KK21, . . *"They ran the wagon over the coffee pot and _____."*) Inf **ME19,** Stove it up. **1975** Gould *ME Lingo* 280, *Stove.* . . "he stove up his truck." **1982** *Smithsonian Letters* **ME,** *Stove up,* broken up. "The hired man stove up my tractor." **1988** *Yankee* May 104 **NEng,** [He] must use a crutch and cane to get around because of an injury sustained when a tree fell on him and "stove him up."

b ppl adj *stove(n) up:* See **stove-up.**

4 To drive, thrust, or hurl with force. **chiefly SE; less freq NEast**

1784 in 1785 Amer. Acad. Arts & Sci. *Memoirs* 1.273 **ceMA,** And a distiller's cistern . . was burst to pieces, by the agitation of the liquor in it; which was thrown out with such force, as . . to stave off a board or two from a fence, at the distance of eight or ten feet from it. **1837**

Knickerbocker 10.408 **NC,** Stove two of his front teeth down his throat. **1860** Claiborne *Life Dale* 124 **VA,** I staved the bayonet through his body. **1879** Twain in *Atlantic Mth.* 43.178 **MO,** He was moving swiftly back and forth among the débris of his furniture, now and then staving chance fragments of it across the room with his foot. **1908** Wasson *Home from Sea* 269 **sME coast,** You could n't never once beat it out of her head that she was the one to blame . . for Bob Henderson's losin' his haul-holt . . and staving the life outen him on deck. **1913** Kephart *Highlanders* 229 **sAppalachians,** I stove a brier in my heel wunst. **c1938** in 1970 Hyatt *Hoodoo* 2.1478 **seGA** [Black], Throw jest as fur towards yore enemies or whosomevah yo' love or anything like dat, dat yo' kin *stave* . . it. **1946** *PADS* 6.28 **eNC** (as of c1905) [Black], *Stave.* . . Mainly in past tense and past participle, *stove:* to stab with a knife; to throw angrily. "He stove a knife in him." "He stove a brick at him." **1952** Brown *NC Folkl.* 1.595, *Stove* . . to thrust in, drive in with great force. "He stove that knife in Lem's back."—General. Illiterate. **1972** *Foxfire Book* 293 **nGA,** A hoop snake, they say, has a spike on their tail; and if they stave that spike in y', it'll kill y'.

5 also with *around, out;* rarely with *it:* To rush, stride vigorously; to work hard; to stamp or storm about—freq in v phr *rip and stave.* [Engl and Scots dial] **chiefly Sth, S Midl** Cf **staver, staving** adj, adv, **stiver 1**

1825 Neal *Brother Jonathan* 2.303 **CT,** "Hold in! . . " cried out a long, slab-sided Virginian, as our adventurers went, staving through Broadway, in Mr. Ashley's go-cart. **1879** (1880) Twain *Tramp Abroad* 368, Other pedestrians went staving by us with vigorous strides. **1887** *Century Illustr. Mag.* 33.709, I thought you couldn't be fool enough to let me rip and stave jus' as I pleased. **1899** (1912) Green *VA Folk-Speech* 416, *Stave.* . . To go or rush along recklessly or regardless of everything, as one in a rage; work energetically; drive. **1902** *DN* 2.246 **sIL,** *Stave.* . . To act violently. 'He jes staved around.' **1909** *DN* 3.375 **eAL, wGA,** *Stave.* . . To go rushing along, making a lot of racket. **1915** *DN* 4.188 **swVA,** *Rip and stave.* . . To rage and scold about. **1934** (1970) Wilson *Backwoods Amer.* 13 **AR, MO,** This dawg slows up and lets the rest of the pack go stavin' on past him. **1935** Hurston *Mules & Men* 202 **FL** [Black], Ah want you to git on it and go 'round de world jus' as fas' as you kin stave it. **1939** Hall Coll. **wNC, eTN,** All the dogs was right with us. They just stove right out at it. . . The dogs they just stove off the road into a little laurel patch. **1950** *PADS* 14.64 **SC,** *Stave.* . . To run, to go in a hurry. "He went staving down the road." **c1960** Wilson Coll. **csKY,** *Stave.* . . To go hurrying. Rare. **1963** *Mt. Life* 39.2.51 **sAppalachians,** Reckon he must'a' drawed a little whiff o' the vin'gar jurg afore he started aout, the way he's a-rippin' and a'stavin' araoun'. **1979** Lewis *How to Talk Yankee* [32] **nNEng,** *Stave . . ,* to move vigorously, often irresponsibly. . . "Henry was here for about two hours, full as a tick and staving around, looking for a fight."

stave in See **stave** v **2**

stave it, stave out See **stave** v **5**

stave plank See **stage plank**

staver n [Perh Engl dial; cf *EDD staver* sb. 3, 6] Cf **ripstaver, stave** v **5**

An extraordinary specimen; a humdinger, whopper.

1852 (1853) Pearson *Cousin Franck's* 158 **VA,** Wal, ef you haint a staver, an' a witch, to boot! **1855** Roe *Long Look Ahead* 356 **CT,** I say, Charley, that colt's a staver. But aint you afraid he will do mischief sometimes? he looks as if he wanted to tear things. **1869** Stowe *Oldtown Folks* 117 **NEng,** She was spoken of with applause under such titles as "a staver," "a pealer," "a roarer to work." **1879** in 1899 *Coronet Memories* 302, A healthier sky and the sea somewhat moderating. It was a staver of a night—cold. **1899** (1912) Green *VA Folk-Speech* 416, *Staver.* . . An active, energetic person. **1904** *DN* 2.429 **Cape Cod MA** (as of a1857), *Staver.* . . Used of a person to express high but undefined praise. 'He's a staver!' **1910** *DN* 3.449 **wNY,** *Staver.* . . A hard, energetic worker. **1912** *DN* 3.591 **wIN,** *Staver.* . . An unusually large or strong person or animal. "Just watch him. Isn't he a staver?" **1915** in 1971 Wyeth *Wyeths Letters* 503 **MA,** Carolyn is a *staver* and keeps us all guessing.

staves, to adv phr [Transf from the literal application to a barrel or other coopered vessel; cf *SND stave* n. 2] **scattered, but chiefly Midl**

To pieces—freq in phr *fall to staves;* also fig.

[**1788** *Weekly Monitor* (Litchfield CT) 25 Aug 1/3 **sePA,** Toasts given by . . Coopers. May the new government prove a binding hoop to the states, and never suffer them to go to staves.] **1846** Rupp *Hist. &*

Topog. 441 **csPA,** "God bless me," says Mr. Cooper, "you were nearly knocked to staves." "Oh yes, (says he very coolly) though you are a cooper, you could not have set me up." **1888** in 2003 *DARE* File—Internet **neTN** [*Cumberland Gap Progress* 30 May], The fellow found himself almost knocked to staves and his stomach for fight all gone. **1903** *DN* 2.331 **seMO,** *Staves, gone to.* . . Wrecked; ruined. 'He got to drinking worse and worse and finally went to staves entirely.' **1940** (1968) Haun *Hawk's Done Gone* 28 **eTN,** "Granny, you're nigh tired to death, hain't you?" And I did feel all at once like I was about to fall to staves. **1956** Gipson *Old Yeller* 16 **TX,** On top of that, he was gun shy. Fire a gun close to Jumper, and he'd fall to staves. **1966–70** *DARE* (Qu. KK20a, *Something that looks as if it might collapse any minute: "That old shed is certainly _____."*) Infs **AR**56, **CO**29, **IL**35, 143, **MS**1, **VA**50, Falling to staves; **LA**2, Going to staves. **1967** Bourne *Woman in Levi's* 208 **AZ,** Your corrals are falling to staves. **1968** in 2002 *DARE* File—Internet [*Mission Messenger* (St. Louis MO)], They are unfortunately perpetuating prejudice and patching up partisan parapets in a world that is coming unglued and falling to staves. **2006** in 2008 *DARE* File—Internet **TX,** Fragile race relations would fall to staves.

stave up   See **stave** v 3a

staving adj [**stave** v 5] Cf *ripstaving* (at **ripstaver**), **staver**
Great, powerful, fine.

1858 in 1875 Rodenbough *From Everglade* 225, He [=a pony] is a staving little fellow. **1861** *Merchants' Mag.* 44.397, He enjoys the reputation . . of one doing a staving business. **1870** *Yale Lit. Mag.* 36.140, I could write you a staving obituary. **1882** *Harper's New Mth. Mag.* 64.921, The wheat crop this year wuz a very stavin' one. **1898** Lloyd *Country Life* 112 **AL,** But all the same I made a stavin, stirrin speech. **1904** [see **staving** adv]. **1907** *DN* 3.207 **nwAR,** *Staving.* . . Excellent. "We had a [rip] stavin[g] time at the dance." **1928** *Ruppenthal Coll.* **KS,** *Staving.* . . fine; excellent, esp. strong, vigorous; a staving young man. **1930** Shoemaker *1300 Words* 54 **cPA Mts** (as of c1900), *Staving*—Big, sturdy, powerful. **c1960** *Wilson Coll.* **csKY,** *Staving time.* . . An unusually big time, an enjoyable time. **1993** *DARE* File **cnIL** (as of 1878), My mother's aunt, living on a farm in Paw Paw, Illinois, kept a diary for part of 1878, and in it she wrote "we had a staving team."

staving adv

Extremely, very.

1864 in 2003 *DARE* File—Internet **NY,** Gilbert is a staving good tent mate when I got up this morning he had a big fire in front of the tent. **1877** in 1937 Ruede *Sod-House* 111 **PA,** Had a staving good supper—fried rabbits, bread and butter, onions, radishes, pie, and coffee ad libitum. **1877** Wright *Big Bonanza* 279 **West,** They fiddled and danced till they all got blind drunk and broke up in a row. But the gal had a stavin' lively weddin' after all! **1892** *DN* 1.232 **KY,** *Stavin'* ['stevɪn]: very [*DN* Ed: also in Michigan]. "That is a stavin' fine horse." Cf. Bartlett [*DN* Ed: who defines it only as 'great,' 'strong.' Both uses are known in New England]. **1893** *Harper's New Mth. Mag.* 87.124 **Nantucket MA,** Oh, you women, specially you staving smart ones, how you do get swamped. **1898** Lloyd *Country Life* 117 **AL,** Rocky Creek went windin by a stavin big majority for Jackson. **1898** Smith *Caleb West* 194 **NEast,** They was stavin' good to her an' kep' 'er till mornin'. **1904** *DN* 2.428 **Cape Cod MA** (as of a1857), *Staving, adj.* and *adv.* Excellent, exceeding. 'We had a staving good time.' **1955** Wheeler–Rives *Dome* 303 **NY** (as of 1904), Mrs. Taft raked up a strong piece of goods, and I retired to an alcove and this time I made a staving good job of it.

stawk   See **stock** n

stay v

1 To dwell, reside; to maintain a home. [Scots, nIr dial] **chiefly Sth, S Midl** *chiefly among Black speakers*

1899 (1912) Green *VA Folk-Speech* 416, *Stay.* . . To remain; especially to remain in a place for an indefinite time; abide; sojourn; dwell; reside. **1951** *AmSp* 26.75 **sIL** [Black], 'Do you stay here?' In common Negro parlance *stay* is used for 'live.' **1962** Faulkner *Reivers* 13 **MS** [Black], Mr Winbush stays a solid eight miles from town. **1967** *DARE* FW Addit **AL, GA, SC** [Black], *Stay*—to live. "Where do you stay?" **1970** *Ibid* **swKY,** *Stay at*—to maintain a permanent residence [at]; e.g., "I stay at [address]." **1971** Mitchell *Blow My Blues Away* 59 **nwMS** [Black], Rosie Hill. . . Oh, yeah, she stay somewhere down the road here a piece. I can tell you near about where she stay at. **1986** Pederson *LAGS Concordance,* 1 inf, **swMS,** He stay a good piece from me—lives; 1 inf, **cnMS,** He used to stay—live, dwell; 1 inf, **csTN,** I stay—young people now use to mean live; 1 inf, **cMS,** I stayed over in the delta—I lived; 1

inf, **swTN,** She doesn't stay far from us; my uncle stays with us—always uses stay for live; 1 inf, **ceTX,** Stay—the majority of Blacks; live; 1 inf, **cGA,** Stays in—lives in; 1 inf, **neMS,** Where I stay—where I live. [All infs Black] **1986** *Atlantic Mth.* 257.48, In the Chicago ghetto poor blacks use the verb stay instead of live, as in "I stay at Robert Taylor Homes." Besides implying an inconstant life, this comes from a perfectly sensible sharecroppers' locution: "I stay at the Smiths' place." **1997** *DARE* File, "Stay" for "live" is normal among both blacks and whites here in South Georgia. *Ibid,* In West Tennessee, "stay" was perfectly normal for blacks, but it was marked (even stereotyped) as such. Very unusual in white speech. *Ibid,* I am an African American from Houston, TX with much of my family from Baton Rouge, LA. We used "stay" for "live" quite regularly. **1998** *Ibid* **MS, MO** [Black], I have heard "stay" used in the sense of "dwell" or "live" among Blacks in both Marks, Mississippi and Fulton, Missouri. **2004** *Ibid* **csWI** [Black], When I met a colleague (who grew up in California) at a local shopping mall, he asked, "Do you stay around here?" It took me a second to realize he was asking if I lived near there. **2009** *DARE* File **cIN,** I hear that [=*stay* for *live*] from older, rural adults in Central Indiana. . . the parents or grandparents of many of these older people immigrated from eastern Kentucky and eastern Tennessee between 1880 and 1903.

2 Used with a pres pple or adj to signify habitual action or usual condition; see quot. *among Black speakers* Cf **be** v **B1(f), steady B1;** cf also *DBE stay 4*

2000 *DARE* File **NYC,** "Stressed *Stay:* A New African-American English Aspect Marker". . . He *stay* flossing. 'He's always/frequently dressed very well.' . . My moms *stay* catching me coming in late. . . He *stay* wearing Vanson jackets. . . She *stay* pregnant. 'She is frequently pregnant.' . . That man *stay* sick. . . *Stay* expresses *frequentative iterative habitual* . . aspect. . . I did not hear stressed *stay* in African-American communities before the '90s. **2007** *Ibid* [Black], It didn't feel much like home, the way she *stayed* snatching the key back from me.

3 Used as a copula or aux verb; see also quots 1942, 1981. **HI** Cf *DBE stay 3, DCEU stay 3, 4*

1934 *AmSp* 9.123 [Engl dial of HI], *Stay* is the chief glory of the Hawaiian dialect, the one endemic verbal auxiliary. It is the Portuguese *esta,* Englished. The sense of *it is* is preserved, though not to the exclusion of other meanings. There is in *stay* something of the force of the progressive forms of the verb, and it supplements them or less often is used in their place. *Us stay sweating* (or *sweat*) *like hell* means, according to the context, "We are sweating" or "We were sweating." *Stay* may also express habitual action. **1942** *AmSp* 17.18 **HI** [English of Hawaiian children], *Stay.* . . Used instead of many forms of the verb *to be* both as copula and as auxiliary, as *He stay sleep,* or *Papa no stay* for *Papa is not at home.* **1966** Morimoto *Hawaiian Dial. Engl.* 98, Eventually mainland Nisei troops adopted many Hawaiian words or pidgin English words. . . I believe I continued to use some of these words long after my separation from the 442[nd Regimental Combat Team] at the end of the war. Examples: . . *"I stay come"* [I'm coming]. **1972** Carr *Da Kine Talk* 150 **HI,** *Stay* vs. forms of *to be.* . . "Where you stay go?" 'Where are you going?' "What you stay eat?" 'What are you eating?' **1981** *Pidgin To Da Max* np **HI,** *Stay*—To be. If Hamlet had come from Waimanalo. . . I stay or I no stay—'Ass da question, yeah?

stay all night   v phr

Used as a formulaic remark on parting.

1924 Raine *Land of Saddle-Bags* 4 **sAppalachians,** The lad conducted me across three fords and bade me good night, adding in response to my hearty thanks—for it would have been an insult to offer him money—"Well, ye better go home with me and stay all night." **1983** *MJLF* 9.1.62 **ceKY** (as of 1956), *You all better stay all night* . . a leave-taking pleasantry. **1999** *Folklife Center News* 21.4.12 **WV,** "You better stay all night, boys." Maggie Hammons Parker's phrase was a regular marker of the visits Alan and I paid to Marlinton, West Virginia, in the 1970s. Something about the emphasis she gave the word all reinforced the ritual aspect of her instruction.

stay-bit   n [*EDD* at *stay* v. 2.(2)] Cf **jack bite,** *DS* H5
See quot 1953.

1953 Randolph–Wilson *Down in Holler* 288 **Ozarks,** *Stay-bit.* . . A snack, a bite of food between meals. **2003** *DARE* File—Internet, [Diet discussion:] Adding the "staybit" I just had: 1/2 Myoplex Lite Cinnamon Roll Crunch Bar.

stay hitched   See **hitched, stand**

stay-place   n   chiefly sAppalachians
A shelter or dwelling.

1917 *DN* 4.417 **wNC,** That shack was put up fer a stay-place for them herders to pass the night in. **1934** in 2003 *DARE* File—Internet **eNC,** When mother is taken away, home may be ever so humble, but it is only a stay place, it is never a real home for what is home without a mother. **1967** Fetterman *Stinking Creek* 83 **seKY,** All a man needs is a stay place, and I'll take this as good as any. **1970** Justus *Tales* 42 **sAppalachians,** Of course, what he and Samson needed most was a home, a sure-enough stay-place, where they could earn their board and keep. **1984** Wilder *You All Spoken Here* 74 **Sth,** *Stay place:* A temporary or overnight shelter, as for hikers on the Appalachian Trail. *Ibid* 208, *Settin' up with:* Keeping the corpse company during the night at the stay place of the deceased. **2004** Montgomery–Hall *Dict. Smoky Mt. Engl.* 568 **wNC, eTN,** *Stay place.* . . A shelter to spend the night.

stay with v phr   Cf *keep company* (at **keep** v B5b), *sit up* (at **set up** v phr **4**)

To associate with as a lover.

1889 (1971) Farmer *Americanisms* 516, *Stay with.* . . Lovers *stay with* one another when courting. **1909** *DN* 3.416 **nME,** *Stay with.* . . To be attentive to; used of a young man or woman who is devoted to one of the opposite sex.

stead   See **bedstead**

steada   See **instead**

steady adj, adv, v   Usu |ˈstɛdɪ|; for varr see **A** below

A Forms.

1 |ˈstɪdɪ|; pronc-spp *stid(d)y.*

1815 Humphreys *Yankey in England* 108, *Stiddy,* steady. **1894** Riley *Armazindy* 52 **IN,** Chicken-hawk a-hangin' / Stiddy 'bove de stable-lot. **1899** Garland *Boy Life* 338 **nwIA** (as of c1870s), Stiddy, Dan. Take hold of it; w-o-oo-p, stiddy! **1899** (1912) Green *VA Folk-Speech* 417, *Stiddy, adj.* A form of *steady.* **1905** *DN* 3.56 **eNE,** In many words, [ɛ] tends to become [ɪ] . . get, steady, etc. **1909** [see **A2** below]. **1910** *DN* 3.449 **wNY,** *Stidy, adj.* and *v.* Steady. **1915** (1916) Johnson *Highways New Engl.* 187, He ain't fast, but he's stiddy. **1923** *DN* 5.222 **swMO,** *Stiddy, adj.* Steady. Also, *Studdy.* **1923** (1946) Greer-Petrie *Angeline Steppin'* 36 **csKY,** Makin' 'em [=walking sticks] is the only thing I ever know'd him to work at stiddy. **1931** Hannum *Thursday April* 193 **wNC,** Some say Joe is too blamed stiddy. **1932** Wasson *Sailing Days* 46 **cME coast,** Same time, the crew's wages is goin' on stiddy. **1933** *AmSp* 8.2.44 **neNY,** *Steady* [ˈstɪdɪ]. **1941** *LANE* Map 399 *(Her sweetheart)* 19 infs, **chiefly ME, NH, neMA,** Proncs of the type [ˈstɪdɪ]. *Ibid* Map 400 *(His sweetheart)* 15 infs, **chiefly ME, NH,** Proncs of the type [ˈstɪdɪ]. **1950** *PADS* 13.23 **sKY,** *Stiddy* [ˈstɪdɪ], studdy [ˈstʌdɪ]. . . *Steady.* Among uneducated. . . "Bill's got a stiddy job drivin' a truck." "Studdy this post while I nail it." **1975** Gould *ME Lingo* 277, *Stiddy*—Steady.

2 |ˈstʌdɪ, ˈstʌdɪ|; pronc-spp *stud(d)y.* **chiefly Sth, S Midl**

1795 Dearborn *Columbian Grammar* 139, *List of Improprieties.* . . Study for Steady. **1843** (1916) Hall *New Purchase* 227 **IN,** He . . kept right study ahead slash through weeds and briars. **1867** [see **B1** below]. **1871** in 1983 *PADS* 70.52 **ce,sePA,** *Study, adv.* Steadily. "She talked study and I don't know when I've laughed as much I am pretty near sick." **1899** (1912) Green *VA Folk-Speech* 425, *Studdy, adj.* For *steady.* **1909** *DN* 3.377 **eAL, wGA,** *Study, adj.* Steady. Also *stiddy.* **1914** *DN* 4.113 **cKS,** *Study, adj.* Steady. **1915** *DN* 4.191 **swVA,** *Study.* Variant of *steady.* **1923** *DN* [see **A1** above]. **1942** Hall *Smoky Mt. Speech* 20 **wNC, eTN,** Very often [ʌ] replaces [ɛ] in *steady* v. (e.g., [hɪ ˈstʌdid hɪzˈsɛf . .]). **1950** [see **A1** above]. **1954** Harder *Coll.* **cwTN,** *Studdy* [ˈstʌdɪ]—steady. **1967** *Mt. Life* Spring 15 **sAppalachians,** He stuck clost to the sides of the rocks for a while, a-studyin (steadying) hisse'f. **1976** Garber *Mountain-ese* 88 **sAppalachians,** *Study* . . steady—All I need is a real study job. **1983** *MJLF* 9.1.58 **ceKY** (as of 1956), *Study* . . steady. **2007** [see **B1** below].

B As adv.

1 Used as an aspectual marker or intensifier; see quots. [Cf *SND steady* adv. "Continuously, all the time"; *DBE study* adv. "regularly"] *among Black speakers*

1867 Allen et al. *Slave Songs* xxvi **seSC,** *Studdy* (steady) is used to denote any continued or customary action. "He studdy 'buse an' cuss we," was the complaint entered by some little children against a large girl. "I studdy talk hard, but you no yearde me," was Rina's defense when I reproved her for not speaking loud enough. **1983** Baugh *Black Street Speech* 86, *Steady* typically occurs with progressive . . verbs in sentences like "Leon be steady trippin," "We be steady hustlin," or "She be steady be runnin her mouth." The noteworthy exception has been observed with

prepositions following *steady,* for example, "You just steady on everybody's case." Used in the preceding ways, *steady* functions as an intensified continuative. **1999** *DARE* File **Sth** [Black], "She steady working," . . and "She steady looking." **2007** *DARE* File—Internet [Black], Back in the day, a person having a good time could be said to be "steady [ˈstʌdɪ] gettin' up / gittin' up."

2 in adv phr *steady by jerks:* Unsteadily. *joc*

1853 Torrey *City & Country* 251 **MA,** You may earn your living, and get along steady by jerks, and enjoy it. **1860** Street *Woods & Waters* 16 **neNY,** 'Oh, stiddy by jerks,' says old Allen. **1872** Bartol *Radical Problems* 105 **NEng,** The workman's proverb, "Steady by jerks," is illustrated by how many a crisis in the world. **1942** McAtee *Dial. Grant Co. IN* 61 (as of 1890s), *Steady by jerks* . . descriptive of progress that is not as smooth as desirable, also facetiously in admonitions to be steady. **1944** *PADS* 2.26 **cwNC,** *Steady by jerks.* . . In an uneven manner. **1983** *DARE* File **ceWI,** Stiddy by jerks—poking fun at one's efforts. **2002** *Bismarck Tribune* (ND) 24 May sec B 1 (Internet), Construction trucks will be moving in and out of regular traffic on the west side of State. . . Strata's Ron Reiswig describes traffic as 'steady by jerks.'

steady bee n   Also *steady John*   Pronc-spp *study bee, ~ John* [Cf *SND steady* v. "Of a hawk . . : to hover in one spot on the lookout for prey"; *EDD steady* v. 7 "To balance."]   **esp sAppalachians**

Either a **hover fly** or a **sweat bee 1.**

1936 Morehouse *Rain on Just* 18 **NC,** Dolly stopped for a moment to hunt for a 'steady bee,' one of the white-faced fellows whose big fat bodies buzzed ever so, but boasted never a sting to lean on. **1964** Reynolds *Born of Mts.* 6 **wNC, eTN,** The natives call it "The Study Bee," or "Study John" from its habit of hovering before one [=a flower] in hummingbird fashion as if it were studying out the situation. **1967** Berry *Place On Earth* 412 **KY,** A small yellow-striped fly, known around Port William as a steady-bee, comes and stands still in the air in front of her. **1967** *DARE* FW Addit **LA**1, Steady John [ˈstʌdɪ ˌdʒɑn]—a mostly black bumblebee that bores holes in wood. [FW: This is the usual pronunciation of *steady.*] **1968** *DARE* (Qu. R10, *Very small flies that don't sting, often seen hovering in large groups or bunches outdoors in summer)* Inf **NC54,** Study bees—yellow; (Qu. R21, . . *Other kinds of stinging insects)* Inf **NC54,** There's another kind of study bee that looks like a bumblebee and doesn't sting. **1997** in 2004 Montgomery–Hall *Dict. Smoky Mt. Engl.* 578 **wNC, eTN,** There's a yellow study bee. I'll have good luck today . . ; . . called thus because it could hang steady in the air like a helicopter . . , *study john.* **2004** in 2008 *DARE* File—Internet **swMS,** I became a great attraction to a hoard of little yellow and black, bee-like flies who couldn't resist sopping up my sweat. . . My father called these insects Steady Bees. . . I've also heard them called Sweat Bees, but at least my father used that name for a smaller, black bee that would sting you. **2008** *Ibid* **KY,** I grew up calling these bugs Steady Bees. You know the ones that hover around you?

steady by jerks   See **steady B2**

steady John   See **steady bee**

steak fish n   Also *steak cod*   **NEast**

Used as the market name for a large cod; see quot 1894.

1880 *Marion Daily Star* (OH) [14 Aug 3]/4 (newspaperarchive.com) **seMA,** Presently he flops a magnificent specimen of a speckled steak cod on deck, a genuine thirty pound white-bellied and grey-backed school fish. **1881** *Macon Telegraph & Messenger* (GA) 15 June 1/6 **NYC,** Fish bait was the best—sea trout, something like our steak fish. **1894** *Outing* 23.404 **Gloucester MA,** Steak fish are cod measuring twenty-two inches or more in length; market fish are those measuring less, but weighing three pounds or more, and scrod are those weighing under three pounds. *Ibid,* The result of the trip was as follows: thirteen thousand five hundred-weight of steak cod [etc]. **1968** *DARE* (Qu. P2, . . *Kinds of saltwater fish caught around here . . good to eat)* Inf **PA66,** Steak cod. **2003** *DARE* File—Internet **PA,** Fresh Cut Fillets. . . Boston Steak Cod fillet. **2003** *DARE* File **Baltimore MD,** Steakfish—seen on a sign in a fish market.

steal v   Usu |stiː(ə)l|; also |stɪl| Pronc-sp *still*   Cf Pronc Intro 3.I.3.c

A Pronc var.

1985 *Jrl. Engl. Ling.* 18.124 **eVA,** In words like *steal, heal,* . . which usually occur with /i/, the high-front vowel, the vowel becomes /ɪ/ which makes *steal* and *still, heal* and *hill,* . . homophones. **2000** Shores *Tangier Is.* 172 **Chesapeake Bay,** *Steal* and *still* have the same vowel, that of the latter. **2002** *DARE* File—Internet 24 **seKY**, Jesus always had to still away and pray. **2005** [see **steel A**]. **2006** *DARE* File—Internet **CA**, If you think . . the American military . . is somehow going to still away in the Arabian night *a la* a Viet-Nam-resembling debacle—forget that. **2007** *Ibid* **NC** [Black], It is so alright to Still Away sometimes. *Ibid* **FL** [Black], During the World War they knew how to still Away and break the weapon.

B Gram forms.

1 Past: usu *stole;* also:

a *stealed, stealt.* Cf **-ed 2**

1846 (1857) Herbert *Frank Forester's Sporting Scenes* 79, No one can say I stealed it. **1856** *Harper's New Mth. Mag.* 13.307 **VA** [Black], I never stealed money in all my life. **1884** *Anglia* 7.253 [Black], To the regular forms of the Irregular verbs as used by the whites, the Negro adds the following forms of his own. . . *Pres.* steal—*Past.* stealed, stealt, stoled, stolened. **1953** Atwood *Survey of Verb Forms* 22 **Atlantic, Steal.** . . The preterite form *stole* is very heavily predominant. . . One S.C. informant uses *stealed.* **1968** *DARE* (Qu. OO42a, *About stealing money: "He admitted that he* _____ *[the money]."*) Inf **NC50**, Stealed. **1993** *Star Tribune* (Minneapolis MN) 26 Nov sec B 1 (Internet), I wouldn't have had turkey unless I stealed it.

b *stol(e)d.* **scattered, but most freq Sth, S Midl, SW** See Map Cf **-ed 3**

1845 Thompson *Pineville* 114 **cGA**, I'll give my Bible affydavy that he stold the horse and cart. **1871** (1892) Johnston *Dukesborough Tales* 37 **GA**, The man that fooled the Tory in the Revolutionary War, and stoled his horse. **1884** [see **B1a** above]. **1893** Riley *Poems Here* 146 **IN**, An' 'at's my little bee-bag the Fairies stold away. **1899** (1912) Green *VA Folk-Speech* 420, *Stold.* . . Past tense and past part. of *steal.* **1903** *DN* 2.332 **seMO**, *Stold, pret.* of steal. 'He stold away my daughter.' **1907** *DN* 3.237 **nwAR**, *Stold, pret.* of steal. **1909** *DN* 3.376 **eAL, wGA**, *Stold, pret.* of steal. **1953** Atwood *Survey of Verb Forms* 22 **Atlantic, Steal.** . . The preterite form *stole* is very heavily predominant . . ; only a scattering of informants give the form *stoled* /stold/ before *my.* . . We might reasonably conjecture that *stoled* would have been of fairly common occurrence if recorded before a vowel. **1955** Roberts *S. from Hell-fer-Sartin* 48 **seKY**, Nippy stold the old man's horses and brought 'em back to that other man. **1965–70** *DARE* (Qu. OO42a, *About stealing money: "He admitted that he* _____ *[the money]."*) 88 Infs, **scattered, but esp Sth, S Midl, SW**, Stoled [Of all Infs responding to the question, 29% were comm type 5, 27% gs educ or less; of those giving this response, 47% were comm type 5, 52% gs educ or less.]; (Qu. V4, . . *Words for stealing something valuable* . . *"Yesterday somebody* _____ *my watch."*) 16 Infs, **chiefly Sth, S Midl**, Stoled; (Qu. U11, *If you buy something but don't pay cash for it* . . *"I* _____ *."*) Inf **MO**19, Stoled it; (Qu. Y26b, *To walk very quietly: "The children filled their pockets and* _____ *out the back way."*) Infs **TX**83, **WI**60, Stoled. **1965–70** *DARE* Tape **CA**197, That was a terrible crime in those days, as bad as it was in the . . plains when somebody stoled a horse there; **MS**1, He stoled a mule; **MS**71, They stoled a car; **NJ**21, He'd tell people how somebody'd drove up there and stoled it. **1989** Pederson *LAGS Tech. Index* 355 **Gulf Region** (Swiped) 62 infs, Stoled.

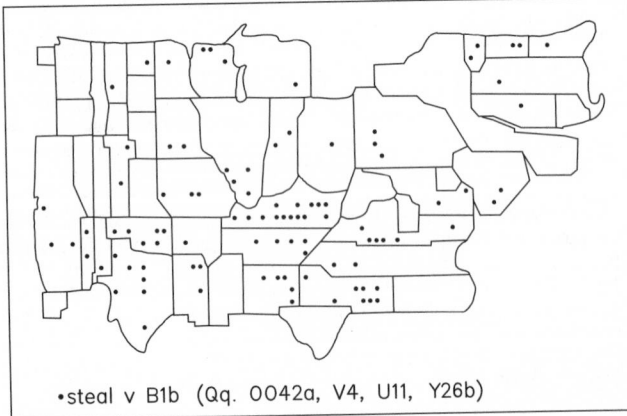

•steal v B1b (Qq. OO42a, V4, U11, Y26b)

c *stolded.*

1900 *Philadelphia Inquirer* (PA) 4 Feb Colored sec 3/7, "That's a big, big story!" the valiant little master of the dog cried indignantly, though his eyes were filled with tears. "You stolded him." **1940** *AmSp* 15.51

sAppalachians, Ozarks, Abnormal preterites abound. . . Superfluous *-(d)ed* is added to the past form of many verbs . . stoled or stolded.

d *stolen(ed).*

1884 [see **B1a** above]. **1967–68** *DARE* (Qu. OO42a, *About stealing money: "He admitted that he* _____ *[the money]."*) Infs **MD**43, **MO**8, Stolen. **2003** *DARE* File—Internet, There apparently was a race horse named Hoof Hearted. I think he stolened the name.

2 Past pple, ppl adj: usu *stolen;* also:

a *stealed.*

1886 *Century Illustr. Mag.* 32.197 **GA** [Black], An' so many been stealed I used to sleep in de stalls at night.

b *stole.* **widespread**

1706 *Boston News–Letter* (MA) 3 June 6/2, There was Stole, A little Moses Boat from the side of the Sloop Larke. **1820** Eastburn–Sands *Yamoyden* 28, As if a beam from the lamp had stole / That burnt within his inmost soul. **1867** (1969) Lanier *Tiger-Lilies* 153 **TN**, You has stole what 's better 'n any rifle or horse. **1876** Barker *Poems* 98 **ME**, Cale McCluer had stole my girl. **1891** *DN* 1.144 **cNY**, *Stole,* participle for *stolen.* **1905** *DN* 3.102 **nwAR**, Preterites occur in the speech of the uneducated or partly educated as perfect participles. . . stole. **1926** Roberts *Time of Man* 9 **KY**, If only some o'nary trash hadn't stole my shoes. **1956** Algren *Walk on the Wild Side* 83 **Chicago IL**, I was mad 'cause I hadn't stole things like the other kids. **1965–70** *DARE* (Qu. OO42b, *About stealing money: "He says it's the first time he has ever* _____ *[money]."*) 227 Infs, **widespread**, Stole; **NH**10, Stole any [Of all Infs responding to the question, 29% were comm type 5, 66% old, 27% gs educ or less; of those giving these responses, 39% were comm type 5, 76% old, 43% gs educ or less]; (Qu. AA4b) Inf **IL**96, Got her nest stole. **1996** Horton *Island Out of Time* 135 **Chesapeake Bay MD**, Some was stole, some was sold.

c *stol(e)d, stolt.* **chiefly Sth, S Midl, SW** See Map

1845 Thompson *Pineville* 109 **cGA**, But who upon yeath [=earth] could went and stol'd 'em right here in broad daylight? **1890** *Harper's New Mth. Mag.* 82.115 **GA** [Black], He had done stolt ole Mis' Twine weddin'-ring. **1899** [see **B1b** above]. **1965–70** *DARE* (Qu. OO42b, *About stealing money: "He says it's the first time he has ever* _____ *[money]."*) 71 Infs, **chiefly Sth, S Midl, SW**, Stoled; **KY**24, **MD**40, Stoled anything. [Of all Infs responding to the question, 29% were comm type 5, 27% less than hs educ, 51% male; of those giving these responses, 45% were comm type 5, 62% less than hs educ, 63% male.] **1966** *DARE* FW Addit **AR**43, [Tape recording from 1958:] I've stoled 'em from the rich and I've gived 'em to the poor. **1979** Melton *'Pon My Honor* 32 **TN**, The other people in the settlement begin to have their corn stold, too.

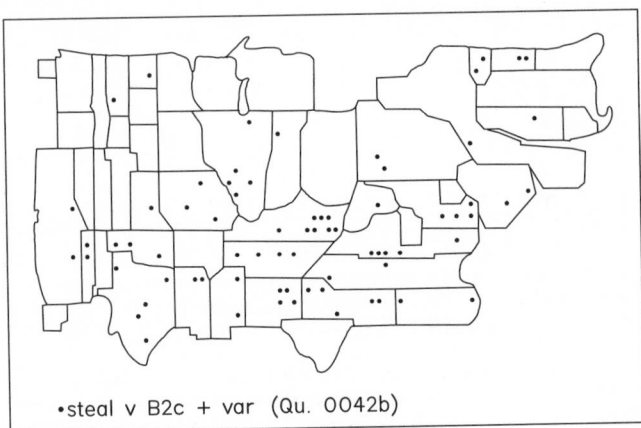

•steal v B2c + var (Qu. OO42b)

d *stolden.* [Cf pret *stoled* at **B1b** above]

1969 *DARE* (Qu. OO42b, *About stealing money: "He says it's the first time he has ever* _____ *[money]."*) Inf **NC**76, Stolden. **2003** *DARE* File—Internet, She has stolden my soul. *Ibid* **MN**, Last time I parked on the street my car got broken into and my CD player and CDs were stolden.

C Sense.

Of a hen: to make (a nest) in a hidden place; also transf; hence adj phr *stole out* made in a hidden place. [*OED2 steal* v.[1] 6.c 1743 →]

1865 *Atlantic Mth.* 15.654, Hens are fond of little mysteries. With tons of hay at their disposal, they will steal a nest in a discarded feeding-trough.   **1885** *Harper's New Mth. Mag.* 70.209 **NEng,** A hen that stole her nest . . was tracked to earth like a fox and cooped triumphantly. **1900** *New Engl. Mag.* 22.338, That speckled hen's stole her nest again. **1943** McAtee *Dial. Grant Co. IN Suppl. 2* 2 (as of 1890s), *Steal* . . hide; "That ole dominicker's stole her nest agin." **1964** Sneller *Vanished World* 252 **cNY** (as of c1900), Sometimes a hen would steal her nest, lay her eggs in it, and never be missed. **1966** *DARE* FW Addit **ME5,** To *steal a nest* (of a hen)—to lay eggs hidden in bushes (instead of in nest) in order to hatch them. **1969** *DARE* (Qu. AA4b, *. . A woman who is very eager to get married. . . "She's _____."*) Inf **IL96,** Got her nest stole out and laying eggs. **1984** Wilder *You All Spoken Here* 135 **Sth,** *Steal nests:* Broody hens do it.

steal n   See **stale 1**

steal a step   See **stealing steps**

steal clothes   See **stealing sticks**

stealed   See **steal B1a, 2a**

steal goods, stealing chips (or goods)   See **stealing sticks**

stealing grapes n   Also *stealing apples*   Cf **graping, go; mossy**

See quots.

1883 Newell *Games & Songs* 167 **NY,** *Stealing Grapes.* A circle of children with arms raised. Enter keeper of garden: "What are you doing in my vineyard?" "Stealing grapes." "What will you do if the black man comes?" "Rush through if I can." **1901** *DN* 2.148 **wMD,** *Stealin' apples. . .* A game like mossy.

stealing partners n   Also *stealing partner game, steal partners* **Sth, S Midl**   Cf **fancy four, play-party, twistification**

Any of var "games" played to music, often as a substitute for dancing.

1883 *Macon Telegraph & Messenger* (GA) 16 Oct 3/4, A young negro offended his sweetheart by selecting another dusky damsel for his partner during a game called "Stealing Partners." **1884** *Atlanta Constitution* (GA) 26 Aug 5/1 **neAL,** A regular game of "steal partners" has been going on secretly between our merchants and clerks. **1891** *Ibid* 1 Aug 4 **csGA,** The evening's pleasures were opened with a game of "stealing partners" and closed with a wild, woolly "jay bird." **1904** (1913) Johnson *Highways South* 101 **GA,** In Stealing Partners, we all have partners but one boy, and he pick out any girl he want and swings. That leave another boy without a partner, and *he* have to pick out a girl and swing her, and so on. **1916** *TX Folkl. Soc. Pub.* 1.25 **TX,** *Steal Partners. . .* You stole my partner at my dislike,/ So early in the morning. . . Reel, reel at my dislike,/ . . So early in the morning. **1943** Writers' Program NC *Bundle of Troubles* 59 [Black], "Let's dance 'steal partners'," she says, a-shaking her bones in music time. **1959** Lomax *Rainbow Sign* 34 **AL** [Black], We played stealin-pardner games like "Rosey Baby". . . If I was stealin partners, I'd have to dance all the way to the other bunch and then sing and act mightily and steal me a partner and take her back to my crowd. I'd keep on till the other bunch would be down to the main one. Then *he* gon' start stealin' his pardners back. **1966–68** *DARE* (Qu. EE2, *Games that have one extra player—when a signal is given, the players change places, and the extra one tries to get a place*) Infs **AL32, TX35,** Stealing partners; **LA12,** Stealing partners—people go around in a ring; (Qu. EE33, *. . Outdoor games . . that children play*) Inf **VA26,** Stealing partners; (Qu. FF4, *Names and joking names for different kinds of dancing parties*) Inf **FL19,** Stealing partners. **1986** Pederson *LAGS Concordance,* 1 inf, **nwGA,** Stealing partners—childhood game.

stealing pegs   See **stealing sticks**

stealing steps n   Also *steal a step, ~ steps* **esp Sth, S Midl** Cf **may I**

A var of the game **red light 1.**

1906 *Macon Daily Telegraph* (GA) 1 Sept 6/5, Merry games of "drop the handkerchief," "snake in the gully," "stealing steps," etc., were played on the lawn. **1957** *Sat. Eve. Post Letters* **GA** (as of c1905), The game you know as "Red Light", we knew as "Stealing Steps". *Ibid* **wKY** (as of c1930), We played "red-light" and its variants "steal-steps" and "Chinese school". **1966** *DARE* (Qu. EE33, *. . Outdoor games . . that children play*) Inf **NC22,** Stealing steps (or blue light)—now one was "it"; he said to take so many giant steps, monkey jumps, scissor steps, etc. You'd have to say "May I?" or else go back. [The object was to] see who could get home first; **NC52,** Steal a step—one person turns back and another rushes the goal; when he turns around, he must be stopped. **1966** *DARE* Tape **AL6,** Stealing steps. . . The children all line

up on the steps and the teacher . . would be very far out, and they would go down the line, and you'd give each one a certain number of steps. "You may take one giant step or one baby step" or one some other kind of step. While she wasn't looking, you could steal steps. But if you stole steps and she caught you, you had to go back to the starting point. But if she didn't see you doing it, you'd keep what you stole, and the first one to gain the position of the teacher was the next one that was "it.". . You had to say "May I," and if you didn't say "May I," you lost your turn; . . you had to go back to . . the starting point.

stealing sticks n   Also *steal stick(s), steal the ~, sticks* **scattered, but more freq Sth, S Midl**

A children's game in which the members of two teams attempt to steal sticks belonging to the opposing team while attempting to elude capture; similarly nouns *steal clothes, steal(ing) goods, stealing chips, ~ pegs,* and varr, games which differ only in the object to be stolen; see quots.

1883 Newell *Games & Songs* 168, *Stealing sticks.* A company of players divide, each having the same number of sticks, which they deposit on each side of a line; whoever crosses the line may seize a stick, but if caught is confined in a prison, marked out for the purpose. **1897** (1952) McGill *Narrative* 30 **SC,** In the game of "Steal Clothes" we divided into two companies chosen by the captains, who, drawing a long line on the ground, claim their respective sides of it as their possession, while the clothes, consisting of the boys' round jackets and the girls' aprons were placed thirty or forty yards in the rear of each company. Any one caught in the act of stealing or pulled over the line was neither paroled nor exchanged, but put into active service on the opposite side to which he first belonged. **1899** (1912) Green *VA Folk-Speech* 416, *Steal-clothes. . .* A boys' game, the players divided in two parts and from a line in the middle of the ground running across to take the "clothes"—jackets or caps, and some distance from the base. **1901** *DN* 2.148 **cNY,** *Steal goods. . .* A game at Ithaca, N.Y. A game known also as steal sticks (Schuyler Co., N.Y.), steal stones (Lowell, Mass.), steal wedges (Gouverneur, N.Y.). Also sticks (Steuben Co., N.Y.). **1905** *DN* 3.96 **nwAR,** *Stealin(g) wood. . .* The name of a game. Common. **1956** McAtee *Some Dialect NC* 43, *Steal-stick. . .* A game between "sides," starting with equal numbers of sticks, won by the side that managed to steal all of the opponent's store. **1957** *Sat. Eve. Post Letters* **TX** (as of c1885), The liveliest game and most commonly played was "sticks." Leaders choose their best and fastest runners first. Then half the group arranges itself around a base and the other half around another base, each supplied with an equal number of sticks. Then the stealing began; one group stealing from the other. The game ended in a victory for the side that got all the sticks. You could steal a stick or catch a person on the opposite side stealing a stick. **c1960** *Wilson Coll.* **csKY,** *Stealing sticks. . .* Also called *Stealing Goods.* **1965–70** *DARE* (Qu. EE33, *. . Outdoor games . . that children play*) Inf **VA26,** Stealing goods; **KY85,** Stealing pegs—old-fashioned; **GA68,** Stealing sticks—draw a line between teams, put sticks in circles; if caught before entering circle, belong to other side; **KY89,** Stealing sticks—same as stealing goods—two sides "choose out"; each side has sticks, try to steal the other side's sticks; **TX99,** Steal sticks—two sides; two circles with sticks from each side; try to steal each other's sticks; if caught, you join opposite side; **WY24,** Steal sticks—each team had pile of sticks; stole from each other; **SC11,** Steal the chips—any number of players—each side guards its chips, and you try to get through to steal chips without being tagged; if you're tagged, you join the team tagging you; whenever one team loses all its chips, the game ends; **NM9,** Steal the sticks—two teams, each defending their pile of sticks and raiding the other's; **ND9,** Steal the sticks—had to run and grab sticks; **TX42,** Steal the sticks; **WI24,** Steal the sticks—two teams, trying to get a stick from the other's pile without being caught; (Qu. EE2, *Games that have one extra player—when a signal is given, the players change places, and the extra one tries to get a place*) Inf **TX36,** Stealing sticks; **FL30,** Sticks—six on each side of a line, a pot of sticks on each side; one runs to grab the sticks from the other side; (Qu. EE12, *Games in which one captain hides his team and the other team tries to find it*) Inf **IN38A,** Steal sticks. **1986** Pederson *LAGS Concordance,* 1 inf, **nwMS,** Stealing chips—childhood game; 1 inf, **ceTX,** Stealing chips—variant of the game "alligator"; 1 inf, **cMS,** Stealing goods; 5 infs, **AL, AR, GA, LA,** Stealing stick(s). **1998** *WI State Jrl.* (Madison) 6 July sec B 3 (Internet), We girls joined the boys in every game—steal sticks, pumpum pullaway, three deep, even a mild form of baseball.

steal partners   See **stealing partners**

steal steps   See **stealing steps**

steal stick(s) See **stealing sticks**

stealt See **steal B1a**

steal the stick(s) See **stealing sticks**

steam n

1 in phrr *bucket* (or *cup, pail*) *of steam* and varr: A nonexistent item used as the basis of a practical joke. [*OED bucket of steam* (at *sell* sb.[2] 2.a quot 1898)] **scattered, but chiefly NEast** See Map

1908 *Anaconda Std.* (MT) 16 Aug 7/6, "I mean where do you get the steam when the clerk sends you for it. He said the guy in 318 wants a bucket of steam." The bellboy held up a tin pail in which he expected to carry the steam. [**1947** Berrey–Van den Bark *Amer. Slang Suppl.* 13.12, [Army:] Fictitious articles (for which raw recruits are sent). . . *bucket of boost.*] **1965–70** *DARE* (Qu. HH14, *Ways of teasing a beginner or inexperienced person—for example, by sending him for a 'left-handed monkey wrench': "Go get me _____."*) 35 Infs, **scattered, but chiefly NEast,** Bucket (*or* bag, cup, pail, potful) of steam; **NJ**33, **SC**21, Bag (*or* bucket) of cold steam; **NY**92, Pail of blue steam. **1980** in 1983 Beyle *How Talk Cape Cod* 26, *Bucket of steam*—Cape Codders are not unknown for their remarkable sense of humor. A bucket of steam is something a native might send a "foreigner" out to look for just to "test his mettle." **2001** *DARE* File—Internet, [Summary of *Hopalong Cassidy* radio program of 19 Mar 1949:] The yard boss . . tells California to get some red signal oil. There is none, and Hoppy jokingly tells him to mix a bucket of steam with some green oil and it will turn red. [*Ibid* **Canada,** I started to work on July 3rd 1941 . . as an engine wiper on the Canadian Pacific Railway. . . Sometimes a machinist would ask you to get them a left handed monkey wrench out of their tool box. I never did find one. Another good one was a bucket of steam to clean up with.]

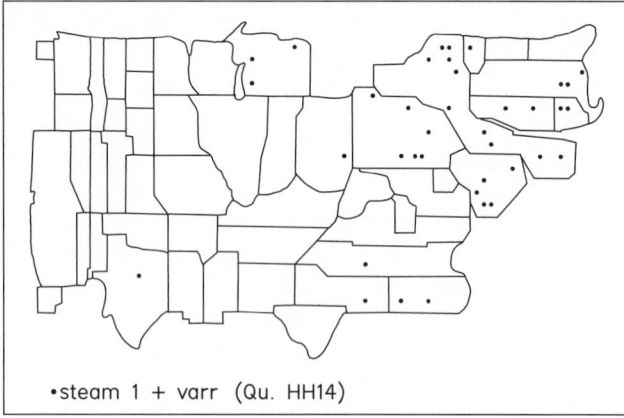

•steam 1 + varr (Qu. HH14)

2 Any of var alcoholic drinks; see quots. Cf **steam up**

1830 Ames *Mariner's Sketches* 23 **MA,** I never felt any inconvenience or sickness during the whole time I was in Batavia, which I attributed in a great measure to my following the advice of the old French pilot . . not to drink too much water, but always qualify it with a little steam. **1865** Crockett *Life* 121, We staid all night with them, and had a high night of it, as I took steam enough to drive out all the cold that was in me, and about three times as much more. **1970** *DARE* (Qu. DD21a, *General words . . for any kind of liquor*) Inf **TN**50, Steam. **1972** Claerbaut *Black Jargon* 81, *Steam.* . . 1. beer. . . 2. wine.

steam beer n Also *steam* [See quots 1899, 1902; but perh orig a trade name meant to associate a cheap type of beer with the then advanced technology of the *steam brewery*] **orig chiefly CA, now widely known**

An especially effervescent lager-style beer; see quot 1957. Note: Since 1978 *Steam Beer* has been a registered trademark of Anchor Brewing Company, San Francisco.

[**1857** *Alton Weekly Courier* (IL) 23 Apr 4/3, [Advt:] A.A. Le Beau & Co.'s Steam Brewery Lagar [sic] Beer.] **1879** *Decatur Daily Rev.* (IL) 3 Oct 1/6, [Advt:] *Harpsrite & Shlaudeman, Steam Brewery and Bottling Works.* . . Pure Standard Lager Beer . . ; and steam beer in quart and pint bottles, prepared for family use. **1889** *Amer. Jrl. Pharmacy* 61.443, It was stated by Prof. Wenzell that picrotoxin had been found only in a cheap variety, commonly called steam beer in San Francisco. **1895** *Overland Mth.* (2d ser) 26.651 **CA,** Cassius . . boasted among the boys that he preferred steam beer. **1899** (1977) Norris *McTeague* 1 **San Francisco CA,** He stopped at Joe Frenna's Saloon and bought a pitcher

of steam beer. [Footnote:] A cheap form of beer which was particularly popular in California. . . The "steam" refers to the strong carbonation in this form of beer. **1902** *Amer. Handy Book Brewing* 699, *Common or Steam Beer,* light in color, hop aroma and bitter taste not very pronounced; very lively and not necessarily brilliant. *Ibid* 776, *California Steam Beer.* . . It is called steam beer on account of its high effervescing properties and the amount of pressure ("steam") it has in the packages. **1919** Kyne *Capt. Scraggs* 285 **CA,** He was homeward bound to his dear old San Francisco—back to steam beer, to all of his old cronies of the Embarcadero. **1926** Riesenberg *Vignettes* 259 **San Francisco CA,** A few fights began between men who were on their fifth and sixth schooners of steam. **1951** *Tap & Tavern* 18 June 13 (*Popik Coll.*), About a year or so ago, this column discussed that almost extinct West Coast institution, *"steam beer."* To know about "steam" is a sure indication that a person's background includes a personal acquaintance with San Francisco or the West Coast 'way back when Steam fell prey to the inroads of lager beer. **1959** *San Francisco Chron.* (CA) 28 June 1/3, There won't be a drop of steam beer in Northern California after a few more days. **1996** *Brew Your Own* Feb (Internet), Steam beer as a generic style had a very poor reputation. . . Anchor reinvented the style. . . Very few people now living can claim to have tasted a steam beer not inspired by or actually made by Anchor.

steamboat n Cf **canal boat, gunboat 1**

A large foot or shoe.

1916 *DN* 4.348 **cTX** (as of 1896), *Steamboat.* . . Shoe. Also Va., La. **1935** *AmSp* 10.9, The resemblance of feet to various forms of water craft seems to prompt the currency of *tugboats, steamboats, gunboats, battleships, canal boats, sailboats, steamers, canoes,* and *submarines.* **1966– 69** *DARE* (Qu. X38, *Joking names for unusually big or clumsy feet*) Infs **MI**81, 103, **NY**84, **OH**20, **WA**6, Steamboat(s).

steamed (up) See **steam up**

steamer clam n

1 also *steamer, steaming clam:* A **soft-shell clam** (here: *Mya arenaria*). **chiefly NEng**

1909 MA Comms. Fisheries & Game *Rept. Mollusk Fisheries MA* 179, Small clams, or "steamers," are shipped in the shell. **1939** *LANE* Map 235 (*Names for the soft clam*) 2 infs, **CT,** Steamer; 2 infs, **CT,** Steaming clam. **1947** Morris *Field Guide Shells Atl.* 65, *Mya arenaria.* . . Known by such names as 'long clam,' 'soft-shelled clam,' 'steamer clam,' and 'long-necked clam,' it lives in the muds and gravels between the tides. **1970** *DARE* (Qu. P18, . . *Kinds of shellfish*) Inf **NJ**67, Steamers. **1975** Gould *ME Lingo* 276, *Steamer*—In this instance, a simply delicious long-neck Maine clam not too small and not too large, just perfect for steaming. **1981** *Seventeen Letters* **NY,** Soft shelled clams here [=in Maryland] are the same as steamers in New York. **1995** *DARE* File **MA,** Steamers are clams sold raw at seafood stores or steamed in restaurants. They are eaten with your fingers and dipped into warm broth and melted butter.

2 A **littleneck 2** (here: *Protothaca staminea*).

1970 *Star–News* (Pasadena CA) 25 Feb [19]/1 (newspaperarchive.com), [Advt:] *Steamer Clams*—Fresh, Littleneck. **1989** Mickelson *Nat. Hist.* 47 **AK,** Gravel intertidal areas in well protected bays [of Prince William Sound] support butter and littleneck (steamer) clams. **1994** Guterson *Snow Falling* 77 **nwWA,** In the evening there were bonfires and steamer clams, mussels, oysters, and perch.

steam hole n

=**smoke hole.**

1898 Chambers *Haunts* 209 **ME,** The steam-hole of a beaver's house might be more easily located than the chimney of Skeene's hut. **2000** [see **smoke hole**].

steaming clam See **steamer clam 1**

steam pot See **pot 3**

steam up v phr Cf **steam 2**

To become intoxicated, get drunk; hence ppl adjs *steamed (up)* intoxicated, drunk.

1927 *DN* 5.464 [Underworld jargon], *Steam up.* . . To get drunk. **1929** M.A. Gill *Underworld Slang* 10/2 (*OED2*), *Steamed up,* drunk. **1931** *AmSp* 7.87 [Prohibition terms], Terms referring to the state of intoxication. . . Steamed up. **1933** *AmSp* 8.3.32 [Prison terms], *Steamed up.* Intoxicated. **1966** *DARE* (Qu. DD13, *When a drinker is just beginning to show the effects of the liquor . . he's _____*) Inf **MT**3, Steamed up. **1971** Terrell *Bunkhouse Papers* 156, A cowman sat next to the houseman, and he was steamed with liquor so that he slumped a little to one side.

steboy See **stuboy**

sted(der) See **instead**

steel n, v Usu |sti(ə)l|; also **scattered, but esp wPA** |stɪl|; hence n *steeler* |'stɪlɚ| Pronc-spp *still(er)* Cf Pronc Intro 3.I.3.c, **steal** v A

A Forms.

1979 *Sociol. Qrly.* 20.383 **nIL,** Several other still mill employees received nominations. **1982** McCool *Sam McCool's Pittsburghese* 32 **swPA,** *Still:* a metal for which Pittsburgh is famous. "Remember the good old days when they used *still* to build cars?" *Ibid* 34, *Stillers:* Pittsburgh's champion football team. **2000** *Lang. Variation* 12.181 **OH,** A similar laxing of the high front vowel in *steel* to produce a merger with *still* is apparently not yet common in Ohio . . , even in the southeast and southwest, the areas closest to the documented presence of the merger in perception if not production. **2000** *DARE* File, It's one of many mergers going on in the Midland, the West . . and, to some extent, in the South. Thus, hail and hell merge to hell . . , fill and feel merge to fill, still and steel merge to still, pool and pull merge to pull, etc. **2004** (acc) *Pittsburgh Speech & Soc.* (Internet), Throughout the U.S., more and more people say "steel" so it sounds like "still." Even the most local of the features of "Pittsburghese" can be heard in a fairly large area of central and southwestern Pennsylvania. *Ibid,* Words like "yinz," "dahn-tahn," and "Stillers" have become symbols of localness in Pittsburgh. **2005** *DARE* File—Internet **swPA,** Steel, still, steal—homophones with different meanings . . as in "still mill." **2006** *Ibid* **swPA,** In the first game . . the Stillers rushed for 143 yards. *Ibid* **swPA,** *You know you're from Western Pa. (and Pittsburgh) if. . .* You know what a still mill is. **2007** *Ibid* **swPA,** Scenes from Pittsburgh. . . Still mill.

B Sense.

See **steelie.**

steel-backed minnow n Also *steelback (minnow), steely-back minnow, steel-backed chub*

A **stone roller 1** (here: *Campostoma anomalum*).

1876 NY Acad. Sci. *Annals Lyceum Nat. Hist.* 11.375 **nGA,** We heard several peculiar vernacular names for fishes on the Rock Castle and Cumberland [including] Steel-backed Minnow . . Campostoma anomalum. **1878** U.S. Natl. Museum *Bulletin* 12.72 **TN,** *List of Fishes of Nashville.* . . Minnow Tribe. . . Stone Toter. Horny Head. . . Steel Back. **1884** *Ibid* 27.480, *Campostoma anomalum.* . . Stone-roller; Stone-lugger; Steely-back minnow. **1896** *Ibid* 47.205, Stone-roller; Stone-lugger; Steel-backed Chub [etc]. **1969** *DARE* (Qu. P7, *Small fish used as bait for bigger fish*) Inf **TX74,** Steel-buck [sic] minnow. **2004** in 2007 *DARE* File—Internet **WI,** "So, wha'cha using? Lindy jigs?" "Sure, Walt, dem and a floatin' jig with big steelback minnows."

steelhead n

1 also *steelhead trout,* ~ *salmon, steelie:* Usu the sea-run **rainbow trout;** occas another trout; see quots.

1882 U.S. Natl. Museum *Bulletin* 16.313 **nCA,** *S[almo] gairdneri* . . Steel-head; Hard-head; Salmon Trout. **1884** Goode *Fisheries U.S.* 1.475, *The Black spotted Trout—Salmo purpuratus* [=Oncorhynchus clarkii]. This fish is known as the "Trout," "Mountain Trout," . . etc., in the mountains, but when in the ocean, full grown, as "Salmon Trout" or "Steel-head." **1900** *Overland Mth.* (2d ser) 35.546 **CA,** That gamiest of all fish, the steelhead trout. **1949** Caine *N. Amer. Sport Fish* 70, In the past it has been a general custom to call any trout that have migrated to sea "steelheads." This includes cutthroat trout, Dolly Varden trout, and even Eastern brook trout. All of this is most confusing. **1965–70** *DARE* (Qu. P1, . . *Kinds of freshwater fish . . caught around here . . good to eat*) 11 Infs, **CA, MI, OR, WA,** Steelhead; **CA23,** Steelhead—a variety of trout; **KS15,** Lake trout—a species of steelhead; **OR13,** Landlocked salmon—steelhead, pinoche; **CA101, 120, 141, 191, MI14,** Steelhead trout; **AK1,** Steelhead trout—our only true salmon; **CA31, 105,** Steelhead salmon; **CA25,** Steelies; (Qu. P2, . . *Kinds of saltwater fish caught around here . . good to eat*) Infs **CA109, 111, 137, 145, WA24, 30,** Steelhead; **CA105,** Salmon: three kinds—chinook, silvers, steelhead; **CA130,** Steelhead is a "sea-run rainbow"—lives in ocean and returns to rivers to spawn; **AK9,** Steelhead salmon; **WA6, 12,** Steelheads; (Qu. P14, . . *Commercial fishing . . what do the fishermen go out after?*) Inf **CA111,** Steelhead. **1966** *Port Townsend Leader* (WA) 1 Dec 9/1, [Advt:] Steelhead Season Opens Sunday, Dec. 4. **1968** *Mt. Home News* (ID) 8 Feb 8/1, Just over 3/4 million eyed steelhead eggs . . were planted in artificial hatching channels last year. **1968** *DARE* Tape **CA100,** You

could catch trout or steelhead, silverside—they were salmon; **CA103,** [Inf:] That's what they do every year, the steelheads. And that's what they're doing now, they're working down the stream to get ready to go out into the ocean. [FW:] The steelhead trout do that? . . [Inf:] Steelhead salmon, I call 'em salmon. **1978** *AK Fishing Guide* 63, A steelhead returns from the sea large and silvery, blue-gray above and white below. It turns color when it spends any time in fresh water. **2003** (acc) WI Univ. Sea Grant Inst. *Fish Gt. Lakes* (Internet), The first rainbow trout planted in the Great Lakes were probably "steelheads." This is a strain of rainbow trout that migrates into the ocean before returning to spawn in their freshwater home streams.

2 =**ruddy duck.** Cf **hardhead 5a, hickoryhead**

1888 Trumbull *Names of Birds* 112 **MD,** William Wagner, a well known Washington gunner, tells of hearing it [=the ruddy duck] called *water-partridge,* and *steel-head,* on the Patuxent River, Md.

steelhead salmon (or trout) See **steelhead 1**

steelie n Also *steel(y)*

1 A ball of steel (or rarely another metal) used as a playing marble. Cf **baldy 2, half-crock**

1915 *Lima Sun. News* (OH) 21 Feb 2/3, Judging from some of the accurate shooting of two of the little chaps . . with their "aggies" and "steelies" they must have been indulging in winter training on their mother's carpets. **1922** *DN* 5.188 **MN,** *Steely.* . . A steel marble. **1934** *AmSp* 9.75 **ND,** *Steelie.* A heavy marble made of steel. **1955** *PADS* 23.31 **cwAL,** *Steelie (steely).* . . A marble made of steel, usually an automobile ball-bearing before the advent of roller-bearings. **1957** *Sat. Eve. Post Letters* **swMO** (as of 1912–16), The following were all in use during my boyhood. . . Agates, Glassies, Pintos, Pottries, Steelies. **1958** *PADS* 29.40 **WI,** *Steel.* . . A steel or ball-bearing marble. . . *Steelie.* . . Ill., Ky., Mass., Mich., Mo., Wis. **1958** *Resp. to PADS 29* **cnOK,** Steelie—a polished steel ball—up to about 1′ [sic] in diameter. Living around the oil field we sometimes used brass check valve balls but these were also known as steelies. **1963** North *Rascal* 51 **WI** (as of 1918), Here were glassies and steelies and one real agate marble. **1965–70** *DARE* (Qu. EE6d, *Special marbles*) 189 Infs, **widespread,** Steelies; **FL33,** Steels; (Qu. EE6a, . . *Different kinds of marbles—the big one that's used to knock others out of the ring*) 12 Infs, **scattered,** Steelie; **PA19,** Big steelie; (Qu. EE6b, *Small marbles or marbles in general*) Infs **GA75, OR13, TN55,** Steelies; (Qu. EE6c, *Cheap marbles*) Infs **IL45, MI19,** Steelies. **1976** *WI Acad. Rev.* June 20 (as of 1920s), Bully types favored "steelies," which actually were steel ball bearings. **1983** *MJLF* 9.1.57 **ceKY** (as of 1956), Steelies . . ball bearings used as marbles.

2 as *steelies:* A marble game; see quot.

1968–69 *DARE* (Qu. EE7, . . *Kinds of marble games*) Inf **WV10,** Steelies—big circle with small circle inside; knock marbles from small circle into big circle; [don't] know why called steelies; **WV18,** Steelies—don't know how it's played.

3 See **steelhead 1.**

4 =**pine mushroom.**

1992 *NYT Mag.* 16 Feb 67 **PA,** As a child, he would shimmy up a . . hillside on his stomach, following a vein of tricholoma (called "steelies" or "pinies [sic]" in his part of the country), . . a basket on his wrist.

steelies See **steelie 2**

steel netting See **netting (wire)**

steelpot n [Folk-etym for **skillpot**] Cf **kettlepot** =**mud turtle 2b(1).**

1967 *DARE* (Qu. P24, . . *Kinds of turtles*) Inf **SC45,** Steelpots—small ones that get your bait when fishing.

steelweed n [See quot 1914]

An aster (here: *Symphyotrichum ericoides* var *ericoides*).

1900 *OH Naturalist* Dec 19, The stems are tough and wiry and this gives the local name "Steelweed," a common designation in Adams County and adjoining regions. It is said by some, however, that this name is given it "because the flowers are the color of bright steel." **1914** Georgia *Manual Weeds* 433, White Heath Aster—*Aster ericoides* [=*Symphyotrichum e.* var *e.*] . . Meadows and pastures infested with this weed are in a bad condition, for as green forage it is worthless, and the hard, woody stems that have given it the name of Steelweed dull or break the mowing knives and "cut the grade" of hay that is intended for market. **1969** *DARE* (Qu. S26a, . . *Wildflowers . . Roadside flowers*) Inf **KY49,** Steelweed—the dead stalk is like steel, is hard.

steely See **steelie**

steelyard bird n

=solitary sandpiper or **spotted sandpiper.**

1870 (1873) Maynard *Naturalist's Guide* 141 **MA,** *Rhyacophilus solitarius* . . —*Solitary Sandpiper,* "Steelyard Bird." **1876** *Forest & Stream* 7.149 **Long Is. NY,** The teeters, or steelyard birds, as some call them, are next. **1910** Gilmore *Birds Yr.* 104, *Spotted Sandpiper.* . . As you move quietly along . . he will start up . . , running rapidly along with a peculiar balancing or teetering motion of the body, which has given him the name of Teeter-up, or Steelyard bird.

steely-back minnow See **steel-backed minnow**

steen adj, n [Prob abbr for *sixteen*] Cf **forty-eleven**

Used as a large or indefinite number; hence adj *steenth.*

1883 *Coshocton Age* (OH) 6 Oct 5/4, No; seven girls gave him the dead march the other day. He caught step with himself 'steen times, he got so rattled. **1900** in 2003 *DARE* File—Internet, A ghastly fracture of his [=a statue's] personality, in the region of his steenth cervical vertebrae, caused his premature demise at the age of 25. **1901** *S. Workman* 30.616, It did not take the news long to go through the length and breadth of 'steenth street. **1909** *DN* 3.375 **eAL, wGA,** *Steen, adj.* An indefinite or large amount of. Also as noun. Slang. **1944** in 1951 *AmSp* 26.65, 'I have steen million things to do.' 'Steen thousand women.' **1949** *AmSp* 24.229, 'Steen. In common usage. 'I've told you that 'steen times.' 'Steenth. 'For the 'steenth time I say No.' '[It is] something that intrigues the listeners of Take It or Leave It, the old $64 Question program now in its 'steenth season.'—Newspaper item of September 12, 1948. **1951** *AmSp* 26.65, *Steen.* One would judge this word to be abstracted from *sixteen.* It has, I think, been familiar to me for many, many years, often in hyperbolical combinations.

steephead n Also *steephead ravine* **chiefly nwFL**

A small valley with steep side and end walls created by erosion by emerging ground water.

1909 FL Geol. Surv. *Annual Rept. for 1908–09* 262, The streams in the western part of Gadsden County and in the northern part of Liberty County head in a characteristic manner. Each tributary terminates in a semi-circular spring head, the descent to which is almost precipitous for 50 to 60 feet from the plateau level. Usually this slope is not too steep to retain soil. . . Occasionally, however, heads occur that are vertical or nearly so. The termination of these streams are spoken of locally as "steepheads." **1962** Kurz–Godfrey *Trees N. FL* 48, *Carya pallida.* . . is known to occur on the slopes of a steephead, Hickory Head, in Okaloosa County. **1998** *News Herald* (Panama City FL) 29 Dec (Internet) **nwFL,** Stan Kirkland had brought me to a "steep-head" north of Bristol. . . A steep-head is an area along a riverbank that can drop off better than 300 feet in a short distance to a canyon. **2003** *DARE* File—Internet **nwFL,** Here the river is fed by a labyrinth of creeks which carve their way eastward . . , creating 100 foot deep V-shaped valleys. . . These . . are filled with a lush growth of forest. These unique Florida canyons even have their own name: "Steephead ravines" (or just "Steepheads").

steeple n¹ See **staple** n¹

steeple n² Pronc-sp *staple* [By hypercorrection; cf **staple** n¹] **chiefly Sth, S Midl** See Map

Std sense, var forms.

1965–70 *DARE* (Qu. CC1, *On a church building . . the part that sticks up high*) 16 Infs, **chiefly Sth, S Midl,** Staple [ste(ɪ)pl, ste(ɪ)pəl]. **1982** *Barrick Coll.* **csPA,** Steeple—staple.

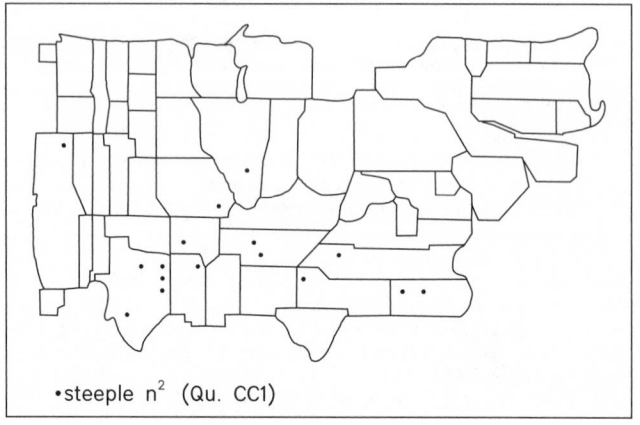

•steeple n² (Qu. CC1)

steeplebush n Also *steeplebrush, steepleplant* **esp NEng**
See Map

A spiraea, usu *Spiraea tomentosa.*

1822 Eaton *Botany* 478, *[Spiraea] tomentosa* (steeple-bush, purple hard-hack, meadow-sweet.) **1854** King *Amer. Eclectic Dispensatory* 902, *Spiraea tomentosa.* . . This plant, known also by the names of *Meadow-sweet, White-leaf,* and *Steeple-bush,* is a small shrub, from two to four feet in hight [sic]. **1915** (1926) Armstrong–Thornber *Western Wild Flowers* 230, *Hardhack, Steeple-bush. Spiraea Douglasii.* . . Wash., Oreg., Cal. **1947** *Sat. Review* 31 May 15 **NH,** The hill pastures . . are in season apt to be full of spiraea tomentosa, alias hardhack, alias steeple bush. **1966–68** *DARE* Wildfl QR Plates 93A, 94A Inf **NH4,** Either steeplebush or hardhack; Pl.94A Inf **MI57,** Steeplebush; **MN30,** Steeplebrush. **1967–70** *DARE* (Qu. S26a, . . *Wildflowers. . . Roadside flowers*) Inf **MA67,** Steeplebush—same as hardhack—a pink, shrubby plant found in pastures; **MA78,** Steeplebush; **RI12,** Steeplebush—blooms in August—got pinkish-purple flower, grows in dry places; (Qu. S26d, *Wildflowers that grow in meadows;* not asked in early QRs) Inf **CT11,** Steepleplant; **RI15,** Hardhack or steeplebush; (Qu. T16) Inf **MA5,** Steeplebush. **1989** Mosher *Stranger* 406 **nVT** (as of 1952), We . . crossed a brushy pasture overrun with dead goldenrod, purple asters, faded pink steeplebush. **2006** *Bangor Daily News* (ME) 28 Aug sec C 6 (Internet), Late summer always surprises me. . . Dusty-pink steeplebush blossoms poke from bushes, and purple loosestrife and Queen Anne's lace come up in droves.

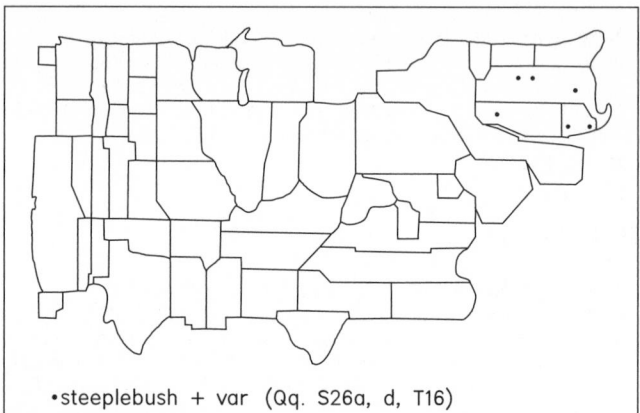

•steeplebush + var (Qq. S26a, d, T16)

steeple-cap n

A **lady's slipper 1.**

1950 Correll *Native Orchids* 22, *Cypripedium arietinum.* . . Common names: Ram's-head Orchid, . . Steeple-cap.

steepleplant See **steeplebush**

steepy adj [*OED2* 1565 →; "*Obs.* exc. *arch.*"]
Steep.

1916 *DN* 4.295 **sAppalachians,** *-y.* . . is found with adjectives which in modern English do not require it, as in steep*y,* salt*y,* etc. **1991** Still *Wolfpen Notebooks* 75 **sAppalachians,** His daddy left him a farm, pretty good land even if it was steepy.

steer n¹ Also *steer cow* **scattered, but somewhat more freq Sth, S Midl** *euphem*

A bull.

1946 *PADS* 5.40 **VA,** *Steer.* . . A bull; on the Eastern Shore, on the lower Rappahannock, in the southern Piedmont, in the presence of women. **1949** Kurath *Word Geog.* 62, *Bull.* . . *Steer* [is used] from southern Maryland to Albemarle Sound. **1965–70** *DARE* (Qu. K22, *Words used for a bull*) 29 Infs, **scattered,** Steer; (Qu. K23, *Words used by women or in mixed company for a bull*) 11 Infs, **scattered,** Steer [10 of 11 Infs comm type 4 or 5, 9 old]. **1966** Dakin *Dial. Vocab. Ohio R. Valley* 2.230, *Steer* [as a euphem for a bull] . . appears in the southern Mountains, the Bluegrass, and in the Indiana hills. **1967** Faries *Word Geog. MO* 89, *Bull.* . . Scattered occurrences of . . euphemistic expressions appear throughout the state: *sire . . steer . . top cow.* **1970** Tarpley *Blinky* 166 **neTX,** *Male cow* (euphemism) . . [13 of 200 infs] steer. **1972** *PADS* 58.17 **cwAL,** *Bull.* . . alternate terms . . *steer* (1 [of 27 infs]) . . and *ox* (1). **1973** Allen *LAUM* 1.244 **Upper MW** (as of c1950), *Bull.* . . Eastern Virginia *steer* is unaccountably reported in this sense by two Minnesotans, one of British parentage and the other of Icelandic parentage. **1986** Pederson *LAGS Concordance* **Gulf Region,** *(Bull)* [Of the 67 infs who gave *steer(s)* as their response, 13 characterized it as a euphemism, a polite term, a word used in the presence of women and the like.]; 1 inf, **neFL,** Steer cow—they called it to avoid bull; 1 inf, **cnMS,** Yearling steer—before women.

steer v, hence ppl adj *steered* [Pronc varr of *stir(red); cf SND steer* v.[1]]

1942 Redding *No Day* 9 **Sth** (as of c1920) [Black], We'se all steered up ever' which way. **2000** Shores *Tangier Is.* 235 **Chesapeake Bay,** Did you *steer* it up (stir). **2008** *DARE* File—Internet **WV,** All this is, is a tactic to get Republican vs. Democrat arguments steered up.

steer n[2]   See **stewer**

steer cow   See **steer** n[1]

steered   See **steer** v

steershead n   Also *steerhead* [Because the petals resemble the head and horns of a steer]

A **bleeding heart 1** (here: *Dicentra uniflora*).

1915 (1926) Armstrong–Thornber *Western Wild Flowers* 170, *B[icuculla]* [=*Dicentra*] *uniflora* is a diminutive alpine plant. . . called Squirrel Corn and Steer's Head. **1936** McDougall–Baggley *Plants of Yellowstone* 64, Steerhead . . a little alpine plant . . with usually a single flesh-colored flower, shaped like those of the bleeding heart. **1959** Barnes *Nat. Hist. Wasatch Winter* 78 **UT,** The Dutchman's breeches, squirrel corn, bleeding heart, or steer's head *(Dicentra uniflora),* as it is variously called. **2003** (acc) U.S. Forest Serv. *ID Panhandle Natl. Forests* (Internet), Related to the gardener's bleeding hearts, steer's head grows in rich, well drained, organic soils throughout the northwest.

stegg n   [Engl dial; var of *stag* a young ox; cf *EDD* steg sb. 8, *stag* sb.[3] 2]

1930 Shoemaker *1300 Words* 54 **cPA Mts** (as of c1900), Stegg—A bullock that has been altered at an age that stops further growth.

Steller's jay n

Std: the western jay *Cyanocitta stelleri.*   Also called **mountain jay 1, pine ~ 2, topknot ~ 2**

stem clam n

A **soft-shell clam** (here: *Mya arenaria*).

1859 (1968) Bartlett *Americanisms* 84, The Soft Clam. . . has a long, extensible, cartilaginous snout, or proboscis, through which it ejects water; whence it is also called Stem-clam and Piss-clam. **1885** *Amer. Naturalist* 19.361 **NJ,** The systematists call our mollusk *Mya arenaria,* but in popular speech, because of its siphon, it is sometimes known as the stem-clam. **1902** *Jrl. Amer. Folkl.* 15.247, The soft-shelled clam *(Mya arenaria),* known also as the "stem-clam." **1953** *Oneonta Star* (NY) 3 Apr 6/3, Mr. and Mrs. George Gregory entertained at a stem clam dinner for the family Sunday. **2003** Carpenter *Laughing* 190 **Long Is. NY,** Fishing with his mouth and eyes open, he [=a dog] grabbed small stem clams, which he chomped upon.

stemper n   Also with *the* Also *stimper(s)* [Aphet forms of *distemper*]   **Sth, S Midl**

1865 (1866) Casseday *Hortons at Home* 208 **C Atl,** I found that pointer pup you lost, out in the woods, pesky bad with the 'stemper. **1954** *Harder Coll.* **cwTN,** Diseases, horse or mule. . . [stɪmpɚ]: "It's in the head; snotty nose." **1970** *DARE* (Qu. K47, . . *Diseases . . horses or mules commonly get*) Inf **MO24,** Stimper—the horse gets poor and his nose runs like people who have a cold; **KY93,** Stimpers. **2005** in 2008 *DARE* File—Internet **cwNC,** He tries to walk, but walks like he is disorented [sic]. I've heard this called the "stimper". Is there a cure? **2008** *Ibid* **ceSC,** Longfellow left us with the stemper when he was a couple of years old. *Ibid* **cnGA,** He had the stimper, he was brain dead so we had to put him down!!

stem-winder n   [From *stem-winder* a watch wound by means of a knob on its stem (rather than by a key), regarded as a markedly superior article]

1 Someone or something excellent or extraordinary, esp an energetic person; a humdinger.

1879 Bond *One Yr.* 81, Mr. Snipe was also the recipient of marked attention, and Mrs. Dewberry affirmed that he was "a stem winder and no mistake," but just what she meant by that assertion Mr. Snipe declared he had n't the remotest idea. **1892** Gunter *Miss Dividends* 68, Ain't he a stem-winder, though? **1895** *Overland Mth.* (2d ser) 26.651, This en-

tertainment is a stem winder. **1897** *KS Univ. Qrly.* (ser B) 6.92, *Stem winder:* a first-class anything.—General. **1941** *AmSp* 16.24 **sIN,** *Stem-winder.* [Footnote:] Cf. *caution.* [*Ibid* 21, *Caution.* Used as a noun, with the meaning of *dandy, corker,* etc.] **1942** Berrey–Van den Bark *Amer. Slang* 29.2, *Something excellent.* . . stem-winder. *Ibid* 395.1, *Superior or admirable person.* . . stem-winder. *Ibid* 412.1, *Enterprising or energetic person.* . . stem-winder. **1958** McCulloch *Woods Words* 181 **Pacific NW,** *Stemwinder.* . . Any very good machine. **1965–70** *DARE* (Qu. HH27a, *A very able and energetic person who gets things done*) 10 Infs, **scattered,** Stem-winder; (Qu. B25, . . *Joking names . . for a very heavy rain.* . . *"It's a regular _____."*) Inf **NY205,** Stem-winder; (Qu. Y11, . . *A very hard blow: "You should have seen Bill go down. Joe really hit him a _____."*) Inf **AL47,** Stem-winder; (Qu. DD16, *To have a drinking bout and get drunk is to go on a _____*) Inf **MT3,** Stem-winder. **a1975** Lunsford *It Used to Be* 170 **sAppalachians,** A "stemwinder" . . means a big one. **1977** *Time* 3 Jan 55, The 1,008 cadres and 24 fraternal foreign delegations . . endured no fewer than 55 speeches, including an eight-hour stem-winder. **2004** Marler *Reflections on Life* 60 **cLA** (as of 1930s), *Stem-winder.* = An active person and somewhat a character.

2   A boy; a baby boy.

1967 *DARE* FW Addit **nwNY,** Stem-winder—a boy. **1982** Barrick *Coll.* **csPA,** Stem-winder—male baby.

stenner n   [PaGer *schtenner*]   **chiefly sePA** *old-fash*   =**stand** n **1.**

1841 Stahle *Descr. Borough of Reading* 32 **sePA,** Butter-Churns, Wash-Tubs, Iron-bound & Painted Buckets, Crout-Stenners, &c., &c. **1916** PA State Lunatic Hospital *Annual Rept. for 1916* 49 **csPA,** Carpet-sweepers. . . Rat- and mouse-traps. . . Cedar stenners. . . Hand truck. **1935** Frederick *PA Dutch* 261 **sePA,** Huge *stenners,* open headed barrels, were filled with it [=sauerkraut]. **1953** *Hist. Rev. Berks Co.* Oct–Dec 6 **ePA,** One of the most widespread and frequently heard PaG loanwords is *stenner,* which is used to designate a round metal or cardboard container. Thus one speaks of a *stenner* of lard or a *stenner* of ice cream. **1987** *Jrl. Engl. Ling.* 20.2.175 **ePA,** Although Schach (1953:6) describes *stenner* as "one of the most widespread and frequently heard PaG loanwords", it is clear that it now has little or no currency. Indeed, only three informants remembered the item after it was presented to them. All three are Mennonite females over 65. Two of them said that *stenner* refers only to lard cans, and thus the rarity of the referent has apparently led to the loss of the word form.

stent n, v   [Var of *stint; OED2* stint sb.[1] a1300 →]   **scattered, but esp NEast**

1833 Smith *Life Jack Downing* 31 **ME,** Father used to say that I did n't love work a bit better than uncle Joshua did, without he'd give me my stent, and then he said I would spring to it and get it done by noon. **1862** (1882) Stowe *Pearl of Orr's Is.* 148 **ME,** Mis' Kittredge has gone shoppin' . . , and left Sally a 'stent' to do. **1863** *Atlantic Mth.* 11.170 **wMA,** Dorcas had nearly finished her "stent" on the little wheel. **1881** Holley *Wayward Pardner* 74 **Upstate NY,** They stent themselves on clothes, and I don't s'pose they allow themselves hardly enough to eat and drink. **1888** *Century Illustr. Mag.* 37.36 **nOH,** If you are weak, and can't finish your stent, you are given twenty blows with the cat. **1899** (1912) Green *VA Folk-Speech* 416, *Stent.* . . Allotted portion. "A stent of tobacco." **1905** *DN* 3.56 **eNE,** The change of *i* to *e,* is seen in *stent.* **1907** *DN* 3.201 **seNH,** *Stent.* . . Allotted or self-imposed task. "I can't leave the shop and go with you; I haven't got my stent done yet." **1909** *DN* 3.417 **nME,** *Stent.* . . Stint. **1928** *AmSp* 3.403 **Ozarks,** The short *i* sound is sometimes replaced by short *e,* as when *stint* and *bin* are pronounced *stent* and *ben.* **1929** *AmSp* 5.123 **ME,** Children were asked "Have you done your stent?"

step across v phr   Also *step on*   **chiefly West**

To mount (a horse).

1926 Santee *Men & Horses* 30 **AZ,** He wished Jimmy and Shorty would happen up as he stepped across the little roan. **1938** (1962) Crawford *West TX Kid* 115 **West** (as of a1905), I don't think the new horse moved a foot while I was saddling him but when I stepped across him, he went after me pretty lively, using what is called the "sunfish" style. **1944** Adams *Western Words* 155, *Step across*—Slang for mounting a horse. **1967** Green *Horse Tradin'* 244 **TX,** I stepped on her and rode on off across the trading square. **2008** *DARE* File—Internet **AL,** "Mr. Pat was nice enough to put me on him this week," Gann said, adding he had never stepped on the horse until the day before qualifying him for the finals Friday morning. *Ibid* **MT,** When he stepped on his horse, with one foot in the stirrup, his horse shied about 10 feet to the side, stretching his leg out to full length.

step ant n *joc*
=piss ant 1.
[**1945** McAtee *Nomina Abitera* 19, A "gag" worth relating avers that a flustered young lady at a picnic made the transposition: "Piss on that step-ant."] **1953** Randolph–Wilson *Down in Holler* 117 **Ozarks,** Piss-ant is sometimes pronounced *peezent,* and the term step-ant is used by some squeamish persons. **1954** *Harder Coll.* **cwTN,** Step-ant. . . Euphemism for *piss-ant.* **1967–69** *DARE* (Qu. R17, . . *Names . . for the big black ants that sting*) Infs **MI**104, **OH**33, Step ants; **VA**15, Step ants—couldn't say piss ant; "There goes a piss ant—step on it"; (Qu. R18, . . *Kinds of ants*) Inf **AZ**9, Step ants; **CA**145, Step ants—same as piss ants; step on to make them smell; **NJ**8, Step ants—so called because you step on them whenever you see them. **1982** *Barrick Coll.* **csPA,** Piss-ant—Euphemistically called step-ant: "There goes a step-ant; piss on it." **1986** Pederson *LAGS Concordance,* 1 inf, **swGA,** Step ants. **2002** in 2008 *DARE* File—Internet **TX,** In Texiz, those tiny little black "sugar ants" are almost always called either "step ants" or "piss ants". At least down in ranching country. The name step ants is usually used by the ladies, and the men just call them piss ants.

step aside v phr [*SND* (at *step* v.) "to err morally, to commit a fault, go astray"]
1952 Brown *NC Folkl.* 1.594, Step aside. . . To commit (sexual) immorality.

stepball n   **C Atl**   Cf **three outs**
A game similar to **stoopball.**
1975 Ferretti *Gt. Amer. Book Sidewalk Games* 135, The most popular form of Stoopball is called Stoopball . . in most parts of the United States, *Home Runs* in Brooklyn and *Step Ball* in Philadelphia. **1975** *Lincoln Star* (NE) 7 July 4/3 **VA** (as of 1939), That summer we played step ball until dark. **1977** *Eve. Capital* (Annapolis MD) 17 Sept 3/6, Debuting at this fair are sports activities . . and distinctly Baltimorean games such as step ball. **1989** *Syracuse Herald–Jrl.* (NY) 28 Mar Metro ed sec D 1/4 **Washington DC** (as of 1951), Thursdays and Saturdays I'd be ripped from the neighborhood, torn from the day's game of stepball or running bases and placed on a streetcar. **1997** *DARE* File—Internet **NJ,** If you grew up in Philadelphia or Baltimore or an eastern city, you probably played stepball. **2003** *Ibid* **Baltimore MD,** Stepball is one game that we played. You threw a tennis ball against a step and your opponent standing in the street would have to catch it. It was played like baseball. Three outs to an inning. If the ball landed beyond a series of lines in the street it would count as a single, double, triple or homerun. **2005** *Ibid* **Philadelphia PA,** Stepball—Similar to halfball in that it had baseball rules but no base running. But in this game, there was no bat. Standing close to the rowhouse, you'd throw the ball against the steps as hard as you could . . to get height and distance. If it landed without being caught it was a hit.

step-drop v phr, hence vbl n *step-dropping*   Cf **drop D1**
To sow seed on foot at the interval of a step; to plant (seeds) in such a way.
1945 Saxon *Gumbo Ya-Ya* 562 **LA,** Step-dropping: dropping a seed, or seeds, with each step. **1968** *DARE* FW Addit **DE,** Step-drop—to plant corn so that it can be plowed both ways. [FW illustr shows corn planted in square grid.] **1986** Pederson *LAGS Concordance,* 1 inf, **nwMS,** Step-drop corn—planting corn on foot.

stepmother n [Engl dial]
A hangnail or roughness of the skin surrounding the nail.
1894 *DN* 1.334 **NJ,** Stepmother: a ragged nail or a roughness of the skin. **1930** Shoemaker *1300 Words* 53 **cPA Mts** (as of c1900), Step-mother—A hang-nail. [**1965** *DARE* File **Winnipeg Canada** (as of c1914), A hangnail on the finger is called a "Stepmother's blessin'."] **2004** *DARE* File **Philadelphia PA** (as of 1950s), My family, native Philadelphians, always used the term "stepmother" for hangnail.

stepmother slice n   Also *stepmother's slice, stepmother bread (slice)*
Usu a thick slice of bread, but see quots 1928, 1976, 2009.
1906 OR Bd. Horticult. *Biennial Rept. 1907* 166, We spent a lot of money in getting out some colored work representing a lad . . in the act of taking his second bite from a luscious big red cherry . . ; much as a youngster would attack a step-mother's slice of bread and butter. **1915** *Warren Eve. Times* (PA) 19 Jan 8/4, This Slicer is Made Like a Mitre Box! and there is now no use of the "Famous Step-mother slice of

bread" that is too thick to bite. **1918** *Eve. State Jrl. Lincoln Daily News* (NE) 2 Sept 4/3 **IN,** "There, I do declare, I've cut you 'stepmother' bread slices—too thick," said the old lady. "Altho why they call thick slices 'stepmother bread' I dunno. Seems to me thin slices and not much of 'em would be what stepmothers would give." **1928** Kearney *Hodag* 108 **cWI,** There was a stack of white bread, which contained no stepmother slices. **1958** in 1969 *Western Folkl.* 28.42 **swID,** Thick slices of bread are called "Step-mother Slices." **1976** *DARE* File **sID** (as of c1920), If one person starts to slice a loaf of bread and another person finishes the job, the first piece cut by the second person will inevitably be uneven. *Stepmother slice* probably just means that someone new has taken over a job or has replaced someone else. **2009** *NADS Letters* **cVA,** I heard the term "stepmother slice" applied to a raggedly cut piece of bread in central Virginia within the last few years. The speaker was a woman of about fifty who has spent most of her life in tidewater and piedmont Virginia, but she is also a voracious reader, and I have no idea where she acquired that term.

stepney n, usu cap [Etym unknown] *among Gullah speakers*
Hunger, hard times; also personified as a malevolent spirit.
1922 Gonzales *Black Border* 34 **sSC, GA coasts,** Stepney ain' fuh come een *my* house. [Footnote to *stepney:*] A Gullah synonym for hunger. **1926** Smith *Gullah* 32 **sSC, GA coasts,** Two words that have not been traced to any known source, and which may be African in origin, are *Stepney* and *Plat-eye*. *Stepney* is used in the sense of hunger or want, or like the proverbial wolf: "Haffuh wu'k haa'd fuh keep Stepney frum de do'." **1930** Stoney–Shelby *Black Genesis* 39 **seSC,** An' when Stepney (hunger) git 'em, dey hunt out all what is fitten to nyam. *Ibid* 76, Dere is a nice lot o' grits right dere to de edge. He turn away, but Stepney pinch him, an' he ease in towards it. **1954** *PADS* 21.39 **SC coast,** Stepney. . . Extremely hard times, starvation times; hunger. . . *Stepney* is also looked upon as an evil spirit or "hant."

step off the carpet v phr   Also abbr *step off*   **scattered, but esp Sth**   Cf **carpet, on the**
To get married.
1843 in 1956 Eliason *Tarheel Talk* 297 **cn,cNC,** Cousin Fanny . . stepped off the carpet. **1865** in 1984 Edmonds *Jrls.* 233 **cnVA,** Friend Douglas stepped off the carpet Wednesday evening. **1884** Baldwin *Yankee School-Teacher* 161 **VA,** An' 't don't look right, someway, f'r a girl to step off in anythin' but silk. **1893** Shands *MS Speech* 60, Step off. . . Used by all classes for *marry;* as, "I think he will step off next fall." **1909** *DN* 3.375 **eAL, wGA,** Step off. . . To get married. **1920** *DN* 5.86 **NC,** Step off the carpet, to marry. **1921** *DN* 5.111 **CA,** To step off. . . To get married. **1937** (1977) Hurston *Their Eyes* 171 **FL** [Black], "Tea Cake don't talk dat way. He's aimin' tuh make hisself permanent wid me. We done made up our mind tuh marry." . . "Well, when you aim tuh step off?" **1942** Warnick *Garrett Co. MD* 14 **nwMD** (as of 1900–18), *Step off* . . get married. **1944** *PADS* 2.26 **cwOH, cwNC,** Step off . . To get married. In N.C. to step off the carpet. **1945** *PADS* 3.12 **cwNY,** Step off. . . Generally known here, though less common than formerly. **1966–69** *DARE* (Qu. AA15a, . . *Joking ways . . of saying that people got married . . "They _____."*) Infs **GA**15, **NJ**4, Stepped off; (Qu. AA15b, . . *Joking ways . . of saying that a man is getting married. . . "He _____."*) Infs **GA**15, **NJ**28, **TX**29, Step(ped) off; (Qu. AA15c, . . *Joking ways . . of saying that a woman is getting married. . . "She _____."*) Infs **GA**15, **NY**152, 219, Stepped off. **1984** Wilder *You All Spoken Here* 99 **Sth,** Step off the carpet: Get married.

step on   See **step across**

step out v phr   **chiefly NEng**
Fig: to die; to disappear; hence adj phr *stepped out* dead.
1843 *Huron Reflector* (Norwalk OH) 7 Feb [2]/3 (newspaperarchive.com), In an evil hour, their true history will become too manifest, and while they have "stepped out" to parts unknown, the people will revel in all the beauties and excellencies of *individual liability.* **1844** *Yale Lit. Mag.* 9.381, Of the other pieces . . which have been sent us, some will be found in the present number . . and the remainder have "stept out." **1851** Burke *Polly Peablossom* 177 **OH,** Ay, dead!—stepped out!—d-d-dead as Tecumsah! **1903** McFaul *Ike Glidden* 277 **NEng,** He is the cause of my ruin. Yes, that is why he stepped out when he did. **1930** Shoemaker *1300 Words* 55 **cPA Mts** (as of c1900), Step out—To die. **1932** Tooné *Yankee Slang* 34, Step out: To die. Brown: Is Mr. Hiram P. Fysh to home? Nar, he ain't, I guess he's "stepped out." Brown: When's he coming back? He ain't, he's gone dead. **1943** *LANE* Map 521 (*Kicked the bucket*) 4 infs, **ME, NH, VT,** Stepped out. **1969**

DARE (Qu. BB56, *Joking expressions for dying: "He _____."*) Inf **RI**15, Stepped out.   **2003** *DARE* File **nwMA**, I have heard the term "stepped out," but only once that I can recall in my lifetime. Years ago a person of my age died of a heart condition and I can remember Cora Nelson saying "Gerald stepped out kind of sudden, didn't he?" It stuck with me because it isn't a term that's usually used around here.

steps n

1 =giant steps.

1975 Ferretti *Gt. Amer. Book Sidewalk Games* 204, Giant Steps as it is known almost everywhere is also called *Steps* in Connecticut.

2 =may I.

1953 Brewster *Amer. Nonsinging Games* 164 **GA**, Steps. . . One girl . . is the leader. The others line up some distance away facing her. One of the latter calls to the leader, "How many and what kind?" The leader replies, for example, "Three baby ones." The others then take three very short steps toward her. In answer to the next question, the leader's order may be "Two giant ones." This continues until one of the players is near enough to the leader to touch her. The first to do so becomes leader in the next game.   **1967** *DARE* (Qu. EE16, *Hiding games that start with a special, elaborate method of sending the players out to hide*) Inf **PA**26, (Mother) may I?—called steps.

3 =red light.

1935 Mason–Mitchell *Social Games* 249, Steps. . . Select an "It" and have him blind against a wall or post. . . "It" calls "Go" and counts ten out loud rapidly, and then turns so that he can see the players. On the word "Go" the players immediately start toward "it" but must not be seen moving by "it" when he turns. All who are seen moving are sent back to the starting line. Continue until some player advances close enough to touch "it." This player wins.

step school n   Also *step teacher*   Cf **step-up, stone school** =school.

2000 *NADS Letters* **cMS**, Rock school. We called it "step school" at First Presbyterian Day School in Jackson, Mississippi (I attended in 1974–1978). . . The game . . didn't require a rock per se. I think anything small enough to be held in the hand sufficed. Correct guessers went up a step and sat down, and the others sat one step lower.   **2001** *Ibid* **nwPA**, You asked about the usage of "rock school, rock teacher, stone school." When I was growing up in Erie, Pennsylvania, we kids would play 'step teacher' just as you describe it. Depending whether you guessed correctly or incorrectly, you moved up or down one step, respectively.

step stove n   orig widespread; later chiefly Sth, S Midl

A wood-burning cooking stove with a low cooking surface over the firebox in front and a raised oven behind.

1900 *NY Herald* (NY) 30 Dec 13/5, If she [=the housewife of 2001] is old and fussy she may grumble at the electric oven, and sigh for the good old days of the gas stove, just as the old lady of to-day yearns back to step stoves.   **1906** *Hist. Encycl. IL* 626 **ceIL**, When, in about 1838 to 1840 Charles H. Nabb brought into old Richmond a "step stove," all the women for miles around came to view the new-fangled contrivance. . . It had the front part above the firebox lower than the back part which was above the oven, and so received its name from its shape.   **1917** Baldwin *Making of a Township* 83 **ceIN**, Father bought the first clock and cook stove in the Township. . . The stove was what they called a step stove.   **1932** Stribling *Store* 85 **AL**, She put two sticks of wood in the kitchen step stove.   **1941** Justus *Cabin on Kettle Creek* 18 **eTN**, Mammy was standing by the step stove taking something . . out of a pan.   **c1960** Wilson *Coll.* **csKY**, Step-stove—A cooking stove with two levels on top.   **1965–67** *DARE* Tape **AL**33, Part of the time we cooked on a little old step stove; **VA**114, We just had. . . a little bitty step stove. . . It had legs, and up here was a little thing called the hearth and the doors opened there and . . there was two eyes here on this step, and then up another step and there was two more eyes and then the oven.   **1982** Ginns *Snowbird Gravy* 39 **nwNC**, Mother cooked on the fire, but we finally got a small stove, wood stove. I think it was what we called a "step stove" in that day. Had two different tops on it, separated. Had two burners down here, and two up here.   **1986** Pederson *LAGS Concordance*, 2 infs, **TN**, (A) step stove.

step teacher   See **step school**

‡step-up n   Cf **steps, step school**

1966 *DARE* (Qu. EE33, . . *Outdoor games . . that children play*) Inf **NC**4, Step-up—one would call out numbers, the others would go up the steps so many at a time, trying to get to top.

step up to v phr   Cf *set* (or *sit*) *up to* (at **set up** v phr **2**)

To court.

1858 Hammett *Piney Woods Tavern* 122 **CT**, It's an undeniable fact that six on 'em was took with the disease [=love] all of a sudent; sot in for the hardest kind of sparkin'. . . But when he got to steppin' up to a most amazin' scrumptious kind of a gal, . . I tell *you*, if we didn't open on him [=play tricks on him].   **1908** Wasson *Home from Sea* 145 **ME**, Land, if 't wa'n't for me being hitched already, Jabez, be jiggered if you would n't see me a-steppin' up to her myself.   **1941** *LANE* Map 404 *(Courting her)* 1 inf, **cwVT**, Stepping up to.

'stericky   See **hystericky**

sterile v

To spay or neuter (an animal).

1967–68 *DARE* (Qu. J3a, *To make a female dog so that she can't breed, she must be _____*) Infs **KY**32, **LA**24, Steriled; (Qu. J3b, *To make a female cat so that she can't breed, she must be _____*) Infs **KY**32, **LA**24, Steriled.

stern n   Usu |stɜ(r)n|; also *old-fash* |stɑrn| Pronc-sp *starn*

Similarly adv *astarn*   **chiefly NEng**   Cf Pronc Intro 3.I.1.f, **earn, learn, servant**

Std senses, var form.

1729 *Amer. Weekly Mercury* (Philadelphia PA) 2 Oct 4/2, [Advt:] They are supposed [sic] to have stole their Indentures, and a Cannoe, Branded on the Starn with *S.W.*   **1839** *S. Lit. Jrl.* 5.432 **ME**, I was setting in the starn, paddling along at a moderate jog.   **1844** *N. Amer. Rev.* 58.219 **NEng**, Pat threw one foot out astarn.   **1858** Hammett *Piney Woods Tavern* 120 **CT**, And . . she open'd the door, and give me a kick on the starn-post, that sent me a tumblin'.   **1894** *Scribner's Mag.* 16.390 **eLong Is. NY**, The Jane Mari'r bein' astarn blazin' fore and aft.   **1899** (1912) Green *VA Folk-Speech* 415, Starn, n. A form of stern.   **1901** *Atlantic Mth.* 87.90 **ME** (as of c1776), Some fools would ha' tried to run astarn.   **1903** *DN* 2.290 **Cape Cod MA** (as of a1857), Old folks still pronounced *er* as *ar* . . starnfomust (=sternforemost).   **1904** Day *Kin o' Ktaadn* 187 **ME**, Santy Claus starn-chase behind us through the snowflakes in the sky.   **1941** Stuart *Men of Mts.* 14 **eKY**, A bumble-bee can't suck the tassels without his starn-end rubbing the ground.

stern sheets n pl

Fig: see quots.

1855 in 1974 Sully *No Tears* 115, The sentinel . . taught him politeness by planting a ball and three buckshot in his stern sheets.   **1883** Twain *Life on Missip.* (Boston) 270 **MO**, He had more selfish organs than any seven men in the world—all packed in the stern-sheets of his skull, of course.   **1885** Porter *Incidents* 334, He [=a dog] run away clean, only stoppin' once to sit up on his stern sheets an' put his paw to his nose.   **1935** Byrd *Discovery* 270, The part of him that stuck out of the tent at that moment, I reflected, was in air -50° cold: his stern sheets in air +80° warm.   **1954** Ratigan *Soo Canal* 63 **nMI**, He's begun to spread out—with his stern sheets glued to a Detroit office chair.   **1965** Gallery *Eight Bells* 83, When it was finally shown that an aviator's brains did not reside in his stern sheets, many people claimed this proved what they had really thought all along. . . that we had no brains at all!   **1975** Gould *ME Lingo* 277, Stern sheets—The seat at the stern of a rowboat, and accordingly almost anything in Maine that is rearward; the back seat of an automobile or somebody's backside: "All he needs is a good boot in the stern sheets!"

sterrup   See **stirrup**

stew n   Also *ginger stew, lemon ~, whisk(e)y ~*   esp Midl, Sth   Cf **Quaker stew, vinegar ~**

A beverage made from whiskey, hot water, sugar, and spice or other flavoring; a toddy.

1846 Gerstäcker *Regulatoren in AR* 1.173, "Nun Gentlemen, kommt das Beste—der Stew." [Footnote: Ein in den westlichen Wäldern sehr beliebtes Getränk aus Whiskey, heißem Wasser, Gewürz, Zucker und Butter bestehend.] [="Now Gentlemen, comes the best part—the stew."] [Footnote: A drink very popular in the western forests, consisting of whiskey, hot water, spice, sugar, and butter.]   *Ibid* 181, Mrs. Roberts und Mr. Rowson sollten nur den gestrengen Herrn Roberts hier sitzen sehen, und Whiskey-Stew trinken, die würden schöne Gesichter schneiden. [=If only Mrs. Roberts and Mr. Rowson could see respectable Mr. Roberts sitting here and drinking whiskey-stew, they would make some fine faces!]   **1847** Howe *Hist. Coll. OH* 275, Early in the afternoon they quitted work, and grew jolly over a bottle of "stew." . . [F]irst, a huge kettle, of gallons' capacity, was placed upon the ground, resting upon three stones, and a fire kindled under it. In it was put two or three buckets of water, a few pounds of maple sugar, a few ounces of allspice . . , a pound of butter, and, finally, two or three gallons of whiskey. **1868** Davis *Dallas Galbraith* 214 **ceNJ,** Old Potter . . was brewing a whisky-stew over the fire. **1875** *OH Farmer* 47.331, When you get sick, get Aunt Betsy to make a ginger stew, or some pennyroyal tea . . ; then if you are not better, send for your family physician. **1883** in 1983 Zeigler *Lexicon Middle GA* 135, You have descended to the very bottom . . and taken to sorghum [whiskey]. . . There you sit even now with an exhausted mug of stew made of sorghum four days old! **1931** Randolph *Ozarks* 66, One favorite Christmas beverage was known as "stew"—a mixture of whiskey and ginger and hot water. **1976** Wolfram–Christian *Appalachian Speech* 173 **sWV,** Now, Dad would make a ginger stew with Whiskey, give it to us kids if we got the flu or something like that. **1996** Stimpson *My Remembers* 56 **TX** [Black] (as of 1930s), Dad would make us a lemon stew—boil the lemon, put Vicks salve in and whiskey, and we would drink it as hot as you could stand it.

stew builder n Also *stew bum*

Esp among loggers: a camp cook.

1925 *AmSp* 1.137 **Pacific NW,** A camp cook is simply a cook until the loggers have graded him; and for each grade of cook they have a name full of meaning. "Gut-burglar," "stomach-robber," "stewbum," "sizzler," "dough-roller," and "star chief." **1927** *AmSp* 2.392 [Vagabond argot], A cook is a *grease-burner, stew-builder* or *mulligan-mixer.* **1942** *AmSp* 17.224 **Nth** [Loggers' talk], *Stew builder.* Camp cook. **1958** McCulloch *Woods Words* 182 **Pacific NW,** *Stew builder*—A camp cook. *Stew bum*—A camp cook, especially on a drive.

stewed Quaker See **Quaker stew**

stewed witch, feel like a v phr Also *feel worse than a stewed witch*

=*feel like a boiled owl* (at **boiled owl 1**).

1863 in 1877 Waddell *Biog. Sketch Linton Stephens* 27 **GA,** With the dirt, and loss of sleep, and cold last night, I am feeling to-day very much like a "stewed witch." **1909** *DN* 3.375 **eAL, wGA,** *Stewed witch.* . . Used to indicate a very uncomfortable bodily condition or state of feeling. "I feel like a stewed witch this morning." **2001** *DARE* File—Internet (as of a1900), One woman said she felt "worse than a stewed witch" after laundry day.

stewer n Also *stewer pan* Pronc-spp *steer, stir* **chiefly Lower Missip Valley, TX, OK** See Map

A deep, usu metal, vessel for cooking food; see quots.

1820 *Baltimore Patriot & Mercantile Advt.* (MD) 11 July 3/4, [Advt:] A great variety of Brass, Copper & Tin Ware. . . Sauce and Stewer Pans. **1862** in 1904 Olnhausen *Advent. Army Nurse* 58 **NEng,** They had to furnish their own food and cook it themselves, so my stewer was always going. **1897** *Delta Herald & Times* (PA) 7 May [4]/4 (newspaperarchive.com), [Advt:] Cooking Crocks at 10c. Two elegant shapes of this favorite cooking vessel. One a stewer and the other a kettle. **1933** *AmSp* 8.1.52 **Ozarks,** *Stewer.* . . A vessel used for stewing meat, a stew pan. **1938** in 2004 *DARE* File—Internet **OK** (as of c1901), He . . removed a large rock, under which was a granite stewer, the bottom had rusted out of the stewer and the money was gone. **1954** *Harder Coll.* **cwTN,** *Stewer.* . . A stewpan, a metal vessel with a handle. Sometimes pronounced like *stir.* **c1960** *Wilson Coll.* **csKY,** *Stewpan.* . . A saucepan; sometimes called a stewer. **1965–70** *DARE* (Qu. F4, . . *The deep metal container used to boil foods*) 19 Infs, **esp Lower Missip Valley, TX, OK,** Stewer; **AR54,** Stewer—what they use nowadays; **KY74,** Stewer—old-fashioned; **OK31,** Stewer—used to call; **OK47,** Stewer—most usual. **1972** *Atlanta Letters* **GA,** I did not know until I was married, moved to Tennessee and worked with a large, national company that had brought in "Yankees" that "stewer" was not a dictionary word for a sauce pan. **1986** Pederson *LAGS Concordance (Pail)* 1 inf, **nwTN,** Mother sometimes milked into [a] stewer; 1 inf, **nwTN,** Stewer—for milking; aluminum, with handle; 1 inf, **cwTN,** Stewer—had a handle; made of aluminum; 1 inf, **nwTN,** Stewer—for milking; *(Kettle)* 1 inf, **neAR,** Stewer; 1 inf, **csTN,** Stewers—old-fashioned kettles with handles; *(Frying pan)* 1 inf, **cwAR,** Stewer; 1 inf, **swAR,** Stewer—a pot with a lid; 1 inf, **cwTN,** Stewers and pots for cooking; 1 inf, **nwTN,** Stewers—old term for saucepan. **2004** *DARE* File—Internet **nwAL,** In a large stewer add 4–5 cups water, 2 cans Chicken Broth [etc]. *Ibid* **cnTX,** Others cooked beans in a stewer, but we used a steer; others cooked by a recipe while we followed a receipt, and we used a monkey ranch to adjust the plow.

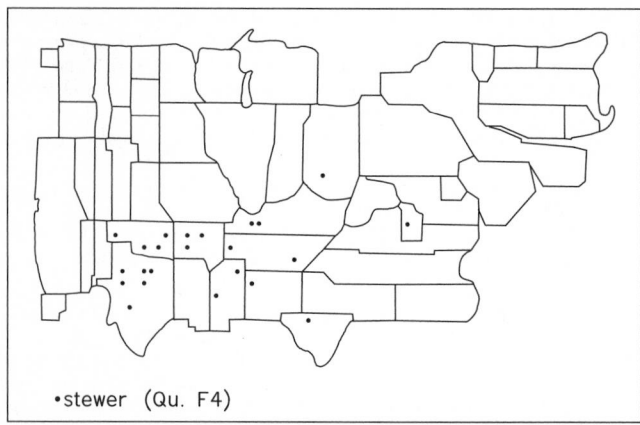

•stewer (Qu. F4)

stew the dishrag v phr Cf *put the big pot in the little one* (at **pot n 11**)

Fig: to go to great lengths to prepare a meal, esp for unexpected guests.

[**1893** *Outing* 23.473 [Black], She announced her intention of putting 'de big pot in de little one—dish-rag and all,' which means great things.] **1936** Rak *Mt. Cattle* 116 **seAZ,** The cooks began 'throwing the big pot into the little one and stewing the dishrag.' **1946** *PADS* 6.41 **swVA,** We'll put the little pot in the big pot and stew the dishrag. (We'll do our best to provide a meal for unexpected company). **1984** Wilder *You All Spoken Here* 82 **Sth,** *Stew the dishrag:* Lay on a lavish repast; cook up a storm; put the big pot in the little one and fry the skillet. **2007** in 2008 *DARE* File—Internet **TN,** I *love* heading into the kitchen to "put the big pot in the little one and stew the dishrag," to quote my grandmother's peculiar—and unfathomable—expression for cooking for a special occasion.

stib n Cf **white-tailed stib**

1 =**red-backed sandpiper.**

[**1852** in 1876 *Forest & Stream* 7.212 **MA,** *T[ringa] alpina.* Stile.] **1876** *Ibid* 245 **MA,** In looking over the "List of Gunner's Names," printed from my manuscript, I notice two errors. . . Against the two trinqas [sic]—*Alpina* and *Bonapartei*—for "stile," as you have it, read "stib." Why stib, I can't make out. **1956** MA Audubon Soc. *Bulletin* 40.20 **MA,** Red-backed Sandpiper. . . Stib (Mass. From the note of this or an associated species.)

2 =**sanderling.**

1923 U.S. Dept. Ag. *Misc. Circular* 13.57 **MA,** Sanderling. . . Vernacular Names. . . *In local use.* . . skinner, stib. **1948** Pearson *Sea Flavor* 143 **NEng,** Shoremen and fishermen, clam diggers and lobstermen have given *Crocethia* a roster of nicknames—beach bird, whitey . . , whiting, stib [etc].

stick n

1 =**tobacco stick;** the amount of tobacco hung on such a stick; hence n *stick rack* a wooden rack upon which the **tobacco sticks** are put; see quots. **S Midl** Cf **stick v 2**

1724 (1865) Jones *Present State VA* 40, It is hung to dry on *Sticks,* as Paper at the Paper-Mills. **1851** *De Bow's Rev.* 11.397 **MD,** *Tobacco sticks* are small round sticks, or are split out like laths, and are about one inch square, or one and a half inches square. . . If the tobacco is of good size, six or seven plants are enough on a four-foot stick. **1869** [see **stick v 2**]. **1940** *AmSp* 15.135 [Tobacco market language], *Stick racks.* Wooden racks on which the packers put the sticks. **1944** *PADS* 2.71 **S Midl,** *Stick.* . . A small (usually) flat piece of timber ((four feet and four inches long)) on which the freshly pulled or cut tobacco is hung before being cured ((and packed away)). **1956** *Hench Coll.* **csVA,** [Postcard caption:] Tobacco leaves have been harvested, bound in small bundles then tied on sticks. When these sticks have been racked in the barn the heat will be continuously applied . . for final curing. **1966** *PADS* 45.24 **cnKY,** Stalks of tobacco are strung on the stick for curing and again for bulking. . . "We put six stalks on a stick." . . A unit of measure. A stick contains six cut stalks of tobacco for curing or a number of tied hands for bulking. **1966–69** *DARE* Tape **DC5,** When you got that 'bacca laid in rows, why then next thing somebody will come along with sticks and judge how many sticks, and they'll drop the sticks along the row of 'bacca; **KY35,** We cut it [=tobacco] and put it on a stick. Ordinarily, about six plants to a stick, say something over four feet long. . . A stick four feet four inches we'll lap on the rails and hang in the barn. After cutting it, we may pile it overnight, maybe twelve or fifteen sticks of tobacco in one pile. **1967** Key *Tobacco Vocab.* 224 **GA, KY, MD, MO, NC, TN,** Stick. . . A slender length of wood. . . Stalks of tob[acco] are strung on the stick. . . A unit of measure. A stick contains 6 cut stalks of tob[acco]. **1986** Pederson *LAGS Concordance,* 1 inf, **csGA,** Strung that stick full (of tobacco).

2 A peculiar, awkward, or incompetent person—freq in phrr *odd* (or *queer*) *stick.* [*OED2 stick* sb.¹ 12 1682 →] **esp NEng** See Map *old-fash; usu derog*

1820 *NY Columbian* (NY) 12 Jan 2/3, Jesse Buel does all he can, but you know he is a poor stick. **1848** Lowell *Biglow* 143 'Upcountry' **MA,** Crooked stick, a perverse, froward person. **1848** Bartlett *Americanisms* 238, Odd stick. An eccentric person; as, 'John Randolph was an odd stick.' **1856** Olmsted *Journey Slave States* 83 **CT,** He had to hire white men to help him, but they were poor sticks and would be half the time drunk. **1857** *Harper's New Mth. Mag.* 15.716 **TX,** During a trial . . he very suddenly stopped the proceedings of the court, and called attention to a certain Ben Van—a queer stick of the bar. **1874** (1969) Coffin *Caleb Krinkle* 105 **NH,** "All my friends on the Porgie side, say that you are an odd stick." "I expect it is so, though I never have been able to get at a satisfactory meaning of that term. I have come to the conclusion, however, that there are several classes of odd-sticks. A person who departs in any considerable degree from notions of what society thinks is proper, is an odd stick." **1899** (1912) Green *VA Folk-Speech* 417, Stick. . . A person who is stiff and awkward in bearing; hence, a stupid, incapable, or incompetent person. **1900** *DN* 2.64 [College slang] **OH,** Stick. . . An uninteresting person. **1905** *DN* 3.15 **cCT,** Odd stick. . . An eccentric person. **1915** (1916) Johnson *Highways New Engl.* 70, He certainly was an odd old stick and a great talker, and I presume he told a good deal that wa'n't true. **1930** Shoemaker *1300 Words* 60 **cPA Mts** (as of c1900), Stick—A dull, uninteresting person. **1946** Driscoll *Country Jake* 78 **KS,** I looked apologetically at boys and men, because I was an odd stick, a cripple, one who was not earning his keep. **c1960** *Wilson Coll.* **csKY,** Stick. . . A dull, stupid person. **1965–70** *DARE* (Qu. II7, *Somebody who doesn't seem to 'fit in' or to get along very well . . "He's kind of a _____."*) 11 Infs, **NEng,** Odd stick; (Qu. AA15c, . . *Joking ways . . of saying that a woman is getting married. . . "She _____."*) Inf **MA**21, Is getting a poor stick; (Qu. HH1, *Names and nicknames for a rustic or countrified person*) Inf **GA**1, Country stick; (Qu. HH4, *Someone who has odd or peculiar ideas or notions*) Infs **MA**5, 35, 55, Odd stick; **MA**89, **RI**15, Queer stick; (Qu. HH16, *Uncomplimentary words with no definite meaning—just used when you want to show that you don't think much of a person: "Don't invite him. He's a _____."*) Inf **NY**69, Old stick; (Qu. HH21, *A very awkward, clumsy person*) Inf **VT**12, Limber stick; (Qu. HH24, *Somebody who doesn't talk very much, who keeps his thoughts to himself*) Inf **MA**35, Odd stick; (Qu. HH40, *Uncomplimentary words for an old man*) Infs **ID**1, **OH**95, Stick; **NJ**15, Old stick. [17 of 20 total Infs old]

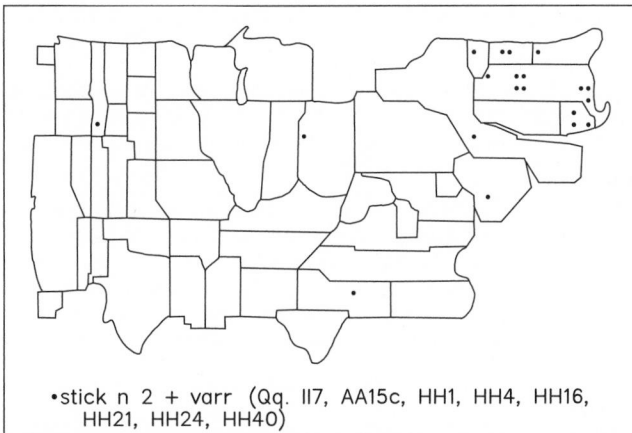

•stick n 2 + varr (Qq. II7, AA15c, HH1, HH4, HH16, HH21, HH24, HH40)

3 Speed; a rate of speed. Cf **cut stick**

1830 in 1939 Thornton *Amer. Gloss.* 3.653, He whirls [the coach] away at a pretty good stick. **1905** Wasson *Green Shay* 44 **NEng,** Bedide ef he did n't up and grab old skipper by the scroff o' the neck, and snake him off in tow, goin' a ten-knot stick [Footnote: Rate] at the least cal'lation. **1914** *DN* 4.80 **ME, nNH,** Stick. . . Speed. "He's goin' full stick." "She was goin' a good stick, when I seen her." [**1925** *DN* 5.343 **Nfld,** Stick on, get a better. Go faster.]

4 also *sticks:* Used as an assent to a proposal of marriage; see quots. Cf **beeswax 2**

1960 Hall *Smoky Mt. Folks* 52 **wNC, eTN,** If a widower said "beeswax" to a widow . . he was proposing marriage. If she wished to marry him, she answered "sticks." **1996** in 2004 Montgomery–Hall *Dict. Smoky Mt. Engl.* 569 **sAppalachians,** If a widower said "resin", he was proposing marriage. If a widow wished to marry him, she said "stick".

5 also *wooden stick:* A toothpick. Cf **finishing stick, hunger ~, quitting ~**

1967–70 *DARE* (Qu. G11, *Other names or nicknames for a toothpick*) Infs **IL**11, **PA**245, **WI**62, Stick; **PA**66, Wooden stick. **1986** *DARE* File **OK,** Stick—a tooth pick.

6 See **stick bug 1.**

stick v

1 To thrust or drive (a sharp object). **widespread, but less freq Inland Nth, N Midl, West** See Map Cf **run v B2** Note: The reflexive phrr *to stick oneself (with a sharp object)* and varr elicited at Qu. Y64b do not show a regional pattern.

1823 [see **stick a pin there**]. **1838** *U.S. Mag. & Democratic Rev.* 2.170, The little man . . stuck his needle into his work. **1965–70** *DARE* (Qu. Y46a, *To get hurt with something sharp . . "He _____ a thorn into his hand."*) 567 Infs, **widespread, but less freq Inland Nth, N Midl, West,** Stuck; **SC**10, Stick; (Qu. V1, *When you suspect that somebody is trying to deceive you*) Inf **OK**18, Trying to stick a knife in my back; (Qu. Y3, *To say uncomplimentary things about somebody*) Inf **CT**11, Stick a knife into him; (Qu. BB51a, . . *Cures for corns or warts*) Inf **NC**16, Scratch it with a pin and stick pin in ground; **MA**73, Stick heated needle through wart; (Qu. BB51b, . . *'Magical' cures for corns or warts*) Inf **CA**94, Stick a needle in wart; **UT**10, Stick a pin through it; **SD**3, Stick needle in wart and apply lighted match to needle; **NJ**16, Stick pins in wart and throw away pins. **1966** *DARE* Tape **FL**19, He pulled his shoes off . . and he stuck a bad splinter in his foot. **1986** Pederson *LAGS Concordance (Stabbed)* 1 inf, **nwTN,** Stuck a knife in him.

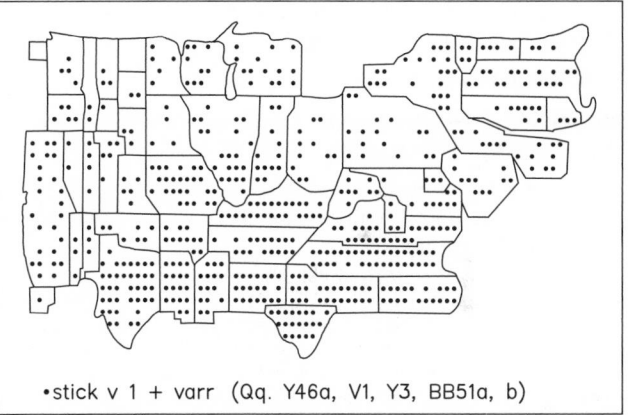

•stick v 1 + varr (Qq. Y46a, V1, Y3, BB51a, b)

2 To pierce tobacco stalks for hanging on a stick; to arrange the stalks on a stick; to insert such a stick in the ground for drying; to hang (tobacco) on a stick; to allow (tobacco) to begin to dry on the stick in the field; hence vbl n *sticking;* n *sticker.* **esp S Midl** Cf **stick n 1**

1841 *Amer. Farmer* new ser 2.332 **MD,** The most careful hands should only be permitted to stick tobacco in this way. **1869** Porcher *Resources* 525 **OH,** Having filled the stick, remove the socket, lay your stick of tobacco on the floor, and go on sticking until the load is all stuck; or it is a good plan to have rails laid on the lower tie and hang for the present as you stick. **1944** *PADS* 2.71 **S Midl,** Stick. . . to arrange tobacco on . . a stick; to punch a hole horizontally through the stalk before hanging. *Sticker.* . . The person who pierces—"sticks"—the stalk. **1967** Key *Tobacco Vocab.* **TN,** Stick. . . To insert sticks in the ground vertically after the stalks have been speared on them—to permit the stalks to wilt down before taking them to the barn. **1969** *NC Folkl.* 17.33 **wNC,** Deliberately leaving tobacco standing on sticks in the field to partially cure in a succession of dry clear days in late August or early September was called *sticking.* Some farmers were proponents of sticking as opposed to *scaffolding* (allowing the tobacco to hang on a temporary scaffold in the open air several days before housing it). . . Some farmers claimed burley "just naturally *kyored* (cured) *up* prettier" if it was stuck or scaffolded before it was housed.

3 See quots; hence ppl adj *stuck.* **esp Mid Atl**

1912 NC Dept. Ag. *Biennial Rept.* 10, A remarkable thing about the land is that one and, sometimes, two crops are made before the land is proved. This was called *stuck corn.* **1919** U.S. Congress House *Homes for Soldiers* 35 **NC,** In the very heart of this swamp I saw what they call stuck corn. . . Boys had passed along the land, in a row, and with a stick made a hole 6 inches deep in the ground and dropped in a couple of seeds of corn; and they had bins full of this corn. **1946** *PADS* 6.28 **eNC** (as of c1900), *Stick corn.* . . To plant corn in holes dug by a grubbing hoe in unplowed ground. ((In s. Va. a stick was sometimes used to make the hole.)) **1994** Mullins *Echoes* 81, Marn and Vann Cornfield had sent the boys and girls to "stick" beans in the richest part of the field. . . Each year, after the second hoeing of the corn, beans were planted next to the hills of corn—pushed into the ground by hand, called "sticking" beans—to grow and climb the corn stalks for support. **2004** *News & Observer* (Raleigh NC) 18 Apr sec D 8 (Internet) **NC [Black],** All my young days I worked hard out in the fields. . . I was sticking corn for 40 cents a day.

4 In marble play; of a shooting marble: to remain in the ring; to spin in place after striking another marble; hence ppl adj *stuck;* vbl n *sticking;* see quots. Cf **sticker 2**

1908 *DN* 3.309 **TX,** In marbles, when one's taw stops inside the ring he is said to be *fat. Stuck* is the term used in Texas. **1955** *Daily Progress* (Charlottesville VA) 10 Mar 24/1, If he knocked one or more marbles from the ring, he might continue shooting, provided his "taw", or shooting marble "stuck," or stayed in the ring. **1957** *Sat. Eve. Post Letters* **OK** (as of 1890s), If the taw were spinning rapidly and in a horizontal spin, (that is if the rotational axis were vertical), and the objective marble was struck exactly center, the taw would stick, (and we called it sticking) and spin without moving beyond the point where the objective lay. **1966** *DARE* Tape **NM9,** [FW:] And, when it sticks, it'll, uh? [Inf:] You shoot again. [FW:] It'll stay in one spot. It won't move around then? [Inf:] Yes. . . You have to grab where the taw sticks. There's where you shoot from the next time. . . If you peg and stick, you've got to shoot down. . . so that the taw'll stick where you want it. **1986** Pederson *LAGS Concordance,* 2 infs, **swGA,** Stuck—of marble(s) remaining in the circle (or pot, ring).

stick-a-knife See **stick-knife**

stickalerio See **stickery-leivo**

stick-a-marie See **stingaree 3**

stick-and-clay chimney n Also *stick(-and-daub) chimney;* for addit varr see quots **chiefly Sth, S Midl** *hist* Cf **cat-and-clay, stack chimney 2**

A chimney framed with sticks and plastered with clay.

1840 *Huron Reflector* (Norwalk OH) 12 May [2]/2 (newspaper-archive.com), On the right . . stood a *Log Cabin,* constructed in the Backwoods style, the crevices between the logs being well plastered with clay, a stick chimney at each extremity, and the door well provided with a latch. **1863** *Ladies' Repository* 23.398 **swTN,** A "stick and clay" chimney on the same ample scale lets out the smoke and lets in the rain. **1880** Durant *Hist. Ingham Co. MI* 307 (as of 1840), It had . . a large stick-and-mud chimney, which let in a good supply of light from the top. **1887** *Century Illustr. Mag.* 34.111 **ceAR,** The water mirrored the Shinault cabin with its . . "stick and dirt" chimney. **1898** Lloyd *Country Life* 11 **AL,** It don't make any difference whether it is one of these clumsy old brown houses, . . with stick chimneys and shed rooms. **1903** *DN* 2.331 **seMO,** *Stick-and-dirt* (chimney). . . A chimney made with sticks laid up 'log house fashion' and plastered with clay. Still common in some localities. **1905** *DN* 3.96 **nwAR,** *Stick-chimney.* . . An outside chimney of short thick sticks daubed with clay or mud. Uncommon in N.W. Ark., which has plenty of rocks for chimneys. **1906** *DN* 3.158 **nwAR,** Stick and mud chimney. **1913** in 2000 *Carmi Times* (IL) 12 Apr (Internet) **seIL,** The chimney was what was called a stick and daub chimney. **1938** in 1976 *Weevils in the Wheat* 82 **VA** [Black], The cabins were covered with boards, nailed on and had stick-and-mud chimneys. **1966** *DARE* Tape **AL1,** Stick-and-dirt chimney, you seen one of them? . . Chimney put up out of mud and sticks. **1967** *DARE* FW Addit **LA1,** *Stick-and-mud chimney*—a fireplace and chimney framed with sticks and caked with a mixture of mud and straw. **1975** McDonough *Garden Sass* 52 **AR,** The stick and daub chimney was built almost exclusively in the pine log cabins of the Ouachita Mountains. **2000** Humphreys *Nowhere* 49 **csNC** (as of c1865), The old

stick-and-clay chimney like ours had been replaced by a sharp-cornered red brick one.

stick a pin there v phr Also *stick a pin here* and varr

Fig: to take careful note of what has just been said—usu in imper, mark my words!

1823 *Adams Centinel* (Gettysburg PA) 10 Sept [3]/2 (newspaper-archive.com), The people . . had sense enough to reject him, as they will the Legislative Caucus candidate in Pennsylvania, come October, Stick a pin there. **1854** (1855) Parton *Ruth Hall* 355, "I must take a phrenological look at you. Bless me! what an affectionate little creature you must be," said he, passing his hand over her head; "stick a pin there now, while I examine the rest of your bumps." **1889** *Mt. Echo* (Clinton AR) 12 July (Internet), If their parents can't control them, which it seems they can't, the law can and will. Now boys, "stick a pin there." **1909** *Daily People* (NY NY) 3 Aug 2/1, Guesde completed his speech saying he by no means meant to deny that the hour for physical force would arrive. . . Stick a pin there. **1910** Raine *Bucky O'Connor* 265 **West,** You butt in once more and you better reach for your hardware simultaneous. Stick a pin in that. **1939** FWP *ID Lore* 242, Stick a pin there—make a note of it. **1948** *Daily Oklahoman* (Oklahoma City OK) 7 June 8/1, It might be a good idea for the voters to stick a pin here and remember a thing or two on next election day. **2007** *DARE* File—Internet **TX,** My kid isn't old enough to be interested in football—I kind of hope he never is, but we'll stick a pin in that idea for a little later.

stick bait n Also *stick-bait worm* [See quot 1876; found in Brit use from early 19th cent on] **sAppalachians** Cf **periwinkle n[2] 2, rock worm, sandstoodle, stick bug 3, stick worm 1**

The larva of the caddis fly; also used as mass noun.

1876 *Forest & Stream* 7.82 **wNC,** During this time our friends were in Big Laurel, turning over flat stones, and procuring what they called "stick bait"—that is, small water-worms—that surround themselves with a tube of little sticks, which they glue together for a covering. **1883** Zeigler–Grosscup *Heart of Alleghanies* 110 **NC,** The best fishing I ever saw done was by a mountaineer, one day in early June, who used a green-winged, yellow-bodied, artificial fly with a stick-bait worm strung on the hook. **1892** *Amer. Angler* 22.23 **wNC,** "Try stick bait; that's what we 'uns fish with." "Stick bait, what's that?" *Ibid,* Smythe was dumbfounded when the Captain let him into the secret of "stick bait." Had never heard of such a thing. Said it was unknown in the Adirondacks and the streams of New England. **1916** Kephart *Camping & Woodcraft* 2.412, From early spring until June, or even July, it is easy to get "stick bait" (the larva of the caddis fly) in almost any trout stream. **1966–69** *DARE* (Qu. P6, . . *Kinds of worms . . used for bait*) Inf **GA72,** Stick bait—build nests in streams; [(Qu. R4, . . *Insect that hatches in . . lakes or rivers . . and is good fish bait*) Inf **NC36,** Mayfly—larva [sic] are called stick bait]. **1986** in 2004 Montgomery–Hall *Dict. Smoky Mt. Engl.* 569 **wNC, eTN,** Here we mountain folk used to fish for the now rare native brook trout; hunting in the shallows for what we called stick bait. (Now I've learned they are called caddis insects.) **1991** Weals *Last Train* 22 **eTN** (as of early 20th cent), When he was old enough to gather stick-bait and help carry trout, Lonnie would go with his father . . on fishing trips. **1996** Houk *Food Smokies* 21 **eTN, wNC,** In the side pools of the creek they gathered "stick bait," caddisfly larvae that build cases of sticks and pebbles around themselves.

stickball n

1 An informal version of baseball usu played in an urban setting such as the street, using a stick and usu a rubber ball; see quot 1977. **chiefly NEast, esp NYC** See Map

1824 *Nantucket Inquirer* (MA) 12 Jan 3/5, It is hereby ordered, that no person shall play Foot-ball or Poke, Stick-ball or Swinger, within the compact part of the Town of Nantucket. **1922** *NY Times* (NY) 3 Sept sec 2 1/4, Games of tag, . . handball, stick ball, whip tag, . . and other games will be carried on daily. **1947** *Commentary* May 464 **NYC,** Sometimes we became so engrossed by a punchball or a stickball game that night would fall without anyone's being aware of it. **1953** *Sun* (Baltimore MD) 1 Apr 12/1, As a South Baltimore boy . . Governor McKeldin can remember romping barefooted in the neighborhood, playing stick-ball . . and otherwise taking his recreation. **1965–70** *DARE* (Qu. EE11, *Bat-and-ball games for just a few players [when there aren't enough for a regular game]*) Infs **MA127, MO7, NY1, 42, 55, 81, 89, 152, 186,** Stickball; **NY118,** Stickballs [sic]. **1969** *DARE* File **MA** (as of c1950), *Stickball*—A rudimentary form of baseball played with a tennis ball and broom handle. **c1970** *Ibid* **NYC** (as of c1925), Stick-ball. **1975** Ferretti *Gt. Amer. Book Sidewalk Games* 185, Stickball is the na-

tional game of American cities. . . Stickball is city baseball. **1977** *Eve.*
Capital (Annapolis MD) 6 Oct 22 **NYC,** Stickball. . . is played with a
rounded stick about three feet long, usually a broomstick. You also need
a pink rubber ball, also known as a "spaldeen." . . Stickball can be
played in the middle of the street. . . The batter tosses the ball straight
up, quickly grasps the stick and tries to cream the ball. **1986** Pederson
LAGS Concordance (Ball . . games) 4 infs, **AL, LA, TN,** Stickball. [3 of
4 infs urban] **1992** *DARE* File **Washington DC,** I grew up in DC, and I
have a vague memory of [an informal game of baseball with less than
nine players] being called *stickball.* **2007** *NY Times* (NY) 1 July 26/6
NYC, Anthony Gigante . . organized a league to play what may be the
most resilient of the traditional games—stickball—although its slow demise has been lamented for years.

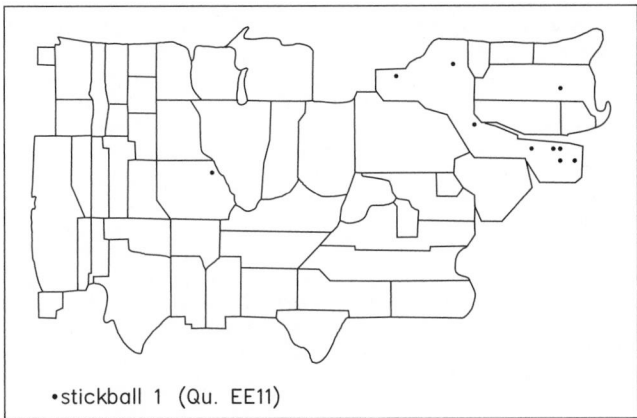

•stickball 1 (Qu. EE11)

2 An American Indian ball game similar to lacrosse played
esp by woodland tribes of the Southeast; see quots.

1907 *Checotah Times* (OK) 19 Apr [5]/6 (newspaperarchive.com), The
Indians have begun playing stick ball. **1919** *Daily Oklahoman* (Okla-
homa City OK) 7 Nov 12/1, *Championship Stick Ball Game*—Between
Eufauloche Town vs. Cheyarha Town—Thrilling, Exciting—A Real
Sport Played by Real Indians. **1946** *Life* 11 Nov 91, On the Cherokees'
Qualla Indian Reservation in North Carolina . . the Wolftown Wolves
met the Wolftown Bears in a crucial game of stickball. . . The game of
stickball . . is a primitive version of modern lacrosse. **1965** *DARE* (Qu.
EE11) Inf **OK9,** Stickball—Indians play stickball using two sticks with
webbed cups on end and two goalposts. **1986** Pederson *LAGS Concor-*
dance, 2 infs, **MS,** Stickball—Indian game. **1995** Williams *Gt. Smoky*
Mts. Folklife 181 **wNC, eTN,** This sport . . has long fascinated anthro-
pologists, including Mooney, who documented Cherokee stickball in the
late nineteenth century. **2003** *Commercial Appeal* (Memphis TN) 2
Aug sec B 2 (Internet), Corn grinding, stick ball games and dancing are
a few ways the local Choctaw Indians will share their culture this weekend at Chucalissa Archaeological Museum. **2004** *DARE* File—Internet,
[Caption:] Photo of a stick ball game, the Choctaw version of lacrosse
in Mississippi, ca. 1900. *Ibid* **FL,** Seminole Indian Village and Cultural Center . . Tampa, FL. . . The grounds include various *chickee*
dwellings, and an area for playing the traditional stick ball game. *Ibid*
OK, A-ne-jo-di, or Stick-ball, is a very rough game played by not only
the Cherokee, but many other Southeastern Woodland tribes including
the Muscogee (Creek), Seminole, and others.

3 See quot. Cf **cat** n **3a**

1966–69 *DARE* (Qu. EE10, *A game in which a short stick lying on the*
ground is flipped into the air and then hit with a longer stick) Infs
MA58, NY86, Stickball; **WA6,** Stickball—stick thrown to you and you
hit it with other stick.

stick bean n   esp Inland Sth, AR   See Map
A pole bean.

1906 *DN* 3.158 **nwAR,** *Stick bean.* . . Pole bean. **1909** *DN* 3.375
eAL, wGA, *Stick-bean.* . . *Pole-bean.* **1967–69** *DARE* (Qu. I14, *Kinds*
of beans that you eat in the pod before they're dry) Inf **TN4,** Stick
beans—same as pole beans; (Qu. I20, . . *Kinds of beans*) Infs **AL27,**
KY5, 17, 24, 34, 37, Stick beans; **AR47,** Stick beans—put a stick beside
them for them to climb on; [**CA24,** Pole beans—called stick peas by
Japanese]. **1983** *MJLF* 9.1.57 **ceKY** (as of 1956), *Stick beans* . . stake
beans. **1986** Pederson *LAGS Concordance (Green beans)* 18 infs, 11
TN, 4 **nAL,** 3 **nwAR,** Stick bean(s); 1 inf, **ceTN,** Stick beans—run on a
stick; 1 inf, **ceTN,** Stick beans—you'd have to stick them. **2003** *DARE*
File—Internet **KY,** That will give me four stick beans, at any rate.

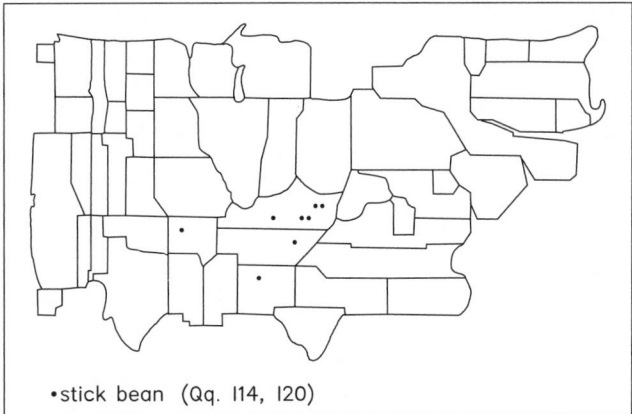

•stick bean (Qq. I14, I20)

stick broom n   [Appar to distinguish it from homemade
brooms that were made without a separate handle]   **chiefly SE,**
esp S Atl   See Map   Cf **kitchen broom**
A broom with a long handle.

1910 *Dothan Eagle* (AL) 13 Dec 2/2, Had there been no pistol, she
would have probably grabbed a fire poker, or a stick broom as a weapon.
c1938 in 1970 Hyatt *Hoodoo* 1.403 **seGA,** Take de *stick broom* an' jest
throw three hands of table salt behin' dem an' take dat *stick broom* . . an'
jest turns de broom up, an' dey won't be botherin' round yo' no mo'.
1939 FWP *These are Our Lives* 45 **S Midl,** He brought a chair from the
porch to the yard, swept clean in country style with a stick broom.
1952 Brown *NC Folkl.* 1.594, *Stick-broom.* . . "A store-bought"
broom—one that has a stick for a handle. **1956** McAtee *Some Dialect*
NC 43, Stick broom. . . A purchased broom with a stick handle. **1965–**
70 *DARE* (Qu. F36, . . *Kinds of brooms*) 19 Infs, **chiefly S Atl,** Stick
broom; **GA2,** Stick broom—with long handle; **LA6,** Stick broom—has
a long handle for sweeping the floor; **SC3,** Stick broom—an ordinary
house broom; **SC6,** Stick broom—what you buy in a store; **SC9,** Stick
broom—like from a store; **SC29,** Stick broom—long-handled broom;
the common one bought in the grocery store; **SC34,** Stick broom—the
kind you'd *buy* (ordinarily) for your house at a grocery store. **1967**
DARE FW Addit **SC,** *Stick broom*—in counterdistinction to a straw
broom—has a stick for a handle. **1986** Pederson *LAGS Concordance*
(Broom) 12 infs, **GA, AL, FL, MS,** Stick broom; 1 inf, **neGA,** Stick
broom—store bought; 1 inf, **seMS,** Stick broom—the kind you buy in
the store. **2002** in 2004 *DARE* File—Internet **swNC,** The lost handcuff
key, which was later found wedged inside the straw part of the stick
broom, doesn't help explain things. **2004** *Ibid* **csAL** (as of 1920s), I realize now the broom sage swept our wooden floors better than the stick
broom. But the idea of a store-bought broom got my attention.

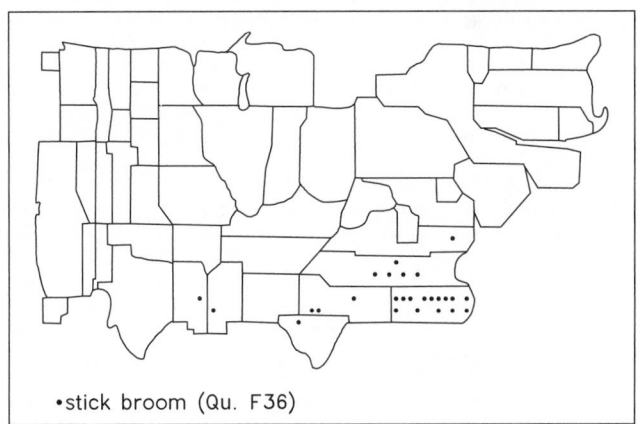

•stick broom (Qu. F36)

stick bug n

1 also *stick:* A **walkingstick 1.** Cf **stick horse**

1868 *Amer. Entomologist* 1.58, The long-bodied, long-legged, slender,
slow-moving, greenish-brown insects . . are the common *Stick-bug*
(*Spectrum femoratum,* Say). This is the best and most appropriate English name for them. . . There are, however, a variety of other local
names. **1890** *Century Dict.* 5943, *Stick-bug.* . . Any orthopterous insect
of the family *Phasmidae:* particularly applied to *Diapheromera femo-*
rata, the commonest insect of this kind in the United States, where it is

also called *wood-horse, stick-insect, twig-bug* [etc.]. **1894** *Harper's New Mth. Mag.* Feb 456, The form [of walkingstick] common over the greater part of the United States, which the country people near Salem, Massachusetts . . call "witches' horses," and which in some other States are dubbed "stick-bugs" and "prairie alligators," our *Diapheromera femorata*. **1965–70** *DARE* (Qu. R9a, *An insect from two to four inches long that lives in bushes and looks like a dead twig*) **CA**181, **GA**76, **MI**14, **MN**34, **PA**165, **VA**21, **WA**15, Stick bug; **KS**3, Stick bug—walking stick is what my children call it; **MI**94, 96, **NY**233, Stick(s). **1968** *DARE* FW Addit **GA**65, Stick bug—[in] Waukegan, Illinois. **1994** Cornwell *Body Farm* 359 **NC**, "I personally couldn't shoot a stick bug." "If that's the same as a praying mantis, you shouldn't shoot a stick bug. It would be bad luck." "It's not the same thing. . . A praying mantis is a whole 'nother insect."

2 =praying mantis B.

1968 *AmSp* 43.53 **KS**, [In a series of names for the praying mantis:] Stick bug [1 inf]. [**1994** see **1** above.] [**1997** *DARE* File—Internet, In Canada they call a praying mantis a stick bug, which confused our kids.] **2007** *Ibid* **CA**, The stick bug (Mantis) was based on a real insect in nature. We spent months on the cg model, textures and on the animation rig. . . We even bought 2 live stick bugs to keep as reference back in California.

3 =stick bait.

1973 *Mt. Democrat & Placerville Times* (CA) 10 May [12]/2 (newspaperarchive.com), Pollywogs wriggled up and down, stick bugs slowly negotiated the "crick" bottom, and dragonflies darted here and there.

stick chimney See **stick-and-clay chimney**

stick devil horse See **devil's horse 4**

sticker n

1 also *sticker burr, stickle ~, stickler:* Any of var clinging seeds or burrs such as **cockleburr** or **beggar ticks 1;** a thorn, spine, or prickle; hence nouns *sticker* (or *sticky*) *bush, sticker grass, ~ weed.* Cf **picker 1, pricker**

1889 *Sun. Oregonian* (Portland OR) 9 June 15/1, Our principal varieties of wild grasses are, native clover, cheet, poverty or sticker grass and in some localities, the renowned bunch grass. **1897** *KS Univ. Qrly.* (ser B) 6.92 **neKS**, *Sticker weed:* one of several weeds, the leaves or seeds of which stick to clothing. **1898** (1908) Atherton *Californians* 231, Trennahan . . plucked the "stickers" from his trousers. **1902** *DN* 2.246 **sIL**, *Sticker.* . . Thorn or brier. **1906** *DN* 3.158 **nwAR**, *Sticker.* . . Thorn, bramble. "There are stickers on those vines." **1908** Johnson *Highways Pacific Coast* 212 **nCA**, The hens . . often stole nests off in the manzanita shrubs and thorny "sticker-bushes." **1909** *DN* 3.375 **eAL, wGA**, *Sticker.* . . A spine, a thorn. "This bush is full of stickers." **1931** U.S. Dept. Ag. *Misc. Pub.* 101.139, Nuttall gilia, locally known as stickerbush, stinkweed [etc.]. **1933** *Amer. Anthropologist* 35.610 **OK**, There were no briar weeds, or stickers, or burrs; so the children as well as their parents were nearly always barefooted. **1935** Sandoz *Jules* 285 **wNE** (as of 1880–1930), Carefully they stepped through the rose-brush thickets, stooping to pull sand burrs and cactus from their feet. . . Jule was whispering about the man's high-laced boots. "He don't have to get stickers, I bet." **1938** Stuart *Dark Hills* 212 **eKY**, There is dew on the sticker weeds around the hog pen. **1950** *WELS* **WI** (*A large round weed seed that clings to your clothing*) 1 Inf, Sticker; (*Small, flat weed seeds with two prongs that cling to clothing*) 2 Infs, Sticker. **1965–70** *DARE* (Qu. S13, . . *A common wild bush with bunches of round, prickly seeds; when they get dry they stick to your clothing*) 24 Infs, **esp NEast**, Sticker(s); **PA**44, Stickers—really burdock; **NY**44, **PA**245, Sticker bush; **NJ**45, **SC**19, Sticker burr; **NJ**55, Stickle burr; (Qu. S14, . . *Prickly seeds, small and flat, with two prongs at one end, that cling to clothing*) 24 Infs, **chiefly Nth, N Midl**, Stickers; **WI**48, Stickers—a general term for any weeds that prick, sting, or cling to your clothing; **NY**2, Sticklers; (Qu. S12b, . . *The sharp points along the stems of rose bushes, berry bushes, and so on . . small ones;* total Infs questioned, 75) 21 Infs, **scattered**, Stickers; **OK**52, Rose-stickers; (Qu. S15, . . *Weed seeds that cling to clothing*) Infs **GA**25, **IL**50, **LA**4, 17, **OR**16, Sticker(s); **KS**3, Sticker—it's a low, crawling plant that blooms and gets stickers on it; **TX**15, 27, Sticker burrs; **VA**2, Sticker burr—little green things, tiny, three-cornered; **MO**32, Sticker grass; (Qu. S9, . . *Kinds of grass that are hard to get rid of*) Inf **CA**136, Sticker grass; **FL**22, Stickers; (Qu. S12a, . . *The sharp points along the stems of rose bushes, berry bushes, and so on . . large ones;* total Infs questioned, 75) Infs **FL**26, **MS**16, Stickers; (Qu. S16) Inf **MS**86, Sticker weed—another name for ['trɛsæl] [*DARE* Ed: =**tread-soft(ly) 2**]; (Qu. S21, . . *Weeds . . that are a trouble in gardens and fields*) Inf **LA**15, Sticker weed—has little stickers on it;

(Qu. T6, *The pointed leaves that fall from pine trees*) Inf **WA**20, Stickers. **1966** *DARE* Tape **OK**31, [Inf:] We used to eat prickly-pear apples. [FW:] What're they like? [Inf:] Oh, they're . . plumb full of stickers. **1997** *DARE* File—Internet cePA [CoalSpeak], *Stickers, sticker bushes, sticky-bushes:* Thorn or brier bushes. "I was up da back drinkin' and I went to take a leak and fell in da sticker bushes!"

2 also *stickie;* In marble play: a marble, usu a shooter, that remains in place after striking (or being struck by) another marble. [**stick v 4**]

1916 *DN* 4.347 **seLA**, *Hitting a sticker.* In marbles, a play in which the marble shot, after striking another marble, remains whirling in one spot. **1955** *PADS* 23.31 **cwAL**, *Stickie.* . . A marble that will remain in the ring instead of rolling out. **1966** *DARE* (Qu. EE6a, . . *Different kinds of marbles—the big one that's used to knock others out of the ring*) Inf **FL**10, Sticker; (Qu. EE6d, *Special marbles*) Inf **FL**10, Sticker—one that stays right where it is; when it hits, it spins. **1966–67** *DARE* Tape **NM**9, A sticker is the taw that you're shooting with. And you use either a heavy lead marble or a glassie; **SC**40, We had shooters and we called 'em stickers. A sticker was a good shooter that when you shot in the bull's-eye, it would just sit and spin and it wouldn't run out of your pot. c**1970** Wiersma *Marbles Terms* **seMI** (as of c1940), A sticker was a marble which when hit by another remained embedded or stayed put on the ground.

3 A store order or scrip issued by a coal company.

1943 Korson *Coal Dust* 72, The same colloquial terms were used for scrip and store orders, such as "stickers," "clackers," "flickers," and "drag." **1973** *PADS* 59.55 **eKY, VA** [Bituminous coal mining vocab], *Sticker.* . . Scrip.

4 See **stick v 2.**

sticker burr (or bush, grass, weed) See **sticker 1**

stickerweed See **stickweed a, b(6)**

stickery-leivo n Also *stickalerio, stick relievo* Cf **relievo, ring-a-levio**

Any of var games; see quots.

1901 *DN* 2.148 **cNY**, *Stickery-leivo.* . . The same game as sic-a-nineten. **1957** *Sat. Eve. Post Letters* **NH**, A class-mate of mine of 65 years ago, has given me his recollection. . . of "Stick Relievo". . . The boy who was "it" leaned a stick against a tree, blinded his eyes while the others hid. After a few moments he opened his eyes, and tried to spot another boy, call this boy's name and throw the stick at him and call "Stick Relievo" and the other boy would be it. **1968** *DARE* (Qu. EE18, *Games in which the players set up a stone, a tin can, or something similar, and then try to knock it down*) Inf **NY**60, Stickalerio.

stick-far-the-red-oak n Also *stick-far-the-white-oak* **=chuck-will's-widow.**

1938 *Oriole* 3.2.9 **Okefenokee GA**, Another local name for the Chuck-will's-widow, current on Billy's Island in days gone by, is the onomatopoeic "Stick-far-the-white-oak." Jack Mizell, of Charlton County, knows this name and a slight variant as well: "Stick-far-the-red-oak."

stick-frog n Also *sticky-frog* **chiefly S Atl** See Map Cf **stick-knife**

Mumblety-peg.

1874 *GA Weekly Telegraph & GA Jrl.* (Macon) 3 Mar 6/5 **swGA**, The only trouble occurred between too Boys, they wear playing Stickfrog on a condition that whichever one lost the game was to root up a peg driven down 2 inches in the ground by the winer. **1912** *Montgomery Advt.* (AL) 27 Nov 4/3, What has become of the old and innocent game of "stick-frog," and who knows how to play it? **1965–70** *DARE* (Qu. EE5, *Games where you try to make a jackknife stick in the ground*) 30 Infs, **chiefly S Atl**, Stick-frog; **NC**1, Sticky-frog. [24 Infs old] **1966** *DARE* Tape **FL**8, [FW:] How about this game where you made the jackknife stick in the ground? . . [Inf:] Well, that was called stick-frog. And you would use a knife with, with one blade open out straight, and pitch it. And if it stuck into the ground, you had to do that a certain number of times. . . And then you'd open out the blade, the second blade, and leave it . . one out and one straight up, see, and then you would stick that into the ground. You just use the blades in different ways. **2002** Puckett *Memories GA Teacher* 91 (as of 1918), The little girls played with dolls, and the small boys played marbles, stick frog, Rolly Holey, or barnyard.

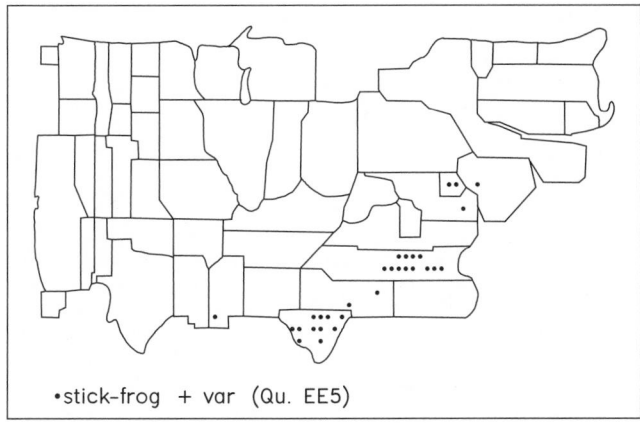

•stick-frog + var (Qu. EE5)

stick gig n   **chiefly NC, VA**   Cf **stick wagon**

A light, two-wheeled, one-horse carriage for a single passenger.

1802 *Democratic Republican & Commercial Daily Advt.* (Baltimore MD) 22 July 4/4, [Advt:] *A new stick Gig—For sale—*Well hung on bars, with a compleat set of plated harness. **1857** *Harper's New Mth. Mag.* 14.744 **NC,** That hoss reminds me of a hoss that old Major Bulbous used to drive in that old stick gig of his'n. **1860** Mordecai *Virginia* 82 **VA,** His style of travelling to and from Raleigh, N.C., about 175 miles each way . . was for many years, in that primitive sort of vehicle, a stick gig (or chair as it was then called), with one horse and no attendant. **a1883** (1911) Bagby *VA Gentleman* 1, Once a month the lawyers, in their stick-gigs or "single-chairs," and the farmers on their plantation mares, chatting and spitting amicably, with switches poised in up-and-downy elbows, jogged on to court. **1912** Green *VA Folk-Speech* 417, *Stick-gig.* . . A vehicle on two tall wheels, with sticks around the body like a chair.

stick horse n   Cf **stick bug 1,** *stick devil horse* (at **devil's horse 4**) =**walkingstick 1.**

1967–69 *DARE* (Qu. R9a, *An insect from two to four inches long that lives in bushes and looks like a dead twig*) Inf **TX**33, Stick horse.

stickie   See **sticker 2**

stick in v phr   Cf **stick me**

In marble play: to place (a marble) in the ring as a stake; to stake a marble; hence n *stick-in* a marble used as a stake.

1909 *DN* 3.375 **eAL, wGA,** *Stick-in.* . . A marble used as a stake in playing for keeps. **1955** *PADS* 23.11 **cwTN, cwAL,** [*Ante.* . . The preliminary wager in a marble game of chance.] *Ibid* 31, *Stick-in.* . . Same as *ante.* **1980** *NADS Letters* **Birmingham AL** (as of 1920s), When two play, each sticks-in a marble and these go at opposite ends of the ring. . . If a player has lost all his marbles but his toy [=taw], he may ask another player to "stick-in on his toy"; in other words, to lend him a marble to stick-in.

stick-in n   See **stick-up 2**

sticking n   [*stick* v to stack freshly-sawn boards with spacers for drying; cf *sticker* strip of wood used for this purpose] **chiefly nNEng**

A strip of wood (usu cut from sawmill offcuts) used to separate freshly-sawn boards for drying; material prepared for this purpose; an offcut regarded as waste or sold for kindling.

1871 Ream *Hist. Trip Saginaw* 48 **MI,** There were men at hand to seize the lumber and dispose of the scantlings, stickings and slabs. **1876** in 2011 (acc) Lexis–Nexis Legal Research *U.S. Supreme Court Cases* (Internet) **VT,** The defendants . . for a long time had maintained a constant fire . . for the purpose of burning the edgings, stickings, slabs, and other waste material from the saw-mill. **1908** *Daily Kennebec Jrl.* (Augusta ME) 26 June 11/5, It [=a fire] spread into the lumber yard . . where it burned lumber, sawdust and stickings. **1928** *Portsmouth Herald & Times* (NH) 23 May 10/4, [Advt:] *Kindling wood—*Slab wood, hard wood, stickings and mill ends. **1944** Shea *Gals Left Behind* 27 **ME,** There was a truck in the mill yard being loaded with stickings (kindling to you). **1966** *DARE* Tape **ME**6, When you get your lumber out in the yard, put down bearings to keep it up offen the ground. Whenever they lay in the water, the plank or whichever it is, they put in a

sticking between 'em to keep 'em from molding and so they'll dry. **1975** Gould *ME Lingo* 277, Boards fresh off a sawmill carriage are tiered to season or dry, and the tiers are separated by *edgings* or *stickings* to allow air to pass through the pile. . . The same edgings are sometimes used for firewood, so a man will buy a load of *stickings* or his wife will burn *stickings.* **1990** Hastings *Last Yankees* 55 **VT,** My first job was cutting sticking for piling lumber. . . I sawed my stickings out of waste, anything you could get an inch piece out of.

sticking ppl adj   Also *stuck* *among Black speakers*   Cf **sticking full,** *stinking rich*

Having plenty of money or another desirable possession or quality.

1954 Armstrong *Satchmo* 212 **LA** [Black], "I know you're sticking." He meant he knew I had plenty of money. *Ibid* 229, What I mean by "sticking" is that she had a big basket of good old southern fried chicken which she had fixed for her trip. **1968** *Current Slang* 3.2.46 [Watts slang; Black], *Stick.* . . To possess large quantities of drugs. To be well endowed with physical beauty.—He is *stuck.*—That broad is *sticking.* **1970** *DARE* (Qu. U37, . . *Somebody who has plenty of money*) Inf **KY**94, He's really sticking. [Inf Black] [**2006** *DARE* File—Internet **FL** [Black], Men who tuck their shirts in and clowns both have something strangely in common. They're both incredibly sticking rich.]

sticking vbl n   See **stick v 2, 4**

sticking full adj phr   [Cf *OED2 stick full* (at *stick* v.¹ 5.b); cf also Ger *stecken voll* to be full of]   Cf **sticking** ppl adj

Very full.

1835 Simms *Partisan* 2.86 **SC,** That farthest one [=a terrapin] . . is a superb fellow, fat as butter, and sticking full of eggs. **1852** *Scientific Amer.* 8.111 **NY,** The article would be acceptable . . short, clear, crisp, and sticking full of facts. **1871** *Harper's New Mth. Mag.* 43.646 **NYC,** And there was kept up the "card rack," sticking full of letters and business notices. **1955** Ritchie *Singing Family* 266 **seKY,** Well, it was coal you know, that the trains come in after. These hills right sticking full of coal.

sticking pin n   Also *stick pin*   Cf **common pin**

A straight pin.

1903 *McClure's Mag.* 21 advt sec 137 **CT,** To every embroiderer ordering our New Embroidery Book this Stick Pin Holder will be sent free until November 1st, 1903. **c1938** in 1970 Hyatt *Hoodoo* 1.465 **neSC** [Black], An' if ah got a wart on me, . . an' ah wanta git rid of it, ah'll go an' git me nine *stickin'-pins.* **1950** *WELS Suppl.* **cWI,** Stick-pin—for common pin. **1994** *DARE* File **nTX,** If disambiguation [between *pen* and *pin*] is needed I would likely say 'writing p_n' (stereotypically contrasted with a 'sticking p_n'). *Ibid* **TX,** It [=*ink pen*] is . . opposed, at times, to a stick-pin. *Ibid* **TX,** I don't recall any of my teachers . . insisting that we say "ink pen" to make sure we weren't asking for sticking pins. *Ibid* **sOH,** It's writin' pin as opposed to a stick pin here in southern Ohio. *Ibid* **MS,** I say 'ink pen' to make it clear that I'm not talking about a 'sticking pin.'

sticking plaster n   [*sticking plaster* an adhesive cloth bandage] *old-fash; joc*   Cf **sticktight 3**

A tagalong.

1908 *Van Wert Daily Bulletin* (OH) 3 Mar [4]/2 (newspaperarchive.com), Well, the other night sister told pa that you was a sticking plaster. **1942** Berrey–Van den Bark *Amer. Slang* 419.1, *Parasitical dependent.* . . sticking plaster. *Ibid* 441.1, *Hanger-on.* . . sticking plaster. **1966–68** *DARE* (Qu. Y9, *Somebody who always follows along behind others: "His little brother is an awful _____."*) Inf **DE**5, Sticking plaster; (Qu. HH16, *Uncomplimentary words with no definite meaning— just used when you want to show that you don't think much of a person: "Don't invite him. He's a _____."*) Inf **NY**43, Sticking plaster; (Qu. II18, *Someone who joins himself on to you and your group without being asked and won't leave*) Infs **DC**8, **MD**33, 39, **NJ**4, 18, **PA**27, Sticking plaster. [7 of 8 Infs old]

stick-knife n   Also *stick-a-knife*   **chiefly NEng**   See Map on p. 280   Cf **stick-frog**

Mumblety-peg; see also quot 1843.

1843 *Gift Christmas 1844* 52 **NY,** The pastime of the moment was mumble-the-peg, and that part of the game euphoniously called "stick-knife," having been played out, the uproar of the moment arose from witnessing the wry faces made by those who had lost, in paying the customary forfeit of drawing the peg from the ground with their teeth.

1853 *Daily Zanesville Courier* (OH) 12 Jan [2]/3 (newspaper-archive.com), Mr. Hatch was over to Mad Fisk's grocery, and was playing stick-knife with the gentlemanly proprietor, on the counter. **1864** *Harper's New Mth. Mag.* 29.328 **MA**, Suddenly her nervous walk was stopped by the apparition of a boy apparently playing "stick-knife" in the grass just at her side. He was making wonderful evolutions in the air at each turn of the knife. **1871** Alcott *Little Men* 94 **MA**, Dan . . proposed that they should play stick-knife. **1957** *Sat. Eve. Post Letters* **wMA** (as of c1920), *Stick-knife*—Two played. A small circular piece of ground was softened up and a routine of throws with a one bladed pen knife followed. **1966–69** *DARE* (Qu. EE5, *Games where you try to make a jackknife stick in the ground*) Infs **ME**5, **MA**1, 11, 58, **RI**15, 17, Stick-knife; **MA**5, Stick-a-knife. [**1969** Opie–Opie *Children's Games* 223, Our English correspondents recall playing the game with a sequence of up to eighteen tossings. . . They knew it . . as 'Stick Knife' or 'Stickie Knife'.] **1982** *Greenfield Recorder* (MA) 22 Apr sec A 4, "Stick-a-Knife" was a spring game. It required only a jackknife and a grassy plot. The large blade was opened, then the player put it in every possible position on the one hand, gave it a carefully studied flip that made the blade stand up in the ground. Each position counted for a certain sum . . the highest scorer won.

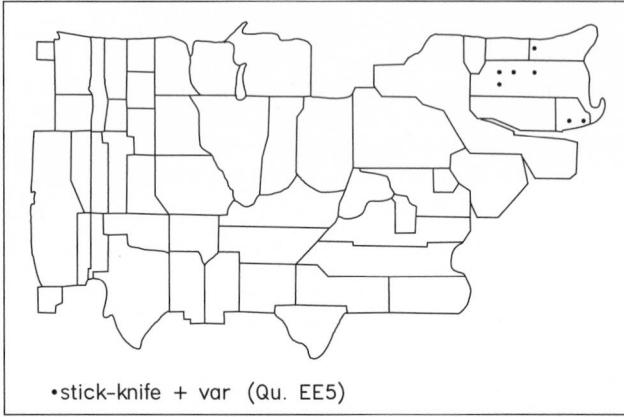

•stick-knife + var (Qu. EE5)

stickleaf n [See quot 1915]

A chiefly western herbaceous plant of the genus *Mentzelia*. Also called **blazing star 4**. For other names of var spp see **candleflower 1, chalk rose, chicken thief, cowboy lily 1, evening star 1, gumbo lily 1, gunebo ~, Mohave comet, moonflower 4, morning star 2, poor man's patches, prairie lily 2, sand ~ 3, scoria ~, sticktight 1**.

1902 Mackenzie *Manual Flora Jackson Co.* 136 **MO**, *M[entzelia] oligosperma*. . . Stick Leaf. **1915** (1926) Armstrong–Thornber *Western Wild Flowers* 300, There are many kinds of Mentzelia, all western. . . The barbed hairs which clothe the stems and leaves make the plant stick to whatever it touches, . . hence the common name Stick-leaf. **1936** McDougall–Baggley *Plants of Yellowstone* 88, *Mentzelia*. . . The genus is commonly known as *stickleaf*. **1961** Wills–Irwin *Flowers TX* 158, Stick-leaf—*Mentzelia nuda*. . has leaves which feel sandpapery to the touch and which become firmly attached to the clothes of those who brush against them. **1967** *DARE* FW Addit **OR**12, Blazing star. . . Stickleaf, locally sand lily. **1975** Zwinger *Run River* 209 **UT**, At the foot of the cliff, minute desert annuals—stickleaf, gilia, camissonia— . . are all a hand width apart and only an inch or so high. **2003** *Assoc. Press State & Local Wire* 12 July (Internet) **UT**, The 20,000-acre Fisher Towers unit of twisted canyons, described by a BLM wilderness inventory as home to bighorn sheep, peregrine falcon and such rare plants as Schultz stickleaf, a blazing yellow star.

stickleback n

Std: a fish of the family Gasterosteidae. For other names of var spp see **needlefish 4, pinfish 3, salmon-killer, thornback 2**.

stickle burr, stickler See **sticker 1**

stick me intj Cf **stick in** v phr

In marble play: see quot 1955.

1890 *DN* 1.66 **KY**, *Stick me*. Put a marble in the ring for me. **1955** *PADS* 23.31 **cwTN, cwAL**, *Stick me*. . . A call made by a player without

marbles requesting another to lend or give him a marble so that he may be eligible to play.

stick-me-tight See **sticktight 1**

stick-nest rat See **stick rat**

stick on v phr [PaGer *aaschtecke* (Ger *anstecken*) to kindle] **PaGer area** Cf **make on 3**, *DS* Y41a, b

To light (a lamp); to turn on (a light).

1908 *German Amer. Annals* 10.44 **sePA**, Stick the light on. (Rare.) Enkindle; light. "Get the lamp and stick the light on." . . fr. Pa. Ger. idiom; also Ger. **1916** *DN* 4.339 **PA**, Stick. . . In stick the light on, light the lamp. **1997** in 1999 Millersville Univ. Center for PA Ger. Studies *Jrl.* Fall 23, Stick the light on. I will have to _____ the light on, because I can't see anything . . [4 of 40 infs] *stick*. **2003** *DARE* File **nwIN** (as of c1969) [Amish], Stick the light on.

stick pin See **sticking pin**

stick rack See **stick n 1**

stick rat n Also *stick-nest rat*

A **wood rat** (here: *Neotoma floridana floridana*).

1924 in 1927 Boston Soc. Nat. Hist. *Proc.* 38.303 **seGA**, In the den were the mother Weasel and three young ones . . ; also three [dead] rats that are known here as Stick Rats [Harper: *Neotoma*] and live mostly in the river swamp. **1927** *Ibid* 356, *Neotoma floridana floridana*. . . The Lees and others of Billy's Island give it the appropriate name of 'Stick-nest Rat.' **1969** *DARE* Tape **GA**51, [FW:] What kind of rat is that? [Inf:] They used to call him the stick rat. . . He'd tote sticks and build a pile of trash as big as a gator's nest. . . He'd have places underground, some old log or stump, and he'll go under all that and go in one place and have another place he'll come out, and he builds nestes out of sticks. Big rat, nearly as big as a cat squirrel.

stick relievo See **stickery-leivo**

sticks n

1 See **stealing sticks**.

2 See **stick n 4**.

stickseed n

1 Either of two closely related plants:

a A plant of the genus *Hackelia*, esp *H. virginiana*; the seed of this plant. For other names of var spp see **beggar's lice 1, beggar ticks 4, devil's tick, dysentery weed 2, forget-me-not 1b, sheep burr, soldier B2, sticktight 1, stickweed b(4), tickweed 6**

1843 Torrey *Flora NY* 2.90, Echinospermum Virginicum [=*Hackelia virginiana*] . . *Broad-leaved Stickseed*. **1873** MO State Entomol. *Annual Rept.* 52, Mr. J.D. Putnam, of Davenport, Iowa . . reports having found the [potato beetle] larvae on Stickseed (*Echinospermum strictum*), common Pigweed [etc]. **1931** Harned *Wild Flowers Alleghanies* 411, Virginia Stickseed (*Lappula* [=*Hackelia*] *virginiana*). **2003** (acc) U.S. Dept. Ag. *Plants Database* (Internet), *Hackelia brevicaula*. . . Poison Canyon stickseed.

b A plant of the genus *Lappula*; the seed of this plant. For other names of var spp see **beggar's lice 1, beggar ticks 4, beggarweed 2, burr forget-me-not, sticktight 1, stickweed b(4), tickseed 4**

1843 Torrey *Flora NY* 2.90, Echinospermum Lappula [=*Lappula squarrosa*] . . *Narrow-leaved Stickseed*. . . Prickles of the fruit barbed. **1848** Gray *Manual of Botany* 339, *E[chinospermum] Lappula*. . . nutlets each with a double row of prickles at the margins. . . A homely weed. **1908** *Bot. Gaz.* 46.97, *Lappula texana*, the hairy stick-seed. . . is an annual and very fertile. **1915** (1926) Armstrong–Thornber *Western Wild Flowers* 422, There are many kinds of Lappula . . [characterized by] nutlets armed with barbed prickles, forming burs, giving the common name, Stickseed. **1968** *DARE* FW Addit **CO**7A, Wild forget-me-not. . . also called stickseed—*Lappula occidentalis*. **2003** (acc) U.S. Dept. Ag. *Plants Database* (Internet), *Lappula occidentalis*. . . flatspine stickseed.

2 =**beggar ticks 1**.

1876 Hobbs *Bot. Hdbk.* 112, Stickseed, Beggars' tick, Bidens frondosa. **1914** Georgia *Manual Weeds* 475, Swamp Beggar-ticks. . . *Bidens connata*. . . Purple-stemmed Stickseed, Harvest Lice.

3 An agrimony, usu *Agrimonia eupatoria*. Cf **beggar ticks 3**

1893 *Jrl. Amer. Folkl.* 6.141 **WV**, *Agrimonia Eupatoria*, stick seed;

beggar's ticks.   **1910** Graves *Flowering Plants* 240 **CT,** Agrimonia gryposepala. . . Stickseed. Cocklebur. Beggar-ticks.

4 =hound's-tongue 1.

   1894 *Jrl. Amer. Folkl.* 7.95 **WV,** *Cynoglossum,* sp., stick-seed, dog-bur, wool-mat.

5 =tickseed 1. [See quot]

   1903 KS Acad. Sci. *Trans.* 18.196, Coreopsis tinctoria. Stickseed. Middle and western Kansas. Expectorant, tonic.   **1931** Clute *Common Plants* 102, The tick-seed *(Coreopsis)* has a striking likeness to a tick, though people unacquainted with this resemblance often call it stickseed and imagine the name refers to the way in which the fruits cling to one's clothing.

sticktail n

=ruddy duck.

   1844 Giraud *Birds Long Is.* 394, Duck, stick-tail.   **1926** (1986) Phillips *Nat. Hist. Ducks* 4.159, Ruddy Duck. . . Vernacular Names. . . Heavy-tail, Stick-tail, Spine-tail [etc].

sticktight n

1 also pl; also *stick-me-tight, sticky-tight:* Any of var plants having clinging seeds, such as **beggar ticks 1, cockleburr 1,** a **hound's-tongue 1, stickleaf,** a **stickseed 1,** or a **sanicle 1;** the seed of such a plant.   **scattered, but chiefly Inland Nth, W Midl** See Map Cf **prickly tight**

   1853 NY State Museum *Catalogue Cabinet Nat. Hist.* 23, Bidens frondosa, *Common Bur-marigold,* or *Sticktight.*   **1863** *Rural Affairs* 3.88, Bur Marigold, Stick-tight, or Spanish Needles, *(Bidens frondosa)*—The seeds of this plant . . adhere when ripe to clothing and the coats of animals.   **1894** *Jrl. Amer. Folkl.* 7.95 **IN,** *Cynoglossum officinale.* . . stick-tights. *Ibid* **IN,** *Echinospermum Virginicum,* stick-tights. *Ibid* **MN,** *Echinospermum . . Virginicum* [=*Hackelia virginiana*] . . stick-tight. *Ibid* **MN,** *E[chinospermum] Redowskii,* Lehm., var. *occidentale,* Watson [=*Lappula occidentalis*], stick-tight.   **1897** IN Dept. Geol. & Nat. Resources *Rept. for 1896* 670, *L[appula] virginiana* [=*Hackelia v.*] . . Beggar's Lice. Stickseed. Sticktight.   **1932** Rydberg *Flora Prairies* 666, *Lappula* [spp] . . Stickseed, Burseed, Stick-tight, Beggar-ticks.   **1937** U.S. Forest Serv. *Range Plant Hdbk.* W101, Stickseeds, also known as burseeds, sticktights, and beggarticks, thus named because the burlike nutlets cling to clothing and the fur of animals.   **1940** *Amer. Midland Naturalist* 23.547 **CA,** *Hackelia californica.* . . Stick-Tight.   **1950** *WELS* **WI** *(Small, flat weed seeds with two prongs that cling to clothing)* 32 Infs, Sticktight; 2 Infs, Stick-me-tight; *(Other weed seeds that cling to clothing)* 8 Infs, Sticktight.   **1951** Voss–Eifert *IL Wild Flowers* 138, Black Snakeroot (Sanicle. Stick-Tights.) [*Ibid,* Sanicle has small, round, hard seeds covered with short, soft, curving prickles. When any fabric or fur brushes past the sanicle fruits they immediately are separated from the plant and go off.]   **1965–70** *DARE* (Qu. S14, . . *Prickly seeds, small and flat, with two prongs at one end, that cling to clothing)* 139 Infs, **scattered, but chiefly Inland Nth, W Midl,** Sticktight(s); **WA**33, Sticktights—but that's Southern; **KY**85, **NC**80, Sticky-tights; **WA**15, Stick-me-tight; (Qu. S13, . . *A common wild bush with bunches of round, prickly seeds; when they get dry they stick to your clothing)* 68 Infs, **scattered, but chiefly Inland Nth, W Midl,** Sticktight(s); **CA**150, Sticktights—new word to community; **IN**48, **MI**69, **TN**31, 33, 34, 35, 36, **WA**15, Stick-me-tights; (Qu. S15, . . *Weed seeds that cling to clothing)* 19 Infs, **scattered,** Sticktight(s); **WI**50, Sticktights—a general category; **KY**5, Sticky-tights.   **2001** in

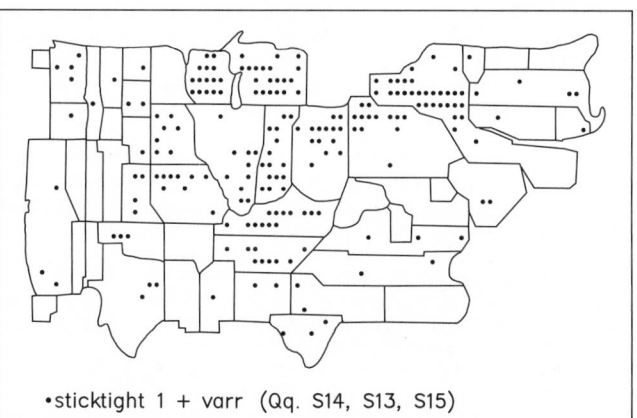

•sticktight 1 + varr (Qq. S14, S13, S15)

2008 *DARE* File—Internet **SC,** But many folks probably wouldn't have a clue until they looked at the fruit . . and suddenly recognized that our little purple bloom is none other than "Beggar-Lice," a plant whose seeds are also called—as we painstakingly pluck them from our pant-legs—"those dad-blamed 'Sticktights'."

2 =clingstone.

   1968 *DARE* (Qu. I52, *The kind of a peach where the hard center is tight to the flesh)* Inf **IN**3, Sticktight.

3 also *sticky-tight:* A tagalong; one who clings to another. Cf **sticking plaster**

   1950 *WELS (Someone who joins you or your group without being asked, and won't leave . . "He's an awful _____.")* 3 Infs, **WI,** Sticktight.   **1965–70** *DARE* (Qu. II18) 10 Infs, **scattered,** Sticktight; **NC**79, Sticky-tight. [8 of 11 Infs female]   **2005** *DARE* File—Internet **GA,** She's been a "stick-tight" today. She sat with me at the 8:30 service snuggling right up under my arm.

4 =bay bed. Cf tick tight

   1983 *MJLF* 9.1.57 **ceKY** (as of 1956), *Stick tight . .* a bay bed.

stick-up n

1 An **oyster B1;** see quot.

   1881 Ingersoll *Oyster-Industry* 249 **NJ,** *Stickup*—A long, thin oyster, growing in mud, etc. (Dennis creek, New Jersey.)   **1894** *DN* 1.334 **NJ,** *Stickup:* a long, thin oyster; so called in Cape May from the fact that it "stickups," as oystermen say, in the mud.

2 also *stick-in:* Mumblety-peg.

   1968–69 *DARE* (Qu. EE5, *Games where you try to make a jackknife stick in the ground)* Infs **LA**34, **NY**205, Stick-up.   **1975** Ferretti *Gt. Amer. Book Sidewalk Games* 162, Mumblety-Peg is also called *Stick In.*

stick-up onion n

=green onion 1.

   1986 Pederson *LAGS Concordance,* 1 inf, **ceTX,** Stick-up onions—used to call green onions this.

stick wagon n chiefly PA, MD Cf road wagon, stick gig
See quot 1908.

   1890 *Daily News* (Frederick MD) 19 Mar [2]/6 (newspaper-archive.com), 3 buggies, 1 good falling top, 1 phaeton, 1 stick wagon or buggy.   **1891** *Herald–Despatch* (Decatur IL) 28 Mar 1/5, [Advt:] The company . . have now in the course of construction a light stick wagon for W.C. Fearn to be finished in natural wood colors.   **1908** *German Amer. Annals* 10.45 **sePA,** *Stick-wagon* or *Road-wagon.* Carriage, no top, for two persons; open box. "We drove over in a stick wagon."   **1908** *Star & Sentinel* (Gettysburg PA) 8 July [3]/1 (newspaper-archive.com), *Horse Ran off; Buggy Upset.* A horse attached to a stick wagon . . became unmanagable [sic] . . and ran away.   **1929** *News* (Frederick MD) 27 July 1/2, A Model T Ford . . crashed into a horse and stick wagon.   **1948** *Ibid* 29 Sept 11/4, [Advt:] Stick wagon, horse collars, 2 five-gallon cans of auto oil.   **1963** in 2003 *DARE* File—Internet **MD** (as of 1898), When Stanley was twenty-one years old, he was given a new buggy and his very own horse. The going was a little easier, and the old stick wagon and spring-wagon were retired for Sunday at least.   **1969** *DARE* (Qu. N41b, *Horse-drawn vehicles to carry heavy loads)* Inf **WV**17, Stick wagon—board side, no top; two seats, four people.

stickweed n esp sAppalachians
Any of var plants noted for their clinging seeds or sticklike stems, as:

a also *stickerweed:* Used generically or in contexts that do not allow firm identification; also fig.

   1705 Beverley *Hist. VA* 1.15, They [=Indians] have no Salt among them, but for seasoning, use the Ashes of Hiccory, Stickweed, or some other Wood or Plant affording a Salt ash.   **1809** Weems *Life George Washington* 4, He will . . stand forth confessed in native stickweed sterility and worthlessness.   **1899** (1912) Green *VA Folk-Speech* 417, *Stickweed.* . . A tall, straight weed that is hard and looks like a stick when it is dry.   **1931** *AmSp* 7.93 **eKY,** The fence-corners were a wonderful yellow with either goldenrod or stick-weeds in bloom.   **1940** (1978) Still *River of Earth* 174 **eKY,** Mother brought out an armload of yellowrods, stickweed blooms, and farewell-summer Euly had stuck around in fruit jars.   **1965–70** *DARE* (Qu. S21, . . *Weeds . . that are a trouble in gardens and fields)* Infs **VA**21, 26, Stickweed; **MD**36, Stickweed—straight, hard stem, grows a yard high; **NC**35, Stickweed—like artichoke weed; **NC**81, Stickweed—grows straight up, roots send up weeds; **NC**67, Stickweeds; (Qu. S26a, . . *Wildflowers. . . Roadside flowers)* Inf **KY**40,

Stickweed; (Qu. S26b, *Wildflowers that grow in water or wet places*) Inf **VA**43, Stickweed; (Qu. S26d, *Wildflowers that grow in meadows; not asked in early QRs*) Infs **KY**40, **TN**13, Stickweed. **1997** *Montgomery Coll.* **wNC, eTN,** Stickerweed. . . any plant with points or stickers, same as stickweed.

b Spec:

(1) A **crownbeard.**

1739 (1946) Gronovius *Flora Virginica* 102, *Verbesina floribus corymbosis, foliis lanceolatis petiolatis.* [=Verbesina with corymbose flowers and lanceolate, petiolate leaves.] . . White Stickweed. **1870** *Amer. Naturalist* 4.400 **sAppalachians,** The universal "stick-weed" (*Actinomeris squamosa* [sic for *squarrosa;* =*Verbesina alternifolia*]) of the Great Valley was rare. **1894** *Jrl. Amer. Folkl.* 7.90 **WV,** *Actinomeris squarrosa* [=*Verbesina alternifolia*]. . . wing-stem, stickweed. **2003** (acc) VA Polytechnic *Weed Identification Guide* (Internet), Stickweed or Yellow Crownbeard: *Verbesina occidentalis.* . . Stems usually persist throughout the winter, which is more than likely where this weed gets one of its common names.

(2) An aster; see quots.

1892 *Science* 19.356, Stickweed, White Devil, *Aster lateriflorus* [=*Symphyotrichum lateriflorum*]. **1894** *Jrl. Amer. Folkl.* 7.91 **WV,** *Aster cordifolius* . . var. *laevigatus* [=*Symphyotrichum lowrieanum*], Blue Devil, stick-weed [etc]. *Ibid, Aster diffusus* . . var. *hirsuticaulis* [=*Symphyotrichum lateriflorum* var. *hirsuticaule*] . . Old Virginia stickweed [etc]. **1996–97** in 2004 Montgomery–Hall *Dict. Smoky Mt. Engl.* 569 **wNC, eTN,** Stickweed . . fall-blooming purple aster . . an aster, tall in the form of a stick, having the texture of wood, used to start a fire.

(3) =**gum succory.**

1895 U.S. Dept. Ag. *Farmers' Bulletin* 28.25, Chondrilla, gum succory, skeleton weed, stickweed . . West Virginia to Maryland.

(4) A **stickseed 1.**

1862 IN State Geologist *Rept. Geol. Reconnoissance IN* 64, A considerable amount of smart weed, rag weed, stick weed, (Echinospermum lappula,) . . indicate their growth by a cool, moist soil. **1897** *Jrl. Amer. Folkl.* 10.51 **CA,** *Echinospermum floribundum* [=*Hackelia floribunda*] . . stick weed. **1930** OK Univ. Biol. Surv. *Pub.* 2.77, *Lappula redowskii* . . var. *occidentalis* [=*Lappula occidentalis*]. . . Hairy Stickweed. **1938** *Amer. Midland Naturalist* 19.359 **CA,** *Hackelia Cusickii.* . . Cusick Stickweed. Always under juniper trees. The flowers resemble Forget-me-not. **1953** *Ibid* 50.481 **nMN,** Ground cover was sparse and mostly of weedy herb such as . . stickweed (*Lappula* sp.) [etc].

(5) A **ragweed 2.**

1799 *Med. Repository* 3.213 **PA,** It feeds upon the prunella vulgaris, or self-heal, and ambrosia trifida, or stick weed. **1900** Lyons *Plant Names* 27, *A[mbrosia] artemisiaefolia.* . . Stick-weed [etc].

(6) also *stickerweed:* =**beggar ticks 1.**

1950 *WELS* (*Small, flat weed seeds with two prongs that cling to clothing*) 1 Inf, **WI,** Stickweed, devil's clothespin. **1970** *DARE* (Qu. S14, . . *Prickly seeds, small and flat, with two prongs at one end, that cling to clothing*) Inf **KY**71, Stickweed—same as sticktights. **1976** Garber *Mountain-ese* 15 **sAppalachians,** Chigger-weed . . stickweed. **1996–97** in 2004 Montgomery–Hall *Dict. Smoky Mt. Engl.* 569 **wNC, eTN,** *Stickerweed* . . same as *beggar lice* or *tick clover.*

(7) A **mullein.**

1969 *DARE* (Qu. S20, *A common weed that grows on open hillsides: It has velvety green leaves close to the ground, and a tall stalk with small yellow flowers on a spike at the top*) Infs **KY**18, 28, Stickweed. [*DARE* Ed: These Infs may refer instead to other senses.]

(8) A **Jerusalem oak 1** (here: *Chenopodium ambrosioides*). Cf **stinkweed 2**

1971 Krochmal *Appalachia Med. Plants* 86, *Chenopodium ambrosioides.* . . Common Names . . stickweed, stinking weed [etc]. **1974** (1977) Coon *Useful Plants* 95, Jerusalem tea . . stick weed, stinking weed [etc]. **1986** Pederson *LAGS Concordance,* 2 infs, **AL, TN,** Stickweed; 1 inf, **TN,** Stickweed or stinkweed. [*DARE* Ed: Some of these infs may refer instead to other senses above.]

stick worm n

1 =**stick bait.**

1890 *Forest & Stream* 27 Nov 376 **wNC,** About two weeks after my arrival at the fishing grounds, the stick worm became plentiful and then we gave up the red worm. . . The stick worm is either white or light lemon-color; it is about three-fourths of an inch in length. **1932** *Daily News* (Huntingdon PA) 20 May 12/5, On examining the stomach of a

brown trout . . Boyden found two stickworms, and remnants of the protective covering, which they had formed. **1948** *N. Adams Transcript* (MA) 22 Apr 10/3, "Ziggy" reports that all of the trout taken were feeding on "stick worms." **1960** *Chicago Tribune* (IL) 24 Apr sec D 7/6, "Stick worms," or caddis fly nymphs, are . . deadly on trout. Yet I've never seen them used in the midwest even tho the streams here are alive with them. **2008** *DARE* File—Internet **WV,** I used small red worms, mud bugs (dragonfly nymphs), golden rod grubs (deer fly larva) and stick worms (not sure just what these are but check it [sic] the eddies along a stream or a slack water area when you see a small stick floating pick it up and see if you find a small green color worm inside).

2 The larva of a geometrid moth.

1890 Packard *Insects* 476, *Eugonia alniaria.* . . The caterpillar is called the stick worm from its habit of holding itself out erect like a piece of twig, to which it bears a close resemblance. **1896** *Harper's New Mth. Mag.* 93.603, The "stick-worm" is one of the most interesting, because he seems always to mimic the leaf-stalk of the tree on which he is. . . Moreover, he always on the least alarm stands out stiffly from the branch at the exact angle at which its leaves grow. **1966–69** *DARE* (Qu. R9a, *An insect from two to four inches long that lives in bushes and looks like a dead twig*) Inf **MI**9, I think you call them stick worm; **NY**219, Stick worm. **2006** in 2008 *DARE* File—Internet **wNC,** And this evening, a "stick worm" just lowered itself from the trees right onto my husband's arm. Looks exactly like a stick.

sticky n

1 Any of var baked goods with a sugary coating or filling; see quots. **esp Sth, S Midl**

c1885 in 1981 Woodward *Mary Chesnut's Civil War* 763 **NC** (as of 1865), Stickies are, as their names denote, cakes which are sticky with sugar—maybe molasses. **1916** *DN* 4.345 **cwFL,** *Sticky.* . . A kind of biscuit made by cooling out the dough large and thin, drawing up the corners over an inclosed bit of butter and sugar, or of jelly, and then baking. **1941** Writers' Program *Guide SC* 155, *Stickies.* . . Roll dough thin. Cut in 12 squares (about 3½ inches). Divide the butter into 12 parts, place on each square, and pour the sugar over. Then fold corners of dough to center. Press edges closely and place in pan just allowing to touch each other. Bake in fairly hot oven. **1958** *PADS* 29.16 **TN,** *Sticky, stickies:* "Cold biscuits split in two, buttered, and molasses poured over them, then put in a hot oven." **2003** *DARE* File—Internet, [Menu item from a restaurant chain located primarily in **swPA, neOH:**] Grilled Stickies—An Eat'n Park tradition. Our sweet'n cinnamon loaf, sliced and grilled in butter and topped with honey sauce.

2 See quot 1913.

1913 *DN* 4.28 **NW,** *Sticky.* . . A clayey mud, formed from a volcanic cinder deposit, that gathers like wet snow, only worse, and forms tenacious lumps of great size on wagon wheels and feet. . . "We got covered with sticky and could hardly walk at all." **1967** *DARE* (Qu. C31, . . *Heavy, sticky soil*) Inf **OR**2, Sticky.

sticky bun n

1 A bun or roll with a sugary coating; esp, also *Dutch sticky bun, Philadelphia sticky (cinnamon) bun, sticky cinnamon bun:* a sweet roll with a filling usu including butter, sugar, cinnamon, and currants or nuts. **orig esp NEast; now more widespread**

1900 Hurd *Bennett Twins* 107 **NYC,** Her foot was on the top step when there came a fusillade of fruit, hard rolls, and sticky buns, sent spinning toward her with triumphant shouts. **1906** *Smith College Mth.* 14.84 **cwMA,** Fancy going down town for sticky buns now! **1918** *Janesville Daily Gaz.* (WI) 30 Nov 8/7, Oddsen Ends . . jumped up on the counter, only mashing seven sticky cinnamon buns. **1939** *Gettysburg Times* (PA) 13 Nov 3/4, [Advt:] Philadelphia Sticky Buns 16c. **1940** *San Antonio Sun. Light* (TX) 1 Sept mag sec [*Amer. Weekly*] 16/2, When Mrs. H.E. Dail, Newport, N.C., had a hankering for old-fashioned Philadelphia Sticky Cinnamon Buns . . , readers all over the country immediately responded with cinnamon bun recipes. **1948** Hutchison *PA Du. Cook Book* 27, *Sticky Buns.* [Recipe includes yeast, lukewarm water, lukewarm milk, sugar, salt, flour, butter, brown sugar, raisins, currants, cinnamon.] **1964** Amer. Heritage *Cookbook* 436, *Philadelphia Sticky Buns*—In the nineteenth century, Sticky Buns—a Philadelphia specialty—were sold fresh every day and were eaten at breakfast, teatime, and dinner. **c1965** Randle *Cookbooks* (Ask Neighbor) 33 **neOH,** *Dutch Sticky Buns.* **1966–68** *DARE* (Qu. H32, . . *Fancy rolls and pastries*) Infs **PA**13, 60, 143, 150, 171, Sticky buns; **MI**9, Sticky buns—cinnamon rolls with brown sugar and nuts in bottom of pan; **NY**94, Sticky buns—brown sugar and nuts, very sticky. **1995** *Denver Post* (CO) 20

July food sec 1 (Internet), A chef friend in Aspen shared this tremendous recipe for homemade sticky buns. It's rolled sweet yeast dough baked over brown-sugar caramel. When the sticky buns are cooked, you invert the pan and let the caramel soak in. **1999** Mariani *Encycl. Amer. Food & Drink* 310, *Sticky bun*. . . Although they are popular throughout the United States, they are often associated with Philadelphia and sometimes called "Philadelphia sticky buns," although in Philadelphia itself, they are called "cinnamon buns." **2004** *San Francisco Examiner* (CA) 16 May sports sec 3 (Internet), A favorite item she and Coughlin enjoy are "sticky buns" from one Berkeley coffee shop.

2 also *old sticky bun:* A **mushroom B1** (here: *Suillus granulatus*).

1980 Marteka *Mushrooms* 144, The granulated bolete *(Suillus granulatus)* has many common names, including butterball and old sticky bun. The latter name was appended to this mushroom because of the sticky coating of its cap. *Ibid* 155, *Granulated Bolete.* . . sticky bun.

sticky bush   See **sticker 1**

sticky cinnamon bun   See **sticky bun 1**

sticky-frog   See **stick-frog**

sticky-handed adj
Larcenous, sticky-fingered.
   1939 *AmSp* 14.92 **eTN,** *Sticky-handed.* Thieving. 'He's sticky handed.' **c1950** *Halpert Coll.* 60 **wKY, nwTN,** To be sticky-handed = describing a thief: "He's sticky-handed." **1965–70** *DARE* (Qu. V6, . . *Words . . for a thief*) Inf **FL**51, Sticky-handed person; [**FL**22, Sticky-hands; (Qu. JJ19, *If somebody has dishonest intentions, or is up to no good . .* "*I think he's got _____.*") Inf **IL**44, Sticky hands]. **2002** *Washington Post* (DC) 13 Mar sec D 1, For every robed charlatan, fringe radical or sticky-handed promoter . . there were far more social workers, religious leaders, businessmen and lawyers.

sticky-heads n
=**gum plant 1.**
   1933 Small *Manual SE Flora* 1337, *Grindelia* [spp]. . . Sticky-heads. **1961** Smith *MI Wildflowers* 385, Sticky-heads. . . *Grindelia squarrosa.* . . The Indians used the species medicinally. They ground the seeds to make a flavoring and used the resin to hold women's hair in place.

sticky laurel n   [See quot 1937]
A **snowbrush 1** (here: *Ceanothus velutinus*).
   1906 U.S. Natl. Museum *Contrib. Herbarium* 11.51 **WA,** Sticky laurel *(Ceanothus velutinus)* and thimbleberry *(Rubus parciflorus),* form dense thickets. **1937** U.S. Forest Serv. *Range Plant Hdbk.* B47, Snowbrush refers to the abundant fluffy masses of white flowers; . . "sticky laurel" to the sticky and rather glossy character of the upper surface of the leathery leaves. **1966** *DARE* Wildfl QR Pl.126 Inf **WA**10, Mountain balm—buckbrush if pink; sticky laurel or mountain balm if white. **2007** in 2008 *DARE* File—Internet **ID,** We climb through an open area, pushing through thick shrubs with globs of small white fragrant flowers (sticky laurel aka mountain balm? mallow leaf nine bark?) growing over the trail.

sticky-tight   See **sticktight 1, 3**

‡sticky-wicky n   Cf **wicket**
   1968 *DARE* (Qu. EE18, *Games in which the players set up a stone, a tin can, or something similar, and then try to knock it down*) Inf **NJ**28, Sticky-wicky—with stick.

stid n   See **bedstead**

stid adv   See **instead**

stidd(i)er   See **instead**

stid(d)y   See **steady A1**

stiffback (perch) n   Also *stiff-backed perch*   **VA**
=**white perch 1.**
   1928 *Ind. Notes & Monogr.* 1.367 **eVA,** At Pamunkey the fish-hunter goes down to one of the ponds or tidal pools . . where he finds the "cow fish" or "stiff-backed perch" guarding their young so the other fish will not eat them. **1970** *DARE* (Qu. P14, . . *Commercial fishing . . what do the fishermen go out after?*) Inf **VA**75, Stiffback. **2001** *DARE* File—Internet **VA,** The white perch or "stiffback" is the next species to start a spawning run. **2003** *Ibid* **seVA,** Caught 20 largemouth, a small pickeral [sic], and a stiffback perch. (White perch).

stiff jacks   See **tough jack**

stiff-starch n   Also *stitch starch*   **Sth, TX**
A game in which two children lock hands, lean back, and spin around as fast as possible; hence v *stiff-starch* to play this game.
   1909 *DN* 3.376 **eAL, wGA,** *Stiff-starch.* . . A children's game. **1948** Harris *Hearthstones* 103 **neNC,** Stiff-starch, the dizzy game in which two playmates whirled on their toes round and round together, had been the nearest to dancing that Henrietta had known. **1960** Williams *Walk Egypt* 89 **GA,** There were young'uns playing Fox-and-Goose and Stiff-Starch. **1969** *DARE* (Qu. EE33, . . *Outdoor games . . that children play*) Inf **TX**61, Stiff starch. **2003** *DARE* File—Internet **cnTX** (as of 1936), In those days we played Red Rover, May I, Hully Gull, Anti-Over, Stiff Starch . . Hoop and Tee, and Hide and Seek. **2004** *NADS Letters* **cnTX,** Stiff starch—we played this in north central Texas when I was a child. . . Stiff starch is played by partners (usually girls). One girl asks, "Wanta play stiff starch?" They then curl their fingers inside the partners' fingers . . with thumbs on the outside. Lean back while stepping almost in place, but gradually turning in a circle with arms stretched out and stiff. The turning is faster and faster until the grip is lost and partners fall, giggling, to the grass. **2005** *Ibid* **ceGA** (as of c1945), Stiff starch is a children's game that I played in Augusta, Georgia, as a girl. . . The way it is played is: 2 children (usually girls) stand facing each other and with one girl's hands facing upward and the other girls hands facing downward they grasp their fingers together. They lean backward hard using each other as an anchor and go around in a circle using short scuffling steps. They go faster, and faster, and faster until they get dizzy or one falls out of the game. My sister was stiff starching with our cousin and our cousin got dizzy, let go, fell, and broke her arm. **2007** *Ibid* **GA** (as of 1950s), I noticed your reference to "stiff starch". I am from GA and we always called it "stitch starch". It is a game for two played mostly by little girls where they hold hands by the bent fingers only (over and under, one girl's hands on top and one on the bottom), no thumbs, and spin in a circle—leaning back as far as possible—until someone can no longer hold on.

stifftail n
=**ruddy duck.**
   1888 Trumbull *Names of Birds* 112, **PA, NJ, DC, GA,** In the vicinity of Philadelphia, at Somers Point, N.J., to some at Washington, D.C., and at Savannah, Ga., [the ruddy duck is known as] stiff-tail. **1917** (1923) *Birds Amer.* 1.152, Ruddy Duck. . . Other Names. . . Stiff-tail. **1921** LA Dept. of Conserv. *Bulletin* 10.62, Another popular name [for the ruddy duck] is "stiff tail."

stiff-tailed widgeon   See **widgeon 2c**

stifftwig gum n
A **gum elastic** (here: *Sideroxylon lanuginosum*).
   1979 Little *Checklist U.S. Trees* 66, *Bumelia lanuginosa* [=*Sideroxylon lanuginosum*]. . . Other common names . . stifftwig-gum, gum elastic [etc].

stifle n   **ME, MA**   Cf **étouffée, smother** n **1**
A stew usu consisting mostly of meat or fish, potatoes, and onions.
   1832 in 1975 Jones *Amer. Food* 4 **Boston MA,** Eel Stifle. **1903** *DN* 2.301 **Cape Cod MA** (as of a1857), *Stifle.* . . Sliced vegetables cooked in a covered spider. **1914** *DN* 4.155 **Cape Cod MA,** *Potato-stifle—spider-stifle.* . . A species of food composed of sliced potatoes, sliced onions, pork-fat, and water, salted, sometimes peppered, and cooked slowly in a frying-pan, or 'spider.' "We're going to have spider-stifle for dinner." **1934** Harwich Pt. Lib. Assoc. *From Cape Cod* 185, *Cape Cod Stifle.* . . salt pork . . onions . . potatoes, cut up and fried. Cover with water and simmer about an hour in a covered pot. Any left over meats may be added. **1939** Wolcott *Yankee Cook Book* 365, *Stifle.* A Cape Cod name for a meat or fish stew. **1952** Tracy *Coast Cookery* 105 **MA,** *Hallelujah* or Cape Cod Stifle, a stew made of salt pork, onions, and potatoes. **1975** Gould *ME Lingo* 278, *Stifle*—Heard in sections of Maine with certain mid-European folks mixed into the population, *stifle* is a meat and gravy dish not unlike a ragout. . . "We're having a stifle for supper." Women at the meat counter will ask for "meat for a stifle." **2001** in 2008 *DARE* File—Internet **NEng,** Now clam chowder well made is very good, but there are much better chowders—fish (especially when made with cod cheeks); corn, made with fresh corn and its "milk"; and eel stifle. . . All these are made pretty much the way clam chowder is made.

stile n¹ **chiefly Sth, S Midl** *old-fash* Cf **stile block**

A mounting block or platform. Note: This sense derives from the use of a stile, once commonly provided for crossing a fence before a house or public building, as a convenient step from which to mount a horse or vehicle.

[**1878** Eggleston in *Scribner's Mth.* 16.637 **IN,** At last she rode up to the fence of what she was sure must be Gid Kirtley's cabin. . . There was no stile, and no one to help her dismount.] [**1887** *Atlantic Mth.* 60.34 **KY,** Passing the "lot," with its great whitewashed barn and stable, we reached the stile which led to the house-yard, and quickly scrambled up the three outside steps and down the three inside ones. *Ibid* 42, After a leave-taking that all tried to make like an ordinary one, he went to the stile to mount his horse.] **1897** *Harper's New Mth. Mag.* 95.764 **KY,** The old church . . , the saddle-horses hitched to the plank fence, the long stiles, with the country girls dismounting in their long black skirts . . — all helped little by little to draw him back to the faith from which he had started adrift. **1933** in 2005 *DARE* File—Internet **swVA,** I remember so well the military bearing of Col. A.J. May, as he would ride down to his office each morning . . and dismount on the stile. **1974** *Ibid* **swMS,** A stile that was built around one of the fine cedars for the convenience of the ladies to mount and dismount their horses. **1976** *Ibid* **cKS,** [Text of a historical marker:] Hitching Post and Stone Stile used in the early days by ladies when mounting their horse. **1980** *Bittersweet* 8.2.56 **csMO** (as of c1900), The ladies all rode sidesaddle. When they reached the church building, there was a platform built where the lady could dismount. . . The platform was built of two-inch oak boards, two and a half feet high with steps and was called a stile.

stile n² Also sp *style* [Malaprop for *sty*]

1824 (1930) W. Sewall *Diary* 96 **VA,** I came home and built me a hog style. **1846** *Hagers-Town Torch Light* (MD) 6 July [3]/1 (newspaperarchive.com), The raving streams poured their noisy floods into our streets . . bearing on their headlong currents numerous small buildings, located on their banks, hencoops, pig-styles, bridges [etc]. **1903** *Dubuque Telegraph–Herald* (IA) 16 Jan 7/7, [Advt:] Nine room house, large barn and cellar . . , pig styles, etc. **1939** *LANE* Map 110 *(Pig pen; hog house)* 1 inf, **ceCT,** [pɪg staɪəl]; 1 inf, **swME,** [pɪg staˣ⁴l]. **1986** Pederson *LAGS Concordance (Hogs)* 1 inf, **swFL,** Stile = sty? **2003** *DARE* File—Internet, The place looked like a pig-stile. *Ibid,* I mean look @ this place, a true *pig stile.*

stile v [Scots dial *stell* (also *stile*) to put in place, station, set up] *relic* Cf **tile**

To fix something (as a gun) so that it is aimed in a particular direction.

1883 Amer. Philol. Assoc. *Trans.* 14.53 **Sth,** Stile. To stile a gun is to aim it, as a cannon, or to direct a small gun by putting it on supports. **1936** *AmSp* 11.372 **VA,** In the discussion of some unpleasantness in the neighborhood of a church, a certain man was accused of having *stiled* his radio on the church while service was being held. . . Another man, whose hen house had been raided, *stiled* a gun in it. Later, he went in and was shot with the gun which he himself had *stiled.* **1947** Humphreys *Of Me* 40 **seWV** (as of 1870s), *Stile*—to place a gun in the proper position beforehand for game or a burglar.

stile block n Also rarely *styles block* **chiefly Sth, S Midl** Cf **stile** n¹

A block usu of stone serving as or forming part of a stile for crossing a fence; a stile; a mounting block.

1846 *Amer. Whig Rev.* 3.318 **TX,** He was sitting on the stile-blocks of his Rancho. **1863** Hill *Myrtle* 33 **KY,** We stood on the old stile blocks, and your brother Will held the bridle of the little pony I was going to ride away from your home. **1893** in 2004 (acc) Lexis–Nexis Legal Research *State Case Law: TX* (Internet), There were no stile blocks nor hitching posts on either side of said gate. **1894** Maury *Recoll. Virginian* 172 (as of c1862), Nothing was left but the stile blocks, over which old Mr. Brooks had been passing for 40 years. **1922** Baily *June Gold* 173 **NC,** Hitching posts outside a tumbling picket fence, a stile-block where equestrians might alight from "side saddles," and a rude tree-branched shelter for "horsebeasts" . . proved that the Holiness church . . took care of its own. **1923** (1946) Greer-Petrie *Angeline Doin' Society* 4 **csKY,** Any stranger that 'ud so much as set foot on our styles-block atter dark. **1935** *Amer. Prefaces* 1.25, At length I reach the stile-blocks, a name given to the wooden steps that lead up like stairs, over the fence. They were built as a courtesy to my mother and women folks . . so they can climb over the fence without tearing their clothes. **1981** *Bittersweet* 9.1.49 **MO,** Meeting Stanley at dusk at the kennels we crossed some

stile blocks to enter what looked like a city of dogs. **2004** *Hannibal Courier–Post* (MO) 31 Jan (Internet), A long stile block stood where the present church stands for those who came on horseback to get off and on their horses.

still adv

1 followed directly or indirectly by redundant *yet:* Now (or then) as before. **esp Sth, S Midl** Cf **yet** adv, conj **B1a**

1833 *Rural Repository* 10.80 **NY,** Thy father's halls still yet resound / To notes of revelry and mirth. **1848** Tubbee *Sketch of the Life* 64 **MS,** I gradually resigned myself into its [=sleep's] friendly arms, as I still yet listened to the old man's voice. **1911** (1999) Lowery *Life Old Plantation* 45 **SC** (Internet), And yet he can recall the most of them and the image of their person still yet lingers in his memory. **a1922** in 1985 *TN Civil War Veterans* 1.9 [I] still work a little at the business yet when I am able to work. **1957** in 2004 Montgomery–Hall *Dict. Smoky Mt. Engl.* 665 **wNC, eTN,** *Yet.* . . The rocks is still there yet. **1957** Taylor *Back Mt.* 42 **swMO,** Hit was still yit rainin' tother day / When a old feller started acrost the street. **1986** Pederson *LAGS Concordance,* 1 inf, **neAL,** People does still yet = people still do it; 1 inf, **ceTX,** There are a few around here still yet; 1 inf, **seGA,** He's still quite young yet. **2001** *DARE* File **OH,** And then there's the (apparently) redundant form "still yet," used along the Ohio River. A student of mine who uses it natively elicited responses in her hometown of Portsmouth . . Ohio to this sentence: "He still yet owns that old car." Maximum responses in three categories ranged from 20% personal use to 63% denial of personal use but recognition of others' use of it to 90% non-recognition—the last by teenagers. So it's disappearing in this area (I've only heard it a couple of times in Athens).

2 Used at the end of an independent clause: Habitually, regularly, from time to time. [Calque of any of several PaGer sentence advs (see quot 1968), appar based on obs *still* continually, invariably, always] **chiefly PaGer areas**

1882 (1971) Gibbons *PA Dutch* 390, "Mind Ressler? He was in Sprecher's;" or, "Do you remember Ressler? He used to be employed in Sprecher's store." **1886** Amer. Philol. Assoc. *Proc.* 17.xiii **ePA,** "Still" expresses habit. When young Miss Society tells young Miss Accomplishments that she practices her piano lesson in the morning "still," she does not mean to say that she still continues to do so . . but simply that it is her habit to perform that task at that time. **1899** (1912) Green *VA Folk-Speech* 418, Still. . . Constantly; continually; habitually; always; ever. "You go there still." **1908** *German Amer. Annals* 10.45 **sePA,** *Still.* Used at end of sentence to denote customary action. "I see him when I go down street still." . . The word is used of the future with no reference to the past at times. Thus, in engaging a new milkman, one would say, "I want you to stop at my house still," although he had never stopped previously. **1939** Aurand *Quaint Idioms* 27 [PaGer], She used to come here *still,* or *yet,* but now she *don't nomore.* **1948** *AmSp* 23.238 [Engl of PA Germans], 'How do you keep from getting frostbitten?' asked the prospective customer. 'Oh, I get in—still—to get warm,' was the answer. . . [This can] be translated as, 'I seem to be outdoors all day in the cold; *nevertheless* or *still* I manage to get indoors from time to time in order to get warm.' **1968** *Helen Adolf Festschrift* 39 **cePA,** *Still* (Pennsylvania German . . *als, dann un wann, ebmols*) . . [is] very often used redundantly. . . "We go to visit them still" (Pennsylvania German *als*). "She goes over to see them still" (Pennsylvania German *dann un wann, ebmols*). **1982** *Barrick Coll.* **csPA,** *Still*—from time to time. . . "I see him go apast still."

3 in phr *still and yet:* Nevertheless. **chiefly Sth, S Midl** Cf *yet and still* (at **yet** adv, conj **B3**).

1902 Young *Plantation Legends* 229 **AL** [Black], Nummine ef he do be little and puny as a Guinea nigger . . , still and yit you don't know whar'r he ain't got fust-class, molly-glaster hair under dat head-handkercher! **1905** *New Engl. Mag.* 31.598, But still and yet, this crape is all I can do for him, and I'm not going to take it off, jest yet. **1987** Kytle *Voices* 162 **NC** [Black], Still and yet, we couldn't feel sure, and anyhow we liked for somebody to be there in case he roused up. **1998** in 2008 *DARE* File—Internet **VA,** Sometimes a player would quit vamping entirely just to listen closely to someone else. Still and yet, after about an hour, I was banjoed-out. **c2006** *Ibid* **MS** [Black], Some drug dealers dont look like drug dealers they help children and old ladies but still and yet in their heart their still drug dealers. **2007** in 2008 (acc) Lexis–Nexis Legal Research *State Case Law: AR* (Internet), Still and yet, she maintains that she loves her son and received extended visitation with him until she refused to take a drug test.

still v¹ See **steal**

still n, v² See **steel**

still and yet See **still** adv **3**

still beer n chiefly sAppalachians
=**beer** n **1.**

  1816 Niles' Weekly Reg. 11.132, Gillespie's improved Steam Still. . . It is divided into two parts. In the lower is placed the fermented liquor (still beer). **1840** Spirit of Times 10.109 **SC,** He . . loved his still beer and potatoes (with now and then a leetle brandy) far better than the military. **1881** Atkinson After Moonshiners 14 **Sth,** He himself could loaf around his still, drink "still beer" and "moonshine," and have forty cents of surplusage to lay by. **1885** Harper's New Mth. Mag. 71.51, Innumerable chicherias—shops in which is made and sold chicha, a cheap but not unwholesome drink of fermented corn, and similar to the "still beer" of whiskey manufacturers—are found. **1940** Hall Coll. **wNC, eTN,** Still beer. . . Same as beer, corn beer. **1949** AmSp 24.8 [Argot of the moonshiner], Beer. Also still beer. . . Fermenting mash, either grain or sugar. **1967** DARE Tape **TN**9, [Inf:] Use one sixty-gallon oak barrel, one bushel of cornmeal to twenty pound of sugar. Fill barrel with warm water for mash or still beer. **a1975** Lunsford It Used to Be 80 **wNC,** Then there's still beer. Just before they get ready to "mash in," they get some of that beer, sometimes drink it. **1985** Wilkinson Moonshine 21 **neNC,** Initially, the mash tastes sweet and is sticky; fermented, it is tangy and sour. While turning, it has a two- or three-inch snowy collar, and when ready it is clear on top and the color of dark beer. It is called still beer, or meal beer, or meal mammy.

stiller See **steel**

still hill See **hill** n **6**

still pond (no more moving) n Also still water; for addit varr see quots

  Any of var children's games in which players must stop moving at a predetermined call; also used as a call in such a game; also fig.

  1881 Goldsmith Peace Pelican 294, Groups of children . . strolled up and down . . occasionally lessening in numbers as the enthusiastic glee in the library over "Still Pond no Moving," grew wilder. **1883** Newell Games & Songs 163, In Cincinnati the game [=blindman's buff] is also played in a dark room, without bandaging the eyes. . . Another variety, also commonly played without blindfolding, goes by the name of "Still Pond," or "Still Palm." The child who is "it," counting up to ten, says [\"]Still proving,/ No moving." . . The catcher must guess by the touch the name of his captive. **1889** in 2008 DARE File—Internet **MD,** Madeline came over and we played still pond. **1909** (1923) Bancroft Games 189, Still Pond; No More Moving! (Still water, still water, stop!) **1917** Canfield Understood Betsy 194 **VT,** During recess . . they were playing still-pond-no-more-moving on the playground. **1931** Time 25 May 18, Mr Baruch learned from experience all about war profiteering. To eradicate it he proposed a Federal command of still-pond-no-more-moving. **1949** MacCracken Family Gramercy Park 88 **NYC,** We played "Still pond no more moving" with the nurses. . . You played blindfold and caught them, but it was very hard to tell which was which . . so you had to make them giggle or something. **1950** WELS (Other outdoor games . . played during your childhood) 1 Inf, **seWI,** Still water. **1950** WELS Suppl. **seWI,** Still Pond—players not blindfolded—people trying to get from one goal to another, and when "Still pond" was said they had to lie flat. **1957** Sat. Eve. Post Letters **cwNY** (as of c1900), One-two-three and so on to ten. . . Stillwater!! Then you had to stand absolutely still (unless the person who was it turned his or her head and while turned you might gain a few steps in order to hide.) If you got home free—and the "It" went hunting, we could call "Onion-onion" or "Tobacco"—words that obviously meant come or go back! **1967** DARE (Qu. EE33, . . Outdoor games . . that children play) Inf **MN**2, Still water—a form of hide-and-seek; all players run to hide except one who is "it"; he counts 1-2-3-4-5. . . still water, then all players must stop; count resumes with stopping until all players are hidden; **SC**5, Stilly pond, stilly water. **1967** DARE Tape **MA**100, Still pond, no more moving. . . Somebody was blindfolded or turned back-to and the other people tried to cover a space, and then you turned round of a sudden and said, "Still pond, no more moving," and of course you'd be caught off balance, and if you had to put your other foot down, why then you were "it."

still-pot n [OED2 1839]

  In moonshining: =**pot** n **2;** also rarely transf: illegally distilled liquor.

  1949 AmSp 24.4 [Argot of the moonshiner], Heat is applied directly to a metal plate beneath the copper still pot, which is set securely in the rocks. **1967** DARE (Qu. DD21c, Nicknames for whiskey, especially illegally made whiskey) Inf **MI**67, Still-pot. **1974** Maurer–Pearl KY Moonshine 126, Still-pot. . . The metal body of the still in which the beer is cooked. " . . old still-pot's about burnt up."

still-tongued adj Also still-tongue [Cf OED2 still a. 2.b "Habitually silent, taciturn. Phrase, to keep a still tongue in one's head"; 1729 →] esp S Midl Cf **shut-mouth**
  Taciturn; tight-lipped.

  1817 Ferguson Abaddon's Steam Engine 45, An honest, still-tongued man, will faithfully take the beam out of his own eye. **1828** in 2003 DARE File—Internet **cnTN,** [From a case heard before the Jackson Co. Circuit Court:] Plff [=plaintiff] was a still tongued man but never hinted any thing to the contrary while she lived there. **1875** Bayard Taylor in Atlantic Mth. 35.26, Weimar . . is like a still-tongued . . person in a gay and talkative company. **1898** (1999) Elliott Durket Sperret 50 (Internet) **sAppalachians,** All the Durkets hes sperret an' Si ain't none o' your soft-walkin'—still-tongued folks like the Warrens. **1933** Miller Lamb in His Bosom 278 **GA,** Solemn-mouthed, still-tongued, they stood about their mother, waiting to see how they must act in this emergency. **1940** AmSp 15.447 **eTN,** Still tongue. Timid or untalkative. 'Malissa is a still tongue woman.' **1966–68** DARE (Qu. HH24, Somebody who doesn't talk very much, who keeps his thoughts to himself) Inf **DE**3, Still-tongue people; **AR**28, Still-tongued. **2008** DARE File—Internet **TN,** You remember the quiet kid in your high school class? Not the one who rarely spoke, but the one who never spoke? That was me. I'm still exceptionally still-tongued, but not nearly as much as back in the day.

still water n¹ See **still pond (no more moving)**

still water n² [Cf EDD still-waters (at still sb.² 3) "distilled waters; home-made illicit spirits"]

  1970 DARE (Qu. DD21c, Nicknames for whiskey, especially illegally made whiskey) Inf **TN**50, Still water.

still yet See **still** adv **1**

stilly pond (or water) See **still pond (no more moving)**

stilt sandpiper n Also stilt, stilted sandpiper
  Std: a long-legged **sandpiper** (Calidris himantopus). Also called **bastard dowitcher, ~ yellowlegs, drumstick 1, frostbird 3, frost snipe 1a, greenleg, long-legged sandpiper, mongrel B1, mottled sandpiper, peep 2, sand peep**

stilts, like hell on See **hell 5**

stimper(s) See **stemper**

stingaree n

  1 also stingamaree, stingeree, stinger ray: A stingray or related fish of the order Rajiformes. [Varr of stingray]
  1838 in 1922 Lamar Papers 2.87 **TX,** Sergeant Bryant was cut on the foot with an oyster shell, and Mr. Edington was stung by a Stingaree. **1860** U.S. War Dept. Rept. Explor. Railroad 12.3.368, A kind of stingaree or skate is not uncommon in Puget Sound. **1862** in 1981 Williams From That Terrible Field 105, I never go in the water without fearing for my feet: what with cat-fish—and "stinger-ees" and oyster-shells on the banks feet is in danger. **1868** Scientific Amer. 8 July 19 **Charleston SC,** The submarine monster recently captured by a fishing boat, and now on exhibition on South Bay . . is what is known as the sea eagle or clam cracker . . also known by the name of eagle ray or stingaree. **1882** Eggleston Wreck Red Bird 24 **eSC,** The creature . . is. . . called by negroes and fishermen, and nearly every body else on the coast, stingarees. **1899** (1912) Green VA Folk-Speech 418, Stingaree . . a stingray. **1927** Jrl. Amer. Folk. 40.168 **LA,** Use the sting of a stingaree for a toothpick and you will never have a toothache again. **1965–70** DARE (Qu. P4, Saltwater fish that are not good to eat) Infs **DE**4, **LA**31, 44, **NC**27, **SC**63, Stingaree(s); **TX**14, **VA**41, Stinger ray; (Qu. P18) Inf **NC**49, Stinger ray. **1966** DARE Tape **FL**14, We have the stingarees. . . They're a kind of a round, flat fish, and you step on him and he sticks his stingy in you, and boy, you really see stars; **SC**18, Cold pile is trash that comes in when the net is brought in and is put on the deck. It has shrimp, fish, crabs, sharks, stingamarees . . pretty well anything you'll find in the ocean. **1968** DARE FW Addit **seLA,** Stingaree = stingray; this fish is not usually eaten, but some people make a soup out of the flaps; the flaps are the wide fins resembling wings. **1986** Pederson LAGS Concordance Gulf Region, 7 infs, Stingarees; 1 inf, Stingarees—dried tails used to whip children.

2 =**horn snake 1.** Cf **stinging snake**

1946 *Scientific Mth.* July 21 **seLA,** In this section of Louisiana the species [=*Farancia abacura*] is invariably referred to as the "stingaree," although this is the accepted common name of a fish, the sting ray.

3 also *stinger marie, stick-a-marie:* See quots.

1957 *Sat. Eve. Post Letters* **NC** (as of c1915), Action games: Kick The Can, Puss-in-a Corner, Stick-a-Marie, Safe in Jail. **1986** Pederson *LAGS Concordance (Ball games)* 1 inf, **seFL,** Stingaree—rubber ball, hit opponent on the ass; 1 inf, **ceGA,** Stinger Marie—form of dodge ball—with baseball.

stingaree bush n

=**chaparral pea.**

1961 Thomas *Flora Santa Cruz* 207 **cwCA,** *Pickeringia . . montana. . .* Chaparral Pea, Stingaree Bush. . . throughout the Santa Cruz Mountains.

stinger n

1 A **bullhead 1b** (here: *Ameiurus melas*).

1951 Harlan–Speaker *IA Fish* 94, Northern Black Bullhead. . . Other Names . . catfish, stinger, and river snapper.

2 A **mosquito** n[1] **B1.**

1965–70 *DARE* (Qu. R15a, . . *Names or nicknames . . for mosquitoes*) Infs **CA111, IL9, MA4,** 122, **NY183, WI50,** 65, Stinger; (Qu. R15b, . . *An extra-big mosquito*) Inf **CA107,** Stinger; **CA111,** Giant stinger.

3 =**porcupine.**

1967 *DARE* (Qu. P31, . . *Names or nicknames . . for the . . porcupine*) Inf **NY10,** Stinger.

4 A **dragonfly.**

1968 *DARE* (Qu. R2, . . *The dragonfly*) Infs **MA7, NJ10,** Stinger. **1971** *AmSp* 46.172 **Chicago IL,** Insect with four long and narrow, transparent wings, often found near ponds . . *stinger 2* [infs]. **1971** Bright *Word Geog. CA & NV* 114 **cwCA,** [Dragon fly:] stingers . . 1 [inf].

stingeree See **stingaree 1**

stinger marie See **stingaree 3**

stinger ray See **stingaree 1**

stinger snake See **stinging snake**

stinging lizard n **chiefly TX, Lower Missip Valley** See Map Cf **lizard, stinging scorpion**

=**scorpion B1.**

1852 *De Bow's Rev.* 12.275 **LA,** *Scorpion,* vulgarly called *stinging lizard,* is the true scorpion of natural history, and is very plentiful in the pine hills. **1855** *Scientific Amer.* 10.334 **TX,** The stinging lizard has no resemblance to any of its relatives, either lizard or alligator; but has a body more the shape of a cricket, with legs like a spider, and a long tail, the largest part being at the greatest extremity from the body, which envelopes the sting which, though very painful, is not very dangerous. **1870** Duval *Advent. Big-Foot* 76 **TX,** He sprang up as suddenly as if a stinging lizard had popped him. **1915** *Jrl. Amer. Folkl.* 28.16 **West,** Even the stinging lizard, the horned frog, the centipede, the prairie-dog, the rattlesnake, are fast disappearing. **1923** *DN* 5.222 **swMO,** *Stingin' lizard. . .* Scorpion. **1926** TX Folkl. Soc. *Pub.* 5.61, The true scorpion is popularly called a "stinging lizard," this misnomer being in common use throughout the state of Texas. **1931** Randolph *Ozarks* 70, The real

scorpion is known as a *stingin'-lizard!* **1965–70** *DARE* (Qu. R21) 12 Infs, 8 **TX,** Stinging lizard; **LA2,** Stinging lizard (occasional) or hot-tail (occasional) or stinging scorpion (most frequent); **OK52,** Stinging lizard—also called stinging scorpion; (Qu. R28) Inf **MO37,** Stinging lizard . . looks like a crawfish. **1986** Pederson *LAGS Concordance,* 3 infs, **Gulf Region,** Stinging lizard(s). **1999** *DARE* File **seMO** (as of c1955), In S.E. Missouri . . I encountered "scorpion" used to refer to a skink (reptile, lizard). Concurrent (and obviously needed) was the use of "stingin' lizard" to refer to the poisonous arachnid. **2001** *Houston Chron.* (TX) 20 Sept sec A 27 (Internet), The other night I found a stinging lizard in the bathtub. A scorpion, that is. But in my growing-up time in West Texas this fellow was known to me only as a stinging lizard.

stinging nettle n

1 Std: a **nettle 1** (here: usu *Urtica dioica*).

2 also *stinging nettle jellyfish, sting nettle:* A stinging jellyfish (here: *Chrysaora quinquecirrha*). [*OED2* 1706 → for a jellyfish] **chiefly Chesapeake Bay** Also called **nettle n 5, poison nettle 2, sea nettle**

1887 *Galveston Daily News* (TX) 2 Sept 8/4, Before he takes a header from the pier now he inspects the water with a powerful microscope to see that the water is not infested with anything in the way of jellyfish or stinging nettle. **1899** (1912) Green *VA Folk-Speech* 364, Sting-nettle. . . The jelly-fish; also called *sea-nettle.* **1958** *Washington Post & Times Herald* (DC) 6 Aug sec B 3/7, That pestiferous dactylometra quinquecirrha [=*Chrysaora g.*] . . Known more familiarly as jellyfish or stinging nettle, this scourge of the beaches has invaded the Chesapeake Bay and its tributaries. **1965** *DARE* (Qu. R23b) Inf **FL22,** Stinging nettles. **1970** *DARE* FW Addit **seVA,** Stinging nettles—jellyfish with poisonous tentacles . . —1 to 8 inches [in] diameter—only tourists call them jellyfish. **1976** Ryland *Richmond Co. VA* 377, (Stinging) nettle—stinging jellyfish in the river in mid-summer. **1998** *NADS Letters* **VA,** In the area around Deltaville, VA where I spent time as a youth, the small jellyfish that come into the Chesapeake Bay in summer are called "stinging nettles" or sometimes "poison nettles." **2002** *DARE* File—Internet **Chesapeake Bay,** Of all the Chesapeake's creatures, the most hated is the stinging nettle jellyfish. **2003** *Ibid,* East Coast sea nettle (*Chrysaora quinquecirrha*)—This stinging nettle is common in the Chesapeake from mid-summer through fall.

3 A **hemp nettle** (here: *Galeopsis tetrahit*).

1914 Georgia *Manual Weeds* 354, Hemp Nettle. . . *Other English names:* Dog Nettle, Bee Nettle, Stinging Nettle [etc].

4 A **spurge nettle** (here: *Cnidoscolus stimulosus*).

1950 Gray–Fernald *Manual of Botany* 959, C[*nidoscolus*] *stimulosus. . .* "Stinging Nettle". **1974** Morton *Folk Remedies* 51 **SC,** Stinging Nettle. . . *Cnidoscolus stimulosus.* **1999** FL Div. Plant Industry *Botany Circular No. 34* 4 **cFL,** *Cnidoscolus stimulosus . .* is called 'tread-softly' and 'finger-rot'. . . However, a common name that has wide usage (at least in central Florida) is 'stinging nettle.'

stinging nettle jellyfish See **stinging nettle 2**

stinging scorpion n **chiefly OK, TX, LA** See Map Cf **scorpion B2, stinging lizard**

=**scorpion B1.**

1870 Duval *Advent. Big-Foot* 294 **TX,** With my tarantula boots made of alligator-skin, and my centipede hunting-shirt made of tanned rattle-

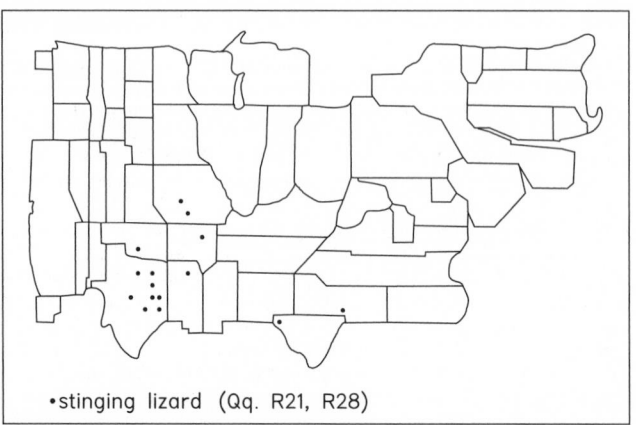

•stinging lizard (Qq. R21, R28)

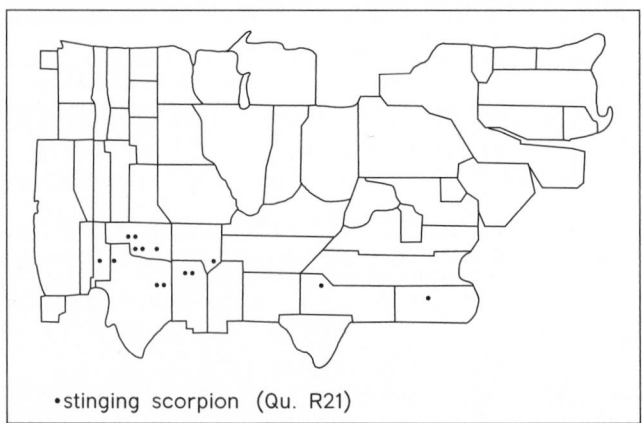

•stinging scorpion (Qu. R21)

snakes' hides, I have escaped pretty well; but these don't protect you against the stinging scorpions, 'cow-killers,' and scaly-back chinches, that crawl about at night when you are asleep! **1956** Ker *Vocab. W. TX* 244, Stinging scorpion—stinging lizard. [1 of 67 infs] **1965–70** *DARE* (Qu. R21) 14 Infs, **esp OK, TX, LA,** Stinging scorpion. **1986** Pederson *LAGS Concordance,* 5 infs, **Gulf Region,** Stinging scorpion(s). **2002** *San Antonio Express–News* (TX) 22 Jan sec D 1 (Internet), "It's just one of the nice things about living in Texas," he jokes. "That, and the stinging scorpion."

stinging snake n   Also *stinger snake*   **chiefly Lower Missip Valley**

Either of two closely related snakes: usu **horn snake 1,** but also **rainbow snake.**

   1887 *Mt. Democrat* (Placerville CA) [26 Nov 4]/1 (newspaperarchive.com) **AR,** I found a very large blunt-tail stinging snake, measuring five feet and about one inch. **1906** *Ft. Wayne Jrl.–Gaz.* (IN) 18 Aug 5/5, When confronted with a veritable stinging snake without any sting, and as "harmless as a dove," a doubt begins to pervade his mind. **1908** *Washington Post* (DC) 11 Aug 6/6, In the snake house at the New York zoo yesterday the superintendents and keepers demonstrated that as a deadly stinger the stinging snake of the mudholes, swamps, and bayous of Louisiana, Mississippi, and other parts of the South is a myth. **1919** *Copeia* 73.73 **nwMS** (as of c1890), The writer came to Clarksdale, Miss. 30 years ago. . . Shortly after, stories were heard about the prevalence of numerous "stinging snakes" in the neighborhood. **1925** TX Folkl. Soc. *Pub.* 4.47 **nwLA,** In northwestern Louisiana, the colored people do not seem to identify *Farancia abacura* with the hoop snake; they prefer to consider it as the "deadly stinging snake." **1949** *Scientific Mth.* Jan 53, When we speak of the hoop snake, horn snake, or stinging snake, a single species, *Farancia abacura,* is implied. The circular position of the snake lying prone and engulfing its prey suggests a "hoop;" the tail spine suggests a "horn;" the sharp end of the spine prodding the human hand suggests a deadly "stinger." **1950** *James R. Basin* 208 **VA,** Another coastal plain snake is the red-bellied snake *(Farancia abacura),* also called the stinger snake and mud snake. **1965–68** *DARE* (Qu. P25, . . *Kinds of snakes*) Infs **MS**63, **NC**21, **TN**26, Stinging snake; **AR**55, Stinging snake—with a tail like a pencil that they hit you with the point of; **LA**18, Stinging snake—I don't think there's any such thing, but some of 'em say they are black with a red stomach; **LA**29, I used to work for a feller, we had lots of hogs. Had a waller down there in the gully. Ever once in a while we'd hear one squeal and they'd come back up and die. There was a big snake in there—what we call a stinging snake, and one day he shot that snake and we never did lose no more hogs. They're a kind of a red spotted snake. **1979** Behler–King *Audubon Field Guide Reptiles* 611, Rainbow Snake *(Farancia erytrogramma). . .* Folk tales have it that the "stinging snake," "hoop snake," or "thunderbolt," bites its tail, rolls like a hoop, and stings a victim to death with the spine on the tail tip. **1982** Ginns *Snowbird Gravy* 142 **nwNC,** I don't know if you've ever heard of a stinger snake or not. A hoop snake. It rolls—a stinger on the end of its tail, and it's got a joint in it just like your finger. They call 'em "stinger snakes." **1986** Pederson *LAGS Concordance* **Gulf Region,** 3 infs, Stinging snake; 1 inf, Stinging snake—rolls like a hoop. **2008** *DARE* File—Internet **MS,** That's a monster! Down here, they are also called a "Stinging Snake" because of the weird tip of their tail.

stinging weed n   Also *stinging weed vine*
Prob =**nettle 1.**

   1954 *Harder Coll.* **cwTN,** Slinging [sic] *weed vine. . .* A weed that causes itching and swelling. " 'At old stanging weed vine'll jis' setchu afar." **1967–69** *DARE* (Qu. S17, . . *Kinds of plants . . that . . cause itching and swelling*) Inf **KY**21, Stinging weed; **CO**15, Stinging nettles or stinging weed; **LA**31, Burning weed or stinging weed—has narrow, dark green leaves, grows in edge of marsh; it'll just naturally burn you up. **2003** in 2007 *DARE* File—Internet **sMO,** We've got a plant here in Southern Missouri called "stinging weed". . . It's a roadside, country field type weed that looks like a slim, green wheat-like plant.

stinging worm n   Also *cotton stinging worm*   **chiefly Sth, S Midl**   See Map
A caterpillar with stinging hairs, esp the **saddleback caterpillar.**

   1862 (1996) Jackson *Experience Slave SC* 22 (Internet) [Black], We were now put to picking cotton. This is not so pleasant a job as might be imagined. The whole field is covered with "stinging worms," a species

of caterpillar. **1879** Comstock *Rept. Cotton Insects* 486 **cGA,** I herewith inclose another insect that is very destructive to cotton. . . They are called here the stinging worm, and their sting is very painful. **1904** Acad. Nat. Sci. Philadelphia Entomol. Sec. *Entomol. News & Proc.* 15.125 **cNC,** *Automeris io. . .* The larvæ of this species seem most commonly to be found on cotton . . and are usually known as the Cotton Stinging Worm. **1925** *Charleston Daily Mail* (WV) 27 Oct 4/3, When a playmate threw a "stinging worm" at the nine-year-old son of John Denis, of Cranberry ridge, the insect struck the boy in the eye, and he is now in a local hospital being treated for blindness. **1965–70** *DARE* (Qu. R27, . . *Kinds of caterpillars or similar worms*) Infs **KY**88, **LA**40, **SC**32, 57, **TX**4, Stinging worm; **AL**32, Stinging worms—packsaddles; **GA**77, Brown stinging worm—on tobacco, has two horns; **KY**28, Packsaddle—a stinging worm; **NC**87, Cotton stinging worm; **TN**26, Stinging worms—get on cotton; (Qu. R9a) Inf **NC**41, Stinging worms; (Qu. R21, . . *Other kinds of stinging insects*) Infs **NC**67, **OH**40, Stinging worm; **NC**54, Stinging worm—a fuzzy caterpillar; **TN**26, Stinging worms—get on cotton. **1986** Pederson *LAGS Concordance* **Gulf Region,** 4 infs, Stinging worm(s); 1 inf, Stinging worm—in cotton field, green and hairy. [**2000** *KY Explorer* Sept (Internet) **seKY** (as of 1940s), Another time, in the late summer, we were working in the cornfield. . . I hated that job, because there was some kind of stinging worm that always managed to get me, no matter how hard I tried to avoid it. . . We just called them "packsaddles."] **2000** *DARE* File—Internet **LA,** Could you please research the Louisian [sic] stinging worm or caterpillar and share the information? I am at a dead end and my yard is full of the little things. They are black long and spiky with the occasional red spot.

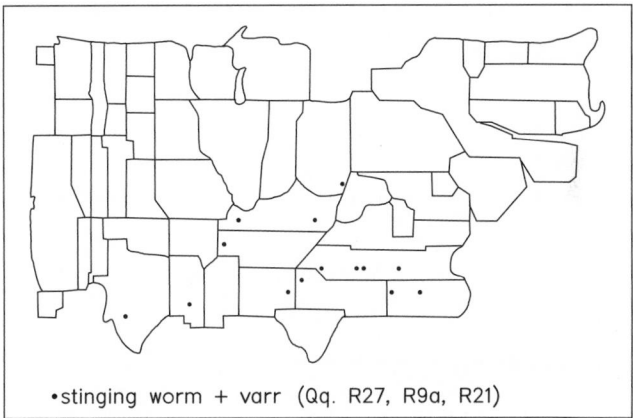

•stinging worm + varr (Qq. R27, R9a, R21)

stingless nettle n
A **richweed 1** (here: *Pilea pumila*).

   1822 Eaton *Botany* 499, [*Urtica] pumila* [=*Pilea p.*] . . stingless nettle, richweed. **1876** Hobbs *Bot. Hdbk.* 220, [Urtica] pumila, Stingless nettle. **1936** Winter *Plants NE* 190, *P[ilea] pumila . .* Stingless Nettle. **1994** *Washington Post* (DC) 24 July sec B 3 (Internet), A black speck on the underside of a stingless nettle leaf was, he noted, a caterpillar of either the red admiral or comma butterfly species.

sting nettle   See **stinging nettle 2**

sting-tongue n   [See quot 1908]
A **prickly ash 1.**

   1897 Sudworth *Arborescent Flora* 265 **AR, FL,** Prickly Ash. . . Stingtongue (Fla. negroes, Ark.) **1908** Rogers *Tree Book* 348, The Negro in the South chews a piece of prickly ash bark to cure the toothache. "Sting-tongue" and "pepperwood" he calls it, for it produces a burning sensation and a copious flow of saliva. **1950** Peattie *Nat. Hist. Trees* 427, *Zanthoxylum americanum. . .* Other Names: Prickly Ash. Wait-a-bit. Sting-tongue.

stingy-gut(s) n
A miserly or selfish person.

   1855 in 2003 *DARE* File—Internet **cNY,** Nancy says she won't give you a thing out of the garden. She is an old stingy gut—that's so and no mistake. **1956** Ker *Vocab. W. TX* 346, Stingy; *a stingy person. . .* stingy gut. [1 of 67 infs] **1961** Folk *Word Atlas N. LA* map 1401, Stingy—Stingy person . . [less freq responses include] stingy gut. **1965–70** *DARE* (Qu. U33, *Names or nicknames for a stingy person*) 10 Infs, **scattered,** Stingy-guts; **GA**77, **IL**114, Stingy-gut; (Qu. U36a, . . *A person who saves in a mean way or is greedy in money matters:* "He's an awful

_____.") Infs **GA**77, **TN**14, Stingy-gut; (Qu. U36b, . . *A person who saves in a mean way or is greedy in money matters: "She certainly is _____.")* Inf **TN**14, Awful stingy-gut. **1970** Tarpley *Blinky* 240 **neTX,** *A person who is too careful with his money . .* stingy gut [rare]. **1986** Pederson *LAGS Concordance (Tightwad)* 3 infs, **FL, GA, TN,** Stingy-gut. **1994** Gray *My New Friends* 14 **nMI** (as of 1920s), He wouldn't let anyone ride on it let alone belly flop it on the boarding house hill. We called him a stingy gut. **2003** *DARE* File—Internet **cUT** (as of c1900), We were back with the horse in just a few minutes and it was so quick he would only give us half a sack, so we nicknamed him "Old Stingy Guts."

stingy vine n

A **sensitive brier** (here: *Mimosa microphylla*).

1905 (1975) Miles *Spirit of Mts.* 39 **seTN,** Pearlybuds of the wild syringa were opening to show the pure pale gold of their hearts. . . This plant is here known as shame-brier or stingy-vine; both names are highly suggestive of its sudden drooping or closing and drawing back.

stink v

To emit an odor; to smell—used in positive contexts; see quots.

1935 *AmSp* 10.167 **PA** [Engl of PA Germans], It stinks good. **1942** (1971) Campbell *Cloud-Walking* 89 **seKY,** This here rose-smelly soap . . stinks pine-blank like flower blooms. . . It pleasured me a heap to stink so pretty for once. **1952** Brown *NC Folkl.* 1.594, Stink. . . That pumgranny shore stinks good. **1953** Randolph–Wilson *Down in Holler* 83 **Ozarks,** My neighbor said of some perfume, "It sure stinks beautiful."

stink apple n

A **jimson weed** (here: *Datura stramonium*).

1971 Krochmal *Appalachia Med. Plants* 108, Jimsonweed, . . stink apple, stinkweed, stinkwort [etc.].

stink bait n

1 An offensive-smelling bait used in fishing for catfish or, rarely, in attracting bees; see quots. Cf **sour bait**

1921 *Wichita Daily Times* (Wichita Falls TX) 20 Mar sec 2 8/2, Some fishermen are using a new kind of bait known as stink-bait[.] It is said to have an ordor [sic] so powerfully disagreeable that the action of the water fails to extinguish it and catfish take kindly to it. **1944** *Portsmouth Herald* (NH) 28 June 6/4 **OK,** It's called "Stink Bait Fishing," and the fish you catch are catfish. **1956** *Atchison Daily Globe* (KS) 12 Feb 11/1, The ice should be off the streams and lakes before too long and then the stinkbait fishermen will start for the early channel cat fishing. **1969–70** *DARE* (Qu. P13, . . *Ways of fishing . . besides the ordinary hook and line)* Inf **IL**81, Stink bait—imported from Minnesota or Wisconsin; **TX**78, Stink bait—as buffalo guts or anything that stinks. **1973** *Foxfire 2* 37 **nGA,** Joe Kilby claims that some old-timers used to put corn cobs and dirt in a bucket, urinate in it, and then leave it for a few days. When they got back, the bees would be there. And Elb agrees, saying the old-timers used to call that "stinkbait." **1986** Pederson *LAGS Concordance,* 1 inf, **cAL,** Stink bait—needed for catfish; 1 inf, **seMS,** Stink bait—for catfish. **2000** *Chicago Sun–Times* (IL) 11 June sports sec 120 (Internet), Catfish catches have taken off with the warmer weather. . . Most action is on night crawlers or stinkbait. **2003** *DARE* File—Internet **IA,** Many catfishers swear by stinkbait, a noxious goo usually based on overripe cheese. **2004** *Ibid* **TX,** *Bells of Hell Stinkbait Recipe.* . . This is not a bait to try and make unless you are part buzzard, this stuff really stinks. . . hog brains . . cheese . . shad or other small baitfish. *Ibid* **TX,** Recipes for stinkbait. . . Raisin bran, stale bread, Big Red sodey pop, overripe bananas, raw chicken livers, an' squeeze cheese spread. . . If it don't make you gag when you stick yore head in to git a sniff, it ain't done yet. **2004** *DARE* File **ceNY** (as of late 1950s–60s), There were catfish in the Hudson River and we fished for them with stinkbait. Stinkbait was used only for catfish. We used to use chicken guts. Put them in a tin can and leave them out in the sun for a while—like a week.

2 See quot. Cf **stinkworm**

1968 *DARE* (Qu. P6, . . *Kinds of worms . . used for bait)* Inf **PA**73, Stink bait—a small red worm found around manure piles, used mainly in winter.

stink ball n[1]

The fruit of the **Osage orange.**

1971 *Today Show Letters* **swPA** (as of c1925), The Osage orange we

called "monkey balls." But [when] we used them as weapons in gang warfare, we called them "stink balls."

stink ball n[2] [Cf *sting ball* an early form of baseball in which a runner could be put out if struck by a ball thrown by a member of the opposite team]

1969 *DARE* (Qu. EE33, *Other outdoor games)* Inf **GA**75, Dodge ball—people in a ring; two teams try to hit each other with a ball; one who is hit is out. Stink ball—same [as dodge ball].

stink base n Also *stinker* [Cf *SND stink* n. 2 "A player who has been made prisoner in the game of *Scots and English* or sim. games. . . Also *stinkard, stinker* . . , *stinky*. . . Hence *stinky-dails, stinkers,* the game itself." (*SND dale, dail* n.[4] 2 "The base or 'home' in hide-and-seek . . and similar games.")] *old-fash* Cf **base** n **B1, black man 2, dare-base**

=**prisoner's base;** the base in the game; hence n *stinker* a player who has been tagged.

1891 *AN&Q* 7.220 **IA,** I remember when I was a small boy at school in Mahaska county, this State, that the game now known as "base" was always called "stink-base." **1894** in 2008 (acc) Lexis–Nexis Legal Research *State Case Law: IN* (Internet), On Sunday, April 12, 1891, . . George Sears, with three other boys near his age, was playing at a game called by them ['·]stink-base,' two of the boys having their base on the north side and two on the south side of Romig street. **1901** *DN* 2.148 **cwNY,** Stinker. . . Another name for prisoner's base. **1905** *DN* 3.96 **nwAR,** Stink-base. . . Prisoner's base. **1906** *DN* 3.158 **nwAR,** Stinker. . . A prisoner in the game of *stinkbase* (prisoner's base). **1915** *DN* 4.191 **swVA,** Stink base. A game at running bases. **1947** Lomax *Advent. Ballad Hunter* 14 **TX** (as of c1880), We children never played games on Sunday, not even . . stink base. **1957** *Sat. Eve. Post Letters* **ceIA** (as of 1890s), Prisoner's base was called stink base and anyone caught was placed in stink which usually called for a holding of noses. **1964** Wallace *Frontier Life* 38 **OK** (as of 1893–1906), At recess and the noon hour, we staged such games as Blackman, Stink-Base, New York, or a ball game we called Two-Old-Cat. **1967–70** *DARE* (Qu. EE33, . . *Outdoor games . . that children play)* Inf **IL**76, Stink base—like black man, but they had to stay on base; you could get your people off the stink base; **IL**130, Stink base—one is on base, another tries to rescue; **OH**82, Stink base—two bases, get to the other base; if you're tagged, go to stink base until teammate frees you; **TX**11, Stink base. [All Infs old] **1983** *MJLF* 9.1.57 **ceKY** (as of 1956), Stink base . . the name of a tag game. **1986** Pederson *LAGS Concordance,* 2 infs, **cnAR, cnTX,** Stink base. [Both infs old] **2004** in 2008 *DARE* File—Internet **AR,** First the Beatles break up, and now no more red rover? Next you'll be telling me there's no more stink base either.

stink beetle n

1 See **stinkbug a.**

2 See **stinkbug b(3).**

stink bells n

A **fritillary** (here: *Fritillaria agrestis*) native to California.

1901 Jepson *Flora CA* 109, F[ritillaria] agrestis. . . Stink Bells. . . Mr. Davy describes the odor as very obnoxious. **1961** Thomas *Flora Santa Cruz* 119 **cwCA,** F[ritillaria] agrestis. . . Ill-scented Fritillary, Stink Bells. **2006** *Bay Nature* Apr–June (Internet) **CA,** There are populations of rarities such as stinkbells (Fritillaria agrestis), [etc.].

stink berry n

1 =**Carolina buckthorn 1;** the fruit of this tree.

1897 Sudworth *Arborescent Flora* 298 **NE,** *Rhamnus caroliniana.* . . Stink Berry.

2 The fruit of *Ginkgo biloba.*

2001 *DARE* File—Internet **Philadelphia PA,** Ever see students walking down City Avenue doing acrobatics and tiptoeing clumsily around and over imaginary barriers? That is the stink berry dance, folks. . . The berries, or nuts, come from the ginkgo, or maidenhair tree. **2005** in 2008 *DARE* File—Internet **DC,** The immature gingko berries have still not fallen as a result of any spraying you are responsible for successfully completing. . . We don't want inches of stink berries on our streets. **2006** *Ibid* **NYC,** Perhaps someday—like 'crisp fall air' and burning leaves—the smell of the stink berries will also remind me of the pleasures of the autumnal equinox, but until then it just makes me sick.

stinkbird n Also *stink sparrow* chiefly Sth

Any of several sparrows supposed to have a scent that causes hunting dogs to point, as **grasshopper sparrow, pinewoods ~,** or **savannah ~.**

1898 Baskett *At You-All's House* 278 **MO,** Once he stopped dead still—moved cautiously up, and a little brown, streaked swamp-sparrow flew out of a tuft of grass. Shan called it a "stinkbird," with a hunter's contempt for anything not game that balks his dog. **1949** Sprunt–Chamberlain *SC Bird Life* 526, Eastern Savannah Sparrow. . . Local Names: Stink Bird. *Ibid* 527, Eastern Grasshopper Sparrow. . . Local Names: Stink Bird. **1952** Carr *Turtles* 144, The only other creature that in my experience consistently causes a trained dog to haul up spasmodically in a rigid point is a small ground-dwelling sparrow which so regularly deludes bird dogs that it is known by quail hunters as "stink-bird." **1953** Randolph–Wilson *Down in Holler* 289 **Ozarks,** *Stink bird. . .* Any small bird which stays close to the ground. A man whose bird dog kept making false points, and finding no quail, told me, "It's them damn' stink-birds a-foolin' him." **1955** *Oriole* 20.1.13 **GA,** Bachman's Sparrow.—Grass Sparrow; Stink Bird (hunting dogs "point" it, hence it is supposed to have a strong scent). **1958** Babcock *I Don't Want* 23 **eSC,** A man may get more pleasure from watching his own fumbling pup do a bang-up job on a stink sparrow than from watching another man's dog give a Grand Junction performance on an entire bevy. **1967** *DARE* (Qu. Q21, . . *Kinds of sparrows*) Inf **TX**33, Stinkbird—because dogs always point them. **2003** *DARE* File—Internet **sAL,** If "Ole Sport" were still around and still sometimes pointing Chipping Sparrows instead of Bobwhites, for the sake of the old days I would still call them "Stink Birds."

stinkbox n   Cf **stinkpot 1**

=mud turtle 2b(1) or **musk turtle 1.**

c1940 Newman–Murphy *Conserv. Notes* 5 **LA,** Among the varieties of turtles are . . land terrapin (stink box) and snapping turtle. **1966** *DARE* (Qu. P24, . . *Kinds of turtles*) Inf **FL**7, Stinkbox. **2004** *DARE* File—Internet **NYC,** My biggest concern is that I need to know what species (if any) can be comfortably housed in a 30G for life. I looked into a stinkbox turtle and not sure if I like it all that much.

stinkbug n

An insect that generates a foul-smelling liquid or that stinks when crushed, as:

a   also *stink beetle:* Used generically or in ref to specific insects not identifiable from the context.   Cf **smell bug**

1851 Lazarus *Compar. Psych.* 214, The hideous furniture of our globe, . . the thirty serpents, the forty-three stinkbugs, the tigers, the wolves [etc]. **1878** Hart *Sazerac Lying Club* 193 **NV,** The earlier birds of the season, such as caterpillars, stink-bugs, mosquito-hawks, and grasshoppers. **1965–70** *DARE* (Qu. R30, . . *Kinds of beetles;* not asked in early QRs) 417 Infs, **widespread,** Stinkbug; **CA**145, **KS**7, 12, **MN**19, 42, **NE**3, **NY**209, **PA**168, Stink beetle; **GA**84, Stink beetle—square-bodied, with long snout; **HI**14, Southern stinkbug; (Qu. R5, *A big brown beetle that comes out in large numbers in spring and early summer, and flies with a buzzing sound*) Infs **CA**119, **OK**25, Stinkbug; **HI**4, Black stinkbug; (Qu. R21, . . *Other kinds of stinging insects*) Inf **TX**73, Stinkbug. **1985** Ladwig *How to Talk Dirty* 37 **Ozarks,** I'm hungry enough to eat a stink bug off'n a dead skunk. **1986** Pederson *LAGS Concordance* **Gulf Region,** 5 infs, Stinkbug(s); 1 inf, Stinkbugs—not chiggers; crab-like faces; four feet.

b   Spec:

(1)   also *stinking bug:* The squash bug *(Anasa tristis).*

1877 Bartlett *Americanisms* 647 **CT,** *Squash-Bug. . .* A small yellow bug, injurious to the vines of squashes, melons, and cucumbers. . . In Connecticut, called a *stink-bug.* **1967–70** *DARE* (Qu. R30, . . *Kinds of beetles;* not asked in early QRs) Infs **AL**30, **SC**63, Stinkbug—same as pumpkin bug; **GA**65, Stinking bug—same as pumpkin bug; **VA**57, Stinkbug—yellow. **1967** *Harder Coll.* **cwTN,** Stinking bug—An insect that emits a strong, distasteful odor; often called a "punkin bug." **1982** *Barrick Coll.* **csPA,** Stink bug—squash bug. Any insect which, when "squashed," emits a pungent odor. **1986** Pederson *LAGS Concordance,* 1 inf, **seMS,** Stinkbugs—eat insides of plants. **2002** *DARE* File—Internet, Squash bugs, *Anasa tristis,* are sometimes mistakenly called stink bugs because they may give off a foul odor when squashed.

(2)   An insect of the family Pentatomidae such as the **harlequin cabbage bug.**   Cf **huckleberry bug**

1897 *Amer. Naturalist* 31.395, Stink bugs *(Pentatomidae),* whose nauseating odor is familiar to every one who has been berrying, were eaten by the catbirds. **1904** *Science* 19.393, When on a collecting trip near College Station, Texas, early in October, I examined the stomach con-

tents of a half-grown toad. In this mass I found two stink-bugs *(Euschistus fissilis).* **1967–69** *DARE* (Qu. R30, . . *Kinds of beetles;* not asked in early QRs) Inf **CT**2, Stinkbug—looks like a small turtle; **CT**13, Stinkbug—in the huckleberries; **MI**51, Stinkbug—found sometimes on raspberries; you can tell by taste a berry it's been on; **NY**71, Stinkbug—they get onto raspberries; **NY**227, Stinkbug—on berries—don't taste too good if you eat one by mistake. **1967** *DARE* FW Addit **neLA,** *Stinkbug* ['stæɪŋk,bʌg] [FW illustr: shield-shaped insect]. **1980** Milne–Milne *Audubon Field Guide Insects* 483, Stink bugs get their common name from the copious amounts of foul-smelling liquid they discharge when disturbed. **2006** *Roanoke Times* (VA) 16 Oct 3 (Internet), If you mash that sucker, the odor will just make you want to die before your time. That's why they're called stinkbugs, Irving. The scientists call them pentatomidae but that doesn't make them respectable.

(3)   also *stink beetle:* **=pinacate bug.   esp CA**

1957 Jaeger *N. Amer. Deserts* 170, *Eleodes armata.* Called circus bugs or stink beetles because of their queer way, when disturbed, of standing with the body raised vertically and because when handled or crushed they give off a strong offensive odor. **1965–70** *DARE* (Qu. R30, . . *Kinds of beetles;* not asked in early QRs) Infs **CA**40, 53, 91, **CO**47, **NV**7, Stinkbug; **CA**20, Black one—called a tumblebug or stinkbug; **CA**26, Stinkbug—not a beetle; sticks his tail up and stinks; **CA**87, Stinkbug or ['pinəkartɛɪ] [sic]; **CA**101, Stinkbug—black—stands with his head down and his little butt up. **2004** *DARE* File **sID** (as of c1965), I first encountered stinkbugs *(Eleodes)* in southern Idaho. When disturbed, they tilt their hind end and emit a foul smell.

(4)   A bedbug.

1966–69 *DARE* (Qu. R24, . . *Names . . for a bedbug*) Infs **IN**14, **NY**219, **OH**53, **WA**6, Stinkbug; **NV**7, Stinkbugs—the red one—people don't have anymore [laughter].

(5)   **=chinch bug 2.**

1967–69 *DARE* (Qu. R30, . . *Kinds of beetles;* not asked in early QRs) Infs **IN**35, 75, **KY**75, 94, **LA**18, **NC**81, **VA**105, Chinch bug is the same as stinkbug; **OR**1, Chintz bug—same as pine beetle or stinkbug.

(6)   **=ladybug.**

1967–68 *DARE* (Qu. R30, . . *Kinds of beetles;* not asked in early QRs) Infs **CT**6, **NJ**1, Stinkbug—same as ladybug.

(7)   **=carrion beetle.**

1969 *DARE* (Qu. R30, . . *Kinds of beetles;* not asked in early QRs) Inf **KY**40, Carrion bug—some say stinkbug.

stinkbush n

1   **=fragrant sumac** or another **sumac B.   Cf stinking hazel**

1881 *Amer. Med. Jrl.* 9.312, I consider that the now famous "Mosuri Stink Bush" did its duty nobly for this old man. **1892** (1974) Millspaugh *Amer. Med. Plants* 39–1, *Rhus aromatica. . .* Com. Names. . . Stink Bush, Skunk Bush. **1958** Jacobs–Burlage *Index Plants NC* 10, *Rhus canadensis* [=*R. aromatica*]. . . Fragrant or sweet-scented sumach; stink bush; skunk bush. **1967** *DARE* (Qu. S26e, *Other wildflowers not yet mentioned;* not asked in early QRs) Inf **SC**32, Stinkbush—*Rhus glabra.*

2   **=Florida anise-tree.**

1880 *Amer. Entomologist* 2d ser 1.228 **cMS,** Should the Cotton Worms make their appearance this season. . . I shall use a decoction of the leaves of what is known as "Stink Bush," which grows abundantly in our swamps. **1885** *Cincinnati Lancet & Clinic* 53.42, The shrub Illicium Floridanum is an evergreen found growing in clumps in swampy places in the Southern States. It is known to farmers as poison bay, horse kill and stink bush. **1933** Small *Manual SE Flora* 534, *I[llicium] floridanum. . .* Purple-anise. Stink-bush. . . Swamps and low hammocks, Coastal Plain, N. Fla. to La. and N. Ala. . . The flowers have the odor of decaying fish. **1979** Little *Checklist U.S. Trees* 151, Polecat-tree, purple anise-tree . . stinkbush.

stink case   See **stink cheese**

stink-cat n   Also *stink-katz*

=skunk 1.

1966–70 *DARE* (Qu. P26, *Names and nicknames . . for a skunk*) Infs **CA**153, **IA**32, **NJ**22, 67, **WI**48, Stink-cat; **OK**52, Stink-cat—used by old-time Germans; **IN**35, Stink-katz; **MI**93, Stink-katz—said by early Germans—the English "stink-cat" said only for a joke. **1986** Pederson *LAGS Concordance (Skunk)* 1 inf, **seFL,** Stink cat. **2003** in 2008 *DARE* File—Internet, I really want to get rid of these things before my wife or daughter gets it while collecting eggs. If that happens I will be in the doghouse for as long as it takes for the smell to wear off of them. I wonder where mamma stink cat is.

stink cheese n Also *stink case* [Calque (and partial calque) of PaGer *schtinkkaes;* see quot 1924] **esp PaGer settlement areas** Cf **cook cheese, hand cheese**

A cottage cheese, esp one which has been allowed to ripen.

[**1924** Lambert *PA Ger. Dict.* 143, *Schtink . . kaes . .* Hand or Dutch cheese.] **1950** *WELS (Different kinds of home-made cheese)* 1 Inf, **ceWI,** Stink cheese. **1957** Showalter *Mennonite Cookbook* 113, *Old-fashioned Stink Cheese . .* allow cheese to ripen 5 days instead of 3 days. It must be kept in a warm place while ripening. **c1965** Randle *Cookbooks* (Plain Cookery) 1.[10] **ceOH,** Stink Case—Let a gal. of milk get thick. Put this on stove, keep stirring constantly till you can press curdles of milk together. Put through cheese cloth or any material that is thin enough to divide the curdles from the whey. After the whey is thoroughly pressed out, get your skillet with butter in size of a walnut, melt this[,] add the curdles, 1 t. of baking soda, salt to suit taste, stir with a potato masher. Cook till smooth, add cream or milk, to thickness desired. Pour in a dish and it's ready to eat. **1966** *Wichita Eagle* (KS) 9 Apr sec B 2/1, I am glad there are still some Pennsylvania Dutch extant, and I hope I can answer all the letters I have received in response to the 'stink cheese' recipe. **1968** *Budget* (Sugarcreek OH) 25 July 13/2, [Amish Pioneer Day demonstration:] Making "Stink" Cheese. **1968** *DARE* (Qu. H60, *The lumpy white cheese that is made from sour milk*) Infs **MD**27, **PA**143, Stink cheese; **OH**81, Stink case. **2003** *DARE* File—Internet **cwIL** (as of c1900), Grandmother made what all her grandchildren called "stink cheese." She mixed cottage cheese with garlic, caraway seeds, salt and perhaps pepper. Then she formed small cakes of it and placed them in a one gallon stone jar and covered them with cream. She covered the jar top with a cloth . . and set the jar on a shelf in the pantry. She stirred it every day and added cream until it became a yellowish stinking mess about the consistency of thick gravy. This was then eaten on the large three-inch "store" crackers. Limburger was as a rose and Roquefort as a geranium compared with this fermented mess!

stink cherry n

=**Carolina buckthorn 1.**

1897 Sudworth *Arborescent Flora* 298 **NE,** *Rhamnus caroliniana. . .* Stink Cherry.

stinker See **stink base**

stink feather n

=**bugbane 1.**

1959 Carleton *Index Herb. Plants* 112, *Stink feather:* Cimicifuga [spp.].

stink grass n Also *stinking grass*

A **love grass** (here: *Eragrostis cilianensis*).

1894 *Jrl. Amer. Folkl.* 7.104 **NE,** *Eragrostis major* [=*E. cilianensis*] . . stink-grass. **1898** *Ibid* 11.283 **KS,** *Eragrostis major . .* stinking grass, stink grass. **1947** *Amer. Midland Naturalist* 38.31 **MD,** *Eragrostis cilianensis* (Stink Grass). . . Common (locally abundant) in cultivated fields. **2003** (acc) U.S. Dept. Ag. *Plants Database* (Internet), *Eragrostis cilianensis . .* stinkgrass.

stinkhorn n [*OED2* 1724 →]

A **mushroom B1** of the order Phallales, usu *Phallus impudicus.* For other names of var spp see **death baby**

1875 *Scribner's Mth.* 10.717, *Phallus impudicus,* which commonly bears the not over-classic, though very expressive name of *stinkhorn.* **1908** Hard *Mushroom Edible* 524, Laced Stinkhorn. . . A few years ago one of these plants insisted upon growing near my house, where a fence post had formerly been, with the effect of almost driving the family from home. **1981** Lincoff *Audubon Field Guide Mushrooms* 831, The stinkhorns are fungi you usually smell before you see. **1987** McKnight–McKnight *Mushrooms* 347, Net Stinkhorn. . . Odor weak to strong, repulsive. *Ibid* 348, Stinkhorns often have no odor. This may lead to occasional deception, due to careless statements in mycological literature suggesting that one always encounters the smell before sighting a stinkhorn. **2007** *Atlanta Jrl.–Constitution* (GA) 25 Jan sec HG 3 (Internet) **SC,** Q: We are inundated with stinkhorn mushrooms. The smell is awful, and all we are able to do is dig them up and throw them away.

stinking ash n

1 A **hop tree** (here: *Ptelea trifoliata*).

1835 Riddell *Synopsis Flora W. States* 36, Ptelea trifoliata. . . Stinking prairie bush. Stinking ash. Swamp dogwood. **1843** Torrey *Flora NY* 1.133, Ptelea trifoliata. . . *Swamp Dogwood. Stinking Ash.* . . Flowers lat-

eral and terminal; the odor disagreeable. **1876** Hobbs *Bot. Hdbk.* 113, Stinking ash, Wafer ash, Ptelea trifoliata. **1930** [see **stinking prairie-bush**]. **1958** Jacobs–Burlage *Index Plants NC* 195, Stinking ash, hop tree [etc].

2 =**box elder.**

1883 Hale *Woods NC* 89 **SC,** Ash-leaved maple. . . In South Carolina I have heard it called *Stinking Ash.* It has the leaves of an *Ash,* and the fruit of a *Maple.*

stinking balm n

A **pennyroyal B1** (here: *Hedeoma pulegioides*).

1828 Rafinesque *Med. Flora* 1.231, *Hedeoma pulegioides. . .* Vulgar Names—Pennyroyal, Tickweed, Stinking balm [etc]. **1911** Henkel *Amer. Med. Leaves* 26, Stinking balm, mosquito plant. [*Ibid,* The odor is very repulsive to insects, and pennyroyal is therefore much used for keeping away mosquitoes and other troublesome insects.] **1971** Krochmal *Appalachia Med. Plants* 138, *Hedeoma pulegioides. . .* squaw mint, stinking balm [etc].

stinking benjamin n **chiefly NEng** Cf **benjamin**

A **trillium** (here: *Trillium erectum*).

[**1892** *Jrl. Amer. Folkl.* 5.104, *Trillium erectum. . .* stinking Benjamin. N[ew] B[runswick].] **1916** Cleghorn *Spinster* 148 **VT,** They came . . upon a little plot of . . ill-smelling crimson trillium, with its ugly, vigorous Vermont name of "stinking Benjamin." **1950** Gray–Fernald *Manual of Botany* 445, *T[rillium] erectum.* . . Stinking Benjamin [etc]. **1955** *Moosehead Gazette* (Dexter ME) Feb 17/3 *(Hench Coll.),* Where but in Maine, would trillium be Stinking Benjamin? **1959** *VT Hist.* 27.160, *Stinking Benjamin. . .* Red trillium. Common. **1966–69** *DARE* (Qu. S2, . . *The flower that comes up in the woods early in spring, with three white petals that turn pink as the flower grows older*) Infs **ME**8, **MA**25, 58, Stinking Benjamin. **1975** Gould *ME Lingo* 278, *Stinkin' Benjamin*—The purple trillium. If brought into the house as an early spring bouquet, it fills the room with a fetid stench.

stinking buckeye n

=**Ohio buckeye.**

1882 IN Dept. Geol. & Nat. Resources *Rept. for 1881* 122, Stinking Buckeye. . . *Æsculus fœtida.* **1897** Sudworth *Arborescent Flora* 293 **AL, AR,** Ohio Buckeye. . . Stinking Buckeye. **1950** Peattie *Nat. Hist. Trees* 477, Ohio Buckeye. . . Fetid or Stinking Buckeye.

stinking bug See **stinkbug b(1)**

stinking camomile n Also sp *stinking chamomile* [*OED2* (at camomile sb. 1.b) 1578 →]

=**dog fennel 1.**

1817 Barton *Vegetable Materia Medica* 1.161, *Anthemis cotula.* Wild chamomile. May-weed. Stinking Chamomile. May-flower. (In England) Mathen. Dog's Fennel. **1894** *Jrl. Amer. Folkl.* 7.91 **NY,** *Anthemis Cotula . .* stinking chamomile. **1961** Smith *MI Wildflowers* 419, Mayweed, Stinking Chamomile, Dogfennel. **1979** Blair & Ketchum's *Country Jrl.* Sept 63 **nNEng,** Stinking Chamomile. **2006** Vizgirdas *Wild Plants* 187, Three species of *Anthemis* are found in California: *A. arvensis* (corn chamomile), *A. cotula* (stinking chamomile), and *A. tinctoria* (golden chamomile).

stinking cedar n **chiefly FL**

1 Either of two trees of the genus *Torreya:* usu *T. taxifolia* of northwest Florida, but also the **California nutmeg** *(T. californica).* The former is also called **gopherwood 2, savin 2** Cf **stinking yew**

1838 *Annals Nat. Hist.* 1.129 **nwFL,** The wood is . . of a strong and peculiar odour . . , hence it is frequently called, in the country where it grows, 'stinking cedar.' **1884** U.S. Dept. Ag. *Rept. of Secy. for 1884* 127 **nwFL,** From the doctor we obtain instructions for finding and permission to cut what he calls savin, which my axman calls stinking cedar, the same being called by botanists *Torreya taxifolia.* **1884** Sargent *Forests of N. Amer.* 186, *Torreya Californica.* . . California nutmeg. Stinking cedar. **1885** [see **2** below]. **1908** Sudworth *Forest Trees Pacific* 191, California nutmeg. . . is locally known as "stinking cedar" and "stinking yew," on account of the disagreeable odor emitted by its green parts and, to some extent, by its green wood when bruised. **1948** Tresidder *Trees Yosemite* 85 **CA,** On account of the disagreeable odor which results from bruising the foliage and even the wood, the tree is sometimes known as "stinking yew" or "stinking cedar." **1954** *Amer. Midland Naturalist* 52.270 **swGA,** Torreya, Stinking-cedar.—Found only in two or three ravines north of the Florida state line. **1979**

Bowden *Always Rivers Flow* 60 **nwFL** (as of 1930s–40s), And characteristic of the age of West Florida is the ancient evergreen Torreya, the oldest tree of all . . . the *stinking cedar* of the Apalachicola valley that became a part of the region's folklore as identical with the gopher wood of which Noah traditionally built the Ark. **1986** Pederson *LAGS Concordance,* 1 inf, **nwFL,** Stinking cedar. **2006** Vizgirdas *Wild Plants* 38, The species is often called "stinking cedar," because of its strong aroma.

2 =**Florida yew.**

1885 *Bot. Gaz.* 10.253 **FL,** It is called *Savin,* or *Stinking Cedar* . . , names also applied, I believe, to the Florida Yew *(Taxus Floridana),* a rarer tree, which is sometimes seen growing with it.

stinking chamomile   See **stinking camomile**

stinking clover n

=**Rocky Mountain bee plant.**

1895 MO Bot. Garden *Annual Rept.* 124, *Cleome serrulata.* . . Has a very fetid odor, on account of which it is called Stinking Clover by the country people. **1930** OK Univ. Biol. Surv. *Pub.* 2.64, *Cleome serrulata.* . . Pink Cleome. Stinking Clover. **1933** *Torreya* 33.83 **MT,** *Cleome serrulata.* . . Stinking clover, Mackelwain Lake. **1967** Dodge *Roadside Wildflowers* 15, Stinking clover. . . the unpleasant odor of the crushed foliage raises question as to flavor of the honey.

stinking daisy n

=**dog fennel 1.**

1914 Georgia *Manual Weeds* 488, *Anthemis Cotula.* . . Stinking Daisy, White Stinkweed. **1936** (1937) Meade *Adam's Profession* 65 **sVA,** Stinking Daisy, the one you used to know, has come to town as *Anthemis cotula.* **1956** *Jrl. Amer. Folkl.* 69.13, The ill-smelling *Anthemis cotula* (which is variously called Dog, Horse, Pigsty, Poison, or Stinking Daisy).

stinking-dog willie   See **stinking willie 2**

stinking fir n   Cf **piss fir**

=**grand fir.**

1909 Jepson *Trees CA* 218, *Abies grandis.* . . The woodsmen of the north coast of California call this species "Stinking Fir," on account of the odorous sap. **1923** Abrams *Flora Pacific States* 1.66, *Abies grandis.* . . Often called Stinking Fir by lumbermen.

stinking fleabane n

A **marsh fleabane 1** (here: *Pluchea foetida*).

1867 Curtis *Botany* 30 **NC,** *Pluchea* . . fœtida, . . (Stinking Fleabane). **1950** Gray–Fernald *Manual of Botany* 1449, *P[luchea] foetida* . . Stinking Fleabane. . . Wet sand, ditches and swamps. **1979** Hallowell *People Bayou* 16 **sLA,** Woven into its [=a marsh's] fabric are over one hundred plant species, bearing such curious names as sensitive jointvetch, rattlebox, floating-heart, and stinking fleabane. **2006** Nelson *Atl. Wildflowers* 119 **FL,** Stinking Camphorweed, Marsh Fleabane, or Stinking Fleabane—*Pluchea foetida.*

stinking grass   See **stink grass**

stinking hazel n   Cf **stinkbush 1**

=**fragrant sumac** or a related **sumac B** (here: *Rhus trilobata*).

1940 Steyermark *Flora MO* 331, Fragrant Sumac, Polecat Bush, Stinking Hazel *(Rhus aromatica). Ibid,* Polecat Bush, Skunk Bush, Stinking Hazel *(Rhus trilobata* Nutt. var. *serotina*).

stinking jenny n   Cf **stinking jim, stinkpot 1**

Either the **mud turtle 2b(1)** or the **musk turtle 1.**

1933 *Copeia* 11 **seGA,** *Sternotherus carinatus* . . , musk terrapin.—Found in eastern portion of Okefinokee and locally known as "Stinkin Jenny." **1986** Pederson *LAGS Concordance,* 1 inf, **cMS,** Stinking Jenny—cooter, small, steals bait. **2003** *DARE* File—Internet **seGA,** The Stinkpot, also called "The Stinking Jenny" or "The Stinking Jim", is about 5½″ long and is of the musk turtle family, easily recognized by their offensive smell.

stinking jim n   Also *jim-stink, stink-jim* [See quot 1909] **Sth, S Midl** Cf **stinking jenny, stinkpot 1**

Either the **mud turtle 2b(1)** or the **musk turtle 1.**

[**1880** (1881) Harris *Uncle Remus Songs* 54, 'Oh, my! You hear dat, gals?' sez Miss Meadows, sez she; 'Brer Fox call Brer Tarrypin Stinkin' Jim.'] **1909** *DN* 3.376 **eAL, wGA,** *Stinkin(g)-jim.* . . A small malodorous terrapin or terrestrial tortoise. **1918** *Copeia* 53.22 **VA,** "Stinking Jim". *Kinosternon odoratum.* **1939** TN Acad. Sci. *Jrl.* 14.86 **nwTN,** *Sternotherus odoratus* . . "Stinkin' Jim", Stinkpot, Musk Turtle. . . often

fed upon dead fish and refuse, but was not observed to catch living fish. **1949** *AmSp* 24.113 **GA,** *Stink Jim.* . . A small, foul-smelling terrapin. [McIntosh Co., Ga.] **1952** Carr *Turtles* 80, A really noteworthy attribute of this stink-jim [=*Sternotherus minor*] is its penchant for high basking perches. **1966–68** *DARE* (Qu. P24, . . *Kinds of turtles*) Inf **GA**65, Stinking jim [laughter]; **OK**52, Stinking jim—small, steals fish bait; **SC**31, Stinking jim—a mud turtle; **TN**24, Striped-head turtles or stinking jims. **1986** Pederson *LAGS Concordance* **Gulf Region,** 1 inf, Stink Jim; 1 inf, Stink Jim, Jim stink = box cooter; 1 inf, Stink Jim—terrapin-looking thing; 1 inf, Stink Jim—resembles loggerhead, longer; 1 inf, Stinking Jim—smells bad, gets all the way in hull; 1 inf, Stinking Jim = water terrapin. **1989** FL State Museum *Bulletin Biol. Sci.* 34.58 **nAL,** We were told by local residents that . . "stinking jims," a local name for both *S. odoratus* and *S. depressus,* had become scarce. **2003** [see **stinking jenny**].

stinking mayweed n   [*OED2* 1670 →]

=**dog fennel 1.**

1869 Porcher *Resources* 454 **Sth,** The common name of dogfennel has been applied . . to the wild chamomile (*Maruta cotula* [=*Anthemis c.*],) or stinking Mayweed. **1916** *Torreya* 16.240 **ME,** *Anthemis cotula* . . Stinking mayweed, Matinicus Id. **1973** Hitchcock–Cronquist *Flora Pacific NW* 482, Stinking m[ayweed] . . *A[nthemis] cotula.*

stinking mustard n

1 A **pennycress** (here: *Thlaspi arvense*).

1914 Georgia *Manual Weeds* 174, Penny Cress. . . *Other English names* . . Stinkweed, Stinking Mustard [etc]. . . When bruised, the plant exhales a most disgusting garlicky odor; if it is eaten by milch cows, the dairy products are spoiled.

2 =**jackass clover.**

1925 Jepson *Manual Plants CA* 409, *Wislizenia refracta.* . . A bee plant in the San Joaquin and often called Stinking Mustard because of its strong odor.

stinking poke   See **poke** n³ **2**

stinking prairie-bush n

A **hop tree** (here: *Ptelea trifoliata*).

1835 [see **stinking ash 1**]. **1876** Hobbs *Bot. Hdbk.* 113, Stinking prairie bush, Wafer ash, Ptelea trifoliata. **1930** Sievers *Amer. Med. Plants* 36, Hoptree. . . stinking ash, stinking prairie-bush.

stinking tom n

1 Either the **mud turtle 2b(1)** or the **musk turtle 1.**   Cf **stinking jim**

1949 *AmSp* 24.113 **FL,** *Stinking Tom.* . . A small, foul-smelling terrapin. [Alachua Co., Fla.] **1986** Pederson *LAGS Concordance (Turtle)* 1 inf, **cwAR,** Stinking Tom—small, bad odor.

2 =**tree of heaven.**

1982 *Barrick Coll.* **csPA,** *Stinkin' Tom*—a type of sumac; Ailanthus altissima.

stinking turtle   See **stink turtle**

stinking weed   See **stinkweed 2**

stinking willie n   Also sp *stinking Willy*

1 A **ragwort** (here: *Senecio jacobaea*). [A Scots name for this species (*SND* 1825 →), used also in eCanada where this European weed was first established in North America]

1876 Hobbs *Bot. Hdbk.* 113, Stinking Willie, Ragwort, Senecio Jacobaea. [**1884** *Bot. Gaz.* 9.58 **Nova Scotia Canada,** In tramping about the vicinity *Senecio Jacobæa* . . was found to be one of the commonest weeds. . . It is locally known as "Stinking Willie."] **1914** Georgia *Manual Weeds* 506, Stinking Willie—*Senecio Jacobea.* . . *Range:* Newfoundland, Prince Edward Island, Nova Scotia, and Quebec; locally in Ontario, Maine, southern New York, and New Jersey. . . The range of this coarse and dangerous weed is not at present very extensive, and every effort ought to be made to prevent its further dissemination. . . When green, the whole plant emits a most disagreeable, fetid odor. [**1941** *Dunkirk Eve. Observer* (NY) 31 May 15/4, Dr. Fernald said an example is the St. James-wort. . . About 70 years ago this species appeared in Nova Scotia, and by 1900 it had become one of the worst weeds of the countryside. Farmers in that locality rechristened it "Stinking Willie" and now it has reached as far south as Massachusetts.] **1964** Kingsbury *Poisonous Plants U.S.* 425, *Senecio jacobaea* . . Stinking willie.

2 also *stinking-dog willie:* A **trillium** (here: *Trillium erectum*). **esp sAppalachians**

1933 Small *Manual SE Flora* 307, T[rillium] erectum. . . Brown-beth. Stinking-Willie. **1939** TN Acad. Sci. *Jrl.* 14.292 **eTN,** Of even greater range and abundance than any of the others named is Stinking Willie (*Trillium erectum,* var. *album*). **1962** Frome *Whose Woods* 96 **wNC,** The moist ground beneath the dogwood would turn white, too, with snow trillium, the flower of the trinity, bearing . . the curious local name of "Stinking Willy." **1964** Campbell et al. *Gt. Smoky Wildflowers* 58, Purple Wakerobin. . . Because of a slightly unpleasant odor, it is sometimes called *stinking willie.* **1968** *DARE* (Qu. S2, . . *The flower that comes up in the woods early in spring, with three white petals that turn pink as the flower grows older*) Inf **PA**99, Stinking-dog willie, wet-dog willie. **1971** Hutchins *Hidden Valley* 57, Here, beside the road, I discover another trillium, this one a wake-robin *(Trillium erectum).* Its three petals are deep purple-red and the plant has a most unpleasant smell, which is the reason it is often known as "stinking Willie."

stinking willow n

A **false indigo 1** (here: *Amorpha californica*).

1931 U.S. Dept. Ag. *Misc. Pub.* 101.83 **CA,** *California indigobush . . often locally known as stinking willow.*

stinking Willy See stinking Willie

stinking yew n Cf stinking cedar

A tree of the genus *Torreya:* usu the **California nutmeg** *(T. californica),* but occas *T. taxifolia.*

1858 Gordon *Pinetum* 326, Gen. *Torreya.* . . The Stinking Yews. . . All small evergreen trees, found either in North America, China, or Japan, and emitting a strong disagreeable smell from all parts when bruised. *Ibid* 328, *Torreya myristica,* . . the Californian Nutmeg. . . [A]ll parts of the tree emit a very disagreeable odour, when either bruised or burned, and is called by the Californian emigrants the Stinking Yew, or Californian Nutmeg. **1876** Vasey *Catalogue Trees* 35, *Torreya taxifolia.* . . Florida. . . It is called by the inhabitants Stinking Yew, from the unpleasant odor of the bruised leaves. . . *Torreya Californica.* . . California. . . It is, like the preceding, called the Stinking Yew. **1910** Jepson *Silva CA* 168, In early days backwoodsmen often selected the trees for their rough bridges on account of the remarkable durability of the wood, which on account of its odor they call Stinking Yew. **1922** IA Acad. Sci. *Proc.* 29.247 **ceCA,** The bull pine . . appears and with it in the moist canyons . . an occasional stinking yew *(Tumion Californicum),* which is a rather rare tree, and unique among the California conifers. **1996** *Scientific Amer.* Mar 22, The number of stinking yew trees, named for the pungent odor of their needles, has been dropping since the 1950s.

stink-jim See stinking jim

stink-katz See stink-cat

stinkpot n

1 Either the **mud turtle 2b(1)** or the **musk turtle 1. scattered, but esp C Atl** See Map Cf **stinkbox, stinking jenny, ~ jim**

1825 Acad. Nat. Sci. Philadelphia *Jrl.* 4.217, The *odorata* is generally known by the name of "stink-pot," from its musky odor. **1842** DeKay *Zool. NY* 3.23, The *Musk Tortoise* or *Mud Turtle, Mud Terrapin* or *Stinkpot,* (with other equally savory popular names,) is to be found in most of our ponds and ditches. **1884** Goode *Fisheries U.S.* 1.154, The exceeding rankness of the odor of one species, *Aromochelys odorata* [= *Sternotherus odoratus*], has gained for it the very expressive appellation of "Stink-pot." **1928** Baylor Univ. Museum *Contrib.* 16.20, Musk Turtle. . . The name *Stink Pot* is throughout the greater part of eastern North America applied to this turtle. **1939** FWP *Guide NJ* 22, There are many types of turtles, including . . the mud turtle (stinkpot) of wood and marsh. **1941** Writers' Program *Guide AR* 17, Reptiles other than snakes are the turtles—mud, snapping, box and musk (or stinkpot). **1958** Conant *Reptiles & Amphibians* 35, Musk and Mud Turtles. . . These are the "stinkpots," the "skillpots," and the "stinking-jims" that often take the fisherman's hook. Such inelegant names derive from a musky secretion exuded at the time of capture from each of two glandular openings on each side of the body. **1965–70** *DARE* (Qu. P24, . . *Kinds of turtles*) Infs **NJ**17, 31, **PA**1, 29, 35, Stinkpot; **DE**3, Stinkpot—a terrapin; **LA**15, Stinkpot—that old green turtle, he's a dry-land turtle; **MD**29, Stinkpot—water turtle, dark shell with light spots; **NJ**53, Stinkpot—small, black. **1981** Vogt *Nat. Hist. WI* 93, When grasped, stinkpots claw and snap with their sharp hooked beak. **2003** *NY Times* (NY) 31 Aug sec 5 3/3

(Internet) **VT,** Visitors are introduced to mudpuppies (a type of salamander) and stinkpots (musk turtles), garter and rat snakes.

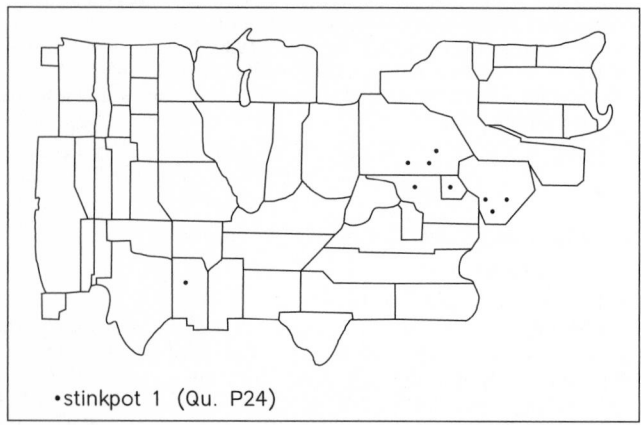

•stinkpot 1 (Qu. P24)

2 A **trillium** (here: *Trillium erectum*). **chiefly nNY** See Map

1967–69 *DARE* (Qu. S2, . . *The flower that comes up in the woods early in spring, with three white petals that turn pink as the flower grows older*) Infs **NY**6, 21, 28, 92, 191, 219, **PA**192, Stinkpot(s); **NY**97, Stinkpot—the red ones. **1968** *DARE* FW Addit **cnNY,** Trillium—when we were kids, we called 'em stinkpots. **2004** in 2007 *DARE* File—Internet **NY,** Red Trillium, we call it Stink Pot around here, is pretty nasty too! **2006** in 2008 *Ibid* **swNH,** Wake Robin, Trillium Erectum (aka "Stinkpot" due to their curiously strong stench). These are the first ones I've seen this year. **2008** *Ibid* **nNY,** I grew up on the Canadian border of NY state and there was a spot in the woods down the road from us that was filled with trilliums. . . The red trilliums we always called stinkpots due to the smell.

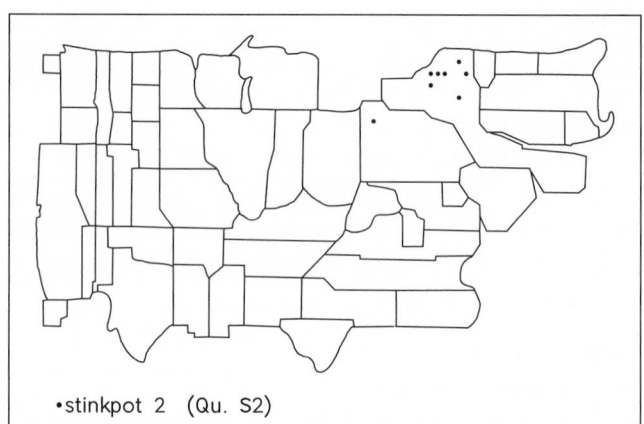

•stinkpot 2 (Qu. S2)

stink shad n chiefly FL

A **gizzard shad 1** (here: *Dorosoma cepedianum*).

1880 Smithsonian Inst. *Misc. Coll.* 19.119 **neFL,** *Dorosoma Cepedianum.* . . Stink Shad. St. John's [River]. **1940** Acad. Nat. Sci. Philadelphia *Proc.* 92.229 **FL,** In 1917 'Stink Shad' were reported in Lakes Okeechobee and Harney, and I saw several fish with such a name that had been taken in either Orange Lake or Lochloosa Lake. I assume that these were *Dorosoma.* **1970** *News Tribune* (Ft. Pierce FL) 12 Jan 2/7, [Caption:] Fish, disoriented by the cold, swam on their backs, as evidenced by this stink shad. **2003** *DARE* File—Internet **FL,** [Caption:] Osprey catching a Stink Shad near Ocala, Florida. **2005** in 2008 *Ibid* **FL,** Whoever told you that about filleting trash fish had never caught a "stink shad"! They are slimey (like phlegm all over them, yak!) have their own unique disgusting odor.

stink-shell turtle See stink turtle

stink sparrow See stinkbird

stink tree n

1 =**tree of heaven.**

[**1878** *S. Med. Rec.* 8.338, The "tree of heaven." . . gives off very disagreeable odors, whence it might more aptly be called "stink-tree."] **1895** NJ Geol. Surv. *Annual Rept. for 1894* 249, *Ailanthus glandulo-*

sus. . . Tree of Heaven, tallow tree, pride of China, stink tree. **1926** *Jrl. NY Bot. Garden* 27.67, Not only will the Tree of Heaven or "Stink Tree," as it is commonly called, thrive in the fertile soil of our forests, but appears perfectly at home in the ash heaps, dumps, and back yards of our crowded city. **1973** Wharton–Barbour *Trees KY* 539, *Ailanthus altissima.* . . The flowers of the male tree are strongly ill-scented, causing it to be called "stink tree," but the flowers of the female tree are unscented. **2002** *Baltimore City Paper Online* (MD) May 29 (Internet), This invasive, weedy import is nowadays known as the weed tree, or the ghetto palm, or the stink tree. **2003** *DARE* File—Internet **KY**, Tree of heaven is also unforgettable; a common moniker around here is stink tree, for the smell when a leaf is broken off or if its stiff stem is snapped.

2   =box elder.   Cf stinking ash 2

1969 *DARE* (Qu. T13, . . *Names . . for . . box elder*) Inf **IL45**, Stink tree.

stink turtle n   Also *stinking turtle, stink-shell* ~
Either the **mud turtle 2b(1)** or the **musk turtle 1.**

1886 Abbott *Upland* 249 **NJ**, The mud turtle, the stinking turtle, the painted and the spotted species, all will seize any salamander that crosses their path. **1890** *Century Dict.* 5950, *Stink-turtle.* . . The muskturtle. **1944** *Jrl. Amer. Folkl.* 57.42 **SC**, Its name [in the Catawba language] denotes . . the shape or odor of the stink-turtle (Sternotherus minor). **1967–70** *DARE* (Qu. P24, . . *Kinds of turtles*) Inf **LA34**, Stinking turtle = a small turtle with hinged undershell; lives in water and sticks; closes up like a box turtle; **GA41**, Stink-shell turtle; **LA14**, Stink turtles—might be same thing as mud turtle; **NJ65**, Stink turtle. **1986** Pederson *LAGS Concordance,* 1 inf, **ceTX**, Stink turtle—lives on land. **2005** *CT Post* (Bridgeport) 5 Aug (Internet), Both box and stink turtles are native to Connecticut and are of special concern.

stink verbena n
=devil's bouquet.

1951 *PADS* 15.31 **TX**, *Nyctaginia capitata.* . . Devil's bouquet; stink verbena.

stink vine n   HI
=maile pilau.

1929 Neal *Honolulu Gardens* 312, Stink vine, maile pilau. . . The leaves look like those of the true *maile* but unlike them have a strong unpleasant odor. **1971** Pukui–Elbert *Hawaiian Dict.* 206, *Maile-pilau.* Stink vine. . . *Lit.,* stinking *maile.* **2003** *Honolulu Advt.* (HI) 14 Oct sec B 1 (Internet) **HI**, Skunk vine, maile pilau, lesser Malayan stinkwort, stink vine. From its various common names, you get the picture that *Paederia foetida* isn't exactly welcome in most gardens.

stinkwater n
Asparagus.

1968 *DARE* (Qu. I29, *Names or nicknames for asparagus*) Inf **CA36**, Stinkwater—because it makes urine smell bad.

stinkweed n
1   A jimson weed, usu *Datura stramonium*.

1798 *Med. Repository* 1.550, The subject of this dissertation is the plant known, in different parts of the United States, by the various names of Jamestown-weed, French chesnut, stink-weed, and moonweed, or moon-wort. **1804** Volney *View Soil U.S.A.* 69, [Translator's note:] These banks, and all the slopes along the Ohio, abound with the stramoneum (stink-weed), which is said to have been brought hither accidentally from Virginia. **1828** Rafinesque *Med. Flora* 1.146, *Datura stramonium.* . . Vulgar Names—Jamestownweed, Jimson, Stinkweed, &c. **1859** (1968) Bartlett *Americanisms* 219, Jamestown Weed. . . The Thorn Apple. . . Its Northern name is Stinkweed. **1869** Roosevelt *Five Acres* 187 **NY**, "Sweet scented! Why, that is a stink-weed. If you don't believe me, just touch it." It was. . . I had succeeded in producing about a hundred stink-weeds. **1894** *Jrl. Amer. Folkl.* 7.95 **WV**, *Datura Stramonium* . . stinkweed. **1966** Peden *Land* 319 **cIN**, The unpleasant odor of its foliage has earned this hardy annual [=Jimson weed] the subtitle "stinkweed." **1971** Krochmal *Appalachia Med. Plants* 108, Jimsonweed . . stink apple, stinkweed, stinkwort [etc].

2   also *stinking weed*: A Jerusalem oak 1 (here: *Chenopodium ambrosioides*).   Cf stickweed b(8)

1828 Rafinesque *Med. Flora* 1.103, *Chenopodium anthelminticum* [= *C. ambrosioides*]. . . Jerusalem Oak, Wormwood, Worm seed, Stinking weed. **1892** (1974) Millspaugh *Amer. Med. Plants* 140, *Chenopodium anthelminticum.* . . American wormseed, Jerusalem oak, Stinkweed. **1933** Small *Manual SE Flora* 466, *A[mbrina] ambrosioides* [=*Chenopodium a.*]. . Mexican-tea. Wormseed. Stinkweed. **1974** Morton *Folk*

Remedies 43 **SC**, Jerusalem oak . . Stinkweed. . . Plant juice or infusion valued as a vermifuge for children. **1986** Pederson *LAGS Concordance (Undesirable grass in a cotton field)* 1 inf, **neTN**, Stinkweed or stickweed.

3   =dog fennel 1.

1856 *Amer. Pharmaceutical Assoc. Proc.* 70 **nwGA**, *Anthemis cotula* is one of our greatest pests. May-weed, stink-weed, dog-fennel, and wild chamomile are its vulgar names. It completely covers waste lands and the commons around our cities and towns. **1929** *Torreya* 29.151 **ME**, *Anthemis Cotula* was "Stink weed." **1935** (1943) Muenscher *Weeds* 451, *Anthemis Cotula* . . Dog fennel, Mayweed, Stinkweed. **1950** *WELS Suppl.* **csWI**, Stinkweeds, stink daisies—wild camomile.

4   =butter-and-eggs 1.

1859 *NY Ag. Soc. Trans. for 1858* 18.403, Snap dragon or toad-flax, known also as stink-weed and butter and eggs *(linaria vulgaris),* one of the greatest pests in some parts of the State, is not found in any field of the farm. **1861** *Amer. Inst. NYC Annual Rept. for 1860–61* 223 **cwMA**, "The plant grows from eight to eighteen inches high, covering the whole ground in a dense mass, to the exclusion of all kinds of grass and grain. . . This weed gives out a very unpleasant smell, and is known here by the name of stink weed." Mr. Carpenter.—It is known in Westchester county as wild flax or butter and eggs. **1968** *DARE* (Qu. S11) Inf **PA104**, Butter-and-eggs—used to call it stinkweed.

5   =poison hemlock 1.

1892 (1974) Millspaugh *Amer. Med. Plants* 68–1, Wild or poison hemlock, Stink-weed. . . This large, unsavory, biennial herb, grows to a height varying from 2 to 6 feet. **1914** *Georgia Manual Weeds* 300, *Poison Hemlock.* . . Poison Stinkweed. . . The whole plant has a very disagreeable "mousy" odor, especially when bruised. **1935** (1943) Muenscher *Weeds* 350, *Conium maculatum.* . . Poison stinkweed.

6   A fetid marigold 1 (here: *Dyssodia papposa*).

1896 U.S. Dept. Ag. *Yearbook for 1895* 598, Fetid marigold, stink-weed.—*Dyosodia* [sic] *papposa.* **1898** *Jrl. Amer. Folkl.* 11.229 **KS**, *Dysodia chrysanthemoides* [=*Dyssodia papposa*] . . stinkweed. **1901** *Science* 8 Nov 723 **Plains States,** The dark green of stinkweed (*Dyssodia papposa*) as seen in the summer is replaced in early winter by a pronounced brick-red. **1914** *Georgia Manual Weeds* 485, Fetid Marigold. . . Yellow Dog-fennel, Stinkweed. **1935** (1943) Muenscher *Weeds* 480, *Dyssodia papposa.* . . False mayweed, Stinkweed.

7   =Rocky Mountain bee plant.

1901 *MT Ag. Exper. Sta. Bulletin* 30.35, *Cleome integrifolia.* . . Indian Pink; Stinkweed. . . Frequent in grain fields and waste places east of the Divide and now spreading westward along the railways, where it threatens to become a bad weed. **1930** *Folk-Say* 4.192 **NM**, Stinkweed, as the bee plant is very commonly called, is an essential to the Indians for many purposes. **1957** Barnes *Nat. Hist. Wasatch Summer* 44 **UT**, We find . . beds of pink cleome, stinkweed or Rocky Mountain bee plant (*Cleome serrulata*). **1967** *DARE* FW Addit **OR**12, Spiderflowers (caper family)—locally called stinkweed.

8   =jackass clover.

1911 *CA Ag. Exper. Sta. Berkeley Bulletin* 217.992, *Wislizenia refracta.* . . Jackass Clover. Stinkweed. **1944** Abrams *Flora Pacific States* 2.326, *Wislizenia californica* [=*W. refracta* subsp *c.*] . . California Stinkweed. **1957** *MO Bot. Garden Annals* 44.78, *W[islizenia] refracta.* . . Jackass Clover, Stinkweed, Spectacle Pod.

9   A gilia; see quots.

1914 *Georgia Manual Weeds* 329, Skunkweed—*Navarretia squarrosa.* . . *Other English names:* Stinkweed, Pepperweed [etc]. **1931** U.S. Dept. Ag. *Misc. Pub.* 101.139, Nuttall gilia [=*Linanthus nuttallii*], locally known as stickerbush, stinkweed. **1967** *DARE* FW Addit **OR**12, Skyrocket (phlox family, gilia)—locally: stinkweed.

10   A pennycress (here: *Thlaspi arvense*).

[**1892** Canada Dept. Ag. *Exper. Farms Rept. for 1891* 215, Penny Cress, "Stink-weed," "French-weed" (*Thlaspi arvense*). This is considered one of the worst weeds in Manitoba.] **1909** *VT Ag. Exper. Sta. Bulletin* 138.15, Stink weed, *Thlaspi arvense.* **1914** *Georgia Manual Weeds* 174, Penny Cress. . . Frenchweed, Stinkweed, Stinking Mustard [etc]. **1935** (1943) Muenscher *Weeds* 281, *Thlaspi arvense.* . . Frenchweed, Stinkweed [etc]. **1937** U.S. Forest Serv. *Range Plant Hdbk.* W187, Field pennycress. . . known locally as bastard-cress, . . stinkweed [etc] . . is now well distributed throughout the United States. **1968** *DARE* (Qu. S21, . . *Weeds . . that are a trouble in gardens and fields*) Inf **MN23**, Frenchweed or stinkweed. **2008** *Houston Chron.* (TX) 7 Sept 2 (Internet), Would he devote an acre of his fields near the Vermont line this fall to grow stinkweed? "It was like, 'What the heck? I've been trying to get rid of these things for 30 years. Now you want me to plant them?'"

11 =velvetleaf a.

1926 IA Geol. Surv. *Bulletin* 4.641, The most outstanding example of this type of annual weed is the velvet-weed *(Abutilon Theophrasti),* sometimes known as button weed, butter-print, velvet-leaf, Indian mallow, stinkweed and skunkweed. **1969** *DARE* (Qu. S21, . . *Weeds . . that are a trouble in gardens and fields*) Inf **IL44,** Velvettweed, stinkweed, elephant's ears, buttonweed—all names for the same plant—big leaves that look like elephant's ears and are [sic] velvety, small, button-like seeds.

12 A marsh fleabane 1, usu *Pluchea camphorata.*

1947 U.S. Pub. Health Serv. *Malaria Control* 336, There are some species against which grazing is not effective. Notable among these are stinkweed (*Pluchea* sp.), whitetop . . , wild cotton [etc]. **1950** Gray-Fernald *Manual of Botany* 1448, *Pluchea* [spp.] . . Marsh-Fleabane. Stinkweed. *Ibid* 1449, *P. camphorata.* . . Camphorweed, Stinkweed. **1975** Duncan–Foote *Wildflowers SE* 206, Camphorweed; Stinkweed— *Pluchea camphorata.* . . Foul-smelling annual or perennial. **2008** *DARE* File—Internet **AL,** *Pluchea odorata*—sweetscent. . . The Stinkweed is a perennial in my zone 7b garden. It is not very attractive but is a magnet for insects.

13 =tree of heaven.

1948 Taylor *Encycl. Gardening* 16, *Ailanthus.* . . *altissima.* Tree-of-Heaven. Stinkweed; also called *A. glandulosa.* . . the odor of the male flower is noxious to many. **1952** Cooper *Late Harvest* 218 **NJ,** And now we turn to things disgraceful. Thus, 'A Stinkweed Grows in Brooklyn,' for that is what we boys called the Ailanthus-tree some fifty years ago in a small town in New Jersey. **1954** *Sun* (Baltimore MD) 4 June 21/1, Due to the fact that its leaves, when crushed, are very disagreeable to get next to, the *ailanthus* is also known as "stinkweed." **1971** Kieran *Nat. Hist. NYC* 187, If you use your hand to strip the leaflets from the long compound leaves . . you will understand why a common name for this Tree-of-Heaven is Stinkweed. **2001** *DARE* File—Internet, Tree-of-heaven, Ailanthus altissima, is also called stinkweed. . . The flowers of the male tree give off a vile, putrid odor.

14 A boneset 1 (here: *Eupatorium purpureum*).

1958 Jacobs–Burlage *Index Plants NC* 52, *Eupatorium purpureum.* . . Quillwort; stinkweed [etc]. **1971** Krochmal *Appalachia Med. Plants* 120, Joe-pyeweed, . . stinkweed [etc].

15 Perh a milk vetch such as *Astragalus mollissimus.*

1966 *DARE* (Qu. S21, . . *Weeds . . that are a trouble in gardens and fields*) Inf **NM9,** Stinkweed—purple flower, "beans" in seedpods, grow[s] up to four feet high in clusters.

16 =skunk cabbage 1a.

1968 *DARE* Wildfl QR Pl.5 (*Spathyema foetida* [=*Symplocarpus foetidus*]) Inf **OH82,** Stinkweed.

17 =Queen Anne's lace 1.

1968 *DARE* (Qu. S6, . . *Queen Anne's lace: [Summertime roadside weed two feet high or so with a lacy white top]*) Inf **NY49,** Stinkweed.

stinkwood n
=Carolina buckthorn 1.

1897 Sudworth *Arborescent Flora* 298 **LA,** *Rhamnus caroliniana.* . . Stinkwood.

stinkworm n

Any of var strong-smelling annelid worms freq used for bait; see quots.

1941 Robinson *Pond Fishing* 63, Use the dark red worms of large size whenever possible. . . Do not use the small ringed worms that are found in manure piles—called "stink" worms. **1950** *USGA Jrl. & Turf Management* Apr 32, The earthworm (*Pheretima* [=*Amynthas*] *hupeiensis* . .), a pest in golf-course greens, originated in the Orient. . . In general it is light grass-green in color on the dorsal surface. . . It is extremely active at all times. . . Furthermore, it discharges a disagreeable secretion, thus the common name "stinkworm." **1962** *Pop. Electronics* July 90, Be ready with your rods and a can of stinkworms about four o'clock tomorrow afternoon, and I'll show you the best channel-cat fishing east of the Mississippi! **1967–69** *DARE* (Qu. P6, . . *Kinds of worms . . used for bait*) Inf **KY23,** Stinkworm; **OH33,** Stinkworm— that's a redworm. **2003** *DARE* File—Internet, Common names for the *Eisenia fetida* are: *Redworm,* Red Wiggler, . . Stink Worm [etc]. **2006** *Ibid* **NE,** Take along a spade and hit the banks for green or "stink" worms. . . They do stink but work wonders for sturgeon. **2006** in 2008

Ibid **OH,** They are excellent channel bait. I've always heard them called stink worms. They are pretty small and skinny, green, and some of the worst smelling things you will ever smell. **2007** *Ibid* **nwPA,** Are you familiar with what I call a stink worm or sewer worm? Will grow to the size of medium red worms and are striped like a tiger. When you put these on you [sic] hook your hands will smell bad (stink).

‡stinky n

c1970 Wiersma *Marbles Terms* **cnIL** (as of c1957), *Stinky* . . any marble you would give up freely. Eg. This chippie is a stinky.

stint n [*OED2* a1466 →]

Also with modifier: A small shore bird, usu the **least sandpiper.**

1834 Nuttall *Manual Ornith.* 2.117, Stint, or Little Sandpiper. . . *Tringa pusilla* [=*Calidris p.*] **1903** Dawson *Birds OH* 2.510, Least Sandpiper. . . Synonyms.—American Stint; Peep. **1956** *AmSp* 31.299, The name *stint* is applied in Great Britain to some of the smaller shore birds and especially to the dunlin, or red-backed sandpiper. Usage in America, if not so frequent, is much the same in its applications.

stint v [*OED2* stint v. I.3 "To cease moving, pause in a journey, to halt, stop, stand still. . . *Obs.*"] *relic*

1975 Gainer *Witches* 17 **sAppalachians,** Stint . . to stop. "Don't stint till you've gone all the way home."

stir n[1] Cf **stir-off** n

1 An occasion at which maple syrup is made.

1967 *DARE* Tape **OH8,** [FW:] I thought . . the Maple Syrup Festival was pretty big. [Inf:] We don't have a festival here. . . *the* Maple Festival is up in Chardon. . . They sell maple products, too, and they have a stir up there.

2 A batch (of sorghum syrup or apple butter).

1976 Garber *Mountain-ese* 76 **sAppalachians,** *Run-a-stir* . . make sorgrum—Come over tonight and help us run-a-stir uv molasses. **1984** Wilder *You All Spoken Here* 85 **Sth,** *Stir:* A quantity of apple butter; three bushels of apples will make a stir.

stir n[2] See **stewer**

stirabout n

1 also *stirabout pudding, stirry, stir-up:* A porridge of cornmeal or oatmeal; **hasty pudding.** [Orig Anglo-Ir]

1853 (1982) Lea *Domestic Cookery* 82, *New England Hasty Pudding, or Stir-about.* Boil three quarts of water in an iron pot; mix a pint of Indian meal in cold water, and make it thin enough to pour easily; when the water boils, pour it in; stir well with a wooden stick kept for the purpose; it takes about an hour to boil; salt to your taste; stir in dry meal to make it thick enough, beating it all the time. Eat it with milk or molasses, or butter and sugar. **1856** in 1937 *Amer. Legion Mag.* July 58 **wIA,** 2 families gave out, being frightened at getting nothing for 3 days but Indian corn stirabout. **1939** Wolcott *Yankee Cook Book* 165, Hasty pudding was a favorite supper dish on New England farms where it was sometimes called Stir-about Pudding. **1941** *LANE* Map 288 *(Corn meal mush)* 1 inf, **cnRI,** Stir-about, an Irish word; 1 inf, **seMA,** Stir-about, 'the genuine old name for it' (The informant is of Irish descent.); 1 inf, **ceMA,** Stir-about, 'because you keep stirring it'; 1 inf, **cMA,** Stir-about, heard from Irish maids; 1 inf, **csCT,** Stir-up, used by a local Irish family. **1941** Justus *Cabin on Kettle Creek* 98 **eTN,** Pudding's like stirabout in one way. You can use just about whatever you have and it's likely to turn out well enough. **1949** Emrich *Wild West Custom* 183 **wMT,** In Butte, the mainstay of the Irish miners was "stirabout." This was no more than old-fashioned oatmeal thinned with milk, and was served by the ton to the miners. **1966** *DARE* (Qu. H24, . . *Names or nicknames . . for boiled cornmeal*) Inf **SC26,** Mush—fry bacon, leave grease, boil water, put in meal—by Whites this is called stirabout or stirry.

‡2 in pl: Pancake batter that is stirred as it is cooked; see quot.

1968 *DARE* Tape **SC56,** We'd put that in the frying pan and just stir it all up, you know, instead of letting it be in a hot, whole cake. That's like pancake dough you're making. And put that and stir it up and they'd eat it for breakfast . . , stirabouts they called that. . . Stir it all up and let 'em brown. . . It'd be just a little more browner and . . just in little lumps instead of whole pancake.

stirabout pudding   See **stirabout 1**

stir off v phr, hence vbl n *stirring off*   Cf **stir-off** n, **sugar off** v phr, **syrup off**

1 To crystallize (a sugar syrup, esp maple syrup) by boiling it to the proper concentration and then stirring it as it cools; to make (a batch of sugar) in this way; to boil down syrup for sugar; hence n *stirring-off (bee)* =**stir-off** n.

1829 *Amer. Farmer* 11.107 **csPA**, If the [maple] molasses is thick it will form a thread in the water, and if this thread will break like glass, when struck with a knife, it must be taken off the fire and is fit to stir off. The kettle is set on the ground and occasionally stirred till it cools and granulates.   **1846** *Knickerbocker* 27.211 **WY**, All . . were there . . to witness the grand 'stirring off.'   **1861** in 2003 *DARE* File—Internet **cIN**, [Diary entry for 3 Apr:] Betty and I went over to Uncle Natties to a stirring off. Eat and [sic] sugar until I was almost sick.   **1862** in 2004 *Ibid* **neOH**, April 1st Tuesday. . . Jane came down, helped stir off two batches of sugar.   **1863** *Scientific Amer.* 8.52 **NH**, Return the sirup, and place it over a brisk fire, and evaporate as quickly as possible to the proper consistence. If it is to be caked, it must be harder than for tub sugar, or to stir off dry.   **1875** Wasson *Annals Pioneer Settlers* 37 **ceIN**, The [maple] sap was boiled down for hours, . . till the sap became diminished in quantity and sweeter, when it was called syrup, and taken out; when sufficient syrup was boiled it was "stirred off" or grained and became sugar.   **1879** [see **2** below].   **1881** *Harper's New Mth. Mag.* 62.649 **VT**, When the contents were reduced to a desired consistency, the hot syrup . . was poured into a large . . kettle for the process of "stirring off."   **1883** *Lippincott's Mag.* 31.303 **OH**, When the Davises were ready to stir off in their sugar-camp, it was the most natural thing in the world for them to invite their neighbors to come and eat the sugar.   **1910** in 2004 *DARE* File—Internet **swIA**, [We] raised cane for sorgum syrup and sometimes stirred off some for sugar.   **1914** Keith *Hist. Watson Family* np **MO**, We were stirring off a big kettle full of sugar when the wolves began to howl.   **c1938** in Lib. of Congress *Amer. Memory: WPA Life Hist.* (Internet) **VT**, The women folk have full charge of the stirrin'-off and making of the fancy sugar cakes. When the men think they have the best run of sap . . they pass the word along and Ma calls a "stirrin'-off bee." All the women gather at the sugar house armed with huge spoons and milk pans. . . [T]hey stand in a busy row, tongues wagging against the clatter of spoon on pan, and beat, beat, beat; the heavy amber syrup smooths to creamy thick stuff which must be poured at exactly the right moment into the ranks of tin molds which are waiting ready. A little is stirred-off earlier, before the syrup gets too thick, to make Ma some maple cream.

2 To complete a batch of (maple or sorghum syrup or fruit butter).

1858 IN State Bd. Ag. *Annual Rept. for 1857* 492, The grape and pear butter was made by adding half a pound of sugar to a pound of fruit and stirred off as above.   **1879** in 2004 *DARE* File—Internet **neIN**, Saturday, March 29, 1879. Boys working & boiling in the Camp to day. . . the women Stir off Molasses & Sugar in P.M.   **1927** *AmSp* 2.365 **cwWV**, *Stirring off* . . to complete a kettle of butter or a pan of molasses. "How soon will that kettle be stirred off?"   **1959** [see **stir-off** n].   **1976** *Bittersweet* Winter 26 **Ozarks**, [Making Maple Syrup:] Near the end of the day my father would begin testing the syrup every few minutes to see when it was the proper consistency for "stirring off." When it reached that stage he pulled the fire out from under the boiler, let the syrup cool a bit, then poured it into various containers.   **2004** *DARE* File—Internet **neOH**, It was in 1937 when the church women started their project of "Apple Butter Making." . . The congregation of the church 'stirred off' many hundreds of gallons.   **2008** *Ibid* **WV**, It generally takes 8–10 hrs to stir off a kettle [of apple butter].

stir-off n [**stir off** v phr] **chiefly sAppalachians, esp eKY** Cf **molasses making, stir** n¹

The completion of a batch of sorghum syrup (or, less freq, of maple sugar or syrup, or apple butter); a communal gathering accompanying this process.

1897 *Werner's Mag.* 19.244 **Sth**, The season here we hold so dear is when the cane we grind./ I[f] you could go to a "stir off," and see a kettle full,/ You would say there was nothing like a good old taffy pull.   **1901** *Independent* 53.1128 **KY**, It was at a "stir off" that we arranged for the debate.   **1923** (1946) Greer-Petrie *Angeline Doin' Society* 7 **csKY**, We have . . log-rollin's, and quiltin's, and in the fall of the year, stir-offs.   **1953** *PADS* 19.14 **seKY**, *Stir-off*. . . A neighborhood social event after molasses is made and the time has come to take it off.   **1954**

in 2004 *DARE* File—Internet **neKY** (as of c1880), This molding of the [maple] sugar and dipping out the residue of syrup was called a "stir off," as at the last there was much stirring of the syrup before it grained and was followed sometimes by an invitation to those present to dip in ("Hep yo'self") with spoons or wood paddles and eat of the syrup in the bottom of the kettle.   **1959** Roberts *Up Cutshin* 31 **seKY**, Everybody raised cane. We would have a stir-off every night when we got to making 'lasses. Get the cane into the mill and grind it into juice of a day, and then it would take us till sometimes two o'clock in the night to get it stirred off.   **c1960** *Wilson Coll.* **csKY**, *Stir-off*. . . The run-off or finishing of a making of sorghum.   **1969** *DARE* (Qu. FF2, . . Kinds of *parties*) Inf **KY**41, Stir-off—for the 'lassy-making.   **1969** *DARE* FW Addit **ceKY**, *Stir-off*—a party where neighbors help make molasses or sorghum.   **1991** AL Coop. Ext. Serv. *Sweet Sorghum Culture*, Cool the strained [sorghum] syrup obtained from each "stir-off" in a large container to about 140 degrees to 160 degrees F as quickly as possible.   **2002** WA Bluegrass Assoc. *Bluegrass Gaz.* Summer 2 (Internet) **VA**, It took me back to my days in Virginia when my parents would make maple syrup and have a sugar stir-off where the entire community came.   **2004** *DARE* File—Internet **cKY**, When I was a boy, stir-off time was one of the highlights of the year. The stir-off was what we had near the end of the day when we made sorghum molasses.   *Ibid* **neTN**, When it was sorghum makin' time it was a community event. Many people would refer to it as the "Stir Off" and would often ask, "Are you a goin' to the stir off tomorrow?"   *Ibid* **swVA**, Big Stone Gap Antique Show. . . Other activities include Apple butter stir-off, pinto bean dinner, . . and much more.   *Ibid* **seOH**, From the Founders Day Festival in April, . . the Apple Butter Stir-Off in October, to the Holiday Lights Festival in December, the Belpre year is full of celebrations and festivals.

stirp See **stirrup**

stirring off vbl n   See **stir off** v phr

stirring-off (bee) See **stir off** v phr **1**

stirring plow n   **chiefly Upper Missip Valley, Plains States**
A moldboard plow for general use in already-broken ground.

1844 *Prairie Farmer* 4.168 **IL**, First Division—Plows for all kinds of plowing, exclusive of breaking prairie. . . Second Division—Stirring plow.   **1871** Hutchinson *Resources KS* 146, By . . following a breaker with a stirring plow, to throw the soil on top of the inverted sod . . as much might be accomplished in one year as . . in . . two years.   **1874** U.S. Dept. Ag. *Rept. of Secy. for 1873* 439 **NE**, With a good plowman I commenced turning over the sod with a strong team, and with another, using a common stirring-plow, followed, turning up the soil six inches deep.   **1896** Hickenlooper *Illustr. Hist. Monroe Co. IA* 194, After the ground had first been broken with the big prairie plow, the ground in later years was turned over by the "diamond" plow or "stirring" plow.   **1908** in 2003 *DARE* File—Internet [*State Herald* (Holyoke CO) 20 Nov], [Advt:] Public auction . . 16 inch stirring plow.   **1929** Bell *Some Contrib. KS Vocab.* 103, *Stirring plow*. . . A plow with a shorter moldboard than that of a *breaking plow*. The *stirring plow* is the ordinary kind of plow, the *breaking plow* being the unusual kind.   **1947** *Maryville Daily Forum* (MO) 25 Feb 8/7, [Advt:] Implements— . . 2 riding cultivators; 16″ stirring plow, riding attachment.   **1967–68** *DARE* (Qu. L18, *Kinds of plows*) Inf **IA**36, Gang plow—same as stirring plow; stirring plow—drawn by horses, two or three plowshares; **KS**5, Stirring plow—you use that on stubble.   **1974** *Muscatine Jrl.* (IA) 13 Apr 9/7, [Advt:] Simplicity tractor with mower. 800 lb. platform scales. 2 section harrow. 16 inch stirring plow.

stirrup n   Usu |ˈstɝ-əp, ˈstɪr-əp|; also |ˈstɪr-əp, ˈstɛr-əp|; occas |stɝp|; for addit varr see quots   Pronc-spp *sterrup, stirp, stur(ru)p*   Cf **squirrel** n, **syrup**
Std sense, var forms.

1676 in 2008 *DARE* File—Internet **seMA**, Item 2 paire of sterrup Irons & Gertts.   **1714** in 1894 Providence RI Rec. Comm. *Early Rec.* 7.174, To a Bridle Sturrup Jrons & leathers.   **1891** *DN* 1.131 **cNY**, [stɝ-əp], or [stɝ-əp].   **1910** *DN* 3.450 **wNY**, *Sturrup*. . . Stirrup.   **1911** *DN* 3.501 **Sth, S Midl**, Stirrup . . [ʌ] 32 [of 158 infs] . . [ɝ] 113 . . [ɪ] 13.   **1941** *AmSp* 16.7 **eTX** [Black], *Stirrup* . . [ʌ:], as the typical, and [ʌɪᵛ], as the occasional, sound.   **1942** *AmSp* 17.31 **seNY**, The centralization of [ɪ] . . [yielding [ɝ] in words like *bird, flurry,* and *scurry*] is now less striking in downstate speech. . . Variations include *stirrup* [strəp] 8 [infs], [stirəp] 2, [stɛˀrəp] 1, [stɝrəp] 20.   **1944** *PADS* 2.30 **eKY**, Sturp [stʌrp]. . . Stirrup. . . Common.   **1954** *Harder Coll.* **cwTN**, *Stirrup* [stʌrp].   **c1960** *Wilson Coll.* **csKY**, *Stirrups* . . /stɝps/ . . /stɝəps/.   **1961** Kurath–McDavid *Pronc. Engl.* 127, In *stirrup* the variants /stɪrəp/ and

/stɛrəp/ are much more widespread [than those vowels are in *squirrel*], though the variants /stɜəp ~ stɜrəp ~ stʌrəp/ occur everywhere and predominate decisively in the greater part of the Eastern States. /stɪrəp ~ stɛrəp/ are common in New England (but not in the usually conservative "Down East") and occur with some frequency in parts of Upstate New York, in Metropolitan New York, and in South Carolina. Elsewhere, as in southeastern Pennsylvania, eastern Virginia, and the Ohio Valley, they are rare. Outside New England, /stɪrəp/ seems to have prestige. . . All American variants have their parallels in English folk speech. **1989** Pederson *LAGS Tech. Index* 143 **Gulf Region** *(Stirrups)* [Of 914 infs, 629 gave proncs of the types [stʌrəp(s), stʌrɪp(s)]; 59 infs, [stɛrəp(s), stɛrɪp(s)]; 52 infs, [stɪrəp(s), stɪrɪp(s)]; 16 infs, [stUrəp(s), stUrɪp(s)]; 6 infs, [stʌrʌp(s)]; 2 infs, [starəps]; 1 inf, [stɔrɪp].] **2006** in 2007 *DARE* File—Internet **AL,** I know it has sturrups but i like sturrups. **2008** *DARE* File—Internet **OH,** [Advt:] Saddle. . . Has Perris Sterrups. *Ibid* **ME,** [Advt:] Its [sic] comes with the matching bridle, white saddle pad, stirp leathers, and bit with the bridle. *Ibid* **AZ,** [Advt:] The kid saddle has a crack in the seat its just a little one and has some cracking by the sturps. *Ibid* **MN,** But they will actually touch there nose to there sides or near the stirps if you have a saddle on. *Ibid* **FL,** [Advt:] Trail saddle comes with sturps brand new leather that is holding sturps.

stirrup oil n   [In ref to a shoemaker's stirrup; cf *OED2 stirrup* sb. 2.b, *EDD stirrup* sb. 1.(6)]   Cf *hickory oil* (at **hickory** n B3), **oil of hazel,** *DS* Y16, HH14
=**strap oil.**

1766 in 1976 Laurens *Papers* 5.120 **SC,** I . . am glad to find that you apply that useful ointment which you call Stirrup Oil when he wants it. **1828** *Reg. PA* 2.287 **Philadelphia PA** (as of 1788), Every trade was preceded by a stage, on wheels, and the business of the shop in full operation. The Cordwainer's Shop stopped at the corner of Vine and Third, when the master, seizing one of the apprentices, gave him a "dose of stirrup oil," . . to the merriment of the beholders. **1866** Comstock *Betsey Jane Ward* 89, It's my advice that yu go strate home 2 yure shop, be4 yu get a dose of stirrup-ile. **1895** *DN* 1.383 **NJ,** *Stirrup oil* . . shoemaker's term for a whipping, or punishment administered with the stirrup, or knee-strap. **1897** *CT Mag.* 3.303 (as of early 19th cent), The Major's apprentices . . occasionally applied sundry "ticket-of-leave" methods of . . getting rid of too long tarrying or troublesome visitors, such as sending them down to Capt. Thomas's shop after "stirrup" oil. **1899** (1912) Green *VA Folk-Speech* 419, *Stirrup-oil.* . . A sound beating; a drubbing with a leather strap. **1936** *El Paso Herald–Post* (TX) 1 Apr 4/1, The day will be full of other foolery, not counting the usual phony phone calls and solemn requests for left-handed monkey-wrenches, stirrup oil, and pigeon's milk.

stirry v   [Cf Engl dial *stirree, sturry* (at *EDD stir* v.)]
To stir.
1857 *S. Lit. Messenger* 24.124 **VA** [Black], He's not able to stirry 'bout much yit awhile. **1911** Cocke *Bypaths Dixie* 46 **Sth** [Black], De chillun an' Abe come er runnin' but de ole man ain' stirry er speck. **1982** *Barrick Coll.* **csPA,** Stirry—stir—"Would you stirry the soup for me." "I stirried it until it boiled." **2003** in 2004 *DARE* File—Internet **seLA,** I . . mixed a tablespoon of sugar in each of the cups and stirred (or as we say in N.O., "stirried them.") **2004** *NADS Letters* **ceTX** [Black], Stirry—"To stir." As a child, i.e. till my early teens, ca. 1950, I used this. It was pronounced as though spelled "steery." I'm black and was born in Marshall, Harrison County, Texas in 1937. It was also used by my maternal grandfather, likewise born in Marshall in 1877, and my maternal grandmother, born in Longview, Gregg county, Texas in 1898.

stirry n   See **stirabout 1**

stir up v phr   Cf *rustle up* (at **rustle** v A1)
To prepare or arrange food or drink in a hurry.
1884 *Anglia* 7.273 **Sth, S Midl** [Black], *To stir up er bobbykew* = to get up a pic-nic. **1927** *AmSp* 2.365 **cwWV,** Stir up some dinner . . to get some food in a hurry. "Stir us up some dinner; we have to go to town." **1954** *Harder Coll.* **cwTN,** Stir up some dinner. **1966** *DARE* (Qu. H73, . . *Preparing coffee: the housewife says, "I think I'll go and _____ some coffee."*) Inf **MS**1, Stir up. **1969** in 2003 *DARE* File—Internet, [From the script for the film *The Wild Bunch:*] Why the hell don't you stir up some grub? **2002** *DARE* File—Internet **TX,** Count on me if you're in the Shepherd, Texas area. . . I'll make coffee anytime and stir up some grub for the weary traveller.

stir-up n   See **stirabout 1**

stitch n

1 also *stitch of work:* The smallest amount of work—usu in neg phrr.   **chiefly Nth**   See Map   Cf **lick** n **4b(2)**
1851 Arthur *Lights & Shadows* 69, I'm angry now—so you had better go home at once; if you don't, I'll never give you [=a seamstress] a stitch of work, so help—. **1872** (1873) Shillaber *Partingtonian Patchwork* 234 **MA,** Got married, and made money by it—needn't do a stitch of work again as long as I live. **1889** *Scribner's Mag.* 6.674 **NY,** Daisy hasn't done a stitch of work all summer. **1939** in Lib. of Congress *Amer. Memory: WPA Life Hist.* **MA** (Internet), Nowadays every darned person is too lazy to do a stitch of work. **1950** *WELS* **WI** (*To do no work at all, not even make any effort: "She hasn't _____ all day."*) 3 Infs, Done a (*or* one) stitch; 2 Infs, Done a stitch of work. **1965–70** *DARE* (Qu. LL18) 13 Infs, **chiefly Nth,** Done a stitch; **CT**4, 12, **IL**46, **ME**19, **PA**167, Done a stitch of work. **1976** Gardner *Oct. Light* 119 **VT,** She wouldn't do a stitch around the house all day, wouldn't even fix breakfast. **2002** *Salt Lake Tribune* (UT) 3 Oct (Internet), Did my child get a D-minus because he knew the content but didn't do a stitch of work?

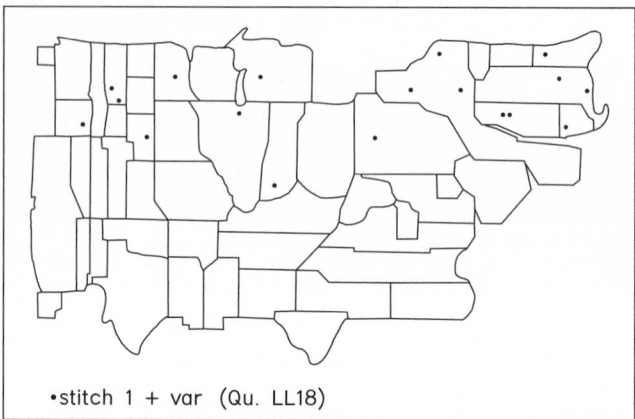

•stitch 1 + var   (Qu. LL18)

2 A short distance or indefinite period of time.   [*EDD stitch* sb.¹ 6]
1939 Wolfe *Web & Rock* 18 **NC,** There was a certain stitch of afternoon while the boy waited. **1958** *VA Qrly. Rev.* 34.245 **wNC, eTN,** The jackass he had passed a stitch back on the road brayed again.

stitcher n   Cf **ear sewer 1, eye stitcher**
A dragonfly.
1969–70 *DARE* (Qu. R2, . . *The dragonfly*) Inf **CA**119, Stitcher; **MA**122, The kids called it stitcher.

stitch of work   See **stitch 1**

stitch starch   See **stiff starch**

stitchwort n   [*OED2* c1265 →]
=**chickweed 1a.**
1784 in 1785 Amer. Acad. Arts & Sci. *Memoirs* 1.446 **NEng,** Stitchwort. Blossoms in panicles; white. **1824** Bigelow *Florula Bostoniensis* 182 **MA,** *Stellaria longifolia* . . Stichwort [sic]. . . A small, starry, white flower. **1876** Hobbs *Bot. Hdbk.* 112, Stitchwort, Stellaria media. **1903** Small *Flora SE U.S.* 421, Alsine [spp]. . . [*Stellaria* L.] Chickweed. Starwort. Stitchwort. **1971** Krochmal *Appalachia Med. Plants* 242, *Stellaria media.* . . Common Names: Chickweed, . . stitchwort [etc].

stived ppl adj   Freq with *up,* rarely *in*   [*EDD stive* v.² 1 "to pen up; to stifle . . ; freq. with *up.* . . *Stivy, adj.* close, stuffy, stifling"; a fusion of two unrelated verbs originally meaning "to pack tightly" and "to stew" (*OED2 stive* v.², v.³)]   **NEng, seNY** *old-fash*
Of a person: crowded (esp in hot and unhealthy conditions), cooped up; of a room, situation, etc: crowded, stifling, oppressive; also fig; hence adj *stivy* stifling, stuffy.
1804 *NY Eve. Post* (NY) 15 Sept 2/5, To shew the manner in which these unhappy workmen were stived up, so that the poor fellows engendered . . yellow fever, Dr Daniel D. Walter is brought forward. **1816** Pickering *Vocab.* 181, *Stived.* (Commonly used with *up.*) New England. A low word. This is an English *provincialism.* **1835** (1956) Crownin-

shield *Diary* 112 **seMA,** The back wall slanted in and Mary had the slanting side to sleep upon, and she thought she would have a hard time stived in behind me. **1836** Withington *Puritan Essays* 1.108 **MA,** We found the sick and suffering victim, in a little stived room, smelling strongly of oakum, . . calculated rather to destroy health, than to restore the sick to health again. **1838** (1839) Thome–Kimball *Emancipation* 316, The air, which the day before had been painfully hot and stived, was cool and fresh. **1844** *Bangor Daily Whig & Courier* (ME) 27 July 2, Our philosophical friend of the New York Tribune recommends to people stived up in cities . . to improve a few days of the present season for a jaunt into the country, to breathe the pure air. **1845** Judd *Margaret* 329 **swME,** "Things are a good deal stived up," answered the Deacon. "People's minds are sour, and I don't know, Molly, what we can do." **1871** Stowe *Pink & White Tyranny* 79 **NEng,** I can't think of anything that would induce me to take a long, hot ride in the sun, and to sit in that stived-up room with those common creatures. **1874** (1875) Alcott *Eight Cousins* 121 **MA,** Does that old noodle think I'm going to stay stived up here much longer? **1884** Jewett *Country Dr.* 13 **ME,** I thought it seemed kind o' stived up here in the kitchen, and I opened the door and looked out. **1927** *AmSp* 3.140 **eME,** When ventilation was very poor or people lived in close, stuffy rooms, they were "all stived up." "Stivy" is a word meaning . . crammed, crowded, stuffy.

stiver v |ˈstɪvɚ| Also sp *stivver* **NEng, esp MA, ME**

1 also with *along, it, off:* To proceed, esp persistently or with vigor; to get going. [Cf *EDD stive* v.³ [staɪv] "To walk energetically and fast; to bustle." Cf also **stave** v 5]

1848 Bartlett *Americanisms* 334, *To stiver.* To run; to move off. A low word used in the Northern States. **1857** (1858) Tripp *Fisher Boy* 59 **MA,** The crew stivered along across the gray old fields. *Ibid* 77, The jib was stowed, the main-sail furled, the fore-sheets hauled abaft, when the obedient craft stivered along by the wind, just of a pace to hold her ground for the morrow. **1859** in 1864 Weiss *Life Parker* 2.364 **ceMA,** I was *stivering* along the road from Montreux, eating grapes. **1875** *Old & New* 11.44 **NEast coast,** The two brothers . . stivered through the city arm in arm. **1903** *DN* 2.301 **Cape Cod MA** (as of a1857), *Stiver* [stɪvɚ]. . . To walk rapidly or busily. 'Come, stiver off to bed now.' *Ibid* 353 **cME,** *Stiver for.* . . Move rapidly; go after quickly, as 'I'll stiver for the doughnuts.' **1904** Day *Kin o' Ktaadn* 126 **ME,** Then stivver it to that poorhouse where she has said they be. **1914** *DN* 4.80 **ME, nNH,** *Stivver.* . . To go, run, hasten. **1934** in 1947 Botkin *Treas. New Engl. Folkl.* 34 **ME,** It must have been an amusing spectacle, those seven housewives each with a hayfork over her shoulder, stivering along the new road through the woods. **1971** *DARE* File **Cape Cod MA,** Stivver . . was . . very familiar . . in my childhood, 1901–1915+. "To stivver along" meant to get yourself to some point as expeditiously as possible. In me it conjures up the picture of a little old man hustling off on some errand or homeward bound as fast as his elderly feet would carry him. **1983** Beyle *How Talk Cape Cod* 26, *Stivver*—Proper command to one in his sitting britches, "Stivver along now."

2 also with *along, off, round:* To move with difficulty; to stagger; to struggle. [*EDD stiver* v. 4 [ˈstɪvə(r)] "to stagger; to struggle; also used *fig.* and with *about.*"]

1870 *Atlantic Mth.* 26.317 **eMA,** We put about and stood out the Bay for her, stivering along ourselves as we might, a close-reefed mainsail and bonnet off the jib being all the pilot-boat would carry. **1903** *DN* 2.353 **MA,** *Stiver round.* . . To move about. I can hardly stiver round this morning. **1908** Wasson *Home from Sea* 219 **sME coast,** Let all them kind stivver, sink or swim, says gov'mint. **1927** *AmSp* 3.139 **eME,** "Stiver," meaning to stagger or walk with difficulty, "so tired I could hardly stiver." **1963** Haywood *Yankee Dict.* 163, *Stivver.* . . Sometimes it was used to describe hard going. An old lady might sigh and say, "Well, I'll manage to stivver along somehow." **1972** *NYT Article Letters* **ME,** If the going is rough, we'll try to "stivver along". **1977** *Yankee* Jan 73 **Isleboro ME,** The cold cripples some folks . . so they can barely *stiver and go.* **2002** *World* (Barre VT) 24 Apr (Internet), Several times I tried to stiver up from my couch du jour. *Ibid* 22 May, When I was finally able to stiver around, I decided that I should drive downtown just to let friends know that I was alive and improving.

3 with *under, (up) to;* Of a ship: to tolerate (a particular spread of canvas or force of wind); hence *fig:* to bear, put up with. [*EDD stiver* v. 5 "*Obs.* To strive against; with *up:* to stand up against."]

1868 *Atlantic Mth.* 21.15 **eMA,** That 's more canvas than I 'd like to stiver under, though. **1901** Wasson in *Ibid* 88.57 **sME coast,** It couldn't been more 'n half an hour after our anchor was broke out 'fore that packet had all she could stivver to under her three lower sails. **1903** Wasson *Cap'n Simeon's Store* 29 **ME,** We got all we can stivver to in any kind o' shape a'ready. **1908** Wasson *Home from Sea* 108 **sME coast,** I see this 'ere bo't headin' in dead afore it, with every mite of wind she could stiver under, and still, she never appeared to git ahead. *Ibid* 293, Wearin' every sol'tary rag of sail the schooner would stivver under, and still stay atop o' water. **1975** Gould *ME Lingo* 278, *Stivver*—A maximum; all that one can accept, stand for, put up with, endure: "That's about all I can stivver up to."

4 with *out:* To endure (something) to the end, "stick (something) out."

1971 *Today Show Letters* **swME,** I don't find the expression "to stiver it out" in the dictionary. My folks would say to us as we were tiring and wanting to give up what we were doing—"Oh, keep on! You can stiver it out!"

stiver along See **stiver 1, 2**

stiver it See **stiver 1**

stiver off See **stiver 1, 2**

stiver out See **stiver 4**

stiver round See **stiver 2**

stiver to (or under, up to) See **stiver 3**

stivver See **stiver**

stivy See **stived**

St. John's wort See **Saint-Johns-wort**

sto n See **store** n

sto v [Cf Du *staa* Stay! Stand!] Cf *DS* K81

Used as a command to a cow; see quots.

1949 Kurath *Word Geog.* 64, Calls to Cows during Milking. . . *sto!* in the Albany [NY] area, doubtless of Dutch origin. **1967** Faries *Word Geog. MO* 92, Calls to cows during milking. . . The Northern calls *sto!* and *kush(ie)!* seem almost unknown in Missouri. *Ibid* 177, Sto ! (6 [of c700 infs]). **1972** McDavid *Coll.* **cnGA,** *Sto!*—Call to cow to stand still.

stoah See **store** n

stob n Pronc-sp *stahb, staub* [*OED2* 1321 →; now nEngl, Scots, nIr dial] **chiefly Sth, S Midl**

1 A stake, post, or peg.

1845 Hooper *Advent. Simon Suggs* 46 **AL,** Prudence is the stob I fasten the grape-vine of *my* cunnoo to. **1855** (2001) Brown *Slave Life GA* 41 (Internet), His body swung by its own weight, his hands being high over his head and his right foot level with the pointed end of the oaken "stob" or stake. **1883** *Amer. Philol. Assoc. Trans.* 14.53 **Sth,** *Stob,* 'a small post *or* stake *or* stump of a shrub,' commonly so used in many, if not all, parts of the South. It is not elegant, however. **1891** *PMLA* 6.3.175 **TN,** A *stob* is a stake driven in the ground, or a tall stump of a tree. "Do you see that peckerwood on that old stob over yonder?" **1901** *DN* 2.148, *Stob.* . . Stake; "tied to a stob." **1902** [see **2** below]. **1903** *DN* 2.332 **seMO,** *Stob.* . . Stake. 'He set a mulberry stob at each corner of his land.' **1906** *DN* 3.158 **nwAR,** *Stob.* . . A short stake driven into the ground. **1907** [see **2** below]. **1907** *DN* 3.237 **nwAR,** *Stob.* . . Stake. "We drove stobs at the corners of the lot." **1909** *DN* 3.376 **eAL, wGA,** *Stob.* . . A stake, a small post. **1914** *DN* 4.160 **cVA,** *Stahb.* . . Stake. "Yo' aint pulled up nairy a stahb, yit." **1915** *DN* 4.191 **swVA,** *Stob.* . . A stake. **1923** *DN* 5.222 **swMO,** *Stob.* . . A short post or stake. **1927** Adams *Congaree* 73 **cSC** [Black], Chain he foots, shackles an' all to a stob in de groun'. **1964** Will *Hist. Okeechobee* 121 **FL,** The "staff" at the net's end, was fastened to a "stob" planted firmly in the lake's bottom. **1966–70** *DARE* FW Addit **LA,** *Stob*—stake; short, sturdy piece of wood; **NM6,** [stob]—a marker point for surveyors, etc. Usually a small cedar post with top level with or just above ground; **VA38,** *Stob*—a wooden fence post. **1970** *DARE* (Qu. EE37, *The game where you try to throw metal rings or something similar over a stake in the ground*) Inf **VA50,** Ring-the-stob. **1984** *WI State Jrl.* (Madison) 20 Dec sec 4 1 **NC,** "I druther have a drink," said my drinkin' uncle, "than a poke in the eye with a sharp stob." **1994** Thomas *Come Go with Me* 63 **S Midl,** Pa drove a good long stob [Thomas: or stake] in the ground. **2004** *Tampa Tribune* (FL) 1 Nov Metro sec 1 (Internet), Gary drives the stob into the ground with the metal, then rubs it across the stob. . . The resulting vibration . . drives the earthworms crazy. **2009** *DARE* File **DE,** "Staub" or "stob" is used instead of "stake" or "stave".

2 A projecting stump or stub.

1883 [see **1** above]. **1891** [see **1** above]. **1902** *DN* 2.246 **sIL,** *Stob.* . . 1. A stub. 2. A short stake driven in the ground. The short stub or stump of a sprout. **1907** *DN* 3.227 **nwAR,** *Stob.* . . 1. A stub. 2. A short stake driven into the ground. **1929** Dobie *Vaquero* 205 **TX,** Patches of the brush hand's bandana hanging on thorns and stobs sometimes mark his trail. **1930** Shoemaker *1300 Words* 58 **cPA Mts** (as of c1900), *Stob*—A dead hemlock tree, left standing by lumbermen. **1932** Randolph *Ozark Mt. Folks* 136, He tuck th' powder-horn off an' hung it up on a big yaller stob he seen a-stickin' out o' th' cedar-tree. **1968** Ferrell *Bear Tales* 24 **sAppalachians** (*Montgomery Coll.*), Oncet one of my hounds was chasin' a fox. . . That dog ran into a staub so hard he drove it right into his breast an' killed hisself. **1969** *DARE* File **WV,** *Stob* [stab] = a piece of stubble (corn, etc.) or other plant material sticking up out of the ground. **1979** Wellman *Old Gods* 129 **sAppalachians,** I put out my ash stick to seek for openings where I might get through. I scraped my shoulder and my cheek on branch stobs. **1982** *Barrick Coll.* **csPA,** *Stob*—stub of a tree lime [sic]; small stump; butt of corn stalk. **1994** NC Lang. & Life Project *Harkers Is. Vocab.* 10 **eNC,** *Stob.* . . A stick or stump protruding out of the ground or along the shoreline. **2002** Proulx *That Old Ace* 65 **TX,** They'd just bush-hogged the damn roadsides, now bristling with brush stobs sharp as punji sticks.

3 A splinter or sliver of wood.

1967 *DARE* (Qu. Y44, *A very small, sharp piece of wood: "His finger is sore—he ran a _____ into it."*) Inf **TX**29, Stob, splinter.

4 in phr *on the stob:* On credit. [*stob* prob in ref to a spindle file] Cf *DS* U11

1973 McCarthy *Child of God* 125 **TN,** Five dollars and ten cents, he said. Just put it on the stob for me. . . How much do I owe altogether? said Ballard. Thirty-four dollars and nineteen cents.

stob v

A Gram forms.

Past and past pple: usu *stobbed;* also *stob.*

1871 [see **B1** below]. **1975** [see **B1** below]. **1986** Pederson *LAGS Concordance* (He stabbed *her with a big knife*) 3 infs, **FL, LA, MS,** Stob (him *or* me); 1 inf, **cAL,** He stob. [3 of 4 infs Black]

B Senses.

1 also *staub:* To stab, jab, poke. [*OED2* 1529 →; "dial."]
Sth, S Midl Cf **job** v² **1**

1860 *Atlantic Mth.* 6.35 **MD,** I have got one tombstone yet to show you . . : it belongs to old Master Rousby, who was stobbed aboard ship. **1871** (1892) Johnston *Dukesborough Tales* 60 **GA,** Seaby have sich a big knife! An' he have stob more saplin's! and more punkins! and more watermillions! **1883** Zeigler-Grosscup *Heart of Alleghanies* 52, I . . staubed him deep in the side with the knife. **1893** Shands *MS Speech* 60, *Stob.* . . Negro pronunciation of the verb *stab.* **1902** *DN* 2.246 **sIL,** *Stob.* . . 1. Stab. 2. To stub, as the toe. **1909** *DN* 3.376 **eAL, wGA,** *Stob.* . . To stab. **1915** *DN* 4.191 **swVA,** *Stob,* Variant of *stab, v.* **1917** *DN* 4.417 **wNC, KY,** *Stob.* Variant of *stab, v.* **1923** *DN* 5.222 **swMO,** *Stob.* . . To stab or jab with a stick. **1927** *DN* 5.470 **sAppalachians,** *Stabbed*—stobbed. **1939** *Hall Coll.* **wNC, eTN,** He run up and stobbed his knife into it [=a bear]. **1969–70** *DARE* (Qu. Y46a, *To get hurt with something sharp . . "He _____ a thorn into his hand."*) Inf **KY**40, Stobbed; (Qu. Y46b, *To get hurt with something sharp . . "She herself up with a needle."*) Inf **WV**16, Stobbed. **1975** Thomas *Hear the Lambs* 190 **nwAL,** I ain't never stob nobody or cut 'em. **1991** Pederson *LAGS Social Matrix* 246 **Gulf Region,** [Of the 46 infs who responded with *stobbed* for *stabbed,* 24 were Black, 22 White.]

2 To stub (a toe).

1888 Mackay *Dict. Lowland Scotch* 217, "I have *stobbed* my toe," said the late President Lincoln, in explanation of his temporary lameness. **1902** [see **B1** above]. **1960** Criswell *Resp. to PADS* 20 **Ozarks,** *Stob.* . . To stub (a toe), etc. Always common. **1990** Smith *Understanding Speaking S. Lang.* 8, *Stob*—A stake, peg, stick or snag protruding from the ground, sometimes causing a person to *stob* a toe or trip and fall when running barefooted. **2005** Williams *Gratitude* 527 **wNC** (as of 1940s), *Stob* also means like when you hit your toe or finger straight on the end of it and *stove* it up. Example: I *stobbed* (stumped) my toe agin' a chair leg.

3 with *out:* To stake out (an animal).

1902 *DN* 2.246 **sIL,** *Stob out.* . . To hitch out or picket, as a horse or cow with a long rope tied to a stob, for the purpose of grazing. **1907** *DN* 3.227 **nwAR,** *Stob out.* **2003** in 2004 *DARE* File—Internet **AR,** I stobbed out two hens and a jake decoy [while turkey hunting]. **2007** in

2008 *Ibid* **cwNC,** When I was growing up out here on the farm in Alexander (in the 1950s) we regularly patronized a *real* chain store in Asheville. . . No matter the kind of chain you needed—from a heavy logging chain to the light chain we used to 'stob out' cows for grazing, Morrison's had it. . . Today, the world has changed. Just try to find a 'stob' chain in Wally Mart, they don't got them.

4 To propel (a boat) with a **stob pole.**

1963 Alter *Shovel Nose* 181 **GA,** Hughie stobbed the leaky old skiff toward the pin-down thicket.

5 also with *out:* To set out (stakes or poles); to provide with stakes; hence vbl n *stobbing,* n *stobber.* [*SND* stob v. 3 "to mark or bound with posts; to prop up with stakes"]

1996 in 2008 (acc) Lexis-Nexis Legal Research *State Case Law: SC* (Internet), Meanwhile, Robison and Moser were "stobbing" out poles for shrimp baiting. **2003** *DARE* File **csOK** (as of 1950s), To *stob* means to set out stakes. I learned this word when I was a teenager in Duncan, Oklahoma in the 1950's from a woman who was born probably in the 1880's. . . I believe she said she *stobbed* her garden—but the word might have been used intransitively—she may have said simply that she *stobbed.* But it means to set out stakes in a garden to use as poles for vine plants such as beans to wind around. **2008** *DARE* File—Internet **Sth,** "Stobbing" is a southern construction term. I picked it up in the 70's when working as a house builder for my father. . . Stobbing is what you do when you start a house. "Stobs" (2 x 4 stakes) are driven into the ground at each corner of the structure. Batterboards are nailed to the stakes and strings are drawn between the boards to show where the foundation walls will go. Stobbing is the first step in transferring an abstraction, the blueprint, into physical reality. . . Not all carpenters can do it. A good stobber must be able to see how patterns on paper translate into lines on the ground and how those lines translate into a house.

stobber n

1 See quots. Cf **jobber**

1912 Cobb *Cobb's Anatomy* 132, A manicure lady could no more do a manicure properly without using an orange wood stobber . . than a cartoonist could draw a picture of a man in jail without putting a ball and chain on him. **1923** *DN* 5.222 **swMO,** *Stobber.* . . Any sharp-pointed instrument used in punching holes.

2 See quot 2004. **CA**

1997 in 2008 *DARE* File—Internet **CA,** 10,000 sq.ft. parking lot for 45 vehicles with barricades; entrance road gate and stobbers or fencing of entrance road. **2004** Rohde-Rohde *Best Hikes* 22 **nCA,** Stobber—a short, thick post, usually about one foot high, often set in rows along park roadsides or parking areas to prevent vehicle encroachment. *Ibid* 59, The trail starts at a row of stobbers next to the parking pullout. **2005** in 2008 *DARE* File—Internet **CA,** We graded gravel in front of the bathrooms at Oak Hollow Campground and Group Picnic. I took one of the kids with me to plant some sign posts and a stobber. **2008** *Ibid* **cCA,** Replace missing or damaged parking area delineators ("stobbers") in approximately 75 campsites.

3 See **stob** v **B5.**

stobbing See stob v B5

stobby adj [*EDD* stobby "Rough, stubbly; . . bristly, unshaven."]

See quots.

1973 McCarthy *Child of God* 71 **TN,** You cain't just grind a axe and grind it, he said. See how stobby it's got? **2004** *AR Times* (Little Rock) 19 Mar News/Politics sec (Internet), She subjected it [=a japonica bush] to every torture in the gardener's inquisitor's kit—chemical, chopping axe, . . everything short of dynamite—and over every winter she built . . fires on top of the stobby butchered remains.

stob chain n

A chain for staking out an animal.

2007 [see **stob** v **B3**].

stob out See stob v B3, 5

stob pole n Cf push pole

A pole for propelling a boat.

1940 (1941) Bell *Swamp Water* 3 **Okefenokee GA,** Ben poled silently, taking great care not to rap the boat with the stob pole. **1953** Randolph-Wilson *Down in Holler* 289 **Ozarks,** *Stob.* . . A *stob-pole* is used in propelling a boat in shallow water; the boatman uses it to prevent collision with *stobs.* **1963** Alter *Shovel Nose* 10 **GA,** Mama gator came up behind the . . skiff. . . *"Lookout!"* Hughie yelled, and he grabbed for the stob pole.

stock n Usu |stɑk|; also |stɔk| Also sp *stalk, stawk*

A Forms.

1887 Kirkland *Zury* 7 **ceIL,** Th'aint no grass h'yer fer the stawk. **1894** *Scribner's Mag.* 15.562 **Sth** [Black], Hafe o' yo' lan's 'u'd be public lan's in no time, an' the res' 'u'd belong to a stawk comp'ny. **1903** *DN* 2.353, *Stock.* . . Pronounced [stɔk], with long open o. **1906** [see **C4** below]. **1913** Johnson *Highways St. Lawrence to VA* 19, But the state won't hardly let you cut a whipstalk on its land. **1914** *DN* 4.113 **cKS,** *Stock* [stɔk]. . . "A hundred head of stock." **1942** Hall *Smoky Mt. Speech* 28 **wNC, eTN,** *Stock* and *mock* always have [ɔ]. **1967** *DARE* (Qu. M11) Inf **TN19,** Stock [stɔk]. **1985** Benes *Amer. Speech* 75 **cME coast** (as of a1847), The vowel of contemporary *bought* occurs in . . *stock* (homophonous with *stalk*).

B Gram form.

Used as count noun rather than mass noun in ref to farm animals.

1986 Pederson *LAGS Concordance* (*Feed [the cattle]*) 1 inf, **cwTN,** Corn was raised to feed your stocks; 2 infs, **FL, MS,** (Feed) the stocks; 1 inf, **cwGA,** Lots of stocks; 1 inf, **seMS,** Stocks; (*Feed [the fowls]*) 1 inf, **cnMS,** Stocks [=horses]. [4 of 6 infs Black]

C Senses.

1 A sawlog; a log used as building material; hence n *stock chimney* a chimney constructed of logs. [Cf *OED2 stock* sb.¹ A.1.a, b *"Obs."*]

1857 *Mag. Travel* 1.285, I turned with depressed spirits and slow step to the house, taking a seat by a dull fire which smouldered in the stock chimney. **1899** (1912) Green *VA Folk-Speech* 419, *Stock.* . . Trunk of a tree. A stock of timber. **1918** in 2003 *DARE* File—Internet **seWA** (as of 1853), [From *Lyman's History of Old Walla Walla County*:], They took up their residence on a small ranch there and the father built a log cabin with a clapboard roof and stock chimney. **1939** Writers' Program *Guide KY* 127, Above the throat of the fireplace the chimney was constructed of "stocks" or logs carefully chinked, at first with clay but later with mortar. In time the "stock" chimneys, always in danger of burning, were replaced with stone. **1966** *DARE* Tape **GA1,** When it was cut, hauled in, it was called stock. That's a log that's just cut up in these joints of twelve and sixteen foot. Was put into the sawmill and sawed up into lumber.

2 also *milking stock, stocks:* A stanchion. [Transf from *stock(s)* any of var devices for restraining a large animal, as a cow or horse, for shoeing or medical treatment]

[**1876** Knight *Amer. Mech. Dict.* 3.2391, *Stocks.* . . 2. *(Farriery and Manege)* A frame in which refractory animals are held for shoeing or veterinary purposes.] **1966–70** *DARE* (Qu. M11, *What do you put the cow's head through when she stands in the barn?*) Infs **GA1, PA187, VA38,** Stock; **TN19,** Stock [stɔk]—in dairy milking shed; **TN24,** Stocks. **2002** in 2003 *DARE* File—Internet **IN,** I ran to the barn. . . One side had several pens. . . On the other side there were milking stocks and stalls.

3 The gross value of fish caught; hence v *stock* to gross. [Cf *OED2 stock* sb.¹ 53.b *"Obs."*]

1856 Reynolds *Peter Gott* 163 **neMA,** They usually stocked from thirty-five hundred to four thousand dollars per year. . . When their stock, or the produce of their year's work, amounted to four thousand dollars, two thousand of it belonged to the vessel. **1884** U.S. Natl. Museum *Bulletin* 27.712, Mackerel schooner Oasis, of North Haven, Me. . . Her catch in 1882 was 1,500 barrels of mackerel; total stock, $9,000. **1952** (1973) Thomas *Fast & Able* 6 **neMA,** Her total stock for 14 years . . was $292,000. One of her best years was 1899, when she was high line of the haddockers with a stock of $25,441. *Ibid* 7, He retired from the sea in 1916. His total stock in 32 years was a little short of $900,000. *Ibid* 11, The first trip, gone 14 days, was 17,000 lbs. halibut, stocking $2,180.

4 also *pen stalk, ~ stock:* =**staff;** hence n *stock pen* a **dip pen. chiefly S Midl, nNEng** See Map

1860 Worcester *Dict.* 1053, *Penstock.* . . The handle of a pen. **1904** Day *Kin o' Ktaadn* 125 **ME,** Then the boss he fetched a pen-stock and thawed the yaller ink. **1906** (1907) Wiggin *New Chron. Rebecca* 78 **ME,** Last night I dreamed that the river was ink and I kept dipping into it and writing with a penstalk made of a young pine tree. **1909** [see **staff**]. **1931–33** *LANE Worksheets* **RI,** *Penstock.* . . Penholder. **c1960** Mathews Coll. **AL** (as of c1891), Penstock. Not rare in my boyhood in

Ala.; only term we used. **1965–70** *DARE* (Qu. JJ10b, *Parts of an ink pen*) 31 Infs, **chiefly S Midl,** Stock; 17 Infs, **S Midl, nNEng,** Pen stock; **AR33,** Point and the stock; (Qu. JJ10a, *Different kinds of pens and pencils*) Inf **AR52,** Pen stock; **GA73, NC45,** Stock pen.

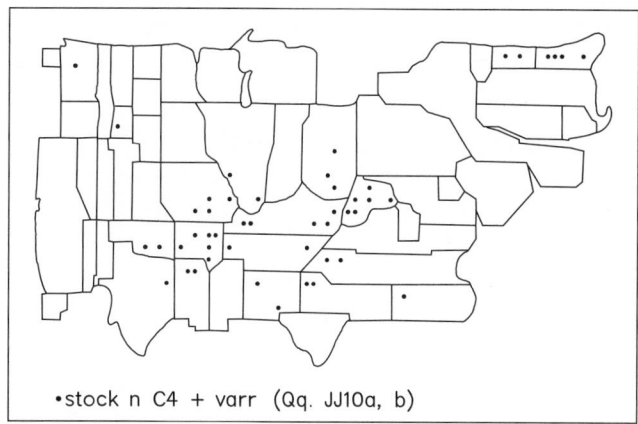

•stock n C4 + varr (Qq. JJ10a, b)

stock v See **stock** n C3

stockamore n

=**hackamore.**

1929 *AmSp* 5.62 **NE** [Cattle country talk], The "hackamore," sometimes called a "stockamore," has knots fitting close to the nostrils and really punishes a "bronc" to submission.

stock-and-rail fence n [Cf *OED2 stock* n.¹ A.1.a *"Obs.* or *arch."*]

1969 *DARE* (Qu. L65, . . *Kinds of fences*) Inf **NY205,** Stock-and-rail fence—stumps of trees and rail laid across the top.

stock barn n **scattered, but esp Midl** See Map Cf **stock house**

A building for housing livestock.

1835 *Genesee Farmer* 5.311 **wNY,** [Advt:] The buildings consist of . . one stock barn, 30 by 40 feet, with a shed 20 by 50 feet, with convenient stabling for 16 head of horses and cattle. **1841** *Farmers' Reg.* 9.596 **neMA,** I have . . one barn built by my predecessor, for sheep, which I have converted into a hay and stock barn. **1860** *Rural Affairs* 2.95, A correspondent in Chester county, Pa., gives the following minute description of a large and commodious grain, hay, and stock barn. **1893** *Manufacturer & Builder* 25.228 **Chicago IL,** The following buildings have been erected in Jackson Park and Midway Plaisance. . . Administration building. . . Stock barn. . . Public comfort. **1939** in Lib. of Congress *Amer. Memory: FSA/OWI* (Internet), [Caption:] Stock barn of Montgomery Mule Company, Alabama, on day of big mule auction. **1940** *Ibid,* Working cowboys cleaning out the stock barns at the San Angelo Fat Stock Show, San Angelo, Texas. **1941** *Ibid,* Dairy cattle and stock barn on farm near Lexington, Nebraska. **c1960** *Wilson Coll.* **csKY,** *Stockbarn.* . . A building where stock, usually horses, are kept. **1965–70** *DARE* (Qu. M1, . . *Kinds of barns . . according to their use or the way they are built*) 91 Infs, **scattered, but esp Midl,** Stock barn; **AL38,** Hay and stock barn; (Qu. M9, *The part of a barn where horses are kept*) Infs **AL11, IN45,** Stock barn; (Qu. M10, *The part of the barn where cows are kept*) Inf **AL11,** Stock barn. **1966** Dakin *Dial. Vocab.*

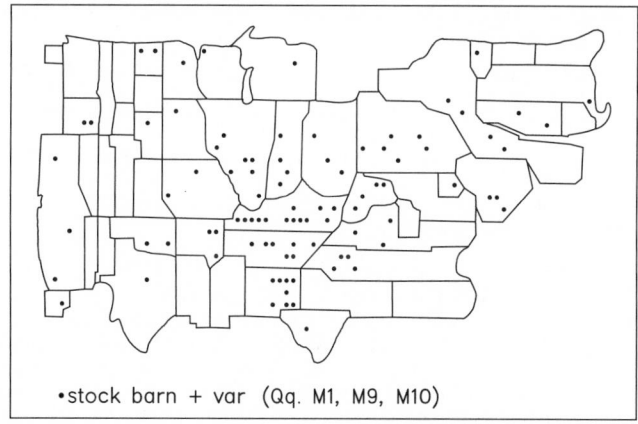

•stock barn + var (Qq. M1, M9, M10)

Ohio R. Valley 2.81, *Cow barn. . . Barn* or occasionally *stock barn* is the newer term.   **1971** Bright *Word Geog. CA & NV* 151, *Barn. . .* The following compounds occurred four times or less: *feed barn, livestock barn . . stock barn.*   **1986** Pederson *LAGS Concordance (Barn)* 9 infs, 5 **TN,** Stock barn; *(Cow barn)* 2 infs, **GA, TN,** Stock barn; *(Corncrib)* 1 inf, **ceGA,** Stock barn.   **2005** *Cleveland Plain Dealer* (OH) 14 Oct sec B 8 (Internet), Seven homes and a market were hit, as well as the stock barn and the silo at David Klingensmith's dairy farm.

stock beast   See **beast B2**

stock chimney   See **stock** n **C1**

stock corn n

A field var of **Indian corn 1,** used as livestock feed.

  1833 (1930) W. Sewall *Diary* 153, Hauling stock corn.   **1854** Wailes *Rept. on Ag. & Geol. MS* 182, As a stock corn, the gourd seed, from its easy mastication, is perhaps generally preferred.   **1889** U.S. Dept. Ag. *Rept. of Secy. for 1888* 656 **MS,** The White Giant Normandy is a favorite stock corn in this State.   **1913** OR Bd. Horticult. *Biennial Rept.* 101, Though Oregon is not considered a corn-growing State, . . soon some one will produce a stock corn suited to Oregon climate.   **1967–70** *DARE* (Qu. I34, *If you don't have sweet corn, you can always eat young* _____) Infs **NC**76, 87, **NV**5, **OR**13, Stock corn.

stock cow n   **chiefly Sth, S Midl**   See Map   *euphem*

A bull.

  1965–70 *DARE* (Qu. K23, *Words used by women or in mixed company for a bull)* 16 Infs, **chiefly Sth, S Midl,** Stock cow; (Qu. K22, *Words used for a bull)* Infs **FL**48, **GA**52, **MS**60, **SC**1, 26, **VA**70, Stock cow.

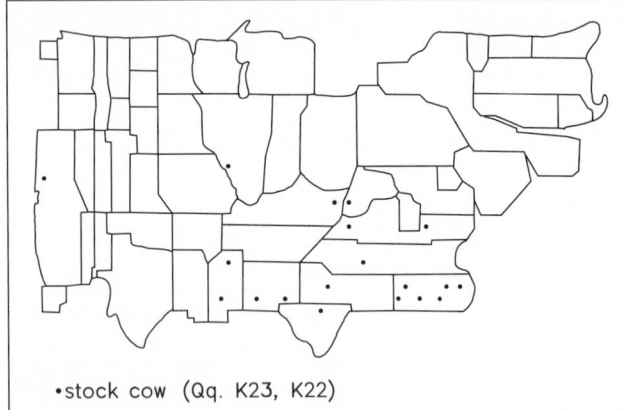

•stock cow (Qq. K23, K22)

stock house n   *esp NC*

=**stock barn.**

  1855 *S. Planter* 15.109, Every planter . . will consult the conveniences of locality, &c., of his plantation in the construction of his stock houses and lots.   **1858** *IN Farmer* 7.163, Now is the time to collect all the Manure about your stock houses.   **1889** *S. Cultivator* 47.92 **neNC,** We have a nice lot of manure from our hogs, cattle and team, the latter being kept in a good dry stock house.   **1899** NC Dept. Labor *Annual Rept. for 1898* 414, We use stock house manure for sweet and Irish potatoes.   **1946** *PADS* 6.28 **eNC** (as of 1900–10), *Stockhouse. . .* A building provided with stables on each side of a central passageway and with a hayloft in the upper part. . . Common.   **1966–70** *DARE* (Qu. M1, . . *Kinds of barns . . according to their use or the way they are built)* Infs **NC**8, 85, Stock house.

stocking cap n   *among Black speakers*   Cf **do-rag**

A woman's stocking used as a head covering; see quots.

  1963 *Freedomways* 3.57 **Harlem NYC** [Black], *Stocking cap:* woman's silk stocking pulled over head to hold hair in place.   **1994** Smitherman *Black Talk* 215, *Stocking cap*—A head covering made by cutting off the lower part of a woman's nylon stocking; fits tight and keeps the hair in place.

stock pea n

1 =**black-eyed pea.**   *esp S Midl*   *old-fash*

  1844 *Amer. Agric.* 3.25 **nAL,** Corn is plowed twice each way . . and thinned to two plants in a place. Stock-peas are planted the third plowing, in the middle of the wide rows.   **1853** *S. Cultivator* 11.356 **TN,** I have been cultivating the common cow or stock pea for the purpose of fattening pork hogs.   **1858** Wells *Farm Pocket Manual* 118, The plant called Cow-pea or Indian pea, and sometimes Stock pea, is extensively

cultivated in some of the Southern States, both as a forage crop and a fertilizer.   **1862** in 1899 U.S. War Dept. *War of Rebellion* 2d ser 4.231, Occasionally small allowances of sugar, rice, stock pease and molasses were made [in an Alabama prison].   **1869** U.S. Dept. Ag. *Rept. of Secy. for 1868* 221 **VA,** The lot intended for peanuts, say next year, has been seeded in stock peas this year.   **1949** *Daily Independent* (Murphysboro IL) 14 Apr sec 2 4/6, [Advt:] Stock peas, Vergennes. And Virginia soybeans, both in top condition.   **c1960** *Wilson Coll.* **csKY,** Peas (that is, cowpeas or stock peas) grown on most farms of other times. Some used for hay.   **1968** *DARE* (Qu. I20, . . *Kinds of beans)* Inf **TN**26, Stock peas or speckled peas; (Qu. L9b, *Hay from other kinds of plants [not grass]; not asked in early QRs)* Inf **NC**80, Stock peas—good hay for stock; grows in low land.   **2005** in 2008 *DARE* File—Internet **TN,** In the fall of the year, our uncle had fields full of what we called "stock peas." They were small brown peas with speckles. I later learned to call them whipporwill peas.

2 The soybean *(Glycine max).*

  1918 U.S. Dept. Ag. *Farmers' Bulletin* 973.3, The *soy bean . . ,* also called . . in North Carolina the stock pea, is an annual leguminous plant.   **1966** *DARE* Tape **NC**8, Round beans, as they call 'em. Soy beans. . . They're for feed and then they are ground. . . Some refer to them . . as stock peas.

stock pen   See **stock** n **C4**

stocks   See **stock** n **C2**

stockyards, at the adj phr   Cf *DS* AA27

Having a menstrual period.

  1948 *Word* 4.183, Indirect allusion to red or blood also is made: *the gal's at the stockyards.*

stodge v   Also sp *stoge*   *esp NEng*

1 also with *up:* To mix (food) into an unappetizing mass; to jumble together; hence ppl adj phr *stodged up.*   [*EDD stodge* v. 10 "To mix into a thick, liquid mass; to stir up"]

  1895 *DN* 1.394 **IN,** *Stodge:* to muss or mix up.   **1902** *Arena* 27.195 **NEng,** That stodged-up mess I ate at the hotel didn't go to the spot at all.   **1910** *DN* 3.455 **seVT,** *Sto(d)ge, v. tr.* To mix foods together incongruously.

2 with *up:* To put together (a meal), cobble (something) up usu in an improvisatory way.

  1909 *Outing* 53.440, Let the rest of the crowd rustle the wood; you . . start the stew or stodge up something *new* for a change.   **1914** Dickinson *WI Plays* 64, Grandma: But look what I stodged up for the little chap. *[She holds up an absurd black doll with a white head.]*   **1944** Holton *Yankees Were Like This* 231 **Cape Cod MA** (as of c1890), No girl who grew up on the Cape in my day . . was incapable of stodging up a fairly acceptable meal.   **1953** Randolph-Wilson *Down in Holler* 289 **Ozarks,** *Stodge. . .* To season, to spice, to flavor. A possum is not very palatable unless it is stodged up with red pepper, spicewood, and so on.   **1966** *DARE* (Qu. KK63, *To do a clumsy or hurried job of repairing something: "It will never last—he just _____."*) Inf **MA**6, Stodge it up.   **1985** *DARE* File **cVT,** I have heard "stodge" used here again— someone had to get a meal for unexpected company—and she said, "I'll stodge up something."   **1999** *Log Cabin Chronicles* Jan (Internet) **nVT,** There was . . rich stuff to eat: Scotch eggs stodged up by a German lassie.   **1999** Perkins *Perk's Path* 420 **MI,** We . . sold every item that could be handed out over a platform we had stodged up in the morning.

3 with *around:* See quot.

  1959 *VT Hist.* 27.161 **neVT,** *Stodge around. . .* 1. To do something without a plan. 2. [T]o prepare a meal. Occasional. Essex Co.

stodge n   Also *stoge*   [*OED2 stodge* n. 1 1825 →]

A mixture, esp one of incongruous or unappetizing foodstuffs.

  1901 *DN* 2.148 **cNY,** *Stodge. . .* Any kind of mixture. . . Potato-stodge. A preparation of sliced potatoes and water.   **1910** *DN* 3.455 **seVT,** *Sto(d)ge. . .* An incongruous mixture of foods.   **1980** *DARE* File **cVT** (as of c1900), Stodge—unappetizing mixture of food.

stodge around   See **stodge** v **3**

stodged up   See **stodge** v **1**

stodger n   Also *stoger*   [**stodge** v]

See quots.

  1910 *DN* 3.455 **seVT,** *Sto(d)ger. . .* A cook with slovenly habits.   **1959** *VT Hist.* 27.161, *Stodger. . .* A lazy person. Rare.

stodge up See **stodge** v **1, 2**

sto-er See **store** n

stog v Also *stug* [chiefly Scots, nIr dial] **sAppalachians**
To walk awkwardly or heavily; to plod.
  1925 Dargan *Highland Annals* 247 **wNC,** They's all skeered to marry
Nathe, an' no wonder when he kept stuggin' round the country lookin'
like the hind wheels o' destruction. **1940** in 2004 West *No Lonesome
Road* 41 **sAppalachians,** He stogged off down a cotton row. **1969**
DARE (Qu. Y25, *To walk heavily, making a lot of noise: "He came
_____ into the house."*) Inf **KY**19, Really setting his feet down;
stoging ['stogɪn]. **1997** in 2004 Montgomery–Hall *Dict. Smoky Mt.
Engl.* 572 **wNC,** He'd go stoggin' around the country.

stoga See **stogie**

stoge v See **stodge** v

stoge n See **stodge** n

stoger See **stodger**

stogie n, also attrib Also *stoga, stogy* [Abbrs of **conestoga 3**]
old-fash
A man's work shoe or boot.
  1830 *Mechanics' Press* (Utica NY) 9 Jan 66/3, In six days they crimpt
and made *forty-five* pairs of Stoga Boots. **1845** (1847) Palmer *Jrl.* 117
OR, I paid for a pair of *stoga* shoes, made in one of the eastern states.
1872 Twain *Roughing It* 22 **West,** Each of us put on a rough, heavy suit
of clothing, woolen army shirt and "stogy" boots included. **1884** in
1938 *DN* 6.654 **NE,** He went down to the store, got a pair of stoga
boots, put on overalls, and went out among farmers as a common cow-
doctor. **1887** (1895) Robinson *Uncle Lisha* 17 **wVT,** He " 'callated his
stogies 'ould turn water like a cabbage-leaf if you gin 'em a dost o' taller
or mushrat ile onct a week." **1892** *DN* 1.237 **cwMO,** *Stogies* . . coarse,
rough shoes or boots. **1893** *KS Univ. Qrly.* 1.142 **KS,** *Stogy:* a sort of
boot. **1905** *DN* 3.96 **nwAR,** *Stogies.* . . Brogans. **1965–70** *DARE* (Qu.
W11, *Men's low, rough work shoes*) Infs **AL**3, **CA**202, **IL**74, 83, **IN**34,
KY59, **NM**12, **OK**1, **OR**13, Stogies; **OK**1, Everyday stogies; **TN**36,
Work stogies; (Qu. W42b, . . *Nicknames for men's square-toed shoes*)
Inf **MI**81, Stogies. [10 of 11 total Infs old] **1982** Brooks *Quicksand* 96
swUT (as of c1908), A little, funny-looking girl came forward to meet
me, her hair braided, her red calico dress trimmed with white braid, her
too-large stogie shoes.

stogie tree n Cf **cigar tree**
=**catalpa B1.**
  1970 *DARE* (Qu. T9, *The common shade tree with large heart-shaped
leaves, clusters of white blossoms, and long thin seed pods or 'beans'*)
Inf **WV**21, Stogie tree. **2002** *AR Lit. Forum* (Internet), Looming in the
back was a tree with broad leaves and long, pencil-thin green pods, a
stogie tree, the only one of its kind in the neighborhood. Years later I
learned the real name for it—a catalpa tree. **2007** in 2008 *DARE* File—
Internet **WV,** It's sometimes called catawba or "stogie tree". It's easily
recognized by the long slender seed pods in late Summer and Fall.

stogy See **stogie**

stoke v, hence vbl n *stoking,* ppl adj *stoked* [Etym unknown]
To divide (game meat) among a group of hunters; see quot
1913.
  1913 Kephart *Highlanders* 102 **sAppalachians,** The mountaineers
have an odd way of sharing the spoils of the chase. They call it "stoking
the meat," a use of the word *stoke* that I have never heard elsewhere. The
hide is sold, and the proceeds divided equally among the hunters, but the
meat is cut up into as many pieces as there are partners in the chase;
then one man goes indoors or behind a tree, and somebody at the carcass, laying his hand on a portion, calls out: "Whose piece is this?"
"Granville Calhoun's," cries the hidden man. . . And so on down the
line. Everybody gets what chance determines for him, and there can be
no charges of unfairness. **c1920** Kephart in 1993 Farwell–Nicholas
Smoky Mt. Voices 159 **sAppalachians,** Boy's [sic] le's stoke this meat.
1957 Combs *Lang. S. Highlanders* **sAppalachians,** Stoke—to divide by
drawing lots. *Ibid,* Stoking meat—"stoked" bear meat.

stoker n [Perh folk-etym for *stogie*]
  1966–70 *DARE* (Qu. DD6a, *Other names or nicknames for cigars*)
Infs **CT**17, **DC**8, **KY**10, **MD**42, **MS**88, **NH**18, **NY**27, **VA**73, Stoker.

stoking See **stoke**

stold See **steal** **B1b, 2c**

stolded See **steal** **B1c**

stolden See **steal** **B2d**

stole See **steal** **B2b**

stoled See **steal** **B1b, 2c**

stolen(ed) See **steal** **B1d**

stole out See **steal** **C**

stolt See **steal** **B2c**

stomach-ache weed n
  =**fire pink 1.**
  1968 *DARE* FW Addit **VA**15, Stomach-ache weed = fire pink—it
likes to grow where dogs or humans have been sick on their stomach
and vomited. . . also called belly-ache weed.

stomach robber n Cf **belly robber**
One who supplies poor or inadequate food, esp a camp cook.
  1910 (1911) Service *Trail of '98* 15 **CA,** Five dollars a week for board:
costs them two-fifty, and they will be stomach robbers at that. **1912**
Whittles *Parish Pines* 63 **MN,** Cooks are "dough punchers" or "biscuit
shooters," and if unskilled, "stomach robbers." **1912** Berkman *Prison
Memoirs* 263 **PA,** But the subjects of common interest are soon exhausted. The oft-repeated tirade against . . the "stomach-robber of a
Warden." **1918** *Daily Courier* (Connellsville PA) 5 Mar 7/2, Our former mess sergeant was 'busted'. . . He was tried [by a "kangaroo court"]
on a charge of being a stomach robber. **1925** *AmSp* 1.137 **Pacific NW,**
A camp cook is simply a cook until the loggers have graded him; and for
each grade of cook they have a name full of meaning. "Gut-burglar,"
"stomach-robber," "stewbum," "sizzler," "dough-roller," and "star chief."
1927 *DN* 5.464 [Underworld jargon], *Stomach robber.* . . A cook.
1958 McCulloch *Woods Words* 182 **Pacific NW,** *Stomach robber*—A
cook. **2004** *DARE* File—Internet **wNC** (as of c1900), Many students
boarded with Schenck's Rangers. . . [Ranger] Gillespie was a "stomach
robber", who "couldn't heat a pot of water," much less cook.

stomp n
1 also *cow stomp:* An area where livestock gather or are
penned; hence n *stomp lot* a pen for animals. **Sth, S Midl**
  a1816 in 1848 GA Hist. Soc. *Coll.* 3.1.45, The owners of horses have
a place called a *stomp*. They select a place of good food, cut down a tree
or two, and make salt logs. Here the horses gather of themselves, in the
fly season. **1917** *DN* 4.421 **wLA,** *Stomp.* . . A place where cattle are
penned. **1952** Brown *NC Folkl.* 1.530, *Cow-stomp:* . . A cool, shaded
place where cows seek refuge during the heat of the day and "stomp"
when attacked by flies.—West. **1967–69** *DARE* (Qu. M13, *The space
near the barn with a fence around it where you keep the livestock*) Infs
LA15, 18, Stomp (lot); (Qu. M14, *The open area around or next to the
barn*) Infs **AR**55, **LA**18, **TX**63, Stomp; **LA**15, Stomp lot. [All Infs old]
1967 *DARE* FW Addit **cnLA,** Stomp [stɔmp] = area around a homestead and in front where the cows congregate at night. **1968** *Ibid* **LA**11,
Cow manure was called cow piles and it stunk like polecats on cow
stomps. **1970** Tarpley *Blinky* 42 **nwTX,** Small enclosure where cows
are kept. . . One informant . . calls this enclosure a *stomp lot* because it
is where cows wait impatiently at milking time. **1974** Fink *Mountain
Speech* 25 **wNC, eTN,** *Stomp* . . clearing with grass trodden of [sic] by
horses or cattle. "They's a big stomp on top of the mountain." **1976**
Garber *Mountain-ese* 88 **sAppalachians,** *Stomp* . . cleared spot—There
was a big stomp by the barn. **1981** Pederson *LAGS Basic Materials,* 1
inf, **ceLA,** Stomp; front stomp; back stomp; place where wood was
kept—cleared area; now called "parking places."

2 A male rustic or someone who dresses like one. **NM** Cf
stomper 3
  1970 *Current Slang* 4.3–4.24 [NM State Univ slang], *Stomp.* . . A student who wears jeans, a coyboy [sic] hat, boots, and a wide leather belt.
1986 *DARE* File, In New Mexico the rural males of Little Texas, the
Southeast corner of the state, are called *stomps*. **1998** *DARE* File **NM,**
In eastern New Mexico the word *stomp* means "a rustic young man who
is easy to get into a fight." *The stomps* used to fight *the chukes*—short for
Pachuco, Mexican-American gang youth.

3 See **stomper 2.**

stomp-down n
A lively party with dancing.
  1927 *Atlantic Mth.* 140.184 **NYC,** And long as you trimmin' me,
lemme have two tickets for the stomp-down tonight. **1957** Parris *My*

Mountains 176 **eTN, wNC,** It's a hoe-down and a stomp-down. **1966** *DARE* (Qu. FF4, *Names and joking names for different kinds of dancing parties*) Inf **SC3,** Stomp-down. **1995–97** in 2004 Montgomery–Hall *Dict. Smoky Mt. Engl.* 572 **wNC, eTN,** *Stomp-down . . = dancing to string music.*

stomp-down adj phr, adv phr Also *stomped down, stomping (down)* **Sth, S Midl**

True, genuine, pure; really, very.

1896 *Chautauquan* 23.87 **GA,** It is not uncommon to hear an extreme specimen of the genus described as "a regular stomp-down corn cracker." **1902** Young *Plantation Legends* 40 **cwAL** [Black], I'm rale stomp-down hongry fer de fresh. **1912** Young *Behind the Pines* 18 **cwAL** [Black], Miss Rabbit gwine to have a rale stomped down weddin'. **c1937** in 1972 *Amer. Slave* 2.1.8 **SC** [Black], De reason they is superstitious comes from nothin' but stomppdown [sic] ignorance. **1938** in Lib. of Congress *Amer. Memory: WPA Life Hist.* (Internet) **Savannah GA** [Black], He's a Democrat in his heart . . but on the ticket voting he's a stomp down Republican. **1940** Harris *Folk Plays* 67 **eNC,** I always favored lettin' Etta have Dan'l, but you was so stomp-down against it. **1940** (1941) Bell *Swamp Water* 217 **Okefenokee GA,** That's a stomp-down good race they're having. **1951** Ross *Jackson Mahaffey* 90 **NC,** He was a crotchety old widower . . and a stomping good carpenter. **1952** Brown *NC Folkl.* 1.594, *Stomping. . .* Very, excellent. "Mr. Charlie is a stompin' good man to work for."—Guilford county. **1953** Brewer *Word Brazos* 72 **eTX** [Black], One rail dark complected boy . . gits stompin' down mad. **1965** Will *Okeechobee Boats* 140 **FL,** There was not much pie in the pioneering, and that's a stomped down fact. **1965–70** *DARE* (Qu. FF17, *. . A very good or enjoyable time: "We all had a _____ last night."*) Infs **AR56, MS63,** Stomp-down good time. **1973** Bontemps *Old South* 152 **Sth** [Black] (as of 1930s), This a stomping down pretty shirt. **1975** Newell *If Nothin' Don't Happen* 47 **nwFL,** I had a real stomped-down belly ache from just one plate. **1984** Wilder *You All Spoken Here* 53 **Sth,** *She's so ugly the tide wouldn't take her out:* Stomp-down ugly. *Ibid* 190, *Stomp down:* Absolute, as "That's the stomp down truth, so help me." **1986** Pederson *LAGS Concordance,* 1 inf, **cwGA,** Stomp down—referring to a good time; 1 inf, **cwFL,** A stomp-down good one [=a first-rate writing pen]. **2004** *DARE* File—Internet **nwFL,** If you should get the urge to go on a real stomp-down good, no-frills, duck-hunting trip, you can contact Catfish.

stomper n

1 also *stumper:* A food masher or compressor; the dasher of a churn.

1910 *Gettysburg Times* (PA) 15 Oct 1/4, They have done away with the old style way of pounding the cut cabbage with what we used to call a "stomper." **1927** Kennedy *Gritny* 30 **sLA** [Black], I up wid my potato-stomper was stannin' on de pot shelf, an' I played de thing all up an' down de back his head. **1942** Warnick *Garrett Co. MD* 15 **nwMD** (as of 1900–18), *Tater-stumper . .* potato-masher. **1955** Johnson *50 Yrs.* 14 **ND,** When we packed butter in the big casks, we first dumped in the firm butter, then poured the soft butter in to fill in the spaces. To complete the packing we made use of a heavy wooden stomper. **1966** *Good Old Days* 2.12.4 **CA** (as of c1890), My mother and father sliced the cabbage very fine, put it in a wooden barrel with salt. There was a stomper which my father made from a piece of wood. **1967** *DARE* Tape **NE7,** She churned the butter in an old crock churn with the stomper up and down. **1976** *PA Folklife* Spring 31, *Stomper,* a wooden sauerkraut or potato masher. **2008** *DARE* File—Internet **WI,** You will need something to "stomp" the cabbage with. I use a "stomper" I bought from Lehman's, but you can use a rolling pin that has no handles, the hitting end of a baseball bat, or a piece of 2″ x 4″.

2 also *stomp:* A man's boot or shoe, esp a heavy one; see quots. Cf **kicker** n[1] **2, waffle stomper**

1899 (1912) Green *VA Folk-Speech* 420, *Stompers. . .* Large, heavy shoes. **1970** Major *Dict. Afro-Amer. Slang* 109, *Stompers:* (1940's) one's shoes. . . *Stomps:* (1940's) one's shoes. **1972** Claerbaut *Black Jargon* 81, *Stompers . .* shoes; footwear: *Got some new stompers.* **1975** *AmSp* 50.67 **AR** (as of c1970), *Stompers. . .* Boots, especially cowboy boots. **2005** *DARE* File **eTX** (as of c1950), In East Texas, "stomps" was used to mean "shoes." The semantic relationship between "stomps" and "kicks" is obvious.

3 See quot. Cf *shit-stomper* (at **shit-kicker**)

1986 *DARE* File **cwCA,** One name I heard from a truck driver in the Bay area for Southern whites is *stompers* (short for shit-stompers, which is also a kind of boot).

stomping (down) See **stomp-down** adj phr, adv phr

stomp lot See **stomp 1**

stone n Usu |sto(ʊ)n|; also esp **NEng** |stən, stʌn, stoʊən| Pronc-spp *sto-un, stun*

A Forms.

1848 Lowell *Biglow* 102 **'Upcountry' MA,** Ware every rock there wuz about with precious stuns wuz blazin. **1878** Hart *Sazerac Lying Club* 16 **NV,** They was throwed back on their ha'nches jest as if they had butted clean up ag'in a stun' wall. **1890** *DN* 1.40 **ME,** *Stone:* [author's pronc] originally [stən]; now [stoʊn]. **1890** Holley *Samantha among Brethren* 175 **NY,** I fell down and hurt my head on a stun. **1892** *New Engl. Mag.* 12.101 **NH,** She see one o' them Barrers children tumble off o' the stun wall, and a big stun roll on top o' its arm. **1902** (1904) Rowe *Maid of Bar Harbor* 57 **ME,** That back pastur' o' his is a master place for that kind o' stun. **1905** *DN* 3.22 **cCT,** *Stun. . .* A stone. **1926** *AmSp* 2.77 **ME,** No alien has ever yet been able to master our so-called short *o*. . . [T]ry to enunciate such words as *road, coat, boat, load,* and *stone*. . . [S]ay very rapidly "ro-ud," "co-ut," "bo-ut," "lo-ud," and "sto-un." **1939** *LANE* Map 35 *(He threw a stone)* **NEng,** [Proncs of the types [sto(ʊ)n, sto(ʊ)n] occur throughout **NEng;** those of the types [stoᵊn, stoᵊn, stoᵊn] occur chiefly in **ME, NH, VT;** proncs such as [stən], with "New England short *o,*" occur occasionally, esp in **VT, eMA.**] **1945** Partridge *January Thaw* 212 **CT,** Uncle Walter smiled. "Well, I guess there's no use waitin' for him. Got a stunboat?" **1959** *VT Hist.* 27.161, *Stone* [stʌn]. . . Common. Rural areas. **1961** Kurath–McDavid *Pronc. Engl.* 111, The dialect of New England possesses a checked mid-back vowel /ə/, traditionally called "the New England short *o,*" in such words as *coat, road, smoke, stone, home, whole,* which does not occur outside the New England settlement area, i.e., the Northern dialect area. . . This vowel phoneme, a hallmark of the New England dialect, is sharply recessive at the present time and has obviously been receding for several generations. **1985** Benes *Amer. Speech* 82 **cwMA** (as of c1845), Rich transcribed . . *stone,* and *throat* with the short *o,* while retaining long *o* in *own, note,* [etc].

B Senses.

The hard center of a fruit, as: see below. Cf **pit** n[2] **1**

a Of a cherry. **widespread, but somewhat more freq NEng** See Map

[**1628** in 1853 MA (Colony) *Rec. of Gov.* 1.24, To send for New England . . Stones of all sorts of fruites, as peaches, plums, filberts, cherries.] **1821** *N. Amer. Rev. & Misc. Jrl.* 12.430, Why is not the acorn, which is planted at the same time with the cherry-stone, regarded as the cause of the fruit-tree? **1941** *LANE* Map 269 *(Cherry stone)* **NEng,** [Stone is the predominant term in the region except for the southwest, where *pit* is more frequent.] **c1960** Wilson Coll. **csKY,** *Cherry seed* is almost universal; *pit* and *stone* are known but rarely used. **1965–70** *DARE* (Qu. I48, *The hard center of a cherry*) 215 Infs, **widespread, but somewhat more freq NEng,** Stone. **1966** [see **pit** n[2] **1a**]. **1970** Tarpley *Blinky* 186 **nwTX,** Hard center of a cherry . . stone [13 of 200 infs]. **1971** Bright *Word Geog. CA & NV* 182, *Pit . .* of a cherry . . *stone* 17% [of 300 infs]. **1972** [see **pit** n[2] **1a**]. **1973** Allen *LAUM* 1.304 (as of c1950), *Seed* (of a cherry). . . *Pit* not only . . dominates all the U[pper] M[idwest] but appears to be gaining in popularity. . . *Stone,* a UM minority form clearly Northern with two-thirds of its occurrences in Minnesota (though with five in the South Midland region of Iowa), seems conversely to be on the wane. **1989** Pederson *LAGS Tech. Index* 180 **Gulf Region** *(Cherry seed)* 51 infs, Stone; 6 infs, Cherrystone. **2005** *Boston Globe* (MA) 20 July sec C 3 (Internet), Almond extract imparts a stronger whiff of almond than a cherry stone ever could.

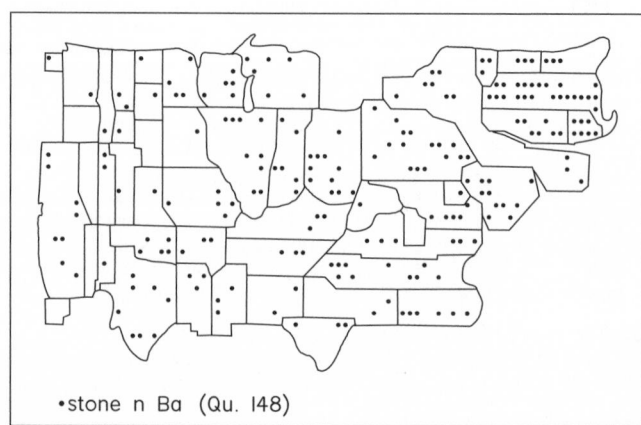

•stone n Ba (Qu. I48)

b Of a plum. **widespread, but more freq Nth, N Midl, esp NEng** See Map

[**1628** see **Ba** above.] **1858** Neill *Hist. MN* 74, A bullet or plum-stone is placed by one party in one of four moccasins or mittens. **1965–70** *DARE* (Qu. I49, . . *The hard center of a plum*) 233 Infs, **widespread, but more freq Nth, N Midl, esp NEng,** Stone. **1986** Pederson *LAGS Concordance,* 5 infs, **GA, LA, MS,** Plum stone.

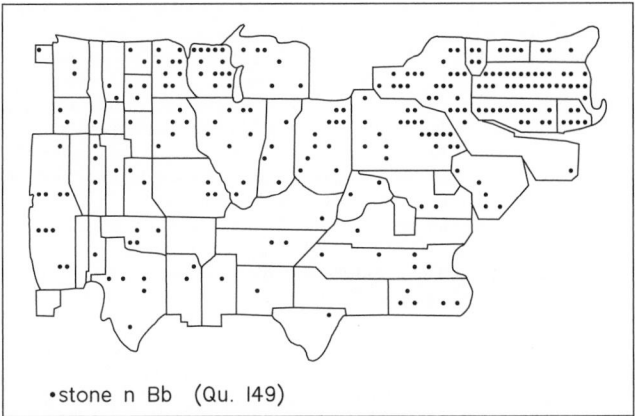

•stone n Bb (Qu. I49)

c Of a peach. **widespread, but more freq Nth, N Midl** See Map Cf **clearstone, clingstone, freestone,** *open stone* (at **open peach**)

[**1628** see **Ba** above.] **1724** Royal Soc. London *Philos. Trans.* 33.195 **NEng,** Our Peach Trees . . bear commonly in three Years from the Stone. **1832** *N. Amer. Rev.* 35.404, Their seeds are generally such as the peach-stone or the apple-seed. **1859** Taliaferro *Fisher's R.* 70 **nwNC** (as of 1820s), There warn't a bullit in it—nothin' but a peach-stone. **1941** *LANE* Map 268 (*Peach stone*) **NEng,** [*Stone* is the predominant term throughout the region.] **1965–70** *DARE* (Qu. I50, . . *The hard center of a peach*) 360 Infs, **widespread, but more freq Nth,** Stone. **1966** Dakin *Dial. Vocab. Ohio R. Valley* 2.357, Stone (*of a peach*)—The endocarp of a peach and its enclosed seed are called *seed* and *stone* throughout most of the Ohio Valley. **1968** [see **seed** n 1]. **1970** Tarpley *Blinky* 184 **nwTX,** Hard center of a peach . . stone [2 of 200 infs]. **1971** Bright *Word Geog. CA & NV* 182, Pit . . of a peach . . *stone* 40% [of 300 infs]. **1973** Allen *LAUM* 1.305 **Upper MW** (as of c1950), Stone (*of a peach*). . . Stone, in contrast with its use for the center of a cherry, is a majority form in Minnesota, Iowa, and Minnesota [sic for *North Dakota*], and nearly that in South Dakota and Nebraska. **1989** Pederson *LAGS Tech. Index* 180 **Gulf Region** (*Peach seed*) 82 infs, Stone; 13 infs, Peach stone.

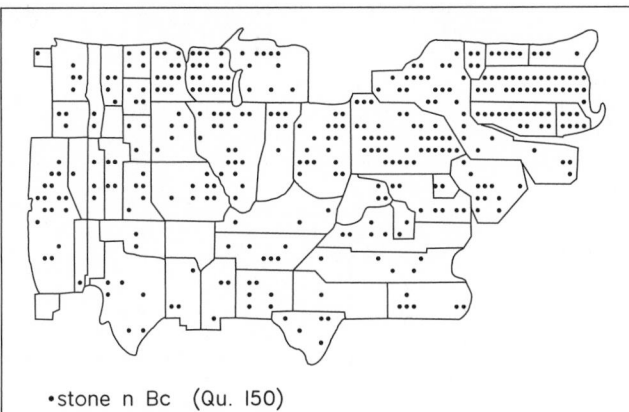

•stone n Bc (Qu. I50)

stone v [*OED2 stone* v. 6 *"Obs."*]
To castrate.

1949 McDavid *Coll.* **swNY,** To stone a pig—castrate. **1950** *WELS* (*Words for castrating an animal*) 1 Inf, **ceWI,** Stone—old-fashioned. **1966–68** *DARE* (Qu. K70) Infs **FL15, LA14, NJ8,** Stone.

stone adj [Cf *OED2 stone* sb. 19.b] *among Black speakers*
Genuine, complete; excellent.

1968 *Current Slang* 3.2.46 **Los Angeles CA** [Watts slang; Black], *Stone fox.* . . An attractive girl. **1970** Abrahams *Deep Down* 267 **Phila-**

delphia PA [Black], *Stone*—An adjective or adverb indicating a greater degree of whatever the noun or verb which it modifies originally meant. A "stone sailor" is a sailor who has all sailors' characteristics. **1972** *AmSp* 47.152 [Black] (as of 1970), Look at those stone calves shake! **1979** Gillespie–Fraser *To Be Or Not To Bop* 377 [Black], My Philadelphia lawyer . . was a genius, a stone genius in a courtroom. **1980** Folb *Runnin' Down* 49 **cwCA** [Black], Dese ain' levis, dis is *stone* alligator! *Ibid* 118, I'ma be a *stone* pimp. Get me a Cadillac. *Ibid* 126, You ain't nothin' but a stone, hope-to-die, strung out nigger! **1986** Pederson *LAGS Concordance* (Caucasian) 1 inf, **cwFL,** A stone cracker—a pure-blooded white. [Inf Black] **1996** McDowell *Leaving Pipe Shop* 122 **AL** [Black] (as of 1950s), Lockhart was a stone preacher.

stone board n
=**stoneboat.**

1939 *LANE* Map 168 (*Stone boat*) 1 inf, **swCT,** Most of the old-fashioned farmers call it a stone board. **1968** *DARE* (Qu. L57, *A low wooden platform used for bringing stones or heavy things out of the fields*) Inf **NJ6,** Stone board.

stoneboat n **chiefly Nth, N Midl, West** See Map Also called **bed** n B5, **boat** 1, **claprack, cradle** 3, **dray** n 1, **flat** n¹ 5, **flatboat** n 2, **float** n 4, **log boat, mud boat** 1, **rock boat, scow** n¹ 1, **skift** n¹ 2, **slip** n² 1, **stone board, stonebolt, stone drag** Cf **drag** n 2, **sled** n, **slide** n 1
A sledge used for transporting stones or other heavy loads.

1822 Hull *Minutes* App 9 **MA,** 1 yoke oxen, and two men hauling stone in stone-boat. **1850** Willis *Life Here & There* 75 **cwNY,** A stone-boat would run glibly over such shallow snow! **1908** *German Amer. Annals* 10.45 **sePA,** Stone-boat. Low sled, drawn by one or two horses. "Bring those barrels on the stone-boat." **1909** *DN* 3.417 **nME,** Stone-boat. . . A drag about three by five feet, made of planks, and used for hauling rocks over the ground. **1910** *DN* 3.449 **wNY,** Stone-boat. . . A sled without runners used primarily for drawing stones. **1922** (1926) Cady *Rhymes VT* 87, [Poem title:] A Vermont Stoneboat. **1929** *AmSp* 5.126 **NY,** We picked rocks . . and piled them on drags, known in New York State as "stone boats," a name I never heard in Maine. **1931** *AmSp* 6.230 **neOR,** The 'stone boat' is a small drag used for hauling away the stones that come to the surface in the fields each spring. *Ibid* 7.120 **eID,** A heavy sled called a *stone boat* is used to haul to the edge of a field the volcanic rocks which work to the surface. **1949** Kurath *Word Geog.* 58, Stone boat. . . The wheelless horse-drawn vehicle made of heavy planks, used for dragging stones from the fields, is known as a . . *stone boat* in the North, except for the coastal area of New England, which has *drag* or *stone drag.* **1958** McCulloch *Woods Words* 182 **Pacific NW,** Stone boat—A small flat wooden sled used in skidding, by some horse loggers; name probably taken from the stone boat used by farmers in picking stones off their fields. **1965–70** *DARE* (Qu. L57, *A low wooden platform used for bringing stones or heavy things out of the fields*) 288 Infs, **chiefly Nth, N Midl, West,** Stoneboat; (Qu. N40a, . . *Sleighs . . for hauling loads*) Infs **MI24, 71, ND3, NY216, OH82, OR3, WA28,** Stoneboat; (Qu. N40c, *Other kinds of sleighs*) Inf **NY183,** Stoneboat; (Qu. N41b, *Horse-drawn vehicles to carry heavy loads*) Infs **CT5, MN19, NY97, 109, 183, WI5,** Stoneboat; (Qu. EE24a, *When there's snow, children go down the hill on a _____*) Inf **WI5,** Stoneboat. **1969** *DARE* Tape **NY223,** They take this on a great big stoneboat, they call it; it doesn't have wheels, it has runners so that it doesn't sink down into the soft earth. **2000** Chamberlain *River Stories* 108 **swWI,** Dad solved the problem by building an old-fashioned sled, which we called a stone boat.

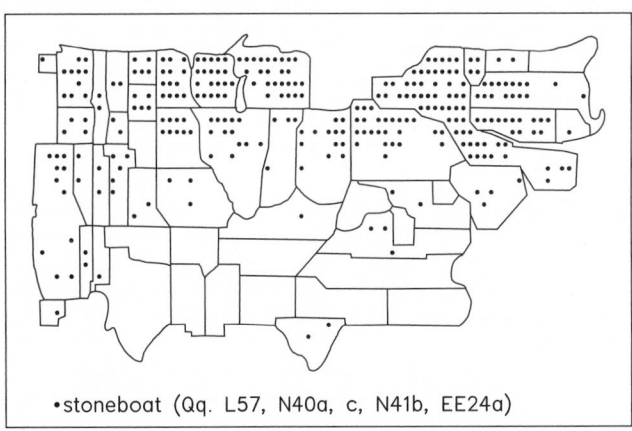

•stoneboat (Qq. L57, N40a, c, N41b, EE24a)

stonebolt n [Var of **stoneboat**] **Nth**

1945 *Syracuse Herald–Jrl.* (NY) 14 Sept 3/3, Lyle Durant's team, weighing 3,800 pounds, dragged the stonebolt weighing 5,221 pounds a distance of 271 feet to win the horse-pulling contest. **1967** *DARE* (Qu. L57, *A low wooden platform used for bringing stones or heavy things out of the fields*) Inf **MI**67, Stoneboat or -bolt—I've heard it pronounced both ways. **1973** Allen *LAUM* 1.219 (as of c1950), *Stone boat. . .* stone bolt [3 infs, **MN**]. **1981** *PADS* 67.26 **Mesabi Iron Range MN,** *Stoneboat. . .* The Northern *stone boat* (or *bolt*) . . is the usual Iron Range expression. . . The *bolt* form, occurring only once among other Minnesota informants, is used by almost half of those on the Range. **1995** *Mt. Democrat* (Placerville CA) 23 Oct sec B 4/1, Several of the men built a stonebolt (a very heavy sled), dragged it with horses through the old Master Place. **2004** *DARE* File—Internet **MT** (as of 1940s), I remember [race]tracks that were made by dragging a stonebolt and harrow around and around in a hay field.

stone bug n

=**sow bug.**

1960 Korson *Black Rock* 430 **PA,** According to Bowman, stone bugs were grey, about ¾ of an inch long. Found under dry stones. They rolled themselves into a grey ball when disturbed.

stonecat See **stone catfish 1**

stone catfish n

1 also *stonecat:* Any of var fishes of the genus *Noturus,* esp *N. flavus.* Also called **madtom, stone roller 3, willow cat d.** For other names of the common *N. flavus* see **doogler, mongrel bullhead;** for other names of var spp see **mudcat 1c, poison catfish, tadpole madtom**

1849 (1851) Heck *Iconographic Encycl.* 2.216, The genus *Noturus,* known provincially as stone cat-fish, embraces but few species, found in the Atlantic streams south of New York, and in those of the Mississippi valley. **1861** *Philp's Washington* 32 **DC,** The latter [=*Noturus*] is called "stone cat." The wound inflicted by its spines becomes excessively painful, and has even been known to produce death. **1868** *Riverside Mag.* 2.373 **VA,** He went . . to fish in a certain pond, said to be full of stone cats. **1899** *Trenton Eve. Times* (NJ) 17 June 1/5, The bass are biting splendidly down in the Susquehanna river. . . Stone catfish is the favorite bait. **1908** Forbes–Richardson *Fishes of IL* 194, *Noturus flavus* . . Stonecat. . . This interesting little fish, commonest under stones in swift waters in the larger creeks and smaller rivers, is rather abundant. **1933** John G. Shedd Aquarium *Guide* 54, The Stone Cats or Mad-Toms are small catfish, rarely over nine or ten inches in length. **1951** *New Castle News* (PA) 21 June 28/4, What species are classified as 'bait fish' . . ? In general, the minnows (except fall fish); also, killifishes and stone catfish. **2008** *DARE* File—Internet **nePA,** [Advt:] Products: . . Shiners in four sizes, fathead minnows in two sizes, stone catfish (plus albino stone cats), [etc].

2 =**brown bullhead.**

1906 NJ State Museum *Annual Rept. for 1905* 169, *Ameiurus nebulosus. . .* Miller's Thumb. Stone Cat Fish.

stone clover n [See quot 1922]

=**rabbit-foot clover.**

1837 Darlington *Flora Cestrica* 406 **sePA,** *T[rifolium] arvense. . .* Field Trifolium. *Vulgò*—Stone Clover. . . It is a worthless species,—and indicative of a poor soil. **1848** in 1850 Cooper *Rural Hours* 125 **NY,** The downy "rabbit-foot," or "stone-clover," the common red variety . . and the "hop clovers," are all introduced. **1914** Georgia *Manual Weeds* 230, Stone Clover usually grows and is able to thrive on very dry, sandy, and gravelly soils. **1922** *Amer. Botanist* 28.34, "Old field clover", "stone clover" and "poverty grass" allude to the habit this plant [= *Trifolium arvense*] has of growing in sterile soil. **1935** (1943) Muenscher *Weeds* 309, Rabbit-foot clover, Stone clover, Old-field clover. **1939** *Arlington Heights Herald* (IL) 30 Mar 10/4, [Advt:] *For Sale* . . 5 ton stone clover and 5 ton timothy hay.

stonecrop n

1 Std: a plant of the genus *Sedum* or the related **roseroot.** For other names of var spp see **hen and chickens 1a(3), orpine, queen's crown 2, rock moss, rose crown, wall pepper, widow's cross** Cf **flowering moss 2**

2 =**bluff lettuce.**

1906 Smithsonian Inst. *Annual Rept. for 1905* 83, 5 specimens of a Stone-crop, *Dudleya,* from Lower California. **1954** CA Div. Beaches &

Parks *Pt. Lobos Wild Flowers* 19, *Dudleya farinosa. . .* Bluff Lettuce, stone-crop, hen-and-chickens are all frequently-used common names. **1961** Peck *Manual OR* 394, *D[udleya] farinosa. . .* Sea-cliff Stonecrop. Very glaucous. **2005** in 2006 *DARE* File—Internet, This beautiful Lycaenid is found in Southern California. I reared these on stonecrop (*Dudleya spp.*)

stone curlew n

1 Either of two similar birds: usu the **willet,** but also the greater **yellowlegs 1.**

1823 James *Acct. of Exped.* 1.374, *Scolopax. . . (Totanus) melanoleucus . .* —Stone curlew. **1828** Flint *Condensed Geog.* 2.515 **Missip Valley,** The following catalogue contains but a small proportion of the number of Western birds; but it is believed that the birds most frequently seen . . are included here. . . Stone Curlew. **1835** Audubon *Ornith. Biog.* 3.510 **Sth,** The Semipalmated Snipe is known . . from the Carolinas southward . . [as the] "Stone Curlew." **1844** DeKay *Zool. NY* 2.251, The *Willet, Semipalmated Snipe,* or *Stone Curlew,* reaches this State about the beginning of May, and breeds from Louisiana to Massachusetts. **1869** (1875) Bumstead *On the Wing* 131, Willet or Stone Curlew (*Scolopax semipalmata*).

2 pronc-sp *stone culoo:* =**white ibis.**

1917 (1923) *Birds Amer.* 1.175, White Ibis. . . Other Names.—Spanish Curlew; Stone Curlew (young) [etc]. **1955** *Oriole* 20.1.3, *White Ibis. . . Stone Culoo* (latter term equals curlew; "stone curlew" probably adopted from some general natural history; the bird rightfully bearing that name [=the Norfolk plover] does not occur in North America). **1969** Longstreet *Birds FL* 29, White Ibis—*Other names:* Spanish Curlew; White Curlew; Stone Curlew.

stone drag n **chiefly NEast, esp eNEng** See Map *old-fash* Cf **drag** n **2**

=**stoneboat.**

1835 (1927) Rodman *Diary* 143 **MA,** Went to the head of the River for planks sawed for my stone drags. **1860** *Scientific Amer.* 2.38, Oxen working on a stone-drag . . should carry their heads up. **1892** *Overland Mth.* (2d ser) 19.418 **CA,** I've heard say . . that "even a stone drag cannot stand everything." **1903** McFaul *Ike Glidden* 26 **ME,** They attached him to a stone-drag. **a1910** in 1979 *AmSp* 54.99 **ME,** *Stone drag. . .* "A man can't stand ev'ything no more'n a stone-drag." **1949** [see **stoneboat**]. **1965–70** *DARE* (Qu. L57, *A low wooden platform used for bringing stones or heavy things out of the fields*) 11 Infs, **esp NEast,** Stone drag. [10 of 11 Infs old] **1966** Dakin *Dial. Vocab. Ohio R. Valley* 2.157, *Stone boat. . .* The eastern New England term *stone drag* is even more common than *stone boat* in the Ohio Company area but appears only once . . outside this region of New England settlement. **1967** Faries *Word Geog. MO* 83, *Stone boat. . . Stone drag* (87 occurrences [from 700 infs]), the least frequent of the North and North Midland terms, seems to follow the Missouri and Mississippi Rivers and is especially frequent in the Northern Plains east of the Chariton River and north of the Salt River. **1984** *MJLF* 10.157 **cnWI,** Stone drag. A conveyance made of planks for hauling off big stones. **1986** *Daily Intelligencer* (Doylestown PA) 29 Apr sec C 10 **ME,** [Caption:] He calls the sled-like device used to haul the rocks to the edge of the field a "stone drag."

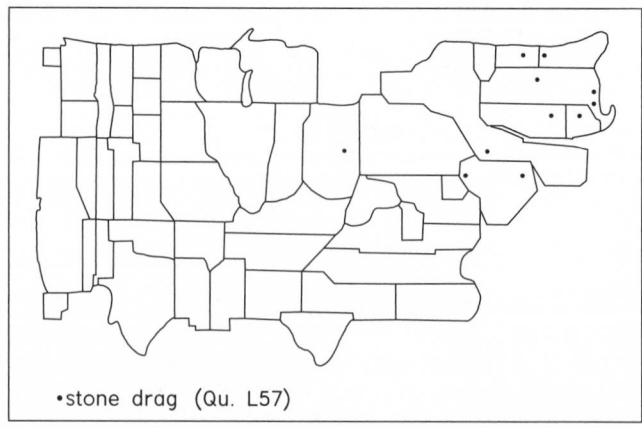

•stone drag (Qu. L57)

stone dray See **dray** n **1**

stonedy See **stonie**

stone fence n widespread, but esp freq Inland Nth, N Midl
See Map Cf **rock fence**
=**stone wall.**
    1682 in 1901 Derby CT *Town Rec.* 305, [Mr. Bowers] is to hav that part of ye fenc . . next his hous namely ye stone fenc. **1844** Stephens *High Life in NY* 1.37, I might as well a been talking to a stun fence. **1946** *PADS* 5.40 VA, *Stone fence.* . . A fence of loose stone; on the Middle Neck, in the Piedmont north of the Rappahannock, and the lower Shenandoah Valley. **1947** *PADS* 8.24 wNY, *Stone fence.* **1949** Kurath *Word Geog.* 55, Fences built of loose stones around fields and pastures are known as . . *stone fences* in the North Midland, and as *rock fences* farther south. *Stone fence* now predominates in all of Maryland, but in West Virginia the Southern *rock fence* is now more common than the Midland *stone fence.* **1965–70** *DARE* (Qu. L60, *A fence made of stone or rock without mortar*) 273 Infs, **widespread, but esp freq Inland Nth, N Midl,** Stone fence; [NY52, VA26, Loose-stone fence; MD32, Dry-stone fence;] (Qu. L65, . . *Kinds of fences*) Infs IL85, 104, KS17, NY230, OR7, PA153, 174, WV10, Stone fence; NJ45, Laid-up stone fence; [(Qu. L60b, *A fence of stone built with mortar;* total Infs questioned, 75) Infs MS9, 21, 28, 40, 60, OK1, 20, 33, Stone fence;] (Qu. L64) Inf CT17, Stone fence. **1981** *PADS* 67.23 **Mesabi Iron Range MN,** The common term for Iron Range informants . . is the North Midland *stone fence,* which is usual for other Minnesota informants. **1982** *Washington Post* (DC) 13 Feb sec B 1 (Internet) **cnVA,** "It takes a long time to build a proper stone fence," said Nalls, who can rebuild about five feet of old fence a day. **1984** *MJLF* 10.157 **cnWI,** *Stone fence.* Fieldstones piled along property lines so as to form a fence. **1989** Pederson *LAGS Tech. Index* 65 **Gulf Region,** *Stone wall.* . . stone fence 71 [of 914 primary infs]. **2005** *Assoc. Press State & Local Wire* 26 May (Internet) **cnKY,** The sounds of 17 professional and recreational stone wallers chipping away at stone rang out . . as they rebuild nearly 100 feet of a historic stone fence.

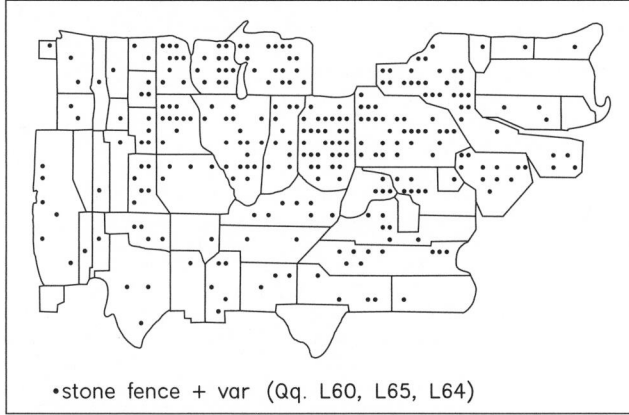

•stone fence + var (Qq. L60, L65, L64)

stone game See **stone school**

stone hedge n Also *stone-hedge fence,* ~ *row* [Cf *EDD hedge* sb. 4 "A wall, *gen.* of granite, occas. of earth or turf."] Nth
=**stone wall.**
    1833 *Cincinnati Mirror* (OH) 5 Oct 3/1 OH, "Giff it to him!" shouted Johannes, who had crawled from his hiding place, and was standing close by on the stone-hedge. **1858** Townsend *While It Was Morning* 314 NEng, The golden rod shook its yellow tassels by the stone hedges. **1927** *Lancaster Daily Eagle* (OH) 15 Apr 4/7, [Serialized novel:] It necessitated stopping the car alongside a crumbling stone hedge. **1933** *WI Rapids Daily Tribune* (WI) 19 Jan 11/6, The decorative scheme gives the room the appearance of a garden. The lower part of the walls are painted to represent a stone hedge. **1950** *WELS (Kinds of fences made of stones . . Not mortared)* 1 Inf, **csWI,** Stone hedge. **1961** in 2009 (acc) Lexis–Nexis Legal Research *State Case Law:* NJ (Internet), He testified that he never crossed over the stone hedge row as Schlett had indicated, but recalled that Schlett "showed me a sign up in the air, when I came out, on a tree, which was between the stone fence and the road, and I probably went underneath it." **1967–70** *DARE* (Qu. L60, *A fence made of stone or rock without mortar*) Infs NJ2, OH75, PA246, Stone hedge; [MI23, Hedge]. **1969** *DARE* FW Addit neIL, Stone hedge—a New England term. **1973** Allen *LAUM* 1.195 (as of c1950), *Stone wall.* . . stone hedge [1 inf, nIA]. **1998** *Frederick Post* (MD) 7 Mar sec D 7/1, [Advt:] No city taxes or HOA. 2 brick FPs. Stone hedge fence.

stone johnny n esp ND, SD
See quot 1938.
    1938 FWP *Guide SD* 87, *Stone johnny:* a monument of piled rocks usually erected by a sheepherder. [**1981** Simpson–Simpson *North of Narrows* 178 ID (as of 1931), A few minutes later the lookout on Stone Johnny Mountain called in.] **2004** *DARE* File—Internet SD, My favorite, though, was a cartoon of my Dad titled, Albert watching the sheep. Einar drew what we called a stone johnny . . a small stone structure on the top of the butte that overlooked the sheep pasture. *Ibid* ND, There will be a Stone Johnny (a pile of scoria rocks) at the descent. Follow the trail along the ridge to the Sully Creek Campground.

stone lily n
A **pasqueflower** (here: *Pulsatilla patens*).
    1898 *Jrl. Amer. Folkl.* 11.221 csWI, *Anemone patens* [=*Pulsatilla p.*] . . wind anemone, Easter-flower, stone-lily.

stone lugger See **stone toter**

‡**stone men** n Cf **hull-gull, stone school**
    1969 *DARE* (Qu. EE33, . . *Outdoor games . . that children play*) Inf MI103, Stone men—people would have to guess which hand the stone was in.

stone mint n
=**dittany.**
    1828 Rafinesque *Med. Flora* 1.136, *Cunila mariana* [=*C. origanoides*]. . . *Vulgar Names*—Mountain Dittany, Stone Mint [etc]. **1854** King *Amer. Eclectic Dispensatory* 417, *Cunila Mariana.* . . This plant, also called *Stonemint, Mountain dittany,* etc., is an indigenous perennial plant. **1941** Walker *Lookout* 51 TN, *Stonemint,* known by the makers of tea as American dittany, makes a thrifty growth. **1974** (1977) Coon *Useful Plants* 156, *Cunila origanoides*—Dittany, sweet horsemint, wild basil, stonemint.

stone on the chest n Cf *DS* BB10
    1929 *AmSp* 5.147 CO [Mining expressions], The disease most feared by miners, tuberculosis, is known as *stone on the chest.*

stone owl n [See quot 1867]
=**saw-whet owl.**
    1867 (1870) Samuels *Birds New Engl.* 577, *Nyctala acadica* [= *Aegolius acadicus*]. . . It generally frequents stone quarries or piles of rocks, beneath which it takes shelter; and it is from this habit that the bird here is known by the name of "stone owl." **1911** *Mansfield News* (OH) 29 July 16/2, He shot a stone owl and is now having the beautiful bird mounted to add to his collection. The stone owl is a very rare bird in this section. **c1940** *LAMSAS Materials,* 1 inf, **MD,** Night owl, stone owl—red; 1 inf, **VA,** Stone owl . . night owl.

stone-pecker n [*OED2* 1731 →]
=**ruddy turnstone.**
    1903 Coues *Key to N. Amer. Birds* 2.785, *A[renaria] interpres.* . . Turnstone. . . Stone-pecker.

stone pine n Also *Mexican stone pine* [*OED2* 1759 → in ref to European species *(Pinus pinea, P. cembra)* with edible seeds]
A **piñon 1** (here: *Pinus cembroides* or *P. monophylla*).
    [**1852** Standish–Noble *Practical Hints* 80, *Pinus cembroides.* . . (Cembran-like Stone Pine.) . . A very handsome tree, indigenous to the mountains of California, at an altitude of 10,000 feet, where it occurs as a dwarf tree twenty to thirty feet high.] **1908** Britton *N. Amer. Trees* 14, *Pinus cembroides.* . . variously known as Mexican piñon or pinyon, Nut pine, Piñon and Stone pine. **1938** Van Dersal *Native Woody Plants* 348, Pine, . . Mexican stone *(Pinus cembroides).* **1968** *DARE* (Qu. T17, . . *Kinds of pine trees;* not asked in early QRs) Inf CA65, Stone pine—goes clear across streets; surface roots. [*DARE* Ed: This Inf may refer instead to *Pinus pinea.*] **1995** Brako et al. *Scientific & Common Names Plants* 204, Stone pine—*Pinus monophylla.*

stone-post rock See **post rock**

stoner See **stonie**

stone roller n [Because in feeding or nesting they push stones about]
1 also *stone-roller minnow:* A **minnow B1** of the genus *Campostoma,* usu *C. anomalum.* For other names of this species see **doughbelly 1, greased chub, hornyhead b, knot-**

head 4, mammy n[2], **racehorse chub, rock-roller 2, slick** n **6, steel-backed minnow, stone toter 2, tallow-mouth minnow**

1876 Jordan *Manual Vertebrates N. U.S.* 275, *C[ampostoma] anomalum, . .* Stone Lugger. Stone Roller. . . Mississippi Valley, everywhere abundant; one of the most curious and interesting of American fishes. **1929** *OK Univ. Biol. Surv. Pub.* 1.2.94, Stone-roller minnow. . . Red River system in Oklahoma. **1933** *AmSp* 8.1.52 **Ozarks,** *Stone rollers. . .* Small sucker-like fish, about four or five inches long, which feed in large schools. **1947** Hubbs–Lagler *Fishes Gt. Lakes* 69, Ohio stoneroller—*Campostoma anomalum anomalum. . .* Showing a preference for clear brooks, creeks and small rivers. **1967** Cross *Hdbk. Fishes KS* 162, The stoneroller inhabits most small streams of Kansas. . . Males prepare nests by digging into the bottom with their snouts, pushing stones aside, and by lifting pebbles in their mouths. **2005** *Copeia* 797, In our surveys, *N[oturus] crypticus* was frequently associated with the Central Stoneroller (*Campostoma anomalum*).

2 =**hog sucker.**

1855 *IL State Ag. Soc. Trans. for 1853–54* 594, *Catostomus nigricans. . .* Stone Roller, Flat-headed Sucker. **1874** *Forest & Stream* 3.203 **IA,** He threw away the first fish of this kind caught by him, thinking it kindred to the mullet, or stone roller, a species of fresh water sucker. **1876** Jordan *Manual Vertebrates N. U.S.* 294, *H[ypentelium] nigricans. . .* Stone Roller. Mud Sucker. **1882** [see **stone toter 1**]. **1904** Kellogg *Boy Fisherman* 38 **wIL,** "And here is another old-timer," pointing to a long round fish, sprinkled with black spots along the sides. "We called them 'stone rollers' when I was a boy. Sometimes they were sold under the high-sounding name of 'channel trout'." . . "We still call them stone rollers, or corn cobs," said Jack, "and they are one of the best selling fish in the sucker family." **1950** *WELS* **WI** (*Kinds of fish not commonly eaten*) 1 Inf, Stone rollers; 1 Inf, Stone rollers. Biggest 10″, much like sucker and redhorse. Scavengers—push the stones aside, only found in streams.

3 =**stone catfish 1.** Cf **poison catfish**

1888 *NY Times* (NY) 8 July 13/7 **csPA,** The stone roller season begins as soon as the Spring floods subside, when men and boys haunt the creeks and other stone roller retreats to lay in stocks of the standard bait. The stone roller is probably a member of the pout family, as is recognized in some localities by calling it the stone cat. **1890** *Forest & Stream* 35.5, The common way of catching the stone catfish, or stone roller, is by striking with a stone the flat rock under which it is supposed to be hiding. **1909** *Outing* 54.225 **nePA,** From my bait box I took two five-inch red catfish, the little "stone-rollers" of the Delaware.

4 =**peamouth.**

1908 Grinnell *Jack Explorer* 154 **Pacific NW,** "Pea mouths?" said Jack. "I think I've heard that name, but I don't know what it means." "Why," replied Hugh, "it's a kind of a brook white fish, I reckon. . . Some people call them stone rollers. I don't know just why, unless, perhaps, they turn over the stones at the bottom of the stream when they're looking for food."

stoneroller minnow See **stone roller 1**

stoneroot n [See quot 1971]
=**horse balm.**

1828 Rafinesque *Med. Flora* 1.111, *Collinsonia canadensis. . .* Vulgar Names—Richweed, . . Stone-root [etc]. **1872** Schele de Vere *Americanisms* 399, The *Stone-Root* (Collinsonia canadensis), the flowers of which have an odor like lemons, is also known as *Rich Weed* from this fragrance. **1892** *IN Dept. Geol. & Nat. Resources Rept. for 1891* 150, Rich-weed. Stone-root. **1930** Sievers *Amer. Med. Plants* 23, Citronella Horsebalm. . . Stoneroot, Collinsonia [etc]. **1971** Krochmal *Appalachia Med. Plants* 100, Stone root. . . Plant rises from a thick, woody rhizome. **1983** *MJLF* 9.1.58 **ceKY** (as of 1956), *Stone root . .* a medicinal herb.

stone row n **chiefly NJ, PA**

A heap of stones along the edge of a field.

1852 in 2009 (acc) Lexis–Nexis Legal Research *State Case Law: NJ* (Internet), He admits that the complainant put a stone row instead of a stone wall along one side of part of the lot, but says that the expense was not $10. **1883** *Century Illustr. Mag.* 26.686 **NY,** A pair of brown-thrashers . . were flitting from bush to bush along an old stone row in a remote field. **1888** in 2009 (acc) Lexis–Nexis Legal Research *State Case Law: MI* (Internet), The road . . encroached upon as follows, to-wit: By rail fence, stone row, rail piles, hay barn and sheds. **1949** Kurath *Word Geog.* 26, On the Jersey side of the Delaware River a number of unique expressions have been noted . . *stone row . .* for the stone fence (only on the upper Delaware). **1962** in 2009 (acc) Lexis–Nexis Legal Research *State Case Law: NJ* (Internet), There was a stone row

and fence along this end of the boundary. **1967–68** *DARE* (Qu. L60, *A fence made of stone or rock without mortar*) Infs **NJ**1, 2, 10, **PA**59, Stone row; (Qu. L65, . . *Kinds of fences*) Inf **NJ**45, Stone row. **1967** *DARE* FW Addit **NJ,** People in Warren and Sussex Cos. often call fences made of unmortared stone *stone rows*. **1977–78** Foster *Lexical Variation* 98 **NJ,** Stone Wall. . . *Stone row,* in LAUS [=Linguistic Atlas of the United States and Canada] restricted to Northwest Jersey . . , is attested . . everywhere [in NJ] except Bergen, Hudson, Essex, and the Philadelphia Suburbs. **1990** *Gettysburg Times* (PA) 17 Nov sec A 4/4, Put out a salt block on a hawthorn stake near the stone row. **1994** *Wellsboro Gaz.* (PA) 13 July Marketplace sec 3/3, Pioneers dumped most stones in rows on the borders of their fields. These stone rows sometimes served as fence lines as well. The industrious farmer built solid stone walls along these rows. **2003** *DARE* File—Internet **NJ,** I have seen ruffed grouse drum . . even while sitting on a large grapevine that was on top of an old stone row.

stone runner n [*OED2* 1681 →]
=**piping plover.**

1876 *Forest & Stream* 7.149 **Long Is. NY,** The stonerunner is white, with a black ring around the neck.

stone school n Also *stone game,* ~ *teacher* **chiefly NEast** Cf **dummy school, rock school, step school**
=**school.**

1945 Boyd *Hdbk. Games* 80, *Stone Teacher*—The players sit on the bottom step of a flight of stairs while one, the "teacher" stands facing them. The teacher puts his hands behind him, and shifts a pebble . . from one hand to the other and then holds his closed fists out in front of the end child, who guesses in which hand the pebble is concealed. If he guesses correctly he moves up a step. . . The teacher repeats this for each child. The one who is first to make the trip to the top and back to the bottom step takes the teacher's place. **1966–69** *DARE* (Qu. EE33, . . *Outdoor games . . that children play*) Inf **NY**130, Stone school—you sit on a step and the teacher holds a pebble in her hand and if you guess which hand holds the stone, you go up a step or a grade; (Qu. EE4) Inf **DC**8, Stone teacher—have stone in one hand or the other, make children guess which. It's done on steps, which are "grades" beginning with kindergarten; if they guess right about the stones, they go up one grade. One at top wins. **1988** *DARE* File **csWI** (as of 1930s), This game [= **dummy school**] was called *stone school* in Cottage Grove, WI. **2000** *NADS Letters* **VA,** As a child, I played "stone school" at recess. *Ibid* **cwNY,** Stone school. . . is the term we used for the game when I was growing up in Buffalo, NY. . . I . . ws [sic] born in 1954. *Ibid* **cwNY,** I used to play "stone school" . . in the mid- to late 40s in upstate (Rochester area) NY. *Ibid* **csMA,** We played Stone School growing up in Central Massachusetts—Auburn—when I was a youngster. . . I was born in 1943. **2001** *Ibid* **seNY,** I played stone school as a child in Poughkeepsie, N.Y., during early to mid '50s. *Ibid* **ceNY,** "Stone School" . . I played this . . when I was little, in the 1950's. . . This was in a village in the northern Catskills in upstate New York. *Ibid* **sePA,** "Chinese school, or rock school." . . My father used to play this game with us. . . He called it the "stone game." He was from Philadelphia (born 1926).

stoneseed piñon n Also *stoneseed piñon pine,* ~ *Mexican piñon*

A **piñon 1** (here: *Pinus cembroides*).

1897 Sudworth *Arborescent Flora* 17, *Pinus cembroides. . .* Stoneseed Mexican Pinyon. **1900** Lyons *Plant Names* 291, *P. cembroides . .* Stone-seed Pinyon. **1976** Elmore *Shrubs & Trees SW* 19, Mexican Pinyon—three-leaved or stoneseed pinyon pine.

stone sturgeon n [See quot 1983] Cf **rock sturgeon**
=**lake sturgeon.**

1882 U.S. Natl. Museum *Bulletin* 16.87, *Acipenser rubicundus* [=*A. fulvescens*] . . Black Sturgeon; Stone Sturgeon; Rock Sturgeon.— Our common fresh-water sturgeon. **1938** Schrenkeisen *Field Book Fishes* 13, The Lake Sturgeon, also called Rock Sturgeon, Stone Sturgeon [etc].

stone tag n Cf **iron tag, stoop** ~ n[2], **tree** ~, **wood** ~
A variation of the children's game of tag; see quot 1935.

1883 Newell *Games & Songs* 158, *Tag. . .* The original form of this game seems to have been "Iron Tag," or "Tag on Iron." . . In like manner, owing to the occasional scarcity of iron objects, *wood-tag* and *stone-tag* have been varieties of the sport in America. **1932–34** Hanley *Disks* **CT,** In stone tag you must stand on a stone and the one that's "it" gits you off your stone, you're "it" in turn. **1935** Mason–Mitchell *Social Games* 248, *Wood Tag. . .* Select one player to serve as "it." He chases the other players who are safe only when touching wood. . . *Vari-*

*ations.—*True Tag . . Plaster Tag . . Grass Tag . . Stone Tag. **1950** *Sedalia Democrat* (MO) 13 June 9/7, Wednesday's program at Liberty park playground includes . . wood, or stone tag. **1968–69** *DARE* (Qu. EE33, . . *Outdoor games . . that children play*) Inf **VT**16, Stone tag; **NY**107, Stone tag—tag where any stone is "home." **1975** Ferretti *Gt. Amer. Book Sidewalk Games* 111, Tag games in which a person touching a designated substance is considered safe: for example . . Stone Tag.

stone teacher See **stone school**

stone toter n Also *stone lugger* Note: The identity of the fish in many of these quots is uncertain, and some may refer instead to other fish of similar habits.

1 =**hog sucker.**

1812 in 1935 Stuart *Discovery OR Trail* 130 **VA,** Our almost only resource for food . . is poor Trout and a species of Sucker which is fat & really excellent, called by Virginians the *Stone-toater.* **1857** in 2009 *DARE* File—Internet **cVA,** We fished at various places along the stream where we had in out [sic] boyhood been accustomed to do. . . We had a good mess, catfish, chubs & stone toters & one eel. **1876** Jordan *Manual Vertebrates N. U.S.* 294, *Hypentelium* [spp] . . Big Stone Luggers. **1878** U.S. Natl. Museum *Bulletin* 12.162, *Catostomus nigricans.* . . Hog Sucker. Hog Mullet. Hog Molly. Crawl-a-bottom. Stone Roller. Stone Toter. Stone Lugger. Hammer-head. Mud Sucker. **1882** U.S. Natl. Museum *Bulletin* 16.130, *C[atostomus] nigricans.* . . Stone Roller; Toter; . . Stone Lugger. **1892** "Bill Nye" in *Mansfield News* (OH) 30 June [2]/1 (newspaperarchive.com), The hog sucker, or stone toter, as it is also called by ornithologists, is so called because it has a flat place on the head on which to carry stones for the purpose of building wing dams for a nest. . . The stone toter makes good eating. **1894** Essex Inst. *Bulletin* 26.55 **KY,** Stone Toter *(Catostomus nigricans . .).* Common everywhere in the eastern half of the State.

2 =**stone roller 1.**

1817 Paulding *Letters from South* 2.4, The most singular fish in this part of the world is called the *stone-toter,* whose brow is surmounted with several little sharp horns, by the aid of which he *totes* small flat stones . . in order to make a snug little circular inclosure [sic], for his lady to lie in safely. **1854** Wailes *Rept. on Ag. & Geol. MS* 336, Three species of small fish found in the clear creeks of our State, and familiarly known as *horny-heads,* or *Stone-toters,* were obtained during the past summer. **1876** [see **stone roller 1**]. **1878** U.S. Natl. Museum *Bulletin* 12.72 **cnTN,** *List of Fishes of Nashville, as given by a Fisherman . . to A. Winchell.* . . "Minnow Tribe." Silver Side. Stone Toter. Horny Head. White Roach. Creek Mullet. Steel Back. **1892** U.S. Fish Comm. *Bulletin for 1890* 251, *Campostoma anomalum.* . . Stone-toter. **1994** (1995) Snead *Hollow Boy* 9 **nVA** (as of c1930), Although I enjoyed fishing in the Keyser Run that flowed out of the hollow, I never caught any big fish, only small "stone toters," "chub," and speckled fish. **2005** in 2009 *DARE* File—Internet **AR,** Stop by the boat ramp and catch ya some of those lil suckers the locals call stone toters. . . [T]hey are a small sucker have seen them up to 6–8 inches but not much bigger.

stone wall n **scattered, but chiefly NEast** See Map Also called **stone fence, ~ hedge**

A barrier of stones laid without mortar serving as a fence.

1651 in 1901 Portsmouth RI *Early Rec.* 54, The aforesayed Earl shall make fforty Rod of stone wall. **1754** (1901) Hempstead *Diary* 626 **CT,** Mr Swan . . hath agreed with me to make Stonewall for 20s a Rod. **1814** *Niles' Weekly Reg.* 7.68 **neNY,** Our troops occupying a strong position behind a stone wall, for some time stopped the progress of the enemy. **1855** *New Engl. Farmer* 7.438 **VT,** Is it the better plan to level the ground where stone wall is to be laid? **1885** *MA Ploughman & New Engl. Jrl. Ag.* 4 July 1, With our improved methods of farming, stone walls are considered very undesirable, and farmers who have farms cut up in small enclosures by stone walls, are exercising their ingenuity to get rid of the rocks. **1907** *DN* 3.201 **seNH,** *Stone wall.* . . Neither *stone fence* nor *rock wall.* The New England stone wall is *sui generis.* It is made of unhewn stones of from six inches to two feet in diameter just as they were removed from the land which they enclose. **1910** *DN* 3.449 **wNY,** *Stone wall.* . . A stone fence built of stones of all sizes, just as they were hauled from the adjacent land. **1926** *DN* 5.389 **ME,** *Stone wall.* . . Fence made of loosely piled rocks. Universal. **1949** Kurath *Word Geog.* 14, In New England, the greater part of New York State, and in northeastern Pennsylvania *stone wall* . . is the regular name for a fence built of loose stone. **1952** Caldwell *Lamp for Nightfall* 51 **ME,** I was sitting out there on the stone wall thinking about everything. **1965–70** *DARE* (Qu. L60, *A fence made of stone or rock without mortar*) 152 Infs, **scattered, but chiefly NEast,** Stone wall; **CT**2, **DC**2, **HI**2, Dry stone wall; [(Qu. X19b, . . *If a person's hearing is very bad . . he's* _____) 9 Infs,

scattered, Deaf as a stone wall; **WI**50, Deaf stone wall; **NC**72, Stone-wall deaf; (Qu. L60b, *A fence of stone built with mortar;* total Infs questioned, 75) 9 Infs, **scattered Sth, SW,** Stone wall;] (Qu. L65, . . *Kinds of fences*) Infs **CT**9, **HI**2, **NY**20, 62, **PA**103, **RI**2, Stone wall; **CT**6, Ornamental stone wall; [(Qu. KK9, *When someone undertakes something too big for him to handle: "This time you've _____."*) Inf **GA**31, You're butting your head against a stone wall]. **1989** Pederson *LAGS Tech. Index* 65 **Gulf Region,** Stone wall 98 [of 914 infs].

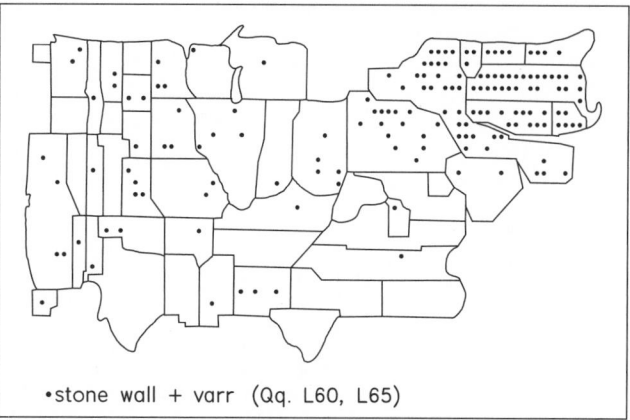

•stone wall + varr (Qq. L60, L65)

stone weed n [See quot 1859]

A **gromwell** (here: *Buglossoides arvense*).

1837 Darlington *Flora Cestrica* 118 **sePA,** Field Lithospermum. *Vulgò*—Stone weed. **1843** Torrey *Flora NY* 2.85, Lithospermum arvense. . . Corn Gromwell. Stone-weed. **1859** (1880) Darlington *Amer. Weeds* 243, *Field Lithospermum.* Stone-weed. Gromwell. . . [F]ormerly a reputed cure for the stone in the bladder, from the stony-like appearance of its seeds. **1898** *Jrl. Amer. Folkl.* 11.275, *Lithospermum arvense,* L., pigeon-weed, stone-weed.

stonewort n [See quot 1976; *OED2* 1816 →]

A **musk grass** (here: *Chara* spp).

1847 Wood *Class-Book* 637, *C[hara] sabulosa.* . . *Stone-wort.* . . thickly encrusted and very brittle. **1933** *Torreya* 33.81, *Chara* sp.— Musk grass . . lime weed, stonewort. **1939** *AmSp* 14.255, *Chara.* . . also called *featherbeds, stonewort,* and *horse watertail.* **1976** Bailey-Bailey *Hortus Third* 258, *Characeae.* . . *Stonewort family.* . . the entire plant body sometimes incrusted with calcium carbonate. **2003** *Post-Std.* (Syracuse NY) 21 May sec B 2/5, "Hmmmm. Chara," Lord said, fingering the stringy stuff, a benign weed—also known as stonewort or muskgrass.

stoney n

1 See **stonie.**

2 See quot.

1997 *DARE* File **IN,** A similar label in Bloomington, Indiana was "stoney," for the kids whose parents worked in the limestone quarries south of town, and for all non-town, non-University kids.

stonie n Also sp *stoney* Also *stonedy, stoner* [Cf *EDD stony* sb. 1, *stonedy* sb. 1, *stoner*] Cf **pottery** n[1]

A playing marble made of or resembling stone.

1889 *Olean Democrat* (NY) 9 May [9]/4 (newspaperarchive.com), Taws or stoneys, of brown marble, streaked with darker tones of the same color, form the third class. **1919** Deutsch *Banners* 25, Glazed potties, blue and green and lavender,/ Gleam near pale stonies' warm eburnean. **1935** *AmSp* 10.159 **seNE,** Stonie. . . A pottery-like marble, very smooth and heavy, coming in all different sizes. Used mostly for *shooters.* **1946** *Mason City Globe–Gaz.* (IA) 11 Sept 2/1, Agates, mibs, . . stonies, tawes [sic] and several with pure gold stripes . . are arranged in the . . Mason City public library. **1955** *PADS* 23.31 **cwTN, cwAL,** *Stoney (stonie, stonedy).* . . A marble made of stone. . . The offensive marble or taw. **1965–70** *DARE* (Qu. EE6d, *Special marbles*) Infs **IL**96, **IN**45, Stonies; **MD**29, Stonies—solid color; **NJ**18, Stonies—resembled stone; **AL**39, Stoners—made of clay or stone, prize marbles; (Qu. EE6b, *Small marbles or marbles in general*) Inf **AZ**8, Stonies; (Qu. EE6c, *Cheap marbles*) Inf **OK**20, Stonies; **FL**48, Stonies—clay, but cost more than glass.

stony head n [From the tubercles that grow on the heads of adults in breeding season]
=**hornyhead c.**

1878 (1880) Hallock *Sportsman's Gaz.* 384, Stony Head.—*Ceraticthys* [sic] *biguttatus*. . . Length six inches. Much esteemed as food. **1884** U.S. Natl. Museum *Bulletin* 27.485, *Ceratichthys biguttatus* [=*Nocomis b.*] . . Horny Head; Stony Head.

stoock See **stook**

stooge n

1965–70 *DARE* (Qu. M2, . . *The small wooden construction on top of a barn with slats for ventilation*) Inf **AL**62, **FL**22, Stooge; **MN**2, Stooge—a slang term.

stook n   Also sp *stoock*   Usu |stuk|; occas |stʊk|

1 A shock of grain or, rarely, flax; hence v *stook* to gather grain into a shock; vbl n *stooking*. [*OED2 stook* n.[1] 1 14 . . →] **chiefly NEng, nNY, Gt Lakes** See Map *old-fash* Cf **shook** n, v[2], **stout** n

1828 Webster *Amer. Dict., Stook,* n. A small collection of sheaves set up in the field. [*Local.*] *Stook,* v.t. To set up sheaves of grain in stooks. [*Local.*] **1844** *New Engl. Farmer & Horticult. Reg.* 22.317, To test the comparative utility of cutting (or topping) the corn, and stooking—or cutting up stalk and butt with the ear on. . . The stooked was bound with straw and carried out on the grass. **1888** *New Engl. Mag.* 6.590, It [= *cap sheaf*] has reference to the putting the last sheaf upon the *stook* or *shock* of bundles in the field. **1898** (1899) Earle *Home Life* 169 **NEng,** Rippling was done in the field. The stalks [of flax] were then tied in bundles called beats or bates and stacked. They were tied only at the seed end, and the base of the stalks was spread out forming a tent-shaped stack, called a stook. **1910** *DN* 3.453 **seVT,** *Corn-stoock* [stuk]. . . A bundle of corn-stalks set up in a conical form. *Ibid* 455 **seVT,** *Stoock*. . . To put corn stalks into bundles, thus forming *stoocks.* **1939** *LANE* Map 126 *(Sheaf; shock)* **NEng,** *Shock, stook* and *shook* are used both of grain and of (Indian) corn. [Proncs of the type [stuwk] are most frequent, but proncs of the type [stʊk] also occur.] **1959** *VT Hist.* 27.161, *Stook*. . . A shock of corn or grain. . . To shock the corn. Occasional among farmers. **1965** Needham–Mussey *Country Things* 27 **sVT,** By the first of October the corn should be stooked and the potatoes and oats all in. **1965–70** *DARE* (Qu. L30b, *Then these sheaves . . are set together in piles called* _____) 10 Infs, **esp NEast,** Stook(s) [stuk(s)]; **MI**2, [stuks]—some people use the term "shock" here, but mostly all say "stook"; **MI**8, We used to call them [stuks], but they said we were Scotchman [sic] for doing it; also call them "shocks"; **MI**78, [stuks]—North Dakota and some parts of Canada; **MA**25, [stuks]—grain or corn is stooked; **MA**37, [stuks]—corn; **NH**5, [stuk]—at least the term is used for corn; **NY**24, [stuks]; [stuk] it up; [**OH**22, [stuk]—in Canada; **WA**1A, Stooks—in Canada;] **MA**75, ['stukɪn] it—when they tied corn in bundles; (Qu. L30a, *When grain is cut it is . . tied up in* _____) Inf **MA**74, Stooked [stukt]; **MI**67, [stuk]; **NY**23, Corn is stooks [stuks]. [22 of 23 total Infs old] **1971** Wood *Vocab. Change* 43 **Sth,** *Piles of stalks*. . . *Shook* and *stook* occur in less than one-tenth of the choices. **1973** Allen *LAUM* 1.274 (as of c1950), *Shock* (of corn, wheat, etc.) . . the uniformly Canadian *stook* [is] found also in Rolette County, North Dakota, just south of the border. **1973** Gawthrop *Dial. Calumet* 77 **nwIN,** *Pile of bundles . . stook* 2 [of 125 checklist infs]. **1986** Pederson *LAGS Concordance (Shock)* 1 inf, **csTN,** Stook. **1997** in 2008 Phelps *Bernardston* 55 (as of 1930s), But we didn't have a silo. The corn we raised was cut and stooked.

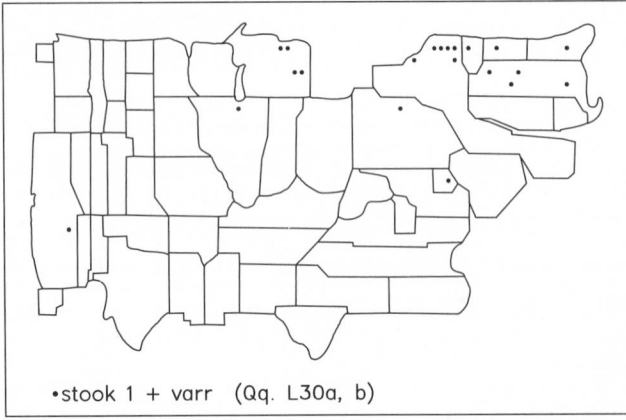

•stook 1 + varr   (Qq. L30a, b)

2 =**cock** n[2].

1958 *AmSp* 33.272 **eWA** [Ranching terms], *Shock; stook* [stuk]. A small pile of hay, forked from the windrow for drying and for ease in loading. **1969** *DARE* (Qu. L12, . . *The small piles of hay standing in the field*) Inf **IL**46, [stuks]—some call them; **IL**65, [stuks] [Inf uncertain]. **1973** Allen *LAUM* 1.186 (as of c1950), *Haycock* (in the field). . . stook [1 inf, **ND**].

stooking See **stook 1**

stool n

1 An invitation. [Prob ult in allusion to the proverb in quot 1992, which can be traced back to the 16th cent] **sAppalachians**

1883 *Century Illustr. Mag.* 26.190 **sAppalachians,** When I ast 'im out with us that night, he went like a man that had a stool to a quiltin' bee. **1891** *PMLA* 6.3.175 **TN,** Stool is an old-fashioned word for invitation; as, a stool to a party or wedding. **1940** *AmSp* 15.448 [TN mountain speech], *Stool.* Invitation. 'I have a stool to the wedding supper.' **1968–70** *DARE* (Qu. FF6, *Expressions . . meaning 'to be asked to go to a party'*: "*Did you get a* _____ *to the party?*") Inf **VA**11, Stool—"Are you going to the party?" "No, my stool didn't have but three legs"; [(Qu. II18, *Someone who joins himself on to you and your group without being asked and won't leave*) Inf **MO**23, Who told you to bring your stool to sit on]. [**1992** Mieder *Dict. Amer. Proverbs* 625 **AL, GA,** The uninvited should bring their own stool.]

2 See quot. [Cf Upton *Surv. Engl. Dial. stool* "the *stem* of a corn plant"; "the *butt* of a sheaf of corn"]

1970 *DARE* (Qu. L30b, *Then these sheaves . . are set together in piles called* _____) Inf **VA**40, Shocks—pile of stools; stools [stuəlz]—a bunch of bundles.

stool-bottom(ed) chair n   **Sth, S Midl**   Cf **stool chair** A chair with a solid wood seat.

1858 in 2004 *DARE* File—Internet **ceAL,** 6 Split bottom Chairs 3.00—2 Stool bottom chairs 1.00. **1864** *Ibid* **cnKY,** D.J. Weller—6 Stool bottom chairs—6.80[;] J.V. Crenshaw—3 Split bottom chairs—1.30—1 Rocking chair 2.00. **1881** *Ibid* **wMD,** Half dozen stool bottom chairs, and one rocking chair. **1906** *DN* 3.159 **nwAR,** *Stool-bottom chair.* . . A chair, all parts of which, including the seat, are of wood. **1922** in 2004 *DARE* File—Internet **cwWV,** As he breeched the gun one barrel fired, contents passing through a stool bottom chair, tearing the lower round out, then hitting the calf of Count's left leg. **1935** *Ibid* **seAR** (as of 1880s), In the hot months there were always cane or stool-bottomed chairs to attract occupants.

stool chair n [Cf *EDD stool chair* (at *stool* sb.[1] 1.(2)) "a four legged stool; a chair without a back"]   **chiefly Mid and S Atl** Cf **stool-bottom(ed) chair** See quots.

1758 in 2004 *DARE* File—Internet **ceVA,** 11 Chaires with Cain Bottoms @ 2/6—1.7.6 / 2 Stool Chairs @ 5/—.10.0 / a two armed Chair £3. **1831** *Ibid* **ceNC,** [Will:] One pine table, one candle stand, one rocking chair, & six other stool chairs, & one buffet. **1855** *Ibid* **ceGA,** 1 split bottom chair . . .62 / 5 stool chairs . . .75. **1874** *Ibid* **DE,** 1 Sett stool Chairs 2.00. **1906** *DN* 3.159 **nwAR,** *Stool chair.* . . Stool. **1940** Stuart *Trees of Heaven* 108 **eKY,** Tarvin sits on a stool chair drying his socks. **1946** *PADS* 6.29 **eNC** (as of 1900–10), *Stool chair.* . . Any chair without rockers; usually an ordinary hard-bottomed, straight-backed chair. . . Common. **1981** in 2004 *DARE* File—Internet **neFL,** Back porches for the reasons that they were more utilitarian than for leisure were usually furnished with straight (or stool) chairs and benches rather than rockers. **2000** *Syracuse Herald–Amer.* (NY) 18 June 19/3 **GA,** When Mr. Pitman started playing, whatever I [=Ray Charles] was doing I'd stop to go in and sit on that little stool chair he had there.

stoop n

1 A flight of outdoor steps leading to an entrance door or porch; a roofed or unroofed porch. [Du *stoep* platform or steps in front of a house] **orig esp NEast; now more widespread** Cf **door stoop, storm ~**

1736 *NY Weekly Jrl.* (NY) 20 Dec 4/2, He . . was so violently hurried against a Stoop or Porch before a Door, that his Scull was fractur'd. **1755** in 1916 Essex Inst. *Coll.* 52.78 **MA,** Houses of one Story & a Stoop to each. **1824** in 1928 MO Hist. Soc. *Coll.* 6.64 **MO,** Set Jo to dressing old plank from stoops. **1872** U.S. Congress *Rept. Joint Select Comm. Insurrectionary States* 6.478 **GA,** Wallace was standing on his stoop, at his office-door. **1878** *Appletons' Jrl.* 5.412 **seNY,** If it is summer, he will be resting after dinner in the cool *stoop* or porch of the Dutch farmhouse. **1891** *Living Age* 190.154 **NYC,** The door is approached by a precipitate flight of steps—a "stoop," as it is called. **1894** *DN* 1.343 **wCT,** *Stoop:* porch or small veranda (with roof). **1901**

DN 2.149 **cNY,** *Stoop.* . . Piazza . . ; never of steps alone; . . in Washington Co., N.Y., always without cover.   **1905** *DN* 3.21 **cCT,** *Stoop.* . . The door steps, or a little porch.   *Ibid* 66 **eNE,** *Stoop.* . . Porch, or step. Very common.   **1908** Fox *Lonesome Pine* 29 **KY,** The mountaineer and the "furriner" sat on the porch while Bub carved away at another pine dagger on the stoop.   **1909** *DN* 3.417 **nME,** *Stoop.* . . A porch.   **1910** *DN* 3.449 **wNY,** *Stoop.* . . Porch; veranda.   **1912** *DN* 3.569 **cNY,** *Stoop.* . . Porch, roofed or unroofed.   **1938** *AmSp* 13.319, In New England, as represented by Massachusetts and New Hampshire, a *stoop* is a short flight of broad steps, sometimes with a small roof over the door.   **1941** *Language* 17.332 **WI** [*LANCS* fieldwork], *Stoop*—29 [of 50 infs]. . . All agree that *stoop* is older than *porch;* it was once 'the usual word' . . 'old-timers always said it' . . 'that was the name when they first began to build them'. . . It is still in use [by 2 infs] . . but some . . say and many others imply, that it is out of use.   **1944** *PADS* 2.13, *Stoop.* . . The steps of a porch. S. and cent. Ala. ((In some parts of Texas: a porch. Reported from S.C.: a small roofless porch at the back of a house.))   **1951** *Chr. Sci. Monitor* (Boston MA) 20 Oct 8/2 **wCT,** Grandmother never spoke of a veranda, piazza, or porch, but always of a stoop.   **1958** *PADS* 29.16 **TN,** *Stoop.* . . A porch. "Real old people say stoop".   **1965–70** *DARE* (Qu. D17, . . *The platform, sometimes with a roof, that's built on the front or the side of a house*) 112 Infs, **widespread,** Stoop; **DC**3, Baltimore stoop; **MO**27, Small stoop; (Qu. D11, *When you go into a house, the part just beyond the front door is the _____*) Infs **MO**17, **NC**81, **UT**13, Stoop; (Qu. D12, *The part that's put on in winter around an outside door to give extra protection from the cold*) Inf **NH**10, Stoop that is closed in; (Qu. D16, . . *Parts added on to the main part of a house*) Inf **NC**55, Stoop; (Qu. Y27, *To go about aimlessly, with nothing to do: "He's always _____ around the drugstore."*) Inf **NY**70, Holding up the stoop; (Qu. II15, *When somebody is passing by and you want him or her to stop and talk a while*) Inf **MA**61, Come up on the stoop a while.   **1985** *DARE* File **cwIN,** The small back porch above the back steps is the "stoop." And one "sets" on it, rather than sitting on it.   **1989** Pederson *LAGS Tech. Index* 43 **Gulf Region,** *Porch.* . . stoop 98 [of 914 infs].   **1999** *WI State Jrl.* (Madison) 25 July sec C 1/4, City kids without a yard big enough to play baseball would wham the ball off the stoop, the concrete stairs leading up to the front door.

2 See quot.

1946 *PADS* 6.29 **wVA,** *Stoop.* . . A sort of stepladder used by women in the 1890's for mounting a horse. Salem.

stoopball n [**stoop 1**] esp **NYC** Cf **Boston baseball, hit-off-the-step, off-the-point, stepball, three outs**

A game in which a rubber ball is bounced off the front steps of a building; see quots.

1909 *NY Times* (NY) 12 May 1/2, The boy . . with some ten or a dozen other boys . . began to play "stoop" ball in the street.   **1924** *NYT Mag.* 15 June 8 **NYC,** Mr. Storey has listed a wide variety of today's diversions and near the head of his list, in frequency, appear stoop ball, hopscotch, . . fencing with sticks and tag.   **1961** Salinger *Franny* 122 **NYC,** Public-school children from Third and Second Avenues came to play jacks or stoopball on its stone steps.   **1967–70** *DARE* (Qu. EE33, . . *Outdoor games . . that children play*) Infs **NY**119, 241, Stoopball; **NY**34, Stoopball—ball thrown hard against a stoop; one tries to catch it; various scoring; **NY**89, Stoopball—threw ball against stoop; rules for runs like baseball.   **c1968** *DARE* File **NYC** (as of c1925), *Stoop ball* . . a form of baseball in which a "batter" threw a rubber ball with some force against the stoop—or front stair, typically of a brownstone house—causing it to fly toward the other players; caught on the fly, the batter was out; a grounder allowed him two or three bases to score runs.   **1969** *DARE* File **Boston MA** (as of 1940s–50s), *Stoopball.* . . game in which a player bounced a rubber ball off the front steps or "stoop" of a house and tried to catch it.   *Ibid* **Akron OH** (as of 1920s), *Stoopball.*   **1975** Ferretti *Gt. Amer. Book Sidewalk Games* 131, *Stoopball.* . . Stoopball calls for a stoop and a spaldeen. . . [T]he best stoops for Stoopball belong to brownstones. The object is to throw a spaldeen against a step and gain points or runs.   **1999** *WI State Jrl.* (Madison) 25 July sec C 1/3, When [they] moved here [= Rock Co., WI] from Detroit, bringing with them the Stoopball League of America, their new neighbors were prone to ask, "What's stoopball?" . . [He] would launch into a historical explanation of this game played by generations of kids from Boston to New York to Detroit to Chicago.   **2000** *NADS Letters* **Brooklyn NYC** (as of 1950s), To play stoopball, the "batter" threw a rubber "Spaldeen" . . against the steps and the "fielder," who stood behind the batter, had to catch the ball on the rebound to get the batter out.   **2003** *NY Times* (NY) 15 June sec 6 17/1, Diplomats do not use ring-a-levio, hopscotch, ring around the

rosie, prisoner's base, Jackie shine a light or stoopball to describe global strategies.

stoop-down n   Also *stoop-low*

1966–67 *DARE* (Qu. DD21a, *General words . . for any kind of liquor*) Inf **MS**71, Stoop-low; (Qu. DD21c, *Nicknames for whiskey, especially illegally made whiskey*) Inf **TX**37, Stoop-down.

stoop tag n[1]

=**squat tag.**

1898 Dunne *Mr. Dooley Peace & War* 195 **Chicago IL,** Little Flora an' little Fauna playin' stoop-tag aroun' a whale.   **1909** (1923) Bancroft *Games* 190, *Stoop Tag* ("Squat" Tag). . . One player is It and chases the others, trying to tag one of them. A player may escape being tagged by suddenly stooping or "squatting"; but each player may stoop but three times.   **1950** *WELS Suppl.* **csWI,** *Squat tag* in my childhood. The kids out home now call it *stoop tag.*   **1968** *DARE* (Qu. EE33, . . *Outdoor games . . that children play*) Inf **MN**33, Stoop tag—can't be tagged if you squat; **VA**13, Stoop tag = squat tag; **WV**10, Stoop tag—one is "it"; he has to hold a base while trying to tag other people; if he tries to catch another person, you can stoop . . for any length of time and he can't catch them; if he goes away from the base, untagged people can go in and recapture tagged people.   **1975** *Ford Times* Mar 22, We played plain tag, stoop tag, freeze tag, free tag.   **1977–78** [see **stoop tag** n[2]].   **2000** in 2004 *DARE* File—Internet **swCA** (as of 1960s), Do you remember the yard games. Stoop tag—Rover Red Rover send blank right over—or something like that.

stoop tag n[2]

A variety of tag in which a **stoop 1** is used as a **base B2** or **goal B.**

1977–78 Foster *Lexical Variation* 120 **NJ,** I have encountered two sets of rules for *stoop tag.* In the traditional game, a player is safe when he is standing on a stoop, but for some New Jerseyans a player is safe if he squats.   **2000** *DARE* File—Internet **Bronx NYC,** Stoop Tag. . . The stoop was the "safe place" you would go so you couldn't be "It". In team versions it was the "jail" where captured opposing team members would be placed, only to be freed by other team members.

stop-and-go n

1 =**red light 1.**

1977–78 Foster *Lexical Variation* 79 **NJ,** *Red Light.* . . Minor responses include . . *Stop and Go.*

2 See **stop-and-go light.**

stop-and-go light n   Also *stop-and-go, ~ (traffic) signal* [*OED2* 1935] **scattered, but esp freq Upper Missip Valley** See Map on p. 310

A traffic signal.

1916 *Frederick Post* (MD) 19 Dec 3/1, Four "Keep to the Right" signs . . displaced the semaphore, otherwise known as the "Stop and Go" signal, at the Square Corner, yesterday.   **1924** *Cedar Rapids Tribune* (IA) 12 Dec 4/1, The stop-and-go traffic signals at Second avenue and Third street . . are intended to control the movement of pedestrians as well as of vehicles.   **1926** *Appleton Post-Crescent* (WI) 21 Oct 5/7, The new system . . includes a stop and go light at each inside of the intersection.   **1929** in 2003 (acc) Lexis-Nexis Legal Research *State Case Law: IL* (Internet), Evidence respecting the existence and traffic movement indication shown by "stop and go" lights . . was admissible.   **1931** *Ibid: WI,* On November 1, 1928, the city of Chippewa Falls . . entered into a contract with Holtz Brothers Electric Company for installing a traffic-control system of stop-and-go lights.   **1965–70** *DARE* (Qu. N9, *The colored lights that control the cars at busy road crossings*) 30 Infs, **scattered, but esp freq Upper Missip Valley,** Stop-and-go lights; 10 Infs, **scattered,** Stop-and-go; **CA**42, 166, **GA**82, **IA**14, **MO**32, Stop-and-go signals.   **1990** *Capital Times* (Madison WI) 30 Apr sec A 9/1, The city . . is planning stop-and-go lights . . to increase safety for pedestrians.   **2003** *DARE* File—Internet **nwIN,** Follow I394 south to Exchange Road, which has a stop and go light.   *Ibid* **WI,** Follow C until you pass through a stop and go light.   *Ibid* **NC,** The Church will be located at the right approximately 100′ from the last stop and go light.   *Ibid* **IL,** Turn right and go to the first stop and go light.   *Ibid* **MN,** At the Stop and Go light for Osgood Ave . . turn left.   *Ibid* **MI,** City of Grand Rapids, Michigan. . . Disregarded Stop and Go Light . . $80.00.   *Ibid* **swCA,** Take the *Sixth St.* exit and go to the 3rd stop-and-go light which is Cedar.   *Ibid* **KS,** The stop and go light at 10th and Main was out of order.

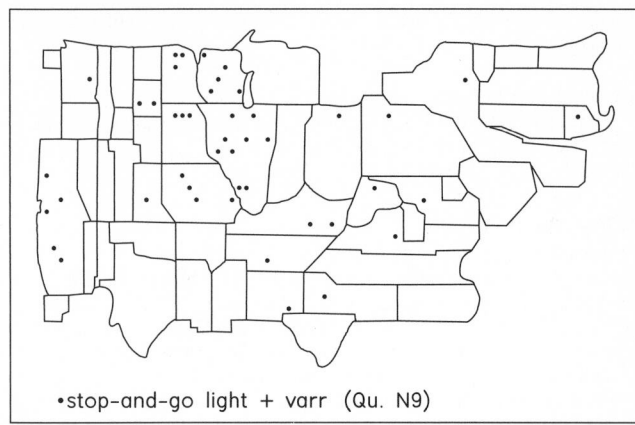

•stop-and-go light + varr (Qu. N9)

stop base n

A children's game; also used as a call in the game.

1968 *DARE* (Qu. EE33, . . *Outdoor games . . that children play*) Inf **TN**27, Stop base—you have two bases; somebody hollers "stop base"; if they catch you while you're running, you're out. If you're stopped, you're safe.

stop by v phr **scattered, but somewhat more freq Midl, Sth** Cf **come by 2**

To make a usu short or passing visit; to make such a visit to (someone's house).

1861 in 1999 Carney *Diary* (Internet) **TN**, They promised to stop by this afternoon but did not. **1905** *DN* 3.96 **nwAR**, *Stop by*. . . To call, to visit. 'I believe I'll stop by and see Bud.' Common. **1923** *DN* 5.244 **LA**, *Stop by*. . . To visit. "Stop by my house." **1944** *PADS* 2.13 **Sth**, *Stop by*. . . To stop in passing by. . . Over wide areas of the South. General colloquial. **1964** in 1970 Johnson *White House Diary* 103 **TX**, I had asked Mrs. MacArthur and her son . . to stop by the White House to warm up and have a cup of tea. **1965–70** *DARE* (Qu. II14, *To pay a short visit: "Last night our new neighbors _____."*) 65 Infs, **scattered, but somewhat more freq Midl, Sth**, Stopped by; **NJ**2, Stopped by a spell; **IN**35, **WI**76, Stopped by for a minute; **SC**10, Stop by; (Qu. II15, *When somebody is passing by and you want him or her to stop and talk a while*) Infs **FL**14, **MI**104, **PA**172, **SC**34, **VA**29, Stop by; **IA**46, Stop by a minute; **GA**77, Stop by and bitch awhile; **LA**2, Stop by and we'll chat awhile; **MO**23, Stop by awhile. **2003** *DARE* File—Internet, I decided to surprise her and stop by a while.

stop, go by and See **go by** v phr **1**

stopper n

1 Any of several trees of the myrtle family, as: see below. [From their use in treating diarrhea]

a Any of several trees of the genus *Eugenia* found chiefly in Florida and the Florida Keys. For other names of var spp see **gurgeon stopper, ironwood c(3), red stopper, redberry ~, Spanish ~, spiceberry 2, white stopper**

1884 Sargent *Forests of N. Amer.* 89, *Eugenia monticola* [=*E. axillaris*]. . . Stopper. . . Florida, Saint John's river to Umbrella Key. *Ibid*, *Eugenia longipes* [=*E. rhombea*]. . . Stopper. . . The small red fruit with the flavor of cranberries. **1908** Britton *N. Amer. Trees* 726, *Eugenia confusa*. . . Garber's stopper. . . grows in hammocks in southern peninsular Florida and the Keys. **1933** Small *Manual SE Flora* 935, *Eugenia* [spp]. . . Stoppers. **1982** *Miami Herald* (FL) 24 Oct sec H 11/2, Most, but not all, of the plants called stoppers are eugenias. . . Oh yes, the name *stopper*. . . The pioneers are said to have brewed an infusion of the leaves and used it to stop diarrhea.

b often with modifier: A closely related Florida tree *(Myrcianthes fragrans)*. Also called **Florida myrtle, nakedwood 2, twinberry 3**

1903 Small *Flora SE U.S.* 832, *Anamonis* [=*Myrcianthes fragrans*]. . . Naked Stpoper [sic]. Naked-wood. **1946** West-Arnold *Native Trees FL* 156, *Eugenia simpsoni* [=*Myrcianthes fragrans*]. . . Simpson Eugenia, Stopper. **1982** *Miami Herald* (FL) 24 Oct sec H 11/3, Like its cousin the guava, Simpson's stopper has pretty, flaking bark. **2003** *DARE* File—Internet **FL**, Simpson's Stopper is becoming more and more commonly used [for landscaping] as people discover its many desirable char-

acteristics. . . The fruits have a sweet, citrusy, pine-like flavor and were traditionally used to treat diarrhea (thus the name "stopper").

c A **spicewood 2** (here: *Calyptranthes zuzygium*).

1982 *Miami Herald* (FL) 24 Oct sec H 11/3, Myrtle-of-the-river, *Calyptranthes zuzygium*, is also often called a stopper.

2 See quots. Cf *DS* DD18

1927 *DN* 5.478 **Ozarks**, *Stopper*. . . A drink of whiskey. "Jes' a leetle stopper now 'n' then aint a-goin' t' hurt nobody." **1984** Wilder *You All Spoken Here* 138 **Sth**, *Stopper:* A drink measure. This from glass stoppers in old decanters that served as shot glasses as well as bottle stoppers.

store n Usu |stor, stɔr, stoə(r), stɔə(r)| Pronc-spp **Sth, S Midl** *sto(ah)*; rarely *sto-er, tore*

A Forms.

c1885 in 1981 Woodward *Mary Chesnut's Civil War* 754 **NC** (as of 1865), Colonel Childs stopped me to present a Mr. Stowe—"Who keeps a sto'," he whispered in an aside. **1905** *DN* 3.96 **nwAR**, *Sto'-bought(en)*. **1909** *S. Atl. Qrly.* 8.52 **seSC**, The elimination of initial *s* in . . *st* as . . *'tore* [etc] . . are all characteristics of Gullah. **1914** *DN* 4.160 **cVA**, *Sto, stoah*. . . Store. "Ceceh, yo' don't p'onounce yo' 'ahs' at aw! Yo' say *'sto'* foah *'stoah'!*" (Cecil, you don't pronounce your r's at all! You say *"sto"* for *"stoah"!*) **1922** Gonzales *Black Border* 329 **sSC, GA coasts** [Gullah glossary], *Sto'*—store. **1934** Carmer *Stars Fell on AL* 162, He goes back in the sto'. **1937** in 1976 *Weevils in the Wheat* 264 **VA** [Black], When we got to Richmond, we went in a sto'. **1975** Gould *ME Lingo* 279, *Store*—Markets, malls, shopping centers, and such modern emporia will be with us a long time before they wean the Mainer from his "goin' to the *sto-er.*"

B Senses.

1 used attrib: Commercially made; purchased rather than home-made. **widespread, but less freq Sth, Lower Missip Valley, TX** See Map Cf **boughten 1**

1806 *Centinel* (Gettysburg PA) 15 Jan 263/1, [Advt:] There will be exposed to sale, by public vendue. . . A Variety of *store goods, house & kitchen furniture, farming utensils*. **1851** Turner *Hist. Pioneer Settlement* 563 **cwNY**, It [=potash] was the first available means that the new settlers had to pay for store goods. **1872** U.S. Congress *Rept. Joint Select Comm. Insurrectionary States* 543 **SC** [Black], It was store-cloth, black and white. **1884** *Anglia* 7.277 **Sth, S Midl** [Black], *Sto'-closze* = 'store-clothes'. **1899** (1912) Green *VA Folk-Speech* 421, *Store-tea*. . . China tea, distinguished from *yarb* tea, sassafras-tea, ginger-tea. **1902** *DN* 2.246 **sIL**, *Store*. . . In certain expressions, as 'store clothes [kloz],' 'store sugar,' to mean something manufactured as distinct from something made at home. **1903** *DN* 2.332 **seMO**, *Store-tea*. . . 'We caint afford store-tea and so make out with sassafras.' **1905** *DN* 3.21 **cCT**, *Store goods*. . . Goods purchased at a store in distinction from those made at home. **1907** *DN* 3.227 **nwAR**, *Store*. . . Manufactured; not domestic. **1952** FWP *Guide SD* 71, Many business establishments combined logs with "store" lumber to save money. **1965–70** *DARE* (Qu. H13, *Bread that is not made at home*) 191 Infs, **widespread, but less freq Sth**, Store bread; (Qu. U2, . . *A piece of clothing not made at home—one that you buy*) 13 Infs, **scattered**, Store clothes; **CT**15, **MD**49, **MA**73, **NJ**56, **NY**57, Store clothing; **MD**34, **MA**37, Store goods; **PA**88, **WI**12, Store suit; **MA**124, Store dress; **VA**8, Store material; **WI**12, Store trousers; (Qu. F36, . . *Kinds of brooms*) Inf **MT**3, Store broom; (Qu. F46, . . *Matches you can strike anywhere; not asked*

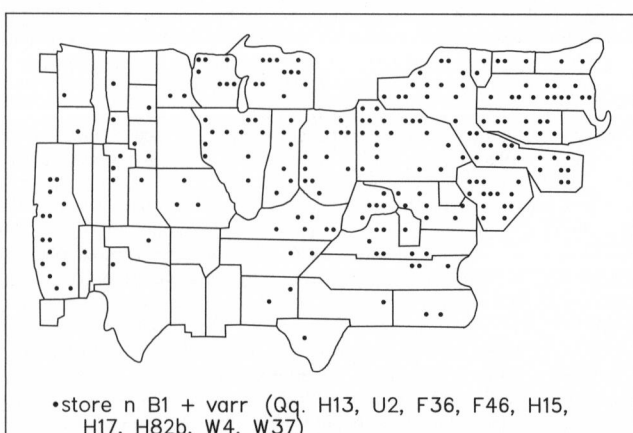

•store n B1 + varr (Qq. H13, U2, F36, F46, H15, H17, H82b, W4, W37)

in early QRs) Infs **NY**99, **OH**76, **PA**128, Store matches; (Qu. H15, *Bread made with wheat flour*) Inf **MA**122, Store bread; (Qu. H17, . . *Kinds [of yeast]*) Infs **CA**22, **MO**3, Store yeast; **VA**9, Store east; (Qu. H82b, *Kinds of cheap candy that used to be sold years ago*) Infs **AZ**8, **MT**3, Store candy; (Qu. W4, . . *Men's coats or jackets for work and outdoor wear*) Inf **NJ**8, Store coat; (Qu. W37, *When a woman puts on her good clothes and tries to look her best . . she's _____*) Inf **NY**41, Got on her store clothes. **2004** *Oregonian* (Portland OR) 26 June Sunrise ed sec B 2 (Internet), Three loaves of store bread would last into next week. Three loaves of home-baked wouldn't last an evening.

2 Spec; of teeth: artificial, false. **widespread, but less freq Sth, Lower Missip Valley** See Map Cf **boughten 2, store-bought 1**

1861 *Vanity Fair* 4.4 **ME,** You must be more careful with them store teeth of your'n, or you'll hav to gum it agin! **1880** *Atlantic Mth.* 45.851, He came near laughing his store teeth out, and said it was all the same whether we drove to the right or to the left. **1965–70** *DARE* (Qu. X13b, *Joking names for false teeth*) 183 Infs, **widespread, but less freq Sth, Lower Missip Valley,** Store teeth. **1975** Gould *ME Lingo* 279, *Store choppers*—False teeth. **1998** *Milwaukee Jrl.* (WI) 24 Oct 1 (Internet) (as of 1906), One day when an elderly gentleman was gathering the skeletons he found a skull containing false teeth. To impress the ever present group of curious children he carefully extricated the store teeth.

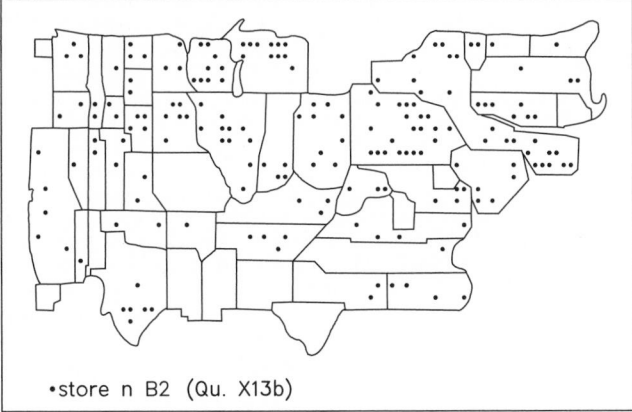

•store n B2 (Qu. X13b)

store v **esp C Atl, sAppalachians** Cf **marketing 1**

To shop; hence vbl n *storing* shopping.

1940 in 1944 *ADD* **swPA, nWV,** Store. . . 'Some says shoppin' an' some says storin'.' Old speaker. **1960** *DE Folkl. Bulletin* 1.36, We did our storing (bought our groceries, etc.) **1967–68** *DARE* (Qu. U1a, *When you are going to a store or several stores to buy things . . "I'm going _____."*) Inf **PA**29, Storing; (Qu. U1b, . . *Buying groceries*) Inf **PA**126, Storing; **NJ**45, Storing—I've never said storing; people do say storing; **PA**7, Go to the store; Dutch—going to do their storing. **1974** Fink *Mountain Speech* 25 **wNC, eTN,** *Store* . . to trade in a store. "I've got a lot of storing to do." **2002** *Sun. News Jrl.* (Wilmington DE) 7 July sec A 6/2, Many of the words and phrases that once made the speech patterns of Delawareans unique have disappeared just since the 1980s. . . People who were on their way to buy groceries would be said to be "gone to do your storin."

store-bought adj phr Note: *Store-bought* in the general sense "bought at a store" is not regional.

1 Of teeth: artificial, false; occas used absol. **chiefly Sth, S Midl, SW** See Map Cf **boughten 2, store n B1b**

1938 in 2003 *DARE* File—Internet, It is store bought food which has given us store bought teeth. **1954** *Harder Coll.* **cwTN,** Store bought teeth. . . False teeth. **c1960** *Wilson Coll.* **csKY,** Store-bought teeth. . . False teeth; used humorously. **1965–70** *DARE* (Qu. X13b, *Joking names for false teeth*) 189 Infs, **chiefly Sth, S Midl, SW,** Store-bought teeth; **MN**2, Store-boughts. **1986** Pederson *LAGS Concordance,* 3 infs, **AL, AR, LA,** Store-bought teeth. **2003** *Tampa Tribune* (FL) 1 July (Internet), West Virginia promised to wear its store-bought teeth when dining in South Florida.

2 in phr *store-bought eyes:* Eyeglasses.

1966–67 *DARE* (Qu. X23, . . *Joking words . . for eyeglasses*) Infs **GA**12, **LA**3, Store-bought eyes. **2003** *DARE* File—Internet, I really like it because instead of a 1000 page book that took my store bought

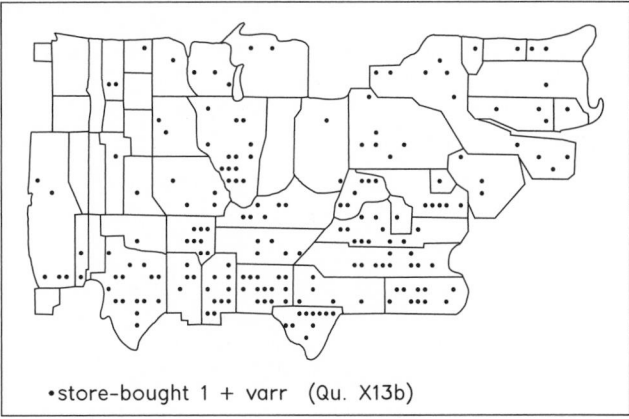

•store-bought 1 + varr (Qu. X13b)

eyes to see it had a keyword database. *Ibid,* Didn't I post an apology about this once before—just my aging & store-bought eyes. *Ibid,* I once had real good eye site and was expert with a firle [sic for *rifle*]. Now that I have to weair these store bought *eyes* shoot groups just dont come up to par.

store-boughten adj phr Note: *Store-boughten* in the general sense is not regional.

=store-bought 1. Cf **boughten 2**

1949 *Billboard* 19 Nov 84/2 **MN,** If the average age is over 50, it's almost a sure-fire bet that most of the plant workers have store-boughten teeth. **1965–70** *DARE* (Qu. X13b, *Joking names for false teeth*) 14 Infs, **scattered,** Store-boughten teeth. [**2003** *DARE* File—Internet **Canada,** He decided he'd better go to town and buy some of those "store-boughten" teeth as replacements.]

store-bought eyes See **store-bought 2**

store eyes n Cf **store-bought 2**

1967 *DARE* (Qu. X23, . . *Joking words . . for eyeglasses*) Inf **OH**12, Store eyes.

store-house n

A shop, retail store.

c1773 in 1845 *S. Lit. Messenger* 11.139 **NEng,** Shops . . are here called Store Houses. **1844** *Madison Express* (WI) 30 May [4]/2 (newspaperarchive.com), [Advt:] *Wanted—10,000 Bushels* of Wheat, delivered at my Ware-House in Racine . ., for which the highest price in cash will be paid, or I will pay in goods if delivered at my Store-House in Madison. **1877** Johnson *Hist. Anderson Co. KS* 63, About this time a store house was built and occupied by a merchant. **1903** *DN* 2.332 **seMO,** *Store-house.* . . Store; a house in which goods are sold. **1907** *DN* 3.237 **nwAR,** *Store-house.* . . A house in which goods are sold. **1915** *DN* 4.191 **swVA,** *Store-house.* . . A house where merchandise is sold. **1984** Wilder *You All Spoken Here* 170 **Sth,** Store house: Grocery or dry goods store.

storify v [**story** v] Cf **-ify**

To tell a lie.

1977 *NADS Letters,* I grew up in Manatee County Florida just after the 2nd WW, and all our neighbors were southern whites, with roots up in Georgia and Alabama. . . They'd go up to Georgia for a family reunion and see a lot of their "shirttail folk"—distant relatives, and an old aunt who was "older than dirt." "B.J.—you're storifying ta me agin (lying)!"

storing See **store** v

stork n

Any of var large wading birds such as the **wood ibis, sandhill crane,** or **whooping crane 1.**

1709 (1967) Lawson *New Voyage* 150, Among them [=cranes] often frequent Storks, which are here seen, and no where besides in *America,* that I have yet heard of. **1791** Bartram *Travels* 190, The silver plumed ganet and stork, the sage and solitary pelican of the wilderness, have already retired to their silent nocturnal habitations. **1805** (1905) Clark *Orig. Jrls. Lewis & Clark Exped.* 3.193 **VA,** Emence numbers of fowls flying in every direction, Such as Swan, geese, Brants, Cranes, Stalks [*Storks*], white guls. **1923** U.S. Dept. Ag. *Misc. Circular* 13.39 **NJ, FL, LA,** Whooping Crane. . . Vernacular names. . . *In local use.* . . stork. *Ibid* 40 **LA,** Sandhill Crane. . . stork. **1955** *Oriole* 20.1.3, Wood Ibis. . . Stork (this bird deserves the name as it is our only representative of the stork family). **1964** Will *Hist. Okeechobee* 149 **FL,** Up in the sky a

Floridy stork, an old Flint Head, comes wingin' along overhead. **1966–69** *DARE* (Qu. Q8) Infs **ME**6, **MO**12, Stork; (Qu. Q10, . . *Water birds and marsh birds*) Infs **FL**4, 39, **MA**15, **MO**4, 18, Stork. **2005** *Assoc. Press State & Local Wire* 25 July (Internet) **FL,** When he was shooting, he noticed many wading birds, including a couple of storks.

storkbill See **storksbill 2**

stork bite n   Also *stork mark*   Cf **mother's mark**
A common type of small, pinkish birthmark that often fades with time.
  1923 Reed *Obstetrics* 319, "Stork Bites" is the popular name applied to the intense red spots which are sometimes found in the vicinity of the hair margin of the scalp, the forehead and eyebrows. **1960** *Post-Std.* (Syracuse NY) 1 Nov 8/3, My 16 month old baby still has stork marks on her forehead and upper eyelids. The pediatrician says they will fade but doesn't say when. **1970** *DARE* FW Addit **MA**83, Stork mark— temporary birthmark, fades out before child grows up. **1993** *DARE* File **nMN,** There is a type of birthmark that fades quickly which is sometimes called a Stork Bite. *Ibid* **sIL,** Around here, the reddish birthmarks on babies (white ones) are called "stork bites"! This is only for the kind that eventually fade. *Ibid* **cNY** (as of 1947–69), Stork bites are the little ones [=birthmarks]. **2006** *Assoc. Press State & Local Wire* 13 May (Internet) **NH,** She pronounced the tiny red birthmarks . . "stork bites" and told Percy not to worry the marks would go away. **2008** *DARE* File—Internet, My baby has a stork mark on the back of her scalp at the neck. How long did it take for your childs to go away?

stork party See **stork shower**

storksbill n   [*OED2* 1562 →]
1 Std: a plant of the genus *Erodium,* esp *E. cicutarium* or *E. moschatum.*   For other names of var spp see **clocks, cranesbill 3, filaree, mayflower 12, musk clover, needle weed (plant), pick needle, pin clover, ~ grass 1, ~ needle 2, pine needle, pinkets, pinweed 2**
2 also *storkbill:* A **cranesbill 1** (here: *Geranium maculatum*).
  1828 Rafinesque *Med. Flora* 1.215, *Geranium maculatum.* . . *Vulgar Names*—Crowfoot, Alum-root, . . Storkbill. **1900** Lyons *Plant Names* 172, *G[eranium] maculatum.* . . Cranesbill, . . Storksbill [etc]. **1939** *Natl. Geogr. Mag.* Aug 231, Wild geraniums are better known by the common names of "storksbill," "cranesbill," and the like, from the resemblance of the tapering seed pods to the slender beaks of birds. **1974** (1977) Coon *Useful Plants* 144, *Geranium maculatum*—Cranesbill, wild geranium, storkbill [etc].

stork shower n   Also *stork party*   **scattered, but esp NEast, Sth, S Midl**   See Map   Cf **variety shower**
A party for an expectant mother or newborn child to which guests bring gifts.
  [**1903** *Daily Northwestern* (Oshkosh WI) 18 July 4/2, Out of the west comes the idea for a new fad in swell society. . . It was devised at Denver and is called a stork party, consisting of a luncheon at which the central table decoration is a mound of peonies, sustaining in all his dignity a stork, bearing in his bill a realistic representation of the little stranger whose prospective advent is thus announced by the smiling, happy hostess.] **1906** *Elyria Republican* (OH) 13 Dec 2/5, A stork shower was given in honor of the little daughter of Rev. Black by the members of the M.E. church. . . Many pretty and cunning presents were brought. **1942** in 2003 *DARE* File—Internet **WV,** A stork shower was given at the home of Mrs. Leo Trent. **1949** Webber *Backwoods Teacher* 79 **Ozarks,** Dear Mrs Nelson a stork shar [sic] is being held for my daughter in town next Tuesday. Of next week. . . If you cant go please leave gift at store if you want to. **c1960** *Wilson Coll.* **csKY,** Stork shower. . . A gift party for an expectant mother. **1965–70** *DARE* (Qu. FF3, . . 'Showers' or 'gift parties') 76 Infs, **scattered, but esp NEast, Sth, S Midl,** Stork showers; **VT**16, Pink and blue stork showers; **KY**24, **VA**26, Stork parties. **1966** *Russell Rec.* (KS) 11 Aug 3/3, Mrs. Irwin was the honored guest of a stork shower given Wednesday. **1967** *Catahoula News-Booster* (Jonesville-Harrisonburg LA) 30 Nov 3/5, A Stork Shower honoring Mrs. Kay McCaver is planned. **1968** *Salem Sunbeam* (NJ) 2 July sec B 9/2, Mrs. Edward Hassler was surprised on Thursday evening at her home . . with a stork shower. **1968** *Harlem Valley Times* (Amenia NY) 1 Aug 15/1, Mrs. Thomas Hussey was guest of honor at a surprise stork shower. **2003** *DARE* File—Internet **AR,** Signs of affection. . . Welcoming the babies of Northwest Arkansas since 2001! . . One Day Stork Shower Rental with "The Shower is Here" Bundle.

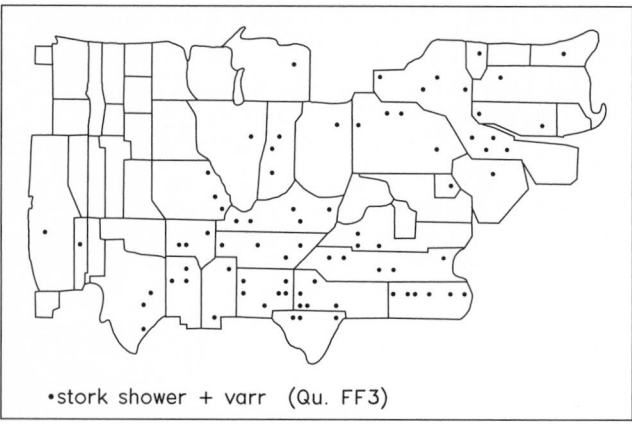

•stork shower + varr   (Qu. FF3)

storm bird n   [See quots]   **Gulf States**
1 also *storm king:* =**man-o'-war bird.**
  1931 *Wilson Bulletin* 43.130 **sLA,** Man-O'-War Bird. *Fregata aquila.* This species . . is known as the "storm bird" by the people of the coast region. **1944** Kane *Deep Delta Country* 162 **sLA,** Now came a sign that they had been taught to recognize as a final warning: far up, black and solemn, winged the hardy man-of-war, or "storm," birds. When they headed steadily inland, fury was not far behind. **1951** *AmSp* 26.270 **FL, LA, TX,** In states bordering the Gulf of Mexico, when those incomparable flyers, the man-o'-war birds, are greatly active, and especially if they head inland in numbers, a hurricane is foretold. In Florida, Louisiana, and Texas they are known both as *storm birds* and *hurricane birds.* **1968** *DARE* File, [Clipping from *Rockport Pilot* (TX):] And what did we see when tropical storm Candy visited our area? Magnificant [sic] frigate birds known as man-o-wars and storm birds by our natives, all along our coastline toward Fulton and back on Highway 35. **1978** Mullen *Old Fishermen* 56 **seTX,** There is another bird, related to the albatross, which is variously called a storm bird, scissortail, storm king, or water turkey. It is always prophetic of a storm or bad weather.
2 Any of var other birds; see quots.   Cf **rainbird, storm crow**
  1951 *AmSp* 26.270 **NC, MD,** At Mattamuskeet, North Carolina, also, when the local *storm bird* (little blue heron) flocks inland, people are sure that bad weather will soon follow. Much smaller birds, each of which in its own way has earned the sobriquet of *storm bird,* are the bank swallow (N.C.) and the tufted titmouse (Md.), the former probably from conspicuous flocking, and the latter from repeated, loud whistling. **1993** Keller-Keller *Birds Indianapolis* 53, *Yellow-Billed Cuckoo—Coccyzus americanus.* . . It was often called the rain-crow or storm-bird by old-time birders because this species frequently calls before a storm or on gray, overcast days.

storm buggy n   Also *storm rig*   Cf **storm front 1**
A fully enclosed buggy.
  1882 *Oshkosh Daily Northwestern* (WI) 15 Sept [4]/5 (newspaperarchive.com), The Oshkosh Carriage company . . is fully represented with an exhibition of eleven styles of buggies and carriages. . . A storm buggy, with top, and a very stylish buckboard. **1912** [see **storm front 1**]. **1913** in 2003 *DARE* File—Internet [*Carriage Monthly* Jan], [Caption:] Storm Buggy Equipped With Electric Lights. **1968–69** *DARE* (Qu. N41a, . . *Horse-drawn vehicles . . to carry people*) Inf **IN**39, Storm buggy; **IL**36, Storm buggy—sliding doors of glass, all closed in; **OH**88, Storm rig. **2007** *DARE* File—Internet **MI,** Amish Storm Buggy. . . $2,500.00 . . Leave windshield and all windows open when the weather is good, drop everything down for warmth or against bad weather.

storm cave n   **esp Plains States, IA**   See Map   Cf **storm pit** =**cyclone shelter.**
  1883 *Atlanta Constitution* (GA) 1 June 4/4 **IA,** Many Iowa houses now have a storm cave connected with the cellar. **1899** *Century Illustr. Mag.* 58.596 **MO,** A strong cellar or a storm-cave of easy access is usually a safe retreat. It is better that the storm-cave should be placed a short distance southwest of the house, and connected with the cellar by a tunnel. **1930** *Lincoln Sun. Star* (NE) 11 May 1/1, [Headline:] Second Tornado Strikes. . . Four Persons At Ed Schernikau's Home Reach Storm Cave Just Ahead of Wind. **1965–70** *DARE* (Qu. D22, *Underground place to go to in case of a violent windstorm*) Infs **CO**19, **GA**13, **IN**54, **IA**11, 31, **KS**8, 14, 16, **NE**2, Storm cave. **2000** *Atchison Daily Globe* (KS)

22 June 8/2, For Sale By Owner. . . Has three sided carport attached & storm cave in backyard.

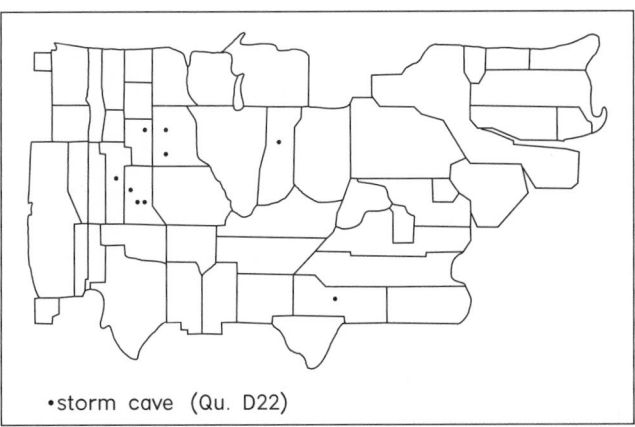

•storm cave (Qu. D22)

storm closet n
=**storm shed 1.**

1895 Allegheny PA *Municipal Rept. for 1894–95* 868 **PA,** Painted storm closet on front porch. . . Put up storm closet at door leading to dormitory above bake house. **1911** *Wellsboro Agitator* (PA) 1 Nov 1/1, In Morris . . they have . . rural schools . . with storm closets before the doors as required by law. **1955** Patton *Piece of Luck* 14 **Sth,** I'm hanging my coat in the storm closet. Now my hat. Now I'm taking off my rubbers! **1968** *DARE* (Qu. D12, *The part that's put on in winter around an outside door to give extra protection from the cold*) Inf **IN**48, Storm closet.

storm crow n
=**yellow-billed cuckoo.**

1903 Coues *Key to N. Amer. Birds* 610, Yellow-billed Cuckoo. Rain-crow. Rain-dove. Storm-crow. Chow-chow. **1946** Stimpson *Book about Things* 55, The American cuckoo is known to country people as the rain or storm crow because its plaintive note . . is regarded as a sign of rain or storm. **2005** *DARE* File—Internet **CA** [*Modesto Bee* (CA) 15 June], The legendary yellow-billed cuckoo, or "Storm Crow" (so called because of its persistent clucking calls, said to increase in volume and frequency before storms) was at one time a common breeding resident of our Central Valley riparian forest.

‡storm dog n

1968 *DARE* (Qu. B11, . . *Other kinds of clouds that come often*) Inf **DE**1, Storm dogs—little white clouds before a storm.

storm enclosure n Also *storm entrance, ~ entry* **scattered, but esp NEast** See Map
=**storm shed 1.**

1880 *Davenport Daily Gaz.* (IA) 31 Dec [4]/7 (newspaper-archive.com), A new sign was visible over the entrance to the Keator House yesterday. It corresponds very well with the other features of the storm entrance. **1889** *Springfield Daily Republican* (MA) 27 Nov 1/1, [Advt:] Just the time to buy Weather Strips. . . No storm entries or windows needed where they are used. **1897** *Salem Daily News* (OH) 22 Feb 8/2, The storm enclosure has been removed from the front of the store room which will be occupied in East Main street by J. George Walz. **1907** *DN* 3.250 **eME,** *Storm-entrance.* . . Outside booth-like house-entrance, generally used only during the winter, and removed at the end of winter. **1908** *Bucks Co. Gaz.* (Bristol PA) 9 Oct 3/6, Thomas Hawkes, Esq., . . is inclosing his porch with a neat storm enclosure. **1923** Cather *Lost Lady* 38 **Plains States,** She drew him through the little storm entry, which protected the front door in winter. **1968–69** *DARE* (Qu. D12, *The part that's put on in winter around an outside door to give extra protection from the cold*) Infs **CT**7, **NJ**21, 39, **NY**90, Storm enclosure; **CT**18, **NY**52, 92, Storm entrance; **CT**29, **IN**76, **ME**5, Storm entry; **MO**15, Storm entrance—a little protection built there to keep the north wind from getting to the other door. [10 of 11 Infs comm type 4 or 5, 9 old] **2003** *DARE* File—Internet **IA,** I got to the stairway, found the snow-covered steps and handrail and pulled myself up step-by-step until I reached the small storm enclosure at the top. I pushed the storm door open, stepped inside, and knocked on the kitchen door. *Ibid* **MA,** [Town of Westford zoning bylaws:] Steps or stoop, bulkheads, window-sill, chimney, roof eaves, fire escape, fire tower, storm enclosure or similar architectural features shall not project more than two (2) feet.

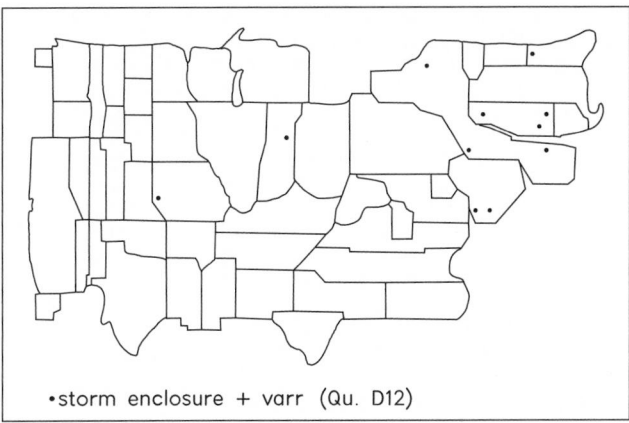

•storm enclosure + varr (Qu. D12)

storm front n

1 A removable enclosure to protect those riding in an open vehicle from inclement weather; a vehicle furnished with such an enclosure; see quots.

1870 *NY Herald* (NY) 28 June 1/3, [Advt:] Barouche for sale. . . unusually light and stylish, with storm front to make it a close [sic] carriage in bad weather. **1903** *Daily Herald* (Delphos OH) 12 Jan 4/8, *Adjustable Storm Front.* . . Completely protects the passengers from rain, wind, cold, etc. Plenty of room inside the buggy. **1907** *Ft. Wayne Jrl.–Gaz.* 10 Mar 23/2, *For Sale*—A one-seated, 15-horse power Winton touring car, . . thoroughly overhauled; canopy top. storm front. **1912** *Decatur Daily Rev.* (IL) 22 Oct 7/2, Storm Fronts. The storm front attachment for the ordinary buggy costs from $5 to $12 or $15. This front is of oil cloth and isinglass and while not making an air tight compartment like the storm buggy, is practically as efficient for wind or rain protection. **1967** Jacobs *Rejoicing* 135 **cIN** (as of c1930), We used the buggy's "storm front"—a patented canvas cover fastened to the top which dropped in front of the occupants to protect them from the rain. **1967** *DARE* (Qu. N41a, . . *Horse-drawn vehicles . . to carry people*) Inf **OH**22, Storm front—enclosed.

2 Prob =**storm shed 1.**

1968–70 *DARE* (Qu. D12, *The part that's put on in winter around an outside door to give extra protection from the cold*) Infs **IL**31, 113, **OH**70, Storm front; **VT**3, Storm front—enclosed whole front of shed and piazza, had windows and doors.

storm gull n [See quot 1951]
=**skimmer 1** or another bird such as **herring gull** or Bonaparte's gull.

1946 Hausman *Eastern Birds* 332, Black Skimmer. . . Other Names—Scissorbill, Cutwater, Shearwater, Storm Gull. **1951** *AmSp* 26.270 **FL, WI, VA,** The name *storm gull* has been given to the herring gull in Florida, to Bonaparte's gull in Wisconsin, and to the black skimmer in Virginia, doubtless from unusual flight behavior.

storm hit it, look like a v phr For addit varr see quots **chiefly Sth, S Midl** See Map
To be very untidy.

1952 in 1956 Mason *Harlan Fiske Stone* 788, His secretary persisted in tidying up his desk, but by mid-morning "it looked as if a storm had

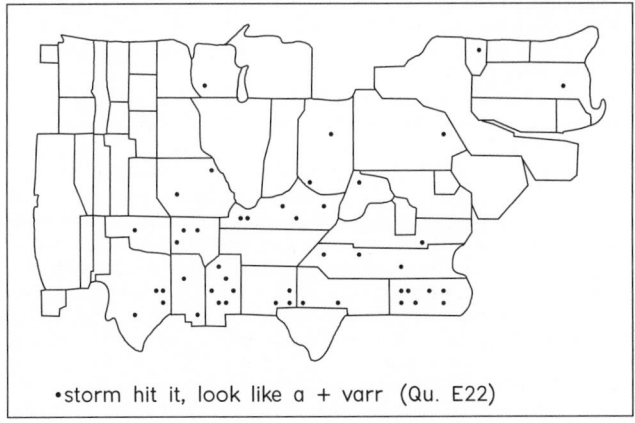

•storm hit it, look like a + varr (Qu. E22)

hit it." **1965–70** *DARE* (Qu. E22, *If a house is untidy and everything is upset . . . "It's a _____!" or "It looks like _____."*) 20 Infs, **esp Sth, S Midl,** A storm hit it; 10 Infs, **Sth, S Midl,** A storm been (*or* blowed, had been, has been, went) through it; **KY**89, **NC**33, **OK**13, **SC**46, **WV**14, A storm (had) struck it; **MS**79, **OH**102, **SC**29, 69, A storm blew (*or* been, had been) through; **KY**84, **MO**20, A storm had hit it; **AL**55, **MA**50, A storm hit; **PA**126, As though a storm has been through; **KY**33, A storm's hit it; **TX**35, There's been a storm through it. **2004** Osteen *Your Best Life* 283 **TX,** Your trunk or backseat may be filled with . . junk. . . and sometimes our car looks like a storm hit it.

storm hole See **storm pit**

storm house n

1 =**storm shed 1. Nth, esp Upstate NY, Gt Lakes** See Map *old-fash*

1829 in 1851 Schoolcraft *Personal Memoirs* 322 **MI,** The winter has passed with less effect from the intensity of its cold and external dreariness, from the fact of my being ensconsed [*sic*] in a new house, with double window-sashes, fine storm-houses, plenty of maple fuel, books, and studies. **1874** Lowell *Antony Brade* 94 **MA,** Come to the storm-house door, and I'll let you in. **1884** in 2004 *DARE* File—Internet **cwNY,** Now if it could only be Joseph Heallot and we could have a storm house to sit in. we have got one over our back door but it would be pretty cold to stay in very long at a time. **1887** *Harper's New Mth. Mag.* 76.119, Two men . . were bending down at the storm-house in front of her parlor door. . . The little piazza was deserted, unless both were hiding in the storm-house. **1907** *DN* 3.250 **ME,** Storm house. . . Outside booth-like house-entrance, generally used only during the winter, and removed at the end of winter. **1949** McDavid *Coll.* **cwNY,** Storm house—door shelter for winter protection. **1964** Sneller *Vanished World* 77 **cNY** (as of c1900), There was a great rattling at the little stormhouse door and a stamping of feet shaking the snow off boots. **1965–70** *DARE* (Qu. D12, *The part that's put on in winter around an outside door to give extra protection from the cold*) 17 Infs, **chiefly Upstate NY, Gt Lakes,** Storm house.

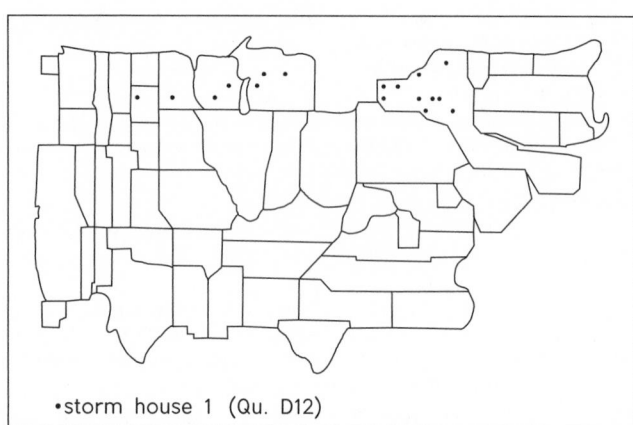

•storm house 1 (Qu. D12)

2 =**cyclone cellar. chiefly Inland Sth, Lower Missip Valley, TX, OK** See Map Cf **storm pit**

1906 *DN* 3.159 **nwAR,** Storm house. . . A pit or cellar made for refuge from tornadoes. **1938** in Lib. of Congress *Amer. Memory: WPA Life Hist.* (Internet) **cTX,** [From an account of a cyclone:] Everything but the storm house and our family were gone. This was due to the fact that the roof [of the storm house] is just above the ground and covered with earth. **1956** Ker *Vocab. W. TX* 195, *Storm house*—a room built underground where all went during a storm. [1 of 67 infs] **1965–70** *DARE* (Qu. D22, *Underground place to go to in case of a violent windstorm*) 32 Infs, **chiefly Inland Sth, Lower Missip Valley, TX, OK,** Storm house; **TX**52, Storm house—not actually in house, thirty or forty yards away; **UT**8, Storm house—but we don't have them here; they have them in Texas; (Qu. D20, *Names for a sloping outside cellar door*) Inf **OK**21, Storm-house door. **1986** Pederson *LAGS Concordance,* 4 infs, **AR, FL, LA, MS,** Storm house; 1 inf, **nwAL,** Storm house—storm shelters underground; 1 inf, **neMS,** Storm house—for protection against windstorms; 1 inf, **swTN,** Storm house—cellar; 1 inf, **swTN,** Storm house—under house for escaping from storms. **1996** Bowerman *Fireclay* (Internet) **AR,** They had a storm house in their back yard that was lined with steel and had food and water stored in it. Everyone else had a storm pit. . . I was very impressed by such affluence. **2004** *DARE* File—Inter-

net **seMO,** [Advt:] Outside on the acre lot you'll find a large storm house, large shop wired for 110 and 220, and a two space car port.

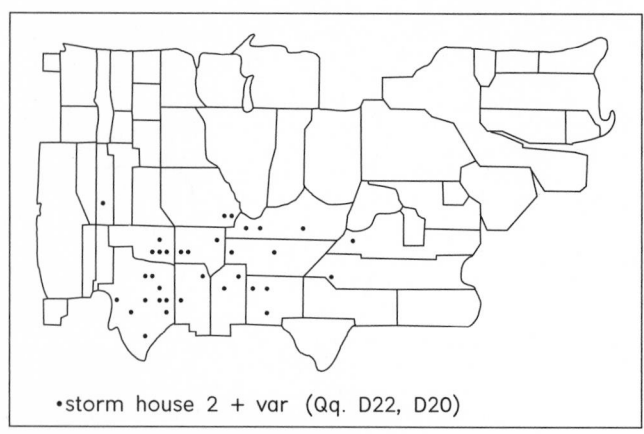

•storm house 2 + var (Qq. D22, D20)

storm king See **storm bird 1**

storm minnow n [See quot 2004]

A baitfish (*Dormitator maculatus*) of marshes along the South Atlantic and Gulf coasts.

1968 *DARE* FW Addit **seLA,** Storm minnows. . . are caught in marshes and ditches. **2001** *DARE* File—Internet **seLA,** I knew this old timer who converted his wife's goldfish pond into a mud pit. . . So this guy could fill it up and fish with the storm minnows until January, when no one had them. **2004** *Ibid* **AL,** *Dormitator maculatus.* . . The only time of the year that their presence is noticeable is when they move in large schools on the surface in connection with winter storms, hence the name storm minnow.

storm petrel n Also *stormy petrel*

Std: an ocean bird of the family Hydrobatidae. For other names of var of these see **fork-tailed petrel, Mother Carey's chicken 1, sea martin**

storm pile n

A thunderhead.

1950 *WELS* (*Names you have for particular kinds of clouds*) 1 Inf, **cWI,** Storm piles—clouds which seem to pile up suddenly before a storm. **1950** *WELS Suppl.* **seWI,** Storm piles . . have heard. **1967** *DARE* (Qu. B9, . . *Big clouds that roll up high before a rainstorm*) Inf **AL**15, Storm piles.

storm pit n Also rarely *storm hole* **chiefly Gulf States, S Atl** See Map Cf **storm cave, ~ house 2, ~ shed 2**

=**cyclone cellar.**

1884 *Atlanta Constitution* (GA) 4 Apr 2/4 **cGA,** We heard the other day of a gentleman who had prepared him a storm pit in this county and used it on last Tuesday night. **1886** in 2003 *DARE* File—Internet **AL** [*Gospel Messenger* Oct], On Easter Sunday, . . a cyclone swept away his house, his family just escaping in time by taking shelter in a storm pit in the yard. **1930** Vines *River Goes* 259 **nAL,** He can fix him up a storm pit. **1939** in Lib. of Congress *Amer. Memory: FSA/OWI* (Internet), [Caption:] Storm pit, shelter built and used by many families in Alabama

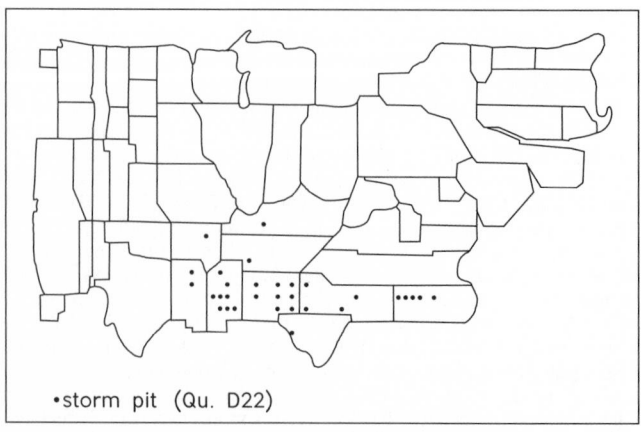

•storm pit (Qu. D22)

during storms or high winds. Coffee County, Alabama.   **1965–70** *DARE* (Qu. D22, *Underground place to go to in case of a violent windstorm*) 31 Infs, **chiefly Gulf States, S Atl,** Storm pit.   **1986** Pederson *LAGS Concordance,* 1 inf, **nwLA,** A root cellar is like a storm pit; 1 inf, **csMS,** Storm pit (=storm cellar?); 1 inf, **cLA,** Underground storm pit—protection against storm; 1 inf, **cnGA,** Storm pits—cellar; under house or porch; 1 inf, **neLA,** Some had storm pits dug in ground.   **1993** Mason *Feather Crowns* 30 **KY** (as of c1900), "What if we did have an earthquake here? What would we do?" "Gather in the wash. . . And run for the storm hole."   **1996** [see **storm house 2**].   **2004** *DARE* File—Internet **cAL,** [Advt:] 3 br, 1½ ba, . . 2 car garage & workshop. All fenced in with storm pit.

storm porch n   **chiefly Nth**
=**storm shed 1.**

   1874 (1875) Gardner *Homes* 168 **MA,** The vestibules—portable storm-porches are not to be tolerated—must also be skilful doorkeepers, proof against hostile storms.   **1889** *Atlantic Mth.* 64.107 **MA,** He [=a woodchuck] may have taken the old farmhouse as a convenient portico for his burrow, a sort of storm-porch, as it were.   **1941** *LANE* Map 351 *(Porch), Porch* usually denotes a small covered platform in front of a door or a small projecting roof (often supported by side pillars) over a door, serving to protect the entry from the weather. It is so defined by 180 informants in all parts of New England. . . 2 infs, **MA,** Storm porch. **1965–70** *DARE* (Qu. D12, *The part that's put on in winter around an outside door to give extra protection from the cold*) Infs **AK**2, **MA**83, 98, **MI**10, 69, **MO**15, **NY**28, **ND**5, **SD**5, Storm porch.   **1973** Allen *LAUM* 1.179 (as of c1950), *Shed. . .* storm porch [1 inf, **MN**].   **1977** *Fairbanks Daily News–Miner* (AK) 10 Sept 7/1, [Caption:] The "Carpenters for the Lord," Lucille and Lee Dale, stand in front of the storm porch they have added to the Methodist parsonage the last two weeks. **2004** *DARE* File—Internet **cwWA,** We had an old storm porch which needed to be replaced. We could have simply removed it, but we like the idea of a windbreak by the front door.

storm rig   See **storm buggy**

storm shed n

1   A small enclosed porch erected either permanently or seasonally to protect an entrance door in cold weather.   **esp Inland Nth**   See Map   Also called **storm closet, ~ enclosure, ~ front 2, ~ porch, ~ shelter, ~ stoop, ~ vestibule**

   1879 *Cedar Rapids Weekly Times* (IA) 13 Nov [3]/2 (newspaperarchive.com), Patch up your broken windows and batten the cracks of your storm sheds.   **1886** *Daily NE State Jrl.* (Lincoln) 3 Feb [8]/4 (newspaperarchive.com), Night before last they [=thieves] entered the storm shed at Capt. Phillips' house and took therefrom two or three pairs of arctics and cheaper rubbers.   **1898** Haskell *2 Yrs.* 181 **AK,** In nearly all [the log cabins] the roof projects from three to five feet over the front entrance, and a storm shed is erected by standing poles upright from the ground to the roof as close together as possible. By having the opening into this storm shed at one side, the entrance to the dwelling is protected from the wind and drifting snow.   **1909** in 2003 *DARE* File—Internet **NYC,** [Item from *Standard Union* (Brooklyn NY):] Climbing to the top of a one story storm shed to reach his bedroom in the rear of the second floor of 1123 Third avenue, Martin Larsen . . lost his balance.   **1920** Lewis *Main Street* 81 **MN,** Storm sheds were erected at every door. **1965–70** *DARE* (Qu. D12, *The part that's put on in winter around an outside door to give extra protection from the cold*) 27 Infs, **scattered, but esp Inland Nth,** Storm shed; **MI**102, Storm shed—was used to

store boots, but was part of the house; found in older houses; **MI**108, Storm shed—a temporary room put onto your porch; **MN**6, Storm shed—don't do this much now; **MN**30, Storm shed—used to call; a little boxlike affair built on; **NY**65, Storm shed—a box; **SC**66, Storm shed [FW sugg]; very seldom used in this section; **WI**47, Storm shed—remembered from time past.   **1973** Allen *LAUM* 1.179 (as of c1950), *Shed. . .* storm shed [2 infs, **MN, ND**].   **2003** *DARE* File—Internet **cnNY** (as of 1889), The woodshed now had its storm shed to shelter the woodshed door from the prevailing west wind, and make a sheltered outside nook to stamp snow or mud off one's boots. In summer the storm shed held a wash stand with soap, wash basin, and towels handy.

2   =**cyclone cellar.**   Cf **storm pit**

   1996 in 2004 *DARE* File—Internet, [Song lyrics:] Dark clouds started turning / Spinning 'round like a top / We went for cover in the storm shed / With no time to stop / When the storm was over / We came up from the ground / Well the house was still standing / But the porch was down.   **1996** *Austin Downtown Arts* 2.10 (Internet) **cTX,** I notice that the storm shed has been broken into, maybe a bum off the highway or some teenagers are to blame.   **2004** *DARE* File—Internet **csLA** (as of 1940s), We would be awakened during the night when a bad storm came up and told to go to the storm shed.   **2006** in 2008 *Ibid* **MS,** When I was a kid in Northern Mississippi, we had a "storm shed" half underground. The neighbors had one, too, but theirs was an old chevy panel truck, fron [sic] end removed and sealed and buried under ground halfway with the rear doors opening out.

storm shelter n
=**storm shed 1.**

   1968 *DARE* (Qu. D12, *The part that's put on in winter around an outside door to give extra protection from the cold*) Infs **PA**134, **VT**7, Storm shelter.

storm stoop n   [**stoop 1**]
=**storm shed 1.**

   1909 *Racine Daily Jrl.* (WI) 12 July [6]/5 (newspaperarchive.com), It was voted . . to build a storm stoop on the front of the school house.   **1967** *DARE* (Qu. D12, *The part that's put on in winter around an outside door to give extra protection from the cold*) Inf **NY**2, Storm stoop.

storm vestibule n   **chiefly Nth**
=**storm shed 1.**

   1912 *NY Times* (NY) 21 Oct 14/1, Sealed proposals for furnishing storm sash and storm vestibules . . for Hospital Addition will be received here.   **1933** in 2003 *DARE* File—Internet, Architectural drawings for an entrance hall ("storm vestibule") for Garfield Hospital, Washington, D.C. Includes preliminary and working drawings showing storm vestibule as plans, elevations, sections, and details.   **1936** in 1986 Deering *Mt. Architecture* (Internet) **OR,** [Entry is through a] storm vestibule, in front of which is a porte cochere to partially protect the sleds when they arrive during snowfalls.   **1966–69** *DARE* (Qu. D12, *The part that's put on in winter around an outside door to give extra protection from the cold*) Infs **DC**3, **NJ**56, **PA**206, **RI**12, Storm vestibule; **NY**34, Storm vestibule—old-fashioned; **OH**34, Storm vestibule—in old houses. [5 of 6 Infs old]   **1998** *DARE* File—Internet **VT,** *Middlebury College President's House Undergoes Renovation. . .* There will be improvements to the storm vestibule arrangement at the front door.   **2002** Kyle *After Shock* 58 **AK,** Dana went through the storm vestibule full of dog harnesses, guns, and parkas.

storm windows n pl   **esp Upper MW, WI**   *joc*
Eyeglasses—also used as a nickname for one wearing glasses.

   1897 *IA State Reporter* (Waterloo) 24 June 1/2, Shippy is all right. He . . wore a large front extension, and had on storm windows, which added much to his dignified appearance.   **1950** *WELS (Nicknames for eye-glasses)* 5 Infs, **WI,** Storm windows.   **1958** Putnam *Theodore Roosevelt* 1.528 (as of 1885), They'd make fun of his glasses—call him 'Four Eyes,' 'Storm Windows.'   **1966–68** *DARE* (Qu. X23) Infs **MN**3, 15, 23, 33, **ND**3, **WI**64, Storm windows.

stormy petrel   See **storm petrel**

story n

1   A liar.   [*OED2 story* sb.¹ 7 1869 →]
   1899 (1912) Green *VA Folk-Speech* 421, *Story. . .* Polite for liar. "What a story you are." "You are a big story."   **1909** *DN* 3.376 **eAL, wGA,** *Story. . .* A liar, a story teller. "You are a story." Euphemism.   **1977** Dillard *Lexicon* 140, In Gullah . . *story* is often used for liar.

2   A television soap opera.

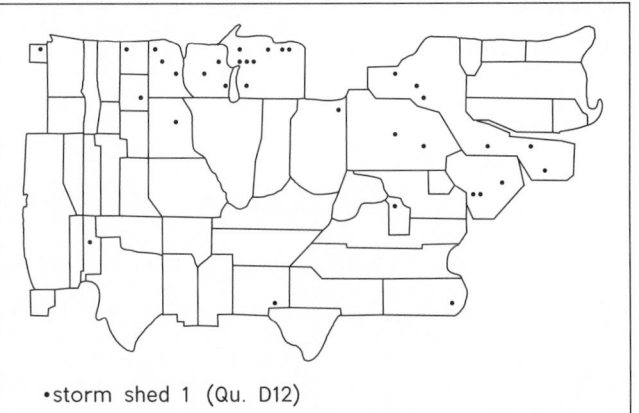

•storm shed 1 (Qu. D12)

1974 Kimmel *Adulthood & Aging* 337 **GA,** I come back here at 2:00 every afternoon and watch my stories on TV. **1986** Pederson *LAGS Concordance,* 1 inf, **seFL,** Stories (=soap operas). [Inf Black] **1992** *DARE* File **Los Angeles CA,** The stories = soap operas . . among Blacks; now so called. *Ibid* **Orlando FL,** I heard . . an Orlando Fla-born hotel maid . . refer to the daytime soap operas as "the stories." . . She was Black. **2003** *DARE* File—Internet, *Soap Operas Poll*—Do you watch talk shows as well as soaps? . . Forget talk! I *only* watch my stories. *Ibid,* I do have a 'guilty pleasure.' I do love to watch my stories in the afternoon. *Ibid* **NYC,** I think I'm going to the gym to watch my stories and run in place. *Ibid* **NJ,** I am off to browse monster . . and watch "my stories" and oprah. **2009** Stockett *Help* 50 **MS** (as of 1960s) [Black], She's taken to laying on the couch while my stories are on. . . I've been tuned in to *The Guiding Light* for twenty-four years, since I was ten years old and listening to it on Mama's radio.

story v [Engl dial] **chiefly Sth, S Midl**
To give a false or malicious account, lie, tattle; rarely, to lie to.
1877 Perrow *Hoosier Ed.* 135 **IN,** "Johny," she continued, "you mustn't do that way. Only naughty little boys story." "Yes'm, but I ain't storying." **1898** *Amer. Practitioner & News* 26.22 **KY,** I remember she remarked, when told that the operation was completed, "Doctor, you are storying." She thought we were trying to fool her, and that no operation had been performed. **1906** *DN* 3.159 **nwAR,** *Story.* . . To lie. "He's storying." **1909** *DN* 3.376 **eAL, wGA,** *Story.* . . To tell a lie. "He storied about it." Rare. **1912** *DN* 3.591 **wIN,** *Story.* . . To lie, fib. Euphemistic or facetious. **1952** Brown *NC Folkl.* 1.594, *Story* . . to tell a falsehood. Generally euphemistic. "You storied to me about going to that dance." **1953** Goodwin *It's Good* 114 **sIL** [Black], Well, it's true. That's what he said. . . I don't have to story. **1966** *DARE* Tape **SC**11, [Inf:] You got this [=a tape recorder] cut off? [FW:] Uh-huh. [Inf:] No, you haven't, you rascal, you! . . Look at the thing running there! . . You did story me; you said you didn't have it on. **1966** *DARE* FW Addit **SC,** He's storying—telling a falsehood. **1971** in 1993 Major *Calling the Wind* 321 **LA** [Black], I'm scared Miss Hebert go'n whip me, that's why I story to her. **1972** *NYT Article Letters* **KY,** Once in a little town in Kentucky when my wife . . saw some nice looking muffins served at the next table and asked for some [she] was told by the waitress that there were no more. Later on some new ones appeared . . and the waitress served them to us, a bit flustered, and said: "Sorry ma'am. I did not mean to story on you!" **1982** *Smithsonian Letters* **WV,** For the past five or six years I have secretly recorded some of the unusual phrases that continually pop up in my mother's conversation. She is seventy years old, grew up in Dodderidge County, W. Va. . . to story = to lie. **1984** Weaver *TX Crude* 128, *To story.* To lie, prevaricate. "I believe you're storying me, son." **1986** Pederson *LAGS Concordance (Children's nicknames for one who tattles)* 1 inf, **cnMS,** [He] storied on him. **2008** *DARE* File **seIA** (as of c1970), If my father suspected I might not be telling him the truth, he would ask sternly, "Are you storyin' to me?"

stoughton bottle n Also *stotin bottle, stot(t)en ~, stote an' ~* [Appar in ref to the bottles in which Stoughton Bitters were sold]
Used in similes as an example of something that sits around uselessly; hence a lazy, unresponsive, or stupid person.
1870 *Waukesha Plaindealer* (WI) 11 Jan 1/6, Me cousin Ulisses next till me right hand, looked like a stoughton bottle, beside a full sized decanter of fishky. **1880** *Marion Daily Star* (OH) 15 Sept 1/2, Hancock's a stoughton bottle, that's what he is. **1885** in 2004 *DARE* File—Internet [*Winfield Courier* (KS) 2 July] **KS,** He has been one of those stoughton bottle Republicans who sit up on a shelf to see others do the work and spend their money. **1887** (1892) Hinman *Corporal Si Klegg* 111, Whar's the fun in them fellers stan'in' like so many stoughton-bottles hangin' on ter that blanket! **1892** *KS Univ. Qrly.* 1.99, *Stoughton-bottle:* an unimpressionable fellow. (From Stoughton's Bitters, common in the 50's.) **1911** Ware *Indian War 1864* 128 **West,** Before that time [=the early 1850s] an old invention called "Stoughton" had been for a long while in vogue. In every saloon was a bottle of "Stoughton bitters". . . It was only occasionally the Stoughton was used, but the Stoughton bottle was always at the bar, and the synonym for an idle fellow, always in evidence and doing nothing, was to call him a "Stoughton bottle." **1911** *DN* 3.540 **eKY,** *Stōtin-bŏttle.* . . A sluggard, or dullard. **1923** *DN* 5.239 **swWI,** *Stoughton bottle, to stand like a.* . . To stand very still or stupidly. . . "He just stood there like a Stoughton bottle." **1942** Berrey-Van den Bark *Amer. Slang* 584.4, Audience. . . *stote an' bottle,* an unresponsive audience. **1954** Carson *Old Country Store* 236, 'There he sat,

like a Stoughton bottle,' people would say to indicate one who was dull, heavy, or unresponsive. **1958** *VT Hist.* 26.261, As silent as a Stoughton bottle. To stand there like a Stoughton bottle. **1968** *DARE* FW Addit **NYC,** "She just sat there like a stoughton bottle" (means: sat there like a poker face). **2002** *DARE* File—Internet, My mother used to say "He sat there like a stotten bottle" which was to say he . . sat there without contributing to the discussion or activity. **2004** *DARE* File—Internet, My grandmother, from Shelbyville, MO, (she would be 117 if she were still alive!) used to say, "Don't stand there like a stotenbottle."

sto-un See **stone** n

stout adj
1 Physically strong; powerful. [*OED2 stout* a. A.6.a c1386 →; "Now only *U.S. dial.*"]
1717 *Boston News–Letter* (MA) 12 Aug 2/2 **eMA,** [Advt:] Arrived in the Ship Globe . . Sundry Servants, Men, Young Lads, Stout Boys; of several Trades . . which are to Serve from 4 to 9 Years. **1803** in 1940 Criswell *Lewis & Clark* 82, One fellow . . was carrying off not only his own horse but that also of his competitor; but the other being the stoutest of the two dismounted him and took both. **1882** Twain *Stolen White Elephant* 269, Your word 'stout' means 'fleshy'; our word 'stout' usually means 'strong.' **1894** *DN* 1.342 **wCT,** Stout: strong (of muscle). Never used = corpulent. **1899** (1912) Green *VA Folk-Speech* 421, *Stout.* . . Strong built man; broad and strong. **1902** *DN* 2.246 **sIL,** *Stout.* . . Strong. The latter is applied only to things affecting the senses, as 'strong light,' 'strong smell,' 'strong coffee.' **1907** *DN* 3.227 **nwAR,** *Stout.* . . Strong. **1912** *DN* 3.569 **cNY,** *Stout.* . . Strong, not *fleshy* as in Illinois and Missouri. **1913** *DN* 4.54 **seNH,** *Stout.* . . "That calf's terrible stout: he pretty near pulled me all over the field." **1941** *LANE* Map 460 *(Strong)* **NEng,** [*Stout* is widespread throughout the region.] The word is used in two different senses (meaning both 'strong' and 'fat' or 'obese') by 141 informants in all parts of our territory. **1958** McCulloch *Woods Words* 182 **Pacific NW,** *Stout*—Strong, rugged. **1966** Dakin *Dial. Vocab. Ohio R. Valley* 2.455, *Strong*—A person with much physical strength. . . *Stout* is the most common . . everywhere except in Illinois. . . Scattered speakers in all parts of Illinois say *stout,* but other words are more common. . . Comments indicate that *stout* = "corpulent" is spreading as a newer meaning for this word. **1967** *DARE* FW Addit **TN**14, "Stouter" used in context of "stronger." **1970** *Foxfire* Spring–Summer 7 **nGA,** If I's stout enough I could pull it out . . , but I ain't. **1973** Allen *LAUM* 1.352 (as of c1950), *Strong,* the common term, is used by seven or eight out of ten infs. . . *Husky,* next most frequent . . , exhibits a very slight Northern bias in the eastern half [of the Upper Midwest] but a significant one in the west. In contrast, *stout* is significantly Midland, with higher frequency in Iowa and Nebraska. **1993** Kingsolver *Pigs in Heaven* 220 **OK,** "We caught a snapping turtle in the mud. Leon poked a stick at it and it bit it and wouldn't turn loose. . . Those things are *stout.*" "They'll give you a stout bite, too, if you don't leave them be."

2 Physically healthy; well; robust. [*OED2 stout* a. A.6.b 1697 → "*Obs.* exc. *Sc.*"] **chiefly S Midl**
1806 *Lit. Mag. & Amer. Reg.* 5.255, Book-learning should be the least concern of the delicately constituted. Living instruction turns out its pupils not only stouter but abler. **1828** in 1956 Eliason *Tarheel Talk* 297 **ce,seNC,** Susan must take care of herself and get perfectly stout before I return. **1871** in 1927 Jones *FL Plantation Rec.* 186 **nwFL,** Glad to hear you are getting Stout again. **1871** in 1983 *PADS* 70.52 **ce,sePA,** M[argary] washed and at noon she got sick and laid down. . . she is going to leave us soon as she's not stout enough for us. **1916** *DN* 4.339 **PA,** *Stout.* . . Healthy; well. "I haven't been very stout lately." **1926** *DN* 5.404 **Ozarks,** *Stout.* . . In good health; never used to mean corpulent or obese. "Them stout gals is allus kinder skinny-like." **1927** *AmSp* 2.365 **cwWV,** *Stout* . . healthy. "Is your woman stout?" **1929** *AmSp* 5.122 **ME,** The complaint was heard, "I don't feel very stout this spring. I guess I've got the spring fever." **1942** (1971) Campbell *Cloud-Walking* 15 **seKY,** Iffen I don't get no sleep I won't be stout to keep my younguns fixed to take learning. **1943** *LANE* Map 497 *(Pretty well)* 1 inf, **cCT,** Fine and stout. **1952** Brown *NC Folkl.* 1.594, *Stout.* . . Healthy. **1953** *Hall Coll.* **eTN,** Daddy wasn't stout, and when hit'd be a big snow on the ground, I had to get out and get the wood. **1965** *DARE* (Qu. KK28, *Feeling ambitious and eager to work*) Inf **MS**61, Stout. **1969** *DARE* FW Addit **swNC,** I'm not too stout—healthy. **1971** *Foxfire* Winter 253 **nGA,** That's th'reason women ain't stout. They make 'em get right up [after childbirth]. **1974** Fink *Mountain Speech* 25 **wNC, eTN,** *Stout* . . strong or well. "I'm feeling purty stout." **1994** in

2004 Montgomery–Hall *Dict. Smoky Mt. Engl.* 574 **wNC, eTN,** *Stout.* . . Reckon you're stout? [=are you in good health?]

3 Strong (in flavor or odor). **west of Appalachians** See Map

1875 *Old & New* 11.378, The men did their simple cooking, drank their stout coffee, . . and turned into their blankets and buffaloes. **1932** *Ogden Std.–Examiner* (UT) 23 Dec 1/2, Round ups . . are here again . . with . . the stout smell of burning hair and hide filling crisp mountain air. **1944** *Sun. Jrl. & Star* (Lincoln NE) 28 Oct comic sec, [*Flyin' Jenny* comic strip:] How's for the old crew chief throwin' about a gallon of stout coffee together? **1965–70** *DARE* (Qu. H74a, . . *Coffee . . very strong*) 9 Infs, **scattered west of Appalachians,** (Pretty *or* too) stout; **CO**40, **OK**1, **UT**4, Stout coffee. **1971** *Today Show Letters* **sw,csMS,** Stout—Referring to strong tasting chewing tobacco. **2008** *DARE* File **seIA, csWI,** If the radishes from his garden are strongly flavored, my father will warn you that they're "pretty stout." If coffee is too strong for her liking, my mother will remark that it's "awfully stout."

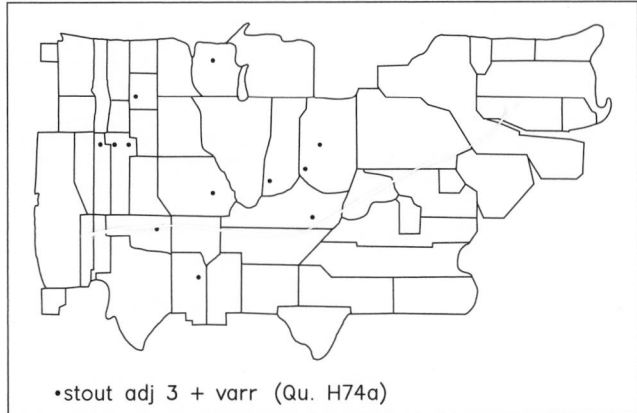

•stout adj 3 + varr (Qu. H74a)

stout n [Prob folk-etym for Engl dial *stowk* or Du dial. *stuik* (both cognate with **stook**)] **chiefly NY**

A shock of grain (or rarely hemp); hence v (phr) *stout (up)* to gather in shocks; vbl n *stouting;* ppl adj *stouted.*

1820 *Plough Boy* 2.75 **ceNY,** I will describe my mode of stacking or stouting it [=rye]. The stacks or stouts are made by placing the beads [sic] of six sheaves together in a double row . . and one sheaf at each end of the row . . : then place on two cap sheaves. **1829** *Amer. Advocate* (Hallowell ME) 7 Feb 1/2 **ceNY,** It [=hemp] is bound in small bundles, and set up on the buts in stouts for curing. **1846** Onderdonk *Documents & Letters* 115 **Long Is. NY** (as of 1776), Kirk was in his corn-field stouting top-stalks. **1850** *Cultivator* 7.278 **MI,** If the crop [of wheat] cannot be cut till nearly or quite ripe, we can then put it in stouts as the stooking is a trifle. **1854** U.S. Patent Office *Annual Rept. for 1853: Ag.* 120 **cnPA,** The corn is cut up and "stouted" in small stouts, or stooks. **1877** *Cultivator & Country Gentleman* 42.682 **cNY,** Once we bound the grain [=barley] into bundles and stouted it up; but this was long ago. **1877** Tullidge *Women Mormondom* 130, I stole down into a corn-field, and crawled into a 'stout of corn.' **1919** *Kingston Daily Freeman* (NY) 21 Oct 13/2, [Advt:] *For Sale*—400 stouts of cornstalks. **1937** *Middletown Times Herald* (NY) 8 Sept 5/1, There will be a lot [of corn] stouted up and husked out. . . Al Booth . . figures on drawing in a load of stouted corn every other day until January first. **1939** *LANE* Map 126 (*Sheaf; shock*), Stout applies only to corn. . . 1 inf, **cwCT,** Stout [ˈsdaʊt]; 1 inf, **cwCT,** *Shock,* 16 bundles; *stout,* of (Indian) corn, consisting of 36 to 46 *hills.* Corn is [ˈstaʊtɪd ˈʌp]; 1 inf, **nwCT,** Three *shocks* of (Indian) corn make a *stout.* cf [stɛˈʔot ˈʌp]. **1968** *Oneonta Star* (NY) 22 Oct 2/5, Our farmer had brought . . the tallest corn stalks and arranged them about the stakes like the old corn stouts.

stout adv [*OED2 stout* adv. B.a "Now *rare*"]

Sturdily, boldly.

1939 *Hall Coll.* **eTN,** Stout. . . And we'd hear 'em talk big and stout, how they'd he'p carry the old bear out. **1975** Chalmers *Better* 66 **Smoky Mts,** Good shoes will wear stout even for this trifling generation.

stouted See **stout** n

stouter n [Var, perh by folk-etym, of swEngl dial *strouter* (*EDD* at *strout* v. 2) "a 'strut' . . or support in the side of a

wagon." Cf *DNE strouter* (also *stouter*) "One of several heavy posts placed vertically to support and strengthen the head of a fishing stage or wharf."]

A wagon or sled stake.

1857 Janvrin *Peace* 73 **NEng,** Chip brought out his sled with strong white ash "stouters," and folding a soft buffalo skin for a cushion seated Peace thereon. **1891** *AN&Q* 7.155, This is a local Americanism. . . In some parts of Essex county, Massachusetts, a *stouter* is any one of the upright stakes of an ox-sled, or other similar vehicle. I think the stakes of an ox-cart would also be called *stouters.* **1918** *DN* 5.17 **Martha's Vineyard MA,** *Stouter.* . . Stake for retaining load, on hay-wagon, etc.

stout house n **TX** *joc*

A jail.

1956 *Amarillo Globe–Times* (TX) 27 Nov 20/1, New York has a new jail. . . We haven't been advised exactly what pastel tints are being used in [the] New York stout house. **1956** Ker *Vocab. W. TX* 406, *Jail* (jocular terms). . . stout-house. [2 of 67 infs] **1967** *DARE* (Qu. V11, . . *Joking names . . for a county or city jail*) Inf **TX**37, Stout house. **1971** *Big Spring Daily Herald* (TX) 15 Feb 12/3, *Shot To Death In Stout House.* . . A detective was shot to death today by a prisoner he was fingerprinting in a Bronx station house.

stouting See **stout** n

‡**stouts** n pl

1932 *DN* 6.284 **swCT,** Stouts. Grandfather's word for the conceited, cocksure way of the adolescent boy. "He has the stouts, or he has a bad case of the stouts."

stout up See **stout** n

stove v[1] See **stave** v

stove v[2] [From *stove* past, past pple of **stave** v]

1 with *in:* =**stave** v **2;** hence ppl adj phr *stoved in.*

1863 in 1890 U.S. War Dept. *War of Rebellion* 1st ser 28.2.354, Four enemy's launches, stoved in, are run on Morris Island beach. **1906** *DN* 3.159 **nwAR,** Stove in. . . To knock in. "Let's stove in that hat." **1944** in 2003 (acc) Lexis–Nexis Legal Research *State Case Law: OH* (Internet), It is evidenced that the front of defendant's car was badly damaged and that plaintiff's car was badly stoved in. **1950** Richter *Town* 146 **OH,** A row boat with a stoved-in side.

2a with *up:* =**stave** v **3a.**

1897 *KS Univ. Qrly.* (ser B) 6.58, Stove up . . to make stiff; as, Such driving will stove up your horse.

b ppl adj *stoved up:* See **stove up 1.**

3 =**stave** v **4.**

1930 *DN* 6.88 **cWV,** Stoving steel, driving grabs into logs.

4 To stub (a finger or toe), sprain (a joint or ligament); hence ppl adj *stoved.* [*SND stave* v. 3 "To sprain, bruise or confuse a joint of the body"] **esp wPA, OH, WV**

1941 *Coshocton Tribune* (OH) 13 Feb [12]/2 (newspaperarchive.com), [Basketball player] Silverthorne . . may be at a slight handicap, owing to a stoved finger which he received at Zanesville Tuesday night. **1982** *DARE* File **cOH,** "I stoved it" = I jammed my finger while playing baseball. **1990** Cavender *Folk Med. Lexicon* 32 **csAppalachians,** Stove . . to jam or stub a finger or toe. **1995** Pittsburgh Univ. *Univ. Times* 3 Dec (Internet), "I think I broke this one," she said . . , indicating a swollen finger, "or at least I stoved it badly." **1997** in 2003 (acc) Lexis–Nexis Legal Research *State Case Law: WV* (Internet), The appellees filed suit for damages . . on January 25, 1989. . . Mrs. Morrison sought damages for a "stoved" right shoulder. **2000** *DARE* File, My wife (age 34, grew up near Akron, OH) says she "stoved" her finger. . . I've asked around and found a 30-something colleague from Morgantown, WV who also uses "stove" in this way. He says you "stub" your toe, but you "stove" your finger. Another colleague says her mother (approx. 50 yrs old, from Eastern OH) also uses this term. **2003** *DARE* File—Internet **WV,** It was all accomplished without one accident more serious than a stoved finger. *Ibid* **neTN,** Two "stoved" fingers on my right hand as a result of trying to field a hot ground smash with my bare hand. *Ibid* **wPA,** I stoved my finger while catching a pass. *Ibid* **OH,** I know it took just one badly stoved thumb, to convince one pitcher that being able to grasp a softball year round . . was more important than playing volleyball. **2004** *DARE* File **swPA** (as of c1960), When I was growing up, I would have said "I stoved my finger" if I had caught the tip of it on a volleyball.

stove catch n esp S Midl
=**stove handle.**

1905 *DN* 3.96 **nwAR,** *Stove-catch.* . . Stove-lifter. 'The baby's lost the stove-catch, and I can't find it.' Rare. **1957** Combs *Lang. S. Highlanders* **sAppalachians,** Stove ketch—lifter for removing caps from a kitchen range. **1960** Criswell *Resp. to PADS 20* **Ozarks,** These [=stove lids] lifted with a stove catch. **1966–70** *DARE* (Qu. F11, *The thing you use to remove the lids . . from a wood-burning stove when it is hot*) Infs **AR**38, **IL**103, **KY**41, **OK**53, **SC**34, **VA**2, Stove catch. [5 of 6 Infs old]

stove cover See **cover B2**

stoved ppl adj See **stove** v² **4**

stoved adj See **stove up 1**

stoved in See **stove** v² **1**

stoved up See **stove up 1**

stove eye See **eye** n¹ **1**

stove handle n esp Nth See Map Also called **stove catch, ~ jack**
A detachable handle for lifting stove lids.

1867 *Scientific Amer.* 16.194, [Advt:] Longshore's Patent Combined Stove Handle and Household Tool, will fit and lift with convenience and safety any stove lid, skillet, frying pan, . . or any other hot vessel or dish. **1888** *Overland Mth.* (2d ser) 12.322 **CA,** He'll jump up, fire the stove handle, rocking chair, and lamp at you . . and clean you out. **1965–70** *DARE* (Qu. F11, *The thing you use to remove the lids . . from a wood-burning stove when it is hot*) 74 Infs, **esp Nth,** Stove handle.

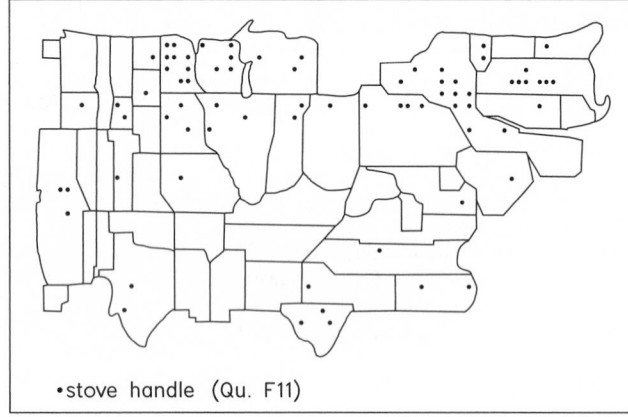

•stove handle (Qu. F11)

stove hearth See **hearth B1**

stove hook See **hook** n **4**

stove in See **stove** v² **1**

stove iron n Cf **charcoal iron**
A flatiron heated on a stove.

1907 in 2004 *DARE* File—Internet **Brooklyn NYC,** One tailor, with a family of seven, brought his stove irons and other tailor accessories over in a cart. **1941** *Ibid* **UT** (as of c1880), All the washing was done on the washboards and the ironing with a stove iron. **1966–68** *DARE* (Qu. F29, *Different kinds of irons—not electric—used . . for smoothing clothes after they're washed*) Infs **ID**5, **VA**2, 9, **WA**27, Stove iron; [**SC**19, Stove iron—burned cobs, coals, etc;] **VA**13, Stove iron = flatiron = sadiron. **2004** *DARE* File—Internet **swWI,** Mother would heat a brick or stove iron and wrap it in a paper sack and place it under the covers at the foot of our bed. *Ibid* **seTN** (as of 1930s), We also had to wash clothes on a wash-board and iron with a stove iron.

stove jack n
=**stove handle.**

1968–70 *DARE* (Qu. F11, *The thing you use to remove the lids . . from a wood-burning stove when it is hot*) Infs **LA**28, **VA**42, Stove jack. **1975** *Lima News* (OH) 20 July sec D 7/3, *Public sale.* . . old stove jack, wooden barrel.

stove key See **key** n **3**

stove lid n

1 The removable circular metal lid of a wood-burning stove. **widespread, but chiefly Nth, N Midl** See Map Cf **cap** n¹ **2a, eye** n¹ **1, stove plate 2**

1866 *Harper's New Mth. Mag.* 32.265 **PA,** One of the party said he had seen a bull-frog as large as the stove lid. **1913** Johnson *Highways St. Lawrence to VA* 238 **DE,** We never had a box of blacking, but we'd turn the stove lid over and rub on soot from it with a brush. That made our shoes black. **1922** (1926) Cady *Rhymes VT* 54, Then Nellie drops her lesson leaf / Inside the fire she's poking,/ And then she drops the stove lid, too,/ The thing is so provoking. **1965–70** *DARE* (Qu. F10, . . *Wood-burning stoves . . the round flat pieces that you take out to put in the wood*) 183 Infs, **widespread, but chiefly Nth, N Midl,** Stove lid; (Qu. F11, *The thing you use to remove the lids . . from a wood-burning stove when it is hot*) Inf **LA**24, Stove-lid handle; **MA**63, Stove-lid holder; (Qu. F12) Inf **OH**72, Stove lid; (Qu. HH22b, . . *A very mean person*) Inf **ME**3, Tighter than a stove lid. **2000** (2001) Thayer *Certain Slant* 14 **ME,** He messes with the stove lids and sets another log in the firebox. . . He rubs his hands over the tilted stove lid.

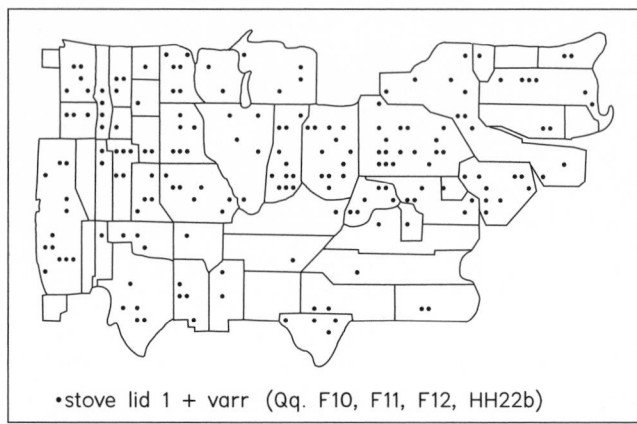

•stove lid 1 + varr (Qq. F10, F11, F12, HH22b)

2 A pancake. [From the shape]

1967 *DARE* (Qu. H20b, . . *Names . . for pancakes*) Inf **OR**1, Stove lids. **1969** Sorden *Lumberjack Lingo* 122 **NEng, Gt Lakes,** Stovelids—Pancakes or griddle cakes.

‡**3** pl: Eyeglasses.

1970 *DARE* (Qu. X23, . . *Joking words . . for eyeglasses*) Inf **TX**95, Stove lids.

stoven ppl adj See **stave** v

Stovepipe City n Also *Stovepipe Village* **chiefly nNEng, NY**
Used as a name or nickname for a shantytown.

[**1882** Becket *Montreal Snow Shoe Club* 7 **Canada,** Charlie Meyer "left a bloody track o'er twenty miles of snow" until they reached a "Stovepipe village."] **1896** *Hornellsville Weekly Tribune* (NY) [30 Oct 8]/5 (newspaperarchive.com), Two colts were killed by the cars last Saturday evening at Stovepipe City, one car was wrecked. **1910** McGovern *When Krag* 52, Algernon's father had become a skilled mechanic of good standing in the local silk factory at Stovepipe Village. **1940** Writers' Program *Guide NY* 537, In the winter, innumerable movable shanties, referred to in local idiom as the 'Stovepipe City,' dot the gleaming sweep of ice on Lake Champlain. Inside them, heavily clothed ice-fishermen sit huddled around kerosene stoves. **1943** *Wellington Leader* (TX) 20 May 1/2, [Caption:] Navy construction battalion Seabees line up for chow at "Stovepipe City," their base at Camp Rousseau, Port Hueneme, Calif. **1949** Hill *Winooski* 181 **VT,** Ugly tenements and shacks to house the influx of workers created "Stovepipe City." **1968–69** *DARE* (Qu. C33, . . *Joking names . . for an out-of-the-way place, or a very small or unimportant place*) Inf **NH**14, Stovepipe Village—name of several small settlements; (Qu. C35, *Nicknames for the different parts of your town or city*) Inf **VT**16, Stovepipe City. **1999** *DARE* File—Internet **ME,** [From the minutes of the Harpswell selectmen's meeting of July 31:] Selectman Weil moved to replace Stovepipe Village with Basin Cove. **2002** *World* (Barre VT) 18 Sept (Internet), Various neighborhoods had interesting names such as Tough End, Stovepipe City, Rabbit Hollow, and Oatmeal Flats.

stove plate n

1 =**hearth B1.**

1886 *Amer. Philol. Assoc. Proc.* 17.xii **ePA,** "Stove-plate" *(Ofenplatte)* for what is called stove-hearth in New England. **1908** *German Amer. Annals* 10.45 **sePA,** Stove-plate. Stove hearth. "Brush the ashes off the stove plate." . . fr. Pa. Ger. *ŭfã blat;* Ger. *ofen platte.*

2 =**stove lid 1.**

1877 *Decatur Daily Republican* (IL) 3 Jan 1/3 **St. Louis MO,** He sat down on a stove plate that Bridget had just taken off the roaring stove. **1967–69** *DARE* (Qu. F10, . . *Wood-burning stoves . . the round flat pieces that you take out to put in the wood*) Infs **AR**47, **IN**66, **PA**2, 22, 88, Stove plate. **1984** *Syracuse Herald–Jrl.* (NY) 14 May sec B 1/5, The husband says he was hit over the head with a stove plate. The wife says it was a pan of macaroni.

stove poker See **poker** n¹ **2**

stove up adj phr Cf **stave** v **3a**

1 also rarely *stoved (up), stoven up;* Of a person or animal: incapacitated, esp by overwork, exposure, or injury; also fig. **chiefly Sth, S Midl**

1855 *Spirit of Times* 25.386 **NY,** Down again on other side, sitting so as to balance wagon on two left wheels along an inclined plane of lines fastened to a pair of "stove up" leaders. **1864** *Morning Oregonian* (Portland OR) 8 Jan 2/1, We [=the Democratic Party] are gone in, stove up, smashed, played out, used up, catawampused—in fact, whipped. **1884** *Anglia* 7.275 **Sth, S Midl** [Black], To look sorter stove up = to look used up. **1896** Harris *Sister Jane* 311 **GA,** Sandy, your cloze is all right, but you look stove up. **1897** *KS Univ. Qrly* (ser B) 6.58 **KS,** Stove up . . the horse is all stove up. **1909** *DN* 3.376 **eAL, wGA,** Stove-up. . . A horse is said to be *stove up* when his legs are stiff, as from overwork or overfeeding. Also used of persons in the sense 'worn out, done up.' "You look sorter stove-up this morning." **1915** *DN* 4.191 **swVA,** Stove up. . . Stiff from overwork. "That horse is mighty bad stove up." **1942** McAtee *Dial. Grant Co. IN* 62 (as of 1890s), Stove up . . with the legs stiff from overwork, especially on hard or very uneven surfaces, applied to both livestock and men; often preceded by "all." **1952** Brown *NC Folkl.* 1.595, Stove up. . . Stiff, sore, lame because of hard work or physical injury. **1964** *Lima News* (OH) 15 Mar sec A 13/5, Many of these animals . . are so badly stoven up that they cannot be shown again. **1965** *DARE* FW Addit **MS,** All stove up—sick in bed or having to stay in because of a fall, etc. **1968–70** *DARE* (Qu. K47, . . *Diseases . . horses or mules commonly get*) Inf **GA**68, Stove up; (Qu. BB8, *When a person's joints and muscles ache and sometimes swell up, especially in damp weather*) Inf **OH**95, All stoved up; (Qu. KK30, *Feeling slowed up or without energy: "I certainly feel _____."*) Inf **LA**17, Stove up. **1972** *Atlanta Letters* **nwGA,** Yes I have been Stove Up from stoopin an Picking up Corn Stalks all day Long. **1975** Gainer *Witches* 17 **sAppalachians,** Stoved (adj.), incapacitated. "That horse got stoved from being rid down hill too fast." **1985** *Amer. Jrl. Med.* Feb 184 **eTN,** The hurting started on Friday and by Sunday he was stoved up in bed. **1986** Pederson *LAGS Concordance (Tired; exhausted)* 1 inf, **cnMS,** All stove up; *(Worn-out)* 2 infs, **GA, MS,** Stove up. **2002** Perry *Population 485* 5 **WI,** As long as I can remember, Stanislaw Jabowski was all stove up. **2003** *DARE* File **ceMO,** The neurosurgeon's nurse told me that I should expect to be "stoved up" for awhile.

2 Congested; clogged; constipated; also fig. **scattered, but esp Sth**

1934 Hurston *Jonah's Gourd Vine* 15 **AL** [Black], Ah don't want mah chilluns all stove-up wid uh bad cold from proagin' 'round in de rain. **1965–70** *DARE* (Qu. BB21, . . *Being constipated*) 10 Infs, **scattered,** Stove up. **1967** *DARE* FW Addit **WA,** [Radio announcer:] *Stove up* (with a cold)—stuffed up. **1986** Pederson *LAGS Concordance (Hoarse)* 1 inf, **seGA,** Stove up. **1989** Gibbons *Virtuous Woman* 107 **NC,** Why couldn't have somebody just as easily said he was mean, mean to the core, and then . . something clicked in that car and he let what was stove up come flying out? **2003** *DARE* File—Internet, I'm from the Carolinas . . and my dad (b. 1919 d. 1983) used to use "stove up" to mean either "stiff and sore" or "constipated." You had to discern his intended meaning from the context. *Ibid* **TX,** My Granny and Grandaddy were from Texas and I remember them saying "stove up" but if I remember correctly they usually used it to mean clogged up. Like having a cold or sinus problems.

stove up v See **stove** v² **2a**

‡**stowed up** adj phr Cf **stove up** adj phr **2**

1968 *DARE* (Qu. BB21, . . *Being constipated*) Inf **MN**19, Stowed up.

strack See **strike** v A1, 2

stracked See **strike** v A2

stracted See **distracted 1**

straddle n esp **S Midl**

The crotch; hence adj phr *straddle-deep* up to the crotch in depth.

1870 in 1938 *MN Hist.* 19.323 **MA,** We have had a pretty good supply of snow this winter. in the woods, it is about straddle deep on a man. **1917** *DN* 4.418 **IL, KY, wMA, wNC,** Straddle. . . Crotch. "Wet up to the straddle." **1939** *Hall Coll.* **wNC, eTN,** Straddle. . . "They poured tar between her straddle." . . "I can see yer straddle through them pants." **1941** *Ibid,* Straddle deep—"We had an awful rain the other day. I waded water straddle deep in the highway in Shiloh." **1949** *PADS* 11.11 **wTX** (as of 1911–29), Straddle. . . The crotch. **1954** *Harder Coll.* **cwTN,** Straddle. . . The crotch. **c1960** *Wilson Coll.* **csKY,** Straddle. . . The crotch. **1968** *DARE* File **MD,** He . . attempted to climb the pole. He got up just far enough before he slipped back, to tear the straddle out of his pants. **1982** Slone *How We Talked* 99 **eKY** (as of c1950), The depth of the snow was described as: a skiff of snow; ankle-deep; knee-deep; straddle-deep; over your head.

straddle board n

1 =**saddle board.** Cf *DS* **D30**

1896 *Cherokee Advocate* (Tahlequah OK) 1 Feb 2/8, *Notice For Bids.* . . new straddle boards to be replaced. **1899** *Pop. Sci. News* 33.127 **KS,** The peak of "the first great roof" [=the carapace of the prehistoric sea turtle *Protostega gigas*] had straddle boards on, and a row of shingles, but its architect forgot to finish shingling. **1900** *Tyrone Daily Herald* (PA) 26 Oct [3]/3 (newspaperarchive.com), The latest vagary which the summer visitors brought to the front in Maine is the erection of wooden cottages having the outside boarding densely coated with . . moss. The abandoned farmhouses were searched for lichened corner and straddle boards, and extravagant prices were paid for bits of ancient wood. **1912** *DN* 3.591 **wIN,** Straddle-boards. . . Ridging; wooden *coping.* "We have all the shingles on the house, but no straddle-boards." **1915** *Kansas City Times* (MO) 23 Aug 1/2, The "straddle board" and a square of shingles were torn off the roof.

2 A school-bus seat consisting of a board running lengthways down the center. **chiefly AR, MO**

1934 WV State Dept. Educ. *Biennial Rept.* 77, Seats. (a) Padded or covered. (b) Straddle board not recommended. (c) There should be a seat for every child. **1985** Arnold *Voices Amer. Homemakers* 70 **seMO** (as of c1936), The school bus was a long dotty thing that had seats down like each side, and a straddle board, we called it, in the center. If you weren't lucky enough to get a side seat, you had to ride the straddle board. **2003** *DARE* File—Internet **AR** (as of c1930), A typical [school] bus about that time was somewhat like this—a continuous seat front to back, one on either side and one called the "straddle board" down the center. **2008** N. AR College *Hall Talk* (Internet) **cnAR** (as of c1935), The first school bus. . . was a 1926 Model T. Ford with a low speed rear axle to which a bus body had been fitted. . . If the bus was packed very carefully it would hold 30 students. . . On each side of the bus there where [sic] wooden seats. . . Going down the center of the bus was a straddle board. When the students sat down they straddled this seat. . . [I]f the students leaned backwards . . the kids sitting on the back of the board would slide off and onto the bus floor. **2008** *DARE* File—Internet **cnAR** (as of c1928), A large [school] bus made with one continuous seat from front to back on either side and one called the "straddle board" down the center was the main, or "big" bus. For shorter routes, similarly made buses were made on the beds of pick-ups.

straddlebug n

1 Any long-legged insect; also fig. Cf **spradling bug**

[**1797** *Time-Piece & Lit. Companion* 1.220, Well then (cries Dermot [=an Irishman]) I've swallowed a straddle bug, for I feel'd it kick.] **1831** Finn *Amer. Comic Annual* 157 **VT,** Out sailed this great he-devil [=a frog] from under the bank. By the living hoky, he was as large as a small-sized man! Such a straddle bug I never seed! **1853** Durivage *Life Scenes* 143 **MA,** Pump water is full of animalculae, and straddle bugs don't exist in pond water. **1856** *Peterson's Mag.* 30.47 **OH,** "Maybe you think Cal Godfrey, the great straddle-bug, looks better." . . "Calvin Godfrey is no more of a straddle-bug than you yourself are a straddlebug." **1859** (1968) Bartlett *Americanisms* 454, Straddle-Bug. The popular name for a beetle. **1867** Twain *Jumping Frog* 10 **CA,** If he even seen a straddle-bug start to go anywheres, he would bet you how long it would take him to get wherever he was going to, and if you took him up, he would foller that straddle-bug to Mexico. **1874** *Harper's New Mth. Mag.* 49.603, Oh, bury Bartholomew out in the woods,/ In a beautiful hole in the ground,/ Where the bumble-bees buzz and the woodpeckers sing / And the straddle-bugs tumble around. **1883** *Littell's Living Age* 159.438, It is touching to observe the intimate relations which the toad at once establishes with the "black bug," the "straddle bug," and the "striped bug, the saddest of the year." **1942** McAtee *Notes Thornton's Gloss.* [4], *Straddlebug.* . . The word is more or less generally used as a variant of the popular term "bug", meaning insects in general.

2 also *straddlebug plow:* **=straddle plow.**

1861 OH State Bd. Ag. *Annual Rept. for 1860* 72, Planted six quarts of Yellow Mad River corn . . , covered it with a "Straddle Bug." **1914** Whitson *Centennial Hist. Grant Co. IN* 1.84 (as of a1870), Some made a straddle bug by using a small forked sapling. A beam similar to a plow beam was inserted into this and a small shovel was bolted to each fork, with handles attached, the operator would straddle the furrow with this implement and the corn would be covered with dispatch. **1947** *Lima News* (OH) 8 Oct 19/2, *Public Sale.* . . Potato digger; straddle bug plow; double shovel plow. **1970** *DARE* (Qu. L18, *Kinds of plows*) Inf **OH95,** Straddlebug—shovels straddle rows of potatoes to cover with dirt.

3 An improvised tripod used to mark ownership of a piece of property.

1917 Garland *Son Middle Border* 303 **WI** (as of 1883), We . . set forth . . to mark the location of our claims with the "straddle-bugs." The straddle-bug . . was composed of three boards set together in tripod form and was used as . . a sign of occupancy. Its presence defended a claim against the next comer. **1948** *Range Riders Western* May 23 **TX,** Always before, the straddle bug had been a symbol of ownership, a pioneer's first notice to Nature that he had come to tame new land, to grow crops and make a home.

4 See quots. Cf **jitney** n **4**

1950 *Western Folkl.* 9.122 **nwOR** [Sawmill workers' speech], *Straddle-bug.* See *Jitney.* [*Ibid* 121, *Jitney.* A motor vehicle that straddles a load of lumber and picks up the load by means of flanges which slide under the ends of the blocks.] **1952** *Daily Inter Lake* (Kalispell MT) 29 Apr 1/6, *Prowler Saw: A straddle bug* nearly depositing its load of lumber on LaSalle road.

5 See quot.

1941 *LANE* Map 285 *(Baker's bread),* Terms for various types of cakes fried in deep fat. . . 1 inf, **eME coast,** Straddle bugs.

6 See quot.

1907 *DN* 3.201 **seNH,** *Straddlebug.* . . A woman with a mannish gait. "She's a regular straddle-bug."

straddlebug plow See **straddlebug 2**

straddle-deep See **straddle** n

straddle jack n

1 **=jack** n[1] **6.**

1969 *DARE* (Qu. L59, *An implement with an X-frame . . to hold firewood for sawing*) Inf **KY23,** Straddle jack.

2 **=straddle plow.**

1890 in 2008 (acc) Lexis–Nexis Legal Research *Patent Files* (Internet) **TX,** Among the objects in view is to provide a plow of cheap and simple construction and adapted to be converted into . . what is commonly known as a "straddle jack." **1913** Branigin *Hist. Johnson Co. IN* 212, The "grasshopper," a small side-bar plow, and later the "straddle jack," two small plows set as to straddle the row, were the first improvements upon the work of the hands in covering corn. **1940** Kennedy–Harlow *Schoolmaster* 229 **IN** (as of c1870), We dropped the seed corn in the crossings [of two furrows], and covered it either with a hoe or a plow with two shovels about ten inches apart, called a "straddle-jack." **1965** *Kokomo Tribune Kokomo Dispatch* (IN) 19 Aug 31/5, *Public Sale.* . . straddle jack plow. **1986** Pederson *LAGS Concordance* **ceMS,** 1 inf, Straddle jack—two sweeps; left no middle to bust; 1 inf, Straddle jack—plow; got weeds out of cotton.

3 See quot.

1991 *DARE* File **cID,** A straddle jack is a type of rock jack, used as a means of keeping a barbed wire fence tight in scab land (i.e., land with a thin layer of topsoil such that the fence posts can't be sunk more than a few inches into the ground).

straddle plow n Cf **straddlebug 2, straddle jack 2**

See quot 1876.

1857 in 2008 (acc) Lexis–Nexis Legal Research *Patent Files* (Internet) **PA,** Figure 1 is a straddle-plow and harrow, which is constructed by putting four pieces of wood . . together in the form of a diamond, with [a] beam . . through the center, underneath of which is attached the cornharrow . . going in front of the plows, pulverizing the ground, preparing it for the plows to follow. **1876** Knight *Amer. Mech. Dict.* 3.2414, *Straddle-plow.* A plow with two triangular, parallel shares, a little distance apart, and used for running on each side of a row of dropped corn, to cover the seed. **1893** *Atlanta Constitution* (GA) 15 Oct 24/4, If corn is to be put in the grain should follow at once; cover with a straddle plow of small capacity, as the grain should be covered very light. **1969** *DARE* (Qu. L25, *The implement used to clean out weeds and loosen the earth between rows of corn*) Inf **PA201,** Straddle plow.

stradways adv

Astride.

c1940 (1997) O'Neill *Story* 67 **sMO** (as of 1880s), All the girls rode sidewise—though few had sidesaddles. . . The shock of the first female riding "stradways" had not yet shaken the community. **1983** *MJLF* 9.1.58 **ceKY** (as of 1956), *Stradways* . . astride.

straggle bush n Also *straggly gooseberry*

A **gooseberry 1** (here: *Ribes divaricatum*).

1901 Jepson *Flora CA* 273, Straggly Gooseberry. . . Common in shaded cañons and flats from Southern California northward. **1938** Van Dersal *Native Woody Plants* 234, *Ribes divaricatum.* . . Straggly gooseberry. **1961** Thomas *Flora Santa Cruz* 193 **cwCA,** *G[rossularia] divaricata* [=*Ribes d.*] . . Straggly Gooseberry, Straggle Bush.

straggy adj Cf **stratty**

Straggly, unkempt.

1872 Tice *Over Plains* 44 **MO,** He [=a prairie dog] indeed resembles a fox squirrel, . . with a short, black, straggy-haired tail. **1909** *Trenton Eve. Times* (NJ) 27 Mar 3/2, The market for fowls ruled very firm. . . The bulk of the receipts, however, was of coarse and straggy stock, which . . had to be sold at inside figures. **1914** *Lincoln Daily Star* (NE) 1 May City Ed 8/3, It [=dandruff] not only starves the hair and makes it fall out, but it makes it stringy, straggy, dull[,] dry, brittle and lifeless. **1963** *Gettysburg Times* (PA) 7 Oct 7/4, My leaflet . . shows you how to overcome such annoyances as . . straggy hair and even stuck zippers. **1983** *MJLF* 9.1.58 **ceKY** (as of 1956), *Straggy headed* . . with mussed up, straggly, hair. **2004** *DARE* File—Internet **sMN,** This will be his last date if he is unshaved or straggy looking.

straight n

1 The truth; the facts—often in phr *the straight of it.* Cf **flat** n[1] **7**

1836 (1861) Tucker *Partisan Leader* 292 **VA,** You don't know what it's going to be; so I must tell you all the straight of it. **1863** (1864) Heard *Hist. Sioux War* 165 **MN,** I am in a hurry to get back, and tell my relatives the straight of it. **1900** Dix *Deacon Bradbury* 266, You've heared th' straight of it. **1905** *DN* 3.96 **nwAR,** *Straight of it.* . . The real situation, the exact truth. 'I haven't found out the straight of it yet.' Common. **1928** *Ruppenthal Coll.* **KS,** *The straight of it.* . . the truth; accurate statement of facts, etc. I want to get the straight of it before I come to any conclusions. We may never get the straight of it. **1951** Giles *Harbin's Ridge* 161 **KY,** I wanted to get the straight about this piece of land. **c1960** *Wilson Coll.* **csKY,** *Straight.* . . The truth, the exact story, "the straight of it." **1966** Barnes–Jensen *Dict. UT Slang* 40, *Straight of it* . . truth. **1967–68** *DARE* Tape **SC46,** I think maybe you bury it; I don't remember the straight of it; **WI22,** We'll get a horse and let's see you put some shoes on it, so we'll know whether you are telling us the straight of it or not. **1986** Pederson *LAGS Concordance,* 1 inf, **swGA,** I just don't think he told me the straight of it; 1 inf, **cAR,** I can't remember the straight of that thing. **1996** McDowell *Leaving Pipe Shop* 30 **AL** [Black], Crockett didn't last long at U.S. Pipe and Foundry, although I never have been able to learn the straight of why he left there to haul furniture. **2005** Thompson *Share No Secrets* 32 **WV,** She had some bad experience . . that people say gave her mind a turn, but I couldn't get the straight of it.

2 A cigarette. Cf **square** n[1] **B3**

[**1923** J. Manchon *Le Slang* 296 (OED2), *A straight = a straighter = a straight cut,* une cigarette en tabac de Virginie.] **1959** *Esquire* Nov. 70 [sic *OED2*—quot not found], *Straight* . . an ordinary cigarette. **1969**

DARE (Qu. DD6b, *Nicknames for cigarettes*) Inf **IN**75, Straights. **1972** Shafer *Dict. Prison Slang* 36 **TX**, *Straight*—a cigarette.

3 See **straight drive (transmission).**

4 See **straight gas.**

straight-billed curlew n
Either of two closely related birds:

a also *straight-bill:* =**marbled godwit.**

1813 (1824) Wilson *Amer. Ornith.* 7.30, Our gunners call it [=the marbled godwit] the *Straight-billed Curlew,* and sometimes the *Red Curlew.* **1844** DeKay *Zool. NY* 2.253, With us it [=the marbled godwit] is generally called the *Marlin,* and less frequently *Red Curlew, Straight-billed Curlew* and *Dough-bird.* **1880** *Forest & Stream* 15.4 **NJ,** Great marbled godwit. . . In New Jersey it is sometimes called the straight-billed curlew. **1923** U.S. Dept. Ag. *Misc. Circular* 13.58, Marbled Godwit. . . Vernacular Names. . . *In local use* . . straight-bill (Miss.); straight-billed curlew (Mass., N.Y., N.J., Va., N.C., S.C., Ill.) **2001** MD Ornith. Soc. *MD Yellowthroat* Mar–Apr 6 **eVA, eMD,** Now birds, that's somethin' else. Lot of them little sandpipers, we got all sorts. The big ones, the Straight-billed Curlew, they used to shoot and eat them.

b =**Hudsonian godwit.**

1923 U.S. Dept. Ag. *Misc. Circular* 13.59 **MA,** Hudsonian godwit. . . Vernacular Names. . . *In local use* . . straight-billed curlew, whiterump.

straight drive (transmission) n   Also *straight (transmission), straight shift (transmission), straight stick*   **chiefly Sth, S Midl**
A manual transmission on a vehicle; hence n *straight shift* the gearshift for a manual transmission.

1944 *Fresno Bee the Republican* (CA) 23 July [63]/2 (newspaperarchive.com), Of exclusive two-cylinder design, with a straight transmission, they give you power that sticks right to the task. **1950** *Abilene Reporter–News* (TX) 15 Sept [30]/2 (newspaperarchive.com), *46 Olds.* . . Straight shift. **1953** *Statesville Daily Rec.* (NC) 27 Feb classified advt sec [6]/5 (newspaperarchive.com), 1951 *Buick* Special 4-door, light gray with straight drive, radio, heater. **1986** Pederson *LAGS Concordance (Gearshift)* 4 infs, **AL, GA, TN,** Straight shift; 1 inf, **csTN,** Straight shift—floor shift; 1 inf, **cnAL,** Straight shift—on steering wheel; 1 inf, **cnAL,** Straight shift—on the floor. **1996** *DARE* File **SC,** My brother and his girlfriend were visiting this weekend, and she told me that she was sick of "straight drive" and wanted her next car to be an automatic; **KY,** In the mid and late 1950's in the Louisville (KY) area, a manual transmission was a 'stick,' 'stick shift' or 'straight stick'; **NC,** In Piedmont North Carolina in the 1950's and 1960's the opposite of automatic (automobile transmission) was straight drive; **NC,** I grew up in the Blue Ridge Mountains of NC, and have always heard a manual transmission referred to as a "straight transmission," or oftentimes simply "a straight"; **MS,** The first term I ever knew for a manual transmission . . was "straight shift." . . The normal term in Mississippi in the '50s was "straight shift"; **OH,** Growing up in southern Ohio during the 1950's, an area influenced by Appalachian transplants, I did hear "straight drive" occasionally . . [for a] manual transmission. **2003** *DARE* File—Internet **GA,** This car was designed to be a straight shift and the automatic suffers from that; **GA,** Ours has straight drive transmission. . . I prefer an automatic transmission; **VA,** [He] . . drives a Ford Probe with a straight shift; **VA,** In the old days . . the straight drive would outrun an automatic; **TN,** Any stock automatic or straight shift transmission; **NV,** In 1958, when I had barely learned to drive with an automatic transmission, my father insisted I run an errand in his straight-transmission '57 Chevy; **NC,** He picked up on the fact that I had ordered a clutch cable and obviously had a straight-drive vehicle.

straight gas n   Also *straight (gasoline)*   **chiefly C Atl, VA**
See Map   Cf **low-test**
Regular (as opposed to high-octane) gasoline.

1910 *Commerce Jrl.* (TX) [21 Jan 3]/3 (newspaperarchive.com), The gasoline is doped with picric acid or some other high explosive, and with the increased power thus obtained the boats are able to win races they would lose if ordinary straight gasoline were used. **1923** *Indianapolis Sun. Star* (IN) 28 Jan sec 5 6/1, [Advt:] One of the several outstanding advantages of a benzol blend (such as Crystal-Pep) over straight gasoline is the absence of "carbon knock." **1927** *Davenport Democrat & Leader* (IA) 11 Nov 26/7 **DC,** He will be counseled that he should . . use "doped" gas, or high-test gas, or straight gas. . . Straight gas—the common, or garden variety—has many staunch advocates. **1947** *Pottstown Mercury* (PA) 11 Aug 8, Both ethyl and straight gas is sold at the Merit service station. **1965–70** *DARE* (Qu. N15a, . . *Gasoline* . .

cheaper kind) Infs **DC**8, 12, **DE**1, **MD**25, **MS**59, **PA**154, **VA**30, 84, 96, Straight; **MD**20, **NJ**56, **VA**27, Straight gas.

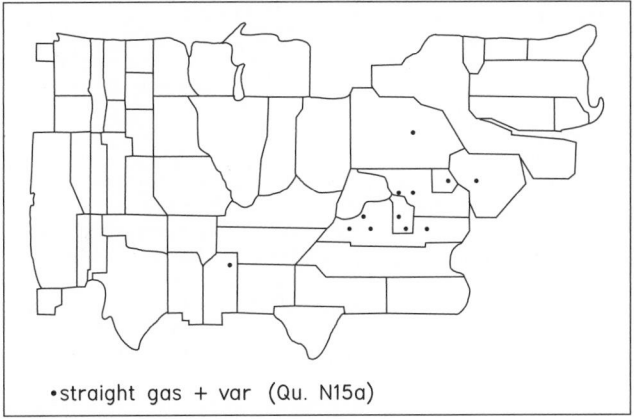

•straight gas + var (Qu. N15a)

straight hard wind   See **straight wind**

straight, out   See **straight, right out**

straight pen n   [Perh orig applied to a pen with a *straight pen-holder;* cf quot 1895]   **chiefly Nth, N Midl, West**   See Map
=**dip pen.**

[**1895** (1969) Montgomery Ward *Catalogue* 114, Straight Penholders, fluted cedar handles, with binding tips, for school use. Per dozen. . . \$0.03.] **1923** *WI Rapids Daily Tribune* (WI) 16 Feb 1/1 **csWI,** The edict of the principal has gone forth that fountain pens shall supercede the straight pen in the hands of pupils. **1942** *Lowell Sun & Citizen-Leader* (MA) 12 Mar 11/3, Using a plain office straight pen and ink, and a piece of cardboard he found in the hangar, he turned out two [posters]. **1955** *Albuquerque Jrl.* (NM) 3 Sept 1/8, Meanwhile, the scratchy, smearing generations-old straight pens will continue in use at Albuquerque [in the Post Office]. **1965–70** *DARE* (Qu. JJ10a, *Different kinds of pens and pencils*) 22 Infs, **chiefly Nth, N Midl, West,** Straight pens; **CT**33, Straight pens—one you dip; **IL**17, Straight pens—pen with point that you dip; **MD**2, Straight pens—used in childhood—pen that is dipped in ink; **NH**14, Straight pens—dipped into inkwell; **PA**81, Straight pens—in an inkwell. [14 of 27 Infs comm type 4, 8 comm type 5, 16 mid aged, 11 old] **1976** *Syracuse Herald–American* (NY) 1 Feb 48/4, He [=a collector of antique tools and household items] said many students do not even know what a straight pen is.

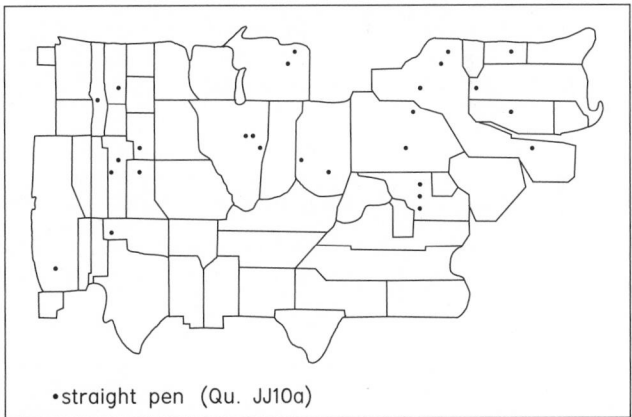

•straight pen (Qu. JJ10a)

straight, right out adv phr, adj phr   Also *out straight*   **NEng, NY**
As fast or hard as possible, full tilt; going or working at the limit of one's capacity, very busy.

1929 *Forest & Stream* 99.16 **MA,** In a short time we were going down the road right out straight, Cox in the lead and Lydia and E. Pinkham [= horses] close behind. **1942** *Fitchburg Sentinel* (MA) 12 Sept 8/5, This year, the [bowling] alleys might be able to handle about 8000 bowlers, but they'll be right out straight doing it. **1947** Gould *House Jacob Built* 21 **ME,** He was never in a hurry. He couldn't stand people who were "right out straight," or "all heifered up." **1947** Coffin *Yankee Coast* 304 **ME,** There followed a hot pursuit across the island, with the baby gull right out straight, going as fast as his short, stiff legs could carry him. **1959** *Portsmouth Herald* (NH) 29 Oct 6/1, "Brother!" exclaimed Doc this morning, "We are out straight. This game is a sellout. They are pestering me for tickets and I am all out." **1960** *VT Hist.* 28.220, To be right out straight. (To be hard pressed with work. From racing horses with fore and hind legs extended 'right out straight.') **1965** *Daily Kennebec Jrl.* (Augusta ME) 29 July 2/1, Weary firefighters chased many small fires in the Augusta area. . . "They've been going right out straight lately. These boys are tired." **1975** Gould *ME Lingo* 60, In late August and early September the *corn shop* was right *out straight.* *Ibid* 198, Anybody bustling about, full of business, too active to do anything else, is right *out straight.* The phrase comes from teaming oxen; as they lean into their yoke and strain every muscle the chain connecting them to the load is right out straight. **2004** Graves *Mallets* 186 **eME coast,** If he needed cash, it's not like he had many other ways of getting it. He's already working right out straight. **2009** in 2010 DARE File—Internet **ceNY,** I had never heard the phrase "out straight" until I moved to Hoosick Falls, NY. . . [L]et me give you an example: "I have a full-time job, I'm writing 2 ebooks, trying to get my new apartment arranged, and keeping up this blog—I'm out straight!" **2010** *Ibid* **neMA,** It's a busy life: We run an organic CSA farm in Rowley, Mass., which keeps me right out straight from May to October.

straights intj   [*straight* + **-s** suff²]

A call used in marble play; see quots.

1922 *DN* 5.188, Straights. . . =Vence ye crooks. [*Ibid* 186 **KY,** If the boy who first knocked the "man" near the edge first cries out "Vence ye crooks," the next player must shoot at it in a diametric line.] **1926** *AmSp* 2.66 [Playground argot], Hear the chatter that comes out of a marble-shooting ring. "Straights," "vent," "knuckle down," "three knuckles down," "in the country," "roundings," "vent everything," the youngsters cry. **1955** *PADS* 23.31 **cwTN,** Straights. . . A call requiring that the player shoot from the required position without taking advantage of "crooks" . . or "rounds."

straights n

A marble game; see quots.

1958 *PADS* 29.41 **WI,** Straights. . . A marble game. **c1970** Wiersma *Marbles Terms, Straights.* . . Game in which players take turns shooting at the opponent's marble.

straight shift (transmission), straight stick (or transmission)   See **straight drive (transmission)**

straight town   See **town ball 2b**

straight up, not to know   v phr   For addit varr see quots   **scattered, but rare Atlantic**   See Map   Cf **B from (a) bull's foot, not to know**

To be stupid or ignorant; to lack common sense.

1891 *Galveston Daily News* (TX) 21 Aug 4/5, He had been down there in the brush and cactus until he did not know "straight up." **1898** in 1921 Thorp *Songs Cowboys* 97 **NM, TX,** Though he didn't know "straight" up about a cow. **1905** *DN* 3.66 **eNE,** Straight up. Phrase used in "didn't know straight up," meaning "knew nothing at all." [*Ibid* 85 **nwAR,** Know straight up. . . To be clever, to be shrewd. 'They thought they knew straight up.' Common.] **1916** *DN* 4.348 **KS** (as of 1896), Straight-up. . . The simplest thing; anything. . . "He doesn't know straight-up." **1927** *AmSp* 3.169 **SW** [Cowboy speech], If one [=a cowboy] gets lost he "don't know straight up." **1929** *AmSp* 5.74 **NE** [Cattle

country talk], When playing cards. . . if one plays stupidly, he "don't know straight up." **1954** *Harder Coll.* **cwTN,** Know straight up. . . "He don't know straight up." Of a person who seems to be stupid. **1965–70** DARE (Qu. JJ15b, *Sayings about a person who seems to you very stupid: "He doesn't know _____."*) 42 Infs, **scattered, but rare Atlantic,** Straight up; **IL**11, **WI**30, From straight up; **AR**13, **NE**11, Straight up from nothing; **MO**11, Nothing from straight up; [**TN**53, Straight up and down]. **1985** Ladwig *How to Talk Dirty* 26 **Ozarks,** He don't know straight up from apple butter. **2002** in 2008 DARE File—Internet **PA,** I . . don't know straight up about computing or burning.

straight wake, make a   v phr   [Transf from naut use]

To go directly over the straightest, quickest course.

1840 *Madison Express* (WI) [11 Apr 4]/2 (newspaperarchive.com) **MO,** The husband [was] seated in front . . driving a pair of skeleton bobtails, and making a straight wake for the western country! **1852** Abbott *Marco Paul's Voyages VT* 23 **Nantucket MA,** We would cut across the country . . till we got to another stage route, and then make a straight wake, till we got to New Bedford. **1853** Hammett *Stray Yankee in TX* 416, A sailor had escaped from some man-of-war at Savannah; fearful of being retaken . . he made a *straight wake* up the river for Augusta. **1868** Longfellow *New Engl. Tragedies* 66 **MA,** Now let us make a straight wake for the tavern. **1883** *Daily NV State Jrl.* (Reno) 17 Aug [3]/2 (newspaperarchive.com), The stranger did not stop to argue the question but made a straight wake for the depot. **1916** Macy–Hussey *Nantucket Scrap Basket* 147, "*Straight Wake*"—A bee line; as "the lad made a straight wake for home." **1942** ME Univ. *Studies* 56.43, To make a straight wake is to go directly and without delay.

straight wind   n   Also *straight hard wind*   **esp Cent**   See Map

A violent or destructive wind that moves in one direction (as opposed to a tornado).

1882 *Star & Sentinel* (Gettysburg PA) 28 June [2]/4 (newspaperarchive.com) **IA,** The centre of the storm was at Independence, where it broke in great fury at 5 P.M., blowing from the northwest a straight wind without the tornado funnel. **1903** *Chillicothe Constitution* (MO) 11 Sept 1/1, The north part of the city got off with a heavy straight wind and rain that came down in sheets. **1933** *AmSp* 8.4.50 **NE** [Pioneer vocab], Often the lands were swept by *straight winds,* strong and continuous. **1960** *Lincoln Eve. Jrl. & NE State Jrl.* (NE) 16 June City Ed 1/1, Many people think that only a tornado can cause this type of severe damage. . . But a 'straight' wind can cause terrific damage. **c1961** *McDavid Coll.* **OK,** Straight wind—as opposed to a twister. **1965–70** DARE (Qu. B17, *A destructive wind that blows straight*) 13 Infs, **esp Cent,** (Hard) straight wind; **AR**47, **OK**1, 18, 25, Straight hard wind; (Qu. B18, . . *Special kinds of wind*) Infs **CA**5, **MO**3, 11, (Hard) straight wind; **MO**35, Straight hard wind. [19 of 21 Infs comm type 4 or 5] **2003** DARE File—Internet **FL,** The tornado . . is a rotational wind. The other, more predominant wind from a thunderstorm is called a downburst, which is a straight wind in Florida.

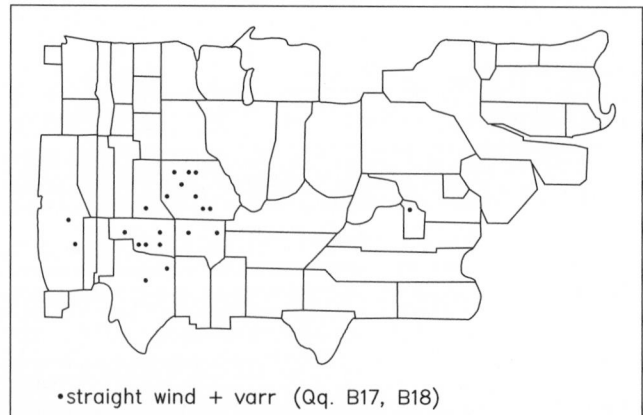

•straight wind + varr (Qq. B17, B18)

strain   n, v   [Cf *OED2 streen(e,* obs forms of *strain*]   Pronc-spp *strean, streen*   Similarly nouns *streaner, streenings* Cf *drean, dreen* (at **drain** v, n¹ **A1**)

Std senses, var forms.

1779 in 1907 *PA Archives* 6th ser 12.623, To a Milk Streaner, . . 5 6. **1906** *Amer. Mag.* 62.172 **ME,** She got up at five A.M., . . streened the milk . . an' fed the shoats. **1912** Green *VA Folk-Speech* 423, *Strean, v.*

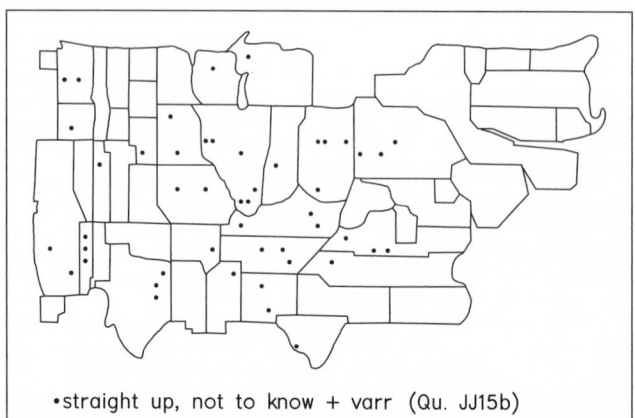

•straight up, not to know + varr (Qu. JJ15b)

For *strain.* To "strean milk." **1914** *DN* 4.80 **ME, nNH,** *Streen, n.* Strain. *Streenin's, n. pl.* Dirty milk or refuse.

stram v   chiefly NEng

1 To thrash or flail about. [Cf *EDD stram* v.[1] 2 "To strike or thrust violently."]

1828 (1970) Webster *Amer. Dict., Stram.* . . To spread out the limbs; to sprawl. [Webster: *Local and vulgar.*] **1890** *DN* 1.19 **seNH,** *Stram:* flourish the limbs. . . 'to stram about in bed' = flounder, kick about. **1927** *AmSp* 3.138 **eME,** A young child crying and displaying temper was said to "kick and stram." This word *stram* means in older English "to recoil with violence and noise," which gives a vivid picture of a child in a tantrum, screaming, kicking, hitting its head, throwing about its arms.

2 To walk vigorously; to strut; to gallivant. [Cf *EDD stram* v.[3] 2 "To walk in a rude, noisy manner."]

1856 Whitcher *Bedott Papers* 306 **cNY,** [She] strammed right across the room and sot down. **1869** Stowe *Oldtown Folks* 142 **NEng,** You might jest as well give young turkey chicks to the old gobbler, and let him stram off in the mowin' grass with 'em. **1890** *DN* 1.19 **seNH,** *Stram:* flourish the limbs. . . 'to go stramming along the street,' 'to stram about the room,' that is, to stride with ado and bustle. **1933** Miller *Lamb in His Bosom* 130 **GA,** A wife has no business a-strammin' around over the country. **1941** *Sheboygan Press* (WI) 18 Sept 17/2, [Advt:] *Children's Cotton Flannel Sleepers* . . with double-soled feet that can take all the "stramming around" that goes on! **1970** (1971) Cooper *One Dragon* 83 **NEng,** Nowadays girls were so independent that carrying their necessities in flight bags over their shoulders, they went stramming off to foreign parts.

stram n

1 A vigorous walk. [**stram** v 2]

1869 Stowe *Oldtown Folks* 567 **NEng,** I hed sech a stram this mornin', 'n' hain't hed nothin' but a two-cent roll.

2 A child. [Cf *EDD stram* sb.[3] 1 "A big person; a 'tripe' of a lad."]

1916 Macy–Hussey *Nantucket Scrap Basket* 167, *"Strams"*—Children; not common, but apparently authentic.

strand n[1]   [Scots, nEngl dial *strand* a stream, channel] **FL, sGA**

A long, narrow, marshy area, often heavily wooded.

1915 *Brooklyn Museum Qrly.* 2.239 **Okefenokee GA** (as of 1912), Between the two islands lies a mile-wide, watery stretch that goes by the somewhat misleading name of 'strand;' and when we set forth into the bog, it soon became of such a depth that the bearhounds with us half waded and half swam. . . We frequently sank almost waist-deep into the holes of the uneven, root-entangled trail, or tottered here and there across a quivering bed of floating sphagnum. After consuming more than an hour in our struggle through the 'strand,' we emerged gradually upon the *terra firma* of Honey Island. **1971** Craighead *Trees S. FL* 126, Included under the term "tree islands" are hammocks, bay heads . . cypress strands . . buttonwood strands . . and pop ash heads. **1975** Newell *If Nothin' Don't Happen* 118 **nwFL,** A strand is a long stretch of cypress timber and can be from a hundred yards to a mile wide and several miles long, like big Fahkahatchee Strand. **1975** Natl. Audubon Soc. *Corkscrew* 6 **FL,** The stand of cypress trees here is in the form commonly known as a "strand." This means that the trees occur in a long, narrow, and somewhat open stand. **2004** *DARE* File—Internet **swFL,** In places, limestone has dissolved, forming elongated sloughs or channels, which have accumulated deep organic soils. These channels or sloughs have been colonized by cypress and other trees, creating swamp forests that stand out on the horizon in contrast to the open prairies and pinelands that occupy the sterile veneer of marl soil, which is on top of the remaining limestone. The local term for these linear swamps is "strand."

strand n[2]   FL

A face cord (of wood); see quot 1954.

1896 *DN* 1.425, *Strand:* a pile of fixed dimensions of *strand wood. Strand wood:* pine wood cut into lengths of about 32 inches for burning in locomotives. Fla. **1942** Hench Coll. **FL,** [A] graduate student told me that at Clearwater, Florida, people call a load, or a small load, of wood, a *strand* of wood. **1954** *AmSp* 29.238 **FL,** The word *strand* is used in Florida to designate a measure of wood equivalent to approximately a third of a cord, or to a pile four feet high, eight feet long, and sixteen to twenty-two inches wide. The term is widely known in Florida.

2004 *DARE* File—Internet **nFL** (as of 1940s), I remember that it took about three or four hours for the two of us to cut and split a "strand" of firewood. . . We loaded it up in the wagon, sold it, and delivered it for the grand sum of $.75 cents to $125 [sic] per strand!

strand snipe n

=sanderling.

1876 *Forest & Stream* 7.149 **Long Is. NY,** The strand or surf snipe . . are good eating. They feed close to the water along the beach where the waves break. **1883** *Trenton Times* (NJ) 21 Dec [2]/3 (newspaperarchive.com), Last Summer two taxidermists settled themselves at Long Beach, N.J. . . Fifteen cents apiece was given for terns, ten cents for strand snipe.

strang   See string

strange adj

1 Coming from another place (for a specified purpose); visiting. [Cf *OED2 strange* a. 2 "Belonging to some other place or neighbourhood" c1290 →] Cf **stranger**

1869 *Harper's New Mth. Mag.* 38.527 **Nantucket MA,** First Day a great many world's people [=non-Quakers] were at meeting on account of the strange Friends [=Friends from England]. **1872** in 1983 *PADS* 70.52 **ce,sePA,** Father Mother & I went to Quarterly Meeting at Abington today had speaking by a strange man from long Island & a strange woman from N York. **1968** *Budget* (Sugarcreek OH) 18 July 2/6 **OH,** David P. Troyer church was at Sam Yoder's today and will be at Em. Raber's in 2 weeks. Strange preacher was Pre. Robert R. Troyer.

2 in phr *make strange (of):* To feel or affect surprise; to be or act surprised at; to pretend ignorance of. [Cf *OED2 strange* a. 13 1456-7 →]

1660 in 1860 Gardiner *Hist. Pequot War* 28 **MA,** So they wakened me as they thought, but I was not asleep, and told me the story, but I made strange of the matter. **1855** Ward *Female among Mormons* 66, I woke from this state to ask for my child, and they made strange of it—laughed, and said I was beside myself—wanted to know what made me imagine such an absurdity. **1856** Adams *Justice By-Ways* 20 **SC,** If you please, gentlemen, . . my house is highly respectable—highly respectable (don't make strange of me tending my own door!) I assure you gentlemen. **1865** *Harper's New Mth. Mag.* 30.268 **WI,** Don't understand, eh? As though leaving me at the Half-way House wasn't enough, but you must send back by D— 'to enquire if you hadn't left something!' and now make strange, as though you didn't know it! **c1950** in 2004 *DARE* File—Internet **IN,** Somebody of course, is ready to make strange of the fact that a man should be buried in water but he is not left there very long for verse 5 says, "planted and raised in the likeness of the resurrection of Christ." **1953** Randolph–Wilson *Down in Holler* 263 **Ozarks,** *Make strange.* . . To be amazed or astonished. Nancy Clemens, of Springfield, Mo., heard a farmer say, "I sure made strange when they showed me them bugs through the microscope." The sentence "she made strange of me" may mean "she didn't recognize me" or "she seemed surprised at my appearance."

3 Shy; afraid of strangers; hence v phr *make strange* to be or act shy or timid. [*SND strange* adj. 2 "shy, self-conscious among strangers, esp. of children. Gen. Sc. Obs. exc. dial. in Eng."] **scattered, but esp PA** Cf **make** v[1] **C17a**

1899 (1912) Green *VA Folk-Speech* 422, *Strange.* . . Shy; reserved; retiring. **1910** *Daily Independent* (Monessen PA) 17 Nov [4]/1 (newspaperarchive.com), [Advt:] Don't make strange with us! Come, see what we have to offer for your benefit! **1940** Hench Coll. **eVA** (as of 1870–1900), To make strange = to be hesitant or reluctant. **1957** *Sat. Eve. Post Letters* **swWI,** We always spoke of a child "making strange"—being afraid of strangers. **1984** *DARE* File **csPA,** Strange—adj., "afraid of strangers". "That dog's a little strange." "She's not strange at all". **1993** *Ibid* **cwPA,** Strange—'afraid of strangers.' "Is your child strange?" *Ibid* **cwPA** (as of 1950s), "He's making strange." For a child (toddler age) retreating from advancing unfamiliar adult. **2004** *Ibid* **Philadelphia PA** (as of 1940s), My mother would say of a baby who cried when approached by anyone other than its own mother, "He's in that stage where he makes strange." **2005** *NADS Letters* **RI,** When talking about her first great-grandchild, she often remarks how friendly and pleasant he is, even with strangers—"so friendly, not strange at all." Everyone in my family knows that "strange," when used to describe kids, means "shy," . . but I have found that many of my friends (from outside Rhode Island) don't understand it. *Ibid* **NH,** In early 1982, when I was visiting relatives in New Hampshire with my seven month old, my relatives complimented me on my son: "He's not strange at all!" The phrase was translated for me as "He's not shy with strangers at all". *Ibid* **sPA,** If the child is shy or doesn't want to speak or interact with someone new, they would say, "She's strange." . . My Mom is 73 and my aunt is about 60. *Ibid* **csIL,** The term "make strange" used by adults in our Dutch/German farming community . . is used specifically to describe a baby/toddler who is shy around others. **2007** *Ibid* **cMN,** She said her daughter was "making strange" when the people would talk to her. Everyone at the table was confused. She later realized that she learned the expression from her grandparents who were both Russian.

strange bee n   Also *strange fly*   Cf **news bee**

1891 *AN&Q* 7.81 **IA,** In this part of the United States there is a small, brown and yellow-banded fly, about one-third the size of a common honey-bee, known as the "Strange Fly" or "Strange Bee;" it being affirmed that his appearance is a forerunner of strange and startling news.

strange floater n

A **freshwater clam** (here: *Strophitus undulatus*).

1982 U.S. Fish & Wildlife Serv. *Fresh-Water Mussels* 2.48, Strange floater. . . *Strophitus undulatus.* . . Shell brown, sometimes with green rays. **1992** Cummings–Mayer *Field Guide Freshwater Mussels MW* 82, Squawfoot. . . Other common names—Strange floater, sloughfoot, creeper.

strange fly   See **strange bee**

stranger n   esp PA   Cf **strange 1**

A visitor, guest.

1869 *Harper's New Mth. Mag.* 38.527, [When I was in Ohio was just when the English Friends, Jonathan and Hannah Purley, were in the country. We met them at Marlborough Quarterly Meeting.] *Ibid* 528, I . . asked Jemima if she would not like some lemon-puddings [for the honored guests]. 'Thy apple-pies and rice-puddings are nice, dear,' I said; 'but Hannah Purley and Jonathan are such strangers, we might go a little out of the common way.' **1872** in 1983 *PADS* 70.53 **ce,sePA,** The strangers expect to visit all the meetings composing this Quarterly Meeting. **1874** *Ibid,* Grand Mother had 15 or 16 strangers to dinner. **1882** (1971) Gibbons *PA Dutch* 390, "We're getting strangers, and I was fetched." (They are expecting company at our house, and they sent for me to come home.) **1899** (1912) Green *VA Folk-Speech* 422, *Stranger.* . . One not belonging to the house; a guest; a visitor. **1907** (1970) Martin *Betrothal* 108 **sePA,** We're getting strangers Thursdays and we've made out to clean the kitchen to-morrow. **1983** *PADS* 70.53 **ce,sePA** (as of c1870), *Stranger.* . . Any person outside of one's immediate circle. The term carries no negative connotation; it could be applied to a member of a family no longer living at home. **2004** *DARE* File **sePA,** In the newspaper *The Budget* you still see the words *strangers,* or the dialectal *Fremmi,* or German *Fremde* used to mean 'visitors.' It doesn't imply strangeness, just the fact that they are guests, whether already acquainted or not.

strangleweed n   Also *strangle vine*   [*OED2* 1863 →]   =dodder.

1898 Britton–Brown *Illustr. Flora* 3.27, *Cuscuta* [spp]. . . Known as Dodder, or Strangle-weed. **1914** Georgia *Manual Weeds* 324, Clover Dodder. . . *Other English names:* Love-vine, Strangle Weed [etc.] **1951** *PADS* 15.38 **TX,** Cuscutaceae . . Love vine; strangle-weed [etc.]. **1967** *DARE* Wildfl QR (Wills–Irwin) Pl.34A Inf **TX44,** Plant is called strangleweed and love vine; grows on *cadillo* and purple nightshade. **1968** *DARE* (Qu. S21, . . *Weeds . . that are a trouble in gardens and fields*) Inf **PA118,** Strangleweed. **1970** Correll *Plants TX* 1255, Additional vernacular names [for *Cuscuta* spp] . . are "angel's hair" . . "strangle vine." **1971** Dodge *100 Desert Wildflowers* 56, Field dodder—choisy, lovevine, strangleweed, devil's hair.

strangth, strank   See **strength**

strap fern n   [From the long, narrow leaves]

A fern of the genus *Campyloneurum,* usu *C. phyllitidis.* For other names of var spp see **hart's tongue 2**

1929 *Amer. Fern Jrl.* 19.114 **FL,** The polypody covered the whole fallen trunk with its arching streamers, flanked at either end by a beautiful plant of the strap fern. **1938** Small *Ferns SE States* 85, *C[ampyloneurum] Phyllitidis.* . . The hammocks of Florida possess many kinds of ferns that would not be recognized as such from their leaves. . . This strap-fern is one of the more common ones of this type. **1975** Natl. Audubon Soc. *Corkscrew* 10, Strap fern (*Campyloneuron phyllitidis*). . . To those accustomed to the ferns of more northern places, the long sword-like leaves do not look like ferns at all. **2004** *DARE* File—Internet **FL,** Narrow strap-fern (*Campyloneurum angustifolium*). . . Tailed strap-fern (*Campyloneurum costatum*). . . Due to its similarity to the common strap fern (*C. phyllitidis*), tailed strap-fern is often overlooked.

strap oil n   Also *strop oil*   [Cf *EDD* strap oil (at *strap* sb.[1] 1)]   Cf **stirrup oil, strop ~**

A beating or whipping; also treated as a tangible item used as the basis of a practical joke; see quots.

1846 *Yale Lit. Mag.* 11.172, White lamp black, soft soap molds, strap oil and doves' milk . . were among the various articles which he inquired for. **1865** *Herald & Torch-Light* (Hagerstown MD) 5 Apr [5]/1 (newspaperarchive.com), On this day [=April 1]. . . a knowing boy will despatch a younger brother . . to the cobblers for a little *strap oil.* **1875** Lewis *Quad's Odds* 381, Old maids jabbed at him with umbrellas, merchants flung pound weights at him, shoemakers dosed him with strap oil. **1887** Hazeltine *Early Hist. Ellicott NY* 168, The shoemakers finally missed their chestnuts and learning that Ira and Niles had taken some of them, coaxed them into the shop and administered "strap oil" in dangerous doses. **1903** *Scandia Jrl.* (KS) [20 Mar 6]/2 (newspaperarchive.com), Bur Oak sports amuse themselves these dull days by sending small boys to borrow "strop oil" and left handed monkey krenches [sic]. **1907** *DN* 3.201 **seNH,** Strap-oil. . . A whipping. It was once, if not now, a favorite joke among shoemakers to send boys from one shoeshop to another for strap-oil. **1921** *DN* 5.95, Strap-oil. A boy is sent for ten cents worth, and the strap is given him more or less gently. **1932** in 2003 *DARE* File—Internet **IN** [*Warsaw Daily Times* (IN) 16 Jan], "Strap oil" was administered to all new frequenters at Ed Ettinger's harness shop. **1965–70** *DARE* (Qu. HH14, *Ways of teasing a beginner or inexperienced person—for example, by sending him for a 'left-handed monkey wrench': "Go get me _____."*) Infs **IN82, NY**1, 219, **OH**37, **VA**50, Strap oil; **NJ**2, Strap oil—from woodworking factory in town; **NY**52, Strap oil—then he would be supposed to get a beating from his father; **NY**70, Strap oil—then they got a whipping with a belt—for kids; **NY**88, Strap oil—when he went after it, he got strapped; **OH**95, Strap oil—on a farm: a "greener" is sent to get it; he is worked over with a strap by the crew he is sent to get it from; **OR**3, Strap oil—a spanking. **1975** Gould *ME Lingo* 280, *Strap oil*—A spanking, as done by a kindly father to his wayward son with a razor strop or a bit of harness. Sometimes called "harness oil." But in addition to that, a fool's errand. Just as people have been sent to get a left-handed monkey wrench and a pail of steam, boys underfoot have been sent to the blacksmith shop for some *strap oil.* **1984** Wilder *You All Spoken Here* 49 **Sth,** A dose of strop oil is applied with a razor strap or a leather belt. **2004** *DARE* File—Internet, From the attitude you have displayed here, young lady . . I think you could use a good dose of strop oil. **2007** Baker *Adult Children* 89, I was like 3 or 4 years. . . and his favorite little saying was, "I'll give you a dose of strap oil." And he took his belt and folded it over and whacked us a couple of good ones with it.

strap oyster n

A long **oyster B1** that grows in mud.

1881 Ingersoll *Oyster-Industry* 249, Strap-oyster. . . The long, slender form which grows in mud.

stratty adj   Cf **straggy**

Of one's hair; unkempt.

1952 *Tucson Daily Citizen* (AZ) 21 June 16/4, You mean you don't know what a stratty head is? Nell does. . . "In my neck of the woods down in Arkansas, stratty is such a common expression I never dreamed Mr. Webster wasn't personally acquainted with same. The term is usually associated with a head of hair that hasn't been on friendly terms with a comb 'n brush over a period of time.—Tousled, bushy,—Stratty, if you please, sir!" **1983** *MJLF* 9.1.58 **ceKY** (as of 1956), *Straggy headed* . . with mussed up, straggly, hair. *Stratty headed* . . same. **2003** *DARE* File—Internet **Charlotte NC,** It is never unusual for us to set an extra plate at dinner or find a few stratty-headed teenage boys asleep on our rec room floor on Saturday morning.

stravage v   [Scots dial]

To wander aimlessly.

1959 *VT Hist.* 27.161 **cn,neVT,** Stravage around. . . To bustle about. Rare. Orleans. **2002** in 2003 (acc) Lexis–Nexis Legal Research *Federal Case Law: Court of Appeals: Ninth Circuit* (Internet) **CA,** The statute speaks with enough clarity to permit . . one to stop with its own words, rather than undertaking to stravage in a wilderness of possible legislative purposes.   **2003** *DARE* File—Internet, They [=the Amish] stravage along the highways at night with no lights or reflectors and then bitch about the traffic passing them.

straw n

1   also *pine straw;* as mass noun: The **needles 1** of a pine or other conifer, esp the dried fallen leaves; rarely used as count noun.   **chiefly S Atl, Gulf States, TX**   See Map

1825 in 1829 *S. Agriculturist* 2.260 **SC,** There is nothing in the southern country more abundant; at least the materials with which to make it [=manure]: nor can we be ever in want of them, until *black-jack* leaves and *pine-straw* become scarce.   **1852** *De Bow's Rev.* 12.536 **Sth,** One of the best methods . . is to shade the whole grounds of the orchard with straw—wheat, oat, or pine straw.   **1856** Olmsted *Journey Slave States* 321 **NC,** There were occasionally young long-leaved pines: . . the leaves, or *straw,* as its foliage is called here, long, graceful, and lustrous.   **1908** *DN* 3.357 **eAL, wGA,** Pine-straw. . . The fallen needles or leaves of pine trees.   **1929** *AmSp* 5.19 **Ozarks,** *Pine straw.* . . Dead pine needles lying on the ground.   **1939** FWP *Guide NC* 277, Juniper tea made from steeped cedar "straw," was once a common beverage in swamp lumber camps and was believed to give immunity from malaria.   **1941** *Nature Mag.* 34.139, Throughout the range of the longleaf pine from extreme southeastern Virginia to Florida and southern Alabama, straws [is the word used for its leaves]. This term is applied chiefly in the collective sense, as straw, and the fallen leaves of the pine are used for the bedding of domestic animals, for packing, and for other things for which grain straw is employed in regions where it is plentiful.   **1946** *PADS* 6.23 **ceNC,** *Pine straw.* . . Pine needles.   **1965–70** *DARE* (Qu. T6, *The pointed leaves that fall from pine trees*) 75 Infs, **chiefly S Atl, Gulf States, TX,** Pine straw; **AL**30, **FL**49, **GA**35, **NC**21, 33, 79, 81, **SC**53, Straw [*DARE* Ed: 23 of these Infs specified fallen needles.]; (Qu. M19, *A place for keeping carrots, turnips, potatoes, and so on over the winter*) Inf **LA**22, You make a pit like, and line it with pine straw and put your potatoes in it.   **1966–69** *DARE* Tape **FL**6, They'd put pine straw in here, put the potatoes in there, and then put the dirt on real good all over; **FL**47, He got pine straw and all kinds of trash and put it in there very deep in between the rows [of pineapples]; **NC**24, One day I saw him [= a quail] . . in just nothing but light straw, pine straw, underneath some trees; **SC**46, Everybody used pine straw in the lots, horse lots and cow lots; **GA**51, It burned the straws out of the tops of them trees, them's the straw, didn't leave no straws.   **1968–70** *DARE* FW Addit **GA**25, Pine needles are still on the tree; pine straw is the dried needles on the ground; **NJ,** Pine tags or shadows—pine straw, branches of pine needles to cover vegetable beds in winter. [FW: Speaker built such beds in Virginia.]   **1992** Kincaid *Crossing Blood* 199 **nwFL** (as of 1950s), The ground was padded with red pine straw.   **2008** *DARE* File—Internet **FL,** [Advt:] *You'll Like Doing Business With Us* . . Clean, Fresh, Quality Pine Straw! . . Overnight Delivery of Pine Straw in the Southeast U.S.!

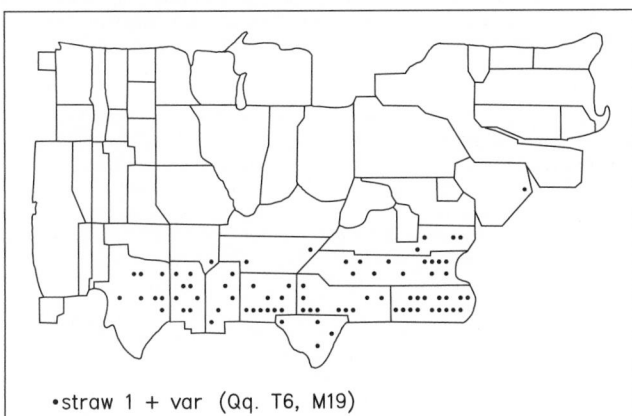

•straw 1 + var (Qq. T6, M19)

2   See **straw boss.**

straw barn   See **straw shed**

straw bass   n   Cf **strawberry bass 1**

Any of var centrarchid fish, esp **largemouth bass** or **crappie.**

1875 *MA Ploughman & New Engl. Jrl. Ag.* 25 Dec 1/7 **nOH,** Fishing with some other boys . . with 'bob and sinker' for 'pumpkin seed' and 'straw-bass,' I happened to be behind on the score.   **1876** *Forest & Stream* 6.266 **NE,** We . . saw a great many fish "in nests" that I called

black bass, but Arnold claimed they were "straw bass."   **1877** Hallock *Sportsman's Gaz.* 323, Straw Bass; Rock Bass; Calico Bass; Goggle-eye; or Croppie.—*Ambloplites rupestris.* . . They are abundant in Lakes Pepin and St. Croix.   **1890** *Newark Daily Advocate* (OH) 30 July [4]/4 (newspaperarchive.com), We have breeding ponds at Chagrin Falls and are arranging for the distribution now or in the fall of small-mouth black bass, straw bass or croppie, and marble catfish.   **1892** Perry et al. *Amer. Game Fishes* 153, Black Bass species are sometimes confounded with the Rock Bass (*Ambloplites rupestris*), the Calico Bass, or Straw Bass (*Pomoxys sparoides*), or the White Bass (*Roccus chrysops*), which are entirely different fishes.   **1902** *Recreation* 17.457, The best common name for this species is the large mouth black bass, but it is known in different parts of the country by many different names, as . . straw bass in Northern Indiana and elsewhere.   **1919** IN Acad. Sci. *Proc. for 1918* 240, Small pinkish parasites . . were found quite common in the stomachs of fishes, particularly the Straw Bass (*Micropterus salmoides*).   **1978** *Outdoor Life* Sept 56, Scientists call the large-mouth bass Micropterus salmoides. . . But there are many lesser-known names too. Some of them are . . straw bass, bayou bass [etc].

straw bell   n

A **bellwort** (here: *Uvularia perfoliata*).

1855 *Putnam's Mag.* 6.573 **CT,** About its base clustered a quaint crowd of brown flowered trilliums, and the delicate straw-bells of May.   **1863** Higginson *Outdoor Papers* 237 **MA,** Anemone may dispute the prize of melody with Windflower, . . Uvularia with Bellwort and Straw-bell.   **1916** Keeler *Early Wildflowers* 12, Straw Bell. . . New England and Ontario to Minnesota and south to Florida and Mississippi.   **1954** *Amer. Midland Naturalist* 52.284 **GA,** *U[vularia] perfoliata* . . Strawbell, bellwort.—Rich woods of ravines and bluffs, frequent.   **2003** *DARE* File—Internet **MA,** *Uvularia perfoliata* (Strawbell) $6.00 qt.

strawberry   n

1   Std: the fruit of a plant of the genus *Fragaria;* the plant itself.   For other names of var spp see **earth mulberry, sheep-tit (berry), sow-tit.**

2   A bean, esp a pinto bean—usu in combs *Alaskan strawberry, Boston ~, Mexican ~, miners' ~, prairie ~;* for addit varr see quots.   *joc*

1878 Campion *Frontier* 323, We had, indeed, *Arizona strawberries* for dinner, fried in bacon grease.   **1884** in 1945 *AmSp* 20.71 **NY,** 'Give me a plate of beans,' he said to the waiter. 'One plate of Boston strawberries,' yelled that functionary.   **1925** *AmSp* 1.137 **Pacific NW,** Chase along that bowl of strawberries (beans).   **1931** *AmSp* 7.51 **Sth, SW** [Lumberjack lingo], Beans are always "camp strawberries."   **1939** Franck *Lure of AK* 123, "Alaskan strawberries," in the Sourdough vernacular, are . . beans, out of a can.   **1943** Korson *Coal Dust* 69 **PA,** Beans and white gravy made a popular combination in hard times, the beans under the name of "miners' strawberries."   **1947** Croy *Corn Country* 278, He [=the prairie pioneer] had to live for great stretches on beans. And so they became "prairie strawberries."   **1956** Almirall *From College* 145 **CO,** It was time for supper, so we ate ours of "Mexican strawberries" (beans, in polite language), right out of cans.   **1967–68** *DARE* (Qu. I17, *Beans . . that are dark red when they are dry*) Inf **CA**90, California strawberries; (Qu. HH30, *Things that are nicknamed for different nationalities*) Inf **TX**1, Mexican strawberries—pinto beans.   **1977** Dunlop *Wheels West* 169, A cook produced suppers of beans, known as "Pecos strawberries".   **2003** *DARE* File—Internet **HI,** So let's hit the trail and tie on the old feed bag, we promise no jerky or prairie strawberries.

3   also *army strawberry:* A prune.   *joc*   Cf **anchor brand strawberry**

1923 in 1972 *AmSp* 47.108 (as of 1917–19) [Slang of Amer Forces in Europe], *Strawberries* for 'prunes.'   **1940** *AmSp* 15.211 [C.C.C. chatter], Common articles of food . . given figurative names . . prunes, *army strawberries. Ibid* 451 [Argot of the sea], *Strawberry.* The wrinkled prune, in the seamen's jargon.   **1941** *AmSp* 16.163 [Army slang], *Army strawberries.* Prunes.

strawberry bass   n

1   Usu =black **crappie** (*Pomoxis nigromaculatus*), but also white **crappie** (*Pomoxis annularis*).   **chiefly Gt Lakes, Upstate NY**

1867 De Voe *Market Asst.* 294 **NY,** *Calico bass, speckled bass,* or *partridge-tailed bass.*—This fish is also known among our fishermen as the "strawberry bass."   **1877** OH Comm. Fisheries *First Annual Rept.* 77,

P[omoxis] hexacanthus. . . Strawberry Bass. **1884** Goode *Fisheries U.S.* 1.336, In Lake Erie, and in Ohio generally, it [=*Pomoxis sparoides*] is the "Strawberry Bass," or "Grass Bass." **1939** Natl. Geogr. Soc. *Fishes* 110 **Gt Lakes,** White Crappie. . . Around the Great Lakes it is called ringed crappie, pale crappie, and strawberry bass. **1968** *DARE* (Qu. P1, . . *Kinds of freshwater fish . . caught around here . . good to eat*) Inf **NY74,** Strawberry bass; **NY71,** Strawberry bass or crappie; **NY75,** Strawberry bass [FW: =crappie]. **2003** *DARE* File—Internet **ceWI,** We always called them [=a kind of sunfish] strawberry bass when I was a kid.

2 =**tripletail 1.**

1928 U.S. Bur. Fisheries *Bulletin 1927* 43.256 **VA,** *Lobotes surinamensis.* . . Virtually the entire catch is marketed in Norfolk, where the species is known either as lumpfish or strawberry bass. **1935** Caine *Game Fish* 138, Tripletail. . . *Synonyms:* Blackfish . . Strawberry Bass.

3 =**bluegill 1.**

1983 Becker *Fishes WI* 844, Bluegill. . . Other common names: bluegill sunfish, . . strawberry bass.

strawberry bird n

1 =**bobolink B.**

1799 Barton *Fragments Nat. Hist. PA* app I 20 **CT,** *Emberiza oryzivora* [=*Dolichonys o.*] If I do not mistake, this bird in Connecticut is called the Strawberry-bird. **1897** Briggs *Reminiscences & Letters* 12 **cwMA** (as of a1851), I remember well the rare walks I took with him . . when the bobolinks were bubbling over with song. . . He called them "strawberry birds," because they came with the first strawberry flowers.

2 =**purple finch.**

1889 Ridgway *Ornith. IL* 1.225 **CT,** *Purple Finch.* Popular synonyms. . . Strawberry Bird (Connecticut).

strawberry blite n

Std: a **goosefoot** (here: *Chenopodium capitatum*). Also called **eye hurt, Indian paint 4, ~ strawberry 2, strawberry pigweed**

strawberry bramble n   Also *strawberry dwarf bramble*

A **raspberry B** (here: *Rubus pedatus*) of the Northwest and Alaska.

1961 Peck *Manual OR* 441, *R[ubus] pedatus* . . Strawberry Dwarf Bramble. . . Woods in the high Cascade and Blue Mts., and to Alaska and Calif. **1973** Hitchcock–Cronquist *Flora Pacific NW* 224, Strawberry b[ramble] . . *R[ubus] pedatus.* **2004** *DARE* File—Internet **WA,** Rubus pedatus—Strawberry bramble.

strawberry bream n

A **sunfish** n 1a; see quots.

1931 Amer. Fisheries Soc. *Trans.* 61.83 **AR,** In addition to the above basses we have the white crappie, bluegill bream, strawberry bream, . . and many other sunfishes. **1932** *Kerrville Mt. Sun* (TX) 20 Oct 10/1, When the draining process began he found . . strawberry bream, which came from the State of Georgia. **1941** Writers' Program *Guide OK* 343, Channel catfish have been successfully bred as have "Texas strawberry bream," a species of game fish new to Oklahoma. **1967** *DARE* FW Addit **cAR,** *Strawberry bream* ['brɪm]—name around Saline County, Arkansas, for a large, blunt-nosed, red-bellied variety of sunfish. **1999** *DARE* File—Internet **FL,** I went down to the Strawberry Bream hole on the creek this afternoon. . . The reason . . for the local name of Strawberry Bream [=*Lepomis marginatus*] I believe to be their reddish color with speckles and small size. Also Flathead catfish will eat them like we eat strawberries if used for bait.

strawberry bush n

1 also *strawberry shrub:* A **burning bush 1:** usu *Euonymus americana,* but also *E. atropurpurea.*

1828 Rafinesque *Med. Flora* 1.195, The *Euonymus Americanus* is also called Strawberry shrub with us; but erroneously, since the berries hardly resemble strawberries. **1848** Gray *Manual of Botany* 84, *E[uonymus] Americanus.* . . Strawberry-bush. **1867** MO State Bd. Ag. *Annual Rept. for 1866* 81, *Euonymus Americana* (strawberry bush). . . Many of our nurserymen sell the burning bush [=*E. atropurpureus*] for the strawberry bush. **1880** (1881) Nickell *Bot. Ready Ref.* 59, *Euonymus americanus. Burning Bush.* Strawberry Shrub. Strawberry Bush [etc]. **1883** Hale *Woods NC* 165, *Strawberry Bush.* . . [is] a shrub 2 to 5 feet high, found in all the Districts, and known by the names of Burning Bush, Fish-wood, and Bursting Heart. **1901** Lounsberry *S. Wild Flowers* 317, Burning Bush. Strawberry Bush. Wahoo. . . *Florida and Texas to New*

York. **1930** Sievers *Amer. Med. Plants* 59, Wahoo—*Euonymus atropurpureus.* . . strawberry tree, strawberry bush [etc]. **1936** *Torreya* 36.39 **NJ,** In season, one may find azalea, strawberry-bush . . and wild grape. **1972** GA Dept. Ag. *Farmers Market Bulletin* 11 Oct 8/1, Hearts-a-Bustin is only one of many common names for Euonymus americanus. Others include "Puppy Toes", "Strawberry Bush" [etc].

2 =**Carolina allspice.** [From the fragrance] Cf **strawberry shrub 2**

1859 (1880) Darlington *Amer. Weeds* 135, Carolina-allspice. . . Strawberry-bush. . . There are several species of this genus cultivated for the fragrance of their rather unsightly flowers. **1893** *Jrl. Amer. Folkl.* 6.141 **eMA,** *Calycanthus floridus* . . strawberry bush. **1964** Batson *Wild Flowers SC* 48, Strawberry-bush. . . Rich woods and bluffs. Spring. Pennsylvania to Alabama. **1974** (1977) Coon *Useful Plants* 85, *Calycanthus floridus*—Sweet shrub, strawberry-bush. . . Native from Virginia southwards, this wonderfully sweet-smelling eight foot shrub is one of the finest wild plants to be brought into cultivation.

strawberry cactus n

1 also *Indian strawberry cactus, Mexican strawberry, strawberry hedgehog:* A **hedgehog cactus 3,** esp *Echinocereus engelmannii* or *E. enneacanthus.* Cf **Mexican strawberry 1**

1854 (1932) Bell *Log TX–CA Trail* 35.233, Eat some—what the mexicans call—Mexican strawberry, these are nothing more than a speices [sic] of *Prickly Pear;* the inside of the pear resembles the strawberry. **1886** Havard *Flora W. & S. TX for 1885* 519, *Cereus stramineus* [=*Echinocereus enneacanthus*]. . . (Strawberry Cactus; Pitahaya.) Very common west of the Pecos. . . The ripe fruit is red, 1½ inches long, 1 inch thick, with thick skin bearing but few spines and easily peeled off. It is equal or superior, in quality and flavor, to the best strawberry. **1941** *Jrl. Amer. Folkl.* 54.66 **cwTX,** For a long, long time the Indians have known that the Strawberry Cactus or Pitaya (Echinocereus stramineus) is good to eat. **1942** Hylander *Plant Life* 322, The Hedgehog Cacti (*Echinocereus*). . . are also known as Strawberry Cacti because the masses of bright red fruits look like strawberries and can be eaten the same way. *Ibid* 324, Indian Strawberry Cactus. . . The clusters of spines can be easily rubbed off from the strawberry-like fruit. **1973** *AZ Highways* Mar 39, Whether you call them Strawberry Hedgehog, Calico Hedgehog, or Purple Torch (Echinocereus engelmannii), everyone finds the blossoms most attractive and delicate. **1985** Dodge *Flowers SW Deserts* 128, *Echinocereus fendleri.* . . Fruits . . may be eaten like strawberries, hence the name strawberry cactus. **2002** *Daily Herald* (Arlington Heights IL) 3 Mar sec 7 6/3 **wTX,** A clump of strawberry cactus has so many scarlet blossoms we hardly can see the thorny stems. In another month, thirsty desert creatures will feast on the succulent fruit.

2 A **pincushion cactus 1.**

1896 *Jrl. Amer. Folkl.* 9.188 **sCA,** *Mamillaria* [sic] *Goodridgii* [=*M. dioica*] . . strawberry cactus. **1897** Parsons *Wild Flowers CA* 24, Strawberry Cactus. . . The handsome scarlet berries . . are easily picked out. . . [T]he flavor is delicious, though I cannot say it resembles that of the strawberry. **1919** Chase *CA Desert* 59, There is a quaint little cactus . . , *Mammillaria tetrancistrus,* usually only two or three inches high, that has an entirely different flower. It is claret-color . . , and bears for fruit a bright coral-red vessel like a tiny *chile.* . . I have heard it called "strawberry" cactus, a puzzling misnomer. **1932** Bentley *Spanish Terms* 122 **SW,** *Chilito.* . . A small variety of cactus (probably *Mammillaria tetrancistrus*) known otherwise as pin-cushion cactus, strawberry cactus and fish-hook cactus. **2004** (acc) U.S. Dept. Ag. *Plants Database* (Internet), *Mammillaria dioica.* . . strawberry cactus.

3 A **barrel cactus** (here: *Thelocactus setispinus*).

1976 Bailey–Bailey *Hortus Third* 475, [*Ferocactus*] *setispinus* [=*Thelocactus s.*] . . *Strawberry cactus.* . . fr[uit] globose, red, . . pulp red. Spring to autumn. S. Tex. and n. Mex.

strawberry dwarf bramble   See **strawberry bramble**

strawberry fly n   chiefly NJ   See Map

A tabanid, esp a **deerfly 1.**

1910 NJ State Museum *Annual Rept. for 1909* 738, These are moderate or large species, popularly known as "horse flies," but locally and referring to special types, also as "gad-flies," "deer-flies," "ear-flies," "golden-eyed flies," "strawberry flies," etc. **1967–68** *DARE* (Qu. R12, . . *Other kinds of flies*) Infs **NJ**16, 17, 21, 22, 31, 39, Strawberry fly; **DC2,** Strawberry fly—most all summer—drives horses crazy. **1998** *DARE* File—Internet **NJ,** But even greenheads and their nearly as notorious relations, strawberry flies and "no-see-um" gnats, may prove inadequate to stop people from swarming to the bay region.

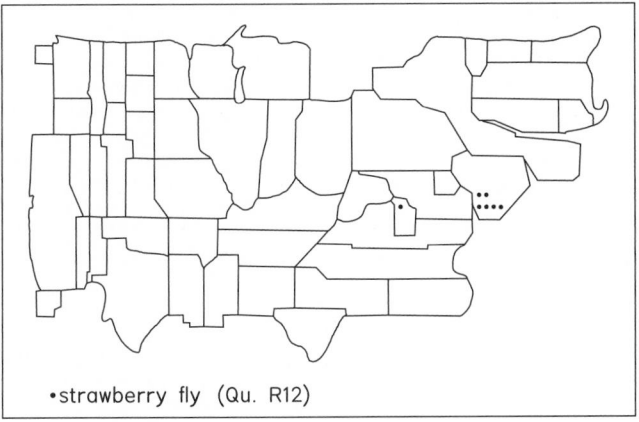

•strawberry fly (Qu. R12)

‡**strawberry friend** n

1953 Randolph–Wilson *Down in Holler* 289 **Ozarks,** *Strawberry friend. . .* A moocher. Many city people visit their backwoods cousins only when strawberries are ripe, to get enough free berries for a year's supply of jam.

strawberry geranium n
=**Indian strawberry 1.**

1883 Chapman *Flora Southern U.S.* 620, *F[ragaria] (Duchesnea) indica . .* Strawberry geranium. **1901** Mohr *Plant Life AL* 541, *Duchesnea indica. . .* Strawberry Geranium. . . Widely spread in damp copses, shaded borders of fields, roadsides.

strawberry hedgehog See **strawberry cactus 1**

strawberry perch n
=**crappie.**

1877 Hallock *Sportsman's Gaz.* 378, *Strawberry perch. . . Pomoxys hexacanthus* [=*P. annularis*]. . . ranges from Lakes Huron and Erie to the Southwestern States. **1887** Goode *Amer. Fishes* 69 **OH,** In Lake Erie, and in Ohio generally, it [=rock bass] is the "Strawberry Bass," "Strawberry Perch" or "Grass Bass." **1933** LA Dept. of Conserv. *Fishes* 333, The Sac-a-lait. . . This species, [sic] popularity is very well attested by the variety of names it has been given [including] . . Strawberry Perch. **1975** Evanoff *Catch More Fish* 90, The white crappie has been called some of the same names as the black crappie and also sac-a-lait, strawberry perch [etc].

strawberry pigweed n
=**strawberry blite** or a similar **goosefoot.**

1917 Rydberg *Flora Rocky Mts.* 242, *Blitum. . .* Strawberry Blite, Strawberry Pigweed. . . *B. capitatum* [=*Chenopodium c.*] . . *B. virgatum* [=*C. foliosum*]. . . *B. hastatum* [=*C. overi*]. **1935** (1943) Muenscher *Weeds* 208, *Chenopodium capitatum. . .* Strawberry spinach, Strawberry pigweed. . . mostly in the northeastern states and the Rocky Mountain states.

strawberry shrub n

1 See **strawberry bush 1.**
2 A **sweet shrub,** usu **Carolina allspice.** Cf **strawberry bush 2**

1881 Church *Home Garden* 24, Children especially delight in another June visitor, the blossom of the sweet-scented shrub, or spice bush, also known as strawberry shrub. **1887** Washburn *To the Pacific* 97 **NY,** The calacanthus [sic], or, with us, the strawberry shrub, lines the road here. **1909** *Century Illustr. Mag.* 78.524 **NEng,** I was standing over there by the strawberry shrub. **1915** (1926) Armstrong–Thornber *Western Wild Flowers* 158, Strawberry Shrub—*Calycanthus occidentalis. . .* resembles the familiar shrub of old-fashioned gardens and the flowers have the same pleasant and elusive aroma, something like strawberries. **1936** Smith–Sass *Carolina Rice* 18 **SC coast,** The shrubbery portions were traversed by wide walks or allees, through the trees, many of them flowering: japonicas, . . strawberry shrub, . . and many others. **1943** Peattie *Great Smokies* 172 **eTN, wNC,** Strawberry shrub, with its . . strange odor, something like fermenting strawberries. **1946** Benét *Last Circle* 274 **NEng,** There weren't any flowers around, but there was a smell like strawberry shrub. **1975** Hamel–Chiltoskey *Cherokee Plants* 58, Strawberry shrub—*Calycanthus floridus. . .* Roots are strong emetics.

strawberry tomato n
=**ground cherry.**

1856 in 1862 Colt *Went to KS* 133 **NY,** The strawberry tomatoes . . are indigenous to the soil. **1873** *Amer. Naturalist* 7.11, The potato, the egg-plant . . [and] the strawberry tomato *(Physalis)* are well known esculent vegetables. **1890** *AN&Q* 6.4, I suppose . . [your correspondent's] *wild tomato* to be some species of *Physalis.* . . The market-men call them *strawberry tomatoes.* **1915** (1926) Armstrong–Thornber *Western Wild Flowers* 460, The common names [of *Physalis* spp], Ground-cherry and Strawberry-tomato, are suggested by the fruit, which is juicy, often red or yellow, and in some kinds is edible. **1937** St. John *Flora SE WA & ID* 365, Physalis pruinosa . . *Strawberry Tomato.* . . Shore of Snake River. **1961** Wills–Irwin *Flowers TX* 183, The Strawberry-tomato or Cape-gooseberry, *P[hysalis] peruviana* . . has bright red-orange calyces when the berries are ripe.

strawberry tree n
A **burning bush 1,** usu *Euonymus atropurpurea.*

1813 Muhlenberg *Catalogus Plantarum* 25, *[Euonymus] Americanus* (burning bush, strawberry tree). **1837** Darlington *Flora Cestrica* 150 **sePA,** American Euonymus. *Vulgo*—Burning Bush. Strawberry-tree. . . This is a very pretty little species, its mature capsules, in autumn, being a bright crimson. **1843** Torrey *Flora NY* 1.142, Euonymus americanus. . . *Strawberry-tree.* **1897** Sudworth *Arborescent Flora* 281 **NY,** *Evonymus* [sic] *atropurpureus.* . . Common names. . . Strawberry-tree. **1930** Sievers *Amer. Med. Plants* 59, Wahoo. . . Other common names.—Burningbush, . . strawberry-tree [etc]. **1960** Vines *Trees SW* 661, Eastern Wahoo. . . Vernacular names are . . Bitter-oak, and Strawberry-tree.

strawbill n
=**hooded merganser.**

1911 *Forest & Stream* 77.172 **AR,** Hooded Merganser. . . Straw-Bill, Mud Lake.

straw boss n Also *straw, straw chief,* ~ *push* Cf **gaffer** n[1], **scratch boss**

An assistant, subordinate, or acting foreman of a crew of workers; also *fig.*

1889 *Union Pacific Employes' Mag.* 4.59 **ID,** [He] is dealing out heavy jobs to the big ones, and little jobs to the small ones in the machine shop, in the capacity of straw boss during the absence of S. Wallace. **1894** (1971) Carwardine *Pullman Strike* 117, These employees. . . [having suffered] the continued oppression of the "straw bosses," . . were in no condition to be trifled with by the Company. **1905** U.S. Forest Serv. *Bulletin* 61.50 [Logging terms], *Straw boss.* . . A subforeman in a logging camp. **1906** *DN* 3.159 **nwAR,** *Straw boss.* . . Assistant foreman. **1920** Hunter *Trail Drivers TX* 298, In a cattle outfit . . the leader of any particular bunch of men is called the "boss," his first lieutenant or right-hand man. **1927** *AmSp* 2.506 [Hobo lingo], A "straw-boss" is very commonly an assistant boss. I understand that the term originated from a joke about the boss "thrasher," who attended to the grain-on-the-stalk going into the thresher while the second-man watched after the straw coming out, and, hence, supposedly had little to do. **1933** *AmSp* 8.1.32 **nwTX** [Ranch diction], *Straw or straw boss.* The person in charge when the foreman is absent; the second in command. **1942** ME Univ. *Studies* 57.134, *Straw Boss.* An assistant foreman. **1945** Hubbard *Railroad Ave.* 363, *Straw boss*—Foreman of small gang or acting foreman. **1950** *AmSp* 25.230 **ceMS,** *Straw boss.* Manager of a plantation. **1958** McCulloch *Woods Words* 183 **Pacific NW,** *Straw boss*—The man in charge of a small crew when the regular foreman is absent. **1965–70** *DARE* (Qu. HH43b, *The assistant to the top person in charge of a group of workmen*) 346 Infs, **widespread,** Straw boss; **OH**95, Straw chief; **MI**120, Straw push; (Qu. HH43a, *The top person in charge of a group of workmen*) 22 Infs, **scattered,** Straw boss; (Qu. L1, *A man who is employed to help with work on a farm*) Inf **CA**161, Straw boss; (Qu. AA21, . . *Joking expressions . . about a wife who gives the orders and a husband who takes them from her*) Inf **MI**75, She's the straw boss; (Qu. HH36, *A careless, slovenly woman: "She's just an old _____."*) Inf **NH**10, Straw boss; (Qu. II20b, *A person who tries too hard to gain somebody else's favor: "He's always trying to _____ the boss."*) Inf **OK**18, Get to be straw boss; (Qu. II23, *Joking names for the people who are, or think they are, the best society of a community: The _____*) Inf **DC**13, Straw boss. **1969** Sorden *Lumberjack Lingo* 122 **NEng, Gt Lakes,** *Straw push*—The man who took the job of the regular woods boss when he was away. Same as straw boss. **2001** *Valley Independent* (Monessen PA) 30 Oct sec B 6/1,

[Horoscope:] Social issues are likely to be at the bottom of your troubles today if you handle relationships like a straw-boss on the line.

straw bottom n   Cf **hay bottom 2**

1958 *AmSp* 33.272 **eWA** [Ranching terms], *Straw bottom.* See *hay bottom. Ibid* 270, *Hay bottom.* . . The last couple of feet of a hay stack.

straw chief   See **straw boss**

straw-field child n   Cf *DS* Z11b

1984 Wilder *You All Spoken Here* 99 **Sth,** *Come-by-chance child:* Illegitimate. . . *Ditch-edge chillun, straw-field chillun, sawmill child, buzzard baby:* Same as above.

strawflower n

1 =bellwort.

1863 (1870) Rand *Flowers Parlor & Garden* 393 **NEast,** A companion of the *Anemone nemorosa* is the pretty Bellwort, or Straw Flower *(Uvularia sessifolia).* **1933** Small *Manual SE Flora* 299, *Uvularia* [spp]. . . Bellworts. Straw-flowers. **1949** Moldenke *Amer. Wild Flowers* 336, *U[vularia] perfoliata,* the strawbell, strawflower, or perfoliate bellwort, is a denizen of rich woods and thickets.

2 =pearly everlasting 1.

1923 Pellett *Amer. Honey Plants* 126 **WA,** In Washington it is commonly called straw-flower by the beekeepers. In the east it is known as life-everlasting, moonshine, ladies' tobacco, silver-button, etc. **1950** *WELS Suppl.* **csWI,** Strawflower, everlasting flower, everlasting—Small flower with bright vari-colored blossoms. . . When flower stops growth it dries—color and all. **1957** Roberts–Nelson *Wildflowers CO* 55, Strawflower, as well as everlasting, is a term used for this flower because it can be dried and kept for a long time without losing its form or color.

straw fly n   Cf **horn fly**

See quots.

1913 U.S. Dept. Ag. *Farmers' Bulletin* 540.5, Many individuals in certain sections speak of the stable fly as the "wild fly," "straw fly," or "biting house fly." **1966–68** *DARE* (Qu. R12, . . *Other kinds of flies*) Inf **AR**28, Straw fly—same as horn fly; **LA**31, Straw fly. **1968** *DARE* Tape **LA**31, We have a straw fly that lights on the back of the cow—big bevies of 'em.

straw, in the adv phr   Cf **called to straw**

In childbed.

1899 (1912) Green *VA Folk-Speech* 240, *In the straw.* . . Lying in; a woman is said to be in the straw when she is lying in, and not ready to get up. **1970** *DARE* (Qu. AA28, . . *Joking or sly expressions* . . *women use to say that another is going to have a baby* . . *"She['s] _____."*) Inf **TN**52, Gonna get in the straw.

strawlily n

A **bellwort,** usu *Uvularia sessilifolia.*

1878 Slosson *China Hunters Club* 201 **CT,** Bess might have added to her bouquet . . the delicate bellworts or straw-lilies (uvularias). **1894** *Jrl. Amer. Folkl.* 7.102 **CT,** *Oakesia sessifolia* [=*Uvularia s.*] . . Straw-lilies. **1940** Clute *Amer. Plant Names* 15, *U[vularia] grandiflora.* Straw-flower. Large bellwort, corn-flower, straw-lily. **1949** Moldenke *Amer. Wild Flowers* 336, The wildoats or strawlily, *O[akesiella] sessifolia* [=*Uvularia s.*] [is] an entirely smooth plant living in moist woods and thickets and on banks from New Brunswick to Georgia and west to Minnesota and Arkansas.

straw mow   See **mow** n[1] **2**

straw push   See **straw boss**

straw ride n   esp Atlantic

A pleasure ride in the country taken in a wagon or sleigh partially filled with straw; a hayride.

1841 *Daily MO Republican* (St. Louis) 15 Dec 2/3 **NJ,** A Straw Ride. . . I . . found standing before the door a pair of fine horses attached to a common farm wagon. The inside of the body . . was partly filled with nice clean straw; over this buffalo skins were spread, altogether the affair looked pretty comfortable. . . [W]e made a party of about a dozen. **1872** *Ladies' Repository* 47.277 **seNY,** I recall the delight of a party of gay girl visitors who had just returned from a merry "straw ride." **1886** *Century Illustr. Mag.* 32.25 **ceMA,** She had gone over to the Pastures with a party of summer-folks on a straw-ride and picked blueberries. **1901** *Atlantic Mth.* 88.460 **MA coast,** "The Methodists' straw ride! I do declare!" A long pung creaked into view from the four corners, with slow horses, big bells clanging, and a crowded party of villagers. [**1932–34** *Hanley Disks* **ceMA,** [Hanley:] What is a straw ride like? [Inf:] We rented an old pung and had it full of straw and then we had the

robes over us and sang songs, then went to a hotel somewhere or restaurant and had a good oyster stew and pickles and then came home.] **1948** Bean *Yankee Auctioneer* 11 **wMA,** Straw ride parties ending with a country church supper in the winter. **1956** *Sun* (Baltimore MD) 22 July (Internet), *Straw Rides in the Moonlight.* . . A country straw ride! For Baltimore's teen-agers in the late 1890's nothing was more fun. . . Everyone sat in the straw, the boys with their legs dangling over the side. Then the team of four mules was whipped up, and away we went, moving slowly along the country lanes. **1966–69** *DARE* FW Addit **ceCT,** Straw ride—hayride; **MA**48, Straw ride = hayride. **2003** *DARE* File—Internet **MD,** We will take a straw ride around the family farm.

straw shed n   Also *straw barn*

1 A farm building in which straw is stored.

1836 *Genesee Farmer* 6.212 **NY,** I frequently brine the straw which I put into my straw barn. **1837** *Ibid* 7.259 **MD,** This building is more convenient, costs less, takes less room, and the business is more easily conducted, than by building corn-house, stable, carriage house, hay and straw sheds, all separate, . . requiring four times the roof. **1858** *Compiler* (Gettysburg PA) 1 Mar [4]/1 (newspaperarchive.com), The straw shed, upon which the shingles above alluded to, were put in roof, was torn down. **1899** *OH Farmer* 95.313 **IN,** I want to build an addition to my barn for a straw shed and a covered barnyard. **1920** *Oxnard Daily Courier & Oxnard Daily News* (CA) 6 Dec [2]/5 (newspaper-archive.com), [Advt:] Modern improvements, large barn, implement sheds, straw shed, garage, bunk house. **1967–69** *DARE* (Qu. M1, . . *Kinds of barns . . according to their use or the way they are built*) Infs **OH**70, **PA**137, Straw shed; **MI**40, Straw barn; (Qu. M22, . . *Kinds of buildings . . on farms*) Inf **OH**10, Straw shed; **NY**224, Straw shed—to store straw for bedding cattle. [*DARE* Ed: Some of these Infs may refer instead to **2** below.] **1992** *Daily News* (Huntingdon PA) 16 July 13/4, [Advt:] *Public Auction.* . . two story frame house, large bank barn, silo, straw shed, wire corn crib.

2 A shelter for livestock or equipment, consisting of a minimal framework covered with straw.   **chiefly Upper MW, N Cent**

[**1853** *Cultivator* 3d ser 1.12 **NY,** He doubled his manure by drawing . . large quantities of muck to his farm-yard, where it was kept comparatively dry till wanted, under a cheap slab and straw shed.] **1859** *Genesee Farmer* 2d ser 20.370 **VA,** I have a common straw shed . . in the summer open all around, in winter open only to the south; they [= sheep] go in and out at pleasure. **1875** *Weekly IA State Reg.* (Des Moines) 8 Oct [2]/5 (newspaperarchive.com), Let . . our farmers . . provide warm straw sheds for all animals for the approaching winter. **1891** in 2003 *DARE* File—Internet **cwWI,** I have a wife & child to support on a little farm and am without means to improve it. . . Nothing but a straw shed for my cow and a poor one at that. **1905** *New Oxford Item* (PA) 13 Oct [10]/1 (newspaperarchive.com), The farm machinery had been placed under a straw-shed . . made of the straw from the August threshing, piled up and over a rude scaffolding of unbarked logs. **1929** *AmSp* 5.55 **NE** [Cattle country talk], The smaller ranches that do not have large barns may have a number of "straw sheds," a winter shelter made of posts and covered with hay. **1936** in Lib. of Congress *Amer. Memory: FSA/OWI* (Internet) **IA,** [Caption:] Straw barn built by Lloyd Sampson for his chickens and livestock near Armstrong, Iowa. **1947** *Joplin Globe* (MO) 13 July sec C 5/7, Many farmers . . are building straw sheds as they thresh this year. . . The framework should be made of posts and poles before threshing. The straw is then blown on the framework. **1947** Forrest *Hist. W. Murray Co.* 29 **MN** (as of c1875), She dug herself out of the house and the stock out of the straw shed after the snowstorms. **1960** *Herald–Press* (St. Joseph MI) 30 Mar 3/1, A board member . . asked Childs if a straw shed for farm animals would be prohibited by a section of the building code which requires roofs to be finished with "a standard roofing material." **1966** Dakin *Dial. Vocab. Ohio R. Valley* 2.82, A *straw shed* is a frame covered with straw and open on one side. **1967** Jacobs *Rejoicing* 17 **cIN** (as of c1930), His lean-to strawshed was now a yellow barn with cupolas and lightning rods. **1973** Allen *LAUM* 1.187 (as of c1950), Shelter for cows. . . *straw shed:* Open on one side and covered with straw [2 infs, **IA**]. . . A lean-to [1 inf, **NE**]. . . Shelter . . for hogs and pigs. . . straw shed [1 inf, **MN**]. **2003** *DARE* File—Internet **ND** (as of 1940), I had to . . make more barn room. I built a lean-to on the barn—a straw shed that consisted of fence posts and woven wire with straw polked [sic] between the wire. *Ibid* **NE** (as of 1881), Their first house was a dugout. Their first barn was a straw shed, but was later replaced with a sod barn.

straw widow n   [Prob calque of Ger *Strohwitwe*]

=grass widow 1.

1883 (1884) Joel–Stegman *Rifle Shots* 270, Little private excursions were often resorted to . . in the immediate vicinity which had been abandoned by their rebel proprietors, but yet held in full possession by their "straw widows" or "orphan daughters." **1968** *DARE* (Qu. AA26, *A divorced woman*) Inf **VA5,** Straw widow. **1969** Stevenson *Ethic for Survival* 11, Finally, my [=the book's editor's] special gratitude is due to my wife . . often a straw widow because of Stevenson. **2003** *DARE* File—Internet **NC,** *Joseph Bedford Smart.* A physician in Forest City, moved to Murphy following a scandal about a "straw widow" (divorcee).

stray adj, also used absol

1 Of a horse: accidentally bred. Cf **field colt 1**

1965–69 *DARE* (Qu. K43, *A horse that was not intentionally bred, or bred by accident*) Infs **AR47, IL77, LA15, 18, MT2, UT3,** Stray.

2 Of a child: illegitimate; born out of wedlock—also used in fig combs *stray colt, ~ goat.* **scattered Sth, S Midl** Cf **field colt 2**

1938 in 1979 *Amer. Slave Suppl. 2* 1553 **WV,** I do not know who my father was, as I was a stray colt and never was told who he was. **1953** Brewer *Word Brazos* 100 **eTX** [Black], Ah calls to min' a sportin' life gal up to Mudville on de ole Pearson farm what hab a stray boy. Don' nobody know his pappy; an' his mammy . . keep a silent tongue 'bout de boy's pappy. But one thing, dis boy, lack mos' stray chilluns, don' relish workin' on de fawm. **1968–69** *DARE* (Qu. Z11b, . . *[A child whose parents were not married]*) Inf **LA31,** Stray; **KY51,** Stray—heard, not used; **LA28,** Stray colt; **SC58,** Stray goat. **1970** Tarpley *Blinky* 220 **neTX,** *Child of an unwed mother* . . stray [rare]. **1986** Pederson *LAGS Concordance* (Bastard) 2 infs, **GA, LA,** Stray colt; 1 inf, **swAR,** Strays.

stray v TX Cf stray man

To search for stray cattle; also in phr *stray the herd* to separate stray cattle from a herd.

1869 *Overland Mth.* 3.126 **TX,** It often happens, in a populated country . . that they are obliged to stop and "stray" the herd. While several herdsmen are stationed around it to hold it fast, another rides in, selects a stray brand, and "cuts it out." **1954** Tolbert *Bigamy Jones* 162 **wTX** (as of 1870s), My uncle "strayed" for my grandfather when he wasn't down in the state legislature making $1 a day as a senator. (By "strayed," I'm not talking about Uncle Blue's morals. I just mean he looked for stray cattle.)

stray colt (or goat) See stray adj 2

stray goose n

A children's chasing game; see quots.

1929 Gordon *Born to Be* 38 [Black], Stray Goose was then their favorite game. . . . The one who was to be the stray goose was the kid who won the block dash. . . The winner was given a half-mile head start on a straightaway. He must turn, holler "Stray Goose!" and then it was up to the mob to catch him. Every time he turned, he had to holler "Stray Goose." If they caught him, they could do anything they wanted to him except perform an operation or kill him. **1995** Heatwole *Shenandoah Voices* 23 **wVA** (as of 19th cent), Stray Goose was a running and hiding game in Augusta County that covered a great area. The children divided up into two teams, usually three or four to a side. One team was designated as the geese. Both sides would spread way out. At a given signal, the geese would scatter in all directions, yelling "stray goose!" The members of the other team pursued them until all the geese were tagged.

stray man n West Cf outside man 1, stray v

A cowhand sent to other outfits' herds to seek his own outfit's stray cattle.

1902 *Out West Mag.* 16.619, The fall roundup was over. A week since, the stray men had cut out their cattle and gone home. **1920** Hunter *Trail Drivers TX* 298, The "stray man" is the cowboy's name for one who goes to the neighboring ranches after stray cattle. **1936** *NV State Jrl.* (Reno) 10 Mar 6/1, Warnecke made the cowboy from Roswell, N.M.—he once was "stray man" for Circle–Diamond outfit—tell how he roped a bald eagle. **1945** Thorp *Pardner* 241 **SW,** The others [= ranches] were invited to send men to represent their brands and work with the wagon. These representatives were called "stray men" . . because they were hunting critters in their brands that had strayed.

streach See stretch

streak n

1 In turpentine production: a cut made into a pine tree to obtain turpentine; hence v *streak* to make such a cut. Cf **face n 4**

1903 *Eve. Post* (NY NY) 1 June 7/1, The freshly exposed surfaces of

sapwood, called the "streak," meet just above the centre of the box, the angle formed by them being known as a "peak." The distance of the streak from the box increases with each weekly chipping. **1941** *AmSp* 16.237 **csGA** [Turpentine industry terms], In order to keep the crude gum flowing it is necessary to make a *streak* or scarification of the tree once a week. **1966** *DARE* Tape **GA7,** If you protect 'em, you don't lose too many of 'em, and don' work 'em, streak 'em too deep. . . The depth that you cut the streak depends on the size of the tree. You have a small tree, you can't cut it too deep. If you did, a large wind might come along and blow it over.

2 See quot.

1926 *DN* 5.389 **ME,** *Streak.* . . Creek. Universal.

3 See **streaked bass.**

streak v See streak n 1

streaked adj Also streaky Pronc-sp streak-id

Stricken with mental or physical distress, agitation, discomfort, or illness—usu in phrr *feel* (or *look*) *streaked;* see quots. **chiefly NEng**

1815 Humphreys *Yankey in England* 57, The good, gracious suzz! how streaked I feel all over! **1834** Davis *Letters Downing* 207 **ME,** Jest then in come Amos and the Globe man, and some more of our folks, and lookin pretty streaked too, and I got a notion right off there was somethin stirrin. **1836** (1838) Haliburton *Clockmaker* (1st ser) 40 **NEng,** And I think, said he, I've seen to day, (turning and looking him full in the face, for he intended to hit him pretty hard,) *I think I have seen to-day the greatest Hog I ever saw in my life.* The neighbours snickered a good deal, and the Elder felt pretty streaked. **1848** Lowell *Biglow* 146 **'Upcountry' MA,** Streaked, *uncomfortable, discomfited.* **1858** Hammett *Piney Woods Tavern* 115 **CT,** Now, you'd cal'late the wimmin would turn red, and feel amazin' streaked. **1859** *Bentley's Misc.* 45.471, "Well," said Colonel Washington M. Snakes, " . . I'll tell you what, though. Loan me a twenty-dollar note till they remit from Snakesville. . . You needn't feel streaky; I shan't slope." **1878** Beadle *Western Wilds* 416, The nearest pursuer was now but two hundred yards behind him. "I felt orful streaked, . . but I knowed 'old blaze' had never failed yet." **1905** *DN* 3.21 **cCT,** *Streaked.* . . In the phrase 'to feel *streaked,*' i.e. in poor physical condition. **1908** Wasson *Home from Sea* 113 **sME coast,** He'd growed to feel kind of streaked like, this last year or two. I seen myself that last winter took it out of him scand'lous, and come to take it this fall, seems's though he'd aged up ter'ble quick, all to once like. **1968** Coatsworth *ME Memories* 155, They say that they are feeling "streaked," or so "waggy" that they can't keep themselves busy. **1975** Gould *ME Lingo* 280, *Streaked*—Used like peaked (peak-id). . . Anybody looking poorly and washed-out is *streak-id.* Sometimes streaky.

streaked and striked adj phr Also ring-streaked and striked

[By assim from *streaked and striped*]

Striped.

1898 in 1993 Harris *Dearest Chums* 200 **GA,** J.C. . . came home . . still wearing his standing-collar, and still allowing his ring-streaked and striked cravat to crawl over the back of his collar. **1902** (1903) Smith *Bill Arp Uncivil War* 208 **GA,** The mantel-piece and jams, and doors, and bedsteads, and sewin' machine, and window-glass were all ring-streaked and striked. **1906** *DN* 3.159 **nwAR,** *Streaked and striked* [DARE Ed: Punct prob suggests proncs ['strikɪd] and ['straɪkɪd].] . . Striped. **1909** *DN* 3.363 **eAL, wGA,** *Ring-streaked and striked.* . . Striped irregularly. . . The *-ed* is always pronounced as a separate syllable.

streaked-back plover n Also streaked-backed plover

=ruddy turnstone.

1888 Trumbull *Names of Birds* 186 **MA,** At Falmouth [the turnstone is called] Sparked-back, Streaked-back, and Bishop Plover. **1923** U.S. Dept. Ag. *Misc. Circular* 13.71, Common Turnstone (*Arenaria interpres*). . . Vernacular Names. . . *In local use.* . . sparked-back, streaked-back [plover] (Mass.); streaked-backed plover (Long Id., N.Y.).

streaked bacon See streaked meat

streaked bass n Also streak, streaker

Any of three closely related fishes: a **striped bass 1** (here: *Morone saxatilis*), a **white bass 1** (here: *M. chrysops*), or a **yellow bass 2** (here: *M. mississippiensis*).

1782 Crèvecoeur *Letters* 129 **Nantucket MA,** Most common, are the streaked bass, the blue fish [etc]. **1810** in 1849 Campbell *Life & Writings De Witt Clinton* 137 **NY,** *White Bass*—In shape like our white perch, but rather longer. The tail resembles that of the streaked bass. **1828** *New Engl. Farmer* (Fessenden) 6.360, A Rock Fish, *alias* Streaked Bass, weighing *one hundred and ten pounds,* was caught in the river Delaware, opposite Billingsport, N.J. on the 26th ult. **1832** in 1997 *Seashore Chron.* 39 **seVA,** The season for Rock and the *streaked* Bass was just commencing. **1859** (1968) Bartlett *Americanisms* 457 **NEng,** Streaked Bass. Striped bass. **1903** Goode–Gill *Amer. Fishes* 23, In the North it is called the "Striped Bass," in the South the "Rock Fish" or "Rock." . . In old books it is sometimes called the "Streaked-bass." **1951** Harlan–Speaker *IA Fish* 102, White Bass. . . Other Names—Silver bass, . . streaker. *Ibid* 103, Yellow Bass. . . Other Names—Streaker [etc]. **1972** Sparano *Outdoors Encycl.* 362, White bass—Common Names: White bass, . . streak. *Ibid,* Yellow Bass. . . streaker. **2000** *DARE* File—Internet **NJ,** The streaked bass was dubbed Perca Mitchilli in his [=Dr. Samuel Mitchill's] honor.

streaked gopher See **striped gopher**

streaked gravy n Also *streakedy gravy, streak(y) gravy* **Sth, S Midl** Cf **striped gravy**
=**red-eye gravy.**

1927 *Amer. Mercury* 12.183 **GA,** Ham and steak, streaked gravy and eggs cooked on one side. **1942** *FL Highways* Feb 11, You'll never get to Washington unless you let your hair down and emit a series of 'news releases' on how to kiss your wife, spank your baby and make streaked gravy. **1969** *Engl. Jrl.* 58.1226 **sAppalachians,** If she has *ham-meat,* she will certainly proffer you *biscuit-bread* to go with it and its *"streakedy"* gravy. **1969** *DARE* (Qu. H37, . . *Words . . for gravy. Any joking ones?*) Inf **KY**62, Brown gravy = streaky gravy—made with greasy meat like ham, shoulder. **1970** Owen *Hillbilly Humor* 60 **Ozarks,** Do you remember the smell of ham and red-eye or streaked gravy? **1984** Wilder *You All Spoken Here* 87 **Sth,** *Streak gravy:* Gravy made from streaker-lean, streaker-fat bacon, or from home-cured bacon grease and water. **1999** *DARE* File—Internet **Sth,** We'd make streaky gravy in the grease. I think after it was good and brown, add hot coffee to the grease, pour over hot biscuits and home-made butter. **2000** *Ibid* **AR,** There was always biscuits in the warming closet and streaked gravy on the back of the wood stove. **2003** *Ibid* **OK** (as of c1903), We always made redeye (sawmill) streaked gravy, by adding a little liquid coffee to the fried ham drippings.

streaked-head turtle n Also *streaked-neck turtle, streaker-head, streaky-head;* for addit varr see quots **Gulf Region**
A **cooter 1.**

1966–68 *DARE* (Qu. P24, . . *Kinds of turtles*) Infs **GA**25, **MS**72, Streaked-head turtle; (Qu. P29, . . *'Gophers' . . other name . . or what other animal are they most like*) Inf **MS**72, Gopher—black but big like a streaked-headed turtle. **1967** *DARE* Tape **LA**5, [Inf:] What we call a streaky-head is a greenback turtle. Got kind of red stripes on his neck. . . [FW:] How big do they get? [Inf:] 'Bout the size of the top of a eight-quart water bucket. [FW:] 'Bout fourteen inches? [Inf:] Uh-huh. . . That's usually a greenback, greenback turtle. **1978** Newell *Trouble* 66 **FL,** Uncle Charlie Dean were settin' on the porch in a rockin' chair . . , just about as unconcerned as a streaked-head turtle asleep on a log. **1986** Pederson *LAGS Concordance* **Gulf Region,** 8 infs, Streaked-head (turtle); 1 inf, Streaked-head terrapin; 1 inf, Streaky-head = Mobilian turtle; 1 inf, Streaker-head—stays in water; 2 infs, Streakedy-head turtle; 2 infs, Streaked-neck (turtle).

streaked meat n Also *streaked bacon, ~ pork, streaky bacon, ~ meat;* for addit varr see quots **chiefly Sth, S Midl, esp sAppalachians** See Map Cf **fatback, white meat**
Salt pork or bacon with alternating layers of meat and fat.

1881 *Marion Daily Star* (OH) 12 Oct [3]/3 (newspaperarchive.com), Three-quarters of a pound of streaked bacon. **1885** *Herald & Torch-Light* (Hagerstown MD) 7 May [4]/1 (newspaperarchive.com), Streaky bacon must be used in the proportion of a quarter of pound of bacon to every pound of meat. **1928** in 1952 Mathes *Tall Tales* 68 **sAppalachians,** Birdeye Collins was the first to sling across his shoulders his snack of corn dodger, streaked middling and home-ground coffee, rolled in an old blanket. **1940** *AmSp* 15.448 [TN mountain speech], *Streaked meat.* Bacon. 'City folks eat streaked meat.' **1966–69** *DARE* (Qu. H38, . . *Words for bacon [including joking ones]*) Infs **AR**38, **GA**75, **NC**30, 36, 37, 44, **TN**5, 11, Streaked meat; **SC**97, Streaked butt; **VA**1, Streaky bacon. **1972** *Atlanta Letters* **cnGA,** When I was growing up in Georgia I used to hear, "Par-bile some turnip salat in a cooking vessel with a piece of streekt middlin from a shoat that has been salted down in a larder." **1973** *Thompson Coll.* **nwAL** (as of 1920s), Streaked (with

two syllables) meat = salt pork from bellies. **1989** Pederson *LAGS Tech. Index* 158 **Gulf Region** *(Salt pork)* 30 infs, Streaked (bacon, lean, meat, pork); 2 infs, Streak meat; *(Side [of bacon])* 4 infs, Streaked *(or streaky)* meat; *(Smoked meat)* 7 infs, Streaked bacon *(or meat). Ibid* 159, *(Bacon)* 3 infs, **Gulf Region,** Streaked bacon *(or meat).* **2002** *Roanoke Times & World-News* (VA) 25 Aug (Internet), Good home (well almost) cooking with real mashed potatoes and real biscuits and green beans that have been cooked all day in streakedy pork. **2003** *DARE* File—Internet **TN,** *Polk County Ramp Tramp Festival.* . . Spend the day enjoying bluegrass music and old time fellowship while enjoying a meal of fried ramps in eggs, fried potatoes, streaked meat, white beans, and corn bread. **2007** in 2008 *Ibid* **wNC,** Extra crispy bacon starts to taste like what we call "streaked meat" (pronounced streak-ed). Some people call it fat-back, but to me fat-back is solid white and streaked meat tastes different and is . . streaked. **2008** *Ibid* **neTN,** Fat back is from the lower part of a pig's belly. First comes the bacon, well streaked with lean meat. Next comes streaked meat, the mid-portion of the pig's belly, not quite lean enough for bacon. . . Finally the fat back. . . All three portions were salt cured and sometimes smoked.

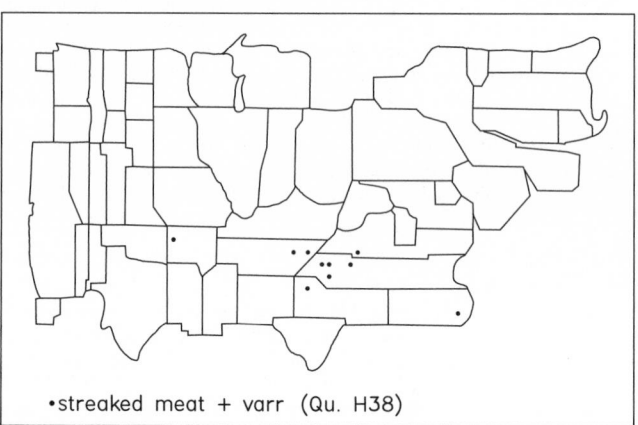

•streaked meat + varr (Qu. H38)

streaked snake n Also *streaker* **chiefly MI, NEast** See Map
Any of var striped snakes.

1791 *Phenix Windham Herald* (CT) 30 July 3/2, A Streaked Snake was last week killed in Scotland society, this town, which being opened was found to contain between eighty and ninety young snakes from four to six inches in length. **1865** in 2004 *DARE* File—Internet **cnNY,** It was quite a large streaked snake. **1908** Johnson *Highways Pacific Coast* 298 **OR,** These pools or the warm neighboring banks were a resort of numerous "streaked" snakes, as they are called in Oregon, but which we in the East speak of as "striped." **1928** Ruthven et al. *Herpetology MI* 122, Garter-snake should apply to this species [=*Thamnophis sirtalis s.*] in Michigan. The more common term Streaked Snake is used for any striped snake. **1965–70** *DARE* (Qu. P25, . . *Kinds of snakes*) 12 Infs, **esp MI, NY,** Streaked snake; **CT**17, Streaker. **1994** *Practical Homeschooling* 2.3.29 **MI** (as of c1925), Sure enough, a little streaked snake was sticking its head out the side of her desk.

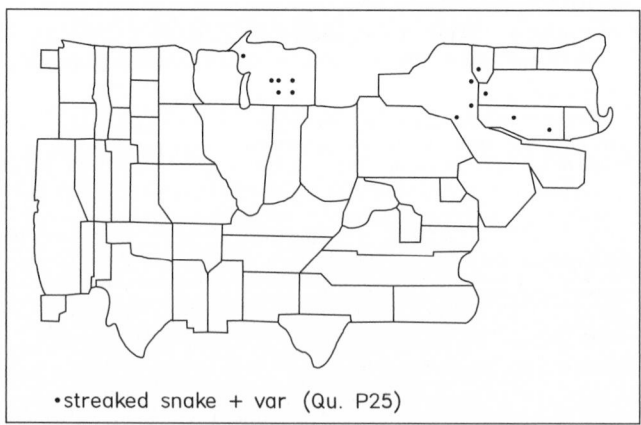

•streaked snake + var (Qu. P25)

streakedy adj |'strikɪdɨ| [Var of *streaked*] **Sth, S Midl** Cf Pronc Intro III.1 See also **streakedy-strikedy**

1949 Marshall *Little Squire Jim* 85 **NC,** Annie was examining the gray streak in her hair before the bit of mirror on the wall. "Wont his maw streakedy in the hair, too?" **1953** Randolph–Wilson *Down in Holler* 34 **Ozarks,** Certain monosyllabic adjectives . . are often pronounced in two syllables. Sometimes such words are made trisyllabic by the addition of *y,* so that . . streaked becomes *streakedy.* **1957** *Oshkosh Daily Northwestern* (WI) 15 Aug 7/1 **NC,** Women, of course, are united in their intolerance of bachelors. The singles, because they want slave labor to guarantee future ease when they're slightly fatter and more streakedy in the hair. **1968** *DARE* FW Addit **GA**22, *Streakedy* ['strɪkɪdɪ]—adjective used to describe the water turkey. **1969** *Engl. Jrl.* [see **streaked gravy**]. **1986** Pederson *LAGS Concordance,* 2 infs, **GA,** Streakedy-head turtle(s); 1 inf, **neGA,** Streakedy—describing thin part of bacon side; 1 inf, **seGA,** Greenish, streakedy-looking thing; 1 inf, **cnLA,** Would look streakedy. **2002** [see **streaked meat**].

streakedy gravy See **streaked gravy**

streakedy-strikedy adj   Also *streakity-strikity*   [Var of **streaked and striked**]   Cf Intro "Language Changes" I.3, **streakedy**

1896 *Amer. Antiq. & Oriental Jrl.* 18.100 **sGA** [Black], He got eyes sorter red roun de lids, and de balls streakedy strikedy wid red. **1906** *DN* 3.159 **nwAR,** *Streakity-strikity.* . . Striped.

streaker n

1   See **streaked bass.**

2   See **streaked snake.**

streaker-head See **streaked-head turtle**

streaker-lean See **streak of lean**

streakfield n   Also *fieldstreak*   [See quot 1909]

Usu a **whiptail 2** (here: *Cnemidophorus sexlineatus*); see quots.

1886 *Amer. Philol. Assoc. Trans.* 17.46 **Sth,** List of common Southern expressions—many of them vulgarisms—that have not, so far as I know, either old English or provincial English authority. . . *scuttler* or *streakfield* (striped lizard). **1909** *Science* new ser 30.123 **nGA,** The blue-tailed skink (*Eumeces fasciatus* Linnaeus). . . In every field and wood, they may be found basking in the sun or running with great rapidity over the ground, until they seem only a streak, hence the common name streak-field. **1948** *Amer. Midland Naturalist* 40.382 **S Midl,** *Cnemidophorus sexlineatus.* . . Racerunner, fieldstreak.—We saw several of these lizards . . but were unable to collect a specimen.

streak gravy See **streaked gravy**

streak-id See **streaked**

streakity-strikity See **streakedy-strikedy**

streak off v phr   [Cf *OED2 strike* v. 16 "To mark off (land, a ridge)"]   **Sth**

To mark out (a ridge, row, or field) with a plow.

1962 Faulkner *Reivers* 89 **MS,** Every spring a middle is streaked off in the best ground on the place, and every stalk of cotton betwixt that middle and the edge of the field belongs to the Christmas fund. **1967** *DARE* FW Addit **LA**1, *Streak it off*—to lay off a row as a guide for planting in a field. **c1974** Jones *Ozark Hill Boy* 8 **AR** (as of c1910), We cut and hauled wood, made and hauled rails, and streaked off the entire place and planted a crop. **1986** Pederson *LAGS Concordance,* 1 inf, **ceGA,** Streaking off (the rows).

streak of lean n   Pronc-sp *streaker-lean*   Similarly n *streak of fat;* often in comb *streak of lean and streak of fat* and varr chiefly **SE**   See Map

=**middling 2** with alternating strips of lean and fat meat.

1874 Campbell *GA Baptists* 490, Instead of cod liver oil, I have been, and am still, taking (for dinner) broiled middling, (streak of lean and streak of fat.) **1884** *Atlanta Constitution* (GA) 16 Mar 14/4, We . . briled some streak of lean and streak of fat on the coals. **1912** Zettler *War Stories* 52 **GA** (as of 1861), We cooked the biscuits and fried the "streak of lean and streak of fat." **1935** Caldwell *Kneel* 245 **GA,** Can't you go up to the big house and ask for a little piece of streak-of-lean? **1950** *PADS* 14.64 **SC,** Streak o' lean. . . Salt pork sides with one or more streaks of lean meat. **1954** *Harder Coll.* **cwTN,** Streak o' lean: middlin' meat with lines of lean meat in it. **1956** McAtee *Some Dialect NC* 43, *Streak o'lean:* . . salt pork sides with one or more streaks of lean meat. **1965–70** *DARE* (Qu. H38, . . *Words for bacon [including joking*

ones]) 11 Infs, 10 **SE,** Streak of lean; **AL**60, **GA**90, 92, Streak of lean ['strɪk ə 'lin]; **NC**84, Streak of lean (salt pork) comes from the same part of the hog as bacon; can be used as bacon; **GA**88, Streak of lean—also called sowbelly; **NC**10, Streak of lean—regular bacon; **FL**8, **NC**52, Streak of lean (and) streak of fat; **GA**85, 88, **MS**54, Streak of fat; **GA**81, Streak of fat—not cured, but salted; **NC**10, Streak of fat—salt pork; **NY**223, Streak of fat—pork, but not smoked; [**MS**25, Strip of lean]. **1971** *Thompson Coll.* **cnAL,** cw,c**GA,** *Streak-o'-lean* . . from "dry salt pork bellies." **1972** *Atlanta Letters* c**GA,** *Streak o' lean and streak o' fat*—salt pork, side meat, and in the market pork belly. **1984** Wilder *You All Spoken Here* 87 **Sth,** *Streak gravy:* Gravy made from streaker-lean, streaker-fat bacon. **1989** Pederson *LAGS Tech. Index* 158 **Gulf Region** *(Salt pork)* 86 infs, Streak of (the) lean; 27 infs, Streak of lean streak of fat; 3 infs, Streak of lean and (a) streak of fat; 4 infs, Streak of fat; 2 infs, Streak of fat (and) streak of lean. *Ibid* 159, *(Smoked meat)* 16 infs, **Gulf Region,** Streak of lean. **2008** *DARE* File—Internet **GA,** I can tell ya what a biscuit with a slice of streak-of-lean is, . . or even grits with red-eye gravy. . . but I simply don't know what a ringding is.

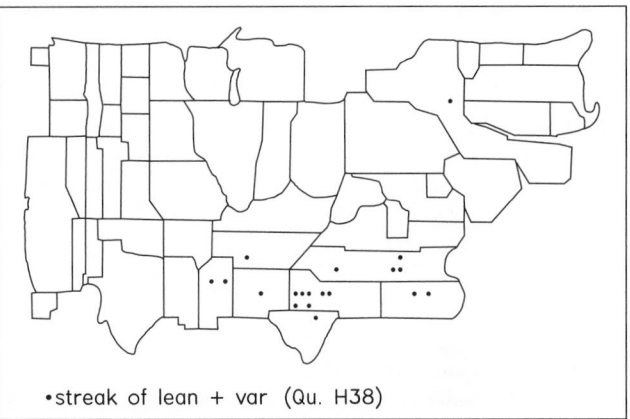

•streak of lean + var (Qu. H38)

streak of rust n   Also *two streaks of rust*

A little-used or poorly maintained railway line.

1869 *Scientific Amer.* 20.395, An engineer resigned his position on a Western railroad in disgust, because, as he said, it consisted of nothing but the right of way and two streaks of rust. **1879** *Chester Daily Times* (PA) [19 Nov] [4]/2 (newspaperarchive.com), It [=the Chicago and Northwestern Railway] was for some time, as its later day and would-be rivals put it, "a streak of rust." **1907** *Daily Rev.* (Decatur IL) 6 Nov 10/2, The most material need . . was . . a man that could change the streak of rust called the Peoria division into something resembling a railroad. **1942** Berrey–Van den Bark *Amer. Slang* 775.1, *Railroad.* . . streak of rust . . *a little-used or discontinued railway.* **1945** Hubbard *Railroad Ave.* 358, Rust or *streak o' rust*—Railroad. **1967–69** *DARE* (Qu. N37, *Joking names for a branch railroad that is not very important or gives poor service*) Infs **IA**19, **PA**193, Streak of rust; **IL**11, **WI**51, Two streaks of rust. **1976** Gould *Blackie's RR Hdbk.* 18, *Streak of rust:* A branch line or seldom used railroad. **2003** *DARE* File—Internet **IA** (as of c1890), Prosperity . . was to be short lived for the "streak of rust," as it was called by many envious citizens of Rock Rapids. When the Northwestern Railroad began its program of retrenchments during the depression . . it started with the retirement of its "curious branch from Luverne, Minnesota to Doon, Iowa in 1934."

streaky See **streaked**

streaky bacon See **streaked meat**

streaky gravy See **streaked gravy**

streaky-head See **streaked-head turtle**

streaky meat See **streaked meat**

stream orchid n   Also *stream orchis*

A western **helleborine** (here: *Epipactis gigantea*).

1901 Jepson *Flora CA* 132, *E[pipactis] gigantea.* . . Stream Orchis. **1950** Correll *Native Orchids* 128, *Epipactis gigantea.* . . Common names: Giant Helleborine, Stream Orchid [etc]. **1966** *Julian Apple Day* 15 **csCA,** She . . still knows where pink ocotillo and stream orchis grow. **1979** Spellenberg *Audubon Guide N. Amer. Wildflowers W. Region* 641, Stream Orchid. . . Deserts to mountains in springs or seeps, near ponds, along streams.

stream shooter n

Either of two **dace:** *Rhinichthys atratulus* or **longnose dace.**

1962 Becker *Intra-Spec. Variation* 3, A minnow dealer, with whom I have spoken. . . had never distinguished between *R[hinichthys] cataractae* and *R. atratulus,* always called both by the names "slipjack", "stoneroller", or "stream shooter", and doubted that they were separate species until I pointed out to him the distinguishing morphological differences.

strean See **strain**

streecar See **streetcar**

streech See **stretch**

streel n [Ir dial; cf *DNE, DPEIE*]

A slovenly woman; hence adj *streely* unkempt, disheveled.

[**1925** *DN* 5.344 **Nfld,** *Streel.* . . A dirty, slovenly woman.] **1967** *DARE* (Qu. HH36, *A careless, slovenly woman: "She's just an old _____."*) Inf **IL**5, Streel—Irish word meaning slovenly woman; used amongst people of Irish descent, used often in Nauvoo. **1982** *Smithsonian Letters* **IA,** "Streel"—(adj. form—"streely")—my grandmother's word for unkempt ("Go comb your hair & pull up your socks—you look like an old streel.")

streen(ings) See **strain**

street apple n

1 =**alley apple 1.**

1995 *DARE* File **Newark NJ** (as of 1960s) [Black], [TV interview:] We looked up and there were street apples coming down from the rooftops and windows, you know, bottles and rocks.

2 =**alley apple 2.** Cf **road apple**

1967 *DARE* FW Addit **sePA,** *Street apples* or *alley apples*—horse droppings. The Amish drive nothing but horses in this area. Strasburg PA—said by men.

street Arab See **Arab** n **B1**

streetcar n Pronc-sp *streecar* **widespread exc NEast** See Map Cf **trolley**

A public conveyance for passengers that runs on tracks on city streets.

1857 Parton *Fresh Leaves* 263, I . . am prepared to scream . . any minute after every seat in a street car is filled. **1862** Trollope *N. Amer.* 1.185 **seWI,** Omnibuses, or street cars working on rails run hither and thither. **1882** *Manufacturer & Builder* 14.219, The cable system . . would appear to have solved the vexed question of supplanting animal power for street-car propulsion. **1901** *Amer. Missionary* 55.91 **MS,** This bill provides that the street car companies shall furnish separate cars for blacks and whites. **1947** Williams *A Streetcar Named Desire* [title] **New Orleans LA.** **1965–70** *DARE* (Qu. N34, *An electric car that runs on tracks in a city*) 421 Infs, **widespread exc NEast,** Streetcar; (Qu. N41a, . . *Horse-drawn vehicles . . to carry people*) Infs **AL**6, **CA**28, **DC**12, **GA**15, **NE**9, **OH**77, **PA**29, **TX**28, (Horse-drawn) streetcar. **1982** McCool *Sam McCool's Pittsburghese* 34 **PA,** Streecar: streetcar or trolley. **2003** *WI State Jrl.* (Madison) 16 Dec sec A 8/1, Don't sidetrack streetcar plan. . . The goal was to offer commuters a rail alternative to car travel.

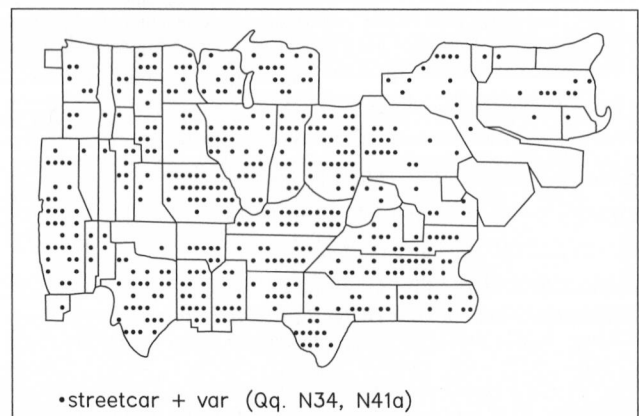

•streetcar + var (Qq. N34, N41a)

street card n

See quots.

2001 *DARE* File **nwKS,** Street card—These cards are hung on the doors of local businesses after a death, to inform the townspeople. [*DARE* Ed: The card lists the name of the deceased along with dates and places of birth and death, plus details of the visitation and funeral.] **2004** *Ibid* **nwKS,** The term "street cards" is probably a funeral industry slang for the window cards that we put up around town when a death has occurred to alert the townspeople to the death and give them the funeral and burial information. Street cards are probably used only in smaller towns and then not every town uses them.

streetch See **stretch**

street checkers n **esp NYC** Cf **skelly**

A children's street game; see quots.

1931 *Jrl. Educ. Sociol.* 4.610, Street checkers is played in much the same way as marbles. A chalk diagram is drawn on the sidewalk with numbered squares, the checker is placed in square number 1 and flipped with the fingers to square number 2 and so on. The checker must slide into the square to assure a consecutive turn. The winner is the player who reaches the last square first. **1975** Ferretti *Gt. Amer. Book Sidewalk Games* 229, *Street checkers.* . . A simple rectangle is chalked off in the street, and a stake of regular checkers (perhaps as many as five per player) is set inside the rectangle. Then, the shooters shoot them out, marbles style, with shooters. . . The shooter is placed flat on the ground shot by flicking the forefinger off the thumb and hitting it straight on. This is a "for keeps" game. **1985** *NY Times* (NY) 17 Feb sec 1 58/1 **NYC** (as of c1930), As an 8-year-old, he invented a lead-filled disk that made him a winner at street checkers—in which a player tries to knock an opponent's checker pieces from an area marked on the street. **2003** *DARE* File—Internet **NYC** (as of 1940s–50s), My Brooklyn was Williamsburg. . . We . . played handball, stick ball, punch ball, potsy, stoop ball, street checkers.

street cleaner n *among Black speakers* Cf **street, in the**

A promiscuous woman; a prostitute.

1982 Walker *Color Purple* 40 **GA** [Black], Everybody know who he mean. He talk bout a strumpet in short skirts, smoking cigarettes, drinking gin. Singing for money and taking other women mens. Talk bout slut, hussy, heifer and streetcleaner. **1998** (2000) Green *Cassell's Dict. Slang* 1149, *Streetcleaner.* . . [1930s–50s] (US Black) *1* a promiscuous woman *2* a prostitute.

street hockey See **hockey** n[1] **1**

street, in the adj phr Also *in the streets* **esp Sth, S Midl** See Map *among Black speakers* Cf *on the road, in the* ~ (at **road** n[1] **B3a**), **street cleaner**

Gadding about, esp in search of pleasure or sexual adventure.

1965–70 *DARE* (Qu. Y29b, . . *About a man [who doesn't stay home much]: "He's always _____."*) Infs **DC**11, **FL**48, 51, **GA**90, **MS**45, 80, **PA**66, 241, **TX**86, In the street(s); [**SC**26, He stay in the street; **MI**72, Staying out in the street]; (Qu. Y29a, *To 'go out' a great deal, not to stay at home much: "She's always _____."*) Infs **FL**48, **LA**8, **MS**80, **MO**23, **NC**88, **SC**66, 70, **TX**86, In the street(s); [**MI**72, Staying out in the street]. [All Infs Black, 14 of 16 total Infs female] [**1986** Pederson *LAGS Concordance (Whorehouse)* 1 inf, swAL, In the street. [Inf Black]]

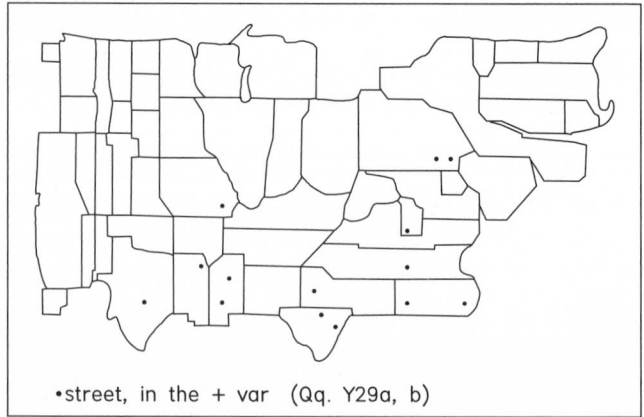

•street, in the + var (Qq. Y29a, b)

street lawn n **scattered, but esp OH**
=**tree lawn.**

1886 in 2008 (acc) Lexis–Nexis Legal Research *State Case Law: MI* (Internet), The company planted one of its guy-posts . . in the street lawn, on the south side of Joy street, in front of the residence of the plaintiff. . . The post was placed in the lawn, which was used for shade trees and ornamental purposes, about midway between the curb and sidewalk. **1938** *Ibid: OH,* His automobile started to skid, finally causing said automobile to go over the curb on the west side of South State Street and against two trees located in the street lawn in front of the premises. **1967** *DARE* (Qu. N44, *In a town, the strip of grass and trees between the sidewalk and the curb*) Inf **OH**29, Street lawn. **2004** *DARE* File—Internet **nwOH,** Rake leaves to the devil strip, the area between the curb and the sidewalk. *Ibid* **nwOH,** No person shall park in the devil strip or street lawn area. *Ibid* **cOH,** No consumption of alcoholic beverages is allowed on the street, city sidewalks, or street lawn. *Ibid* **cND,** This grant offers a direct reimbursement to citizens . . who plant trees in the City's street-lawn area adjacent to their property. *Ibid* **cnOH,** No parking on street lawn area. *Ibid* **swMI,** Please try to keep leaves within the street lawn right-of-way. *Ibid* **neOH,** No person shall drive a vehicle on a street lawn area. *Ibid* **cOH,** The tree lawn, street lawn, or park strip includes the strip of land (usually grassed) lying between the street right-of-way line and the street curb or pavement. [*DARE* Ed: A search of the Internet suggests that while the term *street lawn* is in use in scattered communities elsewhere, it occurs most frequently in **OH,** where it is often the term adopted in city ordinances.]

street runner n   Cf **roadrunner 4; street, in the**
See quots.

1904 in 2004 King *To Find Peace* 113 **LA,** The house-girl . . turned out to be insolent. . . A street runner by day & night—she had become. **1968–70** *DARE* (Qu. Y29a, *To 'go out' a great deal, not to stay at home much:* "*She's always _____.*") Inf **NJ**67, Street runner; (Qu. HH37, *An immoral woman*) Inf **OH**41, Street runner. **2001** Hamer *What It Means* 100 [Black], My daughter, she ain't perfect but she ain't no street-runner.

street sparrow n
=**English sparrow.**

1879 *St. Nicholas* 6.210, She saw nothing but the snow, and two street-sparrows picking up crumbs, and chattering noisily to each other. **1902** Howells *Lit. & Life* 93 **NY,** The street sparrows, pestiferous and persistent as they are, would forsake my sylvan pageant if I spoke of the Bird-foot Violet as the *Viola Pedata.* **1923** Dawson *Birds CA* 1.223, English Sparrow. . . Synonyms . . Domestic Sparrow. Street Sparrow [etc.]. **1967–70** *DARE* (Qu. Q21, . . *Kinds of sparrows*) Infs **ID**5, **KY**94, **TX**96, Street sparrow.

street sweeper n
=**English sparrow.**

1969 *DARE* (Qu. Q22, *Joking names or nicknames for the common sparrow*) Inf **MI**101, Street sweeper.

street yarn n   [Cf *EDD* spin street yarn (at *spin* v. 7.(9))]   *old-fash*

Gossip, idle talk—usu in phr *spin street yarn* to gossip; hence vbl nouns *spinning street yarn, street-yarning* spreading gossip; n *street-yarn spinner* a gossip.

1782 in 1980 Morris *Papers* 5.285 **CT,** It would be out of my Power to neglect my Business having nothing to divert me from it unless to spin Street Yarn. **1808** in 1895 *New Engl. Mag.* 18.244, But now our ships they are unrigged—/ Our sailors spin street-yarn, Sir. **1828** *N. Amer. Rev.* 27.128, Does Mr Droz really mean to tell us, that a tailor, for instance, will best consult his happiness by . . passing most of his precious hours in spinning street-yarn? **1850** *Defiance Democrat* (OH) 20 July 1/2, It does away at once with the tittle tattle, gossip, street yarn, foolish exagerations [sic], scandal, and news mongering. **1856** in 1953 *Post–Std.* (Syracuse NY) 13 Sept sec C 7/5, Feathers, fans, dress, sofa-lolling, scandal-making, wearing kids, talking nonsense, and street-yarning do not make the true woman. **1864** *Harper's New Mth. Mag.* 29.585 **NEng,** She spun more street-yarn than her ancestors had ever footed in the course of their united lives. **c1870** in 2003 *DARE* File—Internet **KY,** He never loitered about the streets, was no street yarn spinner, but was of quiet disposition. **1913** (1980) Hardy *OH Schoolmistress* 56, She . . asked, "Why didn't you tell her you came up here to see her spin street-yarn?" **1959** *VT Hist.* 27.167 **cw,swVT,** Spin street yarns. . . To gossip. Rare. Rutland.

streissler n   [Appar var of PaGer *schtreissel* pretzel, small round cake]   **PaGer area**
A pastry; see quots.

c1910 in 1953 *PA Dutchman* 15 Feb 9, There was one stand that we never saw at any other time. It was from Lititz, and had huge cakes, round, thick, tight as a cork. I have eaten nothing so delicious since. I

think they were called "Streisslers." **1935** *AmSp* 10.170 **PA** [Engl of PA Germans], Other German words used in English are. . . *Streisslers,* a pastry run through a funnel and fried in grease. **1957** *Gettysburg Times* (PA) 28 June 9/6, Farm women . . will preside at the wooden tables . . serving such typical Dutch delicacies as hubba beer, streissler, shoofly pie.

strength n   Usu |streŋ(k)θ|; also freq |striŋ(k)θ, strenθ, strinθ|; for addit varr see quots   Pronc-spp *strangth, strank, stren(g)k, strenth*   Cf Pronc Intro 3.I.4, 20, **length**
Std sense, var forms.

1753 in 2006 Montgomery *From Ulster* 150 **cPA,** Ezekel Strenth of ye lord. **1792** in 1956 Eliason *Tarheel Talk* 318 **ce,seNC,** Strenth. **1834** (1925) Evans *Jrl.* 3.214 **IN,** Some few traits of their . . Herculian strenth appeared in their brawny . . limbs. **1878** *Appletons' Jrl.* 5.413 **PA,** The Pennsylvanian says *strenth* and *lenth.* **1889** *Overland Mth.* (2d ser) 13.631 **NC** [Black], He had n' got dis foot mo' d'n half turnt back befo' his strenk giv out. **1893** Owen *Voodoo Tales* 53 **MO** [Black], Yo' betteh git dat lil ole niggah ter putt fo'th huh strenk. **1899** Chesnutt *Conjure Woman* 26 **NC** [Black], En ef he don't pick up his strenk mighty soon, I spec' I'm gwine ter lose 'im. **1899** (1912) Green *VA Folk-Speech* 423, Strangth. . . For *strength*. . . Strenth. . . A form of *strength.* **1902** *DN* 2.246 **sIL,** Strength. Often pronounced [strenθ]. **1922** Gonzales *Black Border* 329 **sSC, GA coasts** [Gullah glossary], Strengk—strength. **1923** *DN* 5.222 **swMO,** Strenth. . . Strength. **1930** *AmSp* 5.205 **Ozarks,** The hillman nearly always substitutes *n* for *ng* in such words as *length* and *strength.* **1937** *AmSp* 12.126 **Upstate NY,** Strength [occurs] 249 times with [ŋ], 19 times with [ŋk], four times with [n]. **1941** O'Donnell *Great Big Doorstep* 78 **LA** [Cajun], Eight strappin chirren, taking the strank of the ones that died. **1942** *AmSp* 17.156 **seNY,** Strength—[n] 24, [ŋk] 2, [n] 5. **1943** *AmSp* 18.264 **VA,** The raising of [ɛ] to [ɪ] is very common . . [strɪnθ] or [strɪŋθ]. *Ibid* 270, Strength frequently [has] [n] instead of [ŋ] . . [strɪnθ]. [strɪnθ]. **1952** Brown *NC Folkl.* 1.595, Strenth [strɛnθ, strɪnθ]. . . Strength. **1967** *DARE* (Qu. A21, *When someone is in too much of a hurry . . "Now just slow down! Don't _____."*) Inf **HI**8, Use your strength [strɛntθ]. **1973** Gawthrop *Dial. Calumet* 57 **nwIN,** /k/. . . occurs regularly in such words as . . *strength* in the speech of all informants. **1975** Gould *ME Lingo* 280, Strenth—Proper sound for strength: "He don't know his own strenth." **1982** McCool *Sam McCool's Pittsburghese* 34 **PA,** Strenth: strength. **2000** Shores *Tangier Is.* 175 **Chesapeake Bay,** *Length* and *strength* have the vowel of "stray."

strengthy adj   Also *strenthy*   [nEngl, Scots dial]   Cf Intro "Language Changes" III.1
Strong, sturdy; fortifying.

1831 in 1904 *Amer. Hist. Assoc. Annual Rept. for 1903* 1.469 **cGA,** Mr. Wiggins addressed the board in a speech containing some *lengthy, strenthy,* and *depthy* argument. **1851** Wheeler *Rural Homes* 209, Black or bronze are the coverings for iron—the grave, honest, strengthy old substance will only be contented with sober, unchanging negation of gaiety in hue. *Ibid* 278, The prodigal, strengthy giants of younger growth are here hewn away. **1862** *Vanity Fair* 5.47, He saw *Glorianna* emerge from the other room with two cocktails, fragrant and strengthy. **1884** *Bucks Co. Gaz.* (Bristol PA) 14 Feb 1/7, A temperance hotel—nothing stronger than butter, which was rather strengthy when A.W. was there. **1911** *Syracuse Herald* (NY) 2 Nov 8/7, You don't look a very strengthy lady, and I'll fill it [=a hand bellows] with wind for ye. . . [From] Youth's Companion. **1916** *DN* 4.348 **cTX** (as of 1896), Strengthy. . . Strong. **1928** in 1952 Mathes *Tall Tales* 60 **sAppalachians,** They's worse things than killin' a man's body, even the fine, strengthy body of a young man! **1952** Justus *Children Gt. Smoky Mts.* 18 **eTN,** It's tasty and it's strengthy. *Ibid* 53, While you go atter them I'll take some strengthy scantlings and some twenty-penny nails and fix that broken fence. **2002** *DARE* File—Internet **MD,** He's encountered by strengthy apes who enslave him.

strenk, strenth See **strength**

stretch n, v   Usu |stretʃ|; also esp **sAppalachians** |stritʃ| Pronc-spp *streach, stree(t)ch*
A Pronc forms.   [Engl dial]

1837 Sherwood *Gaz. GA* 71, Provincialisms. . . Streetch, for stretch. **1843** (1916) Hall *New Purchase* 146 **IN,** We kin lay in stores enough at Squattertown to last more nor six months on a streech. **1917** in 1944 *ADD* **sWV,** Stretch. . . streach. **1942** Hall *Smoky Mt. Speech* 21 **wNC, eTN,** An Emerts Cove family told, with some amusement, that a neighbor pronounced *stretch* [stritʃ]; an aged informant of Wears Valley said that this was once the usual pronunciation.

B As noun.

A game for two players employing a knife or other sharp-pointed object; see quots. **scattered, but esp NEast** See Map

1965–70 *DARE* (Qu. EE5, *Games where you try to make a jackknife stick in the ground*) 13 Infs, **scattered, but esp NEast**, Stretch; **MA9**, Stretch—two players face each other; **NY98**, Stretch—two guys stand facing in opposite directions with two left or two right feet touching. They take turns sticking the knife. The one who did not throw the knife has to put his free foot next to the knife and pull it out of the ground without moving his foot away from the other guy's; **PA94**, Stretch—stretch as far away as knife stuck. **1967** *DARE* FW Addit **cwCA**, Since the beginning of the current school year, students have been playing a game called stretch on all the campus lawns. Stretch is played by tossing a pencil down into the ground. The pencil must stick up within two feet of the side of your opponent's feet. Your opponent has his feet together up to this point, stretches a leg to the pencil, then takes his turn at throwing. The loser is the person who is already so stretched that he cannot extend his foot to the required length. [**1969** Opie–Opie *Children's Games* 219, The object of the game is to force the opponent to stretch his legs so far apart that he cannot move them further, and gives in, or falls over while attempting the stretch . . In England and Wales the usual names for the game are 'Split the Kipper', 'Splits', and 'Stretch'.] **1983** *DARE* File CO, UT, (*Games where you try to make a jackknife stick in the ground*) Stretch. **1986** Pederson *LAGS Concordance* (*Knife . . games*) 3 infs, **FL, MS, TN**, Stretch; 1 inf, **csTN**, Stretch—knife-throwing game; stretched for knife; 1 inf, **seLA**, Stretch—feet together; knife thrown near; stretch.

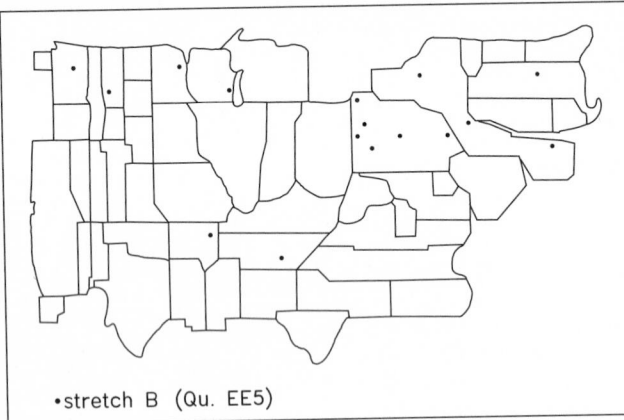

•stretch B (Qu. EE5)

stretchberry n **esp TX**

1 also *stretcher berry*: The fruit of a **greenbrier** (here: *Smilax bona-nox*); the plant itself. [See quot 1888] Also called **bamboo, bamboo brier, ~ vine, bullbrier, catbrier, China brier, Chinaroot 1, false sarsaparilla 2, gumberry 2, saw brier, smilax, tramp's-trouble, wild potato 4a**

1888 Torrey Bot. Club *Bulletin* 15.162 **TX**, It [=*Smilax bona-nox*] is commonly known as 'bramble' or 'stretchberry,' the latter name from the thin, rubber-like covering over the seed, which is often used by children to put with chewing-gum, making the gum stretch like rubber. **1897** *Jrl. Amer. Folkl.* 10.145 **TX**, *Smilax Bona-nox* . . bamboo vine, stretch-berry, Waco. **1920** *Torreya* 20.19 **SC**, *Smilax bona-nox* . . Stretch-berry, Charleston. **1951** *PADS* 15.29 **TX**, *Smilax bona-nox* . . Stretch-berry; gum-berry. **1954** *Harder Coll.* **cwTN**, Stretch berries, put in wax (chewing gum) to stretch it. **1959** Sanders *Echoes* 34 **swAR**, He . . gave me a stick of the chewing gum. It . . had no stretch in it like when I would stop down on the branch and pick some stretch berries and chew in with my gum. **1963** Owens *Look to River* 74 **TX**, Thorns of stretchberry vines pulled his clothes. **1967** *DARE* (Qu. I44, *What kinds of berries grow wild around here?*) Inf **AR55**, Stretcher berries—grow on briers and kids chew 'em like gum. **2004** *DARE* File—Internet **TX**, [Caption:] Young Sprout of Stretchberry Greenbriar.

2 The fruit of a **forestiera** (here: *Forestiera pubescens*); the plant itself. [See quot 1978]

1970 Correll *Plants TX* 1200, Stretch-berry . . Children are known to chew the fruits of this species with ordinary chewing-gum to produce a sort of "bubble-gum." **1978** *Chinquapin* 1.5.59 **eTX** (as of c1920), We would go out and pick it [=sweet gum], and then we would pick these little old black berries we called stretch berries in that day, and we would peel the black outside off . . and take that little white thin, tissue-thin, strippin' that was . . around that seed, and we would put it in our gum. And we would just chew it . . and you could just blow great big old bubbles with it. It was our bubble gum. **2004** *DARE* File—Internet **OK**, *Forestiera pubescens*. . . Common names: elbow bush, stretchberry.

stretcher n

1 =**spreader**; hence n *stretcher rig*; see quot 1986. [*EDD stretcher* sb. 1 "The bar which keeps the chains apart between the horses in plowing &c."] Cf **evener 1**

1814 in 2008 *DARE* File—Internet **IN**, 1 horse stretcher .75—1 set double trees 2 clevises 1.25. **1882** *Star & Sentinel* (Gettysburg PA) 15 Feb [3]/6 (newspaperarchive.com), [Advt:] Single, double and treble Trees, two-horse Stretcher, Feed Trough [etc]. **1943** *Frederick Post* (MD) 20 Mar 8/2, [Advt:] 3 double trees, 3 triple trees, 6 single trees, jockey sticks, 2-horse stretcher, 3-horse stretcher. **1958** McCulloch *Woods Words* 183 **Pacific NW**, Stretcher—A bar to keep the singletrees spread apart when skidding with horses. **1966** Dakin *Dial. Vocab. Ohio R. Valley* 2.153, Evener. . . the pivoted bar with a singletree attached at each end—used when two horses are harnessed abreast. . . Two Kentucky informants . . say *stretcher*—apparently = *doubletree*. **1967** *DARE* (Qu. L47, *The two movable bars behind a team of horses are fastened to a longer piece; this is a* ____) Inf **NV2**, Evener or stretcher. **1967** *DARE* Tape **AR50**, [Inf:] We used stretchers and grabs. [FW:] What's a stretcher? [Inf:] Well, it's a device you hook your team to, then hook your grabs onto that just so you can skid your logs. **1967–69** *DARE* FW Addit **AR**, Stretchers is a chain with a stick in it, and you put it on each end of a log to haul it out; **swKY**, Stretchers—a doubletree (the bar for two horses to be hitched to). **1976** Sublette Co. Artist Guild *More Tales* 159 **WY** (as of c1900), A heavy chain ran down between the horses from the lead team to the front wagon. To this chain were fastened what was called "stretchers". These were similar to a set of singletrees and doubletrees except that an iron pipe was used instead of the doubletree. Also a chain ran down to the main chain from each singletree eliminating a center pin. This long "lead chain" was usually run through a loose loop hanging below the wagon tongue. **1986** Pederson *LAGS Concordance* (*Singletree*) 1 inf, **ceTX**, Stretcher rig—used when 6 horses needed [for] hauling; (*Doubletree*) 1 inf, **cwLA**, Stretcher rig—for more than two; 1 inf, **neMS**, Stretchers; (*Principal parts of drag*) 1 inf, **ceTN**, Stretchers—hooked onto clevis with swivel link.

2 Used in var combs for a nonexistent item used as the basis for a practical joke.

1909 *Fresno Morning Republican* (CA) 3 Oct [20]/1 (newspaperarchive.com), Tommy is asked to find the paper stretcher, quick, for Mr. Jones' stenographer. . . If Tommy Green is a country boy, whose first real job is in a quarry, he will probably come in contact with the stone stretcher before he has been at work many hours. **1912** *NV State Jrl.* (Reno) 24 Sept 9/1, *Wanted Striped Paint*—Tales about left handed monkey wrenches, paper stretcher and feather foundries are outclassed. **1921** *DN* 5.93, Words used in practical jokes upon the uninitiated in crafts, business houses, the army and navy, and doubtless in other relations. . . *bottle stretcher*. *Ibid* 94, *Cable stretcher*. . . *check stretcher*. St. Louis and Cleveland. . . *glass stretcher*. *Ibid* 95, *Paper stretcher*. . . *shoe-string stretcher*. . . *timber stretcher*. *Ibid* 97, *Fly wheel stretcher*. **1922** *Eaton Coll.* **nWI**, Paper-stretcher . . what greenhorns in paper mills are sent to get. **1923** *DN* 5.241, *Envelope stretcher*. *Ibid* 242, *Way-bill stretcher*. **1938** *Appleton Post–Crescent* (WI) 20 June 10/5, He gave one of the lads an armful of boards, stakes and odds and ends which had been tied together and labeled "tent stretcher" and told him to take it to troop No. 14. **1946** *PADS* 6.33 **VA**, Yepping stretcher. . . Quarry sought on a college snipe hunt. Roanoke College, around 1900. **1951** in 1953 Botkin–Harlow *Treas. Railroad Folkl.* 331, Harassed substitutes are sent from one clerk to another, in search of a sack stretcher, case scraper, or similar weird article. **1965–70** *DARE* (Qu. HH14, *Ways of teasing a beginner or inexperienced person—for example, by sending him for a 'left-handed monkey wrench': "Go get me* ____ ") 18 Infs, **scattered, but somewhat more freq Nth, N Midl**, Board-stretcher; 15 Infs, **scattered**, Paper-stretcher; 11 Infs, **esp Lower Missip Valley**, Pipe-stretcher; 8 Infs, **scattered**, Lumber-stretcher; 5 Infs, **scattered**, Plank-stretcher; 60 Infs, **scattered**, Backroom (*or* bacon, bar, bolt, bottle, box, brick, bucket, cable, cat, cement, chain, check, corset, cup, currency, ditch, door, feed, fence, flag, gate, kettle, etc) -stretcher; (Qu. CC17) Inf **FL22**, Get a lumber-stretcher. **1970** *DARE* File **seNC**, Check-stretcher. **1977** *Ibid* **nwIL**, "Go to the walk-in and get me the bacon-stretcher." Used rather frequently between 1967–1973 in a restaurant in Peoria. **1982** Slone *How We Talked* 21 **eKY** (as of c1950), A "lumber stretcher"—An imaginary tool used to stretch lumber when a board has been cut too short. A greenhorn or someone new at the job was always sent to borrow a lumber stretcher. **2007** *DARE* File—Internet, *What does a lumber stretcher look like?* I just started working at a lumber yard part time after school. My boss told me to go find the lumber stretcher.

3 also *stretcher band:* See quot. Cf **stretching leather**
1967–69 *DARE* (Qu. F49, . . *Rubber band;* not asked in early QRs) Infs **KY**34, 41, Stretcher (band).

4 See **stretch worm.**

stretcher band See **stretcher 3**

stretcher berry See **stretchberry 1**

stretcher rig See **stretcher 1**

stretch flow n **SE** *chiefly hist*
In rice-growing: the second flooding of the field; hence n *stretch water* the water constituting this flooding.
1854 *De Bow's Rev.* 16.610 **GA,** Two days after this weeding, the long water will gradually be drawn off. [Footnote to *long water:*] In Georgia and elsewhere, perhaps, this is called the "stretch flow." **1867** *Harper's Weekly* 5 Jan 5 **ceGA,** When it [=rice] has reached two or three inches in height it is again flooded with what is technically called stretch-water. **1897** *Jrl. & Rev.* (Aiken SC) 20 Oct [5]/4 (newspaperarchive.com), After the tender plant has gotten its head well above the ground, what is known as the "stretch flow" is turned on. **1936** Smith–Sass *Carolina Rice* 27 **SC coast** (as of 1850s), As soon as the rice could be "trailed" from bank to bank with the dew on it at sunrise, the water would again be put on for the "point-flow," or, as it was sometimes called, the "stretch-flow" or "long-flow." This time it was quite deep, even to the top of the check banks, and the rice was "stretched" from three to six inches according to the temperature, for one of the reasons for the water at that season was that it kept the rice warm. **1937** Heyward *Madagascar* 37 **sSC coast,** The only object of the stretch-flow was to destroy grasses which had sprouted after the sprout-flow had been withdrawn. **2004** *DARE* File—Internet **SC,** As the rice matures, the water level is increased. This is called "stretch water."

stretch hives n Cf **bold hives 2,** *DS* BB24, 25
See quots.
1970 *Jrl. Amer. Folkl.* 83.139, Informants reported . . that it was generally believed in the southern mountains that all infants should be made to break out in "little red" hives. If the infant did not break out with these hives, the disease would "go in" and turn into the dreaded and fatal, "bold" or "stretch" hives. **1990** Cavender *Folk Med. Lexicon* 32 **sAppalachians,** *Stretch hives*—rash.

stretching vbl n **esp S Midl**
Serving or waiting at table—freq in v phr *do one's own stretching* to serve oneself.
1885 Baker *At the Pastor's* 14, Guda went round with the coffee-pot: Stina had disappeared; for, as she said, "the family always did their own stretching." **1891** *Living Age* 190.152, A friend of mine says that when a parlor-maid came to be interviewed she inquired, "Do you do your own stretching?" Upon inquiry she learnt that this meant, "Do you serve yourselves at table?" **1892** *Jrl. Amer. Folkl.* 5.236 **nMD,** In Baltimore, a candidate for the position of house servant inquired of the lady if she did her own "stretching," meaning if he should be required to *wait* on the table. **1905** *DN* 3.96 **nwAR,** *Stretching.* . . Waiting on oneself at table. 'Do you do your own stretching?' Rare. **1918** *DN* 5.19 **NC,** *Stretching,* waiting on the table. **1942** in 1944 *ADD* **cKY, wPA,** *Stretch.* . . [The maid's away tonight. You'll have to do your own] stretching. [We'll do housework, but no] stretching. **1952** Brown *NC Folkl.* 1.595, *Stretch.* . . To wait on the table. "I'll cook, wash dishes, and do such things; but you'll have to do the stretching." **1954** *Titusville Herald* (PA) 8 Apr 4/2, [Syndicated column:] My secretary . . hired a new maid last week. Salary and hours had been agreed upon when the applicant suddenly inquired, "Do you folks do your own stretching?"

stretching leather n Cf **stretcher 3**
1982 Slone *How We Talked* 36 **eKY** (as of c1950), *Stretching leather*—rubber.

stretching the telegraph wire n
1964 Wallace *Frontier Life* 41 **OK** (as of 1893–1906), We all ate our lunches and then continued our games of Dare-base, Hopscotch, Blackman, and a few of the "kissing" games, such as Painting the Double Shovel, and Stretching the Telegraph Wire, since there was no teacher present to stop us.

stretch the blanket v phr Also *stretch one's blanket* **esp S Midl**
To exaggerate; to lie.
1851 Hooper *Widow Rugby's Husband* 120 **AL,** I have hearn 'stretchin' the blanket,' and 'shootin' with the long bow;' and I always thought we was great on that, in this here Ameriky. **1858** Green *Secret Band* 173, A man who can be excited to bet upon an election, can be excited when upon oath to stretch the blanket; or, in plainer language, to swear to a lie. **1882** *Harper's New Mth. Mag.* 64.927 **sOH,** I wuz glad ter hev Lex Farley appreshiate her, even though he stretched the blanket a little in doin' so. **1911** in 1983 Truman *Dear Bess* 28 **MO,** They were out here last spring and I tell you they ate more than harvest hands. That's saying as much about their gastronomic ability as is possible without stretching the blanket. **1917** in 1944 *ADD* **sWV,** Stretch the blanket. To exaggerate. **1923** (1946) Greer-Petrie *Angeline Doin' Society* 2 **csKY,** Somehow, he'd draw'd up the idy the parson had stretched his blankit. **1927** *AmSp* 2.348 **cwWV,** That man stretched the blanket when he told about Florida. **1953** Randolph–Wilson *Down in Holler* 289 **Ozarks,** *Stretch the blanket.* . . To exaggerate, to tell a tall story. "Don't you reckon Ab was stretchin' the blanket a little?" said one of my neighbors, referring to a man who claimed he had killed a running deer with his derringer. **c1960** *Wilson Coll.* **csKY,** *Stretch the blanket.* . . Exaggerate, lie but usually not viciously. **1985** *DARE* File, Stretch the blanket: Exaggeration, in Appalachia. **1997** in 2004 Montgomery–Hall *Dict. Smoky Mt. Engl.* 575 **wNC, eTN,** *Stretch the blanket.* . . To exaggerate. . . (known to eight consultants). **1999** *DARE* File **ceSC,** My grandmother used to say something when one of us was telling a story with elaborations that went, well, let's say somewhat beyond the facts. She would ask 'Aren't you stretchin' your blanket with that one?' I say that to our kids, and they know I mean they're really exaggerating, but sometimes their friends look at me like I've really started speaking Martian.

stretch water See **stretch flow**

stretch worm n Also *stretcher* **GA, Gulf States**
=earthworm.
[**1856** SC Court of Appeals *Rept. of Cases* 9.382, The said defendant . . did wickedly, maliciously and falsely compose, write and publish, of and concerning the said plaintiff, a false, wicked and malicious libel, . . to wit: 'To de big faced blacksmith,' (meaning the plaintiff,) 'and his stretch worm overseer, the infant, Peter Dickey, hog killer.'] **1958** Browne *Pop. Beliefs AL* 48, Stretch-worms, split up the center, washed and dried in the sunshine, then baked until dry, crushed into powder and taken, will cure chills. **1966–69** *DARE* (Qu. P5, . . *The common worm used as bait*) Inf **LA**12, Stretch worm; (Qu. P6, . . *Kinds of worms . . used for bait*) Infs **GA**1, 14, 72, Stretcher. **1986** Pederson *LAGS Concordance (Earthworms)* 1 inf, **nwAL,** Stretch worms.

strew See **strow**

stribbly See **strubbly**

strick See **strike** v A1, 2

strid See **stride** v A

striddle n Cf **scrid**
A shred, fragment.
1957 Beck *Folkl. ME* 73, One day, as the skipper was driving past her house, the horse balked and the harness fell "all to striddles." *Ibid* 168, This reminds him of a hunting trip he had with "poor" Fred . . when his clothes "was tore clear to striddles," to ribbons. **1975** Gould *ME Lingo* 280, *Striddles*—Tatters or ribbons, rags, small pieces of fabric. You sew enough *striddles* together and you've got a patchwork quilt.

stride v
A Gram form.
Past: usu *strode;* rarely *strid.*
1905 *DN* 3.102 **nwAR,** Abnormal preterites. . . strid.
B Sense.
To ride a horse astride. Cf **stride saddle**
1967 *DARE* FW Addit **TN**16, "Everybody strides now" (meaning: women don't use sidesaddles anymore). . . country people (at least older ones).

stride saddle n [By analogy with *sidesaddle*]

A saddle upon which one sits astride; hence adv phr *stride saddle* astride.

1906 *San Antonio Daily Light* (TX) 9 Dec 10/7, [Advt:] *Nothing* nicer for a Christmas present than a Ben Varga ladies' stride saddle. **1910** *Post-Std.* (Syracuse NY) 10 June 15/3, *For sale—family two-seater . . ;* also a stride saddle cheap. **1956** Ker *Vocab. W. TX* 181, *Kinds of saddles. . .* stride saddle. [1 of 67 infs] **1969** *DARE* Tape **CA**138, Later, when they were riding stride saddle, they had what they call riding skirts. **1976** Wood *What God Blessed* 82 **TX,** I have in my possession a stride saddle with the quilted seat made by Padget Brothers of Dallas, Texas. It won first prize at the Fort Worth Fat Stock Show in 1905.

striffen n Also *scriffen, scrivin, striff(l)in, strifning* [Scots, nIr dial; prob < Scots Gael *streafon, streabhon* (=Ir *sreabhann*) fringe, membrane] **chiefly S Midl**

1 A membrane such as that surrounding viscera or found on the interior surface of an eggshell; broadly, the entrails.

1892 *KS Univ. Qrly.* 1.99 **MO,** *Striffin,* or *strifning:* the membrane surrounding the abdominal viscera. **1897** (1898) Coburn *Swine Husbandry* 107 **ceIL,** The best *way* [of castrating boars] is the way understood by every old farmer, unless the hog is ruptured, in which case the striffen around the seed (called the scrotal sack) should be taken out with the seed. **1902** *DN* 2.246 **sIL,** *Striffin. . .* 1. The diaphragm. 2. Any membranous substance. 3. A niggardly portion. **1905** in 2008 (acc) Lexis-Nexis Legal Research *State Case Law: MO* (Internet), He stated that the man falling on him "bursted a striffin." **1906** *DN* 3.123 **sIN,** *Strifflins. . .* Diaphragm; entrails. Used of hogs at "killing time." **1917** *DN* 4.416 **wNC,** *Scriffen. . .* Membrane inclosing the visceral cavity or the brain. "The scriffen of the brain was cut." **c1926** in 2004 Montgomery-Hall *Dict. Smoky Mt. Engl.* 575 **wNC,** He cut away the striffin from the man's insides so as to be able to see what was wrong with him. **1927** *AmSp* 2.363 **cwWV,** *Scriffen . .* membrane lining the abdominal cavity. To relieve bloat in cattle, stick the point of a sharp knife through the scriffen. **1946** Hench *Coll.* **swVA,** A conversation . . revealed that he had a word in his speech that lots of people do not know the meaning of. It is *striffen,* a thin membrane in an animal that holds its inner organs together. **1953** Randolph-Wilson *Down in Holler* 289 **Ozarks,** *Striffin. . .* This name is applied to the membrane which lines an eggshell, also to the tough skin which protects the body of a mussel. "Pearls always lays at the end of the shell, just under the striffin," a shell-digger told me. Sometimes it means a membrane in the human body. A judge in Christian County, Mo., was asked the meaning of the word *epididymis.* "Oh, it's that striffin around the testicle," said he. **1954** Harder *Coll.* **cwTN,** *Striffin. . .* Any membrane. **c1960** Wilson *Coll.* **csKY,** *Striffen. . .* The membrane inside an egg shell; any membrane. **1963** Watkins–Watkins *Yesterday Hills* 131 **cnGA,** Some broke an egg and used the membrane (which they called "scrivin" or "scriffen") just inside the shell as a medicine for risings. **1984** Woods *WV Was Good* 223, Striffen—a bare covering of connection, such as the fibrous outside layer on skinned beef. It can mean a bare part, just a little bit of connecting tissue or flesh of any creature, such as, "Only a striffen of the crippled squirrel's foot held it to the leg." **1986** Pederson *LAGS Concordance (Yolk)* 1 inf, **neTN,** Striffen—part next to shell. **2007** in 2008 *DARE* File, Is this type of roast suppose to have all this fat through out the entire roast or did I get a bad one? I'm going crazy trying to get all that fat and striffin out.

2 The smallest piece or amount.

1868 (1869) Kellogg *Lion Ben* 68 **ME,** To see how they live! just the least little scriffin of bread and butter, or a little pie. **1875** Thompson *Hoosier Mosaics* 193 **IN,** I'll split ye to the backbone in a second. . . Take every striffin of hide off 'n ye! **1889** Thompson in *Century Illustr. Mag.* 38.896 **cGA,** Hain't yer got a striffin' of sense left? **1902** [see **1** above].

striggle n

A wavy line, squiggle; hence v *striggle* to distribute irregularly, scatter.

1930s in 1944 *ADD* **eWV,** *Striggle. . .* To strew, spread, scatter. 'You have striggled the milk all over your clothes.' Common. **1936** Rowntree *Hardy Californians* 136, *V. sheltonii* grows in the Yellow Pine belt . . in the moist ledges of rocks. . . Its roots are mere striggles. **1942** *Times Recorder* (Zanesville OH) 26 Nov 5/4, If only a fire could be built on the hearth once or twice during the winter, so a striggle of smoke would float out the chimney into the sparkly air.

strike v

A Forms.

1 pres: usu *strike;* pronc-spp **Sth, S Midl** *strack, strick.*

1889 *Harper's New Mth. Mag.* 80.69 **LA** [Black], Des strack a bow 'crost de fiddle, an' ev'y j'int in he's bordy look like hit 'd loosen up an' 'spon' ter de chune. **1930** *DN* 6.84 **cSC,** *Strike,* n. and v. Pronounced [stræk]. Common. **1934** Hurston *Jonah's Gourd Vine* 13 **AL** [Black], Strack uh light, dere, some uh y'all chaps. **c1937** in 1976 *Weevils in the Wheat* 107 **VA** [Black], Massa Nottingham, he never had 'em on his place neider. He didn' never strick one o' his niggers; nobody else better not neider. **1937** *Ibid* 105 **VA** [Black], We didn't use no matches, 'stead we'd strick a rock on a piece of steel. We'd let the sparks fall on some cotton. **1944** *PADS* 2.30 **eKY, nwNC,** *Strack* [stræk]. . . To strike. Wautaugua Co., N.C. Common. E. Ky. Somewhat rare. **1968** *DARE* (Qu. Y41a, . . *To tell someone to light a lamp or lantern: "_____ the lamp."*) Inf **NC**49, Strick a match to the lamp. [Inf Amer Ind] **2005** [see **2** below].

2 past: usu *struck;* also *striked, strucked, strucken(ed), structid, strukt;* pronc-spp *strack(ed), strick, strook.*

1689 (1892) Hammond *Diary* 147 **MA,** A thunder shower . . strook his wife on her face. **1862** *Ladies' Repository* 22.185, I thought likely the maid deserved to be striked, so I striked her. **1873** *Harper's New Mth. Mag.* 48.14 **NY,** The boys striked at Albiany [sic] one spring. **1883** *Century Illustr. Mag.* 26.345 **GA** [Black], Den he strack de slick part. **1884** *Anglia* 7.253 [Black], To the regular forms of the Irregular verbs as used by the whites, the Negro adds the following forms of his own. . . *Pres.* strike. . . *Past.* striked, strukt, strucked, struckened. **1888** *Century Illustr. Mag.* 35.734 **LA** [Black], Dat man trawmp on him in de dark and he strack he wid his hawny tail. **1911** in 1944 *ADD* **VA,** *Strucken. . .* Mr. Bangs never strucken me a lick. **1922** Gonzales *Black Border* 329 **sSC, GA coasts** [Gullah glossary], *Structid*—struck. **1986** Pederson *LAGS Concordance,* 1 inf, **ceTX,** Strick = struck. **2005** Williams *Gratitude* 527 **wNC** (as of 1940s), *Strack, stracked:* strike, struck. The snake stracked at him and missed.

3 past pple: usu *struck, stricken;* also *strike(d), strucken(ed).*

1828 Webster *Amer. Dict.,* Strucken, the old pp. of *strike,* is obsolete. **1862** [see **2** above]. **1883** (1971) Harris *Nights with Remus* 249 **GA** [Black], Maybe she bin strucken down wid some kinder ailment. **1888** in 2004 *DARE* File—Internet **KY,** In 1861 . . I was struckened down with a disease of the bowels. **1957** *AmSp* 32.42 (as of 17th cent), *Stricken . . strucken* [as past pple]. **1991** Greene *Praying for Sheetrock* 47 **seGA** [Black], I have never strike her and she have never strike me and we love each other twenty-five years.

B Senses.

1 To take (fish) with a spear or, rarely, other sharp implement, esp at night with a light; hence vbl n *striking;* n *striker* one who fishes in this way; nouns *striking fork,* ~ *pole* a fish spear. [*OED2 strike* v. 33.c 1697 →, *striker* sb. 3.b 1697 →] **chiefly S Atl, esp SC** Cf **gig** v² **1, torch** v

[**1696** (1945) Dickinson *Jrl.* 35 [Jamaican writer in **FL**], The Casseekey . . sent his son with his striking staff to the inlet to strike fish for us.] **1894** *Whitehall Times & Blair Banner* (WI) 15 Nov Supplement **SC,** Flounder Striking. . . Did you ever "strike" a flounder? Probably not unless you have lived or passed some time on the coast of the southern states. . . Standing . . in the bow, armed with a striking pole, which is simply a heavy rod about 8 feet long, with a two pronged fork at one end, [he] kept his eyes fixed on the water. . . It would be natural to suppose that the "striker" would occasionally mistake some object for a flounder . . but . . I never knew . . any of the . . many negroes whom I . . saw out "striking" to be guilty of failure. **1938** FWP *Ocean Highway* 125 **SC,** The flickering lights from the fire-pans of the strikers, as these night fishermen are called. **1966–70** *DARE* (Qu. P13, . . *Ways of fishing . . besides the ordinary hook and line*) Inf **FL**7, Striking—with light and piece of metal; **SC**4, Striking—with spears for flounder; **SC**9, Striking—flounder; **SC**63, Striking, gigging for flounder; **SC**69, Striking—done in cold weather; striking fork [FW illustr: trident]; **VA**41, Striking—spearing at night with flashlight. **1966** *DARE* Tape **SC**15, And go striking for flounder. **1981** *SC Wildlife* May–June 48, Gigging saltwater fish with the aid of a light is a year-round sport in Beaufort County. If you use the term "gigging" to a native, he'll look at you askance. Down here it is "striking," pure and simple. You go out in a bateau with a strong light, "strike" the fish, and put it into the boat. *Ibid* 49, The striker must be able to drift quietly over the striking area. **1981** Harper-Presley *Okefinokee* 44 **seGA** (as of 1912), The next evening . . was a good one for a novel pastime called "striking." . . We waded slowly about in a stooping position, holding a bundle of blazing light'ood knots in the left hand and a machete in the right hand. When a fish of sufficient size was sighted, one of us would make a swift downward stroke and cut the booty in two. **1986** Pederson *LAGS Concordance,* 1 inf, **nwLA,** Striking—in fishing with gig and torch.

2 Of a larval oyster: to attach to a solid object; hence n *strike* the attachment of larval oysters to solid objects; a crop of young oysters. **esp Delmarva** Cf **set** v[1] **B8, set** n[1] **1**

1877 *Scribner's Mth.* 15.231, The infant oysters begin to be plainly visible in about a fortnight after they strike. **1881** Ingersoll *Oyster-Industry* 249 seNY, *Strike* . . when infant oysters attach themselves to any object they are said to "strike". (Staten Island.) **1912** Green *VA Folk-Speech* 424, *Strike.* . . When the spawn of oysters is plentifull there is a good strike. **1968** *DARE* Tape **MD**43, I'm speaking of a clam or a oyster. . . Where they strike. . . that's where that starts to growing, right there. **1970** *Ibid* **VA**79, And the reason they take 'em [=small oysters] up over there [=the James River] is because of the pollution in the water and also because there is a—the number of strikes they get. What we call strike is the small oysters; they have to attach to something to grow. And they strike so thick that they never mature, so they take 'em up and bring 'em over to the Potomac . . and plant 'em. **1976** Warner *Beautiful Swimmers* 87 **eMD,** Oyster larvae . . "strike" or attach themselves as spat to old shell or other hard objects. **1976** Ryland *Richmond Co. VA* 377, *Strike*—a good strike is when there are plenty of seed-oysters. **1984** *DARE* File **Chesapeake Bay** [Watermen's vocab], Spat / strike.

3 To meet with, come across (a person), esp by chance. Cf **strike up with**

1865 in 1939 Thornton *Amer. Gloss.* 656 **PA,** Coming down Four-and-a-half street, . . I struck the Sergeant-at-Arms, or rather the Sergeant-at-Arms struck me. **1874** Rusling *Across Amer.* 39 **KS,** On Wild-Cat Creek . . we struck a Mr. Silvers. **1878** Beadle *Western Wilds* 29, 'Fore long I struck an ole pard o' dad's. **1890** *DN* 1.66 **KY,** *Strike:* to meet, or to find. "I struck him at Jim Bell's." **1892** *Harper's New Mth. Mag.* 85.404, That's an introduction to the editor of *Every Evening,* and you'll strike him at the office about now, if you'd like to see him. **1940** White *Wild Geese* 91 **NW** (as of 1890s), You see I struck a fellow down at the floats, and we got to talking.

4 also *with off:* To take (a photograph). [By ext from printing or engraving techniques] Cf **make** v[1] **D11**

1874 *Portsmouth Times* (OH) 26 Dec [2]/3 (newspaperarchive.com), The countryman wanted his physiognomy transferred to glass; in other words he wanted his picture struck. **1892** *Newark Daily Advocate* (OH) 28 Mar [2]/3 (newspaperarchive.com) **NH,** I send . . picture of myself. . . Friends say I have greatly improved since this picture was struck off. **1936** *Pt. Arthur News* (TX) 1 Apr 5/2, *Junior Police Will Have Picture Taken*—Port Arthur's junior police . . are going to have their picture "struck." **1995** *Brophy Coll.* 72 swMO (as of c1960), *Strike.* [T]o take (a photo). . . have one's picture struck.

strike n   See **strike** v **B2**

strike a knot   See **hit a knot**

strike a lick v phr   Also *strike a lick of work*   **chiefly Sth, S Midl** Cf **hit a lick 1**

To do any work at all—usu in neg constrs.

1850 *Huron Reflector* (Norwalk OH) 13 Aug 1/7, I have never been on Rose's Bar since, neither have I struck a lick in the mines. **1872** U.S. Congress *Rept. Joint Select Comm. Insurrectionary States* 2.52 **NC,** I got a gentleman to go on and complete it, but I understand he has not struck a lick on it. **1881** in 2004 *DARE* File—Internet **TX** [*Gainesville Weekly Reg.* (TX) 29 Jan], Officer Kitrell arrested a tramp yesterday morning. . . He said that . . he had not struck a lick of work in six years. **1883** *Atlantic Mth.* 52.545 **sAppalachians,** He hain't struck a lick of work fur nigh on ter a month. **1897** in 2004 *DARE* File—Internet, I am totally disabled at this time, and I have not struck a lick of work for three years. [*DARE* Ed: Although the writer was from NJ, he had been a prisoner of war in Belle Isle, Virginia, from 1863–65.] **1953** *PADS* 19.14 **sAppalachians,** *Strike a lick.* . . Used in connection with work. "He's plum lazy. He didn't strike a lick of work." **1954** *Harder Coll.* **cwTN,** *Strike a lick.* **1966–68** *DARE* (Qu. LL18, *To do no work at all, not even make any effort: "She hasn't _____ all day."*) Infs **IN**32, **LA**25, **MS**7, **NC**36, 38, 48, **TN**1, **VA**80, Struck a lick. **1978** *Mt. Democrat & Placerville Times* (CA) 31 Mar [30]/2 (newspaperarchive.com), He was elected to several school offices but once elected he never struck a lick.

2005 Williams *Gratitude* 527 **wNC** (as of 1940s), A person who was too lazy to work at anything *woutn't strack a lick at nuthin'.*

striked   See **strike** v **A2, 3**

strike off   See **strike** v **B4**

strike one's funny bone (or spot)   See **funny bone 2**

striker n   Cf **black striker, gannet ~, little ~**

1 also *striker bird, ~ gull:* =**tern,** esp **royal tern.** [See quot 1938] **esp C and Mid Atl**

1890 Warren *Birds PA* 22 **NJ,** Fishermen on the coast of New Jersey where the Least Tern is a common summer resident know it by the names of "Sea Swallow," "Little Gull" and "Striker." **1917** *Wilson Bulletin* 29.2.75 **NC, VA,** *Gelochelidon nilotica* [=*Sterna n.*] . . Big striker, Wallops I[slan]d, Va. *Ibid, Sterna maxima* . . big striker at Beaufort, N.C. *Ibid* 76, *Sterna hirundo* . . striker, Beaufort, N.C. **1938** Oberholser *Bird Life LA* 294, Sometimes the terns strike the water with such force as to disappear entirely beneath the surface, and the activity of the birds is remarkable. From such behavior this tern [=the common tern, *Sterna hirundo*] has received the name 'striker', which it shares with most of the other smaller terns. **1947** (1962) Henry *Misty* 53 **eVA,** A white striker bird flew up from the ground and perched on Grandpa's gnarled forefinger. **1955** *Oriole* 20.1.7, Royal Tern.—Big Striker (from its plunging into the water while feeding). **1962** Imhof *AL Birds* 275, Terns, known locally as Strikers or Sea Swallows. **1966–70** *DARE* (Qu. Q10, . . *Water birds and marsh birds*) Inf **MD**45, Tern—also called striker; **NC**12, Striker; **NC**27, Striker—small gull with black head; **VA**47, Striker—any tern—because the tern "strikes" the water when feeding. **1969** *DARE* FW Addit **NC,** Striker gull—type of bird. **1996** Horton *Island Out of Time* 240 **Chesapeake Bay MD,** I was born in Ireland in the worst winter the island had ever seen. It was a genuine fuzz cod from nor'west, glass a'fallin' like a striker. [Footnote:] Tern, a bird that dives for fish.

2 =**Cooper's hawk.**

1917 (1923) *Birds Amer.* 2.67, Cooper's hawk—*Accipiter cooperi* . . Other Names. . . Swift Hawk; Striker. **1951** Teale *North with Spring* 132 **GA,** To the Georgia swampmen . . the Cooper's hawk is the "striker."

3   See **strike** v **B1.**

striker bird (or gull)   See **striker 1**

strike up with v phr   **Sth, S Midl** Cf **strike** v **B3**

To come across, meet with (a person).

1884 *Atlantic Mth.* 53.41 **SC,** She wuz 's peart an' purty 's you, miss, w'en I fust struck up with 'er. **1884** *Anglia* 7.263 **Sth, S Midl** [Black], *To strike up wid* = to meet accidentally. **1887** (1967) Harris *Free Joe* 19 **GA,** You er still layin' off for to strike up wi' Lucindy out thar in the woods, I reckon. **1905** *DN* 3.96 **nwAR,** *Strike up with.* . . To meet accidentally. 'I struck up with him down town.' Common. **1909** *DN* 3.377 **eAL, wGA,** *Strike up with.* . . To meet accidentally. **1947** McDavid *Coll.* **ceSC,** *Struck up with*—'met by chance.' **1952** Brown *NC Folkl.* 1.595, *Strike (up with).* . . To meet, to come in contact with. "If you strike up with Jim, let him know I'm here." . . General. **1966** *DARE* (Qu. II17, *If you happen to meet someone that you haven't seen for a while: "Guess who I _____ this morning."*) Inf **GA**1, Struck up with. **1986** Pederson *LAGS Concordance ([I ran] across)* 1 inf, **cGA,** I struck up with someone.

striking, striking fork   See **strike** v **B1**

striking paper n   Also *striking tickets* [Cf *EDD* strike v. 13 "To touch gently; to stroke"] **Sth, S Midl**

Toilet paper.

1984 Wilder *You All Spoken Here* 38 **Sth,** *Strikin' paper:* Toilet paper. **2000** *DARE* File **Sth,** This evening, a friend of mine asked me about the term "striking paper," which her boyfriend recently told her is a euphemism for toilet paper. I've never heard it, but he says that it's a common usage in the south. **2001** *Ibid* **NC,** I'm curious as to the origin of the term "striking paper" or "striking tickets" in reference to toilet paper. I can remember my grandfather, who would be 102 this year if still alive, use this term in my childhood. I've also heard this used several times in recent months, all by 65+ year olds in Northwestern North Carolina. **2001** in 2004 *DARE* File—Internet **seGA,** I went fishing this past weekend and forgot the most important item. *Striking paper.* **2004** *Ibid* **sMS,** Candles and *strikin' paper?* (toilet paper for you flat-landers) Check.

striking pole   See **strike** v **B1**

striking tickets   See **striking paper**

string n, v   Usu |strıŋ|; also **Sth, S Midl** |stræŋ, streŋ| Pronc-sp *strang*   Cf Pronc Intro 3.I.6.d

A Forms.

[**1934** *AmSp* 9.210 **Sth,** A few words having standard [ı] before [ŋ] change [ı] to [e] or [eı]. . . *string.*] **1937** *Frontier & Midland* 18.14 **S Midl,** It got to where a fellow could go to a bean strangin . . without gittin his skull cracked. *Ibid* 16, I heerd Ambrose's fiddle hit the floor and one strang twanged. **1939** Steinbeck *Grapes* 36 **OK,** Me an' some guys had a strang band goin'. **1942** Hall *Smoky Mt. Speech* 16 **wNC, eTN,** [ɛ] often occurs in . . *string.* **1966** *Wilson Coll.* **csKY,** *String* is often /stræŋ/. **1969–70** *DARE* Tape **GA**71, She just strings [stræŋz] the beans; **VA**38, I've had tote 'em [=tobacco leaves] out, lay 'em out in the shade, then maybe we'd go back after lunch and string [stræŋ] 'em. **2005** Williams *Gratitude* 527 **wNC** (as of 1940s), *Strang:* string.

B As noun.

1 The group of horses assigned to a cowhand for his individual use.   [*OED2* a1734 →]   **West**   Cf **mount** n **1**

1888 *Century Illustr. Mag.* 35.656 **MT,** Each of us has his own string of horses, eight or ten in number. **1929** *AmSp* 5.66 **NE** [Cattle country talk], Saddle ponies, "herding horses," the "string," "string of horses," or "cowboy's string" of horses kept in the "pony pasture" or barn so that under any circumstances saddle horses can be obtained when needed, are said to be "kept up." **1936** McCarthy *Lang. Mosshorn* np **West** [Range terms], *String.* . . A number of horses assigned to a cowboy for his individual use while working for an outfit. **1939** (1973) FWP *Guide MT* 416, *String*—Saddle horses kept for the use of a single rider. **1940** *Sat. Review* 17 Aug 9, When I joined a northwestern Colorado roundup I was assigned a "string" from the "cavvy." . . [I]t was a "string" of six "hosses." **1941** Writers' Program *Guide WY* 465, *String*—Horses assigned each rider. **1973** Allen *LAUM* 1.409 (as of c1950), String. Two or more horses owned by one cowpuncher [1 inf, **SD**].

2 A cowhand's rope; a lariat—freq in phr *put one's string on* to rope (an animal).   **West**

1897 Stanley *Life Amer. Cow-Boy* np **TX,** No brags I make,/ Straight goods I give you now,/ I'll put my string on anything / From a locomotive to a cow. **1908** Bronson *Reminiscences Ranchman* 47 **West,** Now, Tender, . . yu shore ha' raised hell droppin' y'r string on ole 'Bars! **1920** Hunter *Trail Drivers TX* 298, Roping a cow is sometimes referred to as "putting your string on her." **1929** *AmSp* 5.63 **NE** [Cattle country talk], Rope is the commonest Nebraska term for the Spanish *reata*, rope[.] It may be called "string," "clothes line," or "throw rope." **1933** *AmSp* 8.1.28 **nwTX** [Ranch diction], *Put your string on.* To rope. **1940** Writers' Program *Guide NV* 77, A rope is sometimes *seagrass, twine, string, Tom Horn,* or *maguey.* **1940** *Cattleman* May 18 **West,** These linen ropes handle and throw very much like the rawhide ropes although they are much stronger and perhaps a little faster than the "skin strings."

C As verb.

1 To attach (tobacco leaves) to a stick for drying; hence n *stringer;* vbl n *stringing.*   **chiefly S Atl**   Cf **stringing horse**

1875 King *Gt. South* 633 **LA,** [Caption:] Tobacco Culture—Stringing the Primings. **1938** in Lib. of Congress *Amer. Memory: FSA/OWI* (Internet) **SC,** [Caption:] Stringing tobacco. Florence County, South Carolina. **1941** Writers' Program *Guide SC* 367, Even the tiniest child can 'hand' tobacco—pass it on, several leaves at a time, to an elder who strings it on a stick. **1948** *AmSp* 23.308 **csWI,** *String* . . the plants, that is, to put them on *lath.* **1966–70** *DARE* Tape **FL**26, But now they're replacing their womenfolks and stringing by their stringing machines, which is done with electricity; **NC**3, The tenant goes out and gets about three or four leaves at the bottom, usually the leaves that are starting to turn into yellow, and he brings them to the barn and they string them on a stick. They put about twenty handfuls to the stick; **SC**24, [FW:] What are some of the people that you have to have to harvest it? [Inf:] . . The stringers and the unstringers; **VA**38, [see **A** above]. **1967** Key *Tobacco Vocab.* 232 **GA, NC,** *Stringing.* **1969** *NC Folkl.* 17.31 **wNC,** In western North Carolina tobacco was always *strung* on the stick with . . a hollow, sharp-pointed piece of steel that fits like a cone over the end of the tobacco stick. Three words for this implement were commonly used in western North Carolina: *stringer, needle* and *gaev.* . . The cutter . . passed the stalk to the *stringer,* who laid the stalk on the sharp point of the *gaev* about eight inches from the butt and pressed down. The stalk was thus split, strung on the stick and pushed to the ground, and the process was repeated until the stick held five or six stalks. **1986** Pederson

LAGS Concordance **csGA,** 1 inf, Stringer—person who hangs tobacco on strings; 1 inf, Stringers—string leaves on sticks; 1 inf, Stringing tobacco. **2001** *Capital* (Annapolis MD) 1 Dec sec D 3/4, I learned to harvest vegetables and string tobacco.

2 also with *up:* To tie (a shoe); hence *string-up (shoe)* a shoe fastened with laces.

1921 in 2010 (acc) Lexis–Nexis Legal Research *State Case Law: FL* (Internet), She would get up in bed at dead hours of the night and put on her clothes and string up her shoes and put all her clothes on the trunks. **1923** Parsons *Folk-lore Sea Islands* 174 **csSC,** If you go along the road and meet a string-up shoes and a button-up, the string-up tells you, "Good-morning!" and the button-up don't. Why is that? **1969** *Blues Line* 445 **LA,** I got up this morning / And I put on my shoes / I strung my shoes / Then I washed my face. **1982** *Grit* (Williamsport PA) 13 June 16/4, Moving west, she found that Ohio residents would "string up" their shoes, while she usually laced them. **1993** *Coast Watch* Sept/Oct 17 **NC,** [Caption to a picture of a laced shoe:] String—to lace up. **2006** West *Survival Man* 276 [Black], He confided that he had never worn string up shoes because his family started him in loafers from the time he was a small child.

3 In marble play: see quot.

c**1970** Wiersma *Marbles Terms, String* . . in certain types of games the goal of the shooting: 'I won 'cause mine was closer to the string.' *Ibid* **swMI** (as of 1960), *String*—The line which defined the playing circle.

string ball n

A bat-and-ball game; see quots.

1970 *DARE* (Qu. EE11, *Bat-and-ball games for just a few players [when there aren't enough for a regular game]*) Inf **FL**48, String ball—just like baseball, and you make believe you have a full team when you don't. **1997** in 2004 Montgomery–Hall *Dict. Smoky Mt. Engl.* 576 **wNC, eTN,** *String ball.* . . a version of baseball using a makeshift ball fashioned from bits of cloth and string.

string bean n   Also *stringed bean*   **widespread, but somewhat less freq W Midl**   See Map   Cf **green bean, snap ~**

A cultivated bean *(Phaseolus vulgaris)* eaten in the pod.

1759 in 1911 Dow *Holyoke Diaries* 20 **MA,** First Str[ing] Beans ys year viz C.W. Beans. **1793** in 1836 MA Hist. Soc. *Coll.* 5.129, I found his . . Indian beans ready to be eaten as stringed beans. **1849** Foster *NY in Slices* 72, His *bella inamorata* is at that very moment "putting in" a slice of roast beef garnished with string-beans and new potatoes. **1907** in 1953 *PA Dutchman* Apr 5, Whenever I see string-beans served with a thin milk or water dressing my thoughts go back to the bean dinners of the days of long ago. **1946** *PADS* 5.41 **VA,** *String beans.* . . North of the Rappahannock, not common. **1947** *PADS* 8.24 **wNY,** *String beans:* The usual term. **1949** Kurath *Word Geog.* 73, Three terms for string beans are current over large areas: *string beans* north of the Potomac, *snap beans* south of it, and *green-beans* in the West Midland. **1962** Atwood *Vocab. TX* 59, The usual terms for fresh beans in the pod are *snap beans* (or *snaps*) (52[% of approx 270 infs]), *green beans* (36), and *string beans* (30). **1965–70** *DARE* (Qu. I14, *Kinds of beans that you eat in the pod before they're dry*) 502 Infs, **widespread, but somewhat less freq W Midl,** String beans; **MD**41, **PA**40, Green string beans; **VA**42, "Move-in-ers" say string beans; (Qu. I20, . . *Kinds of beans*) 36 Infs, **scattered,** String beans; **IN**69, Bush string beans; **AR**52, Giant string beans; **CA**36, Green string beans; **CA**132, Italian string beans; **IN**69, Pole string beans; **CA**36, Wax string beans; **NY**205, Yellow string beans; (Qu. I15, *Some of the beans that you eat in the pod have yellow pods; you call these _____*) 26 Infs, 12 **NEast,** Yellow string beans; 15 Infs, 10 **NEast,** String beans; **MA**47, White string beans; **OH**27, Dried string beans; (Qu. H49, *Dishes made by boiling potatoes with other foods*) Infs **GA**62, **KY**22, **NC**38, **TX**36, Potatoes and string beans; **CA**132, **MS**34, **PA**110, String beans and potatoes; (Qu. H50, *Dishes made with beans, peas, or corn that everybody around here knows, but people in other places might not*) Inf **CA**136, Corn and string beans; **PA**159, Ham and string beans; **PA**136, String beans; **PA**41, String beans and ham; **VA**98, String beans cooked with strips of pork; (Qu. H56, *Names for . . pickles*) Infs **LA**40, **MI**100, Pickled string beans; (Qu. H57, *Tasty or spicy side-dishes served with meats*) Inf **PA**159, Sour string bean; (Qu. I4, . . *Vegetables . . less commonly grown around here*) Infs **CO**45, **CT**2, **NJ**37, String beans; **NY**70, Yellow string beans. **1972** *PADS* 58.21 **cwAL,** *String beans.* Northern and Midland *string beans* (14 [of 27 infs]) is more common than Southern *snap beans* (4) or Midland *green beans* (2). **1973** Allen *LAUM* 1.310 (as of c1950), *String beans* . . has become the majority form in all the U[pper] M[idwest] except Minnesota. **1986** Pederson *LAGS Concordance,* 446 infs, **Gulf Region,** String bean(s). **2004** *Daily News* (Huntingdon PA) 16 Sept 10/1, Commonly called string beans, they are more correctly termed snap beans after the sound of being broken into bite-sized pieces. Fifty years ago, they were truly string beans because they had a tough "string" along the seam edge of the pods.

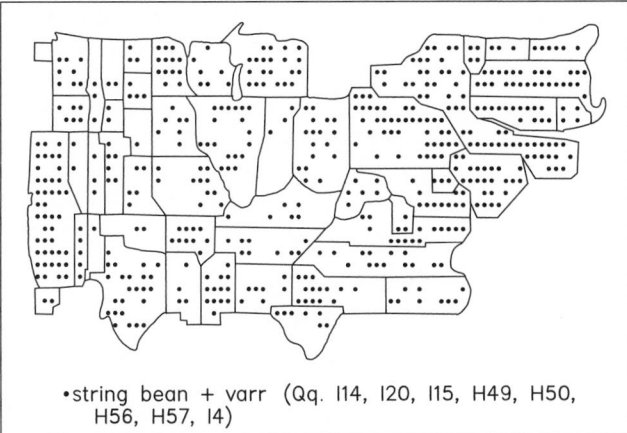

•string bean + varr (Qq. I14, I20, I15, H49, H50, H56, H57, I4)

stringbean tree n [From the shape of the pods]
=**catalpa B1.**

1967–68 *DARE* (Qu. T9, *The common shade tree with large heart-shaped leaves, clusters of white blossoms, and long thin seed pods or 'beans'*) Inf **NJ**21, Stringbean tree or Indian smoker; **OH**2, Catalpa or stringbean tree. **2008** *DARE* File—Internet **AL,** [Caption:] *String Bean Tree*—Actually, it's just a closup [sic] of my catalpa tree.

string bow n
=**mouth bow.**

a1975 Lunsford *It Used to Be* 172 **sAppalachians,** "String bow" is a musical instrument. You take a bow of wood, stretch a cord across it, or a wire, from one end to the other in front of the bow. At one end the wood is turned down flat so the cord will lie close to it. You put that in your mouth and you govern the pitch by it, like playing a Jew's harp. It is one of the oldest musical instruments known.

string doctor n Cf measuring woman
A type of folk healer; see quots.

1912 *IL Med. Jrl.* 21.777, I have not had a case of erysipelas for years without some wise neighbor coming in and insisting that they get a "string doctor." The string doctor, I think, passes a cord over the eruption, says a few magic words, and the cord must be burned by a slow, smouldering fire. **1941** Writers' Program *Guide IN* 119, Children were measured by 'string doctors' for short growth; the string was buried and when it began to rot the child began to grow. The rite was most effective if performed by the seventh daughter of a seventh daughter. [**1965–70** *DARE* (Qu. BB51b, . . *'Magical' cures for corns or warts*) Inf **GA**33, Tie knot in string, throw over shoulder; **IN**35, Tie knots in a string; **KY**51, Rub with walnut leaf, wad leaf up, tie with string, bury under rock; **KY**90, Tie knots in string, bury it, as many knots as warts; **LA**18, Tie string around ankle or finger; **MD**24, Tie a knot in a string, put outside where rain could reach it; **MI**115, String around little finger; **MO**4, Rub a string and put under house eaves; **MO**25, Tie knots in strings and burn; **NV**2, Hide a dishrag on a string; **NJ**35, Put a loop in a string; **OR**4, Tie string around wart; when string dissolves in toilet, wart gone; **TN**16, Knot yarn string for wart, put in house drip, when rots, no wart; **TX**29, Tie a string around your finger and then bury string. [*DARE* Ed: Many Infs simply said to tie a string around the wart.]]

stringed bean See string bean

stringer See string C1

stringer road n
=**fore-and-aft road.**

1899 in 2008 (acc) Lexis–Nexis Legal Research *State Case Law: PA* (Internet), The tramway originally laid was a stringer road with wooden rails—strap iron in places on top of the rails. **1905** U.S. Forest Serv. *Bulletin* 61.50 [Logging terms], *Stringer road. See* Fore-and-aft road. [*Ibid* 37, *Fore-and-aft road.* A skid road made of logs placed parallel to its direction, making the road resemble a chute. (P[acific] C[oast] F[orest]).] **1920** *Lumber Industry & Its Workers* 16 **Sth,** The pole road and the stringer road are still in use in a few localities, but they are not

common. **1958** McCulloch *Woods Words* 183 **Pacific NW,** *Stringer road*—A fore-and-aft road.

stringhalt n Also *springhalt, stringhalter*
A Forms. [The variant *springhalt* is old (*OED2* 1613 →); *stringhalter* (if not an error) is a back-formation from *stringhaltered* (at **stringhalted**).]

1848 *S. Lit. Messenger* 14.726, The clergyman had just arrived in a barouche . . drawn by a meek old horse, with the agitations of a springhalt. **1871** *Morning Oregonian* (Portland OR) [3 Feb 4]/1 (newspaperarchive.com), Ploughing should not be continued later than 10 or 11 o'clock at night. . . We have known plows to acquire springhalt and inflammatory rheumatism from late plowing. **1901** *Landmark* (Statesville NC) 4 Oct 2/3, The prosecution was begun on the ground that the horse had string halter, a disease from which a horse never recovers. . . [T]he counsel for the defendant demanded . . that the jury be permitted by the court to . . see for themselves whether or not the claims . . that he was string-haltered were true. **1923** [see **B** below]. **1959** [see **B** below].

B Sense.
A limp or twitch in a person's leg; a person having such an affliction. [Transf from std *stringhalt* a lameness of horses in which the affected animal jerks up one or both hind legs in an exaggerated fashion at each step] Cf **stringhalted B1**

1857 *Putnam's Mag.* 9.252, I remember one unlucky individual, apparently troubled with the string-halt, who twitched his leg after him in a style that was too much for the gravity of us youths. **1871** *Galaxy* 12.734, Old H. is, it would seem, a most agile old person, having a distinct "string-halt" in each leg. **1923** *Bridgeport Telegram* (CT) 9 June 14/2, I watch them [=golfers] move with sprightly step, no sign of springhalt in their tread. **1940** Harris *Folk Plays* 37 **NC,** Well, I ain't no plug yet, nor string-halt neither, am I? **1958** McCulloch *Woods Words* 183 **Pacific NW,** *Stringhalt*—Man with a limp (from the disability which affects horses). **1959** *VT Hist.* 27.160 **neVT,** *Spring halt.* . . [A] person's tired feet. Occasional. Caledonia.

stringhalt v See stringhalted B2

stringhalted adj Also, appar by folk-etym, *springhaltered, stringhaltered*
A Forms.

1893 *Daily NV State Jrl.* (Reno) [25 Aug 4]/5 (newspaperarchive.com) **CO,** He . . prances about like a string haltered horse, awkward as a Shanghai rooster that wants to light. **1909** Wason *Happy Hawkins* 106 **West,** He always walked like a hoss 'at was string-haltered in all four legs. **1929** *Mt. Democrat* (Placerville CA) 22 Nov 2/3, If the vehicle . . is a wornout . . affair, with a spavined, buck-kneed, stringhaltered means of locomotion, the thing to do is wake up to modern ways of doing things. **1938** Runyon in *NV State Jrl.* (Reno) 27 July 10/2, The idea of the hotel was to provide accomodations [sic] . . for the spavined and stringhaltered who make pilgrimages to "the spa." **c1960** *Wilson Coll.* **csKY,** *String halt.* . . A disease of horses, which causes irregular muscle contraction. Also *string-haltered.* **1966** *DARE* (Qu. K47, . . *Diseases . . horses or mules commonly get*) Inf **NC**15, Stringhaltered; (Qu. BB1, *When a person has been injured so that when he walks he steps more heavily on one foot than the other: "He _____."*) Inf **FL**31, Springhaltered—crippled and he walks on toes—old-fashioned. **1999** *Draft Horse Jrl.* 36.3.71 **IA,** Stringhalt is the condition, and "stringhaltered" is a colloquial term used to name the same condition.

B Senses.
1 Of a person: lame; hence v *stringhalter* to lame. [Transf from std sense *stringhalted* of a horse: afflicted with stringhalt (*OED2* 1687 →)] Cf **stringhalt n B**

1882 *Ft. Wayne Daily Gaz.* (IN) 6 July 2/5, Jimmy Webster [=a baseball player] was a little stringhalted yesterday. **c1945** in 2004 *DARE* File—Internet, He was hit through the calves of both legs by shell fragments; it string-haltered him temporarily and he sat down . . to wait for a medico. **1966** [see **A** above]. **1984** Burns *Cold Sassy* 69 **nGA** (as of 1906), Old Charlie and his mule were both string-halted, each having a tight ligament in the leg that made him limp. **1986** *Wall St. Jrl. Letters* **neOK,** I told my wife: "She walks like she is string-halted." . . She didn't know what I meant. . . It describes a horse who has pulled a leg tendon—and thus would walk with a halting gate [sic].

2 Severely restricted; thwarted, stymied; hence verbs *stringhalt(er)* to restrict severely; to thwart, stymie. [Appar reinterpretation based on folk-etym]

1895 *Courier* (Connellsville PA) 11 Jan 4/1, By all means, let us have simple and speedy methods of administering justice. It is perhaps necessary that the Blind Goddess have a bandage over her eyes, but there's no reason she should be string-halted. **1909** Porter *Roads of Destiny* 269, The powers of my department appear to be considerably string-halted. **1930** *Coshocton Tribune* (OH) 9 Feb 2/4, Such a reduction would stringhalter the United States and make the American navy decidedly inferior to the British navy. **1946** *Lima News* (OH) 10 Nov 25/2, Davis, too, was string-halted and rendered well nigh void by the Notre Dame ends. **1961** *Salisbury Times* (MD) 9 Mar 6/1, Low temperatures and icy gales hurt used-car sales and string-halted new-car business. **1984** Wilder *You All Spoken Here* 190 **Sth,** *String-halted:* Restrained; restricted. **2003** *DARE* File—Internet **OK,** They stymied and string-haltered the working individuals, who are simply wanting to enjoy life, liberty, and the pursuit of happiness.

stringhalter n   See **stringhalt** n

stringhalter v   See **stringhalted B1, 2**

stringhaltered   See **stringhalted**

stringing   See **string C1**

stringing horse n   [**string C1**]

A trestle on which **tobacco sticks** are placed to be strung with tobacco.

[**1939** in Lib. of Congress *Amer. Memory: FSA/OWI* (Internet) **NC,** [Caption:] Stringing tobacco. Note "horses" for holding sticks while stringing. Granville County, North Carolina.] **1948** *AmSp* 23.308 **csWI,** *Stringing horse . .* holds the lath about four feet above and parallel to the ground. **1966** *DARE* Tape **NC7,** You have . . a stringing horse, which is just a frame that'll hold a four-and-a-half-foot stick of tobacco. And you fasten your string at one end of the stick and then, as you loop it over across . . , whoever wants to hands it to you. **2004** *DARE* File—Internet **NC,** On November 30, 2001, Cape Fear Museum presented the opening of Down Tobacco Road. . . The exhibit includes . . artifacts such as . . tobacco sticks, stringing horse, . . and tobacco fertilizer bags.

string of pearls n   Cf **rice B2**

1967 *DARE* (Qu. R25, *Joking names for a head louse, or body louse*) Inf **TX40,** String of pearls.

string of varnish   See **varnished car**

string up (shoe)   See **string C2**

strip v, hence vbl n *stripping*   Cf **pull v 1a**

1 To remove (cured tobacco leaves) from the main stem of the plant and, usu, sort them by grade; to remove and sort tobacco leaves; hence n *stripper* one who does this; comb *tobacco stripping* a cooperative gathering for the purpose of doing this.   Cf **strip house**   Note: This corresponds to *OED2 strip* v.[1] 16.a, but the two earliest quots there, 1688 and 1786, belong rather to 16.b.

[**1724** in 1969 Herndon *Wm. Tatham Tobacco* 109 **VA,** They . . cover it up in *bulk . .* , where it lies till they have leisure or occasion to *stem* it (that is, pull the leaves from the stalk), or strip it (that is, to take out the great fibres). [Tatham's footnote (1800): The terms, *stem,* and *strip,* are here transposed; probably by an oversight of the first printer.]] **1787** *Amer. Museum* 1.136 **MD,** When cured. . . it is taken down, and stripped. This is performed by holding the but-end [sic] of the plant in your left hand, and with your right *culling* off the first leaves . . until you have enough gathered to form *a hand of tobacco* (or bundle). *Ibid* 1.137, The tobacco being stript . . is packed up in bulks. **1800** in 1969 Herndon *Wm. Tatham Tobacco* 38 **VA,** *Of Stripping and Bundling. . .* The sticks, containing the tobacco which may be sufficiently cured, are taken down and drawn out of the plants. These are then taken up one by one respectively, and the leaves being stripped from the stalk of the plant, are rolled round the butts or thick ends of the leaf, with one of the smallest leaves as a bandage, and thus made up into little bundles. **1851** *De Bow's Rev.* 11.397 **MD,** It [=cured tobacco] is first pulled or taken off the sticks and put in piles, then the leaves are stripped off and tied in bundles. . . Stripping should never be done in drying, or harsh weather. **1869** Porcher *Resources* 526 **OH,** *Stripping.*—When the tobacco is sufficiently cured to strip, . . you will have to watch for it to get "in case" for handling. **1872** *Scribner's Mth.* 4.654 **VA,** But there comes a mild damp spell, and the watchful planter seizing the right moment . . musters all the force he can command for the work of stripping and stemming. **1896** *Harper's New Mth. Mag.* 93.772, The black settlement, for the most part, holds its main crop for the spring rise. . . That is

why Smith Stover has a tobacco-stripping this mild, misty November day. **1944** *PADS* 2.71 **S Midl,** *Strip. . .* To pull leaves ((of the cured tobacco)) from the stalk and arrange by grades. *Stripper. . .* A person who strips. **1966** *PADS* 45.24 **cnKY,** *Strip. . .* To remove the leaves from the stalk after curing. . . *Stripper. . .* One who strips tobacco. **1967** *Key Tobacco Vocab.* 233 **CT, KY, MD, MO, TN,** *Strip. . .* To remove the leaves from the stalk after curing. *Ibid* 234 **CT, MD, MO, PA,** *Stripper. . .* One who strips tob[acco]. **1968–70** *DARE* Tape **MD13,** Then you cut it, and hang it in the barn for the cure. And after it cures, why then you go ahead and strip it, get it ready for market; **OH57,** It'd have to be stripped in the grades. . . You have professional men strip it in the grades. . . And of course different grades bring different prices. . . Lately they've been stripping bright leaf and lugs together; **VA43,** Had to go cross the road to a colored gentleman's house . . to use his barn. Dad cured it, and finally we got it all stripped out. I don't remember the pounds of it, but we had some real dark ground leaves. **1969** *NC Folkl.* 17.34 **wNC,** The first phase of working off the crop was *stripping,* pulling the leaves from the stalk and separating them into *grades.* **2004** *DARE* File—Internet **cnKY,** [Caption:] Stripping burley tobacco in Ray Brewer's barn, Shelby County. November 23, 2002.

2 in phr *strip fodder:* To strip blades of corn for **fodder n 2;** hence n *stripped fodder.*   Cf **fodder-pulling**

1830 in 1956 Eliason *Tarheel Talk* 297 **NC,** Stripping foddy. **1862** in 1945 Easterby *SC Rice Plantation* 271, Rain Men striping fodder. **1885** Stroyer *My Life in the South* 62 **cSC,** A man was engaged in stripping fodder and put some green ears of corn in the fire to roast for himself to eat. **1926** *Landmark* (Statesville NC) 15 Nov 3/1, Stock relish the barley straw as well as they relish the blades of stripped fodder from the corn. **1939** in Lib. of Congress *Amer. Memory: WPA Life Hist.* (Internet) **wNC,** A woman of powerful frame . . she . . hired out by the day to do farm work, breaking off corn tops and stripping fodder. **1986** Pederson *LAGS Concordance,* 1 inf, **swTN,** Stripped fodder.

stripe (bass)   See **striped bass 1**

striped adder   See **striped snake 1**

striped-ass (hornet) n   Cf **white-faced hornet, white-tailed ~**

=**bald-faced hornet.**

1939 *LANE* Map 240–41 *(Hornet),* The *white-faced hornet* (vespa maculata [=*Dolichovespula m.*]), a large social wasp, striped black and white. . . 1 inf, **seNH,** ['stræepɪd 'ɑːs hɒˤᵊnɪt]. **1968** *DARE* (Qu. R21, . . *Other kinds of stinging insects*) Inf **WI32,** Striped-ass—big black wasps—make a big round globular nest.

striped-back turtle   See **striped turtle 1**

striped bass n

1 also *stripe (bass), striper (bass):* A fish of the genus *Morone:* usu *M. saxatilis,* but also **white bass 1** or **yellow bass 2. scattered, but chiefly Atlantic, Lower Missip Valley, CA**   See Map   For other names of *M. saxatilis* see **greenhead 1, pebble, rock bass 7, rockfish 1, sea bass 1c, squid-hound (bass), streaked bass**

1787 Gesellschaft Naturforschender Freunde *Schriften* 8.160 **NY,** Rock-Fish. Striked [sic] Bass. **1818** *Amer. Monthly Mag. & Crit. Rev.* 2.295, The striped bass, of New-York, or Rock-fish, . . is another excellent salt-water fish. **1820** *Western Rev.* 1.370, Golden-eyes Perch. *Perca chrysops. . .* Vulgar names Rock fish, . . Gold eyes, Striped bass, &c. It is commonly mistaken for the Rock fish or Striped bass of the Atlantic Ocean. **1854** *Harper's New Mth. Mag.* 9.317 **RI,** You stroll along the cliff to the Bass Rocks, and throw your line for sea or striped bass. **1911** U.S. Bur. Census *Fisheries 1908* 317, Striped bass (*Roccus lineatus* [=*Morone saxatilis*]). . . In the North it is generally called the "striped bass". . . The name is sometimes applied to the white bass (*Roccus chrysops*) of the Great Lakes region. **1940** Weygandt *Down Jersey* 39 **sNJ,** There are those who are worried about the future of striped bass, striped bass as they are called among the descendants of New Englanders on the middle coasts of New Jersey. **1941** Writers' Program *Guide LA* 673, Right on this road to *Jeems* (or *James*) Bayou . . an excellent fishing spot for yellow bass (locally called striped bass). **1965–70** *DARE* (Qu. P2, . . *Kinds of saltwater fish caught around here . . good to eat*) 24 Infs, **chiefly Atlantic,** Striped bass; **CA17, CT39, MA72, NJ16, 22, 39, NY87,** Striper; **NJ28,** Striper bass; (Qu. P1, . . *Kinds of freshwater fish . . caught around here . . good to eat*) 21 Infs, **scattered,** Striped bass; **IL119, TN65,** Stripes; **TN44,** Stripe—white bass; **SC24,** Landlocked striped bass; (Qu. P3, *Freshwater fish* *that are not good to eat*) Inf **KY**16, Striped bass; (Qu. P14, . . *Commercial fishing . . what do the fishermen go out after?*) Infs **LA**8, **NC**80, **NY**48, 118, **VA**55, Striped bass; **NJ**16, Rock or striped bass; **MA**123, **NJ**39, Striper(s).   **1967–68** *DARE* Tape **IL**9, We have quite a few striped bass; **LA**5, [FW: The book name for what . . [the Inf] called striped bass is yellow bass.]; **MD**15, The one fish that is a native Chesapeake Bay fish, the rockfish or the striped bass, is still with us, and they're very plentiful; **MA**97, Too bad we haven't any stripers left in our icebox. . . It's a gamy saltwater fish, a bass. And you can have it anywhere from fifteen pounds to forty, fifty, sixty pounds; **NJ**41, When we used to fish down here for the striped bass, . . why, we used to go out . . before daybreak.   **1975** Evanoff *Catch More Fish* 126, Along the Atlantic Coast . . the striped bass is king. They are also caught in the surf along the Pacific Coast. . . Stripers bite best when the surf is rough. **1986** Pederson *LAGS Concordance* **Gulf Region,** 17 infs, Striped bass; 1 inf, Striped bass—freshwater; 1 inf, Striped bass—saltwater; 2 infs, Stripe bass; 1 inf, Striped basses.   **2004** *DARE* File—Internet **NJ,** One of the most frequently asked questions our guide service receives at this time of year is "When can I catch a striper again?"

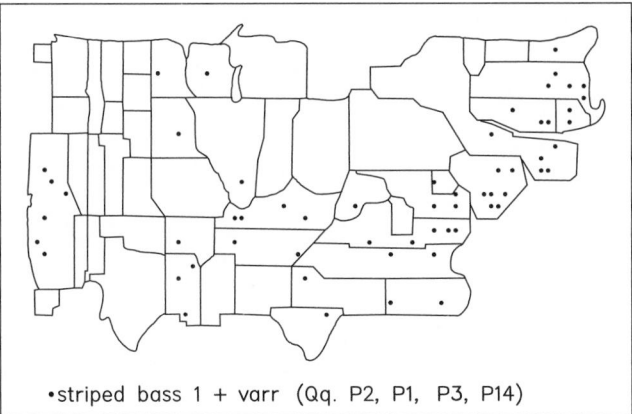

•striped bass 1 + varr (Qq. P2, P1, P3, P14)

2   =largemouth bass.
   1933 LA Dept. of Conserv. *Fishes* 313, Black Bass. . . [Popular names include] Large-mouthed Black Bass; . . Striped Bass [etc].   **1935** Caine *Game Fish* 4, Large-mouthed Black Bass. . . *Synonyms:* Rock Bass . . Striped Bass [etc].

striped dace n   [See quot 1983]
The blacknose **dace** (*Rhinichthys atratulus).*
   1882 *Continent* 2.45, The striped dace erect a pretentious home for their young, working in pairs.   **1899** *News* (Frederick MD) 2 May [3]/1 (newspaperarchive.com), Another simple . . way to ascertain whether trout will live or thrive . . it is only necessary to learn if the creek minnow or striped dace can be found in such stream.   **1906** NJ State Museum *Annual Rept. for 1905* 151, *Rhinichthys atronasus.* . . Striped Dace.   **1943** Eddy–Surber *N. Fishes* 132, Western Blacknose Dace (Striped Dace).   **1983** Becker *Fishes WI* 467, Striped or redfin dace. . . young-of-year with a distinct broad stripe of black chromatophores extending from tip of snout to end of body.

striped dogwood n   Cf **false dogwood 1**
=striped maple.
   1848 Gray *Manual of Botany* 80, A[cer] *Pennsylvanicum* . . (Striped Maple.) . . Also called *Striped Dogwood,* and *Moose-Wood.*   **1860** Curtis *Cat. Plants NC* 52, Striped Maple. . . known under the names . . of *Moosewood* and *Striped Dogwood.* . . The bark is smooth and green, with longitudinal dark stripes, which distinguishes it at all seasons. **1891** Jesup *Plants Hanover NH* 9, A[cer] *Pennsylvanicum* . . Striped Dogwood. Moose-Wood.   **1940** Clute *Amer. Plant Names* 129, Striped Maple. Moosewood, whistle-wood, striped dogwood [etc].

striped fish n
A **greenling** (here: *Pleurogrammus monopterygius*).
   1882 Petroff *Report on the Population, Industries, and Resources of Alaska* (1880 census) 72 (Tabbert *Dict. Alaskan Engl.*), This fish (. . known at present as *Pleurogrammus monopterygius*) is found about the whole of the Aleutian chain, and also among the Shumagin islands, congregating in large schools. At Attoo it is known as the kelp-fish, on the Shumagins as the yellow or striped fish, and from Oonalashka to Atkha as the Atkha mackerel.

striped gentian n
Std: a **gentian** (here: *Gentiana villosa*).   Also called **marsh gentian**

striped gopher n   Also *streaked gopher, striper, stripy gopher* **chiefly Upper Missip Valley**   See Map
A **ground squirrel b** (here: *Spermophilus tridecemlineatus*).
   1849 *Columbian Lady's & Gentleman's Mag.* 10.5, The striped gopher, the "sapper and miner," flies past with a chirp, and disappears. **1860** *Valley Farmer* 12.337 **cnIL,** I found that the little ground squirrel, here called striped gopher, had dug down pretty deep.   **1907** *New North* (Rhinelander WI) 1 Aug suppl 15/7, Every person who shall kill any crow shall be entitled to a reward of fifteen cents . . , or any streaked gopher ten cents.   **1941** *Mason City Globe-Gaz.* (IA) 4 Apr 10/2, North Iowa seems to have an abundant supply of striped gopher and pocket gopher.   **1947** Cahalane *Mammals* 352, On the midwestern prairies the summer sun at noon may drive a shaded thermometer over one hundred degrees, but the striper skips about, the only zestful creature in a broiling, wilted world.   **1961** Jackson *Mammals WI* 130, Striped Ground Squirrel. . . In Wisconsin commonly called gopher or striped gopher. Other names include . . streaked gopher, and whistle sneak.   **1965–70** *DARE* (Qu. P29, . . 'Gophers' . . other name . . or what other animal are they most like) 9 Infs, 8 **Upper Missip Valley,** Striped gopher; **SD**2, Stripy gopher; (Qu. P27, . . Kinds of squirrels) Inf **IA**4, Striper.   **1970** *Western Folkl.* 29.168 **Upper MW,** In a clearly defined area of extreme southeastern Minnesota and northeastern Iowa the regular term is *streaked gopher. Ibid* 169, Striped gopher. . . occurs in northern Iowa, the western two-thirds of Minnesota, almost all of North Dakota, the western one-third of South Dakota.   **1989** Gores *Wolf Time* 209 **MN,** Far down the slope a stripy gopher came out to stand up straight beside its burrow—really the thirteen-lined ground squirrel, . . but everyone just called them stripy gophers.   **2004** *Star Tribune* (Minneapolis MN) 15 Sept (Internet), Koos' earliest education as a hunter came at the expense of striped gophers.

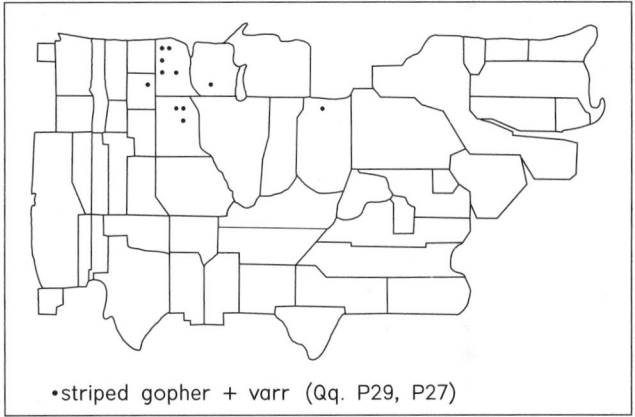

•striped gopher + varr (Qq. P29, P27)

striped gravy n   esp **S Midl**   Cf **streaked gravy**
   1933 *Panola Watchman* (Carthage TX) [12 Jan 11]/2 (newspaperarchive.com), A hogless world would be a dull, insipid and dreary habitation. It would mean no streaked bacon, no aromatic ham or striped gravy [etc].   **1967–70** *DARE* (Qu. H37, . . Words . . for gravy. Any joking ones?) Inf **AR**53, Striped gravy—from fried ham or pork chops, with a little water added; **KY**79, Striped gravy.   **1976** *NW AR Times* (Fayetteville) 12 Dec 1/5, Red-eye gravy also called streaked or striped gravy, was another by-product of the cooking of pork.   **2006** *Aiken Std.* (SC) 27 Feb sec C 2/1, I've heard paeans sung to . . striped gravy.

striped grunt n
A **grunt** n **1,** usu *Haemulon macrostomum*.
   1898 U.S. Natl. Museum *Bulletin* 47.1296, *Haemulon macrostomum,* . . Gray Grunt; Striped Grunt.   **1902** Jordan–Evermann *Amer. Fishes* 423, Striped Grunt. . . Colour in life, body dirty silvery with about 9 dark longitudinal streaks.   **1935** Caine *Game Fish* 83, Gray Grunt. . . *Synonyms* . . Striped Grunt [etc].   **1983** *Audubon Field Guide N. Amer. Fishes* 612, Striped Grunt (*H[aemulon] striatum*) has slender body; yellow with 4 dark brown stripes.

striped-head turtle   See **striped turtle 1, 2**

striped ink   See **striped paint**

striped lake bass n

=**white bass 1.**

1876 Jordan *Manual Vertebrates N. U.S.* 226, R[occus] chrysops [= *Morone c.*] . . White Bass. Striped Lake Bass. Silvery, with six or more dark stripes, sometimes "so interrupted and transposed as to appear like ancient church music." **1887** Goode *Amer. Fishes* 32, The White Bass, or Striped Lake Bass, *Roccus chrysops,* is often confounded with the Striped Bass, which it closely resembles. **1949** Caine *N. Amer. Sport Fish* 122, Striped Lake Bass. . . The white bass.

striped-leg turtle   See **striped turtle 1**

striped mallard n

=**Florida duck.**

1932 Howell *FL Bird Life* 132, Florida Duck: *Anas fulvigula fulvigula.* . . Other Names: Florida Black Duck; . . Striped Mallard [etc]. **1969** Longstreet *Birds FL* 34, Florida Duck—Other names. . . Striped Mallard [etc].

striped maple n   [Because the bark is striped longitudinally]
Std: a **maple** of the eastern US (here: *Acer pensylvanicum*). Also called **dogwood 2, elkwood 1, false dogwood 1, goosefoot maple 1, green ~ 2, moose ~, moosewood 1, mountain alder 2, striped dogwood, whistlewood 2, white maple 3**

striped meat n   Cf **streaked meat, streak of lean**
See quots.

1966 *DARE* (Qu. H38, . . *Words for bacon*) Inf **NC**44, Stripèd meat, streaked meat. **1988** Moore *Mt. Voices* 102 **wNC,** She'd cook a great hunk of lean striped meat, good fresh pork, and then she'd soak that pumpkin and then cook it in that.

striped moccasin n

A **water snake 1** or **3**; see quots.

1928 Baylor Univ. Museum *Contrib.* 16.17 **TX,** Clark's Water Snake is sometimes called Striped Moccasin. *Ibid,* Graham's Water Snake. . . In eastern and central Texas this species is commonly known as the Striped Moccasin. *Ibid* 18, Stiff Snake. . . Like all longitudinally striped water snakes, this species is a Striped Moccasin. **1968** *DARE* (Qu. P25, . . *Kinds of snakes*) Inf **LA**15, Striped moccasin, also called stinging snake. **1986** Pederson *LAGS Concordance,* 1 inf, **cwAL,** Striped moccasin.

striped mouse snake n   Cf **mouse snake 3**

A **patch-nosed snake** (here: *Salvadora grahamiae*).

1928 Baylor Univ. Museum *Contrib.* 16.15 **San Antonio TX,** Patchnose Snake. . . In the San Antonio region, this species is sometimes called the Striped Mouse Snake.

striped mullet n

Std: a **mullet** n[1] **1** (here: *Mugil cephalus*). Also called **ama-ama, black mullet 2, fatback 2a, Indian River chicken, jumping mullet 1, molly** n[1] **7a, pond mullet, popeye ~, sand ~ 1, sea ~ 2**

striped oak n

An **oak** (here: either *Quercus falcata* or *Q. texana*).

1960 Vines *Trees SW* 198, Other names for it [=*Quercus nuttallii* [= *Q. texana*]] are Smooth-bark Red Oak, Tight-bark Red Oak, Yellow-butt Oak, Striped Oak [etc]. **1967** *DARE* (Qu. T10, . . *Kinds of oak trees*) Inf **LA**2, Striped [oak] [FW: Inf identified pictures of southern red oak and pin oak . . as being most like striped oak leaves.]; **LA**10, Striped oak [FW: =southern red oak].

striped paint n   Also *striped ink*   Cf **checkered paint, spotted paint**

A nonexistent item used as the basis of a practical joke.

1876 *Hornellsville Tribune* (NY) 28 July 1/7, A Worcester man was wandering from paint shop to paint shop . . , asking for "striped paint with which to paint a barber pole." **1891** *Middletown Daily Times* (NY) 4 Dec 3/6, It is not true that before painting the barber pole he went to Power & Co. and asked for some "striped paint." **1911** *Indiana Weekly Messenger* (PA) [26 Apr 6/4] (newspaperarchive.com) **KS,** For the red and black lines that lie artistically on the fair pages what could be more appropriate than "striped ink"? **1921** *DN* 5.95 **OH,** Striped ink. Reported from printing office. **1938** in Lib. of Congress *Amer. Memory: WPA Life Hist.* (Internet) **TX,** I was . . sent to buy "striped paint." **1965–70** *DARE* (Qu. HH14, *Ways of teasing a beginner or inexperienced person—for example, by sending him for a 'left-handed monkey*

wrench': "Go get me _____.") 25 Infs, **scattered,** (Can of) striped paint; **IL**80, Bucket of striped paint; **TX**51, Striped ink. **1995** *Mt. Democrat* (Placerville CA) 31 Mar sec A 8/2, No more . . sending your kid to the hardware store for a can of red-and-white striped paint.

striped perch n

1 =**yellow perch 1.**

1870 McClung *MN in 1870* 180, There are also . . perch (striped, yellow and white). **1902** Jordan–Evermann *Amer. Fishes* 366, Wherever found, this species [=*Perca flavescens*] is the perch *par excellence.* Among other names by which it is known are American perch, raccoon perch, red perch, and striped perch. **1939** Natl. Geogr. Soc. *Fishes* 132, *Perca flavescens.* . . Like other fishes of extended range, it has several names in different localities, such as ringed perch, raccoon perch, red perch, or striped perch. **1966** *DARE* (Qu. P1, . . *Kinds of freshwater fish . . caught around here . . good to eat*) Inf **FL**16, Striped perch. **1983** Becker *Fishes WI* 886, *Yellow Perch.* . . Other common names . . red perch, striped perch.

2 A Pacific **surfperch** (here: either *Embiotoca lateralis* or *Hypsurus caryi*).

1939 Natl. Geogr. Soc. *Fishes* 229, [Caption:] Close to the shoreline, the Striped, or Blue, Perch . . raises families of from 21 to 90. **1946** La Monte *N. Amer. Game Fishes* 91, Rainbow Perch—*Hypsurus caryi.* . . Names: Striped Perch, Bugara. *Ibid,* Striped Perch—*Taeniotoca lateralis* [=*Embiotoca l.*]

striped pig n   Cf **blind pig, ~ tiger, piggery 2**   *hist*

A pig painted with stripes and ostensibly exhibited to paying customers who are then given "free" drinks as a way of evading laws against selling liquor by the drink.   Note: The striped pig phenomenon was occasioned by the passage of a law in Massachusetts on July 1, 1838, prohibiting the sale of liquor in quantities less than fifteen gallons; the act was repealed on Feb. 11, 1840.

1838 *Hist. Striped Pig* 5 **Boston MA,** Within the tent below stood the worthy couple . . the 'striped pig' and his associate,—surrounded by all those elements and implements of intoxication. **1850** MI Constitutional Convention *Report* 770, Every man here knows that every drug store and shop in his village would be turned into grog shops [if allowed to sell alcohol for "mechanical, medicinal, and chemical purposes"]. The stuff would be sold as freely as ever. It would be a perfect "striped pig" operation. **1854** Child *Tippletonia* 79, This singular conduct excited my curiosity, and led me to inquire whether cards, dice, or some other unlawful games were not carried on within. The person whom I addressed . . looked very wise, and whispered in my ear that the "striped pig" was kept there. He kindly informed me that for a dime I could be admitted to look at the strange quadruped, and to take a friend in with me; and . . when once in, that we might regale ourselves with such of the mineral waters as we had a fancy for, without any charge whatever. **1858** (1859) Howe *Advent. Americans* 229 **Boston MA,** On a tent at the ground, was a show bill as below: [*DARE* Ed: A picture of a striped pig and the legend:] Great Curiosity./ The Striped Pig./ To be seen here—Admittance 6¼ cts. Crowds flocked to see the wonder, and . . many were not contented with a single visit, but made repeated calls in the course of the day . . and as they came out, were in a jovial humor . . such . . as to draw the attention of the authorities to the spot. On entering, they found a common white pig painted in black stripes, zebra like; near him stood a table well provided with New England rum, brandy, gin, etc., which the owner of the show had provided . . for the refreshment of the curiosity-seekers. There being no law in Massachusetts against exhibiting a common pig daubed with black paint, nor none against giving away alcoholic stimulants, the exhibitor suffered no harm. **1870** *Harper's New Mth. Mag.* 40.294, The law against nine-pins, the tradition says, could not touch ten-pins; and if a man could not lawfully sell a dram there was no law to prevent his giving you a dram if you would pay four pence ha'penny to see his renowned striped pig.

striped skunk n

Usu as *little striped skunk:* =**spotted skunk.**   Note: The term *striped skunk* is also widely used for skunks of the genus *Mephitis.*

1857 U.S. War Dept. *Rept. Explor. Railroad* (Mammals) 6.44, *Mephitis bicolor.* Little Striped Skunk. . . four parallel dorsal stripes interrupted and broken behind. **1873** *Harper's New Mth. Mag.* Aug 469 **FL,** The little striped skunk (*Mephitis bicolor*) is very abundant in certain sections. **1879** U.S. Natl. Museum *Bulletin* 14.4, Spilogale zorilla. . . Little Striped Skunk.—Western United States and Pacific

Slope. **1895** in 1937 Grinnell et al. *Fur-Bearing Mammals CA* 307 **CA,** One of the ladies crept up stairs one night and opening the door softly, found the culprit—a striped skunk *[Spilogale].* **1928** Anthony *N. Amer. Mammals* 120, Spotted Skunk. . . Little Striped Skunk. . . color pattern black and white, arranged in conspicuous stripes or connected spots. **1937** Grinnell et al. *Fur-Bearing Mammals CA* 293, California Spotted Skunk—*Spilogale gracilis phenax.* . . Other Names. . . Striped Skunk. **1961** Jackson *Mammals WI* 369, Prairie Spotted Skunk. . . *Vernacular names.* . . Little spotted skunk, little striped skunk [etc].

striped snake n

1 also *black-striped snake, striped adder:* A **garter snake 1,** esp *Thamnophis sirtalis.* **chiefly NEng** See Map

1778 Carver *Travels N. Amer.* 486, The *striped* or *garter snake* is exactly the same as that species found in other climates. **1792** Belknap *Hist. NH* 3.176, Striped Snake, *Anguis eryx?* **1836** Edward *Hist. TX* 76, The long black snake and the striped or garter snake . . are never failing pests of the barn-yard. **1842** Thompson *Hist. VT* 1.115, *Coluber sirtalis.* . . This is the most common and generally diffused species of snake in Vermont, and is universally known by the name of *Striped Snake.* **1842** DeKay *Zool. NY* 3.45, The Striped Snake . . is known under various popular names, such as *Green Garter-snake, Slow Garter, Swamp Garter, Water Garter, Striped Adder, &c.* **1858** Thoreau in 1878 *Atlantic Mth.* Apr 448 **MA,** I startle a striped snake. It is a large one, with a white stripe down the dorsal ridge between two black ones, and on each side the last a buff one, and blotchy brown sides, darker towards the tail. Beneath, greenish-yellow. This snake generally has a pinkish cast. **1891** Jesup *Plants Hanover NH* 63, E[utainia] sirtalis . . Common Garter Snake. Striped Snake. Abundant. **1908** [see **streaked snake**]. **1926** in 1952 Ditmars *N. Amer. Snakes* 223 **IA,** This [= *Thamnophis radix*] is the commonest species of striped snake or garter snake in most parts of Iowa. **1965–70** *DARE* (Qu. P25, . . *Kinds of snakes*) 10 Infs, **chiefly NEng,** Striped snake; **CT**14, Striped snakes—sometimes called garter snakes; **CT**23, 31, 36, **MA**47, 72, **RI**4, 12, Striped adder; **MA**35, Black-striped snake. [*DARE* Ed: In the 10 cases where a pronc for *striped* was recorded, it was disyllabic, of the type ['straɪpɨd].]

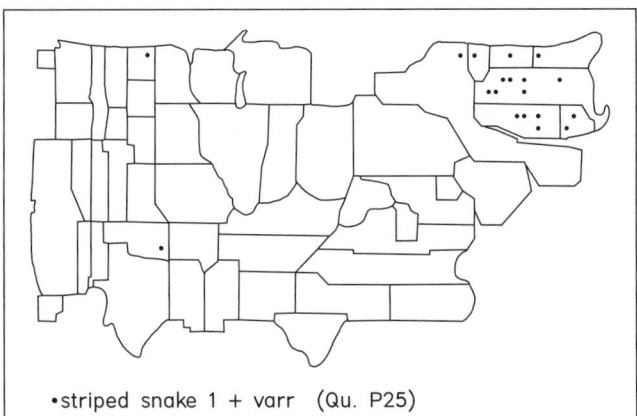

•striped snake 1 + varr (Qu. P25)

2 in phrr *meaner than* (or *as mean as*) *a striped snake:* Extremely mean. **esp sAppalachians**

1941 in 2004 Montgomery–Hall *Dict. Smoky Mt. Engl.* 383 **wNC,** He's as mean as a striped snake. **1966–69** *DARE* (Qu. HH22b, . . *A very mean person . . "He's meaner than _____."*) Infs **GA**77, **IL**96, **NC**36, 37, A striped ['straɪpɨd] snake; **VA**15, Striped snake—most common; [**GA**72, Strappage snake]. **1993** Ison–Ison *Whole 'Nother Lang.* 42 **sAppalachians,** *Mean as a striped snake*—Very, very mean. **1997** in 2004 Montgomery–Hall *Dict. Smoky Mt. Engl.* 383 **eTN,** Joe is meaner than a striped snake.

striped squirrel n

1 A **chipmunk** (here: *Tamias* and *Eutamias* spp). **chiefly NEast** Note: Some of these quots may refer instead to **2** below.

1791 Bartram *Travels* 284, The ground squirrel, or little striped squirrel of Pennsylvania and the northern regions, is never seen here [=in the southeast US], and very rarely in the mountains northwest of these territories. **1792** Belknap *Hist. NH* 3.163, The *striped squirrel (sciurus striatus [=Tamias s.])* . . provides its winter food from the cornfields, and deposits it in holes in the earth. **1842** Thompson *Hist. VT* 1.46, The

Striped Squirrel is . . common in Vermont. . . It is likewise frequently called the *Chipmuck,* or *Chipping Squirrel,* from its note. **1849** (1911) Thoreau *Week on Concord* 241 **MA,** The chipping, or striped squirrel, *sciurus striatus* [=*Tamias s.*], sat upon the end of some Virginia fence or rider reaching over the stream. **1857** U.S. War Dept. *Rept. Explor. Railroad* 8.xxxviii, *Tamias quadrivittatus* [=*Eutamias q.*] . . Missouri Striped Squirrel.—Upper Missouri to Rocky Mountains, and west to the Cascade Range. *Ibid, Tamias dorsalis* [=*Eutamias d.*] . . Gila Striped Squirrel.—Fort Webster, New Mexico. *Ibid, Tamias townsendii* [=*Eutamias t.*] . . Townsend's Striped Squirrel.—From Puget's Sound to Petaluma, California, along and west of Cascade Mountains. **1859** *Hist. Town Dorchester MA* 301, This year [=1735] the town offered a bounty of two pence on the heads of small striped squirrels. **1907** *DN* 3.210 **nwAR, cCT,** Chipmunk. . . The striped squirrel. **1917** *DN* 4.431 **LA,** Ground squirrel. The chipmunk (Tamias striatus): also called *striped squirrel.* **1939** *LANE* Map 229 **NEng,** The following synonyms of *chipmunk* were offered . . *striped squirrel* [9 infs]. **1966–68** *DARE* (Qu. P27, . . *Kinds of squirrels*) Inf **NH**14, Striped squirrel; **ME**6, Striped squirrel—a chipmunk.

2 A **ground squirrel b,** usu *Spermophilus tridecemlineatus,* but also *S. lateralis.*

1857 U.S. War Dept. *Rept. Explor. Railroad* 8.xxxviii, *Spermophilus lateralis* . . Say's Striped Squirrel.—Rocky Mountains to Cascades. **1872** Schele de Vere *Americanisms* 101, A striped squirrel of Wisconsin (Spermophilus tredecimlineatus). **1970** *Western Folkl.* 29.172, *Minnesota striped squirrel,* . . *striped ground squirrel,* . . and *striped squirrel* are names for the thirteen-lined ground squirrel.

striped surf fish n Also *striped surfperch*

A Pacific **surfperch** (here: *Embiotoca lateralis*).

1896 U.S. Bur. Fisheries *Rept. for 1895* 404, Taeniotoca [=*Embiotoca*] lateralis . . *Blue Perch; Striped Surf-fish.* **1946** La Monte *N. Amer. Game Fishes* 91, Striped Perch. . . Names: Blue Perch, . . Striped Surf Fish. **1992** *Ecology* 73.405, Striped surfperch were not evenly divided among the dietary categories.

striped tiger n

A **louse B1.**

1968 *DARE* (Qu. R25, *Joking names for a head louse, or body louse*) Inf **OH**56, Striped tigers.

striped turtle n

1 also *striped-back turtle, striped-head ~, striped-leg ~:* Perh a **red-bellied turtle.** **esp Lower Missip Valley, TX**

1933 *Amer. Midland Naturalist* 14.588 **KY,** Striped Turtle: *Pseudemys concinna.* **1965–70** *DARE* (Qu. P24, . . *Kinds of turtles*) Infs **AR**36, **IN**55, **TX**100, Striped turtle; **SC**57, Striped turtle—orange stripes on his neck and legs—not good to eat; **MS**16, **TX**35, Striped-head turtle; **MS**6, Striped-back turtle—same as striped-head turtle; **LA**8, Striped-leg turtle. **1999** in 2004 *DARE* File—Internet **sFL,** I balanced the typewriter on my chest and swished the water with my free hand, barely evading a striped turtle on a log.

2 as *striped-head turtle:* Perh a **musk turtle 1** (here: *Sternotherus minor*).

1968 *DARE* (Qu. P24, . . *Kinds of turtles*) Inf **TN**24, Striped-head turtle—same as stinking Jim.

striped warbler n

=**black-and-white warbler.**

1917 (1923) *Birds Amer.* 3.112, Black and White Warbler. . . Striped Warbler. . . Plumage, black and white in stripes. **1944** Hausman *Amer. Birds* 497, Black and White Warbler. . . Other Names . . Striped Warbler [etc].

striped wasp n Also *striper* **esp Cent** See Map on p. 344

A **yellow jacket 1** or similar wasp.

1966–70 *DARE* (Qu. R21, . . *Other kinds of stinging insects*) Infs **MO**18, 19, 20, **TN**24, **TX**104, Striped wasp; **MO**39, Striped wasp—yellow stripes; smaller than honeybee; **OK**42, Striped wasp—smaller, yellow-striped in back; **AR**41, Yellow striped wasp; **MO**36, Yellow striper. **1986** Pederson *LAGS Concordance (Wasps)* 6 infs, **inland Gulf Region,** Striped wasp(s); 1 inf, **seAR,** A little striped wasp resembles a yellow jacket; [1 inf, **cnAL,** A little Guinea wasp is a striped wasp].

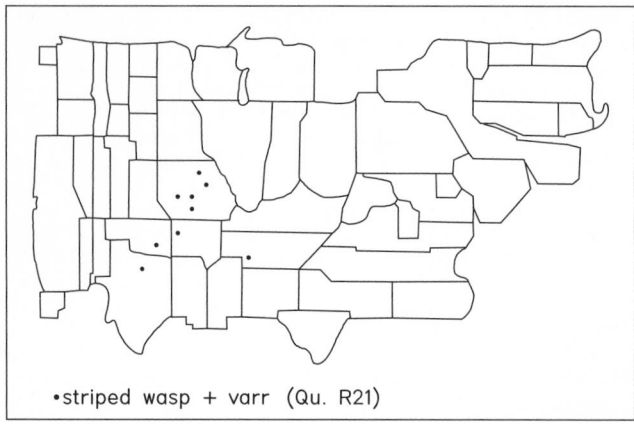

•striped wasp + varr (Qu. R21)

striped water snake n

Usu =**queen snake,** but occas another **water snake 1** or **3.**

1883 WI Chief Geologist *Geol. WI* 1.424, *T[ropidonotus] leberis* [= *Regina septemvittata*]. . . Striped Water Snake. **1928** Pope–Dickinson *Amphibians* 61, *Queen Snake.* . . Other common names are Striped Water Snake, Yellow-bellied Snake and Leather Snake. **1940** *VA Jrl. Sci.* 1.37, The other water snake, *Natrix septemvittata,* the Queen Snake, or Striped Water Snake, does not have the . . reputation for viciousness nor size. **1952** Ditmars *N. Amer. Snakes* 81, Striped Water Snake, *Natrix rigida* [=*Regina rigida*]. **1955** Carr–Goin *Guide Reptiles* 285 **FL,** *Natrix sipedon taeniata* [=*Nerodia fasciata*] . . East Coast Striped Water Snake. . . East Coast of Florida. **1969** *DARE* (Qu. P25, . . *Kinds of snakes*) Inf **RI4,** Striped water snake.

stripedy adj Also sp *stripety* Cf Intro "Language Changes" III.1

Striped.

1885 Thompson *By-Ways* 24, Allus thut 'at a Peckwood wer' a leetle, tinty, stripedy feller. **1937** in 2004 *DARE* File—Internet **OK,** Everything was stripedy cause Mammy like to make it fancy. **1939** *Sat. Eve. Post* 25 Nov 60 **nFL,** Like a stripety polecat. **1967** *DARE* (Qu. R30, . . *Kinds of beetles;* not asked in early QRs) Inf **WA28,** Elm bug—little stripety one. **c1974** in 2004 *DARE* File—Internet **TX** (as of c1930) [John Henry Falk *Christmas Story*], There was an apple and an orange and some stripety candy at everybody's place. **1999** *DARE* File—Internet, I then used paper clips and lengths of wire insulation to add the smaller plumbing (the stripety ones) to finish. **2003** *Cotton Farming* Nov (Internet) **cwMS,** I looked up, and them convicts was comin' outa that cornfield like black 'n white stripedy armyworms. **2004** *DARE* File—Internet **neIL,** Nick brought in stripedy socks and a soft, squishy, smiley shark.

striper n

1 See **striped gopher.**

2 See **striped wasp.**

3 also *striper bass:* See **striped bass 1.**

stripety See **stripedy**

strip fishing n esp **AK**

See quots.

1935 *Reno Eve. Gaz.* (NV) 24 Aug 5/4 **AK,** He had no more than hit Juneau . . when the very next day he was out in what they call "Strip" fishing for what I think they call "Jack Salman [sic]." **1939** FWP *Guide AK* xxviii, Strip fishing for salmon is very popular around Juneau. . . The angler casts and trolls until the fish are located . . then the boat is anchored and the fishing is conducted entirely by casting a hook baited with herring. **1983** Neely *AK Calls* 53, As far as we know my husband introduced strip fishing to the Juneau area. His combination of a limber pole, light weight line and freshly cut bait was unbeatable. The scent of fresh blood from the cut herring was a terrific enticement for salmon. **2003** *DARE* File—Internet **AK,** Strip fishing involves letting the line sink to the bottom of the water and pulling it up with a jerking motion to give the bait life and attract fish. **2004** *Ibid* **CA,** "Strip fishing" is the most popular method for steelhead fishing on the Carmel. Strip fishing is using monofilament instead of fly line and a lead slinky attached no less than 18″ above the lure.

strip fodder See **strip 2**

strip house n Also *stripping house, ~ shed, tobacco-stripping room* [**strip 1**] Cf **grading house**

A place in which tobacco is stripped; see quots.

1872 *Elyria Independent Democrat* (OH) [21 Aug 3]/1 (newspaper-archive.com), The fire alarm on Monday was occasioned by a barrel taking fire in Massey, Kenyon & Co's stripping room, which was filled with leaf tobacco. **1880** *Daily Gaz. & Bulletin* (Williamsport PA) 17 July [4]/2 (newspaperarchive.com), There is a stripping house 34 feet by 14, with a cellar under the whole building in which tobacco can be stripped at any time. **1894** *Bucks Co. Gaz.* (Bristol PA) 1 Nov 4/5, [Advt:] Large frame tobacco building, with stripping room attached. **1939** in Lib. of Congress *Amer. Memory: WPA Life Hist.* (Internet) **cnNC,** [Caption:] Daughter of Mr. and Mrs. Fred Wilkins helping "take off" the tobacco for grading and stripping in the strip house on their farm. **1941** *Press–Gaz.* (Hillsboro OH) 28 Jan 5/2, [Advt:] *Farm for sale*—Two barns, . . garage and tobacco stripping shed. **1944** *PADS* 2.71 **S Midl,** *Strip(ping)-house.* . . A small house in which tobacco is stripped and graded. **1965–70** *DARE* (Qu. M22, . . *Kinds of buildings . . on farms*) Infs **KY62, 64, 72, 75, 93,** Stripping room; **KY68,** Stripping room—attached to tobacco barn usually, but not always; **NC87, PA137, TN53,** Strip house; **DC5,** Stripping house; **PA23,** Stripping shed; **TN37,** Tobacco-stripping room [FW: not a room, but a separate shed about the size and shape of a tool shed]. **1965–70** *DARE* Tape **VA38,** I'd been with her and my uncle to the . . stripping room, we called it, maybe next to the 'bacco barn; take off leaves for 'em, I'll take the stalk tobacco off; **WI1,** Then they take it in the strip house and pull the leaves all off 'n the stems and put 'em in bundles; they weigh about 50, 60 pounds apiece. **1966** *PADS* 45.24 **cnKY,** Stripping room. . . A room or shed where tobacco is stripped. **1967** Key *Tobacco Vocab.* 235 **KY, PA, MO,** *Stripping room.* . . A room or shed where tob[acco] is stripped; **MD,** Stripping house. **2000** *Courier–Jrl.* (Louisville KY) 3 Feb (Internet) **cnKY,** They spent yesterday in the stripping room of their tobacco barn, wondering how they will survive after Tuesday's announcement of a 45 percent cut in tobacco quotas. **2003** *DARE* File—Internet **csWI,** In the winter . . the dried plants become easy to handle and all the laths are taken down, the plants are removed and the leaves removed from the stalks. This is called "stripping" and is done in a special shed called the "strip house."

stripped fodder See **strip 2**

stripper n

1 also *stripper cow:* A cow that gives little or no milk. [Brit dial, esp nIr] **scattered, but more freq Midl** Cf **farrow** adj

1779 *PA Packet Genl. Advt.* (Lancaster) 27 July 4/1, [Advt:] *Strayed* . . a large dun *Cow,* a stripper, and low in flesh. **1829** in 2004 *DARE* File—Internet **IN,** [Estate inventory:] One Stripper Cow $8.00. **1890** *Ibid* **IA,** I leave to Simon Lawlor my stripper cow. **1902** *DN* 2.246 **sIL,** *Stripper.* . . A cow nearly dry. **1905** ME Dept. Ag. *Annual Rept. 1904* 84, The milk of almost every cow . . becomes so affected in flavor during the last of the milking period that it is sufficient, even though you have but one stripper cow in the herd, to influence the flavor of the whole batch of butter from twenty cows. **1906** *DN* 3.123 **sIN,** *Stripper.* . . A heifer, or cow without milk. **1937** *AmSp* 12.103 **eNE** [Farm terms], If she gives little milk or is about to end her period of lactation she is a *stripper.* **1942** Warnick *Garrett Co. MD* 14 **nwMD** (as of 1900–18), *Stripper* . . cow during second year of her milking period. **1944** *PADS* 2.61 **MO,** *Stripper.* . . A milkcow that is almost dry. Middle West. Common. **c1960** Wilson *Coll.* **csKY,** *Stripper.* . . A cow in the second year of her milking period. **1965–70** *DARE* (Qu. K3b, *When a cow stops giving milk . . she's a _____;* not asked in early QRs) 63 Infs, **scattered, but more freq Midl,** Stripper. [Of all Infs responding to the question, 65% were male; of those giving this response, 83% were male.]

2 See **strip 1.**

stripper cow See **stripper 1**

stripping See **strip**

stripping house (or room, shed) See **strip house**

stripy gopher See **striped gopher**

Striver's Row n *among Black speakers*

Used as a nickname for an exclusive residential district.

1926 Van Vechten *Nigger Heaven* 77 **Harlem NYC,** The chauffeur . . drove the pair . . to West One hundred and thirty-ninth Street, dubbed Strivers' Row by all and sundry in Harlem. This block of tan brick houses. . . had been taken over by rich Negroes . . lawyers, physicians, real-estate operators, or opulent proprietors of beauty parlours. **1966–70** *DARE* (Qu. II24, *Names or nicknames for the part of a town where the well-off people live*) Infs **DC3, KY94, SC68,** Striver's Row. [All Infs Black] **1983** Abdul-Jabbar *Giant Steps* 70 **NYC** [Black], Striver's Row . . elegant, light straw-colored brick row houses on 138th and 139th Streets between Seventh and Eighth Avenues. . . In the early 1900s W.T. Handy had lived there, and Eubie Blake, and when the rest of Harlem deteriorated into a ghetto, the people in these houses . . maintained the beauty of their blocks against the hard times. In turn-of-the-century innocence these people were known as "strivers" and the houses came to be called Striver's Row. **2002** *Chron.–Telegram* (Elyria OH) 18 Aug sec G 7/2 **NYC** [Black], Ex-cop Mali Anderson may be fictional, but she does her sleuthing in a very real neighborhood . . : Harlem's Strivers Row.

strollop v Also with *around* [Cf *EDD* strollop v. 4 "To stride or walk about aggressively; to go about in an untidy, slovenly manner"] **esp S Midl** Cf **trollop 1**
To wander or idle about, traipse; to gallivant; hence vbl n *strolloping;* n *strolloper.*

1895 *Davenport Daily Republican* (IA) 5 Oct 4/3, Who wants to buy a run-down farm, with . . hogs rooting around, poultry strolloping on door steps and leaving their cards? **1925** Dargan *Highland Annals* 58 **cwNC,** When I strikes Granny Groom's place she's at the gate wantin' me to talk to her Lizy's girl who's fixin' to leave an' strollop over the country. **1935** *Atlantic Mth.* 156.44 **GA,** I was . . tired of strollopin' around. . . I . . had strolloped on foot all the way from . . Georgia. **1939** *AmSp* 14.92 **eTN,** *Strolloping around.* Traveling about the community for a low or immoral purpose. 'He's been strolloping around fur a long time.' **1953** Randolph–Wilson *Down in Holler* 289 **Ozarks,** Annie knows better than to strollop around with them town fellers. **1969** *DARE* (Qu. Y28, *A person who loiters about with nothing to do*) Inf **GA77,** Strolloper; (Qu. Y29a, *To 'go out' a great deal, not to stay at home much:* "She's always _____.") Inf **GA77,** Strolloping around. **1995–97** in 2004 Montgomery–Hall *Dict. Smoky Mt. Engl.* 577 **wNC, eTN,** *Strollop. . .* She'd be a good mother if she'd forget her strollopin'. . . Here she comes, a-strollopin' down the road.

strollop n [Cf *EDD* strollop sb. 1] **esp S Midl**
An immodest or promiscuous woman.

1936 *AmSp* 11.317 **Ozarks,** *Strollop. . .* A rambling woman of doubtful morals. Probably a combination of *trollop* and *strumpet.* **1940** Stuart *Trees of Heaven* 248 **eKY,** Bad Tussie wimmen atter you, Anse. Bad wimmen. The old low-down strollops! **1952** Brown *NC Folkl.* 1.595, *Strollop. . .* A woman of loose or questionable character.—West. **c1960** *Wilson Coll.* **csKY,** *Strollope* [sic] . . Immoral woman, probably a corruption of trollop. **1967** *DARE* (Qu. AA7b, *. . A woman who is very fond of men and is always trying to know more—if she's not respectable about it*) Inf **IL25,** Strollop. **1997** in 2004 Montgomery–Hall *Dict. Smoky Mt. Engl.* 577 **eTN, wNC,** *Strollop. . .* loose woman.

strollop around, strolloper, strolloping vbl n See **strollop** v

strolloping adj, hence adv *strolloping*
=**larruping** adj **1.**
1927 *DN* 5.478 **Ozarks,** *Strollopin',* adj. Highly satisfactory. "Jeff shore has made hisse'f some strollopin' good licker."

stromp v [Perh blend of *stomp* + *tramp/tromp*] Cf **stromple**
To tread heavily, stomp, tramp.

1922 *Syracuse Herald* (NY) 3 June [12]/7 (newspaperarchive.com), John was home an hour ahead of time. He stromped through to the kitchen. **1969** *DARE* (Qu. Y25, *To walk heavily, making a lot of noise:* "He came _____ into the house.") Inf **CA165,** Stromping. **2000** *DARE* File—Internet **MT,** My husband and I had just spent the last two summers . . stromping through cemeteries. **2004** *Ibid,* After a night of sitting the engine refused to start without stromping on the gas and holding it until the RPMs were at about 2000.

stromp n [Cf **stromp** v]
1907 *DN* 3.201 **seNH,** *Stromp. . .* A woman with mannish gait.

stromple v [Prob **stromp** v + frequentative *-le*]
1908 *S. Atl. Qrly.* 7.346 **seSC,** The *Gullah* negro . . *stromples* when he treads heavily.

strong adj, v Usu |strɔŋ|; also |strɑŋ|; for addit varr see **A** below
See Pronc Intro 3.I.6.c, 3.III.4 Cf **long** adj, n, prep, adv[1] **A**

A Forms.

1942 *AmSp* 17.37 **seNY,** *Strong* . . [ɑ] 0 [infs] . . [ɒ] 2 . . [ɔ] 21 . . [ɔˑ] 2. **c1960** *Wilson Coll.* **csKY,** *Strong* is /strɑŋ/ or /strɔŋ/. **1961** *Language* 37.562 **Pacific NW,** The first form predominates; the second is infrequent to rare. . . [ɒ] in . . *long, strong* . . [ɑ] used . . to some extent, especially in eastern Washington, Oregon, and Idaho. **1961** Kurath–McDavid *Pronc. Engl.* 164, *Long, strong. . .* The North, the North Midland, large sections of the South Midland, and the Lower South have the /ɔ ~ ɒ/ of *law* in *long, strong* almost universally. On the other hand, Virginia east of the Blue Ridge and all of North Carolina have in these words the /ɑ/ of *lot* with similar regularity. Outside this large section of the South, more or less scattered instances of /ɑ/ appear in southern West Virginia, eastern Pennsylvania, northeastern New Jersey, Brooklyn, and western New England. **1973** *PADS* 60.53 **seNC,** *Strong. . .* The Carteret speakers. . . [ɑ] said . . [ɔ] but one lone /ɑ/ user. **1976** Allen *LAUM* 3.265 **Upper MW** (as of c1950), The common Northern and North Midland /ɔ-ɒ/ vowel range in *long* and *strong* is paralleled by its universality in the U[pper] M[idwest]. . . Although fully rounded /ɔ/ occurs generally throughout the five states, weakly rounded /ɒ/ is less common. In *strong* it appears throughout, but less frequently in Minnesota. **1989** Pederson *LAGS Tech. Index* 269 **Gulf Region,** *Strong.* [Of 914 infs, 544 offered proncs of the type [strɒŋ], 125 offered proncs of the type [strɑŋ], and 4 offered proncs of the type [straʊŋ].]

B As adj. [Ger *streng* strict, severe]
1935 *AmSp* 10.170 **PA** [Engl of PA Germans], *Strong.* Strict. 'Though she never used force, she was a very strong teacher.'

C As verb.

1 To cause (one, or one's breath) to smell bad; to overpower with a bad smell. **sAppalachians**
1913 Kephart *Highlanders* 283 **sAppalachians,** Baby, that onion'll strong ye! **1926** Roberts *Time of Man* 358 **KY,** They [=onions] do strong me. . . They strong my breath. **c1940** in 2004 Montgomery–Hall *Dict. Smoky Mt. Engl.* 577 **eTN,** Onion will strong you. **1961** Seeman *In Arms of Mt.* 189 **eTN,** Timo has grown to be the largest goat. . . His smell . . is strong and rank as sea kelp. . . A lank old hunter drawled, "That thar smell will strong ye—hit jest burns my nose!" **1962** *Natl. Geogr. Mag.* July 89 **eTN,** There are "ramps" in the Smokies, namely wild onions. . . The mountain people ate both the leaves and the bulbs in the springtime. . . "That's an onion that'll strong ye. . . One bite'll stay with a man fer days."

2 To strengthen, fortify.
1941 O'Donnell *Great Big Doorstep* 250 **sLA,** 'I guess I'm just tired,' . . 'The coffee gunna strong you soon, darling.'

strong enough to walk See **walk, strong enough to**

stronger adv [Etym unknown]
Earlier.
1943 *AmSp* 18.307, During 1938 and 1939 I lived in Dayton, Ohio. One of my friends there was . . a native. . . One morning I called on the telephone. His mother answered. 'Elvin's already gone. . . He left here at nine-thirty, or maybe a little bit stronger.' My wife and I puzzled over the meaning . . was it 'earlier' or 'later'? . . About two weeks ago I was speaking to . . a production man at Knopf's. . . 'Publication date has been set for September seventh . . so we should have printed copies by the seventh of August, or a little stronger.' I asked what the 'stronger' meant and learned that it meant 'earlier.' I also learned that Mr. Hendrickson is from Missouri.

strong horse n
An athletic contest resembling tug-of-war.
1943 Korson *Coal Dust* 100, Indiana miners had a game like tug-of-war they called "Strong Horse." Two teams took up positions on opposite sides of a chalked line. At a given signal the foreman of one team grabbed the other foreman's hand across the line, and then the two teams tugged at each other until one or the other was pulled over the line.

strong-in-the-log shoe n [Perh alter of *strong-in-the-Lord* + *shoe;* cf Ephesians 6:10]
1965–66 *DARE* (Qu. W11, *Men's low, rough work shoes*) Infs **AL3, MS60,** Strong-in-the-log shoes.

strong man Sampson n Cf **Sampson's snakeroot**
A **tea weed 2** (here: *Sida rhombifolia*).
1974 Morton *Folk Remedies* 143 **SC,** "Strong Man Sampson"—*Sida rhombifolia.* . . Plant is boiled for "tea," drunk as a beverage. . . [T]he liquid is also taken by men to increase their "courage" (potency).

stroobly See **strubbly**

strook See **strike** v A2

stroovly See **strubbly**

strop n, v [*strop* is the expected descendant of ME *strope;* it has been replaced in many senses by the Scots dial form *strap,* but remains std in a few technical senses, esp "strip of leather or other material for sharpening a razor or other edge tool."] **chiefly Sth, S Midl**

A strap; to beat with a strap; hence vbl n *stropping* a beating.

1776 in 1979 *Letters of Delegates to Congress* 5.424, They have made a most violent effort to confine a man in jail for refusing the Continental Currency, and after a week's struggle have stropped him. **1828** (1970) Webster *Amer. Dict., Strop.* . . A strap. . . This orthography is particularly used for a strip of lether [sic] used for sharpening razors and giving them a fine smooth edge; a razor-strop. But *strap* is preferable. **1867** Harris *Sut Lovingood Yarns* 50 **TN,** That night, a neighbor gal got a all fired, overhandid stroppin frum her mam, wif a stirrup leather. **1883** (1971) Harris *Nights with Remus* 114 **GA** [Black], Mars John bawl out lak a man w'at got a strop in he han'. **1884** *Anglia* 7.276 **Sth, S Midl** [Black], *To strop* = to chastise. **1899** (1912) Green *VA Folk-Speech* 424, *Strop, n.* and *v.* For *strap,* in all its senses. **1902** *DN* 2.246 **sIL,** *Strop.* . . A strap. **1907** *DN* 3.227 **nwAR,** *Strop.* . . A strap. **1933** Rawlings *South Moon* 259 **FL,** Hit'll skeer 'em into mindin' their manners more to have twenty men put the strop to 'em easy, than for one man to fram the chitlin's plumb outen 'em. **1936** *AmSp* 11.317 **Ozarks,** *Strop.* . . Strap. **1940** in Lib. of Congress *Amer. Memory: WPA Life Hist.* (Internet) **TX** (as of c1888) [Black], Don't you know to loosen your saddle strops? **1976** Garber *Mountain-ese* 88 **sAppalachians,** *Strop* . . thong of leather—He tied his saddle girth with a leather strop. **1986** Pederson *LAGS Concordance,* 1 inf, **seMS,** Bridle strop; 1 inf, **cnLA,** Flank strop; 1 inf, **eTN,** A pocketbook with two strops on it; 1 inf, **neGA,** Strops—galluses; 1 inf, **cGA,** Strops—used to urge horses on; 1 inf, **swAL,** Strops—on overalls; 1 inf, **csTN,** Suspender strops. [**1989** Pederson *LAGS Tech. Index* 84 **Gulf Region,** *Strap.* [Of 914 infs, 547 responded with *strap,* 243 with *strop.*] [*DARE* Ed: The question was intended to elicit words for razor strop.]] **1995** *Signal Mag.* Dec np **cwTX,** *Strop*—A simple leather strap for torturing children, or threatening to.

strop oil See **strap oil**

stropping vbl n See **strop**

stropping adj

Of a person: robust, sturdily built, strapping.

1899 (1912) Green *VA Folk-Speech* 423, *Strapping.* . . Tall; lusty; robust. *Stropping.* "Two stropping women." **1916** Lardner *You Know Me Al* 48 **csIN,** She is some queen, Al—a great big stropping girl that must weigh one hundred and sixty lbs. **1924** (1946) Greer-Petrie *Angeline Gits an Eyeful* 3 **csKY,** Great big, stroppin' men. **1986** Pederson *LAGS Concordance,* 1 inf, **seAL,** Big-old stropping boy.

stroud n, v Similarly ppl adj *strouded* [Varr of *shroud(ed)*] Cf Pronc Intro 3.I.18

1899 (1912) Green *VA Folk-Speech* 424, *Stroud.* . . A form of *shroud.* **1927** Kennedy *Gritny* 220 **sLA** [Black], Gussie [=a dead man] sho look like somebody diffunt, layin' up there strouded in dem purrade clo'se he got on. **c1938** in 1970 Hyatt *Hoodoo* 1.229 **ceVA** [Black], After she was strouded [Hyatt: shrouded] and laid out, a water dog crawled out of her mouth alive.

strow v, hence past *strowed,* past pple, ppl adj *strowed, strown,* n *strower* |stro, -d, -n, -ə(r)| Also sp *strew* [Var of *strew* [stru]; the two pronc types have competed since ME, but the spelling has not always represented the preferred pronc; many of the 18th-cent orthoepists gave proncs of the type [stro] for both *strow* and *strew.*] **chiefly Sth, S Midl** Note: Only clearly non-literary exx are given here; *strow* also appears as an archaism or relic in formal 19th-cent writing.

1805 (1904) Clark *Orig. Jrls. Lewis & Clark Exped.* 4.66 **VA,** The last [=mountains] excessively bad & thickly Strowed with falling timber & Pine. **1828** Webster *Amer. Dict., Strew.* . . This verb is written *straw, strew,* or *strow; straw* is nearly obsolete, and *strow* is obsolescent. *Strew* is generally used. **1887** (1967) Harris *Free Joe* 224 **GA** [Black], Dey wuz a cap yer, a hat yander, en de groun' look like it wuz des strowed wid um. **1899** (1912) Green *VA Folk-Speech* 424, *Strow.* . . Strowed,

strown, strowing. A form of *strew.* **1931** (1991) Hughes–Hurston *Mule Bone* 118 **cFL** [Black], Nobody bet' not slur my wife in here. Do, I'll strow 'em over de country. **1942** Hall *Smoky Mt. Speech* 38 **wNC, eTN,** *Strew* 'scatter' was quaintly used in the sentence: 'We saw where you [stroud] books . . on the floor.' **1953** Brewer *Word Brazos* 45 **eTX** [Black], When de Sunday comed for de baptizin', Nigguhs was strowed all up an' down bof sides of de rivuh for de cer'mony. **1966–69** *DARE* (Qu. P37b, *Nicknames for a shotgun*) Inf **GA**89, Seed-strower; (Qu. Y37, *To make a place untidy or disorderly: "I wish they wouldn't _____ the room so."*) Inf **NC**37, Strow; **GA**44, Strown about; (Qu. Y38, *Mixed together, confused: "The things in the drawer are all _____."*) Inf **NC**37, Strown. **1967** *DARE* FW Addit **LA**12, Stuff strowed [stroud] all over the room. **1969** *NC Folkl.* 17.29 **wNC,** Fertilizer was *hand-strowed* (strewn). **1979** *DARE* File **cSC,** Strow—scatter gossip. "If she finds out about it, she'll go from house to house strowing it." **1982** Mason *Shiloh* 83 **wKY,** They just strow like you've never seen. Right through the middle of the living room. **1986** Pederson *LAGS Concordance,* 1 inf, **cnGA,** Strow it—strew, of cotton; 1 inf, **cnGA,** We strowed seeds from a horn. **1998** in 2004 *DARE* File—Internet **AR,** "An upright angler wouldn't leave trash strowed all up and down the river," he'd say. **2002** *Ibid* **GA,** They kept . . strowing shit everywhere. **2004** *Ibid* **seAL,** The styrofoam was strown everywhere. **2004** *DARE* File **eTX** [Black], Does "strew, strewed, strewn" rhyme with "sew, sewed, sewn," i.e. "stro, strode, strone," outside of black East Texas?

stroy v, ppl adj [Aphet forms of *destroy(ed)*] **Sth, Midl** *chiefly among Black speakers* Cf **struction**

1862 *Liberator* (Boston MA) 5 Sept 3 **VA** [Black], Tink de Union 'stroy it? **1888** Jones *Negro Myths* 60 **GA coast,** Groun-mole . . bin er root up de tetter patch, an stroy pinder. **1889** *MLN* 4.209 **TN** [Black], She done lost Marse George, and done 'stroy he life. **1922** Gonzales *Black Border* 329 **sSC, GA coasts** [Gullah glossary], *'Stroy'd*—destroy, destroys, destroyed, destroying. **1927** Adams *Congaree* 6 **cSC** [Black], Dey 'stroy your body and if dey ain't 'stroy it, look like dey' 'stroy your soul. *Ibid* 26, He say he think he nerves is 'stroy. **1952** Brown *NC Folkl.* 1.595, *'Stroy.* . . Destroy. **1957** in 1958 Brewer *Dog Ghosts* 121 **TX** [Black], He'd kill 'er an' 'stroy all de property.

strubble v [Prob < **strubbly**]

1916 *DN* 4.329 **KS,** *Strubble.* . . To put (the hair) in disorder.

strubbly adj, adv Also *schtroobly, scroobly, stribbly, stroobly, stroovly, strubly, struwwli* [PaGer *schtruwwlich;* cf Ger *strubb(e)lig* tousled] **chiefly PaGer area**

Of one's hair: untidy, disheveled, straggly; untidily.

1872 Haldeman *PA Dutch* 19, P[ennsylvania] G[erman] 'schtruwlich' (disordered, uncombed, as hair). English of the locality *stroobly.* **1882** (1971) Gibbons *PA Dutch* 390, "Your head is strubly," means that your hair is tumbled. **1896** *DN* 1.425 **cnMD,** *Stroobly* [strʊblɪ]: disheveled. "You got your hair all stroobly now." **1908** *German Amer. Annals* 10.45 **sePA,** *Stroobly.* Tangled, dishevelled; usually of hair. **1916** *DN* 4.280 **NE,** *Scroobly.* . . Mussy, untidy. "My, but my hair is scroobly." Reported as brought from eastern Ohio. *Ibid* 329 **KS,** *Strubbly.* . . Unkempt; shaggy; toused. Also Phila., Pa. **1935** *AmSp* 10.170 **PA** [Engl of PA Germans], Other German words used in English are. . . *Strubbly,* unkempt, hair mussed up. [**1950** *WELS Suppl.* **csWI,** *Strudely* . . [stru·dəli]—in disarray, mussed up. "Jane, your hair are all strudely."] **1952** Brown *NC Folkl.* 1.595, *Stribbly:* adj. and adv. Untidy; untidily.— Catawba county. **1959** George *My Side* 53 **ceNY,** When I awoke my eyes opened on two gray eyes in a white stroobly head. **1965** *DARE* File **DE,** Strubbly—disheveled. **1967** *DARE* Tape **PA**9, [FW:] They use the word strubbly around here, don't they? [Inf:] . . ['strʊbli] hair! . . Well, we used to, but I don't hear it much anymore. . . They do sometimes in the country. **1967** *DARE* FW Addit **sePA,** If hair is messed up, it is [strɪbli]. Very common, all speakers know and use it. **1968** *Helen Adolf Festschrift* 37, Pennsylvania German survivals in . . English. . . *struwwli*—This word, derived from Pennsylvania German *schtruwwlich,* is still used occasionally in describing dishevelled, unkempt hair. **1971** *Today Show Letters* **sePA** [PaGer], In Dutch country, if a person's hair is in disarray, it is *stroobly.* Or, more accurately, *schtroobly.* A great word, still current in usage here. **1987** *Jrl. Engl. Ling.* 20.2.176 **ePA,** *Stroobly/stroovly* 'disheveled, unkempt (esp. hair)'. . . 13.5% (17 [infs]), ages 12–101. **1996** Huth *Famil. Words* 112 **csPA,** *Strubly* /'stɹu:bli/ . . <said of hair> messy, tousled. **1999** Myers *Play It Again* 19 **sePA,** "Samuel Berkey with the straggly beard." "Ah, that Samuel Berkey. *Strubbly* Sam." **2000** *DARE* File **PA,** My grandmother, born in Boynton, PA in 1903 used to say that hair that was messed up was "stribbly."

struck all of a heap See **heap** n **4a**

strucked See **strike** v **A2**

strucken(ed) See **strike** v **A2, 3**

struck on adj phr **chiefly S Midl** See Map Cf *stuck on*

Enamored of, strongly attracted to.

 1892 *Union Pacific Employes' Mag.* 7.36, We have seen others that the expression, "he is struck on himself" might apply and contempt justly go with it. **1914** *Sun. Rev.* (Decatur IL) 9 Aug 15/3, You could tell by the way George had his arm around Susy's waist that he was struck on her. **1918** Whitaker *Hist. Corporal Fess Whitaker* 45 **KY,** All the girls were struck on me because I was a soldier. **1941** *LANE* Map 404 *(Courting her)* 3 infs, **CT, MA,** Struck on her. **1946** *PADS* 6.29 **eNC** (as of 1900–10), *Struck on, to be. . .* To be very fond of one. . . Common. **1947** *PADS* 7.15 **IN.** *Ibid* 26 **wNY.** *Ibid* 29 **MO.** **1954** Roberts *I Bought Dog* 34 **ce,seKY,** They were getting struck on one another by this time and she invited him to their party. **1966–69** *DARE* (Qu. AA5, *If a woman seems to be going after one certain man that she wants to marry: "She's _____ him."*) Inf **AR**24, Struck on; (Qu. AA10, *A very special liking that a boy may have for a girl [or the other way round] . . "He _____ her." or "She _____ him."*) Infs **AR**24, **KY**5, **ME**16, **VA**5, Is struck on; (Qu. GG19a, *When you can see from the way a person acts that he's feeling important or independent: "He surely is _____ these days."*) Inf **LA**11, Struck on; (Qu. HH8, *A person who likes to brag*) Inf **NC**37, Struck on hisself. **1986** Pederson *LAGS Concordance ([He is] courting her)* 7 infs, **AR, LA, MS, TN,** (Getting) struck on her; 2 infs, **swMS, nwTN,** (He's) struck on that girl; 1 inf, **swTN,** Is struck on her; she's struck on him; 1 inf, **csTN,** Struck on the girl. **2004** *DARE* File—Internet **TN** (as of 1920), I told him about my mother being struck on him.

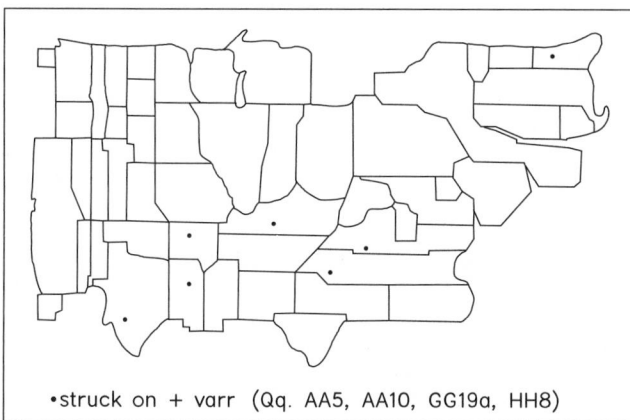

•struck on + varr (Qq. AA5, AA10, GG19a, HH8)

structid See **strike** v **A2**

struction n Also sp *struckshun* [Aphet forms of *construction, destruction*] *among Black speakers* Cf **stroy**

 1880 (1881) Harris *Uncle Remus Songs* 87 **GA** [Black], I hear tell you gwine ter sen' me ter 'struckshun, en nab my fambly. **1922** Gonzales *Black Border* 329 **sSC, GA coasts** [Gullah glossary], *'Struckshun*—destruction. *'Struckshun*—construction. **1927** Adams *Congaree* 6 **cSC** [Black], Every which er way I look I see 'struction. I see sturgeon tangle up in a wire fence. **1966** *DARE* (Qu. HH26, *A person who is always ready to stir up trouble*) Inf **SC**26, Struction maker. [Inf Black]

struggle-buggy n

An automobile, esp one that is old or broken down.

 1924 *Pt. Arthur News* (TX) 19 Nov 1/1, Johnny Rizer sporting a "jelly-bean" struggle buggy. **1925** *College Humor* Sept 20, I'll say you can park in my struggle buggy. **1926** Van Vechten *Nigger Heaven* 286 [Black], *Struggle-buggy:* Ford. **1946** (1972) Mezzrow–Wolfe *Really Blues* 74 [Black], My struggle-buggy was getting to look like a rinky-dink old tin can on wheels. **1960** Wentworth–Flexner *Slang* 526, *Struggle-buggy. . .* An automobile. *Some late 1920's and c1930 use, esp. by students, in ref. to the attempted male use of the automobile as a private place in which one could attempt to neck with a girl.* **1968–70** *DARE* (Qu. N5, *Nicknames for an automobile, especially an old or broken-down car*) Infs **GA**40, **KY**94, **VA**41, Struggle-buggy. [All Infs Black] **1970** Major *Dict. Afro-Amer. Slang* 110, *Struggle buggy:* (1930's-40's) a very old rundown car. **2003** *DARE* File—Internet, [From the song "Barber Shop" by Tom Waits:] i just bought myself a struggle buggy

suckers powder blue. *Ibid* **TX,** I drove back to Waco in a . . white 1996 Ford Explorer. . . I bid a fond farewell to the Struggle Buggy and left it in Austin.

struggle string n

The pull-cord of an outboard motor.

 1975 Gould *ME Lingo* 281, *Struggle-string . .* for the starting cord on an outboard motor . . is now a favorite with all Maine guides who wish the *jeezly* manufacturers would make a motor that will commence. **2004** *DARE* File—Internet, So you have acquired an old outboard! . . Here is what I advise *before* putting fuel in and pulling the "Struggle String."

strukt See **strike** v **A2**

strushled adj [*SND strushle* adj. "[strʌʃl]. . . Untidy, slovenly, disorderly, of persons or things"]

 1959 *VT Hist.* 27.161 **cn,neVT,** Strushled ['strʌ̃šld]. . . Disorderly; mussed. From an unpublished article on Craftsbury speech by Gladys Colburn. Occasional among the Scotch. Orleans.

strut v [*OED2 strut* v.[1] 2.a, c "*Obs.*"] **chiefly Sth, S Midl** Cf **strut** n

To bulge, be stiff or protuberant with swelling; to cause to bulge, distend; hence ppl adj *strutted* swollen, turgid; n *strutting* swelling, turgidity.

 1771 (1961) Adams *Diary* 2.24 **MA,** The Cow, whose Titts strutt with Milk, is unmilked til 9. o Clock. **1883** Amer. Philol. Assoc. *Trans.* 14.53 **Sth,** Strut, 'to be over-full, to swell out.' One of my correspondents from New York marked this as common in that State; two others from there do not know it; nor do any others of my correspondents know it. It is not common, but still used at the South; so said a negro nurse recently. **1926** *DN* 5.405 **Ozarks,** Strut. . . To distend. "Thet feller's eye-ball war strutted plum to a bladder." **1927** *DN* 5.478 **Ozarks,** Strut. . . To swell. "Maw's foot's plum strutted this mornin'. Yes, she jes' swole plum t' a strut." **1958** Randolph *Sticks* 31 **Ozarks,** It looked like the fellow's wife was in the family way, but she pooched out faster than a natural baby ought to strut a woman. **1966** *PADS* 45.24 **cnKY,** Strut. . . Of tobacco leaves curing: To begin to stand out from the stalk as though coming back to life as a result of taking up a lot of moisture. . . "If the leaves start to strut, you know that you'd better start firing." **1966–70** *DARE* (Qu. H9, *If somebody always eats a considerable amount of food, you say he's a _____*) Inf **GA**88, Strut himself; (Qu. K7, *What sickness can a cow get in her udder—for example, if she's left unmilked too long?*) Inf **MS**66, Strutting; (Qu. BB32, *If somebody had a swelling—for example, in his whole face . . "Last week his face was all _____."*) Infs **TX**51, 79, Strutted. **1976** Garber *Mountain-ese* 88 **sAppalachians,** Strut . . swell—Rumatiz causes my joints to strut. **1984** *Annals Internal Med.* 100.6.899 **cwAL,** My feet are strutted means they are tight and swollen. **1985** *Amer. Jrl. Med.* Feb 184 **eTN,** Strutted . . filled to capacity; swollen to maximum volume—"It swolled up and then it got strutted." **1986** Pederson *LAGS Concordance (The pockets)* 1 inf, **swAL,** Strut (=bulge); 1 inf, **seMS,** Strutted (=bulged). **2003** *DARE* File—Internet **AR,** Relaxation of the pelvic ligaments and strutting of the teats usually occur within 24 hours of calving. **2005** *DARE* File **TX,** "He got so strutted, he couldn't move." It means that he ate too much but is, of course, an exaggeration.

strut n [**strut** v]

1 A state of turgidity or distension. [Cf *EDD all in a strut* (at *strout* sb. 4)] **Sth, S Midl**

 1867 Harris *Sut Lovingood Yarns* 196 **TN,** He wer swell'd all over, ni ontu bustin, an' the door wer chock full ove him, all in a strut. His arms stuck out like a settin hen's wings, his hat cocked before, his feet wide apart. **1927** [see **strut** v]. **1956** Gipson *Old Yeller* 78 **TX,** Her bag was all in a strut with milk that the calf couldn't hold. **1958** *PADS* 29.17 **TN,** *Swollen in a strut:* Severely swollen. *Strut* is redundant, meaning swollen or a swelling. Rep. from Henry [Co.] **1966** *Wilson Coll.* **csKY,** Strut. . . A swelled condition. . . My cut finger is in a strut. **1968–70** *DARE* Tape **IN**45, Some tobaccos can be completely ruined. . . It goes into a strut and after it's cured it's a dingy, dark color and it doesn't weigh much; **KY**75, The tobacco will get so wet that it'll just swell out in the barn; we call it a strut. **1990** Cavender *Folk Med. Lexicon* 32 **csAppalachians,** My foot swelled into a strut.

2 Fig: a state of anxiety or stress—in phr *in a strut.* [Cf *EDD strout* sb. 5] **chiefly Sth, S Midl**

 1863 Newell *Orpheus C. Kerr* 2.111, Columbia, young, a giant baby born,/ Aim'd at a manhood ere a child had been,/ And slipping downward in a strut forlorn,/ Learns, to its sorrow, what 'tis good to know. **c1920** in 1993 Farwell–Nicholas *Smoky Mt. Voices* 160 **sAppalachians,** "I'm in a powerful strut this morning.". . "You 'pear to be in a powerful strut this morning." **1935** Murray *Schoolhouse* 14 **eTN,** One hears another man, this one in financial difficulty, speak of himself as "in a strut." **1937** *WI Rapids Daily Tribune* (WI) 10 Sept 5/1, [Syndicated sports column:] Poor Sammy was in a strut trying to make up his mind. **1949** *Hench Coll.* **AL,** I, too, have been in a strut, partly because I am giving Spenser, which I have not given for years. **1952** Brown *NC Folkl.* 1.595, *Strut, in a.* . . To be under strain, hard pressed, usually by work. "I've been in a terrible strut trying to finish my plowing before it rained again."—Granville county. **1956** McAtee *Some Dialect NC* 44, *Strut, in a.* . . To be under strain; hard pressed. **1994–97** in 2004 Montgomery–Hall *Dict. Smoky Mt. Engl.* 577 **wNC, eTN,** *In a strut.* . . in a bind.

3 A party or social event with eating, drinking, and dancing; hence n *pie strut* a party where pies are served. *esp freq among Black speakers* Cf **chitterling strut**

1933 in 1983 Taft *Blues Lyric Poetry* 238 [Black], Up in Harlem : every Saturday night / When the high browns get together : it's just too tight / They all congregates there : in an all night strut / And what they do : is tut tut tut. **1970** *DARE* (Qu. FF1, . . *A kind of group meeting called a 'social' or 'sociable'.* . . *[What goes on?]*) Inf **TN**53, Pie struts. [Inf Black] **1991** Ruff *Call to Assembly* 53 **nAL,** A chitlin strut was a musical frolic with dancing, distinctive food, and the kind of freewheeling entertainment that made Alabama's Saturday nights the best night of the week. . . A good player or singer might drop in at three or four struts in different neighborhoods during the course of an active Saturday night.

strut fart n
See quot 1944.

1944 *PADS* 2.21 **sAppalachians,** *Strut-fart.* . . One who struts around, highly conscious of his own importance. **1987** Klein *T Bone 'n Weasel* 10 **Sth,** Pleez you slapassed slack-twisted strut fart.

strut one's okra See **okra C1**

strutted, strutting See **strut v**

struwwli See **strubbly**

stub v With *along, around*
To walk, esp heavily or awkwardly; also fig.

1845 *U.S. Democratic Rev.* 16.243, No heroine has ever achieved her conquests in slippers of a larger size than number 2 (think of that, poor mortals, who stub about in capacious fives and sixes!) **1868** *Harper's New Mth. Mag.* 37.348, Am I not on foot stubbing along too poor to take a stage? **1875** Lewis *Quad's Odds* 480, The writer will stub along through life with a heart full of joyfulness. **1884** *Overland Mth.* (2d ser) 3.150 **San Francisco CA,** I wished I had the "seven-league boots," but I had to stub along in my little number sixes. **1914** *DN* 4.81 **ME, nNH,** *Stub raound.* . . To get or go around: go. **c1960** *Wilson Coll.* **csKY,** *Stub along.* . . Go along heedlessly or awkwardly.

stub-and-twist n [In allusion to its toughness, from *stub (and) twist* of a gun barrel: made of used horseshoe nails and scrap steel welded together, drawn into a long ribbon, twisted into a helix, and welded edge-to-edge]
=ruddy duck.

1888 Trumbull *Names of Birds* 113 **NC,** Another name at Newberne for the Ruddy [duck], and a very popular one, is *Light-wood Knot.* . . The knot of this "light-wood" is proverbially hard, and the appellation is therefore like "hard-head," "tough-head," "stub-and-twist," etc., and refers to the difficulty sometimes experienced in quieting these creatures. **1917** (1923) *Birds Amer.* 1.152, Ruddy Duck . . Other names . . Stub-and-twist [etc].

stub around See **stub**

stubbed up See **stub up**

stubbleberry n esp **ND, SD**
=deadly nightshade.

1902 Bailey *Cyclop. Horticult.* 4.1678, *Black Nightshade.* . . In the Dakotas . . the plant is often called "Stubbleberry," as it volunteers freely in wheat stubble, and the fruit is much used there for pies and preserves. **1914** *Aberdeen Daily News* (SD) 19 Oct 8/4, *Stubble Berries Dangerous*—William H. Morgan . . just had rather an unpleasant experience from eating liberally of this very pleasing wild fruit. **1919** *Amer. Jrl. Vet. Med.* 14.192 **IA,** A lady used stubble berries for pies, but could not tell the difference between stubble berries and deadly nightshade. . . The

stubble berry is the same as the deadly nightshade *(Solanum nigrum).* **1946** *Daily Huronite & Plainsman* (Huron SD) 8 Sept 4/8, Premium winners in the agriculture department at the 1946 State Fair. . . Native stubble berries or night shades—1st, Alice Arne; 2nd, Mrs. Leonard Reed. **1977** *Daily Jrl.* (Fergus Falls MN) [9 Sept 10]/5 (newspaper-archive.com), Some of the wild foods he and Marguerite know about are inheritances from their families—thorn apple jelly and stubbleberry jelly are among them.

stubble duck n **west of Missip R**
A **ring-necked pheasant** or other game bird, esp when killed illegally.

1888 *Daily Huronite* (Huron SD) 15 Aug 1/3, Stubble duck are fat and plenty, and hunters . . are living high. Evidently Beadle county is chilly on the game and local option laws. **1902** *NE State Jrl.* (Lincoln) 30 Jan 4/4, The hotel and restaurant men in Nebraska and other states are experiencing considerable difficulty in supplying their guests with quail and game. The old dodge of serving these birds under the name of plover, snipe, or stubble duck don't go any more. **1929** *Chron.–Telegram* (Elyria OH) 21 Dec 14/5 **UT,** But stubble ducks, thick in many sections of the state, are protected by game laws under the heading "Chinese pheasants." . . The name 'stubble duck' was coined in an attempt to conceal the real import, and hunters and farmers were wont to hunt the 'ducks' during closed season. **1941** Writers' Program *Guide CO* 366 **cnCO,** Throughout this area ring-necked pheasants, native to China, known locally as "stubble ducks," are seen in the fields and along the highway. **1949** *PADS* 11.26 **CO,** *Stubble duck.* . . A pheasant. A term used to avoid the law. **1966** *DARE* (Qu. Q7, *Names and nicknames for . . game birds*) Inf **OK**18, Stubble duck—quail shot out of season—used to keep kids from knowing. **1975** *Progress–Rev.* (La Porte City IA) 12 Nov [9]/2 (newspaperarchive.com), Pheasant hunters locally had a good opener. . . I met several hunters in the field who had their limit of stubble-ducks. **2003** *DARE* File—Internet **SD** (as of 1940), Grandma had pheasant in gravy (we ate it the year around as the fields were always in motion with their ring-necked beauty; when it was not hunting season we called it stubble duck).

stubble horse n Cf **land-horse**
1968 *DARE* (Qu. K32b, *The horse on the left side in plowing or hauling*) Inf **IA**43, Stubble horse.

stubble jumper n Cf **stump jumper,** *DCan*
Esp among loggers and miners: a farmer; a greenhorn.

1939 FWP *ID Lore* 244, Seeing he was a stubble-jumper (greenhorn), the school mom (forked pole used in loading) gunned (turned) and got me. **1949** Emrich *Wild West Custom* 164, Arizona miners call them [= greenhorns] . . stubble jumpers. **1958** McCulloch *Woods Words* 184 **Pacific NW,** *Stubble jumper*—A part time farmer at work in the woods. **1973** Allen *LAUM* 1.350 (as of c1950), A rustic . . stubble jumper [1 inf, **MN**].

stubborn adj [*OED2* stubborn adj. 3 "Hard, stiff, rigid. *Obs.* exc. of weed or stone."] **esp Sth, S Midl**
1 Of material objects; hard, stiff, unyielding.

1899 (1912) Green *VA Folk-Speech* 425, *Stubborn, adj.* Stiff; thick. "If you cut your beard it will grow very stubborn." **1991** Still *Wolfpen Notebooks* 85 **sAppalachians,** Corn meal that's not dried out proper makes stubborn bread.

2 Of a person: constipated. Note: The combs *stubborn bowels,* ~ *constipation* are widespread and not treated here.

1984 *Annals Internal Med.* 100.6.899 **cwAL,** Grandpa is stubborn means that he is constipated. **2007** *DARE* File—Internet **Sth** [EMA Provider's Guide to Southern Medical Terminology], Stubborn = constipated.

stubborndy adj [Var of *stubborn;* cf Intro "Language Changes" III.1] Cf **loggeredy-headed**

1964 *Mt. Life* Spring 54 **sAppalachians,** A body mightenigh as well whup a gin pole . ., withouten he wants to very near it to cut the blood outen the poor little stubborndy, loggeredy headed mule.

stub camp n **West**
=spike camp.

1933 *Fresno Bee the Republican* (CA) 29 Aug sec B 2/2, This crew will form Stub Camp No. 1 at Gray Meadows. . . An advance crew . . left to establish Stub Camp No. 2 at Little Kern. **1938** *Indiana Weekly Messenger* (PA) 14 July 3/3 **UT,** The notice [at a CCC camp] called for volunteers to carry water pipes to a stub camp about 16 miles away. **1958** McCulloch *Woods Words* 184 **Pacific NW,** *Stub camp*—Same as side camp. [*Ibid* 164, *Side camp*—A small camp set up temporarily away from the main camp, as for timber cruising, engineering parties, etc.] **1993** McClelland *Presenting Nature* 217, At Yosemite, the cables on Half Dome that had been installed about 1920 by the Sierra Club were now replaced and strengthened by the CCC. . . This trail work was done from a stub camp. **2003** *DARE* File—Internet [National Park Service] **csUT,** Efforts . . eventually were rewarded by federal designation of the area as Capitol Reef National Monument in 1937. Soon after, a stub camp of the Civilian Conservation Corps (CCC) was set up just west of Fruita.

stub-headed See **stump-headed**

stubnose buffalo n Also *stub-nosed buffalofish*
=bigmouth buffalo.

   1933 LA Dept. of Conserv. *Fishes* 437, *M[egastomatobus] cyprinella,* the Stub-nosed Buffalofish. *Ibid* 441, The Common Buffalofish or Redmouth Buffalo. . . Stub Nose Buffalo, Chub Nose Buffalo, Pug Nose Buffalo [etc]. **1983** Becker *Fishes WI* 615, Bigmouth buffalo. . . Other common names . . stubnose buffalo [etc].

stub one's toe v phr

1 also *stump one's toe:* To become pregnant. Cf **break one's leg, stump** n[1] **6**

   1965–69 *DARE* (Qu. AA28, . . *Joking or sly expressions . . women use to say that another is going to have a baby* . . "*She['s] _____.*") Inf **IL5,** Stubbed her toe; **LA6,** She stumped her toe; **MS16,** Stumped her toe; burnt her foot.

2 To do something exceptionally well.

   2002 *DARE* File **AL,** "Stub my toe" or "Stub your toe"—"I [or you] really lucked out". This seemingly odd contradiction means one did exceptionally well, as I was told the other evening, "You really stubbed your toe on that chess pie." The speaker was about fifty years-old, and from Wilcox County, Alabama. The other guests from north Alabama, Kentucky and Arkansas had never heard it. I had not heard it used in years, other than by me. It was used by mother, and her family [from Montgomery, and Geneva counties], and neighbors and friends in those places.

stuboy exclam, v |stə'bɔɪ| Also *staboy, steboy;* for addit pronc and sp varr see quots [Prob aphet forms of *hist-a-boy;* cf *OED2* hist int. 2 "Cf. Sc. *hist-a-cat!, 'st-a-cat!,* used in hounding a dog after a cat."] **scattered, but esp NEast** *old-fash* Cf **suboy**

Used as a call to drive, rouse, or sic an animal (or rarely a person); to drive, rouse, or sic; to pursue.

   1811 [see **whooee 3**]. [**1841** in 1870 Emerson *Prose Wks.* 1.174 **MA,** Wherever he sees anything that will keep men amused . . he must cry, "Hist-a-boy," and urge the game on.] **1843** Thompson *Major Jones' Courtship* 25 **GA,** "Thar it is—that black and white thing—on that log," says Tom. "Steboy; catch him!" ses he [to the dogs]. **1845** *Living Age* 4.156 **NEng,** Now folks will stuboy father, and set him on, to make him let out jist for a laugh. **1890** *DN* 1.23 **NEng,** *Steboy* [stə'bɔɪ], an exclamation used in setting a dog on an animal or thing. **1892** *DN* 1.237 **cwMO,** *Steboy* [stɪ'bɔɪ]: used in driving pigs. **1900** *Sun* (NY NY) 9 Nov 6/1, Instead of offering a bounty for the heads of the wolves, he stubboyed them against the sheep. **1903** *DN* 2.347, *Note on "Stuboy."* . . [T]here are nearly as many spellings of this dialectal word as there are correspondents. . . *st'boy, steboy, stiboi,* . . *s'te'boy,* . . *'stheboy, staboy, 'st-a-boy, 'st'boy, stewboy,* . . *stubboy.* . . In Liberty, N.Y., the word is [stəbɔɪ] . . used . . in driving hogs. In Moravia it is also [stəbɔɪ]. Residents of Brooklyn use [stəbɔɪ] as an expression of approval in bowling games and other sports. In Philadelphia [stəbɔɪ] is used in urging on a dog. The word is generally known throughout New England. . . [stəbɔɪ] is used there, as in Philadelphia, in setting an unwilling dog on another dog. In East Conway, N.H., it is a command to set a dog after another animal, or a man; in Concord, Mass., it is also used to dogs. In Biddeford, Maine, [stəbɔɪ] is used to drive cattle or sheep; in Northwestern Connecticut it is a call to dogs, never to pigs. . . In Illinois [stəbɔɪ] is the form to drive hogs. . . In Michigan [stəbɔɪ] is equivalent to "There's the culprit, go for him." . . From this survey . . it is conjectured that [stəbɔɪ] is the form in New England and the Middle Atlantic states. **1908** Day *King Spruce* 219 **ME,** Two crews ste'boyed together by us to capture a State pauper. **1924** *DN* 5.295 **csNH,** *Stuboy.* . . To set a dog on any person or thing.

stub scythe n **NEng, esp MA** *old-fash* Cf **brush scythe, bush hook, ~ scythe**

A stout scythe used for clearing underbrush.

   1650 in 1908 *Mayflower Descendant* 10.174 **MA,** One spade one mattacke one holborne and stub syth. **1719** in 2004 *DARE* File—Internet **RI,** One stub scythe, two nibs and a ring. **1797** *Ibid* **CT,** Two hoes 3s/, one dung fork 3s/, one pitch fork 1s/6d, one rake 1s/, one stub scythe 1s/6d. **1857** (1949) Thoreau *Jrl.* 10.50 **MA,** Who knows not whether he is hacking at the upas tree or the Tree of Knowledge, with axe and stub-scythe. **1860** (1861) Abbot *Stories of Rainbow & Lucky* 69 **MA,** You might help me a good deal by clearing up the underbrush, if I only had another axe for you, or a stub-scythe. **1869** Wells *Water-Power of ME* 54, Wherever the labor of man has made a *clearing,* immediately unless prevented by stub-scythe, fire, and the ploughshare, innumerable shrubs and treelets swarm into its occupancy. **1969** *DARE* (Qu. L35, *Hand tools used for cutting underbrush and digging out roots*) Inf **MA40,** Stub scythe—thicker scythe than used for cutting grass. [Inf old]

stubtail n

=ruddy duck.

   1923 U.S. Dept. Ag. *Misc. Circular* 13.31 **AL,** Ruddy Duck. . . Vernacular Names. . . *In local use.* . . stubtail.

stub up v phr, hence ppl adj phr *stubbed up* [Prob < *stubborn*] **sAppalachians** Cf **sull** v

To become sullen, silent, or uncooperative.

   1946 *AmSp* 21.271 **neKY,** *Stub up.* . . To balk, to become obstinate; also to shut up, to become silent. 'All the way we were talking along, but just as soon as we got near home she stubbed up and never said a word.' **1975** Chalmers *Better* 66 **wNC, eTN,** But should you contrary him, he may sull or stub up. **1999** in 2004 Montgomery–Hall *Dict. Smoky Mt. Engl.* 577 **eTN,** *All stubbed up* = become stubborn, uncooperative. **2005** Williams *Gratitude* 528 **wNC** (as of 1940s), *Stub up:* balk; be stubborn; pout.

stuck ppl adj

1 See **stick** v **3, 4.**

2 See **sticking** ppl adj.

stuck in the cork adj phr

See quot.

   2000 *NADS Letters,* As a child visiting my grandparents in eastern PA in the 40s and early 50s I was familiar with the sense, but not the origin of my grandfather's expression "He's stuck in the cork." One who was "stuck in the cork" had become upset or angered by some untoward turn of events and continued to be angry or upset long after the inciting event or cause had ceased to exist or had been otherwise resolved. . . [A] Penn State Professor and friend . . used the expression. . . His exegesis of the expression was that it derived from the days of steam power and the necessity of keeping track of the pressure in the steam boiler with a pressure gauge. At those times when the pressure dangerously increased rapidly, the needle of the gauge would, with force, be impelled against a cork bumper at the upper end of its permitted excursion. Occasionally the needle would remain "stuck in the cork" even after the boiler pressure had been reduced to a lesser, more safe level, and required a rap with the knuckle to be dislodged and return to an accurate reading of the (lower) pressure. . . Anyway, that seemed to make sense, particularly considering that my grandfather, Lee Washburn, had been a steam locomotive engineer . . just after the turn of the century. The only other user of this expression I recall was an out-of-work coal miner . . from Bluefield, West Virginia, who was working as a farm laborer on the cranberry bogs of south New Jersey in the summer of 1960.

‡**stuck up** adj phr Cf **strike** v **B2**

Of an oyster bed: prepared and seeded; also fig.

   1939 FWP *Guide NJ* 640 **csNJ,** This is an oyster town. A typical sign on a store in its short business block reads, "Garrison's Restaurant, an old bed newly stuck up." The terminology is that used to describe a plot under the waters of Maurice River Cove where oysters had formerly been raised, which had been again prepared and seeded with oyster "spat."

stud n[1] See **studs**

stud n[2] Also *stud-duck*

A **merganser** (here: *Mergus merganser*) or **red-breasted merganser.**

   1923 U.S. Dept. Ag. *Misc. Circular* 13.5 **TN,** American Merganser. . . stud. *Ibid* 6 **TN,** Red-breasted Merganser. . . stud-duck.

stud buzzard See **stud duck 2**

studden, studdin See **study** v[1]

studdle v   [*EDD studdle* v. 1 "To stir up so as to make thick and muddy"]

To roil, muddy (a liquid); hence ppl adj *studdled;* adj *studdly.*

   1918 *DN* 5.16 **Martha's Vineyard MA,** *Studdle.* . . To stir up, to roil. (After upsetting coffee-pot): "Well, I guess that coffee's a little studdled now." **1963** *Word* 19.278 **Martha's Vineyard MA,** We find . . *studdled* for 'dirty, roiled' water. **1968** *DARE* (Qu. KK39, *Stirred up, upset:* "*Because of the storm, the pond was all _____.*") Inf **NJ**20, Studdly.

stud duck n

1   See **stud** n[2].

2   also *stud buzzard, ~ possum:* An influential or important person; a boss, leader.

   1942 Perry *Texas* 198, Sam Houston, who was, as it were, the old stud possum of Texas history. **1959** Ruark *Poor No More* 132 **Sth,** I'm the chief mate and I'm the stud duck on this bucket. Don't you ever forget it. **1967–70** *DARE* (Qu. HH17, *A person who tries to appear important, or who tries to lay down the law in his community: "He'd like to be the _____ around here.*") Infs **IN**42, **WY**1, Stud duck; (Qu. HH43a, *The top person in charge of a group of workmen*) Inf **TX**98, Stud duck. **1984** Weaver *TX Crude* 129, *Stud duck.* . . *(Also Stud buzzard.)* The acknowledged leader of a clique, or community. "Sheriff Buckshot is the stud duck around here, and if he tells you a rooster can pull a freight train, you better get off the track." **1985** Madson *Up River* 244 **Upper Missip Valley,** This is usually a deckhand but in some cases it is the Stud Duck (captain) himself. **2000** *Milwaukee Jrl.* (WI) 3 Dec sec C 8 (Internet), "Warren is supposed to be the stud duck in this whole draft," one scout said. **2002** *DARE* File—Internet, If the Democrats win an extra five or six seats . . doesn't Dick Gephardt become the stud duck in Washington right then?

studdy   See **steady** A2

studfish n   **chiefly S Midl**

A **killifish 1** (here: *Fundulus catenatus* or *F. stellifer*).

   1876 NY Acad. Sci. *Annals Lyceum Nat. Hist.* 11.324 **nGA,** *Xenisma stellifera* [=*Fundulus stellifer*]. . . Its congener, *catenata,* is known as the Stud-fish or Studdy-Pearch. **1882** U.S. Natl. Museum *Bulletin* 16.337, *F[undulus] catenatus.* . . Stud-fish. . . Tennessee and Cumberland Rivers. *Ibid, F[undulus] stellifer.* . . Spotted Stud-fish. . . Alabama River, in clear streams and springs; a beautiful fish. **1929** OK Univ. Biol. Surv. *Pub.* 1.97, *Fundulus catenatus.* . . Studfish. . . one of the forms common to the Tennessee and Ozark uplands. **1967** Cross *Hdbk. Fishes KS* 230, Northern studfish—*Fundulus catenatus.* **2004** (acc) U.S. Dept. Ag. *Integrated Taxonomic Info. System* (Internet), *Fundulus catenatus.* . . Northern studfish. *Ibid, Fundulus stellifer.* . . Southern studfish.

studiment   See **studyment 2**

studin   See **study** v[1]

stud possum   See **stud duck 2**

studs n   Also *stud* [Cf Brit dial *take (the) stunt* (*EDD stunt* sb. 15), *take the sturdy* or *sturdies* (*EDD sturdy* adj. 9.(2))]   **chiefly Sth, S Midl**

A fit of stubborn opposition, balkiness—usu in phrr *take* (or *get, have*) *the studs.*

   1797 in 1882 *PA Mag. Hist. & Biog.* 6.111, Dont you think Mr Ashleys leading Strings may give way, if the Commy should take the Studd. **1830** *VA Lit. Museum* 1.479, "To take the stud"—to be obstinate: originally applied to a horse that refuses to go on. **1843** *Spirit of Times* 7 Oct 378/1 **MS,** We suspect his temper was somewhat "riled," . . and that, to quote an expressive Mississippi term, he "took the studs." His obstinacy or stubbornness . . lost him the race. **1891** *Century Illustr. Mag.* 41.560 **GA,** Pap has taken the studs, and I have made up my mind to leave here for good and all. **1899** (1912) Green *VA Folk-Speech* 426, *Studs.* . . When a person or animal is obstinate and will do neither one thing nor another he is said to "take the studs." **1918** Whitaker *Hist. Corporal Fess Whitaker* 11 **KY,** When I was eight years old my mother . . put me on an old mule named "John," [and] put a spur on my right heel to make the old mule go if he took the studs. **1923** *DN* 5.223 **swMS,** *Take the studs.* . . To balk or refuse to obey, as an animal. To become stubborn or obstinate, as a person. **1936** *AmSp* 11.318 **Ozarks,** *Take the studs.* . . To become stubborn, immovable, unyielding. 'We was doin' all right till ol' Deacon Jones tuck th' studs, but it aint no use talkin' no more t'night.' **1943** Writers' Program NC *Bundle of Troubles* 72, Abe's well liked, 'cept when he gets his spells of stubs [sic]

and his temper gets riled, which is higher than a Georgia pine. **1950** *PADS* 14.64 **SC,** *Studs.* . . A show of temper in a horse, wherein he refuses to move. A horse is said to have the studs, or to take the studs. **c1960** Wilson Coll. **csKY,** *Studs.* . . Contrary spell of horse or mule. **1966** *DARE* (Qu. A11, *When somebody takes too long about coming to a decision . . "I wish he'd quit _____.*") Inf **FL**7, He's got the studs. **1986** Pederson *LAGS Concordance,* 1 inf, **swGA,** Taking the studs—of a mule that won't move.

study v[1]   Also, for *studying,* pronc-spp *studden, stud(d)in', stuttin'*

1   intr: To engage in thought, meditate; to think, reflect, be concerned (about, on, or over something or someone). [*OED2 study* v. 2.a 1340 →]   **chiefly Sth, S Midl, TX**   See Map

   1840 Haliburton *Clockmaker* (3d ser) 30 **NEng,** Who should I meet . . but the Major a-pokin' along with his cocoanut down, a-studyin' over somethin' or another quite deep. **1859** *Atlantic Mth.* 3.104 **MA,** When he heard that your remarks on Dr. Mayhew had come out, Seth . . come up to Newport to get them, and spent all his time, last winter, studyin' on it and makin' his remarks. **1859** *Harper's New Mth. Mag.* 20.140 **KY,** I am always Studying about you it dos me no good at all I have been studying about you ever sense last July. **1863** in 1962 Truxall *Respects to All* 94 **PA,** We rec'd. two months pay yesterday and I have been studying about sending some money in this letter. **1884** *Anglia* 7.262 **Sth, S Midl** [Black], *To study* = to meditate. **1890** Johnston *Widow Guthrie* 218 **GA** (as of 1830s) [Black], Marster, warm night like dis, he ain' studdin' 'bout rogues; whut he studdin' 'bout is keepin' hisself cool. **1899** (1912) Green *VA Folk-Speech* 426, There they all sat silent around the fire studying. **1902** *DN* 2.246 **sIL,** *Study.* . . To cogitate; to be absorbed in thought; to meditate; to reflect. **1903** *DN* 2.332 **seMO,** *Study.* . . To think; to consider. 'I'll study about that and let you know later.' 'I never studied about his treating me thataway.' **1904** *DN* 2.421 **nwAR,** *Study.* . . To reflect, consider. "I'll have to study on that before I can give you an answer." **1909** *DN* 3.377 **eAL, wGA,** *Study, v.i.* To think, consider, ponder. **1914** *DN* 4.160 **cVA,** *Study about.* . . To have in consideration. "Ah'm not studyin' 'bout that!" **1923** *DN* 5.222 **swMO,** *Study.* . . To ponder, to cogitate over a problem. **1938** Rawlings *Yearling* 10 **nFL,** The notion takened me . . afore I studied on the beetree. **1941** O'Donnell *Great Big Doorstep* 17 **sLA** [Black], 'My Papa,' Evvie said. 'Yeah.' 'Where is he, well?' 'Ain studden bout yo paw. Reckon he eatin in de house.' **1942** Faulkner *Go Down* 77 **MS,** What I cant keep from studying about is what we gonter tell Nat about that back porch and that well. **1952** Brown *NC Folkl.* 1.596, *Study (about).* . . To take under consideration; to think about. "I'll study about helping him pay that debt." **1963** Owens *Look to River* 133 **TX,** "Ain't you gonna put the plow back?" "We ain't got time to study none about the plow." **1965–70** *DARE* (Qu. JJ18, *If you want to have time to think about something before you make a decision: "Give me till tomorrow, I'd like to _____.*") 29 Infs, **esp Sth, S Midl, TX,** Study on (or about, over) it; **LA**3, **MO**1, **SC**32, 34, Study; **KY**21, Study about that; **CT**33, Study awhile; **CA**209, Study on this; (Qu. JJ36, *To work out a plan, especially a secret plan: "Mary knows more about that, you and she can _____ together.*") Inf **AR**39, Study about it. **1982** Barrick *Coll.* **csPA,** *Study—think, meditate.* "That made him study." **1989** *New Yorker* 27 Feb 56 **nwTX,** I don't believe you should set down and study on yourself. **1999** *AmSp* 74.246 **ceSC,** Mr. Arnold, he says he bes studying about tearing that old house down. **1999** *DARE* File **WV,**

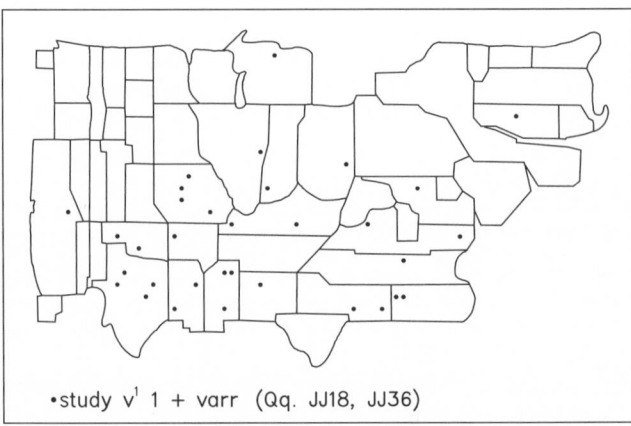

•study v[1] 1 + varr (Qq. JJ18, JJ36)

When my friend told her mother a story about my mother, she replied, "I ain't stuttin' 'bout Travis' momma."

2 also with *out, over;* tr: To think, ponder, reflect on or about (something). **chiefly Sth, S Midl, TX**   See Map

1856 (1968) Drew *Refugee* 260 **VA** [Black], I began to study what I should do for something to eat. **1867** Harris *Sut Lovingood Yarns* 45 **TN,** An' he look'd sorter like he'd been studyin a deep plan tu cheat sumbody, an' hed miss'd. **1935** Wolfe *Of Time* 240 **NC,** Why, you know, I got to studyin' it over tonight and it's just occurred to me—now I'll tell you what *my* theory is. **1939** *Hall Coll.* **eTN,** I studied what was the matter. **1943** Chase *Jack Tales* 127 **wNC,** Jack got his senses back pretty soon and set there a little while tryin' to study what to do. **1955** Roberts *S. from Hell-fer-Sartin* 8 **seKY,** Let me sorter study it out a while. **1963** Wright *Lawd Today* 28 **Chicago IL** [Black], Then I'll study my scheme some. **1965–70** *DARE* (Qu. JJ18, *If you want to have time to think about something before you make a decision: "Give me till tomorrow, I'd like to _____."*) 26 Infs, **chiefly Sth, S Midl, TX,** Study it (out *or* over); **MO**19, **OK**45, Study the situation (*or* matter); **CA**96, **KS**13, Study this; **NM**12, Study it a little; **MN**12, Study that a little; **AR**47, Study that over; (Qu. JJ36, *To work out a plan, especially a secret plan: "Mary knows more about that, you and she can _____ together."*) Infs **KY**36, **SC**65, Study it; (Qu. KK47, *Something that is left undecided or unfinished: "Perhaps we'd better just _____."*) Inf **MS**56, Study that over. **1969** *DARE* FW Addit **KY**65, *Study*—to think about something. "I studied it a bit."

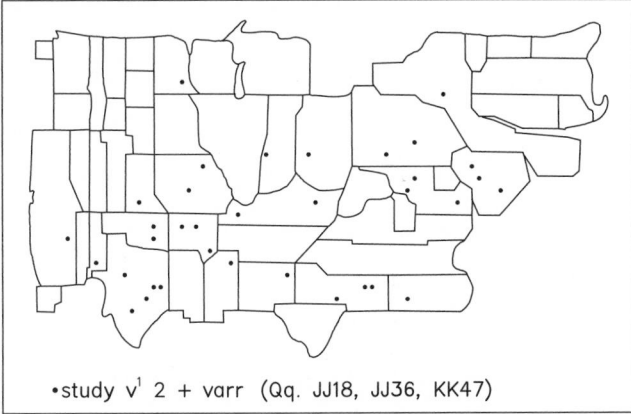

•study v¹ 2 + varr (Qq. JJ18, JJ36, KK47)

3 with *out, up:* To devise, design, formulate. **esp sAppalachians**

1867 Harris *Sut Lovingood Yarns* 67 **TN,** I studied out at las' a plan what I thort wud wake the devil. **1925** Dargan *Highland Annals* 223 **sAppalachians,** I've studied out how I can pay you back. **1939** in 2004 Montgomery–Hall *Dict. Smoky Mt. Engl.* 578 **wNC,** I just decided I'd study up some way to get them turkeys. **1968** *DARE* (Qu. JJ36, *To work out a plan, especially a secret plan: "Mary knows more about that, you and she can _____ together."*) Inf **MD**22, Study it up. **1970** in 2004 Montgomery–Hall *Dict. Smoky Mt. Engl.* 578 **eTN,** But I studies out the matter this-a-way. **1984** Wilder *You All Spoken Here* 152 **Sth,** *Study out:* Formulate, as in "God must to of put more time a-studyin' out oak trees than any other sort."

4 To have any interest in or concern for—used in neg constrs. **Sth, S Midl** *chiefly among Black speakers*

1893 Shands *MS Speech* 76, *Stud'in' yu.* . . A very common negro phrase for *thinking about you;* as, "G'way fum hya, chile; I ain't stud'in' yu." **1931** (1991) Hughes–Hurston *Mule Bone* 81 **cFL** [Black], She ain't studying none of you-all nohow. All she wants is what you got in your pocket. **1946** *PADS* 6.29 **eNC** (as of 1900–10) [Black], *Study one, not to.* . . To ignore one; to wish to have nothing to do with one. "I ain't studyin' you." **1959** Ruark *Poor No More* 16 **Sth** [Black], I just ain't *studyin'* mens. **1965** *DARE* FW Addit **Sth,** I'm not studyin' you—Expression of disbelief used frequently among Negroes and less-educated White people in the South (Alabama and Mississippi, I know). Also used to get across the idea that you are not paying attention to a person. **1969** Emmons *Deep Rivers* 51 **eTX** [Black], "You'll get all o' his proppity and you can make a livin' without work, for the rest o' your life." Tom, he say, "I ain't studyin' that old man's proppity." **1970** *DARE* (Qu. GG21a, *If you don't care what a person does* . . *"You can go ahead and do it _____."*) Inf **FL**48, I ain't studying you; (Qu. KK26, *Something that makes no difference at all to you: "He can think what he*

likes, it _____ me.") Inf **FL**48, I ain't studying him. **1984** Wilder *You All Spoken Here* 169 **Sth,** *I ain't studyin' you:* Leave me be; I'm payin' you no mind. **1998** *DARE* File **Sth** [Black], "I ain't studyin' you!"—i.e. I'm paying no attention to you.

5 See quot.

1895 *DN* 1.374 **seKY, eTN, wNC,** *Study* . . talk, discuss. . . [*DN* Ed: Also reported from Md.] "I studied about her hair to my man when I got home."

6 foll by infin: To plan, intend.

1934 Carmer *Stars Fell on AL* 208 [Black], The colored folks is studyin' to have a parade to make the crops grow. They have it every year. **1943** in 1944 *ADD* **ceWV,** I study to bypass latin names for flora & fauna, but the book name of the red bird . . rolls off the tongue with . . gusto.

7 with *around:* To deliberate indecisively.

1967 *DARE* (Qu. A11, *When somebody takes too long about coming to a decision* . . *"I wish he'd quit _____."*) Inf **MO**38, Studying around.

8 with *at:* To observe, look at intently.

1984 Doig *English Creek* 59 **nMT,** My father was studying across at the burn in the gloomy way he always did here.

study v², adj, adv   See **steady A2**

study around   See **study** v¹ 7

study at   See **study** v¹ 8

study bee   See **steady bee**

studying cap n [*EDD* to put on one's *studying-cap* (at *study* v. 1(1)) to think deeply.]   Cf **study** v¹ 1, 2

A thinking cap—used in var phrr indicating a state of deep thought or reflection; see quots.

1835 in 2004 *DARE* File—Internet **VA,** If I succeed in winning a little Eliza of Woodstock—who is now wearing her studying cap—I am off for Illinois. **1848** *Ibid* **KS,** I have had my studying cap on ever since you were here. **1875** Thompson *Hoosier Mosaics* 162, The remains of departed things . . put one into his studying cap to puzzle over specimens fully as curious and interesting in their way as the *cephalaspis.* **1948** in 2004 *DARE* File—Internet, I just thought I would call your attention to the fact and let you get on your studying cap. **1969** *DARE* (Qu. JJ27, *To give somebody a hint for his own good: "He had no idea that she was up to anything, but I put _____."*) Inf **GA**77, His studying cap on him. **2004** *DARE* File—Internet, I have a pretty thick skin. . . But I'm going to expect you to put on your thinking (and studying) cap when engaged in dialogue with me on a weighty matter such as this.

study John   See **steady bee**

studyment n   Cf **-ment**

1 A state of deep thought or reverie; the subject or result of one's meditation. **sAppalachians**

1913 Kephart *Highlanders* 224 **sAppalachians,** Studyment (reverie). **1917** Kephart in *DN* 4.418 **wNC,** *Studyment.* . . "He sot thar all in a studyment." "Nancy, honey, what's your studyments to-night?" **c1926** in 2004 Montgomery–Hall *Dict. Smoky Mt. Engl.* 578 **wNC,** *Studyment* = dreaming. **1952** Brown *NC Folkl.* 1.596, *Studyment.* . . Consideration, study, reverie. "He's in a powerful studyment trying to figure out how to get the money." Illiterate. Mainly Negroes. **1994** in 2004 Montgomery–Hall *Dict. Smoky Mt. Engl.* 578 **wNC,** Studyment [=reverie, contemplation].

2 sp *studiment:* See quots.

1993 *Coast Watch* Sept/Oct 15 **Outer Banks NC,** [Caption:] Studiments—books. **2004** *DARE* File—Internet **eNC** [Outer Banks Lexicon], *Studiments*—Studies or Lessons. "Missy shore knows her studiments, she does."

study out   See **study** v¹ 2, 3

study over   See **study** v¹ 2

study up   See **study** v¹ 3

stuff n [Cf *EDD stuff* sb.¹ 6 "Live stock, poultry, &c."] **West** Cf **she-stuff**

Cattle.

1920 Hunter *Trail Drivers TX* 378 (as of 1874), These cattle were in good shape and as fine beeves as you ever saw, no she stuff. **1934**

(1940) Weseen *Dict. Amer. Slang* 98 [Western slang], *Grown stuff*—Full-grown cattle. *Ibid* 108, *Stuff*—Cattle. *Ibid* 110, *Wild stuff*—Wild cattle. **1944** Adams *Western Words* 68, *Grown stuff*—Full-grown cattle. *Ibid* 158, *Stuff*—A common reference to general range stock which might include yearlings, bulls, steers, weaners, cows with calves, and dry cows.

stuffie n esp RI

A clamshell (esp that of a **quahog**) filled with a mixture of chopped clams and other ingredients and baked.

1982 Chaika *Speaking RI* [9], *Stuffies* = quahog shells stuffed with various stuffings, often made with farina, sometimes having hot peppa. **1987** *St. Petersburg Times* (FL) 6 Aug sec D 2 (Internet) **RI**, Many of the specialties are unique. . . stuffies (stuffed quahog clams). **2002** *NY Times* (NY) 13 Nov sec F 1/5 (Internet) **RI**, Stuffed quahogs are often called stuffies, and the two terms are used interchangeably throughout the state. **2002** Stern–Stern *Roadfood* 46 **seMA**, So when we ask for stuffed quahogs (clams), she nods approvingly and calls our order by its proper local name: "You want stuffies." **2004** *Milwaukee Jrl.* (WI) 18 Jan Entree sec 3 (Internet), Stuffies are one of the great American dishes contributed by the New Englanders. Stuffies . . are stuffed baked clams. The clams of choice are quahogs. **2005** *DARE* File—Internet **RI**, Stuffies come in as many versions as there are cooks.

stug See stog

stump n[1]

1 The stub of a cigar or cigarette. **scattered, but chiefly C and S Atl, Gulf States, TX** See Map

1845 *Amer. Whig Rev.* 1.83, They gathered up every cigar-stump the passengers threw away. **1878** *Atlantic Mth.* 41.576 **sAppalachians**, Mr. Kenyon rose, threw away the stump of his cigar, and entered the room. **1917** Rice *Calvary Alley* 75 **KY**, [His] lips trembled slightly despite the stump of a cigarette that he manfully held between them. **c1938** in Lib. of Congress *Amer. Memory: WPA Life Hist.* (Internet) **NM**, "What did you find?" I eagerly inquired. "Cigarette stumps, 'bout ten o' 'em." **1965–70** *DARE* (Qu. DD8, *The part left over when a cigar or cigarette is smoked*) 86 Infs, **scattered, but chiefly C and S Atl, Gulf States, TX**, Stump; PA36, Cigar stump; (Qu. DD6a, *Other names or nicknames for cigars*) Infs **PA**42, 195, **TX**86, Stump; **TX**26, Stump—after it's been smoked.

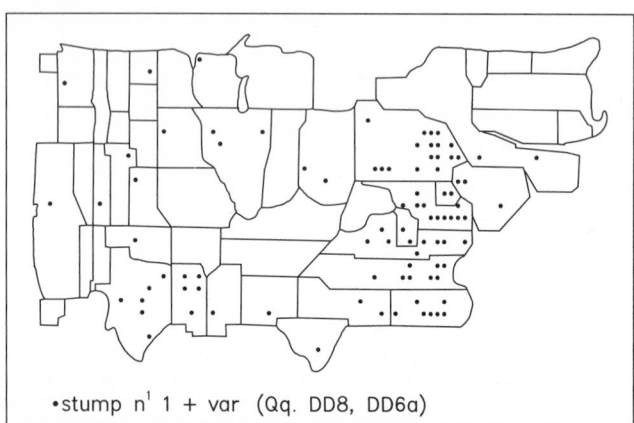

•stump n[1] 1 + var (Qq. DD8, DD6a)

2 In coal mining: see quots. Cf **barrier, entry 2**

1881 Raymond *Gloss. Mining* 85 **PA**, *Stump*. . . A small pillar of coal, left at the foot of a *breast* to protect the *gangway*. **1947** Natl. Coal Assoc. *Gloss.* 23, *Stump*—Entry pillars. **1973** *PADS* 59.56 [Bituminous coal mining vocab], *Stump* . . = barrier (pillar).

3 See quot. Cf **pom-pom-pullaway**

1909 *DN* 3.414 **nME**, *Pullaway*. . . A children's game. One player begins as *stump* or catcher. When he calls *pull away* all the players have to run across a line. Those that he catches come over to his side and help him catch others when *pull away* is called again.

4 See **stump liquor.**

5 in phrr *from the stump (up)*; In ref to building something of wood: from the felling of the tree; hence fig, from the very beginning, from scratch.

1813 *Niles' Natl. Reg.* 4 Sep 12, The Sylph . . schooner rigged, was built and ready for service in *"thirty-three days from the stump."* **1841**

Lynch *RI Book* 315, These . . built and equipped this fleet; and launched the whole . . in about ninety days, after the first blow was struck. They built from the stump, six vessels. **1844** Lee-Frost *10 Yrs. OR* 280, A house must be built from the stump in a few weeks. **1913** (1980) Hardy *OH Schoolmistress* 153, This prize was to be given for the best dinner "from the stump" prepared in the shortest time. "From the stump," it may be explained, implied that every dish must be cooked then and there from the beginning, hot bread and pie included. **1967** *DARE* (Qu. A24, . . *Someone who has always been the same way: "He's been hot-tempered from _____."*) Inf **TN**23, The stump up.

6 in phr *up a stump* and varr: See below.

a At an impasse; in a predicament; perplexed.

1829 Kirkham *Engl. Grammar* 192 **NEng**, I axt him for't, and he sade no; and then ize up a stump. **1853** (1928) Knight *Diary* 41 **MA**, Came to Wood Creek, and are up a stump again. **1896** *Harper's New Mth. Mag.* 93.350 **MO**, We got the di'monds and went aboard the boat. But now we was up a stump, for we couldn't go to bed. We had to set up and watch each other. **1939** *AmSp* 14.266 **swIN**, To be 'up a stump' is to be puzzled about something. **1950** *WELS Suppl.* **cwWI**, *Up a stump*. In a predicament. "Then my line broke and then I was up a stump." Old-fashioned but still current. **c1960** *Wilson Coll.* **csKY**, *Up a stump*. . . Rendered speechless or powerless. **1970** *DARE* FW Addit **NC**75, *Up a gum stump*—meaning reached an impasse, bewildered. **1980** (1987) Syatt *Like We Say* 184, He's up a gump stump. *[A dead end].* **1984** Wilder *You All Spoken Here* 190 **Sth**, *Up against a stump:* In a quandary. **1986** *DARE* File **cIL**, I assumed it [=the phrase *up a gum stump*] meant someone was in a "sticky situation." I once asked my mother-in-law, a native Kentuckian. She said it meant "She's pregnant." **1993** Hassler *Dear James* 21 **MN**, It was no wonder she looked down in the mouth. He'd been told . . that overseeing the breakup of the parochial school had left her up a stump. *Ibid*, Soon Judy would be called to some parish in greater need of her pastoral talents, . . and where would that leave Sylvester? Up a stump.

b Pregnant. **esp NEast** Cf **tree, up a 2**

1930 Shoemaker *1300 Words* 64 **cPA Mts** (as of c1900), *Up the stump*—An unmarried girl who has become pregnant. **1931–33** *LANE Worksheets,* 2 infs, **CT**, Up a stump—pregnant. [2 infs] **1965–70** *DARE* (Qu. AA28, . . *Joking or sly expressions . . women use to say that another is going to have a baby . . "She['s] _____."*) Infs **ME**9, **MI**65, **NH**14, **PA**67, 215, **WI**21, Up a stump; **NY**52, 84, **PA**104, Up the stump. **1971** Brunvand *Guide Folkl. UT* 37, Other commonly heard expressions are euphemistic references to sensitive subjects, like . . "up a stump" for pregnancy. **1975** Gould *ME Lingo* 305, *Up a stump*—Pregnant. The term can be used for a properly married lady's condition, but more often refers to the results of premarital dalliance: "I hear she's only sixteen and up a stump." **1986** [see **a** above].

stump n[2] See **stump v 1**

stump v

1 To dare, challenge (someone) to do something; to threaten (someone); hence n *stump* a dare or challenge, freq in phrr *take* (or *have*) *a stump* to decline a challenge. **chiefly Nth, esp NEng** *old-fash*

1766 in 1850 Adams *Works* 2.204 **MA**, Keen, of Pembroke was warm, and stumped Soule, the moderator, to lay down the money and prevent a tax upon the poor. **1815** Humphreys *Yankey in England* 108, *Stump*, challenge. **a1824** (1937) Guild *Jrl.* 3.266 **VT**, I stump you to touch me with your . . little finger, Sir. **1832** in 1905 U.S. Military Acad. Assoc. Graduates *Bulletin* 4.73 **RI**, So I pushed down [the cliff] . . 'stumping' them to follow me. . . They 'were not the boys to take a stump,' and consequently soon began to try to get down. **1842** *Warsaw* (Ill.) *Signal* 3 Sep. 3/3 *(DA)*, Joe is not good for much, but he said I dare him, and I won't have a stump from any body. **1869** (1870) Kellogg *Ark* 11 **ME**, What a fool I was [for jumping on a skunk]! . . but I'm glad I killed him: who's going to take a stump from a skunk? **1892** *DN* 1.212 **ceMA**, To stump (= challenge). **1894** *Advance* (Chicago IL) 18 Oct 102/3 **eMA**, The bravest thing ye did was to refuse to run the risk fer a mere stump! **1897** *League Amer. Wheelmen Bulletin* 25.688 **ceMA**, Well, we never took a stump;/ So we started [to steal melons], on the jump. **1897** *KS Univ. Qrly.* (ser B) 6.92 **neKS**, *Stump*: to dare; among youths. **1905** *DN* 3.22 **cCT**, *Stump*. . . To challenge. *Ibid* 66 **eNE**, *Stump*. . . Dare or banter. "I'll stump you to walk the fence rail." **1909** *DN* 3.417 **nME**, *Stump*. . . To dare or challenge. **1910** *DN* 3.450 **wNY**, I'll stump you to do it. **1912** *DN* 3.569 **cNY**, I stump you to jump off that stack. **1943** *LANE* Map 696 *(You dare not)* 1 inf, **ceMA**, I'll stump you to do it (= I dare you ~); 1 inf, **ceMA,** I stump you! (= I dare you!); 1 inf, **csVT,** Stumping him to go (= daring him ~); [1 inf, **neCT,** I stunt you to do it (= I dare you ~)]. **1959** *VT Hist.* 27.161, *Stump. . .* To dare; to threaten; to challenge. . . Rare. **1969** *DARE* (Qu. Y5, . . *To urge somebody to do something he shouldn't: "Johnny wouldn't have tried that if the other boys hadn't _____."*) Inf **CT**36, Stumped him. [Inf old] **1979** *DARE* File **cnMA** (as of c1915), When I was a child we never *dared* people to do things, we stumped them. "I stump you to jump off that stone wall."

2a To strike (usu a toe) unintentionally against something fixed; hence ppl adj *stumped* stubbed. **chiefly Sth, S Midl**
   1828 (1970) Webster *Amer. Dict., Stump. . .* To strike any thing fixed and hard with the toe. [*Vulgar.*] **1890** Howells *Boy's Town* 114 **sOH,** This did not prove him a cry-baby; it was allowable, like crying when you stumped your toe. **1899** (1912) Green *VA Folk-Speech* 426, *Stump. . .* To strike unexpectedly and sharply, as the foot or toes against something fixed: as, to *stump* one's toe against a stone. **1905** *DN* 3.97 **nwAR,** *Stump. . .* To stub. 'If we stumped our toes, we thought the Yanks did it.' Universal. 'Stub' occurs very rarely. **1909** *DN* 3.377 **eAL, wGA,** *Stump. . .* To strike against an obstacle. One never hears of *stubbing* one's toes, or the like. **1937** NE Univ. *Univ. Studies* 37.113 [Terms from play-party songs], "And the monkey stumped his toe." . . "Stumped my toe on the table leg." **1949** (1958) Stuart *Thread* 6 **KY,** Many a dark and stormy night,/ When I went home with you,/ I stumped my toe and down I go,/ Because I wanted you. **1956** McAtee *Some Dialect NC* 44, *Stump. . .* To strike the foot against an obstacle. Usage in western Maryland was the same; in Indiana, we said, "stub." **1965** West *Time Was* 7 **nwNC,** He did not have to find everything out after a bloody nose or stumped toe. **1976** Ryland *Richmond Co. VA* 377, *Stump*—as to stump one's toe.

b in phr *stump one's toe:* See **stub one's toe 1.**

stumpblower, old n, freq cap Also *stump puller* [In ref to the use of dynamite to remove stumps] *joc*
Used as a name for a powerful alcoholic beverage; see quots.
   1960 *Daily Inter Lake* (Kalispell MT) 4 Aug 2/6, [Advt:] So grab your jug of Old Stump Blower and your Poke full of Gold and head for Penney's. **1974** Dabney *Mountain Spirits* 25 **sAppalachians,** The names [for corn whiskey] go on . . "stump puller." **1979** *Oregonian Article Letters* **OR,** I know a man out here who makes his own wine. He always speaks of it as "Old Stumpblower". **1984** *MJLF* 10.154 **cnWI,** *Old Stump Blower.* Strong white port wine, bought for hunting to celebrate the shooting of a buck. **1999** *DARE* File—Internet, Pay your bills on time and give your regular driver a . . bottle of Old Stumpblower at Christmas and they will take care of you. **2001** *Ibid* **Sth,** Is Old Underwear real btw? . . Whiskey maybe? . . Don't know for a fact, but wouldn't be surprised if it was. . . Only as real as my favorite: Old Stumpblower. . . Typical of whiskey names, at least here in the south. **2004** *Ibid* **GA,** The guide who serves end-of-the-day libations from a bottle labeled "Old Stumpblower" is probably scrimping on the liquor.

stump-break See **stump-broke**

stump-breaker n Also *stump cock*
=**pileated woodpecker B.**
   1953 *AmSp* 28.284 **TN,** *Cock of the wood* is an almost universal title for the pileated [woodpecker], and it has also been hailed as. . . *stumpcock* [etc.]. **1956** MA Audubon Soc. *Bulletin* 40.83 **ME,** Pileated Woodpecker. . . Stump-breaker. . . Its powerful excavating demolishes decaying tree trunks.

stump-broke adj Also *stump-trained* **scattered, but esp Sth, S Midl, TX**
Of an animal: trained to back up to and stand near a stump for purposes of bestiality; also fig; hence, by back-formation, verbs *stump-break, stump-train.*
   1979 *AR Times* Mar 37 [Arkansas talk], And there is one expression, "a stump-trained mule," that requires a bit of careful elucidation. Now, the idea here is to have the mule back up to the remains of a tree, thus to facilitate the erogenous urge of some gap-toothed country lad whose introduction to the facts of life was somewhat more down to earth than for most of us. **1982** *DARE* File **nwFL** (as of 1941), Stump-broke—(adj.) said of a cow trained to back up for intercourse with a man elevated upon a tree stump. I first heard this mid-1941 from a rural teenager in Escambia County, Fla.; it was generally known to Gonzales/Cantonment area high school boys. *Ibid* **cUT,** I had heard of stumpbreaking horses

in Utah. . . The person I had first heard it from . . came from central Utah (Ephraim), child of pioneer Mormon family. . . She said men in the area referred to stumpbreaking horses. She had heard it only in reference to horses, no other beasts. **1984** Weaver *TX Crude* 129, *Stump-broke.* Unquestionably obedient. A stump-broke mule is a mule which has been trained to back up to and stand before a stump for purposes of passive sexual intercourse. "What's wrong with my nose? I'll tell you what's wrong with my nose. I asked Gunther if he had his girl friend stump-broke yet, and he hit me on it, that's what." **1996** in 2004 *DARE* File—Internet, He remembered all their names, including that of the Hayseed who bragged that he had "stump-trained" his favorite heifer. **2000** *Philadelphia Citypaper.net* (PA) 13 July (Internet), Stump broke. There's a piece of rural slang unfamiliar to most urbanites. Unless you've lived with farm animals, and with certain sorts who like to date outside of their species. . . For me, the phrase recently came up in a card game. A player in our regular group had surrendered his hand somewhat too gracefully, got suckered one more time. "Frankie . . you're stump broke," punned the victor as he swept in his chips. **2002** *DARE* File—Internet **IN,** In Indiana the talk was always about stump-trained mares, kinda hard to teach a cow "giddy up-whoa-back." **2003** *Ibid* **AL,** I grew up in LA (lower Alabama) back when cars were fast and cows were stump broke. *Ibid* **MO,** Them Yankee's [sic] like TH don't know about the finer things in life like Cow Tipping or owning a Stump Broke Heifer! *Ibid* **TX,** Go take out your anger on your favorite sheep. Remember, do not go after the pretty one, get the one that is stump trained. **2004** *Ibid* **nWI,** Canadian Club Hunting Camp . . A Society for the Preservation of Stump Trained Does.

stump-bumper See **stumpknocker 1**

stump city n, freq cap Also *stumptown*
A settlement originally made in recently cleared woodland—also used as a name or nickname for such a settlement.
   1839 *Tioga Eagle* (Wellsborough PA) [12 June 6]/1 (newspaperarchive.com), Proposals are invited to carry two daily mails. . . From Harrisburg . . West Hanover, East Hanover, Jonestown, Stumptown . . to Pottsville. **1857** (1870) Watson *Annals Philadelphia & PA* 2.531 **PA,** Went through Stump town, a small log house town . . in the county of Lebanon. **1859** Sprague *Gloversville* 46 **NY,** In the year 1816, Jonathan Sedgwick proposed to name the place Stump City, which, from its appropriateness, was generally adopted. It bore this name till the year 1828. **1862** *Harper's New Mth. Mag.* 133 **MI,** In one of the many stump cities for which Michigan is noted live two individuals who put 'M.D.' at the end of their names. **1887** *Overland Mth.* (2d ser) 9.616 **MO,** They's a right smart chance of 'em over yander in Stump Town. **1966–70** *DARE* (Qu. C34, *Nicknames for nearby settlements, villages, or districts*) Infs **MA**100, **VA**75, Stumptown; **IA**22, Stumptown—where the Mormons were at one time—because they cleared and left the stumps; **MD**42, Stumptown—a nickname for Williamsburg—a colored town; (Qu. C35, *Nicknames for the different parts of your town or city*) Infs **NC**30, **VA**59, Stumptown; **NJ**25, Stumptown—because [it] had an area of willows which were cut down in swampy land, leaving stumps. **1979** *Washington Post* (DC) 1 Nov sec C 5 (Internet), He was a native of Stumptown, W.Va. **1998** *Seattle Daily Times* (WA) 6 Apr final ed sec B 3 (Internet), Kirkland became known as "stump city" because of the desolation left from the 1890s land clearing. **2003** *DARE* File **Pacific NW,** Stumptown—Portland. Many stumps were left after the early pioneers cut down so many trees. **2004** *Atlanta Jrl.-Constitution* (GA) 15 Jan Cherokee sec 1 (Internet), Homes were also built by the Canton Cotton Mill for black employees on Crisler Street or what was once called Stumptown in the 1940s and 1950s—the first time African-Americans were allowed to live inside the city. That small community . . was called Stumptown because emancipated slaves chopped down trees and built homes on the stumps.

stump cock See **stump breaker**

stump country n, also attrib
A tract of land abounding in tree stumps.
   1892 *Olean Democrat* (NY) [25 Oct 11]/5 (newspaperarchive.com), He . . converted it from a rough stump country into one of the finest farms in Genesee county. **1896** *Home Missionary* July 129 **MI,** Vast tracks of "stump country" are as truly virgin soil as if the region had just been discovered. **1935** Davis *Honey* 16 **OR,** A long-necked man named Moss who turned all his gs into ds after the fashion of stump-country roustabouts. **c1945** in Lib. of Congress *Amer. Memory: Hist. Amer. West* (Internet) **CO,** [Caption:] James Peak from Stump Country.

2001 *DARE* File—Internet **cMI,** For six generations his family has resided in the village of Mecosta, in Michigan's stump country.

stump driver n   Cf pile driver 1, post ~, stumpknocker 2 =bittern.

1959 *Names* 7.119 **MI, VT,** Names suggested by resemblance of the bittern "music" to resonant pounding include . . stump-driver [etc].
1966 *DARE* (Qu. Q8, *A water bird that makes a booming sound before rain and often stands with its beak pointed almost straight up*) Inf **MI**10, Bittern . . other names . . pile driver (more commonly stump driver).

stump ear n

A **gray squirrel 1** (here: *Sciurus carolinensis*).
1961 Jackson *Mammals WI* 155, *Sciurus carolinensis hypophaeus.* . . In Wisconsin usually called gray squirrel. Other names include . . stump ear [etc].

stumped   See stump v 2a

stumper   See stomper 1

stump farm n   chiefly Nth   Cf stump ranch

A farm abounding in trees and stumps, esp one on recently cleared forest land; hence n *stump farmer* one who works or owns such a farm; a rustic.
1862 MI State Bd. Ag. *Annual Rept.* 100, While the surface is covered with stumps, and the unevenness which necessarily accompanies a "stump farm," exists, the implements which can be used are but few.
1888 *Atlantic Mth.* 62.633 **VT,** He remained a boy at home on a stump farm in Canada. **1909** *Stevens Point Daily Jrl.* (WI) 8 May 1/1, He had been . . living in a lonely cabin on a stump farm in a hole in the woods near Pray. **1923** *Ironwood Daily–Globe* (MI) 12 Sept 4/3, We must remember to twit California with having no stump farms as delightfully stumpy as those of Michigan. **1939** in Lib. of Congress *Amer. Memory: FSA/OWI* (Internet) **wWA,** [Caption:] Stump farm. Typical of cut over area of Western Washington. *Ibid* **wWA,** [Caption:] Stump farm seen from the road. Note stump pile in distant field at left, where the bulldozer has just cleared another farm. *Ibid* **nID,** [Caption:] Stump farmer prepares to blow out tamarack stump. *Ibid* **cwMT,** [Caption:] Flathead valley special project, Montana. Stump farm. **1941** Ward *Holding Hills* 69 **IA** (as of early 20th cent), A man must make land on a stump farm. Down must come the native oaks and crabs and elms, and the undergrowth of hazel and buckbrush must be scythed to the ground. **1966–69** *DARE* (Qu. HH1, *Names and nicknames for a rustic or countrified person*) Infs **GA**3, **KY**10, Stump farmer. **1966** *DARE* Tape **WA**1, A stump farm is acreage that is not developed. Your largest crop . . are stumps and trees.

stump fence n   chiefly NEast, Gt Lakes   See Map

A fence made of uprooted tree stumps.
1845 Judd *Margaret* 138 **swME,** They crossed the stump-fence into the herb-garden. **1880** *Scribner's Mth.* 19.508 **NEng,** Long after our people had begun to tire of mowing and plowing about the great pine stumps . . some timely genius arose and invented . . the stump fence. **1902** White *Blazed Trail* 120 **MI,** Southern Michigan was once a pine forest; now the twisted stump-fences about the most fertile farms of the north alone break the expanse of prairie. **1907** *DN* 3.250 **eME,** *Stump fence.* . . A fence made of the uprooted stumps of trees. **1933** White *Dog Days* 37 **CA,** Stubble fields bounded by stump or "snake" fences of rails. **1938** *AmSp* 13.74 **ME,** Homlier [sic] than a stump fence. **1942** Giese *Farm Fence Hdbk.* 12, [Caption:] A Wisconsin stump fence.

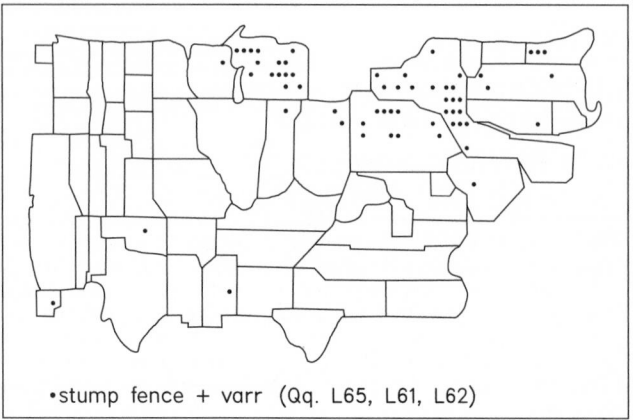

•stump fence + varr (Qq. L65, L61, L62)

1965–70 *DARE* (Qu. L65, . . *Kinds of fences*) 53 Infs, **chiefly NEast, Gt Lakes,** Stump fence; **MI**116, Pine stump fence; [**HI**12, Stump and log fence; **PA**137, Stump row;] (Qu. L61, *Fences made of solid logs, now or in the past*) Infs **MI**107, **NY**142, **OH**6, Stump fence; **MI**97, 101, Pine stump fence; (Qu. L62, *A fence made of split logs*) Inf **NY**164, Stump fence—line the stumps against the road. **1965** Needham–Mussey *Country Things* 16 **VT,** Gramp had often made stump fences. **1967** *PA Game News* Sept 32 **PA,** [Caption:] Stump fence.

stump-fucker n

A female ichneumon wasp or similar insect; see quots.
2003 *DARE* File—Internet **neCA,** Sometimes we'd catch insects we called "Stump-fuckers" which are really Ichneumon Wasps, so-called because of their habits of laying eggs in stumps. **2004** *DARE* File **WI** (as of 1960s), While doing research in the late 1960s, I frequently heard local people as well as some of my entomological colleagues refer to an ichneumon wasp as a "stump-fucker." Recently a friend casually mentioned that he had seen a "stump-fucker" on one of his trees. The "stump-fucker" is a female ichneumon wasp (*Megarhyssa* spp) with a long slender ovipositor which it uses to deposit eggs under the bark of trees. **2004** *Ibid* **csWI** (as of c1975), When I first came to Wisconsin I heard people use the term *stump-fucker* for a large insect with a long, tail-like appendage. [*Ibid* **WI,** There is a type of sawfly we call a horntail—it lays its eggs with the aid of a long ovipositor ("stinger") in dead trees and stumps—sometimes it gets stuck. I have also heard it referred to as a stumpf_____.]

stump furnace n

In moonshining: see quot.
1969 *DARE* Tape **GA**72, A stump furnace . . has a bedrock on it; you build it about sixteen or eighteen inches high and about the same width for your firebox. . . Its back is enclosed with rock, and they are built up in a sloping manner to come to a point at the top of the cap of your still.

stump-headed adj   Also stub-headed

Obstinate, stubborn.
1940 (1978) Still *River of Earth* 120 **KY,** My boys were a mite stubheaded, as growing ones air. But nary a son I had pleasured himself with shooting off guns, a-rim-recking at Hardin Town and in the camps, a-playing at cards and mixing in knife scrapes. **1970** *DARE* (Qu. GG18, . . *'Obstinate': "Why does he have to be so _____."*) Inf **PA**242, Stump-headed. **2004** *DARE* File—Internet **TX,** I have freely admitted to being a . . stump-headed know nothing. . . I'm pig ignorant.

stump-hole liquor n   Also stump-hole, ~ juice, ~ water, ~ whiskey [From the use of stump holes in concealing and distributing liquor illegally; see quot 1926] Sth, S Midl, esp NC, SC   See Map   Cf stump juice, ~ liquor, ~ water 2

Illegally distilled liquor.
[**1926** in 2004 (acc) Lexis–Nexis Legal Research *State Case Law: AR* (Internet), After following a trail quite a distance, appellant found one-half gallon of whiskey in a stump hole. Witness remarked that he wished he could find some more; whereupon appellant resumed the search and soon found another one-half gallon in the ground. Witness placed $11 on a stump and took the whiskey.] *Ibid: NC,* I smelled the odor of liquor on him and it was stump-hole liquor he was drinking. **1950** *PADS* 14.65 **SC,** Stumphole liquor. . . Same as *stumpwater.* **1955** *Statesville Rec. & Landmark* (NC) 29 Jan 2/5 **SC,** George Ridgell . . told a court . . that stumphole water is "bootleg whiskey which some of the deputies brought in on raids." **1956** in 2004 (acc) Lexis–Nexis Legal Research *State Case Law: SC* (Internet), I understood him to say that there was something about two bottles of bottled in bond and two bottles of stump-hole whiskey; they scratched out the stump-hole whiskey and had him charged on the bottled in bond. **1960** Lee *Mockingbird* 15 **sAL,** They experimented with stumphole whiskey. **1966–70** *DARE* (Qu. DD21a, *General words . . for any kind of liquor*) Inf **NC**13, Stump-hole; (Qu. DD21b, *General words . . for bad liquor*) Infs **NC**13, 85, **SC**24, Stump-hole (whiskey); (Qu. DD21c, *Nicknames for whiskey, especially illegally made whiskey*) Infs **NC**49, 85, 87, **SC**40, Stump-hole. **1968** *Foxfire* Fall–Winter 111 **sAppalachians,** Well, I slurped up another sample or two of the stump-hole while I was about it. **1986** Pederson *LAGS Concordance,* 1 inf, **seMS,** Stump-hole juice. **2001** *DARE* File—Internet **Sth,** I managed to fake enough gulps of "stump hole liquor" to convince a few moonshiners that I wasn't from the bureau of Alcohol, Tobacco and Firearms.

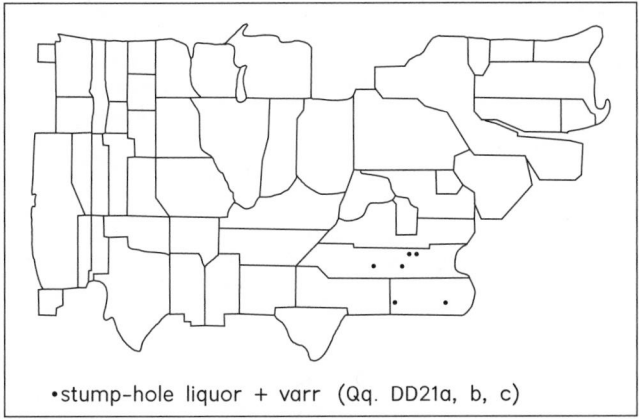

•stump-hole liquor + varr (Qq. DD21a, b, c)

stumpitty adj   Cf Intro "Language Changes" III.1

1930 Stoney-Shelby *Black Genesis* 67 **seSC,** It got four foots wid claws on dem, an' a leetle stumpitty sharp-p'int tail.

stump juice n   **chiefly Sth, S Midl**   See Map   Cf **stump-hole liquor**

Illegally distilled liquor; bad liquor.

1949 *Traverse City Rec.-Eagle* (MI) 30 July 4/1, A lively traffic in various kinds of native "stump juice" is being reported and several imbibers are said to have perished.   **1952** McCall *Cherokees & Pioneers* 101 **sAppalachians,** You are invited to share a little something . . called moonshine . . stump juice . . mountain dew.   **1965–70** *DARE* (Qu. DD21a, *General words . . for any kind of liquor*) Inf **TN**53, Stump juice; (Qu. DD21c, *Nicknames for whiskey, especially illegally made whiskey*) Infs **AL**6, **FL**52, **GA**26, 84, **MS**59, **NJ**33, **SC**19, **WV**7, Stump juice.   **1973** *DARE* File **AR Ozarks** (as of c1910), Bootleg or illegal whisky was stump juice, corn squeezin', or redeye.   **1986** Pederson *LAGS Concordance (Cheap liquor)* 7 infs, **AL, GA, TX,** Stump juice; 1 inf, **cnGA,** Stump juice—not good quality; 1 inf, **seGA,** Stump juice— they hid it behind stumps; 1 inf, **swAL,** Stump juice—heard from a man from Florida.

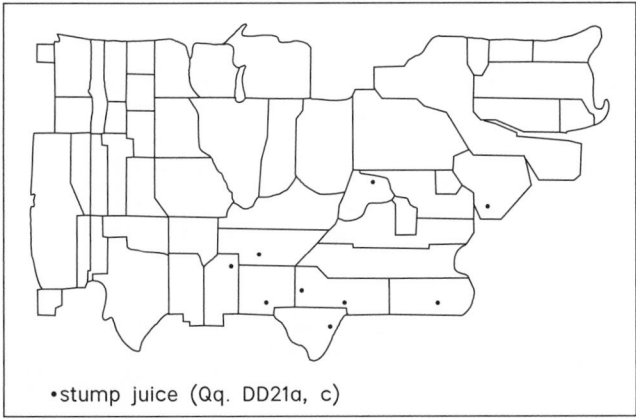

•stump juice (Qq. DD21a, c)

stump-jumper n

1   also *stump-jump, ~-kicker:* A rustic; a hillbilly.   **scattered, but chiefly Sth, S Midl**

1918 *DN* 5.19 **NC,** Stump-jumper, a countryman.   **1936** Street *Look Away* 87 **Ozarks,** That's the home of the hillbillies. Some folks call 'em "stump-jumpers."   **1943** in 1944 *ADD* **nWV,** Stump-jumper. . . She musta been one o' these West Virginia stump-jumpers.   **1964** *PADS* 42.31 **Chicago IL,** The most characteristic feature of Negro terms for Caucasians is the tendency to expand particularized designations for Caucasians to include all members of the race, e.g., terms for poor Southerners . . stump-jumper.   **1965–70** *DARE* (Qu. HH1, *Names and nicknames for a rustic or countrified person*) Infs **IL**11, **LA**37, **MD**9, 49, **MS**88, **PA**199, **WV**7, Stump-jumper; **LA**46, Stump-jump; **NY**73, Stump-kicker; (Qu. L3, *A man who lives on the farm and does the work, but divides the expenses and profits with the owner*) Inf **CT**13, Stump-jumper.   **1967** LeCompte *Word Atlas* 251 **seLA,** North Louisianians. . . stump jumpers [1 of 21 infs].   **1968** *DARE* Tape **LA**34, [Inf:] We have a lot of disturbing-the-peace-by-fighting calls. These young fellas get all wined up, these levee-dwellers come in to town and they—[FW:] These

what? [Inf:] Levee-dweller, stump-jumper. . . it's a little term we have for people that live on the levee. . . And they usually a little more ignorant than we are and they dress sloppy, long hair, greasy-looking kids, and they get liquored up and they speak mostly French and the next thing you know they—they always in trouble.   **1986** Pederson *LAGS Concordance (A rustic)* 3 infs, **GA, MS, TN,** Stump-jumper(s); *(Poor whites)* 1 inf, **csLA,** Stump-jumper—someone from Mississippi; *(Caucasian)* 1 inf, **csLA,** Stump-jumpers.   **1997** in 2004 Montgomery–Hall *Dict. Smoky Mt. Engl.* 578 **wNC,** *Stump jumper.* . . A country person.   **2002** *NY Times* (NY) 18 Apr sec F 4/1 **KY,** Fresh with pride to be from Kentucky again, Mr. Offutt writes, "You won't hear these words spoken anymore: redneck, hillbilly, cracker, stump-jumper, weed-sucker, ridgerunner."

2   See quots.   Cf *stump rancher* (at **stump ranch**)

1979 *Oregonian* (Portland OR) 23 Sept sec A 1, Does he have [the term] "stumpjumper" (a homesteader who has to clear his land of trees before he can farm)?   **2000** *DARE* File **nwMI,** [Pamphlet from restaurant:] *Stump jumper:* . . a Yooper who works in the woods.

stump-kicker   See **stump-jumper 1**

stumpknocker n

1   also *stumpbumper:* A **sunfish** n **1a** such as the **red-eared sunfish 1** or the spotted sunfish *(L. punctatus).* [See quots 1949, 1986]   **esp FL, GA**

1931 *Key W. Citizen* (FL) [21 Dec 34]/6 (newspaperarchive.com), It shall be unlawful for any person to take in any one day more than the following number of each designated species of fresh water fish: . . stump-knocker, 30.   **1934** *Natl. Geogr. Mag.* 65.605 **Okefenokee GA,** The bulk of a day's catch with hook and line is made up of such basses as the warmouth, the "stump-knocker," and the "sand-flirter."   **c1940** Eliason *Word Lists FL* 11 **wFL,** *Stumpknocker:* A small-sized black perch that is found in most of the streams of W. Fla.   **1949** Caine *N. Amer. Sport Fish* 46, Stumpknocker—*Lepomis punctatus.* . . This member of the illustrious sunfishes is purported to have gained its name because of its habit of lying around old stumps watching for insects to approach the water's edge. When one comes within reach, the stumpknocker leaps out of the water and flings itself against the stump, knocking the insect into the water and at the same time, making an audible thump as it hits the stump.   **1951** Teale *North with Spring* 136 **GA,** Negroes were out for the spring fishing, angling for "stump-knockers" in brimming roadside ditches.   **1965–69** *DARE* (Qu. P1, . . *Kinds of freshwater fish . . caught around here . . good to eat*) Inf **FL**17, Stumpknocker—live in and under stumps; **FL**32, Stumpknocker; **GA**25, Stumpknocker—same as black bream; **GA**89, Stumpknockers—similar to perch.   **1972** *DARE* File **FL,** Stumpknocker—a type of panfish, similar to bream.   **1973** *Ibid* **SC,** Stumpknocker—a bream.   **1986** Pederson *LAGS Concordance* **FL, GA,** 8 infs, Stumpknocker(s); 1 inf, Stumpknocker—lives under roots, stumps in water; 1 inf, Stumpknockers— perch, stay around stumps.   **1997** *Mt. Democrat* (Placerville CA) 10 Apr sec A 9/1, Warmer water temperatures will entice the "stumpknockers" (blue gills) to swarm.   **2001** *DARE* File **FL, MS,** In Louisiana the red-ear is a chickapin; in Florida or Mississippi they call it a stump-bumper, a stump-knocker, or a shell-cracker.

2   =**bittern.**   Cf **stump driver**

1959 *Names* 7.119 **NY,** Names suggested by resemblance of the bittern "music" to resonant pounding include . . stump-knocker.

3   also *stumpknock(er) preacher:* An itinerant or inept preacher.   **S Atl**   *esp freq among Black speakers*   Cf **chairbacker, stump sucker 2**

1931 (1991) Hughes–Hurston *Mule Bone* 61 **cFL** [Black], Dat puts me in mind of a Baptist brother that was crazy 'bout de preachers and de preacher was crazy 'bout feeding his face. So his son got tired of trying to beat dese stump-knockers to de grub on the table.   **1942** (1965) Parrish *Slave Songs* 247 **GA coast,** A Negro "stump-knocker"—as itinerant preachers without a regular charge used to be called—frankly told me he wasn't much on preaching, but when it came to singing he always got his people—and a meal.   **1955** *PADS* 23.35 **Sth,** Local terms . . *stump-knocker* . . a part-time voluntary preacher, normally without formal seminary training and generally with a low degree of competence.   **1967–68** *DARE* (Qu. CC10, . . *An unprofessional, part-time lay preacher*) Infs **GA**42, **SC**40, Stumpknocker; **SC**40, Stumpknock preacher.   **1986** Pederson *LAGS Concordance (Jackleg preacher)* 4 infs, **FL, GA,** Stumpknocker—untrained preacher; 2 infs, **FL, GA,** Stumpknocker = jackleg; 2 infs, **cw,nwFL,** Stumpknocker; 1 inf, **cGA,** Stumpknocker—ain't got no church; 1 inf, **swGA,** Stumpknocker—a preacher that's not too good; 1 inf, **cGA,** Stumpknocker preacher. [10 of 11 infs Black]

stump liquor n Also *stump,* ~ *lightning,* ~ *rum,* ~ *whiskey*
Sth, S Midl, esp GA Cf **stump-hole liquor, tussock** ~
Illegally distilled liquor; bad liquor.

1921 *Atlanta Constitution* (GA) 4 Feb 10/2, He thinks this judge with a name that smacks so much of hill-bred stump rum is built along the same lines. **1929** *AmSp* 4.440, Names for intoxicants of various grades and potencies . . stump liquor. **1942** *WI Rapids Daily Tribune* (WI) 26 Sept 7/3 **GA,** What the average drinker of sugarhead or stump rum doesn't realize is that the bottled headache he buys . . isn't as potent as licensed liquor. **1948** Hanna–Hanna *Lake Okeechobee* 201 **FL,** One large laboratory for the production of "stump lightning" was discovered by some lumbermen. **1955** in 2004 Lexis–Nexis Legal Research *State Case Law: MS* (Internet), Appellant was working in the Diamond Playhouse, an establishment commonly known as a "honky-tonk" or "night club," where "stump" whiskey was sold and consumed. **1960** Williams *Walk Egypt* 147 **GA,** He smelled of smoke and sweat and stump-rum. **1967–70** *DARE* (Qu. DD21b, *General words . . for bad liquor*) Inf **GA**59, Stump; (Qu. DD21c, *Nicknames for whiskey, especially illegally made whiskey*) Infs **GA**59, **SC**69, Stump; **SC**43, Stump liquor; **SC**40, Stump rum. **1979** *Antioch Rev.* 37.49 **MS,** You strong as stump whiskey and mean as a yard dog! **1986** Pederson *LAGS Concordance (Cheap liquor)* 6 infs, 5 **GA,** 1 **eMS,** Stump liquor; 1 inf, **csGA,** Stump liquor—homemade; 2 infs, **GA,** Stump rum; 1 inf, **ceGA,** Stump rum—poor-grade moonshine; 1 inf, **neGA,** Stump rum—cheap moonshine; 1 inf, **cwMS,** Stump whiskey. **1999** *NY Times* (NY) 15 Nov sec A 25/1 (Internet) **Ozarks,** I helped make a delivery of stump liquor one time. . . That's white lightning, moonshine, you know.

stump logging n [Cf *DCan stumper* quot 1908 "Many trees . . would drop right into water from the stumps when felled"] Cf **hot logging**
1969 Sorden *Lumberjack Lingo* 123 **NEng, Gt Lakes,** *Stump logging*—A logging operation in which the logs went directly from the woods to the mill, not stored in a pile. Same as hot logging.

stump lot n **chiefly CT, MA, Upstate NY** Cf **stump pasture**
A lot or field abounding in tree stumps.
1864 (1868) Trowbridge *3 Scouts* 1, Around them were all the evidences of desolating war—neglected fields, demolished fences, and orchards converted into stump-lots. [*DARE* Ed: Setting is **TN,** but author was born in **NY** and resided in **MA.**] **1873** Bailey *Life in Danbury* 97 **CT,** If every flying pang had been a drunken plow chased by a demon across a stump lot, I think the observer would understand my condition. **1882** *Harper's New Mth. Mag.* 64.871 **MA,** [Caption:] The Stump Lot. **1899** *New Engl. Mag.* 21.343 **cNY,** A cornfield in a stump lot was a sight that would astonish the farmer who runs gang ploughs. **1949** *McDavid Coll.* **cNY,** Stump lot = cleared field. **1974** *Mt. Democrat & Placerville Times* (CA) 6 June [32]/7 **eOR** (newspaperarchive.com), Turns out this stump lot is 90 miles south. **2008** *DARE* File—Internet **cNY,** [Advt:] Water access on Goodyear Lake stump lot offers fantastic fishing.

stump mover n Also *stump puller,* ~ *washer* **Sth, S Midl** Cf **trash mover 1**
A very heavy rain; a rainstorm.
1891 TN State Bd. Health *Bulletin* 6.192 **ceTN,** That rain was none of your drizzle drazzles; it was a log roller, a stump mover and a gully washer. **1962** Atwood *Vocab. TX* 38, Torrential rain. . . humorous phrases . . [with] limited currency . . *stump mover.* **1966–70** *DARE* (Qu. B25, . . *Joking names . . for a very heavy rain. . . "It's a regular _____."*) Infs **AL**1, **IL**122, Stump mover; **TX**11, Stump puller; **SC**19, Stump washer. **1986** Pederson *LAGS Concordance (Heavy rain)* 1 inf, **csGA,** Stump mover; *(Thunderstorm)* 1 inf, **csTX,** Stump mover.

stump mushroom n Also *stumpy* [Because it grows on the stumps of conifers and hardwoods] **esp N Cent**
An edible **mushroom B1** (here: *Armillariella mellea*).
1966–69 *DARE* (Qu. S19, *Mushrooms that grow out like brackets from the sides of trees*) Infs **MI**26, **OH**5, **WI**37, Stump mushroom(s); **WI**61, Swamp or stump mushrooms; **MI**64, Stumpies. **1985** Ammirati et al. *Poisonous Mushrooms* 234, *Armillariella mellea. . .* Common names. Honey mushroom, stump mushroom. **2003** *Detroit Free Press* (MI) 5 Nov (Internet), Don Kogut affectionately refers to the fungi [held] in his fingers as stumpies. . . "I would say that 99 percent of them grow on the stumps of oak trees," Kogut said. *Ibid,* Formally known as

Armillariella mellea or honey mushroom, the stump mushroom is an edible fall fungus that is popping up in woodlands all over Manistee County. **2004** *Pittsburgh Post–Gaz.* (PA) 22 Sept sec N 5 (Internet), The majority of mushroom nicknames are descriptive and colorful, such as the deliciously edible Honey mushroom, known locally as the Stump mushroom.

stump one's toe See **stub one's toe 1**

stump pasture n Cf **stump farm,** ~ **ranch**
A **stump lot** or **stump country.**
1871 *VT Hist. Gaz.* 2.498 (as of 1821), Passing rapidly along the pathway, on a ridge in the stump-pasture . . they hear a "halloo!" **1890** *Overland Mth.* (2d ser) 15.273, A man . . established himself on a hillock overlooking the rear of the isolated building, while another strolled carelessly about the stump pasture in front. **1908** in 2002 Seattle Municipal Archives *Archives Gaz.* Winter (Internet), We looked over the stump pasture area and Mr. Dawson located the edge of the timber west of it. **1937** *WI Rapids Daily Tribune* (WI) 24 Dec 7/6, About 28.9 per cent of this land was stump pasture which can be plowed. **1967** *WI Conserv. Bulletin* 32.5.23 **WI,** A "stump pasture," this is called—the result of a clear-cut followed by fire. **1984** *Arabian Horse World* July 454 **IN,** Dr. Pettigrew bought Sankirah and her suckling foal Hanad in the winter of 1922–23 without papers for $300 in one-dollar bills plus $100 for help in getting the mare and foal out of a "stump" pasture in which the tree stumps were four feet high. **1995** *Richwood Gaz.* (OH) 28 Jun 5/4, In a cornfield north of the stump pasture was a huge boulder.

stump puller n
1 See **stump mover.**
2 See **stumpblower, old.**

stump ranch n [*DCan stump ranch* 1919, *stump rancher* 1963] **Pacific NW** Cf **rock farm, stump** ~
A ranch abounding in trees and stumps, esp on recently cleared forest land; hence n *stump rancher* one who works or owns such a ranch; a rustic.
1896 *CO Springs Gaz.* (CO) 19 Feb 8/1, Mr. A.M. Ripley has sold his ranch property . . to a syndicate which will start another town site. The land is known as the Stump ranch. **1931** in 2004 Lexis–Nexis Legal Research *State Case Law: WA* (Internet), Plaintiff resided near the town of Auburn upon a twenty-acre stump ranch, upon which he raised a little produce, and where he kept four cows and a few chickens. **1936** in Lib. of Congress *Amer. Memory: FSA/OWI* (Internet) **wOR,** [Caption:] Stump ranches spring up in the wake of the logging company and try to wrest a living from a few acres of forest land. **1937** in 2004 Lexis–Nexis Legal Research *State Case Law: ID* (Internet), In the spring of 1933 the family purchased a small stump ranch of 80 acres, 40 of which were cleared. **1939** in Lib. of Congress *Amer. Memory: FSA/OWI* (Internet) **nID,** [Caption:] Stump rancher and wife. **1941** *AmSp* 16.234 **MT** [Lumberjack jargon], *Stump rancher.* A small farmer in a wooded area. **1949** Peattie *Cascades* 144 **Pacific NW,** Thousands upon thousands swarming all over the dry lands east of the mountains to take up homesteads, thousands more buying "stump ranches" from the lumber companies at four bits an acre. **1950** *NV State Jrl.* (Reno) 24 May 1/2 **WA,** Mrs. Grace Mellick guarded her 43-acre stump ranch with a shotgun today, holding off a swarm of amateur and professional prospectors. **1966–67** *DARE* (Qu. HH1, *Names and nicknames for a rustic or countrified person*) Infs **OR**1, **WA**1, Stump rancher. **2001** *Oregonian* (Portland OR) 18 Dec sec B 1 (Internet), He grew up "on a stump ranch in the Coast Range, where horses were part of life."

stump rum See **stump liquor**

stump sucker n
1 An animal, esp a horse, given to gnawing at or sucking tree stumps or other wood, often accompanied by the swallowing of air; hence adj *stump-sucking.* **esp Sth, S Midl** Cf **cribber, wind sucker**
1811 *Supporter* (Chillicothe OH) 5 Oct 3/3, One bay mare . . blind of the right eye, supposed to be a stump sucker. **1862** in 2004 *DARE* File—Internet **sIL,** One two year old filley more particularly known as the stump sucker. **1890** *Scribner's Mag.* 7.67 **AR,** Parson had been . . wanting for Dick to trade for a horse that was nearly 'bout a hundred years old and a stump-sucker to the bargain. **1901** Harben *Westerfelt* 23 **nGA,** I've been walkin' so blamed fast I've mighty nigh lost my breath. I'm blowin' like a stump-suckin' hoss. **1906** *DN* 3.123 **sIN,** *Stump-sucker. . .* A pig, horse, or any animal that sucks roots. **1923** *DN* 5.222 **swMO,** *Stump sucker. . .* See *Cribber.* **1938** in 2004 *DARE* File—Inter-

net **TX,** Maybe you never heard of a stump-sucking pig. I am told that pigs have been known to develop a mania for sucking stumps. A pig will stand for hours and suck at a knot on a stump. He will not even quit to drink slop or eat corn. **1941** *AmSp* 16.24 **sIN,** *Stump-sucker.* A horse that chews saplings. **1942** McAtee *Dial. Grant Co. IN* 62 (as of 1890s), *Stump-sucker . . a cribber . . ,* a horse that sets its upper teeth on the edge of a manger or other object and gulps air that later may cause it great discomfort. **1954** *Harder Coll.* **cwTN,** *Stump-sucker. . .* A pig that continuously sucks the ground. **1958** Babcock *I Don't Want* 146 **eSC,** He was marvelously set in his ways and as stubborn as a stump-sucking Georgia mule. **c1960** *Wilson Coll.* **csKY,** *Stump-sucker. . .* A horse that catches hold of some fixed object with its teeth and belches air. **1967** Green *Horse Tradin'* 114 **TX,** I asked the old storekeeper what was the difference between a cribber and a stump sucker. He said: "There ain't any difference in the vice—the difference is in the location. If he's in Kentucky, he's a cribber—and if he's in Texas, he's a stump sucker." **1968** *DARE* (Qu. K47, . . *Diseases . . horses or mules commonly get*) Inf **IN**3, Stump sucker. **1995** *Brophy Coll.* 72 **swMO** (as of c1960), *Stump-sucker.* [A] horse which gnaws at the wood of its stall.

2 Fig; see quots. Cf **stumpknocker 3**

1949 *AmSp* 24.113 **SC,** *Stump-sucker. . .* An uneducated, part-time, lay preacher, generally of poor quality. **1971** *Today Show Letters* **cLA,** "Stump Sucker." This refers to a windy politician who wheeses [sic] and bellows emitting nothing but wind. This came from horses that grabbed a hitching post, or small tree and emitted rasping, windy noises. No one would buy a "stump sucker".

3 A person with buck teeth.

1968 *DARE* (Qu. X12, . . *Large front teeth that stick out of the mouth*) Inf **NC**55, Stump sucker. **1998** in 2004 Montgomery–Hall *Dict. Smoky Mt. Engl.* 578 **wNC,** *Stump sucker* [=one having large teeth that stick out of the front of the mouth] applies esp to children.

stump-sucking See **stump sucker 1**

stump swallow n
=**tree swallow.**

1917 (1923) *Birds Amer.* 3.88, *Iridoprocne bicolor. . .* Stump Swallow. . . Dead tree stubs and rotting upturned tree roots in flooded areas are the usual homes of the Tree Swallows. **1956** MA Audubon Soc. *Bulletin* 40.84 **MA, RI,** Tree Swallow. . . Stump Swallow. **1966** *DARE* (Qu. Q20, . . *Kinds of swallows and birds like them*) Inf **ME**14, Stump swallow.

stumptail See **stumptail moccasin**

stump-tail(ed) cow in flytime n Also *stump-tail bull in flytime, stump-tailed bull in fly season, stump-tailed mule in flytime* **esp Sth, S Midl** Cf **flytime 1b**
Used in var similes as an example of ceaseless but futile activity.

1819 *KY Almanac for 1820* 29 **Lexington KY,** [He] has no more chance for the worth of his dollar, than a stump tail bull in fly time. **1899** (1912) Green *VA Folk-Speech* 39, Stand no more chance than a stump-tail bull in fly-time. **1900** *Post–Std.* (Syracuse NY) 6 Sept 4/4 **TN,** A Tennessee stock breeder . . said . . , "Bryan has no more chance of being elected President than a stump-tailed cow in fly time has of taking it easy." **1916** *Syracuse Herald* (NY) 29 Oct 23/1, Their busyness resembles that of a stump-tailed mule in fly-time. It doesn't seem to get them anywhere. **1978** *AP Letters* **neGA,** There are some [words] that are still used by old-timers, such as: . . Busy as a stump-tail cow in fly time. **2004** *DARE* File—Internet **TX,** Busy as a stump-tailed bull in fly season.

stumptail moccasin n Also *stumptail (water moccasin)* **esp Gulf States**
=**cottonmouth.**

[**1878** *Indiana Progress* (PA) [10 Oct 6]/1 (newspaperarchive.com), You all know 'bout de story—how de snake came swooping 'round / A stump-tail, rusty moccasin, a-crawlin' on de groun'.] **1882** *Atlanta Constitution* (GA) 6 Aug 2/4, It is true that sometimes people are bitten by a big stumptail water moccasin. **1894** *Ft. Wayne Gaz.* (IN) 19 Aug 3/4 **cMD,** But his cousin, the cottonmouth, or stumptail moccasin, will bring your last will and testament into service nearly surer than cholera or yellow fever. **1894** U.S. Natl. Museum *Proc.* 17.330 **sFL,** *Agkistrodon piscivorus. . .* "Moccasin," "Watermoccasin," "Stump-tail moccasin," and "Cottonmouth moccasin" are the names by which this much-dreaded snake is known in south Florida. **1928** Baylor Univ. Museum *Contrib.* 16.19 **TX,** The venomous Cottonmouth is the Water

Moccasin and Black Moccasin. On account of its short tail, it is also called Blunt-tail Moccasin and Stump-tail Moccasin. The last-mentioned is the usual negro name for this snake. **1967–68** *DARE* (Qu. P25, . . *Kinds of snakes*) Inf **LA**10, Stumptail moccasin. . . All the moccasins are poison except the fish moccasin; **LA**40, Copperheaded moccasin—there are different kinds—stumptail moccasin (the poisonous kind), [and] another poisonous kind; **LA**3, Rattlesnakes—stumptail has no rattles. **1986** Pederson *LAGS Concordance,* 1 inf, **nwLA,** Stump tail—dry-land moccasin. **2000** in 2004 *DARE* File—Internet **MS,** As the turkey gobbled again, he jumped over into the stump hole, but in the mid air he glanced down to find a stump-tail moccasin about two and a half feet long.

stump-the-leader n Cf **stump** v 1
=**stunt master.**

1874 *Edwardsville Intelligencer* (IL) [17 June 2]/4 (newspaperarchive.com), Who, in their anxiety for fun, play such games as "stump the leader." **1908** *Daily Northwestern* (Oshkosh WI) 29 Dec 3/3, Pull away, stump the leader, "pussy in the corner," . . and nameless other combinations of the games which boys and girls like to play, were carried out. **1932** Farrell *Young Lonigan* 224 **Chicago IL** (as of 1916), Kenny did all kinds of dippy dives, back flaps and rolls. . . He started a stump-the-leader game on the [diving] board but he was too good for them, so they all lost interest. **1957** *Sat. Eve. Post Letters* **swMA** (as of 1921–26), Other games played in the area. . . *Stump the leader.* [*Ibid* **eCanada** (as of 1895–1900), *Stump the leader*—A follow the leader game—if you can do all the stunts he sets—you become it & try to do stunts others can't to see who is champ.] **2004** *DARE* File—Internet **Chicago IL** (as of c1938), We played games like Baseball, Stump the Leader, Card Games, Flip the Ice Wagon . . and Going Junking.

stumptown See **stump city**

stump-train(ed) See **stump broke**

stump tree n
=**Kentucky coffee tree.**

[**1812** Michaux *Histoire des Arbres* 2.273, Coffee Tree. . . [L]es Français Canadiens lui ont donné le nom de *Chicot, Stump tree.* [=Coffee Tree. . . The French-Canadians call it *Chicot, Stump tree.*]] **1846** Browne *Trees* 219, *Gymnocladus canadensis. . .* Nicker-tree, Stump tree, Kentucky Coffee-tree. **1901** Lounsberry *S. Wild Flowers* 263, Stump tree. . . It appears stump-like and weather-beaten [in winter].

stump ugly adj phr
Very ugly; also fig.

[**1956** *Bangor D[aily] N[ews]* 7/20 5 (Whiting *Mod. Proverbs*) **ME,** Homelier than a stump fence built by moonlight.] **1995** Lesley *Sky Fisherman* 55 **OR,** "Your uncle's a pretty decent cook, too," he said. "Make somebody a good wife, if he wasn't stump ugly." **2000** *Car & Driver* June (Internet), The lumpy exterior styling is controversial, stump ugly at first meeting. **2002** *DARE* File—Internet **NC,** The state's budget picture remains stump-ugly. **2004** *Milwaukee Jrl. Sentinel* (WI) 1 Feb Travel sec 1 (Internet), He looks . . all leathery and spotted and anything but pretty (stump ugly, in fact).

stump, up a See **stump** n¹ **B6**

stump-washer See **stump-mover**

stump water n

1a Rainwater that has collected in the hollow of a stump, often used in folk magic and as a home remedy, esp for skin conditions. **chiefly Sth, S Midl** See Map on p. 358 Cf **spunkwater**

1879 *Daily Constitution* (Atlanta GA) 9 Dec 6/3 (newspaperarchive.com), *Stump* water won't kyore de gripes. **1912** Green *VA Folk-Speech* 427, *Stump-water. . .* Rain water that collects in hollow stumps is a cure for warts if the hands are washed in it. **1934** Carmer *Stars Fell on AL* 282, Warts . . may be obliterated; by applying to them three times at intervals "stump water," that is, water which has been concentrated or partly evaporated through exposure to sunlight when held cupped in a rotten stump. **1947** (1964) Randolph *Ozark Superstitions* 109, The skin disease called tetter is treated with spunk water or stump water—simply rain water which happens to be retained in a hollow stump. **1950** *WELS (What special cures for corns or warts do you know of?)* 1 Inf, **cWI,** Stump water—older people believed that warts could be cured by putting nine drops of water found in a stump on the wart, leaving the stump, without looking back; [1 Inf, **csWI,** For warts—water that has been standing in a hollow of an oak tree]. **1954** *Harder Coll.* **cwTN,** *Stump-*

water. . . Water that collects in hollow stumps; used for various ailments, especially to remove warts. **c1960** *Wilson Coll.* **csKY,** *Stump water*. . . Water in a hollow stump; once used for freckles. **1965–70** *DARE* (Qu. BB51a, . . *Cures for corns or warts*) 20 Infs, **chiefly Sth, S Midl, esp WV,** Stump water; (Qu. KK7, *When wood . . is starting to decay inside . . "It's _____ inside."*) Inf **VA**11, Full of stump water. **1968** Kellner *Aunt Serena* 149 **IN,** I told him about Miz Mazey and the doctoring secrets which she had brought from Windy Gap, Kentucky. . . Stump water will take off freckles. **1970** Anderson *TX Folk Med.* xv, Even so, special efficacy is attributed to stump water (sometimes called "spunk" water)—rainwater collected in old tree stumps.

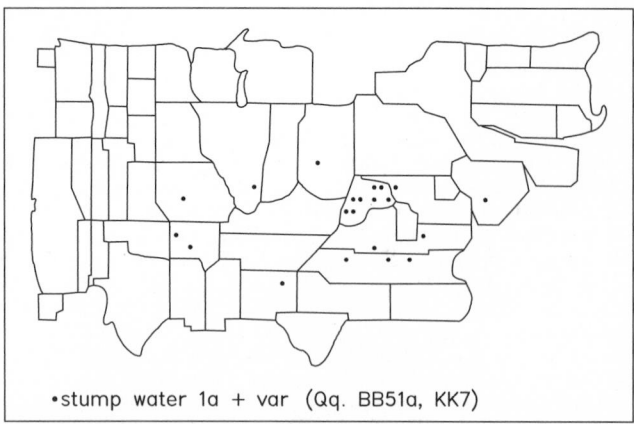

•stump water 1a + var (Qq. BB51a, KK7)

b Used as an example of something weak or unpalatable, freq in ref to weak coffee. **chiefly Inland Sth, sAppalachians** See Map

1892 Nye in *Hornellsville Weekly Tribune* (NY) [29 Jan 6]/2 (newspaperarchive.com), We used to make our writing ink . . of maple bark, which was boiled down till it was a little redder than umbrella juice and a little thicker than stump water. **1896** (1897) Davis *Elephant's Track* 29 **TX,** He cert'n'y is weaker'n stump-water . . but he's sickly an' consumpted. **1907** *Atlanta Constitution* (GA) 29 Nov 8/1, [Advt:] *Luzianne Coffee* . . will make many another kind "taste like stump-water." **1930** *Bee* (Danville VA) 4 July 4/4, Teach us to be thankful for the stump water served and called coffee. **1965–70** *DARE* (Qu. H74b, . . *Coffee . . very weak*) Infs **AR**38, **GA**75, **KY**15, **OH**39, (Like) stump water; **AL**34, 61, **IL**27, **MS**1, **NC**31, 48, **TN**30, **TX**3, Weak as stump water. **2005** Williams *Gratitude* 528 **wNC** (as of 1940s), *Stumpwater:* Poor quality moonshine likker is said to be as weak as *stumpwater*. Also, somebody that *ain't got many smarts* is said to have *a head full of* stumpwater *fer brains*.

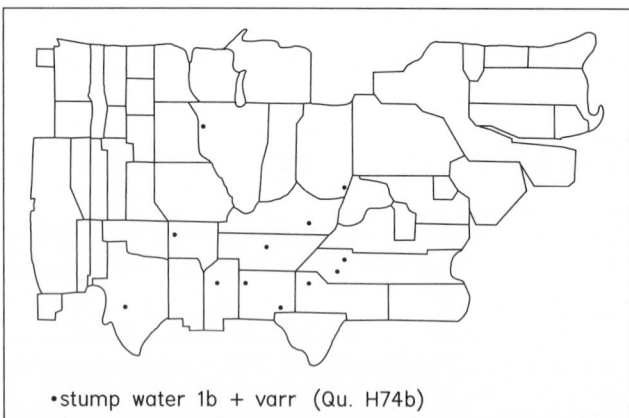

•stump water 1b + varr (Qu. H74b)

2 Illegally distilled liquor; bad liquor. **chiefly Sth, S Midl** Cf **stump-hole liquor, stump juice, ~ liquor**

1878 *Allen Co. Democrat* (Lima OH) 6 June 3/5, Susan had imbibed entirely too much "stump water" for her delicate organization, and succumbed to its enchanting effects. **1890** in 1944 *Herald–Press* (St. Joseph MI) 15 Mar 8/2, Some of the leaders of democracy in Benton Harbor came over to assist with the blowout which consisted chiefly in sampling the different brands of "stump water" on tap in town. **1924** *Middlesboro Daily News* (KY) 23 May 1/4 **AR,** Any alcoholic liquid sold for beverage purposes, even though it was found "on a stump where

money previously had been placed and was purchased under the "trade name" of "stump water" must assume [sic] to be "whiskey," the Arkansas supreme court said recently. **1950** *PADS* 14.65 **SC,** *Stumpwater*. . . Illicit liquor, boot-leg liquor. **1966–70** *DARE* (Qu. DD21a, *General words . . for any kind of liquor*) Inf **TN**53, Stump water; (Qu. DD21b, *General words . . for bad liquor*) Inf **KY**10, Stump water; (Qu. DD21c, *Nicknames for whiskey, especially illegally made whiskey*) Infs **KY**10, **MS**71, **SC**58, Stump water. **1972** *Atlanta Letters* **nwGA,** Stump water = moonshine whiskey. **1975** *Appalachian Jrl.* 2.156 **wNC,** But if one asked for *red eye, sugar head,* or *stump water,* he was referring not to gravy but to mountain *white light'nin'.* **1986** Pederson *LAGS Concordance (Cheap liquor)* 6 infs, **AR, AL, GA, MS,** Stump water. **1999** *NY Times* (NY) 15 Nov sec A 25/1 (Internet) **Ozarks,** "He even delivered stump water," Mrs. Hunter said cheerfully. Stump water? "White lightning. We're talking moonshine."

3 Nonsense, baloney—also used as an exclam.

1933 Williamson *Woods Colt* 22 **Ozarks,** "Reckon Uncle Joe ain't a-hankerin' to have nothin' to do with no Starbucks, an' you know it." "Oh, stump water! Look here, Clint, that feud's older than the State of Arkansas, an' plumb forgot, the way it ort to be." **1960** Hall *Smoky Mt. Folks* 64 **wNC, eTN,** Also very familiar are sayings like . . the uncomplimentary "His head is full of stump water" (that is, he is stupid). **1969** *DARE* (Qu. NN13, *When you think that the thing somebody has just said is silly or untrue: "Oh, that's a lot of _____."*) Inf **GA**72, Stump water. **2005** [see **1b** above].

stump whiskey See **stump liquor**

stump wren n
=**house wren 1.**

1917 (1923) *Birds Amer.* 3.192, House Wren. . . Other Names. . . Wood Wren; Stump Wren. . . The House Wren is famous for the odd kinds of cavities which it selects for its nest [including] . . hollow limbs or trunks of fruit trees. **1946** Hausman *Eastern Birds* 441, Eastern House Wren—*Troglodytes aedon aedon.* . . Other Names . . Stump Wren.

stumpy See **stump mushroom**

stun v
Std sense, var form.
Past, past pple, ppl adj: usu *stunned;* also *stunded.* Cf *drownded* (at **drown 3**), **-ed 1**

1781 in 1973 *Amer. Philos. Soc. Proc.* 117.398 **RI,** Several others struck Captain O'Brien and stunned him and hove him overboard. . . Mr. Howell was hoved in the boat stunded. **1795** Dearborn *Columbian Grammar* 139, *List of Improprieties.* . . Stunded for Stun'd. **1815** Humphreys *Yankey in England* 108, *Stunded,* stunned. **1818** Fessenden *Ladies Monitor* 172 **NEng,** Provincial words . . to be avoided. . . *stunded* for stunned. **1861** Holmes *Venner* 2.177 **wMA,** "Been stunded," Abel said. "He can't tell nothin'." **1883** *Sat. Herald* (Decatur IL) [10 Nov 7]/3 **seNY** (newspaperarchive.com), She was stunded for a moment, but was able to ride with the others to the house of Mr. Belmont. **1901** *Atlantic Mth.* 87.102 **ME** (as of c1776), He fetched me another on my nose here; most stunded me. **1976** in 2004 *DARE* File—Internet **IN,** [Transcript of taped interview:] Something might have hit me. . . Well, I was stunded. **2004** *Ibid* **MI,** I was approved only 2 days after all necessary paper work was faxed. I was stunded. *Ibid* **VA,** I have never really been in a fight before and i was just stunded.

stun n See **stone** n

stunded v See **stun** v

stunt v Cf Intro "Language Changes" I.8
To stun.

1845 Hooper *Advent. Simon Suggs* 197 **AL,** Some on 'em would throw a long log o' wood . . as nigh at me as they could guess, *to stunt the cat.* **1859** *S. Lit. Messenger* 28.144 **Sth,** He [=a fish] wuz a crowder, though, an fit desput, an we wuz ableeg'd to stunt him with rocks. **1885** Holley *Sweet Cicely* 43 **NY,** "Did it strike you senseless, Mr. Gansey?" "No," he said: it only stunted him. **1888** Jones *Negro Myths* 105 **GA coast,** De Ole Man knock um een de head wid de butt er eh whip an stunted um. **1943** Chase *Jack Tales* 156 **wNC,** Jack got him a long pole and whacked 'em all in the head to stunt 'em so's they wouldn't try to fly off no more. **1958** *Julian Apple Day* [14] **csCA,** One of the boys stunted him [=a rooster] with a rock from his slingshot and the Postmaster whacks old red's head off. **2004** *DARE* File—Internet **Chicago IL,** Two days later, I was stunted when I read about something that happened that very night.

stunt n Also *stunter* [*OED2 stunt* n.¹ 2 "A creature which has been hindered from attaining full growth or development"; but perh here a blend of *runt + stunted*]

A pig that is not thriving.
1966–67 *DARE* (Qu. K55, *A pig that doesn't grow well and is not worth keeping*) Infs **MI**64, **SC**32, Stunt; **AZ**5, Stunter.

stunt master n Cf **stump-the-leader**
1891 *Jrl. Amer. Folkl.* 4.228 **Brooklyn NYC,** *Stunt master, or follow the leader,* is a game in which the leader endeavors to *stunt* the others; that is, perform some feat in which they are unable to follow him. One boy is chosen *stunt master* or *leader,* and the others arrange themselves in order behind him. The leader may vault fences, jump, run, etc., and the others must follow him. Three chances are given to them, and those that fail on the last trial are sent down to the end of the line.

stunty adj
Stunted.
1823 Cooper *Pioneers* 2.171 **NY,** I never put my axe into a stunty tree. **1916** *DN* 4.343 **cnMD,** *Stunty. . .* Stunted. **1966** *DARE* (Qu. K55, *A pig that doesn't grow well and is not worth keeping*) Inf **SC**9, Stunty pig. **1974** *Mother Earth News* May/June 18 **OH,** I think my plants have given up. . . [T]hey're short and stunty and just not growing at all. **2000** in 2004 *DARE* File—Internet **KY,** My o[pen] p[ollinated] is always stunty looking, but my silver queen was perfect.

sturgeon n
Std: a large fish of the family Acipenseridae. For other names of var spp see **lake sturgeon, mamoose, shovelnose sturgeon**; for other names of the flesh of this fish see **Albany beef**

sturgeon chub n
A chub (here: *Macrhybopsis gelida*).
1951 Harlan–Speaker *IA Fish* 76, The sturgeon chub is known only from the Missouri River in Iowa. **1967** Cross *Hdbk. Fishes KS* 97, In Kansas, the sturgeon chub is known only from the Kansas River, the lower Smoky Hill River, and the Missouri River. **1971** Brown *Fishes MT* 90, Sturgeon chub—*Hybopsis gelida. . .* Recent collections have all been from the lower Yellowstone River and its tributaries. **1983** *Audubon Field Guide N. Amer. Fishes* 423, Sturgeon chub (*H. gelida*) . . occurs in . . Mississippi River from Missouri to Louisiana.

sturgeon sucker n
=**longnose sucker.**
1926 *MI Univ. Museum Zool. Misc. Pub.* 15.22, *Catostomus catostomus* Forster Sturgeon sucker; long-nose sucker; red or red-side sucker. **1943** Eddy–Surber *N. Fishes* 111, The northern sturgeon sucker ranges from the St. Lawrence and Great Lakes basin westward into the Rocky Mountains and also northward.

sturk n [Scots, nEngl dial *stirk, sturk* a young bull; fig, a stupid or foolish person]
1926 *Appleton Post-Crescent* (WI) 1 June 3/1 **ceKY,** When he [=a boy] grows up, he is an "overgrown sturk".

stur(ru)p See **stirrup**

stuttin See **study** v¹

style n See **stile** n 2

style v Also with *out* among *Black speakers*
To show off, show oneself to be stylish, esp in dress; to show off (one's stylish possessions, esp clothes).
1968 *Current Slang* 3.2.46 [Watts slang; Black], *Style. . .* To show off, to act a part. **1970** *Ibid* 5.2.13 [Black univ student slang], *Style. . .* To conduct oneself in an urbane, "hip" manner, especially in dress and in such activities as dancing. **1970** *DARE* (Qu. W37, *When a woman puts on her good clothes and tries to look her best . . she's _____*) Inf **IL**140, Styling; (Qu. W38, *When a man dresses himself up in his best clothes . . he's _____*) Inf **IL**140, Styling. [Inf Black] **1972** Kochman *Rappin'* 191 [Black], The ritual [of a Black church service] begins with the preacher "stylin' out," which the audience eagerly awaits. ("Stylin' out" means he's going to perform certain acts, say certain things with flourish and finesse.) **1980** Folb *Runnin' Down* 27 **cwCA** [Black], Dese *pimps* walkin' 'round, stylin' 'suits and thangs. *Ibid* 47, Everybody high class. Dese *pimps* walkin' 'round, stylin' 'suits and thangs. **1986** Pederson *LAGS Concordance,* 1 inf, **seFL,** He's not styling right—of pimp without Cadillac [inf Black].

styles block See **stile block**

styptic weed n
A **senna** n¹ **B1** (here: *Senna occidentalis*).
1863 Porcher *Resources* 230 **Sth,** Styptic Weed; Florida Coffee. Common around old buildings; collected in St. John's; vicinity of Charleston; Columbia. . . The negroes apply the leaves, smeared with grease, as a dressing for sores. **1876** Hobbs *Bot. Hdbk.* 156, Cassia [=*Senna*] *occidentalis,* Styptic weed. **1930** *OK Univ. Biol. Surv. Pub.* 2.66, *Cassia occidentalis. . .* Coffee-senna; Styptic-weed. **1974** (1977) Coon *Useful Plants* 166, *C[assia] Caroliniana* [=*Senna occidentalis*] is called styptic weed, used as hinted by the name, for itches and inflammation.

su See **soo** 3

suage See **swage**

suaharo See **saguaro**

sub See **submarine sandwich**

subby See **sob** v

submarine n
1 See **submarine sandwich.**
2 A doughnut. Cf **sinker 2b**
1916 *Independent* Oct 77, Two submarines [=doughnuts] and a mug of murk—no cow! **1942** Berrey–Van den Bark *Amer. Slang* 91.25, *Doughnuts. . .* submarines *("sinkers").* **1967–70** *DARE* (Qu. H30, *An oblong cake, cooked in deep fat*) Infs **KS**16, **MN**1, **WV**20, Submarine; **NY**218, Submarine [FW sugg].
3 A foot. Cf **canal boat, gunboat**
1919 *DN* 5.69 **NM** [Among hs students], *Submarines,* the feet. "What size shoe do you wear on those submarines?" **1934** (1940) Weseen *Dict. Amer. Slang* 405, *Submarines*—the feet. **1935** *AmSp* 10.9, The American imagination is fertile in creating humorous names, usually metaphorical, for human feet and the shoes that protect them. . . The resemblance of feet to various forms of water craft seems to prompt the currency of *tugboats, steamboats, gunboats, battleships, canal boats, sailboats, steamers, canoes,* and *submarines.*
4 also *black pot submarine;* In moonshining: a type of still. [From the shape]
1972 (1978) Carr *Second Oldest Profession* 185 **swVA,** The submarine still has replaced many of the small pot stills of earlier years. The name is derived from the elongated shape of the unit, which is really more like an army tank minus the tracks. **1985** Wilkinson *Moonshine* 23 **neNC,** In North Carolina three kinds of stills are most often found: the pot, the submarine, and the steam plant. [**2001** *Philadelphia Weekly* 11 Apr (Internet) **VA,** The 800-gallon, submarine-shaped stills, blackened from the propane burners that cook the mash, are usually made of galvanized metal or aluminum with wooden sides.] **2002** *DARE* File—Internet **NC,** [From an interview with a moonshiner:] What we call a 'still' in North Carolina is a 'pot' in Tennessee. And here they call it a 'submarine' . . or a 'black pot submarine.'

submarine grinder See **grinder 3**

submarine sandwich n Also *sub, submarine* orig scattered, but chiefly **NEast, N Cent, C Atl; now widespread** See Map on p. 360 Cf **Cuban sandwich, grinder 3, hero, hoagie, Italian sandwich, muffuletta, poor boy n 1, spucky, torpedo sandwich, wedge** n¹ **2, zep**
A large sandwich made with Italian or French bread or a long bun, and a variety of meats, cheeses, and vegetables.
1940 in 2001 *Popik Coll.* **DE,** [Wilmington Classified Telephone Directory:] Arsenios Daniel—Spaghetti and Submarine Sandwiches. . . De Matteis John—Italian Food A Specialty . . Submarine Sandwiches To Take Out. **1943** *Better Homes & Gardens* Mar 38/2, *Submarine Sandwich*—It's long, low, and goes down easily. Split a Coney roll; hollow out. . . Fill fore 'n' aft and in the middle with three different fillings: baked beans with onion; chopped egg and mayonnaise; diced ham with relish. They'll eat straight thru from stem to stern. Oh Boy! **1949** *NY Herald Tribune* (NY) 7 Aug mag sec 24/1 **DE,** Biggest submarine-sandwich fleet . . is built by Jack Twilley's stand-up-and-at-'em snack bar. . . Four Sundays back, we stood there, notebook in one hand . . recording who came to buy "subs". . . Want to introduce the submarine to your town? . . If you can't get . . long rolls, whack off nine-inch cuts of French flute bread or use the long Italian hard rolls. . . Split . . lengthwise. . . Flatten like an open book. . . Lay on the following ingredients . . pressed ham . . provoloni cheese . . lettuce . . tomato. Sprinkle with thyme, celery seed and salt; drizzle over olive oil. . . onion cut into thin

rings . . four one-half-inch-thick slices of dill pickle and a few sliver slices of hot pickled peppers. **1965–70** *DARE* (Qu. H42, . . *[A sandwich] . . in a much larger, longer bun, that's a meal in itself*) 243 Infs, **scattered, but chiefly NEast, C Atl, Gt Lakes, N Midl,** Submarine (sandwich); 10 Infs, **scattered,** Sub; [**CT**33, Submarine grinder;] (Qu. H41, . . *Kinds of roll or bun sandwiches . . in a round bun or roll*) Infs **IN**65, **MA**122, **NY**80, Submarine; **NJ**18, Sub. **1986** Pederson *LAGS Concordance* **Gulf Region** *(Hero sandwich)* 43 infs, Submarine(s); 29 infs, Submarine sandwich(es); 3 infs, Subs.

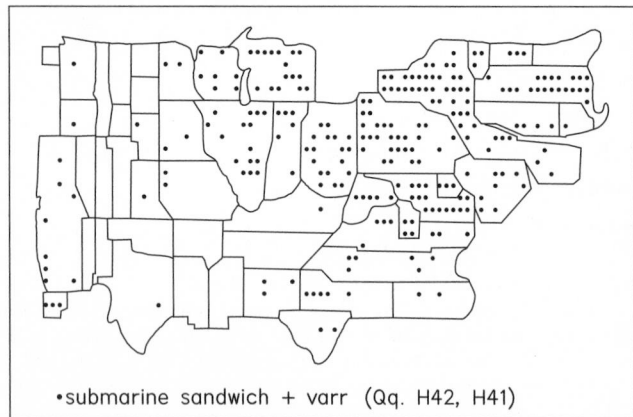

•submarine sandwich + varr (Qq. H42, H41)

suboy exclam, v |sǝˈbɔɪ| Also *sheboy* for addit varr see quots Cf **soo** exclam **3**
=stuboy.
    1831 *Daily Natl. Intelligencer* (DC) 13 Aug 3/2 **GA,** Say but 'su' boy,' and away they will obey your call. **1843** *Republican Compiler* (Gettysburg PA) 16 Oct 1/3 **AL,** Sick, s-i-c-k him, Bull—suboy! suboy! suboy! **1890** *DN* 1.59 **RI,** Steboy. Instead of *steboy* I have often heard *sheboy*, though *steboy* is the proper form. **1903** *DN* 2.347, *Note on "Stub-boy."* . . [T]here are nearly as many spellings of this dialectal word as there are correspondents. . . *st'boy, steboy, stiboi, suboy, su boy, subboy, sooboy, soobboy,* . . *stubboy.* . . The two following pronunciations . . appear to predominate, [stǝbɔɪ] and [sǝbɔɪ]. The latter suggests a possible connection between this word and *su cow*. . . In the Middle West the form appears more often without the *t*. In Central Ohio . . [sǝbɔɪ] is used to drive pigs. People of Cincinnati are said to cry [sǝbɔɪ] when they want to call their hogs, [stǝbɔɪ] when they wish to disperse them. In Illinois [stǝbɔɪ] is the form to drive hogs; in Indiana, [sǝbɔɪ]. . . A few scattered reports from the South reveal the absence of the *t* in the word as a rule. In Savannah [sǝbɔɪ] = "Get there quick and catch him, you measly whelp"—used to fox-hound and corn-dog. In Spartanburg, S.C., [sǝbɔɪ] is a word used "in managing swine." In Gallatin, Tenn., [sǝbɔɪ] is yelled at a hog to drive him from one point to another. From this survey . . it is conjectured that [stǝbɔɪ] is the form in New England and the Middle Atlantic states; [sǝbɔɪ], the prevailing form in the South and in the Middle West. **1912** *DN* 3.591 **wIN,** *Subuoy, interj.* An exclamation used in driving hogs. **1915** *DN* 4.191 **swVA,** *Soo-y.* . . Used in urging on hogs. Also *su-boy.* **1955** Parris *Roaming the Mountains* 68 **wNC,** He caught the familiar cry "suboy! suboy! suboy!" Then a barefoot boy came into sight, scattering shelled corn. Behind came the first of a plodding, grunting drove of hogs.

subpoena n, v Usu |sǝˈpinǝ|; also **widespread exc Sth** |sǝˈpini, -nɪ| and (for past, past pple) |sǝˈpinɪd, -nɪd| (See Map); **chiefly Sth, S Midl** |sǝˈpiniǝ, -jǝ|; for addit varr see quot 1965–70 Pronc-spp *soopeeny, subpeeny, supeen, suppeney, sup(p)eeny, suppe(e)nied;* for addit pronc and sp varr see quots Cf Intro "Language Changes" IV.1.b
Std senses, var forms.
    1769 in 1953 Woodmason *Carolina Backcountry* 158 **SC,** After which comes Warrants, and Suppeneys, and Affadavers, and Recogners, and what not. **1845** in 1956 Eliason *Tarheel Talk* 318 **nw,cnNC,** Suppenied. **1888** *Atlantic Mth.* 62.827 **wNC, eTN,** Let him . . hear mine an' Marcelly's testimony, 'cordin' ter the subpeeny. **1888** *Century Illustr. Mag.* 36.81 **IL,** You needn't soopeeny me. **c1938** in 1970 Hyatt *Hoodoo* 2.1092 **New Orleans LA** [Black], Then I get a supeen [Hyatt: subpoena] from the court what day my son going to be in court. **1940** in 1944 *ADD,* Subpoena. . . [sǝˈpini], -[nɪ]. Radio. **1941** Smith *Going to God's Country* 99 **MO** (as of 1890), When court was set Mr. H.H. Smith was souphened on the jury. **1943** in 1944 *ADD,* Subpoena. . . [sǝˈpinɪd], pret. Radio. **1954** *Harder Coll.* **cwTN,** Subpoena. . . su-

peeny. **1965–70** *DARE* (Qu. V8a, . . *A paper ordering somebody to appear in court*) 222 Infs, **widespread,** Subpoena [proncs of the type [sǝˈpinǝ]]; 14 Infs, **scattered,** Subpoena [no pronc recorded]; 142 Infs, **widespread exc Sth,** Suppeeny [proncs of the types [sǝˈpini, -nɪ]]; **IL**74, **MO**13, **NJ**4, Suppeeny [no pronc recorded]; **IN**45, **MI**13, **MO**18, [(ˌ)sǝbˈpini]; **OK**47, **PA**70, [suˈpini, -nɪ]; **MO**39, **TN**5, [ˈspini, -nɪ]; **IN**26, [ˌsɪsˈpini]; **GA**9, 13, 72, 82, **KY**5, 85, **NE**10, **SC**32, **TX**40, 42, [sǝˈpinjǝ]; **IN**30, **OK**31, [sǝˈpini(j)ǝ]; **GA**74, [sǝˈpinjɚ]; **GA**77, [sǝˈpɪnjǝ]; **KY**13, [ˌsuˈpinjǝ]; **CA**6, **KY**63, **MD**49, **MI**18, **MO**26, **NY**144, **VA**33, [(ˌ)sǝbˈpinǝ]; **MO**7, [ˈsǝb,pinɛ]; **HI**6, **KY**50, **PA**74, [(ˌ)suˈpinǝ, -nɛ]; **TX**26, [ˌsuˈpounǝ]; **FL**8, [sǝˈpinǝd]; **GA**84, [sǝˈpɛinǝ]; **WA**9, [ˈsʌpi,nǝ]; (Qu. V8b, *Of a person who has been given a paper ordering him into court . . "He was _____ into court."*) 106 Infs, **widespread,** Subpoenaed [proncs of the type [sǝˈpinǝd]]; 15 Infs, **scattered,** Subpoenaed [no pronc recorded]; 81 Infs, **widespread exc Sth,** Suppenied [proncs of the types [sǝˈpinid, -ɪd, -ɪd]]; **IL**68, **NM**9, **OK**1, 18, 20, 42, Suppeenied [no pronc recorded]; **MO**3, 13, 19, **WV**13, [sǝbˈpinid]; **ID**4, [suˈpinid]; **MA**37, Suffeenied [sǝˈfinid]; **GA**9, 72, 82, **KY**85, **TN**27, **TX**43, Suppeeniaed [sǝˈpinjǝd]; **IN**30, [sǝˈpiniǝd]; **GA**74, 77, Suppeeniared [sǝˈpinjɚd]; **FL**22, Suppeenered [sǝˈpinɚd]; **LA**13, **MO**2, **NE**3, [sǝbˈpinǝd]; **IL**137, **KY**81, **NY**81, [sǝˈpinǝd]; **PA**76, [suˈpinǝd]; **WA**28, [sǝˈpinɑd]. **1966** *Wilson Coll.* **csKY,** Subpoena. . . Most often called a supeeny.

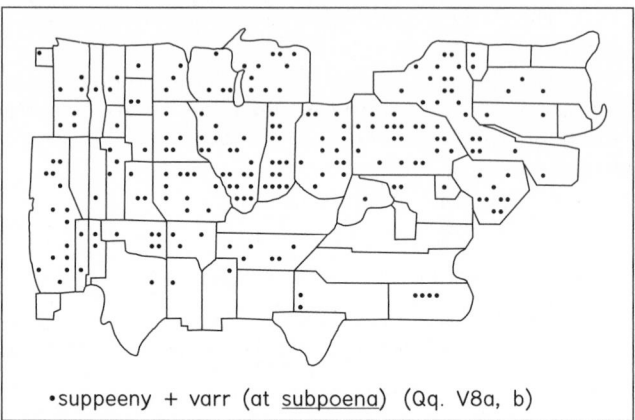

•suppeeny + varr (at subpoena) (Qq. V8a, b)

subscription n
The tuition payment at a **subscription school.**
    1962 Dykeman *Tall Woman* 190 **sAppalachians** (as of 1877), I'm saving for the children's subscriptions, do we get our school started up again. **1986** Scott *Beyond Beauty* 17 (Montgomery–Hall *Dict. Smoky Mt. Engl.*) **wNC,** The school term varied, but normally it ran from November through January. If sufficient funds could be collected, that is "subscriptions," it continued through February and March.

subscription school n [*OED2* 1708] *old-fash* Cf **free school**
A private school.
    1834 *New Engl. Mag.* 6.296, Her summer district school had long since ended, but she was now engaged in a private subscription school for those misses and little children, whose mothers considered that the winter district school had become too crowded and boisterous for the safety of their darlings. **1857** *Adams Sentinel* (Gettysburg PA) [26 Oct 3]/3 (newspaperarchive.com), [Advt:] The Subscription School of Miss Mary M'Clellan . . will not be opened until the *first of November.* Her terms are $1.25 per month. **1866** Fisher *Life Benjamin Silliman* 298 **CT,** In February 1798, I resorted to Wethersfield . . and during nine months I instructed the subscription school. **1893** *Daily Rev.* (Decatur IL) [14 Apr 8]/3 (newspaperarchive.com), Will McIllwain began a subscription school here Monday with about fifty in attendance. **1906** *DN* 3.159 **nwAR,** *Subscription school.* . . Private school. "Miss Robbie Engles is teaching a subscription school here." **1922** in 1985 *TN Civil War Veterans* 1.115, I attended subscription schools, my parents paid $1 per months for each scholar. **c1938** in Lib. of Congress *Amer. Memory: WPA Life Hist.* (Internet) **TX** (as of c1886), We children attended a subscription school while in Grapevine. *Ibid* **SC** (as of c1870), There were no free schools. I . . later attended a subscription school . . schools where the teacher charged a dollar a month per pupil. **1956** *Hall Coll.* **wNC,** I attended school at Gatlinburg, a subscription school. A man who lived there ran the school. . . [We] paid fifteen cents a day for board. It was a three-months school. **1986** Wear *Sugarlands* 79 **eTN,** Sometimes parents paid tuition for extra months of school after Christmas; these were called subscription schools. **2000** Baldacci *Wish You Well* 130

swVA, "They had school when you were little?" Oz asked. Louisa smiled. "They had what was called subscription school, Oz. A dollar a month for three month a year."

subway n

An underpass for vehicles or pedestrians, freq under railroad tracks.

1865 *Atlantic Mth.* 15.83 **NYC,** Central Park . . already contains . . four sub-ways for the passage of trade-vehicles across the Park, with an aggregate length of two miles. **1890** *Lima Daily News* (OH) 10 Apr [2]/1 (newspaperarchive.com), The property owners on Union street were promised . . they would have nothing to pay for the improvement of the street by the subway under the Pittsburgh, Ft. Wayne & Chicago Railroad tracks. **1898** *Fitchburg Daily Sentinel* (MA) 15 Oct 6/2, The plan contemplates . . constructing a subway under the tracks, or a footbridge over the tracks. **1910** *Washington Post* (DC) 18 Aug 2/3, The Baltimore and Ohio will join with the city [=Washington DC] in building . . a pedestrian and vehicle subway at Virginia avenue. **1926** *NV State Jrl.* (Reno) 27 Dec 6/5, The California highway commission already has asked the state railroad commission to issue an order that a subway be built under the tracks at the Truckee end of the new route. **1934** *Syracuse Herald* (NY) 13 Nov 6/2, Vehicular and Pedestrian Subway Under Rails Proposed. **1967** *DARE* Tape **ID**6, Some of the passengers . . they'd get off to stretch their legs. You only had to walk up a block. There was no subway then, you see. There was a pedestrian crossing there. **1983** *Barrick Coll.* **csPA,** Subway—underpass; viaduct. Always called "subway," the underpass is confusing to city folk who can't understand how Pa.'s small towns can have a subway, or why they need one. Curiously, the word is generally applied only to railroad underpasses; expressways have "underpasses." **1992** *Columbus Dispatch* (OH) 20 Oct sec B 4 (Internet), Postle proposed a pedestrian subway to give children living west of High Street a safe passageway to the school. **2002** *DARE* File—Internet **MN,** The Rochester Marriott Mayo Clinic is connected via a pedestrian skywalk to the Mayo Clinic. . . A pedestrian subway connects the hotel to the Galleria Mall. **2004** *Ibid* **NJ,** Construction in the pedestrian subway will continue. . . The stairs leading from the pedestrian subway to the west end of the outbound platform will remain closed. *Ibid* **NC,** The station also has a pedestrian subway, extending from the waiting areas under the tracks and up to the train platforms.

succat See soo cat

succor See sucker sweep

succory n [*OED2* 1533 →]

=chicory 1.

1737 (1911) Brickell *Nat. Hist. NC* 18, The *Sallads* are. . . common *Fennel, Endive, Succory.* **1824** Bigelow *Florula Bostoniensis* 285 **MA,** *Cichorium intybus . . Succory.* . . The large, blue flowers of this elegant plant are extremely common in pastures and road sides every where in the vicinity of Boston. **1897** Parsons *Wild Flowers CA* 312, Succory. . . This is a stranger from over the seas, whose native home is England; and like all English, it is an excellent colonist. **1971** *GA Dept. Ag. Farmers Market Bulletin* 10 Feb 8, Chicory—Cichorium Intybus, or succory, blueweed, blue dandelion or coffeeweed. **1987** Bowers *100 Roadside Wildflowers* 99, Common Chicory—Succory.

succory dock n Also *succory dock cress* [*OED2 succory dock-cress* (at *succory* n 3) 1857]

The nipplewort (*Lapsana communis*).

1876 Hobbs *Bot. Hdbk.* 114, Succory dock cress, Nipplewort, Lapsana communis. **1914** Georgia *Manual Weeds* 523, Nipplewort. . . Other English names: Succory Dock, Ballogan. **1991** in 2004 *DARE* File—Internet, The name "Dock" . . is applied to some other plants, such as . . succory dock (*Lapsana communis,* or nipplewort, a tall, softly fuzzy dandelion cousin).

succoteague See squeteague

such adj, adv, pron Usu |sʌč|; for varr see **A** below [Cf *EDD* for Scots, Ir, Engl dial forms]

A Forms.

1 |sič|; pronc-spp *si(t)ch;* hence *sicher* (for *such a*). **scattered, but chiefly Sth, S Midl**

1795 Dearborn *Columbian Grammar* 138, List of Improprieties. . . Sitch for Such. **1818** Fessenden *Ladies Monitor* 172 **NEng,** Provincial words . . to be avoided. . . *sich* or *sicher* for such. **1843** (1916) Hall *New Purchase* 119 **IN,** If any body hears or sees sich a stray, we'll put him up. **1851** Hooper *Widow Rugby's Husband* 131 **AL,** Coats . . said

"he'd be drot if he liked any sich jokes." **1884** *Anglia* 7.266 **Sth, S Midl** [Black], *'Taint no sicher thing!* = it is untrue. **1887** *Scribner's Mag.* 2.482 **AR,** I fight fair. I wudn't do ye sicher way. **1899** in (1912) Green *VA Folk-Speech* 385, *Sich, adj.* and *pron.* A variant of *such.* **1901** *DN* 2.149 **cNY,** *Such.* Pron. [sič, sɛč] not infrequent. **1903** *DN* 2.332 **seMO,** *Such, pron.* Pronounced sech or sich. 'I won't go with sich.' **1907** *DN* 3.237 **nwAR,** *Such, pron.* Pronounced sech or sich. **1909** *DN* 3.369 **eAL, wGA,** *Sich, adj.* Such. **1915** [see **A2** below]. **1923** *DN* 5.220 **swMO,** *Sich,* adv. Such. Also *Sech.* **1931** *PMLA* 46.1316 **sAppalachians,** *U,* short. . . Sometimes short *i,* as in "sich" (such). **1932** Wasson *Sailing Days* 46 **cME coast,** He's apt to lay in some little eel-rut of a harbor waitin' for jest sich and sich a favorable slant o' wind. **1941** *AmSp* 16.157 **NYC** [New York dialect], *Sich*—such. **1943** *LANE* Map 626 *(Such)* **NEng,** Pronunciations of the type of [sətʃ, sətʃ], occasionally also pronunciations of the type of [sɪtʃ, sɪtʃ], represent unstressed forms recorded in contexts such as ,That's such a 'good one. Pronunciations of the type of [sɛtʃ] are regarded as natural or more common by [5 infs]; pronunciations of the type of [sɪtʃ, sɪtʃ] are so regarded by [4 infs]. Pronunciations of the types of [sɛtʃ, sɪtʃ] are regarded as older though still in use by [28 infs]. **1949** Turner *Africanisms* 266 **seSC** [Gullah], [ɒɪ nɛwə si sɪc [approx = [sič]] tɪŋ]. [=I never see such thing.] **1966** *DARE* Tape **AL**11, Well, have to git sich as coffee, sugar. **1989** Pederson *LAGS Tech. Index* 364 **Gulf Region,** *Such.* [95 of 914 infs gave the pronc [sič].]

2 |sɛč|; pronc-spp *se(t)ch.* **scattered, but chiefly Sth, S Midl**

1848 Lowell *Biglow* 146 'Upcountry' **MA,** Sech, *such.* **1871** Eggleston *Hoosier Schoolmaster* 39 **sIN,** He uses sech remarkable smart words. **1893** Shands *MS Speech* 55, Sech [sɛtʃ]. Negro for *such.* **1899** (1912) Green *VA Folk-Speech* 385, *Sich, adv.* Sech. Forms of *such.* **1901** [see **A1** above]. **1903** [see **A1** above]. **1907** [see **A1** above]. **1909** *DN* 3.367 **eAL, wGA,** *Sech, adj.* Such. **1914** *DN* 4.77 **ME, nNH,** *No sech thing!* Exclamation of indignant dissent. **1915** *DN* 4.190 **swVA,** Setch. Variant of *such.* Also *sitch.* **1923** [see **A1** above]. **1937** in 1976 *Weevils in the Wheat* 207 **VA** [Black], Dat wuz six months gone—March an' setch. **c1940** Eliason *Word Lists FL* 14 **wFL,** Sech [sɛtʃ]: Such. Used among the old. **1943** [see **A1** above]. **1976** Garber *Mountain-ese* 78 **sAppalachians,** I've never seed sech a strong man as he wuz. **1989** Pederson *LAGS Tech. Index* 364 **Gulf Region,** *Such.* [21 of 914 infs gave the pronc [sɛč].]

3 Other varr: see quots. Cf **senkah, sicarum**

1892 (1969) Christensen *Afro-Amer. Folk Lore* 9 **seSC,** Cooter . . beat Deer in de ten-mile race, for all Deer hab shich long foot. **1949** Turner *Africanisms* 286 **seSC** [Gullah], [ʃɪʃə wʌn]. [=Such a one.] **1989** Pederson *LAGS Tech. Index* 364 **Gulf Region,** *Such.* [Of 914 infs, 4 gave the proncs [sʌt(s)]; 2 infs, [suč]; 2 infs, [sʌš]; 1 inf, [šʌč]; 1 inf, [sɪš]; 1 inf, [zuš].]

B As pron.

1 in phrr *any such, no such:* Anything like that; nothing like that; see quots. [Cf *OED2 such* B.27] **sAppalachians**

1926 Roberts *Time of Man* 30 **KY,** He's got no call to be a-tellen any such. *Ibid* 373, Nobody thinks Pap burned it. . . Don't talk about any such. **1937** *Hall Coll.* **wNC, eTN,** They whipped, they feathered the lewd woman. I didn't hold with no such whatever. **1939** *U.S. Natl. Park Serv. Regional Rev.* (Richmond VA) 3.4–5.6 **wNC,** One elderly woman of the Oconaluftee area declined the microphone . . and informed the investigators: "I don't fancy no sich as that and I won't jine up with ye!" **1974** Fink *Mountain Speech* 17 **wNC, eTN,** No sech . . not anything. "I never said no sech." **1997** in 2004 Montgomery–Hall *Dict. Smoky Mt. Engl.* 579 **wNC, eTN,** Such. . . any such (known to nine consultants).

2 in phrr *any such of a, no such of a:* Such a; no such. **orig chiefly Sth, S Midl; now more widespread** Cf **Bg**

1864 Winthrop *Speech* 4 **MA,** Heaven save us from any such of a party. **1893** Shands *MS Speech* 60, Such of a thing. This expression is used by all classes nearly always in the sentence: "It is no such of a thing"; i.e. it is not true. As *such* means *of that kind,* the *of* between *such* and *thing* may be introduced from the idea expressed in saying, it is not that kind of [a] thing, or not a thing of that kind. **1909** *DN* 3.352 **eAL, wGA,** No such of a thing. . . No such thing. **1923** *DN* 5.215 **swMO,** No sich of a damn' thing, indignant denial. **1941** in 1980 Welty *Coll. Stories* 47 **MS,** I did not say any such of a thing, the idea! **1970** *Thompson Coll.* **Sth,** "They ain't no such of a word as ain't"—common in southern vulgate. **1976** Stone–Grey *White Trash* xi **Sth,** Some southern writers. . . will go to great lengths to deny there's any such (of a) thing as a Cracker in their gene pool. **1978** Kalibabky *Hawdaw* 1.[10] **neMN,** No such of a ting: No such thing. "Whatta you talkin' about! There's no such of a ting as gettin' a deal dese days." **1986** Pederson

LAGS Concordance, 3 infs, **AR, GA, TX,** (I didn't say) no such of a thing. **1997** in 2004 *DARE* File—Internet **cNY,** I am pretty sure our Council doesn't have any such of a policy at present. **2001** *Ibid* **AL,** Mother called me and I assured her I hadn't said any such of a thing. **2004** *Ibid* **WA,** Before the "commission" could even make any such of a decision to do so, it would first also take the approval of the "director" to do it. *Ibid* **KS,** Is there any such of a man in existent [sic]? *Ibid* **CA,** [From a case heard before the Superior Court of California, Santa Cruz, on 6 Feb:] That is a lie. The defendant argued no such of a thing.

such a matter   See **matter** n¹ **B2**

suck n

1 also *suck pool:* A whirlpool; a strong current—freq used in place names. **chiefly S Midl** Cf **suckhole 1**

   1778 Hutchins *Topog. Descr.* 32 **seTN,** About 200 miles above these shoals, is, what is called, the *Whirl,* or *Suck,* occasioned, I imagine, by the high mountain, which there confines the River. **1805** (1905) Clark *Orig. Jrls. Lewis & Clark Exped.* 3.180 **VA,** One of the men shot a goose above this Great Shute, which was floating into the Shute, when an Indian observed it, plunged! into the water & swam to the Goose and brought in on shore, at the head of the Suck. **1838** *S. Lit. Messenger* 4.220, There were dangers on the route. The boat might be stove: the shoals of the Tennessee were to be passed, as well as the boiling suck, which even at this day is the terror of all navigators of that stream. **1890** *Scribner's Mag.* 8.611, Its [=the Colorado River's] dashing current is torn up by . . powerful whirlpools, sucks, and eddies. **1939** FWP *Guide TN* 253, When the Cherokee and Creek besieged Fort Loudoun in 1761, the French at New Orleans sent a supply boat up the Tennessee to aid the Indians. The boat could not navigate the "Suck" of the Tennessee, however, and the goods were sold to the Indians near present Chattanooga. **1953** (1977) Hubbard *Shantyboat* 279 **Missip-Ohio Valleys,** In the johnboat it was all I could do to keep out of the way as the whirlpools swung the two boats around like balls on a string. I could see the hull of the houseboat settling down in the sucks, almost to the guards. **1966–70** *DARE* (Qu. C8, *. . A place in a stream where water flows round and round and draws things in toward the center*) Inf **TN26,** Suck; **KY86,** Suck—on the river—will pull in a boat; **OK51,** Suck pool; (Qu. O18, *Different currents or actions of the water that are important when you're in a boat*) Inf **OK52,** Suck pools—in rainy weather, they have currents called suck pools, whirlpools, and twirl pools on big creeks and rivers; **KY86,** Sucks. **1981** Pederson *LAGS Basic Materials (Creek)* 1 inf, **csTN,** ['mɪ^ŋgoˤ ,sʌˤg, 'mɪ^ŋgoˤ ,sɤks]—a curve that drew in water. **2008** *DARE* File—Internet **nWI,** The lower section seemed to fish best this year with the biggest of the big boys coming from the Tunnel Bend and Pool, the Big Suck and the Hoover Pool.

2 also *suck lick, ~ spring:* A wet place frequented by animals where nutrients are secured by sucking rather than licking— also used in place-names. **esp VA, KY** Cf **lick** n **8**

   1792 in 1940 *AmSp* 15.398 **VA,** Crossing a drain by the Suck Lick. **1805** in 1951 *Hench Coll.* **KY,** [From a deposition:] Did it appear to you the game principally sucked the sulphur water in the branch or lick'd the clay in the bank? Ans.—I think the sulphur water was the greatest object. By same:—If you had been directing any person to this place would you have call'd it a suck or Clay Lick? Ans.—I should have told them a good deer suck. **1816** in 1940 *AmSp* 15.398 **VA,** To a Beach and gum by the road side near the suckspring. **1832** Rafinesque *Atl. Jrl.* 74 **KY,** They were called *licks* by the first settlers, because they noticed that buffaloes, elks and deer went *to* lick the saline ground, and *sucks* when they went to suck or drink the saline springs or pools. *Ibid* 76 **KY,** Licks become Sucks sometimes in the Winter and Spring, in rainy weather: and many Sucks become Licks in the dry season. **1936** *Hench Coll.* **VA,** Heard at Douthat State Park Virginia. I asked the custodian what was the meaning of "suck" in the place names "Blue Suck Falls" and "Blue Suck Trail" and was told that a suck was as above [="a lick, a place where deer find salt"]. **1986** Pederson *LAGS Concordance (Creek)* 1 inf, **neLA,** Cow Suck Bayou.

3 A toady; a sycophant, esp a teacher's pet. [*OED2* 1900 →] Cf **sucker 6, suckhole 3**

   1943 Korson *Coal Dust* 52, Coal operators had spies, or "sucks" as they were called, who would report back to the company office the substance of a sermon. **1955** Gaddis *Recognitions* 373, The shade of the boy whom he had not seen since they were boys together (Martin was Father Joseph's "suck") lived on the air as though they had parted only minutes before. **1965–70** *DARE* (Qu. JJ3b, *When a school child makes a special effort to 'get in good' with the teacher in hopes of getting a*

better grade: "She's an awful _____.") 13 Infs, **scattered,** Suck; **MI26,** Teacher['s] suck.

suck-egg adj   **chiefly Sth, Midl**

1a   Of an animal, esp a dog: given to stealing and eating eggs; hence used broadly as an abusive epithet for a dog. **chiefly Sth** See Map Cf **egg-sucker 1, egg-sucking**

   1861 *Harper's New Mth. Mag.* 24.135 **AL,** He'd a gin the good-for-nothing, nasty, suck-egg critters [=dogs] sich a scare that they never would a come back agin. **1882** *Landmark* (Statesville NC) 24 Feb [2]/4 (newspaperarchive.com), Two negro boys . . were searching a barn for a suck-egg cat which they proposed to kill. **1909** *DN* 3.377 **eAL, wGA,** *Suck-egg. . .* Egg-sucking. "I'll have to kill that old suck-egg dog." Common. *Ibid* 404 **nwAR,** *Suck-egg dog. . .* 1. A dog that sucks eggs. 2. A superlatively mean dog. **1941** Stuart *Men of Mts.* 141 **eKY,** I've bought her a twenty-gauge gun to kill suck-egg dogs with. **1965–70** *DARE* (Qu. J2, *. . Joking or uncomplimentary words . . for dogs*) 15 Infs, **chiefly SE,** Suck-egg dog; **IN3, SC4, 9, 23, 26, 38,** Suck-egg dog [FW sugg]; **AL6,** Suck-egg dog—heard; **IL114,** Suck-egg dog—"suck-egg" dogs really do suck eggs; **SC1,** Suck-egg dog [FW sugg; Inf has heard, but restricts it to dogs that do suck eggs.]; **SC3,** Suck-egg dog [FW sugg]—older—not used now, and when it was used, was applied only to egg-sucking dogs; **SC7,** Suck-egg dog—just one that gets eggs; **SC11,** Suck-egg dog [FW sugg]—just one who gets eggs; **SC66,** Suck-egg dog—also a children's insult to each other. [23 of 28 Infs old, 12 gs educ or less] **2003** Hart *Buddies* 52 **nGA,** His egg basket was overturned and shells lay scattered on the ground. . . "Well, Ernie, I won't git no shoes today for shore 'cause of some ole suck-egg dog."

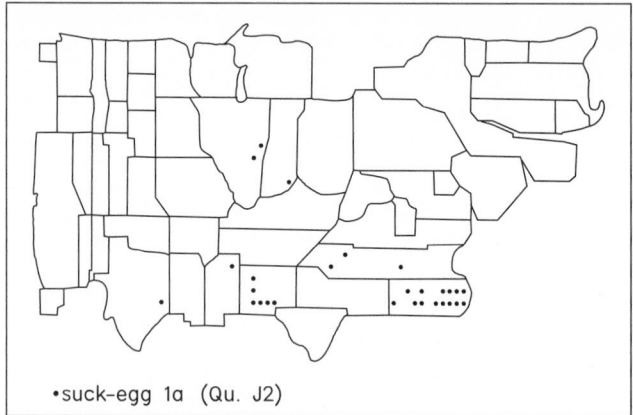

•suck-egg 1a (Qu. J2)

b   in combs *suck-egg dog, ~ son of a bitch:* Fig, and used in var comparisons as an example of one who is contemptible, sneaky, guilty-looking, etc.

   1852 Baldwin *Southern & SW Sketches* 36 **MS,** Sez I, you eternal, yaller faced, pizen-mouthed, suck egg son of er _____! **1860** *Weekly Std.* (Raleigh NC) 11 Apr 1/5, A man who . . would compare our present distinguished Executive to a "suck-egg dog" is beneath the notice of the editor of the *Register.* **1882** *Harper's New Mth. Mag.* 64.244 **GA,** Ef he'll confind hisself to that, he'll never feel like a-prowlin' around his own house, like a suck-egg dog around of hen-nessees. **1892** *DN* 1.232 **KY,** *Suck-egg.* A *suck-egg* dog is a superlatively mean dog. "He is as mean as a suck-egg dog." **1922** Gonzales *Black Border* 33 **sSC, GA coasts** [Gullah], Joe look shameface' ez uh suck-aig dog w'en oonuh [= you] ketch'um een uh hen nes'. **1930** *DN* 6.80 **cSC,** *Dare. . .* "I dee-double-dare-you like a suck-egg dog." **1958** Allen *7 Men* 107 **TX,** I will be a suck-egg son of a bitch. **1959** Ruark *Poor No More* 505 **Sth,** They all a bunch of son of a bitches and suck-egg dogs and . . I'd shoot a suck-egg dog. **1978** *AP Letters* **neGA** (as of c1900), Expressions . . of the pioneers . . from . . mountain and rural areas: . . "He is sneaky as a suck-egg dog." **1984** Wilder *You All Spoken Here* 109 **Sth,** *Like a suck-egg dog:* Shame-faced. **2002** *Sun. News Jrl.* (Wilmington DE) 7 July sec A 1/3, Crooks used to be "guilty as a suck-egg dog"—an old farmer's expression based on farm dogs that would steal eggs straight out of a hen's nest and get caught carrying the eggs in their mouths. **2004** in 2006 *DARE* File—Internet **MD,** So, I slunk off like a suck-egg dog to the bathroom and the shower stall.

c   in comb *suck-egg mule* (rarely *suck-egged ~*): Fig, used esp in phr *I'll be a suck-egg mule,* and in comparisons.

   1925 *Mexia Daily News* (TX) 7 Apr 5/4, The well known "suck-egg mule," is familiar to everyone, in fact it has ever [sic] passed into slang but a farmer . . has unearthed a mule that does more than that—he eats chickens. **1936** *Esquire* Nov 57 **KY,** One fellow knows Pa. "W'y little Mick Powderjay if it ain't I'm a suck-egg mule." And he slaps Pa on the back. **1942** *AmSp* 17.130 **IN,** *I'll be a suck-egg mule!* (said in disgust). **1944** *PADS* 2.11 **AL, MS,** *Mule, suck-egged:* Superlative of surprise or astonishment. "Well, I'll be a suck-egged mule. . . " Ala., Miss. Low popular. Reported. **1954** Tolbert *Bigamy Jones* 159 **wTX** (as of 1870s), I'll be a suck-egg mule! **1967** *DARE* (Qu. NN32, *Exclamations like 'I swear' or 'I vow'*) Inf **TX11,** Be a suck-egg mule. **1999** Garlock *With Heart* 2 **OK** (as of 1938), You stupid-ass woman! I never met one a ya that had the brains of a suck-egg mule. **2001** *DARE* File—Internet **NC,** My dad always uses that expression, along with things such as "meaner than a striped-eyed snake," "lower than a suck-egg mule." **2002** *Ibid* **MO,** I think killin' is too good for the suck-egg mule that crafted this miscegenated piece of scrap metal.

2 Contemptible.

1869 *Coshocton Democrat* (OH) 2 Mar [3]/1 (newspaperarchive.com), Collier is to be rewarded with the office of *"Egg Inspector,"* owing to his natural suck-egg disposition. **1951** West *Witch Diggers* 52 **IN,** This is no suck-egg job, Mary. **2005** *DARE* File—Internet **PA,** We have bemoaned the lack of video evidence of her antics (other than the suck-egg quality 30 sec. clips our Canon G-2 still camera can do).

suck-egg dog See **suck-egg 1b**

suck-egg(ed) mule See **suck-egg 1c**

suck eggs, mean enough to adj phr

Contemptible, low.

1906 *DN* 3.146 **nwAR,** *Mean enough to suck eggs. . .* Low-minded, base. Used both of dogs and of men. **1927** *AmSp* 2.360 **cwWV,** *Mean enough to suck eggs . .* meaner than a dog. "That boy looks mean enough to suck eggs." **1942** McAtee *Dial. Grant Co.* **IN** 42 (as of 1890s), *Mean enough to suck eggs . .* here as in the first example "mean", signifies low, disreputable.

suck-egg son of a bitch See **suck-egg 1b**

suckemstance See **circumstance**

sucker n

1 Std: a fish of the family Catostomidae. For other names of var spp see **black sucker, buffalo fish, chubsucker 1, chunky, cui-ui, flannel-mouth sucker, flatback, harelip sucker, hog ~, humpback ~, June ~ 2, longnose ~, minnow B2e, Missouri sucker, mountain ~, mudsucker 1b, mullet** n[1] **2, red sucker, redhorse 1, ~ sucker 2, Sacramento sucker, shit-house trout, spotted sucker, white ~ 1**

2 A **hagfish** (here: *Myxine glutinosa*).

1873 U.S. Bur. Fisheries *Rept. for 1871 & 1872* 1.814, *Myxine glutinosa. . .* Hag-fish; sucker; slime-fish. Polar regions to Cape Cod.

3 A **kingfish 1** (here: *Menticirrhus undulatus*).

1882 U.S. Natl. Museum *Bulletin* 16.578, *M[enticirrus] undulatus. . .* "Sucker". . . Pacific coast, from Panama north to Point Concepcion; abundant. **1891** *Century Dict.* 6040, *Sucker. . .* (7) A Californian food fish, the sciaenoid *Menticirrus undulatus.*

4 =**bobolink B.**

1923 U.S. Dept. Ag. *Misc. Circular* 13.75 **FL,** Bobolink. . . Vernacular Names. . . *In local use. . .* sucker, wheat-bird, yellow ricebird.

5 also *suck-leech:* A leech.

1966–70 *DARE* (Qu. R23a, *Blood-sucking creatures—in water*) Infs **OH47, 67, TN65,** Suckers, leeches; **RI17, WA1,** Suckers; **SC9,** Suck-leech.

6 A toady, apple-polisher; a hanger-on. **chiefly Nth, N Midl, esp NEast** See Map

1900 *DN* 2.65 [College slang], *Sucker. . .* One who flatters an instructor. **1929** *AmSp* 4.373 **PA** [Mining town terms], *Sucker*—One who hangs around a boss to win his favor. When a man is asked if he is working the next day (when everyone else, with few exceptions, is not working, and he answers affirmatively, he is told he's got a good hose; if not working, "hose is broke." **1932** *AmSp* 7.403 **WA** [Orphanage argot], *Sucker. . .* A toady; a student politician; a teacher's pet. **1965–70** *DARE* (Qu. II20a, *A person who tries too hard to gain somebody else's favor: "He's an awful _____ ."*) 33 Infs, **chiefly Nth, N Midl, esp NEast,** Sucker; [**PA138,** Boss sucker;] (Qu. JJ3b, *When a school child makes a special effort to 'get in good' with the teacher in hopes of getting a better grade: "She's an awful _____ ."*) 9 Infs, **chiefly**

NEast, Sucker; **MA35,** Teacher's sucker; (Qu. HH43b, *The assistant to the top person in charge of a group of workmen*) Infs **MA5, VT12,** (Boss's) sucker; (Qu. II18, *Someone who joins himself on to you and your group without being asked and won't leave*) Inf **PA162,** Sucker.

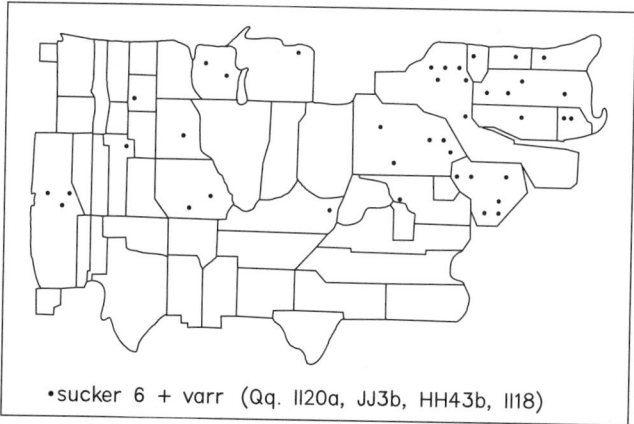

•sucker 6 + varr (Qq. II20a, JJ3b, HH43b, II18)

7 freq in combs: A hard candy, esp a lollipop. **widespread, but less freq N Atl** See Map Cf **lollipop 1a**

1907 *DN* 3.250 **eME,** *Sucker. . .* A kind of hard candy held by a small wooden stick and sucked. "Let's buy suckers." **1965** *Bee* (Phillips WI) 19 Aug [11/3], [Advt:] *Free* Suckers and Balloons for the Kiddies. **1965–70** *DARE* (Qu. H81, *Candy on a stick for children to lick*) 636 Infs, **widespread, but less freq N Atl,** Sucker; 58 Infs, **scattered,** Allday sucker; (Qu. H82a, *Cheap candies sold especially for schoolchildren*) 52 Infs, **scattered, but infreq N Atl,** Suckers; 13 Infs, **esp Sth, S Midl,** All-day suckers; **CA118, IN35, KY81, MD37, NY113,** Penny sucker(s); **IL134,** Big-daddy suckers; **NY70,** Caramel all-day suckers; (Qu. H82b, *Kinds of cheap candy that used to be sold years ago*) 25 Infs, **scattered,** Suckers; 15 Infs, **scattered,** All-day suckers; **MD37, NY226,** Penny suckers; **WA27,** Bat suckers; **NY70,** Caramel all-day suckers; **VA28,** Hand sucker; **NY169,** Peppermint-stick suckers; **PA2,** White vanilla suckers with peanut butter in middle; (Qu. HH22c, *A very mean person . . "He's mean enough to _____ ."*) Inf **WI47,** Steal a baby's sucker. **1968** *Daily Sentinel–Tribune* (Bowling Green OH) 20 May 7/5, The therapy committee reported they would help the Special Education classes . . make planters from milk cartons and sucker sticks. **1994** *DARE* File **nwMA** (as of 1960s), A sucker was always some kind of hard candy, like a butterscotch or a lozenge; not on a stick. If it was on a stick, it was called a lollipop.

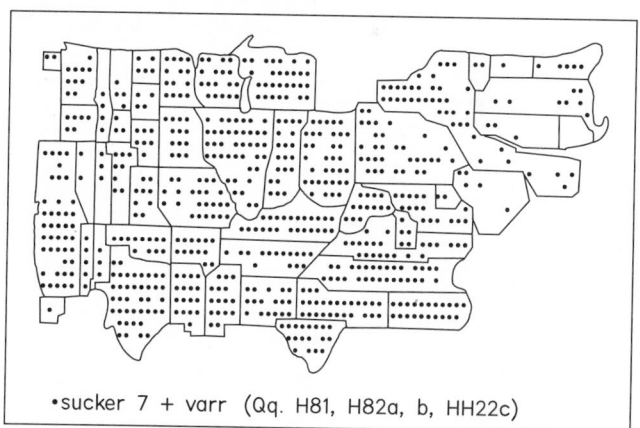

•sucker 7 + varr (Qq. H81, H82a, b, HH22c)

sucker bite n Also *sucker (bite) mark* **chiefly wPA, eOH** See Map on p. 364 Cf **monkey bite 1, octopus ~** =**hickey** n[2] **c;** also transf.

1965–70 *DARE* (Qu. X39, *A mark on the skin where somebody has sucked it hard and brought the blood to the surface*) Infs **OH40, 82, PA93, 94, 134, 167, 214, WV20,** Sucker bite; **OH46,** Sucker bite—you have to suck and bite to get it, and you're a sucker if you do; **PA76,** Sucker bite [FW: This word is the only one ever heard around here [= Pittsburgh].]; **IN66, OH47, PA142,** Sucker mark; **OH44,** Sucker bed [sic—FW sp]. [8 of 14 Infs coll educ, 7 young] **1997** *DARE* File—Internet, How'd you get that sucker mark on your neck? . . Yup, that dawg marked you, honey. **2004** *Ibid*, When she got in the car, she had a big dark sucker-bite on her neck. *Ibid,* The shirt will actually cut you when you bring it down and create some pain. It gives you "sucker bite" marks. *Ibid,* A boy has a "sucker mark" on his neck in a scene after we see him kissing a girl.

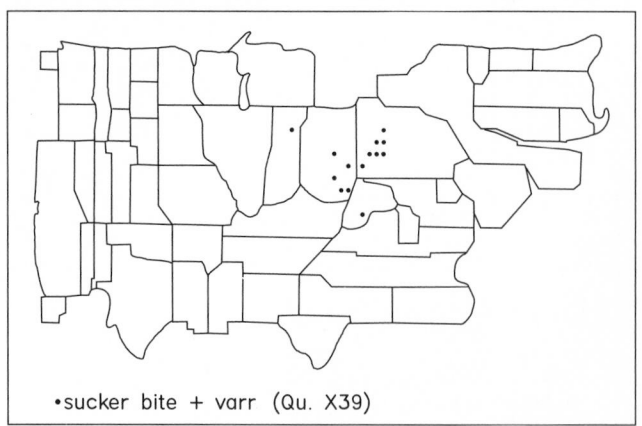

•sucker bite + varr (Qu. X39)

suckerel n

=Missouri sucker.

    1820 *Western Rev.* 2.355, Genus. Suckrel [sic]. Cycleptus. *Ibid,* Black Suckrel. Cycleptus nigrescens [=*C. elongatus*]. . . It is also found in the Missouri, whence it is sometimes called the Missouri Sucker. **1878** U.S. Natl. Museum *Bulletin* 12.189, Cycleptus elongatus. . . *Suckerel.* . . This species is found in some abundance in the larger streams. At the Falls of the Ohio, it is taken in nets, and meets a ready sale.

sucker flax n

A **flax** n (here: *Linum medium*).

    1970 Correll *Plants TX* 899, *Linum medium* . . var *texanum* . . Sucker flax. . . Open fields, meadows and swales, e. Tex. **2004** (acc) TX A&M Univ. *TX Vascular Plant Checklist* (Internet), *Linum . . medium* var. *texanum . .* (texas flax, sucker flax).

sucker mark   See **sucker bite**

sucker minnow   See **minnow B2e**

suckermouth minnow n   Also *suckermouth (dace), sucker-mouthed minnow*

A **minnow B1** of the genus *Phenacobius,* usu *P. mirabilis.*

    1908 Forbes–Richardson *Fishes of IL* 158, *Phenacobius mirabilis.* . . Sucker-mouthed minnow. . . The inferior sucker-like mouth, thick lips, small scales, and black spot at base of caudal fin in this species will, taken together, distinguish it from all other minnows found in Illinois. **1929** OK Univ. Biol. Surv. *Pub.* 1.2.87, Phenacobius mirabilis. . . (Sucker-mouth minnow)—Arkansas River system in Arkansas. . . [and] Oklahoma. **1943** Eddy–Surber *N. Fishes* 146, Suckermouth Minnow. **1956** Harlan–Speaker *IA Fish* 92, The suckermouth reaches its greatest abundance in the Des Moines River watershed. *Ibid,* This minnow . . is used extensively as bait by anglers, who usually refer to it as the suckermouth dace. **1981** (1984) Janovy *Back in Keith Co.* 32 **NE,** What if we used another bait, a trash fish? How many would say, "That's a sucker fry," or "That's a first-year suckermouth minnow"? Not many.

sucker sweep n   Also *succor*

In logging: =**sweeper 1.**

    1956 Sorden–Ebert *Logger's Words* 36 **Gt Lakes,** *Succor,* See *sweeper. Sucker-sweep,* See *sweeper.* [*Ibid* 37, *Sweeper,* An uprooted tree which has fallen into the stream. It could sweep men off a raft or log and it frequently caused a jam.]

suckhole n

1 A whirlpool. **chiefly Sth, S Midl** See Map Cf **suck 1**

    1886 *Daily NV State Jrl.* (Reno) 17 June 2/1, When a man gets into a county office if he isn't a free man, he finds himself in a whirlpool—a perfect suckhole of expense, which drains his purse. **1897** *KS Univ. Qrly.* (ser B) 6.58 **KS,** *Suck-hole:* an eddy; and a fabulous hole in the bottom of a river, believed by boys and some men to go down to the center of the earth, and to suck swimmers in. **1905** Chesnutt *Col.'s Dream* 25 **GA,** Peter had taken care of him, and taught him to paddle in the shallow water of the creek and to avoid the suck-holes. **1909** *DN* 3.377 **eAL, wGA,** *Suck-hole.* . . A whirlpool. Common. **1950** *WELS (A*

place where flowing water goes round and round and draws things in toward the center of it)* 1 Inf, **ceWI,** Suckhole. **c1960** *Wilson Coll.* **csKY,** *Suck-hole.* . . A whirlpool. **1965–70** *DARE* (Qu. C8) 48 Infs, **chiefly Sth, S Midl,** Suckhole; (Qu. C3, *A place in a swift stream where the surface of the water is broken*) Inf **AL**14, Suckhole. **1986** Pederson *LAGS Concordance,* 1 inf, **cnGA,** Suckhole—deep part of stream; 1 inf, **sLA,** Suckhole—whirlpool; 1 inf, **ceAR,** Suckhole—cold places in pond; suck the body down. **2002** in 2010 *DARE* File—Internet **UT,** The river was so fast, and so rough, and so shallow, that . . I was getting sucked into a suckhole, rapid, or waterfall every 1 second or less.

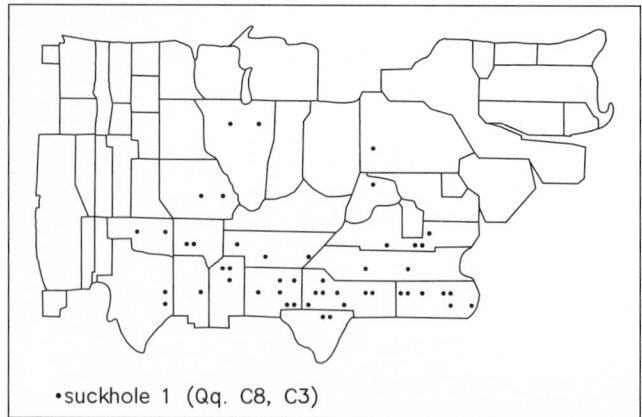

•suckhole 1 (Qq. C8, C3)

2 An area of quicksand; also fig. **esp Mid Atl, SE** See Map Cf **sucksand**

    1928 *Amer. Mercury* 13.343 **OR,** Now the top of the grade was close. But there was a suckhole, a deadly patch of mire, to drive through before the pull could come to an end. **1965–70** *DARE* (Qu. C11, *Soft, wet sand in streams or wet places, that draws people and things down into it*) 13 Infs, **esp Mid and S Atl,** Suckhole; **DC**8, Suckhole—in a branch; **OR**2, Suckhole—on highway signs; **TN**52, Suckholes will draw you down into them, but sinkholes will not draw you all the way down; **VA**82, Suckholes—term used by Black people. **1986** Pederson *LAGS Concordance,* 1 inf, **nwMS,** Suckhole—in bayou; get in, you couldn't get out. **2002** *NY Times* (NY) 3 Feb sec 14 1/2 **NJ,** I began to think of these [=terrifying highway interchanges] as New Jersey's Bermuda Triangles, and started taking nominations. . . A colleague suggested something called the "airport circle" . . which is no longer a circle . . but remains a hopeless suckhole of confusion in South Jersey. [*DARE* Ed: This quot may refer instead to **1** above.]

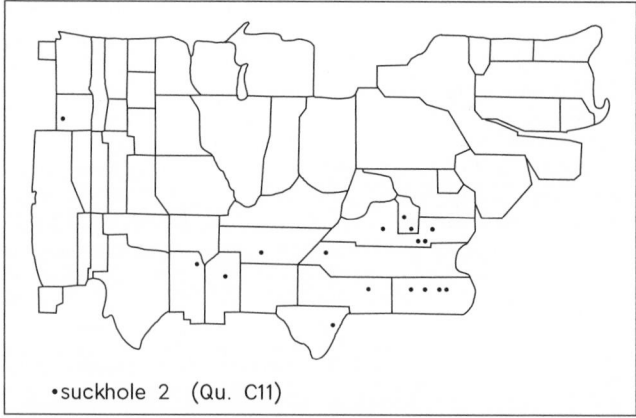

•suckhole 2 (Qu. C11)

3 also *suckholer:* A toady; an apple-polisher; hence v *suck-hole* to curry favor with, toady to; v phr *suckhole around* to be a toady. **chiefly Inland Nth, now more widespread** See Map Cf *AND*

    1939 in Lib. of Congress *Amer. Memory: WPA Life Hist.* (Internet) **Chicago IL,** He never joined the union. He's just a suckhole for the company. He sticks up for Swift & Company like he owned the damn place. **1950** *WELS (When a student tries to be extra nice to the teacher in hopes of getting a better grade. . . "She's an awful _____!")* 1 Inf, **cWI,** Suckhole. **1965–70** *DARE* (Qu. II20a, *A person who tries too hard to gain somebody's favor: "He's an awful _____."*) Infs **ME**1, **MI**28, **MT**1, **NY**2, 27, 96, 131, 224, Suckhole; **LA**20, **MN**33,

ND5, Suckholer; (Qu. HH43b, *The assistant to the top person in charge of a group of workmen*) Inf **OR**3, Suckholer; (Qu. II20b, *A person who tries too hard to gain somebody else's favor: "He's always trying to _____ the boss."*) Infs **MI**28, 108, **ND**3, **NY**96, 227, **OH**22, Suckhole; **MT**4, Suckholing around; (Qu. JJ3a, *When a school child makes a special effort to 'get in good' with the teacher in hopes of getting a better grade: "He's trying to _____ again."*) Inf **PA**130, Suckhole around; (Qu. JJ3b, *When a school child makes a special effort to 'get in good' with the teacher in hopes of getting a better grade: "She's an awful _____."*) Infs **MN**2, **NY**9, 96, 109, 224, **PA**130, **WA**11, Suckhole; **MT**1, Suckholer. **2007** *DARE* File—Internet, Why would anybody be envious of an ass kissing corporate suckhole toady metrosexual like Greenberg? *Ibid,* [He] must be trying for the Clinton suckhole of the year award. Even calling her "dear Senator." **2008** *Ibid,* I think you're a GOP suckhole sycophant.

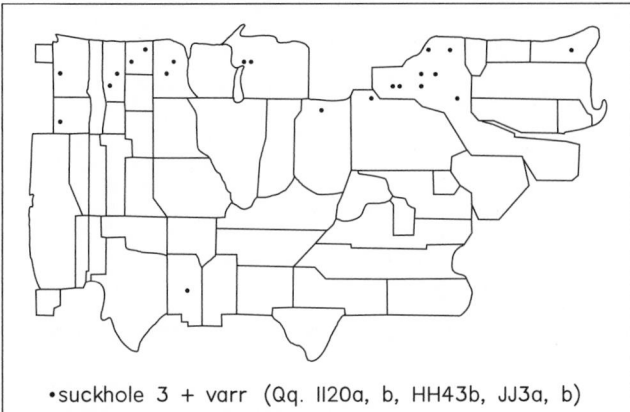

•suckhole 3 + varr (Qq. II20a, b, HH43b, JJ3a, b)

sucking toad n Cf **swelltoad, toadfish a**
A **puffer** n[1] **1** (here: *Sphoeroides maculatus*).
   1891 NY Comms. Fisheries *Report* 19.242 **Chesapeake Bay,** *Swell Fish. . . During the process of inflation the fish makes a sucking sound, from which doubtless comes the Chesapeake bay name of "sucking toad."*

suck-leech See **sucker 5**

suckles n [*OED2* 1475 →]
=**red clover.**
   1900 Lyons *Plant Names* 377, *T[rifolium] pratense. . .* Red Clover, . . Suckles. **1922** *Amer. Botanist* 28.34, *Trifolium pratense* is the "red clover", . . and from its abundant nectar, "honeysuckle clover", "suckles" and "sugar plums".

suckley perch n [After Dr. George *Suckley,* 1830–69]
The white **crappie** (*Pomoxis annularis*).
   1933 LA Dept. of Conserv. *Fishes* 333, [*Pomoxis annularis*'s] popularity is very well attested by the variety of names it has been given. . . [including] Suckley Perch [etc.].

suck lick See **suck 2**

suck one's teeth v phr Also *suck teeth* Cf **cut-eye, cut one's eyes, suck-teeth** n
To make a hissing or sucking sound usu by placing the tongue against or just behind the front teeth and creating a vacuum with the tongue. Note: While this vocal "gesture" is prob widespread, it has a particularly prominent and formalized position in Black cultures in Africa, the Caribbean, and the US, where it is used esp to express indignation or contempt. (See *DCEU* and John R. Rickford and Angela E. Rickford "Cut-Eye and Suck-Teeth: African Words and Gestures in New World Guise" in 1976 *Jrl. Amer. Folkl.* 89.294–309.)
   1835 Longstreet *GA Scenes* 175, They stopped about four feet apart, and looked each other full in the face for about half a minute; during all which time Toby sucked his teeth, winked, and made signs with his shoulders and elbows to the by-standers that he knew Hardy was drunk, and was going to quiz him for their amusement. **1890** *Atlanta Constitution* (GA) 17 Aug 6/4, [Short story:] Dady Cato groaned and shook his head, and Maum Phillis [=a Black woman] sucked her teeth in speechless scorn. "Tryin' tuh do like she wuz w'ite." **1919** *Jrl. Amer. Folkl.* 32.378 **seSC** [Black], If a child sucks its teeth (the upper teeth brought

against the lower lip and sucked), I don't care whose child it is, any old person will slap it in the mouth, will swell his mouth up, and say, "Little no-manner bunter . . , no good will foller you if you do dat." They say, "Devil suck his teeth. Devil would foller you 'til you get to heaven's gate. He done mad now, he lost you. Suck his teeth, go back. Always suck his teeth when he lose a soul." **1922** Gonzales *Black Border* 329 **sSC, GA coasts** [Gullah glossary], *Suck me teet'*—and "suck 'e teet'"—a contemptuous gesture, frequently indulged in by the fair sex. **1928** *Decatur Herald* (IL) 29 Nov 4/1, [Serialized detective novel by S.S. Van Dine:] Heath sucked his teeth wonderingly. "I'm glad I don't run across many of her kind," he remarked. **1928** Peterkin *Scarlet Sister Mary* 287 **SC** [Gullah], You go let dat man what fooled you see how you forgot em [=him]. You go look em straight in de eye, suck you teeth at em, den walk off an' leave em. Walk off proudful. Strut. **1930** Stoney–Shelby *Black Genesis* 155 **seSC,** Cain suck he teet'. He set eye on Abel an' say, slow an' hard, "How you dare to put sich a name on yo' Pa an' you brudder before God?" **1977** Norman *Kinfolks* 3 **eKY,** "Wilgus Collier's my name. I don't have a middle name." The fat man shook his head and sucked his teeth. "Well," he said. "Either way, it's a poor out for a name." **1982** Walker *Color Purple* 45 **GA** [Black], She have the nerve to put one hand on her naked hip and bat her eyes at me. Then she suck her teef and roll her eyes at the ceiling while I wash her. **1988** Naylor *Mama Day* 182 **sSC, GA, coasts** [Black], "I hope you don't think I'm staying in all week to be baking." Cocoa sucks her teeth. "I hope you don't think I'd ask you," Miranda says. "It ain't no secret to anybody at this table the way you cook." **1997** (1998) Morrison *Paradise* 126 **OK** [Black], In the cab, the driver and his wife exchanged looks. Then the driver leaned out the window . . to holler at Sweetie's back, "You need some help?" Sweetie did not turn her head or acknowledge the offer. The couple looked at each other and sucked teeth as the husband shifted into drive. **2004** *DARE* File—Internet [Black], We never suck teeth when we see a black man with a white woman.

suck pool See **suck 1**

sucksand n Cf **suckhole 2**
Quicksand.
   1967–70 *DARE* (Qu. C11, *Soft, wet sand in streams or wet places, that draws people and things down into it*) Infs **SC**43, **VA**38, Sucksand. **2004** *DARE* File—Internet, Now, we'll limit this game to the small wooded area between here and the stream. . . I must warn you that a pool of suck-sand opened up in this area. *Ibid* **LA,** The blackest bog y'ever saw, . . carpeted in a black sludge that'd t'ooze up yer leg if ya stood in one place too long. An' that was the *safe* part t'walk in, coz the rest was all suck-sand.

suck spring See **suck 2**

suck teeth v phr See **suck one's teeth**

suck-teeth n [Cf *DJE, DCEU*] Cf **suck one's teeth**
An act of sucking one's teeth as a sign of disapproval or contempt; the sound made by such an act.
   2004 *DARE* File—Internet **NYC** [Black], The buxom woman, for all the bad eye and suck teeth she gave Puff Daddy next to her, was not really vocal enough to tell her friend to stop talking from his ass. *Ibid* **NYC** [Black], 'Well if it's so dumb why u watching it then?' *sista head turn w/suck teeth sound* Cuz it ain't nothin else on biatch.

sucky rag n Cf **sugar tit**
See quots.
   1993 Mason *Feather Crowns* 122 **KY** (as of c1900), "We'll have to make a sugar tit," said Alma. "Mittens said make a sucky rag," Amanda said. "Same thing," Alma said. **2002** *DARE* File—Internet **MA,** [Caption:] Zella's sucky rag. [*DARE* Ed: Photo shows infant sucking on what looks like a sock.]

sudden adj, adv, n Pronc-spp *sudd(e)nt, sudding, suddint* Similarly adv *sud(d)ently, suddingly* [Forms with final *-t* are widespread in Brit dial; cf also *sarmint* (at **sermon**). For *sudding(ly)* cf **-ing B1**]
Std senses, var forms.
   1675 in 1925 *AmSp* 1.146 **RI,** *Suddingly.* **1804** (1905) Lewis *Orig. Jrls. Lewis & Clark Exped.* 7.35, The Sand being Quick Vanquishd Suddently from Under her. **1835** (1927) Evans *Exped. Rocky Mts.* 14.198 **IN,** Sudently behind a log he heard a noise in the leaves. **1858** Hammett *Piney Woods Tavern* 122, Six on 'em was took with the disease all of a suddent. **1861** Holmes *Venner* 2.296 **NEng,** Sudding 'n' onexpected. **1894** Riley *Armazindy* 47 **IN,** Then come sudden, th'ough

the reeds / . . Them-air woods-hogs. **1897** Hay *Poems* 27 **IN,** I tries to tell him it would n't do,/ When suddingly Golyer growled. **1903** *DN* 2.332 **seMO,** *Suddenly.* **1907** *DN* 3.237 **nwAR,** *Suddenly.* **1909** *DN* 3.377 **eAL, wGA,** *Suddent. . . Suddenly. Often with like.* "She died sorter suddent-like." **1915** *DN* 4.191 **swVA,** *Suddenly.* **1922** Gonzales *Black Border* 329 **sSC, GA coasts** [Gullah glossary], *Sudd'nt*—sudden, suddenly. **1928** *AmSp* 3.404 **Ozarks** (as of 1916–27), Among consonants the letter *t* is always bobbing up in unexpected places. . . *Sudden* is always *suddint*. **1932** Randolph *Ozark Mt. Folks* 58, He allus fixed his stool so one leg was loose, an' then he could pull it out easy if he was t' want a good club right suddint. **1936** in 1952 Mathes *Tall Tales* 208 **sAppalachians,** Ye know he was allus takin' suddent notions. **1937** (1963) Hyatt *Kiverlid* 13 **KY,** All suddent she fetched a lunge and bolted clear out'n the road. **1944** *PADS* 2.21 **sAppalachians,** *Suddent(ly).* **1967** *Mt. Life* 43.1.15 **sAppalachians,** All of a suddent he come smack up to a big openin in the rock.

suds n pl, but sg or pl in constr

1 Beer. **widespread** Cf **foam 2**

1904 Hobart *I'm from MO* 52 **NJ,** Who . . hoists in a few dippers of suds? **1932** *AmSp* 7.436 [Stanford Univ expressions], Sometimes "tiger sweat" is substituted for whiskey, likewise "suds" for beer. **1942** *AmSp* 17.104 [Truck driver lingo], *Load of suds.* Beer truck. **1965** Bradford *Born with the Blues* 91 **Sth** [Black], I walked aroun' to the White Rose Bar & Grill, to get a nip and some cool suds. **1965–70** *DARE* (Qu. DD25, . . *Nicknames . . for beer*) 339 Infs, **widespread,** Suds; **CA**15, **NM**6, **NY**217, Bucket o' suds; **NY**52, Scuttle of suds; (Qu. DD21a) Inf **NY**52, Suds. **2004** *Milwaukee Jrl. Sentinel* (WI) 16 May Entree sec 1 (Internet), According to the Queer Eye guy, it will deliver a more pleasing experience than sipping suds from a Dixie cup.

2 in phr *in the suds:* In the thick of activity.

1833 *New Engl. Mag.* 5.81, I 'm almost afraid now we shall get to Downingville before this letter does, so that we shall be likely to catch you all in the suds before you think of it. [**1859** *Atlantic Mth.* 4.615 **RI,** I dunno how 'tis . . that Miss Coffin can allers be so forehanded with her work, an' do sich a master sight on't too. She don't never seem to be in the suds, Monday nor no time.] **1916** Macy-Hussey *Nantucket Scrap Basket* 136 **seMA,** *"In the Suds"*—In the thick of things, especially in a social way, as "oh, she's right in the suds."

suds intj See **suz**

suel See **sowel**

suelze n Usu |sul(t)s, 'sultsə|; for varr see quot 2005 Also *sul(t)z, sulze(r)* [Ger dial *sülze* brawn] **chiefly Ger settlement areas, esp WI** Cf **sylte**

Jellied pressed-meat; see quots.

1918 *Mansfield News* (OH) 8 Feb 12/3, *Sausages*—Pork sausage—Head cheese—Liver pudding—Pig-foot sulz—Blood sausage. **1920** Kander *Settlement Cook Book* 272 **WI,** *Jellied Veal (Sulz)* [Recipe includes veal shank, water, salt, pepper, carrot, celery root, onion]. . . let boil slowly until meat falls from bones. Strain the liquid. . . pour over the meat and vegetable mixture. Place in mould and set aside to cool and harden. **1940** Brown *Amer. Cooks* 916 **WI,** Suelze, or Jellied Veal. **1949** (1986) Leonard *Jewish Cookery* 207, *Pitcha* (Calf's Feet Jelly—also called *Sulze*). **1968** *DARE* (Qu. H43, *Foods made from parts of the head and inner organs of an animal*) Inf **WI**47, Suelze [suls]—German headcheese; **NY**49, Sulzer—German—made into loaf like headcheese; (Qu. H65, *Foreign foods favored by people around here*) Inf **WI**53, Sultz—German headcheese. **1971** *AmSp* 46.172 **Chicago IL,** 'Loaf of jellied pressed-meat made of flesh from the head of a hog' . . *Sülze* 3 [of 37 infs]. *Ibid* 177, *Sülze:* /'zultsə/ . . /'sɪlsə/ . . /sults/. [*DARE* Ed: First 2 infs German-Amer bilinguals; 3rd a German-Amer monolingual English speaker] **1976** *Sheboygan Press* (WI) 16 June 35/3, *Cold Cuts By The Slice or Pound.* . . Pork Loaf—Dutch Loaf . . Cotto Salami—Turkey Loaf . . Suelze. **1976** *Herald Times-Reporter* (Manitowoc WI) 1 Apr 2/5, I spent a great deal time . . making the traditional Polska Kielbasa at Easter time and sultz at the Christmas season. **1979** *Daily Herald* (Arlington Heights IL) 8 Mar sec 5 8/3, *Deli Counter.* . . Featuring . . Kiske—Homemade Sultz—Potato Sausage . . Pierogi. **2005** *DARE* File **WI,** One of the most common dishes to appear at family gatherings in my 1950s childhood was Sülz; it was still served at a family re-union last summer. Sülz—still pronounced often in the German way ['sultsə], but also commonly [sɪlts] or [sʌlts] and even ['sɪltsə] by some—consists of bits of meat in its own solidified jelly, often made in a loaf pan and served cold.

suffancified adj Also *cironcified, safoncified, seffancified, serancified, serfanciful, sorensified, suffonsified, surencified;* for addit varr see quots [Fanciful formations perh based on *sufficiently satisfied*]

Satisfied—usu in phr *my sufficiency is suffancified* and varr, used as a humorously exaggerated formula of politeness when refusing food, esp at a meal.

1947 *Lima News* (OH) 4 Aug 6/3, I'll be quite suffancified if you give the wheat a good rinsing in plain water. **1978** *DARE* File **nAL** (as of c1903), About 75 years ago I was visiting in the foothills of the Appalachians in North Alabama where I heard this word in general use. A dinner guest, when asked to have more food would sometimes say, "No thank you. I feel myself most highly cironchified." . . All the people in that area were of English and Scotch ancestry, had seen few outsiders, and most had never seen a black person. **1979** *NYT Article Letters* **IA** (as of a1940), My sufficiency is fancified; **neOH,** Safancified; **MT** (as of c1920), Saffonified; **KS,** Safoncified; **KS** (as of c1910), Suffonsified . . saponsified; **OH,** Sequancified; **IL** (as of a1900), Sequencified; **CT, MA, NY, OH, PA, WI,** Serancified; **IL, MI, PA, WI,** Serencified; **IL, MA,** Serensified; **PA,** Sufanciful; **MI,** Sufonsified; **IL,** Sufuncified. **1980** *AmSp* 55.295, I [=F.G. Cassidy] was asked by an elderly lady in West Virginia to explain the word *cironcified* (as she spelled it). . . The formulas typically fall into two parts . . , one part refusing more food, the other explaining the refusal. A common pattern is "My sufficiency is fully surancified; any more would be obnoxious to my fastidious taste." . . Variants have been sent me from nineteen states and three provinces of Canada. *Ibid* 296, Formally the variants fall into distinct groups. . . suffancified, suffencified, suffoncified, suffuncified, suffauncified, suffonified, seffancified, serfancified—suffanciful, serfanciful, so fanciful—surancified, surencified, surrossified—surquancified, surquencified—ferancified. . . The guest may be . . *prodigiously . . suffencified.* **1985** *WI Alumnus Letters* **seWI,** "I am sufficiently safancified and full clear up to my quiddy quoddy." It is used to refuse additional helpings of food at the end of a meal, or to express satisfaction with the meal. I learned this expression from my father. **1985** *ME Sunday Telegram* (Portland) 8 Dec sec A 40/2 **swME** (prob as of c1930), An expression . . pronounced with gusto (perhaps with overtones of regret) at the end of an evening meal: "My sufficiency is suffonsified!" [**1991** *DARE* File **swOH** (as of c1920), He heard her say while declining a dish, "My sufficiency is fanciful."] **1997** *Chattanooga Free Press* (TN) 14 Dec sec B 10 (Internet), A couple of weeks ago, someone commented on the impolite refusal of more food, "I'm stuffed." Two readers were instructed as to alternative responses. Say "No, thank you. I've had a plentiful sufficiency; any more would be a super-abundancy." (The second contains a word we cannot find, but may have been a made-up family word.) "My sufficiency is ?surrensified?; anything more would be obnoxious to my fastidious taste." **1998** *DARE* File **seWI** (as of c1980), My father used to say "My appetite has been surencified," meaning he had had enough to eat. My friend's uncle also said this. Both gentlemen lived on the German side of Milwaukee and worked in the central city. **2002** *Ibid,* A subscriber has written to ask about a puzzling bit of American dialect usage. Can anyone help?—It's from Virginia–North Carolina, an older generation, (maybe a hundred years back) and probably from the Appalachians. Three different older friends remember their grandmother's using it. It means "I'm full", "I've had plenty to eat". . . "My sufficiency is serrancified." **2003** *Ibid* **NE,** My mother . . might ask, "Are you fully sorensified?" Now her children have begun to answer other people who ask us, "Have you had enough to eat?", with, "Yes, I am feeling fully sorensified." **2004** *Ibid* **SC,** [At The Citadel:] All of my sufficiencies have been suffulsified and any further indulgence on my part may well prove to be super sanctimonious.

suffer v [*OED2 suffer* v. 11 "*Obs.* exc. *dial.*"]

To cause to suffer; to harm, mistreat.

1928 Peterkin *Scarlet Sister Mary* 300 **SC** [Gullah], You must be forgot how July done me, Auntie; how July suffered me. I done well to live. *Ibid* 325, Don' be f'aid, honey.—Death ain' gwine to suffer you. **1972** Jones-Hawes *Step it Down* 4 **eGA** [Black], When you get a child or a job, [Hawes: taking care of children] do like I used to do—don't *suffer* the little childrens. . . Treat them like you wish to be treated.

suffling n, adj Also *soofling* [Cf *EDD suffle* v. "*Obs.* Dev. To puff, blow; also to sob, sigh." Cf also *suff* var of *sough* (at *EDD sough* v.[1] 13) "To breathe heavily, esp in sleep; to pant, draw in the breath; to sigh, sob."]

See quot.

1904 Day *Kin o' Ktaadn* 11 **ME,** Moist sufflings of impatient cattle hint that "fodder-time" is at hand. *Ibid* 144, Ginger cookies and swagon stew and a sooflin' chorus spoonin'.

suffon(c)ified, suffonsified, suffulsified, suffuncified, sufonsified, sufuncified See **suffancified**

sug n |šŭg| Also sp *shoog, shug* [Abbrs for *sugar*] **Sth, S Midl**

Used as a term of address, an endearment, or a nickname; see quots.

1887 Kirkland *Zury* 17 **IL,** What 's th' matter, Shoog? Don't 'ee cry. **1935** *Peabody Jrl. Educ.* 13.10 **Sth,** Shug, short for sugar, and her visiting friend Mary L., pronounced as one word, were about six. **1960** Williams *Walk Egypt* 301 **GA,** Two soldiers walked by. "Hi, shug," she called. They grinned and walked on. **1967–70** *DARE* (Qu. AA3, *Nicknames or affectionate names for a sweetheart*) Infs **MO**3, **NC**77, **VA**69, Sug [šŭg]; **AL**34, Sug. **1982** Walker *Color Purple* 98 **Sth** [Black], Wake up Sugar, I say. They back. And Shug roll over . . and git out of the bed. **1989** Gurganus *Oldest Confederate Widow* 351 **Sth,** As they say, sug, it's all relative. Relatives especially. **1999** *DARE* File **NC,** Lunch . . was interesting—in part because of the waitress's form of address to her customers (perhaps only the female ones): "Sug"—as in the first part of "Sugar." **1999** in 2004 *DARE* File—Internet **NC,** Petitioner sometimes referred to others within his employment by such nicknames as "shoog", "baby doll", "honey", "pal", "sugar booger", "friend", "buddy", and "old buddy".

sugan n Usu |'sŭgən|; also |'sʊgən|; rarely |'sŭkən| Also sp *sogin, so-gun, soogan, soogum, sougan, suggan, sug(g)in* [Ir, Scots Engl *suggan* (< Ir, Scots Gael *súgán*) a rope of hay or straw; a collar or pad made of such rope; a bed cover. The last sense is appar known only from a single early 19th-cent Scots source. Perh this and **3** below come ultimately from a joc comparison of coarse cloth to something made of straw rope, but early evidence is lacking.]

1 A protective pad for a draft animal's neck or back. [Cf *Concise Ulster Dict. suggan* 2 "A straw horse-collar"; 5 "A protective straw pad on a horse's or donkey's back for carrying loads."]

1902 *DN* 2.245 **sIL,** Sogin ['sugɪn]. . . The pad under a horse collar to prevent chafing. **1952** Brown *NC Folkl.* 1.593 **nwNC,** Soogan. . . A kind of saddle used on an ox to transport objects on.

2 A coarse blanket, quilt, or comforter. **chiefly West, esp Rocky Mts, SW** See Map

[**1905** *Manitoba Morning Free Press* (Winnipeg) 9 Dec 17/4, We slept upon our sougans, after hours of riding hard,/ With our saddle for a pillow and our broncho for a guard.] **1907** White *AZ Nights* 72, Sitting cross-legged on his "so-gun" in the middle of the floor, he told us the following yarn. **1915** *DN* 4.245 **MT,** Soogan. . . Sheep herder's blanket. "When they move, they just roll up the soogan and are off." **1920** Hunter *Trail Drivers TX* 52 (as of 1882), The contents of the trunk were . . a pair of chaps . . one sugan, a hen-skin blanket. **1933** *AmSp* 8.1.31 **nwTX** [Ranch diction], *Sugin* (the "u" is pronounced as "oo" in *foot,* and the "g" is hard). A quilt or comforter. **1935** Sandoz *Jules* 115 **wNE** (as of 1880–1930), The next day the men slept between soogans in the haymow. **1939** FWP *ID Lore* 244, The following is reported as the talk of a southwest Idaho cowboy: In the mornun the night-herder rolls out of his soogan (bed-roll). **1939** (1973) FWP *Guide MT* 416, *Soogan*—Quilt, blanket. **1940** *AmSp* 15.211 **OK** [C.C.C. chatter], Among the boys from Oklahoma, a comfort or quilt was a *soogan*. **1941** Writers' Program *Guide WY* 465, *Sougan*—Originally small blanket of thick weave, used to keep out rain or cold. With coming of tarpaulin, the word came to mean any cheap or old worn blanket used on the trail. **c1955** Reed–Person *Ling. Atlas Pacific NW,* 1 inf, Soogums. **1958** *AmSp* 33.103 **Rocky Mts,** Sugan. . . ['sʊgən] or ['sugən]. *Ibid* 104 **NM,** My interviews . . take the word back to the 1880s and 1890s when every cowboy had a sugan. **1958** McCulloch *Woods Words* 174 **Pacific NW,** Soogan—A quilt or heavy blanket used in the days when loggers carried their own bed rolls. The soogan was generally cut square and many a logger almost went crazy switching it around and around in a dark bunkhouse trying to find the long end. **1959** *AmSp* 34.73, A few months ago I became acquainted with a number of warehousemen and truck drivers. The latter drive on long-distance runs, e.g., from Los Angeles to Seattle. Recently I heard one of them use *sugan.* I listened for a while until several of them had used it. They assured me that the word

was common, in their shoptalk, for a heavy, quilted wrapping for furniture in transit. One of them said he remembered hearing it first from an older driver when he first entered the occupation in 1928. **1966–67** *DARE* (Qu. E15, *The cloth that is put on top of a bed, mostly for decoration*) Inf **MT**3, Sugan [sugən]—bedroll; (Qu. E16, *A padded covering used on a bed, mostly for warmth*) Inf **MT**5, Quilt—called a sugan ['sugən]—early-day camp talk; **ID**4, Sugan [sugən]—heavy quilt used by lumberjacks in lumber camps; **ID**5, Sugan [sugən]—heavy quilts that loggers took to lumber camps; **SD**8, Sugan [sukən]; **TX**5, Sugan—central Texas—homemade quilt. **1969** Sorden *Lumberjack Lingo* 117 **NEng, Gt Lakes,** *Sougan* or *soogan*—A heavy blanket; name applied generally in the early days when the lumberjacks carried their own bedrolls. **1981** *KS Qrly.* 13.2.70 **nNV** [Cow camp lexicon], *Sougan* . . a quilted blanket, used as part of a bedroll.

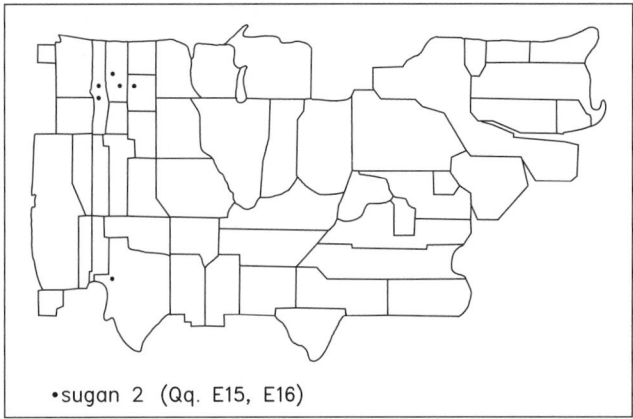

•*sugan* 2 (Qq. E15, E16)

3 also *suggin sack:* A coarse sack; a bag, pouch, or other container for carrying something; hence *suggin cloth* coarse bagging. **chiefly sAppalachians** Cf **soojet**

1904–07 in 2004 Montgomery–Hall *Dict. Smoky Mt. Engl.* 581 **sAppalachians,** Better put a ration in your suggin, Bob. **1913** Kephart *Highlanders* 75 **sAppalachians,** "Suggin" or "sujjit" (the *u* pronounced like *oo* in look) is true mountain dialect for a pouch, valise, or carryall. **1927** Mason *Lure Great Smokies* 98 **wNC, eTN,** There was not a vanity case among the effects of his 'woman' except perhaps a 'sugin' of bear-oil with which . . she anointed her hair. *Ibid* 156, The weapon's shot pouch . . contained . . a gourd for bullets, called a 'sugin.' **1938** in 1974 *Amer. Slave* 13.3.93 **neGA** (as of a1860), Suggin sacks was sewed together to make our mattress ticks and dem ticks was filled wid straw. . . Dem was coarse sacks sort of lak de guano sacks us uses now. *Ibid* 13.4.139 **neGA,** Mattresses were not much; they were made of suggin sacks filled with straw. . . Suggin cloth was made of coarse flax wove in a loom. **1952** Brown *NC Folkl.* 1.596, *Sug(g)an.* . . A bag-wallet. **1997** in 2004 Montgomery–Hall *Dict. Smoky Mt. Engl.* 581 **wNC,** *Suggin.* . . A pouch, carryall. **2003** in 2005 *DARE* File—Internet **PA,** When one went to the local mill, one brought ones [sic] own sturdy bags to be used—if one needed more bags the mill could sell, or in some cases give, cheaper, loosely woven bags—sugans. . . I understand that the suggins (meaning cheap, not well made bed coverings) that I find once in awhile in 'Western' books, particularly Texas, originates from the sugans of Pennsylvania. **2004** *DARE* File—Internet **sAppalachians,** My grandma . . who was raised up in the back of beyond and who wuz a growed up woman before she ever saw a motorcar . . would tell me the story of how they would carry thier sunday "go to meeting" shoes in thier suggin (sack/tote bag) and walk to church barefooted.

sugar n

1 also attrib: A **sugar maple;** hence *sugar wood* sugar maple trees (collectively); the wood of such trees. **esp Midl**

1809 Henry *Travels Indian Terr.* 69 **nMI** (as of c1763), A ridge . . is rocky and covered with the rock or sugar maple, or sugar wood. **1816** in 1916 *MD Hist. Mag.* 11.233, A sugar stump in the Corn which we Imagine nearly south. **1826** in 2004 *DARE* File—Internet **IN,** Where we built our new log cabin, it was a dense forest of beech, sugar, elm, ash, oak and hickory. **1838** in 1839 Plumbe *Sketches IA & WI* 62 **IA,** The prairies are generally . . surrounded with groves of . . sugar, lynn, walnut, &c. **1843** (1916) Hall *New Purchase* 226 **IN,** They goes fust and fassens their hossis to the swinging branch of that thare sugar west o' the place. **1879** *Globe* (Atchison KS) 2 Apr [2]/2 (newspaper-archive.com), [Advt:] You can get good sugar wood at the new wood yard on 3d st. **1883** in 2004 *DARE* File—Internet **OH,** The timber consisted of beech, sugar, elm, hickory, oak and other varieties. **1887** *Ft. Wayne Sentinel* (IN) 11 Jan [4]/5 (newspaperarchive.com), [Advt:] Hickory, beech and sugar wood at the Raccoon Coal and Wood Yards. **c1926** in 2004 *DARE* File—Internet **OH,** There is however but little woodland left on the farm, all the good timber,—sugar, ash and oak, as well as the beech, having been cut down and sold. **1937** *Mansfield News–Jrl.* (OH) 15 Jan 21/5, [Advt:] Beech, oak, ash, hickory, and sugar wood: chunk and fireplace.

2 also rarely *sugars; often with the:* **=sugar diabetes. chiefly east of Missip R** See Map

1965–70 *DARE* (Qu. BB48, *When a person has too much sugar in his blood and may have to take insulin for it . . he has _____*) 59 Infs, **esp east of Missip R,** Sugar; 11 Infs, **scattered,** The sugar; **MI**118, The sugars [Of all Infs responding to the question, 6% were Black; of those giving these responses, 13% were Black.]; (Qu. BB49, *. . Other kinds of diseases*) Inf **NJ**67, Sugar. **1967** *DARE* FW Addit **LA,** Sugar = diabetes. "I didn't know H_____ had sugar." **1982** Heat Moon *Blue Highways* 315 **nwNY,** Now we don't move so good, and I got the sugar. **1990** Cavender *Folk Med. Lexicon* 32 **sAppalachians,** *Sugar*—a diabetic condition: "My sugar has been acting up lately." **1999** Hodges *Tough Customers* 67 **sAppalachians,** It's just going to be . . one thing happening after another, now you got the sugar and all. **2000** *Diabetes Care* 23.332 **VA** [Black], Subjects who consider that they have the condition "sugar" differ in a variety of ways from those who believe they have diabetes or sugar-diabetes. Those with sugar were more likely to say that their condition was not serious and was curable, and were more likely to attribute it to a dietary cause. In addition, this group was older and less well educated than those who said they had diabetes or sugar-diabetes. **2003** *DARE* File **nwMS** [Black], When I was in Quitman County, Mississippi I heard black people there say *to have sugar* meaning to have diabetes, but I had never heard *sugar* used as a simple noun for diabetes. **2004** *Wall St. Jrl.* (NY NY) 10 Nov sec A 12 (Internet) **swPA,** "I was worried about Ed. He's got the sugar real bad," Mr. Van Dyke says.

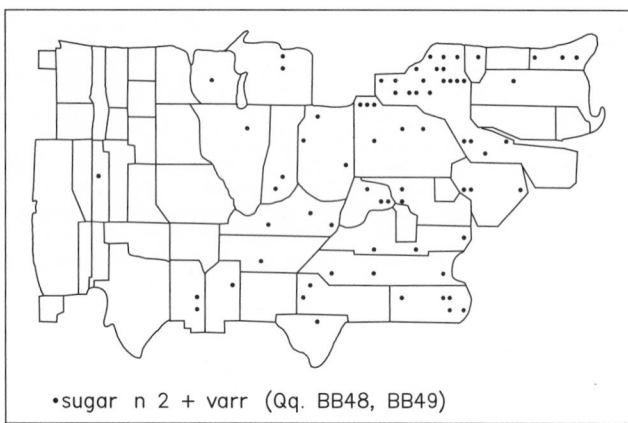

•sugar n 2 + varr (Qq. BB48, BB49)

3 Fig: affection demonstrated through hugs and kisses. **esp Sth, S Midl**

1920 in 2010 (acc) Lexis–Nexis Legal Research *State Case Law: GA* (Internet), He caught her by the arm, "mashed" her arm three times, leaned his face over close to hers, and said, "Give me some sugar." **1967** *DARE* FW Addit **AR**47, How about a little sugar?—way of asking for a kiss. **1983** Abbott *Womenfolks* 163 **AR,** If they wanted a hug from a child they commanded, "Give me some sugar." **1986** Pederson *LAGS Concordance (Kissing)* 1 inf, **cGA,** Give me some sugar; 1 inf, **cnGA,** Trying to get some sugar; 1 inf, **seMS,** Getting some sugar; 1 inf, **ceAR,** Give me some sugar—wouldn't say "give me a kiss." **2001** House *Clay's Quilt* 288 **eKY,** "Give Auntie some sugar," he told the baby. **2001** *DARE* File **cAL,** When I visited relatives in Birmingham I heard something new to me: *sugar* means kisses and hugs, especially from a child. For instance, people would say, "That child is so sweet—she's always giving her granny some sugar."

4 in phrr *too much sugar for a dime* (or *cent, nickel, penny*): Not worth the effort or expense; too much; too good to be true. **esp Sth** *old-fash*

1881 *Reno Eve. Gaz.* (NV) 17 June [3]/3 (newspaperarchive.com), *Too Much Sugar for a Cent.* C.R. Bacon, of the Mastodon Minstrels, visited the *Gazette* office today, to say that he thought of arranging a special train to Carson on Monday. . . [I]t would seem that the troupe might

have stopped here as well as at Carson. **1886** *Daily News* (Frederick MD) [14 May 4]/3 (newspaperarchive.com), We want a railroad it is true, but . . we don't intend to be taxed for anything and then have to pay to have our produce hauled on it; no indeed that's too much sugar for a cent. **1943** McAtee *Dial. Grant Co. IN Suppl. 2* 13 (as of 1890s), *Sugar for a cent,*" *"That's too much.* Saying meaning, "there must be a catch in it'*[.]* **1945** *Lima News* (OH) 1 Oct 1/3 **MO,** I've been nominated three times before for commander in chief [of the GAR]. . . Somebody else can have it. It's too much sugar for a penny. **1956** McAtee *Some Dialect NC* 44, *Sugar for a cent."* *"That's too much:* saying, meaning there must be a catch in the proposition. **1985** *DARE* File **Hattiesburg MS,** "It's too much sugar for a dime" means that it's more trouble than it's worth. **2001** in 2005 *DARE* File—Internet **MI,** I could probably anneal and recut the radius but that's too much sugar for a nickel! These things are "harder than a whores heart!" **2004** *News Courier* (Athens AL) 1 May (Internet), I wore out that little Rambler before I decided that [=working for three radio stations] was just too much sugar for a dime. **2005** *DARE* File—Internet **Sth,** I believe that last is just about too much sugar for a dime, as Mama would say. *Ibid,* Do you know of any "old sayings" that . . young people today might not know the meanings? Example: That is too much sugar for a dime (meaning that what seems like a bargain, may really be to lure you into a bad deal.) *Ibid, They* [=ancestors] *Said:* That's too much sugar for a nickel. *We Say:* That is too hard or to [sic] much trouble to do. *Ibid,* I recall my grandmother saying: "Now that's too much sugar for a dime!" Meaning something was too much effort for what you would get out of it.

sugar v, hence vbl n *sugaring* **chiefly NEast, esp VT**

To engage in the process of making syrup or sugar from maple sap.

1778 (1903) Patten *Diary* 380 **NH,** I went up to the boys where they was Shugaring but it was dull weather. **1864** in 2000 Phelps *Civil War Letters* 41 **VT,** It being some time since I have heard from you, but supposeing you were busy at home about this time of the year, geting ready for sugaring. **1890** Holley *Samantha among Brethren* 125 **NY,** Josiah promised that we would go [on a visit to some relatives] right away after sugerin'. **1947** *AmSp* 22.153 **wPA** [Maple syrup production vocab], *Sugaring.* The whole enterprise of sugar and sirup making. **1959** *VT Hist.* 27.161, *Sugaring. . .* The making of sugar by boiling down maple sap. **1966** *DARE* Tape **MA**5, [Aux Inf:] I sugared, I made sugar just thirty-nine years. . . at the last place where I sugared. **1982** Heat Moon *Blue Highways* 336 **NY,** I'm the fifth generation to sugar on this land. But the sixth generation, all nine of them, come out to help durin' the season. **1989** Mosher *Stranger* 62 **nVT** (as of 1952), We sugared-off the last batch of sap around noon, ate a quick lunch of beans laced with brand-new maple syrup, then gathered up the taps and sap buckets . . and stored them. . . Sugaring was over for another year. **1995** White *Sleeping* 103 **VT,** Dear Tina, I'm fine. I've been maple sugaring. Do you sugar? **2001** *Yankee* Mar 55 **VT,** Sugaring is over. The maple trees have quit working for the sap-gatherers and have begun working for themselves.

sugar ant n [*OED2* 1790 →] **scattered, but chiefly Sth, TX** See Map

An ant (*Monomorium pharaonis*) that is attracted to sugar.

[**1790** Royal Soc. London *Philos. Trans.* 80.346, The Sugar Ants, so called from their ruinous effects on the sugar-cane, first made their appearance in Grenada about twenty years ago.] **1930** (1935) Porter *Flowering Judas* 130 **TX,** Look here, daughter, how do ants get in this

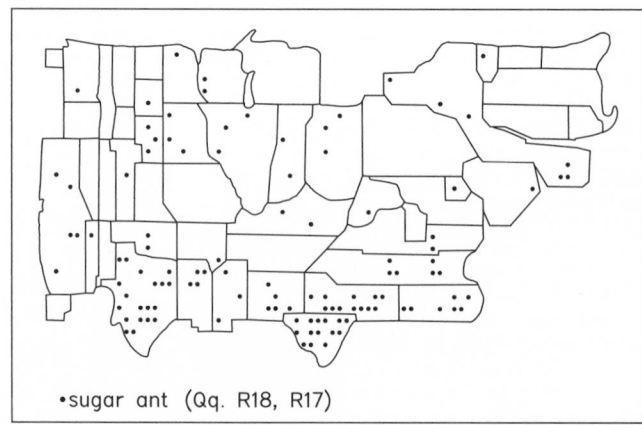

•sugar ant (Qq. R18, R17)

bed? I saw sugar ants yesterday. **1949** *PADS* 11.9 **TX,** *Pissant.* . . A small red ant. Also called *sugar ant.* **1950** *WELS,* 1 Inf, **seWI,** Sugar ant. **1965–70** *DARE* (Qu. R18, . . *Kinds of ants*) 109 Infs, **scattered, but chiefly Sth, TX,** Sugar ant; **OK**11, Sugar ant—little brown feller; **OK**52, Sugar ant . . very small and fast; **TX**39, Sugar ant—polite name for piss ants; (Qu. R17) Inf **TX**11, Sugar ant—small, tiny. **1995** Karr *Liars' Club* 95 **eTX,** The little red ants we called sugar ants were crawling over the glasses. **2004** TX Coop. Ext. *Dealing with Household Pests S. TX* (Internet), *Sugar Ants: Make Your Own Bait At Home.* . . The Sugar Ant and the Crazy Ant . . are especially prone to invading homes in San Antonio and South Texas.

sugar apple n

A **custard apple 1,** usu *Annona squamosa,* of southern Florida and the Keys.

[**1738** Royal Soc. London *Philos. Trans.* 40.347 **West Indies,** Some of these Fruits have, from their Taste, been called *Custard-apple, Sugar-apple,* and *Sour-sops.*] **1837** (1962) Williams *Territory FL* 113, The sugar apple and custard apple grows perfectly well, about the capes, and keys of the southern district. **1933** Small *Manual SE Flora* 533 **seFL,** *A[nnona] squamosa.* . . Sugar-apple. Sweet-sop. . . Hammocks, Florida Keys. **1939** FWP *Guide FL* 327 **seFL,** All Florida fruits grow on the keys. . . Rarer fruits include the spherical roseapple; . . and sugar apples, sweet and custardlike. **1964** Will *Hist. Okeechobee* 35 **FL,** The Anona family of tropical trees includes those with such tasty fruits as Sugar Apple (Anona Squamosa). **1966** *DARE* Tape **FL**23, We have another tropical fruit known as the sugar apple. It's of the soursap family, but more delicate in flavor and quite sweet. It needs no sweetening and can be eaten. In the inside are plugs with black seeds too, but this can be eaten with a spoon. **2008** *DARE* File—Internet **swFL,** *The Sugar Apple* . . *Annona Squamosa*—Have you ever been lucky enough to enjoy a sugar apple? . . They look like WWII knobby hand grenades.

sugar ash n [Because the sap yields sugar]

=**box elder.**

1897 Sudworth *Arborescent Flora* 291 **FL,** *Acer negundo.* . . Common Names. . . Sugar Ash. **1950** Peattie *Nat. Hist. Trees* 472, Box Elder. . . Other Names: Ash-leaved or Manitoba Maple. Sugar Ash. [*Ibid* 474, Odd as it sounds to easterners, the Box Elder yields a sugar, not despised even today by Middle Western farmers.]

sugar bass n

A **rock bass 2** (here: *Paralabrax nebulifer*).

1953 Roedel *Common Fishes CA* 74, Sand Bass—*Paralabrax nebulifer.* . . Unauthorized Names: Ground bass, sugar bass. **2000** in 2004 *DARE* File—Internet **CA,** We also caught a whole mess of shallow water rockfish while we were at it, including chucklehead, sugar bass, and chocolate bass.

sugarberry n

1 A **hackberry**; see quots. **chiefly Midl, S Atl** Cf **sugar hackberry, ~ nut**

1797 Smith *Nat. Hist. GA* 1.71, Taken feeding on the Sugar-berry or Hack-berry. **1818** Barton *Compendium Florae Philadelphicae* 1.151 **swNJ,** *Celtis.* . . *occidentalis.* . . *Sugar-berry Tree. American Nettle Tree.* **1830** Rafinesque *Med. Flora* 2.206 **Sth,** *Celtis* [spp]. . . *Nettle tree, Hackberry* in the West, *Sugar-berry tree* in the South. **1869** *Amer. Naturalist* 3.407 **MT,** Western Sugar-berry (*Celtis reticulata* [=*C. laevigata* var *r.*]) . . grows only about thirty feet high, with a short trunk sometimes a foot thick. **1883** *Century Illustr. Mag.* Mar 676 **NY,** It is plain why the sugar-berry tree *(Celtis)* holds its drupes all winter: it is in order that the birds may come and sow the seed. **1899** (1912) Green *VA Folk-Speech* 428, *Sugar-berry.* . . Same as hackberry. **1908** Rogers *Tree Book* 236, Hackberry, Nettle Tree, Sugar Berry (*Celtis occidentalis*). *Ibid* 237, The little axillary sugar berries. . . are the delight of birds throughout hard winters. **1965–70** *DARE* (Qu. T13, . . *Names* . . *for* . . *hackberry*) 28 Infs, **chiefly Midl, S Atl,** Sugarberry; (Qu. T16, . . *Kinds of trees* . . *'special'*) Infs **SC**63, **TX**11, Sugarberry; **GA**53, Sugarberry tree; (Qu. I44, *What kinds of berries grow wild around here?*) Inf **SC**46, Sugarberries; (Qu. I46, . . *Kinds of fruits that grow wild around here*) Inf **PA**242, Sugarberry. [*DARE* Ed: Some of these Infs may refer instead to other senses below.] **1979** Little *Checklist U.S. Trees* 80, *Celtis laevigata* . . *sugarberry.* . . Other common names—sugar hackberry, . . Texas sugarberry [etc]. **1986** Pederson *LAGS Concordance* **Gulf Region,** 4 infs, Sugarberry (-ies); 1 inf, Sugarberry tree.

2 A **serviceberry** (here: *Amelanchier canadensis*). Cf **sugar pear, ~ plum 1**

1855 [see **sugar pear**]. **1893** *Jrl. Amer. Folkl.* 6.141 **NH,** *Amelanchier Canadensis* . . sugar-plum. Vt. sugar pear. Orono, Me. Sugar berry.

N. Woodstock, N.H. **1966** *DARE* (Qu. T13) Inf **ME**5, Sugarberry—might be wild pear.

3 A **wintergreen 2** (here: *Gaultheria hispidula*). Cf **sugar plum 2**

1897 *Jrl. Amer. Folkl.* 10.49, *Chiogenes serpyllifolia* [=*Gaultheria hispidula*]. . . sugar-berry.

4 A **lowbush blueberry** (here: *Vaccinium angustifolium*). Cf **sugar blueberry, ~ huckleberry**

1867 De Voe *Market Asst.* 393 **NYC,** Another better variety of the *low-bush,* known as the "sugar-berry," being quite sweet, of a bluish coat, or like a coat of flour dusted over them, and with very small seeds. **1945** *Brittonia* 5.231, *Vaccinium angustifolium.* . . This is the common commercial blueberry, or sugarberry, harvested extensively in the northeastern States.

5 =**anaqua.**

1960 Vines *Trees SW* 883, Anaqua. . . Other vernacular names are . . Knackaway, Nockaway, Sugarberry [etc]. **1986** Pederson *LAGS Concordance,* 1 inf, **csTX,** Sugarberry tree—anaqua, white blooms. **1999** in 2004 *DARE* File—Internet **TX,** The trees here were loaded with berries. . . Later we were told that these were Anaqua (Sugarberry) Trees.

6 See quots.

1967–70 *DARE* (Qu. T13) Inf **AL**25, Sugarberry—I thought [it] was an oak tree; **SC**67, Sugarberry—belongs to oak family; sugarstone—dark red berry—alternate name.

sugar birch n

=**sweet birch 1.**

1743 (1751) Bartram *Observations* 27 **PA,** The timber was sugar birch, sugar maples, oak and poplar. **2004** *DARE* File—Internet, The eastern North American tree *Betula lenta,* known variously as sweet birch, black birch, cherry birch, sugar birch [etc].

sugarbird n

1 =**evening grosbeak.**

[**1834** Nuttall *Manual Ornith.* 2.594, Evening Grosbeak. . . This very brilliant and remarkable bird is a common inhabitant of the maple groves which occupy the plains of the Saskatchewan; and hence arises its common aboriginal Cree name of the Sugar-Bird (*Seesebasquit-pethaysish*).] **1917** (1923) *Birds Amer.* 3.2, Evening Grosbeak. . . Other Names.—Sugar Bird; American Hawfinch.

2 The tufted **titmouse** (*Baeolophus bicolor*).

1949 Hadley *Indiana Birds* 43 *(DA),* The tufted titmouse. . . is sometimes called Tom tit also sugar bird and Peter bird. **1951** *AmSp* 26.277 **IN, OH, WV,** Because they are most heard during the season of tapping maples and making tree sugar, the wood wren is named *sugar bird* in West Virginia as is the tufted titmouse also in that state, Ohio, and Indiana.

3 =**house wren 1.**

1951 [see **2** above].

sugar blueberry n

A **lowbush blueberry** (here: *Vaccinium angustifolium*). Cf **sugarberry 4**

1900 Lyons *Plant Names* 386, *V[accinium] Pennsylvanicum* [=*V. angustifolium*]. . . Dwarf, Low-bush or Sugar Blueberry. **1939** Medsger *Edible Wild Plants* 72, Dwarf, Sugar, or Early Sweet Blueberry. . . *Vaccinium angustifolium.* **1952** Blackburn *Trees* 291, *V[accinium] angustifolium.* . . Low sugar blueberry.

sugar bone n

See quots.

1967 *DARE* (Qu. X33, *The place in the elbow that gives you a strange feeling if you hit it against something*) Inf **AL**33, Sugar bone. **1986** Pederson *LAGS Concordance,* 1 inf, **cwGA,** Sugar bone = Adam's apple.

sugar-booger n Also *sugar-bugger* **esp Sth** Cf **bookie-sug**

A sweetheart; also used as a nickname for a sweetheart or as a term of endearment.

1941 Faherty *Big Old Sun* 110 **FL,** [He] tiptoed behind her and pinched her fat upper arm. . . "Don't get gay, sugar booger," she called back. **1976** Garber *Mountain-ese* 88 **sAppalachians,** *Sugar-bugger* . . sweetheart—Jamie took his little sugar-bugger and went to the movin' pitcher show. **1989** *Chron.-Telegram* (Elyria OH) 21 Oct 12/5, [Personal advt:] *Shag*—I love you more each day. *Sugar booger.* **1999** [see **sug**]. **2004** *DARE* File—Internet **TX,** To celebrate this modern love festival with wine, you and your sugar bugger have plenty of choices.

sugar bowl(s) n   **chiefly Pacific NW**

A **virgin's bower,** usu *Clematis hirsutissima.*

   1937 St. John *Flora SE WA & ID* 151, *Clematis hirsutissima . . Sugar Bowls. . .* The leaves taste like strychnine.   **1966** *DARE* (Qu. S23, *Pale blue flowers with downy leaves and cups that come up on open, stony hillsides in March or early April*) Inf **WA**3, Sugar bowl—tends towards lavender, maybe not so early.   **1966–67** *DARE* Wildfl QR Pl.74 [=*Viorna* [=*Clematis*] *ochroleuca*] Infs **OR**12, **WA**10, 15, Sugar bowl(s).   **1979** Spellenberg *Audubon Guide N. Amer. Wildflowers W. Region* 709, Vase Flower; Sugar Bowls; Leather Flower *(Clematis hirsutissima).*   **1990** *Plants SW* (Catalog) 94, *Clematis hirsutissima*—Sugarbowls—Deep purple flowers nod on erect, herbaceous perennials 2 ft. tall.

sugar bread n   **esp S Midl**

=**sweet bread 2.**

   1926 Roberts *Time of Man* 167 **KY,** They sat by the fire during the evening eating the sugar bread that Nellie had baked.   **1936** *AmSp* 11.317 **Ozarks,** *Sugar-bread. . .* Cake.   **1997** in 2004 Montgomery-Hall *Dict. Smoky Mt. Engl.* 580 **wNC,** *Sugar bread. . .* Same as *sweet bread 1.* [*Ibid* 586, *Sweet bread . . 1* A baked good . . that is sweetened, often with molasses.]

sugar bucket   See **bucket 2c**

sugar bug n

=**whirligig beetle.**

   1941 *Nature Mag.* Mar 138 **MD,** Among other characteristics of the whirligig beetle is that of emitting, when handled, an odor that is considered pleasant or the reverse, depending upon the perception of the observer. Those finding it agreeable have been the most vocal for they have called the insects sugar bugs (Maryland), apple bugs (New Jersey, Maryland, Indiana), and mellow bugs (Alabama).

sugar-bugger   See **sugar-booger**

sugar bush n

1 =**maple orchard.** [bush n[1] **B1c** < Du *bos* forest]   **chiefly wNEng, Upstate NY, Gt Lakes**   See Map   Cf **maple bush, sugar wood 2**

   c1755 in 1929 *AmSp* 5.166 **eNY,** Sugarbush.   **1823** Cooper *Pioneers* 2.7 **cNY,** We will stop and see the 'sugar bush' of Billy Kirby.   **1842** Kirkland *Forest Life* 2.206 **MI,** A sugar-bush means from two hundred to a thousand maple-trees, grouped here and there within the circuit of a mile or so.   **1890** Holley *Samantha among Brethren* 183 **NY,** He has got . . a big sugar bush, over 1100 trees, and a nice little sugar house.   **1923** *DN* 5.237 **swWI,** *Sugar bush. . .* A grove of sugar maples.   **1947** *AmSp* 22.152 **wPA** [Maple syrup production vocab], *Sugar bush.* A grove or small forest of maples set aside for the production of sirup.   **1959** [see **sugar wood 2**].   **1965** Teale *Wandering Through Winter* 292 **VT,** In a sugarbush of a hundred trees . . there is as wide a difference in the quantity and quality of the sap produced as among that number of cows in regard to the milk they yield.   **1965–70** *DARE* (Qu. T4, *The place where . . trees grow together and sap is gathered*) 120 Infs, **chiefly wNEng, Upstate NY, Gt Lakes,** Sugar bush.   **1968** Pochmann *Triple Ridge* 80 **cWI,** Most sugarbush farmers now use only plastic tubes.   **1982** *Greenfield Recorder* (MA) 20 Mar sec A 4/1, Do native New Englanders all say "sugar orchard?" "Sugar bush" has crept in these later years, but I don't like it.   **2001** *DARE* File **cVT,** Terms such as *sugar bush* (referring to the stand of rock (hard) maple trees groomed

for that purpose) and *sugar house* (the usually rough hewn building housing the evaporator and other equipment) are most common in Central Vermont.

2 also *sugar sumac:* A southwestern **sumac B** (here: *Rhus ovata*).

   1900 *West Amer. Scientist* Sept 61 **sCA,** *Rhus ovata. . .* The Sugarbush is a handsome evergreen shrub.   **1910** Jepson *Silva CA* 28, Sour Berry *(Rhus integrifolia),* Sugar Bush *(Rhus ovata)* are southern shrubs sometimes arborescent.   **1938** Van Dersal *Native Woody Plants* 230, *Rhus ovata. . . Sugar sumac. . .* A large evergreen shrub.   **1962** Balls *Early Uses CA Plants* 43, The ripe berries of the Sugar Bush, *Rhus ovata . .* are coated with a sour-sweet, sticky substance which both the Indians and the early settlers enjoyed when stirred into water and cooled.   **1975** Lamb *Woody Plants SW* 146 **sCA,** Sugar sumac, also called sugar bush in southern California, is a small, compact, rounded shrub.   **2004** *DARE* File—Internet **CA,** Since Sugar bush is usually a little slow out of the ground, we'll inter-plant with Ceanothus.

sugar camp n   **chiefly N Cent, WV, wPA**   See Map   Cf **camp 2, maple camp, sugar place, sugary, syrup camp**

The place in or near a grove of maple trees where the facilities for the production of syrup or sugar are located; a grove of maple trees from which maple sap is collected.

   1779 (1903) Patten *Diary* 400 **NH,** I went to our shugar Camp.   **1818** in 2004 *DARE* File—Internet **nwPA,** Mr. Moore working at sugar camp, gathered 100 buckets of sap.   **1869** *Harper's New Mth. Mag.* 39.847 **OH,** Widow Holden's sugar-camp made a sorry appearance in contrast with ours, we thought. In place of our huge iron kettles she had a tea-kettle and two small brass pots in which to boil the sap.   **1871** [see **sugar orchard**].   **1901** *DN* 2.149 **OH,** *Sugar-camp. . .* The same as sugar-bush.   **1915** *DN* 4.191 **swVA,** *Sugar camp. . .* An orchard of sugar maples.   **1916** *Ft. Wayne News* (IN) [10 Apr] 9/8 (newspaperarchive.com) **wPA,** To those of us who wrought in the sugar camp, as it was commonly called in this section, or sugar bush as it was termed in New England and the western reserve, these are the days of sweet memories.   **1947** *AmSp* 22.153 **wPA** [Maple syrup production vocab], *Sugar camp.* The locality and all facilities for producing sirup; including *grove, boiling house,* etc.   **1949** Kurath *Word Geog.* 76, *(Sugar) maple grove. . .* In Western Pennsylvania, northern West Virginia, and adjoining parts of Ohio *sugar camp . .* [is] common.   **1965–70** *DARE* (Qu. T4, *The place where . . trees grow together and sap is gathered*) 52 Infs, **chiefly N Cent, WV, wPA,** Sugar camp.   **1966** Dakin *Dial. Vocab. Ohio R. Valley* 2.415, *Maple grove. . . Sugar camp* is very common in Ohio, about as common as *sugar grove* in Indiana, and more common than the latter in Illinois. In Kentucky *sugar camp* is the most common usage between the Mountains and the Green-Barren River. . . [S]ome speakers use *sugar camp* to make a secondary differentiation. This term is used by these speakers only as a name for the place—building(s), etc.— where the sap is brought to be boiled until it becomes maple syrup or maple sugar. It frequently is not, therefore, an exact synonym for . . terms which refer primarily to the stand of sugar maple trees as the place where the sweet sap is collected.   **1982** Powers *Cataloochee* 318 **cwNC** (as of a1940), Neil Sutton had made wooden piggins to catch maple sap out of his sugar camp in Little Cataloochee.   **2004** *Washington Post* (DC) 14 Mar Travel sec 2 (Internet), The few . . and the proud . . of Highland County, Va., expect up to 50,000 people at the Maple Festival. On March 20–21, see syrup tapped right from the tree at five sugar camps.

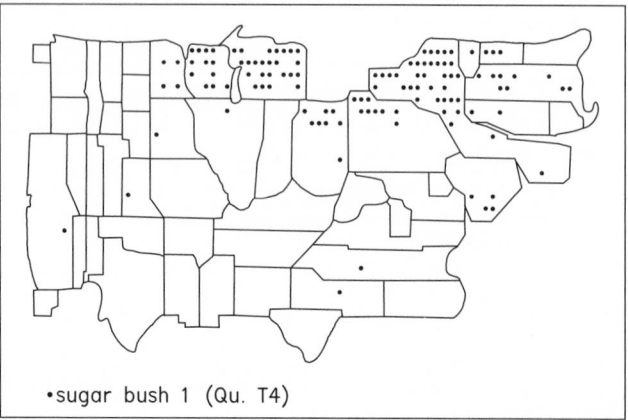

•sugar bush 1 (Qu. T4)

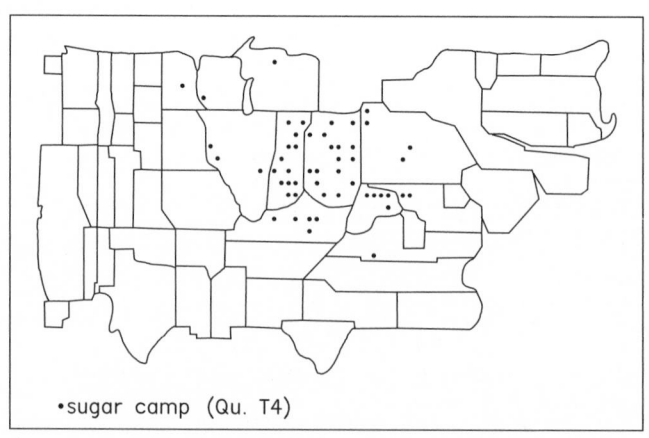

•sugar camp (Qu. T4)

sugar corn n   scattered, but esp C Atl   See Map   Cf **butter and sugar corn, sweet ~**

A var of **Indian corn 1** (here: *Zea mays* var *rugosa*) used as table corn.

1831 *Star* (Gettysburg PA) [12 July 4]/1 (newspaperarchive.com), He planted some of the red cob Tuskarora . . in rows with the largest eared white cob sugar corn he could find.   **1847** *De Bow's Rev.* 4.240 **VA,** There is a variety of Indian Corn produced in the United States, according to Mr. Browne, viz. . . Virginia white gourd seed; early sweet or sugar Corn, or Pappoon Corn.   **1849** Howitt *Our Cousins in OH* 77, Willie assisted his father in planting sweet corn, or sugar corn, in the garden.   **1870** *Harper's New Mth. Mag.* 40.315, In this village [near Portland ME] is located one of the numerous corn-packing establishments . . , which employs all of the available "help" of the locality in canning that delicious article known to the world over as "Yarmouth Sugar Corn."   **1871** (1874) Terhune *Common Sense* 233 **VA,** Boiled Green Corn. Choose young sugar-corn, full grown, but not hard.   **1931** Randolph *Ozarks* 20, They et up ever' last stalk o' sugar-corn even.   **1938** Stuart *Dark Hills* 207 **eKY,** It's that little early sugar corn.   **1941** *LANE* Map 261 *(Sweet corn)* 3 infs, **NH, RI, VT,** Sugar corn.   **1947** *News* (Frederick MD) 26 Aug 1/1, The Japanese beetle has made a "big difference" in the county's sugar corn crop this summer, one canner said today.   **1956** *DE Folkl. Bulletin* 1.24, Pull sugar (*i.e.,* sweet) corn.   **1961** *Press–Gaz.* (Hillsboro OH) 4 Aug 8 (newspaperarchive.com), [Advt:] Home Grown *Sugar Corn* 49c Dozen.   **1965–70** *DARE* (Qu. I33, . . *Ears of corn that are just right for eating*) Infs **NJ56, OH76, PA171, VA33, 74, 78, 108,** Sugar corn; **DE1,** Sugar corn [FW: It is also common to see this on advertisements in grocery stores.]; **MD19,** Sugar corn—same as sweet corn; **VA9,** Eating corn, sugar corn; (Qu. I34, *If you don't have sweet corn, you can always eat young _____*) Inf **TN20,** Sugar corn; (Qu. L34, . . *Most important crops grown around here*) Infs **FL4, NJ22,** Sugar corn.   **1986** Pederson *LAGS Concordance,* 5 infs, **GA, TX,** Sugar corn; 1 inf, **TN,** Some still say sugar corn.

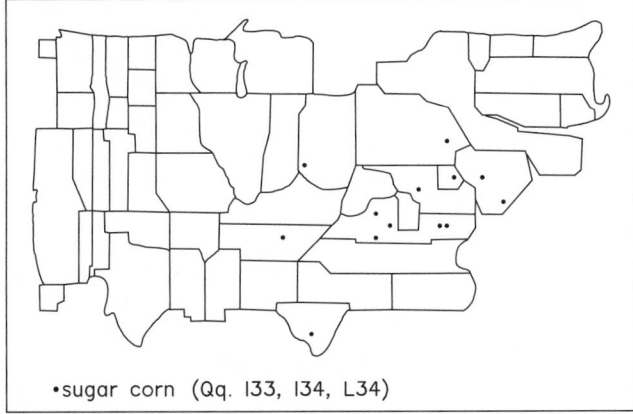

•sugar corn (Qq. I33, I34, L34)

sugar cream pie n   Also *Hoosier sugar cream pie, Indiana (sugar) cream pie*   esp **IN, OH**

A pie in which the principal ingredients are sugar and cream; see quots.

1937 *Logansport Press* (IN) 4 Nov 2/2, Home Tested Recipe—Sugar Cream Pie [Recipe includes sugar, flour, milk, butter, cream, salt, nutmeg or vanilla.]   **1954** *Van Wert Times–Bulletin* (OH) 9 Sept 2/1, [Advt:] Old Fashion Sugar Cream Pie 57c each.   **1959** *Mansfield News–Jrl.* (OH) 6 Apr 5/1, Perhaps this is the old-fashioned cream pie recipe Mrs. J.W.J. is trying to find. *Sugar Cream Pie.* [Recipe includes sugar, flour, heavy cream.]   **1968** Kellner *Aunt Serena* 101 **cIN** (as of c1920), Clara Peters was going to take sugar-cream pies to the church social.   **1969** *DARE* (Qu. H63, *Kinds of desserts*) Inf **IN66,** Sugar cream pie.   **2003** *DARE* File—Internet, I grew up in the Hoosier State. . . outside of Indianapolis. . . no one I meet seems to know what Euchre, Sugar Cream Pie or Detassling Corn are unless they are from Indiana. . . I can't believe you [=a correspondent from sIN] don't know what euchre and sugar cream pie are!   **2004** *Ibid, Sugar Cream Pie* . . or Hoosier sugar cream pie, Indiana cream pie. . . The recipe originated in Indiana with the Shaker community in the 1850s as a great pie recipe when the apple bins were empty.   **2005** *Ibid, Peeper Pie (aka Sugar Cream Pie).* . . This super easy, and oh-so-yummy dessert was introduced to me . . by my Indiana-born husband and his family. *Ibid,* Indiana Sugar Cream Pie.   **2005** *DARE* File **cnIN** (as of 1940s), I first had sugar cream pie in

a diner in Kokomo. . . It's not like a custard or pudding pie; there are no eggs in it. It sets up some but is quite runny. . . [Ingredients: sugar, flour, corn syrup, cream, and melted butter.]

sugar crowder   See **crowder**

sugar day n

A day of **sugar weather.**

1839 Ware *Sketches* 137 **eTN** (as of 1787), It was what people called a good sugar day; and Mrs. Carter . . chose to stay at home for the purpose of making sugar.   **1849** Howitt *Our Cousins in OH* 40, The days became warm and bright, although the nights were still cold and frosty. These were called "sugar days," and people who had sugar camps or woods of sugar-maple were now busied night and day in the manufacture of the delicious maple-sugar.   **1878** *St. Joseph Traveler & Herald* (MI) [27 Apr 4]/3 (newspaperarchive.com) **VT,** Then they must, if a "sugar day" comes, go over the whole labor, if the hole where the sap [sic] was driven in has become seared.   **1898** *N. Adams Transcript* (MA) [2 Apr] 8/3 (newspaperarchive.com), Contrary to general opinion, good sugar weather has been scarce this year. There were a few good sugar days last month, but for the most part there has not been enough change in temperature between night and day for a good flow of sap.   **2001** *Herald* (Randolph VT) 8 May (Internet), Town meeting day has long been the traditional beginning, even though there have been some earlier sugar days in recent years.

sugar diabetes n   [Lat *diabetes mellitus* sweet diabetes]   *esp freq among rural speakers and those with little formal educ*   Also called **sugar** n 2, **~ disease, sweet blood, ~ diabetes**   Cf *DS* BB48

Diabetes.

1862 *Indiana Democrat* (PA) 13 Nov 4/3, In February, 1861, I was afflicted with the sugar diabetes.   **1939** in Lib. of Congress *Amer. Memory: WPA Life Hist.* (Internet) **MA,** He worka hard for many years. Then he geta sick with whata de doctor call-ed sugar diabetes.   **1965–70** *DARE* (Qu. BB48, *When a person has too much sugar in his blood and may have to take insulin for it . . he has _____*) 115 Infs, **widespread,** Sugar diabetes [Of all Infs responding to the question, 68% were comm type 4 or 5, 29% gs educ or less; of those giving this response, 79% were comm type 4 or 5, 44% gs educ or less.]; (Qu. BB49, . . *Other kinds of diseases*) Inf **MO37,** Sugar diabetes; (Qu. DD24, . . *Diseases . . from . . drinking*) Inf **MO18,** Sugar diabetes.   **1986** Pederson *LAGS Concordance,* 4 infs, **LA, MS, TN,** Sugar diabetes.   **2000** [see **sugar** n 2].

sugar disease n

=**sugar diabetes.**

1870 *W. Homoeopathic Observer* 152 **IL,** Her medical advisers diagnosed the sugar disease.   **1914** *Indianapolis Star* (IN) 29 July 6/6, Diabetes, or sugar disease . . is recognized when doctors find sugar to pass out in the kidney fluids.   **1966–69** *DARE* (Qu. BB48, *When a person has too much sugar in his blood and may have to take insulin for it . . he has _____*) Infs **IL46, MA6, MI108,** Sugar disease. [All Infs old]   **2004** *Columbus Dispatch* (OH) 15 June sec A 7 (Internet), Banting and Best had no idea when they discovered insulin how many consequences of "the sugar disease" would arise.

sugar-drip (liquor)   See **sugar whiskey**

sugar eat n   esp **MA**

=**sugar supper.**

1859 G.K. Wilder *Diary* (MS) 7 April *(DA),* I was invited to a party, a sugar eat.   **1871** *Titusville Morning Herald* (PA) 15 Mar [3]/7 (newspaperarchive.com), Grand "Sugar Eat" and Dance.   **1938** *Chron.–Telegram* (Elyria OH) 19 Apr 4/6, Penfield Grange meets . . at 8 P.M. A warm sugar eat will be enjoyed.   **1939** in Lib. of Congress *Amer. Memory: WPA Life Hist.* (Internet) **wMA,** Did you ever go to a sugar eat? . . Well we usually hold the sugar eat at the church. . . Folks get a plate full of snow and then the wax is ladled out of the bi'lers on to the snow and when it hardens a might, you eat it.   **1959** *Berkshire Eagle* (Pittsfield MA) 1 Apr 27/5, The Grange plans a sugar eat following its regular business meeting tomorrow. . . Those attending should bring flat pans for the sugar.   **1969** *DARE* (Qu. FF1, . . *A kind of group meeting called a 'social' or 'sociable'*) Inf **MA58,** Sugar eat.   **1988** Palmer *Lang. W. Cent. MA* 39, *Sugar eat.* . . We took a pan and got good, fresh snow and packed it down. Then we would pour some hot, syrupy maple sugar all over it and let it harden good. Usually you had to have crackers and often, sour pickles with it so you could eat a little more. That's a part of every winter.

sugared liquor See **sugar whiskey**

sugar foot n

1 freq cap; also *Sugarfoots:* Used as a name or nickname; see quots. **esp Sth, West**

1872 Twain *Roughing It* 344 **NV,** It seemed local and meagre when contrasted with the fame of such men as . . Sugarfoot Mike . . Six-fingered Pete, etc., etc. **1878** Hart *Sazerac Lying Club* 161 **NV,** "Smith?" said the boy, "which Smith do you want? . . there's Big Smith and Little Smith, Three-fingered Smith, Bottle-nose Smith . . Sugar-foot Smith . . Hungry Smith, and I don't know maybe one or two more." **1880** *Bismarck Tribune* (ND) 25 June 2/1 **CA,** There was at that time a noted desperado known as Sugar Foot. **1939** in Lib. of Congress *Amer. Memory: WPA Life Hist.* (Internet) **FL** [Black], "Bye Sugarfoots," he calls to Roberta as we drive away. **1966** Barnes–Jensen *Dict. UT Slang* 41, *Sugar foot:* . . a name used for a good man rather wild in nature. **1966** *Coshocton Tribune* (OH) 27 Feb Comics sec 1/3, [*Dick Tracy* comic strip:] Hello, Baby Doll. This is Sugar Foot. **1967–70** *DARE* (Qu. AA3, *Nicknames or affectionate names for a sweetheart*) Infs **GA**77, **SC**32, Sugar foot; (Qu. HH15, *A very inexperienced person*) Inf **TN**65, Sugar foot. **1984** Burns *Cold Sassy* 104 **nGA** (as of 1906), Mama sat me down for a talking-to. "Now, sugarfoot, you got to get something straight," she began. **1986** Pederson *LAGS Concordance* (*I must ask [my husband]*) 1 inf, **cwFL,** Sugar Foot—has heard this; 1 inf, **cwGA,** Sugar Foot—girl friend; 1 inf, **cTN,** Sugar Foot—informant's nickname.

2 A dance; see quots; hence vbl n *sugar-footing.* **esp MD**

1933 *Sun* (Baltimore MD) 4 Aug 10/7, Each of the youngsters were . . employing a step which must have originated on the upper Zambezi. It is locally called the "sugar-foot," and seems to consist in a stamp and shuffle of violence almost incredible even on a cool night. . . The beer-garden management has posted a warning: "No sugar-footing on Saturday and Sunday." **1937** *Frederick Post* (MD) 1 Oct 4/4, In the south, the "Shag" is known as "The Sugar Foot". **1938** *Sun* (Baltimore MD) 24 June 4/3, The Virginia reel, the shag, the sugarfoot and trucking predominate on the dance program arranged by the student sponsors. **1968** *DARE* (Qu. FF5a, . . *Different steps and figures in dancing—in past years*) Inf **MD**39, Sugar foot.

3 Used as an intj; see quots. *euphem* Cf **foot** intj

1995 *DARE* File, My mother always used "sugar foot" in front of us kids, but would occasionally slip up and actually say shit instead. She grew up on the eastern shore of Maryland, but spent all of her adult life in the suburbs of D.C. and Baltimore. **2001** *DARE* File—Internet, Humph! A big strong webmaster like myself? . . Aw, sugarfoot! I want to share my troubles with an understanding reader like you.

sugar-footing See **sugar foot 2**

Sugarfoots See **sugar foot 1**

sugar grape n
=**sand grape.**

1872 *Amer. Naturalist* 6.541 **TX,** *Vitis rupestris.* . . known under the name of *Sugar grape.* **1891** Coulter *Botany W. TX* 63, Rock, or Sand, or Sugar grape. . . In the valley of Devil's River and westward into the mountains west of the Pecos. . . Also called "mountain grape." **1893** *Jrl. Amer. Folkl.* 6.139 **WV,** *Vitis rupestris,* sand grape; sugar grape. **1939** Medsger *Edible Wild Plants* 56, Sand or Sugar Grape. . . Southern Pennsylvania to Tennessee and southward. **1960** Vines *Trees SW* 725, Long's Grape [=*Vitis acerifolia*]. . . Also known by the vernacular names of Maple-leaf Grape, Bush Grape, Sand Grape, Sugar Grape [etc]. **2004** (acc) TX A&M Univ. *Plantanswer Machine* (Internet), [Texas Native Plants Database:] Sugar grape can be found growing on rocky limestone slopes and stream beds on the Edwards Plateau, north to Oklahoma and Missouri, and east to Tennessee and West Virginia.

sugar grass n
Any of var sweet grasses or grasslike plants such as **manna grass,** a **rush** n¹ **B** (here: *Juncus effusus*), or **sorghum C.**

1862 *Scientific Amer.* 6.11 **CA,** Sugar Grasses. . . There is also a certain natural sweet grass, from which the natives press the juice and boil it down into sugar and molasses. **1891** *Century Dict.* 6046, *Sugar-grass.* . . The common sorghum, particularly its Chinese variety. **1920** *Torreya* 20.19 **CA,** *Juncus effusus* . . Sugar grass, Lower Klamath Lake. **1970** Kirk *Wild Edible Plants W. U.S.* 177, *Glyceria* species. . . Manna Grass, Sugar Grass.

sugar grove n Cf **sugar bush 1, syrup grove**
=**maple orchard;** also used as a place name.

1792 Imlay *Western Terr.* 136 **KY,** Settlement of this country . . has expanded into fertile fields, blushing orchards . . luxuriant sugar groves. **1855** *New Englander & Yale Rev.* 13.160, Mr. Edward D. Chapman . . East Sugar Grove, Pa. **1884** *Atlantic Mth.* 54.54 **NH,** It was to be noticed that the hermits were in or near the sugar-grove, while the Swainsons were in the forest. **1917** Eaton *Green Trails* 14 **NEng,** It is a steep way, past a running brook and through a sugar grove. **1947** *AmSp* 22.307 [Maple sugar terms], *Sugar grove* was our term for a stand of sugar trees in east central Indiana. . . The *Century Atlas* of 1897 enters *sugar grove* as a topographic name in Illinois, in Michigan, and in Kentucky. **1949** Kurath *Word Geog.* 36, *Sugar grove* . . for the sugar maple grove, from the Allegheny River to the Kanawha (also in central Pennsylvania and on the upper reaches of the Potomac). *Ibid* 76, In Western Pennsylvania, northern West Virginia, and adjoining parts of Ohio *sugar camp* and *sugar grove* are common. **1965–70** *DARE* (Qu. T4, *The place where . . trees grow together and sap is gathered*) 24 Infs, **chiefly east of Missip R,** Sugar grove. [21 Infs comm type 4 or 5] **1966** Dakin *Dial. Vocab. Ohio R. Valley* 2.415, *Sugar grove* is about as common as *maple grove* in Ohio but appears with decreasing frequency farther west and is quite rare in Illinois. Although it cannot be called common, *sugar grove* is known in all sections of Kentucky. **1986** Pederson *LAGS Concordance (Maple grove)* 4 infs, **AL, TN, TX,** Sugar grove.

sugar hackberry n Cf **sugarberry 1**
A **hackberry** (here: *Celtis laevigata*).

1960 Vines *Trees SW* 203, Sugar Hackberry—*Celtis laevigata.* . . Tree attaining a height of 100 ft. **1988** *Amer. Midland Naturalist* 119.436, We collected termites from traps in red maple, . . sugar hackberry (*Celtis laevigata*) [etc].

sugar haw n
A **hawthorn** such as **pear hawthorn.**

1824 Doddridge *Notes Indian Wars* 86 **PA, VA,** The sugar haws . . were most esteemed. **1901** Mohr *Plant Life AL* 546, *Crataegus spathulata.* . . Sugar Haw. . . Most abundant in the mountains and Lower hill country. **1950** Peattie *Nat. Hist. Trees* 365, Pear Hawthorn. . . Other Name: Sugar Haw. . . New York State . . to Minnesota and Arkansas, and south to the mountains of Georgia. **1967** *DARE* (Qu. T16, . . *Kinds of trees . . 'special'*) Inf **AR**52, Hog haw, sugar haw. **2004** *DARE* File—Internet **cAR,** *Crataegus marshallii* with common names of sugar haw, red haw or parsley leaf haw.

sugar-head (liquor) See **sugar whiskey**

sugar house n Note: The term *sugar house* as a commercial establishment where sugar is sold or stored is not treated here.

1 A building in which maple sap is boiled and made into sugar or syrup. **chiefly NEng, Upstate NY**

1819 in 1821 Dalton *Travels U.S.A.* 102 **cNY,** There being few farms in this part of the country without maple trees and sugar houses. **1890** [see **sugar bush 1**]. **1917** *DN* 4.401 neOH, KY, NY, nNEng, *Sugar-house.* . . The building for housing the furnace, boiling pans, and other appliances for boiling sap in the sugar-bush. **1947** *AmSp* 22.153 **wPA** [Maple syrup production vocab], *Sugar house.* The same as *boiling house.* **1959** *VT Hist.* 27.161, *Sugar house.* . . A small wooden structure in which maple syrup is boiled and made. Common. **1965** Teale *Wandering Through Winter* 296 **VT,** We saw it [=maple sap] boiling and bubbling in Ranney's sugar house. **1966–69** *DARE* (Qu. M22, . . *Kinds of buildings . . on farms*) Infs **MA**5, 31, **NH**5, **NY**92, 200, **VT**2, Sugar house; **OH**75, Sugar house—to make maple syrup; (Qu. T4) Inf **NH**14, Sugar house. **1968** *DARE* Tape **CT**3, I have since built a regular sugar house. **2000** [see **sugar lot**]. **2001** [see **sugar bush 1**].

2 A building in which juice is pressed out of sugar cane and made into sugar or syrup. **chiefly LA**

1814 (1922) Tatum *Jrl.* 7.117 **LA,** The enemy now formed their encampment . . keeping up a strong Picquet at Bienvenue's & Browns Houses and one Regement in the sugar House of the former. **1853** *Harper's New Mth. Mag.* 7.754 **LA,** The engines of the sugar-house . . are lifeless; its kettles are cold, its store-rooms are empty. **1873** *Scribner's Mth.* 7.146 **LA,** Entering from the wharf . . the sugar house, an immense solidly-built building, crammed with costly machinery, greets the eye. **1930** (1972) Cate *Our Todays* 35 **coastal SC,** Practically all of the missions had nearby an octagonal building which was used as a fortress. In ante-bellum days, mills for grinding sugar cane were located in these buildings which came to be known as sugar houses. **1941** Writers' Program *Guide LA* 536, At midnight, at the end of the grinding season, the sugarhouse whistle blows and a bonfire, which can be seen for miles, is made of the cane tops. . . The modern factory is a far cry from the old-fashioned sugarhouse. Use of the centrifugal system has put an end to the colorful but inefficient open-kettle method of syrup and sugar making. **1966** *DARE* (Qu. M22, . . *Kinds of buildings . . on farms*) Infs **FL**7, 20, Sugar house. **1967** LeCompte *Word Atlas* 174 **seLA,** *Place where juice is pressed out of sugarcane and manufactured into sugar. . .* sugar house [7 of 21 infs].

sugar huckleberry n   Cf **sugarberry 4**
=low blueberry or **lowbush blueberry.**
     1837 Darlington *Flora Cestrica* 257 **sePA,** Pennsylvanian *Vaccinium. Vulgò*—Sugar Huckleberry. **1843** (1844) Johnson *Farmer's Encycl.* 1141 **PA,** [*Vaccinium*] *tenellum,* sometimes called sugar-huckleberries, small and rather too saccharine, but a very agreeable fruit, brought in great quantities to the Philadelphia market. **1950** Gray–Fernald *Manual of Botany* 1133, *V*[*accinium*] *vacillans.* . . Sugar-Huckleberry. . . berries dark blue, . . very sweet. **1960** Vines *Trees SW* 822, Blueridge Blueberry. . . locally known under the names of Low Huckleberry, Sugar Huckleberry [etc]. **1968** McPhee *Pine Barrens* 43 **NJ,** Fred explained . . that "hog huckleberries" are huckleberries and "sugar huckleberries" are blueberries. **1976** Bailey–Bailey *Hortus Third* 1143, [*Vaccinium*] *vacillans* . . Sugar h[uckleberry].

‡**sugarinctum** exclam   Cf **spizzerinctum, sugar foot 3**
     1983 *DARE* File **ceWI,** Sugarinctum—exclamation.

sugaring See **sugar** v

sugaring off vbl n   See **sugar off** v phr **2, 5d**

sugaring off n   Also *sugar-off* esp **NEast** Cf **stir-off** n, *sugaring off* vbl n (at **sugar off** v phr **2**), **sugar party, sugar supper**
A social gathering at which maple sugar, usu in the form of **sugar on snow,** is made and eaten, held either in conjunction with the manufacture of maple sugar for future use or as an independent party or "social."
     1855 Abbott *Cone Cut* 46 **CT,** No "sugaring off," was so good as that at which Calick made rude wooden spoons and equally uncouth merriment for the company. **1874** (1969) Coffin *Caleb Krinkle* 309 **cNH,** Perhaps you don't remember me, but I remember you. I met you at Caleb's sugaring off. **1896** *Atlantic Mth.* 77.470 **VT,** There might be a grand invasion of the camp by a score of young folks coming to the feast of "sugaring-off," when the hot syrup was cooled into dabs of waxy sugar in sap-tubs filled with clean snow, and each tub was a centre of love-making and merry-making. **1915** *Newark Advocate* (OH) 11 Dec 7/4, In order thoroughly to understand Mrs. Tight's paper, a real old-fashioned sugaring off was enjoyed by the club. **1917** *Warren Eve. Times* (PA) 20 Apr 2/3, The Homemakers club had a most enjoyable meeting last evening. . . [A]fter the business meeting . . the club had a sugaring off. **1925** *Wellsboro Agitator* (PA) 15 Apr 7/2 (as of 1860s), Frequently the young boys and girls would visit the camp, and this meant a "sugar off" to treat them. **1933** *Frederick Post* (MD) 17 Feb 4/6, A "sugar off" makes a delightful informal spring party. The affair is quite likely to take place in the kitchen and the hostess is sure to have plenty of help.

sugaring-off party n   Also *sugaring-off dinner,* ~ *social* esp **NEast**   Cf **sugar off** v phr **4**
=sugar supper.
     1874 (1875) Coffin *Caleb Krinkle* 428 **cNH,** There came a stripling wearing a purple velveteen coat, tipping from a sled at Caleb's sugaring-off party. **1904** *Fitchburg Daily Sentinel* (MA) 23 Apr 2/1, A real old-fashioned sugaring off party with real this year's sugar, made in Vermont, will be held . . tonight. A small admission fee will insure all the sugar you can eat and a good entertainment besides. **1944** Johnson *As Much* 56 **VT,** They . . were famed for their cooking, their "sugaring-off parties," and their barn dances. **1967** *Syracuse Herald–Jrl.* (NY) 11 Apr 11/2, The annual Sugaring-Off dinner of the First Universalist Church . . will be held Wednesday. **1967–69** *DARE* (Qu. FF1, . . *A kind of group meeting called a 'social' or 'sociable'. . . [What goes on?]*) Inf **OH**5, Sugaring-off party—at maple sugar time; **NY**137, Sugaring-off social—boiled the maple syrup and made a treat of it. **1976** *Kennebec Jrl.* (Augusta ME) 24 Apr 18/4, In old Downeast tradition, there will be a sugaring off party. Pure maple syrup . . will be boiled down to a tacky

consistency and then poured over clean snow. **2009** *Gazette* (Cedar Rapids IA) 14 Mar sec C 1/1, Indian Creek Nature Center . . will hold a "sugaring off" party . . as it boils the last of the season's maple sap.

sugar jack See **sugar whiskey**

sugar lip See **sugar mouth**

sugar liquor See **sugar whiskey**

sugar loaf n
A **grape hyacinth** (here: *Muscari neglectum*).
     1897 *Jrl. Amer. Folkl.* 10.145 **swOH,** *Muscari racemosum* [=*M. neglectum*] . . var. *plumatilis,* feather hyacinth, sugar loaf, Sulphur Grove.

sugar loaf town n   Also *sugar lump time*
=lemonade.
     1923 Harbin *Phunology* 108, Simple children's games, such as "Sugar-Loaf Town," "Farmer's in the Dell," etc. **1956** *KY Folkl. Rec.* 2.130 **wKY,** Sugar Loaf Town (Lemonade)—The players divide themselves into two equal groups and then each group chooses a "home base." . . The first group . . pretends to be doing some chore such as chopping wood, milking, or any other occupation. . . Members of the second group then attempt to guess what occupation the first group are participating in. If they guess correctly, they may chase the first group back to home base. If a member of the first group is touched by a member of the second group, he then becomes a member of the second group. The second group then visits the first group, following the same procedure. This continues until one group has all the players. **c1960** *Wilson Coll.* **csKY,** *Sugarloaf Town.* . . A child's game made up of charades to be guessed, once played in every school. **1966** *DARE* (Qu. EE1, . . *Games . . children play . . in which they form a ring, and either sing or recite a rhyme*) Inf **NC**9, Sugar lump time—divide into two teams; each player does some pantomime, then runs to get back to his team. **2004** Children's Music Network *Pass It On* (Internet) **seKY** (as of 1940s), [Interview with Jean Ritchie:] They loved the one "Sugar Loaf Town." It's an acting-out game: you choose sides, and then one side marches forward and says, "Here we come!" And the other side marches back. "Where you from?" "Sugar Loaf Town." "What's your trade?" "Lemonade." "Come a little closer and get to work!"

sugar lot n   scattered, but chiefly **NEng,** esp **VT**   Cf **sugar bush 1**
=maple orchard.
     1841 *Lowell Offering* 1.225 **MA,** Friend H. called to invite me to visit his sugar-lot. **1859** *Harper's New Mth. Mag.* 19.278 **VT,** [The] applicant had been arrested for wantonly upsetting a churn of sap in his neighbor's sugar-lot. **1896** VT State Bd. Ag. *Rept. for 1895* 15.35, [The sugar maker] will need to watch his opportunity to get his roads made about his sugar lot, and not spend the first week of the sugar season breaking roads. **1939** in Lib. of Congress *Amer. Memory: WPA Life Hist.* (Internet) **VT,** Due to his foresight Ezra's sugar lot was all ready. **1941** *LANE* Map 247 (*Maple sugar grove*) 6 infs, **ME, VT,** Sugar lot. **1967** Faries *Word Geog. MO* 135, Sugar lot 4 [of c700 infs]. **1967–69** *DARE* (Qu. T4, *The place where . . trees grow together and sap is gathered*) Infs **CO**9, **IL**26, **IA**45, **VT**16, Sugar lot. **1967** *DARE* Tape **VT**1, Father bought the place, I guess, before he died. It had a sugar house and a sugar lot. . . Father used to run the . . sugar lot, 'cause the sap was gathered and drawn in by horses in the gathering tub. **1971** Wood *Vocab. Change* 34, A stand of maples. . . [S]ugar lot is reported only in Tennessee and Alabama. **2000** *DARE* File—Internet **VT,** [Advt:] Andover . . 10.53 acre sugar lot with sugarhouse—meadow, views. . . $69,500.

sugar lump time See **sugar loaf town**

sugar maple n
Std: any of var **maples:** usu *Acer saccharum,* but occas **black maple, box elder, chalk maple, Florida maple,** or **silver maple,** whose sap is used to make syrup and sugar; the wood of such a tree.   For other names of *A. saccharum* see **bird's-eye maple, curly** ~, **hard** ~, **hardrock** ~, **honey** ~, **rock** ~, **sap tree 1, sugar 1,** ~ **tree, sweet maple, water** ~ **e, white** ~ **3**

sugar-maple borer See **maple borer**

sugar maple orchard See **maple orchard**

sugar melon n   [*OED2* 1629 →]   **esp N Cent**

A sweet melon: usu a cantaloupe or **muskmelon,** but occas a **watermelon; see** quots.

1887 *Portsmouth Times* (OH) 3 Sept [3]/5 (newspaperarchive.com), [Advt:] *Water and Sugar Melons.* The . . best brands grown of sugar and watermelons kept always on hand. **1901** Mohr *Plant Life AL* 831, *Cucumis melo cantelupa.* . . Cantaloupe. Sugar Melon. **1906** *New Oxford Item* (PA) [29 June 6]/5 (newspaperarchive.com) **IN,** Growing Watermelons. . . I prefer Dixie and McIver sugar melons. **1914** *Newark Advocate* (OH) 21 July 4/2, The Audubon Educational Board is offering four prizes . . to Ohio boys and girls who will save the seeds of water melons, musk melons, sugar melons, cucumbers and squashes, and agree to feed them to the birds next winter. **1929** *Daily Northwestern* (Oshkosh WI) 16 Aug 24/1, [Advt:] *Watermelons* (Sugar Melons)—39c. **1938** *WI Rapids Daily Tribune* (WI) 11 Aug 8/6, [Advt:] Cantaloupe—New Mexico Sugar Melons—Extra Jumbo. **1966–69** *DARE* (Qu. I26, . . *Kinds of melons*) Infs **OH**49, 76, 87, **WI**49, Sugar melon; **IN**76, Ohio sugar melon; **MI**106, Sugar melon—has a white outside; **NM**8, Sweet melons are called sugar melons; **SC**43, Sugar melon—small watermelon, very round, head-sized. **1973** Allen *LAUM* 1.314 **MN, NE** (as of c1950), Twice *sugar melon* appears as a synonym for *muskmelon.* **1986** Pederson *LAGS Concordance* se**AL,** 1 inf, Sugar melon; 1 inf, Sugar melon = mushmelon, cantaloupe. **2000** in 2005 *DARE* File—Internet s**OH,** My family called cantaloupes "sugar melons." **2004** *DARE* File se**WI** (as of c1960), My mother, who is from Milwaukee, refers to muskmelon as "sugar melon."

sugar moon   See **sugar whiskey**

sugar mosey   See **moshey**

sugar mouth n   Also *sugar lip*   **esp S Midl**   Cf **sweet-mouth**

One who avoids saying anything unpleasant or improper; a flatterer, "sweet-talker"; also used as a nickname; hence adj phr *sugar-mouthed.*

1870 Edwards *Hist. IL* 41 (as of c1812), Gomo replied that he . . wished that the chiefs could attend and hear for themselves our father's words; for no communication which he or any other Indian might make would be believed. They would, he said, call him *sugar-mouth,* and charge him with being excited by fear or moved by treachery. **1902** *Ft. Wayne News* (IN) 9 June [8]/2 (newspaperarchive.com) **TN,** Mr. Johnson Kate called "old Sugar Mouth," and she was fond of saying: "How sweet old Sugar Mouth prays." **1912** *DN* 3.591 w**IN,** Sugar-lip. . . A term applied to one who is over-anxious to say complimentary words. **1941** Daniels *Tar Heels* 323 **NC,** Seconding the nomination of Roosevelt in a regular "sugar-mouth" speech. **1952** Brown *NC Folkl.* 1.596, *Sugar-mouthed.* . . Deceitful, "sateful," "sweet-mouthed."—Central and east. **1970** *DARE* (Qu. II20a, *A person who tries too hard to gain somebody else's favor: "He's an awful _____."*) Inf **VA**38, Sugar mouth. **1997** *Atlanta Jrl.–Constitution* (GA) 28 Sept Dixie Living sec 1 (Internet), My father, a staunch Presbyterian, had never used the Lord's name in vain or spoken a faint "damn", as far as I knew. (Muv was not so sugar-mouthed.) **1998** *Ibid* 21 June Dixie Living sec 1 (Internet), I mention it to warn anybody who is in danger of becoming carping and critical that it's no fun. I'm back to being sugar-mouthed. . . if possible. **2004** *DARE* File—Internet, Bush is just a sugar-mouthed idiot who can fool half of this world with his sweet words.

sugar mule n   **chiefly Sth**   Cf **cotton mule, tobacco ~**

A large mule esp fit for work on sugar plantations.

1887 *Wide Awake* Y.128 **LA,** Uncle Joshua led the Procession mounted on mother's own big sugar-mule. **1891** *Bismarck Tribune* (ND) 28 Aug 2/3, There is no reason why we cannot raise the largest and best mules that are to be found in the market, called in the south the sugar mule, which goes to the cities and large plantations for heavy draft work. **1915** *Washington Post* (DC) 8 Aug 44/4, The Southern planter depends almost altogether on Missouri for his mules. Roughly speaking, mules are divided into two classes, the cotton and the sugar mule. The latter is the better grade, the huge, well-built animals which are used on the sugar plantations of the far South. **1941** O'Donnell *Great Big Doorstep* 114 s**LA,** So they had a barge of mule. Big sugar mule, taking them down from New Orleans to Home Place. **1943** Caldwell *GA Boy* 21, Pa always had a good excuse for not going, usually saying Ida, our sugar mule, had the colic. **1948** *Life* 26 June 108, He sells "sugar mules" (tall, weighing 1,100 pounds or more) in Louisiana. **1969** Kantor *MO Bittersweet* 83, Missouri mules used to be bred as sugar mules or cotton mules (depending on whether they were going to work in cane or cotton) and also as all-purpose draft animals. **2004** *DARE*

File—Internet **MO** (as of c1970), It was our belief that if another prisoner risks a beating to ask you a question about, say, the difference between a sugar mule and a cotton mule, you must take the same risk to find the information.

sugarnut n   Cf **sugarberry 1**

A **hackberry** (here: *Celtis occidentalis*).

1937 *Torreya* 37.96 **KY,** *Celtis occidentalis.* . . sugarnut.

sugar off v phr   **chiefly Nth, N Midl, esp NEast**   Cf **stir off** v phr, **syrup off**

1 tr: To convert (maple sap or syrup) to sugar or make (sugar) from maple syrup by boiling it to the point where it will crystallize.

1818 in 2004 *DARE* File—Internet nw**PA,** Grass begins to look green. Mr. Moore sugared off 23# for the first. **1852** Warner *Queechy* 1.397 **NY,** Ha' you got a good big cask, or plenty o' tubs and that? or will you sugar off the hull lot every night and fix it that way? **1863** *Scientific Amer.* new ser 8.52 **NH,** It [=maple syrup] is then strained and set aside until we are ready to sugar it off. **1878** *Oshkosh Daily Northwestern* (WI) 11 Mar [4]/2 (newspaperarchive.com), J.R. Moore of this place sugared off 140 pounds of maple sugar on March 7th, all at once in one kettle. **1880** *Harper's New Mth. Mag.* 61.584 **CT,** She let him make endless work for her in the kitchen with his pans of molasses candy, kittles of syrup to sugar off [etc]. **1889** *Herald & Torch-Light* (Hagerstown MD) 2 May 1/8 **VT,** A quantity of the syrup is pronounced done, and it is dipped into a pail to be carried to the house to be sugared off. . . The syrup is poured into a pan on the kitchen stove and allowed to boil until enough water is evaporated so it will grain. . . When sufficiently done the mass is poured into molds to form cakes, into tubs for tub sugar, or is stirred off dry when it is about the color of coffee. **1989** [see **sugar** v].

2 intr: To convert maple (or rarely sorghum) syrup to sugar by boiling it to the point where it will crystallize; broadly, to engage in the whole process of making sugar, or, in recent usage, syrup, from maple sap; hence vbl n *sugaring off.*

1831 *Genesee Farmer* 1.310 **NY,** I well remember . . the occasional *Parties,* at *sugaring-off-times,* when all the boys and girls came together, to eat, play, and be happy. **1842** Kirkland *Forest Life* 2.211 **MI,** The process called "sugaring-off"—rather an abstruse affair—is, I believe, not considered likely to be quite perfect without the aid of female hands. **1863** *Scientific Amer.* new ser 9.1, [Description of a patent evaporator for making sorghum sugar:] The sugaring-off is completed in the pans over the furnaces. **1876** in 1988 Palmer *Lang. W. Cent. MA* 32, Spent the evening. We sugared off. **1888** *Hornellsville Weekly Tribune* (NY) [5 May 6]/1 (newspaperarchive.com), A few farmers in western Pennsylvania have their boiling houses so equipped that the last process may be gone through with on the premises, but generally the awaiting syrup is loaded in barrels and conveyed to the farm houses, where the farm wives and their daughters take charge of it and "sugar off." **1929** Coolidge *Autobiog.* 26 c**VT,** We . . brought the sap to the sugar house, where in a heater and pans it was boiled down into syrup to be taken to the house for sugaring off. **1947** *AmSp* 22.153 w**PA,** Sugar off. The further treatment of sirup by which it is made into a solid product. **1950** *WELS Suppl.* ce**WI,** Sugaring off—Boiling down maple sap to make sugar or even syrup. **1959** *VT Hist.* 27.161, Sugar off. . . In maple sugaring, to boil the maple sap until it crystallizes into sugar. . . Common. **1966–67** *DARE* Tape **MA**5C, I'd take the syrup over to the house and make that into sugar—at the house, not at the sugar house, but at the house where I lived. . . We had a sugaring-off pan. . . Just put it right on a regular kitchen stove; **NY**1, [Inf:] In fact, my wife takes her fourth-grade class up there each spring to watch the sugaring-off operation. . . [FW:] I don't know anything about the process of sugaring off, as you called it. . . [Inf:] Well, of course the first thing they have to do is tap the trees. . . and then go round . . and gather the sap. **1988** Palmer *Lang. W. Cent. MA* 32, [šugɚ ɔf]—When you take syrup, put it in a big pan, and cook it. . . until [it got to the] candy stage—very thick. **1989** Mosher *Stranger* 60 n**VT** (as of 1952), Sugaring-off! . . It's way too late on into the spring of the year to sugar-off, bub. All's you'll get is . . blackstrap. **2001** *DARE* File **NEng,** Sugaring terms. Much of our maple sugaring (syrup) making comes from the 18th and 19th century when our Vermont and New England maple production was virtually all made into maple sugar. . . Now the term *sugaring off* refers only to the actual making of maple syrup. **2003** *Ibid* nw**MA,** Sugaring off is the term for the whole process of making maple syrup.

3 Of a sugar syrup: to crystallize.

1880 *Decatur Daily Rev.* (IL) [29 Mar 2]/6 (newspaperarchive.com), Put five pounds of . . sugar into a tin pan, and put a very little water into it, and set it on the stove—and boil it until it is ready to sugar off. **1911** *Wellsboro Gaz.* (PA) 21 Dec [7]/2 (newspaperarchive.com), A Troy man poured half a can of maple syrup into the oil cup of his automobile, by mistake, of course. He started for Elmira, the syrup got hot, and sugared off, and the man had a sweet time of it.

4 To make maple sugar candy as part of a social gathering, hold a **sugaring-off party.** Cf **maple cream, sugaring off** n, **sugar on snow**

1862 *Richland Co. Observer* (Richland Center WI) 25 Apr 4/1 **csWI,** The proprietor of the Union House . . procured some maple sirup, invited in a few friends, and "sugared off." Our reporter was present, and got pretty well sweetened. **1883** *Olean Democrat* (NY) [10 Apr 8]/2 (newspaperarchive.com), The A.O.U.W. sugared off Tuesday evening. **1906** *Fitchburg Daily Sentinel* (MA) 22 Mar 2/3, *Will Sugar Off Friday Night*—The Sons and Daughters of New Hampshire will hold their annual maple sugar party in Lincoln hall. **1917** *Warren Eve. Times* (PA) 31 Mar 2/3, All members and their wives or a friend are urged to be present. A committee will "sugar off" so don't miss it. **1922** *Bridgeport Telegram* (CT) 31 Mar 14/8, If you want a real jolly party for either young or old "sugar off" in the evening. . . Four cups fresh maple sirup, 4 tablespoons cream. . . Boil until the sirup forms a soft ball when dropped in cold water. . . Let cool and then stir with a strong plated teaspoon. . . A prize may be given to the person who stirs his sirup to the whitest, creamiest candy.

5 Fig:

a To interpret, extract the meaning of.

1870 *Harper's New Mth. Mag.* 42.157, The Drawer writes down for the general edification the following . . : "Here's to Pands pen / Dasoci al Hou?—Rinhar /. . " Which may be "sugared off" as follows: Then stop and spend a social hour [etc.]." **1923** *NE State Jrl.* (Lincoln) 5 Jan 6/4, It is agreed that after his message is sugared off it means that he would have the code repealed and then restored in such a way that he would be a more absolute master of appointments than "King Samuel the First" was in his most palmy days.

b To come or bring to a conclusion; to "finish off" (in a good or bad sense).

1889 *Salem Daily News* (OH) 11 Nov [2]/1 (newspaperarchive.com) **KS,** Douglas . . has a sorghum "battery," but the company is financially sugared off and the mill is silent. **1895** *Eve. Democrat* (Warren PA) 8 May [4]/2 (newspaperarchive.com), The baseball kaldron is still boiling and from present indications the matter will be ready to "sugar off" this evening . . , when word will be sent to the O. and I. league officials announcing the fact that Warren will go in. **1900** *Daily Northwestern* (Oshkosh WI) 14 July 4/3, He filled the same position in the campaign of 1896 and will undoubtedly be "taken care of" by President McKinley when the thing is "sugared off" in March of 1901. **1957** *Syracuse Herald–Jrl.* (NY) 7 Aug 25/1, We four talked about the coming Basilio–Robinson title bout. "I think Carmen can sugar-off that guy," said Charlie. [*DARE* Ed: Robinson was known as "Sugar" Ray Robinson.] **1959** *VT Hist.* 27.161, *Sugar off.* . . 2. To conclude a business deal. 3. To finish or stop something. A business deal is sugared off.

c To cash in on an investment; to "come off" in respect to profit; to end up being worth (a particular amount).

1902 *Massillon Independent* (OH) [17 Apr 3]/1 (newspaperarchive.com) **IA,** If he works his five acres in the right manner he will sugar off at the end of the year with a better profit than most men with eighty acre farms. *Ibid* 20 Nov [6]/3 (newspaperarchive.com) **IA,** He wishes to know if it is best for him to sell it and buy an eighty acre farm and be free from debt or hang on and try to pay out where he is. . . We would sugar off if we were in his place. **1907** *Daily Independent* (Monessen PA) 18 Jan 4/1, The influence of locality upon speech is illustrated by a reply received from a Vermont farmer and quoted in the Boston Herald. The old man had been questioned in regard to the value of an estate left by one of his neighbors. "Well," said he . . , "We cal'late he'll sugar off about $50,000." **1928** *IA Recorder* (Greene) 16 May 4/2, The way this business sugars off when added up is as follows: 1 case kidney beans, $2.50; 1 case best peas, $3.50; 1 case pork and beans, $2.30, or a total of $8.30, or $1.30 less than the "very generous" offer of this benevolent (?) Muscatine radio merchandising concern.

d as vbl n *sugaring off:* See quot.

1945 Le Sueur *North Star Country* 245 **MN, WI, nIA,** There was "sugaring-off"—buying some portions [of land], holding them, cutting the cream [of the timber] before anybody knew it.

sugar-off n   See **sugaring off** n

sugar on snow n   Also *maple sugar on snow*   **chiefly NEng** Cf **sugaring off** n, **sugar supper, syrup on snow, warm sugar** =**jack wax 1.**

1870 *Ladies' Repository* 43.469 **MA,** The word . . [was] associated with green and brown meadows and an occasional violet, and maple woods and their quite as fragrant tribute of sugar on snow. **1886** *Stevens Point Jrl.* (WI) 8 May 7/2 **VT,** Numerous are the entertainments in the Sunday-school rooms in which "new sugar on snow" is the great attraction. **1895** *Fitchburg Daily Sentinel* (MA) 13 Mar 2/1, The First Spiritual Church will hold a social, Thursday evening. . . Warm sugar on snow will be served. **1898** *Ft. Wayne Sentinel* (IN) 26 Feb sec 2 1/3, An old-fashioned but delicious treat is "maple sugar on snow." **1939** Wolcott *Yankee Cook Book* 346 **VT,** *A Sugar-On-Snow Party.* . . Menu for sugar-on-snow party—Sugar on Snow—Plain Doughnuts—Sour Pickles—Coffee. **1947** *PADS* 8.9 **VT,** *Sugar on snow.* . . The syrup is boiled until it "waxes" or "hairs." . . In earlier days the syrup was then poured out on a snowbank. In modern times it is served with pans of snow, and with sour pickles and doughnuts. **1947** *AmSp* 22.153 **wPA** [Maple syrup production vocab], *Sugar-on-snow.* . . This is often a part of the entertainment at winter parties in sugar-making sections. **1959** *VT Hist.* 27.161, *Sugar-on-snow.* . . Taffy-like ribbons of maple syrup poured over snow before it is eaten. Common. **1966** *DARE* Tape **NH**6, [FW:] And when they put this syrup on the snow to check it, what did they do with it afterward? . . [Inf:] You ate it. Sugar on snow—it was something that in my girlhood days I ate a great deal of. **1969** *DARE* (Qu. H45, *Dishes . . that everybody around here would know, but that people in other places might not*) Inf **MA**58, Sugar on snow. [FW sugg] **1977** *DARE* File **cwMA,** Audrey took me to a sugar-on-snow supper, the old time kind with a real baked bean supper first, then the sugar on snow, doughnuts and pickles. **1979** *Post–Std.* (Syracuse NY) 6 Apr 32/3, *Maple Sugar on Snow Supper.* At Burke United Methodist Church. **2005** *Yankee* Mar 110 **nwMA,** I also tried another sugarhouse delicacy called sugar on snow.

sugar orchard n   Also *maple sugar orchard*   **chiefly nNEng, sAppalachians**   See Map   Cf **sugar bush 1** =**maple orchard.**

1819 (1915) Mason *Pioneer West* 23 **MO,** Salt wells and sugar orchards are common in this country. **1831** *Genesee Farmer* 1.310 **NY,** The men and boys make this excellent and delicious sweet, from our very ample Sugar Orchard. **1857** *Cultivator* 5.299 **NY,** He has a fine maple sugar orchard from which . . he has always derived his whole supply of sweets. **1871** Eggleston *Hoosier Schoolmaster* 32 **sIN,** He got over the fence to go through the "sugar camp" (or sugar *orchard,* as they say at the East). **1901** *DN* 2.149 **ME,** *Sugar-orchard.* . . The same as sugar-bush. **1903** *DN* 2.332 **seMO,** *Sugar-orchard.* . . A grove of sugar-maple trees. **1939** *Hall Coll.* **wNC, eTN,** *Sugar orchard.* . . An orchard of sugar maple trees. **1946** *AmSp* 21.43 **VT,** The present-day Vermonter's name for the area of maples that are tapped for sugar is . . regularly *sugar orchard.* **1949** Kurath *Word Geog.* 76, *(Sugar) maple grove.* . . [T]he greater part of Western New England [has] *sugar orchard. Sugar orchard* is used also on the lower Merrimack and, though less commonly, in other parts of Eastern New England. . . *Sugar orchard* is the characteristic expression in the southern Appalachians from the northern watershed of the Kanawha to the Carolinas. **1959** [see **sugar wood 2**]. **1965–70** *DARE* (Qu. T4, *The place where . . trees grow together and sap is gathered*) 27 Infs, **chiefly nNEng, sAppalachians,**

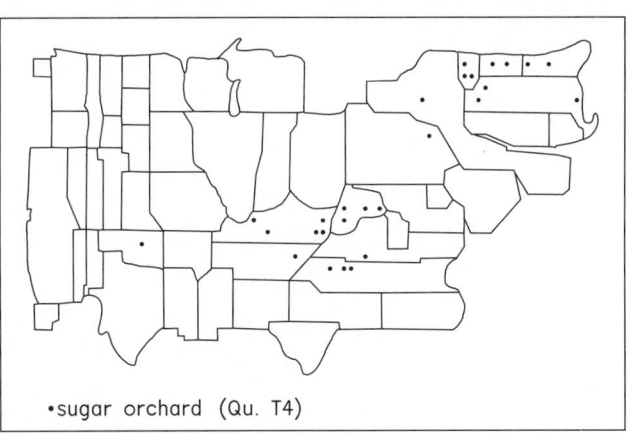

•sugar orchard (Qu. T4)

Sugar orchard. **1974** *Bennington Banner* (VT) 17 July 11/4, He returned to Vermont . . and presently operates . . a 500-acre dairy farm and large maple sugar orchard. **1982** [see **sugar bush 1**]. **1986** Pederson *LAGS Concordance (Maple grove)* 3 infs, **TN**, Sugar orchard. **2001** *Yankee* Mar 102 **VT**, We continued our walk . . and entered the sugar orchard in the thin shade of leafless maples.

sugar party n   chiefly NEast, esp VT
=**sugaring off** n.

1843 *Knickerbocker* 22.167 **VT**, Never did a sugar party terminate more agreeably or profitably for all concerned. **1853** *Country Gentleman* 17 Feb 108, By the way, is there a person in the region of the maple, who never attended a sugar party? **1867** *Hornellsville Tribune* (NY) 7 Mar [3]/1 (newspaperarchive.com), The ladies of the Presbyterian Church and Society have a Festival and Sugar Party at Metropolitan Hall tomorrow (Friday) evening, for the benefit of the Church. **1886** *New Engl. Mag.* 4.215 **VT**, This event [=sugaring off] takes place . . when the syrup has accumulated in sufficient quantities; and, as it presents the first fruits of the harvest, it is usually made the occasion of a sugar-party. **1897** *Living Age* 214.437 **VT**, A good many years ago, . . I was invited to attend a "sugar party"—a vernal festivity, . . at which the guests were to take part in the enjoyment of spreading the hot wax of maple syrup on snow smoothly packed in pans, and partaking of this delicacy. **1907** Howells *Through Eye of Needle* 65 **NH**, I once went to a sugar-party up in New Hampshire. **1931** *Chron.–Telegram* (Elyria OH) 7 Apr [8]/8 (newspaperarchive.com), Ten Oberlin College girl students enjoyed a sugar party at the F.C. Brandt home, Saturday. **1939** in Lib. of Congress *Amer. Memory: WPA Life Hist.* (Internet) **nVT**, When the children were growing up, every year saw sugar parties when the young fry gathered in the sugar house and fed on syrup-on-snow, pickles, raised doughnuts and coffee. **1959** *VT Hist.* 27.161, Sugar party. . . Var. sugar-on-snow party. A party at which maple sugar on snow is served. Common. **1970** *DARE* (Qu. FF2, . . *Kinds of parties*) Inf **NY**232, Sugar parties—making maple-sugar wax, boiled maple sugar poured on snow. **1982** *Post–Std.* (Syracuse NY) 16 Apr sec B 2/5, The American Cancer Society will conduct its annual Old Fashioned Sugar Party in Athol.

sugar pea n
=**garden pea**.

1954 *PADS* 21.26 **SC**, English peas. . . Garden peas, cultivated for table use. Also called *sugar peas . . , green peas, garden peas*. . . Not the variety of pea with edible pods. . . *English peas* are purveyed commercially and widely sold under the name *green peas*. All four of these terms are used generally in South Carolina, with the possible exception of *sugar peas*.

sugar pear n   esp NEng   Cf **sugarberry 2, sugar plum 1**
A **serviceberry**, esp *Amelanchier canadensis*.

1846 Emerson *Rept. Trees & Shrubs* 430 **MA**, The Rowan Tree or Mountain Ash, and the Wild Sugar Pear, so valuable for their fruit and for the beauty and fragrance of their flowers. *Ibid* 442, The Wild Sugar Pear. *Amelanchier.* **c1855** U.S. War Dept. *Rept. Explor. Railroad* (Stevens' Exped.) 1.296, In summer the Indians. . . collect . . a berry, called in some of the eastern States the sugar-berry or sugar-pear. **1892** *Jrl. Amer. Folkl.* 5.95 **ME**, *Amelanchier Canadensis*. . . sugar pear. Washington Co[unty]. **1893** *Ibid* 6.141 **ME**, *Amelanchier Canadensis*. . . sugar pear. Orono, Me. **1896** *Ibid* 9.186 **ME**, *Amelanchier Canadensis* . . sugar-pear, Oxford County. **1966** Grimm *Recognizing Native Shrubs* 131, Swamp Juneberry—*Amelanchier intermedia*. . . Also known as the Swamp Sugar-pear.

sugar pie n   scattered exc Nth, N Midl   See Map
Used as a term of endearment; see quots.

1903 *Century Illustr. Mag.* 66.775 **LA** [Black], Well, heah I is, Sugar-pie. **1911** *NY Times* (NY) 9 Mar 6/5, They were married in November, 1898, in St. Louis. . . Letters introduced as evidence were of an affectionate tenor. In one written . . on Nov. 10, 1910, he referred to her as his "Dear Sugar Pie." **1923** in 2004 Lexis–Nexis Legal Research *State Case Law: FL* (Internet), Listen Sugar Pie how did you injury [= enjoy] your self least night. **1930** *DN* 6.84 **SC**, Sugar-pie. . . Common term of endearment. **1960** Williams *Walk Egypt* 4 **GA**, She's going to be my little play-pretty, ain't you, sugarpie? **1965–70** *DARE* (Qu. AA3, *Nicknames or affectionate names for a sweetheart*) 17 Infs, **scattered exc Nth, N Midl**, Sugar pie. **2002** McLaughlin–Kraus *Nanny Diaries* 107 **NYC**, Come on, sugar pie. Come and dance with Momma.

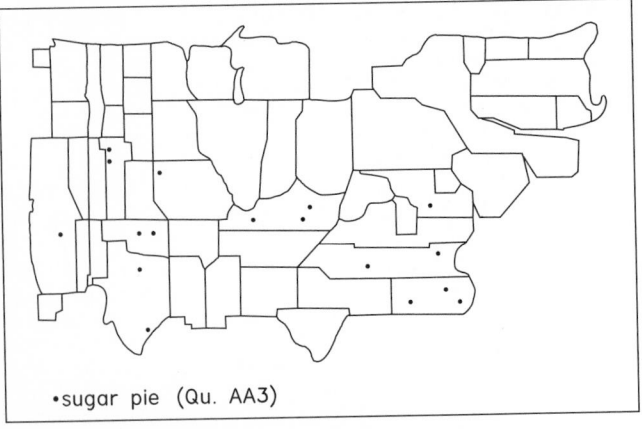

•sugar pie (Qu. AA3)

sugar pie pumpkin   See **sugar pumpkin**

sugar pine n   [Because the heartwood exudes a sweet resin]
Cf **little sugar pine**
A **pine** n 1 (here: *Pinus lambertiana*) native chiefly to California.   Also called **big pine, nut ~ d**

1846 (1932) Johnson–Winter *Route Rocky Mts.* 89 **nCA**, It is called Sugar Pine, from the peculiar quality of its gum, which tastes very much like Sugar saturated with Turpentine. **1854** *Scientific Amer.* 10 June 312 **OR**, The sugar pine in the Rogue river country of Oregon attains a great size, is remarkably straight, smooth, symmetrical and rich colored. . . It gets its name from yielding a rich white sugar, which is said to answer very well for sweetening. **1897** Lewis *Wolfville* 285 **AZ**, I peels some sugar-pines, like I sees Injuns, an' scrapes off the white skin next the trees, an' makes a pasty kind of bread of it, an' I'm all right. **1920** Saunders *Useful Wild Plants* 75, The most esteemed nut-pines are the Two-leaved Pine . . and the stately Sugar Pine (*P[inus] lambertiana* . .). **1947** Peattie *Sierra Nevada* 157 **eCA**, The sugar pine has a very characteristic effect on the skyline. **1965–70** *DARE* (Qu. T17, . . *Kinds of pine trees;* not asked in early QRs) 27 Infs, 22 **CA**, Sugar pine; (Qu. I43, *What kinds of nuts grow wild around here?*) Inf **CA**136, Sugar pine—soft nuts; (Qu. T3, *The tree that produces syrup and sugar*) Inf **CA**105, Sugar pine; (Qu. T5, . . *Kinds of evergreens, other than pine*) Inf **CA**200, Sugar pine. **1969** *DARE* Tape **CA**144, It was built of clear sugar pine lumber. **2000** in 2004 *DARE* File—Internet **CA**, The sugar pine. . . was a useful tree in the life of the Native American tribes, which took the hardened fluid from within the tree bark for something schoolchildren could appreciate: They chewed the sugar sweet white nodules like gum.

sugar place n   chiefly nNEng, esp VT
=**sugar camp**.

1825 *Zion's Herald* (Boston MA) 3 Aug 4/1, He was returning from the sugar place and carrying a ladle. **1847** (1853) Thompson *Locke Amsden* 9 **VT**, I have as good a sugar-place as anybody else in all these parts . . but I can't say much for its management. **1887** *New Engl. Mag.* 4.214 **VT**, In larger orchards, where the ground is not too rough, a barrel or hogshead is fastened upon a sled and drawn through the sugar-place by a yoke of oxen. **1939** in Lib. of Congress *Amer. Memory: WPA Life Hist.* (Internet) **VT**, To Ezra, whose sugar place is a model of up-to-date equipment and efficiency, the syrup and sugar are a fine gift from the gods. **1949** Kurath *Word Geog.* 76, (Sugar) maple grove. . . [N]ortheastern Vermont and the adjoining parts of New Hampshire [have] *sugar place*. **1959** [see **sugar wood 2**]. **1967** Faries *Word Geog. MO* 135, Sugar place 5 [of c700 infs]. **1969** *DARE* (Qu. T4, *The place where trees grow together and sap is gathered*) Infs **MA**58, **VT**16, Sugar place. **1971** Wood *Vocab. Change* 34 **Sth**, *A stand of maples*. . . Scattered instances are given of . . *sugar place* east and west of the Mississippi. **2004** *DARE* File—Internet **cnVT**, The Green Hollow Sugarhouse is located on an old family sugarbush. . . This sugar-place has been in Larry's family for 5 generations.

sugar plum n

1 A **serviceberry**.   esp MI   Cf **sugarberry 2, sugar pear**
1832 Browne *Sylva* 216, June Berry. . . In the northern section of the Union, it is called *Wild Pear Tree* and *Sugar Plum*. **1892** *Jrl. Amer. Folkl.* 5.95 **NH**, *Amelanchier Canadensis*, . . sugar plum; shad-blow. **1893** *Ibid* 6.141 **VT**, *Amelanchier Canadensis*, . . sugar plum. **1930** *Amer. Midland Naturalist* 12.60 **MI**, *Amelanchier Canadensis*. . . In Michigan, Shad Bush and Sugar Plums are the common names for all

the species of this genus. . . Sugar Plum is the most commonly used. **1966–68** *DARE* (Qu. I44, *What kinds of berries grow wild around here?*) Inf **MI**9, Juneberries—same as sugar plums; **MI**19, Sugar plums; (Qu. I46, . . *Kinds of fruits that grow wild around here*) Infs **MI**23, 34, **WI**72, Sugar plums. **1966** *DARE* Tape **MI**36, There was a nice sugar plum tree there or Juneberries.

2 A **wintergreen** (here: *Gaultheria hispidula*). Cf **sugar-berry 3**

1916 *Torreya* 16.239 **ME**, *Chiogenes hispidula*. . . Sugar plum, snow-berry, moxie vine, Matinicus I[slan]d. **1924** *Amer. Botanist* 30.57, "Sugar-plum" is a fanciful name [for *Chiogenes hispidula*] but "ivory-plum" is more descriptive.

sugar pumpkin n   Also *sugar pie pumpkin*   Cf **sweet pump-kin**

=pie pumpkin.

1863 Burr *Field & Garden* 205, Sugar-Pumpkin. . . For pies, it is not surpassed by any of the family; and it is superior for table use to many of the garden squashes. **1905** in 1911 *Century Dict. Suppl.*, Negro or Nantucket *Sugar Pumpkin.* The true old-fashioned black-warted, shelled pumpkin. It is a fine pumpkin for family use, the favorite for making pumpkin pies. It is a dark green when ripe, though the flesh is a rich or-ange yellow, very thick and sweet. **1950** *WELS* **WI** (*Kinds of pumpkins that grow in your neighborhood*) 3 Infs, Sugar pumpkins; 1 Inf, Sugar pie pumpkins—small, fine, light yellow flesh. **1966–68** *DARE* (Qu. I23, . . *Kinds of squash*) Infs **CT**6, 17, Sugar pumpkin(s); (Qu. I24, . . *Kinds of pumpkins;* total Infs questioned, 75) Inf **MS**72, Sugar pumpkin. **1971** GA Dept. Ag. *Farmers Market Bulletin* 24 Nov 1/3 **nwGA**, [Let-ter:] What is the difference in butternut squash, cushaw, and sugar pumpkin? . . [Response:] . . The sugar pumpkin is eight inches long, dark orange, and weighs five pounds. **1986** Pederson *LAGS Concor-dance,* 1 inf, **swTN**, Sugar pumpkins—small ones, used for sweet dishes; 1 inf, **cnMS**, Sugar pumpkins—small variety.

sugar rag n

=sugar tit; also fig.

1835 Necker *Progr. Educ.* (transl. Willard & Phelps) 334 **CT**, The one I have been describing . . was sucking a sugar-rag. [Footnote: I give the term which I have usually heard applied, an invention for the purpose of keeping a child still. Sugar with a little bread or pounded cracker, is tied up in a bit of linen.] **1855** Cooke *Ellie* 203 **VA**, Are you going . . to make a sugar-rag for that baby up there? **1888** *Harper's New Mth. Mag.* 76.230 **VA**, I'm a pore ole fool ez oughter be a-suckin' ov a sugar rag, 'stead o' tendin' ter er beeg place like this. **1928** Peterkin *Scarlet Sister Mary* 185 **SC** [Gullah], Maum Hannah had some butter and brown sugar and was tying it into a cloth, making a sugar rag for Sera-phine to suck. **1931–33** *LANE Worksheets* **MA**, *Sugar rag*—same as sap and sugar tit. **1938** *Daily Progress* (Charlottesville VA) 15 Feb 1/6 (*Hench Coll.*), The lower branch of the bicameral council voted last night . . to deed the lot to the State despite an impassioned plea . . [by the mayor,] who dubbed the concessions . . a "sugar-rag dipped in pare-goric."

sugarro   See **saguaro**

sugars   See **sugar n 2**

sugar scoop n

A **foamflower** (here: *Tiarella trifoliata* var *unifoliata*) of the Pacific and northern Rocky Mountain states.

1959 Munz–Keck *CA Flora* 739, *T[iarella] unifoliata*. . . Sugar-Scoop. **1968** Hultén *Flora AK* 584, *Tiarella unifoliata*. . . Sugar-Scoop. . . Moist, shady places, woods. Described from the Rocky Moun-tains, near the source of the Columbia and Portage Rivers. **1987** Hughes–Blackwell *Wildflowers SE AK* 100, Unifoliate Foamflower, sugar-scoop (*Tiarella unifoliata*).

sugar snow n   esp **NEast, Gt Lakes**

An early spring snowfall associated with **sugar weather.**

1850 *Cultivator* 7.167 **NY**, If a snow falls at this time, . . so great a rush of sap follows, that this is usually termed a sugar-snow. **1861** *At-lantic Mth.* 7.391 **VT**, The snow that actually falls during April is usu-ally only what Vermonters call "sugar-snow," . . taking its name, not so much from its looks as from the fact that it denotes the proper weather for "sugaring," namely, cold nights and warm days. **1871** *St. Joseph Herald* (MI) 18 Mar 1/2, On Sunday it was pleasant until evening, when a sugar snow set in. **1905** *Daily Northwestern* (Oshkosh WI) 16 Mar 4/3, Of course we will have to have our annual sugar snow before we can bank on spring. **1932** *Wilder Little House* 92 **WI**, It's called a sugar

snow, because a snow this time of year means that men can make more sugar. **1967–70** *DARE* (Qu. B39, *A very light fall of snow*) Inf **MA**5, Sugar snow—it came a little cold spell, and it would warm right up and the sap would run; **MI**63, Sugar snow—made maple syrup run good in the spring; depends maybe on what time of year it is; **NY**233, Sugar snow—in spring; **NY**34, **OH**7, Sugar snow. **1985** Mitchard *Mother Less Child* 277 **csWI**, We had the sugar snow late one night, and woke up to its tracery on the windows of our room. **1989** Mosher *Stranger* 36 **nVT** (as of 1952), Charlie had been right about the snow. . . It had al-ready begun, big wet flakes of sugar snow that melted as soon as they touched the street. **2004** *DARE* File—Internet **IN**, Sometimes we get a sugar snow. This happens when rapidly changing air currents bring in a low pressure cell accompanied by a cold front after a warm day. . . The snow continues all night. One would think that sap flow would cease un-der such conditions. But because of the preceding moderate tempera-tures and the substantial drop in barometric pressure, the flow remains prodigious all through the night and into the next day.

sugar stew n   Cf **candy stew**

A party at which pulled candy is made; the candy itself.

1906 *Anaconda Std.* (MT) 28 Oct sec 2 4/1, A candy pull. . . That is what they call it nowadays. In my youth and at the South, it was known familiarly as a "Molasses Stew"—sometimes as a "Sugar Stew." **1970** *DARE* (Qu. H80, *Kinds of candy . . made at home*) Inf **VA**56, Sugar stew—mix, pull, it hardens, break off pieces. **2004** *DARE* File—Inter-net, *Sugar stew* [recipe contains sugar, water, vinegar, and salt]. Mix all ingredients in a *heavy* saucepan and cook over medium heat, constantly stirring, until the mixture reaches a boil. Continue cooking, without stir-ring, to the hard-ball stage on candy thermometer. Pour immediately onto a buttered marble slab or into a buttered metal pan. Let cool slightly. . . Butter your hands and very carefully begin to fold and lightly knead the candy. When it is firm enough to handle, the fun begins. Have everyone butter his hands and have partners pull the candy. The candy is stretched between the partners in thin strands, then folded, twisted and pulled again, until it becomes pearly white and creamy and begins to hold its shape. . . Break off small sections and roll into strands. . . Cut or break into pieces. *Ibid* **NC, VA** (as of c1920s), A crowd of young peo-ple would "storm" one of the crowd's house and have a big sugar stew. Oh, sugar stews have been a delightful entertainment for generations.

sugarstick n

A white saprophyte with reddish stripes (*Allotropa virgata*) native to the Pacific and northern Rocky Mountain states. Also called **barber pole 3, candystick 2, devil's wand**

1940 *Amer. Midland Naturalist* 23.544 **CA**, *Allotropa virgata*. . . Sugar Stick. . . Grows particularly in rotten logs of *Abies magnifica* var. *shastensis*. **1949** Peattie *Cascades* 233, The most striking member of this group is the barber's pole or sugar-stick, Allotropa virgata. . . a dis-tinctive red-and-white striped stalk about six to twelve inches high. **1973** Hitchcock–Cronquist *Flora Pacific NW* 341, *Allotropa*. . . Candy-stick; Sugarstick.

sugar sumac   See **sugar bush 2**

sugar supper n   Also *maple-sugar supper, maple-sugar social* esp **NEast**   Cf **sugar eat, sugaring off n, sugaring-off party**

A party or social at which **sugar on snow** is made and eaten.

1880 *Fitchburg Daily Sentinel* (MA) 14 Apr [2]/4 (newspaper-archive.com), Remember the maple sugar supper at the Methodist church this (Wednesday) evening. **1899** *Centralia Enterprise & Tri-bune* (WI) [1 Apr 5]/2 (newspaperarchive.com), The Ladies' Aid Soci-ety. . . is making arrangements for a maple sugar social. **1939** Berolz-heimer *U.S. Cookbook* 53 **NEng**, Even now, in New England towns, if sugaring off and a fresh fall of snow coincide, the Ladies' Aid is likely to sponsor a "sugar supper." **1967** *DARE* Tape **VT**1, [FW:] Did they ever have sugar suppers at the church? [Inf:] Oh, yes. . . [FW:] What do they usually serve at a sugar supper? [Inf:] . . They often have baked beans and boiled ham, sliced, and potato salad. They fill you up pretty well, so you won't eat so much sugar. Then for dessert, . . sugar on snow. They usually put it on in pitchers, and people can have all they want. **1982** *Syracuse Herald–Jrl.* (NY) 14 Apr sec B 2/5, 41st Annual Maple Sugar Supper of the First Universalist Church, . . 5:30 to 7:30 p.m. **2005** *DARE* File **nwMA**, Yes I have heard of Sugar Suppers. They still have them at churches. You boil the syrup to a certain consis-tency, which when poured by spoonful of the syrup on snow that is packed in soup dishes, it will harden to a taffy.

sugar tit n Also *sugar teat,* euphems *sugar tee,* ~ *thumb,* ~ *treat, S.T.* **scattered, but esp Sth, S Midl** Cf **sucky rag, sugar ~**

A homemade pacifier for a baby, usu consisting of sugar and sometimes other ingredients tied up in a piece of cloth; also fig.

1831 Osborn *60 Yrs.* 1.164 **NY,** "I think an emetic would be of eminent service; don't you doctor?" . . "Doubtless!" answered my uncle . . "and so would a sugar-teat." **1840** *Huron Reflector* (Norwalk OH) 31 Mar 2/6, You were at that time more conversant with your sugar-teats and rattle-boxes. **1874** *Defiance Democrat* (OH) 31 Dec 2/2, 'Tis sad that these three are so mad and awful bad. Give them each a sugar tit. **1892** *DN* 1.232 **KY,** *Sugar-tit* . . sugar-teat. Sugar tied up in a piece of cotton cloth for the fretful child to suck. [*DN* Ed: Also in New England and Michigan.] **1899** (1912) Green *VA Folk-Speech* 428, *Sugar-teat.* . . Sugar tied up in a rag of linen of the shape and size of a woman's nipple, and moistened, given to an infant to suck to quiet it. **1900** *Daily Northwestern* (Oshkosh WI) 28 Sept 4/2, The sugar teat has ever been the offering of peace to soothe the griefs of fools and little children. **1940** *Sun* (Baltimore MD) 20 Sept 11/1 *(Hench Coll.),* Harold L. Ickes . . accuses Mr. Willkie today of employing "sugar-thumb" tactics . . for the purpose of "appeasing" the voters. **1942** Faulkner *Go Down* 50 **MS,** Aunt Thisbe can fix him a sugar-tit. **1951** West *Witch Diggers* 42 **IN,** What this world wants is a sugar-tit to suck on, and a sugar-tit's what I give it. **1959** *Sikeston Herald* (MO) [26 Mar 4]/1, [Advt:] Politicians, like Felker, don't like city manager government because they don't like to turn the old sugar tit loose. **1966–69** *DARE* FW Addit **KY**36, *Sugar tit*—old-fashioned pacifier made by putting sugar and butter into cloth, twisting it into a nipple shape, and moistening it so a baby can suck on it; **Sth,** *Sugar tit*—sugar mixed with whiskey in a white cloth for a child who has a cold to suck. **1990** Cavender *Folk Med. Lexicon* 32 **sAppalachians,** *Sugar tit*—a pacifier for babies made of a piece of soft, absorbent cloth soaked in a solution of sugar and whiskey. **2002** *DARE* File **AL,** "Sugar teat" or "sugar tit" or "sugar-tee" or "sugar treat" or "S.T."—A sugar cube, wrapped in . . a handkerchief and given to a baby for them to suck on. **2004** *DARE* File—Internet **swCA,** But the sugar tit there is so sweet and large that the government created hurdles . . to its endless supply of cash.

sugar toad n **Chesapeake Bay**

A **puffer** n[1] **1** (here: *Sphoeroides maculatus*).

1970 *DARE* Tape **VA**112, [FW:] What kind of a fish is a sugar toad? [Inf:] It's that one with all them little bristles on him, real white and sort of yellowish on top, and he's got teeth almost, well, like a turtle, and he's got a little teeny mouth. And he swells up; he keeps puffing until it blows up. In other words, you call them blow-toads, the old people did. But now they call them chicken of the sea, and they sell them in the market, forty cents a pound. **1984** *DARE* File **Chesapeake Bay** [Watermen's vocab], Sugar toad. **2003** *Nation's Restaurant News* 26 May (Internet), Commonly called sugar toads, the by-catch fish actually is the lower Chesapeake Bay blowfish.

sugar treat See **sugar tit**

sugar tree n Also *maple-sugar tree* **chiefly Midl** See Map

A **sugar maple;** rarely, any of var other trees yielding sweet sap.

1699 Royal Soc. London *Philos. Trans.* 21.438 **MD,** We have also . . a sort of Elm like a *Dutch* Elm, which we call the Sugar-Tree, from the sweetness of its Juice, with which some have made good Sugar. **1716** Petiver *Petiveriana* 11, *Sugar-tree,* grows at the Heads of *Rivers* . . this by tapping yeilds [sic] a *Juice* which they boyl in to a *Sugar.* **1780** in 1916 Mereness *Travels* 634 **KY,** Monday night there was a smart white frost succeeded by a warm clear day, the sugar trees run plentifully but the Juice was of an Acid cast. **1798** Bourbon Co. KY *Rept. Processioners,* At the end of such distance we marked a corner four Bettywoods and sugartree and Buckeye. **1828** in 1936 *KS Hist. Qrly.* 5.265 **PA,** They lament the scarcity of wood, and especially the almost total absence of the sugar tree. **1843** (1916) Hall *New Purchase* 97 **IN,** One day Mrs. Seymour entered the parlour with a cake of sugar-tree sugar in her hands. **1896** *Jrl. Amer. Folkl.* 9.185 **IL, IN, OH,** *Acer saccharinum* . . sugar tree. **1903** *DN* 2.332 **seMO,** *Sugar-tree.* . . Hard maple or sugar-maple. **1904** (1913) Johnson *Highways South* 142 **eTN,** The only trees that looked really springlike were the occasional maples, or "sugar trees," as they are called. **1913** Morley *Carolina Mts.* 19, The sugar-maple,—"sugar-tree" the native here calls it,—abundant in some regions, sweetens the corn-pone of the mountaineer. **1949** Kurath *Word*

Geog. 31, From Western Pennsylvania to the Blue Ridge in North Carolina the sugar maple is called a *sugar tree.* In West Virginia and the southwestern corner of Pennsylvania this is the regular term; elsewhere in the West Midland *sugar maple* is equally common now and is clearly gaining ground. *Sugar tree* is still heard here and there in south-central Pennsylvania. **1965–70** *DARE* (Qu. T3, *The tree that produces syrup and sugar*) 40 Infs, **chiefly Midl,** Sugar tree; **CT**31, **MO**21, **WA**33, Maple-sugar tree; (Qu. H80, *Kinds of candy . . made at home*) Inf **KY**34, Sugar-tree candy—old-fashioned; (Qu. T4) Infs **KY**9, 11, **MO**8, **NH**16, **TN**46, Sugar-tree grove; **MO**4, **WI**23, Sugar tree(s); (Qu. T14, . . *Kinds of maples*) Infs **KY**21, 39, **VA**27, Sugar tree. **1986** Pederson *LAGS Concordance (Sugar maple)* 32 infs, 26 **TN,** Sugar tree(s); 2 infs, **TN,** Sugar-tree orchard; 1 inf, **TN,** Sugar-tree grove.

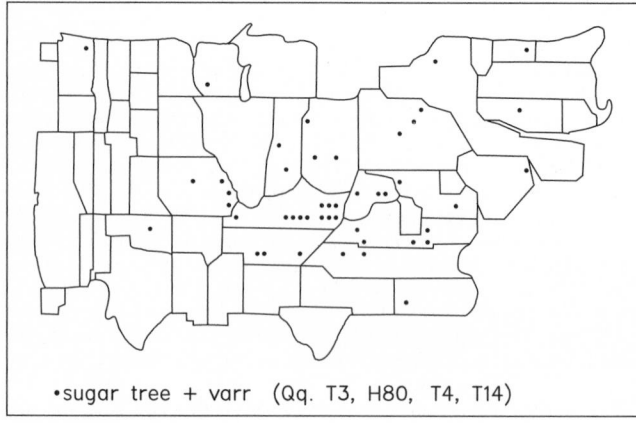

•sugar tree + varr (Qq. T3, H80, T4, T14)

sugar-tree molasses n
=**tree molasses.**

1870 Swift *Robert Greathouse* 233 **MO,** Somebody is going to gobble her up, like a plate of hot buckwheat cakes with sugar-tree molasses on them. **1907** *Daily Kennebec Jrl.* (Augusta ME) 16 May 12/6, Commercialism and greed . . have got in their fell work on sugar tree molasses, just as they have affected everything else. **1912** *DN* 3.591 **wIN,** *Sugar-tree molasses.* . . Maple syrup. **1915** *DN* 4.191 **swVA,** *Sugar tree molasses.* . . Maple syrup. **1957** Combs *Lang. S. Highlanders* **sAppalachians,** *Sugar tree molasses*—molasses made from the juice of the sugar maple.

sugar-trough gourd n [From its use in collecting maple sap; see quot 1921]
=**bottle gourd.**

1873 *Sandusky Reg.* (OH) 22 Oct [1]/7 (newspaperarchive.com), [Advt:] H Q Cooke, sugar trough gourd. **1874** *Amer. Cyclop.* 8.131, A variety [of gourd] is known at the west as sugar-trough gourd, the large flattened-spherical shell of which will hold several gallons. **1890** *Amer. Naturalist* 24.740, In some localities . . under the name of sugar trough gourd, a lagenaria is grown for the use of the shell of the fruit for the purposes of a pail. **1902** *Daily Rev.* (Decatur IL) 20 Oct [4]/5 (newspaperarchive.com), If a huge sugar-trough gourd is to be obtained in the neighborhood, get it and clean thoroughly. **1921** Closz *Reminiscences Newcastle IA* 61, Holes were bored a few inches into the trunks of hard maple trees. . . and the sap caught in sugar-trough gourds or other receptacles. **1958** *Van Wert Times–Bulletin* (OH) 4 Sept 6/3, *Winners In Vegetable Show At County Fair.* . . Sugar Trough Gourd.

sugar water n **chiefly sAppalachians, IN, OH, PA**

The clear, slightly sweet maple sap that rises in early spring and is collected to make sugar and syrup; hence v phrr *to run* (or *drip*) *like sugar water.*

1818 Birkbeck *Letters IL* 63, A range of iron kettles are steaming away; in these the "sugar water" is evaporated to a syrup of proper consistency. **1853** Finley *Autobiog.* 37 **OH,** It was in the night, and we were boiling sugar water. **1890** (1972) Howells *Boy's Town* 161 **sOH,** The boys began to go to the woods to get sugar-water, as they called the maple sap. **1916** *Ft. Wayne News* (IN) [10 Apr] 9/8 (newspaperarchive.com) **wPA,** In the sugar bush country [=New England and the Western Reserve] they call it sap, but in this section it was called sugar water. **1925** Dargan *Highland Annals* 258 **wNC,** I found ever'thing running like sugar-water in sap-time. **1928** *Frederick Post* (MD) 17 Nov 6/1 **nwMD,** Today the "sugar water" is gathered in metal buckets. **1941** Stuart *Men of Mts.* 305 **eKY,** Each spring I tapped the maples and got sugar water. **1947** *Richmond Times–Dispatch* (VA) 17 Mar 8/3 *(Hench Coll.)* **cwVA,** When the folks out here say "sap," they mean only the sap which flows in the trees when the buds begin to swell. Strictly speaking, the crystal-clear liquid which is now dropping into the pails hanging on the maple trees is sap, but now it's called "sugar water" to distinguish it from the milkier substance which will come with spring. **1967** Borland *Hill Country* 335 **nwCT,** Take three barrels of sugar-water (maple sap, to you) and boil it down to one. **1968** *DARE* Tape **IN**36, It takes about a barrel of this sugar water to make a gallon of pure maple syrup. **1970** *Mod. Maturity* June/July 61 **PA,** What Mr. Wolkomir calls . . sap, we call sugar-water. **1972** *NYT Article Letters* **IN,** My mother, who was born and raised in Indiana, always referred to a child's runny nose as, "dripping like a sugar-water tree." **1987** *Frederick Post* (MD) 16 Mar sec A 8/1, Crowds clustered around a boiling caldron of sugar water.

sugar weather n   Cf **sugar day, ~ snow**
Early spring weather marked by warm days and cold nights promoting the flow of maple sap and ushering in the sugaring season.

1823 Cooper *Pioneers* 2.9 **cNY,** This is your true sugar weather . . a frosty night, and a sunshiny day. I warrant me that the sap runs like a mill-tail up the maples, this warm morning. **1836** *Penny Mag.* 5.476 **PA,** About three weeks is a full average of "sugar weather." **1867** *Harper's New Mth. Mag.* 34.713 **OH,** And now their days are fair and fleet / As the days of sugar weather. **1898** [see **sugar day**]. **1938** in Lib. of Congress *Amer. Memory: WPA Life Hist.* (Internet) **VT,** We won't be havin' any sugar weather for a couple of weeks. **1947** *AmSp* 22.153 **wPA** [Maple syrup production vocab], *Sugar weather.* The time when the days are warm (over 32°) and the nights are cold and frosty. Usually the middle or last part of February in most sugar producing areas. **1954** White *Adirondack Country* 303 **Upstate NY,** Adirondack people watch the weather closely in the first weeks, or even at the end of February, waiting for the first sign of "sugar weather," bright sunny days to set the sap running fast in the maples, and cold crisp nights. **2005** *Yankee* Mar 110 **NEng,** Every year, generally in late February, temperatures are likely to fluctuate from below freezing at night to the low 40s during the day. When this "sugar weather" comes, sugar makers can begin to tap their maple trees.

sugar weed n
See quot.

1966–68 *DARE* (Qu. S20, *A common weed that grows on open hillsides: It has velvety green leaves close to the ground, and a tall stalk with small yellow flowers on a spike at the top*) Inf **ME**6A, Sugar weed—similar to a mullein—long, narrow, fuzzy leaves; (Qu. S21, . . *Weeds . . that are a trouble in gardens and fields*) Inf **MD**29, Sugar weed; (Qu. S22, . . *The bright yellow flowers that bloom in clusters in marshes in early springtime*) Inf **MD**20, Sugar weeds.

sugar whiskey n   Also *sugar(ed) liquor, sugar jack, ~ moon, ~-head (liquor), ~-drip (liquor);* for addit varr see quots **chiefly sAppalachians**
Illegally distilled whiskey for which the main raw material is sugar.

1924 *Coshocton Tribune & Times–Age* (OH) 20 May 4/4, Sugar whiskey was confiscated in a raid on the farm of F.H. Kotlachek in Orange Township. **1929** *Bee* (Danville VA) 23 Feb 3/5 **CO,** Raiding the same place three times in 30 minutes, Denver police finally secured a quantity of "sugar moon" and arrested three men. **1939** in Lib. of Congress *Amer. Memory: WPA Life Hist.* (Internet) **NC,** When we searched the place we got eight gallons of "sugar head". (whiskey made of sugar and corn meal.) **1939** Hall Coll. **wNC, eTN,** Sugar liquor. . . "Well, . . old-timers made it with corn, what they make straight corn, and they [Hall: people at the present time] 've been makin' sugar liquor. . . [T]ake maybe a half bushel of meal, fifty pounds sugar to a sixty-gallon barrel, and let it work." *Ibid,* Sugar-drip liquor. . . Whiskey made by the process of adding sugar to the mash (the newer way of making 'moonshine' liquor). **1945** *Landmark* (Statesville NC) 27 Sept 4/1, The moonshiners had apparently short-changed the rumrunners, giving them weak or watered booze instead of the usual run of sugar head liquor. **1949** Arnow *Hunter's Horn* 171 **KY,** There was a smoothness and a kindness to the tongue not to be found in any of the sugar moon he had bought lately. **1952** Brown *NC Folkl.* 1.596, Sugar loaf. . . Whisky. **1962** Hall Coll. **wNC, eTN,** Sugared liquor. Whiskey made from mash to which sugar has been added. . . "But this is not real whiskey, this [is] sugared liquor." **1965–70** *DARE* (Qu. DD21a, *General words . . for any kind of liquor*)

Inf **TN**14, Sugar-drip; (Qu. DD28b, . . *Fermented drinks . . made at home*) Inf **GA**84, Sugar liquor; **TX**68, Sugar wine; (Qu. DD21c, *Nicknames for whiskey, especially illegally made whiskey*) Inf **TN**14, Sugar-drip; **VA**15, Sugar-head—made with sugar; **KY**72, Sugar whiskey; (Qu. DD31, *Joking names for homemade hard liquor;* total Infs questioned, 75) Inf **OK**11, Sugar whiskey. **1969** *DARE* Tape **GA**71, Sugar whiskey, they'd get about, I guess about eight to ten dollars a gallon. . . It's made out of sugar. . . They start off with corn and then they run one run and then they take that beer and pour it back in their boxes and sugar it and pour, put sugar on it, and work it again, rework it; . . they'll run that two or three times. **1974** Maurer–Pearl *KY Moonshine* 25, Today most moonshiners make sugar whiskey. Adding a little cornmeal to the mixture theoretically gives the whiskey a corn flavor. . . When straight sugar is used with very little or no cornmeal added, the resulting whiskey is called *sugar jack.* **1974** Dabney *Mountain Spirits* 24 **sAppalachians,** Most modern-day corn whiskey is really mostly a sugar product called "sugartop." **1986** Pederson *LAGS Concordance,* 1 inf, **neGA,** Sugar whiskey. **1989** *DARE* File **cnNC,** You live in the best liquor country there is when you live in Stokes County. It used to be that they made the best white sugar-head liquor ever.

sugar wood n
1 See **sugar** n 1.
2 usu pl, but sing in const: **=maple orchard.**   Cf **sugar bush 1**

1860 *Scientific Amer.* 7 Apr 235 **MI,** Large preparations are being made for a successful campaign in the sugar woods. **c1890** in 1913 Taber *Stowe Notes* 36 **VT,** I was in the sugar-wood for some time. **1904** *Trenton Times* (NJ) 29 Dec 7/1, "You git th' axe an' we'll start now. . . It's only up in th' sugar woods." **1907** Cockrum *Pioneer IN* 163, Went . . into the sugar woods and prepared to make sugar. **1948** *Sheboygan Press* (WI) 31 Mar 15/3 **VT,** [Headline:] College Has Its Own Sugar Woods. [Caption:] Middlebury College in Vermont spreads its campus to the sugar maple woods for annual "sugaring off" party. **1959** *VT Hist.* 27.162, *Sugar woods*. . . The sugar bush; the trees which give the sap for maple sugar. This term, *sugar place,* and *sugar orchard* are used in Caledonia County. On the other side of the Green Mountains, near Rutland Co., the terms, *sugar bush* and *sap works* are used. Common. **1983** *Syracuse Herald–Amer.* (NY) 6 Mar sec E 11/2, 185 ac[res] are wooded. Including sugar woods with maple sugar house. **2007** *DARE* File—Internet **cnVT,** [Advt:] Approximately half of the land is open pastures & rolling hay fields with the remainder in mixed hard woods, including marketable timber and a mature sugar woods.
3 Wood used as fuel for sugar or syrup making.

1861 in 1961 *VT Hist.* 29.67, Mar. 14—Worked in sugar house, moving and piling sugar wood, washing buckets. **1879** *Decatur Daily Rev.* (IL) [19 July 2]/6 (newspaperarchive.com) **csLA,** Large numbers chop sugar-wood on plantations at 65 to 75 cents per cord. The wood is about 3½ feet long, and they chop two cords a day [to boil sugar-cane juice]. **1907** *Newark Advocate* (OH) 27 Feb 7/2, Mr. Clarence Jones . . is hauling sugar wood to his grandmother's sugar camp. **1917** *DN* 4.401 **neOH,** Sugar-wood. . . Wood fuel for boiling maple sap in the sugar-bush. . . Sugar-coal is a recent formation with analogous meaning (Portage Co.). "I have my sugar-wood all cut." "I haven't got my sugar-coal yet (1917)."[*] **1927** *AmSp* 2.365 **cwWV,** Sugar-wood . . wood to boil sugar. "We have lots of good dry sugar wood this spring." **1939** *Times Herald* (Olean NY) 6 Mar 5/7, Sugar wood [is being] cut for next winter, for the wood must be well seasoned to boil the sap to make the sugar and sirup. **1950** *Wellsboro Agitator* (PA) 12 Apr 1/5, During the season, which lasts 4 to 6 weeks, he burns about 25 cords of "sugar wood" under the evaporators. **2005** in 2007 *DARE* File—Internet **NH,** We're getting our sugar wood in early, so it will be dry by the time we need it in March.

sugary n   [*DCan* 1832 →; transl of CanFr *sucrerie*]
=sugar camp.
1883 (1885) Allen *New Amer. Farm Book* 272 **NEng,** The primitive mode of arranging the sugary, is with large receiving troughs, (or much better, tanks,) placed near the fires. [**1941** *LANE* Map 247 *(Sugar maple grove)* 1 inf, **New Brunswick Canada,** Sugary.] **1968** *DARE* (Qu. T4, *The place where . . trees grow together and sap is gathered*) Inf **CT**15, Sugary.

suggan, suggin n[1]   See **sugan**

suggin n[2]   [Prob from the surname *Suggins*]   **AR** Cf **clapper 2, Goins**

A **poor White 1** from the White River area of northeastern Arkansas.

1953 Randolph–Wilson *Down in Holler* 290 **Ozarks,** *Suggin* ['sʌgɪn]. . . A hillman of inferior stock and low mentality. "Them Hornet Creek fellers is purty nigh all suggins, an' us folks don't neighbor with 'em." **1974** *Bittersweet* 2.2.28 **AR,** Mrs. Graham has recently published recipes of the Suggins, poor folk of Scotch-Irish descent who settled in Northeast Arkansas. **1975** McDonough *Garden Sass* 261 **AR,** One of the most interesting folk terms is the expression "suggins," used to indicate "por folks." This has led to the formation of a Suggin Society to study the humble parts of Arkansas' past. . . It is pronounced soo-gin; it was originally meant as an insult ("Don't act like a suggin" was often said to children); and it is used primarily by people living along the White River. **1999** Ozark Soc. *Pack & Paddle* Summer (Internet) **AR,** The Corps now wants to convert a 258-mile stretch of the White River . . to service the would-be world port up in "Suggins' country." **2003** in 2005 *DARE* File—Internet **cnAR,** My grandmother . . was from the Salem area of Arkansas and used the term "suggins" all her life (born about 1895) to refer to poor white trash or ne'er-do-wells.

suggin cloth, suggin sack See **sugan 3**

sugin See **sugan**

sugkeye salmon See **sockeye salmon**

suh See **say** conj

suit n |sut|

1 A head (of hair), set (of whiskers).

1803 (1965) Lewis *Jrls.* 61 **VA,** Lorimier . . is remarkable for having once had a remarkable suit of hair. **1851** Judd *Margaret* 1.289 **ME,** The face of this gentleman was strikingly marked by a suit of enormous black whiskers. **1886** Amer. Philol. Assoc. *Trans.* 17.46 **Sth,** List of common Southern expressions. . . *Suit* of hair (head of hair). **1914** *Frederick Post* (MD) 3 Nov 4/3 **KS,** Occasionally a man can take a suit of whiskers and let them alone. **1926** Roberts *Time of Man* 107 **KY,** A pretty woman, a beauty with big quick eyes and a heavy suit of hair. **1927** *Bee* (Danville VA) 29 Oct 2/4, [Advt:] Marcel Waving—We have three prices now 50¢, 75¢, and $1.00 according to the suit of hair. **1933** *Syracuse Herald* (NY) 23 July sec 3 7/4, Having only one suit of hair in this life they do not intend to experiment with it. **1948** *News* (Frederick MD) 7 Feb 6/6, [Syndicated story about Babe Ruth's birthday:] He has a full suit of hair, nicked with gray. **1969** *Edwardsville Intelligencer* (IL) 24 Oct 7/8, [Russell Baker column:] Perhaps you have decided that it is essential for humanity that he have his hair cut. Say, "Boy, I don't want to see you with that full suit of hair down on your scapula when I get home from work tomorrow." **1969** *DARE* File **eVA,** Suit (of hair) = a head (of hair), mass of hair on the head. . . Regular usage of an elderly relative.

2 A set of furniture. [*OED2 suit* sb. 18.b "A set of tools, plate, furniture, locks, etc."; 1424 → (of furniture, 1622)] **scattered, but now more freq Sth, Midl**

1852 *NY Daily Times* (NY) [21 May 3]/6 (newspaperarchive.com), [Advt:] Elegant furniture at auction. . . rich parlor suits covered in brocatelle, plush and damask. **1861** *Harper's New Mth. Mag.* 22.473 **NYC,** [They had] a suit of furniture on the second floor that fairly outshone the rosewood in Mrs. Newcome's bedroom. **1897** (1968) Sears *Catalogue* 655, A $35.00 Bed Room Suit for $22.75. *Ibid* 663, Our Special $18.50 Parlor Suit. **1900** *Anaconda Std.* (MT) 15 July 8/2, Special Bedroom Suit Pricing During Our July Unloading Sale. **1949** *New Yorker* 3 Dec 42/2 **TN** [Black], John R. lent Jess the money for the down payment on a "suit" of furniture. **1966** *Cynthiana Democrat* (KY) 9 June 8/1, Public Auction . . Bed room suit; China closet. **1987** Gibbons *Ellen Foster* 31 **NC,** Next they got some camping equipment, a waffle iron, bedroom suits, and some toys. **1988** *Gettysburg Times* (PA) 10–11 Sept sec A 7/1, The company employs 160 men and women at its bedroom suit manufacturing plant in Gettysburg. **1995** *DARE* File **TX, MS, TN, IN, eNM, MN,** Suit [sut] [=a grouping of furniture]. **2004** *DARE* File—Internet **neWV** [Dillon's Furniture], You can find the bedroom suit you are looking for at our store. *Ibid* **cTX** [BedZzz Inc.], What pieces do you want in your bedroom suit? *Ibid* **ceNY** [Upstate Furniture Outlet], We feature . . over 40 different bedrooms on display at all times starting at $399 for a starter set and going up to a full bedroom suit with poster beds.

suitcase n Cf **fiddle case, satchel foot**

1967–69 *DARE* (Qu. X38, *Joking names for unusually big or clumsy feet*) Infs **CT**19, **MN**2, **PA**53, **RI**15, **WI**33, Suitcases.

suitcase farmer n Also rarely *suitcase rancher* **esp Plains States**

A farmer who does not live on the land, but visits it to work or supervise work on it when necessary; hence *suitcase farming* running a farm in this way.

1930 *Billings Gaz.* (MT) 24 Aug mag sec 11/3 **NE,** The corner druggist in a little town in western Nebraska grew eloquent as he traced the sudden fortune of the community's most successful "suitcase farmer." **1931** *NY Times* (NY) 9 Aug mag sec 2/2 **wKS,** Meanwhile this new and greatest of wheat empires has lived upon canned milk, canned beans, canned this and that—a canners' paradise. "Suitcase farming," they call it. **1934** *Sun. Jrl. & Star* (Lincoln NE) 3 June sec C–D 3/1, Nebraska's has-been "suitcase" farmer who used to go out in the western part of the state, put in a section or two of wheat in the fall, go back to so-called sunny California for the winter and then return the next summer to harvest the crop would have a hard time . . in the small republic of Czechoslavakia [sic]. **1939** FWP *Guide KS* 70, The "suitcase farmers" entered the field. They were non-resident owners who had purchased large areas of land and hired farmers in the neighborhood to plow and seed them to wheat. The term, "suitcase farmer," has also been applied to the small-town bankers and business men in the western Kansas wheat country who bought or leased lands and employed farmers to plant and harvest their crops for them. **1941** *AmSp* 16.239 **NE,** "Suitcase farmer" is a term used of farmers on the Great Plains who put in a crop of wheat in the fall and come back to harvest it the next summer, after having spent the winter in their permanent homes elsewhere. **1948** Hanna–Hanna *Lake Okeechobee* 298 **FL,** The "suitcase farmer," as he is frequently called, rents land—and usually machinery—hires seasonal labor, makes and sells his crop and is through. **1954** *Greeley Daily Tribune & Greeley Republican* (CO) 14 July 7/3, The Coloradoan contended, "this hasn't been a case of bad management or suitcase farming. People are just faced with a condition they can't do anything about." **1958** *Washington Post & Times Herald* (DC) 6 Oct sec B 7/3 (Hench Coll.) **wKS,** Absentee operations . . created the term "suitcase farmer" for the producer who comes to the farm from his city home and lives out of a suitcase the days he is seeding or harvesting. **1976** Lynn–Vecsey *Loretta Lynn* 85 **CO,** They moved from Oklahoma because their Daddy was trying to get a better farm and they used to get snubbed when they arrived in Colorado. People used to call them "sod-busters" and "suitcase farmers" and "trailer trash." **1989** Frazier *Gt. Plains* 133 **CO,** And the suitcase farmers. They'd come in and plow up a bunch of ground and when it didn't rain they'd pack up and leave the dust to blow on the rest of us. **2003** *New Yorker* 18 + 25 Aug 129 **WY,** To the new-moneyed suitcase ranchers who had moved in all around him—ex-California realestate agents, fabulous doctors, and retired cola executives—the Harp looked like a skanky run-down outfit. **2004** *DARE* File—Internet **ceKS,** I grew up in the city but our family farm was where we went every weekend, suitcase farmers.

sujjit See **soojet**

suk(e) See **sook** exclam

sukee, sukey See **sookie**

sukkegh salmon See **sockeye salmon**

sukkuh See **senkah**

sukkuhr'um See **sicarum**

sulfur butter n Also sp *sulphur butter*

A **jelly fungus** (here: *Tremella lutescens*).

1987 McKnight–McKnight *Mushrooms* 68, Sulphur Butter *(Tremella lutescens . .)* is usually . . sulphur yellow to pale yellow. **2005** *DARE* File—Internet, *T. lutescens* or Sulfur Butter is paler [than *T. mesenterica*] and the lobes are hollow.

sulfur flower n Also sp *sulphur flower*

A **wild buckwheat 2;** see quots.

1900 *Sunset* July 121 **CA,** We may see the brilliant yellow masses of the sulphur flower, *Eriogonum umbellatum.* **1915** (1926) Armstrong–Thornber *Western Wild Flowers* 94, Sulphur Flower—*Eriogonum Bakeri.* . . There are several other kinds of Sulphur Flower. **1942** Hylander *Plant Life* 202, The Sulphur Flower genus *(Eriogonum)* includes a great number of woolly-leaved plants found on the deserts, plains, mesas and mountain slopes of the western states. **1947** Peattie *Sierra Nevada* 123 **CA,** Whether you go traipsing in the northern or southern Sierra, you will soon see sulphur-flower, the commonest mountain buckwheat. **1987** Bowers *100 Roadside Wildflowers* 29, The name

sulphur-flower is applied to several species of closely related, yellow-flowered buckwheats that grow with pinyons and junipers in northern Arizona, New Mexico, Utah, and Colorado. *Eriogonum umbellatum* . . is perhaps the most common of these.

sulfur shelf n   Also *sulphur mushroom*, ~ *shelf*
A bracket **mushroom** n **B1** (here: *Laetiporus sulphureus*).
   1925 *Book of Rural Life* 6.3722, The *sulphur mushroom*, so-called on account of its sulphurous odor and sulphur-yellow color. It is one of the largest of our common mushrooms, growing sometimes in masses three or four feet in diameter. **1943** Fernald–Kinsey *Edible Wild Plants E. N. Amer.* 397, Sulphur Mushroom, *Polyporus sulphureus* [=*Laetiporus s.*] . . forming large overlapping sulphur-yellow (or orange-shaded) brackets on the trunks or bases of dead or injured deciduous trees or on logs and stumps. **1964** *WI Rapids Daily Tribune* (WI) 13 June 2/6, The "foolproof four", [are] morels, puffballs, sulfur shelf, and shaggy-manes. **1980** Marteka *Mushrooms* 88, Each of these bright objects turns out to be an unusually large fungus, appropriately called the sulphur shelf mushroom . . for the bright yellow underside of the caps. **1987** McKnight–McKnight *Mushrooms* 127, Sulphur Shelf—*Laetiporus sulphureus*. . . Yellow to orange, weathering to nearly white.

sulky n
1 attrib; Of farm equipment: provided with a seat, as:
a See **sulky plow.**
b *sulky (corn-)cultivator*, ~ *harrow*, ~ *(hay-)rake*, ~ *rig.*
   1862 *NY Times* (NY) 13 June 6/5, [Advt:] Patent sulky hay-rakes, revolving rakes, and harvesting tools of every description. **1864** *Alton Telegraph* (IL) 29 Apr [3]/4 (newspaperarchive.com), [Advt:] Gaskell's Patent Sulky Corn Cultivator. **1867** *Scientific Amer.* 10 Aug 92 **IA**, Sulky Harrow And Cultivator. **1868** *Ibid* 25 Jan 55 **IL**, It may be readily converted from a riding or sulky cultivator into a walking cultivator. **1869** *Child Gaz. Monroe Co. NY* 140, Steel-Tooth Sulky Rake. **1942** *Middletown Times Herald* (NY) 3 Mar 2/3, Pictured working on a sulky harrow are Frank Locoteil [etc]. **1951** *Chron.–Telegram* (Elyria OH) 15 Mar 12/1, Auction Sale. . . Sulky cultivator. **1965–67** *DARE* (Qu. L16, *Machines used . . in handling hay*) Inf **OK**1, Mowing machine with sulky rig and buck rake; **MO**38, **OK**43, 52, Sulky rake. **1986** Pederson *LAGS Concordance*, 1 inf, **ceAR**, Sulky rake—buck rake. **1995** *Brophy Coll.* 73 **swMO** (as of c1960), Sulky rake. [A] mechanical rake with a seat for riding.
2 In logging: see quots.   Cf **big wheels, katydid 5, logging wheels**
   1913 Bryant *Logging* 184, In the fir forests of the Northwest where high-wheeled log "sulkies" are sometimes used, a well-graded dirt road 25 or 30 feet wide, with gentle grades and easy curves is required. **1950** *Portland Sun. Telegram & Sun. Press Herald* (ME) 17 Sept mag sec 1/3, No old type drag for these men. A modern hoister sulky is hooked onto one end of the trimmed logs. **1952** *Progress* (Clearfield PA) 12 Nov 22/3, [Advt:] Tractor with logging winch, also log sulky. **1958** McCulloch *Woods Words* 184 **Pacific NW**, *Sulky*—A two-wheeled carrier used in yarding behind a cat in place of an arch. **1969** Sorden *Lumberjack Lingo* 123 **NEng, Gt Lakes**, *Sulky*—A pair of wheels, usually ten to fourteen feet high, used for transporting logs. Same as big wheels, timber wheels, katydid, logging wheels, high wheels.
3 also *baby sulky, sulky baby cart* (or *buggy*), *sulky cart*, ~ *stroller:* A baby carriage or stroller, esp one with two wheels that is designed to be pulled.   *old-fash*
   1910 *NE State Jrl.* (Lincoln) 24 Sept 12/4, Baby Sulky, with rubber tires—1.50. **1919** *Mansfield News* (OH) 4 June 7/3, Baby Carriages—Go-carts, Sulkies and Strollers— . . Folding Sulky—Light weight adjustable hood, back and handle, good springs, a dandy Sulky—$7.65. **1927** *WI Rapids Daily Tribune* (WI) 11 Oct 6/2, For Sale . . Sulky baby buggy $10.00. **1941** *Bismarck Tribune* (ND) 23 Jan 7/6, Two wheel Sulky baby cart with top. **1958** *Berkshire Eagle* (Pittsfield MA) 23 July 33, Sulky Strollers $10.95. **1965–70** *DARE* (Qu. N42, *Vehicles for a baby or small child—the kind it can lie down in*) Infs **AR**52, **IL**26, **TX**9, **VA**6, Sulky; (Qu. N43, *Vehicles for a small child—the kind it has to sit up in*) Infs **IL**26, **IN**3, **KY**23A, **MS**6, **OK**3, **VA**6, Sulky. [7 of 8 total Infs old] **c1965** in 2004 *DARE* File—Internet **cwNY** (as of c1916), Bill was pushing Marion's sulky cart (stroller) back and forth on the side walk in front of the house one day.

sulky adj   [Appar by confusion with *sultry*]
Of the weather: oppressively hot and humid.
   1911 *Daily Independent* (Monessen PA) [29 Nov 4]/1 (newspaperarchive.com), Every green blade had disappeared, . . the brooks were

dried up, . . the air was hot and sulky. **1928** *Woman's Home Companion* Nov 170 **MO**, But when March came, hot and sulky, I had to turn to the village dressmakers and get an adequate wardrobe together. **1965–70** *DARE* (Qu. B3, *If a day is very hot . . it's* ———), Sulky; (Qu. B4, *A day when the air is very still, moist, and warm—it's* ———) Infs **IL**93, 114, **LA**7, **MO**22, **OK**13, **VA**38, Sulky; [**AL**24, Sulfy]. **1994** *DARE* File **seIA**, "The weather's been hot and sulky all week." "Yeah, I don't mind the heat, but the air is so sulky you can't breathe." **2004** *DARE* File—Internet **SE**, We had sulky but slightly cooler weather today, hooray! It rained briefly and then never did get that hot compared to yesterday.

sulky baby buggy (or **cart**), **sulky cart**   See **sulky** n **3**
sulky (corn-)cultivator, sulky harrow (or **hay-rake**)   See **sulky** n **1b**
sulky plow n   Also *sulky*   **scattered, but chiefly Nth, N Midl, West**   See Map
=**riding plow.**
   1864 *Scientific Amer.* 17 Sept 184, Adjustable Sulky Plow. This plow is novel in design and construction and is intended to reduce the fatigue attending the performance of this portion of farm labor. It will be seen that the plowman rides instead of walks. . . A patent for this plow was obtained on the 15th of September, 1858. **1883** GA Dept. Ag. *Pub. Circular No. 27* 8.12, Several farmers have the sulky plow. Not time yet to report their value. **1902** (1969) Sears *Catalogue* 678, Tongueless Sulky Plow. **1922** *Wellsboro Agitator* (PA) 24 May 8/4, Auction Sale. . . 1 Oliver Sulky Plow, 1 P & O Sulky Plow, nearly new. **1937** *AmSp* 12.105 **eNE** [Farm terms], A *sulky* plow has wheels and one *bottom*. It is a *riding plow*, not a *walking plow*. **1944** *PADS* 2.61 **MO, VA**, *Sulky-plow*. . . A plow that has wheels and one bottom. . . Common. **1948** Beston *N. Farm* 119 **cME coast**, He brought with him the rig he uses, a sulky-plough pulled by his cherished team of huge white horses. **1965–70** *DARE* (Qu. L18, *Kinds of plows*) 191 Infs, **esp Nth, N Midl, West**, Sulky plow; **MO**37, Big sulkies; (Qu. L25, *The implement used to . . loosen the earth*) Inf **PA**235, Sulky. **1986** Pederson *LAGS Concordance (Plow)* 2 infs, **TN, TX**, Sulky plow. **1992** Phelps *Famous Last Words* 22 **NEng**, A few years later I learned to plow with a sulky or riding plow which had two bottoms which worked best on level land, as hitting a rock on a side hill could roll them over.

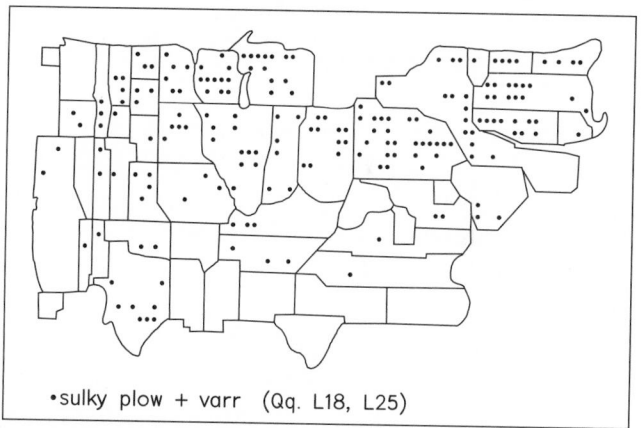

•sulky plow + varr (Qq. L18, L25)

sulky rake (or **rig**)   See **sulky** n **1b**
sulky stroller   See **sulky** n **3**

sull v, hence vbl n *sulling*   Freq with *up*   [Back-formation < *sullen* understood as *sullin(g)*]   **chiefly Sth, S Midl, TX**   See Map on p. 382   Cf **stub up; sulls, the; sully; surl**
To refuse to move or respond; to balk; to sulk, be stubbornly resistant or hostile; hence ppl adjs *sulled (up).*
   1869 *Overland Mth.* 3.127 **SW**, A mustang . . will both "sull," (have the sulks) and "buck." **1902** *DN* 2.246 **sIL**, *Sull*. . . 1. To hold a position with imperturbable obstinacy and a total disregard of surroundings, as a possum, or a hog in a corner. 2. To be in a semi-comatose state through pain. Used only of animals. **1902** *Commerce Jrl.* (TX) [28 Mar suppl] (newspaperarchive.com), Will it . . elevate those to its councils who have fought its nominees and sulled in their tents when the battle was on? **1903** *DN* 2.332 **seMO**, *Sull*. . . To sulk; to balk. 'My oxens sull whenever they get hot.' 'She is a quare child and sulls whenever she is contrairied.' **1906** *DN* 3.159 **nwAR**, *Sull*. **1909** *DN* 3.377 **eAL**,

wGA, *Sull.* **1916** *DN* 4.348 **cTX** (as of 1896), *Sull.* **1920** Hunter *Trail Drivers TX* 152 (as of 1919), Finally, the mule sulled and just stood in the middle of the ring with our rider still on him spurring and whipping him with his hat. **1923** *DN* 5.222 **swMO,** *Sull.* . . To grow sullen, to refuse to talk. Also to balk, as a draft animal. **1933** Williamson *Woods Colt* 171 **Ozarks,** Wal, I don't aim to have no sullin' round hyar. . . Youuns open your trap an' say somethin'. **1950** Stuart *Hie Hunters* 34 **eKY,** Ain't ye ever heard of playin' possum? That's what he's doin'. He's just sulled and when he [=a possum] comes to life, he'll reach up and grab my hand! **1956** in 2004 Montgomery-Hall *Dict. Smoky Mt. Engl.* 582 **wNC,** So mad you're foamin' at the mouth like an old bull when he is sulled up. **1965-70** *DARE* (Qu. GG35a, *To sulk or pout: "It won't do any good to _____ about it."*) 43 Infs, **chiefly Sth, S Midl, TX,** Sull; **FL**48, **KY**17, **NC**69, Sull up; (Qu. GG35b, *[To sulk or pout:] "Because she couldn't go, she's been _____ all day."*) Infs **GA**44, **KY**17, Sulled; **NC**69, Sullin' up; [22 Infs, **scattered, but esp Sth,** Sullin' (*or* sullen)]. **1982** Mason *Shiloh* 160 **wKY,** I get these headaches and I've got this hurtin'. And I can't taste. . . I get all sulled up. **2000** in 2004 *DARE* File—Internet, [Speech given by President Clinton 2 Apr 2000:] I remember, there were just all these guys in their plaid shirts just looking at me kind of sulled up. **2001** *Ibid* **TX,** She sulls up worse than any horse I have ever seen. . . She sulls and won't move. **2003** *Ibid* **TN,** It was much different than the previous years at Hogwarts. Harry is very sulled up this year.

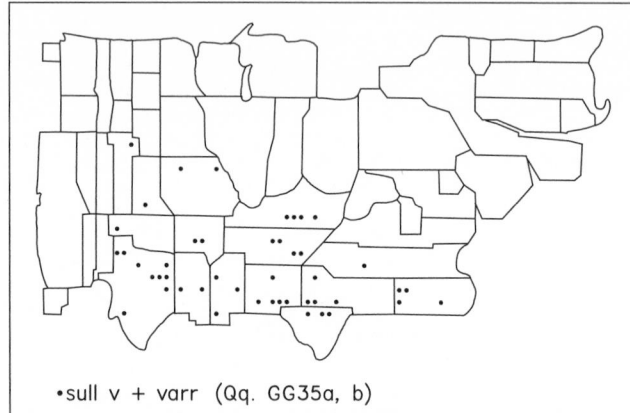

•sull v + varr (Qq. GG35a, b)

sull n
=**sulls, the.**
    1999 Mason *Clear Springs* 227 **wKY,** Chris started to cry. "She's gettin' a sull on," Mose said. "Like a old possum gettin' a sull on."

sulla(r) See **cellar** n¹

sulled (up) See **sull** v

suller See **cellar** n¹

sulling See **sull** v

sulls, the n pl, but sg in constr [**sull** v]
A fit of sulks, rage, or hysterics.
    1954 *Harder Coll.* **cwTN,** The sulls . . a gloomy, sullen state. "Emmer's had the old sulls all day." **1955** Warren *Angels* 154 **KY** (as of c1863), Get the sulks and sulls, or the vapors like they were ladies, and swallow the tongue, or just are melancholy. **2001** *Standard* (Macclenny FL) 2 May (Internet), A cousin of mine had the "sulls" one day [because she couldn't go swimming] and Grandma said she was "a-buttin' and a-stavin'." **2001** *Threepenny Rev.* Fall 8 **wTX,** I myself was prone to sudden destructive angers and what my grandmother would call "the sulls." I have more than one vivid memory of being in my bedroom as one of these angers subsides, books and clothes scattered on the floor, a chair and dresser overturned.

sull up See **sull** v

sully adj
Sullen, sulky.
    1951 Giles *Harbin's Ridge* 64 **eKY,** He did take to drinking mighty heavy, and he got to acting sully and scowly. *Ibid* 83, Ben . . then had come to the house groggy and sully. **1975** Chalmers *Better* 66 **Smoky Mts,** But some of them were awful sully—wouldn't ever talk lessen there was need.

sulphur butter See **sulfur butter**

sulphur flower See **sulfur flower**

sulphur mushroom (or shelf) See **sulfur shelf**

sulta See **sylte**

sulter v [*OED2* *sulter* →1695, but here perh back-formation from *sultry*] **chiefly sAppalachians, Ozarks** Cf **swulter**
To swelter.
    1913 Kephart *Highlanders* 312 **sAppalachians,** I went down into the valley, wunst, and I declar I nigh sultered! 'Pears like there ain't breath enough to go round, with all them people. **1926** *DN* 5.404 **Ozarks,** *Sulter.* . . To smother, to suffocate. "I mighty nigh sultered down in thet 'ar holler." **1954** *Harder Coll.* **cwTN,** *Sulter.* . . "To smother, to suffocate." **1994-97** in 2004 Montgomery-Hall *Dict. Smoky Mt. Engl.* 587 **wNC, eTN,** *Swelter.* . . *sulter* [5 infs].

sul(t)z, sulzer See **suelze**

sumac n Usu |'s(ɪ)umæk| or *esp Nth, N Midl somewhat old-fash* |'š(ɪ)umæk| (represented in *DARE* quots by sp *shumac*); also **esp Sth, S Midl** *chiefly rural* |'šume(ɪ)k| (represented in *DARE* quots by sp *shoemake*) Also sp *shoemac(h), shoemake, shoemate, shumac(h), shumake, shumate, sumach, sumack;* perh by folk-etym, *shoemaker, shumaker;* for addit pronc and sp varr see quots

A Forms.
    1588 (1903) Hariot *Briefe Rept. VA* sig B4ʳ, There is *Shoemake* well knowen, and vsed in England for blacke. **1629** in 1853 MA (Colony) *Rec. of Gov.* 1.384, [I] wishe alsoe yt there be some sassafras . . sent vs, as a[lsoe good st]ore of shoomacke. **1799** *Herald of Freedom* (Edenton NC) 27 Mar [4]/1, 1408 acres . . beginning at a pine stump in the center of a persimmon, sweet gum and shoemake. **c1804** (1905) Lewis *Orig. Jrls. Lewis & Clark Exped.* 6.141 **VA,** Above Bull Island . . in the river bottoms. Shoemate commences. **1805** (1904) Clark *Ibid* 2.236 **VA,** S[h]rubs are arrow wo[o]d red wood . . a Sp[e]cie of Shomake &c. **1805** (1904) Lewis *Ibid* 337 **VA,** I saw near the creek some . . shumate . . of the small species. **1828** Webster *Amer. Dict., Sumac, sumach,* n. shu′mak. **1838** *U.S. Mag. & Democratic Rev.* 3.154 **NEng,** The crimson leaves of the Shumac . . blend . . the Oak's more sombre pink. **1839** (1974) Murray *Travels* 1.452 **West,** [Kinnikinnick] is . . composed of the dried leaves of the shumack and the inner bark of the red willow. **1857** *N. Amer. Rev.* 85.181, The gudewife no longer points to her "shoemake" (as the sumach-tree was formerly called), with its crimson clusters. **1869** Porcher *Resources* 240 **SC,** Your correspondent informs us that it is very beneficial in making shoewax, consequently it was called *shoemach. Ibid,* The shoemac leaf is put into a vat. **1883** *Century Illustr. Mag.* 26.143 **nGA,** My mind is drappin' loose like seed-ticks from a shumake bush. **1884** Baldwin *Yankee School-Teacher* 11 **VA,** Sumake an' sassyfras choke up de good lan' so it's all a waste o' weeds. **1896** *Jrl. Amer. Folkl.* 9.185 **swMO,** *Rhus copallina,* . . black shumack. . . *Rhus glabra,* . . white shumack. **1899** (1912) Green *VA Folk-Speech* 383, Shoemake. **1901** *DN* 2.149 **cNY,** Sumac (pron. ['sumek]). **1905** *DN* 3.58 **eNE,** Shumac for *sumac.* **1909** *DN* 3.369 **eAL, wGA,** Shoemake. . . Sumack. Sometimes pronounced ['šumæk]. **1915** *DN* 4.190 **swVA,** Shoemake [šumek]. Variant [by folk etymology?—*DN* Ed.] of *sumach.* **1918** *Bridgeport Telegram* (CT) 24 Sept 11/2, [Advt:] Gold and red of maple, russet of oak, crimson and green of shumach. **1925** Dargan *Highland Annals* 46 **cwNC,** There's shumake for a swelled throat. **1926** *Torreya* 26.5 **seGA,** *Rhus copallina.* . . Shoemaker berry, Sapelo Id., Ga. **1930** Shoemaker *1300 Words* 59 **cPA Mts** (as of c1900), *Shumake*—The Sumac. **c1938** in 1970 Hyatt *Hoodoo* 2.1102 **cSC** [Black], Take some of dat same *shoemaker* root—some people call it de devil's-shoestring. **1946** Stuart *Tales Plum Grove* 42 **eKY,** Clumps of shoemakes stood here. **1946** *Vidette-Messenger* (Valparaiso IN) 18 Sept 2/6, The Dettman crowd . . have big piles of shumac and locust to show for their efforts. **1949** *WELS Suppl.* **neWI,** On Washington Island, Wis. . . Sumac is "shoemaker bushes." **1961** Kurath-McDavid *Pronc. Engl.* 140, *Sumac.* . . /æ/ is almost universal in cultivated speech, except in parts of the Lower South . . and of West Virginia. Among the middle group, on the other hand, it is largely confined to the North and the North Midland, predominating decidedly over the /e/ of *take* in urbanized areas and only less so in the countryside. It is not common in folk speech, except in parts of New England and New York State. Sumac with the vowel /e/ . . occurs everywhere, except in urban areas of the North and the North Midland. . . In the South and the South Midland it is regular in common and in folk speech, and appears even in cultivated speech in parts of the Lower South and West Virginia. In the North Midland and the North, /e/

is rather frequent in rural folk speech but uncommon among middle-class speakers. . . The vowel /ɛ/ . . occurs with some frequency on both sides of lower Chesapeake Bay and in west-central North Carolina. . . Scattered instances of the /ɑ/ of *dock* occur . . , mostly in the speech of the better educated and the cultured . . , presumably as an over-refinement. *Ibid* 177, *Sumac*. . . This word is generally pronounced with initial /š/. . . However, many cultured urbanites along the Atlantic seaboard . . , and some living farther inland, say /sumǽk/. Among less educated speakers this type is rare outside of New England. **1965–70** *DARE* (Qu. T13, *What other names do you have for . . sumac*) 201 Infs, **widespread,** (Poison *or* red, etc) sumac [no pronc recorded]; 26 Infs, **scattered,** (Poison *or* red) sumac ['sjumæk]; **GA**18, Sumac ['sjumæk]; **MA**1, Sumac ['zumæk]; **WI**37, Poison sumac ['sumɑk]; **IA**8, Sumac ['sʌmək]; 137 Infs, **scattered, but slightly more freq Nth, N Midl,** (Poison *or* red, etc) shumac ['šumæk]; 12 Infs, **scattered,** Shumac [no pronc recorded]; **IN**9, 19, 26, **OH**25, 49, 69, 82, 90, **TX**51, Shumac ['šjumæk, 'šɪu-]; **IL**6, 7, **NY**92, **OH**64, **SD**3, **WI**23, 64, Shumac ['šumak]; **OH**16, 80, (Common *or* poison) shumac ['šjumak]; 132 Infs, **scattered, but more freq Sth, S Midl,** Shoemake (bush) [no pronc recorded]; 34 Infs, **chiefly Sth, S Midl, esp KY,** (English, poison, *or* red) shoemake ['šume(ɪ)k]; **GA**80, Shoemake ['šumɛk]; 22 Infs, **scattered,** Shoemaker [no pronc recorded]; **AR**32, **TN**1, **TX**43, Shoemate ['šume(ɪ)t]; **AR**56, **MS**31, **NC**41, Shoemate [no pronc recorded]; (Qu. S17, . . *Kinds of plants . . that . . cause itching and swelling*) 132 Infs, **scattered, but less freq Sth, S Midl, West,** (Poison *or* wild) sumac ['sumæk]; 22 Infs, **scattered,** (Poison) sumac [no pronc recorded]; **NY**41, 44, 48, 205, **OH**22, 28, 59, **PA**111, **WI**48, (Poison) sumac ['sumɑk, -mak, -mɔk]; **IL**135, **IA**13, **MD**9, **NY**236, (Poison) sumac ['sjumæk, 'sɪu-]; **NJ**12, Sumac ['sjumak]; **MI**102, **TN**39, Poison sumac ['sumɪk]; **NY**20, **TX**32, Sumac ['sʌmæk]; **MD**26, Poison sumac ['sʌmɪk]; **MA**45, Poison sumac ['sɜːmæk]; **IN**3, ['siumɛk]; **MA**3, **NJ**19, Poison sumac ['zumæk]; 102 Infs, **chiefly Nth, N Midl,** (Poison *or* white, etc) shumac ['šumæk]; **MN**23, **NJ**16, Poison shumac [no pronc recorded]; **MS**6, **MO**21, **NY**92, 207, **OH**28, 65, **WI**64, (Poison) shumac ['šumɑk, -mak]; **NY**211, **OH**25, 69, 78, 90, (Poison) shumac ['šjumæk]; **OH**12, 16, ['šjumak]; 47 Infs, **chiefly Sth, Midl,** (Poison) shoemake [šume(ɪ)k]; **GA**77, **NC**37, **NJ**31, **WI**12, 43, Shoemake [no pronc recorded]; **GA**80, **IN**70, **NY**106, 209, (Poison) shoemake ['šumɛk]; **GA**89, Poison shoemake ['šumeɪk]; **MS**31, 70, **MO**20, **SC**7, (Poison) shoemate ['šume(ɪ)t]; **NC**41, Shoemate ['šjumet]; **MO**18, **SC**46, Shoemate [no pronc recorded]; **GA**77, Shoemaker [no pronc recorded]; **IL**135, Shoemaker ['šɪu͵mækɚ]; **MO**8, Shoemaker ['šumekɚ] [Of all Infs responding to Qu. S17, 9% were comm type 1 or 2, 72% comm type 4 or 5, 8% young, 27% gs educ or less, 32% coll educ; of those giving the response *sumac,* 21% were comm type 1 or 2, 56% comm type 4 or 5, 13% young, 11% gs educ or less, 41% coll educ; of those giving the response *shumac,* 3% were comm type 1 or 2, 73% comm type 4 or 5, 2% young, 31% gs educ or less, 29% coll educ; of those giving the response *shoemake,* 1% were comm type 1 or 2, 53% comm type 4 or 5, 4% young, 25% gs educ or less, 15% coll educ.]; (Qu. I44) Inf **OH**22, Sumac [no pronc recorded]; (Qu. S16) Infs **CO**7, **IN**67, Sumac [no pronc recorded]; **IA**3, **PA**235, (Poison) shumac ['šumæk]; **CT**6, **WI**32, (Poison) shumac ['šumak]; **GA**84, Poison shoe-make ['šu<͵mɛɪk]; (Qu. S26a) Inf **MO**18, Shoemates ['šuᵛu·meɪts]; (Qu. S26e) Inf **OH**86, Sumac ['sumæk]; **PA**245, Shumac ['šumæk]; (Qu. T10) Inf **CT**6, Sumac ['sumæk]; (Qu. T15) Infs **IL**17, **MA**100, (Staghorn) sumac [no pronc recorded]; **CT**2, **NY**211, (Poison) shumac ['šumæk]; **MI**65, 112, (Poison) shoemake ['šumek]; (Qu. T16) Inf **MA**6, Shumac ['šumæk]; **IN**27, Shoemake [no pronc recorded]; (Qu. BB25) Infs **NJ**64, **NY**36, Poison sumac [no pronc recorded]; **MI**62, Poison sumac ['sumæk]; **FL**26, Shoemake [no pronc recorded]; (Qu. BB50a) Inf **NY**183, Shumac ['šumæk] tea; **NY**191, Shumac ['šumæk] blossoms and honey; **KY**84, Sumac-berry cough syrup [no pronc recorded]. **1968** *DARE* FW Addit ne**NY**, ['šu͵mæk 'babz, 'šu͵meɪk 'babz] = flower buds of sumac used as source for red dye. Inf seems to use the *mac* pronc more frequently in isolation, the *make* in the combination "sumac bobs." **1974** Morton *Folk Remedies* 127 **SC,** Sumac; "shumaker." **1989** Pederson *LAGS Tech. Index* 220 **Gulf Region,** [The main types of pronc recorded were ['š(ɪ)umek] (226 infs), ['s(ɪ)umæk] (156 infs), ['š(ɪ)umæk] (48 infs), ['š(ɪ)umet] (25 infs), and ['šumekə(r)] (11 infs).] **2004** in 2005 *DARE* File—Internet nw**MO**, Anyway, my feet itch, i shouldnt had been walking in the woods yesterday, i think i got poisensumake on my feet. **2005** *Ibid* ne**TN**, Su-mac. . . The elderly people call it Shumac (shoo-mack and sometimes shoo-mach).

B Sense.

Std: a plant of the genus *Rhus.* For other names of var spp see **agrillo 2, agrito 2, bob sumach, dwarf sumac, fragrant ~,**

kinnikinnick 2a, laurel sumac, lemita, lemonade berry, ma-hogany 2c, mangla, mountain laurel 7, ~ sumac 1, pole-cat bush, quail ~ 2, shoemaker berry, shoestring weed 1, skunkberry 2, skunkbrush 1, skunkbush 1, smooth su-mac 1, sourberry 2, spicebush 7, squawberry 4, squaw-bush 3, squaw-weed 5, staghorn sumac, stinkbush 1, stink-ing hazel, sugar bush 2, threeleaf sumac, three-lobed ~, tobacco ~, white ~ 2 Cf devil's shoestring 14, Indian lem-onade 2, ~ salt 1, poison sumac

sumblesault n   Pronc-spp *sumblesot, summelsault*   **esp Sth** Cf **tumblesault**

A **somersault.**

    1966–69 *DARE* (Qu. EE9a, *The children's trick of turning over rapidly straight forward close to the ground*) Inf **GA**89, **MD**31, Sumblesault(s); **NH**11, Sumblesot; **MS**1, Summelsault. **1986** Pederson *LAGS Concordance (Somersault)* 4 infs, **GA,** 1 inf, ne**FL,** Sumblesault. **2003** *DARE* File—Internet **FL,** I did a double sumblesault and a mid air three time reverse double fold jack knive [sic] dive.

sumbleset n   [Blend of **somerset** + *tumble*]   **esp Sth**   Cf **tumbleset**

A **somersault.**

    1943 *LANE* Map 578 *(Somersault)* 1 inf, ne**MA,** [sʌˀmbɫsɛ^ʚˀ]. **1967** *DARE* (Qu. EE9a, *The children's trick of turning over rapidly straight forward close to the ground*) Inf **SC**40, Sumbleset. **1986** Pederson *LAGS Concordance (Somersault)* 9 infs, **AL, GA, LA, MS, TX,** Sumbleset(s).

sumblesot See **sumblesault**

summage v   [Prob pronc var of **summons;** cf **mange, rein A, running range**]

To summon.

    1874 Armstrong–Ludlow *Hampton* 219 [Black], Death say, "I come on a-dat hebbenly 'cree; De hebben is, &c./ My warrant's for to summage thee." **1893** Shands *MS Speech* 76, *Summage* [sʌmeǰ]. Very often used by negroes for *summon.* **1929** Dungee *Random Rhymes* 47 **VA** [Black], Le's git down to de business dat have summage us to meet.

summelsault See **sumblesault**

summer black duck n   Also *black summer duck*   Cf **summer duck**

A **black duck 1,** usu *Anas rubripes,* but also **Florida duck.**

    1898 Elliot *Wild Fowl* 111, Mottled Duck. . . In Louisiana it is known as Canard Noir d'Eté, or Black Summer Duck. **1917** (1923) *Birds Amer.* 1.116, Black Duck. . . Other Names. . . Summer Black Duck; Spring Black Duck. **1925** (1928) Forbush *Birds MA* 1.195, *Anas rubripes tristis.* . . summer black duck. **1951** *AmSp* 26.272, We hear of the *summer black duck* (black duck, Mass., and mottled duck, La., Texas). . . Some of these names are counterparts, if not reflections, of the Louisiana French names *canard noir d'été* [etc].

summer bluebird n

=**indigo bunting.**

    1822 Latham *Genl. Hist. Birds* 5.345, *Indigo Bunting.* Emberiza cyanea. . . It is rare in Georgia, and there called Summer Blue Bird. **1917** *Wilson Bulletin* 29.2.83 **KY,** *Passerina cyanea.*—Summer blue-bird, Hickman, Ky. **1951** *AmSp* 26.272 **GA, KY, AL,** Passing to other groups of birds, we find. . . *summer bluebird* (indigo bunting . .).

summer canary n   Cf **summer yellowbird**

1   =**goldfinch 1.**

    1940 Trautman *Birds Buckeye Lake* 405 **OH,** Eastern Goldfinches were present during each winter. . . Several of the older residents have told me that the "thistle bird" or "summer canary with black wings" was a common summer resident as early as 1870. **1968** *DARE* (Qu. Q14, . . *Names . . for . . goldfinch*) Inf **NY**48, Wild canary, summer canary. **2002** in 2004 *DARE* File—Internet **NY,** What's a "summer canary" do-ing in the dead of winter?

2   =**yellow warbler.**

    1959 Barnes *Nat. Hist. Wasatch Winter* 68 **UT,** Our summer canary or warbler (*Dendroica aestiva morcomi* [=*D. petechia*]) . . commonly lilts about our brookside willows.

summercater n   Also *summercator*   [Prob blend of *summer* + **rusticator**]   **ME**   Cf **summer complaint 2**

A summer vacationer.

1975 Gould *ME Lingo* 282, *Summercater*—This improvement on *rusticator* gives Mainers another word for the seasonal visitor. An individual may be dubbed a *summercater,* but there is a tendency to use the word in the aggregate: "Saw the first summercaters today!" **1999** *Chr. Sci. Monitor* (Boston MA) 25 June (Internet), Not long ago the TV show Jeopardy! asked what we folks in Maine call our seasonal visitors. I sat up straight in my . . chair . . because here in Maine we have many words for our summer folks that would be a mite rough for a polite evening game show. . . I think nobody gave the right word, which is all to the good, but it turned out the word was "rusticator," which is incorrect. We use the word, but we know what it means, and it is not a summercater, a "summer complaint," and wash your mouth out. **2005** *Down East* Apr 87 **ME,** Almost since tourists began coming to Maine in the middle of the nineteenth century, Mainers have been willing to rent out their homes to them. Some long-time residents of Bar Harbor still talk about moving in with in-laws or other relatives for a few weeks each August to make way for the summercators.

summerce See **somewheres**

summer cohosh n Cf **cohosh**

A **bugbane 1** (here: *Cimicifuga americana*).

  1938 Small *Ferns SE States* 513, *C[imicifuga] americana.* . . Summer-cohosh. . . Woods, Blue Ridge and Appalachian provinces, Ga. to Tenn. and N.Y. **1950** Gray–Fernald *Manual of Botany* 671, *C[imicifuga] americana.* . . Summer-Cohosh. . . Moist woods, chiefly along the mts.

summer complaint n

1 also *summer complaints, ~ sickness:* A severe gastrointestinal infection esp of children in summertime; broadly, diarrhea.

  1819 *Republican Compiler* (Gettysburg PA) [1 Sept 2]/5 (newspaperarchive.com), We have been confidently assured . . that what is called the summer complaint may be cured with gun-powder—a tea spoon full pulverized, and taken with a little water. **1847** *Acad. Nat. Sci. Philadelphia Proc.* 3.232, On the endemic gastro-follicular Enteritis, or Summer complaint of children. **1848** in 2004 *DARE* File—Internet **NY,** Barry, Cordelia [Age] 6. . . Cause of Death. . . summer complaint. **1860** *Ibid* **IL,** Callarant, Alcist [Age] 2 [Died from] Summer complaint. **1909** *DN* 3.377 **eAL, wGA,** Summer complaint. . . Diarrhea: the disease often becomes prevalent in the summer or in fruit season. **1914** Furman *Sight* 46 **KY,** Seven sons of my body have I laid in the grave, three in infancy of summer-complaint. **1937** Sandoz *Slogum* 84 **NE,** He said he had summer complaint, could n't eat a single peanut. Weak as a cat. **1945** Pickard–Buley *Midwest Pioneer* 40 (as of c1820), For "summer complaint" or dysentery would be prescribed a poultice of peppermint and tansy leaves. **1965–70** *DARE* (Qu. BB19, *Joking names for looseness of the bowels*) 10 Infs, 6 **NEast,** Summer complaint; **PA**49, Summer complaint—for babies; **VA**46, Summer sickness; (Qu. BB13, . . *Chills and fever*) Inf **IL**77, Summer complaint; **NJ**3, Summer complaint—old-fashioned; (Qu. BB49, . . *Other kinds of diseases*) Infs **MO**21, **PA**54, Summer complaint; **KS**13, Summer complaint—diarrhea and upset stomach; **KY**41, Summer complaints—baby's disease caused by lack of food, flies, unsanitary conditions—old-fashioned; **PA**36, Summer complaint—diarrhea, vomiting, fever. **1967** *DARE* Tape **PA**64, [FW:] Do you know a disease called the "summer complaint" that children used to get? [Inf:] Oh, yes—diarrhea. . Toasted bread and milk was one of the best things for that. **1970** *NC Folkl.* 18.19, For diarrhea ("summer complaint"), use drink made from bark of peachtree root. **1975** Gould *ME Lingo* 282, There actually is a warm-weather distemper Mainers call the *summer complaint;* it usually means loose bowels and an accompanying lethargy.

2 Fig: a summer vacationer, esp an annoying one. **coastal ME, Cape Cod MA** Cf **rusticator, summercater, summer people**

  1924 *DN* 5.287 **Cape Cod MA,** A 'summer complaint' is not any disease which presents itself during the summer; instead it is a name applied by the natives to summer residents. **1926** *AmSp* 2.82 **ME,** They [=summer residents] wouldn't feel quite so superior if they knew that behind their backs they are "summer complaints." **1975** Gould *ME Lingo* 282, *Summer complaint.* . . Transferring the term to the tourist and recreation clientele undoubtedly involves editorial comment. . . Actually, amongst well oriented summer people, the term is no longer wholly objectionable, because a lady *summercating* on Loud's Island said, "You'll have to ask somebody else for directions. I'm just a summer complaint and I don't know." **1982** Wilkinson *Midnights* 33 **Cape Cod MA,** He called me a summer complaint—what the locals call an annoying tourist. **1999** [see **summercater**]. **2004** *DARE* File—Internet **coastal ME,**

The phrase 'summer complaint' used to be heard along the Maine coast throughout the summer—back in the 1950s and 1960s. . . Years ago you might have been sitting in a local diner minding your business and someone by the window would say—to no one in particular—"Secure the moorin' lines here comes a gang of summah complaints." Everyone in the diner knew right off . . that the place was about to be invaded by a raucous bunch of oddly dressed people 'from away.'

summer complaints See **summer complaint 1**

summer coot n **FL**
=**Florida gallinule.**

  1888 Trumbull *Names of Birds* 123 **FL,** Some distinguish the Gallinule at St. Augustine as *summer-coot,* . . and at Sanford, same state, as the Florida Gallinule. **1923** U.S. Dept. Ag. *Misc. Circular* 13.44 **FL,** Florida Gallinule. . . Vernacular Names. . . summer coot.

summer cypress n [*OED2* 1767 →] Cf **Moses' firebush**
Std: an introduced plant of the genus *Kochia,* usu *K. scoparia* or *K. americana.* For other names of the former see **burning bush 3, Chicago fire, fireball 4, fire bush 2, Mexican fireweed, red-hot poker 2, scarlet cup 2;** for other names of the latter see **fartweed 1, green molly, molly n¹ 8, red molly, red sage 1**

summer duck n Cf **summer black duck, ~ French duck**
1 =**wood duck 1. chiefly Sth**

  1731 Catesby *Nat. Hist. Carolina* 1.97, *The Summer Duck.* . . They breed in *Virginia* and *Carolina,* and make their Nests in the Holes of tall Trees (made by Wood-peckers) growing in Water, particularly Cypress Trees. **1775** (1922) Schaw *Jrl. of a Lady* 175 **NC,** The beauty of the Summer-duck makes its death almost a murder. **1806** (1965) Lewis–Clark *Hist. Lewis–Clark Exped.* 3.918, *March 31st.* . . At the same place we saw a summer-duck, or wood-duck, as it is sometimes called. **1835** in 1836 *S. Lit. Messenger* 2.119 **SC,** The summer duck, with its glorious plumage, skims along the same muddy lake, on the edge of which the d—d bodiless crane screams and crouches. **1844** Giraud *Birds Long Is.* 312, It [=*Anas sponsa*] is called Summer Duck from remaining with us throughout the summer. **1870** *Harper's New Mth. Mag.* 40.436 **MD,** The well-known summer-duck—*Anas sponsa*—claims, and is justly entitled to, the proud designation of the most beautiful of all our waterfowl. . . It is the only duck which remains with us during the summer months and breeds. **1903** Dawson *Birds OH* 2.598, Wood Duck. . . Summer Duck. **1965–70** *DARE* (Qu. Q5, . . *Kinds of wild ducks*) 21 Infs, **chiefly Sth,** Summer duck; **AL**31, Summer or acorn duck; **DE**3, Summer ducks or Pennsylvania wood ducks. [*DARE* Ed: Some of these Infs may refer instead to other senses below.] **1985** Madson *Up River* 161 **Upper Missip Valley,** Within a decade the "summer duck" was out of danger and doing well.

2 Either the blue-winged teal (*Anas discors*) or the **green-winged teal.**

  1891 *Leighton News* (AL) 14 Feb np, Blue-winged Teal. . . This and the above species [=green-winged teal] are known here simply as Teal, and, in common with all the smaller species of this family, are sometimes called Summer Ducks. **1970** *DARE* (Qu. Q5, . . *Kinds of wild ducks*) Inf **TN**24, Summer duck—very much the color of the mallard except for green head, little bitty fellow a size larger than a didapple; **VA**47, Summer duck (blue-wing teal)—in area summer only.

3 =**Florida duck.**

  1911 *Forest & Stream* 77.172 **FL, LA, TX,** Southern Black Mallard. . . Summer Duck, Southern Florida; Vinton and Cameron, La.; Matagorda and Rockport, Texas. **1951** *AmSp* 26.272 **FL, MS, LA, TX,** Of *summer ducks* there are several, as . . mottled duck [etc]. . . Some of these names are counterparts, if not reflections, of the Louisiana French names *canard d'été* [etc]. **1955** Lowery *LA Birds* 165, Mottled Duck. . . This is the "summer duck," a bird well known to residents along our Gulf Coast, where the species nests commonly and occurs in considerable numbers even in winter. **1968** *DARE* (Qu. Q5, . . *Kinds of wild ducks*) Inf **LA**31, Summer duck, which is really a black mallard. [*DARE* Ed: This Inf may refer instead to **7** below.]

4 A **tree duck 1** (here: either *Dendrocygna autumnalis* or *D. bicolor*).

  1923 U.S. Dept. Ag. *Misc. Circular* 13.38 **TX,** Black-bellied Tree-duck (*Dendrocygna autumnalis*). . . cornfield duck, long-legged duck, summer duck. The last three are said to be in vernacular use in Texas. *Ibid* **TX,** Fulvous Tree-duck (*Dendrocygna bicolor*). . . summer duck.

5 =**hooded merganser.**

1923 U.S. Dept. Ag. *Misc. Circular* 13.7 **AL,** Hooded Merganser. . . Vernacular Names. . . summer duck. **1962** Imhof *AL Birds* 160, Hooded Merganser. . . Other names: Summer Duck [etc].

6 =**baldpate 1.**

1955 MA Audubon Soc. *Bulletin* 39.314 **MA,** Baldpate. . . speckle-bellied summer duck, . . summer duck [etc]. **1968** *DARE* Tape **DE**7, The summer duck is a good eating duck. . . He looks more like a baldpate—can't tell them two hardly apart.

7 A **black duck 1** (here: *Anas rubripes*).

1955 MA Audubon Soc. *Bulletin* 39.314 **MA,** Black Duck. . . Summer Black Duck, Summer Duck [etc].

8 =**coot** n[1] **1.**

1966–70 *DARE* (Qu. Q5, . . *Kinds of wild ducks*) Inf **TX**62, Summer duck—small, dark ducks; (Qu. Q9, *The bird that looks like a small, dull-colored duck and is commonly found on ponds and lakes*) Infs **SC**21, **TN**53, Summer duck; **GA**84, Summer duck—only here in summer; **TX**62, Summer duck or water hen or mud hen.

summer-farewell n

1 An aster (here: *Symphyotrichum novi-belgii*). Cf **farewell-summer 1**

1916 *Torreya* 16.240 **cME coast,** *Aster novi-belgii* [=*Symphyotrichum n.*] . . Summer farewell, Matinicus I[slan]d.

2 A southeastern **prairie clover** (here: *Dalea pinnata*).

1944 AL Geol. Surv. *Bulletin* 53.132, *K[uhnistera] pinnata* [=*Dalea p.*] . . sometimes known as "summer farewell," because it blooms in late summer. **1955** *S. Folkl. Qrly.* 19.235, A small thistle that blooms late and signals that summer is gone bears the poetic title *Summer Farewell*. **1975** Duncan–Foote *Wildflowers SE* 74, Summer-farewell—*Petalostemum caroliniense* [=*Dalea pinnata*].

summer flounder n [Because it is abundant near shore in summer]

An Atlantic **flounder** n B (here: *Paralichthys dentatus*). Also called **flatfish 2, fluke** n[1]**, jewfish 3, turbot 1**

1814 in 1815 Lit. & Philos. Soc. NY *Trans.* 1.390, *Flounder of New-York* (*Pleuronectes dentatus* [=*Paralichthys d.*]) . . called the summer flounder. **1859** Goodrich *Illustr. Nat. Hist.* 460, The New York Flounder, *P[latessa] dentata* [=*Paralichthys dentatus*], also called *Toothed Flat-Fish,* is about twenty inches long; is well flavored, and common in our markets under the name of the *Summer-Flounder.* **1906** NJ State Museum *Annual Rept. for 1905* 393, Summer Flounder. **1951** Taylor *Surv. Marine Fisheries NC* 134, North Carolina waters contain several species although the commercial catch is made up largely of the summer or southern flounder. **1969** *DARE* (Qu. P2, . . *Kinds of saltwater fish caught around here . . good to eat*) Inf **RI**4, Winter flounder, summer flounder—eyes on different sides. **1975** Evanoff *Catch More Fish* 105, Another member of the flounder family often caught . . is the "summer" flounder, or "fluke," which . . is caught from Rhode Island to Virginia and the Carolinas, and also in the Gulf of Mexico. **1979** McPhee *Giving Good Weight* 100, Summer flounders are left-eyed. Winter flounders are right-eyed. **2004** *DARE* File—Internet **NJ,** The summer flounder is a bottom dwelling predator that enters our New Jersey waters sometime around late April, early May.

summer folk(s) See **summer people**

summer French duck n Also *summer French mallard* **LA** Cf **summer mallard**
=**Florida duck.**

1911 *Forest & Stream* 77.172 **LA,** Southern Black Mallard . . Summer French Duck, Mississippi Delta, La. **1921** LA Dept. of Conserv. *Bulletin* 10.53, A variety of French and English names are applied to the summer mallard, principal among which are "summer French duck", "Mexican mallard", "canard des isles", "canard d'ete", and "island duck". **1951** *AmSp* 26.272 **LA,** The mottled duck is also dubbed *summer black mallard, summer French duck,* and *summer French mallard.*

summer grape n

Std: a **grape** (here: usu *Vitis aestivalis*) that blooms or matures in summer. For other names of this species see **bunch grape, pigeon ~, post-oak ~, sand ~, swamp ~ 1, turkey ~, winter ~**

summer green snake See **summer snake**

summer grosbeak n
=**rose-breasted grosbeak.**

1917 (1923) *Birds Amer.* 3.65, Rose-breasted Grosbeak. . . Other Names.—Potato-bug Bird; . . Summer Grosbeak [etc].

summer gull n

1 The common **tern** (*Sterna hirundo*).

1844 DeKay *Zool. NY* 2.299, The *Big* or *Common Tern* appears . . about the middle of April. . . It leaves us in the autumn for the south, and hence is generally known here as the *Summer Gull.* **1844** Giraud *Birds Long Is.* 350 **seNY,** The Common Tern is familiar to our bay-gunners, as well as to many sportsmen (who never look for generic distinctions,) by the name of "Summer Gull." **1886** *Science* 26 Feb 198 **Long Is. NY,** An observer at the eastern end of Long Island informs me that the 'summer gulls' (common terns) have greatly decreased in numbers. **1910** *Perry Daily Chief* (IA) 14 June 2/5, The tern is a bird that is sometimes called the sea-swallow or summer gull. **1951** [see **2** below].

2 =**laughing gull.**

1951 *AmSp* 26.272, We find the name *summer gull* specifying the laughing gull (N.J.) and common tern (Maine, N.Y., N.J.)

summer haw n

A **hawthorn:** usu *Crataegus flava,* but also *C. mollis* or a **mayhaw 1** (here: *C. aestivalis*). For other names of *C. flava* see **red haw 1**

1857 Gray *Manual of Botany* 124, *C[rataegus] flava.* . . Summer Haw. . . Sandy soil, Virginia and southward. **1884** Sargent *Forests of N. Amer.* 83, *Crataegus flava.* . . Summer Haw. Yellow Haw. Virginia southward, generally near the coast, to Tampa Bay, Florida, west through the Gulf states to eastern Texas and southern Arkansas. **1920** Saunders *Useful Wild Plants* 92, The Summer Haw (*Crataegus flava . .*), a small tree of the Southern States, bears somewhat pear-shaped, yellowish fruits. **1973** Stephens *Woody Plants* 238, *Crataegus mollis.* . . Red haw, hawthorn, summer haw, turkey haw. **1980** Little *Audubon Guide N. Amer. Trees E. Region* 471, Yellow Hawthorn—"Summer Haw."

summer herring n Cf **fall herring**
=**glut herring.**

1814 in 1815 Lit. & Philos. Soc. NY *Trans.* 1.456, *Summer Herring of New-York.* (*Clupea aestivalis.*) **1896** U.S. Bur. Fisheries *Rept. for 1895* 282, *Pomolobus aestivalis* [=*Alosa a.*] . . Summer Herring. **1973** Knight *Cook's Fish Guide* 382.

summer huckleberry n

A **staggerbush** (here: *Lyonia mariana*).

1967 *DARE* Wildfl QR Pl.155B [=*Neopieris mariana* [=*Lyonia m.*]] Inf **TX**34, Summer huckleberry.

summer kitchen n chiefly **Nth, N Midl, exc NW** See Map on p. 386 Cf **porch n 1**
=**outside kitchen.**

1833 Trollope *Refugee* 1.57 **cwNY,** The other wing . . would be found on that side, open to the heavens, and serving the double purpose of a summer kitchen, and a wash-house. **1851** Wheeler *Rural Homes* 51 **CT,** In many parts of this country, and especially in the Southern States, a summer kitchen is used, which is detached from the house. **1862** *Continental Mth.* 1.614, I . . was exercising myself . . in the summer-kitchen. **1890** Holley *Samantha among Brethren* 53 **NY,** Josiah wuz a-bringin' in the cook stove from the summer kitchen. **1928** Aldrich *Lantern* 3 **NE,** The dining-room, kitchen, and a summer kitchen beyond. **1948** Beston *N. Farm* 114 **cME coast,** The "summer kitchen" is the cooler and more airy. **1965–70** *DARE* (Qu. D16, . . *Parts added on to the main part of a house*) 59 Infs, **chiefly Nth, N Midl, exc NW,** Summer kitchen; (Qu. M22, . . *Kinds of buildings . . on farms*) 12 Infs, **Nth, N Midl,** Summer kitchen; (Qu. D7, *A small space anywhere in a house where you can hide things or get them out of the way*) Inf **IL**113, Summer kitchen; (Qu. D8, *The small room next to the kitchen [in older houses] where dishes and sometimes foods are kept*) Infs **IN**76, **MD**8, **MI**68, **MO**21, **OH**80, **PA**5, 242, Summer kitchen. **1966–68** *DARE* Tape **NH**6, We had a stove . . which was in a room that we just used for summer kitchen. We called it summer kitchen; **PA**126, The outside kitchen . . we had a summer kitchen . . and that was only used in the summer and we had no hot water running out there. **1983** *MJLF* 9.1.58 **ceKY** (as of 1956), *Summer kitchen . .* a screened-in room built onto a house for cooking in the summer. **1986** Pederson *LAGS Concordance* (*Kitchen*) 17 Infs, **Gulf Region,** Summer kitchen. **2005** *DARE* File—

Internet **FL,** We are getting ready to build a summer kitchen. . . I'd love to see some pictures of people's summer kitchens.

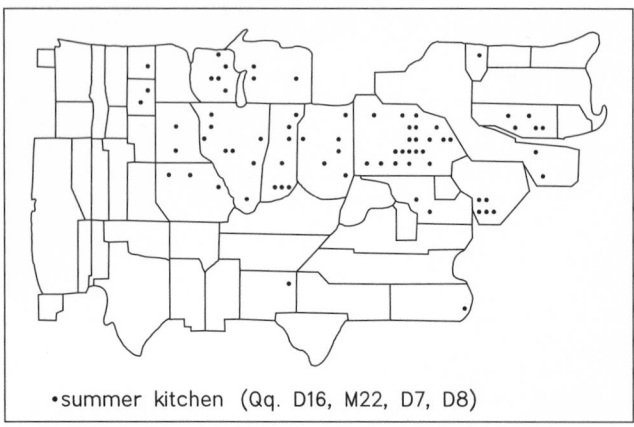

•summer kitchen (Qq. D16, M22, D7, D8)

summer lilac n
=butterfly bush 1.

1923 *Indianapolis Star* (IN) 13 May 37/1, *Butterfly Bush* or Summer Lilac. *Have You Got a Butterfly Bush On Your Lawn?* **1966** *DARE* Wildfl QR Pl.114 [=*Lespedeza frutescens*] Inf **WA**15, Butterfly bush (but butterfly bush is really a summer lilac). **1992** *Capital Times* (Madison WI) 12 Feb sec D 4/5, One of the most successful plants for attracting butterflies is . . the butterfly bush. . . By mid-summer, my "summer lilacs" are 5 feet tall and covered with both purple blooms and beautiful butterflies. **2004** *DARE* File—Internet **sCA,** To attract butterflies to your garden, you'll need colorful nectar flowers such as verbena, geraniums, summer lilacs and lantana.

summer mallard n
=Florida duck.

1911 *Forest & Stream* 77.172 **LA,** (Southern Black Mallard) *Anas fulvigula*. . . Summer Black Mallard, . . Summer Mallard. **1921** [see **summer French duck**]. **1969** Longstreet *Birds FL* 34, Florida Duck—*Other names:* Florida Black Duck . . Summer Mallard.

summer name n
An alias.

1902 *Out West Mag.* 16.392 **NM,** Who is he? Really couldn't say. He comes when you call Bud Keyes. But that may be only his summer name, you know. **1920** *IA City Daily Press* (IA) 14 Sept 8/4, You need have no worry on that score, Mrs. Jenks. I'm General Ruey, Andrew Bowers was just my summer name, as it were. **1944** Adams *Western Words* 159, *Summer name*—When a man chose to give a name other than his true one, the West respected a code of showing no curiosity about his past. The nearest approach to curiosity would be when he was asked, facetiously, "What is your summer name?"

summer onion n Cf **spring onion**
A **scallion** such as *Allium cepa* var *cepa*.

1875 (1881) Duyckinck–Duyckinck *Cyclop. Amer. Lit.* 2.291, Harry contributed his quota in the shape of . . two or three young, green-topped, summer onions. **1966** *DARE* FW Addit **WA**6, *Gloria*—a summer onion, white, somewhat pointed. **1968** *DARE* (Qu. I6, *The kind of onions that come up fresh early in the year, and you eat them raw*) Inf **IN**52, Summer onions.

summer people n pl Also summer folk(s) chiefly **NEast,** esp **NEng** Cf **summer complaint 2**
Summer vacationers.

1870 *Atlantic Mth.* 26.21 **NEng,** There's summer-folks in their ker-ridges comes riding by to see them there hills. **1875** Harris *Perfect Adonis* 14 **NJ,** It's just a little village overflowed by summer people . . and as I said, people come for an economical summer. **1879** Smith *Taghconic* 359 **wMA,** Lenox summer-folk—the most energetic of pleasure seekers—are always trooping to some of them. **1883** *Atlantic Mth.* 50.37 **MA,** There was a fellow here last summer,—a family of summer folks at the Sherman Hotel. **1898** Westcott *Harum* 286 **cNY,** Our friend had met quite a number of the "summer people." **1909** *Daily Gaz. & Bulletin* (Williamsport PA) [27 Jan 7]/6 **MA** (newspaperarchive.com), Among our summer people there is a great demand for 'antiques.' . . All the summer folks was there, and most of the town women and girls. **1938** *Sun* (Baltimore MD) 24 Mar 10/2, New England has been declin-

ing. Her rural areas are given over to a sort of subsistence farming or to the entertainment of "summer people." **1941** *IA City Press–Citizen* (IA) 19 Sept 2/2 **NJ,** Do you summer folks take your country dogs back to town with you? **1941** *LANE* Map 449 *(Tourist)* 2 infs, **CT, NH,** Summer people. **1967** *DARE* FW Addit **neNY,** *Summer people*—the tourist crowd. **1990** King *4 Past Midnight* 625 **ME,** Mr. Merrill made his money "rooking the summer people." **2002** *Portsmouth Herald* (NH) 6 July (Internet) **ME,** When I was a boy many years ago down in Warren, Maine, tourists were known as "summer people."

summer poinsettia n

1 An **amaranth,** usu *Amaranthus tricolor.* Cf **poinsettia B1**

1967 *DARE* (Qu. S26c, *Wildflowers that grow in woods*) Inf **AL**33, Summer poinsettia—smaller than regular size. [*DARE* Ed: This Inf may refer instead to another sense below.] **2002** *Union Daily Times* (SC) 23 July (Internet), One unusual flower at her home is this summer poinsettia. . . Mrs. Neal said she ordered the Amaranthus or summer poinsettias from Park's Seed Co. **2003** in 2004 *DARE* File—Internet **IN,** Flower Show—Annuals—Amaranthus (Summer Poinsettia). *Ibid* **OH,** "I saw a plant called 'Summer Poinsettia'; grows 2 feet with red, yellow and green leaves. Is there another name?"—That's Amaranthus. **2004** *Ibid* **NC,** Occasionally while driving around the county I will see an Amaranthus tricolor. The book [sic] list Tampala and Jacob's Coat as common names but I have heard it called summer poinsettia.

2 A **spurge,** usu *Euphorbia heterophylla.*

2003 in 2004 *DARE* File—Internet **TN,** This species [=*Euphorbia cyathophora*] is not as common as *Euphorbia heterophylla* . . which is also known as "Summer Poinsettia" (as are several varieties of Amaranthus . .).

3 A **hibiscus** (here: *Hibiscus coccineus*).

2004 *DARE* File—Internet **NJ,** Summer Poinsettia Seeds—Seeds selected from Hibiscus coccineus. . . We obtained seeds for our plants from a dear friend in New Jersey where the plants are called 'Summer Poinsettia'.

summer redbird n Cf **redbird c, d, winter redbird**
The male **summer tanager;** rarely, the male **scarlet tanager.**

1731 Catesby *Nat. Hist. Carolina* 1.56, *The Summer Red-Bird.* . . They are Birds of Passage, leaving *Virginia* and *Carolina* in Winter. **1791** Bartram *Travels* [290 *bis*], M[erula] Marilandica, the summer red bird. **1844** DeKay *Zool. NY* 2.175, The *Red-bird*, or *Summer Red-bird*, comes to us from the South, but . . only during the hottest part of the summer. **1895** *Atlantic Mth.* May 607, It was a summer tanager, I told him, or a summer redbird. **1951** *AmSp* 26.272, *Summer redbird* (scarlet tanager, Pa., Mich., and summer tanager, generally). **2004** PA Game Comm. *Wildlife Notes* (Internet), *Tanagers.* . . Summer Tanager—This all-red tanager breeds mainly in the Southeastern U.S., where it is called the "summer redbird." **2004** *DARE* File—Internet **sAL** (as of 1950s), On a summer day we might catch a glimpse of a "Summer Redbird" high in the pecan tree.

summer robin n Cf **winter robin**
=robin 1.

1917 *Wilson Bulletin* 29.2.85 **wOR, wWA,** *Planesticus migratorius propinquus* [=*Turdus m.*] . . Summer robin, western Washington and Oregon.

summer rockets n
A **bugbane 1** (here: *Cimicifuga racemosa*).

1959 Carleton *Index Herb. Plants* 113, *Summer Rockets:* Cimicifuga racemosa.

summer rose-cup n
An **evening primrose a** (here: *Oenothera kunthiana*).

1959 Carleton *Index Herb. Plants* 113, *Summer rose-cup:* Oenothera kunthiana.

summers See **somewheres**

summer salmon n
=rainbow trout.

1953 Roedel *Common Fishes CA* 43, Steelhead rainbow trout. . . Unauthorized Names: Salmon trout, half pounder, summer salmon, hardhead. **1975** Evanoff *Catch More Fish* 79, They [=steelheads] are also called salmon trout, summer salmon, and hardheads.

summer's darling n
A **farewell-to-spring** (here: *Clarkia amoena*).

1911 Jepson *Flora CA* 279, G[odetia] [=*Clarkia*] *amoena*. . . Summer's Darling. . . Very common and showy on shady banks or bushy hillslopes in San Mateo Co., Oakland Hills and Marin Co.   **1949** Moldenke *Amer. Wild Flowers* 93, Summers-darling or farewell-to-spring, *G[odetia] amoena*, has . . lilac-crimson or red-pink flowers, often with a darker central and basal splotch.

summerset   See **somerset**

summer's farewell   See **farewell-summer**

summer sheldrake n
=**hooded merganser.**
   1888 Trumbull *Names of Birds* 73 **CT,** At Essex . . [the hooded merganser is known as] summer sheldrake.   **1951** *AmSp* 26.272 **CT, MI,** *Summer sheldrake* means the hooded merganser in Connecticut and Michigan.

summer shrike n
   A **loggerhead shrike** (here: *Lanius ludovicianus migrans*).
   [**1911** Seton *Arctic Prairies* 302, It [=a northern shrike] flew off much after the manner of the Summer Shrike.]   **1914** Eaton *Birds NY* 2.358, The smaller varieties [of shrike], such as our Migrant or Summer shrike, are mostly beneficial on account of their habit of destroying mice, grasshoppers, and the larger beetles.

summer sickness   See **summer complaint 1**

summer snake n   Also *summer green snake*
   A **green snake,** usu *Opheodrys aestivus.*
   1802 Shaw *Genl. Zool.* 3.2.551, Summer Snake. Coluber Æstivus. . . Native of many parts of North America, residing on trees.   **1876** Jordan *Manual Vertebrates N. U.S.* 179, *Cyclophis* [spp]. . . Summer Snakes. *Ibid, C. aestivus* . . Summer Green Snake. . . a most exquisite little creature.   **1908** NJ State Museum *Annual Rept. for 1907* 196, Opheodrys aestivus. . . Summer snake.   **1918** *Copeia* 58.66 **PA,** Opheodrys aestivus, Summer Green Snake, Green Whip Snake.

summer sores n pl   esp **S Midl**   Cf **dew sore**
   A skin eruption, usu impetigo, typically suffered by children in the summer.
   1928 *Health Bulletin* 43.10.24, Impetigo Contagiosa. . . is most prevalent in warm weather it is sometimes called by laymen "summer sores in children."   **1932** *Educ. Method* 12.33 **ceGA,** A bulletin . . was given each child . . containing information about how to . . prevent the usual epidemic of summer sores.   **1962** TN Folk Lore Soc. *Bulletin* 28.6, The whole herb [=toadflax] chopped and boiled in lard until it is crisp makes a wonderful ointment which is soothing and healing to ulcerous skin eruptions, summer sores, etc.   **1981** *DARE* File **ceKY** (as of c1930), Dew sores or summer sores.   **1983** *MJLF* 9.1.58 **ceKY** (as of 1956), *Summer sores* . . impetigo.   **1985** Tyler *Hoosier Remedies* 140 **IN,** "Summer sores" will heal rapidly after they have been licked thoroughly by a dog.   **2004** *DARE* File—Internet **OK** (as of c1960), Remember summer sores and the alleged cure was eating raisins and the treatment was putting sulfur on the sores?

summer sparrow n
   A sparrow such as the **pinewoods sparrow** or **vesper sparrow.**
   1823 Latham *Genl. Hist. Birds* 6.136 **GA,** Summer Finch. . . is called the Summer Sparrow.   **1876** Jordan *Manual Vertebrates N. U.S.* 187, *Peucaea* [spp]. . . Summer Sparrows. . . *P. aestivalis* [=*Aimophila a.*]   **1906** *Archives of MD* 479.1275, It shall not be lawful to kill in Montgomery county any . . chipping or summer sparrow [etc].   **1951** *AmSp* 26.272 **NC, GA,** *Summer sparrow* (vesper sparrow . .).   **1969–70** *DARE* (Qu. Q21, . . *Kinds of sparrows*) Infs **NC67, VA43,** Summer sparrow.

summer squash n   For varr see quots   **widespread, but less freq C and S Atl, Lower Missip Valley**   See Map
   A **squash** n¹ **B1** (*Cucurbita pepo* varr) whose fruit is used in summer.   For other names of var of these see **long-neck squash, pattypan ~, white ~**
   1815 (1914) Bentley *Diary* 4.346 **MA,** A more free use has been made of the summer squash than ever before known.   **1842** in 1866 Hawthorne in *Atlantic Mth.* July 46, Summer-squashes are a very pleasant vegetable to be acquainted with. They grow in the forms of urns and vases,—some shallow, others deeper, and all with a beautifully scalloped edge.   **1902** *Jrl. Amer. Folkl.* 15.259, Varieties of squash are distinguished as summer-squash, winter-squash, Hubbard squash, crook-neck squash, etc.   **1925** *Book of Rural Life* 9.5251, Summer squashes are

used as a cooked vegetable while very young and before the outer wall or shell has hardened. . . Of summer squashes the chief varieties are the White and Yellow Bush Scallops, or Pattypans, and the Crooknecks.   **1948** Beston *N. Farm* 140 **cME coast,** The old-fashioned "summer squash" has never been so good since the government straightened its neck.   **1949** *Natl. Geogr. Mag.* Aug 162, The small, quick-growing forms that are eaten before the rinds and seeds begin to harden are called summer squash and belong to the species *C. pepo.*   **1965–70** *DARE* (Qu. I23, . . *Kinds of squash*) 321 Infs, **chiefly Nth, N Midl, West,** Summer squash; **CA57,** Summer squash—the oblong yellow one; **CA87,** Summer squash—the scalloped white ones; **IL35,** Summer squash—can be round or long and narrow; green, white, or different colors; **IA24,** Summer squash—big at one end; a long, curly neck; **MN14,** Summer squash—matures early—a general term for one like a long cucumber; **NV7,** Summer squash—all different sizes and shapes—named for [the] ripening time; **MA83,** Straightneck summer squash; **MI19,** Flat summer squash; **CT4, FL31, NY128,** Summer crookneck squash; **NY233,** Crookneck summer squash; **NC3,** Summer yellow squash; **NC10,** Summer straightneck squash; **SC62,** Yellow summer squash; **TX21,** White summer squash; (Qu. I3) Inf **NH16,** Summer squash; (Qu. L34, . . *Most important crops grown around here*) Inf **CT4,** Summer squash.   **1986** Pederson *LAGS Concordance* **Gulf Region,** 20 infs, Summer squash; 2 infs, Yellow summer squash; 1 inf, Summer squash—white; 1 inf, Summer squash—yellow crookneck.

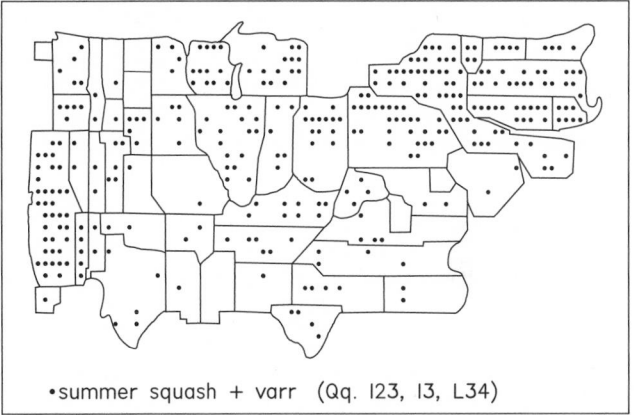

•summer squash + varr (Qq. I23, I3, L34)

summer tanager n
   A tanager *(Piranga rubra)* native chiefly to the South and South Midland.   Also called **bee bird 2, French mockingbird 5, quaker 2, red caille, redbird d, summer ~, yellow caille**
   1783 Latham *Genl. Synopsis Birds* 2.220, *Summer T[anager].* Muscicapa rubra. . . A Little bigger than an House Sparrow. . . Inhabits *Carolina* and *Virginia* in the summer.   **1868** Cronise *Nat. Wealth CA* 459, The Summer Tanager . . , common in the Atlantic States in summer, is also found in the Colorado valley.   **1890** Warren *Birds PA* 252, The Summer Tanager is a very rare and irregular summer visitor in Pennsylvania.   **1913** *Auk* 30.499 **Okefenokee GA,** Summer Tanager. . . Fairly common in the pines on Billy's Island, but not found elsewhere in the swamp except on Floyd's Island.   **1969** *DARE* FW Addit **KY,** *Summer tanager*—also known as bee bird. The summer tanager is the one here accused of eating bees. Common.

summer teal n   Cf **fall teal, spring ~ 2**
   The blue-winged teal *(Anas discors).*
   1888 Trumbull *Names of Birds* 30 **seNY,** *Blue-winged Teal* . . also known as *summer teal*. This latter name is common at Moriches, Long Island, and I am inclined to believe that I have heard it among the gunners of other localities.   **1917** (1923) *Birds Amer.* 1.124, The Blue-wing is the common summer Teal of the open prairie regions of the northwest.   **1944** *Times Recorder* (Zanesville OH) 31 Mar sec B 7/2, Blue-wings, which love warm weather enough to have earned the name of "summer teal" are not expected in great numbers for a few weeks.   **1955** MA Audubon Soc. *Bulletin* 39.314 **MA,** Blue-winged Teal. . . Summer Teal. . . An earlier fall migrant than the Green-wing, it sometimes comes in summer, i.e., August.   **1967** *DARE* (Qu. Q5, . . *Kinds of wild ducks*) Inf **SC40,** Summer teal—stay year-round.   **1969** Longstreet *Birds FL* 34, So many blue-winged teals stay in Florida from the end of August to the latter part of the following April, and come south so early, that they are commonly referred to as "summer teals".

summer time n [Cf *OED2* *summer-time* sb. 2]
=fast time 1.

1937 *Lit. Digest* 1 May 9, Daylight-saving or, as it is now coming to be called, "fast" or "summer" time.

summer titi n Cf **titi 1b**
=he-huckleberry 1.

1968 *DARE* FW Addit **GA**25, Ironwood—old-fashioned nickname for the summer ty-ty tree. **1971** *Sheboygan Press* (WI) 26 Jan 7/4, Naturally green honey is being produced in North Carolina, from the nectar of a shrub known as the summer titi. **2000** *Natl. Honey Market News* June **GA,** Honey producers in the southern portions of the state worked off summer titi during early to mid June.

summer trout n

A **weakfish.**

1909 *Atlanta Constitution* (GA) 30 May sec B 2/6, It remained for Captain Ben White . . to make it possible for the public to enjoy a day's sport catching summer trout weighing from around two pounds up to six and eight and even ten pounds. **1934** *Coshocton Tribune* (OH) 29 May 7/7 **Atlantic coast,** The boys of the salt rod are preparing for the weakfish. . . The fish, sometimes known as . . summer trout . . is an excellent food fish. **1966–67** *DARE* (Qu. P2, . . *Kinds of saltwater fish caught around here . . good to eat*) Infs **GA**11, **SC**43, 63, Summer trout. **1986** Pederson *LAGS Concordance,* 1 inf, **ceGA,** Summer trout. **2004** *DARE* File—Internet, They [=weakfish] are more abundant from North Carolina to Florida in colder months and Delaware to New York as temperatures rise. This led to one of the common names, "summer trout," because anglers in the populated Northeast would only catch them during the summer months.

Summerville Indian n SC Cf **brass ankle, Marlboro blue, redleg 4**

A person of racially mixed ancestry living near Summerville, South Carolina.

1945 *Amer. Jrl. Sociol.* 51.35 **SC,** People . . who do not fit into the biracial caste system. . . These outcastes, whom I call "mestizos," are designated by a wide variety of names, none of them flattering. . . they are called . . "Summerville Indians," [etc]. **1946** *Social Forces* 24.439 **SC,** These [mixed-race] peoples are located mainly on the coastal plain area of the State. . . other nicknames are "Greeks," "Portugese," [sic] . . Yellow-hammers, Summerville Indians. **1963** Berry *Almost White* 35, Sometimes it is the nearby town which gives the people their name. Hence, we have the Summerville Indians in South Carolina. **1966–67** *DARE* (Qu. HH29a, . . *People of mixed blood—part Indian*) Inf **SC**44, Summerville Indian—don't gee-haw with White or Black community, live apart, racial composition a mystery; (Qu. HH29b, . . *People of mixed blood—part Negro*) Inf **SC**21, Summerville Indians—not White or Negro—mestizos, don't fit with either racial community; so called because they live near Summerville. **1995** *Tampa Tribune* (FL) 28 Feb 2 (Internet), She moved to this area two months ago from Summerville, S.C. She was . . active at the Summerville Indian Reservation.

summer warbler n
=yellow warbler.

1842 Thompson *Hist. VT* 1.81, The Summer Warbler. *Sylvia aestiva.* . . Greenish yellow above; crown and beneath bright golden yellow; breast and sides with long spots of reddish orange. **1892** *Atlantic Mth.* Oct 575 **MA,** Our yellow summer warbler is far prettier and more dainty than the [British] yellow-hammer. **1903** Dawson *Birds OH* 1.135, The Summer Warbler's gold is about as common as that of the Dandelion, but its trim little form has not achieved any such distinctness in the public mind. **1957** Barnes *Nat. Hist. Wasatch Spring* 59 **UT,** Flitting about the same willows . . are some real warblers, the yellow or summer warbler and . . the Audubon. **1968** *Daily Times–News* (Burlington NC) 16 Feb sec A 4/2 **seNY,** Some index of change, some certainty of the seasonal sequences, turn the oriole and the summer warbler northward.

summer wood n chiefly **Nth, West** *old-fash* Cf **squaw wood**

Wood (or similar fuel) for summer cooking, usu consisting of quick-burning species or scraps of var sorts.

1875 *Atlantic Mth.* 35.210 **Nth,** We . . [brought] back to the door load after load of sticks and limbs and chips for summer wood. **1893** *Woodland Daily Democrat* (CA) 9 June [2]/3 (newspaperarchive.com), [Advt:] Summer Wood, Gasoline. *Lowest Prices.* **1903** *Ottumwa Daily Courier* (IA) 11 Apr 8/2, [Advt:] Use cobs for summer wood. For sale at our elevator. **1907** *Daily Northwestern* (Oshkosh WI) 2 July 5/6,

[Advt:] *Bass wood bark,* Good Summer Wood. 50¢ per cord at Our Yard. **1915** *Amer. Forestry* Oct 964, Sometimes chestnut is used in rural districts, where the gas range is not, as "summer wood." The fact that it ignites and burns quickly renders it desirable when a light, quick fire is wanted. **1932** *Reno Eve. Gaz.* (NV) 29 Apr 15/7, [Advt:] For Sale—All pine summer wood for quick heating $4.50 cord load. **1949** *Gaz. & Bulletin* (Williamsport PA) 4 Aug 15/1, [Advt:] Summer wood, hardwood blocks, $5 load. **1979** *WI State Jrl.* (Madison) 16 Sept sec 3 1/4, Fast-burning woods like poplar and basswood . . are referred to [in some rural areas] as "summer wood," meaning they were used for quick kitchen-cooking fires on hot summer days. **c1980** in 2005 *DARE* File—Internet **NH** (as of c1905), There is a difference between gray birch and white birch. Gray birch never grows big; it burns readily, green. We had a lot of it, so it became our summer wood.

summer woodpecker n
=red-headed woodpecker 1.

1822 Latham *Genl. Hist. Birds* 3.396 **GA,** It [=the red-headed woodpecker] is called in Georgia the Summer Woodpecker, and Corn-eater.

summer yellowbird n Cf **summer canary**

1 **=yellow warbler.**

1791 Bartram *Travels* 292, P[arus] luteus, the summer yellow bird. **1844** DeKay *Zool. NY* 2.99, This [=*Sylvicola aestiva* [=*Dendroica petechia*]] is a very common species in our State, and is called *Summer Yellow-bird,* to contradistinguish it from the *Common Yellow-bird (Carduelis tristis),* which is seen here at all seasons of the year. **1875** Flagg *Birds Seasons New Engl.* 93, The Summer Yellow-Bird is one of that incomparable tribe of warblers. . . His plumage is not bright yellow, but faintly streaked with olive on the back and wings. **1898** (1900) Davie *Nests N. Amer. Birds* 436, Yellow Warbler. . . Known by several names, such as Summer Warbler, Summer Yellow-bird, Blue-eyed Yellow Warbler and Golden Warbler. **1946** Kopman *Wild Acres* 99 **LA,** The yellow warbler, or summer yellowbird, is another species that has practically disappeared from . . New Orleans.

2 A **goldfinch 1** (here: *Carduelis tristis*).

1899 Howe–Sturtevant *Birds RI* 70, American Goldfinch.—*Summer Yellowbird.* . . An abundant summer, and common winter resident. **1932** Bennitt *Check-list* 61 **MO,** Eastern goldfinch. . . Wild canary; summer yellow-bird; thistle-bird; salad bird. **1966** *DARE* (Qu. Q14, . . *Names . . for . . goldfinch*) Inf **NC**27, Summer yellowbirds.

summons v chiefly **NEast, Sth, S Midl, SW** See Map

To serve with a summons or similar legal order; to take out a summons against.

1659 in 1867 Upham *Salem Witchcraft* 1.433 **MA,** John Godfrey . . shall be legally summonsed thereunto. **1676** in 1868 Sewall *Hist. Woburn MA* 58, The Selectmen mett . . and summonsed Hopestill Foster for inordinate wages. **1729** in 1857 *New Engl. Hist. & Geneal. Reg.* 11.244 **MA,** Then I . . Summonsed Danil Jesham to appeear at ye same time. **1853** Flagg *Venice* 2.451, He had summonsed its officers to justify themselves for disobedience of orders. **1880** *Living Age* 147.507 **TN,** He . . brought up sixteen children, not one of whom, except me, has ever been summonsed before a justice. **1893** Shands *MS Speech* 61, *Summons.* Used as a verb even by educated people; as, "He was summonsed before the court." **1899** (1912) Green *VA Folk-Speech* 429, *Summons.* . . To serve with a summons. **1909** *DN* 3.159 **nwAR,** *Summons.* . . To summon. "They summonsed me." *Ibid* 377 **eAL, wGA,** *Summons.* . . To summon to court. Common. **1946** *PADS* 6.29 **eNC** (as

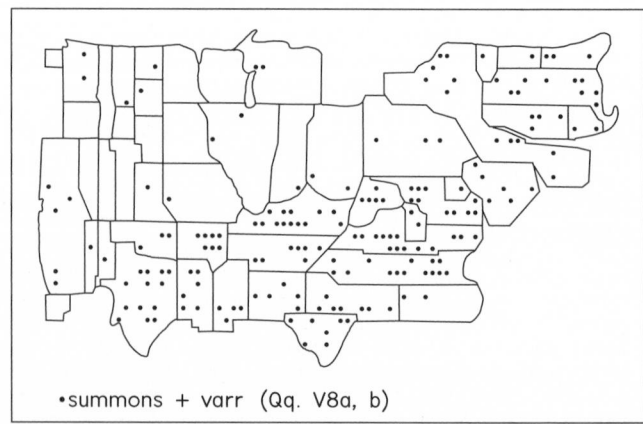

•summons + varr (Qq. V8a, b)

of 1900–10), *Summons.* . . To summon. "I was summonsed to court last week." . . Common. **c1960** *Wilson Coll.* **csKY,** Uncle Ed has been summonsed to serve on the jury. **1965–70** *DARE* (Qu. V8b, *Of a person who has been given a paper ordering him into court . .* "*He was _____ into court.*") 179 Infs, **chiefly NEast, Sth, S Midl, SW,** Summonsed; **CT**30, Summonsed in; **OK**28, Summonsed to appear in; (Qu. V8a) Inf **FL**39, Summonsed. **1992** *NY Times* (NY) 24 May 38/1, "If they're legal, fine," Chief Ryan said, "if not . . , they'll be summonsed." **1997** in 2004 Montgomery–Hall *Dict. Smoky Mt. Engl.* 582 **wNC, eTN,** *Summons.* . . To take out a summons against. . . (known to nine consultants). **2007** *Portland Press Herald* (ME) 8 Feb sec E 2 (Internet), She was summonsed for speed, possession of marijuana and drug paraphernalia.

sumpen See **something A3**

sumpener See **something or other**

sumpin, sump'm, sumpn See **something A3**

sum(p)tin(g) See **something A5**

sumption See **suption** n[1]

sumpweed n
=**marsh elder 1.**
   1936 McDougall–Baggley *Plants of Yellowstone* 128, Sumpweed *(Iva axillaris).*—A low, rather coarse herb with stems 4 to 6 inches high. **1972** *Amer. Anthropologist* 74.335, *Iva annua* . . colloquially known as sumpweed or marsh-elder, is a member of the family compositae. **1990** *Post-Std.* (Syracuse NY) 25 Jan sec D 3/4, *Iva annua*—marsh elder or sumpweed.

sumwheres See **somewheres**

sun and moon n
A children's game: =**Molly Bright.**
   1913 (1980) Hardy *OH Schoolmistress* 37, "Sun and Moon". . . Two of the largest and strongest girls would agree secretly to be Sun and Moon. They would stand eight or ten feet apart facing each other, and the players in a group to one side would come up, one at a time, within eight or ten feet of the line between the Sun and Moon, stop and call out: "How far is it to Briley-Bright?" "Three score miles and ten," answered the leaders. "Can I get there by candle light?" "Yes, if your legs are long and light. But look out for the old witches on the way." Then she would start to run between the two leaders, who would run to catch her. Then both leaders clasped their arms around her, whispering in her ear: "Which will you be, Sun or Moon?" When she had chosen, she was told to stand behind the luminary of her choice. When all had gone through the ordeal and stood behind the two leaders each with her hands clasped round the waist of the one in front, the two leaders grasped hands and there was a trial of strength, the weaker side tumbling over on the grass.

sun-ball n **chiefly sAppalachians, Ozarks** Cf Intro "Language Changes" I.4, **moon-ball** Note: *Sun-ball* has had some currency in (chiefly 19th cent) literary contexts; such uses are not illustrated here.
The orb of the sun.
   1911 *Century Illustr. Mag.* 81.767 **KY,** Geordie . . started off on his long walk, after "giving his hand" to Miss Loring to be back "before the sun-ball drapped" that evening. **1916** *DN* 4.294 **sAppalachians,** *Sun-ball* (the sun). **1918** *Century Illustr. Mag.* 95.396 **sAppalachians,** Let us consider the mountaineers a race apart and dwell lovingly upon such idiosyncrasies as "sun-ball," . . and "man-pusson." **1929** *AmSp* 5.143 **eKY,** The sun-ball was settin'. **1933** *AmSp* 8.1.52 **Ozarks,** *Sun ball.* . . The sun. *When I woke up th' sun ball was jest a-showin' on top o' Dalhart's Bald.* **1940** (1978) Still *River of Earth* 15 **KY,** Father waited, shading his eyes from the sun-ball, trying to see who they were. **1941** Justus *Cabin on Kettle Creek* 6 **eTN,** The sun ball's over the mountain. **1952** Brown *NC Folkl.* 1.596, *Sun-ball.* . . The sun.—Central and east. **1982** Slone *How We Talked* 29 **eKY** (as of c1950), *Sunball*—sun. **1997** in 2004 Montgomery–Hall *Dict. Smoky Mt. Engl.* 582 **wNC, eTN,** *Sun ball.* . . The sun. . . [known to 4 consultants].

sun bass n
A **pumpkinseed 1** (here: *Lepomis gibbosus*).
   1883 *Weekly Hawk-Eye* (Burlington IA) 14 June 11/1, The principle [sic] fish are the pickerel and sun bass. **1938** Schrenkeisen *Field Book Fishes* 246, Common Sunfish—*Lepomis gibbosus.* . . Common names.—Sunfish . . Sun Bass; Sunny. **2004** *DARE* File—Internet **FL,**

There is also some very good freshwater fishing for bass, sun bass and sunfish.

sunberella n Also sp *sunbrella* [Joc blend of *sun* + *umbrella*] Cf **rainberella**
A parasol.
   1957 *Frederick Post* (MD) 26 July 12/6, Sun-brella Days are summer's best! **1966–70** *DARE* (Qu. W1b, *If you use an umbrella . . when the sun is too hot, you call it a _____*) Inf **NY**205, Sunberella; **NJ**3, **VA**2, Sunberella; (Qu. W1c, . . *Joking names . . for an umbrella*) Infs **MS**45, **TN**53, Sunberella.

sunbonnet babies n [After the highly popular *Sunbonnet Babies* textbooks by Bertha Corbett Melcher and Eulalie Osgood Grover (1902 →), featuring drawings of little girls with faces completely hidden by their bonnets]
1 A **blue-eyed Mary 1** (here: *Collinsia grandiflora*).
   1934 Haskin *Wild Flowers Pacific Coast* 323 **OR,** A more distinctive name [for *Collinsia grandiflora*], found in use among the students at Oregon State College, is "sunbonnet babies," a name, which, because of the peculiar shape of the flowers, seems quite appropriate.
2 A **sunbonnets** (here: *Chaptalia nutans*).
   1936 Whitehouse *TX Flowers* 191, Nodding Thistle. . . Sunbonnet Babies *(Thrysanthema nutans)* [=*Chaptalia n.*] . . The leaves form a basal rosette from which grows the slender, leafless flowering stalk bearing the nodding flower head.

sunbonnets n
A plant of the genus *Chaptalia* or the closely related *Leibnitzia lyrata.* For other names of *Chaptalia* spp see **pineland daisy, sunbonnet babies 2**
   1933 Small *Manual SE Flora* 1486, *Chaptalia* [spp]. . . Sunbonnets. **1955** *S. Folkl. Qrly.* 19.233, *Sunbonnets* (Chaptalia tomentosa) bear one purplish blossom on each slender stalk, and as they blow in the breeze remind one of a bevy of sunbonneted girls. **2004** (acc) U.S. Dept. Ag. *Plants Database* (Internet), *Chaptalia albicans.* . . white sunbonnets. *Ibid, Leibnitzia lyrata.* . . Seeman's sunbonnets.

sunbrella See **sunberella**

sunbright n
A **fameflower.**
   1948 Wherry *Wild Flower Guide* 74, Sunbright *(Talinum teretifolium).* . . Flowers ½ in. across, deep carmine-pink, opening for a few hours around midday. **1959** Carleton *Index Herb. Plants* 26, *Cherry sunbright:* Talinum calycinum. *Ibid* 113, *Sun bright:* Talinum calycinum. **2004** (acc) U.S. Dept. Ag. *Plants Database* (Internet), *Talinum parviflorum* . . sunbright.

sun buckle See **sandbakkels**

suncups n Cf **sundrops**
Either of two closely related plants:
a also *suncup:* An **evening primrose b,** esp *Camissonia ovata.*
   1897 Parsons *Wild Flowers CA* 110, Sun-cups. . . The flat rosettes of leaves sometimes measure over a foot across, and are thickly sown with the bright golden flowers, large in proportion to the size of the plants. **1954** CA Div. Beaches & Parks *Pt. Lobos Wild Flowers* 14, Sun-cups thrive throughout the grassland areas, along most of the trails and by the picnic tables. **1967** *DARE* (Qu. S22, . . *The bright yellow flowers that bloom in clusters in marshes in early springtime*) Inf **CA**20, Suncups—not exactly in marshes, but in wet fields. **2004** (acc) U.S. Dept. Ag. *Plants Database* (Internet), *Camissonia boothii* . . ssp *condensata* . . shredding suncup.
b An **evening primrose a.**
   1915 (1926) Armstrong–Thornber *Western Wild Flowers* 330, Suncups—*Lavauxia primiveris (Oenothera).* . . An attractive little plant, in the desert. . . It superficially resembles *Taraxia ovata* [=*Camissonia o.*], the Sun-cups so common on the southwestern coast.

sundae n Usu |ˈsʌnde, ˈsʌndɪ|; rarely |ˈsʌndə| Pronc-sp *sunduh*
Std sense, var pronc.
   1981 Pinckert *Truth Engl.* 18, Take the following sentence: *The chocolate sundae was invented in St. Louis, Missouri.* . . You could say *sunday* or *sunduh*. **1993** Frazer *"Heartland" English* 279 **ceMO,** The "St.

Louis only" category is for the Gateway City's pronunciation of *sundae* as [sʌndə] rather than [sʌnde] or [sʌndi]. As far as I have been able to determine, nowhere else in the country is *sundae* pronounced as [sʌndə], and traditional and popular explanations (mostly by non-St. Louisans) for what is usually perceived as an abberant pronunciation have been less than flattering. . . According to Professor Donald Lance . . Gateway City folklore dictates that turn-of-the-century soda jerks in a particular South St. Louis drug store invented the pronunciation because they received moral objections to the selling of ice cream sundaes [sʌndəz] (which were typically made with Coca-Cola, one of the secret ingredients of which was a derivative of cocaine) on Sundays [sʌndez]. **2004** *DARE* File **St. Louis MO,** The local pronunciation of "sundae" in St. Louis is (or was, when I was a kid) [sʌndə]. *Ibid* **St. Louis MO,** Has DARE completed its entry for 'sundae', including info on the pronunciation (heard hereabouts) 'sunduh'? **2006** *Ibid* **seNE,** I used to hear the pronunciation "sundə" occasionally in Lincoln NE in the thirties. I don't know if the speakers were from STL [=St. Louis]. **2010** *Ibid* **sIL,** We used to pronounce *sundae* more like *sun-duh*. *Ibid* **nwIL,** I was born in 1958 and grew up in Peoria Illinois. There is a pronunciation in Peoria of the word "sundae" as in hot fudge sundae that is distinct and a true localism: sun-duh. The reason I mention it is that it was considered the only proper upper-socioeconomic pronunciation when I grew up, and was deemed correct and standard in that group, whereas the rest of the town called it sundae.

‡**Sunday** n [Perh abbr for *Sunday shine*]
   1995 *DARE* File **nwNC,** *Sunday* = the shine, in phr "to wear the Sunday off"—as said of cheap furniture which ages quickly.

Sunday a week   See **week** n¹ **Ba**

Sunday baby n   Also *Sunday child*   esp **NC**
A child born out of wedlock.
   1944 *PADS* 6.29 **eNC** (as of 1900–10), *Sunday baby.* . . A bastard. . . Common. **1949** Kurath *Word Geog.* 77 **coastal NC,** *Bastard.* . . The playful expression *Sunday baby* or *child* is heard from Albemarle Sound to the mouth of the Neuse. **1967** Faries *Word Geog. MO* 116, *Bastard.* . . *Sunday baby,* and *Sunday child* seem to be practically unknown in Missouri. *Ibid* 146, *Sunday baby* 1 [of c700 infs]—*Sunday child* 1. **1969** *DARE* (Qu. Z11b, . . *[A child whose parents were not married]*) Inf **NC61,** Sunday child.

Sunday below Monday   See **Monday comes before Sunday**

Sunday child   See **Sunday baby**

‡**Sunday cow** n   *euphem*   Cf *DS* K23
   1995 McCormack *Fields Pastures* 129 **cwAL** (as of 1960s), She would never refer to the male cow as a "bull," for instance, because the word "bull" was too coarse for sensitive ears. Instead, she referred to the bull as "the Sunday cow."

Sunday, forty ways till adv phr   Also *forty* (or *six, seven,* etc) *ways for Sunday, seven weeks from ~, forty miles till ~;* for addit varr see quots Cf **Sunday, look both ways for**
In all directions; in confusion, askew; in every way, thoroughly.
   1883 *Overland Mth.* (2d ser) 2.620, The crosses and the wreaths and things flew a dozen ways for Sunday. **1891** Garland *Main-Travelled Roads* 258 **IA,** I expec' that man has jest let ev'rything go six ways f'r Sunday. **1943** *AN&Q* 3.7 **NEng** (as of c1925), Socked it into him seven ways for Sunday. **1948** Sandburg *Remembrance* 890 **IL** (as of c1850), And my hair, instead of every way for Sunday, as they say, was combed down proper. **1951** *AmSp* 26.66, *Forty ways for* (also *from*) *Sunday;* i.e., every which way, in all directions, in confusion. **1952** *AmSp* 27.291 **cIL** (as of c1900), Effective emphasis was achieved by using an expression of time to indicate distance: 'I'll knock him seven weeks from Sunday!' **1960** Criswell *Resp. to PADS 20* **Ozarks,** Every which way, . . forty ways to Sunday or till Sunday. **1965–70** *DARE* (Qu. MM12a, . . *'In all directions'* . . "He shot into a flock of birds and they went _____.") Infs **KS19, NJ16,** Forty ways till Sunday; **DC8, SC40,** Forty ways till Sunday [FW sugg]; **IN22, SC31, VA11,** Forty ways from Sunday; **CO33, TN20,** Forty ways for Sunday; **CA102, MI110,** Four ways for Sunday; **CT12,** All ways for Sunday; **PA126,** Sixty ways for Sunday; (Qu. MM12b, . . *'In all directions'* . . "When she was out on the dance floor, she broke her beads and they went _____.") Inf **VA21,** Forty miles till Sunday; **IN35,** Forty ways from Sunday; (Qu. MM13, *The table was nice and straight until he came along and knocked it _____*) Inf **IN7,** Forty ways for Sunday. **1976** *Newsweek* 10 May 111, For primitive thrills, a man-eating shark gobbling bathers off the

summer beaches of Long Island beats sunken Bermudian treasure six ways to Sunday. **1978** Doig *This House* 210 **MT** (as of c1955), Wouldn't you just know, this thread keeps tangling itself six ways from Sunday. **1984** Wilder *You All Spoken Here* 44 **Sth,** He'd knock you sky west and crooked and four ways from Sunday. **1999** *DARE* File, He tries six ways from Sunday to be nice to her. **2003** Thompson *Nerd* 67 **TN,** Trouble was coming at us six ways to Sunday.

Sunday-go-meeting   See **Sunday-go-to-meeting**

Sunday-go-to-a-meeting throat   See **Sunday throat**

Sunday-go-to-meeting adj phr, also used absol   Also *Sunday-(go-)meeting, Sunday-go-to-church, Sunday-to-go-to-meeting;* for addit varr see quots
Usu of clothes: suitable for attending church, best, most formal.
   1831 (1940) Motte *Charleston to Harvard* 100 **SC,** Rose at 7, and having shaved and dressed myself,—in Sunday-go-to-meeting clothes, started for a walk to Boston. **1831** *Boston Eve. Transcript* (MA) 12 Dec 1/1, They tossed on their "Sunday-go-to-meetings," and crossed into Jarsey. **1859** Taliaferro *Fisher's R.* 171 **nwNC,** His "Sunday go to meetin'" hat is an old-fashioned, smooth, bell-crowned fur hat. **1883** (1971) Harris *Nights with Remus* 264 **GA** [Black], He aint wanter git he Sunday-go-ter-meetin' cloze wet. **1897** *KS Univ. Qrly.* (ser B) 6.92, *Sunday-go-to-meeting:* usually applied to "store clothes." **1909** *DN* 3.377 **eAL, wGA,** *Sunday-go-to-meetin(g).* . . Best. "He has on his Sunday-go-to-meetin' clothes." **1939** Coffin *Capt. Abby* 49 **ME** (as of 1860s), He drove his mother Deborah, in all her jetty Sunday-go-to-meeting best, to the First Parish Church. **1946** *PADS* 6.29 **eNC** (as of 1900–10), *Sunday-go-to-meeting clothes.* . . Best bib and tucker. . . Occasional among young people. **1954** in 1958 Brewer *Dog Ghosts* 62 **TX** [Black], He cain't b'lieve hit's Sandy an' Eerie all diked up in dem fine Sunday-go-to-meetin' clo'es. **1965–70** *DARE* (Qu. W39, *Joking ways of referring to a person's best clothes*) 209 Infs, **widespread,** Sunday-go-to-meeting clothes; 13 Infs, **scattered,** Sunday-go-meeting clothes; **CO27, FL25, GA1,** 13, **KY5, MA64, MI13, NY219,** Sunday-meeting clothes; **IA8, OH6, IL96, NC41,** Sunday-go-to-meeting best (or dress, duds, suit); **CA65, KY19, MO36, VA54,** Sunday-go-(to-)meetings; **ND1, SC10,** Sunday-go-to-church clothes; **MO29,** Sunday-go-to-meets; **NE10,** Sunday-to-go-to-meeting; **NM7,** Sunday-to-meeting clothes; (Qu. W38, *When a man dresses himself up in his best clothes . . he's _____*) Infs **MA1, MI23, MO26,** Got his Sunday-go-to-meeting clothes on; **NC61, PA54,** Got on his Sunday-go-to-meeting clothes; **AL10, MN2, OH43, PA104,** (In his) Sunday-go-to-meeting clothes; **GA1,** Got on his Sunday-meeting clothes; **PA66,** Has his Sunday-go-to-meeting; **CO27,** In his Sunday-meeting clothes; **NY165,** Putting on his Sunday-go-to-meeting clothes; (Qu. W37, *When a woman puts on her good clothes and tries to look her best . . she's _____*) Inf **NC16,** All diked up in her Sunday-go-to-meetin' clothes; **TX1,** Got on her Sunday-go-to-meeting clothes; **PA66,** Has her Sunday-go-to-meetin's on; **AL10,** Sunday-go-to-meeting clothes. **1967** *DARE* Tape **CA15,** But in those days, a man generally had only one good suit, his Sunday-go-to-meeting suit, as it was called. **1980** *DARE* File **IA,** Sunday-go-to-meeting clothes—I was familiar with it in my Dubuque (Ia.) childhood. It was used humorously, always, not only with *clothes,* but with *manners, manner, air, look,* etc. **1985** *NC Folkl. Jrl.* 33.46 **wNC** (as of c1920), Dressed in her best "Sunday-go-to-meetin'" she brought it [=a pie] to the large table near the front of the auditorium. **2004** *Seattle Times* (WA) 7 May Northwest Life sec 2 (Internet), It is a fond, sentimental, Black-sisterhood-is-powerful pastiche of anecdotes and gospel songs, strung together like so many beads in a "Sunday go to meeting" necklace.

Sunday, look both ways for v phr   Also *look forty* (or *six, seven,* etc) *ways for Sunday;* for addit varr see quots   Cf **Sunday, forty ways till**
To look in various directions, freq as a sign of confusion or embarrassment; also used in var joc expressions to imply that one is cross-eyed; to point in all directions, be disordered.
   [**1834** *Life Andrew Jackson* 102 **ME,** They were sitewated something like squint-a-pipes, who was born in the middle of the week and didn't know which side tu look for Sunday.] **1836** (1838) Haliburton *Clockmaker* (1st ser) 67 **NEng,** With their hair looking a thousand ways for Sunday. **1840** Haliburton *Clockmaker* (3d ser) 185 **NEng,** His hair looked a hundred ways for Sunday. **1845** *U.S. Mag. & Democratic Rev.* 16.242, The varied charms of nature fall as delightfully upon that eye that "looks seven ways for Sunday," as upon one that is "in itself a soul."

1867 Paulding *Tales Good Woman* 288, The brow projected exuberantly . . over a pair of rascally little cross-firing, twinkling eyes, that, as the country people said, looked at least nine ways from Sunday. **1898** Westcott *Harum* 345 **nNY,** You'd ought to have seen his jaw go down. He wriggled 'round in his chair, an' looked ten diff'rent ways fer Sunday. **1899** (1912) Green *VA Folk-Speech* 429, *Sunday. . .* To look both ways for Sunday. Often said of a person staring vacantly about. "What are you standing there for, looking both ways for Sunday?" **1912** *DN* 3.582 **wIN,** *Look forty ways for Sunday. . .* To look hastily in every direction. "He rushed around the corner looking forty ways for Sunday." **1922** *DN* 5.170 **NE, WI,** *Look seven ways for Sunday. . .* To be confused. "He looked seven ways for Sunday." **1927** *AmSp* 2.360 **cwWV,** *Look forty ways for Sunday . .* to look in all directions. "Harry looked forty ways for Sunday when I caught him in the chicken coop." **1960** *VT Hist.* 28.226, He looks both ways for Sunday. He looks six ways for Sunday. **1976** Ryland *Richmond Co. VA* 378, Looking both ways for Sunday or six ways for Sunday. **1982** Slone *How We Talked* 39 **eKY** (as of c1950), You look as if you were born on Wednesday and looking both ways for Sunday.

Sunday-meeting n   See **Sunday-go-to-meeting**

Sunday milkshake n   Cf *DS* DD24

1983 Neuffer–Neuffer *Correct Mispronc.* 18 **cnSC,** Her sale of "Sunday milkshakes"—that's a euphemism for beer sold on the seventh day, contrary to South Carolina's variegated blue laws.

Sunday pipe   See **Sunday throat**

Sunday pone n   Cf **Sunday pudding**

1940 Writers' Program *Guide MD* 444 **seMD,** Good cooking is a Snow Hill tradition, whether the food is terrapin in chafing dishes . . or the noted Sunday-pone of Worcester County. The latter is a damp but digestible form of corn bread (also called sweat-pone) that is cooked slowly all night in large iron pots. Nowadays the pone pot and its mixture of meal and molasses is put in the stove oven, but in old times it was set in the fireplace, covered with embers, and left until morning.

Sunday-school word n

A profane utterance; broadly, a taboo word of any sort.

1876 *Hagerstown Mail* (MD) 24 Nov 1/7, His wife discovered that he had tacked down the wrong side. The double process of ripping up the carpet and ripping out Sunday school words was here instituted. **1898** *Bucks Co. Gaz.* (Bristol PA) 23 June 4/3, We stood all day in . . a drizzling rain without tents, blankets or rations . . but under existing circumstances Sunday school words were not so profuse as they might have been. **1903** *Indiana Weekly Messenger* (PA) 11 Feb 4/4, Meanwhile Silas sat astride the log in a pouring rain and thought Sunday-school words. **1906** *DN* 3.159 **nwAR,** *Sunday school words. . .* Oaths, curses. "I felt like going off and saying some Sunday school words." **1909** *DN* 3.377 **eAL, wGA,** *Sunday-school words. . .* Curse words, oaths. [**1917** in 2007 *DARE* File—Internet **VA** (as of 1863), The water came to the level of my shoulders. How ever, we crossed safely, many of the boys prayed and some of them used Sunday School words in the wrong place.] **2004** in 2007 *Ibid* **MN,** Judge Porter told the school lawyer . . " . . If you don't cooperate, I'll throw your ass in jail." People in the courtroom were in shock—first time we ever heard a judge use a Sunday-school word in open court. **2006** in 2007 *Ibid* **AL,** He and I used a few sunday school words to [sic], sometimes the middle finger too!

Sunday throat n   Also *Sunday pipe, ~-go-to-a-meeting throat* joc

One's windpipe.

1894 (1895) Krohn *Practical Lessons* 71, When a dry cracker crumb lodges in one's "Sunday throat," swallowing, coughing, shedding tears, and changes in breathing and circulation inevitably result. **1905** *Stevens Point Jrl.* (WI) 11 Nov 7/1, Well, ma swallowed something crosswise down her Sunday throat and choked, and pa swatted her on the back so she would cough it up. **1907** Sinclair *Lure Dim Trails* 128 **West,** Hank was taken with a fit of strangling that turned his face a dark purple. Afterward he explained brokenly that something had got down his Sunday throat. **1914** Perkins *Eskimo Twins* 36, The water went down his "Sunday-throat" and choked him! **1955** *Post–Std.* (Syracuse NY) 18 Oct 10/4, As a rule, the individual with a mouthful of food is distracted and oops, it goes down the Sunday throat. **1965–70** *DARE* (Qu. X7, . . *The throat:* "*Some food got stuck in his _____.*") 24 Infs, **scattered,** Sunday throat; NY93, WI43, 47, Sunday pipe; MD9, Food went down my Sunday throat; WA1, Sunday-go-to-a-meeting throat. **1982** *Smithsonian Letters* **OH,** Here are a couple of expressions my mother-in-law,

from Wood County, Ohio, used to use: "It's gone down his Sunday throat," when someone choked a bit while eating. **2002** *DARE* File **nwMO,** The expression is alive and thriving in my everyday speech (ultimately NW Missouri), where it refers to matter going down the windpipe when it should have gone down the "other throat." The resultant gagging and sputtering evokes the comment "it/something went down my/your Sunday throat."

Sunday-to-go-to-meeting   See **Sunday-go-to-meeting**

Sunday week   See **week** n[1] **Ba**

sun devil n

1 =**dust devil 1.**

1967 *DARE* (Qu. B16, *A destructive wind that comes with a funnel-shaped cloud*) Inf **TX5,** Sun devil—not destructive; little dust swirls. **1997** *DARE* File—Internet **AZ,** According to the ASU School of Climatology, a "sun devil" is an unusual atmospheric condition caused by a high degree of sunlight, somewhat similar to a dust devil.

2 See **sunfish 1c.**

sundew n

Std: a plant of the family Droseraceae, usu *Drosera rotundifolia.* For other names of *D. rotundifolia* see **dew plant, eyebright 7, flycatch plant, Venus's-flytrap 2**

sundial n

A **lupine,** usu *Lupinus perennis.*

1840 MA Zool. & Bot. Surv. *Herb. Plants & Quadrupeds* 63, *L[upinus] peren[n]is. . .* Sun Dial. Perennial, often growing in splendid clusters. **1892** *Jrl. Amer. Folkl.* 5.94 **nOH,** *Lupinus villosus,* monkey faces; sun-dial. **1901** Lounsberry *S. Wild Flowers* 268, Many of them [=lupines] have the peculiarity of turning to face the sun and are called "sun dials." **1922** *Amer. Botanist* 28.76, *Lupinus perennis. . .* The most descriptive but little used name is "sundial" possibly in allusion to the round pinnate leaves whose leaflets spread out in a circle like the conventional sundial though Wood says the reference is to the leaves which follow the sun all day. **1982** *Plants SW* (Catalog) 21, Sundial Lupine— *L. perennis.*

sun dog n   [*OED2* 1635 →]   **chiefly Nth, N Midl**   Cf **rain dog, water dog 3, weather gall, windgall**

A parhelion or a halo around the sun.

1700 Tulley *Almanack* np **Boston MA,** Also the Sun-dogs (as they call them) appearing in the Morning or Evening, is a sign of Cold, Wet & windy weather, especially in the Winter time. [**1831** *Star* (Gettysburg PA) 9 Mar 1/1, [From an account of a lunar eclipse:] A third declared it was . . an enormous sun-dog, as big as all out doors, carrying away the moon in his mouth.] **1856** U.S. War Dept. *Rept. Explor. Railroad* 4 app 187, Towards evening, about 20° north of the sun, appeared a bright prismatic-colored segment of an arch, a portion of a halo such as sailors call a sun-dog. **1899** (1912) Green *VA Folk-Speech* 429, *Sun-dog. . .* A mock sun. **1938** in Lib. of Congress *Amer. Memory: WPA Life Hist.* (Internet) **NE,** 1 sun dog on north side of sun colder weather. 1 sundog on south side of sun, warmer and dry weather. Sundog on each side of sun, night of [sic] morning sign of storm. **1942** McAtee *Dial. Grant Co. IN* 63 (as of 1890s), *Sun-dogs . .* mock suns, red spots appearing each side of the sun when near the horizon in frosty weather; thought to presage continued cold. **1945** Hamlin *9 Mile Bridge* 175 **nME,** One dark morning there were three suns burning on the horizon—a sign of a heavy storm. Two were sundogs, reflections through the unsettled atmosphere. **1957** *Hand Coll.* **cOH,** Sun dogs, ends of rainbows in the morning, are "weather breeders," i.e., storms are coming. **1965** Bowen *Alaskan Dict.* 32, *Sun dogs*—Pillars of light on either side of the sun. **1968** *DARE* File **IN, IA,** *Sun dog*—Yellow-white spots in western sky in winter. It denotes cold weather or a blizzard. *Ibid* **NJ,** *Sun dog*—like a rainbow as the sun goes down. One big circle of light. If there are small ones with it you say, "The old bitch is out with her pups." This means rain. **1969** *DARE* (Qu. B5, *When the weather looks as if it will become bad . . it's _____*) Inf **WI75,** Weather breeder is a day (in winter particularly) when there are sun dogs in the morning and generally a southeast or northeast wind; bad weather coming; (Qu. B6, *When clouds begin to increase . . it's _____*) Inf **CT25,** Sun dogs—the clouds float against each other; (Qu. B9, . . *Big clouds that roll up high before a rainstorm*) Inf **CT25,** Sun dogs; (Qu. B11, . . *Other kinds of clouds that come often*) Inf **MI100,** Sun dogs—when the sun appears between clouds. **1986** *DARE* File **WI,** Sun dog: A rainbow seen in a cloud near the sun. Does not go to earth like a normal rainbow. **2004** *Milwaukee Jrl. Sentinel* (WI) 14 Mar 20 (Internet), People often confuse the sun dog with the rainbow. . . The rainbow is in the shape of a bow while the sun dog is bright spots of color that appear on either side of the sun when there is a thin layer of high cirrus clouds composed of ice crystals that cover the sky. Sun dogs usually have no rain or snow associated with them.

sundown n [*OED2* 1620 →] **widespread, but more freq Sth, S Midl, SW** See Map
The time when the sun sets.

1712 Tompson *Heaven* 97 **Boston MA,** Work your piece of a day before Sun-down. **1784** in 1908 Mathews *A. Ellicott* 23 **NEng,** About sun down we got to Jackson's. **1832** Trollope *Domestic Manners* (NY) 146, You can hardly get half a mile before "sun-down," as they call it, warns you that you must run or drive home again, . . for fear you should get "a chill." **1870** *Atlantic Mth.* 26.433 **NY,** Before sundown it looked as if we might have fishing again on the morrow. **1894** *DN* 1.334 **NJ,** *Sun down:* sunset; very common. **1899** (1912) Green *VA Folk-Speech* 429, *Sundown.* . . Sunset; sunsetting. **1902** *DN* 2.246 **sIL.** **1903** *DN* 2.332 **seMO.** **1906** *DN* 3.123 **sIN.** **1907** *DN* 3.237 **nwAR.** **1909** *DN* 3.377 **eAL, wGA.** **1910** *DN* 3.450 **cwNY,** *Sundown.* . . Sunset. In such sentences as "I want to finish cutting this piece of hay by sundown." **1927** *AmSp* 3.139 **eME,** The older people. . . referred to dawn as "sun-up," dusk as "sun-down." **1939** *LANE* Map 74 *(Sunset)* **NEng,** [*Sundown* is widespread throughout the region.] Most informants do not distinguish in meaning between *sunset* and *sundown;* but some use the latter term only in adverbial phrases of time (*until sundown, after* ~, *from* ~ *to dark,* etc.) **1965–70** *DARE* (Qu. A4, *The time of day when the sun goes out of sight*) 306 Infs, **widespread, but more freq Sth, S Midl, SW,** Sundown; **OH4,** After sundown; (Qu. A5, *The time right after the sun goes out of sight, before it becomes all dark*) Infs **AZ12, 15, CA207, MS79, NY80,** Sundown; **AR17, OH41, TX29, VA13,** After sundown; **LA27, TN1,** Between sundown and dark; **LA20,** Late in the evening after sundown; **TX5,** Late sundown; (Qu. A3, *The time between the middle of the day and supper time*) Inf **SC51,** Sundown. **1989** Pederson *LAGS Tech. Index* 18 **Gulf Region,** Sundown (497 [of 914 infs])—sunset (253).

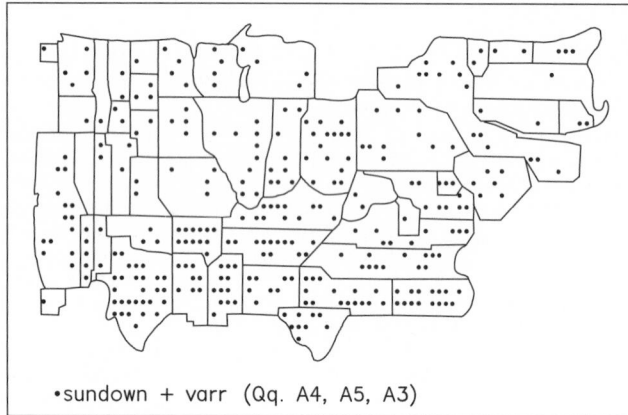

•sundown + varr (Qq. A4, A5, A3)

sundowner n

1 **=opossum.**
1968 *DARE* (Qu. P31, . . *Names or nicknames . . for the . . opossum*) Inf **IN45,** Sundowner.

2 A warm northerly wind that develops in the late afternoon in a short segment of the California coast in the area of Santa Barbara. **sCA** Cf **Santa Ana**
1977 *Capital Times* (Madison WI) 27 July 1, Santa Barbara, Calif. . . The blaze was first reported at 7:42 p.m. Tuesday, burning south of the brush covered hills and whipped by a "sundowner," a hot wind from the northeast gusting the [sic] 45 miles an hour. **2000** *Weatherwise* 53.3.40, A sundowner is a dry, warm California northerly along a 60-mile stretch of the coast near Santa Barbara. It often develops on schedule in the late afternoon or early evening.

sundrops n Cf **suncups**
Either of two closely related plants:

a also *sundrop:* **=evening primrose a.**
1784 in 1785 *Amer. Acad. Arts & Sci. Memoirs* 1.438 **PA,** *Sundrop.* . . They open about eleven o'clock. **1830** Rafinesque *Med. Flora* 2.247, Oenothera biennis. . . *Sundrop.* . . Flowers fragrant and phosphorescent at night. **1840** *MA Zool. & Bot. Surv. Herb. Plants & Quadrupeds* 47,

[*Oenothera*] *fruticosa.* . . Sundrop. Rather shrubby, was found by T.A. Greene, at Plymouth. **1902** (1909) Mathews *Field Book Amer. Wild Flowers* 300, Sundrops—*Oenothera fruticosa.* . . Common in fields and on roadsides everywhere. **1942** (1960) Robertson *Red Hills* 200 **SC,** Wild patches of blazing gold foxglove, . . sundrops, primroses [etc]. **1967** *DARE* Wildfl QR Pl.147A [=*Kneiffia* [=*Oenothera*] *fruticosa*] Inf **SC41,** Sundrop. **1985** Dodge *Flowers SW Deserts* 78, Evening-Primrose—Sundrop. . . *Oenothera primiveris.* . . Texas–New Mexico deserts. Blooms yellow.

b as *sundrop:* **=evening primrose b.**
1985 Dodge *Flowers SW Deserts* 78, Evening-Primrose—Sundrop—*Camissonia brevipes.* . . Arizona and California deserts. Blooms yellow.

sunduh See **sundae**

sunfish n

1 Any of var freshwater fishes, as:

a A fish of the family Centrarchidae, esp of the genus *Lepomis.* **chiefly Nth, Midl, exc NW** For other names of *Lepomis* spp see **bluegill 1, bream B3, dollar sunfish, green ~ 1, Indianfish, johnny roach, kivver, longear sunfish, orangespotted ~, peacock ~ 2, perch n[1] B2, pinfish 2, pottersaw, pumpkinseed 1, redbelly 1, red perch 3, redbreasted sunfish 1, red-eared ~ 1, roach n[1] 2, rock bass 5, shell-cracker, strawberry bream, stumpknocker 1, sun granny, sunny, sun perch, tobacco box 1, yellow perch 4**
1685 Penn *Further Acct.* PA 9, There is the *Catfish,* or *Flathead* . . *Perch black* and *white, Smelt, Sunfish,* &c. **1709** (1967) Lawson *New Voyage* 161 **NC, SC,** Sun-Fish are flat and rounder than a Bream, and are reckon'd a fine-tasted Fish, and not without Reason. They are much the size of Angel-Fish. **1784** (1929) Filson *Kentucke* 26, Suckers, sunfish, and other hook-fish, are abundant. **1814** in 1815 *Lit. & Philos. Soc. NY Trans.* 1.403, Fresh-water Sunfish, or Pond Perch. (*Labrus* [= *Lepomis*] *auritus.*) **1838** *MA Zool. & Bot. Surv. Repts. Zool.* 36, The *Pomotis vulgaris* [=*Lepomis gibbosus*] and *Cephalus brevis* [=*Mola mola*], the one a beautiful little pond fish, a few inches in length, the other a marine species, oftentimes weighing several hundred pounds, are both called "*Sun-fish.*" **1870** *Harper's New Mth. Mag.* 41.305, The sunfish of the interior fresh waters, is a kind of perch, is very different from the sunfish of the coast, which may be either a huge, broad fish, looking as if the posterior half had been cut away, or else a mass of floating, animated jelly. **1884** Goode *Fisheries U.S.* 1.405, The Warmouth—Chaenobryttus gulosus. . . The names "Perch," "Sun-fish," "Goggle-eye," and "Red-eye" it shares with others of its relatives. **1933** LA Dept. of Conserv. *Fishes* 343, The Sunfish family (the Centrarchidae) numbers some thirty-eight American species. . . Here belong such game fishes as the Large-mouthed and Small-mouthed Black Bass, the Spotted or Kentucky Bass, the Long-eared Sunfish, the Warmouth Bass, the Rock Bass and the Sac-a-lait. **1949** Caine *N. Amer. Sport Fish* 29, Rock Bass. . . *Colloquial Names* . . Sunfish[,] Sunfish Bass. **1965–70** *DARE* (Qu. P1, . . *Kinds of freshwater fish . . caught around here . . good to eat*) 193 Infs, **chiefly Nth, Midl, exc NW,** Sunfish; (Qu. P3, *Freshwater fish that are not good to eat*) 23 Infs, **chiefly NEast,** Sunfish; (Qu. P7, *Small fish used as bait for bigger fish*) 9 Infs, **chiefly Midl,** Sunfish; **WV7,** Sunfish minnies. [*DARE* Ed: Some of these Infs may refer instead to other senses below.] **1969** *DARE* Tape **MI**102, He had a few sunfish and that one perch.

b **=golden shiner.**
1933 LA Dept. of Conserv. *Fishes* 444, The Golden Shiner. . . Known under the various names of Roach, Bream, Sunfish [etc].

c also *sun devil:* **=yellow perch 1.**
2001 *DARE* File **swNM,** There is the description of a kind of fish in New Mexico called *sun devil* or *sun fish*[:] "They're real yellow," the informant says[:] "Their fins are real spiky." He is a half Anglo/half Hispanic, born 1982. . . This informant is from here in Silver City.

2 Any of var saltwater fishes, as:

a A **moonfish 2** (here: *Selene setapinnis*).
1878 U.S. Natl. Museum *Proc.* 1.376 **NC,** Vomer [=*Selene*] setipinnis . . *Moon-fish; Sunfish.* **1968–70** *DARE* (Qu. P4, *Saltwater fish that are not good to eat*) Inf **MA**80, Sunfish—same as moonfish; **NC**80, Butterfish—some call them sunfish.

b **=threadfish 3.**
1896 U.S. Natl. Museum *Bulletin* 47.931, *Alectis ciliaris.* . . Threadfish; Cobbler Fish; Sunfish.

c A **filefish** (here: *Aluterus schoepfi*).

1906 NJ State Museum *Annual Rept. for 1905* 359, Alutera schoepfi. . . Orange File Fish. Sun Fish.

3 See **sunfish** v.

sunfish v, hence vbl n, ppl adj *sunfishing* [See quot 1933]
West Cf **swap ends 2a**

Of a horse: to buck violently, usu with a twisting motion; hence n *sunfish* such a style of bucking; n *sunfisher* a horse that bucks in such a manner.

1888 *Century Illustr. Mag.* 35.849 **West,** Sometimes he . . may buck steadily in one place, or "sunfish,"—that is, bring first one shoulder down almost to the ground and then the other. **1913** *DN* 4.28 **NW,** *Sunfisher.* . . A bucking horse that stands straight up on his hind legs. **1921** Thorp *Songs Cowboys* 107 **West** [Black], "I'se got yo' number sure dis time,/ I doan care what yer try!"/ 'Bout den he gimme de ole sun-fish,/ Rail-fence, en do-se-do. **1929** *AmSp* 5.65 **NE** [Cattle country talk], If the "pony". . . twists his body into a crescent and seems to quiver zig-zag fashion in the air, he "sun fishes" and is himself a "sun fisher." **1933** *AmSp* 8.1.29 **nwTX** [Ranch diction], *Sunfish.* A style of pitching—jumping and twisting to alternate sides during each jump, supposedly turning almost to a horizontal position as the sunfish does. **1936** McCarthy *Lang. Mosshorn* np **West** [Range terms], *Sun-fish.* . . A hard type of bucking. Generally high wide jumps taken by a horse in throwing its rider. **1952** FWP *Guide SD* 84, *Sunfisher:* a bucking horse which twists in the air, first to one side and then to the other. **1954** *Julian Apple Day* [21] **csCA,** Around the big pole corral they went, with that cayuse doin' everything in the book, sunfishin', jack-knifin', and just plain hard stiff-legged buckin'. **1987** Doig *Dancing* 317 **MT** (as of c1917), "Watch out for when this sonofabitch starts sunfishing, . . or he'll stick your head in the ground." **1999** Proulx *Close Range* 153 **WY,** The terrain of Scrope himself consisted of a . . ruined back from a pneumatic-drill ride on the back of a sunfishing, fence-cornering, tatter-eared pinto.

sunflower n

1 Std: a plant of the genus *Helianthus*. For other names of var spp see **brown-eyed Susan 4, California sunflower, combflower 3, Indian potato b, Jerusalem artichoke, swamp flower, ~ sunflower 2, throatwort sunflower, wild artichoke 1**

2 also *cutleaf sunflower, wild ~:* A **balsamroot;** see quots. Cf **big sunflower**

1844 (1845) Wilkes *Narr. U.S. Explor. Exped.* 4.434 **cOR,** The seed of the Balsamoriza [sic] (Oregon sunflower), is also used here, being pounded into a kind of meal. **1901** U.S. Dept. Ag. Div. Botany *Bulletin* 26.146 **MT,** Wild Sunflower. . . *Balsamorhiza sagittata*. . . The flowers appear in May and are among the most conspicuous of the season. **1937** U.S. Forest Serv. *Range Plant Hdbk.* W42, Hooker balsamroot, also known as cutleaf balsamroot and cutleaf sunflower. . . The flower stalks . . [bear] a single sunflowerlike blossom. *Ibid* W43, Arrowleaf balsamroot. . . is locally called sunflower, graydock, and breadroot.

3 also *wild sunflower:* A **rosinweed 1.**

1851 (1852) Curtiss *Western Portraiture* 153 **WI,** The mineral flower, the tall, bright purple and red feather, the sun flower [rosin weed] . . render the scene indescribably beautiful. **1967** *DARE* Wildfl QR Pl.251 [= *Silphium perfoliatum*] Inf **OH**14, Sunflowers; **MI**57, Wild sunflower. **1968** *DARE* (Qu. S26a, . . *Wildflowers. . . Roadside flowers*) Inf **KS**16, Rosinweed—a species of sunflower.

4 also *wild sunflower:* A **mule-ear 2;** see quots.

1897 Parsons *Wild Flowers CA* 157, In late spring our open plains and hillsides are often plentifully sown with the large golden flowers of these Californian compass-plants [=*Wyethia angustifolia*], called "sunflowers" by many people. **1902** U.S. Natl. Museum *Contrib. Herbarium* 7.365 **CA,** For remedies in case of poisoning. . . One undoubtedly original cure consists in applying a strong decoction of the root of the sunflower (*Wyethia longicaulis*) to the affected parts. **1957** Barnes *Nat. Hist. Wasatch Spring* 80 **UT,** All the hills are yellowed with sunflowers (*Wyethia amplexicaulis*). **1967** Gilkey–Dennis *Hdbk. NW Plants* 420, Wyethia angustifolia . . *Wild sunflower.* . . heads sunflowerlike. **1967** *DARE* (Qu. S26e) Inf **OR**10, Sunflowers—a mule-ear (fuzzy leaf, large daisy).

5 also *wild sunflower:* =**elecampane.** [*OED2* 1850 →]

1900 Lyons *Plant Names* 202, I[nula] Helenium. . . Wild Sunflower.

1967 *DARE* Wildfl QR Pl.250 [=*Inula helenium*], Infs **OH**14, **SC**49, Sunflower(s); **MI**57, Wild sunflowers.

6 also *wild sunflower:* A **coneflower 1;** see quots. [*OED2* 1763 →]

1901 U.S. Dept. Ag. Div. Botany *Bulletin* 26.123 **MT,** Tall Cone Flower. (*Rudbeckia laciniata* L.) This plant is known in Montana as wild sunflower. . . The flower heads are from 2 to 3 inches across, with yellow drooping rays and a dull yellow disk. **1967–70** *DARE* (Qu. S7, *A kind of daisy, bright yellow with a dark center, that grows along roadsides in late summer*) Inf **CA**185, Sunflower or black-eyed Susan; **CO**4, Black-eyed Susan—a sunflower here [FW sugg]; (Qu. S26d, *Wildflowers that grow in meadows;* not asked in early QRs) Inf **KY**49, Wild sunflower or black-eyed Susan—bigger than yellow daisy.

7 =**goldeneye 4.**

1931 U.S. Dept. Ag. *Misc. Pub.* 101.165 **West,** Some of the woody species of *Viguiera* . . such as *V. helianthoides, V. parishii, V. stenoloba, V. tenuifolia,* and *V. texana*. . . are usually known locally under the comprehensive term sunflowers. **1937** U.S. Forest Serv. *Range Plant Hdbk.* W204-1, Showy goldeneye, a perennial herb with golden-yellow, sunflowerlike flower heads, is sometimes known as rosinweed and as little, small, many-flowered, or mountain sunflower. *Ibid* W204-2, *Viguiera*. . . The species are usually called sunflowers, which name is best restricted to the true sunflowers (*Helianthus* spp.)

8 =**orange sneezeweed.**

1937 U.S. Forest Serv. *Range Plant Hdbk.* W88-1, Orange sneezeweed, sometimes also called Hoopes sneezeweed, owls-claws, sunflower [etc].

9 A **mallow B** (here: *Malva parviflora*).

1949 Curtin *By the Prophet* 80 **AZ,** Malva parviflora. . . No uses for the plant were known at Wetcamp, but I was informed that it is called "sunflower" because the leaves follow the sun and droop at sunset.

10 also *wild sunflower:* An **oxeye 2b;** see quots.

1959 Carleton *Index Herb. Plants* 114, *Sunflower* . . Heliopsis [spp]. **1966–67** *DARE* Wildfl QR Pl.252 [=*Heliopsis helianthoides*] Infs **OH**14, **OR**9, **WA**10, Sunflower; **MI**57, Wild sunflower.

sunflower tree n
=**fringe tree.**

1903 Small *Flora SE U.S.* 920, *Chionanthus Virginica*. . . In rocky soil and along streams, Pennsylvania to Florida and Texas. . . Sunflower Tree. **1955** *S. Folkl. Qrly.* 19.232, *Sunflower Tree* . . is a sheet of pure white color from top to bottom in early March before the foliage appears. **1960** Vines *Trees SW* 849, Vernacular names are . . Snowflower-tree, Sunflower-tree [etc].

sungazer n esp Gulf States Cf **stargazer 3**
Usu =**bittern,** but also **least bittern.**

1916 *Times–Picayune* (New Orleans LA) 2 Apr 5/2, American Bittern. . . Garde-Soleil; Sun-Gazer. **1951** Teale *North with Spring* 132 **GA,** To the Georgia swampmen the bittern is the "sun-gazer." **1957** *Names* 7.117 **AL, LA, TX,** Other cognomens resulting from the bill-pointing attitude of the bittern are: sky-gazer and star-gazer (Ga.), sun-gazer (Ala., La., Tex.), and look-up (N.Y.) **1962** Imhof *AL Birds* 100, Least Bittern. . . Other name: Sungazer. **1968** *DARE* (Qu. Q8, *A water bird that makes a booming sound before rain and often stands with its beak pointed almost straight up*) Inf **GA**35, Sun-gazer—same as bittern.

sunged See **sing** v A2

sun granny n
A **sunfish** n 1a.

1969 *DARE* (Qu. P1, . . *Kinds of freshwater fish . . caught around here . . good to eat*) Inf **KY**28, Sun grannies—small, flat, golden-looking, like a big goldfish. **1993** Kinman *KY Fish* 8, Longear Sunfish. . . Also called: Bream, sun granny, sunperch [etc]. **2001** Ross *Inland Fishes MS* 415, *Lepomis macrochirus* Rafinesque, Bluegill. . . *Local names:* baldface, blue bream . . sun granny, yellow belly.

sun grin n

An involuntary squinting expression caused by bright sunlight; a fixed or humorless grin.

1899 *Werner's Readings & Recitations* 23.116, Some people . . must content themselves with a simple grin: [*Give it in a silly way.*] Then there is the sun-grin. [*Give it.*] **1906** *DN* 3.159 **nwAR,** *Sun-grins.* . . The seeming smiles of a person whose face is not protected against the sun's rays. "Bring my hat around. I've got the sun-grins." **1915** *Cook Co. Herald* (Arlington Heights IL) 1 Oct 1/4, The editor, being meek and lowly, grins a sun-grin as if he liked it. **1929** *Lima News* (OH) 4 June 13/8, [Advt:] We will furnish you a pair of Glasses that will soften the bright rays of the sun and help you avoid the sun-grin and the squinting which results. **1942** McAtee *Dial. Grant Co. IN* 63 (as of 1890s), *Sun-grins* . . squintings to protect the eyes from strong sunlight. **1956** McAtee *Some Dialect NC* 44, Sun-grins. **c1960** *Wilson Coll.* **csKY,** *Sun-grins.* . . A distortion of the face in bright light. **1967–70** *DARE* (Qu. X25, *To close your eyes part way—for example, when looking at the sun*) Infs **IL**135, **KY**11, **MO**20, **TX**32, Sun grin(s). **1988** in 2004 *DARE* File—Internet **neOH,** At the first sight of marching soldiers the crowd broke into applause. . . By the end of the day I had sun-grin from smiling so much. **2003** *DARE* File—Internet **AR,** [Caption:] Me with my usual awful sun grin. **2004** *Ibid* **Cape Cod MA,** [Caption:] Another sun grin pic. *Ibid,* [Caption:] I get in there too but I have a sun grin.

sunhot n *Gullah*

Sunshine, heat of the sun.

1922 Gonzales *Black Border* 179 **sSC, GA coasts** [Gullah], 'E ketch all dem fish, en' 'e couldn' sell'um to de buckruh 'cause dem binnuh leddown all day een de sunhot. *Ibid* 330 [Gullah glossary], *Sunhot—* sunshine, heat of sun. **1928** Peterkin *Scarlet Sister Mary* 87 **SC** [Gullah], "How-come you got de headache?" "I dunno, lessen so much sun-hot to-day done it." That was a poor excuse. Sun-hot could not make July's head ache. **1930** Stoney–Shelby *Black Genesis* 185 **seSC** [Gullah], He find Br' Deer lyin' down in de sunhot in he yard. **1992** Geraty *Bittle* 66 **Charleston SC** [Gullah], Mus' don' cook dead crab, 'kase ef 'e dead een de sunhot, 'e done fuh spile.

sun lotus n

=banana waterlily.

1933 Small *Manual SE Flora* 543, *C[astalia] flava* [=*Nymphaea mexicana*]. . . Yellow Water-lily. Sun-lotus. . . Lakes, ponds, and slow streams, pen[insular] Fla. **1953** Greene–Blomquist *Flowers South* 38, The distinctive yellow water-lily or sun-lotus . . is restricted to peninsular Fla.

sunny n

A **sunfish** n **1a.**

1835 Audubon *Ornith. Biog.* 3.51, The sunny. . . swam to one side, then to another. **1865** Norris *Amer. Angler's Book* 116, This beautiful little fish . . is known in the Middle and Southern States as the Sunfish or "Sunny." Yankee boys call them "Punkin Seeds." **1884** Goode *Fisheries U.S.* 1.405, This [=*Lepomis gibbosus*] is the common "Sun-fish," "Pumpkin-seed," or "Sunny" of the brooks of New York and New England. **1965–70** *DARE* (Qu. P1, . . *Kinds of freshwater fish . . caught around here . . good to eat*) Infs **NJ**27, **NY**118, **PA**89, Sunny (or sunnies)—same as sunfish; **NJ**2, 45, Sunnies; (Qu. P3, *Freshwater fish that are not good to eat*) Inf **NY**32, Sunnies; **NY**51, Sunnies—too small to eat; **PA**141, Sunny. **1982** Barrick *Coll.* **csPA,** Sunny—sunfish. **1989** Gores *Wolf Time* 177 **MN,** The fishermen and hunters who frequented this portion of the Mississippi wetlands could always get from him where the walleyes or sunnies or crappies were hitting. **2004** *DARE* File—Internet **NY,** As winter approaches, most species will feed well and bass, pickerel and sunnies should be easy to catch on a number of baits. *Ibid* **MN,** Lakes that have good spawning habitat but not much food can produce swarms of small adult Sunnies that never grow larger than four or five inches.

sun-pain n **chiefly Sth, S Midl**

A severe headache that begins in the morning and gets better toward evening.

1810 (1908) Drake *Notices Cincinnati* 41 **swOH,** The "sun-pain" or periodical head-ach [sic]. . . consists of a pain in the lower part of the os frontis on one side, near the orbit of the eye, commencing early in the morning, and continuing through a part of the whole of the day. **1834** Baird *View Valley Missip.* 85, A form of winter or relapsing intermittent fever, is 'periodical head-ache,' or 'sun pain,' so called . . from the well known fact, that the fit generally comes on . . about sun-rise and seldom continues after sun-set. **1851** (1856) Dunglison *Med. Lexicon* 434, *Hemicrania*. . . pain, confined to one half of the head. It is almost always of an intermittent character . . at times, continuing only as long as the sun is above the horizon; and hence sometimes called *Sun-pain.* **1899** (1912) Green *VA Folk-Speech* 429, *Sun-pain.* . . Face-ache; neuralgia in the upper part of the face, said to come on with the sun and go off as the sun goes down. Cured by hanging a piece of lead around the neck made of an ounce bullet, with nine holes in it, in the form of a triangle. **1903** *DN* 2.332 **seMO,** *Sun-pain.* . . A kind of headache. Pain over the eyes.

1921 *DN* 5.119 **KY,** *Sun-pain.* . . A pain in the head, at sunrise. Neuralgia, or headache? **1933** *AmSp* 8.1.52 **Ozarks,** *Sun pain.* . . A headache which begins at sunrise and lasts until dark, usually attributed to malaria. **1945** Saxon *Gumbo Ya-Ya* 533 **LA,** In the Delta country there is an affliction called sun pain, which the older people claim is peculiar to that section of the country. Sun pain is a periodic pain located at the back of the head. It grows and wanes with the sun's movements in the sky. [**1952** Brown *NC Folkl.* 1.596, *Sun-pains.* . . Severe pains in the limbs and body, as reported by slaves. The pain began with the rising of the sun and ceased when it set. . . Obsolete.] **1954** Harder *Coll.* **cwTN,** *Sun pain.* . . A severe headache. **1982** Slone *How We Talked* 106 **eKY** (as of c1950), *Hed'dake*—Headache. Said as one word. Some were called "a sun pain." Cure: stay out of the sun.

sun perch n **chiefly S Midl, Lower Missip Valley, Cent** See Map

A **sunfish** n **1a;** see quots.

1749 in 1883 *Century Illustr. Mag.* 26.544 **PA,** June 1st, 1749, received of the Honorable Thomas Stretch, Esquire, & Co., three sun perch. **1804** (1905) Lewis *Orig. Jrls. Lewis & Clark Exped.* 6.174, In this lake there is also . . Sunperch. **1851** *De Bow's Rev.* 11.56 **LA,** *Perch*—Three kinds, Viz., *white, brindled, sun or red-bellied.* **1859** Taliaferro *Fisher's R.* 109 **nwNC** (as of 1820s), Close under the Blue Ridge we had nothing but chubs, hornyheads, pikes, white suckers, sunperch, eels, . . and a few other small varieties of the finny tribes. **1865** Norris *Amer. Angler's Book* 118 **Sth,** The Blue Bream, or Copper-Nosed Bream [=*Lepomis macrochirus*] . . seldom exceeds eight inches in length. The other . . is the Red-Bellied Perch, or Red-Tailed Bream [=*Lepomis auritus*]. There is yet another . . known as the Goggle-Eye, or War-Mouth Perch [=*Chaenobryttus gulosus*]. . . These three species are frequently called Sunfish, or Sun Perch. **1876** NY Acad. Sci. *Annals Lyceum Nat. Hist.* 11.318 **nGA,** *Xenotis sanguinolentus* [=*Lepomis megalotis*]. . . known to the fishermen as Sun Pearch. **1887** Goode *Amer. Fishes* 66 **PA,** *Lepomis auritus.* . . In Pennsylvania it is called "Sun Perch" . . elsewhere it is the . . "Red Bellied Perch." **1916** *Copeia* 36.80 **NC,** Species that occur in the Lumbee between Blue's Bridge and Turnpike Bridge. . . *Eupomotis* [=*Lepomis*] *gibbosus.* Sun Perch. Common. **1933** LA Dept. of Conserv. *Fishes* 349, The Long-eared Sunfish or Blackears. . . has now many common names [including] Sun Perch. **1965–70** *DARE* (Qu. P1, . . *Kinds of freshwater fish . . caught around here . . good to eat*) 17 Infs, **chiefly S Midl, Lower Missip Valley, Cent,** Sun perch; **LA**20, Sun perch—they have a little mouth and bright colors; **MD**20, Sun perch—same as bluegill; (Qu. P2, . . *Kinds of saltwater fish caught around here . . good to eat*) Inf **DE**4, Yellow, red = yellow perch or sun perch; (Qu. P7, *Small fish used as bait for bigger fish*) Infs **KS**17, **MO**20, Sun perch. **1986** Pederson *LAGS Concordance* (Common freshwater fish) 22 infs, **Gulf Region,** Sun perch(es).

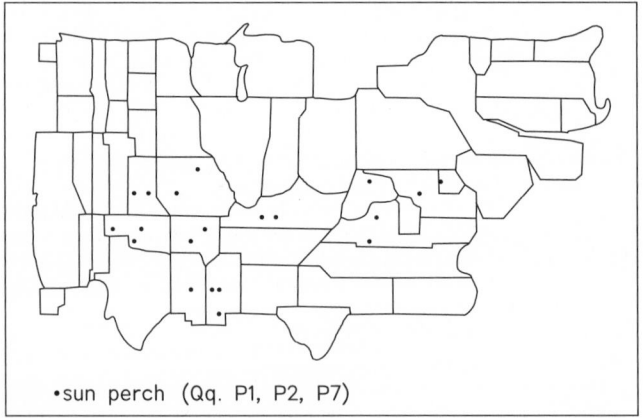

•sun perch (Qq. P1, P2, P7)

sunrising n [*OED2* sunrising "Now *rare* or *arch.*"] **esp Sth, S Midl**

Sunrise, dawn; hence in attrib use, eastern.

1650 in 1849 *Doc. Hist. State of NY* 1.676, No man shall sett any gun, but he shall look to it while the stars appear, and take up the gunn by the sunrising. **1785** (1978) Washington *Diaries* 4.177 **VA,** About Sunrising . . rid up to Keeptrieste. **1807** (1919) Bedford *Tour to New Orleans* 62 **VA,** The barge discovered last night passed us before sunrising. **1966–69** *DARE* (Qu. A1, . . *The time in the early morning before the sun comes into sight*) Inf **LA**12, Before sunrising; (Qu. A2, *The time when the sun first comes into sight*) Infs **GA**4, **KY**5, **NC**60, Sunrising.

[All Infs old]   **1970** *DARE* FW Addit **NJ,** The sunrisin' side of the tree—where to get sassafras for sassafras tea. (Inf . . probably made sassafras tea in Virginia.)

sunset cactus n

A **pincushion cactus 1** (here: *Mammillaria grahamii*).

1912 *Plant World* 15.187 **AZ,** Even the sunset cactus, *Mamillaria grahami* . . becomes decidedly abundant on the desert hills below.   **1942** Hylander *Plant Life* 322, The Sunset Cactus, slightly smaller with grayish-white spines and pink or rose bell-shaped blossoms.   *Ibid* 659, Sunset Cactus—Mamillaria [sic] grahamii.   **2004** *DARE* File—Internet, *Mammillaria grahamii*—Common Name(s): Arizona Fishhook Cactus, . . Sunset Cactus.

sunset flower n   [See quot 2004]

A **milkweed 1** (here: *Asclepias curassavica*).

1992 Wildseed Farms *Wildflowers* (Catalog) 33, Sunset Flower/Scarlet Milkweed. . . The flowers are showy with bright scarlet petals surrounding the orange and yellow hoods.   **2004** *DARE* File—Internet, *Asclepias currassavica—Sunset Flower*. . . Growing to 30″, it carries clusters of orange/red flowers (hence its name) continuously from spring to fall.

sunset lily n

A **leopard lily 1** (here: *Lilium pardalinum* x *humboldtii*).

1938 McFarland *Garden Bulbs* 136, Widely and appropriately advertised as the "Sunset Lily," . . this natural hybrid between two Californian natives, Lilium pardalinum and L. Humboldti, is surely a magnificent plant.   **1976** Bruce *How to Grow Wildflowers* 182, One of the easiest of all to grow is the Sunset Lily, *L. harrisianum* (formerly *L. pardalinum giganticum*), a robust plant with red and yellow turks-caps resembling those of its eastern relatives.

sunshine n

A **gold fields 1** (here: *Lasthenia californica*).

1897 Parsons *Wild Flowers CA* 124, Sunshine. . . *Baeria gracilis* [= *Lasthenia californica*]. . . It literally covers the earth with a close carpet of rich golden bloom.   **1915** (1926) Armstrong–Thornber *Western Wild Flowers* 550, Sunshine, Gold Fields—*Baeria gracilis*.

sunshine bush n

=forsythia.

1902 Earle *Old Time Gardens* 189 **NEng,** In New England gardens the Forsythia is called 'Sunshine Bush.'   **1956** McAtee *Some Dialect NC* 55, Golden candlesticks . . sunshine bushes (Forsythia).

sun spider n

A **wind scorpion;** see quots.

1915 Herms *Med. & Vet. Entomol.* 373 **sCA,** Solpugids. . . Common names applied to this order are "Sun Spider" and "Wind Scorpion."   **1926** Essig *Insects N. Amer.* 13, In the western parts of America they [= Solpugida] are called "solpugids," "sun spiders," and "vinegarones." [*Ibid*, To the Arabs they are known as "akreb-errih" (wind scorpions), to the Spanish as "aranas [sic] del sol" (spiders of the sun).]   **1940** Writers' Program *Guide NM* 19, Wild stories are sometimes heard of the deadly vinegarroon, which is a sun spider *(solpugida)*.   **1947** Dodge *Poisonous Dwellers* 40, The range of the solpugid or sun spider is by no means limited to the desert, but its reputation as a poisonous creature seems to be much worse in the Southwest than elsewhere.   **1969** *DARE* (Qu. R28, . . *Kinds of spiders*) Inf **CA**114, Sun spider. [FW: name gotten out of insect book]   **1980** Milne–Milne *Audubon Field Guide Insects* 935, Although most are nocturnal, these arachnids are sometimes called sunspiders after their sunny desert habitat.   **2004** (acc) U.S. Dept. Ag. *Integrated Taxonomic Info. System* (Internet), Common Name(s): solpugids[,] sun spiders.

sun-squall n   Also sp *sun-squawl*   **NEng**

A **sea nettle** or other jellyfish.

1855 Thoreau in *Putnam's Mag.* 6.161 **Cape Cod MA,** The beach was also strewn with beautiful sea-gillies [sic for *sea-jellies*], which the wreckers called sun-squall, one of the lowest forms of animal life, some white, some wine-colored, and a foot in diameter.   **1859** (1968) Bartlett *Americanisms* 463 **NEng,** Sun-Squall. A term applied, on the coast of New England, to the Medusae, or Sea-Nettles. It appears to be a corruption of the Germ. *Schirmqualle* (lit. umbrella jelly-fish).   **a1862** (1865) Thoreau *Cape Cod* 79 **MA,** He also said that the sun-squawl was poisonous to handle, and when the sailors came across it, they did not meddle with it, but heaved it out of their way.   **1880** *Harper's New Mth. Mag.* 61.503 **ME,** The round, limpid jelly-fish called the sun-squall, occurring sometimes almost numerously enough to stop the way of a boat.

1884 Goode *Fisheries U.S.* 1.169 **NEng,** The jelly-fish, or sun-squalls, which are so abundant along the New England coast in summer.   **1924** *DN* 5.288 **seMA,** Jelly fish are 'sunsqualls' for some unknown reason.

sunthin   See **something A1**

sun time n   [*OED2* 1855]   Cf **God's time, railroad time 2**

Local time (as opposed to standard time).

1887 *Sat. Rev.* (E. Liverpool OH) 7 May 1/3, *The New Time*. Our Broadway neighbor gets badly muddled on the new standard time. . . "Our present time is twenty minutes slower than Pittsburgh time, so that by the change the first bell at the school house, which now rings at 8:40 sun time, will after Monday ring at 9 o'clock sun time. The change will make a difference of 56 minutes between city and railroad time. The change will cause work to begin at 7:20 instead of 7 o'clock, sun time, as at present, and close at 6:20, sun time, instead of 6, as at present."   **1911** (1913) Johnson *Highways Gt. Lakes* 94, Sun time—God's time—is good enough for me.   **1946** Wilson *Fidelity Folks* 42 **swKY,** He said that Fidelity kept sun time rather than railroad time because it was nearer the sun.   **1952** in 1953 Botkin–Harlow *Treas. Railroad Folkl.* 514, The only "time" that existed in this country was local time, commonly called "sun time," which was based upon the transit of the sun across the meridian.   **c1960** *Wilson Coll.* **csKY,** Railroad time. . . Standard time as opposed to "sun time."   **1969** *DARE* Tape **GA**84, At 11:30, which was sun time, and the sun time was twenty minutes ahead of railroad time. Railroad time . . is what standard time is now.   **1976** *DARE* File **MA,** *Railroad time*. . . I have heard old people in the Ohio-Erie, Pennsylvania area tell of having to make the distinction between this and *sun* time.

sun trout n

1 A **weakfish** (here: *Cynoscion regalis*).

1884 Goode *Fisheries U.S.* 1.362 **S Atl,** In the Southern Atlantic States it [=*Cynoscion regale*] is called "Grey Trout," "Sun Trout," and "Shad Trout."

2 **=crappie.** esp **GA**

1966–68 *DARE* (Qu. P1, . . *Kinds of freshwater fish . . caught around here . . good to eat*) Inf **GA**16, Sun trout—same as croppers; **GA**19, 34, Sun trout—same as speckled perch.

sun turtle n   chiefly **NEng**

=spotted turtle or **painted turtle.**

1909 *St. Nicholas* 36.465 **ceMA,** I have three: two painted turtles and one sun turtle.   **1927** *Bridgeport Telegram* (CT) 13 Aug [11]/3 (newspaperarchive.com), There are now a total of five different kinds of turtles included in Pomperaug's collection, wood turtle, musk turtle, painted turtle, sun turtle and box turtle.   **1968–70** *DARE* (Qu. P24, . . *Kinds of turtles*) Infs **CT**36, **MA**80, **OH**84, **RI**6, Sun turtle; **RI**4, Sun turtle—same as spotted turtle.   **1970** *Oshkosh Daily Northwestern* (WI) 22 May 26/7, We have a sun turtle that seems sick.   **2002** *Sentinel & Enterprise* (Fitchburg MA) 2 June sec A 3/2, Sun turtles were spotted basking in the brilliant rays.   **2004** Carroll *Self-Portrait* 8 **PA** (as of c1955), When I asked someone in my neighborhood the next day, I was told that it was a "sun turtle" [*DARE* Ed: **=spotted turtle**].   **2004** in 2005 *DARE* File—Internet **Cape Cod MA,** [I've] had one [=a largemouth bass] regurgitate about a 6 inch diameter shell of a sun turtle.   **2005** *Ibid, Painted Turtle*. . . This is perhaps the most common (or at least the most commonly seen) turtle species in southern New England. It is also known as the Sun Turtle.

sup v   Also with *up*   [*OED2* c1000 →]   *old-fash*

To drink, esp a little at a time; to sip.

1608 in 1895 *Atlantic Mth.* 76.357 **VA,** [They] did long for to sup up that little remnant [of alcohol].   **1881** *Atlanta Constitution* (GA) 8 Oct 8/2, Mr. King succeeded . . in finding Smith quietly supping his mug of beer in a saloon on Marietta street.   **1906** *DN* 3.159 **nwAR,** *Sup*. . . To sip. "He supped his coffee."   **1926** Ferber *Show Boat* 6 **MA,** I try to get you to sup up a little soup.   **1947** *Daily Reg.* (Harrisburg IL) 22 Mar 2/4 **TX,** Frank supped his coffee.   **1949** Hornsby *Lonesome Valley* 112 **eKY,** She took a chicken wing and gnawed on it and supped her coffee.   **1951** *Denton Jrl.* (MD) 28 Dec 8/1 **AR,** He slowly supped his milk, hoping that someone would come and join him.   **1965–70** *DARE* (Qu. H11b, *If he makes a noise with his food, he _____*) 12 Infs, **scattered, Sups; ME**9, Sups his soup; **CO**40, Sups it; (Qu. H11a, *If somebody eats rapidly and noisily, you say he _____*) Inf **NC**51, Sup it—drink. [13 of 15 Infs old, 12 comm type 4 or 5]

sup n   [*OED2* 1570 →]   now esp **Sth, S Midl** *somewhat old-fash*

A sip, swallow (of liquid); a usu small drink.

1871 *Harper's New Mth. Mag.* 42.718 **MA,** To . . eat hard-boiled . . eggs . . "with a sup of Bob's cawfee," was, as the Bos'n says, having "dead loads of comfort." 1892 *Century Illustr. Mag.* 45.315 **NYC,** She "did n't believe in these new-fangled notions that a child must not have a bit or a sup of a thing but milk." 1899 (1912) Green *VA Folk-Speech* 429, *Sup.* . . A small quantity of liquid; he took a *sup* of whiskey. 1913 Wharton *Custom of Country* 105 **NY,** Won't you take just a sup of milk before you go to bed? 1940 Faulkner *Hamlet* 56 **MS,** "I just brought it. Try a sup of it. It's good." The other took the bottle. [1941 *LANE* Map 314 *(A bite [between meals])* 1 inf, **cME,** Sup.] 1949 Hornsby *Lonesome Valley* 321 **eKY,** Uncle Lihugh was walking toward the spring for a sup of water. 1965–68 *DARE* (Qu. BB51b, . . *'Magical' cures for corns or warts*) Inf **TN1,** Nine sups of water; (Qu. DD18, *A drink of liquor, or the amount of liquor taken in one swallow: "He took a good _____.")* Infs **LA11, NC54, VA15,** Sup; (Qu. DD19, *A little drink: "I'll just take _____.";* total Infs questioned, 75) Infs **MS60, OK18,** Sup. [4 of 6 infs gs educ or less, 5 comm type 5] 1972 *Atlanta Letters* **cnGA,** Small Drink—Give me a Sup or Swig of Whiskey. 1975 *Appalachian Jrl.* 2.156 **wNC,** A small portion was a *taddle,* or *tad,* or *sup,* a *dab,* a *skimption,* or a *grain.* 2001 House *Clay's Quilt* 61 **eKY,** "I will, soon's I get me a sup of beer." He grabbed Goody's ice-cold Miller and drank half of it straight down. 2003 in 2005 (acc) Lexis–Nexis Legal Research *State Case Law: TN* (Internet), His father asked the victim for a "sup" of beer but that the victim refused. 2005 *DARE* File—Internet **OR,** You can view some of my work in person at the Portland Coffee House. . . Stop by have a sup of coffee and check out my prints.

supawn n   Also *soupon, suppawn;* for addit varr see quots [Amer Du *sapaen* boiled corn meal < Algonquian; cf Natick *saupaun* softened by water] **chiefly NY** *old-fash* Cf **hasty pudding 1**

Cornmeal mush.

[c1612 (1849) Strachey *Hist. VA Britannia* 183, Asapan, *a hasty pudding.*] [1655 Donck *Beschryvinge* 55, Haer gemeen voetsel en daer sy dit Cooren meest toe gebruycken is *Pap* die men daer te Lande *Sapaen* noemt. [=Their [=the Indians'] staple food, and what they mostly use this grain [=corn] for, is porridge, which the people of that country call *supaen.*]] 1817 *Norwich Courier* (CT) 26 Feb 2/2 **NY,** My soliloquy was interrupted by, *"Sir, your suppawn is ready."* . . Yes Sir, they called our *national dish*—the pride of Connecticut—by the *vile* name of *suppawn.* 1819 (1820) Irving *Hist. NY* 2.110, They [=the Van Bummels of the Bronx] were the first inventors of suppawn or mush and milk. 1835 Hoffman *Winter in West* 1.144 [Writer from NY], I helped myself with an iron spoon from a dish of suppawn. 1847 (1852) Crowen *Amer. Cookery* 236 **NY,** This is the genuine way of making soupon, sometimes called hasty pudding, which however, is a misnomer; few of the old Dutch, around Schenectady or thereabout, would not be disturbed at hearing it called by other than its ancient name, suppon. 1894 *Century Illustr. Mag.* 47.852, Succotash, and supawn are Indian names, but some of them are cut down from their polysyllabled aboriginal resonance. 1904 *DN* 2.401 [Some Lumber and Other Words], Soupon. . . Corn meal pudding. [1907 *Amer. Anthropologist* 9.496, *Suppawn* . . still used in northern New Jersey for corn-soup.] 1949 Kurath *Word Geog.* 24 **NY,** *Suppawn* . ., accented on the second syllable and not infrequently reduced to *spawn,* esp in the phrase *spawn and milk,* is a common name for corn meal mush in the Hudson valley. 1953 Piercy *Shaker Cook Book* 75 **OH** (as of early 1800s), Corn dishes such as their forefathers had learned to concoct from the Indians— suppone (pone) . . and Indian pudding.

supeen(y)   See **subpoena**

super n   **scattered, but chiefly NYC**   [Abbr for *superintendent*]

A resident attendant of an apartment house who performs such functions as janitor, handyman, and porter.

1957 *Post–Std.* (Syracuse NY) 1 Sept mag sec 12/2, [Short story:] He said the park was supposed to be for residents of the Rose Park Apartments, and my old man was just a building super. 1977–78 Foster *Lexical Variation* 33 **NJ,** *Super* 'apartment house janitor' is known throughout New Jersey; . . the term appears to be in common use everywhere except the Philadelphia Suburbs and perhaps Passaic. 1979 *El Super* [title]. [*DARE* Ed: An American independent Spanish language film about the trials and tribulations of a homesick Cuban exile working as a building superintendent in New York City.] 1986 Pederson *LAGS Concordance (Superintendent, janitor, manager)* 2 infs, **GA,** Super—does

(minor) repairs; 1 inf, **csTN,** Super; 1 inf, **ceTN,** Super = janitor; 1 inf, **seLA,** Super not common here, used in big cities; 1 inf, **nwFL,** The super. 1993 Delany–Delany *Having Our Say* 100 **NYC** [Black], You'd have to go from one place to the next, and the super would say, "There's no room now, but come back next month and see." 2004 in 2005 *DARE* File—Internet **seLA,** The super, if you call him that, came by one Monday without warning . . and turned out the electricity so he could work on the problem. 2005 *Ibid* **NYC,** After four calls to management and a few mentions to the Super, I'm beginning to give up on ever having my own little name plate.

superhighway n   Also *super*   **widespread exc West**   See Map Cf **freeway**

A divided highway designed for high-speed travel.

1924 *Atlanta Constitution* (GA) 16 Nov mag sec 3, [Headline:] The Detroit Super-Highway Said to Be the Solution of the Evil That Is Strangling American Communities. 1933 *Natl. Geogr. Mag.* May 549 **NJ,** [Caption:] This structure carries the four-lane "superhighway" over the Raritan River near New Brunswick. 1965–70 *DARE* (Qu. N16a, *Names for a highway with two lanes on each side and a separation down the middle*) 91 Infs, **widespread exc West,** Superhighway; **MS83, SC32, 57, TN53,** Super. 1998 *Los Angeles Times* (CA) 8 Nov 15 (Internet) **wPA,** On the shoulder of America's oldest superhighway, . . a concrete staircase leads up, up, up a hillside into the Pennsylvania sky.

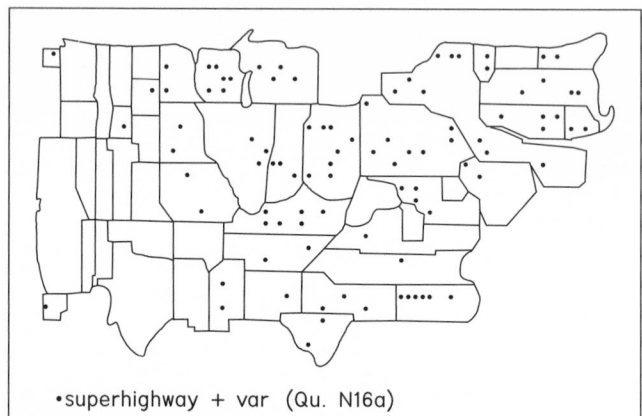

•superhighway + var (Qu. N16a)

suplejack   See **supplejack 2**

supm   See **something A4**

suppawn, suppon   See **supawn**

suppeenied, suppeeny   See **subpoena**

suppen   See **something A4**

suppender   See **suspender**

suppeney, suppenied   See **subpoena**

supper n   **widespread**   Cf **dinner 1b**

The evening meal; the last meal of the day.

1622 *Mourt's Relation Iournall Plimoth* 9 **MA,** Wee got three fat Geese, and six Ducks to our Supper. 1775 (1924) Cresswell *Jrl.* 104 **PA,** Just as the Sun went down we stopped to get our Supper on some Dewberries. 1859 Gosse *Letters from AL* 68, The meal which we are accustomed to call "tea," is by Americans, universally, I believe, called "supper," and it is the final meal; there being but three in the day. 1863 Dodge *Gala-Days* 114 **MA,** If it is nearer noon than morning, we call it dinner. If it is nearer night than noon, we call it supper, unless we have fashionable friends with us, and then we call it dinner, and the other thing lunch. 1900 in 1995 Millersville Univ. Center for PA Ger. Studies *Jrl.* Fall 9, Sunday. . . Geibel's were at Minnie's for dinner and supper. 1937 (1959) Weidman *I Can Get It* 103 **NY,** "Ma!" I said reprovingly, "Not supper. Dinner!" 1965–70 *DARE* (Qu. H3, *The meal that people eat at the end of the day*) 828 Infs, **widespread,** Supper. 1966 *DARE* Tape **FL7,** They would go up and they'd be entertained; they'd take a nap and rest until dinner, which was more likely to be called supper back in that period. 1982 Slone *How We Talked* 10 **eKY** (as of c1950), We did not use the word lunch, the three meals were breakfast, dinner and supper, in that order. Dinner and supper were both large meals and breakfast was almost as large, only a little different, such as hot biscuits while there was cornbread for the other meals. 1994 NC Lang. & Life

Project *Harkers Is. Vocab.* 11 **eNC,** *Supper*. . . The evening meal. General Southern, widespread regional use. **2000** *NADS Letters* **seRI,** *Supper* is still in use in SE New England . . , but in the general population seems to be phasing out toward *dinner*. . . Supper. . . An everyday evening meal. Distinguished from dinner in that dinner is reserved for special occasions like Thanksgiving; supper is the regular meal we eat every night. *Ibid* **neIL,** "Supper" was the same as "dinner" where I grew up around Chicago. In the rural areas of the Upper Midwest, "dinner" is the noon meal and the largest meal. "Supper" is a light meal, like "lunch" was where I grew up, but in the evening. I can't seem to adjust to this one, even after 20 years of trying.

supper club n   chiefly Gt Lakes, esp WI

An independent restaurant that usu serves only the evening meal, offering traditional American food and drink, frequently providing live music, and often having meeting or banquet rooms for community organizations or family celebrations.

    1940 *Rhinelander Daily News* (WI) 20 June 2/2, *Czecho Supper Club* "Famous For Its Home Cooked Food." **1999** *WI State Jrl.* (Madison) 27 June sec C 2/1, [Headline:] *Supper club is one of the things that make Wisconsin what it is.* . . [Text:] Yes, there are restaurants called supper clubs elsewhere, but they're not the same. . . A real supper club has fish on Friday night, prime rib on Saturday and is never open for lunch. It has cloth napkins, waitresses (never waiters) in sensible shoes, relish trays, cracker baskets and a salad bar . . [that] must contain . . cheese spread, three-bean salad, pickled beets and those crinkle-cut carrots in French dressing. **1999** *DARE* File—Internet [Central Florida Green Bay Packer Backers] 5 **WI,** *Supper club:* a restaurant up-nort, no membership required. **2007** in 2009 *DARE* File—Internet, The term "supper club" seems to be a phenomenon of the Upper Midwest, even more specifically of the Upper Mississippi Valley. . . I called up the business directory . . database. . . Thirty-eight states had one or more supper clubs. . . New England, the South and West have relatively few. . . Wisconsin is the absolute *epicenter* of supper clubs. **2009** *WI People & Ideas* Summer 19, Most Wisconsinites just know a supper club when they see it. . . If it serves a trifecta of food, drink, and entertainment, you might have found yourself a supper club. *Ibid* 21, The best supper clubs still insist on homemade, housemade everything. *Ibid* 23, The supper club may have survived and thrived after the Depression due to its long-established niche in community life. Public, religious, and political groups hold meetings . . in supper club banquet rooms . . , and families gather there for anniversaries, graduations . . and other commemorations. **2009** *DARE* File—Internet **seWI,** After prohibition ended, Wisconsin liquor licenses were issued mostly outside the city limits, with the contingency that the establishment must serve food. To make use of the liquor license, establishments started to specialize in dinners, thus *"supper clubs"* were born. *Ibid* **Minneapolis MN,** Because the ceiling was heavy timber Douglas fir, and because Kim was feeling a little nostalgic for northern Wisconsin, they decided to create a contemporized version of a supper club. *Ibid* **nWI,** *Continuing The Tradition Of The Northwoods' Great Supper Clubs*. . . Our comfortable dining room is a gathering place for locals and out-of-towners alike. . . We are a classic Supper Club style restaurant right out of the forties. *Ibid* **nWI,** Situated on quiet Boot Lake. . . a traditional Wisconsin "supper club" . . [offers] a full bar and . . two dining rooms, available for meetings or private group dining.

supper on the ground n   Cf dinner on the ground(s)

A picnic meal, esp in the evening; a communal outdoor meal to which dishes are brought to share.

    1876 *Janesville Gaz.* (WI) 14 June [2]/2 (newspaperarchive.com), The ladies of the new S.D.B. church . . [promised] to furnish the workmen with a No. 1 picnic dinner and supper on the ground. **1887** *Atlanta Constitution* (GA) 12 Oct 5/2, The best thing is to . . go out and look at the exposition, get a light supper on the ground . . and be ready . . to see the fireworks at 8 o'clock. **1916** *Adams Co. News* (Gettysburg PA) 26 Aug 4/5, A number of visitors were in the park on Sunday. Several of the families had dinner and supper on the ground. **1960** Williams *Walk Egypt* 129 **nGA,** Long rows of wooden tables were set up under the trees for homecoming dinners and suppers-on-the-ground. **2004** *DARE* File—Internet **OK,** We held revivals in just about every kind of church that would open the doors for us. . . We had many a 'supper on the ground' provided by some great Christian folk; *Ibid* **AL,** Hawkins Holler was the scene of music and dancing every Saturday night except in the dead of winter. People would come from miles around bringing a cov-

ered dish to enjoy an early evening of supper "on the ground" as they called it.

suppin'   See something A4

supplejack n

1 A sinewy climbing vine *(Berchemia scandens)* of the southeastern US. [*OED2* 1725 →] Also called **coon grape 3, rattan vine**

    1788 Schöpf *Reise* II.286 *(DA),* Ein windendes Staudengewächs dieser Art ist der sogenannte Supple Jack, wovon ich aber weder Blätter noch Blüthe gesehen. Es macht einen hölzernen biegsamen Stamm, einen bis zwey Finger dick, und 40- 50- 60 Fuss lang. [=A twining suffrutescent plant of this sort is the so-called supplejack, of which, however, I have seen neither leaves nor flowers. It produces a woody flexible stem, one to two fingers thick, and 40- 50- 60 feet long.] **1812** Stoddard *Sketches LA* 169, Most of the low lands are covered with underwood, vines, supple jacks, and cane; so that it is extremely difficult . . to penetrate them. **1834** Audubon *Ornith. Biog.* 2.344 **Sth,** The Supple Jack is a species of Smilax extremely abundant in all the swampy portions of the Southern States. **1860** Curtis *Cat. Plants NC* 117, *Rattan. Supplejack*. . . A very tough flexible vine running up trees. . . The berry is dark purple . . with a thin coat and a hard smooth nut. **1930** Stoney–Shelby *Black Genesis* 187 **seSC,** Tis all tangle up wid jasmine an' cat briar, an' smilax, an' supplejack. **1941** Walker *Lookout* 57 **TN,** Occasionally, . . a pert specimen of supple-jack . . has climbed a tree and twisted itself so tightly . . that the host perishes. **1953** Greene–Blomquist *Flowers South* 71, Supple-Jack, Rattan-Vine. . . The common names of this twining vine emphasize its slender, cord-like stems and its vigorous climbing habit. **1993** *Mother Earth News* Aug/Sept 79 **MD,** Supplejack *(Berchemia),* which grows in the South, is actually not too supple, but it makes a delightful, contorted framework [for a basket].

2 also *sooplejack, suplejack:* =**jumping jack 5;** also fig.   Cf **limber jack 3, supple-sawney**

    1776 in 1888 Cutler *Life* 1.55 **MA,** They made us several presents of . . sweatmeets . . supple-jacks . . bread. **1791** (1927) Maclay *Jrl.* 390 **PA,** Schuyler is the supple-jack of his son-in-law Hamilton. **1835** Longstreet *GA Scenes* 13, Bob Simons danced for all the world like a "Suple Jack," (or as we commonly called it, a "Suple Sawney,") when the string is pulled with varied force, at intervals of seconds. **1871** in 1914 Whitman *Complete Prose* 217, Millions of sturdy farmers and mechanics are thus the helpless supple-jacks of . . politicians. **1914** *DN* 4.160 **cVA,** Soople-jack. . . Jumping-jack.

supple-sawney n   [*supple* + *Sawney* var of the name *Sandy;* cf *EDD Sandy* sb.²]   old-fash   Cf supplejack 2

=**jumping jack 5.**

    1835 [see **supplejack 2**]. **1888** *Century Illustr. Mag.* 36.771 **Sth,** Jumping-jacks, or "supple sawneys," were made of pasteboard, and worked their arms and legs through the medium of a cotton string. **1993** Mason *Feather Crowns* 407 **KY** (as of 1900), She picked up the supple-sawney and moved its arms and legs so that it danced.

suption n¹   Also *sumption, supshun* [Etym unknown]   SE, Gulf States   *esp freq among Black speakers; old-fash*

Esp of food: nutritive substance, essence, savor; juice; fig: satisfaction.

    1887 *Atlanta Constitution* (GA) 13 Aug 3/4 [Black], 'Twont do to sturv de sarrl too much, case if you do you lose all the suption (substance) in the lan'. **1922** Gonzales *Black Border* 330 **sSC, GA coasts** [Gullah glossary], *Supshun*—substance, sustenance, strength of food, as of a juicy roast: "Da' meat hab supshun een'um"—that meat has much nourishment. **1927** Kennedy *Gritny* 113 **sLA** [Black], Add the necessary vegetables and seasoning to the chicken soup to "give it supshun." **1930** Stoney–Shelby *Black Genesis* 7 **seSC,** One dem Cherubim put down a plate full o' dem scrap, wid a lot o' spoon bittle an' pot-licker an' sich-like suption on dem. **1940** Faulkner *Hamlet* 27 **MS,** I chew up a nickel [cigar] now and then until the suption is out of it. But I aint never lit a match to one yet. **1941** Faulkner *Men Working* 198 **MS,** I wisht they wouldn't give us so many of them celeries. . . I just cain't learn to stomach 'um somehow. They don't seem to be much suption in 'em. **1941** Writers' Program *Guide SC* 154, The Negro cook who is an artist in preparing food for a white family will often follow quite different methods in her own kitchen. 'White folks' vittles ain't got no suption,' she will say, meaning that they have no flavor. **1942** Kennedy *Palmetto Country* 147 **FL** [Black], "You gotta cook vegetables so they won't loose their sumption" . . meaning that food values should not be destroyed by overcooking. **1950** *PADS* 14.65 **SC**, *Suption.* . . 1. Substance, as applied to food. "The yellow corn has more suption in it." 2. The rich juice or gravy from cooked meat; the drippings from a roast fowl or beef. **1959** Faulkner *Mansion* 48 **MS**, "They—the Judge—is going to give you another trial." "What for? . . I done already had one that I never got much suption out of."

suption n², v [Var of *suction*]
1944 *Sat. Eve. Post* 5 Feb 24 **Sth**, I don't rightly know how we got the fish we ate. Maybe it was a hole in the ship's bottom and a pump that suptioned 'em in. **1949** Webber *Backwoods Teacher* 30 **Ozarks**, My feed line is kind of clogged up, . . so I have to stop ever' once in a while and sipher out some gas to pour in the little tank under the hood to get the suption started up again.

sup up See **sup** v

surancified See **suffancified**

surcy See **sirsee**

sure adj, adv
Std senses, var forms.

1 |šu(ə)r, šuə; šu(ə)r, šuə|; also, esp in informal use, |šɝ|; for addit varr see quot 1989; pronc-spp *shoe-ah, shoo(-er), shure.* **formerly chiefly Nth, N Midl; now more widespread**
1815 Humphreys *Yankey in England* 108, *Shure,* sure. **1914** *DN* 4.160 **cVA**, *Shoo-enough.* . . Real, genuine. **1947** in 1965 *DARE* File **csWI**, That's for sure [ðæts fɚ ʃuɚ]. **1961** Kurath–McDavid *Pronc. Engl.* 119, In *poor, sure* the high vowels /u ~ ʊ/ are in almost exclusive use in the North Midland and the North, except for northeastern New England. . . South of Pennsylvania the high vowels /u ~ ʊ/ are rare. In the South Midland they occur both in folk speech and in the speech of the better educated, in the South mostly in the speech of the cultured (presumably as an innovation). **1965** Carmony *Speech Terre Haute* 65 **sIN**, The most advanced varieties, varying from [ʊˤ] to [ʉ], occur in palatal and alveolar environments, as in . . *sure* [šʉɚ]. *Ibid* 113, /o/, however, does not occur in the records in the pronunciation of *sure*, which was not often elicited. **1974** Gilbreth *Dictionary* 14 **Boston MA**, *Shoe ah:* Certain; i.e., "Victory is a shoe ah thing." **1975** Gould *ME Lingo* 253, *Shoo-er*—Sure. **1976** Allen *LAUM* 3.30 **Upper MW** (as of c1950), *Sure.* . . The lower high-front [ʊ] . . is equally common in all the U[pper] M[idwest] except southern Iowa. *Ibid* 31, But totally assimilated variants with only the retroflex vowel, [ʃɚ] . . turn up in the UM. . . chiefly in the two eastern states [=MN, IA]. **1989** Pederson *LAGS Tech. Index* 339 **Gulf Region**, *Sure.* [Of 914 infs, 511 offered proncs of the type [šur]; 23 infs, proncs of the type [šur]; 72 infs, proncs of the type [šɝ]; 17 infs, proncs of the type [šɪr]; 3 infs, proncs of the type [šʌr].] **1999** *DARE* File—Internet [Boston Online *Wicked Good Guide to Boston English*], *Shoe-ah*—Yes, as in: "Wanna go downa Cape this weekend? Shoe-ah!"

2 |šo(ə)r, šoə, šɔr, šjor|; pronc-spp *sho(ah), shoar, shore;* similarly adv *surely* (pronc-spp *sho(ly), shorely).* **chiefly Sth, S Midl**
1790 in 1956 Eliason *Tarheel Talk* 318 **c,csNC**, Shore. **1795** Dearborn *Columbian Grammar* 138, *List of Improprieties.* . . *Shoar for Sure (certain).* **1882** *Atlantic Mth.* 50.629 **Sth** [Black], "Why, did you ever kill a man?" "I did, shoah," said he. **1890** *DN* 1.70 **LA**, *Shore:* sure. **1892** (1969) Christensen *Afro-Amer. Folk Lore* 43 **seSC**, Oh! sho, go 'long! **1893** Shands *MS Speech* 56, *Sho* [šo]. The common negro pronunciation for *sure. Sholy* is likewise used for *surely. Sho* is sometimes used for *surely. Shore* for *sure* is also common here, as in Louisiana. **1899** Edwards *Defense* 1 **GA**, I sho'ly did cuss. **1902** *DN* 2.246 **sIL**, *Sure, surely.* Often pronounced [šor], [šorlɪ], as if written shore, shorely. **1903** *DN* 2.332 **seMO**, *Sure.* . . Pronounced shore. **1907** *DN* 3.227 **nwAR**, *Sure, surely.* Often pronounced [šor], [šorlɪ]. *Ibid* 237 **nwAR**, *Sure.* . . Pronounced shore. **1909** *DN* 3.369 **eAL, wGA**, *Sho(re)ly.* . . Surely. *Ibid* 377 **eAL, wGA**, *Sure.* . . Usually pronounced [šo]. **1911** *DN* 3.551 **WY**, *Shore,* sure. **1914** *DN* 4.160 **cVA**, *Sho.* . . Sure. **1915** *DN* 4.190 **swVA**, *Shore, shorely.* Variant of *sure, surely.* **1922** Gonzales *Black Border* 326 **sSC, GA coasts** [Gullah glossary], *Sho'ly*—surely. **1923** *DN* 5.220 **swMO**, *Shore.* . . Sure or surely. Shorely. **a1930** in 1991 Hughes–Hurston *Mule Bone* 31 **cFL** [Black], *Sholy,* Dave, sholy. **1935** Sandoz *Jules* 380 **wNE** (as of 1880–1930), "That family shore is tough on womenfolks," Dick Weyant commented. **1938** Rawlings *Yearling* 12 **nFL**, You shore didn't git enough to hurt you. **c1940** Eliason *Word Lists FL* 14 **wFL**, *Sure* [ʃɔɚ]. **1940** *AmSp* 15.50 **sAppa-**

lachians, Ozarks, Not [ʊɚ] but [oʊɚ] occurs in . . shore (sure). **1942** Faulkner *Go Down* 20 **MS**, An unmarried lady will sholy have her door locked with strangers in the house. **1944** *PADS* 2.13, *Sure is* [šoʹɪz]: It certainly is. Term of assent. Deep South. Negro. Low popular. **1961** Kurath–McDavid *Pronc. Engl.* 119, The vowels in . . *sure.* . . All of the South and the South Midland . . have predominantly the mid vowel /o/, so that . . *sure* rime[s] with *four, shore.* Maryland west of Chesapeake Bay agrees with the South. . . In the South and the South Midland the /o/ of . . *sure* / . . šo ~ šo ~ šor/ exhibits the same diaphones as in *four, door.* . . [T]he mid vowel /o/ occurs . . with some frequency in northeastern New England, notably in coastal Maine and New Hampshire. **1965–70** *DARE* (Qu. H11b) Inf **TN**27, Shore does chaw loud; (Qu. R15b, . . *An extra-big mosquito*) Inf **MS**70, Sho' nuff bad skeeter; (Qu. W38) Inf **GA**28, Shore does look sharp; (Qu. X49) Inf **NJ**69, Shore thin; (Qu. AA21) Inf **GA**28, He shore is henpecked; (Qu. HH25) Inf **GA**28, He shore is quiet; (Qu. JJ30a) Inf **VA**46, Shore forgot; (Qu. KK1a, . . *Very good—for example, food: "That pie was _____."*) Inf **MS**88, Sho' good; sho' nuff good; (Qu. NN1, . . *Words like 'yes': "Are you coming along too?"*) Infs **LA**3, 17, Sho' (am); **DE**1, **LA**17, Sho' nuff; **NY**146, **TX**26, Shore; **LA**17, Why sho'; (Qu. NN2, *Exclamations of very strong agreement: Somebody says, "I think Smith is absolutely right," and you reply, "_____."*) Infs **LA**3, **SC**9, **TN**46, Sho' am (or is); **HI**1, Sho' nuff; **LA**17, He sho' is; **MS**64, That's for dang shore; (Qu. NN3) Inf **GA**31, She shore is; (Qu. NN7, *Exclamations of surprise: "They're getting married next week? Well, _____."*) Infs **LA**3, **TN**26, 46, Sho' nuff. **1965–67** *DARE* FW Addit **MS**, *Sho* or *shorely* or *shore*—another way of saying sure or surely. Mostly used by Negroes; **wNC**, *Sure* adj. . . [šjor]. **1976** Allen *LAUM* 3.30 **Upper MW** (as of c1950), *Sure.* . . The U[pper] M[idwest] distribution of these mid- and low-back vowels [=/o/, /ɔ/] . . [shows] only a few instances in Minnesota but a number in southern Iowa. . . This minority form, not favored by educated speakers, may have become recessive, as it has not spread into the more recently settled portions of the UM. **1989** Pederson *LAGS Tech. Index* 339 **Gulf Region**, *Sure.* [Of 914 infs, 221 offered proncs of the type [šo(r)]; 7 infs, proncs of the type [šɔ(r)].] **2000** Metcalf *How We Talk* 89 **sePA**, *Sure* in Philadelphia sounds the same as *shore.*

sure and certain See **certain B3**

sure enough adv phr
1 Really, truly. **chiefly Sth, S Midl**
1884 Smith *Bill Arp's Scrap Book* 77 **nwGA**, There was another sensation in the back piazza and it was sure enough feet this time. **1937** (1977) Hurston *Their Eyes* 15 **FL** [Black], Ah'm liable to have something sho nuff good tomorrow, 'cause you done come. **1938** in 1983 Truman *Dear Bess* 412 **MO**, It has been "sho' nuff" lonesome without any letter or telegram or phone call from you. **c1950** Halpert Coll. **wKY, nwTN**, *Sure enough.* . . "That's a sure 'nough (sho nuff) flucey hat." **1963** Wright *Lawd Today* 69 **Chicago IL** [Black], Do they sure enough believe 'im? **1966–70** *DARE* (Qu. R15b, . . *An extra-big mosquito*) Inf **MS**70, Sho' nuff bad skeeter; (Qu. DD15, *A person who is thoroughly drunk*) Inf **NM**3, Sure nuff drunk; (Qu. II11b, *If two people can't bear each other at all . . "Those two are _____."*) Inf **AR**47, Sure nuff at outs; (Qu. KK1a, . . *Very good—for example, food: "That pie was _____."*) Inf **MS**88, Sho nuff good. **1969** Emmons *Deep Rivers* 94 **eTX** [Black], I said, "Mama, I don't see how come Rosie can just sure 'nough want to die." **1976** Ryland *Richmond Co. VA* 376, *Sho 'nuff*—"You don't say?!"; also, as an adverb, "She was sho 'nuff mad that time!" **2001** *DARE* File **ceOK**, The Cherokee informant from Tahlequah, born in 1918, uses *sure-enough* as an intensive—as in "It's sure-enough small," which may be a general Southernism.

2 For sure—usu used in final position for emphasis; see quots. **chiefly Sth, NEng**
1827 *Norwalk Reporter & Huron Advt.* (OH) 19 May 1/4, I found they had thrown it away sure enough, and there they accused me of throwing it away. **1843** Thompson *Major Jones' Courtship* 12 **GA**, I wouldn't be supprised if we *was* to have a "grate morel revolution" shore enuff. **1861** Holmes *Venner* 1.195 **NEng**, A game little devil she was, sure enough! **1869** Stowe *Oldtown Folks* 71 **NEng**, Aunt Lois thought, with evident anguish, of the best room. Here was the Major, sure enough, and we all sitting round the kitchen fire! **1871** (1882) Stowe *Fireside Stories* 166 **NEng**, Ef they heard a noise in the night, or ef the wind squealed and howled . . , they'd think sure enough there was that horrid yell a comin' down chimbley. **1880** *Scribner's Mth.* 20.427 **FL** [Black], An' I look in you' face and see de tears streamin' down, and distress shore 'nough. **1884** *Anglia* 7.258 **Sth, S Midl** [Black], There are many peculiar intensives in the Negro dialect designed to give emphasis to an

assertion: . . *Sho' nuff.* **1895** *DN* 1.374 **seKY, eTN, wNC,** *Shore nuff:* certainly, without fail. "Are you going, shore nuff?" **1931** (1991) Hughes–Hurston *Mule Bone* 57 **cFL** [Black], Oh, I laks to see gals all mad. But dem boys *is* crazy sho nuff. **1932** (1974) Caldwell *Tobacco Road* 47 **GA,** You ought to do something for her this time, sure enough. **1940** *Sat. Eve. Post* 6 Jan 32 **MS,** Did he, sure 'nuff? **1958** Humphrey *Home from the Hill* 80 **neTX,** Hit's a wile hawg, sho nuff. **1995** *Signal Mag.* Dec np **cwTX,** Sure nough—"I want you to do it; sure nough." Certainly; please.

3 Used as a response to a statement to indicate interest, concern, or surprise; really? you don't say! **chiefly Sth, S Midl** See Map

1897 *Stevens Point Jrl.* (WI) [4 Sept 3]/7 (newspaperarchive.com), "Whar'd yo' git dat load er lumber, Br'er Black?" "Down ter de Healin' Ba'm church." "Sho 'nough? Has dey tord de buildin' down?" **1904** *DN* 2.421 **nwAR,** Sure enough. . . 'I had a good time in St. Louis.' 'Sure enough?' **c1950** *Halpert Coll.* 61 **wKY, nwTN,** Sure enough. . . "Sure 'nough!" as an exclamation = so it is! [Halpert: Something like "Well, I declare!"] As a question, "Sure 'nough?" = do you really mean that? **1965–70** *DARE* (Qu. NN7, *Exclamations of surprise: "They're getting married next week! Well, _____."*) Infs **AR**51, **GA**84, **LA**3, **SC**67, **TN**26, 46, **TX**59, Sho' (*or* sure) nuff; **FL**2, **KY**24, 92, **TX**1, Sure enough. **1976** [see **1** above]. **1986** Pederson *LAGS Concordance,* 13 infs, **scattered Gulf Region,** Sure (e)nough? = is that right?

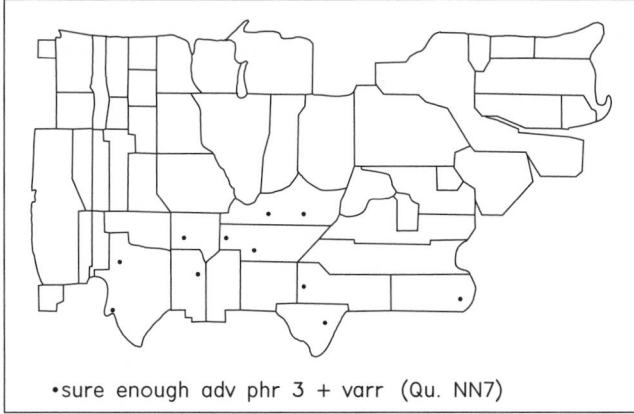

•sure enough adv phr 3 + varr (Qu. NN7)

sure-enough adj **chiefly Sth, S Midl**
Real, genuine, true.

1846 (1973) Porter *Quarter Race* 112 **MS,** It was a man with a sure-enough fence-rail. **1859** Taliaferro *Fisher's R.* 59 **nwNC** (as of 1820s), This that I'm gwine to narrate was a sure-enough bite. **1883** *Century Illustr. Mag.* 26.796 **VA,** Finding herself utterly unable to reconcile the time shown by her usually reliable watch to the varying times shown by the railway clocks at different points, she turned to the writer, and, using a provincial expression, asked appealingly: "Please tell me what is sure enough time?" **1884** *Anglia* 7.263 **Sth, S Midl** [Black], *To year sho' 'nuff cussin'* = to hear passionate words. **1887** (1967) Harris *Free Joe* 187 **GA,** Miss Kingsbury . . had "writ a sure-enough book," as the genial landlady expressed it. **1893** Shands *MS Speech* 56, *Sho nuff.* . . Negro for *sure enough* . . "Dat was sutenly a sho nuff ghos' I seed last night." **1899** (1912) Green *VA Folk-Speech* 430, *Sure-enough.* . . Genuine; real; not imitation: as, *sure-enough* butter. **1903** *DN* 2.333 **seMO,** *Sure-enough.* . . Genuine. 'Hit's a shore-enough gold watch.' **1909** *DN* 3.377 **eAL, wGA,** *Sure-(e)nough.* . . Genuine, real. **1914** *DN* 4.160 **cVA,** *Shoo-enough.* . . Real, genuine. **1929** Ellis *Ordinary Woman* 6 **CO** (as of early 20th cent), You couldn't help feeling it would be a sure-enough success this time. **1932** (1974) Caldwell *Tobacco Road* 83 **GA,** A sure-enough brand-new automobile? **1941** Justus *Cabin on Kettle Creek* 41 **eTN,** Let's get our pine knots in a hurry and then have some sure-enough fun. **1942** McAtee *Dial. Grant Co. IN* 63 (as of 1890s), *Sure enough* . . genuine; "a shore-nuff gold piece". Dial. **1959** Lomax *Rainbow Sign* 44 **AL** [Black], One child would get up and act just like a sho-nuff preacher. **1967** *DARE* (Qu. Y12b, *A real fight in which blows are struck*) Inf **SC**46, Sure-enough fight. **1988** Lincoln *Avenue* 205 **wNC** (as of c1940) [Black], A sho' nuff doctor is what you need. You don't need no jackleg.

sure for certain See **certain B3**

surencified See **suffancified**

surface coal n Also *surface fuel* **West** Cf **prairie coal**
Dried cow dung used as fuel.

1915 *DN* 4.229 **wTX,** *Surface-coal.* . . Cow dung, which is widely used for fuel. **1938** in Lib. of Congress *Amer. Memory: WPA Life Hist.* **TX** (Internet), Cow chips, dried to a crisp in the strong sunshine of the Panhandle, was sometimes gathered to be used on summer days to make a hot, quick fire. Mrs. Britt called the strange fuel appropriately, "surface coal". **1942** Berrey–Van den Bark *Amer. Slang* 915.13 **West,** Surface fuel, *dried cattle dung used for fuel.* **1948** *SW Rev.* 33.238 **TX,** There were other names for the commodity [=cow chips]—surface coal, prairie coal, and Babcock coal are just a few of them. **2004** *DARE* File—Internet **KS** (as of c1887), [From undated *Kiowa County Signal* article:] When the family came to Kansas a definite resolution was made not to use the "surface coal" for which Kansas is noted. They would burn corn stalks, which seemed more refined. *Ibid* **OK** (as of c1905), Food . . was cooked over open fires. . . When the wood was not available for cooking, "cow chips", also known as surface coal, were used for fires.

surf clam n
A marine clam of the genus *Spisula,* esp *S. solidissima,* or the related *Mactromeris polynyma.* For other names of var spp see **dish shell, hen clam 1, sea ~ b;** for other names of *S. solidissima* see **beach clam, dipper ~, run-down** n, **sea clam a, sedge ~, skimmer 2**

1873 Baird *Rept. Condition Sea Fisheries* 358, The "sea-clam" or "surf-clam," *Mactra solidissima* [=*Spisula s.*] . . occurs all along our coast . . from North Carolina to Labrador. **1884** U.S. Natl. Museum *Bulletin* 27.260, *Mactra solidissima.* . . Hen Clam, Surf Clam, or Sea Clam. . . Abundant from Delaware Bay to Cape Cod. **1911** *Trenton Eve. Times* (NJ) 10 July 9/3, The sea clam . . is the hen clam in New England, the skimmer on the Jersey coast, and the beach clam as far down as Little Egg inlet. From there south it is the surf clam, scoop clam . ., and at Ocracoke [sic] and Hatteras it is called the big clam. **1938** *Scientific Mth.* 46.338, *Spissula* [sic] *solidissima* is the "surf clam" of the New England coast. **1968** *DARE* Tape **DE**4, [A] surf clam is a soft-shell clam and with a different shape than a quahog clam. **1979** McPhee *Giving Good Weight* 98, Scooping tons of big surf clams . . the clammers moved slowly. **1981** Meinkoth *Audubon Field Guide Seashore* 570, The Surf Clam lives in relatively clean sand and can be found in the zone of breaking surf.

surf duck n
=**surf scoter.**

1814 Wilson *Amer. Ornith.* 8.49, Black, or Surf Duck. *Anas perspicillata.* . . This Duck is peculiar to America, and . . confined to the shores and bays of the sea. **1834** Nuttall *Manual Ornith.* 2.417, The Surf Duck or Sea Coot breeds also along the shores of Hudson's Bay and in Labrador. **1844** DeKay *Zool. NY* 2.335, The Surf Duck. . . very common on the coast of New-York during the winter. **1926** *Reno Eve. Gaz.* (NV) 1 Dec 8/4, A handsome surf duck, almost bronze in color, in places, was today added to the collection of mounted birds. **1955** MA Audubon Soc. *Bulletin* 39.377 **MA, CT, RI,** *Surf Scoter.* . . Surf Duck.

surfer n
=**surf scoter.**

1852 in 1876 *Forest & Stream* 7.212 **eMA,** *Pelionetta perspicillata.* Surfer.

surf fish n
1 =**surfperch.**

1868 Cronise *Nat. Wealth CA* 489, Embiotocoidae [sic]. . . They have been described by several naturalists under different names . . and from their usual resorts on the open sea beaches, are often called "Surf Fish." **1882** U.S. Natl. Museum *Bulletin* 16.585, Embiotocidae *(The Surf-fishes.)* . . Fishes of the Pacific coast of North America, inhabiting bays and the surf on sandy beaches. **1898** *AZ Republican* (Phoenix) 12 Nov 5/4, Every day, fresh from the coast, a fine assortment of ocean game, including . . white and surf fish. **1919** *Oxnard Courier* (CA) 14 Nov 5/6, J.P. Coute recently caught a surf fish from the Hueneme wharf that weighed four and a half pounds. **2004** *DARE* File—Internet, Barred Surfperch. . . Other Common Names: barred perch, silver perch, surf perch, sand perch, silver surf fish.

2 =**surf smelt.**

1968 *DARE* (Qu. P2, . . *Kinds of saltwater fish caught around here* . .

good to eat) Inf **CA**105, Surf fish; (Qu. P7) Inf **CA**105, Smelt or day fish or surf fish. **1968** *DARE* Tape **CA**104, You ever heard of surf fish? . . Well, they're smelts—I call them smelt. **2005** *DARE* File— Internet **nwCA**, These smelt 6 to 10 inches in length, are called surf fish and night fish by the sportsmen who take them in nets as they approach the beach to spawn.

surfperch n

Std: a fish of the Pacific family Embiotocidae. For other names of var spp see **black perch 2b, blue ~ 2, croaker** n[1] **1c, kelp perch 1, minnow B2c, mojarra 2, niggerlip, perch** n[1] **B5, pile perch, pogy 4, porgy** n[1] **5, rainbow perch, sand ~ 2c, sea ~ d, shiner 2e, squawfish 1, striped perch 2, ~ surf fish, surf fish 1, white perch 6**

surf scoter n

Std: a **scoter** (here: *Melanitta perspicillata*). Also called **baldpate 2, black duck 1, booby** n[1] **3, butter duck 1, buzzard coot, coot** n[1] **2a, deaf duck 2, goggle-nose, gray coot, hollow-billed ~, horsehead 2, Indian duck, iron pot, jew duck 2, king coot, morocco jaw, mussel-bill, nigger duck 2, patchbill coot, patchhead, pictured-bill, pishaug, scooter** n[3], **scovy 2, sea coot 1, ~ duck, skunk coot, ~ duck, skunk- head 1, snuff-taker, speckled-bill coot, spectacle ~, surf duck, surfer, whistling diver, whitehead 3**

surf smelt n

A Pacific **smelt 1** (here usu: *Hypomesus pretiosus*). For other names of *H. pretiosus* see **day fish, surf ~ 2**

1879 in 1881 U.S. Natl. Museum *Proc.* 3.43 **nwWA**, The Quillchute Indians, who collect and dry for winter use a very choice variety of smelt *(Hypomesus olidus),* which I have named the surf-smelt. **1882** U.S. Natl. Museum *Bulletin* 16.294, *H[ypomesus] pretiosus.* . . *Surf Smelt.* . . Pacific coast, from California northward; abundant, spawning in the surf. **1928** Pan-Pacific Research Inst. *Jrl.* 3.3.12, *Hypomesus pretiosus.* . . Surf smelt. **1953** Roedel *Common Fishes CA* 39, Surf Smelt. . . A minor commercial species, comprising a small fraction of the State's "smelt" catch and landed chiefly at San Francisco. **2004** *DARE* File—Internet **CA**, During the summer months you will often see schools of small fish in the water. These are generally surf smelt (day smelt) but at times there are also a few night smelt, jacksmelt, and even anchovies.

surf snipe n

=sanderling.

1881 Hapgood–Roosevelt *Shore Birds* 38, There are the small plovers, called ring-necks, beach-snipe and surf-snipe. **1904** (1910) Wheelock *Birds CA* 68, Sanderling. . . Common names: Surf Snipe; Ruddy Plover; Beach Bird. **1910** Eaton *Birds NY* 1.320, The Sanderling, or Surf snipe, is the whitest of all our sandpipers and our most characteristic beach bird. **1956** MA Audubon Soc. *Bulletin* 40.21 **ME, MA,** *Sanderling.* . . Surf Snipe. . . It closely follows retreating waves in search of food.

surgeonfish n   Also *surgeon* [See quot 1842]

A fish of the family Acanthuridae. For other names of var spp see **convict** n, **doctorfish, kala** n[1], **manini** n **1, unicorn fish 2**

1842 DeKay *Zool. NY* 4.139, The surgeon. *Acanthurus phlebotomus* [=*A. chirurgis*]. . . On each side of the tail is a strong, acute, compressed, lancet-shaped spine. **1858** Redfield *Zoöl. Sci.* 565, The Surgeon-fish, *A[canthurus] phlebotomus* . . is another species found off the coasts of the United States. **1871** *Harper's New Mth. Mag.* June 31 **FL,** The surgeon-fish *(Acanthurus phlebotomus)* is another remarkable indigene of these waters. **1884** Goode *Fisheries U.S.* 1.279, On the coast of Florida, as well as through the West Indies and in the Bermudas, occur two species of this family, *Acanthurus caeruleus* and *A. nigricans,* generally known as "Doctor-fish" or "Surgeon-fish." **1933** John G. Shedd Aquarium *Guide* 124, The tangs, or surgeonfishes, are herbivorous fishes of the warm seas. **1960** Gosline–Brock *Hawaiian Fishes* 242, Surgeonfishes . . represent one of the most abundant families of Hawaiian fishes. **2004** *DARE* File—Internet **HI,** Surgeonfish sport lovely little scalpels at the small of the tail.

‡surl v [Back-formation from *surly*] Cf **sull** v

1914 *DN* 4.81 **ME, nNH,** *Surl.* . . To be surly, ugly, etc.

surly n   Also *surley*   esp **TX, OK** See Map   *euphem*

A bull—also used as a quasi-proper name.

1933 *AmSp* 8.1.30 **nwTX** [Ranch diction], *Surly.* A bull. *Ibid* 52

Ozarks, *Surly.* . . A bull. **1940** in Lib. of Congress *Amer. Memory: WPA Life Hist.* **TX** (Internet), The embryo cattleman could not afford to buy a good bull—Bones said "surly"; he would not use the word "bull" before a lady interviewer. **1956** Ker *Vocab. W. TX* 317, "Surly," a slang term for a bull. **1962** Atwood *Vocab. TX* 57, *Male bovine (with original equipment).* . . Among the euphemisms that still survive [is] . . *surly.* . . distinctly concentrated in the South Plains and a portion of Central Texas . . ; it is definitely archaic. **1965–70** *DARE* (Qu. K22, *Words used for a bull*) Infs **TX**40, 42, 51, Surly; (Qu. K23, *Words used by women or in mixed company for a bull*) Infs **OK**27, **TX**89, Surly; **KY**14, 68, Surly—old-fashioned; **OK**1, Old Surly. [6 of 8 Infs old] **1966** Dakin *Dial. Vocab. Ohio R. Valley* 2.232, *Bull.* . . euphemisms. . . Other polite names mentioned once or twice . . *surly.* **1970** Tarpley *Blinky* 164 **neTX,** *Male cow* . . surly [2 of 200 infs]. . . Four informants, three of them non-city females over 40, substitute *surly, bullie,* or *year-ling,* for they were forbidden in childhood ever to say *bull,* and they still avoid that word. **1986** Pederson *LAGS Concordance (Bull)* 1 inf, **cnAR,** Surly—polite term; 1 inf, **ceTX,** Surlies. **1994** Turnbo *White R. Chron.* 79 **Ozarks** (as of 1842), A negro man and himself, while passing through the prairie one day met three buffalo—a bull or "Surley" as he called him, a cow and a small heifer.

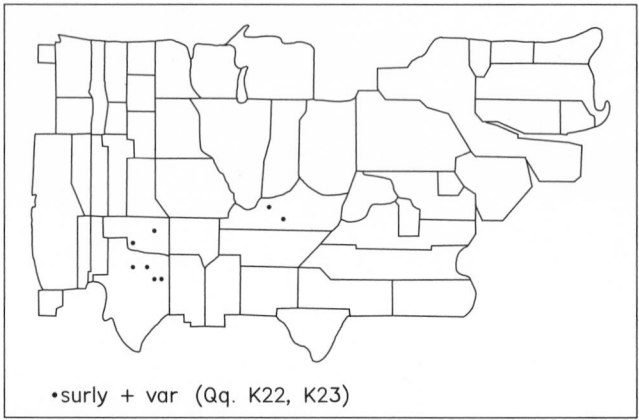

•surly + var (Qq. K22, K23)

surp   See **syrup**

surquancified, surquencified, surrensified   See **suffancified**

‡surrogated adj [Perh blend of *serrated* + *corrugated* or malaprop for *corrugated*] Cf Intro "Language Changes" I.10

1968 *DARE* (Qu. L37) Inf **KS**12, Idiot stick—straight stick, surrogated iron on the bottom; used around here.

surrop   See **syrup**

surrossified   See **suffancified**

surround v   Pronc-sp *sarround* [*OED2* surround v. 4 "To go or travel around . . *Obs.*"]   chiefly **sAppalachians**

To bypass, go around.

1910 in 2004 Montgomery–Hall *Dict. Smoky Mt. Engl.* 583 **wNC, eTN,** Devil Sam Walker's excellent term, "*sarround*" (a peak or a swamp) will always do duty for me. **1917** *DN* 4.418 **wNC,** *Sur-round.* . . To pass by going around. "I couldn't git through the laurel; so I jist surrounded it." **1924** Raine *Land of Saddle-Bags* 102 **sAppala-chians,** You'll have to *surround* them places. **1926** *DN* 5.404 **Ozarks,** *Surround.* . . To go around, to detour. "I surrounded th' house an' snuk in back o' th' barn." **1937** Hall Coll. **wNC, eTN,** *Surround.* . . I would rather surround a snake than kill it. **1940** in 1968 Haun *Hawk's Done Gone* 108 **eTN,** The tree in the yard was blowed up by the roots. . . we had to surround the tree to get up on the porch. **1974** Fink *Mountain Speech* 25 **wNC, eTN,** *Surround* . . go around. *"We surrounded the hill."* **1986** Pederson *LAGS Concordance,* 1 inf, **nwFL,** I done my best t[o] try to surround them = go around/circumvent big cities while driving.

surrow   See **sorry** adj

surrup   See **syrup**

surs   See **suz**

sursie   See **sirsee**

surup   See **syrup**

surveyor n [OED2 surveyor sb. 1.a "Overseer, supervisor. . . As a title of officials in various departments, offices, or works"; 1442 →] **chiefly NEng** See Map Cf **maintainer, patrolman, trustee**

Esp in combs *surveyor of highways* (or *roads*), *highway* (or *road*) *surveyor:* A local official responsible for the upkeep of public roads.

1634 in 1901 Cambridge MA *Records* 10, John White is Chossen surveior to seethe [sic] highways and streete kept cleane and in repair. **1646** in 1857 New Haven (Colony) *Records* 231 **CT,** It was ordered that the surveyours of the highwayes doe view them, & returne the names of those that are defective either for cart or foote. **1770** in 1929 Summers *Annals* 97 **swVA,** Stoval Kettering is appointed Surveyor of the Road. **1839** *Bangor Daily Whig & Courier* (ME) 21 Jan [4]/4 (newspaperarchive.com), They are taxed in bills committed to me to collect as General Surveyor of Highways and Collector of the non-resident proprietor highway tax for the year 1838, by the Assessors of said Town. **1859** White *Hist. Coventry VT* 18 (as of 1803), The town was organized by the choice of officers as follows: *Joseph Marsh, Samuel Cobb, John Wells, Jr.,* and *Daniel B. Smith,* Highway Surveyors. **1886** *Atlantic Mth.* 58.497 **NEng,** A natural border of alder bushes, grape-vines, . . and such like is an inexpensive decoration of the very best sort, such as the Village Improvement Society ought never to allow any highway surveyor to lay hands on. **1904** *Trenton Times* (NJ) 9 Mar 3/1, *Rural Elections Result in Surprises. . . West Windsor Township. . .* Surveyor of the highways, Howard A. Robinson. . . *Ewing Township. . .* Surveyor of highways Frank Croasdale. . . *Hamilton Township (West). . .* Surveyor of highway Charles Anderson. **1913** *Fitchburg Daily Sentinel* (MA) 25 Mar 9/3, Road Surveyor Willard has started in on spring work in this village. **1915** *Daily Rev.* (Decatur IL) 6 July 12/5, Highway Commissioners . . have filed . . a petition for a writ of certiorari ordering Town Clerk Henry Johnson and Preston J. Hicks, county surveyor of roads, to produce in court a transcript of the proceedings in the case wherein the width of Lost bridge road was reduced. **1957** *Newport Daily News* (RI) 23 July 9/1, No person other than the Surveyor of Highways or the caretaker of the dump . . shall ignite or burn any waste deposited at the dump. **1965–70** DARE (Qu. N33, *A man whose job is to take care of roads in a certain locality*) Infs **MA**40, 55, **RI**4, 6, Road surveyor; **ME**5, Road surveyor—years ago, had a district, usually was a selectman; **MA**30, Road surveyor—each has his own district, town divided into several districts; [**FL**48, Road supervisor, road maintenance men, road surveyor—[each] named by his particular job;] **MA**68, Used to have highway surveyors—men who took care of a particular district; **MA**74, Highway surveyor—[same as] road commissioner, road man; **MA**58, **RI**15, Surveyor. **1982** Wilkinson *Midnights* 30 **Cape Cod MA,** His regular job was as the highway surveyor, an elected position that meant he looked after the town's roads—saw, among other things, that they were plowed and sanded after snow, and kept free of potholes. **2006** *Patriot Ledger* (Quincy MA) 26 Jan 11 (Internet), The town had . . $29,000 in snow-removal bills, town Highway Surveyor Paul Foulsham told the board.

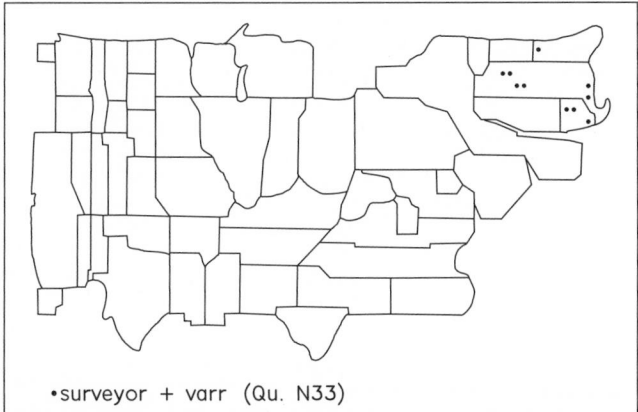

•surveyor + varr (Qu. N33)

survigerous, survigorous, survigr(o)us See **servigrous**

Susan n

=**black-eyed Susan 2.**

1935 Sandoz *Jules* 149 **wNE,** To him a hundred sixty acres of wild Susans was not a field of gold but a field going back to sod, a dead venture. **1953** Nelson *Plants Rocky Mt. Park* 175, The well-known "Su-

san," with its large gold and chocolate flower heads and rough foliage is frequently seen in mountain meadows. **1993** Kingsolver *Pigs in Heaven* 220 **OK,** Taylor has begun picking long-stemmed black-eyed Susans from the roadside. . . Taylor hands Alice a bouquet of orangeyyellow Susans and begins picking another one.

susanside n [Joc var of *suicide*] Cf **kick Sue in the side**

1855 Hannibal *Black Diamonds* 72 [Black], De poor poet . . tuck to drinkin' sweeten'd milk, in order to commit susanside, but, on de contrary, got fits. **1876** Southworth *Self-Raised* 53 **MD,** Youre a killin of yourself jest as fast as ever you can, which is no better nor Susanside, because it is agin natur and agin rillijun. **1928** *Warren Morning Mirror* (PA) 23 June 3/1, The Ramblings is the ambulance service that totes 'em away after they've committed susanside talking back to the editor. **1968–69** DARE (Qu. BB57, *If someone committed suicide . . he _____*) Infs **CT**39, **IN**38, (Committed) susanside.

sushi n [Japanese; OED2 1893 →] **orig HI, but now widely known** Cf **sashimi**

Vinegar-flavored rice rolled up with fish, vegetables, or egg in a square of dried seaweed and sliced into bite-sized pieces.

1894 *NY Times* (NY) 19 Nov 5/5 **NYC,** All Nations At Dinner—A Japanese Feast for Members of the Club and Guests. . . Sushi. . . a preparation of rice, beets, red cabbage, bits of lobster, celery, &c. **1940** Bazore *Hawaiian Foods* 69 **HI,** Sushi—Cooked rice combined with aburage, cooked burdock, carrots, string beans, mushrooms, egg, cooked fish cake, or smoked eel. It is flavored with dried bonito, vinegar, sugar, and salt. **1967** DARE (Qu. H65, *Foreign foods favored by people around here*) Inf **HI**9, Sushi—vinegar, sugar, salt, rice rolled in noli [= nori] (seaweed). **1972** Carr *Da Kine Talk* 91 **HI,** Several varieties of *sushi* are made in Hawaii, all of them using *gohan* 'cooked rice' mixed with vinegar and sugar. **1979** McPhee *Giving Good Weight* 220, For his most recent birthday he was given raw fish . . —mackerel sushi, octopus sushi, fluke sushi, shrimp sushi. **1981** *Pidgin To Da Max* np **HI,** *Sushi* . . Japanese pupu [=hors d'oeuvre]. **1991** Saiki *From the Lanai* 25 **HI,** The Sakura Cafe exceeded its usual excellent service . . with trays of sushi, bits of choice seafood and delectible [sic] condiments too numerous to mention. **2005** DARE File—Internet, Rice cooked for sushi should be slightly harder in texture than for other dishes. *Ibid* **CA,** For those already smitten and those just curious about this unique cuisine, we provide a place to learn more about sushi. *Ibid,* Try these kidfriendly sushi recipes (no fish required).

suspect v Pronc-spp *spec(k), spect* **esp Sth, S Midl** Cf **expect**

Std sense, var forms.

1862 (1864) Browne *Artemus Ward Book* 180, "Who do you spect I air?" sed I. **1883** *Century Illustr. Mag.* 26.614 **GA** [Black], Honey, I speck Miss Sally lookin' und' de bed en axin' whar you is. **1884** *Anglia* 7.275 **Sth, S Midl** [Black], *I 'speck* = I suspect and I expect. **1894** Riley *Armazindy* 48 **IN,** Where, I 'spect, "The Freeport crowd"/ Never *warmed* to us. **1899** (1967) Chesnutt *Wife of Youth* 144 **NC** [Black], I 'spec' . . dat I knows whar dis boy come f'om. **1909** *DN* 3.373 **eAL, wGA,** Speck. . . To suspect. **1986** Pederson *LAGS Concordance* (I think) 5 infs, **AL, GA, MS, TX,** I [su]spect.

suspender n Usu |sə'spendə(r)|; also |sәpendә|, rarely |s(ə)pɪndə-| Pronc-spp *(s)pender, spinder, suppender* Cf "Pronc Intro" I.7, 9

Std sense, var forms.

1937 in 1976 *Weevils in the Wheat* 317 **VA** [Black], I could knit 'spinders, socks an' ev'ythin' you kin think of. **1941** LANE Map 363 (*Suspenders*) 10 infs, **scattered MA, VT, NH,** [sәpendәz]. **1954** Harder *Coll.* **cwTN,** Suspenders [spɪndɚz]. **1965–70** DARE (Qu. W7, *If a man doesn't use a belt, what does he wear over his shoulders to hold up his trousers?*) 45 Infs, **scattered,** Spenders; 38 Infs, **scattered,** Suppender(s). [Of those Infs giving the response *suppender(s),* 24 were gs educ or less.] **1981** Pederson *LAGS Basic Materials,* [4 infs, **AR, GA, LA, TX,** proncs of the types [sә'pendәz, sә'pɪndɚz].] **1989** Pederson *LAGS Tech. Index* 103 **Gulf Region** (*Suspenders*) 80 infs, [Su]spender(s); 1 inf, [Sus]penders. **1990** Smith *Understanding Speaking S. Lang.* 8, *Spenders*—Straps that hold your pants up.

suspicion v Pronc-spp *spicion, spishun* Eye-dial sp *suspishion* **scattered, but esp Sth, S Midl** *old-fash*

To suspect, be suspicious of.

1818 in 1824 Knight *Letters* 107 **KY,** Some words are used, even by genteel people, from their imperfect educations, in a new sense; . . as: . .

to suspicion one. **a1820** in 1845 Cist *Cincinnati Misc.* 1.127 **wPA,** He broke out afresh, accusing me of suspicioning him of a wish to rob me. **1844** Thompson *Major Jones's Courtship* 97 **GA,** They spicioned something. **1863** (1922) Jackson *Col.'s Diary* 98 **PA,** One day I suspicioned a woman . . of being a smuggler. **1867** Harris *Sut Lovingood Yarns* 67 **TN,** I sorter suspishiond hit, but still hed hopes. **1884** *Anglia* 7.269 **Sth, S Midl** [Black], To 'spishun = to suspect. **1893** Shands *MS Speech* 61, *Suspicion. To suspect.* Used by whites, educated and uneducated, to a considerable extent. Negroes say *'spicion.* **1898** Westcott *Harum* 117 **nNY,** I don't know a thing about any outside matters of his'n, though I suspicion he has got quite a few. **1899** (1912) Green *VA Folk-Speech* 430, *Suspicion.* . . To suspect of having done a bad deed. "I suspicioned him at once." **1900** Day *Up in ME* 23, I s'picion how ye never heard of Ebernezer Cowles. **1902** *DN* 2.246 **sIL,** *Suspicion.* . . To suspect. **1903** *DN* 2.332 **seMO,** *Suspicion.* . . Suspect. 'I suspicioned that fellow from the start.' **1905** *DN* 3.97 **nwAR,** No one ever suspicioned that he was losing his mind. **1909** *DN* 3.377 **eAL, wGA,** *Suspicion.* . . To suspect. A very common error. **1911** Porter *Harvester* 513 **IN,** If David has got these fool things counted and misses any, . . he'll s'picion me. **1915** (1916) Johnson *Highways New Engl.* 128, He'd cut a slit or two in them to make sure nobody would suspicion they were new. **1929** Sale *Tree Named John* 90 **MS,** Ah been 'spicionin' dat cat fer a witch ever sence he been comin' roun' hyere. **1949** in 1986 *DARE* File **neOH,** I suspicioned it was not the right thing. Young adult. Male—College student. **1961** Seeman *In Arms of Mt.* 58 **eTN,** The law wouldn't never have suspicioned Tracy. **1965–70** *DARE* (Qu. GG12, *To have an inner feeling that something is about to happen: "There she comes now, I _____ she would."*) 14 Infs, **scattered, but esp Sth, S Midl,** Suspicioned; (Qu. JJ37, *When you have reason to believe that someone is not honest: "I'm not sure, but I _____ that man is a thief.";* total Infs questioned, 75) Inf **FL**14, Suspicion; (Qu. NN7, *Exclamations of surprise: "They're getting married next week? Well, _____.")* Inf **WA**18, I never suspicioned any. [15 of 16 Infs old] **1968** *DARE* FW Addit **LA**40, *Suspicion*—verb. "Make them take it ever time she'd even suspicion they might be constipated." **1975** Gould *ME Lingo* 283, I suspicioned there was chicanery afoot! **1986** Pederson *LAGS Concordance,* 1 inf, **csTN,** They suspicion he did it; 1 inf, **swGA,** Where you might be suspicioned; 1 inf, **cTN,** Suspicioned = suspected; 1 inf, **swAR,** It was suspicioned; 1 inf, **seFL,** They sort of suspicioned that his wife.

Susquehanna salmon n **chiefly PA**
=walleye.

    1851 Herbert *Frank Forester's Fish & Fishing* 105, The fish called *"Trout,"* by the inhabitants of Carolina and the neighboring States, . . is said to abound in the rivers of Pennsylvania. This is, I doubt not, the fish alluded to by a recent writer in the "Spirit of the Times," as the Susquehanna Salmon, unless perchance another nameless fish, the *Perca lucioperca,* is intended. **1871** in 1872 *Fur Fin & Feather* 122 *(DA),* [Game Laws of Pennsylvania:] The species commonly known as Susquehanna salmon, pike, perch, jack salmon . . shall henceforth not be taken . . during their spawning time. **1897** *New Oxford Item* (PA) 7 May [4]/1 (newspaperarchive.com), The opening season for fishing in Pennsylvania is as follows: . . wall-eyed pike, commonly known as Susquehanna salmon, May 30 to January 1. **1901** *Bedford Gaz.* (PA) 7 June 2/5, The following fish are placed in the protection of the act . . Susquehanna salmon or wall-eyed pike [etc]. **1935** Caine *Game Fish* 31, Wall-Eyed Pike. . . *Synonyms.* . . Susquehanna Salmon. **1969–70** *DARE* (Qu. P1, . . *Kinds of freshwater fish . . caught around here . . good to eat)* Inf **PA**199, Susquehanna salmon—walleye pike; **PA**242, Susquehanna salmon.

sussie See **sirsee**

susy adj [Cf *SND susy* (at *shusy* n. 1) "Used for a woman in gen., esp. a silly empty-headed woman"] Cf **durgen** adj, **jakey** adj
See quot 1928; hence adv *susy.*

    1926 *DN* 5.404 **Ozarks,** *Susy.* . . Countrified or uncouth. Usually applied to a woman whose manner or clothing is inferior. **1928** *AmSp* 4.116 [Ozark neologisms], *Susy,* used with reference to persons who are hopelessly inferior, and at the same time ludicrously complacent or conceited. A girl whose clothing is unsuitable or antiquated, but who believes herself quite properly attired, is *dressed plum susy;* an elderly bachelor who imagines that all the girls are in love with him, when they are really laughing behind his back, is a *susy ol' fool.*

sut See **soot**

sutenly See **certainly**

suterberry n
A **prickly ash 1** (here: *Zanthoxylum americanum*).

    1830 Rafinesque *Med. Flora* 2.113, *Xanthoxylon fraxineum* [=*Zanthoxylum americanum*]. *Names.* Shrubby Prickly Ash . . Suterberry. **1900** Lyons *Plant Names* 399, *X[anthoxylum] Americanum.* . . Suterberry. . . *Berries* used to flavor beer, etc. **1960** Vines *Trees SW* 594, Common Prickly-ash—*Zanthoxylum americanum.* . . Vernacular names in use are Angelica-tree, Northern Prickly-ash, Toothache, Suterberry, and Pepperwood.

suthard See **southward**

suthin(g) See **something A2**

su'tinly, sut'n'(e)y See **certainly**

sutthin See **something A2**

sutt(i)n See **certain**

sutty See **soot**

suvigrous, suvvigus See **servigrous**

Suwannee chicken n Also *Suwannee chicken cooter,* ~ *River chicken* Cf **Arkansas chicken, mud hen 3**
A **red-bellied turtle** (here: *Pseudemys concinna*).

    1945 Barbour *Naturalist in Cuba* 69, That member of the group called the "Suwanee [sic] Chicken" is perhaps the best-flavored thing I know in turtle or tortoise form. **1950** *PADS* 14.77 **FL,** *Suwannee River chicken.* . . A fresh water turtle. **1952** Carr *Turtles* 301 **FL,** There used to be a man on an island off the mouth of the Suwannee River who contributed much to the fame of the Suwannee chicken through the extraordinary artistry of the stews he made of it. **1958** Conant *Reptiles & Amphibians* 59, *Suwannee Cooter.* . . This is the "suwannee chicken" esteemed by epicures. **1983** *Audubon Mag.* 85.86 **cnFL,** No bone-strewn riffle or shards of Indian pottery or Suwannee chicken cooter shying at my passing.

Suwannee daisy n
=black-eyed Susan 2.

    1970 *DARE* (Qu. S7, *A kind of daisy, bright yellow with a dark center, that grows along roadsides in late summer)* Inf **OH**95, Suwannee ['swani] daisy.

Suwannee River chicken See **Suwannee chicken**

suwarrow See **saguaro**

suwee See **sooey** v

suwel See **sowel**

suz intj Also *suds, surs, suzz* [Scots, Engl dial *sirs* (also sp *sirse, surs,* etc, and used in var phrr, as *my sirs, sirs a day, sirs alive, sirs me*), usu and prob correctly regarded as developed from the pl of *sir* used as a term of address (but cf *SND ser* v.²); cf the similar development of *man* and *boy.*] **scattered, but esp NEng** *old-fash;* esp *freq among women*
Used as an expression of surprise, annoyance, etc—usu in phrr *dear (me) suz, la(w)* ~, *o* ~ and varr.

    1815 Humphreys *Yankey in England* 109, Suzz! surs! a corruption from sirs. **1845** Judd *Margaret* 37 **NEng** (as of late 18th cent), "How much shall I measure you of this tiffany, Matty?" at length asked Abel. "Oh dear me suz! I don't know," she replied. **1859** (1968) Bartlett *Americanisms* 465, *Suzz!* A corrupt pronunciation of *sirs!* An exclamation much used in New England, as *sirs* is in Scotland. It is sometimes lengthened into *Law, suzz!* i.e. Lord, sirs! **1884** Baldwin *Yankee School-Teacher* 126 **VA,** The mortal suz, Marun! *Ibid* 127, The lawful suz! **1884** *Overland Mth.* (2d ser) 4.275 **MS** [Black], Dear suz! 'pears, chile, like chain-lightnin' ain't quicker on the move'n what you is. **1892** *KS Univ. Qrly.* 1.99 **KS,** *Suz* . . as in, Dear suz, and Law suz. **1903** *DN* 2.299 **Cape Cod MA** (as of a1857), La! la suz! la me suz! suz a day! Ejaculations of women. **1905** *DN* 3.66 **eNE,** *Suz.* Exclamation of surprise or fatigue. "Dear me suz," "O suz," "Law me suz," "O suz alive." **1914** *DN* 4.71 **ME, nNH,** Dear me suz. Common exclamation with women. **1939** in Lib. of Congress *Amer. Memory: WPA Life Hist.* (Internet) **wMA,** Oh suz, I couldn't think that far back. . . Goodness suz, I'm glad he can't see me now. **1959** *VT Hist.* new ser 27.162, *Dear me*

Suz! . . Occasional.   **1967** *News–Jrl.* (Mansfield OH) 29 Jan sec G 14/5, [Headline:] Dear Me Suz—Was Sherman Wrong?   **1976** *DARE* File **cnMA** (as of c1915), *Dear me suz,* common when I was a child. My grandmother might have said, "Oh dear me suz, I forgot to empty the pan under the icebox!" I always heard it as *suds.*

swa   See **swear B1**

swab n   Also *swab stick*
In moonshining: see quots.
   1968 [see **toothbrush 2**].   **1974** Maurer–Pearl *KY Moonshine* 126, *Swab.* . . A long, hickory sapling, well frayed at one end and used along with the mash-stick to keep mash from sticking and scorching in the still. Sometimes to better get at the mash, a rag is tied to the end of the stick.   **1974** Dabney *Mountain Spirits* xxv **sAppalachians,** *Swab Stick:* A hickory stick with the end beat up like an old toothbrush. Used by operators to scrub out the still and to keep the mash from sticking to the still wall before reaching a boil. Sometimes called a stir stick.

swab v   [See quot 1970]
To elicit information from (someone).
   1942 Perry *Texas* 135, Oil has introduced many new words into our diction. To try to get information from someone is an attempt to "swab" him.   [**1970** *DARE* FW Addit **TX95,** *Putting the swab to*—meaning to question, as when a *DARE* FW interviews an Inf. . . Origin: from swabbing out oil wells, i.e., sucking out mud and water to clear passage for oil.]

swab stick   See **swab** n

swad n   [Cf *EDD swad* sb.[10] "A portion, measure, quantity; esp. used of liquids"]   Also sp *swod*
A lump, bunch, crowd; a large quantity; also pl: an abundance.
   1828 (1970) Webster *Amer. Dict., Swad.* . . In *New England,* a lump, mass or bunch; also, a crowd. [Webster: *Vulgar.*]   **1833** in 1834 Davis *Letters Downing* 22 **NEng,** Sargent Joel had put in a leetle too much waddin . . and Enoch Bissel . . slipped in a swad of grass, that hit Mr. Van Buren's horse.   *Ibid* 35, There was a swod of fine folks.   **1869** *Overland Mth.* 3.131 **TX,** A Texan never has a great quantity of any thing, but he has "scads" of it . . or "swads."   **1870** Duval *Advent. Big-Foot* 214 **TX,** Our matted and uncombed locks hung down in "swads" around our faces.   **1899** (1912) Green *VA Folk-Speech* 430, *Swad.* . . A lump, mass, or bunch.   **1906** *IA City Daily Press* (IA) 1 Feb 4/4, I'm older now and have gained swads of tact.   **1935** Davis *Honey* 4 **OR,** He was the scholar of the community, with a great swad of intellectual interests.   **1966–67** *DARE* (Qu. U38b, . . *A great deal of money: "He made a _____ [of money]."*) [Inf **MS23,** Swab;] (Qu. LL8a, *A large amount or number: More than enough . . "He's got _____ of time."*) Inf **PA8,** Swads.   **2004** *DARE* File—Internet, D and I spend great swads of it [=time] on pointless trivia.

swaddle-bill n   *prob obs*
=shoveler.
   1709 (1967) Lawson *New Voyage* [155] **NC, SC,** Swaddle-Bills are a sort of an ash-colour'd Duck, which have an extraordinary broad Bill, and are good Meat.   **1785** Pennant *Arctic Zool.* 2.557, We are to seek for the *Swaddle Bill,* an ash-colored Duck of *Carolina,* with an extraordinary broad bill, said not to be very common there, but to be very good food; we must therefore join it . . to this species [=Blue-wing Shoveler].   **1917** (1923) *Birds Amer.* 1.126, *Shoveller.* . . *Other Names.* . . Swaddle-bill.

swadget n   Cf **swad**
   1944 *PADS* 6.33 **cNC** (as of 1941), *Whole swadget.* . . A large amount.

swag n
1   An area of low, freq damp or marshy, land; hence adj *swaggy.*   [Engl, Scots dial]   **chiefly Sth, S Midl**   Cf **sag 2, swale 1**
   1848 *Holden's Dollar Mag.* Aug 475 **Ozarks,** [Footnote:] "A Swag" is often met with in the Western country. It is a concave spot, sunk in below the level by nature.   **1869** *Overland Mth.* 3.130, In Texas . . a "swag" is a kind of hollow which seems to be peculiar to its prairies—narrow, shallow, and marshy and rush-grown at the bottom.   **1895** *DN* 1.394 **MO,** *Swag:* depression in the ground.   **1905** (1975) Miles *Spirit of Mts.* 91 **sAppalachians,** At another time a hunter followed his dogs over a hill in the Suck region, down across a "swag," and over the breaks of the stream, before finally overtaking his quarry.   **1923** *DN* 5.222 **swMO,** *Swag.* . . Low ground, usually wet.   **1929** Dobie *Vaquero* 233

West, We took our stand in a kind of swag down which we felt sure the horse thieves would come.   **1933** *AmSp* 8.1.52 **Ozarks,** *Swag.* . . A piece of low, swampy ground.   **1943** Chase *Jack Tales* 158 **wNC** (as of 1880s), Got on down the mountain and came out in a wide swag toward the river.   **1949** Arnow *Hunter's Horn* 106 **KY,** He would pick up the rocks in the graveyard field and the three corn swags where he had had corn for the last four years.   **1955** Faulkner *Big Woods* 189 **MS,** We was walking . . when we come on the dogs . . played out, laying in a little wet swag.   **1967–68** *DARE* (Qu. C6, . . *A piece of land that's often wet, and has grass and weeds growing on it*) Infs **LA15, TX13,** Swag.   **1967** *DARE* FW Addit **AR55,** Swag—a low place, often with wet ground.   **1968** *DARE* File **AL,** Swag—Head of a swamp lying between two slopes. Probably became a branch. A swag might need to be ditched.   **1986** Pederson *LAGS Concordance (Gully)* 1 inf, **neTN,** Swag; 1 inf, **ceTN,** Swags—low places in fields where land settles; *(Meadow)* 1 inf, **cnGA,** Swag; 1 inf, **nwAR,** Swag—similar to swamp; *(Swamp)* 1 inf, **nwAR,** Swag—low, standing water; 1 inf, **seAR,** Swaggy places, swampy, low; 1 inf, **cwLA,** A swag—sinkhole, hills on sides, low in center.

2   A low or level place on a ridge or between two hills; a **gap** n[1] **1.**   **chiefly Sth, S Midl**   Cf **sag 1**
   1929 Summers *Annals* 1586 **swVA,** The summit of that part of White Top known at this day as Elk Garden, the long swag connecting White Top and Balsam.   **1939** *Hall Coll.* **wNC, eTN,** *Swag.* . . A low, level place on a ridge.   **1940** Writers' Program *Guide GA* 476 **cnGA,** South of Snake Mountain the crest of the Blue Ridge falls to a relatively low "sag," which in mountaineer dialect is known as the "Swag of the Blue Ridge." In one of the most isolated highland sections, the "swag" is a vantage point for broad, spectacular views.   **1955** Ritchie *Singing Family* 114 **seKY,** At the very head of Clear Creek is some high pretty land in the swag of the mountain, called Hammond's Gap.   **1956** (1964) Fink *That's Why* 3 **wNC, eTN,** Here these lower places between peaks and along ridges are almost invariably known as *gaps,* with an occasional *swag.*   **1969–70** *DARE* (Qu. C15, *A place in mountains or high hills where you can get through without climbing over the top*) Inf **AR56,** Swag; (Qu. C19, . . *Low land running between hills*) Inf **GA84,** Swag.   **1970** Foxfire 4.71 **nGA,** Sometimes men would get on either side of a gap or swag, set the dogs loose, and let the dogs drive the deer through between them.   **1974** Fink *Mountain Speech* 25 **wNC, eTN,** *Swag* . . low spot in the ground, on a ridge.   **1986** Pederson *LAGS Concordance (Notch)* 3 infs, **GA, TN,** (A) swag; 1 inf, **cTN,** Swag—level place heading off a mountain; 1 inf, **cnAR,** Swag = gap.

3   A low point in a roadway.   **chiefly Sth, S Midl**   See Map
   1965–70 *DARE* (Qu. N30, . . *A sudden short dip in a road*) 19 Infs, **chiefly Sth, S Midl,** Swag.

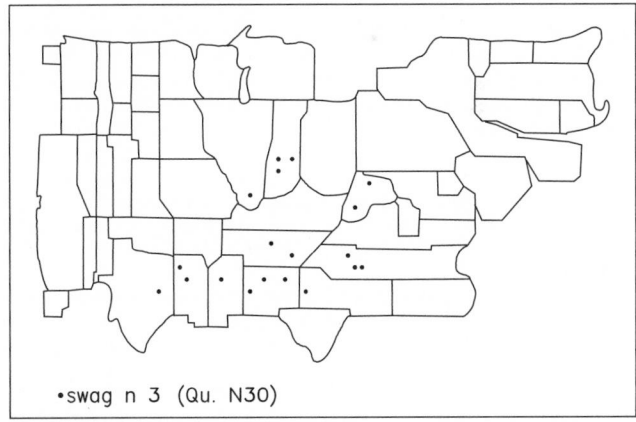

•swag n 3 (Qu. N30)

4   A sag.
   1889 Folsom *Scraps* 128 **GA,** Ah the old log church! With its long roof of clapboards, and the swag in the middle where the back bone had weakened.   **1949** *PADS* 11.11 **wTX** (as of 1911–29), *Swag.* . . A sag.   **1952** Brown *NC Folkl.* 1.596, *Swag.* . . A depression, a *sag.* "This floor has a swag in the center."

5   A swallow, swig.   [*SND swag* n. 4 "A quantity of liquid or liquor, a long 'pull' or draught"]
   1967–69 *DARE* (Qu. DD18, *A drink of liquor, or the amount of liquor taken in one swallow: "He took a good _____."*) Infs **CO15, GA84, MD25, MO21,** Swag.

swag v, hence vbl n *swagging* Also sp *swagg* [*OED2* "Now chiefly *dial*."]

1 To move heavily from side to side, sway; hence ppl adj *swagging* pendulous. [*OED2* 1530 →]

1899 (1912) Green *VA Folk-Speech* 430, *Swag*. . . To move as something heavy and pendent; sway. *Swagging*. . pendulous. **1902** *Atlanta Constitution* (GA) 1 June 26/4, At the rear of the procession came the immense Chinese dragon. . . Swagging from side to side of the thronged thoroughfare, the creature fiercely glared at spectators.

2 also with *down*: To sink, sag, bulge downward; hence ppl adj *swagging*; adj *swaggy*. [*OED2* 1621 →] **chiefly Sth, S Midl**

1792 Belknap *Hist. NH* 3.75, Some [surveyors] allow one in thirty, for the swagging of the chain. **1793** in 1891 Washington *Writings* 12.379 **VA,** The advantage of this latch is, that let the gate swag as it may, it always catches. **1858** *Scientific Amer.* 13.264, Each panel is also braced by a tie, . . which keeps the fence from "swagging." **1891** *Courier* (Connellsville PA) 4 Dec 8/1, The cracking and swagging down of the bridge over the Yough . . while one of Jasper W. Chick's heavy lumber wagons was crossing, caused considerable excitement. **1899** (1912) Green *VA Folk-Speech* 430, *Swag*. . . To sink down by its weight; lean; sag. . . *Swagging*. . . Swaggy. *Swaggy*. . . Sinking, hanging, or leaning by its own weight. **1903** *DN* 2.332 **seMO,** *Swag*. . . Sag. 'The foundations were not good and the house has swagged a right smart.[*] **1907** *DN* 3.237 **nwAR,** *Swag*. . . To sag. **1909** *DN* 3.377 **eAL, wGA,** *Swag*. . . To sag. **1915** *DN* 4.191 **swVA,** *Swag*. . . To sag. **1933** *AmSp* 8.1.52 **Ozarks,** *Swag*. . . To sag. Th' door has got t' swaggin' so bad I caint git it shut no more. **1938** in Lib. of Congress *Amer. Memory: WPA Life Hist.* (Internet) **cNC,** Yonder is my house, that one with the porch ceiling ripped loose and swagging down. **1941** *LANE* Map 362 *(Bulge)* 1 inf, **csRI,** Swag down. **1952** Brown *NC Folkl.* 1.596, *Swag*. . . To sink down, to *sag*.—West. **1979** *AmSp* 54.100 **sME** (as of 1899–1910), *Swag down*. . . Droop or hang loosely. **1986** Pederson *LAGS Concordance (Bulge)* 2 infs, **AL, FL,** Swag; 1 inf, **ceAL,** Swag—hanging down; 1 inf, **nwAR,** She's swagging—about to give birth.

swag down v phr¹ See **swag** v **2**

swag down v phr² See **swage 2, 3**

swage v Also sp *suage* [By-forms of *assuage*. *OED2* swage v.¹ a1300 →; "*Obs.* exc. *arch.* or *dial*." The comb *swage down* (with var *swedge down*) and the var *swag* appear to be US innovations, the former prob infl by the (unrelated) blacksmith's term *swage* (or *swedge*) *down* to reduce in diameter by the use of a swage or die, the latter by **swag** v **2**.] **chiefly Sth, S Midl**

1a To alleviate (a disease); esp, freq with *down*: to shrink (a swelling or swollen member), hence ppl adjs *swag(g)ed down*.

1859 *Weekly Std.* (Raleigh NC) 19 Oct [4]/3 (newspaperarchive.com), [Speech by Sen. James Chesnut Jr. of SC:] The panacea for all the troubles of the Government was applied, and a compromise swaged the distemper for a moment. **1864** in 2001 Barr *Let Us Meet* 247 **SC,** My leg is swagged down a good deal. They poultice it twice a day. **1899** (1912) Green *VA Folk-Speech* 430, *Swage*. . . To make quiet; soothe; assuage. (2) To reduce a swelling in size. **1909** *DN* 3.377 **eAL, wGA,** *Swage*[*b*] suage. . . To assuage. **1931** Goodrich *Mt. Homespun* 56 **sAppalachians,** Her neck was bound up with surgeon's plaster. . . "Poor sister ain't fit to go anywheres till that neck of hers gets swaged down." **1937** (1963) Hyatt *Kiverlid* 81 **KY,** You git yer Granny to tie some fresh pine-tar to hit [=a cut and swollen foot] afore you go to bed, that'll swage it down. **1945** Lyon *Fresh from Hills* 135 **Ozarks,** When I sprained an ankle . . the superintendent of the school said, . . "You'd better put that in hot water and get it swaged down!" **1950** *PADS* 14.65 **SC,** *Swage*. . . To reduce a swelling. **1952** Brown *NC Folkl.* 1.596, *Swage*. . . To assuage. **1984** Wilder *You All Spoken Here* 206 **Sth,** *Swaged down*. . . Reduced in size, as with a boil.

b Spec: to milk or strip (a cow's udder); hence vbl n *swaging*.

1934 Carmer *Stars Fell on AL* 179, Brer Rabbit say: . . 'I kin 'suage your bag, Sis Cow.' . . Then Brer Rabbit . . his ole 'oman and de chillun . . milk Sis Cow and have a big feastin'. **1937** Hench Coll. **VA,** *Suage*—heard orally. Farming people tell me this is a very old expression for milking a cow too thoroughly, so that it goes dry. The expression, they tell me, is never other than "suage the bag", never, e.g. "suage the cow." **1940** Ibid, *Swage*—heard. The expression means to milk the cow and relieve it of any pain it might get from not being nursed or milked. **1950** *PADS* 14.65 **SC,** *Swage*. . . To strip a milch cow. *Swaging*

or stripping is done with a different motion from that of ordinary milking. In stripping or *swaging* the thumb and forefinger are drawn with pressure down the teat. **1969** *DARE* (Qu. K6, . . *Taking the last of the milk from the udder*) Inf **NY**198, Swaging. [FW sugg]

2 with *off*; Of an illness: to abate; esp, also *swedge,* freq with *down;* also *swag down;* of a swelling or swollen member: to shrink.

1702 (1972) Mather *Magnalia* 6.10 **MA,** The Brains left in the Child's Head would swell and swage, according to the *Tides*. **1885** *Newark Daily Advocate* (OH) 4 Aug 1/3 **SC,** Her limbs, which were much swollen and evidently dropsical, have swaged to their normal condition. **1946** *PADS* 6.29 **eNC** (as of 1900–10), *Swage down*. . . To become smaller (said of swellings). . . Common. **1950** *PADS* 14.65 **SC,** *Swage*. . . to become reduced. **1958** *DE Folkl. Bulletin* 1.32, It 'suaged off (said of a pain like rheumatism). **1966** *DARE* (Qu. BB31, *When a swelling begins to get less . . it's _____; total Infs questioned, 75) Inf **GA**8, Swaging, swaging down. **1983** *MJLF* 9.1.58 **ceKY** (as of 1956), *Swaging*. . . going down, as a swelling. **1995–97** in 2004 Montgomery-Hall *Dict. Smoky Mt. Engl.* 584 **eTN, wNC,** *Swag down* = to shrink. *Ibid, Swedge down* = to return to normal, as "My swollen ankle has swedged down since I used Epson Salts on it." **2000** Shores *Tangier Is.* 237 **Chesapeake Bay,** Stay home until the swelling *swages.*

3 with *down;* also *swag down:* To calm, subdue, cow; to become subdued.

1871 (1892) Johnston *Dukesborough Tales* 60 **GA,** You see, Phil, paddlin' me sorter cools and swages him down a leetle bit. **1890** *Atlanta Constitution* (GA) 3 Aug 8/2, ["Bill Arp" column:] The boys got hot over their rights, but they have all swaged down and look as meek and humble as a run-over calf. **1897** Johnston in *Century Illustr. Mag.* 53.761 **GA,** If he'd take the reins in his own hands, and let her understand as the head o' the family he were goin' to keep 'em, she'd swage down and come reason'ble. **1899** [see **1a** above]. **1979** Carpenter *Walton War* 147 **sAppalachians,** Evern (even when) he told me, it sort of swagged down my feelins. *Ibid* 148, "Hit's a sight how a stranger can swagg down a youngun." A stranger had come and a little girl had hidden in the closet.

swaged down See **swage 1a**

swage down See **swage 1a, 3**

swagen See **swagin**

swage off See **swage 2**

swagg See **swag** v

swagged down See **swage 1a**

swagger v Also *swaggers, swags* [Prob reduced from *I shall wager;* cf *SND swag* v.² "Only in fut. tense *I'll swag,* I'll bet" and *wager* v. quot 1918: "I'se waager ta send de Deil edder oot da . . window, or da door, whatever wye ye want."] Cf **swanny** To declare; to swear—usu used as an exclam or in exclam phrs.

1815 Humphreys *Yankey in England* 109, *Swags,* exclamation. **1838** Kettell *Yankee Notions* 132, "I swaggers!" he exclaimed, "this is too bad!" **1996** Horton *Island Out of Time* 228 **Chesapeake Bay MD** The soil there, one said, "is a darn sight marshier than anything that computer's ever seen, swagger it ain't." *Ibid* 241, We got three bushels and sold 'em for three dollars. Swagger die if that warn't the champ. [Footnote:] Swear to die if that wasn't the greatest thing. *Ibid* 253, Hayee, Charruls. . . fair maarnin', I swagger. **2000** Shores *Tangier Is.* 241 **Chesapeake Bay,** *I'll swagger,* if he didn't quit a day later (connotes surprise and disgust).

swagger-tail(ed) coat n Also *swigger(-tail)* **esp Sth** Cf **jimswinger 1**

A long-tailed coat; see quots.

1903 *United Service* 4.111 **Sth** (as of a1860), Almost every city had its Light Guard, whose pride it was at stated intervals to parade the streets in towering bearskins, in swagger-tail coats, in broad white cross-belts, and in pomp and ceremony indescribable. **1908** in 1909 Atl. Deeper Waterways Assoc. *Annual Convention Rept.* 1.22 **NC,** Everyone going to the banquet will be expected to wear his spike-tailed coat . . I don't think there is more than one swagger-tailed coat to the hundred people in the State of North Carolina. **1909** *DN* 3.378 **eAL, wGA,** *Swigger(-tail)*. . . A Prince Albert or cutaway coat; also a dress-coat.

swagging vbl n See **swag** v

swagging ppl adj   See **swag** v **1, 2**

swaggle n, v   [Var of *swagger;* cf *EDD swaggle* v. 1 "To swing; to sway to and fro . . ; to reel and stagger"]   Cf Intro "Language Changes" IV.4, **flitter** n[1], **flustrate**

   1961 *Mt. Life* Spring 7 **sAppalachians,** In a few words. . . *l* is substituted for *r: fluster(at)ed,* (frustrated), *flitter* (fritter), *swaggle* (swagger).

swaggy adj[1]   See **swag** v **2**

swaggy adj[2]   See **swag** n **1**

swagin n |'swegɪn| Also sp *swagen, swagun, swogun* [Etym unknown]   **chiefly ME**

   A soup or porridge; see quots—freq in comb *bean swagin.*

   1909 *DN* 3.408 **nME,** *Bean swāgin.* . . A bean soup.   **1914** *DN* 4.81 **ME, nNH,** *Swagin, swogun.* . . Bean-soup, in lumber-camps. *Ibid* 151 **ceME,** *Bean swagun.* . . Bean porridge.   **1918** *Daily Kennebec Jrl.* (Augusta ME) 19 Mar 6/3, He should use his damaged peas for soup, his beans for swagin, feed the balance to the hens, to the end that nothing may be wasted.   **1950** *WELS Suppl., Bean swagen*—bean soup. Used in Maine lumber camps.   **1966** *DARE* Tape **ME**19, [Inf:] They [= loggers] had baked beans, pea swagin ['pi ˌsweɪgɪn]. [FW:] What's that? [Inf:] Beans and water.   **1967** *DARE* FW Addit **ME,** *Oatmeal swagen*—drink made on farms from molasses, ginger, a little sugar, vinegar, and oatmeal.

swaging   See **swage 1b**

swags   See **swagger**

swagun   See **swagin**

swah   See **swear B1**

swail   See **swale**

swain   See **swan**

Swainson's hawk n   Also *Swainson hawk*

   Std: a large hawk *(Buteo swainsoni)* native to the plains, grasslands, and prairies west of the Mississippi River.   Also called **black hawk 2, brown ~, gopher ~, grasshopper ~ 3**

Swainson's thrush n

   Std: a thrush *(Catharus ustulatus)* with olive-brown back and tail, native chiefly to the northern and northwestern US.   Also called **hermit 2, swamp robin 1c, wood thrush 2**

swale n   Also sp *swail*

   1 also attrib: A low-lying tract of land, as a marsh, swamp, or meadow.   **chiefly Nth, esp NEast, MI**   See Map   Cf **swag n 1, swale grass**

   1667 in 1894 Dedham MA *Early Rec.* 4.135, He may cutt in a place called the Swale, adjoyning to the Ceader Swampe.   **1792** (1806) MA Hist. Soc. *Coll.* 1st ser 1.273, The swamps and swails yield maple, black birch, ash, and some hemlock.   **1834** (1847) Lundy *Life & Travels* 101 **MI,** We crossed a strip of land, about forty rods in width, which reminded me of the "swales" of Michigan.   **1894** *DN* 1.334 **NJ,** *Swale:* low land between sand ridges on the coast beaches.   **1897** Lummis *King of Broncos* 10 **NM,** Indeed the black [horse] swerved to the right and dashed up the swale—and then swerved back and went flying down the valley.   **1899** Garland *Boy Life* 9 **nwIA** (as of c1870s), In the swales . . the crow's-foot, tall and willowy, bowed softly under the feet of the wind.   **1923** *DN* 5.222 **swMO,** *Swale.* . . Low, swampy land.   **1932** *DN* 6.234 **West,** *Swale.* Rather an old-fashioned word for a grassy opening in the forest. It is generally unreported, to me, in the prairie states, as well as in California, but that may be because the thing itself is not common.   **1935** Davis *Honey* 1 **OR,** There were long swales of alder and sweetbrier.   **1940** Faulkner *Hamlet* 209 **MS,** They go on across the swale, toward the woods, and enter them.   **1946** Attwood *Length ME* 17 [Geographical terms], *Swale*—A tract of low, marshy ground, usually rank with vegetation.   **1954** White *Adirondack Country* 38 **NY,** Men will. . . talk about having to hunt "in the swale," using an old English word for lowland.   **1965–70** *DARE* (Qu. C6, . . *A piece of land that's often wet, and has grass and weeds growing on it*) 13 Infs, **scattered Nth,** Swale; **VT**16, Swale bog; (Qu. C19, . . *Low land running between hills*) 10 Infs, **esp Nth, West,** Swale; (Qu. C7, . . *Land that usually has some standing water with trees or bushes growing in it*) Infs **MA**6, 62, **MI**2, 67, 71, **NY**69, 103, 206, Swale (land); (Qu. C14, *A stretch of still water going off to the side from a river or lake*) Infs **CO**41, **MI**23, Swale; [(Qu. L6b, *A piece of land under cultivation—if it's several acres*) Inf

CT2, Swale].   **1985** Benes *Amer. Speech* 41 **ME,** In present-day oral use, *swamp* is the predominant word. There are others, in spoken use roughly synonymous—*bog, fen, heath, marsh, meadow, slough,* and *swale,* all of which, with the exception of *swale,* appear in Maine place names.   **1986** Pederson *LAGS Concordance (Meadow)* 1 inf, **cTX,** Swale—doesn't use; *(Bottomland)* 1 inf, **csTX,** Swale.   **2001** *DARE* File **NM,** I would describe a "swale" as a slight depression or hollow that you can see over a small rise right in front of you. It wasn't wet or swampy or muddy or difficult to cross. . . Some fellow argued with us that this wasn't a swale, it was a swag.

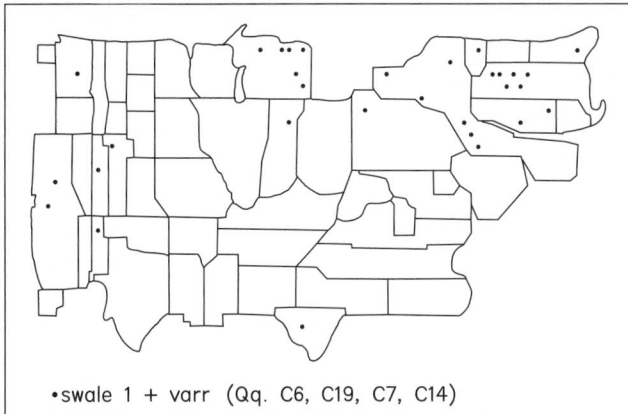

   •swale 1 + varr (Qq. C6, C19, C7, C14)

   2 =**tree lawn.**   [Transf from *swale* grassy depression]   **FL, AL**   Cf *DS* N44

   1986 Pederson *LAGS Concordance,* 1 inf, **seFL,** Swale—strip of grass [between the sidewalk and the street].   **2004** *DARE* File—Internet **FL,** His main advice was . . not to put it [=a political sign] on the swale (the strip of city-owned land between the sidewalk and the street).   **2006** *Ibid* **FL,** This tree was on the publicly owned swale area between the sidewalk and the street.   **2006** *DARE* File **AL,** Swale in AL[,] burm [sic] in FL—I am 91 years old born and raised in the deep woods of Alabama.   **2007** *Ibid* **sFL,** In South Florida . . we call that [=the strip of grass and trees between the sidewalk and the curb] a "Swale."

swale grass n   **chiefly NEng, Upstate NY**   See Map   Cf **marsh hay, slough grass 1, 2b, swamp grass, ~ hay, wild hay**

   Usu a **sedge B1** (here: *Carex* spp), but occas another similar coarse plant that grows in a **swale 1;** often used for hay; hence n *swale hay.*

   1838 MA Ag. Surv. *Rept. for 1837* 19, Considerable quantities of fresh meadow or swale hay is cut.   **1850** Judd *Richard Edney* 459 **ME,** Turf, swale grass, stones, stumps, were brought together, and piled upon it.   **1857** Flint *Practical Treatise* 54 **MA,** The meadow or swale hay was taken from a wet meadow, made up of coarse swale grasses, such as are common in eastern Massachusetts, and pass under the term of "meadow hay." *Ibid* 105, Somewhat over a hundred species [of sedge] are found in New England. . . [T]hey constitute mainly what we term "meadow hay," or more properly swale hay, in eastern Massachusetts. . . It not unfrequently happens . . that there is an admixture of the higher grasses among the carices or sedges, . . possessing higher nutritive qualities, and then . . the hay made from the swale is proportionably improved.   **1874** VT State Bd. Ag. *Rept. for 1873–74* 2.189, [If] the lightest were swale

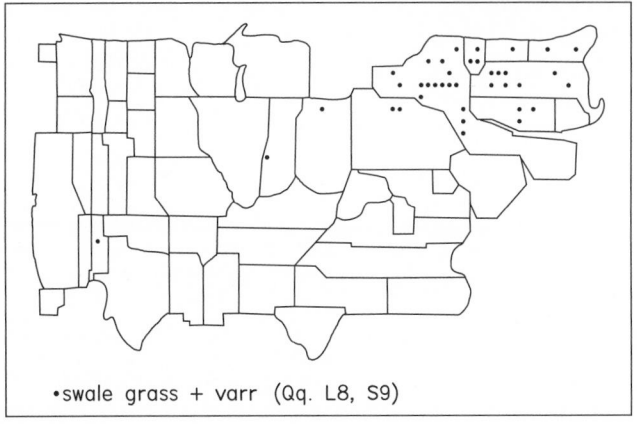

   •swale grass + varr (Qq. L8, S9)

grass, . . I would cut it in June. **1887** *Star & Sentinel* (Gettysburg PA) 15 Nov 4/2, This can be accomplished by horse power, and the entire job be done at once, including any other coarse fodder, such as straw or swale grass. **1922** *Oneonta Daily Star* (NY) 10 Jan 7/3, *Wanted*—At once, a quantity of swale grass or cheap hay for covering ice. **1944** Wellman *Bowl* 83 **KS**, A primitive shed . . roofed over with a slovenly heap of old corn stalks and swale grass. **1965–70** *DARE* (Qu. L8, *Hay that grows naturally in damp places*) 26 Infs, **chiefly NEng, Upstate NY,** Swale (hay); 13 Infs, **chiefly NEng, Upstate NY,** Swale grass; (Qu. S9, . . *Kinds of grass that are hard to get rid of*) Infs NM6, NY109, Swale grass. **2004** *Kennebec Jrl. Online* (Augusta ME) 10 Nov (Internet) **sME,** Hunkered down in the streamside swale grass last Saturday, I waited for a big buck to stop by to dine on wild cranberries.

swaller See **swallow** n[2]

swallerer See **swallow** n[2] **B**

swallop n [Cf *EDD* *swallup* v. "To swallow at a gulp without tasting."]
See quots.
1931 *Bedford Gaz.* (PA) 11 Dec 6/4, The Fairview Ladies' Aid Society will hold a Bazaar. . . Plenty of good eats—Oysters, fried and stewed, chicken swallop, vegetable soup, . . ice cream. **1969** *DARE* (Qu. H36, *Kinds of soup*) Inf **PA206,** Chicken swallop.

swalloping vbl n See **swollop**

swallow n[1]
Std: a bird of the family Hiruninidae or Apodidae. Cf **sea swallow** For other names of var spp see **bank swallow 1, barn ~ 1, chimney swift, cliff swallow, martin, pewee** n[1] **5, purple martin, rainbird 1b, rough-winged swallow, thunder bird 2, tree swallow**

swallow n[2], v Usu |'swalo|; also |'swalə|; **esp Sth, S Midl** |'swalɚ|; for addit varr see quots Pronc-spp *swaller, swalluh* Cf Intro "Language Changes" IV.1.c, **-er 1**
A Forms.
1843 (1916) Hall *New Purchase* 174 **IN,** The prophit . . was chuck'd out and swallered. **1884** *Anglia* 7.265 **Sth, S Midl** [Black], *To done bin an' swallered er thing* = to have swallowed &c. **1899** (1912) Green *VA Folk-Speech* 430, *Swaller.* . . A form of *swallow.* **1903** *DN* 2.301 **Cape Cod MA** (as of a1857), *Swallow* [swalɚ]. . . In expression 'gag and swaller.' To eat large mouthfuls hastily. **1922** Gonzales *Black Border* 330 **sSC, GA coasts** [Gullah glossary], *Swalluh*—(n. and v.) swallow. **1928** *AmSp* 3.403 **Ozarks,** The final *o* sound represented by *ow* is very often replaced by *er* in an unaccented final syllable, giving us such words as . . *swaller.* **1961** Kurath–McDavid *Pronc. Engl.* 172, *Swallow it.* . . In the phrase *swallow it,* a "linking" /r/ occurs chiefly in the South and the South Midland, and again in eastern New England. . . In the South and the South Midland, the linking /r/ is exceedingly common in this phrase. . . In eastern New England . . the /r/ is rather clearly confined to folk speech. . . It has been largely eliminated in urbanized southern New England. . . In Western New England and the New England settlements to the west, /r/ is uncommon even in folk speech, and in Metropolitan New York and Pennsylvania only scattered relics of it have been observed. **1966–69** *DARE* (Qu. H11a, *If somebody eats rapidly and noisily, you say he* _____) Inf **NC37,** Swallers his food; (Qu. H24, . . *Names or nicknames . . for boiled cornmeal*) Inf **CA87,** Gap-an'-swaller; [(Qu. Q20, . . *Kinds of swallows and birds like them*) Infs **GA28, NJ31,** (Chimney) swaller;] (Qu. BB22, . . *Home remedies . . for constipation*) Inf **NY209,** Swaller of castor oil; (Qu. BB50a, . . *Favorite remedies . . for a cough*) Inf **GA33,** Pinch of salt on your tongue and a swaller of water; (Qu. HH25, *One who never has anything to say: "What's the matter with him?* _____?") Inf **VT12,** Swallered his tongue. **1976** Garber *Mountain-ese* 89 **sAppalachians,** *Swaller . . swallow.* **1989** Pederson *LAGS Tech. Index* 196 **Gulf Region,** *Swallow (it).* . . [Of 917 infs, 285 offered proncs of the types ['swalə(ɪt), 'swaləd(ɪt), 'swaləz]; 178 infs, ['swalɚ(ɪt), 'swalərɪt, 'swalɚ(t), 'swalɚɫ, 'swalrɪt, 'swalə‑d, 'swalorɪt, 'swalluɚ, 'swaɚlə]; 81 infs, ['swalo(ɪt), 'swalod, 'swaloz]; 51 infs, ['swalowɪt, 'swalowɪt, 'swaluwɪt, 'swaləwɲ]; 5 infs, ['swalɫ, -ɑ, 'swaluɪt]; 5 infs, ['swælə, -o, -ɚ]; 5 infs, ['swɔlo, -o, ɚ].

B As noun.
Also *swallerer, swallower, swallows, swallow pipe:* The throat, gullet; the Adam's apple. **esp Sth, S Midl** Cf **goozle** n 1
1867 Harris *Sut Lovingood Yarns* 208 **TN,** Jis' then I seed him yerk,

sorter vomitin way, so I straddiled him, an' cotch him by the har, an' pull'd up his head tu straiten his swaller. **1899** (1912) Green *VA Folk-Speech* 430, *Swallow-pipe.* . . The gullet. **1917** *DN* 4.418 **wNC,** *Swallerer.* . . Throat. *Slang.* **1927** *AmSp* 2.365 **cwWV,** *Swallerer . .* throat. "That child has something stuck in his swallerer." **1966–70** *DARE* (Qu. H43) Inf **VA42,** Haslet—kidneys, lights, melts, swaller, liver, and sweetbread; (Qu. X7, . . *The throat: "Some food got stuck in his* _____") Infs **MA6, VA24,** Swallow; **GA72,** Swallow pipe; **KY11, ME21,** Swallower; **GA84,** Swallows. **1983** *MJLF* 9.1.58 **ceKY** (as of 1956), *Swaller . .* the throat. **1986** Pederson *LAGS Concordance (Neck, throat)* 17 infs, **scattered Gulf Region,** Swallow [=Adam's apple, throat, goozle]; 1 inf, **ceFL,** The swallow—Adam's apple; 1 inf, **csTX,** The swallow—inside the throat; [1 inf, **cnGA,** The swallow part;] 1 inf, **cGA,** Your swallow and your google pipe; 1 inf, **cnGA,** Swallow pipe; 1 inf, **cnLA,** Swallower—swallowing mechanism in throat; 1 inf, **csAL,** Swallower means goozle.

C As verb.
In var phrr meaning to become pregnant or to be visibly pregnant, as:
a *swallow a pumpkin (seed)* and varr. **chiefly Sth, S Midl, TX** See Map Cf **eat pumpkin seeds**
c1950 Halpert Coll. 56 **wKY, nwTN,** She swallowed a punkin seed . . = pregnant. **1965–70** *DARE* (Qu. AA28, . . *Joking or sly expressions . . women use to say that another is going to have a baby . . "She['s]* _____.") 34 Infs, **chiefly Sth, S Midl, TX,** Swallowed a pumpkin seed; **AL56, IN26, LA2, SC29, 32, TX98, VA13, 27,** Swallowed a pumpkin; **KY33, TX104,** Swallowed a punkin seed; **AL4,** Swallowed the pumpkin. **1967–69** *DARE* FW Addit **LA11,** Long time ago, Mama said, when you were pregnant, they said, "May has swallowed a pumpkin seed"; **ceNC,** *Swallowed a pumpkin*—meaning pregnant—"She swallowed a pumpkin." **1986** Pederson *LAGS Concordance (Pregnant)* 30 infs, **Gulf Region,** Swallowed a pumpkinseed. [**2004** *DARE* File—Internet **OK,** [From a child's poem:] There once was a lady who swallowed a pumpkin seed./ A few days later her tummy grew bigger and bigger 'til she couldn't see.]

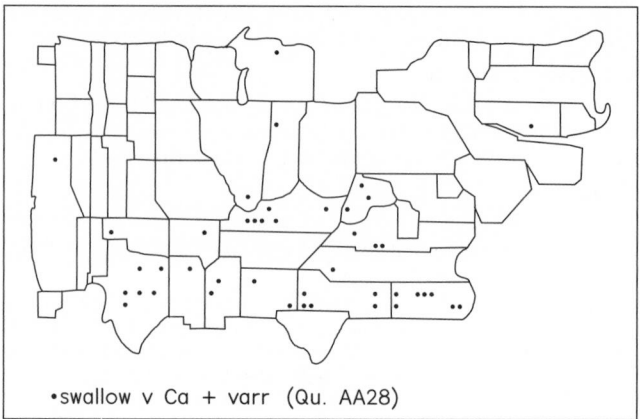

• swallow v Ca + varr (Qu. AA28)

b *swallow a watermelon (seed)* and var.
c1950 Halpert Coll. 56 **wKY, nwTN,** She swallowed a . . watermelon = pregnant. **1965–70** *DARE* (Qu. AA28, . . *Joking or sly expressions . . women use to say that another is going to have a baby . . "She['s]* _____.") 22 Infs, **scattered,** Swallowed a watermelon (seed); **DC8,** Ate a watermelon. **1986** Pederson *LAGS Concordance (Pregnant)* 15 infs, **Gulf Region,** (She) swallowed a watermelon (seed).
c *swallow an olive (seed), swallow a peach* (or *prune*) *seed.*
1967–70 *DARE* (Qu. AA28, . . *Joking or sly expressions . . women use to say that another is going to have a baby . . "She['s]* _____.") Infs **GA81, ID5, OH28, PA245,** Swallowed an olive (seed); **AK8,** Swallowed a prune seed. **1986** Pederson *LAGS Concordance (Pregnant)* 1 inf, **ceTX,** Swallowed a peach seed.
d in var other phrr; see quot.
1966–70 *DARE* (Qu. AA28, . . *Joking or sly expressions . . women use to say that another is going to have a baby . . "She['s]* _____.") Inf **IL63,** Swallowed a coconut; **MD19,** Swallowed an elephant; **OH16,** Swallowed an apple; **PA247,** Swallowed a seed; **SC11,** Swallowed a pill; **VA24,** Swallowed a quarter; swallowed a train.

swallow an olive (seed), swallow a peach (or prune) seed
See **swallow** v **Cc**

swallow a pumpkin (seed)   See **swallow** v Ca

swallow a watermelon (seed)   See **swallow** v Cb

swallower   See **swallow** n² B

swallow fork n   Also *swallow tail* [From the resemblance to a swallow's forked tail] **chiefly Sth, S Midl, SW**   See Map
An **earmark** n consisting of a V-shaped notch cut into the tip of the ear.

   1636 in 1889 Plymouth MA *Records* 1.1, Every mans marke of his Cattle. . . Mr John Weekes a swallow tayle cut out on the left eare. . . Christopher Waddesworth a swallow forke. **1736** in 1975 N. Castle NY *N. Castle Hist. Rec.* B100 seNY, The Ear Mark of *Mosses Quimby* is a swallow fork on the off Ear. **1854** in 1975 *Foxfire 3* 87 nwGA, Jesse Lovel Deposeth and sayeth that his stock mark is a swallow fork in Each year. **1869** *Overland Mth.* 3.126 TX, I had seen a brown-and-white-pied calf, with . . an overslope and a slit in the right, and a swallow-fork in the left. **1906** *DN* 3.159 nwAR, Swallow-fork. . . A triangular incision at the end of an animal's ear leaving two forks resembling the swallow's forked tail. **1907** White *AZ Nights* 149, First, with a sharp knife he cut off slanting the upper quarter of one ear. Then he nicked out a swallow-tail in the other. **1909** *DN* 3.378 eAL, wGA, Swallow-fork. **1915** *DN* 4.185 swVA, Swallow-fork. **1941** Writers' Program *Guide WY* 465, Swallow-fork—A V-shape cut from ear for identification purposes. **1942** Warnick *Garrett Co. MD* 15 nwMD (as of 1900–18), *Swallow-fork* . . an earmark for animals (Chiefly Southern U.S.) **1964** *PADS* 42.16 csKY, *Earmarks. . . swallow fork,* two slits run together to form a *W* or an *M.* **1965–70** *DARE* (Qu. K18, . . *Kind of mark . . to identify a cow*) Infs AL20, GA72, LA40, SC43, TN24, TX5, 6, Swallow fork. **1982** Ginns *Snowbird Gravy* 129 nwNC, Ours was a swallow fork in the left and a overslope in the right. Ears, that is! **1986** Pederson *LAGS Concordance,* 1 inf, ceTN, Swallow fork—in cattle marking; 1 inf, neAR, Swallow fork—part of family brand; 1 inf, ceAR, Swallow fork—a brand on top of the ear; 1 inf, cwAR, Swallow fork—example of brand on hog's ear; 1 inf, swAR, Swallow fork—mark on hog's ear; 1 inf, neFL, Swallow fork—a V cut in the top of cow's ear.

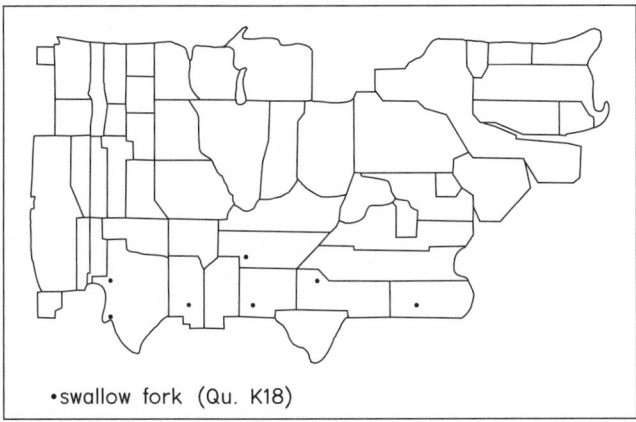

•swallow fork (Qu. K18)

swallow hawk n
=**sparrow hawk 1.**
   1968 *DARE* (Qu. Q4, . . *Kinds of hawks*) Inf MN12, Swallow hawk or bird hawk—will take birds, a smaller hawk. **1999** *DARE* File—Internet eTN, Katie Cottrell returns to the Children's Museum with her fascinating array of birds including the Great Horned Owl, a Kestrel (Swallow Hawk) and a Falcon!

swallow pipe, swallows   See **swallow** n² B

swallow tail n¹   See **swallow fork**

swallowtail n², **swallow-tailed falcon**   See **swallow-tailed kite**

swallow-tailed flycatcher n   Also *swallowtail flycatcher*
A **scissortail 1** (here: *Tyrannus forficatus*).
   [**1783** Latham *Genl. Synopsis Birds* 2.356, *Swallow-tailed fl[fy-catcher]. . .* Inhabits *Mexico.*] **1825** Bonaparte *Amer. Ornith.* 1.15, *Swallow-tailed flycatcher. Muscicapa forficata.* . . Although this bird is very different from the fork-tailed flycatcher . . on account of the form of the tail . . they are apt to be mistaken for each other. **1872** *Amer. Naturalist* 6.484 KS, Milvulus forficatus, Swallow-tail Flycatcher. **1900** U.S. Bur. Amer. Ethnology *Annual Rept. for 1897–98* 1.285 wNC,

It was undoubtedly the scissor-tail or swallow-tailed flycatcher *(Milvulus forficatus),* which belongs properly in Texas and the adjacent region, but strays occasionally into the eastern states. **1955** Forbush–May *Birds* 311, Swallow-tailed Flycatcher. . . In the air it is one of the most graceful and attractive of birds. **2004** *DARE* File—Internet, "Dang, did you know that the Swallow-Tailed Flycatcher is the state bird of Oklahoma?" asked a Dean supporter.

swallow-tailed kite n   Also *swallowtail (hawk or kite), swallow-tailed falcon (or hawk)*
A bird of prey *(Elanoides forficatus)* now native chiefly to the Gulf States.   Also called **fish hawk 2, fishtail ~, forktail ~, fork-tailed kite, scissor-tailed ~, snakebird 4, snake hawk 1, snake-killer 2**
   1731 Catesby *Nat. Hist. Carolina* 1.4, *The Swallow-Tail Hawk.* . . They are said to prey upon Lizards and other Serpents. **1781** Latham *Genl. Synopsis Birds* 1.1.61 NC, SC, *Swallow-tailed F[alcon]* inhabits *Carolina* in the summer months. **1838** Geol. Surv. OH *Second Annual Rept.* 178, *F[alco] furcatus* [=*Elanoides forficatus*]. A few years since the swallow-tailed hawk was to be seen, during the summer, in considerable numbers in Portage and Stark counties. **1853** U.S. Army Corps Topog. Engineers *Rept. Sitgreaves* 60, *Nauclerus furcatus* [=*Elanoides forficatus*]. . . The Swallow-tailed Kite. . . Common in Texas and in the Creek and Cherokee Nations. It appears to have a fondness for frequenting streams; along the Arkansas and its tributaries it was very abundant. **1870** *Harper's New Mth. Mag.* 41.665 FL, It was at Pilatka also we first saw that rare and most beautiful of birds, the swallow-tailed hawk. **1893** *Reno Eve. Gaz.* (NV) 16 Nov 2/4, Fifteen dollars were exchanged evenly for one egg of the swallow-tailed kite. **1917** (1923) *Birds Amer.* 2.60, No other American bird approaches the Swallow-tail in the grace and beauty of its flight. **1946** Kopman *Wild Acres* 187 LA, The swallow-tailed kite is still a characteristic figure in the . . wooded swamplands of southern Louisiana. **1966** *DARE* (Qu. Q4, . . *Kinds of hawks*) Inf FL4, Swallowtail kite. **2004** (acc) *AL Wildlife Federation* (Internet), As you glide beneath a noisy rookery of squabbling egrets and herons, a soaring swallowtail kite gives its klee klee klee cry.

swallowtail flycatcher   See **swallow-tailed flycatcher**

swallowtail hawk (or kite)   See **swallow-tailed kite**

swallowtail stump n
In logging: =**barber chair.**
   1956 Sorden–Ebert *Logger's Words* 36 Gt Lakes, Swallow-tail-stump, A stump with uneven surface because of poor notching. Generally cut by an inexperienced logger. **1958** McCulloch *Woods Words* 185 Pacific NW, Swallow tail stump—A badly cut stump with wood split off the butt log left sticking up in the air; same as barber chair.

swallowwort n
1 Std: =**celandine.** [*OED2* 1578 →]
2 A **milkweed 1** (here: *Asclepias* spp), usu *A. syriaca* or **butterfly weed 1.** [*OED2* 1548 → for *Cynanchum vincetoxicum* of the family Asclepiadaceae]
   1784 in 1785 Amer. Acad. Arts & Sci. *Memoirs* 1.424, *Asclepias. . . Swallowwort. . .* Blossoms white. About fences in moist land. July. **1828** Rafinesque *Med. Flora* 1.74, *Asclepias tuberosa. . . Orange Swallow-wort. Ibid* 76, All the Asclepias. . . produce a fine glossy and silky down. . . The *A[sclepias] syriaca* or Silky Swallow-wort producing more of the down, has been cultivated for the purpose. **1897** *Jrl. Amer. Folkl.* 10.50 West, *Asclepias tuberosa,* . . swallow wort. **1902** *Bedford Gaz.* (PA) 12 Dec 2/7, Honey bees and insects and bugs of less degree find pitfalls and often death in the beautiful blossoms of the milkweed otherwise known as the Virginia swallowwort [=*Asclepias syriaca*]. **1936** Whitehouse *TX Flowers* 101, *Butterfly-weed. . . Asclepias tuberosa. . .* Other common names include orange milkweed . . and orange swallow-wort. . . Several plants are known by the common name of "swallow-wort" and are so called because they bloom in the spring when the swallows appear. **1993** *Intelligencer* (Doylestown PA) 18 June sec C 8/4, Her customers. . . clamor for . . red swallowwort (Asclepias incarnata). **2003** IA Dept. Transportation *Iowa's Living Roadway Plant Profiler* 27, *Butterfly Milkweed . . common names . .* Tuberous Swallowwort.

swalluh   See **swallow** n², v

swamp n, v   Usu |swɑmp|; also freq |swɔmp|; for addit varr see quots   Pronc-spp *s(w)omp*
 A Forms.

1830 in 1956 Eliason *Tarheel Talk* 318 **ne,ceNC,** *Swamp*—somp. **1899** (1912) Green *VA Folk-Speech* 434, *Swomp.* . . A form of *swamp.* **1917** *DN* 4.401 **neOH,** *Swamp* [swɔmp], *n.* and *v.t.* General. **1936** *AmSp* 11.23 **eTX,** *Swamp.* . . the vowel is habitually rounded to [ɒ] or [ɔ]. **1941** *AmSp* 16.5 **eTX** [Black], *Swamp,* [swɔ̃mp]. **1961** Kurath–McDavid *Pronc. Engl.* 163, The regional incidence of /ɔ/ and /ɑ/ after /w/ varies from word to word. The following . . exhibits the predominant usage in selected subareas of the Eastern States along with the usage of substantial minorities. There seems to be no marked social cleavage anywhere. . . *swamp* . . Upstate N.Y.—ɔ ~ ɑ . . Metrop. N.Y.—ɑ . . Phila. area—ɑ . . W. Va.—ɔ ~ ɑ . . Eastern Va.—ɔ . . Eastern S.C.—ɔ. **1976** Allen *LAUM* 3.263 **Upper MW** (as of c1950), In neither the East nor the U[pper] M[idwest] has the rounding effect of the prevocalic /w/ universally yielded a rounded vowel in *swamp.* . . Low-central /ɑ/ seems to carry slightly more prestige . . a situation that holds true if the occurrences of the low-back unround /ɑ/ are also included. The geographical distribution, however, is less clearly defined. A Midland preference for an unround vowel, /ɑ ~ ɑ/, is indicated by its predominance in Iowa and its weakness in Minnesota. . . It is noticeably more frequent in the Midland southern two-thirds of Iowa than in the Northern third. . . A rounded vowel, /ɒ ~ ɔ/, conversely, is the choice of three-fourths of the Minnesota and South Dakota infs. and almost three-fourths of those in Nebraska. **1985** Benes *Amer. Speech* 75 **cME coast** (as of a1847), The vowel of contemporary *bought* occurs in . . *swamp.* **1989** Pederson *LAGS Tech. Index* 107 **Gulf Region,** *Swamp.* [Of 914 infs, 392 offered proncs of the type [swɒmp]; 376 infs, proncs of the type [swɑmp]; 6 infs, proncs of the type [swʌmp]; 4 infs, proncs of the type [swomp].]

B As noun.

1 esp in combs *logging swamp, lumber(ing) ~:* An area of forest where logging is being carried on. **chiefly ME** *old-fash* Cf **daylight in the swamp**

1844 *Bangor Daily Whig & Courier* (ME) 21 Nov 2/5, Five yoke of large working Oxen suitable to put into the lumbering swamp are now offered for sale on fair terms. **1848** Bartlett *Americanisms* 214, *Logging swamp.* In Maine, the place where pine timber is cut. **1857** Bradbury *Flower Forest* 8 **ME,** Bill . . yoked four handsome oxen as could be found in the forests of Maine that winter. He was one of the best teamsters in the swamps. *Ibid,* Henry was delighted with the idea of passing the winter in the 'logging swamps' as they are called. **1860** *Harper's New Mth. Mag.* 20.445 **ME,** There is a pleasure in the ceaseless tramp from the swamp to the landing, and the landing to the swamp, in the companionship of the patient oxen. **1870** Kellogg *Young Ship-Builders* 12 **ME,** I've a lot of axes to make for the logging swamp. **1874** (1875) Coffin *Caleb Krinkle* 35 **NH,** Her husband was a wood-chopper, and worked in the lumber swamp in winter. **1904** *Daily Northwestern* (Oshkosh WI) 27 Aug 7/1, In 1881 John left the lumber swamps and the peanut fields of Virginia and went to Washington, D.C. **1905** *Daily Kennebec Jrl.* (Augusta ME) 25 Oct 5/4, Moore & Burns started 14 horses and about 20 men for the logging swamps, Monday.

2 See **swamp cooler.**

C As verb.

1 also with *out;* In logging: see below. **chiefly Nth**

a To prepare (a tree) for **skidding 2** (as by limbing it); to **skid** v **2a** (a log); to drag or load timber; hence vbl n *swamping (out).* Cf **skid** v **2a**

1784 (1903) Patten *Diary* 480 **NH,** I swampt out 4 small oak logs the boys saved in cuting [sic] wood[.] Ready for hauling out. **1872** (1873) Ball *Lake Co. IN* 353, Getting this timber out in the winter is called "swamping." **1914** *DN* 4.153 **ME,** *Swamp, v.t.* To trim off the superfluous limbs of trees, plants, vines, etc. **1922** *WI Rapids Daily Tribune* (WI) 2 Dec 1/1, Young Koplien was engaged in swamping out logs alone on a wild forty near Auburndale. **1935** *Ironwood Daily–Globe* (MI) 22 Aug 3/5, The pay offered is . . 8 cents per stick for cutting and swamping tie cuts—12 cents delivered to the track. **1967** *DARE* (Qu. OO46a, *Talking about dragging something heavy: "We hitched the log on and _____ it out [of the woods]."*) Inf **NY32,** Swamp it out. **1986** Pederson *LAGS Concordance,* 1 inf, **neLA,** *Swamping*—loading logs on a wagon to haul.

b To clear (an area, esp a path or roadway) of trees, brush, or other obstructions; to remove (brush, etc); to clear the brush from a place; hence vbl n *swamping (out).* Cf **swamper 2**

1851 (1856) Springer *Forest Life* 84 **ME,** An experienced hand . . "spots" the trees where he wishes the road to be "swamped." **1888** *Morning Oregonian* (Portland OR) 1 Dec 2/2, Several miles of the right of way are already swamped and the work has commenced in earnest. **1899** *Century Illustr. Mag.* 57.636 **nWI,** And we'll swamp out the

underbrush / And estimate the stumpage. **1899** *Overland Mth.* (2d ser) 34.253 **Pacific NW,** The feeders, or snake-roads, were simply "swamped out,"—that is, cleared of brush and smoothed down slightly,—and along these the logs were dragged upon the bare ground. **1909** *DN* 3.417 **nME,** *Swamp.* . . To swamp roads is to cut sled roads in the forest for the use of lumbermen. **1920** *DN* 5.84 **Pacific NW,** *Swamp out, to.* To cut brush away. Logging term. **1929** *Indiana Eve. Gaz.* (PA) [15 June] 2/3 (newspaperarchive.com), Another big improvement is the swamping out of the section just to the left of the bridge across the run. This will probably be used as a parking place. **1939** *LANE* Map 122, The expressions *swamped, ~ out, bushed out, brushed* [1 inf] . ., and *slashed out* [1 inf] . ., [were] recorded in the context *We swamped out a road through the woods.* . . They were inquired for systematically only in N.H. and Maine. . . [T]hese terms refer to the cutting of a road or path through the underbrush in the woods, usually in the winter, for the purpose of hauling logs or carrying supplies to a lumber camp or farm. . . *[S]wamp out* . . is once defined [by an inf in **seVT**] as meaning to remove the underbrush from a piece of land. **1942** ME Univ. *Studies* 57.28, Usually the cord cutters swamp their own yards and twitch roads. *Ibid* 134, *Swamp.* To cut trees or brush in a *yard* or a road right-of-way. Also to cut brush around a tree preparatory to felling. **1959** *AmSp* 34.80 **nwCA** [Logger lingo], *Swamp, v.t.* To clear the ground of underbrush, fallen trees, and other obstructions preparatory to constructing a logging road, landing, skid trail, or before falling and bucking. **1961** Seeman *In Arms of Mt.* 38 **eTN,** This very morning we have had two boys swamp out the saplings growing between the bend of the creek and the trail, for our prospective vegetable patch. **1967** *DARE* FW Addit **LA4,** *Swamping*—cutting out a road for teams to haul logs out on. **1968** *DARE* (Qu. L35, *Hand tools used for cutting underbrush and digging out roots*) Inf **CA105,** Swamping ax. **1984** Wilder *You All Spoken Here* 134 **Sth,** *Swamp:* Clear of underbrush, as in "We swamped that ditch in no time a-tall." **2001** in 2005 *DARE* File—Internet **MT,** The sawyer was swamping out around the base of the tree, which was to be fell [sic] in light brush when he rested a moving chain on his left knee. **2005** *Ibid* **sAppalachians,** *Swamp Out the Base*—Clear small trees, brush, and debris from the base of the tree. Remove all material that could cause you to trip or lose your balance. . . Be careful not to fatigue yourself with unnecessary swamping.

2 with *out:* To clean (a place) up; to tidy up; hence vbl n *swamping out.* **chiefly Nth** Cf **swamper 4**

1907 *DN* 3.250 **eME,** *Swamp out.* . . To clear up. Used of a room, yard, garden, etc., that is badly cluttered up. "You'll have to swamp it out." **1928** *Helena Independent* (MT) 17 Jan 6/4, The trousers wet to the knees . . were found to have been in that condition as a result of swamping out a restaurant that day. **1955** *NV State Jrl.* (Reno) 28 Dec 14/2, Reno's weather bureau finished swamping out yesterday. . . The all-important bureau . . got thoroughly flooded along with the rest of the airport last weekend. **1956** Sorden-Ebert *Logger's Words* 36 **Gt Lakes,** *Swamp-out,* Clean up or sweep out a building. **1958** McCulloch *Woods Words* 185 **Pacific NW,** *Swamp out*—To clean out a place, as in sweeping up a bunkhouse. **1963** *Western Folkl.* 22.265 **CA,** *Swamp out* means to clean out a place, such as to "swamp out a room." **1967** *DARE* (Qu. E21, . . *About a room that needs to be put in order* . . *"I'm just going to _____ this room."*) Inf **NY23,** Swamp it out. **1975** Gould *ME Lingo* 283, *Swamp.* . . Transferred [from logging], this term means to clean house: "She heard company was coming, so she swamped out the living room." **1998** in 2005 *DARE* File—Internet **TX,** She did enjoy the new pitchfork when she was swamping out the goat barn though.

swamp adder n
=cottonmouth.

1970 *DARE* (Qu. P25, . . *Kinds of snakes*) Inf **VA70,** Swamp adder. **2004** *DARE* File—Internet, The Cottonmouth probably has more common names than any other North American snake. In the various parts of its range it is referred to as "swamp adder", "gapper", "trapjaw", "chunkhead", "water moccasin", "lowland moccasin", and others. *Ibid* **Sth,** Wrapped around his right leg was coiled the biggest Swamp Adder Travis had ever seen.

swamp alder n **chiefly NEast**
=hazel alder.

1868 (1869) Greeley *Recollections* 297 **NY,** Swamp Alder infested the springy, rocky, boggy ground at the foot of one of my hills. **1871** Lyceum Nat. Hist. NYC *Proc.* 1st ser 201, *Alnus serrulata,* swamp alder. . . Locality Central Duchess Co. **1888** *Jrl. Amer. Folkl.* 1.156, By boiling the bark of the swamp alder in water, the Mud Lake Indians obtained a good red dye. **1912** *Indianapolis Star* (IN) 12/1, Mr. Selder has about forty acres of bottom land covered with a dense growth of swamp alder and underbrush. **1930** Sievers *Amer. Med. Plants* 33, *Alnus rugosa* [= *A. incana* subsp *r.*] . . *Common names.*—Tag alder, common alder, . . swamp-alder. . . Found in swamps and along the marshy banks of streams from New England south. **1950** *Berkshire Eagle* (Pittsfield MA) 25 Apr 13/3, Not only may the sap of such plebian trees like the poplar and the swamp alder be brought into competition but all any little old competitor . . has to do is to dissolve some cane sugar or even beet sugar in water and boil it down. **1967–69** *DARE* (Qu. T15, . . *Kinds of swamp trees*) Infs **PA**29, 104, 223, Swamp alder(s). **2004** *DARE* File—Internet, There were several [turkey] hens roosting in a swamp alder about thirty yards behind the hunter.

swamp angel n

1 =hermit thrush 1. **NEast**

1865 *Atlantic Mth.* May 522, The Hermit-Thrush. . . is quite a rare bird, . . being found in the Middle and Eastern States, . . only in the deepest and most remote forests, usually in damp and swampy localities. On this account the people in the Adirondack region call it the "Swamp Angel." **1912** *Washington Post* (DC) 5 May 12/6, The hermit thrush is called by some of the far Northern people the swamp angel and it was a tribute to the bird under that name that Whitman wrote. **1958** *Progress* (Clearfield PA) 26 Aug 4/2, The hermit is sometimes called the Swamp Angel, for while it enjoys higher woodlands, it also likes swales and swamps. **1997** *Portland Press Herald* (ME) 19 Oct sec E 7 (Internet), Anyone who has heard a hermit thrush will know why Whitman eulogized the singer in "When Lilacs Last in the Dooryard Bloomed". . . The bird is known as the Swamp Angel, but it could as well be the god Pan playing on his pipes.

2 =wood thrush 1.

1883 Nuttall *Ornith. Club Bulletin* 8.72, *Turdus mustelinus* [= *Hylocichla m.*]. Its common names are: *Wood Thrush,* . . *Swamp Angel* (Adirondacks) [etc]. **1929** Forbush *Birds MA* 3.387, *Hylocichla mustelina.* . . *Other names:* swamp angel; wood robin. [*Ibid* 403, Thoreau seems never to have had a clear conception of the vocal differences between the Wood and the Hermit Thrushes, and confused the two.] **1946** Hausman *Eastern Birds* 458, *Hylocichla mustelina.* . . Song Thrush, Wood Robin, Swamp Angel. *Ibid* 459, *Hylocichla guttata faxoni* [= *Catharus g.*] . . American Nightingale, Swamp Angel, Swamp Robin, Solitary Thrush.

3 A **mosquito** n[1] **B1** such as *Aedes sollicitans;* see quots. **esp Sth, S Midl**

1964 Reynolds *Born of Mts.* 9 **wNC**, Mosquitoes, called Swamp Angels or Gallinipers by the natives, cannot breed in running water of mountain streams, so there are few of them. **1992** *St. Louis Post–Dispatch* (MO) 9 Feb (Internet) **FL**, Early arrivals designated the enclave Comfort. Plagued with heat, rain and mosquitoes, called "swamp angels," the island soon renounced that misnomer and took the name Chokoloskee ("old house"). **1993** *St. Petersburg Times* (FL) 24 Oct sec F 1 (Internet) **Everglades FL**, Loren G. "Totch" Brown, Everglades folk hero. . . abandons me at the dock, all alone with the ravenous salt marsh mosquitoes he calls "skeeters" or "swamp angels." **1997** in 2004 Montgomery-Hall *Dict. Smoky Mt. Engl.* 584 **eTN**, Swamp angel. **2002** *St. Petersburg Times* (FL) 18 Aug sec F 1 (Internet) **Everglades FL**, Other people call them mosquitoes, but old-timers have always referred to them as swamp angels.

4 =swamper 1.

[**1855** Ward *Female among Mormons* 10 **NY**, "The Swamp Angel? . . who was that?" "A child died . . and the Mormons gave out that, on a certain night, an angel would come and carry the body to heaven. The time appointed arrived . . , when a figure in white . . appeared. A party of the unbelievers . . immediately gave chase. The figure ran for a neighboring swamp, but was pursued, taken, stripped of its angel robes, and proved to be Pulsifer, the uncle of the deceased."] [**1857** *Hornellsville Tribune* (NY) 20 Aug 1/4, Graceful as a duck, wild as a hawk, pensive as a setting hen, . . like some bright swamp angel she sat.] **1859** White *Hist. Coventry VT* 30 (as of 1813), He was familiarly called "the swamp angel," and if the domains of actual or imaginary zoology contain any such being as that, he was probably not unworthy of the *sobriquet*. He was nearly seven feet in height, broad-shouldered, long-limbed, gaunt, skinny, and crooked; with dark complexion, wide mouth, large teeth, and other features to match. **1860** *Portsmouth Times* (OH) 10 Mar [3]/2 (newspaperarchive.com), *Margaret Jones* a "swamp angel" of some notoriety in the City, of Portsmouth, and vicinity, together with the other defendants . . took possession of a dwelling house . . and broke things up generally. **1860** *Janesville Daily Gaz.* (WI) 29 Oct 1/4 **NY**, The Swamp Angels, as they were called, would come up in troops from the lowlands

along the canal, and Mentz would roll up a tremendous majority against what was called abolitionism and treason. **1903** *DN* 2.332 **seMO**, *Swamp-angel.* . . A young woman from the swamps or backwoods. 'All the young bucks and their swamp-angels came to the circus.' **1906** *DN* 3.160 **nwAR**, *Swamp angel.* . . A countryman from the swampy district. **1931** *AmSp* 7.48 **Sth, SW** [Lumberjack lingo], A true "rosinbelly" detests the "swamp angels" and the cotton pickers who come to his camp after "picking time" with their malaria-stricken families. **1945** Thorp *Pardner* 34 **SW**, A swamp angel was a fellow raised down in the swampy lands, maybe Louisiana or Arkansas. They all had chills and fever, 90 per cent of them chewed snuff sticks, and they generally looked like walking matches. **1968–70** *DARE* (Qu. HH1, *Names and nicknames for a rustic or countrified person*) Infs **MI**76, 78, Swamp angel; **MA**89, Swamp angel—backwoodsy Florida. **1971** Wood *Vocab. Change* 266 **AL, AR, GA, TN**, A rustic. . . *swamp angel.* [Offered by 5 of 1000 infs] **1986** Pederson *LAGS Concordance* (*A rustic*) 1 inf, **csAR**, Swamp angels. **1997** *Midwest Fly Fishing Online* Summer (Internet), A Swamp Angel cuts trees in the U.P. and works long hours. Swamp Angels are tough and can be sudden in their decision-making process.

5 =rutter n[1].

1956 Sorden–Ebert *Logger's Words* 36 **Gt Lakes**, *Swamp-angel,* See rutter. [*Ibid* 28, *Rutter,* A form of plow for cutting ruts in a logging road for the runner of the sleigh to run in, often combined with a snow plow.]

6 See quots.

1950 *WELS* (*A small light that seems to dance over a swamp or marsh by night*) 1 Inf, **ceWI**, Swamp angel. **1969** *DARE* (Qu. CC16) Inf **IL**43, Swamp angel.

7 See quots. Cf **swamp ape**

1967 *DARE* (Qu. CC17, *Imaginary animals or monsters that people . . tell tales about—especially to tease greenhorns*) Inf **NY**23, Swamp angel. **2002** in 2005 *DARE* File—Internet **wKY**, I heard from my mother about shimmering, pale Swamp Angles [*sic*] there who with their very long fingernails hovered above the moldering ground, ready to tear out the eyes of anyone who entered at night.

swamp anise n

=**Florida anise-tree.**

1960 Vines *Trees SW* 278, *Illicium floridanum.* . . Other vernacular names are Polecat-tree, . . Sweet-laurel, Swamp-anise.

swamp ape n **chiefly Gulf States, esp FL** Cf **Bigfoot, Sasquatch, skunk ape, swamp angel 7, ~ gaboon,** DS CC17

A large, hairy, man-like creature reported as living esp in Southern swamps.

1950 *WELS* (*Imaginary wild animals that people tell stories about*) 1 Inf, **ceWI**, Swamp ape—used to hear lumberjacks talking about—old-fashioned. **1999** *Boston Globe* (MA) 10 Jan sec D 2 (Internet) **sFL**, Who knew. . . that the legendary South Florida swamp ape has the physique of a human, the smell of a skunk, and a particular fondness for lima beans? **2000** in 2007 *DARE* File—Internet **FL**, South Florida has for some time been touting it's [*sic*] own version of the famous "Bigfoot" critter that so captures the imagination of the incautious. They call their variety of the species "the Florida Swamp-Ape." **2001** *DARE* File—Internet, The Georgia Swamp Ape Research Center . . was established to collect and study evidence of the cryptozoological creature known as "Sasquatch." **2002** *Star–Telegram* (Ft. Worth TX) 30 Oct (Internet), In the dead of night, they wait for the giant swamp ape they believe lurks along the creek bottoms of Texas, Arkansas and beyond. **2004** *DARE* File—Internet **MS**, *Green Country Hominid Research* regional name checklist. . . Mississippi Swamp Ape.

swamp apple n

1 A gall caused by a fungus (*Exobasidium vaccinii*) on **pinkster 2** (usu *Rhododendron periclymenoides*) or another ericaceous plant. **chiefly NEast** Also called **mayapple 3, pinkster apple, swamp cheese 1,** *swamp pink apple* (at **swamp pink 1**) Cf **huckleberry apple, oak ~ 1**

1846 *Zoologist* 4.1281 **MA**, The galls called swamp-apples . . grow on the small twigs of the swamp-pink, or *Azalea viscosa* [=*Rhododendron v.*] **1859** (1880) Darlington *Amer. Weeds* 214, The *Azalea nudiflo'ra* [= *Rhododendron periclymenoides*], L., or wild Honeysuckle, has often a singular transformation of its flowers, the parts of the flower becoming enlarged and fleshy. . . These succulent excrescences [*sic*] are much sought after by boys who call them "swamp apples" and "swamp cheeses." **1868** *Amer. Naturalist* 2.448 **CT**, The sample of the so-called Swamp-apple, found on the wild Azalia [*sic*] was mislaid in some way.

1890 *AN&Q* 6.56 **MA** (as of c1840), When I was a boy, fifty years ago, we used to gather and eat a kind of fleshy green excrescence from the branches of the *Azalea nudiflora.* We called the excrescences "swamp apples." **1944** Holton *Yankees Were Like This* 145 **Cape Cod MA** (as of c1890), From the wooded end of the swamp we brought in something we called swamp apples. They weren't apples at all, but small, bright-green, semitranslucent globes. **1964** Reynolds *Born of Mts.* 18 **wNC,** On [the azalea's] branches are found abnormal fleshy growths some call swamp apples. **1966–69** *DARE* (Qu. I46, . . *Kinds of fruits that grow wild around here*) Infs **MA**40, 55, Swamp apples; (Qu. S4, . . *May-apple: [Woodside plant, not a tree, with two large spreading leaves; they grow in patches and have a small yellow fruit late in summer]*) Infs **CT**26, **MA**40, **NY**205, **RI**15, 17, Swamp apple. [*DARE* Ed: Some of these Infs may refer instead to **2** below.] **1999** in 2004 Montgomery-Hall *Dict. Smoky Mt. Engl.* 584 **eTN,** *Swamp apple.* . . . it is white, quenches the thirst, tastes somewhat like an apple, and is produced by a chemical reaction to the sting of an insect, also called *azalea gall.*

2 Transf: =**pinkster 2,** usu *Rhododendron periclymenoides.* **NEast** Also called **June apple 2, mayapple 3, swamp cheese 2** Cf **rhododendron**

1805 (1911) Bentley *Diary* 3.166 **MA,** The young ladies furnished themselves with the Kalmia, swamp apples. **1845** Simms *Hist. Schoharie Co.* 163 **ceNY,** The blacks are seen with smiling faces on that day [=Whitsunday], . . going to visit their friends—often bearing flowers called by them Pinkster-bloomies; which are known in New England as blossoms of the swamp-apple. **1871** *Essex Inst. Proc.* 6.38 **MA,** Mr. Perkins . . exhibited several plants which he had there, . . among which were the Azalea or Swamp apple. **1875** *Daily Gaz. & Bulletin* (Williamsport PA) 2 July 1/4 **NY,** He went deeper and deeper into the heart of the forest, picking wild strawberries and the fruit of the swamp apple tree as he went. **1881** *Harper's New Mth. Mag.* 62.526 **ceNY,** Both he and his followers were covered with Pinkster *blummies*—the wild azalea, or swamp-apple. **1892** *Jrl. Amer. Folkl.* 5.100 **eMA,** *Rhododendron nudiflorum* [=*R. periclymenoides*]. . . Swamp apple. **1916** *Daily Northwestern* (Oshkosh WI) 31 May 5/2 **NEng,** We want some [=lilacs] to mix with the pink swamp apple and dogwood branches. **1968–69** *DARE* (Qu. S26b, *Wildflowers that grow in water or wet places*) Inf **CT**26, Swamp apple—four-foot bush, little green fruit, doesn't show much, blossom is pink; **NY**75, Swamp apple or mayflower—not same as mandrake or mayapple; (Qu. S26c, *Wildflowers that grow in woods*) Inf **NY**213, Swamp apple [same as] azalea—a bush; (Qu. T15, . . *Kinds of swamp trees*) Inf **RI**1, Swamp apple; (Qu. S4, . . *Mayapple: [Woodside plant, not a tree, with two large spreading leaves; they grow in patches and have a small yellow fruit late in summer]*) Inf **VT**10, A swamp apple or swamp pink is small and has little apples [*DARE* Ed: cf **mayapple 4**]. **1998** *DARE* File—Internet **cNY,** *Swamp Apple.* . . A fairly common native azalea.

3 =**pond apple. FL**

1966 *DARE* (Qu. S4) Inf **FL**4, Swamp apple—brown fruit; (Qu. T15, . . *Kinds of swamp trees*) Inf **FL**4, Swamp apple. **1989** *Providence Jrl.* (RI) 12 Nov sec H 1 (Internet) **Everglades FL,** We zoomed past yellow swamp apples with huge leaves like waterlilies, through palmettos and saw grass and rushes. **2004** *DARE* File—Internet **FL,** [Caption:] A large clump of plants growing on a Swamp Apple Tree.

swamp ash n

1 Any of three ashes: **green ash,** native to most of the US east of the Rocky Mountains; **black ash 1,** native chiefly to the Northeast and Great Lakes area; or **Carolina ash,** native to the lowland South. Note: It is not always possible to determine which sense is intended in the quots.

1794 in 1914 *Missip. Valley Hist. Rev.* 1.437 **VA,** The face [of the land] is nearly covered with a thick groth [sic] of Shrubbery, Brush, some Beech, Swamp Ash. **1821** Schoolcraft *Jrl.* 76 **AR,** The other forest-trees and plants . . composing the forests of White River [include] . . swamp-ash, (*fraxinus juglandifolia* [=*F. pennsylvanica*];) white oak. **1842** Thompson *Hist. VT* 1.211, *Black ash. Fraxinus sambucifolia* [=*F. nigra*]. . . is commonly found growing . . in and about swamps; and hence it is sometimes called *Swamp Ash.* **1874** *Scribner's Mth.* 9.21 **FL,** Just above Palatka, . . where the magnolia and the water-oak alternate charmingly with the cypress, the swamp ash and the palm, there are also many successful orange groves. **1888** Riley *Pipes o' Pan* 37 **IN,** Clean out o' sight o' home, and skulkin' under kivver / Of the sycamores, jack-oaks, and swamp-ash and ellum. **1897** Sudworth *Arborescent Flora* 325, *Fraxinus nigra.* . . Swamp Ash (Vt., R.I., N.Y.) *Ibid* 330, *Fraxinus lanceolata* [=*F. pennsylvanica*]. . . Swamp Ash (Fla., Ala., Tex.) **1906** *Commerce Jrl.* (TX) 11 May 9/1 **LA,** This swampy

land is covered with stagnant water and dense foliage of swamp ash and cypress growth. **1908** Rogers *Tree Book* 440, The Water, or Swamp Ash (*F[raxinus] caroliniana* . .) grows to 40 feet high in swampy lands skirting the coast from Virginia to middle Florida, and west to the Sabine River in Texas. **1965** Needham–Mussey *Country Things* 85 **sVT,** Black ash or swamp ash was what he used to make baskets. **1967–69** *DARE* (Qu. T15, . . *Kinds of swamp trees*) Infs **IN**26, 31, **IA**8, **KY**6, 53, **NY**148, **WI**12, Swamp ash; **NY**68, The guilders used to make baskets and splints to make chair bottoms—that was swamp ash; (Qu. T16, . . *Kinds of trees* . . *'special'*) Inf **MD**20, Swamp ash—rough bark, grow near swamp, white wood. **1982** *Amer. Jrl. Botany* 69.1316, The most prominent plant species are bald cypress, . . swamp ash (*Fraxinus caroliniana* Miller), and laurel oak.

2 A **forestiera** (here: *Forestiera acuminata*).

1973 Stephens *Woody Plants* 450, *Forestiera acuminata.* . . Swamp privet, swamp ash. . . Swampy ground, stream banks, wet woods, rich or rocky soils in shaded, moist areas.

swamp auger n

1 A nonexistent item used as the basis of a practical joke. Cf *DS* HH14

1969 Sorden *Lumberjack Lingo* 124 **NEng, Gt Lakes,** *Swamp auger*—A mythical tool. It was a common joke among the woodsmen to send a new hand back to the office to get a swamp auger. . . When the foreman wanted to fire a man, he told him to go into town and get a swamp auger. **1984** [see **2** below].

2 An imaginary creature; see quots. **esp WI** Cf *DS* CC17

1922 *News* (Frederick MD) 9 Aug 4/4 **nWI,** *Yarns Of The Big Woods* . . The Swamp Auger. . . To the tenderfoot the tracks are bewildering. . . . "What is that?" asks the tenderfoot. . . "Hmmm," drawls the guide . . "looks like a swamp-auger has passed this way. . . he's a great big bird, kind of built on the order of a duck. And he has a bill that's like a corkscrew. It's mighty handy, too, because he uses it to get his food with. He just bores right down into the swamp for worms, you see." **1939** Tryon *Fearsome Critters* 51, The Swamp Auger . . , often mistaken for an old snag, is found in freshwater lakes. He carries a swivelled proboscis especially adapted to boring three-inch holes in the bottoms of boats. . . But his work can be easily halted by tickling his snout or by sprinkling it with cayenne pepper. Either . . will make the Auger sneeze violently, which he hugely enjoys, and he will then hold his expectant nose tight in the hole until the boat can be beached. **1939** (1962) Thompson *Body & Britches* 299 **NY,** Those numerous creatures of fantasy described by guides, such as . . the Swamp Auger. **1950** *WELS* (*Imaginary wild animals that people tell stories about*) 4 Infs, **WI,** Swamp auger. **1952** *Badger Folkl.* 1.17 **WI** [Logging language], *Swamp auger*—Mythical creature of lumberjack folklore. **1984** *MJLF* 10.158 **cnWI,** *Swamp auger.* A mythical, mole-like creature. In the old days, a mythical tool that greenhorns were sent in search of.

swamp azalea n **esp NEast**

A **rhododendron:** usu *Rhododendron viscosum,* but occas another **rhododendron** such as *R. canescens* or *R. periclymenoides.* For other names of *R. viscosum* see **hammocksweet, honeysuckle 3, June pink, meadow ~ 1, swamp honeysuckle 1, ~ pink 1, wild honeysuckle 1**

1785 Marshall *Arbustrum* 16, *Azalea viscosa palustris* [=*Rhododendron v.*]. *Swamp Azalea.* This is a variety of the white kind, growing naturally in wet low ground. **1874** *Amer. Naturalist* 8.517, As is well known to all botanists, our sweet swamp azalea (*Azalea viscosa*) has its corolla covered on the outside with innumerable clammy and glandular hairs. **1890** *Harper's New Mth. Mag.* 81.625 **MA,** The swamp-azalea shed a slight fragrance from its remnant blossoms, and offered its juicy apples that to me are never offered in vain. **1913** *Torreya* 13.254 **NY,** On the barrens [of Staten Island] several new finds were recorded: . . the white swamp azalea, *Azalea viscosa.* **1934** *Wellsboro Gaz.* (PA) 12 July 3/5, Two other shrubs belonging to the rhododendron family are native of [sic] Pennsylvania, the white swamp azalea whose extremely fragrant white and pink flowers appear from June to August, and the purple azalea. **1970** *DARE* (Qu. S26b, *Wildflowers that grow in water or wet places*) Inf **MA**100, Swamp pink, swamp honeysuckle = swamp azalea. **2004** *Patriot–News* (Harrisburg PA) 17 June sec E 1 (Internet), Audubon Pennsylvania's recommended native plants . . Swamp azalea (Rhododendron viscosum).

swamp bass n

1 A **black bass 1:** a **largemouth bass, smallmouth bass,** or **spotted bass 1.**

1935 Caine *Game Fish* 3 **Sth,** *Large-mouthed Black Bass.* . . Syn-

onyms . . Swamp Bass. *Ibid* 7, *Small-mouthed Black Bass.* . . Swamp Bass. *Ibid* 10, *Spotted Small-mouthed Black Bass.* . . Swamp Bass. **1963** *Oshkosh Daily Northwestern* (WI) 1 Mar 22/6, The prize should go to the South Carolina fisherman out for big swamp bass. **2004** *DARE* File—Internet **MI**, [Caption to photo of largemouth bass:] This is a solid Saginaw Bay backwater swamp bass I caught a few years back in practice. *Ibid* **IA**, I have caught thousands of bass in the weeds, and consider myself an expert in swamp bass.

2 =**bowfin.**

   2002 in 2005 *DARE* File—Internet, Following is a short list of some common names given to some of the different fishes of Texas. . . Bowfin: dogfish, . . swamp bass, cypress trout. **2005** (acc) FL Fish & Wildlife Conserv. Comm. *Other FL Freshwater Fish* (Internet), *Bowfin.* . . Common Names—mudfish, mud pike, dogfish, grindle, blackfish, cottonfish, swamp bass, cypress trout. . . Found throughout Florida. . . Prefers swamps, sloughs and pools, backwaters of lowland streams.

swamp bay n

1 An evergreen tree *(Persea palustris)* native from southern Delaware south to southern Florida and west to southern Texas. Also called **swamp red bay, sweet bay 3, sweetberry tree**

   1843 (1844) Johnson *Farmer's Encycl.* 733, It [=*Gordonia lasianthus*] is very abundant in the branch swamps, and exists in greater proportion than the red bay, swamp bay, and black gum, with which it is usually associated. **1850** Bryant *Letters* 78 **NC**, Tracts of sandy soil . . were interspersed with marshes . . and verdant at their borders with a growth of evergreens, such as the swamp-bay [etc.]. [*DARE* Ed: This quot may refer instead to **2** below.] **1888** *Century Illustr. Mag.* 36.768 **Sth**, We read in the current newspapers . . that "a brilliant yellow" may be obtained by pouring boiling water upon other component parts of "sassafras, swamp bay, and butterfly root." **1897** Sudworth *Arborescent Flora* 201, *Persea pubescens* [=*P. palustris*]. . . Swamp Bay. **1933** Small *Manual SE Flora* 922, *T[amala] pubescens* [=*Persea palustris*]. . . Swamp-bay. . . Swamps and low hammocks, Coastal Plain and rarely adj. provinces. **1947** *Amer. Midland Naturalist* 37.721, *P[ersea] palustris.* . . Swamp-bay. . . The local contrast in appearance of the smooth, mainly scrubby Redbay of our shore woods with the hairy, generally well-developed Swampbay farther inland makes it seem convenient to retain a name for each. **1995** *Sun–Sentinel* (Ft. Lauderdale FL) 15 Oct sec A 1 (Internet) **Everglades FL**, At risk are red bays, swamp bays, strangler figs, Florida maple trees. **2000** *Tampa Tribune* (FL) 28 Sept 2 (Internet), Cypress Creek . . is filled with maples, water hickories, tupelo and swamp bay trees.

2 =**sweet bay 2.**

   1869 Porcher *Resources* 385 **Sth**, Sweet Swamp Bay, or Laurel, (*Magnolia glauca* [=*M. virginiana*].) **1908** Rogers *Tree Book* 250, Swamp bay flowers are globular and small for a magnolia—only two to three inches across—but delightfully fragrant. **1933** Small *Manual SE Flora* 535, *M[agnolia] virginiana.* . . Swamp-bay. . . Swamps and low woods, Coastal Plain and rarely adj. provinces. **1972** Brown *Wildflowers LA* 57, *Swamp Bay. Magnolia virginiana.* . . Common along branch bottoms and in poorly drained sites in the pinelands. **2004** *DARE* File—Internet, The dominant plants [in the Texas Big Thicket] are red bay (*Persea borbonia*) and sweet bay or swamp bay (*Magnolia virginiana*) among the hardwood trees.

swamp beech n esp OH

=**hornbeam 1.**

   1883 in 2003 McConkie *Remembering Joseph* 187 **OH**, They went to a place where there was some beautiful grass and grapevines and swamp beech interlaced. **1897** *Jrl. Amer. Folkl.* 10.144 **OH**, *Carpinus Caroliniana,* . . swamp beech, hornbeam, Sulphur Grove. **1908** *Marion Weekly Star* (OH) 14 Mar 3/6, Beginning at a point in the center of the Williams road where the north line of said survey crosses said road: thence north . . to a hickory and swamp beech.

swamp beet n

A **saxifrage** n[2] (here: *Saxifraga pensylvanica*).

   1898 *Jrl. Amer. Folkl.* 11.226 **ME**, *Saxifraga Pennsylvanica,* . . wild beet, swamp beet.

swamp birch n

1 A **yellow birch** (here: *Betula alleghaniensis*).

   1897 Sudworth *Arborescent Flora* 142 **MN**, *Betula lutea* [=*B. alleghaniensis*]. . . Swamp Birch. **1926** *Gettysburg Times* (PA) 1 May 4/5, The nimble little squirrel . . jumped into a swamp birch to rest a little. **1940** Clute *Amer. Plant Names* 161, *Yellow Birch.* Gray birch, swamp

birch, silver birch. **1969** *DARE* (Qu. T15, . . *Kinds of swamp trees*) Infs **NY**186, 219, Swamp birch. **2003** in 2005 *DARE* File—Internet **MI**, The *Yellow Birch,* also called *Silver Birch* and *Swamp Birch,* is one of the most important timber trees in eastern North America.

2 A low, shrubby birch *(Betula pumila)* native to wetlands in much of the northern half of the US. Also called **dwarf birch, marsh ~, scrub ~, tag alder 2**

   1910 Graves *Flowering Plants* 148 **CT**, *Betula pumila.* . . Low or Swamp Birch. Swamps and wet grounds. Local and apparently confined to the northwestern part of the state. **1941** *Sheboygan Press* (WI) 23 July 14/7, Vegetation along the ditch banks was dense. . . Willow, red-osier dogwood, . . swamp birch, and nightshade was especially abundant. **1975** *Lima News* (OH) 29 Apr sec A 5/2, Equally rare plants, such as the swamp birch, pink lady's-slipper orchid and sundew, grow here [=Cedar Bog State Memorial] as well. **1997** New Engl. Wildfl. Soc. *Wild Flower Notes* 24 **NEng**, *Betula pumila* (swamp birch)—This small shrub is common in limestone swamps in New England. **2005** *DARE* File—Internet **NY**, *Betula pumila* L.—Swamp Birch (rare).

3 =**western birch.**

   1938 Van Dersal *Native Woody Plants* 325, Birch, Swamp (*Betula fontinalis* [=*B. occidentalis*], *Betula pumila*). **1995** Alden *Hardwoods N. Amer.* 21, *Betula alleghaniensis* . . silver birch, swamp birch, . . yellow birch. . . *Betula nana*—swamp birch. . . *Betula occidentalis* . . spring birch, swamp birch.

4 A **dwarf birch** (here: *Betula nana*).

   1995 [see **3** above].

swamp blackberry n Also *running swamp blackberry*

A blackberry (here: *Rubus hispidus*).

   1843 Torrey *Flora NY* 1.217, *Rubus hispidus . . Running Swamp Blackberry.* . . Swamps and wet woods; sometimes in rather dry, but shady situations. **1860** Curtis *Cat. Plants NC* 88, *Swamp Blackberry.* (R[ubus] hispidus . .). A prostrate species . . found in the mountain swamps. . . Fruit black, small and sour. **1903** (1910) Keeler *Our Northern Shrubs* 161, Few trailing plants combine a better effect of flower and foliage than our Swamp Blackberry. **1909** Lincoln *Keziah* 72 **Cape Cod MA**, Opposite its door . . grew a spreading hornbeam tree surrounded by a cluster of swamp blackberry bushes. **1975** *Foxfire 3* 285 **sAppalachians**, Swamp blackberry is found in thickets in low, wet places. **1989** *Amer. Midland Naturalist* 121.306, The most common food in the animal's [=a deer's] stomach was swamp blackberry (*Rubus hispidus* L.) **2004** *Atlanta Jrl.–Constitution* (GA) 4 July (Internet), In addition to the common blackberry . . that grows all over Georgia, the state has several other native blackberry species. . . They include the swamp blackberry and the mountain blackberry.

swamp blackbird n

=**red-winged blackbird.**

   1799 *Amer. Philos. Soc. Trans.* 4.108 **PA**, Red-winged-maize-thief. [Footnote:] Commonly called, in Pennsylvania, the Swamp-Black-bird. **1844** DeKay *Zool. NY* 2.141, The *Red-winged Blackbird* is equally well known in every part of the State under the names of *Swamp Blackbird* and *Corn-thief.* **1855** Thomson *Doesticks* 132 **NY**, The people all . . threw bouquets at her [=a singer] when she made a noise like a swamp-blackbird. **1895** *Outing* 27.75 **NC, VA**, A huge flock of swamp blackbirds covered the ground. **1928** *Warren Morning Mirror* (PA) 16 Apr 9/6, The swamp blackbird is already piping his melodious noises in many a greening meadow. **1955** *Oriole* 20.1.12 **GA**, Red-winged blackbird. . . *Swamp Blackbird* (general; "swamp," a misnomer for marsh). **1986** *Morning Call* (Allentown PA) 6 Apr sec C 16 (Internet), In the meantime, especially throughout April, the welcome sounds of the "swamp blackbird," as it's sometimes called, will greet the visitor to the cattail marsh.

swamp black currant See swamp currant

swamp blackgum See black gum 1

swamp blueberry n

Any of several **blueberries 1**, as:

a =**highbush blueberry. chiefly Nth**

   1848 Gray *Manual of Botany* 262, *V[accinium] corymbosum.* . . Common Swamp Blueberry. . . Swamps and wet copses, common. **1860** in 1906 Thoreau *Writings* 20.299 **MA**, Some ten days later comes the high blueberry, or swamp blueberry, the commonest stout shrub of our swamps. **1892** IN Dept. Geol. & Nat. Resources *Rept. for 1891* 147, *V[accinium] corymbosum.* . . Common High or Swamp Blueberry. **1944** Hyland–Steinmetz *Woody Plants ME* 51, *V. corymbosum.* . . Highbush or Swamp Blueberry. Common and locally abundant. . .

Swamps, bogs, low woods, and rocky pastures. **1949** *Pacific Spectator* Spring 223 **CT,** You had to cross the river . . to find the low swamp blueberries, bright blue and sweeter than any other kind. **1964** *Appleton Post-Crescent* (WI) 17 July 11/3, The highbush or swamp blueberry, which grows in marshes, the vaccinium australe [=*V. corymbosum*], if you want to be technical. **2001** *DARE* File—Internet **VA,** In the streamside wetlands. . . Undergrowth included Fringe Tree (*Chionathes* [sic] *virginica*) and shrubs such as . . Highbush or Swamp Blueberry *(Vaccinium corymbosum),* already heavy with fruit and Dangleberry *(Gaylussacia frondosa),* a coastal plain species.

b A **blueberry 1:** either *Vaccinium uliginosum* or *V. caespitosum.* **AK, West**

1931 U.S. Dept. Ag. *Misc. Pub.* 101.134 **West,** Western bog blueberry (*V[accinium] occidentale* [=*V. uliginosum*]), known also as swamp, or western blueberry, and swamp huckleberry, is a smooth compact bush . . ranging from Montana to southeastern British Columbia, California, and Utah, in moist open meadows or bogs at 4,000 to 10,000 feet, but largely subalpine. **1972** Viereck–Little *AK Trees* 234, *Vaccinium caespitosum.* . . Swamp blueberry. . . Low spreading shrub forming mats to 16 in. . . A common shrub of bogs, subalpine meadows, and open spruce-hemlock stands in the coastal forest. **2004** (acc) U.S. Natl. Park Serv. *Freq. Seen Flora* (Internet) **AK,** Dwarf or Swamp blueberry, bilberry, or huckleberry; *Vaccinium caespitosum,* and Bog or Dwarf alpine blueberry or bilberry, *Vaccinium uliginosum,* are both low spreading *dwarf* species with *cylindrical branches,* and white or pink flowers; with *V. uliginosum* being an alpine species, and the most widespread, best-known, and most-used blueberry in Alaska.

c Another **blueberry 1** such as *Vaccinium virgatum* or *V. elliottii.* **Sth**

1999 in 2005 *DARE* File—Internet **AR,** *Vaccinium virgatum* . . Swamp Blueberry. **2003** *Ibid* **Gulf States,** *Vaccinium virgatum* . . Swamp Blueberry. **2005** *Ibid* **GA,** *Vaccinium elliotti* (swamp blueberry).

swamp bug n **LA** Cf **mudbug**

=**crawfish** n **B1.**

1968 *DARE* Tape **LA22,** You got what you call a crawfish, he's a swamp bug; they either call him crawfish or swamp bug down here. **2005** *DARE* File—Internet **LA,** For many years the Little Swamp Bug (crawfish) was known as poor man's food. *Ibid* **LA,** The Crawfish Festival, in Park Hardy, features . . contests for peeling, racing, and eating the illustrious swamp bug.

swamp buttercup n **chiefly N Cent**

A **buttercup 1** (here: *Ranunculus hispidus*).

1928 *Amer. Midland Naturalist* 11.56 **MI,** *Ranunculus carecitorum* [sic; =*R. hispidus* var *caricetorum*]. . . This Swamp Buttercup usually is found on low, wet, more or less wooded and swampy grounds through which a small stream winds its devious way. **1931** *Chron.-Telegram* (Elyria OH) 7 May 19/4 **OH,** Wildflowers are abundant. . . Among the many flowers . . are: Aster, Black-eyed Susan, Swamp Buttercup, . . and Canada Thistle. **1936** IL Nat. Hist. Surv. *Wildflowers* 99, *Swamp Buttercup.* . . Grows 1–3 feet high in swamps and other moist or shady places. . . New Brunswick to Manitoba and south to Georgia and Texas. **1966** *DARE* Wildfl QR Pl.70 [=*Ranunculus hispidus*] **OR12,** Swamp buttercup. **1996** *Dayton Daily News* (OH) 19 Apr sec C 1 (Internet), Other abundant spring flowers include swamp buttercup. **2005** *DARE* File—Internet **neIA,** The flowering of the swamp buttercup has always been a reminder for me that the ladyslippers will soon be flowering.

swamp cabbage n

1 =**skunk cabbage 1a.**

1792 in 1888 Cutler *Life* 2.292 **PA,** Our Swamp Cabbage (or Dracontium foetidum). **1843** (1844) Johnson *Farmer's Encycl.* 996, *Skunk-cabbage.* Swamp-cabbage; Skunk-weed. . It is the *Symplocarpos foetida* of some botanists. **1880** *Harper's New Mth. Mag.* 61.66 **NEast,** The swamp-cabbage flower . . peers above the ground beneath his purple spotted hood. **1896** *Daily Northwestern* (Oshkosh WI) 22 Feb 8/1 **WI,** The swamp cabbage pushes itself through the ground where the warm sun has made a place. **1934** *Amer. Midland Naturalist* 15.329 **MI,** *Spathyema foetida* [=*Symplocarpos f.*] . . Swamp Cabbage. **1967–68** *DARE* (Qu. S26b, *Wildflowers that grow in water or wet places*) Inf **MD20,** Swamp cabbage—leaves like cabbage, flower white or brown, several inches long; **MD30,** Swamp cabbage—large veined leaf, fleshy hooded flower with yellow tongue inside; **NJ2,** Swamp cabbage—skunk cabbage. **1996** *Boston Herald* (MA) 17 Sept 4 (Internet), A misguided

700-pound bull moose, perhaps with a belly full of swamp cabbage, choice leaves and acorns, showed up in a Fitchburg backyard yesterday.

2 Usu =**cabbage palm** or its edible terminal bud; occas also the bud of **saw palmetto 1.** **chiefly FL** Cf **palmetto cabbage**

1933 Rawlings *South Moon* 250 **nFL,** He cut a low-growing palmetto. He trimmed down the ivory cylinder that was the heart of the palm and cut a shaving from the lower end, where the fan-like sections fitted intricately together. They tasted it. It was crisp and sweet, like chestnuts. "That's a swamp cabbage that's fitten," he decided. **1939** FWP *Guide FL* 479 **swFL,** The swamp cabbage is the bud of the cabbage palm, a delicacy long relished in Florida but only recently known elsewhere. **1966** *DARE* Tape **FL37,** [FW:] Just what is this swamp cabbage? . . [Inf:] Well, some people calls 'em palm trees. . . You cut 'em whilst they're small. . . [FW:] What do they look like? Are they long or round or—? [Inf:] Well, they're round. A cabbage is round, about that big around. . . [FW:] And what kind of palm tree is that that gives you those? . . [Aux Inf:] The cabbage palm. **1975** Newell *If Nothin' Don't Happen* 43 **nwFL,** A feller can worry down a few mouthfuls of that even if he ain't hungry, specially if he's got plenty of grits and pokeberry greens or swamp cabbage to go along with it. **1986** Pederson *LAGS Concordance,* 1 inf, **neFL,** Swamp cabbage—made from swamp cabbage palm; 1 inf, **cwFL,** Swamp cabbage—cut from sable palm; 1 inf, **seFL,** Swamp cabbage. **2005** *DARE* File—Internet **SE,** Both cabbage palm . . and saw palmetto . . provided "swamp cabbage" (heart bud of either plants).

swamp canary n

1 Usu the **prothonotary warbler,** but also the hooded warbler *(Wilsonia citrina).* **Sth**

1890 O'Reilly *Athletics & Manly Sport* 378 **NC, VA,** The wren and swamp canary twined their notes like threads of gossamer through the warp and woof of this marvellous tapestry of sound. **1955** *Oriole* 20.1.12 **GA,** *Prothonotary Warbler . . Swamp Canary* (from a habitat, its coloration and its notable song). *Ibid,* *Hooded Warbler—Swamp Canary* (from its habitat, yellow coloration, and striking song). **1996** *SC River News* 2 **SC,** Commonly known as the swamp canary, the prothonotary warbler is a frequent resident of cypress swamps and heavily wooded stream borders in South Carolina. **1997** in 2005 *DARE* File—Internet **LA,** The bird of the day here was the Prothonotary Warbler or "swamp canary" as it is locally called. **2002** NC Office of Environmental Educ. *Roanoke R. Basin* np **NC,** The brilliant prothonotary warbler is known locally as "swamp canary."

2 A **goldfinch 1** (here: *Carduelis tristis*).

1955 *Oriole* 20.1.13 **GA,** *Goldfinch . . Swamp Canary* (perhaps from confusion with warblers so-called; the goldfinch has no particular affinity with swamps; "canary," from the largely yellow coloration of the breeding male).

swamp candle n

1 also freq *swamp candles:* A **loosestrife 1** (here: *Lysimachia terrestris*). [See quot 2005] **esp NEast** Cf **swamp loosestrife 2**

1894 *Jrl. Amer. Folkl.* 7.94 **NEast,** *Lysimachia stricta* (?) . . , swamp candles. **1919** (1923) House *Wild Flowers NY* 212, *Bulb-bearing Loosestrife; Swamp Candles.* . . Flowers . . chiefly in the axils of the upper and smaller leaves and forming a terminal leafy raceme. **1942** Hylander *Plant Life* 626, Swamp Candles is a species [of *Lysimachia*] with long tapering opposite leaves and a terminal spike of yellow flowers which are often streaked with purple; it is found in swampy woods from New England to Georgia. **1951** Graham *My Window* 176 **ME,** Most of our spring flowers appear in the bogs and marshes: . . swamp candles. **1966** *DARE* Wildfl QR Pl.161B [=*Lysimachia terrestris*] Inf **MI7,** Swamp candle. **1968** *DARE* (Qu. S26b, *Wildflowers that grow in water or wet places*) Inf **PA99,** Swamp candle. **2005** *DARE* File—Internet **seNY,** Swamp Candles (Lysimachia terrestris) in bloom come into view. . . The yellow flowers, with two red spots at the base of each petal, are in a terminal raceme standing prominently above the rest of the plant, hence the reference to candles in the common name.

2 =**culver's root 1.**

1968 Pochmann *Triple Ridge* 224 **cWI,** In July swamp candles, Culver's root, lighten the whole meadow.

3 as *swamp candles:* A **black snakeroot 1** (here: *Cimicifuga racemosa*). Cf **fairy candles**

1999 *News & Rec.* (Greensboro NC) 17 July 12 (Internet), The tall spires of swamp candles, Cimicifuga racemosa, also called black snakeroot, are always a delightful addition to the garden, blooming in late June or early July, depending on location.

4 A **sunnybell** (here: *Schoenolirion croceum*).

2005 *DARE* File—Internet **Sth**, *Schoenolirion croceum.* . . Sunnybells, swamp candle. . . Rock outcrops, moist pinelands; 0–400 m; Ala., Fla., Ga., La., N.C., S.C., Tenn., Tex.

swamp candles   See **swamp candle 1, 3**

swamp cedar n

1 A **white cedar 1** (here: *Chamaecyparis thyoides*).   **esp NEast**

a1817 (1821) Dwight *Travels* 1.39 **NEng**, The *Swamp Cedar.* . . is extensively used for shingles.   **1843** (1844) Johnson *Farmer's Encycl.* 15, In New York it has been found . . that posts for rail-fencing, made of Acacia tree, . . will last as long as those of swamp cedar.   **1865** in 1908 U.S. Navy Dept. *Official Records Union & Confederate Navies* 22.227, The knees supporting the spardeck beams . . are of swamp cedar.   **1868** *Amer. Naturalist* 2.334 **NY**, Stumps of the White, or Swamp-cedar (*Cupressus thyoides* [=*Chamaecyparis t.*]), occur in great numbers, fast in the peaty meadows and salt marshes, which are now permanently covered with salt-water.   **1909** Torrey Bot. Club *Bulletin* 36.341 **NJ**, A new and interesting fungus . . appears to be very destructive to the swamp cedar, *Chamaecyparis thyoides*.   **1968–69** *DARE* (Qu. T5, . . *Kinds of evergreens, other than pine*) Inf **NJ31**, Swamp cedar—also called juniper—and red cedar; (Qu. T15, . . *Kinds of swamp trees*) Infs **MA55, NJ21**, Swamp cedar; (Qu. T16, . . *Kinds of trees* . . '*special*') Inf **NJ55**, Swamp cedar.   **2005** *Westborough News* (MA) (Internet), The solid footing in frozen swamps makes it possible to get closer than usual to Atlantic white cedars which are water-tolerant and often grow with their roots in water. Not surprisingly, the tree is also sometimes called swamp cedar.

2 A **bald cypress** (here: *Taxodium distichum*).

1862 *New Amer. Cyclop.* 15.372 **TN**, In the swamps and lowlands of West Tennessee the cypress, hacmatac, cottonwood, and swamp cedar occur in large quantities.   **1892** *Indiana Co. Gaz.* (PA) 27 Jan 7/2, In the famous West Philadelphia Bartram Botanical gardens there flourishes an enormous Florida swamp cedar, the trunk of which is fully six feet in diameter.   **1937** *Torreya* 37.94, *Taxodium* spp.—Swamp cedar, Southern States.

3 =**white cedar 2**.   **chiefly Gt Lakes**

1924 *Ironwood Daily–Globe* (MI) 2 Oct 4/3, If cedars . . , junipers, pines and spruce are to be taken from the swamp or uplands . . , the last two weeks in August or the first two in September, will bear better results. . . This we have found especially true with the common white swamp cedar of Lower Michigan.   **1949** *Mansfield News–Jrl.* (OH) 6 Dec 7/1 **OH**, A sturdy wire mesh makes a good base for a handsome wreath. Hemlock, juniper or swamp cedar are all suitable greenery.   **1960** *Holland Eve. Sentinel* (MI) 30 Apr 11/1, [Advt:] Wanted—25 to 30 swamp cedar trees, 6 to 8 ft. tall.   **1997** (acc) OH Pub. Lib. Info. Network *What Tree Is It?* (Internet) **OH**, *Thuja occidentalis.* . . Sometimes referred to as the "Swamp Cedar" it typically is found growing on limestone soils in moist to boggy habitats. Although more commonly found to the North, it is native to a few localities in Ohio, most notably Cedar Bog State Nature Preserve.

4 **juniper 1** (here: *Juniperus scopulorum*).   **NV**

1983 *Ecological Monogr.* 53.360 **NV**, The unique valley population of *J[uniperus] scopulorum*, known locally as "swamp cedar" . . , persists there primarily because of subirrigation due to seasonal discharge from the towering, snow-clad Snake and Schell Creek Ranges that enclose the basin on the east and west.   **2005** *DARE* File—Internet **NV**, Swamp Cedar Instant Study Area was designated in 1970 to protect the unusual ecosystem of the area, a low marshy zone which supports a large stand of Rocky Mountain Juniper. The small swamp cedar trees provide vegetative screening in this flat land.

swamp cheese n

1 =**swamp apple 1**.

1859 [see **swamp apple 1**].   **1876** Hobbs *Bot. Hdbk.* 114, Swamp cheeses, Swamp apple, Azalea nudiflora [=*Rhododendron periclymenoides*].   **1931–33** *LANE Worksheets* **RI**, Swamp cheese—wild azalea when the flower goes kernel-like, cheese-like.

2 as *swamp cheese bush*: =**swamp apple 2**.

1931–33 *LANE Worksheets* **RI**, Swamp cheese bush—a bush with bell-shaped blossoms, smells sweet like a honeysuckle.

swamp cherry n

1 A **jack-in-the-pulpit 1** (here: *Arisaema triphyllum*).

1951 *PADS* 15.27 **TX**, *Arisaema triphyllum.* . . Swamp cherries. The corm and fruits were boiled and drained before being eaten by the aborigines; birds also like the "cherries."

2 See quots.

1969 *DARE* (Qu. I46, . . *Kinds of fruits that grow wild around here*) Inf **CT39**, Swamp cherries.   **2005** *DARE* File—Internet **PA**, The willow oak will make a wonderful addition to our two other street trees, a wild swamp cherry with beautiful bark, and a dragons'-claw willow with fascinating twisted branch structure.

swamp chess n

A **bromegrass** (here: *Bromus ciliatus*).

1894 Coulter *Botany W. TX* 548, *B[romus] ciliatus.* . . Swamp Chess. . . Moist land, Texas and northward.   **1894** *Jrl. Amer. Folkl.* 7.104 **NE**, *Bromus ciliatus.* . . Swamp chess.   **1912** Baker *Book of Grasses* 230, *Fringed Brome-grass. Swamp Chess.* . . Damp soil in open woods and borders of thickets. . . Newfoundland to New Jersey, west to Manitoba and Minnesota.   **2002** Shetler–Orli *Annotated Vascular Plants* 31 **MD, VA**, *[Bromus] ciliatus* . . fringed brome, fringed brome grass, swamp chess.

swamp chestnut oak n

1 An **oak** (here: *Quercus prinus* L.) native to much of the US east of the Mississippi River.   Also called **basket oak 3, chestnut ~, chestnut white ~, cow ~, mountain ~ a, rock chestnut ~, rock ~, tanbark ~ a, white chestnut ~**

1852 WI State Ag. Soc. *Trans.* 2.405, [*Quercus*] Prinos, Linn. Swamp Chestnut Oak. Near Janesville.   **1860** Curtis *Cat. Plants NC* 33, *Swamp Chestnut Oak.* . . We have two varieties of this tree. . . They are as follows: *Swamp White Oak.* (var: discolor, Michx. [=*Quercus michauxii*]). . . *Rock Chestnut Oak.* var: monticola, Michx. [=*Q. prinus*]—This is sometimes called *Rock Oak* and *Chestnut Oak,* and is found as far north as New England. . . In the leaves and fruit it differs very slightly from the *Swamp Chestnut Oak.* . . The bark is among the best for tanning.   **1908** Britton *N. Amer. Trees* 329, [*Rock Chestnut Oak—Quercus Prinus* Linnaeus.] *Ibid* 330, The bark is used in tanning. . . It is also known as Chestnut oak, Rock oak, Tanbark oak, Swamp chestnut oak, and Mountain oak.   **1976** Bailey–Bailey *Hortus Third* 935, [*Quercus] prinus.* . . Basket o[ak], swamp c[hestnut] o., rock c. o. . . Furnishes an important wood and tanbark.

2 =**basket oak 1**.   Cf **swamp oak 2b(1), ~ white oak 3**

1801 Michaux *Histoire* 5.1, *Quercus prinus (palustris).* . . *Swamp's chestnut oak* [sic]. . . Cet arbre. . . est remarquable par la beauté de sa forme et la grosseur de ses glands qui sont doux et abondans. . . Son bois est excellent. . . [O]n en fait des corbeilles et des balais. [=*Quercus prinus (palustris).* . . *Swamp's chestnut oak.* . . This tree. . . is remarkable for the beauty of its form and the size of its acorns which are sweet and abundant. . . Its wood is excellent. . . Baskets and brooms are made of it.]   **1812** Michaux *Histoire des Arbres* 2.52, Le *Quercus prinus palustris* . . dans la partie inférieure des Etats du Midi . . est désignée sous les différens noms de *Chesnut white oak,* . . de *Swamp chesnut oak* . . ; et le long de la rivière de Savannah, le plus souvent sous celui de *White oak.* [=*Quercus prinus palustris* is known in the lower parts of the southern states under the various names *Chesnut white oak,* . . *swamp chesnut oak* . . ; and along the Savannah river most often *white oak.*]   **1860** Curtis *Cat. Plants NC* 33, *Swamp Chestnut Oak.* . . Not known north of Pennsylvania, but is pretty common in the maritime parts of the Southern States.   **1870** in 1871 Featherman *Rept. Bot. Surv. LA* 12, On approaching nearer the Amite river, the soil becomes more sandy; the swamp chestnut oak ceases to form the characteristic growth.   **1933** Small *Manual SE Flora* 425, *Q[uercus] Michauxii* Nutt[all]. . . Cow-oak. Basket-oak. Swamp white-oak. Swamp Chestnut-oak. . . Swamps, bottoms, and calcareous hammocks.   **1939** Torrey Bot. Club *Bulletin* 66.376 **MD**, Along the upland border where the soil is less peaty are found a number of oaks, chiefly . . swamp chestnut oak *(Q. michauxii)* and white oak *(Q. alba).*   **1970** *DARE* (Qu. T10, . . *Kinds of oak trees*) Inf **IL119**, Swamp chestnut oak.   **1973** Wharton–Barbour *Trees KY* 453, *Quercus michauxii.* . . Swamp chestnut oak, basket oak, cow oak.   **1999** in 2005 *DARE* File—Internet **AL**, *Quercus michauxii.* . . Swamp chestnut oak can be distinguished from chestnut oak and chinkapin oak by more obovate leaves, a larger acorn, and habitat.

swamp chicken n

1 =**king rail 1**.   Cf **prairie chicken 3**

1953 *AmSp* 28.279 **GA**, Swamp chicken . . King rail.

2 Esp the **purple gallinule,** but also the **Florida gallinule.**

1976 *Syracuse Herald–Jrl.* (NY) 12 Sept 18/4 **NY,** Virginia Billings . . has identified 107 species of birds in the marsh area including the . . common gallinule or swamp chicken. **1986** Pederson *LAGS Concordance,* 1 inf, **seFL,** Swamp chickens—hens in marsh. **2004** *Sun. Telegraph* (London) 8 Aug 5 (Internet) **csLA,** A flock of "swamp chickens" scuttles into a bed of blue water hyacinths. **2005** *DARE* File—Internet **Everglades FL,** This purple gallinule (Porphyrula martinica), or swamp chicken, was working the dock for handouts. **2005** *DARE* File **Everglades FL** (as of 1966), The local guide frequently pointed out the "swamp chickens"—purple gallinules. Watching the birds walk across the bonnets, he said, "They got chicken feet and they ain't much for eatin', but they are purty."

3 A frog; see quot.

1937 *Clearfield Progress* (PA) 29 Jan 1/7, This morning James Powell of Riverview found a lively frog cutting capers and hi-jinks in . . Montgomery Creek. . . Powell caught the "swamp chicken" after a lively chase and now has him imprisoned in a can just to prove his story.

swamp cock   See **swamp woodpecker**

swamp cooler n   Also abbr *swamp*   **chiefly West, esp SW** Also called **swamp fan**

An evaporative air cooler; see quot 2001.

1950 *Newsweek* 14 Aug 51, In dry climates it is possible to rig up a primitive but highly effective cooling system, called a "swamp cooler." It consists simply of a fan blowing over an excelsior mat which is drenched with dripping water. **1958** *Tri-City Herald* (Pasco WA) 14 Aug 14/4, Leave the hot house, the damp muggy swamp cooler and take in the fast action . . of a ball game. **1983** *Daily Herald* (Provo UT) 27 May 33/6, [Advt:] 4 bdrm, 2 bath, fam rm, . . swamp cooler, RV driveway. *Ibid* 34/5, [Advt:] By owner, 3 bdrm rambler, 1-¾ bath, . . swamp, solar. *Ibid* 35/7, [Advt:] Large swamp cooler, good cond, $100. **1987** *DARE* File **csAZ,** Swamp coolers n, Evaporative coolers for dwellings that depend solely on the evaporattion [sic] of water for cooling used in SW desert areas wh[e]re humid[ity] is low. **1998** *NADS Letters* **wTX, wOK,** As the Southwest is very dry, a common and inexpensive method of air conditioning is *evaporative air conditioners* or *swamp coolers.* . . These became common in the 50s before *refrigerated air conditioners* became available. **1998** Hillerman *First Eagle* 79 **AZ,** The swamp-cooler fan roared away at its highest setting, mixing damp air into the dry heat. **2001** *USA Today* (Arlington VA) 23 Aug (Internet), Folks differ on why it's called a swamp cooler. Some say because it makes the house feel like a muggy swamp—but that's only when the late summer rains come and the cooler is less efficient. On dry days . . a swamp cooler works fine. In high humidity areas . . they don't work at all. . . Swamp coolers are popular in the Southwest. **2005** *DARE* File **swID,** My grandparents had a swamp cooler in their home in the 1950s. It was a very effective evaporative cooler, but sometimes a green slime would accumulate in the tray, and the humid air that was produced could begin to smell a bit swampy.

swamp cotton n

1 also *swamp cotton grass:* A **cotton grass 1.**

1861 *Scientific Amer.* new ser 4.171 **NY,** We have the same plant— swamp cotton grass—growing native in most of our swamps, especially in the northern part of the State of New York. **1948** *Indiana Eve. Gaz.* (PA) 11 Aug 7/1, Once within the limits of the seepage we found . . the swamp cotton-grass, each stem bearing a tuft of soft brown wool. **1964** *Newark Advocate* (OH) 28 Feb 12/1, He showed slides of insect-eating plants, swamp cotton, and native orchids that are found in this area only on Cranberry Marsh. **1966** *DARE* Wildfl QR Pl.2A [=*Eriophorum callithrix*] Inf **WI**80, Swamp cotton. **2004** *WI Nat. Resources* Aug 22 **nWI,** My favorite bog weed is a white, puffy cotton-like ball suspended on a delicate branch that our elderly neighbor calls "swamp cotton." It is one of the six species of *Eriophorum* (cotton grass) that grows in Wisconsin.

2 A **hibiscus** (here: *Hibiscus moscheutos*). Cf **wild cotton 3a**

2000 Chester *Wildflowers Land Lakes* 109 **KY, TN,** *Swamp Rose-Mallow* or *Swamp-Cotton—Hibiscus moscheutos.*

swamp cotton grass   See **swamp cotton 1**

swamp cottonwood n

A **cottonwood 1** (here: *Populus heterophylla*) native to much of the eastern half of the US. Also called **poplar B1, river cottonwood, swamp poplar 1**

1882 U.S. Natl. Museum *Proc.* 5.86 **IN,** *Populus heterophylla.* "River

Cottonwood"; "Swamp Cottonwood"; "Stumpy Gum." **1897** Sudworth *Arborescent Flora* 130, *Populus heterophylla.* . . Swamp Cottonwood (S.C., Miss., Del.) **1928** *WI Rapids Daily Tribune* (WI) 5 June 4/7, Swamp cottonwood grows in the southeast. **1939** Torrey Bot. Club *Bulletin* 66.370 **eMD,** Small specimens of swamp cottonwood (*Populus heterophylla*) are occasionally noted. **1996** *Cleveland Plain Dealer* (OH) 12 July sec B 1 (Internet), He recalled discovering 17 rare swamp cottonwoods in a 2-acre wetland in Lake County. The trees are common in Louisiana but had not been seen in northern Ohio in over 100 years.

swamp currant n   Also *swamp black currant, swamp red* ~

A **currant B1** native to the northern US: either the black-berried *Ribes lacustre* or the red-berried *R. triste.*

1910 Graves *Flowering Plants* 218 **CT,** *Ribes lacustre.* . . Swamp Black Currant. **1928** Rosendahl–Butters *Trees MN* 139, *Ribes lacustre.* . . *Swamp black currant.* Low shrub . . , stems and branches . . covered with bristly prickles and somewhat longer, slender spines at the nodes. *Ibid* 142, *Ribes triste.* . . *Swamp red currant.* Low unarmed, straggling or reclining shrub. **1931** Fassett *Spring Flora* 81 **WI,** *R[ibes] lacustre. Swamp black currant; prickly currant.* . . Cold woods and swamps, northern Wisconsin. *Ibid* 82, *R. triste.* . . *Swamp Currant.* . . Wet woods, south to Dunn, Washington and Milwaukee counties. **1937** *Amer. Midland Naturalist* 18.970 **WA,** *Ribes lacustre* . . Swamp Currant. Wet places, 2,000 to 5,000 feet, abundant. **1959** Munz–Keck *CA Flora* 749, *R. lacustre.* . . *Swamp Currant.* . . Wet places like meadows, mostly 5000–6000 ft. **1986** *Flora Gt. Plains* 354 **West,** *Ribes lacustre* . . swamp currant. . . Fruit . . dark purple to black. *Ibid* 356, *Ribes triste* . . swamp currant. . . Fruit red. **2004** *DARE* File—Internet, They [=currants] were in bloom so with our books . . we decided they were Swamp Currant and Skunk Currant.

swamp cypress n   **chiefly Sth**

A **bald cypress** (here: *Taxodium distichum*).

1855 (1856) *Lippincott's Pronc. Gaz.* 682, Florida abounds in forest trees, among which are the live-oak, so valuable in ship-building; the water, and other varieties of oak, swamp cypress, . . and laurel. **1859** Downing *Treatise on Landscape Gardening* 527, *Taxodium distichum.* . . Though not an evergreen, yet this valuable genus is closely allied to coniferous trees, and is well known by all planters as the Southern or Swamp cypress, found along the banks of rivers and swamps in vast quantities; in Georgia, Carolina, Florida, and all the Southern States, it reaches the height of one hundred and twenty feet. **1876** Dennett *Louisiana* 70, On the west side of the Teche, . . there is a forest of swamp cypress. **1878** *Atlantic Mth.* 42.218 **TN,** We get gigantic sweet-gums with their beautiful star-like leaves, Spanish oaks, the swamp cypress, and a host of other forms. **1931** *Bee* (Danville VA) 22 Dec 6/4 **LA,** Six feet tall at 76 and as straight as a swamp cypress, Cap'n Cooley suffered a stroke of apoplexy while loading the "Ouachita" up the river. **1968** *DARE* (Qu. T15, . . Kinds of swamp trees) Inf **MD**36, Swamp cypress. **1990** *Pantagraph* (Bloomington IL) 7 Oct sec C 3 (Internet), At the southernmost part of U.S. 51 in Illinois. . . you can find Southern accents, Civil War history, swamp cypress, magnolia trees and high unemployment. **2005** *Times–Picayune* (New Orleans LA) 22 Jan 2 (Internet), A brown pelican—the state's bird—is featured perched on what appears to be a swamp cypress stump.

swamp dew n   Cf *DS* DD21a, b, c

=**mountain dew.**

1928 *Decatur Daily Rev.* (IL) 7 Feb 10/5, Somebody . . told him that he'd better take another drink of "swamp dew" and go to bed, that KWKH is "nothing but a bootleg station anyway." . . About the drinking charge, Mr. Henderson denied that he drank "swamp dew." We drink good old red whisky, he said. **1940** *Sat. Eve. Post* 3 Feb 15 **sMS,** He never sold his swamp dew. . . If a man wanted a jug of good red-eye, he could call at the cabin and leave a sack of flour or a side of meat.

swamp dewberry n   Also *running swamp dewberry*

A **dewberry 1** (here: *Rubus hispidus*).

1917 *Bot. Gaz.* 63.507 **NY,** Running swamp dewberry. . . *R[ubus] hispidus.* **1942** Tehon *Fieldbook IL Shrubs* 116, The Swamp Dewberry grows near lakes and marshes, especially at the base of wooded slopes. **1973** Wharton–Barbour *Trees KY* 535, *Swamp Dewberry.* . . This species . . can easily be distinguished from the group of common dewberries. It grows in swamp forests and wet meadows. Though infrequent it is locally plentiful in southern and eastern Kentucky. **1999** Torrey Bot. Club *Bulletin* 126.89 **NJ,** Some of the flowers in bloom were bugleweed (*Ajuga reptans*), . . swamp dewberry (*Rubus hispidus*), . . and common blue violet (*V[iola] sororia*). **2005** (acc) Colby–Sawyer College *Virtual Herbarium* (Internet) **cNH,** Like common dewberry, the fruit is black when ripe, but swamp dewberry has a distinctly sour taste.

swamp dogwood n

1 Any of several **dogwoods 1.**

1815 Drake *Natural View Cincinnati* 76 **wOH,** The botanical resources of this. . *Forest of the Miami country* [include] . . *Cornus . . candidissima* [=*C. racemosa*] . . *Swamp dogwood.* **1817** Darby *Geogr. Descr. LA* 353 **LA, sMS, AL,** *Cornus alba* [=*C. sericea*] . . Swamp dogwood. **1891** *Herald–Despatch* (Decatur IL) [9 May 7/2] (newspaperarchive.com) **nwOH,** Your correspondent went through a neighborhood known in Portage county as red brush, so called because of the great abundance of the swamp dogwood or "red-willow" that grows in that region. This is the cornus sanguinea. **1932** *Daily Northwestern* (Oshkosh WI) 16 July 8/2, The oval leaves [of buttonbush] . . somewhat resemble those of the swamp dogwood. **1940** Steyermark *Flora MO* 402, *Swamp Dogwood (Cornus obliqua.)* . . Thickets, wet prairies, bogs, and along beds of small streams. **1964** Batson *Wild Flowers SC* 80, *Swamp dogwood, red willow: C[ornus] stricta* [=*C. foemina*]. . . A medium-sized shrub with red twigs and stems. **1966–68** *DARE* (Qu. T15, . . *Kinds of swamp trees*) Infs **MS**16, **NC**33, **VA**15, 26, Swamp dogwood; (Qu. T16, . . *Kinds of trees . . 'special'*) Inf **VA**15, Swamp dogwood. [*DARE* Ed: Some of these Infs may refer instead to other senses below.] **1989** *Amer. Midland Naturalist* 122.38 **FL,** The den site . . was located . . in a dense thicket of grape vines, bracken fern . . , wax myrtle . . , and swamp dogwood *(Cornus foemina).* **2000** Torrey Bot. Soc. *Jrl.* 127.184 **NJ,** In bloom were *Cornus amomum* (swamp dogwood) and *Lythrum salicaria* (purple loosestrife).

2 A **hop tree** (here: *Ptelea trifoliata*).

1843 Torrey *Flora NY* 1.133, *Ptelea trifoliata. . . Swamp Dogwood. Stinking Ash.* . . Flowers lateral and terminal; the odor disagreeable. **1882** (1897) Hale *Materia Medica* 526, *Ptelea trifoliata. . .* is also known as *Wingseed, Shrubby trefoil,* and *Swamp Dogwood. . .* It is common to this country, growing mostly west of the Alleghanies, in shady, moist hedges, and edges of woods. **1966** *Sun. Jrl. & Star* (Lincoln NE) 9 Jan sec D 17/4, Aguebark. . . is commonly known as pickaway anise or quininetree or wafer ash or swamp dogwood or shrubby trefoil or wingseed. **1974** (1977) Coon *Useful Plants* 238, *Ptelea trifoliata . .* swamp dogwood. **2003** *DARE* File—Internet, *Ptelea trifoliate* [sic]. . . *Common Names:* Water-ash, Stinking-ash, . . Swamp dogwood.

3 A **poison sumac** (here: *Toxicodendron vernix*).

1859 (1880) Darlington *Amer. Weeds* 79, *Poisonous Rhus.* Poison Sumach. Poison Elder. Swamp Dogwood. **1892** (1974) Millspaugh *Amer. Med. Plants* 37–1, *Rhus venenata. . .* Com. Names.—Poison or Swamp Sumach, Poison Elder, Poison or Swamp Dogwood, Poison Ash, Poison Tree, =Poison Wood.

4 =**buttonbush 1.**

1869 Cook *Physio-Med. Dispensatory* 329, *Cephalanthus occidentalis. Button bush, pond or swamp dogwood, globe flower. . .* The *bark* is a slow, but quite decided tonic, of the stimulating and moderately relaxing class. . . Several intelligent gentlemen have told me that it is much depended on as an antiperiodic in the south-western States. **1918** *Dispensatory U.S.A.* 1312, *Cephalanthus occidentalis* L. *Button Bush. Button Wood. Crane Willow. Swamp Dogwood. . .* A common indigenous shrub which grows in moist places.

5 A **burning bush 1** (here: *Euonymus americana*). Cf **swamp willow 3**

1964 Campbell et al. *Gt. Smoky Wildflowers* 78 **wNC, eTN,** Hearts-abustin'. . . Common names include strawberry bush, swamp dogwood, spindle bush, wahoo, and a dozen others. **2005** *DARE* File—Internet, Other names for "hearts-a-busting-with-love" are "strawberry bush," swamp dogwood, "arrow wood," and "spindle bush."

swamp dragon n

=**lizard's tail 1.**

1869 Porcher *Resources* 9 **Sth,** *Swamp Dragon, (Saururus Cernuus).*—The roots of this plant, growing abundantly in the swamps and marshes along the seaboard, boiled and mashed, furnish an easily procurable and highly soothing material for poultices. **1937** *Torreya* 37.96 **SC,** *Saururus cernuus.* . . Swamp-dragon.

swamp duck n

=**wood duck 1.**

1982 Elman *Hunter's Field Guide* 186, *Wood Duck. . . Common & regional names* . . swamp duck. **1987** *Sun. Capital* (Annapolis MD) 15 Nov sec C 17/1, This bird . . is that real show duck, the woody or wood duck, also known as the tree duck, the swamp duck and even the sum-

mer duck. **1994** *Dayton Daily News* (OH) 27 Feb sec D 6 (Internet), With increased development of both industry and agriculture in Ohio, wood ducks (also called woodies, swamp ducks, squealers and summer ducks) have lost many of their natural nesting places.

swamp elder n

1 A **forestiera.** Cf **devil's elbow**

1905 *Atlanta Constitution* (GA) [21 Aug] 10/4 (newspaperarchive.com), Also the bush called swamp elder or button elder or some call it devil's elbow. **2005** *DARE* File—Internet **sLA,** Cypress trees thrive in the swamp areas. . . Others [=trees and shrubs] include ash, elm, . . plum trees, pecan, hackberry, honey locust, sycamore, and swamp elder.

2 An **elder** n[2] (here: *Sambucus racemosa* var *racemosa*).

1967 *DARE* (Qu. T15, . . *Kinds of swamp trees*) Inf **MI**67, Swamp elder. **1973** *Ecology* 54.917 **wPA,** A few woody shrubs of . . devil's walking stick, swamp elder (*Sambucus pubens* [=*S. racemosa* var *racemosa*]), and American chestnut are found. **1974** Peden *Speak to Earth* 83 **cIN,** Swamp elder. . . It is a jungly plant with an attractive, thin, serrated leaf and a stalk that looks like a pale-green glass tube filled with water. It has a tiny, inconspicuous white flower.

swamp elm n   scattered, but esp NEast, N Cent

Usu =**white elm** or **rock elm 1;** rarely **slippery elm;** see quots.

1854 MI State Ag. Soc. *Trans. for 1853* 5.138, The trees indigenous to the soil, were white, red, and swamp oak; . . red and white, or swamp elm; . . with several other varieties in less abundance. **1867** *Scientific Amer.* 16.102 **KY,** At Louisville, the buds of the swamp elm, the swamp maple, and sweet gum, were considerably swollen, and the blossoms of the elm forming. **1872** Knapp *Hist. Maumee Valley* 464 **OH,** A thorough test has established the fact that no timber is better adapted to the production of barrel staves, than this once repudiated swamp elm. **1902** *Daily Northwestern* (Oshkosh WI) 2 Apr 2/3, The best trees to plant are the white elm and swamp elm and the kind commonly called 'slippery elm.' **1950** *WELS* (*Different kinds of elm trees*) 6 Infs, **WI,** Swamp elm. **1953** *Traverse City Rec.-Eagle* (MI) 9 Feb 4/3, This time please leave out the swamp elm stuff. It doesn't burn—just melts a little bit. **1960** Vines *Trees SW* 209, *Ulmus americana.* . . Vernacular names are . . Soft Elm, Swamp Elm, White Elm, and Water Elm. *Ibid* 214, *Ulmus. . . thomasi.* . . is also known under the names of Cork Elm, . . Swamp Elm, . . and Wahoo Elm. **1966–69** *DARE* (Qu. T11, . . *Kinds of elm trees*) Infs **GA**80, **NY**22, 113, Swamp elm; **FL**16, Wild elm or swamp elm; **PA**126, Swamp elm—large tree, large round shape to it; **NY**101, 219, Swamp ellum; **VT**10, Swamp ellum—same as slippery elm and red elm; (Qu. T15, . . *Kinds of swamp trees*) Infs **CT**9, **IN**69, **NY**155, Swamp elm; **NY**24, **VT**10, Swamp ellum. **2000** *Post–Std.* (Syracuse NY) 21 Sept 20/4 (as of 1925), On the farm of Lewis Wheat . . is a tree, commonly called a swamp elm, that is believed to be the largest tree of its kind in New York State. Three feet from the ground the circumference is about 33 feet. **2005** *DARE* File—Internet **NJ,** A dwarf pine forest . . stretches from Monmouth Count [sic] to Cape May. Other plants, aside from the occasional swamp elm or catalpa, rely on their insect trapping abilities to compensate for the bleak soil.

swamper n

1 One who lives in or frequents a swamp. **chiefly Sth, S Midl** Also called **swamp angel 4, ~ hound, ~ rabbit 5, ~ rat 1**

1775 *NC Gaz.* (New Bern) 24 Mar 3/3, Fellow Dismalites and Swampers, are not we the Men whom God hath appointed to curb the Insolence of *Britain.* **1845** *Amer. Penny Mag.* 1.475 **NJ,** Speculating in Jersey Blackberries. . . Great is the excitement among the barefooted Tattamy swampers when the market is 'up.' **1856** *Harper's New Mth. Mag.* 13.447 **NC,** Joe Skeeters holds the office of shingle-counter for the Dismal Swamp Land Company, and in addition is a thoroughbred swamper. **1857** Long *Pictures Slavery* (2d ed) 321 **MD,** This extensive swamp lies between Snow Hill, Worcester County, Md., and Dagsboro', Sussex County, Del. . . It abounds in cypress timber, which is riven into shingles by the "swampers." **1888** *Century Illustr. Mag.* 35.550 **LA,** When the swamps are deep in water the swamper may paddle up to these trees whose narrowed waists are now within the swing of his ax. **1903** *DN* 2.332 **seMO,** *Swamper.* . . An inhabitant of the swamps. **1906** *DN* 3.160 **nwAR,** *Swamper.* . . A man who lives in swampy country. "The swampers and the hill-billies don't hit it off very well." Randolph Co. **1935** Hurston *Mules & Men* 277 **LA,** A swamper is a root-and-conjure doctor who goes to the swamps and gathers his or her own herbs and roots. **1942** Faulkner *Go Down* 222 **MS,** They were swampers: gaunt, malaria-ridden men appearing from nowhere, who ran trap-lines for coons. **1967** *DARE* FW Addit **GA**19, *Swamper*—pronounced [ˌswɔmpɚ]—a native of the Okefenokee area. **1986** Pederson *LAGS Concordance (A rustic)* 1 inf, **seAL,** Swampers.

2 In logging: a worker who clears roadways or removes brush from around trees, trims fallen trees, and assists in skidding or loading them. [**swamp** v C1b] **chiefly Nth** Cf **gutterman**

1842 (1850) Abbott *Cousin Lucy* 68 **ME,** The swamper finds out which the good trees are, and he makes a road to them, so that, when they are cut down, they can haul them out. **1850** Seymour *Sketches MN* 202, One swamper, or road breaker . . is constantly employed in keeping the roads open. **1870** *Overland Mth.* 5.57 **WA,** Then come the swampers, who, under the direction of the "boss," clear the roads. **1892** *Overland Mth.* (2d ser) 20.265 **nwCA,** Before the sawyers begin on the prostrate trees a fire is kindled, to burn off the obstructing brush. During the conflagration the "swampers" are vigilantly at work . . to prevent the destruction of valuable timber other than the redwood. **1907** *DN* 3.250 **eME,** *Swamper.* . . A woodsman who makes roads where lumbering is to be done by felling and removing trees. **1909** *DN* 3.417 **nME,** *Swamper.* . . A man who swamps roads. **1920** *DN* 5.84 **NW,** *Swamper.* One who swamps out a given area. Logging. **1930** *DN* 6.89 **cWV,** *Swamper,* a road builder; a clearer of under-brush. **1952** *Badger Folkl.* 1.17 **WI** [Logging language], *Swamper*—A man assigned to cutting a trail from roads to fallen trees, so that logs may be skidded (dragged) to skidway. **1965** in 2005 *DARE* File—Internet **cMI,** I started in at 15 in 1901. I was what they called a swamper. I knocked the limbs off the logs and made the trails for the skidders. I hitched up the logs and put 'em up to load on the drays. **1966–70** *DARE* Tape **ME**19, When we used to go lumbering, . . we had a swamper. . . A swamper is a guy that tromps the roads; **MI**125, [FW:] On part of the logging crew, were there some of the men who trimmed it? [Inf:] Well, they was what they called a swamper, and he cleaned out the road. . . Cut the brush away . . if there was a limb out on there—[FW:] On the tree you cut down. [Inf:] Yeah. **2004** *DARE* File—Internet, *Swampers*—Swampers must maintain a safe distance from the sawyer when cutting.

3 An assistant to a teamster or truck driver, or on any of var other vehicles. **chiefly West**

1870 *Territorial Enterprise* (VA City NV) 21 Apr 3/1, A "swamper" is a man who goes with the driver of a . . team as his assistant. **1896** *Century Illustr. Mag.* 52.100 **West,** Mr. Harshaw is the "swamper," because he makes himself useful doing things my lord does n't like to do. . . We two sat on the back seat, . . and the "swamper" sat anywhere on the lumps and bumps which our baggage made. **1919** *Oxnard Daily Courier & Oxnard Daily News* (CA) 25 Oct [2]/4 (newspaperarchive.com), *Wanted*—By young man job as swamper on caterpillar. **1922** *DN* 5.181 **NW,** *Swamper.* . . A general assistant to the engineer of a caterpillar traction engine. **1929** *AmSp* 4.345 [Vagabond lingo], *Swamper*—A helper on an auto truck. **1929** *Ibid* 5.147 **CO** [Mining expressions], The helper on the ore train is a *swamper,* one who cleans out the cars. **1931** *AmSp* 7.159 [Newspaper jargon], The papers are taken in trucks away from the building for the other routes. *Swampers* throw the papers off the trucks at the proper destinations. **1950** *Western Folkl.* 9.29, [Footnote:] A "swamper" is a skinner's helper. After helping to load the cars he also serves as a brakeman. **1967** *TX Observer* (Austin) 7 July 2/3 [Oil field lingo], The swamper was the worker who served as a kind of footman or flunky for the truck driver, pulling at the winch line, wrapping it around bundles of pipe or rig timber or junk. **1982** *Syracuse Herald–Amer.* (NY) 15 Aug mag sec 36/1 **UT, CO,** To explore the sandstone canyons of Dinosaur National Monument . . I had signed on as a swamper for Charlie Gibbs. . . The swamper's main duty is to bail out the water that splashes into the raft. **1997** Worsley–Worsley *From Oz to E.T.* 86 **NYC,** New York Teamsters at that time [=1967] were a world unto themselves. . . On some trucks there was a second man called a "swamper" who sat in the cab with the driver; as far as I could see, he did nothing.

4 One who cleans and does other unskilled labor in a saloon or similar establishment. **scattered, but esp West** Cf **swamp** v C2

1907 *Oregonian* (Portland OR) 13 Oct 8/1, He was a swamper in a saloon. **1922** *DN* 5.181 **NW,** *Swamper.* . . A janitor for a saloon, poolroom, etc. **1927** *DN* 5.465 [Underworld jargon], *Swamper.* . . A brothel roustabout. **1929** *Syracuse Herald* (NY) 13 Mar 5/1 **NYC,** From the position of swamper Anton had worked up to the ease and distinction of the position of head barkeep. **1937** *Ironwood Daily–Globe* (MI) 22 Jan

1/5, Marko Vance, operator of the North Star tavern . . , was free today after paying a $75 fine for receiving coal stolen by a . . swamper employed by him. **1965–66** *DARE* Tape **NM**13, He [=the cook on a roundup] might call his helper—swamper, they called it; **UT**1, Saloon bum . . worked in a saloon, probably. . . he was probably a swamper in a saloon. **1971** *Daily Progress* (Charlottesville VA) 29 May 14/8 **CA,** One victim was . . a skid-row figure . . who worked in Marysville as a "swamper," or janitor, when he needed money. **1981** *KS Qrly.* 13.2.70, *Swamper* . . ranch employee or helper performing menial chores. **1984** Wilder *You All Spoken Here* 135 **Sth,** *Swamper:* An old or spavined logger, so stove-up he can't work outside anymore and now swamps, or cleans, the bunkhouses. **1987** *DARE* File **Milwaukee WI,** *Swamper:* an employee in a bar who brings beer kegs, etc up from the basement.

5 A waterproof, usu all-rubber, boot. **chiefly nwMI** Note: This is not the safety-toe boot of the same name.

1921 *Indiana Progress* (PA) 23 Feb 8/2, Did you ever see a pair of *Hood* Red Swampers? They are great for snow-shoeing, hunting, for any outdoor work or play. All rubber uppers, lace snugly over heavy socks. **1950** *Ironwood Daily–Globe* (MI) 4 Oct 9/6, *Just Received! Another Shipment of* Boys'—Youths' and Men's *Swampers*—The wonderful boot with the rubber bottom and leather tops. **1966** *DARE* (Qu. W11, *Men's low, rough work shoes*) Inf **MI**33, Boots, swampers—if they come 2 or 3 inches above the anklebone. **1989** *DARE* File **nwMI,** *Swampers* were used commonly in the 1950s and 1960s to indicate boots used in the bush. They were laced, rubber boots, didn't leak, and were ideal for tramping around in the wet snow in the winter. Loggers and hunters ordinarily wore swampers, as did we children when playing. **2000** *Ibid* **nwMI,** [Restaurant pamphlet:] *Swampers:* Rubber boots worn by Yoopers [=residents of the Upper Peninsula] in the spring during the muddy season. Not a winter boot. **2004** *DARE* File—Internet **nwMI,** Dere's a new pastymatic and snowblower for mother / A steel [sic] chainsaw and some swampers for brother. **2005** *Ibid* **nwMI,** Swampers, Puddle Boots. . . These rubber boots have a distinct advantage . . when compared to molded PVC products.

6 See quot.

1999 *DARE* File—Internet **WI** [Central Florida Green Bay Packer Backers], *Swampers:* hip waders worn while fishing.

7 See quot. Cf *swamping ax* (at **swamp** v C1b)

1967 *DARE* (Qu. L35, *Hand tools used for cutting underbrush and digging out roots*) Inf **MI**56, Swampers.

8 =**varying hare.**

1949 *WELS Suppl.* **neWI,** A snowshoe hare is called a "swamper" because he likes marshes. **1961** Jackson *Mammals WI* 108, *Lepus americanus phaeonotus.* . . *Vernacular names.*—In Wisconsin commonly called snowshoe hare, snowshoe rabbit, or simply snowshoe. . . Other names include . . snow rabbit, swamp jack rabbit, swamper.

9 =**swamp rabbit 1.**

1968 *DARE* (Qu. P30, . . *Wild rabbits*) Inf **MO**34, Rabbits—in the southeast they have what they call the big swampers. **1989** *Sports Afield* Jan 78 **sTN,** When Turkey Newman says "rabbits," . . he means swampers—wetland bunnies that grow twice as big as their upland cousins. **1994** *Evansville Courier* (IN) 13 Feb (Internet), When the Tri-State had miles of cane breaks and low-profile dams, swampers were plentiful. . . Evansville hunter Keith Smith had never seen a swamper until a rabbit-hunting buddy urged him to tag along on a February hunt in Kentucky.

10 also *pineywoods swamper:* =**razorback hog.**

c1970 Pederson *Dial. Surv. Rural GA* **seGA** (*What do you call a long-legged hog that has a thin body and a long snout?*) 2 infs, Swamper; 1 inf, Pineywoods swamper.

11 as *swampuh:* See **swamp Yankee.**

swamp fan n

=**swamp cooler.**

1970 Rosenberg *Art Amer. Preacher* 12, If the congregation is prosperous the church will have a large swamp fan built into the wall, as noisy as an old Ford, which blows warm air around. **1997** *DARE* File—Internet **NV,** This means that U may have a month or two a year where you pay $30 extra to run the swamp fan. Swamp coolers are *not* energy hogs like air conditioning. **1999** Moseley *Grinning* 162 **TX,** I told my van load of passengers about the "swamp" fans that were still in operation when I was born. "You would go out every hour or so, depending on the heat, and water down the straw pads around the unit. The pump was supposed to circulate water, but it was just so hot that the water would evaporate before it could make it to the top of the straw." **2002** *Yale Lit.*

Mag. Spring 11, It was the moth that night in August . . / . . Upstairs, the swamp fan / and through the screen, crickets pulsed.   **2004** *DARE* File—Internet **TX,** The meeting room was to be cooled by an evaporative cooler (swamp fan), but it was making noises which would be disruptive.

swamp finch n

Usu the **song sparrow** (here: *Melospiza melodia*), but also **swamp sparrow 1.**

1801 Latham *Suppl. II Genl. Synopsis Birds* 206, Swamp F[inch]. *Fringilla iliaca* [=*Melospiza melodia*].   **1844** DeKay *Zool. NY* 2.165, *The Swamp Finch. Ammodramus palustris* [=*Melospiza melodia*]. . . This species . . occurs in swamps, wet meadows, and along the margins of rivers.   **1859** Goodrich *Illustr. Nat. Hist.* 169, The *Swamp-Finch* . . makes its nest on the ground; feeds on grass-seeds and aquatic insects.   **1897** Doubleday *Bird Neighbors* 160, Swamp Song Sparrow (*Melospiza georgiana*). . . Called also: swamp sparrow; marsh sparrow; red grass-bird; swamp finch.   **1957** *Hammond Times* (IN) 5 Apr sec C 5/2, Other names for the song sparrow are hedge sparrow . . and swamp finch.

swamp fire   See **fire B1**

swamp flag   n   Sth

An **iris B1** (here: *Iris virginica*).

1827 in 1910 TX State Hist. Assoc. *Qrly.* 13.70 **TX,** These hollow squares are thatched over with the swamp flag and stand ready to receive their inhabitants.   **1912** (1998) Ripley *Social Life New Orleans* 63 (Internet) **LA,** The old shellroad was a long drive, Bayou St. John on one side, swamps on the other, green with rushes and palmetto, clothed with gay flowers of the swamp flag.   **1969** *DARE* (Qu. S24, *A wild flower that grows in swamps and marshes and looks like a small blue iris*) Inf **KY21,** Swamp flags.   **2000** in 2005 *DARE* File—Internet, *Iris virginica. Common name:* Swamp Flag.

swamp flower   n   Cf **swamp sunflower**

Either a **sneezeweed 1** (here: *Helenium autumnale*) or a **sunflower 1** (here: *Helianthus angustifolius*); see quots.

1903 (1910) Miller *How to Make Garden* 349, Swamp-flower, *Helianthus angustifolius.*   **1967** *DARE* Wildfl QR Pl.249A [=*Helianthus angustifolius*] Inf **OH**37, Swamp flower.   **2000** in 2005 *DARE* File—Internet **FL,** *Things to do in July.* . . Cut back fall-blooming perennials such as chrysanthemums, *Salvia leucantha,* swamp flower, pineapple sage, and Mexican mint marigold.   **2005** (acc) KY Univ. *KY Garden Flowers* (Internet), *Helenium autumnale—Sneezeweed, Helen's Flower, False Sunflower, Swamp Flower* . . a reliable perennial for Kentucky gardens and a Kentucky native. It grows best in full sun with moist, well drained soil.

swamp fly   n

1   A biting fly: usu a **black fly** or **punkie 1,** but see quots.

1836 in 1912 Thornton *Amer. Gloss.* 1.165 **NEng,** The down east girls have a droll way of amusing themselves, viz., by *chewing spruce gum,* mingled as it frequently is with dirt, dead mosquitoes, and swamp flies.   **1853** *Harper's New Mth. Mag.* 7.771 **LA,** I was already speckled by the bites of a thousand swamp-flies and musquitoes, that all night long had preyed upon me.   **1898** *N. Adams Transcript* (MA) 4 Apr [2]/3 (newspaperarchive.com), He does not picture himself as left lying in the mud and filth . . , unable to protect himself from the millions of mosquitoes and swamp flies that madden him with their poisonous sting.   **1903** *Auk* 20.438 **GA,** I came to a swamp I had never visited before. . . Birds were singing and darting all around, and the 'swamp-flies' were making my life miserable.   **1917** Wharton *Summer* 7 **Sth,** He reddened, and leaned forward to flick a swamp-fly from the horse's neck.   **1928** *Ironwood Daily–Globe* (MI) 3 Aug 7/2, Holmstedt was near exhaustion and was suffering from the bites of swamp flies when discovered coming out on the state highway.   **1968** *DARE* Tape **WV**12, In Myrtle Beach last year they had some type of fly. . . It bit, stung. . . Swamp fly, I believe.   **1993** *NY Times* (NY) 5 Oct sec C 4/2 **NC,** Wearing coveralls to ward off the swamp flies, he steered the boat toward Durant Island.   **2003** *DARE* File—Internet **nMN,** No-see-ums were moderate on Sturgeon. Canoe Flies (swamp flies, house flies on steroids, whatever. . .) were awful from 10am to 7pm.

2   =**dragonfly.**

1849 in 1911 Lowell *Poet. Wks.* 99 **MA,** There is . . / No rush, the bending tilt of swamp-fly blue,/ But He therewith the ravening wolf can chase.   **c1955** Reed–Person *Ling. Atlas Pacific NW,* 1 inf, Swamp fly.   **1986** Pederson *LAGS Concordance,* 1 inf, **cAL,** Swamp flies = snake doctors.

swamp fly honeysuckle   n   Cf **fly honeysuckle**

A **honeysuckle 2** (here: *Lonicera oblongifolia*).

1848 Gray *Manual of Botany* 172, L[*onicera*] *oblongifolia.* . . Swamp Fly-Honeysuckle. . . Bogs, N. and W. New York to Wisconsin. . . Corolla . . yellowish-white.   **1929** *Amer. Midland Naturalist* 11.421, *Lonicera oblongifolia.* . . Swamp Fly Honeysuckle.   **1977** Torrey Bot. Club *Bulletin* 104.397 **PA,** Flowering dogwood . . was at its best, as were pinxter-flower . . , swamp fly honeysuckle (*Lonicera oblongifolia*), and trumpet honeysuckle.   **2004** ME Dept. Conserv. Nat. Areas Program *Rare Plant Fact Sheets,* Because of the specific habitat requirements of swamp fly-honeysuckle—open areas of cool cedar swamps underlain by limestone—it is not widespread, but populations may be plentiful where it does occur.

swamp fox   n

=**gray fox.**

1923 Biol. Soc. DC *Proc.* 36.123 **DC,** Gray Fox; Tree Fox; Swamp Fox. *Urocyon cinereoargenteus cinereoargenteus.*   **1982** Elman *Hunter's Field Guide* 352, Gray Fox. . . *Common & regional names* . . swamp fox.   **2002** *Gulfshore Life* Feb (Internet) **swFL,** Also called the swamp fox because of its ability to swim and climb trees, the gray fox (Urocyon cinereoargenteus) is curious, wary and sly.

swamp frog   n

1   Either the **pickerel frog** or a **bullfrog 1.**

1855 IL State Ag. Soc. *Trans. for 1853–54* 593, Rana clamata. Large Swamp Frog.   **1869** (1870) Tardy *Southland Writers* 2.890 **Sth,** Soon the chick-will-willow, whip-poor-will, and night-hawk raise their voices, . . and the harsh-throated swamp-frog sends a hoarse cry from the dingle below.   **1892** IN Dept. Geol. & Nat. Resources *Rept. for 1891* 475, *Rana palustris.* . . Swamp Frog.   **1893** *Science* 22.75 **Sth,** The size is about that of a small "leopard frog," *Rana pipilus,* or the "swamp frog," *Rana palustris,* to which last it is closely related.   **1917** *Wellsboro Agitator* (PA) 31 Jan 2/2, Freckled as a thin swamp frog,/ Who sits an' hollers on a log.   **1933** *Bee* (Danville VA) 31 Mar 5/5 **LA,** In this land where a swamp frog's croak is a lullaby[s] . . steam boats are romantic things.   **1957** *Science* 126.559, Even more dramatic changes in serum proteins occurred during the development of the swamp frog, *Rana hecksheri* [sic].   **1981** Pederson *LAGS Basic Materials,* 1 inf, **csTN,** Swamp frog. [*DARE* Ed: This inf may refer instead to **2** below.]

2   A **tree frog 1;** see quots.

1895 *Chicago Tribune* (IL) 15 Dec 41/2, A day all sunny on the steep,/ When lazy swamp-frogs rouse and peep.   **1940** FL Univ. *Biol. Sci. Ser.* 56, *Pseudacris feriarum* . . Baird's swamp-frog.   **1952** *Gaz. & Bulletin* (Williamsport PA) 4 Apr sec H 5/1, You see swamp frog or peepers are different from their cold water cousins, the bull-frog or bully-rumers.   **1956** *Hammond Times* (IN) 17 Oct sec B 2/4 **LA,** Last night I was watching a little rain frog . . whipping up mosquitoes with his long tongue. . . While that swamp frog (his front paws look like human hands with suction cups on his fingers) was entertaining me, along comes Harrison Payne.   **1966** Dakin *Dial. Vocab. Ohio R. Valley* 2.388, Kentucky has *sprat frog, swamp ~,* . . and *peeper toad* [for *spring peeper*].   **1967–70** *DARE* (Qu. P21, *Small frogs that sing or chirp loudly in spring*) Infs **KY**9, 34, **TN**56, Swamp frogs.   **1990** Adamus–Brandt *Impacts Wetlands U.S.* 92 **MN,** Spring peeper (Hyla crucifer) and swamp frog (Pseudacris nigrita) were found in the two zones most distant from the pond, spruce and fir-ash.

swamp gaboon   n   Cf **swamp ape,** DS CC17

An imaginary creature; see quots.

1913 *DN* 4.3 **ME,** *Swamp gaboon.* . . An imaginary animal by which the tracks of snow shoes are said to be made. "I see where a swamp gaboon crossed the tote road last night, boys."   **1955** *Time* 28 Nov 77, The leading lady of the great tradition is expected to resemble the gyascutus, prock, tree squeak and swamp gaboon rolled into one.   **2000** *Village Voice* (NY NY) 25 Jan (Internet), As it turns out, the girl is not a girl at all, but "a prodigious monster, a true swamp gahoon [sic]" with horned feet and strange protuberances.

swamp gallberry   n

A **gallberry** (here: *Ilex coriacea*).

1926 (1949) McQueen–Mizell *Hist. Okefenokee* 144 **seGA,** Swamp Gallberry.   **1932** *Ecological Monogr.* 2.2.138 **Okefenokee GA,** *Ilex lucida* . . "Sweet Gallberry," "Swamp gallberry."   **1968** *DARE* (Qu. T5, . . *Kinds of evergreens, other than pine*) Inf **GA**35, Swamp gullberry [sic]—a kind of holly.

swamp gentian n

1 A **gentian** (here: *Gentiana douglasiana*) native to Washington and Alaska.

1952 Williams *AK Wildfl. Glimpses* 35, In August and September the muskegs from Kenai Peninsula to Southeastern Alaska are starred with the small white blossoms of the *swamp gentian.* **1973** Hitchcock–Cronquist *Flora Pacific NW* 360, Swamp g[entian] . . *G[entiana] douglasiana.* **1987** Hughes–Blackwell *Wildflowers SE AK* 65, Swamp gentian *(Gentiana douglasiana).* . . 2–10″ tall; flowers are pleated like a skirt. **2002** in 2005 *DARE* File—Internet **WA,** Makah Coppers are known to feed upon *Swamp Gentian,* whose bloom peaks with the butterfly's flight period.

2 A **gentian** (here: *Gentiana sceptrum*) native to the Pacific Northwest and California.

2005 *DARE* File—Internet, *Gentiana sceptrum.* . . "King Gentian" or "Swamp Gentian". . . The large flowers. . . are a cobalt blue color with a tubular shape. . . Native from British Columbia down to California.

3 =**soapwort gentian. Cf marsh gentian**

2005 (acc) TX A&M Univ. *TX Vascular Plant Checklist* (Internet), *Gentiana.* . . *saponaria* var. *saponaria* (bottle gentian, swamp gentian, soapwort gentian).

swamp gooseberry n

A **gooseberry 1** (here: *Ribes lacustre*).

1824 Bigelow *Florula Bostoniensis* 91, *Ribes lacustre.* . . *Swamp Gooseberry.* . . In the *Notch* of the White mountains, by the side of the *Saco river.* **1843** Torrey *Flora NY* 1.247, *Ribes lacustre.* . . *Swamp Gooseberry.* . . Fruit dark purple, and ill-flavored. Mountain swamps. **a1862** (1864) Thoreau *ME Woods* 223, I also saw the swamp gooseberry *(Ribes lacustre),* with green fruit. **1895** Gray–Bailey *Field Botany* 169, *R[ibes] lacustre.* . . Lake or Swamp G[ooseberry]. Cold bogs and wet woods. . . Small bristly berries of unpleasant flavor. **1925** Jepson *Manual Plants CA* 470, *Swamp Gooseberry.* . . Cold wet mountain meadows. **1972** Viereck–Little *AK Trees* 150, Swamp gooseberry is an occasional shrub with white spruce and Sitka spruce in the interior and coastal forests. . . Because of . . the skunklike odor, the bristly berries are infrequently used for making jellies and jams. **2004** *Seattle Post–Intelligencer* (WA) 31 Mar sec B 3 (Internet), Volunteers can help at the county's Lake Stevens-area nursery many Fridays throughout the year to nurture swamp gooseberries, . . and other native species.

swamp grape n **Sth**

1 Usu either a **muscadine grape** (here: *Vitis rotundifolia*) or a **fox grape 1**; rarely **summer grape**; see quots.

[**1867** MA State Bd. Ag. *Annual Rept. for 1866* 14.149, I commenced planting the seeds of the wild grape, . . the Labrusca it is called. . . They are quite good for a swamp grape.] **1909** Munson *Foundations Amer. Grape* 25 **TN,** *Vitis labrusca.* . . "Swamp Grape," in Tennessee. **1922** Hedrick *Cyclop. Hardy Fruits* 230, *Vitis aestivalis.* . . Summer Grape, . . Duck-shot grape, Swamp Grape, Pigeon Grape. . . The berries are destitute of pulp, have a comparatively thin, tough skin and a peculiar spicy flavor. **1960** Vines *Trees SW* 722, *Vitis* . . *labrusca.* . . Also known under the names of Northern Fox Grape, . . Swamp Grape, and Wild Vine. **1982** *Boston Globe* (MA) 20 May 1 (Internet), Muscadine is rarely seen in the north. It's a southern grape, the "swamp grape," thick-skinned and meaty like the Concord. **1996** *Times–Picayune* (New Orleans LA) 7 Sept sec B 3 (Internet), The swamp grape, muscadine, may have its day. **2002** *Advocate* (Baton Rouge LA) 15 Aug sec F 1 (Internet), In Texas, muscadines are also called mustang grapes or swamp grapes. **2004** in 2005 *DARE* File—Internet **nGA,** The taste of the Muscadine grape (also known as a bullace or swamp grape), brings back childhood memories to those who grew up in the South.

2 =**false grape 2.**

1920 *Torreya* 20.23 **LA,** *Ampelopsis cordata.* . . Raccoon, or swamp grape.

swamp grass n **scattered, but chiefly Nth, Midl** See Map Cf **marsh grass, meadow ~, swamp hay, thatch grass**

Any of var coarse grasses such as **cordgrass** or **reed 1,** or a coarse plant of the family Cyperaceae such as a **sedge B1** that grows in wetlands, but esp those grasses used for hay or forage.

1821 Willich *Domestic Encycl.* 194, Swamp grass, *cynosuroides.* **1842** Thompson *Hist. VT* 1.69, These [nests] are usually constructed in a thicket of alders, or other bushes, . . and are made of the leaves of flags, swamp-grass, &c. **1849** (1863) Allen *Amer. Farm Book* 103, *American*

or *Swamp Cock's-Foot* (*D[actylis] cynosuroides* [=*Spartina c.*]) is an indigenous swamp grass, yielding a large amount of grass or hay of inferior quality. **1870** *Edwardsville Intelligencer* (IL) [6 Oct 3]/5 (newspaperarchive.com), The *Ohio Farmer* says: . . "[A]ll the sedges which constitute most of what is called swamp grass, require little drying, and will be months in the cocks without decaying." **1901** *Torreya* 1.115 **GA,** *Sporobolus Indicus.* . . Swamp-grass. **1908** Forbes–Richardson *Fishes of IL* xxix, The intervening swamps are fringed with bands of thick-growing swamp grass on a miry, mucky soil. **1943** *Sun* (Baltimore MD) 14 Sept 16/7 *(Hench Coll.),* It is true the cat-o'-nine-tails is a whip but it is also the swamp grass you are talking about. **1944** AL Geol. Surv. *Bulletin* 53.68, *S[porobolus] Poiretii* [=*S. indicus*]. . . I have heard it called "swamp grass," which is not a very appropriate name. **1945** MI Ag. Exper. Sta. *Technical Bulletin* 201.29, *Cyperacea.* . . Superficially the members of this family resemble the true grasses and by many are known as "swamp grasses." **1950** *WELS (Hay that grows naturally in damp places)* 5 Infs, **WI,** Swamp grass. **1960** *Amer. Midland Naturalist* 63.409 **MO,** The plant most commonly eaten by swamp rabbits was *Carex lupulina,* locally called swamp grass. **1965–70** *DARE* (Qu. L8, *Hay that grows naturally in damp places*) 134 Infs, **scattered, but chiefly Nth, Midl,** Swamp grass; **CT6,** Swamp grass—called salt grass along the seashore; **ME5,** Fresh grass—any wild grass like swamp grass, bluejoint, [as opposed to] salt grass; **MA74,** Bluejoint—ordinary swamp grass; (Qu. S9, . . *Kinds of grass that are hard to get rid of*) Infs **KY21, 28, 40, MA6, PA68, WA30,** Swamp grass; **MI34,** Swamp grass—grows about 14 inches tall with a prickly leaf like a turnip, will snag a silk stocking; (Qu. S24) Inf **PA216,** Swamp grass; (Qu. S26b, *Wildflowers that grow in water or wet places*) Infs **KY68, 74, VA40,** Swamp grass. **1968** *DARE* FW Addit **VA,** Swamp grass—narrow-leafed, smooth stem, triangular if cut across; 1–1½ feet tall, grows in marshy or damp places. **1985** *Daily Intelligencer* (Doylestown PA) 30 May sec A 20/1 **NJ,** *City plants swamp grass at sludge beds.* . . A species of swamp grass will help the city solve its sludge disposal problems. . . Phragmites, a tall reedy plant native to seashore areas, are being planted in the sewer department's sludge drying beds. **2004** *DARE* File—Internet **cwCT,** In bright sun the phragmites (swamp grass—reeds) nod in unison with the wind.

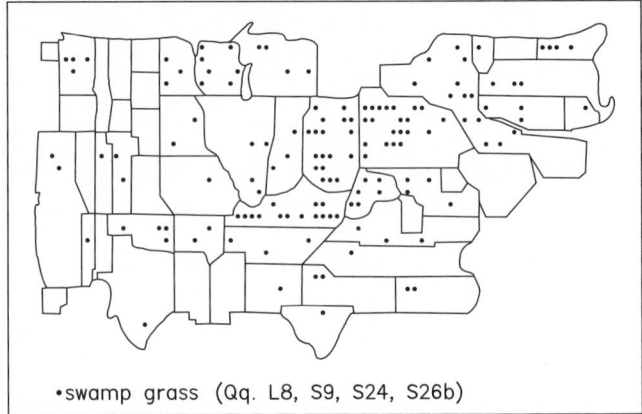

•swamp grass (Qq. L8, S9, S24, S26b)

swamp guinea n **Cf marsh guinea**
=**wood duck 1.**

1953 *AmSp* 28.277 **SC,** Swamp guinea—Wood duck.

swamp gum n

Any of several **tupelos:** a **black gum 1** (here: *Nyssa sylvatica*), a **swamp tupelo** (here: *N. biflora*), or a **tupelo gum** (here: *N. aquatica*).

1802 (1803) Ellicott *Jrl.* 288, In the middle states it is generally found on the common swamp gum, (nyssa integrifolia [=*N. sylvatica*]). **1829** *N. Amer. Rev.* 28.86 **Sth,** The cypress. . . begins to be seen on the wet lands, near the mouth of the Ohio, and is, with the swamp gum, the most common tree in the deep swamps from that point to the gulf of Mexico. **1834** Baird *View Valley Missip.* 265 **MS,** The cypress and swamp gum, are large in the swampy lands. **1891** *Indiana Progress* (PA) 18 Nov 3/7, The swamp gum which grows in Delaware is a very valuable wood. When boiled it can be handled like paper and it is used extensively in the manufacture of boxes. **1935** *Helena Independent* (MT) 17 Mar 3/5 **DE,** He could not burn that wood the Emergency Relief administration dumped in his front yard. It was swamp gum, tough as rubber under the ax and it exuded more moisture than a water-soaked grapefruit rind.

1940 Clute *Amer. Plant Names* 265, *Nyssa aquatica*. White-, swamp-, pawpaw-, yellow-, ladle-, sap-gum. **1958** *Ecology* 39.34 **VA,** Swamp gum (*Nyssa sylvatica* var. *biflora*) prefers the wetter site as a seedling, but does much better as a sub-dominant tree on the drier site. **2003** *Daytona Beach News–Jrl.* (FL) 1 May sec A 1 (Internet), Fyock has made hundreds of songbirds, shorebirds, game birds and birds of prey out of tupelo wood—a light, swamp tree that grows from Savannah, Ga., to Baton Rouge, La. It is also known as swamp gum. **2005** *DARE* File—Internet **FL,** Water tupelo (*Nyssa aquatica*), and black or swamp gum (*N. sylvatica*) are also commonly found growing in swamps.

swamp hare n

1 =**swamp rabbit 1.**

1839 Acad. Nat. Sci. Philadelphia *Jrl.* 8.1.78, *Lepus aquaticus* [= *Sylvilagus a.*] . . Swamp Hare. **1854** Wailes *Rept. on Ag. & Geol. MS* 311, Lepus aquaticus. Swamp hare. *Ibid* 317, The Swamp Hare is much larger and more shy [than the Gray Rabbit]. **1873** *Atlantic Mth.* 31.675 **Sth,** A species much resembling this one is the swamp-hare, also occurring in the Southern States, and which, when hunted, takes to the water. **1920** Burgess *Burgess Animal Book* 18 **Sth,** "Yesterday," said she, "I told you about your water-loving cousin, the Marsh Rabbit. You have another relative down there in the Sunny South who is almost as fond of the water. Some folks call him the Swamp Rabbit. Others call him the Swamp Hare. The latter is really the best name for him, because he is a true Hare." **2005** *DARE* File—Internet, The swamp rabbit goes by many descriptive nicknames. Throughout his range, he is called "canecutter," because of his fondness for young cane shoots. In other areas he's known as cane jake, swamp hare, water rabbit or, simply, swamper.

2 =**varying hare.**

1897 *Field* (London) 6 Feb 167/3 **NEng,** The swamp, or northern hare, is a big strong animal, nearly allied to our jack-rabbit of the prairies. He is usually found in what are locally termed swamps, tracks of cedar, on rough, low ground—not wet, however, as the name would imply. **1938** *Hammond Times* (IN) 9 Jan 14/2 **WI,** I . . set out to see if I could get a rabbit, or rather, hare, for the animals were the large swamp hares.

swamp haw n　Also *swamp-haw viburnum*　**SE**

A **viburnum,** usu *Viburnum nudum* or *V. n.* var *cassinoides.*

1837 (1962) Williams *Territory FL* 90, Swamp Haw. V[iburnum] nudum. **1933** Small *Manual SE Flora* 1272, *V[iburnum] nudum.* . . *Swamp-haw.* . . Swamps and low grounds. **1960** Vines *Trees SW* 960, *Viburnum nudum.* . . Vernacular names in use are Withe-rod . . and Swamp-haw Viburnum. **1999** Dahl *South Carolina's Wetlands* 23, Swamp haw (*Viburnum cassinoides* [=*V. nudum* var c.]). **2002** Gresham *Dark Magic* 17 **eAL,** Her heart floated on the primeval landscape of purple bladderwort and climbing heath and swamp haw and mistletoe festooned high in the cypresses. **2005** (acc) U.S. Natl. Arboretum *Kick the Invasive Habit* (Internet), Swamp haw viburnum, *Viburnum nudum.* . . swamp haw, *Viburnum dentatum.*

swamp hawk n

Either the **marsh hawk 1** or the **red-shouldered hawk;** see quots.

1892 Harris *Uncle Remus & Friends* 5 **GA** [Black], Dey er done broke in ter ketchin' chickens—de goshawk, de swamphawk en de bluedarter. **1908** *Fitchburg Daily Sentinel* (MA) 19 Nov 6/2, A.E. Davidson shot a swamp hawk, Monday, measuring over three feet from tip to tip. **1940** Todd *Birds W. PA* 707, Hawk, Swamp, *see* Hawk, Marsh. **1966–69** *DARE* (Qu. Q4, . . *Kinds of hawks*) Inf **GA6,** Swamp hawk; **ME6,** Heath hawk—a swamp hawk; **NJ52,** Swamp hawk—this is the marsh harrier; **NY191,** Swamp hawk. **1999** in 2005 *DARE* File—Internet **NJ,** Red-shouldered Hawk—(*Buteo lineatus*). . . This hawk is found primarily in Northern NJ . . preferring wooded swamps. . . Feeding heavily on frogs[,] crayfish and snakes, this raptor, formerly known as the Swamp Hawk, hunts in wetlands such as those associated with the Russia Brook.

swamp-haw viburnum　See **swamp haw**

swamp hay n　Cf **marsh hay, meadow ~, prairie ~, salt ~, slough grass 1, swale ~, wild hay**

Hay made from **swamp grass.**

1808 in 2005 *DARE* File—Internet **NJ,** 11 [Aug]. On Thurs I split fifty cosway poles & stackd the swamp hay. **1850** (1968) Taylor *Eldorado* 2.52, As the man's hair happened to be glowing in color and coarse in texture, the mistake of the donkey in taking it to be swamp hay, is not so much to be wondered at. **1872** *Paxton Weekly Rec.* (IL) 24 Oct 4/2, In winter give a pile of leaves, swamp-hay or straw. **1898** IN Dept. Geol.

& Nat. Resources *Rept. for 1897* 67, Many of the prairies . . were wet prairies, and for years yielded only swamp hay and pasture. **1917** *Wellsboro Agitator* (PA) 14 Feb 2/5, Do not for a moment deceive yourself with the belief that a heifer or dry cow may get through on swamp hay or poor pasture and do well. **1950** *WELS* **WI** (*Hay that grows naturally in damp places*) 5 Infs, Swamp hay; 1 Inf, Swamp. **1965–70** *DARE* (Qu. L8, *Hay that grows naturally in damp places*) 79 Infs, **scattered, but less freq Sth, West,** Swamp hay; **MO3,** Swamp. **1991** MN Univ. Ext. Serv. *Beef Cattle Management Update* 3, Not all cows are worth $1,000 and swamp hay shouldn't be priced as if it were alfalfa. **2004** *DARE* File—Internet **TN,** That is more than I need for my cows, but no one will buy swamp hay.

swamp hellebore n

=**Indian poke 1.**

1751 in 1934 Eliot *Field Husbandry* 3.70, *Take the Roots of Swamp Hellebore,* sometimes called *Skunk Cabbage, Tickle Weed, Bear Root. This Root is known by these several Names in different Places.* **1814** Bigelow *Florula Bostoniensis* 246 **MA,** *Veratrum viride.* . . *Poke root. Swamp Hellebore.* . . A large, green, leafy plant, not unfrequent in meadows and swamps. **1840** MA Zool. & Bot. Surv. *Herb. Plants & Quadrupeds* 205, *V[eratrum] viride.* Indian Poke. Itch-weed. Swamp Hellebore. . . A poisonous plant; emetic. **1898** U.S. Dept. Ag. Div. Botany *Bulletin* 20.16, *Veratrum viride.* . . Swamp hellebore . . Grows abundantly in wet meadows and along mountain brooks throughout New England; southward in cold localities through New York and Delaware to Virginia, and in the Alleghany Mountains to Georgia; westward in northern Wisconsin, the mountains of Oregon, Washington, and Idaho, and in Alaska. **1968** *DARE* FW Addit **VA15,** Swamp hellebore = hellebore, *Veratrum viride.* Common, wet places. **2005** *DARE* File—Internet **NY,** *Veratrum viride* (swamp hellebore).

swamp hen n　Cf **water hen 1c**

=**coot** n[1] **1.**

1924 *Amer. Midland Naturalist* 9.73 **IA,** *Fulica americana.* . . Mudhen, Waterhen, Swamp Hen, Black Mudhen. **1927** *Frederick Post* (MD) 27 Sept 8/2, A seldom-seen bird was brought to the office of the News–Post Saturday. . . The bird was identified as a swamp hen, and is said to be fairly common around the fish ponds near Buckeystown. It was about a foot long from tip of bill to tail, of dark, almost black color on the back and light underneath, and had green webbed feet. . . It was said to be very elusive, and was an unusual diver and fighter.

swamp hickory n

Any of var **hickories B1,** usu of moist environments, as:

a　A **pignut 1** (here: *Carya glabra*).

1775 (1962) Romans *Nat. Hist. FL* 28, *Juglans alba aquatica, cortice glabro, arbor humilis; fructu amaro.* White swamp hickory, with a smooth bark being a dwarf tree and a bitter fruit. [*DARE* Ed: Romans may have mistaken the similar scrub hickory, *Carya floridana,* for *C. glabra*]. **1824** Elliott *Sketch* 2.627 **GA, SC,** [*Juglans*] *Porcina.* . . It is found along the margins of swamps, or on the flat knowls with which our swamps are frequently broken, and is commonly known as the Swamp or Pignut Hickory. **1896** *Bucks Co. Gaz.* (Bristol PA) 23 Jan 3/3 **FL,** The swamp hickory, with its peculiar foliage and small but rich, sweet nut, upon which the far famed razor back hog, alike with the beautiful gray squirrel, feasts in profound silence, but doubtless with voracious appetite. **1938** Matschat *Suwannee R.* 161 **neFL, seGA,** They alus stuck togither tightern the bark on a swamp hickory afore saprunnin' time. **1960** Vines *Trees SW* 131, *Carya aquatica.* . . Vernacular names are Bitter Pecan, Swamp Hickory, and Water Pignut. *Ibid* 133, *Carya cordiformis.* . . Vernacular names are Swamp Hickory, . . Pignut Hickory. *Ibid* 135, Swamp Hickory. *Carya leiodermis* [=*C. glabra*]. **1979** Little *Checklist U.S. Trees* 72, *Carya aquatica.* . . Swamp hickory. *Ibid, Carya cordiformis.* . . Swamp hickory. *Ibid, Carya glabra.* . . Swamp hickory. *Ibid* 74, *Carya myristiciformis.* . . Swamp hickory.

b　=**bitternut 1.**

1810 Michaux *Histoire des Arbres* 1.177, *Juglans amara.* . . Cette espèce est généralement connu dans l'État de New-Jersey, sous le nom de *Bitter nut* . . ; tandis que dans la Pensylvanie, et notamment dans le Comté de Lancaster, elle est désignée par celui de *White Hickery* . . et quelquefois encore de *Swamp Hickery.* . . Mais plus au sud elle est confondue avec le *Juglans porcina.* [=*Juglans amara* [=*Carya cordiformis*]. This species is generally known in the State of New Jersey, as *Bitter nut* . . ; while in Pennsylvania, and especially in Lancaster County, it is called *White Hickery* . . and sometimes *Swamp Hickery.* . . But further south it is confused with *Juglans porcina* [=*C. glabra*].] **1884**

Sargent *Forests of N. Amer.* 134, *Carya amara* [=*C. cordiformis*]. . . Swamp Hickory. . . *Carya aquatica*. . . Swamp Hickory. **1960** *Appleton Post-Crescent* (WI) 4 May [editorial page]/7 (newspaperarchive.com) **csWI**, The "Old Bob LaFollette" memorial tree in state capitol park, a swamp hickory, is withering in spite of the best efforts of the statehouse grounds crew. **1960** [see **a** above]. **1979** [see **a** above].

c =**water hickory.**

1817 Darby *Geogr. Descr. LA* 354, *Juglans aquatica*. . . Swamp hickory. **1884** [see **b** above]. **1960** [see **a** above]. **1979** [see **a** above]. **1986** Pederson *LAGS Concordance (Common trees)* 1 inf, **ceAL**, Swamp hickory nut.

d =**nutmeg hickory.**

1881 *Bot. Gaz.* 6.273, *Carya myristicaeformis* . . was observed in great abundance in South-Eastern Arkansas, . . growing with *Carya aquatica* in low situations. The nut of this species is about the size of a pecan, and is edible. It is called swamp hickory by the natives. **1979** [see **a** above]. **1990** Burns *Silvics N. Amer.* 2.215 **Sth**, Nutmeg hickory *(Carya myristiciformis)*, also called swamp hickory or bitter water hickory, is found as small, possibly relict populations across the South . . on rich moist soils of higher bottom lands and stream banks.

swamp hog n **S Atl, Gulf States**
A swamp-dwelling **razorback hog.**

1890 *Indiana Gaz.* (PA) [19 Nov 9/3] (newspaperarchive.com) **MS**, Hamilton S. Beal. . . lives in the Mississippi river bottoms, and having, at an early age, acquired a strong appetite for a sort of pudding made of the giblets of the swamp hog, decided to practice medicine. **1915** *New Smyrna News* (FL) [30 Apr 13]/6 (newspaperarchive.com), Hearing the brush rustle, bruin started to investigate, probably thinking a fat swamp hog was waiting to be dined upon. **1986** Pederson *LAGS Concordance (Wild hog)* 1 inf, **csGA**, Swamp hogs—dangerous; 1 inf, **cLA**, Swamp hogs; 1 inf, **seMS**, Swamp hog. **1997** *Evansville Courier* (IN) 12 Oct sec B 10 (Internet) **SC**, When the waters cover the islands and feeding areas [in the swamp], swamp hogs and deer move across them. **2000** *Bowhunter* 29.84 (Internet) **GA**, And as we hummed by seemingly endless marsh flats and island after island draped in Spanish moss and alive with all sorts of animal life, it was easy to imagine a return trip to hunt wily, wonderful swamp hogs. **2001** *DARE* File—Internet **TN**, I think a boar from Tennessee Mountains that feeds in corn or bean fields would taste better than a swamp hog living off of grubs, roots, and snakes. **2004** *Post-Std.* (Syracuse NY) 6 June sec D 15/6 **Sth**, [Caption:] *Uncle Larry*—Pictured with World Record Cracker Swamp Hog.

swamp holly n

1 A **holly** n[1] **1:** usu **possum haw 2** or a **winterberry 1** (here: *Ilex verticillata*), but also *Ilex amelanchier* or a **yaupon** (here: *Ilex cassine*).

1888 *Amer. Garden* 9.208, The scarlet berries of the Swamp Holly *(Ilex verticillata)* . . are due to come up this spring. **1900** Lyons *Plant Names* 199, *I[lex] decidua*. . . Southeastern U.S. Swamp or Meadow Holly. **1918** Porter *Daughter* 330 **IN**, She . . made a trip up the ravine, where she gathered all the bittersweet berries, swamp holly, and wild rose seed heads she could find. **1938** Matschat *Suwannee R.* 118 **neFL, seGA**, But Manthy and many of the other older women . . preferred a pungent drink brewed from the leaves of yaupon, the swamp holly. **1959** *Sheboygan Press* (WI) 27 May 42/8, There are interesting lowland plants like monseed [sic] vines and swamp holly. **1973** Wharton–Barbour *Trees KY* 281, *Ilex decidua*. . *Swamp holly, possum-haw*. Tall shrub or small tree up to 25 feet in height, with light gray bark. **1976** Bailey–Bailey *Hortus Third* 589, *[Ilex] Amelanchier*. . . *Sarvis h[olly], swamp h[olly]*. . . Hills of coastal plain, se. Va. to Ga. **1994** *Star Tribune* (Minneapolis MN) 5 Dec 4 (Internet), Ilex Verticillata, or winterberry. . . can be found growing wild in swamps from Newfoundland to Minnesota and southward from Georgia to Missouri. Winterberry is also known as swamp holly and as black alder (because the leaves turn black after the first frost). **2002** U.S. Fish & Wildlife Serv. *Bon Secour Trail Guide* [9] **AL**, Dahoon/Swamp Holly *(Ilex cassine)*—Small trees with dull green leaves. **2004** *WI Nat. Resources* Aug 22 **nWI**, When mixed in with swamp holly *(Ilex verticillata)*, it makes a beautiful holiday decoration. The holly bush is four to five feet tall and you won't miss its plentiful bright red berries, it is one of two native hollies in Wisconsin.

2 A **mountain holly 2** (here: *Nemopanthus mucronatus*).

2005 (acc) MN Univ. *Plants Cedar Creek* (Internet) **MN**, *Nemopanthus mucronatus* (Swamp Holly) is a hard-to-find shrub in mixed tamarack-hardwood swamps. Although other locations are more typical, a few can be found in the tamarack-black spruce swamp at Beckman Lake.

swamp honeysuckle n

1 Any of several **rhododendrons**, but esp a **swamp azalea** (here: *Rhododendron viscosum*) or a **pinkster 2** (here: *R. periclymenoides*).

1818 Nuttall *Genera N. Amer. Plants* 134, Azalea. . . (Swamp Honeysuckle.) **1822** Eaton *Botany* 200, *[Azalea] nitida* [=*Rhododendron viscosum*] (swamp honeysuckle . .). **1859** (1968) Bartlett *Americanisms* 200, *Honeysuckle*, or *Swamp Honeysuckle*. A name improperly but commonly applied to the *Azalea viscosa* [=*Rhododendron v.*] and *nudiflora* [=*R. periclymenoides*]. **1894** *Jrl. Amer. Folkl.* 7.93 **MA**, *Rhododendron viscosum*, . . swamp honeysuckle. **1936** Whitehouse *TX Flowers* 92, Thickets of the pink azalea or swamp-honeysuckle *(Azalea nudiflora)* occur in a few places in East Texas. **1966** *DARE* Wildfl QR Pl.154 [=*Rhododendron periclymenoides*] Infs **OH**14, **SC**41, Swamp honeysuckle. **1970** *DARE* (Qu. S26b, *Wildflowers that grow in water or wet places*) Inf **MA**100, Swamp pink, swamp honeysuckle = swamp azalea. **1976** *Daily Times* (Salisbury MD) 12 May 20/3, Swamp honeysuckle and fringetree were in bloom near Snow Hill. **1979** Bowden *Always Rivers Flow* 180 **nwFL** (as of 1930s–40s), The quaint jutting formations share the banks with dark water-choked caverns shaded by the woodland armies . . —tall sweetbays, . . titi, swamp honeysuckle, dense tangles of yaupon and snaking choking vine.

2 A **honeysuckle 2**; see quots. Cf **swamp fly honeysuckle**

1864 NY Univ. *Seventeenth Annual Rept. Condition Cabinet Nat. Hist.* 17.87, *[Lonicera] oblongifolia*. . . Swamp-honeysuckle. **1903** *Rhodora* 5.158 **NEng**, Later these bogs will repeat this show of colors in other fine displays: white in . . the Swamp Honeysuckle, *Lonicera oblongifolia* [etc]. **1934** *Ecology* 15.162 **Adirondacks NY**, Several sturdy bushes of swamp honeysuckle, *Lonicera oblongifolia* . . , grow on slightly elevated spots. **1935** Crater L. Nat. Hist. Assoc. *Nature Notes* Sept (Internet) **OR**, Swamp Honeysuckle *(L[onicera] utahensis)* grows only in wet or boggy places. **1958** Petrides *Trees & Shrubs* 47, *Swamp honeysuckle—Lonicera oblongifolia*. . . A more or less *hairless* honeysuckle. **1961** Douglas *My Wilderness* 17 **CO**, Swamp or bearberry honeysuckle is a coarse shrub with yellow flowers.

swamp hook n **chiefly Nth, esp MI, WI** Cf **swamp** v **C1**
In logging: a large hook with a sharp end, usu attached to a long chain and used in skidding logs.

1874 U.S. Bur. Indian Affairs *Rept. for 1873* 178 **WI**, The blacksmith reports that he has . . made . . 10 cant-hooks, 8 swamp-hooks. **1877** *Lumberman's Gaz.* 22 Dec 418 **MI**, Swamp hooks, pevys, skidding tongs, always on hand. **1885** *Oshkosh Daily Northwestern* (WI) 7 Jan [3]/5 (newspaperarchive.com), A man . . was recently caught in the fleshy part of the arm with a swamp hook and quite severely gashed. **1902** White *Blazed Trail* 13 **MI**, Thus the stick of timber rested in a long loop, one end of which led to the invisible horse, and the other Jim made fast to the top of the pile. He did so by jamming into another log the steel swamp-hook with which the chain was armed. **1905** U.S. Forest Serv. *Bulletin* 61.50 [Logging terms], *Swamp hook*. A large, single hook on the end of a chain, used in handling logs, most commonly in skidding. (Gen[eral]). **1920** *DN* 5.84 **NW**, *Swamp hook*. Large hook used in rolling logs. Horses are hitched to it. Logging. **1958** McCulloch *Woods Words* 185 **Pacific NW**, *Swamp hook*—A large all-purpose open hook on the end of a line or chain, used in animal skidding or on a chunk-out operation. **1964** Clarkson *Tumult* 373 **WV**, *Swamp hook*—a large all-purpose open hook on the end of a line or chain, used in skidding with horses. **1967** *DARE* (Qu. L35, *Hand tools used for cutting underbrush and digging out roots*) Inf **MI**47, Swamp hook—not a hand tool; used in connection with horses. **1984** *MJLF* 10.158 **cnWI**, *Swamp hook*. Hook on the end of a chain, used to load logs or pull them out of mud and snow.

swamp hornbeam See **hornbeam 2**

swamp hound n Cf *DS* HH1
=**swamper 1.**

1945 Thorp *Pardner* 213 **SW**, Ike . . told the boys about it, and warned them whenever they were on guard, to be sure to pack their six-shooters, as you never could tell what mischief those swamp hounds might be up to. **2003** in 2005 *DARE* File—Internet **FL**, Can I say "good'aye" if I'm not Australian? Oh well, cut an old Florida swamp hound some slack. **2005** *Ibid*, I personally loath having my photo taken. I'm not a swamp hound either so it doesn't have anything to do with looks.

swamp huckleberry n Cf **upland huckleberry**

1a A **blueberry 1**: usu *Vaccinium corymbosum* of the eastern and southern regions of the US, occas also *V. fuscatum* or another **blueberry 1** of the same regions; see quots.

1800 (1826) Maude *Niagara* 8 **NY**, The swamp huckleberry, a tall shrub like the alder, an excellent fruit just beginning to ripen. **1837** Darlington *Flora Cestrica* 257 **sePA**, *Corymbose Vaccinium. Vulgò*—Swamp, or Tall Huckleberry. . . Shaded swamps and rivulets; frequent. . . This is often a stout shrub. **a1862** (2000) Thoreau *Wild Fruits* 39 **NEng**, There is a variety growing in swamps, . . commonly three or four feet high, but often seven feet; the berries . . are round and glossy black, with resinous dots as usual, and grow in flattish-topped racemes, sometimes ten or twelve together, though generally more scattered. I call it the swamp huckleberry. **1912** Lincoln *Rise Roscoe* 196 **Cape Cod MA**, A moment more and the tall swamp-huckleberry bushes at the edge of the sandy beach parted and between them stepped gingerly a clean-cut, handsome brown horse. **1926** (1949) McQueen–Mizell *Hist. Okefenokee* 125 **seGA**, Then there is the small blue swamp huckleberry, which grows around the edges of the Swamp or in shrubby places. This berry is about the size of a low mold shot. **1968** *DARE* Tape Inf **NJ**51, You see, there's a swamp huckleberry, that's wild, and then there's an upland huckleberry that's wild—they grow on lower bushes. **2005** *DARE* File—Internet, The latest in the market are the fruits of the High Bush Blueberry [=*Vaccinium corymbosum*] of the northeast states and the High Bush Huckleberry [=*Gaylussacia baccata*], both of them widely known as "Swamp Huckleberry," from their preference for moist woodlands and swampy ground. *Ibid,* *Vaccinium atrococcum*—downy swamp huckleberry; black huckleberry; black highbush blueberry.

b Another **blueberry 1** (here: *Vaccinium uliginosum*).

1931 U.S. Dept. Ag. *Misc. Pub.* 101.134, *Western bog blueberry* (*V[accinium] occidentale* [=*V. uliginosum*]), known also as . . swamp huckleberry, is a smooth compact bush . . ranging from Montana to southeastern British Columbia, California and Utah. **1939** *Amer. Midland Naturalist* 22.258 **OR**, At Boundary Spring the boggy opening is covered with this willow [=*Salix pseudocordata*], associated with swamp huckleberry.

2 A **huckleberry 1**, usu *Gaylussacia dumosa* or *G. baccata*.

1853 NY State Museum *Catalogue Cabinet Nat. Hist.* 26, *Gaylussacia hirtella* [=*G. dumosa*], Dwarf Swamp Huckleberry. **2002** in 2005 *DARE* File—Internet **seNJ**, *Gaylussacia dumosa* (swamp huckleberry). **2005** [see **1a** above].

swamp hyacinth n

A **swamp pink 3** (here: *Helonias bullata*).

1948 Wherry *Wild Flower Guide* 10, Swamp-hyacinth. . . Sepals and petals dull pink, and stamens lavender-blue. **1967–68** *DARE* (Qu. S26b, *Wildflowers that grow in water or wet places*) Inf **PA**99, Swamp hyacinth—grows in New Jersey; (Qu. S26e, *Other wildflowers not yet mentioned;* not asked in early QRs) Inf **TN**22, Swamp hyacinth. **1976** Bruce *How to Grow Wildflowers* 172, The most beautiful of all bunch-flowers . . is *Helonias bullata*, the Swamp-pink or Swamp-hyacinth, a rare inhabitant of sphagnum bogs and shady swamps from Staten Island to Virginia and (upland) to Georgia. **1983** Torrey Bot. Club *Bulletin* 110.384 **PA**, Among the latter [=flowers still in bloom] were . . swamp Hyacinth (*Helonias bullata*), . . and several species of violets. **2005** *DARE* File—Internet, Swamp-hyacinth (*Helonias bullata*).

swamping See **swamp C1a, b**

swamping out See **swamp C1a, b, 2**

swamp iris n Also *swamp Irish* **widespread exc West**

Any of var native **irises B1**, but also occas the introduced *Iris pseudacorus*.

1917 *Gaz. & Bulletin* (Williamsport PA) 24 May 9/1, The smaller sorts—Spanish iris and that dwarf swamp iris that is native in our own south . . need smaller dishes. **1932** *Helena Independent* (MT) 23 July 6/3, I also saw a swamp iris in bloom a few days ago. **1949** *WELS Suppl.* **WI**, Swamp iris = Blue Flag. **1950** *WELS* (*Wild flower that looks like a small blue iris, found in swamps and marshes*) 2 Infs, **WI**, Swamp iris. **1965–70** *DARE* (Qu. S24, *A wild flower that grows in swamps and marshes and looks like a small blue iris*) 35 Infs, **widespread exc Cent, SW, Rocky Mts, Pacific**, Swamp iris; **NY**200, Swamp Irish; (Qu. S26b, *Wildflowers that grow in water or wet places*) Inf **KY**85, Swamp iris. **1966** *DARE* Wildfl QR Pl.26 [=*Iris versicolor*] Infs **AR**44, **WA**30, Swamp iris. **1995** *News* (Frederick MD) 3 Aug sec

B 7/5, Throughout . . their garden, the Avants strive to use native plants such as . . swamp iris. **2005** *DARE* File—Internet **Okefenokee GA**, *Swamp Iris*. The southern blue-flag, *Iris virginica*, is a beautiful purple-blue flower found in the swamp. *Ibid* **AL**, Southern swamp iris or Louisiana iris—Tall iris native to wetlands in the Southeast, including hybrids in many colors and forms. *Ibid* **AR**, *Iris versicolor*—Swamp iris. . . When you'd like some knife-like foliage for . . that boggy spot, consider this eastern native. *Ibid* **UT**, In the early 1990s, we added a group of Yellow Flags (I. pseudacorus, also known as Yellow Water Iris or Swamp Iris).

swamp ironwood See **ironwood b(1)**

swamp jackrabbit See **swamp rabbit 3**

swamp juniper n Cf **juniper 2b**

A **white cedar 1** (here: *Chamaecyparis thyoides*).

[**1889** *Century Dict.* 3254, *Juniper*. . . The name is locally applied to other trees, the so-called juniper swamps of the southern United States consisting of the white cedar, *Chamaecyparis thyoides*.] **1906** *Arboriculture* 5.115, In Southern Alabama and Western Florida we find the swamp juniper in considerable quantities, which is being cut for telegraph poles. **1960** Vines *Trees SW* 9, *Chamaecyparis thyoides*. . . Other vernacular names are . . Southern White Cedar, Swamp Cedar, Swamp Juniper. **2002** *SC Market Bulletin* 3 Oct 6/4, *Atlantic white cedar,* (Swamp Juniper), 1 gal. containers, $5ea. **2005** *DARE* File—Internet, We call it "Swamp Juniper" around the South. It grows in the wetlands of North Carolina and South Georgia and . . boat grade white cedar is hard to find.

swamp laurel n

1 =**sweet bay 2.** **chiefly SE**

1739 (1946) Gronovius *Flora Virginica* 61, Magnolia Lauri folio. . . *Swamp-Laurel.* **a1782** (1788) Jefferson *Notes VA* 38, Swamp laurel. Magnolia glauca [=*Magnolia virginiana*]. **1810** Michaux *Histoire des Arbres* 1.27, M[agnolia] glauca. . . *Sweet bay, White bay* et *swamp's laurel,* noms plus en usage dans la partie maritime des Etats méridionaux. [=M[agnolia] glauca. . . *Sweet bay, White bay* and *swamp's laurel,* names more in use in the maritime portion of the southern States.] **1869** Porcher *Resources* 36 **Sth**, Swamp Laurel, (*Magnolia glauca,* L.) Diffused in damp pine lands. **1939** Torrey Bot. Club *Bulletin* 66.480, *Magnolia virginiana* L. The sweet bay or swamp laurel occurs from Massachusetts and Long Island southward in the coastal plain to Texas. **1979** Little *Checklist U.S. Trees* 167, *Magnolia virginiana*. . . Swamp-bay, southern sweetbay, . . swamp-laurel.

2 A **mountain laurel 1**, usu *Kalmia polifolia* or *K. microphylla*.

1822 Eaton *Botany* 325 **MA**, [*Kalmia*] *glauca* [=*K. polifolia*] . . swamp laurel. . . Plainfield and Hinsdale, Mass. **1843** Torrey *Flora NY* 1.441, *Kalmia glauca.* . . *Swamp Laurel.* . . Sphagnous swamps; from Hudson and Catskill northward; also in the Western part of the State. **1869** Fuller *Uncle John* 138 **NEng**, The farmers around here call it [=*Kalmia polifolia*] 'Swamp-Laurel.' **1906** Rydberg *Flora CO* 260, *American or Swamp Laurel.* . . *Kalmia microphylla.* . . In mountain swamps from Alb[erta] and Alaska to Colo. and Calif. **1921** *Ecology* 2.37 **WA**, Among the erect shrubs may be mentioned . . the swamp laurel (*Kalmia polifolia* [here: =*K. microphylla*]). **1958** Torrey Bot. Club *Bulletin* 85.489, On June 19th the group drove into Vermont and up along the Canadian Border to Island Pond. Here a northern spruce bog was visited, with the usual northern bog vegetation of Leather-leaf, Creeping Snowberry, Swamp Laurel, and Labrador Tea. **1966** *DARE* Wildfl QR Pl.156A [=*Kalmia latifolia*] Inf **WI**80, Swamp laurel; Pl.156B [=*K. polifolia*] Inf **MI**7, Swamp laurel. **1970** *DARE* (Qu. S26b, *Wildflowers that grow in water or wet places*) Inf **PA**245, Swamp laurel. **1992** *Seattle Times* (WA) 9 July sec H 4 (Internet), *West Hylebos Wetlands State Park:* A 70-acre headwater swamp, featuring . . red huckleberry, . . black twinberry, straggly gooseberry, wild roses, swamp violet, swamp laurel, cascara and Pacific dogwood. **2005** *DARE* File—Internet **CO**, *Swamp Laurel.* . . *Kalmia microphylla.* . . It generally likes cold moist places.

3 =**loblolly bay 1.**

1830 Rafinesque *Med. Flora* 2.225, *Gordonia lasianthus.* . . *Swamp Laurel.* Beautiful tree, reaching 100 feet, wood coarse but beautiful. . . Beautiful fragrant blossoms lasting nearly the whole year. **1876** Hobbs *Bot. Hdbk.* 54, Swamp laurel, Gordonia lasianthus.

swamp laurel oak See **laurel oak 2**

swamp leatherwood   See **leatherwood 3**

swamp lily n

Any of several **lilies 1** or plants somewhat resembling a **lily 1**, as:

a   =**lizard's tail 1.**

   1804 Barton *Elements Botany* 268, Saururus (called, in the United States, Swamp lily).   **1821** Elliott *Sketch* 1.432 **SC, GA,** *Saururus.* . . Grows in bogs and ponds; very common. Flowers May–July. *Swamp Lilly.* The fresh root is bruised and applied cold in form of a poultice to inflamed surfaces as an emollient and discutient.   **1837** (1962) Williams *Territory FL* 92, Swamp Lilly. Saururus cernuus—galls.   **1873** Jones *Antiquities S. Indians* 34 **GA,** The emollient and discutient power of the swamp-lily *(Saururus cernuus)* . . [was] communicated to the Europeans by the Indians.   **1913** *Torreya* 13.229 **AR,** *Saururus cernuus.* . . Swamp lily.   **1965** *DARE* (Qu. BB34b, *What is a poultice made with?;* total Infs questioned, 75) Inf **MS**29, Swamp-lily root.

b   Usu a **Turk's-cap 1** (here: *Lilium superbum*), but occas also the similar Carolina **lily 1** *(L. michauxii)* or the **leopard lily 1.**

   1854 Stephens *Fashion & Famine* 95 **NEast,** Near-by was a cloverfield ruddy with blossoms, and broken with clumps and ridges of golden butter-cups and swamp lilies.   **1879** Wallace *Notes Lilies* 167, *[Lilium] Carolinianum* or *Michauxii* is a form allied to *Superbum,* but really larger. It is called the Carolina Swamp Lily.   **1898** *Daily Rev.* (Decatur IL) 4 Feb 4/3 **neMN,** The yellow-red swamp lilies that fringed the marshy ground to the north margin of the [railroad] track seemed to literally burn in the scorching rays of the afternoon sun.   **1928** *Helena Independent* (MT) 7 Oct 15/1, Our native swamp lily, L[ilium] superbum, grows well in some gardens.   **1932** *Sun* (Baltimore MD) 11 Aug 8/9, The swamp lilies leap with a flame and flare.   **1938** McFarland *Garden Bulbs* 116, *Lilium carolinianum.* . . is [a] fine small American Lily, also called the "Southern Swamp Lily." *Ibid* 148, *Lilium superbum.* . . [is] also called the American Turk's-cap and the Swamp Lily.   **2003** in 2005 *DARE* File—Internet, Lilium pardalinum—American Swamp Lily. **2004** *Seattle Times* (WA) 18 Aug sec E 8 (Internet), Native swamp lilies, L[ilium] superbum, face downward from their 8-to-10-foot-tall stalks.

c   A **water lily 1.**   Cf **spatterdock, water chinquapin**

   1857 *Knickerbocker* 49.213 **NJ,** It was a swamp, with green slime, and the swamp-lily moving sluggishly above it.   **1966** *DARE* (Qu. S22, . . *The bright yellow flowers that bloom in clusters in marshes in early springtime)* Inf **NC**21, Swamp lily. [*DARE* Ed: This Inf may refer instead to another sense.]   **2004** in 2005 *DARE* File—Internet **LA,** [Caption of photo of *Nymphaea mexicana:*] Yellow Swamp Lily.

d   A **zephyr lily,** usu **atamasco lily 1.**

   1889 *Century Dict.* 7033, *Zephyranthes.* . . They are known in general as *swamp-lily.*   **1938** McFarland *Garden Bulbs* 292, One of the most satisfactory species for the rock-garden is Zephyranthes Atamasco, the Atamasco- or Swamp-Lily.   **1988** *S. Living* 23.78, The fall flowers of *white swamp lily (Zephyranthes candida)* will remind you of the more familiar atamasco lilies of spring.   **2005** *DARE* File—Internet, [Nursery catalog:] Atamasco Lily. . . Also called Easter Lily or Swamp Lily.

e   =**skunk cabbage 1.**

   1898 *Century Illustr. Mag.* 55.472 **VA,** In the moist places the yellow swamp-lily raised and spread aloft its tiny stars from the cold leaves, mottled like the sides of a swamp-snake.   **1908** *Science* 27.506, *Spathyoema foetida* [=*Symplocarpus foetidus*]. . . The name "skunk-cabbage" does much more to keep it unpopular than anything else. . . They have been seen on sale at the Washington (D.C.) market as "swamp lilies." **1949** Peattie *Cascades* 225, The scientists call it Lysichitum americanum [=*Lysichiton a.*], a few people call it swamp lily, but to everyone else it is skunk cabbage and our noses say this is right.   **2005** *DARE* File—Internet **VA,** Swamp "Lily". . . It has an unpleasant name and an unpleasant odor if disturbed, but skunk cabbage is a handsome rosette of green in the early spring near creeks and wetlands here.

f   also *blue swamp lily:* An **iris B1** such as *Iris virginica.*

   1892 *World* (NY NY) 15 May [9]/3 (newspaperarchive.com), There was a small head-dress . . with yellow narcissus and blue swamp lilies growing out of it.   **1951** *PADS* 15.29 **TX,** *Iris* spp. . . Blue swamp-lilies. **1965–70** *DARE* (Qu. S24, *A wild flower that grows in swamps and marshes and looks like a small blue iris)* 31 Infs, **scattered, but esp SE, sAppalachians,** Swamp lily; (Qu. S3, *A flower like a large violet with a yellow center and small ragged leaves—it comes up early in spring on open, stony hilltops)* Inf **NY**97, Swamp lilies or iris—real name.

g   A liliaceous plant of the genus *Crinum,* esp *C. ameri-*

canum, native chiefly to the Southeast and Gulf States.   For other names of *C. americanum* see **Saint John's lily, spider ~ 3**

   [**1814** Roxburgh *Hortus Bengalensis* 23, *Crinum* . . americanum. Swamp lily. N.S. Wales.]   **1900** Bailey *Cyclop. Horticult.* 1.399 **FL,** The Swamp Lily of Florida—Crinum Americanum.   **1916** Torrey Bot. Club *Bulletin* 43.600, *Crinum americanum.* Florida swamp lily.   **1938** Baker *FL Wild Flowers* 43, *St. John's Lily. Swamp Lily.* . . This beautiful wild crinum blooms chiefly in spring and summer, but flowers are found even in midwinter in the southern part of the state.   **1970** *Auk* 87.492 **FL,** Various plant species . . at 45 nest site were: maidencane . . , white water lily . . , swamp lily *(Crinum americanum)* [etc].   **1996** *Times–Picayune* (New Orleans LA) 21 June sec E 1 (Internet), Crinum americanum, Louisiana's swamp lily, has fragrant white flowers and blooms May–November.   **2004** *Houston Chron.* (TX) 24 July 4 (Internet), Most wildflowers require excellent drainage. . . In this low area, plant crinums (especially the Texas swamp lily) and hymenocallis (giant white spider lilies).

swamp lobelia n

A **lobelia B1,** usu *Lobelia paludosa.*

   1848 Gray *Manual of Botany* 255, L[obelia] paludosa. . . *Swamp Lobelia.* . . Peat-bogs, Delaware . . and southward.   **1901** Lounsberry *S. Wild Flowers* 486, *L[obelia] padulòsa* [sic], swamp lobelia, thrives in the waters of swamps and ponds.   **1953** Greene–Blomquist *Flowers South* 125, *Swamp-Lobelia (Lobelia glandulosa)*—This tall . . species with its deep blue or lavender corolla with a white center stands out conspicuously in . . extensive, wet marshlands of our lower Coastal Plain. . . It ranges from Fla. to Va.   **1995** in 2005 *DARE* File—Internet, Swamp lobelia—Lobelia boykinii.   **2001** *Helen Nash's Pond & Garden* 2.28, *Lobelia paludosa,* swamp lobelia. This wet-soil lover produces . . pale blue flowers in racemes up to 12 inches long.

swamp locust n

=**water locust.**

   1810 Michaux *Histoire des Arbres* 1.34, [Gleditsia] monosperma. . . *Swamp locust* . . dans la partie maritime des Etats méridionaux. [= *Swamp locust* . . in the coastal parts of the southern states.]   **1855** *De Bow's Rev.* 19.411 **IL,** The following list comprehends the forest trees and undergrowth most usually seen: Cotton wood, sycamore, . . honey locust, swamp locust, papaw [etc].   **1901** Lounsberry *S. Wild Flowers* 261, Swamp Locust. . . *Gléditsia aquática.*   **1929** Stemen–Myers *Spring Flora OK* 68, *Gleditsia aquatica.* . . Water or Swamp Locust. A tree, the thorns usually simple. . . In swamps.   **1951** *PADS* 15.34 **TX,** *Gleditsia aquatica.* . . Black-thorn, swamp, or water locust.   **1969** *DARE* (Qu. T15, . . *Kinds of swamp trees)* Inf **TN**33, Swamp locust.   **2005** (acc) TX A&M Univ. *Aggie Horticult.* (Internet), *Water Locust, Swamp Locust*— *Gleditsia aquatica.* . . Grows mainly in east Texas along rivers and swamps or in standing water of lagoons and sloughs.

swamp loosestrife n

1 Std: a tall plant *(Decodon verticillatus)* with arching stems and willow-like leaves native chiefly to the eastern US.   Also called **peatweed, redroot i, redwood 1, slinkweed b, swamp willow 3, ~ willow herb, water willow 2, willow herb 2**

2 A **loosestrife 1:** either *Lysimachia terrestris* or *L. thyrsiflora.*   Cf **swamp candle 1**

   1950 Gray–Fernald *Manual of Botany* 1141, L[ysimachia] terrestris. . . *Yellow* or *Swamp-L[oosestrife], Swamp-candles.* . . Low grounds and wet shores.   **1952** *Amer. Midland Naturalist* 48.763 **neIL,** Lysimachia thyrsiflora—swamp loosestrife.   **1968** Radford et al. *Manual Flora Carolinas* 822, L[ysimachia] terrestris. . . Swamp Loosestrife, Swamp Candles.   **2004** in 2005 *DARE* File—Internet **NY,** *Lysimachia thrysiflora* [sic] L.—swamp loosestrife.

swamp magnolia n

Usu **sweet bay 2,** but also **southern magnolia** or occas another **magnolia 1** (here: *Magnolia ashei*); see quots.

   1755 *Gentleman's Mag.* 25.82, North American *Seeds of Trees, Shrubs, &c. lately imported.* . . Swamp magnolia [etc].   **1813** Muhlenberg *Catalogus Plantarum* 53, *Magnolia.* . . glauca [=*M. virginiana*]. . . swamp.   **1853** Meehan *Amer. Hdbk. Ornamental Trees* 153, *M[agnolia] glauca.* . . Small or swamp magnolia; white bay. Native of the Middle and Southern States. This tree is naturally a native of swampy places. **1872** Schele de Vere *Americanisms* 422, The *Sweet Bay* is the familiar name of a much humbler relative (Magnolia glauca), and not to be compared to the *Swamp Magnolia* (Magnolia grandiflora). **1897** Sudworth *Arborescent Flora* 195, *Magnolia glauca.* . . Swamp Magnolia (N.J., Pa., Tenn.) **1930** *Denton Jrl.* (MD) 21 June 5/7, The southern magnolia / Is proud as she can be,/ She won't even notice / The swamp magnolia tree! **1967–68** *DARE* (Qu. T15, . . *Kinds of swamp trees*) Infs **NJ**21, **TN**11, Swamp magnolia. **2005** *DARE* File—Internet **seMS,** *Magnolia ashei:* (Which I called the "Cowcumber Tree" when I was growing up) Also called the "Swamp Magnolia" or bigleaf magnolia.

swamp mallow n

A **hibiscus** (here: *Hibiscus moscheutos*).

1858 NC State Geologist *Rept. NC Geol. Surv.* 14, Hibiscus. . . Moscheutos. . . (Swamp Mallow.)—Throughout the State. **1901** Lounsberry *S. Wild Flowers* 336, *H. Moscheùtos,* rose mallow, or swamp mallow. **1937** *Ironwood Daily–Globe* (MI) 31 July 4/5, Many colored lillies, swamp mallow, fragrant elderberries, . . and the last of the brown-eyed Susans all challenge you to produce a greater array of beauty or color. **1967** *DARE* Wildfl QR Pl.129 Inf **AR**45, Swamp mallow. **1968** *DARE* (Qu. S26b, *Wildflowers that grow in water or wet places*) Inf **GA**46, Swamp mallow—mostly red, bloom is like okra bloom. **c1979** TX Dept. Highways *Flowers* 39, Native to tropical areas along the Gulf Coast, the Swamp Mallow also inhabits low ground in East Texas. **2004** *Vineyard Gaz.* (Edgartown MA) (Internet), The mallow of which I speak is the swamp mallow (Hibiscus palustris or moscheutos). Also called rose or seaside mallow, this is the large, pink flower that is now blooming in fresh and brackish marshes across the Island.

swamp maple n

1 A **red maple** (here: *Acer rubrum*). **chiefly NEast**

1810 Michaux *Histoire des Arbres* 1.31, Acer rubrum . . *Red flowring* [sic] *maple* . . , *Swamp maple* . . , *Soft maple* . . Dénominations en usage dans tous les États atlantiques. [=Acer rubrum . . *Red flowering maple* . . , *Swamp maple* . . , *Soft maple* . . names in use in all the Atlantic states.] **1869** Stowe *Oldtown Folks* 153 **NEng,** Here and there, a swamp-maple seemed all one crimson flame. **1889** *Overland Mth.* (2d ser) 13.73 **Sth,** Swamp maple gave a clear purple, and poke-berries a bright but not durable solferino. **1897** [see **4** below]. **1899** *Atlantic Mth.* 83.240 **ME,** Here and there at the edge of a dark tract of pointed firs stood a row of bright swamp maples like scarlet flowers. **1941** *LANE* Map 247, Terms denoting other varieties of maples. . . *swamp maple* [9 infs, 7 **wCT**]. **1965–70** *DARE* (Qu. T14, . . *Kinds of maples*) 53 Infs, 43 **NEast,** Swamp maple; **CT**13, Swamp maple—soft maple; **CT**30, Swamp maple—red, soft; **IL**26, Swamp maple or soft; **KY**16, Soft or swamp maple; **MA**100, Soft/red/swamp [maple]—native; **NJ**1, Swamp maple—also bird's eye when dressed; **NY**122, Soft maple = swamp maple; **OH**6, Swamp maple—actually hard maple; (Qu. T15, . . *Kinds of swamp trees*) 33 Infs, 28 **NEast,** Swamp maple; **CT**13, Soft maple = swamp maple; **MA**42, Swamp maple = soft maple. [*DARE* Ed: Some of these Infs may refer instead to other senses below.] **2005** *Sun* (Baltimore MD) 25 Mar sec B 2 (Internet), You know spring is nearby. . . by the swamp maples' red budding even as ice skims the creek.

2 =**box elder.**

1850 Hines *Voyage Round World* 97 **OR,** We arrived at the place on the Wallamette [sic] river where we designed to cross, our trail. . . exceedingly difficult . . as it led us through a dense forest of cottonwood and swamp maple. **1891** *Century Dict.* 6099, *Swamp-maple.* . . The red maple . . ; also, *Acer Californicum* [=*A. negundo* var *californicum*], of the Coast Range in California.

3 =**mountain maple.**

[**1829** Haliburton *Hist. & Statist. Acct. Nova-Scotia* 2.405, *[Acer] Montanum* [=*A. spicatum*]—Swamp Maple.] **1896** *Jrl. Amer. Folkl.* 9.185 **ME,** Acer spicatum . . , swamp maple. **1911** *Century Dict. Suppl., Swamp-maple.* . . 2. The silver maple.—3. The mountain-maple. **1968** *DARE* (Qu. T15, . . *Kinds of swamp trees*) Inf **MD**32, Swamp maple—more like a bush. [*DARE* Ed: This Inf may refer instead to other senses.]

4 =**silver maple.**

1897 Sudworth *Arborescent Flora* 287, *Acer saccharinum.* . . Swamp Maple (W. Va., Md.) *Ibid* 290, *Acer rubrum.* . . Swamp Maple (Vt., N.H., Mass., Conn., R.I., N.Y., N.J., Pa., Del., N.C., S.C., Fla., Ala., Miss., La., Tx., Mo., Ind., Ont., Minn.) **1927** *Ironwood Daily–Globe* (MI) 7 May 7/3, The silver maple, also called the soft maple, white maple and swamp maple, is probably more used for street planting . . than any other tree, though it is one of the least desirable. **1950** *Portland Press Herald* (ME) 30 Sept 8/3, We had in our neighborhood a tree

known as the swamp maple, which always grew in low, swampy land and was not esteemed for anything in particular. Anybody who had to cut swamp maple for firewood spoke sort of apologetically of such an undertaking. **1968** *DARE* (Qu. T14, . . *Kinds of maples*) Inf **WV**4, Swamp maple = water maple—grow quickly and well, used for shade tree. [*DARE* Ed: This Inf may refer instead to other senses above.] **1968** *DARE* Tape **CT**3, Swamp maples will run sap just as sugar maples do, but there's no sweetness to it. **1979** Little *Checklist U.S. Trees* 42, *Acer saccharinum.* . . Swamp maple, water maple, white maple.

swamp marigold n

1 =**marsh marigold. esp NEast**

1902 Chambers *Maid* 183 **NY,** Enormous bunches of peonies perfumed the house, and everywhere masses of yellow and white elderbloom and swamp-marigold brightened the corners. **1969** *DARE* (Qu. S22, . . *The bright yellow flowers that bloom in clusters in marshes in early springtime*) Inf **MA**18, Swamp marigold—good for greens; **NY**227, Cowslip, swamp marigold—eat them for greens with [sic] spring. **1995** *Hartford Courant* (CT) 12 June sec B 3 (Internet), There is an area where students can stroll on a recycled wooden walkway through a swamp and see emergent plants such as skunk cabbage and swamp marigold. **2005** (acc) WA State Univ. Ext. *Gardening W. WA* (Internet), For flowers, herbaceous perennials that grow well in wet soils are astilbe, swamp marigold *(Caltha),* some ferns [etc].

2 A **beggar ticks 1:** usu either *Bidens aristosa* or *B. coronata.* **esp IL**

1901 Mohr *Plant Life AL* 808, *Bidens discoidea.* . . Low Swamp Marigold. **1936** IL Nat. Hist. Surv. *Wildflowers* 372, *Tickseed Sunflower. Swamp Marigold—Bidens tricosperma* [=*B. coronata*]. . . *Bidens coronata* . . and . . *Bidens aristosa* . . are considerably alike. **1952** *Amer. Midland Naturalist* 48.760 **neIL,** Bidens coronata—swamp marigold. **2000** *Omaha World–Herald* (NE) 9 Apr sec B 6 (Internet), It is now possible to find cardinal flowers, Indian grass, Canadian wild rye, little blue stem, great blue lobelias, green dragon, and swamp marigolds—the plants that gave this landscape the mystical quality early explorers remembered long after farmers turning it under with their plows. **2004** *DARE* File—Internet **IL,** *Bidens coronata* . . Tall Swamp Marigold. . . Marshy areas. Disturbed or burned bogs.

3 A **spatterdock;** see quot.

1966 *DARE* Wildfl QR Pl.56 [=*Nuphar lutea* subsp *advena*] Inf **NY**16, Swamp marigold.

4 A naturalized **buttercup 1** (here: *Ranunculus ficaria*).

1999 *Herald* (Rock Hill SC) 23 Feb sec C 1, And the golden dots way over yonder? Yep, lesser celandine (or swamp marigold, as some call it) is starting to bud.

swamp measles n pl *joc*

Splotches of dirt or mud on one's skin.

1978 Massey *Bittersweet Country* 207 **Ozarks,** Swamp measles (dirty): The boys always seemed to have a case of swamp measles.

swamp milkweed n

A **milkweed 1:** usu *Asclepias incarnata;* occas another sp such as *A. perennis;* see quots. For other names of the former see **Indian hemp 3, silkweed, swamp silkweed**

1832 MA Hist. Soc. *Coll.* 2d ser 9.147 **cwVT,** [Asclepias] incarnata,—Swamp milk-weed. **1837** (1962) Williams *Territory FL* 92, Swamp Milkweed. Asclepias parviflora [=*Asclepias perennis*] . . scarlet flower. **1882** *Century Illustr. Mag.* 24.153, The only species of our milkweed *(Asclepias)* that we would recommend for the wild garden are the swamp milkweed *(A. incarnata),* the four-leaved milkweed *(A. quadrifolia),* and the butterfly weed *(A. tuberosa).* **1925** *Decatur Daily Rev.* (IL) 25 Aug 6/4, Swamp milkweed . . adds its delicate color. . . It is listed as a dull light crimson but it blends with almost any thing. **1939** Torrey Bot. Club *Bulletin* 66.605, An interesting case of this [= plant characteristics being overlooked] is the southern swamp milkweed, *Asclepias perennis.* **1966** *DARE* Wildfl QR Plates 172, 173, 174, 175 [=*Asclepias incarnata, A. amplexicaulis, A. quadrifolia, A. syriaca*] Inf **WA**15, Swamp milkweed. **2005** *South Bend Tribune* (IN) 5 Feb 1 (Internet), Swamp milkweed attracts a wide variety of butterflies to your rain garden.

swamp moccasin n Cf highland moccasin

=**cottonmouth.**

1844 *Boston Med. & Surgical Jrl.* 29.42 **LA,** Of all the species of snake that exist among us, none are more formidable than the swamp moccasin. **1861** *S. Lit. Messenger* 32.305 **AL,** She only shrunk again, and shivered, as if the slimy body of the swamp moccasin had touched her. **1861** *Harper's New Mth. Mag.* 23.394 **GA,** Now and then we could see a monster swamp-moccasin, nearly as large as a man's thigh, creeping away at our approach. **1914** Todd *Hiram Young Farmer* 163 **Sth,** Now, a rattlesnake is poisonous, but he gives fair warning; a swamp moccasin lies in wait for the unwary and strikes without sign or sound. **1926** *Crisis* (NY NY) 33.68 **Gulf States,** Ferocious viper snake of the morasses, the swamp moccasin. **1945** *Traverse City Rec.–Eagle* (MI) 23 July 7/6 **FL,** Rev. George Hensley . . ran into trouble with the law in Florida in 1938 when one of his worshippers died from a swamp moccasin's bite.

swamp mosquito n   chiefly Atlantic

A **mosquito** n[1] **B1,** esp *Aedes vexans* or *Culiseta melanura.*

1863 *Harper's New Mth. Mag.* 27.858 **Sth,** It would take a man gifted with considerable imagination to exaggerate the prowess of these Southern swamp mosquitoes. **1900** *NE State Jrl.* (Lincoln) 19 May 4/3, The germ is introduced into the human system through the proboscis of the swamp mosquito, technically known as Anopholes [sic] claviger [= *Anopheles quadrimaculatus*]. **1904** *NY State Museum & Sci. Serv. Bulletin* 79.289, *Culex sylvestris.* . . Swamp mosquito. **1932** *Sun* (Baltimore MD) 23 Aug 4/7 *(Hench Coll.),* The swamp mosquito is only occasionally present in sufficient numbers to cause annoyance. **1938** Rawlings *Yearling* 258 **nFL,** You shore 'twasn't one o' them swamp skeeters you seed after Doc Wilson's liquor? **1964** *Science* 143.361 **MA,** *Swamp Mosquito, Culiseta melanura.* . . The reported restriction of *Culiseta melanura* . . to fresh-water swamps is significant because of the apparent potential of this mosquito as a vector of eastern equine encephalitis. **1968–70** *DARE* (Qu. R15b, . . *An extra-big mosquito*) Infs **IN**35, **NJ**67, Swamp mosquito(es). **2005** *DARE* File—Internet **NJ,** Other important species in Ocean County include *Aedes vexans*—the Swamp Mosquito; *Culex pipiens*—the House Mosquito and *Culex salinarius*—the Unbanded Saltmarsh Mosquito.

swamp moss n

1 A **moss** 1 of the genus *Sphagnum.*   [*OED2* 1785 →] **chiefly Nth**   Cf **seed moss**

1825 Thacher *Amer. Orchardist* 35, In order to preserve them in good condition for grafting . . the whole scion may be enveloped in swamp moss. **1858** Redfield *Zoöl. Sci.* 150, *M[astodon] giganteus* . . was found . . in Burton Co., Missouri, imbedded in a brown sandy deposit, full of the remains of cypress, tropical cane, swamp moss, stems of palmetto, &c. **1871** *Galaxy* 12.426 **ME,** Poynter and Doane packed and sent home some of their trout in boxes . . lined with long, swamp moss. **1903** Long *Little Brother* 165 **CT,** Every soft spot in the earth, every moldering log and patch of swamp moss and muddy place beside the brook, had deep footprints and claw marks. **1929** *Ironwood Daily-Globe* (MI) 27 Dec 4/3, I started to pull the contraption apart and found another row of logs inside and in between the two swamp moss and sheep's wool was packed in. **1947** Grout–Howe *Mosses & Liverworts* 29, Peat is the deposit of dead swamp moss and other bog plants. **1968** *DARE* Tape **NJ**53, I pulled this moss . . this sphagnum moss, this swamp moss. I pulled that and pulled it by the carload and sold it to New York City. **1975** Gould *ME Lingo* 184, In the woods, swamp or sphagnum moss was used to chink log buildings. **2005** *DARE* File—Internet **nWI** (as of c1970), Us boys would have already have [sic] made the snow cave and got out the tarps and dried swamp moss (insulation for the floor).

2 =**Spanish moss.**   **Gulf States**

1843 (1969) Lewis *Odd Leaves* 197 **LA,** The swamp moss was flowing around him [=an owl] in long, tangled masses. **1865** Duganne *Camps & Prisons* 71 **LA,** The bayou is lonesome as before. Its leaden drapery of swamp moss; its wilderness of motionless leaves; its unbroken shadows and unrippled waters; all are lapsed into the lethargy of noon. **1950** Capote *Local Color* 37 **Gulf States,** Tinsel, twinkling in twenty-four-karat sunshine, hangs everywhere like swamp moss. **1994** *St. Petersburg Times* (FL) 7 Mar 1 (Internet), Both had swamp moss draped around various limbs of their body, though he wore considerably more. **2005** *DARE* File—Internet **LA,** See the beautiful trees with swamp moss hanging everywhere.

swamp myrtle n

A **wax myrtle** (here: *Morella cerifera*).

1862 in 2005 *DARE* File—Internet [*Savannah Republican* (GA) 4 Nov 1/3], Myrtle Wax is obtained by boiling the berries of the swamp myrtle, on which it is to be seen as a greenish white cover. **1863** Porcher *Resources* 346 **Sth,** Swamp Myrtle (*Myrica cerifera* [=*Morella c.*]). **1875** Abbott *Leah Mordecai* 188 **Sth,** Uncle Jack, as he walked along, had

broken a green bough from a swamp-myrtle, and gathered a spray of blue winter berries, which he bound together as a nosegay for the child. **1890** *Scribner's Mag.* 7.306 **sFL,** The level monotony of surface is broken here and there by islands bearing dense growths of cypress, bay, . . swamp myrtle, and other heat-and-moisture-loving trees. **1942** TX Ag. Exper. Sta. College Sta. *Bulletin* 609.65, *Myrica cerifera.* Wax Myrtle, Swamp Myrtle. A small bush . . native to the swampy lands along the eastern Gulf Coast and East Texas. **1968** *Daily Times–News* (Burlington NC) 5 Oct sec A 9/3 **MS,** The lush undergrowth of the bayou country, swamp myrtle and palmettos and yaupon, grew close.

swamp needle n

A **darning needle** 1.

1984 Cannon *Popular Beliefs* UT 52 (as of 1950), Devil's darning needles will sew your mouth shut . . ; Swamp needles . . ; Dragonflies, if you get near them.

swamp oak n

1 Any of various unidentified **oaks.**

1681 in 1904 New Castle DE Court *Records* 503, 40 perches to a corner marked swamp oake. **1683** Penn *Letter to Free Soc. Traders* 4, Oak of divers sorts, as *Red, White* and *Black; Spanish Chestnut* and *Swamp,* the most durable of all. **1736** MA Genl. Court *Jrl. House* 55, Plat . . beginning at a Swamp Oak and heap of Stones at the mouth of *Pleasant Brook.* **1766** (1942) Bartram *Diary of a Journey* 40 **eFL,** The east banks being sandy 8 or 10 foot perpendicular, full of live and swamp-oaks. **1790** in 1971 Denny *Military Jrl.* 144 **PA,** March through beech and swamp oak land. **1834** Audubon *Ornith. Biog.* 2.238 **eFL,** Not a single tree of the species did we find, although there were thousands of large "swamp-oaks." **1875** (1876) Hallock *Camp Life* 338 **FL,** Large areas of low-lying land exist, . . with here and there islands of timber, consisting of gum, live and swamp oak, cedar and cabbage palms. **1965–70** *DARE* (Qu. T10, . . *Kinds of oak trees*) 31 Infs, **east of Missip R,** Swamp oak; (Qu. T15, . . *Kinds of swamp trees*) 17 Infs, **chiefly NEast, N Cent, C Atl,** Swamp oak.

2 Spec:

a Any of var **oaks** native chiefly to much of the eastern half of the US, as:

(1) =**swamp white oak 1.**

1814 Bigelow *Florula Bostoniensis* 226, *Quercus bicolor.* . . The wood of the swamp oak is strong, heavy, and flexible, easy to split, and in point of durability approaches the white oak. **1862** *Atlantic Mth.* 9.6, We have, for instance, one name for all the Oaks, but we call the different kinds Swamp Oak, Red Oak, White Oak, Chestnut Oak, etc. . . qualified . . as *Quercus bicolor, Quercus rubra, Quercus alba, Quercus castanea,* etc. **1897** Sudworth *Arborescent Flora* 158, *Quercus bicolor.* . . Swamp Oak (R.I., Pa.) *Ibid* 172, *Quercus palustris.* . . Swamp Oak (Pa., Ohio, Kans.) **1931** Otis *MI Trees* 137, *Swamp White Oak. Swamp Oak. Quercus bicolor.* . . Prefers moist, rich soil bordering swamps and along streams. . . Fairly rapid of growth and reasonably easy to transplant. **2003** *Detroit News* (MI) 30 Aug (Internet), There are many Michigan trees that can replace the ash devastation. . . For areas without restriction on roots: . . Bur oak (*Quercus macrocarpa*) Shingle oak (*Quercus imbricaria*) Swamp oak (*Quercus bicolor*) Sawtooth oak (*Quercus acutissima*) [etc].

(2) =**pin oak 1a.**

1819 (1821) Nuttall *Jrl.* 71 **AR,** *Q. palustris* (the swamp oak). **1862** *New Amer. Cyclop.* 15.719, The Ohio region has but few characteristic trees; the most prominent are . . scarlet and swamp oak (*quercus coccinea* and *palustris*). **1888** *Amer. Naturalist* 22.1151, *Q[uercus] phellos* with *Q. palustris.* . . The largest willow oak in the wood stands close to an equally big swamp oak. **1897** [see **2a(1)** above]. **1980** Little *Audubon Guide N. Amer. Trees E. Region* 403, Pin Oak—"Swamp Oak"—"Spanish Oak"—*Quercus palustris.* . . In nearly pure stands on poorly drained, wet sites.

(3) Any of var other **oaks;** see quots.

1897 *Jrl. Amer. Folkl.* 10.144 **swMO,** *Quercus imbricata,* . . swamp oak, pin oak. **1940** Clute *Amer. Plant Names* 269, *Quercus illicifolia.* Barren oak, scrub oak, dwarf bear oak, water oak, white oak, swamp oak. **1980** Little *Audubon Guide N. Amer. Trees E. Region* 408, *Shumard Oak*—"*Spotted Oak*"—"*Swamp Oak*"—*Quercus shumardii.* . . Moist well-drained soils including flood plains along streams. . . North Carolina to N. Florida, west to central Texas, and north to E. Kansas; local north to S. Michigan and S. Pennsylvania.

b Any of var **oaks** native esp to the South and Midland areas of the US, as:

(1) =**basket oak 1.**

1822 Eaton *Botany* 421, *[Quercus] prinus* [here: =*Q. michauxii*] . . swamp oak. . . Acorn ovate, large, sweet tasted. Large tree. **1876** Hobbs *Bot. Hdbk.* 78, Oak, Swamp, Quercus Prinus [here: =*Q. michauxii*]. **1960** Vines *Trees SW* 153, Swamp Chestnut Oak. . . Vernacular names are Cow Oak, Basket Oak, Michaux Oak, . . and Swamp Oak. **1985** *Frederick Post* (MD) 25 Sept sec B 3/6, Acorns from the oak are usually bitter but those of the swamp oak are edible.

(2) =**willow oak 2.**

1857 (1859) Olmsted *Journey TX* 76, We noticed one group of magnolias and a few willow or swamp oaks *(quercus phellos).* **1947** Collingwood–Brush *Knowing Trees* 198, *Quercus phellos.* . . is so frequently found along wet margins of streams and swamps as to be erroneously known as swamp oak, or water oak. **2005** *DARE* File—Internet **AR,** Willow Oak (pin oak, swamp oak). . . Grows on heavy, better-drained soils of first bottoms in the flood plains of the Mississippi, Arkansas, and larger rivers of south and east.

(3) =**overcup oak 1.**

1901 Lounsberry *S. Wild Flowers* 134, Overcup Oak. Swamp Oak. . . *Quercus Lyrata.* . . Along streams or in ground that is wet throughout the year this oak seems to grow frequently with such companions as . . the cow or basket oak. **2005** *DARE* File—Internet, Quercus lyrata, the Swamp oak or Overcup oak. It's a member of the white oak family that lives in places where people don't normally [sic] like to go: damp lowlands, full of hickory, cypress and gum trees.

(4) Either **red oak 2b** or **cherrybark oak.** Note: *Quercus pagoda* was formerly considered a var of *Q. falcata.*

2005 *DARE* File—Internet **AL,** Cherrybark Oak—*Quercus falcata* var. *pagodaefolia.* . . Other common names: Bottomland red oak, Elliot oak, Red oak, Swamp oak, Swamp Spanish oak. *Ibid, Northern red oak* (several kinds, esp. *Quercus rubra*) grows across the US and eastern Canada. . . The grain is porous and distinctive. *Southern red oak (Q. falcata),* also known as *Spanish* or *swamp oak,* is similar.

c =**valley oak.**

1897 Sudworth *Arborescent Flora* 152 **CA,** *Quercus lobata.* . . Swamp Oak. **1910** Jepson *Silva CA* 209, The wood of the Valley Oak is . . the least valuable hard wood on the Pacific Coast. . . So frequently an inhabitant of the delta lands, it is called "Water Oak," "Bottom Oak," and "Swamp Oak." **1991** Pavlik et al. *Oaks CA* 11, Valley oak has been given a variety of names over the years. The species reminded Spanish explorers of the majestic white oaks of Europe and so the same name *roble* was applied. . . "White Oak," "bottom oak," "swamp oak," and "water oak" are other names that still enjoy regional use. The scientific name *Quercus lobata* is the only one with universal acceptance.

swamp oat grass n Also *swamp oats*

=**oat grass b,** usu *Sphenopholis pensylvanica.* Note: This species was formerly listed as *Trisetum p.*

1901 Mohr *Plant Life AL* 372, *Trisetum pennsylvanicum* [=*Sphenopholis p.*] . . *Swamp Oat Grass.* . . Mountain region. . . Rare. **1933** Small *Manual SE Flora* 108, Trisetum. . . False-oats. Wild oat-grasses. Swamp oat-grasses. **1950** Gray–Fernald *Manual of Botany* 146, T[*risetum] pensylvanicum.* . . Swamp-Oats. . . Springy meadows and wooded swamps. **1995** *Std.–Times* (New Bedford MA) 20 May (Internet), The Apponagansett Swamp also has a rare plant species called swamp oats, a rare form of diminutive grass found in wooded swamps and saltmarshes. **2002** *Daytona Beach News–Jrl.* (FL) 18 Nov sec A 4 (Internet), By also planting sand-holding plants like sea oats, swamp oats, and lyme and sea beach needle grass, we might be able to keep ahead of the ocean's movements.

Swampoodle n scattered, but esp DC

A low-lying, swampy, or poor section of a town or city.

1857 in Lib. of Congress *Amer. Memory: Amer. Time Capsule* (Internet) **DC,** First grand semi-occasional entertainment of the Swampoodle ruins. **1871** U.S. Congress *Congressional Globe* 15 Apr 718 **DC,** Passengers . . will be left out here at this part of the city [of Washington] that . . is known as Swampoodle. **1898** *NE State Jrl.* (Lincoln) 7 Mar 3/2 **AR,** Italian Barbers Engage in an Affray at Texarkana. . . The tragedy occurred in that portion of the city known as Swampoodle. **1960** *Progress* (Clearfield PA) 8 Aug 10/2, Dr. Robert A. Christie . . was reared in Philadelphia's tough "Swampoodle" section. **1967–70** *DARE* (Qu. C34, *Nicknames for nearby settlements, villages, or districts*) Inf **TX**90, Swampoodle; (Qu. C35, *Nicknames for the different parts of your town or city*) Inf **DC**1, Swampoodle—is being drained—low section where Anacostia River goes into Potomac; **PA**200, Swampoodle—east

end of town, because of a swamp located there; (Qu. II21, *When somebody behaves unpleasantly or without manners: "The way he behaves, you'd think he was _____."*) Inf **DC**1, From Swampoodle. **1969** *Coshocton Tribune* (OH) 3 June 7/5 **DC,** We lived in a plumbingless house in Swampoodle, a section of Washington D.C., near Union Station. In today's idiom it would be designated a ghetto. [**1986** Pederson *LAGS Concordance (Names of streams in the neighborhood)* 1 inf, **neTX,** Swampoodle Creek.] **1998** *Washington Post* (DC) 3 Dec sec J 1 (Internet), Munlyn was born in this neighborhood once called Swampoodle. . . They bulldozed the shacks of Swampoodle and erected public housing.

swamp out See **swamp C1, 2**

swamp owl n

1 The barred owl *(Strix varia).* chiefly Sth, esp Gulf States

1853 *Harper's New Mth. Mag.* 7.771 **LA,** With night came new voices—the hideous voices of the nocturnal swamp; the qua-qua of the night-heron, the screech of the swamp-owl, . . the chirp of the savanna-cricket. **1876** *Scribner's Mth.* 11.659 **Sth,** So Inez stopped again, shouted again, and listened, and listened, to hear nothing but a swamp-owl. **1890** Warren *Birds PA* 150, Barred Owls are exceedingly abundant in many of the southern states, where they are known by the names of "Hoot and Swamp Owls." **1914** *Auk* 31.222 **cAL,** *Strix varia alleni.* Florida barred owl.—[Local names:] 'Swamp Owl.' "Hooting Owl."—Very common permanent resident. **1931** *Pt. Arthur News* (TX) 6 Aug 3/5, They shot a swamp owl which had been raiding hen yards in the vicinity of Sabine Pass avenue. **1967** *DARE* (Qu. Q2, . . *Kinds of owls*) Inf **LA**2, Frog or swamp owl; **TX**32, Swamp owl. **1986** Pederson *LAGS Concordance (Hoot owl)* 7 infs, **Gulf Region,** Swamp owl(s); 2 infs, **AL,** Swamp owl—large; 2 infs, **swAL, ceFL,** Swamp owl—same as hoot owl; 1 inf, **ceLA,** Swamp owl—larger, makes "hoo" noise; 1 inf, **cnLA,** Swamp owl—old roundheaded owl. **2005** *DARE* File—Internet **NJ,** Traditionally known as the "swamp owl," the barred owl is a denizen of remote, contiguous, old-growth wetland forests.

2 =**short-eared owl.**

1890 Warren *Birds PA* 149, I have found the Swamp or Short-eared Owl at all times of the year in the Conewago Valley. **1911** *Newark Advocate* (OH) 13 Sept 7/1, The fellow who wants to shoot a red fox . . is further behind the hour than the fellow who is killing the screech owl and swamp owl, which live entirely on the rodents of field, granery [sic] and barn. **1924** *Amer. Midland Naturalist* 9.74 **IA,** *Asio flammeus.* . . Screech Owl, Ground Owl, Swamp Owl. **1940** Todd *Birds W. PA* 708, Swamp [Owl], *see* Owl, Short-eared. **1986** Pederson *LAGS Concordance (Owl)* 1 inf, **cnLA,** Swamp owl—two-foot wingspread, small body.

swamp palmetto n Also *swamp palm*

Usu =**dwarf palmetto 1;** rarely =**cabbage palmetto.**

1812 *Med. & Phys. Jrl.* 27.260, *Sabal Adansoni* [=*S. minor*]; the American Swamp Palmetto. **1849** Lyell *Second Visit* 2.107 **sLA,** The swamp palmetto *(Chamærops adansonia)* raises its fan-shaped leaves ten feet high, although without any main trunk, like the sea-island palmetto. **1852** *De Bow's Rev.* 12.272 **LA,** The *bear grass* is found in the pine woods: this slightly resembles the ordinary swamp palmetto. **1863** Geer *Beyond Lines* 110, For a long time we lay silent and watchful beneath the broad leaves of the swamp palm, close by the roadside. **1898** *Courier* (Connellsville PA) [4 Mar 11]/3 (newspaperarchive.com) **Sth,** There was the newest process of bleaching the swamp palmetto for the plaiting of their own hats. **1901** Lounsberry *S. Wild Flowers* 28, *S[abal] glabra* [=*S. minor*], dwarf sabal, or swamp palmetto, bears from its short, buried stems very large, glaucous leaves. **1950** *Edwardsville Intelligencer* (IL) [11 Mar 5]/2 (newspaperarchive.com) **LA,** The lady from the state university said the baskets and sun-hats Gran'Pere made from swamp palmetto were works of art. **1966** *DARE* (Qu. T15, . . *Kinds of swamp trees*) Inf **FL**20, Swamp palmettos. **2005** *DARE* File—Internet **TX,** Swamp Palm—*Sabal minor.* . . favors the wet alluvial soil in swamps and river bottoms in Texas, Oklahoma, Arkansas and North Carolina.

swamp partridge n

1 =**spruce grouse.**

1828 Bonaparte *Amer. Ornith.* 3.47 **ME, MI, NY,** In these countries the Spotted Grouse is known by the various names of Wood Partridge, Swamp Partridge, Cedar Partridge, and Spruce Partridge. **1842** Thompson *Hist. VT* 1.102, *The Spruce Partridge.* . . This Grouse, which is called, at different places, the Spruce, the Wood or the Swamp Partridge, from its favorite places of resort, is seldom seen in Vermont excepting in the most northerly parts. **1903** Studer *Birds N. Amer.* 142, *Canada Grouse. . . Swamp Partridge. . . (Tetrao canadensis). . .* This species is found in favorable localities, from the northern parts of the United States, from whence it extends its migrations as far north to the limit of the woods, and to the Arctic ocean. **1955** MA Audubon Soc. *Bulletin* 39.442 **ME, VT,** *Spruce Grouse. . .* Swamp Partridge, Wood Partridge.

2 =woodcock 1.

1914 *Auk* 31.218 **cAL,** *Philohela minor.* Woodcock. [Local names:] 'Swamp Partridge.' 'Snipe.'—Permanent resident in rather small numbers in Autauga Co., inhabiting marshes, swamps and wet pastures. **1924** Howell *Birds AL* 95, *Rubicola minor* [=*Scolopax m.*] . . The woodcock . . is sometimes called "hill partridge," or "swamp partridge." **2003** *News & Observer* (Raleigh NC) 16 Jan (Internet), Just what kind of critter is a woodcock? It goes under dozens of names. Old-time Carolinians may recognize it as the night peck, big eyes or swamp partridge.

swamp pine n

1 Any of several **pines,** as:

a **=longleaf pine 1.**

[**1733** Miller *Gardeners Dict.* (at *Abies*), *Species* . . to be found in the *English* Gardens . . [include] Pinus; *Americana, palustris.* The Swamp Pine.] **1797** Smith *Nat. Hist. GA* 83, *Pinus palustris. . .* Long-leaved or swamp pine-tree. **1853** Meehan *Amer. Hdbk. Ornamental Trees* 173, *P. palustris. . .* Southern swamp pine. Native of the Southern States. **1938** Van Dersal *Native Woody Plants* 191, *Pinus palustris. . . Swamp pine. . .* A large evergreen tree; two-needled. **2005** *DARE* File—Internet **FL,** Longleaf pine is also called southern pine, swamp pine, yellow pine, and heart pine.

b **=slash pine b.**

1896 Mohr–Roth *Timber Pines* 77, In Florida, where best known, it [= *Pinus elliottii*] is distinguished as the Slash Pine, or Swamp Pine. **1897** Sudworth *Arborescent Flora* 31, *Pinus heterophylla* [=*P. elliottii*]. . . Swamp Pine (Fla., Miss., Ala., in part). **1926** *Landmark* (Statesville NC) 15 Feb 3/4, A pine of our Southern states, Pinus hetrophylla [sic] . . [is] the slash, or swamp pine. **1946** West–Arnold *Native Trees FL* 6, *Pinus elliotti. . . Slash Pine, Swamp Pine. . .* Lumber manufactured from well-grown trees is of the highest grade. **1980** Little *Audubon Guide N. Amer. Trees E. Region* 288, "Swamp Pine" *Pinus elliottii. . .* Low areas such as pond margins, flatwoods, swamps or "slashes," including poorly drained sandy soils, also uplands and old fields.

c **=loblolly pine 1. esp Mid Atl**

[**1743** Catesby *Nat. Hist. Carolina* 2 [app] xxii, The *Swamp Pine* grows on barren wet Land; they are generally tall and large; the Cones are rather large. These Trees afford little Rosin, but are useful for Masts, Yards, and many other Necessaries.] **1785** Marshall *Arbustrum* 102, Pinus Tæda. *Virginian Swamp, or Frankincence Pine.* This grows to a pretty large size. . . This is useful for boards, and for producing turpentine and tar, as are the other kinds. **1882** Hough *Elements of Forestry* 328, Varieties [of *Pinus taeda*] are known in North Carolina as "Swamp Pine," "Slash Pine." **1896** Mohr–Roth *Timber Pines* 106 **NC, VA,** *Pinus tæda. . .* Swamp Pine. **1960** Vines *Trees SW* 23, *Pinus taeda. . .* Other vernacular names are Frankincense Pine, Black Pine, . . Swamp Pine, . . and Old-field Pine. **1967–70** *DARE* (Qu. T17, . . *Kinds of pine trees;* not asked in early QRs) Infs **AR51, GA77, NC41, PA234,** Swamp pine. [*DARE* Ed: Some of these Infs may refer instead to other senses.] **2005** *DARE* File—Internet **TX,** *Black Pine, Bull Pine, Lowland Pine, Slack Pine, Sap Pine, Indian Pine, Swamp Pine*—The species name, taeda, is for the resinous wood.

d **=shortleaf pine 1.**

1854 Wailes *Rept. on Ag. & Geol. MS* 343, Pine, swamp—Pinus mitis [=*Pinus echinata*].

e **=bishop pine.**

1897 Sudworth *Arborescent Flora* 28 **CA,** *Pinus muricata. . .* California Swamp Pine. . . Swamp Pine. **1910** Jepson *Silva CA* 99, The common name, Bishop Pine, comes from the original locality near San Luis Obispo. . . It is often called "Swamp Pine" because so frequently an inhabitant of boggy hills or flats.

f **=pond pine 1.**

1958 Petrides *Trees & Shrubs* 15, Swamp Pine . . Similar to Pitch Pine. **1993** Silberhorn *Loblolly Pine* 1 **VA,** Another pine occurring almost exclusively in nontidal wetlands is pond or swamp pine *(Pinus serotina).* Pond pine is infrequent in Virginia, but is more common further south along the coast. **2005** *DARE* File—Internet, Swamp pine—*Pinus serotina.*

2 =Douglas fir. Cf Oregon pine

1871 U.S. Army Corps Topog. Engineers *Rept. Explor. 40th Parallel* 5.335, *Abies Douglasii. . .* Tall, pyramidal, with horizontal drooping branches. . . From Washington Territory to Southern California, and in the Rocky Mountains to Colorado and New Mexico. . . known as "Bear River" or "Swamp Pine." **1882** Torrey Bot. Club *Bulletin* 9.156 **eCO,** *Abies Douglasii* . . was quite plentiful at middle elevations, attaining a height of 75 ft., and known as "swamp pine." **1909** in 1914 Stewart *Letters* 7 **WY,** I have a grove of twelve swamp pines on my place, and I am going to build my house there.

swamp pink n

1 A **rhododendron:** usu either **swamp azalea** or a **pinkster 2** (here: *Rhododendron periclymenoides*); hence n *swamp pink apple* =**swamp apple 1. chiefly NEast** See Map Cf **mountain pink 4**

1784 in 1785 Amer. Acad. Arts & Sci. *Memoirs* 1.416 **neMA,** American Honeysuckle. Swamp Pink. . . Common in low, swampy land. June. **1814** Bigelow *Florula Bostoniensis* 52, *Azalea viscosa* [=*Rhododendron v.*] . . *Wild honeysuckle, Swamp pink. . .* A fine flowering shrub, very common among the brushwood in low land. **1847** Wood *Class-Book* 375, *R[hododendron] nudiflorum* [=*R. periclymenoides*]. . . *Swamp Pink. . .* A beautiful and fragrant flowering shrub, 4–6f[eet] high, rather frequent in the forests and thickets of the Northern States as well as the Southern. *Ibid, R. viscosum. . . Clammy Swamp Pink. . .* Less frequent than the last, in rocky woods, Can[ada] to Ga., W[est] to Ky. **1850** (1949) Thoreau *Jrl.* 2.60 **NEng,** The swamp-pink (*Azalea viscosa*), its now withered pistils standing out. **1880** *Atlantic Mth.* 45.418 **NEng,** Can it be possible that Mr. Burroughs does not know the wild white azalea (A. viscosa), familiar to every New England schoolboy as "wild honeysuckle," or "swamp pink"? **1892** *Jrl. Amer. Folkl.* 5.100 **MA,** *Rhododendron viscosum,* swamp pink. *Ibid* **NEast,** *Rhododendron nudiflorum* [=*R. periclymenoides*], . . swamp pink. **1923** *Bridgeport Telegram* (CT) 23 Apr 11/4, *Azalia* [sic]. . . The Swamp Pink is about six feet high with full grown blossoms in May and as its name indicates is pink in color. **1965–70** *DARE* (Qu. I44, *What kinds of berries grow wild around here?*) Inf **MA6,** Swamp pinks also have little fruit; (Qu. S26b, *Wildflowers that grow in water or wet places*) Infs **MA49, 58, 100, NJ55, RI15,** Swamp pink; (Qu. T16, . . *Kinds of trees. . . 'special'*) Inf **MA5,** Wild azalea = swamp pink; (Qu. S4, . . *Mayapple: [Woodside plant, not a tree, with two large spreading leaves; they grow in patches and have a small yellow fruit late in summer]*) Inf **MA39,** Swamp pink; **VT**10, A swamp apple or swamp pink is small and has little apples [*DARE* Ed: cf **mayapple 4**]. **1966** *DARE* Tape **MA6,** We also eat the apple off the swamp pink. **1979** *Greenfield Recorder* (MA) 4 Aug sec A 4/3, Did you ever hear of anybody finding enough swamp pink apples to make any use of them?

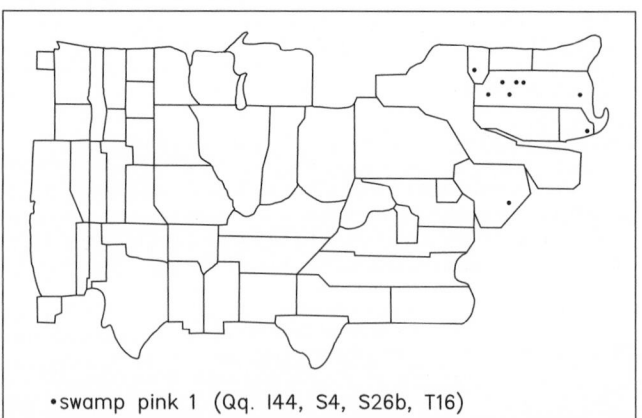

•swamp pink 1 (Qq. I44, S4, S26b, T16)

2 An orchid *(Arethusa bulbosa)* with a showy, pink, scented flower, native from New England south to North Carolina and northwest to Minnesota. Also called **Adam-and-Eve 1, dragon's mouth 1, Indian pink 11, laughing jackass, meadow pink 3, swamp rose orchid, wild pink 3**

1860 *Atlantic Mth.* 5.24 **NEng,** But with June comes the most exquisite of our New England wild-flowers, the arethusa, or swamp-pink, as it is often styled, to the great confusion of its delicate, high-born nature with the great, vulgar, flaunting azalea. **1897** *Jrl. Amer. Folkl.* 10.144

MA, *Arethusa bulbosa*, . . swamp pink, meadow pink. **1961** Smith *MI Wildflowers* 83, *Arethusa, Swamp Pink*. . . This strange little flower has somewhat the appearance of a startled animal. **1979** Niering–Olmstead *Audubon Guide N. Amer. Wildflowers E. Region* 647, *Swamp Pink; Dragon's Mouth.* . . The smooth stalk . . has a *single, bright pink, scented flower* at its summit. **1991** *Morning Call* (Allentown PA) 21 May sec D 1 (Internet), Swamp pink (Arethusa bulbosa) . . and spreading globeflower (Trolius luxus). . . Both endangered. Swamp pink grows in acidic peat habitats in Wayne County.

3 A bog plant *(Helonias bullata)* with a mostly leafless stem topped by a tight cluster of small pink flowers, native from New York south to Virginia and northwest Georgia. Also called **swamp hyacinth**

1889 NJ State Geologist *Final Rept.* 2.243, *Helonias*. . . Swamp Pink. **1897** Creevey *Flowers* 85, Swamp Pink, *Helònias bullàta.* . . A pretty plant, found from New Jersey southward to Virginia. **1911** NJ State Museum *Annual Rept. for 1910* 340, *Helonias bullata.* . . *Swamp Pink.* . . one of the most characteristic plants of the southern half of New Jersey and one of the earliest spring flowers in the region. **1938** FWP *Guide DE* 12, A favorite trek among local and visiting naturalists is made in May to the little known haunts of the "swamp-pink" (helonias), plentiful in isolated districts, chiefly in Sussex County. **1975** Torrey Bot. Club *Bulletin* 102.145 **PA,** We had probably the nicest show of the swamp pink *(Helonias bullata)* that I have ever seen. **2000** *Washington Post* (DC) 11 May sec M 29 (Internet) **MD,** The swamp pink . . looked more like a very bright weed, with its dandelion-like stem and leaves tipped with tiny pale crimson flower clusters.

4 A **grass pink 1,** usu *Calopogon tuberosus.*

1898 *Jrl. Amer. Folkl.* 11.280 **MA,** *Calopogon pulchellus* [=*C. tuberosus*], . . swamp pink. **1940** Writers' Program *Guide TX* 375 **neTX,** The wild rose, shame vine, Virginia creeper, and swamp pink are among the plants that ornament the roadside. **1999** Liggio–Liggio *Wild Orchids TX* 67, *Calopogon tuberosus.* . . Other Common Names: swamp pink, rose wings.

swamp pink apple See **swamp pink 1**

swamp poplar n

1 A **cottonwood 1:** usu **swamp cottonwood,** rarely **Carolina poplar 1.**

1837 (1962) Williams *Territory FL* 90, Swamp Poplar. Populus angulata—river swamp. **1897** Sudworth *Arborescent Flora* 130 **NJ,** *Populus heterophylla.* . . Swamp Poplar. **1943** *Amer. Midland Naturalist* 30.386, Swamp poplar—*Populus heterophylla.* **1969** *Playground Daily News* (Ft. Walton Beach FL) 9 Jan 3/1, A hurricane 2 or 3 years before the tornadohtook [sic] 30 feet out of the top of oqr [sic] swamp poplar. **1970** *DARE* (Qu. T15, . . *Kinds of swamp trees*) Inf **IL**123, Swamp poplar. [*DARE* Ed: This Inf may refer instead to **2** below.] **1980** Little *Audubon Guide N. Amer. Trees E. Region* 324, "Swamp Poplar" "Black Cottonwood". . . Leaves. . . *Densely covered with white hairs when unfolding.* . . Wet sites, often submerged in flood plains and edges of swamps. **2005** *DARE* File—Internet, Among other distinguishing group features are . . the cottony-covered new leaves of the swamp poplar.

2 A **tupelo gum** (here: *Nyssa aquatica*). Cf **swamp tupelo**

1869 Porcher *Resources* 388 **Sth,** Messrs. Howes, Hyatt & Co., shoe and leather dealers, . . manufacture a plantation brogan, differing from the old shoe, in having soles of some light, tough wood—probably the root of the swamp poplar. . . The Black tupelo or black gum, sometimes grows on highlands—the wood is also very light, but it possesses a firmer texture . . —hence the adaptability of the wood of the root for making bowls, shoes, naves of carts, etc. **1958** Jacobs–Burlage *Index Plants NC* 71, *Nyssa aquatica.* . . Tupelo gum; sour gum; swamp poplar. . . This plant grows in swampy forests from Virginia to Florida and west to Texas and Missouri and is found in the low and middle districts of North Carolina. **2004** in 2005 *DARE* File—Internet, The miniatures are . . carved out of "tupelo" (a swamp poplar that grows in Tupelo, MS—and the only part of the tree that can be used is the part that grows under water, because it grows a tighter grain).

swamp post oak n Cf **post oak 1a, swamp ~ 2b(3)** =**overcup oak 1.**

1812 Michaux *Histoire des Arbres* 2.42, La *Quercus lyrata* n'est pas très-multiplié dans la Basse-Caroline et la Basse-Géorgie, ce qui fait que, jusqu'à présent, il n'a été remarqué que des habitans qui demeurent à proximité des lieux où il croît. Ils le connoissent sous les noms d' *Over*

cup oak . . ; de *Swamp post oak* . . ; et plus rarement sous celui de *Water white oak*. . . Le premier de ces noms . . est plus usité dans la Caroline méridionale, et le second l'est davantage sur la rivière Savanah, en Georgie. [=The *Quercus lyrata* is not very common in lower Carolina and lower Georgia, so that it has not been noticed hitherto except by those who live near the places it grows. They know it as *Over cup oak* . . ; *Swamp post oak* . . ; and, less frequently, *Water white oak*. . . The first of these names is used more in South Carolina, and the second on the Savannah river in Georgia.] **1860** Curtis *Cat. Plants NC* 33, Q[uercus] lyrata. . . The foliage has more resemblance to that of the *Post Oak* than of any other, for which reason it is, farther south, called *Swamp Post Oak.* **1897** Sudworth *Arborescent Flora* 155, *Quercus lyrata.* . . Swamp Post Oak (Ala., S.C., Miss., La., Mo.) **1980** Little *Audubon Guide N. Amer. Trees E. Region* 395, "Swamp Post Oak" . . *Quercus lyrata.* . . Wet clay and silty clay soils, mostly on poorly drained flood plains and swamp borders. **2005** *DARE* File—Internet, The large, rough cap on acorns of the swamp post oak are a distinctive feature on this common East Texas tree.

swamp potato n [Perh folk-etym for **swan potato**] =**arrowhead 1,** esp the widely distributed *Sagittaria latifolia;* the edible root of the plant.

1850 U.S. Patent Office *Annual Rept. for 1849: Ag.* 452 **MN,** The *psui-chin-chah,* or *swamp potato,* is found in mud and water about 3 feet deep. **1871** U.S. Dept. Ag. *Rept. of Secy. for 1870* 408, *Sagittaria variabilis* [=*S. latifolia*]. . . Sometimes called swan or swamp potato. The Chippewa name for it is wab-es-i-pinig. It grows in muddy margins of northwestern lakes and rivers, and its tuberous roots furnish an important article of food. **1906** Kephart *Book Camping* 236, *Arrowhead, Broad-leaved.* Swan or Swamp Potato. *Sagittaria latifolia (S. variabilis).* . . Tuberous roots as large as hens' eggs, were an important article of food among Indians. **1964** Batson *Wild Flowers SC* 23, *Swamp-potato, Wampee: S[agittaria] latifolia.* . . Tubers have a high starch content and are edible. **1997** *N. Hills News Rec.* (Allison Park PA) 27 June sec C 3/4, Arrowhead (Sagittaria spp), the swamp potato or duck potato, is an interesting plant recognized by its arrow-shaped leaves. **2005** *DARE* File—Internet, Swamp Potatoes (Tla-Wa-Tsu-Hi-A-Ne-Hi Nu-Nv). . . Directions—Gather and wash swamp potatoes. Bake in oven or in ashes until they are done. Beat the cooked potatoes in the corn beater until they are like any other meal. . . During winter famines, many Cherokees had no other meal except that made from the swamp potatoes.

swamp primrose n esp SE

A **false loosestrife** such as *Ludwigia decurrens, L. leptocarpa,* or *L. palustris.*

1987 Torrey Bot. Club *Bulletin* 114.13 **GA,** Flea beetles . . were the dominant grazing herbivore in this wetland, which is primarily composed of two species of swamp primrose (*Ludwigia leptocarpa* (Nuttall) Hara and *L. decurrens* Walter). **2003** S. FL Water Management District *DuPuis Management Plan* (Internet) **FL,** Strand swamps are shallow, forested, usually elongated depressions or channels dominated by bald cypress. . . Other typical plants include . . swamp primrose (*Ludwigia palustris*).

swamp privet n

A **forestiera,** usu *Forestiera acuminata* or *F. pubescens.*

1901 Mohr *Plant Life AL* 667, Swamp Privet. Forestiera acuminata. . . Carolinian and Louisianian area. **1923** *Reno Eve. Gaz.* (NV) 21 Nov 8/5, [Syndicated column:] Among the kinds of food favored by wild fowl are . . swamp privet. **1942** Tehon *Fieldbook IL Shrubs* 244, *Forestiera . . The Swamp Privets.* The swamp privets are shrubs with opposite, simple, toothed or entire leaves. **1969** *Ecological Monogr.* 39.250, Little Blue Herons build their nests in willow, wax myrtle, and, in northern Florida, in titi. Buttonbush and swamp privet are used in Arkansas. **1992** MO Bot. Garden *Annals* 79.113 **TX,** The area . . consists of a *Spartina* grass prairie plus patches of standing water, with backswamps in which the dominant trees are *Taxodium distichum* . . , *Salix nigra* . . , and *Forestiera acuminata* . . (swamp privet).

swamp-pumper n Also *swamp-pump* Cf **thunder pumper 1**

Either a **bittern** (here: *Botaurus lentiginosus*) or the **least bittern.**

1959 *Names* 7.119, Likening the bittern's vocalization to the sounds made by the operation of an old-fashioned suction-pump has also been a fruitful source of folk-names. Among these allusions are . . swamp-pump (Mich., Calif.), swamp pumper (Wis.) **1963** Gromme *Birds WI*

218, Swamp-pumper (Least Bittern). **1968** *DARE* (Qu. Q8, *A water bird that makes a booming sound before rain and often stands with its beak pointed almost straight up*) Inf **MN**16, Swamp-pump, shypoke—all same. **2005** *DARE* File—Internet **nMI**, Due to its unique call, another name given to the bird [=*Botaurus lentiginosus*] is that of "swamp pumper."

swamp quail n

1 A **meadowlark 1.** Cf **marsh quail**

1778 (1930) Mackenzie *Diary* 1.256 **RI**, No birds have been seen yet, except such as remain here during the Winter, which are the Meadowlark, or Swamp-Quail, the Snow bird, the Quails, and a few Snipes. **2002** *Billings Gaz.* (MT) 24 Mar (Internet), Even when he was a lad in Kansas, back in the '50s, he remembers that people called muskrat "marsh rabbit," and he once sampled [*]"swamp quail," otherwise known as the meadowlark, the state bird of Kansas.

2 =**woodcock 1.**

2005 *Hartford Courant* (CT) 5 Apr sec B 3 (Internet), Woodcock. . . Scolopax minor. . . Here's some of the bird's nicknames: big mud snipe, bog sucker, marsh plover, mud bat, forest snipe and swamp quail. The bird . . can be seen in bogs, swamps, moist upland woodlands and thickets near open fields.

swamp rabbit n Cf **sailor**

1 A large, brownish-gray cottontail rabbit *(Sylvilagus aquaticus)* native from Texas and Oklahoma east to southern Illinois and northern Georgia. Also called **canecutter, swamper 9, swamp hare 1**

1849 White *Statistics GA* 5, Lepus. . . aquaticus. . . Swamp rabbit, Coweta county. **1854** *Living Age* 40.135 **LA**, Thar war the catamount standin' within three feet o' the possum an' the swamp rabbit. **1872** *Amer. Naturalist* 6.771 **TX**, Swamp Rabbit (Lepus aquaticus). . . It abounds in the canebrakes of Alabama, Mississippi, Louisiana, Arkansas and Texas. **1875** *Fur Fin & Feather* 136 **TX**, Other varieties of rabbit—the larger of which, familiarly known as the "swamp rabbit," inhabits the heavy timbered woodlands and river bottoms. **1907** *Ft. Wayne Jrl.–Gaz.* (IN) 28 Dec 9/3 **AR**, On Thanksgiving day they had hanging in their larder venison, . . swamp rabbit, fox squirrel, . . wild hog and rattlesnake. **1956** in 1958 Brewer *Dog Ghosts* 50 **TX** [Black], De swamp rabbit ain't ez pert ez de jack rabbit an' de cottontail. **1965–70** *DARE* (Qu. P30, . . *Wild rabbits*) 53 Infs, **chiefly Lower Missip Valley, wGulf States**, Swamp rabbit(s); **AL**28, 38, Buck (rabbit)—same as swamp rabbit; **FL**48, Swamp rabbit is larger, reddish, long body and tail, longer ear; **FL**51, Swamp rabbit [has] black tail; **GA**34, Swamp rabbit—dark-colored; **GA**65, Swamp rabbit—he's called a canecutter, dark, black, large; **KY**75, Swamp rabbit—in wet marshland, larger than cottontail; **KY**84, Swamp rabbit—larger than gray rabbit; **LA**7, Hill rabbits smaller than swamp rabbits; **LA**44, Swamp rabbit—same size as marsh rabbit but lives in swamp, has a strong taste; **MS**53, Swamp rabbits—canecutters; **OK**15, Swamp rabbit—a little smaller and slower than a jackrabbit; **OK**23, Swamp rabbit—twice as big as a cottontail, lives around water; **OK**52, Swamp rabbit—as big as a jackrabbit but has shorter legs, good eating; **TN**26, An old swamp rabbit, he's bigger again than a hill rabbit; **TX**14, Swamp rabbit—some say marsh [rabbit]. [*DARE* Ed: Some of these Infs may refer instead to **2** below.] **1966** *DARE* Tape **AR**15, [FW:] What kind of rabbits do you have? [Inf:] Well, we have two kinds here. We have what we call the cottonpatch. . . and then we have the swamp rabbit. [FW:] And that's a bigger rabbit? [Inf:] Yeah, that's a larger rabbit. **2005** *Commercial Appeal* (Memphis TN) 6 Feb sec C 16 (Internet), As to the average size of West Tennessee rabbits, Montague said cottontails run 2–3 pounds with swamp rabbits checking in at 5–7 pounds.

2 =**marsh rabbit 1.**

1849 Lyell *Second Visit* 1.228, I had heard much of the swamp-rabbit, which they hunt near the coast in South Carolina and Georgia. **1917** Anthony *Mammals Amer.* 291, The *Carolina Swamp Rabbit*. . . is the smallest, darkest, and most reddish-brown of the Marsh Rabbits. **1927** Boston Soc. Nat. Hist. *Proc.* 38.7.373 **Okefenokee GA**, *Sylvilagus palustris palustris*. . . In the Okefinokee this animal goes by the general name of 'Swamp Rabbit.' **1938** Rawlings *Yearling* 51 **nFL**, The pair of black swamp rabbits was not new. **1965–70** *DARE* (Qu. P30, . . *Wild rabbits*) 34 Infs, **chiefly Mid and S Atl**, Swamp rabbit; **FL**4, Swamp rabbits—black or red; **FL**32, Swamp rabbits—solid brown; **FL**48, Swamp rabbit is larger, reddish, long body and tail, longer ear; **NC**85, Swamp rabbit—brown all over; **SC**19, Swamp rabbit—gray with a stripe; **SC**40, Swamp rabbit—darker, ears are larger, frequents canebrakes, branches; **SC**57, Swamp

rabbit—much larger than cottontail; **SC**69, Brown rabbit—same as swamp rabbit; **VA**70, Swamp rabbit—like plain brown rabbit; **VA**73, Swamp rabbit—plentiful, looks like a jackrabbit, but smaller, brown. [*DARE* Ed: Some of these Infs may refer instead to **1** above.] **1969** *DARE* Tape **GA**51, We got the swamp rabbits, a dark, dark-colored. **1997** *Palm Beach Post* (W. Palm Beach FL) 27 Apr (Internet), Little brown swamp rabbits roam the grounds [of the West Wind Inn on Sanibel Island] along with ibises and pelicans.

3 also *swamp jackrabbit:* =**varying hare.**

[**1879** *Decatur Daily Rev.* (IL) [5 Dec 3]/3 (newspaperarchive.com) **Canada**, Setting snares, she caught swamp rabbits. When she had five of these saved a little store of food she again paddled.] **1935** *Stevens Point Daily Jrl.* (WI) 8 Jan 6/7, In some cases, hunters tell us, the lowland or swamp rabbit appears to be suffering from some sort of disease brought about by the exceptionally heavy rains and snowfall. **1961** Jackson *Mammals WI* 108, *Lepus americanus phaeonotus*. . . *Vernacular names.*—In Wisconsin commonly called showshoe hare, snowshoe rabbit, or simply snowshoe. . . Other names include . . swamp jack rabbit, swamper. **1967–68** *DARE* (Qu. P30, . . *Wild rabbits*) Infs **NY**87, **WA**24, Swamp rabbit.

4 =**muskrat 1,** esp when used for food. Cf **marsh rabbit 2, swamp rat 2**

1906 *NY Times* (NY) 24 June mag sec 5/2, Chicago . . finds room for countless barrels of "swamp rabbit" caught along the famous marshes on Lake Michigan. . . During the trapping season muskrat flesh is on sale in all of the butcher shops along the eastern shore [of MD]. . . The "swamp rabbits" or "black ducks" are served at all the cheap hotels and lodging houses once or twice a week. . . A party of book agents in Captain Cannon's hotel at Cambridge [MD] ate hungrily of the meat. . . Cannon asked them how they liked the "swamp rabbit." . . In New York the knowing patrons of restaurants search down the lists of "game in season" when seeking muskrats. When they come to "swamp rabbit," or "black squirrel," or "Southern rabbits," they know what to expect. It is apt to be just plain muskrat shipped from Baltimore. **1945** *Lowell Sun* (MA) 31 Mar 8/1, Up in my neighborhood they're selling some stuff they call swamp rabbit. I'm almost certain that must be muskrat. **1968–70** *DARE* (Qu. P31, . . *Names or nicknames . . for the . . muskrat*) Infs **MD**31, **NY**76, **PA**147, **VT**16, Swamp rabbit; **IL**29, Swamp rabbit—used in southern Illinois. **2000** Lesley *Storm Riders* 182 **OR**, He was a strange old man who trapped otters and muskrats from the swamp. 'Swamp rabbits,' he called them.

5 =**swamper 1.**

1906 [see **swamp rat 1**].

swamp rat n

1 =**swamper 1.** **chiefly Gulf States, Lower Missip Valley**

1867 Edwards *Shelby & Men* 410, The "higher civilization" folks from the North . . [found] in him a specimen of the *green* Arkansas "swamp-rat." **1906** *DN* 3.160 **nwAR**, *Swamp-angel, swamp-rabbit, swamp-rat.* . . A countryman from the swampy district. **1939** *Frederick Post* (MD) 14 Feb 4/2, When "Jesse James" went into production, [Lon] Chaney [Jr.] was ordered to let his beard grow. . . The foliage is nearly two inches long now, and young Chaney has become a swamp rat in "Mr. Moto in Porto [sic] Rico." **1947** *Pt. Arthur News* (TX) 18 May 18/3, You are nothing but a swamp rat from the swamps of Port Arthur. **1962** Faulkner *Reivers* 102 **MS**, You brought that nephew of yours over here hunting refinement. . . Not looking like a shanty-boat swamp rat. **1986** Pederson *LAGS Concordance (The poor whites)* 1 inf, **ceTX**, Swamp rat; 1 inf, **swAL**, Swamp rat—from river; *(A rustic)* 1 inf, **csGA**, A swamp rat; 1 inf, **cwAL**, Swamp rats. **2004** *Tampa Tribune* (FL) 10 Sept Friday Extra sec 38 (Internet), Gyllenhaal has a small . . role in this surrealistic comedy about disparate twin brothers . . a neurotic writer . . and a shrewd, orchid-thieving swamp rat.

2 =**muskrat 1.** Cf **marsh rat, rat 1, swamp rabbit 4**

1967–69 *DARE* (Qu. P31, . . *Names or nicknames . . for the . . muskrat*) Infs **CA**130, **MN**2, **NY**219, **PA**132, Swamp rat.

3 The nutria *(Myocaster coypus).* Cf **neutral rat**

1952 *Mason City Globe–Gaz.* (IA) 17 Nov 22/1, Quentin Stille . . recently caught a South American swamp rat (Nutria) in the Iowa River. . . The animal weighed 10 pounds. **1999** *Atlanta Jrl.–Constitution* (GA) 21 Feb sec C 1 (Internet) **LA**, Deep in Cajun country between New Orleans and the Gulf of Mexico. . . huge swamp rats, called nutria, dart between the hanging moss and the gnarled trunks of cypress trees. **1999** *Star–Herald* (Scottsbluff NE) 26 Sept 1/5 **MD**, It's a swamp rat as big as a pit bull, and about as affable. A quartet of orange buckteeth jut from its pinched face. . . [and] are good for . . tearing out acres of tender salt marsh plants by the roots. The nutria . . has invaded this tranquil, tawny fringe of Chesapeake Bay. **2002** *Charleston Gaz.* (WV) 28 Dec sec C 4 (Internet) **LA,** Cajun country's No. 1 nuisance—10-pound swamp rats with orange buck teeth and webbed feet—are Kyle Loupe's cash cow.

swamp rattlesnake n Also *swamp rattler*

1 =**massasauga.**

1893 *News* (Frederick MD) [3 June 2]/3 (newspaperarchive.com) **OH,** Of the varieties of rattlers, the black, the yellow and the swamp rattlesnake, he has found the last mentioned the most dangerous, being the quickest to snap and making the lightest noise when it rattles. **1916** *Washington Post* (DC) 27 Aug [44]/5 (newspaperarchive.com) **PA,** The family [of rattlesnakes] has two branches in the state, the mountain variety and the swamp rattlesnake. **1938** *Amer. Midland Naturalist* 20.112 **OH,** *Massasauga; Swamp Rattler; Black Snapper. . .* A stout bodied snake which may attain a length of three feet. **1967** *Fond du Lac Commonwealth Reporter* (WI) 16 June sec 2 8/3, There are only two known poisonous snakes in Wisconsin—the timber rattlesnake and the swamp rattlesnake. . . Swamp rattlers are inclined to be in marshy areas. **1967–69** *DARE* (Qu. P25, . . *Kinds of snakes*) Infs **IL**81, **IN**7, **NJ**53, **OH**16, **PA**168, Swamp rattler. **1990** *Post-Std.* (Syracuse NY) 7 May sec B 2/4, The Cicero Swamp is home to a fragile network of wildlife, including the endangered eastern massauga [sic] rattlesnake known as the pygmy or swamp rattler. **2005** *DARE* File—Internet, Actually a "swamp rattler" is a massasauga. In the Northern states they are still frequently called swamp rattlers. *Ibid* **NY,** Since I'm from NY the Swamp Rattler I know about is the Massasauga.

2 A **diamondback rattlesnake** (here: *Crotalus adamanteus*). Cf **water rattle 2**

1894 *Daily NV State Jrl.* (Reno) [2 May 3]/2 **FL** (newspaperarchive.com), There are two kinds of rattlers in Florida. One is the swamp rattler and the other the highlander. The swamp snake has a larger head and a thicker body and is altogether a heavier snake than his highland brother. His coat, too, is darker and his diamonds brighter. He is more vicious. **1966** *DARE* (Qu. P25, . . *Kinds of snakes*) Inf **SC**19, Swamp rattler—darker than high-hill rattler. **1969** *Chillicothe Constitution–Tribune* (MO) 17 Feb 3/5 **swFL,** *Boy Bitten By Swamp Rattler Has Allergy To Serum. . .* A boy bitten on both ankles by a diamondback rattlesnake in a trackless cypress swamp was in critical condition today.

3 =**timber rattlesnake 1.** Cf **canebrake rattlesnake**

2005 *DARE* File—Internet **GA,** Eastern diamondbacks are declining. . . If you encounter a rattler in south Georgia today, the odds are that it's a canebrake, or "swamp rattler" as they are also known. *Ibid,* In the south the swamp rattlers [sic] is the Canebrake [sic]. *Ibid,* I have also heard the cane called the swamp rattler by older herps.

swamp red bay n esp **FL**
=**swamp bay 1.**

1898 Sudworth *Forest Trees* 66, *Persea pubescens. . .* Swamp Bay. . . *Names in use.*—Swamp Red-Bay (Fla.); Bay (Ga.) **1953** *Ecological Monogr.* 23.117 **nFL,** The characteristic trees of this habitat are almost exclusively different species of bay, the loblolly bay, white bay, and swamp red bay being most common. **2005** *DARE* File—Internet **cFL,** Where the ground is not regularly flooded, the bottomland trees are mostly swamp red bay, water oak, loblolly bay, Florida elm, sweetgum and cabbage palm.

swamp redberry See **redberry a**

swamp red currant See **swamp currant**

swamp red oak n **Sth, S Midl**
Any of several **red oaks,** as:

a =**pin oak 1a.**

1801 Michaux *Histoire* 19, *Quercus palustris. . .* Swamp's [sic] Red Oak. . . Cette espèce est abondante dans . . Illinois. [=*Quercus palustris. . . Swamp's Red Oak. . .* This species is abundant in . . Illinois.]

b =**cherrybark oak.** Cf **swamp oak 2b(4)**

1915 NC Geol. & Economic Surv. *Bulletin* 24.13, Most Important Species Associated With Loblolly Pine. . . Swamp red oak . . *Quercus pagodæfolia.* **1942** *Amer. Midland Naturalist* 28.120, Willow oak is most abundant, swamp red oak is somewhat less so. *Ibid* 122, *Quercus rubra* var. *pagodaefolia* . . Swamp red oak. **1968** *Pt. Arthur News* (TX) 17 Feb 2/4, Champion trees and the counties in which they are growing are as follows: . . shumard oak, Navarro; southern red oak, Leon; swamp red oak, Shelby. **2005** *DARE* File—Internet, *Quercus pagoda* . . swamp red oak . . equally likely to occur . . in wetlands or nonwetlands in the southeast US.

c =**Shumard oak.**

1953 Peattie *Nat. Hist. W. Trees* 224, Shumard Oak. . . *Other Name:* Swamp Red Oak. [*Ibid* 225, Shumard Oak. . . seems closely related to the Red Oak except that its leaves are shining and not dull on the upper surface. . . It also shows points of resemblance to the Pin Oak.] **1977** Torrey Bot. Club *Bulletin* 104.336 **NC,** Beech (*Fagus grandifolia*) may become important in some stands but rarely attains dominance over lowland oaks (e.g., willow oak, *Q*[*uercus*] *phellos;* swamp red oak, *Q. shumardii*). **2005** *DARE* File—Internet, *Swamp Red Oak . . Quercus shumardii. . .* Shumard Red Oak is an upright tree which can attain a height of 120 feet. It is found on rich bottomland soils, moist woods and along streams in the eastern third of Texas.

d =**red oak 2b.**

1980 Little *Audubon Guide N. Amer. Trees E. Region* 388 **Sth,** "Swamp Red Oak"—*Quercus falcata.* **2005** *DARE* File—Internet, Southern Red Oak, Swamp Red Oak, Spanish Oak (*Quercus falcata*).

swamp robin n

1 Any of several birds of the family Turdidae, as:

a =**hermit thrush 1.**

1769 (1906) Smith *Tour Great Rivers* 41 **NY,** The lively Note of the Swamp Robin, the Red Bird and other Birds from the earliest Dawn is entertaining. [*DARE* Ed: This quot may refer instead to another sense below.] **1857** Long *Pictures Slavery* (2d ed) 320 **MD,** The whippowil has struck up his evening song, and the sweet and dying notes of the swamp-robin tell you that he is hanging his harp upon the dark green cypress for the night. **1857** (1949) Thoreau *Jrl.* 9.413 **seMA,** The egg of the *Turdus solitarius* is lettered *"Swamp Robin."* Is this what they so call at New Bedford? **1881** *Cambridge Jeffersonian* (OH) [28 Apr 3]/6 (newspaperarchive.com), The swamp robin is a very scarce bird here. The red bird stays all winter, but we seldom see him on account of his shy habits. **1889** Ridgway *Ornith. IL* 1.62, *Turdus aonalaschkæ pallasii. . . Popular Synonyms.*—Eastern Hermit Thrush; . . Swamp Robin, or Ground Swamp Robin (New England). **1914** Eaton *Birds NY* 2.527, The Hermit thrush is often called the Swamp robin, on account of his beautiful song and his preference for cool, damp forests. . . In the winter he prefers cedar groves and evergreen swamps near the coast. **1929** Forbush *Birds MA* 3.400, *Hermit Thrush. . . Swamp angel; swamp robin. . .* Only New England thrush with rump and tail deep reddish-brown.

b =**wood thrush 1.**

1861 *New Engl. Farmer* 13.171, The Wood Thrush, (*Turdus mustelinus*) . . sometimes called the *Swamp Robin* or *Wood Robin.* **1873** in 1875 Prime *Life Samuel Morse* 596 **NEast,** The singing birds were nearly all silent, for it was July; but the throat of the swamp-robin sent its clear notes far away through the vistas. **1883** Nuttall Ornith. Club *Bulletin* 8.72 **NY,** *Turdus mustelinus.* Its common names are: *Wood Thrush, Wood Robin, Swamp Robin, Swamp Angel* (Adirondacks). **1897** *Oölogist* 14.27 **NC,** Wood Thrush. *Turdus mustelinus.* Commonly called "Swamp Robin" . . is both a summer and winter resident. **1917** Bacheller *Light Clearing* 394 **nNY,** We rode on in silence with the calls of the swamp robin and the hermit thrush ringing in our ears as the night fell. **1948** in a1972 Hench Coll. **VA,** Wood lark, swamp robin, wood thrush—names for the same bird. **1956** *Warren Times–Mirror* (PA) 26 July 4/1, The wood thrush, the swamp robin or the bell bird, has no fine intricate melody, but the simple song it sings has a deep, liquid sweetness. **2000** *DARE* File—Internet **PA,** The wood thrush's genus name Hylocichla is Greek. . . The nicknames, "swamp robin" and "wood robin," refer to its membership in the Thrush family.

c =**Swainson's thrush.**

1876 (1877) Minot *Land-Birds New Engl.* 36, Swainsoni. Swainson's Thrush. . . "Swamp Robin". **1889** Ridgway *Ornith. IL* 1.60 **NEng,** *Turdus ustulatus swainsonii. . . Popular Synonyms.*—Swainson's Thrush; Swamp Robin (New England). *Ibid* 61, The Olive-backed Thrush, or "Swamp Robin" as it is familiarly known in New England, is another of the species which in most parts of the United States where it is found occurs simply as a migrant. **1929** Forbush *Birds MA* 3.397, *Olive-backed Thrush. . . Swainson's thrush; swamp robin. . .* Form similar to that of Veery, but slightly stouter. **1956** MA Audubon Soc. *Bulletin* 40.129 **ME, MA,** *Olive-backed Thrush.* Swamp Robin.

d =**varied thrush.**

1903 *Amer. Anthropologist* 5.332 **Pacific NW,** The month is said to correspond to March. Then the varied thrush or "swamp robin" . . begins to whistle, humming birds and wasps begin to appear. **1926** *Mt. Rainier Nature News Notes* (Internet) **OR,** Two birds fighting on the wing tumbled down almost at my feet. I saw that one was a robin and the other a swamp-robin or varied Thrush. **1953** Jewett *Birds WA* 511, *Ixoreus naevius naevius.* . . Golden Robin; Swamp Robin; Alaska Robin.

e =veery.

1956 MA Audubon Soc. *Bulletin* 40.129 **NEng,** *Veery.* . . Swamp Robin.

2 =rufous-sided towhee.

1810 Wilson *Amer. Ornith.* 2.36, In Virginia he [=*Pipilo erythrophthalmus*] is called the Bulfinch; . . in Pennsylvania the Chewink, and by others the Swamp Robin. **1844** Giraud *Birds Long Is.* 124, *Pipilo erythrophthalmus.* . . This common bird is familiarly known by the appellations of "Ground Robin," "Swamp Robin," and "Chewink." **1916** *Times–Picayune* (New Orleans LA) 23 Apr mag sec 5, *Towhee.* . . Swamp Robin. . . This black and white and brown plumaged bird is a common inhabitant of the alluvial portions of the state and the open wooded sections of lower Louisiana. **1936** *Sun* (Baltimore MD) 17 Feb 7/2 **MD,** If that name [=*go-wank*] fails to strike a responsive chord, they're towhees, bush birds, . . or just plain swamp robins. **1956** MA Audubon Soc. *Bulletin* 40.254 **ME, MA,** *Towhee.* . . Swamp Robin.

3 =wild calla 1.

1849 Amer. Med. Assoc. *Trans.* 2.909 **MA,** *Calla palustris.* Swamp robin; water arum. The properties of this are likewise similar to the arums.

swamp root n

1 Any of var plants used medicinally; see quots. Note: Quots referring to Dr. Kilmer's Swamp Root, a patent medicine widely advertised from the 1880s through the 1940s, are not included here.

1910 Ritter *Mother's Remedies* 680, Poultice the bottom of the feet with blue flag swamp root mashed fine. **1935** in 1937 *Torreya* 37.96 **MO,** *Acorus Calamus.* . . Swamp-root, wild flag, wild iris. **c1938** in 1970 Hyatt *Hoodoo* 2.1157 **seLA** [Black], Yo' boil that together, dis Indian turnip an' dis blackjack vine, an' *swamp-root.* . . It's a root dey call de *swamp-root.* An' yo' make those diff'rent teas of that. That clean all of these insect—any kinda thing dey got in dere, dat clean it all out. **1941** Writers' Program *Guide WV* 140, Teas made from herbs and roots are regarded in high favor: . . swamproot tea for kidney trouble. **1960** *Lima News* (OH) 3 Mar 13/4 **ceNE,** If that mother really wants to help her boys over bed-wetting, tell her to try this recipe an old Indian woman gave my grandmother: Boil up magnolia blossoms with swamp root and chestnuts. **1967–70** *DARE* (Qu. S26b, *Wildflowers that grow in water or wet places*) Inf **CA**65, Swamp root—a white flower; wet places; **NY**10, Swamp root—wet places; (Qu. BB50c, *Remedies for infections*) Inf **CA**206, Swamp root; (Qu. BB50d, *Favorite spring tonics*) Infs **CA**65, **LA**8, Swamp root. [*DARE* Ed: The **CA** Infs are prob referring to **yerba mansa;** **LA**8 may be referring to the patent medicine.] **1986** Pederson *LAGS Concordance (Roots)* 2 infs, **LA,** Swamp root; 1 inf, **csLA,** Swamp root—for fever; 1 inf, **csLA,** Swamp root—with water, drink when cutting teeth; 1 inf, **ceTX,** Swamp root—medicinal, grows near water, vine; swamp root tea—for fever, other ailments. **2005** *DARE* File—Internet, [Caption:] Saururus cernuus—Lizard Tail/Swamproot. *Ibid,* Yerba Mansa. . . This medicinal herb is also called "Swamp Root". An infusion made from the aromatic, peppery roots is used by the native Americans of the southwest, as a general pain reliever and a treatment for stomach ulcers, chest congestion and cold.

2 Illegal liquor, moonshine. Cf *DS* DD21a, b, DD31

1918 *DN* 5.21 **NC,** *Swamp-root,* whiskey made in the woods. **1929** *AmSp* 4.385 **KS** [Wet words], Some of the common names for whiskey—*moonshine* . . *swamproot* . . *mountain dew*—seem to refer to its alleged origin, suggesting that it is manufactured by moonlight in the wilderness. **c1960** *Wilson Coll.* **csKY,** *Swamp-root.* . . Moonshine whiskey, made in the woods and swamps.

swamp rose n

Either of two **wild roses:** *Rosa carolina* or *R. palustris.*

[**1785** Marshall *Arbustrum* 135, Rosa palustris. *Swamp Pennsylvanian Rose.* This grows generally in swamps.] **1814** Bigelow *Florula Bostoniensis* 121, *Rosa Caroliniana.* . . *Swamp rose.* . . grows in swamps and wet grounds. **1822** Eaton *Botany* 451, *Rosa corymbosa* [=*R. palustris*] . . swamp rose. . . Petioles hairy and a little prickly. **1839** *S. Lit. Messenger* 5.45 **TN,** In the summer they [=meadows] are adorned with a profusion of wild flowers, . . among which the swamp rose . . and the beautiful wild honeysuckle (Azalea,) are conspicuous. **1862** *Defiance Democrat* (OH) [5 Apr 4]/1 (newspaperarchive.com), Where the violet grows,/ Or the pale swamp rose,/ . . / Dips her pale petals in the cooling stream. **1902** *Outing* 50.272, The Carolina, or swamp rose, . .

is well known to us all. **1924** Deam *Shrubs IN* 129, *Rosa palustris.* . . *Swamp Rose.* . . In Indiana it occurs throughout the State, growing only in wet places. **1936** IL Nat. Hist. Surv. *Wildflowers* 156, *Swamp Rose—Rosa carolina.* . . Common in swamps and low grounds, and blooms from June to August. **1967–70** *DARE* (Qu. S26d, *Wildflowers that grow in meadows;* not asked in early QRs) Inf **VA**52, Swamp rose; (Qu. S26e, *Other wildflowers not yet mentioned;* not asked in early QRs) Inf **MN**6, Swamp rose. **2005** *York Daily Rec.* (PA) 21 June (Internet), [Caption:] A swamp rose blossoms in JoAnn Babcock's garden.

swamp rose mallow n   Cf **mallow rose**

A **hibiscus,** usu *Hibiscus moscheutos.*

1848 Gray *Manual of Botany* 70, *H[ibiscus] Moscheutos.* . . *Swamp Rose-Mallow.* . . Borders of marshes along and near the coast. **1879** *Eve. Gaz.* (Pt. Jervis NY) 11 Sept [4]/1 (newspaperarchive.com), Professor Forrest Shepard of Norwich has found that the swamp rose mallow—Hibiscus Moscheutos—will yield a fine white fiber, suitable for making cordage. **1930** *Decatur Herald* (IL) 28 Sept 16/1, The swamp rosemallow . . sends forth its bright pink blossoms in August, when it is exceedingly attractive. **1975** *Bucks Co. Courier Times* (Levittown PA) 2 Aug 1/2, [Caption:] Leaf-eaten Swamp Rose Mallow shows the work of Japanese Beetles. **2002** *Intelligencer* (Doylestown PA) 9 May sec E 6/5, *Native plants to attract birds*—Swamp rose mallow (*Hibiscus moscheutos*)[.] Cardinal flower (*Lobelia cardinalis*) [etc].

swamp rose orchid n

=swamp pink 2.

1933 Small *Manual SE Flora* 377, *A[rethusa] bulbosa.* . . *Swamp rose-orchid.* . . Acid bogs. **2005** *DARE* File—Internet, Other terrestrial genera that grow as American wildflowers are the fringe orchids (*Blephariglottis*); . . the wild pinks, or swamp rose orchids (*Arethusa*), of northeastern sphagnum bogs.

swamp sassafras n

1 =sweet bay 2. Cf **sassafras B**

1785 Marshall *Arbustrum* 83, Magnolia glauca [=*M. virginiana*]. *Small Magnolia, or Swamp Sassafras.* This grows naturally in low, moist, or swampy ground. . . The flowers are . . of an agreeable smell. **1810** Michaux *Histoire des Arbres* 1.27, M[agnolia] glauca. . . *Swamp sassafras* . . , nom secondaire à une certaine distance de ces deux villes [=New York and Philadelphia]. [=M[agnolia] glauca. . . *Swamp sassafras* . . , secondary name at some remove from these two cities [=New York and Philadelphia].] **1897** Sudworth *Arborescent Flora* 195 **DE, PA, TN,** *Magnolia glauca.* . . Swamp Sassafras. **1960** Vines *Trees SW* 286, *Magnolia virginiana.* . . Vernacular names are . . Swamp Magnolia, Swamp-sassafras, and Indian-bark.

2 A **dogwood 1** (here: *Cornus rugosa*).

1852 Beach *Amer. Practice Med.* 3.48, Swamp Sassafras, Round-leaved dogwood. . . C.[ornus] Circinata. **1940** Clute *Amer. Plant Names* 256, *Cornus circinata* [=*C. rugosa*]. . . Swamp sassafras.

swamp sauger n   [Perh var of **swamp auger,** or perh *swamp* + **sauger**]   Cf *DS* CC17

1932 Stevens *Saginaw Paul Bunyan* 77 **MI,** Like the swamp sauger and hodag of the hills, the mince was a survivor of the prehistoric period in the Saginaw. **1969** Sorden *Lumberjack Lingo* 124 **NEng, Gt Lakes,** *Swamp sauger*—A mythical, swamp-dwelling animal of great strength. When a log stuck in the mud or in a swamp, the men said it would take a swamp sauger to get it out.

swamp saxifrage n

1 A **saxifrage n²** (here: *Saxifraga pensylvanica*) native chiefly east and north of the Mississippi and Ohio Valleys.

1848 Gray *Manual of Botany* 149, *S[axifraga] Pennsylvanica.* . . *Swamp Saxifrage.* . . Bogs, common. May, June. . . A homely species. **1892** IN Dept. Geol. & Nat. Resources *Rept. for 1891* 142, *Saxifraga Pennsylvanica.* . . Swamp Saxifrage. **1921** *Scientific Mth.* 12.251 **NY,** In the wetter places grow acres of marsh marigold and skunk cabbage interspersed with swamp saxifrage. **1953** *Amer. Midland Naturalist* 50.220 **MI,** The bishop's cap (*Mitella diphylla*), and swamp saxifrage (*Saxifraga pennsylvanica*) are common. **1968** *DARE* (Qu. S26b, *Wildflowers that grow in water or wet places*) Inf **PA**99, Swamp saxifrage. **1988** *Providence Jrl.* (RI) 21 Nov sec A 3 (Internet), The report notes that the Blunders "is considered one of the premier botanical sites in Rhode Island" and the home of the Swamp Saxifrage, a plant on the state's threatened species list. **2003** *Portland Press Herald* (ME) 12 Sept sec B 1 (Internet), *Rare Plants*—Northern blazing star[.] Pale green orchid[.] . . Swamp saxifrage.

2 A **saxifrage** n[2] native chiefly to the Northwest, usu *Saxifraga apetala, S. integrifolia,* or *S. nidifica.*

1973 Hitchcock–Cronquist *Flora Pacific NW* 197, Swamp s[axifrage] . . *S[axifraga] integrifolia.* **2005** *DARE* File—Internet **WA,** [Caption:] Western Swamp Saxifrage blossoms extreme detail [Saxifraga apetala (S. integrifolia var. apetala)]. **2005** *Ibid, Saxifraga nidifica var. claytoniifolia.* . . Swamp saxifrage may be found from the Blue and Wallowa Mts. of southeastern Washington and northeastern Oregon south to the Steens Mt. of southeastern Oregon, and further south to northern Nevada and northeastern California. It may be found eastward to central and southwestern Idaho.

swamp sego n Cf sego lily

=camas 1.

1917 Rydberg *Flora Rocky Mts.* 166, *Quamásia.* . . Camash, Blue Camas, Wild Hyacinth, Swamp Sego. **1963** Craighead *Rocky Mt. Wildflowers* 20, *Camassia quamash.* . . Camash, Swamp Sego. . . This has bright blue flowers. **2005** *DARE* File—Internet, *Camassia quamash* . . Common Name(s): Small camas, Common camass, Swamp sego. . . Description: A bulbous plant with basal clusters of narrow, grass-like, bright green leaves.

swamp shakes n

=shaking ague.

1932 Kelley *Inchin' Along* 223 **AL** [Black], It de bes' stuff dey is fuh de swamp shakes.

swamp sheldrake n

Either the common **merganser** *(Mergus merganser)* or the **hooded merganser.**

1844 DeKay *Zool. NY* 2.318, *Mergus merganser.* . . The female is thought by our sportsmen to be a distinct species, and is called *Weaser,* or *Swamp Sheldrake.* **1888** Trumbull *Names of Birds* 64 seMA, *[Mergus merganser:]* At West Barnstable, Mass., *swamp sheldrake. Ibid* 73 seNY, *Hooded Merganser.* . . On Long Island at Shinnecock Bay, Moriches, and Bellport, *swamp sheldrake.* **1910** Eaton *Birds NY* 1.181, The Hooded merganser, Swamp sheldrake, Hairy-head, or Water pheasant is generally distributed in New York State, occurring in many places where the other mergansers are unknown, because of its habit of frequenting swamps and ponds which are too small to attract the other species.

swamp silkweed n Cf silkweed

A **swamp milkweed** (here: *Asclepias incarnata*).

1843 Torrey *Flora NY* 2.122, *Asclepias incarnata.* . . *Swamp Silkweed.* . . It affords but little milky juice when wounded. It is sometimes employed in domestic practice, and is considered anodyne and diaphoretic. **1887** Bentley *Manual Botany* 618, *A[sclepias] incarnata,* Swamp Silk-weed. **2003** *IA Dept. Transportation Iowa's Living Roadway Plant Profiler* 46 **IA,** *Swamp Milkweed* . . *Other common names* . . Swamp Silkweed. . . A good quality fiber is obtained from the bark and is used in twine and cloth; the seed floss is used to stuff pillows and mixed with other fibers to make cloth.

swamp smartweed n

A **smartweed,** usu *Polygonum amphibium* or *P. hydropiperoides.*

1895 MO Bot. Garden *Annual Rept.* 65 seMO, *Polygonum densiflorum,* the common swamp smartweed of that region . . occurs in dense growths often forming a floating accumulation on which in places a man may walk. **1911** NJ State Museum *Annual Rept. for 1910* 421, *Polygonum emersum [=P. amphibium].* . . *Swamp Smartweed.* . . Borders of swamps and ditches. **1947** *Amer. Midland Naturalist* 38.41 **MD,** *Polygonum hydropiperoides* (Swamp Smartweed). Occasional (locally common) in pools in runs on flood plain. **1966** Torrey Bot. Club *Bulletin* 93.357 **NY,** At Acme pond we saw . . swamp smartweed floating at the surface. **2003** *Post–Std.* (Syracuse NY) 17 Aug sec B 2/1, Among the rare and endangered species scientists are looking for are the bog turtle . . and the swamp smartweed.

swamp snake n

Often with modifier: Any of var water-dwelling snakes, as:

a A usu red-bellied snake *(Seminatrix pygaea)* native from coastal North Carolina to Florida and southeastern Alabama.

[**1709** (1967) Lawson *New Voyage* 135 **NC, SC,** Of the Swamp-Snakes there are three sorts, which are very near akin to the Water-Snakes, and may be rank'd amongst them. The belly of the first is of a Carnation or Pink Colour; his back a dirty brown; they are large, but

have not much Venom in them, as ever I learnt. The next is a large Snake, of a brown Dirt Colour, and always abides in the Marshes. The last is mottled, and very poisonous. They dwell in Swamps Sides, and Ponds, and have prodigious wide Mouths, and (though not long) arrive to the thickness of the Calf of a Man's Leg.] **1924** *Oakland Tribune* (CA) 3 June 17/7 **SC,** An adolescent specimen of the black swamp snake known as seminatrix pygea [sic], hitherto reported only in Florida, was found. **1950** MI Univ. Museum Zool. *Misc. Pub.* 76.5 **FL,** The black swamp snake *Seminatrix* is a monotypic genus of the southeastern United States. . . More than 90 per cent of the specimens available from collections are from a single county (Alachua) in north-central Florida. **1973** *Amer. Midland Naturalist* 89.336 **FL,** A small black swamp snake *(Seminatrix pygaea)* was found scorched and dead under a mat of partly burned grass. **1979** Behler–King *Audubon Field Guide Reptiles* 652, Swamp Snake *(Seminatrix pygaea).* . . Swamps, cedar and cypress ponds, canals, and drainage ditches, especially areas overgrown with water hyacinth. **1995** *Amer. Midland Naturalist* 134.371, The black swamp snake *Seminatrix pygaea* is a small, highly aquatic, natricine snake found along the Atlantic Coastal Plain in the southeastern United States. **2005** *DARE* File—Internet **NC,** *Seminatrix pygaea.* . . Carolina Swamp Snakes are aquatic snakes that range between 10 and 15 in. (25–38 cm) in length. . . They feed on leeches, small fish, worms, and small amphibians such as frogs, Dwarf Salamanders, and tadpoles.

b Either the **horn snake 1** or the related **rainbow snake.**

[**1709** see **a** above.] **c1981** Linzey–Clifford *Snakes VA* 80, *Farancia abacura.* . . Other Common Names . . red-bellied swamp snake. . . Shiny black and smooth above. . . The basic belly color is pink or red. . . These are snakes of the swamps and other lowlands. . . Found on the coastal plain from Virginia to southern Florida and west into eastern Texas. . . Northward in the Mississippi Valley to Missouri, Kentucky, and Illinois. *Ibid* 83, *Farancia erytrogramma* [sic]. . . Other Common Names . . red swamp snake. . . Swamps, marshes (freshwater and brackish), or slow-moving streams and adjacent sandy soils. . . The range of this snake is restricted to the southeastern United States. **2005** *DARE* File—Internet **AL,** Rainbow Snake. . . Other Names . . Red Swamp Snake. . . Occurs across Coastal Plain from Maryland and Virginia to Mississippi and Louisiana, extending southward into central Florida.

c A **water snake 3:** usu *Regina alleni,* but also *R. rigida.* For other names of the former see **mud snake**

[**1709** see **a** above.] **1952** Ditmars *N. Amer. Snakes* 76 **FL, GA,** Allen's Snake, Swamp Snake, Mud Snake, *Liodytes alleni [=Regina a.]* **1958** Conant *Reptiles & Amphibians* 137, Striped Swamp Snake— *Liodytes alleni.* . . Thoroughly aquatic and at home in dense vegetation in shallow water. . At twilight, especially on rainy or humid evenings, Striped Swamp Snakes sometimes travel overland. **1980** *Ecological Monogr.* 50.411, The foraging ecology and trophic dynamics of the striped swamp snake, *Regina alleni,* were studied from 1974–1977 in a south Florida water hyacinth community. **c1981** Linzey–Clifford *Snakes VA* 50, *Regina rigida.* . . Other Common Names: Swamp snake, stiff snake. . . Scales are very shiny, making this the shiniest of the water snakes. **2005** *DARE* File—Internet **FL,** Striped Swamp Snake . . *Regina alleni.* . . Adults are glossy brown. . . The belly is normally uniform yellowish, but can be reddish-orange with a darker smudges [sic] to a well defined row of spots.

swamp snowball n obs

A **hydrangea 1** (here: *Hydrangea quercifolia*).

1834 Audubon *Ornith. Biog.* 2.121 **LA,** The Swamp Snowball. *Hydrangea quercifolia.* . . is found on the broken sandy banks bordering small water-courses, and is abundant in such situations in the uplands of Louisiana. **1854** Wailes *Rept. on Ag. & Geol. MS* 344, Swamp snowball, Hydrangea quercifolia.

swamp song sparrow See swamp sparrow 1

swamp Spanish oak n

1 **=pin oak 1a.** Cf **Spanish oak b(7), swamp ~ 2a(2)**

1810 Michaux *Histoire des Arbres* 1.25, Quercus palustris. . . *Swamp Spanish oak* . . dans les Etats de Pensylvanie et de Maryland. [=Quercus palustris. . . *Swamp Spanish oak* . . in Pennsylvania and of Maryland.] **1897** Sudworth *Arborescent Flora* 172 **AR, KS,** Quercus palustris. . . Swamp Spanish Oak. **1933** Small *Manual SE Flora* 429, *Q[uercus] palustris.* . . Swamp Spanish Oak. . . Woods and swamps, various provinces. **1979** Little *Checklist U.S. Trees* 238, *Quercus palustris.* . . *Other common names* . . swamp Spanish oak.

2 **=cherrybark oak.** Cf **Spanish oak b(5), swamp ~ 2b(4)**

1922 Sargent *Manual Trees* 256, Swamp Spanish Oak. Red Oak.

Quercus pagoda. . . Rich bottom-lands and the alluvial banks of streams. . . [O]ne of the largest and most valuable timber-trees in the river swamps of the Yazoo basin, Mississippi, and of eastern Arkansas. **1947** Collingwood–Brush *Knowing Trees* 197, Because of the resemblance of the bark to that of black cherry, swamp red oak is often known as cherry-bark oak. It is also quite commonly known as swamp Spanish oak. **1979** Little *Checklist U.S. Trees* 231, Cherrybark oak. . . *Quercus pagoda.* . . Other common names . . swamp Spanish oak.

swamp sparrow n

1 also *swamp song sparrow;* Std: a dark-colored sparrow (*Melospiza georgiana*) that frequents low, wet lands.   Also called **grass sparrow f, ground ~ 1e, swamp finch**
2 Either the **hermit thrush 1** or the **wood thrush 1.**

1914 *Auk* 31.235 **cAL,** *Hylocichla mustelina.* Wood Thrush. [Local name:] 'Swamp Sparrow.' Very common summer resident, inhabiting alike moist and dry situations. **1962** Imhof *AL Birds* 402, *Wood Thrush.* . . Other names . . Swamp Sparrow. *Ibid* 403, *Hermit Thrush.* . . Other name: Swamp Sparrow.

swamp spruce n

=black spruce 1.

1870 *Bangor Daily Whig & Courier* (ME) [26 Apr 4]/1 (newspaperarchive.com), Men and dogs followed him [=a bear] until he "treed" somewhere among swamp spruce so dense that they could not see him. **1898** *Amer. Naturalist* 32.213, [In] the Adirondack region, there is now good evidence of . . four species: *P[icea] canadensis,* the white spruce, *P. mariana,* the black spruce, *P. rubra,* the red spruce, . . and what is held to be a new species, the swamp spruce, *P. brevifolia* [= *P. mariana*]. **1929** *Daily Northwestern* (Oshkosh WI) 4 Sept 2/2, Jack pine and swamp spruce have been in the path of most of the fires thus far, but more valuable timber has been threatened. **1950** Grimm *Trees PA* 72, *Picea mariana.* . . often invades the bog mats surrounding lakes, or the cold sphagnum bogs." . . It is therefore often referred to as the "Swamp Spruce." **1967–69** *DARE* (Qu. T5, . . *Kinds of evergreens, other than pine*) Infs **MA62, MN3,** 19, Swamp spruce; **AK9,** Swamp spruce—called fish-trap spruce because the poles were used as supports for fish traps in the sea; (Qu. T15, . . *Kinds of swamp trees*) Infs **AK9, MA62,** Swamp spruce. **2005** *DARE* File—Internet **Nth,** The current common names of this species [=*Picea mariana*] include black spruce, swamp spruce and bog spruce. The latter two names make sense as they relate to the habitat of the species.

swamp sumac n

A **poison sumac** (here: *Toxicodendron vernix*).

1721 Royal Soc. London *Philos. Trans.* 31.145, The Poyson-Wood-Tree grows only in Swamps, or low wet Grounds, and . . is by some called the *Swamp Sumach.* **1749** in 1970 Kalm *Resejournal* 2.145, *Rhus Toxicodendron.* . . Swamp-sumach. **1814** Bigelow *Florula Bostoniensis* 72, *Rhus vernix.* Poison dogwood. Swamp Sumach. . . Grows in bunches in wet swamps. **1885** *Bismarck Daily Tribune* (ND) 31 Oct [4]/2 (newspaperarchive.com), Rhus venenata, the poisonous species, is known in different localities under the several names of poison ash, poison elder, poison dogwood and poison or swamp sumach, and is commonly found in damp or swampy situations. **1941** *LANE* Map 250 *(Sumach),* The terms *swamp sumach* . . [offered by 2 infs] and *upland sumach* . . are applied in Rhode Island to the poison sumach according to the location in which it grows. **1967–70** *DARE* (Qu. T13, . . *Names . . for . . sumac*) Infs **IN69, NJ31, WA30,** Swamp sumac; (Qu. S17, . . *Kinds of plants . . that . . cause itching and swelling*) Inf **VA82,** Thunderwood—swamp sumac.

swamp sunflower n

1 A **sneezeweed 1** (here: *Helenium autumnale*).

1828 Rafinesque *Med. Flora* 1.235, *Helenium Autumnale.* . . Vulgar Names. . . Swamp Sunflower. . . It grows . . in wet meadows, and savannas, damp fields, overflowed grounds, banks of streams. **1898** U.S. Dept. Ag. Div. Botany *Bulletin* 20.54, *Helenium autumnale* . . swamp sunflower. **1934** *Amer. Midland Naturalist* 15.74, *Helenium autumnale* L. False or Swamp Sunflower. **1968** Schmutz et al. *Livestock-Poisoning Plants AZ* 139, Swamp sunflower. **2005** *Los Angeles Times* (CA) 24 Feb sec F 4 (Internet), Japanese anemone, Mexican marigold, liatris and swamp sunflower won't flower until fall.

2 Any of var **sunflowers 1,** but usu *Helianthus angustifolius;* see quots.

1898 Britton–Brown *Illustr. Flora* 3.422, Helianthus angustifolius. . . Narrow-leaved or Swamp Sunflower. **1932** *Ecological Monogr.* 2.199,

Helianthus angustifolius L. Narrow-leaf Sunflower, Swamp Sunflower. **1954** *Ecology* 35.59, The most important forbs are *Chrysopsis graminifolia* . . and swamp sunflower (*Helianthus annuus* L.) **1957** *Mansfield News–Jrl.* (OH) 17 Aug 4/3, In the lowlands and along ditches we are sure to see the golden blankets formed by thousands of plants of the Swamp Sunflower. Helianthus angustifolius is undoubtedly the prettiest of the family. **2005** *DARE* File—Internet, Helianthus simulans (narrow-leaved sunflower, swamp sunflower). *Ibid* **WI,** *Helianthus giganteus* L.—giant sunflower, swamp sunflower, tall sunflower. . . Status: Native.

swamp sycamore n

=buttonbush 1.

1973 Stephens *Woody Plants* 458, *Cephalanthus occidentalis.* . . Swamp sycamore. . . It is common around ponds, lakes, and sloughs.

swamp tea n

1 **=Labrador tea.**

1828 *Pittsfield Sun* (MA) 6 Nov 2/4 **VT,** Cold gander for breakfast, swamp tea and some nut cakes; the latter some consolation. **1876** Hobbs *Bot. Hdbk.* 118, Tea, Swamp. . . Ledum palustre. **1898** *Jrl. Amer. Folkl.* 11.273 **WA,** *Ledum latifolium* [=*L. groenlandicum*]. . . Swamp tea. **1996** in 2005 *DARE* File—Internet **MN,** Lots of people . . on northern reservations here and west into Montana, can show you what they call "swamp tea" though there are two different plants that different kids will show you. Only one of these is what was the traditional swamp tea, . . *Ledum glandulosum,* or Laborador [sic] Tea as its main common English name. The other was known as *Odigadimanido,* a special gift of the spirit or Manido powers. That's *Ceanothus ovatus* [= *C. herbaceus*], or New Jersey Tea in its common English name. *Swamp tea* . . , botanically [sic] named *Ledum glandulosum,* common name Laborador Tea, is found from Greenland to the Rockies, and Northwest coast. . . Most reservation people know about it. It contributes vitamins and minerals, contains both thyeine and caffeine for a pick-up and to still that coffee craving. Tea can be made from crushed green leaves.

2 **=New Jersey tea.**

1996 [see **1** above].

swamp thistle n

A **thistle a** (here: *Cirsium muticum*).

1848 Gray *Manual of Botany* 243, *C[irsium] muticum.* . . Swamp Thistle. . . Swamps and low copses, common. **1880** *Amer. Naturalist* 14.778, In *Cirsium muticum,* or swamp thistle, the crystals of inuline were very small and indistinct. **1892** *Science* 20.333, In southern New York their [=hummingbirds'] favorite flower is the swamp-thistle (*Cirsium muticum*). **1942** *Ecological Monogr.* 12.121 **WI,** Forbs are numerous in this zone, sunflower (*Helianthus giganteus, H. grosseserratus*), swamp milkweed (*Asclepias incarnata*), swamp thistle (*Cirsium muticum*). **1969** *Stevens Point Daily Jrl.* (WI) 1 Oct 16/2, Scattered among them [=annuals] are red osier dogwood and pussy willow, . . stalks of angelica and swamp thistle 12 feet high. **2003** *Chicago Tribune* (IL) 24 Aug 1 (Internet), [Caption:] A patch of swamp thistle, the only plant that swamp metalmark caterpillars will call home, at Bluff Spring Fen Nature Preserve in Elgin.

swamp thrush n

1 **=hermit thrush 1.**

1889 *Ornith. & Oologists' Semi-Annual* 1.43, *Turdus aonalaschkae pallasii,* Hermit Thrush—Swamp Thrush. **1895** Minot *Land-Birds New Engl.* 30, *Aonalaschkae Pallasii* [=*Catharus guttatus*]. . . "Swamp Thrush". . . Common near Boston in April and October. **1956** MA Audubon Soc. *Bulletin* 40.129 **ME, MA,** *Hermit Thrush.* . . Swamp Thrush.

2 **=rufous-sided towhee.**

1866 *Harper's New Mth. Mag.* 32.239, The wax-wing, cedar-bird, and cherry-bird are different names for the same individual; so the bobolink, rice-bird, and rice-bunting; the chewink, swamp-robin, swamp-thrush, and oven-bird [etc].

swamp tupelo n

Either a **tupelo** (here: *Nyssa biflora*) or a **tupelo gum** (here: *N. aquatica*).   For other names of the former see **black gum 1, swamp ~, water tupelo**

1897 Sudworth *Arborescent Flora* 311 **LA, SC,** *Nyssa aquatica.* . . Swamp Tupelo. **1903** *DN* 2.335 **seMO,** Tupelo-gum. . . Swamp tupelo. A tree not related to the gum. **1907** *DN* 3.238 **nwAR,** Tupelo gum. . . Swamp tupelo. **1908** Britton *N. Amer. Trees* 739, *Nyssa aquatica.* . . A water-loving tree . . called . . Swamp tupelo. **1946** West–Arnold *Native*

Trees FL 163, *Nyssa sylvatica biflora* [=*N. biflora*]. . . Swamp Tupelo. . . restricted to shallow water at savannah margins and wet soil adjacent to streams and lakes.   **1979** Little *Checklist U.S. Trees* 178, *Nyssa aquatica.* . . swamp tupelo.   **Ibid** 179, *Nyssa sylvatica* var. *biflora.* . . swamp tupelo.   **1994** *Orlando Sentinel* (FL) 16 Apr 13 (Internet), Wet areas above the normal water level may be inundated for short period of time. At this level, trees such as bald cypress, pond cypress, swamp tupelo or black gum, . . and pond pine are adapted.   **2005** *Richmond Times–Dispatch* (VA) 29 May sec J 1 (Internet), Part of the Beidler sanctuary—roughly 1,800 acres of virgin bald cypress and swamp tupelo trees—represents the largest such stand remaining in the country.

swamp turnip n
=jack-in-the-pulpit 1.
   1880 (1881) Nickell *Bot. Ready Ref.* 22, *Arum Triphyllum*. Indian Turnip. Dragon Root. Wake Robin. . . Wild Turnip. Jack-in-the-Pulpit. Dragon Turnip. Starchwort. Pepper Turnip. . . Marsh Turnip. Meadow Turnip. Swamp Turnip.   **1930** Sievers *Amer. Med. Plants* 37, *Arisaema triphyllum.* . . swamp turnip.   **2005** *DARE* File—Internet, *Special preparation is required* to safely taste why Jack-in-the-pulpit is . . called . . *swamp turnip.*

swamp turtle n
1 A **snapping turtle 1** (here: *Chelydra serpentina*).   **esp NC**
   [**1843** *Tioga Eagle* (Wellsboro PA) 11 Oct [2]/3 (newspaperarchive.com), An Ingenius [sic] *Cradle of Domestic Manufacture,* made by a gentleman in Mississippi, and sent as a present to a friend in Charleston, is described in the following letter which was received with the cradle: "The body or frame of the cradle is manufactured of the shell of what we call the snapping turtle, that weighed 135 pounds, caught by myself, out of my own waters. . . [A]ccompanying the whole is the hide of a panther, dressed after the fashion of the chamois, the animal having been slain by my own hands. . . This is for the stranger to loll and roll upon when tired of his cradle. . . The stranger, whatever may become his name hereafter, may boast that he was rocked to sleep in the shell of a swamp turtle.[*"*]]   **1906** NC Geol. & Economic Surv. *Bulletin* 14.65, *Chelydra serpentina.* . . is the common "swamp-turtle" of the fresh-water ponds.   **1942** *Amer. Midland Naturalist* 28.294 **Ocracoke Is. NC,** *Chelydra serpentina*. Common snapper; "swamp turtle."   **1966–69** *DARE* (Qu. P24, . . *Kinds of turtles*) Infs **NC**12, 27, 60, Swamp turtle; **NC**1, Swamp turtle [tɝ·kḷ].
2 A **red-bellied turtle** (here: *Chrysemys picta bellii*).
   1945 *Jrl. Amer. Folkl.* 58.309 **PA,** The painted turtle [*Chrysemys bellii marginata* (Agassiz)] they [=the Cayuga] speak of in English as the "swamp turtle" and in Cayuga as *kanu'wa ga'hi·* or "shell slanted."

swampuh   See swamp Yankee

swamp violet n   Also *blue swamp violet, purple ~*
A **violet** (here: *Viola palustris*) native to much of the western US and New England.
   1876 *Gardener's Mth. & Horticulturist* 18.149, We have several varieties of the wild violet; first the swamp violet with its shining smooth green leaves and vivid blue flower [etc].   **1916** Meany *Mt. Rainier* 270 **swWA,** *Viola palustris.* . . The common swamp violet was found at Narada Falls.   **1934** Haskin *Wild Flowers Pacific Coast* 221, *Viola palustris.* . Blue Swamp Violet.   **1937** *Amer. Midland Naturalist* 18.974 **Pacific NW,** *Viola palustris.* . , Purple Swamp Violet.   **1967** Gilkey–Dennis *Hdbk. NW Plants* 264, *Viola palustris.* . Swamp violet. . . swampy places.   **1969–70** *DARE* (Qu. S11, . . *Blue violet*) Inf **MA**78, Swamp violet; **RI**15, Swamp violet— deep, purplish hue.   **1993** *Seattle Daily Times* (WA) 27 May 4 (Internet), West Hylebos Wetlands State Park: A 70-acre headwater swamp. . . plants . . include red huckleberry, . . swamp violet, swamp laurel [etc].

swamp wampee   See wampee b

swamp wamper n   Also *swamp womper*
A **king snake 1** (here: *Lampropeltis getula*).
   1951 Teale *North with Spring* 274 **sNJ,** King snakes are "swamp wompers."   **1958** Conant *Reptiles & Amphibians* 167, Eastern kingsnake. . . Habitat is chiefly terrestrial, but it shows a distinct liking for stream banks and borders of swamps. . . Other vernacular names are "thunder snake" and "swamp wamper."   **2005** *DARE* File—Internet **NJ,** *Eastern Kingsnake.* . . This snake, locally called the "swamp wamper," is found only in southern New Jersey from southern Monmouth County southward and is considered common in New Jersey.

swamp wampus   See wampus n² 1

swamp warbler n
1 **=Connecticut warbler.**
   [**1895** Seton in Chapman *Hdbk. Birds* 370, "Connecticut Warbler" is an unfortunate misnomer for this species. "Swamp" or "Tamarac Warbler," or "Bog Black-Throat," would have been much more truly descriptive.]   **1917** (1923) *Birds Amer.* 3.156, *Oporornis agilis.* . . *Other Names.*—Bog Black-throat; Tamarack Warbler; Swamp Warbler.
2 **=prothonotary warbler.**   Cf **swamp yellowbird**
   [**1891** *Century Dict.* 6099, *Swamp-warbler.* . . One of several small sylvicoline birds of the United States . . , as the prothonotary warbler . . , the worm-eating warbler . . , and some related species, formerly all referred to Audubon's genus *Helinaia*.]   **1946** Hausman *Eastern Birds* 498, *Prothonotary warbler.* . . Swamp warbler. . . Habitat—Swampy regions, inundated woodlands, and the marshy, bushy banks of streams.

swamp water n
1 Among loggers: tea.
   1956 Sorden–Ebert *Logger's Words* 36 **Gt Lakes, NEng,** *Swamp-water.* Tea.   **1966** *DARE* Tape **MI**10, Back when I was first becoming seriously interested in . . the activities of some of the older men who had worked in the woods during that period, I couldn't help being impressed by . . an inventive flair that colored their language and their slang. . . Some fellows called tea "swamp water."
2 An alcoholic beverage; see quots.
   1950 *WELS* (Names for any kind of bad liquor) 1 Inf, **cnWI,** Swamp water.   **1970** *DARE* (Qu. DD25, . . *Nicknames . . for beer*) Inf **TN**53, Swamp water.

swamp white cedar n
A **white cedar** (here: *Chamaecyparis thyoides*).
   1904 Torrey Bot. Club *Bulletin* 31.360 **NH,** *Batcheder, F.W.* . . Discusses the occurrence of the swamp white cedar at Manchester, N.H.   **1954** *Progress* (Clearfield PA) 21 Dec 17/1, Outstanding among the evergreens are the Balsam fir, . . Canadian yew, and swamp white cedar.   **1962** *Lima News* (OH) 15 Apr sec A 19/1, [Advt:] We have styles of Early American Rustic Fence—*Swamp White Cedar.*

swamp white oak n   Cf **swamp oak**
1 A large **oak** (here: *Quercus bicolor*) native to much of the northeast quadrant of the US.   Also called **swamp oak 2a(1)**
   1725 in 1896 Cambridge MA Proprietors *Records* 314, We have Settled ye Line . . to a Swamp white Oak tree markd.   **1785** Marshall *Arbustrum* 120, Quercus alba palustris. *Swamp White Oak.* . becomes a pretty large spreading tree.   **1812** Michaux *Histoire des Arbres* 2.46, *Quercus prinus discolor.* . . Dans toutes les parties des Etats-Unis, où existe cette espèce de Chêne, on lui donne le nom de *Swamp white oak.* [=*Quercus prinus discolor* [=*Q. bicolor*]. . . In all parts of the United States where this species of oak exists, it is called *swamp white oak.*]   **1872** *Amer. Naturalist* 6.659 **IN,** The principal trees . . (i.e. which . . are more usually seventy feet and upwards), are hickories . . , swamp white oak (*Q. bicolor*), swamp chestnut oak (*Q. prinos*) [etc].   **1904** *Cambridge Jeffersonian* (OH) 22 Sept 4/5, Thence east to a swamp white oak in a hedge fence.   **1968–70** *DARE* (Qu. T10, . . *Kinds of oak trees*) Infs **CT**4, **OH**92, **PA**99, Swamp white oak; **NJ**39, Swamp white oak—used for ax handles.   **2005** *Post–Std.* (Syracuse NY) 29 Apr sec B 3/1, The swamp white oak is very tall / It does not look small at all.
2 **=overcup oak 1.**
   1817 Darby *Geogr. Descr. LA* 355, *Quercus lyrata.* Swamp white oak.   **1897** Sudworth *Arborescent Flora* 155 **TX,** *Quercus lyrata.* . . Swamp White Oak.   **1963** *Amer. Midland Naturalist* 69.351, *Q[uercus] lyrata.* . . Swamp white oak. Flood-plain forest, frequent.
3 **=basket oak 1.**
   [**1761** in 1941 Woodward *Ploughs & Politicks* 320 **NJ,** It bears very large Acorns. It is by some called Chestnt WO [=white oak] others call ye Swamp WO & some Turkey Oak.]   **1897** Sudworth *Arborescent Flora* 158 **AL, DE,** *Quercus michauxii.* . . Swamp White Oak.   **1943** *Amer. Midland Naturalist* 29.784, *Quercus Prinus* [=*Q. michauxii*]. . . in moist alluvial ground along streams . . is often abundant and of great economic value for lumber. It is sometimes called swamp white oak or swamp chestnut oak or simply white oak by the lumbermen and country people, but over the greater part of its range it is well known as basket oak or cow oak.   **1950** Gray–Fernald *Manual of Botany* 544, *Q[uercus] Michauxii.* . . Swamp-white O[ak]. . . Inundated bottoms, stream-borders and swamps.   **1996** *Advocate* (Baton Rouge LA) 7 Apr sec H 9 (Internet), Trees for wet sites—Sycamore (Platanus occidentalis), . . Overcup oak (Quercus lyrata), Swamp white oak (Quercus michauxii) [etc].

swamp widgeon n

=**European widgeon.**

1911 *Forest & Stream* 77.173 **GA,** *Mareca penelope.* . . The bird is known as Swamp Widgeon on the Savannah River, Ga.

swamp wiggler See **swamp worm**

swamp willow n

1 Any of var **willows 1,** but esp a **black willow 1** (here: *Salix nigra*), a **pussy willow** n[1] (here: *Salix discolor*), or the coastal plain **willow 1** *(Salix caroliniana).*

1765 (1942) Bartram *Diary of a Journey* 17 **NC,** Thay have ye upland willow oak with A hoary leafe, & ye swamp willow with A narrow leafe. **1792** Belknap *Hist. NH* 3.112, *Swamp willow (salix)* is the first tree that shows its blossoms in the spring. In some seasons, its white flowers exhibit a delightful appearance, when all the neighbouring trees remain in their wintry hue. **1814** Bigelow *Florula Bostoniensis* 239, *Salix eriocephala* [here: prob =*S. discolor*]. . . *Swamp Willow.* . . A small tree, common in low, moist grounds. **1853** in 1980 *Jrl. S. Hist.* 46.415 **Sth,** We know a country woman of ours, a farmer's wife, . . who has, during the last season, sold above $200 worth of baskets, manufactured during her leisure hours, out of the common swamp willow. **1880** *Torrey Bot. Club Bulletin* 7.55 **NY,** In a swamp willow found on the 4th of April, 1880. . . The catkins towards the top of the shrub—which was about 7 ft. high—as well as those along the ends of the lower branches, were normally staminate. . . Perhaps I should have stated that the willow (*Salix discolor?*) was growing on the border of a reedy marsh. **1921** Deam *Trees IN* 43, *Salix discolor.* . . Swamp willow. **1933** Small *Manual SE Flora* 413, *S[alix] nigra.* . . Swamp-willow. . . Low grounds, swamps, and river-banks. **1942** *Ecological Monogr.* 12.267 **NE,** [Caption:] Tops of the swamp willow *(Salix petiolaris)* appear in the background above the wild rice. **1966–68** *DARE* (Qu. T15, . . *Kinds of swamp trees*) Infs **MD20, NC27, 79, NH14, PA163,** Swamp willow. [*DARE* Ed: Some of these Infs may refer instead to other senses below.] **1968** Radford et al. *Manual Flora Carolinas* 358, *S[alix] caroliniana* . . Swamp w[illow]. . . stream banks and low, moist areas. **1980** Little *Audubon Guide N. Amer. Trees E. Region* 335, *Black Willow*—"Swamp Willow" . . *Salix nigra.* . . The largest and most important New World willow with one of the most extensive ranges across the country. **2005** *Westborough News* (MA) 5 Mar 5 (Internet), Pussy willow grows in sunny, wet areas, like many other willows. It is sometimes called swamp willow. **2005** *DARE* File—Internet Okefenokee **GA,** Swamp Willow *(Salix caroliniana)*—The inner bark and leaves of many willows, including the bark of the swamp willow, yields [sic] the medicinal extract, salicin (salicylic acid).

2 A **red osier** (here: *Cornus sericea*). *obs* Cf **redwood 1**

1805 (1904) Lewis *Orig. Jrls. Lewis & Clark Exped.* 1.299, The under brush is willow, red wood, (sometimes called red or swamp willow).

3 =**swamp loosestrife 1.**

1858 Amer. Pharmaceutical Assoc. *Proc.* 269, [*Lythrum*] *verticillatum.* Swamp Willow. **1876** Hobbs *Bot. Hdbk.* 189, Lythrum verticillatum, . . Sw[am]p willow.

4 A **burning bush 1** (here: *Euonymus americanus*). Cf **swamp dogwood 5**

1937 Thornburgh *Gt. Smoky Mts.* 25, One of the showiest shrubs in the Great Smokies [is] the evonymous [sic], wahoo or spindlebush. . . It has many descriptive local names—swamp willow, strawberry bush, catspaw, jewel-box, but most descriptive of all is the name given by a mountain man of, "Hearts-bustin'-with-love."

swamp willow herb n

=**swamp loosestrife 1.**

1822 Eaton *Botany* 346, Lythrum verticillatum. . . Swamp-willowherb. **1856** MI State Ag. Soc. *Trans. for 1855* 7.405, Decodon verticillatum. . . Swamp willow-herb. **1866** Hale *Systematic Treatise Abortion* 99, *Decodon verticillatus.* This plant, known to botanists as *lythrum verticillatum,* and by the common people as *swamp loosestrife,* or swamp-willow-herb, has the reputation of causing abortion in brute animals. **1903** Porter *Flora PA* 220, *Decodon verticillatus.* . . Swamp willow-herb or Loosestrife. . . In swamps.

swamp willow oak See **willow oak 3**

swamp wire grass n Cf **wire grass 2a**

A **bluegrass 1** (here: *Poa palustris*).

1751 Eliot *Continuation Field-Husbandry* 13 **CT,** There are Two sorts of Grass which are Natives of the Country, which I would Recommend;

these are *Herd-Grass,* . . the other is *Fowl Meadow,* somtimes called *Duck-Grass,* and somtimes *Swamp-wire-Grass.* . . It is suppos'd to be brought into the Meadows at *Hartford* by the Annual Floods, and called there *Swamp-wire Grass.* **1910** Graves *Flowering Plants* 73 **CT,** *Poa triflora.* . . Swamp Wire Grass. **1977** in 2005 *DARE* File—Internet **CA** (as of 1898), Our cattle had been fortunate to have the spring swamp wire grass to nibble on.

swamp womper See **swamp wamper**

swampwood n

1 =**buttonbush 1.**

1667 in 1889 Plymouth MA *Records* 1.87, On the south side and east end of the said land [I] have bounded it with a swamp wood tree [*DARE* Ed: identity uncertain]. **1828** Rafinesque *Med. Flora* 1.100, *Cephalanthus occidentalis.* . . Swampwood. . . mostly found near streams, ponds, swamps, lakes. **1960** Vines *Trees SW* 938, *Cephalanthus occidentalis.* . . Swampwood.

2 =**leatherwood 1.**

1828 Rafinesque *Med. Flora* 1.158, *Dirca Palustris.* . . Swampwood. . . near streams, and in shady swamps. **1876** Hobbs *Bot. Hdbk.* 115, Swamp wood, Leatherwood, Dirca palustris. **1892** (1974) Millspaugh *Amer. Med. Plants* 146-1, *Dirca palustris.* . . Com[mon] names. . . Rope bark, Swampwood [etc]. **1933** Small *Manual SE Flora* 919, *D[irca] palustris.* . . Swamp-wood. **1983** *Syracuse Herald–Amer.* (NY) 21 Aug sec B 2/3, Most of Smith's pieces are made from alder, cherry wood or whatever he can find in the fields. . . Sometimes seats and the backs of chairs are woven from pliable swamp wood and nailed to the frame of the chair. **2003** Coile–Garland *Notes FL Endangered Plants* 19, *Dirca palustris.* . . Common Names—leatherwood[,] swampwood[,] moose-wood[,] leather-bark[,] eastern leatherwood. . . Descriptions—shrub, to 2 m tall, bark is smooth and pliable (stems difficult to bend and break).

swamp woodpecker n Also *swamp cock*

=**pileated woodpecker B.**

1900 *Anaconda Std.* (MT) 12 Oct 9/2, And the witness nodded like a swamp woodpecker. **1953** *AmSp* 28.284 **FL,** Its [=the pileated woodpecker's] simple *cock* titles include . . *swamp cock.* **1955** *Oriole* 20.1.9 **GA,** Pileated Woodpecker. . . Swamp Woodpecker. **1973** in 2004 Underwood *Bobwhite Quail* 412 **VA,** The sudden raucous yelping of a swamp woodpecker made Chauncey flinch visibly.

swamp worm n Also *swamp wiggler* **GA** Cf **pond worm, wiggler 3**

An **earthworm,** esp one used as bait in fishing.

1860 Walker *Stanley* 110 **MS,** "But see," pointing to a small hole in the ground, surrounded by a deposit peculiar to a certain swamp-worm, "that little untaught insect is my water-gauge." **1878** *Daily Constitution* (Atlanta GA) 1 May [2]/2 (newspaperarchive.com), As the jumping joree gathers the swamp worm to his bosom, so will Ampt lift the character of McLin from the political slough. **1968** *DARE* (Qu. P6, . . *Kinds of worms . . used for bait*) Inf **GA65,** Swamp wiggler. **1986** Pederson *LAGS Concordance,* 2 infs, **GA,** Swamp wiggler(s); 1 inf, **swGA,** Swamp worm—old name for red worm. **2000** *Augusta Chron.* (GA) 3 May sec A 4 (Internet), He . . allowed me to reminisce back to a similar event in my life involving a stringer of bream caught on someone's discarded line, swamp wigglers from under a rotten log and that mad dash back home.

swamp wren n

The long-billed **marsh wren.**

1898 in 2005 *DARE* File—Internet **NE** [*Omaha Sun. World–Herald* 11 Sept 20], The swamp wren piped its insect-like strain. **1946** Hausman *Eastern Birds* 446, Long-billed marsh wren *Telmatodytes palustris palustris.* . . Swamp Wren. . . Seen most commonly in cattail marshes. **2004** in 2005 *DARE* File—Internet **MA,** We . . got a brief glimpse of a house wren, a first for me (at least it was taller and less round than a swamp wren, and had no obvious eye line, so by elimination, I think that has to be correct).

swamp Yankee n Also *swamper* (pronc-sp *swampuh*) **sNEng**

An old-fashioned, rural New Englander; the dialect of such a person; see quots.

1912 *Metropolitan* 36.14 **NEng,** He decided to get a little sailin' dory and go out alone just to show those kings and things around the casino how a native born Swamp Yankee could navigate. **1929** *Outlook & Independent* 153.103, The dregs of white, native stock who remained in hardscrabble, often isolated, communities . . are a social and economic liability. . . In New England these people are called "swamp Yankees." **1931–33** *LANE Worksheets* **MA,** *Swamp Yankee*—person raised in swamp land. Probably derog. **1941** *LANE* Map 450 *(A rustic)* 2 infs, **CT, MA,** Swamp Yankee. **1955** *Lima News* (OH) 7 Sept 6/3 **wMA,** The population here consists principally of what are known as swamp Yankees, folks who came into these hills from Hartford to fight Indians. **1959** *Berkshire Eagle* (Pittsfield MA) 15 Apr 23/4, They need our help, . . but the inherent web-footed, swamp-Yankee thinking that imbues that organization will not bring them to ask us for help. **1963** *AmSp* 38.121 **sNEng,** The term *swamp Yankee* may be defined as 'a rural New England dweller who abides today as a steadfast rustic and who is of Yankee stock that has endured in the New England area since colonial days.' *Ibid* 122, In southeastern Massachusetts . . *swamp Yankee* is used to describe a rural dweller—one of stubborn, old-fashioned, frugal, English-speaking Yankee stock, of good standing in the rural community, but usually possessing minimal formal education. . . [R]ural inhabitants of the . . area do not mind . . being called *swamp Yankees*. . . In central and western Massachusetts . . the term . . has a marked pejorative connotation. **1968** *DARE* Tape **CT**12, A swamp Yankee means just a real Yankee; **CT**13, It's really common. . . It means one that never comes out of the woods, I guess, except but once a year to go to the fair. . . A swamp Yankee is a Yankee Yankee. . . I always thought a swamp Yankee was one who lived back and never had much to do with anybody. . . Wouldn't want to call myself a swamp Yankee. . . Down South, they call 'em crackers—don't amount to much. **1969–70** *DARE* (Qu. HH1, *Names and nicknames for a rustic or countrified person*) Inf **MA**89, Swamp Yankee; (Qu. HH28, *Names and nicknames . . for people of foreign background*) Inf **RI**13, Swamp Yankee. **1969** *DARE* FW Addit **neCT,** *Swamp Yankee*—someone who's stuck in New England—"you can't tell him anything"; **neCT,** *Swamp Yankee*—just born and bred in colonial US [FW: Inf not sure why *swamp*—"maybe once lived off soil"]. **1976** *Lincoln Star* (NE) 1 Mar 4/5, Wallace is talking to "the other Massachusetts"—the forgotten ethnic millworkers, the coastal fishermen, and the "Swamp Yankees" of western Massachusetts whose 18th Century ancestors rose up in Daniel Shays' famous "Rebellion." **1982** *Smithsonian Letters* **RI,** Swamp Yankee—A person of English ancestry, but whose forebears have lived in New England since the start of the Revolutionary War. However, the most important criteria [sic] for being a swamp Yankee is that one's ancestors never amounted to much. **2006** *DARE* File—Internet **RI,** *Swamp Yankee or Swampuh*—A term, specific to eastern Connecticut and South County Rhode Island, used to describe an umpteenth-generation farm-bred denizen of that area who is fiercely independent, stubborn, obstinate, and either ignorant or wily (depending on the prejudices of the source). The *origin* of the name is said to go back to 1776 when almost the entire town of Thompson, Connecticut, hid out in a swamp overnight to escape a British raid that never came. These days the term is generally less derisive. **2011** *DARE* File **seMA,** A guy I went to college with, from New Bedford, said he spoke "Swamp Yankee."

swamp yellowbird n
=**prothonotary warbler.**

1914 *Auk* 31.231 **AL,** Prothonotary Warbler. 'Swamp Yellowbird.'—Common summer resident of swamps. **1962** Imhof *AL Birds* 436, *Protonotaria citrea.* . . Swamp yellowbird. . . It inhabits river swamps and swampy ponds and lakes.

swan v Also sp *swang, swawn, swon;* rarely *swain* [Reanalysis of Scots, nEngl dial *I'se warn* (and varr) I'll warrant, I'll bound (*EDD* warrant v. 1, *SND* warrand v.)] *somewhat old-fash* Cf **snum** v, **swanny**
To swear; to declare—freq used in exclam phrr *I('ll) swan* to express surprise, indignation, or emphasis; also freq in phrr *I swan to man* (or *goodness, gracious*) used euphemistically for "I swear to God."

1823 *MO Intelligencer* (Franklin MO) 20 May 4/1 **OH,** ["Polite Swearing":] I swan it is. **1832** *New Engl. Mag.* 3.190 **VT,** "Well, I swon!" said Saul, . . " 't aint such a mortal poor trade a'ter all." **1836** *Pub. Ledger* (Philadelphia PA) 27 July 4/2, I swan to man it was a mistake. **1843** (1847) Field *Drama Pokerville* 198 **IN,** "Swan to gracious!" exclaimed the old contriver. **1849** [see **thunder** 1]. **1857** *Putnam's Mag.* Sept 350 **NEng,** I swan to man I've done it again! **1892** *KS Univ. Qrly.* 1.99 **KS,** Swan: to vow, as, in exclamation, I swan! **1894** Riley *Armazindy* 45 **IN,** With a dad-burn hook-and-line / And a saplin'-pole—i swawn!/ I've had more fun, to the square / Inch, than ever *any*where! **1895** *DN* 1.397 **c,swNY,** I swan . . exclamation of surprise. **1901** *DN*

2.149 **c,eNY,** Swan [swʌn]. **1902** *DN* 2.247 **sIL,** I swan to man I thought you'd heard of this before. **1905** *DN* 3.22 **cCT,** I swan! *Ibid* 67 **eNE,** I swan to goodness. **1907** *DN* 3.191 **seNH,** I swan. . . I swear. *Ibid* 218 **nwAR,** "I swan," I swear. **1907** Lincoln *Cape Cod* 57 **MA,** They didn't have anything to do but to look "picturesque" and say "I snum!" and "I swan to man!" **1909** *DN* 3.378 **eAL, wGA,** Swan. . . A variant of *swear* as an oath. Sometimes "I'll swan an' be darned" is heard. **1910** *DN* 3.444 **cwNY,** I swan. **1913** *DN* 4.11 **MN,** I swan! **1915** *DN* 4.229 **wTX,** Swan, I'll. **1958** Humphrey *Home from the Hill* 43 **neTX,** I swear, Dick! Excuse me again. I mean, I swan! **1959** *VT Hist.* 27.162, *I swan!* . . Occasional. *I Swan to Goodness!* . . Rare. *I Swan to Man!* . . Rare. **1965–70** *DARE* (Qu. NN32, *Exclamations like 'I swear' or 'I vow'*) 146 Infs, **widespread,** Swan; **KY**91, **MI**67, Swan to goodness; **DE**1, Swan and be durned [Of all Infs responding to the question, 63% were old, 12% young; of those giving these responses, 68% were old, 5% young.]; (Qu. NN7, *Exclamations of surprise: "They're getting married next week? Well, _____."*) Infs **CT**33, **OH**57, **TN**12, **TX**3, I swan; **TX**4, 42, I'll swan; (Qu. NN9a, *Exclamations showing great annoyance: "_____. The electric power is off again."*) Infs **CT**36, **KS**6, **MS**69, **NC**40, **NJ**31, **PA**133, **TX**42, I swan; **SC**45, Well, I'll swan; (Qu. NN25b, *Weakened substitutes for 'damn' or 'damned': "Well, I'll be _____!"*) Inf **MA**73, Swan. **1987** Childress *Out of the Ozarks* 20, "It shore bothers *me*," said Johnny. "A man cook. I swan." **2002** *DARE* File **nwNC,** I hear it here in NW NC "I swain" [with a] long a.

swanee See **swanny**

swanflower n Cf **pelican flower**
A **birthwort 1** (here: *Aristolochia erecta*).

1914 Bailey *Std. Cyclop. Horticult.* 1.393, [*Aristolochia*] *grandiflora.* . . Pelican-Flower. Swan-Flower. Goose-Flower. Duck-Flower. **1942** TX Ag. Exper. Sta. College Sta. *Bulletin* 608.84, *Aristolochia longiflora* [=*A. erecta*]. Swan Flower. . . The large swan-shaped flowers are brown and yellow with dark veining and splotching. Native to Southwest Texas. **1970** Correll *Plants TX* 508, *Aristolochia longiflora.* . . Swan-flower. **2005** *DARE* File—Internet **TX,** The most common pipevine in Austin is the *Swan Flower (Aristolochia erecta)*—It is found in lawns and roadsides east of Interstate 35. Swan Flower looks very much like grass with homely caterpillars covering it. The flowers are green and brown with pouch-like or pipe-like structures.

swang v[1] See **swing** v A, Ba

swang v[2] See **swan**

swanga, swanger adj See **swonger** adj

swanger v, **swangering** See **swonger** v

swan goose n
=**snow goose.**

1955 *AmSp* 30.181, *Swan goose* (snow goose, La.) doubtless alludes to the white color of this bird.

swan grebe n Also *swan-necked grebe* [From its long neck]
The western **grebe** (*Aechmophorus occidentalis*).

1903 Chapman *Color N. Amer. Birds* 44, Western Grebe; Swan Grebe. . . Western North America. **1928** Bailey *Birds NM* 80, The white-throated Western Grebe, or Swan Grebe, [is] the largest and handsomest of this interesting family of divers. **1949** Kitchin *Birds Olympic Peninsula* 13 **WA,** Western Grebe (*Aechmophorus occidentalis*). . . Other common names: Swan Grebe. **1962** Palmer *Hdbk. N. Amer. Birds* 1.94, *Western Grebe—Aechmophorus occidentalis.* . . Also appropriately called Swan-necked Grebe or Swan Grebe. **1971** *Advocate* (Newark OH) 20 Feb 4/3, The Swan Grebe of Clear Lake, Calif., was reduced from 1,000 pairs in 1948 to about 30 in 1960. **1997** in 2005 *DARE* File—Internet **CA,** Our largest grebe, the Western Grebe ("swan grebe") is a common winter resident on coastal bays, lagoons, and along nearshore waters.

swankey n Also sp *swankie, swanky* [*OED2 swanky, swankey* sb.[2] "Small beer, or other poor or weak liquor"; 1841 →]
1 =**switchel.** esp **MA**
1854 Haliburton *Americans at Home* 1.122 **sIL,** [Speaking of a man who has been dipped in molasses and cotton and left to drown:] Thar boys, we'll gin him a chance to pay his rent in Kentuck, and make *swankey* of the Ohio. **1855** Wise *Tales Marines* 159 **NEng,** He deigned to take a full tumbler of the potation, . . observing, at the same time, that he "admired a pull of swanky an all-fired sight better than gin." **1861** *Harper's New Mth. Mag.* 22.459 **MA,** "Fotch along some swankey,

Doctor!" . . But our worthy exile from Guinea was already prepared . . bearing a pail of molasses, vinegar, and water. . . "Tumble up an' git your swankey, boys!" **1878** Upham *Notes Voyage CA* 31 (as of 1849), A fellow-passenger . . caught up from off the deck both hands full of a mixture of brandy, molasses, vinegar and salt water, and after taking a hearty swig, exclaimed, *"Jimminy, boys, this is first-rate swankey."* **1918** *DN* 5.17 **Martha's Vineyard MA,** *Swankie.* . . Water and molasses; sometimes ginger added; also vinegar. . . "When we was whaling we used to dip our hard-tack in swankie." **1932–34** *Hanley Disks* **MA,** *Swankie.* . . Switchel. **1980** *Yankee* Jan 91, When molasses, and sometimes vinegar or "swankey," was mixed into the lobscouse, it was called dandyfunk.

2 A type of low-alcohol beer. **PA, OH** *arch*

1888 *Chr. Union* 37.568 **wPA,** It is reported that some Pittsburg brewers think of going into the manufacture of a beer called "swankey," that will not come within the limits of the Brooks law. . . It contains about 2½ per cent. of alcohol. **1902** *Amer. Handy Book Brewing* 779, Pennsylvania "Swankey." This beer has a local reputation in some parts of Pennsylvania, and is still brewed in Allegheny. It may also be classed as a temperance beverage, containing but little alcohol. Its name is probably a corruption of the German *"Schwenke."* The material employed is malt. Balling of wort, about 7 per cent, hops about one-half pound per barrel, and a flavoring condiment like anise seed. **1903** *Coshocton Daily Age* (OH) 8 Aug 2/2, Swankey, Bishop's beer, No-intox, and all other beverages of that kind are supposed to contain only 2 per cent or less of alcohol. **1911** *Gettysburg Times* (PA) 22 Sept 1/4, Word came to gamblers and "swankey" sellers that the district attorney was on the ground. **2007** in 2008 *DARE* File—Internet, Homebrew Pennsylvania swankey. [A] traditional American style of beer, it's very light in body and alcohol content, with a somewhat unusual brewing adjunct: anise seed. . . [O]ne of my favourite styles of beer to brew and drink.

swanky n [Scots, nEngl dial]

1930 Shoemaker *1300 Words* 57 **cPA Mts** (as of c1900), *Swanky*—Chesty, or self-assertive young fellow.

swan-necked grebe See **swan grebe**

swanny v Also sp *swanee, swanney, swannie, swoney* [Reanalysis of Scots dial *I'se warn ye* (and varr) I'll warrant you (*EDD* warrant v. 1)] **chiefly Sth, S Midl; formerly also NEng** See Map Cf **swagger, swan, swow**

To swear; to declare—freq used in exclam phrr *I('ll) swanny,* rarely *by swanny,* to express surprise, indignation, or emphasis.

1831 Finn *Amer. Comic Annual* 157 **VT,** That are must be the *critter* I heard t'other night in the pond. . . I swanny! he roared louder than a bull. **1832** *New Engl. Mag.* 3.380, One of the most marked peculiarities of the real Yankee, that is, the New-Englander, is in some few instances of the compromise between the disposition to rap out an oath in a moment of excitement, and the check of his conscience. . . Thus, for instance, we have *"I swan"* and *"I swanny"* for I swear . . , and other like creations of the union of wrath and principle. **1861** *Harper's New Mth. Mag.* 22.462 **MA,** She's parted her cable, by Swanney! **1893** Shands *MS Speech* 61, *Swanny.* . . Illiterate white euphemism for *swear.* . . The form *I swanny* is . . [used] only as an expletive in such sentences as, "I swanny! if that ain't so!" **1903** (1984) Ayer *Autobiog.* 3 **NEng,** I went to the village school, and older girls used words that I had been taught were wicked. I called them "swear words." They tried to get me to say them, "I swow, I vow, I swanny, I vanny, good Lord," etc. **1906** *DN* 3.160 **nwAR,** Well, I swan(ee)! **1909** *DN* 3.417 **nME,** Used as a mild form of oath in the ejaculation *I swan* or *I swanny.* **1949** Perry *Granny Van* 197 **TX,** I'll swanny to goodness, . . the regard some people have got for the truth don't amount to a hill of beans. **1959** *VT Hist.* 27.162, *I Swanee!* . . Rare. **1965–70** *DARE* (Qu. NN32, *Exclamations like 'I swear' or 'I vow'*) 72 Infs, **chiefly Sth, S Midl,** Swanny; **MA73,** By swanny; (Qu. NN7, *Exclamations of surprise: "They're getting married next week? Well, _____."*) Infs SC3, 11, 19, 44, I swanny; (Qu. NN9a, *Exclamations showing great annoyance: "_____. The electric power is off again."*) Infs AL30, GA84, I swanny; SC45, Well, I'll swanny. **1984** Wilder *You All Spoken Here* 162 **Sth,** *I swan, I swannie:* Euphemisms for "I'll swear," "I'll be damned," "I'll be kiss my ass." **1994** NC Lang. & Life Project *Harkers Is. Vocab.* 11 **eNC,** Swanny. . . "Swear." *I swanny, I told him to stop.* **2000** *DARE* File **eTX,** I'll swoney is a phrase that my mother used all her life. . . in surprise and exasperation. **2002** Ibid **AL,** "Swanee"—"I swear!" A polite exclamation once much in use, especially by women, but now rarely heard. Friends from southern Arkansas and eastern Tennessee had never heard the phrase.

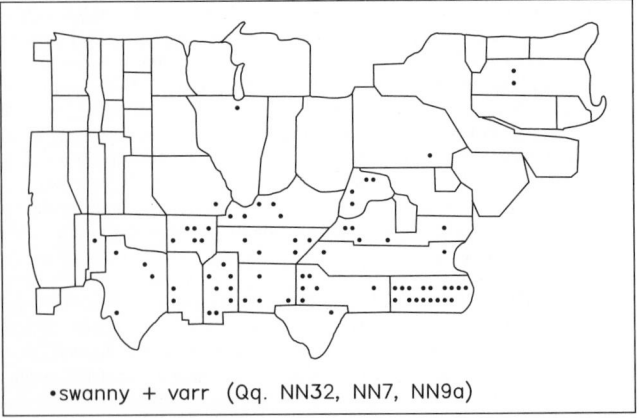

•swanny + varr (Qq. NN32, NN7, NN9a)

swan potato n [Calque of the name in Ojibway (or a closely related lang), prob by way of Fr *pomme de cygne;* see quots 1861 below and 1869 at **swan root**] Cf **duck potato, swamp ~**

=**arrowhead 1,** esp the widely distributed *Sagittaria latifolia.*

1830 Tanner *Narrative* 298, Waw-be-ze-pin-neeg—Arrow head, (swan potatoes). The roots of the common saggittaria, as well as the bulbs of some of the crest flowering lilies, which are eaten by the Indians, receive this name. **1853** *De Bow's Rev.* 15.331 **Gt Lakes,** Nature has also made ample provision for the sustenance of life by a supply of esculent roots, such as the swan potato. **1861** Jones *Hist. Ojebway* 55, There is another plant called *wahbezeepin* or the swan potato, found in bogs or marsh soil. The Indians boil and eat it in cases of extreme hunger. **1870** McClung *MN in 1870* 183, Among the latter [=roots and herbs eaten by Indians] are . . swan potatoe. **1871** [see **swamp potato**]. **1906** [see **swamp potato**]. **1920** *Geogr. Rev.* 9.256, *Sagittaria.* . . There are several American species which under the name arrowhead, swan potato, and swamp potato have given welcome sustenance to pioneers.

swan root n

An **arrowhead 1** (here: *Sagittaria latifolia*).

[**1869** *Amer. Philol. Assoc. Trans.* 1.74, *-Pin* denotes an esculent tuber, or tuberous root; as in (Chip[pewa]) *o-pin,* potato, . . *wawbeze-pin* 'swan root' (a species of Sagittaria), etc.] **1898** *Bot. Gaz.* 26.256 **CA,** Swan root . . used as food by Indians.

swan weed n

=**cocash 2.**

1876 Hobbs *Bot. Hdbk.* 115, Swan weed. . . Aster puniceus. **1914** Georgia *Manual Weeds* 435, *Aster puniceus.* . . Swan weed.

swap day n Also (*horse-*)*swapping day* **scattered, but less freq Nth** Cf **first Monday 1, trade day**

A gathering, often held at regular intervals, for the purpose of bartering or selling goods or livestock; hence spec *swap Tuesday* such a gathering held regularly on Tuesdays.

[**1883** *Landmark* (Statesville NC) 8 June [3]/2 (newspaperarchive.com), There was the usual amount of horse swapping tuesday, and the traders were generally drunk and dressed up.] **1895** *Perry Bulletin* (IA) [29 May 7]/3 (newspaperarchive.com) **TN,** *Swapping Day in Tennessee.* . . Inhabitants Gather in the Towns and Trade Everything. A traveling man thus describes a "horse-swapping day" in Tennessee. . . We were told that these swapping days are held once a month. The men meet at this place and swap everything from a jackknife to a farm, but trading in horses is the favorite fancy with them. **1918** *Oxnard Daily Courier* (CA) 29 June [4]/5 (newspaperarchive.com), "Swap day", when ranchers of the surrounding district meet to exchange anything from automobiles to eggs, has been instituted by the chamber of commerce here. The last Saturday in every month has been set aside as "swap day." **1932** *Mexia Weekly Herald* (TX) 21 Oct 2/3, A two-day "Swap Day" program when farmers . . will be invited to bring their cows, hogs, pigs, wagons, horses, chickens or what have you to swap in a common meeting place and trade to their hearts content is scheduled. **1932** *Appleton Post-Crescent* (WI) 28 Oct 22/8 **WA,** Toppenish, Wash.—Hogs were traded for ducks, sheep for hardware, grain for groceries, and chickens for a load of straw here in an official "swap day." **1933** *Sun* (Baltimore MD) 29 Apr 15/4 **IN,** Indiana Town Finds "Swap Day" Success. . . Duck eggs were swapped for an incubator, a diamond ring was traded for a shot gun, a man secured a truck for a couple of blankets. . . Live stock was exchanged in a corral near by. **1953** *NY Times* (NY) 12 Apr sec X 25, *Hunterdon Hills Garden Club* (N.J.)—Swap Day. Borough Hall, 2 P.M. **1960** Williams *Walk Egypt* 87 **GA,** John Goforth said that on Swap Tuesday in Cardiff you could find a fool for anything. **1970** Owen *Hillbilly Humor* 64 **Ozarks,** One of the first things I remember was the old square in my hometown where we had Swappin' Days, mostly on Saturdays. That day still is the big day for business in the hills. **1984** Wilder *You All Spoken Here* 75 **Sth,** *Sales Monday; swap day; trades day; bone-yard day:* The first Monday in the month and time for trading livestock in sales usually near the county courthouse.

swap ends v phr

1 To turn abruptly through 180°, turn end for end; to reverse course; also fig.

1874 *Overland Mth.* 13.402 **CA,** His foot slipped, and he started head foremost for *terra firma.* When within ten feet of the bottom he touched some scaffolding with his hand, "swapped ends," and lighted on his feet. **1881** *Reno Eve. Gaz.* (NV) 21 May [3]/4 (newspaperarchive.com), The ant stings the hopper, then swaps ends and eats the tender portion of her nephews and nieces. **1895** *Lafayette Advt.* (LA) [19 Jan 3]/3 (newspaperarchive.com), Hard times . . was what brought the prodigal son to his senses and made him swap ends for home. **1895** *S. Hist. Soc. Papers* 23.302 **VA,** I saw a rifle shell almost spent pass close to the head of our column, bounding and "swapping ends" as it went. **1959** *Caribou Co. Sun* (Soda Springs ID) 19 Feb [3]/2 (newspaperarchive.com), The Republicans run the country fer a spell, then the Democrats take over and I reckon as long as we keep swapping ends things will survive. **1967** *Chron.-Telegram* (Elyria OH) 18 Nov 25/4, The dog finds a pheasant's trail and suddenly comes alive. . . He swaps ends and the chase is on. **2005** Williams *Gratitude* 529 **wNC** (as of 1940s), *Swappin' ends:* turning *somersets, end over end; head over heels.*

2 Spec:

a Of a horse or mule: to turn end for end while leaping or bucking; hence vbl n *swapping ends.* **Sth, West** Cf **sunfish** v

1873 *Harper's New Mth. Mag.* 47.317 **LA,** Some wicked sprite of the place gave the paper a flirt, which was no sooner seen and heard than the mule, as mules only know how, instantly "swapped ends," and, leaving the negro sprawling in the dirt, took his departure. **1879** *Scribner's Mth.* 18.888 **MS,** Suddenly, without any warning, Tony's mule performed the evolution known as "swapping ends." **1910** *Sun. State Jrl.* (Lincoln NE) 28 Aug 2/1, [The horse] "sun fished" and swapped ends with such amazing rapidity that Clark was unseated. **1929** *AmSp* 5.65 **NE** [Cattle country talk], If the "pony" turns completely around, "swaps ends" or does an "end for end," he is a "twister." **c1938** in Lib. of Congress *Amer. Memory: WPA Life Hist.* (Internet) **TX,** The hoss bucked, sunfished, swapped ends in mid-air, and put on a big show for about five minutes. **1938** FWP *Guide SD* 86, *Swapping ends:* a horse making a half-circle in the air. **1956** Moody *Home Ranch* 51 **CO,** Clay [=a horse]. . . didn't sunfish, and he didn't swap ends. **2007** Fry *Backyard Horsekeeping* 257, Some bolters like to swap ends like a rodeo horse before they high-tail it home. This movement almost always leaves their rider without stirrups or reins.

b Of a vehicle: to fishtail wildly; to spin out of control.

1925 *Bee* (Danville VA) 7 Apr 12/6, The machine began "swapping ends" until it was entirely out of control. **1952** *Reno Eve. Gaz.* (NV) 19 Nov 16/2, The car . . she was driving . . crashed into a tree, "swapped ends" and then struck another tree. **1966** *Coshocton Tribune* (OH) 28 Aug comic sec [1] (newspaperarchive.com), [*Little Orphan Annie* comic strip:] Hang on, boys! . . The way she [=a boat] swapped ends and slammed through what looked like solid bush! **1970** *News–Jrl.* (Mansfield OH) 15 Aug 9/3, The car swapped ends and went down an embankment. **1993** *Mt. Democrat* (Placerville CA) 27 May sec B 2/4, This axiom came about because of the tendency for tailwheel aircraft to try to "ground loop" or "swap ends" while landing or taxiing them.

swap help (or labor) See **swap work**

swapping day See **swap day**

swapping ends See **swap ends 2a**

swapping work See **swap work**

swap the chair(s) n *old-fash*

Prob =**musical chairs.**

1965–70 *DARE* (Qu. EE2, *Games that have one extra player—when a signal is given, the players change places, and the extra one tries to get*

a place) Infs **AL**3, 20, **IA**36, 41, **IN**14, **MA**58, **MS**59, **NJ**18, **WV**4, Swap the chair; **PA**26, Swap the chairs. [9 of 10 Infs old]

‡**swap the donkey** n

1967 *DARE* (Qu. EE2, *Games that have one extra player—when a signal is given, the players change places, and the extra one tries to get a place*) Inf **PA**26, Swap the donkey—same as swap the chairs.

swap Tuesday See **swap day**

swap work v phr, hence vbl n *swapping work* Also *swap help, ~ labor;* for addit varr see quots **chiefly Sth, S Midl, TX, OK** See Map Cf **exchange work** =**change work.**

1820 in 1854 Jefferson *Writings* 7.190 **VA,** It will . . render them . . sycophants to their Senators, engage these in eternal intrigue to turn one out and put in another, in cabals to swap work. **1859** Taliaferro *Fisher's R.* 218 **wNC,** One neighbor would help another harvest his grain. . . Corn-shuckings were conducted in the same way. . . They "swopped work." **1860** *Janesville Daily Gaz.* (WI) 12 July [2]/3 (newspaperarchive.com) **IL** (as of c1830), We often swapped work in this way. **1862** *Harper's New Mth. Mag.* 25.182 **NC,** 'Squire, I's come to swap work with you. . . It shall never be said that Sol Senter got 'Squire Freeman to marry him fur nothin,' and it mout be swappin' work mout do jist as well. **1896** *Century Illustr. Mag.* 52.622 **ND,** Struggling through the time when they all "swapped work" to get started . . they worked into the time when prosperity arrived. **1929** *AmSp* 5.123 **ME,** The country people still "swap work" or works. **1945** *Harder Coll.* **cwTN,** [Letter:] He has gone to work in hay for Dug Hickerson they are going to swap work. **1949** Hedgecock *Gone Are the Days* 49 **swMO,** We swapped work with him quite a bit, and he always tried to give a little more than he received. **1965–70** *DARE* (Qu. L5, *When a farmer gets help on a job from his neighbors in return for his help on their farms later on*) 204 Infs, **chiefly Sth, S Midl, TX, OK,** Swapping work (or help, labor, jobs, times); 25 Infs, **scattered,** Swap work (or help, labor); **NH**14, Swap work back and forth. **1966** *DARE* Tape **FL**37, Sometimes they'd swap work with the neighbors. . . They'd help them plant . . and then they'd come help them. Just swap work. **1985** *NC Folkl. Jrl.* 33.39 **wNC** (as of c1920), Mother usually "swapped work" or hired a neighbor woman to help prepare them [=apples].

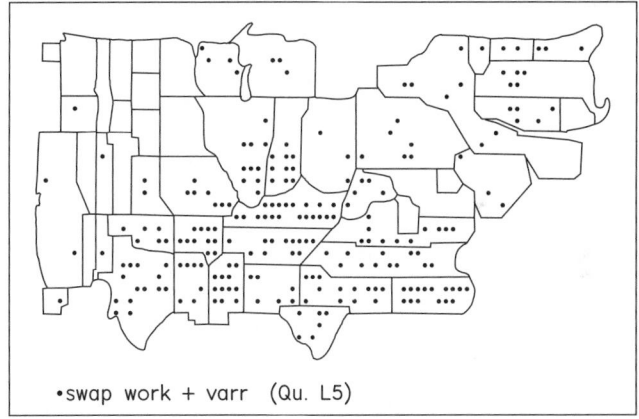

•swap work + varr (Qu. L5)

swar See **swear**

swarp v Also *sworp* [Varr of *swap* in var senses now obs or found only in Engl, Scots dial; for details see etyms at senses below. (The std sense of *swap* derives from the phr *swap a bargain* strike a bargain [*OED2 swap* v. 7.b 1590–1692].)] **chiefly sAppalachians** Cf **swarp** n

1 To strike, beat. [*EDD swap* v.⁴ 1 "*Obsol.* To strike violently; to thrash soundly"; *SND swap* v.¹ "To strike, hit, . . scourge."]

1943 Chase *Jack Tales* 63 **wNC** (as of 1880s), Then he got him a switch and swarped the unicorn a few times to see could it break loose. **1946** *AmSp* 21.272 **neKY,** Climbin' the ridge with the brush swarpin' you in the face. **1950** Stuart *Hie Hunters* 187 **eKY,** Watch that the trace chain don't come loose and swarp old Dinah on the leg. *Ibid* 231, One man rushed in with a pine bough . . and started swarping the flames. **1963** Chappell *It Is Time* 12 **wNC,** He was sworped across the eyes with a sharp chestnut limb when they felled the tree. **1982** in 2004 Montgomery-Hall *Dict. Smoky Mt. Engl.* 585 **wNC, eTN,** We would take an old cane pole, swarp [a bat] down, hold him by the wings, and see his little snapping teeth. **1991** Still *Wolfpen Notebooks* 59 **sAppalachians,** He grabbed off his belt and swarped me, and he swarped me with the wrong end of it. **2003** in 2005 *DARE* File—Internet **KY,** Swarping the water—I guess until I get the rust out of my flyrod I'll be a Creekbank WaterSwarper. **2008** *DARE* File—Internet **WV,** No more limbs swarping my face, no more digging chunks of wood outta the corners of my eyes.

2a To move (something) with a sweeping motion. [*SND swap* v.¹ 3 "To brandish (a weapon), make a swipe with"]

1926 (1930) MacKaye *Tall Tales* **KY** 50, She lipt to her laigs, nosin' us, a-swarpin' her gret tail. **1946** *AmSp* 21.272 **neKY,** His mother swarped the belt at him through the open door. **1946** *Rowan Co. News* 17 Jan (*AmSp* 21.272) **KY,** Then I like to pour a little [molasses] on my plate and swarp a hot bisquit through them. **2002** in 2005 *DARE* File—Internet **neFL,** Love it! swarping that toast around runny yellowness. **2004** *DARE* File—Internet **WV,** They were catching there [sic] fish on jerkbaits with long bills and swarping them down to around 6 ft. of water and let it suspend a little. **2007** in 2008 *Ibid* **eTN,** He was sworping his VW Jetta across 3 lanes at a time for miles. *Ibid* **seKY,** Every kid in walkertown was involved in the picking of the switch. . . i can still hear the kids swarping them thru the air to see if they cracked just right.

b intr; Spec: to cast a fly; hence n *swarper* a flyfisher. [*SND swap* v.¹ 3 "to cast a fishing-rod"]

2003 in 2005 *DARE* File—Internet **KY,** *First time "swarping"*—I went with Billy on Monday to try my hand at flyfishing for the first time ever. . . [Another poster:] I'll let . . one of them other experienced swarpers take it from here.

3 also with *up:* To capture with a dip net.

2007 in 2008 *DARE* File—Internet **eTN,** The fish came to the top and dad swarped it up with the net. *Ibid* **WV,** Sometimes the chicken would have one crab on it and other times we saw up to four crabs. . . The netter (person holding the net) then swarped, as Matt said, the crab off of the chicken and the crab was put into a deep pot.

4 To trail down on, sweep across (a surface); hence ppl adj *swarping* sweeping, trailing. [*SND swap* v.¹ 5 "intr. . . . to swirl, swing, to come down in a forcible sweeping motion"; 6 "Of wind: to blow in gusts, bluster, to sweep down"] Cf **swarpy**

1968 *Hench Coll.* **WV,** Her dress was swarping the floor. **1989** Oliver *Hazel Creek* 31 **wNC,** He cut a large pole and when they would get too close to him he would lash out at them ("swarp" the ground) with the pole to drive them away. **2001** *DARE* File **seWV** (as of c1995), A neighbor talked of a "swarpin' wind," meaning a sweeping wind. **2004** in 2005 *DARE* File—Internet **KY,** I feel as though I should don my sworping dress and get me to the widow's walk.

5 To move erratically; to flap, stagger, weave, flit; hence adj *a-swarp* squirming, wiggling.

1961 *Mt. Life* 37.2.9 **sAppalachians,** Hit won't be five minutes 'till that bag o' fleas [=a dog]'ll be right back in hyar a-swarpin' an' a-swarvin' around. **1968** *Hench Coll.* **WV,** Look, your shirt is swarping. **a1978** (1983) Carpenter *Aunt Arie* 139 **wNC,** Another'n that takes epileptic fits . . goes up and down th'road a lot, swarpin' along. . . She's crazy. **1980** *DARE* File **KY, WV** (as of 1975), If you pick up a snake, it wriggles. Mountaineers will say it's *a-swarp,* or it's *swarping.* I heard this chiefly in West Virginia when I was doing fieldwork with the snake-handlers. **1993** in 2004 Montgomery–Hall *Dict. Smoky Mt. Engl.* 585, *Swarp. . .* move about unsteadily, from one side to another. **2003** *DARE* File—Internet **KY,** Yesterday . . he accused my aunt of being busy "swarping up and down the road." **2005** *Ibid* **swVA,** *Swarp:* Slap, as "Last night I heard a tree limb swarping against the house." **2006** in 2008 *Ibid* **nGA,** Had an [sic] mid 90's mustang swarping all over the road this morning trying to get next to me.

6 also with *around:* To engage in noisy, extravagant, or illicit behavior, esp under the influence of alcohol; to revel, carouse; hence vbl n *swarping;* n *swarper.* [Cf **5** above and *SND swap* v.¹ 7 "tr. To drink in quick long gulps"]

1946 *AmSp* 21.271 **neKY,** *Swarp. . .* In the pple. form *swarping* only, the word has some currency in a sense roughly definable as wenching, hell-raising; or more mildly as skylarking, cavorting, playing: 'The boys was out swarpin' (or 'swarpin' around') last night.' The occurrence of the opprobrious sense appears to be spotty; the word is used in the other senses freely and without embarrassment by native speakers who are

distinctly modest. **1999** DeRosier *Creeker* 44 **eKY,** I never heard anyone back home speak of someone drinking; they always said the person was "drinking and sworping." . . It means wildly running around, cussing and hollering, and in general acting in ways no good, sane, sober person would ever behave. **2002** *DARE* File **eKY,** The sense of "swarper" that I heard in Martin County, Kentucky . . in the 1970s was most definitely opprobrious. A swarper was apt to be any or all of the following: a drunkard, a drug abuser, a gambler, a swearer, and sexually promiscuous! **2003** in 2005 *DARE* File—Internet, You ought to be ashamed of yourself! Encouraging my wife to go a sworping while I'm gone. . . [Later posting:] I was just kidding and I'm amazed that you know what "sworping" is. I thought it was a hill-billyism unknown outside this general area. **2005** *Ibid* **WV,** *Swarping around:* . . It meant that he went out drinking, and chasing women. Grandma Cartie use to say this about some of her sons-in-law, "He's out swarping around again." *Ibid* **WV,** One son is on drugs, drinking[,] sworping, fighting and having unsafe sex. *Ibid* **KY** (as of 1940s), He and I had gone swarping in Baltimore together. We had drunk an inestimable amount of beer together one day. *Ibid* **seKY,** Hazard Community & Technical College hosts its 12th annual Evening with Poets. . . This year, poet, playwright, and sworper Jim Webb returns.

swarp n Also *sworp* **sAppalachians** Cf **swarp** v

1 A blow; a try, go. [*EDD swap* sb.⁵ 9 "A heavy blow; a sudden stroke; a slap."]

1940 Stuart *Trees of Heaven* 168 **eKY,** You can take six rows at a swarp around a newground slope. It'll shore look purty to see where you slice down six rows of weeds. [**1945** *Atlantic Mth.* 176.53 **eKY,** One day he gets too sorry to bend and lace his shoes, and it's a *swarp, swarp* every step.] **1982** in 2004 Montgomery–Hall *Dict. Smoky Mt. Engl.* 585, Dad said that he and a friend were riding one day, and the friend, acting smart, reached over and gave Dad's mule a swarp across the back. **2005** Williams *Gratitude* 529 **wNC** (as of 1940s), Let him take a *swipe* (or swarp) at fixin' it. **2005** *DARE* File—Internet **WV,** I topped the steps and hung a right at the hall barely missing a sworp from the Gravely strap that dad had flung while sliding over the kitchen table.

2 See quot. [*EDD swap* sb.⁵ 11 "An implement used for reaping peas, consisting of part of a scythe fastened to the end of a long handle"; 1875, 1887] *relic*

1969 *DARE* (Qu. L28, *Tools used in the past for cutting grain*) Inf **KY**58, Swarp [swarp].

swarp around See **swarp** v 6

swarper See **swarp** v **2b, 6**

swarping ppl adj See **swarp** v **4**

swarping vbl n See **swarp** v **6**

swarpy adj [**swarp** v **4**]

1946 *AmSp* 21.272 **neKY,** *Swarpy. . .* Full, swinging: 'A little old woman in a long swarpy dress.'

swarther See **swather**

swarthy adj [Transf from the sense "sallow," which was common in the 19th cent.] **Sth, S Midl** Sickly-looking.

[**1875** Palmer *Life Thornwell* 41 **SC,** Pale, swarthy, and sickly in appearance, his voice was strong, and the words flowed from him like a rushing torrent.] [**1903** *DN* 2.332 **seMO,** *Swarthy,* often *swathy. . .* Sallow. 'He has had chills so long, he is right swarthy.'] **1967–69** *DARE* (Qu. BB38, *When a person doesn't look healthy, or looks as if he hadn't been well for some time . . "He looks _____."*) Inf **GA**74, Swarthy—hollow-faced; **KY**28, ['swaθi]—old-fashioned; **NC**55, ['swɔθi]; **TN**14, ['swɑθi]. **1986** Pederson *LAGS Concordance (Peaked)* 1 inf, **neTN,** Swarthy; 1 inf, **cnGA,** Swarthy—puny, sickly; 1 inf, **cnGA,** Swarthy—sick?

swash n Also *swash channel* [*OED2 swash* sb.¹ 3 1670–1 → ("Chiefly U.S."), appar var of earlier *swatch*] **chiefly C and Mid Atl** Cf **drain** n¹ **4**

A narrow stream or channel lying between sandbanks or between a sandbank and the shore.

1681 in 1940 *AmSp* 15.401 **VA,** Downe the side of James river. . . to a marked willow tree in a small swash. **1740** in 1887 *SC Hist. Soc. Coll.* 4.77, There was water Enough in the Swash opposite the Castle for the

Boats to pass. **1775** (1962) Romans *Nat. Hist. FL* app 78, There are several swashes, which though they are narrow, have no less than 11 or 12 feet thro'. **1828** (1970) Webster *Amer. Dict., Swash.* . . In the southern states of America, *swash* . . is a name given to a narrow sound or channel of water lying within a sand bank, or between that and the shore. Many such are found on the shores of the Carolinas. **1895** *Ft. Wayne Sentinel* (IN) 19 Sept 1/2 **NJ**, The Valkyrie . . could be seen following the Defender through the Swash channel with her mainsail set and in tow. **1899** (1912) Green *VA Folk-Speech* 431, *Swash.* . . A narrow sound or channel of water lying within a sand bank, or between that and the shore: as, a *"swash-channel."* **1932** *Natl. Geogr. Mag.* Sept 278 **NC**, Captain Wickes . . was returning to the club through the "swash" channel in a small ducking boat. **1954** *AmSp* 29.252 **VA**, The Swash Hole is the name given to the water between Mulberry Point and the Swash Hole Islands in James River. **1976** Warner *Beautiful Swimmers* 8 **eMD**, Down every tidal gut and through every big "thorofare" and little "swash" or "drain," as the breaks in the marsh islands are called, there comes an enormous and nourishing flow of silage. **2001** *DARE* File—Internet **Staten Is. NY**, The first Elm Tree Lighthouse guided mariners safely through the Swash Channel.

swatch v |swæč|

1 with *around, out:* To show off (clothing); hence ppl adj phr *swatched out* decked out, clothed ostentatiously. [Etym unknown; cf *SND swash* v. 3.(2) "to go about in a showy ostentatious way"]

1911 *DN* 3.549 **NE**, *Swatch* [æ]. . . "She puts on her best clothes, and swatches them out." "She looks swatched out." **1935** *AmSp* 10.158 **NE**, She swatched her skirts around through the halls all day long.

2 also with *around:* To hurry up, move quickly. [Cf *SND swash* v. 3.(1) "to rush to and fro, . . bustle"]

1911 *DN* 3.549 **NE**, *Swatch* [æ]. . . Move violently about. . . "Better swatch round, if you're going to catch that train." **1935** *AmSp* 10.157 **KY**, The verb *swatch* [swætch] in *swatch round*, etc., meaning 'bustle about' or 'get busy,' was used by a Kentucky friend of mine in 1929. It is also heard in Nebraska.

3 To swat.

1916 *DN* 4.281 **NE**, *Swatch* . . [æ]—About the same as *swat*. "The teacher felt like she'd ought to swatch the pupil."

swatch around   See **swatch 1, 2**

swatch(ed) out   See **swatch 1**

swath, carry a v phr   [Cf *OED2 carry* v. 14.a]

To cut a swath; also fig.

1814 in 1965 Fletcher *Letters* 82, I remember how I labored with you in haying the year before I came away. . . I reckon I could carry a swath with Calvin and Miles—and perhaps, Sir, with you. I am not stout and fat but tolerable hearty. **1922** U.S. Congress House *Ag. Appropriation* 93, Some of these fellows . . are able to go almost unerringly to a single currant or gooseberry bush that has been missed by a crew that is working within hand-to-hand touch of each other as they carry a swath through a piece of woodland. **1927** *AmSp* 2.350 **cwWV**, *Carry a swath* . . to be able to carry out an assigned task. "He tried to carry too heavy a swath."

swather n Pronc-sp *swarther* **chiefly Upper MW, West** See Map Cf **tedder**

A mowing machine or attachment that cuts grain and lays it in a swath; see quots.

1860 *Weekly Oregonian* (Portland OR) 14 Apr 5/1, [Advt:] *Wood's Swather*—A new machine. **1876** Knight *Amer. Mech. Dict.* 3.2467, *Swather.* . . A device attached to the front of a mowing-machine for the purpose of raising the uncut fallen grain and marking the line of separation between the cut and uncut grain. **1902** *Hopewell Herald* (NJ) 16 July 4/1, [Advt:] *Oats Swather*—Is guaranteed to lay the grain in a continuous swath better than can be done by the best cradler. **1918** *New Oxford Item* (PA) 7 Nov 10/4, Harvesting can be done with a common mower having a swather attachment. **1929** *Havre Daily News* (MT) 18 Aug 8/4 **KS**, The swather, a new machine in the wheat belt, is used because it cuts grain in an earlier stage than is possible with a combine. Cut stalks are strung out in long windrows by swathers, and combines thresh it a few days later. **1965–70** *DARE* (Qu. L16, *Machines used . . in handling hay*) 9 infs, **esp Upper MW, West**, Swather; **CO**22, Swather—no rake; **MN**40, Swather—lays it in winrows; **OK**33, Hay swar-

thers—now self-powered—cut and even swarth hay at same time (put it into windrows); **OK**27, Swarther; (Qu. L28, *Tools used in the past for cutting grain*) Infs **IA**1, **NY**109, **WI**17, Swather; (Qu. L29, *Machines now used for cutting grain*) Infs **MN**34, 40, **ND**1, 3, **SD**8, Swather; **CA**152, Swather—in big operations; **MN**7, Swather—winnows [*DARE* Ed: prob for *windrows*] your cut grain for the combine to pick up; **MN**31, Swather—used before combine when it has green weeds, etc., in the field. **2004** *DARE* File **NM**, Another word I never came across in my dim and distant farming days in Wisconsin and Vermont [but have heard in New Mexico] was swather—a combination mowing machine and rake that leaves the alfalfa in windrows.

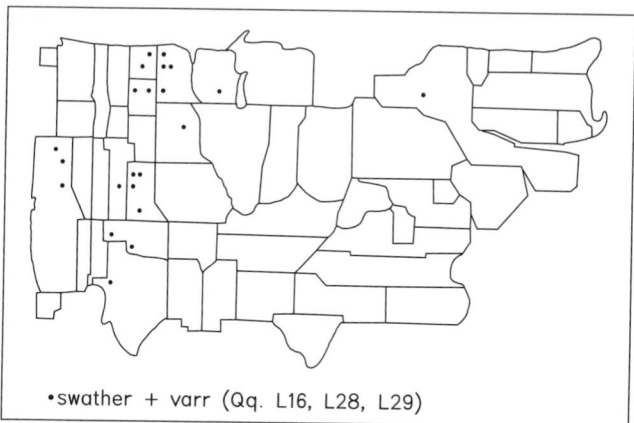

•swather + varr (Qq. L16, L28, L29)

swat'ning   See **sweetening**

swat to the right   See **slap in the back**

swawn   See **swan**

swear v   Pronc-spp *swar, sway(re), sweer*   Cf Pronc Intro 3.I.1.b

A Forms.

1825 Neal *Brother Jonathan* 2.303 **VA**, "Hold in! hold in! or you're jam up, I swar!" cried out a long-slab-sided Virginian. **1871** Eggleston *Hoosier Schoolmaster* 213 **sIN**, You don't swar me [as a witness]. **1887** *Scribner's Mag.* 2.478 **AR**, They's a right smart er folkses kin sw'ar hit's my chile. **1905** *DN* 3.56 **eNE**, *Swear* is sometimes *sweer.* **1922** Gonzales *Black Border* 330 **sSC, GA coasts** [Gullah glossary], *Sway', swayre*—swear.

B Gram varr.

1 past: usu *swore*; also *swa(h), sweared, swo'(d), swored.* Cf *-ed 2, 3*

1857 Southworth *Winny Darling* 307 **VA**, Then he sweared how she shouldn't have you, sir! **1861** *S. Lit. Messenger* 33.134 **MD**, The officers swored they would bring their men on shore and kill everybody. **1869** *Harper's New Mth. Mag.* 38.860 **NY**, Father, was that an agricultural meeting where they passed round a Testament . . and then sweared at it? **1871** Eggleston *Hoosier Schoolmaster* 127 **sIN**, He sweared at me. **1884** *Anglia* 7.253 [Black], To the regular forms of the Irregular verbs as used by the whites, the Negro adds the following forms of his own. . . *Pres.* swear—*Past.* swo', swa' = swah, swo'd (he swo'd he would). **1921** Haswell *Daughter Ozarks* 149 (as of 1880s), One of them miners . . swored that he'd kill me. **1943** *Press–Gaz.* (Hillsboro OH) 10 Sept 8/6 **seNY**, Boyleston sweared he seed it. **1969** *Sheboygan Press* (WI) 4 June sec 4 29/5, Gene sweared in the clubhouse as the Giants romped 9–3.

2 past pple, ppl adj: usu *sworn*; also *sweared, swore(d).*

1805 Shippen *Rept. Trial on Impeachment* 349 **PA**, If he can swear stronger than those who have swore before . . , then he is acquitted. **1855** *Putnam's Mag.* 6.190 **CT**, You know I have swore a solemn oath. **1882** *Harper's New Mth. Mag.* 64.920 **sAppalachians**, He had swore off from tellin' lies. **1891** *Bucks Co. Gaz.* (Bristol PA) 13 Aug 1/2, I had swored an oath. **1927** *DN* 5.478 **Ozarks**, *Sweared.* . . "I'll be sweared t' Gawd ef I ever hyeerd tell o' sich doin's." **1975** Allen *LAUM* 2.79 (as of c1950), *Swear.* [1 inf, **swNE**] has *swore* as the past participle. **1986** Pederson *LAGS Concordance*, 1 inf, **csLA**, You'd have swore and be damned; 1 inf, **cwAR**, You couldn't have swore. **1995** *DARE* File, I could of swore I saw you in it [=a class]. **2001** *Wellsboro Gaz.*

(PA) 18 July sec B 4/2, We could have swore that was a three-legged chicken.

C Senses.

1 in phr *to swear (a child) to:* To attribute, esp under oath, the paternity of (one's illegitimate child) to. [*OED2 swear* v. 9.b "To put *upon* or ascribe *to* a person in a sworn statement"; 1754 →] **chiefly sAppalachians**

1785 in 2005 *DARE* File—Internet **csMD,** On motion for an allowance for the support of her child sworn to him, the same was granted. **1796** *Ibid* **cnTN,** [A bond to indemnify] the parish of Davidson County from any Trouble or Expense concerning Birth, Maintenance or Education of a Bastard child sworn to him by sd. Eleanor Thompson. **1806** in 1993 Rackley-Bradley *Nash Co. NC Court Minutes* 5.72, Ordered that . . Jeremiah Wells to Shew Cause at next Court . . why an allowance Should not be made for Rhoda Pridger for a Bastard Child Sworn to Him. **1890** in 2005 *DARE* File—Internet **seKY,** Soldier left no other children under 16 years that were sworn to him. **1975** Gainer *Witches* 17 **sAppalachians,** *Swear a baby.* . . To name the father of an illegitimate baby. "She never swore her baby to anyone." **1982** Powers *Cataloochee* 202 **cwNC,** You know that (an) ole gal [is] goin' to swear a young'un to us? **1996–97** in 2004 Montgomery-Hall *Dict. Smoky Mt. Engl.* 585 **wNC, eTN,** *Swear to.* . . Of a woman: to claim a certain man to be the father of (her child). . . [4 infs].

2 Used in exclam or parenthetic phrr *I('ll) swear* to express surprise, indignation, or emphasis. **esp Sth, S Midl** Cf **swan, swanny**

1855 *Putnam's Mag.* 6.24 **RI,** "It's a saw-hoss," he murmurs, identifying the printed XX. on the bill. "Well, *I* swear!—If this ain't generous." **1860** *Spirit of Times* 18 Feb 17 **AR,** Well, I'll swear! Why, we have a dog day here every once in a while, and real fun it is too. **1873** Twain-Warner *Gilded Age* 48 **MO,** And just at that moment a red glare appeared . . and the Amaranth came springing after them! "Well, I swear!" **1882** *Century Illustr. Mag.* 24.575 **NEng,** Well, I swear! Why, you infamous old scoundrel, come in out of the wet. **1924** *DN* 5.277 [Exclams], *Swear:* I swear. **1931** *AmSp* 6.204 **MO** [Univ slang], *I'll swear:* an exclamation of surprise or chagrin. **1955** Williams *Cat Tin Roof* 3 **Lower Missip Valley,** Well, I swear, I simply could have di-ieed! **1965–70** *DARE* (Qu. NN7, *Exclamations of surprise: "They're getting married next week? Well, _____."*) Infs **SC**45, **TN**30, 39, **TX**39, I'll swear; **NC**52, **PA**215, I swear; (Qu. NN9a, *Exclamations showing great annoyance: "_____. The electric power is off again."*) Infs **KY**10, **MS**69, **UT**8, I swear; **KY**11, I'll swear; [**TN**33, Swear]. **1970** Tarpley *Blinky* 300 **neTX,** Mild expression of disgust . . I'll swear [rare]. **1986** Pederson *LAGS Concordance* (Damn [it]!) 1 inf, **csGA,** I swear; (Shucks!—exclamations of impatience) 1 inf, **neFL,** I swear; 1 inf, **neTX,** I'll swear—expletive, exclamation. **2002** *DARE* File—Internet **wNC, eTN,** [Title of blog entry:] Well, I Swear!

sweared See **swear B1, 2**

sweat v

A Gram forms.

Past and past pple; see below. Note: As both *sweat* and *sweated* have long been in common use, only quots that give comparative evidence are included here. Also, only the literal sense "to perspire" is treated.

a *sweat,* pronc-sp *swet.* **widespread, but somewhat less freq Sth, S Midl** See Map

1829 Kirkham *Engl. Grammar* 147 **NY,** The following is a list of the *irregular* verbs. Those marked with an R, are sometimes conjugated *regularly.* . . Sweated—swet, R.—swet, R. **1953** Atwood *Survey of Verb Forms* 22, *Sweat.* . The preterite. . . The uninflected *sweat* . . is practically universal throughout the entire Northern area (N. Eng., N.Y., n. N.J., and the northern half of Pa.), where less than one out of 20 informants use the alternate form *sweated.* Beginning in c. Pa., the inflected form *sweated* . . becomes increasingly frequent as one moves southward. It predominates in Md. (two thirds use it) and N.C. (four fifths use it), whereas in Va. and S.C. *sweat* and *sweated* are about equally common. **1955** *PADS* 23.44 **e,sSC, eNC, seGA,** *Sweat* (preterit). As common as *sweated.* **1965–70** *DARE* (Qu. OO47a, *Talking about horses sweating: "It was a warm day and the horses _____ [a lot]."*) 575 Infs, **widespread, but somewhat less freq Sth, S Midl,** Sweat; **NJ**2, Has sweat; (Qu. OO47b, *Talking about horses sweating: "They wouldn't have caught cold if they hadn't _____ [so much]."*) 540 Infs, **widespread, but somewhat less freq Sth, S Midl,** Sweat; **MO**34, 'A' sweat. **1981** *PADS* 67.46 **Mesabi Iron Range MN,** Sweat (pret.) . . *Sweat,*

which is usual with other Minnesota informants . . is used by all of the Iron Range informants. In addition, two Range informants . . also use *sweated.* **1989** [see **Ab** below].

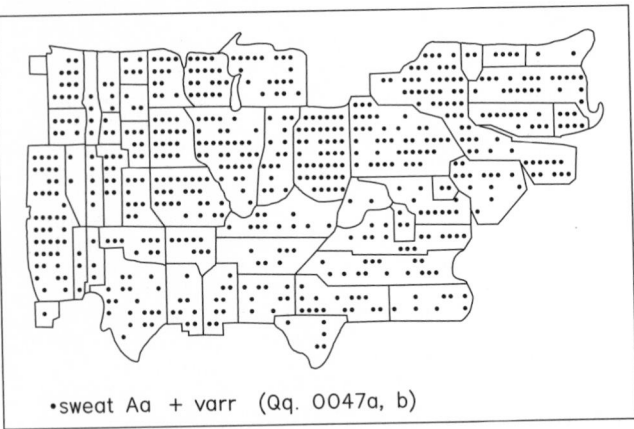

•sweat Aa + varr (Qq. OO47a, b)

b *sweated.* **widespread, but more freq Sth, S Midl, TX** See Map

1829 [see **Aa** above]. **1953** [see **Aa** above]. **1955** [see **Aa** above]. **1965–70** *DARE* (Qu. OO47b, *Talking about horses sweating: "They wouldn't have caught cold if they hadn't _____ [so much]."*) 342 Infs, **widespread, but more freq Sth, S Midl, TX,** Sweated; **NJ**44, Sweated up; (Qu. OO47a, *Talking about horses sweating: "It was a warm day and the horses _____ [a lot]."*) 315 Infs, **widespread, but more freq Sth, S Midl, TX,** Sweated; **NJ**44, Sweated up; **TN**37, Sweated hard; (Qu. X56b, *Expressions about sweating very heavily*) Infs **TN**1, **VA**31, Sweated; **IL**60, Perspired and sweated, too; **OH**78, Really sweated; **LA**14, Sweated like a beef; **MS**50, Sweated like a horse; **TN**37, Sweated through my shirt; **MO**14, Sweated very heavily; (Qu. EE21b, *When boys were fighting very actively* . . *"For a while those fellows really _____."*) Inf **TX**35, Sweated; (Qu. KK44, *To continue doing something even though it is difficult: "For five winters we've _____"*; total Infs questioned, 75) Inf **FL**38, Sweated it out. **1968** *PADS* 50.35 **swTN** [Black], For the past tense of *sweat* four of the ten informants for whom responses were recorded have the uninflected form, /swɛt/. Six have /swɛtɪd/. **1973** *PADS* 60.70 **seNC,** *Sweat.* . . The uninflected preterite *sweat* is practically universal throughout the North, and the inflected *sweated* is increasingly common as one moves South. . . Among our informants, six used the inflected form, while three said *sweat.* **1989** Pederson *LAGS Tech. Index* 282 **Gulf Region,** [For the past of *sweat,* 364 infs gave *sweated* and 58 *sweat;* for the past pple, 141 gave *sweated* and 16 *sweat.*]

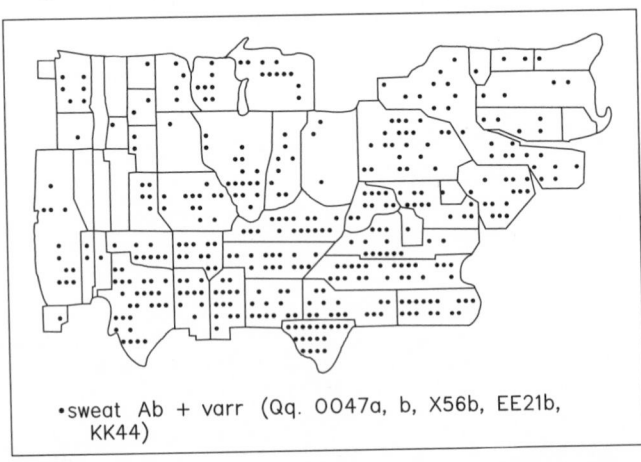

•sweat Ab + varr (Qq. OO47a, b, X56b, EE21b, KK44)

B Sense.

Also with *out;* In moonshining: to extract (the residue of liquor) from empty barrels by heating them; to extract the residue of liquor from (an empty barrel); hence n *sweater.* Cf **barrel-dogging**

1949 *AmSp* 24.8 **KY** [Moonshiner argot], *Bull dog.* . . To heat used barrels . . to sweat out the whiskey which has soaked into the barrel staves. . . Also . . *sweat.* **1954** *Courier-Jrl.* (Louisville KY) 25 Apr mag sec 7/1 **eKY,** They are . . "sweating" . . booze from the charred-oak barrels in which it was once stored for aging at distilleries. **1963** Carson *Social Hist. Bourbon* 109, "Barrel dogging". . . involves "sweating" bourbon out of tightly closed barrels by steaming. **1984** Wilder *You All Spoken Here* 138 **Sth**, *Barrel dogger, steamer, roller, sweater, burner:* One who steams used whiskey barrels, fresh from legal distilleries, to extract whiskey that had been absorbed in the aging process in the white oak barrel staves. **1995** Gold *Odyssey* 69 **sePA** (as of 1950s), He told me that bonded whiskey had aged in the barrels. By "sweating out" each barrel, he said he could get a couple gallons of high-grade whiskey, which he then sold at a high price.

sweat bee n

1 Any of various small bees, usu of the family Halictidae. **chiefly Midl, Gt Lakes, Cent** See Map   For other names of var of these see **hayfield wasp, ice-cream bee, sand ~, steady ~** Cf **sweat fly**

1870 *Putnam's Mag.* 6.48, The little "sweat-bee," that comes about the laborer in the field, alighting on his sweaty hands and arms, and showing his light buff-colored belly at every move, is undoubtedly the holder of the original patent on shears. **1894** U.S. Dept. Ag. Div. Vegetable Pathology *Bulletin* 5.79, The sweat bees of the genus *Halictus* and *Andrena.* **1900** *Ft. Wayne Sentinel* (IN) 14 July 10/5, Sweat bees also haunted that particular portico. The sweat bee looks like a pocket edition of the humble bee, but does not sting, and digs his nest in sound soft wood. **1921** *Sun. State Jrl.* (Lincoln NE) 24 July sec B 7/4, Our hygienic splutter against the fly has deafened us to the music that is in a July meadow fly or sweat bee at noon-day siesta time. **1940–41** Cassidy *WI Atlas*, Sweat bee—grayish, slender, has a little bit of a sharp sting. *Ibid*, Sweat bees sting you when you're sweating—a real bee, not a fly. **1965–70** DARE (Qu. R21, . . *Other kinds of stinging insects*) 161 Infs, **chiefly Midl, Gt Lakes, Cent**, Sweat bee; (Qu. R11, *A very tiny fly that you can hardly see, but that stings*) 25 Infs, **chiefly W Midl, Cent**, Sweat bee; (Qu. R12, . . *Other kinds of flies*) Infs **GA**84, **IL**11, **IN**67, **MN**23, **NE**10, Sweat bee. **1967** DARE FW Addit **LA**8, *Sweat bee*—A small, greenish bee that lights on people who are sweating. It does not sting until you try to brush it off. **1975** Logan *Land Remembers* 120 **swWI** (as of c1920), Some little sweat bees flew around us, but they were after our perspiration, not the anise and sugar water. **2005** *Albuquerque Jrl.* (NM) 31 Aug sec B 1 (Internet), Sweat bees can sting people but the pain is far less severe than a sting from a honeybee or wasp.

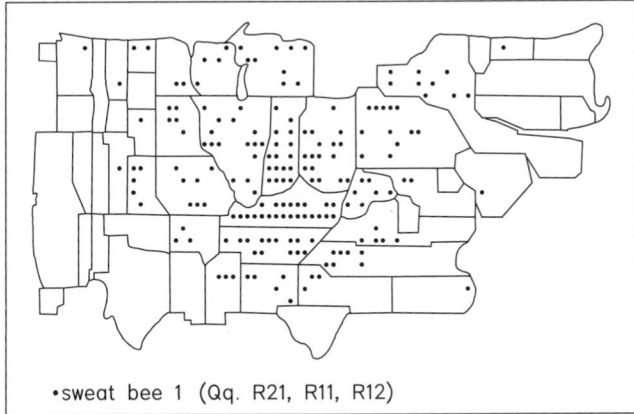

•sweat bee 1 (Qq. R21, R11, R12)

2 A **hover fly** (here: family Syrphidae). Cf **mullein bee, news ~, sweat fly, tassel ~**

1967–68 DARE (Qu. R10, *Very small flies that don't sting, often seen hovering in large groups or bunches outdoors in summer*) Infs **MO**7, 8, 12, **NH**14, Sweat bees. **2004** in 2005 DARE File—Internet, Hover Fly—Flower Fly, Hover Bee, Hover Fly, Sweat Bee, Sweat Fly, Syrphid Fly . . family Syrphidae. . . Adults look like bees or small wasps and are usually seen hovering around flowers. . . Some are very small, others are larger than house flies. . . Hover flies don't bite or sting.

sweated See **sweat Ab**

sweater See **sweat B**

sweat fly n

Usu any of var **hover flies** (here: family Syrphidae); occas also a **sweat bee 1**; see quots.

1843 (1924) Oliver *8 Months* 148 **IL**, The whole earth and air seems teeming with them, and mosquitoes, gallinippers, bugs, . . sweat-flies, . .

join in one continued attack. **1926** Essig *Insects N. Amer.* 566, *Syrphidae.* . . Sweat Flies. **1950** WELS Suppl. **WI**, My mother used to call a certain insect the "sweat fly." It bothered us when we were picking wild raspberries. . . They simply buzzed round and round our heads, seeminly [sic] attracted by the sweaty odor. I do not think they lit. **1953** *Marion Star* (OH) 4 Aug [6]/2 (newspaperarchive.com), In the process of wresting a living from the soil, men learned by hard experience to keep their shirt collars buttoned up tight. Otherwise, hornets, bees, yellow jackets, sweat flies and timothy seed would get inside their shirts. **1965–70** DARE (Qu. R12, . . *Other kinds of flies*) Infs **FL**16, **ID**5, **KS**5, **MA**6, 26, **ME**12, **NY**68, 109, 142, 205, Sweat fly; (Qu. R10, *Very small flies that don't sting, often seen hovering in large groups or bunches outdoors in summer*) Inf **MD**34, Sweat flies; (Qu. R13, *Flies that come to meat or fruit*) Inf **OK**31, Sweat fly; (Qu. R21, . . *Other kinds of stinging insects*) Infs **KY**76, **NY**109, Sweat fly; **NY**211, Mullein bee . . same as mullein fly and sweat fly. **2004** [see **sweat bee 2**].

sweating plant n Also *sweating weed, sweat plant* [See quot 1828]

A **boneset 1** (here: *Eupatorium perfoliatum*).

1828 Rafinesque *Med. Flora* 1.174, *Eupatorium Perfoliatum.* . . Sweating-plant. . . *Properties*—A valuable sudorific. . . The warm infusion causes a copious perspiration. **1876** Hobbs *Bot. Hdbk.* 115, Sweating plant. . . Eupatorium perfoliatum. **1892** (1974) Millspaugh *Amer. Med. Plants* 79–1, *Eupatorium perfoliatum.* . . Sweating weed. . . [It] is diaphoretic only when given in generous doses of the hot infusion. **1944** Wellman *Bowl* 152 **KS**, It's a grand medicine—sweat plant, I call it. When you've got a fever, jest make a tea of this an' drink it. **1953** *Gaz. & Bulletin* (Williamsport PA) 30 Jan sec H 7/1, Boneset grows very profusely throughout our nation. It is sometimes called Sweating Plant . . and Feverwort.

sweating root See **sweatroot**

sweating weed n

1 See **sweating plant.**

2 also *sweatweed*: A **hibiscus**, usu *Hibiscus laevis*, or a **mallow B** (here: *Kosteletzkya virginica*). [See quot 1922]

1813 Muhlenberg *Catalogus Plantarum* 63, *Hibiscus . . Virginicus . .* (sweating weed). **1843** Torrey *Flora NY* 1.114, *Hibiscus virginicus. . .* Virginian Hibiscus. Sweating-weed. . . Borders of salt marshes on the north side of Long Island. **1922** in 2006 DARE File—Internet [*Omaha Sunday World–Herald* (NE) 24 Sept sec E 12], Another branch of this family is the Hibiscus, of which Nebraska has two varieties, one called Sweating Weed, doubtless from properties first discovered by the Amerinds, who used such plants largely in their ceremonies. **1949** Moldenke *Amer. Wild Flowers* 111, Sweating weed, *H[ibiscus] militaris.* **2005** DARE File—Internet, *Sweat weed* or *Virginia saltmarsh mallow* or *Seashore Mallow* (*Kosteletzkya virginica*, syn. *Hibiscus virginicus*) is an herb found in marshes along the east seashore of the United States.

sweat like a dog See **dog n B17e**

sweat like a mule See **mule n¹ 6**

sweat like a nigger (at election) See **nigger n¹ B11**

sweat like a pig See **pig n¹ B16**

sweat like a tiger See **tiger B5**

sweat out See **sweat B**

sweat pad n Cf **blanket 3**, DS H20b

Esp among loggers: a pancake, esp a tough one.

1919 Lockhart *Fighting Shepherdess* 193 **WY**, "Those sweat-pads of yourn would be pretty fair if twant for the lumps of sody a fellers allus bitin' into," the herder commented. **1939** FWP *ID Lore* 244, Lumberjack jargon in the St. Maries area and elsewhere: . . *Sweat pads*— hot cakes. **1956** Sorden–Ebert *Logger's Words* 36 **NEng, Gt Lakes**, *Sweat-pads,* Pancakes. **1969** DARE File **cwWI**, *Sweat pad*—The bottom pancake in a stack. "Do I have to eat the sweat pad, or will you bake me a fresh pancake?" **1972** *Yesterday* 1.2.26, For breakfast the jack settled down before huge mounds of meat, potatoes, and pancakes, sometimes called "sweat pads." **1973** Allen *LAUM* 1.283 (as of c1950), *Griddle cakes.* . . *Sweat pads* is the graphic term of a western Nebraskan familiar with early pioneer days.

sweat plant See **sweating plant**

sweat pone n   esp MD

A variety of corn bread; see quots.

1940 [see **Sunday pone**]. **1971** *Sun. Times* (Salisbury MD) 14 Feb 10/1, Mrs. Francis J. Townsend . . donated her very old recipe for "Sweat Pone" which has its origins in North Carolina. . . *Lil's "Sweat Pone"* [Recipe includes corn meal, molasses, flour, sugar, salt, and canned pumpkin.] . . [L]et stand, covered, for 3 hours. Bake. . . Remove, let stand covered for 12 hours. . . With true corn pone one must plan a day ahead to enjoy this cold weather delight. **2008** *NADS Letters* seMD, What I would call "sweat pone" is a dense, sweet cake of corn-bread that can be eaten as is, or sliced and heated, e.g. for breakfast. The last time I had some, I would have been in my late teens. A few times I bought "sweat pone" from one of the maids at the hotel where I worked. . . I would use the term "corn pone" and "sweat pone" inter-changeably. . . an African-American person would be more likely to say "sweat pone", and an Anglo "corn pone."

sweatroot n   Also *sweating root*

A Jacob's ladder 1 (here: *Polemonium reptans*).

1847 Beach *Amer. Practice Condensed* 689, Greek Valerian, Abscess-root, Blue Bells, Sweat-root—*(Polemonium Reptans)*. **1872** Rudolphy *Pharmaceutical Directory* 27, Sweat root. Polemonium reptans. **1933** Small *Manual SE Flora* 1100, P[olemonium] reptans. . . Sweat-root. **1940** Clute *Amer. Plant Names* 267, *Polemonium reptans,* Sweating-root.

sweatweed n

1 =**marshmallow 1**.

1876 Hobbs *Bot. Hdbk.* 115, Sweat weed. . . Althaea officinalis. **1924** *Amer. Botanist* 30.106, The true marsh-mallow belongs to the genus *Althaea.* . . Further medicinal uses are indicated by such terms as "sweat-weed."

2 See **sweating weed 2**.

Swede n

1 also *Swede turnip:* =**rutabaga B**.   [*OED2* 1812 →]

1822 Woods *2 Yrs. Residence* 215 **sIL**, Swede turnips but little known here. **1856** U.S. Patent Office *Annual Rept. for 1855: Ag.* 262 **KY**, The Swedes were transplanted in drills August 4th. **1864** Randall *Practical Shepherd* 239 **NY**, That acre does very poorly that does not produce 500 bushels of Swedes. **1893** *Edwardsville Intelligencer* (IL) [24 May 6]/5 (newspaperarchive.com), It [=rape] bears a close resemblance to the Swede turnip in the early stages of its growth. **1909** *Gettysburg Times* (PA) [27 July 4]/4 (newspaperarchive.com), A dairyman. . . says it [= kohlrabi] is a better milk producer than the swede turnip. **1950** *WELS* (What names or nicknames do you have for large yellow turnips?) 1 Inf, **WI**, Swede. **1966–69** *DARE* (Qu. I3, . . *The large yellowish root vege-table, similar to a turnip, with a strong taste*) Infs **ID5, IN63, NC72,** Swede turnips; **MI29,** Swede turnips [Inf of Swedish descent]; **NY34,** Swedes. **2004** *DARE* File **MN** (as of c1980), When we visited in north-ern Minnesota, we saw rutabagas in the markets advertized as "Swedes."

2a attrib: Used esp of var tools, devices, or processes assoc with Scandinavian workers; see quots.   See also **Swede fence** Cf **Finn 2b**

1940 Paterson *If It Prove* 197 **MI**, She had picked up. . . raspberries in the sand pits, dug for ballast, by the railway spur. "Swede-holes," the pits were called in local idiom, not quite accurate. . . The foundry-men happened to be Finns. **1942** Beck *Songs MI Lumberjacks* 186, "Swede holes" were holes left along the narrow-gauge tracks in repairing the grade; the name indicates the nationality of the men who did much of the track work. **1958** McCulloch *Woods Words* 186 **Pacific NW**, *Swede car*—A hand-pushed car used for dumping fill dirt along the grade in early logging railroad construction. . . *Swede flag*—Same as swede level. *Swede hooks*—Handled tongs used to carry heavy timbers. *Swede level*—a. Two boards nailed to make a cross, used as a line of lev-els for the shovel runner or cat skinner making a grade. b. Sometimes means a keel mark on a tree or stake at the eye level of the cat skinner, for the same purpose. **1960** *AmSp* 35.270 **cwCA**, Long after a minor-ity group is integrated, or has completely vanished from the trade, the tool name lingers on as a faint reminder of earlier aggression or con-flict. Phrases . . that I have heard in actual usage in San Francisco build-ing construction and waterfront employment are: *German planer, Irish buggy,* . . *Jew nails,* . . *Polack screwdriver,* . . *Portugee pump, Swede hand axe,* and *Swede rule.* **1982** *Smithsonian Letters* **NW**, Swede Trap = Widow Maker (branch caught in a tree). [Local Lumbermen were Scandinavians in the early years.]

b spec, in combs *Swede* (or *Swede's, Swedish*) *fiddle:* A crosscut saw.   **chiefly Nth, esp Pacific NW**   Cf **misery whip**

1930 Williams *Logger-Talk* 30 **Pacific NW**, *Swede-fiddle:* A cross-cut saw. **1938** (1939) Holbrook *Holy Mackinaw* 264, *Swedish fiddle.* Crosscut saw. **1941** Writers' Program *Guide WA* 73, "Fallers" chopped the trees down, while "buckers" cut or "bucked" them into 24, 32, or even 40-foot lengths, using a crosscut saw, or "Swede Fiddle." **1942** *AmSp* 17.224 **Nth** [Loggers' talk], *Swedish fiddle.* A crosscut saw. **1947** Jones *Evergreen Land* 255 **WA**, The fallers and buckers now use power saws instead of "Swede fiddles." **1956** Sorden–Ebert *Logger's Words* 37 **Gt Lakes**, *Swedish-fiddle,* Cross-cut-saw. **1958** McCulloch *Woods Words* 186 **Pacific NW**, *Swede fiddle*—A crosscut saw; particu-larly a bucking saw. **1977** Jones *OR Folkl.* 14, In the case of loggers, not only do they know what a crosscut saw is (the technical term for a type of hand saw once widely used in the woods), they also know that same item as a *misery whip* or a *Swede's fiddle.*

3 in comb *Swede saw:* A bow saw with a tubular metal han-dle; hence v *Swede-saw* to cut with such a saw.   [See quots 1943, 2006; cf *DCan*]   esp **wGt Lakes**

1940 *Brainerd Daily Dispatch* (MN) 18 Dec [7]/7 (newspaper-archive.com), [Advt:] *For Sale:* . . Swede saw. **1943** *Waterloo Sun. Courier* (IA) 7 Feb 9/1, He was proud as he unwrapped the blades and holder, explaining how Minnesotans, near his summer cottage, use the "Swede" saw exclusively to cut trees and firewood in record time. . . The instruction slip—in entirety—was in Swedish. He is still trying to figure it out. **1945** *WI Rapids Daily Tribune* (WI) 2 Oct 7/4, Genuine Sandvik Swede Saw—42 inch blade. **1956** Sorden–Ebert *Logger's Words* 36 **Gt Lakes**, *Swede-saw,* A short saw with bow type handle generally used to cut pulpwood. Same as Finn-saw. **1973** Tabbert *Coll.* **AK**, *Swede saw*—A small saw with changeable blade on an L-shaped tubular metal frame. [**1984** *MJLF* 10.158 **cnWI**, *Swede saw.* The bucksaw.] **2000** Bly *My Lord* 192 **MN**, They stood in the snow . . and swede-sawed up all the trunks. **2006** *DARE* File—Internet **OR**, Bow Saws— . . The original model was probably the bucksaw, with a wooden frame to keep the blade in tension. Earlier this century, though, metal frame saws were imported from Sweden (which is why some still call them "Swede saws").

Swede brain food   See **Swedish condition(er) powder**

Swede brown bean   See **Swedish brown bean**

Swede fence n   Also *Swedish fence*   esp **sePA**   Cf *DS* L62, 65

A type of **stake-and-rider fence;** see quots.

1834 in 2008 (acc) Lexis-Nexis Legal Research *State Case Law: PA* (Internet) **sePA**, A dam in Cassell's time, built by Cassell, swept away; built like a Swede fence. **1867** Martindale *Hist. Byberry & Moreland* 147 **sePA**, Jacob Saurman informs me that it [=a cemetery] had a Swede fence around it when first recollected by him. **1947** *Doylestown Daily Intelligencer* (PA) 9 June 7/1 (as of 1922), Mr. Case, who de-scribed the Swede fence, said this was constructed of stakes and rails. **1961** in 2000 Millersville Univ. Center for PA Ger. Studies *Jrl.* Summer 7 **sePA**, The Swedish and Irish fences were a variation of the stake and rider fence. **1966** Dakin *Dial. Vocab. Ohio R. Valley* 2.104 **KY**, The three point contact with the ground of each section of this fence would clearly give it greater stability on the steep hillsides in this area. The usual name for such a fence is *galloping fence.* . . A Leslie County infor-mant also unquestionably calls this fence a *Swede fence.* . . [A]n Owsley County informant also seems to say *Swede fence* for this same type. **2004** Rehder *Appalachian Folkways* 139, A very rare fence in Appala-chia is called the buck, reindeer, Irish, Shanghai, or Swede fence. Pairs of crossed rails form the vertical support of the fence, while diagonal rails form its linear axis.

Swede fiddle   See **Swede 2b**

Swede mallard n

The common **merganser** (*Mergus merganser*).

1956 *AmSp* 31.181 **MI**, Swede mallard—Common merganser.

Swede saw   See **Swede 3**

Swede's fiddle   See **Swede 2b**

Swede turnip   See **Swede 1**

swedge (down)   See **swage 2**

Swedish brain food   See **Swedish condition(er) powder**

Swedish brown (bean) n   Also *Swede brown bean*

A cultivated bean (*Phaseolus vulgaris* var).

1904 *Tri-City Star* (Davenport IA) 31 Oct 8/1, [Advt:] 3 lbs New Swedish Brown Beans . . 25c. **1940** *Warren Times–Mirror* (PA) 25 Oct 8/4, [Advt:] *New Swedish Specialties*—New Swedish Brown Beans. 2 lb 25c. **1967** *DARE* (Qu. H50, *Dishes made with beans, peas, or corn that everybody around here knows, but people in other places might not*) Inf **MN**11, Swedish brown beans—cooked and combined with cornstarch, vinegar, and sugar; (Qu. I20, . . *Kinds of beans*) Inf **MN**6, Swede brown beans. **1978** *Wanigan Catalog* 20, *Swedish brown*. . . [T]his ochre brown, short oval seed . . has a dark eye ring. A good producer of baking beans. **2005** *Atlanta Jrl.–Constitution* (GA) 30 July 8 (Internet) **Chicago IL,** I am trying to find Swedish foods that my family would prepare when I was a boy in Chicago: Swedish potato sausage, Swedish brown beans, Swedish limpa sweet bread and lingonberries. **2005** *DARE* File—Internet, Settlers from Sweden who arrived in Montana during the late 19th century brought Swedish brown beans to North America. These beans are loved for their mildly sweet flavor and are traditionally prepared as Swedish brown bean soup.

Swedish clover n   Also *Swedish white clover*
=**alsike.**

   1855 *Amer. Inst. NYC Annual Rept. for 1854* 619, *Alsyke or Swedish clover,* (Trifolium hybridum) from England, believed to have originated in the south of Sweden. **1869** *St. Joseph Herald* (MI) [27 Feb 3]/5 (newspaperarchive.com), *Alsike, or Swedish Clover*. . *Alsike Clover* is a hybrid between our common Red and White Clovers. It has of late attained a very high reputation as one of the best clovers for forage. **1897** *Daily Herald* (Delphos OH) 30 Nov 2/6, We were led to try alsike or Swedish clover by Allen, the author of the American Farm Book, and, after a trial of it for some years, would strongly advise anyone wanting a good feeding clover to try it. **1931** *Stevens Point Daily Jrl.* (WI) 25 Apr 9/4, [Advt:] *For Lawn and Garden*— Swedish White Clover seed.

Swedish condition(er) powder n   Also *Swedish* (or *Swede*) *brain food*   **Nth**
Among loggers: =**snoose** n[1].

   1938 (1939) Holbrook *Holy Mackinaw* 264 **Nth,** *Snoose.* Damp snuff for chewing. Also known as *Scandihoovian dynamite* and *Swedish condition powder*. **1956** Sorden–Ebert *Logger's Words* 36 **Gt Lakes,** *Swede-brain-food,* See snoose. . . *Swedish-conditioner-powder,* See snoose. **1958** McCulloch *Woods Words* 186 **Pacific NW,** *Swedish condition powder*—Snoose. **1969** Sorden *Lumberjack Lingo* 125 **NEng, Gt Lakes,** *Swedish brain food*—Snoose.

Swedish fence   See **Swede fence**

Swedish fiddle   See **Swede 2b**

Swedish turnip n   Cf **Swede 1**
=**rutabaga B.**

   1790 Deane *New Engl. Farmer* 468, A treatise upon the Ruta Baga, or Swedish turnip, has been written by William Cobbet [sic]. **1792** in 1939 Washington *Writings* 32.59 **VA,** I had the pleasure a few days ago to receive your letter of the 28th. of September, . . and accompanied with some Seeds of the Swedish Turnip or *Ruta Baga.* **1806** McMahon *Amer. Gardener's Calendar* 427 **PA,** The Swedish turnep, or *Roota Baga,* as it is called, . . requires to be sown in a different season. **1819** *Plough Boy* 1.46 **ceNY,** *Ruta Baga* or *Swedish turnip.* **1929** *Bismarck Tribune* (ND) 26 Nov 4/6, There are many varieties of turnips, the principal three being the white, flat turnip, the yellow globe, and the rutabaga or Swedish turnip. **1950** *WELS* (*What names or nicknames do you have for large yellow turnips?*) 3 Infs, **WI,** Swedish turnip. **1967** *DARE* (Qu. I3, . . *The large yellowish root vegetable, similar to a turnip, with a strong taste*) Inf **MA**5, Swedish turnip; (Qu. HH30, *Things that are nicknamed for different nationalities—for example, a 'Dutch treat'*) Inf **ID**5, Swedish turnips. **2004** *Star Tribune* (Minneapolis MN) 8 Jan sec T 1 (Internet), Occasionally, cookbooks refer to vegetables called Swedes. Some say that's another name for rutabagas, which are also called Swedish turnips. . . Others say the turnip, the rutabaga and the Swede are three distinct vegetables.

Swedish white clover   See **Swedish clover**

Swedish yellow turnip   See **yellow turnip**

sweep n

1   also attrib: A shallow, triangular cultivator blade; a cultivator or plow equipped with one or more such blades; also in var combs; see quots. **chiefly Sth**   See Map   Cf **buzzard-wing sweep**

   1842 in 1969 Turner *Cotton Planter's Manual* 55 **AL,** I have now no

further use for a plough in its subsequent culture, but use the *sweep*—a kind of horse-hoe. **1846** *De Bow's Rev.* 2.136 **MS,** After the cotton is hilled the second time, I use almost entirely the *cultivator,* or the *sweep,* or both. **1941** *Sun* (Baltimore MD) 2 Aug 19/6 **AL,** A sweep plow is mounted behind the tractor to cultivate the middle in the ordinary manner. **1944** Clark *Pills* 160 **AL,** A farmer in Alabama wanted . . 10 weeding hoes no 3, 3 sixteen inch sweeps. **1959** Faulkner *Mansion* 49 **MS,** The mule . . drew the plow and then the sweep. **1965–70** *DARE* (Qu. L18, *Kinds of plows*) 19 Infs, **chiefly Sth,** Sweep; **FL**50, Sweep—shores up sides of a furrow to keep the grass down—"sides it up"; **OH**95, Sweep—wide blade—modern plow; **OK**14, Sweep—shaped like, but larger than, a shovel; **SC**1, Sweep—for working cotton; **SC**7, 26, Sweep—for siding (cotton); **SC**69, Sweep—pushes up sides of a furrow to cut weeds; **TX**32, Sweep—two blades shaped like V; **TX**99, Sweep—modern plow; **TX**32, Half sweep; **MS**66, Heel sweep; **LA**18, Hill sweep; **GA**72, Horse-drawn heel sweep; **GA**17, Side sweep; **FL**36, Single-sweep plow; **OK**14, Solid sweep; **NC**49, **TX**63, Sweep-stock plow; **GA**9, Sweep-wing plow; **AR**51, Twelve-inch solid sweep; **OK**14, Wing sweep; (Qu. L25, *The implement used to clean out weeds and loosen the earth between rows of corn*) 9 Infs, **chiefly Sth,** Sweep; **AL**2, Sweep—a winged instrument; **AL**15, Scooter and a sweep; **GA**17, Side sweep; **GA**5, Sweep cultivator; **FL**34, Sweep tongue; (Qu. L20, *The implement used in a field after it's been plowed to break up the lumps*) Inf **GA**72, Horse-drawn heel sweep. **1986** Pederson *LAGS Concordance Gulf Region* *(Plow)* 13 infs, (A) sweep; 7 infs, Sweep stock; 3 infs, Hill sweep; 1 inf, **cnAL,** Sweep—used last "to lay your crop by"; 1 inf, **cwAL,** Sweep—had "wings" on each side; 1 inf, **cwAL,** Sweep—to bust middles out; 1 inf, **swAL,** Sweep—attaches to scooter stock to kill grass; 1 inf, **nwFL,** Sweep—big-old plow that you laid by corn with; 1 inf, **cMS,** Sweep—small plow to shape rows of cotton; 1 inf, **csMS,** Sweep—V-shaped; 1 inf, **cTX,** Sweep—with a middlebuster; 1 inf, **ceTX,** Sweep—blade on plow; 1 inf, **cTX,** Sweep—throws soil further; 1 inf, **csAL,** A sweep—wide plow; cut under grass; 1 inf, **cnLA,** A sweep—has wings; 1 inf, **swLA,** A sweep—a plow used to clean the middle—cotton; 1 inf, **swTN,** A shovel plow with a hill sweep—used last; 1 inf, **seMS,** Sweep plow; *(Harrow)* 4 infs, **Gulf Region,** Sweep; 1 inf, **cwMS,** Boll weevil sweep—with wings; 1 inf, **cAL,** Sweep—attached to plow; 1 inf, **nwLA,** Sweep—for plowing cotton; 1 inf, **ceMS,** Sweep—turns dirt into middle.

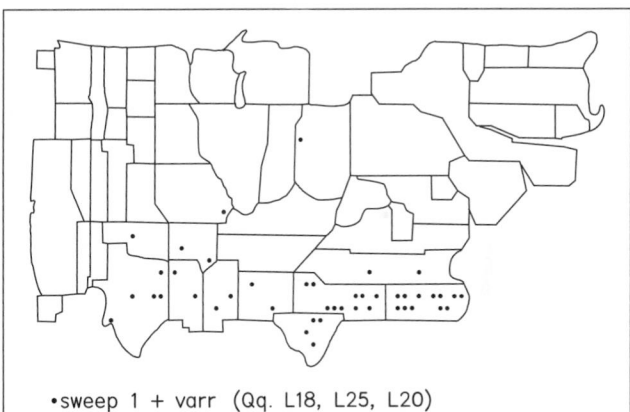

•sweep 1 + varr (Qq. L18, L25, L20)

2   A hazard consisting of a low-hanging tree or branch.   Cf **sweeper 1**

   1952 *Badger Folkl.* 1.17 **WI** [Logging language], *Sweep*—Low hanging branch or tree across road. **1969** Sorden *Lumberjack Lingo* 125 **NEng, Gt Lakes,** *Sweep*. . . A tree branch hanging low across a road or stream.

3   See **sweep rake.**

sweeper n

1   A hazard to navigation consisting of a tree or tree limb leaning over or into the water.   **Nth**   Cf **sawyer 4, sucker sweep**

   1887 Allen *Rept. Exped.* 81 (as of 1885) **AK,** In places the river-bed . . contained fields of lodged timber with roots turned to the current. . . These trees are known to Alaskan pioneers as sweepers, as are those which have the roots fast to the banks, with the trunks and boughs in the water. **1913** *Fairbanks Sun. Times* (AK) 12 Oct [7]/3 (newspaperarchive.com), Mr. Marquam was severely injured while coming downstream. . . While working about the launch, a sweeper knocked him off his feet. **1956** Sorden–Ebert *Logger's Words* 37 **Gt Lakes,** *Sweeper,* An uprooted tree which has fallen into the stream. It could sweep men off a raft or log and it frequently caused a jam. Same as sucker-sweep and succor. **1958** McCulloch *Woods Words* 186 **Pacific NW,** *Sweeper.* . . A tree which has fallen into a river, its roots still fast on the bank; the current sweeps it back and forth. **1966** *DARE* Tape **ME26,** They come to a sweeper, laid there over the brook, and they both laid down . . on the crosspieces on the cat. And one fellow go in under, and course the swell was going down. And the other fellow come, then there it was comin' up. Caught right in the back . . he had a blue sweater on then, and a knot caught right in the back of that, he hung to that. **1977** *New Yorker* 9 May 120 **AK,** Over the cut bank a sweeper had recently fallen, a spruce whose trunk reached into the river. . . Sweepers tend to trap boats. **1994** *Daily Sentinel* (Sitka AK) 22 June 8/3, A Danish tourist was killed after the raft he was in hit a large sweeper and overturned.

2 =**chimney swift.**
1909 *DN* 3.378 **eAL, wGA,** *Sweeper.* . . The chimney-swift.

sweep rake n Also *sweep(-rake reaper)* Cf **go-devil** n **2b**
=**buck rake.**
1854 *Scientific Amer.* 9.235 **MD,** Harvesters of Grain. . . I claim. . . the combination of a continuously revolving sweep rake with a revolving reel, which disposes the grain upon the platform with its stalks converging to the axis of the rake. **1876** *VT State Bd. Ag. Rept. for 1875–76* 3.610, The sweep-rake reaper is now so perfect a machine that it will reap grain so badly lodged that it is with difficulty that it can be mown with a scythe. **1917** *Bedford Gaz.* (PA) 22 June 3/1, Eastern hay growers who are up against the fact of farm labor shortage can get along with fewer men and can reduce the cost of haying by using the sweep rake. . . Any boy capable of driving a pair of horses can operate a sweep rake and handle considerably more hay in a given time than a man pitching by hand. **1946** *Atchison Daily Globe* (KS) 2 Sept 7/5, One Horse Drawn Sweep Rake—One Tractor Drawn Sweep Rake. **1949** *PADS* 11.21 **CO,** *Go-devil.* . . A sweep-rake. **1966–70** *DARE* (Qu. L16, *Machines used . . in handling hay*) Infs **ND9, WA1,** Sweep rake; **CO44,** Go-devil was Kansas for sweep rake; **IL104,** Sweep rake—two horses; **KY75,** Sweep rake—old-fashioned—ten feet wide; a horse on each side pulled it to pick up shocks and carry them to a baler; **MN16,** Sweep rake—for loose [hay]; **WY1,** Sweep or buck rake; **WY5,** Power sweep—the horse-drawn buck rake is usually called a sweep in this region; a power sweep is a mechanized adaptation of this; (Qu. L28, *Tools used in the past for cutting grain*) Inf **TX43,** Sweep. **1986** Pederson *LAGS Concordance,* 1 inf, **cwTN,** Sweep rake—pulled by mules. **2004** *DARE* File—Internet **IA,** Soo Tractor Sweep Rake—2550 Hawkeye Drive, Sioux City.

sweer See **swear**

swee-swee n Also *sweet* [Echoic] Cf **swee-sweet**
=**spotted sandpiper.**
1913 *Auk* 30.493 **Okefenokee GA,** *Actitis macularia. Spotted Sandpiper;* 'Sweet'—The Spotted Sandpiper was a distinct surprise as a summer resident of the swamp. **1916** *Times–Picayune* (New Orleans LA) 2 Apr mag sec 8/3, *Spotted sandpiper.* . . Chevalier de Batture; Swee-swee; Teeter-tail; tip-up.

swee-sweet n [Echoic] **sLA** Cf **swee-swee**
=**solitary sandpiper.**
1916 *Times–Picayune* (New Orleans LA) 2 Apr mag sec 8/2, *Solitary sandpiper* (Helodromas solitarius). Swee-sweet. **1931** LA Dept. of Conserv. *Bulletin* 20.275, A bird of very retiring habits is the "Swee-Sweet," to give the Solitary Sandpiper its best known name in Louisiana. **1936** O'Donnell *Green Margins* 191 **sLA,** While Father Sam chanted in Latin, somewhere a wandering Swee-Sweet (Solitary Sandpiper) was calling busily.

sweet See **swee-swee**

sweet acacia n
=**huisache.**
1901 Mohr *Plant Life AL* 834, *Acacia farnesiana.* . . Sweet Acacia. **1937** U.S. Forest Serv. *Range Plant Hdbk.* B1, The huisache, or sweet acacia *(A[cacia] farnesiana),* native from western Texas south to northern Chile. **1969** *Pt. Arthur News* (TX) 18 July 5/7, A sweet acacia which was ranked as a national champion was torn down long [sic] with the old Uvalde county jail. **2003** *AZ Daily Star* (Tucson) 1 Feb sec B 1 (Internet), We've got sweet acacias and ash trees popping buds that normally wouldn't start growing for over a month, because it's been so warm.

sweet-after-death n Also *sweet-in-death* [See quot 1934]
=**vanilla leaf 1.**
1901 Eastwood *Bergen's Botany* 63, *Achlys,* Oregon Sweet Clover and Deer's-foot, Sweet-in-death. **1915** (1926) Armstrong–Thornber *Western Wild Flowers* 156, *Sweet-after-Death.* . . An attractive perennial, popular on account of its sweet-smelling foliage, which, however, is not fragrant until the leaves are dried. **1919** *DN* 5.59 **WA,** Sweet in death. . . Smell leaves. **1934** Haskin *Wild Flowers Pacific Coast* 119, The names vanilla-leaf and sweet-after-death are given it because the foliage contains a small amount of coumerin [sic], and gives off a sweet fragrance while wilting. **1949** Peattie *Cascades* 231, The plant . . is vanilla-leaf, so named for its odor. When dried, the leaves are even more fragrant and because of this some people call them sweet-after-death.

sweet anise n

1 pronc-sp *sweet anny:* A **sweet cicely.**
1796 Dwight *Short Geog.* 169, Q. What are the vegetable productions of this territory [=Tennessee]? A. . . In the low grounds, cane, snakeroot, angelica, crab-apple, pappaw, sweet-anise, spikenard, and grapes. **1873** in 1976 Miller *Shaker Herbs* 153, *Osmorhiza longistylis.* Anise Root. Sweet Anise. **1885** *Decatur Weekly Republican* (IL) 2 July [3]/4 (newspaperarchive.com), While out in the Dakota timber with a number of companions he said that he thought was sweet anise, a harmless and pleasant tasting root. **1896** *Jrl. Amer. Folkl.* 9.189 **OH,** *Osmorhiza longistylis,* . . sweet anise. . . Odor and taste like true sweet anise. **1900** *Bedford Gaz.* (PA) 8 June 1/4, Walter Miller and Robert Stahl, the 12-year-old sons of two prominent business men, while in the woods today partook of some poisonous herb, mistaking it for sweet anise root. **1927** *DN* 5.472 **Ozarks,** *Anny.* . . Anise. "Swoggle yer worms in this hyar sweet-anny ef you aim t' ketch catfish." [*DARE* Ed: Identification uncertain] **1941** *Press-Gaz.* (Hillsboro OH) 20 May 2/1, Some people chew sweet anise root and rub it over the worm or other bait on the hook and the fish seem to like it. **1950** *Jrl. Range Management* 3.305 **West,** Palatable grasses and weeds must make up at least 70 percent of the plant cover. . . These should include . . sweet anise *(Ozmorhiza occidentalis).* **1982** Slone *How We Talked* 90 **eKY** (as of c1950), *Sweet Anis* [sic]—Dig and chew the roots of this plant, which has a licorice flavor. [**1984** Palmer *Youghiogheny* 70 **nwMD,** Ed shows the sweet anise—a green herb with finely textured leaves—to cronies at the bar. The smell of licorice blends into the Al's Lounge atmosphere. . . Ed says, "You chew 'i up, spit 'i on fishin' worms, then go fishin'."]

2 =**sweet fennel.**
1914 Saunders *With Flowers in CA* 61, By one of the perversions which attends so many popular names, it is generally called sweet anise. It is really fennel *(Foeniculum vulgare).* **1942** *Oakland Tribune* (CA) 14 June sec B 12/8, Included in the school's garden . . are a quarter acre of potatoes, 500 tomato plants, 1000 sweet anise plants and 500 caraway plants being grown for seed. **2003** *Intelligencer* (Doylestown PA) 8 Oct sec D 2/1, Fennel—sold as "sweet anise" in many markets—looks like a plump head of celery topped with a sprig of dill. But the feathery leaves taste of licorice, not dill, and the stalks are stringy and a little tough. Instead, it's the rounded base, or bulb, that people eat and cook with.

3 =**valerian 1.**
1937 U.S. Forest Serv. *Range Plant Hdbk.* W199, *Valeriana spp.* The valerians, also known in the West as tobacco root and sometimes improperly called sweet anise.

sweet annie n
A **wormwood 1** (here: *Artemisia annua*).
1968 *DARE* (Qu. S26e, *Other wildflowers not yet mentioned;* not asked in early QRs) Inf **MD20,** Sweet annie root—grows near water, about a foot high, fine leaves, no flowers—root believed to have medicinal powers. [*DARE* Ed: cf **sweet anise 1.**] **1989** *Frederick Post* (MD) 2 Nov sec D 3/5, Sweet Annie. Leaves, which smell like fresh hay, are a good choice for a potpourri filler. **2003** *Chron.–Telegram* (Elyria OH) 13 Apr sec G 5/4, Sweet Annie (Ardemisia [sic] annua) is a fragrant herb that can help remove odors from antiques.

sweet anny See **sweet anise 1**

sweet apple pickle See **apple pickle**

sweetback n *among Black speakers*
A woman's paramour; a ladies' man; a pimp.
1929 Gordon *Born to Be* 55 [Black], Many a time the conversations became so interesting that I almost died from anxiety had it not been that some bully sweetback would begin to threaten his girl that if she didn't turn in more money, he would import some red hot baby from

Helena or Butte to take her place. **1932** *NY Times* (NY) 1 Jan 30/4 [Black], During a roistering barbecue one of the granddaughters is fatally stabbed by the wife of the "sweetback" with whom she is carousing. **1942** Berrey–Van den Bark *Amer. Slang* 460.11, Friends; lovers. . . *sweet back,* a ladies' man, dandy. **1971** Van Peebles *Sweet Sweetback's Baadasssss Song* [Film title]. **1974** *Black World* Sept 25 **Sth** [Black], *Long Black Song* tells us, here in the 1970's, that the days of darky entertainers, superflies, sweetbacks, and Melindas, if not over, are numbered. **1992** Morrison *Jazz* 119 **NYC** (as of c1926) [Black], He cuts his eyes over to the sweetbacks lounging on the corner. *Ibid* 132, Across the street . . I saw three sweetbacks. Thirty degrees, not even ten in the morning, and they shone like patent leather. Smooth. . . Young. . . One wore spats, and one had a handkerchief in his pocket same color as his tie.

sweet balsam n

1 A **cudweed 1,** usu *Pseudognaphalium obtusifolium*.

1847 Beach *Amer. Practice Condensed* 690, Sweet Balsam, Life Everlasting. **1873** in 1976 Miller *Shaker Herbs* 132, Balsam, Sweet . . *Gnaphalium polycephalum* [=*Pseudognaphalium obtusifolium*]. **1912** Blatchley *IN Weed Book* 159, *Gnaphalium obtusifolium*. . . Sweet Balsam. **1965** (1982) Stupka *Wildflowers* 124 **sAppalachians,** It is sometimes called "poverty-weed" and "old-field balsam," because it thrives in dry areas and waste places. Names such as "sweet balsam" and "sweet life-everlasting" refer to its fragrance. Other names are "rabbit-tobacco" and "cudweed."

‡**2** =**balsam poplar.**

1968 *DARE* (Qu. T12, *The kind of poplar tree that has sticky, sweet-smelling buds*) Inf **MO**12, [FW:] She'd heard of sweet balsam.

sweet basil n

Sweet alyssum *(Lobularia maritima)*.

1954 *Harder Coll.* **cwTN,** Sweet basil—sweet alyssum.

sweet bay n

1 Std: the bay laurel *(Laurus nobilis)*.

2 also *sweetbay magnolia, sweet flowering bay:* A **magnolia 1** (here: *Magnolia virginiana*) native from Massachusetts and New York south to Florida and Texas.   Also called **beaver tree, beaverwood 1, castorwood, dwarf laurel 2, holly bay 2, Indian bark, laurel 1, laurel magnolia, magnolia bay, red ~ 3, small magnolia, spoonwood 2, swamp bay 2, ~ laurel 1, ~ magnolia, ~ sassafras 1, sweet magnolia, white bay 1**

1731 Catesby *Nat. Hist. Carolina* 1.39, The Sweet Flowring Bay. . . In May they begin to blossom, continuing most part of the Summer to perfume the Woods with their fragrant flowers. **1766** (1942) Bartram *Diary of a Journey* 41 **eFL,** On it [=a high bluff] grew great magnolia, sweet-bay, live-oak, palms. **1810** Michaux *Histoire des Arbres* 1.27, M[agnolia] glauca. . . *Sweet bay, White bay* et *swamp's laurel*, noms plus en usage dans la partie maritime des Etats méridionaux. [=M[agnolia] glauca. . . *Sweet bay, White bay* and *swamp's laurel,* names more in use in the coastal areas of the southern States.] **1844** *OH Repository* (Canton) 5 Dec 1/2, Col. Clark remarked . . that the old Indian corn lands at the South are overgrown with magnolia, sweet bay and other trees, forming hammock lands. **1893** *Gettysburg Comp.* (PA) 19 Sept 1/6, The magnolia is a southern tree, but the "sweet bay" grows all along our eastern coast. **1938** Rawlings *Yearling* 217 **nFL,** The sweet bay was still in bloom, filling the sink-hole with its fragrance. **1955** *Lima News* (OH) 29 Apr 26/4, The other kinds include the swamp magnolia, or sweet bay tree, which sometimes reaches a height of 60 feet. **2005** *Roanoke Times* (VA) 6 Jan 5 (Internet), The sweetbay magnolia (Magnolia virginiana). Also called laurel or swamp magnolia, this native usually grows as a loose, open multi-stemmed large shrub or small tree.

3 Either the **red bay 1** or the **swamp bay 1.**

1804 in 1930 Dunbar *Life* 244 **MS,** They [=poor people] have a method of boiling it [=bear fat] from time to time upon sweet-bay leaves which restores it or facilitates its conservation. **1885** *Torrey Bot. Club Bulletin* 12.76, Specimens of beautiful woods are seen in the arbutus, sweet bay (*Persea Carolinensis* [=*P. borbonia*]), Alaska cedar (*Chamaecyparis Nutkaensis*), and the beautifully figured maple burl from Missouri. **1898** (1910) Willoughby *Across Everglades* 123 **sFL,** The Indians use the leaves of the sweet-bay also for making a tea which they consider very wholesome. **1932** *Ecological Monogr.* 2.138 **Okefenokee GA,** *Persea pubescens* [=*P. palustris*] . . "Sweet bay," Red bay. **1961** *Amer. Midland Naturalist* 66.486 **Okefenokee GA,** The principal secondary species are red bay (*Gordonia lasianthus*), white bay (*Mag-*

nolia virginiana), sweet bay (*Persea borbonia*) . . and titi (*Cyrilla racemiflora*). **2004** in 2005 *DARE* File—Internet **TX,** *Persea borbonia*. . . Laurel-like in habit and persistence, the aromatic foliage makes sweet bay a worthy ornamental.

4 =**lancewood.**

1916 *Torreya* 16.237 **sFL,** *Ocotea catesbyana* [=*O. coriacea*]. . . Sweet Bay.

5 =**meadowsweet 2.**

1940 Clute *Amer. Plant Names* 6, F[ilipendula] ulmaria. . . (Sweet bay).

6 =**sweetleaf 1.**

1913 Harper *Economic Botany AL* 301, *Symplocos tinctoria*. . . Sweet-leaf, Sweet Bay. **1971** MO Bot. Garden *Annals* 58.277 **AL,** *S[ymplocos] tinctoria*. . . *Horse-Sugar, Sweet-Leaf, Sweet Bay.* Spring; summer. Rich or alluvial woods, infrequent; throughout.

7 A **wax myrtle** (here: *Morella cerifera*).

1974 Morton *Folk Remedies* 99 **SC,** Sweet Bay. . . *Myrica cerifera* [=*Morella cerifera*].

sweetbay magnolia   See **sweet bay 2**

sweet bean n

=**honey locust 1.**

1900 Lyons *Plant Names* 174, G[leditsia] triacanthos. . . Sweet-bean. **1960** Vines *Trees SW* 532, *Gleditsia . . triacanthos*. . . Sweet-bean. . . Indians ate the fleshy sweet pulp of the young pods. **2005** *DARE* File—Internet **AZ,** *Gleditsia triacanthos*. . . The tree is also commonly known as sweet locust, sweet-bean, or three-thorned acacia. This species has been cultivated since the early 1700s.

sweetbells n

A **fetterbush 3** (here: *Leucothoe racemosa*).

1919 U.S. Natl. Museum *Contrib. Herbarium* 21.223, *Eubotrys racemosa* [=*Leucothoe r.*] . . Sweetbells. Swamps and dry or moist woods. . . Eastern U.S. **1947** *Amer. Midland Naturalist* 38.53 **MD,** *Leucothoe racemosa* (Sweetbells). Common in seepage swamps. **1960** Vines *Trees SW* 809, Sweet-bells . . *Leucothoe racemosa*. **1995** *Virginian–Pilot* (Norfolk VA) 27 Jan 14 (Internet), The tract on Albemarle Drive where the trees grow beside smaller plants—like coastal sweetbells, horse sugar, azaleas and rhododendron—is scheduled to be covered in asphalt. **2005** (acc) TX A&M Univ. *Aggie Horticult.* (Internet), Sweetbells is native to the sandy, acid soils of Southeast Texas, growing in swamps or water edges and other moist areas.

sweet benjamin n   Cf **benjamin, stinking ~**

A **southernwood** (here: *Artemisia abrotanum*).

1894 *Jrl. Amer. Folkl.* 7.91 **MA,** *Artemisia Abrotanum,* . . sweet Benjamin.

sweetberry n

1 A **nannyberry 1** (here: *Viburnum lentago*).

1897 Sudworth *Arborescent Flora* 339 **MN,** *Viburnum lentago*. . . Sweetberry.

2 See **sweetberry honeysuckle.**

sweetberry honeysuckle n   Also *sweetberry*

A **honeysuckle 2** (here: *Lonicera caerulea*).

1929 *Amer. Midland Naturalist* 11.420, *Lonicera caerula* [sic]. . . Sweetberry Honeysuckle. **1936** McDougall–Baggley *Plants of Yellowstone* 115, *Sweetberry honeysuckle* (Lonicera caerulea). **1970** *Daily Courier* (Connellsville PA) 16 Apr 29/6, The new honeysuckle offers edible fruit as well as creamy-white blossoms. And the new honeysuckle is called Sweetberry. **1973** Hitchcock–Cronquist *Flora Pacific NW* 451, Sweet-berry h[oneysuckle]. . . *L[onicera] caerulea.*

sweetberry tree n

=**swamp bay 1.**

1913 *Torreya* 13.233 **SC,** *Persea pubescens* [=*P. palustris*]. . . Sweetberry tree. **2002** in 2005 *DARE* File—Internet **NC,** A yellow-rumped warbler spent some time in the sweetberry tree.

sweet Betsy n

1 also *sweet Betsies, ~ Betty:* =**Carolina allspice.** esp NC, TN   Cf **bubbybush 1**

1889 Murfree *Despot* 464 **eTN,** At the other window a series of straight wands rose up above the sill, and betokened the withered estate of the "sweet Betty" bushes. **1896** *Harper's New Mth. Mag.* 93.774 **TN,** Within the paled garden June-roses grow, along with lilac, sweet-betsy, mock-orange—all the tribe of old-fashioned flowering shrubs. **1896** *Jrl. Amer. Folkl.* 9.180 **AL**, *Calycanthus floridus.* . . Sweet Betsies ([used by] plantation negroes). **1932** *Landmark* (Statesville NC) 15 Mar 2/2, This latter belongs to the calycanthus family, and is first cousin to the sweet betsy. **1988** Edgerton *Floatplane* 41 **NC** (as of 1957), It's a Sweet Betsy bush, come from T.C. Sutton's place about the time they tore it down. **2005** *DARE* File—Internet **NC**, Sweet Betsy is native here in NC and once started will form colonies, grow up to 8 feet tall but still look like a shrub. I think the fragrance is heavenly. **2007** Loewer *Gardens NC* 31, Native and traditional southern shrubs, such as winterberry, fothergillas, Virginia sweet-spire, sweet Betty, rhododendrons, and 'George Tabor' azaleas, form an enclosure that shields the visitor from the noises of the road.

2 also *little sweet Betsy:* A **trillium** (here: *Trillium cuneatum*).

    1968 Radford et al. *Manual Flora Carolinas* 289, *T[rillium] cuneatum* . . Little Sweet Betsy. **2005** *DARE* File—Internet, *T[rillium] cuneatum*, native to a great expanse of the southeastern United States, has several names used here & there. It is called Beth Root & Sweet Betsy, names that are actually plays off the more medicinal-sounding name of Birthroot, which several kinds of trilliums have been called because of alleged value within the pharmacopeia of midwifery. It becomes "Sweet" Betsy because *T. cuneatum* has an unusual fruity odor, which most but not nearly all people find pleasant. It also gets called "Little Sweet Betsy" but the "Little" really ought to be reserved for the true *T. sessile* which looks identical but is less than half the size.

3 See **sweet Betty 2.**

sweet Betty n

1 See **sweet Betsy 1.**

2 also *sweet Betsy:* =**bouncing Bet 1.**

    1896 *Jrl. Amer. Folkl.* 9.182 **IN**, *Saponaria officinalis,* . . sweet Betty. **1958** Jacobs–Burlage *Index Plants NC* 35, *Saponaria officinalis.* . . Sweet-betty. **1991** *Syracuse Herald–Amer.* (NY) 1 Dec 15/2, *Bouncing Bet:* soapwort, bruisewort, sweet Betsy, wild sweet William. **2005** *DARE* File—Internet, Soapwort is also known by the wonderful country names of Bouncing Bet, Soaproot, Wild Sweet William, Sweet Betty and Latherwort.

sweet birch n

1 Std: a birch (*Betula lenta*) native chiefly eastward from the Mississippi and Ohio Valleys. Also called **cherry birch, hogany, mahogany birch, mountain ~ 1, mountain mahogany 1, red birch 1, river ~, spice ~, sugar ~**

2 A **ceanothus:** usu a **deer brush 1** (here: *Ceanothus integerrimus*), but also *Ceanothus parvifolius.*

    1900 *Eclectic Med. Jrl.* 60.512, The bark upon the young branches [of deer brush] is of a sweet aromatic flavor when chewed, and for this reason in many places it is known as sweet birch. **1921** Hall *Hdbk. Yosemite* 252 **ceCA**, A less common species is a close relative, the *Sweet Birch (Ceanothus parvifolius),* which is found . . in the vicinity of Grouse Creek. **1937** U.S. Forest Serv. *Range Plant Hdbk.* B44, *Ceanothus integerrimus. . .* Sweet birch. **1945** *Mt. Democrat & Placerville Republican* (CA) 17 May 5/2, Deerbrush, also called sweet birch and mountain lilac, is the only important forage plant found in the woodlands above 2000 feet. **1974** *Mt. Democrat & Placerville Times* (CA) 4 Apr sec A 10/3, The committee voted to spend $3000 on making browseways through the sweet birch brush on Peavine Ridge to help deer feed during critical winter periods.

sweet bitter n

A **horse gentian** (here: *Triosteum perfoliatum*).

    1787 Schöpf *Materia Medica Amer.* 23, *Triosteum perfoliatum.* . . White Gentian; Sweet-Bitter. **1892** (1974) Millspaugh *Amer. Med. Plants* 74–1, *Triosteum perfoliatum.* . . Sweet-bitter.

sweet blood n

=**sugar diabetes.**

    1969 Dunbar *Will Survive* 29 **MS** [Black], *How about sugar diabetes?* Well, my little boy . . , he was born with this sweet blood the doctor said. **2006** *NY Times* (NY) 9 Jan sec A 1/5 **NYC**, Already, diabetes has swept through families, entire neighborhoods in the Bronx and broad slices of Brooklyn, where it is such a fact of life that people describe it casually, almost comfortably, as "getting the sugar" or having "the sweet blood." **2006** *DARE* File—Internet, My grandmother was cursed with "sweet blood."

sweet blueberry n

A **blueberry 1:** either *Vaccinium angustifolium* or *V. pallidum.*

    1910 Graves *Flowering Plants* 313 **CT**, *Vaccinium pennsylvanicum* [= *V. angustifolium*]. . . Early Sweet Blueberry. **1916** *Edwardsville Intelligencer* (IL) [8 Feb 5]/5 (newspaperarchive.com), Feeding fruit-eating birds is best accomplished by planting selected species of fruit-bearing shrubs and trees, such as . . early sweet blueberry. **1919** *Geogr. Rev.* 7.246 **NH**, Here the Labrador tea . . forms extensive masses of low shrubbery, as likewise do the low and spreading bushes of the bog bilberry . . and the still more dwarfish low, sweet blueberry, *Vaccinium pennsylvanicum* var. *angustifolium* [=*V. angustifolium*]. **1950** Gray–Fernald *Manual of Botany* 1133, *V[accinium] vacillans* [=*V. pallidum*] . . Early Sweet B[lueberry]. . . *V. angustifolium* . . Low Sweet or Late Sweet B[lueberry]. **2003** *Portland Press Herald* (ME) 18 May sec B 1 (Internet), There are several species of wild blueberries in Maine. The most common is the low sweet blueberry with smooth stems that grow on plants four to 15 inches tall. The fruit is dark blue and covered with a waxy coating. There is a black-fruited variety that tends to be slightly larger and sweeter.

sweet bread n   Cf **pan dulce, pão doce**   Note: The std sense of bread with sweetening added either to the dough or to the surface is not included here.

1 Bread made from wheat or other flour (as opposed to corn bread).   Cf **bread n B1, light bread**

    1965 *DARE* FW Addit **NM**, *Sweetbread*—Anything but cornbread. **1984** Joyner *Down by Riverside* 98 **SC coast** (as of a1866), It [=the slaves' diet] occasionally included . . wheat bread (called sweet bread).

2 also *sweet-bread cake:* Any of var kinds of cake, gingerbread, or cake-like cookies; see quots. **Sth, S Midl**   Cf **breadcake, sugar bread**

    1868 Trowbridge *Picture* 380 **TN**, The table was neatly set, with a goodly variety of dishes for a late dinner in a back-country farm-house. I remember . . cold biscuit, cold corn bread, and "sweet bread" (a name given to a plain sort of cake). [**1898** Lloyd *Country Life* 63 **AL**, There was a big bowl of clabber and a hunk of sweetie bread settin on the bottom shelf.] **1903** *DN* 2.332 **seMO**, *Sweet-bread.* . . Cake. **c1940** Eliason *Word Lists FL* 4 **nwFL**, *Sweetbread.* . . Cake. Very rare. **1962** Dykeman *Tall Woman* 122 **NC** (as of 1860), Bring me an egg and I might make us a little sweet-bread cake for supper. **1973** in 2004 Montgomery–Hall *Dict. Smoky Mt. Engl.* 586 **wNC, eTN**, We'd make some sweet bread we called it, or gingerbread. **1982** *Ibid,* *Sweet bread.* . . the term used for cake or sweet cookies, particularly gingerbread. **1983** *MJLF* 9.1.58 **ceKY** (as of 1956), *Sweet bread* . . cake. **1986** Pederson *LAGS Concordance,* 1 inf, **ceMS**, Sweet bread—like gingerbread.

‡**3** French toast.   Cf **lost bread**

    1906 *DN* 3.160 **nwAR**, *Sweetbread.* . . White (wheat) bread dipped in a sweetened egg batter and fried.

sweet-bread cake   See **sweet bread 2**

sweetbrier n

1 A **mountain mahogany 2** (here: *Cercocarpus montanus*). Cf **sweetbrush**

    1937 U.S. Forest Serv. *Range Plant Hdbk.* B51, *True mountain-mahogany—Cercocarpus montanus.* . . bears a number of local names, most of which are indefinite or inaccurate, including . . sweetbrier.

2 See quot.   Cf **China brier, wild asparagus 1**

    2002 *DARE* File **AL**, "Sweet briar" or "chainy briar"—A word for asparagus, used mainly by people of South Carolina extraction. Not much heard anymore. I know what it is but do not use the term, other than to ask others if they know what "chainy briar" is. My father used to sing a little song about "chainy briar", but also called asparagus "sweet briar".

sweetbrush n   Cf **sweetbrier 1**

=**mountain mahogany 2.**

    1911 Jepson *Flora CA* 205, *C[ercocarpus] parvifolius.* . . Common chaparral shrub throughout the Coast Ranges and Sierra Nevada. Often called Sweet Brush and also Mountain Mahogany. **1931** U.S. Dept. Ag. *Misc. Pub.* 101.43, Mountain-mahogany is somewhat cumbersome and none too appropriate a name for Cercocarpus. . . Numerous other, and sometimes quite misleading, local names for these shrubs include . . sweetbrush. **1998** *Wood Mag.* June 27 (Internet), There's a small tree dotting the American West that stockmen like to call sweetbrush. That's because domestic cattle, sheep, and goats (along with deer and other wild creatures) relish its foliage in the warmer months. In winter, after the leaves have fallen, twigs become the main course. This culinary cellulose delight is the mountain mahogany tree *(Cercocarpus spp.)*

sweet bubby See bubbybush 1

sweet buckeye n

=yellow buckeye.

1815 Drake *Natural View Cincinnati* 77 **wOH,** *Æsculus. . . maxima . .* Sweet buckeye. **1847** Wood *Class-Book* 214, *Æ[sculus] flava. . . Sweet Buckeye. . .* A large tree, 30–70f high, common in the Western and Southern States. **1900** *Daily Herald* (Delphos OH) [2 June 2]/5 (newspaperarchive.com), There are distributed in various parts of the estate [= George W. Vanderbilt's "Biltmore" estate in NC] . . sweet buckeye, sugar maple, . . staghorn sumac [etc]. **1943** Peattie *Great Smokies* 155 **sAppalachians,** Sweet buckeye or horse chestnut are found here up to 125 feet in height. **1961** Douglas *My Wilderness* 159 **cwNC,** The sweet buckeye is here, four feet through and ninety feet high. Its shiny dark brown seeds. . . remind the mountain people of a deer's eye because of a scar on them. **2003** *Cleveland Plain Dealer* (OH) 1 Jan sec D 7 (Internet), There are many different variations of the tree: the sweet buckeye (Aesculus octandra), the red buckeye (Aesculus pavia), [etc].

sweet bud n

=balsam poplar.

1970 *DARE* (Qu. T12, *The kind of poplar tree that has sticky, sweet-smelling buds)* Inf **WV21,** Sweet buds.

sweet bush n

1 =sweet fern 1.

1828 Rafinesque *Med. Flora* 1.115, *Comptonia asplenifolia* [=*C. peregrina*]. . . *Vulgar Names*—Sweet-fern, Sweet-bush, Sweet-ferry . . &c. [*Ibid* 117, The whole plant, but chiefly the leaves have a peculiar strong smell, of a sweet and balsamic nature; becoming stronger by pressing or bruising them.] **1911** Henkel *Amer. Med. Leaves* 9, *Comptonia peregrina*. . . Sweet bush. . . The whole plant has a spicy, aromatic odor. **1933** Small *Manual SE Flora* 410, *C[omptonia] peregrina*. . . *Sweet-fern. Fern-bush. Sweet-bush*. . . The pleasant fragrance of the foliage may often be discerned distant from the plant. **2006** *DARE* File—Internet, *Comptonia peregrina*. . . *Common Names*—Sweet fern, . . sweet bush. . . *Description*—A sweet-smelling, many-branched, perennial shrub that grows to 3 feet in height.

2 =Carolina allspice.

1895 *Atlantic Mth.* 75.608, I remember, just beyond the creek, a bank where sweet bush *(Calycanthus),* wild ginger *(Asarum),* rhododendron, laurel, and plenty of trailing arbutus . . were growing side by side. **1955** *Bridgeport Post* (CT) 24 July sec B 1/1, An old-fashioned sweet bush on the lawn, bears fragrant buds. **2001** *Atlanta Jrl.–Constitution* (GA) 26 Apr 7 (Internet), Blooming are dogwood, silverbell, black locust, princess trees, dog hobble, pink azalea, sweet bush, cross vine, . . and many other flowers.

3 =chuckwalla's delight.

1941 Jaeger *Wildflowers* 286 **Desert SW,** *Sweetbush, Chuckawalla's Delight. Bebbia juncea aspera. Ibid* 287, A very common species. . . When for a short period in spring the quite leafless, whitish stems are almost hidden by a mass of fragrant flower heads, the sweetbush is a handsome plant indeed. **1976** *Jrl. Range Management* 29.482 **CA,** Vegetation of the washes is dominated by palo verde *(Cercidium floridum),* . . sweet bush *(Bebbia juncea)* [etc]. **2003** in 2006 *DARE* File—Internet **AZ,** Sweet Bush *(Bebbia juncea)* and Golden Aster *(Heterotheca villosa)* were in bloom and gathering butterflies . . to their offer of nectar.

sweet chervil n Pronc-spp *sweet chevril,* ~ *jarvil,* ~ *javril* [*OED2* 1597 → for *Myrrhis odorata*]

A **sweet cicely** (here: *Osmorhiza longistylis* or *O. claytonii*).

1876 Hobbs *Bot. Hdbk.* 115, Sweet chervil, Sweet cicily, Osmorrhiza longistylis. **1896** *Jrl. Amer. Folkl.* 9.189 **ME,** *Osmorhiza brevistylis* [= *O. claytonii*] and *O. longistylis,* . . sweet jarvil. **1910** Graves *Flowering Plants* 298 **CT,** *Osmorhiza longistylis.* . . Sweet Chervil. **1949** Moldenke *Amer. Wild Flowers* 148, Country boys and girls throughout almost all of North America are usually quite familiar with the thick, clustered, fleshy, aromatic roots of little woodland plants which they call variously *sweetcicely, sweetjavril, sweetchevril, sweetanise,* or *aniseroot (Osmorhiza).* **2004** *DARE* File—Internet **NC,** *Osmorhiza longistylis*—Sweet chervil vs. *Osmorhiza claytonii* seen 5/25 and 5/26 which is sweet cicely.

sweet cicely n [*EDD* 1815]

A plant of the genus *Osmorhiza,* esp *O. longistylis.* For other names of var spp see **anise root, cicel, sweet anise 1,** ~ **chervil, sweetroot 4, wild anise 3**

1832 MA *Hist. Soc. Coll.* 2d ser 9.152 **cwVT,** *Myrrhis dulcis* [here: = *Osmorhiza longistylis*],—Sweet cicely. **1844** Lapham *Geogr. Descr. WI* 80, *Osmorhiza longistylis*. . . Sweet cicely. **1870** Bolander *Catalogue Plants San Francisco* 13 **CA,** *Osmorhiza,* . . —Sweet Cicely.—O. occidentalis, . . —Shady places—O. nuda, . . —Woods. **1908** NM Univ. *Biol. Ser.* 3.1.45, *Osmorrhiza,* . . Sweet Cicely. **1931** *Decatur Herald* (IL) 26 Apr 10/2, We value sweet Cicely not particularly for the beauty of its blossoms, but more for the licorice-like odor and flavor of its root and stem. **1957** Barnes *Nat. Hist. Wasatch Spring* 41 **UT,** The plant, known as sweet cicely *(Osmorhiza occidentalis)* has the rather pleasing delicate scent of vegetables. **1975** *Stevens Point Daily Jrl.* (WI) 27 June 5/3 **WA,** She has thyme and sage and other herbs; sweet cicely grows outside her door for tea. **2004** [see **sweet chervil**].

sweet clematis n

A **virgin's bower:** usu the introduced *Clematis terniflora;* occas another sp such as *C. hirsutissima;* see quots.

1887 *Herald & Torch-Light* (Hagerstown MD) 8 Dec 4/3, Drains and sinks should be neutralized in this way, by having sweet clematis, fragrant honeysuckle and wisteria climb and bloom over them. **1908** *Bedford Gaz.* (PA) 9 Oct 2/2, Sweet Clematis, the Traveler's Joy—Virgin's Bower. . . As autumn advances, its tiny white flowers are replaced by the long feathery down on the seed pods which hangs in graceful tufts like a drapery over hedges and trees. **1928** *Circleville Herald* (OH) 30 Aug 8/1, In the west room were bouquets of large purple, orchid and pink asters, intermingled with fragrant sweet clematis. **2001** *Orlando Sentinel* (FL) 25 Aug sec G 16 (Internet), *Plant Profile: Sweet Clematis.* . . Scientific name: Clematis terniflora. . . Even though it's sometimes called the autumn clematis, plants growing locally open clusters of white fragrant blossoms during July and August.

sweet clover n

1 Std: a clover of the genus *Melilotus,* esp *M. albus.* For other names of the latter see **white sweet clover**

2 A clover of the genus *Trifolium;* esp **red clover,** but also a **sour clover** (here: *Trifolium fucatum*).

1892 *Jrl. Amer. Folkl.* 5.94 **ME, MA,** *Trifolium pratense,* "real sweet clover." **1902** U.S. Natl. Museum *Contrib. Herbarium* 7.360, Indians of Round Valley tell me that they eat clover and that some of the species, especially the sweet clover and the acid clover, are very good and nutritious food. *Ibid* 361, *Trifolium virescens* [=*T. fucatum*]. . . All parts of the plant are sweet, and on this account it is well known as sweet clover. **1974** (1977) Coon *Useful Plants* 170, *Trifolium pratense*—Red clover, trefoil, sweet clover. . . [C]lovers secrete nectar, a source of delicate-flavored honey. **2006** *DARE* File—Internet, Purple clover, aka red clover or sweet clover *(Trifolium pratense . .),* goes by many other common names. . . It is an omnipresent biennial or shortlived perennial, found all around Puget Sound.

3 =vanilla leaf 1.

1898 *Jrl. Amer. Folkl.* 11.222 **OR,** *Achlys triphylla,* . . Sweet clover.

sweet coco n Cf **coco grass, sweet coco** ~

A **nut grass 1** (here: *Cyperus esculentus*).

1850 U.S. Patent Office *Annual Rept. for 1849: Ag.* 156 **swMS,** In wettish flat lands, . . several varieties of *Panicum crus-galli* . . grow vigorously, not unfrequently mixed with *cyperus repens* [=*C. esculentus*], sweet coco, or nut grass. **1941** *Torreya* 41.46 **sLA,** *Cyperus esculentus*. . . Sweet coco.

sweet coco grass n Cf **bitter coco, coco grass, sweet coco**

A bulrush *(Scirpus spp).*

1913 *Torreya* 13.228 **LA,** *Scirpus* spp.—Coco, coco grass, sometimes sweet coco grass, various localities in Louisiana.

sweet coltsfoot n

1 A plant of the genus *Petasites.* Also called **coltsfoot 3.** For other names of var spp see **umbrella leaf 4**

1853 NY State Museum *Catalogue Cabinet Nat. Hist.* 20, *Nardosmia palmata* [=*Petasites frigidus* var *p.*], Sweet Coltsfoot. **1870** Bolander *Catalogue Plants San Francisco* 15 **CA,** *Nardosmia,* . . Sweet Coltsfoot. **1892** Torrey *Foot-Path Way* 227 **NEng,** If you wish me to show you the sweet colt's-foot *(Nardosmia palmata),* you must go with me to one particular spot. **1927** *Torreya* 27.35 **CT,** Sweet coltsfoot. *Petasites palma-*

tus. **1939** *Amer. Jrl. Botany* 26.716 **AK,** Sweet Coltsfoot, *Petasite frigida* [sic] . . , is gathered as greens but to a limited extent only. **2001** *Oregonian* (Portland OR) 17 May 40 (Internet), Alaskan Eskimos relish the cooked young leaves of sweet coltsfoot (*P. frigidus*) and also enjoy the emerging shoots and flowerhead.

2 A **wild ginger 1** (here: *Asarum canadense*).
   1910 Graves *Flowering Plants* 157 **CT,** *Asarum canadense.* . . Sweet . . Coltsfoot. . . The rhizome is used medicinally and an oil from it is used in perfumery.

sweet coneflower n

A **black-eyed Susan 2** (here: *Rudbeckia subtomentosa*).
   1930 OK Univ. Biol. Surv. *Pub.* 2.86, *Rudbeckia subtomentosa.* . . Sweet Cone-flower. **1936** IL Nat. Hist. Surv. *Wildflowers* 363, The Sweet or Prairie Coneflower, *Rudbeckia subtomentosa* . . is an uncommon perennial of prairies and low ground in Illinois. **1948** Stevens *KS Wild Flowers* 373, *Rudbeckia subtomentosa*—Sweet Coneflower. **2006** *DARE* File—Internet, *Sweet Coneflower—Rudbeckia submentosa* [sic]. . . Sweet Coneflower occurs occasionally in the majority of counties in Illinois; it is more common in northern and central Illinois than southern Illinois.

sweet corn n   widespread, but chiefly Nth, N Midl; also West   See Map   Cf roasting corn, sugar corn

=**Indian corn 1,** often when in the milk and esp those horticultural varieties commonly used as table corn.   Also called **green corn 2**
   1646 in 1863 MA Hist. Soc. *Coll.* 4th ser 6.334, Wequash Cooks brother tooke from him . . 2 bushell of sweet corne. **1678** Royal Soc. London *Philos. Trans.* 12.1067, The Indians have another sort of Provision out of this Corn, which they call Sweet-Corn. **1810** in 1944 *Thomas Jefferson's Garden Book* 424 **VA,** Sowed. . . Sweet or shriveled corn in the N.W. corner. **1842** *S. Lit. Messenger* 8.582 **KS,** They now pull much of their corn while it is in the milk, and dry it carefully in the sun: it is then called 'sweet corn.' **1856** in 1862 Colt *Went to KS* 118 **NY,** Found we had sweet corn large enough to boil. **1882** ME Bd. Ag. *Ag. ME* 17, Good corn stalks . . with plenty of sweet corn meal to go with them will make butter that will bring the highest prices. **1941** *LANE* Map 261 *(Sweet corn),* [*Sweet corn* is the most common response throughout NEng.] **1950** *WELS (The kind of corn grown for human beings)* 53 Infs, **WI,** Sweet corn. **c1960** *Wilson Coll.* **csKY,** Sweet corn—the early corn grown in the garden; also called sugar corn. **1965–70** *DARE* (Qu. I33, . . *Ears of corn that are just right for eating*) 281 Infs, **widespread, but chiefly Nth, N Midl; also West,** Sweet corn; [**OR**4, Sweet table corn;] **NJ**24, Jersey sweet corn; (Qu. L22, *When talking about a crop he intends to plant . . a farmer might say, "This year, I'm going to _____ a crop of oats/corn/cotton, etc."*) Infs **H**112, **MI**101, Plant sweet corn. **1995** *Brophy Coll.* 73 **swMO** (as of c1960), *Sweet corn.* [G]arden corn, as opposed to field corn grown to feed livestock. **2006** *Star Tribune* (Minneapolis MN) 15 Feb sec N 1 (Internet), She later worked in a sweet-corn factory and ironed shirts before working her way through school at the University of Northern Iowa.

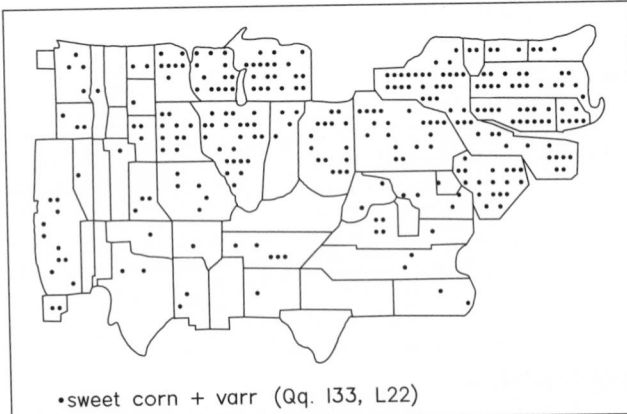

•sweet corn + varr (Qq. I33, L22)

sweet diabetes n

=**sugar diabetes.**
   1893 *Homestead* 13 Oct 10, It was discovered he had sweet diabetes. **1966** *DARE* (Qu. BB48, *When a person has too much sugar in his blood and may have to take insulin for it . . he has _____*) Inf **SC**27, Sweet diabetes. **1972** *Chron.-Telegram* (Elyria OH) 28 Mar 3/1, The most

common type of diabetes (called diabetes mellitus) is what most people think of as "sweet" diabetes—sugar in the urine and too much of it in the blood.

sweet elder n

An **elder** n[2] (here: *Sambucus nigra* subsp *canadensis*).
   1832 Williamson *Hist. ME* 1.107, The *Elder* is of two species, the *black* and *red.* The former, called "Sweet Elder," has handsome blossoms. **1838** Parker *Jrl. Rocky Mts.* 217, There is a new species of sweet elder which I have already described. **1877** *Harper's New Mth. Mag.* 54.908, I take it there's no better sight to be got in the world than in going down through sloping pastures, with . . sweet-elder-blow smells stealing after you from corners of fences. **1896** *Jrl. Amer. Folkl.* 9.189 **West,** *Sambucus Canadensis,* . . Sweet elder. **1951** *PADS* 15.41 **TX,** *Sambucus canadensis* [=*S. nigra* subsp *c.*]. . . Sweet, wine, or tea, elder. Jellies and wines as well as pies are still made from its berries. **2006** *DARE* File—Internet, The most common elderberry in the United States is the American elderberry, or sweet elder *(Sambucus canadensis).*

sweet elm n

=**slippery elm 1.**
   1792 Imlay *Western Terr.* 1.215 **KY,** Sweet elm—*Ulmus saccharina Americana.* **1830** Rafinesque *Med. Flora* 2.271, *Ulmus Fulva* . . Sweet Elm. **1879** in 1894 Duncan *Old Settlers* 11 **cIN,** The principal root on which they [=wild hogs] thus subsisted . . was the sweet or slippery elm. **1933** Small *Manual SE Flora* 441, *U[lmus] fulva.* . . Sweet-Elm. . . The fragrant mucilaginous inner bark is used in medicine. **1968** *DARE* (Qu. T11, . . *Kinds of elm trees*) Inf **IN**9, [swit 'ɛˌləm]. **2004** in 2006 *DARE* File—Internet, I am off to the health store to get some sweet elm, and make some oatmeal with honey for breakfast.

sweetening n   Pronc-sp *swat'ning, sweetning*

1 A substance used to add a sweet flavor to food or drink. **chiefly Sth, S Midl**   Cf **long sweetening, short ~**
   1842 Kirkland *Forest Life* 1.75 **MI,** To them "sweetnin' " is nothing; nor "garden saase;"—nor even whisky itself, unless pork crown the good cheer. **1845** in 1956 Eliason *Tarheel Talk* 298 **NC,** She placed the *sweetening* [for the coffee] as she call sugar before us. **1859** *Ibid,* Father . . is able to raise his own sweetening. **1860** Hundley *Social Relations S. States* 261, A little "swat'ning" to put in their coffee. **1883** GA Dept. Ag. *Pub. Circular No. 26* 8.13, More than half the households have bees. . . The bee product makes up a large percentage of the sweetening of this section. **1895** *DN* 1.374 **seKY, eTN, wNC,** *Sweetening:* sugar. "Will you have some sweetening in your tea?" **1899** (1912) Green *VA Folk-Speech* 432, *Sweetening* . . a substance, as sugar, used to sweeten something. **1902** *DN* 2.247 **sIL,** *Sweetnin.* . . Molasses or sugar. **1903** *DN* 2.332 **seMO,** *Sweetening* or *sweetnin.* . . Sugar. **1905** *DN* 3.97 **nwAR,** *Sweetnin'.* . . Sugar, molasses, syrup. **1909** *DN* 3.378 **eAL, wGA,** *Sweet(e)nin(g).* . . Sugar. **1942** Perry *Texas* 122, The principal "sweetnin'" of many of us Texans is blackstrap molasses. **1949** Graham *Niagara Country* 87, A grove of hard maples was retained for maple-sugaring and "sweetening" for the family. A few hives of bees were added to help provide the "sweetening" supply. **1960** Hall *Smoky Mt. Folks* 60, *Sweetenin':* sugar, honey, or molasses. **1966–70** *DARE* (Qu. H21, . . *The sweet stuff that's poured over these [pan]cakes*) Inf **OH**61, Sweetening; (Qu. H66a, *The sweet liquid that you pour over a pudding*) Infs **NC**72, **OK**53, Sweetening; (Qu. Y40b, . . *Words referring to sticky stuff: "I've got to wash my hands. They're all covered with _____."*) Inf **FL**39, Sweetenings. **1986** Pederson *LAGS Concordance (Sauce)* 2 infs, **AR, LA,** Sweetening; 1 inf, **ceAL,** Sweetening—general term; *(Molasses)* 1 inf, **neMS,** Sweetening—he would let those molasses be his sweetening; 1 inf, **neMS,** Sweetening—Negroes used term for "molasses"; *(Maple syrup)* 1 inf, **csAL,** Sweetening—used by Negroes; 1 inf, **cwTN,** Sweetening—sugar?

2 Candy; a cake or pastry.
   1964 Faulkner *Hamlet* 317 **MS,** Snopes came out of the door carrying a small striped paper bag. . . "Here. . . A little sweetening for the chaps." **1994** NC Lang. & Life Project *Dial. Dict. Lumbee Engl.* 11 **seNC,** Sweetnins. . . Cakes, pastries. *Do you have some sweetnins for after supper?* **2005** Williams *Gratitude* 529 **wNC** (as of 1940s), *Sweet'nin:* . . Anything sweet, such as cake or candy.

3 Fig: punishment.
   1930 Stoney-Shelby *Black Genesis* 112 **seSC,** When I is put all de sweetenin' on him dat his hide will hold up under, I is goin' to teach him sich a good lesson.

sweet everlasting n   Also *sweet life-everlasting*

A **cudweed 1** (here: *Pseudognaphalium obtusifolium*).

1867 *Amer. Naturalist* 1.127, The Marsh Fleabane demands the daily drenchings of the sea, the Dwarf Dandelion affects the dry shelves of rocky uplands, and the Sweet Everlasting is equally pleased with both. **1902** (1909) Mathews *Field Book Amer. Wild Flowers* 504, Sweet Everlasting—*Gnaphalium polycephalum* [=*Pseudognaphalium obtusifolium*]. **1952** *Amer. Midland Naturalist* 47.302, Most of the well-drained fields and clearings were dominated by the flowers of several species of goldenrod, Aster *(Aster pilosus)*, and Sweet Everlasting *(Gnaphalium obtusifolium)*, while many other species were common locally. **1965** (1982) Stupka *Wildflowers* 124 sAppalachians, Names [for *Gnaphalium obtusifolium*] such as "sweet balsam" and "sweet life-everlasting" refer to its fragrance.

sweet fennel n

Std: an introduced and naturalized fennel *(Foeniculum vulgare)*. Also called **ladies'-tobacco d, sweet anise 2, wild ~ 2**

sweet fern n

1 A perennial shrub *(Comptonia peregrina)* with aromatic fernlike leaves, native to much of the eastern third of the US. **chiefly NEng** Also called **fern bush 1, ferngale 1, meadow fern 2, mountain tea 3, sweet bush 1**

1654 (1974) Johnson *Wonder-Working* 81 MA, The sweet Ferne, whose scent is very strong so that some herewith have beene very nere fainting. **1778** Carver *Travels N. Amer.* 504 CT, Juniper, Shrub Oak, Sweet Fern, the Laurel [are native shrubs]. **1828** Rafinesque *Med. Flora* 1.115, *Comptonia asplenifolia* [=*C. peregrina*]. . . *Vulgar Names*—Sweet-fern, Sweet-bush, Sweet-ferry . . &c. [*Ibid* 117, The whole plant, but chiefly the leaves have a peculiar strong smell, of a sweet and balsamic nature; becoming stronger by pressing or bruising them.] **1832** *MA Hist. Soc. Coll.* 2d ser 9.148 cwVT, Comptonia asplenifolia, Sweet fern. **1864** *Catalogue of Herbs* swME, Fern, sweet—Comptonia asplenifolia. **1869** Alcott *Little Women* 2.358 MA, Tommy Bangs *will* smoke sweet-fern cigars under the bed-clothes. **1896** Jewett *Pointed Firs* 213 eME, The darker green of the sweet-fern was scattered on all the pasture heights. **1907** *DN* 3.201 seNH, Sweet fern. . . A shrub (of the sweet-gale family) about two feet high with fragrant leaves, used by young boys as a substitute for tobacco. **1958** Hale *New Engl. Girlhood* 24 **Cape Cod MA**, I could smell the sweet fern up on the moors; the scent came drifting down on the salty breeze. **2005** *Columbus Dispatch* (OH) 6 Nov sec J 2 (Internet), Use plants that grow naturally in a creek setting. . . Biologist Martin Quigley suggests bushes such as sweet fern and Virginia sweetspire.

2 Any of var ferns, as:

a A **maidenhair fern** (here: *Adiantum pedatum*).
1828 Rafinesque *Med. Flora* 1.30, *Adiantum pedatum*. . . Vulgar Names—Maiden-hair, Rock-fern, Sweet-fern. **1892** Torrey *Foot-Path Way* 81 **Cape Cod MA**, Ladies' tresses; bayberry; sweet fern. **1971** Krochmal *Appalachia Med. Plants* 36, *Adiantum Pedatum* . . American maidenhair, hair fern, . . sweet fern.

b A **polypody** (here: *Polypodium virginianum*).
1938 Small *Ferns SE States* 73, Being such a wide-spread fern it [=*Polypodium virginianum*] has received many common names. Some of these are: My Many-feet, . . Sweet-fern, Rock-brake.

3 =**sweet gale.**
1898 *Jrl. Amer. Folkl.* 11.279 wMA, Myrica Gale, . . Sweet fern.

sweet fern plant n

A **wormwood 1** (here: *Artemisia annua*).
1877 *Bot. Gaz.* 2.83 IN, Artemisia annua. . . Escaped from gardens; have found several specimens along road-sides during the past summer. Our amateur gardeners here call it *"Sweet Fern Plant."*

sweet flag n [*OED2* 1640 → for *Acorus calamus*]

Std: a plant of the genus *Acorus,* either the native *A. americanus* or the naturalized *A. calamus.* For other names of these see **beewort, bitter pepper root, calamus, calomel root, cinnamon sedge, citron grass, cotton marais, flagroot, flagrush, muskrat root, pine ~, pneumonia plant, sedge B1, swamp root 1, sweet grass 2, ~ myrtle 2, sweetroot 1**

sweet flowering bay See **sweet bay 2**

sweet gale n

Std: an aromatic shrub *(Myrica gale)* native chiefly in the Northeast, the Great Lakes states, and the Pacific Northwest.

Also called **baybush, Dutch myrtle, ferngale 2, gallbush 2, meadow fern 1, myrtle nut, sweet fern 3**

sweet gallberry n Cf **swamp gallberry**

A **gallberry** (here: *Ilex coriacea*).
1932 *Ecological Monogr.* 2.2.138 Okefenokee GA, Ilex lucida [=*I. coriacea*] . . "Sweet Gallberry," "Swamp gallberry." **1968** Radford et al. *Manual Flora Carolinas* 684, I[lex] coriacea . . Sweet Gallberry. **1979** *Torrey Bot. Club Bulletin* 106.22, Ilex coriacea . . sweet gallberry. **2004** in 2006 DARE File—Internet **FL**, If you find Sweet Bay Magnolias, Sweet Gallberrys [sic] or Black Titis . . , you probably have a wetlands issue.

sweet goldenrod n Also *sweet-scented goldenrod*

A **goldenrod 1** (here: *Solidago odora*).
1822 Eaton *Botany* 466, Solidago odora, sweet-scented golden-rod. . . This is the true golden-rod tea-plant. **1830** Rafinesque *Med. Flora* 2.265, Solidago odora. . . Sweet Goldenrod. . . This [species] easily known by its sweet scent near to aniseed. **1896** *Science* new ser 3.296, Plants contain[in]g mostly volatile oils, making agreeable, fragrant teas: Sassafras, Spice bush . . , Labrador Tea *(Ledum Greenlandicum)*, Sweet Goldenrod *(Solidago odora)*. **1943** *Herald–Press* (St. Joseph MI) 17 Aug 4/8, Catnip is but one of many herbs . . with which the W.C.T.U. [= Woman's Christian Temperance Union] has experimented in making tisanes. . . These herbs include applemint, red clover, sweet goldenrod [etc]. **1969** *News–Jrl.* (Mansfield OH) 10 Aug sec C 7/2, See these seed pods, beginning to develop the indigo color. This is sweet goldenrod. **2004** *Atlanta Jrl.-Constitution* (GA) 17 Oct sec MS 4 (Internet), Georgia has about 40 goldenrod species. Some species—sweet goldenrod (or blue mountain tea), gray goldenrod, tall goldenrod and roughleaf goldenrod—are found throughout the state.

‡sweet grape n Cf **sour grape**

A friend.
1939 *AmSp* 14.92 eTN, Sweet-grape. A friend. 'We've been sweet-grapes all of our born days.'

sweet grass n

1 Any of var sweet-scented grasses, as:

a =**holy grass.**
1805 (1904) Lewis *Orig. Jrls. Lewis & Clark Exped.* 1.323 **ND**, Underneath this scaffold a human body was lying, well rolled in several dressed buffaloe skins and near it a bag . . conta[in]ing sundry articles belonging to the diseased; consisting of . . some dryed roots, several platts of the sweet grass, and a small quantity of Mandan tobacco. **1853** in 1860 U.S. War Dept. *Rept. Explor. Railroad* 12.1.74 **NW**, Some sweet grass, platted, was then set on fire and used in the manner of incense, both to the bowl and the stem. **1886** *Bot. Gaz.* 11.327 **ME**, The Hierochloa borealis [=*Hierochloe odorata*] is known among the Indians as Sweet Grass. There is no Indian name for it, even those Indians who know no other English using this name. **1902** *Science* new ser 16.32, Isolated examples of coiled basketry . . from the Ojibwa Indians of Lake Superior. The coils are of sweet grass and are about one-fourth of an inch in diameter. **1916** *Torreya* 16.236 **ME**, Hierochloe odorata. . . Indian or sweet grass. **1961** Douglas *My Wilderness* 241 nME, The delicate perfume of sweet grass saturated the air. The sweet grass of the Allagash is *Hierochloë odorata.* **1973** Hitchcock–Cronquist *Flora Pacific NW* 644, Hierochloe. . . Sweetgrass. **1989** *Yankee* Apr 20 NEng, Within just a few weeks of publishing his request for a source of sweet grass. . . A couple of readers sent him roots . . others told him . . where he can purchase all he needs to make baskets. **1998** *Intelligencer* (Doylestown PA) 30 Oct sec D 14/1, Muhl will most likely be the only artist at the show who uses sweet grass in her work. Or, to be more precise, Maine sweet grass, which is hand-picked by American Indian tribes who live along the coast of Maine. **2005** *Spokesman–Rev.* (Spokane WA) 17 Sept sec B 1 (Internet), Francis Cullooyah prayed out loud in Salish asking the "Grandfather Creator" to make sacred the ground underfoot. . . Cullooyah also prepared sweet grass and husks. He lit the mix in a shell, and smoke curled from it.

b A native **manna grass** (here: *Glyceria septentrionalis*).
1876 Hobbs *Bot. Hdbk.* 47, Grass[,] Sweet, Manna grass, Glyceria fluitans [=*G. septentrionalis*]. **1933** Small *Manual SE Flora* 131, P[anicularia] septentrionalis. . . Sweet-grass. **1948** Pearson *Sea Flavor* 120, In some spots the feathery-headed, golden-tan sweet-grass blossoms are mixed . . with the goldenrod and blackjack.

c A vernal grass *(Anthoxanthum* spp). Cf **vanilla grass 2**
1968 Hultén *Flora AK* 83, Anthoxanthum odoratum. . . Sweet grass.

1988 Busby et al. *Nat. Resources Mattole R. CA* 33, *Anthoxanthum aristatum*—Sweet grass. **2006** *DARE* File—Internet **WI,** Sweet Grass (*Anthoxanthum odoratum* L.) "wĭckobad mackossu" [sweet grass]. The Forest Potawatomi use the Sweet Grass to make baskets and also to sew with upon buckskin.

2 **=sweet flag.**
   1828 Rafinesque *Med. Flora* 1.25, *Acorus calamus.* . . *Vulgar Names*—Flag-root, Sweet Cane, Myrtle Flag, Sweet Grass, Sweet Root, Sweet Rush. **1911** *Century Dict. Suppl.*, Sweet-grass. . . Same as *sweet-flag*. **1930** Sievers *Amer. Med. Plants* 56, *Acorus calamus.* . . *Other common names.*—Sweet cane, sweet grass, sweet myrtle [etc.].

3 An **arrowhead 1** (here: *Sagittaria subulata*).
   1933 *Torreya* 33.82 **GA,** *Sagittaria subulata.* . . Sweet grass.

sweet gravel See **green gravel**

sweet gum n
Std: a timber tree *(Liquidambar styraciflua)* native chiefly to the southeastern US that produces an exudate or "gum" formerly used medicinally and as a masticatory. Also called **alligator tree, gum ~ 2, gumwood, hazel pine, liquidambar, mountain mahogany 5, opossum tree, red gum 1, sap ~ 1, star-leaved ~, white ~ 1**

sweet haw n
A **black haw 1:** usu *Viburnum prunifolium*, but also *V. rufidulum.*
   1851 in **2006** *DARE* File—Internet **LA,** Beginning at the six dogwoods, . . thence east sixty-seven poles a corner, two hickories and two ash and a sweet haw. **1880** *Hist. Logan Co. & OH* 323, The Wild Grape, Sweet Haw, and Sweet-brier lent delicious odors to the ambient air. **1950** Peattie *Nat. Hist. Trees* 513, *Viburnum prunifolium.* . . Sweet Haw. **1950** Moore *Trees AR* 114, *Viburnum rufidulum.* . . Sweet Haw. **1973** Stephens *Woody Plants* 482, *Viburnum prunifolium.* . . Sweet haw. **2001** WV Assoc. Land Surveyors *WV Surveyor* Spring 9, [Common Name:] Black haw—[Botanical Name:] Viburnum prunifolium—[Other Names:] Sweet-haw.

sweetheart n
1 See quot.
   1899 (1912) Green *VA Folk-Speech* 195, *Gifts.* . . White specks on finger-nails, which have been superstitiously supposed to foreshadow gifts. Sometimes called, also, "a sweetheart."
2 See quot. [Engl dial; cf **4** below]
   1899 (1912) Green *VA Folk-Speech* 432, *Sweetheart.* . . A piece of thorn or briar which becomes attached to a woman's dress and drags along after her.
3 See quot.
   c**1950** Halpert *Coll.* 61 **wKY, nwTN,** Sweetheart = a pig's liver cooked in molasses.
4 as *sweethearts:* A **cleavers** (here: *Galium aparine*). [*EDD* 1876 →]
   1900 Lyons *Plant Names* 167, G[alium] Aparine. . . Sweet-hearts. **1914** Georgia *Manual Weeds* 397, *Galium Aparine.* . . Sweethearts. **1931** Harned *Wild Flowers Alleghanies* 465, G[alium] Aparine. . . Owing to the number of sharp prickles the plant has been given numerous names, among which are, Sweethearts, Loreman, Stick-a-back, etc., all quite suggestive.

sweetheart v, hence vbl n *sweethearting* **chiefly Sth, S Midl**
To court; to pay court to; rarely v phr *sweetheart with* to dally with.
   1885 *Newark Daily Advocate* (OH) 5 Feb 3/1, Men admire the filmy lace and mysteriously shadowed velvet as much after marriage as they did in their sweethearting days. **1899** Chesnutt *Conjure Woman* 73 **csNC** [Black], Wusser'n he wuz befo' he sta'ted sweethea'tin'. **1899** (1912) Green *VA Folk-Speech* 432, *Sweethearting.* . . Courting. "I remember when John used to go there sweethearting." **1930** *VA Qrly. Rev.* 6.246 **S Midl,** Dickie Dye can't sweetheart nobody who aint a proper Primitive Baptist. c**1938** in 1970 Hyatt *Hoodoo* 1.317 **MS** [Black], There was a man, he was—before he married—he was courtin' another lady, and after he married why he still sweethearted with her. **1939** FWP *ID Lore* 242, Sweethearten [sic] a girl. **1972** Cooper *NC Mt. Folkl.* 96, *Sweethearting*—dating or courting a sweetheart. **1974** *Lima News* (OH) 26 Aug 15/5, [Syndicated column:] He was an un-

known who sweethearted one of the world's great beauties. **1986** Pederson *LAGS Concordance (Kissing)* 1 inf, **nwTN,** Sweethearting.

sweetheart bone n Cf **love bone**, *DS* K74
The wishbone.
   1949 *AmSp* 24.114 **cSC,** Sweetheart bone. . . Wishbone. c**1970** Pederson *Dial. Surv. Rural GA,* 1 inf, **seGA,** Sweetheart bone. [Inf Black]

sweetheart buggy n Cf **courting buggy, hug-me-tight 1**
See quots.
   1954 Kramer *Heart* 6 **NC** (as of 1882), His lack of success was emphasized by the swift passage of a trotting bay mare drawing a sweetheart buggy. The top was up and the isinglass-windowed curtains attached against the chilly spring evening. **1966** *DARE* (Qu. N41a, . . *Horse-drawn vehicles . . to carry people*) Inf **ID1,** Sweetheart buggy. [Inf old] **1975** *AZ Daily Sun* (Flagstaff) 30 June 14/3, [Advt:] *For Hire*—Sweetheart Buggy and Hay wagon for parades or weddings. **2003** *DARE* File—Internet **NY,** [Advt:] *Wooden Wheel With Rubber One Seated Sweetheart Buggy*—This is four wheeled with rubber on wooden wheels buggy. They say it is a sweetheart buggy because in the back there is a storage compartment for your lunch.

sweethearting See **sweetheart** v

sweethearts See **sweetheart** n 4

sweetheart with See **sweetheart** v

sweet hickory n Cf **sweet pignut**
A **hickory B1,** such as a **pignut 1;** see quots.
   1855 *Scientific Amer.* 10.187, Mr. Eastbrook believes that oil manufactured from the ordinary shell bark, and large sweet hickory nut, will come into general use for the table. **1873** Beadle *Undeveloped West* 641, In many places . . grows a species of milky weed, with tough, stringy root, in taste resembling the "sweet hickory" the boys used to pull and chew, along the Wabash. **1935** *Science* new ser 81.68, The large number of trees which have been killed by the devastating blight along the Atlantic seaboard. . . include black and Japanese walnuts, butternuts, sweet hickory, shagbark, shellbark, bitternut, pignut hickory [etc.]. **1982** Ginns *Snowbird Gravy* 26 **nwNC,** Sweet hickory. Get the leaves off of 'em just like you'd go and get salet out of your garden. **1993** Kingsolver *Pigs in Heaven* 176 **OK,** Cash is moved by the sight of a little field with . . one small, sweet hickory in the center. **1999** in 2006 *DARE* File—Internet **IN,** Carya ovalis—Sweet Hickory. **2006** *DARE* File—Internet **MI,** We also have sweet hickory trees and at times we have a few hickory nuts for sale. We have two types of sweet hickory trees—the Shagbark and Shellbark. . . Both are excellent tasting.

sweet horsemint n Cf **horsemint**
=dittany.
   1828 Rafinesque *Med. Flora* 1.136, *Cunila mariana* [=*C. origanoides*]. . . Sweet Horsemint.

sweet hurts n [*OED2* hurt sb.³ 1542 → for *Vaccinium myrtillus*]
A **lowbush blueberry** (here: *Vaccinium angustifolium*).
   1940 Clute *Amer. Plant Names* 274, *Vaccinium Pennsylvanicum* [=*V. angustifolium*]. Sweet hurts.

sweet-in-death See **sweet-after-death**

sweet jarvil (or javril) See **sweet chervil**

sweet juniper n Also *sweet juniper berry*
A **lowbush blueberry** (here: *Vaccinium angustifolium*).
   1918 *Daily Kennebec Jrl.* (Augusta ME) [6 Apr 3]/4 (newspaperarchive.com), This pasture has not been used for some years and is grown up to scrub pine, sweet juniper and hock weed. **1922** *Torreya* 22.17 **WV,** *Vaccinium Pennsylvanicum* [=*V. angustifolium*] is called "Sweet Juniper" because the berries are sweeter and ripen about the same time as G[aylussacia] brachycera. **1940** Clute *Amer. Plant Names* 44, *V. Pennsylvanicum.* . . sweet juniper-berry.

sweet knot n
A **mushroom B1** (here: *Globifomes graveolens*).
   1878 *Scribner's Mag.* 16.8, The merest swell of wind brought to our senses the odor of wild-flowers, and that delicious aroma of certain decaying wood called by the . . country-folk sweet-knot. **1904** Torrey Bot. Club *Bulletin* 31.425, *Globifomes graveolens.* . . The heavy odor of the fruiting plant is thought to be responsible for the common name of "Sweet Knot," by which it is known in some sections. **1914** MO Bot. Garden *Annals* 1.132 **OH,** It [=*Globifomes graveolens*] is commonly

known as "sweet knot" from the sweet, powerful odor that it is said to give off. The writer . . has never been able to detect the slightest semblance of a sweet odor. **1952** Torrey Bot. Club *Bulletin* 79.189 **NJ,** The group . . stopped to examine a black oak *(Quercus velutina)* which harbored a growth of sweet knot *(Polyporus graveolens),* one of the few records of this fungus in the State of New Jersey. **1981** Lincoff *Audubon Field Guide Mushrooms* 462, Sweet Knot—*Globifomes graveolens. Ibid* 463, Also known as *Polyporus graveolens.* The Sweet Knot is often odorless, but can still be recognized by its massed, overlapping caps.

sweet lady of the night n

See quot.

2002 *DARE* File **AL,** "Sweet lady of the night"—variant name for moonflower flowers or oddly enough for the sphinx moth.

sweet laurel n

=Florida anise-tree.

1830 Rafinesque *Med. Flora* 2.9, *Illicium floridanum.* . . Florida Anisetree. . . Sweet Laurel. **1922** U.S. Natl. Museum *Contrib. Herbarium* 23.277, *Illicium floridanum.* . . The shrub is reputed poisonous to stock. It is known in Florida as "poison bay" and "sweet laurel." **1960** Vines *Trees SW* 278, *Illicium floridanum.* . . Sweet-laurel.

sweetleaf n

1 A shrub or small tree *(Symplocos tinctoria)* with sweetish-tasting leaves, native chiefly to the southeastern US. Also called **dyeleaves 1, Florida laurel, highbush ~, horse sugar, sweet bay 6, yellowwood 6**

1809 Ramsay *Hist. SC* 2.249, The woods are ransacked for dye-stuffs. . . Sweet leaf, hopea tinctoria [=*Symplocos t.*], imparts an elegant yellow color to the labor of their hands. **1860** Curtis *Cat. Plants NC* 65, *Symplocos tinctoria.* . . *Sweetleaf.* . . The leaves, which are 3 to 5 inches long, are sweet to the taste but rather dry, and greedily eaten by cattle and deer in Winter. **1924** *IA City Press–Citizen* (IA) [5 Apr 2]/1 (newspaperarchive.com) **Sth,** We call it the Sweet Leaf Tree, because of the sweet odor it sends out and the sweet juice we get from chewing the leaves. Some folks call it the Horse Sugar here in the South, but I like the other name better myself. **1968** *Pt. Arthur News* (TX) 17 Feb 2/4 **eTX,** Champion trees and the counties in which they are growing are as follows: White ash, Sabine county; . . common sweetleaf, Montgomery [etc]. **1972** in 1983 Johnson *I Declare* 145 **nwFL,** The small tree we call "horse-sugar" or "sweetleaf," because the main vein of the leaf is sweet, is scientifically *Symplocos tinctoria.* **2006** *Times–Picayune* (New Orleans LA) 22 Jan 1 (Internet), There are several smaller native trees that provide a good understory for the bigger, taller trees and should be considered as part of an urban reforesting, including . . sweetleaf.

2 =vanilla leaf 1.

1925 Jepson *Manual Plants CA* 395, *A[chlys] triphylla.* . . Sweet Leaf. Settlers on the Humboldt coast, prizing the delicate fragrance, hang bunches of the leaves in their houses.

sweet life-everlasting See sweet everlasting

sweet locust n

1 =honey locust 1.

1813 Michaux *Histoire des Arbres* 3.165, Dans ces diverses parties des Etats-Unis, cet arbre [=*Gleditsia triacanthos*] est désigné assez indifféremment par les noms de *Honey locust,* Locust à miel, et de *Sweet locust,* Locust doux. [=In the different parts of the United States this tree [=*Gleditsia triacanthos*] is called rather indifferently *Honey locust,* . . and *Sweet locust.*] **1832** *N. Amer. Rev.* 35.426, The Sweet Locust, or Three-thorned Acacia, . . will be cultivated for its elegant foliage and its rapid growth, though it affords no shelter from the sun. **1884** Sargent *Forests of N. Amer.* 59, *Gleditschia triacanthos.* . . sweet locust. **1957** *Daily Progress* (Charlottesville VA) 29 Nov 19/7, The tree known locally as the honeyshuck, but which botany books list as honey locust, . . or sweet locust, has built-in protection.

2 A **black locust** (here: *Robinia pseudoacacia*).

1930 OK Univ. Biol. Surv. *Pub.* 2.68, *Robinia pseudo-acacia.* . . Sweet Locust.

Sweet Lucy n

1 also *Sweet Luce:* Wine, usu cheap and of poor quality. **chiefly WV, Ohio Valley, wGulf States** See Map

1924 (1970) Kennedy *Black Cameos* 21 **LA** [Black], I'm gwine tell y'all 'bout a stimmalashun wat out-pah'lize all yo' muscat, limmon-gin, sweet-lucy, an' all yo' a'kahol lickuhs po'h'd togethuh. **1958**

Humphrey *Home from the Hill* 7 **neTX,** Still sleeping off their Saddy night Sweet Lucy. **1965–70** *DARE* (Qu. DD27, . . *Nicknames . . for wine*) 21 Infs, **chiefly WV, Ohio Valley, wGulf States,** Sweet Lucy; **KY6,** Sweet Lucy—winos call it; **KY59,** Sweet Lucy—also the name of a local wino; **LA14,** Sweet Lucy—cheap wine, second-run muscatel; **NC85,** Sweet Lucy—hear around the barbershop; **IN49,** Sweet Luce. **1986** Pederson *LAGS Concordance,* 1 inf, **seTX,** Sweet Lucy—generic term [for] wine, may not be cheap; 1 inf, **csTX,** Sweet Lucy—cheap wine; 1 inf, **csAL,** These niggers call it [=wine] Sweet Lucy; 1 inf, **ceTX,** Sweet Lucy—these winos, they wind up on it; *(Wine)* 2 infs, **LA, TX,** Sweet Lucy—cheap grade of wine; not [a] brand name; 1 inf, **csTX,** Sweet Lucy; 1 inf, **ceTX,** Sweet Lucy—any wine; 1 inf, **ceTX,** Sweet Lucy—homemade; 1 inf, **csTX,** Sweet Lucy—nickname for cheap wine.

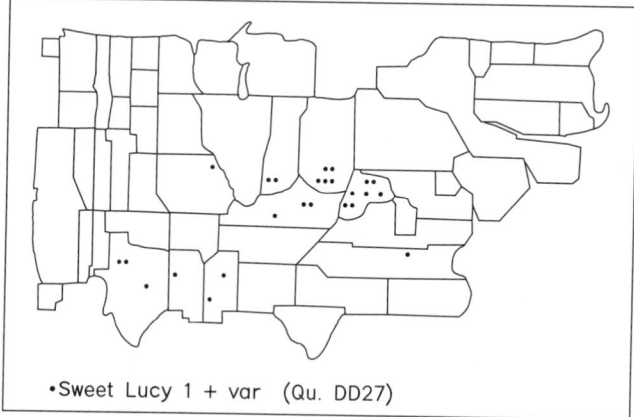

•Sweet Lucy 1 + var (Qu. DD27)

‡2 See quot.

1986 Pederson *LAGS Concordance,* 1 inf, **seLA,** Sweet Lucy—milk with pink syrup; given to children.

sweet magnolia n

=sweet bay 2.

1817 Barton *Vegetable Materia Medica* 1.78, *Magnolia glauca* [=*M. virginiana*]. . . White-bay. Swamp-Sassafras. Beaver-tree. . . Sweet-Magnolia. **1897** Sudworth *Arborescent Flora* 194, *Magnolia glauca* [= *M. virginiana*]. . . Sweet Magnolia. **1945** *Geogr. Rev.* 35.478 **sNJ,** The former [=cedar swamp] is characterized by a mixed growth which includes white cedar, sweet magnolia, laurel [etc]. **1986** Pederson *LAGS Concordance,* 1 inf, **csLA,** Sweet magnolia.

sweet maple n Rarely sweet wood

A **sugar maple.**

1787 in 1793 Amer. Acad. Arts & Sci. *Memoirs* 2.1.156 **Ohio Valley,** Sugar Tree or Sweet Maple . . very beneficial to the country. **1868** Draper *Text-Book Chem.* 393, *Cane Sugar, Sucrose* . . is found in the juices of many plants, as the sugar-cane, beet-root, sweet maple, Indian corn, and date-tree. **1894** *Delphos Daily Herald* (OH) [9 Oct 3]/3 (newspaperarchive.com), Smoke should be made of . . hard wood, such as sweet maple. **1919** *Lima Times–Democrat* (OH) 4 Sept 3/3, [Advt] Sweet Maple Clothes Pins, will fit any size rope or wire. **1924** *Middletown Daily Herald* (NY) [24 Feb 15]/2 (newspaperarchive.com), At the place where the sweet maple trees grew was a log cabin. **1949** *AmSp* 24.114 **eGA,** Sweet maple. . . Sugar maple. **1973** Allen *LAUM* 1.335 **Upper MW** (as of c1950), 1 inf, **IA,** Sweet maple. **1983** *MJLF* 9.58 **ceKY** (as of 1956), *Sweet wood* . . the sugar maple. **1986** Pederson *LAGS Concordance (The kind of tree you tap for syrup)* 2 infs, **cnFL, cAL,** Sweet maple. **1998** *Afr. Amer. Rev.* 32.466, The shed smelled of drying hickory, sweet maple, green pine.

sweet Mary n

A sweet-smelling plant such as costmary *(Balsamita major),* **lemon balm,** or a **horsemint 1** such as **Oswego tea;** see quots.

1894 *Jrl. Amer. Folkl.* 7.96 **NEng,** *Melissa officinalis. . .* sweet Mary. *Ibid* **NH,** *Monarda,* sp., sweet Mary. **1896** Jewett *Pointed Firs* 3 **eME,** The sea-breezes blew into the low end-window of the house laden with not only sweet-brier and sweet-mary, but balm and sage and borage and mint. **1938** Damon *Grandma* 273 **CT** (as of late 19th cent), Our old chest of . . ancient homespun blankets was made fragrant, as well as mothless, by the sprays of sweet Mary she laid in it. **1940** Clute *Amer. Plant Names* 25, *M[elissa] officinalis.* . . Sweet Mary. *Ibid* 79, *C[hrysanthemum] balsamita* var. *tanacetoides.* . . Sweet Mary.

sweet milk n [*OED2* c1420 →] **esp Sth, S Midl** See Map
Fresh milk (as opposed to buttermilk or **sour milk**).

1840 *S. Lit. Messenger* 6.510 **NC,** The centre was filled with pans of clabber, sweet milk, cheese, and various kinds of cornbread. **1869** *Atlantic Mth.* 24.483 **PA,** The [cheese] is made from sweet milk boiled, with sour milk added. **1889** *Century Illustr. Mag.* 35.563 **IL,** Barbara uncovered her basket, which contained . . a bottle of sweet milk. **1909** *DN* 3.417 **nME,** *Sweet milk bread.* . . Bread made of new milk, flour, and salt, set in the morning, and baked in the afternoon of the same day. **1932** Stribling *Store* 256 **AL,** The table before him was loaded with food . . sweet milk . . two kinds of fruit pies. **1937** in Lib. of Congress *Amer. Memory: WPA Life Hist.* (Internet) **TX,** They would come to our place and sit in a row with their cups to get sweet milk. **1939** *Ibid* **NE,** To start: 2 cups of buckwheat flour, ½ cup of cornmeal, 1 cup sweet milk. *Ibid* **SC,** There's a law against country folks selling sweet milk in town. *Ibid* **GA,** A man in the country is . . giving the family a gallon of sweet milk per day. **1965–70** *DARE* (Qu. H19, *What do you mean by a biscuit? How are they made?*) 12 Infs, **chiefly Sth, S Midl,** Sweet-milk biscuit(s); **FL**1, **GA**85, **KY**15, 41, **NC**51, **OK**17, Buttermilk biscuits; sweet-milk biscuits; **NH**6, Sour-milk biscuit—with sody, sweet-milk biscuit—with baking powder; **OK**3, Baking powder, sweet milk; **CO**47, Baking-powder biscuits—baking powder, flour, shortening, salt, sweet milk; **OK**32, [Biscuits are] made with white flour, shortening, salt, and sweet milk and baking powder, or [with] sour milk and soda, or buttermilk and soda; they're all called hot biscuits; (Qu. H37, . . *Words . . for gravy. Any joking ones?*) Infs **KY**85, **TN**66, Sweet-milk gravy; (Qu. H66a, *The sweet liquid that you pour over a pudding*) Inf **KY**84, Sweet milk; **VA**9, Sweet milk and sugar; (Qu. BB22, . . *Home remedies . . for constipation*) Inf **MS**80, Drink sweet milk; (Qu. BB34b) Inf **OK**50, Bread and sweet milk. **1967–69** *DARE* FW Addit **cNC,** Sweet milk—raw milk; **SC,** Sweet milk—whole milk; **ceTN,** Sweet milk—said more commonly than just "milk." If you order a glass of milk, the waitress will say, "Sweet milk?" **1983** Allin *S. Legislative Dict.* 30 **Sth,** *Sweet milk:* fresh from the cow. **1996** *Atlanta Jrl.–Constitution* (GA) 11 Feb sec M 3/3, When a patient asked for sweet milk (the old-fashioned term for the kind that's not buttermilk), she obligingly put sugar in it. **2000** *NADS Letters* **TN,** Dad also called whole milk "sweet milk" (as opposed to buttermilk, which he likes to drink). **2001** *DARE* File **Sth,** "Sweet milk" was used . . to distinguish from buttermilk—this resulted in incomprehension in other parts of the country.

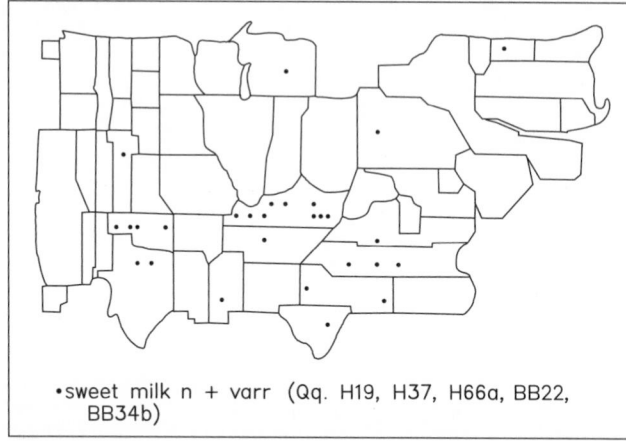

•sweet milk n + varr (Qq. H19, H37, H66a, BB22, BB34b)

sweet milk exclam Cf **cucumber** exclam, **onion** exclam
1968 *DARE* (Qu. EE15, *When he has caught the first of those that were hiding what does the player who is 'it' call out to the others?*) Inf **GA**58, Sweet milk, sweet milk (Waukegan, Illinois).

sweet monkey n
1950 *PADS* 14.65 **SC,** *Sweet monkey.* . . A potent mixture of rum and sorghum molasses.

sweet-mouth v [Prob of Afr origin] Cf **badmouth** v, **sugar mouth** *chiefly Gullah*

To cajole; to persuade with flattery; hence adj *sweet-mouth(ed)* persuasive, verbally seductive; n *sweetmouth* flattery.

1892 (1969) Christensen *Afro-Amer. Folk Lore* 51 **seSC** [Gullah], Yes, Br'er Alligator, I know you is bery sweet mout'. 'E all mealy an' sweet like new pertater. **1922** Gonzales *Black Border* 331 **sSC, GA coasts** [Gullah glossary], *Sweetmout'*—sweetmouth—blarney, flattery. *Sweet-*

mout' talk—soft talk of a philanderer with the gentler sex. **1928** Peterkin *Scarlet Sister Mary* 126 **SC** [Gullah], There he was, running up and down . . peeping through the cracks at those pullets . . talking all kinds of sweet-mouthed talk to them. **1949** Turner *Africanisms* 233, [swit mɛut] 'to flatter,' i.e. 'to sweet mouth'; [i swit mɛut] 'He is a flatterer.' **1950** *PADS* 14.66 **SC,** *Sweet-mouth.* . . To flatter. "You yes' sweet-mouthin' me." *Sweet-mouthed.* . . Flattering, ingratiating. **c1960** Wilson *Coll.* **csKY,** *Sweet-mouthed.* . . Using sweet, sugary talk, often suspiciously sweet. **1986** Pederson *LAGS Concordance,* 1 inf, swAL, "talk nice." [Inf Black] **1987** Jones-Jackson *When Roots Die* 139 **sSC coast** [Gullah], [In a list of idioms "still very much apparent in daily communication":] *Sweetmouth:* flatter.

sweet muffin See **muffin**

sweet myrtle n
1 A **wax myrtle** (here: *Morella cerifera*). **Mid and S Atl**
1705 Beverley *Hist. VA* 2.7 **VA,** They likewise produce great Variety of Evergreens, unknown to me by Name, besides the beauteous Holly, Sweet-Myrtle, Cedar, and the Live Oak. **1863** *S. Lit. Messenger* 37.400 **VA,** Above rose a lofty . . bluff; from its base stretched out an extensive plain of beach, interspersed with marsh weeds and thickets of sweet myrtle. **1880** *Science* 1.264 **sFL,** The same kind of glands is found on the leaves of many other shrubs in Florida—the sweet myrtle (*Myrica* [=*Morella*] *cerifera*), the low-ground blueberry . . and some others. **1926** *Torreya* 26.6 **seGA,** *Iva* spp.—Salt-water myrtle, to distinguish it from the sweet myrtle (Myrica), Sapelo I[slan]d. **1941** Writers' Program *Guide SC* 326 **sSC,** As the highway nears the sea, the air is odorous with sweet myrtle. **1956** Savage *River* 265 **SC,** Nature ordered it that Carolina should sing for her a special song, a song of . . the dense hedgelike masses of sweet myrtle. **1970** *DARE* (Qu. T15, . . *Kinds of swamp trees*) Inf **SC**69, Sweet muckle (myrtle). **1974** Morton *Folk Remedies* 99 **SC,** *Sweet Myrtle.* . . *Myrica cerifera.* . . *Range:* Entire coastal plain of South Carolina and North Carolina; north to southern New Jersey, west to Texas and southeastern Mexico; south to southern Florida and the Keys.
2 =**sweet flag.**
1900 Lyons *Plant Names* 13, *A*[*corus*] *Calamus.* . . Sweet Cane, Sweet Grass, Sweet Myrtle. **1931** Clute *Common Plants* 65, A most un-myrtlelike plant is the common sweet flag or calamus . . though it is often known as sweet myrtle. **1950** *Times Herald* (Olean NY) 27 July 19/1, Other names for it are calamus, sweet root, sweet myrtle, grass myrtle and sweet cinnamon. **1971** Krochmal *Appalachia Med. Plants* 32, *Acorus calamus.* . . Sweet Myrtle. . . In Appalachia, . . the powdered or ground plant is used in sachets.

sweetning See **sweetening**

sweet oak n
1 =**chinquapin oak 1.** [See quot 1921] **esp IN, OH**
1869 *Delphos Weekly Herald* (OH) [8 July 4]/4 (newspaperarchive.com), They will pay $14.00 to $15.00 per thousand for *Sweet* or *White Oak Staves;* $13.00 to $14.00 per thousand for *Bur Oak Staves.* **1879** *Ft. Wayne Weekly Sentinel* (IN) 13 Aug 8/4, The Tierce Staves . . to be made out of White or Sweet Oak. **1894** *Landmark* (Statesville NC) 1 Feb 1/8, Thence [to] . . a sweet oak. **1921** Deam *Trees IN* 104, *Quercus Muhlenbergii.* . . *Chinquapin Oak. Sweet Oak.* . . Kernel sweet, and the most edible of all of our oaks. **1933** *Circleville Herald* (OH) 6 Apr 7/4, East . . 1–2 feet to a sweet oak stump on top of a bank. **1959** *Press-Gaz.* (Hillsboro OH) 21 Apr 5/7, *We* pay cash for white oak, burr and sweet oak. **2006** *DARE* File—Internet **OH,** This mighty oak section is from the Ohio State Champion Sweet Oak (*Quercus mullenbergii* [sic]) that resided just in front of the current main entrance of Pearson Hall.
2 A **wax myrtle** (here: *Morella cerifera*).
1901 *Torreya* 1.115 **GA,** *Myrica cerifera* [=*Morella c.*] . . Sweet oak. **1960** Vines *Trees SW* 118, *Myrica . . cerifera.* . . Vernacular names are Wax-berry, . . Sweet-oak, and Tallow-shrub.

sweet patootie See **patootie 1**

sweet pea n Cf **wild sweet pea**
1 =**garden pea. chiefly Sth, S Midl**
1830 Rafinesque *Med. Flora* 2.252, *Pisum sativum.* . . Sweet Peas. **1905** *AZ Republican* (Phoenix) [25 Jan 7]/1 (newspaperarchive.com), Green Pearls, a delicious sifted sweet pea, fine size, extra flavored. **1950** *WELS* **WI** (*Kinds of peas grown in your neighborhood*) 7 Infs, Sweet pea(s); 1 Inf, Early sweet pea; 1 Inf, Green sweet pea; 1 Inf, Late sweet pea. **c1960** Wilson *Coll.* **csKY,** English peas. . . Garden peas as distinguished from field peas, cowpeas, stock peas, black-eyed peas.

Sometimes called *sweet peas*. **1966–68** *DARE* (Qu. H36, *Kinds of soup*) Inf **SC**26, ['jɪmbo] . . butter beans, corn, tomatoes, okra, sweet peas, carrots; (Qu. I14, *Kinds of beans that you eat in the pod before they're dry*) Inf **NC**50, Sweet peas; (Qu. I20, . . *Kinds of beans*) Inf **KY**5, May peas—small green sweet pea; **SC**26, Sweet peas. **1967** LeCompte *Word Atlas* 308 se**LA**, Small green peas grown in spring gardens. . . sweet peas [4 of 21 infs]. **1986** Pederson *LAGS Concordance*, 9 infs, **Gulf Region,** Sweet pea(s). [*DARE* Ed: 8 of 9 infs Black] **1989** *DARE* File ne**WI** (as of c1963), I remember my grandfather telling me about the various vegetables he planned to plant in his garden, and that he said, "I'm not going to bother with sweet peas this year because they're more work than what you get for the table." **2006** *DARE* File—Internet **Sth,** *Sweet Peas. . . Pisum sativum. . .* Pick the sweet peas regularly to promote growth of new pods. They should be harvested when pods are fully rounded.

2 A **vetchling,** as:

a Std: a commonly cultivated garden plant, *Lathyrus odoratus.*

b Any of several other **vetchlings;** see quots. **widespread, but more freq West**
1914 Georgia *Manual Weeds* 250, *Lathyrus tuberosus. . .* Tuberous Sweet Pea. **1915** (1926) Armstrong-Thornber *Western Wild Flowers* 254, *Narrow-leaved Sweet Pea—Lathyrus graminifolius. . .* This has flowers resembling the cultivated Sweet Pea, but the whole effect is more airy and graceful. *Ibid,* Utah Sweet Pea—*Lathyrus Utahensis.* **1948** Wherry *Wild Flower Guide* 161, *Lathyrus latifolius. . .* Often cultivated under the name of *Hardy Sweet-pea.* **1957** Barnes *Nat. Hist. Wasatch Spring* 85 **UT,** Here we find . . the pretty red-purple sweet pea or vetchling *(Lathyrus brachycalyx).* **1965–70** *DARE* (Qu. S26a, . . *Wildflowers. . . Roadside flowers)* Infs **MI**34, **WA**33, Sweet pea; (Qu. S26c, *Wildflowers that grow in woods)* Inf **MS**6, Sweet peas; (Qu. S26d, *Wildflowers that grow in meadows; not asked in early QRs)* Inf **VA**52, Sweet peas; (Qu. S26e, *Other wildflowers not yet mentioned; not asked in early QRs)* Inf **MA**57, Beach sweet pea—grows in beach sand, bush a foot high; several purple flowers on one stem; **VA**34, Sweet pea; **KY**28, Sweet peas. **1967** *DARE* Wildfl QR Pl.115 [=*Lathyrus maritimus*] Infs **CO**7, **OR**8, Sweet pea. **1970** Correll *Plants TX* 877, *Lathyrus latifolius. . .* Perennial sweetpea. **2006** *DARE* File—Internet **CA,** *Lathyrus vestitus* Nutt. *var. vestitus*—Canyon Sweet Pea. *Ibid* **UT,** Sweet Pea (Lathyrus pauciflorus).

3 A **goat's rue** (here: *Tephrosia virginiana*).
1969 *DARE* Wildfl QR Pl.108B **WI**79, Creeping sweet pea.

sweet pecan n   Cf **bitter pecan**
=**pecan B1.**
1883 *Amer. Jrl. Forestry* 1.209, Water Hickory: Bitter Pecan, *(Carya aquatica). . .* Pecan: Sweet Pecan, *(Carya olivaeformis* [=*C. illinoensis*])*.* This noble and useful tree is decidedly the tree of the Southwest. **1940** *Appleton Post-Crescent* (WI) 22 Nov 24/4, [Advt:] *Bentwood Trays*—Solid Mahogany—Sweet Pecan. . . Beautiful in appearance, very light to handle. **1950** Moore *Trees AR* 28, *Carya illinoensis. . .* Local Name: Sweet Pecan. . . Important commercially for its edible nuts. **1979** Little *Checklist U.S. Trees* 74, *Carya illinoensis. . .* Sweet pecan. **1999** *Times–Picayune* (New Orleans LA) 28 Mar (Internet), Den 3 Webelos II and Den 8 Bears planted a variety of saplings including river birch, native sweet pecan, red maple, wax myrtle, water oak, live oak and Nuttal oak.

sweet pepper n
1 A pepper (here: *Capsicum annuum,* usu Grossum Group). **widespread, but less freq West** See Map   Cf **bell pepper, green ~ 1, mango 2, tomato pepper**
1829 *NY Farmer & Horticult. Repository* 2.202, Sweet pepper of the kingdom of Valencia, Spain . . ; two dishes were served at the dinner, one in salad, the same as in Spain, and the other stuffed, the same as for the Purple Eggplant. **1838** *Mag. Horticult.* 4.35 **DC,** Mr. John Ousely: specimen of sweet pepper, and two fine egg plants. **1892** *DN* 1.189 **TX,** *Chilchóte:* green peppers, sweet peppers. **1903** *Daily Kennebec Jrl.* (Augusta ME) 31 July [6]/1 (newspaperarchive.com), The pepper most commonly used green as a vegetable is the Spanish sweet pepper, also known as the bell pepper and bull-nose. . . This variety of pepper is mild in flavor imparting just enough warmth to be agreeable to the palate and beneficial to the digestive organs. *Ibid, Fried Sweet Peppers.* Select fine large sweet peppers and wash thoroughly. **1919** *Frederick Post* (MD) 30 Oct 2/7, The writer beheld the following delectable articles of food: . . cheese balls rolled in finely minced red and green sweet pepper

[etc]. **1932** *Denton Jrl.* (MD) 23 Apr 8/8, [Advt:] *Plants for Sale.*—Tomato, Sweet Pepper and Egg Plant. **1950** *WELS (What do you call large sweet peppers?)* 12 Infs, **WI,** Sweet pepper(s). **c1960** *Wilson Coll.* cs**KY,** Sweet pepper—the large, mild variety; also called by a few mangoes. **1965–70** *DARE* (Qu. I22d, . . *Peppers—large sweet)* 252 Infs, **widespread, but less freq West,** Sweet peppers; **GA**11, California sweet peppers; **IL**4, **VA**48, Green sweet peppers; **AL**30, **MO**12, **NH**5, **NJ**5, **NY**90, Large sweet peppers; **KY**28, Ruby sweet peppers; **KY**24, Yellow sweet peppers; (Qu. I22c, . . *Peppers—small sweet)* 75 Infs, **widespread, but less freq West,** Sweet peppers; **MA**2, **NC**34, 52, **NY**37, 90, 162, **TX**58, **WA**8, Small sweet peppers; **IN**59, Little sweet peppers; **WA**11, Red and green sweet peppers; (Qu. I4, . . *Vegetables . . less commonly grown around here)* Inf **NY**106, Sweet pepper; (Qu. I28a, . . *Kinds of things . . you call 'greens' . . [Those that are eaten raw])* Inf **SC**43, Sweet peppers. **1982** Slone *How We Talked* 55 e**KY** (as of c1950), Slice two or three large, green sweet peppers. **1983** *Daily Herald* (Arlington Heights IL) 28 Apr sec 5 6/1, Chopped green or red sweet pepper.

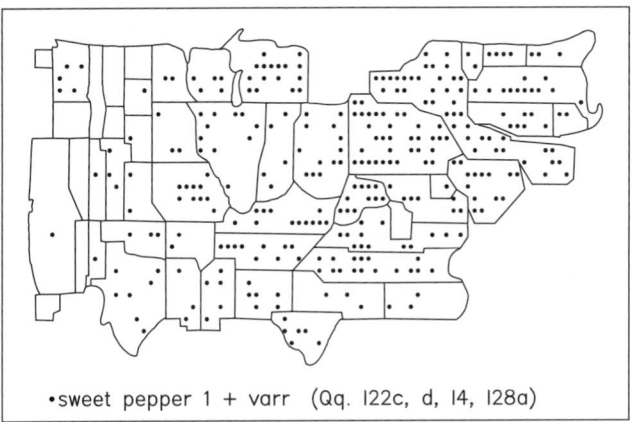

•sweet pepper 1 + varr (Qq. I22c, d, I4, I28a)

2 =**sweet pepperbush.**
1944 Holton *Yankees Were Like This* 84 **MA,** I remember . . the perfume of. . . bush honeysuckle and sweet pepper from the swamps.

sweet pepperbush n
Std: a shrub of the genus *Clethra,* esp *C. alnifolia,* native from New England through the Atlantic states and the southern US. Also called **latherbush, leatherbush 2, pepperbush 3, poor man's soap c, soap bush 2, white alder 1;** for other names of *C. alnifolia* see **puppytail, spicebush 8, sweet pepper 2, white bush 2**

sweet pickle   See **apple pickle**

sweet pignut n   Also *sweet pignut hickory*   Cf **sweet hickory**
A **pignut 1:** usu *Carya ovalis,* but also *C. glabra.*
1908 Larkin *Pioneer Hist. Meigs Co.* 100 **OH,** The Original Forest of Rutland. . . Sweet Pignut. Caya Glabadendroir [sic, prob for *Carya glabra odorata* [=*Carya ovalis*].] **1944** Hyland–Steinmetz *Woody Plants ME* 11, *C[arya] ovalis. . .* Sweet Pignut. . . Indigenous from Massachusetts westward. . . Planted locally in southeastern Oxford County. **1952** Blackburn *Trees* 107, *C[arya] ovalis . .* Sweet Pignut. **1971** Kieran *Nat. Hist. NYC* 172, Three other hickories found in the upland deciduous woods in three of the five boroughs—Queens, Richmond, and the Bronx—are the Pignut . . , the Mockernut . . , and the Sweet or Oval or Red Pignut *(Carya ovalis). Ibid* 173, Possibly the Mockernut and the Sweet Pignut are found in greater numbers in other sectors of the city. **1979** Little *Checklist U.S. Trees* 73, *Carya glabra . . pignut hickory. . . Other common names*—pignut, sweet pignut. *Ibid, Carya glabra* var. *odorata. . . Other common names*—sweet pignut hickory, sweet pignut. **2006** (acc) *MuseumLink IL* (Internet), Pignut hickory *(Carya glabra)* is also commonly referred to as sweet pignut.

sweet pinesap n   [See quot 2004]   Cf **pinesap**
The saprophytic pygmy-pipes *(Monotropis odorata)* native to the southeastern US.   Also called **beechdrops 3, Carolina beechdrops, ~ pinesap**
1857 Gray *Manual of Botany* 261, *Schweinitzia* [=*Monotropsis*], . . Sweet Pine-sap. **1901** Lounsberry *S. Wild Flowers* 376, *Monotropsis odorata,* Carolina beech-drops, or sweet pine-sap . . is more rarely found through shady woods than the Indian pipe and is a rather shorter plant.

1924 *Amer. Botanist* 30.63, *Monotropsis odorata* is the "sweet pine-sap" because of its odor.   **2004** in 2006 (acc) MD Dept. Nat. Resources *Endangered Plants MD* (Internet), The Sweet Pinesap, *Monotropsis odorata*, is not a photosynthetic plant, meaning it does not produce its own food. . . The cinnamon-like scent released by Sweet Pinesap is so strong that it can be used to help locate the plant, which is only a few inches tall and usually hidden under fallen leaves.

sweet pitcher plant n   Also *sweet pitchers*   esp NC, SC

A **pitcher plant 1:** esp *Sarracenia rubra,* but also *S. purpurea* or *S. alata;* see quots.

1928 *Amer. Midland Naturalist* 11.363, *Sarracenia rubra.* . . Sweet Pitcher Plant.   **1934** *Scientific Mth.* 38.85 **NC,** The sweet pitcher-plant, *S[arracenia] rubra,* eluded us for some time, but we finally located it in wet woods on the outskirts of Fayetteville.   **1949** Moldenke *Amer. Wild Flowers* 60, A species with extremely fragrant, reddish purple flowers . . is *S[arracenia] rubra,* the *sweet pitcherplant,* of bogs and low pinelands from southeastern North Carolina to western Florida.   **1976** Bailey-Bailey *Hortus Third* 1007, [*Sarracenia*] *purpurea.* . . Sweet p[itcher] p[lant]. . . A variable sp. of acid bogs, widely distributed in e. N. Amer. . . [*Sarracenia*] *rubra.* . . Sweet p[itcher] p[lant]. . . N.C. to Fla. and Miss.   **1996** *Amer. Jrl. Botany* 83.1017, *Sarracenia jonesii* [=*S. rubra* subsp *jonesii*], the mountain sweet pitcher plant, is known from . . North Carolina and . . South Carolina. . . The fragrant flowers are (usually) maroon and are borne singly on erect scapes from April through June.   **2006** (acc) NC State Univ. *Carnivorous Plants* (Internet), *Sarracenia alata.* . . Sweet pitcher plant; Yellow trumpets. . . Sweet scented maroon flowers.   **2006** *DARE* File—Internet, *Sweet Pitcher Plant—Sarracenia purpurea.* . . The Sweet Pitcher Plant is the only Sarracenia that does not have a hood over the top of the pitcher. Sweet pitchers are native to bogs of the eastern US. and Southern Canada.

sweet pop n   Cf **pape**
=**painted bunting 1.**

1916 *Times–Picayune* (New Orleans LA) 23 Apr 1/5, *Painted Bunting.* . . Pape doux, Sweet "Pop".

sweet poplar n   Also *sweet popple*
=**balsam poplar.**

1824 Monroe *Amer. Botanist* 125, Putrid Fever. . . one handful of bark . . of the Black Ash. . . Wild Cherry. . . Sweet Poplar [etc].   **1850** (1926) Sawyer *Way Sketches* 30 **NY,** We have found no wood since we struck the Platte, except fragments of wagon boxes and a few sweet poplar and cotton wood limbs, brought from the islands by emigrants who have preceded us.   **1948** *WELS Suppl.* **cWI,** Where else besides Waupaca County is the balsam poplar called sweet popple?   **1950** *WELS* (The kind of poplar that has sticky, sweet-smelling buds) 1 Inf, **WI,** Sweet popple.   **1966–70** *DARE* (Qu. T12) Infs **AL**11, **MN**2, **NJ**69, **NY**165, **PA**17, 216, **VA**73, Sweet popple; **SC**21, Sweet poplar.   **2005** in 2006 *DARE* File—Internet **MT,** There are sweet grass, sweet pine, and even sweet poplar, or balsam poplar. They say that the poplar trees smelled so good that rural ladies would gather the buds, soak them in water, and then dip their hankies in it to get the smell.

sweet potato n

1 Std: a thin-skinned, usu yellow- or orange-fleshed root vegetable (*Ipomoea batatas*); also the plant itself.   Also called **Carolina potato, dooley 1, long potato, mother n¹ Bb, music root, nigger killer 1, ~ leg, poot root, potato B2, yam potato**   Cf **wild sweet potato**

2 See **sweet potato squash.**

sweet potato bird n
See quot.

1912 Cobb *Back Home* 39 **wKY,** That huckstering little bird of the dead treetops, which the negroes call the sweet-potato bird . . was calling his mythical wares.

sweet-potato cactus n
=**night-blooming cereus.**

1931 Higgins *Our Cacti* 45 **AZ,** Peniocereus greggi (Cereus greggi). . . comes from a tuber. . . From this fact it is sometimes known as the Sweet Potato Cactus.   **1949** Curtin *By the Prophet* 55 **AZ,** *Cereus Greggii Engelm.* . . Sweetpotato cactus. . . derives this name from the tubers, which ordinarily weigh from five to fifteen pounds.

sweet-potato pie n   Also *potato pie*   chiefly **Sth**   See Map   Cf **potato B2**

Usu a custard-like pie made with **sweet potato 1** and spices; see quots.

1829 Flint *George Mason* 19 **Lower Missip Valley,** There was no . . deficiency of custards, delicious sweet potatoe pies, and various wild fruits.   **1859** (1860) Edgeworth *S. Gardener* 227, *Sweet-Potato Pie.* [Recipe calls for alternating layers of sliced sweet potatoes and spices baked in a puff-pastry crust.]   **1906** Johnson *Highways Missip. Valley* 140 **Ozarks,** There's all kinds [of pies]—apple, peach, blackberry, sorrel, pumpkin, sweet potato, and I don't know what.   **c1965** Randle *Cookbooks* (Ask Neighbor) 98, *Sweet Potatoe Pie, Old Fashioned Southern.* [Recipe includes mashed sweet potatoes, butter, sugar, salt, cinnamon, nutmeg, cloves, milk, eggs.]   **1965–70** *DARE* (Qu. H63, *Kinds of desserts*) 14 Infs, **chiefly Sth,** Sweet-potato pie; **CA**94, Sweet-potato pie—a one-crust pie topped with whipped cream, [made with] butter, sugar, vanilla, eggs, and boiled sweet potato and canned milk; **FL**51, Sweet-potato pie—White people don't go for it; **GA**75, Sweet-potato pie—similar to pumpkin pie; **MO**22, Most famous pie around here is sweet-potato pie; **AL**11, 60, **FL**1, **LA**9, **MS**79, 85, **SC**7, Potato pie; **VA**56, Potato pie (sweet potato).   **1972** Claerbaut *Black Jargon* 82, *Sweet potato pie* . . a soul food dessert popular among black people which is made largely of sweet potatoes or yams and which tastes very similar to pumpkin pie.   **1986** Pederson *LAGS Concordance*, 3 infs, **GA, MS, TN,** Potato pie—of sweet potato(es); 2 infs, **GA, MS,** Sweet-potato pie(s).   **2004** *Washington Post* (DC) 27 Dec sec B 3 (Internet), Judges will evaluate the food and at the end of Kwanzaa declare a winner. . . tonight's course is sweet potato pie.

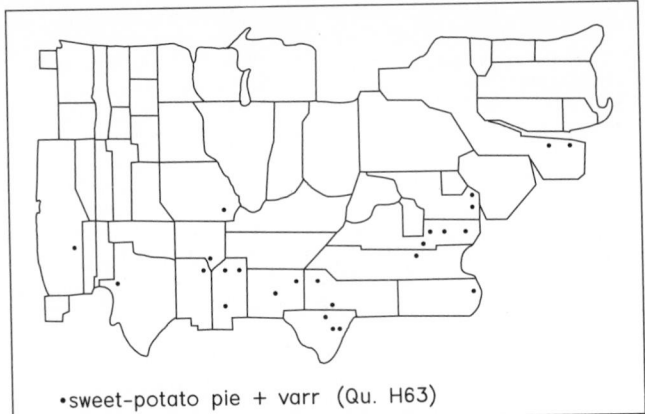

•sweet-potato pie + varr (Qu. H63)

sweet-potato pone   See **potato pone**

sweet-potato pudding n   Also *potato pudding*   chiefly **Sth**   Cf **potato B2**
=**potato pone.**

1827 Leslie *75 Receipts* 21 **PA,** Sweet Potato Pudding. [Recipe includes boiled sweet potato, eggs, powdered sugar, butter, wine-brandy mixture, rose water, spices.]   **1852** Eastman *Aunt Phillis's Cabin* 56 **Sth** [Black], I jist wanted some brandy to put in these potato puddins.   **1859** (1860) Edgeworth *S. Gardener* 212, *Sweet Potato Pudding.* [Recipe includes boiled and grated sweet potatoes, eggs, sugar, butter, nutmeg, lemon peel, brandy.] . . put a paste in the dish, and when the pudding is done sprinkle the top.   **1885** Hearn *Cuisine* 198, *Sweet Potato Pudding.* . . is a Southern dish, and fit to grace the table of an epicure.   **1903** *Fitchburg Daily Sentinel* (MA) 23 Nov 8/6, *Sweet Potato Pudding.* This used to be a favorite Sunday pudding in the South . . "befo de war."   **1933** *Salamanca Republican–Press* (NY) 12 Sept 5/6, *Six September Dinners.* . . Sweet Potato Pudding.   **1950** *PADS* 14.54 **SC,** Potato pudding: . . Same as *potato pone,* except that it has more liquid ingredients and hence a lighter consistency.   **1956** [see **potato pone**].   **c1960** *Wilson Coll.* **csKY,** Potato pudding. . . A pie made of sweet potatoes.   **1965–70** *DARE* (Qu. H63, *Kinds of desserts*) Infs **MS**63, **NC**18, **VA**69, Sweet-potato pudding; **NC**76, Sweet-potato pudding—made like a sheet cake; (Qu. H48, *Baked dishes made of potatoes cut up with meat or cheese*) Inf **SC**1, Potato pudding if made with sweet potatoes.   **2004** *Hartford Courant* (CT) 21 Nov Northeast sec 12 (Internet) **VA,** Someone invariably makes toothache-inducing sweet potato pudding.

sweet-potato squash n   Also *sweet potato, sweet-potato pumpkin*   Cf **potato squash**

A **winter squash,** usu *Cucurbita mixta* cv or *C. moschata* cv.

1852 *W. Horticult. Rev.* 2.223 **sCA,** Among other articles we noticed a sweet potato squash, this vegetable grows to the weight of one hundred pounds. It can be preserved a long while, and be eaten from the time when it weighs but a pound until it attains the large size mentioned. **1854** *Adams Sentinel* (Gettysburg PA) [27 Mar 5]/1 (newspaperarchive.com), *List of Premiums. . . Best Sweet-potato Pumpkin.* **1863** Burr *Field & Garden* 222, *Sweet-Potato Squash.* Plant very similar in character to that of the Hubbard or Autumnal Marrow. **1890** *Amer. Naturalist* 24.738, In 1884 there appeared in our seedmen's catalogues, under the name of Tennessee Sweet Potato Pumpkin, a variety very distinct, of medium size, pear-shape, little ribbed, of a creamy white striped with green color, and the stem swollen and fleshy. **1928** *Decatur Daily Rev.* (IL) 19 Oct 20/3, Hubbard squash are 5 cents a pound and sweetpotato squash are 5 and 10 cents a pound. **1949** *Times Herald* (Olean NY) 27 Sept 4/2, The most resistant varieties . . were Butternut, Green Striped Cushaw, Dickinson Pumpkin, . . and Sweet Potato Pumpkin. **1966–69** *DARE* (Qu. I23, . . *Kinds of squash*) Infs **CO**11, **KY**28, 40, **MO**8, **OR**3, **TN**13, Sweet (po)tato squash; **MD**30, Sweet potato punkin—about two feet long, gourd-shaped, used to make punkin pie; (Qu. I4, . . *Vegetables . . less commonly grown around here*) Inf **IL**50, Sweet potato squash. **1988** Whealy *Garden Seed Inventory* (2d ed) 334, *Cucurbita mixta. . .* Tennessee Sweet Potato Squash. **1990** *Seed Savers Yearbook* 203, *Cucurbita mixta. . .* Tennessee Sweet Potato. *Ibid* 205, *Cucurbita moschata. . .* Sweet Potato. **2003** *Patriot Ledger* (Quincy MA) 29 Oct 17 (Internet), This variety of squash is a disease-resistant heirloom strain. It's also called sweet potato squash, because of its flavor.

sweet pumpkin n Cf **sugar pumpkin**
=**pie pumpkin.**

1848 Emory *Notes Reconnoissance* 590 **MD**, The cooked muscal . . tasted something like sweet pumpkin baked, and looked very much like it. **1852** MI State Ag. Soc. *Trans. for 1851* 3.81, ½ peck potatoes. . . 1 sweet pumpkin. **1855** *Adams Sentinel* (Gettysburg PA) 31 Dec [7]/5 (newspaperarchive.com), *The Ladies' Fair. . .* 1 large sweet pumpkin. **1922** *Syracuse Herald* (NY) 22 Oct mag sec 10/1, *Pumpkin Chips.* This is a delicious conserve. Cut a small sweet pumpkin in halves and the halves in narrow strips. **1969** *DARE* (Qu. I23, . . *Kinds of squash*) Inf **IN**67, Sweet punkin. **1986** Pederson *LAGS Concordance,* 2 infs, **csMS, seAR,** Sweet pumpkin(s). **2005** *Yakima Herald–Republic* (WA) 26 Oct sec C 8 (Internet), The best selection is a pie pumpkin or sweet pumpkin. These are smaller than the large jack-o'-lantern pumpkins and the flesh is sweeter and less watery.

sweet quack See **quack grass 2**

sweet religion n [Folk-etym] Cf **Aunt Jericho, ladies'-streamer**

Sweet alyssum *(Lobularia maritima).*

1926 Smith *Gullah* 31 **sSC, GA coasts,** *Popular Etymologies. . . Sweet religion* for sweet alyssum.

sweetroot n
1 =**sweet flag.**

1828 Rafinesque *Med. Flora* 1.25, *Acorus calamus. . . Vulgar Names*—Flag-root, . . Sweet Root. **1900** Lyons *Plant Names* 13, *A[corus] Calamus. . .* Sweet root. **1950** *Times Herald* (Olean NY) 27 July 19/1, Other names for it [=sweet flag] are calamus, sweet root, sweet myrtle, grass myrtle and sweet cinnamon. **1971** Krochmal *Appalachia Med. Plants* 32, *Acorus calamus. . .* sweetroot. . . In Appalachia, the root is chewed to clear the throat and to cure stomach gas; and the powdered or ground plant is used in sachets.

2 =**wild sarsaparilla 1.**

1828 Rafinesque *Med. Flora* 1.53, *Aralia nudicaulis. . . Vulgar Names*—Spiknard [sic], . . Sweet-root. **1849** Williams *Rept. Med. Botany MA* 4, *Aralia nudicaulis.* Wild sarsaparilla; wild liquorice; sweet root. **1974** (1977) Coon *Useful Plants* 68, *Aralia nudicaulis. . .* shotbush, spignet, sweet root.

3 A **licorice B1** (here: *Glycyrrhiza lepidota*).

1922 *Amer. Botanist* 28.74, Our "wild licorice" (*G[lycyrrhiza] lepidota*) is called "American licorice", "[u]licorice root", "sweet root", and "sweet wood". **1947** *Joplin Globe* (MO) 30 Nov sec B 7/4, Licorice candy is made from juice taken from the roots of the "sweet-root" plant cultivated in southern Europe, Louisiana and California.

4 =**sweet cicely.**

1882 *Amer. Jrl. Pharmacy* 54.149, *Osmorrhiza Longistylis. . .* The roots and rhizoma possess a strong aromatic odor and taste, recalling those of anise. . . The plant is commonly known as Sweet Cicely, Sweet

Root, Paregoric Root, Sweet Anise. **1900** in 1995 Millersville Univ. Center for PA Ger. Studies *Jrl.* Fall 11, In the afternoon I went over to Carrie and we went back to their woods to gather sweet-root. [*DARE* Ed: This quot may refer instead to another sense.] **1937** U.S. Forest Serv. *Range Plant Hdbk.* W137-2, Sweet anise. . . is by far the most important range plant of the sweetroot (*Osmorhiza*) genus. . . The English name most commonly used for plants of this genus is probably sweet cicely, although that name is better restricted to the Old World umbellifer genus *Myrrhis.* Sweetroot is suggested as appropriate and more distinctive for the genus *Osmorhiza,* whose name means fragrant root. **1984** MO Bot. Garden *Annals* 71.1149, *Osmorhiza occidentalis. . .* Root system deep, extensively branched, the roots with a strong, heavy anise-like fragrance. . . *Common names.* Bald cicely, Mountain sweet cicely, Sheep cicely, Sierra sweet cicely, Sweetanise, Sweetroot, Western sweet cicely, Western sweetroot.

5 See quots.

1926 *DN* 5.404 **Ozarks,** *Sweet-root. . .* The tips of seedling hickory roots, often eaten by children. **1963** Allen *Legends & Lore S. IL* 168 **csIL,** Sweet roots were those of young hickory sprouts up to about two feet tall but often having a taproot three feet or more long. . . Pulling sweet roots was done only in spring when the ground was thoroughly water-logged and soft, and the roots had a good stock of sugar stored to start new growth. The gathered roots were roasted in a fire. . . After roasting, the bark was peeled and the roots were chewed.

sweet sage n West
1 Any of several **sagebrushes 1;** see quots.

1851 in 1895 Geographische Gesellschaft Bern *Jahresbericht 1894* 56 **ND,** Ohne Räucherung mit Sweet sage (Wermut, Artemisia) an keinen Schlaf in den Zimmern zu denken. [=There is no hope of sleeping in the rooms unless one smokes them [=mosquitoes] with sweet sage (wormwood, Artemisia).] **1921** *Bot. Gaz.* 71.467 **UT,** Sweet sage (*Artemisia discolor* [=*A. michauxiana*]). **1937** *Mth. Weather Rev.* 65.291 **cUT,** Yellowbrush (*Chrysothamnus lanceolatus*) and "sweet sage" (*Artemisia incompta* [=*A. ludoviciana* subsp *i.*]), together with weeds, sometimes form a complete cover. **1941** *Ecological Monogr.* 11.274 **AZ,** *Artemisia mexicana* Willd. [=*A. ludoviciana* subsp *m.*]—Sweet Sage. **2005** *Indian Country Today* (Oneida NY) 15 June sec B 1 (Internet), **AZ,** Past the twisted juniper trees and sweet sage that scent the breezes after summer rains, the road leads to Monument Valley and the monoliths of red sandstone.

2 =**winter fat.**

1889 Davenport Acad. Nat. Sci. *Proc.* 6.272, This species [of grasshopper] is said . . to feed solely upon *Eurotia lanata* or sweet sage or winter-fat as it is variously known. **1913** (1979) Barnes *Western Grazing* 57, The forage is greatly augmented by the great sage family, especially the sweet sage or 'winter fat' (Eurotia lanata). **2006** *DARE* File—Internet **TX,** *Winterfat, Common Winter Fat, Roemeria, Lamb's Tail, Sweet-sage, White-sage, Feather-sage—Krascheninnikovia lanata.*

sweet salad n Cf **salad B1**
A **Solomon's seal 1** (here: *Polygonatum biflorum*).

2001 *Smoky Mt. News* (Waynesville NC) 28 Mar (Internet), But if you attend a community club potluck in the spring on reservation lands, there's every chance you'll also have an opportunity to try other potherbs as well. . . Stacey salad (small-flowered phacelia, "Phacelia dubia"), sweet salad (Solomon's-seal, "Polygonatum biflorum") . . are collected as young plants, cleaned, and then parboiled or fried or both.

sweet scabious n
1 Std: an introduced and sometimes naturalized **scabious 1** (here: *Scabiosa atropurpurea*). [*OED2* 1789 →]

2 A **fleabane:** either *Erigeron annuus* or *E. philadelphicus.* Cf **scabious 2**

1828 Rafinesque *Med. Flora* 1.162, *Erigeron Philadelphicum. . . Vulgar Names*—Skevish, Scabish, Sweet Scabious. **1843** Torrey *Flora NY* 2.1.355, *Erigeron annuum. . .* Sweet Scabious. Daisy, etc. **1930** *Syracuse Herald* (NY) 15 May 20/7, There is one kind of daisy—known as the sweet scabious or "daisy fleabane"—which is dried and made into flea powder. **1937** U.S. Forest Serv. *Range Plant Hdbk.* W67, Annual wild-daisy (*E[rigeron] annuus*) and Philadelphia wild-daisy, misnamed sweet scabious (*E. philadelphicus*) . . are other wild-daisies with similar properties. **2006** *DARE* File—Internet **nAL,** A close fleabane relative is Sweet Scabious (Erigeron annuus) which has less than 100 rays and stem leaves that are not clasping.

sweet-scented grape n

A **frost grape** (here: *Vitis vulpina*).
1830 Rafinesque *Med. Flora* 2.132, *V[itis] odoratissima.* . . Sweet scented Grape. . . flowers very sweet. **1850** Emerson *Rept. Trees & Shrubs* 470 **MA,** The River Grape. Sweet Scented Grape. **1874** *Daily NV State Jrl.* (Reno) 20 June 1/4, Some twenty years ago there was a variety known as the sweet-scented grape, which never bore fruit, and was valued solely for its exceedingly sweet flowers, but seems unfortunately to have gone out of cultivation. **1903** Porter *Flora PA* 208, *Vitis vulpina.* . . Riverside or Sweet-Scented Grape. . . Along rocky river banks. **2006** *DARE* File—Internet, The most widely distributed of all native North American grapes. . . Sweet-Scented Grape . . botanically . . Vitis Vulpina (Linnaeus).

sweet-scented shrub See **sweet shrub**

sweet-scented sumac(h) n   Also *sweet sumac(h)*
=**fragrant sumac.**
1843 Torrey *Flora NY* 1.131, *Rhus aromatica.* Sweet-scented Sumach. . . Dry rocky hills and gravelly banks. **1847** Wood *Class-Book* 203, *R[hus] aromatica.* . . Sweet Sumac. . . A small, aromatic shrub. . . Drupes red, acid. **1910** Graves *Flowering Plants* 269 **CT,** *Rhus canadensis* [=*R. aromatica*]. . . Sweet-scented Sumach. **1931** *Ecological Monogr.* 1.138 **OK,** The sweet scented sumac (*Schmaltzia crenata*), which is the least common of the sumacs, occur[s] on dry, frequently rocky slopes. **1940** Clute *Amer. Plant Names* 126, *R[hus] Canadensis.* . . Sweet-scented sumach, sweet sumach. **2002** in **2006** *DARE* File—Internet **MO,** Deer will graze on. . . borage, bugle and candytuft through the year; and on lungwort, periwinkle and sweet sumac in the winter months.

sweet shrub n   Pronc-spp *sweet s(w)ub*   Also *sweet-scented shrub*
A shrub of the genus *Calycanthus*, esp **Carolina allspice.** Also called **bubbybush 1;** for other names of var spp see **mountain spicewood, spicebush 4, spicewood 3, strawberry shrub 2, vinegar bush, wild poppy 2**
1786 (1978) Washington *Diaries* 3.53 **VA,** Planted . . 6 of the Sweet scented, or aromatic shrub in my Shrubberies. **1809** Ramsay *Hist. SC* 2.594, Among these are the locust, . . the wild rose, and the sweet shrub. **1830** Rafinesque *Med. Flora* 2.203, Sweet Shrub, Allspice. . . Much esteemed for the blossoms, smelling like Pine-apple. The bark is aromatic, similar to cinnamon. **1893** *Jrl. Amer. Folkl.* 6.141 **eMA,** *Calycanthus floridus,* sweet-scented shrub. **1898** Lloyd *Country Life* 74 **AL,** When we boys and girls went rovin after sweetshrubs. **1899** (1912) Green *VA Folk-Speech* 432, Sweet-shrub. . . Sweet-*swub*. Calycanthus. **1909** *DN* 3.378 **eAL, wGA,** Sweet-s(hr)ub. . . *Calycanthus floridus,* the sweet-scented shrub; also the blossom of this plant. "We got a whole pocket full of sweet subs." . . The children tie the blossoms in their handkerchiefs and keep them until they 'mellow.' **1942** *TX Ag. Exper. Sta. Bulletin* 608.52 **TX,** *Calycanthus floridus.* Sweet-Scented-Shrub, Spice-Bush. . . Fragrant, reddish brown flowers. **1960** Williams *Walk Egypt* 107 **GA,** Why, it was sweet shrub—bubby blossoms, the old folks called them, from their sweet reddish-brown puckers like a woman's nipples. **1968** *DARE* FW Addit **LA**21, Sweet shrub = common local name for *Calycanthus.* **2006** *DARE* File—Internet **NJ,** The fragrance comes from an old shrub that we planted more than 35 years ago. Our Calycanthus floridus or sweet shrub as we call it may also be known as Carolina allspice [etc].

sweet slumber n
=**bloodroot 1.**
1896 *Jrl. Amer. Folkl.* 9.181 **PA,** *Sanguinaria Canadensis,* . . sweet slumber. **1968** *Foxfire* Summer 50, Bloodroot (Sanguinaria) is possibly the most common of the sang-sign plants. . . This is the "red-coonroot" of the mountains. . . Known as "tterwort" [sic for *tetterwort*] or "sweet-slumber" or "she-roots", the dried rootstocks were ground and used in an infusion to relieve pains of burns. **2000** in **2006** *DARE* File—Internet, *Sanguinaria canadensis.* . . It's [sic] common name Sweet Slumber most likely comes from the fact that it is of the Poppy family and contains Protopine, an alkaloid also found in Opium, thus giving it mild narcotic effects.

sweetsop n   [*OED2* 1696 →]
A **custard apple 1** (here: *Annona squamosa*).
1832 (1833) Kenrick *New Amer. Orchardist* 369, Custard Apple. . . Sweet sop (*A. squamosa*). **1859** (1968) Bartlett *Americanisms* 467, Sweet-Sop. (*Annona squamosa.*) **1908** Britton *N. Amer. Trees* 394,

Sweetsop from *A. squamosa.* **1940** Brown *Amer. Cooks* 113 **FL,** Sweetsop or sugar apple. **1964** Will *Hist. Okeechobee* 35 **FL,** The Anona family of tropical trees includes those with such tasty fruits as . . Sweet Sop. **2001** *S. FL Sun–Sentinel* (Ft. Lauderdale) 7 Oct 1 (Internet), Trees that will be available for purchase will include akee, allspice, avocado, carambola, cinnamon, coconut, guava, . . mango, soursop and sweetsop.

sweet soup n   Also *Scandinavian* (or *Norwegian*) *sweet soup* [Norw *søtsuppe*, Sw *sötsoppa*]   **WI, Upper MW**
=**fruit soup.**
1959 *Oshkosh Daily Northwestern* (WI) 21 Dec 28/3, I don't remember that mother ever made any special dishes at Christmas time, but I used to like her sweet soup made with sago and raisins. **1969** *DARE* (Qu. H36, *Kinds of soup*) Inf **WI**76, Sweet soup—cherry or raspberry juice and prunes, raisins, and little round tapioca—now called fruit soup. **1972** *Manitowoc Herald–Times* (WI) 30 Nov sec 2 5/2 **SD,** Since Augustanans are "slightly partial" to Norwegian delicacies, the large Scandinavian booth will appropriately have the largest menu. Lefse, sweet soup, rommegrot . . spritz, and a variety of other cookies and coffee will be served. **1977** Anderson *Grass Roots Cookbook* 204 **nwMN,** Scandinavian Sweet Soup. . . Although called a soup, this is actually a fruit pudding dessert. "It is considered a great delicacy," says Mrs. Kaupang. "In the old days, we always brought a big container of sweet soup to new mothers. Now people just buy gifts." **2004** *DARE* File—Internet **cwWI,** Sot Suppe (Norwegian Sweet Soup). . . I grew up in west central Wisconsin. . . When my mother was a child, sweet soup was a traditional part of Christmas Eve. . . Sweet Soup is made with dried fruit and tapioca.

sweet spire n
=**Virginia willow.**
1928 *Amer. Midland Naturalist* 11.365 **Long Is. NY,** *Itea virginica.* . . Sweetspire [grown under cultivation]. **1939** FWP *Guide NJ* 20, The sweetspire has spikes of bell-shaped white blossoms in summer, and brilliant crimson foliage in autumn. **1953** Greene–Blomquist *Flowers South* 46, Sweet-spire . . *Itea virginica.* **1976** Bruce *How to Grow Wildflowers* 125, Growing in the same sort of locations as Trumpet Honeysuckle is *Itea virginica,* the Tassel-white, Virginia-willow, or Sweetspire, a deciduous shrub of six feet or so. **2005** *St. Joseph News–Press* (MO) 22 Sept (Internet), For a plant that can give you color in the spring and fall, Mr. Hayes suggests Little Henry Itea, also called Sweet Spire. It grows into a shrub 3 feet tall with small scented flowers in the spring.

sweet spirits of cats a-fighting n   Cf *DS* DD21c
Moonshine whiskey.
1969 *DARE* Tape **GA**72, We have a variety of names for this homemade whiskey in this county. . . sweet spirits of cats a-fighting. **1974** Dabney *Mountain Spirits* 25 **GA,** Just about the wildest name for corn whiskey is the expression coined by an old-timer in Rabun County, Georgia: "sweet spirits of cats a fightin'." **1985** Wilkinson *Moonshine* 28 **neNC,** "After that they'd serve you North Carolina Corn." It is called . . sweet spirits of cats a-fighting.

sweet-stem n   Cf *vara dulce* 1
A **bee brush** (here: *Aloysia macrostachya*) native to Texas.
1960 Vines *Trees SW* 887, Sweet-stem . . Aloysia macrostachya. **2003** in **2006** *DARE* File—Internet **TX,** *Aloysia macrostachya,* Sweet Stem, Vara dulce. This is a thornless plant, with soft leaves. **2006** Ibid **TX,** *Vara Dulce,* Sweet-stem . . Aloysia macrostachya. . . Its leaves are larger and more hairy than those of whitebrush (A. gratissima) and have a strong scent reminiscent of thyme or oregano when crushed.

sweet sub See **sweet shrub**

sweet sucker n

1 A **chubsucker 1:** either *Erimyzon oblongus* or *E. sucetta.*
1877 *OH State Bd. Ag. Annual Rept. for 1876* 191, *T[eretulus] oblongus* [=*Erimyzon o.*]. . Creek Fish, Chub Sucker, Sweet Sucker. **1884** Goode *Fisheries U.S.* 1.614, The Chub Sucker—*Erimyzon sucetta.* The "Chub Sucker," "Sweet Sucker," or "Creek-fish" is one of the most abundant and widely diffused of the Suckers, being found from Maine to Texas. **1891** *Newark Daily Advocate* (OH) 16 Feb [4]/4 (newspaperarchive.com), Nearly one-third of the fish caught in these nets are sweet suckers, which never bite at a hook, yet are a fair pan fish. **1943** Eddy–Surber *N. Fishes* 113, *Western Creek Chubsucker* [=*Erimyzon oblongus*] (Sweet Sucker, Pin Minnow). . . A small sucker rarely exceeding 10 inches in length. **2002** in **2006** *DARE* File—Internet **TN,**

Creek Chubsucker—Erimyzon oblongus. . . It is also known as the chubsucker, and sweet sucker.

2 =**Missouri sucker.**

 1902 Jordan–Evermann *Amer. Fishes* 44, Gourd-seed Sucker; Black-horse—*Cycleptus elongatus.* . . Besides the vernacular names given above, it is also known as "Missouri sucker," "sweet sucker," and "suckerel."

sweet sumac(h) See **sweet-scented sumac(h)**

sweet Susan n

=**garden catchfly.**

 1891 *Jrl. Amer. Folkl.* 4.147 **NH,** Silene armeria had only the name *Sweet Susan.*

sweet swub See **sweet shrub**

sweet syringa n Cf **syringa**

A **mock orange 1b;** see quots.

 1845 Page *Prairiedom* 124 **TX,** The . . honeysuckle, passion-flower and sweet syringa, everywhere blossom and diffuse their delicious fragrance through the air. **1871** Colt *Tourist's Guide Empire State* 27 **NY,** The breezes are more odorous of sweet syringa blossoms than any breezes of city or country which you ever enjoyed before. **1886** *Elyria Republican* (OH) 6 May [3]/5 (newspaperarchive.com), The sweet syringa was soon about to open its fragrant petals to the rejoicing world. **1903** Peet *Trees* 7, Mock Orange or Sweet Syringa—*Philadelphus coronarius. Ibid* 34, You will come on your left, after passing a fine bush of the sweet syringa, to a very interesting shrub. **1951** *Traverse City Rec.-Eagle* (MI) 9 Jan 4/3, We can smell the lilac and sweet syringa bushes from our porches come next May. **1967** *DARE* FW Addit **SC49,** *Philadelphus inodorus*—sweet syringa. **1968** *Appleton Post–Crescent* (WI) 30 Jan A/1, The time to do it is when buds appear on the apricot tree, the forsythia bush, . . the sweet syringa bush or any other early-blooming bushes and trees.

sweet tea n chiefly Sth Cf **unsweet tea**

Pre-sweetened iced tea.

 1989 Wier *Place for Outlaws* 123 **AL,** Mama's sweet tea is *real* sweet. She puts the sugar in while the tea's hot and stirs it in good. **1994** *Post–Std.* (Syracuse NY) 27 Sept Orange Insider sec 6/1, There is something likable about this football team. There is also something that drives you to eat grits and drink sweet tea on Sunday morning. **1996** *Syracuse Herald–Jrl.* (NY) 2 June sec AA 1/4 se**AL,** The front porch was a place to sip sweet tea, play card games, braid hair and avoid neighborhood bullies. **1997** Myers *Ming & I* 171 c**NC,** We both asked for sweet tea—the Carolina term for iced tea with sugar. **1999** *DARE* File—Internet **AL,** Tea that isn't in a cup and isn't hot is *sweet tea.* When offered "tea" without a qualifier in northern AL or in Montgomery, the question, "Ice(d) tea?" gets you "Yes Ma'am, sweet tea." *Ibid,* In the Mid-South you will generally hear "ice tea." . . Then if you ask for ice tea, you have to say whether you want sweet tea or not. Sweet tea already has sugar or artificial sweeteners added. [*Ibid,* And sweet tea is the default if you do order 'ice tea,' at least in eastern Georgia and western South Carolina. Only if requested could someone possibly receive unsweetened tea.] **2000** Kingsolver *Prodigal Summer* 410 s**Appalachians,** "I could give you some lemonade or iced tea before you go home." "Sweet tea would hit the spot," he said. **2003** *Marysville Jrl.-Tribune* (OH) 26 Mar 5/6 **GA,** Rep. John Neal, D-Atlanta, and four co-sponsors filed a bill . . that would make it a misdemeanor "of a high and aggravated nature" not to offer sweet tea in any Georgia restaurant that serves iced tea. **2003** in 2005 *DARE* File—Internet **GA,** After getting back from a business trip to Dallas, I was having southern sweet tea withdrawls [sic]. . . Put the water and tea bags in a pot . . and allow to come to a boil. . . remove the pot from the burner, remove the tea bags and as it is cooling add the sugar. Make sure to add the sugar while it is still hot, otherwise you will not get southern sweet tea . . it will taste more like the yankee stuff.

sweet tree n

1 A **black maple** (here: *Acer nigrum*).

 1822 Eaton *Botany* 154, [*Acer*] *nigrum* . . Sweet tree, black maple. . . Large tree, affording almost as much sugar as the last [=*Acer saccharinum*]. **1857** MI State Ag. Soc. *Trans. for 1856* 8.417, Acer. . . nigrum, . . Sweet tree. Black maple.

2 A **sugar maple** that produces sap with a higher than average sugar content; see quots.

 1880 Amer. Assoc. Advancement Sci. *Proc.* 235 **IN,** When I was a boy there was, on my father's farm, a maple tree, which we, in honor of

its excellence, had named the sweet tree. . . I sent for a specimen of the water from this tree and found the percentage of sugar to be 4.30. **1943** *Berkshire Eve. Eagle* (Pittsfield MA) 7 Aug 1/7 **NH,** Two members of the University of New Hampshire's agricultural experiment station are working on . . raising maple trees with a higher percentage of sugar than the average. . . The idea originated from the oft-told farmer's tale of "sweet" trees—trees that gave more sugar than the average. . . A boasted "sweet" tree at Dublin, N.H., tested at 7.5 and another at Georgia Mills, 6.5. **2002** *Washington Post* (DC) 20 Feb sec F 1 (Internet), Sugarmakers are clamoring for "sweet trees"—sugar maple saplings bred by Cornell University to have sap with a higher than usual percentage of sugar.

sweetvetch n

Std: a plant of the genus *Hedysarum.* Also called **jointpod;** for other names of var spp see **Eskimo potato, Indian ~ m, licorice root 1, mashu, wild potato 2c**

sweet viburnum n

A **nannyberry 1** (here: *Viburnum lentago*).

 1824 Bigelow *Florula Bostoniensis* 115, *Viburnum lentago.* . . Sweet Viburnum. . . Fruit sweet to the taste. **1843** Torrey *Flora NY* 1.305, Sweet Viburnum. . . The fruit is rather palatable, especially after having been frozen. **1897** Sudworth *Arborescent Flora* 339 **RI, TN, NE,** *Viburnum lentago.* . . Sweet Viburnum. **1931** Harned *Wild Flowers Alleghanies* 469, *Sweet Viburnum* (V[iburnum] Lentago). **1966** Grimm *Recognizing Native Shrubs* 268, Sweet viburnum—*Viburnum lentago.* **1996** *Orlando Sentinel* (FL) 9 Nov 11 (Internet), Podocarpus, sweet viburnum, anise, cherry laurel [etc] . . make excellent evergreen hedges and screens. **2002** Torrey Bot. Soc. *Jrl.* 129.68, Sweet viburnum.

sweet walnut n NEng, NY

A **shagbark hickory** (here: *Carya ovata*).

 1869 Watson *Military & Civil Hist.* 367 **NY,** The sweet walnut is, however, widely scattered over various sections of the county [=Essex], and flourishes . . in the lovely tract that spreads from the cliffs of Lake George to Champlain. **1897** Sudworth *Arborescent Flora* 113 **VT,** *Hicoria ovata* [=*Carya o.*] . . Sweet Walnut. **1907** in 2003 *Post–Std.* (Syracuse NY) 4 May sec B 2/2, One of the pieces of wood in it [=a clock], a bit of sweet walnut, was taken from a pole that was raised when James K. Polk was nominated for president of the United States. **1924** *Star* (Kansas City MO) 20 Feb 11/7 **NY, NEng,** These timbers must not be confused with the yellow, or shellbark, hickory or the white, or butternut, hickory, which throughout New York and New England are commonly called sweet walnut and bitter walnut respectively. **1941** *LANE* Map 277 (*Walnut shell*) Other terms, not always defined: . . 2 infs, s**VT,** Sweet walnut. **1979** Erichsen-Brown *Med. N. Amer. Plants* 70, *Carya ovata.* . . Sweet or white walnut.

sweetweed n

=**marshmallow 1.**

 1974 (1977) Coon *Useful Plants* 183, *Althaea officinalis* . . Marshmallow, sweet weed, mortification root.

sweet white balsam See **white balsam 1**

sweet William n Cf **mock sweet William, wild ~**

Any of several flowers, as:

a Std: a **pink** n² **1** (here: *Dianthus barbatus*). [*OED2* 1573 →]

b =**phlox.**

 1849 Howitt *Our Cousins in OH* 12, There the children found . . phlox, or sweet-williams, as they were called in America. **1856** in 1862 Colt *Went to KS* 66, Picked another bouquet of . . Japan lilies, . . snake's-head, larkspurs . . prairie roses . . golden coreopsis, sweet William, and a variety of others. **1892** *Jrl. Amer. Folkl.* 5.101 **TX,** *Phlox pilosa,* sweetwilliam. **1897** *Ibid* 10.50 **OH,** *Phlox ovata,* . . sweet William. *Ibid* **MO,** *Phlox pilosa,* sweet William. *Ibid* **IN,** *Phlox* (all species), sweet William. *Ibid* se**MO,** *Phlox pilosa* and related species are confounded with *Verbena Aubletia* [=*V. canadensis*], and all called sweet William. **1929** Bell *Some Contrib. KS Vocab.* 193, Sweet william. . . A prairie flower, same as the *wild phlox.* . . Well known in the eastern part of the State. **1952** Gleason *New Britton & Brown* 3.94, *Phlox.* . . Sweet William. **1967–69** *DARE* FW Addit **AR44,** Sweet William—*Phlox maculata;* **KY,** Sweet Williams—wild blue phlox (*Phlox divaricata*). **1968** *DARE* (Qu. S26a, . . *Wildflowers.* . . *Roadside flowers*) Inf **IN28,** Sweet William = ground phlox; **TN33,** Sweet William—also called blue phlox.

c =Maltese cross.

1847 Wood *Class-Book* 192, *L[ychnis] Chalcedonica.* . . Sweet William. **1884** *Bot. Gaz.* 9.133 **MI**, About one in fifteen [students] discovered that although the leaves were opposite, a bud usually appears only in the axil of one of each pair of those of the Sweet William *(Lychnis).* **1892** *Jrl. Amer. Folkl.* 5.93 **sOH, VT**, *Lychnis chalcedonica,* sweet-william.

d A **meadowsweet 2** (here: *Filipendula rubra*).

1893 *Jrl. Amer. Folkl.* 6.141 **NY**, *Spiraea lobata* [=*Filipendula rubra*], sweet William.

e A **vervain:** either *Verbena bipinnatifida* or *V. canadensis.*

1896 *Jrl. Amer. Folkl.* 9.52 **swMO**, *Verbena Aubletia* [=*V. canadensis*], . . sweet William. . . Flowers have a sweetish taste when eaten, like the flowers of phlox. **1897** [see **b** above]. **1936** Whitehouse *TX Flowers* 117, Wild or Plains Verbena *(Verbena bipinnatifida)* is sometimes called sweet William, a name which properly belongs to the blue woodland phlox *(Phlox divaricata)* or to the clove pink. **1966** *DARE* (Qu. S11) Inf **OK**42, Sweet William—wild verbena (same flower, only one is tame). **1967** Dodge *Roadside Wildflowers* 60, Sweet william. . . *Verbena bipinnatifida.*

sweet William catchfly n   Cf **mock sweet William**

=**garden catchfly.**

1870 in 1871 Featherman *Rept. Bot. Surv. LA* 80, Silene armeria . . Sweet William Catchfly (introduced). **1913** *OH Naturalist* 13.182, *Silene armeria.* . . Sweet William Catchfly. . . flowers in flat cymes with petals rose-colored, white or purple. **1950** Gray–Fernald *Manual of Botany* 633, *S[ilene] armeria.* . . Garden- or Sweet-William-Catchfly, None-so-pretty. **2006** *DARE* File—Internet, Sweet William Catchfly. . . was established in American gardens in the 1820's. The broadside Bernard McMahon published in Philadelphia about 1804 offered seed for both red and white forms.

sweet Wilson n

A **saxifrage** n[2] (here: *Saxifraga virginiensis*).

1896 *Jrl. Amer. Folkl.* 9.187 **MA**, *Saxifraga Virginiensis,* . . sweet Wilson. . . Named by Mrs. Ward fifty years ago, to please Wilson Ward, who complained that there was a sweet William but no sweet Wilson. Name still extant.

sweet winter grape n

=**winter grape 3.**

1885 OH State Horticult. Soc. *Annual Rept. for 1884–85* 203, *Cinerea,* Ashy, or Sweet Winter Grape. **1920** *Torreya* 20.23, *Vitis cinerea.* . . Sweet winter grape. **1938** Van Dersal *Native Woody Plants* 287, *Vitis cinerea.* . . Sweet winter grape. **1969** U.S. Dept. Ag. *Ag. Hdbk. No. 356* 222, Pigeon or sweet winter grape, *V[itis] cinerea* . . has ashy gray leaves. **2003** in 2006 *DARE* File—Internet **TX**, *V[itis] cinerea,* the sweet winter grape, ripens from August through November, but prefers sandy and alluvial soils, not the limestone of Llano.

sweetwood n

1 A **juniper 1** (here: *Juniperus virginiana*); also the wood of this tree.   Cf **red cedar 1**

1891 *Newark Daily Advocate* (OH) 6 Mar [2]/4 (newspaperarchive.com), Each retiring statesman gets three trunks, but those of the senators are better made than those used by representatives, having brass hinges and sweetwood linings. **1940** (1978) Still *River of Earth* 123 **KY**, Grandma reached into the elbow-deep pockets, emptying them of cedar shavings. "Moths live hard where you keep sweetwood," she said. **1953** *Times Recorder* (Zanesville OH) 11 Dec sec B 15/2 **MD**, Then you must go to the marsh to cut sweet-wood switches for the foundation of the wreath. **1953** Randolph–Wilson *Down in Holler* 290 **Ozarks**, *Sweet-wood.* . . Red cedar. "She keeps them fine clothes in a sweet-wood chest, so the moths won't bother 'em."

2 Dried licorice root. [Calque of Ger *Süßholz* (PaGer *siesshols*)]

1900 *NY Teachers' Monogr.* 3.104 **NYC**, It is a very difficult thing to find one . . who would not rate standing in accordance with the amount of candy, sweet-wood or any other esteemed delicacy that is very often used as a weight in the scales of justice. **1913** *Meyer Brothers Druggist* 34.38 **ceMO**, Our older readers will recall the time when sweet wood was a common article for children. It is possible that history will repeat itself and that not only children but grown people as well will form the habit of chewing licorice. **1951** Reimann *Betw. Iron* 108 **nMI** (as of c1910), With what few pennies we were given or earned we bought penny stick candy, horehound, licorice, gum drops, hard mints, rock

candy, chocolate mounds of a doubtful nature, and sweetwood for chewing. **1990** *Reggeboge* 24.17 **sePA** (as of 1880), Licorice root . . was very sweet and we boys could chew a long time on a cent's worth of woody root. It was called "sweet wood."

3 See **sweet maple.**

swell v

Std senses, var forms.

1 infin: usu |swɛl|; also |swol|; pronc-sp *swole.*

c1938 in 1970 Hyatt *Hoodoo* 2.1483 [Black], Yo' gonna put 'em with misery now an' pains with de feet—prob'ly dey will swole where dey can't stand up. **1989** Pederson *LAGS Tech. Index* 283 **Gulf Region,** *Swell* . . [Infinitive:] 4 infs, [swol].

2 past: usu *swelled;* also:

a |swol(d), swʌl(d)|; pronc-spp *swole(d), swoll, swull(ed).* [*OED2 swole* "obs. pa. t. of *swell* v."]

1874 *Old & New* 10.610 **Sth** [Black], My heart heave and swole like it done bust. **1884** *Anglia* 7.253 [Black], To the regular forms of the Irregular verbs as used by the whites, the Negro adds the following forms of his own. . . *Pres.* swell—*Past.* swull. **1934** Hurston *Jonah's Gourd Vine* 125 **AL** [Black], When Ah seen *you*, mah heart swole up. **c1938** in 1970 Hyatt *Hoodoo* 1.228 **sAL** [Black], An' after dat mah legs swoled about dat large. **1940** in 1976 *Weevils in the Wheat* 295 **VA** [Black], Then his legs swoll all up and he couldn't walk none. **1944** [see **3b** below]. **1946** (1972) Mezzrow–Wolfe *Really Blues* 41, I almost busted the buttons off my vest, my chest swole up so much. **1953** Atwood *Survey of Verb Forms* 22, *Swell.* . . The preterite *swole* /swol/ occurs a few times . . in N. Eng., being more common in the Plymouth and Cape Cod areas than elsewhere. It is most common among the older groups, but not entirely confined to them. Elsewhere in the East there are scattered occurrences of *swole,* and in a few areas it shows some concentration. It occurs in about half the communities of e.S.C. (including Charleston); it is found in several contiguous communities (including Richmond) along the lower James Valley; and three informants in New York City use it. There are about 20 occurrences of *swoled* /swold/, widely scattered through all the major areas. . . Other forms that occur . . are . . *swull* /swʌl/, *swulled* /swʌld/. **1989** Pederson *LAGS Tech. Index* 283 **Gulf Region,** *Swell* . . [Preterite:] 118 infs, [swol]; 20 infs, [swold]; 3 infs, [swʌld]. **1997** *Isthmus* (Madison WI) 22 Aug 47/2, One participant said the mosquito "swoll up so big I could see his brand."

b |swoln(d)|; pronc-spp *swollened, swolned.*

1884 *Anglia* 7.253 [Black], *Pres.* swell—*Past.* . . swolned. **1953** Atwood *Survey of Verb Forms* 22, *Swell.* . . *Swollen* /swolən/ (as preterite) shows some 25 occurrences, nearly all in the S[outh] A[tlantic] S[tates]; it indicates some tendency to concentration in the southern Piedmont of Va. . . Other forms that occur . . *swollened* /swolənd/. **1989** Pederson *LAGS Tech. Index* 283, *Swell* . . [Preterite:] 24 infs, [swoln].

c |swɛldɪd|.   Cf **-ed suff 1**

1989 Pederson *LAGS Tech. Index* 283 **Gulf Region,** *Swell* . . [Preterite:] 1 inf, [swɛldɪd].

3 past pple, ppl adj: usu *swelled, swollen;* also:

a |swʌln, swulən|; pronc-sp *swullen.* [Cf *EDD swell* v. I.3]

1914 *DN* 4.113 **cKS**, *Swullen, p[articipial] a[djective]*—Swollen. **1953** Atwood *Survey of Verb Forms* 23, *Swell.* . . [The past participle] *swullen* /swʌlən/ shows a fairly high frequency in the Hudson Valley, n.N.J., s.e.Pa., and along the upper tributaries of the Ohio in w.Pa. **1989** Pederson *LAGS Tech. Index* 283, *Swell* . . [Past participle:] 2 infs, [swʌln]. **1997** *DARE* File, My wife, childhood in Crosby, MN, Michigan's UP, Upstate New York, and northern VT. says *swullen* with the vowel of foot. *Ibid,* My Milwaukee [WI] wife . . pronounce[s] the 'swullen' under discussion here [i.e., as [swulən]].

b |swol(d), 'swoldən|; pronc-spp *swole(d), swoll, swolden, swolt.* **esp Sth, S Midl**   See Map

1864 Wilson *Confederate Private* 44 **VA** (*Montgomery Coll.*), I was glad to heare from you thow sory to heare that you legs was swoled & paned you sow. **1870** Macrae *Americans* 234 **seNC** [Black], Sometimes my feet and ankles would be swole so I could scarce stand. **1895** *DN* 1.376 **seKY, eTN, wNC**, *Swole* = swollen. **1896** *Harper's New Mth. Mag.* 94.110 **LA**, I'd seem like a sort o' swole-up pin-cushion with needles a-stickin' in me all over. **1899** Chesnutt *Conjure Woman* 153 **csNC** [Black], De nex' mawnin' Lightnin' Bug's laigs wuz swoll' up wuss'n befo'. **1909** *DN* 3.405 **nwAR**, *Swole.* . . Swollen. "I hurt my foot yesterday an' its [sic] all swole up this morning." *Swoled.* . . Swollen. "His foot is all swoled up where he stuck a nail in it." **1929** Sale

Tree Named John 38 **MS** [Black], Dat baby's already sick en swole up. **1934** Carmer *Stars Fell on AL* 183 [Black], He had de swole head some seasons frum dat lick. **1944** *PADS* 2.13 **AL, SC, TN,** *Swole* [swol]: pret. and p.p. of *swell.* Deep South. Low popular. **1953** Atwood *Survey of Verb Forms* 23, Nearly all of those who use *swole* as the preterite . . give the past participle as *swollen;* only three use the leveled *swole-swole.* . . Other combinations that occur more or less in isolation are . . *swelled-swolden* /swoldən/, and *swelled-swole.* **1965–70** *DARE* (Qu. BB32, *If somebody had a swelling—for example, in his whole face . . "Last week his face was all _____."*) 39 Infs, **esp Sth, S Midl,** Swole (up); **GA**12, 23, **IL**143, **NY**200, Swoled (up). **1971** in 1993 Major *Calling the Wind* 344 **LA** [Black], I can see where Mama's been crying. Mama's face is swole. **1975** Newell *If Nothin' Don't Happen* 214 **nwFL,** My face were still swoll up and I always will believe one of my face bones had been busted. **1976** Garber *Mountain-ese* 90 **sAppalachians,** *Swolt* . . swelled—The colt's laig was swolt to twice it's [sic] regular size. **1981** Walker *You Can't* 14 [Black], Your lips be too swole to sing. **1983** *MJLF* 9.1.58 **ceKY** (as of 1956), *Swole up* . . swollen. **1984** Burns *Cold Sassy* 288 **nGA** (as of 1906), See yonder? . . Creek must of swole up after the last rain. **1989** Pederson *LAGS Tech. Index* 283 **Gulf Region,** *Swell* . . [Past participle:] 32 infs, [swol]; 4 infs, [swold].

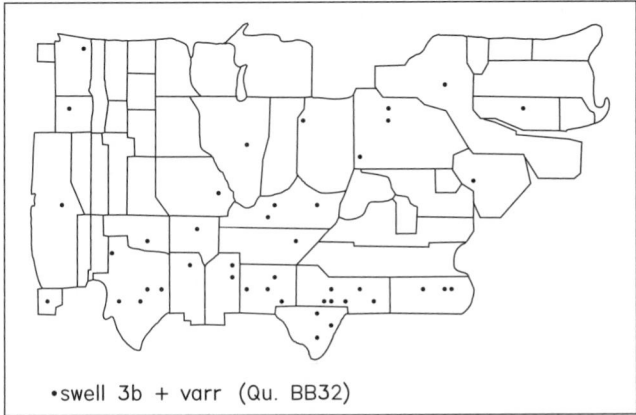

•swell 3b + varr (Qu. BB32)

c |swolņd|; pronc-sp *swollened.* Cf **-ed** suff **1**

    1969 *DARE* (Qu. BB32, *If somebody had a swelling—for example, in his whole face . . "Last week his face was all _____."*) Inf **KY**60, Swollened up. **1989** Pederson *LAGS Tech. Index* 283 **Gulf Region,** *Swell* . . [Past participle:] 1 inf, [swolņd].

swell-back (cutter or sleigh)   See **swell-body sleigh**

swellbelly n   chiefly **Long Is. NY**   Cf **swelltoad**

A **puffer** n[1] **1** (here: *Sphoeroides maculatus*).

    1905 Acad. Nat. Sci. Philadelphia *Proc. for 1904* 56.510 **Nantucket Is. MA,** *Spheroides maculatus.* . . "Swell-belly." . . Taken on the scup grounds. **1952** Cooke *One Man's Amer.* 144 **Long Is. NY,** Swell-bellies, I ought to say, are a pest-fish we catch around Long Island. They are more elegantly known as blowfish. **1991** *DARE* File **seNY,** Swell-belly = blowfish. **2000** in 2006 *DARE* File—Internet **eLong Is. NY,** Terry started serving blowfish occasionally 10 years ago. . . "My family," he said, "has been eating swellbellies since 1640." **2001** Jones *Working* 59 **eLong Is. NY** (as of c1925), I know it was skates because that was my job, to throw them back overboard. . . And swell bellies. Plenty of swell bellies, blowfish. You tickle their bellies; they swell up like a football. It was several years later they found you could eat them.

swell-body (sleigh) n   Also called *swell-back, swell-back cutter,* ~ *sleigh, swell-belly, swell-bodied cutter,* ~ *sleigh* **Nth hist**

=**Albany sleigh.**

    1870 *Hist. & Directory Kent Co. MI* 169, Grand Rapids Carriage Manufactory. . . Pat. Improved Swell Body Sleigh. **1883** *Oshkosh Daily Northwestern* (WI) 19 Sept 4/2, Display of . . carriages and . . sleighs. . . two-seated family swell body sleigh. **1884** *Eve. Observer* (Dunkirk NY) 27 Feb 2/3, When people were gathering at church in Millbrook, N.J., on Sunday night, a stranger, driving a . . pretty little swell-bodied cutter, drove up. **1895** *Newark Daily Advocate* (OH) 16 Jan 5/2, Sleighing parties are in vogue now. All kinds of vehicles are in use from the old pine sled of the farmer to the latest style three seated swell-bodied sleigh of the wealthy. **1928** *Decatur Eve. Herald* (IL) 13 Dec 19/5,

[Advt:] *Closing Out Sale.* . . 1 Swell body sleigh. **1930** Shoemaker *1300 Words* 53 **cPA Mts** (as of c1900), *Swell-belly*—An old-time one horse sleigh. **1943** *LANE* Map 573–74, *Sleighs,* horse-drawn and metal-shod, for passengers: . . *swell-body* [1 inf, **cCT**]. **1964** *Mansfield News-Jrl.* (OH) 2 Aug 12/6, At present he has a stick-seated road wagon . . a swell-body sleigh . . and two pony carts. **1967–70** *DARE* (Qu. N40b, . . *Sleighs for carrying people*) Inf **MI**64, One of the oldest was called swell-back; **NY**233, Swell-back cutter—shaped like swan, runners real high; **NJ**3, Swell-back sleigh; **ID**5, Swell-bodied cutter; (Qu. N40c, *Other kinds of sleighs*) Inf **NY**69, Swell-body—'twas worth anybody's life to ride, because the back was oval and you couldn't lean back in 'em. **1976** *WI Then & Now* Dec 2, The classic Albany (or Swellbody). . . sleighs . . were latter-day city cousins of the homemade, utilitarian sledges that provided most of the winter overland transportation in Wisconsin before railroads and roads.

swell-butt ash n   [See quot]

=**pumpkin ash.**

    1921 Deam *Trees IN* 276, *Fraxinus profunda*—Swell-Butt Ash. . . The preferred habitat of this species is inundated swamps, and when it grows in such situations it generally develops a base swollen to a point somewhat above the water level.

swell-butted adj   Cf *bottle-butted* (at **bottle butt**)

In logging: =**churn-butted.**

    1872 NH Supreme Judicial Court *Reports* 32.154 (as of 1848), That he cut about ten trees, which were small, swell-butted, knotty pines. **1905** U.S. Forest Serv. *Bulletin* 61.50 [Logging terms], *Swell butted.* As applied to a tree, greatly enlarged at the base. . . Syn.: bottle butted, churn butted. **1952** *Humboldt Std.* (Eureka CA) 23 May sec A 3/5, The logger panel could bring up such matters as . . swell butted logs (should they be long-butted). **1958** McCulloch *Woods Words* 186 **Pacific NW,** *Swell butted*—A tree with a large flaring base, such as Sitka spruce.

swellfish n   Cf **swelltoad**

1 A **puffer** n[1] **1,** esp *Sphoeroides maculatus.*

    1807 in 1815 MA Hist. Soc. *Coll.* 2d ser 3.55, The puff fish, or swell fish, or bellows fish, is a cartilaginous fish. It is seven inches long; and . . its proportions are those of a sculpion nearly. **1839** *Boston Jrl. Nat. Hist.* 2.513, Tetraodon turgidus [=*Sphoeroides maculatus*], Mitchell. The Swell Fish. Puffer. **1854** *NY Daily Times* (NY) 10 July [4]/4 (newspaperarchive.com), If you have two hooks to your line, bait one of them with a piece of clam, and you shall have a plenty of porgies, tomcod, flounders, bass to vary the feast, and more swell-fish, we will venture, than you will think to count. **1873** in 1878 Smithsonian Inst. *Misc. Coll.* 14.2.15, Chilichthys turgidus [=*Sphoeroides maculatus*]. . . Swell-fish. . . Cape Cod to Florida. **1899** [see **swelltoad**]. **1903** NY State Museum & Sci. Serv. *Bulletin* 60.621, The swellfish [= *Sphoeroides maculatus*] inhabits the Atlantic coast. . . In most localities the flesh is not eaten, but at Somers Point N.J. certain persons professed to find in it excellent food qualities. **1952** Tracy *Coast Cookery* 296, *Swellfish.* . . Also known as sea squab in some restaurants and fish markets. **1970** *DARE* (Qu. P13, . . *Ways of fishing . . besides the ordinary hook and line*) Inf **VA**47, Pound—used for kingfish, trout, and blowfish or swellfish. **1995** *NY Ed. Newsday* (NY) 24 May sec A 60/2, Whether you know it as puffer, northern puffer, balloon fish, swellfish, bellowfish, globefish, swell toad or just plain blowfish, *Sphaeroides maculatus* is a most uncommon fish. . . During the '50s and '60s they were so numerous that they were rated No. 1 on the pest list.

2 A **burfish,** usu *Chilomycterus schoepfi.*

    1884 Goode *Fisheries U.S.* 1.170, The Porcupine Fishes—*Diodontidae.* . . The best known is the Swell Fish of New England, *Chilomycterus geometricus* [=*C. schoepfi*]. These fishes are commonly known by such names as . . "Toad Fish." **1898** U.S. Natl. Museum *Bulletin* 47.1748, *Chylomycterus Schoepfi.* . . Swell-toad; Swellfish. . . The body is capable of considerable inflation, but less than is the case with the Tetraodonts. **1921** *Copeia* 99.73 **NY,** *Chilomycterus schoepfii.* Spiny Swellfish. Three adults were taken.

swelling toad n   chiefly **MD, VA**

=**swelltoad.**

    1895 *Eve. Bulletin* (Decatur IL) 2 Aug 4/3, *Virginia's Swelling Toad.* . . [T]he greatest natural history oddity to be found along the Atlantic coast of the United States is the swelling toad. . . It . . is most common along the coasts of Virginia, Maryland and North Carolina. **1939** Hench Coll. **VA, MD,** Swelling toad—a fish on the Potomac. **1966** *Eve. Capital* (Annapolis MD) 8 July 15/3, At any time, the rough fish: carp, garfish, skate, . . shark, oyster toads, swelling toads (blowfish), . . may be taken in the tidal waters of Maryland by spear gun and spear. **1972** *Daily Times* (Salisbury MD) 11 Aug 13/3, Puffing, or swelling, toad catches were numerous this week. . . The strip of white meat down this unusual sea creature's back is a delicacy for many. **1976** Warner *Beautiful Swimmers* 13 **Chesapeake Bay,** The blowfish, called "swelling toads" by the watermen. **2002** *Virginian–Pilot* (Norfolk VA) 7 Nov sec E 9 (Internet), We had . . swelling toads, which inflate to amazing dimensions when brought into the boat. **2005** *DARE* File—Internet **VA,** That photo on the 2nd page is a swelling toad. If you get some, don't eat them—they're ugly!

swelltoad n **chiefly Mid and S Atl** Cf **blow-toad, puff ~, sucking ~, swellbelly, swellfish, swelling toad, toadfish a**
A **puffer** n[1] **1,** usu of the genus *Sphoeroides* or *Chilomycterus*.
  1878 U.S. Natl. Museum *Proc.* 1.366 **NC,** *Chilomycterus geometricus* [=*C. schoepfi*]. Swell-toad. . . Sold by small boys as curiosities. **1894** *Eve. Democrat* (Warren PA) 21 Mar [3]/3 (newspaperarchive.com), What is called the "swell" toad on the Carolina and Georgia coast is in his natural state only about six inches in length and four inches across the back, but he is endowed with wonderful expansive facilities. **1899** *Science* new ser 10.880, *Spheroides spengleri.* . . *Swell-fish; Swell-toad.* The normal habitat of this species is Florida and Texas to Brazil; the only northern locality from which it is recorded is Woods Hole, where it was observed only in September and October, 1877. **1919** *Frederick Post* (MD) 29 Oct 3/5 **FL,** During the day they brought up a specimen of the "swell toad" or burfish variety. **1968** *DARE* (Qu. P1, . . *Kinds of freshwater fish . . caught around here . . good to eat*) Inf **MD40,** Swelltoad. **1984** *DARE* File **Chesapeake Bay** [Watermen's vocab], Swell toad. **2000** Hall *Selling Fish* 21 **MD,** Homely as they were, swell toads were always a special fish for me, because my grandfather used to blow them up like balloons, or at least I thought he did. **2006** *DARE* File—Internet **Atl and Gulf coasts,** *[Local Name:]* Swell Toad—*[Common Name:]* Northern Puffer—*[Scientific Name:]* Sphoeroides maculatus.

sweltersome adj, adv [Engl dial; cf **-some** suff]
Sweltering(ly).
  1895 *DN* 1.374 **seKY, eTN, wNC,** *Sweltersome:* sweltering. **1969** *DARE* (Qu. B3, *If a day is very hot . . it's [a]* ———) Inf **KY28,** Sweltersome hot.

swengletree See **swingletree**

swet See **sweat Aa**

swiddle v [Cf *EDD swittle* v.[1] 2 "To twirl like an implement in boring a hole"; v.[2] 1 "To wash or lave gently; to dabble in water"; v.[3] 1 "To . . whittle a stick and leave the pieces lying about."] **esp S Midl**
See quots; hence n *swiddling stick.*
  1913 *DN* 4.44, Swiddle. . . To scatter, dribble. "Don't swiddle the sugar over the table," said a mother to her little girl, who, in attempting to help herself, had scattered sugar over the tablecloth. **1927** *DN* 5.478 **Ozarks,** Swiddle. . . To stir, to dip. "He kep' a-swiddlin' his finger in th' puddin'." **1936** *AmSp* 11.317 **Ozarks,** Swiddle. . . To rinse. A woman often speaks of *swiddlin'* out a few clothes. Near Zinc, Ark., an old woman *swiddled* some molasses off of her finger into a guest's coffee. **1950** *SW Rev.* 35.179 **Lower Missip Valley,** There was no one in the kitchen except Gran, who was swiddling water meaninglessly over some boiling eggs. **1988** Kilgore *Coll. & Recoll.* 1.50 **AL,** Swiddlin' stick— limb used to stir clothes boilin' in the wash pot.

swift n [*EDD swift* sb.[1] 4 "A newt; a small lizard"]
1 also with adj; also *swift lizard:* A **lizard** n **1** of the genus *Sceloporus,* esp a **fence lizard 1** (here: *S. undulatus*). [See quot 1842] For other names of var of these see **pine lizard, rock ~, sagebrush ~, scaly ~, scorpion B2** Cf **sand swift 2**
  1778 Carver *Travels N. Amer.* 489, The Swift Lizard is about six inches long, and has four legs and a tail. Its body which is blue, is prettily striped with dark lines shaded with yellow. . . It is so remarkably agile that . . it might more justly be said to vanish, than to run away. **1837** (1962) Williams *Territory FL* 66, The Swift, lacerta veloxa [sic], is from five to six inches long, of an ash color, striped and dotted with brown. The tail long, of a deep green, and extremely brittle; when broken off it is re-produced in a short time. **1842** DeKay *Zool. NY* 3.31, The Brown Swift . . is also called the *Brown Scorpion,* and its activity has doubtless suggested the name of *Swift.* **1887** Custer *Tenting* 122 **TX,** The lizards the Texans call swifts . . also haunted the tangles of the moss. **1919** *Copeia* 72.64, The common swift (*Sceloporus undulatus*) often "plays

possum" or feigns death when caught. **1941** Writers' Program *Guide AR* 17, Reptiles other than snakes are . . lizards (skinks and swifts). **1946** *Athens Messenger* (OH) 26 July 5/7, Dr. William C. Stehr, Ohio University Zoology Department, said the reptile probably belongs to the "Fence-Swift" lizard species which is common to this section. This particular animal is gray with blue scales and ranges from five to six inches. **1998** *Intelligencer* (Doylestown PA) 2 Feb sec A 3/5, The list of Montgomery County wildlife . . includes . . two kinds of lizards—the fence swift and the five-lined skink. **2005** *Knoxville News–Sentinel* (TN) 25 Apr sec B 1 (Internet), [Caption:] Fence swift.
2 Another small **lizard** n **1:** usu a **whiptail 2** (here: *Cnemidophorus sexlineatus*) or a **skink** (here: *Eumeces fasciatus*); see quots. Cf **sand swift 1, swift-jack**
  1792 Belknap *Hist. NH* 3.174, Swift, *Lacerta fusciata?* [sic; prob = *Eumeces fasciatus*] **1894** U.S. Natl. Museum *Proc.* 17.321, *Cnemidophorus Sexlineatus.* . . This swift . . is so quick and active, running through the shrubs and disappearing "quick as a flash of lightning." **1909** *DN* 3.365 **eAL, wGA,** *Sand-sifter.* . . A small fleet-footed lizard. Also called *racer, swift, swift-jack, swift-jenny.* **1937** *Amer. Midland Naturalist* 18.294 **seOK,** *Cnemidophorus sexlineatus sexlineatus.* . . The swift is equally abundant and as widely distributed as *Sceloporus,* but it is more a form of the open [areas].

swift fox n Also *swift* [See quot 1947]
=**kit fox.**
  1845 *Amer. Whig Rev.* 1.377, He [=Audubon] had several new and curious animals along with him, . . and now they looked like old acquaintances to us, and we soon got up an intimacy with the Swift Fox, the Snarling Badger and the Rocky Mountain Deer. **1879** U.S. Natl. Museum *Bulletin* 14.2 **West,** *Vulpes velox.* . . Kit Fox or Swift Fox. **1905** *Pinedale Roundup* (WY) 3 May 1/2, Of the animals of prey, in search of which the hunter can spend many pleasant hours are to be found the red, gray and silver gray, cross and swift fox . . , wild cat and mountain lion. **1947** Cahalane *Mammals* 235, *Vulpes Velox* and *V. Macrotis.* . . The kit fox has one superiority over the other foxes. It can run faster. . . This ability has been responsible for one of its common names,—"swift fox," or, frequently, just "swift." **1968** *DARE* (Qu. P32, . . *Other kinds of wild animals*) Inf **CA62,** Desert fox—also called a swift—weigh five or six pounds, also called kit fox. **1980** Whitaker *Audubon Field Guide Mammals* 548, The names Kit Fox and Swift Fox are used interchangeably for both species [=*Vulpes macrotis* and *V. velox*]. **2002** *Amer. Midland Naturalist* 148.320, The swift fox (*Vulpes velox*) is a small (<3.0 kg) canid that occurs in the short grass prairie from eastern New Mexico and northwestern Texas to southern Alberta and Saskatchewan.

swift hawk n
=**Cooper's hawk.**
  1874 NY Acad. Sci. *Annals Lyceum Nat. Hist.* 10.380, *N[isus] Cooperi.* . . Cooper's Hawk; "Swift Hawk;" "Quail Hawk." **1944** Hausman *Amer. Birds* 517, Hawk, Swift—see Hawk, Cooper's.

swift-jack n Also *swift-jenny* **chiefly Sth** Cf **jackswift,** *rusty jack* (at **rusty lizard**)
Either a **whiptail 2** (here: *Cnemidophorus sexlineatus*) or a **skink** (here: *Eumeces fasciatus*); see quots.
  1867 *Harper's New Mth. Mag.* 34.333 **VA,** In one [jar] were half a dozen lizards of all sorts, with tails four inches long—lizards blue, green, yellow, striped, spotted. "Hard work I had to catch these swift jacks," said Will, "They run so fast." **1897** CA Acad. Sci. *Occas. Papers* 5.136, The Desert Whiptail Lizard or "Swift Jack" is common in many parts of the Mojave and Colorado Deserts and the Great Basin, but does not range farther west. **1909** *DN* 3.378 **eAL, wGA,** *Swift(-jack).* . . Same as *sand-sifter.* Also *swift-jenny.* **1956** McAtee *Some Dialect NC* 45, *Swift-jack* . . the lizard called "scorpion," which see. [*Ibid* 38, *Scorpion* . . the blue-tailed skink (*Eumeces fasciatus*).] **1959** McAtee *Oddments* 4 **cnNC,** Go about like a swiftjack (a kind of lizard) . . that is rapidly.

swift lizard See **swift 1**

swift water n **scattered, but more freq Sth, S Midl, NEast**
See Map
=**quickwater.**
  1805 (1905) Clark *Orig. Jrls. Lewis & Clark Exped.* 6.7 **VA,** On the river passing several small rapids and swift water the probable decent [sic] in this instance four feet. **1858** *Harper's New Mth. Mag.* 16.494 **CT,** Swift water floods the valleys. **1882** *Ibid* 66.3 **Pacific NW,** The navigation of the Upper Columbia and Snake rivers is difficult but not

dangerous, though to one unaccustomed to swift water it seems perilous. **1915** *Syracuse Herald* (NY) 14 Sept 6/6, She threw herself into the feeder and went through the gates with the swift water from the Mohawk River. **1965–70** *DARE* (Qu. O18, *Different currents or actions of the water that are important when you're in a boat*) 21 Infs, **scattered, but esp Sth, S Midl, NEast,** Swift water; **CA**191, Swift water [FW sugg]—a river channel current; **IN**3, Swift water—hard to handle your boat in; **MS**81, Swift water [FW sugg]—same as undercurrent; swift water and riptide—important to watch in Mississippi River; **NC**63, Swift water—main current, as of a river; **NH**14, Swift water—in a river; **NY**134, Swift water—in the river; **SC**31, Swift water—in a river; (Qu. C3, *A place in a swift stream where the surface of the water is broken*) 10 Infs, **chiefly Sth, S Midl,** Swift water. **1990** *Mt. Democrat & Placerville Times* (CA) 5 Nov sec A 3/1, The mounted patrol is only one segment of the sheriff's Search and Rescue Team, which also includes . . swift-water rescue.

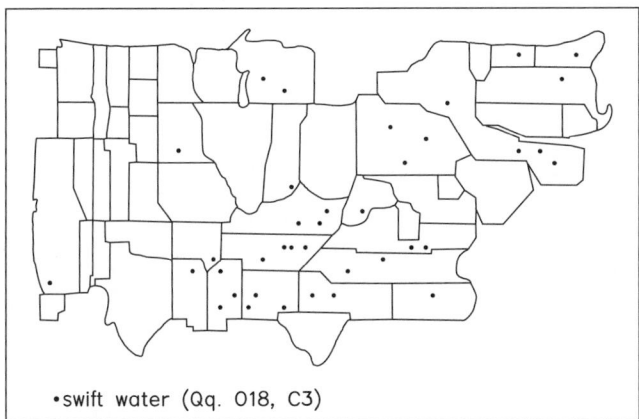

•swift water (Qq. O18, C3)

swiggered, I'll be phr Also *I'll be swiggled, ~ swimdiggled* =**jiggered, I'll be.**

1906 *DN* 3.160 **nwAR,** Swiggered. . . In the ejaculation, "I'll be swiggered." **1912** *Mansfield News* (OH) 7 Dec [10]/3 (newspaper-archive.com), They swore to goodness that . . "hully gee" and "I'll be swimdiggled" were expressions that a mucker might use. **1950** *PADS* 14.66 **SC,** Swigger. . . "I'll be swiggered!" Expression of mild surprise. **1956** McAtee *Some Dialect NC* 45, Swigger: . . euphemism for swearing or for a cuss word. "Well I'll be swiggered." **1970** *DARE* (Qu. NN25b, *Weakened substitutes for 'damn' or 'damned': "Well, I'll be _____!"*) Inf **VA**50, Swiggled. **2002** *DARE* File—Internet, Long Tom said, "I'll be swiggered! There is no wire in that telephone cord." **2003** *Ibid* **CA,** Well, I'll be swiggled! **2005** *Ibid,* Well, I'll be swiggered, the large color pic of my favorite Viking is still in the frame.

swill n esp NEast Cf swill pail 1

Food refuse, esp as collected and prepared for feeding to hogs or other domestic animals.

1818 in 1822 Cobbett *Year's Residence U.S.A.* 174 **Long Is. NY,** The milk and fat pot-liquor and meal are, when put together, called, in Long Island, *swill.* **1899** (1912) Green *VA Folk-Speech* 433, Swill. . . Hogwash. **1909** *DN* 3.371 **eAL, wGA,** Slop. . . Swill, kitchen refuse. **1926** *DN* 5.389 **ME,** Swill. . . Garbage. "Has the swill been collected yet?" Common. **1940** Stong *Hawkeyes* 260 **IA,** [The hired man said] that tomatoes must not be thrown in the swill because they were an aphrodisiac and made the sows rut out of season. **1949** Kurath *Word Geog.* 13, The liquid food given to pigs is called *swill* . . in the North, *slop* elsewhere in the Eastern States. **1966–69** *DARE* (Qu. K60, *When somebody is going to give the pigs food . . "I'm going to _____."*) Inf **NY**41, Feed him his swill; **CT**36, Feed them swill; **PA**242, Give 'em pig swill; **FL**20, Give them swill; **NJ**35, Throw them the swill. **1966–67** *DARE* Tape **ME**26, He was lugging swill to the hogs; **MA**99, We lived in the center of town, and the swill collectors came along and took the swill for the hogs that they raised. You don't hear the word "swill" much nowadays. **1972** *PADS* 57.43 **seOH,** Swill. Only two informants named the liquid food given to pigs. . . [One] used *swill,* a term common to the North. . . [Another] used *slop,* a term common to the Midland and South, sporadic in New England. **1975** Gould *ME Lingo* 284, Swill—Still properly used in Maine rural speech; *swill* and garbage are not synonyms in all respects. Food from the house for the pigs and hens is *swill.* **1980** *DARE* File **cnMA** (as of c1915), *Garbage* was a book word to us. Only people who put on airs would use such a high-brow word for banana

peels and onion skins and table scraps. That was *swill,* which you put in a swill pail for the swill man to dump into one of the town trucks.

swill v chiefly NEast, Gt Lakes See Map

To slop, give **swill** to (a hog).

1852 U.S. Patent Office *Annual Rept. for 1851: Ag.* 213 **NY,** The cheapest method of making pork is to swill the hogs liberally during the summer. **1907** Stacy *Blue Book of Teachers* 80 **IN,** He began life in 1872 near Greencastle, Indiana, and hoed corn, chopped wood, "swilled" the pigs, tilled the soil, . . until he was nineteen years of age. **1948** Manfred *Chokecherry* 44 **nwIA,** He pumped awhile; then for a change, swilled the hogs, watered the chickens. **1950** *WELS Suppl.* **csWI,** Swill hogs—Said by friends of Yankee stock in Marquette Co. **1963** North *Rascal* 154 **WI** (as of 1918), Feeding the calves, and swilling the pigs. **1965–70** *DARE* (Qu. K60, *When somebody is going to give the pigs food . . "I'm going to _____."*) 57 Infs, **scattered, but chiefly NEast, Gt Lakes,** Swill the pigs (*or* hogs). **1974** *Advocate* (Newark OH) 15 June 4/2, It was my fortune . . to know Chuck Colson a little, and perhaps best of all those now genteely [sic] swilling the hogs at Allenwood federal penitentiary.

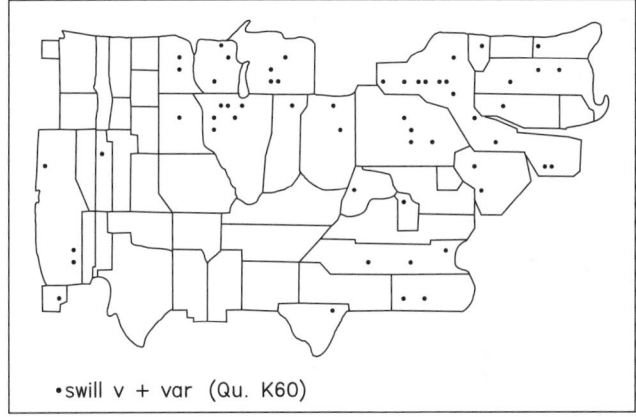

•swill v + var (Qu. K60)

swill pail n

1 also *swill barrel, ~ bucket, ~ can, ~ tub:* =**slop bucket 1;** also fig. **scattered, but esp NEast, MI** See Map on p. 462

1740 in 1741 *Boston News–Letter* (MA) 12 Feb 2/1, Taken up by John Morey, Esq. . . a Swill-Pale, otherwise called a Hog-Pale. **1843** (1916) Hall *New Purchase* 87 **IN,** Swiney becomes wholly savage, and loses all reverence for corn-cribs and swill-tubs. **1862** *Harper's New Mth. Mag.* 25.426 **MN,** The Judge saw the mistress of the pigs, swill-pail in hand, calling them together. **1863** *Ibid* 27.716 **CT,** [The] sort of a man— who . . "looked like a rooster just fished out of a swill-barrel." **1894** *New Engl. Mag.* 16.289, He always resisted the idea that God . . should have everything laid upon him that was attributable to human weakness and error. "Why, . . you would make a swill bucket of him!" **1946** *PADS* 6.29 **eNC** (as of 1900–10), Swill bucket. **1948** Davis *Word Atlas Gt. Lakes* 190, *Vessel for carrying food to hogs.* [*Swill pail* predominates in **MI** (5 of 7 infs); in **IL, IN, OH,** *swill pail, ~ bucket* are minority resps.] **1949** Kurath *Word Geog.* 56, Pail. . . Note . . Northern *swill pail,* and Midland and Southern *slop bucket.* **1962** Morison *One Boy's Boston* 20 **eMA** (as of 1890s), He . . carried wood and coal upstairs for the open fireplaces and grates, set out the ash cans and swill bucket. **1965–70** *DARE* (Qu. F24, *The container for kitchen parings and scraps—inside the kitchen*) 11 Infs, **chiefly NEast, MI,** Swill pail; **ID**4, **MA**7, 43, 72, **NC**36, **PA**242, Swill bucket; **MI**96, **SC**70, Swill can; (Qu. F25, *The container for kitchen parings and scraps—out of doors*) Infs **CT**2, **ME**2, **MI**66, **SC**66, Swill barrel; **MA**14, 98, **ME**5, Swill pail; **MA**83, Swill bucket. **1966** Dakin *Dial. Vocab. Ohio R. Valley* 2.118, *Garbage pail.* . . In the Ohio Valley *slop bucket* predominates overwhelmingly. . . *Swill pail* and *swill bucket* are both rare. **1967** Faries *Word Geog. MO* 79, The Northern *swill pail* and *swill bucket* occur only rarely. **1970** *DARE* FW Addit **MA,** *Swill bucket*—never heard the word *garbage* when I was young. **1973** Allen *LAUM* 1.198 **Upper MW** (as of c1950), *Swill pail* is more frequent in Minnesota, northern Iowa, Nebraska, and South Dakota. But the actually dominant form . . is a combination of the Midland *slop* and the Northern *pail.* **1989** Pederson *LAGS Tech. Index* 67 **Gulf Region** (*Slop bucket*) 599 infs, Slop bucket (*or* barrel, can, jar, pail, pan); 10 infs, Swill bucket (*or* pail). **2003** *DARE* File **csWI** (as of 1930s), *Swill pail*—almost a euphemism; implies pail contains edible garbage.

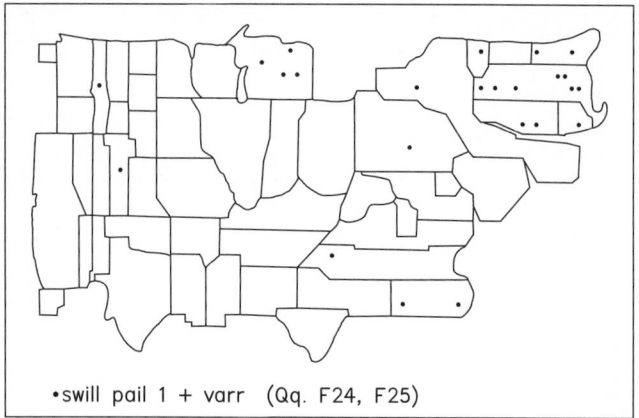

•swill pail 1 + varr (Qq. F24, F25)

2 in phr *swill pail cousin:* See quot.

1959 *VT Hist.* 27.162, *Swill pail cousin.* . . Distant cousin, not highly esteemed. Occasional.

swill tub See **swill pail 1**

swim v

A Forms.

1 past: usu *swam;* also:

a *swim.* **chiefly Sth, S Midl** See Map *esp freq among rural speakers and among speakers with little formal educ*

1953 Atwood *Survey of Verb Forms* 23, *Swim* . . preterite. . . The uninflected *swim* . . is used by only two informants in the M[iddle] A[tlantic] S[tates]; in the S[outh] A[tlantic] S[tates] about 40 informants use it, most of the occurrences being in S.C. and Ga. **1955** *PADS* 23.44 **e,sSC, eNC, seGA,** *Swim* (preterite). Old-fashioned. (Also Virginia Piedmont.) **1965–70** *DARE* (Qu. OO29b, *Talking about swimming: "When we were children we _____ [there too]."*) 15 Infs, **chiefly Sth, S Midl,** Swim. [11 Infs comm type 4 or 5, 12 gs educ or less, 4 Black] **1968** [see **1b** below]. **1989** Pederson *LAGS Tech. Index* 349 **Gulf Region,** *Swim* . . preterit . . [45 of 914 infs, Swim]. **2005** Williams *Gratitude* 529 **wNC** (as of 1940s), *Swim, swum* or *swimmed:* swam.

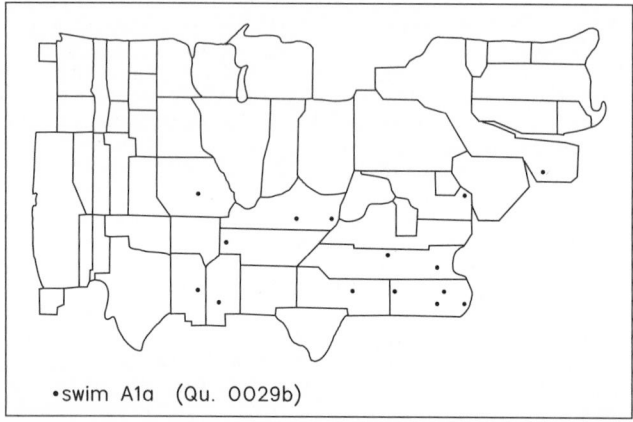

•swim A1a (Qu. OO29b)

b *swimmed, swimt.* **chiefly Sth, S Midl** See Map *esp freq among rural speakers and among speakers with little formal educ* Cf **-ed 2**

1753 in 1836 MA Hist. Soc. *Coll.* ser 3 5.102 **csPA,** Rid to . . the mouth of the Monongahela, where we . . swimmed our horses over Alleghany. **1843** (1916) Hall *New Purchase* 227 **IN,** Thar's where the water is deepish, and jist about where you swim'd your hoss. **1884** *Anglia* 7.253 [Black], To the regular forms of the Irregular verbs as used by the whites, the Negro adds the following forms of his own. . . *Pres.* swim—*Past.* swimmed, swimt. **1921** Haswell *Daughter Ozarks* 141 (as of 1880s), And ye swimmed Finley, ye say! **1953** Atwood *Survey of Verb Forms* 23, *Swim* . . preterite. . . There are two occurrences of *swimmed* . . in N. Eng., four in the M[iddle] A[tlantic] S[tates], and over 35 in the S[outh] A[tlantic] S[tates]. Of the S.A.S. occurrences, 17 are within the eastern two thirds of N.C. **1965–70** *DARE* (Qu. OO29b, *Talking about swimming: "When we were children we _____ [there too]."*) 34 Infs, **chiefly Sth, S Midl,** Swimmed. [29 Infs comm type 4 or 5, 18 gs educ or less, 10 Black] **1968** *PADS* 50.35 **swTN** [Black], For

the past tense of *swim* [6 of 18 infs] . . have /swɪmd/. . . [One] has /swɪm/. **1989** Pederson *LAGS Tech. Index* 349 **Gulf Region,** *Swim* . . preterit . . [27 of 914 infs, Swimmed]. **2005** [see **1a** above].

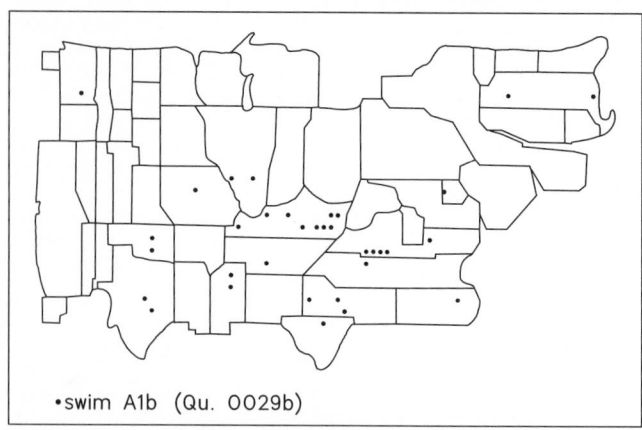

•swim A1b (Qu. OO29b)

c *swum.* **widespread, but esp Sth, S Midl, OK, TX** See Map *esp freq among older rural speakers and among speakers with little formal educ*

1859 Taliaferro *Fisher's R.* 129 **nwNC** (as of 1820s), I duv 'bout one hundred and fifty yards, riz to the top, and outswum like creation, distancin' the sharks, and uvry other vinimus fish. **1893** *DN* 1.278 **nwCT,** *Swim*—[past and past pple:] swum. **1906** *DN* 3.160 **nwAR,** *Swum, v. pret.* Swam. **1953** Atwood *Survey of Verb Forms* 23, *Swim* . . preterite. . . *Swum* . . predominates in n.e. N. Eng., particularly among the older types. In s. N. Eng. about half the older informants use it, and only a scattering of the younger. In e. N.Y. and n. N.J. less than one fourth of the older group use this form. . . Elsewhere in the M[iddle] A[tlantic] S[tates] and in the S[outh] A[tlantic] S[tates] *swum* predominates . . , its frequency varying from slightly over half (Pa.) to nearly nine tenths (N.C.) **1965–70** *DARE* (Qu. OO29b, *Talking about swimming: "When we were children we _____ [there too]."*) 117 Infs, **widespread, but esp Sth, S Midl, OK, TX,** Swum [Of all Infs responding to the question, 68% were comm type 4 or 5, 26% gs educ or less, 64% old; of those giving this response, 83% were comm type 4 or 5, 51% gs educ or less, 74% old.]; (Qu. H74b, . . *Coffee* . . *very weak*) Inf **OK9,** Tastes like it swum the branch. **1968** *DARE* Tape **GA30,** The bear swum out to the other side; **VA9,** He swum across the creek. **1989** Pederson *LAGS Tech. Index* 349 **Gulf Region,** *Swim* . . preterit . . [90 of 914 infs, Swum]. **2005** [see **1a** above].

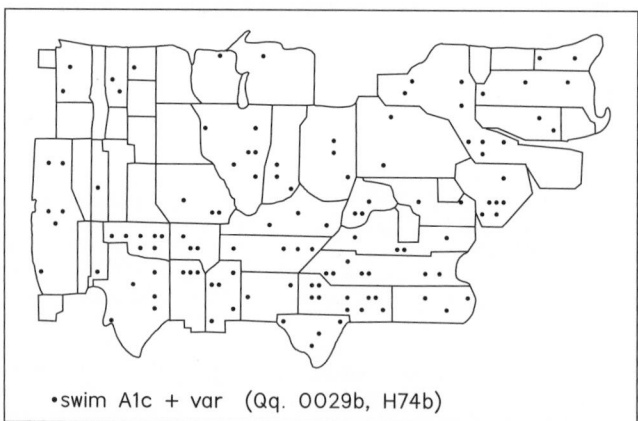

•swim A1c + var (Qq. OO29b, H74b)

d *swummed, swumt.*

1884 *Anglia* 7.253 [Black], To the regular forms of the Irregular verbs as used by the whites, the Negro adds the following forms of his own. . . *Pres.* swim—*Past.* . . swumt. **1892** *Century Illustr. Mag.* 45.318 **IN,** Wunst he shot a deer, one day,/ 'At swummed off, an' got away. **1965** *Tri-City Herald* (Pasco WA) 21 July 18/4, She Swummed It. **1970** *DARE* (Qu. OO29b, *Talking about swimming: "When we were children we _____ [there too]."*) Inf **KY94,** Swummed. **1989** Pederson *LAGS Tech. Index* 349 **Gulf Region,** *Swim* . . preterit . . [2 of 914 infs, Swummed].

2 past pple: usu *swam, swum;* also: see below. Note: *Swam* as a past pple is found throughout the US.

a *swim.* **chiefly Sth, S Midl** See Map *esp freq among rural speakers and among speakers with little formal educ*

1965–70 *DARE* (Qu. OO29a, *Talking about swimming: "The water is clean—we have always _____ [there]."*) 19 Infs, **chiefly Sth, S Midl,** Swim. [15 Infs comm type 4 or 5, 12 gs educ or less, 5 Black] **1989** Pederson *LAGS Tech. Index* 349 **Gulf Region,** *Swim . . past participle . .* [39 of 914 infs, [swɪm]].

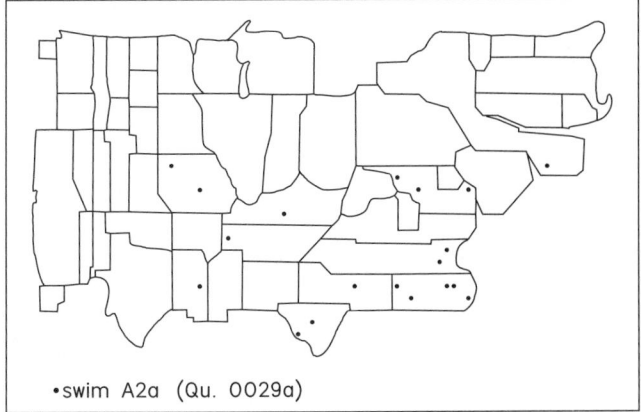

•swim A2a (Qu. OO29a)

b *swimmed.* **chiefly Sth, S Midl** See Map *esp freq among rural speakers and among speakers with little formal educ*

[**1647** in 1835 RI Hist. Soc. *Coll.* 2.103, If one of her sons could not have swimmed, [he] had been left behind her.] **1815** Humphreys *Yankey in England* 19, Had that darned old vessel . . bin a stun's throw furder off from land, I shood never have swimmed to shore. **1947** (1962) Henry *Misty* 72 **eVA,** Current is slack. Time for the ponies to be swimmed across. **1965–70** *DARE* (Qu. OO29a, *Talking about swimming: "The water is clean—we have always _____ [there]."*) 35 Infs, **chiefly Sth, S Midl,** Swimmed. [27 Infs comm type 4 or 5, 21 gs educ or less, 11 Black] **1989** Pederson *LAGS Tech. Index* 349 **Gulf Region,** *Swim . . past participle . .* [43 of 914 infs, Swimmed].

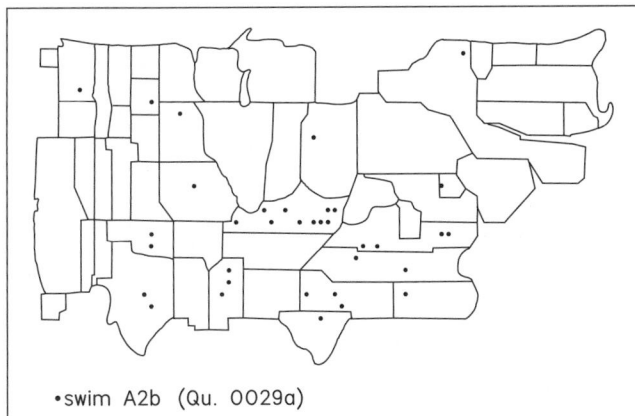

•swim A2b (Qu. OO29a)

B Sense.

Of a liquid: to suffice in quantity or density to float (something). [*OED2 swim* v. 14.a 1669 →]

[**1744** in 1957 Berger–Berger *Diary Amer.* 58 [Scottish writer in VA], [They] welcom'd us into their Province with a Bowl of fine Lemon Punch big enough to have Swimmed half a dozen young Geese.] **1794** (1936) Parry *Jrl.* 34.380 **PA,** Forded Buffaloe Creek, at the mouth, which did not quite swim them [=horses]. **1831** *New Engl. Farmer* (Fessenden) 9.409 **CT,** To prepare the rennet, make 2 quarts of brine that will swim an egg. **1846** (1973) Porter *Quarter Race* 87 **TN,** I had enough liquor plump in me to swim a skunk. **1861** *Atlantic Mth.* 7.151 **NEng,** We've got enough [patent medicine] to swim a ship, on the top-shelf of the pantry to-day, if it was all put together. **1908** *Indianapolis Star* (IN) [15 Oct 7]/5 (newspaperarchive.com), Lay cucumbers in salt water to swim an egg for twenty-four hours. **1944** in 2009 (acc) Lexis-Nexis Legal Research *State Case Law: TX* (Internet), When heavy rains fall the draw becomes very wide and deep enough to swim a horse. **1965–70** *DARE* (Qu. H74a, *. . Coffee . . very strong*) Infs **AL34, GA70, MS55, NC31, TN13,** Swim a(n) iron wedge.

swimdiggled, I'll be See **swiggered, I'll be**

swim-headed See **swimmy-headed**

swimmed See **swim A1b, 2b**

swimmer's itch n **orig Gt Lakes; now more widespread**

An itching skin rash caused by a schistosome parasite that penetrates the skin in both freshwater and saltwater environments.

1929 *WI State Bd. Health Bulletin* 4.23.14, Skin infections among bathers have been reported the past summer from many lake regions in Wisconsin. One of these of considerable prevalence is popularly known as "swimmer's itch." **1947** *Berkshire Eve. Eagle* (Pittsfield MA) 6 Oct 7/4 **seNY,** The scientific name of the affliction is schistosome dermatitis, but it is commonly called water itch on the West Coast and swimmer's itch in the Midwest. Commissioner William A. Holla, of the Westchester County Department of Health, says this is the first time to his knowledge that it has been identified in the East. **1951** *Herald–Press* (St. Joseph MI) 8 Aug 6/4, Thirty bathing beaches on 14 lakes were treated this year in the state's shrunken swimmer's itch control program. **1972** *WI Conserv. Bulletin* 37.3.18, Swimmers' itch is a dermatitis caused by the penetration of a small flatworm or trematode that may be picked up on bathing beaches. **1995** *Syracuse Herald–Jrl.* (NY) 1 July sec A 3/1, Calls about the rash, known as swimmer's itch or duck itch, started Monday. **2005** *Modesto Bee* (CA) 27 Aug sec B 6 (Internet), Swimmer's itch has lots of colorful names—"rice paddy itch," "clam digger's itch" and "duckworms," for instance. . . By whatever name, swimmer's itch is extremely irritating, causing intense itching followed by blisters.

swimmy-headed adj Also *swim-headed* [*OED2* (at *swimmy* a. a) 1881] **Sth, S Midl** Cf **head-swimming**

Dizzy.

1941 Writers' Program *Guide IN* 358 **cIN,** It is in Monroe County that the language of the common folk begins to shade off into the southern Indiana hill country speech. 'Swimmy-headed' means dizzy. **1956** McAtee *Some Dialect NC* 45, Swim-headed . . giddy. [**1986** Pederson *LAGS Concordance,* 1 inf, ceTN, A swimmy head—dizzy.] **1990** Cavender *Folk Med. Lexicon* 32 **sAppalachians,** Swimmy headed—dizzy. **1990** *Daily Herald* (Arlington Heights IL) 1 Aug sec 1 2/2 **GA,** When President Bush said, "Read my lips—no new taxes," he obviously was swimmy-headed. **1990** *DARE* File **wNC** (as of c1920), My aunt, born in 1872, used the term *swimmy-headed* to mean "dizzy." **1991** *DARE* File—Internet **eTN,** I get all swimmy-headed every time I look at you. **2001** *Atlanta Constitution* (GA) 21 Dec sec E 2 (Internet), Southernism No. 2248: "After a couple of beers I get so swimmy-headed I cain't walk straight." **2004** *Columbus Dispatch* (OH) 21 Mar sec C 1 (Internet), He took a couple of steps back, looking a little swimmy-headed, and dropped like a sack of bricks into the grease pit.

swimp See **shrimp**

swimt See **swim A1b**

swinch owl See **squinch owl**

swindle stick n

In logging: =**cheat stick.**

1941 *AmSp* 16.234 [Lumberjack jargon], *Swindle stick.* A log scaler's rule. **1959** *AmSp* 34.80 **nwCA** [Logger lingo], *Swindle stick.* . . A log scaler's rule. **1966** *DARE* Tape **MI10,** And the scaling rule that the scaler used to measure up the camp's output, just as often as not, was called a swindle stick. **1969** Sorden *Lumberjack Lingo* 125 **NEng, Gt Lakes,** *Swindle stick*—A long hardwood ruler used in estimating lumber in logs or timber. Same as log scale rule, cheat stick, money maker, robbers cane, thief stick, scale rule.

swing v

A Pronc varr. Usu |swɪŋ|; also |swæŋ|, |swɛŋ|; pronc-sp *swang.*

1937 *Frontier & Midland* 18.16 **eKY,** It was time to swang, and I swung like my jints was frost-bit. **c1960** *Wilson Coll.* **csKY,** Swing /swæŋ/—often. **1981** Pederson *LAGS Basic Materials,* 1 inf, **seAL,** [swɛˀ·ŋ, swɛ̃ˀ·ŋ]—both may be somewhat facetious.

B Gram forms.

Past: usu *swung;* also:

a *swang.*

[**1806** (1970) Webster *Compendious Dict.* 302, Swing . . swang, swung, *pret.* [*DARE* Ed: This entry was carried over from Webster's English model.]] [**1828** Webster *Amer. Dict.,* Swing . . *pret.* and *pp.*

swung.] **1856** *Harper's New Mth. Mag.* 13.416, The arm . . swang up and down rapidly. **1896** *DN* 1.425 **cwNY,** *Swing:* pret. *swang* [swæŋ], heard in Buffalo. **1899** (1912) Green *VA Folk-Speech* 431, *Swang.* . . Past tense of *swing.* **1906** *DN* 3.160 **nwAR,** *Swang* . . pret. *Swung.* **1909** *DN* 3.378 **eAL, wGA,** *Swang,* pret. of *swing.* **1963** *Julian Apple Day* 1 **csCA,** Remember the swing we used to have, tied way up in a tall tree. . . Belle was kind of plump. So she never swang on it. **1968** *DARE* FW Addit **neOH,** *Swang*—past tense of *swing.* **1969** *DARE* (Qu. FF18, *Joking words . . about a noisy or boisterous celebration or party: "They certainly _____ last night."*) Inf **PA**195, Swang. **1987** *Badger Herald* (Madison WI) 30 July 2/1, My jaw swang wildly in the air. . . I was singing to the radio. **2005** *DARE* File **neNY,** I just heard *swang* . . in an interview on NPR. *Ibid* **TN,** I've heard "swang" in Tennessee on more than one occasion, but certainly not with any frequency.

b *swunged, swungt.* **Cf -ed 1**

1882 *Lippincott's Mag.* 30.64 **LA** [Black], W'en we swunged in de net she bag so, an' I see de mullet beatin'. **1884** *Anglia* 7.253 [Black], To the regular forms of the Irregular verbs as used by the whites, the Negro adds the following forms of his own. . . *Pres.* swing—*Past.* . . swungt. **1899** *Daily IA State Press* (IA City) 30 May 3/4, The boy had been asked to write a composition on the naval battle of Santiago, says the Cleveland Plain Dealer. This is the painful result. . . She swunged the Bruklyn round an' let 'em have it with both barls from the wurd go.

c *swinged, swingt.* **Cf -ed 2**

1884 *Anglia* 7.253 [Black], To the regular forms of the Irregular verbs as used by the whites, the Negro adds the following forms of his own. . . *Pres.* swing—*Past.* swinged, swingt. **1904** *Atlanta Constitution* (GA) 23 Sept 6/4 **GA** [Black], De way he swinged dem sisters was a caution ter behol'! **1909** *DN* 3.378 **eAL, wGA,** *Swinged,* pret. . . of *swing.*

swing n

1 usu attrib in combs *swing dog,* ~ *horse,* ~ *mule,* ~ *steer,* ~ *team:* In a team of six draft animals, the position of the middle pair; in a larger team, the position either of the second pair or of all the intermediate pairs; rarely, an animal in this position.

1857 in 1980 *Ho for CA* 93 **KS,** Then came the "breaking" process, which was accomplished by yoking them [=oxen] up and putting them "in the swing" between old Smut and Snarley (leaders) and Dave and Start (wheelers). **1862** in 1884 U.S. War Dept. *War of Rebellion* 1st ser 11.2.168, Albert Hopkins, the lead driver, unfastened the lead horses from the swing team, one horse of which had also been hit, and brought them from the field. **1863** in 1889 *Ibid* 1st ser 26.2.121 **MA,** Having had two swing horses and drivers killed, I was compelled to retire. **1869** *Overland Mth.* 3.127 **TX,** With the Texan driver all oxen are "steers," and he has his "wheel-steers," his "swing-steers," and his "lead-steers." **1875** *Atlantic Mth.* 35.559 **West,** But that off swing there I would n't ride for a hundred dollars. **1905** U.S. Forest Serv. *Bulletin* 61.50 **Pacific NW** [Logging terms], *Swing team.* In a logging team of six, the pair between the leaders and the butt team. **1929** Willoughby *Trail Eater* vii **AK,** Swing dogs—dogs hitched directly behind the leaders. **1938** in Lib. of Congress *Amer. Memory: WPA Life Hist.* (Internet) **VT,** They'd hitch the three-four yoke oxen on each corner. . . The first yoke that come was the lead team, the ones between was the swing teams and the one on the pole was the pole team. **1965** *AK Sportsman* Oct 13 (Tabbert *Dict. Alaskan Engl.*) My old lead dog was in the team, no longer leading but in the swing. **1967** *DARE* Tape **LA**2, The one next to the leaders is the swing steer; **NV**2, If you were driving six, on one of those Concords, . . there was the wheeler, then the swing team, and the leaders. That made six. **1986** Pederson *LAGS Concordance,* 1 inf, **cwLA,** Swing mules—the middle two in a team of six; 1 inf, **seAR,** Swing team; 1 inf, **nwMS,** Swing team—mules behind lead team.

2 The part of a herd of cattle between the **point B1** and the **flank** n **1;** a position to the side of the herd occupied by a cowhand; hence combs *swing cattle,* ~ *kicker,* ~ *man,* ~ *rider.* **West**

1880 (1883) U.S. Census Office *Rept. Ag.* 974 **TX,** On each side of the lead rides a man on "point". . . Back where the line begins to swell ride two more at "swing". **1903** (1965) Adams *Log Cowboy* 28, The main body of the herd trailed along behind the leaders like an army in loose marching order, guarded by outriders, known as swing men, who rode well out from the advancing column, warding off range cattle and seeing that none of the herd wandered away or dropped out. *Ibid* 312, We swing riders were never out of sight of each other. **1929** *AmSp* 5.72 **NE** [Cattle country talk], Two "hands" "heading" the side lines guarding the cattle on march, are "lead riders" or "point men," and those riders behind

them at long intervals are "swing men" or "flank riders." **1933** (1950) Allen *Cowboy Lore* 36, The cattle in that part of the herd [=following the point] are called swing cattle. **1936** Adams *Cowboy Lingo* 139, About a third of the way back behind the 'point men' came the 'swing riders.' . . Another third of the way back rode the 'flank riders.' . . 'Bringing up the drag' were the 'drag riders' or 'tail riders.' **1952** FWP *Guide SD* 84, *Swing kickers:* horseman on each side, back of the point men, to swing the main body of the herd. **1966** *DARE* Tape **NM**14, [Inf:] We never had over six or eight men with the herd at one time. . . We'd have two in the leads and we'd have two in the swing, and then we'd have—maybe have two in the flank. . . [FW:] Now, the leaders were up in front and the swing was just a little—[Inf:] That's right. The swing was right back behind the leaders.

swing-around n   Also *swing-'em-around*   Cf **play-party, swing Josie**

A party with dancing; a song sung at such a party.

1932 Randolph *Ozark Mt. Folks* 81, Nearly all hill-folk contend that the old-time "swing-arounds" were infinitely more decorous than the modern dances. **1933** *AmSp* 8.1.52 **Ozarks,** *Swing-around.* . . A game-song, as sung by the dancers, at play-parties. **1954** *Harder Coll.* **cwTN,** *Swing-around.* . . "A game song, as sung by the dancers at a play-party." **1969** *DARE* (Qu. FF4, *Names and joking names for different kinds of dancing parties*) Inf **MO**37, Swing-'em-arounds. **1986** Pederson *LAGS Concordance* (A dance) 1 inf, **cnFL,** Swing around.

swing blade n   Also *swinging blade*   **chiefly Sth**   See Map **=sling blade.**

1954 in 2009 (acc) Lexis–Nexis Legal Research *State Case Law: GA* (Internet), The sheriff . . testified that he never saw the defendant around the house with a swing blade. **1960** *News* (Frederick MD) 21 Oct 13/6 **NC,** Raymond Couser, 43, drew an 18-month prison sentence on a charge he chased his wife with a swing blade grass cutter. **1965–70** *DARE* (Qu. L37, *A hand tool used for cutting weeds and grass*) 14 Infs, **Sth,** Swing blade; **LA**15, Swing blade—a twelve-, fourteen-inch blade with little notches on each side; **AL**11, **AR**15, 52, **LA**39, **MO**9, **SC**23, 47, **VA**38, Swinging blade; (Qu. L35, *Hand tools used for cutting underbrush and digging out roots*) Infs **AL**26, **AZ**9, **GA**68, Swing blade. [14 of 26 total Infs gs educ or less] **1986** Pederson *LAGS Concordance* (Lawn mower) 1 inf, **cwFL,** Swing blade; 1 inf, **swAL,** A swing blade— used for cutting hay. **2005** *DARE* File—Internet [Scotts Company Gardening Reference], *Weed and Brush Cutters.* . . The swing blade. . . generally has a straight wooden handle about the diameter of a broomstick. . . [T]he metal straps of the swing blade attach to both ends of the cutting blade. . . The swing blade is held in both hands and used . . with long, looping swings.

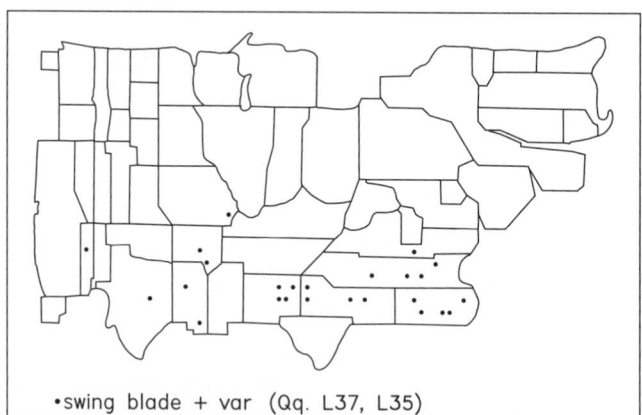

•swing blade + var (Qq. L37, L35)

swing cattle   See **swing** n 2

swing-dingle n   **Nth**

1 A shoulder-yoke for carrying a pair of buckets.

1937 *Daily Kennebec Jrl.* (Augusta ME) 6 Dec 6/6, The purpose of [a] swingdingle is to help pails of water from spring to camp or hovel, and to carry lunches to the men working away from the [lumber] camp. . . About three feet long. . . In the center a space is provided for the neck and shoulders of the user. Two short pieces of rope . . are tied to the ends of the affair. . . and are equipped with small hooks from which pails may be suspended. Swingdingles have been used at the lumber camps for more than 100 years. **1958** *Independent Press–Telegram* (Long Beach CA) 9 Mar mag sec 32/2 **ME,** A swingdingle . . is a sort of yoke once used by farmers to carry two heavy pails. My friend bought one for $3 in a Maine rummage sale.

2 A crude sledge. Cf **lizard** n **3**

1905 U.S. Forest Serv. *Bulletin* 61.50 [Logging terms], *Swing dingle.* A single sled with wood-shod runners and a tongue with lateral play, used in hauling logs down steep slopes on bare ground. (N[orthern] F[orest]). **1939** Mournian *In Those Days* 213 **NY,** He made a swing-dingle. He felled a young tree, split the trunk open and held it with wedges, so'st a hoss could be backed in. Small women and young uns set a-stride behind the critter, whilst beddin' and kettles and sech like was tied onto the branches. **1944** Nute *Lake Superior* 209 **MI, WI, MN,** At noon a cookee brought a hot lunch to them in the woods by means of the "swing-dingle," a rude kitchen, or perhaps buffet service, on runners. **1945** Gould *Farmer Takes a Wife* 43 **ME,** But his real present to Great-grandmother was a swing-dingle—for he wanted her to go calling in style. How America has disintegrated, when a swing dingle must be explained! It was a white maple trunk, the right size, and properly curved in growing so the turned-up end made a runner. The top was split its length, with a treenail at the proper place to stop its splitting all the way. The split part fitted like fills to a steer, and over the runner was erected a bob-sled sort of seat. *Ibid* 62, They rigged up swing-dingles that would hold a couple of barrels, and they hauled water . . for the stock. **2004** Burckhardt *Cook's Tour MN* 148 **MN** (as of c1930), The noon meal was eaten in the woods, served from a one-bob (horse) sleigh called a "swing dingle."

swing dog n

1 See **swing** n **1.**

2 In logging: a cant hook. Cf **cant dog, dog** n[1] **B2**

1938 (1939) Holbrook *Holy Mackinaw* 23 **ME** (as of 1850s), For a century past, rivermen had got along the best they could with a tool as primitive as a stone ax. It was a swing dog. . . Around a short pole, some four feet long, hung an iron collar to which was attached a hook, or dog, for the rolling of logs. It was awkward, and dangerous, for the dog would move up and down and sidewise. **1956** Sorden–Ebert *Logger's Words* 37 **NEng, Gt Lakes,** *Swing-dog,* See cant-hook. **1958** McCulloch *Woods Words* 187 **Pacific NW,** *Swing dog*—A cant hook.

swinge v [*OED2* 1590 →; Engl dial var of *singe*] **chiefly Sth, S Midl** Cf **singed cat**

To singe, burn; hence ppl adjs *swinge(d)* scorched, burnt; shriveled.

1835 Longstreet *GA Scenes* 219, He's a *swinge*-cat. **1844** Thompson *Major Jones's Courtship* 185 **GA,** I don't think I ever did see things jest sprawled out and swinged up so with the sun at this season of the year before. **1890** *Olean Democrat* (NY) 1 May 5/5, South Dakota is the "Swinge Cat state." **1898** Lloyd *Country Life* 52 **AL,** He ought to be took out and smeared all over with tar and feathers and swinged off, and then hung for stinkin. **1899** (1912) Green *VA Folk-Speech* 433, *Swinge.* . . To *singe.* **1909** *DN* 3.378 **eAL, wGA,** *Swinge.* . . To singe. *Ibid* 405 **nwAR,** *Swinge.* . . To singe. "We swinged a rat and turned him loose, thinking he would drive the others off." "He swinged his hair all off." **1914** *DN* 4.113 **cKS,** *Swinged.* . . Singed: as, a swinged cat. **1923** *DN* 5.222 **swMO,** *Swinge.* . . To singe. **1926** *AmSp* 1.420 **Okefenokee GA,** Auter . . wuz swinged all over. . . They had smoked 'im an' swinged 'im. **1927** Kennedy *Gritny* 203 **sLA** [Black], Preachin' ove' 'im now ain' goin' do no good; yonder whah he walkin' munks all dem heavy swingein' flames, tawmentin' his po' soul an' body. **1927** *DN* 5.471 **sAppalachians,** *Swinge.* . . To singe. **1931** *AmSp* 7.91 **eKY,** *Swinge,* to singe. "Dellie, child, take off that cap and swinge the chicken so we can hurry and get it cut up." **1940** Faulkner *Hamlet* 20 **MS,** He's setting at breakfast with a right smart of his eyebrows and hair both swinged off. **1946** *AmSp* 21.97 **sIL,** Older persons *swinge* ('singe') chickens. **1967–70** *DARE* (Qu. LL3a, *Shrunk, dried up: "These apples are all _____."*) Inf **FL**48, Swinged; (Qu. NN20b, *Exclamations caused by sudden pain—a slight burn*) Inf **LA**2, I swinged myself—and they do that to a chicken after they pick him. **1976** Garber *Mountainese* 90 **sAppalachians,** *Swinge* . . singe—You should always swinge a chicken afore you cook it.

swinge cat See **singed cat**

swinged v[1] See **swing** v **Bc**

swinged v[2] See **swinge**

swing-'em-around See **swing-around**

swinger n

1 also *swinging bird:* The **Baltimore oriole** or **orchard oriole.**

1894 *Century Illustr. Mag.* 47.849 **sIN,** This same mellifluous Baltimore oriole. . . the "swinging-bird," as they call him in southern Indiana, will hardly cease to be an oriole because he is no longer an *Oriolus.* **1909** *DN* 3.378 **eAL, wGA,** *Swinger.* . . A bird that hangs its nest so that it swings beneath the forked branch to which it is attached. Common. **1946** Hausman *Eastern Birds* 555, *Orchard Oriole* . . Brown Oriole, Basket Bird, Swinger, Orchard Starling, Orchard Hang-Nest, Bastard Baltimore.

2 A swing. Cf **-er** affix **1**

1899 (1912) Green *VA Folk-Speech* 433, *Swinger.* . . Made by ropes fastened overhead, and with a seat in which children swing backwards and forwards. "He fell out of the swinger and broke his arm." **1986** Pederson *LAGS Concordance (Swing)* 3 infs, **AL, LA, MS,** Swinger; 3 infs, **AL, GA,** Swinger—a swing; 1 inf, **cGA,** Swinger—a yard swing, as from a tree; 1 inf, **cwTN,** Swinger—made from chains; 1 inf, **cwMS,** Swinger—tire on a chain from a tree. [8 of 9 infs Black]

3 also *swinger-go-round:* A homemade merry-go-round. Cf **flying jenny 1**

1986 Pederson *LAGS Concordance (Flying jenny)* 1 inf, **cwGA,** A swinger; 1 inf, **swMS,** Swinger-go-round.

swing horse See **swing** n **1**

swinging bird See **swinger 1**

swinging blade See **swing blade**

‡**swinging jenny** n Cf **swinger 3**

1986 Pederson *LAGS Concordance (Flying jenny)* 1 inf, **cwFL,** Swinging jenny.

swinging statues n Also *swing the statue(s)* Cf **slinging statues**

=**statues 1.**

1967–70 *DARE* (Qu. EE33, . . *Outdoor games . . that children play*) Infs **CO**26, **KY**73, Swing the statue(s); **TX**61, Swing the statue—hold a position until "it" turns back. **1975** Ferretti *Gt. Amer. Book Sidewalk Games* 210, A far simpler version [of statues], which is also considerably rougher, is Swinging Statues. Whoever is "It" simply swings each of the other players around by an arm four times and lets him fly. The players must remain immobile in the positions they land in. Then, he decides which of his creations is best and that statue becomes the swinger. **1982** *Washington Post* (DC) 27 Aug sec F 5 (Internet), Group Games. . . tag, swinging statues, red rover, . . pass-the-orange-under-the-chin. **1986** Pederson *LAGS Concordance (Rough games)* 1 inf, **seFL,** Swing the statue—child swung; stayed in position. **1987** *NADS Letters* **csOK,** The game that *American Regional Dialects* called *statues,* we called *swinging statues* in Duncan. **2000** *DARE* File—Internet **MI,** Day time was filled with games of freeze tag, swinging statues, mother may i . . and grocery store. **2002** *Ibid* **St. Louis MO,** I remember . . games . . such as Red Rover, Swing the Statue.

swing Josie n Cf **swing-around**

A game involving singing and dancing; see quots.

1944 Howard *Walkin' Preacher* 79 **Ozarks,** On the other side of the yard a crowd of young people played "Swing Josie." **1986** Pederson *LAGS Concordance,* 1 inf, **cwLA,** Play swing Josie—involves singing and dancing. **2002** *DARE* File—Internet **TN,** Well, my grandmother and her brother had to go before the church, repent and promise not to dance again. My grandmother said her brother Valva Adams danced all the way to the hen house and back every day. But there were no more "swing Josie" parties.

swing kicker See **swing** n **2**

swingletail n Also *swingtail, swiveltail* [*swingle* a scutcher for beating and cleaning flax; see quot 1884]

A thresher shark (here: *Alopias vulpinus*).

1832 Williamson *Hist. ME* 1.161, The *Shark,* among fishermen, is called the "maneater," "the shovel-nose," and "the swingle-tail;" these being varieties of the species. **1843** DeKay *Zool. NY* 4.349, The Thresher Shark . . is known here under the various popular names of *Thresher, Fox Shark* and *Swingle-tail.* Its principal organ of defence appears to be its long flexible tail: it assails, and literally *threshes* its enemies. **1884** Goode *Fisheries U.S.* 1.672, The *Thresher Shark—Alopias vulpes.* . . known in Europe as the "Fox Shark," and to our fishermen most usually as the "Swingle Tail," . . is one of the most grotesque of sea animals, the upper lobe of the tail being exceedingly long, curving upwards and resembling in form the blade of a scythe. **1946** La Monte *N. Amer. Game Fishes* 3, *Thresher Shark* . . Swiveltail, Swingtail, Fox Shark.

swingletree n Pronc-sp *swengletree* [*OED2* 1483 →] **chiefly C and S Atl, Appalachians** See Map Cf *double swingletree* (at **double singletree**) **=whippletree.**

1774 in 1921 *MD Hist. Mag.* 16.30, The Stallions . . Broke my Swingle Tree, snapped One of my Traces. **1800** (1907) Columbia Hist. Soc. *Records* 10.174 **PA,** The horse . . went off with such violence that it broke the pole & swingletree. **1820** *Amer. Farmer* 2.261 **cnVA,** Swingletrees of three different sizes are made use of; one about four feet long, one rather more than three . . , and three smaller ones to which the traces are fixed. **1838** (1955) *Crockett Almanacks* 115 **wTN,** When I try to write my elbow keeps coming round like a swingle-tree. **1899** (1912) Green *VA Folk-Speech* 433, *Swingletree.* . . A cross bar pivoted at the middle, to which the traces are fastened in a cart, carriage, plough, etc. **1923** *DN* 5.222 **swMO,** *Swingle tree.* . . Singletree or whiffletree. **1927** *AmSp* 2.365, **cwWV,** *Swingle-tree* . . single-tree. "Take those new swingle-trees to the shop and have the blacksmith put the iron on them." **1949** Kurath *Word Geog.* 58, *Singletree.* . . In the North Midland *singletree* is now almost universal. The older *swingletree* does . . survive on the Delaware and in Southern New Jersey. In the South and the Southern Appalachians *singletree* and *swingletree* stand side by side. **1965–70** *DARE* (Qu. L46, *Behind each horse there's a movable bar [the leathers or ropes from the collar are fastened to it]*) 39 Infs, **chiefly C and S Atl, Appalachians,** Swingletree; (Qu. L45, *The long piece of wood that sticks out in front of a wagon, and you put a horse on each side*) Inf **FL**37, Swingletree. **1966** Dakin *Dial. Vocab. Ohio R. Valley* 2.152, *Whiffletree.* . . The regular terms throughout the Ohio Valley are . . *singletree* and *swingletree.* . . *Swingletree* is clearly the older term giving way to *singletree.* . . Among older informants the term is frequently pronounced *swengletree.* **1967** *DARE* FW Addit **swAR,** Swingletree ['swɛnəl,tri]. **1973** Allen *LAUM* 1.215 **Upper MW** (as of c1950), *Whiffletree.* . . Of 1,029 responding by mail, . . *Swingletree* is checked 8 times in Minnesota, and is scattered elsewhere, for a total of 13 instances. **1986** Pederson *LAGS Concordance*, 68 infs, **chiefly eTN, FL, GA,** Swingletree(s).

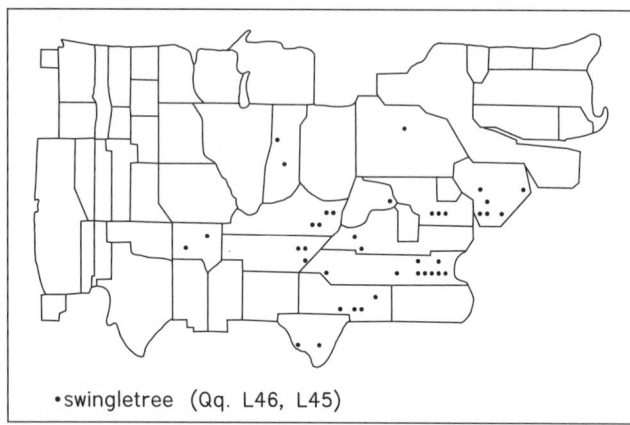

•swingletree (Qq. L46, L45)

swing man See **swing** n 2

swing mule See **swing** n 1

swing rider See **swing** n 2

swing sickle n Cf *DS* L37

Prob a **sling blade.**

1968 *DARE* FW Addit **AR,** Swing sickle ['swæɪŋ ,sɪkəl]. **2001** *DARE* File—Internet **CA,** Tools. . . *Gardening & Digging* . . Swing sickle. **2005** *Ibid* **TN,** Place a check mark next to all the following tasks you have done on a regular basis at work or home. . . used a swing sickle to cut weeds.

swing steer See **swing** n 1

swingt See **swing** v Bc

swingtail See **swingletail**

swingtail dogfish n

A **dogfish 1** (here: *Canis mustelus*).

1917 *Copeia* 41.17 **Long Is. NY,** *Mustelus canis.* . . It is known among the fishers here as "Swing-tail Dogfish."

swing team See **swing** n 1

swing the statue(s) See **swinging statues**

swink See **shrink**

swink owl See **squinch owl**

swipe net n **NC**

A type of seine; see quot 2005; hence vbl nouns *swipe netting, swiping* fishing with such a net.

1968 *DARE* (Qu. P13, . . *Ways of fishing . . besides the ordinary hook and line*) Inf **NC**82, Swipe netting—fish for mullet at night in shallow places. **1969** *DARE* FW Addit **ceNC,** Swipe netting—type of net fishing. *Ibid* **ceNC,** Go swiping—go net fishing. **2005** NC Office Administrative Hearings Register 20.331, Swipe Net Operations. A seine towed by one boat. . . Bunt Net. The last encircling net of a long haul or swipe net operation constructed of small mesh webbing. The bunt net is used to form a pen or pound from which the catch is dipped or bailed.

swish broom n Also *swiss broom, switch (broom)* [Cf *EDD swish* sb. 7 "A switch; a twig" and *OED2 swish-, swish* sb.[1] 3; *swiss-* is prob by folk-etym for *swish-* or *switch-.*] **chiefly Sth, S Midl** See Map *esp freq among Black speakers and among speakers with little formal educ* Cf **whisk broom**

A short-handled broom; similarly n *swish brush.*

1871 *Merry's Museum* 59.296 **ceMA,** Each member is expected . . to carry . . Small Switch Broom, or Duster. **1887** CA State Ag. Soc. *Trans. 1886* 77, *Needle, shell, and waxwork.* . . Mrs. A. Schiemer—Sacramento—Swiss broom holder. **1927** Kennedy *Gritny* 95 **sLA** [Black], I gotta git down on my knees an' brush 'um wid a swiss-broom. **c1938** in 1970 Hyatt *Hoodoo* 1.506 **cwFL** [Black], [Get] chew a swiss [swish] broom. . . [Hyatt: *Swish broom* is a one-handed broom.] **1956** Hench Coll. **cVA,** Billy Davis, colored man who works for us, yesterday several times spoke of wanting a "switch broom" to clean off the mantelpieces, etc. of hemlock needles from Christmas. **1965–70** *DARE* (Qu. F35, *A small broom that you hold in one hand, and use . . in places that are hard to get at*) 30 Infs, **chiefly Sth, S Midl,** Swiss broom; 17 Infs, **chiefly Sth, S Midl,** Swish broom; **KY**77, Swish brush; **AL**1, **GA**4, **MS**79, Switch broom; **AL**14, Switch. [Of all Infs responding to the question, 28% were gs educ or less, 6% Black; of those giving these responses, 57% were gs educ or less, 41% Black.] **1979** *Sports Illustr.* 5 Nov 54 **TN** [Black], I had gone to the trunk to get a swish broom and was sweeping the glass off the seat. **1981** *Chron.–Telegram* (Elyria OH) 22 Nov 10/4 (as of 1940s) [Black], We carried a shoeshine kit, hair brush, and a switch broom to clean the suits. **1986** Pederson *LAGS Concordance*, 1 inf, **neAR,** A switch broom—removes lint from clothes. [Inf Black] **1997** Evers–Szanton *Have No Fear* 100 **MS** [Black], Used a switch broom to brush the dandruff off white folks' leisure suits. **2003** *DARE* File—Internet **sFL,** I don't have a hand vac, but I was thinking of getting one rather than sweeping this mess up with a mini swish broom.

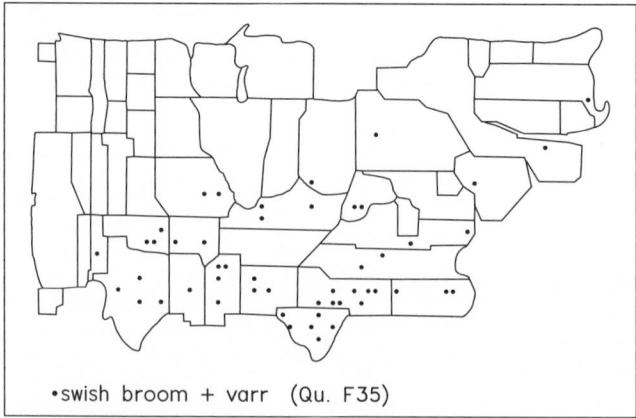

•swish broom + varr (Qu. F35)

Swiss barn n **esp C Atl**

=bank barn.

1832 (1919) Irving *Jrls.* 3.102 **NY,** Entrance, straggling road thro' butternuts. . . gateway built in stone—Swiss barn. **1862** *Adams Sentinel*

(Gettysburg PA) 26 Feb 3/3, *Brick Dwelling House*, containing 12 Rooms and a Kitchen, Out houses, Wash House, . . a good Stone Bank or Swiss Barn. **1884** *Daily News* (Frederick MD) 3 Nov 3/4, The deed was committed in a large Swiss barn which is on the farm where the deceased resided. **1907** *Bucks Co. Gaz.* (Bristol PA) 14 June 3/5, *Sons of America Buy Home in Bucks.* . . It contains a fourteen-room sand stone building, . . large Swiss barn, . . and all necessary outbuildings. **1940** Weygandt *Down Jersey* 42 **sNJ**, The bank barn, or Swiss barn, is far to seek in South Jersey. **1983** *Gettysburg Times* (PA) 24 Dec 25/5, The mid-Atlantic states, particularly Pennsylvania, adopted the Swiss barn to a large extent. Though separate from the house here, the Swiss overhanging barn allowed wagons to be driven into its second level, from where hay could be unloaded and later dropped to the livestock below. Mountainous Switzerland and hilly Pennsylvania worked to the advantage of the farmer in this case. Hills allow for entries on more than one level and eliminate unnecessary lifting.

swiss broom   See **swish broom**

switch v

1 To dowse; hence vbl n *switching*, n *switcher*.

   1929 Dobie *Vaquero* 275, The numerous "water witches" . . have not done a great deal towards watering the land; yet it would be surprising to know how many hard-headed cowmen have drilled at locations made by these "switchers." **1955** TN Folk Lore Soc. *Bulletin* 21.108, The practice of "switching" for water is a rather frequent skill with a believing number of individuals. *Ibid* 110, A Mr. Smith of Cookeville, Putnam County, reports that he switches with one hand by gripping the small end of the switch between the thumb and forefinger. **1958** *Jrl. Amer. Folkl.* 71.524, The term "water divining" is third in popularity. . . "Switching" for water is mentioned in slightly more than one percent of the counties.

2 To strut, swagger, move provocatively. *esp freq among Black speakers* Cf **switch-tail** v **1**, **switchtail** n **2**

   1942 Footner *MD Main* 176, Buena Vista Barnes was ordered to stop "switching" when she passed by Elvira Mearses. **1965–70** *DARE* (Qu. Y22, *To move around in a way to make people take notice of you: "Look at him _____."*) Infs **CA59, MA8, NY237, SC70, TN53**, Switch; **MS60, VA39**, Switching; [7 of 8 Infs Black, 7 female] **2006** *DARE* File—Internet [Black], He looked back just in time to see her switch down the hall to the bathroom. . . He wished she'd walk a little slower, so her high little bottom didn't wiggle so much.

switch (broom)   See **swish broom**

switch-bud hickory n   Also *switch hickory*

A **pignut 1** (here: *Carya glabra*).

   1884 Sargent *Forests of N. Amer.* 134, *Carya porcina.* . . Switch-bud Hickory. . . Dry hills and uplands; common. **1897** Sudworth *Arborescent Flora* 115 **AL**, *Hicoria glabra.* . . Pignut (Hickory). . . Switch-bud Hickory. **1931** Smithsonian Inst. Bur. Ethnology *Bulletin* 103.49 **OK**, In recent times I am told that bows were made of white hickory or "switch hickory," which they [=Choctaws] cut in the fall, allowed to season all winter and made up in the spring. **1960** Vines *Trees SW* 137, *Carya glabra.* . . Vernacular names are Broom Hickory, Switch Hickory, Black Hickory, Red Hickory, White Hickory, Brown Hickory, and Switchbud Hickory.

switch cane n

Std: a cane (here: *Arundinaria gigantea* subsp *tecta*). Also called **mutton cane 1, reed ~**

switchel n   Also *switchell, switzel*   **chiefly Nth, esp NEng** *old-fash*   Cf **belly whistle, ginger water, hayfield drink, swankey** n **1**

A drink made of water and a sweetener, freq molasses, to which vinegar and ginger are often added.

   1790 *Daily Advt.* (NY NY) 22 Mar 3/1, Not wretched *switchel* and vile *hogo* drams. [Footnote to *switchel*: A mixture of molasses and water.] **1825** Neal *Brother Jonathan* 1.256 **CT**, The toddy, egg-nog, and switchell (a drink made of molasses and water—half and half—in use, we believe, at Bunker's Hill), had gone about rather freely. **1894** *DN* 1.343 **wCT**, Switchel: drink made of molasses, water, and ginger (with or without vinegar). **1899** Garland *Boy Life* 111 **nwIA** (as of c1870s), Mr. Stewart kept plenty of "switchel" (which is composed of ginger and water) for his hands to drink. **1899** (1912) Green *VA Folk-Speech* 434, *Switchel.* . . A drink made or [sic] molasses and water, and sometimes a little vinegar and ginger. **1912** *DN* 3.569 **cNY**, *Switchel.* . . A drink made of water, vinegar, molasses, and ginger. **1941** *LANE* Map 312 (*Soft drink*) 3 infs, **CT, MA**, Switchel. **1947** Croy *Corn Country* 282

Plains States, Upper MW, *Switchel:* A drink made of molasses and water, seasoned with ginger and vinegar. The women-folks used to bring it to the men in the field; mighty refreshin'. **1950** *WELS (Unfermented drinks made in your neighborhood)* 1 Inf, **cwWI**, Switchel—vinegar, sugar, water, ginger, and sometimes egg, beaten together and carried in a brown jug to harvest field. **1959** *VT Hist.* 27.162, *Switchel.* . . A drink made of ginger, vinegar, and maple syrup for the haymakers. Obsolescent. **1966** *DARE* Tape **NH6**, My sons say. . . switzel or ginger, ginger water they used to call. It had the vinegar and ginger. . . I think it had about a teaspoonful of ginger and a tablespoonful of vinegar and, oh, about a quarter cup of sugar to a quart or so of water. . . We used cold water. **1968** *DARE* FW Addit **ceNY**, Switchel ['swɪčəl] = beverage made of vinegar and ginger and sugar and water. Especially used in haying time—you could drink all you wanted without getting sick. **1970** *DARE* (Qu. DD28b) Inf **NY234**, Switchel—vinegar, ginger, water, sugar—not fermented. **1994** *DARE* File **nwMA** (as of 1920s–30s), My father always made switchel to have during haying. It was made of molasses and water and ginger. Even if it sat out all day and was lukewarm, it would be real refreshing; cool you right off.

switcher   See **switch 1**

‡switchfoot n   Cf **foot** n **C3, swivel plow**

A reversible bottom on a plow; hence n *switchfoot plow*.

   1969 *DARE* (Qu. L18, *Kinds of plows*) Inf **NC68**, Switchfoot plow—like a boy Dixie, but with a switchfoot on it, a reversible foot to throw dirt downhill no matter which way the plow goes.

switch grass n

1 Std: a **panic grass** (here: *Panicum virgatum*). Also called **feather grass 4, wild redtop 1**

2 A **cordgrass** such as *Spartina spartinae* or *S. bakeri*; see quots. **FL**

   1921 FL Geol. Surv. *Annual Rept.* 13.206, On Merritt's Island the herbaceous vegetation is mostly switch-grass (*Spartina Bakeri*). **1938** Rawlings *Yearling* 348 **nFL**, There was ice everywhere. The switch grass was coated with it. **1943** Pratt *Barefoot Mailman* 43 **FL**, They entered this, striding through tall switch grass and edging carefully around cacti. **1944** *Amer. Midland Naturalist* 32.521 **sFL**, The author describes 68 distinct types of vegetation in southern Florida [including]. . . switch- or cord-grass marshes. **1971** Craighead *Trees S. FL* 103, *Spartina spartinae* or tall cord grass, locally called switch grass. **2000** FL Ornith. Soc. *FL Field Naturalist* 28.98 **FL**, The Cape Sable [seaside sparrow] subspecies was first described as occupying . . less saline marshes dominated by "switch grass" (*Spartina bakeri*).

switch hickory   See **switch-bud hickory**

switch, hide the n   Also *hiding switches, hiding (the) switch*; for addit varr see quots   **chiefly Sth, S Midl**   See Map

A children's game in which players try to locate a hidden switch.

   1867 *Scott's Mth. Mag.* 3.452 **GA**, Oft have I marked the gay and happy scene / Of negroes sporting o'er the mirthful green;/ . . Play hide-the-switch, or in some other play / Prolong the pleasures of the festive day. **1883** (1971) Harris *Nights with Remus* 321 **GA** [Black], Come out yer en less take a game er hidin'-switch. **1892** *DN* 1.230 **KY**, *Hiding the switch* [haɪdɪn swɪč]. This is the name of a game. **1893** Shands *MS Speech* 72, *Hiding the switch* [haɪdɪn swɪč]. This game is played in Mississippi as well as in Kentucky. **1901** in 2005 *DARE* File—Internet **VA** (as of c1860), We played the usual games—marbles & tops . . hide & seek & "hide the switch." **1905** *DN* 3.82 **nwAR**, *Hide the switch*[,] *hidin(g) the switch.* . . The name of a game. Very common. **1908** *DN* 3.320 **eAL, wGA**, *Hide the switch.* . . A children's game. Also *hiding the switch.* **1912** Green *VA Folk-Speech* 223, *Hide the switch.* A children's game. One hides the switch that is sought for by the others; the finder whips any players he can catch before getting to base. **1937** in 1972 *Amer. Slave* 2.1.167 **SC** (as of 1850s) [Black], We had some games we played, like Molly Bright, Hiding Switches, Marbles. We played on Sunday, too, unless the mistress calls us in and stops us. **1965–70** *DARE* (Qu. EE3, *Games in which you hide an object and then look for it*) 19 Infs, **chiefly Sth, S Midl, esp Gulf States**, Hide the switch; **MS15**, Find the switch. **1966** *DARE* Tape **SC26**, A game, hide and switch. I take a switch about that long, or a piece of stick, and carry it, hide it, and the others got to come. . . Yeah, hide and switch. . . Play it, "Bread and butter, come for supper," that's hidin' the switch. **2000** *DARE* File—Internet **KY** (as of 1930s), We played hide the switch. . . We took a switch off a tree and one of us would hide and let the other one try to find it and the one that found it got to whip the other one.

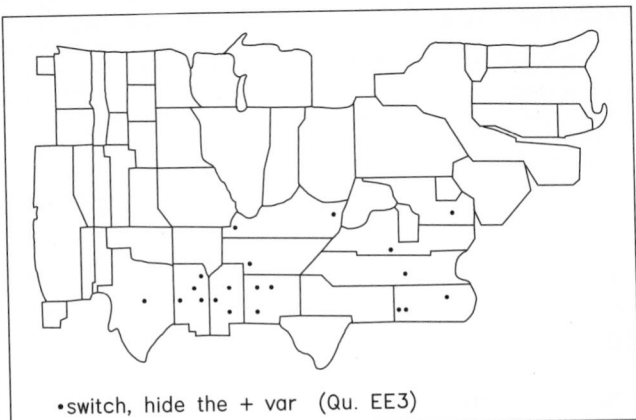

•switch, hide the + var (Qu. EE3)

switchies exclam

In marble play: see quot.

c1970 Wiersma *Marbles Terms* swMI (as of 1960), If you call "switchies" before the game it means that if you lose, you have the option of switching the marble you have to give up for another—usually one not so pretty or precious.

‡**switching** ppl adj [Cf *EDD* switching ppl. adj. 2 "Great of its kind; extensive; superlatively good; noted; fast."]

Fetching, attractive.

1942 Hurston *Dust Tracks* 107 **FL** [Black], "Dat's a switching little gal!" He [=a father speaking of his daughter] used to gloat.

switching vbl n See **switch 1**

switch-ivy n

=**dog hobble 1.**

1933 Small *Manual SE Flora* 1001, *L[eucothoe] Catesbaei.* . . Switch-Ivy. **1953** Greene-Blomquist *Flowers South* 91, Switch-ivy or dog-hobble *(L[eucothoe] editorum).* **1966** Grimm *Recognizing Native Shrubs* 227, *Leucothoe fontanesiana.* . . also called Dog-hobble and Switch-ivy. **2006** (acc) NC State Univ. *Herbarium* (Internet), *Poisonous Vascular Plants.* . . *L[eucothoe] fontanesiana.* . . Dog-hobble, *Leucothoe,* Switch-ivy.

switch mesquite n

A **mesquite B1**; see quot.

1929 Dobie *Vaquero* 201 **TX,** Perhaps no widely dispersed tree growth responds more apparently to climate, altitude, and latitude than the mesquite. In the southern part of Live Oak County . . it develops into great trees; on the Llano River and out on the Edwards Plateau it is gnarled and black-barked, the tops conspicuously thin; on the Plains it is just "switch mesquite."

switch oak n

Usu a **scrub oak** (here: *Quercus* x *pauciloba*), but also a **gray oak 2** of the southwestern US.

1903 Small *Flora SE U.S.* 353, *Quercus undulata.* . . Switch oak. **1908** Britton *N. Amer. Trees* 320, *Quercus undulata.* . . It is also called Scrub oak and Switch oak. **1938** Van Dersal *Native Woody Plants* 347, Oak, Switch *(Quercus undulata).* **1976** Elmore *Shrubs & Trees SW* 23, Scrub, shin, switch or evergreen oak . . *Quercus undulata.*

switch owl See **squitch owl**

switch pie n Cf **peach-tree tea**

A whipping.

1946 in 1958 Brewer *Dog Ghosts* 53 **TX** [Black], Ah was a li'l' shirt-tail boy gittin' switch-pies. **2004** *DARE* File—Internet **MA** (as of 1842), You'd better behave or I'll give ye a taste of switch pie.

switchtail n

1 A **shovelnose sturgeon** (here: *Scaphirhynchus platorynchus*). [See quot 1956] **Upper Missip Valley**

1905 IL State Lab. Nat. Hist. *Bulletin* 7.37 swIL, Mr. H.L. Ashlock . . expressed at this time his belief that a distinct sturgeon . . was occasionally obtained among catches of the common shovelnose locally called the "switch-tail." **1956** Harlan-Speaker *IA Fish* 48, Shovelnose Sturgeon—*Scaphirhynchus platorynchus* . . switchtail. **1983** Becker *Fishes WI* 227, *Scaphirhynchus platorynchus* . . switchtail.

2 also attrib; also *switchy-tail*: A sexually provocative or attractive woman. Cf **switch v 2, switch-tail v 1**

1909 *DN* 3.378 eAL, wGA, *Switch(y)-tail.* . . An immodest or forward girl or woman. **1943** Mitchell *McSorley* 59, At one time I had nine big switch-tail women on my personal payroll, and they all stole from me. **1968** in 1981 James *All Places* 155 **AL,** Everybody was just sort of standing around not saying very much, and then this nice little switchy-tail that Lyndon was particularly interested in, she kind of sidles up to him and says, "Why, Lyndon, honey, that sho is something *else.*" **2009** *DARE* File—Internet, I realized I had reached the age / Between cute young thing and cute l'il-ol' lady / When those switchtails behind the coffee counter / Gave me a Look./ It said, "You are just the wrong demographic."

switch-tail v

1 Of a woman: to waggle the hips; to behave provocatively. Cf **switch 2**

1943 Writers' Program NC *Bundle of Troubles* 121 [Black], All the time I's a-runnin' 'round with her and spendin' the three bucks a week I made at the sawmill on her, she is switch-tailin' 'round with a bunch of other niggers behind my back and takin' what money they got. **1949** Macdonald *Moving Target* 10, She switch-tailed into the house, a pretty piece in a rage.

2 Of a dog: to wag the tail vigorously.

1974 Dumas *Ark of Bones* 86 [Black], It was still a pup, but it was jumpin and switch-tailin round, lickin at strangers so fast it look like it was chasing its tail. **2000** Humphreys *Nowhere* 98 NC, "Here's Girl [= a dog] with Steve Lowrie," I said, switch-tailing across the porch. "Pet me, pet me!"

3 Of a car or driver: to fishtail.

1962 Moody *Shaking Nickel* 111, She [=a car] switch-tailed from side to side, flinging rocks down into the canyon at our left and sideswiping the cut bank at our right. **1996** in 2009 *DARE* File—Internet **ME,** Arthur had recommended we climb over Mt. Tamalpais into Muir Woods, so we put the Owl into low gear and twitched her tail-feathers. Up on Mt. Tam we got tantalizing snapshots of San Francisco Bay and islands through drifting cloud and fog, and switchtailed into the deep pocket of the family woods.

‡**switch twitching** vbl n Cf **switch v 1**

Dowsing; hence n *switch-twitcher.*

1951 Roberts *Henry Gross* 61 ME, I'd rear up, too, if somebody implied that I had been the easy dupe of the village switch-twitchers. *Ibid* 261, This was switch-twitching and necromancy engineered by a shaman wagging a hoodoo stick.

switchy-tail See **switchtail n 2**

swith n [Perh var of *swath*]

See quots.

1982 Slone *How We Talked* 129 eKY (as of c1950), A swith—The width you could reach with your hoe, as you shaved weeds. **1995** in 2004 Montgomery-Hall *Dict. Smoky Mt. Engl.* 589 eTN, Swith. . . the width one could reach with a hoe while cutting wheat or hay.

swither n [Scots, Ir, nEngl dial]

A state of agitation or uncertainty—freq in phr *in a swither;* hence adj *a-swither* excited.

1837 Smith *Col. Crockett's Exploits* 48 **TN,** I . . laughed heartily to think what a swither I had left poor Job in, at not gratifying his curiosity. **1932** *Helena Independent* (MT) 4 Nov 10/4 **NYC,** When it's counting time next Tuesday, and you're all a-swither to know who's elected, don't be too hasty in judging the relative merits of election officials. **1944** *Richmond Times–Dispatch* (VA) 4 Sept 6/2 (Hench Coll.), The designer [of a woman's jacket one inch longer than the War Productions Board allows], in a swither (similar to a dither, but less severe) suddenly had an inspiration. **1946** *PADS* 6.29 swVA (as of 1940), Swither, in a. . . In an emotional storm; excited. "He was all in a swither this morning." **2003** *DARE* File—Internet **NM,** Jim & Vera accepted the award and Jim said he was in a "swither".

‡**swithered** ppl adj [Cf *EDD* swither v.3 2 "To dry up, wither."]

1967 *DARE* FW Addit cLA, Swithered—shriveled—Negro usage passed over to white.

switzel See **switchel**

swivel(ed), swivelled, swivelly See **shrivel v1**

swivel plow n **NEast** *old-fash*

=*sidehill plow* (at **sidehill** n **2b**).

1846 *Amer. Agric.* 5.272, Side-Hill or Swivel Plow. These plows are so constructed that the mould board is easily and instantly changed from one side to the other, which enables the operator to perform the work horizontally upon side-hills, going back and forth on the same side, and turning all the furrow slices with great nicety, downward. **1875** *Bangor Daily Whig & Courier* (ME) 8 Apr 1/3, [Advt:] The Charter Oak Swivel Plow. **1880** *Fitchburg Daily Sentinel* (MA) 23 Sept 2/2, The land is free from large stones, sloping and quite favorable for the swivel plow which was used by all the contestants. **1918** *Middletown Times–Press* (NY) 19 Oct 7/5, [Advt:] Auction. . Wiard swivel plow. **1922** *Frederick Post* (MD) 9 Mar 4/4, [Advt:] Farm machinery . . 1 Wiard swivel plow. **1948** *Coshocton Tribune* (OH) 28 May 2/2, They plow with those cows and a swivel plow. **1966–69** *DARE* (Qu. L18, *Kinds of plows*) Infs **CT**29, **MA**74, Swivel plow; **MA**6, Swivel plow—throws all furrows the same way. [All Infs old, gs educ] **1992** Phelps *Famous Last Words* 22 **sNH** (as of c1926), I learned to plow with a side hill plow or swivell plow as it was called, as at the end of a furrow a latch was released and the mold board could be rolledover and it would turn the other way going back.

swiveltail See **swingletail**

swiveltree n [Engl dial; folk-etym for **swingletree**] =**singletree**.

1858 *Scientific Amer.* 14.48, In case of the horses becoming unruly and running off, they are detached from the swiveltree behind, and in moving forward the hook slips out, and frees the horses from the pole. **1905** *Hopewell Herald* (NJ) 9 Aug [2]/2 (newspaperarchive.com), As Miss Barberia and Burt Drake were driving down Witherspoon street . . the swiveltree broke throwing Miss Barberia out. **1906** *DN* 3.160 **nwAR**, Swivel-tree. . . Whiffletree. **1923** *Hopewell Herald* (NJ) 7 Mar 2/5, [Advt:] 2 sets 4-horse swiveltrees, 1 set 3-horse swiveltrees. **1949** Kurath *Word Geog.* 58, Singletree. . . Only central New Jersey has a local expression, *swiveltree*, several instances of which have been noted also on the upper Ohio. **1956** *PADS* 25.7 **WA**, Swiveltree . . 1 [inf]. **1966–68** *DARE* (Qu. L46, *Behind each horse there's a movable bar [the leathers or ropes from the collar are fastened to it]*) Infs **AL**41, 47, **FL**20, **IN**45, **NJ**50, **NY**1, **VA**7, Swiveltree. **1967** Faries *Word Geog. MO* 137, Swiveltree 3 [of c700 infs]. **1971** Wood *Vocab. Change* 300 **Sth**, 11 [of approx 1000 infs] swiveltree. **1973** Allen *LAUM* 1.215 **Upper MW** (as of c1950), Whiffletree. . . The relic *swiveltree* appears only once, in northwestern Nebraska. **1986** Pederson *LAGS Concordance (Singletree)* 2 infs, **AL**, **MS**, Swivel tree.

swivet n Also *swivit, swivvet, swivvit* [*EDD* swivet "Haste, hurry; a passion"; cf also *EDD* swivetty "Giddy, dizzy."] **chiefly Sth, S Midl**

Rarely pl with *the*: A state of anxiety, excitement, or nervous haste—usu in phr *in a swivet.*

1836 French *Elkswatawa* 1.147 **KY**, Don't be in sich a swivet; if the gal is there, we'll git her. **1872** (1973) Thompson *Major Jones's Courtship* 136 **GA**, All of 'em was in a terrible swivet all the time, for fear I'd git cowed and wouldn't succeed in my oration. **1892** Johnston *Mr. Fortner's* 67 **GA**, Knewed brer Fortner forty year and better. *Never see him in sech a tar'in'* swivit before. **1892** *DN* 1.232 **KY**, Don't be in such a swivet. **1899** (1912) Green *VA Folk-Speech* 434, Swivet. . . Nervous haste; fidgets; a hurry. "Keep still, you are always in such a swivet." **1905** *DN* 3.97 **nwAR**, Swivet. . . Anxiety, eagerness. 'He was in a great swivet to get off.[']' Rare. **1909** *DN* 3.378 **eAL**, **wGA**, Swivet. . . State of excitement. Common. **1917** *DN* 4.418 **LA**, **wNC**, Swivvit. . . Hurry. "He's always in a swivvit." **1937** (1963) Hyatt *Riverlid* 90 **KY**, He drug on in a turrible swivvet to git away. **1946** *PADS* 6.29 **VA**, Swivet, in a: . . Excited. **c1960** Wilson *Coll.* **csKY**, In a swivet (or *swivit*). . . In a state of agitation, or in a hurry, too obviously so. **1966** *Julian Apple Day* [14] **csCA**, Dawn works very hard, and usually has an attack of the swivets and fidgets at the Weed Show, because she doesn't go to bed enough while she's arranging it. **1966–70** *DARE* (Qu. A21, *When someone is in too much of a hurry . . "Now just slow down! Don't _____."*) Infs **AR**38, **FL**1, 11, **MI**122, **TN**4, Be in (such) a swivet; **TX**4, Get in such a swivet; (Qu. GG7, *. . Annoyed or upset: "Though we were only ten minutes late, she was all _____."*) Infs **MI**122, **TX**18, In a swivet. **1969** *DARE* FW Addit **cnNC**, "I'm in a swivet [swɪvət]"—I'm stirred up and have to hurry. **1993** Gibbons *Charms* 103 **NC**, She stayed in a swivet, packing and unpacking, rushing film to the drugstore, pasting snapshots in a new album.

swivveled See **shrivel** v[1]

swivvet, swivvit See **swivet**

swizzled ppl adj[1]

Often in combs *bumswizzled, gumswizzled, hornswizzled;* for addit varr see quots: Used as a euphem for *damned*—freq in phr *I'll be swizzled* and varr.

1840 *Burton's Gentleman's Mag. & Amer. Mth. Rev.* 6.72 **NY**, I'll be swizzled if Uncle Sam ain't got the keownterparts on 'em in one state alone. **1852** Morris *Lights & Shadows* 143 **KY**, He'd larne suthen bout the dratted things [=Freemasonry] fore supper, gawl swizzled eff he didn't. **1860** Street *Woods & Waters* 113 **NY**, Well, I'll be swizzled ef that aire critter . . didn't reach out and ketch hold on a branch. **1868** Paulding *Book of Vagaries* 335, I'll be teetotally rum-swizzled if I am going to let daddy pay you for just the same sort of work. **1881** *Ballou's Mth. Mag.* 53.397, Oh! dad rang the swizzled old gate to the swizzled bow-wows! **1895** *DN* 1.396 **seNY**, Dingswizzled . . expression of surprise, consternation, etc. A person who is at a loss how to act says, "I'll be dingswizzled." **1896** *Harper's New Mth. Mag.* 92.972 **West,** You didn't know that there horn-swizzled Phil Buckminster. **1905** *DN* 3.60 **eNE**, Chawswizzled. . . Confounded. "I'll be chawswizzled." **1911** Saunders *Col. Todhunter* 7 **MO**, I'll be jim swizzled if I don't. **1911** *DN* 3.544 **NE**, Gumswizzled, I'll be . . expressing annoyance, or surprise. "You never went? Well, I'll be gumswizzled!" **1916** *DN* 4.272 **NE**, Bumswizzled. . . Used in "I'll be bumswizzled." [*DN* Ed: In Pa., *gumswizzled.*] **1923** *DN* 5.205 **swMO**, Dad blame, interjection or expletive. Also *Dad burn . . Dad swizzle.* . . All forms frequently end in 'ed.' **1969–70** *DARE* (Qu. NN25b, *Weakened substitutes for 'damn' or 'damned': "Well, I'll be _____!"*) Inf **NY**132, Gumswizzled; **MI**122, Swizzled.

swizzled ppl adj[2] Also with *up* [*EDD* swizzle v. "To shrivel."] **Sth, S Midl** *esp freq among Black speakers*

Shriveled; withered; hence adj *swizzly.*

1917 *Prairie Gold* 139 **IA**, I'm fair swizzled up with the heat. **1936** Davis *Butcher Bird* 155 **neMS** [Black], This little swizzled up parson ain't got what it takes to get you het up with religion. **1956** Dorson *Negro Folktales* 144, He told her he greased himself like she did, till he got all swizzled up, and could go through the keyhole. **1966–70** *DARE* (Qu. LL3a, *Shrunk, dried up: "These apples are all _____."*) Infs **FL**33, **GA**42, 45, **LA**7, **MO**23, Swizzled (up); **LA**7, Swizzly; (Qu. LL3b, *Shrunk, dried up: "He's a little _____ old man."*) Inf **KY**5, Swizzled. [5 of 6 total Infs Black, 5 female] **1989** Pederson *LAGS Tech. Index* 190 **Gulf Region**, Shriveled . . ['swɪz̧l] (1 [inf]), ['swɪzld] (1).

swo' See **swear** B1

swoard See **sword**

swod n See **swad**

swo'd v See **swear** B1

swoggle v [Cf *SND* swaible (also *swabble*) v. 2 "To mop up, swab, wash, scour energetically"] =**wallop**.

1926 *DN* 5.404 **Ozarks**, Swoggle. . . To dip or stir. "Swoggle yer bread in them sogrums oncet!"

swoggled ppl adj Cf **hornswoggle** 3, **swizzled** ppl adj[1]

Used as a euphem for *damned*—freq in phr *I'll be swoggled* and var.

1894 *Short Stories* 17.38 **NY**, "Wal, may I be everlastingly swoggled!" she ejaculated. From a Durkey Points standard this was a fearful curse for a church member. **1908** *New Engl. Mag.* 38.653 **ME**, Well, I'll be swoggled! What a nerve! **1923** Nichols *Trust a Boy* 227 **UT**, "I'll be swoggled!" It was deputy Hawkins' strongest swear word! **1965–70** *DARE* (Qu. NN25b, *Weakened substitutes for 'damn' or 'damned': "Well, I'll be _____!"*) Inf **PA**175, Swoggled. **2004** *DARE* File—Internet, Well Jay I'll be swoggled. . . What a bummer. [*Ibid,* Well, I'll be swoggled by a horn.]

‡**swogon** n

A spirit, spook.

1900 Day *Up in ME* 157, For even in these days P.I.'s shake / At the great Swamp Swogon of Brassua Lake./ When it blitters and glabbers the long night through,/ And shrieks for the souls of the shivering crew. **1908** Day *King Spruce* 195 **ME**, Sure, the witherlicks and the swamp swogons did howl last night, gents, and they all did say as how Tommy Eye ought to be ashamed of the size of his drink.

swogun See **swagin**

swolden See **swell 3b**

swole See **swell 1, 2a, 3b**

swoled, swoll See **swell 2a, 3b**

swollened See **swell 2b, 3c**

swollop n, v [Prob var of *wallop*]

A blow; to strike; hence vbl n *swolloping* (pronc-sp *swalloping*) a beating, thrashing; ppl adj *swolloping* of a blow: strong, powerful.

1850 *Republican Compiler* (Gettysburg PA) 17 June 1/5, A root would catch the nose of the plough; the plough handles would hit John a swollop in the side; and John would commit a breach of the commandment "swear not at all." **1867** Harris *Sut Lovingood Yarns* 119 **TN,** So he snatched a long strip ove the broken ceilin plank, . . an' jis busted hit intu seventeen an' a 'alf pieces at wun swolloping lick ontu the part ove Lum, what fits a saddil. **1999** in 2004 Montgomery–Hall *Dict. Smoky Mt. Engl.* 589 **eTN,** *Swollop.* . . to slap, as a teacher punishing a pupil with a razor strap or belt, as in "Is that all the swalloping you're going to give me?"

swolned See **swell 2b**

swolt See **swell 3b**

swomp See **swamp**

swon See **swan**

swoney See **swanny**

swonger adj Also sp *swanga, swanger, swonga, swonguh* [Of Afr origin; cf **swonger** v] **seSC, eGA** *chiefly Gullah*
Fine, elegant; self-important, proud.

1848 Bartlett *Americanisms* 346, *Swanga.* A word used among the negroes in some parts of the South in connection with *buckra*, as *swanga buckra;* meaning a dandy white man, or literally a dandy devil. *Swanga* is an African word, and belongs to the language spoken near the Gaboon river, where anything gay or elegant is *swanga*. **1852** (1853) McIntosh *Lofty & Lowly* 2.6 **seGA** [Black], I believe sister Auber more swonger [Footnote: Proud] 'dan brudder Cato is of he freedom. [**1859** Mackay *Life & Liberty* 103, Among the pure Americanisms may be cited. . . *Swanger,* a dandy, or "swell."] **1860** Schoolcraft *Black Gauntlet* 201 **SC** [Black], Mr. John Seabrook, ges dun gib him one swanger boat. **1863** *Continental Mth.* 3.291 **seSC** [Gullah], Oh bress de swanga buckra man. *Ibid* 292, In dark room, upstars, am swanga gemman an' anoder buckra man. **1899** *Harper's New Mth. Mag.* 98.421 **GA,** Lizer wuz a settled 'oman, en she nebber hab no swonger way. **1922** Gonzales *Black Border* 163 **sSC, GA coasts** [Gullah], At last they were turned over to Mingo Brown, a pompous corporal, so puffed up with "a little brief authority" that most of the negroes grinned in his face, and some openly guffawed, "eh, eh, Buh Mingo swonguh fuh sowl!" *Ibid* 167, Unruly and insubordinate as a slave, he became "swonguh" with freedom, and was more or less insolent. **1930** Woofter *Black Yeomanry* 29 **seSC** (as of a1861) [Gullah], Next to the driver, in privilege and esteem, were the mechanics and house servants, the "swonga" Negroes who looked askance at the field hands. **1942** (1965) Parrish *Slave Songs* 42 **GA coast,** Many Southerners are familiar with the odd word *swanga* as applied to a proud, boastful Negro. **1954** *PADS* 21.39 **SC,** *Swonger.* . . Exuberant; proud; haughty. Gullah.

swonger v, hence vbl n *swongering* (pronc-sp *swangering*) Also sp *swanger, swongger* [Of Afr origin; cf quot 1949 and **swonger** adj] *chiefly Gullah*
To be proud; to strut, swagger, saunter.

1830 *City Gaz. & Commercial Daily Advt.* (Charleston SC) 13 May 2/4, *Cracker Dictionary—* . . To Swanger, To strut with free negro dignity. **1852** *S. Qrly. Rev.* 6.207 **SC,** He is excruciating, he carries a high head, he is on his p's and q's—or, to use another vulgarism, in this case that of the negro, he "swangers!" **1853** Simms *Sword & Distaff* 456 **SC,** Great was the swangering of Corporal Millhouse, as, with his brother overseers, he reviewed the result. **1926** Smith *Gullah* 34 **sSC, GA coasts,** *Lahgin',* and *swongger,* to assume self importance, to put on airs. Both of these seem pure Negro. **1949** Turner *Africanisms* 201 **sSC, GA coasts** [Gullah], [Words used in conversation:] ['swɑŋɒ] 'to be proud'—M[ende], [suɑŋɒ] 'to be haughty, selfish, evil'; 'to lie in ambush.' Cf. U[mbundu], [suɑŋgula] 'to gloat, to mock'; [esɑŋi] 'exul-

tation, exuberance which may annoy others.' **1954** *PADS* 21.39 **SC,** *Swonger.* . . To saunter, to stroll.

swonguh See **swonger** adj

swoo exclam Also *swook(ie), swooky;* for addit varr see quots **scattered, but esp PaGer area, sAppalachians** Cf **soo, sookie, whook**
Used as a call to cows, rarely to pigs; see quots.

1915 *DN* 4.190 **swVA,** *Sook.* . . Call to cattle at feeding time. Sometimes . . *swook(y), swook-calf(y).* **1941** Stuart *Men of Mts.* 82 **eKY,** Anse calls, "Swookie, swookie, cows! Swookie, swookie, cows!" The cows come to his call. **1965–70** *DARE* (Qu. K80, *The call that's used . . to get the cows in from the pasture*) Infs **IL114, NC53,** Swoo (cow); **CO22, LA2, OH60,** Swook; **OH41, PA207,** Swook [swuk]; **KY39,** Swook-cow; **NC53,** Swook heifer ['swu͜kɛfə·]; **KY84,** Swook-swook-swook. **1966** Dakin *Dial. Vocab. Ohio R. Valley* 2.270, *Calls to cows . . in pasture.* . . [B]lends which developed from the Pennsylvania German calls. . . *swookie!* (Seven Ranges and Muskingum Valley), *swook!* (Mountains, Bluegrass, Dearborn Upland, and Virginia Military District), *swoo!, swoo cow!* (s. Bluegrass and s. Mountains). . . It seems significant that these calls, while not common anywhere, are scattered in the areas that had many early settlers directly from the Pennsylvania German area . . or were settled by the partly German-speaking Cohees who came down the Great Valley. **1967** Faries *Word Geog. MO* 155, [Calls to cows in the pasture] Swook! (2 [of c700 infs]). **1986** Pederson *LAGS Concordance* (Calls to cows) 2 infs, **AR, TN,** Swoo (x2); 1 inf, **cAR,** Swoo, cow, swoo—to get them from pasture; 1 inf, **cwLA,** Swook, sook (x3); Swoo swook—come from pasture; *(Calls to pigs)* 1 inf, **cLA,** Swoo, pig (x2), whoo.

swoon n, v Also *swoond, swound;* ppl adj *swoonding* [Engl dial; cf *OED2, EDD* swound] Cf **drown, -ed** suff **1**
Std senses, var forms.

1684 (1977) Mather *Essay Providences* 101 **MA,** I have read of one. . . that fell into a Swoonding fit at the smell of a Rose. **1815** Humphreys *Yankey in England* 109, *Swound,* swoon. **1831** *Token* 137 **MA,** She was only in a swound, . . but came too, soon after the Doctor had left her. **1836** Paulding *Book St. Nicholas* 85 **NY,** "Maybe, after all," said one, "he is only in a swound." **1838** (1843) Hoffman *Wild Scenes* 2.149, Why, he'd 'a swounded right down on the spot, as I did. **1882** *Harper's New Mth. Mag.* 66.128 **NEng,** I may swoond or lose conscientiousness, but ef yer set it up then, I'll hev it hauled down agin ez soon ez I come to myself. **1904** Martin *Tillie* 283 **PA,** I seen she would mebbe have another such a swoond if she did n't get a long day out in the air. **1933** Miller *Lamb in His Bosom* 82 **GA,** She would have fallen and swounded away if Lonzo's hands had not held her up. **1942** Thomas *Blue Ridge Country* 54 **sAppalachians,** Swoonded dead away! **1957** Combs *Lang. S. Highlanders* np **sAppalachians,** Swound—swoon, v. and n. Ou pro[nounced] like *ou* in *out.* **2004** *DARE* File—Internet, Picture of me and Picture of first guy in eyeliner I ever swoonded over.

swop n [Cf *EDD* swop (at *sope* sb. 1) "A sup; a gulp"; *SND* swap sb.[1] 4 "A pull or swig of liquor"] Cf *DS* DD18

1986 *NADS Letters* **cMD,** swPA, Swop in the sense of 'sip'. Somewhere along the way I picked up the expression, as in "Let me have a swop of that" 'Let me have a sip of that', I know that it wasn't from my childhood in Pittsburgh. I thought it was from the Navy, but my Navy buddies don't know it. I put it on the questionnaire, and got . . clear, unequivocal "yes" answers from only two places, Annapolis, Md. and Greensburg, Penna. ("My grandmother uses it all the time!")

sword n Usu |'sord, 'soə(r)d|; also rarely |swoə·d| Pronc-sp **chiefly sAppalachians** *swoard;* also *swode* [Prob from Scots, Engl dial, though sp-pronc is also possible; cf Intro "Language Changes" I.8]
Std sense, var form.

1806 (1905) Clark *Orig. Jrls. Lewis & Clark Exped.* 4.333 **VA,** I gave him my *Sword,* 100 balls & powder. **1853** [see **you,** pron[2]] **1855** *Harper's New Mth. Mag.* 11.138 **NY,** I was at the the-*a*-ter t'other night, and there a fellow got hoppin' mad. . . when he told a fellow to draw his *swoard.* **1867** Harris *Sut Lovingood Yarns* 38 **TN,** He stole the Romun sword ofen the stone picter ove War thar. **1908** *DN* 3.281 **eAL, wGA,** *Semi-vowels.* w initial disappears in (w)oman, and is retained in sword. **1942** Hall *Smoky Mt. Speech* 88 **wNC, eTN,** In *sword,* [w] has been either retained or restored from the spelling: [swoə·d]. **1943** Chase *Jack*

Tales 85 **wNC** (as of 1880s), Hit's a swoard my grandpa gave me. **1966–67** *DARE* FW Addit **swNC**, *Sword* [swoɚd].

sword fern n

A fern of the genus *Polystichum,* esp a **Christmas fern** (here: *Polystichum acrostichoides*) in the eastern half of the US and *P. munitum* chiefly in the Pacific NW.   Also called **holly fern;** for other names of var spp see **dagger fern, mountain holly ~**

   1896 *Land of Sunshine* 5.113 **CA,** The name sword fern is apt because of the sword-like pinnules.   **1914** *Amer. Fern Jrl.* 4.11 **WA,** *Polystichum munitum. . . Sword Fern.* Leaves 2–5 feet long. . . Alaska to Idaho and California.   **1932** in 1994 Steinbeck *Novels & Stories* 74 **CA,** Sword ferns grew rankly under the alders.   **1939** *Amer. Midland Naturalist* 22.235 **OR,** *Polystichum munitum. . . Sword-fern.* Not abundant except in the heavy forest of Redblanket Creek.   **1967** *DARE* Tape **WA**28, A sword fern is a fern that has the fronds—the fronds are completely covered by a coarser type of leaf on the fern—comes up in a single long leaf and is a graceful long leaf.   **1967** *DARE* FW Addit, Both **MA**5 and **MA**6 use "sword fern" for "Christmas fern."   **1973** Hitchcock–Cronquist *Flora Pacific NW* 53, *Polystichum . . Holly-fern; Christmas-fern; Sword-fern.*   **1976** *Greenfield Recorder* (MA) 23 Oct [Hemenway column], "Ferning." That was the gathering and bunching of sword (Christmas) ferns and . . lady fern for use by florists and decorators.   **1994** Guterson *Snow Falling* 153 **nwWA,** She'd sat among sword ferns six feet tall.   **2006** *Seattle Daily Times* (WA) 28 June sec F 8 (Internet), The native sword fern, Polystichum munitum, endures dry times with stalwart growth.

swordfish n   Cf billfish

1 Std: a fish of the genus *Xiphias,* esp a widely distributed marine fish *(X. gladius)* marked by a long, flat, swordlike bill. For other names of this sp see **au, broadbill 4**

2 Any of var often billed fishes thought to resemble **1** above, as:

a =**longnose gar.**

   1815 Drake *Natural View Cincinnati* 141 **OH,** Perch, pike, eel, yellowcat and sword-fish are most esteemed.   **1852** Lanman *Hist. MI* 29, The principal fish which are found in the surrounding lakes and interior waters of the country are the sturgeon, whitefish, . . muskalunjeh, . . carp, mullet, billfish, swordfish, . . sheep's-head, the gar, and many other kinds.   **1897** *Outing* 30.436, The second of our curious fish was the garpike. . . To the boys they were "swordfish". . . A big gar, with his round, tapering body, stiletto-like jaws, sharp teeth and wicked-looking eyes.   **1911** U.S. Bur. Census *Fisheries 1908* 310, *Gar-pike (Lepisosteus osseus). . .* [is often called] "swordfish."

b The cutlass fish *(Trichiurus lepturus).*

   1842 DeKay *Zool. NY* 4.110, *Trichiurus Lepturus. . .* Tail compressed, tapering very gradually to a fine point. . . This is known here by the fishermen under the name of *Ribbon-fish.* At Jamaica, it is called *Swordfish.*   **1933** LA Dept. of Conserv. *Fishes* 165, In Louisiana the Cutlass Fish is often called the "Swordfish."

c A **needlefish 1** (here: *Strongylura marina*).

   1906 NJ State Museum *Annual Rept. for 1905* 204, *Tylosurus* [= *Strongylura*] *marinus . .* Sword Fish.

d also *marlin swordfish:* The black marlin *(Makaira nigricans).*

   1947 Caine *Salt Water* 23, *Makaira nigricans ampla. . .* Also known as billfish, black marlin, . . marlin swordfish and swordfish.

swore   See swear B2

swored   See swear B1, 2

sworp v   See swarp v

sworp n   See swarp n

swound   See swoon

swow v   Also sp *swowe*   chiefly NEng   Cf swan

To swear; to declare—usu in exclam *I swow!*

   1809 Lindsley *Love & Friendship* 38 **NEng,** I swow I blieve I am raked fore and aft, from stem tewe starn.   **1830** *MA Spy & Worcester Co. Advt.* (Worcester MA) 28 July 4/1, Now I *swow,* Mr. Southerner, you *hadn't ought* to open your mouth about Yankee talk.   **1838** Kettell *Yankee Notions* 148, And it grewe and grewe, till it look'd juste like / I constable, I swowe!   **1853** Simms *Sword & Distaff* 449 **SC,** He's after

the sperrit and the flesh, both! Lawd! I swow! **a1861** in 1930 IL State Hist. Soc. *Jrl.* 23.238 **IL,** Scratching his head, saying "O, I swow, what a damned time this is".   **1894** Frederic *Marsena* 44 **nNY,** Well, I swow! **1900** Day *Up in ME* 5 **ME,** "Did ye break my jug?" she was yellin' still./ "No, durn yer pelt, but I swow I will."   **1903** (1984) Ayer *Autobiog.* 3 **NEng,** Older girls used words that I had been taught were wicked. . . They tried to get me to say them, "I swow, I vow, I swanny, I vanny, good Lord," etc.   **1905** *DN* 3.22 **cCT,** *Swow. . .* To swear. 'I swow.'   **1907** *DN* 3.191 **seNH,** *I swow. . .* Derived by crossing *vow* and *swear.*   **1914** *DN* 4.81 **ME, nNH,** *Swow, I. . .* I swear, I affirm.   **1939** in Lib. of Congress *Amer. Memory: WPA Life Hist.* (Internet) **VT,** I swow, I'd forgot all about it.   **1967–68** *DARE* (Qu. NN32, *Exclamations like 'I swear' or 'I vow'*) Infs **CT**16, **IN**40, **OR**1, Swow.

swrink   See shrink

swub   See shrub n[1]

swull(ed)   See swell 2a

swullen   See swell 3a

swulter v, hence ppl adj *swultering*   Similarly adjs *swult(e)ry* [Prob var of *swelter,* with forms *swult(e)ry* infl by *sultry*]   chiefly S Midl   Cf Intro "Language Changes" I.8, **sulter**

To swelter.

   1864 in 2004 *DARE* File—Internet **IN,** It was the warmest day almost emaginable. & we almost swultered.   *Ibid,* It was a tremendous warm day & very muddy. & so swultry that we could hardly march at tall.   **1888** *Century Illustr. Mag.* 36.772 **csTN,** But aiter stewin' roun' in that swulterin' valley fer nigh onter a week . . I feel ez slimpsy ez a dish-rag.   *Ibid* 777, Blazes, jes ter think er all them nigger folks a-slatherin' roun' through the sun . . —you 'd'a' thought they wus naiterly boun' ter swulter.   **1898** in 2004 *DARE* File—Internet **seGA,** The wind blew verry gently inicitive of what the fourth generraly is verry hot and Swultry.   **1917** in 1944 *ADD* **sWV,** *Sultry. . .* swultry.   **1966–67** *DARE* (Qu. B3, *If a day is very hot . . it's [a]* _____) Inf **AR**1, Swultery; (Qu. B4, *A day when the air is very still, moist, and warm—it's* _____) Inf **AR**17, Swultery; **KY**31, Swultry ['swʌltri].   **1983** *MJLF* 9.1.58 **ceKY** (as of 1956), *Swultry . . .* sultry.   **c1996** in 2004 Montgomery-Hall *Dict. Smoky Mt. Engl.* 587 **wNC,** *Swelter. . .* swulter [1 inf].   *Ibid* 588 **wNC,** Sweltry. . . pronounced *swultry* [1 inf].

swum   See swim A1c

swummed, swumt   See swim A1d

swunged, swungt   See swing v Bb

‡swurge v [*surge* + intrusive *w;* cf Intro "Language Changes" I.8]

   1931 Faulkner in *Scribner's Mag.* 89.585 **MA,** Something come swurging up outen the bushes and jumped the road clean, without touching hoof to it.   **1934** Faulkner in *Sat. Eve. Post* 10 Feb 9 **MS,** He swurged all over me like a barn falling down.

sy n   See scythe n[1]

-sy suff   See -sie

s'y v phr   See say v B1b

sycamore n   Usu |ˈsɪkəmor, -moɚ|; also **chiefly S Midl** |ˈsɪkɪmor, ˈsɪki-|; for addit varr see quot 1965–70   Pronc-spp *sick(e)ymore*

A Forms.

   1940 in 2004 Montgomery-Hall *Dict. Smoky Mt. Engl.* 589 **wNC, eTN,** The trees was silver bell and dog wood sickeymore walnut ash.   **1940** in 1944 *ADD* 619 **swPA, nWV,** [ˈsɪkimor]. 'Sickymore tree.' Old speaker.   **1942** Hall *Smoky Mt. Speech* 60 **wNC, eTN,** A few words are generally sounded with [ɪ] [in the middle syllable]: alcohol, dynamite, miracle, sassafras, spectacles, sycamore.   **1965–70** *DARE* (Qu. T13) Infs **FL**19, **KY**34, **MS**70, 72, **MO**19, **NC**79, **TX**32, **WV**3, [Proncs of the type [ˈsɪkiˌmoɚ]]; **LA**8, **SC**10, 19, 21, 24, 40, [ˈsɪkɪˌmo(ə)]; **LA**22, [ˈsɪkəˌmo]; **NC**55, [ˈsɪkɪˌmoɚ]; **SC**26, [ˌsɪkɪˈmo]; **KY**29, [ˈsɪkəˌməɪn]—some say; **MA**100, [ˈsɪgəmo]; **NJ**69, [ˈsɪklməɚ].   **2006** *DARE* File—Internet **AR,** Hey Mike I sent you an e-mail. Will look through my piles Sunday to look for 5/4 sickymore.

B Sense.

Also attrib: A tree of the genus *Platanus.*   **widespread, but less freq Nth**   See Map on p. 472   Also called **buttonball, buttonwood 1, plane tree 1.**   For other names of *P. occi-*

dentalis, native to much of the eastern two-thirds of the US, see **ballwood tree, buttonbush 2, button tree 1, cucumber tree 3, featherball, fuzzy-ball, gumball tree, ironwood a(4), sevenbark 4, slick-bark tree, water beech 1, whitewood 4, Zaccheus tree;** for other names of var spp see **alamo 2, aliso 1, valley sycamore;** for other names spec to the bristly brown ball-like fruit see **buttonball, buzzard bread, monkey ball 2, porcupine egg**

1709 (1967) Lawson *New Voyage* 106 **NC, SC,** The Sycamore, in these Parts, grows in a low, swampy Land, by River-sides. **1750** (1888) Walker *Jrl.* 56 **sAppalachians,** I Blazed several Trees in the fork and marked T W on a Sycamore Tree. **1855** Newbrough *Lady West* 206 **CA,** In the early days of Sacramento, a number of oak and sycamore trees ornamented nearly every part of the city; but they have long since yielded to that formidable weapon, the ax. **1888** *Century Illustr. Mag.* Sept 770 **Sth,** A favorite lamp . . was a saucer of lard with a dry sycamore ball floating in the midst of it. **1897** Sudworth *Arborescent Flora* 206, *Platanus occidentalis.* . . Common Names. Sycamore [*DARE* Ed: widely reported east of the Missip R]. *Ibid* 207, *Platanus racemosa.* . . Sycamore (Cal.) . . *Platanus wrightii.* . . Sycamore (Ariz.) **1899** (1912) Green *VA Folk-Speech* 434, Sycamore. . . Buttonwood; the plane tree. **1949** Kurath *Word Geog.* 76, The sycamore goes by this name regularly in the valley of the Ohio and its tributaries. East of the Alleghanies *sycamore* is not common except for the Pennsylvania German area. In New England *sycamore* is as distinctly a book word as among the Pennsylvania Germans and in the large urban centers of Philadelphia and New York City. **c1960** *Wilson Coll.* **csKY,** Sycamore. . . the common planetree. Buttonball is unheard of, as is planetree. **1965–70** *DARE* (Qu. T13, . . *Names . . for . . sycamore*) 401 Infs, **widespread, but less freq Nth,** Sycamore; **CA**181, California sycamore; **CA**7, Eastern sycamore, mountain sycamore, Oriental sycamore, valley sycamore; **OH**33, **WV**3, White sycamore, yellow sycamore; **TN**6, Yellow sycamore. **1970** *DARE* Tape **CA**179, My mother was born where that sycamore tree was; **CA**182, At this time of the year the canyon is especially green. We have a lot of native live oak and sycamore; **CA**193, We make tea out of the bark out of the sycamore; **TX**85, Sycamore—local tree. **2005** *DARE* File—Internet **sLA,** Cypress trees thrive in the swamp areas. . . Others [=trees and shrubs] include ash, elm, . . plum trees, pecan, hackberry, honey locust, sycamore, and swamp elder.

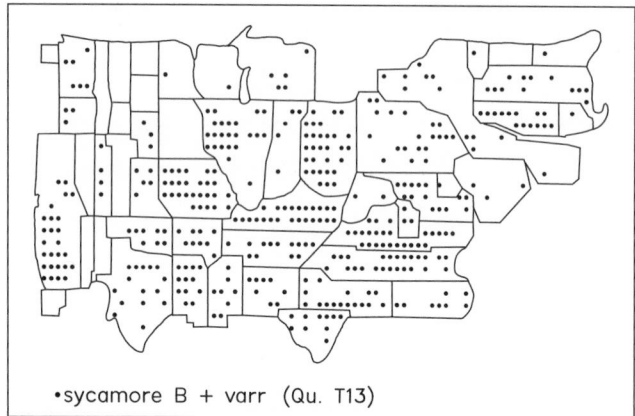

•sycamore B + varr (Qu. T13)

sycamore maple n [*OED2* 1796 →]
Std: a naturalized **maple** (here: *Acer pseudoplatanus*). Also called **plane tree 2**

sye See **scythe** n[1]

sye I See **say** v **B1b**

sylte n Usu |'sɪltə|; for addit varr see quots Also *silta, sulta, sylta* [Dan, Norw *sylte,* Sw *sylta*] **chiefly Scandinavian settlement areas, esp MN** Cf **headcheese 1, suelze**
A dish of pork or veal pressed into the form of a loaf and served sliced; hence nouns *kalfsylta, kalvsylta* spec: such a dish made of veal.

1933 *Southtown Economist* (Chicago IL) 16 Nov 12/8, [Advt:] *Carlson's Famous Homemade Swedish Sausage.* . . Kalf, sylta [sic]— Press sylta—Blood pudding—Lingon berries. **1935** *Racine Jrl.-Times* (WI) 1 Nov 11/5, [Advt:] Home made sylte—Liverloaf—Rullepolse. **1963** *Norw.-Amer. Studies* 22.186 **ND,** The head was boiled with added

lean pieces of pork and all of it then cut up small; this . . was placed in a strong white cloth. . . It was then put away in brine with a weight over it so that it would become solid enough to slice nicely. This pressed meat was called *sylte* and, eaten with *lefse,* it was a Christmas delicacy. **1965–68** *DARE* (Qu. H43, *Foods made from parts of the head and inner organs of an animal*) Inf **KS**7, Kalvsylta—used occasionally = headcheese; **WI**47, Sulta [sul'tɑ]—Swedish; **MN**14, Sylte [sɪltə]—Swedish for "headcheese"—common term here; **UT**3, Sylte—Swedish—headcheese; (Qu. H45, *Dishes made with meat, fish, or poultry that everybody around here would know, but that people in other places might not*) Inf **MN**6, Sylte; (Qu. H65, *Foreign foods favored by people around here*) Inf **MN**1, Sylte [sɪltə]—Scandinavian potted meat; **WY**5, Sylte [sɪltə]—Swedish dish like jellied veal. **1966** Tufford *Scandinavian Recipes* 52 **MN,** Kalvsylta (Pressed Jellied Veal). **1967** *DARE* Tape **MN**6, Sulta ['sul,t'a] is shoulder veal in joints. You boil until cooked and . . run the meat through the grinder. You put it back in the same water and cook it longer and you use salt and pepper for seasoning . . you put it in a pan and gel. You put it in about one and a half inches thick. And that's all, and it just gels all by itself and cut it and most people like it served with vinegar. . . We make it at Christmastime. **1971** *AmSp* 46.172 **Chicago IL,** Loaf of jellied pressed-meat made of flesh from the head of a hog . . *sylte* [2 of 37 infs, both of Norwegian parentage]. **1973** Allen *LAUM* 1.288 **MN** (as of c1950), A . . Minneapolis physician reports that his Swedish parents use *silta,* in an English context, for a product very much like head cheese. **1987** *NY Times* (NY) 17 May sec 4 26/1, The sylte-on-rye . . crowd is apt to be watching the Norwegian parade in Bay Ridge.

‡sympathy v
1923 *DN* 5.222 **swMO,** Sympathy. . . To sympathize with. "I sympathy him f'r his troubles."

sy-reen See **siren**

syringa n [*OED2* 1664 →] Cf **sweet syringa**
=**mock orange 1b.**
1773 in 1943 *Amer. Philos. Soc. Trans.* 33.136 **GA,** The . . Road . . [was] good and o'rshadowed by fragrant Forest Trees . . having their Tall streight Tronks, ornamented with wreaths & Garlands of . . Floriferous Climbers, Woodbines[,] Jassimies, Syringa &c. **1849** Howitt *Our Cousins in OH* 94, A large syringa, studded with its star-like, orange-scented flowers, grew side by side with a sweet-briar in full bloom. **1917** *Science* new ser 46.17, Syringa is a popular name but unfortunately has become attached to mock orange (*Philadelphus*) instead of correctly to lilac. **1951** *Condor* 53.132 **OR,** The understory of this association consists of nine-bark . . , Indian peach (*Osmaronia cerasiformis*), western hazel . . and western valley syringa (*Philadelphus gordonianus*). **1977** *Greenfield Recorder* (MA) 2 Apr 8/1 [Hemenway column] (as of c1900), There was a small sour cherry tree . . , and of course, a syringa bush in front of the parlor window. **c1977** *DARE* File **cnMA** (as of a1930), Syringa—name . . for mock orange. . . I didn't hear *mock orange* until I left here. **1985** *Valley Independent* (Monessen PA) 26 Sept [4]/3 (newspaperarchive.com), It [=the marigold] received no more notice than, well, than syringa. And who outside of Idaho, where it reigns as the state flower, ever speaks of the syringa. **2006** *DARE* File—Internet **ID,** Syringa—Mock Orange—*Philadelphus lewisii.* The Syringa (*Philadelphus lewisii*) was designated the state flower of Idaho by the legislature in 1931. It is a branching shrub with clusters of white, fragrant flowers.

syrup n Usu |'sɪrəp, 'sɝ·əp|; also esp **Sth, S Midl** |'sʌrəp, sɝ·p|; for addit varr see quots Pronc-spp *serup, sir(u)p, surp, surrop, sur(r)up* Cf **stirrup**
Std senses, var forms.
1867 *Harper's New Mth. Mag.* 35.132 **cwWI,** Pownd ital toogether and put init hav of a pint of surp. . . rubarb surrup ecual parts. **1873** *Appletons' Jrl.* 9.139 **GA,** This is prime weather fur bilin' surrup. **1893** Shands *MS Speech* 76, Surup ['sʌrəp]. Syrup is commonly so pronounced by all classes. **1904** *DN* 2.428 **Cape Cod MA** (as of a1857), Surrup. . . Syrup. **1904** [see **syrup cake**]. **1909** *DN* 3.378 **eAL, wGA,** Syrup. . . Pronounced [s3(r)up] or [s3(r)p]. **1910** *DN* 3.450 **cwNY,** Surrup. . . Syrup. **1917** *DN* 4.401 **neOH,** Syrup, [sɝ·əp], *rarely* [sɪrəp]. **1936** *AmSp* 11.32 **eTX,** The usual pronunciations of *syrup* and *stirrup* are ['sɝ·əp], ['stɝ·əp], but less well educated or careless speakers say [sɝ·p], [stɝ·p]. **1937** *AmSp* 12.287 **wVA,** Syrup is ['særəp] (sometimes ['sɝəp]). **1941** *AmSp* 16.16 **eTX** [Black], Syrup. . . [sʌːp]. **1942** *AmSp* 17.31 **seNY,** Syrup [sɪrəp] 66 [of 420 infs], [sɪ·rəp] 8, [sɛrəp] 3, [sɛ·rəp] 1, [sɝ·rəp] 12. **1968** *DARE* (Qu. T4, *The place where . . trees grow together and sap is gathered*) Inf **IN**9, Maple syrup [sɝ·p] grove.

1976 Garber *Mountain-ese* 89 s**Appalachians,** *Surp* . . syrup. **1982** Slone *How We Talked* 26 e**KY** (as of c1950), *S'urp*—syrup. **1989** Pederson *LAGS Tech. Index* 173, *Syrup.* [Of 914 infs, 678 offered proncs of the types ['sʌr(ə)p]; 85 infs, proncs of the type ['sʌrɪp]; 103 infs, proncs of the types ['sɪr(ə)p]; 18 infs, proncs of the type ['sɪrɪp]; 49 infs, proncs of the types ['sɛr(ə)p]; 10 infs, proncs of the type ['sur(ə)p].] **2000** Shores *Tangier Is.* 183 **Chesapeake Bay,** Words typically with the vowel of *bet* before "r" of two syllables *(Mary, merry, cherry, dairy, mirror, syrup)* are pronounced also with the vowel of "bird" as "Mery," "mery," "chery," "dery," "mera," and "serup." **2006** *DARE* File—Internet **WI,** Another example: "My friend says 'sirp,'" says Kristen Kangas of the Eau Claire area. "She's from Wisconsin, too."

syrup biscuit n   chiefly **Sth**
=**molasses biscuit.**

1949 *SW Rev.* 34.248 e**TX,** If we both had a syrup biscuit I would eat mine quick and then say 'havers' and get half of his. **1954** *PADS* 21.39 **SC,** *Syrup biscuit.* . . A biscuit with a hole punched into the edge with a finger and filled with syrup. **2000** *DARE* File—Internet se**GA,** You are very Wiregrass if . . you have ever had a syrup biscuit, where you stick your finger in the biscuit and pour it full of syrup. **2002** *Terry Co. TX* 90 (as of 1939), Mother . . would give me a syrup biscuit (made by making a hole in the biscuit with a finger or thumb and filling it with syrup). **2002** *DARE* File—Internet **SC,** Take your finger and punch a hole in a good hot biscuit, then pour the syrup in. You've got a fine syrup biscuit then. **2005** *Ibid* **AL,** One day He went to school toting his slate in one hand and his lunch bucket in the other, . . containing one syrup biscuit that his mother had poked a hole in and filled with sorghum syrup, a hard boiled egg, . . and a buttered biscuit with sugar in it for des[s]ert.

syrup cake n   chiefly **Sth**
A type of dessert cake made with cane or sorghum syrup.

1897 (1899) Owens *Mrs. Owens' New Cook Book* 512, *Florida Syrup Cake.* [Recipe includes eggs, water, soda, syrup, butter, flour.] **1904** *Atlanta Constitution* (GA) [10 July 22]/4 (newspaperarchive.com), The "booby" [prize] . . was won by Mr. Boyd, it being a sirup cake in a large box. **1970** *DARE* File ne**TX,** Syrup cakes—I've never seen these in any other region. **1984** Hancock *Choestoe* 5 ne**GA,** Hot biscuits and pones of corn bread smeared with fresh butter, a sweet *syrup cake,* milk for us and coffee for the grown-ups. [Footnote to *syrup cake:*] A sort of fruit cake with dried apples, black walnuts and plum jam added to its batter laced with black-strap molasses made from the sorghum cane syrup. **1996** *TX Highway Dept. TX Highways* Dec 49 ce**TX,** *Syrup Cake (Gateau du Sirop)*—This simple, gingerbread-like dessert is adapted from an old Cajun recipe. **2005** *DARE* File—Internet s**AL,** She fixed our sack lunches with oatmeal cookies or syrup cake. This was a special treat because my "Big Daddy" and Dad made the cane syrup. *Ibid,* Old Fashioned Syrup Cake with Sorghum. . . If you substitute molasses, it's not as good.

syrup camp n   Also *maple syrup camp*   esp **N Cent, NEast**
=**sugar camp.**

1895 *Youth's Companion* 69.661 **NH,** Usually they frequent the saloons . . , but these four concluded to loaf at our syrup camp. **1899** *Daily Kennebec Jrl.* (Augusta ME) 8 Mar 10/3, It would do me good to stay there in that syrup camp and assist in making syrup. **1902** *Ft. Wayne Weekly Sentinel* (IN) 12 Mar 5/1, James Morton is running a maple syrup camp. **1921** *Chron.-Telegram* (Elyria OH) 8 Apr 10/3, Irvin . . returned home on Wednesday after spending a month with his cousin . . keeping in the maple syrup camp. **1947** *Bedford Gaz.* (PA) 1 May sec 2 2/6, The Meyersdale Chamber of Commerce . . air-expressed the songstress . . an invitation . . to see what goes on behind the scenes of a maple syrup camp. **1969** *DARE* (Qu. T4, *The place where . . trees grow together and sap is gathered*) Inf **IN**73, Maple syrup camp. **1990** *Daily Herald* (Arlington Heights IL) 7 Aug 2/3, Stephen and Glaida Funk are . . operators of one of Illinois' last remaining syrup camps. . . The first syrup camp was set up on land the family settled in 1824. **2005** *DARE* File—Internet n**IN,** A whole series of events revolve around maple syrup; demonstrations, chain saw carving, a visit to a syrup camp . . and all-you-can-eat pancakes. *Ibid* cs**WI,** We have our maple syrup camp set up at the top of the hill. *Ibid* w**VA,** Enjoy a trip to see a working maple syrup camp.

syrup candy n   chiefly **Gulf States, GA, SC**   See Map
Taffy made from cane syrup.

1933 Miller *Lamb in His Bosom* 81 **GA,** Dicie would make syrup candy and there was much talking and laughing about the fireplace. **1938** Rawlings *Yearling* 325 n**FL,** You figger a fruit cake and a bait o'

syrup candy'll be welcome for my share? **1965–70** *DARE* (Qu. H80, *Kinds of candy . . made at home*) 26 Infs, **chiefly Gulf States, GA, SC,** Syrup candy; **GA**36, Cane syrup candy; (Qu. H82a, *Cheap candies sold especially for schoolchildren*) Inf **GA**3, Black syrup candy; (Qu. H82b, *Kinds of cheap candy that used to be sold years ago*) Infs **LA**16, **TX**104, Syrup candy. **1968** *DARE* FW Addit **GA**28, Syrup candy can be plaited ['plætɪd]—i.e., taffy can be braided. **1971** *Foxfire* Spring–Summer 103 n**GA,** Invite th'young folks in t'make syrup candy. **1986** Pederson *LAGS Concordance,* 3 infs, **GA,** Syrup candy; [1 inf, cn**GA,** Syrup candy—of molasses;] 1 inf, se**AL,** Syrup candy—made from syrup, cooked, pulled; 1 inf, nw**GA,** We cooked this syrup candy what you pull.

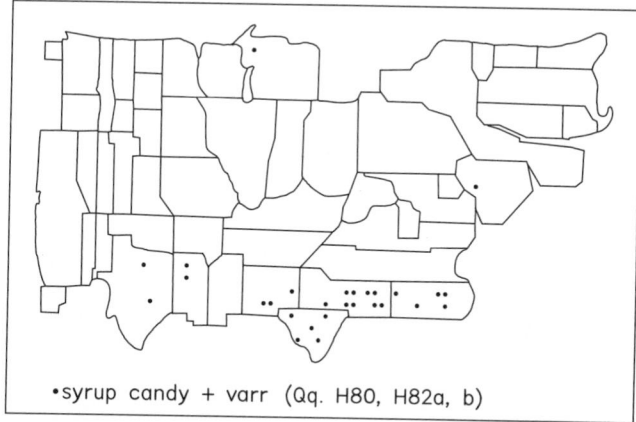

•syrup candy + varr (Qq. H80, H82a, b)

syrup grove n   Also *maple syrup grove*   esp **N Cent**   Cf **sugar grove**
=**maple orchard.**

1966 *Press-Gaz.* (Hillsboro OH) 22 Apr 3/3, There was little damage to the woods, which is part of the Vance maple syrup grove. **1966–68** *DARE* (Qu. T4, *The place where . . trees grow together and sap is gathered*) Infs **IN**9, **MI**27, Maple syrup grove; **OH**18, Syrup grove. **1974** *Stevens Point Daily Jrl.* (WI) 8 Apr 18/1, [Advt:] There is a nice maple syrup grove, and balance pulpwood & lumber. **2002** Independent Organic Inspectors Assoc. *Inspectors' Rept.* Fall 6 (Internet) **VT,** Come visit a Maple Syrup Grove in my back yard.

syrup house n

1 A building in which cane or sorghum juice is boiled down. chiefly **Sth**

1884 *WI State Ag. Soc. Trans.* 21.400, I have ten feet fall from mill to evaporating house; four feet from level of evaporator to floor of syrup house. **1912** Zettler *War Stories* 132 **GA,** The smokehouse stood open, likewise the . . syrup house. **1913** *LA Planter & Sugar Manufacturer* 51.149, Major Glynn is having installed on his Kelson plantation . . a "Webre Closed Evaporator"; great claims are made for the efficacy of this apparatus, which will considerably add to the perfection of this splendid syrup house. **1931** *Dothan Eagle* (AL) 7 Sept 2/3, Let us work for a resurrection . . of the old time Southern farm home, on which we found barns, smoke-houses and syrup houses all full and no locks on any of them. **1966–68** *DARE* (Qu. M22, . . *Kinds of buildings . . on farms*) Infs **FL**6, **GA**33, Syrup house; **SC**24, Syrup house—the place where cane was cooked. **1986** Pederson *LAGS Concordance,* 3 infs, **AL, FL, GA,** Syrup house.

2 =**sugar house 1.**

1903 *OH Farmer* 103.218, *The Maple Sugar Season.* . . If I were asked for a motto to hang up in the syrup house or boiling place, it would be . . "With Neatness and Despatch."

syrup off v phr   chiefly **NEast**   Cf **stir off** v phr, **sugar off** v phr

To draw off completed maple (or rarely sorghum) syrup from the pan or evaporator; broadly, to make maple syrup; hence vbl n, also attrib, *syruping off.*

1859 *Prairie Farmer* new ser 3.130 se**MI,** One of these pans I used as a clarifier, the others as defecators and for "syruping off." **1860** *New Engl. Farmer* 12.245, When the sap arrives at the lower reservoir, it is strained through woolen; they calculate to syrup off once a day. **1872** *VT State Bd. Ag. Report* 1.216, One should make it a point to syrup off quite often. **1893** in 2005 *DARE* File—Internet **Upstate NY,** After dinner, Tim boiled sap. . . Then I took the team & went in the woods. We syruped off & brought up about 35 gallons but not very thick. The women will finish it off on the kitchen stove and bottle it. **1895** *Ibid* **cnPA,** Worked in the bush. . . Syruped off in the morning Had 8 Pails and again at night Had 2 pails. **1917** *DN* 4.401 **neOH,** *Syrup off.* . . Boil maple sap to the consistency of syrup and then remove it from the fire by drawing it off through a cock or similar device. "He syrupped off five times today." Also N.H., Vt., Ky., N.Y. **1922** Burroughs *My Boyhood* 40 **Upstate NY,** At the end of a couple of days of hard boiling Hiram would "syrup off," having reduced two hundred pails of sap to five or six of syrup. The syrupping-off often occurred after dark. **1927** *AmSp* 2.365 **cwWV,** *Syrup off* . . to remove the sap which has been boiled down to syrup. "We syruped off several times to-day." **1950** *Chron.–Telegram* (Elyria OH) 28 Feb 14/5, Be sure your "syruping off" accessories are clean and in good working condition. **1969** *DARE* Tape **VT**7, In the old style, you used to put it all in for a day, and then when it come night you'd syrup off—what they call syruping off—and you would take off all the syrup you had in there.

syrup on snow n Also *maple syrup on snow* esp **NEng** Cf **sugar on snow**

=jack wax 1.

[**1890** Wood *Wilderness MI* 84, "But it needs a habus corpus to git you away when you git to lickin' th' warm sugar," the little justice said. "Er a mixin' syrup on snow," ventured Peg-leg.] **1901** *N. Adams Transcript* (MA) 9 Mar [4]/4 (newspaperarchive.com), A resolution was read favoring a music festival, but an amendment that maple syrup on snow be served in connection with this acted as a rider to defeat the bill. **1939** [see **sugar party**]. **1972** *Portsmouth Herald* (NH) 2 Mar 10/1, Refreshments will consist of syrup on snow, sour pickles and home-made doughnuts.

sythe See **sithe**

Syttende Mai n [Norw "May 17th"] in Norwegian settlement areas

A public celebration of the signing of the Norwegian constitution on May 17, 1814.

1914 *Lincoln Daily News* (NE) 16 May 3/5 **MN,** The keys of the twin cities were given the Norwegians who came for the three days' celebration of Syttende maie [sic], Norway's "Fourth of July," starting today. **1934** *Bismarck Tribune* (ND) 15 May 7/4, Syttende Mai, or Norwegian Independence day, will be celebrated with two events in Bismarck Thursday evening. **1964** *Oshkosh Daily Northwestern* (WI) 22 Apr 34/1, Stoughton—Not everyone in this southern Wisconsin city is Norwegian, but in the middle of May each year, they all act like full-blooded Vikings. For May 17, "Syttende Mai," is Norwegian Independence Day, just as much a holiday in Stoughton as in Oslo, Bergen, or Trondheim. **1968** *DARE* (Qu. FF16, . . *Local contests or celebrations*) Inf **AK**8, Syttende Mai fest. **1969** *Richland Observer* (Richland Center WI) 22 May sec 1 10/3, The hour and a half long Syttende Mai parade . . started on time and each unit was interesting, with many cities, including Iowa and Illinois delegations, represented. **1985** Keillor *Lake Wobegon* 280 **MN,** Crocuses, tulips, and those little blue and yellow flowers, what they call Norwegian incarnations, up by May 17, *Syttende Mai.* **2003** *San Diego Union–Tribune* (CA) 16 May sec E 14 (Internet), Bunads, the festive Norwegian attire reserved for special events, will be much in evidence this weekend as San Diego's Norwegian-American community celebrates Syttende Mai, marking the May 17, 1814, signing of the Norwegian Constitution. **2006** *DARE* File—Internet **wWA,** Seattle's Syttende Mai Committee is very excited to announce that Svein Ludvigsen . . will be our Grand Marshal.

t', (-)ta See **to** prep, adv **A2**

taan See **town** n

tab n

1 =**tablet.** [Abbr]
1899 Thomas *Arizona* 141, Take the back of that writing tab. . . *Tears pasteboard back into two pieces.* **1916** *Lincoln Daily Star* (NE) 18 May 9/1, Hanlon . . grabbed his writing tab and proceeded forthwith to make out a list. **1950** *Chillicothe Constitution–Tribune* (MO) 23 Aug 5/7, [Advt:] *Brush* and *Pencil* Drawing Tab 10¢. **1968** *DARE* (Qu. F48, . . *Pages of writing paper glued together at the top with a cardboard back;* not asked in early QRs) Inf **CT**2A, Tabs. **1968** *La Verne Leader* (CA) 3 July [10]/2 (newspaperarchive.com), [Advt:] 120 Sheets *Writing Tab* 39¢ Val. 4 for $1. **2004** *DARE* File **cwCA** (as of c1955), When I was in grade school we called pads of paper *tabs,* short for *tablets,* I guess. We had writing tabs and drawing tabs.

2 =**ear tag.**
1968–70 *DARE* (Qu. K18, . . *Kind of mark . . to identify a cow*) Infs **MI**83, **OH**78, Ear tab; **NY**52, **PA**135, Tab in the ear; [**SC**69, Tab the ear—put a little metal clamp in the ear].

3 A small amount, dab. Cf **tad** n[1] **2**
1965–68 *DARE* (Qu. LL6b, *A small, indefinite amount* . . *"I'll put in just a _____ of butter."*) Infs **FL**26, **MN**15, **OR**1, **TN**14, **UT**3, **VA**21, Tab; (Qu. LL6c, *A small, indefinite amount* . . *"It still needs just a _____ of cinnamon."*) Inf **GA**11, Tab.

taba n Also *taber, tapaka, tarba, typa* [Varr of **catalpa** or **catawba**]
1967–69 *DARE* (Qu. T9, *The common shade tree with large heart-shaped leaves, clusters of white blossoms, and long thin seed pods or 'beans'*) Inf **IL**71, Tapaka [təˈpɑˌkɑ] tree; (Qu. P6, . . *Kinds of worms . . used for bait*) Inf **LA**7, Taba worm [ˈtɑbə ˌwɜɪm]; **LA**18, Tarba [ˈtɑɚbə] worm. **c1970** Pederson *Dial. Surv. Rural GA* **seGA** (*What do you call large worms used for bait?*) 1 inf, Taber [ˈtʼɑˤˑəbɚ] worms; 1 inf, Taba [ˈtʼɑˑbə] worms; 1 inf, Typa [tʼɑˤˑɪpəˤ].

tabbied rat n [See quot]
=**cotton rat.**
1937 *Boston Soc. Nat. Hist. Proc.* 38.354 **Okefenokee GA**, *Sigmodon hispidus.* . . The Lees of Billy's refer to it more usually as 'Tabbied Rat,' but occasionally as 'Field Rat.' [Footnote to *tabbied:*] This quaint word apparently has the meaning of 'mottled' or 'streaked.'

tabby n, often attrib Also *tappy* [Span *tapia* (wall of) earth tamped in forms. The adaptation of this material defined below was developed in Spanish Florida.] **SE, esp GA, SC**
A concrete made chiefly of lime, sand, and oyster shells and usu tamped in forms.
1745 *London Mag. & Mth. Chronologer* 14.395 **seGA**, The Town [= Frederica, St. Simons Is. GA] is defended by a pretty strong Fort, of Tappy. [Footnote:] A Mixture of Lime, made of Oyster-Shells, with Sand, small Shells, &c. which, when harden'd, is as firm as Stone. *Ibid* 396, Some Houses are built entirely of Brick, some of Brick and Wood, some few of Tappy-Work; but most of the meaner Sort, of Wood only. **1759** *SC Gazette* 7 July (*AmSp* 27.283), Proof of the Goodness of our Fortifications has more than once been made, and Tabby-work is full proved to be the best. **1763** (1770) Johnston *Short Descr. SC* 40, The Harbour is defended by a small Fort, lately built of Tappy, a Cement composed of Oister-shells beat small, with a Mixture of Lime and Water, and is very durable. **1799** (1803) Ellicott *Jrl.* 267 **GA**, That part lying immediately on the water . . was defended by a small battery of tabby

work, (as it is called in that country) which is a composition of broken oyster shells and lime. **1847** *Knickerbocker* 29.455 **eGA**, The borders of the beds are made of 'tabby.' **1885** *Century Illustr. Mag.* 29.874, A concrete of oyster shells, called "tabby," was much used on the southern coast. **1939** Griswold *Sea Is. Lady* 847 **csSC** (as of 1928), Tabby steps, flared at the bottom and flanked by a pair of camellia bushes . . led up to a fine fanlighted doorway. **1966** *DARE* Tape **GA**11, Tabby. . . It's shell that is burned. You burn enough shell to make lime . . and crush it. And then you use the sand . . and they mixed it, made regular . . cement. And then they put it together with shell. **1971** *New Yorker* 20 Mar 56 **seGA**, Its walls were made of tabby—lime, sand, and oyster shells. **1986** Pederson *LAGS Concordance,* 1 inf, **seGA**, Fences made out of tabby; 1 inf, **neFL**, Tabby—roofing material of oystershell and lime; 1 inf, **neFL**, Tabby house—house made of coquina. **2002** *Jacksonville Daily News* (NC) 19 Aug (Internet) **seNC**, When Marcia Main looks at the old tabby wall that stretches through Oceanview Cemetery she sees a dividing line. **2005** *DARE* File—Internet **eGA**, The best way to get a feel for the place [=Savannah's historic district] is simply to wander the "tabby" streets—made from a kind of primitive concrete mashed up with oyster shells.

taber See **taba**

tabernacle n Pronc-sp esp S Midl *tabernickle*
A Forms.
1792 in 1983 *PA Hist.* 50.129, The House . . with Rich Mantles—and Tabernickel frames in the two first storeys. **1880** in 2004 *DARE* File—Internet **swMO**, And when I put of[f] this tabernickle of clay i expect to meet friends and relatives around the thron of God. **1928** *AmSp* 3.402 **Ozarks** (as of 1916–27), One very rarely hears *almanac* and *tabernacle* pronounced correctly in the Ozarks—they usually sound like *almanick* and *tabernickle.* **1931** Randolph *Ozarks* 44, A typical campground is a sheltered cove near a big spring, where a large brush-arbor or "tabernickle" has been set up in a little clearing. **1952** Brown *NC Folkl.* 1.597, *Tabernickle* [ˈtæbəˌnɪkl]: pronc. *Tabernacle.*—Granville county. **1977** Watersons *Sound Sound* (Phonodisc) (Internet), [Liner notes:] *Heavenly Aeroplane*—A Holy Roller jewel of the 1930s, what they call a 'brush arbour hymn' in the backwoods districts of America. Itinerant evangelists . . might select a clearing near a spring and get helpers to build a "tabernickle" consisting of a framework of poles roofed over with leafy branches.
B Sense.
=**sow bug.**
1999 *DARE* File **UT**, I always called it a potato bug. My kids called it a rolie-polie in Minnesota. Someone from Utah told me they called them "tabernacles."

tabi n [Japanese] **esp HI**
See quot 1972.
1969 *DARE* (Qu. W21, *Soft shoes that people wear only inside the house*) Inf **TX**55, Tabis—one-toed socks from Japan. **1972** Carr *Da Kine Talk* 90 **HI**, *Tabi* and *zori* . . known everywhere in Hawaii. . . *Tabi,* socklike foot coverings with a division between the large toe and the other toes, are worn by thousands of non-Japanese women. **1991** Saiki *From the Lanai* 89 **HI**, Then came a rustle . . and soft padded thumps of one wearing *tabis* on a straw mat floor.

table n **esp WV, VA** See Map on p. 476
In var fig phrr referring to weak coffee: See quot.
1968–69 *DARE* (Qu. H74b, . . *Coffee . . very weak*) Inf **MO**25, You have to help this coffee to the table; **WV**1, Set your cup on the floor; [it's] so weak it might fall off the table; **IN**76, So weak that it'll fall off

the table; **WV**4, Too weak to set on the table; **WV**5, Too weak to stand on the table; **VA**13, Weak enough to fall off the table.

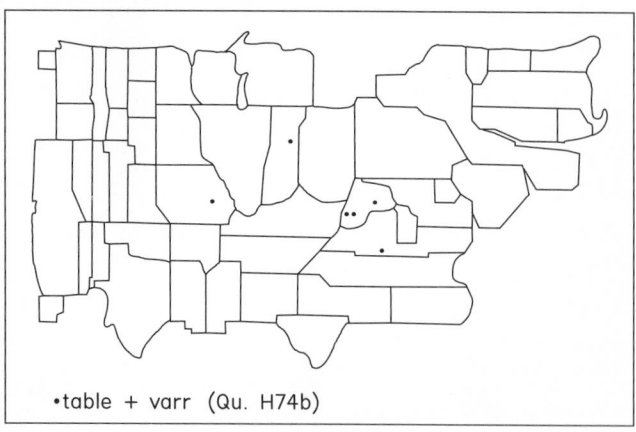

•table + varr (Qu. H74b)

table board n   *old-fash*   Cf **mealer**

The provision of regular meals without, or reckoned separately from, lodging; the amount paid for such provision; hence v *table-board* to provide such meals; n *table-boarder* one who takes such meals.

1859 *Atlantic Mth.* 3.353 **ceMA**, One of the Boys mentioned . . a little trick of the Commons table-boarders, which I, nourished at the parental board, had never heard of. **1861** in 2009 *DARE* File—Internet **OH**, The contract for feeding the soldiers at Camp Taylor was let . . at 50 cents per day per man, for table board. **1869** *Harper's New Mth. Mag.* 39.417 **Philadelphia PA**, Cyrus, who always had table-board on Walnut Street for about the first half of every month, had generally been accustomed from necessity to live in a "bachelor-hall" style for the remaining portion of the month in his rooms on Sansom Street. **1886** *Century Illustr. Mag.* 32.24, "You want table-board or rooms?" "I don't want board at all," began Lemuel again. **1896** *New Engl. Mag.* 20.166 **neOH** (as of early 19th cent), Room rent was from four to six dollars a year; table board was from seventy-five cents to a dollar a week. **1939** in 2003 (acc) Lexis–Nexis Legal Research *State Case Law: NY* (Internet), Ketchum, . . as part of his employment, was furnished with a cottage upon the estate where he and his wife lived and provided table board for three of the estate employees. **1939** *Sun* (Baltimore MD) 8 Apr 18/1 *(Hench Coll.),* It was just one of a number of "eating shifts," Mrs. Hughes explained, since the family is "table boarding" a number of men lodging elsewhere. **2003** *DARE* File—Internet **MD**, This schedule includes [electrical] service to a residence where the occupant has, in addition to his family, roomers or table boarders or a combination of both, not exceeding ten persons.

table garden n   Cf **kitchen garden**

A vegetable garden for home consumption.

1917 Davis *Productive Plant Husbandry* 254, The table garden should be so closely associated with the truck patch that practically no extra work is required. **1926** *Bridgeport Telegram* (CT) 28 Apr 23/1, This would make an ideal location for anyone desiring additional land for flower or table garden. **1939** Griswold *Sea Is. Lady* 687 **csSC** (as of 1912), Without the help of prime hands the work of cotton was too heavy for him now; Linda had been keeping him from attempting anything more than a few acres of corn and a "table" garden. **1968** *DARE* (Qu. I1, . . *The garden where you grow carrots, beans, and such things, to eat at home*) Inf **NY**94, Truck garden—a big one; table garden—a small one. **1986** Pederson *LAGS Concordance (Vegetable garden)* 1 inf, **csLA**, Table gardens.

table legs n pl   Cf *piano legs*

1968–69 *DARE* (Qu. X37, . . *Words . . to describe people's legs if they're noticeably bent, or uneven, or not right*) Infs **NY**66, **PA**182, Table legs; **CA**166, Table legs—thick legs.

Table-Mountain pine n   Also *Table-Rock pine*

A **pine** (here: *Pinus pungens*) native chiefly to the Appalachian region from Pennsylvania south to Georgia and Tennessee.   Also called **hickory pine 2, mountain ~, pitch ~ b(5), poverty ~ 2, prickly ~ 1**

1810 Michaux *Histoire des Arbres* 1.61, *Pinus pungens.* The Table Mountain Pine. . . La montagne de la Table, l'une des plus élevées des

Alléghanys, . . paroît avoir donné son nom à cette espèce de Pin qui couvre presque exclusivement son sommet. [=Table Mountain, one of the highest of the Alleghenies, . . seems to have given its name to this species of Pine which almost exclusively covers its summit.] **1857** Gray *Manual of Botany* 421, *P[inus] pungens.* . . *Table Mountain Pine.* . . Blue Ridge, Virginia, west of Charlottesville . . , and southward. **1897** Sudworth *Arborescent Flora* 28 **DE, MD, PA, SC**, Table-mountain pine. **1933** Small *Manual SE Flora* 6, *Table-mountain pine. Table-rock pine.* . . Has stout leaves and very stout cones with prominently armed scales. **1961** Douglas *My Wilderness* 158 **wNC**, The two-needle Table Mountain pine . . grows tall on the edge of Cades Cove. **1980** Little *Audubon Guide N. Amer. Trees E. Region* 292, *Table Mountain Pine.* . . This tree of mountain ridges is the only pine restricted to the Appalachian Mountains.

table muscle n   *joc*

See quot 1944.

1944 *PADS* 2.36 **NC**, Table-muscle. . . A large girth, "pot belly." Buncombe Co. **1969** *DARE* (Qu. X53a, . . *An oversize stomach*) Inf **CA**140, Table muscle. **2002** *Post* (Centre AL) 8 July (Internet), Speaking of chubby little bellies, if a neighbor should pat your stomach and ask "How long you been buildin' that tool shed?" you shouldn't . . look toward the backyard to see if there's a utility building there you didn't know about. "Tool shed" is often used interchangeably with "table muscle." **2003** *DARE* File—Internet **TX**, I am talking about people whose table muscle is the only muscle in their bodies.

table order, in adj phr

1972 *Atlanta Letters* **GA**, In table order. . . Everyone at home is healthy and feeling good.

Table-Rock pine   See **Table-Mountain pine**

tablet n   **widespread, but less freq NEng, NYC, nNJ**   Cf **block** n **3, pad** n[2] **3, tab 1**

A stack of sheets of paper fastened at one edge so that single sheets can be torn off.

1876 *Defiance Democrat* (OH) 14 Dec [3]/5 (newspaperarchive.com), [Advt:] Hodder's patent Blotter Tablet is a neat, convenient and useful invention for putting up plain or printed stationery. **1894** (1977) Montgomery Ward *Catalogue* 105, *Pencil Tablets.* . . "Penny" Tablets, for pencil use . . ; 64 pages white paper, ruled. *Ibid, Writing Tablets. Notice.*—Writing Tablets are rapidly superceding the ordinary note and letter papers for general correspondence, as they are much more convenient. **1949** Webber *Backwoods Teacher* 92 **Ozarks**, Us kids brung some old'ns to school to write on the backs of till we get our tablets. **1962** Fox *Southern Fried* 79 **SC**, He'd take off his shoes and . . buy a tablet and an envelope, get in the back booth and write. **1963** Edwards *Gravel* 56 **eTN** (as of 1920s), Down the lane we went, fitted out with new clothes, new books, new tablets and pencils. **1965–70** *DARE* (Qu. F48, . . *Pages of writing paper glued together at the top with a cardboard back;* not asked in early QRs) 550 Infs, **widespread, but less freq NEng, NYC, nNJ**, Tablet; 28 Infs, **scattered**, Writin(g) tablet; **IL**31, **KY**44, Ink tablet; **KY**84, Letter tablet; **NY**72, Pencil tablet. **1998** *DARE* File—Internet **csWI** (as of 1930s), We called the cheap paper kind we used in grade school a *tablet;* wrote on it in pencil only.

table tapper n   esp **GA, SC, eNC**   Cf **chairbacker, yard ax 2**

An unprofessional, part-time lay preacher.

1949 Turner *Africanisms* 232 **sSC, GA coasts** [Gullah], [tebl tɑpɑ] 'preacher,' i.e., 'one who taps on the table.' **1951** *AmSp* 26.15 **SC** [Black], *Yard ax,* 'poorly trained irregular preacher,' and its synonym *table tapper* have been recorded chiefly in the Georgetown and Charleston areas and in the Santee Valley. **1966** *DARE* (Qu. CC10, . . *An unprofessional, part-time lay preacher*) Inf **SC**10, Table tapper—teaches a class; **SC**19, Table tapper—fills in for the preacher; **SC**26, Table tapper—I have heard it. **1986** Pederson *LAGS Concordance,* 1 inf, **cnGA**, Table tapper—preacher.

tabs exclam   Cf **dib** n[1] **2**

Used to lay claim to something.

1956 *AmSp* 31.37, I hosie—or . . honie . . or whackie—that. All these assert 'This is mine.' . . And there are its shortened forms. . . *First bores on the apple!* . . *Tabs on the piano!* . . for "First choice!"

tacamahac n   Also *tacamahac tree, tackamahac* [From obs Span *tacamahaca* < Nahuatl, orig applied to an aromatic resin derived from a Mexican tree and thence to other resins of Amer origin used medicinally]

=**balsam poplar.**

[**1739** Miller *Gardeners Dict.* 2 app np, The Tacamahaca. This Tree grows spontaneously on the Continent of *America.*] **1785** Marshall *Arbustrum* 107, Populus balsamifera. *Balsam, or Tacamahac-Tree.* . . The buds abound with a glutinous resin, which is the tacamahacca of the shops. **1843** Torrey *Flora NY* 2.216, Populus balsamifera. . . *Tackama-hac.* . . The buds in the spring are large, yellow, and covered with a fragrant varnish. **1897** Sudworth *Arborescent Flora* 130 **MN**, *Populus balsamifera.* . . Tacamahac. **1928** Rosendahl–Butters *Trees MN* 56, *Balsam poplar, tacamahac.* . . Leaves . . often rusty due to the resinous secretion. **1950** Peattie *Nat. Hist. Trees* 98, *Populus balsamifera.* . . Tacamahac. Balm-of-Gilead. Bam. **1980** Little *Audubon Guide N. Amer. Trees E. Region* 321, "Tacamahac" . . *Populus balsamifera.* . . large, gummy or sticky buds producing *fragrant yellowish resin.* . . [F]rom NW. Alaska . . south to Pennsylvania and west to Iowa; local south to Colorado and in eastern mountains to West Virginia.

tack n

1 A person who is unfashionable or untidy. [**tacky** n **2** or adj¹ **2**]

1893 Shands *MS Speech* 61, *Tacky* [tæki]. Used by all classes for *unfashionable* or *untidy*. It has a corresponding substantive *tack,* which means an unfashionable or untidy person. The word *tacky* is not at all confined to Mississippi, but is heard in almost every part of the Union. I think *tack* is not used so largely.

2 See quot. Cf quot 1958 *PADS* at**tacky** n² **4**

1968 *DARE* (Qu. HH2, *Names and nicknames for a citified person*) Inf **VA**31, Town tack.

3 See quot. Cf **tacky** adj **4**

1972 Claerbaut *Black Jargon* 82, *Tack* . . a clever or smart man.

4 A nickel.

1938 *AmSp* 13.316 **NE** [Black], A *tack* is a nickel. **1947** *True* 32.104 **New Orleans LA** [Black], He . . collects the 'Tack' (I mean the nickle) and returns to the saloon. **1968** *DARE* (Qu. U22, . . *A five-cent piece*) Inf **LA**45, Tack.

5 =**coffin tack.**

1922 *Munsey's Mag.* 76.292 **ceMA**, My goodness! Just wait till mamma sees us smoking a tack! Naughty, Naughty! **1966–69** *DARE* (Qu. DD6b, *Nicknames for cigarettes*) Inf **MO**19, Tacks; **SC**34, Tacks —from "coffin tacks," but coffin left off.

tackamahac See **tacamahac**

tacker n [swEngl dial; now common in Austr Engl] **chiefly DE, MD, NJ, ePA** *old-fash*

A child, esp a boy—freq in comb *little tacker.*

1876 *PA School Jrl.* 25.20 **sePA**, Well do I remember . . the benevolent face beaming down . . upon the "little tackers" who always loved to see the happy owner enter the school-house. **1890** *Cape May Co. Gaz.* (Cape May Court House NJ) 6 June (*DN* 1.76) **MD**, Among a list of so-called 'Jerseyisms,' collected by Mr. F.B. Lee . . , I recognize a number as being in common use in Maryland, viz.: . . *tacker:* a little child. **1894** *DN* 1.334 **NJ**, Tacker: small child. The adjective *little* generally precedes the noun. **1914** *Indianapolis Star* (IN) 31 Jan 6/6, [Syndicated column by a Baltimore MD doctor:] A change of diet . . , massage and correct treatment for the little tacker's legs are then the immediate order of the hour. **1939** *Frederick Post* (MD) 8 Aug 3/3, From a little tacker who donned the gloves in a "paperweight" exhibition match here a few years ago, the youth has developed into a husky, hard-hitting lightweight. **1945** *Gettysburg Times* (PA) 8 Jan 5/3, She stopped and the little tacker said he had lost a dollar. **1955** *DE Folkl. Bulletin* 1.20, Tacker (small child, usually a boy). **2004** *NADS Letters* **Baltimore MD**, "Tacker" or "little tacker." I grew up in Baltimore and we used this form quite commonly. It was often in the expression "cute little tacker," and, I believe was almost always used when speaking of a very young boy. . . I do not hear it often nowadays, and I believe it must be at least obsolescent. *Ibid* **nePA**, Tacker (little tacker), still occasionally used in NE Pennsylvania. Used mostly by over 70's generation, although it does pop up infrequently in their children's speech (50 year olds). **2009** *DARE* File **sNJ** (as of c1960), I have heard the expression "little tacker" referring to a tyke or small child.

tackey n See **tacky** n

tackey adj See **tacky** adj¹

tackey party See **tacky party**

tackie See **tacky** n

tack in one's coffin See **coffin tack**

tackle n Usu |ˈtækḷ|; also **esp NEast** |ˈtekḷ|, **Sth, S Midl, TX** |ˈtɪkḷ| Pronc-spp *tacle, takel, takle, teakle, teckle, teekle, tickle* [The forms with [e] and [i] (implied by spp *teakle, teekle*) continue Brit dial forms (cf *EDD tackle, teagle, SND tackle*); the form with [ɪ] appears to be a US innovation.]

Std sense, var forms. Note: These var forms are appar confined to the sense "a contrivance of ropes and pulleys for hauling or hoisting; one of the elements of such a contrivance."

1778 in 1907 *PA Archives* 6th ser 12.714, Block and Teakle [etc]. **1796** Morse *Amer. Universal Geog.* 1.507 **ceNY**, The cannon were raised by large brass tacles . . from rock to rock. **1804** in 1890 *VA Calendar State Papers* 9.394, One block and teakle. **1846** Worcester *Universal Dict.* 723, *Tackle,* (tăk′kl). . . Pronounced by seamen tā′kl. **1891** *DN* 1.155 **cNY**, [ˈtekḷ] < *tackle.* **1892** *DN* 1.211 **seMA**, Takle [tekḷ]: tackle, as in *block and takle.* **1893** Frederic *Copperhead* 30 **nNY**, I could hear the creaking of the chain drawing up the cans over the tackle, or as we called it, the "teekle." **1893** Shands *MS Speech* 20, *Block* and *tickle.* . . Almost universally used by workmen for *block and tackle.* **1899** (1912) Green *VA Folk-Speech* 436, *T'akel.* . . A device or appliance for grasping or clutching an object, connected with means for holding, moving, or manipulating it. "Block and t'akel." *T'akle. Ibid* 440, *Teakle.* . . Tackle: a "block and teakle." *Ibid* 441, *Teekle.* . . Tackle; block and *teekle,* block and rope for a purchase. **1903** *DN* 2.292 **Cape Cod MA** (as of a1857), Vowels were pronounced long in . . *tackle* [etc]. *Ibid* 333 **seMO**, *Tackle.* . . Pronounced . . [ˈtekḷ]. **1909** *DN* 3.381 **eAL, wGA**, *Tickle.* . . Tackle. Heard only in 'block and tickle.' Sometimes *teckle* is heard. **1918** *DN* 5.17 **Martha's Vineyard MA**, *Tackle* ([e]). . . Ropes and pulleys. **1930s** in 1944 *ADD* **eWV**, Block 'n' tickle. **1933** *AmSp* 8.1.30 **nwTX**, Sick cows not able to stand were . . lifted with a portable block and tackle (pronounced *tickle*). **1942** *ME Univ. Studies* 56.55 [Sea terms], A tackle, a mechanical purchase of blocks and ropes, was always pronounced with a long ā, while *to tackle,* not being nautical, was pronounced with short a, as ashore. **1949** *PADS* 11.12 **wTX**, *Tickle,* block and. . . Uneducated. **1954** Harder *Coll.* **cwTN**, Tickle, block and. . . Occasional. **1954** *PADS* 21.20 **SC**, *Block and tickle.* **c1960** Wilson *Coll.* **csKY**, *Block and tickle.* **1970** *DARE* Tape **TX**96, It was a block-and-tickle outfit. **1975** Gould *ME Lingo* 285, *Tackle and falls*—The pulley arrangement with blocks and line. In Maine, *tackle* in this combination is always pronounced take-'l.

tackweed n

=**puncture vine.**

1935 (1943) Muenscher *Weeds* 312, *Tribulus terrestris.* . . Puncture vine, . . Tackweed. [*Ibid* 313, Mature carpels . . with 2–4 stiff spreading spines up to 7 mm. long. . . The spines are hard enough to stick into automobile tires.]

tacky n Also sp *tackey, tackie*

1 also *tuckey:* A small horse or pony of sturdy but inelegant build; an inferior or broken-down horse. **chiefly Sth** See also **marsh tacky**

1800 Tatham *Communications Ag. & Commerce* 81, At some places, you are thus asked (in local phrase and expression) to *truck* or *trade* for a horse, a cow, or a little *tackie,* &c. (which last term signifies a poney or little horse of small price). **1835** Longstreet *GA Scenes* 25, He's nothing but a tacky. He an't as *pretty* a horse as Bullet, I know; but he'll do. **1839** Hoffman *Wild Scenes* 2.61, A couple of shots, which killed the pedler's fine Kentucky horse, and wounded my Indian tackey. The latter was a tough and spirited little animal, for which I had exchanged a broken-down nag. **1845** Thompson *Pineville* 110 **GA**, Si Perkins had just succeeded in urging his half-famished tuckey up the steps. **1853** *Harper's New Mth. Mag.* 8.20 **VA**, You don't really mean to afflict these wretched tackies with such loads of baggage as we have here. **1858** Hammett *Piney Woods Tavern* 11 **TX**, Let him emigrate to Texas, mount a Spanish tacky, or cane pony, put off into the prairie. **1884** *Century Illustr. Mag.* 27.444, The scrubby little "tackeys" still taken in the marshes along the North Carolina coast are descendants of the wild horses of the colony. **1899** (1912) Green *VA Folk-Speech* 435, *Tacky.* . . An ill-fed or neglected horse; a rough, bony nag. **1903** Murrie *White Castle LA* 40, Hastily saddling his "tacky-pony" he was loping after the sheriff. **1939** Griswold *Sea Is. Lady* 545 **csSC** (as of c1895), Seth also did the trading for a horse, a sturdy little tacky.

2 =**poor White 1.** **Sth, S Midl** Cf **sandhill 2a**

1836 in 1956 Eliason *Tarheel Talk* 298 **nw,cnNC**, I tell them I dont know any better for I'm a mountain tackey *sartin.* a**1883** (1911) Bagby

VA Gentleman 278, D-d-d-dat ar man come cotin' Miss Sally—he—he ain't n-n-nothing but a tackey. **1887** (1967) Harris *Free Joe* 167 **cGA,** That indescribable class of people known in that region as the piney-woods "Tackies." . . Steeped in poverty of the most desolate description, and living the narrowest lives possible in this great Republic. **1888** *Century Illustr. Mag.* 36.799 **GA,** If Mr. Catlett will come to Georgia and go among the "po' whites" and "piney-wood tackeys," he will hear the terms "we-uns" and "you-uns" in everyday use. **1891** *Amer. Missionary* 45.415 **nwAL,** In the foot-hills of the Cumberland Mountains in Northwestern Alabama are a people called "Poor Whites" or "Tackeys." **1907** (1909) Harris *Bishop & Boogerman* 49 **GA,** He had discovered that the vegetables went to the maintenance of a small colony of 'tackies' that had settled near Shady Dale—'dirt-eaters' they were called. **1958** Humphrey *Home from the Hill* 66 **neTX,** His qualities would have been recognized had he been the ditch-edge child of some share-cropping sandhill tacky. **1958** *PADS* 29.17 **TN,** *Tacky, tackies:* Unfashionable, shabby in dress, a person so characterized: "if hicks lived in town they would be town tackies." Rep. from Davidson, Humphreys, Perry, Warren [Counties]. **1986** Pederson *LAGS Concordance,* 1 inf, **cAL,** Pine tacky—epitome of piney-woodsiness.

tacky adj[1]   Also sp *tackey*   [**tacky** n 2]
1 Of poor quality, shoddy, run-down; cheap, common; in poor taste.

1886 *S. Bivouac* 4.343 **sAppalachians,** Tackey (shoddy). **1886** Amer. Philol. Assoc. *Trans.* 17.46 **Sth,** *Tacky* (common). **1915** *DN* 4.217, *Tacky,* common; below par. "My composition sounds tacky." Colloquial. **1925** *AmSp* 1.152 **West,** That expressive word "tacky" is used to describe something slack and run down. **1966–70** *DARE* (Qu. E22, *If a house is untidy and everything is upset . . "It's a _____!" or "It looks like _____."*) Inf **SC26,** Tacky; (Qu. W29, . . *Expressions . . for things that are sewn carelessly . . "They're _____."*) Infs **KS2, TN53,** Tacky; (Qu. KK6, *Something low-grade or of poor quality—for example, a piece of merchandise: "I wouldn't buy that, it's _____."*) Infs **KS2, MI108,** Tacky; (Qu. KK64, *Speaking of the part of a city that was once very fine, but isn't any more: "The neighborhood is sort of _____."*) Inf **CA3,** Tacky. **2001** *NY Times* (NY) 10 June sec ST 6/5, Walking past the soon-to-open Fiorucci store. . . she asked, "Is it one of those tacky home-furnishing stores that sell stuff like glass angel ornaments to rich people?" *Ibid* 11 Dec sec C 1/4, The product being peddled . . can be patriotism itself, in the form of . . tacky "Promise of Freedom" eagle figurines from Franklin Mint. *Ibid* 27 Dec sec F 4/5, "The interior was already getting tacky when I lived there," said Mr. Koch, who left office six years after the 1986 overhaul.

2 Of a person's clothing or appearance: unfashionable, dowdy; untidy; gaudy, tawdry.   **scattered, but chiefly Sth, S Midl**   See Map   Cf *slouchy* (at **slouch** n)

1890 *DN* 1.66 **OH,** *Tacky.* . . Also reported from Cincinnati, with the meaning *slovenly, shabby.* **1892** *KS Univ. Qrly.* 1.99 **KS,** *Tacky:* not fashionably dressed. **1901** [see **tacky** adj[2]]. **1905** [see **tacky** adj[2]]. **1905** *DN* 3.97 **nwAR,** *Tacky.* . . Shabby. 'She looks tacky.' 'She's tacky-looking.' **1906** Casey *Parson's Boys* 121 **sIL** (as of c1860), Never before did their own appearance seem so mean, or their clothes look so old-fashioned and rustic. . . These supercilious dames slightly elevated their noses and seemed to say as plainly as if they had spoken it aloud, "tacky!" **1915** *DN* 4.229 **wTX,** *Tacky.* . . Dowdy, not stylish. **c1950** Halpert Coll. 61 **wKY, nwTN,** *Tacky* = untidy, sloppy. **1960** Carpenter *Tales Manchaca* 149 **cTX** (as of c1915), In a cart just like "Uncle" Tony's . . "will be a tacky wife and a great bunch of runny-nosed, stringy-haired children." **1965–70** *DARE* (Qu. W41, . . *Expressions . . for someone whose clothes never look right or who always dresses carelessly*) 85 Infs, **scattered, but chiefly Sth, S Midl, SW,** Tacky; **AR27, CT20,** Look(s) tacky; **FL48,** Good and tacky; **WI64,** Tacky-looking; (Qu. W37, *When a woman puts on her good clothes and tries to look her best . . she's _____*) Inf **FL2,** Tacky; (Qu. W40, . . *A woman who overdresses or . . spends too much on clothes*) Infs **AL6, 17, GA75, KY59, NC10, TN63,** Tacky; (Qu. X5, . . *Different kinds of men's haircuts*) Inf **SC7,** Tacky; (Qu. HH36, *A careless, slovenly woman: "She's just an old _____."*) Infs **PA239, TN14,** (Looks) tacky. **1967–69** *DARE* FW Addit **swAR,** *Tacky*—unkempt, stringy—"hair down to here, and tacky"; **KY44,** *Tacky*—something that is too gaudy. **1968** *Newark Advocate* (OH) 2 May 30/8, One Southern word I miss, and for which I have never found a satisfactory Northern counterpart, is that useful adjective "tacky." When I was a girl, the Northern work [sic] "jakey" was used to denote lack of style, lack of taste, wrong color, mismatch, ignorant, awkward, shabby, or any fraction thereof. "Tacky" means more or less the same, though if anything, more so. **1974** Fink

Mountain Speech 26 **wNC, eTN,** *Tacky* . . shabby, out of style. "That hat is sortor tacky." **1982** Slone *How We Talked* 30 **eKY** (as of c1950), *Tackey*—ugly or cheap-looking. **1995** *Brophy Coll.* 75 **swMO** (as of c1960), *Tacky* . . slovenly.

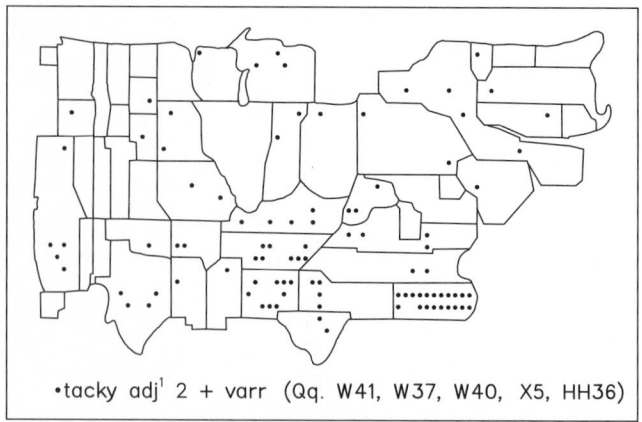

•tacky adj[1] 2 + varr (Qq. W41, W37, W40, X5, HH36)

3 Of a person's behavior: uncouth, ill-mannered.   **chiefly Sth**

1916 *DN* 4.270 **New Orleans LA,** *Tacky.* . . Not quite respectable; 'tough.' **1966–69** *DARE* FW Addit **CO21,** *Tacky*—not well-dressed and also ill-mannered, uncouth, as, "That was tacky of him"; **eNC,** *Tacky:* second-rate, shoddy; e.g., "That sounds mighty tacky," if something doesn't sound like good English; **SC,** *Tacky* . . rude, ill-mannered. **1968–69** *DARE* (Qu. AA7b, . . *A woman who is very fond of men and is always trying to know more—if she's not respectable about it*) Inf **TX61,** Tacky; (Qu. GG19a, *When you can see from the way a person acts that he's feeling important or independent: "He surely is _____ these days."*) Inf **NY69,** Tacky. **1971** *Today Show Letters* **TX,** When an opponent trumps an ace—he is tacky. A dog that is barking to go out—interrupting a conversation is tacky. **1975** *AmSp* 50.67 **AR** (as of c1970), *Tacky.* . . Unattractive or impolite (in behavior)—"She acted so tacky." **1984** Wilder *You All Spoken Here* 13 **Sth,** *Tacky:* Not couth; out of place; improper. **1989** Gurganus *Oldest Confederate Widow* 442 **Sth** (as of 1896), [From a speech by a young girl playing the Virgin Mary in a Christmas pageant:] Ooh, someday folks will look back and say, Boy, was that ever tacky, not letting *them* in! **1991** *NY Times* (NY) 2 June 51/2, There's something particularly inelegant, spelled tacky, about pulling out a calculator to divide the cost of a meal in a restaurant.

tacky adj[2]   [Cf the expression *sharp as a tack* mentally acute] Well prepared, mentally sharp.

1901 *DN* 2.149 **DE,** *Tacky.* . . Usually slovenly. Rarely heard in sense of fine. "I had my lessons right up tacky." **1905** *DN* 3.66 **eNE,** *Tacky.* . . (1) Shabby, untidy; (2) dowdy, the opposite of *chic;* (3) sharp or bright, like *tacks.* Less common in the last meaning, but reported independently by a number of observers. **1911** *DN* 3.548 **NE,** *Tacky.* . . (1) Sharp, bright, to the point. "Oh well, you always were tacky in your answers."

tacky party n   Also sp *tackey party*   [**tacky** adj[1] 2]   **chiefly Sth, S Midl**   See Map
A party at which people dress in unfashionable, dowdy, or ridiculous clothes.

1890 *DN* 1.66 **KY, swOH,** Recently we have had "tacky parties," where the guests dress in the commonest and most unfashionable costumes. **1897** *Atlantic Mth.* 80.244 **eTN,** Their out-of-door attire of knickerbockers and flannel shirts and blazers ought to be deemed . . shabby enough to appease the "tacky" requirements . . for they were pleased to call their burlesque masquerade a "tacky party." **1904** *Charlotte Daily Observer* (NC) 1 Sept 2/2, A tacky party was given . . at the . . home of Mrs. G.W. Smithson. **1905** *DN* 3.97 **nwAR,** *Tacky-party.* **1909** *DN* 3.378 **eAL, wGA,** A *tacky-party* is a party in which the guests dress comically or ridiculously. **1911** in 1983 Truman *Dear Bess* 26 **MO,** I have a "previous engagement" to a tacky party. I am going as I usually go when at home and I bet I take the cake. My very best friends would refuse to recognize me if they ever saw me in my farm rags. **1937** in Lib. of Congress *Amer. Memory: WPA Life Hist.* (Internet) **NM,** The equipment for these schools was purchased by money made from pie suppers, tackey parties and festivals common in this state. **1952** Brown *NC Folkl.* 1.597, *Tacky party.* . . An informal party attended by persons dressed in "tacky" clothes.—Central and east. Obsolescent. **1965** *DARE* FW Addit **NM,** People have tacky parties where they all dress strangely. **1966–67** *DARE* (Qu. FF2, . . *Kinds of parties*) Infs **AL**16, **SC**44, Tacky party; **AL**10, Tacky party—hard times party; **AL**20, Tacky party—dress gaudy; **SC**54, Tacky party—wear old, unattractive clothes; **SC**32, Tacky party—see who could dress up the tackiest; **SC**34, Tacky party—wear unfashionable clothes. **1967** *Chron.-News* (Trinidad CO) 12 Oct 2/5, Plans were made to have a Tacky Party and covered dish supper at the next meeting. **1976** Garber *Mountainese* 90 **sAppalachians,** *Tacky-party* . . costume party—They are havin' a tacky-party at school to celebrate Halloween. **1986** Pederson *LAGS Concordance,* 1 inf, **cnGA,** Tacky parties—dressed in old clothes; 1 inf, **cAL,** Tacky parties—dress as "ugly" as you can; 1 inf, **cnAL,** Tacky party—dressed weird, tried to be tackiest. **2007** *Yale Daily News Insider's Guide Colleges 2008* 674 **NC,** Parties [at Davidson] are open to all and generally adopt themes ranging from toga to boy-band or tacky parties.

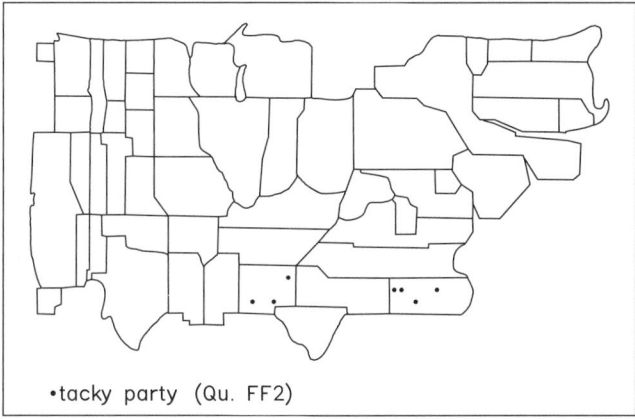

•tacky party (Qu. FF2)

tacle See **tackle**

taco n

1 A folded tortilla filled usu with meat, cheese, tomatoes, and lettuce. **orig SW, but now widespread** See Map Cf **enchilada**

1914 Haffner-Ginger *CA Mex.-Span. Cook Book* 45, *Taco* . . chopped cooked beef and chile sauce in tortilla . . folded, edges sealed together with egg; fried in deep fat. **1934** Franklin School P.-T.A. (Ardmore, Okla.) *Favorite Recipes* 15 *(DA),* To be served with tocos [sic]. **1934** in 2004 (acc) Lexis–Nexis Legal Research *State Case Law: CA* (Internet) **sCA,** He purchased six tacos or tortillas, sometimes called Spanish tamales, at said cafe, paid thirty cents for the same and finally reached the Martinez house with them. **1949** Emrich *Wild West Custom* 168 **SW,** The Southwesterner can scarcely pass a day without the casual use of *adobe, siesta,* . . *frijoles, tacos. Ibid* 179, *Tacos* were made of fine *tortillas* half folded, filled with meat, and fried in deep fat. . . then stuffed from the sides with chopped onions, green *chili*-pepper sauce, shredded lettuce, and grated cheese. **1957** Kerouac *On the Road* 93 **CA,** We went into a Mexican restaurant and had tacos and mashed pinto beans. **1965–70** *DARE* (Qu. H65, *Foreign foods favored by people around here*) 44 Infs, **scattered, but chiefly SW,** Tacos; (Qu. H45, *Dishes made with meat, fish, or poultry that everybody around here would know, but that people in other places might not*) 13 Infs, **sCA, wTX,** Tacos; (Qu. D39, . . *Nicknames* . . *for a small eating place where the food is not es-*

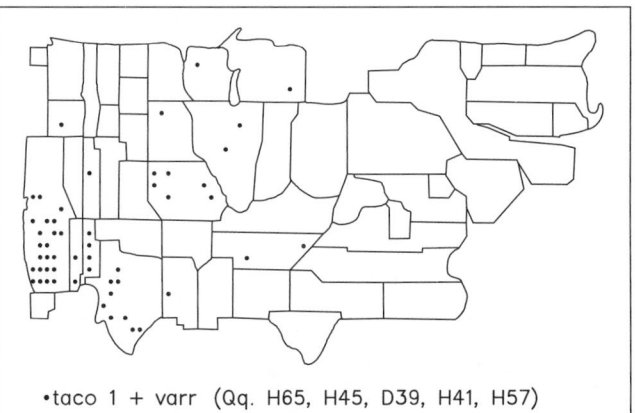

•taco 1 + varr (Qq. H65, H45, D39, H41, H57)

pecially good) Inf **CA**184, Taco joint; (Qu. H41, . . *Kinds of roll or bun sandwiches* . . *in a round bun or roll*) Inf **CA**15, Taco; (Qu. H57, *Tasty or spicy side-dishes served with meats*) Inf **CA**2, Taco sauce. **1986** Pederson *LAGS Concordance,* 4 infs, **swAL, TX.** [2 of 4 infs of Spanish background] **2004** *Valley Independent* (Monessen PA) 31 Jan sec A 7/2, *School Cafeteria Menus.* . . Taco in pita pocket with lettuce, cheese, and taco sauce. . . Taco boat with dinner roll. . . Taco with meat and cheese. **2004** *DARE* File—Internet, Cleaning pennies with taco sauce. *Ibid,* Kauai's own tropical taco. *Ibid,* Easy picnic taco salad. [*DARE* Ed: A search of the Internet yields several million examples of *taco,* many in proprietary names of fast-food restaurants such as *Taco Bell, Taco John's, Taco Time,* etc.]

2 also in combs *taco-bender, ~-eater, ~-roller, ~-twister:* A Mexican or Mexican-American; hence n attrib *taco* inhabited by or characteristic of Mexicans. **esp SW** *derog*

1962 *Western Folkl.* 21.28 **sCA,** A "taco wagon" is a car which has had its leaf springs shackled. *Ibid* 33, *Taco wagon*—among hot rodders, any car which has had its leaf springs shackled, lowering the body. "Taco" may be a substitute for "Mexican." **1968–70** *DARE* (Qu. HH28, *Names and nicknames* . . *for people of foreign background: Mexican*) Inf **CA**177, Taco; **CA**81, Taco-roller. **1969** *DARE* FW Addit **sCA,** Taco . . a Mexican [among high-school age]. **1970** *Current Slang* 4.3-4.25 [NM State Univ slang], *Taco.* . . A Mexican or a Mexican-American (derogatory). *Taco bender.* . . A Mexican or a Mexican-American (derogatory). *Taco town.* . . The Mexican section of a community. *Taco wagon.* . . A modified 1956 (or so) Chevy with much Chrome and with baby booties or sponge dice hanging from the mirror. **1974** *DARE* File **csWI,** Taco-twister—Mexican migrant worker. . . Said by students, Ripon, WI. **1986** Pederson *LAGS Concordance (Mexicans)* 1 inf, **csTX,** Taco eater, taco bender—insult; 1 inf, **csTX,** Taco benders—an insult; 1 inf, **neTX,** Taco benders and greasers and Mexicans.

3 See quot.

1989 *DARE* File **swID,** The act of lifting a person (from behind) by the belt, belt buckles, top of the underwear, the seat of the pants: Taco—2 infs, from Boise, ID.

taco-bender (or -eater, -roller) See **taco 2**

taco telegraph n Cf **moccasin telegraph**

1989 Lesley *River Song* 35 **cnOR,** The man looked at the four empty ladders. "Those wetbacks sure cleared out fast." "The Taco Telegraph," Danny said, and chuckled, because people were always saying Indians got word of things by the Moccasin Telegraph.

taco-twister See **taco 2**

tad n[1]

1 also *tat:* A person, usu a boy or child. *old-fash* Cf **tadwhacker**

1871 *Massillon Independent* (OH) [12 July 3]/1 (newspaper-archive.com), Their No. 1 is . . saucy enough to talk to anybody from the highest priest in politics down to the little tads scarce three feet high. **1877** Bartlett *Americanisms* 688, *Little tads,* small boys. *Old tads,* graybeards, old men. **1892** *DN* 1.232 **KY,** *Tads* . . children. "She had three little tads." **1905** *DN* 3.66 **eNE,** *Tad.* . . Child. "A little tad." *Ibid* 97 **nwAR,** *Tad.* . . Child. 'He's a litle [sic] tad.' Common. **1909** *DN* 3.405 **nwAR,** *Tad.* . . Child. **1913** Johnson *Highways St. Lawrence to VA* 2, The little tads need to dress that way, knocking around in the snow as they do. **1914** *DN* 4.121, *Tad,* Perhaps an abbreviation of *tadpole.* A very small boy, especially a small street boy. **1937** Gardner *Folkl. Schoharie* 77 **ceNY,** When I was a little tad, me and my brothers went to "hook" some plums from the witch woman that lived across the road from our house. **1944** *PADS* 2.29 **eKY,** *Tad, tat* [tæd, tæt]. . . A very small boy. "He was just a tad of a boy when I saw him last." **1962** Salisbury *Quoth the Raven* 96 **seAK,** The tad came down the chimney with his pack on his back and made a great hit. **1965–70** *DARE* (Qu. Z12, *Nicknames and joking words meaning 'a small child': "He's a healthy little _____."*) 23 Infs, **scattered,** Tad. [20 of 23 Infs old] **1986** Pederson *LAGS Concordance (Pet name for a child)* 1 inf, **cnGA,** A cute little tad. [Inf old]

2 also *tat:* A small amount, dab; a short distance; often used adverbially in phr *a tad* slightly, just a bit. **formerly chiefly Sth, S Midl, now widespread** See Map on p. 480 Cf **tab 3**

1915 *DN* 4.191 **swVA,** *Tat.* . . A small amount. **1940** *AmSp* 15.448 [TN mountain speech], *Tad.* A very small amount. 'I want to borrow a tad of salt.' **1960** Williams *Walk Egypt* 110 **GA,** She brushed a tat of mud from his ear. **1961** *AmSp* 36.234 **NC,** *Tad* as meaning a small amount—usage that I have noticed from time to time in North Carolina.

A weather broadcaster was recently heard to speak of 'today being a tad better than yesterday,' and I have one printed example to offer, namely, 'a tad of marshmallow on the look-out's chin.' **1965–70** *DARE* (Qu. LL6b, *A small, indefinite amount . . "I'll put in just a _____ of butter."*) Infs **GA**7, **NC**47, 63, **VA**2, 42, 99, Tad; **KY**36, **LA**12, **MS**60, **NY**107, **SC**31, **TN**30, Tat; **TN**61, Little tat; (Qu. LL6a, *A small, indefinite amount . . "I'll take just a _____ of cream in my coffee."*) Infs **AL**19, **GA**7, 77, **NC**36, 47, 51, **SC**44, **VA**15, 42, Tad; **KY**36, Little tat; (Qu. LL1, *Something very small: "I only took a _____ one."*) Inf **AL**51, A little; tad; **IN**61, Little bitty; a tad; (Qu. LL6c, *A small, indefinite amount . . "It still needs just a _____ of cinnamon."*) Infs **NC**63, **OR**1, **TX**81, Tad; **MS**60, **TN**30, Tat; (Qu. LL7, *In small amounts, by small degrees: "She didn't get the money all at once, they sent it to her _____."*) Inf **GA**7, Little tads at a time; (Qu. LL19, *A few, anywhere from two to four: "Just put in _____ onions."*) Inf **GA**84, Tad; (Qu. MM24, . . *'A short distance': "The river is just a _____ from the house."*) Inf **WA**22, Tad. **1968** *AmSp* 43.237, *More on "tad".* . . I myself first heard the word so used [=meaning a small amount] in the speech of my wife, who has spent most of her life in Wyoming and Nebraska and cannot recall where she learned it. **1975** *AmSp* 50.67 **AR** (as of c1970), *Tad.* . . Small quantity—"I'll have just a tad." "This is just a tad small." **1976** *Time* 27 Sept 39 **GA**, "Pull 'er up a tad, please, mister," said the nonchalant teen-ager pumping gas. **1979** *Capital Times* (Madison WI) 16 Feb 1/2, *Today's Weather.* . . A tad warmer Saturday. **1986** Pederson *LAGS Concordance,* 1 inf, **nwAR**, A tad down the road; *(Better put a sweater on; it's getting _____ cold)* 1 inf, **seAL**, Tad; *(A bite. . . Food taken between regular meals, you call it _____)* 1 inf, **csAL**, Tad. **2004** *DARE* File—Internet, I'm just a tad spoiled. *Ibid,* I'm just a tad excited. *Ibid,* I'm new and just a tad scared. *Ibid,* He was just a tad too emotional about the issue. *Ibid,* Just a tad snowy. [*DARE* Ed: A search of the Internet for adverbial uses of *a tad* yields hundreds of thousands of examples from across the country.]

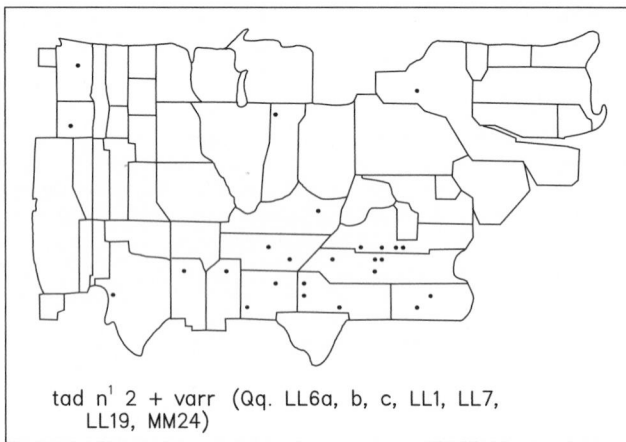

tad n¹ 2 + varr (Qq. LL6a, b, c, LL1, LL7, LL19, MM24)

3 In marble play: a small, cheap marble; a marble game.

1966–69 *DARE* (Qu. EE6b, *Small marbles or marbles in general*) Inf **KY**50, Tads; (Qu. EE6c, *Cheap marbles*) Inf **NC**30, Tads; (Qu. EE7, . . *Kinds of marble games*) Inf **KY**50, Tads—find a smooth place, lay on[e] in the middle and shoot the other at it.

4 See **tadpole 1.**

tad n² [Prob abbr for *Thaddeus*] **esp eNEng**
A person of Irish ancestry.

1914 *DN* 4.146, Among the Irish and their descendants today in this country, one may not infrequently hear in current speech instead of the usual appellative "Irish" such substitutes as: "Paddy", . . "Tad". . . [T]hese expressions . . contain at least a hint of disdain, contempt or ridicule. **1941** *LANE* Map 454 *(Nicknames for an Irishman)* 12 infs, **chiefly neMA, seNH, sME,** Tad. **1967** *DARE* (Qu. HH28, *Names and nicknames . . for people of foreign background: Irish*) Inf **MA**71, Mick, harp, tad.

tad n³ **esp PA**
A person of questionable morals; see quots.

1930 Shoemaker *1300 Words* 63 **cPA Mts**, *Tad*—A girl of questionable character. **1968** *DARE* (Qu. AA6b, . . *A man who is fond of being with women and tries to attract their attention—if he's rude or not respectful*) Inf **PA**131, Skinker, roué, tad; (Qu. HH34, *General words . . for a woman, not necessarily uncomplimentary*) Inf **PA**142, Tad—a fast woman; (Qu. HH37, *An immoral woman*) Inf **PA**142, Tad.

tad n⁴ Also *freshwater tad* Cf **saltwater tad**
=**pied-bill(ed) grebe.**

1917 *Wilson Bulletin* 29.2.74 **VA**, *Podilymbus podiceps.*—Tad, Wallops I[slan]d. **1970** *DARE* (Qu. Q10, . . *Water birds*) Inf **VA**52, Freshwater tad—a pied-billed grebe.

taddick See **toddick**

taddle n
=**toddick.**

1913 [see **toddick**]. **1975** *Appalachian Jrl.* 2.156 **wNC**, A small portion was a *taddle,* or *tad,* or *sup,* a *dab,* a *skimption,* or a *grain,* as in "I need just a grain of salt" or even "I'll have just a grain of water."

taddle fly n
A **mayfly 1.**

1970 *DARE* (Qu. R4, *A large winged insect that hatches in summer in great numbers around lakes or rivers, crowds around lights, lives only a day or so, and is good fish bait*) Inf **PA**247, Taddle ['tæ·dl̩] fly.

tadpole n

1 also *tad, tatpole:* The larva of a frog or toad. [*OED2* 14 . . →] **widespread, but somewhat less freq N Atl, West** See Map Also called **bighead 1, bull tad, mulligrub 1, mullikep, pollywog** n **1**

1709 (1967) Lawson *New Voyage* 138 **NC, SC**, Their [=terrapins'] Food is Snails, Tad-pools, or young Frogs, Mushrooms, and the Dew and Slime of the Earth and Ponds. **1832** *New Engl. Mag.* 2.329, Woe to the luckless lizard, frog, minnow, or tadpole, that approaches his [=a heron's] stand. **1852** *De Bow's Rev.* 12.631 **LA**, *Fishes.*—The only kinds peculiar to these waters is [sic] the *Toad Fish,* . . having a tail and feet resembling the Tadpole in its transition stage. **1950** *WELS* **WI** *(Very young frogs—when they still have tails and no legs)* 42 Infs, Tadpole(s); 1 Inf, Tad. **1965–70** *DARE* (Qu. P20, *Very young frogs—when they still have tails but no legs*) 796 Infs, **widespread, but somewhat less freq N Atl, West,** Tadpoles; **IN**19, Tatpoles; (Qu. B26, *When it's raining very heavily . . "It's raining _____."*) Infs **GA**4, 31, **TX**32, Down tadpoles; **NC**3, **SC**46, Frogs and tadpoles; **NC**62, Pitchforks and tadpoles; **AL**6, Pouring down tadpoles; **FL**33, **GA**13, **SC**29, 46, Tadpoles; **AL**11, Tadpoles and frogs; (Qu. P3, *Freshwater fish that are not good to eat*) Inf **PA**66, Tadpoles; (Qu. P7, *Small fish used as bait for bigger fish*) Infs **MO**1, **SC**40, Tadpoles. **1986** Pederson *LAGS Concordance,* 16 infs, **Gulf Region,** Tadpole(s); 1 inf, **neAL**, Tadpoles = small frogs; 1 inf, **cnAL**, Tadpole frog; 1 inf, **cGA**, Tadpole—develops into frog; 1 inf, **cwLA**, Tadpole = toad; 1 inf, **nwMS**, Tadpoles—these turn into frogs.

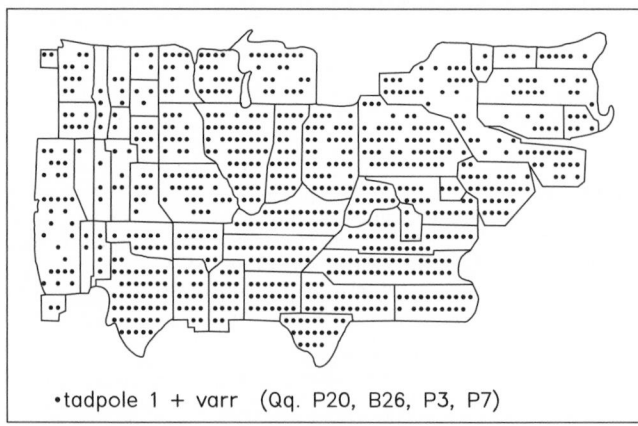

•tadpole 1 + varr (Qq. P20, B26, P3, P7)

2 =**wiggler 1.**

1965–70 *DARE* (Qu. R14, *Small worm-like things [seen in rain barrels or standing water] that hatch into mosquitoes*) 55 Infs, **scattered,** Tadpole(s). [This resp was suggested in 10 instances; 5 Infs were doubtful about this resp.]

3 See **tadpole duck.**

4 An insignificant person; a child. Cf **tad** n¹ **1**

1915 *DN* 4.198, *Tadpole,* insignificant person. "Don't pay any attention to that tadpole. He's not worth your time." **1921** *Amer. Child* 3.265 **Sth** [Black], Don't you marry none of dese little tadpole runts dat 'll make you do nuffin but scrub clothes an' nuss babies all yo' lifetime. **1930** *AmSp* 5.386 [A.E.F. English], *Tadpole.* A small French child.

1966–69 *DARE* (Qu. Y9, *Somebody who always follows along behind others: "His little brother is an awful _____."*) Inf **IN**60, Tadpole; (Qu. Z12, *Nicknames and joking words meaning 'a small child': "He's a healthy little _____."*) Inf **GA**13, Tadpole.   **1986** Pederson *LAGS Concordance,* 1 inf, **ceTX,** When I was a little tadpole (=a small child).

5   A Black person.

1986 Pederson *LAGS Concordance,* 1 inf, **cAR,** Tadpoles—derogatory term for Blacks. [Inf Black]

tadpole cat(fish)   See **tadpole madtom**

tadpole duck n   Also *tadpole*
=hooded merganser.

1888 Trumbull *Names of Birds* 75, Another name . . [for the hooded merganser] commonly heard among the "crackers" of St. Augustine is *tadpole;* the bird having been thought particularly fond of polliwogs, I suppose.   **1955** *Oriole* 20.1.5, Hooded Merganser. . . Tadpole Duck.   **1956** *AmSp* 31.186, Tadpole—Hooded merganser—S.C., Fla. A water-loving creature.

tadpole madtom n   Also *tadpole cat(fish), ~ stonecat*
A **stone catfish 1** (here: *Noturus gyrinus*).

1877 U.S. Natl. Museum *Bulletin* 10.102, *Noturus gyrinus.* . . Tadpole Stone Cat. . . Southern New York to Pennsylvania.   **1908** Forbes–Richardson *Fishes of IL* 197, Tadpole Cat. . . This fish, although distributed throughout the state, is most abundant . . in the branches of the Kaskaskia and the Wabash.   **1918** *Copeia* 53.11 **NY,** About the time of ingress of the pike the successive appearances are . . black bull-head; tadpole cat; mud minnow.   **1933** John G. Shedd Aquarium *Guide* 54, *Schilbeodes gyrinus* [=*Noturus g.*]—Tadpole Catfish.   **1943** Eddy–Surber *N. Fishes* 161, The tadpole madtom ranges from North Dakota to New York and southward to Iowa, Kentucky, and Florida. It . . is probably often mistaken by local fishermen for the young of the bullheads.   **1983** Becker *Fishes WI* 719, In Wisconsin, the tadpole madtom is common in medium to large rivers.

tadpoles, rain v phr   For varr see quots   **chiefly Sth**   See Map
Cf frogs, rain
To rain heavily.

1909 *DN* 3.362 **eAL, wGA,** Rain tadpoles. . . To rain heavily.   **1915** *Atlanta Constitution* (GA) [26 Dec 35]/1 (newspaperarchive.com) **Sth,** I ain't never seen no sorter weather th't could back down this settle*ment from gwine* to a party—they'd go if it rained tadpoles and pennywinkles.   **1941** Street *In Father's House* 117 **seMS,** By that time it was raining tadpoles and nigger babies.   **1965–70** *DARE* (Qu. B26, *When it's raining very heavily . . "It's raining _____."*) Infs **GA**4, 31, **TX**32, Down tadpoles; **NC**3, **SC**46, Frogs and tadpoles; **NC**62, Pitchforks and tadpoles; **AL**6, Pouring down tadpoles; **FL**33, **GA**13, **SC**29, 46, Tadpoles; **AL**11, Tadpoles and frogs.

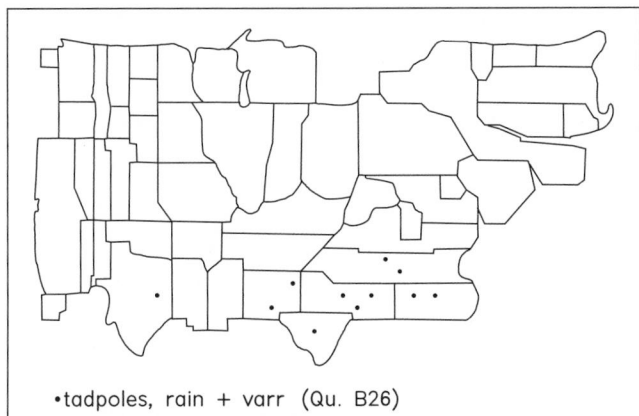

•tadpoles, rain + varr (Qu. B26)

tadpole stonecat   See **tadpole madtom**

tadpole stool n   Cf **frogstool**
A **toadstool.**

1986 Pederson *LAGS Concordance (Toadstools)* 1 inf, **swAL,** Tadpole stools.

tadwhacker n   Also *tadwacker*
=tad n[1] 1.

1941 Still in *Sat. Eve. Post* 10 May 111 **sAppalachians,** I'm fotching . . [a] name for this tadwacker. Long enough he's gone without.

1991 Still *Wolfpen Notebooks* 56 **sAppalachians,** Attending the Old Carr school was a whole heap easier than chopping crabgrass on a hillside in the summer sun. It kept a lot of us tadwhackers in school as long as we could stand it.

tady-wampus   See **wampus** n[2] **1**

taffy n

1   A lollipop.   **scattered, but esp PA, NJ**   See Map

1944 *AmSp* 19.38 **PA,** *Taffy* 'lollipop,' known in some places as a 'sucker.'   **1965–70** *DARE* (Qu. H81, *Candy on a stick for children to lick*) Infs **CA**146, **IL**77, **MA**125, **MO**2, **NJ**15, 18, 21, 23, **PA**248, **VT**16, Taffy; **NC**60, **PA**66, Taffies; **PA**171, Lollipop, taffy—refers to same thing, not saltwater taffy; **PA**239, Apple taffy, lollipop.   **1993** *DARE* File **sNJ,** If one traveled to South Jersey . . a lollipop was a "taffy."   **1998** *NADS Letters* **sePA,** *Taffy* . . a Philadelphia region substitute for *lollipop.*

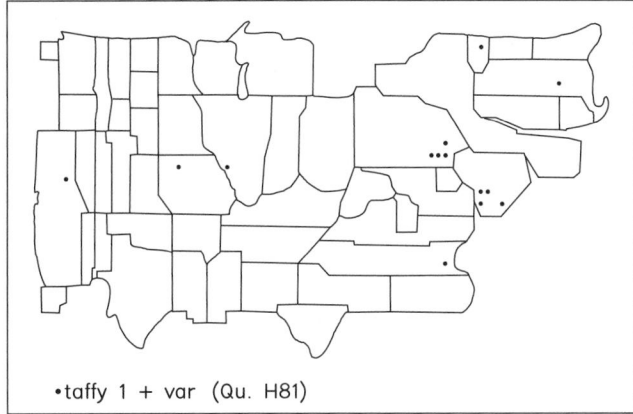

•taffy 1 + var (Qu. H81)

2   in phr *lose one's taffy:* To fail.

1927 *AmSp* 2.360 **cwWV,** Lost his taffy . . to fail. "He lost his taffy on that deal."   **1939** *AmSp* 14.91 **eTN,** Lost his taffy. Defeated. 'He lost his taffy.'

taffy pulling n   Also *taffy candy pulling, taffy party, ~ pull*   Cf **candy pulling, molasses pull(ing)**
A social gathering at which taffy is made.

1858 *Progr. Age & Coshocton Co. Rec.* (OH) 17 Feb [3]/1 (newspaperarchive.com), The "Young America" match hunt, for a "taffy pulling,["] came off on Saturday last.   **1883** (1939) Mayne *Maud* 158 **csIL,** We're going to have a taffy pull at our Y.P.T.A. Friday night.   **1912** *Out West Mag.* 166 **CA,** He wrote with beautiful flourishes, little notes of regret . . declining all socials, taffy pullings and croquet parties.   **1936** (1972) Ise *Sod & Stubble* 22 **KS,** There were frequent social festivities to attend: . . taffy parties, surprise parties, and quilting and sewing parties for the women.   **1938** FWP *Guide IA* 415 **cwIA,** At many mills after the molasses-making has been completed, a big taffy pull is held, the neighbors for miles around gathering for the event.   **1960** in 1984 Gilmore *Ozark Baptizings* 233 **MO,** Now back in the days when I was a boy, people would all meet, and they'd have a party and popcorn, molasses candy, and they would have a "taffy pullin'," they'd call it.   **1965–70** *DARE* (Qu. FF2, . . *Kinds of parties*) Infs **GA**89, **IN**32, **OH**95, **VA**11, 50, Taffy pulling; **MD**26, Taffy pulling, only in old days; **TX**39, Taffy candy pulling; **NJ**33, **OH**18, 98, **VA**1, Taffy pulls; **MI**9, When our children were at home, they loved a taffy pull; **MD**18, Taffy party—people pulled taffy as entertainment in old days; **OK**1, Used to have taffy parties—pull taffy and hang it on clothesline; (Qu. FF1, . . *A kind of group meeting called a 'social' or 'sociable'. . . [What goes on?]*) Inf **IL**82, Used to have sociables all the time—quilting bees, taffy pulls.   **1986** Pederson *LAGS Concordance (Parties)* 2 infs, **cnGA, cnFL,** Taffy pulling (parties).

tag n

1   The pendent staminate ament of an alder (*Alnus* spp) or birch (*Betula* spp). [*OED2 tag* n.[1] 5 1597 →; the only example later than 1597 in *OED2* is 1878 Stowe.]   Cf **tag alder**

1806 Shecut *Flora Carolinæensis* 1.273, The catkins or candles (called in Carolina Alder Tags) of the Alder tree.   **1855** Stowe *May Flower* 451 **MA,** The tags of the alder and the red berries of last summer's wild roses glitter now.   **1869** Porcher *Resources* 307 **Sth,** An astringent decoction may be made of the bark, leaves, or tags [of *Alnus serrulata*].

1877 *Forest & Stream* 9.185 **VT,** Found in crop of ruffed grouse birch tags. **1878** (1977) Stowe *Poganuc People* 182 **CT,** The tremulous tags of the birches and alders shook themselves gaily out in the woods. **c1938** in 1970 Hyatt *Hoodoo* 1.238 **seNC** [Black], Den he got . . some alter [Hyatt: alder] tags. It's a bush grows an' has little *tags* on it jis' about dat long. An' dey . . [boil] it an' got enough water to bathe in. **1970** *DARE* (Qu. BB22, . . *Home remedies . . for constipation*) Inf **VA**41, Alder-tag [ˈɔltɚ ˌtæg] tea—old-fashioned.

2 also *pine tag:* **=needle 1. chiefly VA** See Map Cf **longtag pine, short-tag ~**

1834 *Farmers' Reg.* 1.690 **csVA,** I make a pen in the fallow field . . and litter it almost exclusively with pine tags—(you must allow me the use of this term). **1851** *S. Lit. Messenger* 17.226 **VA,** I was not in the valley to see that bonfire which we made of dead boughs and "pine-tags." **1881** *Harper's New Mth. Mag.* 63.868 **cnVA,** At night they . . lie down on their 'pine-tag' beds, and go to sleep under the stars. **1899** (1912) Green *VA Folk-Speech* 435, *Tag.* . . The long leaves of the pine tree; pine-*tag.* **1935** Glasgow *Vein of Iron* 352 **wVA,** I'd every bit as soon sleep on pine tags, if you'd let me have a foxhound. **c1937** in 1976 *Weevils in the Wheat* 105 **VA** [Black], De mattress wuz stuffed wif straw and pine tags. **c1937** in 1970 Hyatt *Hoodoo* 1.230 **New Orleans LA** [Black], Dey taken dese pine tags—you git dat pine straw while it's green—an' dey wrap mah whole side up in dat. **1965–70** *DARE* (Qu. T6, *The pointed leaves that fall from pine trees*) Infs **VA**43, 46, 47, 57, 73, 82, Pine tag(s); **VA**40, 75, 96, 105, Tags. **1976** Ryland *Richmond Co. VA* 375, *Pine tags*—pine needles (the most common.) **2001** *DARE* File—Internet **VA,** James wants the simple things in life: a pine tag driveway, to earn a living from his land, and for his son to have the same opportunities that he had.

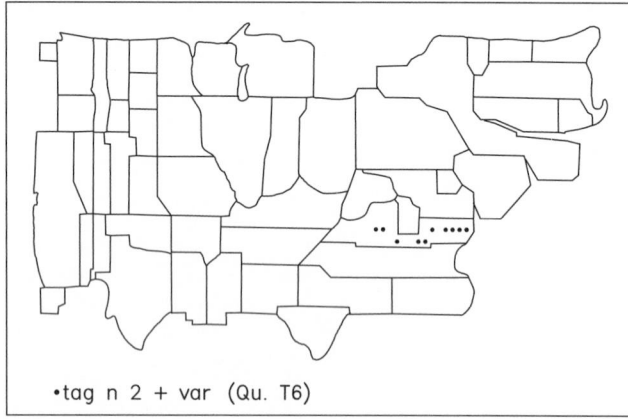

•tag n 2 + var (Qu. T6)

3 A bunch (of grapes).

1967 *DARE* File **cnAL,** Tag (of grapes) = bunch. **2003** *DARE* File—Internet **TN,** Kai chooses a small tag of grapes, nodding her thanks to the knight as she pulls off one and pops it into her mouth. **2007** in 2010 *DARE* File—Internet **csMS,** This is a little art work of mine, a tag of grapes done in watercolor.

4 See quots. See also **ice tag** n[1]

1986 Pederson *LAGS Concordance,* 1 inf, **ceTN,** Soot tag = dust web—get the color of soot. **1991** Beverley *Western NC Almanac* 147, *Tags of ice.* . . icicles.

tag alder n [**tag 1**]

1 An alder, usu *Alnus incana* or *A. serrulata.* **chiefly Nth, esp Gt Lakes** See Map Cf **alder tag**

1831 *Reformed Practice Med.* 76, Piles. *Treatment.* Give a decoction of the root of the tag alder internally. **1876** Hobbs *Bot. Hdbk.* 117, Tag alder, Red alder, Alnus rubra (serratula [sic]). **1910** Graves *Flowering Plants* 148 **CT,** *Alnus serrulata.* . . Smooth or Tag Alder. Frequent or common. **1911** Porter *Harvester* 39 **IN,** He . . made clippings of tag alder, spice brush and white willow. **1940** Steyermark *Flora MO* 126, *Smooth Alder, Tag Alder (Alnus rugosa* [=*A. incana* subsp *rugosa*]). . . Male flowers in drooping slender yellow-brown catkins; female flowers in short upright head-like catkins which become cone-like in fruit. **1965–70** *DARE* (Qu. T15, . . *Kinds of swamp trees*) 19 Infs, 14 **Gt Lakes,** Tag alder; **MN**14, Tag alder—a very small tree—or alder brush, used for smoking fish here; **VA**40, Tag alder or alder tag; (Qu. T13) Inf **NY**148, Tag elder [sic]. **1968** *WI Conserv. Bulletin* 33.5.15 **WI,** Most drumming logs in northern Wisconsin are located in tag alder swamps or on their edges. **1980** Little *Audubon Guide N. Amer. Trees E. Region*

362, *Speckled Alder.* . . "Tag Alder" . . *Alnus rugosa* [=*A. incana* subsp *rugosa*]. . . A low and clump-forming shrub; sometimes a small tree. *Ibid* 363, *Hazel Alder.* . . "Tag alder"—*Alnus serrulata.* . . Large, spreading shrub with several trunks, sometimes a small tree, commonly found at edge of water.

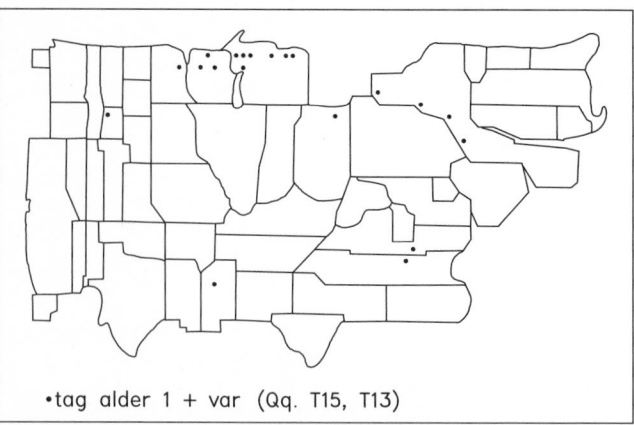

•tag alder 1 + var (Qq. T15, T13)

2 =swamp birch 2.

1894 *Jrl. Amer. Folkl.* 7.98 **MN,** *Betula pumila,* . . tag alder. **1899** MacMillan *MN Plant Life* 246, Of birches there are six species in Minnesota, the black birch, the canoe or paper birch, the river or red birch, the yellow or gray birch, the low birch or tag-alder, and the scrub or glandular birch.

tagger See **tiger**

tag, get one's v phr

1 In the children's game of tag: to tag (someone).

1905 *DN* 3.81 **nwAR,** *Get one's tag.* . . To tag one. 'I'll get your tag.' Common. **1986** Pederson *LAGS Concordance,* 1 inf, **cwAL,** I got my tag—said while playing game of tag.

2 See quots.

1908 *DN* 3.314 **eAL, wGA,** *Get one's tag.* . . To whip or chastise one. **1915** *DN* 4.226 **wTX,** *Get one's . . tag.* . . To get the best of one; to disconcert, or reprove severely. "That teacher will get your . . tag."

tag-goal n Cf **goal**

A children's game.

1888 *Good Housekeeping* 7.153, Gone are the joys of archery and croquet! In vain the delight of "still palm" and "tag goal." **1904** Day *Kin o' Ktaadn* 48 **ME,** Here, there, and yender he ducked and he skun—/ Tag gool with the world and old Brown on the run. **1943** *LANE* Map 584 **seME,** Field workers were instructed to record the name of the children's game in which one, designated as 'it', tries to touch another, who thereupon becomes 'it'. . . [O]ne offered *tag-goal* [ˌtæ·ɹˈguˠul].

tag-heels See **tag-tail**

tag line n

In marble play: **=lag line.**

1967–70 *DARE* [(Qu. EE7, . . *Kinds of marble games*) Inf **GA**42, Tag;] (Qu. EE8, *The line toward which the players roll their marbles before beginning a game, to determine the order of shooting*) Inf **NC**63, Tag line.

tag out exclam

1966 *DARE* (Qu. EE17, *In a game of tag, if a player wants to rest, what does he call out so that he can't be tagged?*) Inf **GA**9, Tag out; [**TX**40, No tag].

tag sale n **chiefly Nth, esp sNEng, NYC**

A sale of used household items, usu held by a private person or by an organization as a cooperative fundraising event.

1919 Alpha Chi Omega *Lyre* 23.287 **CA,** Associated Women Students' Loan Fund netted $355 at a tag sale, to aid women working their way through College. **1968** *Chron.-Telegram* (Elyria OH) 2 July 11/7, [Syndicated column:] These make ideal items for a tag sale. One person's junk can be another person's finds. **1969** *Our Town Reminder* (S. Hadley MA) 23 Apr 28, Garage tag sale: April 24, 25, 26 at 217 Willimansett St. **1982** *Capital Times* (Madison WI) 29 Jan 2/1 **NYC,** A porcelain food stand, which was bought for $2 at a tag sale last year, was sold for $60,000 to an antiques dealer. **1997** Bohjalian *Midwives* 65 **VT**

(as of 1981), She sat upon a firm throw pillow my mother had recently purchased at a tag sale. **1998** *DARE* File **seCT,** I saw signs advertising "tag sales" in Old Saybrook. A friend said that they are the same as garage or yard sales. She hadn't heard the term before moving to Connecticut. **2002** *Ibid* **CT,** There are old Baedeker guides around. . . I've seen them at tag sales, used bookstores, and such. **2004** *Ibid* **nwMA,** Let's clean out the hall closet. I bet we can give a lot of that stuff to the church tag sale. Or, we could combine our things with the Jones family's; they're planning a tag sale on Saturday. **2011** (acc) Vaux–Golder *Dial. Surv.* (Internet), *Terms . . for a sale of unwanted items on your porch, in your yard, etc.* [*Tag sale,* with 3.6% of the responses, is reported chiefly from the **Nth,** esp **sNEng** and the **NYC** metro area.]

tag-tail n   Also *tag-heels* **chiefly Nth, West** See Map *old-fash* Cf **cow's tail 2, horsetail 4, lamb's tail 3, pigtail** n **4, tail** n¹ **6, tailer**

A tagalong, hanger-on; one who lags behind.

1834 Davis *Letters Downing* 311 **ME,** You are surrounded by sich a raft of snuffle-nose, scabby set of tag-tails, that I can't have nothin more to do with you. **1864** (1873) Webster *Amer. Dict., Tag-tail.* . . A person who attaches himself to another against the will of the latter; a dependent; a sycophant; a parasite. **1909** *DN* 3.422 **Cape Cod MA** (as of a1857), *Tagtail.* . . One who brings up the rear or lags behind. **1915** *DN* 4.210, *Tag-tail,* a hanger on. "Mary is such a tag-tail that none of the girls like her." Taunt of school children. **1916** *DN* 4.281 **NE,** *Tagtail.* . . One who "tags along," as a little sister. "Tagtail, tagtail, can't go by herself!" **1917** *DN* 4.437 **NY,** *Tagtail.* **1950** *WELS* (*Somebody who always follows along behind: "He's an awful _____!"*) 9 Infs, **WI,** Tag-tail. **1965–70** *DARE* (Qu. Y9) 71 Infs, **chiefly Nth, West,** Tag-tail; **NY**10, 105, Tag-heels. [Of all Infs responding to the question, 11% were young, 64% old; of those giving these responses, 0% were young, 82% old.]

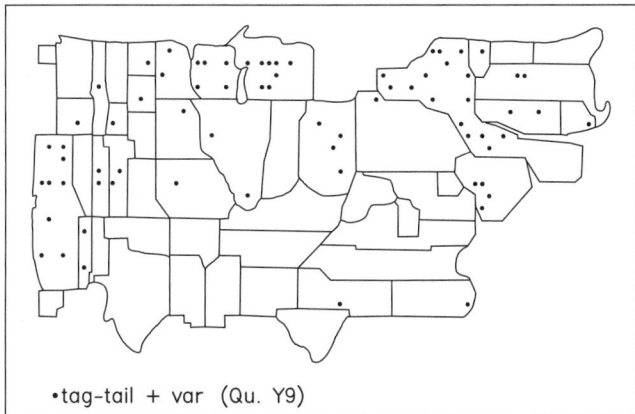

•tag-tail + var (Qu. Y9)

tag ups n   [Cf *tag up* in baseball, to touch a base before running after a fly ball is caught] Cf **work-up,** *DS* EE11

1975 Ferretti *Gt. Amer. Book Sidewalk Games* 189, Another fine three-player Stickball game is *Tag Ups.* In this game, there is only one fielder, a batter, and a runner who stands on third base. The batter hits a fly ball (only fly balls are permitted), and at the moment the fielder catches it, the man on third base races for home. The batter then becomes the catcher and is responsible for tagging the runner out. Each time the runner scores, a run is counted for him; each time he is tagged, he is out. There are two outs to an inning, and after two outs are made, the players rotate, with the runner on third becoming the batter, the batter becoming the fielder, and the fielder going to third base.

tahl See **towel**

tahn See **town** n

tahoka daisy n   [Prob after *Tahoka* city and lake in west Texas] A **tansy aster** (here: *Machaeranthera tanacetifolia*). Also called **dagger flower 1**

1961 Wills–Irwin *Flowers TX* 229, *Tansy-aster—Machaeranthera tanacetifolia.* . . is gaining in favor as a garden annual, and . . is sold by seedsmen under the name "Tahoka Daisy." **1970** Correll *Plants TX* 1585, *Machaeranthera tanacetifolia.* . . *Tahoka daisy.* . . Abundant in sandy soils. **1976** Bailey–Bailey *Hortus Third* 692, [*Machaeranthera*] *tanacetifolia.* . . *Tahoka daisy.* . . Ray fl[ower]s violet-blue or whitish.

tahr See **tire** n

tail n¹

1 in phr *get one's tail over the dashboard* and varr: To become excited, impatient, or angry; in adv phrr *(with one's head up and) tail over the dashboard* and varr: in a high-spirited manner. [See quot 1995]

[**1870** *Harper's New Mth. Mag.* 40.630 **ID,** *Livery and feed stable*— Main Street, Boise City, I.T., Samuel F.P. Briggs, Prop. Fine buggies and as fine horses as ever threw their tails over the dash.] **1876** *Coshocton Age* (OH) 24 Aug [3]/3 (newspaperarchive.com), The few remaining chickens may be seen emerging from the wood-pile, with head up and tail over the dash, looking for a preacher. **1884** *Bismarck Tribune* (ND) [23 May] 6/1 (newspaperarchive.com), The Helena left for Fort Benton at 4:15 yesterday afternoon. She started out with her head up and tail over the dashboard. **1912** *DN* 3.578 **wIN,** *Head up and tail over the dashboard.* . . In a lively, spirited manner. "Ever since election day he has been going around with his head up and tail over the dashboard." [**1927** *AmSp* 2.356 **cwWV,** *Have the tail over the dashboard* . . to be in fine physical condition. "The horses have been standing in the barn for a week. They will have their tails over the dashboard as soon as we hitch them to the buggy."] **1944** Adams *Western Words* 161, *Tail over the dashboard*—Said of one in high spirits. **1946** *Post-Std.* (Syracuse NY) 27 May 4/3, Does he believe that labor has finally gotten its tail over the dash-board? **c1950** Halpert *Coll.* 61 **wKY, nwTN,** *Tail over the dash-board* = describing someone who is miffed. "Oh, she's got her tail over the dashboard about something." [Halpert: The reference is to a horse and buggy, when the horse wants his own way about things.] **1958** McCulloch *Woods Words* 190 **Pacific NW,** *Tail over the dashboard*—A logger on his way to town for the week end. **1967** *DARE* (Qu. A21, *When someone is in too much of a hurry . . "Now just slow down! Don't _____."*) Infs **LA**14, **TX**5, Get your tail (*or* ass) over the dashboard. **1995** (1998) *Brophy Coll.* 75 **swMO** (as of c1960), *Tail over the dash, to get one's.* [T]o become upset or angry (ref. to a horse harnessed to a vehicle with a dashboard). **1998** in 2003 *DARE* File **TX,** When I moved from Louisiana to Houston my immediate boss was a . . woman from East Texas. I learned some very neat regionalisms from her. . . Don't get your tail over the dashboard—don't get upset.

2 in phrr *have* (or *get*) *one's tail over the lines* and varr: To be (or become) stubborn or unmanageable. Cf **line** n¹ **1,** *DS* GG23a, b, c

1912 *DN* 3.578 **wIN,** *Have one's tail over the line.* . . To act stubbornly. "I couldn't do anything with Charley this morning; he had his tail over the line about something." **1927** *AmSp* 2.356 **cwWV,** *To have the tail over the lines* . . to be hard to control. "My sister has allowed her children to get their tails over the lines." **1946** McAtee *Dial. Grant Co. IN Suppl. 3* 10 (as of 1890s), *Tail over the lines,"* "have the . . be contrary, unmanageable. [**1967** *DARE* (Qu. GG23c, . . *Expressions [to tell someone to be patient]*) Inf **CO**21, Don't get your tail over the crupper.] **1968** Adams *Western Words* 316, *Tail over the lines*—A cowboy's description of someone hard to control.

3 in phr *have (something) by the tail on a downhill pull* and varr: To be in an advantageous position with respect to.

1878 *Life & Advent. Sam Bass* 11 **TX,** He assumed his friend in the phraseology of the cattle ranche . . had the world by the tail, with a down-hill pull. **1890** *Atlanta Constitution* (GA) 24 Aug 12/4, Our southern cotton growers will have the world by the tail and a downhill pull on it. **1906** *DN* 3.137 **nwAR,** *Get it by the tail and a down-hill pull on it.* . . To be able to accomplish easily. "Can I do it? Why, I've got it by the tail and a down-hill pull on it." **1950** *Herald–Press* (St. Joseph MI) 13 Jan 8/1, But right now the politicians have the world by the tail on a downhill pull. **1957** *Gt. Bend Daily Tribune* (KS) 7 Mar 12/8, [Advt:] With meat prices like this, you have the high cost of living by the tail with a downhill pull. **1960** Criswell *Resp. to PADS 20* **Ozarks,** Since he was appointed surveyor, he thinks he's got the world by the tail with a downhill pull. **1976** *Walla Walla Union–Bulletin* (WA) 13 Sept 9/6, I don't want to leave Walla Walla. I have a piece of land here. . . The friends, a good job. . . I've got the world by the tail on a downhill pull.

4 in phr *have* (or *get*) *one's tail in a crack* and var: To be (or get) in a difficult situation.

1901 Naylor *Ralph Marlowe* 362 **OH,** He's got his tail in a crack an' he's goin' to git it pinched. **1916** *Daily Kennebec Jrl.* (Augusta ME) 17 May 6/1, The Argus rat got its tail in a crack; the above reprint is its squeal. **1946** *PADS* 6.42 **eNC,** To get one's *tail* in a split stick. (To get into difficulties.) ((Perhaps figurative from the hunter's habit of putting a 'possum's tail in a split stick and letting him "ride" the stick while carrying him.)) Pamlico. Occasional. **1951** Pegler in *Post–Std.* (Syracuse NY) 7 Sept sec 2 17/2, I . . touched him off balance . . by warning . . that a communist was a dirty, traitorous rat who might seem friendly just then because the Russian bear had its tail in a crack. **1971** *Today Show Letters* **cnAL** (as of a1940), My landlady often spoke of people in trouble as having their "tails in a crack." **1972** *Atlanta Letters* **GA,** Get (one's) tail in a crack . . get oneself into a difficult situation. **1988** *Chron.–Telegram* (Elyria OH) 17 Apr sec A 6/3, To employ a crude but colorful expression widely used in political circles, the Democratic Party has got its tail in a crack. **2003** *Kerrville Times* (TX) 18 Jan sec D 7/1, [Letter:] Kim Sung Il . . knows that we have our tail in a crack in the Middle East.

5 in phr *get one's tail in a knot:* To get excited.

   1967 *DARE* (Qu. A21, *When someone is in too much of a hurry . . "Now just slow down! Don't _____."*) Inf **WA**30, Get your tail in a knot. [**1979** *NYT Article Letters,* "I'll jerk a knot in your tail". . . The above all part of the language I grew up with. In McLean County, Illinois.] **1992** *Daily Herald* (Arlington Heights IL) 16 Aug sec 1A 14/3, Don't get your tail in a knot until you've weighed all your options.

6 also in var combs (see quot): **=tag-tail.**

   1965–70 *DARE* (Qu. Y9, *Somebody who always follows along behind others: "His little brother is an awful _____."*) Infs **GA**63, **HI**7, **VA**47, Tail; [**CA**21, Tail-behind;] **DE**2, Tail end; **CA**134, Tailgate; **GA**77, Tail-tagger; **NC**55, Tail-twister.

tail v[1], hence vbl n *tailing*

1 also with *down:* To throw (an animal, esp a cow or calf) to the ground by pulling on its tail. [This and **2** below are specialized uses of *OED2 tail* v. 2 "To grasp or drag by the tail"; 1638 →.] **West, esp TX** Cf **colear**

   1839 Hoffman *Wild Scenes* 1.102 **NY,** "A man that can't tail a deer oughtn't to hunt him." "Why, John, you couldn't hold a fat buck by his tail long enough to cut his throat." [**1887** *Scribner's Mag.* 2.509 **West,** *Tail,* to hold a steer down by the tail after it is lassoed and heeled.] **1895** Remington *Pony Tracks* 95 **TX,** Mr. Bailey . . in the next instant "tailed" and threw the bull as it was about to enter the timber. **1897** Lewis *Wolfville* 203 **AZ,** "What's tailin' a pony?" "It's ridin' up from the r'ar an' takin' a half-hitch on your saddlehorn with the tail of another gent's pony, an' then spurrin' by an' swappin' ends with the whole outfit,—gent, hoss, an' all." **1920** Hunter *Trail Drivers TX* 297, He "bulldogs" them [=cows] by twisting the neck, or "tails" him by giving a sudden jerk on the tail when some of the animal's feet are off the ground. **1929** Dobie *Vaquero* 15 **TX,** The safest and most effective thing to do when an old steer ran off was to tail him. A thorough tailing usually knocked the breath out of him. . . Really, with a fast horse and a certain sleight that comes only from practice it is very easy to tail an animal down. **1929** *AmSp* 5.69 **NE** [Cattle country talk], "Tailing" is the method of throwing a "critter" by seizing its tail and giving it a quick pull to one side, thus throwing the animal off balance. **1933** *AmSp* 8.1.30 **nwTX** [Ranch diction], *Tail down.* To throw an animal, by catching it by the tail. Some cowboys were able to *tail* a big steer *down* without dismounting. **1941** Writers' Program *Guide WY* 465, *Tail.* . . To throw a calf after the rope has dragged the animal near the branding fire.

2 usu with *up:* To force or help (a cow) to its feet by pulling on its tail.

   1868 IA State Ag. Soc. *Rept. for 1867* 129, Shelter and good feeding is a sure preventive, and much cheaper than 'tailing them up' or taking off their hides toward Spring. **1916** *DN* 4.331 **KS,** *Tail.* . . To help (domestic animals, esp. cattle) to rise by seizing the creature's tail. **1917** Garland *Son Middle Border* 116 **WI,** Some of . . [the cows] got so weak that they had to be 'tailed' up as it was called. **1920** Hunter *Trail Drivers TX* 5 (as of c1890), Gradually the cow-puncher, whose delight was to ride his pony "up the trail" was deprived of that privilege, and now instead he goes along with a train load to "tail 'em up" when the cattle get down in a stock car. **1923** *DN* 5.222 **swMO,** *Tail up.* . . To lift an animal or to assist it in rising by seizing it by the tail. **1927** *AmSp* 2.365 **cwWV,** *Tail* . . to help raise an animal that is down. "We had to tail four of the steers this morning." **1928** *AmSp* 4.132 **NE,** To "tail up a cow" is to help a weak cow to her feet. **c1938** in Lib. of Congress *Amer. Memory: WPA Life Hist.* (Internet) **TX,** I was kept busy that winter tailing up old poor cows. **1941** Cleaveland *No Life* 309 **NM,** Unlike a horse, a cow gets up on her hind feet first, so a stout pull on her tail may be just the little help she needs; but if she cannot be 'tailed up,' a sling around her middle and some sort of block-and-tackle may have to be rigged up. **1945** Thorp *Pardner* 246 **SW,** After one of them [=cat-

tle pulled out of a boghole] . . had rested for a while in the sun, then, if you "tailed" it up (gave it a lift by the tail), as like as not it would . . dash straight for the bog from which it had just been rescued. **2002** O'Connor–Day *Lazy B* 249 **AZ,** The cowboys had to go to the corrals three times a day and literally help the thin cows up and make them walk around for a while. The cowboy term for this procedure is "tailing up" the cow.

3 also with *down;* In logging: to retard (a load of logs) on a steep slope with a rope or chain attached to its rear.

   1792 Belknap *Hist. NH* 3.106, Some of the cattle are placed behind it; a chain which is attached to their yokes is brought forward and fastened to the hinder end of the load [of logs], and the resistance which is made by these cattle, checks the descent. This operation is called *tailing.* **1851** (1856) Springer *Forest Life* 104 **ME,** In other instances loads are eased down hillsides by the use of "tackel and fall" or by a strong "warp," taking a "bite" round a tree, and hitching to one yoke of the oxen. In this manner the load is "tailed down" steeps where it would be impossible for the "tongue oxen" to resist the pressure of the load. **1958** McCulloch *Woods Words* 189 **Pacific NW,** *Tail down.* . . To snub the tail end of a turn of logs down a steep pitch when skidding with animals.

4 with *down;* In logging: see quots.

   1905 U.S. Forest Serv. *Bulletin* 61.50 [Logging terms], *Taildown, to.* To roll logs on a skidway to a point on the skids where they can be quickly reached by the loading crew. (N[orthern] F[orests]) **1939** FWP *ID Lore* 244, Lumberjack jargon in the St. Maries area and elsewhere: . . *Tail down*—to roll a log onto a skidway. **1958** McCulloch *Woods Words* 189 **Pacific NW,** *Tail down.* . . To shove the last of a rollway of logs into the river. . . To take down a cold deck of logs and load it out. **1969** Sorden *Lumberjack Lingo* 127 **NEng, Gt Lakes,** *Tailing down*— Rolling logs down a skidway from the rear of the log pile. Rolling logs to the deck pile.

5 freq with *up;* also with *together:* To fasten (a pack animal) to or by the tail. **chiefly West**

   [**1914** Washburn *Two in Wilderness* 289 **Canada,** I am going to tail the horses together.] **1920** Barnes *Tales X-Bar* 39 **West,** Had him tailed up to old Paint. . . Me being tired and sleepy I never sensed the loss till I gits here with the mule's rope a dragging along still tied to Paint's tail. **1948** Keith *Big Game* 394, A pack string will always make better time and arrive in better condition if tailed up. **1959** Back *Horses & Trails* 101 **WY,** When you tail or tie horses together, be sure they are friends, or at least tolerate each other. . . If you happen to have quite a string tied or tailed together, sometimes these whims can raise hell. **2009** *Redoubt Reporter* (Soldotna AK) 1 July (Internet), Eugene Hansen had "tailed up" the horses in his pack . . when the bear hide slipped.

6 as vbl n *tailing up;* In logging: see quot. Cf **sack** v **1a**

   1969 Sorden *Lumberjack Lingo* 127 **NEng, Gt Lakes,** *Tailing up*— Collecting derelict logs left stranded at the close of a river drive.

tail v[2] See **tailor** v

tail n[2] [Prob folk-etym for **stale 1**]

See quots.

   1914 *DN* 4.154 **NH,** *Tail.* . . A rake; *fork tail,* a rake, fork handle.

tail down See **tail** v[1] **1, 3, 4**

tail end n

1 The least desirable segment of a herd of animals; hence n *tailender* a scrawny or poor-quality animal. Cf **tailing** n **1**

   1875 U.S. Comm. Red Cloud Ind. Agency *Report* 268, They were small cattle, but not very poor either; they were good to eat, but small; they were the tail-end of the herd. **1907** Love *Deadwood Dick* 52, Short yearlings were those over one year old and short of two years, long yearlings those two years and short of three years, tail end and scabs mean nearly the same thing, and comprise all the very young stock of all classes not yet reached the dignity of yearlings. These latter were in demand from the cattle men, who took them to feed until they got their growth. **1941** Ward *Holding Hills* 50 **IA** (as of early 20th cent), When, in order to get good cattle, he had to take any tail-enders, he singled them out the first day and told Joe to take "these culls" over to the timber eighty. **1969–70** *DARE* (Qu. K54, . . *The smallest pig in a litter*) Inf **VA**105, Tailender; [**MA**55, Tail pig.]

2 See **tail** n[1] **6.**

tailender See **tail end** n **1**

tail end of nowhere See **end of nowhere(s)**

tailer n

1 =**tag-tail.**

1942 Berrey–Van den Bark *Amer. Slang* 426.16, *Follower. . .* Tailer. *Ibid* 441.1, *Hanger-on. . .* Tailer. **1966–70** *DARE* (Qu. Y9, *Somebody who always follows along behind others: "His little brother is an awful _____."*) Infs **GA**3, **KY**11, **ND**5, Tailer.

2 See quot. [**tail** v¹ **2**]

1928 *AmSp* 4.129 **NE,** If a cow . . is thin and weak because of a barren range and must be helped to its feet, it is a "tailer" because the "sandhiller" must twist its tail to force it to rise.

tailer v See **tailor** v

tailgate n

1 The heel of a loaf of bread. Cf **nibby** n¹

1967 Green *Horse Tradin'* 212 **TX,** I said: "I like the tailgate." He just cut off both ends of the loaf of bread and said: "There's you two tailgates."

2 See **tail** n¹ **6.**

tailgating vbl n Cf **bum-riding, shacking** vbl n², **skitching**

Holding on to the back of a car as it drives over snow or ice.

c1980 *DARE* File **AR,** Charles . . says they called it "tailgating" back in Arkansas.

tail go with the hide, let the See **hide** n² **7a**

tail hold n Pronc-sp *tail holt*

1 A firm grip, often fig.

1874 *Sedalia Daily Democrat* (MO) 16 Mar 1/6, The St. Louis Globe devotes all its time to pulling things through. It tried a tail holt on the social evil, but busted its suspenders and has taken a back seat. **1879** *Portsmouth Times* (OH) 14 Oct 2/3, The two Boss Fosters . . seem to have let their tail hold on Washington township slip. **1916** *Trenton Eve. Times* (NJ) 10 July 11/3, The Cubs open this week with a tail hold on first division, having passed New York and Pittsburgh. **1927** *AmSp* 2.365 **cwWV,** *Tail holt* . . a good hold for lifting. "I got a tail holt, and threw him off his balance." **1930** *AmSp* 6.99 **cNY** [Erie Canal expressions], *Tail-hold on all the winds in time:* A firm grip. "This ain't going to stop" he said; "it's got a tail-hold on all the winds in time." **1956** Gipson *Old Yeller* 2 **TX,** In fact . . all we lack having a tight tail-holt on the world is a little cash money. **1970** *Washington C.H. Rec.–Herald* (OH) 20 Mar 4/1, Those so minded seem to feel that the mere circumstance of being under 25 gives one a tail-hold on the truth.

2 Esp in logging: a solid anchorage, freq a tree or stump, to which a cable is attached; any of var rigging setups involving an anchored cable; hence v *tail-hold* to anchor (rigging). **Pacific NW** Cf **tail tree**

1905 U.S. Forest Serv. *Bulletin* 61.50 **Pacific NW** [Logging terms], *Tail hold.* 1. A means of obtaining increased power in moving a log by tackle. The cable is passed through a block attached to the log and the end fastened to a stationary object, so that hauling on the other end gives twice the power which would be attained by direct attachment of the cable to the log. . . 2. The attachment of the rear end of a donkey sled, usually to a tree or stump. **1950** *Western Folkl.* 9.120 **nwOR** [Logger speech], *Tail hold.* Any secure fastening; usually pronounced "tail holt." **1958** McCulloch *Woods Words* 189 **Pacific NW,** *Tail hold*—a. A line from the tightening blocks on a skyline to an anchor; especially an added line at the tail tree end of the skyline, running to an anchor. b. A hold used to tie the back end of a donkey or a cat to a stump. c. A line anchoring a haulback block to a stump. d. The back end of a snub line. e. To rig a block to something to be moved, running a line through the block from the donkey and out to a tail hold or skyline. **1959** *AmSp* 34.80 **nwCA** [Logger lingo], *Tail holt.* . . The stump or tree to which the baloney [=wire rope] . . is anchored or fastened. **1961** Labbe–Goe *Railroads* 260 **Pacific NW,** *Tailhold:* The point where the end of a line was fastened in a fixed position, as to a stump. **1967** *DARE* Tape **WA**24, Run it back and tail-hold it to another tree back about 2,000 feet. . . That's when you choke on to a tree. That's the end of your . . skyline. **2003** *DARE* File—Internet **Pacific NW,** There are only 2 drums that are used continuously. One that pulls the bucket in and one that pulls the bucket up towards the Skyline, and out towards the tail hold. *Ibid* **CA,** Twister. A line . . that provides additional support for a tailhold stump, guyline stump, or tree used for anchorage in cable logging systems. *Ibid* **WA,** To mobilize materials and construction equip-

ment to the site Sahale used a Madill 071 Yarder, placing it in an old logging cut and erecting a skyline across the canyon to a tailhold anchor more than 2000 feet away.

tail in a crack, get (or have) one's See **tail** n¹ **4**

tail in a knot, get one's See **tail** n¹ **5**

tailing vbl n See **tail** v¹

tailing n

1 The least desirable segment of a herd of animals; a weak or slow animal. Cf **tail end**

1936 McCarthy *Lang. Mosshorn* np **West** [Range terms], *Tailings.* . . Stragglers. **1967** Green *Horse Tradin'* 178 **TX,** It looked to me like he was getting ready to sell me the tailings and him keep the best ones. **2006** Keeble *Nocturnal Amer.* 264 **Pacific NW,** Pascal and Agatha . . hung behind the last tailings of the herd.

2 pl: See quot 1974. Cf **backings, faint**

1892 *Jrl. Amer. Chem. Soc.* 14.48, Fusel oil was discovered by Scheele in the tailings from the rectification of rye whiskey. **1918** Fitch *Dietotherapy* 1.585, [In distilling brandy:] The first part contains the crudities of the wine and is returned to the still; the middle running part is the best part and is used in the second distillation; and the third part or tailings is mingled with the fresh wine to be redistilled. **1974** Maurer–Pearl *KY Moonshine* 126, *Tailings.* . . Faints. [*Ibid* 117, *Faints.* . . (1) Low-proof distillate that comes through the condenser at the end of a run. . . (2) Heated slops used for setting mash.]

tailing up See **tail** v¹ **6**

taillight shiner n

A **shiner 1** (here: *Notropis maculatus*).

1957 Blair et al. *Vertebrates U.S.* 133, *Notropis maculatus.* . . Taillight shiner. Caudal spot conspicuous, large, and round. **1983** *Audubon Field Guide N. Amer. Fishes* 440, *Dusky lateral stripe from snout to caudal fin ends in large, black caudal spot;* breeding males reddish. . . The total lifespan of the Taillight Shiner is 13 to 15 months.

Tail-'n'-horns n

=**horny man.**

1969 *DARE* (Qu. CC8, . . *The devil*) Inf **CA**158, Tail-'n'-horns.

tail on a downhill pull, have (something) by the See **tail** n¹ **3**

tailor n Also sp *taylor* **esp Delmarva**

1 also *tailor herring, ~ shad:* A **hickory shad** (here: *Alosa mediocris*). Cf **freshwater tailor**

1676 Royal Soc. London *Philos. Trans.* 11.625 **VA,** In the Creeks are great store of small fish, as *Perches, Crokers, Taylors, Eels,* and divers others. **1709** (1967) Lawson *New Voyage* 162 **NC, SC,** The Taylor is a Fish about the Bigness of a Trout, but of a bluish and green Colour, with a forked Tail, as a Mackarel has. **1743** Catesby *Nat. Hist. Carolina* 2 [app] xxxii, *A List of the common Names of the Fish of* Carolina. . . Sea Fish. . . Fat-back. Herring. Taylor. Smelt [etc]. **1859** (1968) Bartlett *Americanisms* 469, *Tailor.* A fish resembling the shad, but inferior to it in size and flavor. In the towns on the Potomac, the Blue fish is called a *Salt-water tailor.* **1873** U.S. Bur. Fisheries *Rept. for 1871 & 1872* 811, *Pomolobus mediocris* [=*Alosa m.*] . . Tailor herring *(Potomac). Ibid* 826, *Pomolobus mediocris.* . . The Fall-Shad—The Tailor-Shad. **1884** Goode *Fisheries U.S.* 1.608, In the Potomac the species [=*Alosa mediocris*] is called the "Tailor Shad," or the "Fresh-water Tailor," in contradistinction to the bluefish, which is called the "Salt-water Tailor." **1938** Schrenkeisen *Field Book Fishes* 28, *Pomolobus mediocris* . . has a variety of common names: Hickory Shad, . . Tailor Herring, . . and, in the Potomac, Tailor Shad or Fresh-water Tailor. **1984** *DARE* File **Chesapeake Bay** [Watermen's vocab], Tailor shad.

2 also *tailor blue, tailorfish:* =**bluefish 1.** Cf **saltwater tailor**

1867 De Voe *Market Asst.* 206, This species of mackerel . . is now known in . . the Philadelphia markets as *tailors.* **1873** U.S. Bur. Fisheries *Rept. for 1871 & 1872* 235, The blue-fish. . . is the . . tailor of Maryland. *Ibid* 783, The familiar *Pomatomus saltatrix* . . is also called . . "tailor" (at Philadelphia and along portions of the southern coast). *Ibid* 807, *Pomatomus saltatrix.* . . Tailor *(Maryland and Virginia).* **1874** *Forest & Stream* 1.411 **eMD,** Here they call the . . bluefish taylors. *Ibid, Fish in Season in February.* Southern Waters. . . Tailorfish. **1903** NY State Museum & Sci. Serv. *Bulletin* 60.446 **Ches-**

apeake Bay, *Pomatomus saltatrix*. . . Tailor. **1935** Caine *Game Fish* 46 **Sth**, Bluefish. . . Tailor. **1984** *DARE* File **Chesapeake Bay** [Watermen's vocab], Taylor blue.

tailor v Also *tail* Also sp *tailer* [Cf Ger *Schneider* tailor; player who fails to make a certain score in a card game] **esp S Midl** *old-fash*

To beat (someone) in a game by an overwhelming margin; to **skunk v 1.**

1891 *PMLA* 6.3.173 **TN**, In playing marbles, one boy *tailers (tailors)* another when he wins seven games before the other wins any. **1892** *DN* 1.233 **KY**, *Tailor:* to 'skunk'. . . "We tailored them." **1893** Shands *MS Speech* 61, In Tennessee, a boy is said to *tailer* another when the first wins seven games of marbles to the second's none. The word for this in Mississippi is *tail . . ,* a shortened form, I suppose, for *tailer.* **1915** *DN* 4.191 **swVA**, *Tailor, v.t.* In games = *whitewash.*

tailor bee n Cf **carpenter bee, tailor wasp**

A leaf-cutting bee of the family Megachilidae.

1856 (1949) Thoreau *Jrl.* 9.61 **MA**, The fever-bush is conspicuously flower-budded. Even its spicy leaves have been cut by the tailor bee, and circular pieces taken out. **1867** *Amer. Naturalist* 1.373, The interesting habits of the Leaf-cutting, or Tailor-bee *(Megachile)*, have always attracted attention. **1873** *Harper's New Mth. Mag.* 46.595, Peggy rolled out her paste reflectively, and lined a deep pan as daintily as the tailor-bee lines her nest with a rose leaf. **1887** *Scribner's Mag.* 1.358, The tailor-bee cuts out pieces of rose-leaf, bends them, . . and so makes a thimble-shaped case. **1922** Jenkins *Interesting Neighbors* 15, We had seen and heard of . . tailor-bees which cut out pieces of leaves, like cloth, with which to line their nests.

tailor blue, tailorfish See **tailor** n 2

tailor herring (or shad) See **tailor** n 1

tailor wasp n Cf **tailor bee**

A **paper wasp** (here: *Polistes annularis*).

1884 (1885) McCook *Tenants* 429 **PA**, The branches of these oaks are thickly colonized by ringed wasps—"Tailor wasps," I find they are called by the country-side people. [*Ibid* 430 **PA**, [Caption:] Nest of the ringed or rust-red wasp *(Polistes annulatus* [sic].)] **1896** *Times–Democrat* (Lima OH) 25 Mar 1/4, The tailor wasp, when needing a piece of leaf to line its nest, always cuts its pattern in an exact circle. These wasps have often been watched, but have never been known to mistake the size, to cut the pattern over again or to spoil a leaf.

tail over the dashboard See **tail** n¹ 1

tail over the lines, have (or get) one's See **tail** n¹ 2

tail rider n **chiefly West** Cf **drag driver**

See quots.

1922 Rollins *Cowboy* 253, The foremost one of the punchers in each of these lines was slightly more advanced than the van of the herd and was called a "point man" or "lead rider." Each of the men in line behind him was termed a "swing man" or "flank rider." At the rear of the column came the tail riders. **1926** Branch *Cowboy* 22, "Tail riders," cowboys who rode in the rear of moving cattle-herds to keep the stragglers in the procession, protected themselves from the dust by pulling their bandannas up to their eyes.

tail-tagger See **tail** n¹ 6

tail together See **tail** v¹ 5

tail tree n Cf **home tree, spar ~, tail hold 2**

In logging: a tree used to anchor the rigging at the far end of a cable logging system.

1894 *Amer. Soc. Civil Engineers Trans.* 32.48, On the head tree two sheaves are placed . . , and on the tail tree a 2-ft. steel sheave is chained. **1913** Bryant *Logging* 196, *The cableway system.* This comprises a main wire cable . . suspended between two supports known, respectively, as the "head spar" tree and the "tail" tree. *Ibid* 209, [In the slack-rope system] the far end of the cable passes through a sheave block fastened to a tail tree. **1938** (1939) Holbrook *Holy Mackinaw* 264, *Tail tree.* The No. 2 spar of a skyline hook-up. **1958** McCulloch *Woods Words* 190 **Pacific NW**, *Tail tree*—A spar tree at the outer end of the logging operation, away from the landing. It supports the far end of the skyline in overhead cable systems of logging. **1959** *AmSp* 34.80 **nwCA** [Logger lingo], *Tail tree.* . . A tree at the end of a run, to which the tackle is fastened in power skidding. **1964** Clarkson *Tumult* 373 **WV**, *Tail tree*—In

steam skidding, the tree at the end of the skid-road, to which the rigging used in skidding logs is attached.

tail-twister See **tail** n¹ 6

tail up See **tail** v¹ 2, 5

taint v¹ [*OED2* 1601 →] Cf **blink** v 1, *DS* H46

To become spoiled.

1986 Pederson *LAGS Concordance (The meat is spoiled)* 1 inf, **neTN**, Hit taints; 1 inf, **cnMS**, It'd taint; (*Hit* for *it*) 1 inf, **swGA**, Hit would taint.

taint adj [Abbr for *tainted; OED2* 1620 →]

Spoiled, tainted.

1934 *WV Review* Dec 77, Among these [=words found in central or southern West Virginia] are . . *taint* for *tainted* (as used with milk) [etc]. **1986** Pederson *LAGS Concordance (The meat is spoiled)* 1 inf, **neTN**, Taint; 1 inf, **neMS**, It gets taint.

tain't v² [Contr of *it* + *ain't* v¹] Cf **be C, hain't** v, **twan't**

It is not; rarely, it has not.

1795 Dearborn *Columbian Grammar* 139, *List of Improprieties.* . . Taint for It is not. **1818** Fessenden *Ladies Monitor* 172 **NEng**, Provincial words . . to be avoided. . . *taint* for it is not. [**1843** (1846) Haliburton *Attaché* (1st ser) 2.125 **NEng**, It tante safe to be caged with them in a house out o' town.] **1844** Thompson *Major Jones's Courtship* 48 **GA**, Taint his fault cause he aint got no better sense. **1871** Eggleston *Hoosier Schoolmaster* 188 **sIN**, Taint no use. **1884** *Anglia* 7.266 **Sth, S Midl** [Black], *'Taint no use er* = there is no use in. **1905** *DN* 3.22 **cCT**, *Tain't.* . . It is not. **1907** *DN* 3.219 **nwAR**, *Tain't.* . . It is not. **1929** *AmSp* 5.123 **ME**, Tain't my funeral. **1943** *LANE* Map 685, 1 inf, **swCT**, [tent bɛn ɪn]. . . It has not been in. **1967** *DARE* (Qu. GG21a, *If you don't care what a person does* . . *"You can go ahead and do it* ___.") Inf **CO28**, Tain't any skin off my nose. **1974** Fink *Mountain Speech* 26 **wNC, eTN**, *Tain't* . . *it isn't.* "Tain't what I wanted." **1985** *DARE* File **WV**, Taint worth while: in West Virginia, you don't have time. **1991** *Mt. Democrat* (Placerville CA) 8 Nov sec A 8/2, Being a newspaper writer I fear I too must know a lot. 'Taint so.

tainty adj

Tainted, spoiled.

1966 *DARE* (Qu. H46, *When meat begins to go bad, so that you can't eat it* . . *it's* ___) Inf **AL1**, Tainty; **NC25**, Tainted; fish were tainty. **1973** Allen *LAUM* 1.287 (as of c1950), The meat is *spoiled.* . . tainty [1 inf, **ceMN**]. **1986** Pederson *LAGS Concordance (The meat is spoiled)* 1 inf, **cLA**, Tainty.

tair See **tar** n¹

tairpin See **terrapin**

take v

A Forms.

1 pres: usu *take,* 3rd pers sg *takes;* also:

a *te(c)k.* **chiefly Sth** *esp freq among Black speakers*

1880 Cable *Grandissimes* 414 **LA** [Black], On'y jis teck dis-yeh t'ing off n my laig. **1891** Page *Elsket* 127 **VA** [Black], He teck off he hat . . an' say, 'Good mornin', pa an' ma.' **1906** Casey *Parson's Boys* 211 **sIL** (as of c1860), Teck yerself out of here and see if ye kin meck fer home. **1912** Green *VA Folk-Speech* 441, *Teck.* . . For *take:* "How many did he teck?" **1922** Gonzales *Black Border* 332 **sSC, GA coasts** [Gullah glossary], *Tek*—take, takes, took, taking. **1939** Griswold *Sea Is. Lady* 15 **csSC** (as of 1861) [Gullah], He grabbed his arm and shot at him in Gullah: "Tek you' han' fum dat do'—*yeddy!*" **1989** Pederson *LAGS Tech. Index* 281, [Infin of *take:*] 38 infs, **Gulf Region**, [tɛk]. **1992** Geraty *Bittle* 1 **Charleston SC** [Gullah], Mis' Ginia mus' tek 'e spensul [=pencil], papuh, en' t'ing'.

b *taken.*

1869 Woods *Woman in Prison* 138, I'm sure she had the same as the rest if she had been a mind to taken it. **1897** *KS Univ. Qrly.* (ser B) 6.58 **swMO, eKS**, *Taken:* take. I taken it he is a stranger. **1924** in 1952 Mathes *Tall Tales* 40 **sAppalachians**, I'm goin' to ax him to taken an' read this letter to you-uns. **1941** Smith *Going to God's Country* 173 **MO** (as of 1900), We decided we would taken another chance.

c *tekky, tike, took.*

1883 (1971) Harris *Nights with Remus* 317 **GA** [Black], B'er Rabbit, 'e is bin tekky da chunk y-out da pot; 'e tekky da chunk, un 'e is bin pit Granny Wolf in dey place. **1975** *Appalachian Jrl.* 2.150 **wNC**, *A* is sometimes pronounced as *i:* . . *tike* for take. **1994** Bolton *Gal* 230 **seSC**

[Black], I really wanted to know, did Daddy took her somewhere to take that picture? Did Grandmama take her somewhere?

2 past: usu *took;* also:

a *tu(c)k.* **chiefly Sth, S Midl** See Map *somewhat old-fash*
1805 in 1956 Eliason *Tarheel Talk* 319 **TN,** Tuck. **1830** *Ibid* **NC,** Tuck. **1832** in 1945 Beck *Jersey Genesis* 97 **NJ,** My wife tuck a rattle-snake that . . was six feet long. **1844** Thompson *Major Jones's Courtship* 63 **GA,** I tuck a piece of the Durham. **1871** Eggleston *Hoosier Schoolmaster* 40 **sIN,** I tuck a sheet off the bed. **1884** [see **A2c** below]. **1902** *DN* 2.248 **sIL,** Tuck. **1903** *DN* 2.335 **seMO,** Tuck. **1905** *DN* 3.23 **cCT,** Tuk. **1907** *DN* 3.237 **nwAR,** Tuck. **1909** [see **A2c** below]. **1924** Raine *Land of Saddle-Bags* 207 **sAppalachians,** I tuk the left hand and right heel and they wouldn't touch. **1942** Faulkner *Go Down* 145 **MS,** De Lawd guv, and He tuck away. **1943** *LANE* Map 664 *(Took; taken)* **NEng,** [For the past tense of *take,* the form *took* was recorded from nearly all infs. Two infs gave *tuck* as their only response. *Tuck* was also recorded as a second response from about 25 more infs; in many cases it had been suggested by the fieldworker, and in nearly all cases it was qualified as older, obsolete, or heard from others. One inf gave *taken* as a sole response, and accepted it in addition to *took* at the fieldworker's suggestion.] **1953** Atwood *Survey of Verb Forms* 23, The preterite *tuck* /tʌk/ shows six scattered occurrences in N. Eng., Pa., and N.J. . . In Delmarva, the Tidewater area of Virginia, and nearly all of N.C. it becomes fairly common. . . It also occurs with some regularity in s.w. Va. and throughout W. Va., and is found in a scattered way in S.C. and Ga. . . *Tuck* is primarily a Type I form, over seven eighths of its occurrences being in this group [=infs with little education]. [*DARE* Ed: This survey covers the Atlantic states only.] **1965–70** *DARE* (Qu. OO41a, *About taking too many chances: "He got hurt because he _____ [too many chances]."*) Infs **GA**19, 30, **IL**25, **KY**6, 84, **TN**23, **VA**15, 27, Tuck; (Qu. AA19, . . *A man and woman who are not married but live together as if they were*) Infs **DE**2, **KY**19, Tuck up (together). **1966–68** *DARE* FW Addit **ceTN,** Took [tʌk]—said in conversation. "It [tʌk] a lot of time"; **nwLA,** Took [tʌk]—common, occas among cultivated. **1969** *DARE* Tape **GA**51, She. . . tuck 'em way up in the treetops; **KY**16A, They . . tuck 'em in there. [**1973** *PADS* 60.47 **seNC,** Took. . . All informants gave the vowel in this word the typical [ʊ] or [ʊˁ] which are their allophones for /ʊ/. There was no evidence of the /ʌ/ which PEAS [=1961 Kurath–McDavid *Pronc. Engl.*] found "rather frequently" in the folk speech of the Carolinas.] **1975** [see **A2c** below]. **1989** Pederson *LAGS Tech. Index* 281, [Past of *take:*] 64 infs, **Gulf Region,** [tʌk].

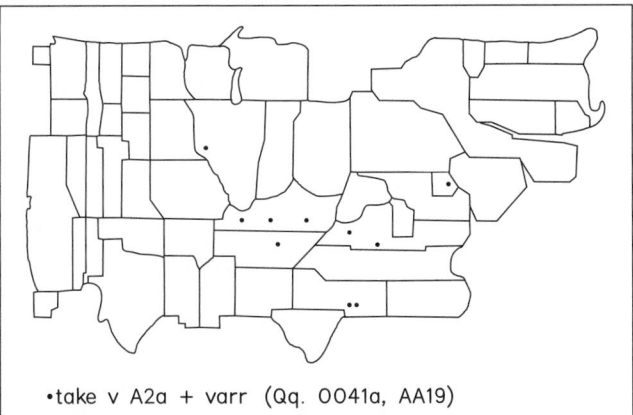

•take v A2a + varr (Qq. OO41a, AA19)

b *taked.*
1860 *Vanity Fair* 2.40 **NYC,** They taked the man up to the scaffold. **1873** [see **A2e** below]. c**1938** [see **A2f** below]. **1953** Atwood *Survey of Verb Forms* 24 **GA,** The following forms occur once each: . . *taked* /tekt/. **1967–69** *DARE* (Qu. OO41a, *About taking too many chances: "He got hurt because he _____ [too many chances]."*) Inf **RI**6, Taked; (Qu. BB44, . . *A person just starting some sickness . . "He _____ pneumonia."*) Inf **KY**34, Taked [FW: used in conv]. **1989** Pederson *LAGS Tech. Index* 281 **Gulf Region,** [Past of *take:*] 2 infs, [tekt]; 1 inf [tɛkt]; 1 inf, ['tekɪd].

c *taken.* **chiefly Sth, S Midl** See Map *chiefly among speakers with little formal educ*
1863 in c1970 *DARE* File **AR,** [Letter from a Confederate Army soldier to his Alabama-born parents:] I have been vaccinated and it taken finely. **1884** *Anglia* 7.253 [Black], To the regular forms of the Irregular

verbs as used by the whites, the Negro adds the following forms of his own. . . *Pres.* take—*Past.* tuck, tucked, taken, -ed. **1893** *KS Univ. Qrly.* 1.142 **ceKS,** Taken: took. **1896** Harris *Sister Jane* 216 **GA,** I taken my axe and went into the timber. **1903** *DN* 2.333 **seMO,** Taken. . . Took. **1904** *DN* 2.421 **nwAR,** 'Joseph's brethren taken him and sold him' [from a student's theme]. **1904** in 2003 *DARE* File—Internet **cnKY,** Harry taken Ades horse home today. Wylder and I takened up my traps up today. **1909** *DN* 3.379 **eAL, wGA,** Taken, pret. of take. A very common error made by illiterate white people, perhaps in an effort to avoid the still more illiterate *tuck,* a form used chiefly by negroes. **1910** *DN* 3.457 **seKY,** Taken. . . Took. **1914** *DN* 4.113 **cKS,** Taken. . . Used as a preterite. **1915** *DN* 4.191 **swVA,** Taken. . . Took.—*takened,* taken. **1916** *DN* 4.341 **seOH,** Taken. . . Took. **1940** Faulkner *Hamlet* 35 **MS,** Ab taken his shoes off. **1943** [see **A2a** above]. **1944** *PADS* 2.13 **seTN,** Taken: pret. of take. . . Rural. **1953** Atwood *Survey of Verb Forms* 24, The preterite *taken* /tekən/ is also confined to the South and South Midland, where it occurs rather commonly in Md. and W. Va., less commonly in Va., N.C., and S.C. This form is demonstrably newer than *tuck.* . . In 16 out of 21 communities where both forms occur the more old-fashioned informant gives *tuck* and the more modern, *taken.* [*DARE* Ed: This survey covers the Atlantic states only.] **1965–70** *DARE* (Qu. OO41a, *About taking too many chances: "He got hurt because he _____ [too many chances]."*) 46 Infs, **chiefly Sth, S Midl,** Taken; **MO**12, **OK**11, (Just) taken down with; **KY**94, He taken sick; (Qu. V4, . . *Words for stealing something valuable . . "Yesterday somebody _____ my watch."*) Inf **MD**42, Taken. **1965–69** *DARE* Tape **GA**8, His parents taken him into that place; **GA**48, It just taken two of us, generally; **MS**61, The doctor taken me off it for a while. **1968** *PADS* 50.36 **swTN** [Black], For the past tense of *take* four of the nine type I informants [=infs with little formal educ] . . have /tekən/. **1975** Allen *LAUM* 2.29 **Upper MW** (as of c1950), Two minor eastern preterit variants survive in the U[pper] M[idwest]. Southern and South Midland *taken* is the form used by six . . infs. . . *Tuck,* dominantly Southern but with a few scattered examples in the northeast Atlantic region, occurs only three times in the UM. **1982** Ginns *Snowbird Gravy* 22 **nwNC,** She canned the apples, and then she taken the peelings and canned those. **1989** Pederson *LAGS Tech. Index* 281 **Gulf Region,** [Past of *take:*] 122 infs, proncs of the type ['tekn̩]; 9 infs, ['tetn̩]; 1 inf ['tɛkn̩]; 1 inf, ['tɛtn̩]; 1 inf, [ten]. **2000** [see **A2d** below].

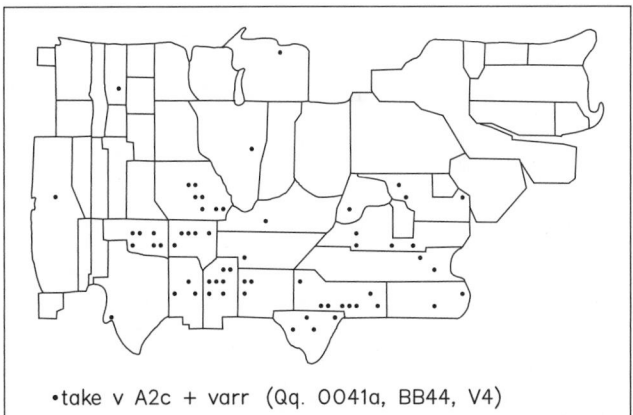

•take v A2c + varr (Qq. OO41a, BB44, V4)

d *takened.* **chiefly Sth, S Midl**
1884 [see **A2c** above]. **1904** in 2003 [see **A2c** above]. **1906** *DN* 3.160 **nwAR,** He takened it from him. **1938** Rawlings *Yearling* 10 **nFL,** The notion takened me. **1953** Atwood *Survey of Verb Forms* 24, There are 26 instances of the preterite *takened* /tekənd/, most of which are in Delmarva, the Tidewater area of Va., and the eastern half of N.C. The greater part (21) of these are in Type I [=infs with little education]. [*DARE* Ed: This survey covers the Atlantic states only.] **1958** Latham *Meskin Hound* 96 **cTX,** [I] damned nigh takened a shot at him then. **1964** Will *Hist. Okeechobee* 96 **FL,** When the notion takened him [= the chizzywink] to migrate, . . you'd be blamed lucky if'n you didn't get smothered in the swarm. **1967–68** *DARE* (Qu. OO41a, *About taking too many chances: "He got hurt because he _____ [too many chances]."*) Inf **AR**51, Takened; **AR**55, Takened—poor White; **LA**2, Takened [FW: used in conv, occas]; **TN**26, Takened [FW: used in conv].

1967 *DARE* FW Addit **AR,** A lot of 'em say "he takened her [to the dance]"; **ceLA,** That little boy took sick and they takened him to Charity. [FW: This was the only time I was able to capture both preterites of *take* in one utterance. Without a lot of data, it would be hard to tell their distribution pattern. I don't think they are in free variation.] **1989** Pederson *LAGS Tech. Index* 281, [Past of *take:*] 9 infs, **Gulf Region,** ['teknd, 'teknd]. **2000** Shores *Tangier Is.* **Chesapeake Bay,** Nonstandard forms showing past times are common: . . taken or takened.

e *tooked, tucked.*

1873 *Our Young Folks* 9.120, "You should n't say 'taked,' my dear," said Cella [=a child], patronizingly; " 'tooked' sounds much bettter." **1884** [see A2c above]. **1890** (1895) Riley *Rhymes of Childhood* 29, An' she tooked me up, an' says / She know where I live, she guess. [*DARE* Ed: Speaker is a small child.] **1898** *Century Illustr. Mag.* 57.158 **SC** [Black], I wuz real glad when . . Tadgeous tooked me back een de baggage-waggin. **1953** Atwood *Survey of Verb Forms* 24 **PA,** The following forms occur once each: *tooked* /tʊkt/. **2003** *DARE* File—Internet **eTN,** Appt. 3 times for liver biopsy—doctor checked & tooked out polyps instead.

f *tooken, tucken.   esp freq among Black speakers*

1891 *Catholic World* 52.483 **MD** [Black], Jes' as soon as I tucken off that yeah voudou, Marse Cla'uns he change his min'. **1892** *Century Illustr. Mag.* 43.582 **TN** [Black], Well, I tucken de letter an' putten de answer in my pocket. **c1938** in 1970 Hyatt *Hoodoo* 1.93 **cSC** [Black], Me an' mah brothah, we tooken de . . cat. . . [H]e git de bone. An' he taked it to a lady dey called *Doctor* Campbell. **1953** Atwood *Survey of Verb Forms* 24 **SC,** The following forms occur once each: . . *tooken* /tʊkən/. **1966** *DARE* (Qu. OO41a, *About taking too many chances: "He got hurt because he _____ [too many chances]."*) Inf **MS**69, Took, tooken—Negro. **1989** Pederson *LAGS Tech. Index* 281, [Past of *take:*] 1 inf, **seMS,** ['tʊgn]. [Inf Black]

g *take.*

1953 Atwood *Survey of Verb Forms* 24, Five informants (three Negro) use the uninflected *take* /tek/ [for *took*]. **1966** *DARE* (Qu. OO41a, *About taking too many chances: "He got hurt because he _____ [too many chances]."*) Infs **SC**10, 26, Take. [Both Infs Black] **1989** Pederson *LAGS Tech. Index* 181, [Past of *take:*] 3 infs, **Gulf Region,** [tek].

h addit varr: See quots.

1953 Atwood *Survey of Verb Forms* 24 **VA,** The following forms occur once each: . . *toke* /tok/. **1989** Pederson *LAGS Tech. Index* 181 **Gulf Region,** [Past of *take:*] 5 infs, [tɪk]; 2 infs, [tɛk]; 1 inf, [tet].

3 past pple: usu *taken;* also:

a *took.*

c1770 in 1953 Woodmason *Carolina Backcountry* 274 **SC,** Ev'rything I have took Possession off by the Provost Marshall. **1858** in 1983 *PADS* 70.55 **ce,sePA,** They had took to many up there. **1861** Holmes *Venner* 2.189 **NEng,** Who's took care o' them things that was on the hoss? **1871** Eggleston *Hoosier Schoolmaster* 99 **sIN,** I must a took a little too much. **1876** in 1969 *PADS* 52.56 **seIL,** Took. . . [T]here was no money took in this week. **1893** *DN* 1.278 **nwCT,** [Pres:] take— [past, past pple:] took. **1898** Westcott *Harum* 266 **nNY,** 'None bein' meant, none will be took,' I says. **1903** *DN* 2.293 **Cape Cod MA** (as of a1857), Many strong verbs use the same form for the past and past participle. . . *take—took.* **1914** *DN* 4.73 **ME, nNH,** Git took down a peg. **1945** FWP *Lay My Burden Down* 99 **MS** (as of c1865) [Black], I was took away. **1953** Atwood *Survey of Verb Forms* 24, The leveled forms *took–took* occur in all major areas, but are not very common . . and show no concentration. Of the informants who use the preterite *tuck,* about half use the same form as a past participle. **1955** Roberts *S. from Hell-fer-Sartin* 141 **seKY,** I guess they scared the girl worse than if he never'd a-took them. **1965–70** *DARE* (Qu. OO41b, *About taking too many chances: "He would be alive today if he hadn't _____ [so many chances]."*) 146 Infs, **widespread,** Took; **NM**11, 'A took; **OK**27, I've ever took—heard; **NC**37, Of took [Of all Infs responding to the question, 29% were comm type 5, 64% old, 25% gs educ or less; of those giving these responses, 48% were comm type 5, 74% old, 55% gs educ or less.]; (Qu. LL23, *Cheated, treated dishonestly: "These apples are wormy, I think you got _____."*) 73 Infs, **widespread,** Took; **IN**8, **NY**28, **SC**39, **TN**52, **VA**15, **WI**61, Took for a ride; **NY**92, Took in; **NE**1, Took on them; (Qu. U8b, . . *"I paid ten dollars for it."*) Infs **NC**16, **IL**58, **KY**18, Got took (for); (Qu. V1, *When you suspect that somebody is trying to deceive you*) Inf **CO**36, I've been took; (Qu. AA15c, . . *Joking ways . . of saying that a woman is getting married. . .*

"She _____.") Infs **IL**29, 110, Got took; (Qu. BB44, . . *A person just starting some sickness . . "He _____ pneumonia."*) Infs **GA**72, **PA**245, **SC**55, Is (*or* was) took (down) with; (Qu. KK1b, . . *'In the very best condition': "His farm is _____."*) Inf **KY**28, Well took care of. **1966–68** *DARE* Tape **AK**9, They thought somebody was gettin' took; **GA**1, The puncheon was took off. **1968** *PADS* 50.44 **swTN** [Black], For the past participle of *take,* /tekən/ is the most commonly used form. /tʊk/ occurs sporadically. **1968** *DARE* FW Addit **csLA,** He said they had took her to the hospital; **cLA,** He might have just took notice of your car there. **1975** Allen *LAUM* 2.29 (as of c1950), Take. . . The single participial variant is *took,* which, though widely scattered in the eastern states, is used by only two U[pper] M[idwest] infs. **1989** Pederson *LAGS Tech. Index* 282, [Past pple of *take:*] 123 infs, **Gulf Region,** [tʊk]. **1999** Morgan *Gap Creek* 33 **NC,** I was took by surprise.

b *tu(c)k.   chiefly Sth, S Midl*

1843 (1916) Hall *New Purchase* 212 **IN,** Tother was tuk out more nor an hour ago. **1845** Thompson *Pineville* 37 **cGA,** I was most ouda-ciously tuck in that time. **1886** *S. Bivouac* 4.348 **sAppalachians,** The man declined it, saying, "he'd never tuck no pay fer nothin' ter eat in his life." **1888** Jones *Negro Myths* 69 **GA coast,** Eh mek um quaintun bout wen de Ring tuk. **1899** Chesnutt *Conjure Woman* 174 **csNC** [Black], She had tuk de ha'rs. **1909** *DN* 3.384 **eAL, wGA,** Tuck, *pret.* and *pp.* of *take.* **1926** *AmSp* 1.412 **Okefenokee GA,** An' I'd tuk around, an' had turned ter come erlong back. **1952** Brown *NC Folkl.* 1.603, *Tuck:* . . Past tense and past participle of *take.* **1953** [see A3a above]. **1967** *DARE* FW Addit **TN**17, It'd'a tuck [tʌk] every bit. **1968–70** *DARE* (Qu. OO41b, *About taking too many chances: "He would be alive today if he hadn't _____ [so many chances]."*) Infs **GA**19, 30, **KY**6, 84, **VA**15, 27, Tuck. [*DARE* Ed: All of these Infs also gave *tuck* at Qu. OO41a.] **1989** Pederson *LAGS Tech. Index* 282, [Past pple of *take:*] 10 infs, **Gulf Region,** [tʌk].

c *takened.*

1857 Wickham *Sea-Spray* 246 **Long Is. NY,** Will He say you are naughty to cry because He's takened her away? [*DARE* Ed: Speaker is a small child.] **1861** in 2003 *DARE* File—Internet **LA,** It has rained Some on us Since we have been here, but I have not takened the least cold from it. **1864** *Ibid* **ME,** There was about nine killed . . and I believe one white Officer takened prisoner. **1894** *Scribner's Mag.* 16.54 **Sth,** I has . . takened out the tucks. **1902** *DN* 2.247 **sIL,** Takened, for took. **1915** [see A2c above]. **1933** Rawlings *South Moon* 45 **FL,** They ain't nary one takened out after you? **1953** Atwood *Survey of Verb Forms* 24, Of those who use the preterite *takened,* two thirds level the preterite and the past participle. . . The following occur from once to five times each: *tuck–take, taken–takened, tuck–takened, toke–takened, took–tooken,* and *take–taken* (Negro). **1968** *DARE* (Qu. AA15c, . . *Joking ways . . of saying that a woman is getting married. . . "She _____."*) Inf **MD**41, Was takened in. **1989** Pederson *LAGS Tech. Index* 282, [Past pple of *take:*] 4 infs, **Gulf Region,** ['teknd]. **2003** *DARE* File—Internet **AL,** This [=photograph] was takened in Escambia County, FL.

d *tooken, tucken.   chiefly Sth*

1856 *S. Lit. Messenger* 23.456 **VA,** Oh! daddy, them light-fingered, what do you call it,/ Has tooken and stolen my watch and my wallet. **1862** Gilmore *Among the Pines* 282 **SC,** Thar's no tellin' how quick the' moight be tooken 'way. **1864** Gilmore *Down in TN* 114, I'se bin a sarchin' fur it . . an hain't found it yit, so ye mus' hev tucken it. **1869** Ward *Men Women & Ghosts* 130 **NEng,** He was "just tooken up all at once into the tree." [*DARE* Ed: Speaker is a small child.] **1870** *Harper's New Mth. Mag.* 41.669 **NC,** The affidavy was to be tooken in camp and on a Saturday night. **1884** *Anglia* 7.268 **Sth, S Midl** [Black], To done bin tooken sick = to have fallen sick. **1884** Baldwin *Yankee School-Teacher* 33 **VA** [Black], All of a suddin I was tooken wid a creepin' ober me. **1886** *Harper's New Mth. Mag.* 72.978 **Sth** [Black], De Lord hab gib, and de Lord hab tucken away. **1941** Daniels *Tar Heels* 211 **NC,** A lot of us mill folks used to be tooken back home for burial. **1953** [see A3c above]. **1989** Pederson *LAGS Tech. Index* 282 **Gulf Region,** [Past pple of *take:*] 5 infs, ['tʊkn]; 1 inf, ['tʊkən]; 1 inf, ['tʊkn]; 1 inf, ['tʌkn]. **1994** Bolton *Gal* 99 **seSC** [Black], She wished that she could have tooken care of me.

e *tooked.*

1866 *Old Guard* 4.652 **Sth** [Black], Take de chances white man; take de chances. I done tooked de chances and I ain't dead yet. [*DARE* Ed: Cf **do** v C5] **1898** *Century Illustr. Mag.* 57.160 **SC** [Black], She had tooked white sand an' de scrubbin'-brush. **1984** Hurmence *My Folks* 15 **NC** (as of c1865) [Black], The Yankees has tooked this place.

f *take(d), tek.*

1848 Drinkwater *Memoir Deborah Porter* 208 **ME,** It is God that has taked her from me. **1922** Gonzales *Black Border* 332 **sSC, GA coasts** [Gullah glossary], *Tek wid'um*—taken with, pleased with him, her, it, them. **c1938** in 1970 Hyatt *Hoodoo* 2.1192 **seGA** [Black], De same way dat dat thing got on yo'—by spirchully devilment work—gotta be taked off. **1966–67** *DARE* (Qu. II2a, *When two people begin to be friendly: "He has just recently _____ with John."*) Inf **SC**26, Take up; (Qu. OO41b, *About taking too many chances: "He would be alive today if he hadn't _____ [so many chances]."*) Inf **SC**26, Take; **SC**10, Take so much chances; **MO**21, 'A take. **1989** Pederson *LAGS Tech. Index* 282 **Gulf Region,** [Past pple of *take:*] 2 infs, [tek]; 1 inf, [teg]; 1 inf, ['tekɪd].

B Senses.

1 Used in var constrs in ref to contracting a disease, as:

a tr: To come down with, become afflicted with (an illness or disease). [*OED2 take* v. 44.b 13 . . →; in ref specifically to disease, 1530 →] **chiefly Sth, S Midl, MO, OK, TX** See Map

1796 Webster *Coll. Bilious Fevers* 151, [Footnote:] Capt. Cochran's crew, however, took the Fever from the French prisoners. **1803** Fessenden *Terrible Tractoration* 20 **NH,** Not one *soul* took small-pox a'ter. **1833** *New Engl. Mag.* 5.473, Some daring rogue of a girl would whisper to mamma her kind fears that she and papa might take cold by riding in the night air. **1843** *S. Qrly. Rev.* 4.149, Nearly all his family took the fever. **1884** *Century Illustr. Mag.* 28.80 **LA,** If I should take the fever, . . Mary will want to come to me. **1938** in Lib. of Congress *Amer. Memory: WPA Life Hist.* (Internet) **NM,** Every one that went to the Henderson home took smallpox. *Ibid* **NE,** I think he took cold that way that finally settled in his kidneys. **1949** Hedgecock *Gone Are the Days* 95 **swMO,** I don't know just why I didn't take pneumonia and die. **1960** Hall *Smoky Mt. Folks* 30, I allowed they might a tuck the Black Tongue and died, just like the cattle tuck it. **1964** Wallace *Frontier Life* 14 **OK** (as of 1893–1906), One of his big brood mares . . "took the fistula" and became practically worthless as a work horse. **1965–70** *DARE* (Qu. BB44, . . *A person just starting some sickness . . "He _____ pneumonia."*) 97 Infs, **chiefly Sth, S Midl, MO, OK, TX,** Took; **FL**49, 51, Took the; **LA**46, **TN**27, Took a cold; **ME**9, Just took; 19 Infs, **chiefly Sth, Midl,** Taken; **AL**30, **FL**26, **GA**9, **KY**28, 35, 40, 90, **TN**3, [He]'s taken; **AL**20, **GA**13, **KS**5, **KY**21, 77, **OK**1, **SC**3, Has taken; **OK**7, [He]'s taken the; **GA**8, **MS**29, **TX**32, Is taking; **IN**82, **NC**37, 79, [He]'s taking; **OK**31, Taking; **KY**34, Taked or take [Of all Infs responding to the question, 29% were comm type 5, 10% young; of those giving these responses, 45% were comm type 5, 4% young.]; (Qu. BB14, *To suddenly become unconscious and fall: "Just as she came to the door she _____."*) Inf **WY**4, Took a fit; (Qu. DD22, . . *Delirium tremens*) Inf **NC**54, Taking drunken streamers; (Qu. JJ15a, *Sayings about a person who seems to you very stupid: "He hasn't sense enough to _____."*) Inf **NC**31, Take a fit; (Qu. NN18, *When somebody sneezes, what do people say to him?*) Infs **GA**5, **OK**14, You're taking cold; **MO**10, You takin' a cold; **NE**3, Are you taking cold? **1966–68** *DARE* Tape **AL**6, He would have stayed in school, but he took typhoid fever and he came home; **IN**23, He took the yellow fever; **OH**51, She took pneumonia; **TX**26, Some men have . . quicked a horse and let him go on limping until he took tetanus; **VA**2, I had been hoeing corn and I tuck a headache and it was real hot. **1968** *DARE* FW Addit **LA**40, He's liable to take gout, too. **1975** *Appalachian Jrl.* 2.158 **wNC,** If a person *took a fit,* he had convulsions. . . One also is said to *take a stroke.* **1982**

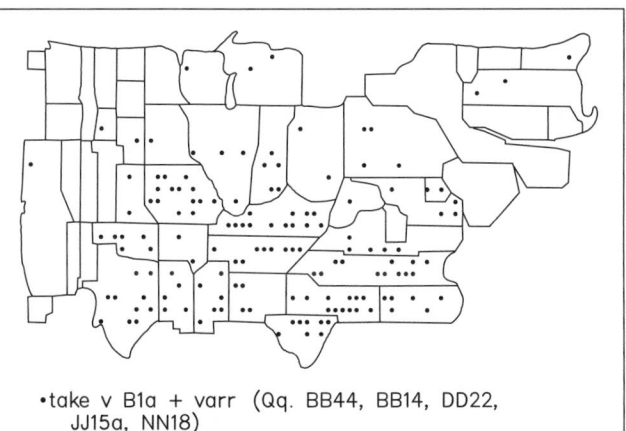
•take v B1a + varr (Qq. BB44, BB14, DD22, JJ15a, NN18)

Chaika *Speaking RI* [9], *Take a fit* = get angry. *[T]ake a hot* [=heart] *attack* = what happens when the ticka goes bad. **1989** Pederson *LAGS Tech. Index* 279 **Gulf Region** (*Caught a cold*) 140 infs, Took a cold; 95 infs, Took cold; 1 inf, Took this cold.

b in passive constrs: To suffer an attack of disease or the onset of labor pains; to come down (with a disease); to fall (sick, ill). [*OED2 take* v. 7.b a1300 →, 7.c 1450–1530 →, 7.d 13 . . →] **scattered, but esp Atlantic** See Map Cf **take down a**

1698 (1911) Mather *Diary* 1.257 **MA,** After my Lecture, I was taken ill. **1768** Hutchinson *Hist. MA Bay* 2.172 **MA,** Some of their number was taken sick of an infectious distemper. **1814** in 1915 *PA Mag. Hist. & Biog.* 39.335 **PA,** I was taken sick on parade. **1820** *N. Amer. Rev.* 10.392, In many instances watering and other parties . . have all been taken sick with the yellow fever, after their return on board. **1839** *S. Lit. Messenger* 5.672 **NEast,** On the day when they were to have sailed, he was taken ill with a fever. **1856** *Putnam's Mag.* 8.126 **NEng,** Nobody would come to help us . . , when Miss Perkins was took. After a while the old lady began to sink. **1872** in 1983 *PADS* 70.54 **ce,sePA,** G[rand] Father was right poorly was taken the 2nd day before with a nervous chill. **1879** *Atlantic Mth.* 44.201 **ME,** If either of you was took sick, why here ye be. **1885** Cable *Dr. Sevier* 281 **LA,** What proportion of those who are taken sick of it die? **1909** *DN* 3.379 **eAL, wGA,** She was taken sick in church last Sunday. **1933** Rawlings *South Moon* 55 **FL,** Must be I'm took, Willy. I ain't never been with nary woman when she was took. I'll see kin I walk the pains off. **1959** *VT Hist.* 27.164, *Took with. . .* Seized with, as a chill. Common. Rural areas. **1965–70** *DARE* (Qu. BB44, . . *A person just starting some sickness . . "He _____ pneumonia."*) 13 Infs, **scattered, but esp Atlantic,** Was (*or* has been) (just) taken with; **GA**72, Is took with, is taken with; **MS**51, Was taken; **NH**16, [Was] taken sudden with; 12 Infs, **chiefly Atlantic,** Was taken sick with; **IN**73, [Was] taken ill with. [1 of 27 total Infs young, 3 mid-aged] **1968** *PADS* 49.14 **Upper MW,** The schools tend to establish literary terms in place of or alongside indigenous folk terms. This influence is also evident in the following examples: . . the decline of *take sick* and *be taken sick* and the rise of *become sick* and *get sick.* **1975** Chalmers *Better* 58 **wNC, eTN,** "Tim's wife is took right bad. Do you reckon you could go?" . . [H]e didn't rightly know what was wrong with her. . . But when they 'didn't know,' it often meant the stork.

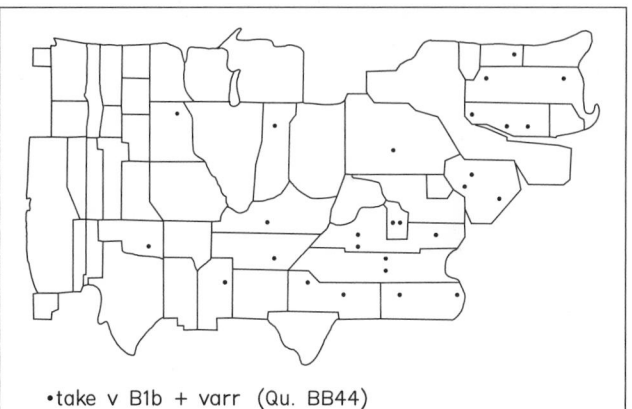
•take v B1b + varr (Qu. BB44)

c intr in phrr *take sick* (or *ill*): To fall sick. [*OED2 take* v. 7.e "*intr.* for *pass.,* with *compl.,* as *to take ill. . . colloq.* and *dial.*"; 1674 →] Cf **take down b**

1775 (1940) Ulster Co. Road Comms. *Records* 2.73 **NY,** The aforesaid Matthias Lafever took Sick and . . Died Soon after. **1843** in 1852 *Living Age* 32.445 **TX,** Lafitte . . crossed over in a fishing boat to Selang, where he took sick and died. **1853** in 1928 OR Pioneer Assoc. *Trans.* 45 **MA,** One of our best oxen took sick. **1885** Twain *Huck. Finn* 138 **MO,** She was at work on what they said was her greatest picture when she took sick. **1893** *Century Illustr. Mag.* 46.305 **NEng,** Ef she hed n't her diseases to talk abaout, I b'lieve she 'd take sick. **1905** *DN* 3.97 **nwAR,** Take sick, v. intr. To fall sick, to be taken sick. **1910** *DN* 3.450 **wNY,** He took sick with a fever. **c1938** in 1970 Hyatt *Hoodoo* 1.3 **swNC** [Black], After we burned that up Witch never came back. Then Witch took sick. **1965–70** *DARE* (Qu. BB44, . . *A person just starting some sickness . . "He _____ pneumonia."*) 23 Infs, **scattered,** (Just) took sick with; **IN**60, **SC**40, Took sick; **KY**94, He taken sick; **CA**144, [He]'s just taken ill with. **1966–70** *DARE* Tape **AL**19, The dog . .

lapped it [=arsenic and milk] up and immediately took sick; **MI**28, Well, my husband took sick, so then we went to the farm and lived with my brother; **MO**38, He took sick and sold his farm; **NY**105, An old farmer had taken sick; **PA**77, She took sick on a . . Saturday morning; **PA**244, We were only in it for about eight or nine months when he took very sick; he had a kidney attack; **TX**31, And McGuire took pretty sick, and when he did, the niece and the nephew got into a squabble. **1989** Pederson *LAGS Tech. Index* 279 **Gulf Region** (*Got sick*) 207 infs, Took sick; 17 infs, Took ill.

2 in phr *take one to do:* To criticize, chide (one), take one to task. **chiefly NEast** [Engl dial *take to do(ing)* (*EDD* at *doing* sb. 4.(2), *take* v. 3.(117), *to-do* v. 2)]

1837 *Qrly. Anti-Slavery Mag.* 2.176 **NEng,** How comes it that a government which never cares for the color of a man's creed should take him to do for the color of his — coat? **1847** *Amer. Whig Rev.* 5.388, No, it is not for pedantry that we would take him to do. **1848** Bartlett *Americanisms* 349, *To take to do.* To take to task; to reprove. **1876** *Ladies' Repository* 3.94 **CT,** Chopping kindlings at his door one Sunday morning, he was taken to do . . for violating the Sabbath. **1877** *Atlantic Mth.* 40.73 **CT,** Land! what a besom he was! his folks never tuned him, nor never took him to do, a mite. **1890** Holley *Samantha among Brethren* 119 **NY,** He goes all over the arguments every time I take him to do about it. **1966** *DARE* FW Addit **ME**19, Took him to do for it = made him account for it. **1977** *Yankee* Jan 73 **Isleboro ME,** When you pick a bone with a man, you *take him to do* for actions of his which don't agree with you. Boys are very often *took to do* when they're caught pulling a raid on the cucumber patch.

3 rarely with *up;* linked to a following verb with *and:* Used without definite meaning, often with a vaguely intensive force; see quots. [*EDD* take v. 4 "in *gen.* colloq. use"]

1795 Dearborn *Columbian Grammar* 136, *List of Improprieties. . .* I took and did it for I did it. **1836** *S. Lit. Messenger* 2.388, "If you do so I will *take and tell* father," such is the constant language of children. . . Is the expression a contraction of some obsolete phrase? Who can tell me if it is to be met with in print? **1873** *Atlantic Mth.* 31.614 **NEast,** I jes' . . took 'n' set 'im down. **1875** (1876) Twain *Tom Sawyer* 23 **MO,** I'll take and bounce a rock off'n your head. **1887** (1967) Harris *Free Joe* 10 **GA** [Black], I tuck'n tu'n de meat over. **1892** *DN* 1.212 **ceMA,** I was familiar in my boyhood with the expressions . . *he up and did it, he took and hit him.* **1893** *KS Univ. Qrly.* 1.142 **KS,** Take and (do anything): proceed to, as 'I took and threw the book away.' **1899** Chesnutt *Conjure Woman* 21 **csNC** [Black], He mus' go en take 'n scrape off de sap. **1909** *DN* 3.379 **eAL, wGA,** Take. . . Used as a quasi-auxiliary, adding an element of intentional or willful action to the main verb: chiefly in the preterit. "He took and hit me." "He took and took my book." **1930** Faulkner *As I Lay Dying* 45 **MS,** "She's gone," Cash says. "She taken and left us," pa says. **c1937** in 1976 *Weevils in the Wheat* 137 **VA** [Black], Purty soon de war come 'long an' Simuel took up an' went to jine up. **c1938** in 1970 Hyatt *Hoodoo* 2.1195 **seGA** [Black], Yo' take an' ketch a black cat, yo' see. Take an' take yo' a pot of hot water. Take yo' nine black hen eggs. Take an' mark yo' a round ring. **1952** Brown *NC Folkl.* 1.597, *Take and* plus another verb: . . Central and east. Illiterate. **1959** *VT Hist.* 27.162, *Take and. . .* Used as a superfluous verb, meaning to proceed to. I'm going to take and milk the cows early. . . Occasional. **1966–69** *DARE* Tape **AL**11, Take and raise them up, fatten 'em, kill 'em; **AK**6, Now they take and dump it in the bay; **CA**128, But a millman, he can take and turn the water on. . . They just take and sprinkle some more amalgam out there; **FL**31, You take and put your water on to boil; **IN**27, All Bertie would do . . is take and scrape the hogs; **MI**14, To make good shingles, they split 'em with a saw, take and throw the knot away; **TX**12, You'd take and put the big wheels . . far enough apart. **1968** *DARE* (Qu. Y18, *To leave in a hurry: "Before they find this out, we'd better _____!"*) Inf **AK**8, Take and make tracks; (Qu. KK66, *When you are showing somebody the right way to do something: "No, not like that—do it _____."*) Inf **MD**26, Take and do it this way. **2003** *DARE* File—Internet **csWI,** Take the broom straw and you take and put a single layer all the way around the stick.

4 To observe, celebrate (a holiday, esp Christmas). [Prob by ext from such phrr as *take dinner*] **chiefly Sth, S Midl**

1871 in 1983 *PADS* 70.54 **ce,sePA,** Margary and her child that lives here went to Waltons yesterday to take New Years. **1876** U.S. Congress *MS in 1875* 1.605 **cwMS** [Black], It was along in that time, because I took Christmas down to Newton. **1890** *Century Illustr. Mag.* 41.297 **nGA,** We 're a-gwine to whirl in an' ast you to stay over an' take Christmas wi' us, sech ez we 'll have. **1906** in 2005 *DARE* File—Internet **WI** [*Tomah Jrl.* 26 Dec], Mr. & Mrs. Byron Johnson & Miss Frances Jonson

[sic] took Christmas at the home of Carr Johnson at Tomah. **1915** *Atlanta Constitution* (GA) 26 Dec sec A 3/3, Both the recall and anti-recall headquarters took Christmas yesterday and both stated that there was no news to give out. **1930** *Mexia Weekly Herald* (TX) 3 Jan 4/3, Mr. and Mrs. Y.C. Anderson and family took Christmas in Turlington. **1979** *DARE* File **cSC,** "I've finished all my shopping; now I'm going to take Christmas." "How are you taking Christmas?"—meaning celebrate or enjoy. "He's taking Christmas"—a discreet way of saying that someone's drinking too much. These expressions . . refer to Christmas only, no other holiday.

5 To pass (a period of time) socially—usu in phrr *take a* (or *the*) *night.* **chiefly Appalachians, esp KY**

1852 Southworth *Discarded Daughter* 1.174 **MD,** I thought you were going to take a night with us. **1917** *Musical Qrly.* 3.382 **eKY,** Strange woman, since you have rid so far, light down and take the night with us. **1919** *DN* 5.35 **seKY,** Take a night with. . . To spend, or pass a night with. Harlan Co. **1940** *AmSp* 15.448 [TN mountain speech], *Take a night.* An invitation to spend the night. 'Git off your horse and take a night with us.' **1942** (1971) Campbell *Cloud-Walking* 73 **seKY,** They had to take the night with her and Nelt. **1949** Guthrie *Way West* 31, There's a preacher takin' the night at the Tuckers'. **1952** Giles *40 Acres* 21 **KY,** Appalachian families visit much together. "Taking the day" with each other, and the church meeting, are the only social affairs. **1955** Ritchie *Singing Family* 10 **seKY,** Why Ollie, I thought you'd come to take the night. **1968** *DARE* FW Addit **MD**12, To take the night, meaning "to spend the night"—remembered by this Inf and other old people as being said by parents and grandparents.

6 in phrr *take a haircut (and shave):* To get a haircut (and shave). [Appar by analogy with *take a bath* and similar phrr] **esp NYC** *esp freq among Jewish speakers*

1917 in 2001 *MI Today* Summer (Internet) **neNJ,** I am attending to all things you spoke about in your letter. I took a haircut and shave. [*DARE* Ed: Writer a Jewish college student] **1971** *DARE* File **NYC,** "I've got to take a haircut today." Heard commonly in New York City. Jewish? **1985** in 2005 *DARE* File—Internet **Chicago IL,** [Tape transcript:] He bought me a second hand suit of clothes. . . And . . sent me to barber, took a haircut and a shave. [*DARE* Ed: Speaker Jewish, born 1890 in Poland; emigrated in 1907 and settled in Chicago 1922] **1996** *Ibid* **Boston MA,** Pretty soon, you forget to eat lunch. Then you forget to take a haircut. [*DARE* Ed: Writer bears an Italian surname] **2003** *Jewish Press* (Brooklyn NY) 15 Oct (Internet) **NYC,** I think that is how they [=the Beatles] actually took a haircut, because they couldn't afford a regular haircut. **2003** *DARE* File—Internet **AZ,** I'm Native American, who lives on the Rez. A week after that photo, I took a haircut, and lost a couple pounds.

7 in interrog phr *what takes (someone or something)?:* What is (someone or something) doing, what does (someone or something) mean?

1952 *DE Folkl. Bulletin* 1.9 [Black], "What takes this great big greazy "T" on this door?" Boy sez, I don' know, sir." **1956** *Ibid* 1.24, Takes (does—as in "What takes that bird in the smokehouse?" or "What takes you with that sack?"). **2009** *DARE* File **DE,** When he ended up slicing his hand . . , my husband's response was "what takes you bangin' on pipes with hammers anyway?"

8 in phrr *take (h)im:* Used to command a dog to attack. **esp Nth** See Map Cf **catch 'im**

1907 *Outing* 50.738 **IA,** She called out to him as though he were a young dog at his first fight. "Whoopee! Git to him, boy, git to him! Take

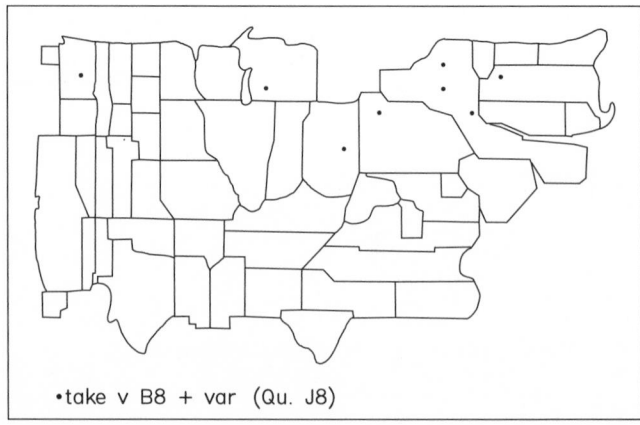

•take v B8 + var (Qu. J8)

him, boy!" **1968–70** *DARE* (Qu. J8, *To tell a dog to attack an animal or a person*) Infs **MI**110, **MA**25, **NY**159, 219, 233, **OH**79, **PA**218, **WA**12, Take him (*or* 'im). [All Infs old, 7 comm type 4 or 5, 6 male] **1986** Pederson *LAGS Concordance* (*Call to a dog to attack another dog*) 4 infs, **neTN, seLA, cwGA,** Take him. [All infs old, 3 male]

take exclam [Prob abbr for *dog take* (at **dog** n¹ **B7**), *plague take* (at **plague B1**), or similar phr]
   1967 *DARE* (Qu. NN8b, . . *Expressions of annoyance: "This jar won't come open, _____ it."*) Inf **OR**13, Take.

take a fall out of   See **fall** n **6**

take a gander   See **gander** n²

take a giant step   See **giant steps**

take a haircut   See **take** v **B6**

take a header   See **header 3**

take ahold   See **ahold**

take a night   See **take** v **B5**

take a pretty   See **pretty C1b**

take a roundance   See **roundance 2**

take a running go   See **running go**

take a spludge   See **spludge** n

take a through   See **through** n **2**

take backwater   See **backwater** n **1**

taked   See **take** v **A2b, 3f**

take down v phr   *somewhat old-fash*   Cf **take** v **B1**
   To come down (with an illness); to fall sick; to become (sick, ill), spec:

a in passive constrs; hence ppl adj phr *taken down* sickened. [Scots, nEngl dial; cf *OED2 take* v. 60.1, *EDD take* v. II.1.(7).(b)]
   1822 Hardie *Acct. Yellow Fever* 44 **NYC,** Mrs. Taylor was taken down with fever, who has since died. **1846** in 1856 Lawrence *Extracts* 261 **MA,** I was taken down with fever the next morning. **1861** *S. Lit. Messenger* 33.190 **VA,** She was tooken down soon after I left. **1870** *Atlantic Mth.* 26.524 **MA,** He was took down with the small-pox. **1889** Copeland *Hist. Clarendon* 210 **NEast,** I . . did not stop work until I was taken down sick at eighty-two years of age. **1937** in Lib. of Congress *Amer. Memory: WPA Life Hist.* (Internet) **NM,** The Spanish influenza broke out and I was taken down with it. **1939** *Ibid* **ME,** The old lady was taken down with appendicitis. **1960** Williams *Walk Egypt* 24 **GA,** The young'uns got no one but me, and dear Lord know what will happen to the poor creatures if I got took down. **1965–70** *DARE* (Qu. BB44, . . *A person just starting some sickness* . . *"He _____ pneumonia."*) Infs **IA**3, **LA**11, **MD**23, **OH**95, **PA**35, **SC**46, 55, Was taken down with; **AR**47, **OK**18, 'S taken down with [*DARE* Ed: This resp is ambiguous; it is here interpreted as "is taken," but might represent "has taken" or even "is taking."]; **PA**245, Is took down with; **SC**55, Was took down with. [All Infs old; 5 of 10 total Infs comm type 5] **1968** Kellner *Aunt Serena* 146 **IN,** Patients were took down, or took bad, or just plain *down*. **1974** Fink *Mountain Speech* 27 **wNC, eTN,** *Took down* or *took down sick* . . sick abed. *"Henry was took down last week."* **1995** in 2004 Montgomery–Hall *Dict. Smoky Mt. Engl.* 592 **eTN,** My grandparents were so took down that they never could get over it.

b in active constrs.   **scattered, but chiefly Sth, S Midl**
   1857 OH Genl. Assembly Senate *App. to Jrl.* 189, I then took down with the erysipelas, and kept my room for ten days. **1889** *Harper's New Mth. Mag.* 78.829, He took down ill that very day,/ And died within a week. **1894** in 2003 *DARE* File—Internet **cwMO** [*Appleton City Jrl.* 14 Mar], But his mother took down with measles shortly after his arrival, and in course of time Eli took them. **c1925** in 1944 *ADD* **nWV,** Last year he taken down with fever. **1927** *AmSp* 3.2 **Ozarks,** The past tense of *to take* is always *taken,* . . except in a few peculiar idioms. For example, the hillman usually says: *Paw he tuck down 'ith pneumonia fever.* **1938** Stuart *Dark Hills* 37 **neKY,** Herbert . . "took down" with pneumonia. **1938** in Lib. of Congress *Amer. Memory: WPA Life Hist.* (Internet) **cNC,** He took down with the consumption and he knowed he didn't have long to live. *Ibid* **NM,** In a few days the whole family took

down with smallpox. **1939** *Ibid* **GA,** There was also an aunt whose husband took down sick and died. **1942** Hurston *Dust Tracks* 91 **FL** [Black], He worked too long in the hot sun one day . . and took down sick. **1960** Williams *Walk Egypt* 296 **GA,** Death do love a back and a bed. If I took down, why, he'd come and cut my toenails. **a1961** in 2003 *DARE* File—Internet **WI,** [Reminiscences of a woman born in 1880:] But Elra took down with typhoid fever so no go, she had to stay home with him. **1965–70** *DARE* (Qu. BB44, . . *A person just starting some sickness* . . *"He _____ pneumonia."*) 14 Infs, **scattered,** Took down with; **MO**12, **OK**11, (Just) taken down with. [12 of 16 Infs old; 14 comm type 3 or 4] **1968** Kellner *Aunt Serena* 97 **cIN** (as of c1920), Bess was sick. Nobody knew why. She just all-of-a-sudden took down. **1976** Garber *Mountain-ese* 95 **sAppalachians,** Hal took down sick and couldn't work. **1982** Slone *How We Talked* 112 **eKY** (as of c1950), *Took down sick*—became ill.

take him   See **take** v **B8**

take ill   See **take** v **B1c**

take 'im   See **take** v **B8**

take in v phr   [*SND tak* v. B.1.(8).(viii) "*intr.* of a church: to assemble, begin service"]   **chiefly Sth, S Midl**   Cf **call** v **6, take out 2, take up 2**
   Intr; Usu of a church service, session (or, less freq, term) of school, or other assembly: to begin; also, less freq, tr in phr *take in school* to open school.
   1875 (1876) Twain *Tom Sawyer* 162 **MO,** She could hardly wait for school to 'take in.' **1890** *DN* 1.59 **Charleston SC,** They say sometimes the *church goes in* at 11 o'clock and *goes out* at 12.30; more often they say the *church takes in* at 11 o'clock and *takes out* at 12.30. **1892** *Amer. Missionary* 46.403 **cAL,** School "took in" with twenty-five more than last year. **1893** Shands *MS Speech* 62, *Take in.* Universally employed for *begin* in reference to schools, and sometimes, in reference to church. **1894** *Amer. Missionary* 48.324 **nwMS,** Here, only two years ago, we, in the dialect of the country, "took in school." **1899** (1912) Green *VA Folk-Speech* 436, The school takes in at 9 o'clock. **1903** *DN* 2.333 **seMO,** *Take in.* . . Of school, to open it in the morning. **1906** *DN* 3.160 **nwAR,** School takes in early and takes out late, seems to me. **1909** *DN* 3.379 **eAL, wGA,** *Take in.* . . Of school, church services, etc., to open; begin. **1910** *DN* 3.458 **FL, GA,** *Take in* and *turn out,* of school. . . To begin and close. **1946** *PADS* 6.30 **ceNC,** *Take in.* . . To begin school by ringing a bell or calling the children in. "School takes in at nine o'clock." Pamlico. Common. **1952** Brown *NC Folkl.* 1.597, *Take in, school.* . . To begin school after a recess or a vacation. "School takes in next Monday."—Central and east. **1966** *DARE* Tape **MS**15, Well, now, if he didn't get many children as he thought round by eight o'clock—he was supposed, the school was supposed to take in at eight—why, he'd take in anytime he got ready. **1986** Pederson *LAGS Concordance* **Gulf Region** (*When does school start?— after vacation*) 27 infs, Take(s) in; 6 infs, Took in; 1 inf, When do they take in school again? **2003** *DARE* File—Internet **swAL,** The officers are present at their stations 30 minutes before school takes in and lets out. *Ibid* **seLA,** Lockport Lower [Elementary School] takes in at 8:40 and lets out at 3:40.

take it time about   See **time about**

takel   See **tackle**

take leather   See **leather 1a**

take low v phr   Also *take low bridge*   **chiefly Sth, S Midl**   *esp freq among Black speakers*
   To humble oneself or accept a lower position.
   1940 Davis–Dollard *Children* 193 **LA,** But he will not take "low bridge" at home, even to escape certain punishment. **1942** *Negro Qrly.* 176, One thing about the old man, he never would take low on his art. **1947** Ballowe *The Lawd* 150 **LA,** The old man's one eye couldn't look you in the face. His whining voice, the fact that he would take low, eat dirt, wouldn't have saved him. *Ibid* 171, They made such a miration over Go-Easy that work on the place almost stopped. Mr. Effingham had to take low on his own plantation. **1966–70** *DARE* (Qu. II19, *When you think somebody has been put ahead of you or has been given something you deserved* . . *"I'd rather quit than _____."*) Inf **FL**1, To take low; **KY**94, Take low, be the underdog; **MO**29, Take low; (Qu. II31, *In an argument between two people, when one of them claims too much and the other shows him up: "He saw that he was wrong, so he started to _____."*) Inf **TN**50, Took low; (Qu. JJ25, *To show somebody that you're the boss: "He thought he could take the place over, but I made him _____."*) Inf **LA**8, Take low. [All Infs Black] **1994** Smitherman

Black Talk 220, *Take low*—To assume a posture of humility in order to defuse conflict and achieve an objective. "Take low and go," that is, Humble yourself, and you'll succeed in whatever you're trying to accomplish.

taken   See **take** v **A1b, 2c**

taken down   See **take down a**

takened   See **take** v **A2d, 3c**

take notice v phr *old-fash*

Of a widow or widower: to be receptive to the idea of remarriage; to be in search of a new spouse.

1875 Howard *One Summer* 48 **NEng,** I am not yet "reconciled," but have recovered from the first crushing effects of my grief. I am "beginning to take notice," as some one said about our friend the pretty widow. **1887** *Scribner's Mag.* 1.721 **VT,** The leader of the opposition remarked that the minister was beginning to take notice a little, . . like every other widower since the world was made. **1891** *Century Illustr. Mag.* 41.515 **VA,** Major Daisy . . said afterwards, with a quizzical smile, that "Josh was taking notice," he presumed. **1894** *Harper's New Mth. Mag.* 90.82 **AR,** A good black alpaca dress . . needed not even to surrender its bands of velvet . . to serve as widow's weeds, a first evidence of her "beginning to take notice" being perhaps not so much the "Valenceens" ruche which was expected to appear at her neck in due season as that which it ushered in. **1899** (1912) Green *VA Folk-Speech* 436, *Take notice*. . . Also, when a widow begins to look at the women with the intention of repairing his loss. **1906** *DN* 3.160 **nwAR,** *Take notice*. . . To look for a wife. "That old widower's takin' notice." **1918** *Eve. State Jrl.* (Lincoln NE) 29 Aug six o'clock sec [2]/3 (newspaperarchive.com), [Short story:] "They say she is beginning to take notice," said Sayre, in a rather cynical tone. "She had some fellow in tow last summer." **1929** *AmSp* 5.123 **ME,** A widow who was ready for another husband was said to be "taking notice," "in the market."

take notice to   See **to** prep **B11**

take off v phr   Cf **cut off** v phr, **make out** v phr **3**

To turn off (an electrical device).

1968 *DARE* (Qu. Y42, *Expressions for putting out a lamp or light*) Inf **MI**75, Take off the light; **WI**66, Blow out—lamp; take off, snap out—light. **1968** *DARE* FW Addit **seLA,** *To take off* = to turn off, said of television. "I wish you'd take that thing off." Grand Isle, LA.

take on v phr, hence vbl n *taking on*   [*OED* c1430 →]   **chiefly Sth; also S Midl, NEast**   See Map

To display strong emotion, "carry on"; to make a fuss or disturbance.

1836 (1838) Haliburton *Clockmaker* (1st ser) 140 **NEng,** When she went on board to sail down to Nova Scotia, all her folks took on as if it was a funeral. **1848** Lowell *Biglow* 146 'Upcountry' **MA,** Take on, *to sorrow*. **1859** Taliaferro *Fisher's R.* 41 **nwNC** (as of 1820s), One day, in class-meeting, Johnson "got happy," and groaned, cried, shouted, and "tuck on no little." **1899** Chesnutt *Conjure Woman* 191 **csNC** [Black], Mars Dugal' tuk on a heap 'bout losin' two er his bes' han's in one day. **1902** *DN* 2.247 **sIL,** *Take on*. . . To grieve; to make a demonstration of pain or suffering. **1905** *DN* 3.22 **cCT,** *Take on*. . . To grieve. **1906** *DN* 3.123 **sIN,** He took on awful at the grave. **1907** *DN* 3.219 **nwAR,** *Take on*. . . To grieve. **1909** *DN* 3.379 **eAL, wGA,** *Take on*. . . To show great emotion either of joy or sorrow: usually with *over*. "She took on terrible at the funeral." **1910** *DN* 3.450 **wNY,** *Take on*. . . To make a display of grief or anger. "Don't take on that way; it won't help matters." **1914** *DN* 4.81 **ME, nNH,** When Sy was laid low, Dell took on mighty hard. **1923** *DN* 5.223 **swMO,** He tuk on suthin' awful when she died. **1923** (1946) Greer-Petrie *Angeline Doin' Society* 14 **csKY,** When we run into Betty Bowles . . and she tuck on over us, and jest baig'd us to go home with her, hit made us happy. **1956** Moody *Home Ranch* 29 **CO** (as of 1911), Didn't reckon a man could sleep in late with you takin' on like a sick calf, did you? **1965–70** *DARE* (Qu. GG33b, *To feel very sad and upset about something: "I never saw a woman _____ so."*; total Infs questioned, 75) Infs **AR**31, **FL**30, **GA**1, 7, 9, **MS**8, 39, 56, 67, **NM**12, **OK**51, Take on; (Qu. AA8, *When people make too much of a show of affection in a public place . . "There they were at the church supper _____ [with each other]."*) Infs **SC**46, **TX**43, Taking on; **TX**29, Taking on over each other; (Qu. FF18, *Joking words . . about a noisy or boisterous celebration or party: "They certainly _____ last night."*) Inf **OK**18, Whoop and holler and take on; (Qu. GG35a, *To sulk or pout: "It won't do any good to _____ about it."*) Inf **NY**102, Take on. **1968–69** *DARE* Tape **GA**74, Any kind of mourning or screaming or

pitiful yelling from the heartbroken relatives—they'd call it taking on; **IN**36, I heard him takin' on and I run and got over there and this pup was running around this coon . . and he's barking and bawling at him so hard. **1986** Pederson *LAGS Concordance* (They are in mourning. . . If the women lost control of themselves, you'd say they were _____) 20 infs, **Gulf Region,** Taking on; 6 infs, **Gulf Region,** Take on; 1 inf, **nwFL,** The little-old calf will bleat and take on.

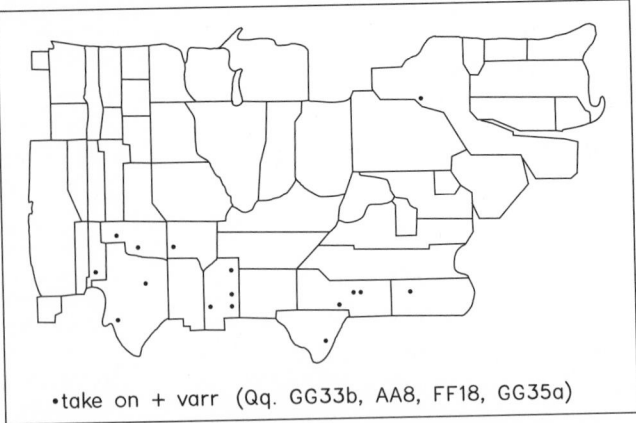

•take on + varr (Qq. GG33b, AA8, FF18, GG35a)

take one's foot in (one's) hand   See **foot** n **C5a**

take (one) to do   See **take** v **B2**

take out v phr

1a   To set out, esp in haste, leave; also fig.

1855 (1940) Chambers *Jrl.* 137 **MT,** When I discovered an Assynaboin camp of about thirty lodges I took out in order to give them the slip. **1867** Twain *Jumping Frog* 18 **CA,** He set the frog down and took out after that feller, but he never ketched him. **1909** *DN* 3.379 **eAL, wGA,** *Take out*. . . To start and run away hastily. "When he make that, he tuck out for home." **1933** Williamson *Woods Colt* 116 **Ozarks,** I told him you jest tuck out, afore he come. **1938** Rawlings *Yearling* 10 **nFL,** How come you to take out such a fur piece? **1938** in Lib. of Congress *Amer. Memory: WPA Life Hist.* (Internet) **NYC,** When they took out after you, there wasn't much use o' running. **1943** McAtee *Dial. Grant Co. IN Suppl. 2* 13 (as of 1890s), *Take out* . . go, leave; "_____ after him." **1952** Brown *NC Folkl.* 1.597, *Take out*. . . To set out; to go. Generally indicates hurry. "He took out to town." "He took out and run." **1963** Owens *Look to River* 133 **TX,** You want him to take out after us? **1967** *DARE* (Qu. X40, . . *Ways . . of saying, "I'm going to bed"*) Inf **TX**43, Take out; (Qu. Y19, *To begin to go away from a place: "It's about time for me to _____."*) Inf **AR**51, Take off, take out; **TX**3, Fade away, take out; (Qu. Y26b, *To walk very quietly: "The children filled their pockets and _____ out the back way."*) Inf **WI**48, Took out. **1968** *DARE* Tape **CA**89, Then they jump off, take out after rabbit with those clubs. **1968** *DARE* FW Addit **IA**29, Taking out after it in the wrong direction = doing things indirectly or round about. **2003** *Chr. Sci. Monitor* (Boston MA) 17 Mar (Internet), "Emmanuel was an LDS (Latter-Day Saint) person, and then he started hearing voices telling he should live polygamy and he took out on his own," said a fundamentalist Mormon who asked that her name not be used. **2003** *DARE* File—Internet **TX,** I checked a pickup truck on radar travelling 50 mph in a 35 mph zone. I turned around and took out after it.

b   Spec: to absent oneself from work or school; to quit a job.

1969 *DARE* Tape **IL**78, One of our ladies that worked for us for years took out, got married and took out and had a little girl. **1984** *Grandfather Tell Me a Story* 55 **OK,** I . . went to school in town, when there wasn't anything to do on the farm. If there was, well, I took out and helped plant whatever there was to be planted. **1999** in 2003 *DARE* File **RI,** Taking out of work to go to doctors [*sic*] appointments twice a week is hard.

2   Of a session of school or a church service: to end.   Cf **take in, turn out 2**

1890 [see **take in**]. **1905** *DN* 3.97 **nwAR,** *Take out*. . . To close. [⸢•⸣]"Do you know when school will take out"? Rare. **1906** [see **take in**].

3a   To unhitch (a horse or team).   **esp S Midl**

1815 *Niles' Weekly Reg.* 7 suppl 17, His carriage was surrounded by the populace, who took out the horses, and dragged him [=a war hero] . . to his lodgings. **1856** Cartwright *Autobiog.* 337 **KY,** I took out my horse, took off the harness, and took the harness and all the traveling appendages into the canoe. **1884** *Harper's New Mth. Mag.* 70.96, In a very few minutes every available hitching-post in sight was taken; many of the men took their horses out and backed the wagons round out of the way, so that the same post might do double duty. **1902** *DN* 2.247 **sIL**, *Take out, v. tr.* To unhitch a team from wagon or plow. **1907** *DN* 3.227 **nwAR**, *Take out, v.t.* To unhitch a team from wagon or plow. *Ibid* 237 **nwAR**, *Take out, v. phr. tr.* To unhitch (horses).

b *intr:* To unhitch a horse or team; hence fig, to stop working, take a break. **esp S Midl**

1899 (1912) Green *VA Folk-Speech* 437, *Take out.* . . Refers to the time of stopping work. "It is 12 o'clock and is time to take out," this is to *take out* the mules from the ploughs or waggons. **1903** *DN* 2.333 **seMO**, *Take out, v. phr. i.* To unhitch (horses). 'He took out and went to the house as soon as the cloud came up.' **1923** *DN* 5.223 **swMO**, *Take out.* . . To quit work. Literally, to take the team out of the field. **1952** Brown *NC Folkl.* 1.597, *Take out.* . . To unhitch an animal.—Central and east. **1958** *PADS* 29.17 **TN**, *Take out:* Stop work; to unhitch a team from farm implements. "Whenever you take out for dinner, stop by here." Rep. from Perry, Warren [Counties].

4 To take (food) from a serving dish; to dig in, help oneself—used chiefly as an invitation to guests. **chiefly S Midl** Cf **take up 1**

1902 *DN* 2.247 **sIL**, *Take.* . . Help yourself, especially at table, as 'take bread,' or 'take out meat.' **1908** Fox *Lonesome Pine* 100 **KY**, Everywhere he found unlimited hospitality. "Take out, stranger," said one old fellow, when there was nothing on the table but some bread and a few potatoes, "have a tater. Take two of 'em—take damn nigh *all* of 'em." **1915** *DN* 4.191 **swVA**, *Take out.* . . Used as a request at table to help oneself to food in a dish. **1918** *DN* 5.21 **NC**, *Take off, take out,* "Take off and help yourself." (At meals.) **1940** Hench Coll. **eVA**, *Take out and help oneself* = make oneself at home, eat and drink hearty. **1955** *DE Folkl. Bulletin* 1.20, Take out and hep yourself (said at the start of a meal). **1987** (1993) Egerton *S. Food* 7 **KY**, As the mother of one of my boyhood friends in Kentucky used to say whenever I happened to show up at dinnertime, "Take out and help yourself."

5 To malfunction, give out. [Presumably fig use of **1b** or **3b** above] **esp Lower Missip Valley**

1968 *DARE* (Qu. KK19, *If a machine or appliance is temporarily out of order: "My sewing machine _____."*) Inf **MO34**, Took out; **MO4**, Took out on me; (Qu. KK20b, *Something that looks as if it might collapse any minute: "Our old washing machine is _____."*) Inf **LA16**, Going to take out on us. **1985** in 2003 *DARE* File—Internet **TX**, March 23: My washing machine took out on me. **1996** *AR Highways* 42.4.24 **MS**, I was on my way to Conway . . when my car took out on me around Exit #130.

taker *n*

In marble play: see quot.

c1970 Wiersma *Marbles Terms* **swMI** (as of c1960), *Taker* . . a shooter which has hit another marble in the playing area, thus giving the player who made the shot either a point or possession of the marble which was hit.

take roundance   See **roundance 2**

take rounders   See **rounders 3**

take sick   See **take v B1c**

take tea for the fever, not to   See **tea for the fever, not to take**

take the gas pipe   See **pipe, take the**

take the libel   See **libel B**

take the night   See **take v B5**

take the rag off   See **rag n¹ 1, 2**

take the rag off(en) the bush   See **rag n¹ 1**

take the studs   See **studs**

take time about   See **time about**

take two rows at a time *v phr* **esp S Midl**

To sleep very soundly; to snore.

1939 *Hall Coll.* **eTN**, I guess Ab was sound asleep that mornin' when he said, "I guess I was takin' two rows at a time when the breakfast bell rung." **1956** McAtee *Some Dialect NC* 48, *Two rows at a time.* . . At a great rate. Sleeping or snoring "two rows at a time." **1967** *DARE* (Qu.

X45, . . *Joking expressions . . about snoring*) Inf **SC29**, I heard you snoring last night. You were taking two rows at a time. **1986** Smith *Wilbur's Tales* 295 **TN**, He's snoring like a log. He's taking two rows at a time. **1997** *DARE* File **seTN**, He fell asleep and was taking two rows at a time.

take up *v phr*

1 To remove (food) from the stove or from the cooking pot in preparation for serving it; to bring food to the table. **scattered, but chiefly Sth, S Midl** Cf **take out 4**

1936 *Amer. Home* 16.1.75, "Take up" the potatoes and peas in their hot dishes which have been in the warming oven with the plates. Carry them all to the table. **1966** *DARE* File **WV**, "Take up" a meal from the stove. **1983** *MJLF* 9.1.58 **ceKY** (as of 1956), *Take up* . . to remove food from the stove and put it on the table. **1997** *DARE* File **cnTX, csOK**, My grandmother and the grandmother of a friend of mine both talked about taking up food—taking it out of the oven. It used to mean putting the food on the closed shelf next to the pipe of a wood stove, but my grandmother and the other woman used it long after they had gas stoves. **2002** *Ibid* **AL, MS**, Vassar Hemphill, [76 years old] of Paloma Plantation, Greenwood, Mississippi, now of Tuscaloosa, uses the phrase, as do I, and as did members of my family in Montgomery. One "takes up food" out of a cooking pot, to put in serving bowls, to place on the table. You "take up pease". **2003** *NADS Letters* **IN**, I was born in 1945 in Brazil, Indiana. . . I use the term "take up the potatoes" or rice, or meat, etc. to mean remove from the cooking pot or pan and place in a serving dish. My daughter (18 years of age) who was born in California and raised in Mexico City and New York City, finds the expression exceedingly quaint and humorous and has never heard it used by anyone but me and my family members in Indiana. *Ibid* **swMO**, We're in Southwest Missouri, and I remember my grandmother—she died about 1980 at age 86—using the term: "Go take up the green beans [from the stove]." **2004** *Ibid* **CA**, "Supper will be ready as soon as I take up the potatoes." . . I've always used this term, as has my mother, now 80 years old. I'm 48, born in Idaho, raised in California. . . My mother was born in Iowa, but grew up in Idaho. It's probable that she got it from her mother, an Iowa native. *Ibid* **cFL**, I still say dinner'll be ready quick as I take up the rice—or let me take up these beans before they burn. *Ibid* **ceMN**, My mother . . would call us to the supper table by saying, "I'm taking up!" This meant she was bringing food to the table. *Ibid* **GA, IN, MO, SC, TX, UT, WI.**

2 *intr;* Usu of a church service, session or term of school, or other assembly: to begin; also, less freq, tr in phr *take up school* to open school. [*SND tak* v. B.1.(14).(vi) "to re-open (a school or college) after a holiday. . . Also *intr.* Gen[eral] Sc[ots]."] **esp Midl, West** Cf **take in**

1858 *Lady's Home Mag. Lit. Art & Fashion* 11.227, Before school takes up, let us all go and join those merry little ones in a round of play. **1865** *Ladies' Repository* 25.626, There are three weeks of it [=holiday vacation] before school takes up again, are there not, Mr. Aikin? **1869** *Lippincott's Mag. Lit. Sci. Educ.* 3.316 **PA**, "Is the meeting taken up yet?" "They take up school at nine." **1871** Eggleston *Hoosier Schoolmaster* 104 **sIN**, And just then there was a murmur: "Meetin's took up." **1875** (1876) Twain *Tom Sawyer* 113 **MO**, The bell for school to 'take up' tinkled faintly. **1878** Eggleston in *Scribner's Mth.* 15.653 **IN**, Meantime the "animal show" at the appointed time, "took up," as the country people expressed it. **1893** *KS Univ. Qrly.* 1.142 **KS**, *Take up:* begin school; tr. and intr. **1905** *DN* 3.97 **nwAR**, *Take up, v. phr. intr:* To reopen. 'When does school take up again?' Common. **1915** *DN* 4.191 **swVA**, The teacher took up school at eight o'clock. **1916** *DN* 4.330 **KS, neOH**, *Take up.* . . To begin (a session as of school or court, or even a lodge): not said of church or lectures or speeches. **1931** Goodrich *Mt. Homespun* 48 **sAppalachians**, Shadrach's "ten" were in the schoolyard every morning when school "took up." **1943** *LANE* Map 539, *When does school begin?* (referring to the date on which a vacation ends, not to the hour of the daily opening). . . 5 infs, **scattered NEng**, Take up [resp sugg by FW in 4 cases]; 1 inf, **CT**, *Take up,* after the Christmas holidays; *start,* after the long summer vacation. **1946** *PADS* 5.41 **VA**, *Take up:* Of school, begin; not common. **1965** *West Time Was* 53 **nwNC**, Meeting was already taking up, and the last talkers were straggling through the front door of the little weatherboarded church. **1965** *DARE* FW Addit **swOK**, "When school takes up . . "—starts. **1966** *DARE* (Qu. OO39b, *Talking about a meeting beginning: "Yes, it _____ [an hour ago]."*) Inf **WA1**, Took up. **1968** *Needles Desert Star* (CA) 29 Feb 6/4, The next Monday morning, school "took up" again. **1986** Pederson *LAGS Concordance* **Gulf Region** (*When does school start?—after vacation*) 24 infs, Take(s) up; 4 infs, Took up.

2001 in 2003 *DARE* File—Internet **OR,** Lodge will be opened and Masters and members from the various Lodges will be introduced. . . Dinner is at 6:30 and Lodge takes up at 7:30. **2003** *Ibid* ne**MO,** 8:10 Bell (students allowed to enter classrooms)—8:30 Bell (school takes up).

3 in phr *take up books:* To begin a session of school; hence intr in phr *books take up* school begins. **chiefly S Midl** Cf **books**

1896 *DN* 1.413 c**TX,** *Books:* school, school-time. "Is it books?" "Has books taken up?" = "Has school taken up (*i.e.* begun)?" Parker Co., Tex. **1903** *DN* 2.333 se**MO,** *Take up books.* . . To resume studies at school in the morning or after recess. **1906** *DN* 3.127 nw**AR,** *Books.* . . School. "When does books take up?" . . "When do books let out?" **1930s** in 1944 *ADD* e**WV,** It's time to take up books. **1942** Warnick *Garrett Co. MD* 15 nw**MD,** *Take up books* . . begin the study period in school. **1951** Giles *Harbin's Ridge* 29 e**KY,** Books took up at eight o'clock. **1976** Garber *Mountain-ese* 95 s**Appalachians,** The teacher took up books an hour later today because uv the snow. **1978** Massey *Bittersweet Country* 207 **Ozarks,** *Take up books* (begin studying): We took up books after the morning prayer. **1983** *MJLF* 9.1.58 ce**KY** (as of 1956), *Take up books* . . to begin recitation hours at school. **1986** Pederson *LAGS Concordance,* 1 inf, ce**TN,** Taking up books.

4 See **take v B3.**

5 To lodge, put up, take up residence. [*OED2 take* v. 93.v.(d) *"Obs.";* 1626–1724] **chiefly S Midl**

1952 Brown *NC Folkl.* 1.597, *Take up at.* . . To live at or with. . . Central and east. **1955** Ritchie *Singing Family* 95 se**KY,** They'd take up nights at whatever house they happened closest to when dark came. **1967** *DARE* File c**SC,** From a newspaper ad in the lost-and-found section: "A hog has took up at my place. Owner please call for." **1976** Wolfram–Christian *Appalachian Speech* 99, Did ever a stray animal come to y'all's house and take up? **2002** *Athens Banner–Herald* (GA) 26 May (Internet), She left us with Skippy, a gray Russian [cat] which took up at our address. **2003** *DARE* File—Internet n**FL,** Patch was a collie who lived on my Uncle Ben's farm. She was a stray that just kind of took up there.

6 in phr *take up for* : To come to the defense of, stand up for. **esp Sth, S Midl**

[**1835** in 1937 *UT Geneal. & Hist. Mag.* 28.122, The congregation were ashamed of him and would not stay to hear, and even some of them who were opposed, took up in our favor.] **1878** *Scribner's Mth.* 15.769 **IN,** To Amanda's surprise, her father took up for Mark. **1884** *Anglia* 7.274 **Sth, S Midl** [Black], *To take up mighty quick fer* = to take sides for. **1930** (1935) Porter *Flowering Judas* 64 **TX,** Who's to take up for Him if we don't, I'd like to know? **1941** *AmSp* 16.25 s**IN,** *Take up for.* To take someone's part. **1942** Warnick *Garrett Co. MD* 15 nw**MD** (as of 1900–18), *Take up for* . . to uphold; to show partiality. **1946** *PADS* 6.30 ce**NC,** *Take up for.* . . To defend one in an argument or a fracas. Pamlico. Common. **1947** *PADS* 8.15 s**IN,** *Take up for.* *Ibid* 23 **KY,** *Take up for.* *Ibid* 26 w**NY,** *Take up for.* *Ibid* 29 **MO,** *Take up for.* **1954** *WELS Suppl.,* In Chicago, and to some degree up here [= Wisconsin Rapids WI] I have heard it used to indicate that someone had taken another person's side in an argument. They say "So-and-so took up for her in court." c**1965** *DARE* File ce**IA,** *Take up for*—In sense of "come to the defense of" I have been familiar with it since my Dubuque (Ia.) childhood. I would label it colloquial. **1977** *New Yorker* 6 June 85 **TX,** "Wouldn't it embarrass *you,* hearing that *your* daddy spent a night in jail?" And Henry said no, it wouldn't—not if he knew his daddy had been taking up for someone. **1996** *AZ Daily Star* (Tucson) 7 Jan (Internet), A boy beat up an uncle of hers who was slow. After Torres "took up for him," some people started saying she was a gang member. **2001** in 2003 *DARE* File—Internet **NYC** [Black], Both of us were from Brooklyn, so I kind of took up for him. **2003** *Ibid* **AR,** Then, they went to criticizing me for various reasons. . . I took up for myself, which I should never do I guess.

7 To make do (with), put up (with). [*OED2 take* v. 93.z.(c) *"Obs.";* 1609–1825]

1771 in 1996 Franklin *Autobiog.* 30, Messrs. Onion and Russel . . had engag'd the great cabin; so that Ralph and I were forced to take up with a berth in the steerage. **1860** in 1890 *Portrait Green L.* 225 **WI,** He lost the best location in town . . and had to take up with about one of the least desirable spots. **1933** Smiley *Gloss. New Paltz* se**NY,** "I can't take up with it" . . meaning that I won't put up with it. c**1938** in Lib. of Congress *Amer. Memory: WPA Life Hist.* (Internet) **NH,** Peo-

ple . . have had to take up with living conditions on the road just as they have had to in their own homes. . . not what they like, but what they can afford.

8 To consort together; esp, to live together without marriage. [Appar abbr for *take up with one another* or *take up together*] **chiefly Sth, esp LA** See Map

1965–70 *DARE* (Qu. AA19, . . *A man and woman who are not married but live together as if they were*) Infs **KY**24, **LA**3, 16, 18, 31, **SC**3, 40, **VA**69, (They) took up; **DE**2, **KY**19, Tuck up; **LA**2, 12, 25, **NC**82, **VA**35, Taking up. **1968** *DARE* FW Addit **LA,** To take up—to begin living together as husband and wife. Negro custom; the expression is used by colored and white. **1986** Pederson *LAGS Concordance,* 1 inf, ce**LA,** Took up—lived together, not married; 1 inf, nw**LA,** Took up—got married; 1 inf, ce**GA,** Take up—live together out of wedlock; 1 inf, ne**LA,** Take up—shack up, not married; 1 inf, cn**LA,** Taken up—got married. **2003** *NADS Letters* ne**AL** (as of 1980s), "Take up" I have heard used without "with" only with pronouns as in: "they took up" or "they're took up" but never "X & Y have taken up." *Ibid* ne**SC,** I have also heard them use "take up" . . , as in "Those two just took up." **2004** *Ibid* **FL,** I have heard "take up" used to mean court or consort without the addition of "with". In Central and North Florida traditional speech you might ask about a possible couple and be told "Lord, yes, they've done took up." I think it is often used in an on again off again romance. "I thought Jesse and Suzy fell out? They had, but they've took up again." *Ibid* cw**NY,** Take up. "They took up." "X and Y have taken up." "They'll take up one of these days."

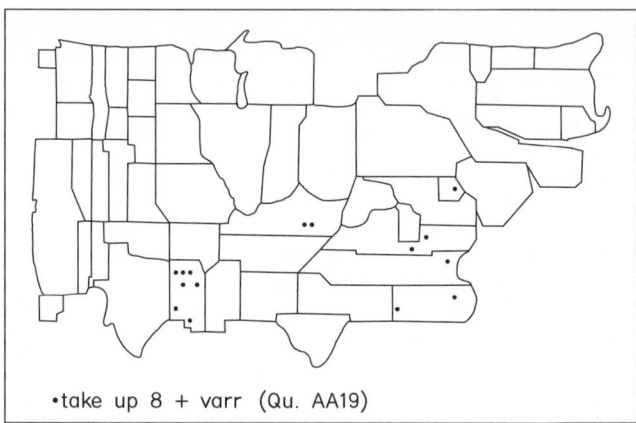

•take up 8 + varr (Qu. AA19)

take up books See **take up 3**

take up for See **take up 6**

take up school See **take up 2**

take water See **water B1**

taking on See **take on**

takle See **tackle**

taku n Also *taku wind* [From the *Taku* valley through which it blows] se**AK**

A strong, cold wind in the Juneau area that blows from the interior.

1904 *Home Missionary* 77.161 **AK,** We dared not stay in the tower room for fear the fierce Taku wind would unroof the tower. **1934** *Anchorage Daily Times* (AK) 12 Nov 2, [Headline:] Taku Hits Old Juneau Hard Swat. **1940** *AK Sportsman* Dec 12, A Taku Wind blows in Juneau whenever there is a strong North or Northeast wind from the Interior. . . It is severest during the winter and it is at this time when it is truly designated as a Taku. **1968** *DARE* (Qu. B17, *A destructive wind that blows straight*) Inf **AK**2, Taku ['tɑˌku] wind—very cold, 60–70 knot (extreme), gusty wind blowing from east and northeast off the ice cap, very turbulent; [ˌtɑˈku]; (Qu. B18, . . *Special kinds of wind*) Inf **AK**7, Taku ['tæˈku]—off mountain (in Juneau area). **1979** *Fairbanks Daily News-Miner* (AK) Feb 15, p4 (Tabbert *Dict. Alaskan Engl.*), We've heard how the Juneau airport is often closed, how the Taku winds whistle through the town on the few clear days. **2006** DuFresne–Spitzer *Alaska* 423 [Glossary:] *Taku wind*—Juneau's sudden gusts of wind, which may exceed 100mph in the spring and fall.

talable See **tolerable**

talala bird n [Cherokee *talala* woodpecker]
A **nuthatch**.

  1966 *DARE* (Qu. Q17, . . *Kinds of woodpeckers*) Inf **NC44**, Talala [tə'lɑlə] bird; (Qu. Q23, *The insect-eating bird that goes headfirst down a tree trunk*) Inf **NC44**, Talala bird.

talayote n
A **vine milkweed**, as:
a *Matelea parvifolia* or *M. cordifolia.*

  1893 CA Acad. Sci. *Proc.* 2d ser 3.152, *Rothrockia cordifolia* [= *Matelea c.*]. . . The rather slender follicles . . when young are eaten raw by the inhabitants. . . Known as "Talayote." **1951** Abrams *Flora Pacific States* 3.373, *Gonolobus parvifolius* [=*Matelea p.*] . . Spearleaf or Talayote. . . California . . and east to western Texas. **1995** in 2004 *DARE* File—Internet **AZ**, *Matelea parvifolia*—spearleaf, talayote. **2000** *Ibid* **sCA**, Though flowering plants are sparse this year, those listed below showed at least some sign of blooming. . . *Matelea parvifolia*—Spearleaf, Talayote (buds).

b *Cynanchum racemosum* var *unifarium.*

  1970 Correll *Plants TX* 1235, *Cynanchum unifarium* [=*C. racemosum* var *u.*] . . Talayote. . . In scrub forests and thickets, climbing over trees and shrubs, mainly on the Edwards Plateau and in the Rio Grande Plains and Trans-Pecos. **1990** in 2004 *DARE* File—Internet **TX**, Cynanchum unifarium—Talayote. **1998** *Ibid* **TX**, *Cynanchum unifarium.* Talayote, swallow-wort. Native perennial herbaceous vine. **2004** *Vascular Plants L.B. Johnson Natl. Park* 16 **TX**, Cynanchum unifarium (Scheele) Woodson (=C. racemosum var. unifarium)—talayote.

tale-idle n *esp* **sAppalachians**
A false story.

  1931 *PMLA* 46.1305 **sAppalachians**, Hit's nary a thing but a tale-idle. (A false report.) **1940** (1968) Haun *Hawk's Done Gone* 97 **ceTN**, Hit's a tale-idle. . . It hain't so. **1957** Combs *Lang. S. Highlanders* **sAppalachians**, Tale-idle—gossip, a false, malicious report, hearsay.

tale packer See **pack** v 2a

tale-tell v [Back-formation from *tale-teller, tale-telling*]
To tell stories.

  1940 (1978) Still *River of Earth* 172 **KY**, Oft we would tale-tell. I told about Uncle Toll's finger-piece, Walking John Gay, and the pigeon-birds. **1980** (2002) Malone *Dingley Falls* 234, Oh, Tracy! . . To tale-tell against our Beanie?

tale-toting See **tote** v A7

talfa See **talpa**

talk v

1 To engage in courtship, contemplate marriage; with *(up) to*: to keep company with, court. **chiefly S Midl**

  1895 *DN* 1.374 **eTN**, Judge Jackson's son has been talkin' to my daughter nigh on a year. **1906** *DN* 3.160 **nwAR**, *Talk up to.* . . To court, to woo. "Bud's talkin' up to her." **1915** *DN* 4.243 **eTN**, *Talk to.* . . To court; woo. **1917** in 1944 *ADD* **swVA**, They are talking. **1924** Raine *Land of Saddle-Bags* 98 **sAppalachians**, When young folk in love with each other make serious plans, they are said to be *talking.* **1927** *DN* 5.478 **Ozarks**, Th' ol' fool was a-talkin' to a widderwoman afore his wife was cold, sca'cely. **1931** *AmSp* 7.91 **eKY**, Matty'n Jim 'ave been talkin' nigh onto a year. **1931** Goodrich *Mt. Homespun* 45 **sAppalachians**, She's fifteen, goin' on sixteen. She's talkin to Jem Taylor. . . It was some minutes before it dawned upon the mind of the Weaving-woman that "talking" to a boy meant "keeping company" with him. **1952** Brown *NC Folkl.* 1.598, *Talk (to).* . . They been talkin' about two years." **1952** Giles *40 Acres* 4 **csKY**, Young couples do not go together. They are said to be "talking" to each other. **1970** *Current Slang* 5.2.13 [Black univ student slang], *Talk to.* . . To have a romantic association with. **1976** Garber *Mountain-ese* 91 **sAppalachians**, Maudie is talkin' to that new hared hand over at Johnsons. **2003** Fought *Chicano Engl.* 103 **Los Angeles CA**, *Talk to,* meaning 'to date'. *We started talking and then I didn't talk to him no more.* (Reina, 17) *I talk to his sister.* (Sancho, 19)

2 in phr *talk to one's plate* (or *food*): To say grace before a meal. Cf **read one's plate**

  1911 *DN* 3.540 **eKY**, *Talk to one's plate.* To "say grace," return thanks at table, e.g., "Stranger, talk to your plate." **1949** *PADS* 11.12 **wTX**, *Talk to (one's) plate.* . . To say grace before meals. **1954** *Harder Coll.*

cwTN, *Talk to ye food:* . . To say grace. *Ibid, Talk to (one's) plate:* . . To say grace.

3 in phr *talk one low:* To speak slightingly of.

  1930 Faulkner *As I Lay Dying* 68 **MS**, And when folks talks him low, I think to myself he aint that less of a man or he couldn't a bore himself this long.

4 in phr *talk to the Lord:* To use profanity.

  1934 Smiley *Gloss. New Paltz* **seNY**, "I had to talk to the Lord this morning".—curse. Spoken after a trip up from the Greenhouse during an ice storm.

talkified adj [*talk* + *-ified*]
Talkative.

  1938 Rawlings *Yearling* 175 **nFL**, You're talkified as a old woman to-day. **1942** Hall *Smoky Mt. Speech* 62 **wNC**, **eTN**, Occasionally the vowel approaches or reaches [i]. Examples: . . *marigold* ['mæri,gould], *talkified.* **1954** *Harder Coll.* **cwTN**, *Talkified.* . . Talking too much, chatty, gossipy.

talking back vbl n Cf **shout** v 1
Responding to a speaker with encouragement.

  1945 Brewer *Humorous Tales SC* 35, Her presence was always helpful to the pastors of the church because she did what they called talkin' back to 'em all the time. **1953** Brewer *Word Brazos* 85 **eTX** [Black], Hit's some sistuhs in de chu'ch what meck de preachuh rail pow'ful in de pulpit by doin' what dey calls "talkin' back to 'im." Ah mean by dat, when a preachuh put ovuh a good lick again' de Devul, dey say, "Preach de Word, son!" or, "You sho' is tellin' de truf now."

talk one low See **talk** 3

talk poor mouth See **poor mouth**

talk to See **talk** 1

talk to one's food (or plate) See **talk** 2

talk to the Lord See **talk** 4

talk up to See **talk** 1

talky See **talpa**

tall n See **taw**

'tall adv See **a-tall**

tallboy n

1 also attrib: A large can of beer. **chiefly Sth, West** Cf **longneck 1**

  1972 *Odessa Amer.* (TX) 28 Dec sec A 3/5, [Grocery advt:] Schlitz Beer 3 Tallboy 24 oz. can $1.00. **1977** *Progress–Rev.* (La Porte City IA) 26 Oct [20]/5 (newspaperarchive.com), Marx Lounge. . . Mon. Special 16 oz. Tallboy 50¢. **1984** Weaver *TX Crude* 64, *Tallboy.* A tall, six-teen-ounce can of beer. **1995** Lesley *Sky Fisherman* 155 **OR**, Seaweed took a tallboy from his bib overalls front pocket and snapped the tab. Warm beer foamed across his hand, but he drank with gusto, then held the can to my lips. **2004** *DARE* File—Internet **TN**, The South was completely foreign to me. The accents, the music, the tallboy beer cans. **2004** *Justice Denied* 23.20 **TN**, I noticed that Linda had a tallboy beer. **2004** in 2005 *DARE* File—Internet **GA**, Never seen without some kind of cheap-ass-tallboy-beer in his hand. **2005** *Ibid* **TX**, "She [=a motor-cycle] oughtta be runnin' by tomorrow," he said as he finished off his Keystone tallboy.

2 A large playing marble. [*tall* var of **taw** + *boy*]

  1992 *DARE* File **eTN**, [From catalog for Smoky Mountain Knife Works:] Playing Marbles is our "National Sport" up here in the Smoky Mountains! . . "*Big Poke*" Contains approx. 300 marbles: 100 Tall Boys + 200 Pee-Dabs.

tall cotton n **chiefly Sth, S Midl** Cf **high cotton 1**
In phr *be in tall cotton* and varr: To be prosperous, do well, be in a good situation.

  1941 TX Bar Assoc. *Proc.* 2.144, Well, I thought I was in tall cotton down there in that city trying a case involving that amount of money. **1949** *PADS* 11.7 **wTX**, *High (tall) cotton, in the:* . . Doing well. **1965** *DARE* FW Addit **OK**, *Tall cotton, to be in:* To have good luck or to be in good spirits. **1984** Wilder *You All Spoken Here* 126 **Sth**, *Shittin' in tall cotton, livin' in tall cotton:* Prosperous; in good financial and/or social position; a good liver. **1985** Ladwig *How to Talk Dirty* 27 **Ozarks**, *She's choppin' tall cotton* . . doing well. **1996** *Atlanta Jrl.–Constitution*

(GA) 11 Feb sec M 3/4, *We're in tall cotton now* (something big just happened). **1999** *Time* 24 Jan (Internet), The Republicans, sitting in tall cotton, relaxed, stretched, and let the presidency continue to unravel. **2002** *Star* (Kansas City MO) 21 Sept (Internet) **ceKS,** When I started out in this business, I thought I was in tall cotton. **2004** *DARE* File—Internet **WV,** Big oil boys in tall cotton now. . . well with the take-over of the Iraq oil fields old Bush's texas oilfrens [sic] have pretty well got things set up the way they want them now.

tall drink of water n
=long drink of water.

1924 Nicholson *Garden Varr.* 119, That tall drink o' water looks like she was sent for and couldn't come! **1935** *NV State Jrl.* (Reno) 16 Mar 4/1, One was short and blond. . . The other was a tall drink of water with a bald spot. **1987** in 1994 Lighter *Random House Dict. Slang* 1.657 [*Sable* (ALC-TV)], My favorite one of your characters is that funny tall drink of water. **1996** *Capital Times* (Madison WI) 4 Sept sec A 11/3 **Chicago IL,** [Mike Royko column:] "My goodness, look at that beautiful tall drink of water." . . "[S]he, like many other lean and lanky lovelies, is here to hit on John-John." **1996** Isaacs *Lily White* 106 **Long Is. NY,** Lee glanced up, but he was standing at the counter, beside his friend, a tall drink of water. **2003** *Boston Globe* (MA) 21 Nov (Internet), [Theater review:] The person you can't take your eyes off of in "Butley" is a tall drink of water named Jake Weber. **2004** *DARE* File—Internet **nwWA,** She will be getting married before you know it. She looks like a tall drink of water, is her dad tall? *Ibid* **MS,** My grandma and mother have drilled these southern expressions into my mind. . . She's a tall drink of water. (tall and skinny).

taller　See **tallow**

talleywhacker　See **tallywhacker 1**

tall hog at the trough n
One who is in a dominant position.

1958 *Tri-City Herald* (Pasco WA) 29 July 4/5, Asked for a few typical Ford phrases he came up with a hefty list, some of Tennessee origin and others coined by Ernie. . . "Tall hog at the trough." **1967** *DARE* FW Addit **cOR,** *Tall hog at the trough*—someone who has all the advantages. **1974** *Bittersweet* 1.3.42 **Ozarks,** When it comes to eating chicken, I'm the tall hog at the trough. **1984** Wilder *You All Spoken Here* 124 **Sth,** *Big dog in the meat house*: The number one guy. . . *Tall hog at the trough, tush hog*: Ditto. **2000** *News* (Kingstree SC) 23 Feb (Internet), Johnny McDaniel is the tall hog at the trough at Farmers Telephone.

talliwhacker　See **tallywhacker 1**

tallman n
=longman.

1887 Walker–Jenks *Songs & Games* 83, Thumbkin says, "I'll dance!" Thumbkin says, "I'll sing!"/ Dance and sing, ye merry little men! Thumbkin says, "I'll dance and sing!"/ Pointer says, "I'll dance!" etc./ Tall man says, "I'll dance!" etc./ Ring man says, "I'll dance!" etc./ Little man says, "I'll dance!" etc. **1965** Ilg–Ames *School Readiness* 171, Show me your middle finger. . . using the child's own naming of "big finger" or "tallman." **1988** *NADS Letters* **csMI,** *Feeble man*—'ring finger': widely known among my students. They attribute the source to the game 'Thumbkin' in which the names of the digits are: thumbkin, pointer, tall man, feeble man, pinkie.

tallow n　Usu |'tælo|; also |'tælə(r)|　Pronc-spp *taller, talluh*　Cf Pronc Intro 3.I.12.d
A Forms.

1840 Haliburton *Clockmaker* (3d ser) 307 **NEng,** I'll jist . . slick up my hair with a taller candle. **1844** Thompson *Major Jones's Courtship* 167 **GA,** Some had long strate greasy hair that hung down in clumps like taller candles. **1856** *Harper's New Mth. Mag.* 12.480 **NEng,** How they did rip the hide and taller off [a whale]. **1863** in 2004 *DARE* File—Internet **IN,** We bought a quarters worth of beef taller to make gravy & shorten our bread with. **1874** (1895) Eggleston *Circuit Rider* 15 **sOH** (as of early 1800s), There was no one present who could "hold a taller dip to Bill's shuckin." **1891** *DN* 1.117 **cNY,** [tælə˞] ([tælə]) . . 'tallow.' **1916** *DN* 4.264 **Cape Cod MA,** Mean enough to skin a flea for the hide 'n taller. **1922** Gonzales *Black Border* 331 **sSC, GA coasts** [Gullah glossary], *Talluh*—tallow. **1927** *AmSp* 3.136 **ME,** A badly cheated one had lost "hide, hoofs and taller." **1936** *AmSp* 11.317 **Ozarks,** *Sink-taller whisky*. . Whisky of a very high alcohol content. **1942** Hall *Smoky Mt. Speech* 80 **wNC, eTN,** The sound [ə˞] . . is the pre-

vailing one in most words spelled with *-o, -ow.* . . tallow. **1967–68** *DARE* Tape **GA30,** Mostly their plan for that was using tallow ['tælə]; **TX40,** But this cold soap, I used to make it with tallow ['tælə˞]. **1976** Garber *Mountain-ese* 91 **sAppalachians,** *Taller* . . tallow.

B Sense.

See **tallow pot.**

tallowberry n

1 also *tallow bayberry:* A **wax myrtle.**

1858 (1864) Coe *Concentrated Organic Medicines* 252, Common Names. Bayberry, Tallow Berry, Wax Myrtle [etc]. **1900** Lyons *Plant Names* 255, *M[yrica] cerifera*. . . Tallow Bayberry. . . *Fruit* source of American vegetable wax or tallow (myrtle wax, bayberry tallow), which is said to have astringent and mildly narcotic properties. **1930** Sievers *Amer. Med. Plants* 10, *Bayberry*. . . *Other common names* . . tallow berry. . . The wax obtained from the berries [is] used for making bayberry candles. **1974** Morton *Folk Remedies* 99 **SC,** *Wax myrtle;* . . *tallow berry*. . . The bony seed is studded with small black particles overlaid with greenish-white wax resulting in a bluish appearance.

2 Appar a **checkerberry** or a **partridgeberry;** see quot.

1867 De Voe *Market Asst.* 392 **NY,** Tallow-berries, or ground-berries. These small red berries are found growing on a small, tender vine resting on the ground, in the cleared woods; and when eaten, they have a sort of sweetish, tallowy taste, but rather pleasant.

3 **=locustberry.**

1884 Sargent *Forests of N. Amer.* 28, *Byrsonima lucida*. . . Tallow-berry. . . Fruit edible.

4 The fruit of the **tallow tree 1;** hence n *tallow-berry tree.*

1829 *S. Agriculturist* 2.526, The foundation of a permanent fence of great utility is easily laid . . by sowing the Tallow-berry either on the bank or alongside of any garden fence, pasture-field, &c. The Tallow Tree is the most difficult to kill after it has sent down its tap-root, of any tree we know. **1901** Mohr *Plant Life AL* 834, *Sapium sebiferum*. . . *Tallow-berry Tree.* Coast plain. **1991** *Houston Chron.* (TX) 16 Nov sec C 12/2, Venture outdoors this weekend . . and experiment with these fall items in dried arrangements for the upcoming holiday: grayish-white tallow berries, [etc]. **2003** *DARE* File—Internet [Spiegel Catalog], Centerpiece. . . Shown with our tallow berry wreath (sold separately). *Ibid* **Charleston SC,** The Orioles have switched to eating a lot of Tallow berries.—I know non-native invaders, those Tallow trees.

tallow bird n　Cf **grease bird**
=Canada jay.

1902 Lord *First Book Birds* (2d ed) 178, The Gray Jay, "Tallow Bird," or "Whisky Jack." **1917** *Wilson Bulletin* 29.2.82 **wWA,** *Perisoreus obscurus*. . . I heard camp-bird, camp-robber, elk-bird, and tallow-bird in western Washington.

tallow brush　See **tallow bush 2**

tallow bush n

1 See **tallow shrub.**

2 also *tallow brush:* **=mountain mahogany 2.**

1931 U.S. Dept. Ag. *Misc. Pub.* 101.43, *Mountain-mahoganies (Cercocarpus spp.)* . . Numerous other, and sometimes quite misleading, local names for these shrubs include . . tallow bush. **1937** U.S. Forest Serv. *Range Plant Hdbk.* B49, *Cercocarpus spp.* . . Many other names, such as . . tallowbush, are applied to these shrubs in various localities.

tallow, let the hide go with the　See **hide** n² **7a**

tallow-mouth minnow n　Cf **doughbelly 1, greased chub**
A **stone roller 1** (here: *Campostoma anomalum*).

1957 Trautman *Fishes* 408 **OH,** Ohio Stoneroller Minnow. . . lips a vivid white, hence the colloquial name of "Tallowmouth Minnow." **1983** Becker *Fishes WI* 476, *Campostoma anomalum*. . . Tallow-mouth minnow. . . Mouth ventral, lower jaw having a distinctive cartilaginous "cutting" edge not covered by skin.

tallow nut n
=hog plum 1.

1791 Bartram *Travels* 94 **FL,** These shelly ridges . . naturally produce Orange groves, Live Oak, . . Tallow-nut, or Wild Lime, and many others. **1884** Sargent *Forests of N. Amer.* 34, *Ximenia americana*. . . *Tallow nut*. . . Common and reaching its greatest development in Florida on the west coast. . . Edible plum-shaped fruit. **1982** Everett *NY Bot. Garden Encycl.* 3571, *Ximenia*. . . Tallow Nut or Tallow Wood or Hog-Plum.

tallow pot n Also *tallow* [From *tallow pot* a container for melted tallow or other lubricant]

In railroading: a locomotive fireman; one who lubricates engines—also used as a nickname.

1888 *Locomotive Firemen's Mag.* 12.425, "Tallow Pot" has some comments on "E.S." and alludes to cyclones.   **1899** *ID Daily Statesman* (Boise) [25 Nov 5/5] (newspaperarchive.com), Extract of report made by head brakeman: . . "Tallow Pot was cracking diamonds in the tank." . . It was translated by an old timer in the office as follows: . . "The fireman was breaking coal."   **1914** *DN* 4.164 **NW,** *Tallow pot.* . . The fireman of a locomotive.   **1916** *DN* 4.357 [Railroad terms], *Tallow-pot.* . . A locomotive fireman. Far West.   **1926** *AmSp* 1.250 **PA,** Here is some of the railroad man's patois: The railroad engineer is known variously as "eagle eye," "hog-head" and "throttle puller"; the fireman as "diamond pusher" and "tallow pot."   **1945** Hubbard *Railroad Ave.* 363, *Tallowpot*—Locomotive fireman, so called from melted tallow used to lubricate valves and shine the engine.   **1953** Botkin–Harlow *Treas. Railroad Folkl.* 326, Back in the engine cab the tallow was leaning on his armrest watching for a signal from the switch crew.   **1962** *AmSp* 37.136 **nwCA,** *Tallow-pot.* . . A fireman on a locomotive. In the early days he used to put the tallow in the pots.   **1966–67** *DARE* Tape **ID**10, I hadn't heard a couple of these terms for the fireman, but my husband tells me that "tallow pot" or "bakehead" is the name for a fireman, particularly on the steam locomotives; **SD**5, [FW:] You were telling me before some of the names that you had for different guys, like what'd you call the engineer? [Inf:] He was the hogger. . . [FW:] Fireman? [Inf:] Tallow pot.   **1968** *AmSp* 43.289 [Railroad vocab], *Tallow pot.* . . The man who oils engines in roundhouses or in car shops. This old term was also once applied to the fireman on a steam engine, as he was responsible for seeing that all the required oil cans were on the engine at the start of a trip.

tallow root n
=**cranefly orchid.**

1862 Hatch *Reminiscences* 80 **NY,** The Ginseng, Sweet Scisley and Tallow roots, were often met with.   **1900** Lyons *Plant Names* 372, *T[ipularia] unifolia* [=*T. discolor*]. . . Tallow-root, Crane-fly Orchis.

tallow shrub n Also *tallow bush*
=**wax myrtle.**

[**1748** in 1970 Kalm *Resejournal* 2.115 **PA,** *Myrica. Candleberry tree.* . . Af de här boende svenska kallades den *talgbuske;* en del af de svenska bruka plåcka bären och göra talglius deraf; och det göra de årligen, emedan dessa lius äro hel goda. [=*Myrica. Candleberry tree.* . . By the Swedes living here called the *tallow bush;* some of the Swedes are in the habit of gathering the berries and making candles from them, and they do that annually, because these candles are excellent.]]   **1778** in 1789 Anburey *Travels* 300 **PA,** Green wax-candles . . were made from the berries of a tree, which is called the tallow shrub, as they produce a kind of wax or tallow.   **1835** Simms *Partisan* 2.136 **SC,** The prisoners . . had been made to file into the grove of tallow bushes.   **1854** Simms *Woodcraft* 87 **SC,** The parties . . separated as before, and once more shrouded themselves among the myrtle and tallow bushes.   **1876** Hobbs *Bot. Hdbk.* 117, Tallow-shrub, Bayberry, Myrica cerifera.   **1933** Small *Manual SE Flora* 409, *Cerothamnus* [=*Morella*]. . . The bark is astringent and wax is obtained from the exudations of the fruits. . . *Wax-myrtles.* . . *Tallow-shrubs.*   **1974** (1977) Coon *Useful Plants* 190, Wax myrtle, candleberry, tallow shrub. This is a shrub of up to 30 feet growing south from zone 7 to Texas.

tallow tree n
1 An introduced tree *(Triadica sebifera)* naturalized in the southeastern US and Gulf States. [*OED2* 1704 →] Also called **Chinese tallow tree, popcorn ~,** *tallow-berry ~* (at **tallowberry 4**)

1814 Pursh *Flora Americae* 2.608, *Stillingia.* . . *sebifera.* . . On the sea-coast of South Carolina; originally a native of China. . . Known by the name of *Tallow Tree.*   **1857** U.S. Patent Office *Annual Rept. for 1856: Ag.* 138 **SC,** [Fish crows] are fond of many kinds of berries, such as the cassena, . . holly, . . and the tallow-tree . . a South Carolina tree of Chinese origin.   **1863** Porcher *Resources* 122 **Sth,** Tallow-tree. . . I have seen it growing abundantly near Charleston, on the King street road. . . In my report . . in 1849, I had, as above, reported the fact of this tree being already naturalized. I have recommended it particularly to the soap manufacturers of Charleston and the Confederate States, as a rich source of oil. The seeds, when burned, give out a great deal of light.   **1886** *Harper's New Mth. Mag.* 73.293 **New Orleans LA,** The long rows of

tallow-trees . . shaded an unpaved street.   **1941** Writers' Program *Guide LA* 22, The tallowtree is a peculiar exotic growing in New Orleans.   **1968** *DARE* (Qu. T16, . . *Kinds of trees . . 'special'*) Inf **LA**28, Popcorn trees or tallow trees . . have long flowers and white seeds that chickens eat. They are used when people want quick shade trees.   **1986** Pederson *LAGS Concordance,* 6 infs, **LA, TX,** Tallow tree(s).

2 See **tallowwood.**

tallowweed n esp **TX**
1 A **bitterweed,** usu *Tetraneuris linearifolia.*

1898 U.S. Div. Agrostology *Bulletin* 10.20 **cTX,** Tallow Weed (*Actinella* [=*Tetraneuris*] *linearifolia*).—Every sheep raiser . . knows the habits and value of this remarkable forage plant.   **1937** U.S. Forest Serv. *Range Plant Hdbk.* W5, The United States species of the *Tetraneuris* . . section, some of which are known as tallowweeds, are rather small plants of distinctive appearance. . . In the Southwest . . the flower heads of a number of the species reputedly [are] . . good sheep and goat forage; local sheepmen in central and western Texas claim that these plants produce a good hard fat both on lambs and sheep. *Ibid* W6, *Tetraneuris linearifolia* . . tallowweed.

2 Any of several **plantains;** see quots.

1903 U.S. Dept. Ag. *Annual Rept. for 1903* 127 **wTX,** Two species of plantain (*Plantago wrightiana* and *P. virginica*) . . [are] locally known as tallow weed. Stockmen report that these species are much relished by stock and that cattle fatten rapidly while grazing on them.   **1936** Whitehouse *TX Flowers* 142, *Tallow-Weed.* . . (*Plantago wrightiana*) is a common plant on prairies from Texas to Arizona. . . It is called tallowweed because cattle fatten on the plants.   **1941** Dobie *Longhorns* 264 **TX,** It was a good season, and tallow weed and grass were coming together. It was the time for the spring cow hunts.   **1967** *DARE* (Qu. S26e, *Other wildflowers not yet mentioned*; not asked in early QRs) Inf **TX**1, Tallowweed—looks like poke; stockmen like this—it puts tallow on cattle.   **1970** Correll *Plants TX* 1477, *Plantago Hookeriana.* . . *Tallow-weed.* . . In sandy, gravelly or rocky soils . . , also on clay flats from e. Tex., along the coast to the Rio Grande Valley and inland w. to the Trans-Pecos.

tallow whacker See **tallywhacker 1**

tallowwood n Also rarely *tallow tree*
=**hog plum 1.**

1908 Britton *N. Amer. Trees* 377, *Tallowwood* . . *Ximenia americana.* . . A thorny small tree or shrub . . in peninsular Florida and the Keys.   **1933** Small *Manual SE Flora* 1251, *Tallow-wood.* . . The tallow tree has become accommodated to a variety of soils and habitats.   **1946** West–Arnold *Native Trees FL* 193, As a tree, the tallowwood occurs in hammocks as far north as Alachua County, but it is most common in the scrubs of peninsular Florida as a low, spiny shrub.   **1962** Harrar–Harrar *Guide S. Trees* 263, *Tallowwood.* . . *Ximenia americana.*   **1982** [see **tallow nut**].

tall pin n
1952 Brown *NC Folkl.* 1.598, *Tall pin.* . . A safety pin.

tall snakeroot See **snakeroot b(4)**

talluh See **tallow**

tall walkers n pl
=**tom walkers.**

1969 *DARE* (Qu. EE35, *Long wooden poles with a footpiece that children walk around on to make them tall*) Inf **OH**89, Tall-walkers—they used to was.

Tally n esp **sAppalachians**
Italy; a person of Italian ancestry.

1904 *DN* 2.402 **cNY,** *Tally.* . . An Italian. "The Tallies are workin' on the railroad."   **1942** Berrey–Van den Bark *Amer. Slang* 49.11, *Italy.* . . Spaghettiland, Tally, Wopland.   **1967–70** *DARE* (Qu. HH28, *Names and nicknames . . for people of foreign background: Italian*) Infs **KY**33, **MD**24, **VA**5, Tallies; **VA**11, Tallies—coalfields of Virginia and West Virginia; **VA**42, Tally—niggers say; **WV**1, 3, Tally.   **1973** *New Yorker* 16 July 37 **WV,** Welch [WV] was just beginning then, and there were a lot of highly skilled Italian stonemasons around. 'Tallies,' they called them. . . The Tallies built this house.   **2008** *DARE* File **sWV,** Ethnic insults used on the playground . . [included] Tally for Italian.

tallyho n Also *tally*
Any of var chasing games.

1893 *Harper's New Mth. Mag.* 86.287 **MA,** They were pretty, pleasant children enough; . . accustomed not to play auction or tally-ho while their parents read or wrote. **1901** *DN* 2.149 **cNY,** Tally-ho. . . A game like hare and hounds. Ithaca. **1966–67** *DARE* (Qu. EE12, *Games in which one captain hides his team and the other team tries to find it*) Inf **GA**12, Tallyho; **NJ**2, Tally.

‡tally-lagger n
1969 *DARE* (Qu. II34, *If you think somebody is trying to use you to his advantage: "I'm not going to be his ———."*) Inf **NC**61, Tally-lagger ['tælilægǝ].

tallywag n
Either the **black sea bass 1** or the related *Centropristis ocyurus.*
1896 U.S. Natl. Museum *Bulletin* 47.1199, *Centropristes striatus. . . Tally-wag.* . . One of the common food-fishes of our Atlantic Coast. **1902** Jordan–Evermann *Amer. Fishes* 397, The tally-wag of the Gulf of Mexico is a distinct species of sea-bass, C[*entropristes*] *ocyurus*, occurring in rather deep water, chiefly on the Snapper Banks. **1946** La Monte *N. Amer. Game Fishes* 48, *Centropristes striatus. . . Tally Wag.* . . Cape Ann, Massachusetts, south to northern Florida. **1993** in 2001 *DARE* File—Internet, *Centropristis ocyurus. . . Vernacular name(s)* Gulf Sea Bass[*], Tallywak. . . *Centropristis striata. . . Vernacular name(s)* Blackfish[*], Rock Bass[*], Black Bass[*], Bluefish[*], Tallywag.

tallywags n pl, but sg or pl in constr [*EDD* tally-wag] Cf **tallywhacker 1**
1899 (1912) Green *VA Folk-Speech* 438, Tallywags. . . A man's privates; the virile member.

tallywhacker n
1 also sp *talleywhacker, talliwhacker, tallow whacker:* The penis. Cf **tallywags**
1941 Hench *Coll.* **seVA,** Talleywhacker = penis. **1942** *Ibid* **NC,** Talleywhacker. . . [Inf] said he had heard it used by negroes and "bad boys" when he was a boy in North Carolina. **1956** *KY Folkl. Rec.* 2.20 **wKY,** In western Kentucky one finds besides *pecker,* . . *jock, talliwhacker,* and *ding-dong.* **1977** Randolph *Pissing in the Snow* 166 **Ozarks** (as of 1922), A woman is mighty lucky to marry a man with a fine big tallywhacker like I got! **1981** Cronkite *On Edge* 175 **TX** (as of c1964), Your mother says she wants me to have a little talk with you about sex. . . You just use that little tallow whacker of yours for peein' through for a while, now. **1982** Heat Moon *Blue Highways* 355 **Philadelphia PA,** "Find a smoother street, captain!" Ron yells. "I'm about to slip with this knife and cut a tallywhacker off!" **1999** Proulx *Close Range* 180 **WY,** The wheat cereal smacking in the pot like a hungry dog, like John Wrench's sap-sticky talley-whacker slapping into Jeri. **2006** Perry *Truck* 81 **nWI,** I have been told the poem is not about a seedling but rather about Dylan's tallywhacker.
2 A hand-held mechanical counter.
1958 McCulloch *Woods Words* 190 **Pacific NW,** Tally whacker—A counter. **1959** *Herald–Press* (St. Joseph MI) 7 Apr 14/1, One experienced game biologist is assigned to each three-man survey team. One man carries a compass, another carries a "Tally-Whacker" which counts his paces. **1986** *DARE* File **nWI,** Toss me the tallywhacker, would you? **2002** in 2004 *DARE* File—Internet **WA,** One person counted [halibut] heads with a tally whacker while another picked up heads and scanned.

talpa n Also *talfa, talky, talpin* [Varr of **catalpa**] **esp KY, TN** Cf **targa, topple, toggle worm**
1900 *MN Horticult.* 28.257, My 'talpa tree, my 'talpa tree;/ 'Tis Minnesota boasts of thee. **1933** *AmSp* 8.1.53 **Ozarks,** Talpa. . . Catalpa. This tree is not native to the Ozarks, I am told, but has been planted in some Ozark towns. In Lawrence County, Mo., there is a settlement called Talpa. Robert Lee Meyers . . says that "*talpa* is a local, rather slangy form of the word." **1954** Harder *Coll.* **cwTN,** Talfa. . . The catalpa tree (*Catalpa speciosa*). **c1960** Wilson *Coll.* **csKY,** Talpin worm. . . Catalpa worm, used for fish bait. ['tælpɪn] or ['tælpɪn]. **1968–69** *DARE* (Qu. P6, . . *Kinds of worms . . used for bait*) Inf **KY**23, Talfa worm ['tæǝlfǝ]; **TN**26, Talfa worm ['tæǝlfɪ ˌwɝˑm]; (Qu. T9, *The common shade tree with large heart-shaped leaves, clusters of white blossoms, and long thin seed pods or 'beans'*) Inf **IN**35, Talky ['tælki]; **KY**21, 43, Talpa ['tælpǝ] (trees).

tamale n[1] Arch spp *tamaule, tamolly, tomale;* freq in comb *hot tamale* [Back-formation from MexSpan *tamales*, pl of *tamal.*

The freq use of *hot tamale* as a fixed comb prob arose from the vendor's cry, "hot tamales!" perh reinterpreted as a ref to the spicy flavor.] **orig chiefly SW, CA, but now widely recognized** See Map
A small portion of cornmeal dough, usu with a spicy meat filling, wrapped in corn shucks and baked or steamed.
1844 (1846) Kendall *Santa Fé Exped.* 2.197, The *tomale* is made of meal, with a slight mixture of red pepper and meat. It is then wrapped in the husks of corn and boiled. **1853** (1854) Bartlett *Personal Narr.* 1.107 **swTX,** *Tamaules* are minced meat, rolled up in corn shucks, and baked on coals. **1854** *Putnam's Mag.* 3.377, Boys with unripe melons, sweet potatoes, cigarritas, eggs, chickens, polonces (sugar in the form of truncated cones about the size of a common tumbler), . . tortillas, tamales, &c. . . were rushing into camp. **1888** Lindley–Widney *CA of South* 89 **swCA,** The *tomale* man is another Mexican feature, who is very similar to the hot-corn hawker of Eastern cities. **1892** *DN* 1.194 **TX,** Tamales are about three or four inches long by one in circumference. It is a favorite dish in Texas, and they are sold on the streets by Mexican pedlers. . . This word is used in Texas as if the singular were *tomale* or *tamale;* it is seldom used except in the plural. **1892** *Overland Mth.* (2d ser) 20.464 **CA,** There is sometimes a picnic, sometimes a fandango, when Mexican friends come from places twenty-five miles distant, where a good deal of whisky is drunk, and many hot tamales eaten. **1896** *Cincinnati Enquirer* (OH) 21 Aug 6/7, Thomas Gates [was arrested] . . on the charge of passing a counterfeit silver dollar on . . an old colored hot tamale man. **1898** *Atlantic Mth.* 81.741 **MT,** The hot tamale (pronounced ta*molly*) . . was introduced by cowboys from the Mexican frontier. *Ibid* 743, There until dawn you lie, hearing at intervals the cry of the hot-tamale man: "Hot tamales! Red-hot tamales! Hot lunch and wiener-wurst! Chickie tamales!" **1913** London *Valley of Moon* 104 **nCA,** They were seated around the table in the kitchen . . making a cold lunch of sandwiches, tamales, and bottled beer. **1932** Bentley *Spanish Terms* 204, The *tamale* is without doubt the most popular with Americans of all Mexican foods. Evidence of this is to be found in the numerous street vendors of *tamales* encountered in American cities and towns. **1939** in Lib. of Congress *Amer. Memory: WPA Life Hist.* (Internet) **Chicago IL,** Then canning hot tamales. That's a dirty job. **1965–70** *DARE* (Qu. H65, *Foreign foods favored by people around here*) 24 Infs, **chiefly SW, CA,** Tamales; **AR**55, **LA**40, **OK**19, 28, 44, **TX**38, Hot tamales; (Qu. H45, *Dishes made with meat, fish, or poultry that everybody around here would know, but that people in other places might not*) 19 Infs, **chiefly SW, CA,** Tamale; **MO**6, 15, **TX**32, Hot tamales; (Qu. H20b, . . *Names . . for pancakes*) Inf **WV**3, Hot tamales; (Qu. H41, . . *Kinds of roll or bun sandwiches . . in a round bun or roll*) Inf **MN**1, Hot tamale. **1995** *News* (Frederick MD) 20 Oct sec C 7/5, *Eating Out.* . . Some choices include a taco and tamale; enchilada and taco; tamale, enchilada and chile relleno. **1995** *N. Hills News Rec.* (Warrendale PA) 17 May sec D 1/2 **MI,** Every day, all year, Serafina makes tamales for . . the main restaurant . . in Detroit's Mexicantown and for the takeout satellites around the area.

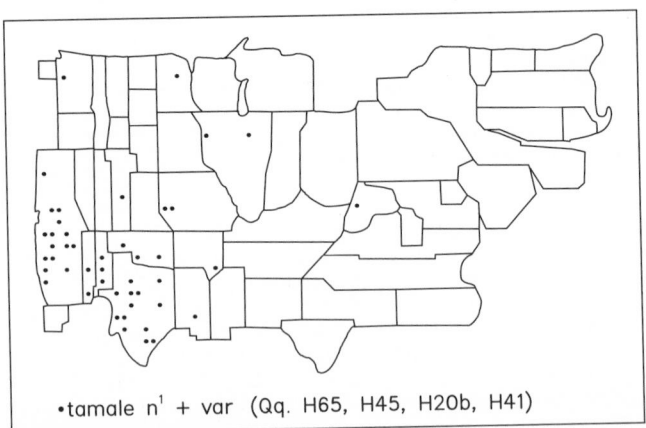

•tamale n[1] + var (Qq. H65, H45, H20b, H41)

tamale n[2] See **tomalley**

tamale pie n **orig chiefly SW, esp CA; now more widely recognized** See Map
A dish made with the same ingredients as a **tamale,** but baked in a casserole rather than in corn shucks.

1911 Williams Pub. Lib. Assoc. *Ariz. Cook Book* 220 *(DA),* Tamale Pie. **1928** *Chicago Tribune* (IL) 12 Aug sec 8 5/6, Lucille Webster Gleason's tamale pie is a perfect meal in itself. **1940** Brown *Amer. Cooks* 584 **NM,** *Chicken tamale pie*—Cut chicken in small pieces and cook in plenty of suet with 2 cloves garlic, 1 small onion, salt, a little chili powder, and 1 can tomatoes, last. Cook 3–4 hours. Line baking dish with cooked white corn meal mush, then chicken meat, alternating with mush until dish is full. Cover with sauce in which chicken was cooked and heat well in oven. **1955** (1956) Clark *Best Cookery Middle West* 99, *Tamale Pie. . .* Cook the corn meal over hot water until stiff and smooth. Now line the bottom of a buttered casserole with the corn meal. . . Pour in the meat mixture, and drop large spoonfuls of mush in a pattern over the top of the casserole. **1965–70** *DARE* (Qu. H45, *Dishes made with meat, fish, or poultry that everybody around here would know, but that people in other places might not*) 9 Infs, 7 **CA,** Tamale pie; **CA**167, Tamale pie—used for potluck suppers; (Qu. H50, *Dishes made with beans, peas, or corn that everybody around here knows, but people in other places might not*) Infs **CA**99, 113, 194, **TX**27, Tamale pie; (Qu. H65, *Foreign foods favored by people around here*) Inf **IL**117, Tamale pie. **1999** *Capital* (Annapolis MD) 6 Oct sec B 1/1, The next two recipes have been sent in by readers. . . The second is for a Tamale Pie. **1999** *Post–Std.* (Syracuse NY) 8 Sept sec D 2/5, *Recipe for diabetics*—Chicken Tamale Pie . . is a contemporary version of tamale pie that uses boneless chicken breasts instead of ground beef and pork sausage. **2002** in 2004 *DARE* File—Internet **AZ,** I was finally able to duplicate Mom's tamale pie, and it would bring back Davey [sic] Crockett from the Alamo.

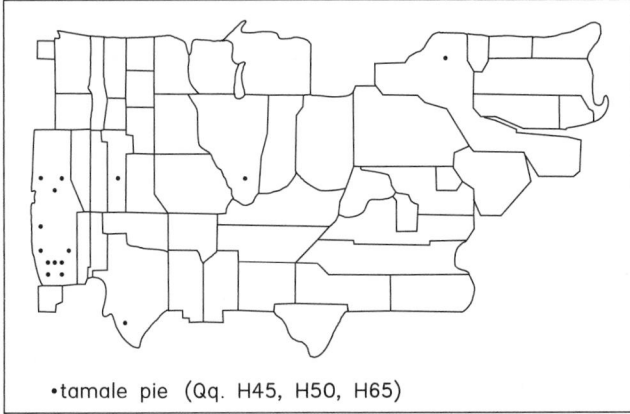

•tamale pie (Qq. H45, H50, H65)

tamalley See **tomalley**

tamarack n   Also *tam(a)rac, tam(e)rack, tamarick, tamarock, termerack*

1 An American tree of the genus *Larix.* **chiefly Nth, West** Also called **hack** n[5] **2, hackmatack 1a, larch 1, tamarisk 2.** For other names of var spp see **juniper 2a, mountain larch, red ~**

1805 (1905) Clark *Orig. Jrls. Lewis & Clark Exped.* 3.66 **VA,** The Mountains which we passed to day . . thickly Strowed with falling timber & Pine Spruce fur Hackmatak & Tamerack. [**1810** Michaux *Histoire des Arbres* 1.29, Larix americana. *American larch. . . Tamarack,* par les Hollandois du New-Jersey. [=Larix americana. *American larch. . . Tamarack,* [so called] by the Dutch of New Jersey.]] **1817** in 1920 *WI Mag. Hist.* 3.351, Crossed a large meadow, a termerack swamp &c. **1842** Barstow *Hist.* NH 453, Boughs of the tamarac and spruce overhang the road. **1869** U.S. Dept. Ag. *Rept. of Secy. for 1868* 176 **AK,** Frames of canoes . . are afterwards covered with its bark, sewed with spruce or tamarack *(Larix)* roots, and the seams calked with spruce gum. **1897** Sudworth *Arborescent Flora* 32, *Larix laricina. . .* Tamarack (Me., N.H, Vt., Mass., R.I., N.Y., N.J., Pa., Del., Ind., Ill., Wis., Mich., Minn., Nebr., Ohio, Ont.) *Ibid* 33, *Larix occidentalis. . .* Tamarack (Oreg.) . . *Larix lyallii. . .* Tamarack (Idaho, Wash., Oreg.) **1945** MI Ag. Exper. Sta. *Technical Bulletin* 201.14, There are numerous swamps, often covered with dense stands of white cedar, tamarack *(Larix laricina),* and black spruce. **1965–70** *DARE* (Qu. T13, *. . Names . . for . . tamarack*) 163 Infs, **chiefly Nth, West,** Tamarack; **CT**4, 23, **NY**30, Tamarack—larch (tree); **ID**5, Tamarack—western larch goes by this name around here; **MA**37, Tamarack—something like larch; **MT**4, Tamarack—really western larch; **NE**3, Tamarack—some call it a

tamarick ['tæmərɪk]; **NY**97, "Tamarack" most common, "larch" occasional; **NY**109, Tamarack [tə'mɛrɪk]; (Qu. T15, . . *Kinds of swamp trees*) 94 Infs, **chiefly Gt Lakes, Upstate NY,** Tamarack; (Qu. T5, . . *Kinds of evergreens, other than pine*) 32 Infs, 25 **MN, MI, WI, Upstate NY,** Tamarack; **ID**4, **MN**19, **OR**13, **VT**10, **WI**58, **WV**2, Tamarack—larch; **MI**10, Tamarack—its needles drop; **MI**14, Tamarack—but is deciduous; **MI**79, Tamarack—coniferous, but not evergreen; **MN**14, Tamarack—a conifer, but not an evergreen, also called larch or western larch in some places—the tamarack is not very thrifty, i.e., it does not do well; **MN**38, Tamarack—it does lose its needles; **NY**6, Tamrck; **NY**68, Tamarack, but it sheds its needles in the fall; **NY**75, Tamarack—they shed their needles; another name is larch, but we didn't ever call 'em larch; **WA**1, Tamarack [tæmræk]; **WI**64, Tamarack—the only one that drops its needles; **WI**78, Tamarack ['tæm,ræk]; **MI**116, **MN**2, Tamarock; (Qu. T16, . . *Kinds of trees . . 'special'*) Infs **MN**29, **NE**8, **OK**32, **WA**33, Tamarack; (Qu. S17, . . *Kinds of plants . . that . . cause itching and swelling*) Inf **WI**17, Tamarack; (Qu. T17, . . *Kinds of pine trees;* not asked in early QRs) Inf **WI**48, Tamarack. [*DARE* Ed: Some of these Infs may refer instead to other senses below.] **1985** Clark *From Mailbox* 203 **ME,** In some parts of Maine people call the tamarack the "juniper tree".

2 also *tamarack pine:* **=lodgepole pine.   esp CA**

1868 (1869) Browne *Resources Pacific Slope* 433, The kinds of timber chiefly used [for telegraph poles is] redwood, pine, cedar, and tamarack. **1871** *Yosemite Guide-Book* 52 **cCA,** That we are respectably high up in the Sierra is rendered evident by the predominance of the *Pinus contorta,* a rather small tree, with its leaves short and in pairs, usually called "tamarack" by the settlers. **1897** Sudworth *Arborescent Flora* 23, *Lodgepole Pine. . . Common Names.* Tamarack (Wyo., Utah, Mont., Cal.) . . Tamarack Pine (Cal.) **1910** Hart *Vigilante Girl* 146 **nCA,** A faint puff of smoke from behind a tamarack tree showed whence it had come. **1910** Jepson *Silva CA* 81, *Pinus murrayana* [=*P. contorta*]. . . Tamrac Pine. *Ibid* 82, The Tamrac Pine, commonly called Tamrac and everywhere readily recognized by its two needles, bur-like cones and very thin bark, inhabits the Sierra Nevada. **1915** Muir *Travels AK* 49, The "tamarac pine" or black pine, as the variety of *P. contorta* is called here, is yellowish-green, in marked contrast with the dark lichen-draped spruce. **1947** Peattie *Sierra Nevada* 160 **CA,** Lodgepole pine . . is plain tamarack to many Californians. **1966** Barnes–Jensen *Dict. UT Slang* 42, *Tamarack* . . a name sometimes given to the Lodgepole or Black Pine *(Pinus murrayana).* **1969** *DARE* (Qu. T13) Inf **CA**120, Tamarack—a pine, grows in the granite—a place here called Tamarack Pines.

3 Either the **red spruce** or the **black spruce 1.**

1892 (1895) Dugger *Balsam Groves* 41 **NC,** Black spruce *(Abies nigra)* which the natives call tamarack. . . is so much like the more abundant balsam that casual observers pass them for one and the same. **1903** Small *Flora SE U.S.* 29, *Picea Mariāna. . .* In moist soil, Newfoundland to the Northwest Territory, New Jersey and Minnesota, and in the mountains of North Carolina. *Black Spruce. He Balsam. Tamarack.* **1933** Small *Manual SE Flora* 7, *P[icea] rubens. . . Red-spruce. . . Tamarack. . .* Often crowns mountain tops with a pure growth.

4 **=tamarisk 1.**   [By confusion of the two similar names] Cf **tamarisk 2**

1904 Kellogg *Forest Planting W. KS* 52.15, The tamarix is often called "tamarack," or "mountain tamarack," but these names do not properly apply to it. **1941** *Torreya* 41.49 **TX,** *Tamarix* spp.—Salt-cedar, tamarack, Texas Panhandle. **1966–69** *DARE* (Qu. T5, . . *Kinds of evergreens, other than pine*) Inf **AZ**10, Tamarack—on river bottoms. (Qu. T13, . . *Names . . for . . tamarack*) Inf **CA**65, Tamarack, [corr to] tamarisk—pink, sweet-smelling, fast-growing; **CO**15, Tamarack—bush, not a tree—along rivers; **CO**22, Tamarack—a bush with purple flowers; **KS**15, Tamarack—used for hedgerows; **OK**7, Tamarack—on the river—not here; **OK**32, Tamarack—a few on the Beaver [River]; [**1971** Dodge *100 Desert Wildflowers* 43, *Tamarisk*—Sometimes confused with tamarack because of the similarity of names.]

tamarack pine See **tamarack 2**

tamarack warbler n

=Connecticut warbler.

[**1895** Seton in Chapman *Hdbk. Birds* 370, "Connecticut Warbler is an unfortunate misnomer for this species. "Swamp" or "Tamarac Warbler," or "Bog Black-Throat," would have been much more truly descriptive.] **1917** (1923) *Birds Amer.* 3.156, *Connecticut Warbler. . .* Tamarack Warbler; Swamp Warbler. **1946** Hausman *Eastern Birds* 534, *Oporornis agilis. . .* Tamarack Warbler.

tamarick See **tamarack**

tamarisk n

1 Std: a plant of the genus *Tamarix* introduced into the US in the mid-1800s, now naturalized and invasive in the Southwest. Also called **salt cedar 1, scrub ~, tamarack 4, tammy**

2 =**tamarack 1;** see quots. [By confusion of the two similar names]

a1817 (1821) Dwight *Travels* 1.36 **NEng,** Hacmontac, or Tamarisk. **1842** *S. Lit. Messenger* 8.657 **WI,** The army . . took up a strong position beyond on the bank of Clear-water creek, not far from its junction with Rock river. Opposite was a very extensive and almost impenetrable tamarisk swamp. **1856** (1857) Parker *MN Hdbk.* 69 **MN,** Above this, from Coon Creek to Fort Ripley, extends an almost continuous tamarisk swamp. . . Where the swamp extends to the [Mississippi] river, the road is almost impassable. **1869** *Ladies' Repository* 3.297 **WA,** This brings the traveler through the mountain range out upon the high mountain prairies which stretch away eastward one hundred and fifty miles, until interrupted by the pine, fir, and tamarisk forests of the Blue Mountains. **1985** Dodge *Flowers SW Deserts* 47, The name tamarisk is often confused with the name of the larch or tamarack tree. There is little similarity except in the name.

tamarock See **tamarack**

tamaule See **tamale**

tambor n

A **rockfish 3** (here: *Sebastodes ruberrimus*).

1881 CA *App. Jrls. Legislature* 2.12.37, S[ebastodes] ruber [=S. ruberrimus]—Large Red Rockfish, Tambor, is probably the largest of all the species, reaching a weight of twelve pounds, or even more. **1884** Goode *Fisheries U.S.* 1.266 **CA,** Red Rock-fish. . . At Monterey it is called by the Portuguese "Tambor," a name evidently transferred from some Atlantic species.

tame ape See **ape** n **2**

tame huckleberry n

A cultivated **serviceberry B;** see quot.

1906 *DN* 3.160 **nwAR,** Tame huckleberry. . . Cultivated service-berry. "You can get three boxes of tame huckleberries for two bits." **1919** Larned *Borderland* 143, The mountain blueberry . . will not grow on low levels or it degenerates there into the tame huckleberry.

tamerack See **tamarack**

tammara See **tomorrow**

tammy n

=**tamarisk 1.**

1992 Ghiglieri *Canyon* 111 **nAZ,** Feathery little tamarisk seeds—a quarter *billion* seeds in a single season from a big tammy—had blown upstream for miles. **1999** in 2005 *DARE* File—Internet **SW,** Today, *Tamarix,* commonly known as "tammies" (Kauffman, personal communication) are some of the most widespread species in riparian areas throughout the Southwest. **2004** *Sierra* July/Aug (Internet) **nwAZ,** It's difficult not to admire the sheer determination of tamarisk, even as you're trying to kill it. . . Across a small stream, one of the larger trees, about 10 or 12 feet tall, starts to creak, then falls with a whump! "Kill tammys!" someone yells. "Boy, that was satisfying," says a fellow tammy warrior.

tamolly See **tamale**

tamoly, holy See **moly, holy**

tamrac(k) See **tamarack**

'tan' See **stand** v

tanbark See **tanbark oak c**

tanbark, like (or quicker than) hell beating See **hell 5**

tanbark oak n [From the use of the bark in tanning]

An **oak** or related tree that produces tanbark, as:

a also *tan oak:* =**swamp chestnut oak 1.**

1883 Smith *Rept. for 1881 & 1882* 296 **AL,** On the high lands or extensive tablelands are . . found . . Q[uercus] Prinus, (the mountain or tan-bark oak) [etc]. **1886** *Harper's New Mth. Mag.* 73.55 **eKY,** On the summits one sees the tan-bark oak. **1897** Sudworth *Arborescent Flora* 156, Quercus prinus. . . Tanbark Oak (Ala.) *Ibid* 169, Quercus velu-

tina. . . Tanbark Oak (Ill.) *Ibid* 179, Quercus densiflora [=Lithocarpus d.] . . Tanbark Oak (Cal.) **1908** Rogers *Tree Book* 203, Tan-bark Oak (*Quercus Prinus . .*). *Ibid* 204, The name. . . "Tan-bark oak" calls attention to the tannin which makes this tree the prey of "peelers" throughout its range. Only the black oak yields as good bark to the tanner. **1939** *Hall Coll.* **wNC,** And [the bears] had been all over the tan-oak trees a-feedin'. . . They had just a little one [=a bear] treed up a little tan oak. **1940** *Ibid,* The tan oak is used for getting tanbark off of. **1999** *DARE* File—Internet **PA,** Oak wilt occurs west of the Susquehanna River in Pennsylvania. The fungus . . attacks most oaks but. . . American . . chestnuts, tanbark oak, and bush chinquapin are also susceptible.

b A **black oak** (here: *Quercus velutina*).

1897 [see **a** above]. **1908** Britton *N. Amer. Trees* 290, It [=Quercus velutina] is also called Yellow oak, . . Dyer's oak, Tan bark oak, and Spotted oak. **1950** Peattie *Nat. Hist. Trees* 225, Quercus velutina. . . Yellow, Dyer's, or Tanbark Oak.

c also *tanbark, tan oak:* An evergreen tree *(Lithocarpus densiflorus)* native to California and Oregon. Also called **hedgehog oak, live ~ 2, peach ~ 2, squaw ~**

1884 Sargent *Forests of N. Amer.* 155, Quercus densiflora [=Lithocarpus d.] . . Tanbark oak. Chestnut oak. Peach oak. . . The bark, rich in tannin, very largely used and preferred to that of any other tree of the Pacific forests for tanning. **1896** *Overland Mth.* (2d ser) 28.347 **nCA,** The abundance of tanbark oak in the county and the comparative inexpensiveness of the bark have rendered the manufacture of leather a profitable industry. **1897** [see **a** above]. **1898** *Jrl. Amer. Folkl.* 11.279 **CA,** Quercus densiflora. . . tan-bark. **1905** U.S. Forest Serv. *Bulletin* 61.40 [Logging terms], *Jay hawk, to.* To strip one 4-foot length of bark from a tanbark oak, leaving the tree standing. (P[acific] C[oast] F[orest]) **1910** Jepson *Silva CA* 237, The bark of Tan Oak furnishes the best tannage known for the production of heavy leathers. **1913** London *Valley of Moon* 526 **CA,** Trees and vines had conspired to weave the leafy roof . . lofty tan-bark oaks, scaled and wrapped and interwound with wild grape and flaming poison oak. **1949** Howell *Marin Flora* 7 **CA,** The laurels and tanbark oaks form a more conspicuous part of the forest. **1967–69** *DARE* (Qu. T10, . . Kinds of oak trees) Infs **CA**101, 137, Tan oak; **CA**105, California tan oak; (Qu. T5, . . Kinds of evergreens, other than pine) Inf **CA**31, Peach oak . . a tan oak laurel [sic]. **2001** *DARE* File—Internet **CA,** As all of us in the Santa Cruz mountains know, the sudden death of tan bark oaks (Lithocarpus densiflora) has left large tan oaks which appeared healthy last year declining and dead this summer.

tanbark tree n

A **hemlock 2** (here: *Tsuga canadensis*).

1900 Lyons *Plant Names* 380, T[suga] Canadensis. . . Tanbark tree. . . *Bark* extensively used for tanning. **1930** Sievers *Amer. Med. Plants* 33, Tsuga canadensis. . . Tanbark tree. . . Found in forests from Ontario south to Virginia and Alabama and west to Michigan and Wisconsin. **1971** Krochmal *Appalachia Med. Plants* 258, Tsuga canadensis. . . Tanbark tree. . . The bark has been used primarily because of its tannin content, which makes it a strong astringent.

tan bay n

=**loblolly bay 1.**

1884 Sargent *Forests of N. Amer.* 25, Tan Bay. . . Gordonia pubescens. . . The bark, rich in tannin, was once occasionally used, locally, in tanning leather. **1897** Sudworth *Arborescent Flora* 273 **MS, FL, LA,** Gordonia lasianthus. . . Tan Bay. **1933** Small *Manual SE Flora* 877, Tan-bay. . . The southern extremity of the range is about Lake Okeechobee in Florida. The bark is some times used for tanning. The red heartwood, close-grained but light and soft, is locally used for cabinet-work. **1976** Bruce *How to Grow Wildflowers* 144, Gordonia lasianthus, the Loblolly-bay (also called Tan-bay, Black-laurel, and, erroneously, Red-bay) has much the same range as Stewartia malacodendron.

tandem adv, n Usu |'tændəm|; also esp **NEng** |'tæntm̩, 'tæntrəm, -trim| Pronc-sp *tantrum*

Std senses, var forms.

1818 Fessenden *Ladies Monitor* 172 **NEng,** Provincial words . . to be avoided. . . *tantrum* for tandem. **1891** *DN* 1.166 **cNY,** *d* becomes *t,* especially after *l, n,* as in . . [tæntm̩] < *tandem.* **1892** *DN* 1.211 **seMA,** *Tantrum:* tandem. **1939** *LANE* Map 174 *(Team)* 1 inf, **RI,** [tæntrɪm tim], two horses driven in single file. **1943** *Ibid* Map 573–4 *(Sled; sleigh)* 1 inf, **neME,** [tæˀntrəm]. **1979** *AmSp* 54.100 **sME** (as of 1899–1910), *Tantrum.* . . Tandem.

tangleberry n
=**dangleberry 1.**

1876 Cooper *Forest Culture* 307, Gaylussacia frondosa. . . The Blue Tangleberry of North America. **1891** *Century Dict.* 6180, *Tangleberry*. . . The dangleberry: same as *bluetangle*. **1903** Porter *Flora PA* 241, *Tangleberry*. . . In moist woods, N.H. to Fla., Ohio and La. **1939** Medsger *Edible Wild Plants* 69, The Tangleberry. . . bears . . berries on slender drooping stems. They are dark blue with a whitish bloom, sweet and pleasing to the taste. . . Generally occurs near the coast. **1972** Brown *Wildflowers LA* 127, *Tangleberry, Dangleberry—Gaylussacia frondosa*. . . Widespread in pinelands of southeastern Louisiana. Also Mississippi.

tangle breeches n   Also sp *tangle britches*   Also *tangled jackets*   Cf **keekling, tangle cake**
=**cruller.**

1858 *Globe* (Huntingdon PA) 8 Dec 4/1, *Tangle Britches.*—Take 3 eggs, a third of a tinful of shortening, a pint of buttermilk, warm the milk and shortening together, make the dough very stiff. **1874** *Harper's Bazaar* 29 Aug 559, *Tangle-breeches*—This is a Western recipe, and especially delights the young folks. Six eggs beaten light, one pound of sugar, a quarter of a pound of butter, and as much flour as will make them thick enough to roll. Cut them into square blocks, slit, tangle, and drop them to fry in hot lard until they are brown. Take them out, drain, and grate on them a little sugar. **1885** *Daily News* (Frederick MD) 17 Feb [4]/1 (newspaperarchive.com), *Local Department. Take Warning.*—The house-keeper who does not make tangle breeches, kinklins, or fans knochts on Ash Wednesday, will have bad luck all year. **1918** *Eve. State Jrl.* (Lincoln NE) 2 Sept 4/3 **IN,** If you're real good I'll come over and cook you some tangle britches. . . Them's what some people call doughnuts, only they're cut different before they go into the hot grease. **1935** Frederick *PA Dutch* 244, *Tangled Jackets*—1 pint of sour milk, 3 eggs, ½ teaspoonful soda, 1 teaspoonful salt, 1 pound flour. Mix and cook in deep fat. **1941** *Sun* (Baltimore MD) 30 Sept 8/1, Associated always with them [=fastnachts] were the strange little confections we called "kinklin's" or sometimes "tangle-britches," which were made of a dough of lard and flour like pie crust, and also twisted before frying. They, too, were sprinkled with powdered sugar and were so delicate and frail they would almost melt in your mouth. **1968** *DARE* (Qu. H28, *Different shapes or types of doughnuts*) Inf **MD**19, Tangle breeches ['tæŋgl ‚brɪčɪz]—long, twisted shape, mother used to make. **1979** *Today Show Letters* **cKS,** In Poughkeepsie, what in Kansas were known as "tanglebritches", a twisted doughnut, were simply called "doughnuts". **1986** Pederson *LAGS Concordance,* 1 inf, **cAL,** Tangle breeches—German relatives made. **2000** in 2004 *DARE* File—Internet **cePA,** The dough was rolled out thin, and cut into pieces 3x4 inches and then 3 slits cut in the center, then deep fat fried. . . I believe my grandmother called them "Hobalscharten"? My mother's generation called them "tangle britches".

tanglebrush n   Also *tanglewood*

A **forestiera** (here: *Forestiera pubescens*).

1923 *Sierra Club Bulletin* 11.88 **CA,** Unless legal measures are taken speedily, the next generation will know only by hearsay the loveliness of California's tanglebrush roadsides in autumn. **1941** Jaeger *Wildflowers* 181 **Desert SW,** *Tanglebrush. Forestiera neomexicana* [=*F. pubescens*]. . . This odd, opposite-leaved shrub. . usually occurs in mountainous areas where ground waters are near the surface. **1960** Vines *Trees SW* 850, *Forestiera pubescens*. . . Sometimes a small tree . . , but usually only a straggling, irregularly shaped shrub. . . Also known under the vernacular names of Devil's-elbow . . and Tanglewood.

tangle cake n   Cf **tangle breeches**
=**cruller.**   Note: The description in quot 1995 appears to be erroneous.

1957 Showalter *Mennonite Cookbook* 346 **MD,** *Tangle Cakes.* . . Roll dough in thin pieces and cut in strips ½ inch wide. Tangle several strips together and fry in deep fat 375°. **1962** *PA Ger. Folkl. Soc. Yearbook* 26.108, In Shenandoah County they made "tangle-cakes" on Shrove Tuesday. If you didn't, you wouldn't have luck with your flax.

tangled jackets   See **tangle breeches**

tangle-eyed adj

Having squint eyes; hence n *tangle-eye* a person with such eyes—also used as a nickname.

1892 *Bismarck Daily Tribune* (ND) 9 Jan 4/3 **MD,** The cross eyed hoodoo remains fixed, as it were, in popular estimation, and nothing will queer you so soon as the blighting glance of the tangle eyed man or woman. **1939** in 2004 (acc) Lexis–Nexis Legal Research *State Case Law: OK* (Internet), A man by the name of Tony Williams, whose nickname was "Tangle-eye," was managing the dancing platform. **1967–70** *DARE* (Qu. X26b, *If a person's eyes look in different directions, looking outward, he's _____*) Infs **TX**37, 92, Tangle-eyed. **1967** *DARE* Tape **TX**19, And a cross-eyed man, they'd refer to him as tangle-eyed. [**1986** Pederson *LAGS Concordance,* 1 inf, **cMS,** Tangle face—cross-eyed [inf Black].]

tanglefoot n

1 also *tanglefoot whisk(e)y:* Inferior or illicit whiskey; other strong drink.   *old-fash*   Cf **busthead, popskull,** DS DD21b, c

1859 *Olney Times* (IL) 4 Mar 2/2, We abandoned the contest, leaving our opponent to enjoy the emoluments of the office, that has been acquired thro' the corrupting influences of tangle-foot whisky. **1859** *Wellsboro Agitator* (PA) 25 Aug 2/2, The immortal Gillis . . has been sent to hob nob, play "seven up" and drink tangle foot whiskey with the King of the Kickapoos. **1867** Harris *Sut Lovingood Yarns* 113 **TN,** I got *two* par ove boots, an' ole tangle-foot whisky enuf to fill 'em. **1885** *Critic* new ser 4.153, I have a brother-in-law who has been a little too fond of tanglefoot whiskey. **1911** *Hunter-Trader-Trapper* 21.93 **TX,** From the music he was making, I knew he had some tanglefoot. **1946** Nelson *Land Dacotahs* 44 **MO,** I can jump higher, hit harder, spit farther, move sideways quicker and drink more tanglefoot whiskey than any son-of-a-bitch on the Missouri River! **1986** *LAGS Concordance,* 1 inf, **cwAR,** Tanglefoot—strong, homemade wine—elderberry.

2 =**hobblebush.**   [See quot]   Cf **tangle-legs, triptoe**

1894 *Jrl. Amer. Folkl.* 7.90 **NH,** *Viburnum lantanoides*. . . Tanglefoot. . . From the fact that the branches often take root at the ends.

3 =**deerweed 1.**

1911 CA Ag. Exper. Sta. Berkeley *Bulletin* 217.997, *Lotus glaber* [=*L. scoparius*]. . . Deerweed. . . Tanglefoot. . . Common everywhere in the Coast ranges in the hill country. . . A very erratic honey producer.

4 as *tanglefoot weed:* A **heath aster;** see quot.

1970 *DARE* (Qu. S21, . . *Weeds . . that are a trouble in gardens and fields*) Inf **KY**83, Tanglefoot weed; (Qu. S25, . . *The small wild chrysanthemum-like flowers . . that bloom in fields late in the fall*) Inf **KY**83, Tanglefoot weed—same as wild asters.

5 See quot.

1910 *DN* 3.455 **seVT, nwMA,** *Tanglefoot*. . . The froth or foam on top of a pail of newly drawn milk. Very rare in W. Brattleboro, Vt., but, I think, very common in Deerfield, Mass.

‡**6** See quot.   Cf **tanglewood 1**

1966 *DARE* (Qu. C28, *A place where underbrush, weeds, vines and small trees grow together so that it's nearly impossible to get through*) Inf **MI**23, Tanglefoot.

tanglefoot weed   See **tanglefoot 4**

tanglefoot whisk(e)y   See **tanglefoot 1**

tangle grass n

A **muhly (grass)** (here: *Muhlenbergia porteri*).

1941 *Torreya* 41.46 **AZ,** *Muhlenbergia porteri*. . . Tangle grass, white grama.

tangle-gut n

1 =**dodder.**

1970 Correll *Plants TX* 1255, *Cuscuta*. . . Additional vernacular names to those above are . . "tangle gut," . . "strangle vine."

2 also *tangle-guts:* A **spring beauty 1** such as *Claytonia caroliniana* or *C. virginica.*   *esp* sAppalachians   [See quot 2001]

1969 *Jrl. Arnold Arboretum* 50.588 **WV,** In parts of West Virginia *Claytonia caroliniana* is known as "tangle-gut." **1982** Slone *How We Talked* 47 **eKY** (as of c1950), [In a list of "salet" plants:] Tangle gut. **2000** OH Dept. Nat. Resources *Nat. OH* Summer (Internet), Many plants have more than one colloquial name. . . Listed below are English names for. . . Ohio natives. . . toothache tree[.] . . tangle-guts. *Ibid,* [Tangle-guts is] Spring-beauty, *Claytonia virginica.* **2001** in 2005 *DARE* File—Internet **swWV,** I remember mom cooking tangle gut. . . The little purple flowers were pretty but the twisted little vines kept reminding you of it's [sic] name. **2003** *DARE* File—Internet **ceKY,** I don't remember tangle gut, but my wife who was born in Martin County and later moved to Floyd, says when she was a girl they picked tangle gun [sic] in to spring time. . . It was served as salad with just hot grease poured over it, the same way some folk fix lettuce. *Ibid* **ceKY,** *Claytonia virginica* (Tanglegut). *Ibid* **swWV,** I have made my fair share of trips to the mountains to pick . . wild greens such as tangle gut, and dandelion greens.

tanglehead n

A forage grass of the genus *Heteropogon,* usu *H. contortus.* For other names of this sp see **pili**

1920 Clements *Plant Indicators* 323 **AZ,** Tangle head *(Heteropogon contortus)* has also made a good showing on the small range enclosure. **1948** Neal *In Gardens HI* 72, *Tanglehead, pili. Heteropogon contortus. . .* It serves as forage in the southwestern United States and Hawaii, preferably before the flowers, with their long bristles, develop. **1970** Correll *Plants TX* 210, *Heteropogon contortus. . . Tanglehead. . .* Local in sandy prairies of extreme s. Tex. and in Trans-Pecos mts. . . *Heteropogon melanocarpus. . . Sweet tanglehead. . .* The plant when fresh emits an odor like that of citronella oil. **1997** Ruyle–Young *AZ Range Grasses* 83, *Tanglehead—Heteropogon contortus. . .* Tanglehead begins growth early in the spring and at this time is readily eaten by cattle and horses.

tangle-legs n [See quot 1860] Cf **tanglefoot 2**
=**hobblebush.**

1818 Eaton *Botany* 489, *Viburnum. . . lantanoides* (hobble-bush, tangle-legs). . . Stem very flexible and crooked, about 5 or 7 feet long. **1860** Curtis *Cat. Plants NC* 91, *Tangle-Legs. . .* A small straggling shrub found in cold damp places in the Mountains. The branches spread upon the ground, and, taking root at their ends, form well secured loops for tripping the feet of inexperienced way-farers. **1901** Lounsberry *S. Wild Flowers* 478, *Tangle-legs. . .* Among the slopes of the high mountains in North Carolina, often where deep shadows fall, this viburnum is most conspicuous among the shrubbery.

tanglement See **-ment B**

tanglewood n

1 Thickly entangled underbrush; also fig. **esp NEast**

1845 *Primitive Expounder* 2.342, He is coming out of the shades and tangle-wood of orthodoxy, and has got a glimpse of the clear field of gospel truth. [**1853** Hawthorne *Tanglewood Tales* [title] **MA.**] **1859** Willis *Convalescent* 322 **NY,** Around and behind, was an impenetrable thicket of logs and tanglewood. **1865** *Atlantic Mth.* 15.521 **NY,** A little zig-zag stream . . which passes through this tanglewood, accounts for many of its features and productions. **1891** *New Engl. Mag.* 11.20 **eMA,** The once scraggy forests, strewn with tanglewood and underbrush, are now as trim as an urban grove. **1966–69** *DARE* (Qu. C28, *A place where underbrush, weeds, vines and small trees grow together so that it's nearly impossible to get through*) Infs **MA**62, **NY**8, **PA**96, **WA**3, Tanglewood.

2 See **tanglebrush.**

tank n[1]

1 A natural or artificial pond used as a reservoir. [This corresponds to the orig sense in which *tank* was borrowed in the 17th cent, appar from the Portuguese in India; the US use, however, was prob reborrowed from, or at least strongly infl by, AmSpan *tanque.*] **chiefly SW, esp TX** Cf **tinaja**

[**1826** in 1924 Austin *Papers* 1.1483 **TX,** In an instant, all the Empty *Tanques* were filled, and there is a supply of water for nearly a year to come.] **1869** *Overland Mth.* 3.130 **TX,** A "tank" in Texas is a pond of fresh water. **1890** *Amer. Antiq. & Oriental Jrl.* 12.201 **SW,** The surface is smooth sandstone, with here and there great hollows filled with rainwater. These places are called "tanks" by the ranchmen. **1896** *DN* 1.426 **TX,** *Tank:* pond. "Drive your horse into the tank." **1897** Hough *Story Cowboy* 14 **sTX,** Across some such small stream the cattle man has thrown a great dam. . . Thus is formed a vast "tank," at which the cattle water. **1915** *DN* 4.229 **wTX,** *Tank. . .* An artificial lake. "Most west Texas towns get their water from tanks." **1941** Writers' Program *Guide OK* 121, A small body of water is a "tank." **1941** Writers' Program *Guide UT* 505, Almost beneath the bridge is a "tank" or pothole in the slickrock such as desert men cherish as sources of drinking water. **1962** Atwood *Vocab. TX* 41, A body of water impounded for the watering of livestock and for other purposes is known throughout most of the state as a *tank . . ;* this term occurs in all but the easternmost extremities of Texas. . . This sort of pool is occasionally referred to as a *stock*

tank . . or *dirt tank. . . Pond . .* is rare except in East Texas, but it is usual in Arkansas and Louisiana. **1965–70** *DARE* (Qu. C4b, *Is there any difference in the size [of a lake and a pond]? For example, would people go fishing or swimming in a pond?*) Inf **IL**5, Tank—small pond, holds water for irrigation; **NM**6, Tank—used for watering stock; some ponds (tanks) might be used for fishing (private) or swimming; **NM**11, Tank = pond; **TX**4, Tank—scraped out and built; surface tank to hold rainwater; **TX**5, Tank—dammed arroyo used for watering stock; **TX**10, Tank—dam up a little riverbed; **TX**13, Tank—dam up drainage area to catch runoff water; **TX**22, Tank—formed by dam across river; **TX**29, Tank—always man-made, one covers 640 acres; **TX**37, Pond, tank (not much used)—about the same; **TX**56, Pond and tank are the same thing; tank used here, farther north they say pond; **TX**64, Tank—small body of fresh water; **TX**84, Tank—smaller than lake, usually artificial, for livestock; **TX**96, Tank—a pond for stockwater, man-made. [*DARE* Ed: Only instances of *tank* that clearly refer to a pond-like body of water are included here; many other instances were recorded in which *tank* has some other sense or where the comments recorded are insufficient to determine the sense intended.] **1969** O'Connor *Horse & Buggy West* 155 **AZ,** [Footnote:] In Arizona lingo a "tank" is a pond created by a dam built across an arroyo to catch and hold rainwater for cattle or for irrigation. **1999** *DARE* File—Internet **TX,** We have very sandy soil. Should I be able to construct a tank myself? If so, is it simply a matter of moving dirt out to form the tank and placing the dirt around it to form a dam?

2 =**peanut gallery.**

1900 *DN* 2.67 [College slang], *Tank. . .* Top gallery of a theatre.

tank v, n[2] See **thank**

tankersome adj [Var of *cantankerous; EDD* has one citation from Suffolk for this form.] Cf **dangersome**

1969 *DARE* (Qu. Z16, *A small child who is rough, misbehaves, and doesn't obey*) Inf **GA**72, Unruly, tankersome.

tanksful See **thank**

tank-stove n Also *oil-tank stove* **AK**

A stove made from a used oil drum.

1904 in 1906 *AK Rept.* 2.271, Tupper Thompson slept bibulously behind the oil tank stove. **1958** Carrighar *Moonlight* 237 **AK,** The cabin was pleasing. . . In the center was that big bellyful of comfort, a "tank-stove"—an oil drum turned on its side with a door cut in one end, the standard stove in north-western Alaska. **1978** *AK Mag.* 44.68 (as of 1900), At the combination bar, gambling room and roadhouse, I thawed out before a roaring wood fire in an oil-tank stove. **2004** *DARE* File—Internet **AK,** Our central heating was an oil tank stove that Papa made into a stove which had an oven and everything.

tank town n Cf **jerkwater** adj

A small or insignificant community, orig one whose main function was to supply water for trains; also used as a nickname for such a community.

1895 *Eve. News* (Lincoln NE) 5 Jan 7/1, [Humor column:] Jerusalem naturally seems to have been located upon a succession of hills and reminds me of Asheville, N.C. in that respect. After David's conquest of Jerusalem it came more into prominence and ceased to be regarded as a tank town. **1918** *Stars & Stripes* (Paris France) 19 July 5/4, A theatrical troupe . . gave its first performance last Friday. . . It . . is already considering flattering proposals to tour the tank towns of the vicinity. There are lots of tank towns in that vicinity. **1927** *DN* 5.465 [Underworld jargon], *Tank town. . .* A town at which a train must stop for water or coal. **1934** *AmSp* 9.319, To the list of names for "hick towns," or synonyms of "Podunk," . . may be added *Tanktown* (a water-tank and no more), *Jumping-off Place, Stop in the Road, One-Horse Town, Jerk-water Town, Painted Post,* and *Spunkyville.* **1945** Street *Gauntlet* 131 **MO** (as of 1920s), The Milford supporters cheered and jeered and Linden was called a jerk-water dump and a tank town and other names, none of them complimentary. **1966–68** *DARE* (Qu. C33, *. . Joking names . . for an out-of-the-way place, or a very small or unimportant place*) Inf **GA**13, Tank town; **WA**12, Tank town—no depot, just water; whistle stop; (Qu. C34, *Nicknames for nearby settlements, villages, or districts*) Inf **OH**49, Tank Town. **1982** *Syracuse Herald–Jrl.* (NY) 10 Feb sec D 1/3, Several years ago, when [Amtrak] passenger service for Syracuse moved to East Syracuse, people joked about how we'd become a tank town. **2001** *Sun. Herald American* (Syracuse NY) [20 May] TV sec 8/5 (newspaperarchive.com), A con man baits a tank town big shot.

tanky See **thanky**

tanky bag See **thanky poke**

tanner crab n, sometimes cap   Also *tanner*   [From Zera L. Tanner (1835–1906); prob first applied to the species *C. tanneri*] **AK**

A crab of the genus *Chionoecetes.*

1947 *Fishery Resources U.S.* 33, The king crab and Tanner crab in the Gulf of Alaska and Bering Sea . . remain a practically untouched resource. **1972** *AK Mag.* Sept 29, We caught 6,000 tanners on the trip I made with the *Voyager.* **1982** *AK Fish Tales* 15.1.9, Approximately 60 percent of the statewide Tanner harvest is taken in the Bering Sea. **1986** Johnson *AK Fisheries Hdbk.* 74, Alaska has two species of Tanner crab, *Chionoecetes bairdi* and *C. opilio.* The former has been the mainstay of the Tanner fishery until recently. **1988** *Kodiak Daily Mirror* (AK) 14 Jan 6, "One hundred and thirty million pounds of Tanners is not a lot for the market demand," said UFMA's Jeff Stephan. **1998** *DARE* File—Internet **AK,** Tanner crabs, once very abundant in the Gulf, are now relatively rare.

tan oak See **tanbark oak a, c**

tansy n

Std: a plant of the genus *Tanacetum.* For other names of var spp see **bitter buttons, double tansy, feverfew 1, golden button 1, hind-heal 2, piss-a-bed 2**

tansy aster n

A plant of the genus *Machaeranthera,* usu *M. tanacetifolia.* For other names of var spp see **goldenbush, goldenweed 1, iron plant, jimmyweed, tahoka daisy, yellow aster 1** Note: Some of these plants were formerly included in the genus *Haplopappus.* The term *tansy aster* has been extended in botanical usage to such related genera as *Psilactis, Rayjacksonia,* and *Xylorhiza.*

1896 KS Ag. Exper. Sta. Manhattan *Bulletin* 57.17, *Aster tanacetifolius* [=*Machaeranthera t.*]. . . Tansy Aster. . . A common weed in sandy fields in western Kansas. **1932** Rydberg *Flora Prairies* 814, *Machaeranthera.* . . Tansy . . Aster. **1936** Whitehouse *TX Flowers* 165, *Tansy Aster (Machaeranthera tanacetifolia).* . . The purple-flowered heads are . . very showy . . It ranges from Nebraska to Mexico and California. **1948** Stevens *KS Wild Flowers* 404, *Machaeranthera tanacetifolia—Tansy Aster.* **1961** Wills–Irwin *Flowers TX* 229, Tansy-aster is gaining in favor as a garden annual, despite the fact that its large asterlike heads are seldom produced in profusion. . . Several additional species . . occur in Texas, all of them in the Trans-Pecos. **2001** *DARE* File—Internet **WY,** The crenulatewinged grasshopper is a grass feeder. . . Small amounts of needleleaf sedge, red threeawn, . . and . . tansy aster, were also found in crop contents.

tansybush n
=**fern-bush 2.**

1931 U.S. Dept. Ag. *Misc. Pub.* 101.55, *Tansybush (Chamaebatiaria millefolium)* . . is an odorous . . and somewhat woolly shrub . . ranging from northwestern California and eastern Oregon . . to western Wyoming, and through Nevada and Utah, into western and southern Arizona. **1967** Dodge *Roadside Wildflowers* 20 **SW,** Tansybush is an aromatic, densely branched shrub which blooms July to November. . . Tansybush is abundant in the Grand Canyon region. **1976** Elmore *Shrubs & Trees SW* 61, Tansybush. . . Small, fernlike leaves—or tansylike leaves, if you are familiar with the garden tansy—should immediately identify this shrub. . . Deer, sheep and goats browse upon its stems and leaves.

tansy mustard n

A plant of the genus *Descurainia,* esp the widespread *D. pinnata.* For other names of var spp see **flaxweed 2, flixweed 1, hedge mustard 1**

1857 Gray *First Lessons* 36, *S[ysimbrium] canescens* [=*Descurainia pinnata*]. . . *Tansy Mustard.* . . Flowers whitish or yellowish. . . Penn. and Ohio to Wisconsin, and southward and westward. **1891** Coulter *Botany W. TX* 16, *S. canescens.* . . Tansy mustard. . . Throughout Texas, and one of the most common of western mustards. **1908** NM Univ. *Biol. Ser.* 3.1.74, Tansy Mustard. . . Common about Albuquerque. March and May. **1937** U.S. Forest Serv. *Range Plant Hdbk.* W182, Tansy-mustards, so called because of their more or less tansylike leaves, and because they belong to the large mustard family . . , are annual, biennial,

or perennial herbs. **1944** Abrams *Flora Pacific States* 2.269, *Descurainia californica.* . . Sierra Tansy-mustard. . . Flowers yellow. . . California east . . and south to northern Arizona and New Mexico. **1959** Anderson *Flora AK* 250, *D[escurainia] richardsonii* [=*D. incana*]. . . Mountain Tansy Mustard. **2000** *DARE* File—Internet, Tansy mustard and flixweed are two similar mustard species common in central and western Kansas.

tansy ragwort n

A **ragwort** (here: *Senecio jacobaea*) common in the Pacific Northwest and New England.

1900 Lyons *Plant Names* 342, *S[enecio] Jacobaea.* . . Tansy Ragwort. **1937** U.S. Forest Serv. *Range Plant Hdbk.* W168, Ragwort *(S[enecio] jacobaea),* . . also known as . . tansy ragwort, has become naturalized in northeastern America. . . The distribution of this aggressive plant, a menace to cattle wherever it occurs, is extending and it will probably reach the range country eventually if, in fact, it is not there now. **1967** *DARE* (Qu. S9, . . *Kinds of grass that are hard to get rid of*) Inf **WA**28, Tansy ragwort; (Qu. S26d, *Wildflowers that grow in meadows;* not asked in early QRs) Inf **WA**28, Tansy ragwort. **1967** *DARE* FW Addit **WA**30, Tansy ragwort—yellow. **2000** *DARE* File—Internet **WA,** When prevalent, tansy ragwort is one of the most common causes of poisoning of cattle and horses, caused by the consumption of the weed found in pasture, hay or silage.

ta'nt See **taunt**

tantibogus n   Also sp *tantibogas*   [Var of swEngl dial *tantarabobus* (and varr)]

The devil; a boogeyman.

1912 Green *VA Folk-Speech* 438, *Tantibogas.* . . *Tantarabobus.* A name for the devil. **1966** *DARE* (Qu. EE41, *A hobgoblin that is used to threaten children and make them behave*) Inf **NC**33, Tantibogus.

tanto, all See **ataunto**

tantrum See **tandem**

tanty-see-bow adj

See quot.

1944 *PADS* 2.61 **MO,** *Tanty-see-bow* [ˌtæntɪ'siˌbo]. . . [*PADS* Ed: Fr. *tant et si beau*?] Now satisfactory after having been otherwise. If a skirt that had been uneven at the bottom was hemmed up until it hung correctly, one would ask, "Does it look tanty-see-bow now?" Or a farmer would kick aside a clod that had prevented a taut string from making a straight line by which to mark the row in the garden, squint along the line, and say, "H'm—I guess it's tanty-see-bow now."

Taos lightning See **lightning** n[1]

taown See **town** n

tap n[1]

1 An indoor or outdoor water faucet. **widespread, but less freq nNEng, Sth, S Midl** See Map on p. 504 Cf **faucet B1, hydrant 1a, b, spigot B**

1865 *Scientific Amer.* 16 Dec 387, Wash the pictures well under the tap. **1875** Johns Hopkins *Hospital Plans* 65 **MD,** The floor should be perfectly tight, and dished, . . and supplied with a water-tap and short hose. **1896** *New Engl. Mag.* 20.4, There will be anathemas profound and unsparing upon the shortsightedness . . which carried sewage away in drain pipes, only to bring it back by the water-tap. **1933** *Syracuse Herald* (NY) 1 Jan [12]/4 (newspaperarchive.com), [Caption:] The police dog. . . shows how he opens doors and how he turns on the water tap when he is thirsty. **1961** Salinger *Franny* 116 **NYC,** Her first, blatantly martyred chore was to turn on the cold-water tap. **1965–70** *DARE* (Qu. F27a, *What you turn on and off inside the house to get running water*) 128 Infs, **scattered, but less freq nNEng, Sth, S Midl,** Tap; **MO**19, Water tap; (Qu. F27b, *What you turn on and off outside the house to get running water*) 77 Infs, **scattered, but less freq nNEng, Sth, S Midl,** Tap; **CO**11, **NJ**55, Outside tap; **CT**7, **IN**54, Water tap; **MI**68, Hose tap. **1966** *Monadnock Regionaire* Summer 14 **swNH,** The taps were all of real gold. **1973** Allen *LAUM* 1.204 **Upper MW** (as of c1950), *Faucet* (as on a water pipe at the kitchen sink). . . Actually more frequent than *spigot* (2.9%) is the variant *tap* (12%), which occurs principally in southern Minnesota and in Canada as a large reflection of its sporadic and rare appearance in New England and southern New Brunswick. . . Data from 1,107 checklists tend to corroborate those from the field records . . although *tap* has only 3.7% and is fairly evenly distributed in the

U[pper] M[idwest]. **2000** *NY Times* (NY) 19 Apr sec A 1, More than 10 million gallons a day of inadequately treated waste water continues to mix with water bound for city taps, said James M. Tierney.

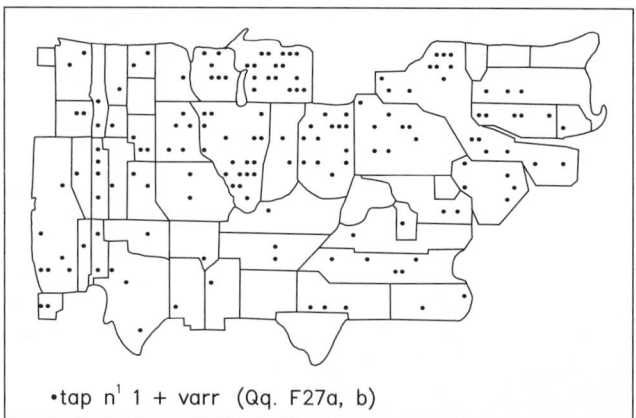

•tap n¹ 1 + varr (Qq. F27a, b)

2 A nut for a bolt. [Appar transf from *tap* tool for cutting a female thread, as euphem substitute for *nut*] **chiefly Sth, S Midl** *old-fash* Cf **tapstick**

1866 Smith *Bill Arp* 154 **GA**, They wouldn't lend a dollar until Mr. Jenkins war inorgarated, for they wanted his name to the note. Thinks says I there's a tap lost about this wagon. **1891** *Courier* (Connellsville PA) 28 Aug 8/2, Honsacker Bros. blew the end out of the cylinder of their engine Tuesday morning. A loose tap was the cause. **1899** (1912) Green *VA Folk-Speech* 438, *Tap.* . . Nut of a screw, the female thread being cut inside. **1903** *DN* 2.333 **seMO**, *Tap.* . . Nut. 'I caint get a tap that will fit this bolt.' **1906** *DN* 3.160 **nwAR**, *Tap.* . . Nut; a small piece of metal provided with an internal screw thread, used on a bolt or screw. **1909** *DN* 3.379 **eAL, wGA**, *Tap.* . . Nut for a bolt. **1930s** in 1944 *ADD* 623 **eWV**, *Tap.* . . Common, as is *nut.* **1946** *PADS* 6.30 **eNC**, *Tap.* . . A nut (for a bolt). *Nut* was never used. (((*PADS* Ed:] Is this another instance of verbal modesty?)) Pamlico. Common. **1947** *PADS* 8.21 **ceIA**, *Tap: Nut* also heard, though *tap* was the common word when I was a boy. *Ibid* 23 **KY**, *Tap:* Not so common now. To the Editor's query: yes. [*DARE* Ed: Ref is to quot 1946 above.] **c1960** *Wilson Coll.* **csKY**. **1962** *DARE* File **KS**, *Tap* . . the nut that screws on to a bolt. Used c1900 . . ; common usage. **1969** *DARE* Tape **KY24**, A little later on they developed . . a nut or a tap, . . an iron contraption that was threaded and corresponded to the same kind of a thread on the axle and they would turn it on with a wrench. **1983** *MJLF* 9.1.58 **ceKY** (as of 1956). **1986** Pederson *LAGS Concordance*, 1 inf, **cGA**, Put a tap on to hold wheel to axle; 1 inf, **swGA**, Tap--part of wheel. [Both infs Black] **2004** *DARE* File—Internet **neTX**, A nut and bolt is a tap and bolt.

3 A hole bored in a maple tree in order to obtain sap; the operation of tapping a maple tree for sap; a **spile** n¹ **2.**

1895 *Olean Democrat* (NY) [11 June 6]/5 (newspaperarchive.com), I must have spiles—elders—of the right diameter, with the pith out and cut so as to fit the tap in the tree. **1899** *New Engl. Mag.* 21.345, The taps or "spiles" were made of elder sticks with the pith pushed out. **1943** *Post-Std.* (Syracuse NY) 24 Mar 26/5, Norm said some 200 taps had been made which is only one-quarter of the normal operation. **1952** *Mansfield News-Jrl.* (OH) 15 Feb 1/5, Syrup producers bore holes through the bark of the trees and insert taps into them. **1987** *Wellsboro Gaz.* (PA) 25 Feb sec 2 4/3, Maple Supplies For Sale. . . tubing, spiles for 125 taps. **1989** Mosher *Stranger* 62 **nVT** (as of 1952), We . . gathered up the taps and sap buckets. **2005** *DARE* File—Internet **NH**, Basic equipment you will need for just a few taps: Drill, hammer, spiles (spouts), buckets with covers [etc]. *Ibid* **cnPA**, When the temperatures are just right, our four tappers get to work, going from tree to tree and inserting taps.

tap v¹ [*EDD* tap v.¹ 3] **NEng, NY** *old-fash*
To half-sole or resole (a boot or shoe).

1746 (1901) Hempstead *Diary* 453 **CT**, I Tapt & nailed Jont Pierpoints Shoes. **1781** in 1882 *Narragansett Hist. Reg.* 1.284 **sRI**, Tapped a pair of shoes. **1817** (1930) W. Sewall *Diary* 8 **ME**, Carried my boots to the shoemaker to be tapped. **1861** in 1961 *VT Hist.* 29.68 **neVT**, April. . . *18* . . paid . . 60c to get boots tapped. **1905** *DN* 3.22 **cCT**, *Tap.* . . To add a new sole to a shoe. **1910** *DN* 3.450 **cwNY**, *Tap.* . . To half-sole boots or shoes. **1936** *AmSp* 11.375, In Rhode Island one always says 'I am going to have my shoes *tapped*' instead of the more customary 'I am

going to have my shoes *soled*.' **1948** Peattie *Berkshires* 323 **wMA**, In Berkshire, shoes are not half-soled—they are "tapped." **1959** *VT Hist.* 27.162, *Tap a shoe.* . . To add a half sole to a shoe. Common. **1967** *DARE* FW Addit **cnNY**, To have shoes resoled is to have them tapped. **1969** *DARE* Tape **CT36**, He bought the leather and tapped my shoes. . . put . . new soles on your shoes. **1969** *DARE* File **cMA** (as of c1915), We never used the word resoled when I was a child. We had our shoes *tapped.*

tap n²

1 A half sole on a boot or shoe. [**tap** v¹] **esp NEng, NY**

1743 (1901) Hempstead *Diary* 12 Dec 418 **seCT**, Nailed on a pr of Tapps on a pr of New Shoes for adam. **1864** (1873) Webster *Amer. Dict.*, *Tăp.* . . The piece of leather fastened upon the bottom of a boot or shoe in tapping it, or in repairing or renewing the sole or heel. **1912** *DN* 3.569 **cNY**, *Taps.* . . Half-soles. To have shoes "tapped" is to have the soles renewed. **1969** *DARE* Tape **CT36**, You could bang them against stuff, you weren't hurting your shoe . . you were hitting the sole . . the tap.

2 A hard plate fastened to the heel or toe of a shoe or boot primarily to prevent wear. **widespread, but esp freq Sth, S Midl, SW** See Map Note: *Tap* is the std form for such a plate intended primarily to make a sharp noise, as on a tap shoe.

1895 (1975) Harben *Land* 12 **GA**, Johnston was a few yards ahead of him and stooped to pick up something glittering in the moonlight. It was the tap from the heel of a shoe and was of solid silver. **c1960** *Wilson Coll.* **csKY**, *Tap.* . . A metal piece worn on the heel of a shoe. **1961** *Post-Std.* (Syracuse NY) 16 Feb 1/5 **NYC**, Some victims of the demonstrators said their attackers used knives, brass knuckles, short lengths of bicycle chain and heavy metal taps on shoe heels. **1965–70** *DARE* (Qu. W12b, *Metal pieces under the tips of shoes to prevent wear*) 346 Infs, **widespread, but esp Sth, S Midl, SW**, Taps; 12 Infs, **chiefly Midl, Sth,** Toe taps; **AR**23, **CO**15, **KY**33, **NC**55, **SC**42, **VA**2, Heel taps; **MO**34, **TN**13, Iron taps; **MS**70, Metal taps; **SC**26, Shoe taps; (Qu. W12a, *Heavy pieces of metal fastened under the soles of boots to keep them from slipping*) 13 Infs, **chiefly Sth, S Midl, SW**, Taps; **FL**31, **KY**5, **NC**1, 6, Heel taps; **MO**34, Iron taps; **NC**22, Steel taps. **1997** in 2004 *DARE* File—Internet **ceMO**, Students are not to wear heel taps or other hardware on the bottoms of their shoes . . , as these mar floor finishes and dent floor tile. **2004** *DARE* File—Internet **CT** [Hale Heel Company], No-Noise Taps. . . Amazing polyurethane taps keep heels perfect for months. Attach with nails . . or use our Professional Cobbler's Glue for fast, long-lasting adhesion.

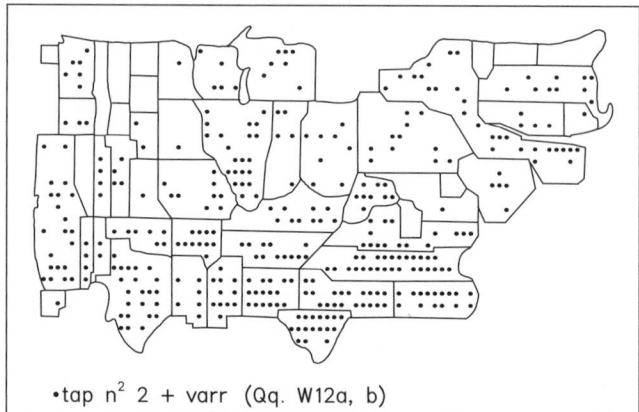

•tap n² 2 + varr (Qq. W12a, b)

3 in neg constrs: The smallest amount of work; the slightest bit—usu in phrr *do a tap (of work)* and varr. Cf **lick** n **4b(2)**

1884 *Daily Gaz.* (Ft. Wayne IN) 5 Aug 8/2, A man could travel clean from Belleville, central Illinois, up into the middle of Minnesota and get all he wanted to eat and drink without doing a tap of work. **1887** in 1950 *AmSp* 25.39 **New Orleans LA**, I understand that Eddie never done a tap of work in his life. **1913** (1975) London *Valley of Moon* 514 **CA**, An' Bridget [=a horse] ain't ever goin' to do a tap of work again. **1950** (1965) Richter *Town* 150 **OH**, Even though she hardly raised her hands to do a tap, Sayward wouldn't have minded having her all summer. **1952** O'Neill *Moon Misbegotten* 10 **CT**, He's nothing but a drunken bum who never done a tap of work in his life. **1965–70** *DARE* (Qu. LL18, *To do no work at all . . "She hasn't _____ all day."*) 23 Infs, **scattered, but esp NEast, Gt Lakes**, Done a tap; 11 Infs, **scattered,**

but esp **TX, Cent,** Turned a tap; **MS**49, **MO**7, **OK**20, **SC**40, Hit a tap; **LA**8, **OH**66, **OK**45, **TX**36, Moved a tap; **IA**5, **NJ**8, Done a tap of work; **NC**35, Struck a tap. **1997** *Abilene Reporter–News* (TX) 25 Dec (Internet), I've been on the payroll 30 years now without doing a tap of work, so it's an ideal situation. **2003** *Sequoyah Co. Times* (Sallisaw OK) 8 Dec (Internet), If a tap of work had been hit in the years since 1948, it was not apparent.

tap v[2]   See **tap-tap**

tap n[3]   See **tapadero**

tapa n   Also *kapa;* pronc-sp *tapper* [*tapa* is the form in many Polynesian languages; *kapa* reflects a typically Haw sound change that was appar still incomplete when the earliest missionaries arrived.] **esp HI**

1 A fabric made by beating the inner bark of various trees; a piece or garment of this fabric.

1798 (1888) New Haven Colony Hist. Soc. *Papers* 4.63, They say when a chief dies his body is rolled up snug in tapper, which is the cloth of the country. **1820** in 1931 Bernice P. Bishop Museum *Special Pub.* 17.32 **HI,** Raspberries and strawberries. . . are raised by the natives, only for painting their tapper. **1825** Ellis *Jrl. HI* 102, Most of the children were naked, or at best had only a narrow strip of tapa fastened round their loins. *Ibid* 116, At the usual time for retiring to rest, these two ladies spread their mats and tapas on the ground in one corner. **1826** Ellis *Narrative HI* 48, Six women, fantastically dressed in yellow tapa's, . . now made their way by couples through the crowd. **1837** *S. Lit. Messenger* 3.421 **HI,** The bodies . . [are] enveloped in numerous folds of a thick kind of *Kapa* called *Pipi.* **1892** Gowen *Paradise Pacific* 38 **HI,** The old industry of beating out *kapa,* or native cloth, from the bark of the paper-mulberry, has been killed through the introduction of prints and calicoes from the outer world. **1951** *AmSp* 26.21 **HI,** Before Captain Cook's discovery of the islands, the main garment was a 'malo' or loincloth of 'kapa' (tapa, or beaten bark cloth). **1967** Reinecke-Tsuzaki *Hawaiian Loanwords* 111, *Tapa, kapa;* /kapa/. . . 1. Barkcloth, formerly made in Hawaii, but now imported from Samoa. 2. A quilt or blanket. V[ery] F[requently used] in first meaning. **1972** Carr *Da Kine Talk* 87 **HI,** *Hawaiian Words Commonly Heard In Hawaii's English. . . Kapa.* Tapa, a cloth made from bark. **2004** *DARE* File—Internet **HI,** Traditional Hawaiian Wedding with Tapa Ceremony by Don Kona Kamakani Atay—$960.

2 usu as *kapa;* Transf: a quilt.

1887 Cincinnati Museum Assoc. *Annual Rept. for 1886* 21, [In a list of donations:] Joseph Mueller, of St. Mary's College, . . Kapa, or bed quilt. Hawaii. **1967** [see **1** above]. **2004** *DARE* File—Internet **HI,** In the early 1940's Jerry Miki was a youngster spending his summers with his "Tutu" (Grandmother) in Kona. He remembers her opening a great camphor chest to show her collection of "Kapas" (Hawaiian quilts) to admiring visitors. *Ibid* **HI,** In the P[arent] E[ducation] S[ervices] component families work with their home visitor to create a kapa (quilt) to welcome their newborn baby.

tapadero n   Also *tapadera, tapidaro, tapidero;* also freq abbr *tap* [MexSpan use of Span *tapadera* cover, lid] **esp West**
A leather hood covering or enclosing the front of a stirrup.

[**1844** (1954) Gregg *Commerce* 150 **NM,** The *estribos* or stirrups are usually made either of bent or mortised wood, . . over which are fastened the *tapaderas* or coverings of leather to protect the toes.] **1857** in 1941 *AmSp* 16.262 **CA** [Span words used in English], Tapadero, a leathern stirrup cover. **1872** Twain *Roughing It* 178 **NV,** It was a Spanish saddle, with ponderous *tapadaros.* **1891** *Century Dict.* 6184, *Tapadera. . .* A heavy leather housing for the stirrup of the Californian saddle. **1892** *DN* 1.195 **TX,** *Tapadéro:* "toe-fender" of Mexican stirrup. Also and more frequently, though incorrectly, *tapidero.* **1929** Dobie *Vaquero* 205 **West,** To work effectively in this brush a vaquero had to have *tapaderos* (toe fenders) on his stirrups. **1929** *AmSp* 5.61 **NE** [Cattle country talk], Some stirrups are covered by leather pieces called "taps" (from the Spanish *tapadero*). These prevent the rider's feet from passing through the stirrups. **1933** White *Dog Days* 197 **CA,** Are we picking the box type, the bulldog, or the long, flapping tapaderos that reach almost to the ground? **1940** Von Tempski *Paradise* 33 **HI,** Dad . . praised the carvings . . twining around the pommel, cantle, tapaderos, and sweat-guards. **1977** Jones *OR Folkl.* 43, *Tapaderos . .* also called taps. **1981** *KS Qrly.* 13.2.70 **nNV,** *Taps . .* leather cover or hood over the stirrups, either snouted or long-pointed. **2003** in 2004 *DARE* File—Internet **csCA,** I don't care for tapaderos for two reasons—they have a tendency to get caught in brush and they are heavy. . . Yes I know

that taps are supposed to protect against brush and in some kinds of brush they probably do. **2004** *Ibid* **TX** [Big Bend Saddlery], *Bulldog Tapaderas*—Built from sole leather to insure a very hard, rigid tap.

tapaka   See **taba**

taparosa n
=**chuparosa 2.**

1931 U.S. Dept. Ag. *Misc. Pub.* 101.144, *Anisacanthus thurberi,* . . known locally as . . taparosa, . . with . . attractive maroon-red flowers, ranges from western Texas to southern New Mexico and Arizona. **1938** Van Dersal *Native Woody Plants* 53, *Anisacanthus thurberi. . . Taparosa. . .* A small shrub with fairly good to very good palatability as stock forage; often closely browsed by sheep and cattle. **1960** Vines *Trees SW* 932, Thurber Anisacanth. . . is also known under the vernacular names of Desert-honeysuckle, Taparosa, and Chuparosa. Palatable to cattle and sheep.

tape caterpillar   See **tape measure**

tape grass n
A grasslike aquatic plant (*Vallisneria americana*). Also called **canvasback grass, celery ~, channel weed, duck celery, eelgrass 2, ox-tongue, poppy** n[1], **riverweed 3, water celery 1, wild ~ 2**

1817 *Amer. Monthly Mag. & Crit. Rev.* 1.430, Two species of *Vallisneria* are noticed as follows. . . *V. Americana* (Tape grass) [etc]. **1822** Eaton *Botany* 505 **NY,** *Vallisneria. . . spiralis* (tape grass . .) leaves floating, linear. **1840** MA Zool. & Bot. Surv. *Herb. Plants & Quadrupeds* 190, Tape Grass. . . The fertile or pistillate flowers are on a long spiral stem or scape rising to the surface. **1894** Coulter *Botany W. TX* 421, *Tape-grass. . .* Submerged stemless plants, with grass-like leaves. **1911** NJ State Museum *Annual Rept. for 1910* 173, *Tape Grass. . .* Larger streams of the North and Middle districts. **1942** Hylander *Plant Life* 596, Tape Grass . . grows in streams and lakes of Florida and Louisiana, where it is the favorite food of ducks and other aquatic birds. **2000** *DARE* File—Internet **FL,** *Tape grass* is a submersed plant that spreads by runners and sometimes forms tall underwater meadows.

tape measure n   Also *tape caterpillar, ~ worm* Cf **measuring worm**
=**looper.**

1967–70 *DARE* (Qu. R27, . . *Kinds of caterpillars or similar worms*) Infs **CT**15, **LA**10, **NY**198, **TX**73, Tape measure; **MI**120, Tape measure [FW sugg]; **LA**10, Tape measure or tape caterpillar; **VA**73, The inchworm is called a tape worm; it is distinguished from the tapeworm found in people.

tap for the simples   See **bore for the simples**

tap hand n   Also *tap (hands)* **chiefly sAppalachians** Cf **duck duck goose, tap the finger, tap the rabbit**
A chasing game similar to drop-the-handkerchief; see quot 1972.

c1930 in 2005 *DARE* File—Internet **cIN** (as of c1865), The little boys and girls played ring around-a-rosy and anty over. The next size played taphand or three corner cat ball. The big boys played bull-pen or town ball, etc. **1960** *Ibid* **cwNC** (as of c1885), At school . . our best games were Tap hand and Base. **1966** *DARE* (Qu. EE1, . . *Games . . children play . . in which they form a ring, and either sing or recite a rhyme*) Inf **NC**33, Tap. **1972** in 1982 Powers *Cataloochee* 167 **cwNC** (as of a1940), We'd play Tap-Hand up there in the old Field. Tap-Hand, one of those old games. Hold hands around this way in a big circle, and one fellow'd tap and went around the ring, and the other'n see if he could catch him. The old Tap Hand Ring. Boys would tap the girls. And the girls would tap the boys. **c1995** in 2005 *DARE* File—Internet **swVA** (as of c1935), Then they would play their favorite games tap hands and drop the hankie. **1996** *Ibid* **swVA,** Didn't have time, much, for fun. . . We would play "Blind Man's Buff[*]" or we would play "Tap Hand" or "Anne Over."

tapidaro, tapidero   See **tapadero**

taping bird n   [See quot 1900]
=**flicker** n[2] **1.**

1887 *Forest & Stream* 28.248 **MA,** I send you a list of the names which I have heard applied to this bird [=*Colaptes auratus*]. . . Taping Bird. . . Mass. **1900** *Wilson Bulletin* 12.2.10, *Taping-bird.* Massachusetts. This epithet was applied because it flies as if "measured [sic] off tape." In the "Audubon Magazine" an error was made in copying from the "Forest and Stream," making it "Tapping-bird," which would of course make it have a very different meaning.

taplin See **tarpaulin**

tap on (the) back n Also *tappy(-hi-spy)* =**tap the icebox.**

1911 *Playground* 5.243, [In a list of games:] Hide and seek, Tap on the back. **1953** Brewster *Amer. Nonsinging Games* 48 **WV**, Tap-on-the-Back. . . This game is an elaboration of Hide and Seek. The player who has been chosen "It" covers his eyes and turns his back upon the others. One of the latter taps him on the back, and "It," turning around, tries to guess which child gave the blow. If his guess is correct, the striker must run to a designated spot and back while the rest of the players hide. If "It" fails to identify the striker, then he must make the run himself. From this point on, the game proceeds as in Hide and Seek. *Ibid* 49, Other names given it are Tappy, Tappy-Hi-Spy. **1966–67** *DARE* (Qu. EE12, *Games in which one captain hides his team and the other team tries to find it*) Inf **MA**71, Tap on the back; (Qu. EE13a, *Games in which every player hides except one, and that one must try to find the others*) Inf **NY**24, Tap on back (not hide-and-seek)—that's the way to choose the hunter; [(Qu. EE16, *Hiding games that start with a special, elaborate method of sending the players out to hide*) Inf **PA**1, Tap-the-finger—run-and-hide].

tap on the icebox See **tap the icebox**

tap over v phr

1917 *DN* 4.401 **neOH, NEng,** *Tap over, v.t. & abs.* Retap maple trees the same season, by boring a new hole or enlarging the old one. "He tapped over all his trees." "He will tap over next week."

tapper See **tapa**

tapping on the icebox See **tap the icebox**

tappy See **tabby**

tappy(-hi-spy) See **tap on (the) back**

tappy on the icebox See **tap the icebox**

tapstick n [**tap** n[1] 2] esp **Sth**

A throwing-stick weighted with a metal nut.

1927 Adams *Congaree* 78 **cSC** [Black], I been back in de woods wid my tap-stick, trying to kill a jay-bird. **1940** Betten *Upland Game* 379 **Sth**, That tap stick is a peculiar weapon; . . ordinarily it is a flexible oak or hickory stick about three feet long. The ammunition consists of discarded nuts or taps picked up along the railroad tracks. A tap is slipped over the reduced outer end of the stick and is flung at a mark with a powerful flip—much like flipping an apple from a stick. **1948** Faulkner *Intruder* 5 **MS**, Aleck Sander already had his tapstick—one of the heavy nuts which bolt railroad rails together, driven onto a short length of broom-handle—which Aleck Sander could throw whirling end over end at a running rabbit pretty near as accurately as he could shoot the shotgun. **1976** Brown *Gloss. Faulkner* 197 **MS**, Tapstick. . . The section of broomstick (or any other tough stick) is whittled down until it can barely be inserted into the opening of the nut, and it is then screwed on. . . We usually called this a throwing-stick. It was used not only for hunting rabbits but also to knock nuts and lodged objects out of trees, etc.

tap-tap exclam

Used as a call by "it" in **hide-and-seek A** to announce that a named hider has been found; hence v *tap* to announce the finding of (someone) in this way.

1968 *DARE* (Qu. EE15, *When he has caught the first of those that were hiding what does the player who is 'it' call out to the others?*) Inf **NY**40, As "it" sees the person, he calls out, "Tap-tap So-and-so, hiding behind the tree," and then he has to touch the base (or post) before the person hiding reaches it; **NY**119, It: "Tap-tap So-and-so behind the tree, one, two, three." Someone who's not tapped and gets home: "Home free all!"

tap the finger n Cf **tap hand**

Prob =**tap the rabbit.**

1934 (1935) Mead–Orth *Transitional Pub. School* 365 **CA**, [In a list of playground games:] Tap the finger. **1948** Jackson *Road Wall* 137 **CA**, After strenuous prisoner's base and wild tap-the-finger, they had settled down on the Donalds' lawn to play some quieter game. **1970** Lebofsky *Lexicon Philadelphia* 218 **sePA**, Tap the finger—game similar to tag, played in a circle. . . was familiar to 18% of those interviewed, none of whom was Age IV [=less than 30 years old]. **2002** *Contra Costa*

Times (Walnut Creek CA) 28 Feb (Internet) **cwCA** (as of 1930s), My memories . . a two-room country school, playing kick the can, tap the finger.

tap the icebox n Also *tap(ping)* (or *tappy*) *on the icebox, tap the iceman, tip the icebox, punch the icebox* (or *iceman*), *wind my icebox* Cf **cut the pie 2, frying pan 3, tap on (the) back, Washington poke**

A guessing game in which one player taps "it" on the back and "it" tries to identify the tapper, often as a preliminary to a game of **hide-and-seek A.**

1949 *Hoosier Folkl. Bulletin* 8.23, Tap the Icebox—I will draw a circle,/ And who will place the dot? (Ill.) The leader draws a circle on the back of a player whose eyes are covered. Another player touches the center of the circle. The player whose eyes are covered tries to guess who has touched him. Variants: 1. I'll be the iceman so I will draw the circle,/ And who'll put in the dot? (Ind.) **1953** Brewster *Amer. Nonsinging Games* 49, Other names given it [=the game *tap-on-the-back*] are . . Tap-the-Icebox, Tap-on-the-Icebox, Tappy-on-the-Icebox. **1957** *Sat. Eve. Post Letters* **cwKY** (as of 1930s), In "tapping on the icebox," the "it" player would hide his eyes on base while another player drew a circle on his back, intoning "I will draw the magic circle and who will punch?" One of the players punched "it" in the center of the circle; "it" then turned around and made a guess as to who had punched. The one named then asked "What shall I do?" "It" then named a task such as running to the oak tree and counting to twenty. The boy named had to do this if "it" guessed correctly; if "it" guessed incorrectly the answer was "Go yourself!" While "it" was doing the task the rest ran and hid, from then on it was like regular hide-and-go-seek. *Ibid* **swMI**, Tap the ice man—One player was "it." He closed his eyes. . . Some one drew a circle on his back with their finger saying "Make a magic circle—sign it with a poke." [*DARE* Ed: The game proceeds as in the previous quot.] *Ibid* **ceIL** (as of 1930s), There was another warm weather favorite called "Tap the Icebox"; one child stood against a tree and hid her head in her arms, while another child drew on the back of the first one and chanted, "Draw a round circle, color it with purple, and somebody put in a dot." Then a third child would comply with this by putting a solid poke with her finger in the imaginary circle. . . If the 'poker' was guessed within three guesses, it was her turn to be the 'icebox tapped.' **1961** *Chicago Daily News* (IL) 4 Apr 18/3, They were playing good old-fashioned "Tap the Icebox," a game Chicago children have played for generations. **1967–69** *DARE* (Qu. EE4, *Games in which one player's eyes are bandaged and he has to catch the others and guess who they are*) Inf **NY**130, Tap the icebox; (Qu. EE12, *Games in which one captain hides his team and the other team tries to find it*) Inf **IN**39, Punch the icebox; (Qu. EE13a, *Games in which every player hides except one, and that one must try to find the others*) Infs **NY**130, **OH**20, **PA**133, Tap the icebox; (Qu. EE16, *Hiding games that start with a special, elaborate method of sending the players out to hide*) Inf **TX**61, Wind my icebox—draw a magic circle on someone's back; someone punches him in the back, then he has to guess who punched him, then everyone runs and hides; **IL**135, Punch the iceman. [All Infs young or mid-aged] **1975** Ferretti *Gt. Amer. Book Sidewalk Games* 112 **Chicago IL**, *Hide-and-Seek.* . . A variation played in Chicago is *Tap the Icebox*, in which the person who is "It" covers his eyes and turns around while the other players stand behind him. One player draws a circle on "Its" back with his finger; then this artist or another player jabs a finger into the center of the circle, "tapping the icebox." "It" then turns and guesses who has tapped him. If his guess is right, the tapper then becomes "It" and the process is repeated. If his guess is wrong, he has to count to 100, eyes covered, and the rules of Hide-and-Seek apply. **1986** Pederson *LAGS Concordance*, 1 inf, **New Orleans LA**, Tip the icebox—a form of "guess who."

tap the rabbit n Also *slap the rabbit* Cf **slap in the back, tap hand, tap the finger**

A chasing game similar to drop-the-handkerchief; see quot 1995.

1865 in 1997 Buck *Shadows* 312 **VA**, We proceeded to the dining room where "tap-the-rabbit," "fox-and-goose," [*sic*]"blindman's buff" and similar dignified games engaged us till after eleven o'clock. **1910** Minton *Rag Weed Rhymes* 53, "Tap the rabbit" 's very good,/ And the "Children of the Wood."/ But I think you all agree,/ "Hide and seek's" the game for me. **1957** *Sat. Eve. Post Letters* **cwPA** (as of c1900), We played "Shinny in your own Hole," . . "Drop the Handkerchief," "Tap the Rabbit" [etc]. **1970** *DARE* (Qu. EE1, . . *Games . . children play . . in which they form a ring, and either sing or recite a rhyme*) Inf **IL**135,

Slap the rabbit; (Qu. EE33, . . *Outdoor games . . that children play*) Inf **VA**30, Tap the rabbit. **1995** Heatwole *Shenandoah Voices* 22 **wVA** (as of 19th cent), Tap the Rabbit was a game played by children. . . They stood in a big ring, facing inward, and a designated child would prowl about behind their backs, outside the ring. He'd tap a child on the shoulder and then take off as fast as he could, trying to circumnavigate the ring. The tapped child would pursue, trying to tag the first child before he got all the way around to the tapped child's vacated space. If he didn't make the tag, he became the new "it." Another informant described the game as being played in the snow, with the circle being about thirty feet in diameter. The variant was that if you were caught by the person you tapped, you had to give him or her a kiss.

tar n[1] Usu |tɑ(r)|; also |tær| Pronc-spp *tair, tare* Cf **jar** v[1] **A, jar** n **A**

A Forms.

1864 *NY Times* (NY) 24 July 6 **NC,** We entered the office room, where some eight or ten natives were gathered around the fire, munching goubers and discussing the capacity of "*Tom Kerr's* mons'ous big tare kiln." **1903** *DN* 2.333 **seMO,** *Tar.* . . Pronounced tair [tær]. 'I always greeze my wagon with pine tair.' **1907** *DN* 3.237 **nwAR,** *Tar.* . . Pronounced tair [tær]. [**1942** Hall *Smoky Mt. Speech* 30, The family name *Tarwater,* usually pronounced with [ɑ] in the first syllable, appears on a disc as ['tæɚwɒtɚ].]

B Senses.

1 =**pitch** n[1]. **widespread, but infreq NEng, West** See Map

c1960 *Wilson Coll.* **csKY,** Tar on pine trees is commonly called gum. **1965–70** *DARE* (Qu. T7, *The sticky stuff that comes out of pine trees*) 37 Infs, **scattered, but infreq NEng, West,** Tar; 11 Infs, **esp N Cent, S Atl,** Pine tar. **1966** *DARE* Tape FL19, They put cups, and then they cut off a part of the tree, the bark . . and they put a cup there and they run two little tin gutters like to this cup to catch the tar; **GA**7, We call it tar, or gum, or turpentine—course, it's not turpentine until it distills. **2004** *DARE* File—Internet, Pine is full of sticky tar and resin which can "gum up" your machine.

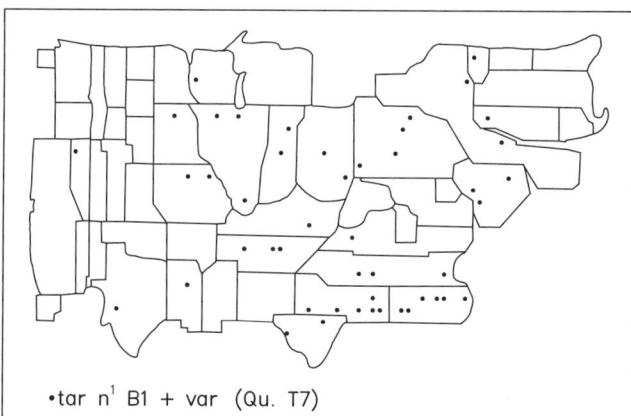

•tar n[1] B1 + var (Qu. T7)

2 Black or very strong coffee. **esp Nth**

1850 Melville *White-Jacket* 15 **NY,** They are an old weather-beaten set, culled from the most experienced seamen on board [a man-of-war]. These are the fellows . . who, when ashore, at an eating-house, call for a bowl of tar and a biscuit. **1942** Berrey–Van den Bark *Amer. Slang* 816.55, Tar, *black coffee.* **1958** McCulloch *Woods Words* 191 **Pacific NW,** *Tar*—Low grade strong coffee. **1966–69** *DARE* (Qu. H74a, . . *Coffee . . very strong*) Infs **IN**74, **MI**9, **MN**14, **OH**71, **PA**1, Tar; [**CA**105, **MI**43, **MN**14, **OH**47, Black as tar; **MN**38, Boiled the tar out of it]. **2004** *DARE* File **AZ,** I remember his big hands slowly stirring his cup of "tar".

tar v See **tear**

tar n[2] See **taw**

tar n[3] See **tire** n

tarabilla n Also *tarabi, tarrabee* [Span *tarabilla*] **esp SW** =**spinner 3.**

[**1901** (1932) Ditchy *Acadiens* 200 **LA,** *Tarabi,* instrument ressemblant à une manivelle, employé pour tordre les torons d'une corde; l'ouvrier qui le tient, lui fait faire une rotation continuelle. [=*Tarabi,* a tool resembling a crank, used to twist the strands of a rope; the worker who holds it

makes it spin continually.]] **1941** *Cattleman* 27.9.73 **TX,** [Caption:] The twisting paddle or "tarrabee" used in making girts. **1953** *Western Folkl.* 12.179, The first *tarabi* . ., as the spinner is called in French Louisiana, was found among the Koasati Indians, who were using it to prepare Spanish-moss yarn, ultimately to be woven into saddle blankets. They later admitted to employing the device in spinning horsehair to make a variety of equipment used with riding horses. *Ibid* 181, [*DARE* Ed: The accompanying map, based on responses from "old timers," shows *tarabilla* as the term used for this device in **sCA, AZ, NM,** and **sTX,** *tarabi, tarrabee* in **swLA** and **seTX.**]

tarantula n Usu |tə'ræntʃələ|; for addit proncs see quot 1965–70 **Pronc-spp** *t(a)rantler, tarentula* Std sense, var forms.

1861 *Harper's New Mth. Mag.* [see **tarantula juice**]. **1887** (1892) Hinman *Corporal Si Klegg* 261, He would start for the doctor's tent shouting that he had been bitten by a "tarantler." **1923** *DN* 5.223 **swMO,** *Trantler.* . . Tarantula. **1927** *DN* 5.479 **Ozarks,** *Trantler.* . . Tarantula, a big hairy spider. **1930** *AmSp* 5.420, Up North folks are learning that educated . . Texans and Oklahomans don't say "trantler" for "tarantula." **1965–70** *DARE* (Qu. R28, . . *Kinds of spiders*) 28 Infs, **chiefly SW, Lower Missip Valley,** [Proncs of the type [tə'ræntʃələ]]; **CA**65, 114, **NY**207, **SD**1, [Proncs of the type [tə'ræntʃulə]]; **OK**23, **TX**66, [tə'ræntʃulə]; **TX**1, [tə'ræntʃlə]; **AR**55, **CA**9, 145, 191, **MO**39, **TX**40, 71, ['træntʃələ]; **TX**27, ['træntʃulə]; **TX**29, ['træntʃlə]; **CA**94, ['tarænčələ]; **CA**107, 191, **LA**18, **TX**9, 42, 59, [Proncs of the type [tə'rænčələ]]; **AR**55, **CA**13, **TX**35, [Proncs of the type ['trænčələ]]; **CA**119, [tə'rænčulə]; **TX**3, **UT**6, [tə'ræntʃulə]; **MD**3, [tɨ'ræntʃulə]; **CO**22, ['tʌræntələ]; **OK**52, [tə'ræntulə]; **CA**87, ['tarəntələ]; **CA**31, ['tarəntulə]; **OK**47, ['tɝæntlə]; **CA**87, 120, 127, **OK**3, [Proncs of the types [tə'rænt(ə)lə]]; **TX**78, ['trænsələ]; **MS**1, **OK**11, ['træns(ə)lə]; **AR**35, Taratula [no pronc recorded]; **OK**25, [tə'rænčulə]; **TX**26, [tə'ræčulə]; **CA**6, ['træčələ]; **MO**9, [traɪ'ænčələ]; **AR**51, [traɪ'ænčələ]; **OK**18, [traɪ'jæntlə]; **CA**53, [traɪ'ænčulə]; (Qu. R21, . . *Other kinds of stinging insects*) Infs **CA**136, **OK**13, [tə'ræntələ]; **TX**68, [tə'rænčələ]; **CA**191, ['trænčələ] hawk; **CA**105, [traɪ'æntlə].

tarantula hawk n Also *tarantula (hawk) wasp, tarantula killer* [See quot 1947] A pompilid wasp of the genus *Pepsis* or *Hemipepsis.* Also called **spider hawk**

1862 *Friend* 35.391 **TX,** To prevent too great an increase of these large spiders, Providence has created an insect of the wasp family (*Pompilius formosus,* Say) called by Texans the tarantula-killer. **1878** Taylor *Between the Gates* 198 **CA,** The tarantula-hawk . . pounces upon his victim and makes a needle-cushion of him. **1886** Van Dyke *Southern CA* 145, The tarantula-wasp is nearly two inches long, with body of deep brilliant blue and wings of deep orange. **1932** *Sun* (Baltimore MD) 8 June 9/1 **cTX** (*Hench Coll.*), A large wasp, known . . as a "tarantula hawk," was victor over a tarantula in a battle. **1947** Carr *Desert Parade* 65 **SW,** Tarantula wasp, tarantula "hawk". . . Its business in life, among other things, is to pounce upon trap-door and tarantula spiders, often much larger than itself, stinging and thus paralyzing them quickly, then removing these motionless but still living spiders to its own burrow to serve as food for its young. **1970** *DARE* (Qu. R21, . . *Other kinds of stinging insects*) Inf **CA**191, Tarantula hawk. **1980** Milne–Milne *Audubon Field Guide Insects* 840, Tarantula hawks are . . found in the Southwest. **2000** *DARE* File—Internet **Desert SW,** *Tarantula Hawk Wasp.* . . Its dark black body shines with a metallic look, providing sharp contrast with its bright orange wings. **2003** *NADS Letters* **cAZ** (as of c1960), In Sedona, AZ, I heard members of my family refer to a rather large wasp as a *tarantula hawk.*

tarantula juice n **West** *hist* Low-grade or adulterated whiskey.

1861 Burton *City Saints* 30 **West,** He [=a teamster] can do nothing without whiskey, which he loves to call tarantula-juice, strychnine, red-eye, corn-juice, Jersey-lightning, leg-stretcher, "tangle-leg," and many other hard and grotesque names. **1861** *Harper's New Mth. Mag.* 21.147 **NV,** We found a large party assembled . . without much to eat and but little to drink, except old-fashioned tarentula-juice, "warranted to kill at forty paces." **1877** Wright *Big Bonanza* 20 **NV,** The liquid refreshment furnished these miners by Nick was probably the first of that popular brand of whisky known as "tarantula juice" ever dispensed within the limits of Virginia City. **1889** Nelson *50 Yrs.* 126 **West,** "Tarantula juice" is two quarts of alcohol, a few burnt peaches, a plug of black tobacco, put in a keg and filled up to five gallons of water. This concoction was a great favourite with both trappers and Indians.

tarantula killer See **tarantula hawk**

tarantula spider n Cf **hunting spider**

Prob a thin-legged **wolf spider** (*Pardosa* spp); see quot.

1901 Fountain *Gt. Deserts* 103 **LA**, In my garden at New Orleans there was a banana plant. . . [T]hese . . bananas were much infested with what are locally called tarantula spiders, which harboured amongst the clusters of fruit . . [and] the leaves. The spiders, with bodies not bigger than a pea, had legs three inches long. . . . They were very nimble and very venomous, their bite causing a large and painful swelling, with feverish symptoms of the system. They are much dreaded by children, and not without reason; but fortunately they rarely infest houses. . . The spiders . . are hunters, and spin no web. . . . They are nocturnal in their habits, hiding away during the day.

tarantula wasp See **tarantula hawk**

tarapin See **terrapin**

tarba See **taba**

tar baby n [From the contrivance of this name by which Brer Rabbit is trapped in the folk tale popularized by Joel Chandler Harris]

1 also *tarheel:* A Black person; see quots. *derog*

1894 *Outlook* 22 Dec 1087 **LA**, I wonder what sort o' white folks dis here tar-baby o' mine done strucken in wid, anyhow? **1919** Kyne *Capt. Scraggs* 243 **CA**, I will scheme up a fittin' form of vengeance on them two tar babies [=Fijians]. **1942** Berrey–Van den Bark *Amer. Slang* 385.17, *Negro child.* . . tar baby. **1947** Lewis *Kingsblood* 348 **MN**, "I didn't know she was a tar-baby." . . "Don't be so dumb. Can't you see it by her jaw?" **1965–66** *DARE* (Qu. HH28, *Names and nicknames . . Negro*) Infs **GA**6, **MS**1, Tar baby; (Qu. HH29b) Inf **SC**3, Tar baby—an especially black Negro. **1970** Tarpley *Blinky* 265 **neTX**, Teasing and derogatory names for Negroes. . . *Other responses* . . tar heels. **1985** Rattray *Advent. Dimon* 33 **Long Is. NY** (as of c1890), Most of these Montauks so-called are no more Indian than I am, or at least not much more, and some of them is real tarbabies. **1986** Pederson *LAGS Concordance,* 1 inf, **cAL**, Tar baby—term for a black; *(Negro)* 1 inf, **csTX**, Tar baby. **2004** *DARE* File—Internet, Some of Kinky's un-PC rambling . . start [sic] to get a little out of hand here. It grows old to hear the same "I'm a Jew so it's okay to drop asides about tar babies, watermelons, and spics," stuff over and over.

2 =**nigger baby 1.**

1950 Prince *S. Heaven* 221 **NC**, There were all kinds of licorice shapes, "Tar Babies," and Teddy bears [etc]. **1975** King *S. Ladies & Gentlemen* 2 **Sth**, The sign on the counter read: *tar babies: 20¢ lb.* Inside the bin was a mountain of little licorice candies shaped like black children. Everyone privately called them "nigger babies." **2004** *DARE* File—Internet **AL**, R.V. . . And Tar Babies—you remember those little black licorice candies? D.V. Except they weren't called Tar Babies. We called 'em "Nigger Babies"—and that was the brand name of the candy!

3 See quot.

2000 Shores *Tangier Is.* 236 **Chesapeake Bay**, We stopped to get a *tar baby* (also *black baby;* refers to Coca-Cola, which years ago came in what looked like a black bottle; no longer current).

tar bowl See **tar bucket 2**

tar bucket n

1 A tagalong. [In ref to the tar bucket that typically hung beneath the rear of a wagon]

[**1909** *RR Trainman* 26.964, Do not be a tar bucket and hang on the coupling pole or walk; but be a willing and conscientious worker.] **1915** *DN* 4.210 **NE**, *Tarbucket,* same meaning as *tag-tail.* The terms are often used together. "A tarbucket tag-tail." **1919** *DN* 5.65 **NM**, *Tarbucket,* a tag-tale [sic], a hanger on. "I hate to go as a tar-bucket.'[?] **1960** Bailey *Resp. to PADS 20* **KS** (*Somebody who always follows along behind: "He's an awful _____."*) A tar-bucket was only a person (usually, I think, a boy) who accompanied a dating couple and was unwelcome. [**1964** in 1971 *Van Wert Times-Bulletin* (OH) 22 June 28/7, Fastened to the rear hounds of these wagons was a tar bucket. . . From these containers arose this old saying: "You might go along and hang on for a tar bucket."] **1967–70** *DARE* (Qu. Y9, *Somebody who always follows along behind others: "His little brother is an awful _____."*) Infs **KS**6, **WV**14, 16, Tar bucket.

2 also *tar bowl,* ~ *pot:* =**scoter.** [See quot 1956]

1876 *Lippincott's Mag. Pop. Lit. & Sci.* 18.233 **DE, MD**, Pied, surf, velvet and scoter ducks (the latter known as "tarpot"). **1923** *U.S. Dept.*

Ag. Misc. Circular 13.27 **MD, IL**, *Scoters.* . . *Collective Vernacular Names.* . . *In local use.* . . Tar-buckets, tar-pots. **1955** *AmSp* 30.182, The scoters . . have names referring to their black color, hardiness, and inedibility, all in one combination, such as . . *bucket* (probably short for *tar bucket,* Md.), *tar-bowl* (Delaware River), and *tarpot* (Del., Md., Wis., Ill.)

3 in exclam phr *your foot in the tar bucket:* See quot.

1996 *DARE* File **cSC** (as of 1950s), My mother, rather than using expressions less genteel, would sometimes say to me, "Your foot in the tar bucket!" Up here [=WI] you might say, "Bullshit!" The expression means "You are not telling the truth," but it could also mean "Go to hell!"

tar bush n Cf **tarweed**

Any of var aromatic shrubs native to the southwestern US such as a **yerba santa,** but esp **mountain misery 1** or *Flourensia cernua.* For other names of the latter see **blackbrush 1, hojase, varnish bush**

1870 Todd *Sunset* 140, Over the hills, and far up too, grows a little bush, called the "Tar Bush," with a beautiful leaf; but it sticks to and defiles whatever touches it. **1884** Miller *Dict. Engl. Names of Plants* 134, Tar-bush, Californian. *Eriodictyon californicum.* **1896** *Jrl. Amer. Folkl.* 9.186 **CA**, *Chamaebatia foliolosa,* . . tar bush, tar weed. **1902** *Out West Mag.* Oct 452 **SW**, Then there were the innumerable cacti . . , and the tar bush, the greasewood, *ocatilla,* mountain mahogany. **1923** Davidson–Moxley *Flora S. CA* 180, *Mountain Misery. Tar-bush.* . . An erect, malodorous shrub with glandular-pubescent foliage. . . *C[hamaebatia] australis.* **1931** U.S. Dept. Ag. *Misc. Pub.* 101.55, *Chamaebatia foliolosa* . . , also known as . . tar-bush, . . is a low, . . resinous, odorous, evergreen shrub. . . indigenous to the Sierra Nevada of California. *Ibid* 165, *Tar-bush (Flourensia cernua)* . . is a resinous, thick-leaved shrub . . ranging from western Texas to southern Arizona and Mexico. **1945** Benson–Darrow *Manual SW Trees* 349, *Flourensia cernua.* . . *Tar bush.* . . Mesas and slopes, often on limestone soils, in the desert and the desert grassland. **1949** *Chicago Tribune* (IL) 29 Feb 30 *(DA),* Cedar and mesquite alone are costing Texas ranchers 115 million dollars a year. Add the sage and cactus, and the . . blue oak, creosote, tarbush . . and prickly pear and the toll is terrific. **1957** Jaeger *N. Amer. Deserts* 270, *Tar bush. Flourensia cernua.* Resinous, bitter-tasting shrub from 3 to 6 feet high with nodding yellow heads of flowers. **1985** Dodge *Flowers SW Deserts* 83, *American Tarbush.* . . *Flourensia cernua.* . . Arizona and Texas deserts. . . The leaves have a hoplike odor and a bitter flavor unpalatable to cattle.

tar candy n Cf **tar baby 2**

c1960 *Wilson Coll.* **csKY**, *Tar candy.* . . Nickname for liquorice candy.

tar-coat See **tear-blanket b**

tard See **tire** v

tare See **tar** n[1]

tared See **tear** B1

tarentula See **tarantula**

tare-up See **tear-up**

tarflower n

A shrub (*Bejaria racemosa*) native chiefly to the pinelands of Florida, Georgia, and Alabama. Also called **flycatcher 4b**

1897 Chapman *Flora Southern U.S.* 288, *[Bejaria] racemosa.* . . Tar-Flower. **1939** FWP *Guide FL* 370 **cwFL**, Pinkish-white tar flowers color the clearings in spring and summer. **1953** Greene–Blomquist *Flowers South* 86, *Tar-flower.* . . is one of the most conspicuous flowering shrubs of the Fla. pinelands. . . The buds and calyces are sticky and catch small insects. **1976** Fleming et al. *Wild Flowers FL* 36, Tarflower grows in sandy soils throughout the coastal plain area from Florida to Georgia.

targa n Cf **talpa**

=**catalpa B2.**

1969 *DARE* FW Addit **seGA**, ['tɑrgɐʔ ˌwɚm]—a kind of caterpillar, as thick as a finger, 3″ long, various colors, spotted, white; used for fish bait.

target n [Abbr for *target rifle*]

A small-bore rifle.

1923 *DN* 5.223 **swMO**, Target. . . A small caliber rifle. **1953** Randolph–Wilson *Down in Holler* 158 **Ozarks**, A target is not a mark to shoot at, but a rifle of small caliber, such as that used in target shooting. "Fetch me the target out of the wagon," a man shouted to his wife, "there's a squirrel in this here tree." **1968–69** *DARE* (Qu. P37a, *Nicknames for a rifle*) Inf **IN**51, Target; **MO**32, Targets—both husband and wife vouch for this term.

target-arse bird n
=**purple gallinule.**

1945 McAtee *Nomina Abitera* 33 **SC**, Purple Gallinule. . . Target-arse bird.

tarheel n Also *tarheeler*

1 A **poor White 1,** esp from the piney woods of North Carolina; a rustic person; any North Carolinian—sometimes applied loosely to people from other parts of the southeastern US. [Presumably in allusion to the importance of tar production in this region, like the earlier-attested nicknames *tar-boiler* (*DA* 1845 →) and *tar-burner* (*DA* 1775 →)] Cf **hoosier B1a, b**

1846 *Emancipator* (Boston MA) 21 Oct 101, There are at this moment at least as many poor whites in the slave states as there are slaves, who are hardly less miserable than the slaves themselves. . . They are never spoken of without some contemptuous epithet. "Red shanks," "Tar heels," &c., are the names by which they are commonly known. The slaveholders look with infinite contempt upon these poor men—a feeling which they cherish for poor men every where. **1863** *Weekly Std.* (Raleigh NC) 3 June [2]/2 (newspaperarchive.com), The troops from other States call us "Tar Heels." I am proud of the name, as tar is a sticky substance, and the "Tar Heels" stuck up like a sick kitten to a hot brick, while many others from a more oily State slipped to the rear, and left the "Tar Heels" to stick it out. **1865** (1867) Moore *Anecdotes* 441, In the command the North Carolinians were better known as the 'Tar heels,' perhaps from their tenacity of purpose as well as their having been enlisted in the piny woods of the old North State. **1878** Eggleston in *Scribner's Mth.* 15.770, Nancy Kirtley was a flower of that curious poor-whitey race which is called "tar-heel" in the northern Carolina, "sand-hiller" in the southern, "corn-cracker" in Kentucky [etc]. **1880** *NY Times* (NY) 3 Sept 4, The ignorant "Tar Heel" of North Carolina, who is making money in the business of illicit distilling of whisky, cannot possibly be made to understand that the officers of the Republic are other than simply his enemies. **1899** *Congressional Record* 26 Jan 32.2.1078 **NC**, [This] amendment we Tar Heels, or a large majority of us, do most heartily commend. **1899** Rahley *The Tar-Heeler's Dream: Characteristic March and Two Step* [title]. **1928** *Builder* 14.264 **NC**, No good "Tar Heeler" figures on living out his allotted span and dying without having been raised to the degree of Master Mason. **1958** McCulloch *Woods Words* 191 **Pacific NW**, *Tar heel*—A name carelessly given to loggers from any southeastern state, not limited to North Carolina. **1966–70** *DARE* (Qu. HH1, *Names and nicknames for a rustic or countrified person*) Inf **AL**11, Hoosier, tarheel; **MD**9, Tarhill [sic]—from South Carolina; (Qu. HH18, *Very insignificant or low-grade people*) Inf **WA**30, Tarheels; (Qu. HH28, . . *People of foreign background*) Inf **WA**3, Tarheels—from Carolinas; (Qu. HH29b, . . *People of mixed blood—part Negro*) Inf **IN**39, Touch of the tarbrush, tarheel; (Qu. HH31, *Somebody who is not from your community, and doesn't belong*) Inf **NJ**69, Tarheel—born Carolina. **1986** Pederson *LAGS Concordance,* 1 inf, **swGA**, Tarheels—from one of the Carolinas; (Caucasian) 1 inf, **cwGA**, Tarheels—people from North Carolina, neutral; (Poor whites) 1 inf, **ceTN**, Tarheel—call a person who left the door open; 1 inf, **seGA**, Tarheels—from North Carolina; (A rustic) 2 infs, **csAL, csMS**, Tarheel—from North Carolina. **1996** *SouthCoastToday* (New Bedford MA) 13 Aug (Internet) **sMA**, "It's the first one that big I've seen up here, but you catch a lot of them off North Carolina," said Frankie Adams, . . a native Tar Heeler. **2004** *DARE* File—Internet **NC**, He knows he'll got [sic] clobbered in the senatorial race in my state and his, North Carolina. We "tarheels" have his number.

2 A turpentine worker.

1966 *DARE* Tape **GA**7, If you see a feller that works it, you call him . . a tarheel . . a tarheeler. **1986** Pederson *LAGS Concordance (A rustic)* 1 inf, **csGA**, Tarheels—live in the swamps, work turpentine.

3 See **tar baby 1.**

taring See **tire** v

tar kiln n Usu |ˈtɑ(r)ˌkɪl|; also |ˈtɑrˌkil, ˈtɑ(r)ˌkɪln| Pronc-spp *tar keel, ~ kill, tarkle*

a A structure used for the destructive distillation of resinous

pine wood, usu consisting of a mound-shaped stack of wood covered with earth, built on a surface that is shaped so that the tar produced as the mound burns is collected and conducted outside the kiln; hence n *tar-kiln bed* prob the base on which a tar kiln is built.   **scattered, but esp NC**

1665 in 1899 Springfield MA *First Century* 2.218, There is granted . . Tenne acres of land . . a little beyond where the Tar kilne was. **1743** Catesby *Nat. Hist. Carolina* 2 [app] ii, Likewise the Smoke of the Tar-Kilns contribute [sic] not a little to deceive Strangers, and possesses them with an ill Opinion of the Air of *Carolina*. **1766** in 1916 Mereness *Travels* 484 **sLA**, We saw several Smokes . . which we were told by our Pilot was as many Tar Kilns. **1812** in 2004 *DARE* File—Internet **seNC**, I wish my executor to sell the lightwood heaped together for the purpose of tar kill, two guns [etc]. **1837** Wetmore *Gaz. MO* 281, He became initiated in . . an acquaintance with whiskey and tar-kilns. **1857** *Putnam's Mag.* 10.329 **NC**, Wal! I'll be smoked in a tar-kill, ef they ain't jest like anybody else, arter all. **1863** *Scientific Amer.* 21 Feb 119 **NC**, In building a tar kiln a small circular mound of earth is first raised, declining from the circumference to the center, where a cavity is formed, communicating by a conduit with a shallow ditch surrounding the mound. Upon this foundation the split sticks are stacked to the height of ten or twelve feet. The stack is then covered with earth as in making charcoal, and the fire applied through an opening in the top. As this continues to burn with smoldering heat, the wood is charred, and the tar flows into the cavity in the center, and thence by the conduit into vessels sunk to receive it. **1864** [see **tar** A]. **1883** *Hist. Tioga Co. PA* 345 **cnPA**, Tar Kilns—In 1838 Isaac Van Zile burned two kilns of tar by the roadside in front of the residence of O.S. Kimball. **1894** *DN* 1.334 **NJ**, *Tar kiln:* place where tar is tried out of pine knots. **1904** (1913) Johnson *Highways South* 293 **NC**, The "sto'keeper" . . said that just where I would find a tar-kiln at that time was uncertain. **1946** *PADS* 6.30 **eNC**, *Tarkle bed; tarkill bed.* . . A tarkiln. Pamlico. Common.

b in phr *smoke like a tar kiln* (or *kettle, pot, wagon*): To emit thick smoke; to smoke tobacco a great deal.   **chiefly S Midl, Gulf States**   See Map

1834 in 1870 *Atlantic Mth.* 26.340 **VA**, Three shot towers . . , the Washington monument . . , and the gas-works smoking like a mountain-sized tar-kiln—are the objects my eye singled out. **1856** in 1931 *KS Hist. Qrly.* 1.30, It dident smoke like a tar kiln, as old Alley said it would. **1901** Burleson *Life & Writings* 88 **TX**, Others stood in the doors and filled the windows, but all smoking like a tar kiln. **1965–70** *DARE* (Qu. DD9b, *Of a person who smokes a great deal* . . "He smokes like a _____.") 13 Infs, **chiefly S Midl, Gulf States,** Tar kiln [ˈtɑ(r)ₒkɪl, ˈtɑrₒkɪl]; **TX**35, [ˈtɔrkɪl]; **GA**77, [ˈtɑrˌkil]; **NC**67, [ˈtɑrˌkɪəl]; **NY**163, [tɑrkɪln]; **TX**18, [ˈtɑrˌkɪln]; **VA**87, [tɑ] kiln; [**TN**16, Tar till;] **NC**35, Tar kettle. **2004** *DARE* File—Internet, I have a 2001 lexus . . and it smoked like a tar kill when started in the morning. *Ibid,* After I finally got it running it smoked like a tar pot. *Ibid,* A brand new engine with new everything will smoke like a tar wagon. *Ibid* **TX**, Erica smokes like a tar keel.

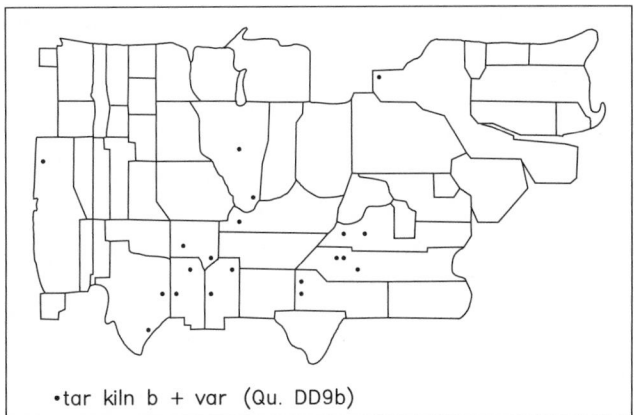

•tar kiln b + var (Qu. DD9b)

tar kiln bed See **tar kiln a**

tarkle See **tar kiln**

tarkle witch See **turtle witch**

tar knot n

A resinous pine knot.

1890 *Congressional Record* 23 June 21.7.6393 **NC,** Burn some North Carolina tar-knots down there. That will destroy your malaria. **1931** (1965) Knittle *Early Palatine Emigration* 174 **NY,** As early as June 16, 1711, Sackett was using horses and wagons rented from Livingston to bring in tar knots for making tar. **1966–70** DARE (Qu. T8, *Joints of pine wood that burn easily and make good fuel*) Infs **IN**35, 73, Tar knots; [**VA**38, Tar lighters; **GA**7, Tar face].

tarnacious adj, adv   Also sp *tarnashus, tarnatious*

=**tarnation** adj, adv; hence adv *tarnaciously.*

1836 (1955) *Crockett Almanacks* 66 **wTN,** They scratched her backsides so tarnaciously they've never itched since. **1859** Taliaferro *Fisher's R.* 44 **nwNC** (as of 1820s), In all the "tight fits" and "tarnatious snarls" he got into, he would outfight, outquarrel, or outwit. **1964** *Mt. Life* 40.1.54 **sAppalachians,** She has "laid off for to ricollect not to whup so tarnashus all-fard hard." **1995** Brophy Coll. 76 **swMO** (as of c1960), *Tarnacious* . . the adjectival form of *tarnation.*

tarnal adj   [Var of *eternal*]   **chiefly NEng; less freq S Midl**
Infernal; damned, damnable—usu used as an intensifier; rarely superl *tarnalest;* also advs *tarnal(ly)* damnably; very much, extremely; n *tarnal* the devil—usu used as a mild oath.

1790 Tyler *Contrast* 29 **MA,** The snarl headed curs fell a-kicking and cursing of me at such a tarnal rate, that I vow I was glad to take to my heels. *Ibid* 67, Laugh by rule! Well, I should like that tarnally. **1836** (1955) *Crockett Almanacks* 44 **wTN,** He heard Jackson making a tarnal strange noise. **1839** *S. Lit. Messenger* 5.432 **ME,** I looked round towards the shore, and there was the tarnalest great overgrown bear that ever I seed in my life. **1846** in 1953 *AmSp* 28.142 **IN,** There was a dozen wagons follerin arter her [=a locomotive], and to save her tarnal black, smoky, noisey neck, she couldn't get clear of them. **1904** *DN* 2.428 **Cape Cod MA,** *Tarnal.* . . For eternal, used to express impatience and dislike. 'There's that tarnal peddler again.' **1905** *DN* 3.22 **cCT,** *Tarnal.* . . Eternal. **1907** *DN* 3.208 **nwAR,** *Tarnal.* . . Confounded. **1911** Shute *Plupy* 32 **NH,** This tarnal son of yours got me this mawnin' to fix him a stick for firin' apples. **1914** *DN* 4.81 **ME, nNH,** *Tarnal.* . . Very, extremely—pejorative, for the most part. **1921** Thorp *Songs Cowboys* 71 **TX,** And I've had a lively russle with a tarnal grizzly bear. **1930** Shoemaker *1300 Words* 61 **cPA Mts** (as of c1900), *Tarnal*—The eternal, an ejaculation. **1943** *LANE* Map 600 *(Shucks! Botheration!)* **NEng,** The word *tarnal,* frequently recorded as an independent exclamation, was offered in a few cases as an adjective, in phrases such as *that tarnal thing!* (equivalent to *that damned thing!*): . . [7 infs, Tarnal]; cf . . ['juᶜw owł 'taˆ·nəł], addressed to a person [1 inf, neMA]. **1947** Botkin *Treas. New Engl. Folkl.* 9, He swore they got so tarnal proud,/ They couldn't do without him. *Ibid* 851, And we didn't care one tarnal bit / For any king or minister. **1959** *VT Hist.* 27.162, *Tarnal.* . . Very. "He was so tarnal mad." . . Rare. **1995** Brophy Coll. 75 **swMO** (as of c1960), *Tarnal.* [E]ternal, everlasting, confounded (mild epithet).

tarnashus   See **tarnacious**

tarnation n, exclam   [Engl dial (though attested earlier in US); blend of **tarnal** + *damnation* or **darnation**]   Cf **thunderation, timenation**
Used alone or in var combs as a euphem for *hell, damnation.*

1790 Tyler *Contrast* 68 **MA,** Tarnation! That's no laughing matter though. **1838** *Hesperian* 1.272 **KY,** Hallo, youngster! What in tarnation are you arter? **1871** Logan *Mimic World* 192, I'd see them in tarnation before I'd take the oath. **1905** *DN* 3.22 **cCT,** *Tarnation.* . . An oath. **1906** *DN* 3.160 **nwAR,** *Tarnation, interj.* Exclamation of anger. **1914** [see **tarnation** adj, adv]. **1934** Faulkner in *Sat. Eve. Post* 10 Feb 76 **MS,** We hadn't no more than turned towards the door, a-asking one another what in tarnation hit could be, . . when hit come busting onto the porch like a harrycane. **1938** Rawlings *Yearling* 49 **nFL,** Git to tarnation! **1942** McAtee *Dial. Grant Co. IN* 64 (as of 1890s), *Tarnation* . . euphemistic swear word, but it did not necessarily mean damnation . . ; might mean fast as in "He ran like all _____" the word was in fact a general purpose intensifier. **1943** *LANE* Map 600, The map shows a great variety of expressions used as exclamations of impatience, irritation, sudden anger and the like. Expressions recorded in two or more communities are here listed in the order of their frequency: *shucks, botheration, tarnation, hell, tarnal, timenation, pshaw* [etc]. **1956** [see **tarnation** adj, adv]. **1958** Humphrey *Home from the Hill* 41 **neTX,** George said, "Oh, tarnation!" We had learned to use innocent cuss words in his presence. **1959** *VT Hist.* 27.162, *What in tarnation!* . . Rare. **1965–70** DARE (Qu. NN8a, *Exclamations of annoyance or disgust:* "Oh _____. I've lost my glasses again.") Infs **KY**84, **MI**108, Tarnation;

(Qu. NN26a, Weakened substitutes for 'hell': "Oh _____!") Infs **GA**31, **MA**98, **OH**59, 76, Tarnation; (Qu. NN26b, . . "Go to _____!") Inf **IL**75, Tarnation; (Qu. NN26c, . . "What the _____!") Infs **FL**16, **ID**6, **MI**10, **NY**230, **NC**41, **OK**48, Tarnation; **CA**170, In tarnation. **2001** *Syracuse Herald–Jrl.* (NY) [13 July Editorial page]/4 (newspaperarchive.com), Why in tarnation did the person who wrote the article feel the need to inject the Jenna Bush incident?

tarnation adj, adv   [Engl dial (though attested earlier in N Amer); cf **tarnation** n, exclam]   Cf **tarnacious**
Used as a euphem for *damned, damnably.*

1783 (1823) Thacher *Military Jrl.* 432 **NEng,** The tarnation fools . . call it a chappeau. **1790** Tyler *Contrast* 66 **MA,** What the rattle makes you look so tarnation glum? **1832** *Political Examiner* (Shelbyville KY) 8 Dec 4/1, I kind a recon none of you ever heard of Deby Snook, caze its a tarnation great secrete. **1836** in 1956 Eliason *Tarheel Talk* 299 **cNC,** So tarnation mean. **1838** Kettell *Yankee Notions* 123, Hannah Downer is apt to be tarnation smart sometimes. **1874** (1937) Nichols *40 Yrs.* 66 **NEng,** [Yankee terms:] An old fashioned Yankee. . . talks of "spunkin' up to an all-fired, tarnation slick gall, clean grit, I tell yeou neow." **1914** *DN* 4.81 **ME, nNH,** *Tarnation, adv.* Same as above [= *tarnal*]. Also used as an exclamation of annoyance, etc. **1932** Tooné *Yankee Slang* 35, *Tarnation:* Expletive—that's too tarnation troublesome. **1945** Partridge *January Thaw* 167 **wCT,** That tarnation pink carpet that's on 'em. It's too soft, too deep. Catches my heels every time I try to come down. **1956** McAtee *Some Dialect NC* 45, *Tarnation:* n., adj., and adv. Euphemistic swear-word and general-purpose intensifier. *Dial. and Slang.* **1965** DARE (Qu. LL37, . . "I was so _____ mad.") Inf **MA**58, Tarnation.

tarnatious   See **tarnacious**

taro n
Std: a food plant *(Colocasia esculenta)* cultivated for the rootstocks, leaves, and stems.   Also called **dasheen, elephant's ear 2**

tarpaulin n   Usu |ˈtɑ(r)ˈpɔlɪn, ˈtɑ(r)pələn|; also |₍ₒ₎tɑrˈpolɪən, ₍ₒ₎tɑrˈpoljən, ˌtɑˈpolɪəm| Pronc-spp *taplin, tarpaullion, tarpoleon, tarpolian, tarpolion, tarpollyon;* for addit varr see quots   [The non-std forms perh continue archaic *tarpaulian* (*OED2* →1719) which, however, is attested only in the sense "(pertaining to) a sailor." Cf also **blasphemious, mischievous**]
Std senses, var forms.

1881 *Sat. Herald* (Decatur IL) [17 Sept 7]/3 (newspaperarchive.com), The tarpolion and light arrangement was good. **1903** *DN* 2.333 **seMO,** *Tarpaulin.* . . Pronounced tarpoleon. This remarkable pronunciation is universal on southern rivers where tarpaulin covers are much used. **1907** *DN* 3.237 **nwAR,** *Tarpaulin.* . . Pronounced tarpoleon (tarpolion). **1921** Thorp *Songs Cowboys* 149 **NM, TX,** And take this old "tarpoleon"/ Too thin to shield my frame. **1930** (1935) Porter *Flowering Judas* 70 **TX,** He can wear your tarpaullion coat. **1931** *AmSp* 6.227 **seNE,** The word "tarpaulin" finds itself curiously pronounced among farmers in southeast Nebraska. Most of them avoid pronouncing the whole word by saying "tarp" or "canvas," but in a show-down I have seldom heard anything but "tarpoleon." This pronunciation has also been reported to me from the opposite corner of the state. **1933** *AmSp* 8.1.30 **nwTX** [Ranch diction], *Tarpoleon.* A tarpaulin; sometimes called *tarp,* never tarpaulin. **1941** in 1944 ADD 624 **WV,** [tɑrˈpolɪən]. Only pron. heard. **1942** Hall *Smoky Mt. Speech* 65 **wNC, eTN,** *Tarpaulin* is [taɚˈpoulɪən]. **c1960** Wilson Coll. **csKY,** *Tarpaulin* is regularly /ˌtɑrˈpolɪən/. **1962** Faulkner *Reivers* 71 **MS,** You laid there under that tarpollyon all the time and let me get out in the mud. **a1966** in 2004 DARE File—Internet **NYC** (as of 1929), A neighborhood youth would climb the . . stairs with a 100-pound block of ice . . wrapped in a tarpaulin (pronounced tarpoleon to rhyme with Bonaparte). **1968** DARE FW Addit **nwLA,** *Tarpaulin*—[ˌtɑrˈpouljən]. "Tarp" is a recent form, prob since WWII. Common. *Ibid* **LA**23, *Tarpaulin*—[ˌtɑrˈpouljən]. **1969** DARE Tape **KY**35, We . . pile it [=tobacco] up and maybe cover it with tarpaulin [ˌtɑˈpolɪəm]. **1969** DARE FW Addit **KY**6, *Tarpaulin*—[tarˈpoljən]. **1975** Newell *If Nothin' Don't Happen* 88 **nwFL,** We stretched a tarpolean in a little clearing. **1976** Garber *Mountain-ese* 91 **sAppalachians,** *Tarpoliun.* **1979** *NYT Article Letters* **NH,** I had to learn the . . meaning of "taplin," . . [which you throw] over the floor or furniture while painting. **1982** Barrick Coll. **csPA,** *Tarpolian.*

tarpentine   See **turpentine** n, v

tarpin   See **terrapin**

tar plant See **tarweed 1b(5)**

tarpn See **terrapin**

tarpoleon See **tarpaulin**

tarpole wagon n [Etym unknown. The term is often connected with the use of *tar* as a lubricant, but the reference of *pole* in this context has not been satisfactorily explained. *DSME* suggests that *tarpole* is a folk-etym for **tarpaulin**.] **chiefly Midl, SW old-fash**

A primitive heavy-duty wagon; a covered wagon; see quots.

[**1909** *Pioneer Days SW* 144, A great many went [to church] in ox wagons. All the wagons were tar pole or wooden axle.] **1910** *Adams Co. News* (Gettysburg PA) 11 June 8/1, *For Sale . .* two four horse tar pole wagons, three inch tread. **1913** Stewart *Indiana Co. PA* 2.848 (as of c1845), At that time all the material for the making and repairing of tarpole wagons was taken from the woods. **1928** *Progr. Farmer & Farm Woman* 14 Jan 26 **neAL** (as of c1850), I used a covered wagon. . . called a tar-pole wagon—had wooden axles with a notch in the hub to allow the linchpin to work through. Tar was used for axle grease. **1937** *Natl. Geogr. Mag.* 71.302 **MS,** From the Piedmont of the Carolinas and Georgia in the decade of 1815 migrated settlers who. . . carved plow-stocks . . and built their "tarpole" wagons—so called because the center poles were greased with tar to make it easier for the oxen to drag them. **1937** in 2004 *DARE* File—Internet **OK,** I was born in Hunt County, Texas, February 20, 1867. We moved to the Indian Territory in 1869 in a tar-pole wagon. The wagon had no thimbles nor skeen [*DARE* Ed: = **skein**] but ran on wooden axles which were greased with tar which Father took out of pine trees. **1939** *Hall Coll.* **eTN,** Axle tree of tarpole wagons made out of hickory; no /skins/ [*DARE* Ed: =**skeins**] over it. **1944** *Gettysburg Times* (PA) 15 Mar 3/5, [Advt:] *Wagons— . .* 2-horse with bed: 2-horse tarpole: three 2-horse spring. **1967** *DARE* (Qu. L13, *The kind of wagon used for carrying hay*) Inf **TN16,** Tarpole wagon—old-fashioned; make tar in a "kittle" and grease wagon with it. **1973** in 1982 *Barrick Coll.* **csPA,** Tarpole wagon—Conestoga wagon, covered with poles and tarp. Uncommon.

tarpolian, tarpolion, tarpollyon See **tarpaulin**

tarpon n[1] Cf **tourist tarpon**

Std: a large saltwater game fish (*Megalops atlantica*) chiefly of South Atlantic and Gulf of Mexico waters. Also called **grande écaille, jewfish 2, silverfish 1, silver king, silverside(s) 4**

tarpon n[2] See **terrapin**

tar pot n

1 See quot. Cf **tar baby 1**

1944 *AmSp* 19.174 **MD,** In the Baltimore of my youth *pickaninny* was not used invidiously, but rather affectionately. So, indeed, was *tar-pot*, also signifying a Negro child.

2 See **tar bucket 2.**

tarrabee See **tarabilla**

tarrapin See **terrapin**

tarred See **tire** v

tarred road n Also *tar road* **chiefly east of Missip R; also MN** See Map Cf **macadam 1, oiled road**

A road surfaced with aggregate coated with or mixed with a bituminous binder.

1904 *Stevens Point Daily Jrl.* (WI) [16 Dec 3]/3 (newspaper-archive.com), Tarred Roads in France. For Banishment of Dust and Preservation of Highways an Effective Process. **1911** *Sandusky Star–Jrl.* (OH) 29 July 5/1, County Commissioners . . went to Toledo Friday to look over tar roads. . . Valuable pointers for work here were discovered. **1915** *Atlanta Constitution* (GA) 21 Jan 9/5, [Advt:] 50-acre dairy, truck farm, 1½ miles Grant Park, tarred road. **1948** *Pottstown Mercury* (PA) 20 Mar 15/8, [Advt:] Located 1 mile southwest of Spring City on tar road. **1950** *WELS* (*Different kinds of unpaved roads*) 1 Inf, **seWI,** Tarred road; (*Roads that are covered with smooth black pavement*) 2 Infs, **cs,seWI,** Tar; (*Other kinds of paved roads*) 1 Inf, **csWI,** Tar. **1965–70** *DARE* (Qu. N21, *Roads that are surfaced with smooth black pavement*) 38 Infs, **chiefly east of Missip R,** Tar; Infs **HI**13, **ME**1, **MI**67, **NJ**60, **RI**6, **SC**26, 57, **VA**78, Tar road; **CT**2, 36, 39, **ME**19, **MN**33, 42, Tarred road; **IN**74, **ME**22, **MN**29, **NC**30, **PA**93, Tarred; (Qu. N23, *Other kinds of paved roads*) Infs **IN**45, **MA**7, 68, 122, **NY**67,

PA66, **RI**1, Tar; **VA**75, Tar road—tar sprayed on gravel; **NC**31, Tarred road; (Qu. N27a, *Names . . for different kinds of unpaved roads*) Inf **OH**63, Tar. **1966** *Post–Std.* (Syracuse NY) 31 July 58/8, [Advt:] 2 creeks, spring, on tar road. **1971** *Daily Kennebec Jrl.* (Augusta ME) 30 Nov 17/3, [Advt:] 200′ frontage on tarred road. **1973** Allen *LAUM* 1.239 **MN, SD** (as of c1950), *Tar road* and *tarred road* turned up in southern Minnesota and on both sides of the Minnesota–Dakota border. **1986** Pederson *LAGS Concordance,* 12 infs, **Gulf Region,** Tar road.

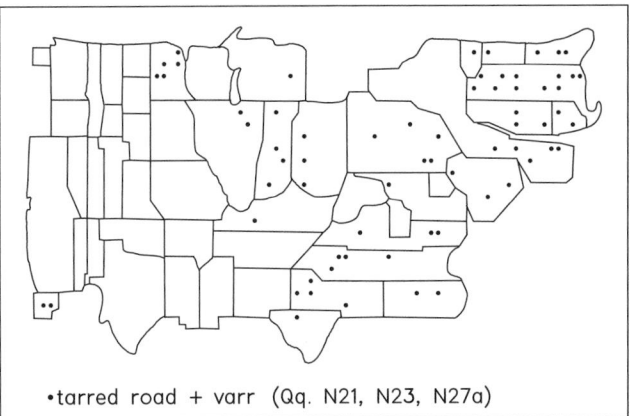

•tarred road + varr (Qq. N21, N23, N27a)

tarrier n [Pronc-sp for *terrier*]

1865 in 1867 Twain *Jumping Frog* 14 **MO,** Well, thish-yer Smiley had rat-tarriers, and chicken cocks. **1893** Shands *MS Speech* 62, *Tarrier* ['tærɪə]. Negro for *terrier*. **1899** (1912) Green *VA Folk-Speech* 439, *Tarrier. . .* Terrier. **1903** *DN* 2.333 **seMO,** *Terrier. . .* Pronounced tarrier. **1907** *DN* 3.237 **nwAR,** *Terrier. . .* Pronounced tarrier. **1917** *DN* 4.398 **neOH,** *Rat tarrier . .* [ræt'tærɪə]. . . Also Ill., IA., Kan. **c1960** *Wilson Coll.* **csKY,** *Terrier* is nearly always /'tærɪə/.

tarrified See **terrify**

tarrified fever See **terrified fever**

tarrify See **terrify**

tar road See **tarred road**

tarruh See **tother**

tarry v [*OED2* tarry v. 4.b 13 . . →; "*arch exc. in U.S.*"] **orig esp NEast; later more widespread** *arch*

To lodge (someplace); to sojourn, abide temporarily. Note: Exx of the sense "linger," as in "Tarry a few minutes longer" or "Don't tarry—we're late" are not included here.

1704 (1825) Knight *Jrls.* 9 **ceMA,** I vissitted the Reverd. Mr. Belcher . . and tarried there till evening, in hopes ye post would come along. **1766** Ingersoll *Letters Stamp-Act* 62 **CT,** I tarried that Night at Mr. Bishop's. **1778** in 1888 Cutler *Life* 1.68 **MA,** I returned to our old quarters and tarried the night. **1816** Pickering *Vocab.* 186, To *Tarry.* To stay, to stop. *New England.* This verb is entirely obsolete in England; and it sounds as strangely to the ear of an Englishman, as *I wist not, I wot not,* and a thousand other antiquated expressions. **1820** Irving *Sketch Book Crayon* 2.351 **NY,** Ichabod Crane . . sojourned, or, as he expressed it, "tarried," in Sleepy Hollow, for the purpose of instructing the children of the vicinity. **1832** in 1936 *UT Geneal. & Hist. Mag.* 27.164 **NY,** May 14. We . . came to the town of Charleston in Vermont; tarried ten days. **1863** in 1889 U.S. War Dept. *War of Rebellion* 1st ser 27.1.723 **OH,** June 15.—Blackburn's Ford to Centreville, 5 miles, where we tarried until Wednesday, June 17. **1875** Twain in *Atlantic Mth.* 35.71 **MO,** He would always manage to have a rusty bolt to scrub while his boat tarried at our town. **1899** (1912) Green *VA Folk-Speech* 439, *Tarry. . .* To stay at a place: "How long do you tarry?" [**c1960** *Wilson Coll.* **csKY,** *Tarry. . .* Stay or wait, sometimes with an idea of staying too long, wearing out one's welcome. [*DARE* Ed: It is not possible to determine whether *stay* in this quot implies "sojourn" or "linger."]]

tarryfied See **terrify**

tarryhoot v, hence vbl n *tarryhooting* Cf **scallyhoot** v

To rush; to gallivant.

1933 Thurber *My Life* 66 **OH,** What was the idea of all them cops tarryhootin' round the house last night? **1940** *Amer. Weekly* (NY NY) 16 June 4/3 **KY,** Her husband was "tarryhootin'" around payin' court to gals on both cricks." *Ibid* 4/4, He took to disappearing and "tarryhootin'" during the ninth year of the marriage. **1950** Moore *Candlemas Bay* 198 **ME,** You're quite a feller for tarryhooting around the woods. **2010** in 2011 *DARE* File—Internet **cVA,** What are you doing in Brazil? . . What does your wife do while you are tarry-hooting about in another country?

tarrypin See **terrapin**

tarvate(d) See **tarvia**

tarve v [Appar *OED2 tirve, tarve* v.² to turn, topple, though the only Brit evidence later than the 16th cent is a single 1824 Scots ex of the form *tirvie*.] *arch*

Tr and intr: To tip, turn.

1895 *DN* 1.394 **Staten Is. NY,** *Tarve:* to turn (trans. and intrans.) to the right or left. "My road tarves off to the eastward." **1899** Garland *Boy Life* 192 **nwIA** (as of c1870s), Say, Link, your stack's tarvin' over. **1917** *DN* 4.401 **neOH,** *Tarve* [tɑrv], *v.t.* and *n.* Same word as *tirve, terve;* cf. O [=*OED*]. The only one I ever heard use the word was a native of R.I. who migrated in 1830, and lived for a time in the Mohawk Valley, N.Y., and later in Western New York. The word may belong to any of these localities. It meant "turn": "You had better tarve your platform a little" = "tilt it down" so as to reap the grain closer to the ground.

tarve n [**tarve** v] *esp* **NEast** *arch*

1 The balance or "hang" (of something to be lifted or maneuvered); a good angle or orientation.

1848 Cooper *Oak-Openings* 1.24 **NY,** "Waal, I can say, I *like* it," answered Gershom, first passing his thumb along the edge of the axe . . ; then swinging the tool, with a view to try its 'hang.' "I can't say much for your axe, *stranger,* for this helve has no tarve to 't, to my mind; but, sich as it is, down must come this elm." **1868** (1869) Roe *Cloud on Heart* 293 **CT,** Then taking a broad grasp there, and stretching the other hand along very knowingly until he thought he had got the right position, [he] just raised him the least, when the doctor called out,—"Stop, stop, my good fellow!" . . "Ay, ay, sir. I wasn't only trying to see if I'd got the true tarve of him." **1900** *New Engl. Mag.* 22.555 **CT,** The massive framework . . rose steadily and swiftly to the perpendicular, and the posts dropped into their mortises, while men on the farther side with long poles "kept the tarve," that is, steadied the frame to prevent a possible overbalancing in that direction. **1917** *DN* 4.401 **neOH,** *Tarve.* . . is reported from Ashtabula Co. as a noun in the sense "proper twist" or "direction"; as, in snaking a log with horses: "Let me get a tarve on it, and then they can pull it."

2 in phr *on the tarve:* See quot.

1910 *DN* 3.437 **wNY,** *Be on the tarve.* . . To be unsteady. "I'm a little on the tarve to-day." Older generation.

tarvia n, freq attrib Also *tarvi, tarv(e)y* [Orig a trademark (registered 1912, first used 1903) for a coal-tar–based road-coating material that was widely advertised in the early decades of the 20th cent; see quot 1919] **chiefly Nth, N Midl, esp MI** See Map

A bituminous material used in road construction to bind or adhere a layer of gravel; a paving material consisting of aggregate mixed with a bituminous binder; a road pavement made with either of these materials; hence verbs *tarvy, tarviate* to surface (a road) with either of these materials; ppl adjs *tarvia'd, tarv(i)ated.*

1907 *Washington Post* (DC) 25 Aug sec S 3/8 **NYC,** It is said that the surface will be covered with tarvia, that the banks will be raised, and that the course will be made the fastest automobile [race]track in the world. **1917** Churchill *Dwelling-Place* 67 **NEng,** The automobiles of the holiday makers swarmed ceaselessly over the tarvia. **1919** *Stars & Stripes* (Paris France) 10 Jan 6/5, [Advt:] *Tarvia Preserves Roads Prevents Dust.* . . Tarvia is a coal-tar preparation for use in constructing new macadam roads or repairing old ones. It reinforces the road-surface and makes it water-proof, dustless, mudless, and proof against motor-trucks. The Barrett Company. **1921** in 2004 *DARE* File—Internet **csKY,** If we had it tarvied all the machines in the country would come to make it a speedway and race track and would kill all our chickens. **1927** *Ibid* **cTX,** That part of said street . . was tarviated or asphalted the first of the week. **1950** *WELS (Roads that are covered with smooth black pavement)* 1 Inf, **seWI,** Tarvia. **1952** FWP *Guide SD* 365, Picture a long, straight tarvia road, shaded by large trees on either side. **1962** Atwood *Vocab. TX* 41, *Paved road.* . . For some reason, *tarv(i)ated road* (one

informant calls it *tarvey*) is confined to Central Texas in the vicinity of Austin. **1965–70** *DARE* (Qu. N21, *Roads that are surfaced with smooth black pavement*) 23 Infs, **chiefly Nth, N Midl, esp MI,** Tarvia; **IN**56, **PA**3, 40, Tarvy; (Qu. N23, *Other kinds of paved roads*) Inf **MI**81, Tarvia; **MI**2, Tarvy. **1967** *DARE* Tape **PA**29, There was two bad roads in there—course, they're all tarvia now. . . You went axle-deep, but today they're all tarvia'd. **a1967** in 1995 *DARE* File **swCT,** [Labels on a rudimentary map:] Dirt Road, Tarvia Road, Concrete Road. **1973** Allen *LAUM* 1.239 **Upper MW** (as of c1950), *Tarvia,* originally a trademark, is the form used by one-fourth of the infs. in both Minnesota and South Dakota. A colloquial variant, *tarvy,* was reported by four infs. in Minnesota and one each in the Dakotas. **1980** *NYT Article Letters* **swIL,** It showed the black of the tarvi (asphalt) road and the black of the twigs. **1986** Pederson *LAGS Concordance,* 1 inf, **ceTX,** Tarvia = blacktop; 1 inf, **csTX,** Tarviated—road, not paved; 1 inf, **csTX,** Tarviated roads—blacktop. **2003** *Princeton Union–Eagle* (MN) 7 Aug (Internet) (as of 1953), The word "tarvia" was used to denote the roads that weren't made of sand. **2003** *Post–Std.* (Syracuse NY) 21 Aug (Internet), What property owners are not allowed to do is lay down tarvia, also known as blacktop, as a cheap way to replace a torn-up sidewalk. [*DARE* Ed: A Lexis–Nexis search of US news turns up 65 recent exx of *tarvia,* all from this newspaper.]

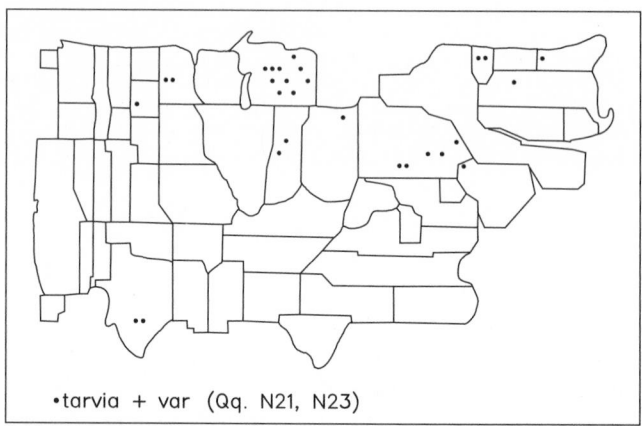

•tarvia + var (Qq. N21, N23)

tar-wadding See **wadding**

tarweed n Cf **tarbush**

1a Any of numerous somewhat resinous or resinous-smelling plants of the western US and esp of California and the Pacific Northwest.

1862 *Atlantic Mth.* 9.172 **CA,** The tar-weed was already thick over her Californian grave. **1872** McClellan *Golden State* 167 **CA,** Blackberries, salmonberries, tar-weed, . . and wild mustard abound all over the coast, valleys, and hill-sides. **1895** *Overland Mth.* (2d ser) 26.102 **CA,** The fragrance of pines and herbs,—sage, thyme, and tarweed,—filled his soul with delight and thanksgiving. **1903** Norris *Responsibilities* 142, The reek of the tar-weed on the Colorado slopes. **1922** Norris *Certain People* 138 **nCA,** The Barbee house was . . set in a waste of crushed dry grass and odorous tar-weed. **1935** Davis *Honey* 169 **OR,** A low hill covered with arrowwood and hazel and tarweed. **1966–70** *DARE* (Qu. S7, *A kind of daisy, bright yellow with a dark center, that grows along roadsides in late summer*) Inf **CA**200, Tarweed; (Qu. S14, . . *Prickly seeds, small and flat, with two prongs at one end, that cling to clothing*) Infs **CA**105, **WA**6, Tarweed; (Qu. S21, . . *Weeds . . that are a trouble in gardens and fields*) Infs **CA**200, **WA**6, Tarweed; (Qu. S26e, *Other wildflowers not yet mentioned; not asked in early QRs*) Inf **CA**65, Tarweed. **1967** Stegner *Little Live Things* 19 **cwCA,** A wall-eyed white horse with . . black feet he had got from wading around in tarweed watched us.

b Spec:

(1) A plant of the California genus *Holocarpha.*

1868 in 1916 Muir *1000 Mile Walk* 209 **CA,** A small unobtrusive plant, *Hemizonia virgata* [=*Holocarpha heermannii*], from six inches to three feet in height, with pale, glandular leaves, suddenly bursts into bloom, in patches miles in extent, like a resurrection of the gold of April. . . The waxy secretion of its leaves and involucres has suggested its grim name of "tarweed," by which it is generally known. **1911** CA Ag. Exper. Sta. Berkeley *Bulletin* 217.1028, *Hemizonia virgata* [=

Holocarpha v.] . . Yellow Tarweed. . . Honey of light yellow color, good flavor and heavy body. This tarweed is a heavy and consistent yielder. **1960** Abrams *Flora Pacific States* 4.184, *Holocarpha virgata*. . . Virgate Tarweed. . . herbage . . strongly resinous and odorous. . . Abundant in hard-baked, valley and foothill soils.

(2) A plant of the genus *Madia.* Also called **mignonette vine 1** For other names of var spp see **gumweed 2, wild coreopsis**

1874 *Amer. Acad. Arts & Sci. Proc.* 9.189 **CA,** *M[adia] capitata* . . the common *Tarweed* of the eastern part of California. **1878** *Amer. Naturalist* 12.605 **CA,** *Madaria elegans* [=*Madia e.*].—The seeds of this species of tar-weed are ground into flour, made into thin cakes, and baked in hot ashes by the California Indians. **1894** *Jrl. Amer. Folkl.* 7.92 **CA,** *Madia sativa,* . . tar-weed. **1898** *Ibid* 11.230 **CA,** *Madia* (sp.), tar weed. **1902** U.S. Natl. Museum *Contrib. Herbarium* 7.395, *Madia densifolia* [=*M. elegans* subsp *d.*] . . An erect, soft-hairy, but only slightly glandular species of tarweed. . . *Madia dissitiflora* [=*M. gracilis*]. . . One of the most typical tarweeds, . . leafy and very viscid throughout. . . The tarry exudation of the easily detachable flower bracts does much damage to clothing and to sheep's wool. **1914** Saunders *With Flowers in CA* 219, I was surprised to see a part of the woodland . . starred with hundreds of lovely daisy-like blooms, yellow-rayed with red centers. Stooping to pick some, I found my hands quickly gummed with a viscid secretion from the plants. . . I had now discovered a . . tarweed. . . It was the species called *Madia elegans,* and as the summer merged into autumn I had an opportunity to extend my acquaintance to half a dozen species both of *Madia* and the kindred genus *Hemizonia.* The latter tribe is exclusively Californian, the flowers often handsome in white or yellow or pink. **1934** Haskin *Wild Flowers Pacific Coast* 373, *Madia sativa.* . . The common tar-weed is such an abundant nuisance in this region that few people recognize its beauty. *Ibid* 374, *Madia glomerata.* . . This abundant tar-weed scents the air over low valley fields with a peculiar semi-acid smell somewhat resembling that of freshly cut rhubarb. **1966** *DARE* FW Addit **WA**10, *Madia*—tarweed. **1973** Hitchcock–Cronquist *Flora Pacific NW* 538, *Madia.* . . Tarweed.

(3) A plant of the genus *Hemizonia.* For other names of var spp see **spikeweed**

1878 *Amer. Naturalist* 12.605 **CA,** *Hemizonia fasciculata,* Tar-weed.— This plant in case of hunger is eaten by the Indians of Southern California after being cooked. . . Its tar-like taste is objected to by some. **1894** *Jrl. Amer. Folkl.* 7.92 **CA,** *Hemizonia pungens,* . . tar-weed. **1896** *Ibid* 9.192 **CA,** *Hemizonia ramossissima,* tar weed. **1898** *Ibid* 11.229 **CA,** *Hemizonia* (sp.), tar weed. **1902** U.S. Natl. Museum *Contrib. Herbarium* 7.394, *Hemizonia luzulaefolia* [=*H. congesta*]. . . The commonest and most prolific representative of the various plants, which on account of their disagreeable exudation, are known as "tarweeds." **1911** CA Ag. Exper. Sta. Berkeley *Bulletin* 217.1028, *Hemizonia fasciculata.* . . Tar-weed. . . Honey dark amber, with strong tarweed aroma. . . The honey is reported to be used largely in the manufacture of chewing tobacco and shoe blacking. **1914** [see **1b(2)** above]. **1961** Thomas *Flora Santa Cruz* 362 **cwCA,** *Hemizonia.* . . Tarweed. Ligules of the ray-flowers yellow.

(4) A **mountain misery 1** (here: *Chamaebatia foliolosa*) native to California.

1873 *Garden* (London) 3.26 **CA,** *Chamaebatia foliolosa.* . . occurs naturally in the hill country of California, where it quite covers the ground, and is named Tarweed by the settlers. **1896** *Jrl. Amer. Folkl.* 9.186 **CA,** *Chamaebatia foliolosa,* . . tar bush, tar weed. **1914** Saunders *With Flowers in CA* 218, *Chamaebatia foliolosa.* . . Anyone walking through the patches of it . . gets his shoes and trousers miserably tarred up with the viscous clothing of the leaves. Sheep and cattle become smeared with the same stuff. . . They call it tarweed, too, which would be good enough except that that name properly belongs to two or three genera of *Compositae,* with similar sticky coats. **1937** U.S. Forest Serv. *Range Plant Hdbk.* B52, Bearmat, also known as . . tarweed, is a low, resinous, heavy-scented, evergreen shrub.

(5) also *tar plant, yellow tarweed:* =**fiddleneck 1.**

1891 CA Ag. Exper. Sta. *Rept. for 1890* 266, The Amsinckias are often called "yellow tar weed," although they are innocent of any tarry matter, but adhere by their hooked bristles. **1914** Georgia *Manual Weeds* 336, *Amsinckia intermedia* [=*A. menziesii* var *i.*] . . Yellow Tarweed. . . An unpleasant hairy weed, with sticky, bristly burs which make it a pest to California wool-growers. **1937** St. John *Flora SE WA & ID* 338, *Amsinckia.* Tar Weed. . . Corolla yellow to orange. **1967**

DARE (Qu. S26d, *Wildflowers that grow in meadows;* not asked in early QRs) Inf **CA**24, Fiddleneck or tar plant—has a yellow flower, grows profusely in fields. **1968** Schmutz et al. *Livestock-Poisoning Plants AZ* 130, *Fiddleneck,* tarweed—*Amsinckia intermedia* and others. Cattle, horses and swine may be poisoned by . . eating large amounts of the seeds of this desert annual. **1973** Hitchcock–Cronquist *Flora Pacific NW* 386, *Amsinckia.* . . Fiddleneck; Tarweed; Fireweed.

(6) =**gum plant 1.**

1900 Lyons *Plant Names* 178, *Grindelia.* . . Gum-plant, Tar-weed. **1936** IL Nat. Hist. Surv. *Wildflowers* 345, *Grindelia squarrosa.* . . The Gum Plant or Tarweed grows on dry banks and prairies from Illinois to Minnesota and Manitoba, south to Texas and Mexico. . . The involucre and upper portions of the stem are exceptionally sticky, giving the plant its common name. **1963** Craighead *Rocky Mt. Wildflowers* 213, *Grindelia squarrosa.* . . Gumplant, Resinweed, Tarweed. . . The heads of this plant, and usually leaves also, are very sticky. **1966** *DARE* Wildfl QR **CO**7, Tarweed—*Grindelia squarrosa.* **1970** Correll *Plants TX* 1570, *Grindelia.* . . Gumweed, Tarweed. Taprooted herbs with leafy stems . . often sticky.

(7) A **blue curls 1** (here: *Trichostema lanceolatum*).

1891 CA Ag. Exper. Sta. *Rept. for 1890* 249, The intensely-scented *Trichostema* (camphor-weed) maintains itself in the . . warmer parts of the State . . defying heat and drought, and playing the part of a "tar-weed" very successfully. **1900** Lyons *Plant Names* 376, *T[richostema] lanceolatum* . ., California, is called Blue Tar-weed. **1902** U.S. Natl. Museum *Contrib. Herbarium* 7.385, *Trichostema lanceolatum.* . . exhales a strong pungent odor, somewhat like that of a mixture of vinegar and turpentine. . . The plant is commonly called blue curls, but it is also known as "vinegar weed" and "tarweed," the latter name being applied to it on account of its sticky exudation. **1911** CA Ag. Exper. Sta. Berkeley *Bulletin* 217.1028, "Vinegar weed" has been applied to a tarweed in the San Joaquin valleys.

(8) A **yerba santa** (here: *Eriodictyon californicum*).

1881 *Can. Pharmaceutical Jrl.* 14.264, *Yerba Santa.* . . is obtained from the region of the Mexican and United States boundary, where by English speaking settlers it is known by the names of . . "tar weed" [etc]. **1902** U.S. Natl. Museum *Contrib. Herbarium* 7.381, *Eriodictyon californicum.* . . The well-known yerba santa . . of California, a dark-green resinous shrub, . . is known under the names . . mountain balm, wild balsam, gum leaves, tar weed.

2 A **waxweed 1** (here: either *Cuphea hyssopifolia* or *C. viscosissima*).

1893 *Jrl. Amer. Folkl.* 6.142 **WV,** *Cuphea petiolata* [=*C. viscosissima*], tar weed. **1929** Pope *Plants HI* 155, *Cuphea hyssopifolia.* . . Clammy *Cuphea* or Tar-weed gets both of its common names from the sticky exudation given out by the glands of the stems when moist with dew or rain. Both names are applicable, the latter being somewhat unsatisfactory as almost every locality has one or more "tar-weeds" of different kinds.

3 =**three-seeded mercury.**

1933 Small *Manual SE Flora* 785, *Acalypha.* . . Three-seeded mercuries. Tar-weeds. Couple-caps.

tarweed canary n

A **goldfinch 1** (here: *Carduelis psaltria*).

1896 *Osprey* 1.29 **cwCA,** Below is a list of "native" tyros' names of some Alameda County birds: . . Arkansas Goldfinch, Tar-weed Canary.

tas See **task**

tasajillo n Also *tasajilla* [MexSpan *tasajillo,* dimin of **tasajo**]

A **prickly pear 1:** usu *Opuntia leptocaulis,* but occas also *O. kleiniae.*

1906 NM Ag. Exper. Station *Bulletin* 60.109, *Tasajilla—Opuntia leptocaulis.* . . The yellow fruited from [sic] is common on the Rio Grande at Laredo. *Ibid* 110, *Tasajilla—Opuntia kleiniae.* . . An open, widely branching shrub 3 to 5 feet high, erect, often growing in tangled thickets but more commonly in isolated impenetrable bunches. . . fruit red. **1929** Dobie *Vaquero* 203 **West,** *Tasajillo* (rat-tail cactus) . . in winter is bizarre and beautiful with a studding of red berries that are fancied by blue topknot Mexican quail and wild turkeys. **1936** Whitehouse *TX Flowers* 77, The pencil cactus or tasajillo (*Opuntia leptocaulis*), conspicuous for its small stems and bright red fruits, is abundant in the state and Mexico. **1967** *DARE* Wildfl QR (Wills-Irwin) Pl.28A [=*Opuntia leptocaulis*] Inf **TX**44, Tasajillo. **1970** Correll *Plants TX* 1091, *Opuntia* leptocaulis. . . Tasajillo. . . Fruit bright-red, fleshy, juicy. . . From Ariz., to N.M., Okla., and w. and s. Tex. . . Opuntia kleiniae. . . Tasajillo. . . Fruit red to green and red, fleshy but only slightly juicy. . . From s. N.M. to Tex. w. of the Pecos River. **1985** Dodge *Flowers SW Deserts* 65, Tasajillo. . . *Opuntia leptocaulis*.

tasajo n Also *tesajo* [MexSpan *tasajo;* see quot 1919] Cf **tasajillo**

A **cactus** n[1] **B1**, usu a **prickly pear 1** (here: *Opuntia leptocaulis*).

1871 *Overland Mth.* 6.555 **TX**, On the Apache Mountains one finds that most singular shrub, the *tasajo*. At a distance, a clump of it looks like a number of green Apache spears planted in the ground, twelve or fifteen feet high. **1919** Raht *Romance* 288 **TX**, Tasajo. Literally "dried" or "jerked" beef. . . Because of the resemblance in shape of the stem of this plant to the long angular strips of meat used for drying, the name became fastened to the plant. . . The plant is a "cereus," probably "Cereus Greggii." **1936** NM Univ. *Biol. Ser.* 4.5.59, Cactus, coyote or turkey, tesajo . . *(Opuntia leptocaulis)*. **1942** Castetter–Bell *Pima & Papago Ag.* 25 **AZ**, Other characteristic chollas of the paloverde belt are the vari-colored or staghorn cholla *(O. versicolor)*, tesajo, . . *(O. leptocaulis)*, the arborescent pencil cholla *(O. arbuscula)*. **1960** Vines *Trees SW* 772, Tasajo Cholla—*Opuntia spinosior*. *Ibid* 773, Tesajo cactus (Tasajillo) . . *Opuntia leptocaulis*. **1975** Lamb *Woody Plants SW* 32, "Tasajo"—*Opuntia spinosior*. *Ibid* 33, Tasajo is found in southwestern New Mexico and in the southeastern quarter of Arizona. **1985** Dodge *Flowers SW Deserts* 65, Tesajo. . . *Opuntia leptocaulis*.

tas'e See **taste A1**

task n Pronc-spp *tas(s)* **GA, SC** *old-fash*

An area of land varying according to local circumstances from one-quarter to three-quarters of an acre; a measure of distance equal to the side of a quarter-acre square.

1786 in 2003 Heuman–Walvin *Slavery Reader* 201 **GA**, One Georgia absentee in 1786 sent a chain "for running out the Tasks" to his plantation manager. "It is 105 feet long," he noted, "and will save a great deal of time in Laying out the field, and do it with more exactness." **1828** (1829) Hall *Travels* 3.219, The [cotton] fields are divided by temporary stakes, into square patches of 105 feet each way, equal to a quarter of an acre. These portions, which are called 'tasks,' are laid off in ridges or beds, five feet apart. **1850** Burke *Reminiscences of GA* 117, In hoeing corn, three tasks are considered a good day's work for a man, two for a woman and one and a half for a boy or girl fourteen or fifteen years old. **1862** in 1906 Pearson *Letters from Port Royal* 78 **SC**, Tirah had planted a task of cow-pease for the Government. **1908** *S. Atl. Qrly.* 7.344 **seSC** [Gullah], A common unit of measure of area . . is a *tass* . . for a hoe-hand generally half-an-acre; for cotton-field hands, three-quarters of an acre; for the rice-field negro, usually a quarter of an acre. **1922** Gonzales *Black Border* 332 **sSC, GA coasts** [Gullah glossary], Tas'—task—a measure of distance as well as of area: 105 feet or 105 feet square. A "tas'," or one-fourth of an acre, being the daily task during slavery on a sea-island cotton plantation, in "listing," "hauling," or hoeing sea-island cotton, a task being frequently completed before noon, when the slave was free for the rest of the day. Used as meaning distance of a shot; as: "My gun kin shoot two tas'"—My gun can kill at 210 feet (70 yards). **1930** Woofter *Black Yeomanry* 92 **seSC**, I jus' try fer plant a tas' [Woofter: ¼ acre]. **1930** Stoney–Shelby *Black Genesis* 104 **seSC**, But Br' Rabbit aint trabble no distance, not so much as a task, before he feel Br' Wolf' hot breat'. **1950** *PADS* 14.66 **SC**, Task. . . 1. A stint of work for a field laborer, especially a hoe-hand; in the rice field, a quarter-acre; in the corn or cotton field, a half-acre. 2. Hence a measure of distance (about 100 ft.). A shotgun will be said "to throw two tas' and kill." Charleston. **1967** *DARE* Tape **SC**43, [Inf:] [We'd get] about seventeen bushels to a row—equals five tasks long. . . [FW:] How long is a task? [Inf:] A task is a hundred and five feet. You get your seventeen bushels from the row. It takes about—a fraction over twenty rows to make an acre, see, so that's a pretty good turnout. [FW:] Would a task be a square piece of land? [Inf:] Well, a task is one hundred and five feet by a hundred and five; that's a fourth of an acre or a task, see. **1968** *DARE* (Qu. L6a, . . *A piece of land under cultivation—less than an acre*) Inf **GA**28, Task would be a quarter of an acre—in "slavery time." **1991** Greene *Praying for Sheetrock* 106 **seGA** [Black], Grandma would give us a tas' [Greene: half acre] of ground to hoe. We work that before breakfast.

tassel n, v Usu |ˈtæsḷ|; also |ˈtɒsḷ|; less freq |ˈtɑsḷ|; rarely |ˈtʌsḷ| Pronc-spp *tawsle, torsul, tossel, tussel;* for addit pronc and sp

varr see quots [*OED2* (at *tassle* n.[1]) records *-o-* spellings from 1609 →. Sheridan (1780) transcribed *tassel* with the *o* of *not,* but most of the later orthoepists recommended the "short *a*" pronc.]

A Forms.

1805 (1905) Clark *Orig. Jrls. Lewis & Clark Exped.* 3.206 **VA**, The womens peticoat is about 15 Inches long made of *arber-vita* or the white Cedar bark wove to a string and hanging down in tossles. **1806** in 1956 Eliason *Tarheel Talk* 319 **NC**, Torsle. **1831** *Ibid* 318 **NC**, Tostles. **1854** in 1995 Bonfield–Morrison *Roxana's* 88 **nwVT**, They [=capes] are large and cut a half round—with collars pointed and a *tussel* on the end of the point. **1856** in 1956 Eliason *Tarheel Talk* 318 **NC**, Tarsels . . torsal. **1887** *Overland Mth.* (2d ser) 10.57 **nAL**, These hyar torsuls . . orter make 'em fetch er power o' money. **1890** *DN* 1.72 **LA**, Tassel (with [ɔ] in the first syllable). **1892** *DN* 1.213 **ceMA**, Tassel. . . My pronunciation was [ˈtɑsl]. *Ibid* 219 **MA**, Tassel. . . The pronunciation [ˈtʌsl] is heard among farmers in Chicopee, Mass. **1893** Shands *MS Speech* 62, Taussle [tɒsl]. . . The ordinary pronunciation of *tassel*. Heard also in Louisiana. **1894** *Century Illustr. Mag.* 47.850, To this day our country people . . preserve the broad vowel of their ancestors: "tossell." **1899** (1912) Green *VA Folk-Speech* 454, Tossel, n. . . Tossel, v. **1903** *DN* 2.334 **seMO**, Tossel, n. and v. **1907** *DN* 3.251 **eME**, Tossel, n. *Ibid* 237 **nwAR**, Tossel, n. **1909** *DN* 3.383 **eAL, wGA**, Tossel, v. and n. . . Very common. **1942** Warnick *Garrett Co. MD* 2 **nwMD** (as of 1900–18), Tossel. **1944** in 1946 *AmSp* 21.53 **nwMN**, We wore 'tossle' caps as children . . , and there were also 'tossles' on the ends of bathrobe cords, but on articles of furniture or other garments they were 'tassles.' **1951** Teale *North with Spring* 32 **FL**, The "tossils" of the canes . . were knotted together. **1961** Kurath–McDavid *Pronc. Engl.* 141, Tassel. . . /æ/ is the usual vowel in cultivated speech throughout the Eastern States. . . Among the other social groups usage varies regionally. The /æ/ of *sack* predominates decidedly in the Upper South, in eastern Pennsylvania, in Metropolitan New York, and in southern New England; it is also common in the Lower South. . . *Tassel* with the vowels /ɔ ~ ɒ/ predominates in western Pennsylvania and the South Midland and is rather common in the Lower South, in Eastern New England, and in parts of New York State (especially the Mohawk Valley). . . The vowels /ɑ/ of *lot* and /ɑ ~ a/ of *father* are not very common . . but occur to some extent in most parts of the Eastern States, apparently without social implications. **1965–70** *DARE* (Qu. I31, *When a corn stalk is well grown, what comes out at the top?*) 611 Infs, **widespread**, Tassel [proncs of the types [ˈtæs(ə)l]]; **GA**75, **IN**7, [ˈtɛs(ɨ)l]; 315 Infs, **widespread**, Tossel [proncs of the types [ˈtɑs(ə)l, ˈtɑs-] and [ˈtɒs(ə)l, ˈtɒs-, ˈtɑs-]]; **LA**12, **NC**50, **SC**3, 32, **TN**26, **TX**36, [Proncs of the types [ˈtɒʊs(ə)l]]; **IN**41, [ˈtɑtsl]; **VA**7, Tussel [ˈtʌsl]; **GA**72, [ˈtaˑɪsl], [ˈtous1]; **MS**1, [ˈtoə,sɒl]; **SC**7, [ˈtausl]. **1968** *DARE* File **DE**, Tossel [tɒsəl] = tufted ornament for mule's bridle. **1969** Wilson *Stars* 114 **Ozarks**, She's emeralds and di'monds and jasmines, whilst I'm only oat heads or maybe corn tawsles. **1979** *DARE* File **cnMA** (as of 1915), When I was six I had some patent leather shoes with tassels on them. A back-woods kind of girl in my school corrected me; she said they were tossels. **1989** Pederson *LAGS Tech. Index* 193 **Gulf Region**, Tassel. [The main varr recorded for the first vowel are [æ] (424 infs), [ɔ] (204), [ɑ] (108), and [ɒ] (47). Minor varr are [ɛ⁽ᴵ⁾] (4) and [e], [aʊ], [ʌ], and [æᴵ] (1 each).] **2009** *DARE* File **seWI** (as of c1960), My mother, who grew up in Milwaukee, spoke of [ˈtɑsl̩z] on our winter caps.

B As noun.

1 also pl: See **tassel flower 2**.

2 pl: =**prairie smoke 2**.

1937 St. John *Flora SE WA & ID* 198, *Geum triflorum* . . var. *ciliatum*. . . Tassels. . . Pilose and silky hirsute throughout. . . The herbage is palatable forage for sheep. [**1966** *DARE* Wildfl QR Pl.100 [= *Geum rivale*] Inf **WA**10, Like tassels, with fruit hanging with fuzzy appendage on seeds, and purplish or rosy-pink flowers. Seed hangs down from flower.]

tassel bush See **tassel tree**

tassel flower n

1 Std: a plant of the genus *Emilia*, esp *E. coccinea*. For other names of var spp see **Flora's paintbrush 2, Indian ~ 2**

2 also *tassel(s);* freq with adj: Any of var **prairie clovers**. [See quot 1922] **esp Sth**

1896 *Jrl. Amer. Folkl.* 9.186 **swMO**, *Petalostemon violaceus* and *P. candidus* [=*Dalea purpurea* and *D. c.*], . . red and white tassel-flowers. **1922** *Amer. Botanist* 28.72, In addition to the general name, *P[eta-*

lostemon] candidum is known as "white tassel flower". *P. purpureum* is the "red tassel flower" the "tassel", be it known alluding to the elongated spikes of flowers. **1933** Small *Manual SE Flora* 696, *P. candidus.* . . *White tassels.* . . Dry soils, prairies, various provinces, Miss. to Tex., Sask., and Ind. . . *P. purpureus* [sic]. . . *Purple-tassels.* . . Prairies, plains, and hills, various provinces, Ala. to N.M., Sask., and Tenn. **1953** Greene–Blomquist *Flowers South* 57, *Purple-Tassel.* . . is the showiest of the prairie-clovers, . . with . . dense spikes of purple flowers. **1975** Duncan–Foote *Wildflowers SE* 76, *Purple-tassels—Petalostemon gattingeri* [=*Dalea* g.] . . Petals rose-purple. . . *P. purpureum* . . is similar. . . *White-tassels—Petalostemum albidum* [=*Dalea carnea*]. . . Petals white. . . Other similar species . . *P. candidum.*

tassel fly n   Also *corn-tossel fly*   esp Inland Sth   Cf **hover fly, sweat bee 2**

A fly of the family Syrphidae.

   1927 Rogers *Bumblepuppy* 11 **AR,** 'Twarn't nothin' but one er them yaller tassel flies. . . A tassel fly ain't got near as much sense as one er these here little black cur flies. **1968–69** *DARE* (Qu. R10, *Very small flies that don't sting, often seen hovering in large groups or bunches outdoors in summer*) Inf **KY5,** Tassel flies; (Qu. R13, *Flies that come to meat or fruit*) Inf **TN26,** Tassel fly—about the size of a housefly, only a little different shape—they hover around corn. **1986** Pederson *LAGS Concordance,* 1 inf, ne**AL,** Tassel flies—small, swarm, yellow-striped bodies. **2003** *DARE* File—Internet **TN,** Tassel fly refers to a small like knat [sic] that you find in the south during hot summer months. It is often seen around gardens and especially in corn fields with roasting ears that are at their sweetest. It was real bothersome especially in the days when farmers would plow their fields with horses and mules. **2004** in 2010 *Ibid* s**IL,** When I was a young lad I would often go fishing with my grandfather and in the hot days of summer we would often encounter "corn-tossel flies." . . [It] has an elongated and flattened body that is striped like a bee (yellow and black) and it has a head like a house fly (two large red eyes being the majority of its head). . . [T]he "corn-tossel fly" (as my grandpa coined it) would hover over a certain location before deciding to land. [Resp: It sounds like you are describing a Flower Fly, Family Syrphidae.]

tassel grass n   Also *sea tassel grass, tassel pondgrass,* ~ *pondweed*

A **ditch grass 2** (here: *Ruppia maritima*).

   1822 Eaton *Botany* 437, *Ruppia.* . . *maritima* (sea tassel-grass . .) floating: leaves pectinate, obtuse. **1840** MA Zool. & Bot. Surv. *Herb. Plants & Quadrupeds* 224, *R[uppia] maritima.* . . Sea Tassel-grass. . . In salt marshes near Boston; a grass-like plant with immersed, linear leaves. **1900** Lyons *Plant Names* 328, *R. maritima.* . . Ditch-grass, Tassel-grass, Tassel Pond-grass, Sea-grass. *Plant* reputed vulnerary. **1933** Small *Manual SE Flora* 15, *Tassel-pondweed.* . . Shallow water, throughout N[orth] A[merica], except the extreme N[orth].

tasselrue n

A **false bugbane** (here: *Trautvetteria caroliniensis*).

   1953 Strausbaugh–Core *Flora WV* 386, *T[rautvetteria] caroliniensis.* . . *Tasselrue.* . . Sepals . . white, very caducous. **1953** Greene–Blomquist *Flowers South* 31, *Tassel-rue (Trautvetteria caroliniensis).* . . The relatively large, palmately-lobed leaves and the white brush-like flowers are the distinguishing marks of this distinctive and attractive plant. **2006** Irwin *Colorado's Best* 3.174, Prepare to meet tasselrue trailside, with its big palmate leaves and little buds that look like folded ivory cups.

tassel-top n   Cf **curly-heads**

A **virgin's bower** (here: *Clematis ochroleuca*).

   1967 *DARE* Wildfl QR Pl.74 [=*Clematis ochroleuca*] Inf **AR44,** Others say tassel-top.

tassel tree n   Also *tassel bush*

A **silk tassel,** usu *Garrya elliptica.*

   1876 Vasey *Catalogue Trees* 16, *Garrya Fremontii.* . . Tassel-tree.—Oregon and California. . . *Garrya elliptica.* . . Satin Tassel-tree.—California. **1931** U.S. Dept. Ag. *Misc. Pub.* 101.122 **Pacific,** *Tasseltree (G. elliptica)* . . ranges from Oregon to California and is grazed to some extent by goats. **1938** Van Dersal *Native Woody Plants* 357, Tassel bush. . . *Garrya veatchii.* . . *Garrya flavescens.* . . Tasseltree. *Garrya elliptica.* **1980** Little *Audubon Guide N. Amer. Trees W. Region* 575, "Tasseltree" . . *Garrya elliptica.* . . Evergreen shrub or small tree with

tassel-like clusters of flowers and fruit. . . W. Oregon south to S. California.

tassel weed n

A **ragweed 2** (here: *Ambrosia artemisiifolia*).

   1892 *Jrl. Amer. Folkl.* 5.98 **MA,** *Ambrosia artemisiæfolia,* tasselweed.

tassel-white n

=**Virginia willow.**

   1933 Small *Manual SE Flora* 300, *I[tea] virginica.* . . *Tassel-white.* . . Swamps and stream-banks. **1950** Gray–Fernald *Manual of Botany* 748, Small white flowers in simple racemes. . . *Tassel-white.* **1973** Wharton–Barbour *Trees KY* 526, This pretty little shrub . . called tassel-white . . grows in swampy woods and along streams in southern Kentucky from east to west, but is infrequent. **1976** Bruce *How to Grow Wildflowers* 125, Growing in the same sort of locations as Trumpet Honeysuckle is *Itea virginica,* the Tassel-white, Virginia-willow, or Sweetspire, a deciduous shrub of six feet or so.

tassel worm n

=**corn earworm.**

   1879 Comstock *Rept. Cotton Insects* 308 **AL,** It is the next, the third brood [of the boll worm] . . which does most damage to corn. This is called the "corn-worm," the "ear-worm," the "tassel-worm." **2003** *DARE* File—Internet **AZ,** There are other great vegetables that produce bushels of abundance in the same small spot of ground as one witless corn stalk, and there are always those damned tassel worms to outsmart.

tasso n |ˈtæso, ˈtɑso| [LaFr *tasso* (also *tassaie, tassao, tasseau*), prob from Span *tasajo* dried salt meat]   chiefly s**LA**

Dried or smoked salt meat or fish, usu highly seasoned and used principally to flavor other foods.

   1841 *S. Lit. Messenger* 7.77 sw**LA,** The evening banquet of gumbo, tasso, and beef, in every variety of form, was shortly served up by their attendants. [**1901** (1932) Ditchy *Acadiens* 200, *Tassaie,* tranche de boeuf salée, séchée au soleil. . . *Tassao,* v. tassaie. [=*Tassaie,* salted sliced meat, dried in the sun. . . *Tassao,* see tassaie.]] [**1931** Read *LA French* 73, *Tasseau,* m. Du tasseau is the equivalent of "jerked beef." Formerly strips of deerskin and fish, too, were dried in the sunshine on a clothes line or wooden support.] **1968** *DARE* (Qu. H44, *Beef that has been dried to preserve it*) Inf **LA28,** Tasso [ˈtæsou]; **LA31,** Tasso [ˈtæsou]—they call dried fish tasso, too. **1968** *DARE* FW Addit **LA26,** Tasso [ˈtɑˌso] = smoked garfish. **1983** *Reinecke Coll.* 10 **LA,** Tasseau, tasso [ˈtɑˌso] . . heavily smoked pork used for seasoning. Cajun. **1991** Kirlin–Kirlin *Smithsonian Folklife Cookbook* 137, The prairies of southwest Louisiana, where ranching is important, provide such beef dishes as tasso, a smoked meat used as seasoning. **2004** *DARE* File—Internet s**LA,** Tasso is a dried smoked product that is seasoned with cayenne pepper, garlic and salt and heavily smoked. . . Although this delicacy is often thinly sliced and eaten alone, it is primarily used as a pungent seasoning for vegetables, gumbos and soups. Today in South Louisiana, tasso is becoming a popular seasoning for new and creative dishes.

taste v, n

A Forms.

1 usu |test|; also |tes|; pronc-sp *tas'e.*   esp **Sth, S Midl**

   1861 Henry *Tell Tale Rag* 1.133 **Sth** [Black], What dat ar fruit wur, dat ole Missa Adam jes tase ob? **1899** Chesnutt *Conjure Woman* 20 cs**NC** [Black], He say it tas'e like whiskey. **1909** *DN* 3.379 e**AL,** w**GA,** *Tase.* . . To taste. **1915** *DN* 4.191 sw**VA,** *Tase,* n. and v. Taste. **1922** Gonzales *Black Border* 332 s**SC, GA coasts** [Gullah glossary], *Tas'e*— taste, tastes, tasted, tasting. **1940–41** Cassidy *WI Atlas* ce**WI,** It tas'es /ˈtesɪz/ the same. (Eau Claire, woman 81 years old). **1981** [see **A2** below]. **1992** [see **B3** below].

2 pres 3rd pers sg: usu |ˈtests|; also |ˈtestɪz, -tɪs|.   esp **Sth, S Midl**   Cf **-es** suff[1] **3a, fist** n[1], **nest**

   1908 *DN* 3.283 e**AL,** w**GA,** Abnormal forms in third singular . . costes, tastes, etc. **1931** *PMLA* 46.1315 s**Appalachians,** *E,* mute, is frequently sounded, as in such words as "tastes." **1942** Hall *Smoky Mt. Speech* 82 w**NC,** e**TN,** *Tastes* [ˈteɪstəs]. **1942** in 1944 *ADD* n**WV,** [ˈtestɪz]. **c1960** Wilson *Coll.* cs**KY,** *Tastes* is often /ˈtestɪz/. **1968** *DARE* Tape **GA39,** It tastes [ˈtestɪz] more like soup. **1974** Fink *Mountain Speech* 26 w**NC,** e**TN,** *Tastes* (2 syllables). . . "Hit tastes sorter bitter." **1981** Pederson *LAGS Basic Materials* **Gulf Region,** [7 infs, proncs of the types ['teɪstɪz, -ɪs]; 7 infs, proncs of the types ['te(ɪ)sɪz, -ɪs].]

B As verb.

1 with *of:* To try the taste of, sample; to eat or drink a small amount of; also fig. [*OED2 taste* v. 12 13 . . →] For addit exx see **of** prep **Ba**

1824 *N. Amer. Rev.* 19.126, There are poets, who have never tasted of Helicon. **1827** *Ibid* 24.405, We have seen many Indians . . who had never tasted of spirituous liquors. **1848** Bartlett *Americanisms* 238, We say *to hear, to see,* to denote an involuntary act; and *to look at, to hearken to* or *to listen to,* to denote a voluntary one. With regard to the other senses we are not so well provided with words; but some people . . endeavor to supply . . [this deficiency] by construing the verbs *to feel, to taste, to smell,* with the preposition *of,* to signify a voluntary act. **1849** *S. Lit. Messenger* 15.414, She barely tasted of the proffered food. **1937** *Hall Coll.* **eTN,** I haven't tasted of it yet. **1949** Dean *Diamond Bess* 196 **TX,** They tasted of the beer that had been brewed in Jefferson. **1969** *DARE* FW Addit **cwNC,** Taste of it = taste it. *Ibid* **cVT,** He tasted of them = he tasted them. **1986** *DARE* File **Sth,** *Taste Of.* . . Used in the South to mean have a taste, or sample, as in "I'm going to taste of this apple pie." I never heard the term used verbally elsewhere.

2 in phr *taste like more('s behind):* To taste very good, making one eager to have more. Cf **moreish**

1869 *Eve. Gaz.* (Pt. Jervis NY) 11 Nov 4/2, [Advt:] For choice Butter—in Port Jervis, go to *H.C. Cunningham's*—just the kind for Buckwheat cakes, always tastes like more. **1897** *Mt. Democrat* (Placerville CA) 2 Jan 5/3, [Advt:] Ohio Buckwheat and Vermont Maple Syrup—will taste like more. **1905** *DN* 3.63 **NE,** Morish. . . "That tastes morish." Cf. "that tastes like more." **1909** *DN* 3.379 **eAL, wGA,** *Tas(t)e like more.* . . A complimentary and facetious expression to indicate that one wishes a second helping. "Them biscuit tase like more." **1942** Warnick *Garrett Co. MD* 15 **nwMD** (as of 1900–18), *Tastes like more* . . a phrase showing fondness for an item of food. **1942** McAtee *Dial. Grant Co. IN* 64 (as of 1890s), *Tastes like more* . . same as "calls for more." **1956** McAtee *Some Dialect NC* 45, *Tastes like more* . . a compliment to food or drink of which one would like a further portion. **1966** *DARE* (Qu. LL35, *Words used to make a statement stronger: "This cake tastes _____ good."*) Inf **ME22,** This cake tastes like more. **1999** *DARE* File **cGA** (as of 1960s), If something tasted really good, we would say "It tastes like more's behind." That would always fool people because they would ask, "Who is Moore?"

3 in phr *taste one's mouth:* To please one's sense of taste. [Scots dial; cf *EDD taste* v. 3, *SND taste* v. 2] *Gullah*

1909 *S. Atl. Qrly.* 8.39 **sSC coast** [Gullah], *Maum Sally,* when gently reproached for dipping into the sugar, says: *"Sho! Miss Suso; yo' ent grutch me sumphm fo' tas'e me mout'?"* **1922** Gonzales *Black Border* 332 **sSC, GA coasts** [Gullah glossary], *Tas'e 'e mout'*—put a taste in his, her or their mouth or mouths. **1992** Geraty *Bittle* 3 **Charleston SC** [Gullah], *Bittle fuh Tas'e 'e Mout'*—Food to Put a Good Taste in the Mouth: Appetizers.

tasted adj [*OED2* 1604 →] **chiefly S Midl** *old-fash*
In var combs: Tasting, having a (specified) flavor.

1709 [see **sunfish** n **1a**]. **1805** (1905) Clark *Orig. Jrls. Lewis & Clark Exped.* 2.77 **VA,** The water of the Missouri will [sic for *well*] tasted not quite So muddy as it is below. **1836** Irving *Astoria* 3.95 **NY,** Their mountain mutton . . extremely well tasted. **1852** *S. Lit. Messenger* 18.211 **VA,** Instead of impressing him with firm faith in some distant and bad tasted water, [the monks] persuaded him that prayers put up to a certain saint . . would work a cure. **1902** *DN* 2.247 **sIL,** *Tasted, adj.* The quality of having a taste, as 'Good tasted fruit.' 'A bad tasted apple.' **1907** *DN* 3.227 **nwAR,** *Tasted, adj.* Tasting. **1909** *DN* 3.379 **eAL, wGA,** *Tasted, adj.* Tasting. **1937** (1963) Hyatt *Kiverlid* 80 **KY,** With tree-sugar sweet'nin' hits better tasted than coffee. **c1960** *Wilson Coll.* **csKY,** *-tasted:* a suffix, meaning tasting or to the taste, used extensively: good-tasted, sweet-tasted, bitter-tasted. **1986** Pederson *LAGS Concordance,* 1 inf, **ceAR,** They was wonderful-tasted pecans.

taste like more('s behind) See **taste B2**

taste of See **taste B1**

taste one's mouth See **taste B3**

tat n See **tad** n¹ **1, 2**

tat v [Abbr for *tattle* v]
To utter by way of gossip.

1953 Randolph–Wilson *Down in Holler* 292 **Ozarks,** *Tat: v.t.* To gossip, to tattle. "You know I don't never tat no tales, Minnie, but I think you orter know how your man's been a-carryin' on whilst you was away." **1954** Harder *Coll.* **cwTN,** *Tat: v.t.* To gossip, to tattle.

ta-ta exclam [Hypocoristic; cf Brit *ta* thanks and *ta-ta* goodbye] **chiefly Sth, S Midl** See Map *esp freq among Black speakers*
Thanks! hence rarely v *ta-ta* to thank.

1884 Baldwin *Yankee School-Teacher* 28 **VA,** Marian had something for each of the children too, including the baby; they shyly grinned and murmured "Ta, ta!" the Virginia form of "Thank you!" **1899** (1912) Green *VA Folk-Speech* 434, *Ta-ta, interj.* Thank you. A child's word. **1965–70** *DARE* (Qu. II39, . . *'Thank you'*) Infs **DC11, MS73, MO23, 29, VA103,** Ta-ta; **LA11,** [ˌtɑˈtɑ]; **LA35,** A child would say [ˌtəˈtɑ]; **MS88,** To kids, [tɑ tɑ]; **VA31,** [təˈtɑ]—old-fashioned, children used to be taught to say this. [8 of 9 Infs female, 6 coll educ, 5 old, 4 Black] **c1977** in 2009 *DARE* File—Internet [Black], [Lyrics to Johnny "Guitar" Watson's "I Want to Ta Ta You, Baby":] I wanna ta ta you, baby—I got to thank you / For bein' mine, mine, mine. **2005** *Ibid* **NY** [Black], Babies were taught to say *"ta-ta"* for thank you as soon as the infant could say *"da-da"* for daddy. . . The frequencies of reminders from parents, grandparents, older Aunties and others to "Say *ta-ta*", was an external stimulant, aiding the learning of saying "Thank You" for baby. [**2008** *DARE* File **Chicago IL,** My father, from Cardiff, Wales, taught me to say *ta* for thank you. I've used it all my life, and I know others (Americans) in the Chicago area who also use it.]

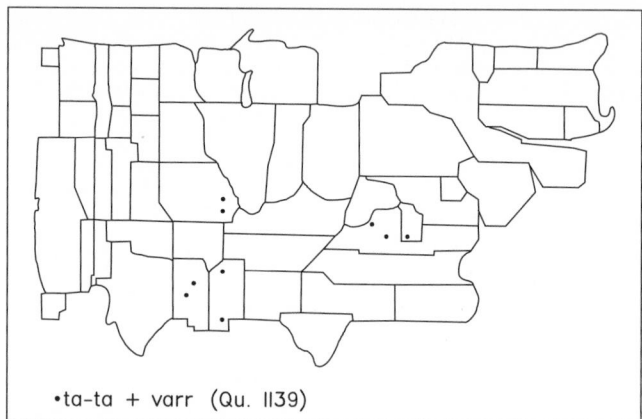

•ta-ta + varr (Qu. II39)

tataba n [Var of **catawba**]
c1970 Pederson *Dial. Surv. Rural GA* **seGA** (*What do you call large worms used for bait?*) 1 inf, [təˈtˈɑᵊbə] worm.

tate See **potato A5**

tater See **potato A3**

tatler See **tattler**

tato See **potato A3**

tatpole See **tadpole 1**

tatter See **tetter** n¹

tattertale n, v [By rhotacism from *tattletale*]
A tattletale; to tattle.

1966 *DARE* (Qu. JJ4, *A child who is always telling on other children*) Inf **NC45,** Tattertale. **2003** *DARE* File—Internet, Being the tattertale that I am, I blurted it out to everyone I knew. **2005** *Ibid* **KY,** I can't believe someone would "tattertale" on somebody for cheating.

tatting-shuttle bird n
A **nuthatch.**
1967 *DARE* (Qu. Q23, *The insect-eating bird that goes headfirst down a tree trunk*) Inf **IA3,** Tatting-shuttle bird.

tattlebudget n Cf **budget** n **3**
A tattletale.
1966 *DARE* (Qu. JJ4, *A child who is always telling on other children*) Inf **ME22,** Tattlebudget [laughter].

tattler n Also sp *tatler* [See quot 1918]
Any of several birds of the family Scolopacidae; now usu the greater or the lesser **yellowlegs 1** or the **willet.**

[**1831** Richardson *Fauna Boreali-Amer.* 2.388, Totanus semipalmatus [=*Catoptrophorus s.*] . . Semipalmated Tatler.] **1834** Nuttall *Manual Ornith.* 2.152, Yellow-shanks Tatler. (*Totanus flavipes* [=*Tringa f.*]). *Ibid* 157, White-tailed Tatler. (*Totanus ochropus* [=*Tringa o.*]). *Ibid* 159, Green-rump Tatler. (*Totanus ochropygius* [=*Tringa solitaria*]). . . The Solitary Tatler of Wilson is, probably, with the change of seasons, a general inhabitant of the whole North American continent. *Ibid* 162, Spotted Tatler. . . (*Totanus macularius* [=*Actitis m.*]). *Ibid* 168, Bartram's Tatler. . . (*Totanus Bartramius* [=*Bartramia longicauda*]). **1844** DeKay *Zool.* NY 2.249, The Solitary Tatler. . . This little bird is, as its name indicates, a solitary and shy species. It is called the *Green-rump Tatler, Wood Tatler,* and the *Jack Snipe,* in various places in the interior. *Ibid* 250, The Varied Tatler. . . This bird is the *Big Yellow-leg,* or *Winter Yellow-leg* of our sportsmen. It appears with us about the middle of May. **1880** *Forest & Stream* 15.4, Tell-tale tattler, or snipe *(Totanus melanoleuca).* . . Yellow-shanks tattler or snipe *(Totanus flavipes)*. **1892** Lee *Hist. Columbus* OH 1.17, Yellow-legged snipe or tattler, then common along the western rivers in autumn. **1911** Howell *Birds* AR 31, *Catoptrophorus semipalmatus inornatus.* This large snipe, or "tattler," breeds on the coast of Texas and Louisiana and from northern Iowa northward and westward. **1917** *DN* 4.430 **LA,** *Tattler.* The western willet (Catophophorus [sic] semipalmatus inornata): also called *vire-vire.* **1918** Grinnell et al. *Game Birds* CA 402, On a marsh or elsewhere in the vicinity of water where other birds are present, the Yellow-legs, by their shrill notes, appear to give warning when a hunter is espied approaching, and the cries so persistently uttered are usually sufficient to put the more desirable game on its guard or even to cause it to take flight. On account of this habit these two birds [=*Tringa melanoleuca* and *T. flavipes*] are often called Tell-tales or Tattlers. **1921** LA Dept. of Conserv. *Bulletin* 10.79, Their biennial visits to Louisiana have always been important stages in the migration of the upland plover, or upland tatler *(Bartramia longicauda).* **1956** MA Audubon Soc. *Bulletin* 40.17 **NEng,** *Upland Plover.* . . Tattler (Conn. As one giving warning by its cries that intruders are present.) *Ibid* 18, *Greater Yellowlegs.* . . Tattler (Mass.) . . *Lesser Yellowlegs.* . . Yellow-shanks Tattler (Mass.) **2007** Lockwood *Basic TX Birds* 377, Wandering Tattler *(Tringa incana).*

tattletale snipe n   Cf **tattler**
The greater **yellowlegs 1.**

    1962 Imhof *AL Birds* 242, Greater Yellowlegs. . . *Other names:* Tattletale Snipe. . . Its *loud whistle,* given in *three* or *four syllables,* usually sounds the alarm to all birds in the vicinity.

taught   See **touch** B

taughten   See **teach** A

taunt   v, n   Usu |ˈtɔnt, ˈtɑnt|; also |ˈtænt| Pronc-spp *ta'nt,* rarely *taynt*   Cf **haunt**
Std senses, var forms.

    1841 (1952) Cooper *Deerslayer* 503 **NY,** Your women begin to ta'nt and abuse me. **1864** (1868) Trowbridge *3 Scouts* 27 **TN,** No, I ain't: it's you that keeps ta'ntin'! I ain't said but that you've been patient. **1891** Riley *Swimmin'-Hole* 6 **IN,** Perfumes / Of harvest dinners seems to rise / And ta'nt a feller. **1893** *Scribner's Mag.* 14.117 **nNY,** Lee Watkins saw 'em with his own eyes, and ta'nted me with it. **1906** Casey *Parson's Boys* 37 **sIL** (as of c1860), Mebbe Louise 'll ta'nt me, and bang me over the head. **1942** Thomas *Blue Ridge Country* 122 **sAppalachians,** It's a plum shame the way that girl taynts him and Mathias. **1969** *DARE* (Qu. GG3, *To tease: "See those big boys trying to _____ [that little one]."*) Inf **PA**206, Taunt [tænt]. **1978** Hiser *Quare Appalachia* 128 **eKY,** Singing about the gal that went ting-a-ling at her true lover's door when he was a-marrying up with a dark skinned gal and tanting her about her skin.

Taunton shag   See **Taunton turkey 2**

Taunton turkey n   [From *Taunton* MA]   **NEng**

1   An **alewife** (here: *Alosa pseudoharengus*).   Cf **Albany beef, Cape Cod turkey**

    1817 Scott *Sorceress* 111 **MA,** These herrings are . . so much superior to all other kinds, that they have dignified them by the name of "Taunton Turkies." **1848** in 1935 *DN* 6.454 **RI,** *Taunton Turkeys.* Herring (fish). **1850** (1851) Allin *Home Ballads* 18 **NEng,** Our Fisheries o'er the world are famed,/ The mackerel, shad, and cod!/ And "Taunton turkeys" are so thick,/ We sell them by the rod! **1859** (1968) Bartlett *Americanisms* 473, *Taunton Turkeys.* The common herring, of which large quantities are taken near Taunton, Massachusetts. **1950** *Chicago Tribune* (IL) 17 Jan 14/3 **MA,** In Massachusetts . . the spring herring [=*Alosa pseudoharengus*] is known as "Taunton turkey."

2   also *Taunton shag:* Either the **double-crested cormorant** or the common **cormorant** *(Phalacrocorax carbo).*

    1899 Howe–Sturtevant *Birds RI* 33, *Phalacrocorax carbo. . .* "Taunton Turkey." "Taunton Shag." . . Migrating up and down Narragansett Bay, generally by the Sakonnet River, to the Taunton, and other rivers to feed. *Ibid* 34, *Phalacrocorax dilophus* [=*P. auritus*]. . . "Taunton Turkey." "Taunton Shag." . . This species migrates like the preceding up and down the Sakonnet and middle passages of Narragansett Bay to the Taunton and other rivers where they spend the day feeding. **1925** (1928) Forbush *Birds MA* 1.160, *Double-crested Cormorant. Other names:* shag, Taunton turkey.

taur   See **tour**

taushents   See **torshent**

tautog n   Usu |təˈtɔg| Also *tautaug,* aphet *tog;* for addit pronc and sp varr see quots   [Narraganset]   **chiefly NEng**
A **wrasse** *(Tautoga onitis)* of coastal Atlantic waters.   Also called **blackfish 1, black porgy, moll** n[1]**, oysterfish 2, saltwater chub, slippery bass, white chin**

    [**1643** Williams *Key into Language* 113 **RI,** Of Fish and Fishing. . . *Taut-auog.* Sheeps-heads.] **1750** (1916) Birket *Cursory Remarks* 31 **NEng,** An ill natured Scold at the ferry house . . gave us Potatoes & Tatogue. **1760** in 1775 Burnaby *Travels* 70 **RI,** Fish are in the greatest plenty and perfection, particularly the tataag or black-fish. **1802** MA Hist. Soc. *Coll.* 1st ser 8.191, A few tautaug are caught in Town cove. **1806** (1970) Webster *Compendious Dict.* 307, Tetaug', n. the rock or black fish. **1839** MA Zool. & Bot. Surv. *Fishes Reptiles* 76 **MA,** At New Bedford, 300 pounds of *fresh* tautog have been sold by a single market-boat in a day. **1846** Worcester *Universal Dict.* 727, Tâu-tŏg' [= [təˈtɑg]]. **1884** Goode *Fisheries U.S.* 1.268, One of the best known shore species of the Atlantic coast is the Tautog or Blackfish. . . East of New York it is usually called Tautog . . ; in New Jersey also . . "Tautog," or "Chub." **1905** NJ State Museum *Annual Rept. for 1904* 344, *Tautoga onitis.* . . Tautog. . . Sea Tog. **1931–33** *LANE* Worksheets **cRI,** Tautog [təˈtɔg]. . . A variety of fish. **1934** Hanley Disks **seMA,** Tautog [təˈtɔg] . . a northern wrasse, called blackfish in New York, not very good. **1968** *Cape May Co. Gaz.* (Cape May Court House NJ) 11 July sec D 3/1, Party boat fishermen are reporting some sea bass and porgies with ling and tautog helping to fill the fish bags. **1969–70** *DARE* (Qu. P2, . . *Kinds of saltwater fish caught around here . . good to eat*) Infs **MA**4, 55, [təˈtɔg]; **MA**80, [totɔg]; **RI**4, [ˈtotɔg] or blackfish; **RI**8, [tɪˈtag]; **RI**15, [tɪtˈtɔg]; **RI**17, [tɪˈtɔg] = blackfish. **1970** *DARE* FW Addit, [Husband of Inf **VA**41 responding to Qu. P2:] [ˈtʌtag]. **2001** *DARE* File—Internet **VA,** Togs, commonly known as blackfish up north, are an ugly fish that fight hard and taste good. **2003** *Ibid* **DE,** *Tautog (blackfish)*—Locally pronounced "tog," these fishes are caught on wrecks and at the breakwaters at Lewes Harbor.

tavern n   [See quot 2002 *Gourmet*]   **chiefly nwIA, seSD**   Cf **spoonburger**
=**loose-meat sandwich.**

    [**1927** *Sioux City Jrl.* (IA) 13 July 13/5, [Advt:] Ye Olde Tavern Sandwich—A Treat to Eat at the Picnic.] **1951** *Le Mars Semi-Weekly Sentinel* (IA) 27 July 1/3 *(Popik Coll.),* When asked about student preferences, Miss Watson replied, "I think they prefer loose meat sandwiches, such as taverns." **1960** *Bethany Cook Book* 248 **seSD,** Taverns. [Recipe includes ground beef, onions, mustard, brown sugar, vinegar, tomato sauce.] **1968** *DARE* (Qu. H41, . . *Kinds of roll or bun sandwiches . . in a round bun or roll*) Inf **IA**41, Tavern—ground-up beef, highly seasoned; **IA**43, Tavern—loose ground meat, highly seasoned; similar to a barbecue. **1972** *DARE* File **seSD,** Tavern—a sloppy-Joe sandwich. **2002** *Gourmet* Aug 50 **nwIA,** Sticklers for historical veracity actually prefer the term "tavern" because that is what David Heglin called it when he first served it in 1924 at Ye Old Tavern, his 25-seat restaurant in Sioux City. **2002** *DARE* File **nwIA** (as of c1960), In my home town in northwest Iowa we used the term "tavern" for a sandwich made with ground beef and tomato sauce. When I went part way across the state to college, no one knew what I meant when I used the term. **2008** *Ibid* **ne,nwIA,** Taverns—sloppy-joe sandwiches.

tavern belly n   Also *t.b.*   **esp WI**
=**Milwaukee goiter** or a person who has one.

    1943 *Amer. Flint* Apr 47, Rudy left so fast that he lost his T.B. (tavern belly) on the way. **1950** *WELS* (An oversize stomach: *If it comes from drinking*) 1 Inf, **ceWI,** Tavern belly; 2 Infs, **WI,** T.b.—tavern belly. **1966–69** *DARE* (Qu. X53a, . . *An oversize stomach*) Inf **NY**33, Tavern belly; **WI**13, T.b. = tavern belly; (Qu. X53b, *An oversize stomach that* *results from drinking*) Infs **NY**33, 221, **WI**13, Tavern belly; **WI**50, Tavern belly or t.b.; (Qu. DD12, . . *A person who drinks steadily or a great deal*) Inf **MI**15, Tavern belly.

taw n Pronc-spp *tall, tawl;* rarely *tar, toar, toe, tor(e)* Cf **toe line, toy**

A Pronc forms.

1848 [see **C2a** below]. **1916** *DN* 4.296 **sAppalachians,** Games at "marvles" (marbles) . . such as . . "long taw(l)." **1922** *DN* 5.188, *Taw.* . . Also *tawl.* **1957** *Sat. Eve. Post Letters* **OK,** Tawl. **1965–70** *DARE* (Qu. EE6a) Inf **CA**73, Tor [tɔr]; **GA**28, Toe; **LA**40, Tall; (Qu. EE8) Inf **MS**1, Tor [toːə] line; **SC**68, Tar [tɑr]. **1966–69** *DARE* Tape **AL**6, [Aux Inf:] The marble you use to shoot with is called, we called 'em taw [tˈɑ·oˆ]. [FW:] A taw [tˈɑ]. Did you use the word "taw" for the marble? **GA**84, [FW:] Do you remember the name of the big marble that you used to knock all the others out? [Inf:] Well, we called it a taw [tˈɛˀɔˇ]. **1968** *DARE* FW Addit seGA, Toe [to]. c1970 Wiersma *Marbles Terms* **MS,** Toar-ball . . either 1) a large marble . . or 2) an extremely small marble. **1982** Slone *How We Talked* 93 **eKY** (as of c1950), *Tall*—the marble used to "shoot" with (hit the other marbles). **1983** *MJLF* 9.1.59 **ceKY,** *Tawl* . . taw, the only pronunciation I ever heard as a child.

B Gram form.

Pl: usu *taws;* also *tawses.* Cf **-es** suff[1] **2**

1916 *DN* 4.347 **New Orleans LA,** *Tawses.* . . Pl. of *taw,* a marble.

C Senses.

1a also *taw man, ~ marble:* A large playing marble, usu used as a **shooter 1;** rarely, also pl: the game of marbles. [*OED2* 1709 →] **widespread exc NEast, Gt Lakes, Upper MW** See Map Cf **alley** n², **~ taw, tallboy 2, toy 1**

1842 *Adams Sentinel* (Gettysburg PA) 24 Oct 1/3 **NY,** See with what a haughty grace he plumps his marble smack against taw. **1861** *Ladies' Repository* 21.627, I won them from Pete Jones. See, I got his glass taw, too. I loaned him one of mine to play with while he put that in the ring. **1869** *Appletons' Jrl.* 1.630, In England, and in some places in the United States, a marble which is almost wholly used to knuckle with, and which is quite often an "alley," is called a "taw." . . Brande . . goes on to say: "*Taw* is the common name of this play in England." He is in error, however, in this last statement, I feel confident, for a taw is "restricted to the marble employed to knuckle with," says a correspondent to the first series of the famous "Notes and Queries;" and, of my own knowledge, I can state that all the boys here of English descent who use the term (and I have known many) apply it according to the extract given from "Notes and Queries." **1875** (1876) Twain *Tom Sawyer* 27 **MO,** I'll give you a marvel. I'll give you a white alley, Jim! And it's a bully taw. **1906** Casey *Parson's Boys* 25 **sIL** (as of c1860), Even his favorite "taw" had been forfeited. **1922** *DN* 5.188, *Taw.* . . The marble shot with. **1955** *PADS* 23.32 **cwTN,** *Taw.* . . The offensive marble, or the shooter. **1957** *Sat. Eve. Post Letters* **wKY** (as of 1930s), The marble used for shooting was a "shooting taw," never "shooter" or simply "taw." **1960** Bailey *Resp. to PADS* 20 **KS,** Shooter: at least more than occasional. Taw: almost invariably used by players. **1965–70** *DARE* (Qu. EE6a, . . *Different kinds of marbles—the big one that's used to knock others out of the ring*) 241 Infs, **widespread exc NEast, Gt Lakes, Upper MW,** Taw; **AR**56, **KY**73, 84, **OK**1, **TN**27, **TX**36, Shooting taw; **MO**32, **OK**1, Taw marble; **GA**77, **NC**41, Head taw (man); **LA**40, Tall; **CA**73, Tor [tɔr]; [**CA**51, Tawnie or tawie [FW: Inf unsure];] (Qu. EE6b,

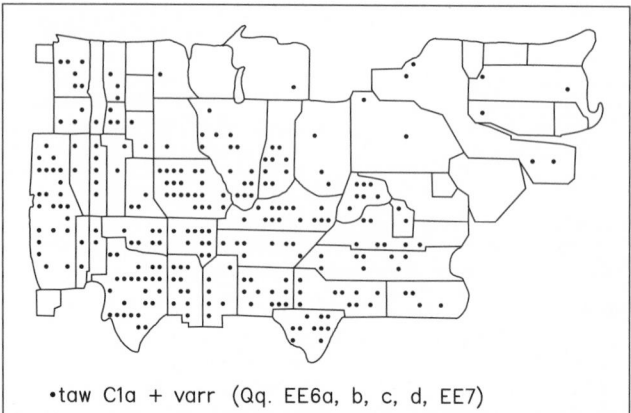

•taw C1a + varr (Qq. EE6a, b, c, d, EE7)

Small marbles or marbles in general) Infs **MO**9, **NC**33, **VA**18, 30, 33, Taws; (Qu. EE6c, *Cheap marbles*) Infs **CO**21, **IN**19, Taws; (Qu. EE6d, *Special marbles*) Infs **MS**30, **MO**36, **VA**1, 13, Taws; (Qu. EE7, . . *Kinds of marble games*) Inf **MS**30, Taw; **IN**41, Taws. **1966–70** *DARE* Tape **AL**3, What you'd . . knock marbles with would be what you called your taw; **AZ**8, Then they stand back of the three holes and lag a taw, or a marble, toward the lag line; **CA**172, You mean the taw? . . That's the one you use to shoot with; **GA**13, We . . drawed a ring . . about two feet in diameter, put the big taw marble . . in the middle; **NM**6, **OK**42, **TX**1, 24, 49, **WA**6, Taw. **c1970** Wiersma *Marbles Terms,* Taw: [tɔ]. . . The shooter in a game of pots.

b in fig phr *lose one's taw:* To lose one's mind. Cf *lose one's marbles*

1895 *Eclectic Med. Gleaner* 6.170 **OH,** Robert Brown of a neighboring town is mentally alienated to a degree. In informing me of this fact, a neighbor of his said, "Bob aint all right no more," then after a little hesitation he added, "he's lost his taw." **1966** *DARE* (Qu. HH6, *Someone who is out of his mind*) Inf **MS**71, Lost his taw.

2a also pl; In marble play: a line from which players shoot or, less freq, toward which marbles are rolled or tossed to determine the order of play; occas a similar line in other games or sports. [*OED2* 1740 →] Cf **lag line, taw line, toe line, toy 2, try line**

1841 *S. Lit. Messenger* 7.698, Master Rough-enough is at first ambitious of "plumping the middle man from taw"—of running the swiftest, or vaulting the highest. **1842** Hawes *Sporting Scenes* 22, Remember how bright and brave was the gallant cavalier who so gracefully reined back his curving charger, before the admiring ladies, up to taw, in front of the Judges' Stand. **1845** *U.S. Mag. & Democratic Rev.* 17.453 **NYC,** Boys who once despised shooting marbles, except "from taw," grovel on the ground in most awkward "knuckles." **1848** Bartlett *Americanisms* 360 **NYC,** *Tore.* The place where one stands to shoot marbles from. Used by the boys of New York. **1893** Shands *MS Speech* 76, *Taws.* . . The place from which the players shoot in the game of marbles called ring-men. **1896** Beard *Outdoor Games* 328, Duck on a Rock. . . The other players stand at a taw or scratch line and throw their ducks at the drake with the purpose of knocking it from its perch. **1899** *Atlanta Constitution* (GA) 22 Sept 9/2, I was playing pool . . and I shot a ball from taw and it jumped the table and went out the window. **1922** *DN* 5.188, *Taw.* . . The place shot from. **1935** *AmSp* 10.159 **seNE,** *Taws.* This term is synonymous with *lag-line* and is perhaps the one more generally used. **1957** *WELS Suppl.* **OK** (as of 1890s), The long axis of the ring pointed toward the shooting line about ten feet away, and five feet or so long. This line was called taws, but was also referred to as the lag line. This was because the players before the game would roll their shooting marble (called a taw) as close to this line as possible. The closest taw to the line had first turn. . . The initial shot was always from taws. Subsequent shots were from the lay, as in golf. **1965–70** *DARE* (Qu. EE8, *The line toward which the players roll their marbles before beginning a game, to determine the order of shooting*) 23 Infs, **esp Sth, S Midl,** Taw; **MO**5, Taws; **VA**35, Head taw. **1966–69** *DARE* Tape **AL**3, You'd go back to this line where you call from taw, and shoot at that ring; **AL**6, [Aux Inf:] The marble that you shot with. [Inf:] It was taw [tˈɑ·oˆ], that was [tˈou], you shoot from taw [tˈɑoˆ]; **IN**83, You stand off about ten feet and shoot the marbles from what they call the taw; **TX**1, You have a big marble right in the center, and whoever knocked that big marble out from taws, if you could hit it the first time, why, you won the game. **1971** [see **taw line**]. **1973** Allen *LAUM* 1.405 (as of c1950), Returns from 740 respondents confirm the evidence in the field data that *lag (line)* is strong in Nebraska and South Dakota but that *taw (line)* is strong in Iowa. Indeed, the checklist shows additionally a Midland leaning in Iowa, with a 48% frequency in the southern half in contrast with a 19% return in the northern. **1976** *WI Acad. Rev.* Mar 9 **seWI** (as of 1920s), About ten to twelve feet away a straight line was marked as the place from which the first shots were to be taken. This line was called "talls."

b hence in var fig phrr:

(1) *come (up) to taw:* To meet expectations or requirements; to come up to scratch, toe the line; similarly *bring one (up) to taw:* to cause one to do this. [*EDD taw* sb. 5.(3), (4)]

1838 *Amer. Turf Reg.* 9.324, Fairfield *(Va.)* Races. . . Produce Stakes of $500 each, . . six subscribers; three 'came to taw.' **1846** *Knickerbocker* 28.359, When they [=Moroccans] do n't 'come up to taw,' and fork over their one, two, or three hundred, . . several large Thomas-cats are placed in these . . breeches. **1866** Pollard *Lost Cause* 288 **TX,**

Changing our front in that direction, we poured in a heavy fire, which soon brought them to taw, as the greater part of two regiments threw down their arms, and ran to us. **1886** *Denton Jrl.* (MD) 7 Sept 4/2 **NYC,** Gramercy Park . . knows good music and insists on having it and the hand-organs coming right up to taw every time. **1898** Lloyd *Country Life* 146 **AL,** All she has got to do is to make a cross mark and spit in it, and Toney he comes to taw. **1899** (1912) Green *VA Folk-Speech* 440, *To come to taw,* to come to a designated line or position; be brought to account. **1909** *DN* 3.348 **eAL, wGA,** *Make one come to taw. . .* To force one to do something he does not desire to do. "When the time comes for him to pay me up, I'll make him come to taw." **1937** in Lib. of Congress *Amer. Memory: WPA Life Hist.* (Internet) **cTX,** He'd ride his hoss into the herd, make it understand which critter was wanted, and that critter was brought to taw. **1938** *Frederick Post* (MD) 10 Sept 9/1 **NYC,** So our hero walked into the manager's office and promised to bring those accumulated arrears up to taw at once. **1956** *Chron.-Telegram* (Elyria OH) 9 Feb 40/1 **NYC,** But then someone discovered we were some months laggard of Russia . . and Bill disappeared into the mists surrounding a program designed to bring us up to taw. **1959** Robertson *Ram* 162 **ID** (as of c1875), He was sure that Obe at least could be brought to taw if she would only say the word. **1984** Wilder *You All Spoken Here* 50 **Sth,** *Bring to taw:* Bring to task; teach one a lesson.

(2) *shoot from taw:* To make a good start, be on the right track; to do all one can.

1913 *Atlanta Constitution* (GA) 9 June 4/5, We're not shooting from taw in trying to find the reason and remedy for this condition. It is popular to blame the laziness and indifference of the farmers. They're not at fault. . . The bankers are the guilty parties. **1937** *NV State Jrl.* (Reno) 4 May 5/1, When he [=a racehorse] won the Paumonok . . , his neck was like a gander's—he was reaching for every inch. He was being whipped for all the jockey had. In short he was shooting from taw. When the company got tougher his neck wasn't long enough, his legs weren't strong enough and his heart wasn't big enough. **1942** Hurston *Dust Tracks* 177 **FL** [Black], The Social Register crowd at Barnard soon took me up, and I became Barnard's sacred black cow. If you had not had lunch with me, you had not shot from taw. **1966** *DARE* Tape **AL6,** [Aux Inf:] That's probably how the expression started, "You haven't shot from taw [t·ɑ]." . . When you haven't begun to do anything successfully . . you say, "You haven't shot from taw [t·ɑʊᵛ] yet."

(3) *from taw:* From the beginning; of the truest sort.

1935 Davis *Honey* 107 **OR,** The only way Mrs. Yarbro could tell anything was to start from taw and tell everything. **1937** in Lib. of Congress *Amer. Memory: WPA Life Hist.* (Internet) **cnTX,** I was sheriff of Jack Co. from 1914 'til 1922, when the Ku Klux finally got me. You see, I fought them all the way from taw, and they tried to get me every year. **1960** Criswell *Resp. to PADS 20* **Ozarks,** "He's a fiddler from taw, nobody can beat him." "Fiddler from way back" means the same thing as "fiddler from who laid the chunks" is the same; are common but less than formerly.

(4) *far from* (or *close to*) *taw:* Far from (or close to) home; also fig.

1875 Wingate *Views & Interviews* 18, His conduct will display . . a sincerity of purpose—which, if he be a man of sense and popular sympathies, is pretty sure to hit the masses of people somewhere not very far from taw. **1937** Gann *Trail Boss* 56 **wTX,** 'Did you make any kind of deal to tie it up?' . . 'No. . . That place is a leetle bit too far from taw for me. I thought I'd better tell you about it first.' **1944** *AmSp* 19.156 **sIN,** *Too far from taw* (usually means too far from home). **1954** in 2004 *DARE* File—Internet **TX,** All of his adult life until a few years ago, Howard Paul was a great, outdoor, going sort of man. . . In later years, he has been kept closer to taw by a thigh bone break, which has given trouble.

(5) *get down to taw:* To apply oneself to the matter at hand, "buckle down"; to get to the heart of the matter, speak bluntly.

1934 *Deming Headlight* (NM) 29 June [4]/1 (newspaperarchive.com), It is true, we do have in Deming a full share of personal, political, and private differences. But that, apparently, doesn't keep us from getting down to taw when there is something to be done for the community. **1941** Street *In Father's House* 65 **MS,** Mr. Martin . . is mighty proud of his farm and hogs and family, but getting right down to taw, his hams ain't as good as Aunt 'Tunia's and he knows it. **1945** Street *Gauntlet* 206 **TX** (as of 1920s), He wouldn't act without consulting his deacons. Getting down to taw, though, he ain't bound to consult with us on revivals.

3 A man's partner at a square dance or **play-party.**

1896 Hickenlooper *Illustr. Hist. Monroe Co. IA* 214, At the common "hoedown" those French terms used by the man who "calls off" are Anglicized into plain English; for instance, the caller will shout the familiar term "Chassez partners!" but in the "hoedown" whirl it is translated into: "Swing your taw,/ Everybody dance to please Grandpa!" **1931** Randolph *Ozarks* 70, A taw is . . a girl—a man's partner at a dance or play-party. **1937** NE Univ. *Univ. Studies* 37.114 [Terms from play-party songs], *Taw,* n. (Dance term.) Partner. (From marble usage.) **1940** *AmSp* 15.221 **cwTX,** When a cowboy prepares for the weekly dance on Saturday night, he 'gets dressed up like a sore toe.' Then he selects his favorite 'taw' (dancing partner). **1974** *Bittersweet* 2.29 **Ozarks,** *Taw*—another term for G[entleman]'s partner.

4 The marker used in the game of hopscotch. Cf **lagger 2, potsy 1**

1988 McBride *Echoes* 21, Young man throws out an imaginary hopscotch taw and hops the imaginary grid. **2000** in 2004 *DARE* File—Internet **swUT,** Hopscotch was another popular girls' game. The game was played on a "board" drawn on the sidewalk. . . Then a taw was thrown into one of the numbered squares. **2001** *Ibid* **seID,** I even remember my great hopscotch taw. It was a Cat's Paw rubber heal [sic] that I'd found on my way to school. **2003** *Ibid* **NYC,** Perhaps they were more interested in making sure every girl got her proper number of jumps, whether or not she could keep time with a rope, or throw a hopscotch taw into the right box. **2004** *Ibid,* No more need for rocks that bounce and roll away. Hoppy Taw flies true and grips when it hits. . . The official Hopscotch marker for tournaments.

tawga worm See **toggle worm**

tawl See **taw**

taw line n chiefly **Sth, S Midl, West** See Map Cf **toe line, toy 2**

=**taw C2a.**

1894 *Daily Rev.* (Decatur IL) 2/4, E.E. Larkins . . and his stepson, Claude Seaton, were playing hop scotch on the sidewalk. Two boys named Morthland came along and stepped on the taw line. **1910** Calhoun *Healthful Sports* 6, *Fat. . .* Make a ring eighteen inches or two feet in diameter; ten feet back draw or scratch a taw line to shoot from. **1955** *PADS* 23.32 **cwTN,** *Taw line. . .* Same as *lag line.* **c1955** Reed–Person *Ling. Atlas Pacific NW,* 8 infs, Taw line. **1957** WELS Suppl. **ceWI,** Baby-In-The-Hole. . . A tennis or soft ball is rolled from the "Taw Line," object being to get the ball in one of the holes. **1965–70** *DARE* (Qu. EE8, *The line toward which the players roll their marbles before beginning a game, to determine the order of shooting*) 106 Infs, **chiefly Sth, S Midl, West,** Taw line; **MS1,** Tor [to:ə] line. **1966–69** *DARE* Tape **FL8,** [Inf:] You had to stay on this line. [FW:] Does that have any special name? [Inf:] Taw line; **GA13,** Between the first and second hole, . . about a foot from . . the first hole, we'd draw . . a taw line. And you stood behind this line and you shot for the first hole; **KY41,** If you shot back here from your taw line . . and shot this middle marble out, . . we call that the middleman; **TX9,** We would throw a marble to another taw line to see . . who was first. **1971** *PADS* 56.35 **AL,** *Used Most by Old [infs] . . taw. . . Used Most by Middle Aged [infs] . . taw line.* **1973** [see **taw C2a**]. **2002** *DARE* File **AL,** "Taw line" or "up to taw" as in "he isn't up to taw"—Refers to the game of marbles, where the outer ring is called the "taw line".

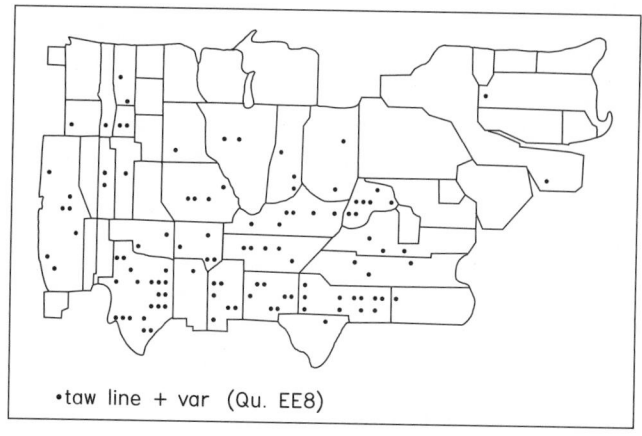

•taw line + var (Qu. EE8)

taw man (or marble) See **taw C1a**

tawny owl n [*OED2* 1768 for *Strix aluco*]
=**barn owl 1.**
1923 Dawson *Birds CA* 3.1070, *American Barn Owl. . . Synonyms.*—
Monkey-faced Owl. Tawny Owl. White Owl. . . *Recognition Marks.*—
Crow size; tawny or white coloration.

tawses See **taw B**

tawsle See **tassel**

tawt See **thwart**

tax v
To charge, make a claim upon (one for an amount); to set the
price; to cost; hence n *tax* the cost.
1848 Bartlett *Americanisms* 351, *To tax.* To charge; as, 'What will you
tax me a yard for this cloth?' **1856** Whitcher *Bedott Papers* 218 **cNY,**
He said 'twas woth double the money he taxed; but seein' he was tradin'
with the clargy, he wouldent charge but half-price. **1858** Hammett
Piney Woods Tavern 259, He was allers plaguy obligin' to us boys—so I
knew he'd help us in this hoss bisniss, and not tax onreasonable. **1905**
DN 3.22 **cCT,** *Tax. . .* To charge. 'What will you tax me for this horse?'
1907 *DN* 3.219 **nwAR,** *Tax, v.t.* To charge. **1929** *AmSp* 5.74 **NE** [Cattle
country talk], When inquiring about the cost of anything, a "ranch hand"
is likely to ask "What is the tax on that?" **1943** *LANE* Map 559–60,
[About 50 infs, **chiefly nNEng, Nantucket MA, Martha's Vineyard
MA,** volunteered or acknowledged *tax* as a synonym of *charge* in the
context "How much do you charge?" Most considered it obsolete or old-
fashioned.] **1966–70** *DARE* (Qu. U8a, . . *"It cost me ten dollars."*) Infs
MO17, **TX**51, Taxed; **NC**18, It taxed me; **CA**207, What did they tax
you for?

tax strip n Cf *DS* N44
=**devil's strip.**
1964 *AmSp* 39.293 **OH,** One informant in Mansfield, Ohio, . . had no
previous knowledge of either *tree lawn* or *Devil's strip.* To him it was either the *tax strip* or the *government strip.* **2009** *DARE* File **neOH,** My
father used tax strip when we we're [sic] young but changed to tree lawn
as we got older. Everyone else in the neighborhood used tree lawn. *Ibid*
sIN, The . . "tax strip" was . . part of your lot/land when you bought it,
you got to pay taxes on it as part of your lot, but you couldn't use it because all the property from the opposite side of the sidewalk to the curb
could only be used by the "govt."

taylor See **tailor** n

taynt See **taunt**

tazzle v Also with *up* [*EDD* "*v.* . . to entangle. . . Hence
Tazzled, ppl. adj. tangled, fuzzy, twisted, knotted. . . *sb.* A tan-
gle; a state of disorder"]
To muddle, mess up, confuse; hence ppl adj *tazzled (up);* n
tizzle-tazzle a state of confusion, a tizzy.
[**a1729** in 1960 Taylor *Poems* 51, In finest Twine of Praise I'm muz-
zled. My tazzled Thoughts twirld into Snick-Snarls run.] **1948** Hurston
Seraph 22 **wFL** [Black], Nothing to do but submit herself to her fate.
But submission tazzled you all up inside. **1957** *Daily Jrl.* (Commerce
TX) 13 Mar 1/1, But Mr. Yarbrough's situation . . has me worried to a
tizzle-tazzle. You know, he ain't got a cow on the place. **1969** *DARE*
(Qu. Y37, *To make a place untidy or disorderly: "I wish they wouldn't
_____ the room so."*) Inf **GA**77, Tazzle up; (Qu. Y38, *Mixed together, confused: "The things in the drawer are all _____."*) Inf
GA77, Tazzled up. **2004** *DARE* File—Internet **TN,** It is in such
moments that God can truly be God. When we are frazzled and tazzled
and ready to crumble, he is there and there in all ways.

t.b. n [Facetious reinterpretations of *t.b.* tuberculosis]
1 See **tavern belly.**
2 See quot.
1967 *DARE* (Qu. BB20, *Joking names or expressions for overactive
kidneys*) Infs **AZ**2, **IL**21, T.b.—tiny bladder.
3 See quot.
1969 *DARE* (Qu. X31, . . *A woman's breasts*) Inf **NY**167, T.b.—two
beauts.

t'baccy See **tobacco** n A2

tchaviche See **tschawytscha**

tea bark n Also *tea box*
A **wax myrtle** (here: *Morella cerifera*).

1974 Morton *Folk Remedies* 99 **SC,** *Tea bark; tea box—Myrica
cerifera* [=*Morella c.*] . . *South Carolina (Current use):* Leaves often
steeped for "tea," drunk as a beverage.

teaberry n
1 also *tea leaves:* A **wintergreen 2,** usu *Gaultheria procumbens;* also the fruit of such a plant. [*DCan* 1796] **esp Mid
and C Atl** See Map
1818 Barton *Compendium Florae Philadelphicae* 1.194, *Gaultheria. . .
procumbens. . . Mountain-tea.* Tea-berry. Partridge-berry. Winter-green.
1828 Rafinesque *Med. Flora* 1.202, *Gautiera* [sic] *repens* [=*Gaultheria
procumbens*]. . . *Vulgar Names* . . Teaberry. **1858** Hogg *Vegetable
Kingdom* 482, The leaves [of *Gaultheria procumbens*] . . when . .
dried . . make an excellent substitute for tea . . and the plant is on that
account called *Tea-berry* and *Mountain Tea.* **1924** *Amer. Botanist*
30.13, Another medicinal plant commonly known as "wintergreen"
[is] . . *Gaultheria procumbens.* . . The pungent oil that permeates all
parts of the plant give [sic] reason for names like . . "tea-leaves" and "tea
berry." **1944** *Advent. Tommy Teaberry* np **PA,** The little old man
pointed at the green bushes nearby and said, "See those? My family and
I grow the finest Teaberry plants on this mountain. . . Here, just taste
that." **1968–70** *DARE* (Qu. I44, *What kinds of berries grow wild
around here?*) Infs **NJ**31, **PA**115, 150, **WV**8, Teaberries; **VA**13, Mountain teaberries; (Qu. S26c, *Wildflowers that grow in woods*) Inf **PA**245,
Tea leaves—two inches off ground, same as teaberry; **VA**28, Teaberry;
(Qu. BB50a, . . *Favorite remedies . . for a cough*) Inf **MD**17, Teaberry
leaves, hemlock branches, wild cherry, apple syrup. **1979** Niering-
Olmstead *Audubon Guide N. Amer. Wildflowers E. Region* 499, *Teaberry . . (Gaultheria procumbens). . .* Teaberry extract is used to flavor
teas, candies, medicines, and chewing gum. **2001** *DARE* File **PA,** I am
familiar with "tea berries," small ground plants with glossy leaves and
edible red berries that grow near Winfield, Pa. They are minty tasting
and used as a local flavoring for ice cream. Tea berry ice cream is a favorite in that area. I have never seen it anywhere else. **2001** *DARE* File
(Internet), Do you remember a gum . . called *Teaberry? . .* We have
Clark's Teaberry Gum available. . . We get our supply from Lowell,
Mass.

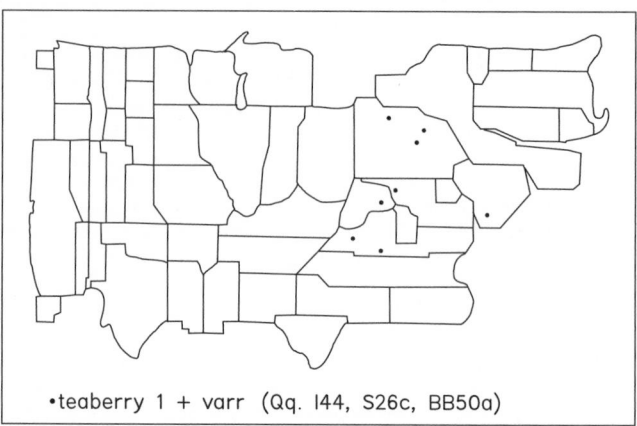

•teaberry 1 + varr (Qq. I44, S26c, BB50a)

2 A **witherod** (here: *Viburnum nudum* var *cassinoides*). Cf
Appalachian tea 2
1916 *Torreya* 16.239 **ME,** *Viburnum cassinoides* . . Tea berry, Matinicus I[slan]d.
3 =**partridgeberry 1.**
1972 Brown *Wildflowers LA* 176, *Tea Berry . . Mitchella repens. . .* An
evergreen, trailing herb. . . Fruit a twin berry, red, edible, about ½ inch
in diameter. Widely distributed in the mixed woods on drier sites.

tea box See **tea bark**

tea cake n **chiefly Sth**
A cookie, usu of a delicate flavor and not heavily sweetened.
Note: In many contexts it is impossible to determine what is
meant by *tea cake;* only exx that clearly refer to a cookie are
included here.
1879 (1965) Tyree *Housekeeping in Old VA* 359, *Tea Cakes.* 2 quarts
of flour. 1 small teacup of lard. 1 small teacup of butter. 3 cupfuls of
sugar. 3 eggs. 1 cupful of cream (sour is best). 2 small teaspoonfuls of
soda. 1 grated nutmeg. Roll out half an inch thick, and bake in a moderate oven. **1932** (1946) Hibben *Amer. Regional Cookery* 313 **MS,** Best

Tea Cakes (Mississippi). . . Chill thoroughly. . . Place on a lightly floured board and roll out to a little less than ⅛-inch thickness. Cut with floured cutter. . . *Approximate yield: 5 dozen cookies.* **1940** Brown *Amer. Cooks* 23 **AL**, Tea Cakes. . . [R]oll thin, cut in rounds, and bake in quick oven. **1956** McAtee *Some Dialect NC* 46, Tea cake . . cookie for between meals snacks. **c1960** *Wilson Coll.* **csKY**, Teacake: . . A kind of cookie, often used as a generic name; cooky is decidedly modern in the area. **1961** Folk *Word Atlas N. LA* 189, Older people gave most of the *tea cake* reponses; young people generally said *cookie.* **1966–70** *DARE* [(Qu. H15, *Bread made with wheat flour*) Inf **SC**19, Tea cake—roll it out, cut it like biscuits—has sugar;] (Qu. H32, . . *Fancy rolls and pastries*) Infs **GA**8, 10, **TX**91, Tea cakes—cookies; **FL**15, Cookies, tea cakes, muffins; **MO**1, Tea cakes. **1966** *DARE* Tape **MS**61, She'd feed us sweetcakes, you know, these molasses cakes. . . We'd call 'em tea cakes. **1967** *DARE* FW Addit **LA**11, Tea cakes—cookies. Hung on the wall in a pillow slip to keep fresh. **1999** *DARE* File—Internet, Also in the south, tea cakes are not at all what they are in other places. . . Tea cakes are cookies—a very particular kind of cookie, at that. . . A good tea cake is round, lightly browned, very slightly chewy, a bit almond-y, a bit vanilla-y, barely sweet—and heavenly.

teach v

A Forms.

Past, past pple: usu *taught;* also *teached, teacht;* rarely *teach, taughten.* [*OED2* "A normalized form *teached* . . has been in partial use since the 14th c., but is not now accepted in educated speech."]

1762 in 1851 *Doc. Hist. State of NY* 4.200, Sr I have been at onidia and had there 18 Scholars and I have teached so long that the [sic] are Come to 4. **1837** Sherwood *Gaz. GA* 71, Teached, for taught. **1872** U.S. Congress *Rept. Joint Select Comm. Insurrectionary States* 5.1973 **nwSC**, It seems to me that men who had good learning and knowledge ought to have teached us better. *Ibid* 11.487 **ceMS** [Black], There was only one school-house that I ever knew burned down. They teached in it about a week. **1893** *DN* 1.278 **wCT**, Teach—[past, past pple:] teached (only in sense of 'keep school.' He uses *learn,* trans., in other senses). **1898** Westcott *Harum* 189 **nNY**, Mebbe I wa'n't only the scum o' the earth, as I'd ben teached to believe. **1908** *DN* 3.283 **eAL, wGA**, Abnormal preterits. . . teacht. **1953** Atwood *Survey of Verb Forms* 24, Those who use *teach* [rather than *learn*] almost invariably give the preterite *taught* /tɔt/. *Teached* /titʃt/ is used, however, by seven N. Eng. informants . . and by four . . informants in Va., N.C., and S.C. **1962** *Mt. Life* 38.1.17 **sAppalachians**, The past and past participle of teach [become] teached. **1965–70** *DARE* (Qu. N8, *If somebody gave you lessons in driving a car* . . *"He _____ me how to drive."*) [905 Infs, **widespread**, Taught;] **AZ**11, **CA**63, **GA**3, **KY**17, 80, **NJ**50, **NY**1, 70, 72, **NC**50, 72, **OK**49, **PA**235, Teached [10 of 13 Infs old, 10 comm type 4 or 5]; **GA**40, **SC**9, Teacht; **MS**60, Taughten ['tɔɔtn̩]; **IN**3, Taughten [*DARE* Ed: This resp may be a FW error for *taught*]. **1969** *DARE* Tape **GA**51, My daddy teached me all this. **1989** Pederson *LAGS Tech. Index* 357 **Gulf Region**, [For the past of *teach*, 529 infs gave [tɔt], 6 [tičt], and 4 [tič].] **2000** Shores *Tangier Is.* 248 **Chesapeake Bay**, Nonstandard forms showing past times are common: . . teached.

B Sense.

With *up:* To educate, bring up.

1924 Raine *Land of Saddle-Bags* 99 **sAppalachians**, The Mountain man uses . . *teach up,* as in teach up the children to have good manners. **1957** Combs *Lang. S. Highlanders* **sAppalachians**, Teach up—teach, educate, bring up. **2003** *Pure Music* (Internet) Sept **neNJ** [Black], Yeah. I mean, that's the way we was taught up to play it [=pedal steel guitar]. **2004** *DARE* File—Internet [Black], The way I was taught up was just strive for the best in all you do and don't care how much people tease you.

teached See teach A

teacher bird n Also *teacher* [Echoic]

=ovenbird.

[**1871** Burroughs *Wake-Robin* 57 **NY**, Commencing in a very low key, . . he [=an ovenbird] grows louder and louder. . . This lay may be represented thus: "Teacher, *teacher,* Teacher, Teacher, Teacher!"—the accent on the first syllable.] **1900** *Birds & All Nature* 7.97, I . . soon found my bird to be the ovenbird, golden-crowned thrush, or teacher bird. But why "teacher" bird? I was constantly asking this question, for to my ears the sound always came as *tichee, ti-chee, ti-chee,* with accent always on the final syllable. **1917** (1923) *Birds Amer.* 3.151, Ovenbird. . . Other Names. . . Teacher. **1924** Howell *Birds AL* 310, Oven-

bird. . . Its song, a vigorous and characteristic utterance, is rendered from a fallen log or a low limb of a tree. Burroughs has translated it as *teach-er, teach-er, teach-er, teach-er,* and has dubbed the bird the "teacher bird." **1938** Oberholser *Bird Life LA* 550, *Seiurus aurocapillus.* . . is called Ovenbird from the shape of its nest, and "teacher-bird" from its ordinary song. **1956** MA Audubon Soc. *Bulletin* 40.130, Ovenbird. . . Teacher Bird (Maine, Vt. The song syllabilizes as *teacher, teacher,* and so on, each repetition becoming louder.) **1990** *Gettysburg Times* (PA) 9 June sec A 4/3, Some people insist on calling the ovenbird a teacher bird because he hollers "teacher, teacher."

teacht See teach A

teach up See teach B

tea clam n

A small **quahog 1.**

1881 Ingersoll *Oyster-Industry* 249, Tea-clam.—The quahaug, *Venus Mercenaria* of small size. **1884** U.S. Natl. Museum *Bulletin* 27.234, Some [quahogs] are taken so small that 2,000 are required to fill a barrel; these, when about one inch in diameter, are called "tea-clams."

teacups n pl *joc*

The hiccups.

1969 *DARE* (Qu. X54, *When a person gets a spell of going 'hic'* . . *he's got the _____*) Inf **GA**72, Hiccups, teacups, hicks. **1969** *DARE* FW Addit **neIL**, Teacups [laughter]. [Inf orig from IA]

tead (up), teaed up See tea up

tea elder n

An elder (here: *Sambucus nigra* subsp *canadensis*).

1951 *PADS* 15.41 **TX**, *Sambucus canadensis.* . . Sweet, wine, or tea, elder. Jellies and wines as well as pies are still made from its berries as is the tea whose virtues were learned from the Indians.

tea fern n

A **cliff brake** (here: *Pellaea mucronata*).

1923 in 1925 Jepson *Manual Plants CA* 33, *P[ellaea] ornithopus* [=*P. mucronata*]. . . Sometimes called Tea Fern. **1970** Kirk *Wild Edible Plants W. U.S.* 218, *Pellaea mucronata* . . Tea Fern. . . The dried fronds may be steeped in hot water for 15 to 20 minutes to produce a fragrant and flavorful tea. In pioneer days an extra strong brew of the tea was used in treating tuberculosis and feverish colds.

tea for the fever, not to take v phr *For varr see quots* esp among Black speakers

Not to put up with any nonsense; not to allow oneself to be intimidated.

a1940 in 1967 Meltzer *In Words* 141 **VA** [Black], They [=the police] didn't do nothing neither. They 'fraid of the women. You can outtalk the men. But us women don't take no tea for the fever. **1953** Fisher *Waiters* 65 **NYC** [Black], "He betta min' his own goddam business. I ain't fixin' to take no tea for the fever this afternoon," he snorted angrily. **1979** *Ms.* Oct 20 **SC** [Black], They said that she didn't take no tea for the fever. Meaning she was outspoken and independent, specially bout the "mens". **1996** Little *Good Hair* 15 **SC** (as of a1940) [Black], Her hair and her stature gave her the appearance of confidence that made many rural Blacks and Whites uncomfortable. People used to say, "Viola don't take no tea for the fever," which means she didn't take any stuff from people. **1996** Mann *Having Our Say* 21 **NC** [Black], But I didn't take tea for the fever! If it wasn't right, I wouldn't do it. **2004** *DARE* File—Internet [Black], The female characters were very, very earthy and Reallll. Oooh man some of them didn't take *any* tea for the fever. . . you rub them the wrong way you'll get hurt! **2007** *BlackPressUSA.com* 20 Feb (Internet) **Baltimore MD**, Theresa is a woman with a "take no tea for the fever" attitude, but behind this façade is a gentle soul full of compassion. **2007** *DARE* File—Internet [Black], Don't take no tea for the fever. [Pseudonym]

tea-hounds n pl

Sideburns.

1972 *AmSp* 47.155 **nwSC**, Some of my earliest memories of childhood . . in Anderson County [SC] . . center upon the hearing of the lively and colorful word *tea-hounds*. It was obviously a slang expression, and it was then, and still is, applied to mean 'the sideburns on a man's face.' Invariably the expression was employed humorously—never derisively. . . The man was normally, I noticed, a fine dresser. **1973** *DARE* File **nw,cnSC**, Tea-hounds = sideburns. This sense used formerly in Anderson and Union Counties, South Carolina. Transf. from use to mean a "ladies'-man," or "lounge lizard."

tea in China, all the n Cf *farm in Texas* (at **farm** n 3)
Fig, in var hyperbolical phrr: something of great value.

   1870 (1871) Terhune *Empty Heart* 337, Shanghai might go to Jericho, and all the tea in China and America to the bottom of the Red Sea, before I would let my Lewis leave me at such a time. **1922** *IA City Press–Citizen* (IA) 9 Sept 6/4 **OH,** If that's not the stuff that'll make a fellow hard you can have all the tea in China. **1953** *NYT Mag.* 25 Jan 17, [Advt:] Leave us face it. We know dozens of women who wouldn't put margarine on their tables for all the tea in China. **1965–70** *DARE* (Qu. KK62, . . *"I wouldn't do that for _____."*) 96 Infs, **widespread, but less freq Sth, S Midl,** All the tea in China; (Qu. V2b, . . *"I wouldn't trust him _____.";* not asked in early QRs) Inf **CA**177, For all the tea in China; (Qu. JJ20, . . *"I'm so sure, I'd _____ it."*) Inf **CA**135, Bet all the tea in China; (Qu. KK55c, . . *Expressions of strong denial*) Infs **NC**36, **NJ**54, **OH**80, Not for all the tea in China; **MN**33, I wouldn't for all the tea in China. **2000** *NY Times* (NY) 5 Mar Business sec 1/6 **cnGA,** You couldn't get me to live in the suburbs for all the tea in China.

teakettle See **kettle** B3

teakettle up v phr
To tidy, put in order.

   1975 Gould *ME Lingo* 287, *Teakittle*—As used in Maine for a quick tidying this word is in the category of *brush out, swamp out, scurryfunge,* and *righten up.* . . "While you're doing the chores, I'll teakittle up the kitchen." **2004** *DARE* File—Internet **RI,** We awoke bright and early the next day, had a quick hearty breakfast, 'tea-kettled up' the cottage, and caravanned to Brown University.

teakle See **tackle**

tealeaf willow n Also *tea-leaved willow*
=**planeleaf willow.**

   1938 Van Dersal *Native Woody Plants* 357, Tealeaf willow (*Salix planifolia*). **1966** Grimm *Recognizing Native Shrubs* 88, Tealeaf Willow. . . A much-branched shrub 8 inches to 10 feet high. . . *Leaves* elliptic to oblong, . . dark green and lustrous above. **1973** Hitchcock–Cronquist *Flora Pacific NW* 69, Circumboreal s to Cal, NM, and N Eng . . tea-l[ea]v[e]d w[illow].

tea leaves See **teaberry** 1

team n

1 A vehicle that is harnessed to one or more draft animals, usu a horse or pair of horses—freq in comb *horse and team*. **chiefly Nth, esp NEng** *hist*

   1779 (1899) Parkman *Diary* 151 **MA,** Mr. Nathan Maynard junr. goes to Boston for Breck and carries in his Team Mr. Eli Forbes' Trunk. **1862** in 1887 U.S. War Dept. *War of Rebellion* 1st ser 19.1.737 **ME,** He was brought in in his team. **1901** *DN* 2.149 **nMA, cNY,** Team. . . Wagon. "Get into the team" = get into the wagon. **1905** *Washington Post* (DC) 3 Sept 19/3 **MA,** Any wheeled arrangement with a single horse is a team in Massachusetts. If it has two horses it is a double team. . . Boston newspapers not infrequently advertise for sale a "perfectly clever horse and team complete." This does not mean three horses, one of them of unusual intelligence. It means merely a wagon, buggy, cart, or some other vehicle, with harness, and a single horse. **1907** *DN* 3.245 **eME,** *Horse and team.* . . Horse and vehicle. *Ibid* 250 **eME,** *Team.* . . A horse and team; or a vehicle. Nearly universal. "Somebody's sacked your team off." "We drove several miles in a team." **1909** *DN* 3.412 **nME,** *Horse and team.* **1916** *Frederick Post* (MD) 21 Nov 3/4, Mrs. Jane Carothers . . is thrown from her team. . . Lewis H. Harwetel . . is hurled from a two-horse team. **1926** [see **3** below]. **1927** [see **2** below]. **1944** *Independent–Rec.* (Helena MT) 20 Feb 10/2, The carrier had to abandon his car and come on later with a horse and team. **1949** Kurath *Word Geog.* 21, In Eastern New England as well as in the lower Connecticut Valley *team* . . often means the draft animal(s) together with the vehicle, in the coastal area sometimes the vehicle alone, as in the phrase *a horse and a team.* **1952** Brown *NC Folkl.* 1.598, In New England a farmer will say: "I will put some apples in my team, hitch up my horses, and drive to town." This same usage occurs in the South. **1967–68** *DARE* (Qu. N41a, . . *Horse-drawn vehicles . . to carry people*) Inf **MA**4, Team; (Qu. N41b, *Horse-drawn vehicles to carry heavy loads*) Inf **MA**4, Team; **MA**7, Low teams; (Qu. N41c, *Horse-drawn vehicles to carry light loads*) Inf **MA**7, High teams—for

iceman, fruit peddlers, delivery; **MA**27, Team. **1976** *Yankee* July 79, [He] drove past in his laundry team, hoping to attract the girl's attention.

2 A single horse and vehicle, regarded (along with the harness) as a single unit. [By ext from *team* two or more draft animals and the vehicle to which they are harnessed] **chiefly NEng** *old-fash*

   1870 *Bangor Daily Whig & Courier* (ME) 19 Dec 2/2, A stolen team, the horse belonging to the firm of Samuel . . & Co., the buggy to Wm. Tibbets, and the harness to some unknown person, is supposed by the tracks to have gone southward towards Dover. **1877** *Harper's New Mth. Mag.* 54.298 **CT,** The colt . . tore the reins out of his hands, and set off at full speed, leaving them three miles from Green's wood . . with a broken wagon, no horse, and an approaching tempest. There was nothing to do but to walk back to the village, hire another "team," and . . drive to Green's wood. **1900** *New Engl. Mag.* 22.659, The traveller drove his team on to the boat. . . The passenger was sitting calmly in his buggy . ., the horse quite heedless of the fact that the waters of the Connecticut were rippling within a few inches of him. **1907** [see **1** above]. **1926** [see **3** below]. **1927** *AmSp* 3.140 **eME,** A single horse and buggy were spoken of as the "team" or "horse and team." **1949** [see **1** above].

3 A single draft animal, usu a horse, that is, or is regarded as potentially, drawing a vehicle. **chiefly NEng** Cf **double team** 1

   1896 *DN* 1.426 **CT,** *Team:* a single horse attached to a carriage. **1926** *AmSp* 2.77 **ME,** The word *team* is about the most misused word you will find in all New England. . . It is common to have it denote a *single* horse. In Maine we seem to employ it for the rig, nay, even for the wagon itself. "I'll hitch up the team and go for the mail," says our farmer friend. Naturally you think he is driving a pair, and you are not disturbed, until you see him driving away one solitary "hoss." A pair he would describe as a "span." **1939** *LANE* Map 174 *(Team)* **NEng,** The informants' definitions are grouped under five heads. . . 1: one horse, usually harnessed or hitched to a vehicle, or otherwise described as working, ready to work, etc. [This sense was recorded from about 45 infs, esp in **nNEng.**] . . 1 inf, **nwCT,** Go and harness your team, 'That means to hitch up your horse and put him to the wagon'; 1 inf, **cMA,** A team may be any number of horses, from one to ten, if they're hitched to something; 1 inf, **cwMA,** If I had a one-horse team, that'd be a team just the same, but it wouldn't be a pair of horses; 1 inf, **swMA,** Team = one horse; double team = two of a kind; 1 inf, **cnVT,** Team—it might mean a pair, or it might mean a horse hitched to a vehicle; 1 inf, **ceNH,** Team—any animal or animals attached to a load. **1968** *DARE* (Qu. K50, *Joking nicknames for mules*) Inf **NC**49, Team—colored fellow used it, even for one.

4 attrib: Belonging to a conservative sect of Mennonites that does not allow members to own automobiles—freq in comb *team Mennonite.* Cf **black-bumper, hook-and-eye, horse-and-buggy**

   1960 *Frederick Post* (MD) 18 June 14/4, A four-bay horse shed . . will be re-erected to house the "Team Mennonite" buggies [at the Kutztown Pennsylvania Dutch Folk Festival]. **1967** *DARE* Tape **PA**30, He'd talk about the Amish and the team Mennonites. . . A black-bumper person will refer to the team person as a plain person, meaning he feels he is no longer plain. . . If you belong to a horse-and-wagon or a team church, then you are plain. **1995** *WI State Jrl.* (Madison) 3 Nov sec A 2/2, Leid says his family came to northern Clark County from Pennsylvania. . . They are so-called "team Mennonites," who shun cars in favor of horse-drawn buggies and bicycles. **2002** in 2004 *DARE* File—Internet **cPA,** I have many personal contacts in the Team Mennonite community, as well as a few in the Old Order Amish community. The main difference between the two, as far as I can see, is that Amish do not use electricity and tractors, whereas the Team Mennonites use both. However, both use only horse drawn buggies for personal transportation.

teamotel See **T-model Ford**

teamster tea n Also *teamster's tea*
=**Mormon tea 1.**

   1878 *Amer. Naturalist* 12.653, Teamster's tea. . . A well-known remedy for gonorrhœa among many Indians and Mexicans. . . a strong astringent. **1931** U.S. Dept. Ag. *Misc. Pub.* 101.12, *Ephedra.* . . Five or six species of this genus commonly occur on semiarid western, or mainly southwestern ranges. All the species are known also as Mormon-tea, . . teamsters' tea, . . and by other local names. **1947** Curtin *Healing Herbs* 49 **SW,** *Teamster's tea.* . . occurs in several species, but it may always be recognized by its numerous and many-jointed twigs. **1970**

Kirk *Wild Edible Plants W. U.S.* 21, *Ephedra* species . . Teamster Tea. . . All of the species make good tea, although some are better than others. . . A surprising number of people in northern Arizona, southern Utah, and eastern Nevada do this [=make such tea] today.

tea plant n

Any of several plants used or formerly used in making a sort of tea, such as **teaberry 1,** a **viburnum** such as a **nannyberry 1** (here: *Viburnum lentago*), or **New Jersey tea;** see quots.

1809 Kendall *Travels* 2.143 **MA,** Where the pine only is found, the ground beneath is nearly bare, sustaining but dwarfish plants, such as the *partridge-berry,* sometimes called the *tea plant* and *Indian tea.* **1886** Ebbutt *Emigrant Life* 72 **KS,** Then there was the wild tea-plant, a small bushy shrub with white flowers and crisp, bright green leaves, which, when picked and dried in the sun, made very good tea. **1894** *Jrl. Amer. Folkl.* 7.96 **LA,** *Lantana,* sp., tea-plant. **1896** *Ibid* 9.190 **csWI,** *Viburnum lentago,* . . tea plant. **1967** *DARE* Wildfl QR Pl.126 [=*Ceanothus americanus*] Inf **AR44,** Tea plant—some kind of tea plant.

tear v Usu |'tɛə(r), 'tæə(r)|; also |tɑ| Pronc-sp *tar*

A Pronc forms.

1859 (1968) Bartlett *Americanisms* 473, *Tear-coat* . . (often pron. *Tar-coat* in the West). **1893** Shands *MS Speech* 62, *Tar* [ta]. Negro for *tear* (verb). **1917** in 1944 *ADD* **sWV,** You'll tar your clothes. **2000** Shores *Tangier Is.* 176 **Chesapeake Bay,** Words like *hair, stairs, there, tear* and *parents* . . have strong *r*-coloring (a prominent *r* sound) and seem to have a sound between that of "haer" and "har," certainly not that of the Appalachian "thar."

B Gram forms.

1 past: usu *tore;* also rarely *tared, tear(ed), to'ne, tored, torn.*

1862 (1864) Browne *Artemus Ward Book* 166 **ME,** I tared myself from her grasp. **1884** *Anglia* 7.253 **Sth, S Midl** [Black], *Pres.* tear—*Past.* tored, teared, to'ne (he to'ne it up). **1903** *DN* 2.293 **Cape Cod MA** (as of a1857), The following forms in *-ed* are in general use: . . teared. **1935** *AmSp* 10.156 **NC,** During a stay in North Carolina it was my good fortune to lodge in the house of a woman whose speech was strikingly rich in local idiom. . . When she brought me a pie, it was with the apology, 'It torn a little, but I knew it would eat all right.' **1966** *DARE* (Qu. Y15, *To beat somebody thoroughly: "John really _____ that fellow!"*) Inf **SC26,** Tear up. **1989** Pederson *LAGS Tech. Index* 362 **Gulf Region,** [For the past tense of *tear,* 3 infs, [tɛəd, tæəd]; 1 inf, [tɔəd]; 1 inf, [tɔən].] **2000** Shores *Tangier Is.* 248 **Chesapeake Bay,** Nonstandard forms showing past times are common: . . teared.

2 past pple, ppl adj: usu *torn;* also:

a *tore;* pronc-sp *toe.* [*OED2* 1387 →] Cf **torn up, torn out, torn down**

1851 Hooper *Widow Rugby's Husband* 92 **AL,** I'd a tore his liver out! **1887** (1967) Harris *Free Joe* 191 **GA,** I git tore up in my mind. **1891** *DN* 1.144 **cNY,** [tɔɚ] . . 'torn.' **1893** *DN* 1.278 **nwCT,** *Tear* [past and past pple:] tore. **1900** *DN* 2.67 [College slang], *Tore, adj.* Worsted; defeated. **1931** (1991) Hughes–Hurston *Mule Bone* 116 **cFL** [Black], This town is bout to be tore up by backbiting. **1936** *AmSp* 11.349 **eTX,** Past participle: . . *tore.* **1941** *AmSp* 16.25 **sIN,** What he don't know's been tore out of the book. **1953** Atwood *Survey of Verb Forms* 24, The form *torn* . . is almost universal in cultured speech. . . *Tore* . . heavily predominates in n.e. N. Eng. among all the noncultured types. In s. and w. N. Eng. it is somewhat scattered and is much more frequent in the older groups. . . In e. N.Y. and n. N.J. *tore* is rather scattered, but elsewhere in the M[iddle] A[tlantic] S[tates] it is used by a majority of Type I [=infs with poor educ] . . and by about half of Type II [=infs with fair educ]. In the S[outh] A[tlantic] S[tates] *tore* . . is all but universal in Type I and in most areas dominates in Type II as well. . . Two W. Va. informants and one Va. informant (Negro) give *tored* . . ; one Ga. Negro uses the uninflected *tear.* **c1960** Wilson *Coll.* **csKY,** Tore up or tored up, for torn up—common. **1965–70** *DARE* (Qu. Y48, *To look in every possible place for something you've mislaid . . "I've _____ [the house looking for them]."*) 24 Infs, **scattered, but more freq Sth,** Tore up; **CO4, MO18, OK18, SC42, TX76,** Tore the house (*or* place, room) up (*or* down, upside down); (Qu. D21, *A small, poorly-built house, or one in rundown condition*) Inf **SC34,** Old tore-up building; (Qu. E22, *If a house is untidy and everything is upset . . "It's a _____!" or "It looks like _____."*) Infs **AR26, FL37, 49,** (All) tore up; **OK26,** Tore-up house; (Qu. W24b, *Sayings to warn a man that his pants are torn or split*) Infs **IN13, MD21, MS72, OK42, TN33,** Your pants (*or* trousers, britches) is (*or* are) tore; **MO5,** He's tore his britches; (Qu. W27, . . *A three-cornered tear in a piece of clothing from catching it on something*

sharp) Inf **TX103,** It's tore out; **VA9,** Tore place; (Qu. Y35, *To spoil something so that it can't be used . . "My new coffee pot—it's completely _____."*) Infs **GA17, 19, KY90, LA6,** Tore up; (Qu. Y38, *Mixed together, confused: "The things in the drawer are all _____."*) Inf **GA6,** Tore up; (Qu. DD15, *A person who is thoroughly drunk*) Infs **NY249, VA39,** Tore up; (Qu. GG2, . . *'Confused, mixed up': "So many things were going on at the same time that he got completely _____."*) Inf **CA110,** Tore up; (Qu. GG4, *Stirred up, angry: "When he saw them coming he got _____."*) Infs **KY70, SC34,** Tore up; (Qu. GG6, *Talking about a person's feelings being hurt: "When she said she wouldn't go with him, he was quite _____."*) Inf **MA58,** All tore out (*or* up); (Qu. GG7, . . *Annoyed or upset: "Though we were only ten minutes late, she was all _____."*) Infs **MA58, TN26, VT12,** Tore out (*or* up); (Qu. GG11, *To be quite anxious about something . . "The letter hasn't come and he's _____."*) Inf **GA72,** Tore up; (Qu. GG13a, *When something keeps bothering a person and makes him nervous . . "It _____ me."*) Inf **OK6,** Gets me tore up; (Qu. GG33a, *To feel very sad and upset about something: "When he got the news he was _____.";* total Infs questioned, 75) Inf **FL14,** Really tore up; (Qu. KK19, *If a machine or appliance is temporarily out of order: "My sewing machine _____."*) Infs **KY28, NC37,** Is tore up; (Qu. KK20a, *Something that looks as if it might collapse any minute: "That old shed is certainly _____."*) Inf **MD47,** Tore up; (Qu. KK20b, *Something that looks as if it might collapse any minute: "Our old washing machine is _____."*) Inf **GA23,** Tore up; (Qu. KK22, . . *Completely shattered: "The jug fell out of the window and was _____."*) Inf **LA6,** Tore all to pieces; (Qu. KK39, *Stirred up, upset: "Because of the storm, the pond was all _____."*) Inf **AL33,** Tore up; (Qu. KK70, *Something that has got out of proper shape: "That house is all _____."*) Inf **DE7,** Tore up. **1968** *PADS* 50.37 **swTN** [Black], For the past participle of *tear* two of the nine type I [=old, with little educ] informants . . and one of the nine type II [=mid-aged, with approx hs educ] . . have /to/ or /tɔə/. **1971** [see **torn up** adj phr 2]. **1975** Allen *LAUM* 2.30 **Upper MW** (as of c1950), Standard *torn* predominates among all speakers and in all states of the U[pper] M[idwest]. The variant *tore,* heavily favored by less-educated infs. in northeastern New England and in Pennsylvania, Ohio, and Kentucky, is likewise more common with Type I speakers in the UM, particularly in Iowa and South Dakota. But even there it is not the majority form, and its weak showing in the more recently settled portions of Nebraska and Minnesota indicates that it is now recessive. **1989** Pederson *LAGS Tech. Index* 362 **Gulf Region,** [For the past participle of *tear,* 130 infs had proncs of the types [tɔ, tɔʷ, tɔə, tɔə].] **2003** Amer. RadioWorks *Hard Time* (Internet) **NC,** This old man . . had tore up camps and beat up guards.

b *tor(e)d, toren.*

1795 Dearborn *Columbian Grammar* 139, *List of Improprieties.* . . Tor'd for Torn. **1927** Adams *Congaree* 31 **cSC** [Black], He look like he all tored up. **1941** O'Donnell *Great Big Doorstep* 23 **sLA,** Her dress is toren. **1953** [see **B2a** above]. **c1960** [see **B2a** above]. **1989** Pederson *LAGS Tech. Index* 362 **Gulf Region,** [For the past participle of *tear,* 3 infs had proncs of the types [tɔʷd, tod, tɔəd].]

c *tear(ed).*

1953 [see **B2a** above]. **2007** *DARE* File—Internet, Foxes had teared it into pieces.

tear-a-blanket See **tear-blanket b**

‡tear a sheet v phr Cf *DS* X55b

1979 *NYT Article Letters* **TX,** My Texas father—born 1886—used. . . "to tear a sheet," meaning to pass wind.

tear-blanket n

Any of var prickly plants, as:

a A **greenbrier** such as *Smilax rotundifolia.*

1836 Latrobe *Rambler in N. Amer.* 1.213, We found . . abundance of green-briar or tear-blanket as it is familiarly called.

b also *tear-a-blanket, tear-coat;* pronc-sp *tar-coat:* =**Hercules'-club 1.** esp **Ozarks**

1859 (1968) Bartlett *Americanisms* 473, *Tear-coat,* or *Tear-blanket* (often pron. *Tar-coat* in the West). The *Arabia* [sic] *Spinosa,* or Angelia [sic] tree, so called because its prickles tear the coats of hunters, or the blankets of the Indians, in passing. **1937** *Torreya* 37.99 **TN,** *Aralia spinosa.* . . Tear-blanket. **1949** Webber *Backwoods Teacher* 264 **Ozarks,** Judas trees burst out everywhere with lavender, and the tear-a-blanket (perhaps some sort of shadbush or hackberry) mingled its whiteness with them. **1950** Moore *Trees AR* 100, *Aralia spinosa.* . . Local Names: Hercules Club, . . Tear-blanket. . . Extremely spiny tree often confused with the prickly ash, the short sharp spines scattered over all the branches. **1986** Pederson *LAGS Concordance,* 1 inf, **nwAR,** Tear-blank(et)—tree, thorns tore blankets.

c A **prickly ash 1** (here: *Zanthoxylum clava-herculis*).

1897 Sudworth *Arborescent Flora* 265 **AR,** *Xanthoxylum clava-herculis.* . . Tear-blanket. **1950** Moore *Trees* AR 90, *Zanthoxylum clava-herculis.* . . Local Names: Prickly Ash, . . Tear Blanket. . . *Tree* usually small. . . *Bark.* . . conspicuously roughened by corky, pyramidal or round-pointed, cone-shaped protuberances an inch or more high which often end in a stout spine. **1960** Vines *Trees* SW 595, *Zanthoxylum clava-herculis.* . . Vernacular names are Toothache, . . Tear Blanket, . . and Wait-a-bit.

d A **cat's-claw** (here: *Acacia greggii*).

1941 Jaeger *Wildflowers* 97 **Desert SW,** *Cat's-claw. Acacia Greggii.* . . It is extraordinarily spiny and most appropriately called "tear-blanket." **1971** Dodge *100 Desert Wildflowers* 27 **SW,** Also known by such descriptive names as "tear-blanket" . . , catclaw acacia is one of the notoriously thorny shrubs or small slender trees of the rocky hillsides and borders of desert washes.

tear-coat See **tear-blanket b**

tear down v phr   **chiefly Sth**   Cf **tear up** v phr **2**

To beat, thrash; hence n *tearing down* a thrashing; ppl adj *tearing-down* of a fight: vigorous.

1892 *KS Univ. Qrly.* 1.99, *Tear-down:* to thrash, as, He gave the boy a good tearing down. **1938** Rawlings *Yearling* 381 **nFL,** I'll tear down all two of you. Now git down and pick up ever' one o' them peas and wash 'em off. **1966–68** *DARE* (Qu. Y12b, *A real fight in which blows are struck*) Inf **MD**44, Tearing-down fight; (Qu. Y16, *A thorough beating:* "*He gave the bully an awful _____.*") Inf **SC**26, Tearing down. **1981** Pederson *LAGS Basic Materials,* 1 inf, **csAL,** Discipline in school: "they'd wear you down, tear you down, give you whippings."

teardown n

1 also attrib: A fierce or destructive person.

1834 Caruthers *Kentuckian* 1.21 **KY,** He's what I call a tear down sneezer. . . He's got no more fear among the Injins than a wild cat in a weasel's nest. **1925** Dargan *Highland Annals* 275 **wNC,** As fer his house, it shore needed a good woman in it, Nan had been sech a tear-down.

2 A violent quarrel.

1941 Wheaton *Mr. George's Joint* 319 **TX** [Black], They gonna have a big tear-down uh a big killin'. **1966** *DARE* (Qu. KK15, *A disagreement or quarrel:* "*They had _____ about where the fence was to be.*") Inf **FL**26, A regular teardown.

teared See **tear B1, 2c**

tear grass n¹
=**Job's tears 1.**

1895 Gray–Bailey *Field Botany* 474, *Coix Lacryma-Jobi.* . . Tear Grass. Plant . . grown for the ornamental clusters of so-called "seeds" . . which are as large as a cherry stone, shining and whitish. **1933** Small *Manual SE Flora* 38, *Tear-grass.* . . Widely cult. and locally escaped, cult. grounds and roadsides, Coastal Plain, Fla. to Tex. . . Employed medicinally, while the hard mature involucres are used as beads. **1961** *Valley News & Green Sheet* (Van Nuys CA) 10 Aug sec B 15/3, Landscaping is magnificent: Camellias, gardenias, tear grass . . cover the grounds.

tear grass n²   See **tearthumb**

tearing-down ppl adj

1 Of a person or occasion: boisterous, rollicking, rip-roaring. **esp S Midl**

1845 Trumbull *Death Nathan Hale* 6 **CT,** Master Hale made a tearing down good speech. **1857** *Emerson's Mag. & Putnam's Mth.* 5.330 **sePA,** Who would think that such a sober old spindle-shanks could be such a tearing-down sinner? **1887** (1888) Smedes *Mems. S. Planter* 55 **MS** [Black], I had a tearin'-down weddin', to be sho'. . . Marster promised de fust one what git married arter he did a tearin'-down weddin', an' I was de fust. **1888** *Atlantic Mth.* 61.550 **eTN,** Racin' an' bettin' air sinful, . . an' that thar tearin'-down, good-lookin' Teck Jepson hev got mighty little religion. **1900** Richardson *Lights & Shadows* 20 **GA,** He was an open infidel. His wife was a "tearing-down" Methodist. **a1954** (1990) Oakley *Rememberin' Roamin' Man* 64 **eTN,** We . . had a tearin

down time listenin to the mountain music. **1986** Pederson *LAGS Concordance,* 1 inf, **neTN,** A tearing down good time.

2 See **tear down** v phr.

tearing down n   See **tear down** v phr

tearing up   See **tear up** v phr **2**

tear-out n   Cf **tear-up** n

See quots.

1929 *AmSp* 5.20 **Ozarks,** *Tear-out.* . . A boisterous or hilarious meeting. "Th' Holiness folks is a-havin' a reg'lar tear-out down t' th' Possum Holler schoolhouse." **1954** *Harder Coll.* **cwTN,** *Tear-out* . . a boisterous or hilarious meeting.

tear out the bone   See **tear the bone out**

tearr n   Also *tee-arr*   [Echoic]

Usu the common **tern** *(Sterna hirundo),* but also the Arctic **tern** *(S. paradisaea)* or the **least tern.**

1792 Belknap *Hist. NH* 3.169, Tee-arr, or fishing gull . . *Sterna minuta.* **1925** (1928) Forbush *Birds* MA 1.105, *Sterna hirundo.* . . Tearr. [*Ibid* 106, *Voice.*—Most commonly *tee' ar-r-r,* uttered harshly, but often more varied in length, enunciation, and pitch, thus expressing different emotions or moods.] **1946** Hausman *Eastern Birds* 321, *Common Tern.* . . *Other Names.* . . Mackerel Gull, Tearr. . . *Notes*—Screams constantly *tée-arr, tée-arrs* and similar tones with variations. Also high, squeaky cries, *keek-keek-keek-keek.* Very vocal. **1956** MA Audubon Soc. *Bulletin* 40.22, *Common Tern.* . . Tearr (Mass. Sonic.) . . *Arctic Tern.* . . Tearr (Mass. Sonic.) . . *Least Tern.* . . Tearr (N.H.)

tear the bone out v phr   Also *tear out the bone*   **esp AR**

To make an extraordinary effort.

1887 in 2004 *DARE* File—Internet AR [*Mountain Echo* 3 Aug], A protracted meeting at Sugar Orchard . . will commence next Saturday. Bro. Mathes(?) is expected to be there to tear the bone out as preacher, while we boys tear the flesh from the chicken legs and wings. **1897** *Ibid* **WA,** When we anxiously peeped through the eye hole in the fly we looked out upon one of the finest audiences ever gathered in Walla Walla. . . We were feeling in excellent spirits and eager to get in and "tear the bone out," as the boys say. **1906** *DN* 3.161 **nwAR,** Tear the bone out. . . To work very hard. "You're just tearing the bone out, aren't you?" **1953** Randolph–Wilson *Down in Holler* 292 **Ozarks,** *Tear the bone out.* . . To do anything thoroughly, to "go the whole hog." Often used in connection with house-cleaning and the like. Sometimes it means simply to throw a noisy party. "We sure did tear the bone out the night Judge Fuller got married." **1966** *DARE* (Qu. FF18, *Joking words . . about a noisy or boisterous celebration or party:* "*They certainly _____ last night.*") Inf **AR**3, Tore the bone out. **1978** *DARE* File **swKS,** To tear out the bone was a customary expression of my grandmother, who grew up in the company of Gaelic-speaking Irish immigrants: "There's a party tonight, and they really tore out the bone getting the house ready."

tearthumb n   Also rarely *tear grass*   [See quot 1837]   Cf **knotweed 1, lady's thumb**

A **smartweed,** usu *Polygonum sagittatum.*   For other names of the latter see **arrowvine, cut-grass 2, saw grass 2, scratch ~ 1**

1837 Darlington *Flora Cestrica* 251 **sePA,** *P[olygonum] sagittatum.* . . Arrow-leaved Tear-thumb. . . *Stem* . . acutely quadrangular, the angles armed with sharp recurved prickles. . . *P. arifolium.* . . Halberd-leaved Tear-thumb. . . This and the preceding commonly grow together, forming large entangled bunches, and are a couple of worthless and often troublesome plants, in swampy meadows. **1868** (1870) Gray *Field Botany* 289, *Tear-thumb.* Stems with spreading branches, the angles and petioles armed with sharp reflexed prickles, by which the plant is enabled to climb. . . *P[olygonum] arifolium.* . . *P. sagittatum.* **1932** Rydberg *Flora Prairies* 290, *Tear-thumb.* Annual or rarely perennial, prickly-armed herbs. **1950** Gray–Fernald *Manual of Botany* 587, *Tear-thumb, Teargrass, Scratchgrass.* . . Arrow-leaved Tearthumb. . . Low grounds, Fla. to Tex., n. to Nfld. [etc.]. *Ibid* 588, *Halberd-leaved Tearthumb.* . . Wet places, oftenest tidal marshes. **1975** Duncan–Foote *Wildflowers SE* 26, *Arrow-vine; Tear-thumb—Polygonum sagittatum.* . . Physical contact with the plant . . readily brings attention because of the sharp backwardly turned prickles on the stems and midveins of the undersides of the leaves. . . *P. arifolium* . . is also prominently prickly. **2003** *Gettysburg Times* (PA) 21 Oct sec B 5/1, Many folks are familiar with mile-a-minute, a very aggressive vine that has tiny thorn-like protrusions on the stem, giving it another name of tear thumb.

tear up v phr

1 To mess up, disorder, muddle up; hence ppl adj *torn* (or *tore*) *up.*

1939 in Lib. of Congress *Amer. Memory: WPA Life Hist.* (Internet) **SC,** Had to go to work this morning and ain't got things cleaned up like I generally keeps them looking. But that's all right—reckon you've seen things tore up before. **1949** Arnow *Hunter's Horn* 278 **KY,** I was all raggedy an my hair all tore up, an I hated fer him to see me. **1952** Brown *NC Folkl.* 1.598, *Tear up the house:* . . To disarrange, throw into disorder, things in a house.—Central and east. **c1960** *Wilson Coll.* **csKY,** *Tear up.* . . Disarrange. **1965–70** *DARE* (Qu. Y37, *To make a place untidy or disorderly: "I wish they wouldn't _____ the room so."*) 85 Infs, **widespread, but less freq Nth, Pacific,** Tear up; (Qu. Y38, *Mixed together, confused: "The things in the drawer are all _____."*) Infs **DE**2, **FL**19, **IN**79, **OH**78, **SC**42, **TX**32, **VA**46, 47, Torn up; **GA**6, Tore up; (Qu. E22, *If a house is untidy and everything is upset*) Infs **AR**26, **FL**37, 49, (All) tore up; **OK**26, Tore-up house; (Qu. KK39, *Stirred up, upset: "Because of the storm, the pond was all _____."*) Infs **AL**6, **FL**25, 52, **TX**1, Torn up; **AL**33, Tore up. **1982** *Barrick Coll.* **csPA,** *Tear up*—jumble together, make a mess of it. "Excuse the way the house is all tore up."

2 To beat, thrash; hence n *tearing up* a beating. **chiefly Sth, Midl** See Map Cf **tear down** v phr

1965–70 *DARE* (Qu. Y15, *To beat somebody thoroughly: "John really _____ that fellow!"*) Infs **AL**8, **DC**11, **DE**5, **IL**140, **KY**61, **MO**29, **PA**94, Tore him up; **CA**94, **GA**7, **SC**40, Tore up; **GA**23, Tore that fellow up; **SC**26, Tear up; (Qu. Y16, *A thorough beating: "He gave the bully an awful _____."*) Inf **MS**86, Tore him up; **GA**7, Tearing up; (Qu. EE21a, *When somebody goes into a fight very actively: "You should have seen Jack _____ Bob."; total Infs questioned, 75)* Inf **MS**52, Tear up. [5 of 14 total Infs Black] **1966** *DARE* FW Addit **MS,** I'm going to tear you up when I get you home. **1986** Pederson *LAGS Concordance* **Gulf Region,** 20 infs, Tear you up (*or* tore him up, etc); 2 infs, (You got) a tearing up; 7 infs, Get our butts (*or* breeches) tore up (and varr); 1 inf, You'd get tore up—you'd get whipped; 1 inf, Get tore up = get a beating; 1 inf, Got tore up—i.e., punished; 1 inf, I'd get my behind tore up; 1 inf, You got tore up = whipped; 1 inf, Daddy tore us up—gave a "severe" whipping; 1 inf, Would have tore us up—i.e., whipped us; 1 inf, I've had my fanny tore up—with a razor strop; 1 inf, I done got tore up with them—of razor straps. **2004** *DARE* File—Internet **ceTX,** Get out of that ditch! If I have to tell you again, I'm going to come out there and tear you up!

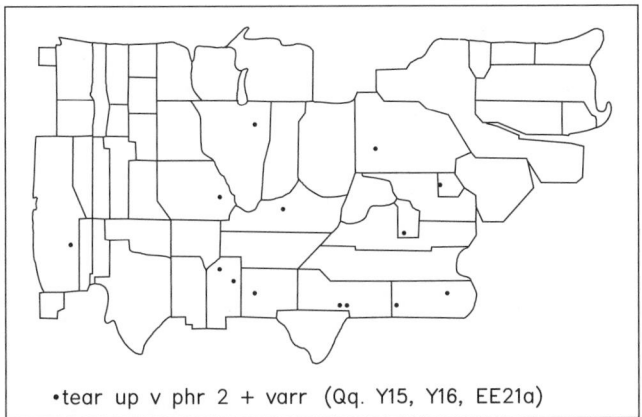

•tear up v phr 2 + varr (Qq. Y15, Y16, EE21a)

3 To break, damage, wreck; hence ppl adj phr *torn* (or *tore*) *up.* **chiefly Sth, S Midl** See Map

1939 in Lib. of Congress *Amer. Memory: WPA Life Hist.* (Internet) **NC,** We had a nice car. Two weeks after he went to Cuba Clyde turned it over and tore it up. **1946** *AmSp* 21.191 **seKY,** *Tear up,* to break. 'Don't set in thet cha'r. One o' hits legs is tore up.' **1965–70** *DARE* (Qu. D21, *A small, poorly-built house, or one in rundown condition*) Inf **SC**34, Old tore-up building; (Qu. Y35, *To spoil something so that it can't be used . . "My new coffee pot—it's completely _____."*) Infs **GA**17, 19, **KY**90, **LA**6, Tore up; (Qu. KK19, . . *Temporarily out of order: "My sewing machine _____."*) Infs **NC**30, 37, **KY**28, **TN**58, **VA**2, Is torn (*or* tore) up; (Qu. KK20a, *Something that looks as if it might collapse any*

minute: *"That old shed is certainly _____."*) Inf **MD**47, Tore up; (Qu. KK20b, . . *"Our old washing machine is _____."*) Infs **GA**23, **NC**45, Torn (*or* tore) up; (Qu. KK21, . . *"They ran the wagon over the coffee pot and _____."*) Inf **OK**27, Tore it up; [(Qu. KK22, . . *"The jug fell out of the window and was _____."*) Infs **LA**6, **VA**69, Torn (*or* tore) all to pieces;] (Qu. KK70, *Something that has got out of proper shape: "That house is all _____."*) Inf **DE**7, Tore up. **1967–69** *DARE* Tape **KY**17, Somebody hit us in the back, tore his car up; **TX**49, There's a little bit of danger in tearing your press up if you ain't watching mighty careful. **1998** *DARE* File **TN,** Tear up the car: My wife uses this to mean it's broken down. "The car's torn up" means it's broken down. **2004** *DARE* File—Internet **eTN,** I went to the McDonald's drive-thru . . once, ordered a milk shake, and was told "the milk shake machine is tore up."

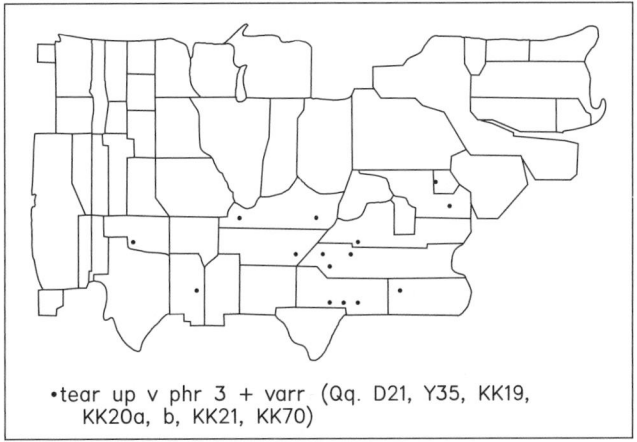

•tear up v phr 3 + varr (Qq. D21, Y35, KK19, KK20a, b, KK21, KK70)

4 Of a machine: to break down. **chiefly Sth, S Midl**

2000 in 2004 *DARE* File—Internet **Sth,** 1978 ford F150, torgue [sic] converter tore up at 18,000 miles, on vacation, 200 miles from home. Transmission tore up 36,000 miles. had rebuilt. Transmission tore up again at 72,000 miles. Had rebuilt. **2002** *DARE* File—Internet **seKY,** Everything in the world goes wrong that day, maybe your car tares [sic] up, your husband starts a fight. **2003** *Ibid* **NC,** I have been using Mozilla ever since my computer tore up a while back. **2004** *Ibid* **csAL,** My computer tore up. *Ibid* **nwSC,** Throughout the day, I'll catch calls if a machine tears up or is not working properly.

5 To upset, anger, or embarrass. Cf **torn up 1**

1959 *Parade* 3 May 9/1 **OH,** I look at those three kids playing and I think, 'If it weren't for me, there'd be four of them.' It just tears me up inside. **1964** *Newark Advocate* (OH) 10 Mar 13/3 **OH,** "I [=Sammy Ellis] should have won more than 12 games," he said ruefully. "It's my obnoxious temper that's to blame. It tears me up when I do something wrong or get what I think is a bad call by the umpire." **1966** *DARE* Tape **NC**24, The thing that upsets you and tears you up and really shocks you is the way they [=quail] take off. **1967–70** *DARE* (Qu. Y2, . . *Upsetting or disturbing somebody: "Losing all that money didn't seem to _____ him a bit."*) Inf **AL**8, Tear him up; (Qu. GG9, *To suddenly embarrass somebody and throw him off balance: "When they told him what she had said about him, it certainly did _____ him."*) Inf **KY**73, Tear him up; (Qu. GG13a, *When something keeps bothering a person and makes him nervous . . "It _____ me."*) Inf **GA**74, Tears me up; (Qu. II29b, . . *To explain the unpleasant effect that person has on you: "He just _____."*) Infs **KY**6, **TX**9, Tears me up. **1999** in 2004 *DARE* File—Internet **seNH,** But it's the cemetery vandals who really tear me up. **2001** *Creative Loafing* (Atlanta GA) 6 June (Internet) **swGA,** This has really tore him up. We talked a couple of weeks ago and he said it's probably one of the most embarrassing things that ever [happened] to him.

tear-up n Also sp *tare-up* Cf **tear-out**

A row, rampage.

1906 *Washington Post* (DC) 5 Dec 3/3 **NYC,** Terry on a tear-up. . . Armed with a revolver and a six-pound shell, Terry McGovern, the former light-weight champion pugilist of the world, became violent today in front of his home . . [in] Brooklyn. **1908** Johnson *Highways Pacific Coast* 132 **sCA,** She [=a bear] found our camp, and she turned over our potatoes and beans and scattered them and our other things all about. Yes, she had a regular tear-up. **1931** Goodrich *Mt. Homespun* 56 **wNC,**

eTN, "It's a regular tare-up of a meetin'," said Hannah, keen for excitement.

tear up jack   See **jack** n[1] **14**

tear weed n   Cf **tearthumb**

Perh a **smartweed.**

1967 *DARE* (Qu. S8, *A common kind of wild grass that grows in fields: it spreads by sending out long underground roots, and it's hard to get rid of*) Inf **CA**31, Tear weed.

teaser n   [*OED2* teaser sb.[1] 2.b "Local name of several birds" 1833 →]   Cf **gull hunter**

=**parasitic jaeger.**

1910 Eaton *Birds NY* 1.116, The Parasitic jaeger is a fairly common or at least a regular transient visitant on the coast of this State. . . Other names for it are . . Marling-spike, Teaser. **1953** Jewett *Birds WA* 289, *Parasitic Jaeger.* . . Other names: Sea Hawk, . . Teaser. . . This jaeger flew straight through the flock, forcing some of the gulls to disgorge recently swallowed fish, the disgorged portions being caught by the jaeger before they reached the water.

teaster   See **tester**

tea towel n   [*OED2* 1863 →]   **widespread, but less freq NEng, Sth**   See Map   Cf **cup towel, drying cloth**

A towel for drying dishes.

1870 *Ladies' Repository* 6.302, Yes, this one is for table linen, and this for kitchen towels and tea towels. **1893** *Harper's New Mth. Mag.* 86.519, She had been washing the dishes as she talked, and she shook the tea towel out of its damp wrinkles and hung it upon the door of the small stove. **1930s** in 1944 *ADD* cwWV, Get another tea towel to dry the glasses. **c1960** *Wilson Coll.* csKY, *Tea towel:* A cloth to dry dishes after they have been warshed and rinched. Very modern: dish towel or drying rag more used, even now. **1965–70** *DARE* (Qu. G16, *What do you dry the dishes with?*) 222 Infs, **widespread, but less freq NEng, Sth,** Tea towel; **IL**47, Linen tea towel; **IA**30, Terry tea towel; (Qu. G17, . . *Kinds of towels*) 25 Infs, **scattered, but esp Nth,** Tea towel; **IL**47, Tea towel made out of old flour sack. **1966** Dakin *Dial. Vocab. Ohio R. Valley* 2.126, *Tea towel* is the older term of those of greater social pretensions and of women. Although it enjoys the same social status, a few who use it regard it as old-fashioned and say that *dishtowel* is "newer" or the name used by the younger generation. **1973** Allen *LAUM* 1.203 **Upper MW** (as of c1950), A newer expression, *tea towel,* has strong Midland orientation with its weight mostly in southern Iowa and Nebraska, but as a term with increasing social prestige it is moving into Minnesota. It is found also in Canada. **2004** *DARE* File—Internet **PA,** In Pennsylvania, where my family is . . from, one washes dishes with a dish cloth, then dries them with a tea towel. In Florida, we wash with a dish rag and dry with a dish towel.

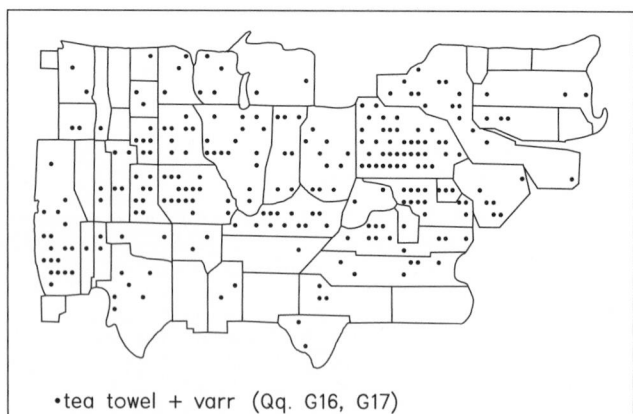

•tea towel + varr (Qq. G16, G17)

tea towel shower   See **towel shower**

tea tree n   **chiefly TX**   Cf **mountain tea-tree, Oregon tea tree, white ~**

=**yaupon.**

1785 Marshall *Arbustrum* 26, *Ever-green Cassine, Yapon, or South-Sea Tea-tree.* This grows naturally in Carolina and some parts of Virginia, but chiefly near the sea. **1836** (1935) Holley *Texas* 88, The Yawpan or tea tree deserves a special notice. Its leaf is very similar, in form and flavor, to that of the veritable Chinese shrub, and

is dried and used as a substitute for the latter, by many of the inhabitants of Texas. **1841** Kennedy *Texas* 1.100, Among the latter [= shrubs], may be enumerated . . red bud, hog wood, the yawpan or tea tree [etc]. **1884** Roosevelt *FL & Game Water-Birds* 44 **FL,** Beaufort was the first thoroughly Southern town, with its fig trees in the open air, the Yupawn, or native Tea tree, . . and its genial air of Southern indolent happiness. **1986** Pederson *LAGS Concordance,* 1 inf, **ceTX,** Tea trees.

tea up v phr   *old-fash*

To drink to excess; hence ppl adjs *tead (up), teaed up* drunk.

1887 in 1950 *AmSp* 25.39 **New Orleans LA,** Bunker Fitz an' his pals buys ten cents er booze . . and gets tead up. **1907** Ade in *Washington Post* (DC) 20 Jan sec 4 5/4, It seems the Habit is comparatively harmless if you listen to music while teaing up. **1912** *DN* 3.591 **wIN,** Tea up. . . To become intoxicated. **1913** *Ft. Wayne News* (IN) 6 Jan 5/2, Albert J. Beveridge had offered in explanation of Colonel [Theodore] Roosevelt's ruffianly remark the statement that the colonel was "tead up" when he made it. **1922** *Stevens Point Daily Jrl.* (WI) 27 Nov 2/3, Nobody's life would be safe if a considerable part of the community were more or less teaed up all the time. **1934** *Monessen Daily Independent* (PA) 14 May 5/8, The fellow who was teaed up the night before has a hard time the next day teeing off. **1941** *Esquire* May 131 **KY,** I was young once and got married. Had a big dance after the wedding dinner. All the boys got tead. Danced all night. **1965–70** *DARE* (Qu. DD13, *When a drinker is just beginning to show the effects of the liquor . . he's _____*) Infs **CT**6, 10, **MS**64, **ND**9, **PA**148, Slightly tead; **IL**29, Tead; **AR**52, **KY**16, **TN**53, (Getting) tead up; **KS**16, Slightly tead up; **WI**59, Bit tead up; (Qu. DD14, *When a person is partly drunk, "He's _____."*) Infs **MS**59, **TN**16, (Getting) tead up. [12 of 13 Infs old]

tea vine n   Cf **Oregon tea 1**

=**yerba buena.**

1897 in 2003 *DARE* File—Internet **cwWA,** The house was beautifully decorated with ivy, tea vines and potted plants. **1937** St. John *Flora SE WA & ID* 360, *Satureja Douglasii* [=*Clinopodium d.*] . . Tea-vine. . . The herbage is aromatic and pleasant. In pioneer times it was steeped to make herb tea. **1968** in 2003 *DARE* File—Internet **seID** (as of 1870), Flowers grew along each side of the path, hollyhocks, bachelor buttons, yellow and pink roses and tea vine climbed the house.

tea weed n

1 A **spirea;** see quots.

1852 MI State Ag. Soc. *Trans. for 1851* 3.197, My timber is generally oak, with some hickory, indigo weed tea weed. **1874** VT State Bd. Ag. *Rept. for 1873–74* 2.775, Common upon flowers of many kinds, especially those of the meadow-sweet or tea-weed.

2 A **mallow B** of the genus *Sida,* esp *S. rhombifolia.* **chiefly S Atl, Gulf States**   For other names of var spp see **false mallow a, Indian ~ 2, ironweed 8, jelly leaf 1, nail grass, strong man Sampson, wireweed 1**

1884 Hilgard *Rept. Cotton MS* 131, The troublesome weeds are crabgrass, morning-glory, coffee-weed, tea-weed, and purslane. **1890** FL Ag. Exper. Sta. *Bulletin* 8.8, *Aggressive Weeds.* . . *Sida stipulata* [=*S. acuta*]. . . Tea weed. *Ibid* 9, *Common Weeds.* . . *Sida spinosa.* . . Tea weed. *Sida rhombifolia.* . . Tea weed. *Ibid* 12, *Occasional Weeds.* . . *Sida cordifolia.* . . Tea weed. **1901** *Torreya* 1.116 **GA,** *Sida rhombifolia.* . . Tea-weed. **1920** *Ibid* 20.23 **GA, SC,** *Sida* sp.—Tea-weed. **1944** AL Geol. Surv. *Bulletin* 53.154, Neal in 1890 applied the name "tea weed" to several species of this genus [=*Sida*] in Florida, and I have heard the same name applied to *S[ida] rhombifolia* in South Georgia about a dozen years later. **1966–68** *DARE* (Qu. S21, . . *Weeds that are a trouble in gardens and fields*) Infs **AR**10, **FL**9, **SC**19, Tea weed(s); **LA**28, Tea weeds—they make a root long as the top. **1974** Morton *Folk Remedies* 143 **SC,** *Tea Weed. . . Sida rhombifolia. . . South Carolina* (Current use): Plant is boiled for "tea," drunk as a beverage. Root is boiled and decoction given to children to relieve fever; the liquid is also taken by men to increase their "courage" (potency). **1986** Pederson *LAGS Concordance,* 6 infs, **Gulf region,** Tea weed(s); 1 inf, **cwMS,** Tea weed = bow vine, tea used as cure for malaria.

3 A **senna** n[1] **B1** (here: *Senna marilandica*).   Cf **coffeeweed 1b**

1895 U.S. Dept. Ag. *Farmers' Bulletin* 28.29, Wild senna, teaweed. . . Cassia marilandica [=*Senna m.*]. Maryland to Texas.

tebar v   Cf *DS* EE17

1895 *DN* 1.397 **cNY,** I tebár (prob. *debar,* though the *t* sound is unmistakable): in children's games when one wishes to withdraw temporarily, in order to avoid being caught, he says, "I tebar."

tech   See **touch**

teched   See **touch B**

techeous, tech(i)ous, techis   See **tetchous**

techy   See **tetchy**

teck   See **take** v **A1a**

teckle   See **tackle**

tecolote n   Also *tecolote owl*   [AmSpan *tecolote* < Nahuatl]
esp TX

Any of var usu small owls; see quots.

1892 *DN* 1.252 **TX,** *Tecolóte:* a species of owl. *Bubo Virginianus.*
1928 Austin *Children Sing* 56 **SW,** Black beetle and the tecolote owl /
Between two winks their ancient forms will take.   **1932** Bentley *Spanish Terms* 206, *Tecolote.* . . From American Indian *tecolotl.* Small owls
of various species in Texas and other parts of the Southwest and northern Mexico are known as *tecolote* owls or merely *tecolotes.*   **1938** *AmSp*
13.119 [Nahuatl words in Amer Engl] **TX,** The great horned owl,
Bubo virginianus subarcticus, is known also in Texas by the name
tecolote, borrowed from Mexican *tecolotl.* . . Also in the Lone Star State
various small species of owls are termed *tecolotes* or *tecolote* owls.
1986 Pederson *LAGS Concordance (Other kinds of owls)* 1 inf, **csTX,**
Tecolote . . large, hoots at night.

ted v   [*OED2* 14 . . →]   **chiefly NEast, N Cent, cAppalachians**
See Map

To spread or stir (drying hay); to operate a **tedder;** hence vbl n
tedding; comb *tedding machine.*

1856 *De Bow's Rev.* 20.536, With the reaping and mowing machines, . . the horse-rakes, hay-tedding machines, . . &c., &c.—it will
soon be practicable to dispense with a greater part of human labor in the
cultivation of the soil.   **1872** *Rural Affairs* 6.286 **NY,** *Tedding.*—In large
meadows, it will be a matter of economy to use either the American . .
or Bullard's . . tedder.   **1892** in 2007 *DARE* File—Internet **cNY,** Then
John took the tedder & tedded the hay till the tedder broke.   **1939**
Chron.-Telegram (Elyria OH) 27 June 12/2, He was tedding hay with a
span of young mules when they ran away throwing him in front of
the tedder.   **1950** *WELS (Tools and machines used for different steps
in handling hay)* 1 Inf, **ceWI,** Tedding machine.   **1951** *Hamburg Reporter* (IA) 29 Mar [8]/3 (newspaperarchive.com), [Advt:] Rotary tedding shortens drying time.   **1965–70** *DARE* (Qu. L11, *What do you do
to hay in the field after it's cut?*) 68 Infs, **chiefly NEast, N Cent,
cAppalachians,** Ted it; NJ29, Tedding [Of all Infs responding to the
question, 70% were old; of those giving these responses, 91% were
old.]; (Qu. L16, *Machines used . . in handling hay*) Inf CT6, Tedding
machine.   **2006** in 2007 *DARE* File—Internet **cOH,** The second field
was not quite dry enough, but I didn't catch it till Haley had already
tedded and raked it for that day. So it was tedded back out and raked
back up the next day. . . Haley . . had been waiting for an hour for me
to come home to set my tractor and tedder up so she could ted while I
plant corn.

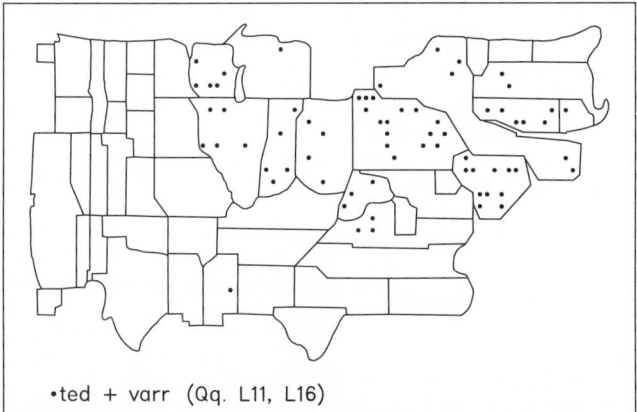

•ted + varr (Qq. L11, L16)

tedder n   Also *hay tedder*   [**ted** + *-er; OED2* 14 . . → for a person performing this function]   **chiefly NEast, N Cent, cAppalachians**   See Map   Cf **fluffer, kicker** n[1] **3b**

A machine for stirring up hay in order to hasten its drying;
hence v *tedder* =**ted;** ppl adj *teddered.*

1846 Colman *European Ag.* 1.463 **MA,** The plough is an immense advance upon the spade; . . the horse-rake and hay-tedder, upon the hand-rake and the common fork.   **1865** *Scientific Amer.* 13.396 **PA,** [Advt:]
Heany's combined hay rake, tedder, and loader—Equal in utility to the
mowing machine.   **1872** [see **ted**].   **1884** *OH Democrat* (New Philadelphia) [12 June 4]/7 (newspaperarchive.com), [Advt:] The only *tedder*
that the wheels do not run on the Teddered hay. . . —Manufactured by—
The Belcher & Taylor Agricultural Tool Co., Chicopee Falls, Mass.
1890 *New Engl. Mag.* 9.12, The farmer's expense is lessened and his
power of production increased, perhaps twofold, by using the mower,
reaper, thresher, hay-tedder, sulky-plough, and grain-drill.   **1892** [see
ted].   **1939** [see **ted**].   **1947** in 2007 *DARE* File—Internet **cME coast,**
July 30. . . I rolled over yesterdays raking and teddered it. Took the
tedder to garage . . to have rear cross piece welded.   **1950** *WELS (Tools
and machines used for different steps in handling hay)* 15 Infs, **WI,**
Tedder.   **1965–70** *DARE* (Qu. L16, *Machines used . . in handling hay*)
104 Infs, **chiefly NEast, N Cent, cAppalachians,** (Hay) tedder [Of all
Infs responding to the question, 70% were old; of those giving these responses, 89% were old.]; (Qu. L11, *What do you do to hay in the field
after it's cut?*) 10 Infs, 8 **NEng,** Tedder it; LA15, Nowdays we tedder it;
MN23, We teddered it—had forks on it that lifted up the hay to dry it
quicker; **MT2,** Teddering—used to say; **MA51,** Tether [sic] it; **MA42,**
NH14, Tedder it out; **NJ58,** Go through it with a hay tedder; **OH17,**
Shake it up with hay tedders.   **1967** *Chateaugay Rec. & Franklin Co.
Democrat* (NY) 13 July [3]/3, [Advt:] P.T.O. Driven *Hay Tedder*—Land
Driven (Reduces Hay Curing Time).   **1968** *DARE* Tape **OH82,** Then
you have what they call a tedder. This doesn't do anything to the drying
stalks except toss them into the air and try to get them off the ground so
they'll dry quicker. This is usually done after a rain.   **2004** *DARE* File—
Internet **NC,** Here are some suggestions to avoid rain damaged hay: . .
Use a tedder or inverter.   **2006** [see **ted**].   **2006** in 2007 *DARE* File—
Internet **MO,** The first of this year's hay is cut and teddered. Today it
will be raked and baled.   **2007** *Ibid* **SC,** I used to work on a farm were
[sic] i was mowing, teddering, raking and baling hay.

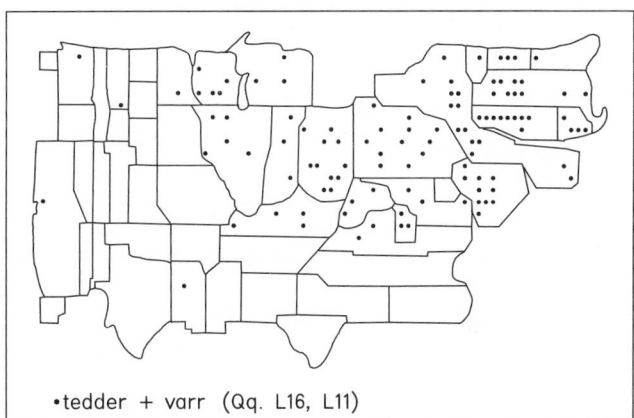

•tedder + varr (Qq. L16, L11)

tedding (machine)   See **ted**

teddy-bear cholla n   Also *teddy-bear (cactus)*   [See quot
1982]

A **prickly pear 1** (here: *Opuntia bigelovii*).

1940 Benson *Cacti AZ* 39, *Opuntia Bigelovii.* . . *Teddy bear cactus.* . .
This is one of the most striking and readily recognized chollas. It is also
the most dangerously spiny, since the numerous spines are barbed and
exceedingly difficult to remove from the skin and flesh.   **1947** Carr
Desert Parade 86 **SW,** Of all the prickly tribe, the teddy bear has the
greatest potential ability to do the most harm to one's person.   **1967–68**
DARE (Qu. S15, . . *Weed seeds that cling to clothing*) Inf **CA4,** A cactus—jumping cholla breaks off easily and clings—teddy-bear cholla;
(Qu. S26e, *Other wildflowers not yet mentioned;* not asked in early QRs)
Inf **CA60,** Teddy-bear cactus—has fuzz on it, a small, round cactus.
1973 *AZ Highways* Mar 29, Teddy Bear Cholla (*Opuntia bigelovii*) is
more thick-set and compact with plump stems formidably aglow with
golden-yellow or greenish-white needles that turn brown-black with age.
1982 *NY Times* (NY) 3 Jan sec 10 17/2 **AZ,** Also present are tangles
of . . teddybear cholla; the teddybear cholla is a cactus so thick with
spines it glistens under the sun as if covered with fur.   **1985** Dodge
Flowers SW Deserts 65, Found in south central and southwestern Ari-

zona and westward into southern California, [and] southern Nevada . . , the teddybear cholla is noticeable at any season.

teddy-bear (hair)cut n   Also *teddy (bear)*   **esp PA, MD**   See Map   *old-fash*

A type of men's haircut similar to a crew cut.

   1943 *Daily Courier* (Connellsville PA) 5 Apr 5/1, Almost every [high school basketball] player had a "teddy bear" haircut.   **1950** *Nashua Telegraph* (NH) 14 July 11/5, When the chips are down . . the guy [=a golfer] with the "teddy-bear" haircut will calmly survey the situation. **1968–70** *DARE* (Qu. X5, . . *Different kinds of men's haircuts*) Inf **LA**15, Teddy bear—old-fashioned; fairly long, it stood straight up; **MD**21, Teddy bear—combed straight back, shingled in back, worn after World War I; **MD**27, Teddy bear—very short, bristly; **PA**154, Teddy bear— short; **PA**202, Teddy bear—used to be common; **PA**216, Teddy bear; **NY**233, Teddy-bear cut—[same as] crew; **MD**17, Teddy—short hair, combed straight back, worn about fifty years ago.   **1984** *Gettysburg Times* (PA) 24 Sept 16/1, Paul H. Ketterman Jr. has been known as "Baldy" since he was five years old. It was that summer when he got a "Teddy Bear" haircut.

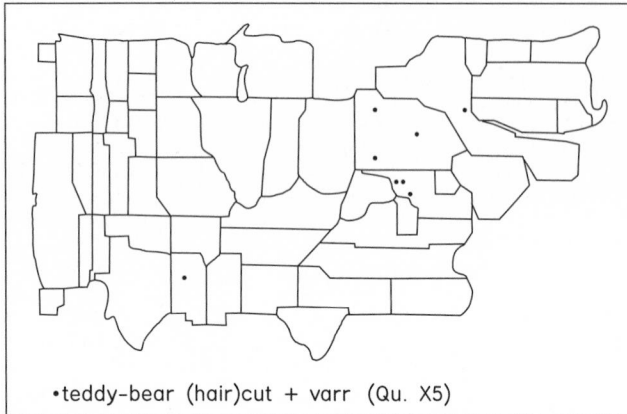

•teddy-bear (hair)cut + varr (Qu. X5)

teder   See **tetter** n¹

tedious adj   Usu |ˈtidɪəs|; also |ˈtijəs| Pronc-spp *teedjus, te(e)jus, teg(g)ious, tegus, tejious*

Std senses, var forms.

   1806 (1905) Clark *Orig. Jrls. Lewis & Clark Exped.* 4.40 **VA,** We find it a very tegious opperation that of makeing salt.   **1835** in 2004 *DARE* File—Internet **cNY,** We had a tegious . . time.   **1878** Hart *Sazerac Lying Club* 60 **NV,** My son, I hope my story aint gittin' teedjus?   **1890** Holley *Samantha among Brethren* 66 **NY,** Truly, it was a wild and harrowin' time, and tegus.   **1899** (1912) Green *VA Folk-Speech* 441, *Tejus. . .* Tedious.   **1913** Kephart *Highlanders* 278 **sAppalachians,** Most hillsmen say . . tejus.   **1931** *PMLA* 46.1317 **sAppalachians,** "Tejious" (tedious). **1936** *AmSp* 11.249 **eTX,** In illiterate speech . . [tidʒəs] [is frequently heard for] *tedious.*   **1940** *NV State Jrl.* (Reno) 2 Oct 4/3, [Walter Winchell column:] "Beyond Tomorrow" is pretty teejus going.   **1942** Hall *Smoky Mt. Speech* 96 **wNC, eTN,** Tedious . . ['tidʒəs].   **c1960** *Wilson Coll.* **csKY,** Tedious is often /ˈtidʒəs/.   **1965–70** *DARE* (Qu. KK11) 8 Infs, **scattered,** Tedious [no pronc recorded]; **IN**32, **FL**48, **OH**95, 99, Tedious ['tijəs]; (Qu. A18) Inf **OH**38, Tedious ['tijjəs].   **1966** *DARE* Tape **SC**17, It's kind of tedious ['tijəs].   **1982** Slone *How We Talked* 31 **eKY** (as of c1950), A "teggious" job.   **2004** *DARE* File—Internet **seOH,** Those are always a little tegious.

tee-arr   See **tearr**

teeayter   See **theater**

teeder   See **teeter** n **4**

teeder-todder (or -totter)   See **teeter-totter 1**

teedjus   See **tedious**

teedle   See **tiddle board**

teedum barrel (whiskey) n

See quot.

   1972 (1978) Carr *Second Oldest Profession* 166 **swVA,** This last name [=*teedum barrel*] comes from a small wooden barrel or cask the moonshiner kept . . for his private drinking likker. . . The real connoisseur of moonshine whiskey knew of . . the teedum barrel and often paid

the premium price required to purchase from this stock.   *Ibid* 236, *Teedum barrel:* Container in which old-time moonshiner kept his private drinking liquor.

teef   See **tooth** n

teefs   See **tooth** n **B2b**

tee-hee's nest with a ha-ha's egg in it, find a v phr   Also *find a haw-haw's nest with a tee-hee's egg in it;* for addit varr see quots   [Cf the expression *find a mare's nest,* which was formerly applied to one who laughed inappropriately]

To giggle or laugh immoderately or inappropriately; hence v phr *look* (or *act*) *like a tee-hee's nest with a ha-ha's egg in it* to be laughable, act laughably.

   1842 Kirkland *Forest Life* 1.116 **MI,** "Steve" laughed loud and long. "Why! a body would think you had found a haw-haw's nest with a te-he's eggs in't" said Mr. Butts, who seemed a little nettled by his friend's ridicule.   **1843** (1846) Haliburton *Attaché* (1st ser) 2.89 **NEng,** I heard such a chatterin', and laughin', and screamin' as I never a'most heerd afore, since I was raised. 'What in natur' is this,' sais I. . . 'There is some critters here I guess, that have found a haw haw's nest, with a tee hee's egg in it.'   **1917** *DN* 4.392 **neOH,** Find a tehee's egg in a haha's nest. . . To have a fit of the giggles. . . Also Vt., N.H., Mass., Ill., Kan., N.Y., Can.   **1939** *AmSp* 14.264 **IN,** A giggler 'has found a Tee-Hee's nest full of Ha-Ha eggs.'   **1958** *VT Hist.* 26.289, They acted like a Tee Hee's nest with a Haw Haw's egg in it.   **1960** *Ibid* 28.207, To find a tee-hee's nest with a ha-ha's egg in it. (To start giggling and not be able to stop.)   **1970** *DARE* File **swWI,** It looks like a tee-hee's nest with a ha-ha's egg in it—something grotesque or laughable. Said by a woman who had lived all her life in Lancaster, Wisconsin.

tee-hinder n   Also *tee-hind, te-hinder*

The buttocks.

   1942 Whipple *Joshua* 285 **UT** (as of c1860), I ain't like some folks who kiss a man's te-hinder like he's the Lord Himself!   **1967–68** *DARE* (Qu. X35, *Joking words for the part of the body that you sit on . . "He slipped and came down hard on his _____."*) Inf **MA**50, Tee-hind; **NY**111, Tee-hinder ['ti,haində˞].   **2004** *DARE* File—Internet **MI** [Black], Amber, you do not have a *bee*hind, you have a *tee*-hind, meaning your booty is so big I could set a *tee*cup on it!

tee-hiney n   Also *tee-hiney-boo*   **esp Sth**   Cf **hiney** n², **tee-hinder**

The buttocks.

   1970 Welty *Losing Battles* 28 **MS,** "Squeezed in tight on his old tee-hiney!" cried Aunt Birdie.   **1990** Smith *Understanding Speaking S. Lang.* 8, *Tee-hiney*—The human posterior.   **2009** in 2010 *DARE* File—Internet **cOH,** They don't give a rat's tee heiny boo about what we do, unless it will increase their revenue and audience.   *Ibid* **AL,** Karma. It always comes back around and bites you on the tee-hiney.   **2010** *Ibid* **VA,** Guess I had better get my tee-hiney-boo on the ball and get busy.

teejus   See **tedious**

tee-kee n

A **tree duck 1** (here: *Dendrocygna bicolor*).

   1916 *Times–Picayune* (New Orleans LA) 26 Mar 2, Fulvous Tree Duck. . . "Tee-kee." . . The long neck and legs, the bill and feet, of a rusty red color throughout, mark this bird at once.

teekle   See **tackle**

teem v   Also *tem,* past *tempt*

1 tr: To pour.   [*OED2* 1482 →]

   1866 *Scientific Amer.* new ser 15.421, The sun during the hottest hours of the day, teems down its rays into the valley.   **1896** *DN* 1.426 **csNY,** Tem . . to pour. "Tem your tea."   **1936** *AmSp* 11.191 **seWY,** To *teem,* past *tempt.* To pour from one vessel into another. 'He tempt the milk into the trough.'   **1953** Randolph–Wilson *Down in Holler* 292 **Ozarks,** *Teem. . .* To pour, to drain. Mary Elizabeth Mahnkey, of Mincy, Mo., quotes one of her neighbors on the best method of pickling beans. "You do thus and so," she said, "an' then you teem the water off." Sometimes it is used to describe a heavy rain: "It sure was a-teemin' about four o'clock. I could hear the water a-pourin' off the roof."

2 intr; with *it* as subj: To rain hard; with *down;* of rain: to fall heavily.   [*OED2* 1828 →]   **scattered, but esp Nth**

   1896 *DN* 1.426 **CT,** Teem: "It teems," it rains hard.   **1909** *Ft. Wayne Sentinel* (IN) 23 Sept 5/6, He simply got into the car . . because the rain was "teeming" down on him.   **1949** in 1986 *DARE* File **MN,** It's teeming outside. Young adult. College student. Minnesota background. **1953** [see **1** above]. **1967–68** *DARE* (Qu. B24, . . *A sudden, very heavy rain*) Inf **NY**43, Teeming; (Qu. B25, . . *Joking names . . for a very heavy rain. . . "It's a regular _____."*) Inf **MA**50, It's teeming out; **NJ**42, It's teeming outdoors—what it means, I don't know. **2005** in 2007 *DARE* File—Internet **NJ**, The rain was teeming down but the wind was less. **2007** *Ibid* **cwCA**, The sky opened, the rains came teeming down, and all work stopped abruptly.

teeming adj   [*OED2* teeming ppl. a. 1 1535 →; "*arch.* and *dial.*"]
Pregnant.

  1953 Randolph–Wilson *Down in Holler* 114 **Ozarks**, If no women are about, a hillman may remark to a comparative stranger that his wife is . . *teemin'*, or with squirrel, . . but these phrases are not for polite conversation between the sexes.

teenchy adj   [Var of **teensy**]   **chiefly Sth**   *somewhat old-fash*
Very tiny.

  1858 *S. Lit. Messenger* 27.423 **VA**, Thar wuz no help fer it, nun, not the leetlist teenchy bit uv a shadder uv it. **1883** (1971) Harris *Nights with Remus* 121 **GA** [Black], A little bit er teenchy sap-sucker run up'n down de tree. **1887** *Scribner's Mag.* 2.367 **sAppalachians**, An' fur off at the een' [of a tunnel] thar's a leetle teenchy speck o' light like the p'int of a needle. **1891** *Century Illustr. Mag.* 42.107 **GA**, It do 'em some of the good they need bad, in . . lettin' 'em git their growth out of the little teenchy things they is. **1905** *Washington Post* (DC) 24 Sept sec 4 4/8, The first time you think you've got a chance to begin one of those continuous performance harp, harp, harps of yours about some teenchy, weenchy, miserable thing, why, away you start. **1909** *DN* 3.382 **eAL, wGA**, *Teenchy* . . commonly heard. **1930** Stoney–Shelby *Black Genesis* 55 **seSC**, He turn, an' he wave he teenchy hank'cher. **1966** *DARE* (Qu. LL1, *Something very small: "I only took a _____ one."*) Inf **SC**5, Teenchy ['tɪnĕɪ]—Negro derivation of tiny. **2004** *DARE* File—Internet **MN**, Aroma is big, fresh hoppiness, . . just a teenchy touch bitter.

teency   See **teensy**

tee-nincy adj   Usu |ˌtiˈnaɪn(t)si|; also |ˌtiˈnaɪnʃi|; for addit varr see quots   Also *tee-nin(e)chy*   Also sp *tee-ninecy, tee-nineshih, tee-nin(e)sy, tee-nintsy*   [Extended forms of **tinesy** (also *tinchy*); cf **tee-niny**]   **chiefly Sth, S Midl**   See Map   Cf **tee-tinsy**
Very tiny—also used as a nickname.

  1898 in 1993 Harris *Dearest Chums* 188 **GA**, He has four *tee-nine-chy* ones [=guinea pigs], and they are very prettily marked. **1909** *DN* 3.380 **eAL, wGA**, Teenincy [tiˈnaɪnsɪ]. . . Tiny. Also *tincy* ['taɪnsɪ]. **1931** (1991) Hughes–Hurston *Mule Bone* 51 **cFL** [Black], Don't you cut dat lil tee-ninchy piece of meat for me and my chillun! **1946** *PADS* 6.30 **eNC**, Teeninsy [tiˈnaɪntsɪ]. . . Very small. . . Girls' word. **1954** in 1958 Brewer *Dog Ghosts* 42 **TX** [Black], Dey looks lack dey be's way yonnuh too big for a tee-ninchy li'l' man lack you. **1966–68** *DARE* (Qu. LL1, *Something very small: "I only took a _____ one."*) Infs **GA**1, **SC**26, **TX**37, **VA**15, Tee-nincy [ˌtiˈnaɪnsɪ, -ɪ]; **FL**28, **TX**29, Tee-nincy ['tiˈnaɪntsɪ, -ˌnaɪntsɪ]; **SC**11, Tee-ninchy [tiˈnaɪnʃɪ]; **SC**34, Tee-nincy [tiˈnɑ·ntsɪ]. **1968** Bradford *Red Sky* 9 **AL**, Frank, honey, would you pass me another slice of that delicious ham, and maybe a tee-ninecy spoonful of okra? **1969** (1970) Angelou *Caged Bird* 147 **AR** [Black], She left me a teenincy note. **1973** McCarthy *Child of God* 98 **TN**, I'd say it would fit her unless she's just teeninecy. **1975** *Lima*

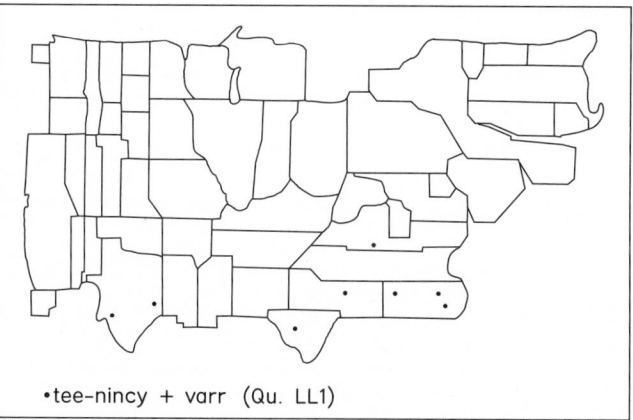

•tee-nincy + varr (Qu. LL1)

News (OH) 11 Aug 4/5, *Johnson, Henry "Tee-Nincy"—Services will be at 1 p.m. Wednesday.* **1981** Pederson *LAGS Basic Materials,* 1 inf, **swAL**, Little tee-ninesy [ˌtˈiˈnaˈ·ˀ˂nsɪ] thing; 1 inf, **swAL**, Tee-nintsy [ˌtˈiˈˀnaˢ·ɪntsɪ]—very small. **1997** *Houston Chron.* (TX) 24 July (Internet), And the men, the czars and princes, they was tee-ninsy. **2000** in 2004 *DARE* File—Internet **TN**, Such copies would certainly be good enough for roller-bladers listening to walkmen on teeninesy headphones. **2005** *DARE* File **TX**, "Tee-nineshih" [ti-naɪnˈʃi] is, in Texas (not just in East Texas and not just by blacks, in this case), used in exclaiming over small objects, whether animate or inanimate, that are—or were once— just too cute for words. . . It can also be used slightingly. "They got 'em a li'l ol' tee-nineshih quarterback'll break half in two, soon's he take a lick."

tee-nine(t)y   See **tee-niny**

tee-nin(t)sy   See **tee-nincy**

tee-niny adj   Usu |ˌtiˈnaɪni|; for varr see quot 1981   Also rarely *teeny-iney, tee-ni(ne)ty*   Also sp *tee-niney, t-niney*   [Extended forms of *tiny;* cf **tee-nincy**]   **Sth, S Midl, esp SC**   See Map   Cf **tee-tiny**
Very tiny—also used as a nickname.

  1870 in 1977 Shepard *1870 Census Floyd Co. KY* 31, [Hamilton,] Teeniny—F[emale]—57—[born] Va. **1909** *Good Housekeeping* 49.500 **Sth**, Strutting around 'cause you most killed a po' little teeniny dog. **1917** Pyrnelle *Miss Tweetty* 166 **AL** [Black], An' dem rooms wuz so little, with sich li'l' tee-ninety winder-panes. **1939** FWP *Guide NC* 98, The "arm baby" is also the "least 'un," the "teeniney," or "teeny chap," her youngest. **1964** Tyler *If Morning Ever Comes* 62 **NC**, I near about lived at their house when I was a teeny-iney girl. **1965–70** *DARE* (Qu. LL1, *Something very small: "I only took a _____ one."*) Infs **NC**4, **SC**2, 9, 21, 39, 44, 45, Tee-niny; **SC**8, 34, 54, Tee-niny [FW sugg]; **LA**17, Tee-niny—this is usually used to describe very small babies; **FL**31, Tee-niny; (Qu. LL6c, *A small, indefinite amount . . . "It still needs just a _____ of cinnamon."*) Inf **AR**47, Tee-niny bit or tee-ninety bit. **1975** *News* (Pt. Arthur TX) 25 Feb 2/3, The undercover agent, Elray "T-Niney" Fontenot, testified in the first trial. **1981** Pederson *LAGS Basic Materials,* 1 inf, **nwTN**, Five or six of those little tee-niny [ˌtˈiˈˀnaˢᵋni] ears; 1 inf, **cwAL**, Tee-niny [ˌtˈiˈˀ·naˑni] peas; 1 inf, **swGA**, A little tee-nin(y) [ˌtˈiˈˀnaˢɛ̃n] [sic] boy. **2004** *TN Tribune* (Nashville) 30 June (Internet), Mary Scales spoke about the local civil rights legacy of her late husband, Robert "Tee-niny" Scales. **2004** *Gwinnett Daily Post* (Lawrenceville GA) 18 July (Internet), Another hiker, they said, had told them there was a T-90 spring somewhere off the trail just ahead. . . "Wait a minute," I said. "Did this guy have a North Georgia accent?" They confirmed that he did, whereupon I informed them that what we were looking for was not a "T-90" spring, but rather a spring that was "tee-niney"—i.e., little bitty. **2004** *DARE* File—Internet **cTX**, D[ust] J[acket] has tee-niny chip at corner tips. *Ibid* **LA**, I don't know how you could get much more than a long-handled teethbrush into those t-niney spaces.

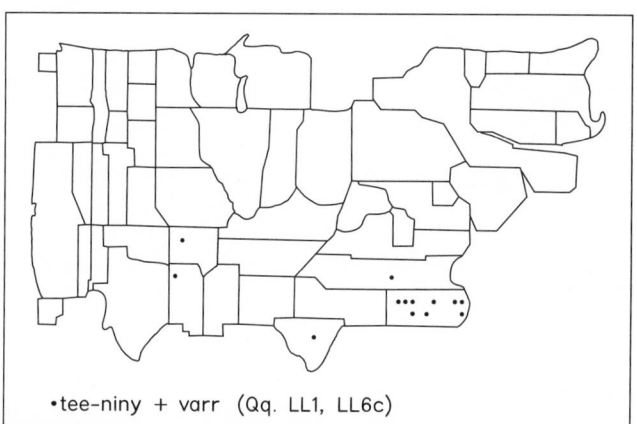

•tee-niny + varr (Qq. LL1, LL6c)

teensy adj |ˈtin(t)si| Also *teency, teentsy, teenzy*   [Prob *teeny* infl by dimin suff *-sy;* cf **tinesy**]   **formerly Sth, S Midl, now widespread, but less freq NEng**   Cf **eentsy, teenchy, teenty, weensy**
Very tiny—also used as a nickname; freq in comb *teensy-weensy* and varr; rarely used absol.

  1856 Cooke *Last Foresters* 283 **VA**, Come, now, tell me the charm in those feet which you young ladies designated, I remember, as 'teensy.' **1872** *Our Young Folks* 8.411 **MD**, Rose was no longer a funny *teensy-weensy* of an infant pig, but was now a half-grown, solid, fat porker. **1896** *Harper's New Mth. Mag.* 93.772 **TN** [Black], Teensy shakes his head, sighing. **1899** (1912) Green *VA Folk-Speech* 441, *Teensy*. . . Small. "Little teensy bit of a boy." **1904** *Washington Post* (DC) 20 Nov 7/2, I wouldn't mind bein' a little, teentsy sick. **1906** *DN* 3.161 **nwAR**, *Tintsy* [sic] ['tɪntsɪ]. . . Tiny. *Tintsy-wintsy* [sic] [tɪntsɪ-wɪntsɪ]. . . Tiny. **1909** *DN* 3.380 **eAL, wGA**, *Teentsy(-weentsy)*. **1949** *Portland Press Herald* (ME) 30 June 18/5, We babbled happily and acted a teensy bit high. **c1960** *Wilson Coll.* **csKY**, Very small—teeny-tiny . . teeny-weeny . . teentsy-weentsy. **1965–70** *DARE* (Qu. LL1, *Something very small:* "*I only took a _____ one.*") 26 Infs, **scattered, but less freq NEast, West**, Teensy-weensy; 20 Infs, **scattered, but less freq NEast**, Teensy; **NY**146, **VA**21, Eentsy-teensy (bit); **GA**68, **NJ**23, Teensy(-weensy) bit; **KY**11, Little teensy; **NC**61, Teensy-tinesy; (Qu. LL2, . . *Too small to be worth much:* "*I don't want that little _____ potato.*") Infs **GA**15, **IN**15, **OR**1, **VA**34, Teensy; **CA**142, **MA**28, ['tɪnsi ('wɪnsi)] [sic]; (Qu. LL6a, *A small, indefinite amount* . . "*I'll take just a _____ of cream in my coffee.*") Inf **TX**5, Teensy bit; (Qu. LL6c, *A small, indefinite amount* . . "*It still needs just a _____ of cinnamon.*") Inf **NY**109, Teensy bit. **1976** Garber *Mountain-ese* 91 **sAppalachians**, *Teency-weency* . . tiny—I'll have jist a teency-weency twist uv lemon in my tea please. **2002** in 2004 *DARE* File—Internet **TX**, A wittle teenzy bit shy. **2005** *DARE* File **cwCA** (as of c1955), We used to say something was teensy ['tɪntsi] or teensy-weensy; but if we said it slowly for emphasis, it was ['ti:nsi].

teensy-tinesy See **tinesy**

teensy-weensy See **teensy**

teenter See **teenter board**

teenter-ass See **teeter** n 1

teenter board n Also *teenter, tinter (board)* [Varr of **teeter** n 4] Cf **tiddle board**
=seesaw 1.

1937 Crane *Let Me Show You VT* 35 **VT**, The word *tinter* (from central Connecticut) occurs once in western Vermont. **1943** *LANE* Map 577 *(Seesaw)* 8 infs, **chiefly lower Connecticut Valley**, Teenter; 2 infs, **cCT**, Teenter board; 2 infs, **cs,swCT**, Tinter; 2 infs, **cs,swCT**, Tinter board; [1 inf, **nwMA**, [tĩnərɪn bɔrd, tĩnərn ~], for *teentering* ~; cf. [tĩntr̩ɪn], adjective, 'unstable or wobbling', of a beam or the like]. **1948** Davis *Word Atlas Gt. Lakes* 245, *Seesaw* . . tinter(board [used by 3 (of 63) infs in **nOH, cMI**]. *Ibid* app qu 82, 3 [of 233] infs, **IL, IN, OH**, Tinter board. **1969** *DARE* (Qu. EE31, *Playground equipment with a long board for two children to sit on and go up and down in turn*) Inf **MA**42, Tinter (board). **1973** Allen *LAUM* 1.223 (as of c1950), *Seesaw* . . Local Massachusetts *tilt* appeared twice . . ; so did Plymouth Colony *tinter board* (Ia. and Nb.) **2006** *NADS Letters*, I first heard "tinter board", which she also referred to as "teeter board" . . from a college friend 30 years ago who had grown up in the Raleigh-Durham area of NC; her parents were actually from western VA, and I believe that most of her quainter language traditions were more reminiscent of that dialect.

teentsy See **teensy**

teenty adj Also in combs *teenty-taunty, ~-tawnty, ~-to(i)nty, ~-weenty* [Prob from Engl dial (*EDD* at *teeny* adj.[1]), though attested earlier in US] **chiefly Nth, esp NEast** *old-fash* Cf **weenty**
Very tiny.

1812 (1838) Burr *Private Jrl.* 2.422, The *sloop Rose* is a *lēētle teenty* thing of about thirty or forty tons. **1844** Stephens *High Life in NY* 2.227 **CT**, A little teenty tointy handful of wood keeps 'em warm as blazes a hull day and night tu. *Ibid* 230, And then she took up one teenty glove. **1851** (1859) Arthur *Stories Housekeepers* 78 **sePA**, I only took a teenty tawnty little piece. **1863** *Harper's New Mth. Mag.* 28.112, A pretty little teenty-taunty babe as ever you see. **1867** *Ibid* 36.67 **MA**, Pickles? . . little teenty, tonty cucumbers, you know, crisp and sharp. **1872** *Appletons' Jrl.* 8.730 **NYC**, It's a little dog! It's a little teenty white live dog! **1890** (1895) Riley *Rhymes of Childhood* 141 **IN**, Noey Bixler ketched him . . / When he's ist a little teenty-weenty baby-coon. **1909** *DN* 3.417 **nME**, *Teentytonty, adj.* Same as *teentytonty*. **1926** Pratt-Stanton *Before Books* 59 **NYC**, He saw a little bit of a teenty weenty fly and he ate him up and that's the end. **1945** *Bismarck Tribune* (ND) 21 Feb 6/6 **CA**, Personally, I wouldn't take even a teenty dose of any sulfa drug unless I were sick abed under the care of my doctor.

teeny-iney See **tee-niny**

teeny tony adj Cf *teenty-tointy* (at **teenty**)
Very tiny.

1909 *DN* 3.417 **nME**, *Teenytony*. . . Diminutive of *tiny*. **2003** in 2004 *DARE* File—Internet **swIN**, Loving the new place. I even like my teeny tony kitchen.

teenzy See **teensy**

tee-o n [Echoic]
=**piping plover**.

1923 U.S. Dept. Ag. *Misc. Circular* 13.70 **MA**, *Piping Plover*. . . *Vernacular Names*. . . In local use. . . Tee-o. **1925** (1928) Forbush *Birds MA* 1.470, *Piping Plover*. . . Tee-o. *Ibid* 471, Some of its local names are derived from its notes as *Peep-lo, Tee-o* and *Feeble*.

teester See **tester**

teet n[1] See **tooth** n

teet n[2]
=**old-squaw**.

1923 U.S. Dept. Ag. *Misc. Circular* 13.24 **OH**, *Old-squaw*. . . *Vernacular Names*. . . Teet.

tee-tally n Also *tee-taddle*
=**seesaw 1.**

1966 *DARE* (Qu. EE31, *Playground equipment with a long board for two children to sit on and go up and down in turn*) Inf **SC**26, Seesaw, tee-tally ['titælɪ]—old-time name. **1967** *McDavid Coll.* **cSC**, Tee-taddle ['ti,tædl]—new name [for] "seesaw." Farmer, 71, 9th grade [educ].

tee-tee v, n **chiefly Sth** *euphem* Cf **thunder mug**
To urinate; urination; by ext, the genitals; hence combs *tee-tee-cloth* a diaper; *tee-tee pot* a chamber pot.

1968–70 *DARE* (Qu. F38, *Utensil kept under the bed for use at night*) Inf **LA**40, Tee-tee pot; (Qu. W19, *Names and nicknames for the folded cloth worn by a baby in place of pants*) Inf **TN**53, Tee-tee cloth; (Qu. BB20, *Joking names or expressions for overactive kidneys*) Inf **GA**42, Tee-tee, pee-pee. **1971** in 1993 Major *Calling the Wind* 312 **LA** [Black child], I get my tee-tee and I wee-wee fast and hard, because I don't want to get cold. **1992** Wells *Little Altars* 6 **LA**, Mama is . . just howling with laughter. Tooty, she yells, quit it! I'm tee-teeing all over myself! **1996** Wells *Divine Secrets* 31 **LA**, They'd laugh until one would accuse the others of making her tee-tee in her pants. **2004** *DARE* File—Internet **MS**, We offered an M&M as a reward when she teeteed. This backfired because she wanted to stay on the potty all day doing nothing just to get the m&m. Almost 6 months later now, she has decided on her own she wants to wear panties and teetee on the potty. *Ibid* **ceTX**, She was in the potty and I was in there with her, and she goes "What is 'prifey'? This?[*] (as she points to her teetee). And I say No. That's your teetee. "*Privacy*" is when you need to be alone.

teeter v, hence vbl n *teetering* Also sp *teter* [Varr of arch and Brit dial *titter* to move unsteadily, *totter* (*OED2 titter* v.[2] c1374 →). First attested in US, but prob of Engl dial origin; cf *teetering pole* in 1975 Viereck *Lexikalische Lowman-Survey* 1.141.] Cf **teetering horse, tiddle board**
To play at **seesaw 1**; hence nouns *teetering board*, ~ *plank*, rarely *tittering board* =**seesaw 1.**

1809 *Something* 1.2 **Boston MA**, Like teetering boys, when one mounts t'other falls. **1843** Stowe *Mayflower* 47 **NEng**, Then he was *tetering* with her on a long board. **1846** Worcester *Universal Dict.* 728, *Teeter*. . . To seesaw on a balanced plank, as children, for amusement. [Worcester: U.S.] **1856** Underhill-Thomson *Elephant Club* 173 **NYC**, We . . 'teetered' in happy sport upon the same board. **a1874** in 1949 *PADS* 11.37 **cME**, D'ye mind it, the place where we teetered, dear Lew.,/ The fence that stood over the run?/ Such teetering, Lew., was an innocent sport,/ For mind it, we teetered for fun. **1884** *Oshkosh Daily Northwestern* (WI) 31 July [2]/1 (newspaperarchive.com), That career . . pulls down still stronger this year because he has got nothing at the other end of the teetering board to hold him up. **1894** *DN* 1.343 **wCT**, *Teeter*: to see-saw, oscillate up and down. Used of the children's sport with plank and fulcrum. **1905** *DN* 3.97 **nwAR**, *Teetering-board*. . . A seesaw. **1907** *Newark Advocate* (OH) 28 Mar 10/3, Miss Mary Peterson fell off a teetering board and severely sprained her left arm. **1909** *DN* 3.380 **eAL, wGA**, *Teeter, v. i.* To seesaw, move up and down, waver. **1910** *DN* 3.450 **cwNY**, *Teeter, v. i.* To seesaw. *Teeter* and *teetering board*. . . A seesaw. **1922** Belknap *Yesterdays of Grand Rapids* 172

MI, Above the swamp where Dick built a robber's roost with a dime novel for a guide, his great-grandson . . teeters on a board with a caretaker to see he does not fall off. **1941** [see **teeter** n 4]. **1943** *LANE* Map 577 *(Seesaw)* 7 infs, **scattered NEng,** Teetering board; 1 inf, **cwVT,** Teetering plank; 1 inf, **ceMA,** Tittering board. **1973** [see **teeter** n 4]. **1986** Pederson *LAGS Concordance (Seesaw)* 1 inf, **csTN,** Teetering plank.

teeter n

1 also *teeter-ass (snipe), teeter-bird, -bob, -butt, -peep, -snipe, -tail, teenter-ass, teeterer:* =**spotted sandpiper.** [See quots]
1805 *Med. Repository* 2.123 **Long Is NY,** *Partial Catalogue of the Birds of New York. . .* Field or teeter snipe. **1844** DeKay *Zool. NY* 2.247, It is known in the books under the names of *Spotted Sandpiper* and *Tattler,* but is better known among the people by the name of *Peet-weet . . ;* or of *Teeter* and *Tiltup,* from its often repeated grotesque jerking motions. **1872** Coues *Key to N. Amer. Birds* 260, *Spotted Sandpiper. . .* [E]xtremely abundant everywhere near water, and breeding throughout the country; familiarly known as the sandlark, . . teeter-tail, . . etc. **1917** (1923) *Birds Amer.* 1.249, *Spotted Sandpiper. . . Other Names. . .* Teeter-peep; Teeter-tail; Teeterer. *Ibid* 250, The Spotted Sandpiper . . is popularly nicknamed "Teeter" . . from its nervous habit of constantly tilting its body. **1925** (1928) Forbush *Birds MA* 1.450, *Spotted Sandpiper. . . Other names . .* teeter-bob; teeter-tail; teeter-peep. **1930** Shoemaker *1300 Words* 62 **cPA Mts** (as of c1900), *Teeter-bird*—The spotted sandpiper. **1936** Roberts *MN Birds* 1.492, This little Sandpiper [=*Actitis macularia*] gets the common name of Teeter Snipe . . from a curious habit of teetering the rear part of the body. **1945** McAtee *Nomina Abitera* 35, Teeter ass. This name [for *Actitis macularia*], seldom if ever seen in print is the most familiar designation of the species in the Northeast (known distribution from Nova Scotia and Long Island west to Illinois and Minnesota; also in Manitoba); teeter-butt, Iowa. **1956** MA Audubon Soc. *Bulletin* 40.17, *Spotted Sandpiper. . .* Teeter (General); Teeter Bird (Vt.); Teeter-bob, Teeter Peep (Mass.); Teeter-tail (General). **1967–69** *DARE* (Qu. Q7, *Names and nicknames for . . game birds*) Inf **MA**42, Teenter-asses ['tɪntɚˌæsəz]; (Qu. Q9) Inf **WI**32, Snipe—called teeter-ass; (Qu. Q10, . . *Water birds and marsh birds*) Inf **MN**18, The teeter or spotted sandpiper; **MI**42, Teeter-ass ['titɚˌæs]—a snipe; **NH**14, Teeter-ass; **NJ**8, Teeter-ass snipe. **1969** Longstreet *Birds FL* 62, *Spotted Sandpiper . .* Teeter-snipe; Teeter Tail.

2 also *teeter-arse, teeter-ass (snipe), teeter-bird, ~-snipe, teetler:* Any of var birds that move in a similar way to **teeter** n **1** above, as the **least sandpiper, solitary sandpiper, killdeer 1, flicker** n[2] **1,** or **water ouzel.**
1867 (1868) Samuels *Ornith. & Oölogy New Engl.* 458, It [=solitary sandpiper] has the habit of nodding its head, and tipping up its body and tail, which has given it the name of "Wagtail," or "Teetler." **1891** IN Horticult. Soc. *Trans. for 1890* 38, *Solitary Sandpiper. . .* Known locally as "Peet-weet," "Teeter Snipe," and "Tilter." **1914** *DN* 4.154 **NH,** *Teeterarse. . .* flicker n[2] 1. Harry wicket [=**flicker** n[2] **1**]. **1945** McAtee *Nomina Abitera* 34, Killdeer. . . Teeter-ass snipe, Pequannock, New Jersey. *Ibid* 35, Solitary Sandpiper. . . Teeter-ass, Illinois. . . This correspondent who . . gave this term for the spotted and solitary sandpipers . . remarked, "You may leave this name out but it is the only common name these two species are known by in this locality." **1954** McAtee *Suppl. to Nomina Abitera* [9] **CO,** Dipper *(Cinclus mexicanus unicolor)*—Teeter-ass. **1956** MA Audubon Soc. *Bulletin* 40.18 **MA,** *Solitary Sandpiper. . .* Teetler. *Ibid* 19 **CT,** *Least Sandpiper. . .* Teeter. **1967–68** *DARE* (Qu. Q14, . . *Names . . for . . killdeer*) Inf **OR**15, Teeter-ass or water ouzel; **NY**52, Teeter-ass snipe. **1971** *Daily Times–News* (Burlington NC) 23 July sec A 7/6, When not singing or feeding, the ouzel often perches on a bank and bobs vigorously. . . This characteristic motion inspired the common name of dipper or "teeter bird."

3 =**harvest mite.**
1968 *DARE* (Qu. R22, *Very small red insects, almost too small to see, that get under your skin and cause itching*) Inf **NJ**8, Teeters ['titɚz].

4 also *te(e)ter board;* rarely *teeder, teeter-beam, ~-pole, titter (board):* =**seesaw 1.** [Cf **teeter** v, **teeter-totter 1.** First attested in US, but prob of Engl dial origin; cf *teeter, teeter-teeter* in 1975 Viereck *Lexikalische Lowman-Survey.*] **scattered, but chiefly NEast, nOH** See Map *old-fash* Cf **teenter board, tiddle board**
1854 *Ladies' Repository* 14.363 **OH,** The pretty wood opposite seemed not to have lost a tree, the "teeters" lay across the logs just as we had left them. **1855** *Knickerbocker* 46.88, We were having a grand time with our 'teeter'-boards upon the highest fence. **1862** *Atlantic Mth.*

9.391 **'Upcountry' MA,** An' *I* tell *you* you 've gut to larn thet War ain't one long teeter / Betwixt *I wan' to* an' *'T wun't du.* **1884** *Sioux Valley News* (Correctionville IA) [25 Sept 2]/1 (newspaperarchive.com), Whenever Ben played teeter-board he always wanted to be the one who stood in the middle and held the balance of power. **1893** *New Engl. Mag.* 15.51 **ME,** Hotels with their paraphernalia of bowling alleys, swings, "teeters," and summer houses find lodgment on prominent points. **1894** *Ibid* 16.670, The plank went up like a teter-board, throwing her forward onto the shore. **1905** *Reno Eve. Gaz.* (NV) 12 Apr 6/3 **cwCA,** [Advt:] Hammock, sand box, children's swing, teeter board. **1909** *DN* 3.417 **nME,** *Teeter. . .* A rocking board. **1910** *DN* 3.450 **cwNY,** *Teeter* and *teetering-board. . .* A seesaw. **1921** *NE State Jrl.* (Lincoln) 20 Aug 7/2, [The park] has swings, teter boards, and other play ground apparatus. **1923** *Fitchburg Sentinel* (MA) 3 Aug 2/1, [He] had both bones of his right forearm fractured yesterday afternoon when he fell off a teeter at the Lowe playground. **1941** *Language* 17.331 **WI** [LANCS fieldwork], *Teeter*—11 [of 50 infs]. . . Primary to . . [9 infs, 2 of whom] use it as vb., with *teeter-board* as sb. . . Secondary to . . [2 infs, 1 of whom said that] 'children say it.' . . Through the state except north and southwest. *Teeter-board*—2 [of 50 infs]. **1943** *LANE* Map 577 *(Seesaw)* [*Teeter* and *teeter board* are the prevailing terms in **nNEng** and most of **MA** and are common in **CT;** only in **RI** and **seMA** are they rare or unknown. The varr *titter* and *titter board* are used by one inf **(ceMA)** and two infs **(wCT, neMA)** respectively; one inf **(cCT)** uses *teeter beam.*] **1965–70** *DARE* (Qu. EE31, *Playground equipment with a long board for two children to sit on and go up and down in turn)* 39 Infs, **esp NEng, Upstate NY,** Teeter board; 38 Infs, **esp NEng, Upstate NY, nOH,** Teeter. [60 of 73 total Infs old, 13 mid-aged] **1966** Dakin *Dial. Vocab. Ohio R. Valley* 2.174, [The variant] *teeter* includes a few instances of *titter* and *teeder. Teeter board* includes *titter board* and *teeter boarding* [sic]. **1973** Allen *LAUM* 1.223 **Upper MW** (as of c1950), *Seesaw. . .* is known as a *teeter-totter* by four out of five U[pper] M[idwest] infs. . . This . . term dominates not only both the New England equivalents *teeter* with its seven instances . . and *teeter board,* preserved only in Minnesota, Iowa, and North Dakota, but also the more literary and urban *seesaw. Ibid,* [Results of mail survey:] 8 [of 1064] infs, Teeter; 13 infs, Teeter board; 1 inf, Teetering board; 1 inf, Teeter pole; 1 inf, Teeting totter. **1989** Pederson *LAGS Tech. Index* 86 *(Seesaw)* 3 infs, **Gulf Region,** Teeterboard. **2005** *DARE* File—Internet **csIL,** [Grade school student handbook:] *Teeter board*—Do not have more than one student on each end of board. **2005** *DARE* File **csOK,** When I was in grade school about 1949 and 1950 in Duncan, Oklahoma I got the impression that *see-saw* was a teacher's word and *teeter-totter* was what the kids called it. Some children called it simply a *teeter.* Long afterward, . . I noticed that a woman teacher talking to the children used the word *teeter-totter* herself.

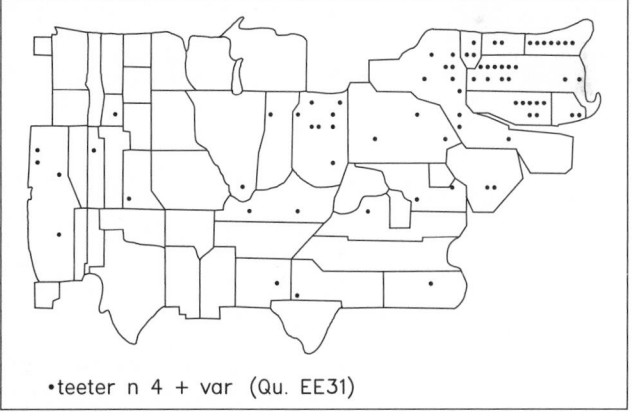

•teeter n 4 + var (Qu. EE31)

teeter-arse See **teeter** n 2

teeter-ass (snipe) See **teeter** n 1, 2

teeter-beam See **teeter** n 4

teeter-bird See **teeter** n 1, 2

teeter board See **teeter** n 4

teeter-bob (or -butt), teeterer See **teeter** n 1

teeter horse See **teetering horse**

teetering (board) See **teeter** v

teetering horse n Also *teeter horse* [Prob blend of *teetering board* (at **teeter** v) + **ridy-horse 2,** but see quot 1973] =**seesaw 1.**

1948 Davis *Word Atlas Gt. Lakes* 245, *Seesaw . .* teetering horse [used by 3 (of 63) infs in csOH, csIN]. **1966** Dakin *Dial. Vocab. Ohio R. Valley* 2.174, Several speakers in south-central Ohio have combined the Northern and Southern regional terms to say *teetering-horse, teeter-horse.* **1973** Allen *LAUM* 1.223 **Upper MW** (as of c1950), *Teetering-horse,* not reported in the East, was checked by three Minnesotans and one northern Iowan [out of 1064 checklist infs]. This term may be a hybrid derived from *teetering board* and the Midland *ridy horse . .* but probably significant is the fact that three of the respondents had parents born in Germany and one had all grandparents born in Germany; the German term for rocking-horse is *Schaukelpferd.* **1973** *Coshocton Tribune* (OH) 17 July 1/5, A swing set and slide have been installed and bases for the teeter horse and for another riding horse have been set.

teetering plank See **teeter** v

teeter-peep See **teeter** n 1

teeter-pole See **teeter** n 4

teeter-snipe See **teeter** n 1, 2

teeter-tail See **teeter** n 1

teeter-tauter (or -tawter) See **teeter-totter 1**

teeter-totter n [Varr of arch and Brit dial *titter-totter* (*OED2* 1530 →). First attested in US, but prob of Engl dial origin; cf *tee-tawter, teetermatorter,* and similar forms in *EDD* (at *titter-totter*), *teeter-totter, teeter-teeter, teetery-tot, teeting board,* etc. in 1975 Viereck *Lexikalische Lowman-Survey* 1.141.]
1 also *teeder-todder, ~-totter, teeter-tauter, ~-tawter, ~-tot, teeting-totter, tee-totter, titter-totter:* =**seesaw 1,** also fig—also used as part of a rhyme to accompany the activity; hence v *teeter-totter* to play at **seesaw 1;** vbl n *teeter-tottering.* **chiefly Inland Nth, Missip-Ohio Valleys, West** See Map

1848 Bartlett *Americanisms* 352, *Teeter-tawter.* The act of see-sawing. In England pronounced *titter-totter.* **1852** Cox *Buckeye Abroad* 218, Europe must play *"teeter-tawter"* over the balance of power for many a year yet. **1869** *Putnam's Mag.* 13.555, "Teeter-tawter, milk and water," [was] accompanied by a concurrent motion at the end of a limb or of a well balanced plank. **1887** *Daily News* (Frederick MD) [28 May 4]/2 **MA** (newspaperarchive.com), Around the wheel extends an elliptical frame, which is adjustable upon the axle much in the manner of a "teeter totter." **1890** (1895) Riley *Rhymes of Childhood* 88 **IN,** Turn to the lane where we used to "teeter totter." **1897** *KS Univ. Qrly.* (ser B) 6.93 **neKS,** *Teeter totter:* to swing up and down on opposite ends of a plank supported in the center. **1905** *DN* 3.66 **eNE,** *Teeter-totter, n.* or *v.* Seesaw. *Ibid* 97 **nwAR,** *Teeter-totter.* . . To see-saw. **1916** *DN* 4.330 **KS,** *Teeter-totter, n.* and *v. i.* A seesaw. Neb. Also, as in Mich., *teeter-tawter.* "In playing at seesaw, the children often keep time with the rime: Teeter-totter,/ Bread and wotter (water)./ Teeter-tawter,/ Bread and water." Also W. Res[erve OH]. **1926** *Elementary School Jrl.* 26.381 **MT,** John _____ was tried for bucking Robert _____ off the teeter-totters and cutting his chin. **1941** *Language* 17.331 **WI** [*LANCS* fieldwork], *Teeter-totter*—35 [of 50 infs]. . . Primary to all but five of these. Distribution general. Used as vb. (with *teeter-board* as sb.) by [1 inf]. . . Used for what children chant while they *teeter* [1 inf]. . . *Teeter-tot*—1 [of 50 infs]. . . *Teeter-totter board*—1 [of 50 infs]. . . Despite some opinion to the contrary, *seesaw* is clearly an innovation: mentioned by only 12 per cent of the oldest but 56 per cent of the middle informants. **1949** Kurath *Word Geog.* 58, On the lower Hudson, on Long Island, and in New Jersey *teeter (board)* is uncommon. Here we encounter *teeter-totter,* an expression that occurs also in the New England settlements of New York State, Pennsylvania, and Ohio. In New England *teeter-totter* can now be heard only on the Housatonic and west of the Green Mountains, but its predominance in northern New Jersey and its widespread use in the New England settlement area lead to the inference that it was formerly more widely current in Western New England. **1956** *Syracuse Herald–Jrl.* (NY) 5 June 27/1, There is a recreation area containing swings, teeter-totter and other equipment now in the park. **1965** *PADS* 43.20 **seMA,** Other names for a seesaw: teeter totter [3 of 9 infs; 1 inf said old term]. **1965–70** *DARE* (Qu. EE31, *Playground equipment with a long board for two children to sit on and go up and down in turn*) 398 Infs, **chiefly Inland Nth, Missip-Ohio Valleys, West,**

Teeter-totter; **IA**29, **MN**12, **NY**70, Tee-totter; **OK**52, Teeter-[tædə]; [54 Infs, **scattered, but esp N Cent, West,** Teeter-tooter [*DARE* Ed: This was a typographical error in the list of likely resps in the QR, which some FWs circled without changing.]; **CA**190, **IL**68, **WA**6, Teeter-toter; **VA**13, Seesaw; titter-teeter—"correct"]. **1966** Dakin *Dial. Vocab. Ohio R. Valley* 2.171, The Northern names [=*teeter, teeter board, teeter-totter*] predominate in the Old Northwest all the way south to the Ohio River. *Ibid* 174, *Teeter-totter . .* includes scattered instances of *teeder-todder, teeder-totter,* and *titter-totter* (fairly common in Indiana). **1968** *PADS* 49.17 **Upper MW** (as of c1950), As a term for the pieces of playground equipment the Northern *teeter-totter* is increasing, while the Southern and Midland *see-saw* is used by a small percentage of each group. **1972** *PADS* 58.16 **cwAL,** *Seesaw.* South and Midland *seesaw* (22 [of 27 infs]) predominates. . . Northern *teeter totter* (2) and *teeter board* (1) were given as alternate responses by middle and cultured informants; two of the informants labeled *teeter totter* a new term. **1973** [see **teeter** n 4]. **1981** *PADS* 67.27 **Mesabi Iron Range MN,** *Seesaw.* . . Sixteen of 17 Mesabi informants responded with the Northern *teeter totter* (rarely *teeting totter*), which is also usual also [sic] among other Minnesota informants (38/53), and one of the Range Type I's [=with little educ] offered *teeter* in addition to *teeter totter.* **1989** Pederson *LAGS Tech. Index* 86 **Gulf Region** (Seesaw) 771 infs, Seesaw; 44 infs, Teeter-totter. **2005** *DARE* File—Internet **OR,** *The correct way of teeter-tottering.* . . Do not teeter-totter with more than one person on each side.

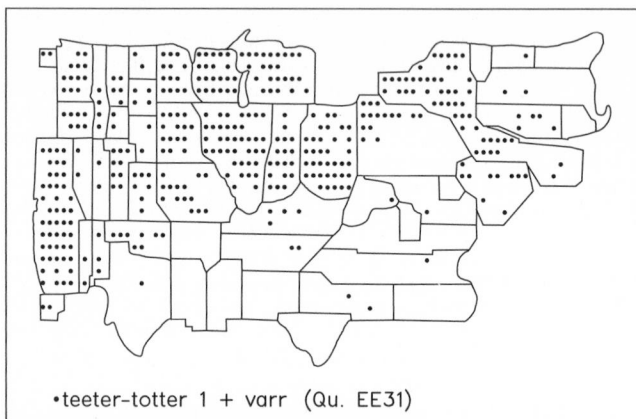

•teeter-totter 1 + varr (Qu. EE31)

2 See quot. Cf **flying jenny 1a**
1968 *DARE* (Qu. EE32, *A homemade merry-go-round*) Inf **MD**49, Teeter-totter—not identical with seesaw. A device with two planks crossing at right angles, on a pole at point where they cross; children can push it with feet so that it moves either around, or up and down, or both; [it] flops around.

teeter-tottering See **teeter-totter 1**

teeth See **tooth** n B1

teethache n Also with *the* [*SND* 1840 →; *EDD* 1898 →] See Intro "Language Changes" II.6
Toothache; a toothache.
1811 *Memoirs CT Acad. Arts & Sci.* 1.264, This kind of weather is very apt to occasion teethache, in dyspeptics. **1848** *WI Democrat* (Madison) [20 May 4]/1 (newspaperarchive.com), "You have the teethache now and then, I perceive," mused the doctor. **1854** in *Worcester Women's Hist. Project* (Internet) **RI,** At home Albert sick with teethache. **1859** (1968) Bartlett *Americanisms* 474, *Teeth-ache.* An attempted improvement in the way of accuracy on the word *tooth-ache.* **1886** in 2005 (acc) *Wayne Co. PA Geneal.* (Internet), I have got the teethache some and will get ready for bed. **1892** *DN* 1.211 **seMA,** *Teethache:* toothache. "She's got the teethache, and so she come down town to have it out." Plymouth and Cape Cod. **1909** *DN* 3.380 **eAL, wGA,** *Teethache. . .* Toothache. Among the negroes, *teefache.* **1911** *Sandusky Reg.* (OH) [9 Dec 15]/4 (newspaperarchive.com), He wouldn't of knowd she was his wife if he had of met her on the street without knowing that she had the teethache, her appearance was that changed. **1922** Gonzales *Black Border* 332 **sSC, GA coasts** [Gullah glossary], *Teet'ache*—toothache.

teeth are floating See **back teeth are floating**

teeth doctor See **tooth doctor**

teethes   See **tooth** n B2b

teeth organ   n   Cf **mouth organ 1**
A harmonica.
1966 *DARE* (Qu. FF7, *A small musical instrument that you blow on, and move from side to side in your mouth*) Inf **SC21**, Mouth organ; as a kid, teeth organ (slang).

teeth-popping   See **pop** v¹ **1b**

teeting-totter   See **teeter-totter 1**

tee-tinsy   adj   Pronc-sp *tee-toncey*   [Extended form of **tinesy;** cf **tee-tiny**]   **esp S Midl**   Cf **tee-nincy**
Very tiny.
1955 *NC Folkl.* 3.2.13 [Black], So often did she speak of a very small baby as a "tee-toncey" thing that he became known as "Tonce." **1965** *Dict. Queen's English* 4 **NC**, (for tiny): I'll have just a tee-toncey piece of pie. **1979** *NYT Article Letters* **Ocracoke Is. NC**, No-see-'ems—Little tee-tinsy gnats that you can bearly [sic] see. Tee-tinsy—extremely small, like the tee-tinsy needle tip. **2004** *DARE* File—Internet **TX**, It was a tee-tinsy kitchen. **2005** *Ibid* **AR**, Tee-toncey. . . Heard recently at an Ozark family gathering when someone said, "I'll just have a tee-toncey helpin' o' them 'taters."

tee-tiny   adj   [Extended form of *tiny;* cf **tee-tinsy**]   **Sth, S Midl**   Cf **tee-niny**
Very tiny.
1941 *Salisbury Times* (MD) 18 Sept 7/8, [Advt:] Tee-tiny tucks ripple a band-bottom blouse. **1945** *Statesville Daily Rec.* (NC) 13 June 2/5, Seven tee-tiny ones just a day or two old . . are certain to give you something to Ohhhhh about. **1966–67** *DARE* (Qu. LL1, *Something very small: "I only took a _____ one."*) Infs **SC3**, 19, 31, 32, Tee-tiny [FW sugg]; **SC24**, Tee-tiny—if you want to emphasize it; **SC26**, Tee-tiny; (Qu. LL2, . . *Too small to be worth much: "I don't want that little _____ potato."*) Inf **SC26**, Tee-tiny. **1987** Kytle *Voices* 14 **NC**, Even as a tee-tiny child, the least little thing would set him off. **2004** *DARE* File—Internet **TX**, When I read the words "tee tiny" together (the way God made them, by the way) I knew I found a weblogger I can relate to. *Ibid* **NC**, We recently moved from a picturesque cabin (tee-tiny) by a mountain stream to an old farm house.

teetler   See **teeter** n 2

teetling board   See **tiddle board**

tee-toe   n   Cf **cricket** n²
1966 *DARE* (Qu. EE10, *A game in which a short stick lying on the ground is flipped into the air and then hit with a longer stick*) Inf **FL10**, Tee-toe ['titoʊ]—you hit a stick on one end so it flips up in the air, and whoever gets it up highest wins.

tee-toncey   See **tee-tinsy**

tee-totter   See **teeter-totter 1**

teets   See **tooth** n B2b

tee-whitie   n   Also *teewity, tee-y-tee, t-witey, t-wyty*
In phr *to a tee-whitie:* To a T, precisely, perfectly.
c1900 in 1944 *ADD* 670 **seOH, nwWV**, [To a] ['tiwaɪtɪ]. **1929** *Sale Specialist* 6, Then he started ape-in' fokes /. . . / He kin take-off you or me / Right down to a tee-y-tee. **1941** in 1944 *ADD* 670 **eWV**, It fits to a T-witey. **1942** McAtee *Dial. Grant Co. IN* 63 (as of 1890s), *Teewity* . . long i . ., in such expressions as "suits me to a _____," "fits to a _____," i.e. entirely, exactly. **1942** Warnick *Garrett Co. MD* 16 **nwMD** (as of 1900–18), *T-wyty,* to a, prep. phr., exactly; sometimes "to a T." **1967–69** *DARE* (Qu. KK3a, . . *The perfect condition—for example, in cooking: "It's done to _____."*) Inf **GA73**, Tee-whitie [ˌtiˈwaɪdiˇ]; (Qu. KK3b, *Something done perfectly—for example, a piece of work: "It's done to _____."*) Infs **GA73, OR3**, Tee-whitie. **1967** *DARE* FW Addit **swOR**, Worked to a tee-whitie [-'waɪtɪ]—i.e., to a T. [**1982** Slone *How We Talked* 38 **eKY** (as of c1950), To fit to a tee-wonk-tum (exactly).]

‡**teewiggin**   n
See quot.
1972 *NYT Article Letters* **cNY**, Her husband . . often invited us to the barns to see a new litter of "little teewiggins" (small pigs).

teewity, tee-y-tee   See **tee-whitie**

teg(g)ious, tegus   See **tedious**

te-hinder   See **tee-hinder**

teither   adv   [Prob by metanalysis of *didn't either*]
1904 *DN* 2.428 **Cape Cod MA**, *Teither.* . . Used by children in contradicting each other. 'I didn't either.' 'Yes, you did teither.'

tejious, tejus   See **tedious**

tek   See **take** v A1a, 3f

tekky   See **take** v A1c

tel   See **till** A1

teld   See **tell** v B2a

telefoam, teleform   See **telephone**

telegraph weed   n   Also *telegraph plant*
=**golden aster 2,** usu *Heterotheca grandiflora.*
1924 Jepson *Flora Economic Plants CA* 158, H[eterotheca] grandiflora. . . Telegraph Weed. **1940** *Jrl. Mammalogy* 21.389 **CA**, Rip-gut grass . . , sheep sorrel . . , and telegraph weed (*Heterotheca grandiflora*) are the main constituents. **1960** Abrams *Flora Pacific States* 4.265, *Heterotheca grandiflora.* . . Telegraph Weed. . . Pappus brick-red. . . Sandy open places. **1974** Munz *Flora S. CA* 187, *Heterotheca.* . . Telegraph Weed. . . Coarse erect herbs. **1987** Bowers *100 Roadside Wildflowers* 44 **SW**, Although telegraph plant is native to the United States, it acts like a weed, and thrives in . . disturbed places. . . *Heterotheca subaxillaris.*

telephone   n, v   Pronc-spp *telefoam, teleform, telephome*
A Forms.
1906 *DN* 3.161 **nwAR**, *Telephome,* v. intr., n. To telephone. "I'd like to know why he telephomed." "I got a telephome message from him." Uncommon both as verb and noun. **1907** *DN* 3.250 **eME**, *Telephome,* n. and v. Telephone. **1914** *DN* 4.81 **ME, nNH**, *Telefoam.* Almost universal form of *telephone.* **1917** in 1944 *ADD* 62 **sWV**, Telephome. **1931** *AmSp* 6.348 **NE**, In the frequent pronunciation *telefome,* the labialization may be owing to a carrying over from the *f* beginning the last syllable, or to vague folk-etymological association with the noun *foam.* **1941** *AmSp* 16.13 **eTX** [Black], ['tɛləfoʊm]. **1942** Faulkner *Go Down* 68 **MS**, It wasn't me that told Mister Roth to telefoam them shurfs! **1979** *AmSp* 54.100 **sME** (as of 1899–1910), *Teleform.* . . Telephone.

B As verb.
To catch fish by stunning them with an electric current, usu generated by an old-fashioned crank telephone; to catch (fish) in this way; hence vbl nouns *telephoning, telephone fishing.* **chiefly SE, S Midl**   See Map   Cf **calling, monkey fishing**
1951 *Dixon Eve. Telegraph* (IL) 21 Sept 3/7 **OK**, You-grind-it-telephones are being used by the folks in these parts to put a mess of fish on their tables. . . They are telephoning for fish. **1954** *Harder Coll.* **cwTN**, *Telephone.* . . To catch fish by electrocuting them. **1956** *Lima News* (OH) 29 July sec D 4/6, Telephoning fish is a method of using old-time magneto telephones as portable electrical generators to stun fish wholesale in handy pools. . . Southern authorities wish the notable Northern lack of interest in the system was nationwide. **1958** in 2005 (acc) Lexis–Nexis Legal Research *State Case Law: OK* (Internet), A motor and boat in which material, devices and, [sic] equipment used in 'telephone fishing' are found is not such property as may be seized and forfeited to the State of Oklahoma. **1965–70** *DARE* (Qu. P13, . .

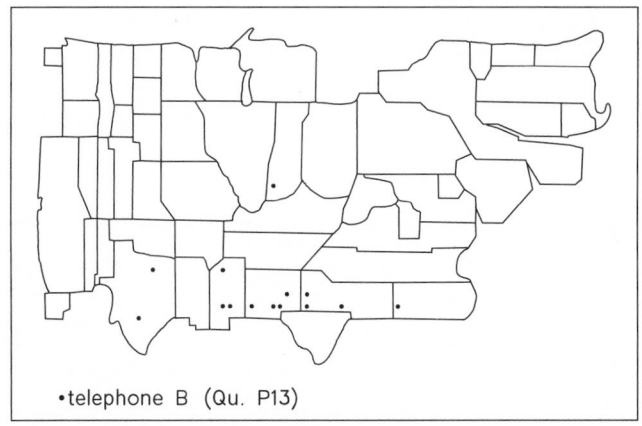

•telephone B (Qu. P13)

Ways of fishing . . besides the ordinary hook and line) Infs **AL**2, **GA**84, 89, **MS**6, Telephoning; **AL**19, **MS**81, 89, **TX**51, Telephoning—illegal; **AL**7, Telephoning—old telephone, crank it; **AL**17, Telephoning—used to—telephone, turn crank; **GA**7, Telephoning—throw line of old wind phone in water and turn crank; **IN**42, Telephoning—electrocute them with a crank telephone; **SC**40, Calling them up, telephoning—two boats: ringing boat drifts along edge, turns the telephone and drags the line; the netting/pickup boat gets the stunned fish—won't work on scaly fish; **TX**11, Telephoning—shock fish with old-time telephone; [**AR**56, Fishing with a telephone]. **2003** in 2005 *DARE* File—Internet **cwMS,** "We were about five or six miles above the Big Black River bridge and encountered two men in a boat telephoning fish," Lt. Long said. **2005** *Ibid* **AR,** When I was a kid, my family controlled access to the Arkansas river for several miles so we locked the game ranger out and telephoned and noodled our way to a huge fish fry every summer.

telephone booth n joc
An outdoor toilet building.

1965–70 *DARE* (Qu. M21b, *Joking names for an outside toilet building*) 9 Infs, **scattered,** Telephone booth; **NV**8, Backyard telephone booth; [**PA**235, Outside Bell telephone;] (Qu. M21a, *An outside toilet building*) Inf **NY**36, Telephone booth. **1986** Pederson *LAGS Concordance (Outhouse)* 1 inf, **cLA,** Telephone booths—joking term.

telephone bug n
=love bug.

1972 *Milwaukee Jrl.* (WI) 24 Sept 27/6, The biological name for the bug is plecia meanctica [sic for *nearctica*]. Along the Texas, Louisiana and Mississippi Gulf Coast, where the insect apparently originates, they are known as honeymoon flies, telephone bugs and double headed bugs. Entomologists say male and female unite when they become adults and live their brief lifetimes flying around that way.

telephone fishing, telephoning See telephone B

tele pole See telly pole

telescope house n chiefly eMD
A house consisting of several sections of graduated size along a single axis.

[**1878** (1977) Stowe *Poganuc People* 166, New England houses have been said by a shrewd observer to be constructed on the model of a telescope; compartment after compartment, lessening in size, and all under one cover.] **1931** Wilstach *Tidewater MD* 69, Another repeated specimen is the so-called "telescope" house, a united series of frame buildings, each smaller than the other. **1940** Writers' Program *Guide MD* 124, The need for space to house an increasing family, or a growing prosperity, also resulted in a type of building Marylanders call a 'telescope house.' These dwellings were extended at one end by an addition slightly higher and wider than its predecessor; third and sometimes fourth units were added, each one a little higher than the one before it. **1964** *Salisbury Times* (MD) 23 Sept 7/4, This telescope house has old handhewn cross doors. **1982** Heat Moon *Blue Highways* 397 **eShore MD,** The telescope house may not be indigenous to the Eastern Shore, but there were more of them here than anywhere else. The name derived from the linking of three houses, each successively larger, so that the two smallest ones look as if they could slide, telescope fashion, into the largest house. **2005** *DARE* File—Internet **neMD,** Prior to being moved, it was a telescope house with three successively smaller parts from front to rear.

tell v
A Pronc forms.

In combs *(I) tell you* |'tɛjə, 'tejə|; pronc-sp *te' you*.

1942 Hall *Smoky Mt. Speech* 103 **wNC, eTN,** In the phrase, 'I want to tell you,' as pronounced by some speakers, *l* is completely vocalized: [a 'wɑnt tə 'tejə]. **1948** Manfred *Chokecherry* 69 **nwIA,** Screech, I te' you what I'll do. **1968** *DARE* Tape **IN**21, I tell you ['tɛjə], I was impressed with it.

B Gram forms.

1 pres:

a infin, usu after *did:* usu *tell;* also *told, tole.* **Sth** *esp freq among Black speakers*

1870 *Punchinello* 1.150 [Black], Thar! Didn't I tole yer? **1890** *Scribner's Mag.* 7.59 **AR,** Didn't you tole me yon was young Rutherford? **1891** *Century Illustr. Mag.* 41.899 **nGA** [Black], Did n' I tole yo' ter call me Mr. Marting? **1928** Peterkin *Scarlet Sister Mary* 80 **seSC** [Gullah], Didn't I told you to stay home tonight? **1929** (1954) Faulkner *Sound & Fury* 22 **MS,** Whyn't you take him on home. *Didn't they told you not to*

take him off the place. **1934** *Sat. Eve. Post* 29 Sept 13 **MS** [Black], If somebody tole you, hit could be a lie. But if you dremp hit, hit can't be a lie case ain't nobody there to tole hit to you. **1953** Brewer *Word Brazos* 30 **eTX** [Black], "Didn' Ah tole you dat if'n you preach dat sermon Ah's gonna whip de hell outen you?"

b (exc 3rd pers sg): usu *tell;* also *tells.*

1778 in 1909 *Mag. Hist. Extra Nos.* 6.27, They tells the wooman that they wanted a Candle and so they gos up Chamber and stands over him. **1806** (1965) Ordway *Jrls.* 388, They tells us that they are determined to Stay up this river. **1945** FWP *Lay My Burden Down* 21 **TX** [Black], They tells me they's coming back if I tells, and I promised not to tell. **1965–70** *DARE* Tape **AL**1, I tells the kids sumpin like that now and they just don't believe it; **MS**1, My people tells me that there was a feller; **TN**51, That's what they tells me to do. [2 of 3 Infs Black]

2 past, past pple: usu *told;* also:

a *tell(e)d, teld.* [*OED2* c1330 →]

1795 Dearborn *Columbian Grammar* 139, *List of Improprieties.* . . Tell'd for Told. **1815** Humphreys *Yankey in England* 109, *Telled*, told. **1836** (1955) Crockett *Almanacks* 52 **wTN,** I . . telled him that I didn't care the fag end of a johnny cake for him. **1843** (1916) Hall *New Purchase* 449 **IN,** I tel'd you to put off a hour ago. **1864** *Harper's New Mth. Mag.* 28.281 **swVT,** Now ef you find that Mr. Thompson telled more truth than Harrison, then you find for the plaintiff. *Ibid* 29.117 **TN,** I'se allers telled Sally sense [=since] thet thet kiverlet ar the flag I means ter live under. **1871** (1882) Stowe *Fireside Stories* 234 **MA,** I telled the deacon he was a gone hoss then. **1899** (1912) Green *VA Folk-Speech* 441, *Teld.* . . Past tense and past part. of *tell.* **1905** *DN* 3.59 **eNE,** *Tell, hear, ketch,* take the regularized preterites *telled, heared, ketched.* **1945** FWP *Lay My Burden Down* 117 **LA** [Black], Young Master's children writ to me once in a while and telled me how they gitting 'long.

b *tole, tol', toll.* [nScots, nIr, and swEngl dial]

1856 *Harper's New Mth. Mag.* 12.340 **VA** [Black], I tole you, Miss Carline, dere is gosisses [=ghosts]. **1872** *Galaxy* 13.485 **SC,** Nan tole me to fetch home suthin'. **1887** Eggleston *Graysons* 91 **IL,** I sh'd thought she'd 'a' tole *you* what kep' 'er. *Ibid* 198, You want to know what Bob tole S'manthy? **1899** Chesnutt *Conjure Woman* 43 **csNC** [Black], Mars Marrabo tol' Sandy fer ter git ready. **1901** Harben *Westerfelt* 8 **nGA,** She ort to know the truth, an' I tol' 'er. **1909** *DN* 3.382 **eAL, wGA,** *Tole,* pret. of *tell.* Common. **1929** Sale *Tree Named John* 13 **MS** [Black], Ah tole her t' git de spade. **1931** (1991) Hughes-Hurston *Mule Bone* 129 **cFL** [Black], Dis is in court an' it's got to be tole. **1933** Rawlings *South Moon* 6 **FL,** The same as on 'tother side o' the river, is what I been tole. **1934** Hurston *Jonah's Gourd Vine* 9 **AL** [Black], You tole 'em not to come till you call 'em. **1941** O'Donnell *Great Big Doorstep* 10 **sLA,** 'I coulda tole you,' said Commodo. **1948** Manfred *Chokecherry* 41 **nwIA,** He's the one that tol' about my brother dyin'. **1974** Gilbreth *Dictionary* 15 **seSC,** *Toll:* Past tense of tell. **2007** Apps *In a Pickle* 40 **cWI** (as of 1950s), It's what he tole me.

c *tolt.* [*EDD* cites a single Ir ex of *towlt.*] **chiefly S Midl**

1887 *Overland Mth.* (2d ser) 10.54 **nAL,** I gin it, Mis' Harjoe, jest ez Sam Parker tolt me. *Ibid* 57, Ye hev tolt me that many er time. **1890** *Harper's New Mth. Mag.* 82.114 **VA** [Black], I tolt her so, an' I tolt her I wuz raise wid quality. **1914** Furman *Sight* 60 **KY,** He tolt me he were aiming to peel them 'ere ingun-skins off my eyes. **1929** *WV Review* Oct 30, Told has been *tolt.* **1933** *AmSp* 8.1.24 **sAppalachians,** In parts of southwestern Virginia, Kentucky and North Carolina certain words have [t] in place of [d]. *Second* is *secont, told, tolt,* and *husband, husbant.* **1999** Proulx *Close Range* 44 **WY,** He didn't ast me. Tolt me to get some guys. **2005** *DARE* File—Internet **nwAR,** Well from what she tolt me she ran all the way back home fast as she had ever ran.

d *toad, tode.* [Similar forms are common in c,sEngl dial, but the US exx perh represent an independent development.] Cf Pronc Intro 3.II.27

1990 Amory *Cat & Curmudgeon* 192 **eTX,** A man at the ranch . . said, . . "He's a real nass fella. . . I toad him how you felt. . . He's in the barn with it [=a burro] rat now." **2004** in 2005 *DARE* File—Internet **MO,** He has tode me that if I had saw what he has saw . . I'd never ever throw a bait without some kind of power bait on it. **2005** *Ibid* **GA,** [Grade-school student's story:] His mom and Dad tode him to go to the farest so he did.

C Senses.

1 To bid, wish; to say to (someone a formula of greeting, farewell, or felicitation). **formerly chiefly Sth, Midl, now widespread**

1838 Gilman *S. Matron* 28 **seSC,** I must tell you all how d'ye and good-bye together, . . for I am going very fast. **1859** (1968) Bartlett *Americanisms* 475, To *tell* one good-bye, is the Southern phrase for to bid one good-bye. **1861** in 2005 *DARE* File **nwTN**, Give my respects to old Uncle Austin and tell him howdy. **1886** *S. Bivouac* 4.343 **sAppalachians**, Tell (say, *e.g.,* "tell good-bye"). **1899** (1912) Green *VA Folk-Speech* 441, *Tell.* . . To tell one good-bye is to bid him good-bye. **1903** *DN* 2.333 **seMO**, Tell the lady good bye! **1903** *Wellsboro Agitator* (PA) 15 July 2/3, [Syndicated short story:] Tomorrer you may tell him merry Christmas from all o' us. **1907** *DN* 3.237 **nwAR**, *Tell (good-bye).* **1908** *German Amer. Annals* 10.47 **sePA**, I must wait and tell him good-by. **1909** *DN* 3.380 **eAL, wGA**, To tell good-bye. **1914** *Daily Rev.* (Decatur IL) 1 May 14/4, He was busy all day Friday with callers who came to tell him 'so long' and 'good luck.' **1915** *DN* 4.191 **swVA**, *Tell goodbye.* **1934** *Oakland Tribune* (CA) 5 Mar 15/7, He did not tell Miss McNamee at the time he told her goodbye at the station that they were "parting forever." **1953** *Holland Eve. Sentinel* (MI) 29 Dec 1/4, I don't know . . whether or not I even told her goodbye. **1998** *Syracuse Herald–Jrl.* (NY) 23 Oct sec B 3/3, He told her goodbye, and he told her to tell mom and dad goodbye. **2005** *DARE* File—Internet **NH**, I should go tell him happy birthday in person.

2 To say—constr with:

a a noun clause without indirect object.

1887 in 2005 *DARE* File—Internet **cNY**, I did not see them married but he told they were married. **1920** *Decatur Daily Rev.* (IL) 6 Nov 7/5, He told that the negroes are often blamed for the horrors of race riots. **1940** (1968) Haun *Hawk's Done Gone* 18 **eTN**, Basil butted in and told that Tiny started it. **2004** in 2005 *DARE* File—Internet **sePA**, I went to the doctor's office on Monday. . . He told that I had some increased ocular pressure. **2005** *Ibid* **ME**, He told that he had given up his car. *Ibid* **FL**, She told she gave up on us. *Ibid* **CA**, They tell that, because of this, I am loosing [sic] students and big money.

b direct quotation. *Gullah, HI creole*

1923 Parsons *Folk-lore Sea Islands* 25 **csSC** [Gullah], Buh Rabbit tell, "My broder, I get all my water out de cow-track." **1949** Turner *Africanisms* 268 **seSC** [Gullah], [tɛl—dɪʃɛ sem mɑn . . sɛ, "unə stɑn stɪl."] [*Ibid* 269, [=Say—this here same man . . say, "You stand still."]] **1972** Carr *Da Kine Talk* 48 **HI**, What I goin' tell *my* mother? My mother tell, "What kind party this goin' be?"

3 To talk, converse. [Engl dial]

1955 Ritchie *Singing Family* 59 **seKY**, Mammy Sally and Pap and t'others seemed like they had a good time talking to him and listening to him tell, but I couldn't open my mouth to save me.

4 with *off on*: To inform on, betray. **chiefly Sth, S Midl**

1963 Edwards *Gravel* 22 **eTN** (as of 1920s), Wes rolled under the bed and she couldn't find him. So Uncle Jeems told off on him. **a1983** in 2005 *DARE* File—Internet **csOK**, I used to say, "Now I'll have to tell off on you when you used to pedal [sic] cabbage." **1998** *Ibid* **cAR**, I have loved the Monkees since 1966 (which tells off on my age a bit). **2002** *Ibid* **ceTX**, I'm glad I didn't act the fool in any form or fashion. He sure would have told off on me. **2004** *DARE* File—Internet **cwLA**, The last several posting [sic] someone is telling off on theirselves. **2005** *Ibid* **neMS**, Jeff [=a mule] told off on her [=a hidden sow], I would not have known otherwise. Whe[n] he would get close to a hog, he would snort.

tell n

1 An account, story—used to give the authority for a statement. **chiefly Nth** *old-fash*

1795 Dearborn *Columbian Grammar* 134, *List of Improprieties.* . . By his *tell* for By his tale. **1815** Humphreys *Yankey in England* 43 **CT**, He is a leetle *twistical,* according to their tell. **1818** (1920) Clark *Diary* 2312 **CT**, They have been 7 or 8 weeks on the road and by their tell had as hard times . . as we had. **1860** Street *Woods & Waters* 45 **neNY**, Twan't nothin' to the way that moose made at Old Ramrod, 'cordin' to his tell, full trot. **1889** Cooke *Steadfast* 386 **CT**, Here's your sellery ain't half-paid, at least, that's the tell. **1898** Westcott *Harum* 241 **nNY**, The' didn't appear to be no one we run across that, accordin' to Price's tell, was wuth under five million. **1916** Howells *Leatherwood God* 144 **OH**, From the tell I've hearn they want you to try him. **1917** *DN* 4.401 **neOH**, *Tell.* . . Account, report. "According to his tell, it was this way." "By your tell, you are a good workman." Also Vt., Mass., Ill., Kan., N.Y. **1929** *AmSp* 5.121, Maine dwellers often said . . in relating a story "I recollect" or "according to his tell."

2 in phr *according to one's tell*: In one's opinion, to one's way of thinking.

1871 Eggleston *Hoosier Schoolmaster* 96 **sIN**, But, laws a me! we're all selfish akordin' to my tell. **1874** (1895) Eggleston *Circuit Rider* 144 **sOH**, See here, mister! Akordin' to my tell, that air's a mighty peart sort

of a hoss fer a feller to ride what don' know . . whar he mout be a travelin'. **1890** *New Engl. Mag.* 8.271 **neMA**, You don't ketch me hirin' out to those kind of folks. Accordin' to my tell, folks that goes a ridin' up and down country in the winter season—! **1966** *DARE* Tape **ME**10, He wouldn't know . . whether he was eating fish or what according to his tell.

tell prep, conj   See **till A1**

tell(e)d   See **tell v B2a**

tell-last   See **trade-last**

tell off on   See **tell v C4**

tell one's pedigree, to   See **pedigree**

tells   See **tell v B1b**

tellsome adj   [*tell* + *-some* suff]
See quots.

1934 (1943) *W2*, *Tellsome.* . . Talkative; esp., officiously forward in offering advice. Local, U.S. **1937** *Forum* 97.129 **ME**, Now, as a Maine guide once said to me, "I don't want to be tellsome," so I forbear laying down the law as to how humorous poetry should be written. **1942** Chevalier *Drivin' Woman* 23 **VA** (as of 1865), Gen'nemen, Mistis Merry nevah meant no hahm. . . She's jest tellsome by nature. **1969** *DARE* FW Addit **ME**, She's tellsome—i.e., forward.

tell someone where to head in   See **head in 3**

telltale n   Cf **tattler**

1 also *telltale godwit, ~ plover, ~ sandpiper, ~ snipe*: The greater or the lesser **yellowlegs 1**. [See quot 1904]

1813 Wilson *Amer. Ornith.* 7.57, This species and the preceding . . are detested [by duck hunters], and stigmatized with the names of the greater and lesser Tell-tale, for their faithful vigilance in alarming the Ducks with their loud and shrill whistle. **1823** James *Acct. of Exped.* 1.4 **swPA**, Among other birds [we] saw . . the tell tale sandpiper. **1842** Audubon *Birds Amer.* 5.316, It is true that the Tell-tale [=*Tringa melanoleuca*] is quite loquacious enough; nay, you, reader, and I, may admit that it is a cunning and watchful bird. **1870** *Amer. Naturalist* 4.547, Tell-tale Sandpiper (*Gambetta melanoleuca*). . . Early in May, these birds in company with other *Scolopacidæ* arrive in the neighborhood of Trenton, New Jersey. **1880** *Forest & Stream* 15.4, *Totanus flavipes.* . . Lesser tell-tale. **1904** (1910) Wheelock *Birds CA* 70, This bird [=*Tringa melanoleuca*] is the sentinel of the game-birds, giving warning of the approach of the hunter in loud, whistling notes repeated rapidly; hence its name "Tell-tale" and "Long-legged Tattler." **1917** (1923) *Birds Amer.* 1.242, Greater Yellow-legs. . . Other Names.—Big Tell-tale; Greater Tell-tale; Tell-tale Godwit. *Ibid* 244, Yellow-legs. . . Other names.— . . Little Tell-tale; Lesser Tell-tale. **1950** *PADS* 14.67 **SC**, *Telltale snipe.* . . The greater yellowlegs; the lesser yellowlegs. **1956** MA Audubon Soc. *Bulletin* 40.18, Greater Yellowlegs. . . Greater Telltale (Mass. Its wariness and shrill cries give all wildlife notice of the presence of intruders.) . . Telltale (Rather general.) . . Telltale Plover (R.I. See note on Greater Telltale.)

2 =**willet. LA**

1899 in 1900 LA Soc. Naturalists *Proc.* 96, *Symphemia semipalmata inornata.* . . *Western Willet; Tell-Tale.* A common resident of the coast. **1911** *Forest & Stream* 77.174 **LA**, *Catoptrophorus semipalmatus.*—Tell Tale. **1923** U.S. Dept. Ag. *Misc. Circular* 13.62 **LA**, *Willet.* . . Telltale, vire-vire.

3 =**killdeer 1**.

1923 U.S. Dept. Ag. *Misc. Circular* 13.69 **seNY**, *Killdeer.* . . Telltale (Long Id., N.Y., Ont.).

telltale godwit (or plover, sandpiper, snipe)   See **telltale 1**

telly pole n   Also sp *tele pole*   **chiefly PA**
A utility pole.

1957 *Sat. Eve. Post Letters* **Philadelphia PA**, "Telepole" instead of telephone or telegraph pole. This is used by everyone in my section of the city. **1970** Lebofsky *Lexicon Philadelphia* 149, *Telly-*—telephone, in combinations such as *tellypole* or *tellywires.* . . *Telly-* was recognized by 39% of the informants (by 49% [of 55 infs] in Philadelphia, by only 14% [of 22 infs] in PMAx [=the rest of the Philadelphia Metropolitan Area]). The clipped form was most familiar to Education 3 Philadelphians [=those with grade-school educ]. . . In addition, more men (48%) had heard of *telly-* than women (29%). Thought of by Philadelphians as a Kensington . . expression, *telly-* is best known by informants in that section of the city. **1976** *Philadelphia Mag.* Mar 126, Tellypole is the correct word of course (for the big wooden poles with wires on them).

What is it—a telegraph pole, a telephone pole, an electric pole? Good usage dictates the word tellypole. **1987** Dillard *Amer. Childhood* 111 **cwPA,** We ourselves used some pure Pittsburghisms. We said "tele pole," pronounced "telly pole," for that splintery sidewalk post I loved to climb. **1997** *DARE* File—Internet **cePA** [CoalSpeak], *Telly-pole:* Telephone pole (possibly just an Ashland phrase—if you said this in Shendo, you'd get beat up). **2001** in 2005 *DARE* File—Internet **neTN,** I was riding my poor half-fixed cat [=motorcycle] 2 weeks after wrapping it around a telly pole. **2002** *Pittsburgh Post-Gaz.* (PA) 26 June (Internet), Yes, the "telly pole," as those of a certain age still call them, belonged to the telephone company.

telly wire n Also *tellypole wire*

A telephone wire or other outdoor utility wire.

1970 [see **telly pole**]. **2004** in 2005 *DARE* File—Internet **GA,** Apparently some of the hard storms we've been experiencing in the Atlanta area . . messed with the telly wires leading to the house. **2005** *Ibid* **Philadelphia PA,** *Tellypole Wire*—Place where you throw your old sneakers.

tem See **teem 1**

tempered adj

Angry, irritated.

1942 (1971) Campbell *Cloud-Walking* 97 **seKY,** Sary would be tempered iffen you didn't know first by seeing it with your own eyes. **1969–70** *DARE* (Qu. GG7, *. . Annoyed or upset: "Though we were only ten minutes late, she was all _____."*) Inf **DC**12, Tempered; (Qu. GG16, *. . Finding fault, or complaining: "You just can't please him— he's always _____."*) Inf **IN**79, Tempered.

tempest n [*OED2 tempest* 1.a "A violent storm of wind" c1250 →; 1.b "A thunderstorm. *U.K. dial.* and *North-Eastern N. Amer.*" c1532 →] **chiefly seNEng** See Map

A violent storm, esp a thunderstorm.

1823 (1922) Anthony *New Bedford* 61 **MA,** In the evening we had quite a tempest. **1877** *Harper's New Mth. Mag.* 54.297 **CT,** Ominous flashes of tempest began to play about the far horizon. **1892** *DN* 1.211 **seMA,** *Tempest:* a thunder-shower. **1893** in 1956 Ritchie *Block Is. Lore & Legends* 62 **RI,** Last Friday we had our first tempest for 1893. **1896** *DN* 1.426 **seMA,** *Tempest:* specifically, a thunder storm. Plymouth. **1908** Freeman *Shoulders* 236 **MA,** "Rose, come right away from that window," cried Sylvia. . . "Only last summer a woman in Alford got struck standing at a window in a tempest." *Ibid* 242, The thunder-tempest, as Sylvia termed it, continued. **1913** *DN* 4.58 **seMA,** *Tempest. . .* An electrical storm only. "We shan't have any more tempests now till next summer." **1916** *DN* 4.336 **seMA,** *Tempest. . .* Thunderstorm. Cape Cod. **1928** Beston *Outermost House* 185 **Cape Cod MA,** A thunderstorm is a "tempest" on the Cape. **1939** *LANE* Map 94 *(Thunder storm)* **chiefly seNEng,** *Tempest* is variously defined. Eleven informants . . use the word only of a severe wind storm, while five others . . mention wind as part of their definition. Eight . . define a tempest as more severe than a thunder storm or a thunder shower, one . . says that a thunder storm may last all day whereas a tempest is shorter and sharper. To three informants . . *tempest* means primarily a display of thunder and lighting [sic]. . . The word is also used of any heavy rain . . , of any severe storm . . , of a storm at night . . and of a storm at sea. **1951** *AmSp* 26.251 **ceNY,** *Tempest* was recorded from a Schuylerville (Saratoga Co.) informant, definitely conscious of his ultimate Nantucket ancestry. **1965** *PADS* 43.17 **seMA,** A destructive windstorm with high wind and rain . . tempest (with thunder); old term [4 of 9 infs]. **1966–**

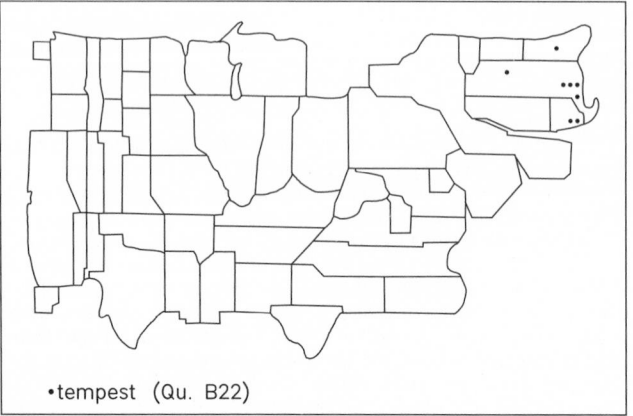

•tempest (Qu. B22)

70 *DARE* (Qu. B22, *Rain accompanied by thunder and lightning*) Infs **ME**22, **MA**55, 100, **RI**15, Tempest; **MA**5, Tempest—has heard in Bridgewater MA, sounds odd here; **MA**40, Tempest [FW: used in conv]; **MA**82, Tempest—Infs [=Inf and two relatives] surprised term wasn't known outside of area; **RI**1, Tempest—all [=Inf and two relatives] have heard tempest, but this is stronger than thunderstorm. **1988** Nickerson *Days to Remember* 133 **Cape Cod MA** (as of c1900), *Tempest*—Today we hear of electrical storms, cloudbursts, heavy rain, etc. Whatever happened to "tempest", meaning a violent downpour with almost constant thunder and lightning?

tempt See **teem**

ten n, adj Usu |tɛn|; also freq **Sth, S Midl** |tɪn|; occas |tæn| Pronc-sp *tin* Cf Pronc Intro 3.I.4.a

Std sense, var forms.

1856 in 1956 Eliason *Tarheel Talk* 318 **c,csNC,** Ten—tin. **1934** *AmSp* 9.210 **Sth,** Many words having standard [ɛn] become [ɪn] in the South. We have, for example, *ten cents* [tɪn sɪn(t)s]. **1937** *AmSp* 12.287 **nwVA,** Towards the southwestern end of the [Shenandoah] Valley there is increasing tendency . . to let the [ɛ] sounds move upward towards [ɪ], in *ten, then, men, any, many.* **1941** *AmSp* 16.5 **eTX** [Black], Before *m, n,* in . . *ten,* [ɛ] becomes [ī]. **1942** Hall *Smoky Mt. Speech* 19 **wNC, eTN,** [ɛ] is often raised to or toward [ɪ] . . [in] *ten. . .* The movement of [ɛ] toward [ɪ] before nasals is very noticeable in children and adolescents, although it is present to a degree in the speech of everyone. **c1960** *Wilson Coll.* **csKY,** *Ten* is nearly always /tɪn/; occasionally it is /tæn/. **1961** Kurath–McDavid *Pronc. Engl.* 103, Before /n/, as in *fence, ten,* the /ɛ/ is often raised in the South, and some speakers in Georgia, South Carolina, and eastern North Carolina have the high vowel /ɪ/. . . Elsewhere /ɪ/ is rare. **1991** Pederson *LAGS Regional Pattern* 20 **Gulf Region,** [Data shows [tɪn] pronc of *ten* used by 429 of 914 infs (47%), esp concentrated in **AR, nMS,** and **AL,** with lesser concentrations in **GA, sMS,** and parts of **eTX.**]

tenable See **tendable**

tenant n[1]

A **louse B1.**

1950 *WELS (Body and head lice)* 1 Inf, **seWI,** Tenants.

tenant n[2] See **tenon**

tendable adj Also *tenable* **chiefly Sth, S Midl**

Of land: arable.

1750 in 2005 *DARE* File—Internet **WV,** The low grounds . . being so very narrow & the chiefest part of the rest being not tendable. **1795** in 2000 Jefferson *Papers* 28.362 **VA,** It would be still better to . . clear the whole body of your tendable lands at once. **1853** *S. Lit. Messenger* 19.275 **SC,** You've got all your tendable lands cleared and in good order. **1863** in 2007 (acc) Lexis–Nexis Legal Research *State Case Law: NC* (Internet), I . . have bargained and sold . . the full and lawful privilege of ponding the water back upon my creek low ground . . , provided the water does not back upon any of my high or tenable lands. **1907** *Oakland Tribune* (CA) 4 Feb 14/7, [Advt:] $1700—35 acres, all tenable; fine vegetables. **1913** *Atlanta Constitution* (GA) [28 July 9]/6 (newspaper-archive.com), [Advt:] 100 *Acres* good, level land, all tenable except about eight acres. **1928** *Frederick Post* (MD) 5 Sept 5/8, [Advt:] *Farm For Sale.*—A fine farm, containing 132 acres, 120 tendable, rest in good wood land. **1965–66** *DARE* (Qu. C29, *A good-sized stretch of level land with practically no trees*) Inf **GA**7, Tendable land; (Qu. L6b, *A piece of land under cultivation—if it's several acres*) Inf **MS**58, Tenable ['tɪnəbl] land. **1976** *Hillsboro Press Gaz.* (OH) 12 Mar 12/5, [Advt:] 24 *Acres* vacant land. . . 12 acre tendable, rest in woods. **1986** Pederson *LAGS Concordance (Loam)* 1 inf, **cTN,** Some good tenable land—manageable. **2005** *DARE* File—Internet **cnTN,** [Advt:] Spring, pond & city water is available. Tendable acreage is on the hilltop.

tender v [*OED2 tender* v.[2] 2.c, d "Now *dial.*"]

To make soft or delicate.

1966 *DARE* Tape FL36A, I got a steam cooker . . it's a great big old high pot is the reason I use it mostly, and then it tenders it good to cook it in. **1979** Carpenter *Walton War* 149 **sAppalachians,** "Women folks hain't much account now-a-days, they have tendered themselves too much." How better to say someone has "gone soft"? Said by an old lady who had always worked hard and thought the younger generation was lazy.

tender n

1907 *DN* 3.250 **eME,** *Tender. . .* Assistant to the catcher or the *thrower* in the game of *round base,* a primitive form of baseball.

tenderfoot n chiefly West

An inexperienced newcomer or visitor in a frontier or rural area; a naive or inexperienced person.

1866 *Atlantic Mth.* 18.246 **swMT,** Awkwardness in comprehending this dialect easily reveals that the hearer bears the disgrace of being a "pilgrim," or a "tender-foot," as they [=miners] style the new emigrant. **1886** *Overland Mth.* (2d ser) 8.613 **swCA,** "The poor thing don't know no better," Mrs. Grimes whispered. . . "Them tenderfeet is awful guys." They could forgive much to a tenderfoot. **1896** *Harper's New Mth. Mag.* 94.95 **MA,** What did cause him to pour forth the vials of his wrath . . was to find that he had harbored in his bosom . . a tenderfoot, a man who did not know enough to refrain from sneezing when ducks were in the pond. **1929** *AmSp* 5.57 **NE** [Cattle country talk], "Ranch hands" generally consider themselves "he-men" when compared with the effete "tenderfoot" or "green horn," one unfamiliar with ranch life. **c1938** in Lib. of Congress *Amer. Memory: WPA Life Hist.* (Internet) **TX,** I began as a tenderfoot of the purest type and ended up as a seasoned rawhide. **1940** *AmSp* 15.221 **cwTX,** When the 'tenderfoot' wife displays her inability to cope with ranch life, her neighbors assert that 'she don't know beef from bull's foot.' **1941** Writers' Program *Guide WY* 465, *Tenderfoot*—A newcomer. One not acquainted with cowboy habits and skills. **c1960** *Wilson Coll.* **csKY,** *Tenderfoot. . .* A greenhorn, a new person at some game or problem. **1965–70** *DARE* (Qu. HH15, *A very inexperienced person, one who is just learning how to do a new thing*) 17 Infs, **scattered, but esp West, NEast,** Tenderfoot; (Qu. HH2, . . *A citified person*) Inf **CA**87, Tenderfoot. **1967** *DARE* Tape **TX**43, The pressure that the cowboys or the city dudes had was to catch a tenderfoot. **2005** *NewsRegister.com* (McMinnville OR) 19 July (Internet), But we got even. When Portlanders came to Eastern Oregon, we often whispered to one another, "Aha, another tenderfoot."

tendful adj esp NEng

Esp of a child: requiring attention.

1833 *New Engl. Mag.* 5.119, When did she . . assist those, whose "sewing had all run behind-hand, because . . the young ones had been so worrisome and tendful with their teething, that their mother could do nothing but see to them?" **1839** in 1940 Drury *Pioneers Spokanes* 260 **ME,** My babe tho very quiet is likewise very tendful so that he demands no small share of my time & is not a very good assistant in writing. **1839** in 1960 Wilbur *Memoirs* 4 **wNY,** I do not feel hardly capeble [sic] of taking care of so small a child. . . My boy is very tendful. **1890** Claflin *Brampton Sketches* 125 **ceMA,** The little girl was reminded that her knitting work was very "tendful," or that she was in "no danger of melting her knitting needles." **1941** *LANE* Map 396 *(Take care of baby)* 1 inf, **csNH,** The baby is tendful, i.e. needs attention. [**2005** *DARE* File—Internet, I gave a small laugh as I heard you speak about Duo and his tendful, messy habit.]

tending out on See tend out 1

tendon See tenon

tend out v phr chiefly NEng

1 usu with *on,* rarely with *for, to:* To attend to, take care of; hence vbl n *tending out on.*

1859 Smith *30 Yrs.* 54 **ME,** I made Stephen tend out for me pretty sharp, and he got my plate filled three or four times with soup, which beat all I ever tasted. **1878** *Harper's New Mth. Mag.* 57.109 **NEng,** He and his men tend out on all the wrecks, and there's many of them on this ugly bit of water. **1890** [see **3** below]. **1902** *Everybody's Mag.* 7.555 **NEng,** She just tended out on Luella as if she had been a baby. **1907** *DN* 3.250 **eME,** *Tend out on.* . . Attend to. "I'll tend out on the ice cream." . . Universal. **1945** *Daily Kennebec Jrl.* (Augusta ME) 14 Apr 6/1, For each one of us, working, shopping, tending out chores—there is another human being "statistically naked." **2004** in 2005 *DARE* File—Internet **CT,** My kids got sick, one with fever, and needed tending out on. *Ibid* **nwNH,** The oldest of three children . . , she was always tending out to her siblings, as well as the children of their surrounding neighbors.

2a To be at hand to render service, stand by; to take care of things.

1871 Hale *How to Do It* 168 **MA,** They two "tended out" in a buggy, but did not do much walking. **1891** Garland *Main-Travelled Roads* 60 **nIL,** Oh, go soak y'r head, old man. If you don't tend out here a little better, down goes your meat-house. **1938** *Daily Kennebec Jrl.* (Augusta ME) 10 Dec 4/1, [Headline:] Randolph's Oldest Business Man Store Proprietor 43 Years . . Tends Out at His Store Every Day. **2004** in 2005 *DARE* File—Internet **cME coast,** In 1970 they moved to Lincolnville where they enjoyed tending out on the farm. **2004** *Lincoln Co. News*

(Damariscotta ME) 7 Jan (Internet), In later years, the station was semi-automatic with two operators tending out as needed.

b Spec; in logging: to watch a section of a river and prevent logs from getting hung up there; to prevent (logs) from getting hung up.

1912 *Amer. Forestry* 18.765 **ME,** The clarion tones of the cookee . . echoed . . until the farthest man "tending out" received the welcome news. **1938** (1939) Holbrook *Holy Mackinaw* 55 **nwNH** (as of c1900), Down at the bend of the river a few men were stationed, "tending out," as they called it, poling the logs from the "off" bank lest they be halted in the eddy and make a jam. **1958** McCulloch *Woods Words* 191 **Pacific NW,** *Tend out*—To get logs moving down the river in good shape. **1963** *Atlantic Mth.* 212.30 **NEng,** Then comes an eddy against the bank where a jam would quickly form if rivermen were not "tending out" there, poling the logs out into the current. **1978** Mosher *Where Rivers Flow* 66 **neVT,** That spring he tended out pulp sticks in the first rapids below the driving dam from iceout in late April.

3 To be in attendance; with *on:* to be present at, attend; to pay attention to.

1861 in 1950 *AmSp* 25.184 **CT,** An Auction Sale . . is advertised in our columns to-day. . . Country merchants should "tend out." **1873** *Overland Mth.* 10.283 **MA,** From the first day I could balance on a bench, I had to tend out on religion. **1890** *DN* 1.22 **Bangor ME,** Another Americanism is one current in this city which I have not observed elsewhere in New England. . . One 'tends out on' church, 'tends out on' the public library for the first opportunity to take the new magazines. Whenever any one is on the alert for any purpose whatever he is 'tending out.' [*DN* Ed: This expression was known to me in Waterville, Me., and I have heard 'tend out on him pretty sharp' used at Southwest Harbor, Me.] **1907** *DN* 3.250 **eME,** *Tend out on.* . . to attend. "Are you going to tend out on the meeting to-night?" Universal. **1915** Day *Landloper* 96 **ME,** "I'm not interested." "You will be, if you tend out. The hearing is before the mayor and the whole city government." *Ibid* 160, He never even tended out on a caucus. **1949** *Portland Press Herald* (ME) 31 Jan 10/5, All of the members are skating enthusiasts and tend out pretty regularly at the community skating rink.

tend out for See tend out 1

tend out on See tend out 1, 3

tend out to See tend out 1

tendriled trumpet creeper See trumpet creeper 2

tenement n [*OED2 tenement* sb. 4.a 1593 →] chiefly NEng old-fash Cf double tenement (at double house 2)

An apartment; hence adjs (also used absol) *two-* (or *three-,* etc) *tenement* divided into two (or three, etc) apartments. Note: *Tenement (house)* in the sense apartment building is not treated here.

1839 *Alton Telegraph* (IL) [13 July 2]/4 (newspaperarchive.com), [Advt:] To rent—A house near the Cave Spring containing two tenements with two rooms and a wash room each with good spring water on the lot. **1844** *Bangor Daily Whig & Courier* (ME) 8 June 1/1, [Advt:] *To Let.* The east tenement of a brick house and stable. *Ibid* 1/2, *Estate of Stephen Goodhue, viz:* . . a lot of land . . with a two tenement house standing thereon. **1845** *Milwaukie Daily Sentinel* (Milwaukee WI) 27 May 1/6, [Advt:] *To rent.*—A tenement in the west ward, on Fourth street. . . Also, a small house in the east ward. **1860** *Atlantic Mth.* 5.676 **Boston MA,** The Directors of the Association proceeded to erect two brick houses, . . each containing separate tenements for twenty families. **1900** *N. Adams Transcript* (MA) 1 Aug [5]/7 (newspaperarchive.com), [Advt:] *For sale.* . . A six-tenement block and a three tenement building on Walnut street. A four-tenement building on Francis street. **1940** *Fitchburg Sentinel* (MA) 19 Nov 12/3, Edwin L. Ramsden and family have moved into the tenement in the F.J. Tenney telephone building. **1941** *LANE* Map 355 *(Tenement),* The map shows the terms *tenement, apartment, flat* and *rent,* denoting usually a part of a house used as a dwelling by one family, sometimes also a whole house occupied by a single family. [*Tenement* is widespread throughout **NEng.**] *Tenement* . . is variously defined as a whole house occupied by a single family . . [5 infs], as either part or all of a house . . [11 infs], as occupying either one or two floors . . [2 infs] or always more than one floor . . [3 infs], or as a rented room in a private house . . [1 inf]. . . A number of informants describe a tenement as 'poor', 'cheap', 'low-class' or 'in the slums' . . [15 infs, 10 **CT, RI**]. Some use the term only of a rented dwelling in the country . . [3 infs]. **1959** *VT Hist.* 27.162, *Tenement.* . . An apartment to rent. Occasional. **1965–70** *DARE* (Qu. D24, *Living quarters in a build-*

ing where several other families live) 34 Infs, **chiefly NEng, NYC,** Tenement; **CT**6, Tenement—smaller than apartments; **MA**5, Tenement—low-priced—no connotation of slum, has to have several in house; **MA**6, Tenement—here no connotation of slums; **MA**10, Tenement—same as apartment in Inf's youth; **MA**34, Tenement—in the poorer districts; **MA**72, Tenement—in the old days; **RI**1, Tenement—used to call it; **RI**9, Tenement—if poor; **SC**20, Tenement—common in the city; [**CT**5, Tenement—more a run-down multiple-family unit; **CT**18, Tenement, I guess, = whole building; unit inside = living quarters [*DARE* Ed: The two bracketed Infs are clearly using *tenement* to mean an apartment building rather than an individual apartment, and it is possible that some of the other Infs are using it in the same way.];] **CT**39, Two-tenement (or three-tenement)—house with two or three apartments; [**NC**3, **NY**2, Tenement house;] (Qu. D23, *A house that is divided in two through the middle so that two families can live in it*) Infs **CT**32, **ME**5, **MA**6, 24, 37, 42, 68, 74, 98, **NH**14, **RI**5, **VT**16, Two-tenement (house); [**ME**15, **MO**27, **NJ**1, **VA**72, Double tenement; **GA**15, **MA**58, Tenement house;] (Qu. D26, . . *Different kinds of apartments*) Infs **IL**85, **MA**44, **NH**10, **OH**66, **PA**131, Tenement(s); [**MA**8, Tenement—three-family house; **MA**98, Tenement—small, run-down apartments]. **2005** *DARE* File **nwMA** (as of 1940s), My mother and father rented the tenement (a small apartment) that was attached to our house. Sometimes, when we were looking for something, we'd say, "Oh, it's out in the tenement."

tenent   See **tenon**

Tenesy   See **Tennessee**

tenet   See **tenon**

ten-gallon hat n   Also *ten-gallon sombrero*   [In humorous ref to its size, but prob based on (perh deliberate) mistranslation of Span *galón* galloon, gold or silver braid; see quot 1939.]   **orig chiefly West; now widely recognized**

A soft, wide-brimmed hat such as cowboys wear.

1920 in 1951 Morrison *Diary* 62 **ID**, A cow puncher with a bandanna around his neck, and wearing chaps, high boots, spurs and a ten-gallon hat, suddenly elevated himself to a standing position on the bar.   **1923** *Mexia Daily News* (TX) 3 Dec 1/7, "Ten gallon" hats are in prominence and every one is wearing clothes of a style in fashion forty or fifty years ago.   **1925** *Oakland Tribune* (CA) 4 June sec A 16/5, Tom Mix. . . paused in Los Angeles long enough to confer upon Mayor George E. Cryer a ten gallon sombrero of the type he used to crown various celebrated heads on his travels oversea.   **1929** *AmSp* 5.59 **NE** [Cattle country talk], His hat is still a "Stetson," regardless of "make." Sometimes one hears "sombrero" and "ten gallon" hat, if the hat is unusually large of crown and brim.   **c1937** in Lib. of Congress *Amer. Memory: WPA Life Hist.* (Internet) **TX** (as of 1879), I had a pair of boots about two months old and they still had the new on them. I had a ten gallon sombrero that I only used for dress purpose, so it was good too.   **c1938** *Ibid* **TX** (as of c1885), The scene is still vivid in my mind. I can see the cowboys with their ten-gallon hats, chaps, high-heel boots, spurs and a bandana around their necks, riding at the side of the herd.   [**1939** *AmSp* 14.201 **SW**, The word 'gallon' had no reference to size at one time; it simply served to describe the braid with which a vaquero's hat was trimmed, and instead of being 'gallon' it should have been 'galloon.' The Mexican vaquero and charro still speaks of his *sombrero galón* or his *galón y toquilla.*]   **1941** Writers' Program *Guide WY* 465, *Ten-gallon hat*—Designation of type of headgear originated by a Cheyenne merchant.   **2005** *DARE* File—Internet **cMA**, A country-western benefit dance and potluck supper will be held at the Social Hall on Sunday. . . Don't forget to wear your ten gallon hat and cowboy boots!

t'engk(ful)   See **thank** v¹, n

ten(g)ky   See **thanky**

ten-holer n   Cf **hole** n **4, holey** n, **rolly-holey**

A marble game; see quot.

1961 Sackett-Koch *KS Folkl.* 222, *Ten-holer.* . . players take turns shooting. As each player reaches the fifth hole, he turns around and retraces his path.

tenion(ing)   See **tenon**

tenner n   chiefly **wPA, Gt Lakes**
=**tennis shoe.**

1932 *Ironwood Daily–Globe* (MI) 16 Sept 6/1, [Advt:] 80 Pairs Boys' Tenners $1.00 value 48¢.   **1965** *Manitowoc Herald–Times* (WI) 2 Aug sec 2 12/1, [Advt:] $2—Women's and children's tenners—$3—Men's

and boys' basketball tenners.   **1967** *DARE* (Qu. W8, *Names and nicknames for low canvas-top shoes with rubber soles*) Inf **MN**2, Tenners.   **1980** *DARE* File **Duluth MN,** *Tenners*—tennis shoes.   **1993** *Valley Independent* (Monessen PA) 13 July sec A 7/1, [Advt:] Women's, Men's & Children's Tenners 20%–50% off.   **2003** in 2005 *DARE* File—Internet **nwMI** (as of 1960s), I started thinking about some words . . unique to the Ironwood area. . . When I went to school below the bridge (the land of the Trolls) I was in for a surprise. . . "What are Tenners?" they asked. How uninformed those Trolls were.   **2004** *Ibid* **NC,** Last shoes worn: new balance tenners.   *Ibid* **PA,** Pittsburg [sic]: Tenors (maybe they spell it tenners?) Took me about 30 minutes to figure out what my college roommate (from Pittsburg) was talking about: sneakers!

Tennessee n   Usu |ˌtɛnəˈsi|; also **chiefly Sth, S Midl** |ˌtɪnəˈsi, ˈtɛnəˌsi, ˈtɪn-| Pronc-spp *Tenesy, Tennes(s)y*   For addit pronc and sp varr see **A** below   Cf Pronc Intro 3.I.4.a, Intro "Language Changes" IV.2

A   Std sense, var forms.

1827 in 1938 *AmSp* 13.263, Tennessee & Michigan . . are Indian names, &, by Indians, are accented on the last syllable. . . and altho' the names of the waters are chiefly retained, the accent is changed.   **1829** *Ibid* 264, Tennessee is accented on the last syllable, but with a strong disposition to throw the accent back to the first. Ten′ne-sy is not an unusual sound.   **1841** in 1934 *AmSp* 9.262 **eTN**, Tennyseeans (Tennesseans). *Tenesee* and *Tennessee* also occur. The interest with this word lies in the tendency to throw the accent on the first syllable, a current pronunciation in the state.   **1883** Zeigler–Grosscup *Heart of Alleghanies* 259 **wNC**, "Tenesy," answered the man, giving the accent on the first syllable, a pronunciation peculiar to the uneducated natives.   **1891** *Century Illustr. Mag.* 41.565 **GA** [Black], It went on dis away plumb till we got ter de Tennyssy River.   **1895** *DN* 1.375 **seKY, eTN, wNC,** *Ténnessee.*   **1903** *DN* 2.333 **seMO,** *Tennyssy.* . . Tennessee, with accent on first syllable.   **1933** *AmSp* 8.4.59 **Delmarva,** I heard only two examples of the common substitution of [ɪ] for [ɛ] in *Tennessee* [tɪnɪsi], *pen,* etc.   **1936** *AmSp* 11.345 **eTX,** [ˈtɪnɪˌsiː].   **1939** *LANE* Map 16 **NEng,** In *Tennessee* the primary stress normally falls on the final syllable, with or without a secondary stress on the first syllable. In emphatic or deliberate utterance, level stress is common. Primary stress on the first syllable, with or without a secondary stress on the third, was recorded [from 21 scattered infs].   **1942** Hall *Smoky Mt. Speech* 55 **wNC, eTN,** *Tennessee,* usually now [ˌtɛnəˈsi], but the older [ˈtɪnəˌsi] is still fairly common.   **1966** *Wilson Coll.* **csKY,** *Tennessee,* among older people in southern Kentucky and northern Tennessee, is often [ˈtɪnəˌsi]. Five generations of my family lived there and called it thus.   **1989** Pederson *LAGS Tech. Index* 321 **Gulf Region,** [In *Tennessee,* 545 infs had the vowel [ɛ] in the first syllable and 308 [ɪ]; 480 accented the last syllable (occasionally with a secondary accent on the first), and 374 accented the first syllable (occasionally with a secondary accent on the first).]

B   Senses.

1   also *Tennessee nine:* A marble game; see quots.

1957 *Sat. Eve. Post Letters* **cwKY** (as of 1930s), "Tennessee" was played on a rectangular ring about six by four feet divided crosswise and lengthwise and surrounded by a larger rectangle leaving an eighteen inch border. Marbles could be "daked" only at the intersections, and all shots were made from the border line. It was usually played for "funs."   **1969–70** *DARE* (Qu. EE7, . . *Kinds of marble games*) Inf **GA**74, Tennessee nine; **1970** *DARE* Tape **TX**99, Tennessee is one of them [=marble games]. And it was played with nine big marbles and draw a square on the ground and put one marble in each corner and one between and one in the center. And then the players would shoot at these marbles, and the one got the most marbles out won the game.

2   =**lemonade.**   Cf **New Orleans B, New York B2**

1968 *DARE* (Qu. EE33, . . *Outdoor games . . that children play*) Inf **PA**133, Tennessee—"Here we come." "Where ya from?" "Tennessee." "What's your trade?" "Lemonade." "Give us some if you're not afraid." (Then a charade.)

Tennessee banana n

The fruit of a **pawpaw** n¹ (here: *Asimina triloba*).

1967 *DARE* (Qu. I46, . . *Kinds of fruits that grow wild around here*) Inf **TN**11, Tennessee bananas—nickname for pawpaw.

Tennessee chicken n   Cf **Arkansas chicken, Cincinnati B1, Georgia chicken**

Used as a joc or euphem term for some meat other than chicken, esp salt pork.

1966 *DARE* (Qu. H38, . . *Words for bacon [including joking ones]*)

Inf **GA**11, Tennessee chicken. **1972** *Atlanta Letters* **cGA,** *Tennessee chicken*—Slices of salt pork containing much lean meat, floured or battered and fried; usually served with milk gravy. **2002** *DARE* File **cOH,** "Tennessee chicken" is basically pet rabbits (or 4H projects raising rabbits) which are served for dinner. When children ask what they're eating for dinner, they're told it's chicken. When they remark that it doesn't taste like chicken, the explanation is that it's "Tennessee chicken."

Tennessee nine   See **Tennessee B1**

Tennes(s)y   See **Tennessee**

tennie n   Also sp *tenny*   **scattered, but chiefly wGt Lakes, IA, West exc NW**   See Map
=**tennis shoe.**

   1920 *Appleton Post–Crescent* (WI) 5 Apr 12/7, [Advt:] Boys' and Girls' Tennies—79c and 98c. **1942** Perry *Texas* 139, Tennis shoes are frequently "tennies." **1954** *WELS Suppl.* **seWI,** Tennys, Sneakers, gymshoes. We hear all three. **1959** *Lincoln Eve. Jrl. & NE State Jrl.* (NE) 10 June 10/7, [Advt:] For Everywhere You Go—*Tennies*—Everything You Do—$2⁹⁹. **1965–70** *DARE* (Qu. W8, *Names and nicknames for low canvas-top shoes with rubber soles*) 40 Infs, **scattered, but chiefly wGt Lakes, IA, West exc NW,** Tennies. [18 Infs young; 4 Infs noted that "kids" use this term.] **1969** *DARE* FW Addit **ceCA,** I heard a teenager say *tennies* (for tennis shoes). **1970** *NV State Jrl.* (Reno) 7 June 22/1, [Advt:] Hop on Down for P.F. Flyer *Tennies*—All Styles Lots of Colors. **1980** *N. Hills News Rec.* (Allison Park PA) 16 May sec A 4/2, On the first day of vacation, we would put our good shoes away and go barefoot or switch to tennies. **1986** [see **tennis shoe**]. **1990** *Mt. Democrat & Placerville Times* (CA) 28 Mar sec A 7/1, Setting a goal gives you a kick in the rump to crawl out of bed and lace on the tennies. **2005** *DARE* File—Internet **WI,** It wasn't until I went out to Wisconsin . . that I heard sneakers called tennies. They all snickered at my calling them "sneakers" of course. . . Them: "What are you going to do in them . . sneak around?" Me: "Well, I'm certainly not playing tennis in them, am I?"

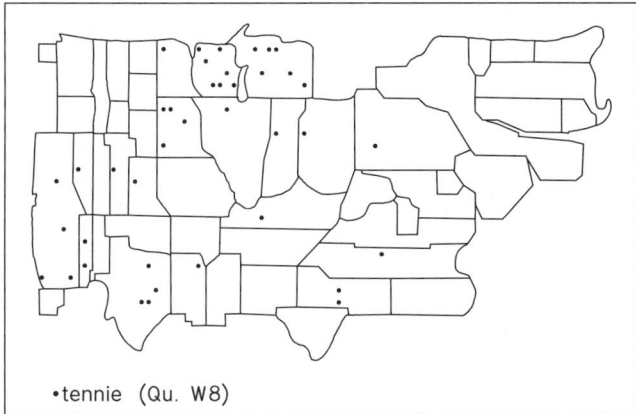
•tennie (Qu. W8)

tennie-pump n   Also sp *tenny-pump*   **chiefly Sth**
=**tennis shoe.**

   1966–67 *DARE* (Qu. W8, *Names and nicknames for low canvas-top shoes with rubber soles*) Infs **AR**52, **FL**28, **GA**11, Tennie-pumps. **1970** *DARE* File **AR, MO,** *Tennie pumps* = sneakers, tennis shoes. Very popular a few years ago. **1972** *Daily Times–News* (Burlington NC) 1 June sec C 11/3, [Advt:] *Infant's canvas tennis shoes*—Tenny-Pumps for Tots! **2003** in 2005 *DARE* File—Internet **neFL,** I once had a load of 6,000 Converse high tops stolen off my yard. Feds found the culprits in 3 days, dancing around a bonfire in the woods, a mountain of tennypumps nearby. **2004** *Ibid* **VA,** Tenny-pumps for wide feet. *Ibid* **cTX,** They were always tennis shoes when I was a kid. . . Now I refer to mine as tennie-pumps. *Ibid* **cNC,** So, shake off the snow, put on your "tennie-pumps" and get going!

tennie-runner n   Also sp *tenny-runner*   **scattered, but chiefly West, esp NW**
=**tennis shoe.**

   1965 *Tri-City Herald* (Pasco WA) 18 July 18, [Advt:] Womens—white & black Tennie runners. **1966–67** *DARE* (Qu. W8, *Names and nicknames for low canvas-top shoes with rubber soles*) Infs **MT**1, **WA**22, 33, Tennie-runners. **1972** *Sun. Jrl. & Star* (Lincoln NE) 10 Dec sec F 12/7, [Personal advt:] Ed—Washed your tennie runners lately? **1975**

AmSp 50.67 **AR** (as of c1970), *Tenny runners*. . . Tennis shoes or similar canvas shoes with rubber soles. **1999** *DARE* File **swID** (as of 1960s), My Idaho relatives (teenagers) called tennis shoes "tennie runners." **2001** *DARE* File—Internet **cOR,** Tennis shoes is marginally acceptable but most of my friends called them tenny-runners when I was a teen. **2002** in 2005 *Ibid* **sUT,** I left myself an "out" in the form of some "tennie-runners" stashed in the pickup from then on! **2004** *Ibid* **WA,** My wife calls athletic shoes tenny runners or tennis shoes. **2005** *Ibid* **WI,** An updated list of Wisconsinisms. . . *Tennies or Tenny-runners:* Known to the rest of the world as tennis shoes or sneakers. *Ibid* **cTX,** *Dallas Slanguage.* . . *Tenny Runners*—A pair of athletic shoes. **2006** *DARE* File **nwPA,** Tennie runners: sneakers, tennies.

tennie shoe   See **tennis shoe**

tennis n   Pl usu *tennises*; also, *esp freq among Black speakers,* *tennis* [For *tennis* appar as pl cf **joist 2, post** n **2b**]   **chiefly Sth**   See Map
=**tennis shoe.**

   1941 Faulkner *Men Working* 22 **MS,** Her feet were . . encased in low tennis shoes—"tennises" she called them. **1965–70** *DARE* (Qu. W8, *Names and nicknames for low canvas-top shoes with rubber soles*) 12 Infs, **chiefly Sth,** Tennises; SC55, Pair of tennis [Inf Black]. **1981** Pederson *LAGS Basic Materials* (*Shoes;* this question was asked chiefly in urban areas) 5 infs, **seFL, seLA, nwMS, swTN,** Tennis [*DARE* Ed: In all these cases, other resps were plural.]; 1 inf, **swAL,** Tennis shoes— just tennis used by blacks; 2 infs, **cnGA, neFL,** Tennises. [7 of 8 infs Black] **2005** *DARE* File—Internet **sLA, eTX** [Black], He looks so good in his shirt and khaki's with my favorite pair of tennis on his feet. *Ibid* **GA,** It's rather unnerving to cross 4 lanes of traffic . . especially when . . you are toting 9 sets of tennises in your hands! *Ibid* **neFL,** *Jacksonville Slanguage.* . . *Tennises*—Any type of athletic shoes.

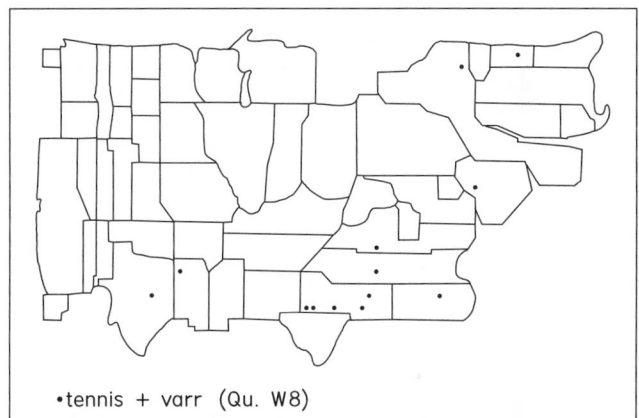
•tennis + varr (Qu. W8)

tennis flannel n   Also *lawn-tennis flannel*   **chiefly Nth, N Midl**

A type of cotton flannel.

   1884 *NY Times* (NY) 20 Apr 16, [Advt:] *Housekeeping* and *White Goods.* . . Lawn-tennis Flannels . . at Twenty-seven cents are the identical quality sold elsewhere at fifty. **1890** *Atlanta Constitution* (GA) 27 July 9/1, [Advt:] *Ladies' Blazers.* . . Those made of Cream Yachting Flannel are particularly pretty; also the Striped French and Tennis Flannel. **1892** *Daily Northwestern* (Oshkosh WI) [20 May 3]/6 (newspaperarchive.com), [Advt:] Good Grade Tennis Flannel Shirts. **1893** *Century Illustr. Mag.* 46.142 **NEast,** Rosina wore another very "knowing" jacket that day. It was of tennis flannel, and the stripes ran over the roundness of her figure in a complication of wondrous curves. **1924** Aldrich *Mother Mason* 4 **NE,** The long figure . . stretched out in its black-and-white-checked tennis-flannel nightgown. **1930** *Oakland Tribune* (CA) 29 Sept sec B 11/4, [Advt:] 'Wade' Tennis Flannel—1250 yards. Neat, clean-looking, striped designs in various colors. **1958** *WELS Suppl.* **wIA,** My mother always used the term, tennis flannel, and I had trouble in later years learning to use "cotton flannel" instead. . . My mother . . grew up near Coshocton, Ohio. *Ibid* **swWI,** 'Tennis flannel' was a common term when I was a child 40 years ago. It is now termed 'outing flannel'. *Ibid* **IA,** At Iowa State College . . outing flannel [was considered] inferior, nap on only one side; tennis flannel [was considered] better quality, nap on both sides. **1969** *Chron.-Telegram* (Elyria OH) [28 Sept 21]/3 (newspaperarchive.com), [Advt:] Bleached white 100% cotton tennis flannel sheet blankets.

tennis shoe n Also *tennie shoe, tenny* ~ **widespread, but less freq NEast** See Map Also called **easy walker, quick start, sneak** n, **sneaker 1, tenner, tennie, ~-pump, ~-runner, tennis**

A rubber-soled shoe, usu with a low canvas upper; an athletic shoe.

1879 *Mt. Democrat* (Placerville CA) [19 July 6]/6 (newspaper-archive.com), [From *N.Y. Home Journal:*] There is little that is new in archery and lawn-tennis shoes. . . [T]he ordinary kind have morocco or common leather tops, are laced or tied with ribbon, and are made with the corrugated India-rubber soles. **1883** *Trenton Times* (NJ) 26 July 7/3, *The Foibles of Fashion.* . . Tennis shoes are fastened by bows of colored ribbon. **1920** *Lancaster Daily Eagle* (OH) 11 May 2/2, A hike about the surrounding country, clothed in sport costumes of middies, bloomers and tennis shoes, added pleasure to the morning adventure. **1942** *Fitchburg Sentinel* (MA) 20 Aug 5/6, [Advt:] Men's, Women's and Children's *Sneakers*—Sturdy Tennis Shoes For Everyone In the Family! **1956** *Reno Eve. Gaz.* (NV) 20 Nov 2/1, Those wearing tennis shoes will not be permitted to rent skates. **1959** *Appleton Post-Crescent* (WI) 7 July sec A 13/6, [Advt:] While they last—Ladies' *White Tennie Shoes.* **1965–70** *DARE* (Qu. W8, *Names and nicknames for low canvas-top shoes with rubber soles*) 470 Infs, **widespread, but less freq NEast,** Tennis shoes; OK20, Tennie shoes. **1986** *AmSp* 61.367, The 110 informants . . were asked: "What do you call the things I'm wearing on my feet?" They were an ordinary pair of rubber-soled, canvas-topped, low-cut, white gym shoes. . . In the Northeast, *sneakers* or *sneaks* was the first response of forty-seven informants. In addition, *tennis shoes* was never considered a synonym in this area, but was defined as a shoe designed specifically for the game of tennis. . . Where *tennis shoes* was the first response (with its diminutive, *tennies*), nine informants indicated that they could use *sneakers* as a synonym, but the remaining fifty-four said they would rarely if ever use the word. . . In the region where the boundary occurs, the following localities fall in the *tennis shoe* area: southern Virginia; Cumberland, Maryland; Wheeling and Charleston, West Virginia; Steubenville, Ohio; and Pittsburgh, Pennsylvania. All of New York State is part of the *sneakers* region, together with eastern Pennsylvania (as far west as York), Baltimore, and Washington with its Maryland suburbs. My four informants for the Cleveland area were divided. **2005** *DARE* File—Internet **MI,** *You Know You're From Michigan When.* . . All your shoes are called "tennis shoes", even though no one here plays tennis anyway. *Ibid* **IA,** Mine are Reeboks, his are Nikes. . . But for me they are "tennis shoes." . . While I do play tennis, I would never wear the Reeboks that I wear for everyday out on the tennis court. . . It comes purely from my Midwestern dialect. Never did I hear anyone at home refer to their Nikes as sneakers, gym shoes, or trainers. They were always "tennis shoes," even if they wore them to play basketball. *Ibid* **TX,** *Tenny Shoes*—Any athletic shoe. (*Never* sneakers).

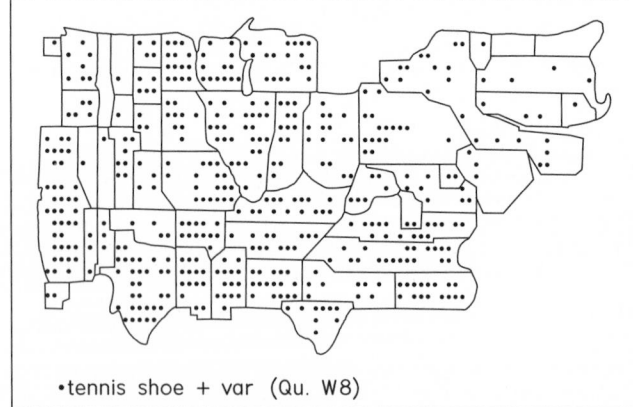

•tennis shoe + var (Qu. W8)

tenny See **tennie**

tenny-pump See **tennie-pump**

tenny-runner See **tennie-runner**

tenny shoe See **tennis shoe**

tenon n Also *tenant, tendon, tene(n)t, tenion* Similarly vbl n *tenioning* [*tenant, -ent* represents an old and once common variant (*OED2* 1549 →); other varr appear to be due to var phonological and folk-etymological influences.]

Std senses, var forms.

1658 in 1922 *Archives of MD* 41.114, One Cros-saw, one Tenant saw, one whip-saw. **1717** in 2005 *DARE* File—Internet **CT,** A Small Cross cut Saw 4/ tenant saw 9/ A square 2/6. **1818** Fessenden *Ladies Monitor* 172 **NEng,** Provincial words . . to be avoided. . . *tenant* for tenon. **1858** in 2005 *DARE* File—Internet **seIN,** 1 tenant saw, keyhole saw. **1899** (1912) Green *VA Folk-Speech* 442, Tenants, *n. pl.* For *tenons.* **1926** *Gettysburg Times* (PA) 12 Mar 5/2, Meat saw; hand saw; tenet saw. **1947** *News* (Frederick MD) 12 Sept 11/6, Compass saw, tenant saw, ice saw. **1967** *DARE* FW Addit **neCO,** Tenoning ['tɛnjənɪn] *plane*—used to pare down the rim-insert end of a spoke for a wagon. **1968** *DARE* (Qu. M1, . . *Kinds of barns . . according to their use or the way they are built*) Inf **NY96,** Mortise-and-tenet ['tɪˣnɪt] barn—made with heavy beams; **NY211,** Tendon-and-pin barn—that's how they're held together. **1970** *DARE* Tape **KY84,** Those ends on the spoke that go through the rim are called tenants ['tɛnnts]. **2003** in 2005 *DARE* File—Internet **WA,** It is way eaiser [sic] to fit a tenion to a mortise than to fit each mortise to tenions. . . After mounting the tenioning jig on the SMT make sure that your tenion jig's fence is 90 degrees to the table surface. **2005** *Ibid* **OR,** The building has mortise and tendon joints and stands three stories tall. *Ibid* **MO,** Sawing the bones off with Joe Hogans tenent saw. *Ibid* **MA,** Timbers are locked by crossing and bracing each other along with mortise and tenion technique.

ten-pounder n

1 A fish of the genus *Elops:* usu *Elops saurus* of Atlantic waters, but also *E. affinis* of Pacific waters. [*OED2* 1699 → for *Elops saurus*] For other names of the former see **bonefish 3, bonyfish 2, ghostfish b, horse mackerel 7, Jack Mariddle, John Mariggle 1, ladyfish 3, liza** n[2] **2, skipjack 1j, tourist tarpon 2;** for other names of the latter see **machete 2**

1884 Goode *Fisheries U.S.* 1.611, The "Big-eyed Herring" or "Ten-pounder", *Elops saurus,* . . occurs all along the coast from Martha's Vineyard southward, but only in the summer in the northern part of its range. . . It is rarely or never eaten in the United States, its flesh being said to be dry and bony. **1915** *Copeia* 25.59 **NY,** The Big-eyed Herring or Ten-Pounder. . . is one of the most primitive of all the . . Teleost fishes. **1955** Carr–Goin *Guide Reptiles* 40, *Elops saurus* . . Ten Pounder. . . A silvery streamlined fish with a deeply forked tail. **1957** Blair et al. *Vertebrates U.S.* 57, *Elops saurus.* . . Atlantic tenpounder. Maximum size 90 cm. . . Enters the mouths of rivers. *Elops affinis.* . . Pacific tenpounder. Known as far up the Colorado River as Laguna Dam, Arizona, and California. **1973** Knight *Cook's Fish Guide* 392, Tenpounder—Ladyfish [=*Elops saurus* and *Albula vulpes*] or see Machete [=*Elops affinis*].

2 A **bonefish 1** (here: *Albula vulpes*).

1935 Caine *Game Fish* 50 **Sth,** Bonefish—*Albula vulpes.* . . Silver Flash, Skipjack, Ten Pounder. . . Shallow banks or bars and mud flats where the water is not over two feet deep. **1973** [see **1** above].

ten step(s) n Cf **stealing steps**

A children's game combining elements of **red light 1** and **I spy** n **1;** see quots.

1909 (1923) Bancroft *Games* 193, Ten Steps—This is a game of hide and seek. . . The distinctive feature of this game is the peculiar limitation put on the opportunity to hide. . . The one who is It . . blinds his eyes and counts to ten while the other players run for hiding places. As soon as the one who is blinding says "Ten!" the players must all stand motionless. . . Any player whom he sees moving must come back to the goal and start over again. The hunter repeats this five times, and any player not entirely out of sight the fifth time the hunter turns must change places with him. . . Having called "Ten!" . . five times, the hunter (or the one taking his place . .) counts one hundred, to give the players time to reach final hiding places, and the game proceeds as in regular I Spy. **1916** in 1969 Frost *Poetry* 114 **NEng,** And your woods / To northward from your window at the sink,/ Waiting to steal a step on us whenever / We drop our eyes or turn to other things,/ As in the game 'ten-step' the children play. **1957** *Sat. Eve. Post Letters* se**WA** (as of 1905–12), *Names of children's games*— . . hop scotch—ten steps—crack-the-whip—hide-and-seek. **1966** *DARE* File **IN,** Ten steps—a type of children's game. **1968** *DARE* (Qu. EE16, *Hiding games that start with a special, elaborate method of sending the players out to hide*) Inf **MN37,** Ten step—blindfolded, object to get as far away as you could without getting caught moving; (Qu. EE33, . . *Outdoor games . . that children play*) Inf **MN37,** Ten step—"it" counts, those caught moving had to stop and go back.

tent caterpillar n Also *tent moth caterpillar, tent worm* [From the tent-like web] **chiefly Nth, N Midl, esp NEast** See Map
A moth larva of the genus *Malacosoma*. Also called **umbrella caterpillar**.
    1837 *Farmers' Cabinet* 1.274, The tent caterpillar . . infests our fruit trees. **1852** Harris *Treatise Insects* 291 **NEng,** *Clisiocampa silvatica,* the tent-caterpillar of the forest. . . lives in communities of three or four hundred individuals under a common web or tent, which is made against the trunk or beneath some of the principal branches of the tree. **1862** *Atlantic Mth.* 10.514 **NEng,** Many . . welcomed the apple-tree to these shores. The tent-caterpillar saddled her eggs on the very first twig that was formed. **1870** *MO State Entomol. Annual Rept.* 7, The Tent Caterpillar *(Clisiocampa Americana)* was more abundant than usual in our orchards, and the Tent Caterpillar of the Forest *(Clisiocampa sylvatica)* also appeared in great numbers both on our orchard and forest trees. **1894** *New Engl. Mag.* 16.60, One third of the apple-trees of Central New York were ruined within the last five years by the tent caterpillar. **1948** Beston *N. Farm* 184 **cME coast,** Autumn tent-caterpillars spinning their destructive webs on various old apple trees. **1965–70** *DARE* (Qu. R27, . . *Kinds of caterpillars or similar worms*) 102 Infs, **chiefly Nth, N Midl, esp NEast,** Tent caterpillar; **ID**1, **KY**65, **NY**28, 88, **OH**47, **TX**33, Tent worm; **NJ**16, Tent capillar; **NJ**39, Tent cat; **KY**94, Tent catepillar; **GA**80, Tent moth caterpillar. **1996** in 2001 *DARE* File—Internet **wWA,** An effective way to control tent caterpillars is to remove their egg cases from trees.

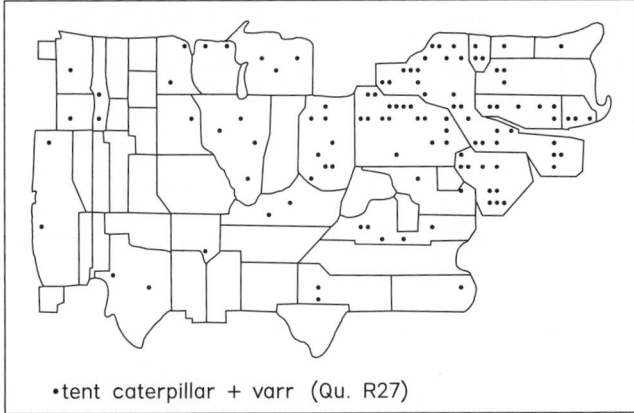

•tent caterpillar + varr (Qu. R27)

tenth month See **first month**

tent moth caterpillar See **tent caterpillar**

ten-toed squash n Also *ten-toes*
    =pattypan squash.
    c1960 *Wilson Coll.* **csKY,** Ten-toed squash—the pattypan type. **1969–70** *DARE* (Qu. I23, . . *Kinds of squash*) Inf **KY**77, Ten-toed squash; **KY**5, Ten-toes—white.

‡**ten-to-two** adv
    ?With one's toes pointed out (as to the numerals on a clock).
    1970 *DARE* (Qu. X37, . . *Words . . to describe people's legs if they're noticeably bent, or uneven, or not right*) Inf **TN**65, He walks ten-to-two.

tent worm See **tent caterpillar**

tepary (bean) n Also *tépari*
A bean *(Phaseolus acutifolius)* native to the southwestern US.
    [**1716** Velarde *Relacion* (1926) 309 *(DA),* Los demás frutos de esta Pimería son maíz, frijol pequeño, llamado *tepari* y otras semillas. [=The rest of the produce of this Pima country are maize, little bean, called *tepari,* and other seeds.]] **1912** *AZ Ag. Exper. Sta. Bulletin* 68.582, The name tepary or tepari (Spanish) originated from the Papago words 'state päve,' 'state' meaning white and 'päve' having reference to the kind of plant to distinguish it from the 'mon' or bean. **1912** Lumholtz *New Trails* 318 **AZ,** He had cooked bones of mountain-sheep with tépari beans for us. **1925** Bryan *Papago Country* 354, The beans known as tépari . . are said to be so resistant to drought that the plants may wither three successive times and then, if enough rain comes, mature a crop. **1942** Castetter–Bell *Pima & Papago Ag.* 92, The cultivated tepary bean antedates the coming of white man in the Southwest. *Ibid* 191, The Papago made only one planting of teparies. **1970** Correll *Plants TX* 888, *Phaseolus acutifolius.* . . Tepary bean. . . Tex., N.M., and Ariz.

2003 *DARE* File—Internet **sAZ,** English Name: *Tepary Beans*—Spanish Name: *Frijol Tepari*—O'odham [=Pima/Papago] Name: *Bavi*—Comcaac [=Seri] Name: *aap. Teepar.* . . Wild teparies were still harvested by the Comcaac and O'odham until World War II. They are one of the best legumes for growing in desert areas, because of their superlative resistance to drought, heat and saline soils.

tepin n [Var of *chilitepin(o), chiltapin* (at **chilipitin**)]
A small hot pepper *(Capsicum annuum* var *aviculare).*
    1967–68 *DARE* (Qu. I22a, . . *Peppers—small hot*) Inf **AZ**8, Red devils, tepini [sic]. **1985** Dent *Feast Santa Fe* 67 **NM,** The hottest among the numerous other dried chilies are the tiny ones. Some are round and the size of peas; others are tapered and thin, miniature versions of large red chilies. As far as Spanish labeling goes, the words *"tepín"* and *"pequín"* appear most frequently on the rounded sort, while the skinniest long ones are called Japanese chiles *(japónes),* or are simply packaged as "hot red chile." **1996** *DARE* File **Madison WI,** [From a list of pepper plants sold at the farmers' market:] *Tepin* . . Fruits are extremely hot. Prolific. **2001** *DARE* File—Internet **CA,** *Capsicum annuum v. aviculare* . . Small round fruit ¼″ across. . . *[T]he tiny Tepín.* . . is five times hotter than the Habanero.

tepopote n [MexSpan < Nahuatl] Cf **popotillo**
    =Mormon tea 1.
    1883 *NC Med. Jrl.* 1 np, *Ephedra antisyphilitica.* . . (Tepopote, Teamster's Tea.) **1937** U.S. Forest Serv. *Range Plant Hdbk.* B73, Jointfir . . is rather descriptive, but as yet only limitedly employed in the range country. . . Local names include Brigham-tea, . . teamsters-tea, and tepopote. **1947** (1976) Curtin *Healing Herbs* 49, *Ephedra torreyana.* . . Tepopote. **1976** Elmore *Shrubs & Trees SW* 92, *Ephedra torreyana.* . . Tepopote [Elmore: little straw]. . . The jointed stems of this ephedra are olive green. **1985** Dodge *Flowers SW Deserts* 70, Mormon-Tea, . . Teposote [sic]. . . *Ephedra trifurca.* . . *Ephedra californica.* . . The harsh, stringy stems . . , when dried, were used with the flowers in making a palatable brew, particularly by the Utah pioneers.

teppentime See **turpentine** n, v

(-)ter prep, adv See **to** prep, adv **A2**

t'er See **tother**

ter See **titty** n¹

terbaccer, terbacker, terbakker, terbarker See **tobacco** n **A1**

terble See **terrible**

tereckly See **directly**

terf See **turf**

tergarruh, tergeer, tergerrer, tergether See **together**

terlet See **toilet 1**

termarter See **tomato A2**

termartusses See **tomato B1**

termater See **tomato A1**

termatter See **tomato A3**

termattusses See **tomato B1**

termenjous See **tremendous**

termerack See **tamarack**

termination dust n **AK**
See quot 1965.
    1957 *Anchorage Daily News* (AK) 30 Oct 4 (Tabbert *Dict. Alaskan Engl.*), Termination dust is due / Almost sled dog racing time. **1965** Bowen *Alaskan Dict.* 32, Termination dust. The first snow, which marks the end of the construction season and the termination of the job. **1999** *Anchorage Daily News* (AK) 8 Sept (Internet), [Caption:] A threesome fishes Cheney Lake recently as termination dust on Ptarmigan Peak hints at the coming of fall. **2005** *DARE* File—Internet **cAK,** By the way the termination dust is here. Was looking at it behind the house while running the snowmachine. Come on snow.

tern n
Std: any of var sea birds of the genus *Sterna* or of related genera. Also called **gull, ~ hunter, gullie, mackerel gull 2, pigeon de mer 1, sea swallow, striker 1;** for other names of var of these see **bass gull, black tern, gannet striker, gull-billed**

tern, Lake Erie gull, least tern, medrick, redbill 1, redshank 1, royal tern, Spanish gull, summer ~ 1, tearr, tide gull, wide-awake

terrace n Also *parking terrace* **chiefly Gt Lakes, Upper Missip Valley** See Map
=**tree lawn.**

1891 *Daily Northwestern* (Oshkosh WI) 10 Sept [4]/3 (newspaperarchive.com), One thing to be decided is the width of the terrace between the sidewalk and the pavement. **1928** *Appleton Post–Crescent* (WI) 27 Apr 4/2, All rubbish . . should b [sic] placed on the terrace so that it can be collected Tuesday. **1946** *Dixon Eve. Telegraph* (IL) 1 Aug 8/1, Papers securely tied in bundles should be placed on the terrace or in case of rain on the porch. **1950** *WELS Suppl.* **csWI,** "Terrace" is the only name I have ever heard for the space between the sidewalk and the street. **1965–70** *DARE* (Qu. N44, *In a town, the strip of grass and trees between the sidewalk and the curb*) 13 Infs, **chiefly Gt Lakes, Upper Missip Valley,** Terrace; **MO26,** Parking terrace. **1979** Stegner *Recapitulation* 6 **Salt Lake City UT,** The terrace rolled down with an unfamiliar smooth nap of grass. **1993** *DARE* File **MI,** In Iowa the strip of ground between the sidewalk & street is called "the parking". My Michigan husband calls it "the terrace". **2005** *Ibid* **KS,** [Brochure from Arkansas City KS Building, Planning, and Codes Office:] Free pickup and disposal of storm damaged tree limbs placed on the terrace *within 7 days of the storm*. **2009** *Isthmus* (Madison WI) 2 Oct 11/1, There are an estimated 300,000 city-owned trees within the city, with about 100,000 of those found on terraces, the strip of green between sidewalks and streets.

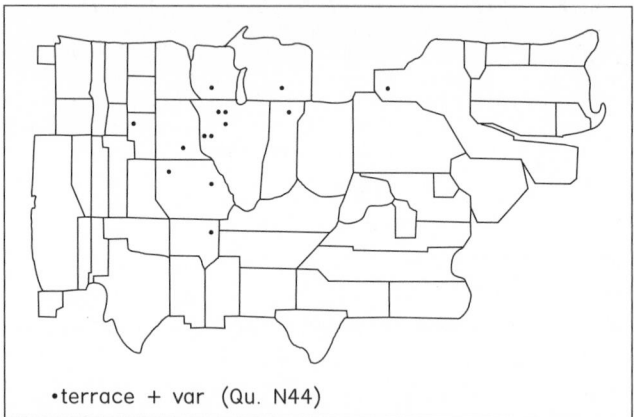

•terrace + var (Qu. N44)

terrapin n, v Usu |ˈtɛrəpɪn, ˈtær-| Pronc-spp *tar(r)apin, tarrypin, tarp(i)n, tarpon, tairpin, terrypin, turpin;* for addit pronc and sp varr see **A** below [Algonquian] Cf **torup**
A Forms.

1672 [see **B1** below]. **1705** Beverley *Hist. VA* 3.14, Their Food is Fish and Flesh of all sorts, and that which participates of both; as . . a small kind of Turtle, or *Tarapins.* **1709** (1967) Lawson *New Voyage* 138 **NC, SC,** The Land-Terebin is of several Sizes, but generally Round-Mouth'd, and not Hawks-Bill'd. **c1738** [see **B1** below]. **1772** in 1916 Mereness *Travels* 517 **FL,** The women danced the Snake dance, the leader haveing her legs Covered with Turpin shells . . filled with small stones on purpose to make a noise. **1784** Smyth *Tour U.S.A.* 1.338 **KY,** These animals are called here *Tarapens.* **1807** (1935) Janson *Stranger in Amer.* 318 **S Atl,** The swamps produce a variety of what may be denominated land turtle. The natives call them loggerheads, tarapins [etc]. **1809** Ramsay *Hist. SC* 2.187, Of the shell fish kind, the soft shelled turtle, terrebin, cray fish. **1849** in 1938 *DN* 6.671 **NC,** His mouth was shut as fast as a highland tarrapin. **1893** Shands *MS Speech* 62, *Tarrypin* [ˈtærɪpɪn]. Negro for *terrapin.* **1903** *DN* 2.333 **seMO,** Terrapin. . . Pronounced tarrapin. **1905** *DN* 3.97 **nwAR,** To shut up like a tarrapin. **1909** *DN* 3.379 **eAL, wGA,** *Tarrapin.* **1915** *DN* 4.191 **swVA,** Terrapin [tɛəˈɪpɪn]. **1922** Gonzales *Black Border* 331 **sSC, GA coasts** [Gullah glossary], *Tarrypin.* **1931** *PMLA* 46.1315 **sAppalachians,** *E* . . often broad, as in: . . "tarpin" (terrapin), and "tairpin" is also heard. **1940** Richter *Trees* 25 **OH** (as of early 1800s), "Kain't ketch a terrypin!" she dared her and sailed off. **1965–70** *DARE* (Qu. P24) 72 Infs, **chiefly Sth, Midl, TX,** [Proncs of the types [ˈtɛrəpɪn, -ɪ-, -ɪ-, -pn̩, -pn̩]]; **AR**52, 55, **LA**18, **MD**24, **MS**1, **NC**49, [ˈtɛrpɪn, -pɪn, -pən]; **KY**28, 35, 76, 86, **VA**47, [ˈtɛɪrpɪn, -pɪn]; 60 Infs, **chiefly Sth, S Midl, TX, OK,** [Proncs of the types [ˈtærəpɪn, -ɪ-, -ɪ-, -pn̩, -pn̩]]; 15 Infs, **scattered Sth, S Midl,** [Proncs of the types [ˈtærpɪn, -pɪn, -pn̩, -pən]]; **FL**32, 35, **NC**21, 24,

[ˈtæripn̩]; **KY**9, [ˈtæɚipin]; 10 Infs, **esp S Midl,** [Proncs of the types [ˈturəpɪn, ta-, -ə-, -pn̩, -pən]]; 14 Infs, **esp S Midl,** [Proncs of the types [ˈturpɪn, -pn̩, -pɪn, -pən]]; **TN**22, [ˈturpɪn]; **TX**74, [ˈtɑrpən]; **IL**78, 85, [ˈteɪrəpɪn]; **IL**86, [ˈteɪrɑpɪn]; **MD**29, [tɛrəpn̩]; **AL**2, [tɛripɪn]; **FL**29, **IN**7, **TX**43, **VA**75, [tɝˈəpɪn, -pn̩]; **AL**17, **GA**7, **MO**16, **SC**7, [tɝˈpɪn, -pɪn]; **NC**44, [ˈtɔrpɪn]; **VA**1, [ˈtɔrpɪn]; **LA**7, [ˈtæːpn̩]; **PA**75, [ˈtɔrəˌpɛpn̩]; **MD**5, [ˈtɛrəfɪn]. **1967** Faries *Word Geog. MO* 129, There are a few write-in expressions . . : *tortoise, terrapin* (and the variant spellings *tarpin* and *tarpon*), and *turtle dog*. **1968** *DARE* FW Addit **DE,** Terrapin—[ˈtɔrpən], reported by old woman, Dover DE. **c1970** Pederson *Dial. Surv. Rural GA* **seGA** (*A creature with a very hard shell that lives in water*) [10 [of 64] infs offered proncs of the types [ˈtærəpɪn, -ɪ-]; 8 infs, proncs of the types [ˈtɛɚəpɪn, -ɪ-]; 2 infs, [ˈtæɚəpɪn(z)]; 1 inf, [ˈtæɚəpuⁿ]; 1 inf, [ˈtæ·pɪn]; 1 inf, [ˈtɛəˈpɪn]; 1 inf, [ˈtɛəpɪnz]; (*A similar creature that lives on land*) 9 infs offered proncs of the type [ˈtɛɚˈəpɪn]; 3 infs, [ˈtɛɚˈpɪn]; 1 inf, [ˈtæɚˈəpɪn]; 1 inf, [ˈtæɚpɪn, tæˈɪˈpɪⁿn, tɛˈɪrpn̩]; 1 inf, [ˈtɝˈpɪn]; 1 inf, [ˈtɛəˈpɪn]; 1 inf, [ˈtæɚpn̩]; 1 inf, [taˈəˈpɪ̃n, taˈpɪn].] **1983** *MJLF* 9.1.58 **ceKY** (as of 1956), *Tarpin.* **1996** [see **C** below].

B As noun.

1 Any of var turtles of fresh or brackish waters, some of which are edible, esp of the family Emydidae, but also of the families Chelydridae and Testudinidae. **chiefly Sth, Midl, TX** See Map

1672 Josselyn *New-Englands Rarities* 34, The *Turtle* that . . is called in *Virginia* a *Terrapine.* **c1738** (1929) Byrd *Histories* 278 **VA,** We catcht a large Tarapin in the River, which is one kind of Turtle. The flesh of it is wholesome, and good for Consumptive People. **1792** (1849) Darlington *Mem. John Bartram* 474, Of these [=tortoises], I have gathered the shells. . . I have the Snapper, Land Turtle . . , Terrapin. **1829** NY Acad. Sci. *Annals Lyceum Nat. Hist.* 3.115, The trivial name terrapin, which Schœpff has affixed to this species [=*Testudo centrata,* Dandin], is by no means appropriate, as the word is a generic term among us, and signifies land or fresh water tortoises as distinguished from marine, which it is well known are ridiculously enough called turtles. **1844** Uncle Sam *Peculiarities* 2.199 **NY,** The fowl and game (including terrapins, or land-tortoises), were in sufficient abundance. **1854** Wailes *Rept. on Ag. & Geol. MS* 327, Cistuda Carolina [=*Terrapene c.*] Terrapin. Cistuda Blandingi [=*Emydoidea b.*] Terrapin. **1894** *DN* 1.329 **NJ,** *Count:* terrapin six inches across belly, fit for market. **1921** U.S. Bur. Fisheries *Rept. for 1919* 7 app 12, Within the Mississippi Basin the word "terrapin" is either a book name or a commercial term applied by market men to such of the hard-shelled turtles as find their way into the trade. **c1938** in 1970 Hyatt *Hoodoo* 2.1494 **seGA,** Yo' take a terrapin, dese ole *box terrapins*—dere's diff'rent kinds, some call 'em de highland terrapin. **1945** McCauley *Reptiles MD & DC* 163, *Malaclemys centrata concentrica.* . . Diamondback terrapin, Salt-water terrapin, Terrapin, Diamondback. . . A moderately large turtle. **1965–70** *DARE* (Qu. P24, . . *Kinds of turtles*) 159 Infs, **chiefly Sth, Midl, TX,** Terrapin; 10 Infs, **scattered Sth, Midl,** Terrapin—on (dry) land (and varr); **CA**11, **KS**6, **LA**14, **OH**33, Terrapin—land turtle; **KY**24, 35, Terrapin—dryland turtle (*or* booger); **FL**35, Terrapin—highland turtle; **IN**27, Terrapin—land tortoise; **SC**3, Terrapin, turtle—both stay in and out of water; live on land much more than cooter; **GA**47, Terrapin = gopher; **FL**26, **IL**119, Terrapin = box (turtle); **FL**32, Alligator [turtle] or terrapin; **LA**31, Terrapin—gets about three or four inches long, stays in marsh; **SC**4, Terrapin—saltwater; **CA**23, Terrapin—a small one; **OK**15, Terra-

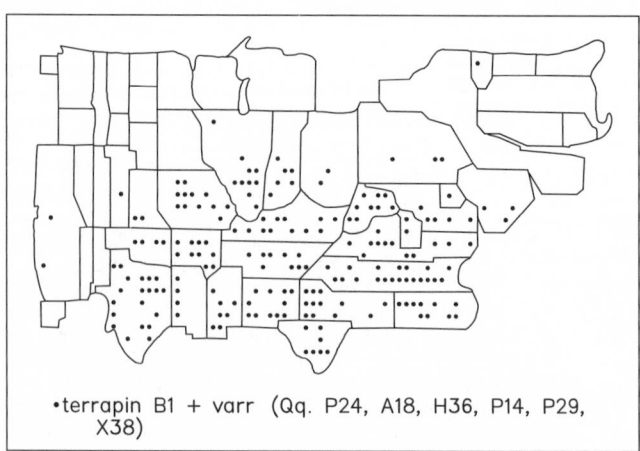

•terrapin B1 + varr (Qq. P24, A18, H36, P14, P29, X38)

pin—small, hard; **TX**9, Terrapin—smaller and flatter than turtle; **MO**8, **NC**49, Terrapin—not (a) turtle; **NC**87, Terrapin—don't eat; looks like a turtle, but isn't really; (Qu. A18, . . *A very slow person: "What's keeping him? He certainly is _____!"*) Infs **KY**36, 84, **VA**22, Slow as a terrapin; (Qu. H36, *Kinds of soup*) Inf **VA**48, Terrapin soup; (Qu. P14, . . *Commercial fishing . . what do the fishermen go out after?*) Inf **SC**34, Terrapin; (Qu. P29, . . *'Gophers' . . other name . . or what other animal are they most like*) Inf **FL**4, Terrapin; **FL**24, Terrapin—small gopher; **GA**84, A terrapin, in south Georgia; **NC**72, Gopher here = terrapin; (Qu. X38, *Joking names for unusually big or clumsy feet*) Inf **GA**77, Feet like a terrapin. **c1970** [see **A** above]. **1970** Tarpley *Blinky* 289 **neTX**, For 91% of the informants, the distinction between a *turtle* and a *terrapin* is that the former lives in water and the latter is chiefly a dry land animal with a high helmet-shaped shell, frequently seen crawling across a highway. **1989** Pederson *LAGS Tech. Index* 211 **Gulf Region**, *Turtle* [i.e., an aquatic testudinate] . . terrapin (42 [infs]). *Ibid* 212, *Terrapin* [i.e., a terrestrial testudinate] . . terrapin (458 [infs]).

2 A person considered to resemble a **terrapin B1** in some way.

1897 Lewis *Wolfville* 102 **AZ**, "Nacherally," says Enright, some sarcastic, "in makin' them schemes you ain't lookin' for no trouble whatever with a band of tarrapins like us." **1906** *DN* 3.160 **nwAR**, *Tarrapin*. . . Shrew. "She's a regular old tarrapin."

C As verb.

To hunt **terrapin B1**.

1970 *DARE* Tape Inf **VA**52A, I terrapinned during the summer. . . And every time you got a big terrapin that was two dollars. **1996** Horton *Island Out of Time* 70 **Chesapeake Bay MD**, You might go . . tarpinin', that's finding where the diamondbacks have buried for the winter. *Ibid* 241, When the ice broke, we went tarp'nin.

terrapin bug n
=harlequin cabbage bug.

1871 *Rural Carolinian* 2.16, Of all the pests the harlequin, or, as we have heard him called, terrapin bug, is the greatest in a garden. **1876** *Eve. Gaz.* (Pt. Jervis NY) 24 June [3]/6 (newspaperarchive.com), *Send $3 and Get a Recipe To* destroy and prevent . . Borer, Locust Bark Louse . . Cut Worm, Canker Worm, . . Terrapin Bug, . . and all destructive insects. **1924** U.S. Dept. Ag. *Farmers' Bulletin* 1371.18, The harlequin cabbage bug, also called the calico bug, fire bug, or terrapin bug, is about half an inch long and red, spotted with black. It is a southern insect, commonly found from Virginia to California, but often works northward. **1938** Brimley *Insects NC* 63, *Harlequin Cabbage Bug. Terrapin Bug.* State-wide, whole season, on cabbages, collards, and related plants. **1948** Wolfe *Farm Gloss.* 154, *Harlequin Bug.* . . Sometimes called "terrapin bug." **1970** *DARE* (Qu. R30, . . *Kinds of beetles; not asked in early QRs*) Inf **VA**46, Terrapin bug—stinks.

terrapin's foot n
=arbutus.

1975 Hamel–Chiltoskey *Cherokee Plants* 23, Arbutus, trailing; . . terrapin's foot. *Epigaea repens*. . . Ingredient for poor digestion.

terreckly See directly

terrible adj, adv
Usu |'terəb(ə)l, -ɪb(ə)l, 'terb(ə)l|; also **esp Sth, S Midl, NEng,** |'tɝəb(ə)l, 'tɝb(ə)l|; for addit varr see quots Pronc-spp *terble, turable, tur'ble, turbul, turrible* Similarly adv *tu'ibly* Std senses, var forms.

1775 (1971) Calk *Jrl.* 35 **VA**, Come to a turable mountain. . . Abrams beast . . made a turrabel flustration amongst the Reast of the Horses. **1884** *Anglia* 7.254 **Sth, S Midl** [Black], *Tu'ibly* (terribly). **1891** *DN* 1.131 **cNY**, [tɝb] < *terrible*. **1892** *DN* 1.242 **MO**, *Terrible*. In Kansas City ['tɝrəbəl] is the popular pronunciation. [*DN* Ed: Is there really a vowel before *l*? The [ɝ] in the first syllable is doubtless common in New England.] **1893** Shands *MS Speech* 65, *Turrible* ['tʌrɪbl]. A pronunciation of *terrible* very common among the illiterate, and sometimes heard in the conversation of the educated. **1903** *DN* 2.333 **seMO**, *Terrible.* . Pronounced turrible. **1907** White *AZ Nights* 25, There's a tur'ble lot of water running loose here. **1909** *DN* 3.380 **eAL, wGA**, *Terrible.* . . Pronounced turrible or tur'ble. **1915** *DN* 4.191 **swVA**, *Terrible* [tɝbl]. **1923** *DN* 5.223 **swMO**, He's a turble worker. **1929** *AmSp* 5.121 **ME,** If it was rough or muddy it was "turrible bad going." **1935** *AmSp* 11.17 **eTX**, *Terrible* is frequently pronounced ['tæːɚbl], ['tʌ.ɚbl], though ['tɛɚbl] also occurs. **1937** *AmSp* 12.286 **wVA**, *Terrible* . . [is] often ['tɝrbl]. **1941** *AmSp* 16.5 **eTX** [Black], *Terrible*, ['tæɚbl]. **1942** Hall

Smoky Mt. Speech 62 **wNC, eTN**, For *terrible*, many old-timers say ['tɝbəl], a pronunciation which illustrates the tendency toward obscuration and loss of the vowel. **1943** *AmSp* 18.265 **VA**, The vowel [ɛ] is often centralized in *terrible* and *buried* . . : ['tɝɪbl] T[idewater] 16%, P[iedmont] 16%, V[alley and Ridge] 3%, A[ppalachian Plateaus] 10%; ['tʌrɪbl] T 5%, P 18%, V 11%, A 10%. [*DARE* Ed: Data based on study of 254 female college students] **1954** in 1958 Brewer *Dog Ghosts* 116 **TX** [Black], Dey ain't nevuh forgit dat turbul night. **1965–70** *DARE* (Qu. LL36, *To make a statement much stronger: "Poor fellow. I think it's a _____ shame."*) 39 Infs, **scattered,** [Proncs of the types ['tɛrəb(ə), -ɪb(ə)l]]; 5 Infs, **scattered,** [Proncs of the types ['tɛrb(ə)l]]; **AL**24, **FL**14, **IL**83, **KY**30, **MA**58, **NC**1, 2, 7, 9, 11, 22, 23, 26, **VA**31, **VT**16, [Proncs of the types ['tɝəbl, -ɪb(ə)l]]; **CA**208, ['tʌrbəl]; **CT**4, ['tarəbəl]; **KY**84, ['tiɚəbul]; **IN**13, **KY**41, [tɝb(ə)l]; **KY**72, ['tɚrbul]; **TN**31, 36, ['turbɪl]. **1966** *DARE* Tape **GA**1, I was terrible [teˀwbl] to climb a tree. **1976** Garber *Mountain-ese* 97 **sAppalachians**, There was a turrible accident. **2000** Shores *Tangier Is.* 187 **Chesapeake Bay,** "Terble" for *terrible*.

terrididdle See tether-devil 1

terrified See terrify B

terrified fever n
Pronc-sp *tarrified fever* [Folk-etym for *typhoid fever*]

1878 McDowell *Like unto Like* 74 **Sth**, He had a spell o' terrified fever las' summer. **1887** *Overland Mth.* (2d ser) 10.69 **nAL**, When ye war tuk with the tarrified fever, hit [=a jack-o'-lantern] usen ter come reg'lar en stan' daown the crick torruds yer 'tater patch. **1906** Johnson *Highways Missip. Valley* 103 **TN** [Black], "What yo' hear from yo' son in Texas, Sister Larkin?" asked the man. "I plumb worried about him," she replied. "De las' news I heard he got de terrified fever." They discussed this typhoid (?) fever, and then the man resumed his journey.

terrify v
Usu |'terə,faɪ|; also |'tæri,faɪ| Pronc-sp *tarrify* Similarly ppl adj *tarrified, tarryfied*

A Forms.

1843 (1916) Hall *New Purchase* 227 **IN**, Darn my leather shirt, if the blasted fool didn't set off agin like a tarrified barr. **1845** (1968) Simms *Wigwam & Cabin* (1st ser) 64 **NC** (as of a1817), And now came a sight to tarrify. As soon as the Indians saw the young prince, they set up a general cry. **1860** *Harper's New Mth. Mag.* 21.481 **Long Is. NY**, The landsman's orfully tarrified at the idea of it. **1883** (1971) Harris *Nights with Remus* 314 **GA** [Black], Don't seem like he bad like some yuther childun w'at I seen. Bless you, I know childun w'at'd keep dish yer whole place tarryfied. **1888** Jones *Negro Myths* 82 **GA coast**, Eh holler down you chimbly an eh tarrify ebry body. **1893** Shands *MS Speech* 62, *Tarrify* ['tærɪfaɪ]. Negro for *terrify*. **1899** [see **B** below]. **1899** Chesnutt *Conjure Woman* 19 **csNC** [Black], He 'uz dat tarrified dat he turn pale. **1922** Gonzales *Black Border* 331 **sSC, GA coasts** [Gullah glossary], *Tarrify*—terrify, terrifies, terrified, terrifying. **c1960** *Wilson Coll.* **csKY**, *Terrify* is sometimes /'tærə,faɪ/. **1978** *DARE* File, [Transcript of Gullah folk tale:] Do, Buh Fox, do don' trow me een da briar patch fuh dem sperrit fuh tarrify me tuh det.

B Sense.

To irritate, torment, harass; hence ppl adj *terrified*. [*OED2 terrify* v. 2 1641 →; "Now only *dial*."] **esp Sth**

1899 (1912) Green *VA Folk-Speech* 439, *Tarrify*. . . To annoy; to tease. "These fleas tarrify me to death." "I can't wear woollen next to my skin, it tarrifies me so." **1984** *Annals Internal Med.* 100.900 **cwAL**, *This rash terrifies me to death* means that the itching is tormenting. **1985** Brooks *Lang. Amer. South* 14 (as of c1915), In my childhood in west Tennessee, one could say that the itch of a chiggerbite "terrified" him. **1998** *DARE* File—Internet, I was able to take a warm bath without being terrified with the intense itch.

territory n

A knife game; see quot 1975.

1934 *Hanley Disks* **cMA**, You mean territory? . . The idea is to get. . . your opponent in a place where he can't stand and throw the knife without going into your own territory. **1970** *DARE* (Qu. EE5, *Games where you try to make a jackknife stick in the ground*) Inf **VA**99, Territory. **1975** Ferretti *Gt. Amer. Book Sidewalk Games* 163, A knife game that requires true throwing skill is Territory. . . The player who is America goes first. He attacks Germany by tossing his knife into that territory, and whichever way the blade sticks becomes the path for a line extended across the country. Once divided, Germany is asked which part of the country he wants. . . A country remains alive as long as the player representing it can hold two fingers flat down in his country. **1986** Pederson *LAGS Concordance,* 1 inf, **cLA,** Territory—game; enlarged by throwing knife.

terrypin   See **terrapin**

terrywuk n

A **Jerusalem oak 1** (here: *Chenopodium ambrosioides*).

1966 Carawan-Carawan *Ain't Got Right* 27 **SC** [Black], My daddy used to cook medicine—herbs medicine: seamuckle, pine top, . . terrywuk. **1974** Morton *Folk Remedies* 43 **SC,** *Terrywuk. . . Chenopodium ambrosioides. . .* Plant juice or infusion valued as a vermifuge for children.

tesajo   See **tasajo**

tesh   See **tush** n **A2**

tesota n

=**desert ironwood.**

1900 Lyons *Plant Names* 264, Tesota. . . A small tree, one species, . . southwestern U.S. **1931** U.S. Dept. Ag. *Misc. Pub.* 101.87, Some difference of opinion exists as to the palatability of the mesquitelike leaves of tesota to livestock. **1947** Carr *Desert Parade* 72, Tesota. . . The seeds . . are edible, tasting something like peanuts. **1975** Lamb *Woody Plants SW* 80, Tesota. . . Lower desert of Ariz. and SE Calif. . . Spiny tree to 30′, short trunk. **1982** *Plants SW* (Catalog) 53, *Tesota* see *Desert Ironwood.*

tester n   Usu |ˈtɛstə(r)|; also **chiefly Sth, S Midl** |ˈtɪstə(r)| Pronc-spp *teaster, teester, tiester* [Spp with *-ee-* or *-ea-* are found from the 15th cent on, and the corresponding pronc was still being recommended for *tester* by Sheridan in 1780.] Std sense [=bed canopy], var forms.

1648 in 1912 MA Essex Co. Court *Records* 2.45, One Bed teaster & vallance. **1719** in 2004 *DARE* File—Internet **seVA,** *Below Stairs. . .* 1 Coverlid 1 blanket 3 pillows & Teaster Cloth -.10.-. **1754** *Ibid* **cMD,** 1 Bed, Bolster, . . a Suit of worked Curtains head Cloth, Teaster Cloth, foot Paces and Vallens. **1827** *Ibid* **swOH,** I will to this said Elizabeth . . a whole set of bed curtains and teester. **1858** *S. Lit. Messenger* 26.189 **VA,** The bed were a good, narrer, high bed, high-postid, but without enny teester and vallins. **1896** *DN* 1.426 **ceMO,** *Tester* (a canopy): pron. [tistɚ]. **1899** (1912) Green *VA Folk-Speech* 441, *Teaster. . .* The frame which connects the tops of the posts of a four-post bedstead, and the material stretched upon it, the whole forming a sort of canopy. **1931** Goodrich *Mt. Homespun* 73 **sAppalachians,** They ain't got no use for them coverlets and county-pins and teesters. **c1937** in 1977 *Amer. Slave* Suppl. 1 1.226 **AL,** The beds were high tiester beds and mattresses about as they use now only more shucks. **1966** *DARE* (Qu. E18) Inf **AL6,** Tester [ˈtistɚ] bed is a high bed with steps up. **1967** LeCompte *Word Atlas* 140 **seLA,** *Canopy over a bed. . .* tester [6 of 21 infs]. . Tester . . , a standard American word, is pronounced [tistə] in Lafourche Parish. **1967** *DARE* FW Addit **swAR,** Teaster [tistə] bed. Half-teaster bed. **1998** in 2004 Montgomery-Hall *Dict. Smoky Mt. Engl.* 597 **eTN,** I don't have any use for those old teesters. **2004** *DARE* File—Internet **New Orleans LA,** The plantation size, full-teaster bed sits against an upholstered floral wall.

tetch   See **touch**

tetched   See **touch B**

tetcherous adj   Cf **tetchous**

=**tetchy.**

1976 Garber *Mountain-ese* 92 **sAppalachians,** *Tetcherous . .* touchy, edgy—She's mighty tetcherous about that subject so don't mention it to her.

tetchie   See **tetchy**

tetchified adj   Cf **-ified**

=**tetchy.**

1944 *PADS* 2.21 **sAppalachians,** *Tetchified. . .* Choleric, fretful.

tetchous adj   Also sp *techeous, techous, te(t)chious, te(t)chis, tetchus* [Prob **touchous** infl by **tetchy**] **Sth, S Midl**

1   =**tetchy.**

1842 *Dollar Mag.* 2.185 **NC,** Why you are as tetchous as a skinned eel. **1857** *S. Lit. Messenger* 25.109 **VA,** He's mighty quick with strangers, powerful tetchous. **1867** Harris *Sut Lovingood Yarns* 96 **TN,** Now

haint hit strange how tetchus they am, on the subjick ove bees? **1890** *DN* 1.66 **KY,** *Tetchus* [ˈtɛčəs]: tetchy. **1893** Shands *MS Speech* 62, *Tetchous* [ˈtɛčəs]. Common among negroes and illiterate whites for *tetchy.* **1899** [see **tetchy**]. **1903** *DN* 2.334 **seMO,** *Touchous. . .* Pronounced techous. Querulous. 'He's getting mighty techous in his old age.' **1907** *DN* 3.237 **nwAR,** *Touchous. . .* Pronounced techous. Querulous. **1909** *DN* 3.380 **eAL, wGA,** *Techous.* **1913** Kephart *Highlanders* 294 **sAppalachians,** A choleric or fretful person is tetchious. **1933** *AmSp* 8.2.29 **eKY,** When Setters's cow transgressed, Obadiah up with the battling stick and drove his neighbor's spotted cow out of the pasture. "Obadiah is techeous," Setters told me afterward. **1952** Brown *NC Folkl.* 1.598, *Techis, tetchis* [ˈtɛtʃɪs]. . . Same as *techious, tetchious; techy, tetchy. . .* General. Illiterate. **1953** Randolph-Wilson *Down in Holler* 292 **Ozarks,** *Tetchous. . .* Tender, sensitive, easily aroused. Usually refers to human beings or domestic animals, but it also means sensitive in a mechanical sense. A hair-trigger rifle is "so Goddamn' tetchous it ain't safe, unless you're used to it." **1966** Dakin *Dial. Vocab. Ohio R. Valley* 2.466, Old variants of both of these terms [=*touchy, tetchy*], touchous and *tetchous,* are usual in the Mountains (*tetchous* in the south) and southern Kentucky and fairly common among older speakers everywhere in this state. . . Relics of *tetchous* appear north of the Ohio in the Hanging Rock region and *touchous* is still known in the southern Virginia Military District, in the Indiana hills, and on the lower Wabash Slope in Illinois. **1990** [see **2** below].

2   Sensitive to touch.

1842 [see **1** above]. **1951** West *Witch Diggers* 30 **IN,** Crowd right up close to me, Ice Rita. I've never been a tetchious man, and I'm willing to hold my breath now to make room for you. **1972** Thomas *Pop. Dict. Ozarks Talk* 86, *Tetchous, touchous: . .* Sensitive; sore; tender to the touch. **1990** Cavender *Folk Med. Lexicon* 33 **csAppalachians,** *Touchous*—[sometimes pronounced "tetchous"] *a.* painfully sensitive to movement or touch: "This toe is so touchous I can hardly walk." *b.* an irritable disposition: "She gets touchous when you talk about politics."

tetchsome adj   Cf **-some** suff

=**tetchy.**

1966 Dakin *Dial. Vocab. Ohio R. Valley* 2.468 **eKY,** *Tetchsome* appears only once, in the Mountains.

tetchus   See **tetchous**

tetchy adj   Usu |ˈtɛči|; also **esp nNEng** |ˈtɪči| Also sp *techy, tetchie;* pronc-sp *tichy* [*OED2* 1592 →; often regarded as pronc-var of *touchy,* but prob of independent origin] **formerly widespread, now esp Sth, S Midl** See Map *old-fash* Cf **tetchous 1, tetcherous, tetchified, tetchsome, touch** v, **touchous 1**

Irritable, fretful, short-tempered; of a subject, situation, etc: sensitive, ticklish.

1815 Humphreys *Yankey in England* 109, *Techy,* easily irritated, froward. **1853** in 1864 Irving *Life & Letters* 4.159 **NY,** When I was a little techy under your bantering at Niagara, it was not the fault of your jokes. **1886** *Century Illustr. Mag.* 31.431 **nGA,** He was what his friends called "a mighty tetchy man" on some subjects. **1899** (1912) Green *VA Folk-Speech* 442, *Tetchy. . .* Peevish; fretful; irritable. *Tetchous.* **1902** *DN* 2.247 **sIL,** *Touchy* [ˈtɛči]. . . irritable. **1904** Day *Kin o' Ktaadn* 74 **ME,** An' he was tetchy 'bout too big a fee. **1907** *DN* 3.227 **nwAR,** *Touchy* [ˈtɛči]. **1924** Raine *Land of Saddle-Bags* 104 **sAppalachians,** "He's a leetle grain *tetchy*" (or tetchous). **1930** *AmSp* 5.205 **Ozarks,** *Touchy* is always *tetchy* in the hill country. **1934** *WV Review* Dec 77, *Tetchy* for *peevish* or *fretful.* **1941** *LANE* Map 470 (*Touchy, quick-tempered*) 34 infs, chiefly **nNEng,** Techy; 12 infs, **nNEng,** Tichy. [11 infs considered proncs of the types [ˈtɛtʃɪ, ˈtɪtʃɪ] to be obsolete; 19 considered them old though still in use.] **1952** Brown *NC Folkl.* 1.598, *Techy, tetchy* [ˈtɛtʃɪ]. . . Of persons or animals: irritable, easily provoked, sensitive; of things, conditions: that which brings about irritation, etc. **1958** Babcock *I Don't Want* 163 **eSC,** As self-willed and "techy" as a prima donna. **c1960** Wilson *Coll.* **csKY,** *Tetchy* (or *techy*). . . Touchy, too easily offended. **1965-70** *DARE* (Qu. GG8, *When a person is very easily offended: "Be careful what you say to him, he's _____."*) 11 Infs, **esp Sth, S Midl,** Tetchy; **AL6,** Tetchy—colored people; (Qu. HH10, *A very timid or cowardly person: "He's _____."*) Inf **DE7,** Sorta tetchy. [12 of 13 Infs comm types 4 or 5, 12 old] **1966** Dakin *Dial. Vocab. Ohio R. Valley* 2.466, A person who is easily offended is called *touchy* everywhere in the Ohio Valley. Some older people along the river in southeastern Ohio, in the Indiana Wabash Valley, and in Kentucky west of the Mountains use the old folk word *tetchy,* but this variant is now rare. **1982** Slone *How We Talked* 71 **eKY** (as of c1950), As we say, it's a very "tetchie" subject.

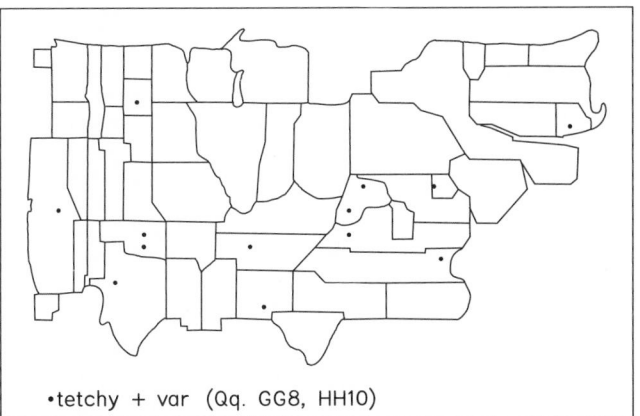

•tetchy + var (Qq. GG8, HH10)

teteet n Also *teteese* [See quot]
=**myrtle warbler.**

1946 Kopman *Wild Acres* 97 **LA,** The myrtle, or yellow-rumped, warbler was once the commonest native bird in New Orleans in winter. It was known under the colloquial name of "teteet," traceable to the local French habit of identifying and lumping together most of the less readily recognized small birds as "petites." To English-speaking boys and some adults, birds so named became "teteets," or even "teteeses," by a kind of alliteration.

teter See **teeter** v

teter-board See **teeter** n 4

tether-devil n

1 also *terrididdle:* A **bittersweet** (here: *Solanum dulcamara*). [*EDD* 1826 →]

1900 Lyons *Plant Names* 349, S[olanum] Dulcamara. . . Tether-devil, Terrididdle. [*DARE* Ed: Lyons marks the latter as a "verbal corruption" of the former.] **1930** Sievers *Amer. Med. Plants* 11, *Solanum dulcamara.* . . Tether-devil.

2 A **matrimony vine 1** (here: *Lycium halimifolium*).

1940 Clute *Amer. Plant Names* 226, *Lycium halimifolium.* . . Tether devil.

tetnit n Cf **titman**

1924 *DN* 5.295 **csNH,** Tetnit. . . A child born of elderly parents.

tetons n pl Cf **high alps**

1968 *DARE* (Qu. X31, . . *A woman's breasts*) Inf **OH**61, Tetons.

tetter n[1] Also *tetters* Pronc-spp *tatter, teder, titter* [*OED2 tetter* sb. 1 a700 →; *EDD tetter* sb. "Also . . *titter*"] **formerly widespread, now chiefly Sth, S Midl, TX** See Map *esp freq among Black speakers*

Any of var diseases of the skin marked by blistering or scaling.

1737 (1911) Brickell *Nat. Hist. NC* 66, The Juice that comes out of the Tree bored, is excellent against Scruffs, Tetters, Ring-worms, Scabs, and sore Mouths. **1828** Webster *Amer. Dict., Tetter* . . In *medicine,* a common name of several cutaneous diseases, consisting of an eruption of vesicles or pustules, in distinct or confluent clusters, spreading over the body in various directions and hardening into scabs or crusts. It includes the shingles, ring-worm, milky scale . . , scald head, etc. **1843** *Adams Sentinel* (Gettysburg PA) [26 June 2]/6 (newspaperarchive.com), [Advt:] *Oakeley's Compound Depurative Syrup,* For the cure of obstinate eruptions of the skin, . . chronic rheumatism, tetter, scrofula or king's evil. **1848** Bartlett *Americanisms* 358, *Titter.* An eruption on the skin. This is merely another pronunciation of *tetter,* used in New England, and, according to Forby, provincial in England. **1856** Edwards *Statist. Gaz.* 134 **VA,** *Carter's Spanish Mixture.* . . An Infallible Remedy for Scrofula, King's Evil, . . Ring Worm or Tetter, . . and all Diseases arising from an Injudicious Use of Mercury, Imprudence in Life, or Impurity of the Blood. **1863** in 1890 U.S. War Dept. *War of Rebellion* 1st ser 29.1.353, The frightful loss among horses is owing to a disease which resembles tetter (called in the army "hoof-rot"). **1919** *DN* 5.35 **seKY,** *Titter.* . . *Tetter,* the disease of the hands. Knott Co. **1930s** in 1944 *ADD*

629 eWV, *Titter* [=tetter]. **c1940** Eliason *Word Lists FL* 11 **wFL,** *Tetter:* Any kind of itching caused by eczema, ring worm, poison ivy, etc. **1965–70** *DARE* (Qu. BB25, . . *Common skin diseases around here*) 21 Infs, **chiefly Sth, S Midl, TX,** Tetter; **AL**61, **NC**88, **OH**103, Tetters; **VA**1, 27, **TX**74, Titter; **MS**1, **TX**86, Tatter; **NJ**53, Dry tatter; (Qu. BB24, . . *A rash that comes out suddenly—from hives or something else: "He's got some kind of _____ all over his chest."*) Inf **NY**105, Tetter rash. [14 of 30 total Infs Black] **1986** Pederson *LAGS Concordance* (*A discharging sore*) 1 inf, **ceGA,** Tetter, not the same as a boil. [Inf Black] **1990** Cavender *Folk Med. Lexicon* 32 **csAppalachians,** *Teder*—a scaly, red skin rash.

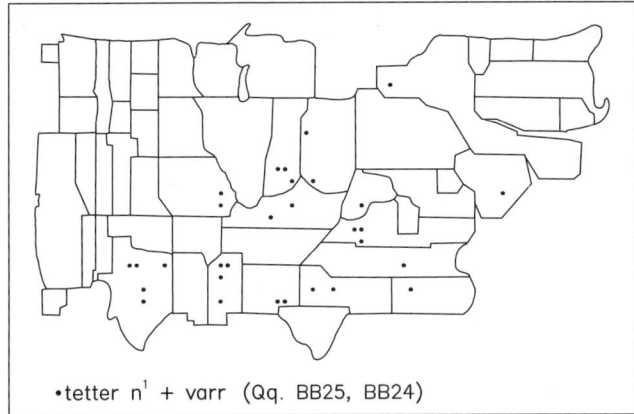

•tetter n[1] + varr (Qq. BB25, BB24)

tetter n[2] See **potato A4**

tetterbush n

A **staggerbush** (here: *Lyonia lucida*).

1869 Porcher *Resources* 417, *Tetter Bush,* (*Andromeda nitida* [= *Lyonia lucida*] . .) Grows in damp, pine land, bogs. **1966** Grimm *Recognizing Native Shrubs* 228 **seGA,** *Lyonia lucida.* . . Coastal plain, Southeastern Virginia south to Florida, west to Louisiana. Also called Tetterbush and Hoorah-bush (Okefenokee region).

tetters See **tetter** n[1]

tetterwort n Also *tetterweed*
=**bloodroot 1.**

1872 Pollock *Bot. Index* 124, Tetterwort. . . Sanguinaria canadensis. **1873** in 1976 Miller *Shaker Herbs* 139, *Bloodroot.* . . Tetterwort. . . When bruised the plant exudes an orange red fluid. The juice is emetic and purgative. **1892** (1974) Millspaugh *Amer. Med. Plants* 22-1, *Sanguinaria canadensis.* . . Bloodroot, . . tetterwort, . . Indian paint. **1933** *Jrl. Amer. Folkl.* 46.5 **Ozarks,** A tea made of bloodroot or tetter-weed is used in the treatment of a skin disease called tetter. **1974** (1977) Coon *Useful Plants* 204, *Sanguinaria canadensis* . . tetterwort. . . Like celandine, the juice may be purgative or mildly sedative, as with the opium poppy, and uses suggested are as for celandine.

tettuh See **potato A4**

teu See **to** prep, adv A2

tew v Also sp *too, tu* [nEngl dial; cf *EDD tew* v.[1] 10. "To fuss over work; to bustle about"] **chiefly NEast** *old-fash* Cf **tew** n, **tewed**

1 often with *round:* To fuss, fret; to bustle (around).

1848 in 1935 *AmSp* 10.41 **Nantucket MA,** *Tuing round.* Going about uselessly. **1871** (1882) Stowe *Fireside Stories* 63 **MA,** Lordy massy! didn't Huldy hev a time on't when the minister began to come out of his study, and want to tew 'round and see to things? **1877** *Atlantic Mth.* 40.75 **CT,** Land of Goshen! . . Do you s'pose I'm goin' to hev a man tewin' round in my way all the time, just cos' he 's my husband? **1878** *Appletons' Jrl.* 5.216, When she got put out she wouldn't go round tewin' and takin' on, but she'd just spunk right up to the biggest on 'em. **1896** (1911) Lowell *Poet. Wks.* 454 **MA,** "Ther's sech a thing ez bein' *tu*" . .; hence the phrase *tooin' round,* meaning a supererogatory activity like that of flies. **1901** *DN* 2.149 **cNY,** *Tew, v.i.* To fret, worry. Otsego Co., N.Y. **1929** *AmSp* 5.119 **ME,** A man who was busy without results was said to be . . "tewing and cutting all over the country." **1959** [see **tew** n].

2 with *at:* To nag at, needle (a person).

1877 Holley *Josiah Allen's Wife* 181 **NY,** And I persume Sarah kep' at him all the time; kep' a tewin' at him about her; kep' him awake nights a twittin' him about her. **1898** Lloyd *Country Life* 140 **AL,** Then they let into pickin and tewin at Andy about this, that and the other jest to see how bad he was muddled and mixed up with himself.

tew n[1] [nEngl dial; cf *EDD tew* sb. 13. "A disturbed state"] **NEast** *old-fash* Cf **tew** v

A state of anxiety or impatience.

1883 Howells *Woman's Reason* 270 **Boston MA,** My wife was always in a tew about the danger. **1895** Brown *Meadow-Grass* 123 **NH,** For the last fortnight, I've been in a real tew to come home. **1901** *DN* 2.149 **cNY,** Tew. . . A worry, fretting. "Don't be in such a tew." N.Y., Otsego Co. **1959** *VT Hist.* 27.163 **nwVT,** Tew [tū]: *n.* A state of nervous excitement or confusion. *v.* to fret. Occasional. Chittenden.

tew prep, adv   See **to** prep, adv **A1b**

tew n[2], adj, pron   See **two**

tew at   See **tew** v 2

tewed adj [nEngl dial; cf *EDD tew* v.[1] 5. "To exhaust . . ; to trouble, harass, bother"] Cf **tew** v

1892 *KS Univ. Qrly.* 1.99, *Tewed:* harrassed [sic], as, I'm tewed and fretted.

tew round   See **tew** 1

tex   See **text**

Texan bird-of-paradise   See **Texas bird of paradise 1**

Texan cabbage bug n
=**harlequin cabbage bug.**

1866 *Practical Entomol.* 1.2, *Strachia histrionica* (Texan Cabbage Bug). **1882** (1903) Treat *Injurious Insects* 41, Hitherto it had been generally supposed by entomologists that the Harlequin Cabbage-bug was confined to the most southerly of the Southern States, such as Texas and Louisiana; and it has consequently been called "the Texan Cabbage-bug."

Texan ebony   See **Texas ebony (tree)**

Texan (green) kingfisher   See **Texas kingfisher**

Texan mimosa   See **Texas mimosa**

Texan mulberry   See **Texas mulberry**

Texan snakeroot   See **snakeroot b(1)**

Texan tortoise   See **Texas tortoise**

Texan white oak   See **white oak 7**

Texan woodpecker   See **Texas woodpecker**

Texas n   Usu |ˈtɛksəs, -ɪs|; also **chiefly Sth, S Midl** |ˈtɛksɪz, -əz|; for addit proncs see **A** below

A Forms.

1934 *AmSp* 9.45 **Sth,** *Texas* is [tɛksɪz] in rustic Southern speech. **1936** *AmSp* 11.164 **eTX,** The vowel in the final syllable of the words listed below is usually [ɪ] or [ɪᵛ]. . All speakers use both sounds indiscriminately in all the words listed. . . Texas. *Ibid* 165, *Dallas* is always pronounced [ˈdælɪs], but *Texas* is sometimes [ˈtɛksəz], sometimes [ˈtɛksɪz], [ˈtɛksɪᵛz]. (The final sound is always [z], never [s].) **1939** *LANE* Map 16 *(Tennessee, Texas),* [Throughout **NEng,** proncs of the type [ˈtɛksəs] occur almost exclusively, with occasional scattered exx of proncs of the types [ˈtɛksɪs, ˈtɛksəz, ˈtɛkzəs, ˈtæksəs].] **1989** Pederson *LAGS Tech. Index* 322 **Gulf Region,** [554 infs pronounced *Texas* with final [-s] (usu as [ˈtɛksɪs], but with a scattering of minor varr, as [ˈtɛksəs, ˈtɛksɪs, ˈtɛkzɪs, etc]), and 218 with final [-z] (usu as [ˈtɛksɪz], but with a scattering of minor varr, as [ˈtɛksəz, ˈtɛkzɪz, etc]).]

B As noun.

1 attrib in var combs: Being a large or impressive example of (the thing in question).

1879 in 1938 *DN* 6.671 **AL,** *Texas northwester.* A violent wind. . . You could not haul [a large vessel] into the harbor of Galveston with all the steam engines that are in the United States today, unless you tore her keel off. She has got to go there and lie out in the roadstead, and when one of these Texas northwesters comes this ship has to sail without unloading. **1965** Teale *Wandering Through Winter* 149 **TX,** Out in a dripping world, after a deluge of "Texas dew" one afternoon, we came to the edge of the bay. **1967** *DARE* (Qu. F39, *A large pocket knife with blades*

that fold in and out) Inf **LA6,** Texas jack. **1984** Doig *English Creek* 247 **nMT,** The hint flew past Good Help by a Texas mile. **1986** Pederson *LAGS Concordance,* 1 inf, **wLA,** Texas jacks—knives. **1996** *DARE* File **AR** (as of 1960s), [I] took my Texas time doing it. **1999** Mariani *Encycl. Amer. Food & Drink* 325, *Texas toast.* Toast that is cut about one inch in thickness, so called because of the popular mythology that everything in Texas is bigger than anywhere else. **2009** *DARE* File **TX,** In my younger days, people spoke of the "Texas fif(th)," a full quart of whiskey, as opposed to the usual 4/5 quart normally referred to as simply a "fif(th)."

2 attrib in var joc combs: Being a poor or makeshift substitute for (the thing in question).   See also **Texas canary bird**

1845 in 1912 Thornton *Amer. Gloss.* 2.794, A Texas feather bed is said to be made of corn cobs and *shucks.* St. Louis *Reveille*, Dec. 29. **1928** *AmSp* 4.127 **NE,** It is a rare road in the "sandhills" that does not pass through a "let-down" or a "Texas gate" or over a "jump over" or "cattle guard." **1936** Adams *Cowboy Lingo* 148, 'Texas butter' was made from the hot lard in which the steak had been fried by putting some flour in the frying-pan and letting it bubble and brown, then adding hot water and stirring until thickened. **1939** FWP *Guide NE* 111, Eloquent of the life of the sandhiller are: . . Texas gate (several bands of wire stapled to sticks attached by wire loops to the fence posts). **1944** Adams *Western Words* 164, *Texas cakewalk*—A hanging. **1958** *Syracuse Herald–Jrl.* (NY) 17 Apr 22/5, Texas caviar is pickled black-eyed peas. It all came about when it fell the lot [sic] of a New York food expert-removed-to-Texas to serve the peas at a fancy New Year's day party. **1962** *AmSp* 37.266 **sCA,** *Texas stop.* . . Slowing down, but not making a full stop at a stop sign. **1970** *Current Slang* 4.3–4.25 [NM State Univ slang], *Texas strawberries.* . . Red beans. **1982** Heat Moon *Blue Highways* 143 **TX,** Poor whites ate them [=armadillos] with greens and cornbread during the Depression and called them "Hoover hogs" or "Texas turkeys" (on the Christmas table.) **1986** *DARE* File **sNM** (as of c1976), *Texas Bridge*—An unbridged crossing in a road where you have to go through the water in the arroyo to get to the other side. **2007** *DARE* File—Internet **TX,** We have a "game room" upstairs in our house. In this part of the country this particular type of room is called the Texas basement. I think that's because almost no houses in Texas actually have basements so they instead build a large multi-purpose room on the second floor to compensate.

Texas ash n
Std: an ash *(Fraxinus texensis)* native to Texas and Oklahoma. Also called **mountain ash 2**

Texas babybonnets n   Also *babybonnets*
A shrub *(Coursetia axillaris)* native to Texas.

1960 Vines *Trees SW* 557, *Texas Baby-bonnets—Coursetia axillaris.* . . A rare, densely branched shrub or small tree. **1970** Correll *Plants TX* 835, *Coursetia axillaris.* . . Baby-bonnets. Rounded shrub . . ; flowers in . . racemes . . ; corolla mostly pale-pink; about 1 cm. long, papilionaceous.

Texas bird-of-paradise n   Also *bird-of-paradise*

1 also *Texan bird-of-paradise:* A **scissortail 1** (here: *Tyrannus forficatus*).

1857 (1859) Olmsted *Journey TX* 313, We had heard it called the tailor-bird; but Woodland said it was known among the rangers as the bird of paradise. If it belong to this particular district, it must have been so denominated in irony; for a more dreary country, of equal extent, I never saw. **1859** (1980) Rhees *Acct. Smithsonian* 63, *Case 18.* . . The Scissortail or swallow-tailed Fly-Catcher or the Texas Bird of Paradise, is an exquisitely beautiful and graceful bird. **1874** Coues *Birds NW* 235, *Milvulus forficatus* [=*Tyrannus f.*]. . . This peculiarly elegant species, not inaptly called "bird of paradise" by the Texans, is merely a straggler to the Missouri water-shed. **1887** *Amer. Field* 27.200 **TX,** In Texas I noticed a bird they call the "scissor-tail," or "bird of paradise;" they are great bee catchers. **1916** *Times–Picayune* (New Orleans LA) 16 Apr 1 **LA,** *Scissor-tailed Flycatcher.* . . Texan Bird of Paradise. . It is a rare bird save in the southwestern portion of the state. **1928** Bailey *Birds NM* 423, That the Scissor-tail . . has not only crossed from Texas—where it is known as the Texas Bird of Paradise—but is slowly spreading, mile by mile, into New Mexico is matter for special gratulation. **1961** Ligon *NM Birds* 178, The Scissor-tailed Flycatcher, often called the "Texas Bird of Paradise," is one of our most beautiful and beneficial birds.

2 =**roadrunner 1.**

1932 TX Folkl. Soc. *Pub.* 10.187, At the business meeting Saturday afternoon the paisano—known also as the road-runner, chaparral cock, and (occasionally) as the Texas bird-of-paradise—was . . adopted as the emblem of the Texas Folk-Lore Society. **1940** Writers' Program *Guide TX* 28 **c,wTX,** The road runner or ground cuckoo, also locally called the chaparral bird, "Texas bird of paradise," and *paisano, . .* is the clown of the highways. **1958** *AZ Highways* 34.2 **swTX,** I have never met "bird-of-paradise" as a name [for the roadrunner] except in the well-worn anecdote of the West Texas real estate agent . . who in answer to his prospective client's question, "What's that bird?" replied, "Bird-of-paradise, some folks call it," whereupon the stranger commented, "He's a hell of a long ways from home, ain't he?"

Texas blazing-star   See **Texas star f**

Texas bluebonnet   n   Cf **bluebonnet 1**

A **lupine,** usu *Lupinus subcarnosus* and *L. texensis.*

1903 *Good Housekeeping* 36.293 (as of c1863) **TX,** Into each [paper] boat went a flower. The wild rose was a royal passenger, Queen Victoria. The Texas bluebonnet was the prince of Wales. **1917** *Oakland Tribune* (CA) 12 Aug 36/2, The violet of Illinois, the Wyoming paint brush and the Texas bluebonnet challenge its [=the California poppy's] delicacy and brilliant coloring. **1936** Whitehouse *TX Flowers* 53, *Texas Bluebonnet (Lupinus texensis)* . . was widely known in pioneer days as buffalo clover. . . Seed-houses sell the Texas bluebonnet under the name of *Lupinus subcarnosus.* . . The bluebonnet was adopted as the state flower in 1901. **1966** *DARE* Wildfl QR Pl.106 Inf **WA**10, Texas bluebonnet. **1967–69** *DARE* (Qu. S11) Inf **SC**36, Texas bluebonnet; (Qu. S23) Inf **MO**9, Texas bluebonnets; (Qu. S26a, . . *Wildflowers*) Inf **NJ**58, Texas bluebonnets. **1970** Correll *Plants TX* 803, *Lupinus subcarnosus.* . . Texas bluebonnet. . . *Lupinus texensis.* . . Texas bluebonnet. . . This is the species that is widely spread by our highway department, garden clubs and other such organizations. **1982** *Plants SW* (Catalog) 21 **TX,** Texas Bluebonnet—*L. texensis.* . . Bright, rich, blue flowers in spring.

Texas blueweed   See **blueweed 4**

Texas boat-tailed grackle   See **Texas grackle**

Texas buckeye   n

1 =Mexican buckeye.

1882 Hough *Elements of Forestry* 255, The Texas Buckeye *(Ungnadia speciosa).* . . forms a small shrub or tree, with brittle wood. **1903** Small *Flora SE U.S.* 746, *Ungnadia speciòsa.* . . Chiefly along streams. . . *Texas Buckeye.* **1960** Vines *Trees SW* 686, *Ungnadia speciosa.* . . Also known under the vernacular names of Monillo, Texas-buckeye. . . The sweet seeds are poisonous to human beings. . . Children in west Texas sometimes use the round seeds for marbles. **1980** Little *Audubon Guide N. Amer. Trees W. Region* 543, "Texas-buckeye" . . *Ungnadia speciosa.* [*Ibid* 544, Although not a true buckeye, it is so called because of the similar large capsules and seeds.]

2 A **buckeye** n **1** (here: *Aesculus glabra* var *arguta*).

1952 Blackburn *Trees* 84 **eTX,** *Aesculus arguta* . . Texas Buckeye. **1960** Vines *Trees SW* 679, *A[esculus] glabra* var. *arguta.* . . Texas Buckeye becomes a tree to 35 ft[.] and 18 in. in diameter on the Texas Edwards Plateau. **1996** *Frederick Post* (MD) 10 Oct sec B 7/6, There may be three leaflets . . like bladdernuts and hop trees; five to seven leaflets, like buckeyes and horse chestnuts, or as many as seven to 11 leaflets, like the Texas buckeye.

Texas buckthorn   n

A **lotebush** (here: *Ziziphus obtusifolia*).

1886 Havard *Flora W. & S. TX for 1885* 508, *Zizyphus obtusifolius.* . . Texas Buckthorn. . . Next to Mezquit, the most widespread and abundant shrub in Western and Southern Texas, on gravelly mesas, slopes and bluffs. **1903** Small *Flora SE U.S.* 749, *Zizyphus obtusifòlia.* . . On plains and prairies. . . *Lotibush. Texas Buckthorn.* **1923** Pellett *Amer. Honey Plants* 191, The . . Texas buckthorn . . is a common chapparel [sic] bush on the plains and prairies of Texas, New Mexico, . . Arizona and adjacent Mexico. **1960** Vines *Trees SW* 695, Vernacular names [for *Zizyphus obtusifolia*] are Texas Buckthorn, Lote-bush, . . and Abrojo. The mealy drupe is edible, but not tasty.

Texas bullfrog   n

Used as a commercial name for a **leopard frog** (here: *Rana pipiens* and *R. sphenocephala*).

1928 Baylor Univ. Museum *Contrib.* 16.6, Thousands of Leopard or Spotted Frogs (*Rana sphenocephala* . . and *Rana pipiens* . .) are shipped north from this State and are served in restaurants and on dining cars as

"Texas Bullfrogs." **1946** *Valley Morning Star* (Harlingen TX) 27 Jan 12/6, A hundred or more sons of the Lone Star State . . are preparing to invade the nation's capital. . . For those whose tastes run that way, there'll be optional meat courses of Texas bullfrog legs, goat's meat and the flesh of Texas rattlesnakes.

Texas canary   n

=painted bunting 1.

1969 Longstreet *Birds FL* 147, *Painted Bunting—Other names* . . Texas Canary.

Texas canary bird   n   Cf **desert canary, Missouri ~, mountain ~**

A mule.

1911 *Wichita Daily Times* (Wichita Falls TX) 29 Nov 2/3, The dweller in the larger cities of Texas who dodged a mule hitched to a wagon . . has failed to appreciate the value of that quadruped, but . . the man who uses draft animals well knows the worth of the long-eared Texas canary bird.

Texas chicken   n   Cf **Arkansas chicken, Georgia ~**

1979 *NC Folkl. Jrl.* 27.88, The importance of fried fatback in the diet of Southern Blacks and poor whites has long been recognized, but a Carolina colloquialism which describes it, *Texas chicken,* seems to have escaped the notice of lexicographers, folklorists and dialect scholars.

Texas crabgrass   n   Cf **crabgrass**

=tumble grass 2a.

1930 OK Univ. Biol. Surv. *Pub.* 2.52, *Schedonnardus paniculatus.* . . Texas Crab-grass. **2000** in 2003 *DARE* File—Internet **TX,** *Schedonnardus paniculatus* . . tumble grass, Texas crab grass.

Texas curly mesquite grass   See **curly mesquite 1**

Texas dandelion   n   [From the yellow flower heads]

A **false dandelion** (here: *Pyrrhopappus pauciflorus*).

1943 *Gleanings Bee Culture* 71.281 **TX,** These were the bees that had collected pollen from the Texas dandelion, a composite in which all of the florets have strap petals. **1961** Wills–Irwin *Flowers TX* 246, *Texas-dandelion—Pyrrhopappus multicaulis* [=*P. pauciflorus*]. *Ibid* 247, Texas-dandelion is a common plant of grassy roadsides, pastures and lawns, found mainly in the southern part of the state. **1967** *DARE* Wildfl QR (Wills–Irwin) Pl.64A Inf **TX**44, Texas dandelion.

Texas dogbane   See **dogbane c**

Texas duck   See **Texas mallard**

Texas ebony (tree)   n   Also *Texan ebony*

A spiny evergreen shrub or small tree *(Ebenopsis ebano)* native to Texas.   Also called **cat's-claw, ebony 2, pilot tree**

1885 *Furniture Gaz.* new ser 23.164 **TX,** The following is a list of the different woods used, . . white elm, Texas ebony, cottonwood [etc]. **1897** Sudworth *Arborescent Flora* 248, *Zygia flexicaulis.* . . Texan Ebony. **1938** Van Dersal *Native Woody Plants* 194, *Pithecolobium* [sic] *flexicaule*—Texas-ebony. . . Wood very durable; locally used for fence posts. **1951** *PADS* 15.33 **TX,** *Zygia flexicaulis.* . . Texas ebony. **1970** Correll *Plants TX* 769, *Texas ebony.* . . Highly prized as an ornamental and shade tree, and also for the very dense red heartwood, which is used to make art objects and small furniture. **1980** *Frederick Post* (MD) 23 May sec B 9/1 **FL,** There are . . mesquite, holly and Texas ebony trees in Frontier Land [in Disney World].

Texas elm   n

=cedar elm.

1883 *Amer. Jrl. Forestry* 1.448 **TX,** *U[lmus] crassifolia* . . (Cedar Elm, Texas Elm). **1938** Van Dersal *Native Woody Plants* 357, Texas elm *(Ulmus crassifolia).* **1960** Vines *Trees SW* 210, *Ulmus crassifolia.* . . Vernacular names are Scrub Elm, . . Texas Elm, . . and Southern Rock Elm.

Texas fly   n

=horn fly.

1888 *Morning Oregonian* (Portland OR) 26 Sept 6/6, It is beyond question true that the range fly—known as the Texas fly o[r] buffalo fly—is . . becoming an alarming pest. The injury this insect does to cattle and stock is considerable. **1889** U.S. Dept. Ag. *Rept. of Secy. for 1889* 346, It [=the horn fly] has also been called the "Texas Fly," the "Buffalo Fly," and the "Buffalo Gnat." These names indicate erroneous popular impressions that the insect came from the West. **1966–69** *DARE* (Qu. R10, *Very small flies that don't sting, often seen hovering in* *large groups or bunches outdoors in summer*) Inf **GA**3, Texas fly; **MA**37, Texas fly—bother the cattle; (Qu. R12, . . *Other kinds of flies*) Inf **NY**71, Texas fly—a little teeny feller—congregate right back of the shoulder blades; **VA**26, Texas fly.

Texas, going to n   Cf **I went to Paris; Jerusalem, going to**

Any of var children's games; see quots.

1940 Harbin *Fun Encycl.* 216, *Going to Texas.*—The leader announces that everyone . . is going to Texas and . . is allowed to take one article. One player . . [says] "I will take my hat." Others decide to take an auto, a lamp, . . etc. . . Number One is asked by the leader what he will do with his hat. He answers that he will wear it. Number Two must now repeat, "I will wear my auto"; Number Three, "I will wear my lamp"; and so on.

Texas golden rainbow n

A **hedgehog cactus 3** (here: *Echinocereus pectinatus*).

1971 Dodge *100 Desert Wildflowers* 52, *Yellow pitaya echinocereus.* Sometimes called "Texas golden rainbow," the yellow pitaya is. . . quite common in portions of Big Bend National Park. . . *Echinocereus pectinatus* var. *neomexicanus*.

Texas goose n

1 =**snow goose. Cf Mexican goose 1a**

1888 Trumbull *Names of Birds* 9 **NJ**, *Snow geese.* . . These birds visit the Delaware regularly, many of them congregating near Bay Side, Cumberland Co., N.J., the species being there known as *Texas goose.*

2 =**white-fronted goose.**

1923 U.S. Dept. Ag. *Misc. Circular* 13.35 **NE**, *White-fronted Goose.* . . Texas goose.

Texas grackle n   Also *Texas boat-tailed grackle*

=**great-tailed grackle.**

1889 Davie *Nests N. Amer. Birds* 284, *Great-tailed Grackle.* . . Called the . . Texas Grackle. It is an abundant bird in southern Texas. **1916** *Times–Picayune* (New Orleans LA) 16 Apr mag sec 9 **LA**, *Texas Boat-tailed Grackle.* . . It is to be found only to the extreme southwestern portion of the state, and may breed within our borders.

Texas green kingfisher   See **Texas kingfisher**

Texas heather n

An **indigo bush 2** (here: *Dalea frutescens*).

1951 *PADS* 15.35 **TX**, *Dalea frutescens.* . . Texas heather; sheep or goat weed. The way sheep or goats devour every morsel of this perfect bouquet of pansy purple, the plant, [sic] will not last very long outside of tightly fenced areas with no "woolies" around.

Texas hot (wiener) n   Also *(hot) Texas wiener, Texas (hot) weiner, Texas hot dog;* for addit varr see quots   **chiefly nNJ, Upstate NY, PA**

A hot dog served with chili sauce and often other condiments.

1927 in 2004 *Popik Coll.* **neNJ**, Texas Hot Weinie Shoppe (Geo Christman) 100 Watchung av [Paterson NJ]. **1967** *DARE* FW Addit **seNY**, *Texas wieners*—same as Texas hots, chili dogs, etc. Poughkeepsie NY. *Ibid* **seNY**, Texas hots—hot dog and chili sauce. Fishkill NY. **1968** *DARE* (Qu. HH30, *Things that are nicknamed for different nationalities*) Inf **NY**80, Texas hot wieners. [FW: Never heard of them, but they're in all diners in this area.] **1968** *DARE* FW Addit **seNY**, *Texas hot wienie*—hot dog with hot chili sauce, mustard, and chopped fresh onion on it. Newburgh NY. **1995** *Folklife Center News* 17.2.10 **neNJ**, According to Chris Betts, the Texas Hot Wiener was invented around 1924 by "an old Greek gentleman" who owned a hot dog "stand" . . in downtown Paterson. . . As Betts's account also suggests, the chili sauce is considered the crucial ingredient in this new food, its invention defining and separating the Hot Texas Wiener from the "old Greek gentleman" was serving before. **2002** Stern–Stern *Roadfood* 98 **neNJ**, According to hot dog historian Robert C. Gamer . . Mr. Patrelis devised a deep-fried frankfurter in a too-short bun, topped with mustard, onions, and spicy meat sauce. . . In 1920 the hot dog stand was renamed the Original Hot Texas Weiner because Mr. Patrelis believed the sauce to be like Texas chili. . . [T]oday Paterson is rich with Texas weiner shops. **2005** *DARE* File—Internet **cwNY**, Zorba's Texas Hots. . . Greek diners have been serving Texas Hots in Buffalo for more than 70 years. It's a cross between a Coney Island Hot Dog and a Chili Dog—it's all in the sauce. *Ibid* **cPA**, Texas Hot Dogs came with an all-meat sauce. . . The first Texas Hot Dog I had was at a drive-in that no longer exists, on a stretch of road south of Altoona. *Ibid,* There seems to be a fairly narrow range where they are called Texas wieners or Texas hot weiners—

north Jersey and southe[a]stern New York. Although last year at Black Mountain NC we had a Texas Hot wiener at a small stand—the proprietor turned out to be recently arrived in the area from north Jersey. *Ibid* **NJ**, I grew up in New Jersey and Hot Texas wieners were always a part of the cuisine.

Texas house n

See quot 1984.

1874 Steele *Dell Dart* 51 **CA**, There is a pleasant house about ten miles from here. Take the left hand road after you cross the ravine. It's the Texas House. *Ibid* 52, As I passed the Texas house I looked all around, . . but seeing no one outside I rode on. [*DARE* Ed: The meaning of *Texas house* here is unclear.] **1955** Harris *Look of Old West* 283, From Texas to Wyoming, it was characteristic, and they still call it a Texas house. It is really two houses, or anyway, two rooms or sets of rooms, semi-annexed to each other by a connecting roof over a long hall open on both sides. **1984** Wilder *You All Spoken Here* 30 **Sth**, *Dog-trot house:* A house of two one-room cabins joined by a roof. . . *Saddlebag house, Texas house:* Same as above.

Texas itch n

A form of mange; see quot 1934.   Also called **buffalo mange**

1880 U.S. Dept. Ag. *Special Rept.* 23.12, West of the Mississippi River about two-fifths of the counties report diseases among horses. . . Some new local names of diseases, Spanish fever, Texas fever, Texas itch, &c., are given for the first time. **1881** in 2003 *DARE* File—Internet **seKS**, [From the *Arkansas City Traveler:*] Carbolic sheep dip will cure Texas itch on horses. **1897** KS Ag. Exper. Sta. Manhattan *Bulletin* 69.103, There have been reports from various parts of the state of a parasitic skin disease of cattle, commonly known among stockmen as Texas itch. I do not know why the disease is called *Texas* itch, unless it may result from the general supposition that most dreaded diseases of cattle originate in that state. **1934** (1943) *W2, Texas itch. Veter[inary].* A form of mange, or scabies, of cattle, usually occurring in winter, caused by a scab mite (*Psoroptes communis bovis*), producing atrophy of the hair follicles, loss of the hair, and desquamation of the epithelium.

Texas kingfisher n   Also *Texan (green) kingfisher, Texas green kingfisher*

A **kingfisher** (here: *Chloroceryle americana*).

1858 U.S. War Dept. *Rept. Explor. Railroad* 9.159, *Ceryle americana.* . . Texas Kingfisher. . . This species is very much smaller than the common northern kingfisher. **1858** *New Engl. Farmer* 10.462, Since the admission of Texas, a handsome little bird, called the Texan green kingfisher, has been discovered. **1881** U.S. Geol. & Geog. Surv. *Bulletin* 6.240, *Ceryle americana cabanisi.* . . —Texan Kingfisher. The occurrence of this diminutive species along the southern border of the United States, and its presence in the Colorado Valley at several points . . , may be sufficient to warrant us in predicting its probable capture within the limits of the State [=NV]. **1915** *Pacific Coast Avifauna* 11.183, *Ceryle americana septentrionalis.* . . Texas Kingfisher Synonyms— . . Cabanis Kingfisher; Texas Green Kingfisher. Status—Recorded twice [in CA]. **1961** Ligon *NM Birds* 165, The little Green, or Texas, Kingfisher, with its exceptionally large and long bill for so small a bird, and its typical Kingfisher ways, is not apt to be confused with any other species. **1964** Phillips *Birds AZ* 67, *Texas Kingfisher.* . . Rare straggler into Santa Cruz drainage (Tucson and above) and San Pedro Valley (Benson and above) in fall and winter.

Texas lantana n

A **lantana** (here: *Lantana horrida*) native chiefly to Texas. Also called **bunchberry 2, calico bush 3**

1960 Vines *Trees SW* 896, Texas Lantana . . bearing varicolored flowers of red, orange or yellow . . grows mostly in sandy soil in Texas, Louisiana, Mississippi, and Mexico. **1961** Wills–Irwin *Flowers TX* 190, Texas Lantana . . is a commoner native species [than *Lantana camara*], . . having 10 to 18 rather coarse teeth on each margin of a leaf and yellow or orange flowers which turn red with age. **1970** Correll *Plants TX* 1327, *Lantana horrida.* . . Texas lantana, hierba de cristo, calico bush.

Texas leopard   See **leopard dog**

Texas loco n   Also *Texas locoweed*

A **milk vetch** (here: *Astragalus mollissimus*).

1900 Lyons *Plant Names* 53, *A[stragalus] mollissimus.* . . Nebraska to Texas. Texas Loco-weed, Loco plant [etc]. **1909** U.S. Bur. Animal Industry *Bulletin* 111.39, *Astragalus mollissimus* is popularly known as "purple loco," "woolly loco," or "Texas loco." **1937** U.S. Forest Serv.

Range Plant Hdbk. W41, Woolly loco, sometimes called . . Texas . . loco, is a low, tufted, perennial herb poisonous to livestock. . . In Arizona, New Mexico, and Texas where this plant is abundant large losses of bees have resulted.   **1970** Correll *Plants TX* 844, *Astragalus mollissimus. . . Texas loco. . .* According to some authorities, this was the first loco weed to be recognized. When eaten, it is especially fatal to horses.

Texas longhorn   See **longhorn 1**

Texas loop n

A type of lariat loop; also fig: see quots.

   1936 McCarthy *Lang. Mosshorn* np **West** [Rodeo terms], *Community Loop.* A lasso loop from six to eight feet in diameter. . . The Texas loop . . is from two and a half to three feet in diameter.   **c1985** in 2005 *DARE* File—Internet **ceTX,** In this final chapter, I will throw a Texas loop, making a gathering of events I have not touched upon.

Texas mallard n   Also *Texas duck*
=**Florida duck.**

   1916 *Times–Picayune* (New Orleans LA) 26 Mar 2/3, Texas Mallard.—Quite like the preceding [=Florida duck], but is mottled on the breast instead of streaked. Found in Southwestern Louisiana near the Texas border.   **1931** LA Dept. of Conserv. *Bulletin* 20.136, It is not strange that we should have thought that our fauna included the "Florida" duck and the "Texas" duck, for the closet naturalists told us that the "Florida" mallard has a *throat nearly clear buff color without the markings* found on the Northern Black Mallards or the female Greenhead; and the "Texas" Mallard *is mottled on the belly with black instead of being streaked* like the other mallards.

Texas mallow n

A **waxmallow** (here: *Malvaviscus arboreus* var *drummondii*).

   1960 Vines *Trees SW* 742, *Malvaviscus drummondii. . .* Vernacular names are Texas Mallow, Mexican Apple [etc].   **1970** Correll *Plants TX* 1028, *Malvaviscus arboreus . .* var. *Drummondii. . . Texas* mallow. Shrub to 3 m. high, . . corolla vermilion-red, . . fruit red, said to be edible either raw or cooked. . . From Fla. to Tex.

Texas millet n

A sometimes weedy grass (*Urochloa texana*) formerly used for forage.   Also called **Colorado grass, concho ~, goose ~ 2c**

   1879 U.S. Dept. Ag. *Rept. of Secy. for 1878* 159, *Panicum Texanum*—Texas Millet. . . This grass has been brought to the attention of the department during several years past.   **1889** Vasey *Ag. Grasses* 25 **TX,** Texas Millet. . . This grass is a native of Texas, and was first described and named in 1866 by Prof. S.B. Buckley.   **1903** Small *Flora SE U.S.* 91, *Panicum Texànum. . .* On plains and prairies, Texas. Summer and fall. *Texas Millet.*   **1930** OK Univ. Biol. Surv. *Pub.* 2.52, *Panicum texanum. . .* Texas Panic-grass. Texas Millet.   **1940** Gates *Flora KS* 134, Texas Millet. Prairies and low open ground along streams and irrigation ditches.   **1970** Correll *Plants TX* 181, *Texas millet. . .* Frequent in disturbed usually sandy ground . . ; Tex., Okla., Miss., Fla.   **2001** *DARE* File—Internet **AL,** Doves are almost 100 percent seed-eaters. . . Choice foods are seeds of barnyard grass, . . Texas millet, and wheat.

Texas mimosa n   Also *Texan mimosa* Cf **mimosa**

A **cat's-claw** (here: *Acacia greggii*).

   1890 CA Ag. Exper. Sta. *Rept. for 1888–89* 175, *Acacia Greggii,* Texan mimosa.   **1914** Bailey *Std. Cyclop. Horticul.* 1.189, *[Acacia] Gréggii. . . Texas Mimosa.* Sometimes a tree 20 ft. high, but usually a shrub of 4–5 ft., growing in thickets along river banks.   **1960** Vines *Trees SW* 499, Vernacular names [for *Acacia greggii*] used are Devil Claws, Texas Mimosa [etc]. . . The fragrant yellow flowers furnish an excellent bee food.   **1984** Vines *Trees Cent. TX* 186, Vernacular names used are Devil Claws, Texas Mimosa, Paradise Flower, Gregg Acacia [etc].

Texas mosquito n   Cf **Jersey mosquito 1**

A large **mosquito** n[1] **B1.**

   1900 *Ft. Wayne Sentinel* (IN) 4 Aug [14]/6 (newspaperarchive.com), Much has been written about the Jersey mosquito. . . With the proper kind of a press agent the Texas mosquito would today be head and heels over his brethren in New Jersey.   **1969–70** *DARE* (Qu. R15b, . . *An extra-big mosquito*) Infs **CA**137, **TX**101, Texas mosquito.   **1986** Pederson *LAGS Concordance* (*Mosquito*) 1 inf, **csTX,** Texas mosquitoes—big ones.

Texas mountain laurel   See **mountain laurel 5**

Texas mulberry n   Also *Texan mulberry*

A mulberry (here: *Morus microphylla*) native to the southwestern US.   Also called **Mexican mulberry 1, mountain ~**

   [**1882** U.S. Geol. & Geog. Surv. *Bulletin* 6.11, *Morus microphylla,* a Texas Mulberry which extends along the southern part of New Mexico and Arizona.]   **1938** Van Dersal *Native Woody Plants* 171, *Morus microphylla. . . Texan mulberry. . .* A large shrub to small or large tree. *Ibid* 357, Texas mulberry (*Morus microphylla*).   **1960** Vines *Trees SW* 219, Texas Mulberry is easily distinguished from Red Mulberry by much smaller leaves and fruit.   **1970** Correll *Plants TX* 497, *Texas mulberry. . .* Fruit . . juicy, edible. In canyons, limestone and igneous slopes in the w. two thirds of Tex.   **1975** Lamb *Woody Plants SW* 87, Texas mulberry. . . The berries are red to black in color and smaller than the domestic varieties.

Texas nettle n   Cf **nettle 2**
=**buffalo burr.**

   1882 *Amer. Naturalist* 16.281, Within a few years a plant has been introduced into Southwestern Iowa, which. . . is commonly called Texas nettle, as it is supposed to have been brought by the herds of Texas cattle.   **1897** IN Dept. Geol. & Nat. Resources *Rept. for 1896* 676, Texas Nettle. Several flowering plants . . were discovered in full bloom in a low, sandy field south of Conover's Pond. . . Undoubtedly a railroad migrant. . . [T]his . . is rapidly spreading eastward from its original home on the plains of Nebraska and Texas.   **1898** *Jrl. Amer. Folkl.* 11.276 **KS,** *Solanum rostratum,* . . Texas nettle.   **1936** Whitehouse *TX Flowers* 129, *Buffalo-Bur. . .* is a common weed . . from Tennessee to Mexico. . . The spreading plants. . . are also called . . Texas nettle.

Texas nightingale n   Cf **Arizona nightingale, Texas canary bird**

   1975 Bagley *Snow Tiger* 97, A Texas nightingale isn't a bird. . . It's a donkey.

Texas oak n

An **oak** (*Quercus texana*) native chiefly to Texas and Oklahoma.   Also called **hill oak 2, mountain ~ c, pin ~ 2e, red ~ 2g, Red River ~, rock ~ 2, Spanish ~ b(4), spotted ~**

   1878 *St. Joseph Traveler & Herald* (MI) 6 Apr [2]/1 (newspaperarchive.com), Sprigs of pine, holly, dogwood, elm, ash, walnut, apple and peach have been grafted on a Texas oak tree, and grow along as though nothing had happened.   **1901** Mohr *Plant Life AL* 61, In the mesophile forests of the bottom lands, cow oak . . , Texas oak (*Quercus texana*), . . and hornbeam . . prevail.   **1950** *Dly. Ardmoreite* (Ardmore, Okla.) 30 April B. 6/3 (*DA*), Trees native to the park include post oak, . . Texas oak, . . and hickory.   **1980** Little *Audubon Guide N. Amer. Trees E. Region* 408, Texas Oak . . has small, usually 5-lobed leaves, small acorns, and hairy red buds.

Texas pink n

1 A centaury (here: *Centaurium texense*).

   1942 TX Ag. Exper. Sta. College Sta. *Bulletin* 609.126, *Centaurium . . texense.* Texas Pink. An annual, branching plant about 10 inches in height that produces . . bright pink, star-shaped flowers.

2 A **marsh pink 1** (here: *Sabatia campestris*).

   1951 *PADS* 15.37 **TX,** *Sabbatia* [sic] *campestris. . .* Texas pink.

Texas plume n
=**standing cypress.**

   1854 in 1856 Parker *Notes Exped.* 55, Throughout our march we found in profusion flowers which, in the North and East, are cultivated with great care as ornaments for the drawing-room or conservatory. The Texas plume—a gorgeous flower of a brilliant scarlet—the red and white rose, [etc].   **1875** *Herald & Torch-Light* (Hagerstown MD) 20 Oct 1/5 **TX,** The most gorgeous flower that I have noticed is the Texas plume: it is a plant about five feet high, the upper half of which is entirely covered with crimson flowers, each plant looks like a plume of fire.   **1897** *Jrl. Amer. Folkl.* 10.50 **TX,** *Gilia coronopifolia* [=*Ipomopsis rubra*], . . Texas plume.   **1936** Whitehouse *TX Flowers* 105, *Standing Cypress. . .* The tall spikes with their masses of red tubular flowers make flaming spots of color on the edges of the post oak woods in May and June. It is sometimes known as . . Texas plume.   **1970** Correll *Plants TX* 1264, *Texas plume. . .* In sun or partial shade in dry sandy or rocky ground. . . From Tex., e. to Fla. and n. to N.C.

Texas porlieria n

Std: a **lignum vitae B** (here: *Guajacum angustifolium*) native to Texas. Also called **guayacan, Indian feather 2, soap-bush 3**

Texas prairie star See **Texas star a**

Texas purple-spike n

A **coralroot 2** (here: *Hexalectris warnockii*).

1970 Correll *Plants TX* 446, *Hexalectris Warnockii. . . Texas purple-spike. . .* The slender maroon or deep-purple stem and the rather large nodding flowers are characteristics of this species.

Texas rattlesnake n

A **diamondback rattlesnake** (here: *Crotalus atrox*).

1900 Stedman *Twentieth Cent. Practice* 20.495, Of the poisonous snakes of North America . . , the best known are: . . of the genus Crotalus . . C. atrox or Texas Rattlesnake, [etc]. **1928** Baylor Univ. Museum *Contrib.* 16.5, The poisonous snakes of Texas are . . Coral Snake . . , Copperhead . . , Texas or Western Diamond-back Rattlesnake. **1952** Ditmars *N. Amer. Snakes* 164, "Texas" Rattlesnake. . . Most of northern Mexico, northward through Texas into Oklahoma, western Arkansas and southern Missouri [etc].

Texas sarsaparilla See **sarsaparilla** B3

Texas snakeroot See **snakeroot b(1)**

Texas sparrow n

A small olive-colored finch (*Arremonops rufivirgatus*) native to southern Texas. Also called **green finch**

1881 U.S. Natl. Museum *Bulletin* 21.26, *Embernagra rufivirgata. . .* Texas Sparrow. **1898** (1900) Davie *Nests N. Amer. Birds* 395, *Texas Sparrow. . .* A common resident on the Lower Rio Grande, in Texas, where it frequents the thickets, brush-fences, and low shrubbery. **1944** Hausman *Amer. Birds* 341, The Texas Sparrow, a dull-colored and unobtrusive little bird, inhabits thickets. . . Its ingenuous little song is uttered from the top of a weed or small bush. **1960** Peterson *Field Guide Birds TX* 249, Olive sparrow—*Arremonops rufivirgata. . .* (Texas Sparrow). **2007** *DARE* File—Internet **TX,** There is no North American bird with a Texan common name (although I guess Olive Sparrow used to be called Texas Sparrow, Scrub Jay was Texas Jay, and Lesser Nighthawk was Texas Nighthawk?).

Texas star n

Any of several plants with flowers, or occas fruits, thought to resemble a star or have the shape of a star, as:

a also *pink Texas star, star of Texas, Texas prairie star:* A **marsh pink 1:** usu *Sabatia campestris,* but also *S. angularis.* Cf **sea star**

1897 *Jrl. Amer. Folkl.* 10.50 **TX,** *Sabbatia* [sic] *angularis, . .* Texas star. **1936** Whitehouse *TX Flowers* 98, *Pink Texas Star. . . Sabbatia campestris. . .* ranges from Missouri and Kansas to Texas and is found on moist prairies throughout Central Texas. **1951** *PADS* 15.37, *Sabbatia campestris. . .* Texas prairie-star. **1959** Carleton *Index Herb. Plants* 112, *Star-of-Texas: Sabbatia stellaris. Ibid* 116, *Texas star: Gilia rubra* [=*Ipomopsis r.*] . . ; *Sabbatia campestris.* **1967** *DARE* (Qu. S26a, . . *Wildflowers . . Roadside flowers*) Inf **TX**12, Texas star. [*DARE* Ed: This Inf may refer instead to another sense below.] **1970** Anderson *TX Folk Med.* 48, Kidney Trouble—Drink tea made from pink "Texas star" plant blossoms.

b A **tickseed 1.**

1907 *Springfield W. Republican* 22 Aug 6 (*DAE*), The fields are dotted with clumps of white golden coreopsis, called the Texas star.

c A cosmos (*Cosmos* spp).

1921 *DN* 5.114 **CA,** Texas star. . . Cosmos.

d also *Texas yellow star, yellow Texas star:* The Lindheimer **daisy 2** (*Lindheimera texana*).

[**1936** Whitehouse *TX Flowers* 170, *Lindheimer's Daisy* (*Lindheimera texana*) shows its star-like flower heads early in the spring.] **1939** Tharp *Vegetation TX* 72, Yellow Texas Star (*Lindheimera*). **1961** Wills–Irwin *Flowers TX* 231, *Lindheimera texana.* . . Texas-star, also known as . . Lindheimer's Daisy, occurs mainly on limestone soils. **1970** Correll *Plants TX* 1625, *Texas yellow star. . .* Abundant in prairies of n.-cen. and s. part of e. Tex. and Edwards Plateau, less abundant in Plains Country.

e also *blue Texas star:* A **blue star 1:** either *Amsonia ciliata* var *texana* or *A. tabernaemontana.*

1936 Whitehouse *TX Flowers* 99, *Blue Texas Star. . . Amsonia texana* [=*Amsonia ciliata* var *t.*] . . The plant is perennial, growing in low clumps on limestone hillsides of Texas. **1949** Moldenke *Amer. Wild*

Flowers 163, The *Texasstar, A[msonia] tabernaemontana,* grows from 2 to 4 feet tall. . . The numerous trumpet-shaped flowers are purplish-blue. . . They bloom . . from Massachusetts to Florida and westward to Kansas and Texas.

f also *red Texas star, Texas blazing-star:* =**standing cypress.**

1936 Whitehouse *TX Flowers* 105, *Standing Cypress* is sometimes known as . . red Texas star. . . The narrow tubular flowers are over an inch long and have broad spreading lobes. **1951** *PADS* 15.38 **TX,** *Gilia rubra* [=*Ipomopsis r.*] . . Texas star; Texas blazing-star. **1959** [see **a** above].

g pl: =**blue-eyed grass 1.**

1951 *PADS* 15.30 **TX,** *Sisyrinchium* spp.—Blue or yellow star-grass; prairie stars; Texas stars.

h =**puncture vine.**

1983 *DARE* File **nCO,** The scientific name of . . "Texas star" . . is *Tribulus terrestris.*

i A **hibiscus** (here: *Hibiscus coccineus*).

2000 *S. Living* Dec 76 **AL,** Texas star (*Hibiscus coccineus*) is one of the showiest and least appreciated species of native hibiscus. **2004** *DARE* File—Internet **NJ,** Summer Poinsettia Seeds—Seeds selected from Hibiscus coccineus. . . We obtained seeds for our plants from a dear friend in New Jersey where the plants are called 'Summer Poinsettia'. It is also know [sic] as 'Texas Star' in the southern states.

Texas strongback n

A **scorpion B1.**

1984 Weaver *TX Crude* 130, *Texas strongback.* A scorpion.

Texas thistle n

1 A **star thistle** (here: *Centaurea americana*).

1895 U.S. Dept. Ag. *Farmers' Bulletin* 28.29, Starthistle, Texas thistle. Centaurea americana. Texas to Oklahoma.

2 =**buffalo burr.**

1898 *Jrl. Amer. Folkl.* 11.276 **KS,** *Solanum rostratum. . .* Texas thistle. **1914** Georgia *Manual Weeds* 368, *Solanum rostratum. . .* Texas Thistle. . . This is one of the weeds frequently transported in baled hay. **1935** (1943) Muenscher *Weeds* 414, Texas thistle. . . Native to the Great Plains from South Dakota to Mexico.

Texas time n Cf **New York minute**

In fig phrr *take one's Texas time* to do something in a leisurely fashion; *on Texas time* unhurried, in an unhurried manner.

1985 in 2008 *DARE* File—Internet, *In a New York Minute. . .* I'd make love to you in a New York minute / And take my Texas time doing it. **2004** *Ibid* **TX,** In the mean time, jus kick back, relax and jus take your texas time perusin the site at your leisure. **2007** *DARE* File—Internet **TX,** You'll need some patience and *forget for a couple of hours, at least, that you have a microwave. . .* because from here on out you'll be cooking on Texas time! **2008** *Ibid,* I'm from *Texas* ((!!!)) and it's a big deal. . . my only bad habit is that I don't call people back . . aand [sic] I live on Texas time, in which I'm usually 10 minutes late to everything. **2009** *Ibid,* Could be that wordpress is on Texas time. . . a little slow.

Texas Tommy n [Perh in ref to the *Texas Tommy* a popular dance c1910]

Prob a **tumbleweed.**

1940 Writers' Program *Guide TX* 663 **wTX,** At midday, weird, heat-created mirages appear and disappear in the distance; heat-devils dance, and the dust-laden weed called Texas Tommy whirls across the highway and beats itself to pieces.

Texas tortoise n Also *Texan tortoise*

A **gopher** n[1] **1a** (here: *Gopherus berlandieri*) native to Texas.

1950 Brown *Annotated Reptiles TX* 235, *Gopherus berlandieri . .* Texan Tortoise. **1956** *Copeia* 177, [List of recommended common names:] Gopherus berlandieri—Texas Tortoise. **1972** Ernst–Barbour *Turtles* 192, Texas tortoises sometimes occupy empty mammal burrows of suitable size. **2001** (acc) TX Parks & Wildlife—Hunting & Wildlife *Wildlife Fact Sheets* (Internet), Features which help in identifying the Texas tortoise are the yellowish-orange, "horned" colored scutes . . on the carapace . . and the elongated . . scute on the plastron. . . The hind legs are cylindrical and columnar, like those of an elephant.

Texas trout n

A **sea catfish** (here: *Arius felis*).

2000 *DARE* File **LA,** Texas trout . . *Arius felis. . .* Average up to 1 pound.

Texas umbrella (tree) n Also *Texas umbrella Chinaberry, ~ China tree* Cf **Chinese umbrella, umbrella tree 2**

A cultivated variety of **Chinaberry 1** (*Melia azedarach* cv *umbraculiformis*) with an umbrella-like form.

1883 *Amer. Jrl. Forestry* 1.440 **TX,** A variety [of Chinaberry tree], *umbraculiformis* (Texas Umbrella Tree). Was first brought to notice about 40 years ago by J. Burke, Sr., of Houston, Tex. **1887** *Fresno Weekly Republican* (CA) [11 Feb 2/5] (newspaperarchive.com), [Advt:] *Fancher Creek Nursery. . .* Pomegranates, Mulberries, . . Texas Umbrella Trees, . . and Ornamental Plants. **1903** NM Ag. Exper. Station *Bulletin* 47.16, [*Melia azedarach*] Var. *umbraculiformis. . .* This is the Texas Umbrella Tree. . . It has a low roundish umbrella-shaped head with a dense foliage. **1960** Vines *Trees SW* 602, There occurs an umbrella-shaped variety known as the Texas Umbrella China-tree, *M. azedarach* forma *umbraculiformis* Berckm., which was reported to be found by botanists originally near San Jacinto Battlefield, Houston, Texas. **1968** *DARE* (Qu. T16, . . *Kinds of trees . . 'special'*) Inf **CA**79, Umbrella trees—Texas umbrella and Chinese umbrella. **2004** *DARE* File—Internet **CA,** The two Texas umbrella trees, on either side of the path, are about 5 years old. In the winter, the bare branches sport small, white, berry-like seed pods. . . In the spring, the trees have fragrant pink flowers. *Ibid* **FL,** Texas umbrella Chinaberry or Texas umbrella tree . . produces upward-arching branches and drooping foliage that make it look like an umbrella.

Texas weiner (or weinie, wiener, wienie) See **Texas hot (wiener)**

Texas white oak See **white oak 7**

Texas winter grass n Cf **winter grass**

A **needlegrass 1** (here: *Nassella leucotricha*).

1949 *Jrl. Range Management* 2.25, Correct grazing has accomplished brush cutting and a vigorous stand of Texas wintergrass, buffalograss, and curlymesquite has taken over. **1957** *Kerrville Times* (TX) 11 Sept 4/2, Some of the grasses on the range are little bluestem, sideoats grama, big bluestem, and Texas winter-grass. **1970** Correll *Plants TX* 121, *Stipa leucotricha* [=*Nassella l.*] . . *Texas winter-grass.* Tufted perennial. . . Abundant in n.-cen. Tex. and Edwards Plateau.

Texas woodpecker n Also *Texan woodpecker*
=**ladder-backed woodpecker 1.**

1872 Coues *Key to N. Amer. Birds* 193, *Texan Woodpecker. . .* Southwestern U.S. and southward. . . [*Picus*] *scalaris.* **1902** Van Vleet *Birds OK* [3], Picus scalaris. Texan Woodpecker. **1917** (1923) *Birds Amer.* 2.145, The Texas Woodpecker shows the ruling characteristic of its family in its choice of food, for the largest item is wood-boring beetle larvae. **1931** OK Univ. Biol. Surv. *Pub.* 3.115, *Texas Woodpecker: Dryobates scalaris symplectus*—Uncommon summer resident in the southwestern corner of the state and in the west end of Cimarron county. . . This little woodpecker has the upper parts including the outer tail feathers barred with black and white except for the middle tail feathers which are black. **1961** Ligon *NM Birds* 172, The Ladder-backed, Texas, or Cactus, Woodpecker is a small black and white bird of arid sections of the state. The color pattern is somewhat like that of the Hairy and Downy, but with red of the male covering entire top of the head. **1970** *DARE* (Qu. Q17, . . *Kinds of woodpeckers*) Inf **TX**84, Texan woodpecker.

Texas yellow star See **Texas star d**

texes See **text**

Texican n [Appar *Texican* Texan (*DA* 1864 →), reinterpreted as blend of *Texan + Mexican*]

A Texan of Mexican or mixed ancestry; hence used, often derog, for a migrant worker from Texas or elsewhere in the Southwest.

1916 Franck *Tramping* 250, Dakin was a boyish man from the Northern States, and Ems a swarthy "Texican" to whom Spanish was more native than English, both wandering southward in quest of jobs, as stationary and locomotive engineers respectively. **1920** *Amer. Child* 2.237 **CA,** Five-year-old children pick [cotton] steadily all day. "Why not?" one hears, "Most of them are Mexicans." Perhaps. But many white American children are among them. . . One hears much in the Valley of "Texicans"—a scornful term other pickers use in speaking of those who come from the Lone Star State. **1945** *Traverse City Rec.-Eagle* (MI) 11 Aug 3/6, *Pickers Depart as Harvest Nears the End*—"Texicans" and Mexican nationals were starting to move out of the region yesterday and today with the bulk of the 1100 nationals and about that many Texans

scheduled to be gone by the middle of next week. **1946** *Kingston Tribune* (WI) 27 June 1/3, *Badger Farmers Count On Help from "Texicans"*—About 2,000 Texas-Mexicans will be working on Wisconsin farms this summer. . . Unlike foreign workers . . the Texans are "free migrants." **1947** U.S. Congress House *Permanent Farm Labor* 53 **MI,** Mrs. *Hepburn.* We have, roughly, about 20,000 migrants coming into the State every year from Texas. They are now getting to call themselves Texicans and not Mexicans. Mr. *Poage.* They are not Mexican citizens; they were born in Texas. **1968** *DARE* Tape **WI**7, These are Mexicans from Texas. . . We call these other boys Texicans; they're the ones with the families. . . When their families are here, it's not so bad. **1971** *Post-Crescent* (Appleton WI) 6 Aug [sec A 4]/1 (newspaperarchive.com), The majority of migrant workers have been Chicanos, usually part Mexican and part Indian. In past years they often were called Texicans since the home base usually was southern Texas or New Mexico. **1993** *Race & Ethnic Relations* 225 **swKS,** Gene Rudd . . offers this shorthand for the town's new demography: "There are the old-timers, the Texicans and the wetbacks." The "Texicans," he says, are longtime Mexican-American residents who moved to Garden City before the recent immigration wave.

text n Usu |ˈtɛkst|; rarely |ˈtɛks, tɛsk|; pl: usu |ˈtɛksts|; also |ˈtɛks|; also **chiefly Sth, S Midl** |ˈtɛks(t)ɪz|; pronc-sp *tex;* pl *tex(t)es* Cf **-es** suff[1] **1a**

Std senses, var forms.

1827 (1939) Sherwood *Gaz. GA* 139, *Textes,* for Texts. **1837** *Ibid* 72, *Provincialisms. . . Tex* and *texes,* for text and texts. **1858** Avery *Harp* 10 **IN,** Ef you'll go and sarch the Scripturs, you'll not only find my tex thar, but a great many other *texes* as will do you good to read. **1861** *S. Lit. Messenger* 32.50 **wNC,** As it arr common ter divide texes inter gennerl heads, I'll divide mine. **1885** *Harper's New Mth. Mag.* 72.167 **VA** [Black], Dey sang de reg'lar shoutin' hymns, what . . is jis made up out o' verses o' old hymns and texes out o' de Bible. **1891** *PMLA* 6.168 **WV,** One minister, a hard-shell Baptist, . . spoke of the *texes* from which he preached his sermon. I need not add that he was from the Tuckahoe valley. **1927** Kennedy *Gritny* 52 **sLA** [Black], Preachin' on Bible texes an' things. **1936** *AmSp* 11.164 **eTX,** The pronunciations [ˈtɛkstɪz], [ˈnɛstɪz] . . occur in illiterate speech and the speech of children. **c1960** Wilson *Coll.* **csKY,** *Texts* is often /tɛks/ or /ˈtɛksɪz/. **1974** Fink *Mountain Speech* 26 **wNC, eTN,** *Textes* . . texts. **1981** Pederson *LAGS Basic Materials,* 1 inf, **cAL,** [tˈɛˑᵊsk] (=text); 1 inf, **swMS,** [tˈɛˑks] (=text).

te' you See **tell** v A

'th See **with** A1

thack See **that** A4

thaeuh See **their**

thaink See **think**

than conj Pronc-spp *(d)an, 'n*
A Forms.

1893 Shands *MS Speech* 62, *Th. . .* is in a large number of instances pronounced by negroes as *d;* as . . *dan* . . for . . *than.* **1894** Riley *Armazindy* 136 **IN,** This-here's gooder'n you *buy!* **1899** (1912) Green *VA Folk-Speech* 66, "I'd rather he'd have it an Tom." "This is better an the other." **1899** Garland *Boy Life* 83 **nwIA,** We don't mind 'em . . any more'n so many garter-snakes. **1901** *DN* 2.183 **neKY** [Black], *Than* . . dan. **1901** Harben *Westerfelt* 15 **nGA,** You'd better have it over with when you're young 'an to suffer when you're a weak old woman like me. **1921** Haswell *Daughter Ozarks* 18 (as of 1880s), Thar ain't nothin' nowhar no better'n this. **1928** Peterkin *Scarlet Sister Mary* 280 **SC** [Gullah], Three ain' no worse dan two. **1936** Greene *Death Deep South* 170 [Black], Some folks is curiouser 'an a cat. **1938** Rawlings *Yearling* 11 **nFL,** Your eyes is bigger'n your belly. **1965–70** *DARE* (Qu. X49, *Expressions . . about a person who is very thin*) Inf **NY**224, Skinnier 'n a rail; **NY**75, Thinner 'n a razor; (Qu. X56b, *Expressions about sweating very heavily*) Inf **VT**8, Wetter 'n a drowned rat; (Qu. DD14, *When a person is partly drunk,* "He's _____.") Inf **IL**135, Higher 'n a Georgia pine; **IL**135, Higher 'n a kite. **1976** Wolfram–Christian *Appalachian Speech* 54 **sWV,** You can't bat more 'n one eye at a time. . . I mean things are gettin' worser anymore 'n what they used to be.

B Sense.

In an equative comparison: As.

1976 Wolfram–Christian *Appalachian Speech* 176, My old woman in there has made as good a biscuits than you ever stuck in your mouth.

thang See **thing**

thank v[1], n Pronc-spp *thang, thenk; esp freq among Black speakers, tank, t'engk* Similarly adj *tanksful, t'engkful*

A Pronc varr.

1851 *Harper's New Mth. Mag.* 3.571 **CT** [Black], I t'ank you. **1861** Jacobs *Incidents Slave Girl* 169 **Sth** [Black], I don't want no tanks, honey. **1881** *Harper's New Mth. Mag.* 62.798 **VA** [Black], T'ank you, sah. **1899** (1912) Green *VA Folk-Speech* 443, *Thang. . .* For thank. "Thang God." **1922** Gonzales *Black Border* 333 **sSC, GA coasts** [Gullah glossary], *T'engkful*—thankful. *T'engk'Gawd*—thank God! **1925** in 1944 *ADD* **swSC, eGA** [Black], *Thank. . .* Everyday speech. 'Thenk you.' **1928** Peterkin *Scarlet Sister Mary* 53 **SC** [Gullah], Tank you kindly, June. *Ibid* 111, Be tanksful, gal. **1940** in 1944 *ADD* **nePA**, [tæŋk] t'ank. Low grade. **2000** *DARE* File **nwMI**, [Pamphlet from restaurant:] *Tanks:* An expression of gratitude.

B Gram form.

Pres 1st pers sg: usu *thank;* also *thanks. esp freq among Black speakers*

1853 Thomas *John Randolph* 93 **VA** [Black], I thanks you, sir. **1856** (1857) Browne *Autobiog.* 208 **KY** [Black], I thanks you for all your kindness to me. **1902** Dixon *Leopard's Spots* 23 **NC**, I thanks you from the bottom of my heart. **1908** Hatcher *John Jasper* 93 **VA** [Black], I thanks de Lord dat mos' enny nice leddy kin git merrid . . ef dey choose. **1939** in Lib. of Congress *Amer. Memory: WPA Life Hist.* (Internet) **GA** [Black], I thanks you for this nickel. **1965** *DARE* (Qu. NN6a, *Exclamations of joy . . when somebody gets a pleasant surprise, he might shout "_____."*) Inf **MS61**, I thanks the Lord. [Inf Black]

thank v[2] See **think**

thankee See **thanky**

thanks See **thank B**

thanky exclam Also *tanky, ten(g)ky, thankee, thonk ee*
Thank you; hence n *thanky* an utterance of the word, an expression of thanks.

1838 *U.S. Mag. & Democratic Rev.* 3.339 **NY,** So the Gen'ral's off without never a thankee. **1850** *Amer. Whig Rev.* 11.169 **NY,** Thanky sir. **1887** Freeman *Humble Romance* 3 **NEng,** Thanky kindly, miss; it's proper good water. **1888** Jones *Negro Myths* 110 **GA coast** [Gullah], Bes plan fuh er man fuh mek sho er eh bittle befo eh say tenky fuh um. **1899** (1912) Green *VA Folk-Speech* 443, *Thanky. . .* "Thank you," for something offered or received. **1909** *DN* 3.380 **eAL, wGA,** *Thanky. . .* Equivalent to *thank you.* "I wouldn't give you thanky for it." **1922** Gonzales *Black Border* 333 **sSC, GA coasts** [Gullah glossary], *T'engky*—thanks, thank you. **1937** in 1976 *Weevils in the Wheat* 62 **VA** [Black], Fer Christ sake A-men an' thanky Jesus! **c1938** in Lib. of Congress *Amer. Memory: WPA Life Hist.* (Internet) **TX** (as of 1859) [Black], These presents the slaves acknowledged with a "Thankee". **1950** [see **thanky poke**]. **1968** *DARE* (Qu. II39, . . *'Thank you'*) Inf **NY92**, Thanky. **1975** *Appalachian Jrl.* 2.151 **wNC,** A may become an *o:* . . *thonk ee* (thank you). **1976** Garber *Mountain-ese* 92 **sAppalachians,** *Thankee . .* I thank you. **1984** Wilder *You All Spoken Here* 24 **Sth,** Them as is friends don't need no thanky.

thanky bag See **thanky poke**

thank you for v phr [Abbr for *I will thank you for* (*OED2* thank v. 3.e 1813 →)] *esp S Midl*
Please pass to me or serve me (something)—used as a polite request at table.

1914 *DN* 4.160 **cVA**, *Thank yo' foah. . .* Please serve me to —. "Thank yo' foah some damsons!" **1958** *PADS* 29.17 **TN**, *Thank you for:* A polite phrase of request. "Thank you for the sorghum molasses" is given as the way to say "Please pass the sorghum." [**1986** Pederson *LAGS Concordance* (*Help yourself*) 1 inf, **neAR**, Thank you—a request for food to be passed.] **1996** *DARE* File **neTX** (as of 1920s–30s), At the table, instead of pass the bread—it was: "Thank you for the bread."

thank-you-ma'am n Also *thank-you-marm;* for addit varr see quots Cf **ma'am** n[1]

1 An abrupt dip or bump in a road or path, either naturally occurring, esp in ice or snow, or deliberately made, esp to divert runoff or, more recently, to slow automobile traffic. [Because it makes the passengers in a vehicle passing over it nod their heads as one might do in uttering this phr. The rhythm of the phr is also imitative, as in many of the synonyms.] Also called **belly-tickler, cahot, dipsy doodle 1, duck-and-dip,**

excuse-me-ma(a)m, how-do-you-do 1, johnny-come-lately, kiss-me-quick 3, tickle bump, whoop-de-do(o), Yankee bump, yes-ma'am Cf **breaker 2, jumper 14, water break** chiefly **Nth,** esp **NEast** See Map

1849 Longfellow *Kavanagh* 56 **NEng,** We went like the wind over the hollows in the snow;—the driver called them 'thank-you-ma'ams,' because they make every body bow. **1867** *Atlantic Mth.* 19.523 **NEng,** Life's a road that's got a good many thank-you-ma'ams to go bumpin' over, says he. **1882** *Harper's New Mth. Mag.* 64.859 **CT,** The old farm coasting path is near by upon the long knoll slope. We see the jouncing "thank you, marm," built up above the wall with rails, and packed with snow. **1890** *Jrl. Amer. Folkl.* 3.311 **MA, NH,** *Thank-ye-marm*—A diphole in the snow, calculated to give a jounce in coasting or sleighing. . . Also, in Massachusetts and New Hampshire, a popular name for the water-bars or open drains which run obliquely across the hill-roads. **1895** *New Engl. Mag.* 18.4 **NEng,** One vigorous trotter . . invariably selects six places of rest on the upward journey, on two of which he is forced to hold his load by main strength, for there is not even the suggestion of a "thank-you-marm." **1917** *DN* 4.402 **neOH, PA,** *Thank-you-ma'am. . .* In Ashtabula Co., a hole in the road when there is snow. **1919** *DN* 5.76 **NEng,** *Thank-you-ma'am.* In New England, not a hole of any sort, but a high, rounded ridge in the road causing a bounce when wheels pass over it. As our buggy struck one, and the bounce reacted, we would cry out: "Thánk-yòu-ma'am!" **1922** *NE State Jrl.* (Lincoln) [4 Dec] 4/2 (newspaperarchive.com), The Lincoln citizen who proposes a "thank-you-ma'am" at each street crossing for the restraining of automobile speed is not voicing a mere vapid dream. **1930** *Oakland Tribune* (CA) 7 Jan 14/2, The low gutter . . , famous for breaking the axles of autoists crossing Broadway without realizing depth [sic] of this thank-you-ma'am, will be ironed out immediately. **1941** Hench Coll. **PA** (as of 1910–12), To keep people from driving fast on the narrow roads of the tannery site, he had bumps put in the road. These I recall him calling "thank-you-marms." **1949** *Berkshire Co. Eagle* (Pittsfield MA) 10 Aug 17/2, There used to be such a trough part way up the long hill from South Egremont to Mount Washington. It was at the top of a steep pitch and every team stopped there, rear wheels braced by a thank-you-marm, while men and beasts rejoiced in the benediction of cold spring water. **1965–70** *DARE* (Qu. N30, . . *A sudden short dip in a road*) 99 Infs, chiefly **NEast,** Thank-you-ma'am; 18 Infs, chiefly **NEast exc NYC, NJ,** Thank-you-mom(s); **CT13, MA30, NY1, TN11,** Thank-you-marm(s); **IL32, NY75, 205, 214,** Thank-you-mum(s); (Qu. C17, . . *A small, rounded hill*) Inf **NY123,** Thank-you-marm; (Qu. N24, *A ditch along the side of a graded road*) Inf **CT2,** Thank-you-ma'am—gulleys right across the road for draining; (Qu. N27b, *When unpaved roads get very rough, you call them _____*) Inf **MA68,** Thank-you-ma'am—when there's a hump in it; **CA87,** Thank-you-moms. **1969** *DARE* Tape **MA30,** Thank-you-marma ['θæŋkjʊˌmɑrmə]. . . It was water bars they put on the hills to divert the water and—that was half of it, half to make an edge or rest for the wheels . . give the horses a rest on the hills. . . When the wheels dropped in, you would dip a head as though you were saying "thank you, marma." **1980** *NADS Letters* **cMO,** Thank-you-ma'am—Usually on road going up a hill to hold the wheels to allow the horses to rest. **1985** *WI Alumnus Letters* **ceWI,** Those built-in bumps on the road to slow one down are now called "silent policemen" but in their early years we called them by that good old term "thank-you-ma'am." *Ibid* **VT,** "Thank you Ma'ams". These were grooves built into the dirt roads on hills, to carry the rain water off of the crown of the road into the ditch.

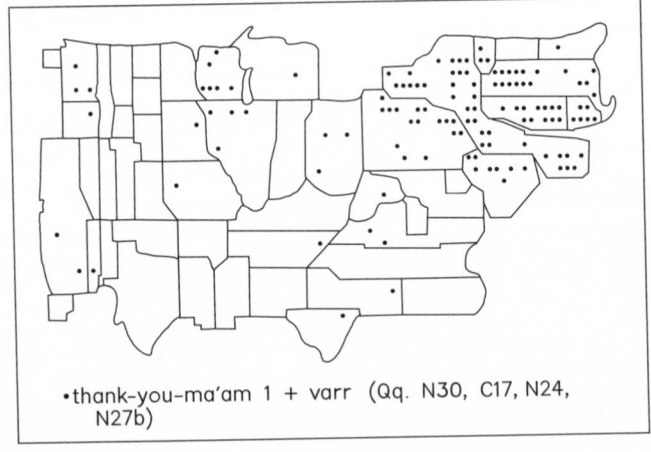

•thank-you-ma'am 1 + varr (Qq. N30, C17, N24, N27b)

2 Transf: a level stretch on a steep road where a team or vehicle can pause. [Cf the similar use of the water bars on steep roads in quots 1895, 1949, 1969, 1980 at **1** above]

1985 *WI Alumnus Letters* **NH**, Regarding "thank-you-ma'am"—in New Hampshire this did not refer to a dip in the road but rather to a flat place when you are going up a hill. According to my grandmother, the derivation came from horses pulling a carriage up the hill. When they got to the flat place they could take a breath and presumably were thinking "Thank you, ma'am." *Ibid* **wMA** (as of c1925), The thank-you-ma'am . . was a level space on a steep slope to rest a team. The farm on which I spent my childhood was a 400-acre shelf half way up a mountain . . in the Massachusetts Berkshires. The road up was very steep and contained four thank-you-ma'ams. When pulled up, the horses always turned in their traces to look back at the wagon, their heads tossing and blowing, saying "Thank you, Ma'am or Sir!" in language entirely clear to anyone who understands horse talk. **1985** *DARE* File **cNY** (as of c1900), Thank-you-marm. A resting place for a loaded wagon on a steep up-hill road to give the horses a breathing place. *Description:* The resting place is a level stretch about 25 ft. long. It is leveled so that the wheels of the wagons need not be blocked. The horses can stand without straining or pulling. They were found in both city and country roads. **2005** *DARE* File—Internet **ceNJ**, "Thank you, Ma'am"s provide the stepped appearance of the road surface . . and are an original feature of its engineering. These level areas connected by sloping risers were built into the road to give relief to horses pulling loads. *Ibid* **cNJ**, The farm was at the top of a hill. Mom tells me that the driveway up the hill had a series of "thank-you-ma'ams"—level spots on the way up the drive.

3 Fig: something of little value.

1952 Brown *NC Folkl.* 1.599, *Thank-you-ma'm.* . . Something of slight worth. "I wouldn't give him a thank-you-ma'm for every dog he has."—Central and east.

thanky poke n Also *t(h)anky bag* [**thanky** + **poke** n¹ **1a, b(1)**] Cf **sanky poke**

A purse, pouch, sack; see quots.

1898 Lloyd *Country Life* 136 **AL**, Aunt Nancy [=a White woman] put her pipe away in her thanky bag. **1950** *PADS* 14.66 **SC**, *Tanky bag.* . . A bag formerly carried by colored retainers when visiting former slave owners, shortly after the end of slavery. The *tanky bag* was filled and the bearers expressed their thanks; *"Tanky, tanky,"* whence the name. **1952** Brown *NC Folkl.* 1.599, *Thanky-poke.* . . A lady's purse.

thanky suit n [Cf *EDD* thank you, sir (at **thank** v. 1.(7)) "a second-hand article of clothing"]

1952 Brown *NC Folkl.* 1.599, *Thanky-suit.* . . A suit given away; hence a rather worthless one.

thanuary n Also *thornuary* [?Varr of *January*] Cf **hill dill**

A children's running game; see quot.

1969 *DARE* (Qu. EE27, *Games played on the ice*) Inf **RI**17, Thornuary ['θɔrnjuˌɛri] or thunder—when played in yard, called hill dill—everybody goes to one end. When "thunder" [is] called, run to far end. "It" has to catch people. All he catches help him catch rest till all caught. Rhyme to go with thornuary: Thornuary, thornuary, three times three / If you don't come now, I'll catch you where you be; (Qu. EE33, . . *Outdoor games . . that children play*) Inf **RI**12, Thanuary ['θænjuˌɛri]—played in yard. We always associated it with January, since you played it then, though not only then [FW: same rhyme as in Jamestown [=community of Inf **RI**17]].

thar adv, adj   See **there A2**

thar(e) pron   See **their**

tharsefs   See **theirselves**

thass   See **that A5**

that pron, conj, adv, art   Usu |ðæt|, unstressed |ðət|; for varr see **A** below

A Forms.

1a pronc-sp *'at.* esp **Sth, S Midl**

1894 Riley *Armazindy* 162 **IN**, He . . mocks the girl 'at scrubs the floor. **1941** O'Donnell *Great Big Doorstep* 17 **sLA** [Black], Evva time at man come heah to wuk Ah godda cook three-fo extry dishes. **1942** Hall *Smoky Mt. Speech* 85 **wNC, eTN**, The omission [of ð] is frequent in such phrases as . . *like that* . . [laᶦkˣˀæt]. **1958** Humphrey *Home from the Hill* 51 **TX**, At's my ole whomper-jawed Rip hound! **1969** *DARE* (Qu. H71) Inf **MO**15, Takin' 'at last piece. **1976** Wolfram–Christian

Appalachian Speech 54, And this boy grabbed a great big cinder block—'bout like *'at* and throwed *'at* in on me. **2000** *DARE* File **seKY** (as of c1950), "I bet At will teach you a lesson". . . "At's the way to do it". **2005** *DARE* File—Internet **Pittsburgh PA**, *Ats*—that's.

b in phrr *that's the boy* (or *girl*): pronc-spp *at(t)a boy* (or *girl*).

1909 *Amer. Mag.* May 40 **IL**, Back of Chance's war cries, "At-a-boy," or "Now ye're pitching," may be hidden a whole command to his team. **1922** *Pt. Arthur Daily News* (TX) 5 May 4/4, "[+]Attaboy, Attaboy!"/ It's a tonic, it's a joy./ It's a phrase of honest praise without alloy. **1924** Marks *Plastic Age* 26 **NEng**, Suddenly one of the girls . . caught the bag deftly. . . Atta girl! **1976** Wolfram–Christian *Appalachian Speech* 54, There are some mainstream varieties where sentence initial ð is deleted. . . Atta boy. **1992** *Mt. Democrat & Placerville Times* (CA) 17 Aug sec A 2/1, Here's an *Atta girl!* for Marci Freeman, director and teacher at the Placerville Preschoolers/Kids' Kampus.

2 |dæt|; pronc-spp *da(t).*   esp freq among **Black speakers**

1823 Cooper *Pioneers* 2.183 **cNY** [Black], "Oh! Worser 'an a dat! worser 'an a dat!" sobbed the negro. **1853** *Harper's New Mth. Mag.* 8.134 **NEng** [Black], Dat year de people call me Mr. Dickson. **1884** *Anglia* 7.258 **Sth, S Midl** [Black], There are many peculiar intensives in the Negro dialect designed to give emphasis to an assertion: . . *I wuz dat tired.* **1887** Page *In Ole VA* 213 **VA** [Black], Ever afterward she blessed the Lord for "dat chile." **1888** Jones *Negro Myths* 3 **GA coast**, From dat day to dis. **1893** Shands *MS Speech* 62, Th is in a large number of instances pronounced by negroes as *d:* as . . *dat* . . for . . *that.* **1908** *DN* 3.282 **eAL, wGA**, [ð] in all positions has, under negro influence, largely become *d*, as in . . [dæt]. **1908** *S. Atl. Qrly.* 7.334 **sSC coast** [Gullah], 'Da' you?' 'Da' me'. **1922** Gonzales *Black Border* 169 **eSC**, Ef uh didn' bin hab 'lij'un [=religion], da' 'ooman' cawpse would'uh gone Jacksinburrah een one oxin cyaa't. **a1930** in 1991 Hughes–Hurston *Mule Bone* 29 **cFL** [Black], There's a heap goin' on 'round heah . . dat Ahm gointer put a stop to. **1930** *AmSp* 6.96 **seVA**, A strong tendency to substitute [d] for [ð] in *that, the,* etc. **1939** Griswold *Sea Is. Lady* 514 **sSC** [Gullah], Miss Em'ly, I been dat worry I ain' pit one drap of food to my mout' dis mo'nin'. **1983** *Daily Intelligencer* (Doylestown PA) 23 Aug 6/6 **Chicago IL**, [Mike Royko column:] But dat's high treason. Dey could be hanged for somethin' like dat, don't dey know it?

3 |ðɛt, ðɑt|; pronc-spp *thet, thot, thut.*

1846 in 1848 Lowell *Biglow* 3 **'Upcountry' MA**, 'Taint a knowin' kind o' cattle / Thet is ketched with mouldy corn. **1858** *Atlantic Mth.* 2.497 **MA**, 'T's mighty plain / Thut the weakes' place mus' stan' the strain. **1869** *Overland Mth.* 3.362 **West**, Thet's it. **1891** *DN* 1.128 **cNY**, The place of [æ] is taken by [ɛ] in many words. . . *'that.'* **1892** *DN* 1.242 **cwMO**, That. Often pronounced [ðɛt] in Kansas City [*DN* Ed: and New England]. "What's thet to you?" **1909** *DN* 3.405 **nwAR**, Thet. . . That. **1930** in 1944 *ADD* **eVA**, That. . . thot [ðɑt]. Several occurrences. **1931** Randolph *Ozarks* 68, Whilst thet 'ar pore susy hippoed woman o' hisn was a-pickin' boogers out'n her yeller tags. **1968** *DARE* FW Addit **MD**20, That [ðɛt] there. **1984** Burns *Cold Sassy* 20 **nGA** (as of 1906), Lord, forgive me for fittin' [=fighting] thet man yesterd'y.

4 pronc-sp *thack.*

1975 Gould *ME Lingo* 289, *Thack*—A curious and unexplained manipulation of "that" by a good many old Mainers: "Thack's just the way he said it."

5 in phr *that's:* pronc-spp *ass, das, thass.*

1858 Hammett *Piney Woods Tavern* 140 [Black], Dey was sparkin' a little, das all. **1934** Hurston *Jonah's Gourd Vine* 305 **AL** [Black], Well, Ah'll give you uh li'l short ride, if thass all yuh want. **1942** *AmSp* 17.17 **HI** [Engl of Hawaiian children], 'Ass (that's). . . As in 'ass mine for *that's* mine. **1949** in 1980 *DARE* File **seMI**, Thassa good one, Wilbur.

B As adv.

Modifying an adj with a following (or rarely preceding) result clause: So, to such an extent.   chiefly **Sth, S Midl**

1883 (1971) Harris *Nights with Remus* 76 **GA** [Black], He wuz dat flat-footed dat, w'en he fine a bee-tree, he can't climb it. **1890** Holley *Samantha among Brethren* 58 **NY**, He had got that wild and reckless in his demeanor and acts, that he went right on with his hollerin'. **1893** *KS Univ. Qrly.* 1.142 **KS**, That: so, as 'He's that sick he can't speak.' **1903** *DN* 2.333 **seMO**, That. . . So. 'I was that tired I could hardly stand up.' **1906** *DN* 3.161 **nwAR**, It was that hard I just couldn't stand. **1922** *DN* 5.184 **GA, KY**, That. . . I'm dat hongry dat my stomach is gittin' ready to go in mo'nin'. **1932** (1974) Caldwell *Tobacco Road* 38 **GA**, He's that lazy he won't get up off the ground sometimes when he stumbles. **1942** McAtee *Dial. Grant Co. IN* 65 (as of 1890s), *That . . so. Dial.* "I was — scairt I couldn't move." **1945** FWP *Lay My Burden Down* 143 **Sth** (as of c1865) [Black], The water come outen these rocks that cold that you can't hold your hand in it for more than a minute. **1946** *PADS* 6.30 **eNC** (as of 1922), *That. . .* I was that tired I couldn't walk. **1952** Brown *NC Folkl.* 1.599, She's that pretty she'll soon be married. **1988** Smith *Fair Ladies* 86 **wNC,** I did not care if it rained or not, nor if I was wet nor dry, I was that sad to be leaving Sugar Fork.

C As conj.

1 Used to introduce a restrictive relative clause that remains formally indistinguishable from an independent sentence, as:

a a clause expressing possessive relation, with:

(1) a possessive pronoun in the relative clause referring to the antecedent. [*OED2 that* rel. pron. 9 "*That* followed by a poss. pron. corresponding to the antecedent . . is an ancient mode of expressing the genitive of the relative. . . *Still common dialectally.*" 1456 →] Cf **that's** pron

1857 in 1927 Jones *FL Plantation Rec.* 173 **nwFL,** I have gote wone [=a mule] thate here winde has bin ingerd [=injured]. **1918** (1920) Tarkington *Magnificent* 106 **IN,** There's a few people that their birth and position, and so on, puts them at the top. **1922** Lewis *Babbitt* 18, There's two fellows that their dads are millionaires. **1936** *AmSp* 11.351 **eTX,** *That* is usually employed as the relative pronoun by the more illiterate speakers, instead of *who. . .* 'They won't hire nobody that their folks ain't on relief.' **1940** Faulkner *Hamlet* 34 **MS,** He was married to his first wife then, the one he got from Jefferson, that one day her pa drew up in a wagon and loaded her and the furniture into it. **1943** *LANE* Map 631 *(Whose father),* [In the context "A boy _____ father is very rich," the response *that his* occurs in all areas of **NEng** except **wMA.** It is the most frequent response (occurring considerably more often than *whose*) in **NH, ME,** and is also quite common in much of **eMA.** Other exx of this construction noted by fieldworkers are: "A lady that her husband died" **(nwCT);** "This old lady that you saw her picture" **(cnCT);** "There's a woman that her name is Sarah" **(seMA);** "A boy that I settled his father's estate" **(seMA);** "My nephew, that I showed you his house yesterday" **(seMA);** "There was a painter made that for me, that his office was down on the wharf" **(cwVT).**] **1975** Allen *LAUM* 2.56 **Upper MW** (as of c1950), *Whose. . .* Many persons . . especially the less educated, find *whose* too difficult to handle and either resort to various unorthodox equivalents or give up completely. . . Both in New England and in the U[pper] M[idwest] the most frequent equivalent in a context with a masculine antecedent is *that his.* Nearly one-third of the Type I [=old, with little formal educ] infs. have this, as does even one Type III [=mid-aged, with coll educ] inf., a Minnesota stock-raiser. **1986** Pederson *LAGS Concordance,* 19 infs, **Gulf Region, esp LA,** [A boy] that his father was rich (and varr); 1 inf, **cMS,** Here's a man that his mother was a train [sic] nurse; 1 inf, **neAR,** This young man that his mother passed away; 1 inf, **swAR,** I've got some cousins that their daddy did that. **2002** *DARE* File—Internet **seKY,** I know a well known minister, that his hair may be an inch longer than some men think it should be.

(2) possessive relation unexpressed but implied by the definite article.

1943 *LANE* Map 631 *(Whose father)* 3 infs, **ceMA, Nantucket Is. MA,** [A boy] that the father [is very rich]; 1 inf, **csCT,** A tree that the branches were hanging low. **1975** Allen *LAUM* 2.56 **Upper MW** (as of c1950), *Whose. . .* The variant *that the . .* appears 11 times in the U[pper] M[idwest] (though not at all in neighboring Wisconsin), also with majority use by Type I [=old, with little formal educ] infs. **1986** Pederson *LAGS Concordance,* 3 infs, **nwAL, ceTX, csTX,** A child that the father was rich (and varr); 1 inf, **neGA,** Lambs that the mother died; 1 inf, **neTX,** I had one that the cotton was grown in Florida.

b a clause expressing other relations, with:

(1) an anaphoric personal pron or adv in the main clause of the embedded sentence referring to the antecedent. Note: From the perspective of std grammar, the anaphoric element in all these exx is simply redundant.

1936 *AmSp* 11.351 **eTX,** Is that the Porters that one of them got killed a few years ago? **1943** *LANE* Map 629 *(Who owns)* 1 inf, **seMA,** [He is the man] that he owns [the orchard]; 1 inf, **cwCT,** I got a cousin that he runs the school; 1 inf, **nwCT,** There's some people that they like to have their children call them . . ; We have a relative by marriage that she says; 1 inf, **seMA,** There's a woman over there that she has a son; 1 inf,

seMA, If a fellow that he uses a lot of wood should ask me; 1 inf, **ceMA,** I had a cook that she had a beau; 1 inf, **cMA,** There are birds that you don't very often see them; 1 inf, **seVT,** There's a man here that she used to work for him. *Ibid* Map 630 *(Who is poor)* 1 inf, **csCT,** There's a boy here that he's 15 years old; 1 inf, **seMA,** We had a schoolteacher that she was an awful bashful girl; 1 inf, **nwMA,** I know many words that they're not used any more. **1962** Steinbeck *Travels* 197, Anybody saw you make a birthday cake for a dog that he don't even know when's his birthday would think you were nuts. **1968** *DARE* (Qu. H27) Inf **LA20,** Doughnut that the lady cut a hole in it with the one tooth. **1975** Allen *LAUM* 2.55 (as of c1950), *Who/that. . .* They had a caller there that he got $600 for callin' one night [1 inf, **ND**]. . . I have a grandson that he is the fourth [1 inf, **NE**]. . . I worked with a man that he had his horses [1 inf, **NE**]. **1986** Pederson *LAGS Concordance,* 1 inf, **neTX,** There was a doctor here in Greenville that he lost his wife; 1 inf, **seLA,** They have a sugar that they cook it into a syrup; 1 inf, **cLA,** A willow pole that they went into the woods and got it; 1 inf, **seMS,** Place that you can't go there; 1 inf, **cAL,** We also had a big walk-in box that we would set our milk in there and keep it good and cold. **1989** in 2004 Montgomery–Hall *Dict. Smoky Mt. Engl.* 599 **wNC, eTN,** *That. . .* There was a couple of brothers that they had a moonshine still. **2001** *DARE* File **cs,ceOK,** Consider *that* plus a subject for "who" as in "you do hear of a man *that* they see one" meaning "you do hear of a man who sees one." . . "McKinnon's was another wealthy people *that* they had a store." . . "He was just a guy *that* he'd do anything for people."

(2) an anaphoric pron in a subordinate clause in the embedded sentence referring to the antecedent. Note: In these exx, omission of the anaphoric pronoun produces a sentence that is either entirely ungrammatical ("He's a man that I don't like the way treats his wife") or marginally grammatical ("They cure a lot of folks that you . . can't seem to find out what's the matter with").

1925 Lewis *Arrowsmith* 149 **ND,** They cure a lot of folks that you regular docs can't seem to find out what's the matter with 'em. **1936** *AmSp* 11.353 **eTX,** Miscellaneous Unusual Constructions: . . He's a man that I don't like the way he treats his wife. Uncle George was the kind of man that you could always tell which side of any question he was on. **1943** *LANE* Map 629 *(Who owns)* 1 inf, **csMA,** There's a lot of them that I don't know if they was born here. **1986** Pederson *LAGS Concordance,* 1 inf, **cTN,** A little mean dog that you can't really tell what it is; [1 inf, **cMS,** Brooms that you went out in the field and would bring broomstraw and make a broom out of it].

2 Used immediately after a conj, relative, or dependent interrogative. Note: Not illustrated here are such combs as *now that, seeing that,* in which *that* is optional in std grammar. [*OED2 that* conj. 6.a c888 →; 7 c1200 →] **chiefly Sth, S Midl**

1862 in 2010 Montgomery–Ellis *Corpus Amer. Civil War Letters* **VT,** I halve had it offered to me a good many times since that I Came here. **1915** *DN* 4.229 **wTX,** *That* is often used pleonastically in such phrases as "Because that (or since that) I couldn't go." **1946** *AmSp* 21.272 **neKY,** *That . .* (superfluous). . . 'It does look like that college students shouldn't have any difficulty . . ' ' . . how that education may improve rural life in the South. . . ' These . . constructions, *like that* and *how that,* are heard on all levels. **1954** *Hall Coll.* **wNC, eTN,** *Because that. . .* So not just because that I'm born and raised here, but I'm just telling ye what other people tells me. **1956** *Ibid, How that. . .* Tell us how that you would find and get the sheep in. *Ibid, Why that. . .* Maybe you can explain then why that it does that. **1978** in 2004 Montgomery–Hall *Dict. Smoky Mt. Engl.* 643 **wNC, eTN,** *When that. . .* I don't remember exactly when that they started building in White Pine. *Ibid, Where that. . .* That's where that I went to school. **1982** Ginns *Snowbird Gravy* 91 **nwNC,** It's just as much glory to him because that if they'd look at it like that, it proves to 'em that it's not me. **b1982** *DARE* File **wTX,** Don't feel *like that* you're being forgotten. I didn't know *whether that* I ought to decline. He didn't understand *why that* others thought differently. Common. **1986** Pederson *LAGS Concordance,* 1 inf, **swGA,** She don't know where that she came from; 1 inf, **swGA,** Hit has got to where that you are never on time; 1 inf, **cwMS,** Unless that he had gone in to shave or something; 1 inf, **swMS,** I feel like that the Lord has given me and her a wonderful life together; 1 inf, **cwLA,** To hold the plate down to where that the hot tamales wouldn't rise to the top; 1 inf, **csTX,** He just felt like that he wanted to preach. **1986** Wear *Sugarlands* 80 **ceTN,** I wondered why that my father called it the lumber room. **1999** in 2004 Montgomery–Hall *Dict. Smoky Mt. Engl.* 649 **wNC, eTN,** I can see why that that would be so. **2007** *DARE* File **nwTX,** If you're about ten years older than I am and from Lubbock, TX, "wh-that" sentences are still possible. The guy sounded like a cowboy extra in a '40's horse opera, eg. ". . . who that I was a-tellin' y'all about." Since ten years older than I am would place him in his 80's, there may not be many such speakers left.

3 Repeated before the main clause of an embedded sentence when a subordinate clause precedes.

1946 *AmSp* 21.272 **neKY,** That . . (superfluous). . . I said that if it rained that the road would be bad.

4 So, so that. [Cf *OED2 that* conj. II.4.b →1868; "*arch.*"]

1914 in 1944 *ADD* **sePA,** We like our pie piping hot that it steams. **1934** *Language* 10.4 **cPA,** *That* is often used in result clauses where normal English would have *so that: I cut my finger that it bled, [the] grade crossing. . . has been reconditioned that vehicular travel is smooth again* (Selinsgrove *Times,* July 20, 1933).

D   As pron.

1   The like, others of the same sort.

1852 Warner *Queechy* 1.397 **NY,** Ha' you got a good big cask, or plenty o' tubs and that? **1966–70** *DARE* Tape **IN**17, The older people and that were all hepped up about the idea; **MI**12, Some of the bigger cities like Detroit and that; **WI**75, That's . . for fishing off piers and that. **1978** *DARE* File **csWI,** You have to have a car to get into town to do your shopping or that. **1979** *Ibid* **swWI,** In high school we never had parallelism and balanced sentences and that. **2003** *NY Times* (NY) 7 Jan sec C 7/4 **wPA,** From a "You Know You're From Pittsburgh If. . ." list on an online chat room about the city: If you add " 'n'at" to the end of every other sentence. **2005** *DARE* File—Internet **Pittsburgh PA,** Maybe some pigs in a blanket or a perogie n'at. . . Let's git some chipped chopped ham . . n'at too.

2   That which. [*OED2 that* rel. pron. 3.a c888 →; "Very common down to 16th c.; now *arch.* and *poetic*"]

1972 *Foxfire Book* 205 **nGA,** Lot'a people throwed away that they called th' rooter.

E   As def art.

Used without demonstrative or emphatic force as equiv to *the.*

1850 in 1999 *AmSp* 74.274 **ceSC,** I war of the mine that i war blest with him lik abraham en that bible. **1944** *PADS* 2.50 **NC, VA,** That: def. art. The; used when not demonstrative or emphatic. "Give that feed to that cow." **1986** Pederson *LAGS Concordance* **Gulf Region,** 1 inf, He really knew that Bible; 1 inf, Home to that base; 1 inf, Across that bay; 1 inf, I say that cow found that calf; 1 inf, A-standing out there in that hall; 1 inf, That ground wasn't no good, if them worms wasn't in that ground; 1 inf, She took me, ga-zip, and hit me in that eye; etc. [*DARE* Ed: Some of these exx may be intended as demonstrative or emphatic.]

thataway adv   Also *thataways*   Cf **a** inert vowel **4, there-away(s), thisaway, whichaway(s),** *yonaway* (at **yonway**)

(In) that direction, way, or manner; like that.

1823 Cooper *Pioneers* 1.196 **nNY,** They are carryin on a great stroke of business that-a-way. **1843** (1916) Hall *New Purchase* 395 **IN,** I thought I might as well fire that a way as any other. **1890** *Overland Mth.* (2d ser) 15.287 **sCA,** There is a little woman lives up our street that a ways. **1899** *Catholic World* 69.793 **Appalachians,** If any of you fellows in store-clothes went down thataways now, you'd be shot first and they'd ask who you might be afterwards. **1901** Harben *Westerfelt* 15 **nGA,** It looked that away to me. **1903** *DN* 2.301 **Cape Cod MA** (as of a1857), *That a way.* . . That way. **1909** *DN* 3.381 **eAL, wGA,** *That-a-way.* . . In that way. **1910** *DN* 3.457 **seKY,** *That-a, this-a.* . . That, this. "You should not talk that-a way." **1916** *DN* 4.330 **KS,** *Thataway.* . . Combination of *that way,* in that manner. **1918** *DN* 5.21 **NC,** *That-a-way, this-a-way,* that way, this way. **1923** *DN* 5.223 **swMO,** *That-away.* . . That way, in that manner, in that direction. **1927** Adams *Congaree* 68 **cSC** [Black], I axe him wuh make he act that-a-way. **1946** *AmSp* 21.53 **nMN,** 'A-going' sounded quite foreign to us, as did 'that-a-way,' both of which were used by a Nebraska family which moved into the community. **1965–70** *DARE* (Qu. MM5, . . *"The house is over _____."*) 25 Infs, **scattered,** Thataway; (Qu. BB40, . . *"All of a sudden he got up and left. What do you suppose _____ him?"*) Inf **KY**11, Made him act thataway; (Qu. KK66, . . *"No, not like that—do it _____."*) Infs **MI**82, **ND**3, Thataway; (Qu. MM12a, . . *'In all directions' . . "He shot into a flock of birds and they went _____."*) Inf **MI**97, Thataway; (Qu. MM22, *If you are talking to a friend who lives in another place and you want to inquire about his neighbor-*

hood . . *"How are things _____?"*) Inf **DE**1, Up thataway. **1966** *DARE* Tape **MS**68, I don't guess you've been up thataway; **NM**3, About nine o'clock in the morning to eight, something thataway, til right about noon. **1991** Greene *Praying for Sheetrock* 243 **seGA,** The State Tourism Department posted signs that urged, "Stay and See Georgia." But the coast listed toward Disneyworld, the quarters and half-dollars rolling thataway.

thataway adj   See **that way**

thataways   See **thataway** adv

thatch grass n   Also *thatch, thatchy grass*   **N Atl**   Cf **creek thatch, salt ~**

Any of var tall, coarse grasses, but usu **cordgrass;** a mass of such grasses.

1622 Mourt's Relation *Iournall Plimoth* 25 **MA,** Some of our people being abroad, to get and gather thatch, they saw great fires. **1682** in 1899 Providence RI Rec. Comm. *Early Rec.* 15.238, Sume kare may be takun Consarning the thach beeds. **1704** in 1894 *Ibid* 5.224, The . . Cove is a place of salt Grass called Thatch. **1704** in 1896 *Ibid* 11.90, Care might be taken for the orderly Cutting of the thatch Grass on the Thatch beds which are within our Towneship of Providence. **1818** Trumbull *Complete Hist.* CT 1.37, Where lands were thus burned there grew bent grass, or as some called it, thatch, two, three and four feet high. **1863** (1864) Mitchell *My Farm* 49 **NEng,** I . . gave them [=bees] a warm shelter of thatch. **1910** Graves *Flowering Plants* 68 **CT,** *Spartina Michauxiana* [=*S. pectinata*]. . . Thatch Grass. **1911** *Century Dict. Suppl., Creek-sedge.* . . A salt-marsh grass, *Spartina glabra* [=*S. alterniflora* var g.] . . Also called *thatchy grass.* **1916** *Torreya* 16.237 **ME,** *Ammophila arenaria.* . . Thatch. **1948** Pearson *Sea Flavor* 118 **NH,** Thatch is an interesting grass. Often it grows to 6 feet or more in height, its jaunty plumes of tan-colored flowers and seed waving in the breeze. **2001** *DARE* File—Internet **eMA,** Saltmarsh cordgrass or thatch grass (Spartina alterniflora). . . was used by the early settlers to thatch the roofs of their houses.

thatch-leaf n

Bay cedar *(Suriana maritima).*

1933 Small *Manual SE Flora* 762, *S[uriana] maritima.* . . *Thatch-leaf.* . . The bay-cedar is usually a shrub with many stems, growing in coastal sands, often just back of the tide line. **1979** Little *Checklist U.S. Trees* 280, *Suriana maritima.* . . Thatch-leaf. . . Shores of c. and s. Fla. incl. Fla. Keys.

thatchy adj   [*thatch* (at **thatch grass**) + *-y*]   Cf **grassy,** *DS* K14

1890 *DN* 1.20 **seNH,** *Thatchy:* said of milk. The milk tastes 'thatchy' because the cows eat 'thatch.' A long, coarse grass, growing in the salt marshes, is known as 'thatch' on the New Hampshire and Massachusetts seacoast. . . The 'thatch' which the New Hampshire cows eat seems to be different from this. It is described as a sort of weed, growing in low places.

thatchy grass   See **thatch grass**

that out adv phr   [Prob *that* pronc-sp for *'thout* (at **without**) + *doubt* with assim of d; cf Pronc Intro 3.II.14]

Without doubt; certainly.

1969 *DARE* FW Addit **seVA,** *That out*—to be sure; certainly. "That out, it isn't gonna rain again." Common. **1991** *DARE* File **eVA,** "That out she's not too *chinchy* to buy a new spider" translates to "You can't mean she's too cheap to buy a new frying pan.["] "That out" means without doubt or doubt out.

that's phr   See **that** A5

that's pron   [Prob a reinterpretation of *that's* contraction of *that his;* cf **that** C1a(1) and *SND that* pron. I.1]

Used as a possessive relative: Whose, of which.

1943 *LANE* Map 631 *(Whose father)* 2 infs, **cnMA, swME,** [A boy] that's father [is very rich]; 1 inf, **swMA,** That's, whose, both unnatural. **1986** in 2004 Montgomery–Hall *Dict. Smoky Mt. Engl.* 599 **wNC, eTN,** We need to remember a woman thats child has died. **1986** Pederson *LAGS Concordance,* 1 inf, **nwFL,** [The boy] that's father was rich; 1 inf, **neFL,** That's mother's a nurse; 1 inf, **seAL,** The boy that's father have [sic] plenty of money. **2004** Adams *My Old Love* 12 **wNC** (as of c1865), I've knowed some that's passion for each other turned to hate.

2011 *DARE* File **TX**, [Heard on television news:] A megachurch that's waistline is growing as fast as its congregation.

that's a horse on one See **horse B9**

that's your mammy See **your mamma**

that there See **there B**

that way adj phr Also *thataway* Cf **like that**
Also in phr *in that way:* Pregnant.

1940 (1968) Haun *Hawk's Done Gone* 103 **TN**, "I guess I might as well tell you now. I'm that way, Ma." . . I tried to think it would be a girl baby. **1954** *Harder Coll.* **cwTN**, *That(a)way.* . . Pregnant. **1965–70** *DARE* (Qu. AA28, *. . Joking or sly expressions . . women use to say that another is going to have a baby . . "She['s] _____."*) 22 Infs, scattered, That way (again); **MA**123, Is that way; **MO**16, Thataway. [16 of 22 total Infs mid-aged] **1986** Pederson *LAGS Concordance (Pregnant)* 3 infs, **AL, LA, MS,** (In *or* she's) that way; 1 inf, **cwAL,** Got his wife thataway. **2002** *DARE* File **KY**, My east-Kentuckian grandmother (1904–1986) used "that way" as a euphemism for "pregnant": e.g., "That was when I was that way with [her child's name]."

thaught, thaut, thawt See **thwart**

thay pron See **they** pron[2]

thay exclam See **they** exclam

thayer See **their**

the def art Usu |ðə, ði|; also |də, di|, rarely |i| Cf Pronc Intro 3.I.17 Pronc-spp *da, de, duh, ee*
A Forms.

1844 *Living Age* 3.362 [Black], No find but one puddle from de fust. **1858** in 1956 Eliason *Tarheel Talk* 319 **ne,ceNC**, De. **1893** Shands *MS Speech* 62, *Th* is in a large number of instances pronounced by negroes as *d:* as . . *de* . . for *the.* **1894** Riley *Armazindy* 52 **IN**, 'Possum in de 'tater-patch. **1899** Chesnutt *Conjure Woman* 13 **csNC** [Black], W'en de season is nigh 'bout ober. **1901** *DN* 2.183 **neKY** [Black], The . . de. **1908** *DN* 3.282 **eAL, wGA**, [ð] in all positions has, under negro influence, largely become *d,* as in . . [di] . . the. **1930** *AmSp* 6.96 **seVA**, A strong tendency to substitute [d] for [ð] in *that, the,* etc. **a1930** in 1991 Hughes–Hurston *Mule Bone* 29 **cFL** [Black], Put dis town on de map! **1930s** in 1944 *ADD* **eWV**, The. . . [i]. Used by only one woman. 'When 'ee moon comes over 'ee mountain.' **1941** *AmSp* 16.10 **eTX** [Black], 'Through the fence,' . . [θu də fīns]. **1942** *Time* 1 June 58 **seNY**, In da good old Brooklyn way. . . and de old pawk ain't da same. . . and da Bums wuz in da cellar. **1980** *NY Times* (NY) 11 Aug sec B 4/4 (Internet), Among the thousands roving about at the Garden will be "de Mayah" or "Hizzoner" (in Chicago it's "duh Mare") as well as "de Guvnah." **2004** *DARE* File **Upper Peninsula MI**, "What would a bad Yooper sound like?" "Yah, I went up to da store yesterday." *Ibid,* [Bumper sticker:] Say yah to da U.P., eh!

B Senses.

1 This, the current—used before a division of time; see quots. [Chiefly Scots dial; cf *EDD the* 12 "*Comb.* with *day, morn, night,* &c.: this, 'to-.'"]

1851 Hooper *Widow Rugby's Husband* 159 **AL**, No, sir, I'm with me House, sir; and if any man gits more'n that out ov me the night, he'll rise betimes in the mornin'. **1895** *DN* 1.394 **swPA**, The year: for *this year.* **1914** *DN* 4.112 **cKS**, The. Used for *to,* in *the day, the night, the morrow.* **1915** *DN* 4.229 **wTX**, Th' evening. This pronunciation of "this evening" is common even among educated people. **1978** Hiser *Quare Appalachia* 25 **eKY** (Montgomery Coll.), My blue hounds can tree more coons from seven o'clock to ten the night, twicet as many, as yourn. *Ibid* 27, Tell that John Bill what you've seen me do the day. *Ibid* 43, I'm a goin to the trustees the morrow and lay a complaint.

2 Used before numbers denoting highways.

1998 *DARE* File **wNY**, The first time I drove to Buffalo, NY from my native NW Pennsylvania . . I heard "the n" (n = a highway number) for the first time. With the two speakers I heard, it applied to all numbered highways—the small local ones as well as the major ones. *Ibid* **neNY**, The correspondent. . reported the use of articles before numbered roads in western NY and southern Ontario. *Ibid* **wNY**, I find the claims of "the n" for western new york to be very weird. . . the first time I met a southern Californian, her use of "the 80" was something I made fun of for years because it was so absolutely foreign to me! *Ibid* **CA**, Recently I heard someone from Bakersfield tell me about a dangerous freeway intersection "where the 52 meets the 53." This didn't surprise me . . , but

shortly thereafter (in the same conversation) I heard someone else from the SF Bay Area mirror that usage in another context. That surprised me. **1999** Guterson *East of the Mts.* 146 **eWA**, It was all the same to him, he said, if he hit the 97 at Wenatchee or followed the 28 to Soap Lake and caught the 17 to Brewster. **1999** *DARE* File **KY**, When I lived in northern Kentucky near Fort Knox during the late sixties, my landlady, who was born and raised near there, always referred to highway 60 as *the sixty.* **2000** Metcalf *How We Talk* 140 **sCA**, In referring to highways, Southern Californians use *the* with numbers, as in *the 101* for U.S. 101, the main coastal route.

theater n Usu |ˈθiətə(r), ˈθɪə-|; also freq **Sth, S Midl** |ˈθiˌetə(r), θiˈe-|; for addit varr see quots Pronc-spp *teeayter, theayter, theaytre, thi-eyter*
Std sense, var forms.

1902 *DN* 2.247 **sIL**, Theatre. Pronounced [θiˈeətr], as if spelled theay'ter. **1906** *DN* 3.161 **nwAR**, Theatre [θiˈeɪtə]. . . A common pronunciation in spite of the tendency toward recessive accent, in most words. **1908** *DN* 3.280 **eAL, wGA**, Processive accent is . . frequent in . . words of more than two syllables; as [θiˈetə]. **1926** Ferber *Show Boat* 363, Your songs are too much like church tunes, see? They're for a funeral, not a theaytre. **1942** Hall *Smoky Mt. Speech* 61 **wNC, eTN**, *Theater* usually has secondary stress on the medial vowel: [ˈθiˌetə]. **1944** *PADS* 2.15 **AL**, Theater [θiˈetə, -ə, ˈθiˈetə, -ə]: Widely used, but usually willingly changed to the standard pronunciation of other American dialects. . . [*PADS* Ed: Second pronunciation common in Va., N.C.] **c1955** Reed–Person *Ling. Atlas Pacific NW*, 4 infs, Thi-eyter. **c1960** *Wilson Coll.* **csKY**, Theater is nearly always [ˈθiˌetə]. **1966–70** *DARE* (Qu. FF24, *The place or building where people go to see motion pictures*) Infs **AL**10, 20, **MI**18, Theater [ˌθiˈetə]; **MS**67, Theater [ˈθiˌetə]; **NY**241, Theater [ˌθiˈedə]. **1966** *DARE* Tape **FL**42, I built that Milton theater [ˌθiˈetə] there. **1969** *DARE* FW Addit **cCA**, Theater [ˈθiˌedə]. **1976** Allen *LAUM* 3.289 **Upper MW** (as of c1950), Theater. . . The majority variant is /ˈθiətə/. . . This pronunciation is used by two-thirds of the U[pper] M[idwest] infs. . . There is no clear geographical pattern. . . The variant /ˈθɪətə/, with /ɪ/ instead of /i/, is twice as frequent among the cultivated speakers as among the others. The reverse is true with respect to the third variant, /ˈθiˌetə/, with a stressed /e/ in the second syllable. Of the infs. with this variant slightly more than one-half have primary stress on the first syllable /θi/ and secondary stress on /e/; the others have secondary stress on /θi/ and primary stress on /e/. This variant is a clear social marker. Three-fourths of its users are in . . the uneducated group. **1989** Pederson *LAGS Tech. Index* 308 **Gulf Region**, Theater. [Of 914 infs, 384 offered proncs of the types [ˈθiˌ(j)edə, -tə]; 87 infs, proncs of the types [ˈθiˌədə, -tə, ˈθiˌɪdə, -tə]; 73 infs, proncs of the types [ˌθiˈedə, -tə]; 48 infs, proncs of the types [ˈθiˌdə, -tə]; 33 infs, proncs of the types [ˈθiˌədə, -tə]; 31 infs, proncs of the types [ˈθiˌdə, -tə]; 23 infs, proncs of the types [ˌθiˈedə, -tə]; 14 infs, proncs of the types [ˈθiˌ(j)edə, -tə]; 12 infs, proncs of the types [ˈθiˌɛdə, -tə]; 5 infs, proncs of the type [ˈtiˌedə]; 4 infs, proncs of the types [ˌθiˈedə, -tə]; 3 infs, proncs of the types [ˌθiˈjedə, -tə]; 3 infs, proncs of the type [ˌtiˈedə].] **1997** *DARE* File—Internet **cePA** [CoalSpeak], Tee-ay-ter: Theater, as in movie theater.

thee See **three**

their pron Usu |ðɛə(r)|; less freq |ðæ(r), ðeə(r), ðar|; infreq |dɛə(r)|; unstressed, often |ðɜ(r)|; for addit varr, and proncs of *theirs,* see quots Pronc-spp *deir, dere, thaeuh, thar(e), thayer, ther* Cf Pronc Intro 3.I.1.b, 3.I.17, **they** pron[1]
Std sense, var forms.

1843 (1916) Hall *New Purchase* 144 **IN**, Folks was a little dubus and didn't want thare company. *Ibid* 331, You'r all servunts of the people and hain't the right . . to give away their . . money without thar consent. **1851** Hooper *Widow Rugby's Husband* 38 **AL**, They was but a little ways from the river—leastways thar camp-fire was. **1866** in 1884 Lanier *Poems* 172 **GA**, Wastin' ther time on the cussed land. **1893** Shands *MS Speech* 62, Th. . . is in a large number of instances pronounced by negroes as *d:* as . . *deir* for . . *their.* **1899** Chesnutt *Conjure Woman* 19 **csNC** [Black], Some . . had gone out wid dere guns en dere dogs. **1909** [see **there A1**]. **1917** *DN* 4.402 **neOH**, Their [ðeə]. . . [ðɛə] and [ðæə] are also common. **1923** (1946) Greer-Petrie *Angeline Steppin'* 31 **csKY**, If he would jest go to the trouble of cutting his mark in thar years [=ears]. **1927** Shewmake *Engl. Pronc. VA* 42, Their. Virginians generally say *thae-uh.* **1928** Peterkin *Scarlet Sister Mary* 69 **SC** [Gullah], Whilst shep-herds watched dere flocks by night. **c1960** *Wilson Coll.* **csKY**, Their /ðɜ/ or /ðar/, older people. **1981** Pederson *LAGS Basic Materials* **Gulf Region**, [For *theirs,* proncs of the types [ðɛəz,

ðɛəz] occur most frequently; those of the types [ðæɚz, ðæəz] are also common; proncs of the types [ðɛəʳz, ðeəz] are somewhat less frequent, while those of the types [ðɚz, ðɪɚz, ðɪəz] are infrequent; proncs of the types [dɛɚz, dɛəz, deⁱz] occur rarely.] **1995** *Brophy Coll.* 76 **swMO** (as of c1960), *Their.* [P]ronounced with diphthong, almost "thayer." **2000** Shores *Tangier Is.* 183 **Chesapeake Bay,** Words with the vowel of *bat* before "r," such as *bear, stairs, their, where, hair,* and *fair,* are pronounced without any glide at all. *Bear,* for example, would pronounced as "baer."

theirn pron   Also *thern, they'rn;* rarely redund *theirns, theirs'n* [Engl dial] Cf **hern** pron, **hisn, ourn, yourn** esp **NEng, Sth, S Midl**
Theirs.

   1795 Dearborn *Columbian Grammar* 139, *List of Improprieties. . .* Theirn for Theirs. **1843** (1916) Hall *New Purchase* 147 **IN,** There was no reglar town of theirn. **1890** Holley *Samantha among Brethren* 10 **NY,** Our deacons seemed to jest flourish on this skeme of theirn. **1907** *DN* 3.250 **eME,** *Theirn. . .* Theirs. **1909** *DN* 3.380 **eAL, wGA,** *The(i)rn. . .* Theirs. **1913** Johnson *Highways St. Lawrence to VA* 257 **wMD,** We are all done with ourn and ready to go to the field before the hands come for theirn. **1930** *AmSp* 5.267 [Ozark dialect], Such possessive forms as *ourn, yourn, hisn, hern* and *theirn* are almost universal in the Ozarks. **1938** in Lib. of Congress *Amer. Memory:* WPA Life Hist. (Internet) **NC,** All they got to do is say the word and I'd hafta get outa this house o' theirn. **1940** Faulkner *Hamlet* 35 **MS,** That was a good swap for anything that could get up and walk from Beasley's lot to theirn by itself. **1943** *LANE* Map 617 **NEng,** [*Theirn* occurs frequently throughout the region.] **1945** FWP *Lay My Burden Down* 145 **Sth** (as of c1865) [Black], Us kept them cleaned and ironed just like the master and the young masters done theirn. **1952** Brown *NC Folkl.* 1.599, *Theirn* [ðɝn]. . . Theirs. . . General. Illiterate. *Theirns* [ðɝnz]. . . Theirs.—General. Illiterate. **1971** *Foxfire* Winter 254 **nGA,** And they done better at home than they do these that went and had they'rn at th'hospital. **1975** Allen *LAUM* 2.54 **Upper MW** (as of c1950), The *-n* forms, *hisn, hern, theirn. . .* survive largely as remembered or locally heard. They are clearly nonstandard relics. *. . hern* and *theirn* occur in the observed speech of only one inf [in **cIA**]. **1986** Pederson *LAGS Concordance (Theirs)* 2 infs, **FL, TN,** Theirn; 1 inf, **csTN,** Folks say theirn; 1 inf, **cwGA,** Theirn—associates form with Negroes; 1 inf, **cnAR,** They could talk our language and theirn; *(You-all's)* 1 inf, **csTX,** Theirn—in "cute, kidding" conversation. **2000** Shores *Tangier Is.* 249 **Chesapeake Bay,** The possessive forms *hisn, hern, ourn, yourn* and *theirn* are frequently used. **2001** *DARE* File **nwMS** [Black], I also heard *theirs'n* for *theirs* among Black people in Quitman county Mississippi—(But *not* "theirn.")

theirs all See **they-all**

theirselves pron   Also *tharsefs, theirselfs, theirselve, therselves;* less freq *theirself* [*OED2* (at *themselves* pron. pl. III) a13 . . →; "prevalent dialectally"] chiefly **nNEng, Sth, S Midl**
See Map
Themselves.

   1843 (1916) Hall *New Purchase* 174 **IN,** They . . didn't . . grow of theirselves out of forty atims by chance. **1866** in 1983 *PADS* 70.54 **ce,sePA,** They played and seemed to enjoy theirselves. **1867** Harris *Sut Lovingood Yarns* 128 **TN,** They . . hed lef the pint ove the steepil stickin out, fur a . . warnin tu the uther chu'ches how tu kery tharsefs. **1871** Eggleston *Hoosier Schoolmaster* 118 **sIN,** Them as says it is liars and thieves theirselves. **1886** *Harper's New Mth. Mag.* 74.103 **ME,** Folks keep to theirselves pretty much. **1898** *Century Illustr. Mag.* 55.833 **GA,** It hurt a body's feelin's . . , a-knowin' what 's goin' on in their own mind about theirself. *Ibid,* They . . al'ays helt theirselfs ready to give their adwices about sech things. **1902** *DN* 2.247 **sIL,** *Theirselves.* **1903** *DN* 2.333 **seMO,** *Theirselves.* **1904** *DN* 2.422 **nwAR,** *Theirselves.* **1906** *DN* 3.123 **sIN,** *Theirselves.* **1909** *DN* 3.380 **eAL, wGA,** *The(i)rselves.* **1942** Hall *Smoky Mt. Speech* 25 **wNC, eTN,** *Theirselves* (for *themselves*) [ðɛɚ'sɛfs]. **1943** *LANE* Map 619, [In the context "They must look out for themselves," 52 infs, chiefly **neMA, sNH, swME,** responded with *theirselves* or, less freq, *theirself.* In only 11 cases, however, was this the inf's only or first response, and 17 were responding to the fieldworker's suggestion. Six indicated that this was obsolete, 4 that it was "older though still in use," and 2 that it was uncommon.] **1952** Brown *NC Folkl.* 1.599, *Theirself, theirselves.* **1965–70** *DARE* (Qu. AA8, . . *"There they were at the church supper _____ [with each other]."*) Inf **MD**19, Making a fool of theirself; **IA**30, **KY**85, **VT**8, Making a fool (out) of theirselves; **KY**85, Making a

monkey out of theirselves; **LA**18, **PA**134, Making a show of theirselves; **MD**32, Making fools of theirselves; **KY**40, Showing theirselves; (Qu. W36, *What . . people say . . about a woman who uses a lot of cosmetics*) Inf **KY**5, Paints theirselves; (Qu. FF18, . . *"They certainly _____ last night."*) Inf **KY**66, Overdid theirselves; (Qu. II18, *Someone who joins himself on to you and your group without being asked and won't leave*) Inf **MO**15, Stuck theirselves in; (Qu. II23, *Joking names for the people who are, or think they are, the best society of a community: The _____*) Inf **TN**15, Proud of theirselves; (Qu. JJ7, . . *Cheating in school examinations*) Inf **TN**13, They're just hurting theirself; (Qu. OO35a, . . *"Last year we fertilized the garden, and the plants really _____."*) Inf **MO**2, Outdid theirselves. [11 of 14 total Infs old, 10 gs educ] **1966–67** *DARE* Tape **AZ**5, Our missionaries. . . earn their money to go on their missions theirself; **FL**32, In about four years they'll be taking care of theirselves. **1976** Wolfram–Christian *WV Coll.* 153 *(Montgomery Coll.),* They slipped out and wrote the excuses theirselve and signed our names to it. **1989** Pederson *LAGS Tech. Index* 150 **Gulf Region** *(Themselves)* 125 infs, Theirself; 135 infs, Theirselves. **2000** Shores *Tangier Is.* 249 **Chesapeake Bay,** The possessive forms. . . *hisself* and *theirself* are common as well. **2002** *DARE* File—Internet **seKY,** Sheep can't see very far, by their selfs. *Ibid* **seKY,** They give their self a name, over their church door, different than, the one where they was at. **2003** Fought *Chicano Engl.* 95 **Los Angeles CA,** [They] have to start supporting theirselves at early ages. *(James, 18).*

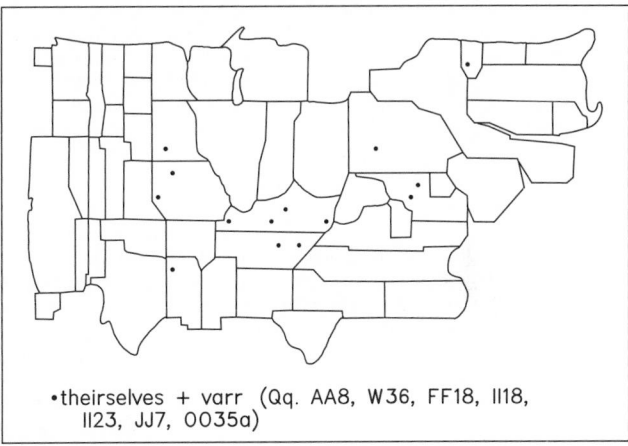

   •theirselves + varr (Qq. AA8, W36, FF18, II18,
   II23, JJ7, OO35a)

theirs'n See **theirn**

them pron, adj   Usu |ðɛm|, unstressed |əm|; also esp **Sth, S Midl** |ðɪm|; *esp freq among Black speakers* |dɛm|; for addit varr see quot 1981 Pronc-sp *dem*
A Forms.

   1899 Woerner *Rebel's Daughter* 70 **Ozarks** (as of c1850) [Black], Food to dem w'at's hungry; drink to dem w'at's thirsty. **1901** *DN* 2.183 **neKY** [Black], *Them*—dem[·] *Themselves*—demsels. **1908** *DN* 3.304 **eAL, wGA** [Black], *De. . .* The. So also *. . dem, . .* etc. These forms . . are . . distinctive of the negro dialect. The use of these forms is rapidly increasing among the white people, however. **1908** *S. Atl. Qrly.* 7.346 **sSC coast** [Gullah], *Dem* for *them.* **1931** (1991) Hughes–Hurston *Mule Bone* 59 **cFL** [Black], Dem boys been de best of friends all they life. **1936** Reese *Worleys* 14 **MD** (as of 1865) [Black], Dem chillun right up in Heben now. **1981** Pederson *LAGS Basic Materials* **Gulf Region,** [For *them,* proncs of the types [ðɛ(ə)m] occur most frequently; those of the types [ðɪ(ə)m] are also common; proncs of the types [ðæᵋm, ðeəm] occur infrequently; those of the types [dɛm, dɪᵊm] occur rarely.]
B As pron.
1 These, those, they—used as a demonstrative pron without distinction between near and far. [*OED2* them B.I.3.a "Now only *dial.* or *illiterate*"; c1489 →] chiefly **Sth, S Midl;** also **NEng**

   1835 Crockett *Account* 99 **wTN,** The old saying, "them that don't work should not eat," don't apply to them. **1840** *New Engl. Farmer & Horticult. Reg.* 18.397, During my stay at Pittsburg nothing appeared to me so peculiar and foreign as the . . phraseology of the people. . . the objective for the nominative in phrases like . . *them's the best.* **1850** in 1999 *AmSp* 74.275 **ceSC,** Them ware me grands. **1899** (1912) Green *VA Folk-Speech* 443, *Them,* pron. These; those. "*Them's 'em,* these are them." **1907** *DN* 3.208 **nwAR,** *Them. . .* Those. "Where are your trunks?" "Them's them." **1908** *S. Atl. Qrly.* 7.346 **sSC coast** [Gullah],

Dem drap t'rue intuh de element; dem scace is mek de sho'. [=They dropped through into the water; they scarcely made it to the shore.] **1933** Rawlings *South Moon* 137 **nFL,** Them's pretty. **1939** FWP *ID Lore* 243, Them's the by Goddest horses that ever be damned! **1942** McAtee *Dial. Grant Co. IN* 65 (as of 1890s), *Them . .* those . . "Them are nice pigs". Now Dial. (Ala., Md., Va.) **1943** LANE Map 620 *(These are)* **NEng,** These are the kind I like. . . About 65% of those who responded to this question offered *them are, ~ is.* . . The same informants without exception also offered *them* as equivalent to *those* in the sentence *Those are the fellows I mean* (see the following map). It is possible, therefore, that some of the cases of *them* entered on this map may mean 'those' rather than 'these', or may be demonstrative pronouns indifferent to the distinction between *these* and *those*. *Ibid* Map 621 *(Those are)* **NEng,** [*Them are, them is,* and *them's* are widespread throughout the region.] *Ibid* Map 622 *(Those were)* **NEng,** [*Them was* and *them were* are widespread throughout the region.] **1966** DARE Tape **ME**26, Them was tote sleds. **1968** DARE (Qu. N70, Them that curl around. **1989** Pederson *LAGS Tech. Index* 94 **Gulf Region,** [In the phrase *Those were the good-old days:* 21 infs, Them was; 12 infs, Them's; 7 infs, Them is; 3 infs, Them; 2 infs, Them were; 1 inf, Them be.]

2 Themselves—used as indirect object. **esp Sth, S Midl** Cf **her B1, him** pron **B1**

1906 *DN* 3.161 **nwAR,** Them. . . Themselves. "They are building them a storm house." **1953** Hall *Coll.* **wNC, eTN,** He . . killed one of them so's't they'd have them some turkey meat. **1969** in 2004 Montgomery–Hall *Dict. Smoky Mt. Engl.* 601 **wNC, eTN,** Them. . . Well, they'd get them a preacher and let him preach a while. **1979** *Ibid,* They'd get 'em out honey. **1986** Pederson *LAGS Concordance,* 1 inf, **nwLA,** They done got them another road. **2002** DARE File—Internet **seKY,** So people move on and start them another church.

3 =and them. *esp Gullah, HI creole*

1922 Gonzales *Black Border* 296 **sSC, GA coasts** [Gullah glossary], *Dem.* . . used for "and them," as "Sancho dem," meaning Sancho and his companions. **1968** Moody *Coming of Age MS* 2 [Black], As soon as Mama them left the house, he would sit up in the rocking chair and fall asleep. **1971** Cunningham *Syntactic Analysis Gullah* 29, The group plural, *them,* which occurs with human nouns only . . indicates that the noun head is accompanied by some socially defined human group. . . Richard-them [=Richard and the others] is my mother brother. . . My mother-them move off Edisto. **1972** Carr *Da Kine Talk* 153 **HI,** Q: "You go library wid Alice-dem?" 'Are you going . . with Alice and her pals?' **1981** *Pidgin To Da Max* np **HI,** *-dem*—Them. You can add this word on when you want to describe a whole bunch of people and you don't want to name them all. . . [Q:] Excuse me, Marlene! Can you find out where Stanley, Arthur, Eric, George, Michael and John are? [A:] Shuah! 'Ey Lorraine! Wheah Stan-dem went?!!? **1988** Naylor *Mama Day* 187 **sSC, GA coasts** [Black], See, my sisters and cousins, them, they married on off beyond the bridge.

C As adj.

1 Those, these; rarely, that—used as a demonstrative adj without distinction between near and far. [*OED2 them* B.III.5 "Now only *dial.* or *illiterate*"; 1596 →] **scattered, but chiefly Sth, S Midl; also NEng**

1806 in 2007 Davis *Co. Line Baptist Minutes* 55 **TN** (Montgomery Coll.), Any Dealings between two Brs touch Temporal Matters Each one Shall Schoose one Member & ym two Shall Schoose one More & they Solution Shall be ye Solution of ye Church. **1850** in 1999 AmSp 74.275 **ceSC,** Them foks cum al the ways to hep me. **1884** Smith *Bill Arp's Scrap Book* 79 **nwGA,** I would give a quarter to paddle them boys. **1899** Garland *Boy Life* 15 **nwIA** (as of c1870s), S'pose I didn't see them fish? **1904** *DN* 2.428 **Cape Cod MA** (as of a1857), *Them, adj.* Those. **1908** *S. Atl. Qrly.* 7.346 **sSC coast** [Gullah], Dem cloud roll up. **1909** *DN* 3.380 **eAL, wGA,** *Them, pron. adj.* Those. Painfully common. **1909** *S. Atl. Qrly.* 8.46 **sSC coast** [Gullah], Dem chillen too pretty. **1936** Reese *Worleys* 8 **MD** (as of 1865) [Black], It's dem Yankees . . dat sets Miss Emly cryin'. **1943** LANE Map 624 *(These fellows)* **NEng,** Sixteen informants offered also the phrase *them fellows,* presumably as an equivalent of *these fellows.* . . Nineteen informants offered only the phrase *them fellows.* Note that of the thirty-five informants . . all but four offered the phrase *them boys* as equivalent to *those boys. Ibid* Map 625 *(Those boys)* **NEng,** [*Them boys* is widespread and appears to be about as frequent as *those boys.*] **1949** Turner *Africanisms* 266 **seSC** [Gullah], [aftə dɛm stɔm, dɛm wɔt ɹit we . . slip ɪn ʊd]. *Ibid* 267, [Transl:] After them storm, them what get away . . sleep in wood. **1952** Brown *NC Folkl.* 1.600, *Them: dem. adj.* . . Those. . . Illiterate. **1966–69**

DARE Tape **AK9,** In them days . . we'd build a school, and . . before we got it built it was too small; **AZ**7, In them days, well, pret' near every settlement there was in Utah was a Mormon settlement; **CA**137, Them days they didn't make any money at all; **SC**9, Tote dem rain. **1967** in 1982 *Barrick Coll.* **csPA,** Them. . . Them blame things is expensive. **1967–68** DARE (Qu. K8, *Joking terms for milking a cow: A farmer might say, "Well, it's time to go out and _____."*) Inf **LA**39, Pull them tits; (Qu. FF21a, *A joke that is so old it doesn't seem funny any more*) Inf **TN**6, Pull off them old socks; (Qu. HH16) Inf **MI**47, One of them windjammers. **1975** Allen *LAUM* 2.58 **Upper MW** (as of c1950), *Those.* . . *those* boys. . . Two demonstrative adjectivals appear in this context to designate objects at some distance—*those* and *them.* As in New England, the contrast between them in the U[pper] M[idwest] seems social, not regional. None of the cultivated infs. . . use *them,* but 60% of the least educated speakers use it. . . The persistent attack of the schools upon this use of *them* is reflected in the fact that 17% of the infs. whose probable normal term is *them* shift to *those* in careful or guarded speech. **1986** Pederson *LAGS Concordance* **Gulf Region,** [There are hundreds of instances of constructions such as *them animals, (shovel out all of) them ashes, them boys, (in) them days, them people,* etc throughout the region.]

2 Their. *Gullah*

1908 *S. Atl. Qrly.* 7.340 **sSC coast** [Gullah], Plantation negroes delight, though not appearing to do so, to watch a visiting stranger talk: "Dey use dem mout' so funny!" **1922** Gonzales *Black Border* 296 **sSC, GA coasts** [Gullah glossary], *Dem'own*—theirs, their own. **1992** Geraty *Bittle* 37 **Charleston SC** [Gullah], Lap chillun en' bed chillun haffuh 'pen'pun dem own Mammy fuh dem supshun.

them there See **there B**

them-uns pron [Scots, nIr dial; cf *SND them yins* (at *yin* pron. 3)] Cf **they-uns, you-uns** pron¹
Them, they, those.

1865 (1866) *Cotton Stealing* 22 **AR,** We need them 'ar, a heap mor'n them uns [do]. *Ibid* 26, "I fixed them 'uns," said the brute, pointing to the two dead men. **1891** Perley *From Timber Town* 189 **sIL,** Recon he's one o' them uns out thar a tryin' ter holler his he'd off! **1902** (1904) Rowe *Maid of Bar Harbor* 166 **ME,** Mebbe if you . . hed yer canvas all clean an' whole as them uns has, *you 'd* look kind o' smart. **1918** *DN* 5.19 **NC,** Themuns, them. Probably due to analogy to *we'uns, you'uns,* which are much more common than *themuns.* **1927** in 1944 *ADD* **WV,** Them-uns. . . them ones. **1969** Doran *Folkl. White Co.* 115 **TN** (Montgomery Coll.), Themens. . . those.

then adv Usu |ðɛn|; for pronc and sp varr see **A** below
A Std senses, var forms.

1 den. *esp freq among Black speakers*

1875 *Scribner's Mth.* 10.240 **GA** [Black], Den, Lord, please take ole Jim. **1884** *Anglia* 7.263 **Sth, S Midl** [Black], *Right den an' dar* = on the spot. **1893** Shands *MS Speech* 15, Th [ð] is nearly always pronounced as *d* at the beginning of words, by negroes; as . . [dɛn] for *then.* **1899** Chesnutt *Conjure Woman* 13 **csNC** [Black], Den de scuppernon' make you smack yo' lip. **1901** *DN* 2.183 **neKY** [Black], Then . . den. **1908** *DN* 3.304 **eAL, wGA** [Black], *De.* . . The. So also . . *den,* . . etc. These forms . . are . . distinctive of the negro dialect. The use of these forms is rapidly increasing among the white people, however. **1928** Peterkin *Scarlet Sister Mary* 124 **SC** [Gullah], If e don' work, den I'll quit makin' love-charms. **1934** Carmer *Stars Fell on AL* 179 [Black], So den Sis Cow git mad. **1958** Humphrey *Home from the Hill* 52 **neTX** [Black], Oh, ver' well den. I see it ain't no help for it. **1980** *Ger. Qrly.* May 358 [Engl of PA Germans], /ð/ realized as [d] as in *then, mother.*

2 |ðɪn|.

1937 *AmSp* 12.287 **wVA,** There is increasing tendency . . to let the [ɛ] sounds move upward towards [ɪ], in . . *then.* **1941** *AmSp* 16.14 **eTX** [Black], [ðɪn] [=then].

3 in comb *and then:* also |nɛn, nɪn|; pronc-sp *nen.*

1890 (1895) Riley *Rhymes of Childhood* 1 **IN,** An' nen—ef our hired girl says he can—/ He milks the cow. **1904** Day *Kin o' Ktaadn* 99 **ME,** An' 'nen she blabbed it all erround. **1941** *AmSp* 16.14 **eTX** [Black], [n n̩ɪn]. . . [n n̩ɛn] [=and then]. **1941** O'Donnell *Great Big Doorstep* 41 **sLA** [Black], Nen de yudda day Ah was passin Chippy's Saloon up de levee an dey's playin a piece on de reckid.

B Used as a weak intensifier in interrogative contexts. **esp MN, WI** Cf **once B**

1987 Mohr *How Minnesotan* 75, So what'd ya think of this weather then, huh? *Something, isn't it?* *Ibid* 76, So, you havin' a little tire trouble then, are you, maybe? *Ibid* 77, Say, long time no see, how's she goin' then, huh? **2001** Keillor in *NY Times* (NY) 26 Aug (Internet) **cMN,** And then you go on to talk about Norwegian bachelor farmers sitting [in] . . the Chatterbox, where large phlegmatic people sit at the counter talking in their singsong accent. *So how you been then?* Oh, you know, not so bad, how's yourself, you keeping busy then? **2006** *Green Bay Press–Gaz.* (WI) 26 Feb (Internet), Among those [characteristics of Wisconsin speech] frequently mentioned by readers: . . Attaching "then," . . or "and that" to the ends of sentences. Example: "Did you like the fish boil then?" **2007** *DARE* File **Upper MW,** When I hear people say things like, "Well, are we going to eat, then?" when they mean "right now," I assume they are from the Upper Midwest. **2008** *Ibid* **WI,** I remember a real Wisconsin bloke in Oshkosh years ago asking me, "You wanna beer den, or what now?" *Ibid* **cwWI,** I hear "then" as a tag quite often. . . One [example] that I regularly hear in service encounters: "Can I get you anything else, then?" I noticed this when I moved here, and it still stands out to me somewhat. Other newer faculty . . have remarked on it as well. **2008** *DARE* File—Internet **MN,** Welcome to Minnesota, then. . . How ya' doin', then? . . Notice how you can add the word *then* to almost any sentence?

theng See **thing**

thenk v¹ See **think**

thenk v² See **thank**

theodore See **fiador**

‡**theotious** adj

1969 *DARE* (Qu. KK1a, . . *Very good—for example, food: "That pie was _____."*) Inf **GA**72, Theotious [ˌθiˈoʊʃɪs].

ther pron See **their**

there adv, adj, pron   Usu |ðɛr, ðɛ(ə), ðær, ðæ(ə)|; for varr see **A** below

A Forms.

1 |ɜ(r), ðʌr|; pronc-spp *ther, thurr.*
1867 Lowell *Biglow* lxi **'Upcountry' MA,** Ther's sech a thing ez bein' *tu.* **1871** Eggleston *Hoosier Schoolmaster* 135 **sIN,** Ther's my brother over in Jackson Kyounty. I mout go there. **1909** *DN* 3.380 **eAL, wGA,** *Ther,* pronunciation of *there* and *their.* **1910** *DN* 3.450 **wNY,** There [ðɜ˞] *haint.* . . There is not; there are not. **1942** Hall *Smoky Mt. Speech* 25 **wNC, eTN,** [ɜ˞] or [ɚ] is also very frequent in . . *their, there* (as an expletive). . . [ðɜ˞z ə 'oʊl 'hæ·ʊs ʌp hɪɚ]. **1943** *LANE* Map 707 *(Over there)* 1 inf, **seMA,** [ðɜ˞ˑ]. **1981** Pederson *LAGS Basic Materials* **Gulf Region,** [Proncs of the type [ðɜ˞] occur very rarely.] **1985** Benes *Amer. Speech* 85 **cwMA** (as of c1850), Rich's transcriptions of *there* and *their* are inconsistent. He sometimes transcribed *there* with [æ] and sometimes with [ə]. Presumably he used [ə] in both words when they were unstressed, but different vowels in them when they were stressed—[æ] in stressed *there*, but [ɛ] in stressed *their.* **2008** *DARE* File **St. Louis MO,** Aw, man! That's cold-blooded, right thurr [ðʌr].

2 |ðɑ(r), ðɑə(r)|; pronc-sp *thar;* also *esp freq among Black speakers,* da(r), dah. **chiefly Sth, S Midl** *old-fash*
1783 in 1956 Eliason *Tarheel Talk* 319 **cnNC,** Thar. **1843** (1916) Hall *New Purchase* 438 **IN,** Thar's no snakes. **1858** Hammett *Piney Woods Tavern* 140 **TX** [Black], And da's no body da, only de ole gempleman. **1867** Allen et al. *Slave Songs* xxxvi **seSC,** Ebery step he take seem like he say, 'Look out dah, groun', I da [=am] comin'. **1890** *DN* 1.69 **KY,** There. . . Sometimes thar [ðɑ·]. **1893** Shands *MS Speech* 63, There. . . Thar, dar, and *dere* are used for *there. Thar* is used mostly by illiterate whites; *dar* and *dere,* by negroes. **1903** *DN* 2.333 **seMO,** There. . . Pronounced thar. . . A very common pronunciation among old-fashioned people. **1907** *DN* 3.237 **nwAR,** There. . . Pronounced by old-fashioned people [ðɑr]. **1909** *DN* 3.380 **eAL, wGA,** Thar. . . There. **1914** *DN* 4.159 **cVA,** Da. . . There. "Da he!" There he (or it) is. **1923** *DN* 5.223 **swMO,** Thar. **1936** in 1976 *Weevils in the Wheat* 193 **VA** [Black], Don' know efen yo' kin see it or not but its dah. **1942** Hall *Smoky Mt. Speech* 25 **wNC, eTN,** A number of old people, and a few others, still say [ðɑə˞] *there.* **1942** Faulkner *Go Down* 136 **MS** [Black], You dont wants ter go back dar by yoself. **1943** *LANE* Map 707 *(Over there),* [Most infs offered proncs of the types [ðɛə, ðɛə, ðæ(ə)r, ðɛ(ə)r]. 15 infs, **scattered nNEng, eMA,** offered proncs of the types [ðɑ, ðɑ, ðɑə, ðɑə(r)].] **1968–69** *DARE* FW Addit **csMD,** There: [ðær] or [ðɑr] on Smith Island, Maryland; **Hatteras Is. NC,** There [ðɑə˞]. **1981** Pederson *LAGS Basic Materials* **Gulf Region,** [Proncs of the type [ðɑə˞] occur only occasionally, those of the type [ðɑə˞] rarely.] **2003** in 2005

DARE File—Internet **wNC, eTN,** My life is complete; thar ain't nuttin' I lack.

3 |dɛə(r), dæə(r)|; pronc-spp *dare, dere.* *esp freq among Black speakers*
1829 Tenney *Female Quixotism* 1.120 **Philadelphia PA** [Black], Dare dare de debil; dare de ghos; all de ghos Betty see. **1837** Sherwood *Gaz. GA* 69, *Dare,* for there. **1899** Chesnutt *Conjure Woman* 14 **csNC** [Black], Dere wuz ole Mars Henry Brayboy's niggers. **1908** *DN* 3.304 **eAL, wGA** [Black], *De.* . . The. So also . . *dere,* etc. These forms . . are . . distinctive of the negro dialect. The use of these forms is rapidly increasing among the white people, however. **1934** Carmer *Stars Fell on AL* 270 [Black], I won't believe it till one of yuh takes dis here red bandanner out in . . [the] pasture where dem Jersey bulls is an' comes out o' dere alive. **1981** Pederson *LAGS Basic Materials* **Gulf Region,** [Of approx 30 exx of proncs of the types [dɛə˞, dɛə, dæə˞, dæə], just under half were offered by Black infs.]

4 |ɑ(r), ɛɑ(r), æ(ə)r, æ(ə)|; pronc-spp *ah, air, ar(e), ere, urr—*usu in close comb with a preceding demonstrative pron or adv. **chiefly Sth, S Midl; also NEng**
1825 Neal *Brother Jonathan* 1.244 **CT,** Is that 'air fellow gone yet? **1834** *Life Andrew Jackson* 122, If 'em are fellers cross this rampart, give 'em plenty of cold iron in his beef. **1841** *Spirit of Times* 27 Mar 42 **AR,** That ar hat cost Sam a mortal sight of Peltry. **1889** Edwards *Runaways* 211 **nGA,** Somehow he could n't work thet ar peg leg edzactly right. **1891** Page *Elsket* 126 **VA** [Black], Consortin' wid some o' dem urr free-issue niggers roun' dyah. **1894** *Century Illustr. Mag.* 47.851 [Black], I smack yeh 'n de mouf widda cawn-hus' yeh doan shet up dattah [=that there] foolin' roun' me. **1909** *DN* 3.380 **eAL, wGA,** That there, pron. or adj. phr. That. Pronounced [ðæt-æə] or [ðæt-ɑr]. **1918** *DN* 5.21 **NC,** That thar, that ar, that there, that (demonstrative). **1931** *AmSp* 7.20 **swPA,** That 'ere one is what I mean. *Ibid* 94 **eKY,** That-air dommer rooster belongs to me. **1932** Randolph *Ozark Mt. Folks* 38, Gawdamighty! Sich doin's as that 'ar 'd skeer anybody! **1940** Faulkner *Hamlet* 18 **MS,** Take that ere rug and wash it. **1942** Hall *Smoky Mt. Speech* 25 **wNC, eTN,** Over there [ˈovɚ,ɑɚ], heard on Cosby Creek. *Ibid* 85, The omission [of ð] is frequent in such phrases as . . *back there, over there, up there:* . . [bæk æə˞], [ˈovɚ ɛ̈ə˞]. . . Children have been observed to drop the [ð] even in a stressed form, as in the sentence: [ˈɑɚz ə 'bɪg oʊl 'spa·dɚ] 'There's a big old spider!' **1943** *LANE* Map 623 *(That tree)* 1 inf, **cwCT,** [ðæt ɛ·ʔər]; 1 inf, **cVT,** [ðæt æ·]; 1 inf, **swME,** [ðæt æ˞·ɔ̆]; 1 inf, **eME,** [ðæt a˞·]. [All of these resps were qualified as obsolete or heard from others.] *Ibid* Map 625 *(Those boys),* [In the comb them 'ere boys, common in **ME, NH, eMA,** most infs offered proncs of the type [æə]; less freq proncs were [æ(ə)r, ɛɑ(r), a, ɑ(ə˞)].] *Ibid* Map 707, 1 inf, **neCT,** [ˈʌp 'æ·ə weɪz]—up there a ways. **1976** Garber *Mountain-ese* 92 **sAppalachians,** That air son-in-law of yourn has done and left our Lucindy. **2000** *NY Rev. Books* 19 Oct 5/1 **TN,** They are indeed hillbillies, fully capable of asking for the borry of a chaw of that-air tobacky.

5 addit varr (see quots); pronc-sp *thore.*
1960 Carpenter *Tales Manchaca* 125 **cTX** (as of c1903), She fell and broke her wrist. "Where does it hurt, Grandma?" I asked. "Well, honey," she drawled, "it hurts right thore, right thore, and right thore," pointing to the various aching spots. **1981** Pederson *LAGS Basic Materials* **Gulf Region,** [Proncs of the types [ðɪɚ, ðɪə] occur rarely.]

B   As adj.

In combs *that* (or *them, those*) *there:* Used for emphasis in indicating a thing at a distance, or a person or thing under discussion.   For addit exx see **A4** above   Cf **here C**
1781 *PA Jrl. & Weekly Advt.* (Philadelphia) 16 May 1/2, [Vulgarisms:] *This here* report of *that there* committee. **1795** Dearborn *Columbian Grammar* 139, *List of Improprieties.* . . That there for That. **1832** *Political Examiner* (Shelbyville KY) 8 Dec 4/1, I put on a spanking new hat . . and slid into them are new seelskin pumps. **1841** *Daily Picayune* (New Orleans LA) 3 Jan 2/4, Vere's the propriety . . of celebrating the 4th of July . . and all them 'ere days, by firing off cannon. **1871** Eggleston *Hoosier Schoolmaster* 28 **sIN,** Them there days. **1899** (1912) Green *VA Folk-Speech* 443, *That-there.* . . That; that one, person or things. . . *Them there.* . . Those. **1922** Gonzales *Black Border* 296 **sSC, GA coasts** [Gullah glossary], Da'dey—that there. **1927** *AmSp* 3.7 **Ozarks,** Thet 'ar licker aint fitten t' drink. **1934** Hurston *Jonah's Gourd Vine* 16 **AL** [Black], Is dat air supper ready yit? **1942** Faulkner *Go Down* 148 **MS,** Come home, son. Dat ar cant help you. **1943** *LANE* Map 621 *(Those are),* A few informants offered more emphatic or more explicit expressions beside the simple demonstrative pronoun: . . 1 inf,

csCT, [ðɛm ðæ·ᵻr, -æᶦə]; 1 inf, cCT, [ðɛm ðɛə]. *Ibid* Map 623 *(That tree)* **NEng,** 4 infs, That 'ere tree. *Ibid* Map 625 *(Those boys),* [*Them 'ere boys* is **widespread throughout ME, NH, eMA,** though often characterized as old-fashioned or obsolete; there are scattered instances of *them there boys,* and one of *those 'ere.*] **1952** Brown *NC Folkl.* 1.599, *That 'air.* . . That there. **1967** *DARE* (Qu. HH18) Inf **MI**67, Them there people. **1968** *DARE* FW Addit **MD**20, That there . . them there. **1991** Still *Wolfpen Notebooks* 83 **sAppalachians,** Listen at that air peckerwood driving nails. **1996** Bell *Biggie Poisoned Politician* 102 **TX,** I say start with that there Crabtree.

thereaway(s) adv [Scots, Ir, nEngl dial] Cf **hereaway, thataway** adv

In or towards that place, thereabouts; hence phr *or thereaway* used to qualify a preceding (often numerical) statement as approximate.

1770 in 1945 *Archives of MD* 62.389, You may as well pay it, there's not above two hundred and fifty due, or thereaway. **1800** in 1815 Dunlap *Life of Charles Brockden Brown* 2.101 **sePA,** The C.'s are gone to Lancaster or thereaway. **1826** Cooper *Last of Mohicans* 1.113 **NY,** Hereabouts, it [=a river] pitches into deep hollows, that rumble and quake the 'arth; and thereaway, it ripples and sings like a brook. **1844** in 1860 Hodgson *Selections* 213, My love to R. Gardner, and all our dear suffering friends thereaway. **1851** *S. Lit. Messenger* 17.689 **VA,** They put three vessels . . on the line to Liverpool, to sail on stated days regularly once a month or thereaway. **1854** *Harper's New Mth. Mag.* 10.84 **MA,** I didn't guess yo' meant to steer for the shop, when yo' p'inted thereaway yonder. **1874** *Oakland Daily Eve. Tribune* (CA) 13 July 3/3, Quite a number of good church-going people were present yesterday, having been inveigled thereaways perhaps just as we were. **1899** (1912) Green *VA Folk-Speech* 443, *Thereaway.* . . In those parts; there; thereabouts. **1929** Macdonald *Fifty Yrs.* 1.163 **NH,** She seated herself by my knee on a footstool none too broad for a person of her amplitude thereaways. **1969** Wilson *Stars* 194 **Ozarks,** I was sort of a orphling. Borned down about Red Star. Ever been thereaways? **2007** *DARE* File—Internet **GA,** Does anyone know if any pizza place, especially in Wisconsin or up thereaways, dares to offer a . . bratwurst pizza?

there's no occasion See **occasion B**

there's snow down South (or on the ground, on the mountain) See **snowing down South, it's**

the rigors See **rigor**

therm n Also *thum-gut* [nEngl dial *tharm* an animal intestine prepared for stuffing] Cf **tom thumb**

1899 (1912) Green *VA Folk-Speech* 443, *Therm.* . . The *therm, thumgut,* the coecum of an animal stuffed full of sausage-meat and smoked. Tharm.

thern See **theirn**

therreckly See **directly**

therselves See **theirselves**

thes See **just 5**

these pron, adj Usu |ðiz|; also *esp among Black speakers* |diz| Pronc-spp *dese, deze*

Std senses, var forms.

1875 in 1884 Lanier *Poems* 179 **GA** [Black], And what for waste de vittles, now . . / Jes' for to strength dese idle hands. **1884** *Anglia* 7.269 **Sth, S Midl** [Black], *Deze days* = at present. **1893** Shands *MS Speech* 62, *Th* is in a large number of instances pronounced by negroes as *d:* as, *dis, dat, dese* [etc]. **1901** *DN* 2.184 **neKY** [Black], *These* . . dese. **1922** Gonzales *Black Border* 297 **sSC, GA coasts** [Gullah glossary], *Dese*—these. **1928** [see **they** adj]. **1942** *Time* 1 June 58 **NYC,** Dese woids I hoid him say. **1981** Pederson *LAGS Basic Materials* **Gulf Region,** [Of 6 instances of proncs of the type [diᵛiz], 3 were by Black infs.]

these here See **here C**

these-uns pron Also *thesens* [Varr of *these ones;* cf *EDD* these 4.(2)] Cf **one A, them-uns, you-uns** pron¹

These.

1863 in 1879 Beatty *Citizen-Soldier* 367 **TN,** As the column approached, said one of the women to a soldier: "Is these uns Yankees?" **1872** Webb *Buffalo Land* 367 **West,** These uns 'ud reach inter ther pockets. **1884** (1885) McCook *Tenants* 171 **PA,** I think, however, them 's a

differt sort o' bees from these uns, ain't they? **1938** in 1974 *Amer. Slave* 12.1.152 **GA** [Black], Lawdy, chile, them wuz tryin' days. Ah sho is glad God let me live to see these 'uns. **1938** Rawlings *Yearling* 182 **nFL,** They'll take a notion to it and they'll try to nest in the hole. The bees has done drove these uns out. **1951** *Mansfield News–Jrl.* (OH) 5 Jan 20/4, [Advt:] These 'uns will save you real money! Don't delay— buy today. **1973** McCarthy *Child of God* 131 **TN,** Is them all the watches you got? Just them three is all. Here. Hand him thesens back. **2000** in 2005 *DARE* File—Internet **cwNC,** Well, I can tell you that's the last time I'll wear these uns in the river. . . I wear 'em long though to cover a scar I don't want to get much sun on.

thet See **that A3**

thew v See **throw A1**

thew adv, prep See **through** adv, prep **1**

thewed See **throw A1, B1c, 2b**

they pron¹ Usu |ðe|; also *esp freq among Black speakers* |de, di| Pronc-sp *dey*

Std senses, var forms.

1850 (1852) Lossing *Pictorial Field-Book* 2.404 **MD** [Black], I reckons dey is pretty tick, dey is, twixt here and Uncle Josh's. **1875** in 1884 Lanier *Poems* 177 **Sth** [Black], Dese ears, *dey* sees the world. **1908** *DN* 3.282 **eAL, wGA,** [ð] in all positions has, under negro influence, largely become *d,* as in . . [di] (they or the). **1922** Gonzales *Black Border* 230 **eSC** [Gullah], Dey berry 'f'aid fuh git dem foot wet, en' dey does climb high 'puntop de tussock. **1928** Peterkin *Scarlet Sister Mary* 162 **SC** [Gullah], A pipe is good to help people when dey is worried in dey mind. **1935** in 1944 *ADD* 636 **NYC,** They. . . Dey. Dial. var. still common among 'toughs.' **1937** in 1976 *Weevils in the Wheat* 215 **VA** [Black], Dat what dey say. **1942** *Time* 1 June 58 **Brooklyn NYC,** All dey do is win. **2005** *DARE* File—Internet **wPA,** Who dey? Dey is da Steelers, dummy!

they pron² Pronc-spp *de(y), thay* [Prob from Scots *the(y)* in similar contexts (*SND there* adv. 1). The US idiom differs, however, in tending to prefer a sg verb, even when the logical subject is pl, whereas Scots idiom leans toward a pl verb even with a sg subject.] **scattered, but chiefly Sth, S Midl** Cf **it** pron **C1**

Esp with existential *be:* Used in place of *there* to anticipate a postponed subject.

1801 in 1956 Eliason *Tarheel Talk* 319 **nw,cwNC,** They. **1843** (1916) Hall *New Purchase* 228 **IN,** If they warn't a mighty powerful heap of laffin. **1845** *Millsaps Letters* 2 (Montgomery Coll.), They has nuthing accurd of importance since you left here. **1852** in 1956 Eliason *Tarheel Talk* 319 **cs,seNC,** De. **1871** Eggleston *Hoosier Schoolmaster* 28 **sIN,** They was a powerful sight of money. **1894** Frederic *Marsena* 60 **nNY,** They ain't no more to this. **1904** Day *Kin o' Ktaadn* 99 **ME,** They's lots of folks. **1909** *DN* 3.380 **eAL, wGA,** They. . . Sometimes used for *there* as an introductive word. "They was six of 'em." **1915** *DN* 4.191 **swVA,** They's lots o' berries over in the big field. **1930** *VA Qrly. Rev.* 6.242 **S Midl,** They's not much in it, but I reckon they's enough. **1932** Randolph *Ozark Mt. Folks* 115, They warn't nothin' she could do 'bout it. **1936** *AmSp* 11.355 **eTX,** They ain't nare one. **1937** in 1976 *Weevils in the Wheat* 297 **VA** [Black], Dey bugs in de wheat. **1942** Hall *Smoky Mt. Speech* 26 **wNC, eTN,** *There* often appears as [ðe] in such uses as, [ðez 'bɪn ə 'ledɪ 'hɪɚ] 'There's been a lady here'; [ðe kʌm ə 'snou 'ðæt 'deɪ] 'There came a snow that day.' **1952** Brown *NC Folkl.* 1.600, "They's a sight o' fruit this year."—Illiterate. **c1955** Eaton Coll. **Washington Is. WI,** They didn't no paper come today nor yesterday neither. **1959** *VT Hist.* 27.163, They . . for *there.* Are they any cookies? Rare. **1967–68** *DARE* (Qu. GG19b, *When you can see from the way a person acts that he's feeling important or independent: "He seems to think he's _____."*) Inf **NY**96, All they is of it; (Qu. LL17, . . *There's no more of something: "The potatoes are _____."*) Inf **KY**33, All gone, they hain't no more. **1967–69** *DARE* FW Addit **cnLA,** "Not anything in there, are they?" Heard in post office; **MA**14, They was = there was/were; they used to be = there used to be; **NY**68, Best paper then is; **seTX,** There are—usually pronounced ['ðe,aɚ] or [,ðe'aɚ] in uninhibited conversation. **1968–70** *DARE* Tape **AR**56, They [ðe] was a still on that; **GA**35, They [ðeɪ] real lucky if they [ðeɪ] five of 'em left; **MO**1, Unless somebody stops at some of these stations and asks if they's [ðez] a trailer court, . . they don't know. **a1978** (1983) Carpenter *Aunt Arie* 94 **NC,** They never did all th' mushmelon seed ever come up neither.

1979 Lewis *How to Talk Yankee* [33] **nNEng,** I hear where thay's going to be a new preacher over to the Methodist Church. **1991** Heat Moon *PrairyErth* 75 **ceKS,** Out would come some Sharp's Crick moonshine, or else they was home brew. **2004** Adams *My Old Love* 116 **wNC** (as of c1865), I believe they ain't nothing that will stop this war.

they adj [Cf **he** pron **2, she** pron **2;** but in this case the substitution may be phonetic rather than grammatical.] **Sth, S Midl** *esp freq among Black speakers*
Their.

    1806 [see **them** C1]. **1843** (1916) Hall *New Purchase* 374 **IN,** I rather allow Johnny Calvin's boys . . ain't likely to have they idees physicked out of them. **1899** Chesnutt *Conjure Woman* 71 **csNC** [Black], Go ter dey wuk fresh en strong. **1928** Peterkin *Scarlet Sister Mary* 111 **eSC** [Gullah], My lil blue hen . . hatched dese beedies, all blue like dey mammy. **1931** (1991) Hughes–Hurston *Mule Bone* 116 **cFL** [Black], Any man that treats they wife bad as you can't tell nobody else they eye is black. **1934** Carmer *Stars Fell on AL* 180 [Black], Dem lil' rabbits set . . thinkin' . . 'bout what dey pa say. **1945** FWP *Lay My Burden Down* 74 **GA** (as of c1865) [Black], After . . the slaves taken out of they bondage, some of the very few white folks give them niggers what they liked the best. **1946** Tallant *Voodoo* 105 **New Orleans LA** [Black], Nobody never did know who they fathers was. **1959** Lomax *Rainbow Sign* 31 **AL** [Black], They could play there till dark. They mothers wouldn't care. **1967** *DARE* (Qu. KK13, . . *Arguing: "They stood there for an hour _____."*) Inf **SC34,** Poppin' they gums. **1973** Walker *In Love* 62 [Black], She were working for some good white people that give her they old clothes. **1988** Lincoln *Avenue* 179 **wNC** (as of c1940) [Black], They leave they trucks, they whiskey, they shotguns, an' everythin'.

they adv Pronc-spp *day, dey* Gullah
There.

    1888 Jones *Negro Myths* 3 **GA coast,** Buh Alligatur, eh day in de middle fas tersleep. *Ibid* 64, Buh Rabbit . . git er hebby dinner day too. **1908** *S. Atl. Qrly.* 7.334 **sSC coast** [Gullah], Me no know hoonah dey. Wuh yuh do dey? [=I didn't know you were there. What were you doing there?] **1992** Geraty *Bittle* 70 **Charleston SC** [Gullah], Uh set tuh de do'step duh ebenin' time./ Set dey en' nyam me bittle.

they exclam Also sp *thay, day* [Prob alter of *there*] **esp NC, GA**
Used as an expression of surprise—also in var combs; see quots.

    1967 *DARE* FW Addit **swNC,** *They*—exclamation of amazement or disbelief. **1975** *DARE* File **GA,** *They*—Exclamation of surprise; apparently euphemism for and abbr. of "The Lord have mercy"; fairly common, rural Ga. **1997** Frazier *Cold Mountain* 126 **NC** (as of c1866), He soon stumbled over an old man sitting on a low stool and knocked him onto the floor. The man on the floor said, They damn. *Ibid* 353, The boy sat and looked at him and then looked at the pistol in his hand and said, They God. As if he had not reckoned at all on it functioning as it had. **2003** Ross *Miss Julia Hits Road* 19 **NC,** "Thay Lord," I said, holding my aching head, "I know how that man drives a car. No telling how he drives a motorcycle." **2003** Dumas *Lita* 44 **GA,** Everything they said was prefaced with "They God!" which is basically a Southern way of saying "Oh my gosh, you guys aren't going to believe this!" **2004** *DARE* File **eTN** (as of c1950s), My mother used to express surprise by saying *They!* For instance, she would say, "They, it's 6:00 already." **2005** Williams *Gratitude* 531 **wNC** (as of 1940s), *They* . . an exclamation to express surprise or amazement, as: *"They!", "They, gosh!"* or *"They, Lordymercy!"* **2005** *DARE* File—Internet, As soon as I looked at the brand spanking new 48mm (1–7/8″) open end "wrench" I said "Thay Lord; would you look at that!" **2010** *DARE* File **KY,** I had a cousin from Clay county, KY who would say, "Day, law. . . "

they-all pron **sAppalachians, Ozarks**
They, all of them; hence poss *theirs all.*

    1913 Kephart *Highlanders* 78 **sAppalachians,** I disremember which buryin'-ground they-all planted ye in. **1927** *AmSp* 3.6 **Ozarks,** *Third Person.* . . [Plural:] they, they-all. **1934** (1970) Wilson *Backwoods Amer.* 68 **Ozarks,** There are double-barreled pronouns . . [in] the mountain language: *we-all, you-all,* and *they-all.* **1969** in 2004 Montgomery–Hall *Dict. Smoky Mt. Engl.* 602 **wNC, eTN,** Old man Lon and Will all, they all went with him. **1976** *Ibid,* Cades Cove nearly took theirs all to Gregory Bald. **1986** Pederson *LAGS Concordance,* 1 inf, **neTN,** Though they-all's connected together.

they'ns See **they-uns**

they'rn See **theirn**

theyselves pron Also *deysef(f), deyse'fs, deyself, deyselves, theyself* [Also found occas in Engl dial, but the US exx prob represent phonetic varr of **theirselves;** cf **they** adj] **chiefly Sth, S Midl** *esp freq among Black speakers*
Themselves.

    1845 Hooper *Advent. Simon Suggs* 133 **AL,** They're peart at the snap game, theyselves. **1851** Hooper *Widow Rugby's Husband* 150 **AL,** There's other people knows something, besides theyselves. **1867** Allen et al. *Slave Songs* xv **eSC** [Black], Dese yere worry deyseff—we don't worry weseff. **1874** Twain in *Atlantic Mth.* 34.592 **VA** [Black], Dat's what folks dat's bawn in Maryland calls deyselves. **1887** *Harper's New Mth. Mag.* 75.585 **GA** [Black], Dey divided me an' sis' Moll an' de lan' twix deyself. **1887** (1967) Harris *Free Joe* 41 **GA** [Black], He ax me w'at de reason dey don't git free deyse'f. **1888** *Overland Mth.* (2d ser) 12.141 [Black], Deys allus . . peekin' 'bout contin'lly whar dey done got no business ter poke deyse'fs. **1889** *Harper's New Mth. Mag.* 78.915 **GA,** Wimming . . is a kind o' creeters, I don't keer how skeery they make out theyselves, they want them they goin' to take up with to be feared o' nothin'. *Ibid,* She hold her own now along with any of 'em yit, as people can see for theyself. **1909** *DN* 3.380 **eAL, wGA,** *Theyselves.* . . Themselves. **1930** Dobie *Coronado* 133 **SW,** Then they got cleaned up theyselves. **1937** (1977) Hurston *Their Eyes* 17 **FL** [Black], Most of dese zigaboos is so het up over yo' business till they liable to hurry theyself to Judgment to find out about you if they don't soon know. **1945** FWP *Lay My Burden Down* 144 **Sth** (as of c1865) [Black], The missus let the womenfolks bake pies, cakes, and custards for the barbecue, just 'zackly like it was for the white folks' barbecue theyself! **1967** *DARE* (Qu. HH8, *A person who likes to brag*) Inf **TN15,** He brags on theyself [ðɛs'sɛ·f]; (Qu. II18, *Someone who joins himself on to you and your group without being asked and won't leave*) Inf **TN15,** Push theyself. **1968** *PADS* 50.34 **swTN** [Black], *Themselves.* . . Two type I informants [=infs with little formal educ] . . have /ðɛsɛlvz/ [=theyselves]. **1974** *Black World* Apr 8, He was presenting the street nigguhs in all they glory without no overt exhortation to them to git theyselves togetha.

they-uns pron Also sp *they'ns* **esp sAppalachians** Cf **one** A, **them-uns**
They, them, their.

    1864 in 1904 Northrop *Chron. from War Prisoner* 137 **SC,** They thought Yankees "rich enough to buy niggers if they'ns wanted any." **1866** *Atlantic Mth.* 18.2 **TN,** Theyuns is agoin' to take you away. **1895** Dromgoole *Heart* 47 **neTN,** They-uns flocked ter me like crows flockin' ter a corn-field; an' me it war . . ez dealt the world o' politics ter they-uns. **1898** (1999) Elliott *Durket Sperret* 97 (Internet) **TN,** Them folks never stir 'thout books in they uns' han's. *Ibid* 151, Hev theyuns got ary dorg? **1898** Remington *Crooked Trails* 117 **FL,** We-uns are expectin' of they-uns to-day. **1927** *AmSp* 2.287 **Ozarks,** *We-uns* and *you-uns* are common . . and even *us-uns* is not unknown, but *they'ns* is not often heard in the Ozarks. **1996** in 2004 Montgomery–Hall *Dict. Smoky Mt. Engl.* 602 **wNC,** *They'uns* [1 inf]. **2005** *DARE* File—Internet **nGA,** Wayull, they'uns got that thang 30–40 year ago.

thick n Pronc-sp *tick* [*OED2* →1836]
A thicket.

    1853 Simms *Sword & Distaff* 80 **SC,** Let us round this thick, and git across the road above. **1856** Simms *Eutaw* 215 **SC** [Gullah], Fuss t'ing, we must hide away de carriage and hoss in some good tick [Simms: thick, or thicket], for we doesn't know, any minute, who's aguine to come 'pon we. **1968** *DARE* Tape **GA51,** These here little thicks all over the Okefenokee Swamp, we call them houses. Just little thicks surrounded by water, there's thousands of them in the swamp, in the prairies. . . My daddy learned me to call them that.

thick as three in a bed adj phr, adv phr For varr see quots **orig more widespread; now chiefly S Midl** See Map on p. 562
Of people: very close, intimate; crowded; in crowded conditions.

    1844 Stephens *High Life in NY* 165, The President and I went to the Theatre, and slept together, and are as thick as three in a bed jest now. **1854** St. Clair *Six Days* 7 **NEng,** Finding that . . they would not offer her a seat [in a bus], she remarked half inquiringly, "All full, I suppose." . . "We're as thick as three in a bed," added another. **1855** *Prescott Tran-*

script (WI) 5 Oct [2]/4 (newspaperarchive.com), The great desideratatum . . is *Lumber* to build houses with. People are living out there as thick as five in a bed. **1868** *Harper's New Mth. Mag.* Mar 412 **MN,** I had heard the saying, "Thick as three in a bed," but here [=in a logging camp] it was literally as thick as a dozen in a bed. **1873** *Ibid* Apr 677 **WV,** A single bed of moderate dimensions was assigned for the accommodation of our party. . . 'As thick as three in a bed,' has become a byword. Four in a bed surpasses the limits of proverbial philosophy; and . . I yielded my share of the couch and took the floor. **1942** Clark *Kentucky* 114 **KY,** When a man says men are intimate friends, he says, "They are as thick as four in a bed." **1946** *PADS* 6.43 **VA,** As thick as three in a bed. (Quite friendly.) . . Rare. **1965–70** *DARE* (Qu. II3, *Expressions to say that people are very friendly toward each other: "They're _____."*) Infs **AR**35, **IA**9, **IL**16, **KY**84, Thick as three in a bed; **TX**104, As thick as three in the bed; **AR**41, As thick as three in a bed as big as I am; **KY**6, 74, **MD**26, **VA**11, Thick as two in a bed; **AR**3, 18, 33, Thick as six in the bed. **1967** in 1968 Haun *Hawk's Done Gone* 302 **eTN,** They always seemed to be about as thick as two in a bed. Pa always took up for him.

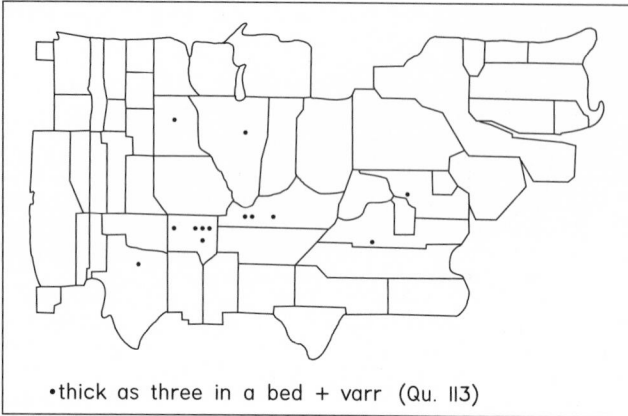

•thick as three in a bed + varr (Qu. II3)

thickened gravy n   Also *thick(en) gravy, thickening ~*   Pronc-sp *thickning gravy*   **chiefly Sth, S Midl**   See Map   Cf **red-eye gravy**

=**flour gravy.**

1864 Bowling Green State Univ. *Center Archival Coll.* (Internet) **TN,** We have just been to supper and we had good biscuits and potatoes and thickened gravy and coffee and meat. **1888** *Dunkirk Observer–Jrl.* (NY) 2 Feb 3/5, In making thickened gravy proceed thus: Take a tablespoon of flour to each pint of liquid desired. **1946** in 2005 *DARE* File—Internet, [Song in the film *Gunning for Vengeance:*] Or shut my mouth with a great slab of that sugar-cured ham / And about a half a gallon of this old thickened gravy. **1963** Watkins–Watkins *Yesterday Hills* 12 **cnGA,** The Watkins children rose at four-thirty, ate salt mackerel and biscuits and "thickning" gravy for breakfast. **1965–70** *DARE* (Qu. H37, *. . Words . . for gravy. Any joking ones?*) Infs **GA**81, **KY**15, 90, **LA**2, **TN**27, **TX**52, Thickened gravy; **LA**19, Thickened gravy—served with chicken, etc—thickened with flour; if milk is added, it's called cream gravy; **TN**30, Thickened gravy—"white gravy" (or thickened gravy) is made by browning slightly some flour in this fat in pan and adding milk; **AR**47, **KY**85, **MS**60, Thickening gravy; **CA**91, Thickening gravy—butter in pan, browned flour in pan; keep this moving so it doesn't burn; salt it a little, add milk and keep stirring it till it thickens; **AR**52, 55, **GA**85, **MS**1, **NJ**54, **SC**46, Thick gravy; (Qu. H25) Inf **KY**5, Thickened gravy. **1975** McDonough *Garden Sass* 74 **AR,** Thickenin' gravy (directions given by Lillie Sugg)—"Cook your sausage. Take it up and leave the grease in the pan. Put flour in the pan and brown it. Cook it for a long time. Put milk in it and cook it a good while—until it's good and thick." **1986** Pederson *LAGS Concordance,* 3 infs, **GA,** Thickening gravy; 1 inf, **ceAL,** Thickening gravy— meat gravy; 1 inf, **seAR,** Thickening gravy—milk, flour, salt, chicken grease; 1 inf, **nwMS,** Thicken gravy—thickening, thickened; 1 inf, **cLA,** Thicken gravy—thickened gravy; 1 inf, **cAR,** Thicken gravy—made from flour, water, salt. **2001** *Standard* (Macclenny FL) 11 July (Internet) **FL** (as of 1930s), Mama wouldn't have enough eggs to feed us all. So she'd make a batch of what we called thickened gravy, just grease and flour and salt and pepper. **2003** *DARE* File—Internet **MS,** That sounds like something my mom would have eaten. She liked thickening gravy on a tomato. **2005** *Ibid* **TX** (as of 1930s), We went as long as

three months eating day-old bread and what we called "thickened gravy." Flour and water—hot!

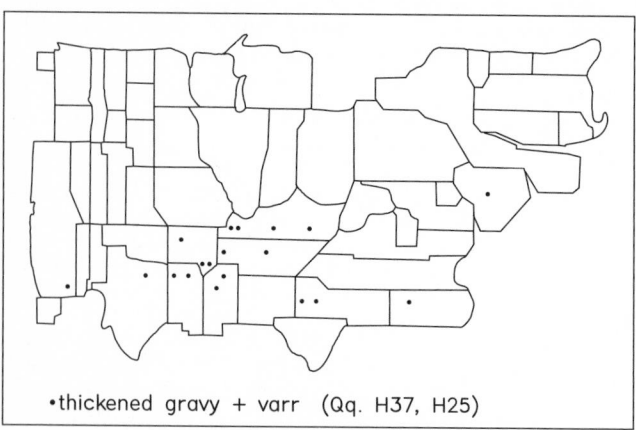

•thickened gravy + varr   (Qq. H37, H25)

thicket creeper n

A **Virginia creeper 1** (here: *Parthenocissus vitacea*).

1930 *Ironwood Daily–Globe* (MI) 19 July 5/3, Other vines well suited for growing on trellises are the Virginia creeper. . . In the same group is the hardier thicket creeper. **1960** Vines *Trees SW* 710, *Thicket Creeper—Parthenocissus vitacea.* . . Woody vine. **1968** Barkley *Plants KS* 232, Parthenocissus vitacea. . . Thicket Creeper. Open woods and thickets along streams. **1970** Correll *Plants TX* 1022, *Thicket creeper.* . . In woods, thickets and on banks in w. Tex.

thick gravy   See **thickened gravy**

thick milk n   [Prob calque of PaGer *dickemilich* or Ger *Dickmilch,* but cf similar compounds in other Germanic langs]   **chiefly Nth, N Midl, esp PA**   See Map
=**clabber** n[1] **1.**

1859 (1860) Edgeworth *S. Gardener* 180 **GA,** *Griddle Cakes, No. II.*—Take a pint of thick milk, or a quart of sour; to the thick add a pint of sweet milk. **1859** Storke *Family Farm* 3.145 **NY,** When the casein is precipitated or the milk coagulated, it is ready to churn. . . The thick milk should always be emptied with the cream into the churn. **1878** *Bucks Co. Gaz.* (Bristol PA) [21 Mar 4]/1 (newspaperarchive.com), [Reprinted from *American Poultry Journal:*] *Feeding Young Turkeys.* . . Thick milk can follow this, with an admixture of scraps of bread, after which cheese (thick milk with the whey drained off) can be given. **1913** *Lincoln Daily News* (NE) 31 Mar sec A 4/4, *Waffles.* One and one-fourth cups flour, one-fourth teaspoonful salt, one-half teaspoon soda, one cup of thick milk, two eggs well beaten, three tablespoons of melted butter. **1914** *DN* 4.114 **cKS,** Thick milk. . . Curdled milk. **1934** Merrill's *Golden Jubilee* np **cWI,** Out in the clearings, breakfast consisted of bread spread with lard, and coffee made from barley. The noon meal would be thick milk, and potatoes with their jackets on. **1948** Davis *Word Atlas Gt. Lakes* app qu 34, 8 (of 233) infs, **MI, IN, OH,** Thick milk. **1949** Kurath *Word Geog.* 70, *Clabber.* . . Pennsylvania has a number of local terms. . . *Thick-milk,* modeled on Pennsylvania German *Dickemilich,* is also extensively used in Pennsylvania from the Delaware River to Pittsburgh. Relics of *thick-milk* appear also in the Mohawk Val-

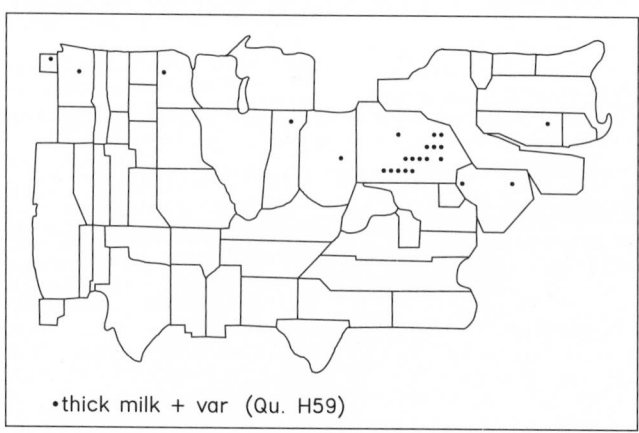

•thick milk + var (Qu. H59)

ley, probably as a legacy of the Palatine settlers of pre-Revolutionary days. **1962** Atwood *Vocab.* TX 62, *Curdled milk.* . . the Pennsylvania German *thick milk* occurs but five times [among 273 infs]. **1965–70** *DARE* (Qu. H59, *Milk that becomes thick as it turns sour*) 23 Infs, 15 **PA**, Thick milk; **PA**40, Think [sic] milk. [20 Infs comm type 4 or 5] **1973** Allen *LAUM* 1.291 **Upper MW** (as of c1950), *Curdled milk.* . . *Thick milk* . . is the usage of sparsely scattered infs. of widely varied parental background. **1985** *AmSp* 60.235 **sePA,** *Thick milk*—Milk which has soured to the point of becoming dense (*sour milk* 55.5% [of 60 infs], *curdled milk* 29%, *thick milk* 12.5%, no response 1.5%, other responses [*buttermilk*] 1.5%. . .) **1986** Pederson *LAGS Concordance* (*Curdled milk*) 1 inf, **seMS,** Thick milk. **2005** *DARE* File—Internet, *Thick milk pie!* It's the pie of the month . . but what the heck is thick milk? . . [I]t's unpasteurized milk that has gone sour and thickened, but somehow it's still yummy. . . This particular pie recipe is Amish.

thickning gravy See **thickened gravy**

thick of fog n **ME coast** Cf **fog mull,** *DNE*

A dense fog that restricts visibility; similarly nouns *thick of snow, ~ vapor* a heavy snow (or mist) that restricts visibility.

1839 in 1999 Lunt *Hauling* 76 **ME,** Thick of snow the forenoon. Clear'd off after dark with northerly wind, but moderate. **1932** Wasson *Sailing Days* 126 **cME coast,** Weeks of dense fog, weather always known as "thick-o'-fog," often continued in the summer. Even more obscuring than fog were winter days when driving wind, "thick-o'-snow," shut out all view except within a few feet. *Ibid,* Impenetrable masses of steam, constantly rising and blowing in clouds over the water, made fair and cold winter days of "thick-o'-vapor," most detested and paralyzing of all. **1947** *Portland Press Herald* (ME) 29 Dec 8/6, When he was 20 years old, he was aboard another fishing vessel which crashed on Cape Cod rocks "in a thick of fog." **1963** Haywood *Yankee Dict.* 172, *Thick of snow*—The mariner's term for a snow fall with big, wet flakes and plenty of them, blowing and swirling so visibility ahead is nearly zero. **1966** *DARE* File **ME coast,** It come up a thick of fog. **1975** Gould *ME Lingo* 289, *Thick o' fog*—See *mull.* *Ibid* 185, *Mull*—The word most often used in Maine for *thick o' fog; a fog mull.*

thick of hearing adj phr Also rarely *thick on hearing* [*OED2* 1526 →; "Now *dial.*"] *old-fash*

Hard of hearing.

1692 in 2005 *DARE* File—Internet **VA,** Shee then made a replye that I could not well hear haveing a could and somthing thick of hearing. [**1720** in 1852 PA Prov. Council *Minutes* 3.97, But we find their Ears are thick.] **1868** NY Constitutional Convention *Proc. & Debates* 4.3090 **NY,** The gentleman must have been very thick of hearing. **1873** Warfield *Miriam Monfort* 182 **sePA,** Old Morton . . was a "little thick of hearing." **1899** (1912) Green *VA Folk-Speech* 443, *Thick-of-hearing.* Slightly deaf. **1970** *DARE* (Qu. X19a, *When a person's hearing is not very good* . . *he's* _____) Inf **VA**46, Thick on hearing. [Inf old]

thick of snow (or vapor) See **thick of fog**

thick on hearing See **thick of hearing**

thicky adj [*OED2* "*Obs.*"] Cf Intro "Language Changes" III.1

Thick, viscous.

1986 Pederson *LAGS Concordance,* 1 inf, **cwMS,** Thicky—of gumbo . . land; 1 inf, **cwAR,** Thicky and wet—of "gumbo."

thief n, v Usu |θif|; also *chiefly among Black speakers* |tif| Pronc-sp *tief*

A Forms. For addit exx, see **B** below.

1829 Tenney *Female Quixotism* 1.116 **Philadelphia PA** [Black], "Dare he be—dare de tief; catch him." **1855** Hammond–Mansfield *Country Margins* 165 **NY** [Black], Old Shadrach . . said to the occupant of the tree, "Look hea, you brack tief, you come down, and Drive [=a dog] eat you head off sartain." **1869** *Harper's New Mth. Mag.* 38.396 **Sth** [Black], Come out, tief! Is dis de way you treats lonesome women? **1893** Shands *MS Speech* 63, *Tief* [tif]. Negro for *thief.* **1970** *DARE* (Qu. V6, . . *Words* . . *for a thief*) Inf **SC**68, Tief. [Inf Black]

B As verb.

Rarely with *up:* To steal, rob; to commit theft; hence vbl n *thiefing. esp freq among Black speakers*

1838 Gilman *S. Matron* 254 **SC** [Black], He tief one sheep. **1853** Simms *Sword & Distaff* 374 **SC** [Black], Ingin Bet good hand for tief, but he nebber guine tief rotten shu't. **1883** *Century Illustr. Mag.* 26.777 **GA** [Black], You no is ketch-a-me! I t'ief you' green pea,—I t'ief um

some mo',—I t'ief um till I dead! **1888** Jones *Negro Myths* 69 **GA coast,** Eh mek um quaintun bout wen de Ring tuk, an who eh tink tief um. **1892** (1969) Christensen *Afro-Amer. Folk Lore* 46 **seSC,** Br'er Rabbit him bring 'e bag 'cause 'e gwine for tief cow-pease. **1922** Gonzales *Black Border* 333 **sSC, GA coasts** [Gullah glossary], *T'ief*—(n. and v.) thief, thieves; steal, steals, stole, stolen, stealing. "T'ief iz bad, but t'ief en' ketch iz de debble"—It is bad to steal, but to steal and be caught is worse. *T'iefin'*—thieving. **1939** in Lib. of Congress *Amer. Memory: WPA Life Hist.* (Internet) **SC** [Black], I ain't never have white or black to point hand at me and say, 'Gabriel you did tief so and so from me.' **1950** *PADS* 14.67 **coastal SC** [Black], *Tief.* . . To steal. **1950** *Dixon Eve. Telegraph* (IL) 12 Apr 1/2, They charged me $4,000.00 in the other case. I pleaded guilty, I didn't need a lawyer to do that. I paid $2,300.00. That is why he pulled out, they thiefed me all along. **1960** *Salisbury Times* (MD) 21 Dec 33/2, Larry Wingate put the tribe back in business thiefing an interception. **1966–68** *DARE* (Qu. V4, . . *Words for stealing something valuable* . . *"Yesterday somebody* _____ *my watch."*) Inf **GA**28, Tiefin' [Inf White]; (Qu. OO42a, *About stealing money: "He admitted that he* _____ *[the money]."*) Inf **SC**26, Steal, thief [tif]; (Qu. OO42b, *About stealing money: "He says it's the first time he has ever* _____ *[money]."*) Inf **SC**26, Steal, thief [tif] [Inf Black]. **1971** Cunningham *Syntactic Analysis Gullah* 44 **seSC,** Them girls tiefed them hen and thief up my sleeping pills. **1977** *Chron.- Telegram* (Elyria OH) 12 June sec E 6/1, But James [Earl Ray] was always interested in money. I bet if they let him out that's what he'd go back to—thiefing.

thief ant n [See quot 1972] Cf **grease ant**

A small ant (*Solenopsis molesta*) native to the US. Also called **kafir ant**

1902 *Amer. Naturalist* 36.952 **IL,** The walls of the galleries in some of the formicaries were tenanted by teeming colonies of the . . thief ant. **1905** Kellogg *Amer. Insects* 544, The thief-ant is so small and obscurely colored that it seems to live in the nest of its host practically unperceived. **1926** Essig *Insects N. Amer.* 858, *The thief ant* . . is known as the kafir ant in Kansas and destroys kafir and Indian corn as well as the larvae of insects. **1958** *Appleton Post–Crescent* (WI) 31 July 38/3, The hundred and more species . . range in size from the shiny black half-inch long carpenter ant to the colorfully named Thief ant and Pharoah's [sic] ant, both . . scarcely a sixteenth of an inch long. **1972** Swan–Papp *Insects* 555, *Thief Ant.* . . It is named for its habit of robbing the food and brood of other ants. **1996** in 2001 *DARE* File—Internet, Grease ant is a name commonly used for one of the smallest ants found in homes in Iowa. These ants are technically known as thief ants.

thiefing See **thief B**

thief stick n

In logging: =**cheat stick.**

1956 Sorden–Ebert *Logger's Words* 37 **Gt Lakes, NEng,** *Thief-stick,* See scale-rule. [*Ibid* 29, *Scale-rule,* A long heavy hardwood ruler marked in inches and feet used in estimating the lumber in standing timber or in logs.] **1958** McCulloch *Woods Words* 192 **Pacific NW,** *Thief stick*—A scale stick.

thief up See **thief B**

thi-eyter See **theater**

thigamy See **thingum 2b**

thill n [*OED2* c1325 →] **chiefly Nth** See Map on p. 564 Cf **fill** n[2]

One of the pair of shafts on a buggy or other vehicle.

1785 in Lib. of Congress *Amer. Memory: G. Washington Papers* (Internet) **VA,** At first I was . . as restive under the operation, as a Colt is of the Saddle. . . Now, no dray moves more readily to the Thill, than I do to the painters. **1834** *Huron Reflector* (Norwalk OH) 9 Sept [4]/4 (newspaperarchive.com), One of the screws fastening the shafts to the axletree dropping off, one side of the thills fell upon his horse's legs, as he was going quite fast down a hill. **1858** *Atlantic Mth.* 2.497 **MA,** There is always *somewhere* a weakest spot,—/ In hub, tire, felloe, in spring or thill. **1877** *Harper's New Mth. Mag.* 54.298 **CT,** This would not have mattered if a sudden jolt had not broken one side of the thills short off, whereupon the colt kicked and plunged till he broke the other. **1912** *Daily Northwestern* (Oshkosh WI) 21 Sept [14]/1 (newspaperarchive.com), He discovered that both thills were snapped off. **1925** *Syracuse Herald* (NY) 20 Apr 4/6, At the Jefferson Street intersection the thills suddenly dropped from the vehicle freeing the frightened steed. **1949** Kurath *Word Geog.* 17, From New England to Lake Erie *fills* or *thills* . . is a common name in rural areas for the shafts of a buggy. *Fills* predominates over *thills* in the more conservative parts of New England and in the settlement area beyond the Hudson. **1965–70** *DARE* (Qu. L44, *On a buggy, two long pieces of wood stick out in front and the horse goes between them. You call them the* _____) 40 Infs, **chiefly Nth,** Thills. [36 Infs comm type 4 or 5, 32 old] **1973** Allen *LAUM* 1.214 **Upper MW** (as of c1950), *Shafts* (of a buggy). . . The *thills* and *fills* reveal their New England and Hudson Valley origin by occurring chiefly in southern Minnesota and northern Iowa.

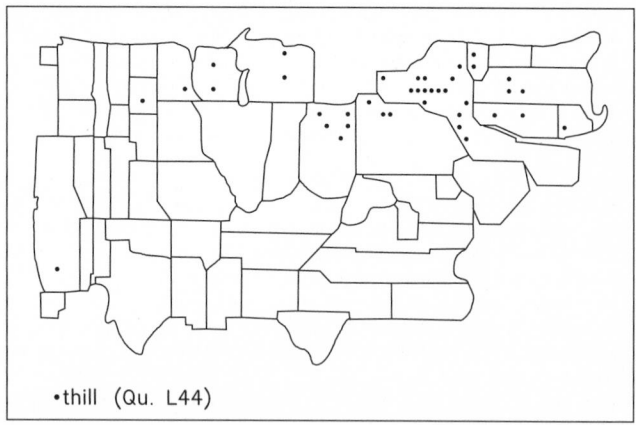

•thill (Qu. L44)

thimble n

1 also *(thimble, thimble,) who's got the thimble; sell the thimble; weave the thimble;* for addit varr see quots: A game in which players try to guess whose hands conceal a thimble. Note: The game of *hide the thimble* in which players search for a hidden thimble is widespread. **chiefly Sth, S Midl** See Map Cf **button B2, hold fast what I give you**

1833 *Sketches D. Crockett* 49, Plays which had been fashionable when their grandmothers were girls, such as Sell the Thimble . . were called up, and wearied out. **1897** (1952) McGill *Narrative* 136 **ceSC,** "Weave the Thimble," all are standing in a circle with partners, each holding the right wrist of his neighbor with his left hand, weaving or passing the thimble with the right hand, while one person stands alone in the centre to find the thimble on its weaving way, quickly passing from right hand to the other. **1905** *DN* 3.92 **nwAR,** Rise, thimble, (and) go to work. . . The name of a game. *Ibid* 100, Weave the thimble. . . The name of a game. **1909** (1923) Bancroft *Games* 194, Thimble Ring. . . The odd player stands in the center of the circle, and tries to detect who holds the thimble that is passed from hand to hand. **1909** *DN* 3.380 **eAL, wGA,** Thimble. . . The name of a guessing game. **1911** *Lincoln Eve. News* (NE) 1 Aug 4/2, Transmigration is generally supposed to mean that when one dies his soul passes into a cat or dog or some other animal, which dying in turn hands the soul on, very much like who's-got-the-thimble. **1935** in 2006 *DARE* File—Internet (as of c1860) **wTN,** When a youth he attended a party, and engaged in playing "weave the thimble." **1945** *Dothan Eagle* (AL) 18 Mar 9/4, Paraphrasing the old children's game of "Thimble, thimble, who has the thimble?"—What the people are now saying is "Ring, ring, what candidate has the ring?" **1953** Brewster *Amer. Nonsinging Games* 9 **IN,** Thimble. . . The child who is "It" goes to each of the others in turn, placing his own clasped hands over those of the others and saying, "Hold fast all I give you." Finally he drops the thimble into one of the pairs of hands. When he reaches the end of the line, he calls to the first player, "Thimble, thimble, who's got the thimble?" The player questioned makes his guess. Then the one who dropped the thimble cries, "Rise up, thimbler!" If the other's guess was correct, the guesser wins the right to drop the thimble next time; if not, he must guess again and the player who received the thimble is the next to drop it. **1965–70** *DARE* (Qu. EE3, *Games in which you hide an object and then look for it*) 11 Infs, **Sth, S Midl,** Thimble; **LA2,** Thimble or Who's got the thimble—everybody clasps their hands and the players have to guess whose hands the thimble is in; **AL29, IL30, KY5,** 40, **TN14, VA54,** (Thimble, thimble,) who's got the thimble; **SC3,** Who's got the thimble—one stands with palms together and presses a thimble between them, rest are seated; he goes along the line and drops the thimble in some person's hand. The standing one then will ask another, "Who's got . . ?" If he fails to guess, he's penalized—made to sing, dance, etc. If several fail to guess correctly, the standing one says, "Rise,

thimble, and go to work," and the one holding it then starts it all over again. He asks several people, according to how many are playing. Whoever guesses right gets the thimble; **AL37, NC2,** Who has the thimble; **FL10, GA33,** Sell the thimble; **NC77,** Dodge the thimble; (Qu. EE1, . . *Games . . children play . . in which they form a ring, and either sing or recite a rhyme*) Inf **NC82,** Thimble—maybe get in circle and pass a thimble; guess who has it; (Qu. EE33, . . *Outdoor games . . that children play*) Inf **VA18,** Thimble; **GA75,** Thimble—pass on a thimble in folded hands; one child had to guess who has the thimble; **NC23,** Weave the thimble—handed it around a ring till one dropped it or guy in center discovered who had it; **SC24,** Sell the thimble—hold hands clasped and one person goes from player to player, then guess who has it. **1982** Slone *How We Talked* 96 **eKY** (as of c1950), We also played Thimble, Thimble, Who Has the Thimble (sometimes called, Button, Button, who has the Button). **1990** in 2005 *DARE* File—Internet **sAppalachians** (as of c1950), Often neighbors joined us in games like "Who's got the Thimble?"

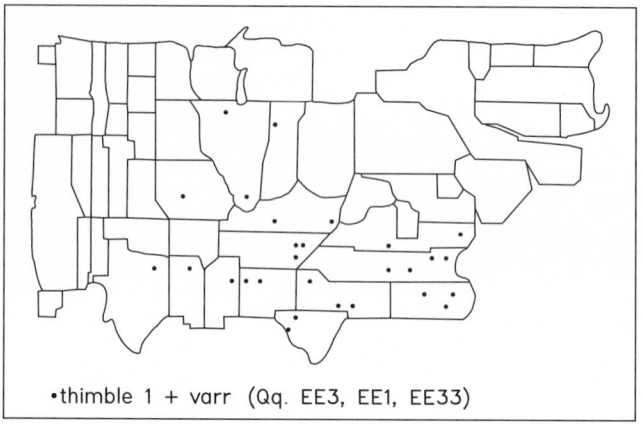

•thimble 1 + varr (Qq. EE3, EE1, EE33)

2 See **thimble fish.**

3 also pl: A **milkwort:** usu *Polygala nana, P. rugelii,* or **orange milkwort.**

1938 Baker *FL Wild Flowers* 121, The most noticeable polygalas in winter and early spring are those that Floridians call thimbles, or bachelors' buttons; *P[olygala] Rugelii,* which blooms in lemon-yellow, and the lower *P. lutea* with orange-yellow flowers. These polygalas, whose flowers are in thimble-like heads, are common in low pinelands and the borders of marshes. The dwarf *P. nana* [is]. . . [v]ery low . . , with a greenish tinge in its pale yellow thimbles, which are close to the basal leaves. **1955** *S. Folkl. Qrly.* 19.232 **FL,** Members of the Pilostaxis [= *Polygala*] family are known as *Small Thimbles* (Pilostaxis nana) or *Orange Thimbles* (Pilostaxis lutea). **1976** Fleming et al. *Wild Flowers FL* 50, *Polygala nana.* . . Look for yellow thimbles in the low, moist pinelands, where it blooms in late summer and throughout the growing season along the coastal plain.

thimble anemone n Cf thimbleflower e, thimbleweed 1

An anemone (here: *Anemone virginiana*).

1948 Wherry *Wild Flower Guide* 52, *Thimble Anemone (A[nemone] virginiana).* . . Carpels numerous, woolly, in a thimble-shaped group. . . Over our area [=NEast, N Cent] and adjoining regions. **1958** Sharpe–Sharpe *101 Wildflowers Shenandoah* 6 **VA,** *Anemone virginiana.* . . Fruiting head tightly compacted into a thimble-shaped cluster. . . Also called thimble anemone. **1965** *Native Plants PA* 54, *Anemone virginiana*—Thimble Anemone. **1969** *Daily Courier* (Connellsville PA) 14 Mar 19/4, Late-June: Yarrow, cow parsnip, . . flowering raspberry, thimble anemone.

thimbleberry n Also *thimble blackberry* [From the thimble-shaped fruit] chiefly NEast, Gt Lakes, NW, nCA See Map Cf cupberry

Any of several American **raspberries B,** but usu *Rubus occidentalis, R. odoratus,* or *R. parviflorus.* For other names of these see **blackcap 1, capberry, flowering raspberry, maiden's tit, red-flannel berry, salmonberry b, Scotch cap, white-flowering raspberry**

1789 in 1941 Howay *Voyages Columbia* 60 **MA writer in Pacific NW,** We frequently meet with gooseberrys rausberries currants blackberries strawberries and thimble berries. **1814** Bigelow *Florula Bos-*

toniensis 121 **MA**, *Rubus occidentalis. . . Black raspberry. Thimble-berry. . .* Fruit black, sprightly and pleasant to the taste. **1853** *Harper's New Mth. Mag.* 6.582 **MI**, The thimbleberry is a large and luscious species of raspberry, destitute of briars. **1883** *Century Illustr. Mag.* 26.681 seNY, The tall thimble blackberries grew in abundance. **1895** *DN* 1.399 **MA**, *Raspberries* means in Mass. only the red; the black are *thimbleberries.* **1907** *DN* 3.202 seNH, *Thimbleberry.* Black raspberry. **1941** *LANE* Map 276 *(Raspberries),* Except as noted below, these terms refer to black (or purple) raspberries only, especially the large cultivated variety. . . 15 infs, **CT, eNEng,** Thimbleberries; 1 inf, swCT, *Thimble-berry,* a large red raspberry; 1 inf, ceCT, Thimbleberries, red, 'the same as raspberries'; 1 inf, seMA, *Thimbleberries,* less common name; 1 inf, ceMA, *Thimbleberries,* black or white; 1 inf, seNH, *Blackcaps =* thimbleberries, the older term; 1 inf, swME, Thimbleberries are called black raspberries here; 1 inf, csME, *Thimbleberries,* red, wild. **1950** *WELS (What kinds of berries grow wild in your neighborhood?)* 3 Infs, **WI,** Thimbleberry. **1965–70** *DARE* (Qu. 144, *What kinds of berries grow wild around here?)* 45 Infs, **chiefly NEast, Gt Lakes, NW, nCA,** Thimbleberries; **AK**3, **MI**68, Thimbleberry. **1966** *DARE* Tape **MI**34, Thimbleberry grows wild, and it's about three to four feet high, and it has a white flower the size of a quarter, and it has a flat berry the size of a quarter, and it's thin like a quarter. Very juicy. . . They are very expensive, but they make very good jam. . . They're very tarty. They're a red berry like the raspberry, and they're very seedy like a raspberry. **1968** *DARE* FW Addit **NY**, In Boonville . . this [=*Rubus odoratus*] is called a thimbleberry. **1987** Hughes–Blackwell *Wildflowers SE AK* 92, Thim-bleberry *(Rubus parviflorus . .).* **2001** *DARE* File—Internet **WA**, Apparently the taste of thimbleberries varies from bland and mealy to sweet, juicy and tart according to growing conditions and individual preference.

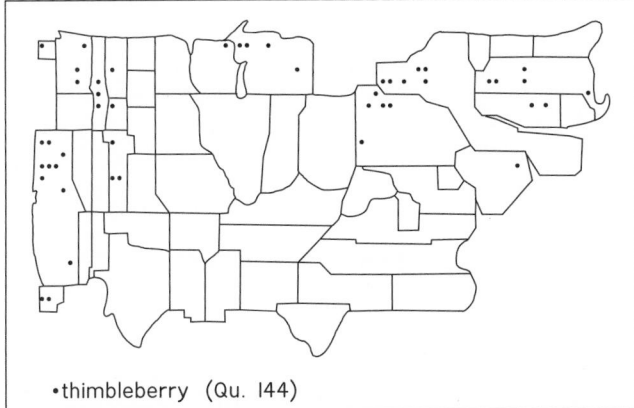

•thimbleberry (Qu. 144)

thimble clover n

A clover (here: *Trifolium microdon*).

   1973 Hitchcock–Cronquist *Flora Pacific NW* 275, Thimble c[lover]. . . *T[rifolium] microdon.*

thimble-eye See **thimble-eyed mackerel**

thimble-eyed ling n

A **squirrel hake** (here: *Urophycis chuss*).

   1905 NJ State Museum *Annual Rept. for 1904* 420, Thimble Eyed Ling. *Phycis* [=*Urophycis*] *chuss.* . . Eye large, a little elongate and well anterior.

thimble-eyed mackerel n Also *thimble-eye (mackerel), thimble mackerel* **NY, NJ**

=**chub mackerel.**

   1814 in 1815 *Lit. & Philos. Soc. NY Trans.* 1.422, *Thimble eyed, bull eyed, or chub mackerel.* . . Comes occasionally in prodigious numbers to the coast of New-York, in autumn. **1884** Goode *Fisheries U.S.* 1.303, The Chub Mackerel, or, as it is also called, the "Thimble-eye," . . closely resembles in general appearance the common Mackerel. *Ibid* 304, Captain Oakes states that the "Thimble-eye Mackerel" . . were very plentiful from 1826 to 1830. **1897** NY Forest Fish & Game Comm. *Annual Rept. for 1896* 236, *Thimble-Eye Mackerel.* . . in 1896 . . abounded in all the little creeks. **1917** *Copeia* 41.19 **Long Is. NY,** *Scomber colias.* Thimble Mackerel. **1998** in 2001 *DARE* File—Internet **NJ,** That evening the seas turned flat and large schools of Thimble Eye Mackerel

showed up. **2001** *Ibid* **NY**, Thimble eye mackerel. . . look just like boston mackerel but have a much larger eye.

thimble fish n Also *thimble*

A jellyfish; see quots.

   1885 Kingsley *Std. Nat. Hist.* 1.93, One of the most abundant medusae at times in the neighborhood of the Florida Keys is a Discophore, called by naturalists *Linerges,* and known to fishermen there as the "thimble-fish," "mutton-fish[," "]thimble" [etc]. **1891** *Sandusky Daily Reg.* (OH) 30 Mar [3]/6 (newspaperarchive.com) **Gulf States,** Beautiful little jelly fish called thimble fish, floating or swimming near its [=the Gulf Stream's] surface in such countless numbers that at times the waters are brown with them. **1901** Arnold *Sea-Beach* 139, *L[inerges] mercurius,* the thimble-fish. The English name indicates the form as well as the size of this little brownish jellyfish, which is found near the Florida Keys, extending in lines for considerable distances.

thimbleflower n Cf **thimbleweed**

Any of several plants, as:

a A **coneflower 1** such as a **black-eyed Susan 2** (here: *Rudbeckia bicolor*) or **goldenglow.**

   1840 MA Zool. & Bot. Surv. *Herb. Plants & Quadrupeds* 140, *R[udbeckia] laciniata.* . . Often called Thimble Flower, from the length and size of the cone-part of the flower. . . This is a handsome plant, and is introduced into some yards and gardens. **1933** Small *Manual SE Flora* 1427, *R[udbeckia] bicolor.* . . *Thimble-flower.* . . Ala. to Tex., Ark., and Tenn. **1947** *Mexia Weekly Herald* (TX) 20 June [5]/2 (newspaperarchive.com), In this particular latitude the gold-petaled thimble flower is symbolic of June. Some call it black-eyed Susan, or cone flower. . . [T]he scientific name is Rudbeckia.

b =**self-heal.**

   1900 Lyons *Plant Names* 306, *P[runella] vulgaris.* . . Thimble-flower.

c A **prairie coneflower 1** (here: *Ratibida columnifera* or *R. peduncularis*).

   1936 Whitehouse *TX Flowers* 173, *Thimble Flower (Ratibida colum-naris* [=*R. columnifera*]) is also called . . long-headed or prairie cone-flower. . . The small tubular flowers are brown and are borne on a thim-ble-shaped or columnar disk which varies greatly in size on different flowers, sometimes being nearly two inches long. **1939** *Gettysburg Times* (PA) 13 July 13/1, One of the finest plants for hot, dry places is the obelish [*sic*] flower or thimble flower (Lepachys columnaris [= *Ratibida columnifera*]), a native of our west. . . [T]he yellow daisies centered with brown cones are showy in the garden from June until frost. **1942** Friend *Plants Rio Grande* (Internet), *Lepachys peduncularis* var. *pitca* [*sic;* =*Ratibida peduncularis* var *picta*]—Long Headed Cone-Flower, Thimble Flower. Plants of this species produce slender, greenish colored cones.

d A gilia (here: *Gilia capitata*).

   1955 *Pasadena Independent* (CA) 9 Oct Garden sec 15/2 sCA, Going to the taller natives we have fuzzy blue Thimble Flower (another Gilia). **1959** Carleton *Index Herb. Plants* 16, *Blue thimbleflower:* Gilia capitata.

e An anemone (here: *Anemone virginiana*). Cf **thimble anemone**

   1966 *DARE* (Qu. S26e, *Other wildflowers not yet mentioned;* not asked in early QRs) Inf **MI**31, Anemone—thimbleflower.

thimble mackerel See **thimble-eyed mackerel**

thimble, thimble, who's got the thimble See **thimble 1**

thimbleweed n

1 Any of var anemones, but usu *Anemone cylindrica* or *A. virginica.* [See quot 1912] Cf **thimble anemone, thim-bleflower e**

   1833 Eaton *Botany* 19, [*Anemone*] *virginiana,* (wind-flower, thimble weed . .). **1843** Torrey *Flora NY* 1.8, *Anemone Virginiana.* . . *Thimble-weed.* . . One of the numerous plants supposed to possess the power of curing the bite of the rattlesnake. **1891** *Jrl. Amer. Folkl.* 4.147 **MA,** Anemone Virginiana was Thimble Weed, as also probably some other species. **1893** *Ibid* 6.136 **WV,** Anemone Virginiana, thimble-weed. **1912** Mathews *Amer. Wild Flowers* 130, *Thimble-weed.* . . [T]he flower-head usually 1 inch or less across, is succeeded by the enlarged fruit-head similar in shape to, and about as large as, a good-sized thimble. **1951** Voss–Eifert *IL Wild Flowers* 120, *Thimbleweed—Anemone cylin-drica.* . . When the petals drop away at last, this seed-cone remains and grows larger. **1967** *DARE* FW Addit **AR**44, Thimbleweed or anemone—*Anemone virginiana.* **2002** *Chron.–Telegram* (Elyria OH) 29 Aug sec C 4/1, McGregor loves Thimbleweed (Anemone virginiana), which is grown not only for its anemone-like flower but also for its thimble-shaped (and sized) seed pod.

2 =**goldenglow.**   Cf **thimbleflower a**

    1848 Bartlett *Americanisms* 354, *Thimble Weed.* (Lat. *Rudbeckia.*) A tall plant six or eight feet high, resembling the sunflower. It is one of the herbs prepared by the Shakers, and is used in medicine for its diuretic and tonic properties. **1910** Graves *Flowering Plants* 393 **CT,** *Rudbeckia laciniata.* . . Tall Cone-flower. Thimble-weed. . . The plant is medicinal.

3 A **prairie clover,** usu *Dalea purpurea.*   [See quot 1922]

    1896 *Jrl. Amer. Folkl.* 9.186 **MO,** *Petalostemon violaceus* [=*Dalea purpurea*] . . thimble-weed. **1922** *Amer. Botanist* 28.72, The "prairie clovers" are found in the genus *Petalostemum.* . . After the petals have fallen, the close-set seed-pods give the plants the name of "thimbleweed".

4 A **vervain** (here: *Verbena stricta*).

    1897 *Jrl. Amer. Folkl.* 10.52 **MO,** *Verbena stricta* . . thimble-weed.

thin as a snake   See **snake** n 1a(1)

t'hind   See **tohind**

thing n   Usu |θɪŋ|; also *esp* **Sth, S Midl** |θæn, θɛŋ, θɪŋ| Pronc-spp *thang, theng, ting*   Cf **nothing, something A**

A   Forms.

    1777 in 1900 Clinton *Pub. Papers* 2.415, The ganerels would not a fout if had not Been for the Speech of peopele and Severl other thangs. **1803** Davis *Travels* 175 **DC** [Black], Where de *Tiber,* Mossa ask? Me . . never see such a ting. **1823** Cooper *Pioneers* 2.182 **cNY** [Black], Such a ting! such a ting! **1880** *Scribner's Mth.* 20.813 **LA** [Black], Don' spill all my wash'n t'ings! **1893** Shands *MS Speech* 10, All classes frequently give [ɪ] the sound of [ɛ] in such words as *sing* . . *thing* . . *sting.* **1922** Gonzales *Black Border* 333 **sSC, GA coasts** [Gullah glossary], *T'ing*—thing, things. **1927** Shewmake *Engl. Pronc.* VA 42, A rather widespread pronunciation of *thing* in Virginia is *theng.* **1931** *Folk-Say* 49 **sLA** [Black], Cotton rows ain' de only thangs what ends at dat ole river. **1934** *AmSp* 9.210 **Sth,** *Thing* . . [θæɪŋ]. **1942** Hall *Smoky Mt. Speech* 16 **wNC, eTN,** [i] may sometimes be heard in . . *thing.* . . In Emerts Cove . . *thing* . . [was] transcribed . . [θeɪŋ]. **1942** in 1944 *ADD* **WV,** *Thing.* . . [θeŋ]. **1943** *AmSp* 18.264 **VA,** The lowering of [ɪ] to [ɛ] is fairly common throughout the state in words like *since* . . *thing* . . *dish.* **c1960** Wilson *Coll.* **csKY,** *Thing* is often /ðæŋ/ or /ðɪŋ/ [sic]. **1966–67** *DARE* FW Addit **cwNC,** *Thing*—[θeŋ]. **1969** (1970) Angelou *Caged Bird* 161 **AR** [Black], Naturally, I believed in hants and ghosts and "thangs." **1971** *AmSp* 46.82 **Chicago IL,** *Thing* /θæŋ/. **1971** Roberts *Third Ear* np [Black], *Thang* . . a stylish way to pronounce 'thing' to indicate identification with Southern blacks. **1984** Burns *Cold Sassy* 5 **nGA** (as of 1906), Loma, they ain't a bloomin' thang you can do bout it. **1994** *Houston Post* (TX) 4 Sept sec F 4/1 **LA,** Dat's the thang of it. **1998** *DARE* File—Internet **cePA** [Language of the Hayna Valley], *Bot tings* [=bought things]. **2000** *DARE* File **seKY** (as of c1950), *Thang*— (Thing) "Brang me that Thang".

B   Sense.

Pl: Livestock; see quots.   [Engl dial]

    1899 (1912) Green *VA Folk-Speech* 444, *Things.* . . Cattle; sheep; live stock. "Its [sic] nearly night, and time to feed the things." **1928** Peterkin *Scarlet Sister Mary* 91 **SC,** He had gone off and left her with supper to cook, all the things to feed and the cow to milk.

thinga(ma)bob   See **thingum 2a**

thingamagig, thingamajig   See **thingum 2c**

thingamie, thingamy   See **thingum 2b**

thing(-em-a-)doodle   See **thingum 2d**

thing-em-a-dudgeon   See **thingum 2e**

thingemajig   See **thingum 2c**

thingembob, thinging-bob   See **thingum 2a**

thingm-a-dodger   See **thingum 2e**

thin grass n

Any of var **bentgrasses 1,** esp *Agrostis perennans.*

    1814 Bigelow *Florula Bostoniensis* 22, Trichodium laxiflorum [= *Agrostis scabra*], Thin grass. . . is readily known by its very thin, spreading, capillary panicle. **1843** Torrey *Flora NY* 2.442, *Agrostis laxi-*

flora. . . *Thin-grass.* . . Old fields and exsiccated swamps; very common. **1848** Gray *Manual of Botany* 577, *A[grostis] perennans.* (*Thin-grass.*) . . Damp shaded places. **1894** Coulter *Botany W. TX* 525, *A[grostis] perennans.* . . *Thin grass.* . . Rare in northern Texas, common northward. **1937** U.S. Forest Serv. *Range Plant Hdbk.* G8, Leafy redtop (*A[grostis] diegoensis* . .), often called thin grass, . . is a moderately tall, fine-leaved grass with a narrow panicle. **1952** Davis *Flora ID* 88, *A. diegoensis.* . . *Thingrass.* . . Mont. to B.C., south to Calif. and Nev.

thingum n

1 A thing (or person) whose name the speaker cannot recall, does not know, or is reluctant to speak.   [*OED2* 1680 →]

    1824 *Old Colony Mem.* (Plymouth MA) 6 Mar 180/1 **NEng,** I'll be souzed in a butter tub, if ever I seed such curiosity thingums in all my born days! **1850** Mitchell *Lorgnette* 176 **NYC,** I do wish that odious Miss Thingum wouldn't be so familiar in the street. **1873** Hartley *Gentlemen's Etiquette* 308, But there is likewise an awkwardness of the mind, that . . with care may be, avoided; as, for instance, to mistake names; to speak of Mr. What-d'ye-call-him, or Mrs. Thingum. **1931** *AmSp* 6.258, Indefinite names current in the Central West of the United States. . . thingum. **1933** *Van Wert Daily Bulletin* (OH) 1 Mar 4/2, But where do we find Mr. Thingum?

2 in var combs in the same sense as above, as:

a   *thingumbob;* also *thinga(ma)bob, thingembob, thingingbob, thingumabob, thingumybob.*   [*OED2* 1751 →]   Cf **jiggumbob**

    1843 (1916) Hall *New Purchase* 349 **IN,** "Romance!—what, a curtain of corduroy thinging-bobs?" Yes, corduroy breeches modestly hung as wall between ladies and gentlemen. **1844** *S. Lit. Messenger* 10.719, [Title:] The Literary Life of Thingum Bob, Esq. **1854** (1855) Stephens *Hagar* 335 **Sth,** We an't any on us perfect, unless its old mother thingumbob there. **1890** *DN* 1.66 **KY,** Thing-um-a-bob. . . "Give me that thing-um-a-bob." Used when the name of the thing cannot be at once recalled. [*DN* Ed: In New England . . thingembob.] **1897** *Atlantic Mth.* 80.716, You don't know anything about Thingabob. **1897** *KS Univ. Qrly.* (ser B) 6.58, *Thingumbob.* **1899** (1912) Green *VA Folk-Speech* 444, *Thingamy.* . . Thingumbob. . . An indefinite name for any person or thing which a speaker is at a loss, or too indifferent, to designate more precisely. **1905** *DN* 3.66 **eNE,** *Thingumbob, thingumabob, thingabob.* . . Indefinite expression applied to something, the name of which is not recalled. **1907** *DN* 3.203 **seNH,** *Thingumbob.* **1909** *DN* 3.380 **eAL, wGA,** *Thingumybob.* **1927** *AmSp* 2.366 **cwWV,** *Thingumbob* . . a mechanical contrivance which is not understood. "We saw a thingumbob at the fair which the man said could milk a cow." **1930** Shoemaker *1300 Words* 62 **cPA Mts** (as of c1900), *Thing-a-bob*—A person whose name one has forgotten. **1967–69** *DARE* (Qu. NN12b, *Things that people say to put off a child when he asks, "What are you making?"*) Infs **CT**22, **GA**89, **NY**83, 169, **OH**61, **PA**69, Thingumabob; **MI**46, Thingabob. **1982** Barrick *Coll.* **csPA,** *Thingamabob*—whatchamacallit, unidentified object.

b   *thingum(m)y;* also *thingamie, thi(n)gamy, thingummie.*   [*OED2* 1796 →]

    1823 Cooper *Pioneers* 2.188 **cNY,** This here thingum'y, . . that maybe looks sum'mat like a rat, is the beast. **1843** (1916) Hall *New Purchase* 210 **IN,** Dressed thus in the husband's boots as well as his thingamies . . our fair lady . . bade defiance to wet grass, running briars . . and all and every evil incident to cow-hunting! **1890** *DN* 1.66, *Thing-um-a-bob.* . . In New England . . thingamy . . also thigamy . . in Massachusetts. **1899** (1912) Green *VA Folk-Speech* 444, *Thingamy.* . . Thingummy. An indefinite name for any person or thing which a speaker is at a loss, or too indifferent, to designate more precisely. **1931** *AmSp* 6.259, Indefinite names current in the Central West of the United States. . . thingummie. **1956** *AmSp* 31.193 [USMC slang], *Gizmo.* . . Any gadget; also *thingummy, whoziz.* Often applied to a person whose name is unknown or difficult to pronounce. **1974** Tyler *Celestial Navigation* 239 **MD,** That explains all those weird thingummies you're sticking in.

c   *thingumajig;* also *thingamagig, thingamajig, thingemajig, thingumajiggen, thingumajigger, thingumajiggus, thingumajing(ie), thingumajjie, thingumyjig.*   [*OED2* 1824 →]   Cf **majig**

    1824 *Old Colony Mem.* (Plymouth MA) 6 Mar 180/1 **NEng,** I'd a lot of cousins, that "com'd all the way down from Varmount to . . see all the cute and curious thingumajigs of the Old Colony." **1890** *DN* 1.66 **NEng,** *Thing-um-a-bob.* [*DN* Ed: In New England . . thingemajig.] **1899** (1912) Green *VA Folk-Speech* 444, *Thingamy.* . . Thingumajig. . . An indefinite name for any person or thing which a speaker is at a loss, or too indifferent, to designate more precisely. **1905** *DN* 3.66 **cNE,** Thingumbob, . . thingumajing, thingumajig, thingumajigger. **1909** *DN* 3.380 **eAL, wGA,** *Thingumybob, . . thingumyjig.* **1912** *DN* 3.592 **wIN,** *Thing-a-ma-jig.* **1931** *AmSp* 6.258, Indefinite names current in the Central West of the United States. . . thingumajjie, thingumajiggen, thingumajiggus, thingumajingie. **1942** Warnick *Garrett Co. MD* 15 (as of 1900–18), Think-a-ma-gig. **1952** Brown *NC Folkl.* 1.600, *Thing-um-a-jig.* . . General term for some object whose name the speaker does not know or cannot recall; or a name for an object regarded jocularly or with ridicule. **1956** Almirall *From College* 129 **CO,** Both of us had on . . the usual open vests, which held matches, tobacco, and maybe some other small thingamajigs. **1965–70** *DARE* (Qu. NN12b, *Things that people say to put off a child when he asks, "What are you making?"*) 147 Infs, **widespread,** Thingumajig; **PA**27, 138, Thingumajig for (a) what-you-may-call-it; **LA**17, Thingumajigger; (Qu. F6, *The kitchen utensil with holes punched through the sides and bottom, to drain off liquid from foods*) Inf **GA**32, Thingumajig; (Qu. EE34, . . *A child's toy*) Infs **LA**34, **MA**2, Thingumajig; (Qu. NN12a, *Things that people say to put a child off when he asks too many questions: "What's that for?"*) Inf **GA**72, That's a thingumajig. **1986** Pederson *LAGS Concordance,* 1 inf, **neTX,** Those iron thingamajigs—he can't recall term.

d *thingumadoodle;* also *thing-em-a-doodle, thing(um)doodle.*

1890 *DN* 1.66 **KY,** *Thing-doodle.* . . "What do you call that thing-doo-dle?" **1893** Shands *MS Speech* 63, *Thing-em-a-doodle.* . . Used by all classes for the name of anything that cannot be readily recalled. **1897** *KS Univ. Qrly.* (ser B) 6.58, *Thingumdoodle.* **1906** *DN* 3.161 **nwAR,** *Thingumadoodle.* **1931** *AmSp* 6.258, Indefinite names current in the Central West of the United States. . . thingumadoodle. **1941** in **1944** *ADD,* What do all those gold thingumadoodles on your arm mean? Radio.

e *thingumydoochy;* also *thing-em-a-dudgeon, thingm-a-dodger, thingumadoogy.*

1890 *DN* 1.66 **KY,** *Thing-em-a-dudgeon.* . . "Where is that thing-em-a-dudgeon?" **1905** *DN* 3.97 **nwAR,** *Thingm-a-dodger.* . . Applied to an object when the speaker does not know or has forgot its name. 'Give me that thingm-a-dodger.' Common. **1909** *DN* 3.380 **eAL, wGA,** *Thingumybob, thingumydoochy.* **1986** Pederson *LAGS Concordance,* 1 inf, **csTN,** Thingumadoogy—a what-you-may-call-it.

f Addit varr; see quots.

1897 *KS Univ. Qrly.* (ser B) 6.58, *Thingamagummer.* **1931** *AmSp* 6.258, Indefinite names current in the Central West of the United States. . . thingumading. *Ibid* 259, Thingumaree, thinkumthankum. **1968** *DARE* (Qu. NN12b, *Things that people say to put off a child when he asks, "What are you making?"*) Inf **NY**69, Thingumawhatsis.

thingumabob   See **thingum 2a**

thingumadoodle   See **thingum 2d**

thingumadoogy   See **thingum 2e**

thingumajig(gen), thingumajigger, thingumajiggus, thing-umajing(ie), thingumajjie   See **thingum 2c**

thingumaree   See **thingum 2f**

thingumbob   See **thingum 2a**

thingumdoodle   See **thingum 2d**

thingummie, thingum(m)y   See **thingum 2b**

thingumybob   See **thingum 2a**

thingumydoochy   See **thingum 2e**

thingumyjig   See **thingum 2c**

think v   Usu |θɪŋk|; also **esp Sth, S Midl** |θe(ɪ)ŋk, θæŋk|; occas |tɪŋk| Pronc-spp *thaink, thank, thenk, tink*   Cf Pronc Intro 3.I.6.d

A   Pronc varr.

1823 Cooper *Pioneers* 2.182 **cNY** [Black], I nebber tink a could 'appen! nebber tink he die! **1858** Hammett *Piney Woods Tavern* 27 [Black], "Ki! ole Mossa," answered the boy—"tink Ned's a fool, and neva see you afore?" **1893** Shands *MS Speech* 15, *Th* . . initial frequently, but not always, has the sound of *t* in the negro dialect; as [tɪŋk] for *think.* **1905** *DN* 3.56 **eNE,** The change of *i* to *e*, is seen in . . *thenk.* **1922** Gonzales *Black Border* 333 **sSC, GA coasts** [Gullah glossary], *T'ink*—think. **1934** *AmSp* 9.210 **Sth,** A few words having standard [ɪ] before [ŋ] change [ɪ] to [e] or [eɪ]. The diphthong is perhaps heard more often than the simple vowel. The number of words is small, but the

sound is rather general and decidedly noticeable. *Bring* . . *spring* . . *think.* **1936** *AmSp* 11.13 **eTX,** [ɪ] before *nk* . . is usually pronounced [ẽ] [eɪ̃]. . . think. **1943** *AmSp* 18.264 **VA,** The lowering of [ɪ] to [ɛ] is fairly common . . in words like . . *think.* **1954** Harder Coll. **cwTN,** Got another thank a-comin': . . Mistaken. **c1960** Wilson Coll. **csKY,** Think is often /θeŋk/ or /θæŋk/. **1961** *Mt. Life* Spring 8 **sAppalachians,** The mountaineer's tendency to . . [have] such pronunciations as . . *thānk* for think. **1967** *DARE* FW Addit **seAR,** Think [θæɪŋk]. **1997** *DARE* File—Internet **cePA** [CoalSpeak], *Tink:* Think. "I tink I spelt dat right." **2000** *DARE* File **nwMI,** [Pamphlet from restaurant in the Upper Peninsula:] *Tinking:* Yooper mental process.

B   Gram forms.

1   pres exc 3rd pers sg: usu *think;* also *thinks,* often in inverted phr *thinks I.* Cf **say B1a**

1781 *PA Jrl. & Weekly Advt.* (Philadelphia) 16 May 1/3, I thinks it will not be long before he come. This is a London vulgarism, and yet one of the grossest kind. **1843** (1916) Hall *New Purchase* 55 **IN,** I allow the stranger and his woman-body thinks themselves mighty big-bugs. *Ibid* 149, And with that idea, thinks I, may be she's out now! **1858** *Harper's New Mth. Mag.* 16.729 **eTN,** Them fellers often talks 'bout you; but they thinks you've deserted 'em. **1879** *Ibid* 59.81 **NEng,** I'm a kind ov a flosofer myself, folks thinks raound here. **1897** Riley *Rubaiyat Doc Sifers* 76 **IN,** Doc's jes a *leetle* too inclined, *some* thinks, to overlook / The criminal and vicious kind we'd ort to bring to book. **1914** Denison *Beside the Bowery* 55 **NYC,** An' I thinks to meself, 'There's somethin' queer about this business,' . . And thinks I, 'There's a woman at the bottom of this.' **1917** in **1944** *ADD* **sWV,** *Thinks.* . . Thinks I. **1926** Eppes *Through Some Yrs.* 115 **FL** [Black], I done tole her what I thinks er her an' her doings. **1953** Atwood *Survey of Verb Forms* 29, *People think.* . . In N. Eng. the plural form *think* . . is almost universal . . in the southern and western areas, including all of Vt. Northeast of the Merrimack, however, as well as on Nantucket and Martha's Vineyard, the singular *thinks* . . is used by nearly all the noncultured informants. In s.e. N.H. and n.e. Mass. there is a small transition area where the two forms are about equally common. . . In the M[iddle] A[tlantic] S[tates] and the S[outh] A[tlantic] S[tates] the singular *thinks* is the universal popular form. . . In the M[iddle] A[tlantic] S[tates] this form has some currency in cultured speech . . ; in the S[outh] A[tlantic] S[tates], as in N. Eng., it is rare in this type of speech. **1967–69** *DARE* Tape **AR**47, A lot of other people thinks the same way; **TN**30, Some thinks that maybe we still have a split. **1986** Pederson *LAGS Concordance,* 7 infs, **AL, GA, MS,** People (who) thinks; 4 infs, **AL, GA, LA, MS,** Lot(s) of people thinks; 2 infs, **AL, GA,** There are (a lot of) people who thinks; 2 infs, **GA, MS,** People thinks he done (did) it; 1 inf, **neTN,** Many people thinks so; 1 inf, **cAL,** There are many people who thinks so; 1 inf, **cnGA,** Lots of people thinks they're frogs; 1 inf, **neTN,** There is a lots [sic] of people thinks; 1 inf, **neGA,** There are people who thinks; 1 inf, **neTN,** Some people thinks it is; 1 inf, **nwFL,** People thinks I'm crazy; 1 inf, **csTN,** Lots of people thinks he will be elected; 1 inf, **ceGA,** Some people thinks he should be; 1 inf, **ceGA,** Some people thinks he did; 2 infs, **MS,** I thinks.

2   past, past pple: usu *thought;* also:

a *thunk.* **chiefly Sth, S Midl**   Note: The catchphrase *Who'd have thunk it?* and varr as well as intentional joc uses of *thunk* have not been recorded.

1845 *Amer. Whig Rev.* 2.611 **TX,** Don't ye know Bill Johnson thunk o' all that? **1881** *Scribner's Mth.* 22.244 **GA** [Black], W'en de hoss feel Brer Fox hangin' dar onter his tail, he thunk sump'n cu'us wuz de marter. **1893** Shands *MS Speech* 63, *Thunk.* . . Negro for *thought.* This past is formed upon analogy with such words as *sink, slink,* etc. **1945** Saxon *Gumbo Ya-Ya* 230 **LA** [Black], Sometimes I thunk I wanted to be free. **1958** Latham *Meskin Hound* 84 **cTX,** "Well, fan my britches!" he exclaimed. "I've thunk up a dilly!" **1976** Garber *Mountain-ese* 94 **sAppalachians,** I thunk about it fer a long time and finally made up my mind. **1986** Pederson *LAGS Concordance,* 1 inf, **neMS,** I thunk like I told you [inf Black]. **1991** Still *Wolfpen Notebooks* 51 **sAppalachians,** I'd had it in his head many a thought his way of think. **1997** in 2004 Montgomery–Hall *Dict. Smoky Mt. Engl.* 603 **wNC, eTN,** Think . . variant past-tense form *thunk* (usu jocular) [5 infs]. **1999** *Ibid* **eTN,** Think. . . I thunk me a thought.

b *thoughted.* Cf **-ed 1**

1910 *Stevens Point Jrl.* (WI) [6 Aug 8]/6 (newspaperarchive.com) [Black], I thoughted every minute dat my time wuz comin' next. **1919** *Woodland Daily Democrat* (CA) 25 July 7/3, *Looking Forward.* You may shake, you may flatter the slops as you will, but the scent of our noses will cling to the still. *Not What We Thoughted.* **1952** Brown *NC*

Folkl. 1.600, *Thoughted.* . . Past tense and past participle of *think.* "I thoughted he'd come back."

C Senses.

1 To remind. **Sth, S Midl**

1913 Kephart *Highlanders* 297 **sAppalachians,** You think me of it in the mornin'. **1930** *VA Qrly. Rev.* 6.246 **S Midl,** There are idioms . . quaint and variable: . . think me of it. **1946** *PADS* 6.30 **eNC** (as of 1900–10), *Think.* . . To remind. "Think me to go by the post office tomorrow." . . Common. **1952** Brown *NC Folkl.* 1.600, *Think* . . to remind one. "Jim, think me to go by your grandma's and get that pig." **1957** Combs *Lang. S. Highlanders* **sAppalachians,** Think—remind. "Think me on (of) it tomor'." **1960** *DE Folkl. Bulletin* 1.36, Think (remind—as in "I'll think you of it"). **1966–68** *DARE* (Qu. JJ28, *If you are afraid you may forget something, you might tell another person, "Before I leave tonight, be sure and _____ [me to do it]."*) Inf **NC**1, Think me of it; **DE**7, Think me of that. **1975** *Appalachian Jrl.* 2.153 **wNC,** "Think me of it" means "Remind me of it." **1997** in 2004 Montgomery–Hall *Dict. Smoky Mt. Engl.* 603 **wNC, eTN,** *Think.* . . To remind [2 infs].

2 in phrr *(I) thinks, says I* and varr, foll by direct statement: I thought to myself. Cf **say v B1b**

1839 *Freeman & Messenger* (Lodi NY) 5 Dec 1/1 **CT,** [Reprinted from *New York Express:*] I had a notion to write for it from the first, because, thinks, sez I, that prime feller Major Jack Downing, writes a good deal for it. **1862** *S. Lit. Messenger* 34.472 **NC,** I stepped round and went into the Baggage Kar, and found sevrul civiluns in thar. 'Thinks,' says I, 'mebby thar's a chance fur old Si yit.' **1866** Smith *Bill Arp* 119 **GA,** Thinks, says I to myself, this is a big thing certain, and I will invest my bottom dollar in this kind of money. **1878** *Harper's New Mth. Mag.* 56.615 **CT,** I held my tongue, for Lowisy's sake. But thinks, sez I, now's your time, Roxanny Keep; pitch in an' do your dooty. **1889** *Century Illustr. Mag.* 38.613 **GA,** That's what old Major Jimmy Bass said he heard, an' I thinks, says I, he 'll have to be monst'us peart ef he gits ahead of Squire Underwood. **1910** *DN* 3.450 **wNY,** Think says I. . . I said to myself. **1917** *DN* 4.402 **neOH,** Thinks 'z I ['θɪŋksəz,aɪ]. . . I thought to myself. Is this a blend between *thinks I* and *says I?* Also N. Eng., Ky.

think box n Also *think piece,* ~ *tank* **chiefly West** *joc* Cf **knowledge box, thinker**

The brain, mind.

1888 *Fitchburg Daily Sentinel* (MA) 8 Dec suppl 1/6, [Bill Nye column:] How does a thought first come to you? . . [I]s it born with a full set of teeth and side whiskers, as it comes to the think tank of Lord Tennyson? **1892** *Eve. News* (Lincoln NE) 30 Mar 2/2, This happy thought flew from a nook in the seething think box of Cy Warmon, poet of the Rockies. **1897** *KS Univ. Qrly.* (ser B) 6.93, Think tank: the intellect.—General. **1910** Raine *Bucky O'Connor* 277 **West,** It hadn't penetrated my think-tank that this was your hacienda. **1913** London *Valley of Moon* 58 **CA,** You want to get them ideas out of your think-box. **1914** *DN* 4.114 **cKS,** Think tank. . . he had a think-piece behind that withered skin. **1949** Guthrie *Way West* 290, A knobby skeleton of a man, . . he had a think-piece behind that withered skin. **1956** *Tri-City Herald* (Pasco WA) 18 Dec 1/1, Start that idea in your little old "think box" now. Let it soak in good and deep. **1971** Roberts *Third Ear* np [Black], *Think piece* . . brain; mind. . . What does she use for a think piece?

thinker n

=**think box.**

1886 *Denton Jrl.* (MD) 29 May 1/6, When he is awake he must think. If his thinker would only keep quiet, he could be comparatively happy. **1936** *Sun* (Baltimore MD) 3 Feb 16/8, There was a slight stir . . when the general said that Philadelphia judges . . "sat on their thinkers when they sat down." **1942** Berrey–Van den Bark *Amer. Slang* 121.15, *Brain.* . . *thinker.* . . *extended to mean the . . intellect.* Ibid 56, *Head.* . . thinker. **1944** Adams *Western Words* 77, His thinker is puny—Said of a weak-minded person. **1949** Chandler *Little Sister* 109 **CA,** What's on the thinker, pal? **1967** *DARE* Tape **TX**38, I can't think. . . My thinker is rusted. **1968** *DARE* (Qu. X28, *Joking words . . for a person's head*) Inf **KS**7, Thinker. **1986** Pederson *LAGS Concordance,* 1 inf, **cnAL,** My thinker's asleep = I can't remember.

think long See **long adv¹ D1**

think one hung the moon See **hang the moon**

think piece See **think box**

thinks (I) See **think B1**

think tank See **think box**

thinkumthankum See **thingum 2f**

thins, the n pl Cf *thin dirties* (at **dirties**)

1947 McDavid Coll. **ceSC,** The thins—dysentery.

third and fourth n Also *thirds and fourths;* for addit varr see quots **chiefly Sth** Cf **halves 1, share-tenant, third cropper**

A payment of one-third of the grain crop and one-fourth of the cotton crop traditionally paid as rent by a tenant farmer who provides his own equipment; a contract made on this basis; hence combs *third-and-fourth cropper,* ~ *farmer,* ~ *system.*

1912 Hickey *Land?* 16 **TX,** These renters of Texas, for two generations, have been accustomed to pay the landlord the traditional third and fourth, which means that of every three bushels of corn and grain they produce, the landlord takes one, of every four bales of cotton . . , the landlord takes one. To the intense disgust of the renter this third and fourth system is passing away. The landlords have commenced to demand a third all round. **1912** in 2005 (acc) Lexis–Nexis Legal Research *State Case Law: GA* (Internet), According to the plaintiff's own testimony, she paid "rent every year, . . one third and a fourth." **1913** *Ibid: AL,* M.V. Smith, the landlord, stated . . that he had rented Guff Smith land upon the third and fourth and was not going to advance him any supplies to make a crop. **1926** *Ibid: TX,* The land was cultivated by tenants, who paid as rent one-third of the grain and one-fourth of the cotton when the tenant furnished the teams and tools. . . "I cultivated it by tenants in 1921. Some of them worked on third and fourth, and some of them were half hands. . . My contract with third and fourth croppers was that they were to leave the fourth dollar in the bank. . . They always sold their own cotton." **1940** Faulkner *Hamlet* 10 **MS,** "I heard you got a farm for rent. . . What do you rent for?" "Third and fourth." **1941** Writers' Program *Guide AR* 204, Throughout the route small farms are the rule, owner-operated or rented on "thirds and fourths." **1944** *Cullman Banner* (AL) 26 Oct [4]/3 (newspaperarchive.com), *Farm for rent*—35–40 acres on halves or thirds and fourths. **1965–69** *DARE* (Qu. L3, *A man who lives on the farm and does the work, but divides the expenses and profits with the owner*) Inf **GA**84, Third-and-fourth farmer—got a third of cotton and [a] fourth of corn; **MS**58, Third-and-fourth cropper—gets three-fourths of cotton and two-thirds of corn; this man furnishes his equipment. **1976** Brown *Gloss. Faulkner* 198 **MS,** *Third and fourth.* . . One who pays at this rate is a "share tenant" rather than a sharecropper. He supplies his own equipment. . . Then he pays one third of the seed and fertilizer for his corn crop, and pays one third of the crop as rent. He pays one fourth of the seed and fertilizer for cotton, and pays one fourth of his crop as rent. **1986** Pederson *LAGS Concordance,* 1 inf, **cwLA,** A third and fourth—tenant pays in sharecropping.

‡**third base** n

1973 *Thompson Coll.* **cAL** (as of 1920s), Cow pile, cow flop, third base = names for adornments left on landscapes by cattle. 'You cayn't hardly go down that way no more thout steppin own third base own accounta how the cows like to hang out there.'

third cropper n Also *third hand,* ~ *man* Cf **fourth hand, third and fourth**

See quot 1968–70.

[**1946** Stuart *Tales Plum Grove* 58 **eKY,** Pa rented it for the third.] **1968–70** *DARE* (Qu. L3, *A man who lives on the farm and does the work, but divides the expenses and profits with the owner*) Inf **NC**49, Third cropper, third man—doesn't have his own tools so gets only a third of profit; **TN**53, Third hand.

Third day See **first day 1**

thirded bread n Cf **rye and Indian (bread)** **NEng**

A bread made with equal amounts of wheat flour, rye flour, and cornmeal.

[**1830** Child *Frugal Housewife* 82 **NEng,** Some think the nicest of all bread is one third Indian, one third rye, and one third flour, made according to the directions for flour bread.] **1853** (1973) Chadwick *Home Cookery* 3 **MA,** *Thirded Bread.* Take two quarts of boiling water and scald your Indian meal. . . One pint bowl of Indian, one of rye, and one of flour. If this quantity makes it too stiff, add more lukewarm water, until the consistence of flour and Indian bread. **1883** (1884) Lincoln *Mrs. Lincoln's Boston Cook Book* 67, *Thirded Bread.* 1 cup white flour . . 1 cup rye flour . . 1 cup yellow corn meal. **1904** *News* (Frederick MD) 2 July 4/1, *Thirded Bread.* A request is made for a recipe for thirded bread. Take one cup of white flour, one cup of rye flour, one cup of yellow cornmeal. **1947** Bowles–Towle *New Engl. Cooking* 69, *Thirded Bread*—4 cups white flour, 4 cups yellow corn meal, 4 cups rye flour [etc].

third hand (or man)   See **third cropper**

third month   See **first month**

third-party bug n

=**harlequin cabbage bug.**

1901 Howard *Insect Book* 313, The harlequin cabbage bug . . is a well-known species in cabbage fields south of New Jersey. It is a serious enemy to cruciferous vegetables. In parts of Georgia it is still known as the "Abe Lincoln bug," and in Texas as the "third-party bug."

third-party fly n   Cf **Texas fly**

Prob = **horn fly.**

1967 *DARE* (Qu. R12, . . *Other kinds of flies*) Inf **TX**1, Third-party fly—gets on cows in patches; **TX**36, Third-party fly—came to this country when the third political party (Bull Moose) was formed.

third rail n   Also *third-rail beer,* ~ *liquor,* ~ *whiskey* [From the extra rail that conducts electricity in an electric railway system]

Cheap, potent liquor or, rarely, wine.

1909 *Lima Times–Democrat* (OH) 4 Feb 7/3, Just plain "third rail" whiskey was the comment of a "paralyzed" fellow picked up near the depot. **1913** *Ft. Wayne News* (IN) 17 Mar 6/2, Those who did not care for beer could get plenty of 'third rail' whiskey, the kind that would eat the signs off an iron post. **1915** *Dothan Eagle* (AL) 20 Sept 2/4 **NYC,** The poor man's "third rail" whiskey and beer. **1921** (1973) Campbell *Southern Highlander* 109 **NC,** This recipe is for fourteen and one-half gallons of the 'third rail' liquor. **1926** *AmSp* 1.653 [Hobo lingo], *Third-rail*—strong wine. **1929** *AmSp* 4.385 **KS** [Wet words], Such terms as *rookus juice, third-rail,* . . *pop-skull,* and *bust-head* are evidently references to the potency or the effect of the liquor designated. **1967** *DARE* (Qu. DD21b, *General words . . for bad liquor*) Infs **IL**11, **NY**1, Third rail.

thirds and fourths   See **third and fourth**

third-shift mosquito n

Appar a **firefly 1.**

1969 *DARE* (Qu. R1, . . *The small insect that flies at night and flashes a light at its tail*) Inf **GA**77, Third-shift mosquiter [laughter].

thirty n, adj, pron   Usu |ˈθɜ(r)ti|; also *esp among Black speakers* |ˈtɜti|; **esp NYC** |ˈθɜɪti| Pronc-spp *t(h)oity, thortey, thutty, tirty, turdy*   Similarly n, adj, pron *t(h)oid*   Cf "Pronc Intro" 3.II.12, **girl** n **A**

Std senses, var forms.

1806 in 1956 Eliason *Tarheel Talk* 319 **nw,cnNC,** Thirty—thortey. **1884** *Century Illustr. Mag.* 27.541 **LA,** I muz baw fawty dollah. . . aw thutty-five. **1894** *Brooklyn Daily Eagle* (NY) 25 Feb 18/7, All he wus ketchin' was thoity cents a day an' his board. **1895** *Ibid* 22/2, When the sound of r should be distinctly heard it is frequently omitted in such words as world, first, third, pronounced woild, foist and thoid. This peculiarity is, however, more characteristic of New Yorkers than of Brooklynites. **1900** Day *Up in ME* 3, He'd tackle that cellar door,/ As he had for thutty years or more. **1902** *Grand Rapids Tribune* (WI Rapids WI) [8 Oct 8]/2 (newspaperarchive.com) **sePA,** Messenger— Hello, Thoity-nine, where's yer uniform? **1922** Gonzales *Black Border* 333 **sSC, GA coasts** [Gullah glossary], T'irty—thirty. **1926** Ryan *Down on 33rd & 3rd* (Musical Score) **NYC,** Thoity-thoid And Thoid. **1933** in 2009 (acc) *Ling. Atlas Projects [AFAM]* (Internet) **SC, GA** [Black], [11 of 69 Infs offered proncs of the type [ˈtɜti] for *thirty.*] **1941** Faulkner *Men Working* 106 **MS,** A man . . could git his thutty days cut down some. **1946** in 1999 Popik Coll. **NYC,** [Song title:] *Moitle From Toity Toid and Toid.* **1961** Kurath–McDavid *Pronc. Engl.* 107, *The Vowel in thirty. . .* /ɜti . . /—This mid-central vowel has striking regional variants. (1) It may be fully constricted . . or it may be only slightly constricted or entirely unconstricted. (2) Both constricted and unconstricted /ɜ/ may be monophthongal or diphthongal. (3) Both types may be pronounced without or with rounding of the lips. . . Unconstricted [ɜ ~ ɞ ~ ɜᶥ ~ ɞᶥ] are confined to . . Eastern New England, Metropolitan New York, Eastern Virginia, and South Carolina–Georgia. *Ibid* 108, Metropolitan New York has unconstricted diphthongal [ɞɪ] [in *thirty*], in cultivated speech also monophthongal or ingliding [ɜ, ɜᵊ]; but slight constriction also occurs. **1998** *DARE* File—Internet **cePA** [Lan-

guage of the Hayna Valley], *Turdy-ate*—WOLF-TV, Channel 38. **2005** *DARE* File **Brooklyn NYC,** Growing up in Brooklyn in the '50s one would hear *thoity* and *thoid.* Those pronunciations were recognized as lower-class and uneducated even by those who *were* lower-class and uneducated.

this pron, adj   Pronc-spp, *esp freq among Black speakers, di(s)s, dish*   Cf Pronc Intro 3.I.17

Std senses, var forms.

1738 in 1974 Franklin *Sayings Poor Richard* 97 **PA,** *Mercury* will have his share in these affairs, and so confound the speech of the people, that when. . . a New Yorker thinks to say *this* he shall say *diss.* **1888** Jones *Negro Myths* 3 **GA coast,** Me know who mek all dis trouble fur me. **1899** Chesnutt *Conjure Woman* 44 **csNC** [Black], Ti'ed er dish yer gwine roun'. [=Tired of this here going around.] **1922** Gonzales *Black Border* 297 **sSC, GA coasts** [Gullah glossary], *Dishyuh*—this, this here. **1930** Woofter *Black Yeomanry* 50 **seSC,** *Dis* for *this.* **a1930** in 1991 Hughes–Hurston *Mule Bone* 29 **cFL** [Black], Ah . . laid down *two hun'ded dollahs wid dis right hand.* **1997** *DARE* File—Internet **cePA** [CoalSpeak], *Dis, dat, dese, dem, dose:* this, that, these, them, those.

this adv   See **just 6**

thisaway adv   Also *this er way, this he(r) way* [*OED2* 1832 →] **scattered, but more freq Atl, Sth, S Midl, TX** See Map *esp freq among rural speakers and those with little formal educ*   Cf **a** inert vowel, **thataway** adv

(In) this direction, way, or manner.

1840 *S. Lit. Messenger* 6.507 **GA,** He seems to be constant *a-usin* about this *away,* and I suspicion he's *arter* you. **1843** (1916) Hall *New Purchase* 161 **IN,** Hold your left hand here . . lettin the loose hand run up agin tother this away. **1893** Shands *MS Speech* 63, This er way and That er way [ðɪs ə weɪ] *and* [ðæt ə weɪ]. . . are, of course, shortened forms of *this here way* and *that there way.* **1895** *DN* 1.374 **seKY, eTN, wNC,** This he(r)-way . . for *this way.* **1899** (1912) Green *VA Folk-Speech* 444, This-away. **1903** *DN* 2.333 **seMO,** Was he coming this-a-way when you seed him? **1905** *DN* 3.98 **nwAR,** 'Do it this-a-way.' Common. **1909** *DN* 3.381 **eAL, wGA,** This-a-way. **1923** *DN* 5.223 **swMO,** This-away. **1932** Toone *Yankee Slang* 36, Thisaway. **1944** *PADS* 2.30 **wNC,** This a-way and that a-way. . . In all directions. . . Also, reported from Va., elsewhere in N.C., upper S.C. **1950** *PADS* 14.67 **SC,** Thisaway. . . "He went thisaway." "Do it thisaway." **1965–70** *DARE* (Qu. KK66, *When you are showing somebody the right way to do something: "No, not like that—do it _____."*) 55 Infs, **scattered, but more freq Atl, Sth, S Midl, TX,** Thisaway [45 of 55 Infs comm type 4 or 5, 22 Infs gs educ or less]; (Qu. MM16, *If you're walking with somebody to the other corner of a square, and you want to save steps . . "It'll be shorter if we _____."*) Inf **LA**8, Go thisaway [Inf comm type 5]. **1966** *DARE* Tape **AR**41, You pull them back and forth thisaway and card it. **1978** Michener *Chesapeake* 728 **MD,** He hadn't oughta behave thisaway. **1989** Pederson *LAGS Tech. Index* 177 **Gulf Region** (*This way*) 237 infs, Thisaway.

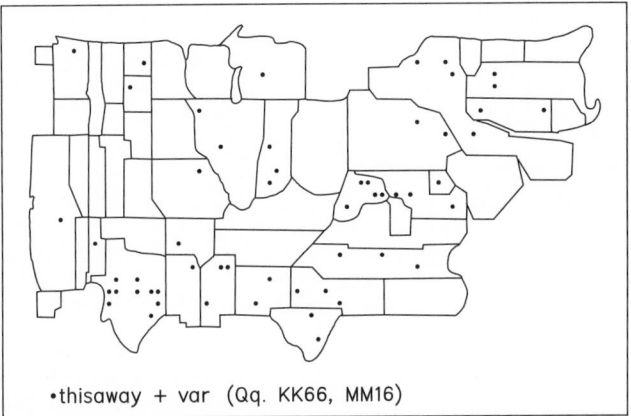

•thisaway + var (Qq. KK66, MM16)

this child   See **child B1**

this er way   See **thisaway**

this here   See **here C**

this he(r) way   See **thisaway**

thist   See **just 6**

thistelow See **fistula**

thistle n

Std: any of numerous prickly plants, as:

a Any of var composites of the family Asteraceae, esp of the genera *Carduus* and *Cirsium*. [*OED2* c725 →] For other names of var of these see **bitter thistle, bull ~, burr ~, button ~ 1, Canada ~, chicken lettuce, Chinese thistle, cotton ~, elk ~, horse ~, Indian ~ 2, milk ~ 1, pasture ~, sow ~, Spanish ~ 1, star ~, swamp ~, Texas ~ 1**

b usu with modifier: Any of var plants of families other than Asteraceae. [*OED2* 1398 →] For var of these see **bee thistle, blue ~, button ~ 2, coyote ~, devil's ~, English ~, false ~, flowering ~, hedgehog ~, Indian ~ 1, Kansas ~, Mexican ~, milk ~ 2, purple ~, Russian ~, Texas ~ 2, yellow ~**

thistle bird n

1 A **goldfinch 1** (here: *Carduelis tristis*).

1808 Wilson *Amer. Ornith.* 1.21, [Goldfinches] pass by various names expressive of their food, color, &c. such as Thistle-bird, Lettuce-bird [etc]. **1858** U.S. War Dept. *Rept. Explor. Railroad* 9.421, *Chrysomitris tristis.* . . *Yellow Bird; Thistle Bird.* . . North America generally. **1914** Eaton *Birds NY* 2.278, The nest is. . . lined with thistledown, a fact almost universal in this species, which has given it [=*Carduelis tristis*] the name of "Thistle bird" in many portions of the State. **1926** *DN* 5.404 **Ozarks,** *Thistle-bird.* . . The goldfinch, a small yellow bird which feeds upon the seeds of thistles. **1939** Harris *Purslane* 90 **cNC,** She heard the familiar "Per-chic-o-ree, per-chic-o-ree" and recognized a thistle bird. **1950** *WELS (Goldfinch)* 3 Infs, **WI,** Thistle bird. **1966–70** *DARE* (Qu. Q14, . . *Names . . for these birds . . goldfinch*) Infs **MN**18, **NH**5, **VA**43, Thistle bird.

2 =**yellow warbler.**

1925 Bailey *Birds FL* 124, *Yellow Warbler.* . . *Dendroica aestiva aestiva* (Wild canary, Yellow bird, Thistle bird)—A few Yellow Warblers breed in our northern area, but . . go farther north and west to spend their summers.

thistle-digger n Cf **scissorbill 2a**

See quots.

1880 Swisshelm *Half Cent.* 37 **wPA,** I should have all the work and privation for which I had bargained—should be a thistle-digger in the vineyard . . , but in no trial could I ever be alone. **1916** *DN* 4.330 **KS,** *Thistle-diggers* . . =*scissors-bills.* [*Ibid* 328, *Scissors.* . . Applied to persons in disparagement. Also *scissors-bills.*]

thistle poppy n Cf **flowering thistle, milk ~ 2**

A **prickly poppy,** usu *Argemone hispida* or *A. polyanthemos.*

1896 *Jrl. Amer. Folkl.* 9.181 **CA,** *Argemone hispida,* . . thistle-poppy. **1908** Hornaday *Camp-Fires* 32 **AZ,** We also noted . . three white thistle-poppies (*Argemone platyceras* [=*A. polyanthemos*]). **1947** Carr *Desert Parade* 76 **Desert SW,** *Thistle poppy:* The large, somewhat fragrant, cup-shaped white flowers of this truly prickly plant are often seen beside desert roads in spring and early summer. . . The plant appears superficially like a tall thistle with erect stems. **1968–69** *DARE* (Qu. S26a, . . *Wildflowers.* . . *Roadside flowers*) Inf **AZ**15, Thistle poppy; **CA**60, Prickly poppy . . also called thistle poppy. **1997** in 2001 *DARE* File—Internet **Desert SW,** Prickly Poppies are also called Thistle Poppy [etc].

thistle sage n

A **sage 1** (here: *Salvia carduacea*) native to California.

1897 Parsons *Wild Flowers CA* 307, *Salvia carduacea.* . . Upon the dry, open plains of the south, the charming flowers of the thistle-sage make their appearance by May. **1898** *Jrl. Amer. Folkl.* 11.277 **CA,** *Salvia carduacea,* . . thistle sage. **1947** *S. Sierran* May 4, On the desert we noted . . the exquisite beauty of the thistle sage. **1968** *DARE* (Qu. S26e, *Other wildflowers not yet mentioned;* not asked in early QRs) Inf **CA**60, Thistle sage—a beautiful orchid flower (color and shape). **1974** Munz *Flora S. CA* 536, *Thistle Sage.* . . Sandy and gravelly places below 4500 ft.

thive n [Var of *chive*]

1950 *WELS (The small plants like onions with hollow green leaves that are cut up in salad)* 1 Inf, **WI,** Thives. **1969** *DARE* (Qu. I7) Inf **NY**209, Thives [θaɪvz].

thoat See **throat**

thob v, n |θɑb| [Var of *throb*] **Sth, S Midl**

1917 in 1944 *ADD* **sWV,** *Throb.* . . thobs. **1941** *Ibid* **WV,** *Throb.* . . th'ob. . . Said of an injured eye. **c1960** Wilson *Coll.* **csKY,** *Throb* is sometimes /θɑb/. **1969** *DARE* File **OK,** *Thob* [θɑb] = throb. "My head thobs so!" **1984** *Annals Internal Med.* 100.900 **cwAL,** Throbs and tolerable have lost their *r*'s and become *thobs* and *tolable.*

thoid, thoity See **thirty**

thole v [Scots, Ir, nEngl dial]

To bear, endure.

1940 in 1944 *ADD* **WV,** *Thole.* . . Can you thole the pain? **1968** Haun *Hawk's Done Gone* 55 **TN,** It went up and down till I thought I couldn't thole it any longer—e'er a bit longer.

tholepin, suffer like a v phr [Perh orig by assoc with **thole,** but the words are unrelated.] **ME, MA coasts**

To suffer excessively.

1904 *DN* 2.428 **Cape Cod MA** (as of a1857), *Suffer like a thole-pin.* . . To suffer extreme pain. **1916** *DN* 4.264 **Cape Cod MA,** I have heard . . the phrase "to suffer like a thole-pin." Since a thole-pin, unlike a metal row-lock, rarely creaks or groans, the figure indicates a survival of the root-meaning of "thole," "to suffer." **1932** Wasson *Sailing Days* 112 **cME coast,** Any old resident of the coast can easily understand the force of the ancient simile, "suffering like a blamed tholepin." **1942** ME Univ. *Studies* 56.72, Thole, meaning a wooden peg, is of Norse origin. It was evidently confused with the early English verb *thole,* to suffer, for the expression *to suffer like a thole pin* was common. The folk etymology was helped by the fact that the thole pin not only bore the strain from oars but expressed its torture in anguished squeaks. **1975** Gould *ME Lingo* 289, To suffer like a tholepin.

thong bark n

A **leatherwood 1** (here: *Dirca palustris*).

1892 (1974) Millspaugh *Amer. Med. Plants* 146-1, *Dirca palustris.* . . *rope bark,* . . *thong bark.* . . *Bark* remarkably tough and fibrous. [*Ibid* 146-2, The Leatherwood is indigenous to North America. . . The fibrous bark afforded material for ropes, thongs, cordage, and baskets, to the American aborigines.]

thonk ee See **thanky**

thoo See **through** adv, prep **1**

thore See **there A5**

thorn n Also *thorn bush* [*OED2* c700 → for any of var plants that bear thorns, esp of the genus *Crataegus*] **formerly N and C Atl, now widespread** Cf **thorn apple, ~ plum, ~ tree** =**hawthorn.**

1785 Marshall *Arbustrum* 88, Mespilus Crus galli [=*Crataegus crus-galli*]. *Pear-leaved Thorn.* This rises with a strong stem to the height of fifteen or twenty feet. **1805** in 1944 *Thomas Jefferson's Garden Book* 299 **VA,** I went immediately to Mr. Main & brot. the 4000 thorns. **1807** Irving *Salmagundi* 311 **NY,** [He carried] a gold-headed thorn cane, bequeathed him by his uncle John. **1814** Bigelow *Florula Bostoniensis* 118, *Crataegus crus galli.* . . *Common Thorn bush.* . . A strong, branching, thorny shrub. . . About fences and thickets. **1822** (1972) Deane *New Engl. Farmer* 191, American Hedge Thorn (*crataegus cordata*). . . The seedling thorns 10,000, were imported in March 1808, from the nursery of Thomas Main, near Georgetown. **1824** Doddridge *Notes Indian Wars* 86 **PA, VA,** Red haws grew on the white thorn bushes. **1844** Lapham *Geogr. Descr. WI* 79, Crataegus punctata, . . thorn. **1893** *Jrl. Amer. Folkl.* 6.141 **ME,** *Crataegus coccinea,* thorn-bush. **1897** Sudworth *Arborescent Flora* 215, *Crataegus douglasii.* . . Thorn (N. Mex., Mont., Idaho). *Ibid* 216, *Crataegus crus-galli.* . . Thorn (Pa., Ky.) *Ibid* 219, *Crataegus coccinea.* . . Thorn (Vt., N.Y., Ky., Mont.) *Ibid* 230, *Crataegus tomentosa.* . . Thorn (N.Y., Ky.) *Ibid* 232, *Crataegus cordata.* . . Thorn (Ky.) **1963** Craighead *Rocky Mt. Wildflowers* 80, *Crataegus rivularis* [=*C. douglasii*]. . . is well known to outdoorsmen, even if only by the general name of Thornbush. **1968–69** *DARE* (Qu. S4, . . *Mayapple:* [*Woodside plant, not a tree, with two large spreading leaves; they grow in patches and have a small yellow fruit late in summer*] Inf **MA**42, Thorn bush; (Qu. I46, . . *Kinds of fruits that grow wild around here*) Inf **NY**52, May apples—grow on a thorn bush, but we don't eat them. **1999** *DARE* File **wID** (as of 1940s), With any scraps left from fence-building, we made arrows for our mighty bows. Actually, we did make one bow from a thorn branch ("hawthorne" [sic]) that was a very powerful one.

thorn apple n

1 Std: a plant of the genus *Datura*, usu *D. stramonium;* also the fruit of such a plant.   For other names see **Indian apple 6, jimson weed**

2 =**hawthorn;** also its fruit.   **widespread, but esp Gt Lakes** See Map

1817 Brown *Western Gaz.* 322 **Gt Lakes,** The plants and shrubs [include]. . . pennyroyal, thorn apple, wild hops.   **1844** Lee–Frost *10 Yrs. OR* 89, The natural fruit of this valley is much the same . . as that upon the Clatsop Plain . . with the addition of wild cherries, red and black, and the thorn-apple.   **1844** Lapham *Geogr. Descr. WI* 79, Crataegus coccinea, . . thorn apple.   **1892** *Jrl. Amer. Folkl.* 5.95 **OH,** *Crataegus,* thorn-apple.   **1897** Sudworth *Arborescent Flora* 215, *Crataegus douglasii*. . . Thorn Apple (Cal., Utah, Wash., Idaho, Nev.)   *Ibid* 216, *Crataegus crus-galli*. . . Thorn Apple (N.Y., W. Va.)   *Ibid* 219, *Crataegus coccinea*. . . Thorn Apple (Vt., Mont.) Thorn Apple Tree (Minn.)   *Ibid* 221, *Crataegus mollis*. . . Red Thorn Apple (Mich.)   *Ibid* 230, *Crataegus tomentosa*. . . Thorn Apple (Ill.)   **1901** Lounsberry *S. Wild Flowers* 250, *C[rataegus] punctata* . . produces . . very large globose pomes, either clear red or bright yellow. These thorn-apples, as they are popularly called by the children, are very palatable when fully ripe and many are gathered by them.   **1910** Wright *Black Bear* 98, Their [=black bears'] favorites everywhere are blueberries and huckleberries, and the red and black haws, called thorn-apples in New England.   **1950** *WELS (Kinds of apples grown in your neighborhood)* 2 Infs, **WI,** (Wild) thorn apple.   **1965–70** *DARE* (Qu. I46, . . *Kinds of fruits that grow wild around here*) 46 Infs, **chiefly Gt Lakes, Upstate NY,** Thorn apples; (Qu. S4) Inf **MI**15, Thorn apple; (Qu. S13) Inf **WI**32, Thorn apple; (Qu. S17) Inf **MI**42, Thorn apple; (Qu. T16, . . *Kinds of trees . . 'special'*) Infs **MI**76, **NH**5, **WI**22, 48, Thorn apple.   **1966** *DARE* Tape **MA**6, We have thorn apples. They have burrs on them after the blossoms have come on. And if the apples come on first, you can pull 'em off and eat 'em.   **1980** Little *Audubon Guide N. Amer. Trees E. Region* 458, *Crataegus,* commonly known as Hawthorn, Haw, Thornapple, . . is a large genus of many difficult-to-distinguish species.

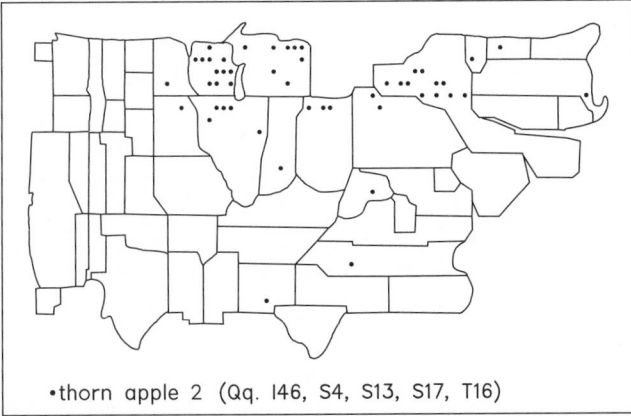

•thorn apple 2 (Qq. I46, S4, S13, S17, T16)

3 A **horse nettle 1** (here: *Solanum carolinense*).

1922 *Amer. Botanist* 28.41 **KY,** Prof. J.C. Nelson writes: The word "Thorn-apple" seems very elusive. I never heard it applied to either *Crataegus* or *Datura;* when we used it in Kentucky, it meant *Solanum carolinense*, a very bad perennial weed of sandy fields. . . I wonder if this application of the name is only local? The books call this plant "horse-nettle," but I never heard this applied to it.

4 =**prickly poppy.**

1953 Greene–Blomquist *Flowers South* 39, *Prickly-Poppies* and *Thorn-Apples* (*Argemone*)—Waxy, leafy-stemmed, usually spiny annual or biennial herbs with flowers which resemble those of poppies, but with sepals and capsules more or less spiny.

thornback n

1 =**cunner** n[1] **1.**   *obs*

1832 Williamson *Hist. ME* 1.163, The *Thornback*, or *Cunner*, is a brown coloured, scaled salt water fish, as large as a white perch, and is a good pan-fish. It has a horny, or thorned back, and is found in Casco bay and westward; and weighs from 1 to 6 pounds.

2 The nine-spined **stickleback** (*Pungitius pungitius*). [*OED2* 1859 → for a stickleback]

1903 NY State Museum & Sci. Serv. *Bulletin* 60.339 **seNY,** This stickleback [=*Pungitius pungitius*]. . . in Great South bay [NY] is known as the thornback.

thornback shark n   [From the dorsal spines]

A **dogfish 1** (here: *Squalus acanthias*).

1905 NJ State Museum *Annual Rept. for 1904* 67, *Squalus acanthias*. . . Spiny Dog Fish. . . Thorn Back Shark.

thornberry n   [*OED2* 1766 →]   Cf **thorn apple 2**

The fruit of a **hawthorn.**

1966 *DARE* (Qu. I44, *What kinds of berries grow wild around here?*) Inf **WA**3, Thornberries.   **1994** *DARE* File **ID,** The Chokecherry puts out berries in grape-like clusters, while the Hawthorne [sic] puts them out in clumps like cherries. . . And, since the "Thornberries" look more like a person imagines "cherries" to look, more than one unbanite [sic] has made a bad mistake when "gathering."

thorn bush   See **thorn**

thornhead   See **thornyhead**

thorn locust n   Also *thorny locust*

=**honey locust 1.**

1859 (1968) Bartlett *Americanisms* 477, *Thorny Locust*. See *Honey Locust*.   **1893** *Jrl. Amer. Folkl.* 6.140 **NY,** *Gleditschia triacanthus*, thorn locust.   **1897** Sudworth *Arborescent Flora* 254, *Gleditsia triacanthos*. . . Thorn Locust (N.Y., Ind., La.) . . Thorny Locust (N.J.)   **1950** Peattie *Nat. Hist. Trees* 403, *Gleditsia triacanthos*. . . Thorny . . Locust.   **1966–69** *DARE* (Qu. T9) Inf **OK**52, Black locust and thorny locust also have pods; (Qu. T16, . . *Kinds of trees . . 'special'*) Inf **IL**62, Thorny locust—grows good along the cricks.   **1974** (1977) Coon *Useful Plants* 167, Thorn locust. . . The wood of large trees is especially valuable for posts . . , as they practically never rot.

thorn oak n

Prob a **pin oak.**

1969 *DARE* (Qu. T10, . . *Kinds of oak trees*) Inf **CT**28, Black, red, yellow, thorn [oaks].

thorn plum n

1 Any of several **hawthorns** or their fruit.   **chiefly NEast** Cf **thorn apple 2**

1897 Sudworth *Arborescent Flora* 216, *Crataegus crus-galli*. . . Thorn Plum (Me.)   *Ibid* 219, *Crataegus coccinea*. . . Thorn Plum (Me., Vt., N.Y.)   *Ibid* 230, *Crataegus tomentosa*. . . Thorn Plum.   **1900** Lyons *Plant Names* 121, *Fruit* of several species [of *Crataegus*] called red haws, occasionally thorn-plums or thorn-apples.   **1943** Fernald–Kinsey *Edible Wild Plants E. N. Amer.* 232, Haw, Thorn, Thorn-Plum, Hawthorn, *Crataegus* (many species). . . The fruits of several species have a juicy pulp from which a delicious marmalade or jelly can be made.   **1945** *NY Folkl. Qrly.* 1.215, The thorn plums were our apples when the mandrakes were all gone,/ The little grapes we used to eat when frosty nights came on.   **1967–68** *DARE* (Qu. I46, . . *Kinds of fruits that grow wild around here*) Inf **NY**9, Thorn plums; (Qu. S14) Inf **NH**14, Thorn plum—has little berries.   **1970** Kirk *Wild Edible Plants W. U.S.* 99, *Crataegus species* . . Hawthorn, Haw, Thorn Plum. . . All species produce edible berries but some produce fleshier fruit than others.

2 A **wild plum 1** (here: *Prunus americana*).

1933 Small *Manual SE Flora* 648, *P[runus] americana*. . . Red-plum. Thorn-plum. . . Fr[uit] ripe late sum. or fall.   **1960** Vines *Trees SW* 404, Other vernacular names [for *Prunus americana*] are. . . Wild Yellow Plum, Red Plum, and Thorn Plum.   **1987** Kindscher *Edible Wild Plants* 170, Wild plum, American plum, . . thorn plum. . . *Prunus americana*. . . Shrubs or small trees, . . small branches sometimes spiny.

thorn poppy n

A **prickly poppy** (here: *Argemone mexicana*).

1858 Amer. Pharmaceutical Assoc. *Proc.* 245, *Argemone Mexicana*. Thorn-poppy. . . This beautiful shrubby tree is in full flower in our wet, swampy woods around Detroit, early in May.   **1876** Hobbs *Bot. Hdbk.* 119, Thorn poppy, Prickly poppy, Argemone Mexicana.   **1936** Whitehouse *TX Flowers* 34, *Argemone mexicana* is also called . . Mexican thorn poppy.

thorn toad n

=**burfish.**

1976 Warner *Beautiful Swimmers* 225 **Chesapeake Bay,** Much rarer were the bizarre species variously called burrfishes or spiny boxfishes. Known as "thorn toads" among watermen, these little fish have been described in scientific literature as "a solid bony box with holes for the mouth, eyes, fins and vent, more or less inflatable." . . Top and bottom it is encased in sharp spines. **1984** *DARE* File **Chesapeake Bay** [Watermen's vocab], Thorn toad.

thorn tree n

Any of var spiny trees, as:

a =**hawthorn.**

1822 Eaton *Botany* 255, *[Crataegus] punctata* . . common thorn tree, . . thorny or unarmed. . . *[Crataegus] crus-galli*, . . thorn tree . . thorny. . . Berries small, red. **1830** Rafinesque *Med. Flora* 2.213, *Crataegus*. . . Hawthorn, Thorn trees. Many species. Fruits of several edible, red or yellow, acid or sweetish, making fine stomachic preserves. **1852** Watson *Nights Block-House* 214 **N Cent,** He provided himself with a stout switch, taken from a thorn-tree. **1908** Britton *N. Amer. Trees* 443, The Thorn Trees . . Genus *Crataegus*. . . are usually spiny, much-branched shrubs or small trees. **1953** Peattie *Nat. Hist. W. Trees* 518, *Douglas Hawthorn*. . . *Other Names* . . Douglas Thorntree. . . East to northern Michigan and western Ontario.

b =**honey locust 1.**

1887 *Amer. Druggist* 16.201 **LA,** The *Gleditschia triacanthos* has several local names in this State. In the northern portion it is called *Thorn Tree.* **1897** IN Dept. Geol. & Nat. Resources *Rept. for 1896* 644, *G[leditschia] triacanthos*. . . Honey Locust. Thorn Tree. **1897** Sudworth *Arborescent Flora* 254, *Gleditsia triacanthos*. . . Thorntree (N.Y., Ind., La.) **1950** Moore *Trees AR* 83, *Honeylocust*. . . Local Names. . . Thorn Tree. . . Tree may attain height of 90 feet in well-stocked stands. **1950** Grimm *Trees PA* 254, The Honey Locust is also known as the . . Thorn Tree. **1960** Vines *Trees SW* 532, *Gleditsia triacanthos*. . . Vernacular names are . . Thorn-tree, Thorny Locust, . . and Sweet-bean. **1967** *DARE* (Qu. T16, . . *Kinds of trees* . . *'special'*) Inf **LA8,** Thorn tree.

c =**Osage orange. Cf hedge**

1968 *DARE* (Qu. T13, . . *Names* . . *for* . . *osage orange*) Inf **NJ45,** Osage orange—thorn trees or thorn fence.

thornuary See thanuary

thorny acacia n

=**honey locust 1.**

1857 (1927) Rodman *Diary* 333 **MA,** Made arrangements for lopping the top branches of the thorny acassia tree at the east of the house. **1897** Sudworth *Arborescent Flora* 254 **TN,** *Gleditsia triacanthos*. . . Thorny Acacia. **1950** Peattie *Nat. Hist. Trees* 403, *Gleditsia triacanthos*. . . Thorny . . Locust. Thorny . . Acacia. . . *Bark* . . sometimes very thorny. . . *Twigs* . . thornless or beset by simple or branched thorns. **1960** Vines *Trees SW* 534, *Gleditsia aquatica*. . . Vernacular names are Swamp Locust and Thorny Acacia. This tree is generally separated from Common Honey-Locust [=*G. triacanthos*], which it resembles, by its generally smaller leaves, slender thorns, and by the much smaller pulpless fruit.

thorny bill n

=**granjeno.**

1931 U.S. Dept. Ag. *Misc. Pub.* 101.25, *Spiny hackberry (C[eltis] pallida)*, sometimes called . . thorny bill, while often common in the Southwest, . . [is] browsed only under overgrazed conditions.

thornyhead n Also thornhead

A fish of the genus *Sebastolobus* native in Pacific waters from Alaska to California. For other names of *S. alascanus* see **idiot B, red rock cod 2, scorpion B4c**

1953 Roedel *Common Fishes CA* 136, *Sebastolobus alascanus*. . . Thornhead. . . A smaller, very similar species, *Sebastolobus altivelis* . . is taken occasionally along with *S. alascanus* in deep water. **1973** Knight *Cook's Fish Guide* 383, Thornhead—Rockfish, Channel [=*Sebastolobus alascanus*]. Thornhead. **1993** *Capital Times* (Madison WI) 25 Aug sec D 6/4 **Los Angeles CA,** Now he turns to something labelled "red ocean perch," a beautiful fish with mottled red skin. . . "It's short-spine thornyhead—fishermen call them 'idiots'—and they're hard to find because the big ones are all sold to Japan." **1997** in 2001 *DARE* File **Pacific,** Once trawl fishermen tossed short-spine and long-spine thornyheads overboard. Now they may get $1 a pound for the fish, which are shipped to Japan. The catch of live thornyheads has increased from 36 pounds in 1991 to 22,000 pounds last year.

thorny locust See thorn locust

thoroughfare n Also thorofare, thoroughfair, thorowfare Atlantic Cf drain v, n¹ C4

A waterway connecting two larger bodies of water; a channel; see quots.

1699 in 1940 *AmSp* 15.402 **VA,** Three thousand acres of Land . . bounded . . by part of Watchepeag then by Islands of Sunken Marshes then by the broad water then by a Thorowfare then by a great bay or Sound into a gutt. **1725** *Ibid,* At ye mouth of a Small branch of Patowmack river Side at a Thoroughfair between two Islands. **1848** Thoreau in *Union Mag.* (NY NY) 3.132 **ME** (as of 1846), After one mile of river, or what the boatmen call "thoroughfare,"—for the river becomes at length only the connecting link between the lakes,— . . we entered the North Twin Lake. **1895** *Outing* 26.484 **ME,** Mr. Iselin sent Captain Haff down among the "thorofares" of the Maine Islands. **1899** (1912) Green *VA Folk-Speech* 444, Thoroughfare. . . Long, narrow body of water through mudflats connecting two bodies of water. **1935** *AmSp* 10.154 **eMD** [Water terms in MD], Thorofare. **1940** Weygandt *Down Jersey* 145 **sNJ,** The dunes of Absecon Island, the thoroughfare and salt marsh behind it . . must have been welcome indeed to the sea-tired eyes of the master of the homing ship. **1946** Attwood *Length ME* 17 [Geographical terms], Thoroughfare, thorofare— A waterway, as between two coast water areas or between two lakes. **1976** Warner *Beautiful Swimmers* 8 **eMD,** Down every tidal gut and through every big "thorofare" and little "swash" or "drain," as the breaks in the marsh islands are called, there comes an enormous . . flow of silage.

thoroughgrow n Also throughgrow Cf thoroughwort 1

A **boneset 1** (here: *Eupatorium perfoliatum*).

1896 *Jrl. Amer. Folkl.* 9.192 **ePA,** *Eupatorium perfoliatum*, . . throughgrow. . . Evidently from the perfoliate leaves. **1949** Moldenke *Amer. Wild Flowers* 219, *Eupatorium perfoliatum*. . . Its pubescent stems . . bear pairs of opposite leaves, the lower of which . . are united by their bases around the stems so that the stem seems to grow right through the leaves. This has given rise to the names of *thoroughwort, thoroughwax, thoroughgrow,* and *thoroughstem.*

thoroughstem n

A **boneset 1** (here: *Eupatorium perfoliatum*).

1818 Barton *Vegetable Materia Medica* 2.125, *Eupatorium Perfoliatum.* Bone-Set. Thorough-Wort. Thorough-stem. **1837** Darlington *Flora Cestrica* 451 **sePA,** *E[upatorium] perfoliatum*. . . Thorough-stem. Bone-set. Indian Sage. . . This species is generally well known for its valuable medicinal properties—being either tonic, cathartic, or emetic, according to the dose, or mode of exhibition. **1876** Hobbs *Bot. Hdbk.* 119, Thorough stem. . . Thorough wax. . . Thoroughwort, Eupatorium perfoliatum. **1911** Henkel *Amer. Med. Leaves* 36, *Eupatorium perfoliatum*. . . Thoroughwort, thorough-stem, thorough-wax. **1949** [see **thoroughgrow**]. **1975** Hamel–Chiltoskey *Cherokee Plants* 26, Thorough-stem. . . Tea for cold, sore throat, flu.

thoroughwax n

1 Std: a plant of the genus *Bupleurum*. [*OED2* 1548 → for *Bupleurum rotundifolium*] Also called **thoroughwort 2**; for other names of *B. rotundifolium* see **modesty 1**

2 A **boneset 1** (here: *Eupatorium perfoliatum*).

1817 Bigelow *Amer. Med. Botany* 1.33, *Eupatorium Perfoliatum*. . . Common names . . *Thorough wort, Thorough wax, Cross wort, Bone set.* **1892** (1974) Millspaugh *Amer. Med. Plants* 79–1, *Eupatorium perfoliatum*. . . *Thorough-wax.* [Footnote:] The true Thoroughwax is *Bupleurum rotundifolium*. **1911** Henkel *Amer. Med. Leaves* 36, *Eupatorium perfoliatum*. . . Thoroughwort, thorough-stem, thorough-wax. **1958** Jacobs–Burlage *Index Plants NC* 52, *Eupatorium perfoliatum*. . . Thoroughwort, thorough wax. . . through-stem. . . thoroughstem. . . This herb is found in swamps, marshes, low grounds, and near streams throughout the United States and North Carolina.

thoroughwort n

1 =**boneset 1;** also any of var other plants formerly included in the genus *Eupatorium.* **esp NEast**

1814 Bigelow *Florula Bostoniensis* 190, *Eupatorium perfoliatum*. . . Thoroughwort. . . Known . . by its long, acute leaves, alternately crossing, and perforated by the stem. **1845** Judd *Margaret* 146 **NEng** (as of 18th cent), She came to the stream . . near it grew . . purple thoroughwort. **1864** Randall *Practical Shepherd* 150 **NY,** The tonic contained in half a dozen teaspoonfulls of . . thoroughwort (*Eupatorium perfoliatum*) tea, has an excellent effect. **1890** Holley *Samantha among Brethren*

197 **NY,** The old lady took thoroughwert [sic] for 'em [=spells of "tightening" in the chest], and Trueman's wife insisted on't that thoroughwert wuz tightenin'. **1906** *Harper's Mth. Mag.* 113.712 **NEng,** [To] the boggy place . . she came in all warm seasons of the year for one thing or another: the wild marsh-marigold, . . thoroughwort, and the root of the sweet-flag. **1931** Harned *Wild Flowers Alleghanies* 502, *Tall Thoroughwort (E[upatorium] altissimum [=Ageratina a.] . .*) A tall, finely pubescent species. . . Woods and sandy soils. **1950** *WELS (What kitchen herbs are used in your neighborhood)* 1 Inf, **WI,** Thoroughwort. **1966** *DARE* Wildfl QR Pl.230 [=*Eupatorium perfoliatum*] Inf **NH4,** Thoroughwort. **1968–69** *DARE* (Qu. S21, . . *Weeds . . that are a trouble in gardens and fields)* Inf **VT4,** Thoroughwort; (Qu. S26b, *Wildflowers that grow in water or wet places)* Infs **MA68, VT13,** Thoroughwort; (Qu. BB50d, *Favorite spring tonics)* Infs **MA29, MI96, NY68, 102,** Thoroughwort. **2001** *Atlanta Jrl.–Constitution* (GA) 26 July 5 (Internet), Other *Eupatoriums* . . include . . whitish-flowered *thoroughwort.*

2 =**thoroughwax 1.** [*OED2* 1597]
1900 Lyons *Plant Names* 72, *B[upleurum] rotundifolium.* . . Thorough-wax or Thoroughwort. **1959** Anderson *Flora AK* 357, *B. americanum.* . . American Thorough-wort. . . Flowers yellow or purplish. **1974** Welsh *Anderson's Flora AK* 469, *Bupleurum triradiatum* [=*B. americanum*] . . *Thorough-wort.* . . In much of Alaska . . and in western Yukon; south to Montana, Idaho and Wyoming.

3 A plant of the genus *Brickellia,* usu *B. eupatorioides.*
1921 MO Bot. Garden *Bulletin* 9.90, *Brickellia grandiflora* . . Large-flowered thoroughwort. **1932** Rydberg *Flora Prairies* 777, *Brickellia.* . . Thoroughwort. Herbs or shrubs. **1942** Hylander *Plant Life* 472, Another plant known as Thoroughwort (*Brickellia* . .), found on hillsides and in canyons from Kansas and Nebraska to Wyoming and Arizona, has umbels of nodding white or pink flowers. *Ibid* 675, Thoroughwort—Brickellia umbellata. **2005** *DARE* File—Internet **West,** *Asteraceae.* . . *Brickellia* . . thoroughwort.

thorowfare See **thoroughfare**

thort See **thwart**

thortey See **thirty**

those pron, adj   Usu |ðoz|; also **chiefly Sth, NYC** *esp freq among Black speakers* |doz| Pronc-spp *dose, doze, t'ose*
Std senses, var forms.
1888 *Century Illustr. Mag.* 35.353 **LA** [Black], You see . . Claude git doze new mash-in all right, he go to ingineerin' ag'in. **1893** Shands *MS Speech* 62, *Th.* . . is in a large number of instances pronounced by negroes as *d:* as . . *dose* . . for . . *those.* **1934** Carmer *Stars Fell on AL* 227 [Black], Where'd you git t'ose shoes so fine? **1939** in 1944 *ADD, Those.* . . pseudo N.Y.C. [doz]. Radio skit. **1941** *Time* 21 July 49 **NYC,** Jimmy obeyed, not sparing a single dese, dem or dose. **1942** *Treasury Star Parade* 33 **NYC,** Remember, just a little bit of the "dese, dem and doze" in your reading. **1981** Pederson *LAGS Basic Materials* **Gulf Region,** [31 infs, proncs of the type [do‹uz]; 13 infs Black.]

those there See **there B**

thot See **that A3**

thote See **throat**

thotty See **thoughty**

though prep¹, adv   Usu |ðo|; also **chiefly Sth** *esp freq among Black speakers* |do| Pronc-spp *do(ugh)*
Std senses, var proncs.
1887 (1967) Harris *Free Joe* 87 **GA** [Black], She say dat dough she spize um all dez bad az she kin, dat man mus' be brung away from dar. **1893** Shands *MS Speech* 26, *Do* [do]. Negro for *though.* **1899** Chesnutt *Conjure Woman* 18 **csNC** [Black], He wuz a peart old nigger, do', en could do a big day's wuk. **1909** *S. Atl. Qrly.* 8.44 **sSC coast** [Gullah], An' dough tarruh mahn dash 'e yat erway, grease bun ron pon topper um. [=And though the other man thrust his hat away, grease ran on top of it.] **1922** Gonzales *Black Border* 297 **sSC, GA coasts** [Gullah glossary], *'Do'*—though. **1934** Hurston *Jonah's Gourd Vine* 35 **AL** [Black], Hit sho look frightenin' . . But hits uh pretty thing do. **c1937** in 1976 *Weevils in the Wheat* 228 **VA** [Black], I was strong den, let 'lone what I is now, even do I dozen look like hit.

though prep²   See **through** adv, prep **1**

thought See **thwart**

thought coming, have another v phr   For varr see quots [Varr of *have another think coming*]   **scattered, but chiefly Sth, S Midl**   See Map
=**guess coming, have another.**
1907 *Atlanta Constitution* (GA) 2 June sec B 2/1, [Advt:] If you are one who thinks a gleety discharge is a trifling matter, you have another thought coming. **1910** *Indianapolis Star* (IN) 25 Oct 8/5, Those deep-browed prophets who see in their mind's eye the insurgents combining with the Democrats . . have another thought coming. **1928** *Ironwood Daily-Globe* (MI) 9 Jan 8/5, If anyone has the idea that the Birdies are the weak sisters of the league this season they have another thought coming. **1949** *Waukesha Freeman* (WI) 28 Feb 2/5, If they think it's going to be easy to pass, they have another thought coming. **1965–70** *DARE* (Qu. KK59, *To have a mistaken idea, or to be quite wrong about something:* "*If he thinks she'll help him, he's _____.*") 20 Infs, **chiefly Sth, S Midl,** Got another thought coming (to him); **MD39, PA113,** Has another thought coming (to him); **GA80,** Another thought coming; **VA46,** Got a thought coming; **KY40,** Got another thought a-coming. **1975** *Post-Std.* (Syracuse NY) 13 Jan 10/1, Anyone expecting the Syracuse African Violet Society to be a stodgy group has another thought coming. **1998** *Valley Independent* (Monessen PA) 28 Oct 4/1, If Governor Ridge thinks we forgot about him giving himself a big raise as soon as he got into office, he has another thought coming.

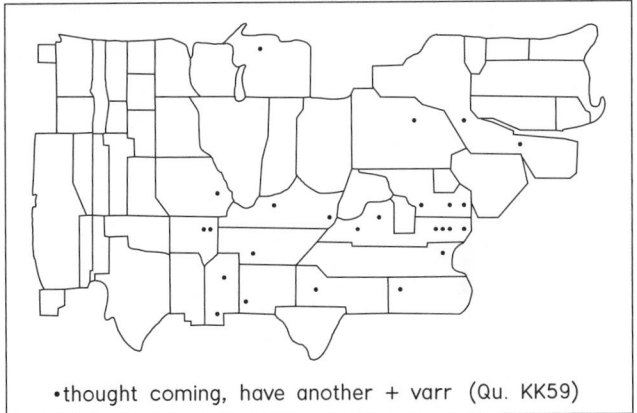

•thought coming, have another + varr (Qu. KK59)

thoughted v   See **think B2b**

thoughted adj   See **unthoughted**

thoughten See **withouten**

thoughty adj   Pronc-sp *thotty*
1 Thoughtful, considerate, kind; hence adj, adv *unthoughty* thoughtless(ly). [Scots dial; cf *OED2* "*Obs.* exc. *Sc.*"] **chiefly S Midl** Cf **unthoughted**
1941 Justus *Cabin on Kettle Creek* 113 **eTN,** You are a mighty thoughty person. **1946** *Hench Coll.* **AR,** [*Lum and Abner* radio show:] It's mighty thoughty of you to call up. **1952** Brown *NC Folkl.* 1.601, *Thoughty.* . . Thoughtful, kind.—Illiterate. **1952** *Hench Coll.* **cVA,** I was talking to George Walker about how kind a certain person had been to his family. . . "Yes, she's been mighty thoughty of us," George said. Was George intentionally using a non-standard form? . . I suspect [not] for he deals a great deal with auto mechanics, gas service men, to whom "thoughty" is a normal word. **1972** *Atlanta Letters* **neGA,** "Southernisms". . . T'was mighty thoughty of you. *Ibid* **nwGA,** Unthoughty—Not thinking—careless. **1979** Carpenter *Walton War* 174 **sAppalachians,** It shore is thoughty of you to do this. **1982** Ginns *Snowbird Gravy* 98 **nwNC,** "I wouldn't do you a wrong if I knowed it with my mind." And I said, "Or I'd just do it unthoughty if I did." **1982** *Smithsonian Letters* **WV,** Thotty = thoughtful. **1986** *WI Alumnus Letters* **Ozarks,** That was a thoughty thing to do. **1998** in 2004 Montgomery-Hall *Dict. Smoky Mt. Engl.* 628 **eTN,** Unthoughty. . . She's an unthoughty person.

2 Ingenious.
1968 Kellner *Aunt Serena* 162 **sIN,** They had a real thoughty plan, they told me. . . If they just stood in front of a stand [at the county fair] and looked sad and penniless, some of the kinfolks were *bound* to come past and buy them something.

thousand-and-one (bean), thousand for one See **thousand-to-one (bean)**

thousand-leg See **thousand-legs**

thousand-legged fence n
=**shadback fence.**

1917 *DN* 4.402 **neOH,** *Thousand-legged fence* = shad-belly fence.

thousand-legs n Also *thousand-leg (worm), thousand-legged worm(ie), thousand-legger* [*OED2* 1807 →] **scattered, but esp freq Sth, Midl** See Map
Either a millipede (Diplopoda) or a **centipede.**

1807 *Med. Repository* 4.164, The insects without wings . . are disposed in six families . . [including] thousand-legs, *scolopendra*. **1811** *Rural Visiter* (Burlington NJ) 1.84, Once in his spite he overset a harmless thousand legs. **1850** *Scientific Amer.* 6.107 **OH,** A small boy was poisoned to death in Munson last week, by eating a part of a worm in an apple. . . His parents picked up the apple, and upon examination, found in it a portion of a worm, known in common parlance as the thousand legged worm. **1885** Hodge *Memoir* 90 **NY** (as of 1805), I was once, a little creeping, toddling boy, discovered by my mother munching a "thousand-legged worm." **1918** Grinnell et al. *Game Birds CA* 530, Some beetles, bugs, caterpillars, grasshoppers, flies, spiders, "thousand-leggers," and snails were also found in the [quail] stomachs examined. **1919** *DN* 5.35 **KY,** *Thousand-legged worm*. . . Centipede. **c1930** Brown *Amer. Folkl. Insect Lore* 5, A "thousand-legs" crawling into a child's ears would "drive it crazy." **1941** O'Donnell *Great Big Doorstep* 200 **sLA,** I never saw a roach lak here. I never saw a thousan-laig. **1950** *PADS* 14.77 **FL,** *Thousand-legger*. . . The millipede. **1954** Harder *Coll.* **cwTN,** *Thousand-leg*. A millipede. **c1960** Wilson *Coll.* **csKY,** *Thousand-leg*. Millipede. **1965–70** *DARE* (Qu. R27, . . *Kinds of caterpillars or similar worms*) Infs **AL2, AR16, KY84, SC57, 63, TX3,** Thousand-leg(s); **AL17,** Elwig [sic] like a thousand-leg; **GA84,** Thousand-legs—same as centipede; **NC6, 47,** Thousand-leg worm(s); **GA17, MD22, MO19, NY12,** Thousand-legged worm; **MI2,** Thousand-legged worm—something like measuring worm, but bigger; **MI65,** Thousand-legged worms—flat—row of legs on each side, sometimes called centipedes; **MI65,** Thousand-legged worm—millipedes, I guess, is the real name for 'em; **OH84,** Thousand-legged worms—same as centipedes; **CA31,** Thousand-legged wormie; **PA58, 112,** Thousand-legger; **MI54,** Thousand-legger—can go like mad; **PA92,** Thousand-leggers—centipede; (Qu. R9a) Inf **NC49,** Thousand-legs; **NY12,** Thousand-legged worm; (Qu. R21, . . *Other kinds of stinging insects*) Inf **TX84,** Centipede—thousand-legs; **WV8,** Centipede is called a thousand-legged worm; **DE4,** Centipede or thousand-legger; (Qu. R28) Inf **MD9,** Thousand-legger—another name for a centipede; **MD26,** Thousand-legger—long, countless number of legs, harmless; **MO26,** Thousand-leggers. **1986** Pederson *LAGS Concordance* **Gulf Region,** 3 infs, Thousand-leg(s); 2 infs, Thousand-leg(ged) worm. **1995** Adams *Come Go Home* 2 **wNC,** We had a run-in with a huge thousand-legs. Granny capped her hand over my mouth when we saw the thousand-legs, because if you show them your teeth, they'll every one rot out.

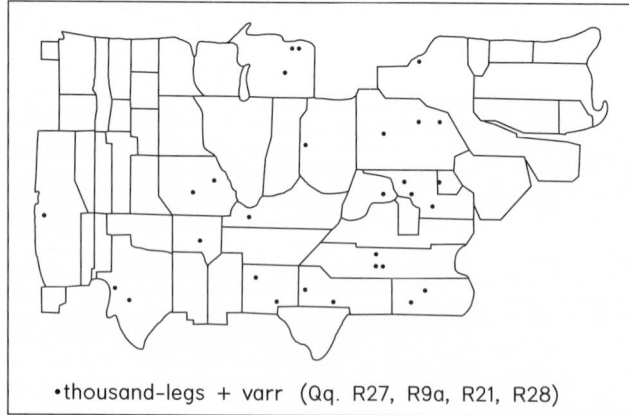
•thousand-legs + varr (Qq. R27, R9a, R21, R28)

thousands adv
Extremely.

1926 *DN* 5.404 **Ozarks,** *Thousands*. . . A large size or amount rather than a large number. "Them britches is thousands big, but they aint noways long 'nuff."

thousand-to-one (bean) n Also *thousand-and-one (bean), thousand for one*
A variety of kidney bean; see quots.

1820 Nicholson *Farmer's Asst.* 17 **NY,** Of those [beans] which have vines, the caseknife bean, the cranberry, and the thousand for one, so called, are very good. **1847** NY Ag. Soc. *Trans. for 1846* 6.603, The crop of beans presented for premium was grown on five-eights [sic] of an acre of land, measured. The variety, the white bean, called thousand to one. **1855** U.S. Patent Office *Annual Rept. for 1854: Ag.* 337, *Kidney Dwarfs, or Snaps*. . . *Refugee or Thousand-to-One*.—This is a late, round-podded variety . . sometimes called "Purple-speckled Valentine." **1870** *New Engl. Farmer* 4.91, Last year I raised a stalk from one bean which bore 230 pods. . . This shows what the Thousand and One bean can do. **1895** *Gleanings Bee Culture* 23.326, Everybody in Florida was planting beans; and it was just one kind of bean, too: the Refugee, or Thousand-to-one. **1970** *DARE* (Qu. I18, *The smaller beans that are white when they are dry*) Inf **NY233,** Thousand-and-one; (Qu. I20, . . *Kinds of beans*) Inf **NY233,** Thousand-and-one. **1999** *Goldenseal* 25.3.11 **WV,** As far as the little Thousand-to-One beans she had when I was a lot younger. I have them, but it took me awhile to get them back.

thout(e)n, 'thoutn' See **withouten**

thow See **throw A1, B1b**

thowed See **throw A1, B1a, 2c**

thown See **throw A1, B1d**

‡**thrap** v Cf **frap**
1957 Beck *Folkl. ME* 168, A man "thraps," thrashes around, to keep warm.

thrash n[1] Also *thrash bird, thresh* [Varr of **thrasher** or *thrush*] **chiefly Sth** See Map Cf Intro "Language Changes" III.4, **brown thrush**

1906 *DN* 3.161 **nwAR,** *Thresh*. . . Thrush. "Jes' lis'n at the thresh sing." **1909** *DN* 3.381 **eAL, wGA,** *Thrash*. . . The thrush. . . *Thresh*. . . Thrush. Rare. **1962** Imhof *AL Birds* 397, *Brown Thrasher*. . . *Other names* . . Thrush. . In Alabama . . a common to abundant permanent resident. **1965–70** *DARE* (Qu. Q14, . . *Names* . . *for these birds:* . . *brown thrasher*) Infs **GA84, LA3, MS11, 87, NC67, 82, TN22, VA40,** Thrash; **GA1, MS60, NC10, VA46,** Brown thrash; **MS47,** Thrash bird; **IA24,** Brown thresh; (Qu. Q14, . . *Names* . . *for these birds:* . . *thrush*) Infs **GA13, 35, LA3, MS11, NC67, TN22,** Thrash; **MS60,** Thresh; [101 Infs, Thrasher; **LA40,** Thrasher—no distinction between thrush and thrasher; **MD4,** Thrasher—Inf has heard, but doesn't know what it is; **TN24,** Thrasher—these [=*thrush* and *thrasher*] are interchangeable, but thrush is more common].

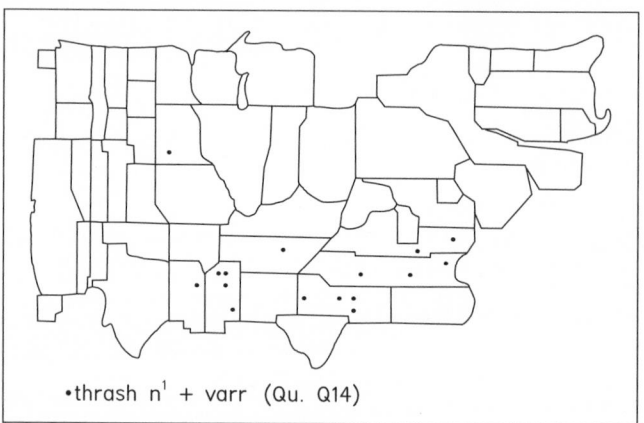
•thrash n[1] + varr (Qu. Q14)

thrash n[2] **esp GA**
=**thrash machine.**

1909 *DN* 3.381 **eAL, wGA,** *Thrash*. . . A threshing machine. **1966–69** *DARE* (Qu. L32a, *In early days, how was the grain separated from the straw?*) Inf **GA9,** Steam-powered thrash; (Qu. L32b, *In early days, how was the grain separated from the chaff?*) Infs **GA9, 87,** Fan in the thrash. [Both Infs old, gs educ] **1966** *DARE* Tape **GA1,** [FW:] How did you separate the grain . . ? [Inf:] . . There was a thrash, back . . in my day. It was pulled around by a pair of mules, a yoke of steers.

thrash n[3] Also rarely, prob by hypercorrection, *thresh* [Varr of *thrush* a fungal infection esp of the mouth in infants; a bacterial infection of the frog of a horse's hoof] **chiefly Sth, S Midl**

1852 Thompson *Major Jones's Courtship* 204 **GA,** Maybe it's nothing but the hives, or the yaller thrash, or some other baby ailment. **1860**

Harper's New Mth. Mag. 20.715, Why, Sir, the baby has got the thrash; Joe never saw his daddy. I thought every body knowed that if Joe *would blow his breath in that baby's mouth* that thrash would be blowed into Kingdom come! **1906** *DN* 3.161 **nwAR,** *Thrash. . .* Thrush; a disease affecting the mouth, lips, and throat of children. **1909** *DN* 3.381 **eAL, wGA,** *Thrash. . .* A baby's disease, an eruption in the mouth. **1912** Green *VA Folk-Speech* 445, *Thrash. . .* A skin and mouth disease of young children. **1915** *DN* 4.192 **swVA,** *Thrash. . .* An eruption of the mouth (in children). **1934** Carmer *Stars Fell on AL* 284, When the baby takes thrash (sore mouth), brew tea of nine saw bugs and make him drink it. **1961** Seeman *In Arms of Mt.* 34 **eTN,** Pity the puny infant with the "thrash." Its throat would be subjected to a wash of green persimmons and sugar, or a decoction of rusty nails and vinegar. **1964** Wallace *Frontier Life* 67 **OK** (as of 1893–1906), When our baby had a bad case of thresh (sore mouth), a neighbor insisted in complete good faith that a person who had never seen the father should blow his breath directly into the child's mouth. **1967–70** *DARE* (Qu. K47, *. . Diseases . . horses or mules commonly get*) Inf **VA43,** Hoof thrash; **MN15,** Thrash; **SC34,** Thrash in their feet; (Qu. BB25, *. . Common skin diseases around here*) Inf **KY34,** Thrash—mouth and chest. **1968** *DARE* Tape **GA30,** You have a young baby that take the thrash, you could write him a card. **1970** *NC Folkl.* 18.8, When the baby has thrash (thrush), let it drink water from the shoe of a black-eyed woman. **1986** Pederson *LAGS Concordance (Diphtheria)* 1 inf, **cwFL,** Thrash [FW: =thrush]. **2005** Williams *Gratitude* 531 **wNC** (as of 1940s), *Thrash.*

thrash n[4] [Var of *trash*]
    c1940 [see **thrash hut**]. **1959** *VT Hist.* 27.164 **nVT,** The French Canadians along the northern border of Vermont have difficulty pronouncing the *th* sound and frequently interchange it with the *tr* sounds. Heard commonly are pronunciations such as the following: Throw [tro] the trash [thrăsh] in the wastebasket. **1965–70** *DARE* (Qu. F25, *The container for kitchen parings and scraps—out of doors*) Inf **MI34,** Thrash can; (Qu. HH18, *Very insignificant or low-grade people*) Infs **IL128, NJ30, NY27, 59, PA24, WI65,** Thrash; **KY59,** White thrash; **AK8,** Dirty White thrash—said by Eskimo woman to Inf, referring to men who were trying to take advantage of her. **1968** *DARE* FW Addit **seMN,** *Thrash pail*—advertised on a store window in Red Wing.

thrash bird See **thrash** n[1]

thrasher n
    Std: any of several birds of the family Mimidae: usu those of the genus *Toxostoma,* but also **sage thrasher.** For other names of var of these see **brown thrasher, cactus thrush, desert ~, Mexican mockingbird, mockingbird 2, pretty-quick, sicklebill 2**

thrash hut n [Cf **thrash** n[4] and *DCEU trash* n[1] 2 "The dried leaves esp of the sugar-cane or banana plants used for thatching huts"]
    c1940 Eliason *Word Lists FL* 4 **nwFL,** *Thrash. . .* Built of palmetto fans. "He built himself a thrash hut close to the road."

thrashing rock See **thrash rock**

thrash machine n Also *thresh machine* **scattered, but esp Upper Missip Valley, N Cent** See Map
    A threshing machine.
    1859 Brace *Norse-Folk* 179 **CT,** They had the usual thresh-machine, turned by cattle or horses. **1905** *Newark Advocate* (OH) 14 Nov 7/3, A kind of press and thrash machine and cook stove all in one. **1915** *Adams Co. News* (Gettysburg PA) [20 Feb 3]/1 (newspaperarchive.com), [Advt:] Old thresh machine for grinding hen manure and shredding fodder. **1927** *Daily Northwestern* (Oshkosh WI) 13 Sept 4/4, John Murphy had his thumb crushed while setting up a thresh machine. **1946** *Oxnard Press–Courier* (CA) 23 Mar 5/3, [Advt:] *Farm Machinery. . .* One C.B. Hay Thrash machine. **1953** *Holland Eve. Sentinel* (MI) 23 June 15/6, [Advt:] Used Wood Bros. thresh machine. A-1 shape. **1965–70** *DARE* (Qu. L28, *Tools used in the past for cutting grain*) Inf **IN63,** Thresh machine, thrash machine; (Qu. L32a, *In early days, how was the grain separated from the straw?*) Infs **DC5, MN7, OH86, 89, UT3,** Thrash machine; (Qu. L32b, *In early days, how was the grain separated from the chaff?*) Infs **CO19, UT3,** Thrash machine; (Qu. L33, *How is the grain separated from the straw nowadays?*) Infs **IA12, 26, 39, MN4, 12, OH45,** Thrash machine. **1993** in 2005 *DARE* File—Internet **csND,** [Transcript of oral history interview:] Then in 1932, I got married and we stayed with my mother four years and I worked for her. Worked on the thresh machine. **2001** *Frederick Post* (MD) 31 Mar sec F 10/7, Auction. . . Several buggies & harness; thrash machine.

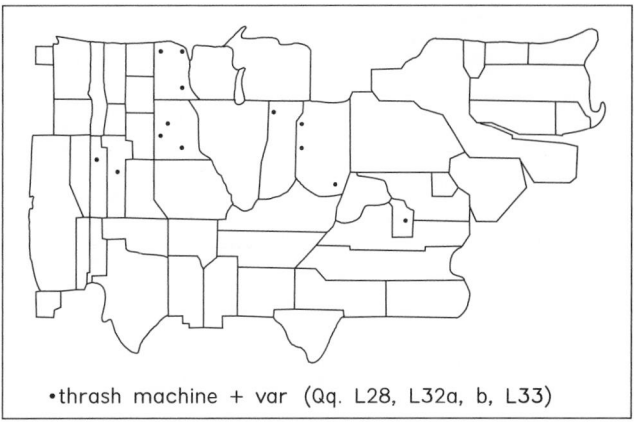

•thrash machine + var (Qq. L28, L32a, b, L33)

thrash rock n Also *thrashing rock*
    See quot 1983.
    1944 Smiley *Gloss. New Paltz* **seNY,** [He] spoke of the "thrash rock", which evidently was a large flat rock in a field. The grain was taken to it to thresh. **1969** *DARE* (Qu. L32a, *In early days, how was the grain separated from the straw?*) Inf **KY16,** Thrashing rock—bundles beat on the thrashing rock. **1983** *MJLF* 9.1.59 **ceKY** (as of 1956), *Thrash rock . .* a large, flat rock for threshing wheat. The wheat was piled on the rock where a horse trod on it.

thread and needle See **needle and thread 2**

threadfin n

1 A fish of the family Polynemidae, in the US *Polydactylus* spp. Also called **threadfish 2;** for other names of var spp see **moi**
    1882 U.S. Natl. Museum *Bulletin* 16.412, *Polynemidae. . . The Thread-fins. . .* Pectoral fins moderate, placed low, divided into two parts, the lower and anterior portion composed of several filiform articulated appendages, free from each other, organs of touch. **1903** NY State Museum & Sci. Serv. *Bulletin* 60.373, *Polydactylus octonemus . .* Threadfin. *Ibid* 374, The threadfin is found on the east coast of the United States from New York to Texas, occurring northward in summer only. **1933** LA Dept. of Conserv. *Fishes* 270, Two species of Threadfins may occur commonly in Louisiana salt water. **1960** Gosline–Brock *Hawaiian Fishes* 154, The threadfins are characterized by the divided pectoral with the upper and lower portions entirely different.

2 See **threadfin shad.**

threadfin shad n Also *threadfin*
    A **gizzard shad 1** (here: *Dorosoma petenense*).
    1955 Carr–Goin *Guide Reptiles* 44, *Dorosoma petenense . .* Florida Threadfin Shad. . . A silvery fish with the last ray of the dorsal fin very long. **1957** Blair et al. *Vertebrates U.S.* 60, Threadfin shad. . . Color silvery. **1967** Cross *Hdbk. Fishes KS* 55, The threadfin . . cannot tolerate temperatures lower than 54° F. **1983** *Audubon Field Guide N. Amer. Fishes* 384, Threadfin Shad . . occurs along coast south from Florida to Central America and in associated freshwater streams; introduced in W. United States.

threadfish n

1 A **thread herring 1** (here: *Opisthonema oglinum*).
    1842 DeKay *Zool. NY* 4.265, It [=*Opisthonema oglinum*] has also the names of *Thread Herring* and *Thread-fish,* in allusion to its last filamentous dorsal ray. **1867** De Voe *Market Asst.* 297 **NYC,** *Spotted thread herring, thread fish.*—This is rather a scarce fish, although occasionally seen here.

2 =**threadfin 1.**
    1862 Acad. Nat. Sci. Philadelphia *Proc. 1861* 40, *Trichidion plumieri* [=*Polydactylus virginicus*] . . "Thread Fish." **1873** in 1878 Smithsonian Inst. *Misc. Coll.* 14.2.23, *Trichidion plumieri. . .* Thread-fish. . . *Trichidion octofilis* [=*Polydactylus octonemus*]. . . Eight-threaded thread-fish. **1884** Goode *Fisheries U.S.* 1.279, *The Thread-fish Family—Polynemidae. . .* Remarkable by reason of the elongate filaments which are developed in connection with the pectoral fin. . . There are two or three species upon our coast, one of which . . [is] the "Thread-fish" of Pensacola [FL], *Polynemus octonemus* [=*Polydactylus o.*] **1926** Pan-Pacific Research Inst. *Jrl.* 1.8 **HI,** *Polynemidae. . . The Thread-Fishes.*

3 A fish *(Alectis ciliaris)* of Atlantic and Gulf waters, the young of which have threadlike extensions on the dorsal and anal fins. Also called **cobblerfish, shoemaker** n[1] **2, sunfish** n **2b**

1873 in 1878 *Smithsonian Inst. Misc. Coll.* 14.2.25, *Blepharichthys crinitus* [=*Alectis ciliaris*]. . . Thread-fish. Cape Cod to Florida. **1921** *Copeia* 91.9 **MA,** Rudderfishes. . . sought the protection of a threadfish *(Alectis ciliaris)* only 5 inches long. **1946** La Monte *N. Amer. Game Fishes* 42, African Pompano. . . is suspected of being the adult of another fish called the Threadfish, *Alectis ciliaris.*

threadfoot n
=**riverweed 1.**

1822 Eaton *Botany* 397, *Podostemum. . . ceratophyllum* (threadfoot . .) stem filiform, floating. . . Attached to rocks and large loose stones in shallow waters. **1861** Wood *Class-Book* 657, *Threadfoot. River Weed. . .* St[em] a few inches long, usually destitute of roots and attached to stones by lateral, fleshy processes. **1933** Small *Manual SE Flora* 584, Plant olive-green, glabrous. . . *Thread-foot.* **1950** Gray–Fernald *Manual of Botany* 731, *Threadfoot. . .* A small olive-green plant, of firm texture, resembling a Seaweed, tenaciously attached to loose stones by fleshy disks or processes in place of roots. **1970** Correll *Plants TX* 714 **OK,** *Thread-foot. . .* is extremely abundant in some sections of the Mountain Fork River in . . Oklahoma.

thread grass n
=**bear grass 1b.**

1951 *PADS* 15.29 **TX,** *Nolina* spp. . . Thread . . grass. These are employed to weave mats for household use or for burial purposes.

thread herring n
1 A fish of the genus *Opisthonema,* usu *O. oglinum.* For other names of this sp see **menhaden 2, shad herring, threadfish 1**

1842 DeKay *Zool. NY* 4.264, The Spotted Thread Herring. *Chatoessus signifer* [=*Opisthonema oglinum*]. *Ibid* [see **threadfish 1**]. **1873** in 1878 *Smithsonian Inst. Misc. Coll.* 14.2.33, *Opisthonema thrissa. . .* Thread-herring. . . Newfoundland to Florida. **1896** U.S. Bur. Fisheries *Rept. for 1895* 283, *Opisthonema. . .* Thread Herring. . . *Opisthonema oglinum. . .* Thread Herring. **1953** Roedel *Common Fishes CA* 34, Pacific Thread Herring—*Opisthonema libertate. . .* Distinguished from other California clupeoids by the extremely elongate last dorsal ray. **1983** *Audubon Field Guide N. Amer. Fishes* 384, Atlantic Thread Herring . . occurs only in saltwater from Cape Cod to Brazil, including Gulf of Mexico.

2 A **gizzard shad 1** (here: *Dorosoma cepedianum*).

1884 Goode *Fisheries U.S.* 1.610, *Dorosoma cepedianum. . .* is known . . in North Carolina as the . . "Thread Herring."

‡thread-hill plow n Cf sidehill n 2b

1966 *DARE* (Qu. L18, *Kinds of plows*) Inf **NH3,** Thread-hill plow—could plow back and forth and throw dirt all on same side.

threading the needle n Also *thread the needle*
=**needle's eye.**

1845 Felt *Annals Salem* 1.364 **MA** (as of 1762), In resuming our list, we come to puss in the corner, . . threading the needle . . walking on stilts and wrestling. **1858** *S. Lit. Messenger* Dec 429, Blind-man's buff, and threading the needle,/ Hunt the slipper, shoe the mare. **1883** Newell *Games & Songs* 91 **MA,** *Threading the Needle.* A boy and a girl, standing each on a stool, make an arch of their hands, under which an endless chain passes, until the hands are dropped, and one of the players is enclosed. The needle's eye / That doth supply / The thread that runs so true;/ Ah! many a lass / Have I let pass / Because I wanted you. **1889** Carleton *City Legends* 16 **MI,** Those games, whose names I now forget. . . Green grow the rushes, Oats peas beans and barley, Threading the needle, Jack-straws. **1907** *DN* 3.202 **seNH,** *Thread-the-needle. . .* A kissing game. Players circle under the arch formed by the outstretched arms and clasped hands of a couple standing on two chairs. The stanza is sung: "The needle's eye that doth supply / The thread that runs so true,/ It has caught many a shining lass,/ And now it has caught you." Hereupon a player is caught. The couple standing on the chairs kiss, and the prisoner relieves the player of the same sex on one of the chairs. **1912** Green *VA Folk-Speech* 445, Thread the needle. A children's play. **1939** in Lib. of Congress *Amer. Memory: WPA Life Hist.* (Internet) **Chicago IL,** [Children interviewed in a schoolyard on the subject of singing games:] *Threading the Needle.* (A boy and a girl, each standing on a stool, make an arch of their hands, under which the children in the game

pass. On the last line the hands are dropped and the two players enclosed). [First stanza:] The needle's eye / That doth supply / The thread that runs so true;/ Ah! many a lass / Have I let pass / Because I wanted you. [Second stanza:] The needle's eye / You can't pass by,/ The thread it runs so true;/ It has caught many a seemly lass,/ And now it has caught you. **1969** *DARE* (Qu. EE33, . . *Outdoor games . . that children play*) Inf **CA**142, Threading the needle. **2006** *DARE* File—Internet, *Thread the Needle. . .* Best suited for younger children. . . To play, several people stand in two rows, and each person holds hands with the player opposite her. The last pair forms an arch with their hands. Then the other players pass under the arch and re-form the two rows. The game continues at least until everyone has had a chance to form the arch—but can continue endlessly. While playing, . . chant the following: The needle's eye / That doth supply / The thread that / Runs so true;/ Ah! many a lass / Have I let past / Because I wanted you.

thread palm n
A **fan palm** (here: *Washingtonia robusta*).

1976 Bailey–Bailey *Hortus Third* 1168, [*Washingtonia*] *robusta. . . Thread palm. . .* L[ea]f blades brilliant green, . . segm[ent]s stiffer and mostly less deeply cut and less slender-pointed, bearing few or no fibers except on very young trees. **1999** *Chr. Sci. Monitor* (Boston MA) 3 Feb (Internet), *Thread palm (Washingtonia robusta):* If you have a sun room, this houseplant will make a striking addition.

thread the needle n See threading the needle

threbble See thribble

three n, adj Usu |θri|; also occas |fri, θi, tri|; for addit varr see quots Pronc-spp *free, thee, tree*
Std sense, var forms.

1853 in 1956 Eliason *Tarheel Talk* 319 **cnNC,** Thee. **1891** *DN* 1.163 **cNY,** [θi] < three. **1899** Chesnutt *Conjure Woman* 32 **csNC** [Black], It wuz th'ee er fo' year. **1901** *DN* 2.184 **neKY** [Black], Three . . free. **1930** *AmSp* 6.95 **VA,** With, three [wɪf], [fri]. **1989** Pederson *LAGS Tech. Index* 1 **Gulf Region,** Three. [Of 914 infs, 25 offered proncs of the type [tri], 8 [sri], 2 [šri], 2 [fri], 1 [θre], 1 [θi].] **1997** *DARE* File—Internet **cePA** [CoalSpeak], Tree: Number between 2 and 4. **2000** *DARE* File **nwMI,** [Pamphlet from restaurant:] Tree and a turd: One-third of ten. **2001** *Ibid* **neWI,** My relatives in Pound and Coleman Wisconsin, in Marinette County, pronounce "three" as "tree." . . My family is of German descent. **2002** Popik *Coll.* **Chicago IL,** Tree. The number between two and four.

three a cat See three old cat

three-awn n Also *three-awn(ed) grass, triple-awn, triple-awn(ed) grass*
=**needlegrass 2.**

1843 Torrey *Flora NY* 2.434, *Aristida. . .* Three-awned Grass. . . *Aristida dichotoma. . .* Dichotomous Three-awned Grass. . . Sandy fields and dry sterile hill sides; common. . . *Aristida gracilis* [=*A. longispica*]. . . Slender Three-awned Grass. . . It never occurs except in the poorest lands. **1848** Gray *Manual of Botany* 584, *Aristida. . .* Triple-awned Grass. . . Lower palea tipped with a triple awn. **1937** U.S. Forest Serv. *Range Plant Hdbk.* G16, Three-awns . . are widely distributed throughout the Western States, being especially well represented in the Southwest. **1946** Reeves–Bain *Flora TX* 50, Aristida. . . Triple-awn Grass. *Ibid* 51, *A. oligantha. . .* Prairie Three-awn. **1963** IL Nat. Hist. Surv. *Biol. Notes* 50.11 **IL,** The prairie . . possesses sizable blowouts. . . These blowouts tend to be stabilized by . . three species of three-awn grass. **1968** Barkley *Plants KS* 38, *Aristida ramosissima. . .* Triple-awn. S. Curve Three Awn. Dry prairies. **2001** *DARE* File—Internet **TX,** Bluestem, three-awn, and grama grass often are found in the shade of the oaks.

three-bird(s) orchid n Also *three birds*
An orchid *(Triphora trianthophora)* native to much of the eastern half of the US. Also called **little-bird orchid**

1900 Lyons *Plant Names* 297, *P[ogonia] trianthophora* [=*Triphora t.*]. . Eastern U.S. . . Three-birds. **1901** Lounsberry *S. Wild Flowers* 84, So quaint and dainty are these blossoms that . . the . . mountaineers through the Alleghanies. . . call the plant, "the three birds." **1933** Small *Manual SE Flora* 378, Three-birds. . . Rich woods, various provinces, rarely Coastal Plain. Fla. to Kans., Wis., and Me. **1968** Radford et al. *Manual Flora Carolinas* 341, *T[riphora] trianthophora. . .* Three Birds Orchid. . . Inflorescence composed of 1–6 (usually 3) flowers. . . Flowers pale pink to almost white, veined or suffused with purple and green. **1979** Wellman *Old Gods* 2 **sAppalachians,** Under some pines, pouchy and pink moccasin flower and three-bird orchids, red and white with a white gape like the mouths of baby birds. **1987** Case *Orchids* 147 **wGt Lakes,** One of their rare finds . . was the three birds orchid . . in a low mixed woodland with much American beech.

three-card monte n
Std sense, var forms.

1 *three-card molly* (or *mollie*). *chiefly among Black speakers*

1947 *Charleroi Mail* (PA) 29 Aug 1/7, "Three card Molly" . . returned to the district with many persons falling victims. . . State and district police are conducting an investigation after five Negroes were reported to have "stripped" victims near Brownsville. **1965** Brown *Manchild* 156 **Harlem NYC** [Black], He showed me the trick in three-card mollie. I used to always think that the trick was to keep your eye on the card. But Reno showed me that I couldn't possibly beat three-card mollie, nor could anybody else, because the card was never there. You had to palm the card. **1966** *DARE* (Qu. DD35, . . *Card games*) Inf **FL1,** Three-card molly. [Inf Black] **1966** *DARE* Tape **AL**13 [Black], You all ever played catch a three-card molly? . . You take two black cards and put 'em on and have a red card and the one who gets the red card is the lucky. . . You take three cards and you take 'em and throw 'em like this and you have your red card in the middle and you 'tend to pull a card, you . . 'tend to pull the red card and that's the lucky card. . . They keep betting on that. **1980** *Eve. Capital* (Annapolis MD) 5 Sept 13/6, The musical imagination of modern jazz pioneer Elvin Jones is explored by focusing on a single composition, 'Three Card Molly'. [*DARE* Ed: Jones is Black.] **1994** *Capital* (Annapolis MD) 7 Apr sec A 12/2, *State workers.* . . We know that we're playing against a stacked deck. We know that we're being victimized in a slick game of three-card molly. **1998** in 2005 *DARE* File—Internet [Black], [From the album *40 Dayz & 40 Nightz* by Xzibit:] 3 Card Molly. . . pick a card any card, I bet you can't pull it . . golden state, number one with a bullet . . it's three card molly.

2 *three-card mounty.*
1967 *DARE* (Qu. DD35, . . *Card games*) Inf **MN2,** Three-card mounty. **2004** *DARE* File—Internet, I like to party with the babes, cruisin' craves, play three card mounty on crazy streets.

three-cornered britches See **three-corner(ed) pants**

three-cornered cactus n
=**night-blooming cereus.**
1896 *Jrl. Amer. Folkl.* 9.188 **AZ,** *Cereus Greggii,* . . three-cornered cactus.

three-cornered cat n Cf **four-cornered cat, two-cornered ~**
=**three old cat.**
1866 in 1946 *Council Bluffs Nonpareil* (IA) [23 June 14]/1 (newspaperarchive.com), When we stated the other day that we were unacquainted with the kind of game which the boys call baseball, we erred greviously [sic]. Little did we know when we wrote that baseball is but another name for two-cornered or three-cornered or four-cornered cat. **1888** *Cosmopolitan* 5.443, "One-cornered cat" . . was, therefore, forced to give way to a further development called "three-cornered cat," which in turn was followed by "four-cornered cat," and from this finally was developed the primitive "base-ball." **1890** Howells *Boy's Town* 83 **sOH,** Three-cornered cat was, I believe, the game which has since grown into baseball, and was even then sometimes called so. **1917** Baldwin *Making of a Township* 391 **ceIN** (as of 1860s), The games played at school in those days were "three-cornered cat" [etc]. **1940** Kennedy–Harlow *Schoolmaster* 228 **IN,** When this game [=two-cornered cat] was enlarged by the appearance of more players to Three- or Four-cornered Cat, it resembled Town Ball in some respects. In each, the runner could be either touched or crossed out; in each a batter could be retired either on a fly or first bounce, and a ball could be knocked in any direction; there were no fouls. **1966–68** *DARE* [(Qu. J5, *A cat with fur of mixed colors*) Inf **NH**14, Three-cornered cat—meaning three-colored;] (Qu. EE11, *Bat-and-ball games for just a few players*) Inf **AR**39, Three-cornered cat.

three-cornered fly n Also *triangle fly*
A **deerfly 1** (here: *Chrysops* spp).
1966–69 *DARE* (Qu. R12, . . *Other kinds of flies*) Inf **IN**3, Three-cornered fly; **ME**20, Deer fly—also called three-cornered fly by older folks; **MA**37, Three-cornered fly—a yellow fly, they bite like the devil; **VT**13, Three-cornered fly or triangle fly—one-half inch, light-colored, bites. [**2002** *DARE* File—Internet **Canada,** When we got there the ranch man person dude was telling us about this triangle fly aka a horsefly that can

eat us and suck our blood.] **2003** *Ibid* **ceVA,** Yet even here, among the swampside Endicott roses and the territorial triangle flies . . we find life!

three-cornered grass n **LA** Cf **three-square**
A bulrush such as *Schoenoplectus americanus* or *S. robustus.*
1921 LA Dept. of Conserv. *Bulletin* 10.35 **LA,** If an examination shows deer tracks, one may be sure that the ground has been turned by deer with their sharp hoofs to get the tender roots of the saw-grass and the goose grass (three-cornered grass, or three-square), of which they are very fond. **1933** *Torreya* 33.82 **swLA,** *Scirpus americanus* [= *Schoenoplectus a.*] . . *Scirpus olneyi* [=*Schoenoplectus americanus*]. . . Three-cornered grass. **1942** *Ibid* 42.158 **LA,** *Scirpus robustus* [= *Schoenoplectus r.*] . . Three-cornered grass. **1979** Hallowell *People Bayou* 50 **sLA,** Someone examined the muskrats' diet and discovered that their favorite food was three-cornered grass, a common marsh species named for the triangular shape of its blades. **1986** Pederson *LAGS Concordance (Marshes)* 1 inf, **nwLA,** Three-cornered grass—tall, in marshes.

three-corner(ed) pants n pl, also sg in constr Also *three-cornered britches,* ~ *panties*
Diapers, a diaper.
1933 *QST* 22.59, Some were active in radio before W2GTW wore three-cornered pants. **1935** *Chron.–Telegram* (Elyria OH) 15 Aug 13/1 **GA,** [*Back Home Again* cartoon:] That was before I knew the minute a blonde got near you you'd turn handsprings, do cart-wheels . . an' act like you were still in three-cornered pants! **1938** Berger *Bowleg Bill* 148 **NEast,** You think that because you ain't out o' yer three-cornered pants long enough to know better. **1949** *Edwardsville Intelligencer* (IL) 27 Apr 13/8, *Inventor Perfects Overnight Diaper.* . . A wealthy Cleveland inventor . . has come up with something new in three-cornered pants. **1951** *Sheboygan Press* (WI) 24 Aug 9/3, Gen. Mark Clark sent the four stars he wore in World War II to a 20 day-old namesake here yesterday, but warned they "might scratch" if used to hold up three-corner pants. **1965–70** *DARE* (Qu. W19, *Names and nicknames for the folded cloth worn by a baby in place of pants*) 18 Infs, **scattered,** Three-corner(ed) pants; **RI**12, Three-cornered britches; **MI**23, Three-cornered panties. **2005** *DARE* File—Internet **ID,** Mitch is a native Idahoan, born in Boise, but moved to Emmett while still in three cornered pants.

three-decker n, also attrib Also *triple-decker* **NEng, esp c,eMA**
A three-story dwelling with one apartment occupying each floor.
1899 MA Medico-Legal Soc. *Trans.* 3.344 **ceMA,** He owned a three-decker house and occupied the lower apartment with his wife. **1905** *Fitchburg Daily Sentinel* (MA) 28 Apr 5/4, A.L. Walker has sold . . a building lot on Cottage street . . to George A. Peck, who will erect a three-decker on the same. **1925** *Fitchburg Sentinel* (MA) 10 Nov 13/8, *South Side*—Three-decker, six-room flats, two-stall garage. Home and investment. **1941** *LANE* Map 355 (*Tenement*) 1 inf, **cMA,** Three decker—a three-story house for three families. **1949** *Portland Sun. Telegram & Sun. Press Herald* (ME) 18 Sept sec A 2/5 **neMA,** Police said [they] . . hid out . . in a three-decker tenement block close to the county jail. **1961** Mumford *City in Hist.* 465 **NEng,** Vast wooden firetraps called three-deckers in New England, happily blessed with open air porches. **1974** *Newport Daily News* (RI) 25 Sept 28/3 **Boston MA,** Residents sat on the stoops of their three-decker houses. **c1975** *DARE* File **NEng,** Three-decker: Houses made up of three flats, one on each floor, are called three-deckers in New England. They usually have a front porch . . on each floor. There are many of these in the Worcester MA area. **1999** *DARE* File—Internet [Boston Online *Wicked Good Guide to Boston English*], *Three-decker*—Originating in Worcester, this quickly became a staple of Boston residential architecture: a narrow, three-story house, in which each floor is a separate apartment. Sometimes also called "triple decker." In Dorchester, though, they'll tell you that "triple decker" is a Yuppie affectation; but in Winthrop, that's what everybody calls them. **2005** *DARE* File **Providence RI** (as of 1950s), Triple-decker was common for a three story apartment house. I never heard three-decker. **2006** *Ibid* **nwMA,** Triple-deckers. Three story tenements. Squarish boxy buildings, identical apartments one above the other. . . They had those in North Adams, Lewiston [ME], Lowell, Lawrence and in all the mill towns.

three-deer n [Echoic]
The olive-sided **flycatcher 1a** (*Contopus cooperi*).
1925 (1928) Forbush *Birds MA* 2.344, *Nuttallornis borealis.* . . *Three-deer; pitch-pine flycatcher.* . . *Voice.*—A two-syllabled call supposed to

resemble the words *three-deer* or *three cheers,* or a three syllabled call *"tuck three beers."*

three dot See **three horn**

three-eyed cat n Also *three-eyed kitten* Cf **one-eyed cat 1** =**three old cat.**

1968 *DARE* (Qu. EE11, *Bat-and-ball games for just a few players [when there aren't enough for a regular game]*) Inf **IN**39, One-eyed cat, two-eyed cat, three-eyed cat. **1969** *DARE* Tape **GA**84, We had one baseball game called three-eyed kitten that we played. . . You had a pitcher and a batter and a catcher. . . He threw the ball and you swung at it so many times, you were out, . . and if the ball bounced and the catcher caught it on the first bounce, you were out. **1996** Williams *Joyful Trek* 81 **TX,** About 1905 in Abilene I found that a ten-or-twelve-acre pasture immediately behind our lot was not patrolled by the sheriff at all. Some boys were out there playing three-eyed cat.

three-faces-under-a-hood n [Brit dial] Note: It is doubtful that this name was ever in popular use in this country.

A **johnny-jump-up 1** (here: *Viola tricolor*).

1835 *Amer. Gardener's Mag.* 1.21, It has been called, in addition to the names already given, *Love in Idleness, Live in Idleness, Call me to you, Three faces under a Hood, Herb Trinity, Flower of Jove, Ladies' Delight, Sparkler, Flamy,* with many others. **1867** *New Engl. Farmer* 1.292, The plant is really a violet, and is sometimes called the *tri-colored* violet. It also bears the names herb-trinity, three-faces-under-a-hood, ladies'-delight, kit-run-about, and heart's-ease.

three feet off to Germany See **Germany**

three-fingered doughnut n

1976 *DARE* File **cnMA** (as of c1915), Three-fingered doughnuts, made by his mother, with dough less sweet than regular (i.e., made with eggs, not yeast) doughnuts, in the shape of a three-fingered hand; the fingers are intended to be broken off and dipped in maple syrup, preferably warm.

three-finger poi See **one-finger poi**

three flies up n Also *three flies (in);* for addit varr see quots Cf **flies and grounders, ~ skinners, fly-up** n

A bat-and-ball game in which a fielder who successfully catches three fly balls becomes the batter; rarely, a similar game in which a ball is kicked.

[**1898** Shivell *Ashes* 83, Choose up sides, er one o' cat,/ Tap flies,— hyere, gimme the bat!/ Scatter out there, fur's you kin—/ Watch your business—three flies in!] **1957** *Sat. Eve. Post Letters* **Chicago IL,** "Three flies or six grounders" was a game where a batter hits balls to fielders and the first one to achieve either the flies or grounders was the batter. [*Ibid* **eCanada,** 3 flies, you're up (baseball).] **1967–68** *DARE* (Qu. EE11, *Bat-and-ball games for just a few players [when there aren't enough for a regular game]*) Inf **CA**32, Three-flies-and-you're-up—catch three flies and you become batter; **LA**23, Three flies in—when you caught three flies, you got to go to bat. **1967** *DARE* Tape **CA**68A, We play three flies up. . . Well, you get a kickball. . . I think there's three or four people out, trying to catch the ball, and then there's pitcher. Then he kicks it. . . [**CA**68:] Whoever catches it three times gets to be up. **1970** Lebofsky *Lexicon Philadelphia* 205, *Three flies* . . round robin game of baseball in which whoever accumulates a certain number of catches bats next. **2001** *San Diego Union–Tribune* (CA) 2 Sept sec C 1 (Internet), We played pickup baseball. . . When there weren't enough of us, we played three-flies-up. **2002** *DARE* File—Internet **FL,** In addition to hide-n-seek, we would play three flies in, baseball, kickball, and capture the flag. **2005** *Ibid* **CA,** We met two little girls who played three flies up with us.

three-foot n Pl *three-foot(s)* [Calque of PaGer *Dreifuss*] **PA**

A three-footed stand for a large kettle.

1893 *Star & Sentinel* (Gettysburg PA) 21 Mar 1/1, [Advt:] Copper Kettle, Coal Oil Stove three-foot, Table 8 feet long [etc]. **1913** *Gettysburg Times* (PA) [15 Mar 3]/1 (newspaperarchive.com), [Advt:] Pots and pans, brass kettle, iron kettle 2 three foot, 2 large parlor lamps. **1916** *Star & Sentinel* (Gettysburg PA) 26 Feb 4/6, [Advt:] 2 iron kettles and three-foots. **1965** *New Oxford Item* (PA) 25 Mar 2/8, [Advt:] 4 iron kettles with three foots. **1973** *Gettysburg Times* (PA) 22 June 11/2, [Advt:] Iron kettles and three foots. **1982** *Barrick Coll.* **csPA,** Three-foot—tripod, esp. used to hold kettles at butcherings. pl. *three-foots.*

three-foot plow See **foot** n **C3**

three-foots See **three-foot**

three-hole(d) cat n Cf **hold** n **B2** =**three old cat.**

1847 *Dwight's Amer. Mag.* 3.642, In the first of these [=Roman ball games] were three players, who stood in a triangle, as in the game of "three-hole cat." **1883** [see **three old cat**]. **1894** *Century Illustr. Mag.* 47.854 **IN,** There is a game of ball played with bats called simply "cat"—sometimes "two-hole cat," "three-hole cat," and so on; or, "two old cat," "three old cat," in the East, according to the number of holes, or bases. **1912** *Oakland Tribune* (CA) 29 May 14/3, Professor W.E. MacLaughlin, who is some ball player himself, figures on changing the game into "three-hole-cat" for the benefit of the seniors, but when he learned . . that the high school lady teachers wished to whale the life out of the seniors with a baseball bat instead of with the usual ruler or strap, he withdrew his "three-hole-cat" idea. **1912** *DN* 3.568 **seNY,** One-old-cat. . . Called *three-holed* on Long Island. **1950** *WELS* (Bat-and-ball games for a few players [when you don't have enough for a regular game]) 1 Inf, **ceWI,** Three-hole cat.

three-holer See **-holer**

three-holes See **hole** n **4**

three horn n Also *threehorn(ed) wartyback, three dot, ~ knot*

A **freshwater clam** (here: *Obliquaria reflexa*).

1941 *AmSp* 16.156, There is . . a three horned warty-back. **1982** U.S. Fish & Wildlife Serv. *Fresh-Water Mussels* [Wall chart], Threehorn . . *Obliquaria reflexa.* . . Each valve has a radial row of several (usually three) large, rounded tubercles ("horns") that alternate with those on the opposite valve. **1992** Cummings–Mayer *Field Guide Freshwater Mussels MW* 100, Threehorn wartyback . . *Other common names*—Hornyback, three dot, three knot.

three hundred n Cf **five hundred 2**

1967 *DARE* (Qu. EE11, *Bat-and-ball games for just a few players [when there aren't enough for a regular game]*) Inf **CO**47, Three hundred—100 fly, 75 first bounce, 50 second bounce, 25 grounder.

‡**three-kitten-mitten** n Cf **kittenball, mitten-kitten,** *three-eyed kitten* (at **three-eyed cat**)

1969 *DARE* (Qu. EE11, *Bat-and-ball games for just a few players [when there aren't enough for a regular game]*) Inf **GA**86, Three-kitten-mitten.

three knot See **three horn**

three-leaf(ed ivy) See **three-leaved ivy**

three-leafed sumac See **threeleaf sumac**

threeleaf hop tree See **three-leaved hop tree**

three-leaf ivy (or poison vine) See **three-leaved ivy**

threeleaf sumac n Also *three-leafed sumac, three-leaved ~* Cf **three-lobed sumac**

A **sumac B:** usu *Rhus trilobata,* but also **fragrant sumac.**

1900 Evans–Stivers *Hist. Adams Co. OH* 14, I made a catalogue of what I saw there. . . Red oak, . . three-leaved sumac [etc]. **1904** NM Ag. Exper. Station *Bulletin* 51.27, Three-leaved Sumac. (*Rhus trilobata*). **1947** (1976) Curtin *Healing Herbs* 112, Rhus trilobata. . . Coahuilla Indians. . . gave a deep black color to the strands of the three-leaf sumac by soaking them for about a week in an infusion of the berry stems of the elder. **1957** Jaeger *N. Amer. Deserts* 37, The most noticeable large plant of the almost snow-white dunes is the vigorously growing, aromatic three-leafed sumac (*Rhus trilobata*), a shrub that is widespread in desert lands. **1990** *Plants SW* (Catalog) 71, *Rhus trilobata*—Three-Leaf Sumac. . . Tart, red berries are used to make a lemon-flavored drink. Attractive to birds.

three-leaved hop tree n Also *threeleaf hop tree*

A **hop tree** (here: *Ptelea trifoliata*).

1900 Lyons *Plant Names* 309, *P[telea] trifoliata.* . . Three-leaved Hop-tree. **1930** OK Univ. Biol. Surv. *Pub.* 2.69, *Ptelea trifoliata.* . . Three-leaved Hop-tree. **1960** Vines *Trees SW* 593, *Ptelea trifoliata.* . . Vernacular names are Three-leaf Hop-tree [etc].

three-leaved ivy n Also *three-leaf (ivy), ~ poison vine, three-leafed ivy, three-point ~, three-leaved poison ivy*

A **poison ivy 1** (here: *Toxicodendron* spp).

1871 *Our Young Folks* 7.687, The three-leaved ivy threatened to kiss our cheeks with poisonous touch. **1898** U.S. Dept. Ag. Div. Botany

Bulletin 20.35, *Poison Ivy. Rhus radicans* [=*Toxicodendron r.*] . . *Other names:* Poison oak; poison vine; three-leafed ivy; poison creeper. **1938** FWP *Guide CT* 13, The three-leaved poison ivy, often called mercury, should be avoided. **1960** Vines *Trees SW* 641, *Toxicodendron radicans.* . . Also known under the vernacular names of Three-leaf Ivy [etc]. **1966** Dakin *Dial. Vocab. Ohio R. Valley* 2.411 **IL,** *Poison ivy.* . . Miscellaneous usages include . . *three point ivy* in . . Edwards County. **1968** *DARE* (Qu. S16, *A three-leaved plant that grows in woods and countryside and makes people's skin itch and swell*) Inf **PA**70, Three-leafed ivy. **1986** Pederson *LAGS Concordance,* 1 inf, **csLA,** Three-leaf, poison; 1 inf, **neTN,** Three-leaf poison vine—not as bad as five-leaf; 1 inf, **neTN,** Three-leaf poison vine; 1 inf, **neTN,** Three-leaf poison vine = poison ivy.

three-leaved maple n
=**box elder.**

1897 Sudworth *Arborescent Flora* 291 **PA,** *Acer negundo.* . . Three-leaved Maple. **1936** *Torreya* 36.79 **NY,** Only the three-leaved maple is strictly wind pollinated. **1950** Moore *Trees AR* 95, *Boxelder.* . . Local Names . . Three Leaved Maple.

three-leaved nightshade n   Cf **nightshade 2**
=**trillium.**

1794 Forsyth *Bot. Nomenclator* sig Y2[r], Trillium—Three-leaved Nightshade—North America. **1837** Darlington *Flora Cestrica* 235 **sePA,** *T[rillium] pendulum* . . Vulgo—Three-leaved Nightshade. **1843** Torrey *Flora NY* 2.295, *Trillium.* . . Three-leaved Nightshade. . . *Trillium erythrocarpum* . . Red-berried Three-leaved Nightshade. . . *Trillium cernuum* . . Nodding Three-leaved Nightshade. **1922** *Clearfield Progress* (PA) 20 Feb 5/3, A variety of trillium is called squaw-flower. It is also called bath-flower, birth-root and three-leaved nightshade. **1949** Moldenke *Amer. Wild Flowers* 338, Because of this very conspicuous arrangement of all their organs in 3's or multiples thereof, these plants [=*Trillium* spp] are often known as *three-leaved nightshades, herb-trinity,* or *trinitylilies.* **1971** Krochmal *Appalachia Med. Plants* 256, *Trillium Erectum* . . three-leaved nightshade.

three-leaved poison ivy   See **three-leaved ivy**

three-leaved sumac   See **threeleaf sumac**

three-lobed sumac n
Any of var western **sumacs B;** see quots.

1914 *Amer. Naturalist* 48.419, The leaf-beetle *Blepharida* . . [eats only] leaves of the three-lobed sumac. **1931** U.S. Dept. Ag. *Misc. Pub.* 101.96, The most valuable of the sumacs from a forage viewpoint are the . . three-lobed sumacs, of which about six or eight valid species occur in the West. **1937** U.S. Forest Serv. *Range Plant Hdbk.* B129, Six or eight species [of *Rhus*] . ., of which skunkbush . . is the most familiar example, occur in the West. These shrubs have divided (compound) leaves with mostly three leaflets, and the group as a whole fairly closely resembles *R[hus] trilobata* . ., the commonest and most widely distributed species. They are known by various vernacular names, including . . three-lobed sumacs. **2001** McGreevy *Ind. Basketry* 37 **SW,** Before the twentieth century, Jicarilla utilitarian baskets were frequently made of natural willow or three-lobed sumac splints.

three o cat   See **three old cat**

three o'clock (at the button factory), it's   See **one o'clock, it's**

three-off-the-curb n
A variation of the children's game **giant steps.**

1957 *Sat. Eve. Post Letters* **cWV** (as of c1917), "Three Off the Curb" . . was always played . . from curb to opposite curb of the street. . . It was a "tag" game. . . The "it" stood in the middle of the street and gave the "go" signal. All the players took three running steps off the curb and stopped. Then the "it" directed each player to take three more steps of "Lady Steps, Baby Steps or Giant Steps." . . Once moving after that, they had to try for the goal. When all were either "in free" or tagged . . the "it" was next counted out from among the "tagged" ones.

three old cat n   Also *three a cat, ~ o cat;* for addit varr see quots   **chiefly Nth**   See Map   Also called **three-cornered cat, three-eyed ~, three-hole(d) ~**
A variation, involving more players, of the bat-and-ball game **one old cat 1.**

1871 *Galaxy* 12.114, The base-ball season has come again. . . If we, inspired by memories of "Three-old-cat," . . should undertake to wield

the bat-stick with some of yonder toddlers, the little blackguards would cry out "butterfingers!" **1883** Eggleston *Hoosier Schoolboy* 12 **IN,** "Four old cat," "two old cat," and "five old cat" are . . played the same way, the number of bases or holes increasing with the addition of each pair of players. It is probable that the game was once—some hundreds of years ago, maybe—called "three hole catch," and that the name was gradually corrupted into "three hole cat," as it is still called in the interior States, and then became changed by mistake to "three old cat." **1907** *DN* 3.195 **seNH,** *Old cat.* . . A simple game of ball with two, three, or four players; hence called *two old cat, three old cat,* and *four old cat* respectively. **1908** *DN* 3.297 **eAL, wGA,** *Cat, one (two, or three) ole.* . . A ball game in which the batters stand at one, (two, or three) points or holes. **1911** Spalding *America's Natl. Game* 35, "What's the matter with having a three-cornered game? then we all can play." The game is tried three-cornered. It works all right, and Three Old Cat, with Six Boys, Three Bats, Three Bases and a Ball has added another step in the evolution of our American game. **1950** *WELS* (*Bat-and-ball games for a few players [when you don't have enough for a regular game]*) 2 Infs, **WI,** Three old cat; 1 Inf, **nwWI,** Three old cat—has three players. **1957** *Sat. Eve. Post Letters* **MA,** [In a list of games played as a child:] 3-o-Cat. *Ibid* **NE,** In S.E. Nebraska, 1900–10, we played . . "One, Two or Three Old Cat" depending on how many bases beside home plate. **1965–70** *DARE* (Qu. EE11, *Bat-and-ball games for just a few players [when there aren't enough for a regular game]*) Infs **AK**5, **CT**6, **MA**38, 100, **NY**219, Three old cat; **MA**24, Three old cat—had only one base; **CA**105, Three old cat my knocks—"my knocks" means he gets to bat first if he says "my knocks" first; **ME**5, Three old cats—just had one base; **CT**3, **WY**5, Three a cat; **CT**9, **MT**3, Three o cat [10 of 12 Infs old]; [**SC**24, Three cat and a bat]. **1982** *Greenfield Recorder* (MA) 22 Apr sec A 4, Some lucky boy might have a ball made of very tightly-wound discarded wool yarn, . . and a whittled down stick for a bat to play "three old cat."

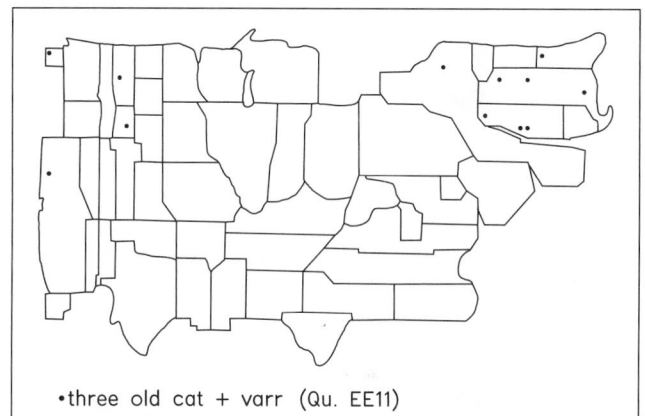

•three old cat + varr (Qu. EE11)

three old cats n
1   See **old cat 1.**
2   See **three old cat.**

three outs n
A game similar to **stoopball** and **off-the-point.**

1995 *DARE* File **Chicago IL,** We played a similar game [to "off the corner"] on the southside of Chicago in the late '40s and early '50s. I think we simply called it "Three Outs." It was meant to simulate a baseball game, and anywhere from two to x number of players could participate, though we usually reserved it for the times when only a few could play. We used a soft rubber ball, the exact equivalent of the inner core of a baseball. . . One threw the ball at a cement ledge which lined the lower portion of the school wall. If any other player caught it, one was out—three outs per inning, nine in a game. If the other player failed to catch it, the "batter" would run the bases—pieces of cardboard or any other available debris which was placed on the ground in advance in simulation of a base path. After an inning, the other "side" was up. As I recall, the point of winning was to avoid getting punched in the arm three times; this was the penalty enacted.

three-point ivy   See **three-leaved ivy**

three-ridge n
A **freshwater clam:** usu *Amblema plicata,* but also *A. costata.* Also called **bluepoint 2**

1908 Kunz–Stevenson *Book of the Pearl* 72 **Upper Missip Valley,**

Two species of Unios, *Quadrula undulata* [=*Amblema costata*] and *Q. plicata* [=*A.p.*], are known among the fishermen as "three-ridges." **1966** *WI Conserv. Bulletin* 31.3.27, By far the most important mussel is the three-ridge or bluepoint. . . These names, which have evolved over the years among local fishermen, are fairly descriptive of the clam itself—if you use a little imagination. **1982** *U.S. Fish & Wildlife Serv. Fresh-Water Mussels* [Wall chart], *Threeridge—Amblema plicata. . . Adult shell with several (usually three) wide, low ridges. . . Three-ridge. . .* One of the two most abundant Upper Mississippi River mussels. **1992** Cummings–Mayer *Field Guide Freshwater Mussels MW* 40, *Threeridge . . Other common names*—Blue-point, purple-tip, fluter.

three-seeded mercury n   Also *three-seed mercury*
A plant of the genus *Acalypha,* esp *A. virginica.*   Also called **copperleaf, couple-cap, mercury weed, tarweed 3;** for other names of var spp see **Jacob's coat**

1814 Bigelow *Florula Bostoniensis* 236, Acalypha Virginica. . . *Three-seeded Mercury.* **1832** *MA Hist. Soc. Coll.* 2d ser 9.146 **cwVT,** Acalypha virginica, . . Three-seed mercury. **1848** Gray *Manual of Botany* 407, *Acalypha. . . Three-seeded Mercury. . .* Pod separating into 3 globular carpels which split into 2 valves. **1869** Porcher *Resources* 145, *Three Seeded Mercury, (Acalypha Virginica . .).* Employed . . successfully in cases of humid asthma, ascites and anasarca. **1923** Davidson–Moxley *Flora S. CA* 221, *Three-seeded Mercury. . .* Fruit a 3-celled, 3-seeded capsule. **1936** IL Nat. Hist. Surv. *Wildflowers* 181, The Three-seeded Mercury, *Acalypha virginica . . ,* is . . common in fields and waste places. . . The plant ranges from Nova Scotia to Minnesota, south to Florida and Texas. **1975** *Chron.–Telegram* (Elyria OH) 19 Jan 10/5, Korschgen is . . probably the nation's leading authority on what wild animals eat. . . Next to grapes, Korschgen found Korean lespedeza 9.7 per cent, . . three-seeded mercury 2.1.

three sisters n
=**trillium.**

c1938 in 1970 Hyatt *Hoodoo* 2.1128 **seGA** [Black], We got anothah one heah dey calls de *Three Sisters. . .* We put dem three *roots* together, de *Daddy Graybeard, Indian Herb* an' *Three Sisters.* We put dem three *roots* together—we puts a name on dere. **1940** Steyermark *Flora MO* 78, *Wake Robin, Three Sisters* (Trillium).

three-square n   Also *three-square (bul)rush*   [*OED2* *three-square* a. "Having three equal sides"; c1440 →]   Cf **three-cornered grass**
A bulrush, usu *Schoenoplectus americanus* or *S. robustus.*

[**1766** (1942) Bartram *Diary of a Journey* 47 **PA,** We then soon came to Forbes's bluff, where grows a good sort of rush to bottom chairs with, or make matts, much better than the common bull-rush or the three-square ones.] **1819** in 1826 *Amer. Farmer* 8.186 **NJ,** From thence up the [Delaware] river, (the water being fresh,) grow the bull rush, three square, . . and the water lily. **1889** *AN&Q* 3.255 **Cape May NJ,** The coarse 'three square,' the noted grass with the odd name, is cut in 'winrows' or rows through which the wind may blow. **1894** *DN* 1.334 **sNJ,** Three-square: a kind of grass found on . . meadows. **1914** *Bot. Gaz.* 58.471, The plants . . would stand in order of evaporating power thus: pickerel-weed:cat-tail:arrow-head:great bulrush:three-square rush:water lily. **1921** [see **three-cornered grass**]. **1950** Stevens *ND Plants* 90, *Scirpus americanus* [=*Schoenoplectus a.*] . . *Chairmakers Rush. Three Square. . .* One of the commonest species, often forming beds along pond margins. **1973** Hitchcock–Cronquist *Flora Pacific NW* 601, Three-square b[ulrush]. . . *S[cirpus] americanus.* **1999** in 2001 *DARE* File—Internet **FL,** *Scirpus pungens* [*Scirpus americanus*]—Three-square bulrush. Three-square might first be encountered as a stand of dark-green triangular stems growing in the mud of a lake shore.

three-step n   [*OED2* 1909]   **chiefly Gt Lakes, NW, CA**   See Map
A dance or dance step done to a three-count rhythm; see quots.

[**1919** 'Monsieur Pierre' *How to Jazz* 7 *(OED2),* The Jazz is a three-step dance done to four-beat time.] **1939** in Lib. of Congress *Amer. Memory: WPA Life Hist.* (Internet) **OR** (as of c1900), As for dances. . . the Old Square Schottische . . was a three-step. **1965–70** *DARE* (Qu. FF5a, . . *Different steps and figures in dancing—in past years*) 24 Infs, **chiefly Gt Lakes, NW, CA,** Three-step. **2004** *DARE* File—Internet, Most people call C&W dancing two-step, no matter what dance they're actually doing. But most people are really doing a three-step. *Ibid* **CA,** The "Three Step" you refer to. . . around here is the Triple Step, otherwise known in some countries as the Polka.

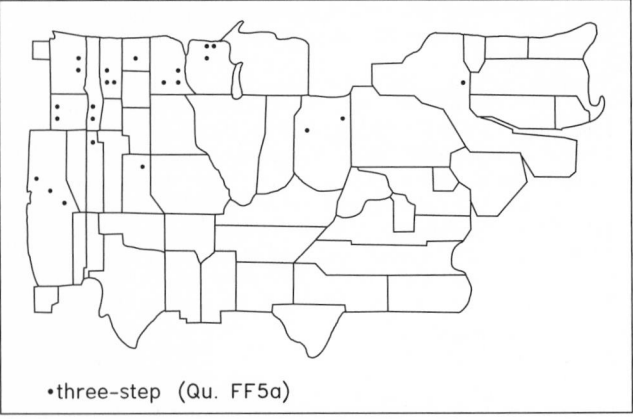

•three-step (Qu. FF5a)

three steps to Germany   See **Germany**

three-teater   See **three-titter**

three-thorned acacia n   Also *triple-thorned acacia*
=**honey locust 1.**

1785 Marshall *Arbustrum* 54, *Triple-thorned Acacia, or Honey Locust. . .* The pods, from the sweetness of their pulp, are used to brew in beer. **1884** Sargent *Forests of N. Amer.* 59, *Gleditschia triacanthos. . . Three-thorned Acacia. . .* The characteristic tree of the "barrens" of middle Kentucky and Tennessee. **1897** Sudworth *Arborescent Flora* 254, *Gleditschia triacanthos. . .* Three-thorned Acacia (Mass., R.I., La., Tex., Mich., Ont., Nebr.) **1950** Peattie *Nat. Hist. Trees* 403, *Three-thorned Acacia. . . Twigs . . thornless or beset by simple or branched thorns.* **1960** Vines *Trees SW* 532, *Gleditschia triacanthos. . .* The species name, *triacanthos,* refers to the commonly 3-branched thorns. Other vernacular names are . . Thorny locust, Three-thorned-acacia, and Sweet-bean.

three-titter n, also attrib   Also *three-teater*   **scattered, but chiefly Nth, Midl**   See Map   *esp freq among men*
A cow with three functioning teats.

1896 *Jrl. Compar. Med. & Vet. Archives* 17.818 **PA,** Made good recovery, except being a "three teater." **1916** *Grand Rapids Tribune* (WI Rapids WI) 3 May 8/1, Five of them were heifers and one other was a three teater. **1937** *AmSp* 12.103 **eNE** [Farm terms], If she [=a cow] has lost the use of a teat she is called a *three-titter.* **1950** *WELS* **WI** (If one quarter of a cow's udder does not give milk, you say she is _____) 26 Infs, [A] three-teater; 10 Infs, [A] three-titter. **1965–70** *DARE* (Qu. K9) 196 Infs, **scattered, but chiefly Nth, Midl,** Three-titter (cow). [Of all Infs responding to the question, 65% were male; of those giving these responses, 77% were male.] **2001** *DARE* File—Internet **VT,** Not all our treatments have been totally successful. I have come to accept the reality of a few "three teater" cows.

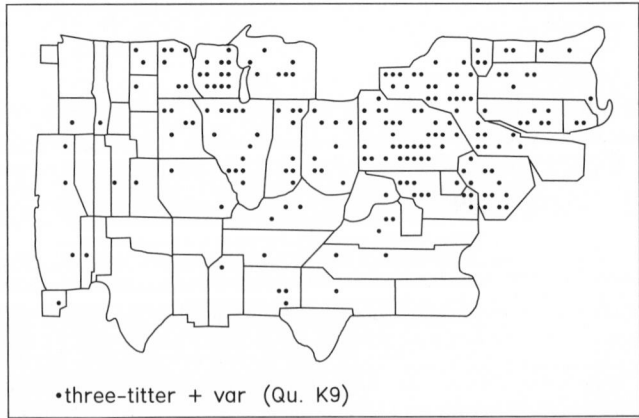

•three-titter + var (Qu. K9)

three-toed plover n   Also *three-toes*
=**golden plover.**

1870 (1873) Maynard *Naturalist's Guide* 138, *Charadrius Virginicus . .* "Three-toed Plover" [etc]. **1888** Trumbull *Names of Birds* 195 **ME,** American Golden Plover. . . In Maine . . at Bath, *Three-toed Plover.* **1917** (1923) *Birds Amer.* 1.257, *Golden Plover. . . Other Names. . .* Three-toed Plover; . . Three-toes. . . Bill small and slender; *no hind toe.* **1955** MA Audubon Soc. *Bulletin* 39.444, *American Golden Plover. . .*

Three-toed Plover (Maine, Mass.); Three-toes (Mass. This species lacks the rudimentary hind, or 4th, toe, possessed by the closely similar Black-bellied Plover.)

three-toed woodpecker n

Either the **black-backed woodpecker** *(Picoides arcticus)* or another **woodpecker B1** *(P. tridactylus),* both native chiefly to Alaska, the Rocky Mountains, and the northern Great Lakes area of the US.   For other names of the latter see **ladder-backed woodpecker 2**

   [1772 Royal Soc. London *Philos. Trans.* 62.334 **Ontario Canada,** Three-toed woodpecker. . . Severn river.] **1831** Richardson *Fauna Boreali-Amer.* 2.311, *Picus . . tridactylus. . . Common Three-toed Wood-pecker. . .* It would be tedious . . to show in what manner all preceding ornithologists have confounded the northern three-toed Woodpeckers; since no two species can be more distinct than those here described and figured. *Ibid* 313, *Picus . . arcticus. . . Arctic Three-toed Wood-pecker. . .* This is in every respect a larger species than the preceding. . . It was observed only on the eastern declivity of the Rocky Mountains, where the common species was also procured. **1839** MA Zool. & Bot. Surv. *Fishes Reptiles* 338, The *three-toed woodpecker, Picus tridacty-lus,* . . is distinguished by . . that peculiar formation of the feet from which it derives its name. **1843** *Amer. Jrl. Science* 44.263, The three-toed woodpecker has been seen in Massachusetts, and Audubon saw it as far south as Pennsylvania; and probably it visits the northern parts of Connecticut. **1887** Ridgway *N. Amer. Birds* 287, *P[icoides] arcticus. . .* Arctic Three-toed Woodpecker. . . *P. americanus* [=*P. tridactylus*]. . . American Three-toed Woodpecker. **1937** Natl. Geogr. Soc. *Book of Birds* 2.62, Along the northern border of our States and in Canada, when floods or fires kill the coniferous trees, look for the three-toed wood-peckers. . . The best way to distinguish it [=*Picoides tridactylus*] . . is to look for the pattern of numerous bars of white that traverse its back, and to remember that the back of the Arctic three-toed [=*P. arcticus*] is solid black. **1966–69** *DARE* (Qu. Q17, . . *Kinds of woodpeckers*) Inf **ME**8, American three-toed woodpecker; **ME**8, **MI**42, Arctic three-toed wood-pecker; **IN**69, **MI**108, **NC**44, **NY**106, Three-toed woodpecker. **1998** Amer. Ornith. Union *Check-list N. Amer. Birds* 341, *Picoides tridac-tylus. . .* Three-toed Woodpecker. . . *Picoides arcticus. . .* Also known as Arctic Three-toed Woodpecker, Black-backed Three-toed Woodpecker.

three-toes   See **three-toed plover**

three-up adj   Cf **eight-up, four-up 1, six-up**
Involving a team of three draft animals.

   1910 *Engin.–Contracting* 33.49 **WY,** [Advt:] Also eight dollars ($8) per day for "three-up" teams.   **1929** in 2007 (acc) Lexis–Nexis Legal Research *State Case Law: AR* (Internet), The defendant employed the teams of plaintiff, known as "three-up teams," at the rate of 75 cents per hour per team for 417 hours. [**1966–67** *DARE* (Qu. K26, *If six oxen are hitched together two and two, you have three* _____) Inf **AR**4, Three-up team; **CA**11, Three-up.] **1967** *DARE* Tape **IA**8, There was fifteen or twenty wagons, what they call three-up wagons. Either had three horses or three mules or a mule and two horses on each wagon; . . they call 'em a three-up wagon.   **1986** Pederson *LAGS Concordance,* 1 inf, swMS, Three-up team—if three animals.

three-way (chili) n   **orig Cincinnati OH, now more widely known**
A dish consisting of chili, spaghetti, and another element, usu grated cheese.

   1952 Nichols *Good Home Cooking* 383 **IN,** Chili three-way starts out with the layer of beans, then one of spaghetti, and lastly the sauce. [**1968** *DARE* (Qu. H45, *Dishes made with meat, fish, or poultry that everybody around here would know, but that people in other places might not*) Inf **OH**76, Chili spaghetti.] **1971** *Press–Gaz.* (Hillsboro OH) 5 Nov [7]/7 (newspaperarchive.com), [Advt:] The buyers are . . owners and operators of several Gold Star Chili Parlors located over a large area. Specializing in three way chili and serving a variety of food.   **1985** *Chron.–Telegram* (Elyria OH) 23 Jan sec B 9/5, *Cincinnati Chili. . .* For basic three-way chili, serve chili on spaghetti and top with cheese. **1994** *Syracuse Herald–Jrl.* (NY) 24 Jan sec C 3/4, In Cincinnati, chili is not made with beans. But in some restaurants you can order it with ex-tras. Two-way means you want the chili over spaghetti. Three-way adds shredded Cheddar cheese. **1999** *DARE* File swOH, I grew up in Cincinnati, and I get Cincinnati Chili every time I return. The two big-gest restaurants that serve it have 3-ways, 4-ways, and 5-ways (1 and 2 are the chili and the spaghetti). The 3-way includes cheese, the 4-way includes onions, and the 5-way add[s] red beans. **2002** *Home & Away*

(WI ed.) Nov–Dec 10 **sOH,** [Headline:] *Three-way Chili is Cincy's Signature Dish. . .* Three-way: chili, spaghetti[,] plus grated cheddar cheese. . . The most popular chili [in Cincinnati] is the three-way.

three-way sedge n
=**galingale 2.**

   1920 U.S. Dept. Ag. *Bulletin* 794.43 **NE,** Three-way sedge *(Dulichum arundinaceum).*   **1950** Gray–Fernald *Manual of Botany* 248, *Three-way Sedge. . .* Swamps and margins of pools and streams.   **1952** Straus-baugh–Core *Flora WV* 156, A tall perennial sedge with terete hollow jointed culms. . . *D[ulichium] arundinaceum. . . Three-way sedge.* **1961** Peck *Manual OR* 150, *Three-way Sedge. . .* Swamps along the coast, to B.C., Calif. and across the continent.   **1970** Correll *Plants TX* 262, *Three-way sedge. . .* Wet places and in shallow water over much of the lowlands of U.S.

thresh n[1]   See **thrash** n[1]

thresh n[2]   See **thrash** n[3]

thresh machine   See **thrash machine**

threw   See **throw B2a**

threwed   See **throw B1c, 2b**

thribble adj, adv, n, v   Also *threbble, thrible, thrip(p)le* [Varr of *triple* or *treble,* infl by *three;* cf *EDD thribble, SND threeple*] *old-fash*   Cf **fourble, tribble, tripletree**

   1765 in 1876 *Harper's New Mth. Mag.* 53.319 **neMA,** To a Double bowl punch, 22/9—To a Thribble bowl ditto, 33/9.   **1835** Kennedy *Horse Shoe Robinson* 27 **SC,** 'I'll warrant him a true man, Galbraith.' 'I'll thribble that warrant,'—replied Galbraith. **1881** *Marion Daily Star* (OH) 12 Feb 1/3, We would not do without one for double or thribble its cost.   **1895** *New Era* (Humeston IA) 27 Feb 5/3, You can thribble your production and get a better quality of fruit.   **1899** (1912) Green *VA Folk-Speech* 445, *Thribble. . .* Treble; triple; threefold.   **1908** Wasson *Home from Sea* 13 **sME coast,** You'll get the rote double and thribble as plain as what we do here.   **1909** *DN* 3.381 **eAL, wGA,** *Thribble. . .* To treble. *Thribble, adj.* Treble. Common. *ibid* 422 **Cape Cod MA** (as of a1857), *Thriple.* . . Triple.   **1932** *AmSp* 7.271 [Oil field language], *Thrible. . . A* stand of three joints of pipe. **1935** Hurston *Mules & Men* 70 **FL** [Black], He won from so many mens till he had threbbled his money.   **1936** *AmSp* 11.190 **NE,** Some of my friends nicknamed a cousin of theirs *Thribble-lip* because his lips were rather thick.   **1941** *AmSp* 16.25 **sIN,** *Thribble.* Triple or treble.   **1949** *Bradford Era* (PA) 3 Oct 4/2, Gauntlets were matching and the bouffant skirt held thripple scallops caught in clusters.   **1949** *PADS* 11.12 **wTX,** Thribble-disc.   **1952** Brown *NC Folkl.* 1.601, *Thribble:* vb. and adj. . . Treble. c**1960** Wilson Coll. **csKY,** Thribble.   **1966** Dakin *Dial. Vocab. Ohio R. Valley* 2.154, Evener. . . *thribbletree, thrippletree.* **1984** *DARE* File **KY,** *Thribling,* probably from Tripling, verb, to charge exorbitantly or deal excessively.

thribbles n pl, exclam   Also *thribs* [*EDD thribs* "Three . . in playing marbles."]   Cf **dubs** n pl **1**, exclam
In marble play: three marbles; also used as a call to lay claim to three marbles.

   1890 *DN* 1.24 **KY,** "Thribs," "thribbles" is three marbles.   **1905** *DN* 3.98 **nwAR,** *Thribs. . . A* term used in playing marbles.   **1909** *DN* 3.381 **eAL, wGA,** *Thribs, n. A* term used in marbles when three men are knocked out of the ring. "Vence you thribs."   **1912** Green *VA Folk-Speech* 445, *Thribs.* . . Three, used in playing marbles.   **1935** *AmSp* 10.159 **seNE,** *Thribs* . . must be cried for three . . marbles.   **1955** *PADS* 23.32 **cwAL,** *Thribs.* . . Three marbles.

thribbletree   See **tripletree**

thrible   See **thribble**

‡**thriblet** n   [Cf *SND threeplet* (at *threeple* n. II)]
A triplet.

   1941 in 1950 Faulkner *Stories* 55 **MS,** The three of them might have been thriblets.

thribletree   See **tripletree**

thribs   See **thribbles**

thrift n

1 Std: a plant of the genus *Armeria.*   For other names of *A. maritima* subsp *sibirica* see **foxflower**

2 also *wild thrift:* =**moss pink 1.   esp NC, GA**

1941 Hart *Official Hist. Laurens Co.* 133 **GA,** [In a list of plants:] Ground or moss pink (wild thrift) [etc]. **1966** *DARE* Wildfl QR Pl.178 [=*Phlox subulata*] Infs **NC**28, 36, Thrift. **1969** *DARE* (Qu. S26a, . . *Wildflowers. . . Roadside flowers*) Inf **GA**80, Thrift—pink or blue, fernlike leaves; (Qu. S26c, *Wildflowers that grow in woods*) Inf **NC**72, Wild thrift or pinks.

thrin n [Prob blend of *three* + *twin*] **esp NEast**
One of three children born at one birth; also fig.

1805 in 1895 Concord MA *Concord Births* 424, [From a church record:] Three female children of Mrs. Abigail Dix, *Thrins,* 2 days old, [died] December 6, 1805. **1838** (1949) Thoreau *Jrl.* 1.51, Truth, Goodness, Beauty,—those celetial thrins,/ Continually are born. **1852** Townsend *Fancies* 57 **NYC,** Mrs. Smithers presented her lord with twins, or thrins, last week. **1881** Greene *Cape Cod Folks* 40 **seMA,** She had thirteen children, three of 'em was twins and one of 'em was thrins. **1910** *Oakland Tribune* (CA) 24 July 26/2 **MI,** Twins, doc? Better'n that—there's thrins in there, sir! **1978** Hiser *Quare Appalachia* 35 **eKY,** What's a thrin? I asked. You know what a twin is, Granny said . . when two are born together, one of them is a twin. Well, when three comes at once, one is a thrin.

thrip n [Abbr of *threepence*] **esp Sth, S Midl**
Something of little or no value—usu in neg phrr.

1890 GA Bar Assoc. *Report* 20, There is not anything but justice that is worth a thrip. **1903** (1904) Churchill *Crossing* 257 **KY,** "My God," cried Ray, pointing angrily at the swarms about the land office, "what trash we have got this last year! Kentucky can go to the devil, half the stations be wiped out, and not a thrip do they care." **1909** *DN* 3.381 **eAL, wGA,** Thrip. . . The original idea of a small coin is lost, but the negative expressions 'not worth a thrip,' 'don't care a thrip,' are very common. **1939** *Time* 6 Nov 15 **VA,** [Quoting VA senator Carter Glass:] The only person on earth who may drag this nation into war is Hitler. . . His pledged word is not worth a thrip. **1966** *DARE* (Qu. KK17, . . 'Worthless': "It isn't worth _____."; total Infs questioned, 75) Inf **GA**9, Thrip.

thrip(p)le See **thribble**

thrippletree See **tripletree**

thriv See **thrive 1, 2**

thrive v
Std senses, var forms.

1 past: usu *throve, thrived* also *thriv(e), thruve.*
1862 *Atlantic Mth.* 9.793 **'Upcountry' MA,** Three-story larnin' 's pop'lar now; I guess / We thriv' ez wal on jes two stories less. **1893** *DN* 1.278 **nwCT,** Thrive . . [past, past pple:] thriv, throve. **1966–70** *DARE* (Qu. OO35a, *Talking about vegetables thriving: "Last year we fertilized the garden, and the plants really _____."*) Infs **FL**49, **SC**26, **VA**71, Thrive; **MS**87, Thriv; **NE**11, Thruve [θruv]. [4 of 5 Infs Black]
2 past pple: usu *thrived, thriven;* also *thriv(e), throve(n).*
1829 *Niles' Weekly Reg.* 39.211 **FL,** The trees pruned have throve beyond my expectation. **1862** *Ladies' Repository* 31.199, If Buchanan had ordered Major Anderson to shell the city of Charleston . . this rebellion would never have throve as it has. **1893** [see **1** above]. **1965–70** *DARE* (Qu. OO35b, *Talking about vegetables thriving: "That land is poor—nothing has ever _____ there."*) 40 Infs, **scattered,** Throve; **AL**6, **FL**49, **OK**42, **SC**26, **VA**71, Thrive; **NE**7, Thriv; **NJ**5, Throven. **1982** Heat Moon *Blue Highways* 31 **cTN,** That's why I keep at farmin', although the crops haven't ever throve.

throat n Usu |θrot|; also **esp Sth, S Midl** |θot|; occas |trot|; for addit varr see quots Pronc-spp *thoat, thote, throurt, t'roat, trophe*
Std sense, var proncs.

1845 in 1958 *AmSp* 33.74 **NC,** Soar thoats. **1890** *DN* 1.41 **csME,** *Throat* . . originally [θrɛt]; now [θrout]. **1893** Shands *MS Speech* 63, Thote [θot]. Negro for *throat.* **1909** *DN* 3.381 **eAL, wGA,** Thoat. . . Throat. **1922** Gonzales *Black Border* 335 **sSC, GA coasts** [Gullah glossary], T'roat—throat. **1923** (1946) Greer-Petrie *Angeline Doin' Society* 5 **csKY,** My stummick thinks my thoat's been cut. **1927** Kennedy *Gritny* 18 **sLA** [Black], Got his th'oat cut clean thoo. **1942** Hall *Smoky Mt. Speech* 90 **wNC, eTN,** Postconsonantally, *r* is commonly elided in *throat* [θot]. **c1960** *Wilson Coll.* **csKY,** *Throat* is sometimes /θot/. **1968** *DARE* (Qu. X7, . . *The throat:* "*Some food got stuck in his*

_____.") Inf **MI**75, [trot]. **1975** Gould *ME Lingo* 290, Throurt—Throat. Listen for this, it comes warmly on the Maine tongue: "Little Teenie has a saw throurt." **1985** Benes *Amer. Speech* 75 **cME coast** (as of c1795), The so-called New England checked *o* occurs in many words in Fisher's speech. These are *bone . . coat . . throat . . wholly.* **1989** Pederson *LAGS Tech. Index* 263 **Gulf Region,** Throat. [Of 914 infs, 63 (more than half of them Black) offered proncs of the type [θot]; 11 infs, proncs of the type [trot].] **1998** *DARE* File—Internet **cePA** [Language of the Hayna Valley], Trophe—I gadda whisper onnakowna I gadda sore trophe.

throat botfly n Also *throat bot*
Std: a botfly (*Gasterophilus nasalis*) that, in the larval stage, is a gastrointestinal parasite of horses. Also called **chin fly**

throat-cut n
=**rose-breasted grosbeak.**
1908 Knight *Birds ME* 439, Rose-breasted Grosbeak; Throat-cut. **1946** Hausman *Eastern Birds* 572, *Hedymeles* [=*Pheucticus*] *ludovicianus.* . . Throat-cut.

throat dog n **West**
A hunting dog trained to kill a game animal, esp a coyote, by biting its throat.

1915 *Outing* 66.316 **ND,** Sired by a blue-blooded Russian wolfhound, mothered by a fair runner and stanch fighter,—a throat dog, Ned called her. **1972** *Jrl.–Tribune* (Marysville OH) 4 Apr 4/2, This dog, in addition to being a good throat dog on coyote [in NE], also killed fox here in Ohio. **1975** *Lincoln Star* (NE) 15 Oct 49/1, [Advt:] Coyote throat dog & 3 greyhound 7 mos old dogs. **1991** Heat Moon *PrairyErth* 152 **ceKS,** Usually, the younger and faster cross-breeds catch the quarry [=a coyote] and turn it to fight as the older ones, the throat dogs, close in to pin it and finish things off. **2005** *DARE* File—Internet **AZ,** I never saw a yote live more than a few seconds with this bunch here. The big black dog is Bull a super sprint dog and a throat dog. *Ibid* **cKS,** He turned into one of the best throat dogs I . . ever saw. A coon would come down out of the tree and old Cody would spar back and forth until he had an opening, then in he'd go and clamp down on the coon's throat until it was dead.

throatroot n
An avens, usu **water avens** or *Geum virginianum.*
1784 in 1785 Amer. Acad. Arts & Sci. *Memoirs* 1.454, Water Avens. Throatroot. Cureall. . . The root is powerfully astringent. **1789** in 1793 Amer. Philos. Soc. *Trans.* 3.xix, In New-England a species of Geum, *water-avens, throat-root, cure all,* is an esteemed remedy for ulcerated [sic] sore-throat. **1828** Rafinesque *Med. Flora* 1.220, *Geum virginianum.* . . Throatroot. [*Ibid* 221, The *Geum rivale,* or water Avens, . . is more commonly employed in the north, and this species in the south; they are both equivalents.] **1876** Hobbs *Bot. Hdbk.* 119, Throat root, White avens, Geum Virginianum.

throatwort n
1 A **blazing star 3,** usu *Liatris spicata.*
1739 (1946) Gronovius *Flora Virginica* 92, *Serratula* [here: =*Liatris*] *foliis linearibus, floribus solitariis sessilibus. . . Radix est discutiens, hinc* Throat-wort. [=*Serratula* [here: =*Liatris*] with linear leaves and sessile solitary flowers. . . Root discutient, hence Throat-wort.] **1830** Rafinesque *Med. Flora* 2.237, *Liatris.* . . Throatwort. . . All have a tuberous medical root. . . Very useful in dropsy, gonorrhea, angina, croup and hives, sore-throat, scrofula, gravel, pains in the breast, after pains of women and bites of snakes, both internally and topically. **1876** Hobbs *Bot. Hdbk.* 119, Throat wort, Button snakeroot, Liatris spicata.
2 A **harebell 1,** usu the naturalized *Campanula trachelium.* [*OED2* 1578 →]
1900 Lyons *Plant Names* 77, *C[ampanula] Trachelium.* . . Throatwort. **1970** *NC Folkl.* 18.32, Canterbury bell, or throat-wart [sic], was used for swellings of throat.

throatwort sunflower n
A **sunflower 1** (here: *Helianthus decapetalus*).
1848 Gray *Manual of Botany* 227 **OH, PA,** *H[elianthus] tracheliifolius* [=*H. decapetalus*]. . . Throatwort sunflower. **1903** Porter *Flora PA* 332, *Helianthus tracheliifolius.* . . Throatwort Sunflower. . . In dry soil, Pa. to Ohio to Wis. **1930** OK Univ. Biol. Surv. *Pub.* 2.85, *Helianthus tracheliifolius.* . . Throatwort Sunflower. **1937** Stemen-

Myers *OK Flora* 585, *Helianthus tracheliifolius.* . . Throatwort Sunflower. . . Dry soil. August–September.

throddy adj [Engl dial]
Plump; sleek.

　　1910 Univ. NC *Mag.* 40.3.8 **Hatteras Is. NC,** Throddy (plump), sleek, in good condition, as applied to a steer or to a mullet. **1938** Matschat *Suwannee R.* 289 **neFL, seGA,** *Old English and Scotch Words.* . . *Throddy:* well grown, plump. **1939** *Fredericksburg News* (IA) [11 May 3]/4 (newspaperarchive.com) **Hatteras Is. NC,** A plump, good-looking girl is a "throddy may."

throde See **throw B1a**

throng adj [Scots, Ir, nEngl dial] **esp PA** *old-fash* Cf **thronged**
Crowded, busy, occupied with work.

　　1781 in 1854 *PA Archives* 1st ser 9.160, Our deficulty in raising them [=teams] were very great, as it was a throng time with the farmers. **1840** in 2005 *DARE* File—Internet **neIN,** I have a vary throng time I have sowed about 60 bushels of oats and i have cleared a hepe of ground. **1848** *Republican Compiler* (Gettysburg PA) 20 Mar [4]/2 (newspaperarchive.com), A letter from Harrisburg informs us that there are strong doubts whether the necessary business will be disposed of by that time, this being a very throng session. **1863** in 1962 Truxall *Respects to All* 93 **PA,** I have no doubt that you are very throng at present harvesting. **1885** *OH Democrat* (New Philadelphia) 19 Nov [3]/3 (newspaperarchive.com), Our mines are all running at present, but not very throng. **1887** *Atlantic Mth.* 60.331 **VA** [Black], It 's throng-time wid 'em . . ; dey ain't got no ledger minutes for ter stop for an ole nigger. **1893** *Indiana Weekly Messenger* (PA) 8 Mar [2]/3 (newspaperarchive.com), One hundred and sixty-four diners at the Clawson House on Monday made things very throng about that popular establishment. **1903** *Landmark* (Statesville NC) 3 Apr [3]/1 (newspaperarchive.com), City Tax Collector Parks had a "throng time" the first three days of the week. **1916** *Indiana Weekly Messenger* (PA) 17 May 1/3, Monday last was a very throng time for 'Squire Crossman and proved a long day for the worthy 'squire. **1924** Raine *Land of Saddle-Bags* 101 **sAppalachians,** I've been very throng today. (A Scottish usage.)

thronged adj [*OED2 thronged* 2.b "Chiefly *dial.*"] **esp OH** *old-fash* Cf **throng**
Busy, occupied (with work).

　　1776 in 1893 *Archives of MD* 12.12, We are so thronged with business that we cannot now write you fully. **1840** *Lorain Std.* (Elyria OH) 13 Oct [2]/1 (newspaperarchive.com), Their voters never fail to be at the polls—while the Democrats are very often too thronged with work to go to the election. **1882** *Athens Messenger* (OH) 9 Mar 5/1, Our local hotels are both seemingly thronged with business. **1888** *Newark Daily Advocate* (OH) 7 Jan 2/3, The people are discovering that the finest work is being done at Smith's Gallery at cheap rates, and he is now thronged with work. **1912** *DN* 3.593 **wIN,** *Thronged.* . . Busy. "He was awfully thronged while I was in his office." **1931** *AmSp* 7.20 **swPA,** *Thronged.* Pressed. . . "I was thronged with work."

thro other See **throughother**

through adv, prep Usu |θru|; for varr see below
Std senses, var forms.

1 |θu, θɪu|; pronc-spp *thew, thoo, though, thu(e).* **chiefly Sth, S Midl**

　　1849 in 1956 Eliason *Tarheel Talk* 319 **nw,cnNC,** Through—though. **1852** *Ibid* **cnNC,** Thew. **1893** Shands *MS Speech* 63, Thoo [θu]. Negro for *through.* **1894** Riley *Armazindy* 54 **IN,** Gimblet-holes up thue his desk. **1896** Harris *Sister Jane* 311 **GA,** You look much as if you'd been drug into a hot sandbank feet foremost. **1906** *DN* 3.161 **nwAR,** *Though* [θu]. . . Through. "I can't get th'ough." Rare. **1909** *DN* 3.381 **eAL, wGA,** *Thu* [θu]. . . Through. Common. **1927** Kennedy *Gritny* 170 **sLA** [Black], Soaked clean thoo to de skin. **1933** Rawlings *South Moon* 105 **nFL,** The buck crashed thu like a lumber-cart. **1934** Hurston *Jonah's Gourd Vine* 233 **AL** [Black], Sho hope mah boy come thew awright. **1940** Writers' Program *Negro in VA* 146 [Black], Ole paddy-rollers got wise an' used to tie dey horses an' come creepin' thew de woods on foot. **1942** Hall *Smoky Mt. Speech* 90 **wNC, eTN,** Postconsonantally, *r* is commonly elided in . . *through* [θu]. . . On a speech record, *through* is once [θ¹u], in which the front glide is perhaps the

remnant of an old [r]. **1958** Humphrey *Home from the Hill* 126 **neTX,** I never seen you laffin when she got thoo with me and started in on you. **1984** Burns *Cold Sassy* 35 **nGA** (as of 1906), If'n she don't pull th'ew, I ain't go'n say it was Thy will. **2001** *DARE* File **seOH,** I do hear r-less "through" often in African-American English.

2 |fru|; pronc-spp *frough, fru.* *esp freq among Black speakers*

　　1849 (1850) Poe *Works* 1.64, "How high up are you?" asked Legrand. "Ebber so fur," replied the negro; "can see de sky fru de top ob de tree." **1893** Shands *MS Speech* 15 [Black], In some cases *th* [θ] initial, has the sound of *f*; as [fru] for *through.* **1901** *DN* 2.184 **neKY** [Black], *Through* . . fru. **1901** *Century Illustr. Mag.* 62.903 **neAR** [Black], Hit all come erbout frough Marse Oscar wantin' ter tu'n dis . . lan' wrong side out. **1925** in 1944 *ADD* **swSC, eGA** [Black], *Through.* . . 'He walk speng fru de wall.' Everyday speech.

3 |tru|; pronc-spp *tru(e).*

　　1852 in 1956 Eliason *Tarheel Talk* 319 **cs,seNC,** *Through* . . true. **1922** Gonzales *Black Border* 335 **sSC, GA coasts** [Gullah glossary], *T'ru*—through. **1925** in 1953 Botkin-Harlow *Treas. Railroad Folkl.* 231, Man! he was sure dead when dey got tru workin' on 'im. **1940** *AmSp* 15.370 **nePA,** *Through* [tru] (very common). **1998** *DARE* File—Internet **cePA** [Language of the Hayna Valley], *True*—Through, as in "Dee bat'rumm is right true dat door."

through n

1 A single pass across a field made by a machine or one or more hands in plowing, sowing, harvesting, etc; the path or swath made in a single pass—freq in phrr *at a* (or *one, two,* etc) *through(s).* [*EDD through* sb. 17 "*Obs.* A slip or width of corn which a set of reapers, &c. drive before them at once. . . 1796"]

　　1835 *Farmers' Reg.* 2.728, I selected four strong, careful hands, to cut and lay down, taking eight rows at a through. **1859** (1968) Bartlett *Americanisms* 477, *Through,* is used in the West for swathe, or the cut of the cradle through grass or grain. **1860** Todd *Young Farmer's Manual* 334 **cNY,** When a team goes from one end of the plowing to the other, it is called a *through.* *Ibid* 356, It is better to sow such a strip at *five* throughs instead of four. **1868** Todd *Amer. Wheat Culturist* 204 **cNY,** Gang-plows . . usually cut from three to four feet in width at one through. *Ibid* 210, Such a cultivator . . cuts a through four or five feet in width. **1890** *DN* 1.66 **KY,** *Through* [θru]: the number of rows worked by a set of hands through a tobacco field. To illustrate: Seven hands will take fourteen rows at a *through,* working from one side of a field to the other. "Did you finish that last through?" **1909** *DN* 3.417 **nME,** *Through.* . . A cutting of grain by a sickle, like a swath. **1941** Stuart *Men of Mts.* 179 **eKY,** Twenty men gathered to hoe Wilburn's corn. We took twenty rows of corn at a time. . . "Twenty rows of corn at a through," said Uncle Hankas. **1992** Williams *S. Mt. Speech* 114 **KY,** He cut two rows of corn at a through. **1995–97** in 2004 Montgomery-Hall *Dict. Smoky Mt. Engl.* 604 **wNC, eTN,** *Through.* . . A pass from one end of a field to the other in harvesting grain [3 infs].

2 A spasm, paroxysm, fit, esp of religious excitement at a revival meeting—freq in phrr *cut* (or *take*) *a through* to become excited or angry; to experience a fit of religious excitement.
sAppalachians

　　1905 (1975) Miles *Spirit of Mts.* 3 **eTN,** Confinement for an hour or two, with songs and the imminent expectation of somebody's "takin' a big through" of religious excitement to break the monotony, is not supportable. **1913** Kephart *Highlanders* 283 **sAppalachians,** "Nance tuk the biggest through at meetin'!" (shouting spell). **1917** *DN* 4.418 **wNC,** *Through.* . . Spasm. "I take a big through o' sneezin' every day." **1952** [see **withouten B**]. **1968** Haun *Hawk's Done Gone* 240 **sAppalachians,** He fussed if she made big biscuits, and he cut a through if she made little biscuits. **1975** *Appalachian Jrl.* 2.157 **wNC,** When asked what he meant by *a big through,* one man responded, "It's when you git happy, git shoutin'." **1996** in 2004 Montgomery-Hall *Dict. Smoky Mt. Engl.* 604, *Through.* . . What if I was to cut a through like that at preachin' again.

3 A course of medication, esp laxatives.

　　1901 Keith *Keith's Domestic Practice* 381, Unfortunate human being in the power of the pagan doctor has to take a dose of physic. A through of calomel being the "regular" thing prescribed. **1927** *DN* 5.478 **Ozarks,** *Through.* . . A series of doses of medicine, particularly applicable to purgatives. "I taken a through o' calomel las' week, an' now Doc's done fixed me up a turrible through o' physic." **1969** *DARE* (Qu. BB22, . . *Home remedies . . for constipation*) Inf **TX**65, A through of calomel. **2005** *DARE* File—Internet **TX,** My grandmother's view on medicine seemed to be, "If it tastes good, it's not medicine!" . . I always looked forward to part of her visit with dread. Almost like clock-work, about the second day, she would . . say, "How long has it been since these kids have had a through of medicine?"

through another See **throughother B**

through cut n   Cf **near cut, nigh ~,** *DS* MM16

A shortcut.

1898 *Scribner's Mag.* 24.238 **VA,** Farther back is a through cut to the Bend. **1932** *Univ. CA Chronicle* 34.53 **CA,** There we left the highway and for a mile or more followed a "through-cut," rough and winding, that leads up Cocyade Gulch and Bear Creek. **1957** in 2004 Montgomery–Hall *Dict. Smoky Mt. Engl.* 604 **wNC, eTN,** Through cut. . . My daddy used to come through here. They had a through cut, a road through there.

through each other See **throughother B**

throughgrow See **thoroughgrow**

throughother adv, adj, n   Pronc-sp *thro other* [Scots, Ir, nEngl dial *throughother, throughither,* but also (esp the longer forms at **B** below) from PaGer *darrich(e)nanner,* Ger *durcheinander,* literally "through one another, through each other"]

A   As adv.

In disorder.

1843 Thompson *Major Jones' Courtship* 9 **GA,** The fust thing I knowed they was all twisted up in a snarl, goin both ways at both ends, and all marchin thro other in the middle, in all sorts of helter skelter fashion.

B   As adj.

Also *through another, through each other:* Mixed up together, in disorder; confused, befuddled.

1843 Thompson *Major Jones' Courtship* 11 **GA,** Thar they was, . . five or six in a heap, rollin over and crawlin out from under, bitin and scratchin, gougin and strikin, kickin and cussin, heads and heels all through other. **1866** *Nation* 2.208, Everybody was in a tumult, and they were all "through other" with their secessionism. **1872** Haldeman *PA Dutch* 57 [English influenced by German], When a person whose vernacular is English says, "I am through another" (I am confused), he is using a translation of the German *durch einander,* P.G. 'dárich ənánnər.' **1872** U.S. Congress *Rept. Joint Select Comm. Insurrectionary States* 3.374 **SC,** I don't know which one it was. They was all through other until they went to eating down on the hearth. **1903** *DN* 2.353 **sePA,** *Through-other* (with accent on first syllable), *adj.* Confused, bothered. 'I feel all through-other.' 'The things in the drawer are all through-other.' **1908** *German Amer. Annals* 10.47 **sePA,** *Through other.* Confused. "Oh, you're through other." . . The form "through another" is also found. **1939** Aurand *Quaint Idioms* 30 [PaGer], Everything is *through each other.* **1950** *WELS* (Confused, mixed up: "The things in the drawer are all _____.") 1 Inf, **ceWI,** Through each other—local community—German.

C   As noun.

A state of disorder.

1929 *AmSp* 4.303 **IA,** The children had left their playthings "in a through-other."

through steady exclam   Pronc-sp *through study*

In marble play: see quot.

1980 *NADS Letters* **cAL** (as of 1920s), Another order is "through steady" (or "through study"), which means that the one about to shoot may not shoot into the ring (which sets him up for a subsequent win), but must shoot completely through the ring (from which point he might hit the stuck-in marble, but is less likely to oust it from the ring).

throughway n   Also *thruway*   **chiefly wNEng, NY** See Map

An expressway; also used as a proper name.

1942 *Syracuse Herald–Jrl.* (NY) 13 Mar 16/2, $200,000,000 Super-Road Is Projected. . . The connecting highway facilities are inadequate for modern highway traffic and . . it will be cheaper to lay out a modern throughway . . than attempt to widen and change the existing highways. **1944** *Sun* (Baltimore MD) 16 Feb 9/1 *(Hench Coll.),* Through-Way Views Listed. . . the Retail Merchants Association of Baltimore were reported favoring the construction of an express highway through the city.

1946 *Syracuse Herald–Jrl.* (NY) 10 July 14/3, Thruway entrances will take incoming vehicles on to the acceleration lane, which will parallel the three-lane highway long enough for the new arrival to pick up Thruway speed and merge gently into the flow of traffic. **1965–70** *DARE* (Qu. N16a, *Names for a highway with two lanes on each side and a separation down the middle*) 48 Infs, **chiefly wNEng, NY,** Throughway; (Qu. N16b, *Names for a highway with two lanes on each side and a separation down the middle—if you have to pay to drive on it*) 15 Infs, **chiefly NY,** Throughway; (Qu. N18, . . *Roads that have numbers or letters. For example, if someone asked directions . . "Take _____."*) Inf **VT**16, Throughway + [number]. **2003** *CT Post* (Bridgeport) 9 Feb sec J 2/5, Once I was up on the throughway, I was stopped near the (Stratford) tolls. **2003** *Post–Std.* (Syracuse NY) 24 May sec C 1/2, A groundbreaking truck stop electrification program . . is being expanded on the state Thruway.

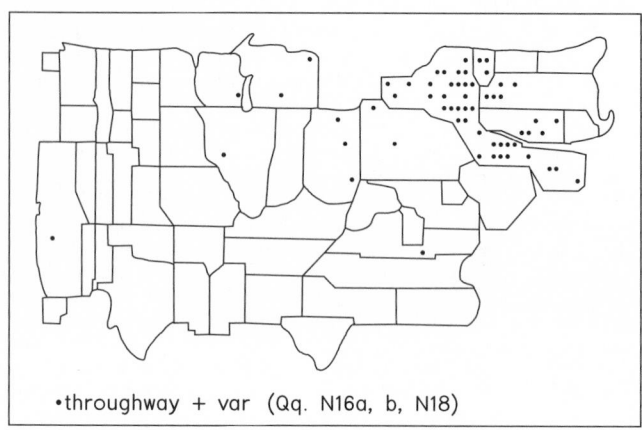

•throughway + var (Qq. N16a, b, N18)

throurt See **throat**

throve(n) See **thrive 2**

throw v

A   Pronc varr.

1   pronc-sp *thow* (similarly *thew,* etc).   **chiefly Sth, S Midl** For addit quots see **B** below

1875 *Scribner's Mth.* 10.240 **AL** [Black], Th'ow away de bread. **1884** [see **B1a** below]. **1890** *DN* 1.69 **KY,** Th'ow [θou]: throw. "He can't th'ow any distance." **1893** Shands *MS Speech* 63, Thow [θo]. Negro for *throw.* The past tense of this verb in negro parlance is *thowed* [θod]. **1894** Riley *Armazindy* 54 **IN,** When the Teacher wuzn't lookin',/ He'd be th'owin' wads [of paper]. **1906** *DN* 3.161 **nwAR,** Thow [θo]. . . To throw. "Why don't you th'ow it?" Rare. **1909** *DN* 3.381 **eAL, wGA,** Thow. . . To throw. . . *Throwed, pret.* and *pp.* of *throw.* Usually *thowed.* **1936** *AmSp* 11.245 **eTX** [Black], Throw . . [θou]. **1947** Williams *Streetcar* 11 **LA,** What was that package he th'ew at 'er? **1949** Webber *Backwoods Teacher* 10 **Ozarks,** I was 'feared to th'ow it at his head lest he'd dodge an' somebody else would get it. **1966** *DARE* Tape **MS**72, The short man . . took my picture just as I went to throw [θou] some corn out to 'em [=chickens]. **1967–69** *DARE* (Qu. C24b) Inf **MS**60, Thowed; (Qu. V2b, *About a deceiving person, or somebody that you can't trust . . "I wouldn't trust him _____.";* not asked in early QRs) Inf **LA**6, As fur as I could thow [θou] a mule; (Qu. Y10) Inf **GA**63, Thowed; (Qu. CC14) Inf **GA**42, Thowed at you; (Qu. OO30a, *Talking about a horse throwing the rider: "John got a bad horse and was _____ [off]."*) Inf **PA**198, Thown. **1973** McCarthy *Child of God* 9 **TN,** It must have thowed his neck out someway or another. **1989** Pederson *LAGS Tech. Index* 117 **Gulf Region,** Throw . . infinitive . . [proncs of the type [θo], 103 of 914 infs] . . present 3rd singular . . [[θoz], 5 infs] . . present participle . . [[θon], 1 inf]. *Ibid, Throw* . . preterit . . [[θod], 87 of 914 infs . . [θu], 21 infs]. *Ibid* 118, *Throw* . . past participle . . [[θon], 1 of 914 infs]. **2001** *DARE* File [Black], Likewise, threw is pronounced [θu] and throw [θo].

2   pronc-sp *trow* (similarly *trew, true, truh,* etc).   *esp freq among Black speakers*   Cf Pronc Intro 3.I.17   For addit quots see **B** below   Note: For the form *trun,* see **A4, B1e, 2d** below

1851 [see **B1b** below]. **1864** (2000) *Songs of Love & Liberty* 38 (Internet) **NC** [Black], We trowed de dogs de head and feet. **1909** *S. Atl. Qrly.* 8.41 **seSC** [Gullah], Fo' God's sake! who truhwy [=threw away] de pot-hook? **1922** Gonzales *Black Border* 335 **sSC, GA coasts** [Gullah glossary], T'row—throw, throws, threw, thrown, throwing. . .

T'ruh'way . . threw . . away. **1922** [see **B2c** below]. **1933** *N. Amer. Rev.* 236.541 seSC [Gullah], What you goan trow on me? **1968** *DARE* Tape **LA**42, They was throwing ['t'roʊɪn] things and everything. **1974** Gilbreth *Dictionary* 15 seSC, *True:* Hurled, i.e., "He true the ball." **1989** Pederson *LAGS Tech. Index* 117 **Gulf Region,** *Throw* . . infinitive [[tro], 10 of 914 infs] . . present participle [[troŋ], 1 inf] . . preterit [[trod], 3 infs; [tru], 7 infs]. **1997** *DARE* File—Internet **WI** [Speak 'Scansin], *Th* should frequently be pronounced *T*—"Trow da cow over da fence some hay." *Ibid* c**PA** [CoalSpeak], *Trow, trew:* Throw, threw. "I trew it to him, but he was too wasted to catch it!"

3 pronc-spp *fro(w).* *esp freq among Black speakers* Cf Pronc Intro 3.I.17

1871 *Galaxy* 12.584 **SC** [Black], Adam was a tryin' to sneak out of it by frowin' all de blame on de Lord hisself! **1885** *Century Illustr. Mag.* 31.99 **VA** [Black], An' den she frows it at his head. **1901** *DN* 2.184 ne**KY** [Black], *Throw* . . fro.

4 pronc-spp *t(h)run.* [See **B1e** below]

1896 *DN* 1.426 c**NY,** *Trun,* also *trun down* . . : to get a person out of one's way. Often equivalent to "sit down upon." **1900** Lewis *Sandburrs* 62 **NYC,** Now d' sucker's nutty. Dey's thrunning dice for him at Bloomin'dale right now. **1918** *Bookman* 48.140 **NYC,** But take turns and don't crowd or I'll trun yez all upstairs. **1959** Powell *Pioneer* 232 **NJ,** All I could do was thrun up a hand. *Ibid* 209, He decided I was afraid to win a lot right away on seven and had tried to thrun away my first bet. **2007** *DARE* File **Cent,** I grew up in central Illinois. My mom grew up in Albany, Texas. . . My dad grew up in the teens and twenties in Kansas City, Little Rock, Butler Missouri, and then Chicago. I'm thinking he brought the word into the family. . . "[Y]ou need to get into that garage and trun some things"; or "I would trun that if I were you".

B Gram forms.

1 past: usu *threw;* also:

a *throwed;* also sp *throde;* pronc-spp *thowed, trowed.* *esp freq among speakers with little formal educ* Cf **-ed** suff **2** For addit quots see **A** above

1848 (1855) Ruxton *Life Far West* 73 **Rocky Mts,** They indulged their appetites—or, in their own language, "throw'd" the meat. **1862** in 1962 Truxall *Respects to All* 23 **PA,** They only throwed one shell and it went over our camp. **1864** [see **A2** above]. **1884** *Anglia* 7.253 [Black], To the regular forms of the Irregular verbs as used by the whites, the Negro adds the following forms of his own. . . *Pres.* th'ow (throw)—*Past.* th'owed, th'own, th'ewed—*Pass. Part.* [same as past]. **1893** *DN* 1.278 nw**CT,** Throw [preterit and past participle]—throwed. **1909** [see **A1** above]. **1911** *DN* 3.551 **WY,** I throwed twenty cattle into the next pasture. **1931** (1991) Hughes–Hurston *Mule Bone* 83 c**FL** [Black], De man thowed dat shotgun dead on him. **1942** Faulkner *Go Down* 56 **MS,** Then I throwed the razor away. **1946** *AmSp* 21.98 s**IL,** *Throde,* threw. **1953** Atwood *Survey of Verb Forms* 25, *Throw* . . preterite. . . *Throwed* /θrod/ (or often in the S[outh] A[tlantic] S[tates] /θod/) exists in all parts of the East. It is scattered through N. Eng., except for c. Mass. and part of c. Conn. In n.e. N. Eng. it is used by the majority [of aged and middle-aged informants with little education]. **1965–70** *DARE* (Qu. OO30b, *Talking about a horse throwing the rider: "Last week the same horse _____ [his brother]."*) 190 Infs, **widespread, but somewhat less freq Pacific,** Throwed; (Qu. Y10, *To throw something* . . "The dog came at him, so he picked up a stone and _____ it at him.") 81 Infs, **scattered, but esp Midl, Sth,** Throwed; **GA**63, Thowed; (Qu. C24b, *"The dog wouldn't go away, so he took a stone/rock and . . _____ [it at it.]"*) 74 Infs, **scattered, but esp Midl, Sth,** Throwed; **MS**60, Thowed [Of all Infs responding to Qq. OO30b, Y10, and C24b, 39%, 27%, and 32% respectively were gs educ or less; of those giving these responses, 62%, 58%, and 66% respectively were gs educ or less.]; (Qu. KK63, *To do a clumsy or hurried job of repairing something: "It will never last—he just _____."*) 32 Infs, **esp Sth, S Midl,** Throwed it together; **GA**73, Throwed it up; **ME**19, Throwed that together; (Qu. BB18, *To vomit a great deal at once*) Inf **SD**5, Just about throwed up my guts; **TN**16, Throwed up a bushel; **KY**11, Throwed up a hatful; **PA**135, Throwed up a lot; **AR**51, Throwed up a sluice of it; **NY**150, Throwed up all but your shoes; **WI**44, Throwed up his shoes; **GA**72, **SC**34, Throwed up his socks; **TX**35, Throwed up your toenails; **WY**4, Throwed your stomach up; (Qu. U15, *When you're buying something, if the seller puts in a little extra to make you feel that you're getting a good bargain*) Infs **ME**6, **MS**59, **NM**7, He throwed in (something); **CT**20, He throwed it in; **AR**23, Something he throwed in; **OK**1, They just throwed that in; **MD**26, They throwed this in; **OK**51, Throwed in something extra; **CO**22, Throwed it in; (Qu. U8a, . . *"It cost me ten dollars."*) Inf **SC**42, Throwed me back; (Qu. U8b, . . *"I paid ten dollars*

for it.") Inf **NH**14, Throwed; (Qu. Y17, *When two people agree to stop fighting and not be enemies any more* . . "I hear they _____.") Infs **MA**15, **NC**33, Throwed in the hatchet (*or* sponge); (Qu. AA11, *If a man asks a girl to marry him and she refuses, . . she _____*) Infs **AL**34, **MI**47, Throwed him over; (Qu. AA12, *If a man loses interest in a girl and stops seeing her . . he _____*) Inf **AL**34, Throwed her over; **VA**24, Throwed her overboard; (Qu. BB56, *Joking expressions for dying:* "He _____.") Inf **NC**61, Throwed in his hat; (Qu. BB57, *If someone committed suicide . . he _____*) Inf **TX**37, Throwed ace-deuce; (Qu. CC14) Inf **GA**42, Thowed at you; (Qu. DD10, *When somebody gives up smoking:* "He isn't smoking any more—a month ago he _____.") Inf **AZ**6, Throwed 'em away; **GA**30, **NC**49, Throwed it down; (Qu. EE28, *Games played in the water*) Inf **NY**75, They throwed mud; (Qu. FF18, *Joking words . . about a noisy or boisterous celebration or party:* "They certainly _____ last night.") Inf **SC**34, Throwed a big one; **MO**16, Throwed a storm last night; (Qu. GG13a, *When something keeps bothering a person and makes him nervous . .* "It _____ me.") Inf **MO**1, Throwed; (Qu. GG15, . . *A person who became over-excited and lost control,* "At that point he really _____.") Inf **AR**51, Throwed a hissy; **TX**37, Throwed ace-deuce; **MO**1, Throwed one; (Qu. GG20, . . *'Very much surprised':* "When those two got married, I was certainly _____.") Inf **KY**6, Throwed me for a loop; (Qu. JJ27, *To give somebody a hint for his own good:* "He had no idea that she was up to anything, but I put _____.") Inf **IA**22, Throwed a hint or two at him; (Qu. KK11, *To make great objections or a big fuss about something:* "When we asked him to do that, he _____.") Infs **AL**3, **AR**56, **LA**2, **MS**56, **TX**4, Throwed a (duck) fit; **TX**37, Throwed a shoe; **ME**19, Throwed up his hands. **1966** *DARE* Tape **MS**72, I went to put my chickens in the chicken yard. . . And I throwed [θoʊd] the corn out. **1989** Pederson *LAGS Tech. Index* 117 **Gulf Region,** *Throw* . . preterit . . [[θrod], 122 of 914 infs; [trod], 3 infs].

b *throw;* pronc-spp *thow, trow.* *esp freq among Black speakers*

1851 Hooper *Widow Rugby's Husband* 33 **AL** [Black], Ketchin' de white boy and fetchin' um to ole missus, what trow rock at de young duck. **1922** [see **A2** above]. **1953** Atwood *Survey of Verb Forms* 25, *Throw* . . preterite. . . The uninflected *throw* . . is used by five informants, including two Negroes. **1966–67** *DARE* (Qu. OO30b, *Talking about a horse throwing the rider:* "Last week the same horse _____ [his brother].") Infs **SC**9, 26, **WA**30, Throw. [2 of 3 Infs Black] **1989** Pederson *LAGS Tech. Index* 117 **Gulf Region,** *Throw* . . preterit . . [[θro], 3 of 914 infs; [Thow] [θo], 1 inf].

c *threwed;* pronc-sp *thewed.* Cf **-ed** suff **3**

1863 in 2000 Hall *Appalachian OH & Civil War* 152, The rebels fell on our right and left as we threwed their ranks in confusion. **1884** [see **B1a** above]. a**1900** (1934) Robinson *Along 3 Rivers* 226 **VT,** 'Zarve was borned the year I hed the startin' hoss. Threwed me off, bags an' all. **1931** in 1977 Randolph *Pissing in the Snow* 57 **Ozarks,** When he give her the flowers she threwed them in the fireplace. **1957** Amer. Philos. Soc. *Proc.* 101.288 **ME,** So he took his pants off and threwed them away. **1965–69** *DARE* (Qu. C24b, *"The dog wouldn't go away, so he took a stone/rock and . . _____ [it at it.]"*) Inf **OK**46, Threwed; (Qu. OO30b, *Talking about a horse throwing the rider:* "Last week the same horse _____ [his brother].") Inf **MO**39, Threwed. **1966** *DARE* Tape **NC**22, You took all the bobjacks in your hand and threwed your ball up and laid 'em down and catch your ball. **1989** Pederson *LAGS Tech. Index* 117 **Gulf Region,** *Throw* . . preterit . . [[θrud], 1 of 914 infs].

d *thrown;* pronc-sp *thown.*

1884 [see **B1a** above]. **1934** Carmer *Stars Fell on AL* 58, My old man was one of 'em till he took to pickin' on the *guitar* an' they thrown him out. **1953** Atwood *Survey of Verb Forms* 25, *Throw.* . . preterite. . . *Thrown* . . occurs once in N.C. **1965–70** *DARE* (Qu. OO30b, *Talking about a horse throwing the rider:* "Last week the same horse _____ [his brother].") 9 Infs, **scattered,** Thrown; (Qu. AA12, *If a man loses interest in a girl and stops seeing her . . he _____*) Infs **IA**3, **MA**3, Thrown her over; (Qu. BB56, *Joking expressions for dying:* "He _____.") Inf **TX**65, Thrown in the sponge.

e *t(h)run.* [Ir dial *threwn, thrun,* which appear freq as past and past pple, and occas as present, of *thrown* in 19th-cent representations of Ir Engl] Cf **A4** above, **B2d** below

1894 Ford *Lit. Shop* 141 **NYC,** "He trun up bote hands!" said the eastsider, earnestly. **1896** *DN* 1.426 **NY,** *Trun.* . . "She trun him," said of a girl who threw a fellow over. . . a vulgar pron. of *thrown.* **1898** Dunne *Mr. Dooley Peace & War* 236 **Chicago IL,** They thrun him out. **1909** *DN* 3.405 nw**AR,** *Trun down.* . . "She trun me down cold." **1918** Mulford *Man from Bar-20* 238 **West,** I got four bits that says he wasn't aimin' at no fire when he thrun them little ones. **1942** in 1944 *ADD, Trun. . . Threw. . .* De monkeys, dey trun all de coconuts dey had. . . Dey trun me right out on my head. . . Dey trun him out too. Radio. **1968–69** *DARE* (Qu. C24b) Inf **CA**36, Threw; [trʌn]—hear occasionally; (Qu. Y10, *To throw something . . "The dog came at him, so he picked up a stone and _____ it at him.")* Inf **CA**36, Threw; trun—hear once in a while; **MA**58, Thrun [θrʌn]—old-fashioned.

2 past pple and ppl adj: usu *thrown;* also:

a *threw.*

1781 *PA Jrl. & Weekly Advt.* (Philadelphia) 16 May 1/3, Had not a gentleman *threw* out. **1833** in 1931 Jackson *Correspondence* 5.12 **TN,** On yesterday the tariff bill would have passed the House of representatives had it not been for a very insulting and irritating speech by wilde of Georgia which has threw the whole of Pennsylvania, New York and Ohio into a flame. **1897** [see **throw off 2**]. **1924** *McClure's Mag.* 56.4.64, I've threw 'em off the track. **1965–70** *DARE* (Qu. OO30a, *Talking about a horse throwing the rider: "John got a bad horse and was _____ [off].")* 29 Infs, **scattered,** Threw. [11 Infs gs educ or less] **1969** *DARE* Tape **RI**4, He got threw before he went out the yard, his first time he used it [=a snowmobile]. **1971** Jennings *Cowboys* 62 **MT, WY** (as of 1877), You lost your horse! The best rider we got, and you did the worst thing a man can do on the range! You got yourself threw! **1989** Pederson *LAGS Tech. Index* 118 **Gulf Region,** *Throw . .* past participle . . [[θru], 2 of 914 infs].

b *threwed;* pronc-sp *thewed.*

1766 in 1995 Waselkov–Braund *William Bartram on SE Indians* 5, I am afraid all will be threwed away upon him. **1884** [see **B1a** above].

c *throwed;* pronc-spp *thowed, trowd.* *chiefly among speakers with little formal educ* Cf **-ed** suff **2, horsethrowed**

1840 *S. Lit. Messenger* 6.506 **Sth,** The torn-down limb of Satan . . has *throwed* me into a mighty *flustrification.* **1884** [see **B1a** above]. **1895** *DN* 1.376 **seKY, eTN, wNC,** *Throwed* = thrown. **1903** *DN* 2.333 **seMO,** He wouldn' give up the farm till he was throwed out by the sheriff. **1909** [see **A1** above]. **1916** Howells *Leatherwood God* 14 **sOH** (as of 1830s), These . . two rooms was th'owed together. **1922** Gonzales *Black Border* 335 **sSC, GA coasts** [Gullah glossary], *T'row'd . .* thrown. **1933** Rawlings *South Moon* 93 **nFL,** They comes ever' day a-fillin' their bellies with my th'owed-out mash. **1939** *Sat. Eve. Post* 10 June 122 **AZ,** Anybody caught stackin' brush in his pile will be th'owed out er the runnin'. **1956** Moody *Home Ranch* 198 **CO** (as of 1911), What's got you throwed? **1965–70** *DARE* (Qu. OO30a, *Talking about a horse throwing the rider: "John got a bad horse and was _____ [off].")* 190 Infs, **widespread,** Throwed; **GA**77, **MI**78, Got throwed [Of all Infs responding to the question, 39% were gs educ or less; of those giving these responses, 63% were gs educ or less.]; (Qu. W29, . . *Expressions . . for things that are sewn carelessly . . "They're _____.")* 37 Infs, **scattered,** Throwed together; (Qu. C6, . . *A piece of land that's often wet, and has grass and weeds growing on it)* Inf **NJ**69, Throwed-away land, throwed-out land; (Qu. D21, *A small, poorly-built house, or one in rundown condition)* Infs **FL**49, **MS**72, Throwed-away house; (Qu. K43, *A horse that was not intentionally bred, or bred by accident)* Inf **TN**26, Throwed; (Qu. N5, *Nicknames for an automobile, especially an old or broken-down car)* Infs **FL**48, **MS**63, Throwed-away (car); (Qu. U15, *When you're buying something, if the seller puts in a little extra to make you feel that you're getting a good bargain)* Infs **MA**37, **NY**96, **SC**32, (It was) throwed in; **OK**18, It's throwed in; **MO**4, Something throwed in; **SC**7, Throwed in extra; (Qu. W41, . . *Expressions . . for someone whose clothes never look right or who always dresses carelessly)* Inf **IL**96, Look like their clothes been throwed at them; **OK**47, Looks like she was throwed together; **MI**104, Looks like they were throwed at her; **MS**83, Throwed together; (Qu. BB18, *To vomit a great deal at once)* Inf **NY**82, Had an awful calf throwed up; (Qu. GG2, . . *'Confused, mixed up': "So many things were going on at the same time that he got completely _____.")* Inf **MO**23, Throwed off; (Qu. II2a, *When two people begin to be friendly: "He has just recently _____ with John.")* Inf **MT**5, Throwed in; (Qu. OO3a, *Speaking about drinking coffee: "The coffee's all gone—we must have _____ [a lot].")* Inf **PA**165, Throwed. **1973** [see **A1** above]. **1989** Pederson *LAGS Tech. Index* 118 **Gulf Region,** *Throw . .* past participle . . [[θrod], 16 of 914 infs; [θod], 7 infs]. **2002** *DARE* File—Internet **seKY,** Cause you are going to be called devils, and be throwed out of some places.

d *t(h)run.* [See **B1e** above]

1896 *DN* 1.426 **NY,** *Trun. . . trun down . .* means "squelched." . . This *trun* appears to be . . simply a vulgar pron. of *thrown.* **1898** Dunne *Mr. Dooley Peace & War* 130 **Chicago IL,** He ought to be impeached an' thrun out. **1901** *Bookman* 14.425 **NYC,** The Tammany leader of one of

the crowded and illiterate East Side districts [said]. . . "When a party gets the big head, . . it always gets trun down." **1906** *Overland Mth.* (2d ser) 47.365 **San Francisco CA,** Jest when yuh think yer 'it' yer get trun down. **1934** Farrell *Young Manhood* 346 **Chicago IL,** I'd maybe fall asleep . . and get thrun out of church on my tail. **1968–69** *DARE* (Qu. OO30a, *Talking about a horse throwing the rider: "John got a bad horse and was _____ [off].")* Infs **IL**78, **OH**43, **TN**31, 33, 34, 36, Thrun.

e *throwned.* Cf **-ed** suff **4**

1861 *Harper's New Mth. Mag.* 22.854 **VA,** The united states. . . has throwned of the york of england. **1989** Pederson *LAGS Tech. Index* 118 **Gulf Region,** *Throw . .* past participle . . [[θrond], 1 of 914 infs].

f *throw;* pronc-sp *trow.*

1922 [see **A2** above]. **1966–67** *DARE* (Qu. OO30a, *Talking about a horse throwing the rider: "John got a bad horse and was _____ [off].")* Infs **IL**14, **OR**2, **SC**9, 26, **WY**5, Throw.

C Senses.

1 To trade or exchange objects sight unseen—usu in phr *throw knives;* hence vbl n *throwing (knives);* n *throw trade* a trade made sight unseen. **Sth, S Midl** See Map

1909 *DN* 3.381 **eAL, wGA,** *Throw knives. . .* To swap sight-unseen. . . "I'll throw knives with you." **1919** *DN* 5.35 **seKY,** *Throw knives, to. . .* To trade, or swap knives. The usage seems to be confined to knives. **c1960** *Wilson Coll.* **csKY,** *Throw knives. . .* Exchange knives "sight-unseen." **1968–69** *DARE* (Qu. U14, . . *Exchanging with somebody when neither one has seen what the other has)* Inf **NC**55, I'll throw knives—where you swap knives sight unseen; **GA**74, Throw knives—if you exchanged knives with another person, you'd say, "Whole blade or no trade"; **NC**30, Throwing knives; **SC**34, Throwing knives—what schoolboys did; neither saw the other's knife—say, "Let's throw knives"; **TX**98, Throwing knives—exchange of knives sight unseen; **AL**2, **MS**1, Throwing; **GA**77, Throw trade. **1984** Wilder *You All Spoken Here* 189 **Sth,** *Throw knives:* Swap knives.

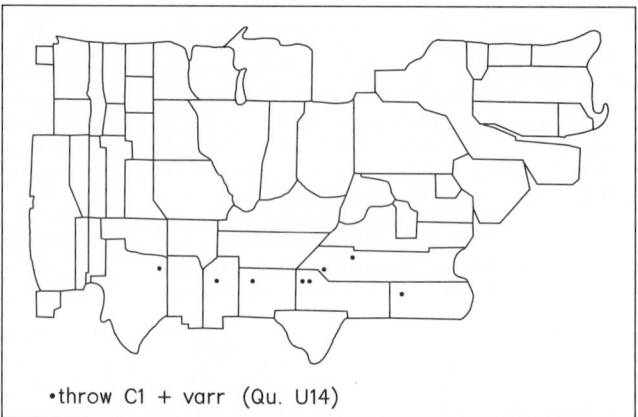

•throw C1 + varr (Qu. U14)

2 in phrr *throw papers, ~ a (paper) route:* To deliver newspapers to subscribers on a regular route. **chiefly Sth, S Midl** Cf **pass** v **4**

1945 *Maryville Daily Forum* (MO) 24 Nov 1/1, B.J. Alcott was in charge of city circulation, and he vowed he'd never throw papers. **1950** *AmSp* 25.302 **nwMO,** After I get out of school I have to throw a paper route and then eat supper. **1975** *Gt. Bend Tribune* (KS) 28 Apr 1/7, Kids still work around the house for spending money. Some mow lawns or throw papers. **2001** *DARE* File **nwMO** (as of c1930), When I used to throw papers we used to have to be sure to get them on the porch. . . My best friend used to throw papers, and I'd go along when he would throw the rural route. **2003** in 2005 *DARE* File—Internet **wTN,** When I was a boy throwing a paper route in a small West Tennessee town, I chanted nonsense poems to the morning air. *Ibid* **AZ,** I throw a paper route to help pay for the horses. **2005** *Tampa Tribune* (FL) 21 Nov (Internet), When both Al and Karen were throwing papers, they worked eight years straight without a day off. **2005** *DARE* File—Internet **seTX,** I throw a paper route every day 365 days a year. *Ibid* **GA,** While throwing papers at 4am, I was shot at by a man in a small truck. **2009** Grisham *Ford Co.* 270 **MS,** His nephew threw the Tupelo daily each morning at sunrise.

3 In **hoodoo** n **1a:** tr, often with *after, for:* to throw symbolically (something believed to have magical power) with the intention of harming someone; intr, often with *after, at, for:* to throw something or perform some other magical ritual intended to harm someone.   *among Black speakers*

1935 Hurston *Mules & Men* 232 **LA** [Black], Somebody had done throwed at her, but they didn't b'lieve in nothin'. **c1938** in 1970 Hyatt *Hoodoo* 1.257 **NYC** [Black], "I'm goin' to throw for you." That means I'm goin' to *cunjure* you to kill you in some way. *Ibid* 433 **neSC** [Black], Ah wus *throw'd aftah* once an' mah mouth wus round dataway an' de nose wus dataway. *Ibid* 509 **New Orleans LA** [Black], Yo' takes a can of lye tuh cut out all devilment dat anybody would *throw*, 'cause if dey goin' *throw* dey goin' always mostly *throw* undah. . . Yo' takes dat can of lye . . an' sprinkle so much all around undah dere. . . Den yo' take that can an' yo' bury it upside down, an' that ketches all de devilment that's *throwed* around. *Ibid* 647 **cwFL** [Black], A woman had a 'fliction on her right side . . an' she thinks somebody had *throwed after*—whut de' called *throwed after* yo'—*throwed* a shoe *after* her or done something like dat. *Ibid* 788 **cwMS** [Black], I couldn't walk right. He told me that somebody had *throwed* something *for me* and so he would rub me. *Ibid* 2.1422 **neFL** [Black], Den yo' write on dat candle with a needle jest what you want it to cover. . . When it burn down, yo' ball up all dat wax; if it's fer good yo' keep it, if it's fer bad yo' *throw it*. Ef yo' is at a distance an' a woman wanta *throw* fer yo' or a man wanta *throw* fer yo', she take gunpowder and she roll it up in a corn shuck and dey . . take a ole pot and put dat shuck in dere, and he'll stand back aside and he'll cuss at it and tell it jest what he want it tuh—whether he want it to hit chew—and he throws some fire in there at dat and dat thing go off, it will hurt chew. **1953** Goodwin *It's Good* 128 **sIL** [Black], You know folks are sayin' somebody done throwed at Big Chick.

4 To turn (a jump rope); to turn a jump rope; hence n *thrower.*

1956 *Western Folkl.* 15.47 **TX,** In this activity, one child is thrower, and doubles the rope so that she is holding both ends of the rope in her hands. She then throws the doubled rope out in such a manner as to describe a circle on the ground. As the turning rope comes around, several children attempt to jump in. The first child to miss must then throw. **1975** McDonough *Garden Sass* 223 **AR,** We played jump the rope with a long thick muscadine vine that we cut in the woods. It took two big girls or boys to throw it. **2001** in 2005 *DARE* File—Internet **TX,** We could even do the "double jump", that is jumping two ropes at a time. . . Then the throwers would whip those ropes as fast as they could until we missed. **2005** *Ibid* **TN,** *Hot Pepper:* Throwing the rope faster than normal, perhaps as fast as the thrower can throw. *High Water:* Throwing the rope so the rope does not touch the ground.

throw a brick and hide one's hand(s) v phr   *among Black speakers*

Fig: to do someone an injury while concealing or denying one's responsibility; see quots.

1986 *Washington Post* (DC) 17 July sec A 3 (Internet) **Chicago IL** [Black], The mayor has reacted sharply to the petition drive, denouncing it and blaming his council opponents. "They want to throw a brick and hide their hand." **2003** Hot Boy$ *Let 'Em Burn* (Sound Recording) [Black], I don't throw a brick and hide my hand / If I make a statement I can stand up actin' like a man. **2003** *DARE* File **nwMS** (as of 1960s) [Black], *Throw a brick and hide your hand*—which I heard a lot from middle aged and older Black people in Quitman County, Mississippi in the 1960's. It means—to do someone harm in secret—often this means to spread gossip about them. **2003** *DARE* File—Internet [Black], It people like you who sits behind the scenes and throw a brick and hide his hand. **2004** *Ibid*, [From a writer called AceBoon:] I agree with Dremond yo. Shit, hiphop is political. Why throw a brick and hide your hand. Its all love over here anyways! **2005** *Ibid* [Black], Then you should have shown the [White] chick on the bike. but thats your tactic, throw a brick and hide your hands. then spin it on the injured party.

throw after   See **throw C3**

throw a hook   See **hook, shoot a**

throw a (paper) route   See **throw C2**

throw at   See **throw C3**

throwback n   **West**

1 A cow or group of cattle separated at a **roundup 1** and sent back to the home range; the process of driving such cattle back.

1936 McCarthy *Lang. Mosshorn* np **West** [Range terms], *Throwbacks.* . . Cattle owned by the ranch which employs the rep. He generally starts these heads back toward their own range. **1958** Blasingame

Dakota Cowboy 18 **SD** (as of c1905), The reps gathered this stock [= strays] from our roundups and drove them back to their owners. Such a drive was known as a "throw-back." *Ibid* 223, Bird Rose sent a man to help take my throw-back [=a large group of cattle] and my string of saddle horses to Ben Lone Man's wagon.

2 Of a horse: the act of rearing up and falling over backwards; hence n *throwbacker* a horse that does this.

1936 Adams *Cowboy Lingo* 99 **West,** The 'throw-back' was when the horse hurled himself backward intentionally, and this was a trick of a 'killer.' **1956** Almirall *From College* 25 **CO,** Goldie St. Claire was killed by what is known as a "throw-backer." The real four-legged outlaw she attempted to ride went over backwards and, before she could clear her feet from her stirrups, pinned her underneath.

throwboard n

The bangboard of a wagon.

1889 NE State Bd. Ag. *Annual Rept. for 1888* 164, I hear from every quarter the measured thwack of ears against the husker's "throw board." **1907** Bailey *Cyclop. Amer. Ag.* 2.411, Large quantities [of corn] are husked from the shocks in the field, while a greater quantity is husked from the standing stalks and thrown into wagons that precede the huskers in the field. A high sideboard or throw-board is placed on one side of the wagon-bed to catch the ears and cause them to fall into the wagon. **1929** CA Ag. Exper. Sta. Berkeley *Bulletin* 477.11, In the harvesting of small acreages, the heads [of grain sorghum] may be thrown into a wagon equipped with a stop or "throw" board. **1936** *Time* 14 Dec 8, [Letter:] I'm an old corn-hand from the corn land—have husked corn many a day—and we always call it the "throw-board" as it is in southern Missouri and in the South. . . Never that fancy city-made word [=bang-board]. **1949** *PADS* 11.12 **wTX** (as of 1911–29), *Throwboard.* . . An extra side-board on a wagon against which corn or maize is thrown from the opposite side.

throw down v phr   Freq with *on, upon*   **esp Gulf States, SW**

1 tr: To lower (a gun) into firing position, draw (a gun) on.

1882 in 2005 (acc) Lexis–Nexis Legal Research *State Case Law: TX* (Internet), The witness caught at the pistol, and as he did so, the defendant threw the pistol down on him and snapped it. The hammer caught on the witness' shirt, and it did not explode. **1897** *Ibid: OK,* Deceased had on another occasion "throwed a shotgun down on him, and started to kill him." . . Just a moment after, he raised his pistol, . . and, with an oath, threw his gun down, and fired towards Williams. **1898** Canfield *Maid of Frontier* 183 **TX,** He . . threw his pistol down on Chisholm at three feet distance. **1909** *Pioneer Days SW* 303 **TX** (as of 1860), I drew my gun down to fire. I thought that I could hit him, but I missed. . . I went through the motion of loading right quick and threw my gun down on him again, and he ran into the brush. **1914** in 2005 (acc) Lexis–Nexis Legal Research *State Case Law: AL* (Internet), I saw he was going to get me anyhow, and threw the gun down on his body, and then I threw it down and shot his leg.

2 intr: To lower a gun into firing position, draw a gun on.

1897 Lummis *King of Broncos* 241 **NM,** He carried it [=a shotgun] on his shoulder, grasping it at the guard "throwing down," just as one would a six-shooter. **1905** in 2005 (acc) Lexis–Nexis Legal Research *State Case Law: OK* (Internet), Well, just as he got his rope on him [=a horse] the deputy threw down on him. **1942** Faulkner *Go Down* 252 **MS,** Boon . . sprang up and threw down upon them with the old gun. **1963** *NY Times* (NY) 12 Mar 4 **NV,** I jumped out of the car and threw down on this cop before they had a chance to take us. **1976** Brown *Gloss. Faulkner* 199 **MS,** *Threw down upon them with the old gun.* . . pointed the gun at them quickly. The expression comes from the situation of a hunter who, for safety's sake, carries his gun (in any of several ways) with the muzzle aimed upwards, and who literally throws the muzzle down onto the line of his game as he aims. **1997** *Atlanta Jrl.-Constitution* (GA) 5 Oct (Internet), One of them pulled out a gun and stuck it in this guy's mouth. I jumped out and threw down on him. **2004** in 2005 *DARE* File—Internet **NY,** The buck broke into an opening about 30 feet across. I threw down on him, saw brown and pulled the trigger.

throw-down hole n   Also *throw-down*

=**hay chute.**

1950 WELS (The hole for throwing hay down below) 1 Inf, **cwWI,** Throw-down hole. **1950** WELS Suppl. **cwWI,** Throw-down hole— division line between hay bays. **1966–70** DARE (Qu. M5) Infs **IL**66, **IN**19, **MS**4, **NJ**22, **OH**48, **SC**69, Throw-down hole; **NY**205, Throwdown.

throw down on (or upon)   See **throw down** v phr

throwed See **throw B1a, 2c**

thrower See **throw C4**

throw for See **throw C3**

throwing (knives) See **throw C1**

throwing the hatchet See **throw the hatchet**

throw knives See **throw C1**

throw line n   scattered, but esp Lower Missip Valley, Missip-
Ohio Valleys, TX   See Map   Cf **setline**

A **trotline** n **1,** esp one that is relatively short and anchored to
the bank at only one end.

　　1890 *Decatur Morning Rev.* (IL) 21 June [4]/3 (newspaper-
archive.com), One catfish weighed 20 pounds, another 15, another 10,
and 3 others from 6 to 8. They were caught on a throw line. **1900** in
1995 Millersville Univ. Center for PA Ger. Studies *Jrl.* Winter 16 **sePA,**
Papa put the rods and throw lines in down at the Forks. **1922** *Mexia
Eve. News* (TX) 30 Jan 5/2, According to the story a throw line baited
with small perch had been put out into the river. **1944** *NE State Jrl.*
(Lincoln) 28 Sept 7/7, Members decided to hold a discussion open to
the public on "Shall We Abandon Throw-line Fishing on Nebraska
Streams?" **1965–70** *DARE* (Qu. P13, . . *Ways of fishing . . besides the
ordinary hook and line*) 13 Infs, **scattered, but esp Lower Missip Valley, Missip-Ohio Valleys, TX,** Throw line(s); **CA65,** Throw line—put a
triangular sinker, three or four hooks, thrown out beyond; **CO4,** Throw
line—a trotline; **IA11,** Throw line—across rivers; **IA29,** Throw line—
weight on one end; **IN35,** Throw line—an unanchored trotline; **IN40,**
Throw line—a short trotline, not anchored; **LA7,** Throw line—a long
line with a number of shorter lines near the end, where a heavy sinker is
attached; **LA10,** Throw line—a heavy weight at end, several hooks and
a bell to warn fishermen; **MN19,** Throw lines—tie one end and throw
the other end out with a weight; **MO39,** Throw line—where a line with
hooks is tied to a tree on the bank; **NV8,** Throw line—had four or five
short lines on one line, not legal now; **OH47,** Throw line—like a
trotline, but on the bottom; **OK52,** Throw line—five, six hooks, throw
out with big weight; **TX81,** Throw line—a trotline tied only at one end;
IA4, Throw-line seining—for catfish, illegal; a line with several hooks
attached is tied to a rock and thrown across a river so four or five hooks
are in the water; [**LA34,** Throw line—no pole; a line with heavy weight
just thrown and held; **MI93,** Throw line—weight would carry bait to
bottom, then you would drag it in; **PA168,** Throw line—also called
handline;] (Qu. P17, . . *When . . people fish by lowering a line and
sinker close to the bottom of the water*) 11 Infs, **scattered,** Throw line
(fishing); **KY75,** Throw line—for catfish; **LA29,** Throw line—attached
to the bank, a heavy sinker at the end of a long line, one or more hooks;
the heavy weight is thrown into the middle of the stream; **MS18,** Throw
lines. [*DARE* Ed: The three bracketed Infs, and perh some of the others,
appear to be referring to a handline rather than a type of trotline.] **1966**
DARE Tape **AR36,** Then you have a throw line that have maybe four,
five hooks on it. You'd tie it to a limb at the bank and bait it up and then
have a weight on it and just throw it out. **1968** *Oshkosh Northwestern*
(WI) 25 Apr 29/3, Drop or throw line fishing shall not be allowed.
1998 *Mother Earth News* Feb/Mar (Internet), A throwline is simply a
trotline that's baited up on shore and thrown out from the bank with a
weight attached.

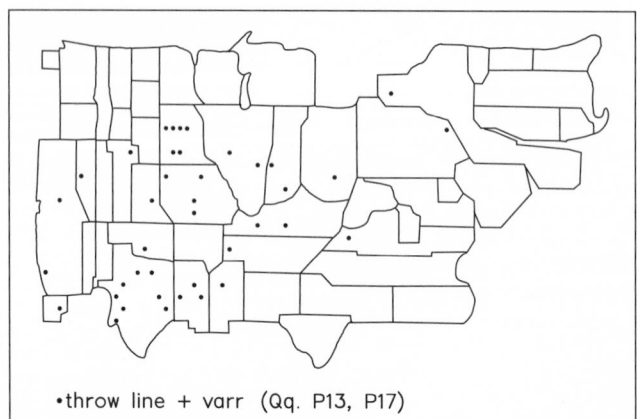

•throw line + varr (Qq. P13, P17)

thrown See **throw B1d**

throwned See **throw B2e**

throw off v phr

1　To fail to exert oneself, shirk.   **chiefly SW**

　　[**1857** *Porter's Spirit of Times* 10 Oct 85 **MO,** It had been stated that
this was a throw off match; it was not so—each man would do his best.]
1867 Twain *Jumping Frog* 18 **West,** I do wonder what in the nation that
frog throw'd off for—I wonder if there an't something the matter with
him. **1875** *Harper's New Mth. Mag.* 50.927 **NM,** Rusty broke for the
fence, and the on-lookers shouted "Run, Rusty, run!" Rusty ran, and as
he climbed the stockade, the steer tilted full against it. . . Once upon the
other side . . he turned to them . . and said, "You fellows must think I am
a darned fool to throw off on such a race as that!" **1956** Gipson *Old
Yeller* 137 **TX,** I knew he wasn't throwing off. Jumper was full of a lot
of pesky, aggravating mule tricks; but when you called on him to move a
load, he'd move it or bust something. **1967–69** *DARE* (Qu. BB27,
When somebody pretends to be sick . . he's _____) Infs **TX**29, 65,
Throwing off; (Qu. JJ26, *If somebody has been doing poor work or not
enough, the boss might say, "If he wants to keep his job he'd better
_____."*) Infs **TX**11, 29, Quit throwing off.

2　with *on:* To neglect, ignore, abandon.

　　1858 (1930) DeLong *Jrls.* 9.263 **NY,** Partially made up my mind
from her statement's that Elida was throwing off on me. **1872** Twain
Roughing It 337 **NV,** What I was a drivin' at, was, that he never *throwed
off* on his mother—don't you see? No indeedy. He give her a house to
live in, and town lots, and plenty of money. **1875** Harte *Tales of Argonauts* 164 **CA,** It won't do . . to let that there gal go back to San Francisco and say, that when she was sick and alone, the only man in Five
Forks under whose roof she had rested . . ever threw off on her. **1885**
Howells in *Harper's New Mth. Mag.* 72.25, They gave him frumps to
take out to supper, mothers and maiden aunts, and if the mothers were
youngish, they threw off on him, and did not care for his talk. **1897**
Higginson *From Land* 197 **WA,** If you want to know so bad, . . I'll tell
you. He's threw off on me.

3　with *on:* To shift blame or responsibility onto.

　　1868 *Putnam's Mag.* 12.569 **nMI,** When I do git into a scrape, I won't
plead a baby-act, and throw off on my friends. **1920** Hunter *Trail
Drivers TX* 334 (as of c1880), This [=willingness to work overtime on
night guard duty] shows the generous disposition of those old trail boys,
in that they would not throw off on their comrades.

4　with *on:* To disparage, ridicule, cast aspersions on.   [Cf
EDD throw off v. II.1.(6).(c) "to make fun"]   **Sth, S Midl**
See Map

　　1887 *Century Illustr. Mag.* 33.612 **sAppalachians,** Now, I ain't a-
meanin' ter throw off on 'em, an' I don't say as they ain't all steddy
enough when they settle down, but a gal in love is the oncertainest
creetur that ever lived. **1915** *DN* 4.243 **eTN,** *Throw off on.* . . To make
fun of; also, to say uncomplimentary things about. "He threw off on me
something awful when I wore them." **1931** (1991) Hughes–Hurston
Mule Bone 94 **cFL** [Black], Jim always tryin' to throw off on me. But
you can't joke him. **1937** *Hall Coll.* **wNC, eTN,** *Throw off.* . . To censure or revile—"She was throwing off on me." **1942** Rawlings *Cross
Creek* 157 **nFL,** Now you're throwin' off on my sister. . . She's a good
woman. Don't you go callin' her boy a bastard. **c1960** *Wilson Coll.*
csKY, *Throw off on.* . . Make fun of. **1965–70** *DARE* (Qu. Y3, *To say
uncomplimentary things about somebody*) 12 Infs, **scattered Sth, S
Midl,** Throw off on; **GA72,** Throwing off on; [**SC58,** Throw on; **VA24,**
Throw one off on;] (Qu. Y4, . . *A very uncomplimentary remark*) Inf

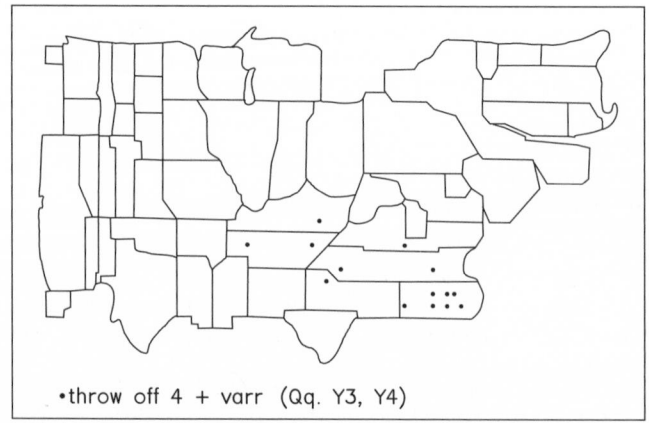

•throw off 4 + varr (Qq. Y3, Y4)

NC11, She's always throwing off on him. **1966** *DARE* FW Addit **SC,** Don't be throwing off on me. **1968** *DARE* Tape **GA**31, I explained to 'em that they were so much safer in a boat here in the Okefenokee than they were in that bus coming in here. . . Some of 'em thought I was throwing off on the bus driver, but I didn't mean that. **1975** Newell *If Nothin' Don't Happen* 152 **FL,** This was a story that Ma didn't like at all. She said it weren't only sacrilegious but that it throwed off on the womenfolks. **1984** Burns *Cold Sassy* 30 **nGA** (as of 1906), She . . didn't throw off on people who said "I seen" or "I taken," like Aunt Loma. **1986** Pederson *LAGS Concordance,* 1 inf, **swGA,** To throw off on—to deprecate. **2000** in 2005 *DARE* File—Internet **AR,** [Speech by President Clinton:] Voters are not stupid. They know, when politicians are throwing off on each other, they're trying to help themselves.

throw off on See **throw off 2, 3, 4**

throw papers See **throw C2**

throw the by See **throw the stick**

throw the dog See **dog** n[1] **B5a**

throw the goal See **throw the stick**

throw the hatchet v phr, hence vbl n *throwing the hatchet* Also *fling the hatchet* [*OED2* throw (fling, sling) the hatchet (at *hatchet* sb. 2) 1780 →] **esp sAppalachians** Fig: to make exaggerated or false statements.
   1841 Mercier–Gallop *Life Man-of-War* 14, Garnet, . . knowing the simplicity of his auditor, was now determined to *fling the hatchet,* as sailors call it. **1899** (1912) Green *VA Folk-Speech* 446, *Throwing the hatchet.* . . Telling lies. "He is given to throwing the hatchet." **c1940** in 2004 Montgomery–Hall *Dict. Smoky Mt. Engl.* 605 **eTN,** He can't open his mouth without throwing the hatchet. **1984** Wilder *You All Spoken Here* 116 **Sth,** *Throw the hatchet:* Exaggerate; tell lies; extend the truth. **1996–97** in 2004 Montgomery–Hall *Dict. Smoky Mt. Engl.* 605 **wNC, eTN,** *Throw the hatchet.* . . To tell a lie [2 infs].

throw the stick n Also *throw the by,* ~ *goal,* ~ *wicket,* ~ *wicky* Cf **bye, kick the can 1, wicket, yards off** A hide-and-seek game that involves sending out or freeing players by throwing a stick.
   [**1883** Newell *Games & Songs* 160, *I Spy.* . . In a variety of the game, a stick is set up against a tree. One of the players seizes it, and throws it as far as possible. The children hide. . . If any of the hiders can reach the tree and throw down the stick, all prisoners are released, and the seeker must begin over again. A similar game, in New York, is called "Yards off."] **1891** *Jrl. Amer. Folkl.* 4.227 **Brooklyn NYC,** *Throw the stick.* One player throws a stick as far as he can, and the one who is "it" must run after it, and put it back in its place. In the mean time the others hide. "It" then looks for those in hiding, and when he spies one of them, he cries out and touches the wicket. The players may run in from hiding, and if they touch the wicket before "it," they are free. The first spied becomes "it" for the next game. **1935** Mason–Mitchell *Social Games* 229, *Green Wolf (Throw the Stick, Yards Off).* . . Lean a stick up against a tree or wall. . . One of the players throws the stick as far as possible and all run and hide. "It" recovers the stick, sets up the goal, and sets out in search. When he sees a player . . "it" and the runner dash for the goal. If "it" reaches it first the player is a prisoner. . . If the runner reaches the goal first he throws the stick and "it" must recover the stick before further searching. . . The game continues until all the players are prisoners. **1953** Brewster *Amer. Nonsinging Games* 48 **IL,** *Throw the Wicket.* . . One of the players is designated wicket-keeper and . . leans the piece of broomstick against a tree or lamp post. Then he covers his eyes . . until the rest have had time to run away and hide. . . [T]he wicket-keeper starts out to find the hiders. If he finds a player and tags him, the latter must go to the wicket and remain there until another player can slip out of his hiding place, seize the wicket, and throw it away without being tagged by the keeper. While the latter is retrieving the wicket, the others in hiding may change their hiding places . . and . . all . . who have been captured are now able to run away and hide again. The game ends only when the keeper holds all the others captive. **1957** *Sat. Eve. Post Letters,* We also played "throw the by"; the one who was "it" hurling a dead stick, "the by," while the others went and hid. *Ibid* **PA,** A stick throwing game was known as "throw the wicky" in Pennsylvania from where my wife came. We knew it in Downers Grove, Illinois as "sheep's in, stick's out." **1968–69** *DARE* (Qu. EE10, *A game in which a short stick lying on the ground is flipped into the air and then hit with a longer stick*) Inf **RI**17, Throw the stick—throw stick, whoever [is] "it" has to retrieve it; others hide, "it" must catch all; (Qu. EE33, . . *Outdoor*

games . . *that children play*) Inf **IA**34, Throw the goal—a form of hide-and-seek. You throw a stick; the person who is "it" must chase the stick while the others hide; [**RI**1, Throw the stick—go out and get first]. **2007** Kalish *Little Heathens* 218 **IA** (as of 1930s), We took this mighty bat . . and used it . . as a goal when we got together spring nights to play throw-the-goal.

throw trade See **throw C1**

throw up v phr **NEng** Of a governing entity: to give up ownership of and responsibility for (a road under its control).
   1720 in 1888 Sheldon *Doc. Hist. Suffield* 205 **MA,** At a Lawfull Town Meeting of the Inhabitants of Suffield. . . It was voted to throw up the highway that runs through James King Junr, his lot; provided there be a way to the Grismill. **1774** in 1922 Hadley *Hist. Goffstown* 1.207 **NH,** Voted to throw up the old road from John Pattee's to Plummer Hadley's and accept one laid out in lieu thereof. **1978** *Yankee* Mar 123 **NH,** I took a walk down Taggert Road the other day. The road's been "thrown up" and now it's a private way. [Footnote to *thrown up:*] Term meaning that when a town gives up a road, that property reverts to the owners on either side of the road to the road's center. The town, by vote, may take the road back if not otherwise stated in the deeds, and then only with the permission of the landholders. **1989** *News & Citizen* (Morrisville VT) 6 Apr 14, The Selectmen . . direct that a hearing be held to determine if the . . public good require that the following highways be reclassified and thrown up and discontinued. **2003** *Burlington Free Press* (VT) 28 Feb (Internet), *Top 10 reasons why you should attend town meeting.* . . Free heat. . . Good conversation. . . Comfort yourself that the term to "throw up a road" isn't as gross as it sounds. **2005** *DARE* File—Internet **VT,** Roads dominated the agenda of the Warren Select Board meeting, . . followed by discussion on whether or not to "throw up," or discontinue, the two roads as public highways.

throw up one's socks See **socks, throw up one's**

throw weight n =**hitching weight.**
   1967 Lanham *Paste-Pot Man* 27 **TX** (as of c1900), They would stop their wagons or buggies on the street in front of the house, toss down a mound of iron with ringbolt and tether-rope called a throw-weight, or drop-weight, and stand by the picket fence.

thrun See **throw A4, B1e, 2d**

thrush blackbird n =**rusty blackbird.**
   1889 Davie *Nests N. Amer. Birds* 1281, The Rusty Grackle or Thrush Blackbird is only . . seen in small flocks in the spring and fall during its passages north and south. **1917** (1923) *Birds Amer.* 2.263, *Rusty Blackbird.* . . *Other Names.*—Rusty Grackle; Thrush Blackbird. [*Ibid* 264, In flight and in the shape of its bill this bird somewhat resembles a Thrush.] **1955** Forbush–May *Birds* 471, *Rusty Blackbird.* . . *Other names:* Rusty Grackle, Thrush Blackbird.

thrusher n [*thrush* infl by *thrasher*]
   1966 *DARE* (Qu. Q14, . . *Names . . for . . brown thrasher*) Inf **MS**21, Thrushers; (Qu. Q14, . . *Names . . for . . thrush*) Inf **AR**42, Thrusher.

thrust n [Perh by folk-etym from *thrush*]
   1966–69 *DARE* (Qu. Q14, . . *Names . . for . . brown thrasher*) Inf **MD**15, Brown thrust [θrʌst]—brown, slightly larger than robin [FW: Inf doesn't know another name for it.]; **MO**37, Brown thrust; **LA**15, Thrust [θrʌst]; (Qu. Q14, . . *Names . . for . . thrush*) Inf **FL**9, Thrust.

thruve See **thrive 1**

thruway See **throughway**

thu(e) See **through** adv, prep **1**

thulé See **tule 1**

thumb v, hence vbl n *thumbing* **West** To poke or jab (a horse) with the thumb to provoke bucking; to treat a horse in such a way.
   1933 *AmSp* 8.1.29 **nwTX** [Ranch diction], *Thumb.* To run one's thumbs up the side of the horse's neck to make him pitch. **1936** Adams *Cowboy Lingo* 104 **West,** 'Thumbing' was jabbing a horse with the thumb to provoke further bucking. **1937** *DN* 6.620 **swTX,** Sometimes the *bronc-* or *bronco-buster* decides to *thumb his mount;* that is, after the wild horse stops pitching, the rider sticks his thumbs into the animal's shoulders in order to goad it on to its final pitches; and thus he tames or

breaks the horse more readily.   **1958** Blasingame *Dakota Cowboy* 204 **SD,** He leaned over and "thumbed" Nigger Heathen on both sides of his neck, from his shoulders to his ears. A dig like that—poking the thumbs into his neck and raking to his ears—was a definite insult to a cow pony.

thumb-ball n

The thumb.

1946 *PADS* 6.13 **eNC** (as of 1900–10), *Thumb-ball: . .* thumb. . . Common among children.   **1950** *PADS* 13.17 **TX** (as of c1920), *Thumb-ball.*

thumb, go all around one's   See elbow, go (all) around one's

thumbing   See thumb

thumb-pounder n   Also *thumb-knocker*

An inexpert carpenter.

1951 *Tri-City Herald* (Pasco WA) 20 Feb 7/3, "How to Expand and Improve Your Home." . . The author's step-by-step directions will be a revelation to every neophyte thumb-pounder.   **1959** *VT Hist.* 27.164, *Thumb-pounder. . .* An awkward carpenter. Common. Vermont.   **1962** *McDavid Coll.* **OK,** Thumb-knocker—jackleg carpenter.   **1988** *Post-Std.* (Syracuse NY) 14 June sec D 3/2, You buy, without browsing, a copy of Home Carpenter & Thumb Pounder magazine and you get it home and nowhere in it is an article on how to build a Nuclear Particle Accelerator.

thumbprint cookie n   Cf robin's nest

A cookie with a depression in the center filled with jam or other sweet substance.

1950 *Eve. Telegraph* (Dixon IL) 30 Nov 19/1, *Thumbprint Cookies. . .* Remove from oven. Quickly press thumb gently on top of each cookie. Return to oven.   **1969** *Daily Times–News* (Burlington NC) 1 May sec C 3/3, Ever since Great Grandma's time, kids have doted on thumbprint cookies.   **1970** *Odessa Amer.* (TX) 2 Jan sec A 4/3, Refreshments of thumbprint cookies with purple centers . . were served to guests.   **1976** *Times Recorder* (Zanesville OH) 5 Dec sec C 3/2, *Thumbprint Cookies. . .* Remove from oven. Quickly press thumb gently on top of each cookie. Return to oven. . . My fondness for Thumbprint Cookies . . [d]eveloped during my college days at Muskingum. A nearby bakery supplied them for our teas and receptions.   **1999** *Mt. Democrat* (Placerville CA) 18 Nov sec A 9/1, Third-place was Nancy Noble for her delicate Thumbprint Cookies.   **2003** *Popik Coll.* **NYC** (as of c1950), I remember as a child helping my mom make thumbprint cookies. My job was pressing my thumb into the center of each ball of dough to make a hole big enough for that sweet jam filling.

thumb weed n   Also *Mary's thumb weed*   Cf lady's thumb, tearthumb

See quot.

1968 *DARE* (Qu. S21, *. . Weeds . . that are a trouble in gardens and fields*) Inf **NC**49, Mary's thumb weed; thumb weed.

thum-gut   See therm

thump barrel n   Also *thump(er), thumper barrel, thump(er) keg, thump tank, thumping keg, thump(ing) chest* [From the noise it makes]   **chiefly sAppalachians**   Also called **doubler 5b**

In moonshining: a closed vessel containing **backings** (or fresh **beer 1**) through which steam from the **still-pot** is passed before it reaches the condenser; hence nouns *long thump rod, thump post* the pipe conveying steam to the bottom of the thump barrel; n *short thump rod* the pipe conveying steam from the thump barrel.

1912 *Recreation* 35.199 **TN,** Some cut wood, others stirred mash, while one well-known desperate character plastered the "thumper" and retort ready for business.   **1913** Kephart *Highlanders* 138 **sAppalachians,** Two and a half gallons is all that can be got out of a bushel by blockaders' methods, even with the aid of a "thumpin'-chist."   **1922** in 2005 (acc) Lexis–Nexis Legal Research *State Case Law: NC* (Internet), The officers found a still site . . , three or four barrels, fermenters filled with beer, and a thumping keg used to put the low wine in.   **1924** *Ibid: AL,* There was evidence that the "thumper keg" smelled strong of whisky.   **1936** *Ibid: AL,* The first witness, testified that . . he saw him take the connection down off the still that runs from the cap to the thumper barrel.   **1939** *Hall Coll.* **eTN,** I don't like a thump a-tall. I would rather have singlin's and doublin's.   **1939** in 2004 Montgomery–Hall *Dict. Smoky Mt. Engl.* 606 **wNC, eTN,** The first run is known as

"singlin's": the second is "doublin's." The second run is by-passed by the use of the "thump tank."   **1967–69** *DARE* Tape **GA**72, The thump barrel was also known as the doubling barrel or the doubler. . . The thump barrel sets between your condenser and your still—it doubles the whiskey; you put backings or beer in this barrel; **TN**9, Use five- or ten-gallon thump keg. Use copper tube for connection from cap still to thumper. . . Sometimes when you're boiling a still . . it pukes over . . through the worm and it makes strings in the whiskey. Well, if you use a thumper, it goes down in the bottom of the thumper and it won't go up in your coil.   **1972** *Foxfire Book* 325 **nGA,** From this barrel . . the steam moves into the long thump rod . . which carries it to the bottom of the fifty-gallon thump barrel . . and releases it to bubble up through the fresh beer. . . Picked up again at the top by the short thump rod . . the steam moves into the heater box.   **1974** Dabney *Mountain Spirits* xxv **sAppalachians,** *Thump Barrel:* Also known as the doubler, thumper, or thump keg. This container is charged with fresh beer or backings. Vapors from the pot bubble through, giving a second distillation called "thump likker."   **1986** Pederson *LAGS Concordance,* 1 inf, **cTN,** A thump—part of the still.   **1995** Parce *Twice-Told* 41 (*Montgomery Coll.*), Normally blockaders did not run doublings. But to ensure good whiskey with singlings, they used a "thump chest" or "barrel."   **c1999** in 2004 Montgomery–Hall *Dict. Smoky Mt. Engl.* 606 **wNC, eTN,** *Thump post. . .* A pipe that goes down in the thump keg with a notch cut out to let the steam through. You put about 4 or 5 gallons of backins in the thump keg for vapors to filter through on the first run.

thumper n

1   See **thump barrel.**

2   A still that employs a **thump barrel.**

1949 Webber *Backwoods Teacher* 125 **Ozarks,** The enterprising fellow who supposedly was running a "thumper"—a "lightnin'" still—at the fork of Little and Big Piney creeks.

3   Prob a **bittern** (here: *Botaurus lentiginosus*).   Cf **thunder pumper 1**

1965 *DARE* (Qu. Q8, *A water bird that makes a booming sound before rain and often stands with its beak pointed almost straight up*) Inf **UT**3, Thumper.

thumper barrel (or keg), thumping chest (or keg), thump keg   See thump barrel

thump liquor n   Also *thump whiskey*

Whiskey made using a **thump barrel.**

1968 *Foxfire* 2.3.101 **nGA,** Names given moonshine include . . thump whiskey.   **1974** [see **thump barrel**].

thump post   See thump barrel

thumps n pl   With *the*   [Transf from *thumps* an affliction of domestic animals marked by contractions of the diaphragm similar to hiccups]   Cf **buck fever**

Palpitations of the heart; see quots.

1878 *Harper's New Mth. Mag.* 58.38 **MA,** No railroad accidents to give you the thumps jest readin' of 'em.   **1903** *DN* 2.333 **seMO,** *Thumps, the. . .* Palpitation of the heart.   **1945** *MD Conservationist* 22.3.14, Campbell told young Skinner that he had been a victim of the "thumps" and that older and more experienced hunters had been worse afflicted in their first deer hunt.

thump tank   See thump barrel

thump whiskey   See thump liquor

thunder n

1   in phr *play thunder:* To wreak havoc; to err, blunder.

1849 *Adams Sentinel* (Gettysburg PA) 27 Aug [4]/3 (newspaper-archive.com) **cwPA,** One "swanged" that Col. McCandless looked like a General that would "play thunder and break things."   **1862** *NY Times* (NY) 9 July 3/3, The lightning on Monday night played thunder with those who deal in beef and mutton. We were informed at the market that whole stocks were discolored and spoiled by the effects of the electric spark.   **1886** *New Era* (Humeston IA) [18 Feb 8]/2 (newspaper-archive.com), You have played thunder; you got the wrong man down to the wrong woman; you have got them crossed. Fix it up quick.   **1905** *Altoona Mirror* (PA) 10 June 4/1, Whether the appointment of Dr. Dixon as the head of the new state health department smashed any big machine slate or not is not certainly known, but it has played thunder with some little ones.   **1931** *Burlington Daily Times* (NC) 22 Apr [3]/2 (newspaperarchive.com), The boll weevil is busy in old Alabama—and it looks like cotton won't be worth a darn; but if you want to make a living, just plant lots of corn, raise a few shoats and toot your own horn. Don't sell, as you are sure to play-thunder. **1952** Brown *NC Folkl.* 1.601, *Thunder, to play.* . . To commit an error or a blunder.—Central and east. **1984** Wilder *You All Spoken Here* 45 **Sth,** *Played thunder:* Played hell; erred, and no two ways about it.

2 in phrr *not to hear (it) thunder* and varr: To be deaf. **chiefly Sth, S Midl** See Map Cf **deaf** adj **B1c, d**

1885 *Marion Daily Star* (OH) 15 June 1/6, [Reprinted from *Puck:*] He's as deaf as a clam. He can't hear it thunder. **1886** *Lima Democratic Times* (OH) 13 Nov 2/7 **GA,** [Patent medicine testimonial:] I was so deaf I couldn't hear thunder. **1900** *Wellsboro Agitator* (PA) 7 Feb 6/5, Pa, that man going yonder can't hear it thunder. . . Is he deaf? **1935** Caldwell *Kneel* 219 **GA,** "Oh, Pa!" he said loudly. "Oh, Pa!" He stopped under the bedroom window when he realized what he had been doing. "Now, that's a fool thing for me to be out here doing. . . Pa couldn't hear it thunder." *Ibid* 223, I'm scared Pa might stray off into the swamp and get lost for good. He couldn't hear it thunder, even. **1956** in 2005 *DARE* File—Internet **SC,** Now, Louise I must quit. I'm nearly blind and can't hear it thunder, and at present I'm tired. **1965–70** *DARE* (Qu. X19b, . . *If a person's hearing is very bad . . he's* _____) Infs **AZ**1, **KY**24, **MD**36, **MS**60, **NC**40, **SC**42, **TN**23, Can't hear (it) thunder; **AR**40, **KY**19, **TN**13, Couldn't hear it thunder; **TN**1, **TX**54, Can't even hear it thunder; **KY**94, **MO**18, He couldn't hear it thunder; **1967** Bourne *Woman in Levi's* 45 **AZ,** I had to . . yell at the top of my voice that *that was the place.* He couldn't hear it thunder, but he would not watch to see if I motioned to him. **1977** Randolph *Pissing in the Snow* 164 **Ozarks,** My old woman is so deaf she can't hear it thunder. **1986** Pederson *LAGS Concordance (Deaf)* 1 inf, **swGA,** He can't hear thunder—really deaf; 1 inf, **csAL,** Couldn't hear thunder—very deaf—commonly used; 1 inf, **nwLA,** That old bastard couldn't hear it thunder. **2005** *DARE* File—Internet **TX,** John is almost deaf and can't hear it thunder. *Ibid* **KS,** [He] could sing like an angel, but couldn't hear it thunder.

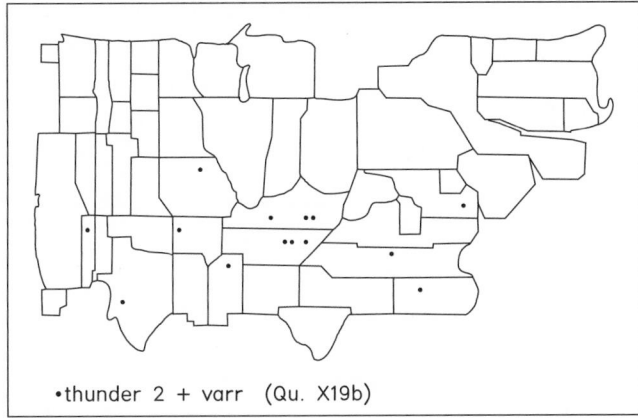

•thunder 2 + varr (Qu. X19b)

3 A children's running game; hence exclam *thunder* used as a call in the game.

1969 [see **thanuary**].

thunder-and-lightning snake See **thunder snake 1**

thunder and Tom Walker exclam Cf **devil and Tom Walker, the**

1932 Stribling *Store* 431 **AL,** "Why, thunder and Tom Walker!" roared Augustus.

thunderation n, exclam Cf **flinderation 2, tarnation** n, exclam See Intro "Language Changes" III.1
Used as a euphem for *hell, damnation.*

1845 Thompson *Pineville* 181 **GA,** I'll blow 'em all to everlastin' thunderation. **1856** (1928) Twain *Advent. Snodgrass* 23 **MO,** Thunderation. It [=the "iron horse"] wasn't no more like a hoss than a meetin house. **1877** *Harper's New Mth. Mag.* 54.294 **CT,** Ketch his head, can't ye? Thunderation! I'm a-tippin', sure's ye live! **1887** *Century Illustr. Mag.* 35.44 **IL,** Everybody wants to know who in thunderation Rache will marry. **1899** (1912) Green *VA Folk-Speech* 447, *Thunderation.* . . An exclamation. **1936** *WV Review* Aug 346, The short expletives that can be shot out for any reason, or for no particular reason, . . [include] Thunderation. **c1938** in Lib. of Congress *Amer. Memory: WPA Life Hist.* (Internet) **TX,** Who in thunderation wouldn't quit most anything to get a trip overseas? **1943** *LANE* Map 600, The map

shows . . expressions used as exclamations of impatience, irritation, sudden anger and the like. . . 3 infs, **ME, MA,** Thunderation. **1956** McAtee *Some Dialect NC* 46, *Thunderation!* . . exclamation of annoyance. **1966** Barnes–Jensen *Dict. UT Slang* 42, *Thunderation:* a vague expletive or intensive; often a mild swear word. **1967–70** *DARE* (Qu. NN8a, *Exclamations of annoyance or disgust:* "Oh _____. *I've lost my glasses again.*") Inf **TN**26, Thunderation; (Qu. NN9a, *Exclamations showing great annoyance:* "_____. *The electric power is off again.*") Infs **KY**84, **MA**71, Thunderation; (Qu. NN26a, *Weakened substitutes for 'hell':* "Oh _____!") Inf **H**11, Thunderation; (Qu. NN32, *Exclamations like 'I swear' or 'I vow'*) Inf **OR**1, Oh thunderation. **1986** Pederson *LAGS Concordance (Land's sakes!)* 1 inf, **ceLA,** Thunderation. **1991** *Intelligencer* (Doylestown PA) 7 Feb sec C 1/1, But how in all thunderation did a Cunard ship wind up with a name like the Vistafjord?

thunderation adv
Used as a euphem for *damnably;* see quots.

1835 *Crockett's Yaller Almanack* 21 **TN,** I don't know as I can say he was so all darned thunderation fat. **1852** (1970) Bennett *Mike Fink* 28 **OH,** And all fur your good, too, ef you warn't so thunderation blind you couldn't see it. **1907** McCutcheon *Daughter* 276 **NY,** The agent fer the troupe left 'em here an' hired Mark, but he's so thunderation slow that he won't paste 'em [=posters] up 'til after the show's been an' gone.

thunder bird n

1 A **bittern** (here: *Botaurus lentiginosus*). Cf **thunder pumper 1**

1959 *Names* 7.120 **FL,** A miscellaneous lot of names [for *Botaurus lentiginosus*], each with a different reason for being, includes . . thunder bird.

2 A **swallow** n[1]. Cf **rainbird 1b**

1986 Pederson *LAGS Concordance,* 1 inf, **cLA,** Thunderbirds = rainbirds, live in chimney.

thunderblust n Cf **thunderbuster**

2000 Launspach *ID Dial. Project* 1 **seID,** (*A very heavy rain which doesn't last long*) 1 inf, Thunderblust.

thunderbolt snake n Also *thunderbolt* Cf **thunder snake =rainbow snake.**

1966 *DARE* (Qu. P25, . . *Kinds of snakes*) Inf **SC**26, Thunderbolt snake. **1979** Behler–King *Audubon Field Guide Reptiles* 610, [*Rainbow Snake (Farancia erythrogramma).* . . Glossy black or blue-black snake with 3 narrow red stripes running length of body. Yellow or reddish-yellow stripe on sides along margins of belly scales. Underside red.] *Ibid* 611, Folk tales have it that the "stinging snake," "hoop snake," or "thunderbolt," bites its tail, rolls like a hoop, and stings a victim to death with the spine on the tail tip. In fact, the Rainbow Snake is usually docile and the spine is quite harmless.

thunderboomer n Cf *DS* B25, **thunderbuster**
A thundercloud, thunderstorm; also fig.

1984 *Daily Herald* (Arlington Heights IL) 23 July sec 2 1/1, No, the sun-kissed schedule isn't the dark cloud in Frey's life. His personal thunderboomer is the mere subject of day baseball. **1986** *DARE* File **Sth,** (*Joking names for a very heavy rain: you might say, "It's a regular _____."*) Thunderboomer. **1987** *Frederick Post* (MD) 20 Aug sec A 2/4, The town is getting the occasional thunder boomer that it missed last summer. **1987** *Syracuse Herald–Jrl.* (NY) 17 Oct sec B 2/6, Mary read last week's note about the lightning hit at Fire Control during the scary thunder-boomer. **2000** *DARE* File **MO,** [I remember] "Rubbernecking on [Interstate] Seventy and thunderboomers on the way; the news in two minutes in ten minutes" from a small radio station I used to work for in Missouri. *Ibid* **NH,** We call thunderstorms "thunderboomers." **2001** *Ibid* **csWI,** That was quite a thunderboomer we had last night.

thunder bowl (or bucket) See **thunder jar**

thunderbuster n Cf **thunderblust, thunderboomer, thundergust**
A thundercloud, thunderstorm.

1950 Reeves *Man from SD* 29, Every day big thunderbusters . . loomed above the line of the Black Hills to the west and promised rain. **1998** *DARE* File—Internet **NH,** Hazy hot and humid today mid to upper 90's! Possible thunderbuster late in the day could be big! **2001** *Ibid* **MS,** Thunderbuster—Thunderstorm; Rainstorm; etc. **2005** *Ibid* **wTX,**

And West Texas gave me a proper sendoff: a muddy, blustering, West Texas thunderbuster. . . A storm as good as any I'd ever seen.

thundercap n

=thunderhead. esp Nth

1857 *U.S. Democratic Rev.* 40.511, The farmer gazes with unalloyed joy at the thunder-caps of the distant clouds. **1877** *Harper's New Mth. Mag.* 54.297 **CT,** All day long great "thunder-caps" had rolled their still and solemn heights of rounded pearl and shadow upward. **1920** *Chron.–Telegram* (Elyria OH) 25 Feb [4]/3 (newspaperarchive.com), Often in summer in a clear blue sky, you will see, in the west, bunches of white, bulbous clouds forming. Soon the lower part turns dark, but the tip remains glistening white. These are called *thunder caps.* **1950** *WELS (Names you have for particular kinds of clouds)* 2 Infs, **WI,** Thundercaps. **1966–69** *DARE* (Qu. B6, *When clouds begin to increase . . it's _____*) Inf **CO2,** Thundercaps rising; (Qu. B9, *. . Big clouds that roll up high before a rainstorm*) Infs **CO2, FL29, IL36, OH78, SD8,** Thundercaps; (Qu. B11, *. . Other kinds of clouds that come often*) Inf **SD8,** White thundercaps. **2002** *DARE* File—Internet **WA,** I spotted some nice cumulus thundercaps over the east side of the Oly Mountains tonight from Seattle.

thunder cooter n Cf cooter n, thunder frog

See quot.

1981 Pederson *LAGS Basic Materials,* 1 inf, **neFL,** I guess why they called them the thunder cooters, I reckon, it's on account of they really would travel around when it was thundering more so than any other. And a lot of them would say that if they bite you, they wouldn't turn you loose until it quit thundering.

thunder dog n Also *thunder puppy* sAppalachians

A **water dog 1** (here: *Necturus* spp).

1969 *DARE* FW Addit **GA,** Thunder puppy—a salamander; said to be the term used in Rabun Co., Ga. **1982** Slone *How We Talked* 111 **eKY** (as of c1950), *Water dogs or thunder dogs*—A small, worm-like animal that lives in the water. We were told that if one bites you, it would not let go until it thundered or a cow bawled. I don't think they bit at all. **1997-98** in 2004 Montgomery–Hall *Dict. Smoky Mt. Engl.* 606 **eTN,** *Thunder dog. . .* = a large salamander often two feet in length . . ; = a large salamander. It was believed that they came to the surface after a thunder storm. A more common term than *water dog . . ;* = so called because it made a loud splash where entering the water.

thunder egg n chiefly West, esp OR

A geode.

1938 *Chicago Heights Star* (IL) 11 Nov 19/5 **OR, WA, WY,** Thunder eggs are a unique type of agate. . . They are rock formations of comparatively roughly spherical nodules varying in size from one inch to one foot in diameter. **1940** Writers' Program OR *Mt. Hood* 391, *Madras . .* is the seat of Jefferson County. . . In this area are many of the colorful agate and opal-filled nodules, commonly termed "thunder eggs." An old legend of the Warm Springs Indians relates that they were cast out of the craters of Mount Jefferson and Mount Hood by the Spirits of Thunder who inhabited the mountains. **1962** Lucia *Klondike Kate* 187 **cOR,** She never returned empty-handed, hauling back . . petrified woods, huge agates . . thunder eggs. **1967–68** *DARE* (Qu. C25, *. . Kinds of stone . . about . . [. . size of a person's head], smooth and hard*) Inf **WI58,** Thunder egg—would be used out West; (Qu. C26, *. . Special kinds of stone or rock*) Inf **OR2,** Thunder eggs—crack open egg shape and it's filled with agate; **OR**10, Thunder egg. **1967–69** *DARE* FW Addit **MO,** Thunder eggs—meaning geodes; term used as a boy in Joplin; **swOR,** Thunder egg—a stone that is rough on the outside but inside is solid, brightly colored agate. **2001** *DARE* File—Internet **NE,** Thunder eggs are agates that have formed in welded ash-flow tuffs. . . This thunder egg may have originated near Grand Marais, Minnesota, . . and have been transported by [sic for *to*] Nebraska by glaciers of Pleistocene age. *Ibid* **OR,** Prineville is home of the famed thunder egg, a ball-shaped chunk of lava concealing an agate or agate and crystal center. **2003** *NYT Mag.* 3 Aug 13/3, I thought everyone knew what a *thunder egg* was. I didn't know it was an Oregon colloquialism.

thunder frog n Cf rain frog 1, thunder cooter

Perh a **tree frog 1.**

1981 Pederson *LAGS Basic Materials,* 1 inf, **seMS,** Thunder frog—when he was a child they told him if the frogs got on you they'd stick to you and wouldn't come off until it thunder [sic]. [Inf Black]

thundergust n Rarely *thundergush* chiefly NEast, esp PA, NJ Cf gust n

A violent thunderstorm.

1734 (1901) Hempstead *Diary* 276 **CT,** Sund[ay] 7 hot a Thunder gust & Shower as the Last Sermon Ended. **1774** (1957) Fithian *Jrl. & Letters* 106 **NJ,** Last Evening was the first thunder Gust we have had this Season. **1810** in 1965 *AmSp* 40.200 **NY,** Went to York to bring up Jersey people Bot a Bomasett Jacket at FlatBush of R. Fish as black as a Thunder Gust. **1825** in 1929 *ND Hist. Qrly.* 4.32, Proceeded at 2 o.c. and ran till ½ past 5 & came to on the right bank in consequence of a thunder gush wind. **1874** in 1983 *PADS* 70.54 **ce,sePA,** There was a thunder gust and pretty hard wind in the afternoon doing much damage in some places. **1899** (1912) Green *VA Folk-Speech* 447, *Thundergust. . .* A thunder-storm, with wind. **1930** (1972) Cate *Our Todays* 102 **NY** (as of 1805), About that hour came up suddenly a thunder gust Which was severe for a short time. **1930** Shoemaker *1300 Words* 61 **cPA Mts** (as of c1900), *Thundergust*—A sudden electrical storm. **1935** *AmSp* 10.172 **PA** [Engl of PA Germans], A sudden shower, accompanied by wind and lightning, is called a *thundergust.* **1951** Swetnam *Pittsylvania Country* 85 **PA,** Most of the pine was sawed into boards on little up-and-down "thunder gust"mills, run by flutter wheels on the rapid, mountain streams [after a thunderstorm]. **1968–70** *DARE* (Qu. B12, *When the wind begins to increase . . it's _____*) Inf **PA**242, Blowing up a thundergust; (Qu. B22, *Rain accompanied by thunder and lightning*) Infs **NJ**15, 20, **PA**242, Thundergust. [All Infs old] **1976** Garber *Mountain-ese* 93 **sAppalachians,** It shure got scarry when it came that big thunder gust afore the rain. **1982** *Barrick Coll.* **csPA,** *Thundergust*—thunderstorm.

thunderhead n Cf anvil head, niggerhead 6, thundercap

A cumulonimbus cloud presaging a thunderstorm.

1849 *Burlington Hawk-Eye* (IA) 18 Jan [2]/4 (newspaperarchive.com), Before noon masses of dark clouds began to appear in the south and west and gradually extend toward the zenith, mostly assuming that form familiar to every denizen of the prairies, called *thunder heads.* **1899** Garland *Boy Life* 111 **nwIA** (as of c1870s), Vast domes of dazzling white clouds . . appeared. . . The farmers kept an anxious eye on these "thunder-heads," regulating the amount of cutting by the signs of the sky. **1906** Casey *Parson's Boys* 181 **sIL** (as of c1860), A few puffy white clouds, known to the boys as "thunder-heads," were slowly rising in the West. **1912** *DN* 3.569 **cNY,** *Thunder heads. . .* Thick, black clouds preceding a thunder storm. Called sometimes *nigger heads.* Used in Connecticut and Vermont. **1935** Sandoz *Jules* 148 **wNE** (as of 1880–1930), A man on Box Butte Creek fortunate enough to get a shower from a June thunderhead won first prize for winter wheat at the state fair. **1965–70** *DARE* (Qu. B9, *. . Big clouds that roll up high before a rainstorm*) 429 Infs, **widespread,** Thunderhead(s); **MO**15, **OK**4, Dark (*or* white) thunderheads; (Qu. B11, *. . Other kinds of clouds that come often*) 20 Infs, **scattered,** Thunderhead(s). **2003** *Star–Herald* (Scottsbluff NE) 11 May sec A 4/6, Big fluffy thunderheads boiled around above us.

‡thunder hole n Cf fraid hole, DS D22

1916 *DN* 4.348 **nwTX** (as of 1896), *Thunder hole. . .* A storm cellar.

thunder jar n Also *thunder bowl, ~ bucket, ~ pot* =thunder mug.

a1954 (1990) Oakley *Rememberin' Roamin' Man* 51 **wNC, eTN,** Heare was the order my dady give me, 2 pounds of Arbuckle green coffee, 5 pounds of sugar, 15 cts. box of matches and a thunder pot with lid. **1966–70** *DARE* (Qu. F38, *Utensil kept under the bed for use at night*) Infs **GA3, OR10, TX51, VT16,** Thunder jar; **DE4, KY77,** Thunder bowl; (Qu. F37b, *Joking names for an indoor toilet; total Infs questioned, 75*) Inf **MS1,** Thunder pot. **1968** Pochmann *Triple Ridge* 62 **cWI,** My mother had crochet on everything from the top of the piano to the thunder bucket. **1968** *Chron.–Telegram* (Elyria OH) 5 Apr 38/1, *Public Auction. . .* thunder bucket. **2001** *DARE* File—Internet, Then they began bringing in old pieces of furniture. A small bed, a chest with a mirror over it and this giant pot that Ryan said was my thunder jar.

thunder jug n esp NEng See Map =thunder mug.

[**1859** Smith *30 Yrs.* 440 **ME,** You don't mean to say he has took our Commodore and shut him up in the Moro [=Morro Castle in Havana, Cuba]? If he has I'll go right in with the Two Pollies [=a ship] and blow the old thunder-jug into the ocean.] **1862** in 1996 Silber–Sievens *Yankee Corresp.* 63 **NH,** One was looking *under* the Bed to take the value of the *thunder jug.* **1947** Gould *House Jacob Built* 44 **ME,** When the bidding [at an auction] dulls off a country gathering always likes the old thunder-jug routine. **1950** *WELS (Utensil kept under a bed for use at* *night)* 5 Infs, **WI,** Thunder jug.   **1965–70** *DARE* (Qu. F38) 16 Infs, **scattered, but esp NEng,** Thunder jug.   **1971** *Frederick Post* (MD) 12 Jan sec A 4/3, Take for example such a highly utilitarian article as that humble but essential bedroom artifact . . the lowly "thunder jug" or chamber pot.   **1973** *Portsmouth Herald* (NH) 2 Nov 4/4, I am . . appalled at the conditions I saw today at the York County Jail in Alfred. . . I saw cells where four inmates are confined . . with no toilet facilities other than a so-called "thunder-jug."   **1975** *Gt. Bend Tribune* (KS) 14 Sept sec A 19/1, *Antique Auction. . . Primitive & Collectible . .* Thunder Jug.

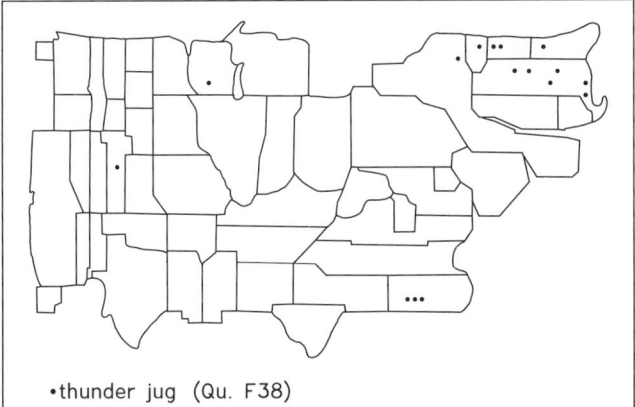

•thunder jug (Qu. F38)

thunder mug n   Also *ker-thunder mug*   **widespread, but chiefly NEast, Upper Missip Valley, West**   See Map   Cf **badger 4, bed pot, betty 1, chamber B4, chamber bucket, ~ mug, charlie 3, commode 4b, curtsy mug, ginny** n[2]**, jar** n **B1c, jimmy-john 3, King Henry, left-handed sugar bowl, mug** n[1]**, night glass, nighthawk** n **6, peggy** n[2]**, polly 2, po-po, pot chamber, slop jar 1,** *tee-tee pot* (at **tee-tee**)**, thunder jar, ~ jug, vessel, white owl 3**

A chamber pot.

1851 Byrn *Life AR Dr.* 24, I . . laid hold of the first thing I could get (which was a thunder mug), and let him have it right in the face and eyes.   **1897** Barrère–Leland *Slang* 2.347, *Thunder-mug* (American low), a chamber utensil.   **1909** *DN* 3.381 **eAL, wGA,** *Thunder-mug.* . . A chamber-pot.   **1912** *DN* 3.592 **wIN,** *Thunder-mug.* . . A chamber-pot.   **1912** Green *VA Folk-Speech* 447, *Thunder-mug.*   **1942** McAtee *Dial. Grant Co. IN Suppl. 1* 9 (as of 1890s), *Thunder-mug.*   **1946** *PADS* 6.30 **eNC** (as of 1900–10), *Thunder mug.* . . A euphemism for *chamber pot.* . . Common among boys and men.   **1965–70** *DARE* (Qu. F38, *Utensil kept under the bed for use at night*) 74 Infs, **widespread, but chiefly NEast, Upper Missip Valley, West,** Thunder mug; **NY**11, Kerthunder mug; **CO**47, Left-handed thunder mug; [(Qu. DD5, *A metal or earthenware receptacle on the floor that tobacco-chewers use*) Inf **TN**53, Thunder mug].   **1976** Garber *Mountain-ese* 93 **sAppalachians,** *Thunder-mug* . . chamber—Maudie fergot to empty the thunder-mug.   **1982** *Barrick Coll.* **csPA,** *Thundermug.*   **1986** Pederson *LAGS Concordance,* 1 inf, **seMS,** Thunder mug = slop jar; 1 inf, **cTX,** Thunder mug—old-fashioned slop jar, bedpan, etc.   **2007** Kalish *Little Heathens* 164 **IA** (as of 1930s), There was a heavy ceramic chamber pot . . ; the men referred to it as the "thunder mug."

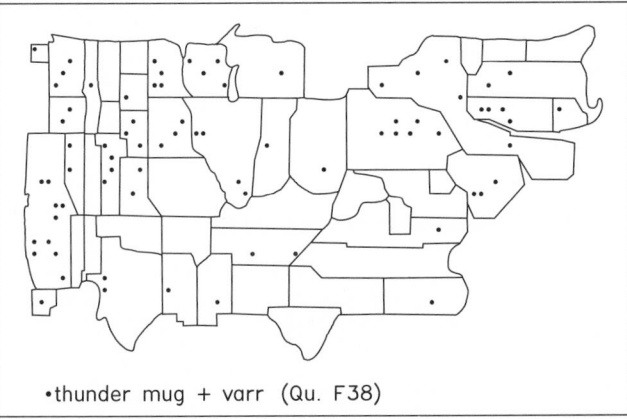

•thunder mug + varr (Qu. F38)

thunder oak n   Cf **poison oak 1, thunderwood 1**

A poison sumac.

1981 Pederson *LAGS Basic Materials,* 1 inf, **ceAL,** Thunder oak—A bush that grows on ground, doesn't get very high. Causes worse rash than poison ivy.

thunder pot   See **thunder jar**

thunder pumper n

1 also *pump-thunder, thunderpump:* A **bittern** (here: *Botaurus lentiginosus*).   **scattered, but esp wGt Lakes, Upper MW**   Cf **pumper, slough-~, swamp-~, thumper 3, thunder bird 1**

1876 *Forest & Stream* 6.338 **IL,** On June 3d I secured seven eggs of the bittern *(Botaurus lentiginosus)* known here as "thunder-pump."   **1877** *Scribner's Mth.* July 285 **IL,** The natives call these bitterns by the very appropriate if not euphonious name of 'thunder-pumper.'   **1890** *Century Dict.* 4845, *Pump-thunder.* . . The American bittern. . . Local, U.S.   **1897** *Oölogist* 14.81 **IL,** When singing the performer goes through a surprising series of motions, making peculiar snakey movements with its head and neck with each sound uttered. These movements, together with the sounds, which are hollow and reverberating, give the species [=*Botaurus lentiginosus*] the name of Thunder Pumper.   **1899** Garland *Boy Life* 123 **nwIA** (as of c1870s), They mocked the kingfishers, and the giant "thunder pumpers" in the reeds.   **1923** *DN* 5.237 **swWI,** *Thunder pumper.* . . According to tradition, the great bittern, not the bittern, thrusts his bill into the water and "pumps" before a thunderstorm. In this notion there may have been at one time, if not at present, an association of cause and effect.   **1937** Sandoz *Slogum* 75 **NE,** He . . lay awake until the frogs in his pond and the thunderpump in the marsh below were silenced by the dawn.   **1938** Matschat *Suwannee R.* 216 **GA,** "Bittern," she said absently. . . "Thunderpump," Ben said. . . he explained that the bird makes a noise like rolling thunder and also pumps up water from small pools, so that it may feed . . on the fish and frogs.   **1950** *WELS (A small heron that makes a booming sound before rain, and often stands with its head pointed up)* 1 Inf, **WI,** Thunderpump; 1 Inf, **WI,** Thunder pumper.   **1959** *Names* 7.119, Likening the bittern's vocalization to the sounds made by the operation of an old-fashioned suction-pump has also been a fruitful source of folk-names. Among these allusions are. . . pump-thunder (Vt., Mass., N.C., Ill., Man.), thunder pump and thunder pumper (general).   **1967–69** *DARE* (Qu. Q8, *A water bird that makes a booming sound before rain and often stands with its beak pointed almost straight up*) Infs **KS**6, **WI**58, Thunder pumper; **CA**136, Thunderpump; **MN**18, American bittern or thunderpump.   **2001** *MN Conserv. Volunteer* Mar–Apr (Internet), *American Bittern.* . . The male's resounding breeding call of *pump-er-lunk* sounds more mechanical than biological and has earned it nicknames such as thunder-pumper, slough-pumper, and stake-driver.

2 =**freshwater drum.**

1882 U.S. Natl. Museum *Bulletin* 16.567, *H[aploidinotus] grunniens.* . . *Thunder-pumper.* . . Great Lakes to Texas.   **1884** Goode *Fisheries U.S.* 1.370, *Haploidinotus grunniens.* . . The name . . "Thunder-pumper," also used for the bittern, *Botaurus lentiginosus,* is heard along the Mississippi River.   **1903** NY State Museum & Sci. Serv. *Bulletin* 60.591, The fresh-water drum has received a great number of common names. . . In the southern states . . the terms thunder pumper, gaspergou and jewel head are used. . . The names drum, croaker and thunder pumper have reference to certain sounds produced by the fish either by means of its air bladder or by grinding together the large molarlike teeth in the pharynx.   **1973** Knight *Cook's Fish Guide* 392, Thunder-pumper—Drum.

thunder puppy   See **thunder dog**

thunder snake n   Cf **thunderbolt snake**

1 also *thunder-and-lightning snake:* Either a **king snake 1** such as *Lampropeltis getulus* or a closely related **milk snake 1** (here: *Lampropeltis triangulum*).   [See quot 1899]

1800 in 1935 Lamb *Letters* 1.219, There is an exhibition quite uncommon in Europe . . *live rattlesnake.* . . whip-snakes, thunder-snakes, pignose-snakes, American vipers.   **1842** DeKay *Zool. NY* 3.39, In this State, its most popular name is *Milk Snake,* although. . . it is called *Chicken Snake, Thunder and Lightning Snake, House Snake,* and *Chequered Adder.*   **1851** *De Bow's Rev.* 11.54 **LA,** *Thunder and Lightning or Brick Wall Snake*—Small, harmless. Red, with checkers of white, causing it to resemble a brick wall, brightly painted and pointed; not numerous.   **1853** Baird–Girard *N. Amer. Reptiles* 86, *Ophibolus getulus* [=*Lampropeltis g.*] . . Thunder Snake; King Snake; Chain Snake.   **1867**

Atlantic Mth. 19.276 **NC,** Back to a late dinner with our various experiences, and perhaps specimens to match;—a thunder-snake, eight feet long [etc]. **1899** Bergen *Animal Lore* 62 **IN,** Thunder-snake. Probably milk-snake, *Ophibolus triangulus.* A snake marked similarly to a rattlesnake, which crawls in cellar walls for mice, etc., and is supposed to foretell thunderstorms. **1928** Baylor Univ. Museum *Contrib.* 16.7 **TX,** *Thunder Snake.* This name is used most commonly with reference to the red varieties of king snake (*Lampropeltis triangulum amaura . .* and its near relatives), but I have frequently heard it applied to the Coral Snake and Copperhead. The Thunder Snake owes its origin to the negro myth that if one will kill one of these bright-colored snakes and turn its belly upward, there will be a heavy thunder storm, followed by much rain. . . Any bright-colored snake, especially if its underparts are also highly colored, is likely to be recognized as a "thunder snake." *Ibid* 16, *Lampropeltis triangulum amaura. . .* In northeastern Texas, this subspecies is the *Thunder Snake* par-excellence. . . *Lampropeltis triangulum gentilis. . .* is also known as the *Thunder Snake.* **1966–67** *DARE* (Qu. P25, *. . Kinds of snakes*) Inf **GA**16, Thunder snake; **LA**10, Thunder snake—stripes around the body—not poison; **SC**19, Thunder snake—same as king snake—catches other snakes; **TX**32, Thunder snake [FW: really a king snake from description]; **TX**35, Thunder snake. **1986** Pederson *LAGS Concordance,* 1 inf, **csAL,** Thunder snake.

2 A **worm snake 1a** (here: *Carphophis amoenus*).

1885 Kingsley *Std. Nat. Hist.* 3.362, The genus *Carphophis* is very generally distributed; in the United States, the species *amoena . .* as the thunder, ground, or worm-snake, is most familiar. **1891** *Century Dict.* 6321, *Thunder-snake. . .* The little worm-snake, *Carphiophis* [sic] (formerly *Celuta) amoena,* common in the United States: apparently so called because forced out of its hole by a heavy shower.

3 **=coral snake 1a.**
1928 [see **1** above].

4 **=copperhead snake 1.**
1928 [see **1** above].

thunderstick n *joc* Cf **rainstick**
An umbrella.
1966–68 *DARE* (Qu. W1c, *. . Joking names . . for an umbrella*) Infs **NC**45, **WI**50, Thunderstick.

thunderwood n

1 A **poison sumac** (here: *Toxicodendron vernix*). **Sth, esp GA** See Map Cf **burn thunderwood, thunder oak**

1842 *S. Planter* 2.194, Poison sumach. Thunder wood. *Rhus vernix,* is very common in and about swamps. It should be most carefully avoided as to the touch—it is the most severe poison, by far the worst of any of our plants. **1885** Canova *Life in S. FL* 57, The arboreal Rhus toxicodendron . . , and the dreaded Rhus vernix, or "thunderwood," were pointed out to us as being worse than the terrible upas tree. **1898** U.S. Dept. Ag. Div. Botany *Bulletin* 20.36 **GA, VA,** *Poison Sumac. . .* Other names: Swamp sumac, dogwood (Mass.) . . thunderwood (Ga., Va.) . . The wood has a faint sulphurous odor, which, together with the leaf scars, which are very prominent, enables one to distinguish the plant from other shrubbery in winter. **1905** Harris *Told by Uncle Remus* 287 **GA** [Black], When she got close ter de pot de steam fum de thunderwood hit her in de face an' eyes an' come mighty nigh takin' her breff away. **1907** in 1931 Harris *Joel Chandler Harris Ed. & Essayist* 350 **GA,** Materialism . . is as infectious as the fumes of burning thunderwood. **1966–70** *DARE* (Qu. S17, *. . Kinds of plants . . that . . cause*

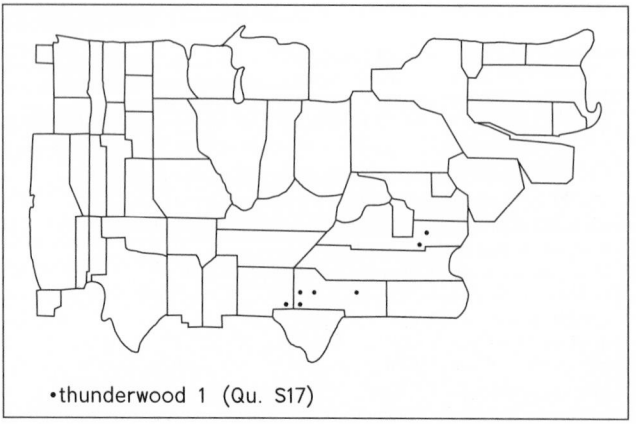

•thunderwood 1 (Qu. S17)

itching and swelling) Inf **AL**58, Thunderwood—has white blooms, grows in swamp; **GA**9, Thunderwood—a vine much like poison oak; **GA**80, Thunderwood—bush, leaves like elm leaves; **GA**84, Thunderwood—in swamps; **GA**89, Thunderwood; **VA**82, Thunderwood—swamp sumac; **VA**71, Thunderwood—a bush. **1986** Pederson *LAGS Concordance,* 27 infs, 21 **GA,** 6 **AL,** Thunderwood. **2001** *DARE* File—Internet **GA,** On a night as clear as good corn liquor / hung bright by a Georgia moon./ Hoar frosted mud that cracks underneath you,/ and ice on the thunderwood's thorn.

‡2 **=sassafras B1.**
1937 (1963) Hyatt *Kiverlid* 60 **KY,** Be keerful, Shad, about fetchin' in that thunder-wood out thar. The smoke o' thunder-wood is shore to draw lightnin'. [Footnote:] thunder-wood—sassafras.

‡3 **=oil nut 2.**
1940 Clute *Amer. Plant Names* 228, *Pyrularia pubera.* Thunder-wood.

thunderworm n
=worm lizard.
1882 *Forest & Stream* 19.45 **FL,** The Florida "Thunder worm." . . is not a true serpent at all, but a lizard-like snake. . . common in Florida, emerging . . after thunder showers. **1891** *Century Dict.* 6322, *Thunderworm. . .* An amphisbænoid lizard of Florida, *Rhineura floridana:* so called as forced out of its burrows by a thunder-shower.

thunk See **think B2a**

thunnel See **tunnel**

thurr See **there A1**

thut See **that A3**

thutty See **thirty**

thwart n Usu |θwɔrt|; also |θɔ(ə)t| Pronc-spp *tawt, thaught, thaut, thawt, thort, thought* [The varr actually represent *OED2 thought* sb.[2], *thaught,* an earlier word that was gradually replaced by *thwart* (presumably through folk-etym) beginning in the early 18th cent.]
Std sense, var forms.
1755 *NY Gaz.* (NY) 24 Mar 2/2, The fifth with difficulty saved himself by standing upon one of the Thoughts of the Boat. **1838** (1970) Fanning *Voyages S. Seas* 96 **CT,** These strokes of white wave force were so great . . that they dashed the yawl boat, in her tackles against the stern, . . driving the ends of her thawts, or plank seats through her sides. **1846** Denison *Old Ironsides* 43, There he was, . . a pale corpse, on a thaught in the little bark he had helped to row through the waves. **1849** Wise *Los Gringos* 319, The crew were doubled up on the thawts, sound asleep. **1890** *DN* 1.24 **ME, Cape Cod MA,** *Thwart . .* (of a boat), pronounced [θɔət]. **1894** *DN* 1.334 **NJ,** *Thwart:* for thwart; rower's seat. Used to a limited extent. **1899** (1912) Green *VA Folk-Speech* 445, *Thort. . .* Thwart, the seat in a boat on which one sits to row. **1903** *DN* 2.291 **Cape Cod MA** (as of a1857), The *w-* sound frequently assimilated or disappeared after a consonant . . *thawt = thwart.* **1942** ME Univ. *Studies* 56.72 (as of 19th cent), She was manned by a crew of sailors who took their seats upon *thwarts* (pronounced thauts). **1945** *Amer. Neptune* 5.87 **MA** (as of a1887), The pronunciation of after was arter when I was young . . as housen for house, cheer for chair, tawt for thwart. **1946** *PADS* 6.30 **eNC** (as of 1900–10), *Thought* [θɔt]. . . *Thwart,* the seat that one sits on when rowing a small boat. . . Common. **2000** Shores *Tangier Is.* 210 **Chesapeake Bay,** The middle seat of a skiff was called by oldtimers a *thaught,* a variation of *thwart.*

'thwartships See **athwartships (of)**

ti n Also *ki, tii* [Haw *kī,* earlier, and in many other Polynesian langs, *ti*]
A woody plant *(Cordyline fruticosa)* with edible roots.
1825 Ellis *Jrl. HI* 79, Two large heaps of *tii* root, (a variety of *Dracæna,* a sweet root, of which an intoxicating drink is made,) . . were, during the day, thrown away at this place. **1864** Anderson *Hawaiian Is.* 134, Then came gigantic ferns, and an extensive tract covered with the *ti* trees. **1933** Bryan *Hawaiian Nature* 83, The large, tuberous, saccharine root of the *. . ti . .* was baked in the *imu* as a sweet food. . . Under the tutelage of certain escaped Botany Bay convicts, the famous ti spirits or original "oke" was distilled. **1954** *Ellery Queen's Mystery Mag.* 4.38 **HI,** As we pushed through thick growth of *ti* and ginger we heard the waterfall. **1980** Bushnell *Water of Kane* 371 **HI** (as of 1876–77), The men of Japan . . were sent into the woods to gather ferns, ti leaves, strands of maile, and other greenery for decorating the tables. **2001**

Tarleton *Potluck* 161 **HI,** *Ti*—(tee). . . The rarely used Hawaiian word is "ki." A woody plant in the lily family, extremely important to early Hawaiian life.

ticalah   See **ticular**

tichy   See **tetchy**

tick n¹

1   Std: usu a parasitic acarid of the family Argasidae or Ixodidae, but also a similarly parasitic dipterous insect of the families Hippoboscidae and Nycteribiidae.   For other names of var of these see **bear tick, cow ~ 1, dog ~ 1, fever ~, garapata, glade tick, lone star ~, seed ~ 1**

2   Usu a weed seed such as those of **tick trefoil,** but occas also the plant itself; see quots.   **esp Nth**   See Map

1925 *Book of Rural Life* 9.5521, *Tick trefoil* and *ticks* are common names for a number of plants contained in . . *Meibomia* [=*Desmodium*]. . . They are distinguished by the sharp-bristled pods which usually break into sections. . . The presence of the pod sections (commonly called *ticks*) in wool or mohair is very damaging, since they are difficult to remove.   **1950** *WELS Suppl.* **ceWI,** Ticks—weed seeds that are flat and have two prongs which stick to clothing.   **1966–68** *DARE* (Qu. S13, . . *A common wild bush with bunches of round, prickly seeds; when they get dry they stick to your clothing*) Inf **OH**87, Ticks; (Qu. S14, . . *Prickly seeds, small and flat, with two prongs at one end, that cling to clothing*) Infs **ID**4, **SD**2, Tick(s); (Qu. S15, . . *Weed seeds that cling to clothing*) Inf **NY**65, Tick—very small; **MI**34, Ticks—a plant; **MS**23, Ticks, sticktights—these are little lice; **PA**176, Ticks—spurs; **WA**24, Ticks.   **1968** *DARE* File **Brooklyn NYC** (as of 1920s), Tick—small flat weed seeds with two prongs that cling to clothing.

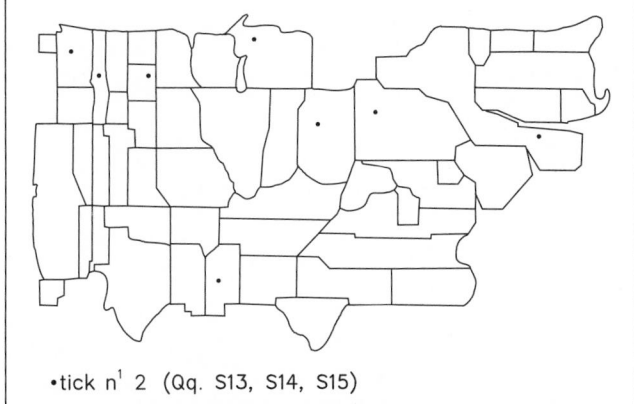

•tick n¹ 2 (Qq. S13, S14, S15)

3   also *bed tick:* A bedbug (here: *Cimex lectularius*).

1966–69 *DARE* (Qu. R24, . . *Names . . for a bedbug*) Infs **NC**37, **NY**107, 165, Tick; **OH**61, Bed tick [Inf doubtful].   **2000** Shores *Tangier Is.* **Chesapeake Bay,** If crabs eat certain kinds of marine bottom animals, they may put off a strong unpleasant odor, for which they are called *ticky crabs,* possibly because the odor is similar to that of bedbugs or bed ticks.

4   Used as a derog, or rarely affectionate, term for a person; see quots.   [*OED2 tick* sb.¹ 1.b 1631 →]

1940 (1978) Still *River of Earth* 118 **KY,** Boone came in laughing, and said it was a boy-child. Hit was Toll, our first-born. He brought the little tick to the bed, and I couldn't wait to look.   **1952** O'Neill *Moon Misbegotten* 17 **CT,** Everyone says you're a wicked old tick, as crooked as a corkscrew.   **1958** McCulloch *Woods Words* 193 **Pacific NW,** *Tick.* . . A man too lazy to work and too shiftless to move.   **1975** *AmSp* 50.68 **AR** (as of c1970), *Tick* . . 1: Overweight person "Tom's date is a real tick." 2: One who is greedy or selfish "He was such a tick about the whole thing."

tick n² [*OED2 tick* sb.⁴ 1642 →]   **chiefly Nth, Midl**   See Map   *old-fash*

Credit; a credit account—freq in phr *on tick;* hence v *tick* to buy on credit; vbl n *ticking.*

1775 (1922) Schaw *Jrl. of a Lady* 179 **NC,** All her little commodities are contrived so, as not to exceed one penny a piece, and her customers know she will not run tick. [1922 footnote:] To "run tick" was, and still is, to give credit.   **1848** Bartlett *Americanisms* 355, *Tick.* . . trust,

credit. . . *To buy on tick, to go on tick,* are the common phrases wherein this now vulgar word is heard. Like many other words once used in good society and by learned men, '*tick*' has almost had its day, and is fast sinking into obscurity.   **1851** Burke *Polly Peablossom* 50 **MO,** Them fellers down in Mechanicsburg wouldn't sell on 'tick.   **1899** (1912) Green *VA Folk-Speech* 447, *Tick.* . . Credit; trust: as, to buy on *tick.*   **1906** Johnson *Highways Missip. Valley* 117 **AR,** From March to October the farmers have little cash, and during this period they very generally "go on tick" at the stores.   **1937** Sandoz *Slogum* 156 **NE,** Big homes . . , put up on tick in the first high optimism of rain on virgin soil, stood gray and deserted now.   **1938** (1964) Korson *Minstrels Mine Patch* 320 **nePA,** *Tick:* Credit.   **1946** Driscoll *Country Jake* 42 **KS,** Mother took the lamp on tick, and paid Mrs. Palmer, the storekeeper, with blackberries.   **1955** *Valley News & Valley Green Sheet* (Van Nuys CA) 5 July 1/1, *A lot of business on tick*—Americans continue to have a whale of an appetite for buying on time.   **1965–70** *DARE* (Qu. U11, *If you buy something but don't pay cash for it . . "I _____."*) 33 Infs, **chiefly Nth, N Midl,** Bought (*or* got, put) it on tick; **SC**4, Bought it on tick terms; **IN**45, Bought on tick; **MD**16, Got it on a tick; **VT**13, On tick; **UT**7, Ticked it. [31 of 36 total Infs old]   **1968** *DARE* Tape **CA**100, They bought their timber on tick—on credit. . . On tick—that means . . you don't pay for it.   **2000** Shores *Tangier Is.* 202 **Chesapeake Bay,** Because of the seasonal nature of a waterman's work, which used to require weeks away from home, the families were offered credit by the local stores. They called the practice *ticking* or *give tick.*

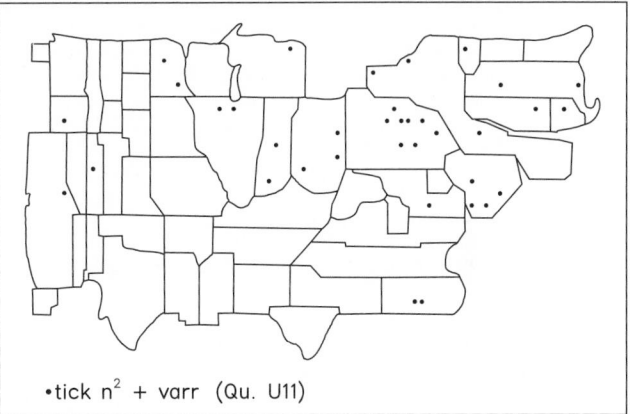

•tick n² + varr (Qu. U11)

tick n³

1   In marble play: a hit between two marbles, esp a light one; hence n *ticks* a marble game based on hits; exclam *ticks* a call entitling a player to multiple shots.

1968–69 *DARE* (Qu. EE7, . . *Kinds of marble games*) Inf **IA**29, Ticks—let's play ticks—a small ring, each player shot from taw line.   **c1970** Wiersma *Marbles Terms* **swMI,** Tics [*sic*]. . . [A] "tic" occurs when a shooting marble hits its target marble. *Ibid,* Tick(s). . . Game in which the player can win the opponent's marble without moving it the required distance. Opponent's marble must be hit on three successive shots. *Ibid,* Ticks. . . A call entitling a player to five chances to hit the target marble out of the pot. *Ibid, Tick* . . sound made at collision of glass or steel marbles, considering the value of the marble; if it was a steelie, boy, was it valuable; the player would make an agreement as to how many times that marble had to be hit or "ticked" to be won for "keeps." Needless to say that you could spend a whole day trying to win a steelie while its owner smashed your glass marbles to bits. The usual phrase was, "two ticks take." [**2006** *DARE* File—Internet **Ontario Canada,** Kids would yell "No ticks allowed" meaning the marble had to be smacked and not just touched to win.]

2   A unit of value for a marble.

1968 *DARE* (Qu. EE6a, c, d, . . *Different kinds of marbles*) Inf **IA**29, Ticks—each marble had a trading value in ticks; taw of onyx—a thousand-tick; jumbo—a fifty-tick marble; ten-tick—a pretty crockery marble; hundred-tick—a glass marble.   **1968** *DARE* Tape **IA**40, These marbles sometimes have various values. . . Then there's a two-tick. It's a little different type of material, usually had two stripes around it. Then they would go up to a ten-tick, which was more of a crockery-type material and of various colors.

tick exclam

In phrr *tick the goal on (name), tick up:* Used as a call in the game of hide-and-seek; see quot.

1969–70 *DARE* (Qu. EE15, *When he has caught the first of those that were hiding what does the player who is 'it' call out to the others?*) Inf **MI**103, At the beginning, the one who was "it" called out, "All 'round goal is caught." If the "it" person saw a player and touched goal, he'd say, "Tick the goal on _____ (person's name)"; **GA**90, Tick up, tick up.

tick n[4] See **thick**

tick v See **tick** n[2]

tick-a-lock exclam   **esp Sth, S Midl**
Used (often along with a gesture representing the turning of a key in a lock) to represent the locking of a metaphorical lock, spec:

a Used to mean that one will remain silent or that another should do so; "mum's the word," "my lips are sealed."
2000 *DARE* File—Internet **TX**, "Now, just wait one doggone minute. . ." "Hsh! Tick-a-lock! Your doggone minute's gone!" **2002** *Ibid*, [Query:] I am wondering if anyone knows the origin of the expression "tick-a-lock"? Sometimes it is accompanied [sic] by a hand gesture of a hand turning an invisible "key" near the lips, and means . . "I'll never tell" or something like that. I get the "lock" part, but why "tick"? (T.V. reference: I've heard many of the denizens of Mayberry [*DARE* Ed: on the *Andy Griffith Show*] use it, as well as Archie Bunker.) [Reply:] On *All In The Family*, it was Edith's way of saying "shut your mouth" or "I'll keep my mouth shut". . . I assume you've never encountered the old-fashioned locks mounted on a plate below the doorknob? There's a definite tick or click when the lock sets into place. **2005** *Ibid*, [Query:] When aunt bee and otis does not want to tell anyone about the others secret, are they saying pick a lock or is it Tick a lock. can't quite make it out. [Reply:]. . . To "tick" (or "tic") a lock is to close it, or clamp it shut, thereby locking it. The "tick a lock" phrase is the one used by Otis and Aunt Bee (and Barney on a couple of occasions), because they want to tell someone to "lock their lips". **2006** *AR Times* (Little Rock) 12 Jan (Internet), I'm Mr. Sunshine for the rest of the year, y'all. If I can't say something good about a person or topic, I'll just zip it. Tickalock. OK? **2006** *DARE* File—Internet **AZ**, In the meantime it's mum, zip, and tick a lock on the "f" word. Okay?

b Used in var children's games esp to indicate that the speaker claims a time out or immunity, or that others are excluded from the game, or that another player is "in jail." Cf *DS* EE17
1943 (1964) *Poetry* 63.132 **IL**, We passed the children crying tick-a-lock / And writing their names with sticks. **1949** Logan *Cousins & Commissars* 76, The wide gate that sealed the city after curfew seemed as protective as the "tick-a-lock, door-is-locked," that I used to pronounce when I was playing house. [**1959** (1967) Opie-Opie *Lore Schoolchildren* 152 **England,** At South Elmsall, and at Alfreton in Derbyshire, several [children] give 'lick-lock' or 'lick-lock, I'm in my den'.] **1968** *Panama City News* (FL) 18 July 4/7, "Hazardous duty, hazardous duty, ha, ha, ha!" I could shout. "Tickalock! I'm in my clause." [**1976** Knapp-Knapp *One Potato* 19, Tick tock, the game is locked,/ Nobody else can play./ And if they do, we'll take their shoe,/ And we'll beat them black and blue.] **1991** in 2005 *DARE* File—Internet **neTX** (as of 1930s), Before television and not much radio we kids made our own fun. . . Cops and Robbers was the easiest to play. . . The jail could be anywhere—you just had to say, "tick-a-lock you're in jail" and "un-tick-a-lock you're out." **1992** *DARE* File **TX**, *Tickalock* or *tick-a-lock*(?): A variation, semi-onomatopeic, of "time out" or "times" (New Jersey) used in children's games to call for a temporary suspension of the game or to temporarily exempt a player. Accompanied by the movement of turning an imaginary key in an imaginary door lock located between the speaker and the other players. As a child, I apparently learned the term from children in suburban St. Louis (they were originally from Texas). . . [S]everal years ago, an old friend used the term in animated conversation. . . He grew up in Corpus Christi, Texas. **2003** *Springfield News–Leader* (MO) 26 July (Internet), Would they be at a loss for words like such wonderful childhood disclaimers as "time out," "tick-a-lock" or "king's X"? **2005** *DARE* File—Internet, Tick a lock, the game is locked, nobody else can plaaay, todaaaay, hooraaaaay!

tick a lock v phr   [**tick-a-lock** exclam **a**]
To be silent.
2003 *DARE* File—Internet **MD**, [After a recitation of annoying events:] I think I'm going to tick-a-lock now. **2005** in 2006 *Ibid* **IA**, Before I could embarrass him, my father . . would look at me, shake his finger and say "Angie, tick a lock." **2006** *Ibid* **LA**, [City Council min-

utes from Shreveport:] I'm not asking them to tick a lock and not say a thing. **2007** *Ibid* **MN**, Norm Coleman is on the radio. He doesn't have the good sense to tick-a-lock.

tick-a-lock n   [**tick-a-lock** exclam **a**]
The gesture representing turning a key in a lock that indicates that one will remain silent.
2003 *Richmond Times–Dispatch* (VA) 9 May sec A 20 (Internet), If it's that funny then you should share it with the entire class. . . Or would you prefer to go to the principal's office? No? Then I'll thank you to put a tick-a-lock on your mouth and throw away the key. **2004** *Dawson News & Advt.* (Athens GA) 7 July (Internet), Chestatee State Bank President Philip Hester motioned the "tick-a-lock" when asked if the winning bid satisfied the multi-million dollar debt on the facility and quietly walked down the courthouse steps.

tick-a-lock adj phr   [**tick-a-lock** exclam **a**]
Silent.
2003 *DARE* File—Internet **cwCA**, Last time I bragged on him I think I jinxed him. So. I'm Tick A Lock until I find out how his endeavor turns out.

tick-a-lock adv phr   [**tick-a-lock** exclam **b**]
Inaccessibly.
1998 Burleith Citizens Assoc. *Newsletter* (Washington DC) Jan (Internet), With regard to out-of-state licensed vehicles that are stowed ticka-lock out of reach behind rental (or other) houses, these comprise an attempted scam avoidance of car registration.

tickbird n   [*OED2* 1850 → for other birds]

1 A **flycatcher 1a**: *Empidonax virens*, a **wood pewee** (here: *Contopus virens*), or a **phoebe** (here: *Sayornis phoebe*). **chiefly AL, GA**
1913 *Auk* 30.498 Okefenokee GA, *Empidonax virescens*. . . 'Tickbird.'—Common. This Flycatcher finds a congenial haunt in the gloom of the cypress 'bays,' where one often hears its note. **1924** Howell *Birds AL* 189, In the South, the phoebe is said to alight on the backs of cattle and to catch insects which live on the animals—a habit which has given it the local name of tick-bird. *Ibid* 190, Tick-bird: *Myiochanes* [= *Contopus*] *virens*. . . One of our commonest and best known flycatchers, found in summer in all parts of the State. **1938** Matschat *Suwannee R.* 26 **neFL, seGA**, The yellow-tailed bee bird and the tickbird, both flycatchers, sing from some shady retreat on the hottest day in summer. **1955** *Oriole* 20.1.10 **GA**, *Eastern Phoebe*. . . *Tick Bird* (from its associating with and alighting upon cattle, as if in search of ticks). **1962** Imhof *AL Birds* 349, *Eastern Phoebe—Sayornis phoebe*. . . Tick Bird. . . This phoebe. . . lacks the eye ring of the smaller *Empidonax* flycatchers. *Ibid* 355, *Eastern Wood Pewee—Contopus virens* . . Tick Bird. **1969** Longstreet *Birds FL* 97, *Phoebe*—Other names: *Bridge Phoebe; Tick Bird.*

2 =**cowbird 1.**
1955 Forbush-May *Birds* 477, *Eastern Cowbird*. . . Other names . . Tick Bird. [*Ibid* 479, During the Summer, Cowbirds gather about pasturing cattle and search for the insects stirred up by the beasts, or, as the cows lie tranquilly chewing their cud, the birds may be seen walking about on their backs, engaged in ridding them of flies and other pests, or merely resting quietly there in perfect security.] **1967** *DARE* (Qu. Q11, . . *Kinds of blackbirds*) Inf **TX**26, Tickbird; (Qu. Q14, . . *Names . . for . . cowbird*) Infs **TX**26, 35, Tickbird.

tick brush n
A **California lilac** (here: *Ceanothus thyrsiflorus*).
1968 *DARE* (Qu. T16, . . *Kinds of trees . . 'special'*) Inf **CA**105, Tick brush—blue blossom—full of wood ticks in spring.

tick clover n
=**tick trefoil.**
1940 Clute *Amer. Plant Names* 257, *Desmodium* spp. Tick clover. **1970** Correll *Plants TX* 855, *Desmodium*. . . Tick-trefoil. Tick-clover. Beggar's-ticks. **1987** Bowers *100 Roadside Wildflowers* 77, The tick clovers are named for the ticklike way the stems and pods cling to clothing. Their adhesive quality comes from numerous small hairs tipped with microscopic barbs.

tickely-bender See **tickly-bender(s)**

ticket n
A trading card; hence n *tickets* a game played with such cards; see quots.

1975 Ferretti *Gt. Amer. Book Sidewalk Games* 95 **Brooklyn NYC,** *Tickets*—Out in Flatbush, Brooklyn, trading cards are used in Tickets. Packs of trading cards . . held together with rubber bands are used almost like pucks. . . A court using three sidewalk squares, is set up, and the first player sails or skims his pack of cards toward the back line of the third square. His opponent does likewise. The player whose pack is closest to the line then puts his knee down at the spot where his pack has landed and uses the pack to touch first the line and then his opponent's pack. Obviously, if packs are close by, it is an easy game to win. . . But it is also easy to see that a good deal of strategy is involved. **1977** *NY Times* (NY) 6 July sec B 1/5, Nobody really knows why. . . "baseball cards" in Queens is "tickets" in Brooklyn.

tick grass n Cf **chiggerweed, redbug plant**
See quot.

1966 *DARE* (Qu. S15, . . *Weed seeds that cling to clothing*) Inf **DC**5, Tick grass—have real ticks on it, [they] get on your privates, tiny red things—can hardly see 'em.

ticking See **tick** n²

tickle n See **tackle**

tickle v [*OED2* 1601 →] Cf **grabble** v **2, noodle** v¹
To touch (a fish) lightly with the fingers in preparation for seizing it and pulling it out of the water; to catch (a fish) with the hand; hence n *tickler;* vbl n *tickling.*

1846 *Knickerbocker* 27.406, Thomas Stubbs thrust his arm into the wave softly, until his crooked fingers were brought to bear, with a seductive tickling, under the immediate belly of the fish. **1850** *Scientific Amer.* 5.323 **ME,** [From the *Hallowell Gazette:*] He took sixteen fine trout out of a brook by tickling their tails. **1860** *S. Lit. Messenger* 31.237 **VA,** It is stated on good authority . . that in Stafford county the practice prevails of catching fish by tickling them. Can this be so? **1941** Writers' Program *Guide SC* 462, Tickling and pegging fish are not only illegal, but unsportsmanlike: tickling consists of hemming game fish into a hole where, escape impossible, they may be pegged with a sharp stick, or taken from the water with the hands. **1957** *Amer. Legion Mag.* Mar 19 **OH,** Some of my catfishing friends still take them by a primitive process called "tickling." Their fishing tackle . . is nothing but bare hands. The time for "tickling" (where it's legal) is in late spring when the catfish begin to spawn. . . While he's on the nest, the "ticklers" simply go into the river and feel around under the rocks with bare hands until they feel a catfish, then they capture him and throw him out on the bank. **1966** *DARE* (Qu. P13, . . *Ways of fishing . . besides the ordinary hook and line*) Inf **MI**32, Tickling them—in spring when rainbow [trout] are spawning, reach hand into water, start at tail, tickle belly, get up to gills, grab 'em. **2005** *DARE* File—Internet **IN,** My brother-in-law used to tickle catfish in the Wabash near Mt. Vernon. They'd crawl along the shallows . . , looking for holes in the steep mud banks where the catfish would lair tail first. They reach into the holes and grab the catfish and hurl it up on the bank.

tickle-backed adj phr [Cf *OED2* tickle a. 7]
1967 *DARE* FW Addit **SC**19, *Tickle-backed*—of an animal that is sensitive to a load or rider on its back—of an ox, horse, cow, etc.

tickle bone n **chiefly Sth, S Midl**
=**funny bone 1;** fig: a sense of humor.

1921 *Eve. Gaz.* (Cedar Rapids IA) 5 Apr 6/1, Trixi, you know, has a little bag o' trix that titillate the 'tickle bone.' **1938** *Appleton Post-Crescent* (WI) 7 Jan 6/6 **NYC,** Does he laugh? If he doesn't there's something wrong with his tickle bone. **1946** Stuart *Tales Plum Grove* 121 **neKY,** "Now, Lizzie, that's not all you's laughin' about," Grandpa said. "I know you too well. I know the things that touch your tickle bone." **c1960** *Wilson Coll.* **csKY,** Tickle-bone. . . The crazy-bone, the funny-bone. **1965–70** *DARE* (Qu. X33, *The place in the elbow that gives you a strange feeling if you hit it against something*) Infs **MS**60, **NC**31, **TN**42, **VA**13, Tickle bone. [**1967** *DARE* Tape **TX**26, [FW:] How'd you get him to raise his leg? [Inf:] Pinch him on a tickle bone near the pastern joint.] **2005** *DARE* File—Internet, A collection of fourteen of Cross' funniest songs were compiled . . in 1994. However, not all of Cross' songs aim at the tickle bone.

tickle box n **esp Sth, S Midl** *joc*
1 An imaginary organ of the body that causes uncontrollable laughter when turned over, tilted, or otherwise affected.

1905 *DN* 3.98 **nwAR,** *Tickle-box.* . . Used with the predicate verb 'turn over,' of an uncontrollable fit of laughter. 'Her tickle-box has

turned over.' 'I had my tickle-box turned over in school the other day. I thought sure I'd have to set out in the hall.' Common. **1909** *DN* 3.381 **eAL, wGA,** *Tickle-box.* . . In the sense reported [in quot 1905]. **1912** *Eve. News* (Ada OK) [6 Nov 2]/3 (newspaperarchive.com), Rube Martin hasn't got his tickle box turned back yet. He was seen still grinning Sunday. **1934** *Denton Jrl.* (MD) 1 Dec 5/6, "Miss Blue Bonnet," a three act musical comedy . . will be staged . . at the Tri-County auditorium. . . "It tilts your tickle box." **1950** *Statesville Daily Rec.* (NC) 28 Mar 5/5, *Peeping Thru the Keyhole,* . . Mr. Hiatt running out of front seats for certain girls whose "tickle boxes" insist upon turning over. **1958** Latham *Meskin Hound* 87 **cTX,** Jim didn't say anything. He couldn't trust his voice. Let him ever open his mouth, and he knew he'd never get his tickle box straight again. **1963** *Oakland Tribune* (CA) 7 June 27/6, Believe me . . it was a test of physical endurance to summon enough strength to turn off the switch to my "tickle box" after . . reading the rantings of the man from Walnut Creek. **1977** *Coshocton Tribune* (OH) 30 Nov 9/2 **cwIL,** A waitress laughed. "You got your tickle box turned over?" Mrs. Smith shouted. **1979** Bowden *Always Rivers Flow* 141 **nwFL** (as of 1930s–40s), She's always fun . . teaching you the meaning of the funnybone, upending your tickle box. **2004** in 2006 *DARE* File—Internet **MS** [Black], My mom bless her heart kept looking back at me trying to hold in laughter so I started coughing to clear my throat and it really made my mom tickle box turn on. *Ibid* **cTX,** I just realized something. . . it set off my 'tickle box' HaHaHaHaHa.

2 See quot.

1969 *DARE* (Qu. X9, *Joking or uncomplimentary words for a person's mouth . . "I wish he'd shut his _____."*) Inf **GA**72, Tickle box.

tickle bump n Cf **belly tickler,** *DS* N30
=**thank-you-ma'am 1.**
1969 *DARE* FW Addit **NH,** *Tickle bumps*—another word for thank-you-ma'ams. Primarily children.

tickle grass n [See quot 1937 at **a**]
Any of var grasses, as:

a also *tickle-mouth*: A **bentgrass 1,** usu *Agrostis hyemalis* or *A. scabra.*

1819 *Amer. Farmer* 1.280 **CT,** It is known, generally among our farmers, by the name of *"tickle mouth"*—although some call it *"wire grass."* . . cattle refuse to eat it. **1832** Williamson *Hist. ME* 1.124, Our *Grasses* constitute a numerous family, . . such as *knot, may, sweet-scented, tickle,* . . and *star-grass.* **1840** MA Zool. & Bot. Surv. *Herb. Plants & Quadrupeds* 234, T[richodium] laxiflorum. Mx. [=*Agrostis scabra*]. Tickle-grass. Spread on dry and rather poor pastures. . . Should be kept down by feeding, as its stem otherwise becomes too wiry for cattle to eat. **1857** MA State Bd. Ag. *Annual Rept. for 1856* 29, *Hair Grass,* or *Fly Away Grass, Tickle Grass,* (agrostis scabra,) is another species. **1924** Croy *R.F.D.* 30 **MO,** The hated barbed ticklegrass was stuffed down trousers. **1937** U.S. Forest Serv. *Range Plant Hdbk.* G11, Winter redtop [=*Agrostis scabra*], a slender, fine-leaved open-ground species, is also called ticklegrass and hairgrass because of its large, open panicles with their widely spreading hairlike branches. . . Ticklegrass is a term loosely applied to a number of grasses which have fine panicles. **1946** C.H. Knowlton (in a letter to the editor 9 July) *(DA)* **ME,** I asked Dr. Merritt Lyndon Fernald of the Gray Herbarium about the name Tickle-mouth. He said that in his boyhood they always called the [tickle] grass by that name, presumably in Orono, Maine. **1950** *WELS* (Other kinds of grass that are hard to get rid of) 1 Inf, **WI,** Tickle grass. **1965–70** *DARE* (Qu. S15, . . *Weed seeds that cling to clothing*) 23 Infs, **scattered, but esp Midl,** Tickle grass; **LA**28, Tickle grass—gets up your clothes; **MI**96, Tickle grass—real fine, reddish, crawls into clothes; **NV**83, Foxtail or tickle grass—death on dog's feet and sheep's mouth; (Qu. L9a, . . *Kinds of grass . . grown for hay*) Inf **AR**47, Tickle grass; (Qu. S8, *A common kind of wild grass that grows in fields: it spreads by sending out long underground roots, and it's hard to get rid of*) Infs **CO**20, 22, **IN**38, **MO**8, 32, Tickle grass; (Qu. S9, . . *Kinds of grass that are hard to get rid of*) Infs **IL**25, 143, **OK**18, Tickle grass; **IL**135, Tickle grass—rolls up in a ball and blows like tumbleweed; (Qu. S17, . . *Kinds of plants . . that . . cause itching and swelling*) Inf **WI**32, Tickle grass; (Qu. S21, . . *Weeds . . that are a trouble in gardens and fields*) Inf **KS**1, Tickle grass. **1968** Barkley *Plants KS* 34, Agrostis hyemalis. . . Hairgrass, Ticklegrass. Open places. . . Agrostis scabra. . . Ticklegrass. Sandy places and open woods. **1973** Hitchcock–Cronquist *Flora Pacific NW* 619, Tickle-grass . . A[grostis] scabra. **1974** Welsh *Anderson's Flora AK* 552, Agrostis scabra . . Ticklegrass. . . This is apparently our most common bentgrass species. It produces pleasing pinkish or purplish filmy margins along roadsides in mid-summer.

b A **panic grass,** usu *Panicum capillare.*

1892 IN Dept. Geol. & Nat. Resources *Rept. for 1891* 157, *P[anicum] capillare.* . . Old-witch Grass. Tickle-Grass. **1894** *Jrl. Amer. Folkl.* 7.104 **NE, WV,** *Panicum capillare,* . . tickle-grass. **1897** *Ibid* 10.147 **OH,** *Panicum capillare,* . . tickle grass. **1912** Blatchley *IN Weed Book* 53, *Panicum capillare.* . . Tickle-grass. . . The spreading tops, being very brittle, break off in autumn and are blown into fence corners or against some barrier where they form great piles. **1912** Wooton–Standley *Grasses NM* 48, *Panicum barbipulvinatum* [=*P. capillare*]. . . Children call it "tickle grass." A common field and garden weed. **1940** Gates *Flora KS* 132, Panicum capillare. . . Ticklegrass, Witchgrass. **1952** Strausbaugh–Core *Flora WV* 80, *P[anicum] gattingeri.* . . Ticklegrass.— Annual grass bearing stiff hairs all over. **1970** *DARE* (Qu. S15, . . *Weed seeds that cling to clothing*) Inf **VA**69, Tickle grass—grows four feet high, with fuzzy head, two inches long; kids would break them off and tickle each other.

c A **dropseed 3** (here: *Sporobolus buckleyi*).

1897 *Jrl. Amer. Folkl.* 10.147 **TX,** *Sporobolus Buckleyi,* . . tickle grass.

d =**love grass.**

1898 *Jrl. Amer. Folkl.* 11.283 **KS,** *Eragrostis major* [=*E. cilianensis*], . . tickle grass. **1912** Baker *Book of Grasses* 172, One of the most common species, Purple Eragrostis [=*Eragrostis pectinacea*], called by children "Tickle-grass," grows in low tufts on dry and sandy soil, where the gauzy flowering-heads, a foot long or more, spread above the dark green, hairy leaves. **1944** AL Geol. Surv. *Bulletin* 53.72, *E[ragrostis] capillaris.* . . "Tickle-grass." Conspicuous in the fall for its stiff, but delicate feathery panicles, more or less purplish, which break off at maturity, forming tumble-weeds. **1948** Blomquist *Grasses NC* 48, *Eragrostis.* . . Lovegrass or ticklegrass. *Ibid* 51, *Eragrostis spectabilis.* . . Purple lovegrass or ticklegrass.

e A **wild barley** (here: *Hordeum jubatum*).

1914 Georgia *Manual Weeds* 64, *Hordeum jubatum.* . . Tickle Grass. Native. . . The long, barbed, reddish-golden awns become very brittle when ripe, and break into small bits which work between the teeth and into the jaws of animals that eat the grass, causing such ulcerations and swellings as sometimes to be mistaken for the disease called "Big Jaw" or "Lumpy Jaw." **1915** Bailey *Std. Cyclop. Horticult.* 1500 **NV,** *H[ordeum] jubatum.* . . Squirrel-tail Grass . . called Tickle-Grass in Nev. **1963** Craighead *Rocky Mt. Wildflowers* 7, *Hordeum jubatum.* . . Ticklegrass. This attractive perennial grass grows in bunches and is quickly noticed because the flower head is densely covered with very slender reddish-golden awns.

f A **muhly (grass)** (here: *Muhlenbergia torreyi*).

1937 U.S. Forest Serv. *Range Plant Hdbk.* G84, Ring muhly [= *Muhlenbergia torreyi*], also called . . ticklegrass, get it [sic] common names from its unusual and characteristic growth habit. As each tuft enlarges, the center dies, leaving a border of tufted grass 2 to 4 inches wide which forms a ring. . . The panicle is 2 to 9 inches long, open and spreading.

tickle-mouth See **tickle grass a**

tickle-my-fancy n Cf **come-tickle-me**

A **johnny-jump-up 1** (here: *Viola tricolor*).

1902 Earle *Old Time Gardens* 135, *Viola tricolor.* . . has a score of folk names . . : Bird's-eye; Garden-gate; Johnny-jump-up; None-so-pretty; Kitty-come; Kit-run-about; Three-faces under-a-hood; Come-and-cuddle-me; . . Tickle-my-fancy. **1959** Carleton *Index Herb. Plants* 117, *Tickle-my-fancy*: Viola tricolor.

tickler n[1]

1 A liquor flask, esp one holding a half-pint; a drink of liquor. **chiefly Sth, S Midl** *old-fash*

1809 (1814) Weems *F. Marion* 170 **SC,** [The old man held] up a stout tickler of brandy. **1851** Burke *Polly Peablossom* 149 **MS,** Then he tuck out er tickler of whisky, and . . tuck three er four swallers out'n it. **1859** Taliaferro *Fisher's R.* 94 **nwNC** (as of 1820s), He was fond of the "tickler," but not to excess. **1867** Harris *Sut Lovingood Yarns* 86 **TN,** He brought up near me, banteringly shaking the half-full "tickler," within an inch of my face. **1872** Schele de Vere *Americanisms* 642, In one of the side-streets of New York the following advertisement used to hang . . : "Pocket-pistols charged, and *ticklers* supplied, on Saturday night up to 12 o'clock, for use next day." In the South the phrase, to "take a *tickler*," is often used as an invitation to "join in a drink." **1889** *Harper's New Mth. Mag.* 79.388 **KY,** Whiskey. . . was not usually bought by the drink, but by the tickler. The tickler was a bottle of narrow shape, holding a half-pint—just enough to tickle. **c1937** in 1976 *Weevils in the Wheat*

32 VA [Black], Well, ol' marse poured dis tickler full fer my young marster and sed, "Run along gal." **1944** *PADS* 2.50 **csVA,** *Tickler.* . . A flat pocket flask, generally used for whisky. . . Older persons. **1960** Hench Coll. **cVA,** *Tickler.* . . a small flask for whiskey (or brandy). [Miss C.M.] (Charlottesville, Va) called me and asked me if "tickler" was an unusual word. She said she had used it in front of some New Englanders and they had laughed and asked "What is that?" She said also that "Every gentleman in my father's generation had a tickler."

2 See **tickle** v.

tickler n[2], adj See **ticular**

tickle-tail n Cf **tickleweed 2**

See quots.

1851 *De Bow's Rev.* 11.50 **LA,** There is a kind of *tassel* grass here which was very abundant last year after the overflow, and is known as *"tickle-tail"* amongst the people. It makes good hay. **1966** *DARE* (Qu. S15, . . *Weed seeds that cling to clothing*) Inf **SC**3, Tickle-tail.

tickle-tongue n Also *tingle-tongue* **chiefly TX** Cf **sting-tongue**

A **prickly ash 1** such as *Zanthoxylum clava-herculis* or *Z. parvum.*

1928 Dormon *Forest Trees LA* 65, The aromatic inner bark, with its strong juice which bites the tongue, has given this tree a number of local names, such as "tingle tongue". **1930** TX Folkl. Soc. *Pub.* 8.70, Chew the bark from a prickly ash bush. The bush is found all over South and West Texas; it is often called "tickle-tongue." **1968** *Dallas Morning News* (TX) 10 Aug sec C 9/2, Toothache tree. . . *Tickle-tongue* tree is what it's often called in East Texas. **1970** Anderson *TX Folk Med.* 76 **TX,** Fill the mouth with tickle-tongue . . leaves. **1990** Guenther *Della Hudson* 140 **LA** (as of 1940s), If we became bored with smoking or chewing pine resin, we could always go next door . . for a real dicey taste treat—tickle tongue bark. **2003** Sitton *Harder Than Hardscrabble* 59 **cTX,** There was a bush that grew right by the side of our outhouse. It had thorns on it, and the leaves were kind of a light green. We called it a "tickle tongue bush," chew the leaves and tickle your tongue. It'd numb it, you know. **2006** in 2007 *DARE* File—Internet **eTX,** Yesterday my wife and I were clearing some brush from a fence line. The brush was tickle tongue tree, that is what it is known [sic] here in East Texas, I have heard of it being called toothache tree, hercules war club. I think maybe it may be prickly ash.

tickleweed n

1 =**Indian poke 1.**

1751 in 1934 Eliot *Field Husbandry* 70 **NEng,** Take the Roots of Swamp Hellebore, sometimes called Skunk Cabbage, Tickle Weed, Bear Root. **1876** Hobbs *Bot. Hdbk.* 120, Tickle weed, American Hellebore, Veratrum viride. **1942** *Land Policy Rev.* 5.1.16 **SD,** Underneath a cover of tickle-weed is the soft and swelling line of soil drifts that choked to death the trees of the windbreak.

2 See quots. Cf **tickle-tail**

1967 *DARE* (Qu. S14, . . *Prickly seeds, small and flat, with two prongs at one end, that cling to clothing*) Inf **TX**33, Tickleweed; (Qu. S15, . . *Weed seeds that cling to clothing*) Inf **TX**33, Tickleweed. **2006** *DARE* File **eTX,** I observed what we in East Texas call a "tickle" weed. It is neither as large nor magnificent as the "tumble weed" of West Texas. However, its personality is much the same: that of a wandering vagabond searching for a place to come to rest.

tickley-benders See **tickly-bender(s)**

tickling See **tickle** v

ticklish adj **NJ** Cf **tickly-bender(s)**

Of ice: rubbery, flexible.

1900 *Trenton Times* (NJ) 15 Dec 4/2, The first skater on the ticklish ice may win the admiration of the whole small-boy tribe, but that will not amount to much when he is being drugged out from a watery grave. **1941** Jones *Small-Town Boy* 109 **ME,** We ventured out on thin ice in the early freeze-up of the lake, daring one another to see who could carry a stone the farthest out on the ticklish bending ice. **1968–69** *DARE* (Qu. B35, *Ice that will bend when you step on it, but not break*) Infs **NJ**8, 22, 31, 56, Ticklish (ice).

ticklish-bender n **chiefly NJ**

=**tickly-bender(s).**

1894 [see **tickly-bender(s)**]. **1909** Ingersoll *Conquest North* 31, The men with snowshoes on their feet . . were content to scuff along while the block ice bent beneath them like rubber. It was two miles across this ticklish bender. **1912** Crumrine *Centennial Washington PA* 89 **swPA,** To skate, we walked out to Ewing's and skated on the creek. Ticklish benders put more than one of us in cold water to our arm pits. **1930** Cole *Stagecoach Tales* 74 **WI,** When the stage over the line extending between Baraboo and Madison crossed the Wisconsin river at Merrimack on the ice, it was sometimes necessary to go on a gallop to keep from breaking through—a magnified "ticklish bender" of one's boyhood days. **1968–69** *DARE* (Qu. B35, *Ice that will bend when you step on it, but not break*) Infs **NJ**20, 39, 55, Ticklish-bender. **1968** *DARE* Tape **NJ**18, We used to have a game named ticklish-bender. . . That's when you're skating on thin ice. . . You'd skate across that and see the ice rock—go up and down.

tickly adj Also *ticky* Cf **tickly-bender(s)**
=**ticklish.**

1967 *DARE* (Qu. B35, *Ice that will bend when you step on it, but not break*) Inf **NY**2, Tickly; **PA**126, Ticky.

tickly-bender(s) n Also *tickely-bender, tickley-benders* **chiefly NEast, esp PA, NJ** Cf **kittly-bender, rubber ice, ticklish bender, tiddlies, tiddly-bender(s), tiddlywinks**

Thin or broken ice on a body of water; the act of running or skating on such ice.

1850 (1854) Kane *Grinnell Exped.* 179 **PA,** The sound presented a novel spectacle to us; the young ice glazing it over, so as to form a viscid sea of sludge and *tickly-benders,* from the northern shore to the pack. **1886** Abbott *Upland* 52 **NJ,** How quickly crows learn to know when the ice will bear them. . . I have even seen them play at "tickle-y benders." **1890** *DN* 1.75 **MA,** *Tittly benders* . . pl.: sallies out on thin ice. . . In Barnstable, Mass., [tɪkl-ɪ] (three syllables) [bendə]. "Let's make it tickly-bender." **1894** *DN* 1.334 **NJ,** *Tickly (tickely, ticklish) bender:* running on yielding ice. **1912** *S. Jersey Republican* (Hammonton NJ) 17 Feb 8/4, Several young folks broke thro' the ice, on the Lake, this week. In every case that we know of, it was because the skater carelessly or foolishly ventured upon newly made ice—"tickly-benders" they call them. **1918** Pennypacker *Autobiog. Pennsylvanian* 42 **sePA** (as of 1850s), When playing "tickly benders" on the thin ice of the canal, the ice gave way and I fell into the water. **1961** Tolman *North of Monadnock* 229 **NH,** Tickly-benders . . is one of those indigenous sports. The skaters form a circle which at one point passes close to the open water at the mouth of a brook, where the ice is thin as cardboard. The first skater gets up as much speed as possible, so as to coast over the thin spot with feet apart and weight evenly distributed. One by one the others follow. . . until the ice is so weakened somebody goes through. **1967–70** *DARE* (Qu. B35, *Ice that will bend when you step on it, but not break*) Inf **NJ**25, Tickly-bender; **IL**81, Tickly-bender—great for skating on; (Qu. EE27, *Games played on the ice*) Inf **CT**42, Tickly-bender—running from one side to the other without falling. **1996** Horton *Island Out of Time* 205 **Chesapeake Bay MD,** In the winter we'd play tickly bender, which is racing across the ice when a thaw has made it limber.

ticks n, exclam See **tick** n[3] 1

tickseed n

1 A plant of the genus *Coreopsis*. For other names of var spp see **dye flower, egg dye, goldenwave, old-maid's-breast-pin, sea dahlia, stickseed 5, Texas star b, tickweed 3, turpentine weed 2**

1830 Rafinesque *Med. Flora* 2.213, Coreopsis. . . Tickseed. The flowers of nearly all the species afford a red dye to the Indians. **1901** Lounsberry *S. Wild Flowers* 525, C[oreopsis] nudata, tickseed, . . occurs mostly along the coast from Florida to Georgia. . . With Coreopsis rosea, the pink tickseed, which also grows in open swamps along the coast, it is the only one with other than yellow or particoloured rays. **1931** Harned *Wild Flowers Alleghanies* 582, Lance-leaved Tickseed (*Coreopsis lanceolata* . .). *Ibid* 583, Star Tickseed (*C. pubescens* . .). Tall Tickseed (*C. tripteris* . .) [etc]. **1940** Steyermark *Flora MO* 538, *Tickseed (Coreopsis)*—Flower-heads large and showy, in the spring flora yellow. **1961** Wills–Irwin *Flowers TX* 236, Golden-wave, also called Tickseed or Coreopsis, is found as a wildflower in East Texas west to Denton and Colorado counties. **1966** *DARE* Wildfl QR Pl.260A [= *Coreopsis lanceolata*] Inf **WA**10, Tickseed. **1970** Campbell et al. *Gt. Smoky Wildflowers* 92, *Coreopsis major*. . . Also known as *tickseed,* this species grows to a height of about 3 feet. **1982** *Miami Herald* (FL) 24 May sec B 1/2, The root from this plant, she says, holding up a bright yellow tickseed, will cure headache.

2 =**tick trefoil.**

1891 *Century Dict.* 6329, Tickseed. . . Same as tick-trefoil [=*Desmodium*]. **1975** Hamel–Chiltoskey *Cherokee Plants* 59, Tickseed . . *Desmodium perplexum* . . *D. nudiflorum*.

3 =**beggar ticks 1.**

1914 Georgia *Manual Weeds* 474, Leafy-bracted Tickseed—*Bidens frondosa* [=*B. tripartita*]. **1931** Harned *Wild Flowers Alleghanies* 585, Leafy-bracted Tickseed. . . Achenes pale brown, . . nearly smooth, with 3 awns, the middle one usually shorter, all barbed downward. **1936** IL Nat. Hist. Surv. *Wildflowers* 372, Thirteen species of *Bidens* are known to occur in Illinois. . . They go by various names, such as . . Tickseed. **1939** Tharp *Vegetation TX* 72, Tickseed (*Bidens* spp.); all regions. **1979** Niering–Olmstead *Audubon Guide N. Amer. Wildflowers E. Region* 368, Two similar species, differing in minute fruit characteristics, are B[idens] polylepis . . and the Southern Tickseed (*B. coronata*).

4 A **stickseed 1b** (here: *Lappula occidentalis*).

1951 *PADS* 15.39 **TX,** *Lappula texana* [=*L. occidentalis*]. . . Tick- or stick-seed.

5 A **pennyroyal B1** (here: *Hedeoma pulegioides*). Cf **tickweed 1**

1940 Clute *Amer. Plant Names* 24, H[edeoma] pulegioides. . . Tickseed.

6 =**lopseed.**

1966–67 *DARE* Wildfl QR Pl.208 [=*Phyrma leptostachya*] Infs **MI**31, 57, Tickseed.

tickseed sunflower n [*OED2* 1786 →]

A **beggar ticks 1,** usu *Bidens aristosa* or *B. coronata*.

1814 Bigelow *Florula Bostoniensis* 315, Coreopsis trichosperma [= *Bidens coronata*]. . . Tickseed Sun flower. . . Flowers large, erect, yellow. **1857** Gray *Manual of Botany* 220, C. trichosperma. . . Tickseed Sunflower. . . Swamps, Massachusetts to Virginia near the coast. **1936** IL Nat. Hist. Surv. *Wildflowers* 372, The Southern Tickseed Sunflower, *Bidens coronata* . . , and the Western Tickseed Sunflower, *Bidens aristosa* . . , are considerably alike but the most noticeable difference is the hairy stems of the latter. **1970** Correll *Plants TX* 1662, *Bidens aristosa*. . . Tickseed sunflower. . . Spring-early summer; most of the e. U.S. **1979** Niering–Olmstead *Audubon Guide N. Amer. Wildflowers E. Region* 368, Tickseed Sunflower (*Bidens aristosa*). . . Slender, leafy, much-branched stems bear several Daisy-like flower heads with yellow ray and disk flowers. . . The fruits of this plant are the very common, 2-pronged stickers that cling to one's clothing during autumn walks.

ticktack n Also *tic(k)-tac(k)-toe, tick-tack-too, tick-tack-tow, tic-toc* See also **ticktack night** Cf **dumb bull 1**

Any of var homemade noisemakers used to make a rapping or other annoying sound against a window or door as a prank, esp at Halloween; the prank itself.

1879 *Stevens Point Jrl.* (WI) [2 Aug 4]/7 (newspaperarchive.com) **cMN,** Some roguish boys were playing "tick-tack" on the front door of Lawyer O.K. Chance's house, in Monticello, Minn. **1882** *Morning Rev.* (Decatur IL) 31 Oct [8]/4 (newspaperarchive.com), Ye fairy tick-tack (composed of one railroad spike and forty rods of twine) [shall] beat ye little pitty-pat upon ye pane. . . Aye, thus and more thusly, shall ye little boy enjoy ye fairy eve of Hallowmas. **1884** Jewett *Country Dr.* 60 **ME,** She rigged a tick-tack here the other night against the window. . . They tie a nail to the end of a string, and run it over a bent pin stuck in the sash, and then they get out of sight and pull, and it clacks against the winder. **1905** *DN* 3.98 **nwAR,** *Tick-tack*. . . A horse-fiddle attached to a door-knob and operated at a distance. **1909** *DN* 3.381 **eAL, wGA,** *Tick-tack*. . . A horse-fiddle . . attached to a window and operated at a distance. **1926** *WI Rapids Daily Tribune* (WI) 29 Oct 12/1, So they got some soap and wrote all over the windows of the stores on the main drag. Then they made a tick-tack-toe and scared all the little pre-historic children until they cried for Castoria. **1932** *Oakland Tribune* (CA) 31 Oct [26]/3 (newspaperarchive.com), Halloween. . . Night of mystery, fun and frolic,/ Tick-tack-tow and tricks diabolic. **1945** [see **ticktack** v]. **1957** *Sat. Eve. Post Letters* **IA** (as of 1890s), In the fall we put tick-tacks on people's window frames at night. They were a string tied around a sharp pointed tack that could be pushed into the wood of the top of [a] window frame. **1967–68** *DARE* (Qu. AA18) Inf **PA**25, Ticktack—cut a spool of thread with notches against window; (Qu. EE33, . . *Outdoor games . . that children play*) Inf **WI**24, Ticktack—a prank with a noisemaker made with spools; (Qu. EE38a) Inf **ME**5, Ticktack—a pin, shingle nail, and piece of string. Stick pin in wood over window, tie nail to string and pull and release string, making "tick tack" on a window.

1977–78 Foster *Lexical Variation* 76 **NJ,** The prankster ties a spool near one end of a piece of string, loosely tapes the short end to a window, and retires to the bushes. Soft jerks on the string will cause the spool to tap against the window, while a hard pull will dislodge the device, enabling escape without discovery. This device . . [is] called a *tick-tack.* **1981** *DARE* File **csMA** (as of c1935), We used to make Halloween "tic-tac-toes". . . Take a large . . spool of thread. Remove thread. Notch the ends of the spool around their circumferences. . . Tip loop of small twine around spool, wind balance, 2–4 feet, around spool. Put pencil through spool. Place against outside of window. Pull! The noise is awful. **1986** *WI Alumnus Letters* **cWI** (as of a1917), "Tic Toc". . . a common wood spool of thread (empty of thread) notched at each end (small notches) then wound with string, a dowel or stick through hole and held against window pane, pulled the string and then culprit ran. We did this only at *Halloween.* **1993** *DARE* File **MA** (as of 1950), The true tick-tack . . was made of a flat piece of rubber inner-tube . . with a wood screw stuck through its center. . . The other form . . was a large empty thread-spool with notches cut into its flanges at each end.

ticktack v, hence vbl n *ticktacking;* also *tick-tack-tooing* [**ticktack** n]

To apply a **ticktack** to, afflict (one) with a **ticktack;** to use a **ticktack.**

   1909 *DN* 3.381 **eAL, wGA,** *Tick-tack, v. tr.* To use the tick-tack to frighten one. "We tick-tacked old Jones last night." **1945** *Fitchburg Sentinel* (MA) 1 Nov 6/2, We can understand . . how children still get a thrill out of tick-tack-tooing windows. . . Once upon a time a tiny girl child who was too young . . to work a tick-tack-too, stood on tiptoe before a store window and made a little mark with a piece of soap. **1970** *DARE* (Qu. AA18) Inf **KY**74, Ticktacking. **1972** Wooden *They Call Me Coach* 27 **IN** (as of 1920s), We pulled all the usual tricks. One of the best, however, was what we called "ticktacking." That's where you grooved an empty spool of thread, put it on someone's door and spun it by pulling the string from thirty or forty feet away. . . There was one person in town who seemed to be quite a crank, so naturally one year we decided to ticktack him. **1975** McDonough *Garden Sass* 200 **AR,** Ticktacking was another form of harassment. . . "You first take a good strong sliver of hardwood and trim it down very thin so's it'll stick into a crack or under a siding board or any place around. And you take a coarse thread and you tie it to this little splinter. . . And you get up and find a place to stick this splinter in under a window casing, or anywhere you can to stick it in there. And then he lets this spool of thread unwind and he gets out there behind some bushes . . and he pulls it tight. And he has some pine resin or beeswax on his fingers and he pulls it and he runs his hand up and down that string—and the tighter he pulls why the higher it goes. It goes *whoooooo-eeeeeee-eeee.*" **1986** Pederson *LAGS Concordance,* 1 inf, **cnAR,** Tick-tacking houses—tying string to houses. **1994** *Valley Independent* (Monessen PA) 10 Oct sec A 5/2, Three male juveniles . . were each charged with criminal mischief, disorderly conduct and curfew violation . . after they were allegedly breaking pumpkins and tick-tacking in various locations in the borough.

ticktack bird n [**ticktack** n]

A **woodpecker B1;** see quot.

   1950 *WELS (Joking and nicknames for woodpeckers)* 1 Inf, **WI,** Ticktack bird.

ticktacking See **ticktack** v

ticktack night n   Also *ticktacking night, tic-tac-toe ~* [**ticktack** n, v]

Usu =**cabbage night;** occas Halloween night.

   1899 *Davenport Daily Leader* (IA) 31 Oct 6/4, Tonight [=Halloween] is the night of all the year when the small boy gets in his work. . . Last night was supposed to be tick-tack night and tonight the general tear up. **1907** *Newark Advocate* (OH) 31 Oct 4/5, It was tick-tacking night, and the youngsters labored under the mistaken idea that they were privileged characters. **1924** *News* (Frederick MD) 30 Oct 1/2, The juvenile element will be active on Friday night [=Halloween], which is known as tick-tack night. **1929** *Circleville Herald* (OH) 1 Nov 1/5, Hallowe'en stunts seem still to last a week, but in the old days there used to be a doorbell night, a cabbage night and a tick-tack night. The eve of all Saints' Day would be the climax to the sally of the spooks. **1977–78** Foster *Lexical Variation* 76 **NJ,** Mercer County is the home of *Tick Tack Night.* Younger informants, who sometimes reinterpret the name as *Tic Tac Toe Night,* believe that they are called upon to draw tic tac toe diagrams on houses and walks, but their elders recall the venerable and far more nefarious true source of the phrase. **1982** Slone *How We Talked*

36 **eKY** (as of c1950), *Tick-tack night*—Halloween. **1993** *DARE* File **swOH,** Forty-four years ago in North Bend, Ohio we participated in tick-tack night. The night before Halloween (for younger kids) we would run up on porches and throw corn at the windows making tick tack sounds—thus the name. Older kids did "damage" night—damage then was considered soaping windows. **2002** *Ibid* **sePA,** The evening of October 30th was known locally as "Tick-Tack Night."

tick-tack-toe n

1 also *tic-tac-to, tic-toc-to:* A game in which typically two or more players, blindfolded or with their eyes shut or averted, take turns stabbing with a pencil or similar implement at a pattern of numbered subdivisions, and the number of the subdivision hit is the player's score for that round. [*OED2* 1884 →] Also called **tip-tap-toe, tit-tat-toe 2, tit-tat-too 1**

   1949 *WELS Suppl.* **seWI,** The game we know as "Tic-Tac-to" or more commonly as "Tic-toc-to" is a game played with pencil and paper. . . A circle is drawn and divided into as many segments as desired. These segments are then numbered and each player takes a pencil in hand, and while either blindfolded or turning the head in such a way so as to make the circle invisible, he repeats these lines: "Tic-toc-to, here I go,/ If I miss, I'll stop on this." . . [O]n the last word, "this," he rests his pencil within the circle at whatever spot the pencil has reached. If the player lets his pencil rest on a number, he gets another "turn." This goes on until he "misses." To score, the player counts each number he has captured. Each captured number is crossed out so that it will no longer be available. . . Sometimes a small circle is made in the center . . and a very large number may be written in. . . This game . . is a very old one. It was very common when my grandmother (now 92 years old) was a young lady. **1953** Brewster *Amer. Nonsinging Games* 130 **TX,** *Tick-Tack-Toe.* . . A picture of a wheel with several spokes is drawn on a sheet of paper or on the blackboard. Numbers are written between the spokes. With eyes closed, each player in turn taps the wheel in time with the following rhyme: Tick-tack-toe,/ Here I go;/ Hit or miss,/ I'll take this! At the word "this," the point of the pencil or crayon is pressed firmly against the last spot touched. . . The game continues until someone reaches whatever score has previously been agreed upon.

2 Std: a game in which two players take turns making a mark in a three-by-three grid and the first to get three marks in a row wins. Also called **cat and mouse 1, crisscross, cross out n 2, jack n[2] 2a, noughts-and-crosses, old cat 1, tick-tack-too 1, tit-tat-toe 1, tit-tat-too 2, tip-tap-toe, X's-and-O's**

3 See **ticktack** n.

tick-tack-too n

1 =**tick-tack-toe 2.** esp **NEng** See Map

   1967–70 *DARE* (Qu. EE38a, *A game played with pencil and paper where the players try to get three X's or three O's in a row*) Infs **MA**42, 69, 100, **RI**1, 12, **TX**31, 97, Tick-tack-too; **CT**23, Tick-tack-too—old-fashioned.

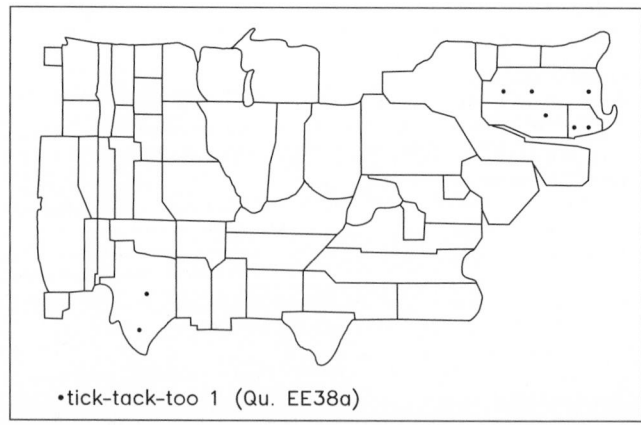

  •tick-tack-too 1 (Qu. EE38a)

2 See **ticktack** n.

tick-tack-tooing See **ticktack** v

tick-tack-tow See **ticktack** n

tick tag n [Scots, nEngl dial *tick* to touch lightly, esp in a children's game of tag]

A children's game; also fig.

1986 Pederson *LAGS Concordance,* 1 inf, **cAL**, Tick tag—a hiding game; 1 inf, **swAL**, Tick tag. [Both infs Black] **2005** in 2006 *DARE* File—Internet **TN**, I called the people who booked the hotel and they all played it off in tick tag call this one call that one about the lie that it was renovated and the filthy state it was in.

tick the goal on   See **tick** exclam 1

tick-tick n

A **click beetle.**

1968 *DARE* (Qu. R8, . . *Kinds of creatures that make a clicking or shrilling or chirping kind of sound*) Inf **LA**37, Tick-tick—lives in under the grass—a beetle that bends its back and snaps it straight with snapping sound.

tick tight n   Cf **sticktight 4**

=**bay bed.**

1983 *MJLF* 9.1.59 **ceKY** (as of 1956), Tick tight . . a bay bed.

tick trefoil n   Cf **fuzzy 3**

Std: a plant of the genus *Desmodium.* Also called **beggar patches, beggar's lice 2, beggar ticks 2, beggarweed 1, devil's fritters, nigger lice, patches, seed tick 2, tick clover, tickseed 2, tickweed 2.** For other names of var spp see **devil's lice, ~ shoestring 11, ~ thistle, dollarleaf 2, groundnut B9, hive vine 2, peavine 1b(6)** Cf **tick** n¹ **2**

tick up   See **tick** exclam 1

tickweed n

1   A **pennyroyal B1** (here: *Hedeoma pulegioides*). [See quot 1828]

1828 Rafinesque *Med. Flora* 1.231, *Hedeoma pulegioides.* . . *Vulgar Names*—Pennyroyal, Tickweed, Stinking Balm, Squaw-mint, &c. *Ibid* 234, This plant [=*H. pulegioides*] is also frequently used to kill the Ticks, *(Ixodes)* which attach themselves to men, dogs and cattle, in summer. These troublesome animals are found wherever the Hedysarums and Lespedezas or true Tickweeds grow, upon which they breed, but both are unknown in the limestone plains. By rubbing the legs or boots with this plant or its oil, these insects will avoid you, or if they have taken hold, the oil kills them. A strong decoction of the plant is equally convenient, and a strong decoction of Tobacco as good likewise. [*DARE* Ed: Those "Hedysarums and Lespedezas" referred to are now included in *Desmodium* spp.] **1869** Porcher *Resources* 487 **Sth**, Pennyroyal; tickweed, (Hedeoma pulegioides . .). . . It is said that the plant, or the oil extracted from it, is an effectual remedy against the attacks of ticks, fleas and mosquitoes. **1892** (1974) Millspaugh *Amer. Med. Plants* 118-1, *Hedeoma pulegioides.* . . Tick-weed. [*Ibid* 118-2, The oil has been recommended as an ointment to keep off gnats, ticks, fleas, and mosquitoes; many who have camped in the northern woods, have anointed their hands, neck, and face with this body, to guard against the pests of that region, but with only partial success.] **1911** Henkel *Amer. Med. Leaves* 26, Tick-weed. . . has a strong mintlike odor and pungent taste. . . The odor is very repulsive to insects. **1930** Sievers *Amer. Med. Plants* 7, *Hedeoma pulegioides.* . . Tickweed. . . The distillation of oil of pennyroyal is a limited industry carried on in scattered sections in the eastern part of the country. **1971** Krochmal *Appalachia Med. Plants* 138, Tickweed. . . A tea is used in Appalachia for treating pneumonia.

2   =**tick trefoil.**

1828 [see **1** above]. **1889** Vasey *Ag. Grasses* 94, *Desmodium.* . . There are about forty species native in the United States. . . There are often called beggar-lice, beggar-weed, or tick-weed. **1966–67** *DARE* Wildfl QR Pl.110 [=*Meibomia michauxii,* now called *Desmodium rotundifolium*] Inf **AR**44, Tickweed family; **MI**31, Tickweed.

3   =**tickseed 1.**

1833 Eaton *Botany* 106, Coreopsis. . . rosea . . (tickweed . .) small, smooth: . . rays unequally 3-toothed. **1876** Hobbs *Bot. Hdbk.* 120, Tickweed, Coreopsis. **1967** *DARE* Wildfl QR Pl.261B [=*Coreopsis rosea*] Inf **SC**41, Tickweed.

4   A **crownbeard** (here: *Verbesina virginica*).

1933 Small *Manual SE Flora* 1443, P[haethusa] virginica [=*Verbesina v.*] . . Frost-weed. Tickweed. Indian-tobacco. **1950** Gray–Fernald *Manual of Botany* 1495, *V. virginica.* . . Tickweed, Frostweed.

5   A **mullein** (here: *Verbascum thapsus*).

1940 Clute *Amer. Plant Names* 274, *Verbascum thapsus.* . . Tick-weed.

6   Any of var **stickseeds 1a** (here: *Hackelia* spp).

1961 Peck *Manual OR* 664, H[ackelia] Cusickii . . Cusick's Tickweed. . . H. setosa . . Bristly Tickweed. . . H. Jessicae [=*H. micrantha*] . . Jessica's Tickweed. . . H. floribunda . . Many-flowered Tickweed. *Ibid* 665, H. hispida . . Rough Tickweed.

ticky adj

1   Finicky, fussy; touchy. **chiefly Sth, S Midl** See Map Cf **ticular**

1894 *Harper's New Mth. Mag.* 89.613 **WV**, They ain't nothin' like's ticky as some. When I see the young folks that's so awful nice about hevin' kyarpets on the floor . . and that all, I often say to 'em, 'Ef you all could see how yer fathers lived without none of them things, you all wouldn't be so ticky.' **1965–70** *DARE* (Qu. HH11a, b *Someone who is too particular or fussy*) 14 Infs, **chiefly Sth, S Midl**, Ticky; (Qu. H12, *If somebody eating a meal takes little bits of food and leaves most of it on his plate, you say he _____*) Infs **GA**75, **IL**134, Ticky; **GA**88, Ticky eater; (Qu. GG8, *When a person is very easily offended: "Be careful what you say to him, he's _____."*) Inf **MO**29, Ticky; (Qu. GG16, . . *Finding fault, or complaining: "You just can't please him—he's always _____."*) Inf **MS**25, So ticky. [8 of 17 total Infs Black] **1972** *Atlanta Letters* **cnGA**, She is so ticky about everything. . . The ones who use this word mean the person is precise, particular & wants things right. **1986** Pederson *LAGS Concordance,* 1 inf, **cnMS**, Ticky = sensitive; 1 inf, **seAR**, Ticky = picky; particular [used of a] fastidious relative. **1999** *DARE* File, "Ticky" and "nitpicky" were synonyms in 1940's in north Florida. **2003** *Dade Co. Sentinel* (Trenton GA) 10 Dec (Internet) **neAL**, She also said she's a stickler for neatness. "My granddaughter says, "Nana, why do you have to be so ticky?" " **2004** in 2006 *DARE* File—Internet **cnMS**, [Transcript of taped interview:] We were so careful and so ticky, . . we watched every plate that went out of the kitchen. . . And . . everything that was made, we would taste. **2005** *Ibid* **GA**, You cannot just plop the President down anywhere in the world. The Secret Service is very ticky about those things.

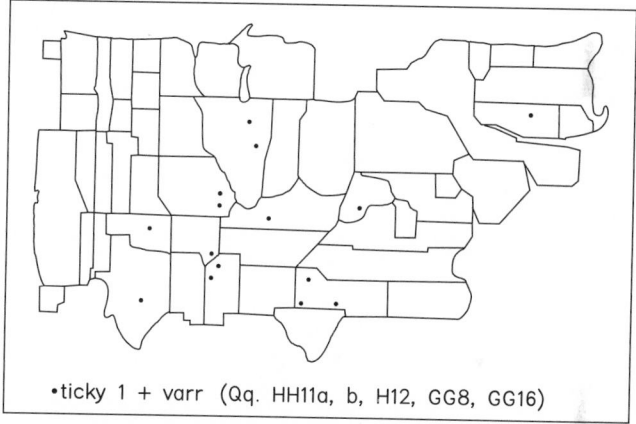

•ticky 1 + varr (Qq. HH11a, b, H12, GG8, GG16)

2   Untidy, rough, shabby. Cf **tacky** adj **1**

1886 *Amer. Philol. Assoc. Trans.* 17.46 **KY**, Tacky (common), *ticky* in Kentucky. **1899** (1912) Green *VA Folk-Speech* 448, Ticky. . . Used of persons in a rough or unpolished condition. **1950** *WELS Suppl.* **seWI**, Ticky—Messy, not neat, a little on the shabby side.

3   See **tickly.**

tic-tac n   Cf DS EE10

1966 *DARE* File **Boston MA**, Tic-tac—Played with old broom handle cut to 5 inch length and tapered at both ends. Object: To strike with another 30 inch length of broom handle and see which could send short length the greatest distance. Three whacks allowed.

tic-tac-to   See **tick-tack-toe 1**

tic-tac-toe   See **ticktack** n

tic-tac-toe night   See **ticktack night**

tic-toc   See **ticktack** n

tic-toc-to   See **tick-tack-toe 1**

ticular n, adj   Also sp *ticalah, tickler* [Aphet forms of **particular**] Cf **ticky**

1844 Thompson *Major Jones's Courtship* 108 **GA**, That paper . . has got them letters in it what you rit to your tickler frend mister Tomson. **1909** *DN* 3.381 **eAL, wGA**, Tickler. . . Particular. "I wasn't doin' nuthin' in tickler." A negroism. **1914** *DN* 4.160 **cVA**, 'Ticalah. . . Particular. "A ticalah fren'," (a particular frend [sic]). **1937** in 1972 *Amer. Slave* 2.90 **SC,** Dat show me dat I done forgot to be particular. I got mo' 'ticular and pray mo' often. **1954** *Harder Coll.* **cwTN,** *Ticular.* . . Particular. . . Said especially of one who is very fussy. . . "She's jis' . . too ticular fer own [sic] good. Even picks at 'er victuals."

tiddely See **tiddlies**

tiddle board n Also *teedle, teetling board, tiddle, tiddling ~, tittling ~* **neMA, seNH** Cf **teeter** v, n **4, teenter board, tiddly-bender(s)**

=**seesaw 1.**

1933 *AmSp* 8.2.18 **MA, NH,** *New England Words for the Seesaw.* . . One of our informants in Rockport on Cape Ann offered *tiddle board* and *tiddlin' board,* another *teetlin' board.* In Seabrook, N.H., just across the Essex County line, *tiddle board* is in use, and one of our informants in Haverhill . . calls the seesaw a *teedle.* We are here obviously dealing with an Essex County word, which has not been discovered elsewhere. **1943** *LANE* Map 577 *(Seesaw)* 2 infs, **neMA,** Tiddle board; 1 inf, **seNH,** Tiddle board—older term; 1 inf, **neMA,** Tiddling board—usually; 1 inf, **seNH,** Tittling board; 1 inf, **neMA,** Teedle; 1 inf, **neMA,** Teetling board. **2007** *DARE* File **neMA,** My mother who was born in 1900 in Gloucester, Massachusetts, always referred to it [=a seesaw] as a "tiddle".

tiddledewinks See **tiddlywinks**

tiddledies See **tiddlies**

tiddledy-benders See **tiddly-bender(s)**

tiddlies n Also *tiddledies, tidd(e)ly* **esp MA**
=**tickly-bender(s)**—usu in phr *run tiddlies.*

1877 Bartlett *Americanisms* 704, *Tiddlies.* Boys say, "run tiddlies," *i.e.* run over ice after it has begun to break up on a sheet of water. [*DARE* Ed: Bartlett was from Rhode Island.] **1887** (1893) Grant *Jack Hall* 42 **ceMA,** Some of the "crowd" . . had gone down to the Frog Pond on the Common to see if there were any "tiddledies," which, as all Boston boys know, are cakes of floating ice formed during the first stages of a thaw; the sport being to jump from one to another, until *terra firma* is reached, without tumbling in. *Ibid* 48, He started off to warn their friends, who were running tiddledies. **1888** [see **tiddly-bender(s)**]. **1900** *New Engl. Mag.* 22.674, What a flood of memories rushed through my mind . . of "running tiddlies" near the shore when the south wind began to blow in early March. **1902** (1903) Lorimer *Letters* 70 **Chicago IL,** While I tried to pass it off with something about your still being green and raw, the ice was mighty thin, and you had the old man running tiddledies. **1915** Lincoln *Thankful's Inheritance* 192 **Cape Cod MA,** Kenelm's like a young one runnin' 'tiddly' on thin ice. **1927** in 1953 Holmes–Laski *Letters* 2.1006 **MA,** When we were boys we used to run tiddledies on the frog pond in the Common—that is jump from piece to piece of the ice, each being enough to jump from but sinking under you if you stopped. **1931–33** *LANE Worksheets* **MA,** *Tiddlies*—the game played on thin ice. To play tiddlies is to slide on ice and feel it bend under you. **1962** Morison *One Boy's Boston* 35 **ceMA** (as of 1890s), During school recesses, when the ice began to break up, we enjoyed the sport of "tiddledewinks," or "running tiddely," . . crossing the pond by running over floating ice cakes and jumping from one to another. . . [T]he Public Garden rang with cries of "Hey, tiddely!" as the boys dared each other. **2008** *DARE* File—Internet, Tiddledies: soft flexible ice, or chunks of floating ice.

tiddling board See **tiddle board**

tiddly See **tiddlies**

tiddly-bender(s) n Also *tiddledy-benders, tittly-bender(s)* **MA**
=**tickly-bender(s);** one who crosses **rubber ice** safely.

1888 *Boston Morning Jrl.* (MA) 17 Dec 3/6, Running tiddledies, or "tiddledy-benders," is a great test of character. **1890** *DN* 1.75 **MA,** *Tittly benders* . . pl.: sallies out on thin ice. "He cuts a tittly bender" is a possible phrase. Possibly applied to the ice itself. **1892** *DN* 1.213 **ceMA,** *Tittly benders.* . . The expression was applied to the ice itself. "Running benders" was a common phrase. **1905** Shute *Real Boys* 210 **seNH,** The crisp singing of the rocker blades was punctuated by the dull thud of small craniums on the hard ice, and the shrill shouts of "Shinney on your own side," "Who yer hittin'?" "No fair holdin'," "Tiddly benders, tiddly benders!" and other cries appropriate to the season. **1943** *LANE* Map 575, Sliding on thin ice. . . 1 inf, **seMA,** ['tɪdlɪ ˌbɛndəz]. **1958** *Sat. Eve. Post Letters* **MA,** *Tiddely-bender* [sic]—In the spring . . there would be small areas of water . . covered with ice. . . A group

would gather on one side—One at a time would skate across—the ice would bend. . . The last one safely across was a Tiddley-bender [sic]. **1970** *DARE* (Qu. B35, *Ice that will bend when you step on it, but not break*) Inf **MA**100, Tiddly-benders.

tiddlywinks n Also *tiddledewinks*
=**tickly-bender(s).**

1962 [see **tiddlies**]. **1967** *DARE* (Qu. B35, *Ice that will bend when you step on it, but not break*) Inf **MA**27, Tiddlywinks—we called it that when we were kids.

tiddy See **titty** n[1]

tiddy baby See **titty baby**

tide n Cf **freshet 2** **chiefly sAppalachians**
An often sudden rising or flooding of an inland river or stream; hence combs *log tide, tie ~, raft ~* a rise sufficient to float and transport logs or log rafts.

a1782 (1788) Jefferson *Notes VA* 9, In common winter and spring tides it [=the Ohio River] affords 15 feet water to Louisville. **1896** (1897) Brodhead *Bound in Shallows* 104 **KY,** A hope of early fall "tides" began to enliven the loggers' conversation. **1905** U.S. Forest Serv. *Bulletin* 61.51 [Logging terms], *Tide.* . . A freshet. In the Appalachian region logs are rolled into a stream and a "tide" awaited to carry them to the boom. **1913** Kephart *Highlanders* 21 **sAppalachians,** The only roads follow the beds of tortuous and rock-strewn water courses, which may be nearly dry when you start out in the morning, but within an hour may be raging torrents. . . A spring "tide" will stop all travel. **1915** *DN* 4.188 **swVA,** *Raft tide.* . . Tide sufficient to float rafts. **1924** Raine *Land of Saddle-Bags* 24 **sAppalachians,** The most sudden tides are the result of heavy rains back in the mountains, when there are a few inches of snow. Then, overnight, creeks will swell to ten times their volume of water and rush down, a strong sullen stream. **1927** *DN* 5.470 **Appalachians,** *Tide.* . . A sudden rise in a stream; freshet. **1929** in 1952 Mathes *Tall Tales* 141 **sAppalachians,** The freeze killed the fruit, the big tide washed the hay away, the drought ruined the tobacker, an' the cholery killed most of the fattenin' hawgs. **1952** Giles *40 Acres* 224 **csKY,** Come a freshet, or what we hereabouts call a tide, in the spring or summer . . Chelf Branch is not to be fooled with. **1958** *PADS* 29.17 **TN,** When enough rain fell to cause the river to rise to a stage that the rafts [of recently cut logs] lying on its banks would float—that was a tide. **1969** *DARE* (Qu. B27, *A sudden rush of water coming from heavy rain*) Inf **KY**41, Tide—comes in the river; **KY**28, Quick tide; (Qu. C9, *Water from a river that comes up and covers low land when the river is high*) Inf **KY**39, Tide; **KY**18, June tide; tie tide; **KY**16, Log tide. [*DARE* Ed: Only resps that clearly point to the flooding of an inland waterway are included here; other Infs giving the resp *tide* at these and other qq were referring to ocean tides.] **1976** Garber *Mountain-ese* 73 **sAppalachians,** The loggers are waitin' for a raft-tide to market their logs. **1978** in 2003 (acc) KY Univ. Oral Hist. Program *Frontier Nursing Serv. Oral Hist. Project* 10 (Internet) **KY,** We ridden come across here on a tide in the river. **1983** *MJLF* 9.1.59 **ceKY** (as of 1956), *Tide* . . a flooding of the river, a freshet. **1997** in 2004 Montgomery–Hall *Dict. Smoky Mt. Engl.* 607 **wNC, eTN,** Tide.

tide gull n
Either the common **tern** *(Sterna hirundo)* or the Arctic **tern** *(S. paradisaea).*

1951 *AmSp* 26.278, Connecting bird movements with those of the tide are the names . . *tide gull* (common tern, Mass., N.Y.) [etc]. **1956** MA Audubon Soc. *Bulletin* 40.22 **MA,** *Common Tern.* . . Tide Gull. . . *Arctic Tern.* . . Tide Gull.

tide hole n **NEng** Cf **hole** n **1b**
An inlet or channel subject to dangerous tidal currents.

1906 *Washington Post* (DC) 11 Feb 6/7 **seNH,** This large basin is now emptied at each tide causing a very swift current in the river. This has resulted in many disasters to shipping and has helped give Portsmouth Harbor a reputation among seafaring men as a "tide hole." **1932** Wasson *Sailing Days* 16 **ME,** Among mariners in the lumber trade, the anchorage at Bucksport obtained an evil reputation as a "tide hole." *Ibid* 145, The lower harbor, itself noted for its depth of water and also for being a tide hole, very rarely froze over. **1956** Teller *Search for Slocum* 204 **seMA,** He said that Slocum depended on him to tow the *Spray* in and out of Menemsha Creek, a worse tide hole then than now. **1967** Duncan–Ware *Cruising Guide* 92 **NEng,** Avoid it [=this harbor]. Either your anchor drags or it fouls among the lobster pots and it's a damn tide hole. **1985** Benes *Amer. Speech* 36 **ME coast,** Maine coastal localities have an array of terms for minor inlets—*cubbyhole, dodge-*

hole, eel-rut[s], gunkhole, hole-in-the-beach, pocket, puddledock, tide-hole. **2004** *Working Waterfront* (Rockland ME) 19 Dec (Internet) **cME coast,** He explained that there are tide holes, places where the tides run so strongly that buoys will run under the surface. To make sure they can find their traps, he said, fishermen "will tie on a second flotation device on the very tip end of the line."

tideland deer n

A **white-tailed deer** (here: *Odocoileus virginianus leucurus*).

1940 *Jrl. Mammalogy* 21.271 **OR, WA,** The existence, near the mouth of the Columbia River, of a population of Pacific white-tailed deer, *Odocoileus virginianus leucurus . . ,* has been recently called to our attention. . . To the farmers and fishermen . . of the river, the "tideland deer" or "cottontail deer" are well known.

tideland spruce n   Also *tidewater spruce*

=Sitka spruce.

1884 Sargent *Forests of N. Amer.* 206, *Picea Sitchensis. . . Tide-land Spruce. . .* A large tree of great economic value, . . reaching its greatest development in Washington territory and Oregon near the mouth of the Columbia river. **1884** U.S. Dept. Ag. *Rept. of Secy. for 1884* 142, *Tidewater Spruce.*—This variety grows 200 feet high and 8 to 10 in diameter. **1897** Sudworth *Arborescent Flora* 41, *Picea sitchensis. . .* Tideland Spruce (Cal., Oreg., Wash.) **1923** in 1925 Jepson *Manual Plants CA* 51, *Tideland Spruce. . .* Forest tree 80 to 190 ft. high. . . Extensively lumbered. In cultivation called Sitka Spruce. **1940** Writers' Program *Oregon* 20, A large area is covered with Douglas fir, interspersed with cedar, yew and hemlock, while along the coast grow gigantic tideland spruce and contorted thickets of lodgepole pine. **1972** Viereck–Little *AK Trees* 54, *Picea sitchensis. . .* Tideland spruce. . . The largest and one of the most valuable trees in Alaska, also the State tree.

tide runner n

1 A **weakfish** such as *Cynoscion regalis.*

1877 Hallock *Sportsman's Gaz.* 244 **Long Is. NY,** In deeper water along the edges of channels and tide-races, . . the weakfish run singly and much larger in size. . . These big fellows are designated as "tide-runners." **1972** Sparano *Outdoors Encycl.* 381, Tiderunner. . . *Cynoscion regalis. . .* Basically a school fish (though large ones are often lone wolves), these weakfish are a coastal species, being found in the surf and in inlets, bays, channels, and saltwater creeks.

2 =hardtail 1.

1935 Caine *Game Fish* 48 **Sth,** *Caranx crysos. . .* Tide Runner. . . *Water Frequented:* Outside and inner reefs around rocks.

tide walker n   **coastal ME**   Cf **deadhead** n **4, sawyer 4**

A log floating, often with only one end at the surface, in coastal waters.

1918 *Daily Kennebec Jrl.* (Augusta ME) 29 June 6/3, The "submarine" reported as being off West Quoddy last Monday turned out to be floating rockweed with a "tide walker" sticking up in it. **1932** Wasson *Sailing Days* 27 **cME coast,** A large number of logs were not salvaged and buffeted about by tide and wind, became water-soaked and partially sank. These nearly hidden dangers to navigation, with one end only slightly showing above water, formed the dreaded "tide walkers" infesting the river and to some extent the Bay. **1941** Williams *Strange Woman* 116 **ME,** The master, alert to his marks, brought them past the Three Fingers; and a tide-walker thumped the packet's bottom. **1942** ME Univ. *Studies* 56.69, In the rivers and bays of Maine vessels were often bothered by water-soaked logs floating with one end out of water. These were called *tidewalkers.* **1981** *DARE* File **eMA,** A tide-walker is a log so heavy that it never fully comes ashore. It's always walking with the tide. **2002** *Yankee* Mar 56 **ME coast,** At the helm, Executive Petty Officer Tim Chase keeps an eye out for deadheads and tidewalkers, the pieces of wood and upright logs that can wreck a small ship.

tidewater crow n

=northwestern crow.

1953 Jewett *Birds WA* 470, *Northwestern Crow. . .* Other names . . Tidewater Crow. . . Great numbers of northwestern crows are to be observed along the ocean beaches, the Strait of San Juan de Fuca, and in the Sound region. . . They are not ordinarily observed far from the salt water, though they sometimes repair to fir forests as much as 3 miles distant to roost at night.

tidewater spruce   See **tideland spruce**

tidy n   *old-fash*

An ornamental covering, esp of fancywork, used to protect the

back, arm, or headrest of a piece of furniture from soiling; an antimacassar.

1848 MA Charitable Mechanic Assoc. *Exhibition* 185, Miss. S.J. Farnsworth, *Bedford, Mass.* Chair tidy. **1850** *Knickerbocker* 36.255 **MA,** One cane-seated rocking-chair . . the back of which is covered with an unapproachable netting of spotless white, called a 'tidy.' **1857** MI State Ag. Soc. *Trans. for 1856* 8.414, M.J. Pattridge, best chair tidy. **1880** *Harper's New Mth. Mag.* 61.656, She . . carries home an embroidered "chair-back"—the more dignified name that she gives nowadays to her "tidy." **1899** (1912) Green *VA Folk-Speech* 448, *Tidies. . .* A more or less ornamental covering for the back of a chair, the arms of a sofa, or the like, to keep them from becoming soiled. **1899** (1977) Norris *McTeague* 144 **San Francisco CA,** The clean white matting and the gay worsted tidies over the chair backs. **1913** Wharton *Custom of Country* 114 **NY,** How'd they expect her fair young life to pass? Playing 'Holy City' on the melodeon, and knitting tidies for church fairs? **1965–70** *DARE* (Qu. E10, *Knitted or crocheted pieces placed on the back and arms of a chair for decoration and cleanliness*) 128 Infs, **widespread,** Tidies; 20 Infs, **scattered,** Chair tidies. [Of all Infs responding to the question, 70% were old; of those giving these responses, 86% were old.] **1983** *MJLF* 9.1.59 **ceKY** (as of 1956), *Tidies . .* doilies.

tidytips n

1 also *tidytip:* A plant of the genus *Layia,* esp *L. platyglossa,* native to the western US.   For other names of var spp see **daisy 2f**

1888 Lindley–Widney *CA of South* 330, The children call it [=*Layia platyglossa*] "tidy-tips," each golden petal being daintily fringed with white. **1898** *Jrl. Amer. Folkl.* 10.230 **CA,** *Layia* (sp.), tidy-tips. **1915** (1926) Armstrong–Thornber *Western Wild Flowers* 554, *Yellow Tidytips—Blepharipappus elegans* [=*Layia platyglossa*]. . . This is common and a very handsome kind. *White Tidy-tips—Blepharipappus glandulosus* [=*Layia g.*] . . This grows in mountain canyons and is very widely distributed. **1949** *Desert Mag.* May 29/2 **sCA,** An abundance of senecio, white tidytips, . . and sand blazing star are among the flowers in bloom. **1966–68** *DARE* (Qu. S7, *A kind of daisy, bright yellow with a dark center, that grows along roadsides in late summer*) Infs CA20, 24, Tidytips; (Qu. S26e, *Other wildflowers not yet mentioned;* not asked in early QRs) Inf CA2, Tidytip; CA60, Tidytips; (Qu. S26a, . . *Wildflowers. . . Roadside flowers*) Infs CA79, 87, Tidytips. **1982** *Plants SW* (Catalog) 29 **CA,** *Tidy-tips—Layia platyglossa. . .* Bright yellow, 2 inch daisies with tidy white tips on the "petals".

2 A **milk vetch** (here: *Astragalus cibarius*).

1957 Barnes *Nat. Hist. Wasatch Spring* 45 **UT,** By the side of the oaks are flowers that resemble clover blooms, with unattractive whitish corollas with purplish keels; they are tidy tips (*Astragalus cibarius*).

3 as *tidytip:* See quot.

1968 *DARE* FW Addit **LA,** Tidytip—yellow lawn weed that looks a little like a dandelion but makes no fuzzy head.

tie-down n   **chiefly West**

A martingale.

1941 Writers' Program *Guide WY* 466, *Tie-down*—A strap to hold down the head of a horse that habitually carries head so high he might fall into a hole without seeing it. **1950** *Statesville Daily Rec.* (NC) 1 Apr [5/3] (newspaperarchive.com) **West,** [Syndicated cartoon:] Th' sorrel I rode th' other day throws his head, so I put on a tie-down. **1959** Martin *Gunbarrel* 235 **WY,** I hope you have no objection to the tie down, Miss Jamison. 'What-the-Hell' throws his head without it. **1967** Green *Horse Tradin'* 123 **TX,** I didn't see any lariat ropes or hackamores or halters or tiedowns or any walking W's, things that would help a cowboy handle a rough bronc. **1967** *DARE* Tape **TX25,** A tie-down, well, that's . . just a leather band that fits around . . his nose and . . goes down to your cinch underneath the horse and . . keeps him from throwing his head up. **1995** in 2005 (acc) Lexis–Nexis Legal Research *State Case Law: SD* (Internet), He often used a "tie-down" bridle on Krissy. . . A tie-down is used to limit the upward mobility of the horse's head and neck. **2005** *DARE* File—Internet, There are two basic types, the standing martingale—known as a tie-down in the western-riding world—and the running martingale or training fork.

tief   See **thief**

tie-hacker n   Also *tie-hack*   Also called **tie-whacker**

One who makes railroad ties, esp one who cuts and hews them by hand; similarly vbl n *tie-hacking.*

1904 *Forest & Stream* 62.56 **cMO,** There lay the valley, a wreck of tree stumps and decaying limbs. The tie-hacker had been at work in my absence. **1910** *IA Recorder* (Greene) [9 Feb 2]/2 (newspaper-archive.com) **MO,** Information given by a tie hacker who witnessed the hold-up from behind a bush betrayed the desperadoes. **1933** Williamson *Woods Colt* 91 **Ozarks,** The hills is chuck full o' pore critters from the towns these days, a-hackin' out railroad ties. . . A tie-hacker, an' a little ways farther on a mess o' fox squirrels. **1941** Writers' Program *Guide AR* 305, Next to farming, tie-hacking is perhaps the most common occupation in rural Arkansas. **1944** *PADS* 2.61 **MO,** *Tie-hacker.* . . A man who hacks (hews) railroad ties with a broad-ax. Douglas Co. Rural. Common. **1953** *Council Bluffs Nonpareil* (IA) 19 Mar 5/5 **WY,** He relates the story of the mighty tie hack who traveled . . to challenge a man called Big Thor to a production duel. . . The tie hacks still come down off the slopes on pay day to play as hard as they worked. **1954** *Harder Coll.* **cwTN,** *Tie-hacker* . . one who hacks ties. **1958** McCulloch *Woods Words* 193 **Pacific NW,** *Tie hack*—A tie cutter, one who makes ties by hand, hewing them out of small timber. **c1960** *Wilson Coll.* **csKY,** *Tie-hack* (or *tie-hacker*). . . A professional maker of cross-ties, often a pretty skilled vagabond, roaming wherever there was timber to be worked. **1963** Owens *Look to River* 63 **TX,** He heard the sound of a broadax striking a log and came to where a tiehacker was hewing out a railroad tie. **1973** Allen *LAUM* 1.349 **Upper MW** (as of c1950), In southwestern South Dakota a retired cattle rancher still uses *tie hacks* and *woodticks* as mildly contemptuous terms for homesteaders who about 1913 and 1914 settled in the foothills south of the Black Hills, where they cut the small timber and sold it for railroad ties. **1999** Proulx *Close Range* 119 **WY,** Old Red, born in Lusk in 1902, . . walked off when he was fourteen to work in a tie-hack camp.

tie loose v phr [Calque of Ger *losbinden* (PaGer *losbinne*)]

To untie, turn loose (a dog, horse, etc), cast off (a vessel); of a vessel or those on it: to cast off moorings, set off; in fig phr *tie loose from:* to "let loose," utter.

1865 in 2002 Nanzig *Badax Tigers* 328 **WI,** We embarked on a fleet of steamers . . on the morning of the 6th and tied loose down the river passing Cincinnati on the evening of the 7th. **1872** *Our Boys & Girls* 12.730 **wPA,** The next morning they "tied loose," as the raftsmen say. **1875** *Burlington Weekly Hawk-Eye* (IA) 1 July 9/2 **CO,** Now . . we want you to treat our boys well; don't crowd them, but "tie them loose," and they'll keep up their corner against the world. **1884** *Freeborn Co. Std.* (Albert Lea MN) 15 Oct 3/3, But they [=thieves] are doubtless about the city and it would be well for every well regulated family to tie the dog loose. **1894** (1895) Hoover *Enemies* 67 **sePA,** He tied his horse loose and rode away like wild in the dark. **1916** *Harper's Mth. Mag.* 133.138 **WY,** It was as true a remark as I ever tied loose from. **1919** *Deming Headlight* (NM) 28 Mar [4]/1 (newspaperarchive.com), When he comes, tie the dog loose and call the police. **1935** *AmSp* 10.167 **PA** [Engl of PA Germans], He tied the dog loose (he untied the dog). **1936** *Sheboygan Press* (WI) 19 Aug [16]/3 (newspaperarchive.com), *The King's English*—This was quite common about 1900 to 1915: "Tie the dog loose and let him run the alley out." **1948** U.S. Congress House *AK Hearings* 333 **AK,** The local citizens are acting as a more or less vigilante committee to tie the ships as they come . . and tie them loose when they leave. **1952** *PA Hist.* 19.486 **cPA,** I tied her [=a lumber-raft] loose for the trip at about 2 p.m., March 14, 1938. *Ibid* 488, The next morning . . we tied loose at about daybreak. *Ibid* 492, The Last Raft first tied loose. **1963** Burroughs *Head-First* 74 **wCO,** It was thus that Mother found me when, her guests having departed, she came to tie me loose. **1969** *DARE* Tape **NY209,** "Going down cellar to tie the dog loose?" That was an old expression that they used. People come in and say, "Well, where's your wife?" or "Where's your husband?" "Oh, they're down cellar tyin' the dog loose." But when they didn't have a dog a-tall.

tie one's mouth v phr   Also *tie up one's mouth*   Gullah

To be silent.

1922 Gonzales *Black Border* 333 **sSC, GA coasts** [Gullah glossary], *Tie up 'e mout'* . . meaning held his, her, or their speech. **1949** Turner *Africanisms* 233, [tɒɪ unə mʊut] 'Hush, stop talking,' i.e., 'Tie your mouth,' being a translation of the Mende sentence *bi lei yili* 'Stop talking,' lit. 'Your mouth tie.' **2005** Kidd *Mermaid Chair* 89 **SC** [Gullah], "Tie yuh mout'," Hepzibah said, switching into Gullah, and everyone fell instantly silent.

tie pass   See **tie ticket**

tier pole n   Also *tier stick*   Cf **pole** n **2**

In tobacco curing: =**rail** n[1] **2.**

1835 *Farmers' Reg.* 2.600 **VA,** As soon as the tobacco is thoroughly

cured by fire, it should be . . removed to the pressing house, . . and crowded away on the tier poles as close as possible. **1868** *OH Democrat* (New Philadelphia) 2 Oct 1/4, I proceeded west until I came to Mr. Woodland's tobacco field. . . [A]cross the broken fence lay what I took to be a broken log about the size of an ordinary tier pole. **1928** *Landmark* (Statesville NC) 7 June 2/5, [He] was found dead last night in a tobacco barn on his farm . . his body dangling from a strand of binding twine, one end of which had been fastened to a tier pole in the barn and the other end around his neck. **1944** *PADS* 2.72 **S Midl,** *Tier-pole, tier-stick.* . . Of several wooden beams upon which the smaller "loaded" sticks of tobacco are hung. **1950** Stuart *Hie Hunters* 110 **eKY,** After he had handed many sticks of tobacco down to Peg, Did dropped down from one tierpole to another. **1965** Davis *Summer Land* 94 **cnNC,** Those logs made a kind of rack in the barn for hanging tobacco sticks; we called them tier poles. **1966** *DARE* (Qu. M4a, . . *The spaces or sections between the joists in a barn;* total Infs questioned, 75) Inf **FL26,** Tier poles—only in barns. **1967** Key *Tobacco Vocab.* 248 **GA, MD, KY, NC, TN,** *Tier.* . . One layer of rails. . . *[T]ier-pole.* **1968** *KY Folkl. Rec.* 14.41 **KY,** *Tier-poles* were placed in the tobacco barns about four feet apart horizontally and two and one-half to three feet apart vertically. The sticks of tobacco were hung on these tier-poles. **1968–70** *DARE* Tapes **KY9, 21, 75, 84, NC51, VA38, 40,** Tier pole. **1986** Pederson *LAGS Concordance,* 1 inf, **csGA,** Tier poles—in tobacco curing.

tiester   See **tester**

tie-ticket n   Also *cross-tie ticket, tie pass*   joc; old-fash

An imaginary ticket entitling one to walk along a railroad track.

1878 *Allen Co. Democrat* (Lima OH) 14 Mar [3]/3 (newspaperarchive.com), He was provided with a ticket . . but evidently thought, in his intoxicated state, that it was a tie-ticket. About three quarters of a mile east of the station he became "tired" and sat down on the track to rest and fell asleep. **1879** Peck *Peck's Fun* 160 **WI,** The burglar could take a tie pass that is in the safe, and walk to Philadelphia. **1893** *Daily Rev.* (Decatur IL) 6 May [8]/1 (newspaperarchive.com), Millard Hoggart attended the meeting of the board of assessors at Sullivan Saturday. He took a tie ticket as no train was going that way. **1896** *Century Illustr. Mag.* 52.622, He had started "The Doddville Weekly Boomer" by offering a tramp editor going from the "Soo" to St. Paul on a "tie pass" the privilege of a room rent-free. **1904** Payne *20th Cent. Fables* 42, At the first Water Tank our friend bought a Cross Tie Ticket and began to Make Tracks toward the Metropolis. **1906** *DN* 3.161 **nwAR,** *Tie-ticket.* . . "To take a tie-ticket," means "to walk the railroad ties," "to walk." **1909** *Humeston New Era* (IA) 21 Apr [8]/3 (newspaperarchive.com), W.H. Davis went to Humeston on business Wednesday and the train got ready to come before he did so he took a tie ticket home. **1914** *DN* 4.112 **cKS,** *Tie pass.* . . Pass to use the railroad ties; privilege to walk. **1966–67** *DARE* (Qu. Y24, . . *To walk, to go on foot:* "I can't get a ride, so I'll just have to _____.") Inf **OK42,** Get a tie-ticket—when walking along railroad tracks; [**TX36,** Get a sand ticket].

tie tide   See **tide**

tie-up n   chiefly **nNEng**

A building or section of a building with stalls for cattle, esp milk cows; a stall or stanchion.

1839 *Farmers' Reg.* 7.134 **ME,** A board from the bottom of the partition that separates the "tie-up" from the barn floor, should be removed, and the hay placed against the aperture within their reach. **1851** (1856) Springer *Forest Life* 82 **ME,** At the further end of the "tie-up" he thinks he hears a little clattering noise. **1883** *ME Dept. Ag. Annual Rept. for 1882* 26.50, The farmers throw the dressing out of the tie-up windows. **1894** *VT State Bd. Ag. Report* 14.112, Think you she will rest until the cobwebs are swept from the tie-ups? **1909** *DN* 3.417 **nME,** *Tie up.* . . See *linter* [=*lean-to*]. **1913** *DN* 4.55 **ME,** *Tie-up.* . . Cow barn; cow stable. **1924** *DN* 5.295 **csNH,** *Tie up.* . . See *stanchel.* **1926** *DN* 5.389 **ME,** *Tie up* (accent on first word). . . Stanchion in collective sense. "The cows are in the tie-up." Common. **1930** Faulkner *As I Lay Dying* 117 **MS,** The cows were still in the tie-up. **1932–34** *Hanley Disks* **neMA,** The hay bays on one side of the barn door and the cow tie-ups on the other. The old-fashioned name is cow-in; **seMA,** I had her in the tie-up and I had to move her to the bull stable. **1949** Kurath *Word Geog.* 21, *Lean-to* . . and *tie-up* . . are common names in eastern Massachusetts, New Hampshire, and Maine for the shed-like addition to the barn in which cows are housed. *Lean-to* predominates in Massachusetts, *tie-up* in New Hampshire and on the coast of Maine. **1959** *VT Hist.* 27.163, *Tie-ups.* . . Stanchions. Common among dairymen. **1964** (1965) Gould *You Should Start* 132 **ME,** True, the figures show that we have more cows than ever before, but the figures also show that the tie-up that had two, three, four cows, maybe ten, is empty. **1966–68** *DARE* (Qu. M10, *The part of the barn where cows are kept*) Infs **ME**5, 19, Tie-up; **NH**14, Cow tie-up. **1995** in 2006 *DARE* File—Internet **seNH** (as of 1930s), After the kitchen and milkroom in the ell came the outhouse, the woodshed, the carriage garage, a 3 or 4 horse stable, and the barn with tie-up for 20–25 cows. **1998** *Ibid* **ME,** Helen is still in heat but this morning I was prepared for her antics and got her into her tie-up more quickly.

tie up one's mouth See **tie one's mouth**

tievine n

1 Any of several similar plants of the family Convolvulaceae, such as a **bindweed 1,** a **morning glory 1,** or *Jacquemontia tamnifolia.* **scattered, but esp TX, LA, MS** See Map

1835 in 1976 Rose *Doc. Hist. Slavery* 319, The "tie-vines" . . are sometimes very troublesome: the tie-vine is nothing more or less than the morning-glory, so carefully cultivated in gardens at the north. **1854** Wailes *Rept. on Ag. & Geol. MS* 344, Tie vine, *Morning glory* Convolvulus arvensis. **1896** (1897) Davis *Elephant's Track* 42 **TX,** Her slight, spare form could be seen, hoe in hand, . . accompanied by Lodelia and the two little boys—all patiently and manfully . . fighting grass and tie-vine. **1936** Whitehouse *TX Flowers* 103, *Purple Morning-Glory, Bindweed, Tie-Vine (Ipomoea trifida* [=*I. cordatotriloba*]) is a lovely but pernicious vine. . . The roots are perennial and very difficult to eradicate from cotton and corn fields. **1951** *PADS* 15.38 **TX,** *Convolvulaceae.* . . Wild morning-glories; bind-weeds; devil's shoe strings; tievines. **1965–70** *DARE* (Qu. S5, . . *Wild morning glory*) 32 Infs, **scattered, but esp TX, LA, MS,** Tievine; **LA**2, Tievine—a little different; it has smaller blooms than wild morning glory; **LA**12, Tievine—these are different from wild morning glory; tievine doesn't bloom; **LA**20, 28, Tievine [FW sugg: Infs say it's different from morning glories]; **NY**211, Tievine—heard—I don't use; **TX**40, There is a tievine, but it has no bloom; **TX**101, Tievine—flower smaller; (Qu. S21, . . *Weeds* . . *that are a trouble in gardens and fields*) Inf **AR**10, Tievine; (Qu. S25, . . *The small wild chrysanthemum-like flowers* . . *that bloom in fields late in the fall*) Inf **MS**82, Tievine. **1968** *DARE* Wildfl QR Pl.176 [=*Convolvulus sepium,* now called *Calystegia s.*] Inf **LA**21, Wild morning glory or tievine—rural. **1972** Brown *Wildflowers LA* 150, *Tie Vine—Jacquemontia tamnifolia.* . . The common name refers to the tangle that stems make in row crops. . . Also Texas, Arkansas, and Mississippi. **2001** *DARE* File—Internet **LA,** *Tie Vine—Jacquemontia tamnifolia.* . . These plants are called tie vine because they gwet [sic] tangled in neighboring plants.

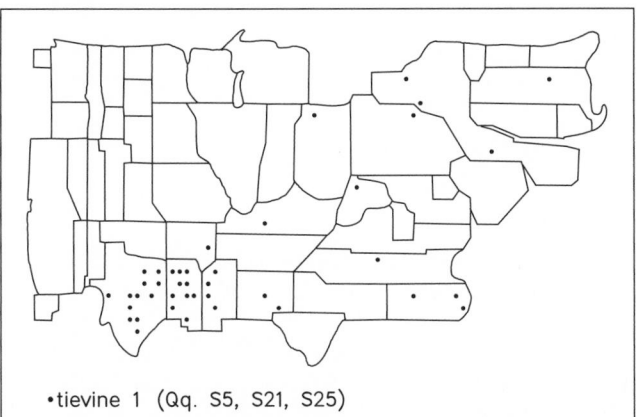

•tievine 1 (Qq. S5, S21, S25)

2 A plant resembling **1** above, as a **heliotrope 1** (here: *Heliotropium convolvulaceum*) or **moneywort 1.**

1951 *PADS* 15.39 **TX,** *Heliotropium convolvulaceum.* . . Baby or dwarf white, morning-glory; bind-weed or tie-vine. **1968** *DARE* Wildfl QR Pl.164A [=*Lysimachia nummularia*] Inf **LA**21, It's shaped like a wild morning glory; farmers call them tievines.

tie-whacker n **esp MO**

=**tie-hacker;** hence adj **tie-whacking.**

1907 *Eve. News* (Ada OK) 11 Oct 1/4, They encountered each other on the sidewalk whereupon this exchange of greetings was overheard— Hello! Cotton-picker—Go to the devil you tie-whacker! was the quick retort. **1923** *DN* 5.223 **swMO,** Tie whacker. . . A tie maker. **1931** Randolph *Ozarks* 68, He aint nothin' on'y a tie-whackin' sheer-crapper noways. **1931** *AmSp* 7.47 **Sth, SW** [Lumberjack lingo], Lumberjack

society is stratified. . . "Tie whackers" are the "boobs" of the logging camp. **1941** Writers' Program *Guide MO* 486 (as of 1880s), Crimes were committed against "tie whackers," who cut timber and shaped logs into railroad ties. **1969** Sorden *Lumberjack Lingo* 129 **NEng, Gt Lakes,** Tie whacker—A man who cuts ties in the woods. **1969** Kantor *MO Bittersweet* 23, Many of those 'tie-whackers,' as they were called, didn't want to live off a small garden patch and a hillside cornfield and what they could hunt and fish for.

tiff n [Prob < Fr *tuf* [tʏf] travertine] **esp MO**

Any of several whitish crystalline minerals typically found associated with lead and zinc ores; esp barite, which is also mined for its own sake.

1814 Brackenridge *Views of LA* 148 **ceMO,** The potter's ore, or galena, has always adhering to it, a sparry matter, which the miners call tiif [sic]. **1819** Schoolcraft *Lead Mines MO* 70, *Tiff, cawk,* and *sulphate of barytes,* are therefore one substance, consisting of the earth *barytes* united to the *sulphuric acid.* **1855** MO Geol. Surv. *Report* 1.199, Instead of the calcareous spar, which occurs in the mines of the South-West, heavy spar or tiff is very abundant. **1858** IA Geol. Surv. *Report* 1.443, The galena is found associated with other metalliferous ores. . . The mineral most frequently found in this connection is calcareous spar, or *tiff,* as it is usually called by the miners; and heavy spar is not uncommon. **1873** *Daily Democrat* (Sedalia MO) 24 Oct 1/6, Several fine specimens of lead ore and tiff are to be seen in the Central Bank, taken from lead mines located 7 miles southeast of Hermitage, Hickory county. **1874** MO Geol. Surv. *Report* 395, *Dolomite.* Brown Spar, Bitter Spar, commonly called "Soft Tiff" by the miners of Southwest Missouri. . . is composed of Carbonate of Lime and Carbonate of Magnesia. . . Missouri miners often mistake it for Barytes, which also they call "Soft Tiff" or "Bald Tiff," and which somewhat resembles it in general appearance. **1920** Fay *Gloss. Mining* 686, *Tiff.* 1. A common name for calcite in Wisconsin and Missouri zinc fields. 2. Barite in southeast Missouri. **1938** *Machinists' Mth. Jrl.* 50.918 **ceMO,** The Tiff miners in this county [=Washington Co.] are the descendants of early French pioneers who settled the western shores of the Mississippi three hundred years ago. **1968–69** *DARE* (Qu. C25, . . *Kinds of stone* . . *about* . . [. . *size of a person's head], smooth and hard*) Inf **MO**16, Tiff; (Qu. C26, . . *Special kinds of stone or rock*) Infs **MO**10, 25, 32, Tiff. **1994** *St. Louis Post–Dispatch* (MO) 9 June sec B 1 (Internet), A locked gate and an 8-foot, chain-link fence surround the kingdom, 2,000 acres of disturbed land that was once a tiff mine.

tiger n Usu |ˈtaɪɡə(r)|; also **esp S Midl** |ˈtæɡə(r), ˈtɛɡər| Pronc-spp *tag(g)er*

A Forms.

1880 *Marion Daily Star* (OH) [24 June 2]/4 (newspaperarchive.com), These are little Johnny's observations on the "Roil Bengol Tagger," as communicated to the San Fraccisco [sic] *Argonaut.* **1898** *Century Illustr. Mag.* 55.832 **GA,** He dodged him the same ef he been a tagger or some 'nother wild varmint. **1912** Green *VA Folk-Speech* 436, *Tagger.* . . Tiger; a dog's name. **1914** *DN* 4.113 **cKS,** *Tager.* . . Tiger:— among children. **1930s** in 1944 *ADD* **eWV,** Tiger. . . tagger [ˈtæɡr]. Always so pron. **1931** Patterson *Road to Canaan* 173 **Sth,** He could hear the frenzied yelps of Tiger, urged on by the dancing figure on the brink: "Sic 'im Tager!" **1943** *Ibid* **nWV,** Tiger. . . [tæɡr]. 'My dog Tagger.' [How do you spell it?] 'T-i-g-e-r.' Boy age 10. **1959** Ruark *Poor No More* 15 **NC** [Black], She fierce lak a tagger cat. **c1960** *Wilson Coll.* **csKY,** Tiger is sometimes /ˈtæɡə/. **1965** *AmSp* 40.226, *Tagger* for *tiger,* frequent in Pittsburgh and Youngstown and apparently also in the surrounding parts of western Pennsylvania and eastern Ohio. **1968** *DARE* (Qu. T10) Inf **GA**65, Tigerfoot [ˈtɛɡɚˌfut] oak.

B Senses.

1 also *tiger cat:* Any of var wild felines native to the US, esp the **mountain lion** or **ocelot;** see quots. **chiefly Sth, SW**

1709 (1967) Lawson *New Voyage* 124 **Carolinas,** Tygers are never met withal in the Settlement; but are more to the Westward, and are not numerous on this Side the Chain of Mountains. **1778** Carver *Travels N. Amer.* 442, Tyger of America. . . I saw one on an island in the Chipeway River. . . It sat up on its hinder parts like a dog; and did not seem either to be apprehensive of our approach, or to discover any ravenous inclinations. **1797** in 1916 Hawkins *Letters* 86 **GA,** The tygers killed his hogs, cattle and sometimes horses. **1806** (1905) Clark *Orig. Jrls. Lewis & Clark Exped.* 4.113, Capt Lewis [has] a Tiger cat skin coat. **1834** Pike *Prose Sketches* 14 **AR,** Imagine, also, here and there a lonely tiger-cat, lying crouched in some little hollow, or bounding off in triumph, bearing some luckless little prairie-dog. **1858** *TX Almanac for 1859* 186, The game of the country [=Webb Co.] consists of leopards, (here called tigers,) cougars, or South American lions, wild cats [etc]. [*DARE* Ed: The "leopard" referred to here is *Felis onca.*] **1927** *Boston Soc. Nat. Hist. Proc.* 38.320 **Okefenokee GA,** *Lynx rufus floridanus* [=*Felis rufus*]. . . There is a widespread local opinion to the effect that there are two kinds . . of Wildcats in the swamp. . . Allen Chesser distinguishes the 'Wildcat' from the 'Tiger-cat' or 'Catamount,' the latter being the larger, and having a white spot back of the ear. It stands about 2 feet high, and has a tail about 5 inches long. The 'Wildcat' is smaller, shorter-tailed, 'darker-tabbied,' and not so common. . . It may be rather safely assumed that there is but a single species in the region. Aside from purely individual variations, some of the differences referred to . . may be due to age or sex. **1940** Writers' Program *Guide TX* 26, The ocelot, also called the tiger-cat, is found in the brush of the Rio Grande. **1966** *DARE* (Qu. P31, . . *Names or nicknames . . for the . . wildcat*) Inf **SC**9, Tiger cat. **1967–69** *DARE* Tape **GA**48, Now this old panther . . I've seen those, but didn't ever see any tigers; **GA**51, Tiger, now, and panther . . I think is what in our way of speaking is the same thing.

2 See **tiger muskellunge.**

3 See **tiger rattlesnake.**

4 See **tiger salamander.**

5 in phr *sweat like a tiger:* =**mule** n[1] **6.**

1852 *Adams Sentinel* (Gettysburg PA) 21 June 7/1 (newspaperarchive.com) **ME,** It's been about the toughest week's work ever I did. I've sweat like a tiger all the week. **1968** *DARE* (Qu. X56b) Infs **NC**79, **TN**27, Sweat(ing) like a tiger. **2002** Tartt *Little Friend* 201 **MS,** He was fine, just dandy, only sweating like a tiger, too hot and a little edgy.

6 in phrr *buck* (or *fight*) *the tiger:* To play against a gambling establishment, esp at faro; hence occas n *tiger* a gambling establishment; the game of faro. *hist* Cf **buck** v[1] **B5b**

1837 *Spirit of Times* 7.368 **AR,** Well, . . some went to fight the tiger, and the way the tiger scratched their eyes out was spiteful. **1838** *Ibid* 8.6 **AR,** "Now," says one, "I'll shew you the tiger." . . Well, what do you suppose they meant by the Tiger? why it was a *'Faro Bank'* on one side, and a 'Roll the Bones, and fair play,' on the other. **1845** Hooper *Advent. Simon Suggs* 55 **AL,** Of these tables the "tiger" claimed three—for faro was predominant in those days. **1851** *Internatl. Mag.* 4.57 **NYC,** The boys went to fight the tiger, and Edwards lost 1400 dollars. **1854** in 1903 WI State Hist. Soc. *Coll.* 2.487 **swWI,** The unwary . . could . . avail themselves of opportunities voluntarily to dispose of their accumulated means, either in drowning their sorrows in the bowl, or "fighting the tiger" in his den. **1857** *Graham's Mag.* 50.560 **DC,** In the second story of nearly every house from the National to Third street, you can buck the *tiger,* see the pi*ctures,* and get a feed. **1865** *Prairie Farmer* 16.263 **cIL,** There was also . . several sweat boards, where the young farmers learned to fight the "tiger," so that they will be posted when they come to see the city. It is a disgrace to any society to allow gambling upon its grounds. **1877** Wright *Big Bonanza* 438 **West,** It is he that bucks at *monte;* plays draw-poker; fights the tiger; patronizes the Hurdies; sings like a "Washoe canary." **1900** *Daily NV State Jrl.* (Reno) 4 Dec 1/5, [Advt:] Square games for those who Buck the Tiger. **1907** Mulford *Bar-20* 91 **SW,** I calculates as how me an' him'll buck th' tiger for a whirl. **2002** *DARE* File—Internet **NV,** Faro is no longer played in Nevada or anywhere else. . . Today it's mostly remembered, when it's remembered at all, for its colorful slang. . . [M]ost famous of all was "bucking the tiger," the term for hitting the faro tables, because all faro establishments advertised on the street with a sign displaying a tiger.

7 also *tiger house:* =**blind tiger 1.**

1905 *DN* 3.98 **nwAR,** Tiger. . . Illicit saloon. **1965–69** *DARE* (Qu. DD30, *Joking names for a place where liquor is [or was] sold and consumed illegally*) Infs **FL**22, **TX**54, **WV**18, Tiger house.

8 in combs *tiger juice, tiger's milk, tiger piss, ~ spit, tiger('s) sweat:* =**panther C2.**

1879 Denison *Exhibition Dramas* 128, I cac'late he *will* break that pledge of his'n in two minutes, . . when that tiger's milk touches bottom. I've felt jes' so, and it always takes more of the same stuff to set a feller right. **1928** Shay *More Pious Friends* 10, And when Mother feels a bit low she takes a shot of tiger milk and feels a lot better for a few moments. **1932** *AmSp* 7.436 [Stanford Univ expressions], Sometimes "tiger sweat" is substituted for whiskey, likewise "suds" for beer. **1942** Berrey–Van den Bark *Amer. Slang* 99.1, Liquor. . . tiger milk. **1949** *Council Bluffs Nonpareil* (IA) 29 Dec 10/5, [*Our Boarding House* cartoon:] I'm . . fighting to shake off the recoil of that tiger sweat you gargle at the Owls Club. **1950** *WELS (Names and nicknames for liquor in general)* 1 Inf, **cwWI,** Tiger sweat; *(Nicknames for whiskey)* 1 Inf,

cWI, Tiger sweat; 1 Inf, **cwWI,** Tiger juice. **1958** McCulloch *Woods Words* 194 **Pacific NW,** *Tiger juice*—A strong drink. **1968** *DARE* (Qu. DD21b, *General words . . for bad liquor*) Inf **WI**48, Tiger piss; (Qu. DD21c, *Nicknames for whiskey, especially illegally made whiskey*) Inf **NY**36, Tiger sweat. **1974** Dabney *Mountain Spirits* 24 **sAppalachians,** Frontiersmen of the 1700s and 1800s referred to corn whiskey as "tiger spit," "black betsy," and "forty-rod." **1985** Wilkinson *Moonshine* 28 **neNC,** "After that they'd serve you North Carolina Corn." It is called . . tiger's sweat.

9 See **tiger-eye.**

tiger bass n

A **black bass 1,** usu a **smallmouth bass** or a **spotted bass 1** (here: *Micropterus punctulatus*).

1880 *IL State Lab. Nat. Hist. Bulletin* 1.3.40, *Small-mouthed Black Bass.* This species, called also tiger bass, river bass, etc., is the black bass *par excellence.* **1888** *Wildwood's Mag.* June 64, In the north and west both species are known as "bass," with the addition of various adjectives expressive of gameness, coloration, or habitat, as "tiger-bass," . . black, green, or yellow-bass; . . marsh-bass, or Oswego-bass. **1908** Forbes–Richardson *Fishes of IL* 265, The young of the small-mouthed bass have a dusky bar crossing the caudal fin, and lack the dark lateral stripe which characterizes the young of the large-mouthed species. This fish is often called "tiger bass" in the East and North. **1958** Latham *Meskin Hound* 25 **TX,** He'd pull his bait from the water, whip it behind him, then flick it forward again to drop gently . . against a lily pad where the spotted tiger bass or blue channel cat lay in wait. **1975** Evanoff *Catch More Fish* 73, The small-mouth bass (*Micropterus dolomieui*) is also called the bronzeback, yellow bass, brown bass, redeye, and tiger bass. **1987** *Cadence* 13.10.26 **Chicago IL,** That was one time I had never seen so many bass in one lake in my life. They had tiger bass, black bass, red bass, green bass. You never saw nothing like it.

tiger brant See **tiger goose**

tiger cat See **tiger B1**

tiger-eye n Also *tiger, tiger's eye* esp **Nth** Cf **cat's-eye 1**

A kind of playing marble; see quots.

1950 *WELS (Names and nicknames for different kinds of marbles)* 1 Inf, **cWI,** Tiger-eyes. **1958** *PADS* 29.41 **WI,** Tiger eye. . . An agate marble. **1966–69** *DARE* (Qu. EE6d, *Special marbles*) Infs **OR**4, 15, **PA**1, 194, Tiger-eyes. **c1970** Wiersma *Marbles Terms, Tigers*—striped marbles. *Ibid* **neNJ,** *Tiger's eye*—marble with black and yellow center. *Ibid* **swMI** (as of c1960), *Tiger eyes* . . in order to designate cat-eye shooters from regular cat-eyes, tiger-eyes is used; so a tiger eye is a large (shooter) cat eye, while a cat eye is used to denote the smaller regular sized marbles. **2007** Bergin *Endings* 84 **NY,** They found a marble. A single tiger eye marble. . . Leslie had not seen marbles in years. . . The one tiger eye was the coveted prize.

tigerfoot oak n

An unidentified **oak.**

1968 *DARE* (Qu. T10, . . *Kinds of oak trees*) Inf **GA**65, Tigerfoot oak.

tiger frog n

A **pickerel frog** or other **leopard frog** such as *Rana pipiens.*

1825 *Acad. Nat. Sci. Philadelphia Jrl.* 5.339, *Rana palustris.* . . Vulgo, *Leopard, Zebra,* or *Tiger-frog.* . . a row of dark-green spots on each side of the spine, extending the whole length of the back: two longitudinal rows on the flanks. **1842** DeKay *Zool. NY* 3.63, This [=*Rana palustris*] is one of our most beautiful frogs, and is remarkably active. It has a strong and disagreeable odor; and from being used as bait, it is called, in various districts, *Pickerel Frog,* and also *Tiger* and *Leopard Frog.* **1889** *Century Dict.* 6334, *Tiger-frog.* . . Same as *leopard-frog* [= *Rana pipiens*]. **1928** Pope–Dickinson *Amphibians* 39, *Rana palustris.* . . Other common names are Marsh Frog, Tiger Frog, Yellow Legs and Grass Frog. **1970** *DARE* (Qu. P23, *Names for the animal similar to the frog that lives away from water*) Inf **MI**112, Tiger frog. **1997** *DARE* File—Internet (as of c1973), It might lead to a friendly challenge of . . "Anny, Anny Over[*]" with our favorite projectile; A Tiger frog, courtesy of a pond across from my house.

tiger goose n Also *tiger brant* [See quot 1955] =**white-fronted goose.**

1910 *Amer. Breeders Mag.* 1.137, One of the most singular cases of the crossing of wild geese I have accomplished was by mating a Canada gander with a female Tiger Brant (White-fronted Goose). **1936** Roberts *MN Birds* 1.212, White-fronted Goose. . . "Tiger Brant". . . An ashy-gray or grayish-brown bird with a white band across the forehead, and underparts whitish blotched with black. **1955** *AmSp* 30.178, On entirely different grounds, the crossbarring of its underside, the white-fronted goose has been dubbed *tiger goose.*

tiger grouper n Also *tiger rockfish*

A **grouper 1b** (here: *Mycteroperca tigris*).

1903 Amer. Museum Nat. Hist. *Annual Rept. for 1902* 63, *New York Aquarium.* . . 1 Tiger Rockfish. **1916** NY Zool. Soc. *Annual Rept. for 1915* 114 **FL,** Tiger rockfish . . like some other species of groupers, . . probably reaches a much larger size in deep water. **1933** John G. Shedd Aquarium *Guide* 100, *Mycteroperca tigris—Tiger Rockfish.* The Tiger Rockfish gets its name from the dark stripes on the body. **2008** *DARE* File—Internet, The *Tiger Grouper* live [sic] in the Western Atlantic from southern Florida . . South to Brazil. It is . . quite numerous at the Flower Banks off the Louisiana coast.

tiger house See **tiger B7**

tiger juice See **tiger B8**

tiger leech n

See quot 1982.

1982 Sternberg *Fishing* 63, Tiger leeches are smaller and slimmer than ribbon leeches. They twist and turn violently in the hand. The tiger leech has two to four rows of faint black spots extending down the back. **2008** *DARE* File—Internet **OR,** *Fly Tying Demonstrations.* . . Tiger Leech.

tiger lily n Also *marsh tiger lily, wild tiger ~* [*OED2* 1824 for *Lilium lancifolium*] **chiefly Nth, N Midl, nCA** See Map Cf **dwarf tiger lily, leopard lily**

Any of var usu spotted, usu orange, red, or yellow **lilies 1;** less commonly a liliaceous plant such as *Fritillaria* or *Hemerocallis* spp.

1836 (1840) Phelps *Lectures on Botany* 111, [*Lilium*] *tigrinum* [=*L. lancifolium*] . . tiger lily . . flowers in whorls; dark orange, spotted with black. . . A very showy plant, of easy culture. **1873** (1874) Aldrich *Cloth* 22 **NEng,** *I like* not lady-slippers,/ . . I like . . / The gorgeous tiger-lilies,/ . . For they are tall and slender;/ Their mouths are dashed with carmine. **1888** Lindley–Widney *CA of South* 170 **swCA,** In August we found . . gorgeous tiger-lilies. **1894** *Jrl. Amer. Folkl.* 7.102 **NJ,** *Lilium Philadelphicum,* . . tiger-lily. *Ibid* **MN,** *Lilium superbum,* . . wild tiger-lily. **1898** *Ibid* 11.281 **WA,** *Lilium Columbianum,* . . tiger lily. *Ibid* **CA,** *Lilium Humboldtii* . . tiger lily. . . *Lilium pardalinum* . . tiger lily. . . *Lilium parvum* . . small tiger lily. **1937** Thornburgh *Gt. Smoky Mts.* 21, Great fields of wild tiger lilies of brilliant orange-red are to be found on the summits. **1940** Clute *Amer. Plant Names* 12, *H*[*emerocallis*] *fulva.* . . Orange day-lily, tiger-lily. . . *L. Philadelphicum.* . . Tiger-lily. *Ibid* 13, *L. superbum.* . . Tiger-lily, nodding tiger-lily. . . *L. tigrinum.* Tiger-lily. **1961** Thomas *Flora Santa Cruz* 118 **cwCA,** *L*[*ilium*] *pardalinum* . . Panther, Leopard, or Tiger Lily, California Tiger Lily. **1963** Craighead *Rocky Mt. Wildflowers* 24, *Fritillaria atropurpurea.* . . Tiger Lily. . . Flowers are dull purplish brown, with greenish-yellow spots. **1965–70** *DARE* (Qu. S26a, . . *Wildflowers.* . . *Roadside flowers*) 30 Infs, **chiefly Nth, Midl,** Tiger lily (*or* lilies); **ME7,** Tiger lily—also called freckle lilies; **NY97,** Tiger lilies—no spots or stripes; **OH2,** Tiger lilies—orange; **MD9, OH28,** Wild tiger lily (*or* lilies); (Qu. S26b, *Wildflowers that grow in water or wet places*) 10 Infs, **esp Nth, nCA,** Tiger lily (*or* lilies); **MD42,** Tiger lily—speckled; **MI9,** Spotted lily, or tiger lily; **CA200, IA8, MA57, MI2, MN42,** Wild tiger lily (*or* lilies); (Qu. S26c, *Wildflowers that grow in woods*) Infs **CA31, 99, FL31, PA231, WI12,** Tiger lily (*or* lilies); **MI42,** Wild tiger lily; (Qu. S26d, *Wildflowers that grow in meadows; not asked in early QRs*) 8 Infs, **chiefly Nth,** Tiger lily; **CA167, WI37,** Wild tiger lily (*or* lilies); (Qu. S26e, *Other wildflowers not yet mentioned; not asked in early QRs*) Infs **IA36, VT16,** Tiger lily (*or* lilies); (Qu. S24, *A wild flower that grows in swamps and marshes and looks like a small blue iris*) Inf **CA105,** Marsh tiger lily; **NY219,** Tiger lily; (Qu. W36, *What . . people say . . about a woman who uses a lot of cosmetics*) Inf **AR18,** Painted like a tiger lily. **1965–70** *DARE* Wildfl QR Pl.13 [=*Lilium philadelphicum*] 13 Infs, **esp Nth,** Tiger lily; Pl.14 [=*Lilium canadense*] Infs **IA25, LA21, MI57, NC28, OR9, 12, WA10, 15,** Tiger lily; Pl.12 [=*Hemerocallis fulva*] Infs **IA25, WI79,** Tiger lily; **NY91,** Day lily, but people are more likely to call it tiger lily; Pl.11 [=*Veratrum viride*] Inf **MN30,** Tiger lily. **1976** Bailey–Bailey *Hortus Third* 660, [*Lilium*] *Catesbaei.* . . Fl[ower]s . . red, yellow toward base, brown-spotted. . . N.C. to Fla. and La. Also called *tiger l*[*ily*] where it is native. *Ibid* 661, [*Lilium*] *lancifolium.* . .

Tiger l[*ily*]. . . Fls . . orange or salmon-red, spotted with purple-black. **1988** Dyer *Farmstead Yards* 87 **eTN,** Turk's-cap lily (*Lilium superbum*), known to [Cades] Cove residents as "tiger lily," [is] often transplanted into farmstead yards from its habitat near "Blue Springs." **2006** *Daily Herald* (Arlington Heights IL) 14 May sec 4 8/5, Species lilies are a good choice for later flowering. The . . orange flowers of the Tiger Lily (*L. tigrinum*) appear in August.

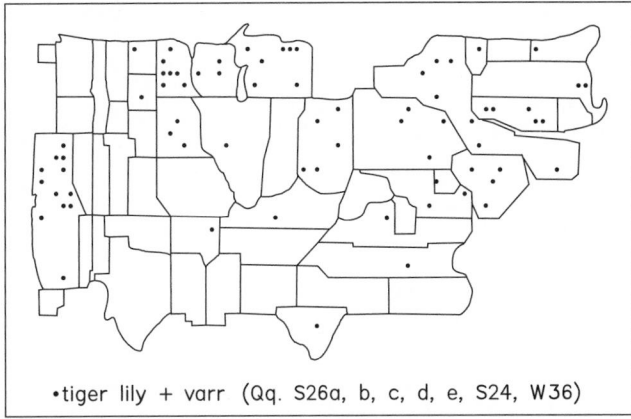

•tiger lily + varr (Qq. S26a, b, c, d, e, S24, W36)

tiger lizard n

A **whiptail 2.**

1857 *U.S. Mag.* 4.18, The tiger lizard (*cnemidophorus tigris*) is . . described. **1873** CA Acad. Nat. Sci. *Proc.* 4.71 **cCA,** *Cnemidophorus tigris* . . Tiger Lizard. **1882** U.S. Natl. Museum *Bulletin* 24.8, *Cnemidophorus Tessellatus Tigris.* . . Tessellated Tiger Lizard. **1928** Baylor Univ. Museum *Contrib.* 16.13 **nwTX,** *Cnemidophorus grahamii.* . . This species, on account of its beautiful buff and black mottlings, is sometimes called *Tiger Lizard.* **1936** Ditmars *Reptiles N. Amer.* 102, Graham's Lizard; Tiger Lizard, *Cnemidophorus grahamii.* . . Differs in the much coarser light and dark markings. The limbs are vividly blotched.

tiger milk See **tiger B8**

tiger moth n

Std: any of var often boldly patterned moths of the family Arctiidae. For other names of var of the larvae of these moths see **harlequin caterpillar, hedgehog ~, salt-marsh ~, woolly bear 1, yellow ~ (caterpillar)**

tiger muskellunge n Also *tiger (muskie)*

A **muskellunge 1** (here: *Esox masquinongy immaculatus*) or a hybrid of the **muskellunge 1** and the **northern pike 1** marked with prominent stripes.

1918 St. John *Practical Bait* 134 **MN, WI,** Specimens showing the dark cross-shades are usually called "tiger muskellunge." **1921** *Forest & Stream* Sept 423, [Caption:] 40 pounds o' Tiger Muskie on a *South Bend Buck-tail.* **1927** Weed *Pike* 31, Occasional specimens [of *Esox masquinongy immaculatus*], locally called "Tiger Muskalonge," may have the spots or bars very distinct. *Ibid* 43, *Esox immaculatus* [=*E. masquinongy i.*] . . Tiger; Wisconsin. Tiger Muskalonge; Wisconsin. Tiger Musky; Wisconsin. **1946** La Monte *N. Amer. Game Fishes* 130, *Esox masquinongy immaculatus.* . . Tiger Muskellunge. . . Another subspecies of the Muskellunge, found in lakes of Wisconsin and Minnesota. **1972** Sparano *Outdoors Encycl.* 366, The tiger (northern) muskie is common in Wisconsin, Minnesota, and western Michigan. **1983** Becker *Fishes WI* 405, *Esox masquinongy.* . . Tiger muskellunge, the muskellunge x northern pike hybrid, is a naturally occurring form in several large lakes. . . An estimated 40–50% of the "muskellunge" caught annually from Lac Vieux Desert on the Wisconsin–Michigan boundary are natural hybrids. **2001** *DARE* File—Internet, The tiger muskie [=*Esox lucius* x *E. masquinongy*] has a distinctive look and should not be confused with the true muskellunge, which has been called a tiger muskie in some areas. *Ibid* **NY,** While they occasionally occur naturally, most tiger muskellunge found in New York State's waters have been stocked. . . In appearance, the tiger musky is a real cross between its two parents. Tigers have the cheek and gill cover scale pattern of northern pike, but the barred dark body markings on a light background like the muskellunge.

tiger of the sea See **sea tiger**

tiger piss See **tiger B8**

tiger rattlesnake n Also *tiger (rattler)* [See quot 1895]
A **rattlesnake 1** (here: *Crotalus tigris*) of the southwestern US.

1868 Cronise *Nat. Wealth CA* 483, The "Tiger Rattlesnake" (. . *C. tigris*) is found in the Colorado desert regions, of large size. **1895** U.S. Natl. Museum *Annual Rept. for 1893* 450, The Tiger Rattler which has received its name . . from its tawny color and marked cross stripes, seems partial to the barren mountain ranges with their rocks and crevices in preference to the desert valleys surrounding them. **1952** Ditmars *N. Amer. Snakes* 257, Tiger Rattlesnake. . . Usual length 2 ½–3 feet; seldom in excess of a yard. **1974** Shaw–Campbell *Snakes West* 228, Several features distinguish the tiger rattlesnake *(Crotalus tigris)*. Most obvious are the thirty-seven to fifty-two dark gray brown tiger stripes that cross its back from head to tail, stripes normally more distinct than those of any other rattlesnake. **2001** *DARE* File—Internet **AZ,** The tiger rattlesnake . . is largely endemic to the Arizona Upland bioregion of the Sonoran Desert.

tiger rockfish See **tiger grouper**

tiger salamander n Also *tiger (triton)*
A **salamander 1:** usu *Ambystoma tigrinum,* widespread except in New England, the Appalachian Mountains, and the far West, but also *A. californiense* of California. For other names of the former see **alligator** n[1] **B1, lizard** n **2, mole salamander, mud puppy** c, **water dog 1**

1842 DeKay *Zool. NY* 3.83, The Tiger Triton. . . Color. Above bluish black. . . The spots on the upper surface pale ochre or lemon yellow. **1892** IL State Lab. Nat. Hist. *Bulletin* 3.373, *Ambystoma tigrinum.* . . Tiger Salamander. . . Very large, total length from six to eleven inches. **1914** *Copeia* 8.4 **NJ,** Tiger Salamander. . . Reported . . from Rancocas. **1926** TX Folkl. Soc. *Pub.* 5.63 **wTX,** The large tiger salamander is a common animal. **1947** Pickwell *Amphibians* 7, *Ambystoma tigrinum californiense* [=*A. californiense*], the California Tiger Salamander, has a restricted range, from Sonoma and Sacramento to Monterey and Kern counties. It is similar to . . the more easterly . . Tiger Salamander [=*A. tigrinum*] in having large yellow spots on a dark bluish or blackish ground color. **1966** Wheeler–Wheeler *Amphibians & Reptiles ND* 31, Tiger Salamander. . . Entirely harmless, and, in fact, if treated properly . . will make interesting (if stupid) pets. **1981** Vogt *Nat. Hist. WI* 47, There may be hundreds of tiger salamanders under your feet, but you will never know it unless you see the fall or spring hordes. . . Ken Lange, naturalist at Devil's Lake State Park, feeds his "tigers" bits of sirloin dangled on a string. **1992** Martone *Townships* 77 **swMN,** The odds were even that [as you explored a farm cellar] you would . . scare up one of the tiger salamanders that had wintered there in the warmth.

tiger's eye See **tiger-eye**

tiger's milk, tiger spit See **tiger B8**

tiger squirrel n
The golden-mantled **ground squirrel** n b *(Spermophilus lateralis).*

1929 Seton *Lives of Game Animals* 4.218 **Rocky Mts,** Golden-Mantled Ground-squirrel . . Two-striped Chipmunk, Rock Squirrel, Tiger Squirrel . . On each side are two parallel black stripes . . with a dull, yellowish white stripe between them. **1943** Gordon *W. Chipmunk* 8, The mantled ground squirrels are now placed in the genus *Citellus,* and most of them in the species *lateralis.* . . Among . . [its] common names are big chipmunk, golden chipmunk, copperhead, copper chip, yellow head, callico [sic] chip, Callo, bummer, rock squirrel, and tiger squirrel.

tiger('s) sweat See **tiger B8**

tiger tail n
=**mountain lion.**

1930 Shoemaker *1300 Words* 63 **cPA Mts** (as of c1900), *Tiger tail*—The Pennsylvania lion or panther.

tiger triton See **tiger salamander**

tight adj *orig esp freq among Black speakers, young speakers, and male speakers; now more widespread*
Of friends: very close.

1965–70 *DARE* (Qu. II3, *Expressions to say that people are very friendly toward each other: "They're _____."*) 10 Infs, **scattered,** (Real) tight; **NH14,** Tight friends; **PA247,** Tight with each other;

CA177, Very tight; **FL48, TN50,** Up tight; (Qu. II1, *. . A close friend . . "He's my _____."*) Inf **FL48,** Tight-gal; tight-man; (Qu. II2a, *When two people begin to be friendly: "He has just recently _____ with John."*) Inf **FL48,** Got tight; (Qu. II2b, *When two people have become friendly . . "It's been quite a while that Mary and Jane have been _____."*) Infs **CA177, FL48,** 52, **WV21,** (Got) tight; (Qu. II20b, *A person who tries too hard to gain somebody else's favor: "He's always trying to _____ the boss."*) Infs **NC84, PA76,** Get tight with; **PA247,** Get in on tight with. [11 of 16 total Infs young, 11 male, 10 Black, 7 coll educ] **1984** in 1988 Donaldson *John Cheever Biog.* 265 **NYC,** Cheever didn't seem to have any "tight friends," Lang thought. **1992** Morrison *Jazz* 121 **NYC** (as of c1926) [Black], It's not a thing you tell except maybe to a tight friend, somebody you knew from before. **1994** Smitherman *Black Talk* 225, *Tight.* . . Describes people who are intimates, close friends or associates. **2005** *DARE* File—Internet **CA,** My home town is berkeley! my dog's name is mac, and my hella tight friend is beebe! **2008** *Ibid,* Chris was a really tight friend of theirs. *Ibid,* A tight friend one can read like a book.

tight adv

1 Quickly; vigorously—usu in phr *as tight as.* [Orig obscure; this sense is hard to relate to other senses of *tight.* Obs or Brit dial *tite* "soon, readily, willingly" has been suggested, but here too the semantic fit is poor; cf *EDD tight* adv. 17 "Tightly; smartly, quickly; strenuously, soundly"] **scattered, but esp NEng**

1833 Smith *Life Jack Downing* 200 **ME,** The President shook hands with all his might an hour or two, till he got so tired he couldn't hardly stand it. . . I . . stood behind him and reached my arm round under his, and shook for him for about a half an hour as tight as I could spring. **1835** *People's Press* (Gettysburg PA) 4 Dec 2/4 **NEng,** It occurred to him . . to run round a small birch tree . . as tight as he could spring. **1861** *Zanesville Daily Courier* (OH) 29 June [7]/2 (newspaperarchive.com), We saw a man, supposed to be a cavalryman; he was on horseback, however, going up the rail road as tight as his horse could jump. **1885** Twain in *Century Illustr. Mag.* 29.544 **MO,** Here comes a couple of men tearing up the path as tight as they could foot it. **1914** *DN* 4.81 **ME, nNH,** Tight. . . Fast. "He come a-stivverin' as tight's he could leg it." *Tight's ye can jump fer luck.* . . As fast or hard as you can go, work. **1926** *DN* 5.389 **ME,** Tight. . . Fast and hard, strenuously. "I worked as tight as I could all the morning." Common. **1941** *LANE* Map 474, 1 inf, **cCT,** He scampered home as tight as he could go. **1949** in 1986 *DARE* File **MI,** He was running as tight as he could go. **1975** Gould *ME Lingo* 291, *Tight.* . . Mainers use the expression "tight as he can jump or run" for full speed ahead. **1978** *DARE* File **WI** (as of c1920s), She really ran tight.

2 Intently. [Cf *SND ticht* adv. "attentively, closely"]

1985 Wilkinson *Moonshine* 110 **neNC,** Then I walked around his car—what I was doing was trying to get the license plate—and he said, 'Why're you looking at that so tight?' I said, 'I'd be a fool if I wasn't looking at a brand new Ford automobile.'

tight n **chiefly SE, TX, OK** See Map
A difficult situation, esp financial straits—usu in phr *in a tight.*

1903 *SE Reporter* 43.769 **GA,** Heery always said, when demand was made upon him for payment, that "he was in a tight right then." **1909** *DN* 3.381 **eAL, wGA,** Tight. . . Same as *tight place.* Often used of financial stringency. "I'm in a tight for a little money." **1916** *DN* 4.348 **cTX** (as of 1896), Tight, n. . . A difficult or precarious position. **1920** Hunter *Trail Drivers TX* 126, We all had our guns and knew how to use them if we got in a tight. **1939** *AmSp* 14.263 **IN,** One temporarily in straitened circumstances is 'in a tight.' **1965–70** *DARE* (Qu. U40, *Somebody who is temporarily out of money . . "At the moment he's _____."*) 13 Infs, **chiefly SE, TX, OK,** In a tight. **1967** Green *Horse Tradin'* 149 **TX,** If you want to get a real picture of a man or a horse, get him in a tight and see what he does under the stress and strain. **1967** Williams *Greenbones* 5 **GA** (as of c1910), You know when the barn burned down last year, it put me in a tight. **1967** *DARE* FW Addit **AL,** Get in a tight—meaning, to run into difficulty, any. Also, to run low of funds as a specialized meaning. **1972** Thomas *Pop. Dict. Ozarks Talk* 87, Tight, in a: . . with back to the wall. "Th' dogs 'ud git in a tight with a big wolf." **1972** *Atlanta Letters* **GA,** I got my tail in a crack (meaning to be in a tight). **1982** *DARE* File **NC** [Black], When you get in a tight, you can borrow some money from me. **1986** Pederson *LAGS Concordance,* 1 inf, **cnAR,** A tight; 1 inf, **nwLA,** Get in a tight = get in a jam; 1 inf, **cTN,** Got in a tight; 1 inf, **ceAR,** Got in a tight—needed food; 1 inf, **csGA,** I was in a tight—needed money badly; 1 inf, **neMS,** We were in a tight—money was scarce; 1 inf, **ceAR,** When, see, welfare get in a tight. [3 infs Black] **1996** McDowell *Leaving Pipe Shop* 51 **AL** (as of 1950s) [Black], Mr. Odell Richards was about the only person in the neighborhood who wasn't forever in a tight. He lent money, stashed throughout his house.

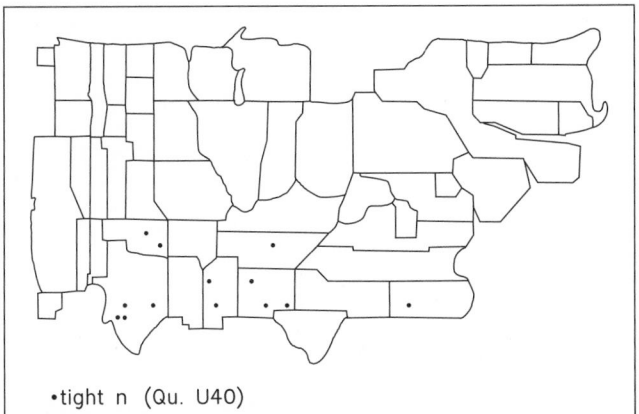

•tight n (Qu. U40)

tight-bark hickory n   Cf **hard-bark hickory, shagbark ~, shellbark ~**

A **hickory** n **B1** with adherent bark, esp **bitternut 1** or **mockernut hickory.**

1899 *Appleton's Annual Cyclop. 1898* 719 **TN,** Oak, tight-bark hickory, ash, . . abound in the forests to which it [=Nashville] looks for its supply. **1914** Wyeth *With Sabre* 435 **AL,** There stood in our grove a slender, graceful, tight-bark hickory sapling, toughest of all tough timber, bending but never breaking. **1986** Pederson *LAGS Concordance* (*Common trees*) 1 inf, **nwTN,** The little old tight-bark hickory. **1997** in Lib. of Congress *Amer. Memory: Tending the Commons* (Sound Recording) (Internet) **WV,** See, there's a tight-bark hickory and a scaly-bark; the scaly-bark usually was [=bore nuts] right before the tight-bark. **2001** Perkey–Wilkins *Crop Tree Field Guide* 128 **cAppalachians,** The shagbark hickory is easily distinguishable. . . To assist in the tougher job of distinguishing between the three tight-bark hickories covered in this guide, the following can be used to help refine identification. . . Mockernut. . . Pignut. . . Bitternut.

tight-eye n[1]   **Sth**
Sleep.
1938 Bell *Tommy Lee Feathers* 55 **sKY** [Black], Better snatch a little tight eye yourself, Feathers. **1942** *Cullman Democrat* (AL) 1 Jan 1/6, What more could a boy want than good clothes, good chow three times a day, eight hours of tight eye each night and an opportunity to help keep "Old Glory" flying. **1967** *DARE* (Qu. X40, . . *Ways . . of saying, "I'm going to bed"*) Inf **SC55,** Get some tight-eye. **1972** *Atlanta Letters* **nwGA,** After that, we'd lay down on our pallet and get some tight eye.

tight-eye n[2]   See **titi**

tight line n   esp **Missip-Ohio Valleys, Gulf States**   See Map
A fishing line kept taut in the water by a heavy sinker; hence nouns *tight-line fishing, tight-lining* fishing with a taut line.
1882 Eggleston *Wreck Red Bird* 17 **IN,** "We fish with tight lines." "What are they?" "Why, long lines with a sinker at the end and no poles." **1959** *Lima News* (OH) 5 Apr sec D 12/8, The casting-rod. . . was good for large-plug casting, for trolling and for tight-line fishing. **1964** *Times Recorder & Zanesville Signal* (OH) 24 June sec B 7/1, The caller told us that . . each time he would cast he would "haul in six pounds of seaweek [sic] while fishing with a 'tight line'." In case you are not aware of it, tight line fishing simply means fishing on the bottom, generally with live bait and sometimes with artificial nightcrawlers. **1965–70** *DARE* (Qu. P17, . . *When . . people fish by lowering a line and sinker close to the bottom of the water*) 19 Infs, **chiefly Missip-Ohio Valleys, Gulf States,** Tight-line fishing; **LA20,** Tight-line fishing—that's with a heavy lead at the bottom; **TX19,** Tight-line fishing—this is sometimes used, means line without a cork; **LA26, MO7,** Tight-lining; **OK25,** Tight-lining—without a cork; they use a slip-lead—a lead sinker that will allow line to slip through for a short way so fish will not feel weight while nibbling; (Qu. P13, . . *Ways of fishing . . besides the ordinary hook and line*) Inf **TX33,** Tight line; (Qu. P15, . . *Fishing that's done from a slowly moving boat*) Inf **TN53,** Tight-lining. **1968** *Pt. Arthur News* (TX) 21 Apr sec E 2/7, I like a cane pole about 12 to 13 feet

long . . with an eagle claw 1-0 hook, and one fairly heavy lead sinker. This is for "tight" line fishing. The tight line has several advantages. **1968** *DARE* FW Addit **csLA,** *Tight line* = fishing rig with a heavy sinker at the end of a line and a hook above it. "That's fishing a tight line, that." **2002** *Chron.-Telegram* (Elyria OH) 21 June sec B 7/5, He caught the prize with a croppie rig baited with a worm while tight-line fishing in Sandusky Bay.

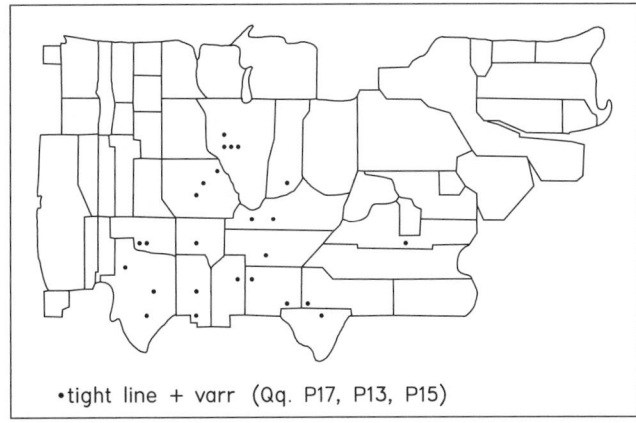

•tight line + varr (Qq. P17, P13, P15)

tight peach n   Also *tight-rock peach, tight-stone*
=**clingstone.**
1967–69 *DARE* (Qu. I52, *The kind of a peach where the hard center is tight to the flesh*) Inf **KY34,** Tight-rock peach; **KY40,** Tight-stone. **1986** Pederson *LAGS Concordance* (*Kind of peach where the flesh is tight against the stone*) 1 inf, **cGA,** Tight peach.

tight-shoe day n   **chiefly Sth, S Midl**
Saturday; market day.
1950 Lenski *TX Tomboy* 72, It's Tight-Shoe day, sugar. . . All the hoe farmers will be there with their best clothes and new tight shoes on— shoes that pinch their feet. **1958** *Lima News* (OH) 14 June 1/1, A little humor on tight-shoe day (as they call Saturdays back in the hills) might help someone get through the weekend. **1965** *DARE* (Qu. U1a, *When you are going to a store or several stores to buy things*) Inf **OK7,** Tight-shoe day—wore good shoes. **1965** *DARE* FW Addit **OK7,** "*Tight-shoe day*"—the day a farmer goes to town (he wears his newest shoes). **1970** Owen *Hillbilly Humor* 118 **Ozarks,** To find out what a hillbilly is, Rosenthal said, "You can talk to the real thing by driving through backwood villages on Tight Shoe Day—that's Saturday—when the mountain people put on their good shoes to come to town." **1973** *TX Mth.* Feb 59, I grew up in the city so I didn't know what "tight shoe day" meant. It seems that you don't plow and seed and milk in your new Brogans. These are saved for the once-a-week Saturday trip into town where you loaded up supplies for the next six days. **1998** Green *Images Santa Rosa* 44 **FL** (as of c1910), Saturdays were the busiest days in downtown Milton because the farmers came to town to buy their week's groceries and supplies, to catch up on the latest political gossip at the courthouse, and perhaps to see a show. . . The kids called it "Tight Shoe Day."

tight-stone   See **tight peach**

tightwad n
1918 *DN* 5.28 **NW,** *Tight-wad.* . . A meat dish: a thin cut rolled up with strips of bacon and fried.

tignon n   [LaFr < Fr *chignon*]   **LA**   Cf **head rag**
A brightly colored handkerchief worn as a head covering by women.
1884 *Bismarck Tribune* (ND) 8 Aug 4/6, [From *New Orleans Times-Democrat:*] Seated on the floor . . were about twenty-five negro men and women . . the women with their heads adorned with the traditional handkerchief, or tignon. **1894** *Harper's New Mth. Mag.* 89.919 **New Orleans LA** [Black], I had to put on a tignon and apron. **1933** *Atlantic Mth.* 151.382 **LA,** She always wore a bandanna handkerchief on her head, tied in a mysterious and beautiful way which in Louisiana was called a tignon. **1945** Saxon *Gumbo Ya-Ya* 364 **LA,** Negro mammies, resplendent in blue calico, red *tignons* and starched white aprons and *fichues,* sold steaming bowls of *gumbo.* **1984** Stall *Proud New Orleans* 172, *Tignon:* A turban-like, brightly-colored Madras handkerchief, formerly worn by women of color in accordance with a city ordinance.

'tigo See **impetigo**

tike See **take** v A1c

tikiteet n [Prob joc alter of *tête-à-tête* a type of sofa designed to allow two persons to converse face to face]
See quots.

1932 *DN* 6.284 **swCT,** *Tikiteet.* A sofa (tête-à-tête). **1947** *Sun* (Baltimore MD) 20 June 1/2 *(Hench Coll.),* A nimshi on the tikiteet—as any New Englander schooled in rare Yankee expressions knows—means a girl on the sofa.

til See **till**

tile v [Var of **stile** v]
To position a set gun; see quots.

1933 Rawlings *South Moon* 103 **nFL,** The old man had killed many hundreds of deer in his day . . "tiling" a gun on a trail that led to a water-hole, gauging the proper height by the size of the tracks, so that the deer, tripping a line connected with the trigger of the concealed gun, fired the shot that killed it. **1946** *PADS* 6.30 **eNC** (as of 1902), *Tile a gun. . .* To place a gun in position to fire automatically when a door or window is opened, as by a thief. . . Rare.

tilefish n
Std: a marine fish of the family Malacanthidae, esp *Lopholatilus chamaeleonticeps.* For other names of var spp see **sand fish 2b**

tile rat n
=**muskrat 1.**

1969 *DARE* (Qu. P31, . . *Names or nicknames . . for the . . muskrat*) Inf **OH88,** Tile rat.

tilikum See **tillicum**

till prep, conj Also sp *til;* for addit varr see **A** below Cf **until**
A Forms.

1 *tel(l), tull.* **chiefly Sth, S Midl**
1692 in 1977 *Salem Witchcraft Papers* 1.263 **MA,** She contienued hurting of me by times tell the 21 march. **1813** (1939) Hartsell *Memora* 11.103 **eTN,** As I pased throw the horses nickered for my cane tell my hart aked for them. **1834** [see **B2** below]. **1845** in 1956 Eliason *Tarheel Talk* 319 **nw,cwNC,** *Till . .* tell. **1848** Lowell *Biglow* 146 **'Up-country' MA,** *Tell, till.* **1851** in 1956 Eliason *Tarheel Talk* 319 **cnNC,** *Till. . .* tull. **1871** Eggleston *Hoosier Schoolmaster* 99 **sIN,** I'll fight them thieves tell the sea goes dry. **1884** *Anglia* 7.276 **Sth, S Midl** [Black], *Tell de middle er nex' munt'* = an indefinite future. **1899** (1912) Green *VA Folk-Speech* 442, Wait tell next week. **1909** *DN* 3.380 **eAL, wGA,** *Tell. . .* Till, until. **1915** *DN* 4.191 **swVA,** *Tell.* Variant of *till.* **1921** Haswell *Daughter Ozarks* 21 (as of 1880s), "Jest keep straight ahead on the main travelled road," said the native, "t'el ye comes to Swan." **1922** Gonzales *Black Border* 332 **sSC, GA coasts** [Gullah glossary], *'Tell*—till, until. **1965** *Dict. Queen's English* 11 **NC,** *Tell:* Till; until. We'll be there tell morning.

2 *twel(l), twill.* **esp Sth, S Midl** *esp freq among Black speakers* Cf Intro "Language Changes" I.8
1837 Sherwood *Gaz. GA* 72, *Twell,* for till;—twell night—twell next week. **1851** Hooper *Widow Rugby's Husband* 38 **AL,** I didn't want to tell you about him twell we'd passed him. **1886** Edwards in *Century Illustr. Mag.* 32.383 **ceGA** [Black], Jes' wait twell we git er mess er red-belly en' brim. **1887** (1967) Harris *Free Joe* 216 **cGA** [Black], We ain't none un us know it twel we er done dar. **1893** Shands *MS Speech* 65, *Twel. . .* Negro for till. **1896** *Amer. Antiq. & Oriental Jrl.* 18.100 **Sth** [Black], Dar dey gwinter stay twill he kin cotch em an cut em out, or twill he kin fine de bag. **1899** (1912) Green *VA Folk-Speech* 464, He won't come twell tomorrow. **1909** *DN* 3.385 **eAL, wGA,** *Twel. . .* Until: chiefly among negroes. **1914** *DN* 4.114 **cKS,** *Twell, twill. . .* Till. **1927** in 1944 *ADD* **WV,** *Till. . .* twill. **1929** Sale *Tree Named John* 20 **MS** [Black], Let it hang hyere twel hit drap off. **1967** *Mt. Life* 43.1.15 **sAppalachians,** He was a-wonderin at that, too, 'twill all of a sudden hit struck him betwixt the eyes. **1972** *Atlanta Letters* **cGA,** Southernisms. . . Hilt him twel he hollered.

B As prep.

1 To (a place of arrival); as far as. [Scots, nIr, nEngl dial]
Cf **until B1**
1829 Kirkham *Engl. Grammar* 207, He went till Pittsburgh. **1878** *Appletons' Jrl.* 5.413 **PA,** *Till* is often substituted for *to* in the Pennsylva-

nia dialect. A horse comes *till* the stable, or a boy *till* the schoolhouse. **1893** Shands *MS Speech* 64, *Til. . .* Negro for *to* used with reference to place. **1908** *German Amer. Annals* 10.47 **sePA,** *Till.*—To (limit of distance). "We walked out till the toll-gate." **1934** *AmSp* 9.127 [Engl dial of HI], The preposition may be . . confused in meaning with another preposition. . . *Till* and *until* for 'to' in space (possibly an imported Scotticism): We walked till Haina. **1966** *DARE* (Qu. V2b, *About a deceiving person, or somebody that you can't trust . .* "I wouldn't trust him _____."; not asked in early QRs) Inf **AL6,** Till the end of your elbow.

2 To—used when the object is not a location. [Scots dial]
1834 *Life Andrew Jackson* 213, Those who don't support your measures say they more than earnt it . . in jumpin from one cause tell another without any reason. **1914** *DN* 4.114 **cKS,** *Till. . .* To. "I object till this thing."

3 In expressions of time between the half hour and the hour: before, until. **widespread, but less freq Nth** See Map *somewhat more freq among those with little formal educ* Cf **of** prep C4, **to** B13
1866 Hosmer *Ten Yrs.* 358 **NEast,** Twenty minutes till twelve—that gave her just time. **1904** *DN* 2.422 **nwAR,** *Till. . .* To. 'It's ten minutes till twelve.' **1911** *Hampton's Mag.* 27.388 **sePA,** "A quarter to five." "A quarter *'to'?*" she repeated uncertainly. "Does that mean a quarter over or a quarter till?" Miss De Ford considered. "A quarter 'till'," she decided. "We couldn't possibly catch the five o'clock car." **1949** Kurath *Word Geog.* 30, In the greater part of the Midland the phrase *quarter till eleven . .* is current. In south-central Pennsylvania and the entire Midland area lying to the south of Pennsylvania *till* is the usual preposition in this phrase, which has also found acceptance in a wide corridor leading from the North Carolina piedmont down the Cape Fear River to the sea. *Till* is used also on the upper Susquehanna and on the Alleghany River. **1965–70** *DARE* (Qu. A6, *What time is this? [. . clock face at 10:45]*) 161 Infs, **widespread, but less freq Nth,** Quarter till eleven; 79 Infs, **chiefly Midl, Sth, TX,** Fifteen (minutes) till eleven; **WV**12, Fifteen minutes till [Of all Infs responding to the question, 31% were gs educ or less; of those giving these responses, 49% were gs educ or less.]; (Qu. A7, . . *What time is this? [. . clock face at 10:30]*) Inf **TN36,** Thirty minutes till eleven [Inf gs educ]. **1975** Allen *LAUM* 2.67 **Upper MW** (as of c1950), Quarter of eleven. . . More than one-half of the informants have *to;* one-third use competing *of. . .* Midland *till . .* is found in southern Iowa and, sparsely, in Nebraska and South Dakota [in the speech of 16 infs]. **1989** Pederson *LAGS Tech. Index* 21 **Gulf Region,** *(Quarter of [eleven])* 295 infs, (A) quarter till; 97 infs, Fifteen (minutes) till; *(Half past [seven])* 8 infs, Thirty minutes till (seven); 1 inf, Half an hour till (seven).

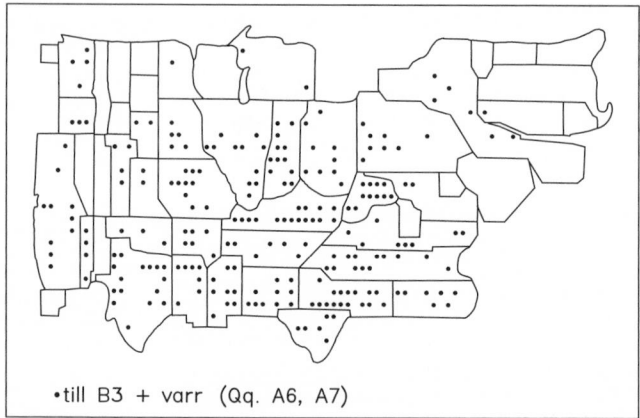

•till B3 + varr (Qq. A6, A7)

4 By, before (a point in time). [Mostly calque of (Pa)Ger *bis* (prep, conj) till, by (the time that), but also Sw *till* (prep) till, by (and perh also Dan, Norw *til* till, by)] **esp PaGer area** Cf **gin** prep, C2 below, **until B2**
1862 in 1976 *Johannes Schwalm* 262 **cePA,** I hope I can exspect you at home to See till Spring. **1879** in 2003 *DARE* File—Internet **sePA,** Started white-washing and till evening had done fence, pig stable, and privy. **1902** *DN* 2.247 **sIL,** *Till. . .* By. 'We'll git this done till twelve.' 'We must git there till sundown.' **1904** Martin *Tillie* 5 **sePA,** Pop he's went to Lancaster, and he 'll be back till half-past three a'ready. **1908** *German Amer. Annals* 10.47 **sePA,** *Till.*—By (in expressions of time). "I do not know my lesson now, but I will know it till to-morrow." **1916** *DN* 4.339 **OH, KS,** *Till. . .* By. "I expect to finish my work till to-mor-

row." Summit Co., Ohio; Kan. **1931** *AmSp* 6.217 **IL, MN, WI,** A collection of Swedish idioms which have influenced the language of English speaking people of Swedish descent. . . collected in the states of Minnesota, Wisconsin, and Illinois. It is to be ready *till Christmas.*—It is to be ready by Christmas.—Det skall vara färdigt *till jul.* **1937** [see **C2** below]. **1980** *Ger. Qrly.* May 359 [Engl of PA Germans], Use of the lexical item *til* to mean "by the time" as in "I hope that changes til tonight."

C As conj.

1a foll expressions of degree: So that—used to indicate a result. **chiefly Sth** Cf **so till, until C1**

1893 Shands *MS Speech* 64, *Til* or *till* has another peculiar use in the negro dialect in sentences like the following, where it is used in the place of *that:* "It hurt me so till I cried." **1927** Kennedy *Gritny* 117 **sLA** [Black], Flowers so natchal till they looked artificial. **1935** Hurston *Mules & Men* 201 **FL** [Black], He moves so fast till Ah don't remember much except seeing him turning somersault. **1944** *PADS* 2.13 **Sth,** *Till, until: conj.* with degree-result clauses. " . . the necessity of the peasants' working so hard till they almost drop." Deep South. Up to high popular level. [*PADS* Ed: Also, reported from upper S.C., mid. Tenn.] **1954** in 1958 Brewer *Dog Ghosts* 124 **TX** [Black], De preachuh was so mad at de tap dancer 'till he say out loud, "If Gawd don't git you, de devil mus'." **1966** *DARE* (Qu. GG26, *A feeling of weakness from fear: "When she saw the dog coming at her she got _____."*) Inf **MS**45, So scared till she could hardly stand up. [Inf Black] **1970** *Thompson Coll.* **cnAL** (as of c1920), Swan's been there enough till he knows his way aroun jus like he was maybe born an raised there. **c1970** Pederson *Dial. Surv. Rural GA,* 1 inf, **seGA,** I haven't seen any of that in so long till I don't remember what they call it. **1986** Pederson *LAGS Concordance,* 1 inf, **ceAL,** There was such a big family of us till they took every room for bedrooms and eating places; 1 inf, **cwAL,** The ticks been so bad in my pasture till you couldn't hardly go down there; 1 inf, **swAL,** It's so expensive till people don't buy them; 1 inf, **neAR,** Been so long till I can't even think about it; 1 inf, **ceFL,** It got so thin till it cracked open; 1 inf, **swGA,** The dogs killed his calves so bad over there till they built some pen traps; 1 inf, **cnLA,** It's been so long till I've forgotten it; 1 inf, **cnLA,** Man, through his science, has got so smart till he thinks he can operate God's work; 1 inf, **cwLA,** He lives so far back there till they have to pump daylight to him; 1 inf, **eTX,** Sugar is so sweet till it makes you sick. **1996** Harrell *Fetch It* 230 **nwNC,** These observers were people who lived close enough to the river till from their residences they could look out on the river.

b So that, in such a way that.

1946 Stuart *Tales Plum Grove* 59 **eKY,** I can't write my name till you can read it.

2 By the time that. [Calque of (Pa)Ger *bis;* see at **B4** above] **PaGer area** Cf **until C3**

1934 *Language* 10.3 **cPA,** That baby'll walk till he's nine month old. **1937** *AmSp* 12.288 **wVA,** The word *till* may mean 'by the time,' or 'by,' as 'I'll be ready till you are' and 'I hope I'll be able to go till next Tuesday.' **1949** Kurath *Word Geog.* 79, *By the time I get there.* . . from the Pennsylvania German area to the Alleghanies one hears *till I get there.* **1985** *AmSp* 60.235 **sePA,** *Till*—By the time. . . The expression *till* in the sense of 'by the time' [e.g., *Till I get there, the game will be over*] remains current in the Pennsylvania German area among people of all ages and educational backgrounds. **2004** *DARE* File **ePA,** In German-influenced English, "till" and sometimes "until/'til" are used in place of "by the time that": "She'll need to get new glasses till school starts," and such like.

tilley hawk See **tilly hawk**

till hell wouldn't have it See **hell 7**

tillicum n Also sp *tilikum* [Chinook Jargon *tilikum* people < Chinook *tilxam*] **chiefly WA** Cf *DCan*

A person, esp an associate or friend.

[**1843** *Chr. Advocate & Jrl.* 18.50 **OR,** Slaves are not considered fillicum [sic], that is, people, but as dogs.] **1868** Natl. Commercial Convention *Proc.* 233 **OR,** In every Indian speech, whatever remark the Indian may make, when he points to a white man, he calls him a "Boston tillicum." **1878** *Pt. Townsend* (Wash.) *Wkly. Argus* 22 March *(DA),* The other day, a school-boy having committed an offense, he was tied up, and some of his 'tillicums,' who do not belong to the church party, set up a howl and finally cut him loose. **1919** *DN* 5.59 **NW,** Tillicums. . . Folks. James Poland of Carrolls was in Kalama Saturday, renewing his acquaintance with old *tillicums.* Kalama Bulletin. **1938** (1939)

Holbrook *Holy Mackinaw* 265, Tillicum. People, a man, a person, but ordinarily a friend. **1939** FWP *Guide AK* xli, Tillicum. . . (C[hinook]) friend. **1947** Jones *Evergreen Land* 173 **WA,** The moving spirits of the Potlatch were "Tilikums" which is the Chinook word for friends. **1959** Hart *McKay's AK* 34, [Glossary:] *Tillicum:* A friend or partner, usually of long association. **1966** *DARE* (Qu. II1, . . *A close friend* . . "He's my _____.") Inf **WA**11, Tillicum—Indian word. **1967** *DARE* FW Addit **cwWA,** Tillicum—friend (Chinook Jargon). High-assed tillicum—good friend.

tillie hawk See **tilly hawk**

tillpot n Cf **skillpot**

A **mud turtle 2b(1).**

1970 *DARE* (Qu. P24, . . *Kinds of turtles*) Inf **VA**96, Tillpot.

till the water gets hot See **water B3**

till who laid the chunk See **who laid the chunk 2**

till who laid the rail(s) See **who laid the rail 2, 3**

till yet See **yet** adv, conj **B2**

tilly hawk n Also *tilley hawk, tillie ~, tilly* [Echoic] **chiefly SE** See Map Cf **chilly hawk, killy ~**

A **sparrow hawk 1** (here: *Falco sparverius*).

1901 *Recreation* 14.304 **TX,** A correspondent . . claims that the sparrow hawk, or tilly hawk, is the worst enemy of our smaller birds. **1913** *Auk* 30.495 **Okefenokee GA,** *Falco sparverius sparverius.* . . 'Tilly Hawk.'—Not common within the swamp. One or two were noted on Honey Island. **1932** Howell *FL Bird Life* 190, Little Sparrow Hawk. . . Other Names: Killy-hawk; Tilly. . . Resident and locally common throughout the State, except on the Lower Keys. [*Ibid* 191, The alarm notes of this species are loud and shrill, *killee, killee,* sharply accented.] **1932** *Scribner's Mag.* 91.281 **FL,** You hadn't orter wasted a shell on a ol' tillie-hawk. **1958** Babcock *I Don't Want* 126 **eSC,** He was wiry . . and as curious and keen-visioned as the tilley hawk that ceaselessly studied the landscape from the chinaberry trees along the ditch row. **1965–70** *DARE* (Qu. Q4, . . *Kinds of hawks*) Infs **FL**4, **GA**16, 35, **SC**26, Tilly hawk(s); **FL**35, ['tɪli]—small; **GA**25, Tilly hawk—here all year; **LA**12, Tilly hawk—old-fashioned [FW: local word for sparrow hawk]; **LA**29, Tilly hawk [FW: =sparrow hawk]; **SC**40, Tilly hawk—size of a blue jay—gets rats, birds. **1969** Longstreet *Birds FL* 48, Killy-hawk; Little Sparrow Hawk; Tilly. . . They often . . sing their loud call note of *killy-killy-killy-killy-killy* to every passer-by. When alarmed the note changes to a sharply accented *killee.*

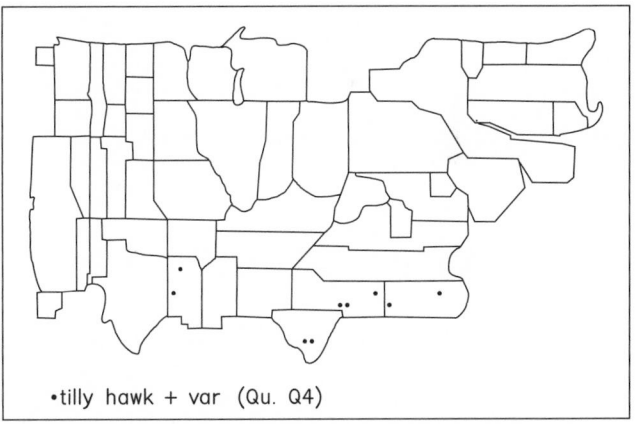

•tilly hawk + var (Qu. Q4)

tilly-i-over n Cf **keely-over 2, tippy-i-over,** *DS* EE22 **=Antony-over.**

1983 *Lutz Coll.* **seNY,** *Anthony-over.* . . a man who played the game near Kingston, New York, calls it *Tilly-I-Over.*

tilt n

1 =**black-necked stilt.**

1813 (1824) Wilson *Amer. Ornith.* 7.54 **NJ,** The names by which this bird is known on the seacoast are the Stilt, Tilt, and Long-shanks. **1844** DeKay *Zool. NY* 2.266, It [=*Himantopus mexicanus*] is known under the various popular names of *Tilt, Stilt, Longshanks* and *Lawyer.* **1918** Grinnell et al. *Game Birds CA* 344, Black-necked Stilt. . . Other names—Lawyer; Tilt. **1923** U.S. Dept. Ag. *Misc. Circular* 13.48 **CA,** Black-necked Stilt. . . Vernacular Names. . . In local use. . . Tilt.

2 =**spotted sandpiper.** Cf **tilter 3, tilt-up 1**

1923 U.S. Dept. Ag. *Misc. Circular* 13.64 **MD, PA,** *Spotted Sandpiper. . . Vernacular Names. . . In local use. . .* Tilt.

3 also *tilt-up;* In ice fishing: a device to which a baited line is attached, all or part of which tips up to signal when a fish has taken the bait. **esp sNEng** Cf **tip-up 3**

1891 *Fitchburg Daily Sentinel* (MA) 14 Jan [4]/2 (newspaperarchive.com) **CT,** On sunny days in winter there are rarely less than from three to a dozen parties of sportsmen . . on its frozen surface, which is dotted all over with flipping tilt-ups. One group of fishermen . . have a couple of hundred tilts in the ice of Avery's pond, day and night, all winter. . . A tilt is rigged like a "teeter board" so that when a fish takes the bait the balanced piece flies into the air and notifies the fishermen . . that they have "got a bite." **1899** (1900) Van Dyke *Fisherman's Luck* 128 **PA,** Over each hole you set a small contrivance called a "tilt-up." **1958** *Lima News* (OH) 28 Dec sec D 5/3, Probably the best kind of tilt for perch fishing is an ordinary green sapling shoot. The thick end should be burried [sic] in the ice and the narrow sensitive end should extend out over the open hole. **1964** *Daily Progress* (Charlottesville VA) 4 Jan 11/7 *(Hench Coll.),* Fishing through the ice "New England style". . . Tie two sticks together in the form of a cross, one of them to lay over the hole, the other is the business part of the machine with a hook, leader and line attached to one end and a rag tied to the other, brightly colored preferably. . . When . . a fish bites, this flag will rise up . . as a signal for us to skate there as fast as we can. . . Make a dozen or two of these "tilts" . . and we are in business. **1968–69** *DARE* (Qu. P13, . . *Ways of fishing . . besides the ordinary hook and line)* Inf **CT**13, Tilt—for ice fishing—red flag pops up when a fish bites; **MA**62, Tilt—has red flag when there's a bite; **MA**74, Tilt—ice fishing; **CT**31, Tilts—through the ice. **1969** *DARE* FW Addit **MA**68, Tilts . . a kind of equipment used in ice fishing; they pull up a red flag when the fish bite. **2005** *DARE* File—Internet **MA,** The most common technique for us is to use what is called a tilt or tip-up. . . What is nice about this system is that you can set your tilts out and sit around a fire or something similar.

4 also *tilting board, tilts, tilt-tot:* =**seesaw 1;** hence v *tilt.* **esp MA** Cf **tilter 1**

1855 Swan *Amer. Comprehensive Reader* 83, Sister Lucy and I were playing with Thomas Watts. We had fixed a tilting-board on a log. **1880** *Helena Independent* (MT) 9 May 1/5 **MA,** Every child knows that the boy on the center of the tilting board can make either end, if the ends are equally weighted, go up or down at pleasure. **1901** *Atlantic Mth.* 88.419 **MA,** There is nothing in the whole political process . . but the dreary ups and downs of a tilting-board. **1917** in 1920 *Negligence Cases* 18.325 **eMA,** "Helen was watching us on the seesaws. I did not say anything to her after I got on the tilts." "I don't know how long Helen stayed near the tilting boards while we were tilting." **1937** Crane *Let Me Show You VT* 35, Tilt (a Cape Cod word) occurs once in eastern Vermont. **1943** *LANE* Map 577 *(Seesaw),* [Tilt and *tilting board* occur freq in **seNEng,** from Narragansett Bay eastward and up the coast of **MA;** *tilting board* also occurs in **c,sNH;**] 1 inf, **neMA,** We call it a tilts; 1 inf, **neMA,** We children always called it a tilts; 1 inf, **cMA,** Nowadays children say *tilts;* but we never did; 1 inf, **seMA,** We always called it a tilt-tot. **1973** Allen *LAUM* 1.223 **MN, IA** (as of c1950), *Seesaw. . .* Local Massachusetts *tilt* appeared twice.

tilt-ass See **tilt-up 1, 2**

tilter n

1 also *tilter(ing) board:* =**seesaw 1;** hence v *tilter* to play on such a device.

1713 in 1893 RI Hist. Soc. *Coll.* 8.17, I was playing a childish play on a tilter . . with one *Power Merit.* . . I fell. **1877** Bartlett *Americanisms* 706 **MA,** Tilter. . . To see-saw on a plank. In common use in Eastern Massachusetts. **1943** *LANE* Map 577 *(Seesaw),* [On the coasts of **NH** and **ME,** *tilter* and *tilter board* are frequent;] 1 inf, **seVT,** Tilter; 3 infs, **seNH, sME,** Tiltering board.

2 =**bluestocking 2.**

1879 *Forest & Stream* 13.625 **TX,** Avocets are called tilters.

3 Either the **solitary sandpiper** or the **spotted sandpiper.** Cf **tilt 2, tilt-up 1**

1891 IN Horticult. Soc. *Trans. for 1890* 38, *Solitary Sandpiper.* Summer resident in some numbers, most common northward. Breeds. More often found along the streams and about the ponds in the woods. Known locally as "Peet-weet," "Teeter Snipe," and "Tilter." **1923** U.S. Dept. Ag. *Misc. Circular* 13.64 **MD,** *Spotted Sandpiper. . . Vernacular Names. . . In local use. . .* Tilter.

tilter(ing) board See **tilter 1**

tilting board, tilts See **tilt 4**

tilt-tail See **tilt-up 1**

tilt-tot See **tilt 4**

tilt-up n

1 also *tilt-ass, tilt-tail:* =**spotted sandpiper.** [See quots] Cf **tip-up 1**

1844 [see **teeter** n 1]. **1890** Warren *Birds PA* 94, *Actitis macularia.* . . The Tilt-up, as this sandpiper is universally known in this section, arrives in Pennsylvania about the middle of April. . . It is common and indigenous. **1895** Kirkwood *List Birds MD* 381, Tilt-ass. **1923** U.S. Dept. Ag. *Misc. Circular* 13.64, *Spotted Sandpiper. . . Vernacular Names. . . In local use. . .* Tilt-tail (Pa.); tilt-up (N.Y., N.J., Pa.) **1940** Todd *Birds W. PA* 710, Tilt-up, *see* Sandpiper, Spotted.

2 also *tilt-ass:* =**killdeer 1.** Cf **bobble-ass, teeter** n 2, **tip-up 2**

1968 *DARE* (Qu. Q14, . . *Names . . for . . killdeer)* Inf **WV**2, Tilt-ass; **WV**7, Tilt-up.

3 See **tilt 3.**

timage n [Prob blend of *timothy* + *silage*] Cf **haylage**
See quots.

1966 Hamilton *Total Dry Matter* 56 **WI,** Timothy varieties and experimental synthetics exhibited different trends. . . Common timothy maintained a uniform production in the first three paddocks, while Timage showed a drop in the second paddock. **1966** *DARE* (Qu. L9a, . . *Kinds of grass . . grown for hay)* Inf **MI**8, Timage ['tɪməj]—form of timothy, but better, more nutritional; **MI**12, ['tɪmɪj]—of course, mostly nowdays it's timage that's grown.

timber n Also *timber sauce, ~ stick joc* Cf **cordwood 2, lumber** n[1] **2**
A toothpick.

1946 *AmSp* 21.36 ceTX [TX A&M Univ slang], *Timber.* . . Toothpick. **1950** WELS *(Names and nicknames for a toothpick)* 1 Inf, **cwWI,** Timber sauce. **1954** *Chron.–Telegram* (Elyria OH) 22 May 15/8, A toothpick is timber sauce in lumber camp country. **1965–70** *DARE* (Qu. G11, *Other names or nicknames for a toothpick)* Infs **AR**47, **MD**17, 24, **VA**13, Timber; **IA**2, **KS**1, **WI**58, Timber sauce; [**AR**47, Stick of timber;] **IL**94, Timber float—expression used with reference to restaurants: to "order" water and a toothpick is to have a timber float; **SC**70, Timber stick. **1970** Major *Dict. Afro-Amer. Slang* 115, *Timber:* (1940's) a toothpick.

timber ant n
A **carpenter ant** such as *Camponotus laevigatus.*

1898 Bailey *Birds Village* 213, Wood-boring beetles, tree-burrowing caterpillars and timber ants make their excavations in a small spot of decay. **1924** Felt *Manual Tree Insects* 234, The large black carpenter ant, *Camponotus herculeanus* . . is the common timber ant of dwellings and forests. **1967** *DARE* (Qu. R18, . . *Kinds of ants)* Inf **CO**37, Black timber ant—in timber, ¾ inch long; **WY**5, Timber ant—drill holes in wood. **1992** Meck–Hoover *Gt. Rivers* 258, The Mamba [=a fishing fly] resembles a big timber ant and has proven to be extremely effective on the river.

timber beast n Also *timber wolf* **Nth, esp Pacific NW**
A logger; rarely, a lumber-mill worker.

1916 *Internatl. Socialist Rev.* 16.463, You scorn him [=the lumberjack] and call him "Timber-beast." **1918** *DN* 5.28 **Pacific NW,** *Timberbeast.* . . A lumberman. Coast of Washington and Oregon. **1925** *AmSp* 1.135 **Pacific NW,** Never call the worker in the woods of the Pacific Northwest "lumberjack." In certain humors he may admit being a timber beast or a savage, but "logger" is the name he has made for himself. **1926** *AmSp* 1.653 [Hobo lingo], *Timber-wolves*—Lumberjacks. **1927** *AmSp* 2.392 [Vagabond argot], A logger [is] a *timber-beast.* **1938** in Lib. of Congress *Amer. Memory: WPA Life Hist.* (Internet), I've been a timber beast up in the North West. **1941** Writers' Program *Guide MI* 352 **swMI,** The Timber Beasts—river drivers and mill men—earned for Muskegon the reputation of 'Lumber Queen,' 'Red Light Queen,' 'Gambling Queen,' and 'Saloon Queen.' **1945** Hamlin *9 Mile Bridge* 45 **nME,** Many of the lumberjacks have families and homes . . but the real "Timber Wolf" is generally a bachelor. He has always been a lumberjack and always will be. **1958** McCulloch *Woods Words* 194 **Pacific NW,** Timber beast—Any guy who works in the woods; but outsiders better not use the expression. **1968** *DARE* (Qu. HH1) Inf **MN**36, Timber beast—the toppers in logging. **1969** Sorden *Lumberjack Lingo* 129 **NEng, Gt Lakes,** *Timber beast*—A lumberjack or logger. **1992** *Mt. Democrat & Placerville Times* (CA) 29 Oct sec A 9/3, Your letter implies that we're in cahoots with 'timber beast pals' (totally false).

timberberry n
=**dogberry j.**

1938 (1958) Sharples *AK Wild Flowers* 40, *C[omandra] livida* [= *Geocaulon l.*]. "Timberberry." . . Grows in open dry places.

timber cart n chiefly Mid and S Atl
=**timber wheels** or occas a four-wheeled vehicle for moving logs.

1796 in 2006 *DARE* File—Internet **DE,** I give and bequeath to my son Ebenezer Hearne . . my plantation cart and timber cart and my yoke of oxen. **1799** *Ibid* c**sNC,** Also I give to Neill Beard and Joseph Beard the 2 youngest yoke of oxen and one timber cart and timber chain, also one saw mill. **1884** Knight *New Mech. Dict.* 894, *Timber Cart.* . . a high wheeled cart for drawing timber. The timber, after the cart is driven over it, is raised to the axle by crank-gearing and tackle. **1887** *Delta Herald* (PA) [23 Dec 4]/2 **SC** (newspaperarchive.com), The twelve year-old son of Mrs. M.A. Pemberton was killed at Bellwood by the lever of a timber cart falling on his head. **1903** *Denton Jrl.* (MD) 24 Oct [2]/3 (newspaperarchive.com), [Advt:] Farm Machinery, &c. . . One pair of Timber Wheels. One pair of Front Wheels for Timber Cart. **1946** *PADS* 6.30 e**NC** (as of 1900–10), *Timber cart.* . . A log cart with wheels about five feet high used for hauling logs about one foot in diameter. The tongue is used for a lever in loading. . . Common. **1956** *AmSp* 31.282 **AL,** About the beginning of this century in southern Alabama timber carts were of two kinds—roller carts and terry-rig carts. . . A roller cart was a two-wheeler. . . Both . . soon passed out of use. **1965–70** *DARE* (Qu. N41a, . . *Horse-drawn vehicles . . to carry people*) Inf **SC**19, Timber cart; (Qu. N41b, *Horse-drawn vehicles to carry heavy loads*) Infs **GA**30, **SC**43, Timber cart; **DE**1, Timber cart—for logs; **LA**15, Timber cart—diameter of the two wheels was eleven feet; the tongue was thirty feet long; **MD**13, Timber cart—for hauling logs; two wheels, axle bows upward, hauled by horses, steers, or tractors; **SC**19, Timber cart—for hauling logs, with real high wheels; **SC**26, Timber cart—two-wheeled; **SC**40, Timber cart—two wheels, wheels backed over a log, a pair of "tongs" gripped the log, back end of log would drag.

timber cat n
A **wildcat** (here: *Lynx rufus*).

1967 *DARE* (Qu. P31, . . *Names or nicknames . . for . . wildcat*) Inf **IL**25, Timber cat. **2000** in 2001 *DARE* File—Internet, [Poem:] I must have seemed cougar or timber cat hissing out a nervous whispered hhhiii!

timber cellar n Cf *DS* M19
1958 Carrighar *Moonlight* 62 **AK,** Root vegetables, as well as the wild roots, were stored in sand in the "timber cellers," dugouts beneath the warm cabins.

timber cock n [Prob blend of **timberdoodle** + **woodcock**] Perh =**ruffed grouse**
[**1940** (1948) Seton *Trail of Artist* 220 **Canada,** In many places, the forest fires had left a stretch of bare and blackened masts that were the ideal homeland of timber cock, redhead, sparrow hawk, and scores of lesser birds.] **1961** *Mt. Democrat & Placerville Times* (CA) 27 Apr 2/4, Somewhere in the heavy wood, a timber cock beat a thunderous roll on an old snag.

timber crappie n
The white **crappie** (*Pomoxis annularis*).

1900 IA *Legislative Documents* 5.52, Among the many names which have been applied to the crappie are . . white crappie and timber crappie. **1933** LA Dept. of Conserv. *Fishes* 333, *Pomoxis annularis.* . . Names it has been given. . . are as follows: Crappie, . . Timber Crappie. **1938** Schenkeisen *Field Book Fishes* 259, *Pomoxis annularis.* . . Timber Crappie. **1971** Walker *Sport Fishing USA* 75, "Tipoff names" . . are: crapet, pale crappie, . . and timber crappie.

timber cruiser n Cf cruise v, n, cruiser 1, landlooker 2, timber looker, tree ~
One who surveys a tract of forest to estimate the quantity and value of marketable timber on it; similarly n *timber cruise* a survey made for this purpose; vbl n *timber cruising* surveying for this purpose.

1888 *Morning Oregonian* (Portland OR) 6 Dec 6/5, This place has lately experienced quite a boom in timber lands. The valley at times seems to be infested with timber cruisers. **1899** *Bismarck Daily Tribune* (ND) 26 Apr 1/5 **OR,** That the entire party which left Seaside April 7 on a timber cruise are dead is an assured fact. **1905** *Stevens Point Daily Jrl.* (WI) 1 Feb [4]/2 (newspaperarchive.com), Hinman returned a few days ago after spending several months in Texas with a timber cruising party led by his father. **1930** *Ironwood Daily–Globe* (MI) 7 Aug 7/4, P.A. Twomey and Thomas Kilroo are at present engaged in a timber cruise of a large section of hardwood timber . . for the Soo Lumber Co. **1942** ME Univ. *Studies* 57.3 nw**ME,** If the area has been gone over by timber cruisers and a plan of the township has been made . . the development will be facilitated. **1946** Waters *Colorado* 223, For twenty years he had . . dealt poker to every timber cruiser, surveyor and cattle buyer. **1950** *New Oxford Item* (PA) 30 Mar 9/4, Robert Rump . . began a timber cruise on the Ira Naugle farm. **1990** *Chron.-Telegram* (Elyria OH) 1 Apr sec A 7/4, Four members of my family . . through FFA have learned many life skills like . . timber cruising, welding and woodworking. **1997** *Post–Std.* (Syracuse NY) 2 Apr sec B 2/3, Previously, he taught forestry at Michigan State College. He also worked as a timber cruiser for Mead Corp. **2001** *Capital* (Annapolis MD) 8 Feb sec A 11/1, The best way . . is to hire a licensed professional forester to conduct a detailed forest inventory called a timber cruise.

timberdoodle n [Perh humorous or euphem alteration of woodcock; cf doodle n¹ 2] chiefly NY, wGt Lakes
=**woodcock 1.**

1839 *Corsair* (NY NY) 13 July 275 **NY,** Nine timber-doodles and five quail, and only one shot missed. **1859** [see **top** n 4]. **1872** *Huntingdon Jrl.* (PA) 14 Aug [3]/1 (newspaperarchive.com), T.C. Fisher and H. Clay Saxton bagged twenty "timber doodles" one day last week, and it wasn't a good day for woodcock either. **1884** *Forest & Stream* 23.207 **MA,** Wilson's snipe and some woodcock are taken, the old "timber-doodles" having those rich colors only found on an October or November bird. **1933** *AmSp* 8.1.53 **Ozarks,** *Timber-doodle.* . . The woodcock. **1950** WELS (*Names and nicknames for other kinds of game birds in your section*) 2 Infs, **WI,** Timberdoodle. **1954** White *Adirondack Country* 31 **NY,** The game birds of the Adirondacks, the woodcock, called locally the timberdoodle, the partridge, and the pheasant exist in no great number. **1965** *DARE* File, *Timberdoodle*—woodcock, area of Belfast NY. **1966** *Newberry News* (MI) 29 Sept 1/1, Woodcock hunters should chalk up another high kill, close to last season's take of nearly 83,000 timber doodles in the upper and northern lower peninsulas. **1967–68** *DARE* (Qu. Q7, *Names and nicknames for . . game birds*) Inf **MI**42, Timberdoodle—that's the woodcock; **NY**97, Woodcock or timberdoodles or whistle-bicky. **1968** *WI Conserv. Bulletin* 33.2.27 **WI,** The better worm population attracts timber doodles. **1985** Madson *Up River* 186 **Upper Missip Valley,** I took the brace of the grouse and the timberdoodle from my game pocket, smoothing their feathers and fanning the tails of the grouse in admiration. **1998** in 2001 *DARE* File—Internet **MN,** *American Woodcock*—An ode to the timber doodle.

timber fly n esp WV See Map Cf black fly, punkie n¹
Appar a **midge.**

1968 *DARE* (Qu. R12, . . *Other kinds of flies*) Infs **WV**3, 4, 5, 7, 8, 10, 16, Timber fly; **CT**2, Timber fly [FW sugg]—same as wood fly.

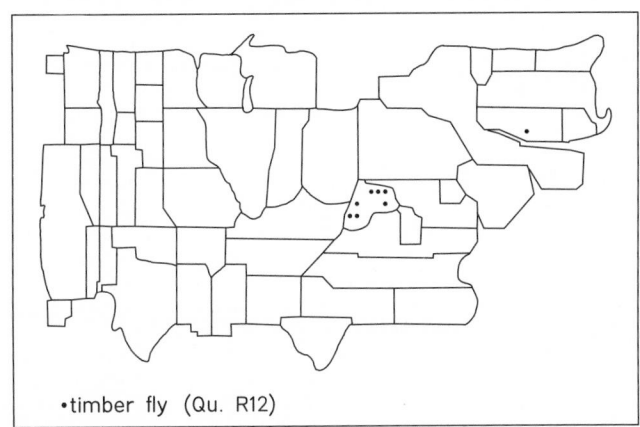

•timber fly (Qu. R12)

timber goose n
A **white-fronted goose** (here: *Anser albifrons* subsp).

1918 *CA Fish & Game* 4.87, The new "tule goose" or "timber goose" is distinguished from its relative, the common white-fronted goose by its greater size, its call notes, its browner tints, its yellow eye ring, and the possession of a greater number of tail feathers. **1982** Elman *Hunter's Field Guide* 298, *Tule Goose (Anser albifrons gambelli)—Common & Regional Names:* tule whitefront, timber goose.

timber grouse n   Also *timber partridge*
Any of var grouse inhabiting woodlands, such as the **dusky grouse, ruffed grouse,** or **spruce grouse;** see quots.

1878 U.S. War Dept. *Annual Rept.* 2.3.1533 **ID,** Prairie chickens, timber grouse, and sage hens abound generally. **1888** Trumbull *Names of Birds* 141, *Wood grouse,* (this term, like that of "timber-grouse," being sometimes broadly used to indicate grouse which inhabit woods, as opposed to those of the "open" or prairie). **1894** *Outing* 24.305 **CO,** We . . had great fun with the timber-grouse and the sage-hens. **1982** Elman *Hunter's Field Guide* 15, Ruffed Grouse . . & Related Timber Grouse. *Ibid* 19, Two crestless, ruffless, but closely related northern and western "timber partridges". . . are the blue grouse (*Dendragapus obscurus*) and spruce grouse (*Canachites canadensis*).

timber honeysuckle n
A **honeysuckle 2** (here: *Lonicera utahensis*).

1931 U.S. Dept. Ag. *Misc. Pub.* 101.147, *Utah honeysuckle . . ,* known locally as . . timber honeysuckle, is a low thin-leaved shrub. . . Its palatability usually varies from worthless or almost worthless to low.

timber hook n
See quot 1956.

1859 *Cent. City Daily Courier* (Syracuse NY) [22 Mar 4]/5 (newspaperarchive.com), 1 timber hook, [$]2,00. **1936** *Lima News* (OH) 20 Oct 15/2, Public Sale. . . one cant hook; one square timber hook. **1956** Sorden–Ebert *Logger's Words* 38, **Gt Lakes,** *Timber-hook,* See lughook. [*Ibid* 22, *Lug-hooks,* A pair of tongs attached to the middle of a short bar and used by two men to carry small logs or railroad cross ties.] **1962** *Brainerd Daily Dispatch* (MN) 6 Oct 7/5, [Advt:] Two timber hooks.

timber jay n   Cf **lumberjack**
Perh =**Canada jay.**

1974 Harris *Barbed Wire* 10 **UT,** Above the caw of the timber jay,/ Above the buzz of the mountain flies,/ Alone with the unremitting breeze,/ He stood. **1984** *DARE* File **UT,** Kinds of jays: timber [jay].

timber looker n   Cf **landlooker 2**
=**timber cruiser.**

1893 MN State Horticult. Soc. *Annual Rept. for 1892* 160, Even the timber-looker, who makes it his business to go out and determine how much wood there is per acre, will often make a mistake of fifty to one hundred per cent one way or the other. **1904** *Atlanta Constitution* (GA) 14 Feb [80]/6 (newspaperarchive.com) **ME,** A timber looker recently told the writer that he knew of but one township in all northern Maine where there were trees worth cutting. **1914** *CO Springs Gaz.* (CO) 22 Mar [7]/1 (newspaperarchive.com), The old-time "timber looker," who could see only the present value of woods and forests, has been replaced by the forest engineer. **1958** McCulloch *Woods Words* 195 **Pacific NW,** *Timber looker*—A timber cruiser, especially one interested in speculation.

timber lot n   esp **NEast, N Cent**   See Map
A piece of land covered with timber.

1723 in 1898 Pelletreau *Early Wills* 46 **NY,** Executors are to sell a lot in the Neck, and a lot in the Field, and my half timber lot. **1781** MA *Acts & Laws Commonwealth* 62, Thence West three Hundred and Twenty-six Rods to the Southwest Corner of Lot Number *Ninety-four,* being the Northwest Corner of the Pine Timber Lot. **1845** *Adams Sentinel* (Gettysburg PA) 8 Dec [2]/2 (newspaperarchive.com), Another tract of Mountain Land . . is also an excellent Timber Lot. **1894** *New Engl. Mag.* 16.620 **NH,** They never yet had sold one acre of their timber lot, though the lumbermen at Stumpville had offered good prices time and again. **1923** *Daily Kennebec Jrl.* (Augusta ME) 31 Oct 7/3, Steam Saw Mill—First class one wanted to operate good pine timber lot in Bennington, N.H. **1965–70** *DARE* (Qu. T2b, . . *A piece of land covered with trees . . a large acreage*) 13 Infs, **esp NEast, N Cent,** Timber lot; (Qu. T2a, . . *A piece of land covered with trees . . only a few acres*) Infs **IA**8, **KY**16, **NY**1, Timber lot. **1993** *Post–Std.* (Syracuse NY) 20 Dec sec E 6/10, Seasoned Firewood. . . Also wanted timber lot.

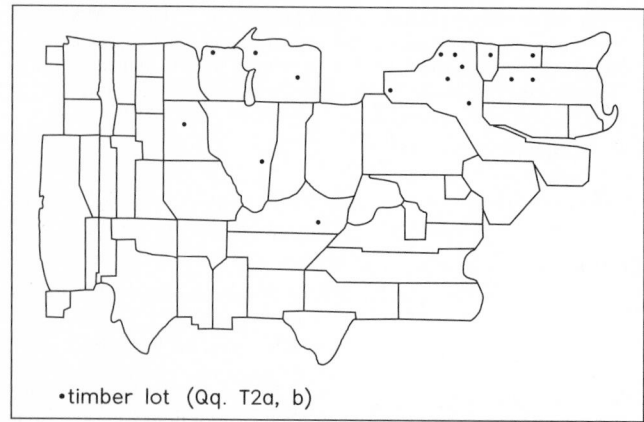

•timber lot (Qq. T2a, b)

timber marten n
=**pine marten.**

1945 *Chem. Abstracts* 39.4194, Data for oils from fox . . , mink . . , timber marten (*Martes martes* L.), [etc]. **1967** *DARE* (Qu. P32, . . *Other kinds of wild animals*) Inf **CO**41, Marten of two types: rock marten—fur not as good, always in rocks; timber marten.

timber match n   Cf **cordwood 1, lumberjack match**
A wooden match.

1967 *DARE* (Qu. F46, . . *Matches you can strike anywhere;* not asked in early QRs) Inf **OR**1, Timber matches.

timber owl n   Cf **tree owl**
Prob the barred owl (*Strix varia*).

1903 *Atl. Slope Naturalist* 1.82 **IL,** [Title:] The Timber Owl of the Mississippi Valley. **1910** Davenport *Country Boy* 29 **OR,** I was in bed, safe from an awful, dark night, a coyote, and some barn and timber owls. **1965–70** *DARE* (Qu. Q2, . . *Kinds of owls*) Infs **SC**41, **WV**13, 17, Timber owl; **IL**114, Timber owl [FW sugg]; **OK**46, Timber owls— make a lot of racket. **2002** Buckley *Standing Ground* 289 **nwCA,** The cry of the timber owl itself is an ill omen, but the bird may also be a transformed human sorcerer, come to "devil" people. Either way, it's bad news.

timber partridge   See **timber grouse**

timber rabbit n
=**varying hare** or other **jackrabbit 1.**

1896 IA *Legislative Documents* 4.94, *Lepus americanus*. . . Timber rabbit. **1904** MN Univ. Ag. Exper. Sta. *Bulletin* 85.149, In the timber we get the Northern or varying hare, *Lepus americanus,* sometimes called "Timber Rabbit." **1924** MI Univ. Museum Zool. *Occas. Papers* 7.15 **OR,** In Tillamook County, Oregon it [=a hare] is locally called "timber rabbit," "snowshoe rabbit," or "red rabbit." **1926** *Forest & Stream* 96.666 **neOK,** In this country we have three distinct species of rabbits. The timber rabbit, which is a large, dark-brown variety, inhabits the timber lands and heavy brushy places. **1967** *DARE* (Qu. P30, . . *Wild rabbits*) Inf **KS**5, Timber rabbit.

timber rattlesnake n   Also *timber rattler*
1 also *timber rattle:* A large **rattlesnake 1** (here: *Crotalus horridus*) native to much of the eastern half of the US.   Also called **banded rattlesnake, black ~, canebrake rattler, mountain ~, pine ~, rattler 1, rock rattlesnake a, Seminole rattler, swamp rattlesnake 3, timber snake a, velvet-tail 1** Cf **brush rattler**

1892 IL State Lab. Nat. Hist. *Bulletin* 3.311, *Crotalus horridus*. . . Timber Rattlesnake. . . Large, reaching a length of six feet. **1928** Baylor Univ. Museum *Contrib.* 16.19 **TX,** *Crotalus horridus*. . . inhabits the forested regions of eastern Texas and is therefore known as the *Timber Rattlesnake.* **1930** *Copeia* 1.37 **OK,** *Crotalus horridus* . . timber rattler. Occasionally killed in the hills. **1938** Matschat *Suwannee R.* 27 **neFL, seGA,** Snakes known to live in the hammocks and piney woods. . . [include] three kinds of rattlesnakes—the diamondback, the timber or Seminole . . , and the small ground rattler. **c1940** Newman–Murphy *Conserv. Notes* 5 **LA,** Among the poisonous snakes may be mentioned the timber rattlesnake. **1965–70** *DARE* (Qu. P25, . . *Kinds of snakes*) 40 Infs, **chiefly east of Missip R,** Timber rattler; **GA**65, Pine rattler—same as timber rattler; **TX**33, Timber rattlesnake; **TX**37, Timber rattle. **1968** *DARE* Tape **GA**35, This one here is a timber rattler, or

Seminole, or often called canebrake. **1974** Dillard *Pilgrim* 223 **VA,** The only other poisonous snake around here is the timber rattler. **2001** *DARE* File—Internet **WI,** Timber rattlesnakes tend to shy away from areas where people are about. . . Timber rattlers are listed as a Protected Wild Animal in Wisconsin.

2 A **prairie rattlesnake** (here: *Crotalus viridis*).   **chiefly CA**
1956 Klauber *Rattlesnakes* 23 **CA,** The snake that I shall call the northern Pacific rattlesnake *(Crotalus viridis oreganus)* is variously known, in different parts of California, as the black, black diamond, diamondback, green, gray, mountain, rock, and timber rattlesnakes, to mention only a few of its names. **1965–70** *DARE* (Qu. P25, . . *Kinds of snakes)* Infs **CA**117, 120, 147, **CO**12, Timber rattler; **CA**36, Timber rattler—a blacker snake; **CA**87, Timber rattler—the black ones; **CA**130, Western timber rattler—up in mountains; a small rattlesnake, very dark in color.

timber sauce   See **timber**

timber snake n
Any of var snakes that frequent woodlands, as:
a =**timber rattlesnake 1.**
1843 *VT Phoenix* (Brattleboro) 4 Aug 1/3 **IL,** These snakes differ in size and appearance from the large or timber snake as much as the prairie wolf does from the large ones.—They are equally vicious . . though being much smaller, they inject into the wound a smaller volume of poison. **1869** Gillmore *Accessible Sports* 227, He [=a large rattlesnake] belonged to the variety which generally goes by the name of timbersnake, much larger and totally different in colour from the prairie rattlesnake or massasauga. **1933** *N. Adams Transcript* (MA) 22 May 12/5, His skin is plainly marked with the diamond-shaped figures that are characteristic of New England rattlers. He is what is known in these parts as a banded or timber snake. **1943** *Daily Capital News* (Jefferson City MO) 9 May 1/3, I would rather see a Pike county timber snake come into my home. **1966–70** *DARE* (Qu. P25, . . *Kinds of snakes)* Infs **KY**82, 93, Timber snake; **NH**18, Timber snake—kind of rattler. **1998** in 2001 *DARE* File—Internet **MI,** Populations of timber snakes are rapidly being depleted across the species' range. **1999** Barnett–Russell *Granny Curse* 81 **eTN,** They heard the sound of timber snakes sounding their rattles underneath the rock.
b =**fox snake.**   Cf **pine snake 2, wood ~**
1938 Conant in *Amer. Midland Naturalist* 20.60 **OH,** *Elaphe vulpina . . Fox Snake; Timber Snake. . .* A medium to large snake attaining a length in excess of five feet. **1958** Conant *Reptiles & Amphibians* 157, *Elaphe vulpina. . .* A serpent with many aliases—a "timber snake" in Ohio and parts of Michigan. **1997** in 2001 *DARE* File—Internet, Fox snakes. . . Elaphe vulpina. . . Range includes the northern Midwestern states for Western Variety. [E]astern Fox has a much more limited range, along the great lakes and Michigan. Known as timber snake, pine snake, spotted adder, and many other names.
c A **rat snake 1** (here: *Elaphe obsoleta*).
1957 in 1993 *Carmen Headlight* (OK) 24 Apr (Internet) **OK** (as of 1895), As I went into my lean-to kitchen, I saw a timber snake crawling through my long handled frying pan which hung on a nail just back of my cook stove. **2001** *DARE* File—Internet **IN,** *Elaphe obsoleta obsolete* [sic]. . . The black rat snake can be found throughout Indiana in rocky hillsides, open woods, dry prairies and stream valleys. . . Other names include cow snake, chicken snake, timber snake, black snake, and black climber. *Ibid* **MO,** We did see a snake. Not a coiled up rattler ready to strike, but a little gray timber snake about 18 inches in length.
d =**rubber boa.**
1936 *Amer. Midland Naturalist* 17.644 **swOR,** At Fish Lake a man described as the "timber snake," a snake evidently of this species [= *Charina bottae*], which occurred locally.
e =**bull snake.**   Cf **pine snake 1**
1970 *DARE* (Qu. P25, . . *Kinds of snakes)* Inf **KY**84, Timber snake = bull snake.

timber squirrel n   esp Upper MW, KS, NE
A **gray squirrel 1** (here: *Sciurus carolinensis*).
1876 Shallenberger *Stark Co.* 124 **IL,** Of squirrels we have the well known western fox squirrel . . , the grey timber squirrel (S. Carolinensis) [etc]. **1902** Wells *Frontier Life* 47 **KS,** The prairie-dog is a very interesting species of marmot. It is about the size of a timber squirrel. **1923** U.S. Dept. Ag. *Farmers' Bulletin* 1375.26 **NE,** *Open seasons:* . . Squirrel (gray, red, fox, timber). . . Sept. 16–Dec. 31. **1966–67** *DARE* (Qu.

P27, . . *Kinds of squirrels)* Infs **IA**4, **KS**5, **NE**8, **SD**5, **WY**5, Timber squirrel.

timber stick   See **timber**

timber wart n   Also *tree wart*
A burl.
1908 *Pop. Mechanics* Feb 82, A real walnut burl, or timber wart, as it is known among lumbermen, . . ranks high in commercial value. **2003** *KentuckyLiving.com* June (Internet), What Ramsey identifies as "perfect" [for wood turning] is called a tree wart among foresters and loggers.

timber wheels n pl   Cf **big wheels, carry-log 1, katydid B5, timber cart**
Two large-diameter wheels connected by an axle under which one end of a log can be suspended for hauling by a team of animals.
1776 in 1912 NC Secy. of State *NC Wills* 47, I give and Bequeath to my son, Richard, . . Two yoak of Oxen, Two peare of Timber wheels [etc]. **1791** Bartram *Travels* 312 **GA,** The logs . . [are] dragged by timber wheels to this yard, and landed near the brink of this high bank as possible. **1849** (1850) Parke *Lectures* 222, Timber wheels being designed to have pieces of timber suspended below the axle, are made high. **1877** *Chester Daily Times* (PA) 20 Oct 1/4, Thomas Sharpless of Edgmont was severely injured on Wednesday by being thrown from timber wheels. **1894** *Scribner's Mag.* 15.561 **LA,** A man pressed close to the side of the halted buggy, to avoid a huge telegraph-pole that came by quivering between two timber wheels. **1903** [see **timber cart**]. **1929** *Denton Jrl.* (MD) 26 Jan 5/1, He had loaded two logs on timber wheels . . when his feet became entangled in some brush. **1952** *Ibid* 4 Apr 9/5, [Advt:] Rope harness, chain harness, 1 set light timber wheels. **1969** Sorden *Lumberjack Lingo* 130 **NEng, Gt Lakes,** *Timber wheels—* A pair of wheels, usually ten to fourteen feet high, used for transporting logs. Same as big wheels, katydid, logging wheels, sulky.

timber wolf n
1 =**gray wolf 1.**   [*DCan* 1860 →]   **chiefly Nth, West**
1856 *Ballou's Pictorial* 10.54, From every direction the prairie wolves were answering to the calls of their companions, and now and then the baying of the more formidable timber wolf fell dismally on the ear. **1872** Webb *Buffalo Land* 292 **West,** Twenty-three dead wolves were found, and the even two dozen was made up by a large specimen of the gray variety—or timber-wolf, as it is called in contradistinction from the cayote [sic]. **1875** U.S. Army Corps Topog. Engineers *Rept. Reconnaissance Black Hills* 79 **SD,** *Gray Wolf; Timber Wolf. . .* One of the most common animals in the Black Hills. . . They were generally observed singly or by twos and threes, sneaking along the mountain sides or crossing the narrow valleys. **1888** *Century Illustr. Mag.* 36.208 **ID,** Occasionally we saw the foot-marks of the great timber wolf. **1917** Anthony *Mammals Amer.* 68, *Gray Wolf, or Timber Wolf. . .* Color usually light, white to grizzled gray. Color variable sometimes through different degrees of gray to all black. **1946** Dufresne *AK's Animals* 82, Alaska timber wolves are among the largest of their kind in America. **1958** Blasingame *Dakota Cowboy* 72 **SD,** The gray wolf, buffalo runner, timber wolf—name or color mattered little, for the animal was the same. **1961** Jackson *Mammals WI* 290, *Canis lupus lycaon. . .* In Wisconsin commonly called gray wolf or timber wolf. **1965–70** *DARE* (Qu. P32, . . *Other kinds of wild animals)* 20 Infs, **chiefly Nth, West,** Timber wolf. **2000** Mech *Wolves MN* 51, Locally the animal is called the "timber wolf" to distinguish it from the coyote, which is also known as the "brush wolf." [*Ibid,* [Caption:] *The specific geographic race of wolf occupying Minnesota was thought to be the eastern timber wolf,* Canis lupus lycaon, *until about 1995. Then new studies indicated that the animal is the great plains wolf,* Canis lupus nubilus.]
2 A **coyote** n **B1** (here: *Canis latrans lestes*); see quot.
1937 Grinnell et al. *Fur-Bearing Mammals CA* 476, Because it [= *Canis latrans lestes*] is large for a coyote, has a heavy coat of fur, and is gray in color, the mountain coyote is often known locally as gray wolf or timber wolf. However, there should be no confusion between even the largest mountain coyote and the smallest true timber or plains wolf.
3 See **timber beast.**

time n
A Form.
Pl: usu *times;* also *time.*   Cf **foot** n **B2b(1)**
1940 in 1970 Hyatt *Hoodoo* 2.1070 [Black], An' yo' take de fellah's

name an' yo' write his name nine time all aroun' dat aig—all aroun' nine times. **1966** *DARE* Tape **MS**72, He come here two or three time.

B Sense.

Wages due, esp at the cessation of employment—freq used in ref to quitting, firing, or being fired.

1887 *Courier-Jrl.* (Louisville KY) 12 Jan 6/3, All that remained for the brakemen and switchmen to do was to go to the office . . and call for what is known in railroad parlance as their "time," otherwise the money due them for services they had rendered before they went on strike. **1902** White *Blazed Trail* 56 **nMI,** So Pat and Henrys were not discharged—were not instructed to "get their time." Fabian Laveque promptly demanded his. **1904** *AZ Republican* (Phoenix) 30 Aug 1/6 **OK,** Thirteen women clerks . . struck today when informed that they could either remain after closing hours, assist in the sweeping and place things in readiness for the next day, or get their time. Each clerk walked to the cashier's desk, drew her pay and quit. **1920** Hunter *Trail Drivers TX* 211 (as of 1877), On the night of August 20, this being 1877, I went to call on Col. J.F. Ellison . . to get my "time," which really means wages, about $180.00, then a small fortune for a young cow boy. *Ibid* 213, Mr. Withers gave him his time and told him to "light a shuck." **1925** in 1953 Botkin–Harlow *Treas. Railroad Folkl.* 227, When they pulled me off muh meat, I had 'im bloody as a hawg. Course then I had to get muh time and beat it. **1935** Cronin *Stars* 608, It broke his heart to give these fifty their time, to send them to join the six hundred men . . already on the dole. **1958** McCulloch *Woods Words* 70 **Pacific NW,** *Get your time*—You're fired. *Ibid* 195, *Time*. . . Pay. **1971** *Foxfire* Spring–Summer 13 **nGA,** I mean you can't come out here and give my men orders t'do things I wouldn't put'em into myself. And if that don't suit'cha, you gimme my time.

C In var phrr:

1 *at the time:* At a time, on each of several occasions. **scattered, but chiefly Sth, S Midl**

1823 Nutting *Practical Gram. Engl.* 73 **VT,** Simply, *one at the time,* doubly, *two at the time.* **1852** *New Engl. Farmer* 4.65, The whole fence may be moved . . by beginning at one end and moving a section or two at the time. **1871** Holden *Trial Gov. NC* 1.845, There were several hundred who were furnished with drinks. I saw them go in two at the time. **1915** Healy *Individual Delinquent* 396, He worked only for a week or two at the time, and at irregular intervals. **1966–68** *DARE* (Qu. BB20, *Joking names or expressions for overactive kidneys*) Inf **GA**44, Tablespoon at the time; (Qu. LL7, *In small amounts, by small degrees: "She didn't get the money all at once, they sent it to her _____."*) Infs **AR**3, 22, **DE**3, **GA**30, **SC**9, 19, 26, Little (bit) at the time. **1983** *MS Writers Talking* 119, I came back quite a bit and stayed sometimes for a month or two at the time. **2003** in 2009 *DARE* File—Internet **NC,** I only use it for a day or two at the time, if I feel I *have* to. *Ibid* **nwSC,** Before I found them, it was almost impossible for me to leave home for longer than a day or two at the time. **2007** *Ibid* **LA,** I was catching them two at the time on tandem ¼ oz. sparkle beetles fished freeline. **2009** *Ibid* **seMI,** Selling just one or two at the time diminishes their value to someone who has a large project to accomplish.

2 *by times:* See **by times.**

3 *in time:* At some time in the past; formerly. **sAppalachians**

1939 in 2004 Montgomery–Hall *Dict. Smoky Mt. Engl.* 322 **wNC,** They had came a water spout in time and drifted in . . a big lot of timber . . and stuff. **1941** Stuart *Men of Mts.* 311 **neKY,** Somebody had tapped 'em [=maple trees] in time. They have made maple syrup from them. **1973** in 2004 Montgomery–Hall *Dict. Smoky Mt. Engl.* 322 **wNC,** The trail went around, well they had in time took a sled and wagon maybe around it. **1974** Fink *Mountain Speech* 13 **wNC, eTN,** *In time* (adv): once. "A house stood there in time." **1975** in 1976 Lindsay *Hist. Grassy Balds* 49 **eTN,** Maybe the Indians might have cut them balds in time. I don't know. They might have raised corn there. **1976** Garber *Mountain-ese* 46 **sAppalachians,** *In-time* (adv) previously—In time this was the best fishin' hole in the whole country.

4 As a euphem: see below. **chiefly NEng** *old-fash* Cf **timenation**

a *in time:* Used after an interrog pron or adv for *in Hell* or similar expletive.

1844 *Bangor Daily Whig & Courier* (ME) 1 Feb 1/4, What in time ail, [sic] you, Massa? [*DARE* Ed: From a short story of undetermined origin that was widely reprinted in newspapers. Several versions, including the earliest located (1841), read "What de debble (*or* debbil)"; "What in time" was evidently an editorial bowdlerization.] **1849** in 1898 Gris-

wold *Corresp.* 250 **MA,** Why in Time don't you come our way and see the boys? **1878** *Atlantic Mth.* 42.612 **MA,** "Well, who in Time"—the expression was strong, but she used it without hesitation, and was never known to repent it—"*will* she go to, then?" **1895** *Atlanta Constitution* (GA) 23 June 9/5, [From *Boston Transcript:*] Isn't drinking any more! Of course not, how in time could he? **1901** *Atlantic Mth.* 87.102 **ME** (as of c1776), What in time's been the matter amongst ye? **1918** Lincoln *Shavings* 191 **MA,** Why in time . . didn't you tell me right out that 'twas Mrs. Armstrong's brother you had in mind? **1943** *LANE* Map 600, 1 inf, **csNH,** What in time is that thing. **a1969** (1982) Langley *Swamp* 161 **seMO** (as of 1920s), Why in time don't you put some wood on that there fire?

b *by time:* Used for *by God* or similar oath.

1848 Lowell *Biglow* 15 'Upcountry' **MA,** I don't ollers agree with him, ses he, but by Time, ses he, I *du* like a feller that ain't a Feared. **1864** (1868) Trowbridge *3 Scouts* 160, By time, don't that taste good! **1916** Lincoln *Mary-'Gusta* 63 **MA,** Helped me do the dishes. Yes, sir, by time, that's what she done. *Ibid* 76, By time! . . that kid's a reg'lar born mother. **1959** *VT Hist.* 27.164 **neVT,** *By Time!* . . Obsolete.

time conj **chiefly Sth, S Midl**
At or by the time that; as soon as.

1887 (1967) Harris *Free Joe* 85 **GA,** I speck dat hoss mus a-bin use'n ter niggers, kaze time I holler at 'im he lay right still. **1890** Johnston *Widow Guthrie* 42 **GA** (as of 1830s), I heerd him a-ex'cisin' his voice time I put my foot on the tavern step. **1926** Ferber *Show Boat* 146 **Sth,** I was keelboatin' time you was runnin' around. **1938** Rawlings *Yearling* 78 **nFL,** I'll foller time I've skinned out your 'coon hide. **1949** Guthrie *Way West* 20 **MO,** You'll stand in need of fun, time you eat a bushel of dust. **1950** Moore *Candlemas Bay* 11 **ME,** Time Joel Walls had his net, one night he caught seven hogsids. **1955** *PADS* 23.42 **e,cSC, eNC, seGA,** Church will be over) *time I get there.* (Also upstate New York.) **1960** Lee *Mockingbird* 19 **sAL,** He was gone time Atticus got there. **1989** Pederson *LAGS Tech. Index* 336 **Gulf Region** *(By the time)* 17 infs, Time. **2009** Littlefield *Bad Day* 264 **MO,** They took you to surgery . . , but time I got over here, you were in recovery.

time exclam See **time out**

time about adv phr [Scots, nEngl dial] **chiefly S Midl, esp sAppalachians**

By turns, alternately—freq in phrr *take (it) time about* to take turns.

1838 in 2004 Montgomery–Hall *Dict. Smoky Mt. Engl.* 608 **eTN,** [T]he male members agree to git wine time about. **1852** Byrn *Rattlehead's Travels* 71 **AR,** We then went on our way, taking it time about riding. **1864** (1997) Edmondson *Diary* 35 (Internet) **TN,** We . . have taken it time about standing Picket, with the horses hidden in the wood. **1917** Rudd–Bond *From Slavery* 34 **AR,** The hands on our place would divide themselves into squads and take time about hunting with Slade at night until he had killed a man or killed the dogs, and they would then carry them home. **1937** in 2006 *DARE* File—Internet **ceOK** (as of 1875), The four men took time about building feeding pens and herding the longhorns. **1969** Green *Wild Cow Tales* 206 **TX,** We all took time about cookin' and this happened to be one of the days I wasn't cookin'. **1974** Fink *Mountain Speech* 27 **wNC, eTN,** They go to her church and his'n, time about. **2000** *Star* (Shelby NC) 30 Oct (Internet), "At first, deacons and their wives took time about cleaning the church," she said. "Now we pay someone." **2005** in 2006 *DARE* File—Internet **csKY,** My oldest daughter and I are taking time about staying with them to help out. **2006** *Ibid* **ceGA,** With four of them taking time about driving, each one only had to drive one week out of each month.

time-loser See **lose time**

timenation n, exclam **NEng** Cf **darnation, tarnation, time n C4**

Used as a euphem for *damnation.*

1892 *Bucks Co. Gaz.* (Bristol PA) 4 Feb 1/4 **ME,** What in timenation you doin with that oxcart? **1943** *LANE* Map 600 *(Shucks! Botheration!)* 21 infs, **ME, NH,** Timenation.

time out exclam Also *time(s), times out; rarely times ex* [Prob transf from *time out* a brief suspension of play in var organized sports (*OED2* time out [at *time* sb. 38] 1896 →)] **widespread, but more freq east of Missip R** See Map Cf **T's =king's ex.**

1950 *WELS* **WI** *(In a game of tag, if you want to rest, what do you call*

out so that "it" can't catch you?) 15 Infs, Time out; 6 Infs, Time(s).
1965–70 *DARE* (Qu. EE17, *In a game of tag, if a player wants to rest, what does he call out so that he can't be tagged?*) 385 Infs, **widespread, but more freq east of Missip R,** Time(s) out; 135 Infs, **widespread, but more freq east of Missip R,** Time(s); **NC**77, Call "time"; **IA**46, Times ex; **NY**250, I got "time"; (Qu. EE20, *When two boys are fighting, and the one who is losing wants to stop, he calls out, "_____."*) 21 Infs, **chiefly east of Missip R,** Time(s) out; 17 Infs, **chiefly Atlantic,** Time(s). **1984** *DARE* File **CO,** When two boys are fighting, and the one who is losing wants to stop, he calls out, "_____": Time out. **1996** *Focus USA* 72, [1994 survey using *DARE*'s Qu. EE17:] The picture has changed among the younger people questioned this year. Sixty-one percent of them [=of 296 total infs] responded with *time out,* almost twice the percentage of informants found by *DARE;* 20% said *time. . . Times* was reported 20 times, *times out* not at all. *Time* is no longer confined to mostly East Coast states, but has spread across the country, while *times* has spread as far west as Texas, Oklahoma, Colorado, and Minnesota, as well as one response in Arizona.

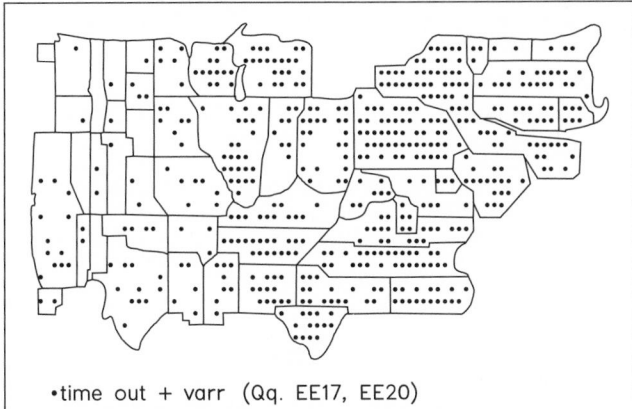

•time out + varr (Qq. EE17, EE20)

timer n   Cf **tick** n[3] **2**

In combs *one-timer, two- ~,* etc: A playing marble valued at one, two, etc times that of the least valuable type.

1966–70 *DARE* (Qu. EE6c, *Cheap marbles*) Inf **NC**84, Two-timers—worth two commas; commas—made of clay, little brown marbles; (Qu. EE6d, *Special marbles*) Inf **OK**52, Gumbos are one-timers; agates and aggies are five-timers; flints and red flints are twenty-five-timers.

times, times ex (or out)   See **time out**

timid adj   **Sth, S Midl**   See Map
=**mincy.**

1881 *Med. Rec.* 20.299, *Dyspepsia: How to Avoid It. . .* A pleasantly written treatise, containing much information for the careful and timid eater.   **1965–70** *DARE* (Qu. H12, *If somebody eating a meal takes little bits of food and leaves most of it on his plate, you say he _____*) 10 Infs, **Sth, S Midl,** Timid eater; **AL**34, **GA**1, (Was) timid; **AR**53, **LA**2, Timid with his eating; (Qu. H10, *If somebody never eats very much food . . he's a _____; total Infs questioned, 75*) Inf **MS**1, Timid eater; [(Qu. H11b, *If he makes a noise with his food, he _____*) Inf **AL**20, Timid]. [9 of 15 total Infs gs educ or less]   **2005** in 2006 *DARE* File—Internet ceMO, If you happen to be a timid eater, don't let our account

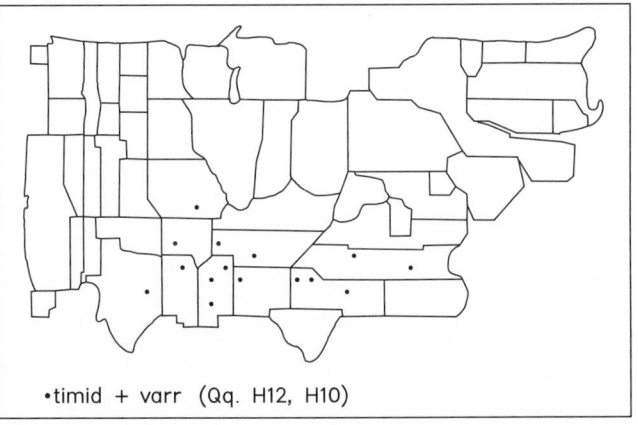

•timid + varr (Qq. H12, H10)

of blissful gluttony scare you off: the menu does include smaller dinner platters as well as solo sandwiches.

timothy n   Also *timothy grass*   Cf **wild timothy**
Std: an introduced and cultivated grass *(Phleum pratense)* used esp for hay.   Also called **herd's-grass 1, hedge grass**

timothy bean n

1800 in 1913 Alderman *NC Colonial Bar* 19 **NC,** The Timothy Beans . . turned out extremely well but unless your black-eyed peas are better I could send you some superior.   **1925** Ashe *Hist. NC* 2.164 (as of early 19th cent), They talked about "Timothy beans" and "Black-eyed peas."   **1968** *DARE* (Qu. I18, *The smaller beans that are white when they are dry*) Inf **DE**3, Timothy beans—old-fashioned—smallest [among soup beans and navy beans].

timothy grass   See **timothy**

timp n   [Du]   Cf **kink, nibby** n[1]

1991 *DARE* File **cWI,** In my family of origin, it [=the end slice of a loaf of bread] was always the "timp". . . I returned to Wausau, my hometown, and conducted the same survey, among my relatives mostly, and of course they answered "the timp". . . My family was half English/Scotch-Irish and half German.

timpiute n
=**scarlet gilia.**

1961 Douglas *My Wilderness* 17 **CO,** Here is a scarlet-colored gilia known as timpiute *(Gilia aggregata).*

tin n[1], adj   See **ten**

tin n[2]   See **tin tin**

tinaja n   [AmSpan *tinaja* water jar]   **SW**   Cf **resaca, tank** n[1] **1**
A depression in solid rock where water accumulates; a water hole—also used in place names.

1835 Royal Geogr. Soc. London *Jrl.* 5.65 **CA,** The only water to be had is found . . in excavations called Tinajas, made by the Indians.   **1856** (1928) Jaeger *Diary Fort Yuma* 14.128 **AZ,** No water at the Tule Tinaja & Tinajas Altas.   **1859** (1968) Bartlett *Americanisms* 480, *Tinaja. . .* is applied on the Mexican frontier to water-holes or cavities in rocks on the sides of mountains, where water accumulates.   **1892** *DN* 1.195 **TX,** *Tinája. . .* [A] water hole or pocket.   **1919** Chase *CA Desert* 347, Somewhere near the mouth of the cañon is a *tinaja* known as Granite Tanks.   **1932** *DN* 6.234 **West,** *Tinaja.* The usual word for *rock-basin* at the time of the Spanish explorers, and still used in place-names on the Mexican border. Probably heard now and then in the Southwest, from Texas to the coast.   **1966** *DARE* (Qu. C4a, *. . A fairly large body of fresh water*) Inf **NM**11, Tank—tinaja [is] Spanish for tank.   **2003** *Post-Std.* (Syracuse NY) 6 Sept sec C 1/2 **AZ,** Two excavators, a track loader and three off-highway trucks work Thursday at Caterpillar Inc.'s Tinaja Peak training area.

tin can alley n

1 A poor or shabby street or section of town.

1898 Brann *Brann the Iconoclast* 1.436, *Town Topics* is what is known as [sic] the terse vernacular of Hungry Hill and Tin-can Alley as a journalistic "nancy"—a trifle too dirty for decency and too epicene for aggressive immorality.   **1915** *Mansfield News* (OH) 13 Aug 5/1, Thomas Jefferson then left his bed and board and cast his lot in with the roughneck cats down in Tin Can alley.   **1928** *Bee* (Danville VA) 12 Jan 13/2, The Latest Out In Records: . . Tin Can Alley Blues.   **1950** *Lima News* (OH) 18 Dec 14/2, Mrs. Nettie Lyle gave a reading, "Christmas in Tin Can Alley."   **1968–70** *DARE* (Qu. II25, *Names or nicknames for the part of a town where the poorer people, special groups, or foreign groups live*) Infs **KS**15, **MI**111, Tin can alley.

2 also *tin can hidi:* A hide-and-seek game.   Cf **kick the can 1**

1929 *Playground & Recreation* 467, Diamond Ball, Volley Ball, Horseshoe, Croquet, Swimming, Track Meet, Tumbling, Tin Can Alley. [*DARE* Ed: This quot may refer instead to **3** below.]   **1957** *Sat. Eve. Post Letters* **swMI,** Tin Can Alley—One person was "it." A large tin can was placed in a small circle. One person ran up and gave the can a good kick. All scattered and hid. "It" had to run and put the can back in the circle and start out hunting. Without being seen one or another of the players would sneak out and kick the can and run and hide again. . . Each time the can was kicked "it" had to run back and set it in the circle before going back to hunt again.   [**1969** Opie–Opie *Children's Games* 166 **Gt Britain,** *Seeking games. . .* 'Tin Can Alley' (Croydon and St. Ives, Cornwall), 'Tin Can Annie' (Knighton).]   **1995** in 1999 Millersville Univ. Center for PA Ger. Studies *Jrl.* Fall 5 (as of 1930s), Playing games was never too much a part of my life. I do remember as a youth playing nipper, the parts made from an old broom stick, "nutzers" (marbles) and tin can "hidi" (hide and seek) on Maple Street. **2004** *DARE* File—Internet **WV,** As a child in my neighborhood, I would play Tin Can Alley with my friends outside until well after dark. For us in the hills of West Virginia, Tin Can Alley was a sophisticated form of Hide and Seek. **2005** *Ibid,* When I was a little boy, one of my favorite games to play on a summer's night after dark was a game we called ["]Tin Can Alley." We'd take three empty cans from the garbage and stack them in the middle of the driveway. One person would be "it," meaning that that person had to guard the cans. Everyone else would hide. . . The person who was "it" would stand in the single spotlight in the driveway and shout, *"Come out, come out, wherever you are!"* The object of the game was for the people hiding, to try to get to the cans and kick them over without being tagged.

3 also *tin can annie,* ~ *willie:* Any of var other games; see quot. Cf **duck on a rock, hockey** n[1] **1**

1965–70 *DARE* (Qu. EE18, *Games in which the players set up a stone, a tin can, or something similar, and then try to knock it down*) 15 Infs, **chiefly Missip Valley, sAppalachians,** Tin can alley [no description of game]; **LA**28, **MS**6, **TX**40, Tin can alley [FW sugg]; **MN**11, Tin can ['ʊli]; **PA**213, Tin can annie; **MD**8, Tin can willie, tin can on the dump—same thing [*DARE* Ed: Some of these Infs may refer instead to **2** above.]; (Qu. EE27, *Games played on the ice*) Inf **IN**56, Tin can alley— like regular hockey only played with brooms and a tin can.

tin can hidi See **tin can alley 2**

tin can hockey See **hockey** n[1] **1**

tin can willie See **tin can alley 3**

tin cloth(es) (or coat) See **tin pants**

tincy See **tinesy**

tin dog n [Cf *AND tin dog* (at *dog* n.[1] 2.d) 1924 →; also *DCan tin dog* 1953] **esp NW**

An improvised noisemaker used to drive sheep; see quots.

1968 Adams *Western Words* 326, *Tin dogs*—A sheepherder's string of empty tin cans on a wire, they can make a frightening noise and are used to get sheep moving when they balk at something. **1978** Doig *This House* 201 **MT** (as of c1955), I had made, each for Grandma and for myself, a noisemaker called a *tin dog*—a ring of baling wire with half a dozen empty evaporated milk cans threaded on so that it could be shaken, tambourine-like, into a clattering din. **1992** Attebery *Sheep* 5 **swID, eOR,** At the end of the band came a herder, probably carrying a "tin dog" and accompanied by real ones.

tinesy adj |ˈtaɪn(t)si| Also rarely *tintchy* Also sp *tincy, tinsey, tin(t)sy, toncey* [Prob *tiny* infl by dimin suff *-sy;* cf **teensy**] **chiefly Sth, S Midl** Cf **tee-nincy, tee-tinsy**

Very tiny—also used as a nickname; freq in combs *teensy-tinesy, tinsy-winsy* and varr.

1851 Gregory *Bertie* 201 **neNC,** "Tinsey, bring me a coal of fire." "Ya-a-s, maussa." **1870** Walworth *Forgiven* 176 **Sth** [Black], Dr. Tilman's been lovin' our Missy ever since she's a little tinsy, winsy gal. **1905** *DN* 3.98 **nwAR,** *Tintsy* ['taɪntsɪ]. . . Tiny. 'O, what a tintsy baby.' 'Little bit of a tintsy baby'—addressed to a two-year-old child to make him ashamed of something babyish. Common. *Tintsy-wintsy* ['taɪntsɪ-ˈwaɪntsɪ]. . . Minute, tiny. 'The Texas fever tick's a tintsy-wintsy bug.' Common. **1909** *DN* 3.380 **eAL, wGA,** *Tincy* ['taɪnsɪ]. *Ibid* 382 **eAL, wGA,** *Tintsy(-wintsy)* ['taɪntsɪ-ˈwaɪntsɪ]. . . Very small, tiny. . . *Tintchy* and *teenchy* are also commonly heard. **1909** *Eve. News* (Ada OK) 15 Jan 1/5, [Despite] Ada's little tinsey name, maidenly modesty and limited political influence, it became a fact to be reckoned with. **1936** *AmSp* 11.276 **eTN,** *Tinsey.* Tiny or small. 'She is a tinsey bantling.' **1936** Morehouse *Rain on Just* 13 **NC,** Even for nine Dolly was uncommon tinsy. **1943** in **1944** *ADD* **NC,** ['taɪntsɪ]. **1955** [see **tee-tinsy**]. **1965–70** *DARE* (Qu. LL1, *Something very small: "I only took a _____ one."*) Inf **NC**61, Teensy-tinesy ['taɪnsɪ]; **PA**50, Tinsy [no transcr]; (Qu. LL3b, *Shrunk, dried up: "He's a little _____ old man."*) Infs **IL**138, **MS**30, 80, **TN**30, 61, 66, Tinesy; **MS**88, Tinesy-weensy. **2003** in **2004** *DARE* File—Internet **NC,** Having seen a snapping turtle grow from a tintsy wintsy quarter size, to the dimensions of a football in a year. *Ibid* **NYC,** If you go in with . . a tinsy bit of polish, you will be treated accordingly. *Ibid* **CA,** There's usually some sort of teensy tinsy symbol to indicate that it's now pm. *Ibid* **TX,** You might be a teensy tinsey bit addicted to exercise! *Ibid* **Ozarks,** Perhaps now

the Toy Fairy will allow me to locate the teensy tinesy piece. **2004** *Ashland Daily Tidings Online Ed.* (OR) 1 Sept (Internet), But, couldn't one tinsy, winsy little hour be given to the award-winning . . reporting of "Democracy Now!"

ting See **thing**

ting-a-ling n [Echoic] **esp LA**

In music: a triangle.

1941 Writers' Program *Guide LA* 93, At the genuine *fais-dodo* the music of the fiddle, the accordion, and the triangle (sometimes called the "ting-a-ling") is always featured. **1982** Heat Moon *Blue Highways* 112 **LA,** Inside, under dim halos of yellow bug lights, an accordion (the heart of a Cajun band), a fiddle, guitar, and ting-a-ling (triangle) cranked out chanky-chank. **2005** *DARE* File—Internet **LA,** Their music blends the tones of French violin, Spanish guitar, ("tity fer" or "ting-a-ling") triangle, and German accordion.

tingle bone n Also *tingling bone*

1968 *DARE* (Qu. X33, *The place in the elbow that gives you a strange feeling if you hit it against something*) Inf **VA**24, Tingle bone—some call it; **NC**55, Tingling bone.

tingle-tongue See **tickle-tongue**

tingling bone See **tingle bone**

ting-tang n [See quot]

Either the **horned grebe** or the **red-necked grebe.**

1902 Job *Among Water-Fowl* 39 **NEng,** I was surprised to find that I had secured, not a Duck, but a Horned Grebe. . . More often, under similar circumstances, it has been the large fellow [=Holboell's grebe]—"Ting-tang," as the gunners name it—that I have observed. **1955** MA Audubon Soc. *Bulletin* 39.309, *Holboell's Grebe* [=*Podiceps grisegena*]. . . Ting-tang (New England. In Scotch and in dialectic British, this word may be applied to anything inferior; it may refer to the grebe's inedibility; on the other hand, the term may be a facetious reply to the question, "What's that?" "Oh! a Ting-tang.") *Ibid* 310, *Horned Grebe.* . . Ting-tang (Mass.)

tin hat See **tin pants**

tin Henry See **Henry B1**

tin horn n **esp TX, OK**

A metal culvert.

1959 in **2005** (acc) Lexis–Nexis Legal Research *State Case Law: OK* (Internet), He said they sold all kinds of building materials, road supplies, grader blades, tin horns, lumber and gravel. **1964** in **2006** (acc) *Ibid: MO,* Since then he had made some minor repairs, including the installation of a "tin horn" (we don't know what that is) and the graveling or regraveling of the driveways. **1965** *DARE* FW Addit **OK,** Tin horn—a culvert pipe, generally of galvanized metal, used to connect two ditches separated by a driveway, etc. **1996** in **2005** (acc) Lexis–Nexis Legal Research *State Case Law: AR* (Internet), Access to the home was gained by a circular driveway off a tin-horn. **2003** *Clinton Daily News* (OK) 17 May (Internet), Workers removed the 40-foot-long culvert. . . "Once we got the crane there and got it set up and figured out how to lift the tinhorn, I think it went real well." **2005** *DARE* File—Internet **TX,** This letter is a reminder . . to have headers or retainers installed on each end of a culvert (tinhorn).

tin horning See **horning** n 1

tink See **think**

tinker n

1 See **tinker mackerel.**

2 A **silversides 1** (here: *Menidia notata*).

1890 *Century Dict.* 5635, *Silversides.* . . The most abundant species along the coast of the United States is *Menidia notata*, also called . . *tinker.*

3 See **tinker loon.**

tinkerbell n

A **wild columbine** (here: *Aquilegia canadensis*).

1980 *Our Smokies Heritage* 3.153 **eTN,** [My father] told them the flower names that local people used, such as ivy for laurel, tinkerbell for columbine and so forth. **1983** Patterson *Spring Wildflower* 18 (Montgomery–Hall *Dict. Smoky Mt. Engl.*) **wNC, eTN,** Lucinda and her late husband Earnest, hiked local trails, gathering specimens like "Tinker

Bell", "Doll's Eye", "Dog Hobble", "Fairy Wand", and "Black-Eyed Trillium".

tinker loon n   Also *tinker*   Cf **loon 2**
=horned grebe.

1877 Bartlett *Americanisms* 799, *Water-Witch.* . . A name applied to the whole family of grebes. They are also called *Hell-divers* and *Tinker-loons.* **1884** Newport Nat. Hist. Soc. *Proc. 1883–84* 43 **RI,** Great Loon, Red-necked Loon, Tinker Loon, Pied-bill Grebe, Red-necked Grebe, [etc]. **1888** Newport Nat. Hist. Soc. *Proc. 1887–88* 17 **RI,** In the grebe family, there are three varieties in this vicinity, namely, the American Red-necked Grebe, which is very rare; the Horned Grebe (locally called the Tinker), and the Pied Grebe or Dabchick. **1899** Howe–Sturtevant *Birds RI* 25, *Horned Grebe.* . . *Tinker Loon, Tinker.* . . It is without doubt our most common Grebe. [**1996** *Cliff Is. Seagull* (ME) 44.1.4, Three quarters of a century ago John Coyle and I used to go sailing. We went in his family's Friend Sloop . . "Tinker Loon" so when John offered to take me sailing recently I was delighted.]

tinker mackerel n   Also *tinker*   **chiefly NEng** Cf **blink** n², **spike 1**

A small or young **mackerel 1:** either *Scomber scombrus* or **chub mackerel.**

1848 Bartlett *Americanisms* 356, *Tinker.* Small mackerel. New England. **1856** in 1884 Goode *Fisheries U.S.* 1.298, Fish of this size [= 6.5–7 inches long] . . are the 'Tinkers,' two years old, and the year after they return to us as the second size, three years old. . . The mackerel . . are denominated as follows: Large ones, second size, "Tinkers," and "Blinks." **1873** U.S. Bur. Fisheries *Rept. for 1871 & 1872* 184 **NEng,** [He] had a number of tinker-mackerel. . . He thought they belonged to a different race from the round mackerel. **1902** Jordan–Evermann *Amer. Fishes* 275, Small mackerel are known among fishermen as . . "tinkers." . . Tinkers are under 9 inches long and are supposed to be about 2 years old. *Ibid* 276, Chub Mackerel; Tinker Mackerel—*Scomber japonicus.* . . This mackerel is widely distributed, occurring in both the Atlantic and Pacific. **1904** *DN* 2.428 **Cape Cod MA** (as of a1857), *Tinker.* . . An undersized mackerel. **1928** Beston *Outermost House* 206 **Cape Cod MA,** I occasionally see birds flying bow-down with tinker mackerel. **1965** *PADS* 43.16 **seMA,** Fish common in this area . . tinker mackerel [1 of 9 infs]. **1968–69** *DARE* (Qu. P2, . . *Kinds of saltwater fish caught around here . . good to eat*) Inf **RI17,** Tinker mackerel—small; (Qu. P14, . . *Commercial fishing . . what do the fishermen go out after?*) Inf **CT14,** Tinker mackerel. **2000** *DARE* File—Internet **Cape Cod MA,** *Preserved Tinker Mackerel.* . . For each jar of preserved fish: 7 to 8 tinker mackerel. . . The preserved tinkers can stay on the shelf for months.

tinker's penny n

A **Saint-John's-wort** (here: *Hypericum anagalloides*) native to the western US.

1925 Jepson *Manual Plants CA* 637, *H[ypericum] anagalloides.* . . *Tinkers Penny.* . . Springy places and streamlets in the hills and mountains, almost throughout Cal. **1937** St. John *Flora SE WA & ID* 258, *Tinker's Penny.* . . Prostrate and mat-forming or ascending. **1966** *DARE* FW Addit **WA10,** Tinker's penny—a *Hypericum* of Washington. A little shrubly [sic] plant—not noxious. **1979** Spellenberg *Audubon Guide N. Amer. Wildflowers W. Region* 542, Tinker's Penny (*Hypericum anagalloides*). **2001** (acc) CA Acad. Sci. *CA Wildflowers* (Internet), If a ground cover is literally supposed to cover the ground, then Tinker's Penny is a prime example.

tinker's weed n   Also *tinker weed*   Cf **Doctor Tinker's weed**

A **horse gentian,** usu *Triosteum perfoliatum.*

[**1691** Plukenet *Phytographia* pl. 104, Periclymenum herbaceum rectum Virginianum Dr. Tinkars weed ibi vulgo vocatum.] **1808** *Med. Repository* 5.130, *Catalogue of Plants collected at Plandome, on Long Island.* . . Triosteum perfoliatum . . fever-root, or tinker's-weed. **1830** Rafinesque *Med. Flora* 2.269, Triosteum perfoliatum . . *Tinker weed.* . . Root purgative, emetic, diuretic, tonic, &c. . . *Tr. angustifolium* . . is equivalent. **1892** (1974) Millspaugh *Amer. Med. Plants* 74–1, *Triosteum perfoliatum.* . . Tinker weed. [*Ibid* 74–2, It was in all probability the Southern species *T. angustifolium* . . that was principally used as an emetic in earlier days, and this is doubtless the plant sent to Pluckenet as *Dr. Tinker's Weed.*] **1910** Graves *Flowering Plants* 367 **CT,** *Triosteum perfoliatum.* . . Tinker's Weed. . . Frequent in dry fields and copses in the shore towns. . . Medicinal. **1961** Smith *MI Wildflowers* 363, *Tinker's-weed—Triosteum perfoliatum.* . . Coarse, hairy perennial . . ; globose drupe superficially resembling a small, hard tomato. **1996** in 2001

DARE File—Internet **LA,** *Triosteum angustifolium*—yellowleaf tinker's-weed. . . *Triosteum perfoliatum*—perfoliate tinker's-weed.

tinky n   Cf **pinkletink**

A **spring peeper.**

1970 *DARE* (Qu. P21, *Small frogs that sing or chirp loudly in spring*) Inf **VA75,** Tinkies—in early spring.

tinmouth n   Also *tin perch*   Cf **papermouth**
=crappie.

1887 Goode *Amer. Fishes* 71, *Pomoxys* [sic] *annularis.* . . has other names of local application as "Tin Mouth," "Bridge Perch," [etc]. **1902** Jordan–Evermann *Amer. Fishes* 334 **nIN, IL,** The crappie. . . is called . . tin-mouth or paper-mouth in northern Indiana and Illinois. **1933** LA Dept. of Conserv. *Fishes* 333, This species[*] [=*Pomoxis annularis*] popularity is very well attested by the variety of names it has been given. . . They are . . Crappie, . . Tinmouth, Tin Perch, White Crappie [etc]. **1938** Schrenkeisen *Field Book Fishes* 259, *Pomoxis annularis.* . . Common names. . . Tin Perch; . . Tinmouth. . . *Pomoxis sparoides* [=*P. nigromaculatus*] . . is a very similar species generally frequenting colder, clear water. . . These two species are often confused, and various common names are applicable to both.

tin-panning n
=horning n 1.

[**1885** *South Fla. Sentinel* (Orlando) 22 July 1/6 (*DAE*), The parties were tin-panned Monday night.] c**1938** in Lib. of Congress *Amer. Memory: WPA Life Hist.* (Internet) **Bronx NYC,** I remember the 'tin-pannings' at weddings. The boys with their pans would make a great racket until someone came out and gave them money for a treat, or else invited them into the house for refreshments. **1949** Kurath *Word Geog.* 79 **MD,** *Serenade.* . . The serenading of newlyweds. . . Regional and local terms are numerous. . . *tin-panning* in Maryland on both sides of the Bay (one of the few expressions confined to Maryland). **1966–68** *DARE* (Qu. AA18, . . *A noisy neighborhood celebration after a wedding, where the married couple is expected to give a treat*) Inf **FL2,** Tin-panning; **NY43,** Tin-panning [FW sugg]. **1971** Wood *Vocab. Change* 302 **Sth,** 36 [of approx 1000 total infs] Tin panning.

tin pants n pl   **chiefly Pacific NW**

Among loggers: water-repellent trousers of heavy fabric; similarly nouns *tin cloth(es), ~ coat, ~ hat.*

1911 *Pacific Mth.* Feb 190, The tin pants, which were quite popular with everybody, were made of heavy, dark brown duck, thoroughly soaked with a waxy substance, probably paraffine, which rendered them absolutely waterproof and as stiff as stovepipe. **1938** *MN Hist.* 19.197, Once in the new forest, he discarded his husky woolens and took on different attire—tin pants and tin coats to keep out the ever pouring rain. **1940** Writers' Program *Oregon* 371, Loggers . . are identified by their chewing tobacco and "snoose" (snuff), by their boots and "tin pants" (water-proofed canvas trousers cut short or "stagged"). **1941** Writers' Program *Guide WA* 345 **cnWA,** The loggers are colorful in their woods garb: mackinaws and waist overalls, "stagged" at the boot tops; oilskins and tarpaulin trousers, or "tin pants." **1950** *Western Folkl.* 9.120 **nwOR** [Logger speech], *Tin clothes.* Water-proofed clothing made of heavy cotton drill. **1956** *AmSp* 31.152 **nwCA** [Logger lingo], *Tin pants.* . . Heavy canvas trousers which loggers coat with paraffin during the rainy season. **1967** *DARE* (Qu. W4, . . *Men's coats or jackets for work and outdoor wear*) Inf **OR1,** Tin coat—logging term. **1968** *Intermountain Observer* (Boise ID) 27 Jan 11/3, Tin Coats and Pants. **1968** Adams *Western Words* 326, *Tin hat*—A logger's water-repellent hat. **2009** *DARE* File—Internet [Filson Website] **WA,** *Double Tin Pants*—The toughest of the tough. . . Double layer of Oil Finish Tin Cloth from waist to knee on front and back of legs.

tin perch   See **tinmouth**

tin plant n

A small composite plant (*Acourtia runcinata*) native to Texas.

1942 TX Ag. Exper. Sta. College Sta. *Bulletin* 609.134, *Perezia runcinata.* Devil's Shaving Brush, Tin Plant. A perennial plant up to 10 inches high that produces a rosette of rough, dark green, thistle-like leaves and thistle-like, rosy-lavender flowers.

tin rooster n   Also *metal rooster*

1950 *WELS* (Joking names for an alarm clock) 1 Inf, **csWI,** Rarely "metal rooster," and I don't remember where. **1953** *PADS* 20.35, Joking names for an alarm clock: tin rooster [etc]. **2003** *DARE* File **csWI** (as of 1930s), Tin rooster. . . Alarm clock. That was in Sauk

County, too, and . . it was very commonly used. "I forgot to set the tin rooster last night."

tinsey, tinsy(-winsy), tintchy   See **tinesy**

tinted adj   [Prob folk-etym for *tainted*]

[**1925** *DN* 5.345 **Nfld**, *Tint*, v.t. Taint.]   **1967–69** *DARE* (Qu. H46, *When meat begins to go bad, so that you can't eat it . . it's _____*) Inf **NY**45, 75, Tinted; spoiled; (Qu. H58, *Milk that's just beginning to become sour*) Inf **NY**75, Tinted; (Qu. K14, *Milk that has a taste from something the cow ate in the pasture . . "That milk is _____."*) Infs **IN**69, **OR**4, Tinted; tainted; **IN**63, Tainted; tinted; **NJ**1, **TN**42, Tinted.

tinter board   See **teenter (board)**

tin tin n   Also *tin, tin tin come in*   Cf **forfeit** n, **Uncle Tom 2**

A game similar to **forfeits**; see quots.

1898 *McClure's Mag.* Aug 350, A little later the games began. First, there was "forfeits." Then came "tin-tin." "Clap in and clap out," followed.   **1932** Farrell *Young Lonigan* 166 **Chicago IL** (as of 1916), That evening they played tin-tin with the girls, and Studs kissed Lucy.   **1936** (1972) Ise *Sod & Stubble* 252 **KS** (as of c1890s), Then they played "Tin Tin."   **1937** Gardner *Folkl. Schoharie* 249 **NY**, *Tin Tin. . .* The players sit down in a circle. . . The one who is "it" asks: "Do you want to buy any tin?"   **1938** in Lib. of Congress *Amer. Memory: WPA Life Hist.* (Internet) **NE** (as of c1890s), We played such games as . . "Tin, Tin, Come in."   **1945** Boyd *Hdbk. Games* 14, *Tin*—This is a game for boys. The tinman goes around among the players and says to each in turn, "How many pounds of tin do you want?" . . The tinman goes around again, saying, "Where's the money for my tin?" and collects a forfeit from each. He then calls out any one of the players and holds a forfeit behind him saying, "How many pounds of tin behind your back?" whereupon that player guesses the name of the owner. If his guess is correct, the guesser gives the owner as many "punches" as he bought pounds of tin. If it is not correct, the owner of the forfeit runs to a goal previously agreed upon, and the guesser tries to catch him. If he catches him, the tinman throws the forfeit as far as he can, and the owner goes and gets it. If . . he gets to the goal without being tagged, the tinman hands him the forfeit. This is repeated until all forfeits are redeemed.   **1953** Brewster *Amer. Nonsinging Games* 23 **IN**, *Forfeit Games. . . Tin-Tin. . .* All the players except one are seated. . . The latter player, carrying a stick or a cane, goes to each of the others in turn, tapping vigorously on the floor in front of him and calling, "Tin-tin, do you want to buy some tin?" The player who is addressed replies, "Yes, I want enough to make a laundry tub (bucket, dipper, etc.)." After the peddler has completed his sale, he says to each of the other players, "Now, when I come back to get my pay for this tin, you must neither smile nor grin, but keep saying (name of the boy's or girl's sweetheart)." He soon makes his reappearance and, going to the first player, announces, "I've come to get the pay for my tin." The other must then reply, "Tom Jones," "Sally Brown," or whatever other name was assigned. Then follow questions (the more ridiculous the better). . . If a player laughs while being questioned, he must pay a forfeit.   **1957** *Sat. Eve. Post Letters* **WI**, *Tin tin. . .* If a person laughs he must give a forfeit; **ceWI** (as of 1890s), *Tin tin*—Parlor game; better known as *forfeits*; **IL**, *Tin tin*; **MI**, *Tin tin come in.*

Tiny Tim n

A **pricklyleaf** (here: *Thymophylla aurea, T. pentachaeta,* or *T. tenuiloba*).

1915 (1926) Armstrong–Thornber *Western Wild Flowers* 556 **AZ**, *Tiny Tim—Hymenathèrum Hartwègi* [=*Thymophylla pentachaeta*]. . . A neat little evergreen, shrubby plant, only about three inches high. . . The flowers are three-eighths of an inch across . . with bright yellow rays and deeper yellow centers.   **1936** Whitehouse *TX Flowers* 184, *Tiny Tim . . (Thymophylla polychaeta* [=*T. aurea*]). . . There is something appealing about the tiny Tim, as the name would indicate. . . *Tiny Tim (Thymophylla pentachaeta). . .* The flower heads are about half an inch broad. Tiny Tim ranges from Texas to Arizona and Mexico.   **1942** *TX Ag. Exper. Sta. College Sta. Bulletin* 609.128 **TX**, *Dyssodia (Thymophylla) tenuiloba.* Tiny Tim. Small annual plants that produce dark green, finely cut foliage having a carrot-like odor.   **1965** Teale *Wandering Through Winter* 150, All across Texas, a host of . . picturesque names have been bestowed on the wild plants of the state. They run from angel's trumpet, . . [to] tiny Tim . . and widow's tears.   **1995** Richardson *Plants Rio Grande* 301, *Thymophylla Lag.* Tiny Tim—Annual or short-lived rounded perennial herbs to ca 20 cm tall.

tiny trumpet n

A **gilia** (here: *Collomia linearis*).

1926 (1955) Clements *Flowers* 26 **Rocky Mts**, *Tiny Trumpet Collomia*

linearis. . . They come into bloom in the spring and blossom throughout the summer.   **1963** Craighead *Rocky Mt. Wildflowers* 150, *Collomia linearis. . .* Tiny Trumpet. . . The flowers are dark to light pink, tubular, and ¼–½ in. long.   **2001** *DARE* File—Internet **cID**, *Collomia linearis,* Tiny trumpet, or narrow-leaf collomia.

tip n[1]

=**foothold**.

1889 *Century Dict.* 2311, *Foothold. . .* A kind of light india-rubber overshoe, leaving the heel unprotected; a sandal. Sometimes called *tip*.   **1894** (1899) Ford *Peter Stirling* 347 **NYC**, "It's very different," he was told. "I put on tips and a mackintosh. You didn't put on anything. And it was pouring torrents."

tip n[2]

See quot.

1967 *DARE* (Qu. EE11, . . *Ball games*) Inf **MI**49, Tip—a soft ball, maybe made of yarn, pitcher would toss it, batter hit it with his hand; there were three bases and home, just like baseball.

tip v   [*OED2 tip* v.[1] 1819 →]   **scattered, but chiefly Sth, S Midl, TX**   See Map   *esp freq among Black speakers*

Also with adv: To tiptoe; to walk or move, esp lightly or furtively; also fig.

1850 *Eclectic Mag.* 10.259 **VA**, I used to tip along on the points of my toes like a French dancer.   **1866** Cooke *Surry* 37 **VA**, I remembered the faint footfalls on the floor of my chamber, as though delicate feet without slippers were tipping along.   **1883** (1971) Harris *Nights with Remus* 149 **GA** [Black], He fine Miss Motts dar, en he tipped in, ole Brer Rabbit did, en he galanted 'roun' 'mungs um.   **1912** Green *VA Folk-Speech* 449, *Tipping, pres. part.* Moving noisily about: "She went tipping about on the point of her toes."   **1931** (1991) Hughes–Hurston *Mule Bone* 149 **cFL** [Black], Well, I'm not going tippin' down no railroad track like a Maltese cat.   **1934** *AmSp* 9.27 [Prison terms; Black], *Tipping grand.* Walking fast; running; leaving quickly.   **1942** (1971) Campbell *Cloud-Walking* 57 **seKY**, He tipped around looking at the doctor-books on the shelves in Doc's front house.   **1946** *AmSp* 21.307 **VT**, *Tipping* ('I saw you come tipping along!'). Possibly for 'tiptoeing.'   **1959** Ruark *Poor No More* 329 **Sth**, She follows me foot to foot. I can't hardly go to the bathroom without her tippin' behind me.   **1965–70** *DARE* (Qu. Y26a, *To walk very quietly: "She came _____ to the baby's bed."*) 71 Infs, **scattered, but chiefly Sth, S Midl, TX**, Tipping; **TX**4, Tipping along; **SC**10, Tipping in; (Qu. Y26b, *To walk very quietly: "The children filled their pockets and _____ out the back way."*) 30 Infs, **chiefly Sth, S Midl**, Tipped; **SC**10, Tip; (Qu. Y29a, *To 'go out' a great deal, not to stay at home much: "She's always _____."*) Inf **NY**240, Tipping; (Qu. BB2, *If a person is careful not to put much weight on his injured leg, you might say he was _____ that leg*) Inf **VA**46, Tipping on; (Qu. II14, *To pay a short visit: "Last night our new neighbors _____."*) Inf **NY**238, Tipped over. [41 of 82 total Infs Black, 53 female]   **1968** *DARE* Tape **GA**25, A real nice-looking young woman walked out and come tipping across the floor.   **1970** *Current Slang* 5.2.13 [Black univ student slang], *Tip. . .* To leave. . . To sneak in or out to meet someone.   **1976** Ryland *Richmond Co. VA* 378, *Tipping*—tiptoeing.   **1986** Pederson *LAGS Concordance,* 1 inf, **nwGA**, Tipping (a)round—of a rabbit. [Inf Black]   **1988** Naylor *Mama Day* 113 **SC, GA coasts** [Black], Remember when Baby Girl could barely tip. . . And we had to hold her by the scruff of the neck to keep her from falling over.   **1998** *DARE* File **MS** [Black], Words I have heard from Blacks in the Mississippi Delta—tip—to walk quietly (but not on tiptoes).

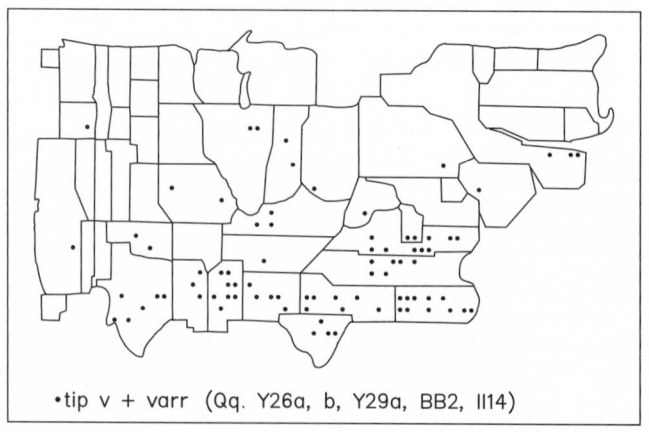

•*tip* v + varr (Qq. Y26a, b, Y29a, BB2, II14)

tip intj   Also *tippy*   Cf **kip,** *DS* K79

Used as a call to chickens.

    1973 Allen *LAUM* 1.267 **Upper MW** (as of c1950), Calls to chickens at feeding. . . *tip* [1 inf, **MN**]; *tippy* [2 infs, **IA, ND**].   **1981** *PADS* 67.31 **Mesabi Iron Range MN,** *Calls to chickens.* . . Infrequent responses on the Range are *tip* . . used by a Swedish-Finn informant.

tipcart n   **NEng, esp MA**

A cart having a body that tips backward in order to empty its contents.

    1855 Burnham *Hist. Hen Fever* 316 **MA,** Defunct Hucksters, in a tip-cart.   **1867** *Scientific Amer.* 16.367 **ME,** [Patent application:] *Tip-Cart Body Fastening.*   **1890** *Atlantic Mth.* 66.117 **MA,** The next bony animal that the reader sees pulling a tip-cart may be a once proud and petted fire horse.   **1907** *DN* 3.202 **seNH,** *Tip-cart.* . . Dump cart; a cart for hauling earth, manure, etc., so made that the body may be detached from the forward wheels and tipped back, thus emptying the load.   **1919** (1921) Lowell *Pictures* 88 **MA,** Why does the clanking of a tip-cart / In the road / Make me so sad?   **1931–33** *LANE Worksheets* **MA,** Tip cart—cart for hauling manure.   **1967–70** *DARE* (Qu. N40a, . . *Sleighs . . for hauling loads*) Inf **MA76,** One-horse tipcart; (Qu. N41a, . . *Horse-drawn vehicles . . to carry people*) Inf **MA72,** Tipcart; (Qu. N41b, *Horse-drawn vehicles to carry heavy loads*) Inf **MA74,** Tipcart; (Qu. U6) Inf **MA50,** Tipcart.   **1969** *DARE* Tape **MA68,** Tipcart was one of two wheels. . . You could lift up the front of it and dump the stuff out of it.   **1976** *Kennebec Jrl.* (Augusta ME) 2 June 19/5, [Advt:] Bolen's rubber tired tip cart . . $50.00.   **2005** *DARE* File **ceMA,** The only distinct knowledge I have of "tipcart" is that our next door neighbor in Lincoln from 1964–1975 . . had one. . . After he died, it was kept on our place for a while, and we used it as a farm stand.

tipcat n   Also *tippy(-cat)*   [*OED2* tip-cat 1801 → (in the sense **cat** n 3b 1676 →)]   Cf **catty** n[1] 1, **kitty** n 4, *DS* EE10

=cat n 3a; hence *tippy* **=cat** n 3b.

    1866 *Play Ground Games for Boys* 117, Tip Cat. . . is a dangerous game. . . It is played with a club resembling a ruler. Its name is derived from a piece of wood called a "Cat," of about six inches in length. . . [W]hen the cat is laid upon the ground, the player with his stick tips it at one end . . high enough for him to strike it as it falls.   **1869** *Atlantic Mth.* 23.282 **NYC,** Everywhere . . the boy may be seen engaged in the winsome game called "tip-cat," . . he tips featly from the ground the odious, conical chunk of wood from which the pastime derives its name.   **1899** Champlin–Bostwick *Young Folks' Games* 727, Tip-cat.   **1906** Lovett *Old Boston Boys* 46, "Tip-cat" was also a popular game. One occasionally sees it played to-day, but not to the extent that it was then. Not content with small soft wood cats, two or three inches in length, we made them of a section of broom handle and about six or eight inches long, using the remainder of the handle for the cat-stick.   **1917** Driggs *Live Lang.* 124, *Spring Sports.* . . These are a few of the old outdoor games and sports: . . Two-old-cat . . Townball . . Rounders . . Tippy Cat.   **1940** Harbin *Fun Encycl.* 788, *Tip cat.*   **1950** *WELS Suppl.* **ceWI,** *Tippy-cat*—game played with long stick and a short stick.   **1953** Brewster *Amer. Nonsinging Games* 160 **IN,** *Tippy.* . . Equipment needed consists of the "tippy" and a paddle or bat for each of the players. The "tippy" is a wooden block an inch thick, about four inches long, and cone-shaped at each end.   **1957** *Sat. Eve. Post Letters* **MI,** I remember the boys playing a game with 2 pieces of wood—They'd hit the end of the smaller with the bigger; this they called "Tippy."   **1986** Pederson *LAGS Concordance,* 1 inf, **cwFL,** Tippy or kitty—4″ sticks projected by striking.

tipover, fruit basket   See **fruit basket d**

tippet n   **Chesapeake Bay**   Cf **twitchet 1**

See quots.

    1968 *DARE* (Qu. K73, . . *Names . . for the rump of a cooked chicken*) Inf **MD43,** Tippet ['tɪpɪt].   **1983** *DARE* File **eVA,** Have you come across "twitchet" and "tippet" for the female genital organ? I heard these words on Tangier all the time in my younger days.   **1996** Horton *Island Out of Time* 106 **Smith Is. MD,** Ma, she joked about it. Ain't you the boss tippet now, she said. [Footnote:] Tippet—a risqué way of saying queen bee; tippet is a local name for the genital area of a female crab.

tippety-bounce n   Cf *DS* EE31

    1933 Kurath in *AmSp* 8.2.18 **Block Is. NY,** Block Island has its own term [for *seesaw*], *tippety-bounce,* which was offered independently by three informants in different parts of the island. [*DARE* Ed: *LANE* Map 577 shows four infs from Block Island using the term.]

tippy n[1]   See **tipcat**

tippy n[2]   Cf **nibby** n[1], **ribbly**

The end piece of a loaf of bread.

    1989 *NADS Letters* **nDE,** My wife and I discovered that we used different words for the end slice of a loaf of bread. She used the word "heel", while I used the word "tippy" (as did the rest of my family).

tippy intj   See **tip** intj

tippy-and-over n   Cf **tippy-i-over**

=Antony-over A.

    1967 *DARE* (Qu. EE22, . . *The game in which they throw a ball over a building . . to a player on the other side*) Inf **PA26,** Tippy-and-over.

tippy-cat   See **tipcat**

tippy-i-over exclam   Cf **tilly-i-over, tippy-and-over**

=Antony-over B.

    1967 *DARE* (Qu. EE23a, *In the game of andy-over . . what . . you call out when you throw the ball*) Inf **PA26,** Tippy-i-over.

tippy-up n   Also *tip-up*   Cf **tipcat**

A ball batted up for others to catch; an informal game in which one player bats balls for other players to catch.

    1897 *KS Univ. Qrly.* (ser B) 6.93, Tippy up: a ball knocked up easily to be caught.   **1917** Butler *Dominie Dean* 227 **eIA,** Once a day or so Roger came in from the sandy ball ground, weighed a load of coal, jotted down the figures and went back to his "tippy-up" game.   **1955** Martin *Sojourn* 77 **ND,** We played tippy-up (as we called it, one batting the ball high in the air and the others catching it).   **1957** *Sat. Eve. Post Letters* **sIN** (as of c1910), If there was an acute shortage of boys and you had to play with the girls the games were usually London Bridge, Whoopee hide, or Tippy-Up. This last was like knocking out flies except a small rubber ball was hit up in the air with a paddle.   **1966–68** *DARE* (Qu. EE11, *Bat-and-ball games for just a few players [when there aren't enough for a regular game]*) Infs **IN30, WI66,** Tippy-up; **FL6,** Tip-up—with a flat bat; you hit it up to the others and whoever caught [it] would be batter.

tipsinna n   Also *tipsin(ah), tipsini*

An **Indian breadroot** (here: *Pediomelum esculentum*).

    1853 *Planters' Banner* (Franklin LA) 24 Mar 3/2 **MN,** Turnips . . grow wild and are much used by the Indians for food. One . . [is] named, the *tipsinna.*   **1859** (1968) Bartlett *Americanisms* 481, Tipsinah. The wild prairie turnip, used as food by the North-western Indians.   **1860** *Harper's New Mth. Mag.* 21.596 **ND,** An Indian had trudged along before us, digging with his tipsini-stick.   **1896** *Jrl. Amer. Folkl.* 9.186 **SD,** *Psoralea esculenta* [=*Pediomelum e.*] . . tipsin, Dakota tipsinah.   **1910** Hodge *Hdbk. Amer. Indians* 2.760, Tipsinah. . . This plant is also known as the Dakota turnip, and tipsinah is derived from *tipsinna,* its name in the Sioux language.   **1932** Vestal *Sitting Bull* 6, How savory the steaming soup in the kettle, the big wooden bowls of crisp white tipsin!   **1950** Stevens *ND Plants* 98, *Arisaema atrorubens* [=*A. triphyllum*]. . . Sometimes called Indian Turnip but should not be confused with Tipsin. *Ibid* 188, *Psoralea esculenta.* . . Tipsin. . . Frequent to common on prairie. The starchy root was a main food for the Indians.

tiptail n

=tip-up 1.

    1891 *Forest & Stream* 37.331 **swIA,** On these boggy bottoms is the home of these palatable and sprightly little grallatores known to our gunners as jack snipe, tiptail, yellow legs, etc.   **1897** Knight *List Birds ME* 50, *Spotted Sandpiper.* . . When on land it seems very uneasy and is constantly tipping, bowing, and teetering. From this habit it is locally known as Teeter-up, Tip-tail, Tip-up, etc.

tip-tap-toe n   Also *tip-tat-toe* [*EDD* at tip sb.[3] 9.(7) "the game of noughts and crosses"]

=tick-tack-toe 1 or **2.**

    1909 (1923) Bancroft *Games* 237, Tip Tap Toe. . . A circle is drawn on a slate or paper. . . This circle is intersected with straight lines, so that it is divided into a series of wedge-shaped spaces. . . In each of these spaces numbers are written in consecutive order. . . The one whose turn it is shuts his eyes, takes a pencil, circles it around over the diagram while he says the following verse:—"Tip, tap, toe, here we go,/ Three jolly sailor boys all in a row." At the close of the verse the player places the point of the pencil on the diagram. . . He then opens his eyes, and should the pencil have touched one of the numbered spaces he marks down to his score the number written in that space, and crosses out that figure on the diagram.   **1927** *WI Rapids Daily Tribune* (WI) 28 Oct 4/5, Here's a novel variation of the Tip, Tap, Toe or Three in a Row game.

1969 *DARE* (Qu. EE38a, *A game played with pencil and paper where the players try to get three X's or three O's in a row*) Inf **NY**200, Tip-tat-toe. **2006** *DARE* File—Internet **cnAL**, "Tip, Tap, Toe"—"Tip, Tap, Toe / Round I go. / Hit or miss / I stop at this." On the white board, draw a pizza shape circle. In each section, write a different sight word. Choose a child to come to the board. The child spins around twice with their eyes closed while saying the Tip, Tap, Toe rhyme. After spinning, he/she points to a word and reads it.

tip the icebox See **tap the icebox**

tip-top n

The tufted **titmouse** *(Baeolophus bicolor)*.

    1917 *Wilson Bulletin* 29.2.84 **KY**, *Baeolophus bicolor*. . . Tip-top.

tip-up n [See quots]

1 Any of var **sandpipers** noted for their frequent bobbing or teetering behavior, as the **least sandpiper, solitary sandpiper, spotted sandpiper,** and greater **yellowlegs 1.** Cf **teeter** n **1, 2, tilt-up 1, tiptail**

    1842 Thompson *Hist. VT* 1.105, *Solitary Tattler*. . . It is generally seen running along upon the shore, frequently stopping, and often nodding, or balancing its head and tail, and hence its vulgar appellation is *Tip-up.* **1848** Bartlett *Americanisms* 247, *Peet-Weet*. . the spotted Sandpiper. . , better known . . by the name of . . *Teeter* and *Tilt-up* or *Tip-up,* from its often repeated grotesque jerking motions. **1873** *Scribner's Mth.* 6.573, Of the sandpipers there are many varieties, . . the smallest of the species, commonly called the "tip-up," going up all the mountain-brooks and breeding in the sand along their banks. **1881** Hapgood–Roosevelt *Shore Birds* 13 **NEng**, The little solitary sandpiper, "tip up", is common here as in most other parts of the country. **1899** Howe–Sturtevant *Birds RI* 53, *Actitis macularia*. . . *Tip-up*. . . An abundant summer resident throughout the State. **1900** *Congressional Record* 30 Apr 33.6.4872/2 **NY**, The killdee and plover flew over the hills and the kingfisher and the little tip-up were seen upon the shores of the river. **1917** Eaton *Green Trails* 255 **MA**, It is like a sand bar, . . a playground for the sandpipers and the plovers. You may often come upon a flock of these birds . . running back and forth and bobbing their heads up and down. "Tip ups," some boys call them. **1923** U.S. Dept. Ag. *Misc. Circular* 13.60 **CA**, *Greater Yellowlegs*. . . *Vernacular Names*. . . *In local use*. . . Tip-up. **1949** Sprunt–Chamberlain *SC Bird Life* 228, *Spotted Sandpiper*. . . *Local Names:* Tip-up; Spotty. **1954** Sprunt *FL Bird Life* 174, *Eastern Solitary Sandpiper*. . . *Local Names:* Tip-up; Wood Sandpiper. **1956** MA Audubon Soc. *Bulletin* 40.17, *Spotted Sandpiper*. . . Tip-up (Universal). *Ibid* 19 **CT**, *Least Sandpiper*. . . Teeter, Tip-up. **1965–70** *DARE* (Qu. Q5, . . *Kinds of wild ducks*) Inf **MI**67, Tip-ups; **NY**231, Tip-up—small, long-legged, tip up as they walk, not duck but on lakeshores; (Qu. Q10, . . *Water birds and marsh birds*) Inf **MI**53, Tip-up is the sandpiper; **NY**10, Tip-up—walks around shore with tail end going up and down; **NY**231, 233, **PA**192, Tip-up(s); **OH**67, Tip-up—same as snipe; **PA**104, Snipe or sandpipers called tip-ups.

2 =**killdeer 1.**

    1951 *WELS Suppl.,* 1 Inf, **WI**, Killdeer = *Tip-Ups*—source unknown.

3 =**tilt 1.** **chiefly NEast** See Map

    1848 in 1850 Cooper *Rural Hours* 42 **NY**, The boys call these contrivances "tip-ups," from the bit of stick to which the line is attached, falling over when the fish bite. **1880** *Harper's New Mth. Mag.* 60.517 **NEng**, Yonder . . in the ice, we chopped our fishing holes, and with baited lines and tip-ups set, we waited. . . With eager eyes we watched the line play out, or saw the tip-up give the warning sign. **1926** *Daily Courier* (Connellsville PA) 30 Dec 10/3, Fishing through the ice. . . All you need to do is prepare half a dozen simple "tip-ups." **1938** *WI Rapids Daily Tribune* (WI) 27 Dec 5/3, The ice-fishing I loved in the good old days, was with "tip-ups". **1965–70** *DARE* (Qu. P13, . . *Ways of fishing . . besides the ordinary hook and line*) Infs **CT**10, **NH**4, Ice fishing with tip-ups; **NY**92, Tip-up; **MA**42, Tip-up—used for ice fishing—has a red flag on one end that goes up when a fish bites; **MA**58, Tip-up—for ice fishing; **NH**14, Tip-up—used in ice fishing; **NJ**41, Tip-up—a trigger-like device to lift fish up for ice fishing; **NY**52, Tip-ups—through the ice—has a flag on one end, line on other that works a gadget similar to a teeter-totter; **NY**75, Tip-up—through the ice; **NY**82, Tip-up—fishing through the ice; **NY**219, Tip-up—through the ice—when fish starts to "run" with hook, a flag comes up; **NY**207, Tip-up fishing—piece of wood with line and flag that's released when the fish bites. **1967** *WI Conserv. Bulletin* 32.1.12 **ceWI**, The styles and types of tip-ups and fish boxes stagger the imagination: underwater tip-ups, heated box tip-ups, tip-ups with mousetraps. . . If it's ever been made, and if it will signal a fish bite, you can bet it's been used on Winnebago. **1982** Stern-

berg *Fishing* 53, Tip-ups have a wooden frame, a flexible steel spring with a small flag on the end, and a reel that operates under water so it will not freeze up. When a fish grabs the bait, a trip mechanism releases the bent spring which pops up to display the flag. **2001** *Post-Std.* (Syracuse NY) 14 Nov 28/2, In Central New York. . . The following are some of the best places in the region to rig a tip-up this winter.

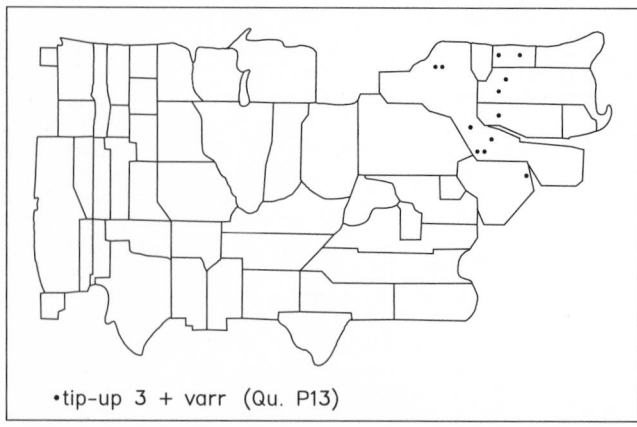

•tip-up 3 + varr (Qu. P13)

4 See **tippy-up.**

tip-up warbler n

The palm **warbler** *(Dendroica palmarum)*.

    1889 Ridgway *Ornith. IL* 1.154, *Palm Warbler*. Popular synonyms. Wagtail Warbler . . Tip-up Warbler. **1917** (1923) *Birds Amer.* 3.150, The Palm Warbler is the ever-tilting Warbler that comes into the Northern States in April. . . The tilting or waving of the tail up and down attracts the casual observer to the bird and it has given the names Tip-up Warbler and Yellow Tip-up to the bird.

tire v Usu |taɪ(ə)r, taɪə|; also **chiefly S Midl** |tar|; for addit varr see quots Similarly adjs *tar(re)d, taring, tord* Cf **fire A** Std senses, var forms.

    1792 in 1956 Eliason *Tarheel Talk* 319 **nw,cwNC**, *Tiring*—taring. **1861** in 1998 *Bone Rattler* 14.3.25 **wNC**, I am giting tard of riting. **1891** *DN* 1.156 **cNY**, [tard] < tired. **1923** (1946) Greer-Petrie *Angeline Steppin'* 35 **csKY**, He 'lowd if Mr. Seelback got tord fiddlin', he'd be glad to play fur 'em hisse'f. **1933** *AmSp* 8.1.32 **wTX**, I warshed this mornin' and arned this evenin'. . . I shore am tard. **1941** Faulkner *Men Working* 35 **MS**, Thought we might run over to The Lake tonight. . . If Stan ain't too tard. **1955** Roberts *S. from Hell-fer-Sartin* 37 **seKY**, Here, you dig a while. I'm tard. **c1960** *Wilson Coll.* **csKY**, Tire /tar/—n. or v. **1961** Kurath–McDavid *Pronc. Engl.* 122, Three different vowel phonemes are current in *wire, tired, fire*. . . The phoneme /ai/ . . (1) has general currency in the North, in the Hudson Valley with Metropolitan New York, and in East Jersey, (2) is nearly universal in the South . . , (3) predominates decidedly in Pennsylvania east of the Susquehanna . . , and (4) is rare in the South Midland, from West Virginia to the South Carolina line, though apparently preferred by cultured speakers. In Eastern New England, Metropolitan New York, and the Upper South—areas in which postvocalic /r/ does not occur—*wire, tired* are disyllabic /waiə, taiəd/; wherever the /r/ is preserved, these words are predominantly monosyllabic /wair, taird/, as in Western New England, Upstate New York, and Pennsylvania. In the piedmont of South Carolina and adjoining parts of Georgia . . *wire, tired* are often pronounced as monosyllabic . . phonemically /wai, taid/. . . It is important to note that in this area *wire, tired* do not rime with *car, tarred*. . . The phoneme /a/ . . occurs in *wire, tired* /war, tard/ throughout the Midland. . . In the South Midland . . it is nearly universal. . . The merging of /ai/ with /a/ before tautosyllabic /r/, which makes *fire, tired* homophonous with *far, tarred*, is a characteristic feature of Midland speech. **1966** *DARE* FW Addit swNC, *Tired* [tard]. **1981** Pederson *LAGS Basic Materials*, 4 infs, **seAL, cwMS, nwAR, ceTX**, [Proncs of the types [tˈaˑəd, tˈaˑə̣d]]; 1 inf, **csGA**, [tˈaᵊˑd, tˈaˑəd]; 1 inf, **cTN**, [tˈaˢəd, tʰaˬˑᵌˑd, tˈeɪd]; 1 inf, **ceAL**, [tˈaˑɚt]; 1 inf, **cnLA**, [tˈaᵋəd]; some say [tˈaˑɚd]; [1 inf, **nwAR**, Got a tired [tˈaˑɚd] on—facetious?] [*DARE* Ed: Infs selected based on pronc reference in *LAGS Concordance*.] **1990** Amory *Cat & Curmudgeon* 192 **eTX**, On the way to our first pasture I kept thinking about that East Texas accent. . . "tarred" for tired. **1999** Mason *Clear Springs* 21 **wKY**, I played jacks and Old Maid with a neighbor girl, but she made fun of the way I said "fire." I said "far." And I said "tard" for "tired." **2000** Shores *Tangier Is.* 172 **Chesapeake Bay**, They say "far" for *fire* and "tard" for *tired*. *Ibid* 184, Words like *wire, tire, tired,* and *fire* are pronounced as if one is hearing two syllables: "war-er," "tar-er," "[']tar-erd," and "far-er."

tire n   Usu |taɪ(ə)r, taɪə|; also **chiefly S Midl** |tɑr| Pronc-spp *ta(h)r, toir*

Std senses, var forms.

1940 *AmSp* 15.214 **TX**, Frequently I hear some Southerners, generally those of the lower social brackets, pronouncing *fire* . . and *tire* as if they were spelled *foir* . . and *toir.* **c1960** [see **tire** v]. **1970** *DARE* FW Addit **ceTN**, *Tire* [tɒ⁊]—for car or truck. **1976** Wolfram–Christian *Appalachian Speech* 65, In a number of varieties of English, . . items like *tire* . . may be pronounced something like *tayer* (phonetically [taᵎər] . .). In A[ppalachian] E[nglish]. . . *tire* . . may be pronounced more like *tahr.* . . Items like *tire* and *fire* are distinguished from *tar* and *far* by differences in the vowel. For one, the vowel of *tire* and *fire* is produced more front in the mouth. . . In addition, the vowel in *tire* and *fire* is usually of slightly longer duration. **1976** Garber *Mountain-ese* 91 **sAppalachians**, *Tar-iron* . . tire iron. **1982** Barrick *Coll.* **csPA**, *Tire*—pron. tar. **2000** Shores *Tangier Is.* 176 **Chesapeake Bay**, Words typically ending in "r" or "l" and preceded by the vowel of the word *die*, such as *wire* and *file*, have the "ah" sound of *father* resulting in "tar" for *tire* [etc].

tired as a dog   See **dog** n[1] **B17c**

tired blood n   Also *lazy blood*

Anemia; also fig.

1912 *Nashua Reporter* (IA) 7 Nov [9]/6 (newspaperarchive.com), [Advt:] *Tired Blood Exposes the Lungs.* . . The purpose of Tonitives for Tired Blood, is to . . help the blood to absorb more nutriment. **1936** *Monessen Daily Independent* (PA) 12 May 5/7, [Advt:] *Tired Blood—Spring Fever—Logy, Tired Feeling.* . . signs of iron-starved blood. **1953** *Indiana Eve. Gaz.* (PA) 23 Mar sec 2 1/1, [Advt:] After an illness you may feel weak and tired because the iron in your blood has been depleted. You may have iron poor, tired blood. . . iron deficiency anemia. **1968–70** *DARE* (Qu. BB5, *A general feeling of discomfort or illness that isn't any one place in particular*) Inf **WI**62, Tired blood [laughter]; **FL**51, Lazy blood [FW: used by Inf's grandmother]; (Qu. BB38, *When a person doesn't look healthy, or looks as if he hadn't been well for some time* . . *"He looks _____."*) Inf **LA**31, Looks like he's got tired blood. **1981** *Frederick Post* (MD) 5 Jan sec B 6/1, Women in the childbearing years need. . . more iron than the "older" person who is often advised to take an iron preparation for "tired blood." **1990** Cavender *Folk Med. Lexicon* 33 **csAppalachians**, *Tired blood*—a condition of fatigue or having no energy. **2004** *Post-Std.* (Syracuse NY) 19 June sec E 4/2, 'Salem's Lot' suffers from *tired blood*—The film lacks any emotional connection to the characters and has an absurd ending.

tiresome weed n

=**eelgrass 1.**

1894 *Jrl. Amer. Folkl.* 7.103 **eNJ**, *Zostera marina* . . , tiresome weed. [Footnote:] From the obstruction which it offers to the oars of boats.

tirty   See **thirty**

tissic(k)   See **phthisic**

tisswood n

1 =**red bay 1.**

1823 Vignoles *Observations Floridas* 88, In the more southern latitudes the torch tree is found, also the gum guiacum, . . sea grape, tiswood, &c. **1897** Sudworth *Arborescent Flora* 201, *Persia borbonia.* . . Tisswood.

2 also *tizwood:* =**silver bell 1.   chiefly wNC, eTN**

1897 Sudworth *Arborescent Flora* 323 **TN**, *Mohrodendron carolinum.* . . Tisswood. **1898** *Pop. Sci. Mth.* 53.428 **TN**, Among the indigenous trees are . . pecan, linden, spruce, dogwood, tiswood, etc. **1910** Guerrant *Galax Gatherers* 105 **cwNC**, I found a rare tree of most beautiful white and pink bell-shaped flowers, and called by the natives the Tizwood. **1913** Gibson *Amer. Forest Trees* 602 **eTN**, In the Great Smoky mountains in Tennessee, where the species [=*Mohrodendron carolinum*] reaches its greatest development, it bears a variety of names, among them being tisswood, peawood, bellwood, and chittamwood. **1926** in 2009 (acc) Lexis–Nexis *Legal Research State Case Law: NC* (Internet) **wNC**, The tracks came down and then croseed the trail and went out between the road and trail to a 'tizwood' bush. **1954** McAtee *Suppl. to Nomina Abitera* [4], Silverbell (*Halesia monticola*)—Peewood, rarely piss-wood, Great Smoky Mountains, North Carolina. The name tiss-wood of books, thus is probably an enphemism [sic]. **1973** in 1982 Powers *Cataloochee* 339 **cwNC**, The house was built . . using native stone and timber which were abundant in the area—hemlock, poplar, chestnut, locust, and tizwood (or silverbell).

tit v, hence vbl n *titting*   Cf **pull** v **3**

To milk (a cow).

1916 *DN* 4.330 **KS**, *Tit, v.t.* To milk (a cow). **1948** *WELS Suppl.* **cwWI**, For milking cows—pailing, titting. **1966–70** *DARE* (Qu. K8, *Joking terms for milking a cow: A farmer might say, "Well, it's time to go out and _____."*) Infs **MI**116, **MO**38, **MA**58, **NY**140, **PA**163, **TN**44, **WV**2, 4, 8, 13, Tit (the cow *or* the cows); **WA**18, Tit [FW sugg]; **ND**3, Titting time.

tita n   **HI**   Cf **titty** n[1]

See quots.

1967 *DARE* (Qu. Z6, *Nicknames and affectionate words meaning 'sister'*) Inf **HI**6, Tita; (Qu. HH37, *An immoral woman*) Inf **HI**13, Tita. **1981** *Pidgin To Da Max* np **HI**, *Tita* (TEE dah) Mokette. [*Ibid, Moke.* . . Local boy whose idea of a good time is to broke some body's face. Male counterpart of *tita.*] **1998** Bernstein *Close Listening* 345 **HI**, The word "Tita" refers to a large woman with a loud voice, who is brash and often funny; she is a stock character in routines by such comedians as the late Rap Replinger and more recently by Frank DeLima. Titas gain their authority through their voices. **2005** *DARE* File—Internet **HI**, *Tita* (TIT-ah). Usually large, always tough, very local female version of moke. *Eh, brah, nevah mess wid dat tita, she go'n bus you up.*

tit for tat adj phr   Also *tit (and) tat* [By ext from *tit for tat* immediate retaliation]   **esp Sth, S Midl**   See Map   Cf **nick and tuck**

Usu of a competition or competitors: close, even, neck and neck.

1898 *Lima News* (OH) 30 Nov [5]/4 (newspaperarchive.com), The pugs [=boxers] seemed evenly matched and it was tit for tat for the first few rounds. **1912** *Oakland Tribune* (CA) 15 July 8/7, It was tit for tat from start to finish. First one side was ahead and then the other. **1916** *Middletown Times–Press* (NY) 30 Oct 8/1, During the second quarter, the playing was tit for tat. **1965–70** *DARE* (Qu. KK54, *Just about equal, very close: "They were both fast runners and it was _____ all the way."*) 26 Infs, **chiefly Sth, S Midl**, Tit for tat; **SC**32, Tit-tat; **MO**19, Tit-tat to go; **TN**12, Tit and tat [ˌtɪtn̩ˈtæt]; (Qu. KK54b, *Just about equal, very close: "It doesn't matter to me—it's _____."*; total Infs questioned, 75) Inf **GA**7, Tit for tat; (Qu. KK65, . . *'The same sort': "If you like Bob, I'm sure you'll like his brother—they're _____."*) Inf **VA**75, Tit for tat. **1977** *Valley Morning Star* (Harlingen TX) 4 Sept sec D 7/2, For a while there, it was tit-for-tat whether [Hurricane] Anita was going to Corpus Christi or the Valley. **2005** *Thomasville Times* (AL) 28 Apr (Internet), The Aggies and Tigers were tit for tat in the first four innings. **2006** *DARE* File—Internet **swVA** (as of c1910), In the third graduating class . . were the Remmer girls and my brother . . , and it was tit for tat who was going to be the valedictorian.

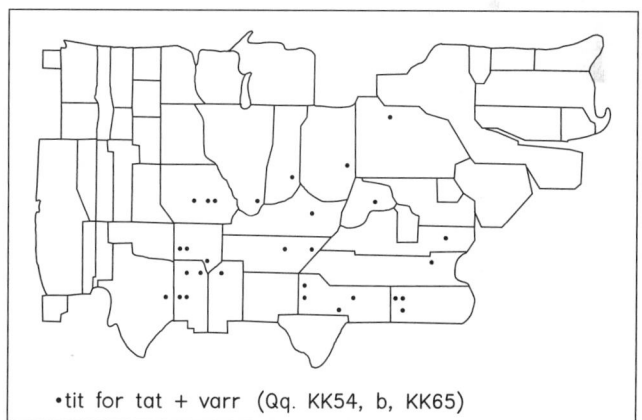

•tit for tat + varr (Qq. KK54, b, KK65)

tit gull n   Cf **tit sparrow**

=**least tern.**

1928 Beston *Outermost House* 208 **Cape Cod MA**, I saw that they were least terns or "tit gulls," rare creatures on our coast. . . A miniature tern, the "leastie," scarce larger than a swallow, and you may know him by the lighter grey of his plumage, his bright lemon-yellow bill, and his delicate orange-yellow feet.

titi n |ˈtaɪ₁taɪ| Pronc-spp *tight-eye, ty-ty*

1 A shrub or tree of the family Cyrillaceae:

a =**buckwheat tree.   Cf black titi 1, spring ~**

1827 Williams *View W. FL* 53, These galls are usually covered with titi and other andromedas. **1837** (1962) Williams *Territory FL* 90, Titi. . . grows from six to twelve feet high. . . In March, their racemes of white flowers are abundant and very ornamental, and their singular strings of three cornered seeds often hang on the bushes till winter. **1880** *Lib. Universal Knowledge* 1.366, *Buckwheat Tree* . . an evergreen shrub in the gulf states. . . Its local name is "titi." **1896** *Garden and Forest* 9.302, *Titi,* or *Ty Ty.* . . The name has been applied . . to *Cliftonia ligustrina.* **1898** Lloyd *Country Life* 267 **AL,** He had . . [been] plungin and tearin through canebrakes and tighteye thickets till you mought think he had rid a whirlwind through Cyclone Streak. **1953** Greene–Blomquist *Flowers South* 68, *Titi* . . *Cliftonia monophylla.* . . This small evergreen tree is distinguished from *Cyrilla* by its . . winged nut-like drupes. . . Swamps and bays, n. Fla. to La. and Ga. **1965–68** *DARE* (Qu. C28, *A place where underbrush, weeds, vines and small trees grow together so that it's nearly impossible to get through*) Inf **LA**27, Titi or a titi swamp; (Qu. S26c, *Wildflowers that grow in woods*) Inf **FL**22, Titi [tɑtɑ]—clusters of little white flowers, very fragrant; (Qu. S26e, *Other wildflowers not yet mentioned; not asked in early QRs*) Infs **AL**15, 20, 30, Titi; (Qu. T15, . . *Kinds of swamp trees*) Inf **FL**7, Titi [taɪtaɪ]—bush; **GA**46, Titi ['taɪˌta]. [*DARE* Ed: Some of these Infs may refer instead to other senses below.] **2001** *DARE* File—Internet **FL,** *Gallberry/Saw Palmetto Compositional Group.* . . Gallberry (*Ilex glabra* and *I. coriacea*) . . and titi (*Cyrilla racemosa* and *Cliftonia monophylla*) are representative species.

b A plant of the genus *Cyrilla,* esp **he-huckleberry 1.** Cf **black titi 2, red ~, summer ~, white ~**

1901 *Torreya* 1.116 **GA,** *Cyrilla racemiflora.* . . Titi. . . *Cliftonia monophylla.* . . Titi. . . In southeast Georgia, where these two species occur together, no distinction is made between them by the natives. **1933** Small *Manual SE Flora* 811, *Cyrilla.* . . Shrubs or small trees. . . *Titis.* **1938** Baker *FL Wild Flowers* 128, *Cyrilla.* In spring and summer the titi shrubs bloom profusely, decorating their branches with many slender white racemes. **1940** (1941) Bell *Swamp Water* 3 **Okefenokee GA,** The little frogs peeped, and a wildcat scratched the bark of a titi tree and yowled. *Ibid* 33, Instead of tupelo bushes, there were runty bays, and titi bushes, and paintroot. **1962** Kurz–Godfrey *Trees N. FL* 197, The cyrillas, commonly called titi, . . are shrubs or small trees. . . often associated with the buckwheat-tree, which they resemble somewhat . . , but from which they differ markedly in time of flowering and appearance of the fruits. . . *Cyrilla parvifolia* . . little-leaf titi. *Ibid* 200, *Cyrilla racemiflora* . . titi. **1968** *DARE* FW Addit **GA**25, Ironwood—old-fashioned nickname for the summer ty-ty tree. **2001** [see **1a** above].

2 Any of var ericaceous plants, as:

a Either of two closely related plants: the Florida hobblebush (*Agarista populifolia*) or a **fetterbush 3** (here: *Leucothoe axillaris*).

1869 Porcher *Resources* 417 **Sth,** *Leucothea* [sic] *acuminata* [=*Agarista populifolia*]. . . Dr. J.H. Mellichamp, of Bluffton, writes me: "This is the true 'Ti-ti.' The best pipe stems are made from this shrub." **1901** Lounsberry *S. Wild Flowers* 391, *L[eucothoe] acuminata,* pipe-wood, titi, inhabits the swamp margins from eastern Florida to the Carolinas. **1945** Coker–Totten *Trees SE U.S.* 278, This is locally called "Titi," but so are a number of other shrubs, as *Leucothoe acuminata, L. axillaris.*

b A **staggerbush** (here: *Lyonia ferruginea* or *L. lucida*). Cf **highland ti-ti**

1897 Sudworth *Arborescent Flora* 313 **FL,** *Andromeda ferruginea* [= *Lyonia f.*] . . Titi. **1968** *DARE* Tape **GA**30, It's a bush that grows here in the [Okefenokee] swamp. It grows thick in some places you have to cut your way through it. . . A gentleman . . from the government come down here to tag these bushes. . . When he come to that he put *titi* on it . . when he came to that hurrah bush. **1979** Little *Checklist U.S. Trees* 164, *Lyonia ferruginea.* . . Staggerbush, titi, rusty lyonia.

c =**sourwood.**

1860 *Harper's New Mth. Mag.* 21.493 **FL,** They gathered great handfuls [of violets] and bound them with white star-like flowers, and the pink bells of the tight-eye. **1897** Sudworth *Arborescent Flora* 314 **SC,** *Oxydendrum arboreum.* . . Titi. **1933** Small *Manual SE Flora* 1002, *O[xydendrum] arboreum.* . . Sorrel-tree. Titi. . . Woods, various provinces, N Fla. to La., Ind., and S Pa. **1960** Vines *Trees SW* 812, Vernacular names [for *Oxydendrum arboreum*] are Sorrel-tree, Sour-gum, Elk-tree, and Titi. The flowers produce a good honey. **1980** Hudak *Trees* 181, Oxydendrum arboreum . . (Sourwood, Sorrel tree, Titi).

3 A **holly** n[1] **1** (here: *Ilex myrtifolia*).

1933 *Torreya* 33.84 **FL,** *Ilex myrtifolia.* . . Titi.

4 A dense thicket.

1905 Fleming *Civil War & Reconstruction* 123 **AL,** The country near the Gulf coast was infested with tories, deserters, and runaway slaves, concealed in caves, "tighteyes," canebrakes, swamps, and the thick woods of the sparsely settled country. [Footnote to *tighteye:*] Thickets which the eye could not penetrate. **1968** *DARE* (Qu. C28, *A place where underbrush, weeds, vines and small trees grow together so that it's nearly impossible to get through*) Inf **LA**27, Titi or a titi swamp.

titlark n [*OED2* 1668 → for *Anthus* spp]

A **pipit:** usu *Anthus spinoletta,* but also *A. spragueii.*

[**1823** Latham *Genl. Hist. Birds* 6.278, In the Collection of Mr. Francillon was one [=a titlark], sent from Mr. Abbot, of Savannah, in Georgia, somewhat larger than the European one, but answering in so many particulars, as to give cause for thinking it the same, or a very slight Variety. It is there called the Brown Lark.] **1831** Audubon *Ornith. Biog.* 1.49, The Brown Titlark . . *Anthus Spinoletta* . . is met with in every portion of the United States which I have visited. **1844** DeKay *Zool.* NY 2.76, The American Titlark. *Anthus ludovicianus* [=*A. spinoletta*]. *Ibid* 77, The *Little Brown Titlark* winters in Louisiana. **1883** Nuttall *Ornith. Club Bulletin* 8.78, In my long list of local American names for this species [=*Anthus spinoletta*] occur the following: *Titlark, . . Lark* [etc]. **1894** Torrey *FL Sketch-Book* 38, Behind me are sharp cries of titlarks. **1916** *Times–Picayune* (New Orleans LA) 30 Apr mag sec 5, *American Pipit.* . . Titlark.—These far-Northern nesting birds are among the common wintering birds in Louisiana. *Sprague Pipit.* . . Like the preceding "Titlark." **1917** (1923) *Birds Amer.* 3.171, We have two of them [=wagtails] in the United States. We call them Pipits or Titlarks. **1962** Imhof *AL Birds* 415, *Anthus spinoletta.* . . Titlark. . . Resembles a sparrow in color and size, but it is distinguished by its family characteristics. **1969** Longstreet *Birds FL* 123, *Titlark.* . . One of the few small land birds that walks with a mincing tread instead of hopping.

title n   *among Black speakers*   Cf **entitle**

A person's name; see quots.

1892 (1893) Botume *First Days* 46 **seSC** (as of 1864), I then explained that we all have two names; but she still replied, "Nothing but Phyllis, ma'am." Upon this an older girl started up and exclaimed, "Pshaw, gal! What's you'm [=your] title?" whereupon she gave the name of her old master. **1936** in 1976 *Weevils in the Wheat* 193 **VA** [Black], What's yo title, huh? I mean what's yo' name? **c1937** in 1972 *Amer. Slave* 2.115 **SC,** From yout (youth) I been a Brown and marry a Brown; title never change. **1939** Griswold *Sea Is. Lady* 140 **csSC** (as of 1865) [Gullah], You ain' know you'-own title, tittie? Shuh! He name Annie K, ma'am. [=You don't know your own name, sister? Shuh! Her name's Annie K, ma'am.] **1950** *PADS* 14.68 **SC,** *Title.* . . A name. Negro usage.

titlement See **entitle**

titling n [Cf *SND titlin* n. 2 "The smallest and weakest in a brood, esp. of pigs in a litter."]

=**titman 1.**

1959 *VT Hist.* 27.164, *Titling.* . . The smallest pig in the litter. Occasional among farmers. **1967** *DARE* (Qu. K54, . . *The smallest pig in a litter*) Inf **NY**9, Titling ['tɪtlən].

titman n [*EDD tit* sb.[1] 2 "A very small person or thing"]

1 also *tit(man) pig, tit one:* The runt of a litter of pigs. **chiefly Nth, esp NEng, Upstate NY** See Map Cf **titling**

1854 Child *Tippletonia* 66 **IN,** And it ever happened that when a new customer came, he rooted away those he found at the forward nipples, who would always in turn greedily snatch at those next below, as the "titman" does when a larger pig drives him away from the dug he has . . appropriated to his own especial use. **1892** *DN* 1.213 **ceMA,** I . . am reminded of the word *titman,* applied to the last born and often weakest and smallest pig in a litter. I have known two schoolmasters who applied the term to their weakest and least promising pupil. **1897** *KS Univ. Qrly.* (ser B) 6.58, *Titman:* suckling pig. **1903** *DN* 2.334 **seMO,** *Titman.* . . The smallest of a litter of pigs. **1910** Davenport *Domesticated Animals* 131 **N Cent,** The "titman," or "runt," in the litter of pigs is really a dwarf, the dwarfing process often being due to insufficient food at the start. **1913** Becker *Larkin of Cotton Run* 40 **NY,** Little, round-shouldered, thin-chested fellers they was, always makin' yeh think of a titman pig. **1947** Croy *Corn Country* 281 **Upper MW,** *Titman:* The runt in a litter of pigs. Usually there is not a place for it to suckle; if not watched, the sow will kill it. **1950** *WELS* (The undersized pig in a litter) 6 Infs, **WI,** Titman. **1965–70** *DARE* (Qu. K54, . . *The smallest pig in a litter*) 71 Infs, **chiefly Nth, esp NEng, Upstate NY,**

Titman; **NY**13, 20, 142, 230, Tit pig; **CT**10, **MI**78, **NY**13, Tit one; (Qu. K55, *A pig that doesn't grow well and is not worth keeping*) 10 Infs, **NEng, Upstate NY,** Titman; (Qu. K51, *. . Pigs, a very young one*) Inf **NY**213, Titman. [65 of 79 total Infs old, 62 male]

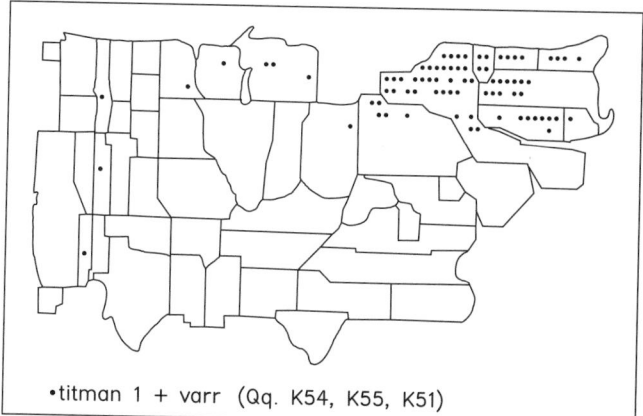

•titman 1 + varr (Qq. K54, K55, K51)

2 A person (usu male) that is literally or figuratively stunted; the smallest or youngest or least significant in a family or other group—also used as a nickname. **chiefly Nth**

1818 Fessenden *Ladies Monitor* 113 **NEng,** But vanity oft prematurely calls,/ Her titman-votaries to your *baby-balls,/* Where tiny belles, and Lilliputian beaux . . / Strut round the hall. **1838** *OH Common School Director* 80, Who would not rather be first in a useful employment than to be titman in one which the world calls honorable? **1845** (1949) Thoreau *Jrl.* 1.373 **MA,** They [=mankind] are the titmen of their race,/ And hug the vales with mincing pace / Like Troglodytes. **1857** *Harper's New Mth. Mag.* 15.767, Jim was the youngest—mother's baby; I know we used to call him "Titman." **1863** in 2006 *DARE* File—Internet **OH,** I have grown some taller since you saw me. . . All the boys in the company have stretched up amazingly, all but George who is bound to be a titman anyhow. **1892** [see 1 above]. **1900** Garland *Eagle's Heart* 101 **ND,** This yer little man [=a boy] must be the tit-man. **1949** in 2006 *DARE* File—Internet **UT,** Henry said, "Lady, I am a polygamist child, the titman of the family of twelve." He was over six feet tall. **1950** *WELS* (*The youngest child in a family:* "There are four children in our family; Johnny is the _____.") 1 Inf, **cwWI,** Titman. **1981** Coon *Adventures* 163, I was the only civilian—in their esteem the titman of the litter. **1989** Mosher *Stranger* 72 **nVT** (as of 1952), According to Titman (so-called because he was the runt of the . . litter), Gilson had . . kicked him.

titman pig See **titman 1**

titmouse n
Std: any of several small birds of the family Paridae and, in the US, of the genera *Poecile* and *Baeolophus.* For other names of these see **chickadee** n[1] **1, creeper 2, Peter bird, tip-top, tomtit a, tuffy** n[2]

tit one, tit pig See **titman 1**

titravate See **titrivate**

‡**titrified** adj Cf **titrivate**
1977 *Yankee* Jan 113 **coastal ME,** But island men when they curse can set your mouth to watering. I calate if I was to explain you'd be titrified.

titrivate v Also sp *titravate* [Varr of *tittivate (up)* to dress oneself up; to adorn, fix up] **chiefly ME**
1 also with *about:* To adjust the personal appearance of; to primp, go (about) ostentatiously; hence ppl adj phr *titrivated out* dressed up.
1854 Smith *Bertha & Lily* 321, Pretty wife she'd make for a minister; titrivating about, belaced and bejewelled, ready to kill. [*DARE* Ed: Set in seNY, but author from **ME.**] **1905** Day in *Amer. Mag.* 60.185 **ME,** It flashed up before my memory, the whole thing; . . the girls giggling and primping and titrivating themselves in the corners and the fellows all red and shiny and nudging each other. **1917** Day *Where Treasure Is* 41 **ME,** I'll be cussed if I see any sense in being titrivated out like this the whole afternoon.
2 also with *up:* To fix up, adjust, manipulate; hence nouns

titrivating, titrivation adjustment, "tinkering"; n *titrivator* a tool used to move a heavy object. [Cf *EDD titivate* 2 "To tidy, clean, put in order; to restore, renovate; to repair a building."]
1903 Wasson *Cap'n Simeon's Store* 228 **ME,** O' course that meant putting of her [=a ship] on the blocks so 's to titrivate her up fit for a fresh start ag'in. **1950** Moore *Candlemas Bay* 213 **ME,** You fixed that wick yourself. . . You know as well as I do that them things don't titrivate themselves up and down. **1996** Proulx *Yankee Magazine's Make It Last* 144 **NH,** The customer didn't care, so my father told me, "Titrivate it!"—which was his expression for "make it work." **1999** in 2006 *DARE* File—Internet **ME,** Have an NC20 to sell. Completed, works, but not well! Needs some titrivating. **2004** *Ibid,* It's a terrific instrument, though in need of titrivation out of the box. *Ibid* **ME,** Everything is going to get unscrewed, rescrewed, titravated, and calibrated anyway. **2005** *DARE* File **coastal ME,** One . . who lives on the coast of Maine and is a sailor said he had a word that . . no one else knew the meaning of—"titrivate." . . I did. I picked it up from my father, who grew up in Harrington, Maine. When you are moving something heavy such as a boat by means of levers, you "titrivate" it this way and that into the desired position. The tool used would be called a "titrivator." **2006** *DARE* File—Internet, It again started to smoke. More adjustments and with more titrivating, got it settled out smoke free once again.
3 See quot.
2003 *DARE* File—Internet **ME,** There are no better people on this earth than Downeast fisherpeople, but they tend to mistrust the State and the[y] obfuscate and titrivate as a default position.

titrivate about, titrivate(d) out See **titrivate 1**

titrivate up, titrivating, titrivation, titrivator See **titrivate 2**

tit sparrow n Cf **tit gull**
Any small sparrow.
1915 Speck *Nanticoke Comm.* DE 41, "Tit sparrow," any small sparrow—English, chipping, or song sparrow. **1968** *DARE* (Qu. Q21, *Kinds of sparrows*) Inf **DE**4, Tit sparrows—like tiny sparrows; **MD**34, Tit sparrow—smaller than English sparrow; **MD**42, Tit sparrow—smaller than English sparrow, stays in woods.

titta See **titty** n[1]

tit-tat See **tit for tat**

tit-tat-toe n
1 also sp *tit-tat-to(w);* for addit varr see quot 1965–70: = **tick-tack-toe 2.** Note: Some of these quots may refer instead to **2** below. [*EDD tit-tat-toe* sb. 1] **widespread, but less freq NEng, Gt Lakes** See Map
1820 Picket–Picket *Academician* 91 **NY,** One boy who is acquainted with . . *tit-tat-to, hop skip and jump,* and a thousand other childish amusements, will communicate all he knows to his school companions. **1850** Foley *Romance Ocean* 28 **NY,** I taught him tit-tat-toe, and several other of my old school-games. **1861** Floy *Bible Morality* 159, When he saw that his father's attention was turned in another direction, he commenced playing with himself a game of tit-tat-toe on his slate. **1879** *Harper's New Mth. Mag.* 59.152, Freeland . . has described a machine constructed by himself for playing automatically the well known game of tit-tat-to. **1895** *Atlantic Mth.* 75.468 **VT,** Even checkers and tit-tat-toe . . and games like those she couldn't play at on account of her

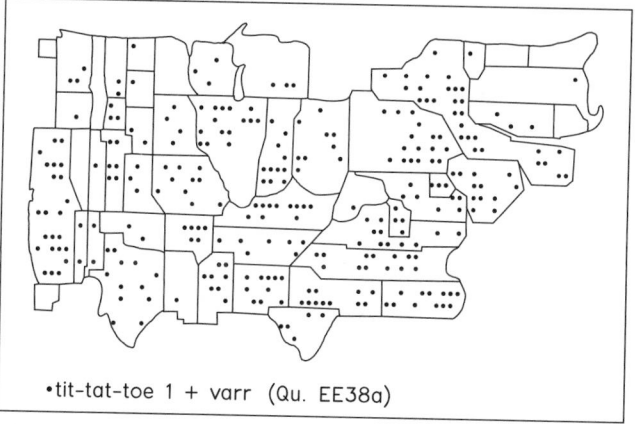

•tit-tat-toe 1 + varr (Qu. EE38a)

poor helpless hands. **1899** (1912) Green *VA Folk-Speech* 450, *Tit-tat-toe*. . . A child's game. "Tit-tat-to, all in a row." **1913** (1980) Hardy *OH Schoolmistress* 114, Various slate games, "Puzzle," "Tit-tat-tow," "Guess the Name," were played with impunity in school time. **1923** Acker *400 Games* 289, *Tit-Tat-Toe*—This familiar game is good for two players. . . The object is to place three of one's marks in a row. **1939** *Clearfield Progress* (PA) 31 Oct 4/1, Propaganda writers are the only ones working while generals twiddle their thumbs and play tit-tat-toe on the backs of their field maps. **1965–70** *DARE* (Qu. EE38a, *A game played with pencil and paper where the players try to get three X's or three O's in a row*) 291 Infs, **widespread, but less freq NEng, Gt Lakes,** Tit-tat-toe; **DE**2, Tit-tat-toe, three in a row; **SC**2, 68, Ti-ta-toe; [**MO**39, Tat; **MS**15, **NY**235, Tat(-tat)-toe; **CA**94, Tick-tat-toe; **NY**200, Tip-tat-toe; **MS**6, Tit-tack-toe; **MO**17, **SC**46, Tit-tat(-taw)]. **1976** *Frederick Post* (MD) 24 Mar sec A 7/4, 1 ¼ carat total weight cluster ring, modern "tit-tat-toe" design.

2 =**tick-tack-toe 1.** [*EDD tit-tat-toe* sb. 3]

1905 *DN* 3.98 **nwAR,** *Tit-tat-tô'*. . . The name of a game commonly played with slates and slate pencils. . . 'Tit-tat-tô,/ Around I go,/ And if I miss / I'll stop at this.' At the close of the game: 'Tit-tat-tô,/ Three in a row.' **1923** Acker *400 Games* 269, *Circular Tit-Tat-Toe*. . . A circular diagram is drawn. . . The compartments may be numbered by 1's or by 5's or 10's. The center compartment is always the smallest. Each player takes a turn, *with eyes shut,* in moving his pencil around in the circle while he says, "Tit-tat-toe, here we go,/ Ten jolly sailormen, all in a row." His pencil stops on the last word. Whatever space is touched by the pencil gives him his count. . . Touching the center compartment wins the game. **1947** *Middletown Times Herald* (NY) 20 Aug 4/5, [Westbrook Pegler column:] Down in my league they score baseball by the tit-tat-toe system, in bunches of fives. **1947** *Waterloo Sun. Courier* (IA) 2 Nov sec 1 4/2, The unlucky man who tries to wade through this mass of statistical material [about different life-insurance policies] is soon so confused that he usually ends up by using the "tit, tat, toe" method of making a decision. **1968** *DARE* (Qu. EE38a) Inf **WI**24, Tit-tat-toe, around you go—played by a group with one blindfolded and a circle of numbers.

tit-tat-too n [*EDD tit-tat-too* (at *tit-tat-toe*)]

1 Prob =**tick-tack-toe 1.**

1857 Train *Amer. Merchant* 364 **MA,** Shuffleboard was most resorted to—a game . . played . . on a chalked plan like children's "tit tat too," counting fifteen each way.

2 also sp *tit-tat-two:* =**tick-tack-toe 2.** **chiefly Sth, S Midl, TX** See Map

1871 Holbrook *School Management* 23 **OH,** If Miranda is detected playing tit-tat-too with her seat-mate . . it is a sad instance of waywardness. **1909** *DN* 3.382 **eAL, wGA,** *Tit-tat-too.* . . The name of a children's game. It is played by two players on a drawing of two parallel lines crossing two others as #, the object of the game being to get three of one's marks in a line. **1911** Shute *Plupy* 201 **NH,** Evenins when we wuz playin' "Red Lion," 'n "Run Sheep Run," 'n "How Many Miles to Barbaree," 'n "Tit-Tat-two" on peoples winders with a brick. **1925** *Oakland Tribune* (CA) 1 Nov mag sec 8, [Cartoon:] Gather round me, kidlets, and get Pop's big idea of teaching the young . . how to shoot craps. Time enough when you grow up to play such rough games as croquet, baccarat, stud poker and tit-tat-too. **1965–70** *DARE* (Qu. EE38a, *A game played with pencil and paper where the players try to get three X's or three O's in a row*) 37 Infs, **chiefly Sth, S Midl, TX,** Tit-tat-too.

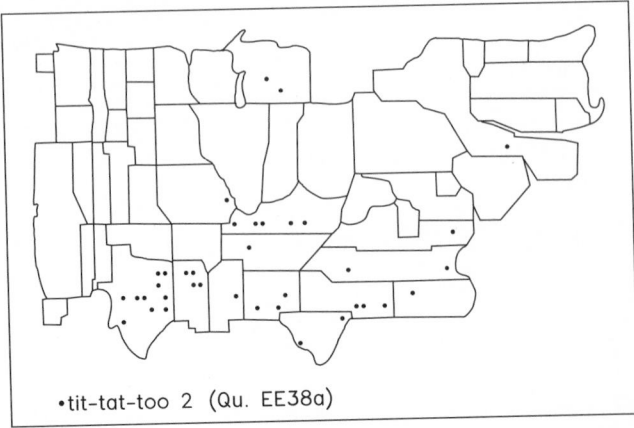

•tit-tat-too 2 (Qu. EE38a)

tit-tat-tow See **tit-tat-toe 1**

tit-tat-two See **tit-tat-too 2**

titter n¹ See **tetter** n¹

titter n² See **titty** n¹

titter(board) See **teeter** n **4**

tittering board See **teeter** v

titter-totter See **teeter-totter 1**

tittie n¹ See **titty** n¹

tittie n² See **titty** n²

titting See **tit**

tittling board See **tiddle board**

tittly-bender(s) See **tiddly-bender(s)**

titty n¹ Also *ter, tiddy, titta, titter, tittie, tittuh* [Perh Scots, nEngl colloq or hypocoristic *titty* sister, but for possible Afr lang analogues cf *DBE*] *esp freq among Gullah speakers*

A sister; also used as a title or term of address for a woman.

1864 *Atlantic Mth.* 13.594 **SC** [Gullah], "Tiddy Rosa, hold your light!/ Brudder Tony, hold your light!" . . This is one of the most spirited shouting-tunes. "Tiddy" is their word for sister. **1867** Allen et al. *Slave Songs* xxvi **seSC,** *Titty* is used for mother or oldest sister; thus Titty Ann was the name by which the children of our man-of-all work knew their mother, Ann. **1883** *Harper's New Mth. Mag.* 69.111 **VA** [Black], Termahta. [Footnote:] Sister Martha, sister being Titta, abbreviated to Ter. **1883** (1971) Harris *Nights with Remus* 345 **GA** [Black], Me 'tan' 'pon a log fer ketch-a da fish fer me lil titty. [Footnote: Sissy.] **1892** (1893) Botume *First Days* 48 **seSC** (as of c1864) [Gullah], The terms "bubber" for brother, and "titty" for sister . . were so generally used. **1897** (1952) McGill *Narrative* 303 **SC,** To each and every one of them their "Titter Sarah" and "Saah" was a sister they embraced, as worthy of their most tender affections. **1922** Gonzales *Black Border* 334 **sSC, GA coasts** [Gullah glossary], *Tittie*[,] *Tittuh*—sister, sisters (informal). **1949** Turner *Africanisms* 247 [Gullah], The following pronunciations of English words . . are common . . ['tɪtə] 'sister.' **1955** *PADS* 23.48 **e,cSC, eNC, seGA** [Gullah vocab], *Titta* 'sister.' **1966** *DARE* (Qu. Z6, *Nicknames and affectionate words meaning 'sister'*) Infs **SC**10, 26, Titty. [Both Infs Black]

titty n² Also sp *tittie* **chiefly Sth, S Midl**

Breast milk.

1827 in 2006 *DARE* File—Internet **NC,** Robert Neil's hair is white as flax, blue eyes, articulates smartly and 20 times in the day is heard to say sometimes Ma Neil have titty—child have—baby have—pretty boy have titty. **1909** *DN* 3.382 **eAL, wGA,** *Titty.* . . milk from the breast. **1915** *DN* 4.192 **swVA,** *Titty.* . . Breast milk. [*DN* Ed: Also heard in New England.] **1923** *DN* 5.223 **swMO,** *Titty.* . . Pap. "Mammy, give that young-un some titty," *i.e.,* let it nurse. **1931** (1991) Hughes–Hurston *Mule Bone* 84 **cFL** [Black], We been palling around together ever since we hollered titty mama, ain't we, boy? **1931** Randolph *Ozarks* 86, Women of the very best families *give tittie* to their babes in public, even in church, without the slightest embarrassment. **1950** *PADS* 14.68 **SC,** *Titty.* . . Milk from the breast. Child's speech. **1954** Harder *Coll.* **cwTN,** *Titty.* . . Milk from the breast. **1958** Humphrey *Home from the Hill* 264 **TX,** She gave the baby titty. . . Then she put the baby to bed. **c1960** Wilson *Coll.* **csKY,** *Titty.* . . milk from the breast. **1982** Barrick *Coll.* **csPA,** *Titty*—breast, teat, by extension milk, esp. human.

titty baby n Also sp *tiddy baby* Also *titty child* **Sth, S Midl** Cf **knee baby, lap child**

A nursing infant; also fig, a whiner, crybaby.

1973 *Patrick Coll.* **cAL,** *Titty child*—suckling child. **1996** Wells *Divine Secrets* 54 **LA,** She turns around at one of the other little girls and sticks her tongue out. Well, that makes that little sissy start crying. "Titty-baby! Little sissy titty-baby!" **1999** Haynes *Mother of Pearl* 80 **MS,** One of the disciples was leaning on marble Christ, crying like a titty-baby and Joleb hated him for such a show of weakness. **2005** *DARE* File—Internet **MO,** The greens must be hard to putt. Tiger shot 4 under, and . . was crying like a titty baby. *Ibid* **FL,** The Tampa Tribune has its Daniel "Titty Baby" Ruth. Ruth is a resident columnist whose lone talent is calling people names when they do not agree with his point of view. **2006** *Ibid* **TX,** When we got married he was crying like a titty baby before he could ever see me walking down the aisle. *Ibid* **TX,** Our fat-assed, lazy, titty baby kids haven't the mettle for 8+ years of intense study, followed by a grueling internship require[d] to become a good doctor. *Ibid* **TX,** You need a pacifier, don't you you big tiddy baby.

tituree n [Prob echoic]
=**killdeer 1.**
    1923 *U.S. Dept. Ag. Misc. Circular* 13.69 **VA,** *Killdeer. . . Vernacular Names. . . In local use. . .* Tituree.

tizic(ky) See **phthisic**

tizwood See **tisswood 2**

tizzerrizzin n Also sp *tizza-rizzen* [Echoic]
See quots.
    1859 Taliaferro *Fisher's R.* 209 **nwNC** (as of 1820s), My head is gwine round and round, and a ringin' in my ears sorter like tizzerrizzin! tizzerrizzin! **1913** (1980) Hardy *OH Schoolmistress* 99, *Tizza-rizzen—* "I have a tizza-rizzen in my head," which meant a feeling like the beginning of a sick headache.

tizzic(k), tizzicky See **phthisic**

Tizzie Lish See **Miss Lizzie Tish**

tizzle-tazzle See **tazzle**

tizzy See **phthisic**

‡**tizzyrinctum** n Cf **spizzerinctum**
    1989 *DARE* File **RI** (as of c1900), Tizzyrinctum = spunk, a fit, [when a person is] giddy, [in] confusion.

t.l. See **trade-last**

T-model Ford adj, also used absol Also *T-model (car), tea-motel* [Metath] **chiefly Sth, S Midl** See Map
A model-T Ford automobile.
    1923 *Lake Co. Times* (Hammond IN) 22 June 19/6, [Advt:] For Sale— 1921 T-model Ford. **1942** in 1973 Dundes *Mother Wit* 28 **FL,** Way after a while a T-model Ford came along full of Negroes. **1963** Edwards *Gravel* 173 **eTN** (as of 1920s), T-Model Tales. **1965–70** *DARE* (Qu. N5, *Nicknames for an automobile, especially an old or broken-down car*) 11 Infs, **Sth, S Midl,** T-model; **AR**51, Jitney—for hire; T-model— for private use, the general term; **KY**86, 91, T-model Ford; (Qu. N6, *An old car that has been fixed up to make it go fast or make a lot of noise*) Inf **MO**9, Just a T-model. **1968** *Foxfire* Mar 9 **neGA,** It was a teamotel ford—tom mitchel was driving it. **1986** Pederson *LAGS Concordance* **Gulf Region,** 16 infs, T-model car (or Ford, truck); 13 infs, T-model(s). **1995** Heatwole *Shenandoah Voices* 31 **wVA** (as of early 20th cent), People would come from all over, in T-models and with horses and buggies.

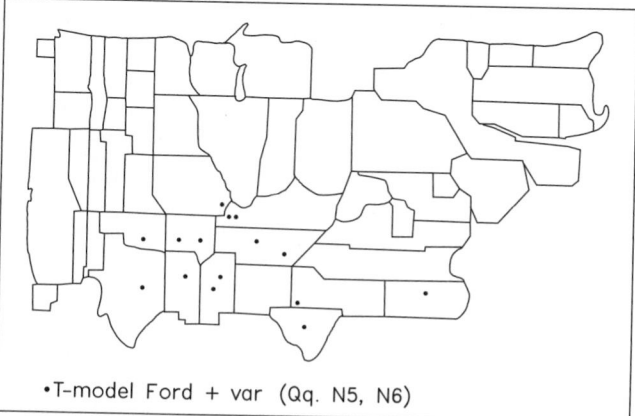
• T-model Ford + var (Qq. N5, N6)

t'morrah, t'morrow See **tomorrow**

t-niney See **tee-niny**

to prep, adv

A Forms. Cf **do** v **A1**

1 in stressed position: usu |tu|; also:

a |to|; pronc-sp *toe*. **chiefly Sth, S Midl, esp VA**
    1865 *Daily Index* (Petersburg VA) 14 Aug 5/2, *Conundrum for Black-smiths.*—Why is an ugly man like an anvil? Because he has a hard face to be (Toby) stricken. [*DARE* Ed: Cf **toby-struck**] **1867** Lowell *Biglow*

lxx 'Upcountry' **MA,** *Too,* when emphatic, changes into *tue* and *to,* sometimes, in similar cases, into *toe,* as, "I did n't hardly know wut *toe* du!" [*DARE* Ed: This pronc-sp is not used anywhere in the text of *The Biglow Papers.*] **1890** *PMLA* 5.198 **VA,** The pronunciation of the preposition *to (too)* [*DARE* Ed: appar =[to]] is now obsolescent. **1914** *DN* 4.159 **cVA,** Ah don't choose toe (to). *Ibid,* Gin it toe me. *Ibid* 160, Hit don't suit me toe go. **1919** *DN* 5.40 **VA,** *To,* prep., pronounced with long o. Good Early English—and Virginian. **1927** Shewmake *Engl. Pronc. VA* 43, The word *to . .* is sometimes called *toe* by the careless and uneducated. **1931** *AmSp* 6.164 **seVA,** Occasionally [to] is heard for *to.* Though not common, [to] may appear almost anywhere in the South. It is old-fashioned. **1933** *AmSp* 8.1.23 **Appalachians,** One hears *toe* for *to* in North Carolina and Virginia; in Kentucky and West Virginia the word has most frequently the vowel in *took.* In sections of Tennessee one hears both. **1934** *WV Review* Dec 78, *Toe* for *to.* **1942** Hall *Smoky Mt. Speech* 38 **wNC, eTN,** For *to,* [tou] appeared only in the phrase *to and fro,* spoken by a lady in dictating a ballad. **1955** *PADS* 23.46 **e,cSC, eNC, seGA,** /o/ in *to.* **1974** Gilbreth *Dictionary* 15 **seSC,** *Toe:* Preposition meaning toward, i.e., "I went toe the Oil of Pams."

b |tju, tiu|; pronc-sp *tew*.
    1861 Holmes *Venner* 2.173 **NEng,** Yeou lay still, 'n' wait t'll that man comes tew. **1887** Kirkland *Zury* 151 **IL,** He . . would wish t' have somebody of his own blood t' leave all his truck tew. **1917** Garland *Son Middle Border* 94 **NY,** Honors tew your pardners—right and left *four!* **1943** *LANE* Map 700 *(Did not use to)* 1 inf, **seNH,** [dɪ^vnt j^ʲ ɪu^s tɪu^w]. *Ibid* Map 734 *(Whether I want to)* **NEng,** [34 infs, proncs of the type [wɒnt t^lu]; 3 infs, proncs of the types [wɒ^ntɪw, wɔ^v·əntɪ^ru].] **1968** *DARE* FW Addit **Baltimore MD,** *To,* two, too pronounced [tju]—especially when stressed. **1982** *AmSp* 57.192, Words in which /u/ is preceded by an alveolar have an *ew* spelling for the vowel [in 1887 Kirkland *Zury*], thus . . *tew* ('to,' 'too,' 'two'). . . This spelling probably indicates the diphthong /iu/ or /ju/ in these words, a pronunciation now rare in Pennsylvania and the Inland North, but still quite common in the South and South Midland.

2 in unstressed position: freq |tə, tu|; also rarely |tɪ, tu|; foll consonants often |ə|, esp in combs such as *had to* |'hædə|, *going to* |'gɒnə|, *want to* |'wɒnə|, etc; pronc-spp *(-)a, -ah, -er, t', (-)ta, (-)ter, teu, tew, (-)tu(h), -(t)y, -uh*.
    1834 *Life Andrew Jackson* 238 **ME,** I . . was jist a gwine tu tell all about it. **1840** *S. Lit. Messenger* 6.771, He oughter have had a lightnin' rod. **1844** Stephens *High Life in NY* xii, *Tu.* To; frequently used for at: *tu hum*—at home. **1852** *Yankee Notions* 1.354, Tew gals, slick critters, asked me teu treat. **1857** *Putnam's Mag.* 9.45 **ME,** He'd wintered twice in the woods, wus sober, and smart tew work. **1881** *Atlantic Mth.* 47.738 **eTN,** Suthin' will happen ter ye afore ye kin git away. **1883** Harris *Nights with Remus* 188 **GA** [Black], He hatter hug a tree fer ter keep fum drappin' on de groun'. **1889** *Lima Daily Times* (OH) 22 May 4/7, *English as She Is Talked.* "Hey, Bill Whyd'nt chu kumtus kool yistaft noon?" "Cozza hadda stateom coz mummuthers sick." **1893** Shands *MS Speech* 35, Hattuh [hætə]. Negro for *have to,* in the sense of being under obligation to do. *Ibid* 65, Tuh [tə]. There is no sound of *r* in the negro pronunciation of *to,* and it should not be written *ter,* as it generally is by dialect writers. **1899** Garland *Boy Life* 161 **nwIA** (as of c1870s), I hope t' God we won't be late. **1904** *DN* 2.423 **Cape Cod MA** (as of a1857), Short final unaccented vowels have a tendency to become short i . . [as] in the preposition *to* in such phrases as *ought to* (oughty), *want to* (waⁿty), *going to* (guⁿty) [etc]. **1904** *Lafayette Advt.* (LA) 20 Apr suppl np, Now that ma's gone pa's gotta take keer o' hisself. **1909** *Syracuse Herald* (NY) 12 Dec sec B 4/3, This 'ere concrete edifice is gonna remain anchored to the landscape. **1922** (1926) Kephart *Highlanders* 123 **sAppalachians,** We haffter pack on muleback or tussle it on our own wethers. **1922** Gonzales *Black Border* 143 **sSC, GA coasts** [Gullah], Now uh haffuh tek me two foot en' walk! *Ibid* [Gullah glossary], *Oughtuh.* **1926** *Syracuse Herald* (NY) 8 Mar comic sec np, Have ya got something good for me ta eat? **1928** *AmSp* 3.403 **Ozarks** (as of 1916–27), *Two* and *too* are pronounced as in standard English, but the *o* in *to* is often elided, or given a sound pretty much like *er.* **1939** Faulkner *Wild Palms* 214 **MS,** Maybe I awda sockm, Pete. **1943** *LANE* Map 572 *(To tell)* **NEng,** [The most common pronc is [tə]; there are scattered instances of [tu] and [tʊ].] *Ibid* Map 699 *(I want to get off)* **NEng,** [Proncs of the types [wɑntə, wɒntə, wɒntə] are most frequent; proncs of the types [wɒnt tu, wɒnt tə] and [wɑ^vnə, wɒnə, wʌnə] are scattered throughout the region.] **1952** Brown *NC Folkl.* 1.543, Goin' a get me a fram-pole and beat you up. **1953** Atwood *Survey of Verb Forms* 35, In *going to* there are almost innumerable phonetic reductions of the types [gɔɪntə, gɔɪnə, gɒnə, gʌnə, gənə].

1978 Kalibabky *Hawdaw* 2.[1] **neMN,** If I find out dat you drank da las' beer, aminah kill you! **1985** Benes *Amer. Speech* 75 **cME coast** (as of c1800), The vowel sound of contemporary *put*. . . is found in [Fisher's representations of] the words *broom*, . . *root, soon, to* (versus the vowel of *boot* in *too* and *two*), . . and *tooth*.

B As prep.

1a At, in (a definite place). [*OED2 to* prep. A.4 925 →; "Now only *dial.* and *U.S. colloq.*"] **scattered, but esp freq Nth** See also *to home* (at **home B4a**) Note: Exx of *be to* with the contextual sense "make a visit to" (as in "I have been to Philadelphia") are not included here.

1814 in 1947 *AmSp* 22.275 **NH,** To for at—he lives to York—he is to his store—I have even heard he isn't to home. **1818** (1920) Clark *Diary* 2321 **CT,** Stayed to Canfields all night. **1839** in 1940 Drury *Pioneers Spokanes* 257 **ME,** Mr. Walker . . having business to Walla Walla left home on the 6th. **1848** (1855) Ruxton *Life Far West* 14, 'Twas about calf-time . . that the biggest kind of rendezvous was held 'to' Independence. **1850** McCallum *ME Letters* [1], I boarded with some of the rest over to the *White House.* **1871** Eggleston *Hoosier Schoolmaster* 97, "They's preachin' down to Bethel Meetin'-house to-day," said the Squire at breakfast. Twenty years in the West could not cure Squire Hawkins [=a New Englander] of saying "to" for "at." **1897** *KS Univ. Qrly.* (ser B) 6.93, *To:* at or in; as, "It's to Lawrence."—General. **1910** *DN* 3.440 **wNY,** He was sent as assemblyman, and died down to Albany. *Ibid* 446 **wNY,** We're over to Garbuttsville often. *Ibid* 450 **wNY,** He was to our house this morning. *Ibid* 451 **wNY,** *Up to, prep. phr.* Up at. I saw him up to the Roberts's yesterday. **1913** *DN* 4.3 **ME,** I wouldn't wonder an you could get some down to Jordan's. **1918** *DN* 5.19 **NC,** He is over to Mrs. Jones' house. **1933** Rawlings *South Moon* 319 **nFL,** He ate hot dinner to my house nigh ever' day. **1935** Sandoz *Jules* 135 **wNE** (as of 1880–1930), We ain't got no pull to Rushville, no friends where they counts. **1939** *Hall Coll.* **eTN,** Ever' bone [of a man's body] was to its place but one. **1963** *PADS* 40.18, [In the Linguistic Atlas materials:] *To* with a place name, as in "He lives up to Hartford," is so widespread in the East that it is almost easier to say where it is not the most common form than where it is. In New England it is practically universal, and it is found all the way south to Virginia, after which it becomes less common. **1966–70** *DARE* (Qu. C33, . . *Joking names . . for an out-of-the-way place, or a very small or unimportant place*) Inf **OK**56, Down to the dump; (Qu. P9, *When you're fishing but not catching any*) Inf **VT**16, Shoulda stayed to home; (Qu. MM11, *When you're trying to find something—you don't know where it is . . "I must have left it _____."*) Inf **NY**68, To home; (Qu. MM22, *If you are talking to a friend who lives in another place and you want to inquire about his neighborhood . . "How are things _____?"*) Inf **AR**55, Up to Little Rock; over to Dermott; down to Hamburg; **NE**11, Up to McCook; down to Lincoln; **CT**42, Down to the "Y"; **MA**14, Over to your house; **ME**9, Over to your place. **1966–68** *DARE* Tape **CA**103, [They] got my father to run that store and keep the books up to Newport; **IN**18, I . . took Bebe to a dance, up over to the Western Auto place; **MA**6, One of the head fellows down to Enfield . . patrolled there two or three times a day; **MI**27, We have a small garden up to our cabin up there in the woods; **MI**49, Every horse trader in the country would always stop out to our house. **1967–69** *DARE* FW Addit **eMD,** My cousin from up to New Jersey, he keeps his boat to the wharf; **ceNY,** He's up to the shop; **NY,** Stop to my house; **NC,** She works to the office at Nago Head; **VT,** He's down to Windsor; **OR,** I had to stay to bed; **VT,** He's down to Windsor. **1992** Scott *Cajun Vernacular Engl.* 43, Mais, cher, Maw-maw got you that to the Walmart. **2001** *DARE* File **NEng,** The use of "over to" where "over at" would normally occur (as in "we had dinner over to Jackson's Restaurant") is fairly common among members of my father's family (who currently live in northeastern MA and southern NH, but whose parents came from southern VT). It has a straightforwardly "down-home," nonstandard flavor in context. *Ibid* **csMO,** I got this new chair over to Wal-Mart. **2004** *Ibid* **swWI,** South and west of Monroe, in rural Lafayette County, people will say, "He lives over to Monroe," but the city people don't say that.

b Used redundantly at the end of a *where* clause. Cf **at prep 4**

1949 *WELS Suppl.* **csWI,** Now to the Cornish [of Mineral Point]. "Where is he to?" means simply "Where is he?"

c Spec in phr *sick to one's stomach* and varr: Nauseated. **scattered, but chiefly Nth, N Midl, CA** See Map and Map Section Cf **at prep 2, of prep C10, on B9, with B2**

1834 Smith *Life Jack Downing* 36 **ME,** Rum, if they take tu much of it, makes folks *sick to the stomach.* **1894** *Harper's New Mth. Mag.* 90.86 **AR,** It's enough to make a person sick to his stummick! **1899** *Daily Northwestern* (Oshkosh WI) 10 Sept 6/3, Mr. Sparks says the electricity made him weak in the joints and sick to his stomach. **1910** *DN* 3.448 **wNY,** Sick to one's stomach. **1929** *AmSp* 5.121 **ME,** A nauseated person was described as "sick to the stomach." **1949** Kurath *Word Geog.* 78 **NEng, NY, PA,** The New England settlement area has predominantly *to the stomach,* northern New England, Upstate New York, and northern Pennsylvania almost exclusively so. **1965–70** *DARE* (Qu. BB16a, *If something a person ate didn't agree with him, he might be sick _____ his stomach*) 463 Infs, **scattered, but chiefly Nth, N Midl, CA,** To; **WV**3, To stomach; **TX**51, To the; (Qu. BB16b, *If something a person ate didn't agree with him, he might just feel a bit _____*) Infs **GA**54, **MO**17, Sick to his stomach; (Qu. H69, *When food is hard on your stomach, you say that it _____*) Inf **MI**72, Made me sick to the stomach; (Qu. BB17, . . *Vomiting*) Infs **MI**69, **MA**125, Sick to his stomach; **IL**43, Sick to the stomach; **NY**69, **OH**8, (Get) sick to your stomach; **OH**98, Be sick to your stomach; (Qu. II29b, . . *To explain the unpleasant effect that person has on you: "He just _____"*) Infs **NJ**1, **WI**34, Makes me sick to my stomach. **1975** Allen *LAUM* 2.64 **Upper MW** (as of c1950), *To [one's stomach]* not only dominates Minnesota and the Dakotas and is quite strong in Iowa and Nebraska but also is especially favored by the most highly educated. **2000** *Gettysburg Times* (PA) 30 Oct 1/3, As Heidi approached the corner of the room, she started to feel sick to her stomach.

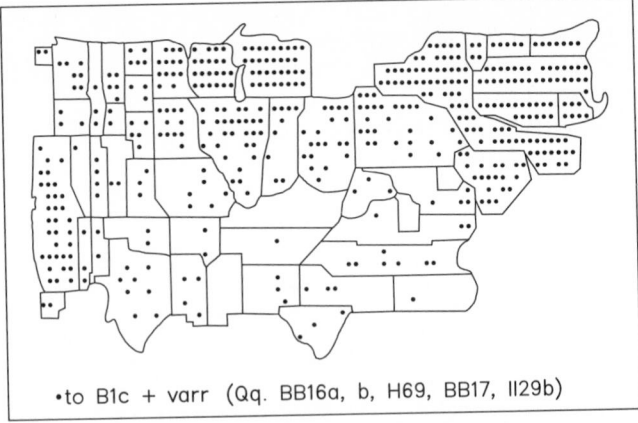

•to B1c + varr (Qq. BB16a, b, H69, BB17, II29b)

2 At (a time); at (once); in or by (a single action). **esp NEng**

1839 *S. Lit. Messenger* 5.432 **ME,** Then all to once I fetched an everlasting spring. **1854** Smith *'Way Down East* 243 **ME,** He's been kind o' edging round the deacon this three weeks, a little to a time. **1856** in 1862 Colt *Went to KS* 147 **NY,** I had the fowl disrobed of feathers and skin, all to one pull by a strong man's hand. **1859** *Knickerbocker* 53.206 **Upstate NY,** I reckon . . [she liked] *me,* too, but not to-once, I expect. **1866** Andrews *South* 174 **cNC,** He did n't take no 'count of these men who was sich good Union men all to once. **1881** *Atlantic Mth.* 48.21 **ME,** He said we could feed him a little to a time. **1896** *DN* 1.421 **NY,** *Once:* to oncet [təwʌnst]. For *at once.* **1907** White *AZ Nights* 290, I'll make her keep her eyes on the ground . . and then I'll let her look up all to once. **1908** Johnson *Highways Pacific Coast* 259 **OR,** I've dipped out three bluebacks to a lick. **1933** Rawlings *South Moon* 37 **FL,** Makin' ten gallons to a time. **1933** (1934) Cushman *Swing* 100 **sAppalachians,** We used to study, all to once't, out loud. **1939** *LANE* Map 52 *(One; once)* 11 infs, **esp s,wNEng,** To once; 1 inf, **cnMA,** To oncet. **1950** Moore *Candlemas Bay* 99 **ME,** A family of eleven could eat a peck of potatoes to a lick. **1963** *PADS* 40.14, *All to once* shows up [in Linguistic Atlas materials], not with any great frequency in New York and northern Pennsylvania and occasionally in Ohio and Michigan, becoming less frequent as one goes west. **1966** *DARE* Tape **MA**86, They used to grind about . . two hundred, two hundred and fifty bushels of apples to once. **1966–69** *DARE* FW Addits **ME, NY,** One to a time; **neNY,** All to once, meaning all at once—common; **ceNY,** "Can't think of anything to the minute"—i.e., "at the minute." Older folk. **1968–69** *DARE* (Qu. LL7, *In small amounts, by small degrees: "She didn't get the money all at once, they sent it to her _____."*) Inf **VT**6, A little to a time; **MA**14, A little bit to a time. **2002** in 2005 *DARE* File—Internet **VT,** If these tips help, try and use them a little to a time. **2003** *Ibid* **ME,** Only get on computer a little to a time.

3 Used to indicate the object of an emotion, where *of* or another prep would be std; see quots. [*OED2 to* prep. 30.b]

1794 (1914) Clark *Jrl.* 425 **VA,** I am now lead to a reflection which if indulged, would perhaps give me two great a disgust to a Military life. **1935** in 1944 *ADD* **WV,** I have a fear to water. **1965–70** *DARE* (Qu. HH10, *A very timid or cowardly person: "He's _____."*) Infs **AL**16, **OH**81, (A)fraid to the dark; (Qu. II11b, *If two people can't bear each other at all . . "Those two are _____."*) Inf **OK**13, Envious to each other.

4 For the benefit of, on behalf of—used in contexts where *for* is std. [Scots, nIr dial; cf *SND* tae prep. 6.(4).(i), *EDD to* prep. 4]

a1863 (1885) Green *Memoir Otey* 118 **VA,** They are ambitious of getting to themselves a name in the world. **1871** in 1983 *PADS* 70.55 **ce,sePA,** I got home at four o'clock and got my supper to myself. **1986** Pederson *LAGS Concordance* **Gulf Region,** 1 inf, Pour it in the trough to him; 1 inf, Cook to three people.

5 With, in addition to. [Calque from Ger *zu; OED2* c897 →] **PaGer area**

1908 *German Amer. Annals* 10.48 **sePA,** *To.* With. "I want some butter to my bread." **1914** *DN* 4.158 **ce,sePA,** We had string beans boiled to a ham. **1935** *AmSp* 10.167 **PA** [Engl of PA Germans], You can wear this color to black.

6 With, under (a teacher). **chiefly WV** Addit exx in *ADD*

1928 in 1944 *ADD* **cwWV,** He has a class to Dr. Brown. **1935** *AmSp* 10.314 **WV,** One of its [=*to*'s] most frequent uses is as a substitute for *with* or *under* when a college student speaks of his classes, courses, or professors. . . 'Last semester I had a course to Professor Blank'. . . 'Professor Blank, to whom I took a course in chemistry.' Apparently this expression is all but restricted to the larger college communities of West Virginia. **1939** *AmSp* 14.156 **WV,** *To.* Under or with (an instructor). Thus: 'I had a class in German to Professor C.' Most of my students could not imagine any other way of stating this sentence. **1996** in 2004 Montgomery–Hall *Dict. Smoky Mt. Engl.* 591 **eTN,** I'm going to take a class to Miss Jones. **2000** *DARE* File—Internet **WV,** I remember the first time I took a class to him I couldn't stand him, but he kinda grows on you.

7 In var uses where *with* would be expected. **Sth, S Midl**

1903 *DN* 2.332 **seMO,** *Swap my nag to his'n.* . . Swap horses with him. **1918** *DN* 5.20 **NC,** *Popular to,* popular with. Johnson Co. **1935** in 1944 *ADD* **WV,** He spent a profitable day to us. **1939** McGuire *FL Cracker Dial.* 110, I was raised to bird dogs. **1945** FWP *Lay My Burden Down* 69 **SC** [Black], I signed up to the government, but they ain't give me nothing. **1969** *DARE* Tape **KY**9, And that [quantity of tobacco plants] . . , to good luck, will set about an acre of ground.

8 Used with vbl n after inceptive verbs such as *begin, get, start;* see quots. **scattered, but somewhat more freq Sth, S Midl** Cf **go** v C2 Note: With *get* in the sense "come to be," this constr is widespread (as in "they got to thinking") and is not illustrated here.

1906 *Atlanta Constitution* (GA) 12 Apr 11/2, In the ninth inning . . Atlanta bats had started to working in great shape. **1929** *Daily Northwestern* (Oshkosh WI) 15 Jan 15/3, Well, filling stations started to tying up in chains, and still I never started to beating out my brains; I merely said, "They'll sell us some cheaper gasoline." **1931** James *Big-Enough* 155 **West,** He begin to using his rope and a running iron, and claiming cattle that wasn't his. **1945** FWP *Lay My Burden Down* 90 **AL** (as of c1860) [Black], Then she grab that broom and start to beating me over the head with it and calling me low-down nigger. **1966–69** *DARE* (Qu. A19, *Other ways of saying "I'll have to hurry": "I'm late, I'll have to _____."*) Inf **KY**20, Get to going; (Qu. A20, *Joking ways of telling somebody to hurry*) Inf **NY**68, Get to going; **NJ**2, Let's get to going. **1968–70** *DARE* Tape **CA**172A, Then he started to milking cows, and raised up a nice herd of cattle; **IN**3, That one evening . . they started to digging in; **KY**75, When you start to stripping a crop, you just don't know . . how many grades you will have. **1978** Dance *Shuckin' & Jivin'* 218 **MS,** These white guys . . got this Black guy . . and they just started to shooting around his feet. **1989** Gurganus *Oldest Confederate Widow* 349 **Sth,** Strange, his straight-facedness had begun to working on me. **1999** *San Angelo Std.-Times* (TX) 3 Nov (Internet), She commenced to squalling.

9 Used as infin marker in var constrs where bare infin is std, as:

a Following causative *have.* **chiefly Sth, S Midl**

a1836 in 1845 *S. Lit. Messenger* 11.552 **NC,** The greater part of them had rifles, but to a part of them he had them to fix a large knife they usu-

ally carried. **1841** *Ibid* 7.200 **MI,** The boys . . had him to keep tally when they were playing ball. **1903** *DN* 2.334 **seMO,** I'll have a man to examine the land. **1904** *DN* 2.418 **nwAR,** *Have* in the sense of *cause* is followed by *to* before the infinitive. 'I had him to bring me the book.' **1925** Hunter *Trail Drivers TX* 150, That noon he had me to trim his hair and whiskers. **1926** *DN* 5.393 **KS,** "I'll have him to call you when he comes in" (said to me by a salesman). "We wish to have every reader of the paper to see it and to think about it."—Editorial statement in the Lawrence Journal-World. **1942** in 1944 *ADD* **WV,** He once had a neighbor lady to come some . . vegetables. **1967** Green *Horse Tradin'* 34 **TX,** That is good Southern English, I'll have you to know! **1968–69** *DARE* Tape **GA**61, The government have you to list priorities; **RI**1, I had my sister-in-law to make me a couple of rhubarb pies. **1986** *AmSp* 61.184 **Sth, S Midl,** At least for college students, *have* followed by *to* (causative *Have him* to *call me;* existential *They had a tornado* to *touch down in Raleigh last night!*) is commonplace in the South and South Midland states but virtually unknown elsewhere. **2003** *DARE* File **AL,** If I could I would contact an elephant handler and have him to bring every . . one he would find and march them into her parking lot.

b Following experiential *have.* **chiefly Sth, S Midl**

1845 *Amer. Whig Rev.* 2.504 **TX,** I wouldn't have him to hear this for a horse! **1877** *Harper's New Mth. Mag.* 55.921 **nePA,** A superintendent says, "I have had them to come at six, and their mothers with them, to get them taken on." **1903** *DN* 2.334 **seMO,** This use of *to* is quite common in country newspapers, as 'Mr. Jones had a barn to burn yesterday.' **1906** *DN* 3.139 **nwAR,** *Have . . to.* . . In such expressions as, "I had a good sister to tell me," i.e., "A good sister told me." "I have had grown chickens to eat strychnine without hurting them." Common. **1908** *DN* 3.319 **eAL, wGA,** I have had watermelons to keep till Christmas. **1936–41** in 1944 *ADD* **neKY,** I've never had a dog to bite me in my life. . . I've had birds to come down out'n the air. **1941** *Ibid* **WV,** The woman who had had 5 husbands to die. **1946** *PADS* 6.18 **ceNC,** "He had a horse to die last night." Pamlico. Common. **1960** Criswell *Resp. to PADS 20* **Ozarks,** *Have.* . . To suffer (a calamity). "He had his house to fall down in that storm." Still very common. **1965–70** *DARE* Tape **KY**85, But one time I had a whole swarm [of bees] to land—to settle on my bee cap, all over my face; **VA**46, We haven't had water to come over the highway. **1971** GA Dept. Ag. *Farmers Market Bulletin* 19 May 8/2, Last summer we had lizards to bed around our patio and steps. **1986** [see **9a** above]. **2004** in 2005 *DARE* File—Internet **NC,** I have never had any [meringue cookies] to fall—I have had them to be chewy.

10 in phrr *different(ly) to:* Different(ly) from. [*OED2* (at *different* adj. 1.b) 1603 →; "*to* . . is found in writers of all ages, and is frequent colloquially, but is considered incorrect"] **esp Sth, S Midl**

1825 (1833) Brown *Institutes Engl. Gram.* 175, [In a list titled "False Syntax":] I will tell you a story very different to that. **1843** *S. Lit. Messenger* 9.278 **eVA,** William's feelings were different to what they had been on any previous visit. **1863** in 1886 U.S. War Dept. *War of Rebellion* 1st ser 16.1.712 **IL,** The effect of this division would have been but little different to that of concentrating at Sparta. [**1891** *Harper's New Mth. Mag.* 83.219, Perhaps the two most frequent Briticisms and the most obvious are the use of *different to* where the American more appropriately and logically says *different from,* and the employment of *directly* and its synonyme *immediately* for *as soon as.*] **1908** *Chillicothe Constitution* (MO) 12 Dec 10/5, I have also received a small lot of fine . . spectacle cases which are quite unique and entirely different to *anything* you have ever seen before. **1923** *Syracuse Herald* (NY) [7 Apr] 3/3 (newspaperarchive.com), The effect is highly interesting since that type of music is quite different to that generally played by the Polish pianist. **1968** *DARE* Tape **GA**69, The Georgia peach industry is entirely different to the California peach industry. **1969** *DARE* (Qu. II11b, *If two people can't bear each other at all . . "Those two are _____."*) Inf **NC**72, Different to each other. **1986** Pederson *LAGS Concordance* **Gulf Region,** [20 exx of the type *A polecat's different to a skunk*]; 1 inf, The kitchen was furnished quite differently to now; 1 inf, Different colored to that.

11 in phr *take notice to:* To take notice of.

1829 Kirkham *Engl. Grammar* 193 **PA,** [In a list of Pennsylvania provincialisms:] I never took notice to it. **1847** Hurd *Grammatical Corrector* 69, *To,* for *of;* as, "He passed me, but I never took any notice to him." "Did you take notice to the eclipse?" This perversion appears to be chiefly restricted to the Middle States. **1874** Lowell *Antony Brade* 195 **MA,** I want you to take notice to the way that left ear is split down. **a1925** in 2005 *DARE* File—Internet **Ozarks,** Every one present took notice to it and could not help smiling every time they saw him do so.

1926 Roberts *Time of Man* 121 **cKY,** How many times do we ever take notice to it? **1931** *Mexia Weekly Herald* (TX) 9 Jan [4]/6 (newspaperarchive.com), Will appreciate all my customers taking notice to this change. **2002** in 2004 *DARE* File—Internet **PA,** That which is condemned by God and once brought horror to God fearing people the world doesn't even take notice to it. **2002** in 2005 *Ibid* **nwFL,** I was shocked when he took notice to "Donkey" from the movie Shrek. **2005** *Ibid* **swNJ,** Then I really took notice to her and I realized that she had lost a lot of weight.

12 in phrr *plant* (or *seed, sow*) *to:* To plant (a field) with. [*OED2 to* prep. 8.d 1799 →; "Chiefly *U.S.*"] **esp Nth**

1833 in 1834 Smith *Life Jack Downing* 28 **ME,** He . . planted the ground all over to corn, and potatoes. **1851** Turner *Hist. Pioneer Settlement* 382 **NY,** The brothers and Springer built a cabin, and clearing six acres, and without the use of a plough, planted it to corn. *Ibid* 176, During the summer, he cleared ten acres and sowed it to wheat. **1865** IL State Ag. Soc. *Trans. for 1861–64* 5.154, The land . . was . . mostly planted to potatoes. **1919** Anderson *Winesburg OH* 103 **nOH,** When the land was drained he planted it to cabbages and onions. **1945** (1946) Macdonald *Egg & I* 54 **WA,** The garden . . was planted to peas, beets, beans, corn [etc]. **1966** *DARE* (Qu. L22, *When talking about a crop he intends to plant . . a farmer might say, "This year, I'm going to _____ a crop of oats/corn/cotton, etc."*) Inf **ME5,** Seed it to oats. **2004** *DARE* File—Internet **ME,** We managed to turn over two acres here, and seed it to a cover crop.

13 In expressions of time between the half hour and the hour: before, until. [*OED2 to* prep. 6.b 1519 →] **widespread, but somewhat less freq NEng, Midl** See Map and Map Section Cf **of** prep **C4, till B3**

1849 *Ladies' Repository* Dec 374, At about ten minutes and a quarter to twelve o'clock . . we started by steamboat. **1906** Lovett *Old Boston Boys* 9, I remember a weather-beaten driver of one of these omnibuses, who, upon being asked the time of starting upon the trips, invariably droned out, "Quarter a'ter, half a'ter, quarter to, and at." **1940** Cottrell *Railroader* 5, The young call-kid who says "ten minutes to nine" instead of "eight-fifty" . . immediately feels the cutting edge of ridicule. **1945** *Middletown Times Herald* (NY) 24 Dec 12/7, Santa Claus. . . always comes down this chimney at a quarter to thirteen. **1949** Kurath *Word Geog.* 50, *Quarter of eleven.* . . In the Northern area, on Delaware Bay, and on Chesapeake Bay *of* and *to* stand side by side in this expression. . . The greater part of the Southern area (Eastern Virginia, northeastern North Carolina, and the Low Country of South Carolina) has exclusively *quarter to.* **1950** *WELS* **WI** (*What time is this*) 38 Infs, Quarter to eleven; 29 Infs, Fifteen (minutes) to eleven. **1965–70** *DARE* (Qu. A6, *What time is this? [. . clock face at 10:45]*) 361 Infs, **widespread, but somewhat less freq NEng, Midl,** Quarter to eleven; 50 Infs, **scattered exc NEast,** Fifteen (minutes) to eleven; **CA87,** Quarter to. **1989** Pederson *LAGS Tech. Index* 21 **Gulf Region,** 222 infs, (A) quarter to; 44 infs, Fifteen (minutes) to; 1 inf, Quarter of an hour to.

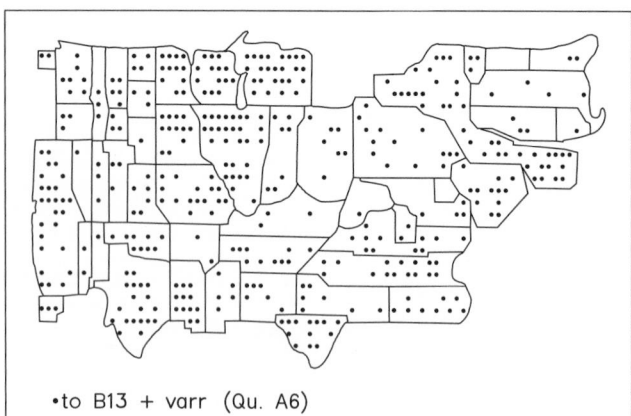

•to B13 + varr (Qu. A6)

14 in phr *trust one to:* To trust (one) to bear the cost of; to trust (one) with. [Prob < Ger *jemandem etwas zutrauen* to trust someone with something]

1869 Keeler *Gloverson* 152, By a great deal of eloquence he had prevailed upon a painter to trust him to a notary's sign. **1968–69** *DARE* (Qu. U11, *If you buy something but don't pay cash for it . . "I _____."*) Inf **NJ53,** Got trusted to it, got credit [Inf's parents German]; (Qu. V2b, *About a deceiving person, or somebody that you can't*

trust . . "I wouldn't trust him _____."; not asked in early QRs) Inf **IN66,** To a nickel [Inf's parents Swiss]. **2004** *DARE* File **cwWI** (as of c1970), My German aunt would say, "I wouldn't trust him to a dollar."

15 in phr *to one's age:* In comparison to the norm for one's age. **Gulf States, sAppalachians**

1882 in 2005 *DARE* File—Internet **csMS,** She a [sic] a gowing on 6 years since Feb the 9. She is small to her age. **1887** *Atlanta Constitution* (GA) 12 Nov 3/3, Tram is only a lad of sixteen summers, and small to his age. **1937** *Hall Coll.* **eTN,** Small to one's age. Small *for* one's age. "That bear was small to his age." . . Cf **stout** (=strong) *to one's age:* "She's stout to her age." (i.e. sturdy considering her age.) **1970** Green *Ely* 82 **csTN** [Black], I am small to my age. **1986** Pederson *LAGS Concordance* **Gulf Region,** 1 inf, Spry to her age; 1 inf, He's big to his age; 1 inf, He's awful pertly to his age; 1 inf, He's still quite active to his age; 1 inf, Quite young-looking to his age. **2002** *McKenzie Banner* (TN) 12 June (Internet), He was small to his age; he didn't start growing 'til he was 16 or 17 years old. **2004** *DARE* File—Internet **nwTN,** Pa was not old enough to be in the army during the Civil War. Well if he had been big to his age he might have got in but he was little.

16 in phrr *get (a)hold* (or *(a)holt*) *to* and varr: To get hold of. **esp Sth, S Midl**

1915 in 2010 (acc) Lexis–Nexis Legal Research *State Case Law: AR* (Internet) [Black], I stepped up on the first step, but they didn't have any stool there, so I caught a-hold to the rod on this side next to the baggage car. **1942** Redding *No Day* 254 **KY** [Black], He'd went for a swim an' one o' them big ol' turtles had got a-holt to him. **1961** Garrett *In Briar Patch* 162 **FL,** It was a crazy idea. . . I let it get a hold to me and started to care too much. **1966–70** *DARE* (Qu. BB40, *If you're inquiring about somebody acting strangely: "All of a sudden he got up and left. What do you suppose _____ him?"*) Inf **NJ69,** Got ahold to; (Qu. NN5, *Ways of saying 'Do you understand?': "You take hold of it this way, _____?"*) Inf **TN46,** Do you get hold to it; (Qu. V5b, *If you take something that nobody seems to own . . "Before anybody else gets it, I'm going to _____ this."*) Inf **SC26,** Grab hold to. **1966–69** *DARE* Tape **GA1,** The dogs would get aholt to her; **OH69,** The younger women don't take aholt to it. They'd rather do other things than quilt. **1986** Pederson *LAGS Concordance* **Gulf Region,** 1 inf, They'd get hold to a stove; 1 inf, It's hard to get aholt to; 1 inf, Anything he could get ahold to; 1 inf, Get ahold to it; 1 inf, Every job I get hold to, they cut me off. **2001** in 2005 *DARE* File—Internet **seSC,** The paint crew that got aholt to my screw probably had some real choice words. **2002** Whack *Meant to Be* 3 **Chicago IL** (as of 1967) [Black], The Spirit had "gotten a holt" to Mother Brock and she was pew-stepping, bench-hopping happy. **2002** in 2005 *DARE* File—Internet **csVA,** You should be able to get ahold to your company employee handbook. **2003** *Ibid* **MS,** His phone waz messed up, but i finally got a holt to him today. **2004** *Ibid* **cLA,** I do hope that the good Lord grabs a holt to her quick. **2005** *Ibid* **ceTX,** The best way to get ahold to me is e-mail.

17 in phr *to oneself:* Alone. [Perh by ext from std *leave to oneself* leave alone]

1986 Pederson *LAGS Concordance,* 1 inf, **LA,** Some likes to eat the cracklings separate to theirselves = by itself/themselves; 1 inf, **MS,** Boil it to himself = boil the meat by itself.

C As adv.

1 So as to become or remain closed or in contact. [*OED2* c1200 →; but cf Ger *zumachen* to shut, close] Cf **make v[1]** **D32**

1847 *Scientific Amer.* 2.281, It [=a carriage] . . is furnished with all the modern improvements, such as . . handles on the inside to pull the door to when shut. **1856** Kelly *Humors* 281 **sePA,** Down rush the girls— slam to the door and bar it! **1886** *Atlantic Mth.* 57.817 **TN,** The sheriff . . pulled the door to. **1908** *German Amer. Annals* 10.33 **sePA,** Make to. (Rare.) "Make the door to." **1930** *NY Times* (NY) 26 Aug 16, He jumped inside [a safe] and pulled the door to behind him, but could not lock it from the inside. **c1938** in Lib. of Congress *Amer. Memory: WPA Life Hist.* (Internet) **VT,** Ezra and Ed draw the door too [sic] and hasp it with a leather thong fastened with a wooden pin. **1939** *Ibid* **neFL,** No, we just push the front door to, and don't bother to lock up nothin. **1940** (1968) Haun *Hawk's Done Gone* 35 **TN,** I batted my eyes. They flopped to and open—like a frog in a hail storm. **1966–69** *DARE* FW Addits **cwAL,** Put the door to—close the door (completely); **ceTN,** Put the door to—shut the door; **neMD,** Push the door to—push the door shut; **swNC,** Pull it to—close it; **GA33,** To make the gate come to = make the gate close. **1970** Thompson *Coll.* **cnAL** (as of 1930s), The crack wouldn't stay to. **1983** *DARE* File **nwMS,** In these parts when we close a door, we "push it *to*", not necessarily fastening the mechanism fully, but just enough to keep the room from being "too airish." **1986** Pederson *LAGS Concordance (Shut the door)* 1 inf, **cwGA,** Pull it to; 1 inf, **swTN,** The wind blew it to. **2004** *DARE* File **csTX** (as of c1954), When my father said "Pull the door to," he meant to close the door and pull it until the latch clicked.

2 foll noun: In front, facing forward or toward something implied by the context—used to form var adv phrr describing orientation. **chiefly Nth, esp NEast; also Pacific** See Map *somewhat old-fash* See also **ass-end-to, back-end-to, backside-to, hindside-to** Cf **scuppers to**

1835 *New Engl. Mag.* 8.11, At this moment she touched—rubbed—faltered for a few seconds, and then broached broadside to, and grounded! **1856** Underhill–Thomson *Elephant Club* 109 **NYC,** The engine . . was now lying by the side of the road with its head in the mud, wrong end to, bottom side up, roasting itself brown. **1894** *Newark Daily Advocate* (OH) 18 Sept 7/4, I should judge it [=a necktie] was securely tied, but it is back side to. **1927** *Decatur Herald* (IL) 4 Jan sec 2 1/3, The girder was loaded on the flat cars so that when they arrived at the bridge site, it was "wrong end to." **1950** *WELS* **WI** *(With the back part forward: "She had her dress on _____.")* 11 Infs, Hindside-to; 3 Infs, Backside-to; 1 Inf, Hind-end-to; 1 Inf, Hind-to; *(The truck was coming down the road _____)* 1 Inf, Hindside-to. **1965–70** *DARE* (Qu. MM2, *Suppose a little girl accidentally gets her dress on wrong so that the back part is turned around . . "Look, you've got your dress on _____.")* 48 Infs, **chiefly Nth, West, esp NEast, NY,** Hindside-to; 23 Infs, **chiefly Nth, esp NEng, NY,** Backside-to; 21 Infs, **chiefly Nth, West,** Wrong-side-to; **AL3, CT25, NY155, WI13, WY5,** Back-end-to; **CA102, 114, IL92, 96,** Hind-part-to; **MA24, NY220, SD5,** Hind-end-to; **ME19, NM9,** Wrong-end-to; **CT36,** Arse-end-to; **NC88,** Hind-to; **MI117,** Hind-way-to; **MA5,** Tother-end-to; **NY24,** Wrong-way-to [Of all Infs responding to the question, 63% were old; of those giving these responses, 74% were old.]; (Qu. MM3, *When someone does something the wrong way round . . "This is the front, you've got the whole thing turned _____.")* 21 Infs, **chiefly Nth,** Ass-end-to; **AK8, CT8, MA2, 61, 98, NY67, 88, 205,** Backside-to; **AK5, CA164, MA40, NH1, NJ39, NY130, 234, OH80,** Hindside-to; **ME12, NE10, NH5, 13, NY185, OH44, PA193, 216,** Wrong-side-to; **CT19, MA61, 73, NY136, 155, PA190,** Back-end-to; **MA11, 14, NM9, NY109, PA177,** Wrong-end-to; **MI76, WA20,** Hind-end-to; **CT36,** Arse-end-to; **WI11,** Front-end-to; **MI117,** Hind-way-to; **NY126,** Tail-end-to; **MA5,** Tother-way-to; **CA189,** Wrong-way-to. **1966** *Daily Times* (Salisbury MD) 14 May 4/3, Head to—a waterman's expression that came ashore and grounded into our language. It's the proper way to bring a boat to beach with the occupants reasonably safe and dry and being the exact opposite of "broadside to." **1973** *Daily Kennebec Jrl.* (Augusta ME) 5 Mar 12/1, Edwin H. Kinney said "the planning is back end to." **1985** *Chron.-Telegram* (Elyria OH) 10 Mar mag sec 2/1, Science is wonderful, but it has yet to develop a carbon paper that can't be used in the typewriter wrong-side-to. **2004** *DARE* File **seWI** (as of c1960), If something was turned around or backwards, my father would say it was "ass-end to." **2004** in 2006 *DARE* File—Internet **ME,** As usual they have their priorities ass-end-to.

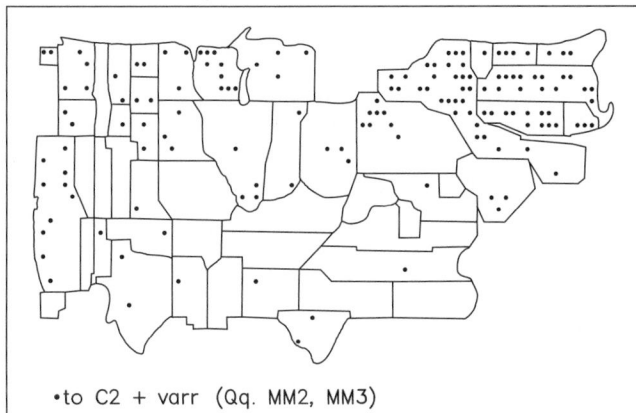

•to C2 + varr (Qq. MM2, MM3)

t.o. exclam [Abbr]
Time out.

1967–69 *DARE* (Qu. EE17, *In a game of tag, if a player wants to rest, what does he call out so that he can't be tagged?*) Inf **MA8,** Times out or t.o.; **NY161,** T.o.

toad n

1 Usu a batrachian of the genus *Bufo,* but also of the genera *Scaphiopus* and *Rhinophrynus.* [*OED2 toad* sb. 1.a c1000 →] **widespread, but chiefly Nth, N Midl, West** See Map Cf **toad-frog 1** For other names see **bull toad, dirt frog, dryland ~, flytrap** n 7, **frog** n B1, **grenouille, ground frog, highland ~, hoptoad 1, humptoad, land frog, ~ toad, piss toad, toad-frog 1, wart frog 1, warty toad;** for other names of *Scaphiopus* see **rainfrog 2;** for names of the larva see **pollywog** n 1, **tadpole 1**

1743 Catesby *Nat. Hist. Carolina* 2.69, *Rana terrestris* [=*Bufo t.*] *The Land Frog. . .* Their bodies are large, resembling more a Toad than a Frog, yet they do not crawl as Toads do, but leap. **1792** Belknap *Hist. NH* 3.174, Toad, *Rana bufo?* **1832** Williamson *Hist. ME* 1.169, The *Toad* is harmless. **1839** MA *Zool. & Bot. Surv. Fishes Reptiles* 50, With us, the habits of the *Bufo Americanus, Common Toad,* are becoming better understood. **1883** WI Chief Geologist *Geol. WI* 1.425, Toads. *Bufo. . .* A common and beneficial animal. **1899** Bergen *Animal Lore* 88 **NEng,** Handling a toad will cause freckles. **1918** *Copeia* 60.78 **swUT,** The call of this toad [=*Scaphiopus hammondii*] was heard both on the Pine Valley Mountains and on the Kolob Plateau . . during June. **1947** Pickwell *Amphibians* 14 **West,** Family *Scaphiopodidae* [= Pelobatidae] . . includes Toads characterized by a horny scraper, or shovel, on the sole of the hind foot. *Ibid* 15, *Bufo alvarius. . .* These great, lumbering, kindly looking Toads live in the desert but are almost aquatic! **1965–70** *DARE* (Qu. P23, *Names for the animal similar to the frog that lives away from water*) 575 Infs, **widespread, but chiefly Nth, N Midl, West,** Toad; (Qu. B26, *When it's raining very heavily . . "It's raining _____.")* Infs **CO4, MS65, NM8,** Toads; **FL37,** Toads and frogs; **MO39,** Toads and pitchforks; (Qu. P20, *Very young frogs—when they still have tails but no legs*) Infs **IN78, MO9, PA240,** Toads; (Qu. BB51a, . . *Cures for corns or warts*) Inf **NY35,** Toad pee; (Qu. BB51b, . . *'Magical' cures for corns or warts*) Infs **CT42, PA36,** Rub a toad on wart; **IN28, MI75,** Put a toad on it; **CO27,** Split a toad; **CT31,** Get water at midnight and dip a toad in it; **PA126,** Rub it with a toad; **WA28,** Keep away from toads. **2002** *DARE* File **swUS,** The Bufonids are commonly known as toads.

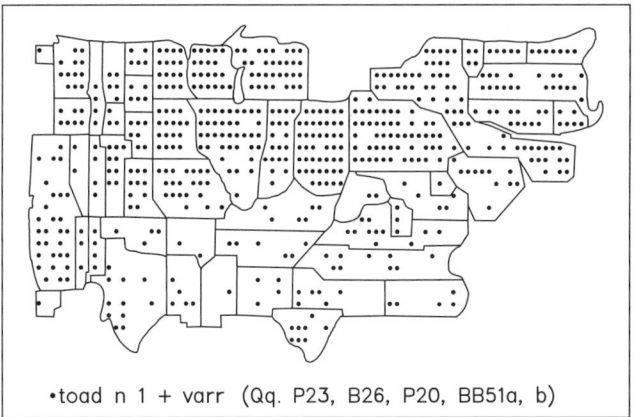

•toad n 1 + varr (Qq. P23, B26, P20, BB51a, b)

2 Usu a **tree frog 1,** but occas also a **bullfrog 1** or other frog. [*OED2 toad* sb. 2. "Used erroneously for the frog *(obs.)*" a1300, 1602] Cf **toad-frog 1, tree toad 1**

1917 *Copeia* 40.13 **OR,** *Ascaphus truei. . .* The "toad" was found at the edge of the creek which is here a cold, swift mountain-stream. **1950** *WELS (Small frogs that sing or chirp loudly in the spring)* 1 Inf, **WI,** Toads. **1965–70** *DARE* (Qu. P21, *Small frogs that sing or chirp loudly in spring*) 11 Infs, **scattered,** Toads; **CA52, PA92,** Toads [FW: Infs uncertain]; (Qu. P22, *Names or nicknames for a very large frog that makes a deep, loud sound*) Inf **CA111,** Toad; **SC21,** Bullfrog = toad; toad-frog—any frog of size; **CA52, WI78,** Toad [FW: Infs uncertain].

3 =**horned toad 1.** Cf **sand toad**

1893 Brit. Museum *Guide Reptiles* 11, [Caption:] Californian "Toad" *(Phrynosoma cornutum).* **1901** Fountain *Gt. Deserts* 158, The "Californian toad," which is really a species of lizard. **1926** TX Folkl. Soc. *Pub.* 5.64 **SW,** If the strange and interesting horned lizard, or "toad," as it is called in the vernacular, were an inhabitant of the bayou counties of Louisiana and Eastern Texas, instead of the drier regions to the westward, . . folklorists would have much more material to place on record. **1928** Baylor Univ. Museum *Contrib.* 16.12 **TX,** *Phrynosoma cornu-*

tum. . . Many of the cowboys simply call it "Toad." **1957** Barnes *Nat. Hist. Wasatch Summer* 39 **UT**, As we trudge over a dry rocky hillside on the way to a canyon, we unexpectedly come upon a desert horned lizard (*Phrynosoma platyrhinos*), and soon get the inoffensive "toad" in hand. **1967** *Refugio Timely Remarks* (TX) 30 Mar 1/1 **TX**, We're in the market for horned frogs again this year. A prevailing price of five cents each is being established for toads six inches and under in length.

4 See **toadfish a**.

5 also *tree toad*: A **mushroom B1** or a **toadstool**. Cf **toad-frog stool, tree frog 2**

1968–69 *DARE* (Qu. I38, *Small plants shaped like an umbrella that grow in woods and fields—which are not safe to eat*) Inf **NY45**, Toads; (Qu. S19, *Mushrooms that grow out like brackets from the sides of trees*) Inf **NY209**, Tree toads.

6 A small child—used affectionately. [*SND* 1768 →] **esp NEng** *old-fash*

1836 (1838) Haliburton *Clockmaker* (1st ser) 262 **NEng**, Two little orphan children, the prettiest litle toads I ever beheld. **1865** *Harper's New Mth. Mag.* 31.313, The little toad was jest as cross and as passionate as he could be all the time. **1868** *Alton Daily Telegraph* (IL) 25 Feb [2]/2 **NY** (newspaperarchive.com), A chap was in here just now and wanted to see Bob's baby, and looked at me and said I was a funny little toad and looked just like Bob. **1894** *Atlantic Mth.* 74.383 **WA**, She interrupted herself, when her husband came in, to tell him how "the little toad" had picked two hops. **1941** *LANE* Map 379 (*Kid, tot*) 1 inf, **sME coast**, [ə lɪˀtl tɔˑᵊd]. **1969** *DARE* (Qu. Z12, *Nicknames and joking words meaning 'a small child'*: "*He's a healthy little _____.*") Inf **RI**12, Toad. [Inf old] **2005** *DARE* File, I asked my lunchmates at the table at the Senior Center if they'd ever used "a little toad" to refer to a small child. They are all in their eighties, and all spoke right up saying that yes, it was commonly used when they were young, but they hadn't heard it used lately. They are from: Georgia; Dover, Mass.; Kansas City, Missouri; Long Island, New York.

7 A female dog. **SC, GA coasts** *Gullah*

1922 Gonzales *Black Border* 334 **sSC, GA coasts** [Gullah glossary], *Toad*—a young female dog. **1930** Stoney-Shelby *Black Genesis* 48 **seSC**, She dot de tail o' de leetle spotty toad (female dog) jus' like she coat.

8 In railroading: a device used to derail a car; see quots. [From its shape and its use in making cars "hop" the rails] Cf **hoptoad**

1931 *Writer's Digest* 11.64 [Railroad terms], *Toad*—Derailer. **1932** *RR Mag.* Oct 370 [Railroad lingo], *Toad*—Derailer. **1940** Cottrell *Railroader* 138, *Toad*—Derail iron.

9 See quot. Cf **frog n 6, joe frog(ger)** (at **joe flogger 2**)

1931–33 *LANE Worksheets* **seCT**, Toads—Rye dough dropped in deep fat—a Rhode Island expression. **1941** *LANE* Map 284 (*Doughnut*) 1 inf, **seRI**, Toads, of raised bread dough.

toad v See **tell v B2d**

toad-belly n

The leaf of **orpine** or a related **stonecrop 1**.

1931 Clute *Common Plants* 112, The only really characteristic name relating to toads is toad-bellies, applied to the leaves of *Sedum telephium* and allied species. These, under proper manipulation, may have the under epidermis loosened and, when inflated with air, present an appearance which the common name accurately describes.

toad bird See **toadhead**

toad bug n [See quots]

A bug of the genus *Gelastocoris*.

[**1895** Comstock-Comstock *Manual Insects* 133, The Toad-shaped Bugs. There is sometimes found on the muddy margins of streams or in marshes . . a curious bug, which on account of its short and broad body and projecting eyes reminds one of a toad; this is *Galgulus* [= *Gelastocoris*] *oculatus*.] **1901** Howard *Insect Book* 281, The Toad Bugs. . . The short, broad body and the projecting eyes, as well as the dull mottled colors, are toad-like. **1949** Swain *Insect Guide* 45, Toad Bugs. . . Very small hopping insects. **2002** (acc) TX A&M Univ. *Discover Entomol.* (Internet), Toad bugs. . . are brownish and about ½ inch long. They hop much like toads and are typically found along rocky shores of lakes or ponds.

toad-choker See **toad-strangler**

toadfish n

Any of var fish supposed to resemble a **toad n 1**, as:

a also *toad*; A tetraodontiform fish: usu a **puffer n¹ 1** of the genus *Sphoeroides* or a **porcupine fish** of the genus *Chilomycterus*. **chiefly Mid and S Atl** See Map Cf **blow-toad, puff ~, sucking ~, swelling ~, swell ~**

1612 Smith *Map VA* 15, The Todefish which will swell till it be like to brust, when it commeth into the aire. **1709** (1967) Lawson *New Voyage* 258, Toad-Fish are nothing but a Skin full of Prickles, and a few Bones; they are as ugly as a Toad, and preserv'd to look upon, and good for nothing else. **1743** Catesby *Nat. Hist. Carolina* 2 [app] xxxii, *Sea Fish*. . . Toad-fish. **1787** *Gesellschaft Naturforschender Freunde Schriften* 8.189, *Tetrodon hispidus*. . . Toadfish, in Neu-York und Rhode-Island. [=*Tetrodon hispidus* [here: =*Sphoeroides maculatus*]. . . Toadfish, in New York and Rhode Island.] *Ibid* 192, *Diodon Atringa*. . . Toadfish, zu Neuyork. [=*Diodon Atringa* [here: =*Chilomycterus schoepfi*]. . . Toadfish, at New York.] **1884** Goode *Fisheries U.S.* 1.170, The Porcupine Fishes—Diodontidae. . . The best known is the Swell Fish of New England, *Chilomycterus geometricus* [=*C. schoepfi*]. These fishes are commonly known by such names as . . "Toad Fish". **1905** NJ State Museum *Annual Rept. for 1904* 364, *Spheroides* [sic] *maculatus*. . . Toad Fish. **1928** Peterkin *Scarlet Sister Mary* 234 **SC**, She just swelled up like a toad-fish and sat and looked at the fire without cracking her teeth. **1965–70** *DARE* (Qu. P4, *Saltwater fish that are not good to eat*) 24 Infs, **chiefly Mid and S Atl**, Toadfish; **DE**1, Toadfish—some people eat these; **NC**60, Toadfish tastes very good; **NY**36, Toadfish—ugly-looking thing; **NC**80, Toad (toadfish); **MD**45, Black toad; (Qu. P2, . . *Kinds of saltwater fish caught around here . . good to eat*) Infs **VA**55, 75, Toad(s); **MD**45, Black toads, swimming toad; (Qu. P3, *Freshwater fish that are not good to eat*) Infs **DC**8, 12, Toadfish; **NJ**67, Toads [FW: Inf queries]; (Qu. P14, . . *Commercial fishing . . what do the fishermen go out after?*) Infs **VA**55, 75, Toad(s). **1969** *DARE* File **NC**, Toadfish—type of fish, horny on underside, which can be eaten but must first be skinned. Also called "horny toad."

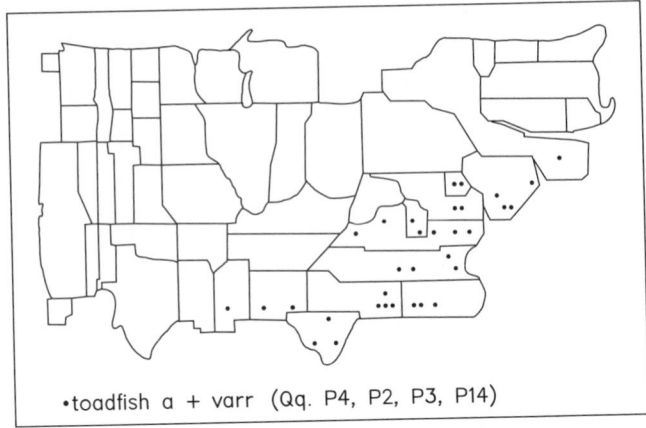

•toadfish a + varr (Qq. P4, P2, P3, P14)

b A batrachoidid fish usu of the genus *Opsanus* of the Atlantic and Gulf coasts, but also a **midshipman** (here: *Porichthys notatus*) of the Pacific coast. For other names of *Opsanus* spp see **oysterfish 1, sea robin 1b**; for other names of *O. tau* see **dogfish 8, grubby 1, mud toad, oyster-cracker 2, oyster toad, sea ~ 2, slimer, toad-grunter**

1787 *Gesellschaft Naturforscher Freunde Schriften* 8.141, *Gadus Tau* [=*Opsanus t*.]. . . Toadfish in Carolina und Virginien. **1814** in 1815 *Lit. & Philos. Soc. NY Trans.* 1.463, Toad-fish. (*Lophius bufo* [= *Opsanus tau*].) . . Brown, clouded, and mottled complexion. . . An inhabitant of our salt water. **1855** Smithsonian Inst. *Annual Rept. for 1854* 340 **NJ**, *Batrachus variegatus*. . . The toad-fish, or, as it is called at Beesley's point, the oyster-fish, . . is one of the fishermen's pests. **1884** U.S. Natl. Museum *Bulletin* 27.433 **wFL**, *Batrachus tau* L. subsp. *beta* [=*Opsanus beta*]. . . Oyster-fish; Toad-fish. . . Gulf of Mexico. This is the common form of toad-fish in shoal water, replacing the typical *B. tau* of more northern waters. . . *Batrachus pardus* [=*Opsanus p*.]. . . Toad-fish. . . West Florida. **1884** Goode *Fisheries U.S.* 1.253, The Toad-fish is very abundant throughout the whole extent of its range, and is easily captured with hook and line. In the Gulf of Mexico many are taken with seines. . . The *Batrachidae* are represented on the Pacific coast by the . . "Toad-fish," *Porichthys porosissimus* [=*P. notatus*]. **1915** [see **c**

below]. **1955** Zim–Shoemaker *Fishes* 157, Toadfish: Opsanus beta.
1967 *DARE* (Qu. P4, *Saltwater fish that are not good to eat*) Inf **DC**2,
Toadfish—big mouth, bites, slimy. **1984** *DARE* File **Chesapeake Bay**
[Watermen's vocab], Brown toad fish, oyster toad. **1986** Pederson
LAGS Concordance (Fish) 2 infs, **FL**, 2 infs ce**GA**, Toadfish.

c =**goosefish.** [*OED2* 1668 for *Lophius piscatorius*]
  1891 *Century Dict.* 6361, Toad-fish. . . 2. A lophioid fish, *Lophius
piscatorius,* so called from its uncouth aspect. **1915** *Copeia* 25.60 **NY**,
Lophius piscatorius [here: =*L. americanus*]. . . Many Long Island
fishermen loosely call it "Toadfish," although probably realizing that it is
different from the smaller *Opsanus tau,* for which the name is also used
and to which it properly belongs.

d as *rock toadfish:* A **sculpin 1** (here: *Hemitripterus americanus*). Cf **sea toad 1, toad-grunter, toad sculpin**
  1884 Goode *Fisheries U.S.* 1.258, Cottidae. . . On our Atlantic coast
are found several species of this family, generally known by the name
"Sculpin," and also by such titles as . . "Sea-toad." . . There is . . a large,
brilliantly colored form, known as the . . "Rock Toad-fish," . . which is
found as far south as the entrance to Chesapeake Bay [and] is abundant
throughout New England. . . This fish, *Hemitripterus . . americanus,* . .
is conspicuous . . by its warted body, its grotesquely elongated fins, and,
above all, by its peculiar habit of swallowing air until its belly is inflated
like a balloon.

toadflax n
  1 Std: a plant of the genus *Linaria,* esp **butter-and-eggs 1.**
  2 A plant of the genus *Nuttallanthus* (formerly *Linaria*), esp
blue toadflax.
  1843 Torrey *Flora NY* 2.32, Linaria Canadensis [=*Nuttallanthus c.*]. .
Canadian Toad-flax. **1897** Parsons *Wild Flowers CA* 304, *Linaria
Canadensis.* . . The delicate blue flowers of the toad-flax are not uncommon in spring. **1915** (1926) Armstrong–Thornber *Western Wild
Flowers* 474, Toad Flax—*Linaria Canadensis.* . . This is found in dry
soil across the continent. **1931** Fassett *Spring Flora* 143 **WI**, *L[inaria]
canadensis. Toadflax.* . . Corolla . . blue. Sandy ground, local. **1970**
Correll *Plants TX* 1426, *Linaria texana* [=*Nuttallanthus texanus*]. .
Texas toad-flax. . . Mostly in e. two thirds of Tex. **1979** Ajilvsgi *Wild
Flowers* 263, *Texas toad-flax.* . . *Flower:* pale blue to violet.

  3 =**dogberry j.**
  1866 Lindley–Moore *Treas. Botany* 2.1154, Toadflax. Bastard, *The-
sium linophyllum;* also an American name for *Comandra* [=*Geocaulon*]. **1966** Heller *Wild Flowers AK* 97, Dogberry, Toadflax—*Geocaulon lividum.* . . Flowers minute, greenish-bronze . . ; fruit an orange
or red, round to oblong berry, edible but not tasty. **1966** *DARE* Wildfl
QR Pl.28B [=*Geocaulon lividum*] Inf **MI**31, Toadflax. **1987** Hughes–
Blackwell *Wildflowers SE AK* 97, Toadflax (*Geocaulon lividum . .*). The
inconspicuous flowers grow out of the mid-upper leaf axils.

toad-floater See **toad-strangler**

toad-frog n
  1 also *toady-frog,* pronc-sp *toadge-~:* A **toad** n **1** or a frog,
esp a **tree frog 1. chiefly Sth, S Midl** See Map Cf **frog
n B1, toad** n **2**
  1827 *Amer. Farmer* 9.44 c**MD**, When chickens go amongst the trees,
they often eat . . insects that spoil the fruit; but they do not half so much
good as the toad frogs. **1861** *Harper's New Mth. Mag.* 23.421 **Sth**, Every body is a pitching into this matter like toad-frogs into a willow
swamp on a lovely evening in the balmy month of June. **1893** *Ibid*
88.59 **LA**, He turned out his toes, 'n' said 'ma'am' an' 'sir,' when he
warn't no mo'n knee-high to a toad-frog. **1902** *DN* 2.230 s**IL**, Bullfrog. . . Considered to be of a different species from a younger one of
the same kind, called a toadfrog. The difference between toads and frogs
not recognized, or, at the most, the distinction is very vague. Toads are
sometimes called hop-toads, but more generally *toadfrogs,* the same as
frogs. *Ibid* 247, Toad frog. . . Term used alike for toad or frog. Toad not
used by itself. **1903** *DN* 2.334 se**MO**, Toad-frog. . . Toad. **1905** *DN*
3.98 nw**AR**, Toad-frog. . . Toad. . . Common. **1909** *DN* 3.382 e**AL**,
w**GA**, Toad-frog. . . Toad. Universal. **1915** *DN* 4.192 sw**VA**, Toad
frog. . . Toad. [*DN* Ed: Also N. Car., La., Kan.] **1927** *DN* 5.478 **Ozarks**, Toad-frog. . . Toad. The word
frog is used with reference to both frogs and toads. **1931** *AmSp* 7.94
e**KY**, Toad-frog. a tailless, jumping amphibian, resembling the frog and
often mistaken for a toad. "If you play with toad-frogs, you'll git warts
on yo'r hands 'n' yo'r cows'll give bloody milk." **1936** in 1970 Hyatt
Hoodoo 1.441 **FL**, Well, he took dat shoe and he took two *toadyfrogs . .*

and he cut dat toadyfrog wide open. **1944** *PADS* 2.13, Toad-frog. . . 1.
A tree-toad. Marshall Co., Ala.; sections of Mo. 2. Almost any kind of
toad or frog except the bullfrog. (Also *toady-frog.*) Deep South. **1949**
PADS 11.26 **CO**, Toad-frog. . . A frog. **1950** *PADS* 14.68 **SC**, Toadge
frog. . . A toad. **1955** Roberts *S. from Hell-fer-Sartin* 119 se**KY**, "Why,
that's a toad frog." **1960** Carpenter *Tales Manchaca* 30 c**TX** (as of
c1880), "Look at that wart on your hand," she'd say. "Been playing with
toad frogs again." **1964** Will *Hist. Okeechobee* 220 **FL**, Nine new mills
have suddenly sprung up here like toadyfrogs after a rain. **1964** *PADS*
42.24 cs**KY**, Toads are *toad-frogs* in the region. **1965–70** *DARE* (Qu.
P23, *Names for the animal similar to the frog that lives away from water*) 284 Infs, **chiefly Sth, S Midl**, Toad-frog; **GA**65, Toad-frog—the
highland frog; **MD**31, Toad-frog, land frog; **SC**21, Bullfrog = toad;
toad-frog any frog of size; **VA**70, Land frog, toad-frog—no difference;
GA77, **SC**9, Toady-frog; (Qu. B26, *When it's raining very heavily . .
"It's raining _____.")* 19 Infs, **scattered Sth, S Midl**, Toad-frogs;
SC34, Down toad-frogs; (Qu. P21, *Small frogs that sing or chirp loudly
in spring*) 12 Infs, **chiefly Sth, S Midl**, Toad-frogs; (Qu. P22, *Names or
nicknames for a very large frog that makes a deep, loud sound*) Infs
SC21, **TX**67, Toad-frog; (Qu. X24, *When a person opens and closes his
eyes quickly, he _____*) Inf **OK**7, Bats his eyes like a toad-frog in a
hailstorm; (Qu. BB51a, . . *Cures for corns or warts*) Inf **TX**43, Tie split
toad-frog to corn, frog turns green, pull both off; (Qu. BB51b, . .
'Magical' cures for corns or warts) Inf **GA**42, Get a toad-frog and rub it
on wart. **1969** *DARE* Tape **GA**48, He said he wanted to get 'em [=
beehives] high enough that the toads couldn't get up and eat 'em, so
little toad-frogs couldn't. **1986** Pederson *LAGS Concordance (Toad)*
Gulf Region, 664 infs, Toad-frog(s); 19 infs, Toady-frog(s); 1 inf,
se**GA**, Scalyback = horn back, toad frog. **1988** Kingsolver *Bean Trees*
23 **KY**, The kid was splashing like a toad frog. **1991** Still *Wolfpen
Notebooks* 94 s**Appalachians**, I figure you know it's the worst kind of
bad luck to kill a toady-frog.

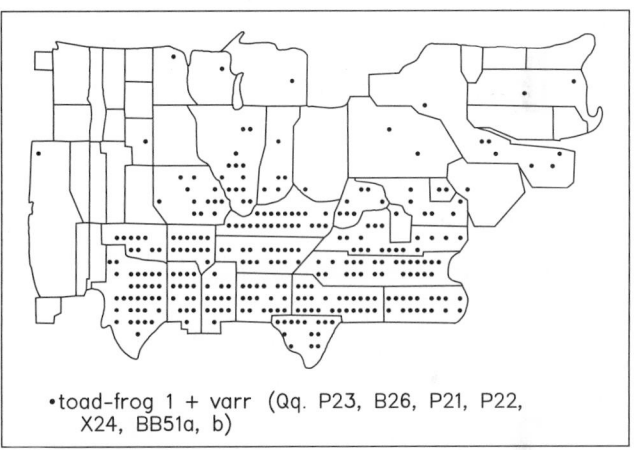

•toad-frog 1 + varr (Qq. P23, B26, P21, P22,
    X24, BB51a, b)

  2 See **toad-frog stool.**

toad-frog bread See **frog bread**

toad-frog house See **toad-frog stool**

toad-frogs, rain v phr Also *rain toads;* for addit varr see quot
1965–70 **chiefly Sth, S Midl** See Map on p. 634 Cf **bullfrogs, rain; frogs, rain**
To rain heavily.
  1908 *Washington Post* (DC) 29 Mar mag sec 9/8, [Children's poem:]
Come, 'tis raining toads and pitchforks,/ And a horse is in each tree.
[**1927** *Sheboygan Press* (WI) 22 Mar 5/6, When the little toads leave the
home of their infancy and start inland, there is such a vast army of them
as to give rise to the popular belief that it has been raining toads.]
1965–70 *DARE* (Qu. B26, *When it's raining very heavily . . "It's raining
_____.")* 19 Infs, **chiefly Sth, S Midl**, Toad-frogs; **MS**65, **NM**8,
Toads; **FL**37, Toads and frogs; **IN**49, Hop-toads; **MD**19, Hump-toads;
MO39, Toads and pitchforks; **NY**34, Frogs and happy [sic] toads; **SC**34,
Down toad-frogs; **TX**33, Hoppy toads; [**CO**4, There come up a rain,
toads so bad, one couldn't stop without killing a toad for over a mile; it
rained toads]. **1986** Pederson *LAGS Concordance* **Gulf Region**, 5 infs,
Rain toad-frogs. **2004** *DARE* File—Internet **TX**, Automatic levelers are
great, right up till the moment they won't retract, and it's raining
toadfrogs.

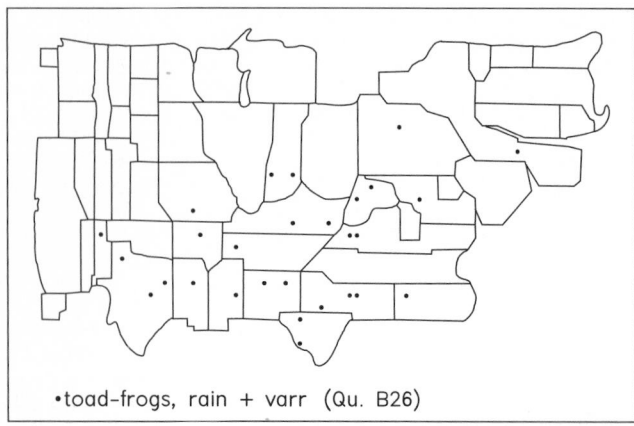

•toad-frogs, rain + varr (Qu. B26)

toadfrog-sticker See **toadstabber 1**

toad-frog stool n Also *toad-frog (house)* **esp Gulf States, GA** *esp freq among Black speakers* Cf **frogstool, toad** n **5, tree frog 2**

A **mushroom B1** or a **toadstool.**

1966–68 *DARE* (Qu. I38, *Small plants shaped like an umbrella that grow in woods and fields—which are not safe to eat*) Infs **GA**17, 19, Toad-frog stools; **GA**32, Toad-frogs. 1986 Pederson *LAGS Concordance* **Gulf Region,** 6 infs, Toad-frogstool(s); 3 infs, Toad-frog houses. [6 infs Black]

toadfrog-strangler See **toad-strangler**

toadge-frog See **toad-frog 1**

toad-grunter n Cf **toadfish d**

A **toadfish b** (here: *Opsanus tau*) or a **sculpin 1.**

1858 Ricketson *Hist. New Bedford MA* 403, Salt water: smelt, . . toad-grunter, shark [etc.]. 1877 Bartlett *Americanisms* 708, *Toad-grunter.* The toad-fish, so called from the noise it makes. 1914 *DN* 4.156 **eMA,** *Toad-grunter.* . . A sculpin. (Reported by a student as current at Woods Hole.)

toadhead n Also *toad bird*
=**golden plover.**

1871 *Our Boys & Girls* 10.744 **NEng,** "Any birds yet, Captain?" "Well, I heerd some toad heads squealin' this mornin' afore daybreak." 1886 *Forest & Stream* 27.287 **MA,** [Letter from John Murdoch:] A thoroughbred Cape Cod gunner from Orleans or Chatham calls the golden plover a "toadhead." *Ibid* 343, [Letter from J.C. Cahoon:] Mr. Murdock [sic] is mistaken . . I am aware that one or two gunners call the golden plover a "toadhead," but I am sure that nearly all of the gunners of Orleans, Chatham and other towns along the Cape call the golden plover the "green plover." *Ibid* 382, [Letter from John Murdoch:] Most of my shore bird nomenclature for Cape Cod was learned in the town of Orleans in the seasons of 1869–'72, and chiefly from the older generation of gunners. . . In those days the golden plover was quite often called "toadhead." 1955 *AmSp* 30.184, *Toadhead* for the golden plover (Mass., N.Y.) . . means only 'big head.' *Toad bird* . . (Mass.) doubtless has the same significance.

toadhide See **toadskin**

toad-hopper n Cf **hoptoad 1**

A **toad** n **1.**

1967–68 *DARE* (Qu. P23, *Names for the animal similar to the frog that lives away from water*) Inf **IN**35, Toad-hoppers; **MO**12, Toad-hopper . . childhood term.

toad in the puddle, biggest n For varr see quots **chiefly Nth**

An important or self-important person.

1851 *Indicator* 3.227 **MA,** The man who has been the 'biggest toad in the puddle,' quite likely will have to be a very small toad. 1855 *U.S. Rev.* 36.40, The imaginarily stalwart editor of "Fish's Money-Box," fortified in his judgment . . that he was "the tallest toad in the puddle" . . estimated his intellectual merit by the gigantic stature of his own fancy. 1869 Adams *Switch Off* 268 **MA,** Being the biggest toad in the puddle did not agree with his constitution. 1898 *Portsmouth Herald* (NH) 3 Sept [4]/3 (newspaperarchive.com), A jealous minded city official who promptly throws cold water on everything at which he is not the only toad in the puddle. 1922 *DN* 5.178, *Toad in the puddle.* . . "He thinks

he's the biggest toad in the puddle," i.e., the most important person in the affair. 1927 *AmSp* 2.366 **cwWV,** *Toad in the puddle, the biggest* . . the most important person. 1929 *AmSp* 5.119 **ME,** Someone conceited. . . "is one of the big bugs," "the biggest toad in the puddle." 1938 *AmSp* 13.74 **OH,** So and so is (or thinks he is) . . the biggest toad in the puddle. 1945 FWP *Lay My Burden Down* 238 **Sth** [Black], In the old days, if the niggers wants the party, Massa am the big toad in the puddle. 1968–69 *DARE* (Qu. HH17, *A person who tries to appear important, or who tries to lay down the law in his community: "He'd like to be the _____ around here."*) Infs **MI**78, **NY**206, **RI**15, Biggest toad in the puddle.

toad lily n

1 =**spatterdock;** see quots. Cf **frog lily**

1784 in 1785 Amer. Acad. Arts & Sci. *Memoirs* 1.456, *Nymphaea* [here: =*Nuphar lutea*]. . . Water Yellow Lily. Toad Lily. . . In ponds and rivers. 1933 *Torreya* 33.83, *Nymphaea advena* [=*Nuphar lutea* subsp *advena*]. . . Toad lily, yellow waterlily.

2 A **white water lily** (here: *Nymphaea odorata*).

1830 Rafinesque *Med. Flora* 2.44, *Nymphaea odorata.* . . White Pond Lily, Toad Lily. . . One large white floating flower. 1872 Rudolphy *Pharmaceutical Directory* 28, Toad lily. Nymphaea odorata. 1891 *Century Dict.* 6361, *Toad-lily.* . . The white water lily, *Castalia* [=*Nymphaea*] *odorata:* an old American name. 1931 Clute *Common Plants* 111, The toad-lily . . is the white water-lily *(Castalia odorata),* apparently named from the belief that toads frequent it.

3 A **miner's lettuce** (here: *Montia chamissoi*).

1914 Frye–Rigg *Elementary Flora NW* 88, M[ontia] chamissonis (toad-lily). 1923 in 1925 Jepson *Manual Plants CA* 347 **seCA,** M[ontia] chamissoi. . . Toad-lily. 1949 Moldenke *Amer. Wild Flowers* 72, Numerous . . plants occur in the West, including the . . pink-flowered *toadlily, Crunocallis* [=*Montia*] *chamissoi.* 1974 Welsh *Anderson's Flora AK* 331, *Montia chamissoi* . . Toad-lily. . . Marshes, seeps, springs or streams in coastal and insular southern Alaska and less commonly in interior southern Alaska.

4 A **fritillary** (here: *Fritillaria agrestis*). [*OED2* 1884 for *Fritillaria pyrenaica*]

1959 Carleton *Index Herb. Plants* 117, Toad-lily: Fritillaria agrestis.

toadmaroon n [Perh blend of *toadstool* + *musheroon* (at **mushroom A**)] Cf **bizmaroon**

A **toadstool.**

1940–41 Cassidy *WI Atlas,* Toadmaroon ['todmɚun]—couldn't be eaten—[FW: Inf (75-year-old Appleton WI farmer) never heard "toadstool."]

toadroot n
=**baneberry 1.**

1830 Rafinesque *Med. Flora* 2.186, *Actea alba* and *rubra. White and Red Cohosh,* or *Baneberry, Toadroot.* . . Plant and berries poisonous, said to be liked by toads. 1876 Hobbs *Bot. Hdbk.* 120, Toad-root, Red cohosh, Actaea rubra. 1892 (1974) Millspaugh *Amer. Med. Plants* 10-1, *Actæa pachypoda.* . . Toad root.

toad rush n
Std: a **rush** n[1] **B** (here: *Juncus bufonius*). Also called **frog rush**

toads See **toward A**

toad sack n [Folk-etym for **tow sack** or **tote sack,** perh infl by **croker sack**] **chiefly Sth, S Midl**
=**tow sack.**

1989 Pederson *LAGS Tech. Index* 76, *Tow sack* . . toad sack (1 [of 914 infs]) . . towed [sic] sack (1). 1996 in 2005 *DARE* File—Internet **neMS,** They had gone off . . and made, my daddy said, "A toad sack full of money," is what he said. 2001 *Ibid* **ceTN,** [Title of a review of a baby-carrier:] Save Your Money And Buy A Toad Sack Instead. 2003 *Ibid* **ceTX,** Put'em [=armadillos] in my toad sack carry them home and get Ma to cook'em up with some rice. 2004 *Ibid* **IL,** We took 3 large burlap "toad sacks" and cut holes in the top of them for our heads. 2005 *Ibid* **csIL,** This pattern is on burlap fabric, or what we used to call toadsack fabric.

toad sculpin n Cf **toadfish d**

A **sculpin 1;** see quot.

1957 Beck *Folkl. ME* 167, Should one become angry he "swole up like an old toad sculpin."

toadshade n   Also *toad trillium* [Appar from the mottling of the leaves thought to resemble the mottled skin of a **toad n 1**]

A **trillium:** usu *Trillium sessile,* but also *T. cuneatum.*

1933 *Small Manual SE Flora* 307, *T[rillium] sessile.* . . Blades oval to suborbicular, often mottled. . . *Toad-shade.* . . The flowers have a penetrating scent resembling that of . . *Calycanthus.* 1953 *Greene–Blomquist Flowers South* 12, *Toadshade (Trillium sessile).* . . has conspicuously mottled leaves. 2002 *DARE* File—Internet, There are two Trilliums known as Toadshade or Toad Trillium. Both have molted [sic], stalkless leaves and maroon or sometimes greenish petals.

toadskin n   Also *toadhide* Cf **frogskin**

A piece of paper money, esp a dollar bill; a dollar.

1857 *Ballou's Dollar Mth. Mag.* 6.275, You'll give a five, you say? . . It's a bargain. Let's see the toad-skin! 1903 Patten *Frank Merriwell at Yale* 197, You made a fool of yourself when you failed to break his wrist, after paying twenty-five toadskins to learn the trick. 1922 *Chron.-Telegram* (Elyria OH) 13 Sept 3/3, The skin the average man loves to touch is the old toadskin, with a president's picture on it. 1927 *DN* 5.465 [Underworld jargon], *Toadskin.* . . Paper currency. Apparently from "greenback." 1935 *Hammond Times* (IN) 19 June 15/1, You can't get by in 1935 with an ancient sports belt. . . Get modern for one toadskin ($1). 1941 *Hall Coll.* eTN, *Toad-skin.* . . A dollar bill, a greenback. . . Common. 1941 *AmSp* 16.25 sIN, *Toad-hide.* Paper money. 1950 *WELS* (*Joking names and nicknames for a paper dollar*) 2 Infs, WI, Toadskins. 1965–70 *DARE* (Qu. U26, *Names or nicknames . . for a paper dollar*) Infs KY84, MO19, 36, NC35, NY66, 219, Toadskin; KY5, Toad hide; (Qu. U20, . . *Dollars . . "It cost a hundred _____."*) Inf NY66, Toadskins; (Qu. U28b, . . *A ten-dollar bill*) Inf IN19, Toadskin. 2003 *DARE* File—Internet CA, [He] won the Badge Raffle, 25 fresh toad skins, and he still refused to buy his mom and dad dinner after the meeting.

toad's-mouth n

A **false dragonhead 1** (here: *Physostegia virginiana*).

1959 Carleton *Index Herb. Plants* 117, *Toad's mouth* . . Physostegia virginiana.

toad snake n   Cf **adder 1**

Perh a **hognose snake.**

1968 *DARE* (Qu. P25, . . *Kinds of snakes*) Inf NJ53, Toad snake—same as adder. 1968 *DARE* Tape NJ53, Once in a while a toad snake comes here too. [1979 Behler–King *Audubon Field Guide Reptiles* 615, Enlarged teeth on rear upper jaw are believed to inject mild venom into toads and frogs upon which it [=*Heterodon platyrhinos*] feeds. It rarely bites people.]

toad sorrel n   Also *toad's sorrel*

A **sheep sorrel** (here: *Rumex acetosella*) or **wood sorrel 1** (here: *Oxalis stricta*).

1892 *Jrl. Amer. Folkl.* 5.102 NH, *Rumex acetosella,* toad's sorrel. 1896 *Ibid* 9.184 ME, *Oxalis corniculata,* var. *stricta* [=*O. stricta*], . . toad sorrel.

toadspit n   [*EDD* 1866 for *Lemna minor*] Cf **frog spit 2**

=**duckweed 1.**

1900 Lyons *Plant Names* 218, *Lemna.* . . Duckweed. . . Toadspit.

toads, rain   See **toad-frogs, rain**

toad's sorrel   See **toad sorrel**

toadstabber n

1   also *toad(frog-)sticker:* A large knife, sword, or bayonet, now esp a large folding knife. **chiefly Nth, N Midl** See Map Cf **frogsticker (knife), pigsticker 2**

1847 *Yankee Doodle* 11 Sept 221 NY, I made a dive for the door—but he out with a darned long toad-sticker, and swore orful . . he'd make a hole in my in'ards. 1858 *Calif. Spirit of Times* (S.F.) 7 Aug 1/8 *(DA),* The Judge put his toad sticker atween his teeth, tuk a pistol in won hand, and a slung shot in the other, and sez thru his nose, 'cum on.' 1877 Bartlett *Americanisms* 708, *Toad-Sticker.* A term for a sword, almost universal among our soldiers during the late war. 1887 (1892) Hinman *Corporal Si Klegg* 581, An officer's . . sword was a "toad-stabber" or "cheese-knife." 1899 (1977) Norris *McTeague* 83 **San Francisco CA,** Frenna drew the knife from the wall. "Guess I'll keep this toad-stabber," he observed. 1910 *DN* 3.450 cwNY, *Toad-stabber—Toad-sticker.* Pocket knife; jack-knife. 1917 *DN* 4.402 neOH, *Toad-stabber.* . . A large pocket-knife. "Yours is a regular old toad-stabber." Also Vt.,

Mass., Ia., Cal., N.Y., Min. [*DN* Ed: In Ill., also *frog-sticker.*] 1923 *DN* 5.237 swWI, *Toad-stabber, toad-sticker.* . . A jack knife. 1950 *WELS WI* (*Names and nicknames for a large pocket-knife with blades that pull in and out*) 20 Infs, Toadstabber; 1 Inf, Toadsticker. c1960 *Wilson Coll.* csKY, *Toad-frog-sticker.* . . Pocket-knife; usually humorous. 1965–70 *DARE* (Qu. F39, *A large pocket knife with blades that fold in and out*) 24 Infs, **chiefly Nth, N Midl,** Toadstabber; CA101, IN35, PA235, 242, Toadsticker. 1982 *Barrick Coll.* csPA, *Toad-sticker*—pocket-knife. Humorously, any knife; bayonet. 1984 Lesley *Winterkill* 273 neOR, He used the Buck knife Pudge had given him. . . "That's a fancy toad stabber you got there. It's so shiny you could shave in it."

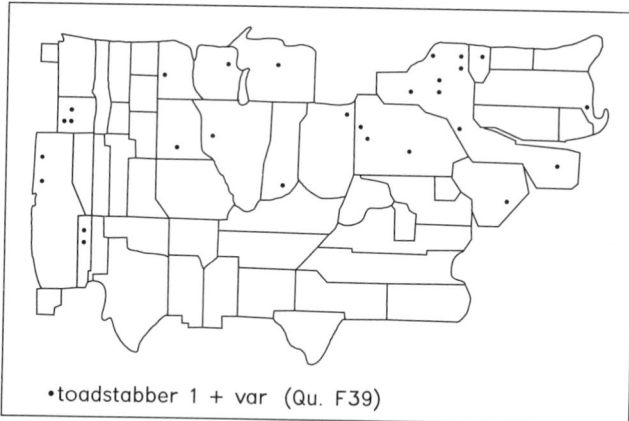

•toadstabber 1 + var (Qu. F39)

2   A sharp-pointed shoe or boot. Cf **frog spayer, pig-stabber 1, snake-kicker (boot)**

1968–69 *DARE* (Qu. W42a, . . *Nicknames . . for men's sharp-pointed shoes*) Infs MI92, NY75, 99, OH82, Toadstabbers.

toad-sticker   See **toadstabber 1**

toadstool n

Std: a **mushroom B1** or other similar fungus such as those of the genera *Agaricus* or *Craterellus,* usu considered to be inedible or poisonous. For other names of var of these see **bull-toad's umbrella, devil's bread 2, ~ nose, devil stool, fairy umbrella, field mushroom, frog bench, ~ bread, ~ house 2, ~ pillow, ~ plant 2, frogstool, frog table, ~ umbrella, hoptoad-stool, platter ~, tadpole ~, toad n 5, ~-frog stool, toadmaroon, toad umbrella**

toad-strangler n   Also *toad-choker, ~-floater, toadfrog-strangler, toad-stringer, ~-washer* **chiefly Gulf States, S Midl** See Map Cf **frog-strangler**

A very heavy rain.

1906 *Landmark* (Statesville NC) 1 June [4/5] (newspaperarchive.com) TX, Have had several rains in the past two weeks and last night a regular toad strangler fell. 1938 Rawlings *Yearling* 228 nFL, Hit's a toad-strangler of a rain. 1944 *PADS* 2.61 swMO, *Toad-strangler.* . . A heavy rain. Greene Co. Rare. . . [*PADS* Ed: Also Va., N.C., S.C.] 1950 *PADS* 14.77 FL, *Toad-floater.* . . A downpour of rain. 1965–70 *DARE* (Qu. B25, . . *Joking names . . for a very heavy rain. . . "It's a regular _____."*) 32 Infs, **chiefly Gulf States, S Midl,** Toad-strangler; GA73,

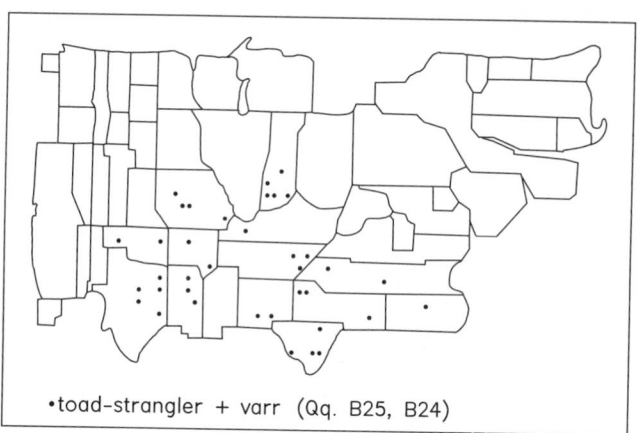

•toad-strangler + varr (Qq. B25, B24)

77, Toadfrog-strangler; **SC**29, Toad-washer; (Qu. B24, . . *A sudden, very heavy rain*) Infs **FL**7, **LA**7, Toad-strangler; **FL**29, Toad-strangler—a quick, very heavy rain—over quite fast. **1985** Ladwig *How to Talk Dirty* 15 **Ozarks**, It was a log-roller and a toad-choker . . (heavy rain). **1986** Pederson *LAGS Concordance* **Gulf Region**, (Heavy rain) 17 infs, Toad-strangler(s); 2 infs, Toad-stringer; 1 inf, Toad-frog strangler; (Thunderstorm) 4 infs, Toad-strangler; 1 inf, Toad-stringer. **2001** *DARE* File **Indianpolis IN**, "A sudden, very heavy rain." In Indiana it's called a "toad-strangler."

toad's umbrella See **toad umbrella**

toad trillium See **toadshade**

toad umbrella n Also *toad's umbrella* Cf **frog umbrella**

A **mushroom B1** or a **toadstool.**

1941 *LANE* Map 280 (Toadstool) 1 inf, **seNH**, Toad's umbrella. **1986** Pederson *LAGS Concordance*, 1 inf, **cwGA**, Toad umbrellas.

toad-washer See **toad-strangler**

toady-frog See **toad-frog 1**

toar See **taw**

toards See **toward A**

toat See **tote** v

toat-road shagamaw See **tote-road shagamaw**

tobac See **tobacco** n 3

tobacco n Usu |təˈbækə|; for varr see **A** below Cf Pronc Intro 3.1.2.d

A Forms.

1 |tə(r)ˈbækə(r)|; also aphet |ˈbækə(r), ˈbækə|; pronc-spp *bacca, baccer, bacco, baccur, backer, baker, terbaccer, terbacker, terbakker, terbarker, tobaccer, tobacker, tobakker, torbarker, tuhbackuh.* [*OED2* 1601 →] **chiefly Sth, S Midl**

1831 Finn *Amer. Comic Annual* 1.53, 'Baccer 'intment 'll cure that are. **1832** *Atkinson's Casket* 443, Why I'd as lieves [sic] touch two old chaws of tobacker. **1838** Gilman *S. Matron* 50 **SC** [Black], Mammy Phillis send missis some egg for buy, ma'am; she an't so berry well, and ax for some 'baccer. **1841** *S. Lit. Messenger* 7.54, Oh! Colonel, gives us a chew of your tobacker! **1846** (1973) Porter *Quarter Race* 158 **MS**, Jones, give me your tobacker. **1847** in 1941 *AmSp* 16.109, Die Patriarchen des schwarzen Volkes saszen, ihren 'bacca rauchend. [=The patriarchs of the black folk were sitting, smoking their 'bacca.] **1848** (1855) Ruxton *Life Far West* 18, Any bacca in your bag, Bill? **1851** Burke *Polly Peablossom* 50 **MO**, That feller . . sold me a pint of red-eye whiskey—an' half ov it backer juice!—for a coon-skin. **1858** Bagby in *S. Lit. Messenger* 26.386, He . . went intoo the terbaker hous and shet the dough. *Ibid*, Po ole Wrankin . . staid in his terbacker hous. *Ibid* 251, Prizin uv tobakker. **1872** Webb *Buffalo Land* 367, They was going ter take a chaw o' terbaccer. **1873** *Appletons' Jrl.* 9.139 **GA**, Dat muss be er new-fashioned way dem fur-away folks has uv fixin' baccur fur people as hain't got no teeth. **1884** Smith *Bill Arp's Scrap Book* 73 **GA**, The devil's race horse . . chaws tobakker like a gentleman. **1893** Shands *MS Speech* 23, |təbækə|. . . terbacker. **1900** Day *Up in ME* 26 **ME**, Shook their fists and hollered round and spit torbarker juice! **1908** *DN* 3.288 **eAL, wGA**, Backer. **1915** *DN* 4.180 **swVA**, Backer. **1915** in 1944 *ADD* **swVA**, Tobacker, 'backer. r is always heard. **1922** Gonzales *Black Border* 335 **sSC, GA coasts** [Gullah glossary], Tuhbackuh—tobacco. **1928** *AmSp* 3.403 **Ozarks** (as of 1916–27), Words like *tomato* and *tobacco* . . are nearly always pronounced *termater* and *terbacker*. **1947** Steed *KY Tobacco Patch* 14, Tobacco, often mispronounced "terbakker." **1950** Stuart *Hie Hunters* 8 **eKY**, I hep Peg a little with the terbacker patchin'. **1950** *PADS* 14.12 **SC**, Baker [ˈbæːkə, ˈbækə, ˈbæki]. . . "I was so skeerd I swallowed my baker." **1965–70** *DARE* (Qu. K27, . . *The sharp-pointed stick used to get oxen to move*) Inf **KY**27, Tobaccer stick; (Qu. L22, *When talking about a crop he intends to plant . . a farmer might say, "This year, I'm going to _____ a crop of oats/corn/cotton, etc."*) Inf **KY**34, Set my [ˈbækɚ] out; (Qu. M22, . . *Kinds of buildings . . on farms*) Inf **TN**19, [ˈbækɚ] barn; (Qu. R6, . . *Names . . for grasshoppers*) Inf **VA**47, [ˈbækɚ] chewer; (Qu. R27, . . *Kinds of caterpillars or similar worms*) Inf **KY**80, [ˈbækɚ] worm; (Qu. DD2, *The portion or quantity of tobacco chewed at one time: "He's always got a big _____ in his cheek."*) Inf **GA**44, Chew o' baccer [ˌʧuwəˈbækɚ]; (Qu. DD4, *Moisture in the mouth, colored brown by snuff or chewing tobacco*) Inf **GA**28, Tobaccer juice; **LA**8, **MD**40,

['bɑekə] spit; **MD**42, Baccer juice; **MD**48, [ˈbækə] juice; **NC**85, Bacco juice; **SC**31, Bacco spit. **1966–70** *DARE* Tape **DC**5, A butterfly. . . He's the one that gonna fly on the 'bacca [ˈbækə] leaves and put the eggs on the 'bacca leaves; **FL**9, They'd pull those leaves off of those tobacco [təˈbækɚ] stalks; **KY**60, They'd catch a farmer . . half-drunk and didn't know the value of his tobacco [təˈbækə]. They'd buy his 'bacca [ˈbækə], tobacco [təˈbækə], and if it hadn't been handled correctly they'd hire people to rehandle it; **VA**75, I believe they did say they had a place down there called a 'bacco [ˈbæko] lot. **1968** *DARE* FW Addit **MD**13, [ˈbækə]. **2003** *Smoky Mt. News* (Waynesville NC) 30 Apr (Internet), Every 'baccer grower gots a good, sharp, pocket knife.

2 |təˈbæki|; also aphet |ˈbæki|; pronc-spp *baccy, backy, t'baccy, tobaccy, tobacky.*

1689 in 1849 *Doc. Hist. State of NY* 2.169, Give them [=the Indians] 6 belt of wampum[;] Some Duffells Tobaccy[;] and some baggs with Provision. **1821** Cooper *Spy* 1.30 [Black], He . . bring you a little good 'baccy from York. **1838** *S. Lit. Messenger* 4.206 **VA**, Ive got of 'baccy a pound. **1846** *Spirit of Times* 4 July 228/2, Carrying my backy pipe with me to smoke. **1852** Olmsted *Walks* 1.18 **NY**, He'd like to . . make a trade with yer for some tobaccy. **1901** Jewett *Tory Lover* 106 **NH**, I . . come upon this old piece o' callamink I'd wrapped some 'baccy in. **1933** Rawlings *South Moon* 46 **nFL**, [Song:] Git along down to Richmond town / To lay my t'baccy down. **1945** FWP *Lay My Burden Down* 21 **TX** [Black], He was mean-looking and chewing a quid of t'baccy. **1950** *PADS* [see **1** above]. **1988** Kingsolver *Bean Trees* 57 **KY**, "I don't see how a body can grow no tobaccy if it don't rain," Granny Logan said.

3 Pronc-sp *tobac.*

[**1847** Howe *Hist. Coll. OH* 303 (as of 1812), Me chaw heap tobac.] **1861** Victor *Maum Guinea* 134 **LA** [Black], A gentleum wid a big chaw of tobac' in his mouf. **1908** *Shields' Mag.* 6.190, I jest took a fresh chaw of tobac. **1950** *WELS* 1 Inf, **WI**, Tobac. **1967** Will *Dredgeman* 39 **FL**, He'd give you his last chaw of tobac even though the truck might not bring another for a week.

B Sense.

Std: a plant of the genus *Nicotiana*, esp the cultivated *N. tabacum*. Cf **British tobacco, devil's ~, false ~, ladies'-~, rabbit ~, sheep ~** For other names of var spp see **black tobacco 1, bull-face ~, coyote ~, dark ~ 1, Indian ~ 5, Indian weed, tree tobacco, tronadora 1**

tobacco exclam [From homophony of 2nd syllable and *back*] Cf **cucumber** exclam, **onion** exclam

In the game of **hide-and-seek A:** a warning by one player to others to get back; see quot 1957.

1957 *Sat. Eve. Post Letters* **Rochester NY** (as of c1900), If you got home free—and the "It" went hunting, we could call "Onion-onion" or "Tobacco"—words that obviously meant come or go back! **1967** *DARE* (Qu. EE15, *When he has caught the first of those that were hiding what does the player who is 'it' call out to the others?*) Inf **PA**16, Cucumber means "come in, come in." *Tobacco* means "go back and hide."

tobacco basket n Also *basket* **chiefly S Midl**

A large, flat tray, usu of woven slats, on which tobacco is piled for transport and display at a warehouse; the quantity of tobacco piled on such a tray.

1909 *Lexington Herald* (KY) 6 Nov 8/7, Tobacco Market Closes on $20 Price—High Figure Offered For a Few Baskets. **1925** *Book of Rural Life* 9.5539, On arrival at the warehouse the tobacco is unloaded and placed on large, flat baskets each capable of holding 1000 pounds of leaf. The baskets are arranged on the floor of the warehouse convenient for inspection. **1930** *Bee* (Danville VA) 30 May 13/6, H.E. Winkler . . was in South Boston, today showing a new patented all steel tobacco basket. . . It is 40 inches square. **1952** *Sun* (Baltimore MD) 19 June 26/4 (Hench Coll.), Warehousemen paid $73 for individual baskets of fine thin crop. **1967** Key *Tobacco Vocab.* 8, Basket. . . A shallow wooden container approximately four feet square in which tobacco is piled in preparation for auctioning. . . A basket of tobacco. **1968** *KY Folkl. Rec.* 14.43 **KY**, Tobacco came to be shipped by wagon to *loose-leaf* markets located in the river towns or a short distance away. It was . . bulked directly on wagons or on *tobacco baskets* (nearly flat lattice-work devices made of thin strips of wood) and was hauled to market. **1969** *DARE* Tape **KY**60, A basket is . . about four by four, but the most that they [=sellers at auction] can put on a basket is . . 700 pounds of tobacco. **2003** *Smoky Mt. News* (Waynesville NC) 30 Apr (Internet), As you tied more hands [of tobacco leaves], you'd go all the way around that basket to where you're stackin' them up higher than my belly button but not as high [as] my shoulders and that's a basket of tobacco.

tobacco bean n

A cultivated bean (*Phaseolus vulgaris* var); see quots.

1970 *DARE* (Qu. I17, *Beans . . that are dark red when they are dry*) Inf **KY**90, Tobacco beans; (Qu. I20, . . *Kinds of beans*) Inf **KY**74, Tobacco bean—big white bean with a red spot—not eaten in the pod—a "hull-out."

tobacco-bed fly   See **tobacco fly 2**

tobacco box n

1   Usu a **pumpkinseed 1** (here: *Lepomis gibbosus*), but also a **longear sunfish** (here: *Lepomis megalotis*) or the **red-breasted sunfish 1,** or other **sunfish n 1a.**

1859 (1968) Bartlett *Americanisms* 482, Tobacco-Box. A small freshwater fish, called also Sunfish and Pumpkin Seed.   **1877** Hallock *Sportsman's Gaz.* 379 **Sth,** Black Perch, sometimes called 'tobacco-box'; found in ponds.   **1884** U.S. Natl. Museum *Bulletin* 27.463, *Lepomis gibbosus. . . Tobacco-box. . .* This is a beautiful little fish, the cherished victim of the youthful angler.   **1903** *Outing* Apr 134, He is content to lure to the surface . . the 'sunny,' 'tobacco box,' or 'pumpkin seed'.   **1938** Schrenkeisen *Field Book Fishes* 244, *Lepomis auritus. . .* Tobaccobox.   *Ibid* 246, *Lepomis gibbosus. . .* Tobaccobox.   *Ibid* 248, *Lepomis megalotis. . .* Tobaccobox.   **1976** Tryckare et al. *Lore of Sportfishing* 102, *Lepomis auritus*—Other common names . . tobacco box.

2   A **skate** n[1] (here: *Leucoraja erinacea*).

1882 U.S. Natl. Museum *Bulletin* 16.40, *R[aja] erinacea. . . Tobacco-box.* Form rhomboid, with all the angles rounded. . . The smallest and commonest of our skates; abundant on our coast, especially northward.   **1917** *Copeia* 41.17 **Long Is. NY,** *Raja erinacea.* Common Skate. A permanent resident. . . Known as "Tobaccobox" and less frequently as "Old Maid."   **1999** (2000) Carey *Against Tide* 30 **NEng,** A common skate. . . Known otherwise and variously as a little skate, . . and tobacco box.

tobacco brush n   Also *tobacco bush* [See quot 1937]

A **snowbrush 1** (here: *Ceanothus velutinus*).

1925 Jepson *Manual Plants CA* 619, *C[eanothus] velutinus. . . Tobacco Brush.*   **1937** U.S. Forest Serv. *Range Plant Hdbk.* B47, *Ceanothus velutinus. . .* Snowbrush refers to the abundant fluffy masses of white flowers; . . tobacco-brush to the Indians' use of the leaves for tobacco.   **1940** Writers' Program *Guide NV* 12, Also in this zone [=the belt converging into the sub-alpine] are the glossy-leafed snow bush or tobacco bush (*Ceanothus velutinus*).   **1961** Thomas *Flora Santa Cruz* 235 **cwCA,** *C[eanothus] velutinus. . .* Sticky Laurel, Tobacco Bush.   **1973** Hitchcock–Cronquist *Flora Pacific NW* 290, Tobacco-brush. . . *C[eanothus] velutinus.*

tobacco budworm   See **budworm**

tobacco bug n

1   Any of several insects that attack the growing **tobacco B** plant such as a **hornworm,** the tobacco flea beetle *(Epitrix hirtipennis),* or the leaf bug *(Dicyphus minimus).*   Cf **tobacco fly**

1880 in 2005 *DARE* File—Internet **ceKY,** The tobacco bug is playing havoc with the tobacco in this county [=Montgomery Co.].   **1890** *E. Reflector* (Greenville NC) 19 Feb (Internet), The tobacco bug, an insect which by a popular misnomer is called "The Fly", . . makes its appearance about the first of April, and for which when it once gets into possession of a plant bed, no remedy has yet been found. . . Against the ravages of the horn-worm there is no remedy short of extermination.   **1911** *Century Dict. Suppl.,* Tobacco-bug. . . A small American capsid bug, *Dicyphus minimus,* which damages the leaves of tobacco in Florida. Also called *suck-fly.*   **1967–70** *DARE* (Qu. R27, . . *Kinds of caterpillars or similar worms*) Inf **OR**1, Tobacco bug; (Qu. R30, . . *Kinds of beetles; not asked in early QRs*) Inf **FL**48, Tobacco bug.

2   A **grasshopper 1.**   Cf **tobacco spitter**

1966–68 *DARE* (Qu. R6, . . *Names . . for grasshoppers*) Infs **IL**50, **MO**35, **WI**48, Tobacco bug(s).

tobacco bush   See **tobacco brush**

tobacco buzzer n

The white-lined **sphinx moth** (*Celerio lineata*).

c1930 Brown *Amer. Folkl. Insect Lore* 4, The common hawk moth (Celerio lineata) is still called a "tobacco buzzer" by some country folk. Its presence in a tobacco field or garden is a bad omen. It is struck down with a shingle paddle.

tobacco chewer   See **tobacco spitter**

tobacco, chew one's   See **chew one's tobacco**

tobacco damp n   Cf **case weather, season** n[1] **1**

A period of humid weather that allows cured tobacco to be handled without damage.

1919 MA Ag. Exper. Sta. *Bulletin* 193.183, A tobacco damp lasts only a short time, and the farmers must get down as much tobacco as possible.   **1948** Bean *Yankee Auctioneer* 73 **wMA,** When dry the [tobacco] leaves are brittle. They break to dust when handled. . . But when damp, they become tough, and . . may be handled without damage. A "tobacco damp" arrives with fog or rain when the temperature reaches about 60 degrees.   **2002** U.S. Dept. Ag. New Engl. Ag. Statistics Serv. *Crop Weather* (Internet), Prolonged rainy weather provided excellent tobacco damp conditions for growers to take down the crop in Connecticut and Massachusetts last week.

tobacco dove n   esp **FL, GA**

=ground dove.

[**1891** *Century Dict.* 6362, Tobacco-dove. . . The small ground dove, *Chamæpelia* (or *Columbigallina*) *passerina.* [*Century* Ed: Bahamas.]]   **1925** Bailey *Birds FL* 63, Ground Dove. . . *Chaemepelia* [sic] *passerina passerina* (Mourning dove, Tobacco dove) This, the smallest of the dove family, is found all over Florida, and is particularly abundant in the coastal area. Its mournful note and small body, make it easily distinguishable from others of the family.   **1932** Howell *FL Bird Life* 281, *Columbigallina passerina passerina* [=*Columbina p.*] . . *Tobacco Dove.* . . Very gentle and unsuspicious.   **1955** *Oriole* 20.1.8 **GA,** Ground Dove. . . Tobacco Dove (from its frequenting tobacco fields).

tobacco eater   See **tobacco spitter**

tobacco flower n

A **wild carrot 1** (here: *Daucus carota*).

1969 *DARE* (Qu. S6, . . *Queen Anne's lace: [Summertime roadside weed two feet high or so with a lacy white top]*) Inf **IL**47, Wild carrot; tobacco flower—we called it that because we chewed the flower—it tasted good.

tobacco fly n   chiefly **Sth, S Midl**

1   also *tobacco miller:* A **sphinx moth** (here: *Manduca quinquemaculata* or *M. sexta*).   Cf **hornworm fly**

[**1688** in 1693 Royal Soc. London *Philos. Trans.* 17.947 **VA,** There be various Accidents and Distempers, whereunto Tobacco is liable, as the Worm, the Flie, . . and the like.]   **1825** *Amer. Farmer* 7.44, I am totally ignorant of the value of the following prescription for destroying the tobacco fly.   **1904** Glasgow *Deliverance* 125 **VA,** "Oh, I don't mind the sun," he answered. . . "I'm too much taken up just now with fighting those confounded tobacco flies. They were as thick as thieves last night." . . Big green moths hovered presently around him, seeking the deep rosy tubes of the clustered flowers, and alighting finally to leave their danger-breeding eggs under the drooping leaves.   **1944** *PADS* 2.72 **sVA,** *Tobacco-fly.* . . Same as *miller. Ibid* 67, Miller, tobacco miller. . . A moth (sometimes as large as a humming bird) which . . deposits on the green tobacco its eggs, which hatch into tobacco worms.   **1957** *KY Folkl. Rec.* 3.61, [Tobacco] *Miller.* . . Adult of the tobacco worm. . . Known also as the hawk moth, sphinx moth . . tobacco fly.   **1966** *PADS* 45.26 **KY,** *Tobacco fly.* . . The mature stage of the tobacco hornworm.   **1966** *DARE* (Qu. R12, . . *Other kinds of flies*) Inf **NC**10, Tobacco fly.   **1980** Milne–Milne *Audubon Field Guide Insects* 780, *Manduca quinquemaculata.* . . These moths are known in southern tobacco-growing states as "tobacco flies." *Ibid* 781, *Manduca sexta.* . . In southern tobacco-growing states the adult is called a "tobacco fly."

2   also *tobacco-bed fly:* The tobacco flea beetle *(Epitrix hirtipennis).*

1807 (1935) Janson *Stranger in Amer.* 345 **VA,** The devastation produced by the *"tobacco-fly,"* which is of the beetle species, black, and large enough to be seen committing its depredations.   **1895** AL Ag. Exper. Sta. *Bulletin* 64.126, The flea beetle, commonly called tobacco fly in the old tobacco States.   **1966** *DARE* Tape DC5, [FW:] Would the flies attack these plants? . . What kind of flies would do that? [Inf:] Well, some be a tobacco fly, a tobacco-bed fly be a little small fly. . . When the leaves get big as a dime, sometimes you can see where they eat holes into 'em. **1968–70** *DARE* (Qu. R10, *Very small flies that don't sting, often seen hovering in large groups or bunches outdoors in summer*) Inf **IN**45, Tobacco fly; (Qu. R30, . . *Kinds of beetles;* not asked in early QRs) Infs **KY**49, 75, 80, Tobacco fly.

tobacco gum n   Also rarely *tobacco wax*   **Sth**

A sticky dark-colored exudate produced by many varieties of **tobacco B.**

1944 *PADS* 2.72 **sVA,** *Tobacco-gum, gum. . .* The dark, bitter, sticky gum on the surface of tobacco. . . *Tobacco-wax. . .* Same as *tobacco-gum.* **1998** *Fayetteville Online* (NC) 22 July (Internet), They leave the farm at 8 or 9 p.m. coated with sweat and the black, sticky gum that oozes from the tobacco plants. By 7 the next morning, they're back in the fields. . . The workers wear long-sleeve shirts and long pants to keep off the sun and keep the tobacco gum from knotting into the hairs of their arms and legs. **2002** *DARE* File (Internet) **KY** (as of c1935), During the summer . . the tobacco plants . . had to be "suckered". . . It was dirty, time consuming work to . . check for a sucker and break it out if there. After a few hours work, your hands would be covered with dust and tobacco gum.

tobacco hawkmoth n   Also *tobacco moth*

A **sphinx moth,** either *Manduca quinquemaculata* or *M. sexta,* the larva of which feeds on the foliage of var solanaceous plants.   For names of the larva see **potato worm, tobacco ~ 1, tomato ~ 1**

1819 Warden *Statist. Political Hist. U.S.* 484, The tobacco hawk moth . . *Sphinx Carolina.* **1859** Gosse *Letters from AL* 66, This is the Tobacco Hawk-moth (*Sphinx Carolina* [=*Manduca sexta*]), a large but sober-coloured species. The usual food of the larva is the tobacco plant, on which it is found in considerable numbers. **1874** U.S. Dept. Ag. *Rept. of Secy. for 1873* 157, The tobacco hawk-moth or "horn-blower" of Maryland, *Macrosila (Sphinx) carolina,* Linn., is a large moth, the caterpillar of which, commonly known as the tobacco-worm . . in the Middle States, is very destructive to the leaf of the tobacco-plant. **1966–68** *DARE* (Qu. R4, *A large winged insect that hatches in summer in great numbers around lakes or rivers, crowds around lights, lives only a day or so, and is good fish bait*) Inf **GA**46, Tobacco moth—almost as large as a hummingbird; (Qu. R27, . . *Kinds of caterpillars or similar worms*) Inf **WA**12, Tobacco moth larva.

tobacco hornworm   See **tobacco worm 1**

tobacco juice n   Also *tobacco spit*   [From the resemblance to **ambeer**]   Cf **molasses C3**

A dark brown, mostly liquid substance regurgitated by a **grasshopper 1.**

1877 Rusling *Gt. West* 36 **MO,** They [=grasshoppers] eat up all my corn, and tobacco. And then when I cussed 'em for it, they coolly sat on the Shanghai-fence that, and squirted tobacco juice at me! **1888** Cox *Hist. Seward Co. NE* 51 If the few tobacco patches furnished each [grasshopper] a chew, at least they took the last vestige of it, and our observation showed that they all spit tobacco juice, or something like it. **1912** *Perry Daily Chief* (IA) 16 Aug 4/5, Everyone has been startled, on seizing a grasshopper, by having the animal throw off a quantity of "tobacco-juice" from his mouth. **1940** Stong *Hawkeyes* 276 **IA,** The largest grasshoppers were retained to spit tobacco juice, which they would, a droplet at a time every time their noses were touched. **1960** Criswell *Resp. to PADS 20* **Ozarks,** Juice from a grasshopper's mouth was frequently called tobacco spit and ambeer. **1961** Cook Co. IL Forest Preserve *Nature Bulletin* (Internet), To get rid of warts, we rubbed them with a grasshopper's "tobacco spit." **2001** *DARE* File—Internet, When I was a kid in our neighborhood we would each catch a grasshopper and hold it in our closed palm for a count of ten. Whoever had the biggest "tobacco spit mark" in their hand got to be first. **2002** *Purcell Reg.* (OK) 26 July (Internet), All I know about a grasshopper is that they spit tobacco juice. Well, it's really not tobacco juice, but that is what grandpa always called it. **2004** *DARE* File **WA** (as of c1963), We called it [= grasshopper "spit"] tobacco juice; **seWI** (as of c1960), By "tobacco juice" we meant the brown "spit" produced by grasshoppers when we handled them; **Bronx NYC** (as of 1955), Tobacco juice was what we kids called the brown stuff that grasshoppers would "spit" on our hands when we caught them.

tobacco knife n

A long-handled blade used in harvesting tobacco; see quots.

1851 *De Bow's Rev.* 11.396 **MD,** It [=tobacco] is cut off close to the

ground by turning up the bottom leaves and striking with a tobacco knife, formed of an old scythe—such knives as often are used for cutting corn. **1966–70** *DARE* Tape **DC**5, Most tobacco knives are made from . . a handsaw. . . And you have a handle on it. . . It would be on more or less like a forty-five degree angle, the blade would be about six inches long. . . It's a straight blade; **KY**84, You had what they called a tobacco knife. It was a piece of metal, sharp, with a iron rod attached to it, and the blade was on one end of the rod and a wooden handle on the other end; **WV**5, You take . . a tobacco knife, . . split it [=a tobacco plant] down the center, cut it off at the bottom. **1967** *Tobacco Vocab.* 130 **MD,** Tobacco knife; **KY,** Tobacco knife, Burley knife—looks like a hatchet; **MO,** Tomahawk, tobacco knife. **1997** Hallman *Handtools Trail Work* 27, Corn Knives—These tools, also called tobacco knives, come in a variety of shapes and sizes. They are commonly used for hand brushing on tree and tobacco plantations. *Ibid,* The tobacco knife blade is tough alloy steel that is 12 inches long. . . It is beveled and sharpened with an ax stone only on one side. **2003** *Smoky Mt. News* (Waynesville NC) 30 Apr (Internet), Bolden described going through the field stalk by stalk, one person cutting with a tobacco knife the shape of a quarter moon. **2004** *Washington Post* (DC) 16 May (Internet) **MD,** The truck's driver knelt on the ground and gently lifted the tobacco knives, which were used to separate the tobacco leaves from the stem.

tobacco ladder n   **sePA**

A frame on a wagon for holding laden **tobacco sticks.**

1887 in 2010 (acc) Lexis–Nexis Legal Research *State Case Law: [PA]* (Internet), Defendant's personal property, viz.: 3 iron hog-troughs, . . 2 sets of tobacco ladders [etc.]. **1967** Key *Tobacco Vocab.* 255 **PA,** Tobacco ladder—An upright framework on the tobacco wagon which holds from 100 to 125 laths, taking them to the shed. **1967** *DARE* Tape **PA**6, We have wagons made with just—ladders—tobacco ladders we call 'em—just for these two rails . . four feet apart so the laths just fit in there. **1974** Reist *Tobacco Lore* [24] **sePA,** A wagon [was] designed with a special rack placed horizontally above the running gear of a farm wagon. Somewhat resembling a ladder because of its cross pieces and hooks, it evolved into what is known as a tobacco ladder. Some in use today were used by Grandfather near the turn of the century. **2004** *DARE* File—Internet **sePA,** [Auction listing:] 3 tobacco ladder wagons w/steel & wooden wheels. . . Lanc[aster] Co.

tobacco lath   See **tobacco stick**

tobacco-leaf n

=**bloodroot 1.**

1940 Clute *Amer. Plant Names* 271, *Sanguinaria Canadensis.* Tobacco-leaf, coon-root, Indian plant.

tobacco miller   See **tobacco fly 1**

tobacco monkey flower n   Cf **wild tobacco 2**

A **monkey flower 1** (here: *Mimulus bolanderi*).

1949 Moldenke *Amer. Wild Flowers* 280, The *tobacco monkeyflower, M. bolanderi,* of California, has dark red flowers, the lower lip sometimes dotted red and white.

tobacco moth   See **tobacco hawkmoth**

tobacco mule n   Cf **cotton mule, sugar ~**

A medium-sized mule used in tobacco farming.

1948 *Life* 26 Jan 108 **MO,** He sells "sugar mules" (tall, weighing 1,100 pounds or more) in Louisiana, "tobacco mules" (medium tall, 1,000 pounds) in Georgia and "banana mules" (small and wiry, 600 to 800 pounds) to the West Indies and Central America. **1950** *Sun* (Baltimore MD) 26 Apr 5/7 **MO,** A tobacco mule weighs 1,100 to 1,200 pounds. They're worked with a single plow in the tobacco fields. Not as big and rugged, of course, as the mules to work around logging or on highway construction, but they're handier. **1967** Wilkinson *Killing Frost* 86 **NC,** He was a sawmill mule not a tobacco mule.

tobacco pipe n   [See quot 1843]   **esp NEast**

=**Indian pipe 1.**

1824 Bigelow *Florula Bostoniensis* 175, *Monotropa uniflora. . .* Tobacco pipe. . . The whole plant is of a clear white, turning black at the tips as it decays. **1843** Torrey *Flora NY* 1.456, *Monotropa uniflora. . .* Indian-pipe. Tobacco-pipe. [*Ibid* 457, The singular form of this plant, much resembling that of a tobacco-pipe, and its pure white color when fresh, make it an object of interest even to persons unaquainted with botany.] **1845** Judd *Margaret* 143 **NEng** (as of 18th cent), In these dark crevices she found . . the curious mushroom-like tobacco-pipe.

1851 (1949) Thoreau *Jrl.* 2.340 **eMA,** The button-bush in blossom. The tobacco-pipe in damp woods. **1892** (1974) Millspaugh *Amer. Med. Plants* 105–1, *Monotropa uniflora. . . Tobacco pipe. . .* Grows in deep, rich, shady woods.

tobacco-pipe fish   See **pipefish 2**

tobacco plant n

1 A **mullein** (here: *Verbascum thapsus*).   Cf **devil's tobacco 3, false ~, Indian ~ 3, sheep ~, wild ~ 3**

1965–70 *DARE* (Qu. S20, *A common weed that grows on open hillsides: It has velvety green leaves close to the ground, and a tall stalk with small yellow flowers on a spike at the top*) Infs **CA**189, **MS**31, Tobacco plant; **ID**5, Mullein—used to call it tobacco plant; **NY**28, Tobacco plant or wild tobacco.

2 A **cudweed 1** such as *Pseudognaphalium obtusifolium.*   Cf **Indian tobacco 9, ladies'-~ c, rabbit ~ 1a**

1968–69 *DARE* (Qu. S11) Inf **RI**1, Tobacco plant—white blossom; (Qu. S26a, . . *Wildflowers. . . Roadside flowers*) Inf **VA**26, Life-everlasting = rabbit tobacco = tobacco plant.

3 =**Indian pipe 1.**   Cf **Indian tobacco 12, tobacco pipe**

1970 *DARE* (Qu. S26e, *Other wildflowers not yet mentioned;* not asked in early QRs) Inf **PA**245, Tobacco plant—whitish stalk 8″, chewed like tobacco, fungus, no green. [FW: sounds like Indian pipe]

tobacco pouch n

A **lady's slipper 1** (here: *Cypripedium fasciculatum*).

1891 Victor *Atlantis Arisen* 225 **NW,** In the shadowy edges of the forest one may find the Indian pipe shooting up its colorless stem, and the pretty "tobacco-pouch" *cypripedium,* with its striped white, brown, and purple pocket held invitingly open.

tobaccoroot n   **West**

1 A **valerian 1,** usu *V. edulis.*   [See quots]

1843 in 1845 Frémont *Rept. Rocky Mts.* 135 **CO,** I ate here, for the first time, the *kooyah,* or tobacco root, *(valeriana edulis,)* the principal edible root among the Indians. **1871** U.S. Dept. Ag. *Rept. of Secy. for 1870* 409, *Wild valerian, (Valeriana edulis,)* called kooyah or tobaccoroot by the Indians of the Northwest, and *raceme de tabac* by the French trappers. The root of this plant is remarkable for a very unpleasant taste and odor, which resemble those of chewing-tobacco. . . The stench of this root is much more offensive when fresh, especially if made into bread or cooked in soup. **1896** *Jrl. Amer. Folkl.* 9.190 **CA,** *Valeriana edulis,* . . tobacco root. **1937** U.S. Forest Serv. *Range Plant Hdbk.* W199, The valerians, also known in the West as tobacco root and sometimes improperly called sweet anise, belong to the relatively small valerian family. . . A dozen or more species grow on the western ranges. . . [and] can be recognized by the characteristic odor of their roots, which, according to a certain old timer, smell "like dirty feet." **1956** St. John *Flora SE WA* 397, *Valeriana edulis. . . Tobacco Root. . .* The baked roots are nutritious. They are brown and smell and taste like chewing tobacco. **1973** Hitchcock–Cronquist *Flora Pacific NW* 455, Tobacco-root. . . *V[aleriana] edulis.*

2 A **bitterroot 2** (here: *Lewisia rediviva*).   [See quots]

1864 *Chambers's Encycl.* 6.109, *L[ewisia] rediviva. . .* is called *Tobacco Root* because, when cooked, it has a tobacco-like smell. **1906** (1918) Parsons *Wild Flowers CA* 230, *Tobacco-root. Lewisia rediviva. . .* This was the "racine-amère," or "bitter-root," of the early French settlers. It is also known as "tobacco-root," because when boiled it has a tobacco-like odor.

tobacco sick adj

1 Of people and animals: ill from contact with tobacco; hence nouns *tobacco sick(ness)* the illness so caused.

1835 *Huron Reflector* (Norwalk OH) [2 June 2]/3 (newspaperarchive.com) **ME,** Tobacco juice will kill the old ones [=lice] and hatch the eggs if put on warm, to our certain knowledge, and oftentimes make the animal tobacco sick—no pleasant feeling. **1887** *Marion Daily Star* (OH) 5 Jan [2]/3 (newspaperarchive.com), I was working in a tobacco factory and the smell of the tobacco leaves used to make me deathly sick every day. Finally one old hand suggested that in the morning when I came to work I put a piece of a tobacco leaf in my mouth as an antidote. I accepted the suggestion and was never tobacco sick again. **1967** Key *Tobacco Vocab.* 257, Tobacco sick. . . Condition caused by heat, smell of tobacco oil, and movement back and forth between plants in budding and topping the plants. **2003** *Jrl. Occupational & Environmental Med.* June (Internet), A syndrome known as Green Tobacco Sickness . . has

been reported in workers who cultivate and harvest tobacco.   **2003** *DARE* File—Internet, The prevalence of Green Tobacco Sickness (GTS) among shade tobacco farm-workers in Connecticut is unknown.

2 Of land: exhausted or infested with pests as a result of growing tobacco: rarely *n tobacco sick* this condition itself.

1864 *Cultivator* 3d ser 12.305 **MD,** These old fields are not only tobacco-sick and "clover-sick," but sick of all other plants except a little hen-grass, sorrel and sassafras bushes. **1920** *WI Rapids Daily Tribune* (WI) 10 Nov [2]/3 (newspaperarchive.com), Already this one type of work [=breeding of disease-resistant plants] on "cabbage sick" and "tobacco sick" has restored these crops to areas that could no longer grow them. **1925** *Bridgeport Telegram* (CT) 25 July 17/2, Dr. James Johnson, of Wisconsin, will give a talk on "Tobacco Sick Soils." **1941** *Daily Progress* (Charlottesville VA) 27 Mar 18/7, Growers who have had trouble with burley on "tobacco sick" land are strongly advised to plant only the resistant strain . . which will grow even on land affected by the root rot. **1967** Key *Tobacco Vocab.* 258 **TN,** The ground was tobacco sick. . . tobacco wouldn't grow.

tobacco sickness   See **tobacco sick 1**

tobacco spit   See **tobacco juice**

tobacco spitter n   Also *spitter, tobacco chewer,* ~ *eater* [See *tobacco spit* (at **tobacco juice**)]   **scattered, but less freq N Atl, Gulf States, West**   See Map

A **grasshopper 1.**

1896 Abbott *Bird-Land* 229 **NEast,** Big brown grasshoppers—the "tobacco-spitters" of boyhood days. **1950** *WELS (Other names for the grasshopper)* **WI,** 1 Inf, Longhorn hopper known to young farm boys as "tobacco spitter"; 1 Inf, Tobacco spitter; 1 Inf, Tobacco chewer. **1965–70** *DARE* (Qu. R6, . . *Names . . for grasshoppers*) 51 Infs, **scattered, but less freq N Atl, Gulf States, West,** Tobacco spitter; **AZ**10, **MO**29, **PA**58, **SC**32, **WI**58, Tobacco spitter [FW: Infs described as children's word]; **IL**64, Tobacco spitter—heard that as a kid; **PA**34, Tobacco spitter—as kids; **MS**53, **NY**41, **SC**21, Tobacco spitter—heard (old-fashioned); **IA**22, Tobacco spitter—old-fashioned; **IL**37, Spitters; **IA**21, **MO**38, Tobacco chewers; **VA**47, Bacco [ˈbækɚ] chewer; bacca-chewing son-of-a-bitch; **PA**68, Tobacco eater; (Qu. R9a) Inf **GA**3, Tobacco spitter. **1970** *DARE* FW Addit **VA,** I heard the term *tobacco spitter* pronounced [ˈbækə ˈspɪdə] from an old woman.

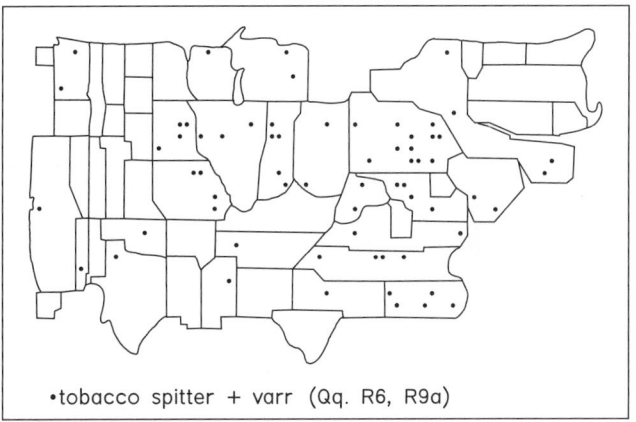

•tobacco spitter + varr (Qq. R6, R9a)

tobacco spud   See **spud** n **1**

tobacco stick n   Also *tobacco lath*   **chiefly S Midl**   Also called **stick** n **1**   Cf **stick** v **2**

A wooden rod or lath on which tobacco is hung for curing; also fig.

1676 Royal Soc. London *Philos. Trans.* 11.635 **VA,** They . . drive into the stalk of each plant a peg, and as fast as they are pegg'd, they hang them up by the pegs on Tobacco-sticks, so nigh each other that they just touch, much after the manner they hang Herrings in *Yarmouth.* **1776** (1924) Cresswell *Jrl.* 166 **VA,** About 600 men appeared under-armed, with Tobacco sticks in general. **1800** in 1969 Herndon *Wm. Tatham Tobacco* 26 **VA,** Timber is . . split . . into pieces of four feet in length, and about an inch and a half diameter. These are termed the *tobacco sticks;* . . their use is to hang the tobacco upon. **1851** [see **stick** n **1**]. **1872** *Scribner's Mth.* 4.653 **VA,** Commencing at a safe distance from the fire, up to the top of the tall building, reach beams stretching across for the reception of the tobacco-sticks, thick pine laths, from which are suspended the heavy plants. **1922** *Bee* (Danville VA) 20 Jan 1/6, [Headline:] Aged Seventy, She Slays Hawk With A Tobacco Stick. **1967–70** *DARE* Tape **KY**56, We'd tie this hand [of tobacco leaves], and then we'd put that on a tobacco stick, and we'd put twelve or . . fourteen hands to a stick; **MA**108, There was a grist mill and they sold grains, and they made tobacco lath and they made shingles; **VA**38, We use what we call tobacco sticks, something like strips about four and a half foot long. . . If they're large leaves you won't want over twenty-six bundles to the stick. You put three leaves in each bundle; **WV**5, They got what they call tobacco sticks. It'll hold, oh, four or five plants. **1968** *KY Folkl. Rec.* 14.40, Tobacco sticks were usually *rived out* with a *froe* from logs of oak or hickory four feet long. They were roughly square in cross section and long enough to hold approximately six stalks of tobacco for curing. **1969–70** *DARE* (Qu. K27, . . *The sharp-pointed stick used to get oxen to move*) Inf **KY**27, Tobaccer stick; (Qu.X37, . . *Words . . to describe people's legs if they're noticeably bent, or uneven, or not right*) Inf **VA**102, Tobacco sticks (for skinny legs). **2003** *Smoky Mt. News* (Waynesville NC) 30 Apr (Internet), Folks used to go to the woods and cut small saplings about the size of a broom stick. Take a hatchet and sharpen it on both ends. That's a tobacco stick.

tobacco stripping See **strip 1**

tobacco-stripping room See **strip house**

tobacco sumac n Cf **kinnikinnick 2a**

A **sumac B** (here: *Rhus virens*) native to Texas.

 1960 Vines *Trees SW* 632, *Rhus. . . virens. . .* Vernacular names . . are Tobacco Sumac [etc]. . . Tamaichia was the name given by the Comanche Indians, who gathered the leaves in the fall, sun-cured them, and mixed them with tobacco for smoking. **1979** Little *Checklist U.S. Trees* 252, *Rhus virens. . .* Tobacco sumac. . . Commonly a shrub less than 10 ft (3 m) high.

tobacco wax See **tobacco gum**

tobaccoweed n

1 =**devil's-grandmother**.

 [**1830** Rafinesque *Med. Flora* 2.217, *Elephantopus,* L. One of the Indian tobaccoes.] **1894** *Jrl. Amer. Folkl.* 7.92 **WV**, *Elephantus* [sic] *tomentosus . .* tobacco weed. **1970** Correll *Plants TX* 1538, *Elephantopus tomentosus. . . Tobacco-weed. . .* Infrequent in wooded sandy lands, . . s.e. U.S.

2 A composite plant (*Atrichoseris platyphylla*) native to the southwestern US. [See quot 1941] Also called **parachute plant**

 1908 *Amer. Naturalist* 42.684 **CA**, The composite *Atrichoseris platyphylla* is called "Tobacco weed" by the boys of Palo Verde. **1925** Jepson *Manual Plants CA* 989, *Atrichoseris platyphylla. . . Tobacco Weed. . .* Gravelly valleys or rocky slopes. **1941** Jaeger *Wildflowers* 306 **Desert SW**, *Atrichoseris platyphylla. . .* Sometimes called tobacco-weed because of the broad, brown-spotted, somewhat tobacco-like leaves, which lie flat to the earth. **1974** Munz *Flora S. CA* 123, *Tobacco-Weed.* Low scapose annual with basal rosette of broad thick l[ea]v[e]s. **2002** *DARE* File—Internet **sCA**, *Atrichoseris platyphylla*—tobacco-weed, gravel ghost, parachute plant.

3 Appar a plant such as a **mullein** (here: *Verbascum thapsus*) or a **cudweed 1** such as *Pseudognaphalium obtusifolium.* Cf **tobacco plant 1, 2**

 1968 *DARE* (Qu. S21, . . *Weeds . . that are a trouble in gardens and fields*) Inf **WI**68, Tobacco weed. **1986** Pederson *LAGS Concordance* (*What do people smoke?*) 1 inf, **cnMS**, Tobacco weed—smoked.

tobaccowood n Also *wood tobacco*

A **witch hazel** (here: *Hamamelis virginiana*).

 1876 Hobbs *Bot. Hdbk.* 120, Tobacco wood, Hamamelis Virginica [sic]. **1930** Sievers *Amer. Med. Plants* 64, *Hamamelis virginiana. . .* Snapping hazel, . . tobacco wood. **1974** Morton *Folk Remedies* 69 **SC**, *Witch-hazel; . .* tobacco wood. . . *South Carolina* (*Current use*): Fresh leaves stuffed up nose to clear passages. They are also rubbed on bleeding gums. . . Bark decoction is taken as a remedy for diarrhea and applied to swellings. **1974** (1977) Coon *Useful Plants* 149, Wood tobacco. . . Rather tall-growing shrub which blooms . . with yellow, thread-like flowers in late autumn. **1979** Erichsen-Brown *Med. N. Amer. Plants* 177, Tobacco wood. . . The wood is hard, weighing 43 lbs per cu. foot.

tobacco worm n

1 also *tobacco hornworm:* A **hornworm** (here: either *Man-*

duca quinquemaculata or *M. sexta*). Cf **potato worm, tomato ~ 1**

 [**1688** in 1693 Royal Soc. London *Philos. Trans.* 17.947 **VA**, There be various Accidents and Distempers, whereunto Tobacco is liable, as the Worm, the Flie, [etc].] **1737** (1911) Brickell *Nat. Hist. NC* 168, The Tobacco-worm . . has two sharp horns on its Head, the Body is white and Black. **1800** in 1969 Herndon *Wm. Tatham Tobacco* 21 **VA**, That which is most destructive . . is the *horn* worm, or large green tobacco worm. **1848** in 1850 Cooper *Rural Hours* 202 **ceNY**, The common green potato, or tobacco-worm, is said to become a moth of this kind. **1874** [see **tobacco hawkmoth**]. **1884** (1885) McCook *Tenants* 69 **PA**, This is the potato-worm, the tomato-worm, or the tobacco-worm, just as you choose to call it. You all know it—a large green caterpillar, with a kind of thorn on the tail, and oblique, whitish stripes on the side of the body. **1924** U.S. Dept. Ag. *Farmers' Bulletin* 1371.38, Tomato worms or hornworms. Certain large green caterpillars are also called tobacco hornworms or tobacco worms. **1944** *PADS* 2.72 **sVA**, *Tobacco-worm. . .* A large green worm that feeds on green tobacco. Same as *horn-worm.* **1965–70** *DARE* (Qu. R27, . . *Kinds of caterpillars or similar worms*) 134 Infs, **scattered, but chiefly Midl, SE**, Tobacco worm; **KY**80, Bacco worm; **HI**14, Horned tobacco worm; **VT**13, Tobacco hornworm; (Qu. P6, . . *Kinds of worms . . used for bait*) Infs **IN**18, 83, **KY**11, 23, 93, **NC**85, **VA**38, 89, Tobacco worm; (Qu. K76, . . *Kinds of poultry . . raised around here*) Inf **SC**23, Guinea—like a big quail, but flecks and white speckles; also a white guinea; ate tobacco worms. **1966–70** *DARE* Tape **FL**26, [FW:] Is there any other kind of a bug or anything that gets, that really goes for it? [Inf:] Just the aphids and the worm, tobacco worms; **KY**75, We have hornworm, which we call the tobacco worm. That is the same worm that is the tomato worm; **OH**58, [FW:] What kind of bugs can get on the tobacco? [Inf:] Well, they have, after it's out in the field, they have tobacco worms. They look something like a tomato worm, and they're different sizes they grow. **1986** Pederson *LAGS Concordance,* 1 inf, **cwAL**, Tobacco worm—crop pest; 1 inf, **ceAR**, (To)bacco worm; 1 inf, **neAR**, Tobacco worm—attacks tobacco; 1 inf, **nwFL**, Tobacco worm; 1 inf, **ceGA**, Tobacco worm—only useful with catfish. **2002** *DARE* File—Internet **csWI**, Often, another pest, the tobacco worm, must be removed [from tobacco].

2 One who chews or smokes tobacco to excess.

 1906 *DN* 3.161 **nwAR**, *Tobacco-worm. . .* One who uses tobacco to excess. **1967–69** *DARE* (Qu. DD3a, . . *A person who uses snuff*) Inf **GA**77, Tobacco worm [laughter]; (Qu. DD9a, . . *A person who smokes a great deal. . . "He's a _____."*) Infs **AL**16, **GA**77, Tobacco worm; **GA**74, Tobacco worm—also used for chewers.

tobaccy See **tobacco** n A2

tobacker See **tobacco** n A1

tobacky See **tobacco** n A2

tobakker See **tobacco** n A1

tobe See **toby 2**

Tobey's behind, as black as See **Toby's heel, blacker than**

toboggan n

1 often *toboggan cap,* ~ *hat;* also aphet *boggan, boggin;* rarely *tobogganing cap:* A stocking cap. **chiefly Sth, S Midl; also Inland Nth** Cf **tuque**

 1870 (1871) Coffin *Seat of Empire* 90 **MN**, A brown toboggan cap of indescribable shape which old Aunt Rachel had knitted for me. **1886** *Marion Daily Star* (OH) 26 Nov 3/1, Practical, Pleasing Presents For Christmas. . . A Toboggan Cap. **1908** *Sandusky Star-Jrl.* (OH) 17 Jan 2/5, The cap or hood . . is peaked like a toboggan hat. **1911** *Century Dict. Suppl.* 1355, *Toboggan-cap. . .* A knit woolen cap, made in a long, bag-like form, the top of which falls down over the head: now commonly called a *toque.* **1929** *AmSp* 5.152 **cNY**, *Toboggan:* a woolen cap. "Take off your toboggan." **1929** Ellis *Ordinary Woman* 89 **CO** (as of early 20th cent), The toboggan cap . . followed, a wool cap fitting close to the head with three large pompons in front. **1942** Hall *Smoky Mt. Speech* 57 **wNC, eTN**, Toboggan 'a knit cap with a tassel,' seems to be known only in its reduced form [ˈbɑɡən]. **1948** *Pacific Spectator* Winter 83 **SC**, He had . . a knitted blue toboggan on his head, against the cold. **c1960** Wilson *Coll.* **csKY**, Toboggan. . . A knitted cap; often just boggan or toboggan cap. **1975** *News & Observer* (Raleigh NC) 6 Jan 24/4, He was wearing a red toboggan and light pants, police said. **1981** *DARE* File **WV**, A woman in her fifties reports that when she was a child in West Virginia stocking caps were always referred to as toboggans. **1995** *News & Observer* (Raleigh NC) 16 Dec, What once were tobogganing caps became, over the years, simply "toboggans." Except we pronounce them, in our own uniquely Southern way, "*toe*-boggins" or sometimes, in the privacy of our own homes, merely "boggins." **1995** *DARE* File **OH, MI,** Students from Toledo, OH and Michiganders use this term [=*toboggan*] for a knit cap. *Ibid* **KY,** I grew up in KY in the 50s using this term [=*toboggan*] . . for a knit cap. . . I check the term regularly with my students [in East Lansing, MI], and none have ever heard it in the meaning 'knit cap,' only as a sled. *Ibid* **nwNC,** I grew up with the word "toboggan" meaning knit cap. *Ibid* **seNY,** A long-time local resident of . . the lower Hudson Valley reported it [=*toboggan*] was familiar to him even from his childhood. *Ibid* **TX,** I learned the word [=*toboggan,* for a knit cap] from my mother when I was a wee thing in Texas. *Ibid* **nGA,** In my family we call it just a "boggin." **1996** Horton *Island Out of Time* 70 **Chesapeake Bay MD,** I picked up this old cedar root and I thought, dast if it isn't shaped like Tom in that toboggan hat he wore when he was livin' here a few years ago. **2000** *NADS Letters* **TN,** In Chattanooga I have heard numerous people using the word Toboggan to mean a ski cap/stocking cap worn in the winter. I never heard it back in Michigan. **2000** *DARE* File **AL,** Amanda, like me, is a native Alabamian, and thought everyone called the cap a toboggan. We were amazed that northerners did not know the term (for a hat). **2004** *DARE* File—Internet **sOH,** I am currently living in southern Ohio and I have heard many people refer to a knit cap as a toboggan.

2 usu as *toboggan scarf:* A long winter scarf. **esp Nth**
    1887 *IA State Reporter* (Waterloo) 22 Dec 1/5, [Advt:] Knit Toboggan Scarf. **1930** *Ogden Std.-Examiner* (UT) 9 Dec 3/5, [Advt:] Toboggan Scarf and Tam Sets. **1962** *Oshkosh Daily Northwestern* (WI) [18 Oct 27] (newspaperarchive.com), [Advt:] Charcoal or gray coat with a toboggan scarf. [*DARE* Ed: Picture shows a long scarf.] **1967** *DARE* (Qu. W3, *A piece of cloth that a woman folds over her head and ties under her chin*) Inf **NJ**3, Toboggan. **2004** *DARE* File **seWI** (as of c1960), A "toboggan scarf" was a long one—five or six feet long. *Ibid* **WI** (as of c1950), When I was a child, my father often wore a long scarf around his neck when he went ice-skating. He called it a "toboggan scarf" and showed me a photo of himself wearing this same "toboggan scarf" in a photo from about 1930. I also heard my Mother's family in Plymouth WI and other local people refer to such winter scarves as "toboggan scarves."

3 A single bobsled or a **double-runner.** [Transf from std sense] **NEng**
    1943 *LANE* Map 573–74 **n,eME,** The following terms for "double sled" are given on the map. . . Toboggan [6 infs]. **1965** *PADS* 43.20 **seMA,** Other names for a bobsled . . toboggan . . [2 of 9 infs] (one sled).

toboggan cap (or hat), tobogganing cap   See **toboggan 1**

toboggan scarf   See **toboggan 2**

tobosa (grass) n
A **galleta,** usu *Pleuraphis mutica.*
    1908 Wooton in NM Ag. Exper. Station *Bulletin* 66.12, The grasses of this society are . . the tobosa grass *(Hilaria mutica)* [=*Pleuraphis m.*] . . , the drier region equivalent of the galleta grass [etc]. **1912** Wooton–Standley *Grasses NM* 34, The name *Galleta Grass* . . is applied locally by the Mexican people to one or sometimes to two species of *Hilaria,* (*H. jamesii,* and *H. mutica* [=*Pleuraphis j.,* and *P. mutica*]) usually and possibly more properly to the former, while the latter is more frequently called *Tobosa. Ibid* 35, The *Tobosa Grass* occupies a position of the same relative importance in the southern third of the State as the Galleta does in the cooler plains and mountains. It closely resembles the other species [=*P. jamesii*] but is coarser, drier and toughter; it is distinctly a bunch grass. **1937** U.S. Forest Serv. *Range Plant Hdbk.* G71, *Tobosa. . . Pleuraphis mutica.* . . Tobosa is an erect perennial very similar in general appearance to galleta *(H[ilaria] jamesii)*. It ranges from western Texas to Arizona and south into Mexico. **1957** Jaeger *N. Amer. Deserts* 47, Tussocks of coarse "tobosa" grass *(Hilaria mutica . .)* and other grasses quite often cover the ground as an open sod. *Ibid* 66, Grasses . . often are in bloom . . after the summer rains. Among the important kinds are . . several species of tobosa. **1967–70** *DARE* (Qu. L9a, . . *Kinds of grass . . grown for hay*) Inf **TX**4, Tobosa [tə'bousə]; (Qu. S9, . . *Kinds of grass that are hard to get rid of*) Inf **CA**208, Toboose [sic] grass; (Qu. S21, . . *Weeds . . that are a trouble in gardens and fields*) Inf **CA**208, Toboose [sic]. **1970** Correll *Plants TX* 252, *Hilaria mutica. . . Tobosa.* **1970** Humphrey *AZ Range Grasses* 93, *Hilaria mutica. . .* The forage value of tobosa grass varies from good during the summer months when it is green, to very poor during the winter months.

toby n
1 also *Pittsburgh toby:* A thin, inexpensive cigar; rarely, a cigarette. **chiefly wPA, nMD** See Map
    1862 in 1962 Truxall *Respects to All* 36 **PA,** Send me a plug of tobacco and a hundred tobys. **1883** *Indiana Democrat* (PA) 22 Mar [3]/1 (newspaperarchive.com), The present price of 100 tobies, outside the revenue, may be given at 60 cents. **1884** *Catholic World* May 276 **cnMD,** Tobias—or Uncle Toby, as he had been christened by the people of Emmittsburg [sic], whither he went now and again to sell cigars, or "Tobies," as the college boys called them long after the Indian himself had gone to the Happy Hunting Ground. **1887** *Newark Daily Advocate* (OH) 24 Sept 4/1, A kind of cigar is very popular in certain sections of the country known as Wheeling stogies or Pittsburg tobies. These are made from Southern or hogshead tobacco, soaked until all the nicotine is washed out of it and then roughly rolled into a long, thin shape of cylindrical form to resemble a cigar. . . Pittsburg furnishes a great many tobies of the kind described, which are smoked and enjoyed alike by the millionaire mill-owner and the humble factory hand. **1908** in 2004 (acc) *Emmitsburg Area Hist. Soc.* (Internet) **cnMD,** (as of c1850), You could buy two cigars or four tobies for a cent. *Ibid,* Often a store would keep a box of tobies on the counter free to everybody. A good deal of tobacco was raised here and people made their own tobies. **1944** *Gettysburg Times* (PA) 12 May 1/1 **cnMD,** In 1847 James Storm opened a store [in Emmitsburg]. . . The cheap cigars, called tobies, sold for 16 cents a hundred. **1965–70** *DARE* (Qu. DD6a, *Other names or nicknames for cigars*) Infs **MD**22, **PA**71, 74, 197, 209, Toby; **PA**76, Tobies are skinny; (Qu. DD6b, *Nicknames for cigarettes*) Infs **FL**22, **PA**185, Toby; (Qu. DD7, *Different names for cigars . . according to size, shape, or the way they're made*) Infs **PA**74, 182, Toby; **PA**132, Tobies—long. **1986** Pederson *LAGS Concordance,* 1 inf, **swGA,** Toby—half-smoked cigarette.

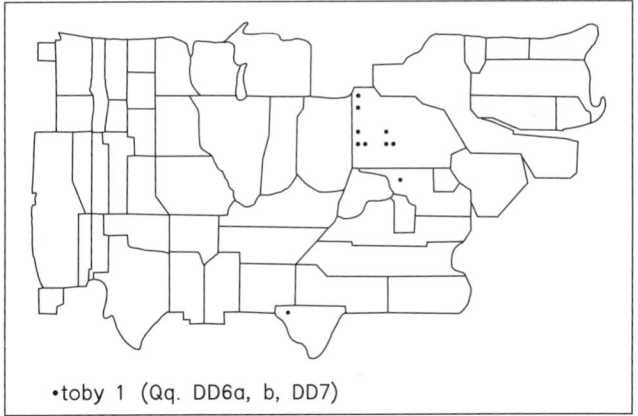

•toby 1 (Qq. DD6a, b, DD7)

2 also *tobe;* In **hoodoo** n **1a:** an amulet or good-luck charm. **chiefly Sth, S Midl** Cf **hand** n B4, **jack** n[1] **15, mojo** n **1**
    1926 Puckett *Folk Beliefs S. Negro* 19 **New Orleans LA,** The term *mojo* is often used by the Mississippi Negroes to mean "charms, amulets, or tricks". . . In New Orleans the term *tobe* or *toby* is used in the same sense. **1930** in 1992 Macleod *Yazoo* 21–83 361 **wTN,** I'm goin' to New Orleans to get this toby fixed of mine / I'm havin' trouble, trouble, I can't keep from cryin'. **c1938** in 1970 Hyatt *Hoodoo* 1.529 **New Orleans LA** [Black], Any time a man have a *toby* or anything of the kind that way he have to be very careful, and if it isn't *charged up* with the right material, it don't do him any good. *Ibid* 558 **Memphis TN,** Yo' takes a frog an' yo' kill him an' lets him dry, takes an' sews him up in a shammy skin, an' *feed* him with whiskey. Well, that's supposed to be a very, very nice *toby* fo' gamblin'. **1938** FWP *Guide MS* 28, Perhaps the "papa toby" of them all, one which is sure to possess the virtue or vice necessary to drive away the hoodoo, is the ever useful piece of red flannel thrust inside of a hollowed-out pecan hull. **1939** FWP *Guide TN* 139 **wTN** [Black], Cunjur doctors will sell you "hands" or "tobies" enabling you to detect witches and ward off their spells. **1980** Banks *First-Person America* 185 **OK** (as of 1939), A toby helps people to be lucky. If you want something real bad, you don't get what you want without some help. That's where my tobies come in. I sell them for just one dollar. . . You put all these things [=*miscellaneous plant leaves and powders*] in a little fancy colored bag, known as a lucky bag.

3 cap: A stock comic character in tent shows; hence n *Toby (show)* a comic tent show.

1940 *Lime Springs Herald* (IA) 20 June [3]/4 (newspaperarchive.com), Several from this way attended the Toby show in Lime Springs last week. **1941** Writers' Program *Guide AR* 118, "Toby shows" also tour the crossroads villages and county seats, playing in tents, schoolhouses, or rented halls. The small cast is headed by "Toby," usually an aging professional who spiels at the gate, sells the tickets, and peddles the candy boxes . . before he takes his place on the stage to play the comedy lead. **1943** *Hammond Times* (IN) 27 Jan 8/3, Tent shows are repertory stock of a more rural type. They're called Toby shows. *Ibid*, I also played in John D. Winninger's repertory show, which is slightly more sophisticated than a Toby. **1964** TN Folk Lore Soc. *Bulletin* 30.49, Bisbee's Comedians . . is one of the two surviving Toby Shows left in the entire country. **1967** *Coshocton Tribune* (OH) 29 Mar 12/1, Mrs. Dibble. . . is 85 and a hearty type, used to own and boss a carnival and used to act in a Toby Show. She drinks brandy and smokes cigars in bed. **1973** *Sun. Times* (Salisbury MD) 1 July sec D 1/4, Robert Cloyd. . . has produced a "Toby Show for Children". . . Toby, a comic takeoff of the medicine man show huckster so prevalent in 19th century rural America, serves as host.

Toby's heel, blacker than adj phr Also *as black as Tobey's behind, dirtier than Toby's ass;* for addit varr see quots
Very black.

1901 *DN* 2.149 **cnNY**, *Toby's heel*. . . In expression, "Blacker'n Toby's heel" = very black. **1928** Fisher *Toilers* 294 **ID**, You can think about life till you're blackern Toby's heel and you won't never see it clear like it is. **1958** *VT Hist.* 26.290, As black as tobey's behind. (boot, foot.) **1997** *DARE* File **swWI**, My former mother-in-law found a dried up peach pit on the ground and remarked that it was "black as Toby's Hill [sic]." I had never heard that phrase, so asked another family member, who said that it was used of any piece of old fruit. **2009** *DARE* File **CO**, He repeatedly used another expression, dirtier than Toby's a**.

Toby show See **toby 3**

toby-struck adj Also *toby-stricken* [Cf **toby 2**] **chiefly VA**
Congenitally malformed or peculiar; see quots.

1865 [see **to** prep, adv **A1a**]. **1933** *Sun. Times–Signal* (Zanesville OH) 11 June sec 2 7/2 **VA**, When she was born—in Richmond, Va., 17 years ago—she wasn't a very attractive child. Down there, it seems, they say an ungainly colt, one that appears certain never to amount to much, is Toby-struck. **1941** Hench Coll. **VA**, Today Virginia . . was describing a colored woman. She has a hideous face. "She was terribly toby-struck," she said. When I asked her what she meant she said "What? You never heard that? A toby-struck person looks as if the devil had ruined her looks." **1942** *Ibid* **VA**, Mrs. Sage of Charlottesville, Va. told me . . of the word toby-struck. . . Mrs. Sage's meaning is "queer, odd, peculiar." "She does such curious things. I think she's toby-struck." **1952** *Ibid* **VA**, Her mother the other day spoke of a droll-looking person as "toby-struck." **1952** Brown *NC Folkl.* 1.601, *Tobystruck:* . . (EDD: "*toby-trot*, a half-witted person.") Ugly; mentally unbalanced.—Central and east [NC].

toby tree n Also *Indian toby tree* [**toby 1**] **esp PA**
=**catalpa B1**.

1967–69 *DARE* (Qu. T9, *The common shade tree with large heart-shaped leaves, clusters of white blossoms, and long thin seed pods or 'beans'*) Infs **PA**70, 74, 95, Toby tree(s); **IL**97 ['tobi] tree; **PA**134, Indian toby tree.

tocalote n
A **star thistle.**

1896 *Jrl. Amer. Folkl.* 9.191 **CA**, *Centaurea Melitensis*, . . tocolote [sic]. **1925** Jepson *Manual Plants CA* 1168, *C[entaurea] melitensis*. . . *Tocalote*. . . One of our most widespread and objectionable grain-field weeds. **1961** Peck *Manual OR* 846, *Tocalote*. . . A weed in cultivated and waste ground west of the Cascade Mts., more common southward. **1967** *DARE* (Qu. S9, . . *Kinds of grass that are hard to get rid of*) Inf **CA**20, Tocalote—a weed, low ground cover. **1970** Correll *Plants TX* 1714, *Tocalote*. . . Abundant in disturbed calcareous soil especially along roads. **2002** (acc) CA Univ.–Davis Coop. Ext. *Weed Research & Info. Center* (Internet), Tocalote and sulfur starthistle do not have cotton-tip seedheads after senescence.

toch See **touch**

toch(e)d, tocht See **touch B**

Tocko n [See quot] Cf **keskydee**
A person of Yugoslavian descent.

1944 Kane *Deep Delta Country* 93 **LA**, When one Slav met another, his greeting was *"Kako ste?"*—"How are you?" The answer was *"Dobro"*—"Good." The amused French called them "Kako ste's"; eventually the word became "Tocko", and it has never been lost.

tod n [Abbr for *toddy*] **esp Sth, S Midl**
1797 Prentiss *Coll. Fugitive Essays* 67 **MA**, Whether thou exercisest thy power in the full bowl of *punch*, . . or the circling mug of *tod*. **1853** Wharton *New Orleans Sketch Book* 53, My acquisition in knowledge gave me a relish for tods and oysters. **1862** (1864) Browne *Artemus Ward Book* 114 **ME**, He liked his tods too well, howsever, & they floored him, as they have many other promisin young men. **1872** Burnham *Memoirs U.S. Secret Service* 98, He had long been possessed with a love of liquor, and he never "shirked his tod" among boon companions. **1885** *Harper's New Mth. Mag.* 71.399 **GA**, He swallowed the drink as unconcernedly as though his morning tod had never been suspended. **1899** (1912) Green *VA Folk-Speech* 451, *Tod*. . . A drink; toddy. **1965** Davis *Summer Land* 234 **cnNC**, Grandpa ate like a bird. The only thing he said was about whiskey. "I'll have my tod now," he said. When they went downstairs to fetch the liquor he said, "Damn a place where they forget a body's tod."

today (a) week See **week** n[1] **Ba**

todder See **tother**

toddick n Also *taddick* [EDD *taddick* (at *tad* sb.[1]) "a small quantity of anything; a measure, &c., partly filled," dimin of *tad* "A quantity; a burden, load," which is prob var of *tod* a measure of wool (usu 28 lbs); a load, bundle] **chiefly NC** Cf **taddle**
A small quantity; a small measure or measuring vessel.

1913 Kephart *Highlanders* 292 **sAppalachians**, Who knows what a toddick or taddle is? I did not until my friend Dargan reported it from the Nantahala [=wNC]. "Ben didn't git a full turn o' meal, but jest a toddick." When a farmer goes to one of our little tub-mills . . he leaves a portion of the meal as toll. This he measures out in a toll-dish or toddick or taddle (the name varies with the locality) which the mill-owner left for that purpose. Toddick, then, is a small measure. **1943** Peattie *Great Smokies* 149, Women borrow a "toddick" of wool, as they did in *The Winter's Tale*. [*DARE* Ed: The ref is appar to *WT* IV.iii, where, however, the word used is *tod,* for a definite measure of wool.] **1946** *PADS* 6.29 **eNC**, *Taddick*. . . A small amount—coffee, sugar, etc., not water or money. Pamlico. Old people. **1952** Brown *NC Folkl.* 1.597, *Taddick*. . . A small amount. Same as *toddick, q.v. Ibid* 601, *Toddick*. . . A small amount. . . —General. **1974** Fink *Mountain Speech* 27 **wNC, eTN**, *Toddick* . . small measuring vessel used in taking toll at a grist mill, hence—small amount.

todduh See **tother**

tode See **tell** v **B2d**

toder See **tother**

todes, todge, tods See **toward A**

toe prep, adv See **to** prep, adv **A1a**

toe n[1]
1 A clove (of garlic). [Prob calque of Ger *Zeh* toe, clove (of garlic)]
1921 *Galveston Daily News* (TX) 18 Dec 34/7, Chop together three dozen oysters . . , one onion, one toe of garlic, [etc]. **1943** *Lima News* (OH) 26 July 3/3, Add sprig of dill, medium sized toe of garlic, and alum . . to each jar. **1951** Brown *Southern Cook Book* 113 **TX**, *Texas kubabs* . . 4 "toes" garlic, crushed. **1953** *Post-Std.* (Syracuse NY) 5 Aug 8/1, Drain and fill the jars with pickles, dill and a few toes of garlic. **1974** *Delta Democrat–Times* (Greenville MS) 4 July 25/5, Brush each cut surface with olive oil in which you have lightly sauteed a toe of garlic. **1993** *DARE* File **Upstate NY**, Saute three large toes of garlic, minced. **2004** *DARE* File—Internet **New Orleans LA**, New Orleans Red Gravy. . . 10–15 cloves garlic, sliced in half lengthwise (if you're from New Orleans, you'll say "toes" of garlic).

2 See **niggertoe 7**.

toe v[1], hence ppl adj *toed*, vbl n *toeing* Cf **tread 1**
Also with *for:* To feel with one's toes for (clams).
1867 *Peterson's Mag.* 51.190, Nothing living was in sight, but two or three women toeing for clams in the clear waters of the inlet. **1984** Wilder *You All Spoken Here* 169 **Sth**, Stomp clams; tread clams; toe clams: Find clams in shallow water by feeling them with your feet. **2003** *DARE* File—Internet, Would you think toed clams better than

raked clams? **2004** *DARE* File—Internet, Vance leads her readers ever so gently and enthusiastically from foraging for wild cattails, to toeing for clams [etc].

toe n² See **taw**

toe v² See **tear B2a**

toe-biter n
1 =**giant water bug.**
    1895 Comstock–Comstock *Manual Insects* 132, In the far West there is a common species [of giant water bug] which is . . *Serphus dilatatus* [=*Abedus d.*] . . These insects are known to California children as "Toe-biters," owing to the great interest they are supposed to take in the feet of waders and swimmers. **1926** Essig *Insects N. Amer.* 367, The name "toe-biter" [for Belostomatidae] comes from the vise-like grip they give if stepped on with bare feet. They also inflict a severe bite and inject poison in the wounds of their victims. **1980** Milne–Milne *Audubon Field Guide Insects* 464, Eastern Toe-biter . . *Benacus griseus*. . . Underwater, they often stab or seize a person's bare foot, earning the name "Toe Biter." . . "Toe-biter" . . *Lethocerus americanus*. . . Shallow freshwater ponds and pools, among bottom vegetation. **1998** *Dermatology Online Jrl.* (Internet), *Lethocerus americanus* is a large water bug commonly found in ponds and slowly moving fresh water. Also known as the "toe biter" for its encounters with swimmers, it has the reputation of inflicting painful bites when carelessly handled.
2 =**hellgrammite 1.**
    1943 KS State Bd. Ag. *Report* June 205, "Dobson flies" are large insects with a wingspread of 1½ to 4 inches. . . The larvae which are known as "hellgrammites," "crawlers" and "toe biters," are aquatic and predacious.

toed See **toe** v

toe-drops n, intj Cf **eye-drops**
In marble play: a shot in which a player drops a marble from his raised foot onto another marble; the call claiming the right to do this.
    1958 *PADS* 29.41 **WI,** Toe-drops. . . A call claiming the right to drop one's marble from one's cocked-up toes (the heel being kept on the ground) in the game of *chase.* **1968** *DARE* Tape **IA**27, And you can say "eye-drops" and "toe-drops." . . And then toe-drops, you get it up here like that [*DARE* Ed:=balance the marble on your foot] . . and then just let it go.

toe for See **toe** v

toe gem See **toe jam**

toeing See **toe** v

toe itch n
1 =**ground itch. chiefly Sth, S Midl**
    1798 Barton *Coll. for an Essay* 47, This complaint is very common, particularly among the negroes, and the poorer sort of white people, in Carolina, Georgia, &c. It is called "Toe-Itch,[*] and [*]Ground-Itch." It is a kind of ulcerous excoriation between the toes, sometimes extending as high as the instep, and is attended with most intolerable itching. **1863** *Weekly Std.* (Raleigh NC) 11 Mar 1/5, A friend of ours has been using the ointment for toe-itch only a few days with decided benefit. **1912** Green *VA Folk-Speech* 465, Toe-each. . . For *toe-itch.* A disease that comes from walking about bare-footed on the wet grass in the morning; from which is said to come *hook-worm.* **1917** *DN* 4.411 **wNC,** Eetch. Variant of *itch.* "That's eetch-weed; it's good for toe eetch." **1928** *Lima News* (OH) 27 Sept 6/3, Ground itch, toe itch, dew itch, hookworm dermatitis, the form of toe itch produced by the invasion of the skin of the feet by the larvae of hookworms, prevalent in the polluted soil of many of the more primitive southern regions. **1929** *Appleton Post–Crescent* (WI) 16 July 6/4, After using remedies to destroy the fungus or ring-worm of toe itch or gymnasium itch, it is important to disinfect the linings of the shoes. **c1960** *Wilson Coll.* **csKY,** Toe-itch. . . Dew poison, ringworm, hookworm, ground itch. **1967–68** *DARE* (Qu. BB25, . . Common skin diseases around here) Infs **LA**15, **SC**31, 46, Toe itch; **SC**32, Toe itch—same as dew itch—breaking out on feet; **SC**34, Toe itch—from being in water too much. **1986** Pederson *LAGS Concordance,* 2 infs, **GA,** Toe itch; 1 inf, **GA,** Toe itch—athlete's foot; 1 inf, **TX,** Toe itch—athlete's foot or ground itch. **1998** in 2003 *DARE* File—Internet **KY,** I am like a bare footed boy in a muddy barn yard. I have a calf by the tale [sic] . . and I am going so fast I am afraid to turn loose for fear of falling on my face in the mud. At the best, I will end up by getting the darndest case of the toe itch you ever saw. **2003** *Advo-*

cate (Baton Rouge LA) 24 July (Internet) **MS,** Kerosene was also used for a nail in the foot, toe itch, rashes, boils and bruises.
2 A **richweed 1** (here: *Pilea pumila*). [See quot]
    1975 Hamel–Chiltoskey *Cherokee Plants* 52, Rich weed, toe itch—*Pilea pumila.* Infusion to reduce excessive hunger in children; rub stems between the toes for itching.

toe jam n Also *toe gem* Cf **foot jelly, jelly** n **5**
See quot 1942.
    1866 *OH Democrat* (New Philadelphia) 7 Sept [4/2] (newspaper-archive.com), The following excellent article . . we publish for the benefit of those of our readers who are peculiarly troubled with "toe jam." **1879** *Atchison Daily Globe* (KS) 10 Mar [4/1] (newspaper-archive.com), Who ever saw a breast pump? . . Or a jumping rope? Or a toe jam? **1942** McAtee *Dial. Grant Co. IN Suppl. 1* 10 (as of 1890s), Toe-jam. . . viscid dirt collecting between the toes of shod, but unwashed feet. **1968** *DARE* FW Addit **FL,** Toe jam—heard from young White man from Vero Beach. *Ibid* **FL,** Toe jam—heard from Negroes from north central Florida. *Ibid* **Ozarks,** Toe jam—this is the common word in my part of the Ozarks—the SW corner of Missouri and NW corner of Arkansas. **1973** *DARE* File swPA (as of 1920s), Your feet would perspire and you'd get dirt between your toes. This dirt was called "toe gems." **1979** Gillespie–Fraser *To Be Or Not To Bop* 310 [Black], I hear Lips play the blues, and it's different from me. Mine ain't the real blues with toe jam between your toes, come in and bend a note around the corner. **1983** *DARE* File seMI (as of c1950), My parents used to call the fuzzies that stuck between your toes "toe jam." **1998** Hillerman *First Eagle* 97 **AZ,** It's 'breakthrough of the month' season. If it isn't a new way to clone toe-jam fungus, it's rediscovering life on Mars.

toe line n Also *toe mark, tow line* [Folk-etym for **taw line**]
    [**1940** *Recreation* (NY) 34.110, A list of the many games of marbles played throughout the country follows: . . Tow line.] **c1955** Reed–Person *Ling. Atlas Pacific NW,* 2 infs, Tow line [for "starting line"]. **1966–68** *DARE* (Qu. EE8, *The line toward which the players roll their marbles before beginning a game, to determine the order of shooting*) Infs **GA**44, **NC**35, **TN**8, Toe line; **AR**51, Toe line is where they must stand. **1971** Wood *Vocab. Change* 316 **GA,** [Volunteered word list:] Toe line. **1971** Bright *Word Geog. CA & NV* 205, *Starting line* . . in marbles. . . There were 5 scattered responses, 1 urban, of *toe line/mark.* **1973** Allen *LAUM* 1.405 **Upper MW** (as of c1950), 8 [of c200] infs, **esp ND,** Toe line; 1 inf, **ND,** Toe line—"Because you had to get your toes up there."

toe mold See **mold** n¹

toenail it v phr Cf *DS* Y24
To walk, "hoof it."
    1965 *DARE* FW Addit **ceMS,** I couldn't get a ride, so I just had to toe-nail it. [Black]

toenails, vomit up one's v phr For varr see quots Cf **heels, throw up one's, toes, throw up one's**
To vomit violently.
    1836 *Waldie's Lib.* 26 Apr supp [1], I vomited so terribly that one of the men [on a US naval vessel] expressed it as his opinion, if I continued, that "I must throw up my boots and toe nails." **1905** *DN* 3.98 **nwAR,** Throw up one's toenails[b] throw up one's toes. . . To vomit vehemently and copiously. 'It made me so sick at my stomach, I threw up my toenails.' **1942** McAtee *Dial. Grant Co. IN* 65 (as of 1890s), Throw up one's toe nails . . vomit severely. **1965–70** *DARE* (Qu. BB18, *To vomit a great deal at once*) 15 Infs, **widespread,** Vomit up your toenails; **MD**17, **MI**19, **OH**38, **PA**216, **VA**33, Throw up your toenails; **AL**33, **CA**170, **CT**12, Heave up your toenails; **CO**27, **IA**47, **MI**65, Threw up his toenails; **CA**36, **SC**19, Heaved up his toenails; **TX**35, Throwed up your toenails; **NY**27, Bring up my toenails; **NY**123, Cough up your toenails; **CO**27, Heaved up my toenails; **KS**15, Puke up your toenails; **MI**55, Threw up everything but my toenails; **WI**68, Throw up his toenails; **TX**18, Toss up your toenails; **MI**10, Tried to throw up your toenails; **OH**66, Turn up your toenails; **OK**25, Urped his toenails up; **GA**59, Vomit my toenails up; **MS**1, Vomit up my toenails; **MS**51, Vomit your toenails up. **2008** in 2010 *DARE* File—Internet neGA, "I'm fine!" he's been known to protest, right before he vomits up his toenails.

toe party See **toe social**

toe rubber n Cf **foothold**
A light rubber overshoe which protects the toe and sole and is held in place by a strap around the heel.

1889 *Marion Daily Star* (OH) 27 June [4/7] (newspaperarchive.com), Summer Rubbers—Light Weight Toe Rubbers. . . For High and Low Heeled Shoes. **1903** *Bedford Gaz.* (PA) 16 Jan 4/7, Rubber goods are a necessity and here is a big stock to pick from—all kinds from the dainty toe-rubbers to the big felt boots. **1948** *Sun* (Baltimore MD) 16 Jan 7/7, Keep dry, head to toe with new "rubberella". . . Its smart plastic handle holds a pair of excellent quality toe-rubbers that fit any size foot. **1950** *WELS* **WI,** 6 Infs, Toe rubbers; 1 Inf, Toe rubbers—ladies' heel-less shoe protector; 1 Inf, Toe rubbers—no heels. **1986** *Daily Herald* (Arlington Heights IL) 27 Feb sec 5B 8, Women's Toe Rubber $7.99.

toe sack See **tow sack**

toe social n Also *toe party,* ~ *touching*
See quots.
1896 *Stevens Point Jrl.* (WI) 21 Nov [9/4] (newspaperarchive.com), A "Toe" social will be given at the Baptist church, Buena Vista . . for the benefit of Rev. L.E. Palmer. All are cordially invited to come. **1935** Hurston *Mules & Men* 31 **nFL,** "Good gracious, Zora! Ain't you never been to a toe-party before?" "Nope. They don't have 'em up North where Ah been. . . " "Well, they hides all the girls behind a curtain and you stick out yo' toe. . . When all de toes is in a line, sticking out from behind de sheet they let de men folks in and they looks over all de toes and buys de ones they want for a dime. Then they got to treat de lady dat owns dat toe to everything she want. Sometime they play it so's you keep de same partner for de whole thing and sometime they fix it so they put de girls back every hour or so and sell de toes agin." **1947** *Sun* (Baltimore MD) 10 Oct 12/2 **MO,** "Toe touchin'" is the name of a new game. . . At the Lincoln School here the girls prepared a meal, the boys put up the cash which went for benefit of the library. Then the girls took off their shoes, covered up with a sheet, and let only their bare feet stick out. The boys went by and touched the foot they wanted next to their own at the dining table. **1966–70** *DARE* [(Qu. EE4, *Games*) Inf **FL**33, Selling toes at a party—all stand barefooted behind a blanket with only toes exposed. The others buy the toes and find a partner that way;] (Qu. FF1, . . *A kind of group meeting called a 'social' or 'sociable'. . . [What goes on?]*) Inf **PA**234, Toe social—women stood behind curtain and stuck their toes out and the men would bid on the toes. **1975** *O'Fallon Flashbacks* (Internet) **MT** (as of c1950), I recall one party where the ladies lined up behind a blanket curtain, extending their toes from under the lower edge of the curtain, then the men bid on their choice of toes! This was called a "Toe Party" or "Toe Social."

toes, throw up one's v phr For varr see quot **esp Nth** Cf **heels, throw up one's; toenails, vomit up one's**
To vomit violently.
1905 [see **toenails, vomit up one's**]. **1965–70** *DARE* (Qu. BB18, *To vomit a great deal at once*) Infs **CA**137, **KY**24, **MA**5, 48, **NY**94, **OH**95, **WI**24, Throw up your toes; **MI**68, Heave up my toes; **CA**209, Heave up toes; **NY**42, Heaved up my toes; **WI**24, Heaved up to his toes; **IL**63, Threw up clear down to his toes; **IN**54, Threw up his toes; **ID**5, Threw up one's toes; **CT**8, Throwing up your toes; **OH**29, Turn up your toes, or something; **IL**39, Vomit clear from their toes; **SC**2, Vomit up your toes. **1986** Pederson *LAGS Concordance* (Vomit—crude and jocular terms) 1 inf, **cTX,** Urp my toes up; 1 inf, **cwAR,** Throws his toes up.

toe touching See **toe social**

tofore prep, adv [*OED2* →1649] **esp S Midl** Cf **tohind**
Before.
1911 *DN* 3.540 **eKY,** Tofore, adv. and prep. Before. **1916** *DN* 4.288 **sAppalachians,** Tofore and afore are frequently found for before. E.g., "It rained tofore we ploughed the corn." **1967–68** *DARE* (Qu. MM2, *Suppose a little girl accidentally gets her dress on wrong so that the back part is turned around . . "Look, you've got your dress on _____."*) Inf **VA**21, Hind-part-tofore; **KS**2, Hind-tofore. **1986** Pederson *LAGS Concordance,* 1 inf, **nwLA,** [tĭ'foˤɚ].

tog See **tautog**

to galore See **galore**

together adv, adj Usu |təˈgɛðə(r)|; also |təˈgæðə|, |təˈgjɛðə(r)| Pronc-spp *tergeer, tergarruh, tergether, tergerrer, togather, togedder, togither, tuhgedduh*
A Forms.
1673 in 1885 *Bay State Mth.* 2.273 **cMA,** Being moved vpon considerations aforesaid togather with advis of Christian friends to set his house in order. **1789** in 1956 Eliason *Tarheel Talk* 319 **cnNC,** Togather. **1820** *Ibid* nw,cwNC, To gather. **1861** *Vanity Fair* 4.93, Miss Bissel and

me sot tergether in the car comin down here. **1863** *Continental Mth.* 3.643 **Sth,** Why, he an' ole Roye ar tergether. **1883** (1971) Harris *Nights with Remus* 237 **GA** [Black], B'er Rabbit un B'er Wolf dey come pit bote 'e head tergerrer. **1887** (1967) Harris *Free Joe* 12 **GA** [Black], We 'uz raise tergeer. **1892** *DN* 1.234 **KY,** Together. Often pronounced [tʌgæðə]. [*DN* Ed: [ʌ] in the first syllable, or [ə]? The accent is doubtless on the second syllable.] **1893** Shands *MS Speech* 76, Togæther [təgæðə]. Illiterate whites very frequently so pronounce *together.* In a number of exercises handed to me by my freshman English class, I have seen the word spelled *togather.* **1906** *DN* 3.162 **nwAR,** Together, adv. Together. *Togather* was found by an instructor in the preparatory school of the University of Arkansas, written in eight themes at one time. **1909** *S. Atl. Qrly.* 8.43 **sSC, GA coasts** [Gullah], Together. . . tergarruh. **1922** Gonzales *Black Border* 335 **sSC, GA coasts** [Gullah glossary], Tuhgedduh—together. **1928** Peterkin *Scarlet Sister Mary* 161 **SC** [Gullah], Den dey gone an' married togedder. **1936** *AmSp* 11.244 **eTX,** Hill-Type . . [təˈgjɛðɚ] *Negro* . . [təˈgjɛðə]. **1940** Stuart *Trees of Heaven* 291 **neKY,** Let's git our heads togither here and come to some settle-ment.

B As adj.
Organized, in or under control; composed, poised, stylish. *orig among Black speakers, now more widely used*
1941 in 1983 Taft *Blues Lyric Poetry* 80 **FL** [Black], Uncle Sam called the men down : name by name / He ain't together : but they ready just the same. **1967–70** *DARE* (Qu. W37, *When a woman puts on her good clothes and tries to look her best . . she's _____*) Inf **CT**43, All together; **DC**11, **TN**50, Together; (Qu. W38, *When a man dresses himself up in his best clothes . . he's _____*) Infs **OH**102, **TN**50, Together; (Qu. HH27b, *Of a very able and energetic person who gets things done*) Inf **CA**187, He's got his head together; (Qu. KK1b, . . *'In the very best condition': "His farm is _____."*) Infs **MO**30, **NY**238, **PA**240, Together; (Qu. KK4, *When things turn out just right . . "Everything is _____ now."*) Infs **NY**238, **PA**236, **TN**46, Together; **AL**62, All together; (Qu. KK8, . . *Succeeding, especially in spite of difficulty: "He had a hard time, but at last he _____."*) Inf **IN**75, Got himself together; **MO**30, Got it together; (Qu. KK27, *A very lively, active old person: "For his age, he's _____."*) Inf **MO**30, Together; (Qu. KK29, *To start working very hard: "He was slow at first but now he's really _____."*) Inf **IN**75, Getting himself together, getting together; **FL**52, Has himself together; (Qu. KK34, . . *Very neat and clean: "Her house always looks _____."*) Infs **MO**30, **NY**241, Together; (Qu. KK43, *When the hardest part of a task is finished: "We've still a long way to go, but at least we _____."*) Inf **MO**30, Got most of it together; (Qu. KK50, *When something is planned out carefully, down to the last detail: "He had it all worked out _____."*) Inf **MA**127, Had his program together—very popular new expression. [13 of 15 total Infs Black; both White Infs young] **1968** *Current Slang* 3.2.48 **CA** [Watts slang; Black], Together. . . Prepared.—His program is together. **1969** *Daily Times–News* (Burlington NC) [6 Mar sec B 8]/1 (newspaper-archive.com), [Clothing advt:] Very together. . . these mixers! **1969** *Current Slang* 3.3.11 **OH,** Together. . . Cool and collected.—College students, both sexes, Ohio. **1970** *Ibid* 5.2.13 [Black univ student slang], Together. . . Aware; having one's affairs in order. **1972** *AmSp* 47.152 [Black] (as of 1970), Seems to me you ought to get together before you off yourself. *Ibid* 153, Get together. . . Be in harmony with one's self. **1977** Smitherman *Talkin* 70 [Black], Since . . *hip* was picked up so readily, it was quickly replaced by *together,* which in turn was replaced by *cold* and *mean.* **2001** *DARE* File—Internet **CO,** I was very together. . . I didn't lose my cool.

togga worm See **toggle worm**

togged (down), togged out, togged up See **tog out**

toggle v Usu with *up*
1 also with *together:* To repair, esp in a makeshift way, cobble up, patch together; also fig; hence ppl adj phr *toggled up.* [Prob from *toggle* to fix with a pin or toggle, in ref to this as a temporary way of repairing a broken chain] **chiefly Nth, now esp NY**
1837 *Torch-Light & Pub. Advt.* (Hagers-Town MD) 3 Aug 1/4 **NY,** He used to wear an old grey coat,/ All toggled up before. **1841** Cobb *Green Hand's Cruise* 2.81, His slouching treble-patched-jacket, ducks without waistband, toggled together with spun-yarn [etc]. **1869** *OH Democrat* (New Philadelphia) 10 Dec 1/6 **GA,** [He] was mounted on a skinny . . horse, with an old toggled up saddle under him. **1871** (1872) Barrett *Spiritual Pilgrim* 145 **NEast,** The system of evangelical religion, toggled up in the dark ages of popery, is purely a *policy* religion. **1871**

Elyria Independent Democrat (OH) 5 Apr 3/1, The buggy pole, which had been broken and mended with straps of iron, fell to the ground. . . He will have some damages to pay as a punishment for using a toggled up buggy pole with such spirited horses. **1893** in 2005 *DARE* File—Internet **cNY,** I broke the new sleigh's short tongue in turning around empty but toggled it up with a chain. **1906** *Washington Post* (DC) 22 Apr sec 3 15/6 **MT,** "Shorty" . . found a pole that could be used as a sled tongue, and we toggled up matters and continued our trip to Bannack. **1914** *DN* 4.154 **NH,** *Toggle up.* . . To put in a broken link in such a way as to hold the chain in place, to fix up anything. **1917** *DN* 4.402 **neOH,** *Toggle up.* . . To repair in a bungling and temporary fashion. **1939** *LANE* Map 152 *(Repair)* 19 infs, **chiefly NH, VT,** Toggle up; 2 infs, **ME, CT,** Toggle; [6 infs, **CT,** Toggle [in ref to std sense of repairing chain]; 2 infs, **MA,** Toggle up [in ref to repairing chain]; 1 inf, **cnCT,** You might toggle a chain, but that wouldn't be mending on it]. **1967–70** *DARE* (Qu. KK63, *To do a clumsy or hurried job of repairing something: "It will never last—he just _____."*) Infs **NY**88, 123, 205, **OR**6, **PA**234, Toggled it up. **1991** *Syracuse Herald–Amer.* (NY) 7 July sec C 4/5, The so-called $51.9 billion state budget Gov. Mario M. Cuomo and the two top legislative leaders . . finally toggled together is only precariously balanced. **2002** in 2005 *DARE* File—Internet **cwNY,** [He] said it [=a street sweeper] is used pretty extensively and that it is unfortunate it broke down on the heels of a difficult budget. He asked if it can be toggled together.

2 also with *out:* =**tog out.**

1919 McEvoy *Slams* 102 **Chicago IL,** As 'round the loop I daily snoop / I see a curious sort of goop,/ All toggled out and walking in / Some fair-haired muskrat's favorite skin. **1941** *LANE* Map 358 *(Dress up)* 1 inf, **seMA,** Toggle out; 1 inf, **cME,** Toggle up. **1950** *WELS Suppl.* **WI,** Toggle it up. . . To fuss it up. **1970** *DARE* (Qu. W30, *When a woman adds decorations to make something more attractive . . "It's too plain—I think I'll put on a few flowers to _____ it up."*) Inf **AR**56, Toggle.

toggle n

1 A block of wood or similar encumbrance attached to an animal's foot or neck to prevent it from straying.

1907 Adams *Reed Anthony* 94 **West,** A wooden toggle was fastened with rawhide to its neck, so it would trail between its forelegs, to prevent running. **1930** Shoemaker *1300 Words* 62 **cPA Mts** (as of c1900), *Toggle*—A log fastened to a cow or steer's neck to . . prevent it from jumping pasture field fences. **1968** Adams *Western Words* 326, *Toggle*—A block of wood about 4 inches wide, 3 inches thick, and 10 to 12 inches long, or a chain about the same length, used to keep a horse or a wild cow from running away. It was attached to a front foot by a piece of rope, rawhide, or hame strap; thus it would trail behind the animal, and if he tried to run, he would step on it with a hind foot. But if the animal merely walked, he soon learned to miss it with his hind foot or feet.

2 In lobstering: a small float attached to the pot warp below the marker buoy, serving to keep the warp off the bottom at low tide. **ME**

1949 *Portland Press Herald* (ME) 12 Aug 1/4, The usual procedure [in a "lobster war"] is to cut the lines holding the buoys and toggles to submerge the traps. **1957** Beck *Folkl. ME* 127, Each pot was equipped with a "pot warp" (line), a "toggle" and a buoy so that it could be found later. The toggle was a watertight glass bottle fastened onto the line at about the distance from the pot as the pot was below low-water mark. **1975** Gould *ME Lingo* 293, In lobstering, another kind of *toggle* is the secondary buoy on the line. A few fathoms below the gayly painted pot buoy whose colors identify ownership, the fisherman attaches a smaller floating device, often a spent whiskey bottle but otherwise made of wood or Styrofoam. Its purpose is to catch up slack line at low tide so the *warp* won't foul on the ocean bottom, and to keep strain off the colored buoy so it will float freely and be easily spotted. **2005** *DARE* File—Internet **swME,** Many of the lobster strings further east of here have a "toggle" to keep the individual trap lines off the bottom in 20+ foot tides. . . Fortunately, this is most prevalent "down east" but it seems to be making some inroads further south.

toggled up See toggle v 1

toggle fence n Cf bunk-and-toggle fence
=**log-and-block fence.**

1907 *DN* 3.250 **eME,** *Toggle fence.* . . A heavy log fence. [**1932** in 1967 *Dict. Canadianisms* 789 **Ontario Canada,** These [=logs in a log fence] were bound by a wooden toggle—a grooved piece, shaped above and below to lie across the logs and hold them in place.] [**2002** *DARE*

File—Internet **New Brunswick Canada,** We built a new bed along the lower line and installed cedar toggle fence in September.]

toggle out See toggle v 2

toggle together See toggle v 1

toggle up See toggle v

toggle worm n Also *tawga worm, togga ~* [Varr of **catawba + worm**] **Sth** Cf **topple, worm tree**
=**catalpa B2;** hence n *toggle-worm tree* =**catalpa B1.**

1966 *DARE* (Qu. P6, *. . Kinds of worms . . used for bait*) Inf **SC**26, Tawga ['tɔugə] worm. **1978** *Paris News* (TX) 5 June 1/4, Sometimes called toggle worms, catalpa worms feed on the broad leaves of catalpa trees. **2003** in 2009 *DARE* File—Internet **nwFL,** I . . had walked under the toggleworm tree near the shed, when something hit me in the forehead. . . Hundreds of toggleworms were sitting on the bottom of hundreds of leaves, eating the leaves. **2006** *Ibid* **seAL,** I caught a bunch of those tomato caterpillars aka tawga worms. . . My uncle found them and went fishing with them. **2008** *Ibid,* We were out looking at our togga worm tree and saw this worm. **2009** *Ibid* **seMS,** The leaves on these trees are *huge* and resemble Toggle Worm Tree leaves, kind of heart shaped.

togither See together

tog out v phr Also *tog up* [*OED2 tog* v. a 1793 →] **chiefly Nth, N Midl** See Map *old-fash* Cf **toggle v 2**
To dress, deck out; to dress oneself up; hence ppl adjs *togged (down), ~ out, ~ up.*

1878 *Scribner's Mth.* 16.910, Them fellers / Togged out in blue shirts and big boots,/ With plug hats an' umbrellers. **1887** in 1950 *AmSp* 25.39 **New Orleans LA,** Tog you up in one of his model shaped suits. **1898** in 1921 Thorp *Songs Cowboys* 37 **NM,** The room was togged out gorgeous—with mistletoe and shawls. **1900** Anson *Ball Player's Career* 148, I had togged him out in a suit of navy blue with brass buttons, at my own expense. **1909** *DN* 3.417 **nME,** Togged out. . . Dressed up. **1916** Lincoln *Mary-'Gusta* 137 **MA,** I'd look like a plain fool togged out in one of them things. **1940–41** Cassidy *WI Atlas,* 1 inf, **seWI,** Tog up, dress up. Dancing party—they togged up. **1941** *LANE* Map 358 *(Dress up)* **NEng,** 8 infs, Tog out; 4 infs, Tog up. **1942** *Amer. Mercury* 55.94 **Harlem NYC** [Black], Draped down—dressed in the height of Harlem fashion; also *togged down.* **1947** *True* 32.102 **New Orleans LA** [Black], [I] togged him out from head to feet. **1960** Criswell *Resp. to PADS 20* **Ozarks,** All decked out, all togged up, cutting a big swath. **1965–70** *DARE* (Qu. W38, *When a man dresses himself up in his best clothes . . he's _____*) 14 Infs, 13 **Nth, N Midl,** (All) togged out; **IN**19, **WA**4, Togged out to kill; 7 Infs, 5 **Nth, N Midl,** (All) togged up; **NJ**67, All togged down; **NC**87, Togged; (Qu. W37, *When a woman puts on her good clothes and tries to look her best . . she's _____*) Infs **MO**15, **MA**5, 72, **NY**96, **WI**43, 64, (All) togged out; **IL**32, **MN**12, **NJ**3, **NY**105, (All) togged up; **NY**240, Togged; (Qu. W30, *When a woman adds decorations to make something more attractive . . "It's too plain—I think I'll put on a few flowers to _____ it up."*) Inf **MA**5, Tog it out; (Qu. W43) Inf **OH**11, All togged up. [Of all Infs responding to these questions, 11% were young, 65% old; of those giving these resps, 0% were young, 87% old.] **1982** Brooks *Quicksand* 151 **swUT** (as of c1909), For us the expression "all togged up" meant not only wearing your best clothes, but wearing a little too much in the way of decoration.

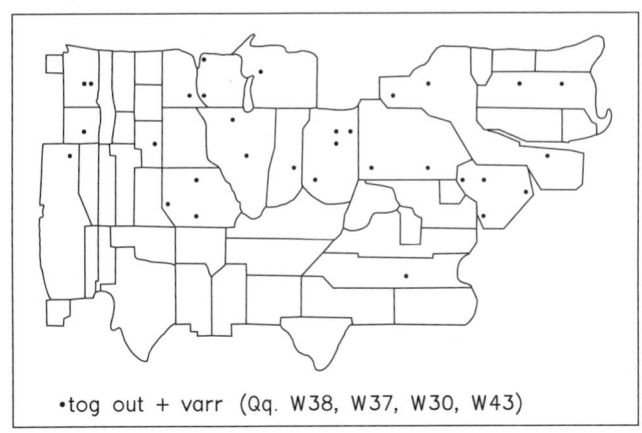

•tog out + varr (Qq. W38, W37, W30, W43)

togs n pl [*OED2 tog* sb.¹ 2.a 1779 →] *somewhat old-fash; esp freq among women*

Clothes.

1849 (1855) Melville *Redburn* 130 **NEng,** In *Madagasky* there, they don't wear any togs at all, nothing but a bowline round the midships. **1865** (1867) Moore *Anecdotes* 286 **NY,** I'm goin' home to New York, and . . I'm goin' to some up-town clothing store, and buy me a suit of togs. **1893** *Overland Mth.* (2d ser) 21.360 **CA,** When everything was shipshape, they plunged below to put on "shore-going togs." **1930** Shoemaker *1300 Words* 62 **cPA Mts** (as of c1900), *Togs*—Sunday togs, best clothes. **1950** *WELS* (*When a woman puts on her good clothes and tries to look her best*) 1 Inf, **WI,** All fixed up in Sunday-go-to-meeting togs. **1965–70** *DARE* (Qu. W43, . . *Joking words . . for clothes in general*) 126 Infs, **widespread, but somewhat less freq S Midl,** Togs [Of all Infs responding to the question, 65% were old, 60% female; of those giving this response, 83% were old, 71% female.]; (Qu. W39, *Joking ways of referring to a person's best clothes*) Infs **CT5, IN73, MA18, 29, WI56, WY2,** Best togs; **CA22,** "Fauncy" togs; **PA67, VA18,** Sunday togs; **MA18, NC79, NY69,** Togs; **LA13,** Tugs [sic] [11 of 12 total Infs old, 10 female]; (Qu. W38, *When a man dresses himself up in his best clothes . . he's* _____) Inf **SC46,** Got on his Sunday togs [Inf old, female]. **1986** Pederson *LAGS Concordance,* 1 inf, **cnGA,** Practice togs—for football team; secondhand; 1 inf, **swTN,** Super togs—referring to well-dressed person; 1 inf, **csTX,** Swanky togs. [2 of 3 infs old] **2005** *Down East* July 106 **ME,** On the oceanfront porch, tourists dressed in togs ranging from campground casual to haute couture pick and sample from the abundant seafood on the menu.

togue n [Cf *DCan*] **chiefly ME**
=**lake trout 1.**

1839 Holmes *Rept. Aroostook R.* 33 **ME,** The large lake trout, or togues, as they are sometimes called, abound here. **1864** ME Dept. Ag. *Annual Rept.* 9.132, The White Fish will live where the trout will, especially the lake trout, or 'togue.' **1879** *Forest & Stream* 12.409 **seNH,** I landed several trout in Lake Winnipiseogee, weighing from three to six pounds each. . . These trout are classified under lake trout, red trout or lake salmon, not togue, as I have been informed, togue inhabiting larger bodies of water, and are less gamy and palatable, and have been known to tip the balance at 42 pounds. **1902** Jordan–Evermann *Amer. Fishes* 204, In Vermont it [=*Salvelinus namaycush*] is called "longe," in Maine it is the "togue." **1937** FWP *Guide ME* 411 **cME,** The thoroughfare between Sugar Island and the eastern shore of the lake is good trolling ground for 'lakers' (togue). **1945** Hamlin *9 Mile Bridge* 124 **nME,** I had never heard them called anything but togue until a party of fishermen proudly showed us their catch of "gray trout." **1966** *DARE* (Qu. P1, . . *Kinds of freshwater fish . . caught around here . . good to eat*) Inf **ME8,** Togue—a lake trout; **ME10,** Lake trout or togue; **1966** *DARE* Tape **ME8,** We have the trout, salmon, and togue. A togue, of course, is a lake trout, and are considered to be the ones to eat. **1985** McPhee *Table of Contents* 288 **ME,** Fish are near the surface—even, to some extent, the togue (as lake trout are called in the region). **1996** *ME Fish & Wildlife* Summer 27, William Day of Kezar Falls holds his prize . . lake trout, believed to be the largest ever caught in Sebago Lake. The monster togue . . played . . for nearly 30 minutes in the early morning of June 3.

tog up See **tog out**

Togus bread n [From *Togus,* name of a town, a stream, and several ponds in Maine]

A steamed bread; see quots.

1880 (1881) Parloa *Miss Parloa's Cook Book* 384 **NEng,** *Togus Bread.* Three cupfuls of sweet milk and one of sour, three cupfuls of Indian meal and one of flour, half a cupful of molasses, one teaspoonful of saleratus, one of salt. Steam three hours. **1940** Brown *Amer. Cooks* 320 **ME,** *Togus Bread.* . . This bread is as native to Maine as Brown Bread is to Boston.

tohind prep, adv Also sp *t'hind* [Prob by analogy with **tofore**] **esp sAppalachians**

Behind.

1911 *DN* 3.540 **eKY,** Tohind. . . Behind. **1944** *PADS* 2.50 **wNC,** Tohind, t'hind. . . Behind. "Look t'hind ye, and ye'll see the snake." **1957** Combs *Lang. S. Highlanders* **sAppalachians,** Tohind—behind, adv. and prep. **1996–97** in 2004 Montgomery–Hall *Dict. Smoky Mt. Engl.* 609 **eTN,** Tohind [confirmed by three infs].

to home See **home B4**

toid See **thirty**

toilet n Usu |ˈtɔɪlɪt|; for varr see **A** below Cf **twilight 1**

Std sense, var forms.

1 |ˈtɜɪlɪt|; pronc-sp *terlet.* **esp NYC**
1934 in 1944 *ADD* Brooklyn **NY,** [t[ɜ]ɪlət]. Supposedly refined. **1937** *AmSp* 12.170 **NYC,** The pronunciation of [ɜɪl] for *oil* is so common that speakers of General American often humorously use *earl* [ɝl] for the New Yorker's [əɪl] as they do *terlet* for his *toilet.* Sometimes . . *r*-speakers, who frequently come into contact with New Yorkers, imitate unconsciously (and incorrectly . .) this pronunciation of [əɪl] by saying [ɝl]. **1940** *AmSp* 15.374 **NYC,** Words which are pronounced with [ɔɪ] in the standard dialects of English are divided into two groups in the speech of certain less-educated New Yorkers. In the first, a variety of [ɔɪ] is found . . [as in] *toy, boy, enjoy.* . . In the second group is . . [əɪ] . . [as in] *spoil, oil, toilet.* . . For this diphthong there is occasionally substituted an *r*-colored vowel or a diphthong whose first element is *r*-colored. **1968** Walter Winchell in *Syracuse Herald–Jrl.* (NY) 25 Jan 24/2 **NYC,** The movie sheik earned five million in five years, owned a yacht, . . and had a gold-rimmed terlet seat. **2005** *DARE* File—Internet **NJ,** Born and bred in Hoboken (ie says terlet instead of toilet, cern instead of coin), he's been a Sherriff's [sic] Officer for 25 years and every year shows.

2 |ˈtɔrlɪt|; pronc-sp *torlet.*
1937 *AmSp* 12.286 **wVA,** Occasionally [tɔrlət] . . [is] heard for . . *toilet.* **1941** *AmSp* 16.120 **VA,** In the Valley may occasionally be heard such grim pronunciations as . . [tɔɚlət] for *toilet.* **2004** *DARE* File—Internet **AL,** We are the Alabama Crimson Tide. . . *We say Roll Tide* and some of us have been known to have sticks with a roll of torlet paper and a box of tide affixed. **2005** *Ibid* **TN,** If'n you can't burn or shred, try using it as torlet paper.

3 |ˈtɔəlɪt, ˈtɔɛ-, ˈtɔ-|; pronc-sp *tollet.* **chiefly Sth, NEng**
1941 *LANE* Map 354 (*Privy*) **NEng,** [18 proncs of the type [ˈtɔəlɪt]; 3 proncs of the type [ˈtɔɛlɪt], 2 proncs of the type [ˈtɔlɪt].] **1967–68** *DARE* (Qu. M21a, *An outside toilet building*) Infs **LA2, 7, 8, MD13, 38, 43,** [Proncs of the types [ˈtɔlɪt, ˈtɔlɪt]]; (Qu. F37, . . *An indoor toilet*) Inf **AR55,** [ˈtɔlɪt]; **MD41,** [ˈtɔlɪt]. **1975** Gould *ME Lingo* 293, Toilet. . . It is not "tawl't" and it is not "toll't" as in toll-road, but it hovers between the two and is definitely not tigh-l't. **1976** Garber *Mountain-ese* 94 **sAppalachians,** They built a two-hole tollet out back uv the house. **2005** *DARE* File—Internet **FL,** I basicly [sic] got called a liar by one of my managers at work and got a empty tollet paper roll thrown at me at home. **2006** *DARE* File **Sth** (as of 1970s), I remember stopping at a not-too-fancy restaurant while traveling in the South, and finding a sign in the ladies' room that instructed me not to throw tampons in the "tollet."

4 |ˈtaɪlɪt, ˈtɑɪlɪt|.
1966–67 *DARE* (Qu. M21a, *An outside toilet building*) Inf **SC9,** [ˈtaɪlɪt]; **SC43,** [ˈtɑɪlɪt].

toir See **tire** n

toity See **thirty**

token n Also rarely *toten* [From *token* an indication, proof; a miraculous sign] **chiefly S Midl**

An apparition or other apparently supernatural omen, esp of death or disaster.

1899 (1912) Green *VA Folk-Speech* 451, Token. . . Apparition, or other sign. "He will not live long as he has seen a token of his death." **1930** Shoemaker *1300 Words* 63 **cPA Mts** (as of c1900), *Token*—The banshee, or warning of death. **1940** Haun *Hawk's Done Gone* 60 **eTN,** She thought she seed something rising up from the bottom [of a spring]. It was Enzor's face. . . Then she thought she heard something. A horse. Enzor's horse. She thought it was a token, maybe. . . She saw something forming in the spring again. A coffin. Somebody in the coffin. **1942** (1971) Campbell *Cloud-Walking* 172 **seKY,** Mort looked like he'd seen a token when Ishmael told him, for Lexie was his favoritest youngun. **1950** Stuart *Hie Hunters* 214 **eKY,** "A voice on the wind as plain as one of yer voices around this table said to me: 'That barn will be set on fire. Take heed.' . ." "Oh, a real token, Peg." Arn spoke with a trembling voice. "What is a token?" . . "It's a warnin' of something to come. When a body gets a token, he'd better take heed." **1953** Randolph–Wilson *Down in Holler* 170 **Ozarks,** The Ozark people do not use the word token in its modern sense. In the back hills, a token is an omen or portent of something supernatural, a sign of some impending calamity. When an albino deer was seen near Forsyth, Missouri, in 1939, many of the old folks "figgered it must be a token." **1968–70** *DARE* (Qu. CC16, *A small light that seems to dance or flicker over a marsh or swamp at night*) Inf **VA50,** A token—a sign of future evil;

[**NJ**53, A token for something]. **1970** *DARE* Tape **VA**52B, They talked about ghosts, tokens and all that. . . My mother told me one time just before one of her children died that she heard a token. . . It was just like somebody had brought a load of lumber in her yard and dumped it out. She called that a token. **1994** NC Lang. & Life Project *Dial. Vocab. Ocracoke* 12 **seNC**, Toten. . . Unusual sound, smell or sighting which indicates the presence of a ghost or spirit. Probably derives from *token*. . . The appearance of a toten may indicate that someone is about to die. *I heard a noise that sounded just like hundreds of children running across the floor, and I said, that's his toten.* Ibid 16 **eNC**, Token. . . A sign or presage of something to come; an omen or portent, often referring to death. . . *The haint was a token of death.*

tol' See **tell** v **B2b**

tol(a)ble See **tolerable**

told See **tell** v **B1a**

told, get one v phr   chiefly **Sth, S Midl**   See Map
To speak one's piece to someone, tell someone off.

1929 McKay *Banjo Story* 151 [Black], Don't ask me ef I didn't done get him told jest as Jesus wanted me to. **1933** Rawlings *South Moon* 224 **nFL**, "I'm goin' on home," he announced, "and git my old woman told." **1935** in 1983 Taft *Blues Lyric Poetry* 192 [Black], I woke up this morning : got on a stroll / Met my baby : got her told. **1965–70** *DARE* (Qu. JJ22, *To express your opinion . . "I went to the meeting, and _____."*) 16 Infs, 13 **Sth, S Midl**, Got them told; **AR**28, **KY**84, **MO**9, **TX**77, **VA**15, Got 'em told; **DC**8, Get 'em told; (Qu. Y6, . . *To put pressure on somebody to do something he ought to have done but hasn't: "He's a whole week late. I'm going to _____."*) Inf **CA**144, Get him told; (Qu. JJ24, *To refuse firmly: "He wanted to get some more money, but this time I _____."*) Inf **LA**2, Got him told; (Qu. JJ35b, . . *Expressions [. . when you have just about reached the point of telling somebody what you think of him]*) Inf **TX**97, For two cents I'd get him told; (Qu. LL27, . . *'Thoroughly': "The boss bawled him out _____."*; total Infs questioned, 75) Inf **FL**26, Got him told. **1983** Mebane *Mary Wayfarer* 224 **NC** [Black], You know she always would get anybody told. She'd tell them exactly what was on her mind. Saturday night she was probably drinking and started getting somebody told and he couldn't take it. **1995** in 2004 *DARE* File—Internet **NC**, When they went out the old drunk come by and says, preacher, you really got them told today. **2001** *DARE* File—Internet **AR** (as of c1900), If one of her daughters said something she didn't like, she sure got them told about it right quick!

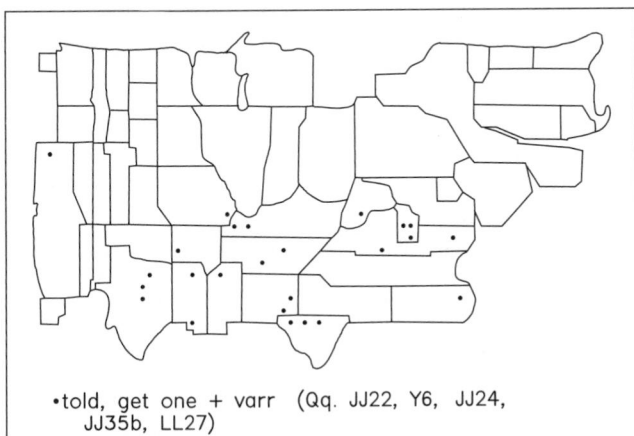

•told, get one + varr (Qq. JJ22, Y6, JJ24, JJ35b, LL27)

tole v¹   See **toll** v¹

tole v²   See **tell** v **B1a, 2b**

tole n   See **toll** v¹ **1**

toleble See **tolerable**

toler See **toller** n

tolerable adj, adv   Usu |'tal(ə)rəbl|; also |'talə(r)bl, 'tarəbl| Pronc-spp *tol(l)able, tol(e)ble, tollible, tol(l)uble;* for addit pronc and sp varr see **A** below
A Forms.
1818 in 1830 Royall *Letters* **AL** 102, "Have you any corn to sell up your say?" "Why, it's purty tol'able sca'ce." **1837** [see **B** below]. **1841** in 1934 *AmSp* 9.263 **eTN**, Tolable. **1848** Lowell *Biglow* 146 'Up-

country' **MA**, Tollable, *tolerable.* **1858** in 1956 Eliason *Tarheel Talk* 319 **c,csNC**, Tolurbel. **1859** Taliaferro *Fisher's R.* 75 **nwNC** (as of 1820s), I were in a lather uv sweat, fur it was tollule hot. **1887** (1967) Harris *Free Joe* 109 **nGA**, "Fine day this." "Well, what little I've saw of it is purty tollerbul." **1890** *DN* 1.69 **KY**, Tol'ble ['talb]: tolerable. "I'm tol'ble well." [*DN* Ed: ['taləb] is a New England pronunciation.] **1902** *DN* 2.247 **sIL**, Tollable. Pronunciation of tolerable or tolerably. **1907** *DN* 3.227 **nwAR**, Tollable, adj., adv. **1914** *DN* 4.114 **cKS**, Tolable, adj. Short for *tolerable.* Ibid 160 **cVA**, Toleble, adv. Tolerable. **1915** *DN* 4.192 **swVA**, Tolable. Short for *tolerable.* **1921** Haswell *Daughter Ozarks* 53 (as of 1800s), He knows pretty tolule durn well what'll happen to him. **1938** Rawlings *Yearling* 150 **nFL**, He's purty tol'able sober. **1943** [see **B** below]. **1966–69** [see **B** below]. **1969** Wilson *Stars* 58 **Ozarks**, But Michael himself went no further than to admit that he was a "tol'able" bee man. **1982** [see **B** below].
B Sense.
In ref to one's health or well-being: moderately good, **fair to middling 1**; not badly, moderately well.   chiefly **Sth, S Midl; also NEng**

1832 Trollope *Domestic Manners* (NY) 95 **OH**, When the visiter entered, they would say, "How do you do?" and shake hands. "Tolerable, I thank ye, how be you?" was the reply. **1837** Sherwood *Gaz.* **GA** 71, Tollible, tolerable;—*sorter tollible,* for tolerably well. **1899** (1912) Green *VA Folk-Speech* 451, Tolerable, *adj.* In fair health; passably well. **1903** *DN* 2.334 **seMO**, Tolerable (often *tollable*). . . The almost invariable reply to the salutation 'how do you do?' It is hardly good form among the country people to say one is well. In nine cases out of ten the reply to an inquiry as to health will be 'tolerable,' or 'just tolerable,' or 'only tolerable.' It is not to be inferred that they are out of health; it is simply the fashionable response. **1907** *DN* 3.237 **nwAR**, Tolerable, *tollable, adj.* The usual reply to the salutation, "How do you do?" or "fair to middlin'." **1909** *DN* 3.382 **wGA**, "How are you to-day?" "Jes' tol'able." **1923** *DN* 5.223 **swMO**, Tol'able. . . Tolerable, in fair health. "I'm a-feelin' jist tol'able." **1940** (1941) Bell *Swamp Water* 74 **Okefenokee GA**, "How y'all gitting along?" Silas asked. "Just tol'able," Thursday said. "How y'all gitting along?" "Just tol'able," Silas answered. **1942** McAtee *Dial. Grant Co.* **IN** 67 (as of 1890s), Tollable (i.e. tolerable) . . as to health, it meant fair to middling, as good as could be expected. **1943** *LANE* Map 497 *(Pretty well)* chiefly **eNG**, 78 infs, Tolerable; [18 infs, Tolerable well]. [*DARE* Ed: Proncs of the type [tɒˑrɪˑbl] were most frequent, followed by [tɒˑlrɪˑbl] and [tɒˑlɪˑbl].] **1946** *PADS* 5.41 **VA**, Tolerable (see *middling*): Fair, in answer to "how are you?"; common everywhere. **1946** *AmSp* 21.99 **sIL**, To an enquiry about his health, a rural person is likely to say *tol'able.* **1956** McAtee *Some Dialect NC* 47, "How're you doin?" "Oh jest tollable." It meant fair to middling, or as well as could be expected. **1966–69** *DARE* FW Addit **cnLA**, Tolerable ['taləbl]—answer to "How are you feeling?" (Country and old-fashioned usage); **nwNC**, Tolerable ['tɔləbl]—in answer to "How are you?"; **cNC**, [taˑəbəl]—tolerably well, as in response to "How are you?" **1974** Fink *Mountain Speech* 27 **wNC, eTN**, Air ye feelin' tolable? **1982** Slone *How We Talked* 28 **eKY** (as of c1950), Tal-a-ble—feeling well. **1986** Pederson *LAGS Concordance* **Gulf Region** *(How are you?)* 15 infs, Tolerable; [6 infs, Tolerable well;] 1 inf, Doing tolerable; [1 inf, Some pretty tolerable good patches;] 1 inf, Just tolerable; 1 inf, Very well or tolerable; 1 inf, They used to say just only tolerable.

tolguacha See **toloache 1**

toll v¹   Also *tolld, tole*
1 To induce (one) to come or follow; to lure, entice, decoy; hence vbl n *tol(l)ing;* rarely n *tole* an inducement. [*OED2 toll, tole* v.¹ 1 "In literary use in England down to 1690; in 18–19th c. in midl. and south. dialects . . and U.S. literary use."]   chiefly **NEng, Sth, S Midl**   Cf **toll bait, toller** n, v
1801 in 1830 Jefferson *Memoir* 3.467 **VA**, To toll us back to the times when we burnt witches. **1814** Wilson *Amer. Ornith.* 8.105 **MD**, The dog, if properly trained, plays backwards and forwards along the margin of the water. . . This method is called *tolling them in.* **1830** *Cabinet Nat. Hist.* 1.44 **Chesapeake Bay**, He had *toled* to within a space between forty to seventy yards off the shore, a bed of certainly hundreds of Ducks. **1850** *Deseret News* (Salt Lake City UT) 17 Aug 73/2 **NJ**, They . . didn't think any more of tolling a ship ashore, than a city sharper would think of cheating a country green horn. **1850** Garrard *Wah-to-yah* 39 **sCO**, The mountaineers spin long yarns of their exploits in hunting and *toling* game. **1864** *Harper's New Mth. Mag.* 28.616 **NEng**, When there ain't nothing else to toll you off from your work it's

always flowers. **1866** Smith *Bill Arp* 8 **GA,** They are . . tolling them [= laborers] off to parts unknown under false pretenses. **1881** *Scribner's Mth.* 22.248 **GA** [Black], De nex' man w'at he meet is a black gal tollin' a whole passel er plantation shotes, en w'en de gal see Brer Rabbit come prancin' 'long, she fling down 'er basket er corn. **1900** Day *Up in ME* 139, Here's a tole to tease Maud to come into the garden / —These rich, rosy lumps o' spruce gum. **1908** Day *King Spruce* 268 **ME,** Toter heard him hootin' out in the swirl of snow on the Dickery pond and toled him ashore by hootin' back at him. **1914** *DN* 4.81 **ME, nNH,** *Tole.* . . To lead or bring along; to induce; to decoy. **1917** *DN* 4.418 **wNC, IL,** I could tole that pig around anywhere. **1923** *DN* 5.223 **swMO,** "Tole up the hogs" (by feeding or calling them). **1929** *AmSp* 5.121 **ME,** We were sent to "tole," "toll" (to lure along, go entice, as most country children have done) by shaking grain or corn, in the endeavor to persuade a reluctant horse to leave the field when we were trying to catch him. *Ibid* 124, If making the advances herself, she "made a dead set for him" or she "toled him into her pen." **1947** Ballowe *The Lawd* 155 **LA** [Black], "Doan' go, Jasper," pleaded Aun' Hattie. "Them's body snatchers. They always sends a mullader [=mulatto] to tole you outer yo' house." **1953** Randolph–Wilson *Down in Holler* 83 **Ozarks,** *Tole,* to entice, is a rather unusual word in most sections of the United States, but is very commonly used in the Ozarks. **1957** Combs *Lang. S. Highlanders* **sAppalachians,** Tolld—var. of *toll,* to entice, induce, invite (of animals). **1966–70** *DARE* FW Addit **KY**84, They tolled him out into the field; **NM**13, *Toll 'em in*—to lead cattle in . . with an empty . . feed sack, etc. **1967–70** *DARE* (Qu. P16, *When fishermen throw bits of bait in the water to attract fish*) Inf **VA**96, Tolling; **TN**53, Tolling fish; (Qu. P35b, *Illegal methods of shooting deer;* not asked in early QRs) Inf **TN**22, Tole 'em up. **1975** Gould *ME Lingo* 294, Children are *tolled* home to supper when Mother yells from the doorway; garbage will *toll* rats; chumming (see *chum*) tolls fish. **2004** in 2005 *DARE* File—Internet **neTX,** I finally . . tolled them [=chickens] out 2 or 3 at a time & shooed them over to the chicken house. **2005** *DARE* File **wTN,** The word tole was used when my father or grandfather were talking about getting an animal or animals (usually cows) to come into a pen. I think this usage will become, if it has not already, obsolete.

2 Of game birds: to admit of being lured; to be attracted to a decoy, duck call, or the like.

1830 *Cabinet Nat. Hist.* 1.43 **Chesapeake Bay,** The *Black-heads* toll the most readily, then the *Red-Heads*. **1984** Russell *For Whom the Ducks Toll: A Select Gathering of Memorable Waterfowling Tales* [title]. **1999** in 2005 *DARE* File—Internet **NH,** We saw thousands of birds, and 14 tolled beautifully. **2005** *Ibid* **MD,** Then we'd put out seve[r]al hundred decoys (a stool) right in front of us. . . Then the Ducks would come flying in and come Tolling right into the Stool. *Ibid* **Upstate NY,** Even the most savvy waterfowlers would have been impressed by the number of ducks tolling to the call. *Ibid* **NC,** Nearly every time a flock would start to toll to my decoys, another hunting party would open up on another flock.

toll v² See **tell** v **B2b**

tollable See **tolerable**

toll bait n [**toll** v¹ **1**] **esp NEng** Cf **chum** n¹
Chopped bait thrown into the water to attract fish; also fig.

1867 *80 Yrs. Progress U.S.* 2.383 **MA,** The "toll-bait," as it is called, is generally menhaden, or porgies. . . It is finely ground in a mill provided for the purpose, then mixed with water, and it is ready for use. Upon the appearance of a school of mackerel . . the vessel is "hove to," and the "toll-bait" thrown. The fish will generally follow this bait to the side of the vessel. **1886** *Century Illustr. Mag.* 32.824 **Gloucester MA,** The first [boat] that arrives rounds to under the lee of the fortunate craft, the crew heaving the toll-bait. **1891** *Salem Daily News* (OH) 24 Sept [3/5] (newspaperarchive.com) **NY,** If he does not believe it, but voted for the resolutions merely as a cheap toll bait for the cranks of the Farmers' Alliance, . . he ought to be ashamed. **1921** *Nation* 12 Oct 400 **ME,** [Youngsters] find a cookie or a piece of cake / Left there like toll-bait to be sure they came.

tolld See **toll** v¹

toller n Also sp *toler* [**toll** v¹ **1**]
A decoy used in duck hunting.

1853 Krider *Krider's Sporting Anecdotes* 234 **MD,** The false ducks were not all imitations of canvass-backs. . . The outside duck at the tail of the rank was a veteran canvass-back, facetiously called the toller. **1874** Long *Amer. Wild-Fowl* 72, For deep-water ducks, three or four de-

coys as tolers may be set out to leeward. **1947** Coffin *Yankee Coast* 180 **ME,** Old Captain Hamilton carved tollers so much more like wild ducks than they were themselves that the ducks gladly sculled up to them and died adoring. **1975** Gould *ME Lingo* 294, While inland sportsmen set decoys to attract ducks and geese, coastal gunners set out tollers. **2005** *DARE* File—Internet **MD,** These [duck] Decoys were also called *"Tollers."* *Ibid* **NJ,** All the Toller Trader Classifieds in Decoy Magazine are offered on its Website.

toller v
=**toll** v¹ **1.**

1975 Gould *ME Lingo* 294, In certain usages toller is interchangeable with *toll;* mothers will "toller" their young ones home.

tollerbul See **tolerable**

tollet See **toilet 3**

tollible See **tolerable**

tolling See **toll** v¹

tollon (berry) See **toyon**

tolluble See **tolerable**

tolo n, also attrib [Cf quot 1949 and Chinook Jargon *tolo* to earn, win] **chiefly WA** Cf **turnabout (dance)**
A dance to which women invite men.

1947 *Walla Walla Union–Bulletin* (WA) 28 Feb 6/2, Whitman's annual Leap week festivities are climaxing with the Mortar Board Tolo formal dance Saturday evening. **1949** in 2004 *DARE* File **Seattle WA,** The girl-dates-boy type of dance was introduced about 30 years ago [c1919] by members of the Tolo Club, founded in 1909 as the upper-class-women's activity and scholastic honorary [society]. . . The club was given the name of 'Tolo,' an Indian word for 'achievement of success.' The annual Tolo informal [dance] was changed to reverse dating procedure, became traditional at the University, and spread across the country carrying the name 'Tolo' with it. **1960** *Perrin Coll.* **Seattle WA,** *Tolo* is used on the University of Washington campus and I believe elsewhere in Seattle as n and adj for a dance or party for which the girls do the inviting and paying. I have noticed it since coming here in 1947. **1998** *DARE* File **wWA** (as of c1940), A friend told me that when she was in high school, the dances where the girls asked the boys were called *tolos* ['to,loz]. **2003** *DARE* File—Internet **nwOR,** Now i just have to get you to go to tolo with a guy. Hey you know i'm going to bug you about this in class. **2004** *DARE* File **Seattle WA** (as of c1960), They seemed to have tolos several times a year at the (Seattle) high school I attended.

toloache n [MexSpan < Nahuatl *toloatzin*] **chiefly SW**

1 also *tolguacha:* A **jimson weed,** usu *Datura inoxia* or *D. wrightii.*

1892 [see **2** below]. **1897** Parsons *Wild Flowers CA* 54, Tolguacha. . . *Datura meteloides*. . . It shares with Jamestown-weed its narcotic poisonous qualities, and is a famous plant among our Indians. **1912** Lumholtz *New Trails* 280 **AZ,** Close to my tent toloache (*datura*) was in flower. **1915** (1926) Armstrong–Thornber *Western Wild Flowers* 458, *Tolguacha, Large-flowered Datura.* **1968** Schmutz et al. *Livestock-Poisoning Plants AZ* 80, Sacred datura, Indianapple, tolguacha (*Datura meteloides*). . . Throughout the state at 1,000 to 6,500 feet. . . Poisoning of both livestock and humans can occur from the ingestion of any part of the plant, including the seeds. **2002** *DARE* File—Internet **Desert SW,** *D. inoxia* is usually referred to as *Toloache.*

2 A **unicorn plant 3** (here: *Proboscidea louisianica* subsp *fragrans*).

1892 *DN* 1.252 **TX,** Toloáche. . . The Mexicans think this plant has the property of developing gradual and permanent insanity. *Martynia fragrans* [=*Proboscidea louisianica* subsp *fragrans*]. . . It is a strong narcotic. From the Mexican *toloatzin*. [*DARE* Ed: The two senses are conflated here; the dangerous properties mentioned here belong to *Datura.*] **1908** NM Univ. *Biol. Ser.* 3.1.33, M[artynia] fragralls [sic]. . . "Toloache." . . Quite common in Tijearas Canon and occasional in arroyos of the mesa.

tolt See **tell** v **B2c**

toluble, tolurbel See **tolerable**

tom n¹

1 In mining: a trough used for gold washing; hence v *tom* to use such a trough. **chiefly West** *old-fash* Cf **long tom 2**
1839 *Amer. Railroad Jrl.* 8.98 **nGA,** The "Rocker" is a somewhat dif-

ferent machine, consisting of a "Riffler," as in the Tom, except that the bars are concave. **1854** in 1942 *CA Folkl. Qrly.* 1.287, I dug, I panned, and tommed awhile. **1863** Hittell *Resources CA* 384, *Tom,* a wooden trough, from ten to fifteen feet long, for washing pay-dirt. **1877** Wright *Big Bonanza* 20 **NV,** He was working with a "tom" (a contrivance for washing auriferous gravel which combines the principles of the rocker and the sluice-box). **1878** Hart *Sazerac Lying Club* 67 **NV,** I've knowed men to take out as much as six hundred dollars to the pan, and a long ways to bed-rock, to say nothin' of what's bin taken out with rockers, and toms, and sluice-boxes. **1906** Canfield *Diary Forty-Niner* 101 **CA,** We ran two Toms and three rockers steady, wheeling dirt to the Toms and using the rockers wherever we found gravel.

2 usu cap: **=Uncle Tom 1;** hence v (phr) *tom (out)* to be servile or ingratiating; vbl n *tomming. among Black speakers*

1963 *Negro Digest* 12.3.70 **MS,** They say you are going to chicken out, Papa. . . They're betting you'll 'Tom.' **1965** Brown *Manchild* 164 **Harlem NYC** [Black], They had an old, dumbhead waiter who was a real Tom. If you said anything to one of the customers and didn't put a "Sir" on it, he'd run up there and say, "Boy, what's wrong wit you?" and all this kind of simple shit. **1968–70** *DARE* (Qu. II19, *When you think somebody has been put ahead of you or has been given something you deserved . . "I'd rather quit than _____."*) Inf **WV**21, Be a Tom; **IL**139, Tom; (Qu. II20a, *A person who tries too hard to gain somebody else's favor: "He's an awful _____."*) Infs **IL**139, **WV**21, Tom; (Qu. II34, *If you think somebody is trying to use you to his advantage: "I'm not going to be his _____."*) Inf **WV**21, Tom; (Qu. JJ4, *A child who is always telling on other children*) Inf **OH**103, Tom. [All Infs Black] **1970** *Current Slang* 5.2.13 [Black univ student slang], *Tom.* . . To yield to white influence (merely because it is white). **1971** Roberts *Third Ear* np [Black], *Tomming* . . acting like Uncle Tom. i.e. behaving in a self-denigrating and self-effacing manner toward a white person; ingratiating oneself with a white person. **1972** Claerbaut *Black Jargon* 83, *Tom* . . a black male who is a disgrace to fellow black people: *He ain't no Tom!* **1986** Pederson *LAGS Concordance,* 1 inf, *ceAL,* A Tom (insulting). **1992** in 1993 Adero *Up South* 37 [Black], Some nigger there . . told the boss that I kissed this black girl. He was a tom. **2009** *DARE* File **TX** [Black] (as of c1960), A lot of other black people would have said that I was tomming out by continuing to associate with a white man who thought nothing of using "black boys" in his casual conversation, back in that day.

3 A Black man.

1968–69 *DARE* (Qu. HH28, *Names and nicknames . . for people of foreign background: Negro*) Inf **GA**83, Nigger, blacky, Tom; (Qu. II25, *Names or nicknames for the part of a town where the poorer people, special groups, or foreign groups live*) Inf **GA**61, Tom Town—the colored section—named after Tom Brown. [Both Infs White]

tom v See **tom** n[1] **1, 2**

tom n[2] See **tommytoe**

tomahawk knife n   Cf **hack knife, jerk ~, tobacco ~**
See quot.
  1966 *PADS* 45.26 **cnKY,** *Tomahawk knife.* . . A tomahawk-shaped knife used to harvest tobacco. . . "You can cut a stalk in one chop with a tomahawk knife." **1967** Key *Tobacco Vocab.* 130 **TN, MO,** *Tomahawk knife.*

tomahtuh See **tomato A2**

tomale See **tamale**

tomalley n   Also sp *tamalley* and, by folk-etym, *tamale* [*OED2* 1666 →]   **esp ME**
The hepatopancreas (the so-called liver) of the lobster or crab; also fig.
  1864 (1873) Webster *Amer. Dict.,* Tŏm'-ăl'ley. . . The liver of the lobster, which becomes green when boiled. **1894** *Daily Rev.* (Decatur IL) 16 Aug [7/4] (newspaperarchive.com), The coral and tomalley may be placed on top, or served on a separate dish—but not mixed in with the [lobster] meat. **c1900** C.W. Greene *Lett. to Sir J.A.H. Murray (DA)* **MA,** When I was a youngster in Massachusetts, we called the gelatinous part of a baked maize pudding, the *tom-alley.* It somewhat resembles in appearance the *tom-alley* of the lobster. **1950** Moore *Candlemas Bay* 259 **ME,** The lobsters boiled to a fine, even red. Grampie ate five. Then he wiped the tomalley off his jackknife. **1973** Knight *Cook's Fish Guide* 251, Save the soft crab butter (tomalley). **1975** Gould *ME Lingo* 294, Your favorite lobster fisherman will probably say *tom-alley.* **2005** *DARE* File—Internet **ME,** Bar Harbor Deluxe Crab Dip. . . All natural

ingredients: Cream Cheese, Crab Tomalley, Crab Meat [etc]. **2005** *DARE* File **ME** (as of 1970s), "What do you call the greenish stuff inside a lobster?" "In Maine it was always called tomalley [tə'mɑli]. I liked it." *Ibid* **ME,** "What do you call the greenish stuff inside a lobster?" "I [from nwMA] always called it the lady. . . My friend Dick, originally from the Portland, Maine area, calls it tomalley." *Ibid* **Boston MA,** The green liver or "tamale" may be eaten and is considered a delicacy by many lobster gourmets. *Ibid* **ME,** Remove all meat and tamalley from lobster shell.

tomalley box n
The cephalothorax of a lobster.
  1966 *DARE* Tape **ME**24, [FW:] And where do you measure the lobsters? [Inf:] By the length of his—well, we call it the tomalley box—of his body.

Tom and Jerry n
=Pat and Charlie.
  1967 *DARE* (Qu. Y24, . . *To walk, to go on foot: "I can't get a ride, so I'll just have to _____."*) Inf **SC**40, Go on Tom and Jerry, use Tom and Jerry.

tomarter, tomarto, tomartus See **tomato A2**

tomata, tomater See **tomato A1**

tomatilla See **tomatillo 2**

tomatillo n   [Span dimin of *tomate* tomato]   **chiefly SW**

1 A **ground-cherry** (here: *Physalis philadelphica* var *immaculata*).
  1897 Britton–Brown *Illustr. Flora* 2.128, *Physalis ixocarpa* [=*P. philadelphica* var *immaculata*]. . . Tomatillo. . . It is often cultivated for its fruit and frequently escapes from cultivation. **1925** Jepson *Manual Plants CA* 894, *P[hysalis] ixocarpa.* . . Tomatillo. . . Orchard weed, nat[uralized] from Mex. **1930** OK Univ. Biol. Surv. *Pub.* 2.79, *Physalis ixocarpa.* . . Tomatillo. Mexican Ground Cherry. **1946** Reeves–Bain *Flora TX* 139, *P[hysalis] ixocarpa.* . . Tomatillo. . . Corolla yellow with a purplish spot in the center. . . Sometimes a weed. **1968** Barkley *Plants KS* 305, Tomatillo. . . Waste ground. **2007** *NY Times* (NY) 9 Sept sec O 12/2, We were served . . chips with three salsas: a mild salsa verde, a lively tomatillo and a fiery habañero.

2 also *tomatilla:* **=wolfberry 2.**
  [**1920** Saunders *Useful Wild Plants* 86 **SW,** The red berries of two shrubs [=*Lycium pallidum* and *L. Andersonii*] of the deserts and semi-deserts of Arizona, New Mexico, and Utah resemble tiny tomatoes and go among the Spanish-speaking population under the name of *tomatillo.* . . They may be eaten raw, if perfectly ripe, or boiled and consumed.] **1925** Jepson *Manual Plants CA* 890, *L[ycium] pallidum.* . . Tomatilla, Rabbit Thorn. . . Densely branched excessively thorny shrub, . . berry . . dull or greenish-white. . . Central Mohave Desert. **1931** U.S. Dept. Ag. *Misc. Pub.* 101.142, About 16 valid species of the . . genus Lycium occur in the West—mainly on warm dry open plains and foothills of the Southwest. These bushes are common and characteristic and a wealth of vernacular names has been bestowed upon them, including . . tomatilla (-o). **1947** (1976) Curtin *Healing Herbs* 59 **NM,** This *tomatillo* is frequently dried and stored away for winter use. **1967** Harrington *Edible Plants Rocky Mts.* 244, *Lycium pallidum* . . Tomatilla. . . The fruits of this plant were much used by the Indians of the Southwest. . . These berries are said to have a bitter astringent quality; the ones we tried certainly lived up to their reputation. **1976** Elmore *Shrubs & Trees SW* 58, Tomatillo. . . *Lycium pallidum.* . . Easily identified when in fruit by its tomato-shaped and tomato-colored, marble-sized fruits. **1985** Dodge *Flowers SW Deserts* 110, Tomatillo. . . Attractive in late spring and summer due to the numerous tomato-colored berries hanging from their stiff, thorny stems. **2002** *DARE* File—Internet **AZ,** Tomatillo (*Lycium* spp).

tomato n   Usu |tə'me(ɪ)to|; for varr see **A** below

A Pronc varr.

1 |tə'meto(r), tə'metɨ| and varr; pronc-spp *termater, tomata, tomater, tomaty, tomayda, tomayta.* **chiefly Sth, S Midl** See Pronc Intro 3.I.12.d
  a1782 (1788) Jefferson *Notes VA* 40, The *gardens* yield musk-melons, water-melons, tomatas, okra [etc]. **1892** [see A3 below]. **1909** *DN* 3.382 **eAL, wGA,** Tomato. . . Pronounced [tə'metə], [tə'mɑtə], [tə'mætə], and sometimes [tə'meto]. From the plural a new form has arisen among the negroes and illiterate whites, *tomatus* [tə'mætus], pl. *tomatuses.* **1922** (1926) Cady *Rhymes VT* 273, And on the shelving . .

boxes for tomater plants. **1928** *AmSp* 3.403 **Ozarks** (as of 1916–27), Words like *tomato* and *tobacco* . . are nearly always pronounced *termater* and *terbacker*. **1936** *AmSp* 11.161 **eTX,** In addition to the usual sound of [ə] in the final syllable, some of the words . . have [ɚ] in less literate speech. They [include] . . *tomato*. **1939** in 1944 *ADD* **eWV,** Tomater plants . . tomaties. **1940** *AmSp* 15.49 **sAppalachians, Ozarks,** Final [o] commonly becomes [ɚ]: winder . . termater [etc]. **1942** Hall *Smoky Mt. Speech* 80 **wNC, eTN,** The sound [ɚ] . . is the prevailing one in most words spelled with *-o, -ow*. . . *Potato, tobacco,* and *tomato* display little evidence of correction to [o], though they are heard fairly often with [ə]. . . An informant of Waldens Creek (Sevier Co., Tenn.) reports that some of the less schooled families of his section say ['teɪtiz] and ['meɪtiz] for *potatoes* and *tomatoes*. **1961** Kurath–McDavid *Pronc. Engl.* 170 **Sth, Midl,** The variant [of *tomato*] ending in [ə] predominates decisively among all social classes in the South and the Midland, except for parts of North Carolina, where constricted /ɝ/ is common in folk speech. *Ibid* **nGA, NC, SC,** Tomato ending in constricted [ɚ]. . . is also current in the northern and western margins of South Carolina and in the hill country of northern Georgia. **1966–67** *DARE* Tape **AL4,** Later on . . we'd plant . . tomatoes [təmeɪtɚz]; **SC46,** [tə'meɪtɚz]. **1989** Pederson *LAGS Tech. Index* 187 **Gulf Region,** [The vowel in the second syllable of *tomato(es)* is almost universally [e] or [eᴵ]; in the last syllable, 684 infs have [ə] and 33 have [ɪ]; 103 infs have [ɚ] and 59 infs have [o].] **1997** *DARE* File—Internet **cePA** [CoalSpeak], *Tamayta* or *tamayda:* Tomato.

2 |tə'mɑto| and varr; pronc-spp *termarter, tomahtuh, tomarter, tomarto, tomartus*.

1847 in 1956 Eliason *Tarheel Talk* 319 **ne,ceNC,** Tomartoes. **1879** [see **B1** below]. **1909** [see **A1** above]. **1917** in 1944 *ADD* **sWV,** Tomartus. **1927** Shewmake *Engl. Pronc. VA* 34, *Tomah-tuh* is a very general Virginia pronunciation. **1929** [see **B1** below]. **1935** [see **A3** below]. **1961** Kurath–McDavid *Pronc. Engl.* 151 **eNEng, neVA,** *Tomato* with the . . /a ~ ɑ/ of *car* has widespread currency only in two subareas of the Atlantic coast, Eastern New England and Eastern Virginia north of the James River.

3 |tə'mæto| and varr; pronc-spp *termatter, tomatus*. **NEast, SE**

1866 in 1885 Handford *Pleasant Hours* 99 **TN,** Sarah Ann says she would like a few improov *termatter* seads. **1891** *DN* 1.121 **cNY,** [tə'mæto], [tə'mætɚ] . . (sometimes [tə'meto]), 'tomato.' **1908** Lincoln *Cy Whittaker* 104 **MA,** Fact is, we ain't got nothin' but termatter and beef broth. **1909** [see **A1** above]. **1930** in 1944 *ADD* **ceSC,** [təmeto], [təmæto]. **1935** *AmSp* 10.293 **Upstate NY,** *Tomato* normally has [e] in the stressed syllable; this appears 183 times as against 57 instances of [æ] and 14 of [ɑ]. **1955** *PADS* 23.46 **e,cSC, eNC, seGA,** /æ/ in *tomatoes* (also Northern). **1959** *VT Hist.* 27.164, *Tomato* [tə·mă'tō] . . pronc. Common. **1961** Kurath–McDavid *Pronc. Engl.* 151 **NEng, NY,** *Tomato* with the vowel /æ/ of *mat* is predominantly a folk pronunciation of the Northern area. . . it is doubtless old folk pronunciation in all of New England. **1968** *DARE* FW Addit **NY,** Tomato [tə'mæto]. **1970** *DARE* File **nPA, wNY,** Tomato [to'mæto].

4 |'meto, 'metə(r)| and other aphet varr; pronc-spp *martis, mat(t)er, mat(t)is, mata, mato, mortas* **chiefly Sth, S Midl**

1895 *DN* 1.394 **KY,** Tomato: plur[al] . . *martisses*, Winchester, Ky. **1915** *DN* 4.185 **swVA,** *Mortases, n. pl.* Tomatoes. **1929** [see **B1** below]. **1942** [see **A1** above]. **1944** *PADS* 2.58 **MO, NC, SC, TN, VA,** *Maters* ['metɚz]. . . Tomatoes. . . Popular. **1950** [see **B1** below]. **1954** Harder *Coll.* **cwTN,** *Maters* . . tomatoes. **1963** Edwards *Gravel* 131 **eTN** (as of 1920s), Along come Toody Lines agoin to the fair to take some maters and things. **1966–68** *DARE* (Qu. I21, *Names or nicknames for tomatoes; total Infs questioned, 75*) Infs **AR27, 39, GA1,** Maters; (Qu. L34, . . *Most important crops grown around here*) Inf **NC54,** ['meɪdɚz]; (Qu. P13) Infs **GA5, 7,** Mata worm. **1970** *AmSp* 45.77 **NC,** *Tomato*. I saved you a fresh 'mato. **1976** Wolfram–Christian *Appalachian Speech* 51, *'Taters* for *potatoes* and *'maters* for *tomatoes* can certainly be considered to be stereotypes, and they are sometimes the topic of comment. . . In fact, one of the informants in our sample responded . . as follows: Fieldworker: What are some of the things people grow here in their gardens? Informant: Oh, potatoes and tomatoes—or did you want me to say 'maters and 'taters? **1982** Slone *How We Talked* 26 **eKY** (as of c1950), *Matters, matoes* . . tomatoes. **1989** Pederson *LAGS Tech. Index* 187 **Gulf Region,** [20 infs gave proncs of the types [medəz, -ɪz], [medɚ, -ɪz], [mɚ, -ɚ].] **1997** Andrews *Dude's Mt. Vittles* 31 **sAppalachians,** The last of the maters had to be canned and a few more jars of vegetable soup mix, too.

5 |pə'metə|; pronc-spp *pemater, pomato*.

1939 in 1944 *ADD* **FL,** Pomatoes [pəmetəz]. Reported heard. **1972**

Atlanta Letters **nwGA,** Pemater. **1989** Pederson *LAGS Tech. Index* 187 **Gulf Region,** 1 inf, [pə'meɪtə].

B Gram forms.

1 double pl: pronc-spp *termartusses, termattusses, tomatoeses, tomattus(s)es, tomattusus, tomatuses, martisses, mat(t)ises, mortases* **chiefly Sth, S Midl** Cf Intro "Language Changes" II.3, *-es* suff[1] 2

1879 *New Haven Reg.* (CT) 22 Aug 2/2, The tomato is masquerading about the market stalls under more aliases than you can shake a stick at. There are tomaytoes, tomarters, tommytoes, tomattuses, tommatoes, tormatoes. **1881** *Godey's Lady's Book* 102.447 **PA,** I went out in the garden and begun lookin' for some late tomatoeses. **1883** (1971) Harris *Nights with Remus* 15 **GA** [Black], Dar wuz Brer Rabbit . . mashin' down de termartusses. **1895** *DN* 1.394 **wPA, cKY,** *Tomato:* plur. *tomattusses.* Springdale, Pa.; *martisses,* Winchester, Ky. **1896** *DN* 1.426 **cNY,** *Tomatoes:* plu. *tomatoeses* [tə'metəsɪz] sometimes heard. **1909** [see **A1** above]. **1912** Green *VA Folk-Speech* 451, *Tomattusses, n. pl.* For *tomatoes.* **1915** [see **A4** above]. **1917** Hill *McAllister's Grove* 86 **FL,** "T-o-m-a-t-o, termattusses," spelled Tallahassie proudly. **1927** Kennedy *Gritny* 163 **sLA** [Black], I'm a plum fool w'en it come to mixin'-up shoe-pick [=**choupique**] an' tomattusus an' seas'nin an things. **1929** Sale *Tree Named John* 145 **MS** (as of c1890) [Black], Chillun tryin' t' tell ole folks mattises ain't mattises, dey is *ter-mar-ters!* **1950** *PADS* 14.46 **SC,** *'Matos, 'matises* ['metəs, 'metɪsɪz]: *n. pl.* Tomatoes. **1986** Pederson *LAGS Concordance,* 2 infs, **sGA,** Tomatoeses.

2 pl: usu *tomatoes;* rarely *tomato.* Cf **cabbage n A2**

1913 Kephart *Highlanders* 297 **sAppalachians,** Tomato, cabbage, molasses and baking powder are always used as plural nouns. . . "I'll have a few more of them cabbage."

C Sense.

Std: the red to yellow fruit of a widely cultivated plant *(Solanum lycopersicum);* also the plant itself. Also called **icebox tomato, marble ~, paradise apple, poison ~, poor man's orange 1, running tomato, tommytoe**

tom-a-toe See **tommytoe**

tomatoeses See **tomato B1**

tomato flower n

Prob a **globe mallow 2.**

1967 *DARE* (Qu. S26a, . . *Wildflowers. . . Roadside flowers*) Inf **CO15,** Tomato flower—like a miniature hollyhock, blooms all the way up stem.

tomato fruitworm See **tomato worm 2**

tomato hornworm See **tomato worm 1**

tomato pepper n Cf **mango 2**

A **sweet pepper 1.**

1914 *Lettuce Misc. Crops* 28, The *Squash,* or *Tomato,* pepper is a flat, somewhat tomato-shaped, thick-fleshed, mildly pungent pepper. **1968** *DARE* (Qu. I22c, . . *Peppers—small sweet*) Inf **NJ17,** Tomato pepper; (Qu. I22d, . . *Peppers—large sweet*) Inf **MO4,** Tomato peppers—also called the little mangle [sic] peppers.

tomato pie n esp **CT, NJ, NY, PA**

Pizza; a pizza.

1942 in 2001 *Popik Coll.* **New Haven CT,** [Telephone directory:] *Frank Pepe* Old Reliable Neapolitan Tomato Pies. **1946** *Post–Std.* (Syracuse NY) 11 Oct 17/7, [Advt:] Oven-Hot Tomato Pie Better Known As "Pizza." **1950** *Progress* (Clearfield PA) 27 Apr 7/1, Pizza (tomato pie) 50c and 75c. **1951** *Traverse City Rec.–Eagle* (MI) 22 June 10/1, Now Serving Pizza—Our famous Italian Tomato Pie which is being served from coast to coast. **1964** *Citizen-Advt.* (Auburn NY) 12 May 7/4, [Advt:] Special Pizza / Tomato Pie / Angelo's. **1982** *Daily Intelligencer* (Doylestown PA) 28 Apr 19/1, [Advt:] Vecchione Italian Bakery-Deli. . . Stromboli—Tomato Pies. **2002** *DARE* File **NJ,** "Pie" is used by non-Italians. Short for "pizza pie" or "tomato pie." (This last is an old usage. I haven't heard it since my early childhood, but you can still see painted signs advertising "tomato pies" on the Jersey Shore.) **2003** *DARE* File—Internet **NJ,** Where I grew up near Trenton, NJ it was always tomato pie. . . In Trenton at least, tomato pie is distinct from pizza, the distinction being the use of smushed canned tomatoes on the pie rather than a pizza sauce. Even in Trenton, though, many people don't make the distinction. *Ibid* **CT,** They still call it *tomato pie* in New Haven. *Ibid* **FL,** There's [a] vastly popular Italian restaurant called "Nick's Tomato Pie" . . in Jupiter, FL. **2004** *Ibid* **PA,** I . . miss the cold tomato pie (pizza) from the Norristown, PA, and surrounding areas. It was rectangular with a simple tomato sauce, romano cheese grated on top, served at room temperature. *Ibid* **NY,** I am from upstate New York and now live in Florida. I miss the tomato pies. *Ibid* **NJ,** Tomato pies are built the opposite of pizza pies. First the cheese, then the toppings, then the sauce.

tomato worm n

1 also *tomato hornworm:* A **hornworm** (here: either *Manduca quinquemaculata* or *M. sexta*). Also called **joe bucks** Cf **potato worm, tobacco ~ 1**

1845 *Amer. Penny Mag.* 1.447, Ichneumons kill millions of noxious insects every year. I have seen a queen tomato-worm with twenty of their beautiful little cocoons upon it. **1868** MI State Bd. Ag. *Annual Rept.* 7.167, In many parts of Michigan, the tomato worm—larvae of the *Sphinx quinqua* [sic]-*maculata*—have been frightfully abundant. **1884** [see **tobacco worm 1**]. **1892** Kellogg *Common Insects KS* 64, *Tomato-Worm (Phlegethontius carolina* [=*Manduca sexta*]). . . Infesting tomatoes; a large, "ugly," green worm. **1915** Essig *Injurious Insects CA* 386, *The Tomato Worm—Protoparce sexta* [=*Manduca s.*] . . The caterpillars are exceedingly large, often attaining a length of nearly 4 inches. They are light green with showy oblique white stripes and highly colored markings around the spiracles on the sides. . . The larvae feed largely upon tomato plants, often defoliating large areas. **1925** *Book of Rural Life* 9.5542, *Tomato worms* . . [are] two closely related . . *hornworms,* that feed on . . tomato leaves. **1954** *Harder Coll.* **cwTN,** Tomato worm. . . Lives on green tomato plants. **1962** Atwood *Vocab. TX* 58, In any case, several other worms are mentioned as usable for fish bait: *catawba worms, grubworms,* . . *tomato worms,* and so on. **1965–70** *DARE* (Qu. R27, . . *Kinds of caterpillars or similar worms*) 306 Infs, **widespread, but less freq NW,** Tomato worm; **VT**13, Tomato hornworm; (Qu. P6, . . *Kinds of worms . . used for bait*) Inf **MO**19, Green tomato worm; **WA**28, Tomato worm; (Qu. P13, . . *Ways of fishing . . besides the ordinary hook and line*) Infs **GA**5, 7, Mata worm. **2000** in 2002 *DARE* File—Internet **CA,** The bad news? Courtney saw a tomato worm for the first time. She was disgusted.

2 usu as *tomato fruitworm:* =**corn earworm.**

1904 U.S. Dept. Ag. *Farmers' Bulletin* 191.6, It need hardly be explained that the larva known variously as the budworm of corn, the tassel worm, corn earworm, or tomato fruitworm, is identical with the cotton bollworm. **1915** Essig *Injurious Insects CA* 396, *The Corn Earworm.* . . This insect is also known as the tomato worm and the cotton bollworm. **1924** U.S. Dept. Ag. *Farmers' Bulletin* 1371.39, The tomato fruitworm . . , also called the corn earworm, is the cause of much trouble to tomato growers, as it eats into the ripening fruit and destroys it. **1972** Swan–Papp *Insects* 279, *Corn Earworm.* . . Also known as the bollworm (on cotton) and the tomato fruitworm (on tomato). **2001** in 2002 *DARE* File—Internet **NC,** The tomato fruitworm is potentially the most damaging pest of tomatoes.

tomattus(s)es, tomattusus, tomatuses See **tomato B1**

tomatus See **tomato A3**

tomaty, tomayda, tomayta See **tomato A1**

tomb n

A tombstone.

1972 *McDavid Coll.* **ceGA,** Tomb = tombstone. "People didn't put no tombs to people's graves."

tombouille n |ˌtɔmˈbuɪ| [LaFr, Fr *tambouille* stew]

A thickened stew; see quots.

[**1901** (1932) Ditchy *Acadiens* 199 **LA,** *Tambouille,* cuisine, pot au feu. [=*Tambouille,* cooking, stew.]] **1968** *DARE* (Qu. H45, *Dishes made with meat, fish, or poultry that everybody around here would know, but that people in other places might not*) Inf **LA**33, Tombouille [tɔmˈbuɪ]—boil fish and take it off the bones. This is cooked with a roux. **2003** *Daily Advt.* (Lafayette LA) 17 Sept sec D 1/1, Their family recipe for tombouille (tom-BOO-wee) . . has been a pre-game favorite for more than 20 years. *Ibid* 8/1, Pork and Sausage Tombouille. [Recipe includes pork sausage, Boston butt roast, chopped onions, light roux [etc.]] **2006** *NADS Letters* **sLA,** Down here in south Louisiana, a Tombouille is great for tailgating before the football games. [Recipe includes pork, pork sausage, and vegetables.]

tomb rock n Also *tombstone rock* **chiefly S Midl** Cf **rock** n¹ **1**

A tombstone.

1932 *Daily Times–News* (Burlington NC) 29 Jan 4/3, Somebody had been cleaning up and cementing the cracks in Mr. Hurry Can's tomb-

rock and had left a white sheet over it. **1942** (1971) Campbell *Cloud-Walking* 168 **seKY,** He painted all the home made tomb rocks in the graveyard blue to match Sam's grave house. **1946** *McDavid Coll.* **nwSC,** Tombstone rock. **1967** *DARE* File **seIL,** "Tomb-rock" for tombstone. **1976** Whitmire *Presence of Past* 2 **nwSC,** The expression "tomb rock" is still a standard name for field stone markers in upper Greenville County. **2001** in 2005 *DARE* File—Internet **TN,** Tomb rock covered with fungus, very difficult to read. **2005** *Ibid* **TN,** He fixed his own tomb rock with just what he wanted on it before he died.

tombstone n

1 also *tombstone tooth:* A tooth, esp a large or prominent one. Cf **gravestone**

1873 Biddle *Glances at World* 293, With ass's ears, and bulldog's groveling brow;/ And mouth with tombstone teeth, in broken rows [etc]. **1889** *Amer. Mag.* 27.474, The vision of his tombstone teeth, disclosed in an honest, unstinted smile of good-will, was my parting salute. **1909** *Hampton's Mag.* 23.542, [Caption:] Where "Billy" loses his "tombstones" [false teeth] and makes a farce. **1916** *Harper's Mth. Mag.* 133.671, He had large, white, tombstone teeth. **1925** Dickson *Old-Fash. Senator* 19 **MS** (as of 1860s), "Yas, suh, Marster. Sholy, suh!" The boy opened his mouth very wide, and showed every tombstone tooth in his head. **1968–69** *DARE* (Qu. X12, . . *Large front teeth that stick out of the mouth*) Infs **CT**15, **MD**44, Tombstones; (Qu. X13a, . . *Joking names . . for teeth*) Infs **MD**31, **NY**214, Tombstones. **2009** Burke *Rain Gods* 192 **TX,** Bobby Lee had screwed up at the convenience store, his eyes as self-righteous and mindless as a moron's, his tombstone teeth too large for his mouth.

2 See quot. Cf **barber chair**

1923 Bryant *Logging* 513, *Tombstone.* . . A slab torn from the bole, which adheres to the stump when a tree is felled. (S[outhern] F[orest]).

tombstone rock See **tomb rock**

tombstone tooth See **tombstone 1**

tomcat v, hence vbl n *tomcatting* Also with *around* **widespread, but esp freq Sth, S Midl** Cf **alley-cat, cat** v **2, eave cat, wild hog** v phr

Of a man: to go out at night, esp in search of sexual adventure; hence nouns *tomcat, tomcatter* one who does this.

1927 *DN* 5.478 Ozarks, Tom catting. . . To seek illicit sexual adventure. "Jeff he's out a-tom-cattin' 'roun' some'ers." **1937** *Hall Coll.* **eTN,** Tom-cat around. . . To be on the loose. . . used of the male on the hunt. **1940** Faulkner *Hamlet* 161 **MS,** He was too old, he told her baldly and plainly, to be tomcatting around at night. **1941** Writers' Program *Guide MO* 135, A young hillman may do a little "tom-cattin' around," but when he "sets up" to a girl, he usually intends to marry her. **1947** Ballowe *The Lawd* 105 **LA,** The Duppy . . made it so hot for the tomcatters that even legitimate sweethearting was given up. **1949** *Joplin Globe* (MO) 28 Dec 7/4, If men would stay home and stop tomcatting around, there wouldn't be any shakedown cases. **c1950** *Halpert Coll.* 63 **wKY, nwTN,** Tomcattin' = living a mildly loose life, chasing after the opposite sex or just continually going out at night. "They've been tomcattin' every night this week." "Oh, he's out tom cattin' around somewhere." (Less favorable) "He's tomcattin' around with somebody else's wife." **1952** Brown *NC Folkl.* 1.601, Tom-cat. . . To call on the ladies at night. **1965–70** *DARE* (Qu. Y29b, . . *About a man [who doesn't stay home much]: "He's always _____."*) 63 Infs, **widespread exc NEng,** Tomcatting (around). **1966–67** *DARE* FW Addit **OK**21, Tomcatting around—traveling, "running around"; **TN,** He's been a-tomcattin' [FW: =running around] again. **1970** *Major Dict. Afro-Amer. Slang* 115, *Tomcat:* a well-dressed dude who is out searching for a willing sexual companion. **1973** *DARE* File Ozarks (as of c1910), Boys with a bad reputation were tomcats or rounders. **1986** Pederson *LAGS Concordance,* 1 inf, **LA,** Tomcatting; 1 inf, **AR,** Tom-catting—promiscuous behavior; 1 inf, **AR,** A-tomcatting—of a young man out late at night. **1998** *Chron.–Telegram* (Elyria OH) 23 Aug sec C 3/1 **AR,** President Clinton talked about his tomcatting and his Tomahawking last week.

tomcat clover n

A clover (here: *Trifolium willdenowii*) native to the far western US and Texas.

1925 Jepson *Manual Plants CA* 538, *T[rifolium] tridentatum* [=*T. willdenowii*]. . . *Tomcat Clover.* . . Our most abundant and widely distributed clover, exhibiting many ecological variations. **1951** Martin *Amer. Wildlife & Plants* 402, Among the native western species of importance to wildlife are tomcat clover . . , clammy clover . . , and foothill clover. **1973** Hitchcock–Cronquist *Flora Pacific NW* 275, W Cas[cades], BC to Cal; Sand c[lover], tomcat c[lover] . . *T[rifolium] tridentatum.* **2002** *DARE* File—Internet **CA**, In spring, you might see blue-eyed grass, tomcat clover, bluedicks, lupines, California poppy, and California buttercup on the sides of the trail.

tomcatter, tomcatting (around) See **tomcat**

tomcod n

1 also *tommycod:* Any of several fishes of the family Gadidae, as:

a A saltwater fish *(Microgadus tomcod)* of North and Central Atlantic coastal waters. **chiefly ME, MA, NH, NY** Also called **frostfish 1**

1722 *New-Engl. Courant* (Boston MA) 1 Oct 1/2, Some *Fishermen* in *Boston* made me pay *Two Pence* for the Sight of a *Tom-Cod* instead of a *Maremaid.* **1787** Gesellschaft Naturforschender Freunde *Schriften* 8.140 **NY**, *Gadus.* [Footnote: Ist eine neue Gattung, die der flach gedrückte Kopf und die borsten artigen Zähne charakterisiren.] *Tom Cod* in New-York genant. [=*Gadus.* [Footnote: [This] is a new species, characterized by the flattened head and the bristle-like teeth.] Called *Tom Cod* in New York.] **1814** in 1815 Lit. & Philos. Soc. NY *Trans.* 1.368, *Tom cod, (Gadus tomcodus.)* The length is about ten to twelve inches. Snout round and blunt. **1838** Kettell *Yankee Notions* 51, Nothing for dinner tomorrow? what! all the tom-cods gone? **1864** Lowell *Fireside Travels* 168 **MA**, I once ventured the horse-mackerel theory to an old fisherman, browner than a tomcod. **1910** *Sat. Eve. Post* 13 Aug 7 **NYC**, On another [day] I'd stroll down to the dock . . and try my luck on the tomcods and lafayettes. **1966–68** *DARE* (Qu. P1, . . *Kinds of freshwater fish . . caught around here . . good to eat)* Inf **ME**20, Tomcod—come upriver from ocean; (Qu. P2, . . *Kinds of saltwater fish caught around here . . good to eat)* Inf **ME**20, Tomcod—come upriver; **NY**66, Tomcod; **NY**76, Tommycods; (Qu. P7, *Small fish used as bait for bigger fish)* Inf **MA**72, Tomcod—used in ice fishing; **ME**6, Tommycods; **NH**14, Tommycod—from salt water, used for freshwater ice fishing. **1978** *Yankee* Mar 92, To Maine people the tomcod is the tommycod. Tommycods are of no particular value, although they were once used for fertilizer when alewives and pogeys were scarce. **2001** *Hudson R. Almanac* (Internet) **seNY**, Although most fauna will be either flying or swimming south for the winter, . . [t]he Atlantic tomcod will be nosing its way upriver in the opposite direction.

b In Pacific waters:

(1) A similar fish *(Microgadus proximus)* of Pacific coastal waters. Also called **smelt 2d**

1852 *San Francisco Herald* (CA) 29 Nov 2/1, A silent vow of meditation, portentous of death to tom-cods and other imprudent little fishes that come darting around the city wharves to spend their Sundays. **1879** U.S. Natl. Museum *Bulletin* 14.29, *Microgadus proximus.* . . *Tom Cod.*—Coast of California. **1905** U.S. Dept. Commerce Bur. Fisheries *Document* 603.44 **AK**, Along the shores of Norton Sound occurs the tomcod *(Microgadus proximus),* or wachna of the natives. This fish, which is very abundant in the fall and spring, is of immense importance to the natives. **1928** Pan-Pacific Research Inst. *Jrl.* 3.3.16 **OR, WA**, *Microgadus proximus.* . . Tom-cod. **1967** *DARE* (Qu. P1, . . *Kinds of freshwater fish . . caught around here . . good to eat)* Inf **OR**4, Tomcod—like a little trout or a fish smelt; (Qu. P3, *Freshwater fish that are not good to eat)* Inf **WA**20, Tomcod. **1997** in 2002 *DARE* File—Internet **CA**, From the mid-pier area out to the end, try a high/low set up for white croaker, Pacific tomcod, sand sole [etc].

(2) Any of various other fish found chiefly in Alaskan waters, such as Pacific cod *(Gadus macrocephalus),* polar cod *(Boreogadus saida),* saffron cod *(Eleginus gracilis),* or **walleye pollock.**

1850 in 1900 Nelson *Eskimo* 25 **AK**, These people had united there and were living peaceably together in order to fish for crabs and tomcods and to hunt for seals. **1870** Dall *Alaska* 484, The tomcod or *waúkhni* of the natives is a permanent resident of the more northern coasts. It is more plenty in the fall than at other seasons. **1886** Turner *Contribs. AK* 90, *Tilesia gracilis* [=*Eleginus g.*] . . Many of the white traders give this fish the English name of "Tom-cod." **1982** *Juneau Guide* 44 (Tabbert *Dict. Alaskan Engl.*) **AK**, Ignored or worse by local fishermen, the tomcod is in fact a pollock. **1991** Tabbert *Dict. Alaskan Engl.* 145, Tomcod is used in Alaska to name at least two other fishes [besides *Microgadus proximus*]. One is the small (about 12 inches) *Boreogadus saida* of the Bering Sea and Arctic Ocean. . . Some of the citations . . probably refer to . . the Pacific cod, *Gadus macrocephalus,* and the saffron cod, *Eleginus gracilis. Ibid,* The name tomcod . . is

also used in the Southeast [of AK] for the large (up to 36 inches), commercially important bottom fish *Theragra chalcogramma.* **2002** *DARE* File—Internet, *Species Name:* Alaska Pollock *(Theragra chalcogramma).* Regional names include . . Pacific tomcod. . . *Geography:* Central California coast to Bering Sea.

2 Any of several other fish resembling **1** above in some way, as:

a In Atlantic waters:

(1) A **kingfish 1** (here: *Menticirrhus saxatilis).* **CT**

1884 Goode *Fisheries U.S.* 1.375, *The King-Fish—Menticirrhus nebulosus* [=*M. saxatilis*] . . , also known as . . the "Tom-cod" on the coast of Connecticut, . . ranges from Cape Ann south at least as far as the mouth of the Saint John's River, Florida. **1911** U.S. Bur. Census *Fisheries 1908* 317, Tomcod. . . The name is also applied to the kingfish *(Menticirrhus saxatilis)* on the Connecticut coast, and to the bocaccio *(Sebastodes paucispinus* [=*Sebastes p.*]) on the California coast.

(2) also *tommycod:* A **hake 2**, usu *Urophycis floridana.*

1882 U.S. Natl. Museum *Proc.* 5.616 **SC**, *Phycis* [=*Urophycis*] *earlii.* . . "Tom-cod." . . Said by fishermen not to be uncommon in the [Charleston] harbor during the winter. **1966** *DARE* (Qu. P2, . . *Kinds of saltwater fish caught around here . . good to eat)* Inf **NC**12, Tommycod or link [sic for ling]. **1973** Knight *Cook's Fish Guide* 393, Tomcod . . or Hake, Southern.

b In Pacific waters:

(1) A **rockfish 3** (here: *Sebastes paucispinus).*

1884 Goode *Fisheries U.S.* 1.266 **CA**, Boccaccio *(Sebastodes paucispinus* [=*Sebastes p.*] . .) . . American fishermen use the name "Jack," and those who fish for the young from the wharves call them "Tomcod." . . This species is one of the largest of the group, reaching a weight of twelve to fifteen pounds. . . It ranges from the Santa Barbara Islands to Cape Mendocino. It inhabits reefs in deep water, only the young coming near the shore. **1911** [see **2a(1)** above].

(2) also *tommy(cod):* =**little roncador. CA**

1919 *CA Fish & Game* 5.13, When *Genyonemus,* the kingfish, is called "tomcod" the name kingfish is transferred to *Seriphus,* the queenfish, or white croaker. **1946** La Monte *N. Amer. Game Fishes* 82, *Kingfish—Genyonemus lineatus.* . . *Names:* White Croaker, . . Tomcod, Shiner, Herring. . . North to San Francisco, California. **1953** Roedel *Common Fishes CA* 100, *White Croaker—Genyonemus lineatus.* . . Not considered a game fish, though it is caught in huge quantities by anglers in Southern California, who usually refer to it as "tomcod" or "tommy." **1968–70** *DARE* (Qu. P2, . . *Kinds of saltwater fish caught around here . . good to eat)* Inf **CA**177, Tomcod = white croaker; (Qu. P4, *Saltwater fish that are not good to eat)* Inf **CA**36, Tomcod—these are wormy; **CA**52, Tomcods—full of worms and bony; **CA**65, Tomcod or roncador . . they're wormy. . . Chinamen eat [them]. **2002** *DARE* File—Internet **sCA**, I had anchored up on a school of Kingfish or as we call them down south, "Tomcod". *Ibid* **sCA**, I now target coastal pelagics, tommycod (kingfish) and perch.

(3) =**queenfish 1.**

1953 Roedel *Common Fishes CA* 94, *Seriphus politus.* . . Central California south at least to San Juanico Bay, Baja California. . . Taken commercially chiefly with bait nets. . . *Unauthorized Names:* Herring, tomcod, shiner, seatrout.

tom fuller n [Folk-etym for Choctaw *tahfula* hominy] **chiefly OK**

Fresh, dried, or fermented hominy; a Choctaw dish made with hominy.

[**1844** in 1863 Goode *Outposts of Zion* 209 **sOK**, In his grave were deposited articles of value . . with a supply of sugar, coffee, tah-ful-lah—sour hominy—and all other things deemed needful for his journey to another world.] **1848** *Ladies' Repository* Sept 275 **OK**, Some [squaws] were beating corn for *tom-fuller* (a kind of hommony). **a1873** (1998) Gaines *Reminiscences* 100 **AL, MS**, The miller having returned home busied himself with preparing meal. The delegations enjoyed both bread and "tom fuller," the night of their arrival. *Ibid* 196, [Footnote:] Tom fuller, or "tuh-fulla," an important national dish of the Choctaw, was hominey made by boiling corn in a lye solution. The fermented hominey became known as "tom fuller" on the southern frontier. **1900** *Daily Rev.* (Decatur IL) 9 Sept 9/5 **seOK**, Over in another part of the grounds will be a big kettle where the 'Tom Fuller' is made. . . You must eat some 'Tom Fuller' before you go away or they [=the Choctaws] will feel insulted. **1939** in 2003 *DARE* File—Internet **OK**, The foods one could prepare out of corn was wanderful [sic]. Hog & Hominy Tamfuller [sic], Peshofa, Corn Light bread, Tambutter, Corn & beans. **1953**

Randolph–Wilson *Down in Holler* 293 **Ozarks,** *Tomfuller.* . . The old name for hominy. . . Taylor Livers, a Cherokee who lives near Stilwell, Okla., tells me that *ta-fu-la* is Choctaw for "a kind of hominy, with pieces of meat mixed in." **1966** *DARE* FW Addit **OK**24, Tom fuller patch—a small patch of corn, usually on a small field in the woods—term used chiefly by Indians. **c1974** Jones *Ozark Hill Boy* 18 **AR** (as of c1920), There was a hollowed out block of wood and a mallet where, Ben explained, tom fuller, a crushed hominy food product had been prepared. **2005** *DARE* File—Internet **OK,** It's made with dried hominy corn that I haven't seen except in Oklahoma. It's also called Tom Fuller if you can find it.

tommatoe See **tommytoe**

tommie See **tommyhawk 2**

tomming See **tom** n[1] **2**

tommy See **tomcod 2b(2)**

tommycod n
1 See **tomcod 1, 2a(2), 2b(2).**
2 The creek chub *(Semotilus atromaculatus).*
1983 Becker *Fishes WI* 437, Creek Chub—*Semotilus atromaculatus.* . . Other common names: horned dace, . . tommycod, . . mud chub. **2002** (acc) IA Dept. Nat. Resources *IA Fish & Fishing: IA Fishes* (Internet), *Creek Chub. . . Semotilus atromaculatus.* . . Other names—horned dace, blackspot chub, brook chub, northern creek chub, silvery chub, . . tommycod, mud chub. . . widely distributed in all major drainage basins in this state.

tommy-cod house n
=**sand collar.**
1901 Arnold *Sea-Beach* 12, Collar-like sandy rings contain the eggs of *Polynices (Lunatia),* which are cemented together in this shape. The boys of Cape Cod call them "tommy-cod houses."

tommyhawk n [Partial folk-etym for *tomahawk;* cf Intro "Language Changes" IV.1.b]
1 A tomahawk; also fig.
[**1813** (1932) Schillinger *Jrl.* 41.66 **OH,** One of our Men Accidently got Cut with A tomihawk in the knee very bad.] **1844** Poe in *S. Lit. Messenger* 10.725, He assured me that he employed the words "Thomas Hawk" to avoid the colloquialism, Tommy, which was low—but that the true idea was Tommy Hawk—or tomahawk. **1854** in 2005 *DARE* File—Internet **OH,** The only evidence of their crossing were marks of feet, or of tommyhawk. **1860** Street *Woods & Waters* 166 **NY,** But when he got rum aboard, look out! Why, he'd dance and kick about, and keep his tommyhawk a-goin'. **c1890** in 2005 *DARE* File—Internet **Ozarks,** The Indians were all afoot and carried their bows and arrows and tommyhawks. **1916** Howells *Leatherwood God* 9 **OH,** When the elder stopped short and sudden, and the other exhorters held back their tommyhawks, and all the saints and sinners left off their groanin' and jerkun' . . it was a great sight. **1920s** in 1944 *ADD* **cNY,** ['tɑmɪ,hɔk]. Usual. **1930** Shoemaker *1300 Words* 60 **cPA Mts** (as of c1900), Tommyhawk—A small hand-forged hatchet carried at the belt by surveyors and hunters. **1967** *DARE* FW Addit **ceTN,** They buried the ['tɑmɪ,hɔk]. **1968** *DARE* Tape **IN**3, They [=Indians] had at one time camped in through here, and we have evidence of that. . . Indian relics, tommyhawks ['tɑmɪ,hɔks] and peace pipes and arrowheads and corn-crackers and lots of things. **1969** *DARE* (Qu. Y17, *When two people agree to stop fighting and not be enemies any more* . . "*I hear they _____.*") Infs **KY**19, 68, Buried the tommyhawk.
2 also *tommie:* The penis.
1886 *Cincinnati Lancet & Clinic* 55.505, A stout motherly-looking Irish woman came into my office. . . "Docther," says she, "can yez do anything wid a bye that has a ring around his tommy?" **c1938** in 1970 Hyatt *Hoodoo* 2.1737 **VA** [Black], Suppose that he is fooling around with her. He'll take and get a little wax from his ear and he rub his *tommie* [Hyatt: tomahawk] wit dat. And if he goes with her, it'll burn—she can't stand him. **1939** Hall Coll. **eTN,** Buryin' a tommy hawk. . . Copulating.
3 pl: =**tom walkers.**
1968 *DARE* (Qu. EE35, *Long wooden poles with a footpiece that children walk around on to make them tall*) Inf **SC**58, Tommyhawks—same as tom walkers.

tommyknocker n Also *tommyknacker* [See quots; cf *OED2* knocker 1.b "A spirit or goblin imagined to dwell in mines and to indicate the presence of ore by knocking" (1747 →), *EDD*

tommyknocker a hammer used to break ore (1824 →)] **chiefly West**
A ghost or spirit said to live in mines; the noise made by such a spirit.
1910 Goodwin *Up Grade* 304 **AZ,** Those are 'Tommy knockers'. . . They are the ghosts of men who were killed in an explosion here, tapping steadily for help. **1938** (1964) Korson *Minstrels Mine Patch* 140 **West,** In our Western mines, the knockings are believed to be the work of mischievous gnomes known as "tommy-knockers." **1939** (1973) FWP *Guide MT* 416, Tommy-knocker—Ghost of a man killed in a mine. Miners say he returns to work the shift on which he was killed. They thus explain the creaking of timbers and similar sounds. **1942** *CA Folkl. Qrly.* 1.128, Tales of Tommy Knockers, or Tommy Knackers, as they are properly called, were originally introduced into western mines by the Cornishmen with the development of quartz mining after 1850. These denizens of the deep, dark chambers of the earth are conceived in different forms: as disembodied spirits of dead miners hovering in a working as patrons, or as little men, elflike, bewhiskered, and wizened. They are usually thought of as benign, occasionally even assisting in the location of ore bodies. If they are not so well disposed, their conduct tends to be mischievous rather than malignant. **1945** *Ibid* 4.322 **CO** [Mining terms], *Tommy-knockers are working again:* This expression is still heard but I could find no evidence in the district of any real belief in their existence among the younger men and only fragmentary survivance among the older. **1959** *Berkshire Eagle* (Pittsfield MA) 27 Mar 13/1 **CA,** When a Cornish miner of the old school tells you how his life was saved by a Tommyknocker's warning . . he is not being facetious. **1968** *DARE* FW Addit **CA,** Tommyknocker—a mine-shaft ghost. Any strange noise is put onto the tommyknocker and the noise itself is called a tommyknocker. "Cousin Jacks wouldn't work a mine with tommy-knockers in it." Common. Mining term. **1972** *NV State Jrl.* (Reno) 6 Oct 17/1, It's like a 'tommy knocker'—a spook that haunts tunnels. **1977** Jones *OR Folkl.* 37 (as of early 20th cent), Tommy knockers are little people that live in the mines. They are mischievous and do things like throwing rocks down on the miners' heads or digging holes under the timbers so that they cave in.

tommytoe n Also *tom-a-toe, tommatoe, tommytoe (to)mato, tom(toe), tom tomato, tommy's toe, tom-tom (tomato)* [Joc or folk-etym var of **tomato**] **now chiefly Sth, S Midl** Cf **marble tomato, running ~**
A **tomato** C, usu a small, round one.
1854 *Knickerbocker* 43.105, The same little darling, desiring some tomatoes at table, which she had heard pronounced 'Tommy-toes' in sport, being puzzled to remember the name, said she wanted some *'Tommy-Footies.'* **1879** [see **tomato** B1]. **1949** *AmSp* 24.13 **IN,** The pronunciation 'tommy-toes' for *tomatoes* has a certain local currency. It probably began as a facetious mispronunciation, but now has the status of a folk-etymological form. **1950** *PADS* 14.68 **SC,** Tommytoe ['tɑmɪ,to]. . . A small variety of tomato. **1950** *WELS* **WI** (*Other names or nicknames for tomatoes*) 5 Infs, Tommytoes; 1 Inf, Tommy's toes; 1 Inf, Toms. **1954** *Harder Coll.* **cwTN,** Tomatoes . . various names: tommy-toes (small, marble-sized tomatoes). **c1960** *Wilson Coll.* **csKY,** Tommytoes. . . Nickname for tomatoes. **1965–66** *DARE* (Qu. I21, *Names or nicknames for tomatoes;* total Infs questioned, 75) Infs **FL**37, **MS**1, 2, **OK**1, 43, Tommytoes; **MS**59, Tommytoes—these are very small, little round tomatoes; **MS**65, Tommytoes—children's term. **1968** *DARE* FW Addit **wTN,** ['tɑmə,touz]—small tomatoes the size of cherries. **1982** Slone *How We Talked* 26 **eKY** (as of c1950), Matters, matoes, tom-a-toes—tomatoes. **1986** Pederson *LAGS Concordance* **Gulf Region** (*What do you call the small tomatoes*) 183 infs, Tommytoes; 5 infs, (Little) tommyto [sic] (to)mato; 2 infs, Cocktail tomatoes = tommytoes; 1 inf, Little tom-tom tomato—bite-size, like quarter; 1 inf, Tomtoes; 1 inf, Tomtoes, tom-tom—little ones, came up volunteer; 1 inf, Tom or cherry tomatoes—little old tommytoes; 1 inf, Tom tomatoes—small ones; 1 inf, Tom tomato—small; 1 inf, Cherry tomatoes—smaller than tommytoes; 1 inf, Tommyto [sic]—only as a joke, pronouncing it stupidly; 1 inf, Tommytoes—has heard for any size; 1 inf, Tommytoes—mother used for all home-grown tomatoes; 1 inf, Tommytoes—has heard for all tomatoes; 1 inf, Tommytoes—called them this for short; 1 inf, Tommytoes—jocular term for all tomatoes; 1 inf, Tommytoes—those who say mean tomatoes, period; 1 inf, Tommytoes—facetious for "tomatoes"; 1 inf, Tommytoes—not necessarily small ones; 1 inf, Tommytoes—any tomatoes, joking; 1 inf, Tommytoes—slang term for all tomatoes; 1 inf, Tommytoes—father's jocular term for all tomatoes; 1 inf, Tommytoes—joking name for large tomatoes. **1999** *Jrl. MultiMedia Hist.* 2 (Internet) **KY,** And we've got our own language here. . . But see "tomatoes" is "maters". . . And them

little um, salad tomatoes, that's "tommy toes." **1999** in 2002 *DARE* File—Internet **MO**, My little bag also had an apple the size of a tom tomato. I guess it was a tom apple. **2000** *Domicile* Mar (Internet) **NC**, This story comes to us from Miss Annie, who is 92 years old. . . We grew almost everything ourselves. . . We got, from the hardware store, tomato plants like June Pink, Early Anna, Mary Globe and Tommy Toes. **2002** *DARE* File—Internet **OH** (as of c1850), In those days people grew in their gardens and flower beds 'Tommytoes' (tomatoes), just for the reason that they looked nice, no one hardly dare to eat them. *Ibid* **TN**, Then in the summer of my life,/ life was sweet as ripe tommy toes on the vine. **2005** Williams *Gratitude* 106 **wNC** (as of 1940s), They had to be transplanted, or they made "tommy-toes" 'stid of maters.

tommy walkers See **tom walkers**

Tommy woodpecker n
=**downy woodpecker.**
  1917 (1923) *Birds Amer.* 2.141, *Downy Woodpecker. . . Other Names. . .* Tommy Woodpecker. **1944** Hausman *Amer. Birds* 532, Woodpecker, Tommy—see Woodpecker, Downy.

tomorrow n, adv Usu |tə'mɑrə, -o|; also |tə'mɔrə, -o|; less freq |tə'mɑri|; for addit varr see quots Pronc-spp *tammara, t' morrah, t'morrow, to-morra(h), tomor(rer), tomorry, to-mor-uh, tuhmar, tuhmorrer* Cf Pronc Intro 3.I.12.d, **borrow** v **A, sparrow** Std senses, var forms.
  1845 *Knickerbocker* 26.277 **MS**, Our kounti taksgathur is a kalkerlatin tu put for ure diggins tomorrer. **1860** Holmes *Professor* 129 **NEng**, So, the old fellah's off to-morrah. **1871** Eggleston *Hoosier Schoolmaster* 81 **sIN**, Pap wants to know ef you would spend tomorry and Sunday at our house? **1895** (1969) Crane *Red Badge* 2 **NY**, We're goin' t' move t' morrah—sure. **1914** *DN* 4.160 **cVA**, To-morra week. . . A week from to-morrow. **1915** *DN* 4.192 **swVA**, Tomor. Short for *tomorrow*. **1923** *DN* 5.223 **swMO**, T'morrow week. . . A week from to-morrow. **1937** (1977) Hurston *Their Eyes* 120 **FL** [Black], You . . won't be able tuh git out de bed tuhmorrer. **1938** Rawlings *Yearling* 99 **nFL**, We'll be back tomorrer. **1948** Manfred *Chokecherry* 89 **nwIA**, Tomorry you'll run like a brand-new top. **1954** *Harder Coll.* **cwTN**, Tomorrow [təmɑr]. **1961** Kurath–McDavid *Pronc. Engl.* 125, *Tomorrow* has either the stressed vowel of *forty*, that is /ɔ ~ ɒ/, or that of *barn*, namely /ɑ ~ a ~ ɑ/; in some areas it is not clear whether *tomorrow* has an allophone of the vowel of *forty* or of *barn*. An unrounded low vowel /ɑ ~ a ~ ɑ/ occurs in nearly all parts of the Eastern States, though with varying frequency, a rounded low-back vowel /ɔ ~ ɒ/ only in certain areas. . . New England predominantly has a more or less rounded [ɒ] sound . . , less commonly a well-rounded [ɔ]. In Eastern New England . . *tomorrow* clearly has /ɒ/. In Western New England . . the variants [ɔ] and [ɑ] are phonemically unambiguous; but the phonically intermediate variant [ɒ] can be as readily assigned to /ɔ/ as to /ɑ/, since these vowels do not appear in contrast before intersyllabic /r/. . . Western and central Pennsylvania usually have sounds ranging from [ɒ] to [ɔˆ]. . . [T]he [ɒ ~ ɑ] phones . . belong to the /ɒ/ phoneme of *law, lot, barn*, the [ɔ ~ ɔˆ] phones to the /o/ of *forty, four, road*. The [ɒ]-like phones occurring . . along with [ɑ ~ ɑ]-like phones in the Low Country of South Carolina and along the coast of Georgia and Florida belong to the /ɑ/ phoneme of *lot*. **1961** *Mt. Life* 37.1.6 **sAppalachians**, Among the uneducated, words ending with open vowels and diphthongs (vowel combinations) have *r* added . . *tomorrer*. **1969** Wilson *Stars* 81 **Ozarks**, Comes tomorry, we'll be far gone in new country. **1982** *Barrick Coll.* **csPA**, *Tomorrow*—pron. tuh-már. **1989** Pederson *LAGS Tech. Index* 19 **Gulf Region**, [For the second syllable of *tomorrow*, 701 infs had the vowel [ɑ], and 66 infs had [ɔ]; for the last syllable, 604 infs had proncs of the type [tə'mɑrə], 129 had [tə'mɑro], and 27 omitted the last syllable; 10 had [tə'mɑri], and one had [tə'mɑrɚ].] **1997** *DARE* File—Internet **cePA** [CoalSpeak], *Tammara*: Tomorrow. **2000** Shores *Tangier Is.* 180 **Chesapeake Bay**, *Wheelbarrow* and *tomorrow* are good examples: "wheel-bare-uh" and "to-mor-uh. . . " More often than not, "mor" or "mora" are used for *tomorrow*.

tom out See **tom** n[1]

Tom show n
  A traveling production of *Uncle Tom's Cabin*, a melodramatic stage adaptation of Harriet Beecher Stowe's novel.
  1890 *Daily Independent* (Monroe WI) 10 Mar 1/4, The only feature of the Tom show was Litte [sic] Maud Sutton, who acted as Eva. **1910** *Washington Post* (DC) 12 Feb 6/3, There is a nimbus about the Tom show which has given many a youth his first glimpse of histrionic glory. **1912** Marquis *Danny's Own* 53 **IL**, I haven't had such rotten luck since I

played the bloodhound in a Tom Show. **1925** *Scribner's Mag.* 77.350 **MA**, In the patter of *Dramatic Mirror* and *Clipper* advertising they were U.T.C. Companies, but when actors spoke to one another they were Tom Shows. **1932** *Syracuse Herald* (NY) 4 Dec sec 3 7/2, It is a fact . . that 90 per cent of all the Tom-show managers came from New York State and a majority of them from Syracuse and its adjacent territory. **1981** in 1995 Ellison *Invisible Man* xvi **VT** (as of c1940), I had seen . . a poster announcing the performance of a "Tom Show," that forgotten term for blackface minstrel versions of Mrs. Stowe's *Uncle Tom's Cabin.*

tomtate n
  Usu a **redmouth** n **1** (here: *Haemulon aurolineatum*), but occas another small **grunt** n **1**; see quots.
  1884 U.S. Fish Comm. *Bulletin* 4.78 **FL**, Among the Grunts . . we find . . the Tom-tate *(H[aemulon] aurolineatum)* [etc]. **1933** John G. Shedd Aquarium *Guide* 109, *Bathystoma striatum* [=*Haemulon s.*]—*Tom-tate; White Grunt.* A small grunt of the West Indies and the Florida Keys, this fish is often mistaken for the young of other similar species. . . *Bathystoma rimator—Tom-tate; Red-mouth Grunt.* This Tom-tate is very abundant at Charleston, North [sic] Carolina, where it is an important food fish. **1935** Caine *Game Fish* 81, French Grunt—*Haemulon flavolineatum*. . . Tom Tate[*]; Yellow Grunt. . . *Average size:* ½ to 1 lb. **1955** Zim–Shoemaker *Fishes* 114, Tomtate is a small grunt, not more than 8 or 10 in. long. It has the same range as the White Grunt [here: =*Haemulon plumieri*], from the West Indies (where it is very common) to the Carolinas. *Ibid* 157, Tomtate: Bathystoma aurolineatum. **1983** Audubon *Field Guide N. Amer. Fishes* 611, Tomtate *(Haemulon aurolineatum). Ibid* 612, The Tomtate is common over shrimping grounds in the Tortugas and the Gulf of Mexico, as well as around reefs and oil platforms. **2002** *DARE* File—Internet **wFL**, Tomtate, Grunt, Spot tail, pain in the a—. The last name is usually what you call Haemulon aurolineatum when you start catching them.

tom thumb n
  1 A large pork sausage usu cased with the stomach or large intestine of a hog and dried and smoked. [Cf **therm,** but perh in allusion to the folk tale of Tom Thumb stuffed in a sausage] **chiefly NC**
  1830 in 1832 *Gem* 4.131 **NJ**, Our repast . . consisted of . . an enormous species of sausage, called a Tom Thumb [etc]. **1871** Mason *Young Housewife's Counsellor* 159 **NC**, On the inside of the leaf-fat . . is a broad sheet of skin, which . . will make a capital case for tom-thumbs, or large sausage. So also will the large intestine. *Ibid* 160, Your tom-thumbs should not be used till thoroughly dried, and then boiled; after which to be divested of their cases, and served either hot or cold. These should always be smoked. **1939** Harris *Purslane* 148 **cNC**, There was an abundance of old bacon ham, barbecued shoat, mutton, tom-thumb, boiled custard, and cake. [Footnote to *tom thumb:* Sausage stuffed into big intestine casing] *Ibid* 295, I went to the smokehouse for a tom-thumb to cook with the turnip salad. **2004** *Metro Mag.* (Raleigh NC) (Internet), I knew I had to come back when I saw rows of "Tom Thumbs" hanging in the cooler—pig's stomachs ("maws," as we called them) stuffed with sausage. . . On the farm, they hung in the smokehouse until special folks came, and you sliced and fried the dried sausage. **2004** *DARE* File—Internet **NC** (as of 1943), Some of the meat was stuffed into the prepared stomachs of the hogs, which were called "dandoodles" or "tom thumbs," for slow oven cooking later. **2005** *Ibid* **ceNC** (as of 1920s), Sometimes, they stuff large intestines [of a hog] and they are called "Tom Thumbs". The sausage is dried and smoked. *Ibid* **VA**, A *Dan Doodle* (or Tom Thumb) is a unique, hickory-smoked sausage with natural casing we still sell today, mostly in rural areas.
  2 The intestines of a hog; see quots.
  1887 U.S. Bur. Animal Industry *Annual Rept. for 1886* 300 **SC**, In some cases the descending colon or "Tom Thumb" was highly inflamed. . . The inflammation generally appeared more severe near the end of the "Tom Thumb," or attachment of appendix vermiformis. **1913** McCulloch–Williams *Dishes* 57 **Sth**, The "Tom Thumbs" were in great request for chitterlings—I never saw them served to white folks but have smelled their savoriness in the cabins. **1940** Brown *Amer. Cooks* 633 **NC**, Chitterlings, or "chittlin's," sometimes called "Tom Thumbs," are the intestines of the hog, also used everywhere for sausage casings.
  3 The thumb.
  1972 Jones–Hawes *Step it Down* 12 **GA** [Black], You call 'em Tom Thumb, dog finger, middle finger, no finger, and little finger. We had a teacher taught us that back in Dawson, Georgia.

tomtit n

Any of several small birds, as:

a A bird of the family Paridae, esp the tufted **titmouse** (*Baeolophus bicolor*) or a **chickadee** n[1] **1** (here: *Poecile atricapilla* or *P. carolinensis*).

1709 (1967) Lawson *New Voyage* 149 **Carolinas,** The Tom-Tit, or Ox-eyes, as in *England.* **1789** in 1941 Howay *Voyages Columbia* 63 **MA,** In the woods we find several sorts of woodpickers, Robbins, . . long tailed thrush[s] ground birds, tomtits. **1792** Belknap *Hist. NH* 3.173, Tom teet [sic], *Parus atricapillus* [=*Poecile a.*]. **1838** Geol. Surv. OH *Second Annual Rept.* 164 **OH,** *Parus bicolor* [=*Baeolophus b.*] . . *Tomtit.* **1843** (1916) Hall *New Purchase* 1.106 **IN,** In vain do flocks of black-birds and robbins, and tom-tits rise! **1872** *Harper's New Mth. Mag.* 45.810 **PA,** Frogs, cray-fish, tomtits, ground-squirrels—all . . went in [the stew] without question. **1910** KY Hist. Soc. *Register* 8.14, Tufted Titmouse, "Tomtit." **1919** Burns *Ornith. Chester Co. PA* 108, *Penthestes atricapillus atricapillus* [=*Poecile a.*]—Chickadee, . . "tomtit." *Ibid* 109, *Penthestes carolinensis carolinensis* [=*Poecile c.*]—Carolina Chickadee, . . "tomtit." **1929** *Wilson Bulletin* 29.2.84, *Baeolophus bicolor.*—Tom-tit, Ossining, N.Y. . . ; Hickman, Ky. . . *Penthestes carolinensis.*—Tom-tit, Hickman, Ky. **1950** *PADS* 14.68 **SC,** *Tomtit.* . . The tufted titmouse; Worthington's marsh wren. **1952** Giles *40 Acres* 158 **KY,** Actually the peter-bird is a titmouse. . . We also call him the tomtit. **1968** *DARE* (Qu. Q23, *The insect-eating bird that goes headfirst down a tree trunk*) Inf **VA**15, Tomtit—book word is titmouse. **2002** *DARE* File—Internet, The Tufted Titmouse, sometimes called a Sugar Bird, or Tomtit, is active and agile.

b A **nuthatch:** usu the **white-breasted nuthatch** or the **brown-headed nuthatch** (*Sitta carolinensis*). Cf **sapsucker 2**

1874 NY Acad. Sci. *Annals Lyceum Nat. Hist.* 10.366 **IL,** *S[itta] Carolinensis.* . . White-bellied Nuthatch; "Tom-tit." Resident. **1883** Nuttall Ornith. Club *Bulletin* 8.76, In *Tomtit* (Ohio Valley) and *Sapsucker* (Maryland) for these birds [=nuthatches], other errors are indicated. **1913** *Auk* 30.502 **Okefenokee GA,** *Florida White-breasted Nuthatch;* 'Tomtit.'—Rather common in the pine barrens. . . *Brown-headed Nuthatch;* 'Tomtit.'—Very common in the pine barrens. . . In habits and note they resemble the Titmice as much as they do the other Nuthatches. **1955** *Oriole* 20.1.11 **GA,** Tufted Titmouse. . . White-breasted Nuthatch. . . Brown-headed Nuthatch.—Tomtit. **1966–68** *DARE* (Qu. Q17, . . *Kinds of woodpeckers*) Inf **GA**3, Tomtit—very tiny; **GA**25, Tomtit—same as nuthatch; **MS**6, Tomtit—little, black and white; (Qu. Q21, . . *Kinds of sparrows*) Inf **UT**5, Tomtit; (Qu. Q23, *The insect-eating bird that goes headfirst down a tree trunk*) Inf **CA**40, Tomtit—a small bird, builds an elongated nest. **1986** Pederson *LAGS Concordance (Woodpecker)* 1 inf, **cwFL,** Tomtit; 1 inf, **csGA,** Tomtits; 1 inf, **swGA,** Tomtit—very small woodpecker.

c The long-billed **marsh wren** (*Cistothorus palustris*).

1883 Nuttall Ornith. Club *Bulletin* 8.77, *Telmatodytes palustris* [=*Cistothorus p.*] is *Tomtit* in South Carolina. **1910** Wayne *Birds SC* 186, *Worthington's Marsh Wren.* . . I have been well acquainted with this little bird ever since my boyhood days, and it was my delight to bog in the marshes . . near Charleston . . in search of the nest and eggs of the "Tom Tit," as this wren was known. **1950** [see **a** above]. **1954** Sprunt *FL Bird Life* 334, *Long-billed Marsh Wren.* . . *Local Names:* Tomtit. . . About the size of the House Wren.

tomtoe, tom-tom, tom(-tom) tomato See **tommytoe**

tom-troller See **troll** v

Tom tumbleturd See **tumbleturd 1**

tom walkers n pl Also *tommy walkers* **chiefly Sth, S Midl** See Map Also called **cow-walkers, george walker, high walkers, jack** n[1] **8, jake walkers, jay ~, jerry ~, johnny ~, jump sticks, long john 4, tall walkers, tommyhawk 3, walking toms** Cf **walking horse**

Stilts.

1899 (1912) Green *VA Folk-Speech* 452, *Tom-walkers.* . . Stilts on which boys walk; in the country usually made of saplings, a limb being used for the footrest. **1909** *DN* 3.382 **eAL, wGA,** *Tomwalker.* . . A stilt. The latter word is rarely heard. **1916** *DN* 4.302 **csVA,** He went all over the town on tom-walkers. **1923** *News* (Frederick MD) 24 Dec 11/5, We are going to give to the first one hundred boys that call at our Market Street Store a pair of "*Tommy Walkers.*" **1946** *PADS* 6.31 **ceNC** (as of 1900–05), *Tomwalkers.* . . Stilts. **1952** Mathews Coll. **SC,** As a boy I never knew they were stilts. They were known to us in Abbeville and

Greenwood Counties as Tom Walkers only. **1954** Harder Coll. **cwTN,** *Tommy-walkers* . . wooden stilts. **1961** Deal *It's Always 3* 233 **nAL** (as of 1939), They could see the place where the Negro houses began, . . and the children with their rubber tires and tin-can tommy-walkers. **1965–70** *DARE* (Qu. EE35, *Long wooden poles with a footpiece that children walk around on to make them tall*) 95 Infs, 91 **Sth, S Midl,** Tom walkers; 10 Infs, **Sth, S Midl,** Tommy walkers; **AL**3, Tom walkers—yes, string on cans, bush with limb on one side—one foot to ground; **AL**20, Tom walkers—when cans; **GA**6, Tom walkers—also tin cans under feet; **NC**38, Tom walkers—country; **NC**84, Tom walkers—old name. **1966** *DARE* Tape **AL**6, The tom walkers were poles with things nailed on them for your feet. . . We called 'em tom walkers; they were stilts. **1974** *Daily Times–News* (Burlington NC) 19 Apr sec B 1/1, Kenneth klops around on stilts, or some people still call them Tom-walkers. **1981** *Boston Globe* (MA) 16 Mar 6/2 **GA,** He [=Jimmy Carter] already has . . made stilts—called "tom walkers" in Plains—for his daughter Amy. **1986** Pederson *LAGS Concordance,* 11 infs, **Gulf Region,** Tom Walkers. **2000** *DARE* File—Internet **seGA,** You are very Wiregrass if . . you ever fell off a pair of Tom Walkers.

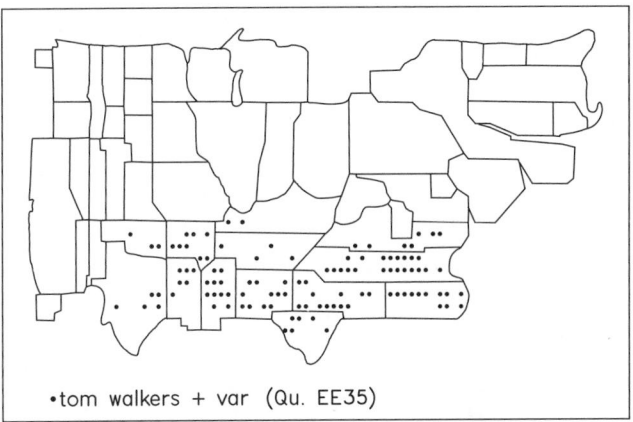

•tom walkers + var (Qu. EE35)

ton n

Pl: usu *tons;* also, chiefly when preceded by a number, *ton.* [*OED2* 1485 →] Cf Intro "Language Changes" II.7, **foot** n **B2b(1), mile B, month B, pound** n[1] **B**

1804 Marshall *Life Washington* 2.426, Two ton of powder . . augmented the booty of the captors. **1859** Judson *Seawaif* 56 **MA,** We'd make some thunder blowin' up with full six ton of powder aboard! **1865** *Atlantic Mth.* 16.623 **PA,** They got about two ton of hay from me. **1866** *Sacramento Daily Union* (CA) 22 May 3/4 **HI,** But in Honolulu, if Smith offends Jones, Jones asks . . "How much do you weigh?" . . "Sixteen hundred and forty pound—and you?" "Two ton to a dot . . peel yourself; you're my blubber!" **1943** *LANE* Map 556 **NEng,** [12 infs responded with plural *ton* preceded by a number; 1 inf responded *several ton.*] **1949** *Mansfield News–Jrl.* (OH) 7 Aug 13/2, The giant pump . . weighed two ton and took much space. **1960** *Lima News* (OH) 22 Nov 11/3, [Caption:] He feared a storm would topple it on his home. It weighed two ton. **1966–69** *DARE* Tape **CA**128, Some of 'em will hold four ton; **MI**21, The tugs used to come in with six to eight ton a day of herring; **MI**47, They hauled as high as . . nine thousand seven hundred and twenty-eight feet of mixed timber, which would be equivalent to about sixty-seven ton; **MN**10, Each pocket would hold . . five cars of ore at about seventy-five ton a car. **2003** *DARE* File—Internet **MN,** My son and I . . picked up at least two ton of rock.

tone v[1] **chiefly Sth** *esp freq among Black speakers* To toll (a bell), usu softly; hence n *tone* a tolling stroke.

1932 Dobie *Tone the Bell* 60 **TX,** All Ah wan' my frien's to do / Is give dat bell a tone./ Well, well, well, tone de bell easy. **1937** *Hall Coll.* **eTN,** She was the first the bell was toned for. Bells [were] toned down for funerals. **c1990** in 2005 *DARE* File—Internet **TX** [Black], If somebody died they'd sit up with 'em. They had what they called 'toning' the bell. Someone died, they'd tone the bell. . . There was a certain sound. For funerals, there was a different tone. I'll never forget that sound. [**1998** in 2004 Montgomery–Hall *Dict. Smoky Mt. Engl.* 611 **eTN,** [In toning a bell:] The bell was rung so its clapper hit the bell softly. Sometimes the clapper was covered with cloth or burlap to tone down the sound.] **1999** MS Univ. Center Study S. Culture *Voices Perthshire* (Video recording) **nwMS** (as of c1940) [Black], See him swing that bell. . . He toning that bell, he ain't ringing it. **2002** *DARE* File—Internet **nVA,** Career fire fighters . . along with volunteers . . came together in unity to form an honor guard that lowered the flag and toned the bell. **2005** *DARE* File—Internet **seTX** [Black], A bell was located in the bell tower section over the ante-room. The bell was toned when someone passed in the neighborhood, for a disaster (fire), or church services. **2006** *DARE* File (as of 1952) [Black], The "story" of the song is the funeral, with concomitant "toning" of the "death-bells" . . of the leadsinger's beloved.

tone v[2]   See **tear B1**

tongs n pl, but sg in attrib use   Also *oyster tongs*   **chiefly Chesapeake Bay**

Also *hand tongs, shaft* ~: A tool resembling a pair of longhandled rakes hinged together used to harvest shellfish, esp oysters, in shallow water; also *patent tongs:* a similar device raised and lowered by means of a derrick rather than handles; hence v *tong* to operate one of these devices; to harvest (shellfish) in this way; vbl n *tonging* (also in var combs); nouns *tonger* (also in var combs), *tongman.*

   1714 in 1894 Providence RI Rec. Comm. *Early Rec.* 6.161 **RI,** To Iron Teeth for Oyster Tongs & Carpenters Adds.   **1805** in 1815 Sutcliff *Travels N. Amer.* 129 **NJ,** These instruments, which are called tongs, are opened wide when the heads are let down from the boats.   **1869** U.S. Dept. Ag. *Rept. of Secy. for 1868* 342 **Chesapeake Bay,** Eleven million bushels [of oysters], taken in the legitimate way of dredging and tonging.   **1870** Davidson *Rept. Oyster Resources MD* 4, The dredgers are strong and comparatively rich; the tongmen are weak and poor.   **1899** (1912) Green *VA Folk-Speech* 452, *Tong. . .* To handle or use tongs, to catch something, as oysters, with tongs. *Tonger. . .* One whose occupation is catching oysters with tongs. *Tonging. . .* The use of oyster-tongs; the method or practice of taking oysters with tongs. *Tongman. . .* One who uses the tongs in taking oysters; a tonger.   **1906** *Forest & Stream* 67.897 **Chesapeake Bay,** I took a lesson in tonging from Bruce Murphy. . . [H]e handed me a forty pound pair of tongs with one hand. I got the 30-inch rakes down to the bottom fifteen feet below the surface and spread the two half-round handles far apart and began to jounce them on the bottom. When the handles were together, I hauled up and found one oyster.   **1947** (1962) Henry *Misty* 127 **eVA,** The people cheered madly when an oyster-tonger . . stayed on his bronco for a matter of minutes.   **1956** *Salisbury Times* (MD) 31 Oct 17/2, Shaft-tonging is done by hand. Then there are patent-tongs, which are operated by the boat's motor.   **1959** *Ibid* 8 Jan 8/2, At present, oystering in the Potomac is restricted to shaft tongs.   **1968** *DARE* Tape **NY**43, Oysters. . . always had to be in deep water. . . They had to be tonged with about eighteenfoot tongs the men had to use.   **1982** *Frederick Post* (MD) [25 Oct sec C 6]/5 (newspaperarchive.com), Maryland fishermen are allowed to use crane-like "patent tongs" to bite the bay floor and bring up oysters, while Virginia residents can only use hand tongs.   **2000** *Forgotten Coastline* (Internet) **FL,** The best oysters in the world are "tonged" from Apalachicola Bay and the area "bars."   **2004** *Washington Post* (DC) 18 July sec C 9 (Internet), He did not outwardly mourn the loss of the sail-powered schooners of his boyhood on which he had hand-tonged for oysters.   **2005** *DARE* File—Internet **MD,** Patent Tong boats can work with one or two men, as everything works with hydraulics. The oysterman works the winder and the tongs by foot pedals. . . Patent Tonger's [sic] work from sunup to three p.m., five days a week.

tongue n

1 also *tongue piece,* ~ *tree:* A shaft that projects from the front of a wagon or other vehicle on each side of which a draft animal is harnessed; hence n pl *tongue-cattle* and varr, draft animals that are harnessed beside the tongue.   **now widespread exc NEng** See Map and Map Section Cf **pole n 1a**

   1748 (1901) Hempstead *Diary* 22 Dec 511 **seCT,** I was at home all day Making a New Tongtree for the Trucks.   **1792** Belknap *Hist. NH* 3.106, The most dangerous circumstance, is the passing over the top of a sharp hill, by which means, the oxen which are nearest to the tongue are sometimes suspended.   **1828** Cooper *Prairie* 1.27 **West,** The men . . applied their strength to the wagon, pulling it, by its projecting tongue.   **1851** (1856) Springer *Forest Life* 106 **ME,** The tongue cattle, pressed by the leaders, . . threw the teamster under the runner.   **1853** (1855) Northup *12 Yrs. Slave* 283 **LA,** Why, he's a reg'lar genius; can make a plough beam, wagon tongue—anything.   **1912** Green *VA Folk-Speech* 452, *Tongue-steers, n. pl.* The yoke of steers that support the tongue of the cart on their necks.   **1939** *LANE* Map 170 *(Wagon tongue)* **NEng,** Nine informants describe a pole as lighter than a tongue. . . Three infor-

mants restrict *pole* to the attachment on a light carriage, using *tongue* or *neap* or both of the attachment on heavier vehicles. . . Often a single term designates both the tongue of a horse-drawn wagon and that of an ox cart. Sixteen informants call the attachment on both kinds of vehicle a *tongue* . . ; thirteen call it a *pole* . . ; and seven call it a *neap.* . . This use of the terms is doubtless more widespread than our records show, since terms for the tongue of an ox cart were not regularly asked for by all the fieldworkers. A few [=six] informants use *tongue* of the attachment of a horse-drawn or ox-drawn sled. [In reference to "the tongue of a horse-drawn wagon or carriage," the response *tongue* (also in combs *wagon tongue, draw tongue*) appears throughout **NEng,** but often as a second or third response; as a first response, it is much less common than *pole* except in **wCT.**]   **1960** Bailey *Resp. to PADS 20* **KS,** "Tongue" was the usual word but I heard "pole."   **1965–70** *DARE* (Qu. L45, *The long piece of wood that sticks out in front of a wagon, and you put a horse on each side*) 779 Infs, **widespread exc NEng,** Tongue; 24 Infs, **scattered exc Nth,** Wagon tongue; **OK**10, Buggy tongue; **FL**15, Center tongue; **MS**19, Hinge tongue; **KY**34, Tongue piece; [**TX**16, Tongue pole;] (Qu. L44, *On a buggy, two long pieces of wood stick out in front and the horse goes between them. You call them the* _____) Infs **AK**8, **FL**37, **LA**43, **OR**4, Tongue(s); **LA**14, Tongue [Inf doubtful]; **OH**43, Tongue, [corr to] shavs; **MO**4, Tongue on a surrey; **PA**71, Tongue between two horses; **TN**62, With two horses you had a tongue and a breast yoke; **WV**7, Tongue [with two horses]; (Qu. L47, *The two movable bars behind a team of horses are fastened to a longer piece; this is a* _____) Infs **IA**33, **MI**86, **NY**2, **WA**4, 18, Tongue.   **1968** Adams *Western Words* 326, *Tongue horses*—In mountain country, the *wheel horses*—those directly before the vehicle—of a wagon team.   **1973** Allen *LAUM* 1.213 **Upper MW** (as of c1950), For the shaft extending from a wagon between the two horses of a team the common term is *tongue,* ranging from 78% in Minnesota to 100% in Iowa and South Dakota. Competing with it is *pole,* which reveals its New England and Hudson Valley provenience by a strong Northern speech zone correlation.   **1981** *PADS* 67.25 **Mesabi Iron Range MN,** For both Iron Range and other Minnesota informants the general *tongue* is usual . . and the Northern *pole* is frequent.

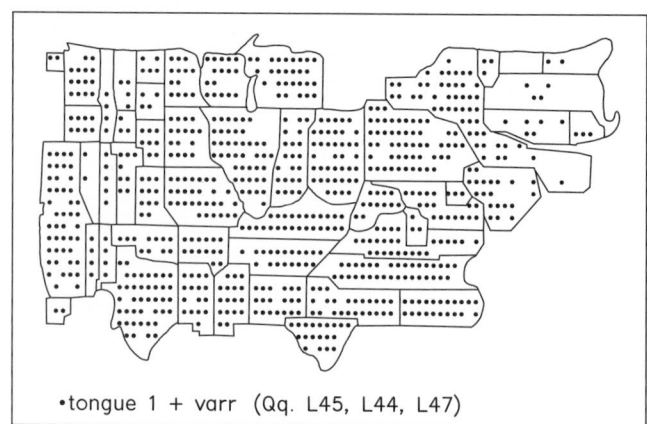

•tongue 1 + varr (Qq. L45, L44, L47)

2 in phr *make one's tongue slap the roof of one's mouth* and varr; Of food: to taste good.   **chiefly Sth**

   1967 *DARE* Tape **TN**16, There's an old saying—it'll make your tongue slap the roof of your mouth. Yeah, good stuff.   **1986** Mickler *White Trash Cooking* 35 **Sth,** So good it'll make your tongue slap your jaw teeth out.   **2003** Popik *Coll.* **AL,** But there isn't a dish that would, as they say in Alabama, make my tongue slap my brain.   **2004** *DARE* File—Internet **GA,** Simple and will make your tongue slap the roof of your mouth.   **2005** *Ibid* **FL,** Makes your tongue slap the roof of your mouth.   **2008** *DARE* File **GA,** That tastes so good that it will make your tongue slap you in the forehead before you can get the second bite to your mouth.   **2009** *Ibid,* The Virginia-Tennessee variant is "make your tongue slap your tonsils".   **2009** Maeder *When I Married* 137 **NC,** Boy howdy, this burger's so good it'll tongue-slap yer brains out.

3 An aster (here: *Symphyotrichum cordifolium*).

   1896 *Jrl. Amer. Folkl.* 9.191 **ME,** *Aster cordifolius* [=*Symphyotrichum c.*], . . tongue.   **1929** *Torreya* 29.151 **ME,** A[ster] cordifolia was known as "*Tongue*" and used as greens.

tongue-bush n

A **prickly ash 1** (here: *Zanthoxylum clava-herculis*).

   1960 Vines *Trees SW* 595, *Zanthoxylum clava-herculis. . . Leaves. . .*

stinging the mouth when chewed. . . Vernacular names are . . Tongue-bush, Rabbit-gum, . . Sting Tongue [etc].

tongue-cattle See **tongue 1**

tongue fight n esp **N Midl** See Map Cf **lip battle, mouth ~**
A quarrel.

1877 *Chester Daily Times* (PA) 2 Oct [4]/1 (newspaperarchive.com), Yesterday afternoon, two colored men commenced a tongue fight at Third street and Edgmont avenue, and a crowd began to collect, thinking from the terrible oaths and rough language it would end in blows. **1880** *Ibid* 28 Aug [3]/3 (newspaperarchive.com), Rosanna Martin and Maria Sophia Anderson . . became involved in a tongue fight on Thursday afternoon. **1900** *Daily Herald* (Delphos OH) 5 May 2/1, One hundred and twenty-three languages are spoken in the Philippines. It might be more serious for us if it was a tongue fight. **1903** *Reno Eve. Gaz.* (NV) 15 Apr 4/4, They left the place reluctantly, but continued their tongue fight as they went up the street. **1965–69** *DARE* (Qu. Y12a, *A fight between two people, mostly with words*) Infs **CA**127, **IN**32, **MD**33, **NE**8, **OK**7, **OR**10, **PA**40, 76, Tongue fight. **2005** *DARE* File—Internet, Revisiting the Leavis–Snow "Two Cultures" tongue fight is like chewing sawdust.

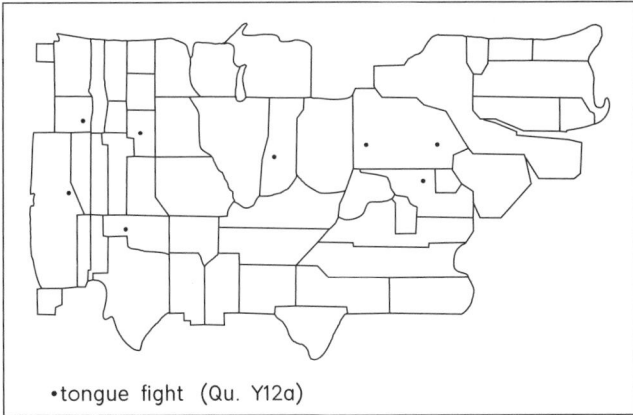

•tongue fight (Qu. Y12a)

tonguefish n [*OED2* 1655 for the family Cynoglossidae; from the shape] Cf **flatfish 1**
A saltwater fish of the genus *Symphurus,* esp *S. plagiusa* of coastal Atlantic and Gulf waters.

1672 Josselyn *New-Englands Rarities* 30, *Soles,* or *Tonguefish,* or *Sea Capon,* or *Sea Partridge.* **1882** U.S. Natl. Museum *Proc.* 5.618 **SC,** *Aphoristia plagiusa* [=*Symphurus p.*] . . *Tongue-fish.* Not rare. **1898** U.S. Natl. Museum *Bulletin* 47.2704, *Symphurus.* . . Tongue-Fishes. *Ibid* 2710, *Symphurus plagiusa.* . . *Tongue Fish.* . . Very common on the sandy shores of our South Atlantic and Gulf States. **1953** Roedel *Common Fishes CA* 70, *California Tonguefish—Symphurus atricauda.* . . It is the only California representative of the family. **1955** Carr–Goin *Guide Reptiles* 117 **FL,** *Symphurus plagiusa* . . Tonguefish. . . A lanceolate, very flattened fish with both eyes on the left side. . . A small fish, less than a foot in length. **1991** Amer. Fisheries Soc. *Common Names Fishes* 68, *Symphurus atricauda* . . P[acific] . . California tonguefish. *Symphurus civitatus* . . A[tlantic] . . offshore tonguefish [etc]. **2002** *DARE* File—Internet **SC,** [The] Captain has been running the dredge. . . It is always a great surprise to discover what he has caught. . . Horseshoe crabs, whelks, tonguefish, shrimp and the occasional seahorses.

tongue grass n

1 A **peppergrass 1,** usu *Lepidium sativum* or *L. virginicum.* [*OED2* 1726 → for *Lepidium sativum*]

1804 (1904) Clark *Orig. Jrls. Lewis & Clark Exped.* 1.40 **VA,** My Servent York . . returned with a Sufficent quantity wild *Creases [Cresses]* or *Tung [Tongue]* grass. **1837** Darlington *Flora Cestrica* 380 **sePA,** *L[epidium] sativum.* . . *Tongue-grass.* . . A pleasant antiscorbutic Cress; and often cultivated for the table. **1861** Wood *Class-Book* 238, *L[epidium] Virginicum.* . . *Tongue-grass.* . . Taste pungent, like that of the garden peppergrass. **1893** *Jrl. Amer. Folk.* 6.137 **IA, IN,** *Lepidium Virginicum,* tongue grass. **1896** *Ibid* 9.181 **swMO,** *Lepidium intermedium* [=*L. densiflorum*], . . wild tongue-grass. **1910** Graves *Flowering Plants* 200 **CT,** *Lepidium virginicum.* . . Tongue Grass. Common. . . *Lepidium apetalum* [=*L. densiflorum*]. . . Tongue Grass. **c1910** in 2003 *DARE* File—Internet **nAR** (as of 1865), For days they lived upon salads, made of the young shoots of polk stalks, tongue grass and other edible

vegetation, without salt, simply boiled. **1925** Jepson *Manual Plants CA* 440, *L. nitidum.* . . *Tongue-grass.* . . Common everywhere on the Cal. plains, low hills and in the valleys. **1954** *Harder Coll.* **cwTN,** You mean you don't know what tongue grass is? Eat that stuff—it's good, eat it before stalk gets hard, about as tall as ye finger is long. **1976** *Bittersweet* 3.3 (Internet) **Ozarks,** Late spring gave us lamb's quarters, wild mustard, sharp tongue grass, wild sage and shepherd's spray. **1982** *Goshen Trails* 18.2.9 **sIL,** We would gather dandelions, sour dock, tongue grass, lamb's quarter, wild lettuce, wild mustard, poke and speckle dick.

2 A **chickweed 1a,** usu *Stellaria media.* [*EDD* 1878–86]

1900 Lyons *Plant Names* 25, Stellaria media. . . Tongue-grass. **1910** Graves *Flowering Plants* 176 **CT,** *Stellaria media.* . . Tongue Grass. . . Common. . . Naturalized from Europe. Sometimes a troublesome weed, especially in damp soil. **1935** (1943) Muenscher *Weeds* 236, *Stellaria media.* . . Tongue-grass. . . Common throughout North America wherever gardens or cultivated fields are planted. **1967** *DARE* (Qu. S21, . . *Weeds . . that are a trouble in gardens and fields*) Inf **AL**37, Tongue grass.

tongue piece See **tongue 1**

tongue pole See **pole** n **1a**

tongue tree See **tongue 1**

tonguey adj [*OED2* 1382 →; "now *U.S.* and *dial.*"]
Loquacious.

1806 *Port Folio* (Oldschool) 2.123 **NEng,** Then if they go to *argufy,*/ I rather *guess,* they'll find too,/ We've got a set of *tonguey blades,*/ T'out-talk 'm, if *'they're mind to.* **1823** Cooper *Pioneers* 1.210 **nNY,** I don't think that . . they are sitch tonguey speakers. **1835** (1836) Gilman *Life on the Lakes* 1.54 **NY,** We had on board the Thomas Jefferson yesterday, a very tonguey Yankee lawyer, who resides at Toledo. **1865** Bowles *Across the Continent* 118 **MA,** His discourse was a rambling, unimpressive exhortation, such as you may hear from a tonguey deacon in any country Baptist or Methodist meeting-house. **1867** Lowell *Biglow* 105 **'Upcountry' MA,** He jes' ropes in your tonguey chaps an' reg'lar ten-inch bores / An' lets 'em play at Congress, ef they'll du it with closed doors. **1899** (1912) Green *VA Folk-Speech* 452, *Tonguey.* . . Loquacious; garrulous. **1915** Cather *Song Lark* 127 **CO,** There was, indeed, only one woman who talked because she was, as Mr. Kronborg said, "tonguey." **1916** *DN* 4.291 **sAppalachians,** Them Joneses is a tonguey (gossipy) set o' people. **1942** Whipple *Joshua* 100 **UT** (as of c1860), I ain't a tonguey woman and I never talk and it's none of my business.

tonic n chiefly **nNEng** See Map on p. 658 and Map Section Cf **dope** n **4**
A carbonated soft drink.

1888 *Boston Daily Globe* (MA) 25 June 3 (Internet), Hugh McIntire was . . arrested . . for the alleged larceny of 10 bottles of tonic and a quantity of raisins and sugar from the store of Mark Rudeman. **1891** *Ibid* 2 Aug 7 (Internet), While opening a bottle of tonic . . George W. Scott . . was struck in the eye by a stopper. **1912** *Fitchburg Daily Sentinel* (MA) 10 Oct 7/4, The child may spend . . a nickel for a sandwich or a bottle of tonic. **1942** *Portsmouth Herald* (NH) 13 Aug 5/8, At times when the men find themselves at the beach without any money a bottle of tonic and a smoke are most welcome. **1945** *Lowell Sun* (MA) 26 Oct 15/1, A bottle of tonic emerging from a soft-drink machine exploded and cut her hand. **1949** Kurath *Word Geog.* 21, *Tonic* . . for soda water is a distinctive Boston trade word which in the last two or three generations has spread southward to Cape Cod and Nantucket, up the Merrimack Valley into New Hampshire, and along the coast of Maine to the Penobscot. **1965–70** *DARE* (Qu. H78, *Ordinary soft drinks, usually carbonated*) 25 Infs, **chiefly nNEng,** Tonic. **1966** *Carroll Co. Independent & Pioneer* (Center Ossipee NH) 22 Apr 5/1, [Advt:] Lampron's Grocery—Cold Tonic—Ale & Beer. **1967** *DARE* File **neMA,** *Tonic*—soda or pop (pop would not be understood and soda would refer either to carbonated water—soda water—or to an ice cream soda). **1975** Gould *ME Lingo* 294, *Tonic*—Proper Maine word for a soft drink from a bottle; a *sody* such as Coke, ginger ale, root beer. **1978** *DARE* File **nwMD,** Carbonated beverages such as Coke are known as "tonic" to natives of Frostburg, Md. **1979** *NYT Article Letters* **nwMD** (as of 1951), I spent a summer in 1951 along the Potomac River west of Cumberland, Maryland, on the Maryland–West Virginia border. Everyone I met there called all carbonated beverages "tonic". **1998** *DARE* File **Boston MA,** I was extremely gratified to observe that at South Station (the main train station in Boston) the big board over the snack shop dispenses its soft drinks . . under the general label "tonics." **2000** *Ibid* **wMD,** My mother grew up in the mountains of western Maryland and when she was a child in the 20's and 30's . . it was called tonic. They mostly call it pop there now. **2007** *Ibid* **ceMA,** In the Boston area, I have only one local friend, a fifty-ish native of Haverhill, MA, who uses *only* "tonic" as his term for carbonated drink.

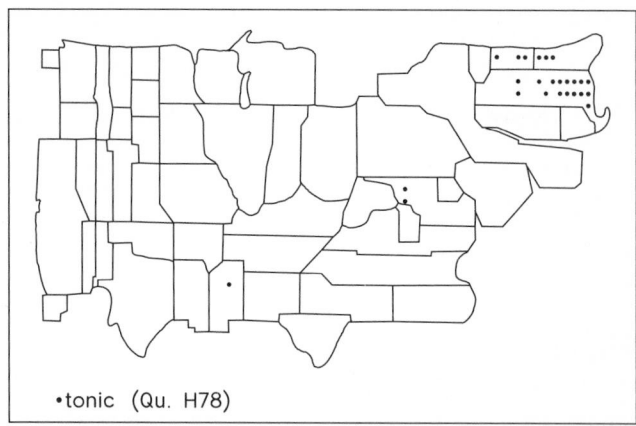

•tonic (Qu. H78)

tonic root n
=**goldenseal 1.**
    1968 *Foxfire* Summer 15, Best known as sang-sign is . . the golden seal (Hydrastis canadensis). Other names for Hydrastis include . . tonic-root.

tonight n, adv   Cf **evening B**
A time from late afternoon of the present day on; during this time.
    1901 *DN* 2.144 **ceNY,** *Night.* . . In the language of school children, four to six p.m. "What are you going to do after school tonight?" . . Common. **1966** *DARE* File **WV,** To-night—anytime after 4:00 p.m.

tonk n[1]   Also *tunk*
1 also *tonk rummy:* A game of rummy for two to five players. *chiefly among Black speakers*
    1908 Moulton *Blue Jeans* 118 **MI,** There was quite a sensational game of tunk in the back room of the drug store. **1937** in 1973 Himes *Black on Black* 125 **OH,** Harold Price . . was just leaving the house for his afternoon tonk session down at the smoke shop. **1939** in Lib. of Congress *Amer. Memory: WPA Life Hist.* (Internet) **NYC** [Black], There sat Fatso playing Tonk with Pretty Boy Matthews. **1942** *Vidette–Messenger* (Valparaiso IN) 17 Oct 6/7, Hank Sanders, . . the post champion Tonk Rummy player. **1965–70** *DARE* (Qu. DD35, . . *Card games*) 11 Infs, **scattered,** Tonk; **DC**12, **MO**30, Tunk; **SC**64, Tunk—like gin rummy; [**WI**40, Tonk—rap poker]. [12 of 14 Infs Black] **1969** (1970) Angelou *Caged Bird* 214 **CA** [Black], Daddy Clidell taught me to play poker, blackjack, tonk and high, low, Jick, Jack and the Game. **1996** McDowell *Leaving Pipe Shop* 87 **AL** (as of 1950s) [Black], During those two weeks, he kept mainly to himself. He wouldn't even play tonk with me, or gin rummy, or anything.
2 See quots.   [Abbr for *honky-tonk*]
    1939 in Lib. of Congress *Amer. Memory: WPA Life Hist.* (Internet) **cnFL,** Every [turpentine] camp has its 'jook', as they are now called, but the original name of this kind of a joint was a 'tunk'. This is a house where the men and women gather on Saturday nights to dance, drink moonshine, gamble and fight. **1948** *Common Ground* 8.38 **AR,** The man who owned the little country tonk was named Hamp. . . It was a one-room shanty store that doubled as a country bar room at night. **1954** Armstrong *Satchmo* 58 **LA,** Saturday the tonk stayed open all night. **1960** Pudney *Pick* 11.138 **CA,** None of the other rundown bars and tonks had anyone remotely like Lia. **1989** Grisham *Time to Kill* 202 **MS** [Black], Everybody at the tonk starts easin' up on her, buyin' drinks, wantin' to dance.

tonk n[2]   See **tunk** n[1] 2

tonk rummy   See **tonk 1**

Tonto n   [From *Tonto*, the "faithful Indian companion" of the (White) title character in the long-running radio (1933–54) and television (1949–57) serial *The Lone Ranger*]

1 An American Indian or Black man who is submissive towards White culture.
    1972 Claerbaut *Black Jargon* 84, Tonto . . a black male who is untrue to his race. See also *handkerchief head, Uncle Tom.* **2005** *DARE* File—Internet, *Being Indian Is* . . listening to all the middle-class Tontos and Uncle Tomahawks tell you we must do things the "American Way."
2 Used as a derog nickname for an American Indian man.
    1982 Heat Moon *Blue Highways* 294, "Say, who's the creep in my room?" "The jigaboo?" "No. Tonto." **2005** *DARE* File—Internet **IL,** The Potters have a player . . who is of Native American heritage. A small group of Dunlap students thought it clever to taunt [him] with chants of . . "Tonto" or any other Indian slur of which they could think.

tonton n   [Fr]   Cf **nuncle**
An uncle—used as a title or term of address.
    1969 *DARE* (Qu. Z7, *Nicknames and affectionate words for any other relatives*) Inf **NY**223, Tonton, tata—French Canadian uncle and aunt. **1983** *Reinecke Coll.* 12 **LA,** Tonton [tɔ̃'tɔ̃]. . . Uncle, usually before given name. N[ew] O[rleans], but not Cajun. Obsolescent.

tony n
1 cap: Used as a nickname for an Italian or Mexican man. [From the common name *Antonio*]
    1907 White *AZ Nights* 253, The newcomer shrugged his shoulders and cast his glance searchingly over the fringe of the crowd. It rested on a Mexican. "Hi Tony! come here," he called. The Mexican approached, flashing his white teeth. **1941** *LANE* Map 453 *(Italian)* 1 inf, **VT,** Tony. **1956** Ker *Vocab. W. TX* 365, Italian (nicknames). . . Tony. [1 of 67 infs] **1968** *DARE* (Qu. HH28, *Names and nicknames . . for people of foreign background: Italian*) Inf **PA**138, Tony.
2 See quot.
    1985 *WI Alumnus Letters* **csWI,** Our . . son, presently a student on campus in Madison, calls the crust or end slice of a loaf of bread the "tony."

Tony Marzetti   See **Johnny Marzetti**

Tony-over exclam
=**Antony-over B1.**
    1968 *DARE* (Qu. EE23a, *In the game of andy-over . . what . . you call out when you throw the ball*) Inf **NJ**16, Tony-over.

too adv   *chiefly Gullah; also HI Creole*   Cf *DJE*
Very, extremely.
    1838 Gilman *S. Matron* 171 [Gullah], Ki! if dem ting an't shine too much! **1867** Allen et al. *Slave Songs* xxviii **seSC,** Too much is the common adverb for a high degree of a quality; "he bad *too* much" was the description of a hard master. **1888** Jones *Negro Myths* 2 **GA coast** [Gullah], Buh Rabbit bin der watch um all de time. Buh Rabbit too scheemy. **1892** (1969) Christensen *Afro-Amer. Folk Lore* 33 **seSC,** Rabbit, I feel too bad. **1922** Gonzales *Black Border* 335 **sSC, GA coasts** [Gullah glossary], Tummuch—too much, intensely, ardently, fervently. **1923** Parsons *Folk-lore Sea Islands* 24 **csSC** [Gullah], But she forgot all her promise dat she made to de ol' man. She was too happy now. **1926** Smith *Gullah* 23 **seSC,** Too long buffo' me shum, me yerre um. [*DARE* Ed: =Very long before I saw it, I heard it.] **1928** Peterkin *Scarlet Sister Mary* 136 **SC** [Gullah], Lord, town had a fine restaurant. The fish there tasted too good. Ibid 157, "I too sorry for you, Si Maye," they'd say. **1930** Stoney–Shelby *Black Genesis* 5 **seSC** [Gullah], De he-males an' de fre-males is goin' to mek out too much better wid each other when dey aint a chance neither for bitin' nor back-bitin'. **1942** *AmSp* 17.21 **HI** [Engl of Hawaiian children], So[ḅ] very . . for these two words *too* is a common substitute. **1965** *DARE* FW Addit **nMS,** Too much better—Very strong term meaning something like the very best. **1971** Cunningham *Syntactic Analysis Gullah* 115, Too—'very'. **1972** Carr *Da Kine Talk* 155 **HI,** "Long time befoah, you firs' come Hawaii, fish too much?" 'When you first came to Hawaii, were there a great many fish?'

too v   See **tew** v

‡**toodlum squaw** n
=**doodl(e)y squat.**
    1968 *DARE* (Qu. JJ15b, *Sayings about a person who seems to you very stupid: "He doesn't know _____."*) Inf **LA**16, Toodlum squaw [ˌtudləm 'skwɒ].

toof   See **tooth** n

toofs See **tooth** n B2a

took v See **take** v A1c, 3a

took n See **tugue**

took-bird n
See quot.
  1981 Harper–Presley *Okefinokee* 70 **seGA** (as of 1930), You know what a took-bird is? It's a little yellow bird that runs ahead of you. Runs along and picks up worms. And he hollers 'tick, tick' [Harper–Presley: possibly a water thrush].

tooked See **take** v A2e, 3e

tooken See **take** v A2f, 3d

tool n Cf *eating tool* (at **eating iron**)
An eating utensil.
  1925 *AmSp* 1.137 **Pacific NW** [Logger talk], His plate, cup and saucer are his "set-up." Knife, fork and spoon are "tools." **1936** *AmSp* 11.45 [Soda jerker jargon], *Tools*. Table utensils. **1942** Berrey–Van den Bark *Amer. Slang* 96.3, *Silverware; knives, forks, and spoons*. Tools, weapons.

tooley See **tule** 1

toolies See **tule** 2

tooly See **tule** 1

too much sugar for a dime (or cent, nickel, penny) See **sugar** n 4

Toonerville trolley n Also *Toonerville (express),* ~ *(trolley) line, Tooneyville car, Tooterville trolley* [From the comic strip *Toonerville Trolley* (1920–55) by Fontaine Fox (1884–1964)] **chiefly Nth, N Midl, Pacific** See Map Cf **hooterville (trolley)**
A small, run-down, or unreliable railroad, train, railcar, or trolley.
  1919 Crowe *Pat Crowe Aviator* 97, We inquired and found that . . there was an electric line. We also found that the Toonerville Trolley had made its one trip and the Skipper had called it a day. **c1938** in Lib. of Congress *Amer. Memory: WPA Life Hist.* (Internet) **VT,** I . . took a train out of North Station. . . I woke up outside Montpelier. I had to ride that gasoline Toonerville Trolly [sic] to [B]arre. **1950** *WELS* **WI** *(Names for a train that stops at every station along the way)* 7 Infs, Toonerville (trolley); *(Joking names for a branch railroad that is not very important or that does not give the best of service)* 7 Infs, Toonerville (trolley); 1 Inf, Toonerville trolley line. **1951** *Chron.–Telegram* (Elyria OH) 13 Sept 11/1, Alaska's "Toonerville Trolley" is fast gaining the stature of a high-balling main line vitally important to the defense of the territory. **1957** Battaglia *Resp. to PADS 20* **eMD** *(Joking names for a branch railroad that is not very important or does not give the best of service)* Toonerville Trolley (recent usage). [**1964** *Appleton Post–Crescent* (WI) 10 Aug sec A 2/3, The cartoonist hit upon the idea of the Toonerville Trolley—ramshackle and late, but folksy. It became the symbol of broken-down transportation everywhere.] **1965–70** *DARE* (Qu. N37, *Joking names for a branch railroad that is not very important or gives poor service*) 114 Infs, **chiefly Nth, N Midl, Pacific,** Toonerville trolley; **MA68,** Toonerville trolley—small local trolley, not a railroad; 16 Infs, 13 **Nth, N Midl,** Toonerville; **MI67,** If it's a trolley, it used to be called a

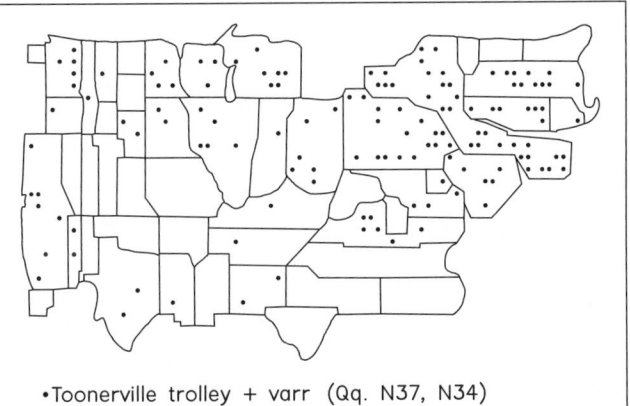

•Toonerville trolley + varr (Qq. N37, N34)

Toonerville; **CT29,** Toonerville express; **VA33,** Toonerville line; **CT5,** Tooneyville car; **NY105, 148,** Tooterville trolley; (Qu. N34, *An electric car that runs on tracks in a city*) Inf **MN36,** Toonerville trolley. **2004** *DARE* File—Internet **MA** (as of 1930s), To get to Boston from Chatham required first taking a "Toonerville Trolley"—a gasoline bus on rail-car wheels. **2005** *Ibid* **NY,** In 1928, due to a lack of riders, the train ended at Port Jefferson and a "Toonerville Trolley" took passengers on to Wading River.

to one's age See **to** prep B15

to oneself See **to** prep B17

toopler See **tupelo**

Toosday See **Tuesday**

tooser See **twoser**

toosh n Also *tush*
A small amount.
  1903 *New Engl. Mag.* 27 Jan Book Notes sec 10, There is profanity of the sailor sort, and "just a tush" of drunkenness. **1999** *DARE* File **CA,** In answer to "Would you like any more dessert?" a friend answered, "Yes, please; just a [tuš]." She said that that was a word she learned from her parents, who were from Tennessee. She thought it might be from *touch.* **2005** *DARE* File—Internet, If the company was founded by Ken Lay it may cost a toosh more than one founded by Alan Greenspan. *Ibid* **swIL,** Very lite . . —overall just a tush too sweet.

toot n[1]
1 A codger, coot—used derogatorily or affectionately of a person; see quots. Cf **poot** n 2
  1888 Pool *Tenting* 15 **MA,** Folks kinder likes him. I do myself. But of all shif'less toots he's the shiflessest. **1892** *Wellsboro Agitator* (PA) 27 July 1/8, The bride lost all patience with her future spouse and burst out with, "Go on, you old toot!" **1923** *DN* 5.217 **swMO,** Pore toot. . . A shiftless, lazy person. **1955** Warren *Angels* 51 **KY** (as of c1855), "You old black toot," Mr. Marmaduke said, calmly, "I'm going to sell you off, you the first one." *Ibid* 299 **LA** (as of c1865), Just think, that old toot sorting garbage all these years and a fortune stacking up for him. **2005** *DARE* File—Internet **TX,** By the last week, I'll be a grumpy old toot!
2 Something of the smallest value, a "hoot"—often in phr *not worth a toot.*
  1905 *Los Angeles Times* (CA) 13 Oct 7/2, His [=Grover Cleveland's] "Horn of Alarm"—the recent attack upon woman suffrage written by the ex-President and published in a woman's journal—is scarcely worth a toot. **1923** *NE State Jrl.* (Lincoln) 24 Jan 4/8, For some very flabby individuals the Brady symphony may keep down fat but for the fat ones it isn't worth a toot so far as reduction is concerned. **1950** *Washington Post* (DC) 16 July 1/1, [Headline:] Stickup Is Not Worth a Toot as Driver Honks, Too. **1966–70** *DARE* (Qu. GG21b, *If you don't care what a person does . . "Go ahead—I don't give a _____."*) Infs **GA77, NY59, VA39,** Toot; (Qu. KK17, . . *'Worthless': "It isn't worth _____."*; total Infs questioned, 75) Inf **MS69,** Toot. **1998** *Syracuse Herald–Jrl.* (NY) 7 July sec B 4/2, When she was young Lena Horne couldn't quite cut the song "Stormy Weather." "I couldn't do it worth a toot," she says.
3 A state of agitation or nervous haste—usu in phr *in a toot.*
  1943 Flint *Dress Right* 151, Heading for reveille on the double, all in a toot to be perfect in every respect, I came face to face with the Commanding Officer. **1966–67** *DARE* (Qu. A21, *When someone is in too much of a hurry . . "Now just slow down! Don't _____."*) Infs **GA1, NE10,** Be in such a toot. **1973** *DARE* File **csWI,** We don't want to do that in such a toot. **1995** *Brophy Coll.* 77 **swMO** (as of c1960), *Toot.* [A] hurry. . . "[W]hat's your toot?" **2004** *DARE* File—Internet **Chicago IL,** We were in such a toot to hit the road by noon on Sunday that we didn't have much time to socialize. *Ibid* **NE,** Why are you in such a toot over registration?

toot n[2] |tʊt| Also sp *tut(t)* [PaGer *tutt, dutt,* Ger *Tüte*]
1 A usu small paper cone or bag used as a container; an ice-cream cone. **chiefly PaGer area** See Map on p. 660
  1890 *DN* 1.75 **ePA,** *Toot* [tʊt]: a conical paper bag of grocers. . . Common in Eastern Pennsylvania. **1908** *German Amer. Annals* 10.49 **sePA,** *Tut* [tʊt]. Small paper bag. "Shall I put the candy in a tut?" . . Pa. Ger. *tud;* Ger. *Düte.* **1935** *AmSp* 10.169 **PA** [Engl of PA Germans], *Tut* (pronounced with the vowel sound of English *look*) is the word generally used for 'paper bag.' **1947** Weitenkampf *Manhattan Kaleidoscope*

47, There were however in those eighteen-seventies, sheets of rough, straw-colored paper in which grocers wrapped your purchases, often deftly turning the sheet into a cornucopia, or "toot," as the children of the East Side called those paper cones. **1949** Kurath *Word Geog.* 56 **PA, MD,** In the bilingual Great Valley of Pennsylvania (from Reading to Frederick in Maryland), the Pennsylvania German term *toot,* rhyming with *foot,* is in common use in the English spoken there. **1952** *AmSp* 27.292 **Bronx NYC,** Forty or more years ago in the Bronx, . . *toot* might signify any receptacle made by twisting paper into the shape of a cone. Beyond that, *toot* had two special applications: (1) a paper cone of colored paper filled with candy and hung on Christmas trees; (2) 'the conical wafer, usually about five inches long, made to hold ice cream'—to quote Webster's definition of ice-cream cone. In the latter sense the receptacle might be called an ice-cream *toot.* The pronunciation was [tʊt]. . . In contemporary New York City these uses of *toot* do not seem to be known except to relics like the present writer. **1952** *Reading Times* (PA) 19 July 11/1 *(Mathews Coll.),* The word "toot," meaning a paper bag, is a perfectly legitimate word. **1965–70** *DARE* (Qu. F21, *A cloth or paper container that you buy flour in*) Inf **MD**19, Flour [tʊt]—old word; (Qu. F22a, *A smaller paper container for bringing groceries home from the store*) Inf **PA**5, Paper toot; **PA**242, Paper [tʊt]—old-fashioned; **MD**19, **PA**136, 242, Toot; (Qu. F22b, *A smaller paper container for carrying a lunch: "He had his lunch in a _____."*) Inf **MD**19, Paper toot; **MD**28, Paper [tʊt]—refers only to small bag; **MD**30, Toot—generally not very large. **1982** *Barrick Coll.* **csPA,** *Tut*—pron. [tʊt]. *[S]ack, paper bag.* Common. **1985** *AmSp* 60.236 **sePA,** *Toot*—Paper container for groceries, etc. . Although many informants reported to the fieldworkers a knowledge of the term, only two persons listed it as a lexical item that they ordinarily use. **2004** *Ger. Life* (Internet) **PA,** Bethlehem, PA. . . Tutt (Brown Bag) Talk: Pennsylvania German Barn Stars and Hex Signs.

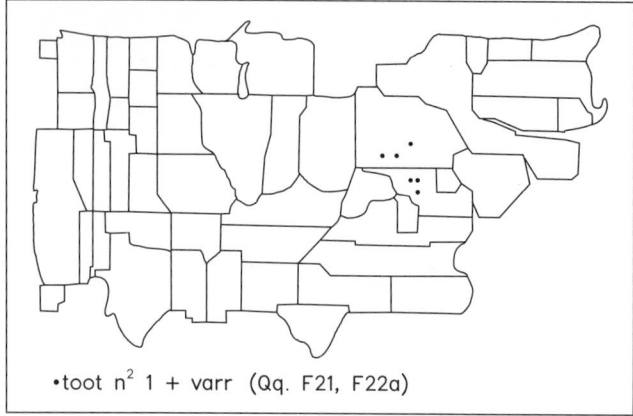

•toot n² 1 + varr (Qq. F21, F22a)

2 See quot.

1970 *DARE* File **nMI,** Toot [tʊt] = the fat sack under a chicken's tail. Said to be said by French-and-Indian people in DeTour, Mich.

toot v, n³

To break wind, fart; as n, also *tooter:* the act of breaking wind; a fart. **chiefly N Cent, W Midl, Gulf States** See Map Cf **poop, poot** v¹ **1, poot** n **1**

1965–70 *DARE* (Qu. X55b, *Words for breaking wind from the bowels*)

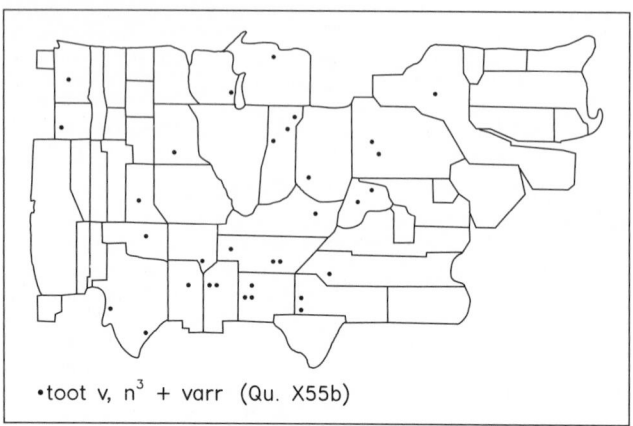

•toot v, n³ + varr (Qu. X55b)

30 Infs, **chiefly N Cent, W Midl, Gulf States,** Toot; **MS**1, Let a toot; **OR**3, Tooter; [(Qu. K73, . . *Names . . for the rump of a cooked chicken*) Inf **CO**47, Toot box]. **1981** Spears *Slang & Euphem.* 398, *Toot.* . . A breaking of wind. [Spears: U.S., 1900s] **2005** *DARE* File **NYC** (as of c1955), Beans, beans, the musical fruit:/ The more you eat, the more you toot;/ The more you toot, the better you feel,/ So eat your beans at every meal.

toot n⁴ See **tooth** n

tooter See **toot** v, n³

Tooterville trolley See **Toonerville trolley**

tooth n Usu |tuθ|; also *chiefly among Black speakers* |tuf, tut|; rarely |tʊθ, tʌθ|; for addit varr see quots Pronc-spp *toof, toot,* pl *teef, teet*

A Pronc varr.

1 sg: See quots.

1852 Hannibal *Professor Hannibal's Discourses* 78 [Black], I kotched a cole in my head and got de toofake. **1872** *Harper's New Mth. Mag.* 44.549 **sOH** [Black], It'll be dis as smove an' fine an' strong as ibory—as a fine-toof comb. **1899** Chesnutt *Conjure Woman* 16 **csNC** [Black], She . . put it all in a big black bottle, wid a snake's toof. **1922** Gonzales *Black Border* 334 **sSC, GA coasts** [Gullah glossary], *Toot'*—tooth, teeth. **1959** *VT Hist.* 27.164, *Tooth* [tʌθ] . . pronc. Common. Rural areas. **c1970** Pederson *Dial. Surv. Rural GA (One tooth)* 2 infs, **seGA,** [t'ʊuf]. **1985** Benes *Amer. Speech* 75 **cME coast** (as of a1847), The vowel sound of contemporary *put* also has an interesting distrubtion [sic] in Fisher's speech. It is found in the words *broom* . . and *tooth.* **1989** Pederson *LAGS Tech. Index* 263 **Gulf Region,** [For the singular *tooth,* 609 infs gave proncs of the type [tuθ], 58 of the type [truθ], 21 of the type [tuf], 10 of the type [tut], 4 of the type [tʊθ], and 1 of the type [tu].] **1997** *DARE* File—Internet **cePA** [CoalSpeak], *Teet, toot:* teeth, tooth. **2000** Metcalf *How We Talk* 161 [Black], To get back to specific African-American pronunciations. . . *this* can be *dis,* . . and *tooth* can be *toof.*

2 pl: See quots.

1852 Hannibal *Professor Hannibal's Discourses* 68 [Black], Her gum elastic lip open and shut on a row ob teef dat shine like bull dogs in a thunder shower. **1855** Bowen *Rambles* 227 [Black], What makes you teef chatter so, boy? **1883** Harris *Nights with Remus* 154 **GA** [Black], He toof look so long en shine so w'ite, . . dat Brer Rabbit hush up en stay still. **1905** Chesnutt *Col.'s Dream* 149 **GA** [Black], Den de black cat open his mouf an' showed 'is teef. **1933** *Chr. Sci. Monitor* (Boston MA) 16 Oct 9/7 (Internet) [Black], Vegetables . . am pow'ful skase right now—skaser dan hen's teef. **1956** *Edwardsville Intelligencer* (IL) 6 Apr 4/5, My ole man done cut his nails wid an ax, and brush his teef wif a file. **1989** Pederson *LAGS Tech. Index* 263 **Gulf Region,** [For the plural *teeth,* 774 infs gave proncs of the type [tiθ], 20 of the type [tif], 9 of the type [tit], 2 of the type [ti], and 1 of the type [teθ].] **1997** [see **A1** above].

B Gram forms.

1 sg: usu *tooth;* also *chiefly among Black speakers teef, teet, teeth;* for addit var see quot 1989. Cf Intro "Language Changes" II.6

1888 Jones *Negro Myths* 142 **GA coast** [Gullah], Old Jack exclaimed: "Haw, Boy! when I graff [=grasp] my han on er teet [=tooth], eh bown fuh come, er de jaw pop,—one or tarruh." **1922** Gonzales *Black Border* 332 **sSC, GA coasts** [Gullah glossary], *Teet'*—tooth, teeth. **1963** *Negro Digest* Aug 76, "You the one getting a teef pulled," he say. **c1970** Pederson *Dial. Surv. Rural GA* **seGA** *(One tooth)* 18 [of 64] infs, Teeth. [16 infs Black] **1989** Pederson *LAGS Tech. Index* 263 **Gulf Region,** [For the singular *tooth,* 12 infs gave proncs of the type [tiθ], 2 of the type [tif], and 1 each of the types [tit, tiš].] **1994** Bolton *Gal* 114 **seSC** [Black], I mean every teeth in her mouth was rotten. There was not one white teeth in her mouth. Every teeth was rotten.

2 pl: usu *teeth;* also *chiefly among Black speakers:*

a *toot(s), tooth(e)s, toofs;* for addit varr see quot 1989.

1899 Edwards *Defense* 212 **GA** [Black], Charley, look like dem 'taters mus' hab toofs an' toe-nails ter hol' on wid. **1902** *Atlanta Constitution* (GA) 8 June 24/2 [Black], Jedge Briles, . . I had dat dirk ter pick mer toothes wid. **1922** [see **A1** above]. **1967–70** *DARE* (Qu. K57, *The big teeth that stick out of a boar's mouth*) Inf **OK**53, Tooths [Inf Black]; (Qu. X13a, . . *Joking names . . for teeth*) Inf **MI**67, Toofs; **MI**42, Toots. **1989** Pederson *LAGS Tech. Index* 263 **Gulf Region,** [For the plural *teeth,* 4 infs gave proncs of the type [tuθ], 4 of the type [tus], 1 each of the types ['tuθɪz, tufs].]

b double pl: *teefs, teethes, teets, tootses;* for addit varr see quot 1989. Cf Intro "Language Changes" II.3

1929 Sale *Tree Named John* 37 **MS** [Black], De onliest way you ever *is* t' git loose is fer me to break dem teethes. **1933** Hurston in *Story* Aug 62 **FL** [Black], Dat heavy-set man wid his mouth full of gold teeths? **c1938** in 1970 Hyatt *Hoodoo* 2.1043 **SC** [Black], Yo' kin take de haid outa hit [=a turtle] an' yo' see dem tootses [Hyatt: teeth] dat is in dere, in his mouf'. . . Yo' take dem two tootses out an' when yo' pull dem two tootses out a leetle bit of blood come. **1939** in Lib. of Congress *Amer. Memory: WPA Life Hist.* (Internet) **Chicago IL** [Black], She jes look in his face reel sweet an show all huh teefs. **1968** *DARE* (Qu. X13a, . . *Joking names . . for teeth*) Inf **OH**70, Big teets. **1989** Pederson *LAGS Tech. Index* 263 **Gulf Region,** [For the plural *teeth,* 7 infs gave proncs of the type ['tiθɪz], 4 of the type ['tifɪz], 2 each of the types [tits, tič, tiz], and 1 of the type ['tisɪz].]

tooth v

To examine a horse's teeth to determine its age; hence vbl n *toothing.*

1920 Hunter *Trail Drivers TX* 298, To tell the age of an animal, the cowboy "tooths" him, meaning to make an examination of the teeth, as is commonly done in the case of horses, which gives fairly accurate indication of their ages. **1933** *AmSp* 8.1.30 **nwTX** [Ranch diction], *Tooth.* To examine a horse's teeth to determine his age. **1968** Adams *Western Words* 327, *Toothing*—Looking into a horse's mouth to tell his age.

toothache bark See **toothache tree 1**

toothache berry n

=**blue cohosh 1.**

1899 *Plant World* 2.198 **PA,** *Toothache berries* for fruit of *Caulophyllum thalictroides* Michx. The berries used to be strung and hung about the neck, as a remedy for that ache which philosophers could never yet endure patiently.

toothache bush See **toothache tree**

toothache grass n [See quot 2002]

A grass of the genus *Ctenium* native to the southern U.S. For other names of *C. aromaticum* see **wild ginger 3**

1837 (1962) Williams *Territory FL* 82, Tooth-ache Grass. Monocera aromatica [=*Ctenium a.*].—This is a singular grass. . . It affects the breath and milk of cows, who eat it when young and tender. The root is bitter, and affects the salivary glands. **1901** Mohr *Plant Life AL* 124, Toothache grass . . [has a] stout aromatic rootstock deeply buried in the compacted sand. **1933** Small *Manual SE Flora* 114, *Ctenium.* . . Toothache-grasses. **2001** *Times–Picayune* (New Orleans LA) 24 Oct (Internet), Standing . . at the edge of a large field of waving toothache grass, parish, state and Nature Conservancy officials joined forces . . to dedicate a nearly mile-long hiking trail. **2002** *DARE* File—Internet **Sth,** *Toothache Grass—Ctenium aromaticum.* . . Chewing parts of the grass has been used to alleviate toothache.

toothache tree n Also *toothache bush* esp SE

1 also *toothache bark,* ~ *plant:* A **prickly ash 1,** usu *Zanthoxylum americanum* or *Z. clava-herculis.* [See quots 1830, 1860]

1731 Catesby *Nat. Hist. Carolina* 1.26, *Zanthoxylum spinosum.* . . The *Pellitory,* or *Tooth-ach Tree.* . . The leaves smell like those of Orange; which, with the Seeds and Bark is aromatic, very hot and astringent, and is used by the People inhabiting the Sea Coasts of *Virginia* and *Carolina* for the Tooth-ach. **1762** Gronovius *Flora Virginica* 47, *Zanthoxylum foliis pinnatis* . . the pellitory or *Toot-ash* [sic] Tree. **1775** (1962) Romans *Nat. Hist. FL* 22, *Zantoxylum* [sic] *spinosum album.* . . Tooth ach tree. **1822** Eaton *Botany* 519, [*Zanthoxylum*] *fraxineum* [=*Z. americanum*] . . tooth-ache bush. . . Taste very pungent. **1830** Rafinesque *Med. Flora* 2.113, *Xanthoxylon fraxineum.* . . Toothache Bush. **1860** Curtis *Cat. Plants NC* 103, *Toothache Tree.* (Zanthoxylum Carolinianum [=*Z. clava-herculis*] . .) . . The bark, leaves and fruit, are aromatic and intensely pungent, producing a rapid secretion of saliva, and are a popular and useful application for toothache. **1876** Hobbs *Bot. Hdbk.* 120, Toothache bark. . . Toothache tree. **1897** Sudworth *Arborescent Flora* 265, *Xanthylum clava-herculis.* . . Toothache-Tree (N.C., S.C., Fla., Miss., La., Ark.) **1965** *Native Plants PA* 30, *Prickly-ash* . . *Xanthoxylum americanum.* . . Also known as "Toothache Plant", its bark was once chewed for this malady. **1980** Little *Audubon Guide N. Amer. Trees E. Region* 536, "Toothache-tree"—"Tingle-tongue"—*Xanthoxylum clava-herculis.* **1993** *Harbinger* (Mobile AL) 7 Dec (Internet),

Over near the corner . . there was a vacant field with one tree in it: The Prickly Ash also known as the Toothache Tree. . . Chewing the bark of the Toothache Tree did not produce hallucination, but local anesthesia. **1993** in 2003 *DARE* File—Internet **ceTX,** Then he [=a bull] went under the toothache tree there across the ditch and when a limb drug across his back, all the hair came off 'en it, too.

2 =**Hercules'-club 1.** [See quot 1945]

1762 Gronovius *Flora Virginica* 48, *Aralia arborea aculeata* [=*Aralia spinosa*]. . . Nostratibus Prickly-ash vel Toot-ash-tree [sic]. **1828** Rafinesque *Med. Flora* 1.56, *A[ralia] spinosa* or Spinard Tree, called also . . Tooth-ache Tree. . . From New-York to Georgia, and west to Missouri, &c. **1869** Porcher *Resources* 51, *Toothache Bush* . . *Aralia spinosa.* . . Plant often confounded with the *Xanthoxylon;* properties somewhat similar. **1933** Small *Manual SE Flora* 960, *A[ralia] spinosa.* . . *Toothache-tree.* . . The bark and fruits are occasionally used for medicine. **1945** Saxon *Gumbo Ya-Ya* 535 **LA,** *Toothache.* . . Rub the gums with the bark or seed of a Prickly Ash (known on Pecan Island as the Toothache Tree), or insert some in the cavity. **1974** Morton *Folk Remedies* 29 **SC,** *Toothache Tree.* . . *Aralia spinosa.* . . Scattered throughout South Carolina and North Carolina; also north to New York, south to northern Florida, and west to Texas.

tooth and toenail adv phr, adj phr Also adv phr *by tooth and toenail* [Var of *(with) tooth and nail* (*OED2* tooth sb. 7.a 1534 →)]

With all one's strength, in earnest; completely; fierce, intense.

1828 *Amer. Farmer* 10.203, An agricultural tyro . . would dash at the culture of wheat and onions, hip and thigh, tooth and toe nail. **1843** *Lorain Republican* (Elyria OH) 30 Aug 1/3, We shall oppose them "tooth and toe nail." **1851** *NY Daily Times* (NY) 12 Nov 1/3 (Internet) **Boston MA,** The Whigs, the Democrats, the Free-Soilers, the Coalitionists, all were up and doing—tooth and toe-nail. **1872** (1973) Thompson *Major Jones's Courtship* 58 **GA,** I'm a revolutioner, and go agin King Alkohol tooth and toe nail. **1909** *DN* 3.383 **eAL, wGA,** *Tooth and toenail.* . . With great energy, severity, activity, etc. "We went at it (fighting) tooth and toe-nail." Very common. **1923** *DN* 5.239 **swWI,** *Tooth and toe nail, by.* . . With the greatest difficulty; fiercely. "He only got it done by tooth and toe nail." "They fit tooth and toe nail." **1940** *AmSp* 15.221 **cwTX,** The ranch spouse may be 'dead set' and 'tooth and toenail' against it.' **1941** Writers' Program *Guide WV* 342, The crest can be reached by a stiff climb through dense thickets of rhododendron and laurel around the south face of the crags and a 'tooth-and-toenail' climb for the last 80 feet to the cleft summit. **c1960** *Wilson Coll.* **csKY,** *By tooth and toenail.* . . With all one's might. **1965–70** *DARE* (Qu. EE21b, *When boys were fighting very actively . . "For a while those fellows really _____."*) 17 Infs, **scattered,** Went at it tooth and toenail; **IL**113, **TX**53, (Fought) tooth and toenail; **CA**166, **IA**22, Going at it tooth and toenail. **1994** *Daily Herald* (Arlington Heights IL) 10 Mar sec 3 3/4, It was a tooth-and-toenail battle to the end.

toothbrush n

1 A twig chewed on one end until frayed and used for applying snuff to the inside of the mouth. **chiefly Sth, S Midl** See Map on p. 662 Cf **dipping stick 1, snuff ~**

1853 *Putnam's Mag.* 1.143 **VA,** Mrs. Braxley was . . an independent go-ahead dipper. . . Mrs. Braxley would brandish her tooth-brush in the President's face, if provoked to it. *Ibid* 2.151 **TX,** Some had strayed off to gather a peculiar root, much used here for tooth-brushes. Several of the larger girls had brought big black bottles of snuff, and . . were blackening their ruby lips and pearly teeth with the disgusting dust. **1895** *DN* 1.374 **seKY, eTN, wNC,** *Tooth-brush:* snuff-stick (used in "dipping"). **1905** *DN* 3.98 **nwAR,** *Tooth-brush.* . . Snuff-stick. **1909** *DN* 3.383 **eAL, wGA,** *Tooth-brush* (or *-bresh*). . . A snuff-stick. **1913** Kephart *Highlanders* 244 **sAppalachians,** The narrow mantel-shelf holds . . a twig or two of sweet birch that has been chewed to shreds at one end and is queerly discolored with something brown (this is what the mountain woman calls her "tooth brush"—a snuff stick, understand). **1926** *DN* 5.404 **Ozarks,** *Tooth-brush.* . . A chewed twig used in dipping snuff. **1946** *PADS* 6.31 **ceNC** (as of 1900–10), *Toothbrush.* . . The mop chewed on the end of a blackgum twig, usually for snuff-dipping but sometimes for cleaning the teeth. **1965–70** *DARE* (Qu. DD3b, *How . . people take snuff*) 11 Infs, 9 **Sth, S Midl,** Rub it on the gums with (a) toothbrush; **MO**4, Rub it on the gums with a snuff stick or toothbrush; **AL**32, **TN**26, **TX**101, 104, (On) toothbrush; **NC**80, Take it with a toothbrush—make their own; **LA**12, Most of 'em got a little brush—toothbrush, you know—they get it off a tree; **NC**82, Some used a toothbrush—made of little gum twigs; you frazzle out one end; **SC**3, Use it on a toothbrush—not a bought toothbrush, but one you get out of the woods. **1966** *DARE* FW Addit **cwNC,** Toothbrash . . ['tuθ‚bræš]—a chewed stick used by snuff dippers. **1975** *Appalachian Jrl.* 2.158 **wNC,** A *toothbrush* is a small twig of birch used to convey snuff to the mouth where it is then rubbed on the teeth.

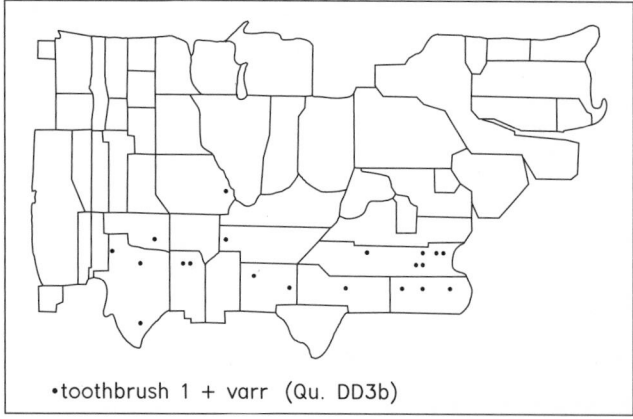

•toothbrush 1 + varr (Qu. DD3b)

2 =swab n.

1968 *Foxfire* 2.3.50 **nGA,** *Swab Stick* or *Toothbrush*—a hickory stick half as thick as your arm and long enough to reach from the top to the bottom of the still. One end is beaten up well so that it frazzles and makes a fibrous swab. This is used to stir the beer in the still while waiting for it to come to a boil, thus preventing it from sticking to the sides of the still, or settling to the bottom and burning.

tooth carpenter n   *usu joc*

A dentist.

1846 *Freeman's Jrl.* (Cooperstown NY) 31 Oct 137/2 **TX,** How horribly shocked the gentlemen aforesaid would be, if they heard . . one of their brethren, a dentist, called a "tooth-carpenter." **1870** *Galaxy* 9.696, The dentist has received the titles of "tusk-hoister" and "tooth-carpenter." **1906** *DN* 3.162 **nwAR,** *Tooth carpenter.* . . Dentist. Facetious. **1927** *WI Mag. Hist.* 10.413, I had the feeling that he could not afford to go to a regular dentist, and so was not offended by his cautious and persistent inquiry as to my ability to pose as a sure enough tooth carpenter. **1950** *WELS,* 2 Infs, **WI,** Tooth carpenter. **1965–70** *DARE* (Qu. BB52, . . *Joking words . . for a dentist*) Infs **IL96, LA28, MD12, 15, MA12, NY27, VA30, WI44,** Tooth carpenter; **WI34,** Tooth carpenter [FW: Her husband is a dentist, and sometimes refers to himself as a tooth carpenter]. **1975** Gould *ME Lingo* 295, *Tooth carpenter*—Upstate Maine-ism for a dentist.

tooth, clean as a hen's   See **hen's tooth 2**

tooth dentist n   [Redund; cf Intro "Language Changes" I.4] **chiefly Sth, S Midl**   See Map

A dentist.

1880 *Dental Jairus* 1.447, Any one desiring to know the whereabouts of the "tooth dentist" referred to, can do so by addressing the editor. **1906** *DN* 3.162 **nwAR,** I've got to see the tooth-dentist. **1914** Furman *Sight* 62 **KY,** And straightway he sont for a tooth-dentist, that tuck a pictur' of my gums in wax then and thar. **1915** *DN* 4.192 **swVA,** *Tooth dentist. Ibid* 229 **wTX,** Tooth-dentist. **1924** Raine *Land of Saddle-Bags* 105 **sAppalachians,** This desire for exactness has given such expressions as . . tooth-dentist. **1949** Webber *Backwoods Teacher* 105 **Ozarks,** A generation which . . put more faith in the "satchel doctor" and "tooth dentist." **1965–70** *DARE* (Qu. BB52, . . *Joking words . . for a dentist*) 36 Infs, 33 **Sth, S Midl,** Tooth dentist. **1986** Pederson *LAGS Concordance,* 2 infs, **nLA,** Tooth dentist. **1995** *DARE* File **MS,** I have a relative who refers to dentists as tooth dentists.

tooth doctor n   Also *teeth doctor*   [*OED2* 1767]   **scattered, but chiefly Sth, Midl**   See Map

A dentist.

1844 Haliburton *Attaché* (2d ser) 42 **NEng,** You've heern tell of Doctor Ivory Hovey . . the tooth doctor of Slickville? **1856** Kelly *Humors* 383, "Doctor," said a gay Southern blood, to a famed "tooth doctor," "look into my mouth." **1884** *Defiance Democrat* (OH) 17 July [2/5] (newspaperarchive.com), By golly, I'm going to learn the tooth doctor's trade. **1909** *DN* 3.383 **eAL, wGA,** *Tooth-doctor.* . . Dentist. **1939** in Lib. of Congress *Amer. Memory: WPA Life Hist.* (Internet) **SC,** The tooth doctor is treating Henry with X-ray. **1950** *WELS* (*Joking and nicknames for a dentist*) 3 Infs, **WI,** Tooth doctor. **1960** Criswell *Resp. to PADS 20* **Ozarks,** *Tooth doctor.* . . Once used to some extent for *dentist.* If heard now at all, it is humorous. **1965–70** *DARE* (Qu. BB52, . . *Joking words . . for a dentist*) 100 Infs, **chiefly Sth, Midl,** Tooth doctor; **SC10,** Teeth doctor. **1973** Allen *LAUM* 1.409 (as of c1950) 1 inf, **SD,** Tooth doctor. A dentist.

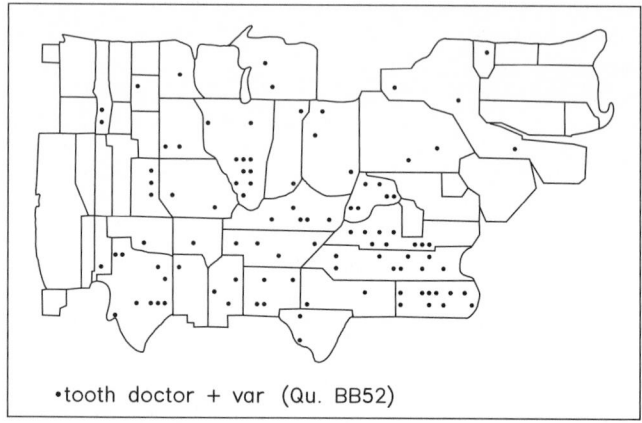

•tooth doctor + var (Qu. BB52)

toothed herring n

1 =mooneye 1.   [See quot 1983]

1842 DeKay *Zool. NY* 4.266, It [=*Hiodon tergisus*] is known under the popular names of *Herring, River Herring,* and *Toothed Herring.* **1902** Jordan–Evermann *Amer. Fishes* 91, *Toothed Herring.* . . *Hiodon alosoides.* . . Of considerable interest to the anglers of the upper Mississippi Valley states. **1908** Forbes–Richardson *Fishes of IL* 44, *Hiodon tergisus.* . . The toothed herring—a name given this species by way of contrast with the "thread-herring" or gizzard-shad *(Dorosoma)*—has been taken by us only some half dozen times in Illinois. **1983** Becker *Fishes WI* 279, The mooneyes or "toothed herrings" superficially resemble the herrings. . . They differ in having . . prominent teeth.

2 A gizzard shad 1 (here: *Dorosoma cepedianum*).

1873 in 1878 Smithsonian Inst. *Misc. Coll.* 14.2.33, *Dorosoma cepedianum.* . . Toothed herring. Cape Cod to Cape Hatteras.

toothes   See **tooth** n **B2a**

toothing vbl n   See **tooth** v

tooth jumper n   **sAppalachians, Ozarks**

One who extracts teeth with a mallet and punch; also vbl n *tooth jumping.*

1913 Kephart *Highlanders* 228 **sAppalachians,** "I have heard of tooth-jumping," said I, "and reported it to dentists back home, but they laughed at me." "Well, they needn't laugh; for it's so. Some men git to be as experienced at it as tooth-dentists are at pullin'. They cut around the gum, and then put the nail at jest sich an angle, slantin' downward for an upper tooth, or upwards for a lower one, and hit one lick." **1931** Randolph *Ozarks* 39, There are no dentists in the hills, but every country physician is provided with a forceps of sorts, and can extract an aching tooth on occasion. There are also a few of the old-time "tooth-jumpers" who do their work surprisingly well with a specially made punch and mallet. **1949** Webber *Backwoods Teacher* 209 **Ozarks,** Her brother Hi had been a tooth-jumper of renown in the old days, being able, it was said, to jump out a tooth in just a second with his punch and mallet.

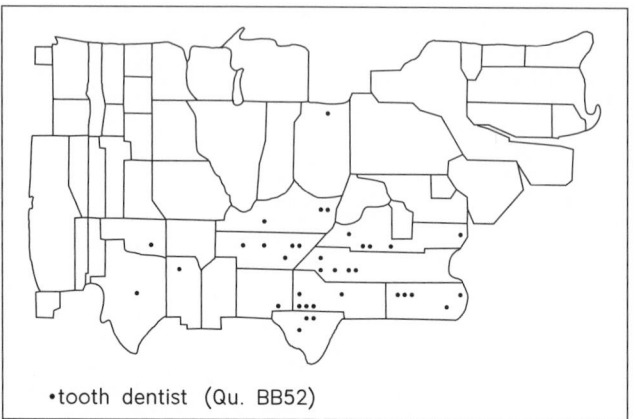

•tooth dentist (Qu. BB52)

1961 Seeman *In Arms of Mt.* 35 **eTN,** A toothache could have led to an ordeal. Imagine going to a mountain "tooth-jumper," who was armed with hammer and nail and kept a pair of home-forged pliers handy!

tooth mouse n [Fr *la petite souris,* literally "the little mouse"] An imaginary creature supposed to leave money in exchange for baby teeth that have been shed.

   2004 *DARE* File—Internet **LA,** Although this is no longer used, I was always told that a tooth mouse, not a tooth fairy, took my teeth and left money. . . [My other friend . . told me she had spoken to *her* mother (who is 75 years old). Her mother remembered the Mouse.] **2005** *Ibid* **LA,** Cajun children used to wait for the tooth mouse to take their teeth from under their pillows and leave money.

toothpick n, also attrib *joc*

1 A large bowie knife; a sword.   Cf **Arkansas toothpick**
   1843 (1916) Hall *New Purchase* 508, Oh! Bloduplex! had it been a dirk! a Spanish blade! a Mississippi tooth-pick! **1848** Cooper *Oak-Openings* 2.43 **NY,** We got our own tooth-picks. **1861** *Hartford Daily Courant* (CT) 26 July 1/1 **Sth,** He saw a company armed with large bowie knives and rifled pistols, who called themselves the "Toothpick Company." **1862** *Mt. Democrat* (Placerville CA) 28 June 1/6, He [=a Hoosier] drew forth the largest, longest, brightest, and most savage-looking bowie-knife I had ever seen. . . "I paid twenty dollars in clear . . gold for this yer toothpick. Give me fifteen dollars on it an' I'll go." **1881** *Morning Rev.* (Decatur IL) 7 Dec [2/3] (newspaperarchive.com) **West,** Buckskin Joe drawed his eleven inch toothpick, and the bar keeper subsequently swept up two fingers. **1910** Hart *Vigilante Girl* 135 **CA,** James Bowie. . . loaned him his toothpick, and it did the business for the other fellow. **1939** *AmSp* 14.31 [Citadel argot], *Toothpick.* . . Cadet officer's sword. *Rare.*

2 also *toothpicker:* A person from Arkansas.
   1846 *Warrock's VA & NC Almanack for 1847* [22], Arkansas . . Tooth Pickers. **1872** *Harper's New Mth. Mag.* 44.317, Below will be found a careful compilation of the various nicknames given to the States and people of this republic . . Arkansas, Toothpicks [etc]. **1886** *Chicago Weekly News* (IL) 29 Apr 4/3, Arkansas is called the Bear state and its people toothpicks from their structure. **1946** McWilliams *S. CA Country* 172, People from Arkansas are "toothpicks." **1949** Mencken in *AmSp* 24.28, *Toothpicker* for an Arkansan was derived from *Arkansas toothpick,* a frontier name for the bowie knife.

3 See quot.
   1946 McDavid *Coll.* **swSC,** Toothpick—hexagonal coffin [term used by] Negro male [type] IA [=folk speaker with least sophistication] age 68 handyman & jackleg preacher. *Ibid,* [Toothpick] (heard from Negroes) [reported by] White man [age] 39 [type] IIB [=common speaker with some sophistication] in same co. [=Allendale] and adjacent one.

toothpick bug n
Prob a **walkingstick 1.**
   1967 *DARE* (Qu. R9a, *An insect from two to four inches long that lives in bushes and looks like a dead twig*) Inf **AZ**2, Toothpick bug.

toothpicker See **toothpick 2**

toothpick grasshopper n   Also *toothpick hopper*
Any of several usu slender and elongated short-horned **grasshoppers 1,** such as *Leptysma marginicollis* or *Stenacris vitreipennis* or those of the genera *Achurus, Mermiria,* or *Paropomala.*
   1980 Milne–Milne *Audubon Field Guide Insects* 426, *Toothpick Grasshopper (Stenacris vitreipennis).* . . *Spine between forelegs.* . . North Carolina to Florida. **2001** Capinera et al. *Grasshoppers FL* 125, *Stenacris vitreipennis.* . . *Glassywinged toothpick grasshopper.* . . This very slender, elongate grasshopper has a distinctly pointed head. . . [I]n all respects, the glassywinged toothpick grasshopper is similar to the cattail toothpick grasshopper, *Leptysma marginicollis.* **2002** (acc) Fauske *Orthoptera N. Gt. Plains* (Internet) **Upper MW,** "Toothpick" hoppers. (*Mermeria* [sic], *Pseudopomala, Parpomala* [sic] and *Sybrula*)—Body extremely slender and elongated, length > 3 cm. **2002** *DARE* File—Internet **eTX,** Hilliard's Toothpick grasshopper. . . This insect receives its name from the habit of aligning parallel to a grass stem with its antennae extended forward, closely resembling a toothpick.

tooth quill See **quill** n **4**

toothroot n
A **toothwort,** usu *Cardamine diphylla.*
   1818 Eaton *Botany* 74, *Dentaria* [spp]. . . Roots always fleshy with tooth-like processes . . tooth-root. **1832** *MA Hist. Soc. Coll.* 2d ser

9.149 **cwVT,** 'Dentaria diphylla, *(Willd[enow])*—Tooth-root; trickle. **1876** Hobbs *Bot. Hdbk.* 120, Tooth root, Dentaria diphylla. **1897** Britton–Brown *Illustr. Flora* 2.131, *Dentaria.* . . The species are called Pepper-root and Tooth-root, from the tooth-like divisions of the rootstock. **1910** Graves *Flowering Plants* 208 **CT,** *Dentaria diphylla.* . . Tooth-root. . . The fresh rootstocks are sometimes eaten as a relish.

tooths See **tooth** n **B2a**

toothwort n
Std: any of several bittercresses of the genus *Cardamine,* esp *C. diphylla.*   For other names of var of these see **creece, crinkleroot, crowfoot 5, milkmaids, pepperroot 1, rainbells, salad B1, spring beauty 4, toothroot, trinkle root, turkey mustard, turkeyfoot 4**

toothy gum n
Prob =**tupelo gum.**
   1967 *DARE* (Qu. T15, . . *Kinds of swamp trees*) Inf **TX**35, Toothy gum.

too-tight n
A **tree frog 1.**
   1969 *DARE* (Qu. P21, *Small frogs that sing or chirp loudly in spring*) Inf **KY**47, Tree frogs—too-tights—sing, "Too-tight, too-tight."

tootses See **tooth** n **B2b**

tooty adj
Small or insignificant.
   1857 Copcutt *Edith* 23 **NYC** [Black], You knock down ole Dinah 'cause she nuss you when you war little tooty baby, you do. **1939** *Coshocton Tribune* (OH) 25 Sept 4/5, She is going to marry a rich man some day off somewhere away from her tooty little town. **1999** Mason *Clear Springs* 212 **wKY,** I'm used to big rooms. Look at that tooty dining room. I couldn't have one of my family dinners in that little hole.

too yet adv phr [See quot 1940]   **MI**
See quots.
   1940 *AmSp* 15.82 [Dutch in MI Engl], *Too yet.* An intensive from the Dutch *ook nog.* 'I have to go there too yet.' Perhaps the most prevalent of Dutchisms in Holland, it is constantly attacked in the local schools. **1958** *AmSp* 33.303 **MI,** Hollanders, even after being here many years, still like to insert the superfluous *too yet.* They will say, 'He married an American girl, too yet,' or 'I do not like popcorn, too yet.' *Too yet* means likewise, as well, or something additional. **2005** *DARE* File—Internet **MI,** Imagine that and with a Democrap [sic] in office (gov'ner) too yet. . . what this world coming to? **2005** *DARE* File **Holland MI,** The phrase [=*too yet*] is familiar to me, and I still use it myself a bit, albeit (I think) only in parody, and always with the thought of my freshman English teacher . . at Calvin [College] in 1966 complaining that the Dutch people in the Roseland area of Chicago used the barbarism "too yet." . . My mom (born in 1925 in Zeeland, MI . .) said: "We would say something like, 'Are you going along too yet?' I don't hear it as much as I used to do it. We say that once in a while but not like years ago. Our folks talked Dutch yet." *Ibid* **Grand Rapids MI** (as of c1935), We were warned by junior high teachers against saying "too yet." And my Ma, language purist immigrant that she was, knieped [=pinched] us for saying it.

toozer See **twoser**

top n

1 A mountaintop; a high elevation.   **sAppalachians**   Cf **top jack**
   1937 *Hall Coll.* **eTN,** A plagued pant'er run me from the top into the field. I had downhill and nothing in the way. *Ibid* **wNC,** I was captured by the Union soldiers just a little inside the top when I was bringing a family from Tennessee. **1943** Peattie *Great Smokies* 40, The word peak is found on our maps and might be understood in this region but it is really not native to it. The equivalent is top, or knob. **1960** Hall *Smoky Mt. Folks* 59, *Top:* a mountain top, as in Rocky Top. [**1968** Powell *NC Gaz.* 427, *Round Top,* mountain in ne Alexander County, an almost perfect cone.] **1999** McNeil *Purchase Knob* 55 **wNC,** Low land might be called "bottoms," and high land "tops."

2 The green leaves at the top of a strawberry; hence v *top* to remove these leaves.   esp **Nth, N Midl**   See Map on p. 664   Cf **cap** n[1] **5, hull** n **B1**
   1965–70 *DARE* (Qu. I47, *When you pull the stem out of a strawberry, what do you call the green part that comes off with the stem?*) 40 Infs,

30 **Nth, N Midl,** Top; **KY**40, Topping 'em or taking the top offen 'em, I reckon. **2005** *DARE* File—Internet **TX,** Choose berries that still have their green tops and show no sign of mold. *Ibid* **IA,** It's quite pretty when it's sitting there on the kitchen counter, filled with coffee grounds, eggshells . . , potato peels, tea bags, strawberry tops [etc].

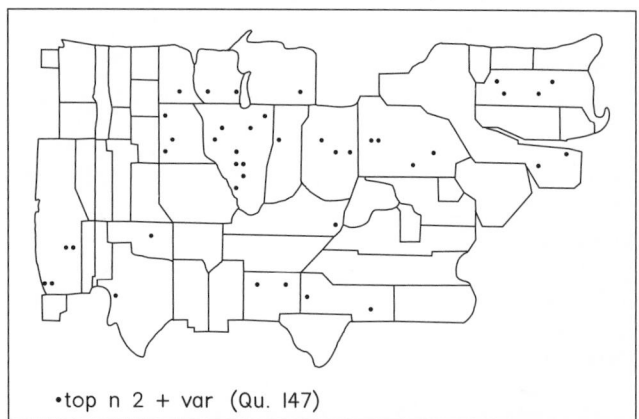

•top n 2 + var (Qu. 147)

3 attrib; Of a horse-drawn vehicle: having a roof or cover. **chiefly NEast, N Cent** See Map *old-fash*

1849 *Knickerbocker* 34.266 **NY,** An ordinary 'top-buggy' wagon. **1852** Bristed *Upper Ten Thousand* 205 **NY,** I have a top-wagon. **1868** *NY Herald* (NY) 18 July 1/2, [Advt:] Fine Top Gig For Sale. **1875** *Ladies' Repository* 2.347, The new top carriage, shining with varnish and silver plate. **1894** *Harper's New Mth. Mag.* 88.381 ceMA, But grocers don't drive round in top-buggies! **1910** *DN* 3.450 wNY, Top-buggy, top-carriage. . . Buggy with a top. "Hitch on to the top-carriage." **1957** *Sat. Eve. Post Letters* cIN, As a child we use to travel in a "top wagon" to my grandfathers at Houghton Lake Mich. a journey of 400 miles by "top wagon" and horses. **1959** *VT Hist.* 27.164 cwVT, Top buggy. . . A carriage. Obsolete. **1965–70** *DARE* (Qu. N41a, *. . Horse-drawn vehicles . . to carry people*) 15 Infs, **chiefly NEast, N Cent,** Top buggy; **MA**68, Top carriage. **1986** Pederson *LAGS Concordance,* 1 inf, **neTX,** Top buggy—with a cover, a roof.

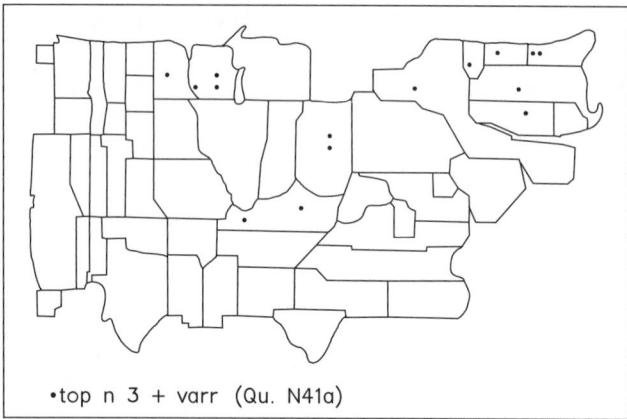

•top n 3 + varr (Qu. N41a)

4 attrib; Of an animal: being a male used for breeding. **esp NEast; also S Midl** *euphem*

1840 Todd *Notes Canada & U.S.* 71 **NEng,** [They] never mention a cock and hen by any other name than a *he* and *she rooster;* and a bull is more delicately lisped forth a *top cow!!!* **1859** *London vs. New York* 46, The fastidious lady of our continent . . with whom the woodcock is a timber doodle, and the parish bull a top cow. **1929** *AmSp* 5.20 **Ozarks,** *Top cow.* . . A bull. The Ozarker regards both *bull* and *top cow* as vulgar, and does not use them in the presence of ladies. **1939** *LANE* Map 190 *(Bull)* 6 infs, 4 **NH,** Top cow; 2 infs, **NH,** Top ox; 1 inf, **MA,** Top steer; Map 197 *(Stallion)* 3 infs, **seNH,** Top horse; Map 206 *(Boar)* 1 inf, **seNH,** Top hog. **1949** Webber *Backwoods Teacher* 134 **Ozarks,** I even heard of a deacon in a church, nonplussed at failing to find the husband at home when he took a cow to a neighboring bull, say to the woman: "Well—uh—which pasture is your top-cow in?" **1953** Randolph–Wilson *Down in Holler* 96 **Ozarks,** In one backwoods district the polite name for bull is *surly.* I . . asked an unusually intelligent schoolmarm what it meant. "That's our name for male animal," she told me. "We're

kind of old-fashioned down here, you know. We couldn't come right out an' say *top-cow* like you-all do up north." **1958** *PADS* 29.17 **TN,** *Top hog:* A boar. **1966–69** *DARE* (Qu. K22, *Words used for a bull*) Inf **CA**157, Top cow; **NY**72, Top ox; (Qu. K23, *Words used by women or in mixed company for a bull*) Inf **CA**157, Top cow; **MI**23, Sire is used by educated women, father cow or top cow by the common woman; (Qu. K52, *A male pig kept for breeding*) Inf **TX**35, Top hog. **1967** Faries *Word Geog.* MO 89, *Bull.* . . Scattered occurrences of a variety of other euphemistic expressions appear throughout the state: . . *top ox, top steer,* . . and *top cow.* **1986** Pederson *LAGS Concordance,* 1 inf, **neFL,** Top cow—old women; 1 inf, **cTN,** Some would say top cow; 1 inf, **cTN,** Top cow—less polite than "male cow."

5 See **top hog 1.**

top v

1 with *off, out;* In building: to reach the top of (a structure); to mark reaching the top of (a structure), usu by affixing a green branch or a flag to the highest point; also intr: to reach the top of a structure; hence vbl nouns *topping off,* ~ *out.*

1834 (1930) W. Sewall *Diary* 160 **IL,** Topped out house chimney. **1950** *NY Folkl. Qrly.* 6.152, At about two o'clock, the masonry foreman climbed to the highest point on the building and there placed a tree sprig, an announcement to all that we had "topped out." **1959** *Herald–Press* (St. Joseph MI) 29 May 5/7, [Caption:] Traditional among ironworkers is a flag-raising ceremony marking the end of major construction. These members of South Bend Local No. 292 . . "topped out" the Huron cement plant yesterday. **1966** Goldstein–Byington *Two Penny Ballads* 151 **PA,** While building a house, put a branch in the highest part. The wood spirit brings you good luck. . . ([Ed (Wayland Hand):] This is the "topping off" ceremony.) **1975** Gould *ME Lingo* 295, Top off—Off is used with *top* in all Maine expressions except to *top* "out" a chimney. **1975** *Sheboygan Press* (WI) 21 July 9/1, [Caption:] The building with the crane on top, to be known as Water Tower Place, was topped off Tuesday at Chicago. **1998** *DARE* File—Internet **GA,** We then topped out the building with a sprig of evergreen which is a tradition in timber frame construction. **2001** *DARE* File **cwCA,** My interest in "topping out" involves the custom of Ironworkers. . . [who] top new high rises with a tree and a flag. **2004** *DARE* File—Internet **NM,** Workers building Los Alamos' new National Security Sciences Building . . "topped out" the building at a ceremony on Thursday by placing an American flag and decorated Christmas tree on a steel beam at the top of the structure.

2 with *off, out, up:* To finish building (a stack or wagonload of hay or grain); also intr: to complete such a stack; hence vbl n *topping off.*

1845 *Amer. Farmer & Spirit* 1.76, Fine long hay, or rye straw, should be used for topping off. **1889** *Indiana Progress* (PA) 9 Oct 2/3, It is a good plan to wait two or three days after putting up the greater part of a stack before topping it up. **1899** Garland *Boy Life* 185 **nwIA** (as of c1870s), He came to "top out" for his father, being light and agile, and able to cling like a chicken to the high stack after it was far above the ladder, but he had never been able to put up a full stack. **1905** *Massillon Independent* (OH) 19 Oct 7/1, This crop should have been all put into one stack, should have been built high and well topped out with wild hay. **1949** Hedgecock *Gone Are the Days* 66 swMO, I felt quite a responsibility when I put up those first wheat stacks. . . For a while we thought we would never get the stack topped out. But we finally made it, although I think it took about two or three more loads than we had anticipated. **1969** *DARE* (Qu. L31) Inf **MA**40, Haystack was topped off—might call that topping off. **1975** Gould *ME Lingo* 295, A load of hay is *topped off,* made neat so it will ride to the barn.

3 usu with *off, out;* Among cowboys: to ride (a difficult or unbroken horse) until it becomes manageable. **West**

1906 *Out West Mag.* 24.317, There was not a better bronco-buster than Nelson. . . Nelson topped off the broncs. **1924** James *Cowboys N. & S.* 86 **West,** Four broncs are tied up and getting "eddicated" and another's saddled ready to be "topped off." **1929** Dobie *Vaquero* 137, Frequently one of the boys would get him to "top off" (ride first) a bad horse. **1929** *AmSp* 5.66 **NE** [Cattle country talk], On cold days a horse might be frisky and an "hostler" . . will "top 'im off," ride him until he can be ridden by one less experienced. **1939** FWP *ID Lore* 244, He throws on the kak (saddle) and screws hisself on tight (assumes a firm position) and tops him off (lets the horse go). **1939** (1973) FWP *Guide MT* 416, *Top a horse*—To ride an unbroken horse, partly taming him. **1958** *AmSp* 33.272 eWA [Ranching terms], *Top.* To ride a bucking horse successfully. *Top out.* To break a horse. Usually the term implies that the horse has merely had the 'rough' taken out of him, but is not actually broken. **2000** *DARE* File **West,** I'm reminded . . of another piquant westernism made of a perfectly ordinary word: top, as in to top a horse—ride an unbroken bronc and partially tame him.

4 See **top** n 2.

top cotton v phr   Also *top the cotton*   Cf **top the brush, top timber**

To be very excited or agitated; to go very fast.

1942 Perry *Texas* 136, If he leaves in a particular hurry, his neighbors may remark, . . "he was mortally toppin' cotton." **c1950** *Halpert Coll.* **wKY,** He topped cotton = got mad and blew his top. **1954** *Harder Coll.* **cwTN,** Talkin' bout mad, man, 'e's toppin' the cotton since 'at gal o' hisn run off. *Ibid,* She was topping the cotton about aunt Minnie deserting her. **1956** *KY Folkl. Rec.* 2.20 **wKY,** *To top cotton,* to become so mad that an individual cannot contain himself, to become whopping mad. . . "I thought he was topping cotton." **1977** Raines *Whiskey Man* 3 **AL,** What's got Ozro topping cotton, son, is that Roosevelt's coming through here.

top cow   See **top** n 4

top crop n

The latest-maturing crop of cotton, gathered from the tops of the plants.

1849 U.S. Patent Office *Annual Rept. for 1848* 154 **AL,** The fall has been very favorable for the top crop, which is now making very rapidly. **1854** in 1927 Jones *FL Plantation Rec.* 97 **nwFL,** The top crop of cotton will be short. **1868** *De Bow's Rev.* 5.875 **AL,** The boll worm is taking all the top crop, so that nothing is left but a very small bottom crop. **1903** *DN* 2.334 **seMO,** *Top-crop.* . . The last picking of cotton. The lower bolls are first to open and are the best. The top bolls are late to open and the cotton in them is not as well matured. **1909** *DN* 3.383 **eAL, wGA,** *Top-crop.* . . The last part of the cotton crop, namely that near the top of the stalks. **1967** *DARE* File **TX,** *Top Crop*—a second crop from the same plants from which the first crop was taken. Common with hand-picked cotton. **1981** *McDavid Coll.* **cnOK** (as of c1960), Bob Van Riper heard "doctor's crop" as meaning a "top crop" of cotton. **1986** Pederson *LAGS Concordance,* 2 infs, **GA,** Top crop (of cotton).

toper n   [*OED2* 1673 →; "Now chiefly literary"]   **scattered, but chiefly Nth, N Midl, West**   See Map   *somewhat old-fash* Cf **boozer, sot** n

A heavy drinker, alcoholic.

1797 *NY Weekly Mag.* 2.323, A veteran toper complained to the celebrated Doctor W. of Boston. [**1826** *Wilmingtonian & DE Advt.* (Wilmington DE) 12 Dec 2/5 **NY,** The heart of the poor lama [sic] was soon, drunk dry by these two feline topers [=two escaped circus tigers].] **1841** *Huron Reflector* (Norwalk OH) 20 Apr 4/2, He had been exhorting the toper to leave off the pernicious habit. **1899** (1912) Green *VA Folk-Speech* 453, *Toper.* . . One who habitually drinks alchoholic [sic] liquors to excess; a hard drinker; a sot. **1930** Shoemaker *1300 Words* 62 **cPA Mts** (as of c1900), *Toper*—A steady drinker. **1965–70** *DARE* (Qu. DD12, . . *A person who drinks steadily or a great deal*) 89 Infs, **scattered, but chiefly Nth, N Midl, West,** Toper; CT23, PA245, Old toper. [Of all Infs responding to the question, 65% were old; of those giving these responses, 78% were old.] **1994** *DARE* File **WI,** I've also heard two occurrences of "toper" both from women over 65. . . The first time I heard it the woman said "oh, I'm not a toper" and I had to ask the woman for a definition. She said "when you go out and drink a lot, you're a toper." A second woman said . . "I'm not a toper, I can't drink that much."

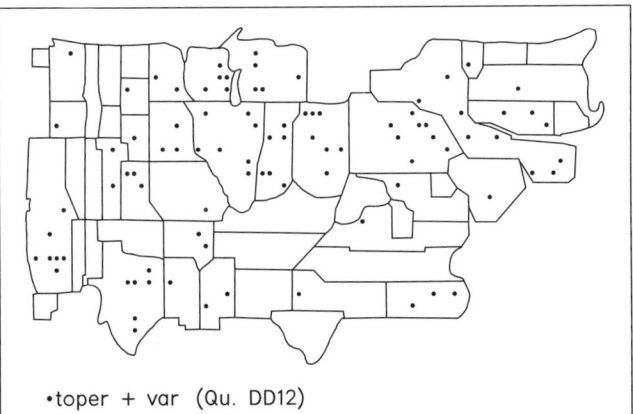

•toper + var (Qu. DD12)

top eye n

1 in phr *keep (one's) top eye open* and varr: To keep a sharp lookout.

1828 *Amer. Farmer* 10.230 **neMD,** Perhaps it would be as well to keep our top-eye open a little sharper toward those smaller items of family expenses. **1851** in Lib. of Congress *Amer. Memory: Amer. Time Capsule* (Internet) **MA,** Caution!! Colored People of Boston. . . Keep a Sharp Look Out for *Kidnappers,* and have *Top Eye* open. **1866** Taylor *Story Kennett* 44 **PA,** I know what I'm about; I have my top eye open, and when there's a good chance, you won't find me sneaking behind the wood-house. **1879** *Chester Daily Times* (PA) 6 Mar 3/3, Cadet Wren was busy blocking up [a cannon], while his comrades kept a top eye open from the lookout. **1914** *School Jrl.* 81.133, It is not doing very well yet and needs to keep top eye open to improve. **2004** *DARE* File—Internet **PA,** I will definitely be keeping "top eye open" (jeez, guess I can close the bottom eye and take a little nap) for a 65 Acugon.

‡**2** See quot.

1970 *DARE* (Qu. X23, . . *Joking words . . for eyeglasses*) Inf **SC**70, Top eye.

topgallant n   [*topgallant (sail)* highest sail on each mast of a moderate-sized square-rigged ship]   **chiefly wCT**   Cf **spindle B2**

The tassel of a corn plant; hence v *topgallant (out)* of corn: to tassel out.

1920 Storm *Minstrel Weather* 45 **NEng,** The corn is out in topgallant. **1941** *LANE* Map 262 *(Corn tassel)* 9 infs, **sw,cwCT,** Topgallant [as n] [proncs of the types ['tɑpg⁽ᴵ⁾ælənt, tɑp'g⁽ᴵ⁾ælənt] or with equal stress]; 5 infs, **sw,cwCT,** Topgallant out; 1 inf, **swCT,** First it *tossels out;* after it's full-fledged, it's all *topgallanted out;* 1 inf, **swCT,** Topgallant [as v].

top hat n   Cf **big hat 2**

An important person, "bigwig."

1946 *Forbes* 1 Oct 24, Employees knew their chief not as a "top hat," remote and inaccessible, but as a flesh-and-blood boss who had a genuine personal interest in the welfare of each one of them. **1958** Blasingame *Dakota Cowboy* 194 **SD** (as of 1906), Smedley, . . curbing his anger and desire to trim the "top hat's" toenails with his .38 automatic, rode over and asked the man from Washington to get away from in front of the heifers. **1967–69** *DARE* (Qu. GG19b, *When you can see from the way a person acts that he's feeling important or independent: "He seems to think he's _____."*) Inf **MA**73, Top hat; (Qu. HH17, *A person who tries to appear important, or who tries to lay down the law in his community: "He'd like to be the _____ around here."*) Infs **IL**16, **MI**78, **NE**9, Top hat.

Tophet n   [*OED2* 1388 →]   **chiefly NEast**

Used as a euphem for hell.

1811 *Centinel* (Gettysburg PA) 12 June [2/1] (newspaperarchive.com), Washington gave it his signature in spite of such clamour, threats and violence, as seemed as tho' half Tophet were let loose. **1820** Eastburn-Sands *Yamoyden* 109 **seNY,** To Tophet flies the howling ghost! **1835** *New Engl. Mag.* 8.474, The water absolutely hisses down your red-hot gullet, and is converted quite to steam, in the miniature tophet, which you mistake for a stomach. **1863** Gilmore *S. Friends* 61 **NC,** It gits a feller's stumac used to Tophet 'fore the rest on him is 'climated. **1899** *Fitchburg Daily Sentinel* (MA) 27 Nov 1/4, How should we get through Tophet? We've done it. . . This Tophet was only a swamp, but it wasn't the worst Tophet we had to go through. **1908** Day *King Spruce* 168 **ME,** "She [=a forest fire] can't be stopped!" moaned Britt. "She's headed for the Notch, and then tophet's let loose!" **1941** *LANE* Map 473, 1 inf, **MA,** Mad as Tophet. **1957** *Sat. Eve. Post Letters* **MA,** Hot as the hinges of Tophet—very warm. **1960** *VT Hist.* 28.223, To be flogged through Tophet in a flour sack. (To be punished.) **1968–70** *DARE* (Qu. HH22b, . . *A very mean person . . "He's meaner than _____."*) Inf **NY**88, Tophet; **CA**197, Tophet—means hell. **1978** *Blair & Ketchum's Country Jrl.* Sept 82 **NEng,** What in Tophet ails her?

top hog n

1 also *top:* A hog that has reached the optimum weight for slaughter.

1874 *Coshocton Democrat* (OH) 8 Dec 3/3, The market has been rather unsteady, top hogs going down on last Saturday to 7¼c. **1910** *Indianapolis Star* (IN) 4 Feb 11/1, Good light hogs sold steady, but the medium and heavy kinds suffered in the discrimination, top hogs showing a decline of 10c. *Ibid* 22 Feb 11/2, Hogs. . . top, $9.25; bulk, $8.90@9.20; heavy, $9.20@9.35; packers and butchers, $9@9.35; light, $8.70@9.10. **1954** *Harder Coll.* **cwTN,** *Top hog.* . . A full-grown hog that is ready for market. **1969** *Independent* (Hawarden IA) 13 Mar [2]/3 (newspaperarchive.com), [It is] the favorite among thousands of top hog producers, purebred raisers and agricultural colleges. **1970** *DARE* Tape **KY**93, Shoats . . that's a small type of a hog. . . He's not a top, he's not large enough to be a top. He's 'tween a top hog and a feeder pig. **1986** Pederson *LAGS Concordance* (A hog ready to slaughter) 4 infs, **TN, AL, TX,** Top hog. **2004** *DARE* File—Internet **KY,** Packing houses that buy Top Hogs will only pay market values for Barrows . . and Gilts. . . Top weight for a Top Hog is 260 Lb.

2 See **top** n **4.**

top horse See **top** n **4**

top jack n Cf **top** n **1**
See quot.
   1967 *DARE* (Qu. HH14, *Ways of teasing a beginner or inexperienced person—for example, by sending him for a 'left-handed monkey wrench': "Go get me _____.")* Inf **TN**1, A top jack—to jack the mountain up.

top knocker See **knocker 7a**

topknot n
1 The head. [*OED2* 1869 →] *joc*
   1870 *Punchinello* 24 Dec 203, Ide nock the foolishness out of your nozzles, or break your pesky old topknots in the atemt. **1893** *Daily Rev.* (Decatur IL) 8 Jan [3]/2 (newspaperarchive.com), The badly scared constable . . felt the two bumps that were already beginning to rise on his topknot, and handed over the rocks. **1926** *Syracuse Herald* (NY) 11 Feb 22/8, The husband . . goes serenely . . on his way, his life fairly full of a number of things and no psychological problems assailing his topknot. **1950** *Chron.–Telegram* (Elyria OH) 7 Nov 3/4, So long as he has chew money, the price of a scuttle of suds and a pillow for his topknot, he's a nappy [sic] man. **1965–70** *DARE* (Qu. X28, *Joking words . . for a person's head*) 24 Infs, **scattered,** Topknot. **1991** *DARE* File **nwAR,** Head—noggin, topknot.
2 =**hooded merganser.**
   1901 OH Acad. Sci. *Annual Rept. 1900* 36, Hooded Merganser. . . Saw-bill, Topknot [etc]. **1923** U.S. Dept. Ag. *Misc. Circular* 13.7 **MI,** *Vernacular Names* [for hooded merganser]. . . *In local use.* . . topknot.
3 See **topknot quail.**

topknot blue jay See **topknot jay 2**

topknot jay n [From the crest]
1 also *blue topknot jay:* A **blue jay 1** (here: *Cyanocitta cristata*).
   1861 *Home Mth.* 4.84, The "top-knot" jay came o'er the moor. **1965–67** *DARE* (Qu. Q16, . . *Kinds of jays*) Inf **FL**22, Blue topknot jays; **SC**34, Blue jay, topknot jay, jaybird—only one kind, three names.
2 as *topknot blue jay, topknotted jay:* =**Steller's jay.**
   1928 Libby–Bryant *Bird Study CA* 56, In forested areas . . the California jay is replaced by the Steller jay, sometimes called "topknotted jay." **1967** *DARE* (Qu. Q16, . . *Kinds of jays*) Inf **CA**31, Topknot blue jays—have black head.

topknot quail n Also *topknot*
=**California quail 1.**
   1875 Royal Geogr. Soc. *Proc.* 19.307 **AZ,** The principal game is bear, deer, antelopes, . . and the peculiar top-knot quail. **1918** Grinnell et al. *Game Birds CA* 514, *Lophortyx californica vallicola* [=*Callipepla c.*] . . *Other names . .* Topknot Quail. **1935** Davis *Honey* 1 **OR,** Blue grouse and topknot-quail boarded in all the brush-piles and thorn-heaps by the hundreds all the year round. **1966** *DARE* (Qu. Q7, *Names and nicknames for . . game birds*) Inf **WA**3, Topknots or California quail. **1982** Elman *Hunter's Field Guide* 92, *Callipepla californica.* . . *Topknot quail.* . . What the hunter sees first is a loose covey . . , their black head plumes bobbing as they skitter through openings in sage, cat's-claw, thornbush, cactus, manzanita, under scrub oak or piñon, into thick chaparral. **2002** *DARE* File—Internet **CA,** The California quail. . . is also known as the Valley quail . . and the Topknot quail. It's a plump bird about 9½–11 inches long with a downward curving black plume on the top of its head.

topknotted jay See **topknot jay 2**

topknot woodpecker n Also *red topknot woodpecker*
Perh the **pileated woodpecker.**

1969–70 *DARE* (Qu. Q17, . . *Kinds of woodpeckers*) Inf **KY**56, Red topknot woodpecker; **TN**65, Topknot woodpecker.

topliner n
=**highline** n **5.**
   1950 *Boston Daily Globe* (MA) 30 July sec A 1/4 *(Mathews Coll.),* Capt Archie MacLeod, at 65, has long been known as a 'top-liner' in Gloucester where he makes his home.

top milk n esp Nth *old-fash*
The upper, cream-rich portion of milk that has not been homogenized.
   1866 *Atlanta Med. & Surgical Jrl.* new ser 7.538, The milk must stand for four or five hours in a cool place. The top milk should then be taken for the child. **1892** *Olean Democrat* (NY) 25 Nov (newspaperarchive.com), "Top milk" is the upper half of milk which has been allowed to stand for a time, say three hours. It should be dipped, not poured off from the under milk. **1901** Sachse *How to Cook* 26 **sePA,** Siphon cream or top-milk may be obtained as follows: Allow milk to stand in a glass jar or bottle (on ice) for four hours. . . Siphon off all but the number of ounces desired, according to the table given. [**1945** Hamlin *9 Mile Bridge* 26 **nME** [FrCan speaker], *Oui,* Mademoiselle, have three or four [cookies], and have a glass of top milk, nice and cold and right off the ice.] **1959** *Syracuse Herald–Jrl.* (NY) 19 Nov 26/6, *Scalloped Oysters—*1½ pints oysters. . . Top milk or light cream [etc]. **1976** *Fond du Lac Reporter* (WI) 16 Sept 10/2, Coffee cream or top milk can be used.

topminnow n [See quot 1908] Cf **topwater 1**
Any of var small fishes of the families Fundulidae and Poeciliidae: usu a **killifish 1** (here: *Fundulus* spp) or a **mosquito fish.**
   1848 Boston Soc. Nat. Hist. *Proc.* 2.51, *Paecilia olivacea* [=*Fundulus olivaceus*] Caught at all seasons, swimming on the top of the water, catching at floating objects. Commonly called *Top minnow.* **1882** U.S. Natl. Museum *Bulletin* 16.338, *Zygonectes* [here: =*Fundulus*]. . . *Top Minnows.* . . Surface swimmers, feeding upon insects. **1884** *Ibid* 27.471, *Zygonectes notatus.* . . *Top Minnow.* Michigan, and southward through the Mississippi Valley to Alabama and Texas. Abundant in ponds and canals. . . *Gambusia patruelis* [=*G. affinis*] . . *Top Minnow.* . . Southern United States, from Virginia to Texas; . . abounding in lowland streams. **1908** Forbes–Richardson *Fishes of IL* 210, Family Poeciliidae [*DARE* Ed: here includes Fundulidae]. . . Many of the species of this family are surface swimmers, "top-minnows," inhabiting canals, ponds, swamps, and sluggish or stagnant streams, where they feed on insects and other life found swimming or floating at the surface of the water. *Ibid* 211, *Fundulus.* . . The three species found in Illinois are typical "top-minnows," feeding on surface-swimming insects, etc. **1933** LA Dept. of Conserv. *Fishes* 451, The Top Minnows [here: =*Gambusia affinis*] are of such small size that they can readily rush into very shallow waters and thus escape from larger fishes. **1964** Lowe *Vertebrates* 147 **AZ,** Family Poeciliidae: Topminnows. **1965** IL Nat. Hist. Surv. *Biol. Notes* 54.9, Cyprinodontidae [here: =Fundulidae]—topminnows. **1968** *DARE* (Qu. P7, *Small fish used as bait for bigger fish*) Inf **NC**49, Topminnow. **2002** (acc) IL Dept. Nat. Resources *Wild about IL Fishes* (Internet), *Family Fundulidae.* . . Often found swimming near the surface, . . Topminnows are small fishes with large eyes, a flattened head and back, upturned mouth, one dorsal fin far back on the body and no lateral line.

top off See **top** v **1, 2, 3**

top of the pot n
1 The highest position, esp in social or economic standing; one who is in this position; hence adj *top-of-the-pot* of the highest standing. **chiefly Sth, S Midl**
   1824 Tucker *Valley Shenandoah* 1.298 **VA,** Old Steener, Mr. Fawkner's father, was overseer to your grandpa—my old master—and now they are at the top of the pot. **1840** Haliburton *Clockmaker* (3d ser) 96 **NEng,** Why don't them patriots (for some on 'em are at the top of the pot) why don't they clap 'em into a coffin, bury 'em decently, and put a monument over them. **1843** (1969) Lewis *Odd Leaves* 24 **LA,** To sum up the whole, the city physician lives at the top of the pot, the swamp doctor scarcely at the rim of the skillet. **1882** *Helena Independent* (MT) 17 Sept [3]/5 (newspaperarchive.com), "Jack" has been twice at the top of the pot and many times at the bottom, since leaving Montana, but is now opening a mine and expects to make a big stake. **1891** Harris *Balaam* 221 **GA,** I can't tell you the time when I ever seed a likelier gal than that one wi' the Judge this evenin'. As we say down

here in Georgia, she's the top of the pot and the pot a bilin'. **1909** *DN* 3.383 **eAL, wGA,** *Top of the pot.* . . A person or thing of the highest value, the most excellent one. **1912** Green *VA Folk-Speech* 453, *Top-of-the-pot.* . . Applied to people of the best sort: "They go about with the top of the pot." **1946** *PADS* 6.31 **ceNC,** *Top of the pot.* . . The highest social or economic class. **1947** Ballowe *The Lawd* 38 **LA,** Even in those days Duppies were scarce over the sea, Duppies of class. The one that the chief had sent behind the slaver to wait on his boy was top-of-the-pot. *Ibid* 66, He a top-o'-the-pot in juju, whar he comed f'um. **1962** *Oshkosh Daily Northwestern* (WI) 19 Jan 6/3, A privileged few have always lived at the top of the pot, monopolizing "la Vita Dolce". **1965–70** *DARE* (Qu. II23, *Joking names for the people who are, or think they are, the best society of a community: The _____*) 9 Infs, 8 **Sth, S Midl,** Top of the pot.

2 Among whalers: the grease that rises when salt-cured meat is boiled.

1916 *DN* 4.336 **Nantucket MA,** *Top o' the pot.* . . Grease left after boiling beef. **1980** *Yankee* Jan 88 **CT,** The "slush," also called "top of the pot," was grease that was skimmed from the surface when boiling salt meat. Slush was saved in barrels for cooking, and at the end of the voyage the excess barrels of slush were sold for making soap.

top onion n Also *topper, toppy, topset (onion), topset scallion* **chiefly Nth, esp NEast** See Map Cf **onion button**

An **onion B:** usu *Allium cepa* var *cepa,* occas *A. c.* var *viviparum;* also the bulbils of such an onion. For other names of *Allium cepa* var *cepa* see **Egyptian onion, multiplying ~, tree ~, walking ~, winter ~**

1831 in 1832 *Genesee Farmer* 19 Feb 51 **wNY,** *Potato-onions* . . each onion will produce from three to six large onions, and a cluster of small ones . . resembling the top-onion seed in appearance, excepting their location being at the bottom of the stocks, instead of the top. **1852** MI *State Ag. Soc. Trans. for 1851* 3.347, *Vegetables.* . . Sample of Dutch top onion seed. **1863** Burr *Field & Garden* 139, *Top or Tree Onion.* . . Bulb large, a little flattened; producing, instead of seeds, a number of small bulbs, or onions, about the size of a filbert, which serve as a substitute for seeds in propagation. **1931–33** *LANE Worksheets* **CT,** Top onions . . scallions. **1965–70** *DARE* (Qu. I5, *. . Kind of onions that keep coming up without replanting year after year*) Infs **MI23, SD3,** Top onions; **CT4,** Egyptian or top onion; **ME5,** Top onions—onions are up on top, above ground; **NY209,** Toppies; **NJ31,** Topset scallions; (Qu. I6, *The kind of onions that come up fresh early in the year, and you eat them raw*) Infs **CT4, NY83,** Top onion(s); **NY220,** Toppies; [**VA**40, Red top—a red onion]. **1976** Bailey–Bailey *Hortus Third* 49, The Proliferum Group [=*Allium cepa* var *cepa*] includes *tree o[nion], Egyptian o., top o., Catawissa o.,* and is prop[agated] by large bulbils borne in infl[orescence]. *Ibid* 787, Other races of the same species [=*A. cepa*] are propagated asexually, as by (a) sets, (b) multipliers, (c) top sets or bulbils. . . Top set onions are little bulbils that appear in the flower cluster in the place of flowers; they are handled in the same way as sets. **1986** Pederson *LAGS Concordance,* 1 inf, **nwTN,** Green top onion—eaten raw; 1 inf, **csTX,** Green top onions. **1988** Whealy *Garden Seed Inventory* (2d ed) 255, *Egyptian Onion* (Tree Onion, Walking Onion, Top Onion, Topper, Everlasting, Egyptian Multiplier). **1990** *Seed Savers Yearbook* 147, *Egyptian.* . . A.k.a. Multiplier, Walking, Topset, Winter or Tree. **2002** *DARE* File—Internet, Top Onion. . . Interesting ornamental onion. Grows bulbs on the tips of the stalks, which eventually fall off and sprout. Does not flower.

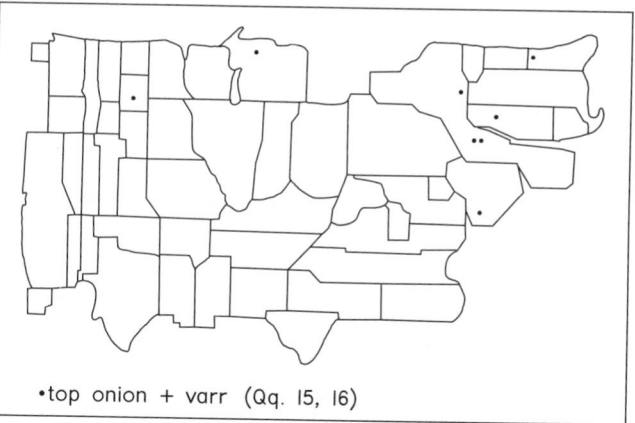

•top onion + varr (Qq. I5, I6)

top out See **top** v **1, 2, 3**

top ox See **top** n **4**

topper prep Also sp *toppuh* [Pronc-spp for *(on) top of*] *Gullah* Cf **pontop**
Upon; on.

1888 Jones *Negro Myths* 46 **GA coast** [Gullah], Now you see de jedgment wuh come topper you. In try fuh chop me head off, you cut you own foot off. *Ibid* 68, Dem wunt tell topper one anurrur. **1909** *S. Atl. Qrly.* 8.42 **seSC** [Gullah], *On, on top of, upon the top of,* become simply *top, topper, p'n top, pan tap, 'pon topper; (top of, top o').* To play on the organ is *fuh play topper oggin.* **1922** Gonzales *Black Border* 334 **sSC, GA coasts** [Gullah glossary], *'Toppuh*—on, on top of.

topper n

1 See **topping shock.**

2 A wig, toupee. Cf **hair topper**

1967–70 *DARE* (Qu. X1a, *Names . . for false hair, worn by men*) Infs **IL9, MO27, NY210,** Topper; **NE11,** Topper—in the last few years; **NJ63,** Topper, hair topper.

3 See **top onion.**

topping adj Also *toppy* **NEng** *arch*
Exhibiting a superior air; assertive, conceited.

1790 Tyler *Contrast* 36 **MA,** You a waiter! by the living jingo, you look so topping, I took you for one of the agents to Congress. **1815** Humphreys *Yankey in England* 30 **NEng,** She's lofty—topping—has her highs—sometimes. **1851** (1852) Stowe *Uncle Tom's Cabin* 2.147 **CT,** She said that she'd bring me down, and have me know, once for all, that I was n't going to be so topping as I had been. **1885** *Harper's New Mth. Mag.* 70.595 **NEng,** He was awful toppin' at first. **1902** (1904) Rowe *Maid of Bar Harbor* 311 **ME,** She's been so toppin' sense she got back that you can't touch 'er with a ten-foot pole. Thinks she's head an' shoulders above good, nice, stay-at-home girls. **1908** Wasson *Home from Sea* 227 **sME coast,** Them folks over there to the office has been gittin' too blame' toppy and independent like of late.

topping n Also *top taste*
Dessert; a dessert.

1926 *AmSp* 1.653 [Hobo lingo], *Toppings*—pastry or cakes. **1927** *AmSp* 2.389 [Vagabond argot], *Toppings* refers to pastry, because it is used to top off a meal. **1944** *AmSp* 19.103 [Vocab of sailors], *Toppings* are dessert, or any bakery stuff. **1986** Pederson *LAGS Concordance,* 1 inf, **AL,** For pudding he would say topping; 1 inf, **MS,** Dessert, topping. **1991** *DARE* File **KS,** When I was growing up we had a neighbor who was originally from Kansas. If a meal had not included dessert, she still had to finish with a bit of something sweet—maybe just bread and jelly—for "top taste."

topping off See **top** v **1, 2**

topping out See **top** v **1**

topping shock n Also *topper* Cf **top** v phr **2**

1965–70 *DARE* (Qu. L31, *. . The top bundle of a shock*) Infs **AL11, 43, IL29, 59, MN2, TN31, 34, 35,** Topping shock; **CO19, NC36,** Topper.

topple n [By metath from **talpa**]

1969 *DARE* (Qu. P6, *. . Kinds of worms . . used for bait*) Inf **IL67,** Topple worms—worms that are found in topple [=**catalpa**] trees.

toppuh See **topper** prep

toppy adj See **topping** adj

toppy n See **top onion**

top screw n **West** Also called **top waddy** Cf **screw** n **2**
The foreman of a group of cowboys.

1920 Hunter *Trail Drivers TX* 298, The leader of any particular bunch of men is called the "boss," his first lieutenant is called the "straw boss," or right-hand man, sometimes called the "top screw" or "top waddy." **1927** *Daily Northwestern* (Oshkosh WI) 24 Sept 2/3 **TX,** A "top screw" is a ranch hand who has been on the ranch for years and knows the business of that particular ranch from top to bottom. **1933** *AmSp* 8.1.30 **nwTX** [Ranch diction], *Top-screw.* Man in charge of a detail of cowboys. **c1937** in Lib. of Congress *Amer. Memory: WPA Life Hist.* (Internet) **TX** (as of c1868), Soon as the waddies finished the job of lining their flue, the top-screw would yell, 'ride you rawhides.' **1941** Writers' Program *Guide WY* 459, *Big boss*—the owner of a cattle outfit. His first lieutenant is called the 'right-hand man,' sometimes 'the top screw.' **1942** [see **top waddy**].

topset (onion), topset scallion   See **top onion**

topside adj, adv   [Transf from nautical *topside* on deck]
Upstairs.
  1914 *DN* 4.164 **NW**, *Topside, adv.* Upstairs.   **1960** Bailey *Resp. to PADS 20* **KS**, Upstairs. . . "Topside" is used by Navy people, but such personnel, from enlisted men to a lieut[enant], a captain and an admiral are close relatives of mine and their families do not say "topside."   **1969** *Cape Cod Std.–Times* (Hyannis MA) 22 Jan 28/8, West Hyannis Port. 2 *bedroom* Cape, living room with fireplace, expansion topside.   **1972** *Oakland Tribune* (CA) 13 Aug sec C [21]/2 (newspaperarchive.com), [Advt:] 1 little topside walk-up studio $130.   **1983** *Capital* (Annapolis MD) 3 Sept 28/5, [Advt:] 2 bedrooms topside are spacious.

topside of earth n
In phr *on topside of earth* and varr: On earth, in creation.
  1868 *Weekly GA Telegraph* (Macon) 24 Jan 4/6, He [=a greenhorn] might be gobbled up by some of the horned beasts as the greenest thing on the top side of earth.   **1886** *Century Illustr. Mag.* 31.434 **nGA**, What upon the top side er the yeth ails you?   **1892** *KS Univ. Qrly.* 1.100 **KS**, *Topside:* on top of, as in, The best man topside o' God's green earth. [**1924** in 1943 Wolfe *Letters Mother* 71 **NC**, [Asheville was] the greatest place upon the top of the earth, in which to live.]   c**1950** Halpert Coll. 64 **wKY, nwTN**, He will believe anything you tell him on topside of earth.

top smelt n
A **silversides 1** (here: *Atherinops affinis*).
  1892 U.S. Bur. Fisheries *Rept. for 1888* app 25 **swCA**, Of the two species of smelt, *A[therinops] californiensis* is locally known as the "bottom smelt." . . The other (*A. affinis*), [is] called the "top smelt."   **1953** Roedel *Common Fishes CA* 77, *Topsmelt—Atherinops affinis.* . . Common inshore fishes which enter brackish and even fresh water.   **1955** Zim–Shoemaker *Fishes* 82, *Topsmelt* and *Jacksmelt* are actually silversides, not Smelts.   **2002** (acc) CA Dept. Fish & Game *San Francisco Bay Fish List* (Internet), Topsmelt range from Vancouver Island, British Columbia to the Gulf of California. Topsmelt are a pelagic, schooling species found in shallow bays, estuaries, sloughs and kelpbeds.

top steer   See **top** n 4

topsy stove n   chiefly **KS, NE**
A small stove with an overhanging top.
  1908 *NE State Jrl.* (Lincoln) 12 Dec sec A 7/6, For Sale—Topsy stove, oven and pipe, $5.   **1914** *DN* 4.114 **cKS**, *Topsy-stove.* . . A heater with two holes on top for cooking.   **1946** *NE State Jrl.* (Lincoln) 8 Feb 1/1, Fire thought to have originated from an overheated topsy stove . . gutted the room.   **1981** Stratton *Pioneer Women* 164 **KS** (as of 1888), A little Topsy Stove, on which the bachelor claim holder had baked his morning flap-jacks, was the final piece of furniture.   **2005** *DARE* File—Internet **NE** (as of 1918), They fixed a stove pipe . . so we could use a little "Topsy Stove" for cooking. The stove had 4 stove lids and a small fire box for fuel. *Ibid* **KS** (as of 1897), The wagon was complete with a four-lid topsy stove andd [*sic*] a bake oven in the stovepipe.

topsy-turvy bird n   [See quots]
=**nuthatch.**
  1918 (1927) Chapman *Our Winter Birds* 30, Nuthatches—The Topsy-turvy Birds.   **1929** Forbush *Birds MA* 3.356, *White-breasted Nuthatch.* *Other names* . . topsy-turvy-bird. . . Creeps up and down the trunks and limbs of trees, often head downward. *Ibid* 361, *Red-breasted Nuthatch.* . . Topsy-turvy bird. . . Moves up or down a tree trunk head first; a very nimble, active, nervous bird.   **1946** Hausman *Eastern Birds* 433, *White-breasted Nuthatch.* . . Topsy-turvy Bird. . . Crawls about on tree trunks and the larger branches, mouselike, head upward or downward.   **1956** MA Audubon Soc. *Bulletin* 40.127 **MA**, *White-breasted Nuthatch.* . . Topsy-turvy Bird. . . *Red-breasted Nuthatch.* . . Topsy-turvy Bird.

top tall timber   See **top timber**

top taste   See **topping** n

top the brush v phr   Cf **top cotton**
See quot.
  1953 Randolph–Wilson *Down in Holler* 169 **Ozarks**, "Pore Andy sure did top the brush gettin' away from there," said one of the bystanders,

who laughed till the tears rolled down his face. To top the brush is to leap or run through undergrowth, as a deer does sometimes.

top the cotton   See **top cotton**

top timber v phr   Also *top tall timber, ~ the trees*   Cf **top cotton**
To make a commotion, "blow one's top."
  1965–70 *DARE* (Qu. KK11, *To make great objections or a big fuss about something: "When we asked him to do that, he _____."*) Inf **AR**56, Topped tall timber; **MS**30, Topped timber; **NY**83, Topped the trees.

top up   See **top** v 2

top waddy n   Cf **waddy 1a**
=**top screw.**
  1902 *Out West Mag.* 17.446, He had worked his way up the cowboy's painful promotion. He had been night-wrangler, day-herder, bog-rider, water-mason, full hand, bronco buster, outside man—and now he was "top waddy"—or, if one wanted to be disrespectful, "straw boss."   **1920** [see **top screw**].   **1942** *AmSp* 17.75 **NE**, The boss is the ranch foreman or manager. . . The assistant to the manager is the *straw boss, top screw,* or *top waddie.*

topwater n
1 also *topwater minnow:* A small fish such as a **killifish 1**, a **mosquito fish**, or a **silversides 1** (here: *Labidesthes sicculus*); also fig.   chiefly **Missip Valley**   Cf **topminnow**
  1854 Wailes *Rept. on Ag. & Geol. MS* 335, *Zygonectes olivaceus* [= *Fundulus o.*] . . Top water.   **1906** Johnson *Highways Missip. Valley* 119 **AR**, They told me about . . "the little topwaters, which stay near the surface and take your bait."   **1929** Sale *Tree Named John* 72 **MS** [Black], You swolly dis'n. Ef you swolly a li'l un, you'll jes swim lak a li'l ole pyetch or a topwater.   **1953** Randolph–Wilson *Down in Holler* 293 **Ozarks**, *Top-water.* . . A little minnow (*Gambusia affinis*) which swims on the surface, eats mosquito larvae, and brings forth its young alive. The word is applied humorously to teen-age youngsters of either sex. Spider Rowland (*Arkansas Gazette,* June 23, 1948) uses *top-waters* to mean small-timers, second-raters.   **1954** Harder Coll. **cwTN**, *Top-water.* . . A small fish (*Gambusia affinis*).   **1965–67** *DARE* (Qu. P7, *Small fish used as bait for bigger fish*) Inf **TX**19, Topwaters; **FL**17, Topwater minnows.   **1985** *New Yorker* 3 June 81 **KY**, See these little minnows? It looks like they've got one eye on the top of their heads. They're called topwaters.   **2002** *DARE* File—Internet **MO**, The golden topwater minnow that was previously thought absent from Missouri was encountered in an upper reach of the St. James Ditch.
2 A **water strider.**
  1954 Harder Coll. **cwTN**, *Topwater.* . . A small water insect that zigs and zags on the surface of the water.

topwater minnow   See **topwater 1**

toque   See **tuque**

tor   See **taw**

torbarker   See **tobacco** n A1

torch v, hence vbl n *torching*   **scattered, but esp ME**   Cf **flounder** v[1], **shine** v, **strike** v B1
To catch (fish or rarely turtles) at night with the aid of a light; to fish in such a way.
  1839 MA Zool. & Bot. Surv. *Fishes Reptiles* 111, [The] scarcity [of herring] has been attributed by the fishermen to *torching* them at night.   **1887** Goode *Fisheries U.S.* 2.503 **SC, GA**, As the fisheries have declined a method known as "torching" has been extensively adopted by the negroes of the locality, who visit the sandy beaches at night with large fire-brands, and catch the terrapin as they crawl out on the sand to deposit their eggs.   **1900** *Daily Herald* (Delphos OH) [22 Feb 2]/5 (newspaperarchive.com), The preparation for torching was simple . . a pole with a grate attached was lashed across the bow and the grate filled with cotton, over which was poured petroleum. . . As soon as they got into shoal water the torch was lighted, and . . the man in the bow stood ready to dip when the fish came to the surface in response to the light.   **1932** Wasson *Sailing Days* 116 **cME coast**, "Torching" herring by night was a common way of taking the little fish.   **1965** *Down East* Oct 18 **ME**, [Title:] Torching Herring by the Dark of the Moon.   **1975** Gould *ME Lingo* 295, *Torching* is fishing at night with flares that attract herring.   **2004** *Natl. Fisherman* Sept 6 **ME** (as of 1954), Annie C. of Kennebunkport is the only boat *torching herring* along the Maine

coast. . . Years back many Mainers torched herring, but today it is legal only for catching bait. **2005** (acc) *ESPN Outdoors* (Internet) **Lake Erie,** Torching involved mounting two large Coleman lanterns on the stern of a flat-bottom rowboat and venturing out after dark with one guy in the bow poling the boat along and another standing up in the stern with a big spear on a 10-foot handle at the ready.

torch n   See **torch cactus 2**

torch cactus n

1   A **cactus** n[1] **B1** of the genus *Cereus.*
[**1731–33** Miller *Gard. Dict.* s.v. *Cereus (OED2),* The Torch-Thistle. Call'd Cereus, because it is, as it were, a kind of taper or torch . . because when these plants have been cut down and dry'd upon the ground, they dip them into oil, and burn them as torches.] **1897** *Lippincott's Mth. Mag.* 409 **seCA,** You may ride through orchards of the torch cactus, its thick trunk supporting bare arms, jointed by like bare perpendicular branches. **1925** Jepson *Manual Plants CA* 658, *Cereus. . . Torch Cactus. . .* (Latin cereus, waxen, referring to the candle-like stem of some species.) **1942** Hylander *Plant Life* 316, A most distinguished group is that of the Torch Cacti which includes the Night Blooming Cereus and the giant Sahuaro. [DARE Ed: The latter is no longer included in the genus *Cereus.*]
2   also *torch:* A **hedgehog cactus 3** (here: either *Echinocereus engelmannii* or *E. viridiflorus*).
1949 Curtin *By the Prophet* 57 **AZ,** *Echinocereus engelmannii. . .* Torch Cactus. . . The blossoms are a brilliant rose-purple, averaging three inches in diameter, and are very showy. **1967** Dodge *Roadside Wildflowers* 44, The green-flowered torch is a small, inconspicuous representative of . . the cactuses. . . Green torch belongs to the group called strawberry cactuses. . . *Echinocereus viridiflorus.* **1973** *AZ Highways* Mar 39, Whether you call them Strawberry Hedgehog, Calico Hedgehog, or Purple Torch *(Echinocereus engelmannii),* everyone finds the blossoms most attractive and delicate. **2002** *DARE* File—Internet **NM,** Cacti are represented by prickly pear, candelabra cholla and dagger cholla, and the green-flowered torch cactus.

torches   See **torchweed 2**

torch flower n

1   A **prairie smoke 1** (here: *Geum triflorum*).
1844 Fuller *Summer Lakes* 63, An elegance . . as different . . as that of the prairie torch-flower from the shopworn article that touches the cheek of that lady within her bonnet. **1863** *Atlantic Mth.* 11.344, Mr. Wharton kissed the bride, and said to the bridegroom,—"She is handsome as a wild tulip." "Bright as the torch-flower of the prairies," added Uncle George. **1950** Stevens *ND Plants* 171, *Geum triflorum. . . Torch Flower. . .* Fruiting head erect, plumes 2–6 cm. long, delicate, bronze or purplish. **1956** in 1969 *DARE* File **swMN** [Flora of Pipestone Natl. Monument], Torch Flower (Avens) (Prairie Smoke) Geum triflorum. **1995** Kantrud *Native Wildflowers ND* (Internet), Also called "torch flower," "maidenhair," "prairie smoke," and "old mans [sic] beard," purple avens is common on native prairies in all but extreme south central North Dakota. . . The distinctive appearance of the plant is due to the styles . . , which greatly elongate in fruit to form purplish-bronze plumes nearly three inches long.
2   An **Oswego tea** (here: *Monarda didyma*).
1966 *DARE* Wildfl QR Pl.189 Inf **TX34,** Torch flower.

torching   See **torch** v

torch pine n **Sth** Cf **ocote**

1   =**pitch pine a(1).**
1890 *Century Dict.* 4496, *Pitch-pine. . .* In America, *Pinus rigida,* a moderate tree of stiff habit, found from New Brunswick to Georgia. . . Also called *torch pine.* **1908** Britton *N. Amer. Trees* 31, It [=*Pinus rigida*] is known by many names, such as . . Torch pine. **1950** Peattie *Nat. Hist. Trees* 20, *Pinus rigida. . .* Black, Torch, or Sap Pine. **2002** *DARE* File—Internet, *Pinus rigida. . .* southern pine, black pine, torch pine. . . High resin content in this species produced the name "pitch pine". Early American settlers would often ignite pine knots for torches.
2   =**loblolly pine 1.**
1878 *Amer. Pharmaceutical Assoc. Proc.* 26.318, *Botanical Synonyms of Pinus taeda. . .* In America, White Pine . . , Torch Pine [etc]. **1896** Mohr–Roth *Timber Pines* 106, *Pinus taeda. . .* Torch Pine. **1908** Rogers *Tree Book* 35, There is probably no pine tree that has more nicknames than this [=*Pinus taeda*]. . . "Sap," "frankincense" and "torch pine" mean that it is rich in resin. **1960** Vines *Trees SW* 22, Loblolly

Pine. . . Other vernacular names are . . Torch Pine [etc]. **2002** *DARE* File—Internet, *Pinus taeda. . .* Torch pine.
3   The wood of **1** or **2** above or a similar **pine 1** used either as kindling or as a torch; see quots.
1925 in 2002 *DARE* File—Internet **TX** (as of 1862), We had to supply a good supply of pitch pine for torches. It was dark as midnight in the cave. . . By this time our torch pine was nearly exhausted. **1929** *Ibid* **GA,** Then the boys. . . would build a fire in the woods and camp while the dogs trailed the opossum, coons, fox, others or whatever the dogs happened to scent. Sometimes they would have to cut down two or three trees. They always carried an ax and plenty of torch pine. **1934** Vines *Green Thicket* 15 **cnAL,** Even Asbury forgot that he wanted to be at home in bed and was ever at hand with torch pine and tow sack.

torchweed n

1   =**snakeweed b(6)** (here: *Gutierrezia* spp). [See quot 1924]
1907 *Amer. Anthro. Assoc. Memoirs* 2.334 **UT,** The torchweed, *Gutierrezia,* abounds almost everywhere. **1924** *Amer. Botanist* 30.33, *Gutierrezia. . .* The common name all over the west . . is "torchweed" or "matchweed", not as one might suppose from the abundance of bright yellow flowers but from the readiness with which the dry stems and resinous buds burn in the spring.
2   also *torches:* A **mullein,** usu *Verbascum thapsus.* [Cf *OED2 torch-weed* (at *torch* sb. 3) 1706]
1900 Lyons *Plant Names* 389, *V[erbascum] Thapsus. . .* Torches. **1904** Henkel *Weeds Used in Med.* 24, *Mullein. . . Other common names. . .* Torches. **1935** (1943) Muenscher *Weeds* 420, *Verbascum Thapsus. . .* Torches. . . Widespread throughout the United States and southern Canada. **1947** Curtin *Healing Herbs* 166, *Verbascum thapsus. . .* Torch Weed. [*Ibid* 167, The early Greeks and Romans made lampwicks from the dried mullein stalks by dipping them in tallow, and it may have been through remembrance of this Roman custom that . . the English [named the plant] torchweed.] **1974** Morton *Folk Remedies* 155 **SC,** *Torchweed; candlewick; flannel leaf. . .* Flowers fragrant, yellow, . . in erect, dense, club-shaped spike.

torchwood n **esp FL**
A shrub or tree of the genus *Amyris* or its wood.   Also called **candlewood 2;** for other names of var spp see **gum elemi 2**
1833 *Niles' Weekly Reg.* 44.394 **FL,** The torchwood tree . . burns bright like lightwood; and in combustion emits a pleasant odour resembling frankincense. **1884** Sargent *Forests of N. Amer.* 33, *Amyris sylvatica* [=*A. elemifera*]. . . Torch Wood. . . Wood very heavy, exceedingly hard and strong, close-grained, compact, resinous. **1897** Sudworth *Arborescent Flora* 267 **FL,** *Amyris Elemifera. . . Common Name.* Torchwood. **1908** Britton *N. Amer. Trees* 575, *Torchwood—Amyris elemifera. . . Balsam Torchwood—Amyris balsamifera. . .* The wood is similar to the preceding species, and its branches are also used for torches. **1938** FWP *U.S. One* 292 **FL,** *Big Torch Key . .* was so named because of the quantity of torchwood on the island. **1960** Vines *Trees SW* 577, The genus name, *Amyris,* refers to the balsamic properties of the genus. . . The name Torchwood was given because the wood ignites easily. **1996** *Audubon Mag.* Nov–Dec 58 **FL,** Emmel's research team placed 760 pupae near torchwood and wild trees . . at seven different sites.

tord v[1]   See **tear B2b**

tord v[2]   See **tire** v

tords   See **toward A**

tore v   See **tear B2a**

tore n[1]   See **taw**

tore n[2]   See **store** n

tore n[3]   See **tour**

toreckly, torectly   See **directly**

tored   See **tear B1, 2b**

tore-down(dest)   See **torn down 1**

toren   See **tear B2b**

torenament   See **tournament**

tore out   See **torn out**

tore up adj phr   See **torn up** adj phr

tore up ppl adj phr   See **tear up** v phr **3**

torge   See **towards A**

to rights adv phr   [*OED2* (at *right* sb.¹ 14.b) 1663 →]   **chiefly NEng** *obs*
Immediately, at once.
   1795 Dearborn *Columbian Grammar* 139, *List of Improprieties. . .* T'writes for Immediately. **1815** Humphreys *Yankey in England* 109, *To-rights,* immediately, instantly. **1829** Kirkham *Engl. Grammar* 192, *New-England. . .* He'll be here, derights. **1835** *Amer. Mth. Mag.* 4.327 **Long Is NY,** T'rights the old man felt the skiff shaken under 'im. **1850** Herbert *Warwick Woodlands* 187 **seNY,** Take a drink, Frank, and you'll feel slick as silk torights, I tell you. **1896** *Harper's New Mth. Mag.* 93.563 **NEng,** Now don't beat about the bush; the men folks'll be back torights. **1903** *DN* 2.300 **Cape Cod MA** (as of a1857), 'To rights,' directly, presently. When the pig was killed it was said, 'If you eat the liver you'll live forever, if you eat the lights, you'll die to rights.'

torkle   See **turtle**

torlet   See **toilet 2**

torment n   **chiefly Sth, S Midl**   See Map
Used as a euphem for *hell.*
   1823 *Baptist Missionary Mag.* 4.302, If I die—Well, I must go to torment. **1851** (1852) Stowe *Uncle Tom's Cabin* 1.310 [Black], I knows I'm gwine to torment. . . I's gwine straight to torment. **1917** *Stevens Point Daily Jrl.* (WI) 26 May 3/5 **AR,** What in torment is going on over there? **1954** *Harder Coll.* **cwTN,** Torment . . for *hell* or *devil.* **1965–70** *DARE* (Qu. CC9, *. . Words or expressions for hell: "That man is headed straight for ____."*) 105 Infs, **chiefly Sth, S Midl,** Torment; **IL**14, Torment—we don't say it much now; **NJ**68, Torment—that's a Southern expression; [**KY**10, Everlasting torment; **OK**42, Place of torment;] (Qu. NN26b, *Weakened substitutes for 'hell': "Go to ____!"*) 12 Infs, 11 **Sth, S Midl,** Torment; (Qu. NN26a, *Weakened substitutes for 'hell': "Oh ____!"*) Infs **GA**3, 28, **MS**1, Torment. **1986** Pederson *LAGS Concordance,* 1 inf, **neAL,** Torment—hell.

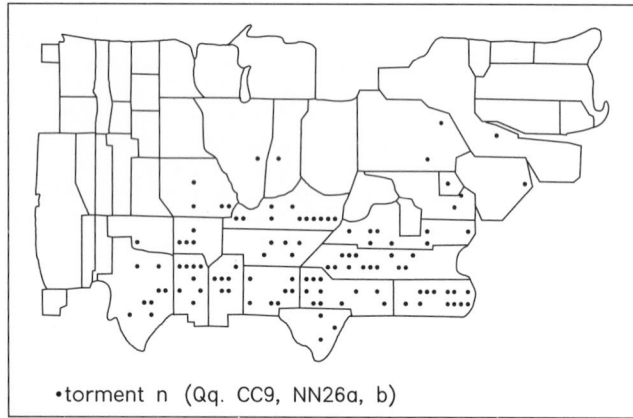

•torment n (Qq. CC9, NN26a, b)

torment v
Used as a euphem for *damn;* hence adj, adv **tormented.**
   1825 Neal *Brother Jonathan* 1.138 **CT,** They hadn't come sich a tormented long piece. **1867** Lowell *Biglow* lix **'Upcountry' MA,** *Tormented:* euphemism for damned, as, "not a tormented cent." *Ibid* 240, Then dogs an' shepherds, after much hard dammin',/ . . Turned tu an' give 'em [=wolves] a tormented lammin'. **1924** *DN* 5.278 [Exclams], Torment it, torment the luck. **1938** Rawlings *Yearling* 179 **FL,** He's so tormented black. Ezra, he's black as a buzzard. **1943** *LANE* Map 599 *(Damn it!)* 3 infs, **sME, neNH,** Torment it. **1950** *WELS* **WI** *(Something that keeps on annoying you . . "That ____ clock has stopped again!")* 1 Inf, Tormented; *(What do you say about a person who enjoys dressing up, or who spends too much on clothes?)* 1 Inf, Stylish, tormented nice. **1967** *DARE* (Qu. LL37, *To make a statement as strong as you can: "I could have wrung her neck, I was so ____ mad."*) Inf **MI**66, Tormented.

torn   See **tear B1**

tornament   See **tournament**

torn down adj phr   Superl *torn-downdest*   **chiefly Sth, S Midl**

1 also *tore down* (superl *tore downdest*): Dissolute, disreputable, unruly, wild; hence adv phr *torn down* violently, very. [Scots, Engl dial]
   1836 Thomas *East & West* 131, They say that old Beckford is a torn down miser. *Ibid* 223, I'm in a torn down hurry. **1861** Adams *Sable Cloud* 94 **Sth,** He is what we call a torn-down character. **1866** Trowbridge *South* 315 **TN,** They was a torn-down bad set of men; bad as the Rebs. **1872** U.S. Congress *Rept. Joint Select Comm. Insurrectionary States* 12.812 **neMS** [Black], *Question.* Did these men pass for respectable young men? *Answer.* No, sir. Whitfield, there nobody didn't like him. He has always been a torn-down man. **1891** Johnston *Primes & Neighbors* 24 **GA,** Mr. Sprowls was not very much of what people called a "reg'lar-built, tore-down cusser." **1899** (1912) Green *VA Folk-Speech* 454, *Torn-down. . .* Rough; violent; turbulent[;] rebellious; ungovernable; hence, overpowering of its kind. **1903** *DN* 2.335 **seMO,** *Torn-down. . .* Violent. 'He is a torn-down fellow when he is drinking and everybody is afraid of him.' **1913** Kephart *Highlanders* 169 **sAppalachians,** "How about the revenue officers? What sort of men are they?" "Torn down scoundrels, every one." **1923** *DN* 5.223 **swMO,** He's the torn downdest fool on airth. **1933** Williamson *Woods Colt* 213 **Ozarks,** Joe Darby is the tore-downdest danged turkey hunter between hell an' breakfast. **1944** *PADS* 2.31 **eKY, nSC,** *Torn-down. . .* Mischievous. "What can a body do with a gang of torn-down younguns under her feet?" *Ibid* 50 **NC, SC,** I was one of the torn downdest tomboys you ever heard of. **1986** Pederson *LAGS Concordance,* 1 inf, **neTN,** A torn-down good time—a riproaring good time; 1 inf, **swGA,** Torn-down good time. **1995–97** in 2004 Montgomery–Hall *Dict. Smoky Mt. Engl.* 597 **wNC, eTN,** She ain't nothing but a tore-down woman [Montgomery: =morally bankrupt].
2 Run down, dilapidated.   Cf **-est** suff **1b**
   1916 *DN* 4.294 **sAppalachians,** The following phrase compounds are found . . *torn-downdest* fence [etc]. **1919** *DN* 5.32 **seKY,** That's the torn-downdest ole shack of a house aroun' here. **1926** Roberts *Time of Man* 107 **cKY,** She herself lived in the torn-downdest place you'd ever see, just a plumb shanty. **1974** Fink *Mountain Speech* 27 **wNC, eTN,** That's the torn-downdest house I ever seen.

tornillo n   Also *tornilla*   [MexSpan *tornillo* < Span *tornillo* screw]
=**screw bean** or its fruit; hence n *tornial* a thicket of this plant.
   1844 Gregg *Commerce* 2.78 **TX,** In the immediate vicinity of El Paso there is another small growth called *tornillo* (or screw-wood), so denominated from a spiral pericarp, which, though different in shape, resembles that of the *mezquite* in flavor. **1847** (1973) Ruxton *Advent. Rocky Mts.* 174 **sNM, nwTX,** The mezquite is now becoming scarce, the tornilla or screw-wood taking its place. **1873** Arny *Interesting NM* 21, Pecan and walnut with considerable hackberry, mezquit, manzanilla and tornillo, were found. **1892** *DN* 1.195 **TX,** *Tornillo:* a tree or large shrub closely related to the *mesquite. . .* The beans are used as food by men and animals *(Prosopis pubescens).* **1945** Thorp *Pardner* 259 **SW,** These thickets were of two kinds. In one, the brush was mostly mesquite and catclaw. Such thickets were called the *matorral.* In another, the prevailing brush was the *tornillo,* and these thickets were known as the tornial. **1970** Correll *Plants TX* 784, *Prosopis pubescens. . .* Screwbean, tornillo. . . Pod 25–50 mm. long overall but tightly spirally coiled. . . *Prosopis reptans. . .* Tornillo. . . Pod 15–37 mm. long overall but tightly spirally coiled. **1985** Dodge *Flowers SW Deserts* 85, Tornillo. . . *Prosopis pubescens.*

torn out adj phr   Also freq *tore out*   **esp NEng**
=**torn up 1.**
   1903 Wasson *Cap'n Simeon's Store* 251 **ME,** Wal, don't go to work and keep us all tore out that way, Job. . . Out with it, and let 's we know the wust right off! **1921** *Med. Pickwick* 7.17 **VT,** 'Doesn't it bring feelings of gratitude to your heart that God made this world so lovely?' Her eyes was a-shinin' and her voice almost broke she was that tore out about it. **1941** *LANE* Map 476–77 *(Excited, all nerved up)* 1 inf, **seVT,** All tore out; 1 inf, **neMA,** Tore out. *Ibid* Map 472 *(Angry)* 1 inf, **cwNH,** Tore out. **1950** Moore *Candlemas Bay* 240 **ME,** Jeb, poor lamb, he was so tore out about you that he never said nothing. **1969** *DARE* (Qu. GG6, *Talking about a person's feelings being hurt: "When she said she wouldn't go with him, he was quite ____."*) Inf **MA**58, All tore out (or up); (Qu. GG7, *. . Annoyed or upset: "Though we were only ten minutes late, she was all ____."*) Inf **MA**58, Tore up (or out); **VT**12, Tore out. **2003** in 2004 *DARE* File—Internet **GA,** I *really*

need to go get a different job . . before I'm so torn out and bitter I can't stand to do anything.

torn up adj phr   Also freq *tore up*   [**tear up** v phr **5**]

1   In an emotionally aroused state; excited, upset, troubled. **chiefly Sth, S Midl**   See Map   Cf **torn out**

   1855 *Coshocton Age* (OH) 4 Aug [2]/2 (newspaperarchive.com), The Democracy of Ohio, like the Pennsylvanian's mind, seems to be all "torn up." **1867** (1868) Meline *2000 Miles* 63 **KY**, The entire bed of the stream [is] in the condition of the Kentuckian who was "uneasy in his mind." It was all "tore up." **1887** (1967) Harris *Free Joe* 191 **ceGA**, Sometimes, when I git tore up in my mind, and begin to think that every thing's wrong-end foremost, I jess think of Hallie Garwood. **1889** *Union Pacific Employes' Mag.* 4.347 **WI**, I will add for the benefit of those "all tore up" on base ball that every quarter of the United States does not . . [so enthusiastically support] the National game. **1895** *Harper's New Mth. Mag.* 91.623 **NYC**, Never mind if your heart's broke, or if a man hits you—never mind if you're all tore up an' crazy— you must talk as if your mouth was chuck full of butter. **1925** Dargan *Highland Annals* 264 **wNC**, He said there wuzn't anybody to blame but him, an' it 'ud kill Ann to be disgraced, which wuz what he ortn't 'a' said to Lu, but Nathe wuz so tore up I reckon he couldn't think o' pickin' his way. **1940** (1968) Haun *Hawk's Done Gone* 107 **eTN**, I was so tore up I didn't care what washed away. I made up my mind to pull myself together. **1965–70** *DARE* (Qu. GG2, . . *'Confused, mixed up':* "So many things were going on at the same time that he got completely _____.") Inf **CA**110, Tore up; (Qu. GG4, *Stirred up, angry:* "When he saw them coming he got _____.") Infs **KY**70, **SC**34, Tore up; (Qu. GG6, *Talking about a person's feelings being hurt:* "When she said she wouldn't go with him, he was quite _____.") Inf **MA**58, All tore out (*or* up); **TX**81, Torn up; (Qu. GG7, . . *Annoyed or upset:* "Though we were only ten minutes late, she was all _____.") Inf **GA**74, Torn up; **TN**26, Tore up; **MA**58, Tore up (*or* out); (Qu. GG11, *To be quite anxious about something* . . "The letter hasn't come and he's _____.") Inf **GA**72, Tore up; (Qu. GG13a, *When something keeps bothering a person and makes him nervous* . . "It _____ me.") Inf **OK**6, Gets me tore up; (Qu. GG33a, *To feel very sad and upset about something:* "When he got the news he was _____."; total Infs questioned, 75) Infs **AR**31, **MS**71, (All) torn up; **FL**14, Really tore up; (Qu. GG33b, *To feel very sad and upset about something:* "I never saw a woman _____ so."; total Infs questioned, 75) Infs **FL**38, **NM**9, (So) torn up. **1985** Edgerton *Raney* 12 **NC**, I said: (now I was really tore up) "Charles, I have told you for months about the condition Uncle Nate has put our family in with alcohol . . and here you are, drunk." **2001** in 2004 *DARE* File—Internet **NC**, I have never in my life been so tore up over anything all I could see was horns, my heart was beating so loud I could hear it and I was shaking like a dog crapping persimmon seeds. **2004** *Ibid* **eTN**, I said, "no sweat, no need to get all tore up about it, just come get it tomorrow."

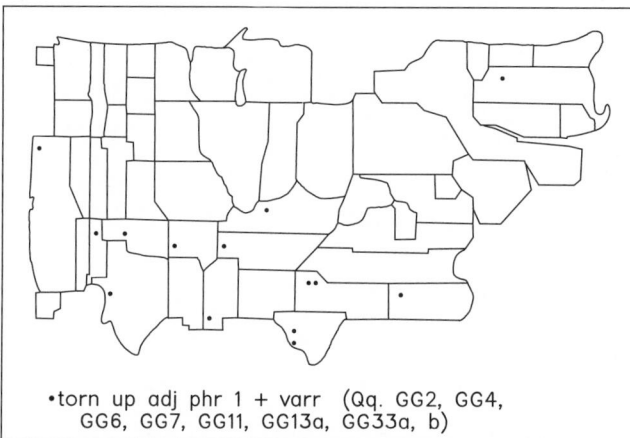

   •torn up adj phr 1 + varr (Qq. GG2, GG4, GG6, GG7, GG11, GG13a, GG33a, b)

2   Drunk.   *chiefly among Black speakers*

   1968 *Current Slang* 3.2.49 [Watts slang; Black], *Tore up*. . . Drunk, intoxicated.—He got *tore up* at that party. **1970** *Ibid* 5.2.14 [Black Univ student slang], *Tore up*. . . Intoxicated. **1970** *DARE* (Qu. DD15, *A person who is thoroughly drunk*) Infs **NY**249, **VA**39, Tore up. [Both Infs Black] **1971** Roberts *Third Ear* np [Black], *Toe (torn) up*. . . completely intoxicated. *Syn*. wasted. **1998** *Columbus Dispatch* (OH) 18

Nov sec C 3/2 [Black], I sat on my porch and drank that brandy and got tore up. **2003** *DARE* File—Internet **TX**, I love the Continental Club, but can never afford to actually get all tore up there.

torn up ppl adj   See **tear up** v phr **1, 3**

toro n   [Span *toro*, perh in New England and Louisiana also Fr *taureau*, bull]

1   A bull; formerly also a bull bison.

a   In general use.   **esp TX**   See Map

   1892 *DN* 1.195 **TX**, *Tóro*: a bull, buffalo bull. **1896** *DN* 1.426 **NY**, *Toro*: a bull. St. Lawrence Co. **1909** *DN* 3.418 **nME**, *Toro*. . . A bull. **1939** *LANE* Map 190 *(Bull)* 5 infs, **VT, NH, MA**, Toro. **1941** *AmSp* 16.265 **CA** (as of 1857) [Span words used in Engl], *Toro*, Bull. **1946** in 1958 Brewer *Dog Ghosts* 56 **TX** [Black], Y'all oughta see dat fine red toro mah boss-man got; he de onlies' red toro Ah done evuh seed. **1962** Atwood *Vocab. TX* 57, *Male bovine (with original equipment)*. . . A Southwest Texas word which still has a limited currency is *toro*. **1966–69** *DARE* (Qu. K22, *Words used for a bull*) Infs **TX**4, 6, 22, Toro; **CA**23, **NY**32, **TX**102, Toro [laughter]; **NM**3, **TX**66, Toro—Mexican. **1986** Pederson *LAGS Concordance (Bull)* 8 Infs, **FL, GA, LA, TX**, Toro. [*DARE* Ed: Of these infs, three spoke Spanish and one spoke French.]

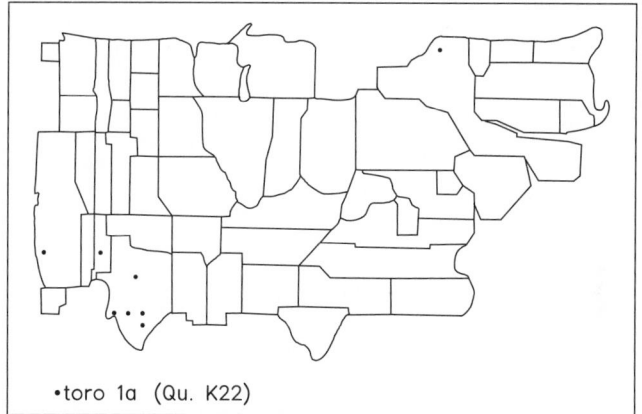

   •toro 1a (Qu. K22)

b   Used as a euphem.   **esp VT, NH**

   1889 Robinson *Sam Lovel's Camps* 4 **VT**, A bull, when not a "toro," is as politely called a "crutter." **1939** *LANE* Map 190 *(Bull)* 15 infs, **VT**, 7 infs, **NH**, 1 inf, **ME**, Toro [as euphem]. **1967** *DARE* (Qu. K23, *Words used by women or in mixed company for a bull*) Infs **TX**4, 37, (Old) toro. **1986** Pederson *LAGS Concordance (Bull)* 1 inf, **GA**, Toro—what the ladies would call him.

2   A **crevalle a** (here: *Caranx hippos*).

   1896 U.S. Natl. Museum *Bulletin* 47.920, *Caranx hippos*. . . Crevallé; *Toro*. . . Head large and deep. Mouth large, low. . . A large and well-known food fish. **1935** Caine *Game Fish* 59, *Caranx hippos*. . . Skipjack[s] Toro. **1972** Sparano *Outdoors Encycl.* 377, *Jack Crevalle—Common names* . . jack, toro. . . The crevalle is short, husky, and slab-sided. **2000** in 2002 *DARE* File—Internet **CA**, We can see him [=a fish] as he circles and he appears to be a large "Toro" (Crevalle).

3   =**cowfish 1**.

   1898 U.S. Natl. Museum *Bulletin* 47.1724, *Lactophrys quadricornis* [=*Acanthostracion q*.] . . *Toro*; *Cow-fish*. . . A stout spine directed forward over each eye. . . Very common from Carolina to Brazil, ranging northward in the Gulf Stream to Charleston and Chesapeake Bay.

torop(e)   See **torup**

torosa n   [Span *toroso, -a* robust]

=**California poppy**.

   1896 *Jrl. Amer. Folkl.* 9.181, *Eschscholtzia Californica*, . . torosa (Span.) **1898** *Ibid* 11.222 **CA**, *Eschscholtzia* (sp.), . . *torosa*. **1915** (1926) Armstrong–Thornber *Western Wild Flowers* 164, *California Poppy*. . . It is the State flower of California and has many . . names, such as Torosa.

torote n   [MexSpan]

=**elephant tree**.

   1945 Benson–Darrow *Manual SW Trees* 216, *Bursera microphylla*. . .

Elephant tree; torote; copal. **1979** Little *Checklist U.S. Trees* 67, *Bursera microphylla.* . . Small-leaf elephant tree, copal, torote (Spanish).

torpedo   See **torpedo sandwich**

torpedo grass n   [See quot 2002]

A **panic grass** (here: *Panicum repens*).

    1948 FL Univ. Ag. Exper. Sta. *Annual Report* 242, Two areas of five acres each were planted to Torpedo grass *(Panicum repens).* **1952** U.S. Bur. Animal Industry *Rept. Chief 1952* 22, With cattle on a mixture of Pangola grass . . and Torpedo grass *(Panicum repens),* total gains of 252 pounds per acre were produced. **1966** *DARE* (Qu. S9, . . *Kinds of grass that are hard to get rid of*) Inf **FL**35, Torpedo grass. **c1967** GA Univ. *Weeds S. U.S.* 26, *Panicum repens*—torpedograss. . . Found on sandy soils, beaches, citrus groves, cultivated fields and wastelands. **2002** (acc) FL Univ. *Center for Aquatic & Invasive Plants* (Internet), Torpedograss *(Panicum repens)* is one of many panic grasses in Florida—except that this one is an invasive exotic that is environmentally and economically damaging. . . Torpedograss *spreads* from underground *rhizomes* that have hard, pointed torpedo-like tips.

torpedo sandwich n   Also *torpedo*   orig **NEast**, now esp **Nth, N Midl**   See Map

A **submarine sandwich.**

    1950 *Newport Daily News* (RI) 7 Mar 12/5, [Advt:] Torpedo Sandwich. A meal in itself. **1950** *Post–Std.* (Syracuse NY) [10 Nov 35]/2 (newspaperarchive.com), [Advt:] Giant Torpedo Sandwich. **1953** *Lowell Sun* (MA) 17 May 23/5, [Advt:] Toni's . . Sandwich Shop. . . Famous for Torpedo Sandwich. . . Ham—Cheese—Lettuce—Onion Pickle. **1965–70** *DARE* (Qu. H42, . . *[A sandwich] . . in a much larger, longer bun, that's a meal in itself*) 24 Infs, **chiefly Nth, N Midl**, Torpedo; **CT**39, Torpedo sandwich. **1967** *AmSp* 42.282, Terms Used for Submarine Sandwich in . . American Cities. . . Torpedo—San Antonio, Manchester, San Diego, Reno, Gary. **1967** *DARE* FW Addit **NC**, Torpedo sandwiches. **1971** *Today Show Letters* **CT**, Another chap with Connecticut background says in Bridgeport they are torpedoes or grinders. . . Yesterday I asked [another person] . . what was the precise locale for use of the word *torpedo.* . . He said along Long Island Sound from Bridgeport to New Haven.

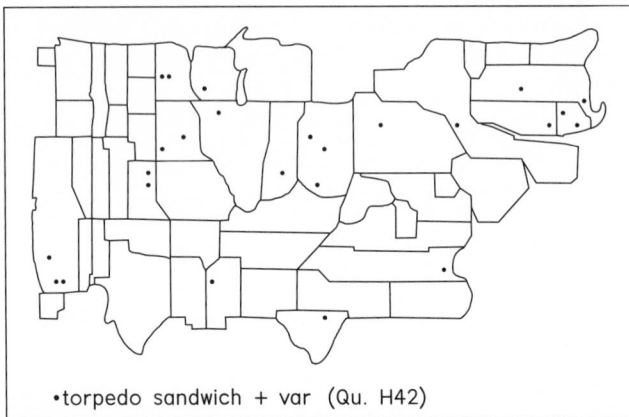

    •torpedo sandwich + var (Qu. H42)

Torrey pine n

Std: a **pine 1** (here: *Pinus torreyana*) native to California. Also called **Del Mar pine, pitch ~ c(7)**

torruh   See **tother**

torshent n   Also *taushents, torsh, tortience, toshens, toshuns, tossance, tossiance, tossion* [Of Algonquian orig; see quot 1908] **chiefly MA** *arch*

The youngest child in a family; hence v phr *tossion up* to indulge or coddle (a child).

    1802 MA Hist. Soc. *Coll.* 1st ser 8.97 **NEng**, The Indians of New England had . . [a] word, which in the dialect of the Nauset Indians was *taushents.* It has been adopted by the descendants of the English in many parts of the Old Colony of Plymouth, and is applied as a term of endearment. **1888** Morse *Chezzles* 36 **MA**, Bob . . is your father's torshent, and the little Barnes girl is her father's; every one in Nipsit calls her little Torsh Barnes. [Footnote to *torshent:*] A word much in use on Cape Cod, meaning the youngest member of a family. **1890** *DN* 1.75 **MA, ME,** The youngest child of a family is called a 'tortience.' South Yarmouth,

Mass. . . Used by old people in Barnstable, Mass., fifty years ago, and not yet extinct. Both ['tɔšəns] and ['tɑšənz] are pronunciations given me. "You're the tortience," *i.e.,* the pet or "baby" of the family. "That's my toshuns" = that's my youngest. The latter pronunciation is also reported as known in Northfield, Me., forty or fifty years ago. **1903** *DN* 2.301 **Cape Cod MA** (as of a1857), *Tortience. . .* The youngest and hence the spoiled child of a family. **1908** *Jrl. Amer. Folkl.* 21.88 **MA,** The word *tâcánt,* "child" . . is evidently the reduced correspondent of Natick . . *muttasóns,* "the youngest child (son)," as the term *toshens* or *torshent,* once in use in the English of certain parts of Massachusetts, proves. **1912** *Boston Herald* (MA) 2 Oct 2/5, Capt. F.M. Howes . . inquired into the origin of . . Tossance or Tossiance as a baptismal name on Cape Cod. *Ibid,* Mrs. Chapman said that we were both Tossions, and explained that the word meant an only child, one who had been brought up as a pet, or allowed to have his own way. . . She said that a certain person would never amount to much, because as a child, he was 'Tossioned up' too much. **1930** Smith *Our Heritage* 91 **Cape Cod MA,** You are twenty years older than she. She is my torshent.

torsk n   [*OED2* 1776 →]

=**cusk 1.**

    1955 U.S. Arctic Info. Center *Gloss.* 22, Cusk. . . A large edible marine fish, *Brosme brosme,* related to the cod. Also called 'torsk,' 'tusk.'

torsul   See **tassel**

tortience   See **torshent**

tortilla n |ˌtɔr'tijə| [MexSpan; *OED2* 1699 →]   orig **SW**, but now **widespread**   See Map

A thin, round cake of wheat or corn flour, usu cooked on a griddle.

    [**1824** Poinsett *Notes on Mexico* 42, Four damsels are industriously employed making tortillas of Indian corn.] **1831** (1973) Pattie *Personal Narr.* 42 **NM**, She then brought forward some tortillas and milk. **1854** (1932) Bell *Log TX–CA Trail* 35.293, Had no regular supper but eat a piece of bacon and flour Tortilla. **1887** *Scribner's Mag.* 2.509 **West,** You will probably find him [=a cowboy] inside . . regaling himself with a scanty breakfast of *tortillas* (diminutive of *torto,* cake). In Mexico, it is a pancake made of Indian meal, mashed, and baked on an earthen pan. **1910** Hart *Vigilante Girl* 221 **nCA,** Those are *enchiladas . . tortillas* or pancakes with chile peppers rolled inside and cooked in milk. **c1938** in Lib. of Congress *Amer. Memory: WPA Life Hist.* (Internet) **TX** (as of 1891), George looked around and said 'Miss Mattie, here is some bread,' and he brought out a plate of tortilla [sic]. I tried one but it was just like buckskin to me. **1965–70** *DARE* (Qu. H65, *Foreign foods favored by people around here*) 12 Infs, 6 **SW**, Tortillas; **TX**102, Corn tortillas, flour tortillas; (Qu. H18, . . *Special kinds of bread*) Infs **CA**94, 113, 118, **NM**5, **TX**5, 29, 43, Tortilla(s); **CA**64, **NM**12, Corn tortillas, flour tortillas; (Qu. H14, *Bread that's made with cornmeal*) Infs **CA**113, **TX**41, Tortillas; (Qu. H15, *Bread made with wheat flour*) Inf **TX**41, Tortillas; (Qu. H25, . . *Names or nicknames . . for fried cornmeal*) Inf **WA**11, Tortillas; (Qu. H45, *Dishes made with meat, fish, or poultry that everybody around here would know, but that people in other places might not*) Inf **TX**73, Tortillas; (Qu. HH28, *Names and nicknames . . for people of foreign background*) Inf **CA**56, Tortilla-eater. **1967–70** *DARE* Tape **AZ**8, Tortillas is the corn, very thin, pancake-type bread that is used. If it's made from just plain white flour, it has a softer, more biscuit-like texture; **CA**90, My board was, all it was, was Mexican tortillas; **CA**193,

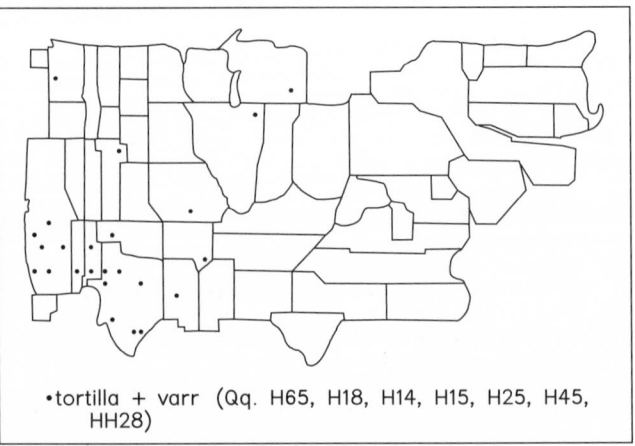

    •tortilla + varr (Qq. H65, H18, H14, H15, H25, H45, HH28)

When I was in the hills over there, I used to make tortillas myself; **TX**28, We have women that sell tortillas; **TX**31, Tortillas, Mexican tortillas. . . are made from ground corn; **TX**41, Around here we have a tortilla made out of corn. We have beans on it . . mayonnaise and cheese and tomatoes. **1989** *Parade* 12 Nov 9, The Mexican food boom has everyone eating burritos, quesadillas, homemade tortilla chips and salsa.

tortoise collar n   [Folk-etym for *torticollis*]
    2000 *DARE* File **MA**, I heard an acquaintance (educational level high school only, I think) say "tortoise collar" for "torticollis" (a medical condition in which the neck is more or less permanently twisted so the head is not facing forward). **2008** in 2010 *DARE* File—Internet **UT**, Hadley had her two month check-up, where she was diagnosed with tortoise collar, a.k.a. torticollis.

torup n   Also *torop(e)*   [Prob of Algonquian orig]   **esp Long Is. NY** Cf **terrapin**
    A turtle, usu a **snapping turtle 1** (here: *Chelydra serpentina*); hence vbl n *toruping* hunting snapping turtles; n *toruper* one who does this.
    1613 (1976) *Early Accts. Colonial VA* 42, I have caught with mine angle . . the Torope or little Turtle. **1874** *Atlantic Mth.* 34.449 **MD**, Then there were crabs to scoop and ducks to shoot, and always, besides, the enchanting possibility of catching a "torop." . . These sea-turtle, at certain seasons, come clawing clumsily up the margins of the sandy coves to lay their eggs on the shore. [*DARE* Ed: Both the region and meaning of *torop* implied here may be inaccurate; it is notable that the author of this story, "Olive A. Wadsworth" (Katherine Floyd Dana), grew up in Utica NY and inherited a considerable estate in Mastic, Long Is. NY.] **1894** *Critic* 27 Oct 268, Farmers and sailors call the big 'snapper' the torup or torop. **1916** *Copeia* 33.58 **Long Is. NY**, *Chelydra serpentina*. . . The name by which the snappers are known along the south shore is "torup." At Mastic, according to Mr. Francis Harper, at least one fisherman used to capture them to sell to the Poospatuck Indians, who prize the flesh. **2003** *DARE* File—Internet **eLong Is. NY**, "Torup". . . is the local name for a large (for our area) snapping turtle. . . Any local resident would be familiar with the term. "Local" in this case, refers to the little town of Eastport and some of the surrounding area. . . [T]he strategy was to row along slowly until a progressing trail of bubbles was sighted. . . As the "duck mud" was disturbed, it caused bubbles to rise, and a progressing trail would indicate that a torup was crawling forward through it. I don't know if they ever crawled backwards, but I never saw a "toruper" with missing fingers, so I presume they didn't. . . In talking to Arthur recently, I learned that he not only went out toruping alone, but on occasion had ten or a dozen torups crawling around in the bottom of the boat with no restraint.

toryweed n   Also *tory-bur(r)*
    A **hound's-tongue 1**, usu *Cynoglossum officinale*.
    1834 *Genesee Farmer* 4.266 **cwNY**, Some years ago when our lands were new, the *Tory Weed (Cynoglossum officinale)* was very troublesome, sticking its hooked seeds on every animal that could receive one. **1864** Randall *Practical Shepherd* 142 **NY**, The large and small Hounds-tongue, or Tory-weed . . and the wild Bur-marigold . . are peculiarly injurious to wool. **1875** (1876) Todd *Story Life* 24 **VT**, After a time [he] returned with some leaves of a plant called "tory weed." **1894** *Jrl. Amer. Folkl.* 7.95 **NY**, *Cynoglossum officinale*, . . Tory-bur. . . Name perhaps now obsolete. **1898** *Ibid* 11.275 **KS**, *Cynoglossum officinale*, . . Tory-burr.

t'ose   See **those**

tosey n
    See quots.
    1926 Smith *Gullah* 29 **sSC, GA coasts**, *Tosey*, as a diminutive of "toad," as a humorous nickname for man or woman. **1950** *PADS* 14.68 **SC**, *Tosey*. . . 1. An affectionate name for a *toad*. An old Scottish usage. Cf. *toadge frog*. 2. A she-dog. 3. A woman.

tosh   See **tush** n **A5**

toshens, toshuns, tossance   See **torshent**

tossel   See **tassel**

tossel-top n   Cf **devil's paintbrush 1, tassel**
    A **hawkweed.**
    1966 *DARE* (Qu. S20) Inf **ME**12, Devil's paintbrush—red, yellow—also called tossel-top; (Qu. S21, . . *Weeds*) Inf **ME**12, Tossel-top for devil's paintbrush.

tossiance, tossion (up)   See **torshent**

toss one's cookies   See **cookie** n[1] **3**

tostada n   Also *tostado*   [MexSpan *tostada* < Span *tostado* toasted]   **orig SW, but now widespread**
    A fried or toasted **tortilla,** often served with beans or other toppings; hence v *tostado.*
    [**1934** *NM Univ. Lang. Ser.* 5.28 **NM** [New Mexican Spanish], *Tostadas, tostaditas.* . . toasted tortillas.] **1936** *Marion Star* (OH) 18 May 9/2, When fried, the tortilla becomes a tostado. **1939** Berolzheimer *U.S. Cookbook* 604 **SW**, Tostadas (Toasted Corn Cakes). . . Fry tortillas. . . Over the tostada place fried sausage and beans and cover with grated cheese. Place in hot oven to melt cheese and just before serving place shredded lettuce on top. Serve hot. **1966** *Roswell Daily Rec.* (NM) 11 Mar 15/2, [Advt:] *Mexican Dinner Special.* . . Tostadas & Hot Sauce. **1966–69** *DARE* (Qu. H65, *Foreign foods favored by people around here*) Inf **CA**2, Tostados; **CA**107, Tostadas. **1967** *DARE* Tape **AZ**8, Some of the names that are used for these various [tortilla] dishes are tostado, burrito, . . enchiladas. **1986** Fussell *I Hear Amer. Cooking* 27, Tostados, those crisp wedge-shaped wafers that are to a bowl of salsa as pepper is to salt, originated in the need to use up all those left-over tortillas at the end of the day. . . Any store-bought tortillas will taste better when tostadoed.

tot   See **tote** v

totch(ed)   See **touch**

tote v   Also sp *toat, tot*   [Perh of Afr orig; cf 1949 Turner *Africanisms* 203]
A Senses.
    1 To carry (a significant load) by personal effort; also intr: to do the carrying for someone; hence n *freight toter.* **widespread, but somewhat more freq Sth, S Midl** See Map on p. 674 Cf **pack** v **1**
    1677 in 1894 *VA Mag. Hist. & Biog.* 2.168 **VA**, [Certain men were] commanded to goe to work, . . and mawl and toat railes. **1781** *PA Jrl. & Weekly Advt.* (Philadelphia) 23 May 1/3 **Sth**, *Tot* is used for *carry,* in some of the southern states. **1816** in 1824 Knight *Letters* 82 **VA** [Black], *Tote,* a slave word, is much used; implying both sustentation and locomotion, as a slave a log, or a nurse a babe. **1816** Pickering *Vocab.* 189, A reviewer of Mr. Webster's dictionary says—"Tote is marked by Mr. Webster, *Virg. (Virginia)* but we believe it a native vulgarism of *Massachusetts.*" . . It is a mere vulgarism, and is much more used in the *Southern* than in the *Northern* States. **1825** Neal *Brother Jonathan* 1.414 **CT**, "I'll not be cotch again, by your tricks." "Cotch!—I reckon!—clear nigger that, I guess. Might as well say fotch, or holp—or tote." **1862** *Continental Mth.* 1.196 **SC**, That cursed Moye sent him to the swamp to tote for the shinglers. It killed him. **1883** Twain *Life on Missip.* (Boston) 304 **MO**, You've got to admire men that deal in ideas of that size and can tote them around without crutches. **1886** *Amer. Philol. Assoc. Trans.* 17.35 **sOH**, Words that were imported during or after the war from the South into Southern Ohio. . . tote (carry). **1894** *Century Illustr. Mag.* 48.874 **VA**, In Virginia English, the negro "carries" the horse to water by making the horse "tote" him. **1909** *DN* 3.383 **eAL, wGA**, *Tote, v. tr.* To carry. Universal. **1911** *DN* 3.540 **eKY**, *Tote v., tr.* To carry. Supposed to be of Negro origin, but common in districts in the Cumberland Mountains where Negroes have never lived. **1915** *DN* 4.229 **wTX**, *Tote, v.t.* To carry, to "pack." **1918** *DN* 5.19 **NC**, *Tote,* carry. **1923** *DN* 5.223 **swMO**, *Tote.* . . To carry. Less frequently used than Pack. **1929** *Sat. Eve. Post* 17 Aug 11 **Sth**, These freight toters are not regular roustabouts. . . Most of them are middle aged negroes. **1939** *LANE* Map 165 **NEng**, The map shows . . the verbs *lug, tote . . ,* recorded in the context *I lugged that suitcase all the way to the station.* [23 scattered infs used *tote(d)* in this sense; 1 commented that it was "quite a common word," while 4 described it as rare.] **1965–70** *DARE* (Qu. Y30a, *To take something up and move it from one place to another—for example, a paper sack of groceries*) 207 Infs, **widespread, but somewhat more freq Sth, S Midl,** Tote; **MO**4, The Southerners would say "tote it out"; (Qu. Y30b, *To take something heavy up and move it from one place to another—for example, a bushel of apples*) 181 Infs, **widespread, but somewhat more freq Sth, S Midl,** Tote; (Qu. F30, *What is a pail . . used for?*) Inf **VA**88, Toting water; (Qu. F31, *What is a bucket . . used for?*) Inf **FL**49, For toting water to the hogs; **VA**88, Toting water; (Qu. Y31, *If a child asked his father to carry him on his back*) Infs **AR**51, **LA**8, **VA**69, Tote me (on your back); (Qu. AA15c, . . *Joking ways . . of saying that a woman is getting married. . . "She*

_____ .") Inf **SC**26, Get somebody to tote that bag; (Qu. LL24, *To keep firewood neat you have to cut it, split it, and* _____ *it up*) Inf **MD**38, Tote it in; (Qu. OO16b, *Talking about bringing tools: "I did bring the hammer, and I also* _____ *[a saw]."*) Inf **IL**31, Back in the old day they might have said fetch or tote. **1965–68** *DARE* Tape **AL**1, Somebody else would tote the juice over there to a big pan where they . . made the syrup; **AL**13, We stayed out in the country where the springs was, and each one of us would tote water in our hands; **AL**33, I was the baby of nine girls, and I always had to tote water and help my mother; **GA**7, If you get too much of it on your hands, your hands'll get so where you can't tote it, or carry it; **GA**30, He had knowed 'em to tote water for a hundred yards; **IL**26, And I toted that all the way back; **MS**1, Joe would've had to tote the coon; **SC**9, Tote them rice. Some tote to the river and some tote to the creek; **SC**16, Put 'em on your head and tote 'em to the flat; **VA**38, We used to tote 'em out in our arms. **1985** *Amer. Jrl. Med.* Feb 184 **eTN**, *Tote* . . to carry—"I was so stoved up they had to tote me."

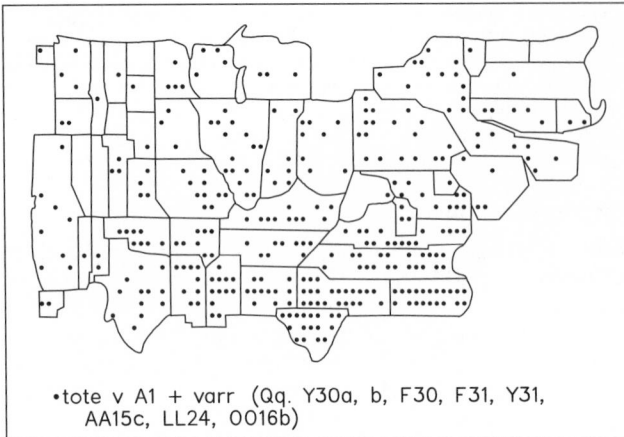

•tote v A1 + varr (Qq. Y30a, b, F30, F31, Y31, AA15c, LL24, OO16b)

2a To transport (a load) with external aid, haul in a vehicle. Cf **carry B3**

1803 Davis *Travels* 389 **VA** [Black], I . . cart all the wood, *tote* the wheat to the mill. **1803** in 1857 Dow *Hist. Cosmopolite* 173 **GA**, I came to a camp where some negroes were *toting* tobacco to market. . . The mode of toting tobacco . . is by rolling it in casks, with a wooden axle through the midst, on the ends of which are fastened the shafts for the horse to draw it by. **1838** Gilman *S. Matron* 50, Fayther says as how he wants Master Richard's horse to help tote some tetters [=potatoes] to tother field. **1907** *DN* 3.251 **eME**, *Tote, v.t.* . . [T]o transport. **1932** (1974) Caldwell *Tobacco Road* 151 **GA**, It's bad luck to carry something to town to sell and then tote it back home. **1939** *LANE* Map 165 *(Lugged)* **NEng**, [Two infs] distinguish between *lug*, 'carry in one's hand', and *carry* . . or *tote* . . , 'carry by team', i.e., on a vehicle; and one distinguishes further between *carry*, 'carry by team on a long haul' (as in hauling provisions through the woods to a lumber camp) and *tote*, 'carry by team on a short haul'. **1946** *Harper's Mag.* 193.308 **MO**, The manure in the feed lots is scraped up by a bulldozer and toted away to the field in a spreader. **1966–68** *DARE* (Qu. L54, *If someone was transporting firewood [or dirt] in a wagon . . he was* _____ *firewood*) Infs **CT**7, **SC**19, **WI**51, Toting; (Qu. OO46a, *Talking about dragging something heavy: "We hitched the log on and* _____ *it out [of the woods]."*) Inf **KS**5, Years ago we'd have said tote. **1974** (1975) Shaw *All God's Dangers* 383 **AL** [Black], There'd be two watergals totin water for that squad of women and only me totin for the men. **2005** *DARE* File—Internet, We were impressed with the new V-10's performance. It toted the load with ease.

b Spec; in logging: to haul (supplies) to a camp; to haul supplies; hence n *toter;* vbl n *toting.* **Nth, esp ME, WI** Cf **tote road, ~ sled, ~ team, ~ wagon**

a1862 [see **tote road**]. **1864** *Wilkes' Spirit of Times* 10 Dec 225 **ME**, It was not an agreeable thought, that near our last tip-over an unfortunate "toter" [=one who uses a tote road] lost his life by being thrown upon a tree, and thereby breaking his neck. **1887** *Stevens Point Jrl.* (WI) [8]/1 (newspaperarchive.com), H.H. Moore is "toting" supplies to Bean's logging camp. **1891** *AN&Q* 6.190 **ME**, Roads . . over which the supplies for the camps are carried, are always called "tote roads" and the teamsters are called "toters." **1895** *Century* [see **tote road**]. **1905** U.S. Forest Serv. *Bulletin* 61.51 [Logging terms], *Tote.* . . To haul supplies to a logging camp. (N[orthern] F[orest]). **1930** *Stevens Point Daily Jrl.*

(WI) 15 Mar 4/3, In his callow days in the lumber camps, [he] prodded a pair of oxen in toting supplies to the Meehan camps. **c1938** in Lib. of Congress *Amer. Memory: WPA Life Hist.* (Internet) **WI**, Then I was put to toting hay, grain, and all camp supplies from Two Harbors, even drunk and fighting lumberjacks. **1942** ME Univ. *Studies* 57.5, Roads for the toting of supplies must be over the easiest grades. . . In this region, it has seldom been necessary to tote over seven miles. *Ibid* 15, All of these materials must be toted to the camps as required. **1968** *DARE* Tape **WI**45, They wanted to buy some Indian horses for—used for toting. You know, that's for hauling provisions back and forth from the logging camps.

3 To convey (a person) in a vehicle.

1769 *Boston Gaz. & Country Jrl.* (MA) 7 Aug 2/2, The next Morning he was toated on board the *Rippon,* in a Canoe . . or some other small Boat. **1807** in 1869 Irving *Life & Letters* 1.140, At Baltimore . . I was *toted* about town and introduced to everybody. **1852** Peterson *Cabin & Parlor* 69 **VA** [Black], "If she ain't gone I kin tote her home, as I go to de village," said the slave. As he spoke, he lifted the board from the bottom of the wagon, to place across the top, in order to form a seat. **1863** Gilmore *S. Friends* 194 **NC**, There's a two-thousand-dollar turnout, and two fifteen-hundred-dollar niggers to tote a woman who ought to go afoot. **1965** *DARE* FW Addit **OK**6, *Toted him*—toted him into town— if a person picked up a hitchhiker, he might say this. **1975** Gould *ME Lingo* 296, "I've got to tote the women to the store" means they will be driven in an automobile. **2005** *DARE* File—Internet **TX**, He . . bought an RV simply so he could tote the [soccer] team back and forth.

4 To have on one's person, carry about so as to have at hand; hence n *toter,* adj *toting* (in combs such as *pistol-toter, ~-toting*). **chiefly Sth, S Midl** See Map

1823 in 1860 Claiborne *Life Quitman* 1.85 **MS**, The belles . . 'tote' their fans with the air of Spanish señoritas. **1845** Thompson *Pineville* 65 **GA**, Did you ever see a woman as tall as the one that toated the hickory [=a buggy whip]? **1856** Arrington *Rangers Tanaha* 89 **TX**, I wish I were a man, so I mout tote big guns too. **1859** *Unsworth's Burnt Cork Lyrics* 55 **NEast**, You'll see a creature on the street,/ . . / Who toats a little cane about,/ To keep the dogs away. **1867** Harris *Sut Lovingood Yarns* 77 **TN**, Sich an 'oman cud du more devilmint nur a loose stud hoss et a muster groun', ef she only know'd what tools she totes. **1905** *DN* 3.90 **nwAR**, *Pistol-toter.* . . One who habitually carries a pistol. **1909** *DN* 3.383 **eAL, wGA**, *Pistol-toter* is common. **1912** *Daily Northwestern* (Oshkosh WI) 17 Oct 6/1, One effect of the Roosevelt shooting has been to start a widespread discussion of the dangers attending promiscuous gun "toting." **1938** in Lib. of Congress *Amer. Memory: WPA Life Hist.* (Internet) **VT**, John was holding the plow and Jim was toting the gad stick. **1955** *Tri-City Herald* (Pasco WA) 19 Apr 1/7, Schoolmates said the youth habitually toated a "switch blade" knife with a seven- or eight-inch long blade. **1966–70** *DARE* (Qu. V9, . . *Nicknames . . for a policeman*) Inf **MS**88, Pistol-toters; Pistol-toting Pete; (Qu. V10a, . . *Joking names . . for a sheriff*) Inf **WI**68, Badge-toter; (Qu. BB53a, . . *Joking names . . for a doctor*) Infs **GA**17, **NC**41, Pill-toter; **NC**4, Black-bag toter; (Qu. DD3b, *How . . people take snuff*) Inf **GA**77, Tote it in the lower lip; (Qu. DD12, . . *A person who drinks steadily or a great deal*) Inf **SC**45, Jug-toter. **1966** *DARE* Tape **FL**39, He was . . one of about three Republicans. And he almost had to tote a pistol when he said he was a Republican; **SC**26, You can keep it [=a horse bone to cure warts] in your pocket or you can throw it away. . . If you tote it, I think you're supposed to tote it a while. **1986** Pederson

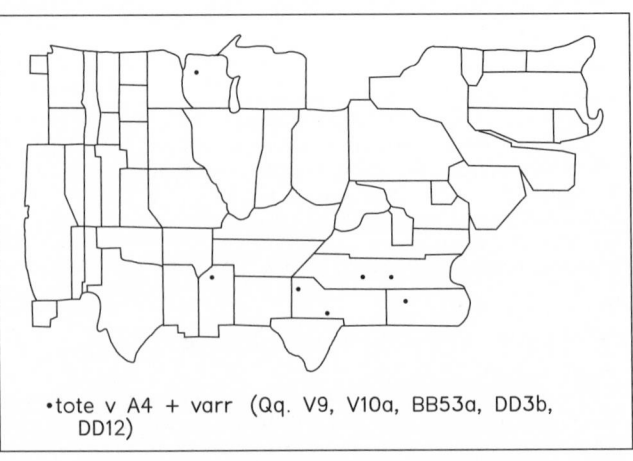

•tote v A4 + varr (Qq. V9, V10a, BB53a, DD3b, DD12)

LAGS Concordance, 1 inf, **seGA,** Toter's license = handgun permit. **1990** *Intelligencer* (Doylestown PA) 27 Mar sec C 1/1, Gangs of thugs toting knives, chains and iron bars. **1999** in 2005 *DARE* File—Internet **GA,** Jerry Falwell actually finds what he considers evil in a Teletubbie that wears purple and totes a purse.

5 To lead (an animal); to take, conduct (a person), esp by authority or force. **chiefly Sth, S Midl   Cf carry B1, 4**

1837 Bird *Nick of Woods* 1.133 **KY,** I say, captain, if your men will fight, just tote 'em back. *Ibid* 145, I wants to ax of you . . whether its a wiser and more christian affa'r, when thar's Injuns in the land a murdering of your neighbour's wives and children . . , to send an able-bodied man to fight them; or to tote him off, a day's journey thar and back ag'in, to track a road that a blind man on a blind horse could travel. **1846** Corcoran *Pickings* 120 **LA,** The watchman "toted" him off to the calaboose. **1851** Burke *Polly Peablossom* 182 **IL,** Wall, old hoss, trot along into the cabin, and I'll yell for Sucker to tote your hanimals to the crib. **1856** Arrington *Rangers Tanaha* 151 **TX** [Black], But ain't you a gwin' to let us tote our women and children with us? **1856** Willcox *Shoepac Recoll.* 97 **MI,** Dick the Sheriff, on catching an urchin, always inquired "Mason or Anti-mason?" and let the prisoner go free, or *toted* him off to the jail, according to his reply. **1860** *Ladies' Repository* 20.307, I have frequently heard a negro inquire, "Shall I tote this horse to the water?" **1863** Gilmore *S. Friends* 84 **NC,** Wall, wen the ole feller wus pooty well primed, Dick stuck his arm inter his'n, toted him off ter the stable, and fotched out a ole, spavin'd . . broken-down critter. **1876** *Harper's New Mth. Mag.* 53.196 **AR** [Black], I took him by de eah an' toted him up to de house. **1979** *Syracuse Herald–Amer.* (NY) 2 Dec mag sec 5/4, [Caption:] *Take him away.* Dudley Moore as George Webber is toted away by two policemen after he crashes into their car.

6 also with *along, around, off:* To head out, take off, depart. *obs*

1857 Wickham *Sea-Spray* 331 **Long Is. NY,** I'll go and see him as I tote along back. **1858** Denison *Old Hepsy* 22 **Sth** [Black], "Come, honey, we'll tote along together." . . She clung close to her protector . . and . . the two left the market. **1858** Hammett *Piney Woods Tavern* 40, Evry one knows that I wer raised in old Tennessee, then toted off to Alabam, . . and then put out for Texas. **1859** Wilson *Our Nig* 89 **NH,** Do n't you know that every night she will want to go toting off to meeting? **1865** *Atlantic Mth.* 15.387 **PA,** Nothing would do but to tote down here to the Crik and make his fortin. **1867** Lowell *Biglow* 16 **'Upcountry' MA,** An, Gin'ral, when you've mixed the drinks an' chalked 'em up, tote roun' / An' see ef ther's a feather-bed (thet's borryable) in town.

7 To carry, pass on (news, gossip), now esp with malicious intent; hence n *gossip-toter;* adjs *gossip-toting, tale-toting.* **Sth, S Midl   Cf pack v 2a**

1867 Harris *Sut Lovingood Yarns* 269 **TN,** Wudn't he be great in a new country to open out roads, ur tote news ove the cumin on the Injuns? **1878** Vaughan *Kate Weathers* 32 **eNC,** I'll risk that, too, . . for I tell her now . . if she does tote news off to Ike, she'll never tote no more to him or anybody else. **1897** *Landmark* (Statesville NC) 7 Dec [3]/4 (newspaperarchive.com), We now have telephone poles to Longisland ready for the wire; so now our poor mouths and feet that get so tired "toting" news will be sent on the wire. **1901** Harben *Westerfelt* 27 **nGA,** I never was much of a hand to tote tales. **1928** *News* (Frederick MD) 16 May 11/3, Carnival folks usually mind their own business and spend damn little time toting tales. **1935** Hurston *Mules & Men* 191 **cFL** [Black], De two-faced heifer! Been hangin' 'round me so she kin tote news to Ella. **a1938** in 1977 *Amer. Slave Suppl. 1* 8.1045 **MS** [Black], Sometimes de slaves toted news back and forth, but dey had to be mighty careful not to let de white folks hear 'bout it. **1965–67** *DARE* (Qu. GG36b, *The kind of person who is always poking into other people's affairs: "She's the _____ person I know!"*) Inf **MS**63, Tale-totingest; (Qu. JJ4, *A child who is always telling on other children*) Inf **LA**12, Gossip-toter. **2004** *DARE* File—Internet **neGA,** They give coverage to every left-leaning, Bush-hating "Gossip-Toting" character that comes down the pipe. *Ibid* **LA,** You are a little immature snitch . . who totes tales without telling the whole story.

8 also with *off:* Of a domestic servant: to take home, surreptitiously or as an acknowledged perquisite, (leftover food or other goods) from one's employer; also in phr *tote the crooked arm:* to engage in this practice; hence vbl n *toting;* pl nouns *totes, totings* food so taken. **chiefly Sth   Cf sling pans**

1905 *Sewanee Rev.* 13.8, Negro cooks . . have been paid from $4.00 to $5.00 a month in cash, with the tacit understanding by both mistress and servant that the latter is going to supplement her wages by carrying away

various articles of food and perhaps other small things that attract her fancy. . . [S]eldom does the mistress remonstrate with or in any way punish the servant for "totin' off" what the latter considers her informal wages. **1923** *DN* 5.244 **LA,** *Tote. . .* To carry home (victuals). **1933** *Hench Coll.* **VA,** A negro servant who totes is one who goes home every night after supper and secretly pilfers food from the refrigerator . . to take home for her children. . . Toting is usually blinked at if done infrequently. **1941** Writers' Program *Guide MO* 132, Negro cooks will sometimes demand the right to "tote" (carry home left-over food) as part of their wages. **1944** *PADS* 2.13 **LA,** *Tote. . .* To take home (left-overs of food). Said of the practice of some Negro servants, permitted or not. *Ibid* **Sth,** *Toting. . .* The practice of taking home food from the employer's kitchen. "I don't allow toting, remember." **1946** Driscoll *Country Jake* 66 **KS,** While Knight was extremely religious and righteous, he followed the custom of toting, common to his people, in the South. Toting is the taking home of the master's or employer's goods, to such value and in such quantities as may seem good to the servant. **1952** Brown *NC Folkl.* 1.602, *Toting. . .* The surreptitious carrying home of food by a servant.—Durham county. **1954** *PADS* 21.23 **SC,** *Carry. . .* The amount of meat . . given to each person engaged in hog killing, to be taken home. Also called *totin's.* Sometimes applied also to what the cook takes home daily. Charleston and environs. **1969** *DARE* FW Addit **NC,** *Totin' privileges*—privilege White ladies extend to their maids, permitting them to take home extra or leftover food. **1984** Wilder *You All Spoken Here* 89 **Sth,** *Totin' the crooked arm:* Heading home with purloined vittles in a vessel tucked close to the body. **1992** *DARE* File **VA** (as of 1916), My mother had interviewed a black woman as a prospective cook, and I overheard her tell my father that the woman would work for *x* dollars a week if she "toted" and . . slightly more . . if she didn't "tote." **2003** *Ibid* **NC** (as of c1950s), When you hired a [Black] cook, you'd say, "We'll pay you x dollars a day plus totes." When the cook had figured out how much the family was likely to eat, she would cook more than that to be sure there would be plenty of totes. The word isn't used as much as it used to be, but you can still hear it.

B In var phrr, as:

1 *tote double;* Of a horse: to carry two riders; also fig, to be very strong. **Sth, S Midl**

1861 *Godey's Lady's Book* 62.112 **GA,** I reckon you can ride behind papa, for our horses all tote double. **1878** *Harper's New Mth. Mag.* 57.951 **Sth,** He discovered that *that horse wouldn't tote double.* **1887** (1888) Smedes *Mems. S. Planter* 51 **TN** (as of 1835), He is as gentle as a cat. But he won't tote double. Me and my old 'oman wants to go to meetin', . . and he won't tote us both. **1903** *DN* 2.334 **seMO,** Will this horse tote double? **1967** *DARE* (Qu. H74a, . . *Coffee . . very strong*) Inf **LA**12, Strong enough to tote double [laughter]. **1986** Pederson *LAGS Concordance,* 1 inf, **nwLA,** My horse will tote double—carry two riders; 1 inf, **cwTN,** Strong enough to tote double and kick up—coffee.

2 *tote fair* (or rarely *tote right,* ~ *square*): To do one's fair share; to act fairly. **chiefly Sth, S Midl**

1866 Smith *Bill Arp* 147 **nwGA,** I don't think you tote fair. **1886** Amer. Philol. Assoc. *Trans.* 17.35 **sOH,** Words that were imported during or after the war from the South into Southern Ohio. . . *tote fair* (deal squarely). **1903** *DN* 2.334 **seMO,** *Tote fair. . .* To do the right thing; to play fair. 'We'll get along all right if he'll tote fair.' **1905** *DN* 3.99 **nwAR,** *Tote fair. . .* Act fairly. 'Tote fair, if you're going to play with me.' Common. **1909** *DN* 3.383 **eAL, wGA,** *Tote fair. . .* To act squarely, do one's full share of work in any common undertaking. **1917** *DN* 4.418 **KY, wNC, SC,** *Tote fair with. . .* To deal fairly with. **1919** Kyne *Capt. Scraggs* 255 **CA,** I was fooled by that doggone mate. I thought he'd tote square with the syndicate. **1933** *AmSp* 8.1.53 **Ozarks,** *Tote right. . .* To be fair, to conform to the local ethics. *I shore do aim t' tote right with ever'body.* The phrase *tote fair* is used with the same meaning. **1950** *PADS* 14.35 **SC,** The dialect phrase "tote fair" . . means originally to hold the handstick the same distance from the log as your partner does. The bearer who is farther away from the burden has a lighter load, and is not "toting fair." **c1960** *Wilson Coll.* **csKY,** *Tote fair. . .* To do one's own part honestly and willingly.

3 *tote guts* (or *vittles*) *to a bear, tote victuals to a nigger:* To do the most rudimentary or distasteful task. **esp Sth   Cf carry guts to a bear, pack v 2b**

1863 Gilmore *S. Friends* 85, Get up, and 'tend to the stranger. You aren't fit to tote victuals to a nigger. *Ibid* 283, Ye're set uv d—d sneakin' hounds, every one on ye. Ye're wuss than the parsons; an' the' hain't fit ter tote vittles ter a bar. **a1930** in 1991 Hughes–Hurston *Mule Bone* 114 **cFL** [Black], Joe Lindsay, don't you know no better than to strain wid folks ain't got sense enough to tote guts to a bear? If they ain't born wid no sense, you can't learn 'em none. **1960** Williams *Walk Egypt* 179 **GA** [Black], Boss, I jes can't hold out to do nothing like that. . . Can't tote guts to a bear. **1973** *Vidette–Messenger* (Valparaiso IN) 8 Feb 6/6, [Syndicated column:] Our caterer is not fit to tote guts to a bear. **2005** *DARE* File **eTX** [Black], Then she came out with "That woman ain't fit to tote guts to a bear," with the emphasis on "bear."

4 *tote milk to:* To curry favor with.

1967 *DARE* (Qu. II20b, *A person who tries too hard to gain somebody else's favor: "He's always trying to _____ the boss."*) Inf **LA**8, Tote milk to.

5 *tote one's own skillet:* To look out for or be responsible for oneself. **esp Sth**

1885 in **2005** *DARE* File—Internet [*Arkansas City Traveler* (KS) 10 June, copied from the *Butler* (Georgia) *Herald*], "Tote Your Own Skillet." The above phrase that is being so often quoted by speakers and writers is not of modern date, but is said to have originated in the early settling up of this country. **1898** Lloyd *Country Life* 199 **AL**, Tote your own skillet and take things easy. **1909** *DN* 3.383 **eAL, wGA**, *Tote one's own skillet. . .* To take care of one's own interests, paddle one's own canoe: a political phrase. **1989** Chariton *This Dog'll Hunt* 117 **TX**, *Independent. . .* Totes her own skillet.

6 *tote the mail:* To run quickly; to move in a hurry. **esp Sth** Cf **pack** v **2d**

1893 Shands *MS Speech* 64, *Tote the mail.* A negro expression for *run swiftly;* as "When I seed dat ghos', I farly toted de mail." **1909** *DN* 3.383 **eAL, wGA**, *Tote the mail. . .* To run away from something very rapidly; 'hit the grit,' 'get up and get.' "I made him fairly tote the mail out of my cane-patch." **1947** Ballowe *The Lawd* 151 **LA**, If Jasper and Cricket were made to tote the mail off the place she would follow. **1972** *Odessa Amer.* (TX) 25 Nov sec B 1/8, Chandler toted the mail 25 times for 70 yards, including a 25-yard romp near the end of the first half [of a football game]. **a1975** Lunsford *It Used to Be* 167 **sAppalachians**, You say, "I made him tote the mail," and it means I made him run.

tote n

1 A load to be carried; a job of carrying; broadly, a task.

1884 Hill *Tales Pioneers* 207 **CO**, I ain't got no wagon, and fo' fowls jist like dat ar, would be a big tote, so I will fotch one at a time. **1909** *DN* 3.383 **eAL, wGA**, *Tote. . .* A burden or load. "That basket of cotton is too big a tote for me." **1950** *Pacific Discovery* Mar–Apr 9 **AZ**, Tuffy loaded our gear into the jeep in order to save the animals the nine-mile tote to the takeoff point. **1958** *Salisbury Times* (MD) 17 Oct 15/3 **Delmarva**, Deals Island people, I heard tell,/ Must haul in dirt to dig a well,/ The land's so low, it's an easy tote / To pick their butter beans from a boat. **1986** Pederson *LAGS Concordance* (*The amount of wood you can carry in your arms*) 1 inf, **nwFL**, A tote; 1 inf, **cnLA**, A tote—the amount you could handle or tote. **2005** *DARE* File—Internet, It was quite a tote of our luggage from the parking garage.

2 A piggyback ride.

1967–70 *DARE* (Qu. Y31, *If a child asked his father to carry him on his back . . "Give me a _____."*) Infs **DC**1, **GA**89, **VA**101, Tote; **CA**97, Tote [FW: Inf used this because his mother was from the South].

tote along (or around) See **tote** v **A6**

tote double See **tote** v **B1**

tote fair See **tote** v **B2**

tote guts to a bear See **tote** v **B3**

tote milk to See **tote** v **B4**

toten See **token**

tote off See **tote** v **A6, 8**

tote one's own skillet See **tote** v **B5**

toter n

1 See **tote** v **A2b, 4.**

2 A **hog sucker** (here: *Hypentelium nigricans*). Cf **stone toter 1**

1820 Rafinesque *Ohio R. Fishes* 68, Ohio Toter. *Hypentelium macropterum* [=*H. nigricans*]. . . Its vulgar name is Toter or Stone Toter. **1836** Mellen *Book U.S.* 223, The Ohio [River] 'toter' is two or three inches in length; its name is derived from the barbarism 'tote,' meaning to 'carry,' because this fish makes itself a cell by surrounding a place with pebbles. **1882** U.S. Natl. Museum *Bulletin* 16.130, *C[atostomus] nigricans* [=

Hypentelium n.] . . Hog Sucker; Stone Roller; Toter. **1896** *Ibid* 47.181, *Catostomus nigricans. . . Toter. . .* Abundant in swift or rocky streams, which it ascends to spawn; never found in muddy or warm waters.

toter pron, adj   See **tother**

tote right   See **tote** v **B2**

tote road n   Also *toting road, tow* ~   [**tote** v **A2b**]   **chiefly Nth, esp ME**

A road used primarily for transporting goods, esp supplies to a logging camp or other remote work site; now also used for transporting logs by truck.

a1862 (1864) Thoreau *ME Woods* 222, The Indian was greatly surprised that we should have taken what he called a "tow" (i.e. tote or toting or supply) road, instead of a carry path. **1874** *Stevens Point Jrl.* (WI) 10 Jan [3]/2 (newspaperarchive.com), The [railroad] track has been completed to Section 101, and all work suspended for the winter, with the exception of the party at work on the Tote road. **1894** *New Engl. Mag.* 15.696 **neNC**, Here is the broad, main highway, . . and the numerous "tote roads" which seem to meander aimlessly here and there, but eventually concentrate at the granaries, gins, factories, and warehouses at the landings. **1895** *Overland Mth.* (2d ser) 25.315 **WA**, Getchell was the distributing point for the "tote-roads" leading to the Monte Cristo mining camps. **1895** *Century Illustr. Mag.* 50.478 **ME**, He would find each one [=logging camp] furnished with its separate "tote road," "tote-team," and "toter." In fact . . , I have never heard any other word used to signify the conveyance of supplies to the camps. **1907** *DN* 3.251 **eME**, *Tote-road. . .* A road in the Maine woods used for the transportation of provisions. **1914** *DN* 4.81 **ME, nNH**, *Tote-road. . .* The road leading from a lumber-camp to the settlement, or to the "landing" on the river. **1935** *Ironwood Daily–Globe* (MI) 9 May 2/6, The body . . was found hanging in a balsam tree near an old tote road leading to the Charcoal Iron Co. mine. **1939** *LANE* Map 44 (*Side road; lane*) 1 inf, **swCT**, Tote road = wood road; 1 inf, **ceMA**, Tote road, on private land; 1 inf, **seME**, Tote road, for taking supplies to a lumber camp. **1940** (1947) Writers' Program *Guide VA* 89, Moving in single file along the narrow trails called 'tote-roads,' . . the horses carried traffic between the older towns and the frontier posts. **1942** ME Univ. *Studies* 57.8, Before camp construction can begin, the tote road to the camp-site from the main depot of supplies . . must be provided. **1945** Hamlin *9 Mile Bridge* 37 **nME**, The tote road is used solely for the transportation of men, materials and supplies to the camp site, and only during the winter . . can anything heavier than a horse go over it. **1950** *WELS* **WI**, 1 Inf, Tote road—logging road; 1 inf, Tow road. **1958** McCulloch *Woods Words* 197 **Pacific NW**, *Tote road. . .* A road supplying a camp. **1966** *DARE* (Qu. N27a, *Names . . for different kinds of unpaved roads*) Inf **ME**9, Tote road—used to haul supplies into camp; (Qu. N29, . . *Names . . for a less important road running back from a main road*) Inf **ME**1, Tote road—old roads for horses—go to lumber camp. **1968** *DARE* Tape **NH**14, A tote road . . used to go clear up through to the pond. . . They used to tote groceries, what they called tote. Stop up to the camps way up. **2001** *DARE* File—Internet **WI**, In the 1870's, the 101 Tote Road was the only land route north of Chippewa Falls along the Flambeau River. **2005** *DARE* File **ME** (as of 1981), Tote road is the standard term for a logging road. The logging companies built the network of gravel tote roads for hauling logs out of the woods.

tote-road shagamaw n   Also *shagamaw, shagimaw*   Also sp *toat-road shagamaw*   **Nth**

A mythical beast of the woods that haunts the **tote roads**, walking alternately on its front feet (those of a bear) and hind feet (those of a moose), and that pilfers and devours clothing; hence v *shagamaw* see quot 1997.

1910 Cox *Fearsome Creatures* 23 **ME**, *The Tote-Road Shagamaw. . .* Gus Demo, of Oldtown, Maine . . once came upon what he recognized as the tracks of a moose. After following it for about 80 rods it changed abruptly into unmistakable bear tracks; another 80 rods and it changed to moose tracks again. . . [It] always followed a tote road or a blazed line through the woods. Coming up within sight of the animal, Gus saw that it had front feet like a bear's and hind feet like those of a moose, and that it was pacing carefully, taking exactly a yard at a step. Suddenly it stopped, looked all about, and swung as on a pivot, then inverting itself and walking on its front feet only, it resumed its pacing. **1921** *Bismarck Tribune* (ND) 26 July 8/3 **MN**, The Toat-Road Shagamaw, an animal which, according to lumbermen's lore, inhabited the lumbering sections of Maine, has invaded the sacred precincts of Minnesota's northwoods. **1948** *Edwardsville Intelligencer* (IL) 9 Apr [6]/5 (newspaperarchive.com), [Caption:] The "shagimaw" is another queer animal—this beast has a sweet tooth—for lumbermens' [sic] clothing. *Ibid* [6]/7, Can they compare . . with the Shagamaw[?] **1972** *Sun* (Lowell MA) 13 May [8]/3 (newspaperarchive.com), When our woodsmen [from Maine] moved west'ard with the lumber harvest, they knew a tote-road shagamaw in Wisconsin, just as they were again to known [sic] them in Oregon and Washington. **1997** MN Pub. Radio *Monsters Lumber Camps* (Internet), I grab the axe and turn for my mittens and they're *gone!* I kid you not. He hangs around the tote roads, and he shagamaws the mittens.

totes See **tote** v **A8**

tote sack n [Folk-etym for **tow sack**] **chiefly Sth, S Midl** Cf **toad sack**

=**tow sack.** Note: Exx of *tote sack* in same sense as std *tote bag* are not recorded here.

1945 *Post–Std.* (Syracuse NY) 15 Aug 6/7, Some friends and I have been discussing the correct name of the large bag called (they say) a "toe sack." I'm from the South, and I think it should be "tote sack"—a sack in which one totes (carries) things. **1957** *Sat. Eve. Post Letters* **KY,** My grandmother was from Ky. . . and any bag was a "poke" except a gunny sack which was a "tote sack." **1958** *PADS* 29.17 **TN,** *Tote sack.* . . A fusion of the widespread *tote* with the similar sounding *tow.* **1961** *Valley News & Green Sheet* (Van Nuys CA) 28 Nov sec A 5/4, *Burlap tote sack.* Ideal for grass and leaves—39¢. **1965–69** *DARE* (Qu. F20, *A cloth container for feed*) Inf **MS60,** Tote sack; (Qu. F23, *A container made of rough, loosely-woven, brown cloth; commonly used for potatoes, etc*) Infs **AL**14, **MS**60, **NC**72, **TN**30, **VA**2, Tote sack; (Qu. F19, *A cloth container for grain*) Inf **NC**72, Tote]. **1989** Pederson *LAGS Tech. Index* 76, *Tow sack* . . tote sack (12 [of 914 infs]). **2005** *DARE* File—Internet **neLA** [Black], He pointed toward a wall at something in [sic] the floor covered with a tote sack. [Author: A burlap sack.] He said, 'Pull that tote sack off'n that pot.' *Ibid* **cTX,** [Item for sale:] Planters Peanut Collectible Burlap Tote Sack.

tote sled n Also *tote sleigh* [**tote** v **A2b**] **chiefly NEng, Gt Lakes**

A sled drawn by horses (or rarely oxen) used for hauling goods, esp supplies to a logging camp.

1880 *Daily Free Press* (Eau Claire WI) 6 Dec [4]/1 (newspaperarchive.com), We noticed quite a number of loaded "tote sleds" headed for the woods this morning. **1885** *Current* 3.40 **MI,** At this point we take a "tote" sleigh, and drive into camp. **1887** in 1962 *Brainerd Daily Dispatch* (MN) 7 Mar 1/1, *For Sale:* Two yokes of heavy work oxen and three sets of tote sleds. **1905** U.S. Forest Serv. *Bulletin* 61.51 [Logging terms], *Tote sled. See* Jumper. [*Ibid* 40, *Jumper.* . . A sled shod with wood, used for hauling supplies over bare ground into a logging camp. (N[orthern] F[orest]).] **1907** *DN* 3.251 **eME,** *Tote-sled.* . . A sled used to "tote" or convey provisions and supplies in the Maine woods. **1930** *Portsmouth Herald* (NH) 8 Apr 7/2, Oxen are still used on the Henderson farm to draw the tote-sleds to the sap-house. **1941** (1988) Writers' Program *Guide MN Arrowhead Country* 200, *Tote Sleigh:* In lumbering, a sleigh on which supplies are hauled. **1950** *WELS* (Sleighs . . *for hauling loads*) 1 Inf, **WI,** Tote sled. **1966** *DARE* (Qu. N40a, . . *Sleighs . . for hauling loads*) Inf **ME**1, Tote sled—one set of runners. **1966** *DARE* Tape **ME**26, They had two sleds, one hooked behind the other. Them was tote sleds.

tote square See **tote** v **B2**

tote team n [**tote** v **A2b**] **Nth, esp NEng, Gt Lakes**

A **team 1** used to haul goods, esp supplies to a logging camp; hence n *tote teamster.*

1864 *Wilkes' Spirit of Times* 10 Dec 226/1 **ME,** A two-horse "tote team" arrived, and with it an old man and an Indian boy. **1884** MN State Bd. Health *Rept. for 1883–84* 63, Quarantined a "tote" teamster, making number thirty-three. **1892** *Bucks Co. Gaz.* (Bristol PA) 7 Jan 1/1 **wWI,** All the supplies for the men and the teams were hauled from home. The team which did this hauling—the "tote team" as it was called—made one trip each week. **1895** *Century* [see **tote road**]. **1902** White *Blazed Trail* 84 **MI,** Thorpe never knew . . how tenderly the tote teamster drove his hay-couched burden to Beeson Lake. **1907** *DN* 3.251 **eME,** *Tote-team.* . . Horse or horses and conveyance for provisions and supplies in the Maine woods. **1914** *Daily Kennebec Jrl.* (Augusta ME) 27 Apr 10/7, If luck favors and he is invited to ride upon a tote team he accepts. **1914** *DN* 4.81 **ME, nNH,** *Tote-team.* . . A supply-team, in lumber-camps. **1923** *Bismarck Tribune* (ND) 18 Feb 3/2 (as of 1873), To reach their prairie home they had traveled miles behind

a team of army mules with the bride riding on piles of tote team dunnage. **1926** Rickaby *Ballads Shanty-Boy* 237 **MI, MN, WI** (as of a1920), *Tote team.* The team used in bringing supplies overland by sled from the trading centres to the camps. **1939** (1962) Thompson *Body & Britches* 131 **NY,** When we asked who Paul Bunyan was, she replied: "O, he was the big lumberjack who had a big ox. . . He came through here with some tote-teams on the way to some camps he had." **1940** *Portsmouth Herald* (NH) 5 Jan 4/2 **ME,** In his years as a warden, Orcutt has . . ridden on horseback, in tote teams, on dog sleds, in automobiles and in airplanes over his territory. **1941** *Sheboygan Press* (WI) 7 Nov 13/6, The tote team had to be helped in many a spot. Everyone walked but the driver. **1958** McCulloch *Woods Words* 197 **Pacific NW,** *Tote team*—A team used in freighting supplies to camp. **1969** Sorden *Lumberjack Lingo* 131 **NEng, Gt Lakes,** *Tote team*—Horses used to take supplies into camp. *Tote teamster*—Driver who brought supplies into camp.

tote the crooked arm See **tote** v **A8**

tote the mail See **tote** v **B6**

tote victuals to a nigger (or vittles to a bear) See **tote** v **B3**

tote wagon n [**tote** v **A2b**] **esp NEng, Gt Lakes**

A horse-drawn wagon used for hauling goods, esp supplies, to a logging camp.

1888 (1889) Fitzmaurice *Shanty Boy* 10 **MI, WI,** The toil hardened woodsmen . . would occasionally wait for the "tote" wagons to catch up to them. **1902** *Daily Northwestern* (Oshkosh WI) 23 Aug 6/6 (as of 1850), I started out, one of four passengers in a return-tote-wagon from the little city of Milwaukee. **1938** in 1971 *Pioneer* (Bemidji MN) [30 June 33]/4 (newspaperarchive.com) (as of 1880s), In order to bring in supplies [to a trading post] it was necessary to haul them in tote wagons over a rough wilderness trail. **1942** *AmSp* 17.105 [Truck driver lingo], *Tote wagon.* Light truck used to haul supplies in a construction camp. **1942** ME Univ. *Studies* 57.134, *Tote Wagon.* A wagon of various types used in *toting.* **2003** *3 Rivers News* (Milo ME) 14 Jan 6 (Internet), Some of the camps . . had a resident with a pair of horses and a tote wagon to haul you over.

tother pron, adj [*OED2* c1250 →] Pronc-spp *tarruh, t'er, todder, todduh, toder, torruh, toter, tudder, tudduh, turr(ah), turrer, turruh, tuther, tutter* **chiefly NEng, Sth, S Midl** Cf **other A**

A Forms.

1837 Sherwood *Gaz. GA* 71, *Tuther,* other. **1847** *Rural Repository* 23.133 [Black], One or todder ob us'l hab to go. **1855** Haliburton *Nature* 2.160 **VA** [Black], It was one or toder. **1867** Harris *Sut Lovingood Yarns* 87 **TN,** I passed 'em a-pas' each uther tuther day. **1884** *Anglia* 7.276 **Sth, S Midl** [Black], *Same ez t'er (tother) one* = like the other one. **1887** Page *In Ole VA* 29, One o' de lieutenants got kilt de same day, an' turr one . . wan' no 'count. **1888** Jones *Negro Myths* 2 **GA coast** [Gullah], Eh lick back an try tarruh side. *Ibid* 4, You cant tell one turr. *Ibid* 190, Tarruh[s] Turruh—the other. **1899** (1912) Green *VA Folk-Speech* 461, *Tudder.* . . The other. **1922** Gonzales *Black Border* 334 **sSC, GA coasts** [Gullah glossary], *Todduh[,] tudduh*—the other, t'other, the others. . . *Torruh*—(also tarruh . .) t'other; the other, the others. **1930** Stoney-Shelby *Black Genesis* 164 **seSC** [Gullah], People down Sawannah-way talk different from de turrah buckra. **1939** in 1976 *Weevils in the Wheat* 306 **VA** [Black], If one want good dey w'uld use de 'toter one. **1939** McGuire *FL Cracker Dial.* 74, More sophisticated Crackers often say of a less-sophisticated friend who still speaks considerable dialect, "He speaks with a 'hain't, a 'tain't and a 'tutter." However, the form *'tutter* never occurs in isolated usage. **1952** Brown *NC Folkl.* 1.601, *Toder, todder, tudder.* . . The other.

B Senses.

1 Other. [*OED2* c1250 → (as pron); a1300 → (as adj)]

1795 Dearborn *Columbian Grammar* 139, *List of Improprieties.* . . The tother for The other. **1821** in 1830 Royall *Letters AL* 121 **NC, TN,** He said if we voted for that there 'tother man, I forgot his name, that government would come and take away our land. **1846** in 1953 *AmSp* 28.142 **IN,** I just walked right through that barrel and come out the other end so quick that it really looked ashamed of itself. **1851** Hooper *Widow Rugby's Husband* 81 **AL,** My t'other daughter, Betsey. **1858** Hammett *Piney Woods Tavern* 289, He had the cases of right-hand gloves shipped to a man in London, and ordered the tothers to be sent on to Liverpool. **1903** *DN* 2.301 **Cape Cod MA** (as of a1857), *Tother.* . . Other. **1939** in 1976 *Weevils in the Wheat* 303 **VA** [Black], I always wus a stickin pins in de tother chil'en. **1966** *DARE* (Qu. X35, *Joking words for the part of the body that you sit on . . "He slipped and came down hard on his _____."*) Infs **ME**10, 21, Tother end. **2003** in 2005 *DARE* File—Internet **TX**, I just replied to your tother thread too and told you to do this. **2004** *Ibid* **CA**, Lars on one side, Oly on the 'tother.

2 The other. [*OED2* 1587 → (as pron); 1627 → (as adj)]
1790 Tyler *Contrast* 29, When I came where they was, one [statue] had got no head, and t'other wer'nt there. **1825** Neal *Brother Jonathan* 1.106 **CT**, Watty, he throws 'em all, one arter tother. **1829** *Adams Sentinel* (Gettysburg PA) [21 Jan 2]/1 (newspaperarchive.com) **KY**, He was talking French to a woman on t'other side of the table. **1843** (1916) Hall *New Purchase* 136 **IN**, One penny is the law; and tother's the gospel. **1852** Beardsley *Reminiscences* 67 **NY**, He says as how in t'other war,/ He ran right at the bullets. **1867** Harris *Sut Lovingood Yarns* 179 **TN**, Wun full ove quilt scraps an' pipes, an' tother es full ove deviltry. **1894** *DN* 1.342 **wCT**, *Tother:* the other. A good old form, still in common use. **1912** Green *VA Folk-Speech* 454, I saw him tother-day. **1936** Jesse Stuart in *Esquire* Nov 226 **KY**, Killed it plum over yander at that rock on tother hill. **1965–70** *DARE* (Qu. MM1, . . *'Opposite to' . . "The shed is _____ the barn."*) 10 Infs, **esp Sth, NEng**, Tother side; **NH**14, Tother side of; (Qu. W29, . . *Expressions . . for things that are sewn carelessly . . "They're _____."*) Inf **NY**220, Which and tother; (Qu. Y20, *To run fast: "You should have seen him _____!"*) Inf **TX**35, Put one in front of tother; (Qu. KK33, . . *'In succession': "He had a cold, then the measles, then chicken pox _____."*) Inf **VA**15, One right after tother; (Qu. KK54, *Just about equal, very close: "They were both fast runners and it was _____ all the way."*) Infs **NY**75, 96, Which and tother; (Qu. KK66, *When you are showing somebody the right way to do something: "No, not like that—do it _____."*) Inf **NH**14, Tother way; (Qu. MM4, . . *A short distance past . . "The mail box is just _____ the pine tree."*) Inf **MS**71, Tother side; **SC**39, Tother side [FW sugg]—that's hillbilly talk; **MS**7, Tother side of. **1976** Garber *Mountain-ese* 95 **sAppalachians**, *Tother* (adj) the other—I wanted the white horse but I had to settle for tother one.

3 See **other B2**.

tother-end-to adv Also *tother-end-backwards, ~-first, ~-foremost, tother-side-fore(most), ~-to, tother-way-which* **chiefly NEast** Cf **back-end-to, backside-to, hindside-to**
Backwards, the wrong way around.
1843 Thompson *Major Jones' Courtship* 19 **GA**, So up I pulls my feet and twisted 'em round through my arms over backwards, and was lettin my body down tother side foremost. **1852** *U.S. Postal Guide* 2.319, The scale ought to have been turned 'tother end foremost. **1856** *U.S. Democratic Rev.* 37.458 **NY**, The blade of a scythe curves in exactly the opposite direction from a sabre, and . . its handle is put on 'tother side foremost into the bargain. **1868** Clift *Tim Bunker* 137 **CT**, But Fred Olmstead has got things turned tother end foremost. **1868** (1869) Pomeroy *Nonsense* 237, I used to enjoy teachin', till they got to makin' boys pants t'other side to! That rather busted me! **1881** *Century Illustr. Mag.* 23.137 **NEng**, A roller . . shouldered the boat over, t'other end first, and slung me into the water. **1898** Westcott *Harum* 191 **nNY**, He had a faculty fer gettin' things t'other-end to that beat all. **1944** *ADD* 656 **cNY** (as of 1900), Your dress is on t'otherside fore. **1966–67** *DARE* (Qu. MM2, *Suppose a little girl accidentally gets her dress on wrong so that the back part is turned around . . "Look, you've got your dress on _____."*) Inf **MA**5, Tother-end-to; (Qu. MM3, *When someone does something the wrong way round . . "This is the front, you've got the whole thing turned _____."*) Inf **ME**16, Tother-end-backwards; **MA**5, Tother-end-to; **MA**6, Tother-way-which.

tother-end-up See **tother-side-up**

tother from which See **which from tother**

tother-side-fore(most), tother-side-to See **tother-end-to**

tother-side-up adv Also *tother-end-up* **chiefly NEast**
Upside down.
1844 (1973) Catlin *Letters Indians* 2.208 **PA**, We committed our bodies . . to the narrow compass of a modest canoe . . that required *us* . . to be exactly in the bottom . . , or it was *"t'other side up"* in an instant. **1854** (1969) Thoreau *Walden* 175 **MA**, He'll turn himself t' other side up and be as green as a leek in two days. **1863** Morford *Sprees* 36 **NY**, T-t-turned it the t-t-tother end up, . . and then y-y-you ought to have s-s-seen how it drawed! **1869** Stowe *Oldtown Folks* 530 **MA**, When he got through the year he turned his bar'l t'other side up, and begun at t'other end. **1878** *Harper's New Mth. Mag.* 56.615 **CT**, He don't read the

golden rewl t'other side up, as you do. **2003** in 2005 *DARE* File—Internet **VT**, My hoss is t'other side up!

tother-way-which See **tother-end-to**

totherwise adv
Otherwise.
1871 Pomeroy *Brick-Dust* 127, I think she was hugged by three thousand men whose habits were good, and by seventeen thousand whose habits were t'otherwise. **1939** in Lib. of Congress *Amer. Memory: WPA Life Hist.* (Internet) **FL**, I hears a lot about the world that-a-way that I wouldn't never know totherwise. **1951** Craig *Singing Hills* 204 **sAppalachians**, The idea of anybody believing totherwise! **2004** in 2005 *DARE* File—Internet **IN**, Good thing I didn't, totherwise I'd be typing to you all from jail. **2005** *Ibid* **TX**, Bottom drivers seat needs fixed totherwise truck is in good running condition.

to the (or this) world See **world, in the**

toting vbl n See **tote v A2b, 8**

toting adj See **tote v A4**

toting papers n [**tote v A5**]
1952 Brown *NC Folkl.* 1.602, *Toting-papers. . .* A warrant. "The sheriff was here looking for you. He had toting-papers for you."

toting road See **tote road**

totings See **tote v A8**

tottle v **chiefly NEng**
1 To totter, rock; to cause to totter; hence adjs *totlish, tottl(e)ish*.
c1820 in 1833 *New Engl. Mag.* 4.439, Before thy name each doctor's practice tottles;/ And 't is mere *fudge* for any to pretend / To ape thee, Prince of gallipots and bottles. **1835** *Knickerbocker* 6.6 **ME**, Had she not been obliged . . to steady her tottleish bark with the paddle which now loitered behind the stern. **1844** Haliburton *Attaché* (2d ser) 1.60 **NEng**, I had to stand her on the foot-stool, and that was so tottlish I had to put one hand on one side of her waist, and one on t'other. **1849** Lanman *Letters Alleghany Mts.* 51, As the rock started from its tottlish foundation, he seized the limb, and thereby saved his life. **1880** Cross *Fifty Yrs.* 128 **OH**, It is distressing to see a trim and handsome boat swayed, tottled and jammed about by an awkward boatman. **1887** (1895) Robinson *Uncle Lisha* 163 **wVT**, Them Injin canews is tottlisher 'n a board sot up aidgeways! **1890** Holley *Samantha among Brethren* 27 **NY**, The last day at my house had tottled her faith, and her own married experience had finished the work [of disillusionment]. **1896** Ballou–Heywood *Autobiog.* 8 **RI**, My brother . . persuaded me to attempt following him over a tottling plank or slab . . across the flume to the dam beyond. **1980** *DARE* File **nwMA**, Is *totlish* a commonly used form of tottery, teetery etc.? I've heard it used only in the region of North Leverett, Mass. . . . I'm sure it was local, not just family.

2 To fall, topple; to cause to fall; hence ppl adj *tottled* tipped. [Scots, nEngl dial; *OED2 tottle* v.¹ 3 1830 →; *EDD tottle* v. 2] **esp Sth, S Midl**
1838 Gilman *S. Matron* 253 **SC**, I strolled to the poultry-yard, and heard Maum Nelly's stories of how twenty fine young turkeys had just tottled backward and died so. **1840** *U.S. Mag. & Democratic Rev.* 7.299, Our eight hundred banks . . resembled as many pyramids standing on their pinnacles, and the first breath of disaster tottled them over. **1847** *De Bow's Rev.* 3.399 **ceGA**, That gigantic tree that the persevering cutter has with so much labor "tottled from its base," . . has vanished. **1855** Adams *Our World* 482 **SC**, The careless porter set it on a pile of baggage, from where it tottled over under the feet of an astonished gentleman. **1882** Dahlgren *S.-Mt. Magic* 68 **wMD**, All on a suddint a big Injun . . run agin him that hard, he jist tottled over. **2004** Russell *Riding with Magi* 9, The old genius is tottled over in the seat with his feet in the air over his head. **2009** *DARE* File—Internet **cnTN**, I would ask Charles later that afternoon how many farmers were killed each year when their tractors tottled over while plowing the steep wheat fields.

tottl(e)ish See **tottle 1**

touch v, n Usu |tʌč|; also **chiefly Sth, S Midl** |tɛč|; for addit varr see **A** below Pronc-spp *te(t)ch, to(t)ch*
A Pronc forms.
1791 in 2005 *DARE* File—Internet **PA**, [Diary entry:] Light Showers till noon then sunshine plowing for buckwheat, Rees's hors[e] not tetch the hay. **1848** Lowell *Biglow* 3 **'Upcountry' MA**, He told Hosee he didn't want to put his ore in to tetch to the Rest on 'em. **1862** *Conti-*

nental Mth. 2.568 **Sth,** Ary nother white man couldn't toch 'em [= slaves] fur less'n two thousand. **1867** Harris *Sut Lovingood Yarns* 78 **wNC,** I hed all the feelins mix'd up, ove the litenin, the river, an' the snake, wif a totch ove the quicksilver sensashun a huntin thru all my veins. **1868** Towle *Stories Fireside* 369 **AL,** She come pretty nigh burning her hand once, but I didn't let her quite *toch* it. **1871** Eggleston *Hoosier Schoolmaster* 112 **sIN,** You jest tech one of these ere fastenings. **1893** [see **B** below]. **1895** *DN* 1.376 **eTN,** I'll be dad gummed if I tech that! **1905** Chesnutt *Col.'s Dream* 80 **GA,** That . . teches me in a sof' spot. **1906** [see **B** below]. **1907** *DN* 3.237 **nwAR,** *Touch, v. tr.* Pronounced tech. **1909** *DN* 3.380 **eAL, wGA,** *Tetch, n.* and *v.* A variant spelling of *tech,* touch. **1922** Gonzales *Black Border* 333 **sSC, GA coasts** [Gullah glossary], *Tetch*—(n. and v.) touch, touches, touched, touching. **1931** (1991) Hughes–Hurston *Mule Bone* 51 **cFL** [Black], I ain't a going to tetch it! **1940** Faulkner *Hamlet* 396 **MS,** The old man spoke: "Tech my elbers," he said. **1961** Kurath–McDavid *Pronc. Engl.* 146, *Touch* . . commonly has the vowel /ɛ/ of *fetch* in the folk speech of the South and the South Midland and not infrequently in that of northeastern New England (Maine). . . Two other pronunciations occur sporadically: (1) an [ɜ]-like sound in western New York State (here clearly a fronted allophone of the vowel /ʌ/ . .) and in the Carolinas and Georgia (here either an allophone of /ʌ/ or of the /ɜ/ of *hurt*); (2) an [ɪ] or [ɨ]-like sound (only two instances in New Hampshire and one in South Carolina). **1978** Massey *Bittersweet Country* 207 **Ozarks,** He has just a tetch of rheumatiz. **2000** Shores *Tangier Is.* 175 **Chesapeake Bay,** Words like *brush, hush, touch,* . . are commonly pronounced among the older Islanders with the vowel of *fresh,* giving us "bresh," "hesh," "tech."

B Gram forms.

Past, past pple: usu *touched;* also **chiefly Sth, S Midl** *te(t)ched, to(t)ch, to(t)ched, tocht, toch'd,* rarely *taught.* Cf **catch** v A3, **fetch** v A2

1835 Paulding *Letters from South* 2.201 **VA** [Black], When de footboat totch de shore, de gin'ral slung he great-coat to Tom Bishop. **1844** Thompson *Major Jones's Courtship* 137 **GA,** I never tetched one of 'em in my life. **1851** Hooper *Widow Rugby's Husband* 90 **AL,** Jim gits on the roan, and tetched him in the flank with the heel. **1852** Byrn *Rattlehead's Chron.* 138 **TN,** The licker . . wer not to be toch til ten o'clock that nite. **1857** Strother *VA Illustr.* 174, "Done gone by, and never toch us!" quoth the coachman. **1860** (1861) Caldwell *Thurstons Old Palmetto* 118 **SC,** The Cap'n was perfickly sober. He hadn't toch'd a drap. **1867** Harris *Sut Lovingood Yarns* 189 **TN,** An' the nigger . . cotch his fiddil in bof hans afore hit toch the yeath. **1882** *Century Illustr. Mag.* 24.877 **GA** [Black], I tole him ef he toch dat chile, I gim de wust whippin' ever he toted. **1883** (1971) Harris *Nights with Remus* 164 **GA** [Black], He aint mo'n totch his head on de piller tel he year de yuther fuss. **1886** *Harper's New Mth. Mag.* 74.37 **Sth,** He had not "tetched a drap in Gord knows how long." **1893** Shands *MS Speech* 64, *Toch* [tắč]—Negro for *touch. Tech* [tɛč] is also used for *touch* by negroes. *Toch* sometimes forms a regular past tense, *tochéd,* and sometimes is itself used as past. **1897** Murfree in *Atlantic Mth.* 80.119 **TN,** Two p'ints had been teched through with a knife-blade. **1899** (1912) Green *VA Folk-Speech* 454, *Totch, v.* For *touched.* **1903** *DN* 2.334 **seMO,** *Toch, pret.* of touch or tech. Touched. 'I never toch him.' Dialect writers often get this expression *tochéd,* which is a double preterite and would be considered incorrect by any 'native.' *Ibid, Touch, v. tr.* Pronounced tech. 'He never teched me.' **1906** *DN* 3.162 **nwAR,** *Totch, v. tr.* To touch, hit. "He never totched the man." **1907** *DN* 3.237 **nwAR,** *Toch, pret.* of touch or tech. **1909** *DN* 3.382 **eAL, wGA,** *Toch(t), pret.* of *tech* or *touch.* **1922** *DN* 5.184 **GA,** *Totch, v.* Touched. "But he hadn't no mo'n totch me 'fo' I flung deze hyer bones in his face." **1952** Brown *NC Folkl.* 1.601, *Totched.* . . Past tense and past participle of *touch.* . . General. Illiterate. **1960** *AmSp* 35.239 **cwCA** [Black], *Toch* [tɒtʃ] or *taught* [tɔut], past tense of 'to touch'. . . Every informant that I interviewed had heard this form [=*taught*] used at one time or another by the 'old folks,' but only three of them . . had ever used it themselves. . . I heard one eleven-year-old girl, the daughter of rural Georgians, . . use the term. While playing a game of jacks, she said, 'The jacks taught. I saw 'em.'

C As verb.

1 with *up:* To steal fish or lobsters from (a trap or net).

1905 Wasson *Green Shay* 57 **ME,** You'd think fish was some dear jest now, to see how fierce them Thrumbcappers are now'days to 'touch up' every trawl they can run afoul of within reach of the Island! **1975** Gould *ME Lingo* 296, *Touchin' up*—A strange Maine euphemism for stealing, perhaps deriving from *touchin' up* somebody in the sense of borrowing. Specifically, it means taking fish or lobsters from another

man's nets or traps. "Somebody's touchin' up my traps, and he just better not let me find out who!"

2 To offend, hurt the feelings of; to become offended or hurt. [Cf *OED2 touch* v. 25.a "To grieve, vex; to injure, harm: esp. in a slight degree"; 1535–1608] **esp Sth, S Midl, IL** See Map Cf **touchous 1**

1959 Lomax *Rainbow Sign* 112 **AL** [Black], Women are just easy to touch, I reckon. They're more easy to feel anything than a man. **1965–70** *DARE* (Qu. GG8, *When a person is very easily offended: "Be careful what you say to him, he's _____."*) 12 Infs, **esp SE, IL,** Easily touched; **AR**51, **MS**56, **NC**31, Easy touched; **SC**58, Touches easy; [(Qu. GG6, *Talking about a person's feelings being hurt: "When she said she wouldn't go with him, he was quite _____."*) Inf **NC**17, Touched to the quick;] (Qu. GG33b, *To feel very sad and upset about something: "I never saw a woman _____ so.";* total Infs questioned, 75) Inf **OK**13, She was touched. [15 of 17 Infs old] **1966** Dakin *Dial. Vocab. Ohio R. Valley* 2.468, *Easy touched* (sometimes *easily*) and *easy tetched* are used by some older speakers in the Mountains, Knobs, and Bluegrass. . . Some of these terms regularly have either or both of two related meanings: (1) easily offended and quick to anger (2) easily offended—"feelings hurt"—weeps, etc. **1986** Pederson *LAGS Concordance (Touchy),* 1 inf, **swMS,** Easy to touch; 1 inf, **neFL,** Easy to touch—means "make angry." [Both infs old]

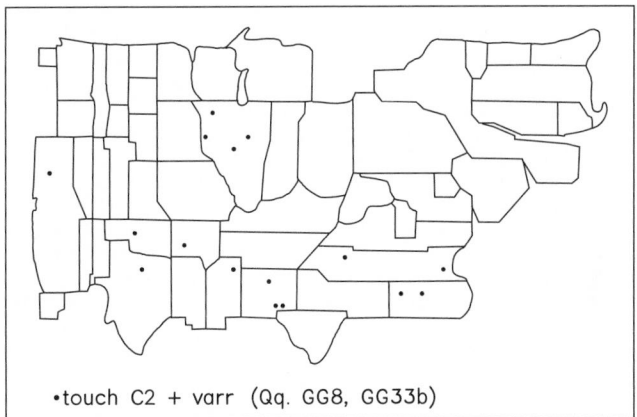

•touch C2 + varr (Qq. GG8, GG33b)

touch berry n Cf **touch-me-not 1**

A **jewelweed 1** (here: *Impatiens pallida*).

1966 *DARE* Wildfl QR Pl.122B [=*Impatiens pallida*] Inf **SC**41, Touch berry—touch-me-not.

touch bug n

1969 *DARE* FW Addit **NC,** *Touch bug*—some type of stinging bug, apparently not a worm. Said to like oak trees.

toucheous See **touchous 1**

touch-hole n [*OED2* 1664 →; by analogy with a cannon, which has a touch-hole at the breech] **esp NEast**

The anus.

1942 McAtee *Dial. Grant Co. IN Suppl. 1* 10 (as of 1890s), *Touch-hole* . . anus. **1966–68** *DARE* (Qu. R11, *A very tiny fly that you can hardly see, but that stings*) Inf **MA**6, Touch-hole flies—husband's term; (Qu. X35, *Joking words for the part of the body that you sit on . . "He slipped and came down hard on his _____."*) Inf **NH**14, Touch-hole. **1966** *DARE* FW Addit **ME**19, Touch-hole—the anus. **1991** Hoagland in Safire *Coming to Terms* 318 **NY,** In my previous communication I drew your attention to the trappers' and hunters' term "touch-hole" for an animal's anus.

touch leather See **leather 1a**

touch-me-not n

1 =**jewelweed 1.** [*OED2* at *touch-me-not* 1.b 1659 →]

1782 in 1793 Amer. Philos. Soc. *Trans.* 3.224, The *orange-colour* employed by the Indians, is obtained . . from the plant called *Touch-me-not.* **1843** *Amer. Pioneer* 2.451 **NC,** We had . . to chop down the nettles, the water-weed, and the touch-me-not. **1895** *Atlantic Mth.* 75.464 **NEng,** Other seeds were gathered as the children's spoils: those of . . the jewelweed, to watch them snap violently open,—hence its country name of touch-me-not and snapweed. **1927** Kennedy *Gritny* 91 **sLA** [Black], Who goin' buy tetch-me-not flow'rs, w'en dey got 'um growin' wil' like grass, all up an' down de railroad track? **1961** Douglas *My Wilderness* 173 **NC,** We found the touch-me-not in seed. I learned that its seed pods are under tension. For when I touched one, it would burst, sending its seeds out in a radius of eighteen inches or more. Its appropriate scientific name is *Impatiens*. **1965–70** *DARE* (Qu. S11, . . *Wild snapdragon*) Infs **IL**16, **IN**30, 35, 38, **VA**28, Touch-me-not(s); (Qu. S26b, *Wildflowers that grow in water or wet places*) Inf **NY**30, Touch-me-not—shoulder height—they pop at the slightest touch in fall; **TN**11, Jewelweed or touch-me-not; **VA**11, Some call balsam touch-me-not; **VA**43, 46, Touch-me-not; (Qu. S26c, *Wildflowers that grow in woods*) Inf **DC**5, [tɛtʃmɪnət]; **ME**8, Touch-me-not; **MI**53, Touch-me-not—grows along lakeshore edges—when you touch it, it explodes; (Qu. S26d, *Wildflowers that grow in meadows; not asked in early QRs*) Inf **KY**28, Tetch-me-nots; (Qu. S26e, *Other wildflowers not yet mentioned; not asked in early QRs*) Inf **MD**18, Touch-me-not—something like snapdragon, yellow with brown speckles, fewer flowers on bush than snapdragon; bruised plant with flower bound onto poison ivy rash as cure; **IN**14, Touch-me-nots. **1966** *DARE* Wildfl QR Pl.122A [=*Impatiens biflora*] 10 Infs, **scattered,** Touch-me-not(s); Pl.122B [=*Impatiens pallida*] Infs **AR**44, **MI**57, **NC**28, **OH**14, 37, **WA**15, Touch-me-not(s). **2002** *DARE* File—Internet, The early morning dewdrops on these spotted touch-me-not leaves glisten in the sunlight. . . There are five species of jewelweed. Two . . are known as touch-me-nots, because when touched, the ripe seed pods "explode" as a means of scattering their seeds.

2 Usu a **sensitive plant 1,** but occas a related plant of similar habit such as a **partridge pea.**   Cf **sensitive plant 1, 2**

    1839 *S. Lit. Messenger* 5.827, He [=Love] skipp'd away with merry bound,/ And soon a Lily stalk he found / To represent her [=a woman's] form,/ . . /The Damask-Rose he mingled then / With Snow-drops gathered from the glen,/ To give her cheek its hue;/ . . /Her heart . . / . . here is a Touch-me-not—/ . . /But all in vain his bow he strung;/ No shaft [=Love's arrow] could reach the lady's heart,/ The Touch-me-not had done its part. **1875** *Appletons' Jrl.* 14.617, Besides, the girl's heart was as sensitive as a touch-me-not, and it quivered at the hint of a something unmaidenly which the hide-and-seek figure seemed to imply. **1899** Woerner *Rebel's Daughter* 301 **Ozarks,** "Have you ever seen the plant commonly called Touch-me-not? . . Or a Mimosa?" . . She led the way to a secluded part of the garden. . . "Now sir," she said, . . "you are in the presence of the . . *Mimosa Sensitiva* [=*M. pudica*]." . . He boldly grasped the topmost branch of the little plant. . . The effect startled him. . . He was surprised to see the little plant close up its leaves pair by pair, with deliberate regularity, . . within a few seconds. **1905** *DN* 3.23 **cCT,** Touch-me-not. . . The sensitive plant. **1907** *DN* 3.219 **nwAR,** Touch-me-not. . . The sensitive plant. **1966** *DARE* Wildfl QR Pl.105A [=*Chamaecrista nictitans*] Inf **MN**37, Touch-me-not. **1976** Bailey-Bailey *Hortus Third* 734, [*Mimosa*] *pudica*. . . Touch-me-not. . . Often grown in the greenhouse as a curiosity, the l[ea]v[e]s being sensitive and closing when touched. **2002** *DARE* File—Internet, The *mimosa pudica* is a sensitive plant whose leaves close at the slightest touch. . . [T]o see it actually responding to your touch, to see the leaves fold and droop . . tickled me. . . We used to call them *touch-me-nots* precisely because of the way the leaves responded.

touchmonk n   Also *tutchmonk, tutchmunk*   Cf **pegmonk**
=**red-throated loon.**

    1875 *Fur Fin & Feather* 119, The smaller species of loon I have heard variously called the spike-bill, the cape-race, the touch-monk, the gun-greaser, the pegging-all [sic], etc. **1925** (1928) Forbush *Birds MA* 1.28, *Gavia stellata*. . . Other names: red-throated diver; . . tutchmunk. **1955** MA Audubon Soc. *Bulletin* 39.309, Red-throated Loon. . . Touchmonk, also spelled Tutchmonk. (Mass. Meaning unknown.)

touch one's pin v phr   [Cf *OED2 pin* sb.¹ 13 "A piece at chess. . . *Obs.*"]
To commit oneself.

    1967 *DARE* FW Addit **LA** [Black], You can't back out now; you've done totched your pin.

touchous adj

1 also sp *toucheous:* =**tetchy;** also fig.   [Ir, nEngl dial] **chiefly Sth, S Midl**   See Map

    1880 *Decatur Daily Rev.* (IL) 21 Jan [2]/5 (newspaperarchive.com), That "touchous" little [rat] trap. **1899** (1912) Green *VA Folk-Speech* 454, *Touchous*. . . Touchy. Apt to take offence on slight provocation; irritable; irascible; peevish; testy; techy. **1901** *Atlanta Constitution* (GA)

22 Nov 7/1, He said that the depot matter "seemed to be the most touchous question in the world." **1946** *PADS* 5.42 **VA,** Touchous. . . Easily angered; common everywhere. *Ibid* 6.31 **ceNC,** Touchous. . . Ill-tempered; resentful of being touched or interfered with. Pamlico. **1960** Lee *Mockingbird* 72 **sAL,** He said Atticus was still touchous about us and the Radleys and it wouldn't do to push him any. **1965–70** *DARE* (Qu. GG8, *When a person is very easily offended: "Be careful what you say to him, he's _____."*) 16 Infs, **chiefly Sth, S Midl,** Touchous; (Qu. GG41, *To lose patience easily: "You never did see such a _____ person."*) Inf **TN**65, Touchous. **1975** *Appalachian Jrl.* 2.159 **wNC,** A person who is *tetchious* or *toucheous* is unusually sensitive and difficult. **1986** Pederson *LAGS Concordance (Easily offended; irritable)* 78 infs, **scattered Gulf Region, but esp TN, MS,** Touchous. **2000** Berry *Jayber Crow* 57 **KY,** It was a touchous moment. I felt like I was on top of a tall pole, ready to fall off.

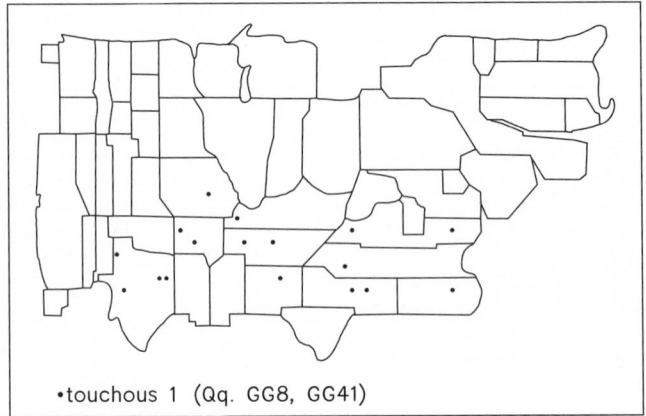

•touchous 1 (Qq. GG8, GG41)

2 Physically sensitive; tender, painful to the touch.   **Sth, S Midl**   Cf **tetchous 2**

    1894 Firebaugh *Physician's Wife* 159 **ceIL,** "Look out, Doc.! It's touchous right thar!" . . "Look out! It's touchouser thar!" **1923** *DN* 5.223 **swMO,** Touchous. . . Tender, sensitive. . . "My bile's [=boil's] right touchous." **1966** *PADS* 46.30 **AR,** Touchous. . . Sensitive.—"It's very touchous. If you touch it, it'll bleed." **1966** *Daily Times* (Salisbury MD) 14 May 4/3 **MD, Delmarva,** Touchous—for sensitive, as a tooth when the drill gets to [sic] near the nerve ending. **1970** *DARE* File **sGA, nFL,** Touchous ['təčəs]—Tender, sore. Used by Negroes in southern Georgia and northern Florida to describe a bruised or inflamed or infected place on the body. **1985** *Amer. Jrl. Med.* Feb 184 **eTN,** Touchous . . painful, tender, sore to touch. "It's sortie touchous to press." **1986** Pederson *LAGS Concordance,* 1 inf, **swAL,** Touchous—sensitive, of a sore place on skin; 1 inf, **csMS,** Flesh is touchous; 1 inf, **cnLA,** Touchous—one who does not like being touched. **1990** [see **tetchous 2**].

touch up   See **touch C1**

tough as whang   See **whang** n¹ **2**

tough as whang leather   See **whang leather**

tough as whitleather   See **whitleather 1**

tougher than whang   See **whang** n¹ **2**

tough-head n
=**ruddy duck.**

    1888 Trumbull *Names of Birds* 111 **MA,** Ruddy duck. . . to some at Martha's Vineyard, *tough-head.*

tough jack n   Also *stiff jacks*   **esp KY**
A kind of molasses candy.

    1957 Combs *Lang. S. Highlanders* **sAppalachians,** Toughjack—a tough candy made by boiling molasses at a "candy pulling." **1969** *DARE* (Qu. H80, *Kinds of candy . . made at home*) Inf **KY**15, Tough jack—a molasses candy, old-fashioned. **1982** Slone *How We Talked* 57 **eKY** (as of c1950), Stiff Jacks, or molasses candy. **1983** Farr *More Moonshine* 193 **seKY,** We always called molasses taffy "Tough Jack"—I was never sure why, unless because it was hard work pulling, doubling back, twisting, and pulling again until the candy was taffy colored and firm. **2004** *DARE* File—Internet **eKY,** I remember popping popcorn at

Grandma Couch's and making cracker jacks and also "tough jack" candy.

tough sledding See **sledding**

toughy (minnow) n Also *tuffy (minnow)* esp S Midl
A **fathead 1,** usu *Pimephales promelas.*

1982 Sternberg *Fishing* 20, Fatheads, also called *tuffies* or *mudminnows. . .* live in lakes and rivers throughout most of North America. *Ibid* 25, In the South, fatheads may be sold as *tuffies* or *mudminnows.* **1986** Pederson *LAGS Concordance (Minnows)* 1 inf, **cnAL,** Toughy minnows, toughies; 1 inf, **cnAL,** Toughy—type of minnow; 1 inf, **ceAL,** Toughies—shipped in from L[ouisian]a, grow in rice paddies. **1998** GA Univ. Warnell School Forestry *Aquaculture Newsl.* Feb (Internet), The fathead minnow is a small dark plump minnow that is popular as bait for crappie fishing. Some fishermen call it the "Tuffy" minnow because it is able to survive a long time in a bait bucket or on a fish hook. **2003** *DARE* File—Internet **nAL,** One of my favorites is a heavy hair jig tipped with a tuffy minnow. *Ibid* **MD,** Rosy red minnows and fathead minnows *are* the exact same species, *Pimephales promelas.* There are many strange names given to rosy red minnows with tuffy or tuffies being pretty common in large chain aquarium stores.

toula See **tule 1**

tour n, v Usu |tu(ə)r, tur|; also |tau(ə)r, tor, tɜ˞| Pronc-spp *taur, tore, tower* Similarly *towerist* [*OED2* 1643 →]
Std senses, var forms.

1794 in 1907 *PA Archives* 6th ser 5.808, The Bearer . . served . . in the Rifle Company . . as a full tower of Duty. **1827** (1939) Sherwood *Gaz. GA* 139, *Tower,* for tour pr[onounced] toor. **1834** *Life Andrew Jackson* 85, James, a boy of sixteen years of age, enrolled himself tu serve a tower of duty. **1847** Hurd *Grammatical Corrector* 90, *Tour* ["incorrect" pronc = [taur]; "correct" pronc = [tur]]. **1855** (1873) Burgess *Five Hundred Mistakes* 36, Pronounce *tour* so as to rhyme with *poor.* Be careful to avoid saying *take a tower.* **1859** Shillaber *Knitting-Work* 360 **NH,** We were out in the country . . on a bit of a "tower," as the landlord of Hardscrabble "guessed," as we stopped there for the night. **1862** (1864) Browne *Artemus Ward Book* 206, My fust perfeshernal tower threw New Englan. **1899** (1912) Green *VA Folk-Speech* 455, *Tower. . .* A turn round some place; a going round from place to place; a continued ramble or excursion; a short journey: as a wedding *tower.* **1903** *DN* 2.334 **seMO,** *Tour. . .* Pronounced tower. Journey. 'They have gone on their weddin' tower.' **1907** *DN* 3.237 **nwAR,** *Tour. . .* Pronounced tower ['tauə]. **1907** White *AZ Nights* 225, At the railroad one of them towerist trains had just slowed down to a halt as I come up, and the towerists was paradin' up and down. **1915** *DN* 4.192 **swVA,** *Tower.* Variant of *tour.* **1932** *AmSp* 7.271 [Oil field language], *Tour. . .* (Pronounced "taur") A shift, usually of eight hours. **1950** *WELS Suppl.* **ceWI,** The *tour* [tɑur] *boss*—man in charge of one shift. [Inf] heard while working in a paper mill. He got a stiff neck looking for a *tower* with a boss in it. **1966** *DARE* Tape **MT3** (as of 1920s), You would have to climb the derrick once or twice during a shift, which they called a ['tauɚ], t-o-u-r, at that time; **OK29,** [FW:] What are these towers? [Inf:] [tauɚz], that is a eight-hour shift. I don't know where they come up with the, the way they spell [tauɚ], but it's t-o-u-r; it's not t-o-w-e-r. **1980** *DARE* File **VT** (as of c1900), If something was wrong he'd have his driver pull up, then he'd lean out the side of the car and shout to a passerby, "We're 'towering' the country. Can you tell us where there's a 'garidge'?" **2000** *Ibid* **IA,** In my pronunciation, *tour* usually has the vowel of *boot* (sometimes, in rapid speech, that of *girl*), but I notice easterners (?) who use the vowel of *boat* or even *bought. Ibid* **MN,** My mother did say both /tɚ/ and /tɚd/ [for tour(ed)] (b. Minnesota 1906). **2007** *DARE* File—Internet **OH,** My next tore of duty in Korea. **2009** *AmSp* 84.441 **NJ,** Informants were asked if *tour* and *door* rhyme. Almost the entire state reported that they did. Only 12 of 427 informants said they did not, 11 of whom were in the north.

tourister n chiefly Sth, S Midl Cf **-er** affix **1, residenter 1**
A tourist.

1923 *DN* 5.223 **swMO,** *Tourister. . .* A tourist. **1930** *AmSp* 5.269 [Ozark dialect], The hillman's common use of *tourister* for *tourist* and *musicianer* for *musician* seems inexplicable at first, but *er* was once a commoner suffix for agent nouns than it is now. **1933** Williamson *Woods Colt* 117 **Ozarks,** To keep them touristers from finding it out. **1964** Will *Hist. Okeechobee* xi **FL,** *Tourister*—a tourist. **1966** *DARE* (Qu. HH28, *Names and nicknames . . for people of foreign background*) Inf **FL28,** Tourister. **2004** Montgomery–Hall *Dict. Smoky Mt. Engl.*

615 **wNC, eTN,** *Tourister . .* (a facetious term, largely introduced to the mountains in recent times).

tourist tarpon n **TX**
1 A **crevalle a** (here: *Caranx hippos*).
1941 TX Acad. Sci. *Trans. for 1940* 24.22 **TX,** *Caranx hippos . .* Crevalle, toro, . . *tourist tarpon* (Port Aransas). **1946** La Monte *N. Amer. Game Fishes* 36, Common Jack Crevalle—*Caranx hippos . .* Names: Crevalle, . . Tourist Tarpon. . . Two or 3 pounds; up to 20.

2 A **ten-pounder 1** (here: *Elops saurus*).
2002 *Corpus Christi Caller-Times* (TX) 18 May (Internet) **sTX,** My San Antonio buddy . . began hooking skipjacks (ladyfish), one of the more acrobatic species of the Texas coast. Some people call them tourist tarpon. **2002** in 2009 *DARE* File—Internet **TX,** I had similiar [sic] trip in Mata. surf last weekend Ladyfish (tourist tarpon) were every where. **2006** *Ibid* **TX,** We had trout in there, but were also treated to healthy rod bending from some hungry Snot Tops (Gaff Top) and some really aggressive Tourist Tarpon (Skip Jacks). **2007** *Ibid* **TX,** They seem perfectly suited to hit any and everything you *dont* want them to hit. For me, if I really want one, all I have to do is find a good tailing red, make that one perfect cast . . and whammo, guaranteed tourist tarpon.

tournament n Usu |'tɜ˞nə,mɪnt, 'turnə,mɪnt|; also |'tɔrnə,mɪnt| Pronc-spp *tor(e)nament, tunament* Cf **tour**
A Forms.
1878 *Marion Daily Star* (OH) 31 Aug [4]/2 (newspaperarchive.com), A Base Ball tornament will be given at Delaware, commencing September 3rd. **1891** Page *Elsket* 128 **VA** [Black], I say, 'P'laski, what air a tunament?' . . 'A tunament . . is whar you gits 'pon a hoss wid a pole, an' rides hard as you kin, an' pokes de pole at a ring.' **1966–67** *DARE* (Qu. FF16) Inf **MI25,** Winter Queen—in connection with the ski tournament ['tornəmənt]; **MI44,** Fireman's tournaments ['tɔrnəmənts]. **2001** *DARE* File **MI,** I have noticed that tournament seems to have two pronunciation[s,] tour-nament and turn-ament. The tour sounds so weird to me. *Ibid* **MN,** As a Northerner, I . . have turn-ament; but the Philadelphia and Baltimore area has tore-nament. **2009** *AmSp* 84.442 **NJ,** The vast majority of New Jerseyans report *tore-* as the first syllable of *tournament.*

B Sense.
A contest in which riders on horseback (rarely, bicycles) attempt to spear a suspended ring; hence nouns *tournament pole* (or *arch*) the pole or structure from which the ring is suspended. **MD, VA, WV**
1888 *OH Democrat* (New Philadelphia) 19 July 1/3 **VA,** [Headline:] A Joust in Virginia. The Annual Tournament on the Rappahannock. The Great Event of the Year. **1891** [see **A** above]. **1897** *News* (Frederick MD) 4 Aug [3]/4 (newspaperarchive.com), Tournament poles have been erected at the park and equipped with rings. Those [bicyclists] who expect to enter the tournament are at liberty to begin practicing at any time. **1933** *Sun* (Baltimore MD) 11 Aug 20/6 *(Hench Coll.),* Reversing the customary procedure, the women of St. James' parish at My Lady's Manor next week will set their lances in rest and ride in a tournament while the men watch from the side of the lists. **1945** *Ibid* 3 Aug 13/2, The parish staged its annual "tournament," a Talbot county tradition of over a hundred years' standing, and virtually an unofficial county holiday. **1968–70** *DARE* (Qu. FF16, . . *Local contests or celebrations*) Infs **VA44, 101,** Jousting tournament; **WV8,** Tournament rides. **1968** *DARE* Tape **WV8,** [FW:] Is there anything to the tournament at all besides just riding and then crowning the queen? [Inf:] They generally have a picnic, the old-time tournament ['tɜ˞nəmɪnt] picnic. You went and took your basket and then put the tables all together and everybody'd eat together. Then, after that was over, then they rode, see? Then when the crown, carnation [=coronation] was over, you went home. [Aux Inf:] Well now, before this picnic starts, they have a charge [=a speech] to the knights. *Ibid,* [Inf:] When you start, you take and put up these three arches. . . Then you put a ring on each arch. [FW:] Now, is that what they're called, arches? [Inf:] . . I think they are. . . We always called 'em a tournament ['tɜ˞nə,mɪnt] pole, but they're arches, I think. **1968** *DARE* FW Addit **ceWV,** I asked several people about the local jousts and no one knew what I was talking about. Most people refer to it as the tournament. The older folk . . call it the picnic. ("There are going to be two picnics in Virginia this week.") In earlier days, the tournament was a more important social event than it is now. Everyone brought his picnic basket and when the rides were over, everyone ate together. **1970** *Frederick Post* (MD) 16 July sec A 16/1, The annual Petersville Jousting

Tournament sponsored by the Silver Bit Riding Club will be held on this Saturday. **2002** *Capital* (Annapolis MD) 11 July 1/2, There have been ring tournament arches at St. Margaret's, where Mr. Ridout is a warden and helps run the tournament, for more than 80 years.

tournament pole   See **tournament B**

touse n   Also sp *touss, towse*   [*OED2* 1795 →]   **chiefly NEng, esp ME**   Cf **catouse**

A commotion, disturbance; a state of agitation; hence v *touse* to make a fuss.

   1836 (1838) Haliburton *Clockmaker* (1st ser) 56 **NEng,** Marm Lecain makes such an eternal touss about her carpets, that I have to go . . to the street door to spit. **1854** (1923) Holmes *Tempest & Sunshine* 22 **MA,** 'Pears like somebody's been tousing round the house all night. **1878** *Harper's New Mth. Mag.* 56.226 **NEast,** She wanted to keep my house./ . . . / I gave her a dollar, and told her to pack;/ At which she made such a touse—/ You never did see such a touse! **1890** *DN* 1.20 **seNH,** *Touse:* ado, fuss. 'To make a touse.' **1894** Jewett in *Atlantic Mth.* 73.45 **ME,** There, what a touse I be in! **1902** (1904) Rowe *Maid of Bar Harbor* 14 **ME,** Half the headaches an' backaches that folks make such a towse over are just clear imagination. **1909** *DN* 3.418 **nME,** *Touse.* . . An outcry or ado. "He is making a great touse over his injury." **1914** *DN* 4.76 **nNH, ME,** *Make a touse.* . . To make a row, or fight; "take on." **1929** *AmSp* 5.128 **ME,** A "towse" . . was a noisy disturbance, "What is all this towse about?" **1950** Moore *Candlemas Bay* 93 **ME,** I can just remember the touse that went up when Jebron wanted to call Marilyn Susan, after her mother.

tow v   Cf **pump** v **2,** *DCEU*

To give (someone) a ride on one's bicycle.

   1968 *DARE* FW Addit **ceSC,** *Tow.* . . Give someone a ride on your bicycle. . . "Tow . . me to the corner." **1973** *DARE* File **ceGA,** *Tow.* . . To ride someone (i.e., a second person) on a bicycle. Current in Savannah, Ga. **2006** *Ibid* **seSC,** I also noted *tow* [meaning "to give (someone) a ride on your bicycle"] in my study in Charleston incidental to the pronunciation data I was collecting.

toward prep   Also *towards*

 A Forms. Usu |tord(z), tɔrd(z), 'toəd(z), 'tɔəd(z)|; also |təˈwo(ə)d(z), təˈwɔ(ə)d(z), tword(z), twɔrd(z)|; also occas |two(ə)d(z), twɔ(ə)d(z)|; **esp Sth** |tod(z)|; **esp S Midl** |tɔrǰ, təwɔrǰ, twarǰ|; pronc-spp *toads, toards, todes, todge, tods, tords, torge, towar(d)ge, toze, twar(d)ge, twarg, twoge;* for addit pronc and sp varr see quots

   1843 (1916) Hall *New Purchase* 115 **IN,** Lee-e-tle tor'ds rite corner of dimind—jeest grazed centre! **1859** Taliaferro *Fisher's R.* 41 **nwNC** (as of 1820s), A heap uv groanin' . . goes a grate ways toads settin' off a meetin'. *Ibid* 56, Right toards me. **1883** (1971) Harris *Nights with Remus* 244 **GA** [Black], Brer Fox crack he whip, un off dey wen' toze town. **1890** *DN* 1.40 **csME,** *Towards* . . [tɔədz], *not* [tɔdz]. **1894** Riley *Armazindy* 69 **IN,** And he whispered, as they driv / Tords the country, *"Now we'll live!"* **1899** (1967) Chesnutt *Wife of Youth* 143 **NC** [Black], Dat kinder weavin' come f'om down to'ds Souf Ca'lina. **1909** *DN* 3.382 **eAL, wGA,** *Tôd(s)* [=[tod(z)]], . . Towards. **1912** Green *VA Folk-Speech* 455, *Towa'rds.* **1928** Bradford *Ol' Man Adam* 6 **cwTN** [Black], Eve see a great big highland moccasin crawlin' long twarg her. **1929** Sale *Tree Named John* 46 **MS,** He sa'ntered off down de road twoge Brer Li-yon's house. **1937** (1963) Hyatt *Riverlid* 87 **KY,** Oncet a pant'er run Gran'pap an' another feller mor'n a mile, as they lit out one night goin' torge home. **1941** *AmSp* 16.6 **eTX** [Black], *Towards,* [toːdz]. **1943** *LANE* Map 722 *(Toward[s])* **NEng,** [Proncs of the types [toəd(z), tɔ(ə)d(z)] occur most frequently (approx 300 times); proncs of the types [tord(z), tɔrd(z)] occur approx 50 times; proncs of the types [təwoəd(z), təwɔ(ə)d(z), two(ə)d(z)] occur occasionally, as do those of the types [təwo(ə)rd(z), təwɔrd(z), tward(z)]; other proncs, such as [tʊ(ə)rdz, tuədz, tɜdz, toə(r)dʒ] occur infrequently.] **1944** *PADS* 2.41 **nwNC,** *Towardge, twardge* [təˈwardʒ, twardʒ]. . . Toward(s). Wautauga Co., N.C. Children. Common. **1950** *PADS* 14.68 **SC,** *Todes, todge.* . . Towards, in the direction of. He went off todge home. **1954** Roberts *I Bought Dog* 29 **seKY,** It come right straight towarge the red bull. **1963** Edwards *Gravel* 16 **eTN** (as of 1920s), Down the little sandy road twarge the spring. **1967–69** *DARE* FW Addit **swAR,** Towards [təˈwɔrǰ]; **AR54,** Towards [təˈwɔrǰ]—heard from others in community [=Murfreesboro], too; **seAR,** Towards—[tɔrǰ] or [tɔrǰ]; **cLA,** [touə˂ˆdz]. They never would let us pronounce the *w;* we always had to pronounce it as if it were spelled t-o-e-r-d-s. The pronunciation of that word placed you [in terms of social class]; **MA**14, [ˌtəˈwɝdz] = towards. **1989** Pederson *LAGS Tech. Index* 119 **Gulf Region,** [Proncs of the types

[tord(z), tɔrd(z)] occur most frequently (approx 250 times), and those of the types [to(ə)d(z), tɔ(ə)d(z)] occur approx 100 times; proncs of the types [təˈword(z), təˈwɔrd(z)] occur approx 100 times, and those of the types [təˈwo(ə)d(z), təˈwɔ(ə)d(z)] approx 60 times; proncs of the types [tword(z), twɔrd(z)] occur approx 60 times, and those of the types [two(ə)d(z), twɔ(ə)d(z)] approx 50 times; proncs of the types [tɔrǰ, tɔrǰ, torč, tworč] occur rarely.]

 B Sense.

In comparison with. **PaGer area**

   1934 *Language* 10.4 **cPA,** *Towards* for *in comparison with: longer towards what it used to be still.* **1935** *AmSp* 10.167 **PA** [Engl of PA Germans], It was very lonesome toward living in a family of five (as compared with living). **1968** *Helen Adolf Festschrift* 38 [English of PaGer area], *Towards* (Pennsylvania German *geeich*) for 'in comparison with'; for example, "I am nothing towards him." **1987** *Jrl. Engl. Ling.* 20.2.176 **ePA,** *Toward(s)* 'in comparison with' (cf PaGer *geeich*). . . 3% [of 100 infs], ages 51–68.

towardge   See **toward A**

towards   See **toward**

towarge   See **toward A**

towba n   [Var of **catawba**]   Cf **toby tree**

=catalpa B1.

   2004 *DARE* File—Internet **neTX,** A catalpa tree is a towba.

tow bag n   **formerly widespread, now esp NC**   See Map

=tow sack.

   1807 (1874) Adams *Memoirs J.Q. Adams* 1.458 **MA,** The President [=Thomas Jefferson] . . told some of his customary staring stories. Among the rest, he said that before he went from Virginia to France he had some ripe pears sewed up in tow bags, and that when he returned six years afterwards he found them in a perfect state of preservation—self-candied. **1839** *Alton Telegraph* (IL) [5 Jan 4]/2 (newspaperarchive.com), [Advt:] Tea Kettles; Tow Bags; Bed Cords; Plow Lines. **1866** *Atlantic Mth.* 18.19 **OH,** The white heifer she had always called hers was sold, and the money tied up in a tow bag. **1878** *St. Joseph Traveler & Herald* (MI) 27 Apr 1/7 **Boston MA,** Yes, it is a deal better than the old one at home, so she tucks it into the old tow bag. **1924** *Landmark* (Statesville NC) 4 Sept 3/4, Tom [=a cat] was taken in a tow bag to Oak bridge and left. **1941** Writers' Program *Guide SC* 236, Assembly Street stores . . line their curb with smelly tow bags, the tops rolled down to show fuzzy cotton-seed. **1943** Writers' Program NC *Bundle of Troubles* 9, When it come time to harvest the taters, we all got baskets and towbags. **1965–70** *DARE* (Qu. F23, *A container made of rough, loosely-woven, brown cloth; commonly used for potatoes, etc*) Infs **NC**8, 10, 20, 23, 25, 88, **TN**30, **VA**47, 69, Tow bag; **MD**37, Tow bag—old folks used to say; (Qu. F19, *A cloth container for grain*) Infs **NC**50, 55, Tow bag. **1966** *DARE* Tape **NC**25, Get a tow bag and put a fifty-pound or a hundred-pound cake [of ice] in a tow bag. **1984** Joyner *Down by Riverside* 114 **SC coast,** Grandchildren of slaves told me of their having heard of . . having to improvise shoes of wooden soles and feet wrapped in tow bags. **1986** Pederson *LAGS Concordance,* 10 infs, **AL, AR, GA, FL, TN,** Tow bag.

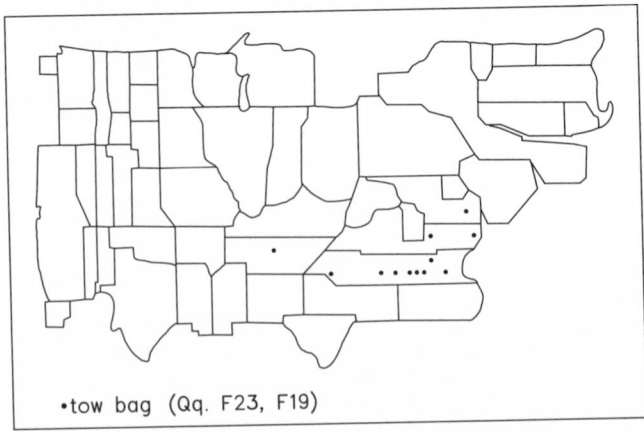

•tow bag (Qq. F23, F19)

towboat n

1 A tugboat used to push or pull barges or other boats; hence n *towboating;* also fig. **chiefly Missip-Ohio Valleys, Lower Missip Valley** See Map

1815 (1823) MA Laws *Private & Special Statutes* 5.42, His patent steam tow boats . . said patent, bearing date the 2d day of April in the year 1814. **1825** *OH Repository* (Canton) 22 Apr [3]/2 (newspaperarchive.com), The steam boat fare . . from New-York to Albany, 140 miles, by the slow or tow boat line . . one dollar. **1843** *U.S. Mag. & Democratic Rev.* 12.342 **OR**, Good pilots would be able at all times to take vessels into the safe harbor behind Cape Hancock, especially if assisted by a steam tow-boat. **1887** *Courier–Jrl.* (Louisville KY) 7 Feb 3/3 **KY**, Theodore Brooks . . will try his hand at towboating this season. **1905** *DN* 3.23 **cCT**, Tow-boat. . . A small steamer for towing larger craft. **1918** *Daily Courier* (Connellsville PA) 22 Mar 8/3, Not in years has the activity been so great in coal barge and tow boat building as at present along the Monongahela river near Pittsburg. **1952** Bissell *Monongahela* 16 **WV**, Oh, we had some hair-raisers—it wouldn't be towboating otherwise. **1965–70** *DARE* (Qu. O10, . . *Kinds of boats*) 16 Infs, **chiefly Missip-Ohio Valleys, Lower Missip Valley,** Towboats; [(Qu. Y9, *Somebody who always follows along behind others: "His little brother is an awful _____."*) Inf **ME**22, Towboat]. **1967–68** *DARE* Tape **IL**9, We have awful large towboats with big tows, mostly coal, grain; **IN**18, We had to call the boat in . . she was sinking. . . When the towboat found out how it was, they just blew the whistle, cut the line loose, and went back to Kentucky; **LA**5, They call them towboats, actually they push loads. . . You don't ever tow, pull, anything. **1969** *DARE* FW Addit **cwIL**, Towboats—barges that push loads up the river—even though they push the loads, never tow it after. Also called "push boats." **2002** *DARE* File **Missip Valley,** In the Mississippi valley a boat which maneuvers unpowered barges around is a "towboat". . . Also, a towboat *always* "tows" barges, although in fact it pushes them.

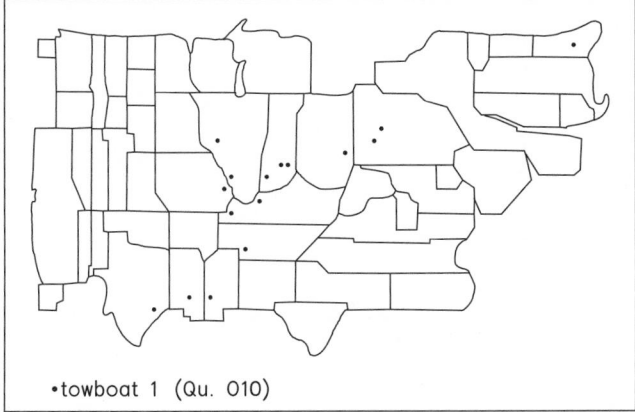

•towboat 1 (Qu. O10)

2 Transf: see quot. Cf **canal boat, gunboat 1**
1968 *DARE* (Qu. W42b, . . *Nicknames for men's square-toed shoes*) Inf **OH**44, Towboats.

towel n Usu |ˈtauəl, ˈtau(ɪ)l|; also **esp Sth, S Midl** |tæl, tɑl, tɔl|; for addit varr see quots Pronc-spp *tahl, towl*
Std sense, var forms.
1854 *Putnam's Mag.* 4.623 **Missip Valley,** "Captain, can't you give me a clean towel?" inquired a passenger recently on board a Mississippi steamer. "Go to h—, stranger. Fifty people have used that towl, and you are the first man I have heard complain of it." **1937** *AmSp* 12.288 **cnVA**, [tɑl] ['tɑrəl] for *towel*. **1939** *LANE* Maps 140, 142, [Proncs of the type [tawɪl] are common in **nNEng** and **MA**; proncs of the type [tæwɪl] are also common in **nNEng,** but not in **MA**; the type [tauwɪl] occurs chiefly in **s,seNEng,** and the types [tao(ɪ)l] are found chiefly in **wNEng** and **MA**.] **1941** *AmSp* 16.10 **eTX** [Black], In *funeral, . . towel,* the final vowel is crowded out: [ˈfjũnl], . . [tɑːl]. **1944** *PADS* 2.31 **NC,** *Towel* [tæl]. . . Usual meaning. Wautauga Co., N.C. All classes. Common. **1961** Kurath–McDavid *Pronc. Engl.* 168 **Atlantic,** *Unstressed Vowels.* . . [T]he New England settlement area and the entire South checked /ɪ/, usually articulated as a high-central /ɨ/. . . When *mountain, towel,* etc., do not have /ɪ/, they end in /-ən, -əl/, articulated as [-ən, -əl] or as syllabic [n̩, l̩]. **1973** *PADS* 60.55 **seNC,** *Towel* was given the typical Southern pronunciation [tæ³l] in most cases. **1982** McCool *Sam McCool's Pittsburghese* 35 **PA,** *Tahl:* towel, as in the "terrible tahl." **1982** Barrick Coll. **csPA,** *Towel*—pron. towl. **1989** Pederson *LAGS Tech. Index* 71 **Gulf Region,** [644 infs gave proncs of the types [tau, ˈtauʊ]; 115 of the types [tauɯ, ˈtau-ɯ]; 10 of the type [ˈtɔl]; 8 of the types [tæ(ɯ)]; 5 of the types [tau, tauɯ]; 3 of the types [tæl, tɛl].] **2006** *DARE* File **ceWI,** If I don't think about it, I pronounce *towel* as one syllable, rhyming with *owl.*

towelhead n Cf **raghead**
One who wears a turban, kaffiyeh, or hijab—used as a derog term for a person from India or the Middle East.
1981 Spears *Slang & Euphem.* 51, *Buddhahead* (also *towel-head*) an Oriental. Mildly derogatory or jocular. **1986** *Gettysburg Times* (PA) 30 Apr 5/1, [Syndicated column:] The best tip on how to avoid such [=terrorists], . . is to stay home where the towel heads can't get you. **1987** *Daily Intelligencer* (Doylestown PA) 5 Apr sec C 6/2, Gibson says he's being treated by a Sikh doctor whom he calls "Dr. Towelhead" because of his turban. **1994** Wormser *Amer. Islam* 46 **NJ,** Sadeck, a ninth-grade student in New Jersey, remembers how painful it was for her to go to public school after the World Trade Center bombing. "The kids would call me towel-head," she says. **1997** *DARE* File—Internet **NYC** (as of c1982), Not forgetting the "immortal" towelhead, which I have heard on occasion in NY City for 15 years or more. *Ibid* **NYC** (as of c1987), So I began to hear some women friends who used to shop there say they didn't go down there anymore because all the fabrics were "towelhead taste." **2001** *Ibid* **CA,** At Berkeley on Thursday, Tejinder Singh was walking when two drunk guys approached him and called him "Terrorist!" and "Towelhead!" **2006** *WI State Jrl.* (Madison) 19 Oct sec A 9/1 **FL,** I never told people I was Indian because people would make fun of it. You know, 'Dot on your forehead,' 'Towelhead.'

towel shower n Also *dish* (or *kitchen, tea*) *towel shower* **chiefly Nth**
A party, usu for a bride or a charitable organization, at which towels are given as gifts; see quots.
1900 *Anaconda Std.* (MT) 7 Oct 23/2, On Monday a "towel shower" was given. . . About 40 ladies were present, each bringing a dainty towel, hemstitched or embroidered. . . [A]t the close of the afternoon all surrounded the bride and showered them upon her. **1940** *NE State Jrl.* (Lincoln) 27 Oct sec C 6/3, Mrs. Raymond Anderson was the honoree at a towel shower arranged for Friday evening. **1949** *Sun. Jrl. & Star* (Lincoln NE) 4 Dec sec C 4/3, There will be a tea towel shower for the [Sigma Chi] chapter house. **1963** *Valley Independent* (Monessen PA) 29 May [28]/4 (newspaperarchive.com), *Fire Auxiliary Holds Kitchen Towel Shower*—A dish towel shower for the kitchen of the Belle Vernon fire hall was planned at the May meeting of the Ladies Auxiliary. **1965** *Appleton Post–Crescent* (WI) 9 Oct sec A 8/6, The Nov. 4 meeting [of Ladies Aid] has been designated a dish towel shower. Members will bring towels for use in the church kitchen. **1967–68** *DARE* (Qu. FF3, . . *'Showers' or 'gift parties'*) Infs **OH**29, 70, **PA**122, Towel showers; **NJ**29, Towel showers for the church kitchen.

tower(ist) See **tour**

tower-of-Babel n
The American featherfoil *(Hottonia inflata).*
1951 *PADS* 15.37 **TX,** *Hottonia inflata.* . . Tower-of-Babel.

towhead n [Appar from the resemblance to a tousled head of light-colored hair]
1 A small sandbar in a river, esp one with a growth of willows or cottonwoods on it. **chiefly Missip-Ohio Valleys**
1822 Cumings *Western Navigator* 7 **Ohio Valley,** Avoid a large bar on the left with a small willow island or tow-head on it. [**1841** Steele *Summer Journey* 223 **Ohio Valley,** Fairy isles are . . fringed with the soft bushy willow called here [=on the Ohio River] *tow.*] **1847** *De Bow's Rev.* 3.429, Between Pittsburg and the mouth of the Ohio there are . . a great number of sand bars and tow-heads. These last are low, sandy islands incapable of cultivation, and covered with willows. **1862** *N. Amer. Rev.* 94.495, Where the current [of the Mississippi] becomes dead, . . the sediment is deposited in gently sloping, sandy mud banks, called willow battures, or, if on an island, tow heads, from the growth of willows on them. **1885** Twain *Huck. Finn* 93 **Missip Valley,** A towhead is a sand-bar that has cotton-woods on it as thick as harrow-teeth. **1950** Bissell *Stretch on River* 89 **eMO,** The big broad stream [=the Mississippi] would roll very wide and slick, on down between islands and towheads as wild as the Magdalena. **1967–68** *DARE* (Qu. C13, *A piece of land that sticks out noticeably into a body of water*) Inf **IN**42, Towhead—in a river; **TN**7, Towhead—projects out of a creek bank, formed when water overflows. **2001** in 2005 *DARE* File—Internet, Lee had saw in the guide book that there was a courtesy dock in Mt Vernon IN but there is no way it was made for a boat our size. We duck in behind a towhead . . and tie to a sunken barge.

2 Transf: a grove of cottonwoods surrounded by open prairie.
1878 *Hist. Jasper Co. IA* 342 (as of 1846–47), They reached a "towhead," or clump of brush on the prairie. **1899** Garland *Boy Life* 97

nwIA (as of c1870s), Scattered over the clay lands were small groves or clumps of popple trees, called "tow-heads" by the settlers. They were commonly only two or three hundred feet in diameter, though in some cases they grow along a ridge many acres in extent.

3 =**hooded merganser.**

1888 Trumbull *Names of Birds* 75, I find also in my memorandum-book the name *tow-head* for this species [=*Lophodytes cucullatus*]. . . I remember distinctly . . that the name was heard in one of our Southern States.

towhee n

1 Std: an emberizid bird of the genus *Pipilo*, esp *P. erythrophthalmus.* For other names of var of these see **brown towhee, green-tailed ~, rufous-sided ~**

2 =**bobolink B.**

1917 (1923) *Birds Amer.* 2.241, Bobolink. . . *Other Names.* . . Towhee (mistake).

to where See **where C1**

to who laid the chunk See **who laid the chunk 2**

to who laid the rail(s) See **who laid the rail 2**

towl See **towel**

tow line See **toe line**

town n Usu |taun|; also esp **Sth, S Midl** |tæun|; for addit varr see quots Pronc-spp *taan, tahn, taown, townd*

A Forms.

1795 Dearborn *Columbian Grammar* 139, *List of Improprieties.* . . Townd for Town. **1810** *Mirror of Taste* 155 **sePA,** It would not be at all impossible to hear a very fine lady say that she was daown in taown, to buy a gaown. **1858** Holmes *Autocrat* 296 **NEng,** But the Deacon swore . . / . . . / He would build one shay to beat the taown. **1890** *PMLA* 5.198 **neVA,** The sound ([au], as in German Haus) is heard among a select few in *house, now,* etc., though the usual pronunciation is here [ɛu], never [əu]. This latter diphthong [ɛu] is long [ɛu] in *town, cow* and some other words, and short [ɛu] in most words. **1905** *DN* 3.103 **nwAR,** [au] has a decided tendency, especially among women, to become [æu]. Cf. [hæudi, næu, tæun, kæu]. **1931** *AmSp* 6.167 **seVA,** The diphthong [au] appears as . . [æu] in . . *down, town, now.* **1936** *AmSp* 11.34 **eTX,** If a norm may be said to exist for this diphthong in East Texas, it is [æu], but variations in the first element produce also [au] and [æˇu]—all of these with various degrees of lengthening and nasalization. . . [tãun], [tæ̃un], [tæˇũn]; [tã:ũn], [tæ̃:ũn], [tæˇ:ũn]. **1937** *AmSp* 12.286 **wVA,** The diphthong [au] is normally [æu] in *town, round* [etc]. **1937** Crane *Let Me Show You VT* 30 **VT,** This twisting of the vowel, as in *taown* for town, *baout* for about, and *daown* for down, is not so common as it once was, but it still survives with some Vermonters. **1942** Hall *Smoky Mt. Speech* 45 **wNC, eTN,** The following words almost always have [æu] rather than [au]. . . town. **1959** *VT Hist.* 27.164, *Town* [tæoun] . . pronc. Common, especially in rural areas. **1982** *AmSp* 57.192 **ceIL** (as of 1887), The most prominent and interesting distinctly regional pronunciation feature is the treatment of the diphthong /au/, rendered in standard spelling as *ou.* . . But Kirkland's dialect spelling of this diphthong has an *a* preceding the *o.* . . *taown* ('town'). . . The letter *a* added here undoubtedly represents the vowel of *cat,* which is the first element for /au/ throughout the South Midland. **2000** *DARE* File **Pittsburgh PA,** The most distinctive pronunciation oddity is /au/ > /a/, the usual Pittsburgh examples being "downtown" /dantan/ ('daan-taan' or 'dahntahn'). **2006** *DARE* File—Internet **Pittsburgh PA,** Every tahn has its own flavor. . . So if you are planning to visit Dahntahn . . we suggest you learn the language.

B Sense.

The home base in the game of **town ball 1;** hence phr *in town* at bat.

1967–69 *DARE* Tape **TN37,** Town ball. . . One boy would knock the ball out, say into the outfield, and whoever caught that ball got to come to . . plate or we call it town. Come in and then he would bat; **TX40,** [Inf:] We used to play town ball. [FW:] How'd that go? [Inf:] . . I don't remember so much about how it went. . . They changed sides. . . Go back and forth . . and say, "We're in town now." **1983** *MJLF* 9.1.44 **ceKY** (as of 1956), *In town* . . at bat.

‡town v

To do something in a stylish way, "go to town."

2004 *DARE* File **eTN** (as of c1965), When my mother said she was

going to go to Europe, she [=a neighbor] said, "You really know how to town!"

town ant n Also *red town ant*

A leaf-cutting ant (*Atta texana*) native to Texas and Louisiana; see quots.

1937 *LA Conserv. Rev.* Jan 14 **LA,** The leaf-cutting or parasol ant (*Atta texana* Buckley). . . is locally called the "red town ant." **1938** U.S. Dept. Ag. *Leaflet* 159.8, Other causes of injury are rabbits; leaf-cutting red ants ("town ants," very serious in parts of Louisiana and Texas) [etc]. **1967–68** *DARE* (Qu. R17, . . *Names . . for the big black ants that sting*) Inf **LA15,** Town ant; (Qu. R18, . . *Kinds of ants*) Infs **TX**35, 36, 37, Town ant. **1986** Pederson *LAGS Concordance,* 1 inf, **nwLA,** Town ants—build tall mounds. **2002** *DARE* File—Internet **TX,** The Texas leaf cutting ant has several common names including the town ant, cut ant, parasol ant, fungus ant and night ant as well as some which cannot be printed. . . The leaf cutting ant lives in large colonies that may exceed 2 million ants.

townat See **town ho**

town ball n

1 A bat-and-ball game similar to baseball; see quots. **chiefly Sth, S Midl** See Map *somewhat old-fash* Cf **five hundred 2, scrub 2, work-up**

1813 (1940) Hartsell *Memora* 12.134 **PA,** Several of the majors and Several of the Docters and my Selfe Commenced that game Coled town ball. **1852** *California Dispatch* 18 Jan 2/4 (*OED2*), A game of 'town ball' which was had on the Plaza during the week, reminded us of other days. **1864** Longstreet *Master William* 98 **GA** (as of c1805), All their amusements are running, jumping, wrestling, playing town-ball, and bull-pen. **1879** *Scribner's Mth.* 17.751 **IN** (as of c1850), Eastern youth played field-base, and Western boys town-ball. **1892** Smith *Farm & Fireside* 267 **GA,** Base-ball has grown out of town-ball; it is no improvement. The pitcher used to belong to the ins and threw the best ball he could, for he wanted it hit . . , but now he belongs to the outs and wants it missed. We used to throw at a boy to stop him running to another base, and we hit him if we could, but these modern balls are hard and heavy and dangerous. **1909** *DN* 3.405 **nwAR,** *Town-ball.* . . A boys' game. **1917** Baldwin *Making of a Township* 391 **ceIN** (as of 1860's), "Town ball." Instead of a baseball bat, a paddle made of oak timber one inch thick and six to ten inches wide, made with a handle, was the bat. There were bases. . . No one ever caught the ball. Instead of a pitcher he was known as the one "giving balls." If he threw a ball so the batter with his big, wide paddle could not hit it, he was immediately fired. **1932** Randolph *Ozark Mt. Folks* 46, We played marbles an' blackman an' dare-base an' two-eyed-cat an' townball an' pig-in-a-hole. **1946** *Greenville Advocate* (AL) 26 Sept [7]/2, The same game [as *four-hole cat* and *one-er-scrub*], with variations, was known in other Alabama communities as "Town Ball." **1947** Lomax *Advent. Ballad Hunter* 14 **TX** (as of c1880), We children never played games on Sunday, not even . . town ball. **1953** *PA Dutchman* Oct 7 **sePA,** There was nothing so distinctive of a remote countryside that retained much of yesterday . . as the game of townball still played in the valley. They did not thank us for trying to introduce baseball at Waterford, they preferred the older game. **1963** Watkins–Watkins *Yesterday Hills* 17 **cnGA,** Boys and girls played town ball, the country version of baseball. The batter could strike at the ball until he hit it or until he missed and the catcher caught it. A base runner was out if a fielder threw the ball at him and hit him while he was running the bases. **1965–70** *DARE* (Qu. EE11, *Bat-and-ball games for just a few players [when there aren't enough for a regular game]*) 37 Infs, **chiefly Sth, S Midl,** Town ball; **FL**26, **GA**18, **TN**14, 65, **TX**32, Tan ball [sic]; **CA**158, **PA**28, Tom ball [sic]; **FL**8, Softball—town ball, she called it as a child; **GA**89, Town ball or patter-cat—played with a rubber ball; **KY**70, Town ball—three or four batters, players rotated positions as batters were put out; **LA**11, Town ball—bat and then run to where the pitcher was before he gets the ball and throws it back; **MD**18, Town ball—variant of baseball—player can be put out by ball thrown between him and the base he's trying to reach; **NY**130, Tan ball [sic; FW sugg]; (Qu. EE33, . . *Outdoor games . . that children play*) Infs **GA**75, **TN**16, Town ball. [37 of 52 Infs old] **1966–69** *DARE* Tape **AL**4, Town ball is . . referred to as "push-up" sometimes. . . You'd start in the field. Now if you caught a fly . . [you'd] immediately go to bat. . . If you caught a ball and threw it to the first baseman . . If he failed to catch the ball you moved to first. . . The man who's on first would go to second, and on to third. Then you became pitcher, then you was catcher. . . Then he got to be . . at bat. . . I've heard it called town ball; **FL**8, Town ball. . . That was played . . the same as softball is today;

TN37, Another game . . related to baseball was called town ball. . . It was . . also a game that was played when [we] probably didn't have quite a large enough group of boys to play baseball.

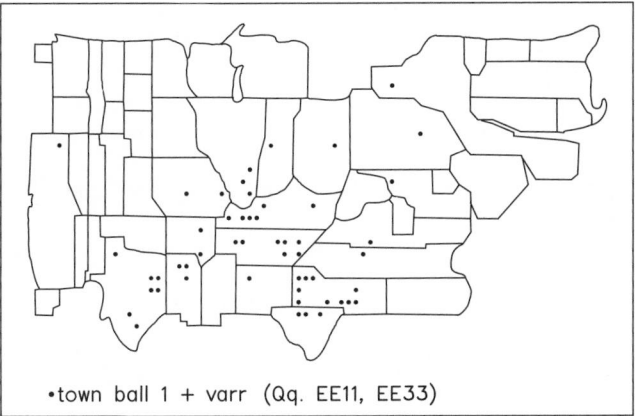

•town ball 1 + varr (Qq. EE11, EE33)

2   in var combs:

a   *round-town (ball):* Such a game played with the bases arranged in a circuit.   **chiefly S Midl**   See Map

1848 *Youth's Friend* 2.146 **OH,** A number of boys . . were engaged in a grove, back of a country school house, in playing what they called "Round Town Ball." **1914** Lambert–Reinhard *Hist. Catasauqua PA* 364 **cePA,** In the game of "Round-town" were four or five bases, placed in the form of a square, diamond, or pentagon, and basemen guarded these safety spots. . . In Round-town more than one man was privileged to share safety at the same base; and a whole bunch was permitted to run bases simultaneously. **1914** [see **b** below]. **1915** [see **b** below]. **1938** Stuart *Dark Hills* 237 **eKY,** The dead were now being buried on the ground where we used to play Fox and Dog, . . London Bridge, and Round-town Ball with a twine ball. **1965–70** *DARE* (Qu. EE11, *Bat-and-ball games for just a few players [when there aren't enough for a regular game])* Infs **KY**40, 41, 72, **OH**48, 74, **VA**30, Round-town; **NC**69, Round-town—pitcher and catcher and a fielder or several—like work-up. **1978** [see **b** below]. **1982** Slone *How We Talked* 94 **eKY** (as of c1950), A game we played which we called "round town" was very much like baseball, with a batter, pitcher, and first, second and third base, homeplate and striking out. **2000** [see **b** below].

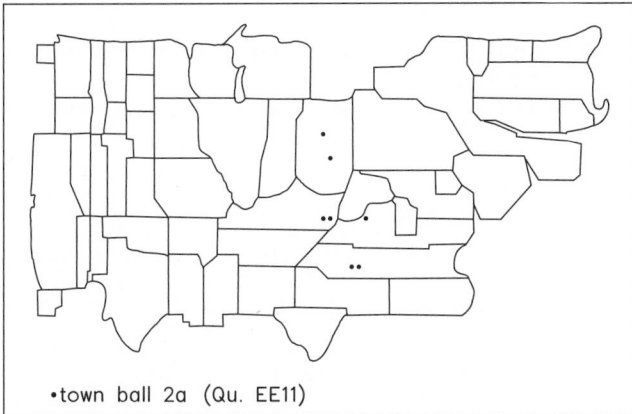

•town ball 2a (Qu. EE11)

b   *straight town:* Such a game played with the bases arranged in a straight line.   **swVA**

1914 Addington *Old-Time School* 30 **VA,** The chief difference between Round Town and Straight Town was in the arrangement of the corners or bases. They made a circular track in the former and a straight track in the latter. **1915** *DN* 4.192 **swVA,** *Town ball.* . . Of two kinds— straight-town and round-town—according to the position of the bases. **1978** in 1994 Reedy *School Hist. Dickenson Co.* 482 **swVA,** Round-town had four bases in a circle, as baseball does today. . . Straight-town had four bases in a row and you used the same rules as you did in Round-town. **2000** in 2005 *DARE* File—Internet **swVA** (as of c1950), Of course, straight town, round town, tag, volleyball, ice skating, whip-crack, mumbly-peg and marbles were some of the fun games we played during my time at Yates.

c   *long-town (ball):* Such a game played with two bases (including "home").   Cf **long ball**

1908 *Friends' Intelligencer* 65.171 **IL,** As he passed the school house at recess or noon-spell . . and caught me in a game of "long town" or "corner ball," it was one excuse to pick me up and take me with him. **1910** *CO Springs Gaz.* (CO) 27 Sept 3/5, In Europe a game involving some of the ideas of tennis was plays [sic] by the kings and nobles of feudal times. It seems to have been to tennis what the old-fashioned long-town game of ball was to modern baseball. **1914** Lambert–Reinhard *Hist. Catasauqua PA* 363 **cePA,** Long-town had only one base which usually was a stone, stump or tree about twenty-five strides from the batting point. . . If the ball was batted over or through the bunch of fielders the batter ran to the goal. . . If a fellow picked up the ball before the runner reached the tree or stump, and threw the ball so as to hit the runner then the runner was out; if he missed the runner so that the ball flew far away, the runner could touch the tree and run "home." When all the batters had safely reached the tree, but none dared risk to run home, and a last man would bat the ball far over the crowd, then there was merriment when everybody ran home. **1933** Long *Forty Letters* 30 **cPA,** A modification of the foregoing game [=Round-Town-Ball] was Long-Town-Ball. There were just two bases about twenty-five feet apart, two batters, one on each base, and two catchers, one behind each bat, and the fielders. The catchers were also the pitchers and the runs were made by the two batters exchanging bases. **1954** *Chillicothe Constitution-Tribune* (MO) 3 Mar 2/6 (as of 1890s), Ball was the favorite game, usually "Long Town" or "Rounder's." **1957** *Sat. Eve. Post Letters* **cIL** (as of c1885–92), Games we played at a country school. . . *Town ball* or *Long town ball.* **1967** *DARE* (Qu. EE11, *Bat-and-ball games for just a few players [when there aren't enough for a regular game])* Inf **MO**38, Long-town—sides, two bases. **2005** *DARE* File— Internet **cWV** (as of c1929), The games I remember are Red Rover, Prisoner and Draw Base and a ball game called "Long Town".

town bird n

1   See **town sparrow.**

2   =**phoebe.**

1955 *Oriole* 20.1.10 **GA,** Eastern Phoebe. . . Town Bird.

townd   See **town** n

town dude n   Pronc-sp *town dood*   **scattered, but esp Sth, S Midl**   See Map

Used as a joc or derog name for a city person.

1886 IA *State Horticult. Soc. Trans. for 1884* 392, With such a farm the common farmer may be as independent as the business man, the banker, or the town dude. **1891** *New Era* (Humeston IA) 29 July [6]/1 (newspaperarchive.com), A good hand on the farm will get all the way from $15 to $20 per month. That may seem little, when some town "dude" is getting maybe $35 or $40 per month. **1894** *Lafayette Advt.* (LA) 3 Nov [3]/2, Trying to farm without an agricultural paper is as absurd as . . a town dude without a mustache. **1901** *Massillon Independent* (OH) 22 Aug [6]/3 (newspaperarchive.com), If he does not thus get the birds some town dude will bag every last one of them. **1950** *Dothan Eagle* (AL) 17 July [1]/4 (newspaperarchive.com), He went out on the lake dressed in his Sunday clothes, . . and the fish thinking him some town dude who didn't know how to land a fish, they went right after his minnows. **1965–70** *DARE* (Qu. HH2, *Names and nicknames for a citified person)* Infs **FL**35, **GA**7, 23, 77, **KY**85, **MO**37, **SC**3, **TN**14, Town dude; (Qu. II23, *Joking names for the people who are, or think*

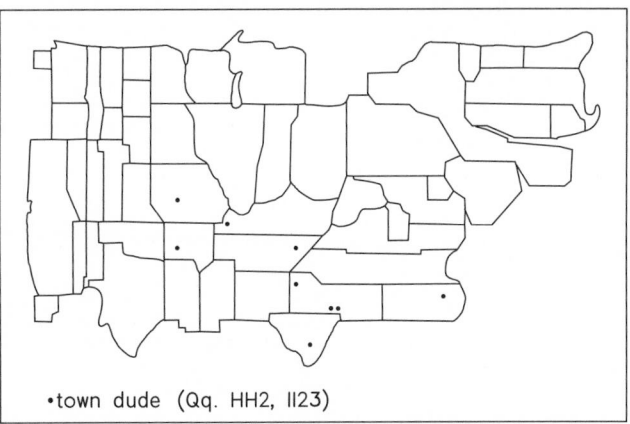

•town dude (Qq. HH2, II23)

they are, the best society of a community: The _____) Inf **AR**51, Town dudes. **1986** Pederson *LAGS Concordance,* 7 infs, **GA, LA,** Town dude(s). **2005** Williams *Gratitude* 169 **wNC** (as of 1940s), Some of the outdoor games I remember us a-playin' was *Whoopee Hide,* which the *town doods* at school called "Hide And Seek."

town farm n   **NEng**   Cf **home farm 2, infirmary, poor farm**

A farm where poor people are maintained at public expense.

1832 (1927) Rodman *Diary* 103 **MA,** Attended . . a meet'g . . in relation to the erection of a Cholera Hospital on the town farm at the point. **1841** *Bangor Daily Whig & Courier* (ME) 16 Aug [2]/5 (newspaperarchive.com), Miss Luce's school on the Town Farm. **1880** *Harper's New Mth. Mag.* 62.86 **CT,** She would rather have taken her children to the town farm, cold as corporative charity is. **1902** Day *Pine Tree Ballads* 32 **ME,** He sat in his cold, bare, town-farm room and patiently spelled and read. **1922** (1926) Cady *Rhymes VT* 165, There's only you and Little Joe,/ The townfarm boy you took, to hoe. **1931–33** *LANE Worksheets* **cMA,** *Home farm—Infirmary. Same as town farm.* **1967** *DARE* Tape **MA**114, [Inf:] It's what they call a town-farm cemetery. . . [FW:] Is that the one that has only a few graves marked? [Inf:] Yeah, that's right. **1978** *DARE* File **cnMA** (as of c1915), When I was a small child people with no means of support were taken to the *poor farm.* But a few years later the Massachusetts poor farms became town farms, by official decree, I presume. **1986** Brewer *Easthampton Town Lodging House* 1 **cwMA,** The history of Easthampton's home for the poor and homeless, known variously as the Almshouse, the Poor Farm, the Town Farm, the Town Infirmary and finally the *Town Lodging House,* is . . a dual concern.

town ho exclam   Also *townat, towno(r)*   **esp Nantucket MA** *arch*

In whaling: used as a cry when a whale is sighted or as a cry for help; also transf.

1791 in 1810 MA Hist. Soc. *Coll.* 1st ser 3.154 **Nantucket MA,** The boys, as soon as they can talk, will make use of the common phrases, as *townor,* which is an Indian word, and signifies that they have seen the whale twice. **1848** in 1935 *AmSp* 10.40 **Nantucket MA,** *Town-at.* Exclamation when a whale is seen. **1851** (1976) Melville *Moby-Dick* 242 **Nantucket MA,** It was not very long after speaking the Goney that another homeward-bound whaleman, the Town-Ho, was encountered. [Footnote to *Town-Ho:*] The ancient whale-cry upon first sighting a whale from the mast-head, still used by whalemen in hunting the famous Gallipagos [sic] terrapin. **1874** Davis *Nimrod* (Internet), 'Zekiel was shouting "Town ho!" for the necessary help to tote this great meat-chest [=a terrapin] to the shore. **1879** in 1887 Goode *Fisheries U.S.* 4.154 **Cape Cod MA** (as of c1820), He sent me aloft to look out. . . I kept looking, and discovered, away to the northward, whale spouts. I sung out, "Towno!" The captain wanted to know where, and I told him off the weather bow. **1926** Ashley *Yankee Whaler* 144 **Nantucket MA,** *Towno! Towno!* An old cry of the whaleman when he wanted assistance, usually voiced when in trouble ashore.

town house n

1 A town hall.   [*OED2* 1530 →]   **chiefly NEast**

1657 in 1881 Boston Registry Dept. *Records* 2.134, A committee [was chosen] to consider of the modell of the towne house, to bee built. **1707** Pemberton *Funeral Sermon* [title page] **Boston MA,** Printed . . for *Benj. Eliot,* & Sold at his Shop under the West end of the Town House. **1718** in 1880 Brookhaven NY *Records* 1.109, Ye Towne at thare owne cost & charge hath ingaged to Repaire what building the sd Phillips hath made for his perticheler convenience joyneing to ye Towne house. **1834** Gordon *Gaz. NJ* 193, On the 23d October, 1676, a warrant was granted by the Governor, for . . so much [land] as was necessary for landing places, school house, town house, market place &c. **1867** Hill *Homespun* 197 **CT,** The chief centre of all attraction in the village is the town-house, where are to be seen the various articles of female ingenuity and industry. **1907** *DN* 3.203 **seNH,** *Town-house. .* Town hall. General. **1917** *DN* 4.402 **neOH,** *Town. .* On W[estern] R[eserve] almost obsolete in the sense "township," but preserved in *town-house = town-hall* (often standing alone in the country) and *town line.* **1950** *WELS Suppl.* **swWI,** Town house—town hall. (Used in town of Dayton, Richland County. Settlers chiefly Scotch, came by way of Ohio.) **1975** Gould *ME Lingo* 297, *Town house—*Preferred in most smaller Maine communities for the town hall. It is not only the seat of municipal government, but is the social center where dances, basketball games, art shows, and many another attraction is held; hence, *town house* encompasses the general activities of a community.

2 An outside toilet building.   Cf **courthouse 2,** *DS* M21b

1959 Sanders *Echoes* 29 **swAR,** We couldn't even go out to the townhouse; that's where we kept our oldest catalogue.

townified adj   [*OED2* 1777 →]

Having the style or manners of a town; citified.

1966–68 *DARE* (Qu. HH2, *Names and nicknames for a citified person*) Infs **NC**35, 82, Townified. **1998** in 2004 Montgomery–Hall *Dict. Smoky Mt. Engl.* 615 **wNC, eTN,** Mountaineers often make adjectives/adverbs from practically any noun or other part of speech by simply adding "fied." . . It would not be uncommon for a person who exhibited characteristics of a town resident to be called "townified."

town meeting n, also attrib   Also *towns meeting*   **chiefly NEng** Cf **March meeting**

A formal assembly of the voters in a town for the transaction of public business.

1636 in 1869 Essex Inst. *Coll.* 9.1.16 **MA,** At a generall Court or towne meeting of Salem held the second of . . May A[nn]o 1636. **1683** in 1882 Southold NY *Town Rec.* 1.129, Stephen Bayly [shall] be the Town Clerk to keep the Town meeting book. **1790** John Adams in 1816 *N. Amer. Rev. & Misc. Jrl.* July 154 **MA,** Your Boston town-meetings, and our Harvard College, have set the universe in motion. **1801** (1898) Hunt *Diary* 5 **PA,** I went to the towns meeting at Eli Shugart's in West Caln. **1806** (1904) Roe *Diary* 26 **NY,** I have attended Townmeeting. **1835** Emerson *Hist. Discourse* 15 **ceMA,** In a town-meeting, the great secret of political science was uncovered, and the problem solved, how to give every individual his fair weight in the government, without any disorder from numbers. **1907** *DN* 3.190 **seNH,** *Hog-reeve. .* An official (usually the most recently married man) chosen at the annual town meeting, whose duty it is to impound stray hogs. **1929** *AmSp* 5.124 **ME,** We heard much of . . "town meeting" with its discussions where those paying only a poll tax were said to "vote taxes for others to pay." **1959** *VT Hist.* 27.148, *Town meeting. .* A meeting for the officers and residents of a town for the purpose of carrying on the town business, held the first Tuesday in March. Common. **1966–68** *DARE* Tape **CT**9, There are regular town meetings to approve the budget and such as that annually. And there are special town meetings when some special issue comes up; **ME**1, Every town meeting, they collect the taxes on every person that pays a tax. **1980** *Verbatim Letters* **cwVT,** Town Meeting Day is a current term for March 3 election day. The traditional town meeting is still held in many towns; and even in Rutland, which is an incorporated city and does not hold town meeting, the term is often used to refer to the day, as in 'My office is closed for Town Meeting Day'. **2005** *DARE* File **MA,** At a Winchester town meeting I saw that direct democracy, which tends to go in every direction at once, benefits from a strong and tactful moderator.

town meeting cake n   **NEng, esp MA**   Cf **election cake, March meeting ~**

A cake or loaf of raised dough formerly sold at **town meetings.**

1837 Haven *Hist. Address* 59 **MA,** In 1637, the Gen. Court ordered that no cakes or buns should be made or sold, except for burials or weddings. [Note: This license having been extended to other public occasions was probably the origin of what is called 'Town meeting cake.'] **1884** Albee *New Castle Hist.* 136 **seNH,** I . . began to go to town-meetings when the good red buns, and town-meeting cake and outside assemblage of boys, were the chief attractions. **1886** *Good Housekeeping* 4.90, Can you give a recipe for making the old fashioned Muster Cake, since called Election Cake and Town Meeting Cake? It is different from and better than Buns. **1941** *LANE* Map 283 *(Bun, roll)* 1 inf, **ceMA,** Town meeting cake, baked in large cakes, formerly sold at town meetings. **1948** Coatsworth *South Shore* 64 **MA,** There are hot cross buns in the bakery window before good Friday, although they no longer display Election Cake or Town Meeting Cake, a sort of larger raisin bun once eaten for the noonday meal in the times when town meeting was an all-day affair. **1969** *DARE* Tape **MA**40, The bakers always used to bake up a batch of town meeting cake and take it out and sell it at these town meetings, and most everybody that came to town meeting would take home a loaf of town meeting cake.

towno(r)   See **town ho**

town road n   [*town* unit of local government + *road*]   **NEng, Upstate NY, wGt Lakes**   See Map

A secondary road built, maintained, or controlled by a town.

1813 Spafford *Gaz. State NY* 326, There are no great leading roads, but the common Town roads are sufficiently numerous. **1838** *Bangor*

Daily Whig & Courier (ME) 4 Dec [2]/5 (newspaperarchive.com), A stake and stones on the line of the town road leading from the Thompson farm. **1850** MI *Constitutional Convention Report* 327 **MI,** The towns have only the power to lay out town roads. **1879** *Fitchburg Daily Sentinel* (MA) 12 June [2]/3 (newspaperarchive.com), There will be another special meeting . . to see if the town will accept the report of the selectmen in locating a new town road. **1896** *Daily Kennebec Jrl.* (Augusta ME) 25 Apr 11/6, [Advt:] Good school on one corner of farm and town road on three sides. **1965–70** *DARE* (Qu. N18, . . *Roads that have numbers or letters. For example, if someone asked directions . . "Take _____."*) Inf **WI**18, Town road; (Qu. N27a, *Names . . for different kinds of unpaved roads*) Infs **CT**23, **NY**32, 127, 210, 220, Town road; (Qu. N28, *A road that connects a big highway with stores and business places set back from it*) Inf **NY**80, Town road; (Qu. N29, . . *Names . . for a less important road running back from a main road*) Infs **CT**5, **NY**233, Town road; (Qu. N26, Town road—maintained by the town; **WI**5, County trunk or town road; (Qu. N33, *A man whose job is to take care of roads in a certain locality*) Inf **NY**233, Town road crew. **1973** Allen *LAUM* 1.241 (as of c1950), 2 infs, **MN,** Town road. **1978** *Blair & Ketchum's Country Jrl.* Aug 97, [Advt:] 32 acres—Jaffrey, N.H., 1400 ft. frontage on old town road. **2004** *Post–Std.* (Syracuse NY) 3 June 24/5, An unfortunate situation occurred . . when the road from the library to the twin rinks was not a town road. I am sure you remember that snow removal ceased in the winter of 2004 until the town accepted ownership.

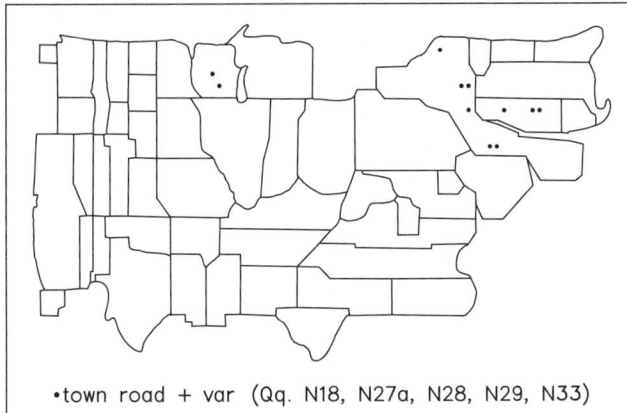

•town road + var (Qq. N18, N27a, N28, N29, N33)

town sack n
See quot.
1972 *Thompson Coll.* **cwGA,** Town sack—light paper bag with colored design, printing, or both. "Be sure to save any town sacks you get for me." Lighter paper than "grocery bags."

towns meeting See **town meeting**

town sparrow n Also *town bird* esp **Sth** Cf **city sparrow**
=**English sparrow.**
1910 *TX Almanac for 1910* 131, All sorts of persistent warfare should be waged against the town sparrow. **1913** U.S. Bur. Educ. *Bulletin* 42.18 **SC,** The children called the English sparrow "town bird." **1962** Imhof *AL Birds* 495, *Passer domesticus* . . *Other Names:* . . Town Sparrow. **1967–69** *DARE* (Qu. Q21, . . *Kinds of sparrows*) Inf **LA**2, English sparrow or French sparrow or town birds; (Qu. Q22, *Joking names or nicknames for the common sparrow*) Inf **KY**11, Town bird—common.

tow road See **tote road**

tow sack n Folk-etym sp *toe sack* [*tow* coarse fiber of flax, hemp, or jute + *sack*] **chiefly Sth, S Midl, TX, OK** See Map and Map Section Cf **burlap bag, crocus sack, croker ~, guano ~, gunny ~** n, **toad ~, tote ~, tow bag**
A large bag usu of burlap or other coarse fabric.
1883 *Hist. St. Clair Co. MI* 688, I was born in what is now known as the township of Cottrellville the 18th day of October, 1808. . . Up to the time I was five years old my whole wardrobe, for winter and summer wear, was a tow-sack with a puckering string about the neck and arms, belted down with a string. **1889** *Salem Daily News* (OH) 23 Nov [6/2] (newspaperarchive.com), I'll whale you till all that is left of you would ooze through a tow sack. **1923** *Atlanta Constitution* (GA) 9 June 20/4, One old darkey carried a tow sack, with the head of an old rooster protruding. **1941** Justus *Cabin on Kettle Creek* 41 **eTN,** Mammy smiled as

she handed them a tow sack apiece for carrying pine knots. **1942** Faulkner *Go Down* 21 **MS,** Uncle Buddy had some cold bread and meat and a jug of buttermilk wrapped in damp towsacks waiting when he waked up. **1946** *PADS* 5.42 **seVA,** Tow sack. . . A large bag made of coarse canvas; in the Norfolk area. **1947** *Deming Headlight* (NM) 11 July 1/5, There will be, perhaps, an old fashioned potato race . . or a toe sack race. **1957** *Atchison Daily Globe* (KS) 9 May 9/1, My mind fell to wondering where I'd put those toe-sack costumes Sis and Sally had during an Indian project. **1958** Humphrey *Home from the Hill* 14 **neTX,** As his man Chauncey put it, he had to fight the women off with a wet towsack. **1965–70** *DARE* (Qu. F23, *A container made of rough, loosely-woven, brown cloth; commonly used for potatoes, etc*) 105 Infs, **chiefly Sth, S Midl, TX, OK,** Tow sack; (Qu. F19, *A cloth container for grain*) 21 Infs, **chiefly Sth, S Midl, TX, OK,** Tow sack; (Qu. F20, *A cloth container for feed*) 18 Infs, **chiefly Sth, S Midl, TX, OK,** Tow sack; (Qu. FF16, . . *Local contests or celebrations*) Infs **KY**89, Tow-sack races. **1989** Pederson *LAGS Tech. Index* 76 **Gulf Region,** Tow sack (315 [of 914 infs]). **1993** *Houston Chron.* (TX) 5 Oct (Internet), The mistake I made was leaving my supply of peanuts on the back porch in that tow sack. **1994** NC Lang. & Life Project *Dial. Dict. Lumbee Engl.* 12 **seNC,** Tow sack. . . A burlap or paper container for carrying objects, often groceries. **2005** *Herald* (Rock Hill SC) 3 July (Internet), There are all types of seines, from homemade ones using tow sacks to rather pricey ones you can buy.

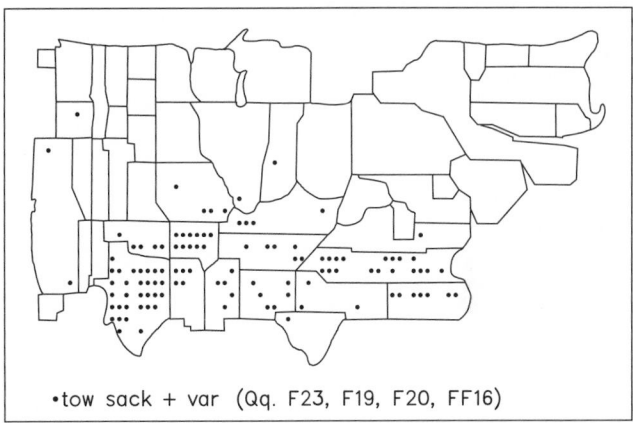

•tow sack + var (Qq. F23, F19, F20, FF16)

towse See **touse**

Towser n [*Towser* a common name for a large dog (*OED2* 1678 →)]
In phr *since Towser was a pup:* =**Hector 1.**
1911 *RR Telegrapher* 28.1328, Things are different "since Towser was a pup." **1926** *NV State Jrl.* (Reno) 3 Sept 6/5, I haven't had so much fun since Towser was a pup. **1955** *Tri-City Herald* (Pasco WA) 18 Feb 10/8, The question about foxes climbing has been making the Hot Stove Circuit ever since Towser was a pup. **1959** *VT Hist.* 27.164, Since Towser was a pup. . . A long time. Occasional.

toy n [By folk-etym]
1 also *toy marble:* =**taw C1a. chiefly Sth, S Midl** See Map
[**1843** (1916) Hall *New Purchase* **sePA** 42, [Cries in marble play:] Knuckle-down!—toy-bone!—go to baste!(?)] **1890** Howells *Boy's Town* 82 **sOH,** A great many points were always coming up: whether a boy took-up, or edged beyond the very place where his toy lay when he shot. **1892** *DN* 1.220 **DC,** Toy: the marble with which you shot. **1942** McAtee *Dial. Grant Co. IN* 68 (as of 1890s), Toy (taw) . . this peculiar pronunciation of a-w was used not only in this name for marble but also in that of an Indian of the Miami tribe that was spelled Atawataw and called " 'toy-toy". **1965–70** *DARE* (Qu. EE6a, . . *Different kinds of marbles—the big one that's used to knock others out of the ring*) 29 Infs, **chiefly Sth, S Midl,** Toy; (Qu. EE6d, *Special marbles*) Infs **MO**23, **OH**103, Toy; **DC**3, Steel toy; (Qu. EE7, . . *Kinds of marble games*) Inf **KY**36, Players stand ten feet back and knock out the middler by pitching or tossing the toy; (Qu. JJ15b, *Sayings about a person who seems to you very stupid: "He doesn't know _____."*) Inf **GA**93, Shot from a toy. **1966–70** *DARE* Tape **NC**22, [FW:] What did you say they used to call the one that you shot with? [Inf:] That was our toy, shooting toy; **NC**85, [FW:] So you call the main marble the toy? [Inf:] Toy marble; **SC**58, [FW:] Did you refer to your marble you shot with—your shooter or your toy? [Inf:] Toy, I believe we called 'em, as well as I remember;

we called 'em our toys; **VA**71, We would have a steel toy, as we would call it, a steel shooter. . . that we would shoot the marbles out of the ring. **1975** in 1981 *NC Folkl. Jrl.* 29.33 **nwNC,** The ones we really prized were glassies or steelies from which we chose our toys (taws) or shooters. **1980** *NADS Letters* **Birmingham AL** (as of 1920s), The marble with which one shoots is . . called a toy (or taw). **1986** Pederson *LAGS Concordance,* 1 inf, **neFL,** Toy—glass, store-bought marbles.

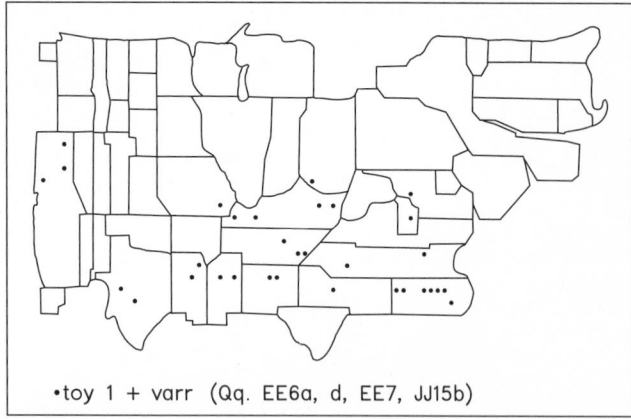

•toy 1 + varr (Qq. EE6a, d, EE7, JJ15b)

2 also *toy line:* =**taw C2a.** **chiefly Sth, S Midl** See Map Cf **taw line, toe ~**

1965–70 *DARE* (Qu. EE8, *The line toward which the players roll their marbles before beginning a game, to determine the order of shooting*) 13 Infs, **chiefly Sth, S Midl,** Toy (line); **NC**52, Head toy. **1970** *DARE* Tape **KY**75, [FW:] When you were playing rolly-hole, was there a place where you had to shoot from? [Inf:] Yeah, we had . . the line, toy line, back at the first hole to start on. **1971** Wood *Vocab. Change* 368 **Sth, S Midl,** Additional volunteered words [for *taw line*] . . *toe line, toy line, throw line.*

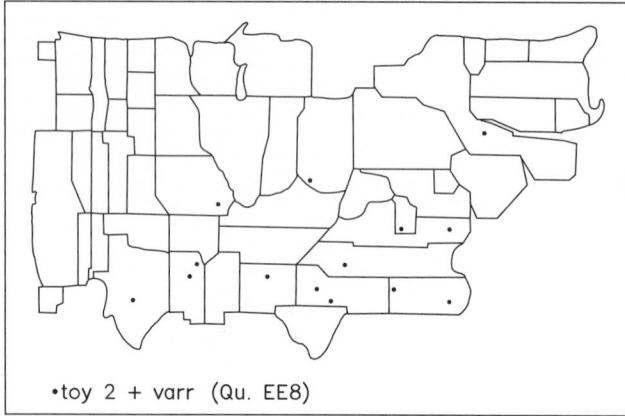

•toy 2 + varr (Qu. EE8)

toy marble See **toy 1**

toyon n Also *tollon (berry)*

An evergreen shrub or small tree *(Heteromeles arbutifolia)* native to California. Also called **California holly, chamise 2, Christmasberry 1, Christmas holly 2, wild holly;** for names of the fruit see **redberry h**

1848 *Californian* (San Francisco) 26 Apr 2/1, Woods, . . willow, madrona, tyon [sic], laurel, ash, cotton-wood, &c. **1876** *Geol. Surv. CA Botany* 1.188, *H[eteromeles]* arbutifolia. . . Toyon or Tollon. **1893** *Overland Mth.* (2d ser) July 39, There was plenty of those red toyon berries and some manzanita. . . This toyon is a smaller berry that grows on a big shrub in the cañons down there, and they call it holly, and make great times over it Christmas in the city,—sell wagon loads. **1893** *Jrl. Amer. Folkl.* 6.141 **CA,** *Heteromeles arbutifolia,* tollon; toyon. **1923** Pellett *Amer. Honey Plants* 87, The Christmas berry is known also as toy-on or tollon berry, as well as California holly. **1947** Peattie *Sierra Nevada* 142 **CA,** Toyon (California's redberry which substitutes for holly). **1967–70** *DARE* (Qu. S26a, . . *Wildflowers. . . Roadside flowers*) Infs **CA**4, 65, Toyon; (Qu. T5, . . *Kinds of evergreens, other than pine*) Inf **CA**70, Toyon; (Qu. T16, . . *Kinds of trees . . 'special'*) Infs **CA**20, 79, 204, Toyon. **2005** *DARE* File **cwCA** (as of c1965), I always looked

forward to a hike on New Year's Day, for then the sky was likely to be a clear bright blue highlighting the brilliant red of the toyon ['tɔɪˌjɑn] berries.

to yonder See **yonder Db**

toze See **toward A**

T.P. and W. v phr [Appar a pun on Toledo, Peoria and Western Railroad, known as the TP&W]

To go on foot, "take pains and walk."

1967–70 *DARE* (Qu. Y24, . . *To walk, to go on foot: "I can't get a ride, so I'll just have to _____."*) Infs **LA**8, **MS**86, T.P. and W.; **NJ**21, T.P. and W. [FW sugg]; **DC**6, Take patience and walk—T.P. and W. **2000** *San Francisco Chron.* (CA) 2 Jan (Internet) **TN** (as of c1910), I remember how as kids we complained about walking the 20 blocks to school and my mother would say, 'TP and W' which meant 'Take pains and walk.' **2000** Mason *Beaches & Ballots* 200 **MS,** They now had to either pay for bus transportation or take pain and walk (TP and W, as black folks say).

tra(b)-ball See **trapball**

trace n[1]

1 A path, trail.

1783 in 1916 Mereness *Travels* 668 **VA,** On the trace to Boons station they were fired on. **1807** in 1810 Pike *Expeditions* 2 app 24, We . . took the large Spanish beaten trace for the Arkansaw river. **1825** (1933) Sibley *Santa Fe Diary* 140, There is a very plain trace all the way & the ground hard & good tho a little hilly. **1859** (1965) Marcy *Prairie Traveler* 19, Another road. . . strikes the Arkansas River near old Fort Mann, on the Santa Fé trace. **1927** Adams *Ranch on Beaver* 1 **KS,** The only landmark in the country was the . . cattle trail. This trace passed some six miles to the eastward. **1982** *Smithsonian Letters* **TX,** Trace—country road. **1998** in 2004 Montgomery–Hall *Dict. Smoky Mt. Engl.* 616 **wNC, eTN,** A trail from Cosby Tn. to the Cherokee nation is still called by some the "Moonshine Trace" because much moonshine whiskey was carried over this trail. **2002** *DARE* File **Ozarks,** Trace = trail.

2 A branch of a stream.

1924 Raine *Land of Saddle-Bags* 6 **sAppalachians,** In one day's journey you may ford the river a hundred times; or you may "take up" a "branch" or "fork" or "trace" to its source in a spring. **1997** in 2004 Montgomery–Hall *Dict. Smoky Mt. Engl.* 616 **wNC, eTN,** Trace. . . A branch of a stream [confirmed by three infs].

trace n[2] Also rarely *trace line, ~ strap, tracer* [*OED2 trace sb.*[2] 13 . . →] **widespread, but less freq Inland Nth, Cent, Rocky Mts, nCA** See Map Cf **trace chain, tug**

One of the two ropes, straps, or chains of a harness connecting the collar to the **singletree** or other part of the vehicle; hence v *trace* to attach the traces to.

1651 in 1908 *Mayflower Descendant* 10.162 **MA,** A Cartrope & trace & Coller. **1783** in 1929 Summers *Annals* 377 **swVA,** 25 lbs. [shall] be allowed Thomas Read for a horse bridle, collar, hames, & traces. **1863** *Continental Mth.* 4.330, Then the traces all gave way. **1879** *Davenport Daily Gaz.* (IA) 18 Nov [4]/4 (newspaperarchive.com), The traces snapped short off, but the momentum of the wagon . . hurled Steffen high up into the air. **1889** *Overland Mth.* (2d ser) 14.242, She took the horse from the traces. **1940** Faulkner *Hamlet* 149 **MS,** Through the long drowsing afternoons the trace-galled mules would

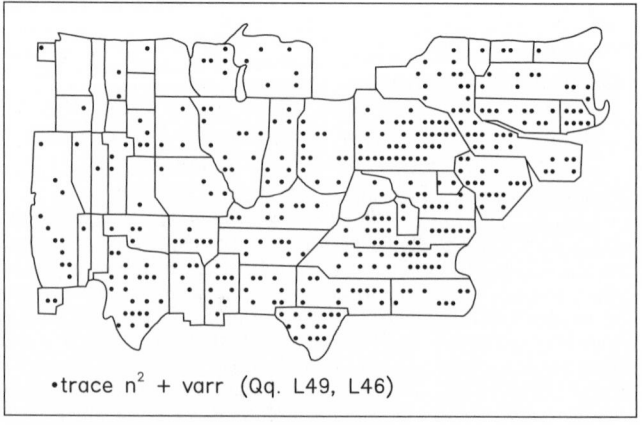

•trace n[2] + varr (Qq. L49, L46)

doze. **1965–70** *DARE* (Qu. L49, *Leathers or ropes, fastened to the collar, that a horse or mule pulls by*) 343 Infs, **widespread, but less freq Inland Nth, Cent, Rocky Mts, nCA,** Trace(s); **CO2,** Traces = tugs [FW: Inf would use both.]; **DC8,** Traces—mostly chains; **FL17,** Traces—made out of cowhide; **GA19,** Traces—iron; **KY53, 86,** Traces if chains, tugs if leather; **NJ58,** Traces—metal—between harness and singletree; **OH56,** Traces—either leather or chains; **OH95,** Traces if chains; **WI77,** Traces—they were tugs here; **MA51, NE9,** Tracer(s); **NC49,** Iron trace; **NC49,** Leather trace; **LA20,** Trace straps; (Qu. L46, *Behind each horse there's a movable bar [the leathers or ropes from the collar are fastened to it]*) Inf **FL1,** Trace holder. **1983** *MJLF* 9.1.59 **ceKY** (as of 1956), *Traces . . tugs made of chains.* **1986** Pederson *LAGS Concordance* **Gulf Region,** 46 infs, Trace(s); 2 infs, Double trace; 1 inf, Trace line; 1 inf, Trace him—put traces on a horse; 1 inf, Trace it, hook the traces.

trace v[1]   Also with *up*   [swEngl dial (*EDD trace* v.[2] 3 "To plait")]   **NEng** *old-fash*   Cf **trace** n[3]

To braid (ears of corn) together by their husks; hence vbl n *tracing.*

1678 [see **trace** n[3]]. **1772** (1903) Patten *Diary* 290 **NH,** I gathered and traced some corn. **1884** VT State Bd. Ag. *VT Ag. Rept. for 1883–84* 285, The ears thus selected should be "traced up" and hung away to dry. **1898** in 2006 *DARE* File—Internet **nwVT,** Thurs 6. . . We traced up corn after supper. **1940** *Old Farmer's Almanac for 1941* 70 **NEng,** In the early fall the farmers would speak of "tracing up" the yellow ears of corn to hang from the beams of the woodshed.

trace n[3]   [swEngl dial (*OED2 trace* sb.[3] 1 "A tress . . of hair," 3.b "A rope . . of onions"; *EDD trace* sb.[2] 2)]   **chiefly NEng** Cf **trace** v[1], **wrist**

A string of ears of corn made by pulling the husks back and braiding them together; hence comb *trace corn* corn put up in this way.

1678 Royal Soc. London *Philos. Trans.* 12.1066 **NEng,** After 'tis gather'd, it [=corn] must, except laid very thin, be presently stripped from the Husks. . . The common way (which they call Tracing) is to weave the Ears together in long Traces by some parts of the Husk left thereon. **1840** *New Engl. Farmer & Horticult. Reg.* 12 Oct 116/3 (*Matthews Coll.*), He expressed a desire that I should send a small trace of the corn to Boston. **1858** in 1966 Boller *MO Fur Trader* 136, 657 traces corn. **1876** *Atlantic Mth.* 38.282 **ME,** I saw the bunches of herbs hanging up and a trace of corn. **1892** *Stevens Point Jrl.* (WI) 24 Sept 1/4, *List of Premiums.* . . Best . . trace pop corn Mrs E Felch. **1926** *Daily Kennebec Jrl.* (Augusta ME) 14 Aug 2/6, The float of the Winthrop Grange was next in line. . . Stacks of grain, bundles of corn stalks, traces of corn, flowers and evergreens combined to make a most attractive picture. **1927** *AmSp* 3.141 **eME,** "A trace of corn," . . several ears of corn plaited or braided together by the husks, then hung from the rafters. **1937** Weygandt *NH Neighbors* 193 **NH,** "Trace corn" is seed corn bound together in a long string by the plaiting together of the husks turned back from the ears. Twenty such strung ears make a "trace." **c1938** in Lib. of Congress *Amer. Memory: WPA Life Hist.* (Internet) **VT,** Ma an' I got that corn all off the traces. **2005** *DARE* File—Internet **NH** [Rochester Fair Exhibitor Handbook], A trace corn [sic] is three (3) ears husked back and braided together. . . Best trace of field corn—[first prize] $5.00.

trace v[2]   See **trace** n[2]

trace chain n   **chiefly Sth, S Midl**   See Map   Cf **tug chain**

Either a chain used as a **trace** n[2] or a short chain at the end of a leather trace used to secure it to the **singletree.**

1781 in 1787 Tarleton *Hist. Campaigns* 469 **VA,** 123 pair of trace chains. **1815** *Niles' Weekly Reg.* 9.94/2 **DE,** Trace chains and other chains. **1837** *Bangor Daily Whig & Courier* (ME) 30 Oct 1/5, The Southern and Western Merchant will find in this stock Log and Trace Chains. **1877** *Reno Eve. Gaz.* (NV) 20 Nov [4]/1 (newspaperarchive.com), One of the spectators said he thought he heard a trace chain rattle. **1899** (1912) Green *VA Folk-Speech* 455, *Trace-chain.* . . A chain used as a harness trace. **1909** *DN* 3.418 **nME,** *Trace chain.* . . The *chain trace* running from the lug [sic for *tug*] strap to the whiffletree. **1949** *WELS Suppl.* **cwWI,** *Tug* is almost entirely used in this community. But the links at the end are always called trace chains. **1965–70** *DARE* (Qu. L49, *Leathers or ropes, fastened to the collar, that a horse or mule pulls by*) 83 Infs, **chiefly Sth, S Midl,** Trace chain(s); **AL33,** Trace chains on buggies—leather for a wagon is a chain; **CO33,** Trace chains—often called if chain; **MI20,** The trace chain is at the end

of the tug; **MI67,** If it ended in a chain, . . the whole thing was called a trace chain; [**OH60,** Chain trace; **ME5,** Chain traces;] (Qu. L46, *Behind each horse there's a movable bar [the leathers or ropes from the collar are fastened to it]*) Inf **AL31,** Trace chain; **LA39,** On a dump cart, the trace chains were hooked to rings. **1967** *PADS* 47.29 **Sth,** The trace chains are hooked to a ratchet on the *hames,* then attached to the backband, and then hooked by rings at the ends of the chains to the hooks of the singletree. **1986** Pederson *LAGS Concordance,* 22 infs, **Gulf Region,** Trace chain(s).

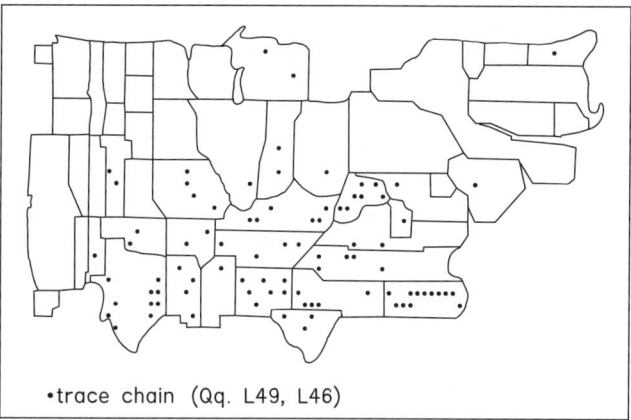

•trace chain (Qq. L49, L46)

trace corn   See **trace** n[3]

trace line, tracer, trace strap   See **trace** n[2]

trace up, tracing   See **trace** v[1]

track n

In hoodoo: a footprint; the dirt from a footprint.

c1938 in 1970 Hyatt *Hoodoo* 1.10 **seNC** [Black], And he said that if he didn't get a piece of her clothes and wrap it up with some sulphur and her track—just one would be all right, the right track, a tablespoonful of her right track—he said that there was no way to cure him but dat. **2004** Bird *Sticks* 35, Materials . . such as dirt from human or animal footprints, are placed in a flannel bag, which is referred to simply as a *flannel* or, more commonly, a *mojo bag.* (This practice, called *foot track magick,* survived slavery and is alive in American Hoodoo.)

tracks n

1 in var combs, esp *hen* (or *chicken*) *tracks:* Illegible handwriting.   **chiefly Nth, N Midl**   See Map

1836 Weld *Corr. Proofs* 185 **MA,** To be well bred, Never be astonished, except at a prodigy of a child, who . . makes turkey-tracks on paper, for the alphabet. **1854** *DE State Reporter* (Dover) 2 May 1/3, There couldn't a man in Worcester read your old hen tracks. [**1857** (1858) Smith *Early IN Trials* 185, He scratched off some caricatures looking like Greek, or turkey tracks.] **1874** (1969) Coffin *Caleb Krinkle* 133 **NH,** He remembered . . how . . he . . wrote as fast as he could, without paying any attention to the hair strokes and shaded lines; and how Miss Hyssop, as a punishment for making such crow's tracks, reset it on the next page. **1928** Andrews *Recollections* 48 **swNH,** He wrote with a quill pen and used a great deal of ink, making regular hen's tracks. **1965–70** *DARE* (Qu. JJ11, *Joking names for handwriting that's*

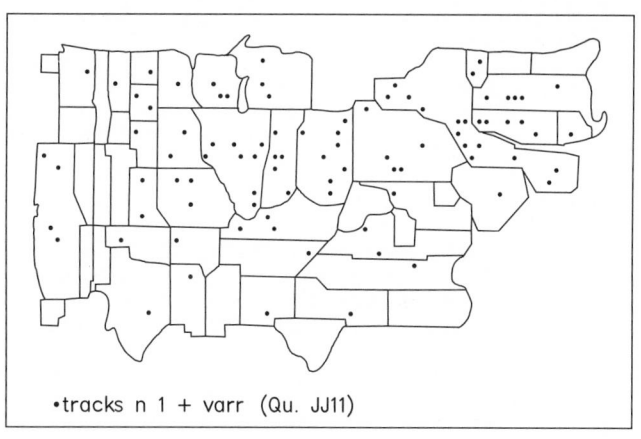

•tracks n 1 + varr (Qu. JJ11)

hard to read: "I can't make anything out of his _____.") 44 Infs, **chiefly Nth, N Midl,** Hen('s) tracks; 38 Infs, 30 **Nth, N Midl,** Chicken tracks; **KS**5, **KY**70, **NY**105, Cat tracks; **IL**53, **MN**21, **RI**17, Crow tracks; **KY**5, **MA**48, Dog tracks; **IN**30, **NY**34, Duck tracks; **AR**39, **IL**11, Pig('s) tracks; **KY**90, Rabbit tracks; **MO**1, Turkey tracks; **WI**5, Goose tracks. **2005** *Gettysburg Times* (PA) 31 Dec 4/1, For one thing, the chicken tracks are getting harder to decode. Either my handwriting is getting lazier or the chicken feed is starting to ferment.

2 also *tracks-out, track(s)-up:* A marble game in which two players shoot at each other's taws; see quots. [Etym uncert; see quot 1958] **esp S Midl**

1897 *McClure's Mag.* 8.322 **KS,** Piggy Pennington went off with the boys . . and fought, or played "tracks up." **1909** *DN* 3.383 **eAL, wGA,** *Tracks.* . . A game at marbles played with taws by boys as they walk along. The one who is behind has the shot, but if one fails to strike his opponent's taw, the turn passes no matter who is behind. **1922** *DN* 5.188 [Marbles terms], *Tracks,* n. = *long-taw.* **1955** *PADS* 23.33 **cwTN,** *Tracks.* . . A game in which two players use one marble each; see *boss out.* **1958** *Resp. to PADS 29* **MO** (as of c1914), *Tracks Out.* Two players. Starting home from school, each player in turn would shoot as far as possible but if an opponents marble was hit you received one marble. If you could get an opponents marble in a wagon track or rut (no paved roads then) you could *wind* [sic] *a handful* by gently hitting his marble and being careful not to go ahead so that it would be his turn. **1963** *KY Folkl. Rec.* 9.60 **eKY,** Game played by shooting at opponent's marble, his shooter, no boundaries . . *tracks:* Perry, Pike, Johnson, Carter, Greenup, Boyd [Counties] . . *tracks-up:* Carter . . *tracks-out:* Morgan. **1969** *DARE* (Qu. EE7, . . *Kinds of marble games*) Inf **IL**96, Track-up—players try to hit each other's taw going to town. Each hit you get a marble from the other guy. [**1973** Ferretti *Marble Book* 66, In Great Britain . . it [=boss-out] has also been known as *boss and span,* and a variation of it . . is called *long-tawl.* In Australia it is . . *black track, track taws, tractor kelly, tractor taw* and *kiss and span.*]

tracks v, hence vbl n *tracksing* (pronc-sp *traxn*) Also sp *trackse, trax*

In marble play: see quots.

1905 *DN* 3.99 **nwAR,** *Trax_{[?]} traxn.* . . 'I'll trax 'em out with you.' Term used in playing marbles. **1909** *DN* 3.383 **eAL, wGA,** *Tracks.* . . To strike a marble so as to make one's taw go in a desired direction. "I can tracks sideways." "I tracksed right up to him." **1922** *DN* 5.188, *Trackse,* v.i. In case of "riders," to shoot so as to push the lone man from the ring. If successful, the player may then shoot at the opposing taw. Also *tracksing,* v.n. **1967** *DARE* Tape **TX**1, Well, you have to learn how to tracks. We call it tracksing. . . You'd hit that marble on this side, knock it out, and tracks down to close to that other one, see?

tracks-out, track(s)-up See **tracks** n **2**

tractor and trailer See **tractor-trailer**

tractor pull n Also *tractor pulling (contest)* Cf **horse pulling**
A contest in which tractors compete to pull a weighted sled the greatest distance.

1938 *Wellsboro Gaz.* (PA) 29 Sept 9/4, The fair officially opening at 2 o'clock with the tractor pulling contest. **1951** *Herald–Press* (St. Joseph MI) 10 Aug 8/1, *Add Driving Skill Test To Youth Fair Tractor Pull*—The tractor-pulling contest scheduled at the Berrien County Youth Fair next week will have a couple of new wrinkles. **1965–70** *DARE* (Qu. FF16, . . *Local contests or celebrations*) Infs **MO**5, 18, **PA**144, **WI**44, Tractor pulling contest; **IL**135, **KY**73, Tractor pulls; **IA**12, Horse and tractor pulling contest; **IL**37, Tractor pulling. **1967** *Roseville Independent* (IL) 3 Aug 7/2, Four big days this year with two tractor pulling contests. **1968** *Rev.–Times* (Oxford NY) 4 July sec A 3/1, Saturday's activities will begin at noon with a tractor pull. **1993** *DARE* File **MA,** Tractor pulls, which don't do much for me. **2011** *DARE* File—Internet **KS,** Activities include, tractor pulls (steam, gas and diesel).

tractor tire (doughnut) n
A large raised, twisted doughnut.

1997 in 2009 *DARE* File—Internet, *You Know You Own an Old Tractor When.* . . Your 7 year old daughter calls crueller [sic] style doughnuts: "Tractor tire doughnuts." **2006** Devoti *Love Is All* 12 **MO,** "How about a tractor tire? They're the freshest." The waitress filled Del's cup and . . retrieved a three-inch high doughnut. **2006** *DARE* File—Internet, A bike a blanket and some tractor tire doughnuts. **2007** *DARE* File **csMN** (as of 1980s), We called round, glazed doughnuts that had bumps tractor tires because that's what they looked like.

tractor-trailer n Also *tractor and trailer, trailer-tractor* **scattered, but more freq Atlantic** See Map and Map Section Cf **semi**
A tractor truck and attached semitrailer.

1914 Genl. Contractors Assoc. NY *Bulletin* 5.85, The vital problem of satisfying this ever-increasing demand for larger units has led to the advent of the three-axle tractor trailer method of transportation in which all the propelling mechanism is carried entirely separate from the load carrying portion. **1925** *Oakland Tribune* (CA) 4 Oct sec O 8/5, That is the principal [sic] of the tractor trailer combination. **1951** *News* (Frederick MD) 19 Jan 1/1, [Headline:] Tractor-Trailer And School Vehicle In Accident. **1965–70** *DARE* (Qu. N11, *A very large truck used to haul freight, new cars, and other big loads*) 73 Infs, **scattered, but more freq Atlantic,** Tractor-trailer; **CA**87, **IN**69, **NJ**44, **OH**45, 61, **VA**75, Tractor and trailer; **GA**23, 54, **OH**77, **SC**57, Tractor-trailer truck; **SC**21, **VA**33, **WI**51, Trailer-tractor; **MA**58, **WV**8, Tractor-trailer outfit; **FL**15, Tractor-trailer rig; **GA**77, Tractor-and-trailer rig; (Qu. L42, *Do you use the word 'rig' around here? What kind of thing do you call a 'rig'?*) Infs **OH**50, **TN**1, Tractor and trailer; **IA**45, **PA**204, Tractor-trailer outfit; **PA**163, Tractors and trailers. **1977–78** Foster *Lexical Variation* 58 **NJ,** [45 (of 166) infs offered *tractor trailer.*] **2003** *DARE* File **cwMA,** [I] have heard *semi*—used on NPR interviews with locals describing accidents—and it's always a midwesterner when they use that term, even though they understand *tractor trailer.* **2005** *Post–Std.* (Syracuse NY) 20 Aug sec B 2/1, [Headline:] Tractor-trailer, mower collide.

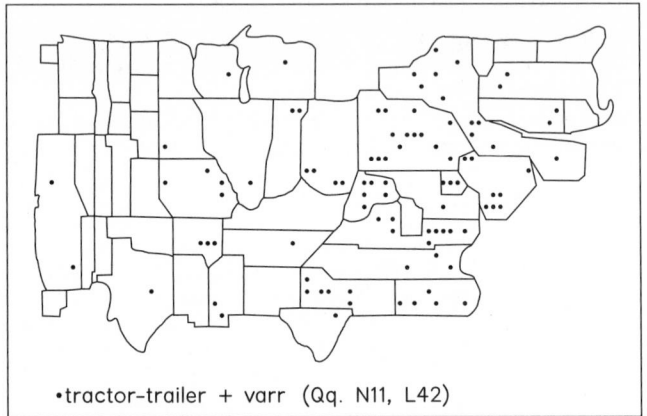

•tractor-trailer + varr (Qq. N11, L42)

trade v [Spec application of an old and otherwise obs sense "to follow a path, go" (*OED2 trade* v. 2 1591–1651, *EDD trade* v. 9)]
Chiefly of game birds: to pass, usu over a regular route, between nearby points; to go (back and forth).

1876 *Scribner's Mth.* 13.152 **seNY,** Sometimes they . . shoot from the sand-pits on the main at red-head and canvas-back, as they are trading in and out of the creeks and coves. **1877** *Ibid* 15.7 **MD,** After that hour the ducks ceased "trading," as flying from one point to another is termed. **1941** *NY Times* (NY) 21 Nov 28, We could see a raft of more than a thousand black ducks in the [Long Island] Sound . . , and broadbill were trading back and forth. **1954** *Chillicothe Constitution–Tribune* (MO) 16 Dec 2/3, There were a few ducks or geese trading along the waterways and sloughs to keep the sportsmen's eyes peeled. **1965** *Lowell Sun* (MA) 5 Nov 18/7, The winds kept the ducks trading from slough to slough. **1969** *Mt. Democrat & Placerville Times* (CA) 5 June sec B 4/1, A bit of wind . . improved fishing. . . I ran across an assemblage of males [=bluegills] that were trading back and forth outside a nesting, though the nests had not yet been dug. **1997** *Abilene Reporter-News* (TX) 31 Aug (Internet), You could see the heavy dove traffic . . , the birds trading back and forth in numerous groups. **2004** *DARE* File—Internet **NJ,** The birds would trade back and forth between this area and the refuge. **2006** *DARE* File **NEast,** "We haven't seen many ducks trading around out here today." This is a standard term used by duck hunters in the northeast US.

trade day n Also *trading day;* also with a day of the week specified, as *trading Monday* Cf **sale day, swap ~, trades ~**
A day fixed in a particular community, usu at regular intervals, for the buying, selling, or bartering of goods; broadly, a flea market.

1887 Eggleston *Graysons* 35 **IL,** Rachel might come to town next Saturday, which was the general trading-day of the country people. **1888** *New Era* (Humeston IA) 30 May [6]/2 (newspaperarchive.com), Seymour had an experimental sale and trade day last Saturday. . . Should it be a success Seymour will probably continue them once or twice a month in the future. **1895** *Atlanta Constitution* (GA) 25 May 2/4 **seGA,** *A Baby Show, Foot Races and a Greasy Pole Entertain the Crowd.* . . One thousand visitors were here today and the trade day was a success. **1905** *DN* 3.99 **nwAR,** *Tradin(g)-day.* . . The citizens of Hackett have organized a trading-day for that town. **1906** Johnson *Highways Missip. Valley* 129 **Ozarks,** This is trading day, and he's got a basket on his arm and is carryin' his eggs and butter up to the village. **1931** *Woodland Daily Democrat* (CA) 19 Mar 6/1, [Advt:] We have some extra fine, large shrubs priced especially low for trade day. **1938** *Wellsboro Agitator* (PA) 9 Nov 6/4, A weekly trade day, when unexpected bargains are offered, is better than "Dollar Days" . . and will, in the course of a year or two, create the habit of visiting Wellsboro on that day each week. **1962** Faulkner *Reivers* 14 **MS,** There were plenty of them; Boon sure picked his day for witnesses; First Saturdays were trade days even then, even in May when you would think people would be too busy getting land planted. **1967** Green *Horse Tradin'* 275, The next morning was Monday, and it would be a Trading Monday. **1971** *Press-Gaz.* (Hillsboro OH) 16 Apr 24/1, [Advt:] Bill Boatman brings back "Old Fashioned Trade Day" to Bainbridge, Ohio. Thousands of dogs and gun traders gather here to swap and sell. **1976** Brown *Gloss. Faulkner* 202 **MS,** *Trade days* . . special days (usually once a month) set aside for auctioning and trading in livestock. The Lafayette County Live Stock and Trade Day Association was organized in 1912. Some north-Mississippi communities to this day have signs on the highways saying "Trade Days: second Saturdays" (of the month) or something similar. **1993** Frazer *"Heartland" English* 219 **nWI,** Barter or the direct exchange of labor for goods continues, even though Saturday "trade days" in Crandon are a thing of the past. **1999** Mason *Clear Springs* 176 **wKY,** He had been trading antique guns for some time, locating the parts he needed to restore guns for collectors. The old trade days had now become flea markets.

trade-last n   Also abbr *t.l.;* for addit varr see quots **widespread, but less freq Atlantic**   See Map   Also called **Alaskan trade, bid** n 2, **last-go-trade**

A compliment given or reported to another on condition of receiving one in exchange; hence v *trade-last,* v phr *trade lasts* to make such an exchange.

1891 Kipling in *Harper's Weekly* 4 July 504, Saidie tells Maimie that Hattie's new frock is pretty. Maimie repeats the compliment to Hattie, who tells Maimie that Saidie is "just too Sweet to live." This is a trade-last. It is also called Criticism. **1893** *KS Univ. Qrly.* 1.142 **KS,** *Trade-lasts:* an exchange of compliments. **1896** *DN* 1.426 **MI, NY, OH,** *Trade-last, -lassie, -me-lass:* a complimentary remark reported by one person to another. "I've got a trade-last for you" (the speaker then reports the complimentary remark made by a third person). Sometimes also a somewhat uncomplimentary remark. **1900** *DN* 2.67 [College slang], *Trade-last.* . . 1. An exchange of compliments. 2. A quoted compliment. . . [T]*rade-last, v.i.* To exchange compliments. **1904** *Ft. Wayne News* (IN) 2 May 5/4, [Advt:] *A Bookful of Trade Lasts* from our customers *could* be published, *if* our business was not confidential. **1905** *DN* 3.66 **eNE,** *Trade-last.* . . A compliment reported by a third party. Generally one is expected in return. **1909** *DN* 3.383 **eAL, wGA,** *Trade-last.* . . A compliment reported from a third party. "I've got a trade-last for you." . . To exchange compliments made by third parties. "I'll trade-last with you." *Ibid* 405 **nwAR,** *Trade-last.* . . A complimentary remark reported by one person to another in exchange for a compliment. **1914** *Syracuse Herald* (NY) 9 Aug [92]/7 **AK,** "What are you going to do?" said the prisoner. "Just trade lasts and exchange philopenas, as it were," Boyd laughed grimly. **1934** Stribling *Unfinished Cathedral* 23 **AL,** I can trade lasts with you! **1937** *AmSp* 12.77 **NE,** *Trade last.* . . The younger generation still uses the expression, usually in its abbreviated form *'T.L.,'* at least in rural Nebraska. *Ibid* 134 **IN** (as of 1890s), 'I have a trade-last for you.' 'What is it?' 'I said it was a trade last. You give me yours *first.*' **1939** in Lib. of Congress *Amer. Memory: WPA Life Hist.* (Internet) **NE,** "T.L.'s" or "Trade Lasts" were always popular and they usually were sincere, genuine compliments from other[s], exchanged or traded. **1965–70** *DARE* (Qu. KK35, *When someone wants to pass on a compliment about you, in exchange for one about himself* . . *"I have a _____ for you."*) 203 Infs, **widespread, but less freq Atlantic,** Trade-last; **CT9,** Trade-last—when somebody offers to give you a compliment, you *have* to reciprocate; **HI1,** Trade-last—I'll *trade* information with you, but I'll give mine *last* (you must

give yours first, or I won't give any); **KY50,** Trade-last—it's a trade. . . they wouldn't tell you something nice 'til you said something nice about them, so you made something up right quick; **OH95,** Trade-last—Inf says he hasn't thought of this for fifty or sixty years; **TX102,** Trade-last—you give me a compliment and I'll trade you last [Of all Infs responding to Qu. KK35, 62% were old, 12% young; of those giving these responses, 82% were old, 2% young.]; 116 Infs, **widespread, but less freq Atlantic,** T.L. [Of all Infs responding to Qu. KK35, 54% were female; of those giving this response, 72% were female.]; **IL72A,** I'll trade last; **KS8,** Trades-last; **MD8,** Trade-for-your-last-go; **MS73,** Trade-for-you-my-last; **TX51,** Trade-last compliments; **UT3,** T.L. [or] tell-last; **VA31,** Trade-last-go; **MN39,** Trade-lash; **MO15,** Trade-latch. **1996** *DARE* File, Many years ago my stepmother said she had a "trade-like" for me. I'd never heard of this, and she explained that it was a compliment someone had paid me, which she offered to repeat if I would tell her something complimentary I'd heard about her. **2006** *DARE* File, A "T.L." is a "tell last." It refers to a protocol regarding second-hand compliments. If A overhears—or is simply told—something complimentary about B, A tells B of the existence of this "t.l." meaning that B must come up with a compliment of some sort for A before the "t.l." will be told to B.

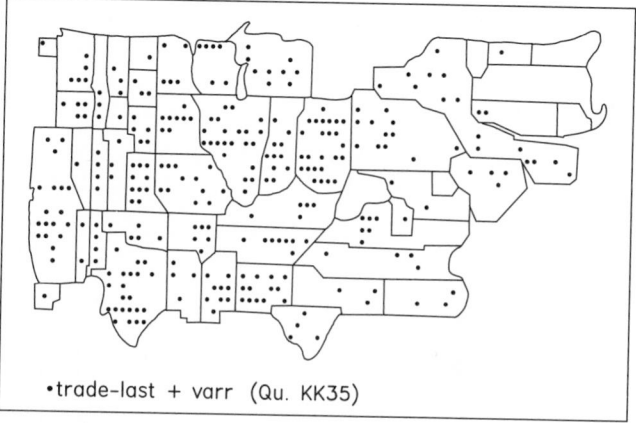

•trade-last + varr (Qu. KK35)

trade out v phr

To accept goods or services to the value of a sum due; to barter; hence n *trade-out.*

1853 (1860) Taylor *January & June* 95, The wife was going in to help her husband 'trade out' a portion of the proceeds of the wheat. **1890** Holley *Samantha among Brethren* 183 **NY,** I meekly carried it back, and begged the smirking clerk to take it again, promising to trade it out in some other way. **1911** *Forestry Qrly.* 9.176 **AZ,** The total payroll amounted to $1,039, out of which $207.80 was paid in cash while the remainder was traded out in the commissary. **1928** Aldrich *Lantern* 173 **NE,** When Isabelle took her lesson, Abbie traded out the butter and eggs she had brought to the Lutz store. **1967** *DARE* (Qu. L5, *When a farmer gets help on a job from his neighbors in return for his help on their farms later on*) Inf **LA14,** Trade-out [FW: noun]; **IN54,** Trading out. **1967** *DARE* Tape **IL15,** We took our produce, our eggs and stuff, to Champaign, to the stores and trade [sic] 'em out for groceries. **1971** *Sun. Dominion–Post* (Morgantown WV) 5 Sept Panorama sec 4/3, If the purchase was less than the worth of the produce, the farmer traded it out over a period of weeks or months. **2005** *DARE* File—Internet **NC,** I'd prefer to do some trade out and keep Uncle Sam out of the loop. . . I normally charge 75–100/hr and would trade out hour/hour.

trade rat n   Also *trader rat, trading rat*   **West**   =**wood rat.**

1881 *Amer. Mag.* 11.35, Among the many strange animals one meets in the Rocky Mountains, the hairy-tailed or trading rat is perhaps the most unique and interesting to the naturalist. **1885** *Pop. Sci. Mth.* 27.831, The Trading-Rat. . . These interesting rodents are dwellers in the Rocky Mountains and adjacent hills. **1908** Johnson *Highways Pacific Coast* 20 **AZ,** About the funniest creature we've got in this country . . is the trade rat. . . The way the rats get their name is that when they take anything of yours they always put something in its place—a stick or burr or whatever comes handy. **1958** McCulloch *Woods Words* 198 **Pacific NW,** *Trader rat*—See pack rat. **1959** Martin *Gunbarrel* 123 **WY,** Whenever a pack rat takes anything, he always leaves something in its place. That's why they're sometimes called trade rats. **1973** *AZ Highways* Mar 29, The Kangaroo Rat as well as the Pack or Trade Rat line their tunnels and runways with the spiny stems . . of the Chollas. **2001** *DARE* File—Internet **TX**, In seeking construction material, a trade rat carrying a stick will eagerly discard it for a glittering ring or a bright coin. Thus there is a trade only when the rodent is forced to discard its current cargo in favor of a more desirable item.

trades exclam   Also *tradies*   Cf **keeps 1, keepsies 2**

In marble play: a call that allows a player to substitute a marble of his choice for one he has lost; hence phr *for trades* on condition that marbles taken may be traded; exclam *no trades* used as a call preventing such substitution.

[**1914** Hubbard in *Harper's Mth. Mag.* 129 advt sec np, Keep Your Car! . . It means first, careful buying—a clinging to conservatism, propriety in outline, in your selection because you are going to buy for keeps and not for trades.] **1958** *PADS* 29.41 **WI**, *Trades.* . . A call entitling a player to exchange a less-valued marble for one he has just lost— perhaps a favorite or lucky marble. **c1970** Wiersma *Marbles Terms* **swMI** (as of c1965), *Trades* . . playing marbles where the winner is allowed any marble the loser wants to give him. . . This time we will play for trades so I can keep my better marbles. *Ibid* **swMI** (as of c1960), *Tradies*—a call which is made by a player before his shot, which enables him, if he loses the shot, to replace the marble being shot with one of inferior value. *Ibid* **swMI** (as of c1955), *No trades* . . phrase called out when the player doesn't want to trade marbles at the end of the game.

trades day n   **chiefly TX**

=trade day.

1896 *Democratic Std.* (Coshocton OH) 6 Nov [5]/4 (newspaper-archive.com), [Advt:] Coshocton Street Fair! Market and Trades Day, Friday and Saturday. . . Traders and buyers are invited from all over the country. **1904** *Galveston Daily News* (TX) 17 Mar 3/5, The trades day committee . . has held its first meeting and arrangements are on foot for . . monthly trades days. **1929** Dobie *Vaquero* 187 **TX**, In many towns Saturday, the first Monday in each month, or some other day, was designated as tradesday. On that day the town would be filled with men and horses. **1932** *Ada Eve. News* (OK) 22 June 2/5, Orel Busby of Ada, candidate for justice of the supreme court, spoke to the trades day crowd of 3,000 persons here today. **1954** *Kerrville Times* (TX) 7 July 7/4, The number of volunteer blood donors were considered satisfactory in view of the dates following so closely upon . . the regular monthly Trades Day shopper's event. **1967** Green *Horse Tradin'* 267 **TX**, I took some saddle horses to Decatur one trades day. **1975** *Commerce Jrl.* (TX) 26 June sec B 2/6, [Advt:] First Annual Delta County Trades Days and Carnival. **2006** *DARE* File—Internet **TX**, My dad's garage looks like a country store. . . On weekends he loads his things up and goes to trades day w[h]ere he haggles with the best of them.

tradies   See **trades**

trading day (or Monday, etc)   See **trade day**

trading rat   See **trade rat**

traffic v   Also with *about*   [*EDD* traffic(k sb. 8]   **esp sAppalachians**

To wander, move idly about.

1913 Kephart *Highlanders* 203 **sAppalachians,** Jist traffickin' about. **1952** *Think* Aug 7, Just the same, rain or shine, half of Paris spilled out of their houses to laugh and traffic along its 900-odd streets. **1954** *Harder Coll.* **cwTN,** *Traffic.* . . Wander aimlessly. **1994** in 2004 Montgomery–Hall *Dict. Smoky Mt. Engl.* 616 **eTN,** Traffic about. **2003** *DARE* File—Internet **DE,** Higher in the sky . . there were even more geese . . trafficking about in flocks.

traffic circle n   Also *circle, ~ drive, ~ crossroad*   **chiefly Atlantic, Gulf States, SW**   See Map   Cf **rotary** n

A road junction in which traffic moves in one direction around a circular island.

1916 Folwell *Municipal Engin.* 161, Traffic circles at intersections of busy thoroughfares have been recommended. **1924** *Middletown Daily Herald* (NY) 21 Nov 1/1, On the highway itself, in order to simplify the movement of automobiles, a traffic circle has been installed. **1927** *Oakland Tribune* (CA) 22 Oct 12/2, The principle of the traffic circles . . is as follows: "The circles would be built at each end of the dam with the streams of automobiles entering them from the abutting streets mingling in the constantly moving whirl to the left and leaving it at any other street. Small circular park plots, each with a central fountain, could be built to center these circles." **1942** *Policy on Rotary Intersections* Amer. Assoc. State Highway Officials 1 (*OED2*), The name 'traffic cir-

cle' is commonly applied to any intersection design based on the one-way movement of vehicles around a central area. **1965–70** *DARE* (Qu. N20, . . *A circular arrangement on one level at a big intersection, where cars can go around till they come to the road they want*) 167 Infs, **scattered, but chiefly Atlantic, Gulf States,** Circle; 115 Infs, **scattered, but chiefly Atlantic, Gulf States, SW,** Traffic circle; **SC**32, Miracle Circle near Seneca—four roads come together with islands, lots of wrecks, a miracle if you can come through without being killed; **TX**12, Circle—signs say this; **GA**45, **MD**40, **OR**3, **VA**38, Circle drive; **GA**40, Circle crossroad. **1969** *Courier–Gaz.* (Rockland ME) 22 June 2/2, Fort McClary Memorial is located two and a half miles south on Kittery Point Road from the traffic circle in Kittery. **2005** *Post-Std.* (Syracuse NY) 10 Feb 11/2, There had been talk about creating a roundabout . . like a small traffic circle.

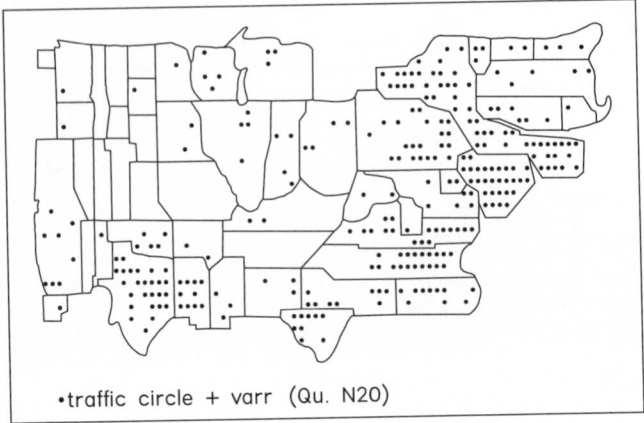

•traffic circle + varr (Qu. N20)

trail v

1   In logging:

a   To drag (logs), esp along a prepared track; hence vbl n *trailing*. [Prob spec use of *OED2 trail* v.[1] 1 "To draw behind one; to drag along upon the ground" c1375 →; cf **trail** n]

[**1832** Murdoch *Epitome Laws Nova-Scotia* 142, Penalties are enacted for encumbering, or injuring roads, for trailing logs on them except over the snow [etc.].] **1877** *Daily Gaz. & Bulletin* (Williamsport PA) 10 Oct [3]/3 (newspaperarchive.com), Logging is not done on quite the same plan here [=WI] as in Pennsylvania. . . All the logs are handled on sleds—no trailing nor sliding, and very few are skidded ahead of the teams, but are mostly loaded with teams and rolling chain. **1883** *Indiana Weekly Messenger* (PA) 14 Feb [3]/3 (newspaperarchive.com), To visit a log camp and see them trailing logs on a slide, we imagine would be worth seeing. . . The slide is built of timber in the shape of a trough. . . One team of horses will pull fifty to sixty logs at once. When the logs get started on a down grade they go at lightning speed. **1911** *Gaz. & Bulletin* (Williamsport PA) 13 Dec 6/6, While Charles Yeagle and one of his men were trailing logs the former's two dogs run a rabbit down the road ahead of them. **1941** *McKean Co. Democrat* (Smethport PA) 13 Nov 4/3, Today girl and woman teamsters are employed in trailing logs from the cutting operations to the sawmill. **1956** Sorden–Ebert *Logger's Words* 39 **Gt Lakes,** *Trailing-down,* Bringing logs from piles in the woods. **1958** McCulloch *Woods Words* 198 **Pacific NW,** *Trail.* . . To skid logs down a road with horses or tractors. . . To skid logs down the track behind a steam engine. **1977** *Foxfire 4* 271 **sAppalachians,** If you was on steep ground, you could take six head of cattle and in places trail as many as fifteen logs behind them. Just looked like a freight train.

b   with *up, together:* To chain (logs) together to form a **trail** n; hence ppl adj phrr *trailed up, ~ together.*

1977 *Foxfire 4* 271 **sAppalachians,** And then whenever I got them logs all trailed up together, I wouldn't have to do nothing only just get the slack all pulled out of them. *Ibid* 272, Take half a day to get'em. Maybe be two o'clock before you got'em all trailed together and ready to go out with'em.

2   To drive (livestock) overland; hence vbl n *trailing.*   **chiefly West**

1885 Nimmo *Rept. Cattle Business* 100, When herds are trailed from Texas, the cattle of Indian Territory and Kansas suffer [from "Texas fever"], if allowed to graze on the Texas trail. **1897** Craig (Colo.) *Courier* 2 Jan *(Mathews Coll.),* Cattle were trailed in from all the ranges of the West, and even from Texas. **1904** Adams *TX Matchmaker* 96, This herd was to be trailed to Abilene, Kansas, and possibly sold beyond that point. **1920** Hunter *Trail Drivers TX* 294 (as of c1880), He spent his young manhood in trailing cattle in Montana and the Northwestern ranges. **1929** *AmSp* 5.74 **NE** [Cattle country talk], To "trail 'em" means to drive cattle a considerable distance, as from a Kansas to a Nebraska ranch. **1941** Writers' Program *Guide WY* 466, *Trail.* . . To follow a herd of cattle; to drive a herd of horses on any dim path or road. **1954** Jordan *Hell's Canyon* 11 **ID,** Our summer range . . would have to be reached by "trailing" the sheep a hundred miles. **1959** Lahey–Hogan *As I Remember It* 81 **swKS** (as of early 20th cent), They trailed that herd through, about twelve miles east of Liberal. **1966** DARE Tape **NM**13, Some of them had followed the ranching business from the time they were youngsters. And some of them trailed cattle in from Texas, into various parts of the country; **SD**8, The last cattle we trailed to Belle Fourche in thirty-eight. . . We trailed them to the railroad up here. **1978** Doig *This House* 212 **MT** (as of c1955), Big strappin' son-of-a-buck, he . . says, "I got a right to trail these sheep through here. . . " I says, "Then why don't ye trail 'em?"

3 To entice or lead. [*OED2* a1717 →]

1930 Stoney–Shelby *Black Genesis* 63 **seSC** [Gullah], If Ebe had catch up an' tame creeter an' fowl what hang roun' de house, dis chile gots for gone out in de woods for git mo', an' trail 'em in wid corn.

4 To carry on a trail.

1969 Wilson *Stars* 112 **Ozarks,** Me and Marthy was gabbin' about how we might get Uncle Billy Rutherford to bottom them chairs that Grandpa Rudolph trailed overland from Alabamy back in the 1840's.

trail n [Spec use of *OED2 trail* sb.¹ 6 "Anything drawn behind as an appendage . . ; a train"] **esp PA** Cf **trail v 1**

A number (of logs) chained end-to-end for hauling.

1880 *Furniture Gaz.* 14.346 **PA,** When a trail is coming down the slide, it is better to be out of the way, as, if a log does strike you, there will be some trouble in making a respectable corpse out of your remains. **1884** Sargent *Forests of N. Amer.* 510 **PA,** When a sufficient number [of logs] . . have been placed end to end in the slide, the hook of a chain is driven into the rear log . . and horses are attached which walk a tow-path formed on one side of the slide, and push ahead of them the 'trail' of logs. **1890** *McKean Democrat* (Smethport PA) 21 Nov [3]/2 (newspaperarchive.com), It appears that Hoffman had a trail of logs in tow. **1909** *Indiana Progress* (PA) 22 Dec 1/2, The young man, who was engaged in driving, was caught by a trail of logs. **1917** *Clearfield Progress* (PA) 18 Oct 3/5, A big buck deer jumped out of the brush into the road along which his team was plodding, with George walking behind just ahead of the trail of logs. **1938** *Helena Independent* (MT) 2 Aug 10/2, Two men escaped injury . . when they jumped from a runaway motor truck carrying 2,000 feet of logs. . . "Because the grade was 35 and 25 per cent down the slope we had seven logs in two sets of trails behind the truck to hold it back. . . All went well until one set of the trails . . broke. The remaining trail was not sufficient to hold the truck back." **1958** McCulloch *Woods Words* 198 **Pacific NW,** *Trail of logs*—A turn of logs being brought to the landing in the days of animal skidding; logs arranged end to end like a bunch of sausages, not bunched as with modern chokers. **1964** Clarkson *Tumult* 373 **WV,** *Trail of logs*—See *tow of logs.*

trailed together (or up) See **trail v 1b**

trailer n

1 See quot; hence n *trailers' row* =**mourners' bench.**

1921 *DN* 5.121 **NY,** *Trailer.* . . One who goes up in church in response to the call for penitents to come up and testify. "There were a good many trailers at the last service." . . [T]*railers' row.* The front row in church; mourners' row.

2 One who rides behind a herd of animals.

1937 Sandoz *Slogum* 32 **NE,** A lone rider pointed the lean, horn-weary herd, two shambled along each side, and the trailer, the dirt eater, limbered up the drags with voice and knot-ended rope.

3 See **trailer truck.**

trailer rig See **trailer truck**

trailers' row See **trailer n 1**

trailer-tractor See **tractor-trailer**

trailer truck n Also *trailer (rig)* **chiefly east of Missip R, esp NEast; also TX, Cent** See Map and Map Section Cf **semi**

A truck-and-trailer rig for hauling freight on roads; now usu spec a semitrailer and tractor truck.

1914 NC Geol. & Economic Surv. *Economic Paper 39* 27, This truck hauled stone at a cost of twenty-five cents per ton mile. With one trailer

truck the cost was fifteen cents per ton mile. **1919** *Ft. Wayne News & Sentinel* (IN) 12 July 4/2, In Los Angeles recently a trailer-truck transported a forty-ton load over a distance of twenty-three miles. **1921** *Syracuse Herald* (NY) 4 Dec 14/4, Owners of trailers, whether it is a small two-wheeled affair in which the family packs tent and camping outfit for a week-end trip, or whether it is a heavy trailer truck for commercial purposes, are warned that a separate license is necessary for this vehicle. **1930** *Decatur Daily Rev.* (IL) 1 Aug 22/5, The horse . . was hit by the big auto trailer truck driven by White. **1940** *Vidette–Messenger* (Valparaiso IN) 12 Dec 1/2, The car they rode in was demolished by a trailer truck. **1965–70** DARE (Qu. N11, *A very large truck used to haul freight, new cars, and other big loads*) 175 Infs, **chiefly east of Missip R, esp NEast; also TX, Cent,** Trailer truck; **TN**11, Trailer rig; 80 Infs, **chiefly east of Missip R,** Trailer; **GA**74, Trailer—the entire truck; **MI**67, Trailers—if they have a double section; **PA**76, Mack trailer; (Qu. L42, *Do you use the word 'rig' around here? What kind of thing do you call a 'rig'?*) Inf **TN**37, Big trailer truck. **1986** Pederson *LAGS Concordance,* 1 inf, **nwFL,** Trailer truck; 1 inf, **cAL,** Used to, you take a trailer truck; [1 inf, **cAL,** Trail trucks].

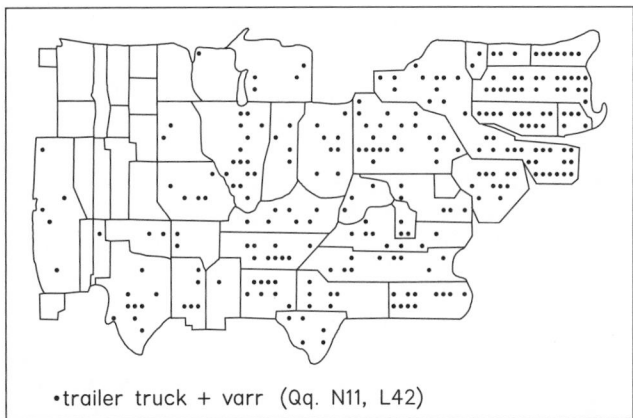

•trailer truck + varr (Qq. N11, L42)

trailing See **trail v 1a, 2**

trailing arbutus See **arbutus**

trailing Charley n Cf **creeping Charlie 2**
=**ground ivy 1.**

1940 Clute *Amer. Plant Names* 265, *Nepeta glechoma.* . . Trailing Charley.

trailing evergreen n Cf **evergreen 2, trailing vine**
=**club moss.**

1874 NH Geol. Surv. *Geol. NH* 1.413, L[ycopodium] dendroideum. Club-Moss. Trailing Evergreen. **1899** Going *Field Flowers* 251 **NEng,** The lycopodiums . . under the names of . . "club-moss", or "trailing-evergreen", are familiar to almost every one who has summered in New England. **1907** *DN* 3.203 **seNH,** *Trailing evergreen.* . . One of two kinds of evergreen plants that run on the ground. **1938** Small *Ferns SE States* 402, L[ycopodium] lucidulum [=Huperzia l.] . . Trailing-evergreen. Staghorn-moss. . . Low, cool, often damp woods. **1950** Gray–Fernald *Manual of Botany* 15, L[ycopodium] complanatum. . . Trailing Evergreen. . . Elongate stem creeping on or near surface of ground. **2002** DARE File—Internet **VA,** Lycopodium complanatum. Also called . . Trailing Evergreen, this creeping evergreen grows in tangled masses that produce fanlike branches resembling juniper.

trailing hollyhock n
=**flower-of-an-hour.**

1900 Bailey *Cyclop. Horticult.* 2.742, [Hibiscus] vesicarius. . . Trailing Hollyhock. **1942** Hylander *Plant Life* 379, The Trailing Hollyhock, or Flower-of-an-hour, . . is an interesting plant with yellow or white flowers which open in the sun and close in the shade.

trailing pea n
=**groundnut B1.**

1900 Lyons *Plant Names* 39, A[pios] Apios. . . Trailing Pea. . . Tubers edible. **1922** *Amer. Botanist* 28.75, Apios tuberosa. . . is also known as "trailing pea."

trailing vine n Cf **trailing evergreen**

A **club moss** (here: *Lycopodium complanatum*).

1897 *Jrl. Amer. Folkl.* 10.147 **VT,** Lycopodium complanatum, . . trailing, running, or creeping vine.

trailing yew n
=creeping juniper.

1916 *Torreya* 16.236 **seME,** *Juniperus horizontalis.* . . Trailing yew, Monhegan I[slan]d. **1978** *U.S. 1979* 623 **seME,** Among the many woodland trails are no less than 600 varieties of flowering plants—including the trailing yew, unique to this island [=Monhegan].

trail together (or up) See **trail** v 1b

train v   chiefly NEng

To romp, "carry on"; hence n *train* a romp; n *trainer* one who romps.

a1861 (1880) Eastman *Poems* 153 **VT,** A very temperate man is he,/ Though it is true, no doubt,/ He had his "train," when, years ago,/ The "Flood-wood" was called out. **1874** *NY Times* (NY) 25 Oct 4/7, "Touse" . . has become obsolete almost everywhere in this country; though I have heard it used in New England as the expressions "training" and "carrying-on" are elsewhere used to designate the capers and pranks of exuberant young people. **1877** Bartlett *Americanisms* 717 **NEng,** Almost peculiar to girls in New England. "She's an awful one to train." **1889** (1890) Howells *Hazard* 53 **NYC,** The girl broke into a fondly approving laugh at his drolling. "Oh, I guess you love to train!" **1890** *DN* 1.20 **seNH,** *Train:* frolic, romp. 'He's training' (of a child). Also 'he's on a train,' or 'a great trainer.' Widely used. **1903** *DN* 2.353 **cMA,** *Train.* . . To carry on, especially said of a young man fond of tricks, flirting, etc. 'John is always training.'

trainasse n [Cajun Fr *traînasse*] **LA**
A shallow, navigable channel through marshland.

1946 Kopman *Wild Acres* 160 **LA,** Along certain parts of the route, hunters, guides, and camp owners have made what the French natives of Louisiana call "traverses" and "trainasses." These are mere ditches in which only the shallowest pirogue may be propelled by a pole. . . At some points these ditches are too shallow to float the pirogue, and only vigorous pushing will keep it moving over the . . ooze. **1976** Assoc. Amer. Geogrs. *Annals* 66.3.349 **LA,** Louisiana's marsh-swamp complex is criss-crossed by artificial waterways. The earliest type of canal excavated in the region was the *traînasse*, a trapping ditch hacked out by trapper-fisher folk to provide marsh access. . . Once a *traînasse* is cut, it remains for years, often enlarging into a bayou. **1979** Hallowell *People Bayou* 42 **sLA,** Most nutria trappers now merely cruise along a bayou or trainasse in their outboards, plucking animals from the traps on the banks. **1986** Pederson *LAGS Concordance,* 1 inf, **seLA,** *Trainasse*— narrow channel [in a] marsh, 2–3 feet wide, shallow. **2007** Dunn *Crossing Trinity* 32 **LA,** Missing the old cabin was easy if one did not know exactly how to find the *trainasse,* or boat trail, through the marsh that lead [sic] to it.

traineau n   Also sp *traineaux, trainneau* Pl *traineaux* [Fr *traîneau*] Cf *DCan*

A sled or sledge; in Canada and around the Great Lakes, a vehicle to be pulled over snow; in Louisiana, a sled to be pulled over land; see quots.

1832 Cooper *Pioneers* 1.3 **NY,** A single track, barely wide enough to receive the sleigh, denoted the route of the highway. [Footnote to *sleigh:*] Sleigh is the word used in every part of the United States to denote a traineau. **1833** in 1835 Hoffman *Winter in West* 1.166, Did you ever see a *jumper?* . . It is a primitive kind of sledge or *traineau.* [**1873** *Forest & Stream* 1.273 **Canada,** Our traineau, heavily loaded, follows behind.] **1891** *Harper's New Mth. Mag.* 82.860, As the patient ass to the follower of the Prophet, so is the travaux (or traîneaux) pony to the Indian. *Ibid,* A dog hitched to a diminutive traîneau. **1900** *Atlantic Mth.* 85.101 **MI** (as of c1850), Once a week the United States mail, in charge of a couple of half-breeds, came through on *traîneaux* drawn by dogs. **1911** (1913) Johnson *Highways Gt. Lakes* 192, Besides the mail, we had on our trainneau blankets and a little camp equipage and grub. **1986** Pederson *LAGS Concordance,* 1 inf, **seLA,** *Traineau*—sledge, for hauling. **2005** *DARE* File—Internet **nwMI** (as of 1861), In the winter . . the mails were hauled for thirty miles on a traineau, a sled with very broad runners that was pulled by a large dog, while the mail carrier on snowshoes beat a path. *Ibid* **LA,** A "traineau" is (was?) actually a sled, but for use on land, as opposed to ice or snow. It was generally used on the farm to transport small tools, like plows, etc., to different parts of the field.

trainer See **train**

trainneau See **traineau**

train, smoke like a v phr   Also *smoke like a freight train;* for addit varr see quot 1965–70 **chiefly Sth, S Midl** See Map
To emit thick smoke; to smoke tobacco a great deal.

1933 *Middlesboro Daily News* (KY) 26 July 4/7, Hubert's car smokes like a train when it runs, and makes very little noise considering the fact that there are no tires on the front wheels. **1965–70** *DARE* (Qu. DD9b, *Of a person who smokes a great deal . . "He smokes like a _____."*) 22 Infs, **chiefly Sth, S Midl,** (Freight) train; **VA**35, Train blowing smoke; **GA**16, Train engine. **2005** in 2006 *DARE* File—Internet **CA,** Just in[s]talled BBR high compression big bore piston and now the bike smokes like a train. *Ibid* **OK,** He smokes like a train and so does his wife. **2006** *Ibid* **ceGA,** Motor will crank but has very bad blow-by and smokes like a freight train.

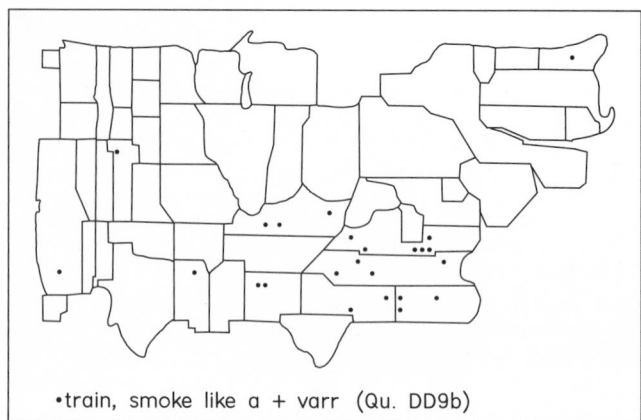

•train, smoke like a + varr (Qu. DD9b)

tramp n
=English sparrow.

1889 Davie *Nests N. Amer. Birds* 294, The House Sparrow. . . is called English Sparrow, . . Parasite, Tramp, Hoodlum, Gamin. **1895** (1907) Wright *Birdcraft* 136, *Passer domesticus.* . . *Tramp.* . . Here in America, the Sparrow is an absolute and unmitigated nuisance.

trampoose v   Also *trampouss, trampooze* arch

To tramp, trudge, wander about; to traverse; hence nouns *trampoose, trampoosing.*

[**1697** in 1905 Gt. Brit. Pub. Rec. Office *Calendar State Papers Colonial Ser. Amer. for 1697–98* 45, It is ruin for any ships to lade here so long as they have such encouragement to run to your parts, whence they are allowed to go "Trampuseing" . . where they please.] **1725** *New-Engl. Courant* (Boston MA) 22 Feb 1/2, It would save the *latter* [= country people] the Toil and Disgrace of trampoosing thro' all the Streets and Lanes in the Town to sell their Pork, Butter, Eggs. **1768** in 1914 Bronson *Hist. Brown Univ.* 37, I took a cold in November which stuck to me all winter, owing to my trampoosing the streets in all weathers. **1815** Humphreys *Yankey in England* 100 **CT,** Som years ago, I landed near to Dover,/ And seed strange sights, trampoosing England over. **1828** Royall *Black Book* 2.287 **VA,** The ladies and myself trampoozed the whole of it. **1840** Cooper *Pathfinder* 1.118 **NY,** I was with him in one of his trampooses. **1843** (1846) Haliburton *Attaché* (1st ser) 1.41 **NEng,** I feel as lonely as a catamount, and as dull as a bachelor beaver. So I trampousses off to the stable. **1845** Thompson *Pineville* 108 **GA,** I wonder if I wasn't trampoosin' all over the place to find you. **1884** Smith *Bill Arp's Scrap Book* 11 **nwGA,** Suddenly we discovered Ben McGinnis trampoosing around. **1887** (1895) Robinson *Uncle Lisha* 117 **wVT,** "Them 'ere long laigs o' his'n hain't gin aout, hev they?" "I sh'd think not. . . [H]e went trampoosin' off on 't the North Hill airly this mornin' arter a fox." **1899** (1912) Green *VA Folk-Speech* 456, *Trampoose.* . . To tramp; walk or wander about. **1947** Sandoz *Tom-Walker* 130, Dakota had burned out two years hand-running, so he trampoosed back to Cincinnati. **1995** Banks *Rule Bone* 291 **NY,** He'd done a lot of trampoosing since he left Au Sable.

tramp room n

A room in a house, often with a door to the outside only, for the accommodation of vagrants.

1913 Frost *Annals Watkins Family* 146 **sOH,** I wonder if . . anyone thinks now to keep a sort of tramp room for strange wayfarers. Uncle Jimmie and Aunt Betsy prepared such a refuge in the upstairs of the frame part of their house. **1933** *Atlantic Mth.* 152.100 **IL,** Thus, because in Matthew there is a verse that reads 'Give to him that asketh thee,' there was in my grandfather's house a room called the Tramp Room.   **1933** Reist *Peter Reist & Descendants* 36 **sePA** (as of c1850), There was a large room above the kitchen . . which was known by his children and grand-children as the "Tramp Room." It contained three beds and in a great many instances all were occupied on the same night.   **1945** Eichner–Tibbets *When Our Town Was Young* 51 **seNY,** The room above the water room was called the "tramp room," where strangers were allowed to sleep. But before the tramps were allowed up there, they were searched, and if they carried any matches, these were taken away. When at last they did get into the room, the door was locked after them.   **1970** *DARE* FW Addit **OH95,** *Tramp room*—a special room maintained in old-fashioned farmhouses for "trampers" to sleep in after eating and exchanging news with the farm family. You couldn't get into the rest of the farm house from the tramp room (for protection of farm family). Also called *traveler's room* and *drover room.*   **1994** Vogt *My Mother's LA Family* 65, Tramps often came to the back door for a handout. They were always given something to eat, and could spend the night in the tramp room. It had only one outside door, so was separate from the rest of the house.   **2006** *DARE* File—Internet **neGA,** [Advt:] Believed that the house was built in the early 1840's. The original back porch and tramp room have been converted to a laundry room, butler's pantry . . , bathroom and large cedar storage closet.

tramp snow v phr   Also *tread snow*   **esp Sth, S Midl**
Of a fire: to make a peculiar sound thought to presage snow; see quots 1899, 1984.

   1845 Kirkland *Western Clearings* 149 **MI,** This bright, soft-singing wood fire, crackling occasionally with that mysterious sound which the good vrouws call "treading snow," and which they hold to foretell sleighing.   **1899** (1912) Green *VA Folk-Speech* 46, When the fire "treads snow" a sign of snowfall.   *Ibid* 457, *Tread-snow, v.* Fire is said to *tread-snow* when a blowing noise is made by the escape of steam from the burning wood caused by the heat.   **1949** Arnow *Hunter's Horn* 304 **KY,** His old daddy . . had smelled more snow in the air the day before, and all night the fire had tramped snow, and sure enough it had started snowing before they'd gone five mile.   **1984** Wilder *You All Spoken Here* 141 **Sth,** *Tramp snow:* Term for an elusive "pat, pat" sound in fireplaces when fires are low; a sign of falling weather.   **1997** *DARE* File—Internet **TX,** And think back to those early days,/ To hear old backlogs tramping snow.

tramp's spurge n   [See quot 2002]
=flowering spurge.

   1892 (1974) Millspaugh *Amer. Med. Plants* xxi, *Euphorbia corollata.* . . Flowering spurge, Tramp's spurge.   **1933** Small *Manual SE Flora* 799, *T[ithymalopsis] corollata* [=*Euphorbia c.*] . . *Flowering-spurge. Tramp's-spurge.* . . Woods, fields, thickets, and roadsides.   **1968** Radford et al. *Manual Flora Carolinas* 672, *Tramps Spurge.* Perennial from stout, deep seated rootstock, freely branched above. . . Stems glabrous or pubescent.   **2002** *Natl. Gardener* (Internet), White Spurge, E[uphorbia] corollata, sometimes called Tramp's Spurge because of its proclivity for growing abundantly along railroad sidings.

tramp's-trouble n
=stretchberry 1.

   1933 Small *Manual SE Flora* 313, *S[milax] Bona-Nox.* . . *Tramp's-trouble. Stretch-berry.* . . Woods, thickets, hammocks, and fence-rows.   **1950** Gray–Fernald *Manual of Botany* 450, *S[milax] Bona-nox.* . . Tramp's-trouble.

transfer truck n   **chiefly SE, S Midl**   See Map and Map Section   Cf **semi, trailer truck**
A wagon or truck used to carry heavy loads on roads.

   1886 *Davenport Gaz.* (IA) 2 Apr 1/7 **MO,** This morning the different freight depots . . present an animated appearance. Transfer trucks and wagons are heavily laden.   **1889** *Ft. Wayne Sentinel* (IN) 29 Apr [6]/2 (newspaperarchive.com), One of Brudi's ice cream wagons and a transfer truck collided on Lafayette street yesterday, and the ice cream wagon was considerably damaged.   **1908** *Des Moines Capital* (IA) [9 Oct] 5/6 (newspaperarchive.com), [Advt:] *One of the Vee Transfer Trucks*—We never send a "joke" after your furniture, but a real wagon like this. One load hauls the average man's goods.   **1914** *Ogden Std.* (UT) 27 June 11/3, He was picked up by the driver of a local auto transfer truck and brought into town.   **1917** *Stevens Point Jrl.* (WI) 17 June 1/4, Shaurette's automobile transfer truck was badly damaged when upset in a ditch.   **1930** *Athens Messenger* (OH) 17 Jan [8]/1 (newspaperarchive.com), [Caption:] This is what happened when an interstate transfer truck collided with a steel telegraph pole at Kansas City, Mo.   **1946**

Landmark (Statesville NC) 24 Jan 1/5, An automobile was demolished Wednesday night after it hit a big transfer truck.   **1965–70** *DARE* (Qu. N11, *A very large truck used to haul freight, new cars, and other big loads*) 52 Infs, **chiefly SE, S Midl,** Transfer truck; [**KY26,** Transfer trailer].   **1986** Pederson *LAGS Concordance,* 1 inf, **cnAL,** Transfer trucks—semis, large.   **2000** in 2006 (acc) Lexis–Nexis Legal Research *State Case Law: NC* (Internet), The trooper noted that the vehicle was what generally people . . call transfer truck, tractor trailer truck that you see on the major highways. It, however, did not have a trailer attached to it at that time. It was just what people commonly say bobtail.

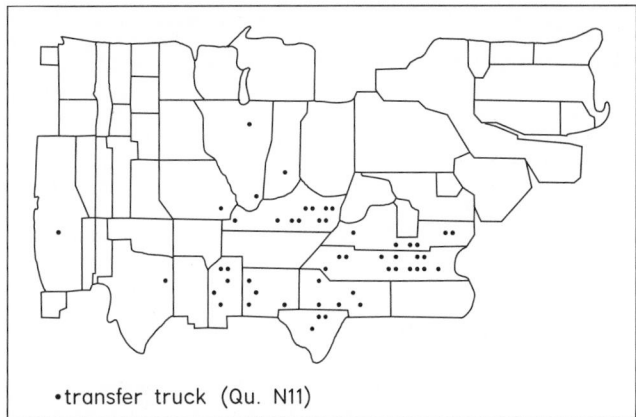

•transfer truck (Qu. N11)

transformation n   [*OED2* 1901 →]   **chiefly Atlantic, N Cent**
See Map   *old-fash*
A hairpiece usu worn by a woman.

   1905 *Oakland Tribune* (CA) 3 June [7]/6 (newspaperarchive.com), The transformation is a dear, delicate, wavy, all-around pompadour, which, put on over hair that is stubby or doesn't grow gracefully, certainly succeeds in completely transforming a woman.   **1914** *Syracuse Herald* (NY) 24 Mar 15/3, Exclusiveness of style and beauty of hair and workmanship show our productions in Pompadours, Outside Transformations, Front Pieces, Switches, etc. to be the only ones possible to women of taste and refinement.   **1948** Faulkner *Intruder* 60 **MS,** He thought [he] remembered an old lady, dead now, a spinster, a neighbor who wore a dyed transformation.   **1948** *Portland Press Herald* (ME) 9 May sec D 3/3, The bachelors and unhappily married . . are anxious to disguise their baldness as much as possible. Which brings us to grips with toupees, transformations and wigs.   **1960** Criswell *Resp. to PADS 20* **Ozarks,** Rats, switches, transformations.   **1965–70** *DARE* (Qu. X1b, *False hair worn by women*) 27 Infs, **chiefly Atlantic, N Cent,** Transformation; (Qu. X1a, *Names . . for false hair, worn by men*) Inf **CT30,** Transformation. [23 of 27 total Infs old, 22 female; 12 Infs remark that the term is old-fashioned.]

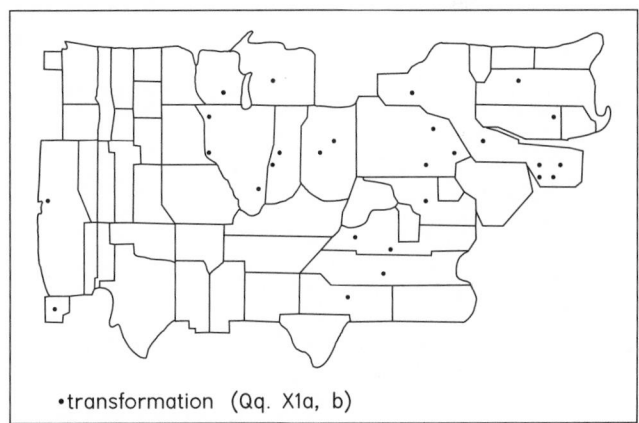

•transformation (Qq. X1a, b)

transparent pudding n   **chiefly S Midl, esp KY**
A pudding made with a mixture of eggs, butter, and sugar, variously flavored; hence nouns *transparent pie,* ~ *tart* a pie or tart filled with such pudding.

   [**1786** Raffald *Experienced Engl.* 175, A Transparent Pudding. . . It will cut light and clear.]   **1847** (1979) Rutledge *Carolina Housewife* 126, *Transparent Pudding.* Half a pound of sugar, half a pound of fresh butter, the yolks of eight eggs [and] any kind of dried sweetmeat. **1879** (1965) Tyree *Housekeeping in Old VA* 389, *Transparent Pudding.* Yolks of 10 eggs; whites of 2. 1 pound of sugar. ½ pound of butter. Season with nutmeg. **1890** James *Mother James' Cooking* 263, *Transparent Pudding.* . . flavor with vanilla or lemon; bake in a buttered dish half an hour, and serve cold. **1914** in 1983 Truman *Dear Bess* 158 **MO,** I got onto a new brand of pie down in Marshall the other day. . . They called it transparent pie. Why I don't know because it looked like pumpkin and tasted like sugar and water with clay or something to give it body. It had a mussy top—one of the kind with a French name that goes on a "leming pie." **1947** Bowles–Towle *New Engl. Cooking* 168, *Transparent Pudding.* [Recipe includes butter, sugar, eggs, brandy or sherry, lemon rind, lemon juice, nutmeg.] **1969** *DARE* (Qu. H63, *Kinds of desserts*) Inf **KY**52, Transparent pie. **1970** *DARE* FW Addit **KY,** *Transparent Pie.* [Recipe includes egg yolks, butter, sugar, cream.] . . Put raisins or little gobs of jelly in unbaked pie shell. Add filling and bake. Beat egg whites for top. **1997** in 2006 *DARE* File—Internet **sOH, nKY,** In my experience, Transparent Pie is Chess Pie, just depends on where you're from. . . Where I grew up (southern Ohio border with Kentucky), it was called Transparent Pie on both sides of the river. . . I found out about Chess Pie when I went to Texas. **2004** *Cincinnati Post* (OH) 14 Jan (Internet) **KY,** From country ham to transparent pie, burgoo and barbecue to blackberry dumplings, Kentucky home cooking is second to none. . . According to the Maysville Chamber of Commerce, even Kroger stores, convenience food marts and multiple bakeries in town stock transparent pies and tarts.

transport n Also *transporter* **chiefly Missip Valley, West, Gulf States, Gt Lakes, Upstate NY** See Map Cf **semi, trailer truck, transfer ~, transport ~**

A large truck capable of hauling a heavy load, often a load of automobiles.

1916 *Amer. Oxonian* 3.20, I heard the buzz of a motor transport that was coming in late. **1937** *Edwardsville Intelligencer* (IL) 26 Nov 1/3, A motor transport and five passenger automobiles figured in the crash. The transport was undamaged. **1952** *Oshkosh Daily Northwestern* (WI) 3 Dec 4/6, [Headline:] Transport Tips, but New Cars Unharmed. **1965–70** *DARE* (Qu. N11, *A very large truck used to haul freight, new cars, and other big loads*) 144 Infs, **chiefly Missip Valley, West, Gulf States, Gt Lakes, Upstate NY,** Transport [12 of these Infs said it was specifically for hauling cars.]; **AR**22, **CA**3, **IA**27, 47, **MN**15, **NJ**19, **NY**75, Car transport; **MD**29, **MI**73, Auto transport; **NV**8, Automobile transport; **MS**1, Motor transport; **MN**42, Transport carrying cars; **NY**92, Transporter. **2003** *DARE* File—Internet **TX,** A transport of 22 tons of [nuclear] waste en route to the WCS site was lost for nearly a month in 2001. . . The driver of the transport was nowhere to be found.

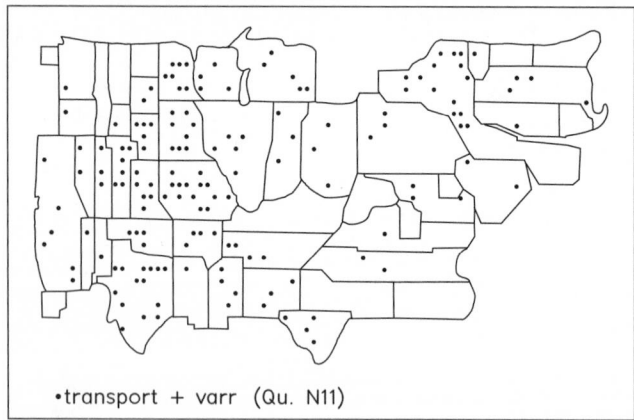

•transport + varr (Qu. N11)

transportate v [Back-formation from *transportation;* cf Intro "Language Changes" III.3] Cf **botherate, perspirate**

To transport.

1871 *Indiana Progress* (PA) [5 Oct 7/3] (newspaperarchive.com), Eighteen beeves recently slaughtered . . were transportated to refrigerating cars . . and found to be as fresh and good as at the hour of starting. **1888** *Newark Daily Advocate* (OH) 15 Nov 1/1, The third assistant . . [recommends]: That . . the pneumatic tube or some equivalent underground system of transportating the mails be adopted. **1930** Shoemaker *1300 Words* 48 **cPA Mts** (as of c1900), *Packer*—One who made a business of transportating goods on horses along the Jersey Shore. **1976** *Syracuse Herald–Jrl.* (NY) 30 Nov sec A 21/1, Students . . will have

regular classes and be transportated as usual tomorrow. **2005** *DARE* File—Internet, Where can I find information on clinical specimens that must be transportated from our hospital to another laboratory?

transporter See **transport**

transport truck n Also *transport van, ~ trailer;* for addit varr see quot 1965–70 **scattered, but esp Sth, S Midl** See Map Cf **transport**

A large truck capable of hauling a heavy load.

1916 *Sandusky Star–Jrl.* (OH) 24 Mar 9/2 **NM,** After replenishing his gasoline supply from an army transport truck, Gorrell soared away toward the field base. **1922** *Decatur Daily Rev.* (IL) 11 Sept 9/5, A large transport truck . . caught fire Saturday . . and was destroyed. . . The truck was loaded with loose hay. **1938** *Reno Eve. Gaz.* (NV) 6 Aug 2/6, The caboose . . left the rails and plunged over a Rock Island trestle, near Des Moines, Iowa, narrowly missing a transport truck on the highway below. **1965–70** *DARE* (Qu. N11, *A very large truck used to haul freight, new cars, and other big loads*) 42 Infs, **scattered, but esp Sth, S Midl,** Transport truck; **TN**1, Car transport truck; **UT**3, Transport van; **MD**31, Transport trailer; **CO**3, Trailer transport; **IL**85, Transport trailer truck. **1996** *Chron.–Telegram* (Elyria OH) 12 Oct sec C 4/3, We drove to Akron where her son Kirt's transport truck was being repaired.

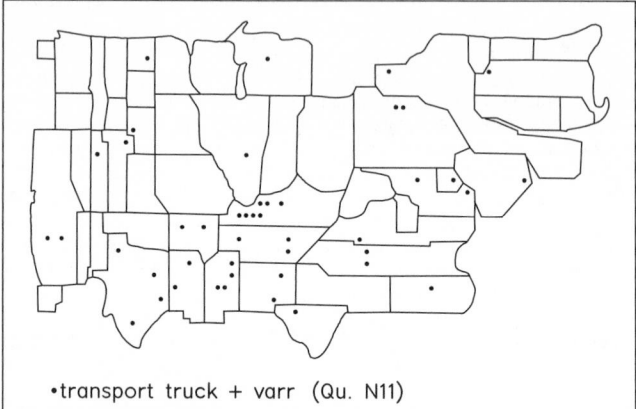

•transport truck + varr (Qu. N11)

trantler See **tarantula**

trap n **chiefly TX** See Map

A fenced enclosure for animals; see quots; hence combs *cattle trap, cow ~, horse ~.*

1926 *Overland Mth.* (2d ser) 84.175 **TX,** The tracks they had been following brought them bang up against the north line of the Seven Up horse trap . . and there in the corral . . stood the peculiarly marked horse they wanted. **1951** *Kerrville Times* (TX) 7 Jan [3]/1 (newspaper-archive.com), Will Auld says he's used to a Horse Trap consisting of something like a hundred acres. **1956** Ker *Vocab. W. TX* 158, *Pasture, cow pasture* and *trap* refer to grassy enclosures smaller than the rest of the pastures on the ranch. **1962** Atwood *Vocab. TX* 49, *Place to enclose horses. . . (horse) trap . . ,* which denotes a much larger enclosure than a *lot,* is confined to the western ranch country . . and occurs most consistently in the Trans-Pecos area. *Ibid* 142, [Map shows 27 instances of *horse trap* or *cow trap* in west Texas, two in southeastern New Mexico.]

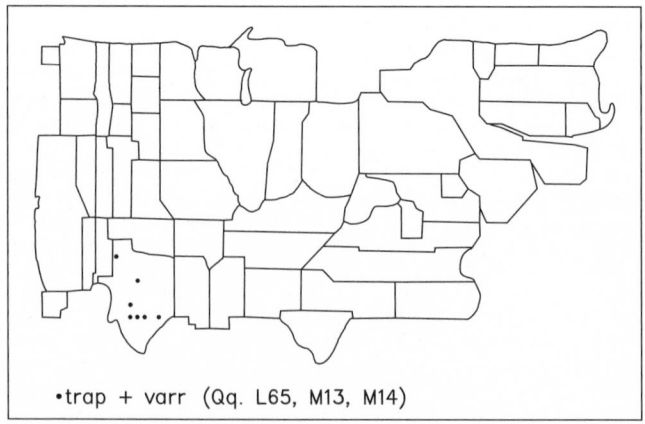

•trap + varr (Qq. L65, M13, M14)

1967–69 DARE (Qu. L65, . . *Kinds of fences*) Inf **TX**22, Cattle trap; trap fence; (Qu. M13, *The space near the barn with a fence around it where you keep the livestock*) Inf **TX**66, Trap; **TX**11, Trap—small area where animals are kept easily accessible; **TX**39, Horse trap [FW: A horse trap, though enclosed, is usually quite large, i.e., many acres.]; (Qu. M14, *The open area around or next to the barn*) Inf **TX**4, Cow trap; **TX**3, horse trap [FW: Sometimes these are enormous.]; **TX**16, Trap—small pasture to keep one horse. **1967** DARE Tape **TX**25, [Inf:] Get my horse . . to keep him in a trap there. [FW:] Well, what'd you mean by trap? [Inf:] Well, it's just a small pasture, you know. . . It runs right into the barn there. It's right there close to the house. **2002** DARE File—Internet **TX**, Ezer provides his working horses some relief from the maddening insects by burning a round bale of poor quality hay in a 40-acre horse trap.

trapball n Pronc-spp *tra(b)-ball* **chiefly Mid Atl**
The ball used in the old game of trapball; hence a small, elastic ball used in various games.
  1713 (1879) S. Sewall *Diary* 2.388 **MA**, [He] came down a Spit, and clear'd the Leaden-throat [of a downspout] by thrusting out a Trap-Ball that stuck there. **1834** *S. Lit. Messenger* 1.181 **VA**, Simon found it impossible to keep up with me, mounted as he was on a high trotting, raw-boned devil, that made the old man bound like a trapball. **1840** *Ibid* 6.773, They dusent know what wimins hearts are made of; but goe on, bandyin' an' kickin' 'em about, jist like they war *trab*-balls. **1851** *Ibid* 17.690 **VA**, We all recollect when the only uses to which India-rubber was applied, were to rub out pencil marks and make trapballs for boys. **1873** (1875) Wolfe *Startling Facts* 22 se**PA**, It made a bound that sent him flying through the air like a trap-ball. **1878** *Forest & Stream* 11.257 **DC**, I would as soon dine off stewed and boiled india-rubber trab-balls as a tough old roasted wild goose. a**1883** (1911) Bagby *VA Gentleman* 49, He must . . cut up his father's gum shoes, to make trap-balls, composed of equal parts of yarn and india-rubber. **1899** (1912) Green *VA Folk-Speech* 455, Trab-ball. . . Trap-ball. An old game played by two or more persons with a ball, bat and trap. . . The ball used in the game of trab ball. **1901** Worthington *Broken Sword* 159 **NC** [Black], Dat ar boy has been scrougin me lak I wus a trabball. **1940** Hench Coll. **NC**, The ball [in the game of rolly-polly] was always called [træ bol]. **1952** Brown *NC Folkl.* 1.234, "Tra-ball" made of yarn or cotton usually ravelled from worn stockings. The name is from the ancient game of trap-ball or trap-bat. **1999** in 2006 DARE File—Internet **MD**, Folks tossed around frisbees, horseshoes, footballs, trap balls and foxtails during the day.

trapdoor n Also *trap hatch* (pronc-sp *trappatch*) **esp NEng**
=**barn door 1.**
  1890 DN 1.20 se**NH**, Trappatch (trap-hatch): trap-door; rent in clothes. 'You've torn a trappatch in your dress.' **1892** DN 1.211 se**MA**, Trapdoor: a triangular rent in cloth. **1969** DARE (Qu. W27, . . *A three-cornered tear in a piece of clothing from catching it on something sharp*) Inf **RI**1, Trapdoor.

trapdoor turtle n Cf **hinge turtle**
Prob a **box turtle.**
  1917 *Phi Beta Pi Qrly.* 14.115 **IA**, He has, however, picked up a pet grouch and is inclined to be as snappy as his "Trap door turtle" at times. **1938** Pratt *Navy Hist.* 265, Porter . . produced from a box a kind of iron pot with square corners and slanting sides, all closed in like a trapdoor turtle asleep. **1968** DARE (Qu. P24, . . *Kinds of turtles*) Inf **KS**17, Trapdoor.

trap hatch See **trapdoor**

trapjaw n Also *trapjaw water moccasin*
=**cottonmouth.**
  1931 (1936) Ditmars *Snakes* 103, The Ozark Mountain people call this snake the "Trap-Jaw" owing to its habit of lying motionless, with jaws widely extended in threatening fashion when disturbed. **2000** in 2006 (acc) *Linnaean St.* (Internet) **TN**, Curled on top of the tiles was the big trap-jaw water moccasin that Baxter Dawes brought in from the woods just yesterday. **2002** DARE File—Internet **AR**, *Strange Trapjaw Experience.* . . My friend and I were doing a little canoeing down the Buffalo River here in Arkansas today and. . . I saw. . . a young cotton about 15″ or so in length. *Ibid,* [Caption:] Some updated pics of Tiny the Trapjaw. **2008** Sanders *Hanging Woods* 132 **AL**, Papa had always vigorously warned me about the poisonous snakes in our area. Especially cottonmouths, or "trap-jaws" as he called them.

trappatch See **trapdoor**

trapper's rat n Also *trapping rat* [**rat** n **1**]
=**muskrat 1.**
  1966–69 DARE (Qu. P31, . . *Names or nicknames . . for . . muskrat*) Inf **MA**32, Trapper's rat; **MI**32, Trapping rat.

trapper's tea n
A **Labrador tea** (here: *Ledum glandulosum*).
  1973 Hitchcock–Cronquist *Flora Pacific NW* 345, Trapper's tea. . . *L[edum] glandulosum.* **2002** DARE File—Internet, Trapper's tea (*L[edum] glandulosum*) is found in the Cascades, the Northwest interior and Oregon, and can be distinguished from other Ledums by its oval leaves, which are mealy white or gray underneath and non-lanate.

trapping rat See **trapper's rat**

traps n pl [*OED2* 1813 →] Cf **truck** n[1] **4**
Belongings, personal property; things, "stuff."
  1835 *New Engl. Mag.* 8.109 **CT**, Let's see your traps. . . open that 'ere pack. **1835** (1906) Bradley *Jrl.* 267 **NH**, Met Mr. Fletcher in as great haste as myself, who fearing to be left behind had sent my "traps" on board with his own. **1858** (1930) DeLong *Jrls.* 9.251 **NY**, Found my bed covered with trap's that some of the women had thrown on it. **1864** in 1981 Woodward *Mary Chesnut's Civil War* 640 **LA**, Then he told her [to] pack up his traps. It was time for him to leave Shreveport. **1864** (1922) Jackson *Col.'s Diary* 163 **PA**, We found hid a barrel of molasses, plenty of salt and other traps. **1865** in 1983 PADS 70.55 ce,se**PA**, All the citizens had packed up traps and left. **1878** Hart *Sazerac Lying Club* 18 **NV**, Uncle John knows all about horses, and harness, and buckboards, and Concord wagons, and such traps. **1899** (1912) Green *VA Folk-Speech* 456, Traps. . . Goods; furniture. **1906** Casey *Parson's Boys* 132 s**IL** (as of c1860), "There, now," he said finally; "put the traps by. . ." The boys . . hastened to stand the gun in a corner and hang the accouterments up by it. **1941** LANE Map 346 (*Rubbish*) 1 inf, **ME**, Traps, first response, of rubbish in the house. **1942** Faulkner *Go Down* 219 **MS**, Get your traps together. Cass says for you to come on home.

'trary See **contrary** v

trash n Also *trash tobacco* **chiefly S Midl, esp KY** Cf **flyings 2**
Formerly any low or impure grade of tobacco; now a trade term used chiefly for leaves near the bottom of the Burley tobacco plant.
  1705 Beverley *Hist. VA* 1.49, When one Colony goes about to prohibit the Trash of that Commodity [=tobacco], . . the other . . pours into England all they can make, both good and bad, without Distinction. **1732** in 1945 *AmSp* 20.275 **VA**, Some of the most turbulint among the planters, rather than their tobacco should be inspected burnt some of the warehouses, upon the presumption that . . their trash which would not pass under the law, they might sell as usual. **1772** in 1919 *MD Hist. Mag.* 14.281, Two Trash hgds [=hogsheads of tobacco] . . are not yet sold. **1849** *Defiance Democrat* (OH) 9 June [4]/2 (newspaperarchive.com), Fill the cup thus formed [=a shallow ditch around a peach tree] with trash tobacco from the shops, and envelop the ball of the tree to the height of three or four inches, with the stems or leaves. **1858** *S. Lit. Messenger* 26.123, Smokt a fine seegare at 4pens to keep up my cackter, but had ruther uv had a pipe with some plane trash at nuthin atall. **1911** *Century Dict. Suppl.* (at *tobacco*), White Burley tobacco. . . The leaves are thus classified: lowest two, 'fliers'; next two, 'common lugs' ('trash' apparently the same) [etc]. **1924** *Kingsport Times* (TN) 4 Jan 1/5, The new schedule of advances . . includes an added grade in the flyings, trash, lugs, bright leaf and red leaf. **1965–70** DARE Tape **KY**9, They used to, way back yonder, make five grades of it [=tobacco], but now they only make about three. And those grades, next one to the bottom to the ground is called a trash; **KY**23, We make three grades out of our tobacco. You take off the trash, then the lugs, and then the tips; **KY**35, Well, we have the flyings and trash we put together; they're just the light, chaffy part of the tobacco, the first part that comes off . . from the ground; **KY**56, The bottom leaf . . is called the flying or trash; **KY**64, The grades are: flyings or trash, which are the most ragged leaves [etc]; **KY**72, Mostly it's trash or flyings; **KY**84, Trash—that's the bottom leaves, and worm-eaten leaves, and leaves that're not too good; **KY**93, First class [of tobacco leaf] is what we call the . . trash, some say it's trash . . and the other is bright leaf, red, and the tip; **OH**58, When the farmer brings the tobacco into the warehouse after he's stripped it, why, they have graders there that grade it out into different—like trash and flyings and the leaf and the lugs and the tips. **1966** PADS 45.27 **KY**, The trash is the higher flyings. **1967** Key *Tobacco Vocab.* 137 **NC**, My

bad trash brought 64 cents, and my good tob[acco] 73 cents. *Ibid* **GA,** They make snuff out of the trash. *Ibid* **MO,** Trash is a fine tobacco. . . one of the better qualities. **2004** *DARE* File—Internet **KY,** The trash grade average less than 15% of the total yield.

trash mover, n

1 also *trash breaker, ~ floater, ~ lifter, ~ toter, ~ washer:* A sudden heavy rain. **chiefly Mid and S Atl, Lower Missip Valley** See Map Cf **earth mover, fence lifter, leaf mover, stump ~**

1879 *Daily Constitution* (Atlanta GA) 26 July 1/6, The rain yesterday was a regular trash mover in some parts of the county. **1895** *Landmark* (Statesville NC) 1 Nov [3]/3 (newspaperarchive.com), The kind of rain the old darkey prayed for—a "redland soaker" and not a "gully-washer and trash mover." **1905** *Atlanta Constitution* (GA) 4 Dec [5]/4 (newspaperarchive.com), What the country people call a 'trash-lifter[1]' is often less than 3 inches. **1913** in 1983 Truman *Dear Bess* 125 **MO,** It looks very much like we were going to have a trash mover. **1941** *Pt. Arthur News* (TX) 30 May 3/3 **AL,** Gov. Eugene Talmadge. . . said that during the day Tuesday, June 3, "we'll have a trash-floater" and a rainy spell which will last about two weeks will begin. **1950** Williams *Rocky Mts.* 248 **CO,** Very often, though, these miraculous downpours would do as much damage as good, washing out furrows, breaking the wheat, and then running off before the hard ground could adequately absorb it. 'Trash-movers' they were called. **1952** Brown *NC Folkl.* 1.602, *Trash-breaker, trash-washer.* . . A big and sudden downpour of rain, a *gully-washer.*—General. **1965–70** *DARE* (Qu. B25, . . *Joking names . . for a very heavy rain.* . . "It's a regular _____") 24 Infs, **chiefly Mid and S Atl, Lower Missip Valley,** Trash mover; **GA**27, **SC**1, **VA**100, Trash floater; **SC**43, Trash lifter; **VA**44, Trash lifter—Negro usage; **NC**31, Trash mover and gully washer; (Qu. B24, . . *A sudden, very heavy rain*) Infs **AR**56, **IL**128, **NC**62, Trash mover; (Qu. C2, *After a heavy rain or a quick thaw, when you see the water in a stream getting higher;* total Infs questioned, 75) Inf **FL**17, Trash mover. **1971** Wood *Vocab. Change* 33 **Sth,** Informants volunteered *(bull) frog strangler, cloud break, deluge, flood, trash toter* [etc]. **1986** Pederson *LAGS Concordance* (Heavy rain) 12 infs, 6 **GA,** Trash mover(s); 1 inf, **AL,** Gully washer and trash mover (single expression). **2005** *DARE* File—Internet **GA,** Let's just say it was a real trash mover of a storm. Georgia gets a whole heap of rain in the spring time.

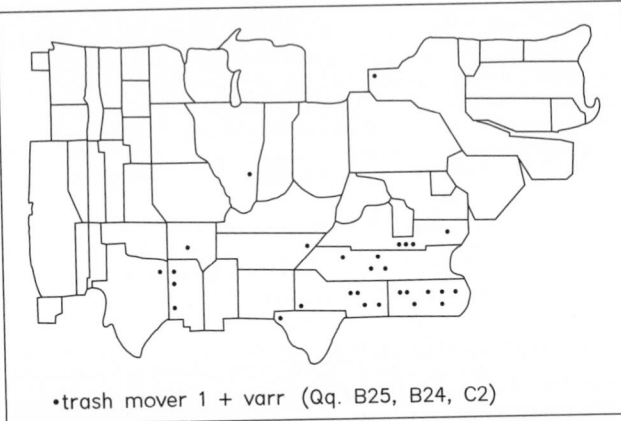

•trash mover 1 + varr (Qq. B25, B24, C2)

2 Fig: an energetic person or thing. **SE, esp NC, SC**

1903 *Landmark* (Statesville NC) 28 Aug 1/2, The speech of Chief Justice Walter Clark . . delivered before the Virginia State Bar Association . . was a "trash mover and gully-washer." **1929** *Carolina Play-Book* 2.3.29, Them high-tempered women are trash-movers, but I'd as soon come in a boat, or did you travel?" *Travel,* in this case, means to walk. **1950** *PADS* 14.68 **SC,** *Trash mover.* . . An energetic, hustling person, a "go-getter." **1966–67** *DARE* (Qu. HH27a, *A very able and energetic person who gets things done*) Infs **NC**33, 37, **SC**32, Trash mover; **SC**34, Trash mover—just like a big rain. **1984** Wilder *You All Spoken Here* 121 **Sth,** Rat killin's nowadays are gatherings of ardent and fun-loving political partisans—political workers known with affection as "trash-movers." **1998** *DARE* File—Internet **AL** (as of c1930), My grandmother . . was known as a trash mover. She saw to it that things got done.

trash tobacco See trash

trash toter (or washer) See trash mover 1

---

traspass See trespass

travel v esp NC

To walk, go by foot.

1880 *Ballou's Mth. Mag.* 52.565 **ME,** No, we did n't travel all the way: we rid as fur as Brother White's 'n' traveled from there over. **1910** *Univ. NC Mag.* 40.3.5 **Hatteras Is. NC,** "How did you come? Did you come in a boat, or did you travel?" *Travel,* in this case, means to walk. **1939** FWP *Guide NC* 292 **neNC,** In Old Trap and all through the district that borders the broad mouth of the Pasquotank River is heard frequently the colloquialism: "Did you travel or come by boat?" "Travel" is the old Elizabethan word for walk. **1952** Brown *NC Folkl.* 1.602, *Travel.* . . To walk, to go by foot. **1993** *Coast Watch* Sept/Oct 15 **Outer Banks NC,** Words such as . . "travel" for walk . . convinced him of that connection [with Elizabethan English].

traveler n Cf galloping dandruff

A louse **B1.**

1939 *AmSp* 14.92 **eTN,** *Travelers.* Head lice. 'The baby's head is full of travelers.' **1957** Combs *Lang. S. Highlanders* **sAppalachians,** Traveler—louse. **1968** *DARE* (Qu. R25, *Joking names for a head louse, or body louse*) Inf **LA**20, Travelers.

traveler's-delight n

=**groundnut B1.**

1892 *Jrl. Amer. Folkl.* 5.94 **MS,** *Apios tuberosa,* traveller's-delight. **1922** *Amer. Botanist* 28.75, The plant [=*Apios tuberosa*] is also known as . . "travellers delight". The last name seems like a book name, but the fragrant chocolate-colored flowers perhaps deserve it.

traveler's-friend n

A **barrel cactus,** usu *Ferocactus emoryi.*

[**1932** Thornber–Bonker *Fantastic Clan* x, The Barrel cactus is the Indian's friend in time of drought, the traveler's friend when lost.] **1942** Hylander *Plant Life* 326, All of the Barrel Cacti can be used as sources of drinking water by thirsty desert travellers, but one species in particular is known as the Traveller's Friend; this is a species found in southern and western Arizona. By cutting off the top of the cylindrical stem and crushing the pulpy mass with a stick, one can get a watery solution which tastes refreshing. Valuable also is the peculiarity of this cactus in always leaning to the southwest—a veritable desert compass as well as a storage tank of water. *Ibid* 660, Traveller's Friend—Echinocactus covillei [=*Ferocactus emoryi*]. **1973** *AZ Highways* Mar 33, The Barrel Cactus, scientifically classified under the name of *Echinocactus,* is the simplest of the cactus shapes. . . The early settlers knew it as "The Traveler's Friend."

traveling agent See agent 1

traveling dandruff See galloping dandruff

traveling pains n pl [Perh folk-etym for *travailing/traveling pains* labor pains, obs exc as an occas metaphor in theological lit]

See quot.

1918 *DN* 4.82 **ME, nNH,** "Travelin' pains" are pains, such as toothache, which cause a man to walk the floor.

travel on one's face See face, run one's

traverse n Also *traverse runner,* rarely *traverse sled* Pronc-sp *travis* [Derivation from CanFr *travois* or *travail* (for which see etym at **travoy** n) has been suggested, but this is unsatisfactory both phonetically and semantically. A more likely source is *OED2 traverse* sb. 18 "Anything laid or fixed athwart or across; a cross-piece," in ref to the crossbar or bolster that connects the runners and on which the body of the vehicle rests.] **chiefly nNEng** See Map Cf **pung**

A short sled designed to support one end of a vehicle; hence nouns *traverse, traverses* (pl, but sometimes constr as sg), *traverse pung, ~ sled, ~ sleigh, traverse runner pung, ~ sled, ~ sleigh* any of var sleds for hauling or coasting supported by a pair of runners at each end; a bobsled, **double-runner.**

1807 in 1847 U.S. Patent Office *List* 210 **MA,** Sleigh, traverse. . . Levi Rogers . . Berwick, Mass. . . Feb. 4, 1807. **1835** *Jrl. Franklin Inst.* new ser 15.98 **VT,** The term traverse sleigh is new to us, although . . it seems to be familiarly used in the part of the country [=Vermont] where the patentee resides. . . It appears to be a kind of double sleigh, intended for the carrying of country produce. . . The platform, or bed, has under it two sets of runners. **1846** *Madison Express* (WI) 19 Mar [3]/4 (newspaperarchive.com) **nwMA**, Twenty-five of the young men and young ladies of our village loaded themselves upon a large traverse sleigh at the top of the hill. **1850** in 2006 (acc) Lexis–Nexis Legal Research *State Case Law: VT* (Internet), The defendant came upon the brow of the hill . . with a load of bark, drawn by two horses on a traverse sleigh. . . The horses and the forward traverse passed the boy without touching him, but the rear traverse did not track after the forward one and ran over him. **1871** *Bangor Daily Whig & Courier* (ME) [7 Dec 4]/2 (newspaperarchive.com), [Advt:] *Elegant Trotting Sleighs* . . also *Double Sleighs, Light Family Sleighs,* . . Also Single and Traverse Runner Pungs. **1882** *Fitchburg Daily Sentinel* (MA) 8 Feb [3]/1 (newspaperarchive.com), A pair of horses attached to a traverse sled made a lively run down Main and Water streets, this morning. **1905** *Ibid* 6 Jan 2/1, The Cleghorn baker . . had trouble with his traverse runner sleigh . . this morning, the forward runners being completely smashed by catching in street car tracks. **1911** *Daily Kennebec Jrl.* (Augusta ME) 19 Oct 8/3, [Advt:] A Set of Traverse Runners. **1915** *Ibid* 15 Jan 8/3, [Advt:] A light one-horse traverse runner sled, new. **1922** Stephens *Busy Yr.* 270 **ME**, Addison and I set a hayrack on two traverse sleds, and with two of the work-horses drove up the winter road. **1943** *LANE* Map 573–74, On the map are presented terms for 'double sleds', consisting of two sets of short runners joined by a reach or plank. . . 42 infs, **chiefly VT, NH, cnMA, swMW,** Traverse; 22 infs, **chiefly eVT, NH, swME,** Traverse sled; 10 infs, **chiefly wVT,** Traverses; 1 inf, **cVT,** A traverses; 1 inf, **cwNH,** A set of traverses; 5 infs, **seNH, neMA,** Traverse runner(s); 3 infs, **ceNH, swME,** Traverse pung; 1 inf, **swVT,** Traverse sleigh. [The usu proncs are of the types ['trævəs, -ɪs] or, less freq, ['trævəs].] **1965–70** *DARE* (Qu. N40a, . . *Sleighs . . for hauling loads*) Inf **MA**58, Traverse; **MA**5, Traverse ['trævəs] had two runners; **MA**23, Traverse ['trævəs]; **MA**59, Traverse runner ['trævəs 'rʌnə]—two sleds hitched to body; **VT**4, Traverse sled; (Qu. N40b, . . *Sleighs for carrying people*) Inf **MA**5, Traverse—for kids sliding—two sleds joined by one board (called also rippers); **MA**6, Traverse sled . . used for people—not horse-drawn; **MA**30, Traverse sleigh—for carrying people and light goods; **MA**58, Traverse sled; traverse sleigh—single-seated sleigh, seldom covered; **VT**4, Two-seater traverse (sleigh); [**NH**5, Traveler's sleigh—two to three seats and a pair of bobsleds beneath;] (Qu. N40c, *Other kinds of sleighs*) Inf **VT**12, Traverse ['trævə·s] sleigh—two small sleds, one under each end; **NY**27, Travis sleigh—two sleighs with a box; **NY**176, [trə'vɔɪs] sleigh; (Qu. EE24a, *When there's snow, children go down the hill on a _____*) Inf **VT**16, Traverse; **MA**38, Traverse ['trævəs]; **NH**5, Traverse—two sets of runners, steered by forward step. **1972** *Portsmouth Herald* (NH) 20 Oct 20/1, [Advt:] Traverse sled 12' long, excellent for family sliding. **1976** *Bennington Banner* (VT) 3 Feb 3/1 **ME,** The two-sled was, of course, the double-runner. If both sleds pivoted on the stretchers, and had cross-chains to make them "track," the device was known as "traverse runners." If the rear sled were bolted to the stretchers, no pivot, the term was simply double-runner. **1979** *DARE* File **cnMA** (as of c1915), My sister and I were never allowed to use the traverse in our barn. . . Sometimes my father would take us and other children sliding on the traverse. **1983** *Greenfield Recorder* (MA) 22 Jan 6, The real work sleds had two traverses instead of long continuous runners like a pung. . . The boy's "double rippers" for pleasure sliding were called traverses also. **2001** VT Dept. Ag. *Agriview* 5 Jan 3/3 **VT,** [Advt:] Two (2) horse traverse sleds, $500. Child's traverse sled, $50. **2006** *Ibid* 10 Mar 5/3 **VT,** [Advt:] Antique, 3 beam travis sled w/4 seats and brake. **2006** *DARE* File—Internet **VT,** [Advt:] Karl

•traverse + varr (Qq. N40a, b, c, EE24a)

Pfister Sleigh Rides. Travis sleigh with bench seats; 12 passengers. Day and eve.; 45 min. ride.

travois See **travoy** n

travois road See **travoy road**

travoy n Also sp *travois* [CanFr in ref to a vehicle consisting of two poles with their hind ends dragging on the ground, used esp by the Plains Indians; var of CanFr *travail* [trə'vaɪ] shafts of a vehicle; cf *OED2* etym note at *travois*] **esp MI, WI** Cf *DCan travois* 3b

A crude sled, esp one used in logging to support one end of a log while the other drags on the ground.

1878 *Lumberman's Gaz.* 20 Apr 353 **WI**, L.O. Rummery and Wm. Pendleton are still putting in logs—the former on travoys and the latter on trucks. **1902** White *Blazed Trail* 52 **eMI**, Earlier in the season, a number of pines had been felled out on the ice, cut in logs, and left in expectation of ice thick enough to bear the travoy "dray." **1905** U.S. Forest Serv. *Bulletin* 61.51 [Logging terms], *Travois. . .* See Dray. **1923** *Appleton Post–Crescent* (WI) 12 June 9/2, Chopping, hauling, piling and burning the logs, digging out stumps, breaking the land with no better tools than axes, handspikes, spades and ox-drawn travois [etc]. **1940–41** Cassidy *WI Atlas* **ceWI**, *Travois. . .* A small triangular device to support the front end of a log (the back end dragging on the ground) in skidding logs. **1950** *WELS* (*A low wooden platform used for hauling stones or heavy things out of the fields*) 1 Inf, **WI**, Stoneboat or travoy. **1956** Sorden–Ebert *Logger's Words* 39 **Gt Lakes**, *Travois*, A drag used to haul logs from woods to skid-way. Generally made from the natural fork of a tree with a cross piece bolted midway in the V. In using, one end of the log rested on travois the other end dragged on snow on the ground. **1966–67** *DARE* (Qu. N41b, *Horse-drawn vehicles to carry heavy loads*) Inf **MI**27, Travois ['trævɔɪ]—more like a dray—on runners; **MI**47, Travois ['trævɔɪ]—used in the woods to haul the log from the tree site to the skidway; the travois was also called a dray around here; [(Qu. N40c, *Other kinds of sleighs*) Inf **NY**219, Tri-boys—heavy log sleigh].

travoy v, hence vbl n *travoying* **MI, WI** Cf **bob** v 2, **sloop** n, v[1]

To haul by means of a **travoy** n.

1878 *Lumberman's Gaz.* 20 Feb 86, Travoying can be carried on to good advantage. *Ibid* 20 Apr 353 **WI**, Evans & Smith and Wescott & Montelius are still at work travoying logs on Red river. **1879** *Oshkosh Daily Northwestern* (WI) 6 Jan 1/5, Travoying has been the order of the day and with good results. **1902** White *Blazed Trail* 52 **eMI**, Owing to the fact that the shores of Pike Lake were extremely precipitous, it had been impossible to travoy the logs up over the hill. *Ibid* 144, He told of the building of the camps, the making of the roads; the cutting, swamping, travoying, skidding.

travoy road n Also *travois road, travoy trail* **esp MI** Cf **drag road, dray ~, gutter ~, runway** 1 **=skid road** 1.

1902 White *Blazed Trail* 10 **MI**, The trails were perhaps three feet wide, and marvels of smoothness. . . They were called travoy roads (French *travois*). Down them the logs would be dragged and hauled. **1905** U.S. Forest Serv. *Bulletin* 61.51 [Logging terms], *Travois road.* See Skid road. **1908** White *Riverman* 132 **MI**, The straightest trees they felled, trimmed, and dragged, down travoy trails they constructed, on sleds they built for the purpose. **1969** Sorden *Lumberjack Lingo* 132 **NEng, Gt Lakes**, *Travois road*—A long skid road used to drag logs from woods to skidway.

traw See **trough** A5

trawft See **trough** A1

trawth See **trough** A2

trax(n) See **tracks** v

treacleberry n *obs*

A **false Solomon's seal** (here: *Maianthemum racemosum*).

1634 Wood *New Engl. Prospect* 14, There bee . . Treackleberies, Hurtleberries, Currants. **1672** Josselyn *New-Englands Rarities* 45, *Salomons-Seal,* of which there is three kinds; the first common in *England,* the second, *Virginia Salomons-Seal,* and the third, differing from both, is called *Treacle Berries,* having the perfect tast of Treacle when they are ripe; and will keep good along while; certainly a very wholsome Berry, and medicinable.

tread v

1 also with *out:* To hunt (clams) by feeling with one's feet; to feel (for clams) with one's feet; hence n *(clam) treader.* **N and Mid Atl** Cf **toe** v[1]

1884 Roosevelt *Superior Fishing* 293 **seNY,** He clambered overboard and set to work treading out clams. **1890** *Middletown Daily Press* (NY) 11 Aug [4]/4 (newspaperarchive.com), Mr. Odell was wading neck deep in the tranquil waters of the Sound treading for clams. **1893** *Reno Eve. Gaz.* (NV) 16 Nov [2]/4 (newspaperarchive.com) **Long Is. NY,** *Treaders in Jamaica Bay.* . . These men are "treading clams"—that is, feeling for these shell-fish with their feet. . . The clam treader thus has in his avocation an excitement akin to that of a lottery. **1905** Hull *Fishing Continent* 33, Now we begin to tread out the clams. We push the bare toes and feet down into the black and slimy mud on the bottom. When a clam is struck, the toes work under it and pry it out. **1914** *DN* 4.156 **Cape Cod MA,** *Tread, v.i.* To step heavily, forcing the heels into the sand. "I cut my foot on a shell treadin' for cohogs." **1947** (1962) Henry *Misty* 50 **eVA,** Most exciting of all, they "treaded for clams." In flannel moccasins to protect their feet, and wide-brimmed hats on their heads, they plunged into Chincoteague Bay. . . They would feel the thin edge of a clam with their feet and remember that they were clam treaders. **1970** *DARE* Tape **VA**47, [FW:] How do you gather clams? [Inf:] Well, there's three or four methods. You either what they call tread 'em with your feet, walk on 'em, feel 'em; they feel right round under your feet. **2005** *DARE* File—Internet **NY** (as of 1930s), We would also tread for clams there [= Gerritsen Beach] when the tide went out and the muddy bottom was exposed. *Ibid* **NJ** (as of 1930s), We go out in the bay to catch some fish or tread for clams. **2006** *Ibid* **seNJ** (as of c1930), At age 14, he got a sneakbox. Using his sneakbox, he would tread clams and sell them to Pole Kelly.

2 To copulate; to cohabit. **chiefly Ozarks, sAppalachians** Note: In ref to birds, *tread* is std and is not illustrated here.

1929 *AmSp* 5.20 **Ozarks,** *Tread* . . to copulate. **1931** *PMLA* 46.1322 **sAppalachians,** "Tread" is also a dangerous word in highland speech, meaning to cohabit.

treader See tread 1

treadfast See tread-soft(ly) 2

treadle n Also *tread* [*OED2 treadle* sb. 3.a "Now *dial.*"] **esp VA**

The chalaza of an egg.

1899 (1912) Green *VA Folk-Speech* 456, *Tread.* . . The thread-like embryo in an egg. *Ibid* 457, *Treadle.* . . The tough ropy or stringy part of the white of an egg; the cholaza [sic]. So called because formerly thought to be the male sperm. **1944** *PADS* 2.50 **sVA,** *Treadle.* . . The chalaza of an egg.

tread out See tread 1

treadsaft(er) See tread-soft(ly) 2

treadsalve See tread-soft(ly)

treadsave See tread-soft(ly) 2

tread snow See tramp snow

tread-soft(ly) n Also *treadsalve* [See quots] **S Atl, Gulf States**

1 A **spurge nettle** (here: either *Cnidoscolus stimulosus* or *C. texanus*).

1814 Pursh *Flora Americae* 2.603, *Jatropha stimulosa* [=*Cnidoscolus s.*] . . is a very injurious weed . . , as it ruins the Negroes' feet when they tread upon it; from which it is known by the name of *Tread-softly.* **1859** (1880) Darlington *Amer. Weeds* 289, *C[nidoscolus] stimulosa.* . . Tread-softly. . . A troublesome weed in light sandy soils. . . The prickles produce great irritation for a short time. **1876** Hobbs *Bot. Hdbk.* 121, Tread-softly, Cnidoscolus stimulans. **1899** (1912) Green *VA Folk-Speech* 457, *Tread-softly, n.* Treadsoft. A low weed armed with white nettles half an inch long that sting severely. **1901** Lounsberry *S. Wild Flowers* 303, In the quaint, common name of this plant [=*Cnidoscolus stimulosus*], "tread-softly," there is breathed a wise precaution, for so beset is it with lustrous hairs as fine and sharp as spun glass that it might well cause annoyance to those who would ruthlessly trample it down.

1934 *Torreya* 34.131 **FL,** Scattered among the sunflowers one often sees small white flowers on very prickly stems. . . If we step on them with bare feet . . we realize that the name, Tread-softly, is well applied. The scientific name of this plant is *Bivonea stimulosa* [=*Cnidoscolus s.*] **1936** Whitehouse *TX Flowers* 65, Bull Nettle (Cnidoscolus texanus), also called tread-softly, spurge-nettle, and "mala mujer" . . , is a vicious plant thickly clothed with stinging hairs and bearing clusters of tubular white flowers. **1949** *PADS* 11.12 **wTX** (as of 1911–29), *Treadsalve.* . . A spurge nettle. **2002** *DARE* File—Internet **TX,** Texas Bull Nettle (Tread-Softly, Spurge Nettle)—*Cnidoscolus texanus.* . . Pay attention to the name. *Do not touch this plant!*

2 also *treadsaft(er), treadfast, treadsave:* Usu a **horse nettle 1** (here: *Solanum carolinense*), but also the related **buffalo burr.**

1832 *Amer. Turf Reg.* 3.282 **NC,** Nothing more was done to her [=a horse], except the fixing in her mouth during the night, a portion . . of horse nettle root, or by some called *tread soft.* **1841** Darby *Manual Botany* 1.xi **Sth,** As another example, let us take the Tread Softly, or Horse Nettle. **1883** *Century Illustr. Mag.* 26.150 **nGA,** "Well," said Teague, by way of condolence, "the man what's stabbed by a pitchfork haint much better off 'n the man that walks bar'footed in a treadsaft patch." **1909** *DN* 3.384 **eAL, wGA,** *Treadsaft, treadsalve.* . . A prickly herb of the night-shade family. **1912** Blatchley *IN Weed Book* 125, *Solanum carolinense.* . . Tread-soft. . . Leaves armed with numerous short, stout, awl-shaped yellow prickles. . . A very common and pernicious weed. . . It is a southern species which has spread widely. **1914** *Jrl. Amer. Folkl.* 27.246 **SC** [Black], A necklace of lengths of "treadsaft" [=horse nettle] roots strung on a thread makes teething easy. **1925** *Book of Rural Life* 9.5593, Tread softly, commonly called *horse nettle,* a pernicious weed infesting cultivated crops over the greater part of the United States. **1944** AL Geol. Surv. *Bulletin* 53.188, *S[olanum] Carolinense* . . horse-nettle, or "tread-saft." . . In Alabama it is common. . . Its flowers are pretty enough, but it is a coarse weed, armed with prickles which are annoying to barefooted children, whence one of its common names, "tread-saft." **1950** *PADS* 14.68 **SC,** *Treadfast.* . . The nettle-like, prickly leafage of the wild potato. "To walk as if he had treadfast under his feet"—to walk quickly, lightly, gingerly. *Ibid* 69, *Treadsalve.* . . The sand-bur; the North American nightshade (tread softly). **1967–70** *DARE* (Qu. S15, . . *Weed seeds that cling to clothing*) Inf **MS**82, ['trɛdsæz]; **MS**86, Stickerweed—common name for ['trɛsæl]; **TX**42, Treadsalve. **1968** *DARE* FW Addit **LA,** Treadsafters ['trɛd,sæftɚz]—a bush about two feet high; it has thousands of stickers. Very old-fashioned around Crowley, La. **1972** *Foxfire Book* 240 **nGA,** *Hives.* . . Take any of a variety of teas to break them out. These teas include . . a tea made from the mashed up berries of the tread-save, red alder leaves, raw alder bark scraped uphill, or a tea from cockle burrs.

treasure bird n [See quot]

=**anhinga.**

1950 Writers' Round Table *Padre Is.* 119 **csTX,** Alexander Singer in a 1927 interview for the Houston Chronicle said that these birds [=sharp-billed water turkeys] were called "treasure birds" on the Island because an early legend accredited them with locating buried treasure and hovering about the spot to invite searchers.

treasure light n Cf **money light**

=**jack-o'-lantern 1.**

1945 Saxon *Gumbo Ya-Ya* 548 **LA,** If you are walking alone in the country on a dark night and you suddenly see lights bobbing up and down trying to attract your attention, do not follow them, for they are treasure lights and very dangerous things. If you follow them, you will not be able to stop until daylight, and they will take you through such a maze that you will be lost. **1964** Brown *NC Folkl.* 7.180, Treasure lights are flashes of light, as of lightning, that spring up from the ground where treasures lie. **1970** in 1988 West *Mex.-Amer. Folkl.* 88 **TX,** She had barely mentioned money when the light went away. If you see a treasure light, you must never mention a treasure. You will never find it.

treasure of love n

=**wall pepper.**

1896 *Jrl. Amer. Folkl.* 9.188 **MA,** *Sedum acre,* . . treasure of love.

treasure vine n

An **evening primrose a.**

1900 *Black Cat* 53.xxi, [Advt:] Our Catalogue for 1900. . . Fragrant Calla, Treasure Vine, Gooseflower [etc]. **1959** Carleton *Index Herb. Plants* 118, *Treasure-vine:* Oenothera (v).

treat v
Form.
Past: usu *treated*, also *tret*. [*OED2* "Sc. and *n. dial.*"]
   1936 *AmSp* 11.192 **seWY,** *Tret.* Past of treat. 'He tret me fine.' **1943** in 1944 *ADD* **WV,** 'He tret me fine.' Reported. **1950** *WELS Suppl.* **csWI,** *Tret*—used as past tense of treat. "He tret me to a bottle of beer."

treat one clever See **clever** adv

trebletree See **tripletree**

tree v

1 Of a hunted animal: to seek refuge, esp in a tree. Note: The tr sense "to drive up a tree, cause to take refuge in a tree" is more widespread and not treated here.
   1769 (1925) Washington *Diaries* 1.321 **VA,** Chased the above fox for an Hour and 45 Minutes when he treed again. **1848** Bartlett *Americanisms* 364, *To tree.* To take refuge in a tree, said of a wild animal. . . This hunter's word is purely American. **1913** Kephart *Highlanders* 81 **sAppalachians,** Finally he [=a bear] gits so tired and wet up that he trees to rest hisself. **1923** *DN* 5.237 **swWI,** *Tree,* v. int. To take refuge, as in a tree, . . used without reference to what affords the refuge. "The wildcat treed in the rocks." "He treed in a hole." **1932** Randolph *Ozark Mt. Folks* 180, The timber along the Ozark streams is full of little gray squirrels, but they do not tree well; fire at a gray squirrel once, and he is very likely to jump out of his tree and run like a rabbit. **1938** Rawlings *Yearling* 297 **nFL,** They won't tree like a cat, they won't turn at bay like a bear. **1939** *Hall Coll.* **wNC, eTN,** Me and my first cousin follered it [Hall: a bear] on down there and finally it treed—went up a tree. *Ibid,* [The bear] tore loose from the dogs and run away down on the flat and treed up another tree. *Ibid,* A bear will tree just as quick as a possum at night. **1939** *Daily Kennebec Jrl.* (Augusta ME) 28 Oct 2/5, Then two wild raccoon treed in a telephone pole at the rear of the postoffice. **1954** *Sportsman* 2.4.64, The smart redbone, a mixture of Irish hound and English bloodhound, is primarily known for his fine work on game that trees. **2002** *DARE* File—Internet **CO,** He [=a cougar] jumped, ran a hundred yards up the hill and treed in a fifteen foot high cedar. **2006** *Ibid* **WI,** One crew ran a bear which provided an exciting chase. It treed just like expected.

2 also v phr *bark tree(d);* Of a dog: to indicate by barking that it has treed an animal; hence adj *treed* of a dog: being at a tree or other site of capture and indicating that an animal is cornered there; also fig.
   1838 *S. Lit. Messenger* 4.405 **GA,** So we call'd the dogs and started off down the vranch [sic] round the corn-field, and fresently [sic] Touze treed. **1882** *Atlanta Constitution* (GA) [18 Oct 1]/1 (newspaperarchive.com), Old Growler treed up a long slim poplar in the swamp. **1895** *Outing* 26.439 **Sth,** The old man advised that we should wait till the dogs treed. **1908** Roosevelt *Outdoor Pastimes* 7, He was not a very noisy dog, and when "barking treed" he had a meditative way of giving single barks separated by intervals of several seconds. **1939** *Hall Coll.* **wNC, eTN,** The dog went across the river and treed. I could see both of 'em [Hall: opossums] up in the tree. *Ibid,* Dogs struck, treed [up] a big hem-pine. *Ibid,* A common expression applied to a dog adept at treeing is: "He'll tree!" **1948** Camp *Hunter's Encycl.* 115 **ME,** A hound that is never let down by his master will stay treed for hours. **1950** Stuart *Hie Hunters* 34 **eKY,** Before he reached midway of the slope . . , he barked treed. **1966–69** *DARE* Tape **GA9,** If he done what they call just walked the tree and went on, he don't tree there; **IN13,** We'd go out in the woods and that dog, and he'd tree up a tree. . . I'd take a shotgun, shoot the coon out; **KY16,** Back them days . . they had an all-purpose hound. And I'd, say, take him out at night, he'd tree. **1970** *Foxfire* Spring-Summer 16 **nGA,** A hunter would. . . follow his dogs as best he could when they "struck," and when they had "treed" (which could be in any place from a hole in the ground to a rock cliff to the top of a real tree) he'd hurry to the spot, call the dogs off, and make his kill. **2002** *DARE* File—Internet **cPA,** It . . was Digger, and by the sound of his chopping bark I could tell he was treed! . . I shouted a few words of encouragement up to the dog . . and he treed harder. **2003** *Ibid,* It would definitely be a game to bark tree on someone, say, standing on a bed. **2004** *Ibid* **MN,** The big question for me is this; "Can I train this dog to stay treed?" **2005** *Ibid* **OH,** It's hard to hear them dogs tree when you are sitting in the truck with the heater blowing on you.

3 tr: To corner or capture (an animal). [By ext from *tree* to drive (an animal) up a tree] **esp Sth, S Midl**
   1868 *Scientific Amer.* 19.376, He "treed" a rabbit in the angle of a

stone wall. **1938** in Lib. of Congress *Amer. Memory: WPA Life Hist.* (Internet) **TX,** I saw a wild hoss off in the distance, and asked the bunch to help me catch him because I needed another hoss. . . There were so many of us that we had him treed in less than three hours. **1953** Randolph-Wilson *Down in Holler* 157 **Ozarks,** The term [=*tree*] is quite correct even when no tree is involved, and one often hears of coons or wildcats *treed* in dens under the limestone cliffs. . . A woman in Crane, Missouri, told me that her terrier would "*tree* moles, then dig 'em out an' kill 'em right in the front yard." **1960** Hall *Smoky Mt. Folks* 61 **wNC, eTN,** *Tree in the ground:* to drive an animal into a hole in the ground. **1972** *Foxfire Book* 274 **nGA,** When an animal is "treed," it is not necessarily "put up a tree," but holed up anywhere.

tree n, adj See **three**

tree bank n Also *bank* **esp IL, WI**
=**tree lawn.**
   1901 in 2009 (acc) Lexis-Nexis Legal Research *State Case Law: IL* (Internet), The sidewalk on South Liberty street stood several feet above the grade for the travel of teams, on what was called the tree bank. **1914** *Chicago Tribune* (IL) 17 Dec 6/6, Can something be done to open a drain from the sidewalk through the tree bank on the north side of Irving Park Boulevard? **1926** *Daily Northwestern* (Oshkosh WI) 15 Apr 5/2, Mayor L.G. Kellogg discussed the subject of planting trees in the tree bank surrounding the new postoffice building. **1950** *WELS* (The narrow area between the sidewalk and the curb or street) 2 Infs, **sWI,** Tree bank. **1951** Johnson *Resp. to PADS 20* **DE** (The narrow area between the sidewalk and the curb or street) Bank. **1958** in 2009 (acc) Lexis-Nexis Legal Research *State Case Law: NY* (Internet), At no point did any sidewalk cross the tree bank along Pennsylvania Avenue so as to give a pedestrian . . a readily apparent method of crossing that heavily travelled street. **1968–70** *DARE* (Qu. N44, *In a town, the strip of grass and trees between the sidewalk and the curb*) Infs **IL35, WV16, WI51,** Tree bank; **AR25,** Bank [Inf uncertain]. **1971** *AmSp* 46.76 **Chicago IL,** Grass strip between curb and sidewalk: *fairway, parkway, tree bank, tree lawn.* **2005** *DARE* File—Internet **neIL,** Those who do not have a driveway or other off-street parking area may park on the tree bank. *Ibid* **WI,** Trees should be placed on the tree bank with all lights and ornaments removed.

tree bark n Also *tree yelp* [Cf **tree** v **2**]
The bark of a hunting dog when it has treed its quarry.
   1889 *Littell's Living Age* 67.506 **VA,** Suddenly the experienced ears of all the 'coon hunters caught a different note in the canine music. 'Dat ar's a tree bark,' exclaimed one. **1923** in 2004 Montgomery-Hall *Dict. Smoky Mt. Engl.* 617 **wNC, eTN,** We heard the furious race, the well-known tree bark, and Mark's shots. **1939** *Hall Coll.* **wNC,** [The dogs] bayed and commenced barkin' the tree bark. **1948** Camp *Hunter's Encycl.* 115 **ME,** While most coonhounds have a distinct tree bark . . , there are some who change very little when the trail has reached its destination. **1960** Burnett *This Was My Valley* 31 **wNC,** As soon as Fan and Glass, Lead, Sooner, and Ring got their second breath, they settled down to their coarse tree bark. **1969** *DARE* Tape **GA74,** We'd hear him give the tree yelp. That tree bark was entirely different because in making it, the dog would point his head upward 'n' it would be a entirely different sound. So by the second time Old Riley'd made his tree bark, Sam would say he's treed. **2003** Hulet *Born under Stump* 31 **WA,** If the bear trees, the dogs' voices change to a different tune. It's hard to describe but I recognize it as soon as I hear it. I call it a tree bark. **2003** *DARE* File—Internet, I've known beagles who would use their tree bark on cookies on the kitchen counter. Got your attention, which is their whole intention.

tree barnacle See **barnacle mushroom**

tree belt n **NEast, esp MA**
=**tree lawn.**
   1898 Boston Park Dept. *Annual Rept.* 14 **ceMA,** Additional [tennis] courts were made on the Blue Hill-avenue end, using up all the level ground to the tree belt. **1913** Newark (NJ) Shade Tree Comm. *Annual Rept.* 10.54, [Elms] should only be planted on streets having a tree belt, i.e., a strip of ground from three to eight feet wide between the curb and the walk dedicated to the trees. **1948** Bean *Yankee Auctioneer* 119 **wMA,** In the old days many homes had . . a post set in the tree belt next the sidewalk for the use of company who came visiting in horse-drawn rigs. **1954** in 2009 (acc) Lexis-Nexis Legal Research *State Case Law: CT* (Internet), The complaint alleges that the sidewalk was "so made or raised above the level of the adjoining surface of the tree belt as to be

unsafe for travel." **1966** *PMLA* 81.2.14 **csMA,** The grass strip between the sidewalk and the curb, . . is a *tree belt* locally in Springfield, Massachusetts. **1967–69** *DARE* (Qu. N44, *In a town, the strip of grass and trees between the sidewalk and the curb*) Infs **MA**5, 23, 58, Tree belt. **1978** *Greenfield Recorder* (MA) 6 May sec A 8/6 (as of c1900), At my mother's home on Central Street, Montague Center, there in the tree belt, were two nice granite posts with rings [for hitching horses]. **1989** in 2009 (acc) Lexis–Nexis Legal Research *State Case Law: NJ* (Internet), Red brick tree belts have been laid along much of the length of Westfield Avenue and trees planted. **2005** *DARE* File—Internet **csMA,** Place leaf bags on the tree belt, *not in the street.* **2006** *DARE* File **cnMA,** In the town where i [sic] own my business, . . these strips are termed "tree belts".

tree bender n Also *tree mover* Cf **trash mover 1**
A sudden heavy rain.

1969 *DARE* (Qu. B25, . . *Joking names . . for a very heavy rain. . . "It's a regular _____."*) Inf **MA**36, Tree bender; **NC**67, Tree mover. **2005** *DARE* File—Internet **TX,** This one was a "tree bender" for sure. Lots of rain, lots of wind, thunder and lightening [sic].

tree border n **WI, CT**
=**tree lawn.**

1946 Milwaukee *Charter Ordinances* 11 **seWI,** That portion of the street lying between the curb and the sidewalk, also known as the tree border. **1961** in 2006 (acc) Lexis–Nexis Legal Research *State Case Law: WI* (Internet), The complaint does not expressly allege that Allied Investment Company . . owns the "tree border" between the sidewalk and the curb. **2004** *Bristol Press* (CT) (Internet) **CT,** A West Street woman was charged Thursday with illegal dumping when she placed "a large amount of trash on the tree border outside her property." **2004** *DARE* File—Internet **CT,** Ahh Bristol and trees . . I once went to a City Council meeting and had Stretch Norton tell me that trees dont belong in the tree border. **2005** *Ibid* [Stevens Point WI Forestry Specifications], The top one (1) foot of all excavations in the tree border (between the curb and sidewalk/property line) . . shall be backfilled *only* with clean, viable soil. **2006** *DARE* File **csWI,** In late years, I have heard "tree border" used for the strip between the sidewalk and the street, but I don't think I even had a word for this when I was growing up in the 50s and 60s. **2008** *DARE* File [see **tree terrace**].

tree box n, also attrib **chiefly DC**
=**tree lawn.**

1906 in 2009 (acc) Lexis–Nexis Legal Research *State Case Law: DC* (Internet), This manhole was the middle one of three of the same kind on the south side of the street. There were tree boxes there, and this sewer trap was out in the tree space surrounded by grass and dirt, and not in the paved portion of the sidewalk. **1970** *DARE* (Qu. N44, *In a town, the strip of grass and trees between the sidewalk and the curb*) Inf **DC**12, Tree box. **1994** *Wellsboro Gaz.* (PA) 27 July 3/4, Soil surrounding the tree box is often compacted to allow for street paving and sidewalk placement. **2000** *DARE* File—Internet **DC,** Mr. Brown also mowed the "tree box" area along the curbs surrounding the park. **2003** *Ibid* **DC,** They are . . bricking over the tree-box strip of ground between the concrete sidewalk and the curb. **2004** *Ibid* **DC,** This will also be a good time for you tree stewards to clean up and spruce up your tree boxes.

tree buckthorn n
=**Carolina buckthorn 1.**

1953 Little *Native Trees U.S.* 363, *Rhamnus caroliniana.* . . Indian-cherry, tree buckthorn.

tree cactus n

1 A **prickly pear 1** (here: *Opuntia imbricata*). Cf **tree cholla**

1848 *Curtis's Bot. Mag.* 74.38 **SW,** It is nearly allied to *Opuntia furiosa . .* , but well distinguished from it; and as it appears to be undescribed, I can give it no more appropriate name than *O. arborescens,* the *tree* Cactus, or *Foconoztle* [sic for *joconostle* or *soconostle*], as called by the Mexicans. **1880** Hayden *Gt. West* 128 **sCO,** At least thirteen species of cactus abound, from the familiar prickly-pear . . , up to the tree-cactus with its large purple flowers and sharp thorns, growing twelve feet in height in favorable localities. **1890** *Chivington* (Colo.) *Chief* 17 Jan. 1/2 *(DA),* The canes referred to . . were of a species of tree cactus that grows in our Colorado mountains; and were just as Nature had 'designed' and 'carved' them. **1896** *Jrl. Amer. Folkl.* 9.188 **AZ,** *Opuntia arborescens* [=*O. imbricata*], . . tree cactus. **1930** OK Univ. Biol. Surv.

Pub. 2.73, *Opuntia arborescens.* . . Tree Cactus. Cholla. **1968** Barkley *Plants KS* 246, *Opuntia imbricata.* . . Tree Cactus. Foothills and plains. Native, but often cultivated in western Kansas. **1976** Elmore *Shrubs & Trees SW* 59, Tree . . cactus. . . *Opuntia imbricata.* . . This usually grows to 6 feet high, but in favorable locations it will grow up to 15 feet tall with a trunk diameter to 10 inches, qualifying it as a small "tree." **1992** Kirkpatrick *Wildflowers W. Plains* 26, *Opuntia imbricata.* . . Tree Cactus grows tall and upright, sometimes bushy but usually treelike. . . Tree Cacti are pretty common on the Western Plains, but especially below the Caprock area of Texas.

2 =**saguaro.**

1849 *Amer. Jrl. Sci. & Arts* 2d ser 7.453 *West,* The great tree Cactus which makes such a striking appearance, as figured by Major Emory, and which is described by Dr. Engelmann under the name of *Cereus giganteus.* **1876** U.S. Dept. Ag. *Rept. of Secy. for 1875* 163 **wTX, AZ,** *Cereus giganteus.* . . Tree Cactus. . . grows 50 to 60 feet in a straight column, and finally divides into several naked-looking branches. **1905** *Jrl. NY Bot. Garden* 6.149, Regarding the distribution of the tree cactus in California Mr. Brown also says "The saguaro does not grow in the hills back of Picacho." **1921** MO Bot. Garden *Bulletin* 117, One of the most interesting plants in the semi-arid regions of Arizona and Mexico is the giant tree cactus (suwarro). **1977** (1985) Lamb *Climatic Hist.* 181, Saguaro, the giant tree cactus of Arizona *(Carnegiea gigantea).*

3 A **cactus** n[1] **B1** (here: *Pilosocereus robinii*) native to the Florida Keys.

1933 Small *Manual SE Flora* 916, *Cephalocereus* [=*Pilosocereus*]. . . Succulent shrubs or trees with fluted stems and branches. . . *Tree-cacti.* . . *C. Deeringii* [=*P. robinii* var *d.*] inhabits the Key Largo limestone, *C. keyensis* [=*P. r.* var *r.*] the Key West oölite. **2002** (acc) N. Prairie Wildlife Research Center *Biol. Resources* (Internet) **FL,** An inventory of tree-cactus populations by a Florida Atlantic University team indicates the number to be almost 500 clumps.

tree cholla n Cf **cholla, tree cactus 1**

A **prickly pear 1** (here: either *Opuntia imbricata* or *O. versicolor*).

1908 Hornaday *Camp-Fires* 224 **AZ,** The Tree Choya is . . less of a curse than Bigelow's. **1940** Benson *Cacti AZ* 31, *Opuntia versicolor.* . . Staghorn or tree cholla. Green or purplish-green arborescent cholla usually 3 to 7 or rarely 12 feet high; stems intricately branched, . . branches cylindrical. **1947** Carr *Desert Parade* 83, Staghorn or tree cholla. . . Tree cholla prefers the vicinity of arroyos and other areas where there is a growth of shrubs and grass. **1960** Vines *Trees SW* 772, *Opuntia versicolor.* . . is also known as Tree Cholla. **1970** Correll *Plants TX* 1091, *Opuntia imbricata.* . . Tree cholla. . . usually a small tree 1–2 m. high. **2002** *DARE* File—Internet, Staghorn Cholla/Tree Cholla . . *Opuntia versicolor.* . . With forked branches resembling deer antlers this tree-like cactus hybridizes easily. . . *Tree Cholla—Opuntia imbricata.* . . Prevalent from desert flats to Pinyon and Juniper stands.

tree claim n **Upper MW, Plains States**

A parcel of treeless public land allotted to a settler on condition that a certain proportion of it be planted with trees; the area so planted; broadly, any grove of trees in a largely unwooded area.

1876 *Freeborn Co. Std.* (Albert Lea MN) 15 June [2]/1 (newspaperarchive.com), C.H. Funk, of Nobles county, has set . . 8,000 of the trees, and all the cuttings . . on his tree claim. **1887** Nye *Remarks* 496 **ND, SD,** Do you think I ought to bury myself on a tree claim with a woman far my inferior, while I have talents that would shine in the best of society? **1929** Bell *Some Contrib. KS Vocab.* 107, Tree claim. . . The same as a *timber claim.* **1930** *Bismarck Tribune* (ND) [31 Jan 9]/3 (newspaperarchive.com), Charles Bleckreid has purchased the trees and other wood on the tree claim east of town belonging to the Spangberg estate. **1959** Lahey–Hogan *As I Remember It* 8 **swKS** (as of 1886), Uncle Johnnie and Uncle Tommie each took up a tree claim just over the line in Grant County. **1967** *DARE* (Qu. T2a, . . *A piece of land covered with trees . . only a few acres*) Inf **CO**3, Tree claim—in order to "prove up" on your land. **1973** Allen *LAUM* 1.334 (as of c1950), *Clump* (of trees). . . tree claim [3 infs, **MN, SD**]. *Ibid* 333, Tree claim, originally a quasi-legal designation, has its origin in the Timber Culture Act of Congress in 1873. Under the provisions of that act, title to 160 acres of public prairie land was transferred to anyone who planted 40 acres of trees on the land and then kept them growing for ten years. **2002** *DARE* File **nwMN,** When the farmer bought his quarter section, he was given the 160 acres free providing he planted 10 acres of it to trees, which were always cottonwoods in this area. They were important landmarks. When

I talk to my brothers about the area we still use them to orient our selves: "The Tree Claim" (the one along the north edge of our quarter), . . "the tree claim next to the railroad," etc. **2002** in 2006 *DARE* File—Internet **ND,** I watch how the growth of the city has finally reached the distant tree-claim where I would often drive out to when I was 16 to watch the hawks soar on the hot summer winds. **2003** *Bismarck Tribune* (ND) 10 Dec 2 (Internet), Some [memorable experiences] took place 25 years ago in the middle of dad's pasture, on a work weekend of hoeing and weeding a new tree claim. . . Some of us enjoyed it so much; we planted three more tree claims over the next 15 years. **2006** *DARE* File—Internet **NE,** [Advt:] This Acreage also includes a submersible well, 1 windmill and a tree claim.

tree climber n

=**pilot black snake.**

1945 McCauley *Reptiles MD & DC* 81, *Elaphe obsoleta obsoleta.* . . Tree climber, Cowsucker. [*Ibid* 83, Although not a truly arboreal snake, *Elaphe o. obsoleta* is perfectly at home in trees, ostensibly climbing in search of birds or their eggs.]

tree cotton n

The cottony hairs of the **cottonwood 1** seed.

1935 Davis *Honey* 301 **OR,** The cottonwood was seeding, and a deep haze of blue-gray tree-cotton floated on the surface of the spring.

tree court n

=**tree lawn.**

1950 *WELS Suppl.* **seWI,** The name used in our locality [=Dodgeville] most frequently for the strip of lawn between sidewalk and street is "Tree Court."

tree cranberry   See **cranberry tree**

tree creeper n   [*OED2* 1814 →]   Cf **creeper 2, creeping warbler**

A small creeping bird such as the **white-breasted nuthatch** or the **black-and-white warbler,** but esp the **brown creeper 1.**

1839 Audubon *Synopsis Birds* 72, *Certhia.* . . *Tree-Creeper.* . . *Certhia familiaris.* . . Brown Tree-Creeper. . . Upper parts reddish-brown. **1917** *Wilson Bulletin* 29.2.84 **KY,** *Mniotilta varia.*—Tree creeper. . . *Sitta carolinensis.* . . tree-creeper. **2002** (acc) IL Dept. Nat. Resources *IL Nat. Hist. Surv.* (Internet), The brown creeper, *Certhia americana.* . . Other names, American brown creeper, common creeper, little brown creeper, tree creeper.

tree-creeping warbler   See **creeping warbler**

tree cricket n

A usu pale green cricket of the genus *Oecanthus.*   For other names of *O. fultoni* see **greenbug 2**

1858 *Acad. Nat. Sci. Philadelphia Proc. for 1857* 177, Dr. Leidy stated that a few evenings since, in the yard attached to his residence, he for the first time had the opportunity of observing the male Tree-cricket, *Oecanthus,* while chirping. **1860** Hooker *Nat. Hist.* 256, The Tree Cricket . . is a very delicate insect. Its color is pale ivory; its antennæ and legs are very long, and its wing-covers are thin. Its familiar shrill sound is produced only by the male Cricket. . . These differ decidedly from other members of the Cricket tribe in living wholly on trees. **1877** VT State Bd. Ag. *Report* 4.154, The tree cricket . . is sometimes very troublesome to the raspberry. **1905** Kellogg *Amer. Insects* 160, The snowy tree-cricket. . . [is] common all through the East and Middle West. **1926** Essig *Insects N. Amer.* 101, Tree Crickets. . . are . . small, delicate crickets which are arboreal in habits and pale yellowish green or brownish in color to match their surroundings. **1966–69** *DARE* (Qu. R7, *Insects that sit in trees or bushes in hot weather and make a sharp, buzzing sound*) Infs **GA**89, **IN**69, Tree cricket; (Qu. R8, . . *Kinds of creatures that make a clicking or shrilling or chirping kind of sound*) Inf **MS**16, Tree crickets. **1986** Pederson *LAGS Concordance (Insects, some green and some brown)* 1 inf, nwGA, Tree crickets. **2002** (acc) Clemson Univ. Entomol. *Clemson* (Internet) **SC,** Although generally considered a minor pest of tobacco in South Carolina, at times the tree crickets have caused damage.

treed   See **tree v 2**

tree dare-base   See **dare-base**

tree dog n   Cf **catch dog**

A hunting dog trained to tree game.

1889 *Littell's Living Age* 182.504 **VA,** "A perfectly elegant tree-dog he has." "Tree dog!" I said. "Do you mean it climbs?" "No, he doesn't

do that way. He just marks the tree the 'possum's in." **1916** *Lincoln Daily Star* (NE) 22 Nov 11/1, [Advt:] For Sale—Two coon and varmint hounds, trained excellent, tree dogs; reasonable. **1923** *DN* 5.223 **swMO,** Tree dog. . . Any dog that barks when his quarry has been brought to bay. **1927** *AmSp* 3.163 **wKY,** Not long ago a country weekly in western Kentucky carried an advertisement for a tree dog. The odd expression probably conveys no meaning to people in general, but to hunters, at least in certain parts of Kentucky, it characterizes a dog that will tree a hunted animal. **1933** *AmSp* 8.1.53 **Ozarks,** *Tree dog.* . . A dog used in hunting coons, possums and the like, as distinguished from a foxhound. **1933** *Sheboygan Press* (WI) 17 Oct 14/6, [Advt:] Old Coon Hound—A-1 tree dog, for sale cheap. **1954** *Harder Coll.* **cwTN,** *Tree-dog.* . . A dog use[d] in hunting coons, possums. **1969–70** *DARE* Tape **KY**16, We had what . . we called tree dogs, you know, would hunt every night to catch possums, coons, skunks and that; **KY**75, Sometimes he'll make a real good tree dog. **1976** Garber *Mountain-ese* 96 **sAppalachians,** If you want a good tree-dog you've got to train him properly. **1977** *Bennington Banner* (VT) 16 Aug 14/4, [Advt:] Good hunter, good tree dog.

tree duck n   [From the habit of often nesting in natural tree cavities]

1 Std: a duck of the genus *Dendrocygna.*   Also called **cornfield duck, fiddler ~ 1, long-legged ~;** for other names of *D. autumnalis* see **black-bellied tree duck, summer duck 4;** for other names of *D. bicolor* see **Mexican duck 1, ~ squealer, squealer 5, summer duck 4, tee-kee, wood duck 3**

2 =**wood duck 1.**

1785 Latham *Genl. Synopsis Birds* 3.547, *Anas sponsa.* . . *American Wood Duck.* . . Appears at *New York* early in the spring, and breeds there: makes the nest in the decayed hollows of trees, or such as have been made by *Woodpeckers,* and often between the forks of the branches; whence by some called *Summer Duck,* and *Tree Duck.* **1874** NY Acad. Sci. *Annals Lyceum Nat. Hist.* 10.389, *A[ix] sponsa.* Summer Duck; Wood Duck; Tree Duck. **1938** Oberholser *Bird Life LA* 122, It [=*Aix sponsa*] is one of the relatively few . . ducks that do not nest on the ground. For this purpose the bird selects a cavity in a tree, and from this habit is called 'Wood Duck' or 'tree duck'. **1966–69** *DARE* (Qu. Q5, . . *Kinds of wild ducks*) Inf **MI**36, Tree ducks; (Qu. Q23) Inf **IL**33, Tree duck—hatches eggs in hollow trees. **1969** Longstreet *Birds FL* 35, *Tree Duck; Acorn Duck.* . . Found from Labrador to Florida.

3 =**hooded merganser.**

1888 Trumbull *Names of Birds* 75, Mr. Ridgway told me that he had heard "Wood-duck," and also *tree-duck* . . commonly applied to this species [=*Lophodytes cucullatus*], in lower or more southern portions of the Wabash valley, Ill. and Ind. The application . . is natural enough, of course, as the Merganser breeds in woods, nesting in the hollow of a tree like the "Wood-duck" [=*Aix sponsa*] of people generally.

tree fern n

1 An arborescent fern of the genus *Cibotium* native to Hawaii.   Also called **hapuu 1, pulu**   [*OED2* 1846 → for related genera]

1841 *Penny Cyclop.* 20.391 **HI,** The underwood is tree-fern, from four to forty feet high. **1873** in 1966 Bishop *Sandwich Is.* 71 **HI,** I notice that the foreigners never use the English or botanical names of trees or plants, but speak of *ohias, ohelos* . . *pulu* (tree fern) [etc]. *Ibid* 89, He . . put down a shake-down of *pulu* (the silky covering of the fronds of one species of tree-fern). **1933** Bryan *Hawaiian Nature* 122, In the neighborhood of Kilauea Crater . . there are large forests made up of tree ferns. *Ibid* 123, These three kinds [=*Cibotium chamissoi, C. glaucum, C. menziesii*] of giant tree ferns are found nowhere else in the world except the Hawaiian islands. **1970** Carlquist *Hawaii* 328, *Cibotium glaucum,* with whitish waxy undersides of leaves, is the hapuu, or tree fern, which can be found at Kilauea. **1994** Stone–Pratt *Hawai'i's Plants* 189, Tree ferns typically reach heights of 20 ft.

2 A fern usu growing on or about trees, as:

a =**royal fern.**

1900 Lyons *Plant Names* 270, *O[smunda] regalis.* . . Tree Fern. **1938** *Small Ferns SE States* 342, The extensive geographic distribution has . . allowed this fern to accumulate a rather large number of common names. Besides royal-fern we find . . tree-fern . . and others.

b =**polypody.**

1901 Clute *Our Ferns* 199, Among its common names are hoary polypody, scaly polypody, tree fern and resurrection fern. Tree fern is from its habit of growing in the treetops. **1920** *Torreya* 20.91, *Poly-*

podium polypodioides [=*Pleopeltis p.*] . . Common local names are . . "tree fern"—from its epiphytic habit of growing on the trunks of trees—and more generally, "resurrection fern." **1941** Walker *Lookout* 56 **TN,** The polypodiums, or tree ferns . . seek out the rough bark of the forest trees. **1951** *PADS* 15.26 **TX,** *Polypodium polypodioides.* . . Tree fern, i.e. one that grows on trees.

treefish n

A **rockfish 3** (here: *Sebastes serriceps*) native to California.

1881 CA *App. Jrls. Legislature* 2.36 **CA,** *S[ebastodes] serriceps,* the Saw-head or Tree fish, . . is abundant in rather deep water about Santa Catalina Island. **1884** Goode *Fisheries U.S.* 1.263 **CA,** *Sebastichthys serriceps.* . . Wherever this species receives a distinctive name, it is known as the "Tree-fish," an appellation originating with the Portuguese at Monterey, and without obvious application. **1953** Roedel *Common Fishes CA* 135, *Treefish.* . . Central California south into central Baja California. . . Of very minor significance. **2002** (acc) U.S. Natl. Oceanic & Atmospheric Admin. *Channel Is.* (Internet) **CA,** Many species of rockfish inhabit the waters of the Channel Islands. Treefish *(Sebastes serriceps)* generally live in rocky crevices and caves of depths up to 46 meters (150 feet).

tree fly n

A **cicada.**

1954 *Harder Coll.* **cwTN,** *Tree fly.* . . Insect that sits in a tree or bush and makes a sharp buzzing sound in hot weather.

tree fox n

=**gray fox.**

1916 *Natl. Geogr. Mag.* 30.420 **West,** In some parts of the west they [=gray foxes] are called "tree foxes," because when pursued by dogs they often climb into the tops of small branching trees. **1937** Grinnell et al. *Fur-Bearing Mammals CA* 2.437, The gray fox is sometimes called. . . "tree fox." This is fairly descriptive, since the gray fox is the only member of the . . dog family . . living in California which climbs trees.

tree frog n

1 An anuran of the family Hylidae, esp of the genus *Hyla,* but also of another genus such as *Pseudacris,* a **cricket frog,** or **thunder frog. widespread, but less freq NEast** See Map For other names of var of these see **bell frog, cheeper, coat bet, crut** n[3]**, fry-bacon frog, granite toad, grass frog b, green ~ a, greenhead 5b, hyla, jeeper, katydid B4, knee-deep, leaf frog, March peeper, marsh frog 2, ~ peeper, mud quacker, night peeper, ~ toad, peedee 2, peeper** n[1]**, pinewoods tree frog, piper, pond frog 2, rainbird 2, rain-frog 1, rainmaker 1, scraper** n[2]**, snipe 6, spring frog 1, ~ peeper, squealer 8, swamp frog 2, toad** n **2, toad-frog 1, too-tight, tree toad 1, ~ trat, water frog**

1738 Royal Soc. London *Philos. Trans.* 40.348 **NC, SC,** *Rana viridis arborea. The green Tree Frog.* These *Frogs* are always found sticking to the under Sides of Leaves of Trees, and other Plants. **1792** Belknap *Hist. NH* 3.174, Tree Frog, *Rana arborea.* **1837** (1962) Williams *Territory FL* 66, The Little Tree-Frog . . is of a fine pale green color. . . They are very musical reptiles, and rejoice at the fall of rain. **1854** Hammond *Hills* 154 **NY,** Just listen to the tree-frog, how merrily he pipes all along the shore. **1890** IL State Lab. Nat. Hist. *Bulletin* 3.189 **IL,** *Chorophilus triseriatus* [=*Pseudacris t.*] . . This is the characteristic prairie "tree-frog." . . The most nearly musical of all our amphibians. **1906** *DN* 3.121 **nwAR,** Tree-frog. **1918** *Copeia* 60.79 **swUT,** *Hyla arenicolor.* . . This tree frog was found most abundant on rocks and cliffs along swift running streams. . . The frogs are most vociferous in the late afternoon. **1950** *WELS* **WI** (*Small frogs that sing or chirp loudly in the spring*) 9 Infs, Tree frog; (*Names for the animal like a frog that lives away from water*) 3 Infs, Tree frog; (*Insects that sit in trees or bushes and make a sharp buzzing sound in hot weather*) 3 Infs, Tree frog; (*Other creatures that make a clicking, shrilling, or chirring sound*) 2 Infs, Tree frog. **c1960** *Wilson Coll.* **csKY,** *Tree frog.* . . sings loudly for such a small animal, and is supposed to prophesy rain. **1965–70** *DARE* (Qu. P21, *Small frogs that sing or chirp loudly in spring*) 262 Infs, **widespread, but less freq NEast,** Tree frogs; (Qu. R7, *Insects that sit in trees or bushes in hot weather and make a sharp, buzzing sound*) 48 Infs, **scattered,** Tree frogs; (Qu. P23, *Names for the animal similar to the frog that lives away from water*) 17 Infs, **chiefly Midl,** Tree frog; (Qu. P22) Inf **NY35,** Tree frog; (Qu. R8, . . *Kinds of creatures that make a clicking or shrilling or chirping kind of sound*) Infs **AR41, PA132,** Tree frog. **2002** (acc) Sa-

vannah R. Ecology Lab. *SREL Herpetology* (Internet) **GA,** Treefrogs spend most of their time high in trees or in bushes, but they come down to breed on spring and summer nights.

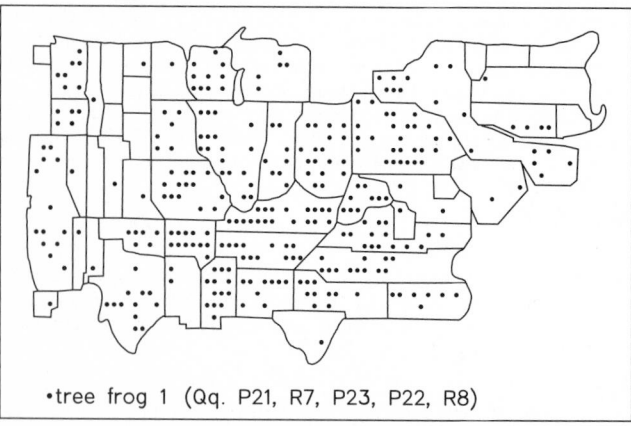

•tree frog 1 (Qq. P21, R7, P23, P22, R8)

2 A **mushroom B1.** Cf **toad** n **5, toad-frog stool**

1969 *DARE* (Qu. S19, *Mushrooms that grow out like brackets from the sides of trees*) Inf **KY11,** Tree frog.

tree gum n

See quot.

1965 *Good Old Days* Nov 12 **WI** (as of c1910), The picture on the front of the July issue reminds me of chewing the pitch on the Norway Pine in Wisconsin when I was a girl. My Dad would chop into the bark to make the pitch run because it took about five years for it to cure it to be so one could chew it. Since I've tried the pitch from the Bull Pine—it's much the same. So "tree gum["]—is the same now as in "The Good Old Days.["]

tree haw n

The green **hawthorn** *(Crataegus viridis).*

1897 Sudworth *Arborescent Flora* 232, *Crataegus viridis.* . . Tree Haw (Ala., Miss., La., S.C.) **1901** Mohr *Plant Life AL* 546, *Crataegus viridis.* . . *Tree Haw.* . . A pretty tree, 20 to 25 feet high. Most frequent in the bottoms of the Alabama and Tombigbee rivers, occasionally subject to overflow.

tree-hole mosquito n [See quot 1911]

A **mosquito** n[1] **B1:** either *Aedes triseriatus* in the eastern US or *Ochlerotatus sierrensis* in the western US.

1904 NJ Ag. Exper. Sta. *Rept. Mosquitoes* 272, *Culex triseriatus* [= *Aedes t.*] . . The Tree-hole Mosquito. **1965** Blickenstaff *Insects* 303, *Aedes sierrensis* [=*Ochlerotatus s.*] . . western tree-hole mosquito. **1980** Milne–Milne *Audubon Field Guide Insects* 641, *Tree-hole Mosquito (Aedes triseriatus).* . . Of all mosquitoes that breed in tree holes, this is the most widely distributed. **2002** *DARE* File—Internet **CA,** The treehole mosquito is widely distributed in western North America . . and throughout California.

tree huckleberry n

=**farkleberry** or **highbush cranberry.**

1845 PA College Linnaean Assoc. *Lit. Rec. & Jrl.* 1.62, *Vaccinium corymbosum.* . . Tree Huckleberry. **1897** Sudworth *Arborescent Flora* 312 **SC,** *Vaccinium arboreum.* . . Tree Huckleberry. **1936** Whitehouse *TX Flowers* 92, The tree-huckleberry is a shrub or small tree, very abundant in the woods of East Texas and the Southern States. **1972** Brown *Wildflowers LA* 133, *Tree Huckleberry.* . . Widely distributed in the pinelands of Louisiana. . . Also Texas, Arkansas, and Mississippi. **2002** *DARE* File—Internet **cnMS,** Beech saplings and tree huckleberry were negatively affected by fire.

tree-knocker See knocker 1

tree lawn n chiefly Gt Lakes, esp OH See Map Also called curb 2, devil's strip, parking n 2, parkway 3, street lawn, swale 2, terrace, tree bank, ~ belt, ~ border, ~ box, ~ court, ~ plot, ~ strip, ~ terrace

The strip of grass and trees between the sidewalk and the curb.

1895 Cleveland OH Bd. Park Comms. *Annual Rept. 1894* 89, A sidewalk and tree lawn will be built on the easterly side of the drive during the next season. **1943** *Herald–Press* (St. Joseph MI) 17 July 10/4, The tree is on the Leyis avenue side of the property, on the south tree lawn. **1950** *WELS Suppl.* **ceWI**, *Tree lawn*—Strip between sidewalk and street; **csWI**, It is called the *tree lawn* in Lake Mills; **seWI**, His father always told him to cut the tree lawn; **MI**, My husband's family (from St. Joseph, Mich.) call it "tree lawn." **1964** *AmSp* 39.293 **OH**, *Tree lawn* appears to be the common term in Cleveland. **1965–70** *DARE* (Qu. N44, *In a town, the strip of grass and trees between the sidewalk and the curb*) 14 Infs, **chiefly Gt Lakes**, Tree lawn. **1967** *PADS* 47.12 **nOH**, Tree lawn—'curb strip.' **1968** *DARE* FW Addit **Cleveland OH**, *Treelawn*—Strip of grass between the sidewalk and the road. **1971** *Wood Vocab. Change* 53 **Sth**, *Tree lawn.* [Offered by 48 of 1000 infs] **1971** [see **tree bank**]. **1972** *DARE* FW Addit **Toledo OH**, *Tree lawn*—The lawn between the sidewalk and the street. **1986** Pederson *LAGS Concordance (Strip of grass between the sidewalk and the street in town)* 1 inf, **seAL**, Tree lawn—common term in his family; 1 inf, **ceTN**, Tree lawn—guessing. **1996** *DARE* File **MI, OH**, *Tree lawn.* . . seems to have a MI/OH thin distribution; my wife, originally from Cleveland/Lakewood, OH also knows it. **2004** *Cleveland Plain Dealer* (OH) 4 Nov sec E 4/1, Lynne Gill rescued an old window from a neighbor's treelawn right before trash day. **2006** *DARE* File **neOH**, A (locally born) nurse noted in a record that the pedestrian "was struck while standing on treelawn" and one of my coworkers—from Pennsylvania—had no idea what that meant. . . Three of my co-workers—the ones that grew up in town in northeast Ohio—used the term familiarly; three others, from Kentucky, Pennsylvania, and rural Ohio, had no name for it.

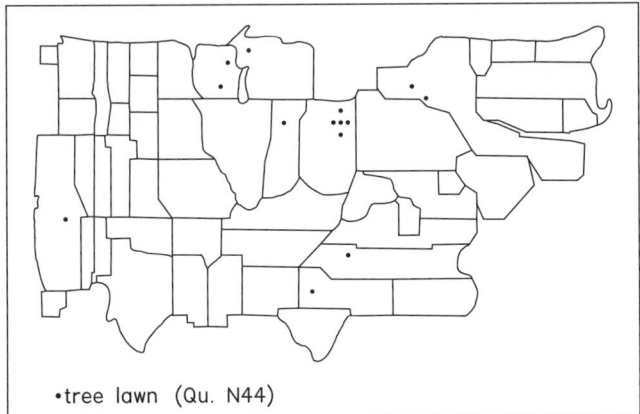

•tree lawn (Qu. N44)

tree lizard n

A small brown or gray **lizard 1** (here: *Urosaurus ornatus*) native chiefly to the Southwest.

1947 Pickwell *Amphibians* 30, *Urosaurus ornatus symmetricus,* the Arizona Tree Lizard, resembles somewhat the Pacific States species of the next genus, *Uta.* **1958** Humphrey *Home from the Hill* 48 **neTX**, There he could find not just boy's game—butcher birds and tree lizards and jays. **2002** (acc) AZ State Univ. *Ask Biologist* (Internet), Tree lizards *(Urosaurus ornatus)* are among the most common lizards in the southwestern United States. You can often find them warming themselves in a sunny spot on a tree, fence, or wall.

tree looker n   Also *tree spotter*

=timber cruiser.

1913 *DN* 4.28 **NW**, *Tree looker.* . . A timber estimater [sic], cruiser, etc. Also in the Lake states and South. "The crew of tree lookers camped for the night." **1958** McCulloch *Woods Words* 200 **Pacific NW**, *Tree spotter.* . . A timber cruiser.

tree molasses n   Cf **molasses C1, maple molasses, sugar-tree molasses, tree sugar, ~ sweetening, ~ syrup**

Maple syrup.

1859 (1968) Bartlett *Americanisms* 488, *Tree molasses.* Molasses made from the Sugar-maple tree; a term very common in the West. **1880** *Harper's New Mth. Mag.* Sept 582 **CT**, We'd hed buckwheats an' tree molasses for breakfast that day. **1907** in 2006 *DARE* File—Internet **AR**, The syrup or tree molasses, is one of the rarest dishes ever eaten and the ingenuity [of] man has never devised a syrup that will compare with tree molasses for deliciousness. **c1937** in 1974 *Amer. Slave* 16.14 **cKY**, The water [=sap] was then dipped out and placed in different kettles to boil until it became the desired thickness for "Tree Molasses". **1947** *AmSp* 22.306 **ceIN**, My grandparents (I am a former Hoosier) made hundreds of gallons of tree molasses in some seasons from our

sugar grove in Henry county. **1952** Brown *NC Folkl.* 1.602, *Tree-molasses.* . . Maple syrup. **1961** *Morgantown Post* (WV) 8 Apr 5/6, With the ramps the diners had bacon, fried taters, corn pone, tree molasses and sassafras tea. **1964** Smith *PA Germans* 108 **nwVA**, We made a meal of fried cakes and hog meat an [sic] Shrove Tuesday, we put tree molasses (maple syrup) on them. **1974** [see **tree sugar**].

tree moss n

1 Any of several plants having a form that resembles a very small tree, as:

a A **moss** n **1**, esp of the genus *Climacium*. [*OED2* 1611 at *tree-moss* sb. a]

1822 Eaton *Botany* 241, *Climacium.* . . *dendroides* . . (tree moss) stem branching, tree-form. **1852** WI State Ag. Soc. *Trans.* 2.419 **WI**, *Climacium.* . . Tree Moss. **1907** Marshall *Mosses* 271, *Tree Mosses.* . . The species of the *Genus Climacium* are large, resembling miniature evergreen trees. They are common in shady woods, in damp places on decayed logs, on roots of trees and on hummocks in swamps. **1942** Hylander *Plant Life* 98, The Tree Moss *(Climacium)* is . . often confused with the Running Pine *(Lycopodium).* . . The erect tree-like shoots form dark green clumps on the damp earth in woods and swamps. **1951** Dunham *How to Know Mosses* 181, The distinguishing characteristic of *Climacium* is the manner of branching, which gives it its popular name of "Tree-Moss." If a number of plants are examined, some are quite sure to be found that at once suggest tiny trees, as the *branches spread all around the stem* and point upwards. **2002** (acc) OH Univ. *Bryophyte* (Internet), *Climacium.* Common name: tree moss. . . *Climacium dendroides* lives within a broad northern band in eastern North America. This habitat overlaps with *Climacium americanum*'s habitat, which tends to be more towards the south. . . The most obvious characteristic is an overall tree-like appearance.

b A **club moss**.   Cf **fir club moss**

1681 Grew *Musæum* 235, The *Creeping Tree Mosse* of *America.* 'Twas found betwixt *Virginia* and *Florida.* **1832** MA Hist. Soc. *Coll.* 2d ser 9.152 **cwVT**, [Lycopodium] dendroideum, Tree-moss. **1898** Britton–Brown *Illustr. Flora* 3.574, [Index:] *Moss.* . *Tree* [=Fir Club-moss. . . *Lycopodium selago;* Cypress Spurge. . . *Euphorbia Cyparissias*]. **1938** Small *Ferns SE States* 402, In addition to the common name, fir-clubmoss, the plant [=*Lycopodium selago*] is known as *Firmoss, Tree-moss* [etc].

c   **=cypress spurge.**

1892 *Jrl. Amer. Folkl.* 5.102 **OH**, *Euphorbia Cyparissias,* tree-moss. **1898** [see **1b** above].

2 Any of several plants with a "mossy" or mosslike appearance that are often pendent from trees, as:

a   **=Spanish moss.**

1766 (1942) Bartram *Diary of a Journey* 46, We encamped . . on a bed of long tree-moss, to preserve us from the . . damp ground. **1866** Trowbridge *South* 448 **AL**, All through the lower half of the State, the long tree-moss grows with great luxuriance. **1881** *Harper's New Mth. Mag.* Apr 729 **Sth**, He made a little ugly ridikilous baby out o' *tar.* . . Dar was watermillion seed fur teef, and glow-worms fur eyes, an a' toad-stool fur a nose, an' de gray tree-moss fur hair. **1895** Smithsonian Inst. *Smithsonian Contrib.* 32.187.477, Neither do the grass-woven nests of the Arizona Hooded Oriole resemble the common type of its near relative found in Texas. I refer to the nests built of tree moss, which are usually located in bunches of the same material. **1958** in 2002 *DARE* File—Internet **TX**, Such trips, on foot or on horseback, would necessitate camping out over night, sleeping on a bed made of tree moss! **1974** Morton *Folk Remedies* 153 **SC**, "Tree Moss". . . *Tillandsia usneoides. Ibid* 154, A Johns Island woman says that as a premature baby she was carried on a pad of "tree moss" and always slept on a bed of the moss. **2001** *DARE* File—Internet **MS**, Gathered and bailed [sic] tree moss for mattress stuffing, 1916–early 1920s.

b A lichen of the genus *Usnea* or *Bryoria,* or a spike moss (here: *Selaginella oregana*).   Cf **moss** n **2c**

1822 Eaton *Botany* 501, *Usnea.* . . *florida.* . . On trees. This and the following species [=*U. strigosa*] of lichen are usually called tree moss. **1866** Lindley–Moore *Treas. Botany* 1197, *Usnea.* . . The species grow on rocks or trunks of trees, from which latter circumstances they are often called Tree Moss or Tree Hair. **1872** Schele de Vere *Americanisms* 411, The *Long Moss* or *Spanish Moss* (Tillandsia usneoides) forms one of the most striking features in the Southern landscape. . . At first sight it resembles the Tree-moss (Usnea) of the North; but that is a lichen, while this is a phenoganeous plant. **1884** *Century Illustr. Mag.* 28.846 **ID**,

Pedestrianism in this somber twilight realm of dense foliage and trailing tree-moss has an especial charm when it leads out toward light and civilization. **1885** *Ibid* 29.838 **OH,** Fallen trees and often the trunks and lower limbs of live ones were thickly sheathed in moss—not the trailing tree-moss of the Rocky Mountain forests, but a thick, tufted, carpet-like moss.

3 Appar a polypore or other shelflike **mushroom B1; see** quot.

1966–68 *DARE* (Qu. S19, *Mushrooms that grow out like brackets from the sides of trees*) Inf **MN**28, Tree moss; **SC**3, Tree moss—looks like ears on the tree, right frilly-like.

tree mouse n

1 =**nuthatch.**

1895 (1907) Wright *Birdcraft* 74, The Nuthatches. . . seldom . . stay in one spot long enough to be examined. In fact "tree-mice," the local name our farmers give them, is quite appropriate. **1946** Hausman *Eastern Birds* 433, White-breasted Nuthatch. . . Tree Mouse. . . Crawls about on tree trunks and the larger branches, mouselike, head upward or downward.

2 =**brown creeper 1.** [*EDD* 1893]

1955 *AmSp* 30.179 **WY,** *Tree mouse* . . is not a surprising name for the brown creeper, which so closely sticks to the bark of the trees it seems forever clambering.

3 An arboreal vole (*Arborimus longicaudus*) native to California and Oregon.

1915 CA Acad. Sci. *Proc.* 5.156, The tree mouse is dependent on the trees in which it lives for food, drink and shelter. **1928** Anthony *N. Amer. Mammals* 408, Red Tree Mouse.—*Phenocomys longicaudus.* . . Rather large in size; tail long, somewhat hairy. *Ibid* 409, There is reason to believe that the Tree Mouse is rather more plentiful in its chosen habitat than its scarcity in collections would indicate. **1947** Cahalane *Mammals* 519, The tree mouse . . looks like a small meadow mouse. **2002** *DARE* File—Internet, The red tree mouse (*Phenocomys longicaudus* [=*Arborimus l.*]) is an arboreal rodent that lives high in the canopy of the coniferous forest.

tree mover　See **tree bender**

tree mushroom n　Cf **tree frog 2, ~ moss 3**

A polypore such as an **oyster mushroom** or similar **mushroom B1.**

1907 WI State Horticult. Soc. *Annual Rept.* 37.43, No doubt you have all noticed the oyster mushroom. . . Another tree mushroom which is easily identified is the sulphirus polyporus. **1953** *Pop. Sci. Mth.* May 65, [Advt:] Tree-Mushroom! Logs, stumps sprout top price crops. Spawn, instructions, $1.00 bill. **1965–70** *DARE* (Qu. S19, *Mushrooms that grow out like brackets from the sides of trees*) 19 Infs, **scattered,** Tree mushroom(s); **OH**66, Tree musheroon; (Qu. S18) Inf **IL**63, Tree mushroom—grow on tree stumps, red in color. **2003** *DARE* File—Internet **MT,** We occasionally ate tree mushrooms, also known as oyster mushrooms (*Pleurotus ostreatus*), which could be found growing on dead cottonwood trees about the same time the morels were popping up in the soil below.

tree of Christ n

=**crucifixion thorn 3.**

1931 U.S. Dept. Ag. *Misc. Pub.* 101.116, Canotia . . , also called crucifixion thorn . . and tree of Christ, . . is a shrub or small tree . . occurring in Arizona and southern California. **1972** Costello *Desert World* 104, Thorniness is one of the keys to the survival of. . . canotia (*Canotia holacantha*), called Mohave-thorn and tree of Christ.

tree of heaven n

Std: an introduced tree (*Ailanthus altissima*).　Also called **Chinese sumac, ~ tree of heaven, devil's walkingstick 1, false varnish tree, heaven tree, smoke ~ 3, stinking tom 2, stink tree, stinkweed 13, varnish tree b**

‡**tree of paradise** n

See quot.

1968 *DARE* (Qu. T16, . . *Kinds of trees* . . '*special*') Inf **NC**55, Tree of paradise—a mimosa.

tree onion n

=**top onion.**

[**1797** Salisbury *Hortus Paddingtonensis* 4, Allium . . canadense. . . Tree-Onion.] **1827** in 1828 *New Engl. Farmer* (Fessenden) 6.11, Cana-

dian, or tree onion. This is remarkable for producing a bulb or onion at the top of the stalk. **1840** MA Zool. & Bot. Surv. *Herb. Plants & Quadrupeds* 210, A[llium] proliferum [=A. cepa var cepa]. . . Tree Onion. Bears its bulbs on the stem, and among the flowers, or instead of them. **1919** Sturtevant *Notes Edible Plants* 31, A[llium] canadense. . . Tree Onion. Wild Garlic. . . It is found throughout northern United States and Canada. **1986** *Seed Savers Exchange* 98, Allium x proliferum . . tree, top, walking, winter or Egyptian onion. **2000** (acc) MI State Univ. Ext. *Home Horticult.* (Internet), Tree onions are used mainly for green onions.

tree orchid n

Std: any of var orchids that grow on trees, such as those of the genera *Encyclia* and *Epidendrum.*　For other names of var of these see **clamshell orchid, cowhorn ~, dollar ~, green-fly ~, onion ~, penny ~**

tree owl n　Cf **timber owl**

Prob the barred owl (*Strix varia*).

1965–70 *DARE* (Qu. Q2, . . *Kinds of owls*) 22 Infs, **scattered, but esp Cent, Upper Missip Valley,** Tree owl; **OK**11, Hoot owl (or tree owl); **VA**73, Tree owl—same as hooping owl. **1986** Pederson *LAGS Concordance* **Gulf Region,** 6 infs, Tree owl; 1 inf, Tree owl = hoot owl.

tree palmetto n

A **palmetto B,** usu **cabbage palm.**

1759 Garden in 1821 Smith *Selection Corresp. Linnaeus* 1.432 **SC,** I never saw any other than the tree Palmetto and swamp Palmetto, between which I know very little difference but in the size. *Ibid* 433, The tree Palmetto on the sea side grows to 30 or 40 feet high without a branch, and bears a fruit just like the *Chamaerops,* or swamp Palmetto. **1765** (1942) Bartram *Diary of a Journey* 39 **FL,** We now came to plenty of the tree palmetto, which the inhabitants call cabbage-tree, and is much eaten both raw and boiled. **1861** U.S. Patent Office *Annual Rept. for 1860: Ag.* 421 **NC,** Chamaerops palmetto, Tree palmetto. **1897** Sudworth *Arborescent Flora* 104 **LA,** Sabal palmetto. . . Tree Palmetto. **2002** *DARE* File—Internet **TX,** Sabal texana [=*S. mexicana*]—Tree Palmetto—Palm.

tree plot n　Rarely *tree plat*

=**tree lawn.**

1907 in 2009 (acc) Lexis–Nexis Legal Research *State Case Law: IN* (Internet), In the construction of said street at said point, a brick sidewalk, six feet wide, was constructed along the north side thereof, . . immediately south of said sidewalk . . and abutting the south side of said sidewalk at said point, was a tree plot or grass plot about six feet in width, and extending westwardly along the south side of said sidewalk. **1929** *WI Rapids Daily Tribune* (WI) 6 Nov 2/1, It was voted to grade at city expense the tree plot between the sidewalk and curb on Second avenue. **1940** in 2009 (acc) Lexis–Nexis Legal Research *State Case Law: NC* (Internet), The water meter box was located on the grass or tree plot between the paved portion of the sidewalk and the curb. **1958** *New Oxford Item* (PA) 24 Apr 1/4, The sidewalk ordinance . . was amended to include the construction of grass and tree plots between curbing and sidewalk. **1972** in 2009 *DARE* File—Internet **swIN,** Each container shall be placed . . on a tree-plat near a street in a convenient, accessible location for the collection of the refuse. **2005** *Ibid* **cIN,** Frank Nierzwicki explained there will be a tree plot between the sidewalk and street.

tree poppy n

1 Std: a plant of the genus *Dendromecon* native to California.

2 =**matilija poppy. CA**

[**1893** *Yr.-Book Pharmacy 1892–93* 322, One other poppy before I pass on deserves special notice, this is the Californian or tree poppy, *Romneya Coulteri.*] **1898** *Jrl. Amer. Folkl.* 11.222 **CA,** Romneya . . , California tree poppy. **1976** Bailey–Bailey *Hortus Third* 974, *Romneya. . . Coulteri. . . California tree poppy.* To 8 ft. **2002** *DARE* File—Internet, The Matilija poppy, *Romneya coulteri,* is also known as the California tree poppy. . . This native of southern and Baja California, is a true member of the . . poppy family.

tree-pounder n　Also *tree-tapper*　Cf **nail-pounder**

A woodpecker **B1.**

1966 *DARE* (Qu. Q18, *Joking names and nicknames for woodpeckers*) Inf **ME**6, Tree-pounders; **ID**1, Tree-tappers.

tree primrose n

An **evening primrose a** (here: *Oenothera biennis*).

1629 Parkinson *Paradisi* 264, The tree Primrose of Virginia. **1814** Bigelow *Florula Bostoniensis* 148, *Œnothera biennis. . . Tree primrose. . .* Stem from three to five feet high. . . This plant, originally American, is now naturalized, and very common throughout Europe. **1892** (1974) Millspaugh *Amer. Med. Plants* 60–1, *Tree Primrose. . .* Attains a growth of from 2 to 4 feet. **1935** (1943) Muenscher *Weeds* 345, Tree Primrose. . . Widely and locally common throughout eastern North America and also on the Pacific Coast. **2002** (acc) *OH Perennial & Biennial Weed Guide* (Internet), *Oenothera biennis*—tree primrose. . . In the U.S., its range includes an area between the east coast and North Dakota and it is located on the West Coast as well.

tree snake n   Cf **green tree snake**

A **green snake, rat snake 1,** or similar snake of arboreal habits; see quots.

1965–69 *DARE* (Qu. P25, . . *Kinds of snakes*) Infs **AL**31, **CA**160, **OK**15, Tree snake(s); **FL**32, Chicken snake or tree snake; **MI**2, Pine snake—at Escanaba—also called tree snake; **OK**18, Whip snake or tree snake; **TN**26, Tree snake = green [snake], doesn't get too big. **1986** Pederson *LAGS Concordance,* 1 inf, **nwAR,** Tree snake—in limbs, hollow tree.

tree sparkleberry   See **sparkleberry**

tree sparrow n

1   Std: a sparrow *(Spizella arborea)* native to the northern half of the US.   Also called **Canada sparrow, Canadian ~, winter chippy**

2   =**chipping sparrow.**

1956 MA Audubon Soc. *Bulletin* 40.255 **ME,** *Chipping Sparrow. . .* Tree Sparrow.

tree spotter   See **tree looker**

tree squeak n

1   A mythical animal of the woods whose call sounds like the squeaking of tree branches.   **chiefly ME**

1911 *Hunter-Trader-Trapper* 22.50, Have you heard that story of . . how two of the city chaps started to capture a tree squeak[?] **1913** *DN* 4.3 **ME,** *Tree squeak. . .* An imaginary bird or animal. Really the noise made by trees rubbing in the wind, and resembling the cry of a bird or wild animal. **1939** Tryon *Fearsome Critters* 55, *The Tree-Squeak*—Built something like a weasel, . . he is chameleon-like, and can wrap himself around a tree-trunk and match the bark exactly. . . Has a variety of calls; a whine like a panther, a squeal like a young pig, and sometimes a roar like a bunch of cannon crackers at a shotgun wedding. **1973** *Daily Kennebec Jrl.* (Augusta ME) [27] Mar 7/5 (newspaperarchive.com), My spouse, who likes to tell me he was "hatched, not born" in the Washington County woods, . . has introduced me to many of his forest friends including the Tree Squeak and the Swamp Sauger. **1973** *Post-Std.* (Syracuse NY) 30 July 15/1, George Fullmer, North Syracuse, has returned from Maine with up-to-date information on a rare Tree Squeak captured there. **2006** *DARE* File—Internet **ME,** Click on over to the authorized, official *Maine Tree Squeak* site to order T-shirts.

2   A nonexistent item used as the basis of a practical joke.

1966 *DARE* (Qu. HH14, *Ways of teasing a beginner or inexperienced person—for example, by sending him for a 'left-handed monkey wrench':* "Go get me _____.") Inf **MI**10, Tree squeak; (Qu. NN12b, *Things that people say to put off a child when he asks, "What are you making?"*) Inf **ME**12, Tree squeak.

tree squirrel n   **chiefly west of Missip R**   See Map   Cf **ground squirrel** n, **prairie ~**

An arboreal squirrel, esp one of the genus *Sciurus* or *Tamiasciurus.*

1822 Woods *2 Yrs. Residence* 193 **sIL,** Tree-squirrels are of two or more sorts, and are eaten here. **1868** Cronise *Nat. Wealth CA* 443, The Grey Ground-Squirrels (. . *Spermophilus Beecheyi,* and . . *S. Douglassii*). . . are of the size of a half-grown cat, and have a long, bushy tail, like the tree squirrel; but do not ascend trees, except occasionally for food. **1928** Anthony *N. Amer. Mammals* 244, Genus *Sciurus.* Tree Squirrels. **1965–70** *DARE* (Qu. P27, . . *Kinds of squirrels*) 39 Infs, **chiefly west of Missip R,** Tree squirrel; **CA**65, 80, 87, 160, 211, Tree squirrel = gray squirrel; **CA**7, Mountain tree squirrel—California gray [squirrel]; **CA**23, Tree squirrel is a variety found in the mountains; **IA**41, Tree squirrel—brown, climb trees; gray squirrel—a gray tree squirrel; **IL**71, Tree squirrel—ours are all brown; **MA**5, Tree or flying squirrel—same; **WI**62, Tree squirrel—a little browner than the

gray squirrel. **1982** Elman *Hunter's Field Guide* 396, Tree squirrels and their closest relatives are the most hunted of American game. **2002** *DARE* File—Internet **CA,** The California Ground Squirrel. . . The tail is longer than half the head and body length, and is almost as bushy as a tree squirrel's tail.

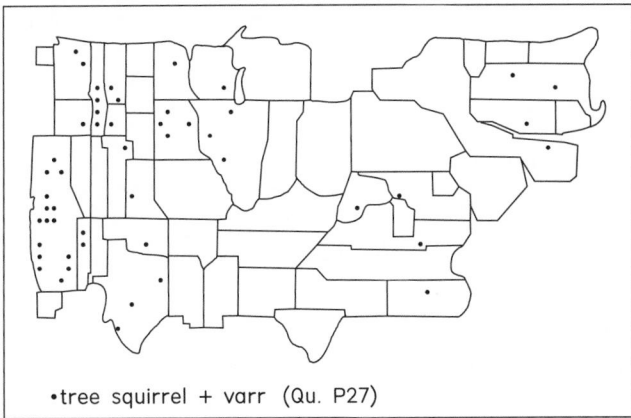

•tree squirrel + varr (Qu. P27)

tree strip n   esp **N Cent**
=**tree lawn.**

1908 *Yr. Book Charleston 1907* 81 **SC,** Macadam road, 30 ft. wide, with tree strip on each side. . . $5,200. **1909** *Fall R. Park Comms. Annual Rept.* 7 **MA,** The persistent cross-cutting in the South Park playground was . . overcome by placing a five foot iron picket fence on the outside of the tree strip bordering Bradford Avenue. **1938** *Oshkosh Northwestern* (WI) 13 Apr 2/3, Circuit Judge Arold [sic] Murphy took under advisement the question: Is a tree strip between the curb and sidewalk part of the street? **1950** *WELS Suppl.* **cWI,** Tree strip—Only term known [in] New London [WI]. **1951** *Post-Std.* (Syracuse NY) 16 Nov 8/5, An iron pipe . . had been driven into concrete near the curb . . to bar parking from the paved tree strip. **1955** *Chron.–Telegram* (Elyria OH) 3 Jan [2]/6 (newspaperarchive.com), Residents should put the Christmas trees on the tree strip in front of their homes. **1963** *Hammond Times* (IN) 10 Nov 15/3, Refrain from planting specimens that will compete with the tree strip for nutrients and moisture. **1968–70** *DARE* (Qu. N44, *In a town, the strip of grass and trees between the sidewalk and the curb*) Infs **OH**82, **TN**53, Tree strip. **1974** *Times Recorder* (Zanesville OH) 2 Nov sec A 2/4, Officials have asked residents to bag leaves and replace them in the tree strip area where street crews will pick them up.

tree sugar n   **chiefly S Midl**   Cf **tree molasses**
Maple sugar.

1824 *Amer. Farmer* 3.22 **swPA,** I send you a small sample of our *tree sugar.* . . It is from a parcel that took the first premium last fall. **1835** Martin *New Gaz. VA & DC* 383, There is in Lee county, probably more tree sugar made, than in any other county in the S.W. **1859** (1968) Bartlett *Americanisms* 488, *Tree-Sugar.* Sugar made from the Maple-tree. Western. **1901** *Everybody's Mag.* 4.333 **IN,** Coffee. . . was new to the Western settler at the time of which I write, milk and water sweetened with "tree-sugar" being the usual table-drink. **1903** *DN* 2.335 **seMO,** *Tree-sugar, and tree-syrup.* . . Maple sugar and syrup. **1932** [see **tree syrup**]. **1951** *AmSp* 26.277, Because they are most heard during the season of tapping maples and making tree sugar, the wood wren is named *sugar bird* in West Virginia. **1952** Brown *NC Folkl.* 1.602, *Tree-sugar.* . . Maple sugar. **1974** Fink *Mountain Speech* 27 **wNC, eTN,** *Tree sugar* . . sugar made by boiling down the sweet sap of [the] hard maple tree. Also called tree syrup and tree molasses. **1982** Ginns *Snowbird Gravy* 39 **nwNC,** Bore a hole in a tree with a bit. Then drive a elder spout in there for the water to run out. Catch it in a trough. Carry it in and make tree sugar out of it. Boil it down, you know. **1998** in 2004 Montgomery-Hall *Dict. Smoky Mt. Engl.* 618 **wNC, eTN,** Tree sugar.

tree-sugar sweetening   See **tree sweetening**

tree surgeon n

A **woodpecker B1.**

[**1911** Mills *Spell Rockies* 193, Dr. Woodpecker, Tree Surgeon. *Ibid* 194, Though the woodpecker gives general attention to hundreds of kinds of insects, he specializes on those which injure the tree internally,—which require a surgical operation to obtain.] [**1937** Natl. Geogr. Soc. *Book of Birds* 2.73, The ivory-bill is a particularly efficient tree surgeon.] **1967** *DARE* (Qu. Q17, . . *Kinds of woodpeckers*) Inf **ID5,** Tree surgeon.

tree swallow n

Std: a **swallow** n[1] (here: *Tachycineta bicolor*) with white underparts, native chiefly to much of the northern half of the US. Also called **blue swallow 1, eave ~ 2, house ~ 2, martin, little ~, stump swallow, white-bellied swallow, white-breasted martin**

tree sweetening n Also *tree-sugar sweetening* Cf **tree molasses**

Maple sugar or syrup.

1893 Leland *Memoirs* 294 **IN,** There was no sugar at his supper-table, but he had three substitutes for it—"tree-sweetnin', bee-sweetnin', and sorghum"—that is, maple sugar, honey, and the molasses made from Chinese maize. **1937** (1963) Hyatt *Riverlid* 80 **KY,** With tree-sugar sweet'nin' hits better tasted than coffee. **1944** Blair *Tall Tale America* 206 **WV,** And bring me thirty-three buttermilk biscuits and tree-sweetnin' for them, for to finish off with.

tree syrup n esp S Midl Cf **tree molasses**

Maple syrup.

1901 Lloyd *Warwick of Knobs* 157 **KY,** The smoke from the fire that boiled the tree syrup curled from many hillside camps. **1903** [see **tree sugar**]. **1932** *Randolph Enterprise* (Elkins, W. Va.) 18 Feb. 5/2 *(DA),* The weather hasn't been cold enough yet to make much success in making tree syrup and sugar. **1974** [see **tree sugar**].

tree tag n esp Gt Lakes Cf **stone tag**

A variation of the children's game of tag; see quots.

1899 Champlin–Bostwick *Young Folks' Games* 701, Tree Tag. Each player chooses a tree as his goal, and cannot be captured while touching it except by some other player's going around it three times. **1907** *Oakland Tribune* (CA) 17 Dec [11]/2 (newspaperarchive.com) (as of c1860), We played tree-tag among the oaks covering what is now the commercial center of this city. **1913** *Mansfield News* (OH) 23 June 5/1, [Headline:] *Child Injured by Motorcycle. . .* Children Playing Tree Tag. **1935** [see **stone tag**]. **1957** *Sat. Eve. Post Letters* **seMN** (as of 1890–97), When I was a child . . we called the games we played by these names. . . Tag: face-tag, wood tag, tree-tag, squat-tag, skip-tag. *Ibid* **cwMN** (as of 1903–10), "Tag"—Wood-tag, Tree-tag, Squat-tag, Last tag. *Ibid* **Chicago IL** (as of 1910–20), "Tree tag" as the name implies, was tag played in trees and many times in trees that had limbs intertwining so we could cross from one tree to another without grounding. **1968–70** *DARE* (Qu. EE33, . . *Outdoor games . . that children play*) Infs **MI109, NY107,** Tree tag; **MI106,** Tree tag—if you . . touched a tree, you were safe; **MI118,** Tree tag—tag played *in* trees; **NY120,** Tree tag—run from one tree to the other—each tree is a goal. **1975** [see **stoop tag** n[1]].

tree-tapper See **tree-pounder**

tree terrace n esp WI Cf **terrace**

=**tree lawn.**

2005 *DARE* File—Internet **neWI,** If you are shoveling or blowing snow from the public sidewalk in front of your property, . . that snow should be deposited onto the tree terrace, . . *not* into the street. **2007** Beaver Dam Bd. Pub. Wks. *Minutes* 18 June (Internet) **csWI,** An ordinance . . relative to *exemptions* of signs permitted in the tree terrace. **2008** Cedarburg Common Council *Minutes* 14 Jan (Internet) **csWI,** In Columbus we used the term *tree border* for the strip of grass between the sidewalk and the street. Sometimes we said *tree terrace.* **2008** *DARE* File—Internet **seWI,** An underground gas main ran directly underneath the stump in the center of the tree terrace.

tree toad n

1 =tree frog 1. chiefly Nth See Map

1778 Carver *Travels N. Amer.* 489, Among the reptiles of North America there is a species of the toad termed the *tree toad,* which is nearly of the same shape as the common sort, but smaller and with longer claws. **1785** in 1888 Cutler *Life* 2.229 **MA,** Dr. Hill says the tree-toad, or tree-frog, as he calls it, is peculiar to North America, and to some few places in the North of Europe. **a1828** in 1841 Brainard *Poems* 23 **CT,** I am a jolly tree toad upon a chestnut bough;/ I chirp because I know the night was made for me. **1845** Judd *Margaret* 14 **swME,** The tree-toad chimed in with his loud trilling chirrup. **1886** Bynner *Agnes Surriage* 196 **MA,** Tree-toads filled the air with twilight clamor. **1899** *Mth. S. Dakotan* 1.165, They were content to spend their days . . listening as evening approached, to the orchestra of beetles and tree toads. **1914** *Copeia* 10.4, The Swamp Tree Toad (*Pseudacris triseriatus* [sic]). . . In

New York it does not appear to have been noticed except in the southern part of the state. **1931–33** *LANE Worksheets* **seCT,** A ground toad is distinct from the rainbird or tree toad. **1939** *LANE* Map 231 *(Frog)* 1 inf, **neVT,** Peeper = tree toad = hyla—the smallest kind of frog. **1950** *WELS* **WI** *(Names for the tree frog)* 21 Infs, Tree toad(s); *(Other creatures that make a clicking, shrilling, or chirring sound)* 6 Infs, Tree toad(s); *(Small frogs that sing or chirp loudly in the spring)* 5 Infs, Tree toad; *(Insects that sit in trees or bushes and make a sharp buzzing sound in hot weather)* 4 Infs, Tree toad(s); *(How can you tell when it's going to rain?)* 2 Infs, Tree toads sing; *(What actions of birds or animals help to foretell the weather?)* 1 Inf, Tree toad chirping—rain. **1951** *PADS* 15.62 **ceIN** (as of 1890s), Tree toad. . . The tree frog (*Hyla versicolor).* **1965–70** *DARE* (Qu. P21, *Small frogs that sing or chirp loudly in spring*) 31 Infs, **chiefly NEast, N Cent,** Tree toad; (Qu. P23, *Names for the animal similar to the frog that lives away from water*) 24 Infs, **chiefly NEast, N Cent,** Tree toad; **CT2C,** A tree toad can change colors; a hoptoad can't; **ME6,** Tree toad changes color according to bark he's on; **NY71,** Tree toad—has a slick coat, lives in trees; (Qu. R7, *Insects that sit in trees or bushes in hot weather and make a sharp, buzzing sound*) 19 Infs, **chiefly NEast, N Cent,** Tree toad; **CT15,** Tree toad—sounds like a policeman's whistle; (Qu. R8, . . *Kinds of creatures that make a clicking or shrilling or chirping kind of sound*) 9 Infs, **NEast, N Cent,** Tree toad; (Qu. R9a, *An insect from two to four inches long that lives in bushes and looks like a dead twig*) Inf **MA40,** Tree toads. **1986** Pederson *LAGS Concordance,* 10 infs, **Gulf Region,** Tree toad(s). **2001** Keillor *Lake Wobegon Summer* 18 **MN,** I look like a tree toad who was changed into a boy but not completely.

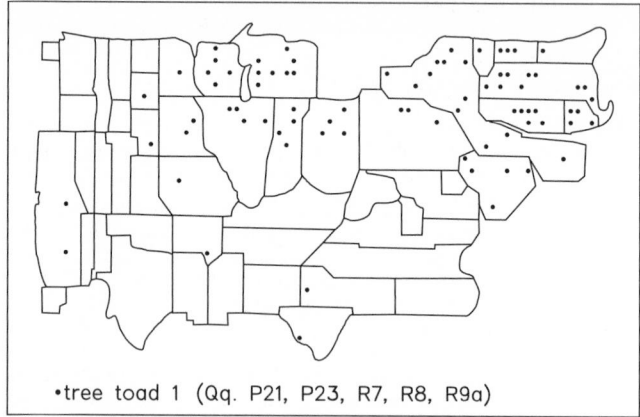

•tree toad 1 (Qq. P21, P23, R7, R8, R9a)

2 See **toad** n **5.**

tree tobacco n

A **tobacco** B (here: *Nicotiana glauca*) naturalized chiefly in the Southwest.

1894 *Jrl. Amer. Folkl.* 7.95 **CA,** *Nicotiana glauca,* . . tree tobacco. **1931** U.S. Dept. Ag. *Misc. Pub.* 101.142, *Tree tobacco.* . . has widely escaped from cultivation and become well established from western Texas to southern California (occasionally elsewhere northward and eastward, especially in the South). **1967** *DARE* Wildfl QR (Wills–Irwin) Pl.38B Inf **TX44,** Tree tobacco. **1985** Dodge *Flowers SW Deserts* 66, Tree tobacco is conspicuous because of its rank growth, its large leaves, and the spectacular clusters of tubular, yellow flowers. **2002** *DARE* File—Internet **TX,** Tree Tobacco. . . forms a small tree, reputedly up to some 20 feet tall.

tree-top v

See quot 1953.

1953 Randolph–Wilson *Down in Holler* 294 **Ozarks,** *Tree-top.* . . To land a fish with unnecessary force, throwing it into the tree-tops. Figuratively, to attack any project with unusual vigor or enthusiasm. Of a girl who quite obviously "set her cap" for a village preacher it was said: "Minnie figures on tree-toppin' him!" **1957** *TX Game & Fish* 15.6.29, A little girl. . . had her father put it [=wiener] on a hook, pitched it into the pool and. . . wham! . . tree-topped a flopping trout into the crowd behind her. **1965** SE Assoc. Game & Fish Comms. *Proc.* 388 **MO,** To. . . the young fisherman who has just "tree topped" a wiggling bullhead. . . ask these people what monetary value is placed on lifetime memories. **1999** in 2004 Canfield *Chicken Soup Fisherman's Soul* 93 **OK,** We'd go to a farm pond, hook on a dab of earthworm, throw Parker's line into the water, and in about three seconds the bobber would go under and Parker would tree-top a three-inch bluegill.

tree trat n

A **tree frog 1.**

1983 *MJLF* 9.1.59 **ceKY** (as of 1956), *Tree trat . . a tree toad.*

tree, up a adj phr

1 also *up the tree:* Drunk.

1856 Kelly *Humors* 184 **OH,** But when he was "up the tree," a little sprung, or *tight,* as you may say, he was . . chock full of wolf and brimstone! **1970** *DARE* (Qu. DD15, *A person who is thoroughly drunk*) Inf **TN**66, Up a tree.

2 Pregnant. [By ext from std *up a tree* in a difficult position] **Nth**

1941 *LANE* Map 392, **MA, NH,** *Pregnant. . .* 2 infs, Up a tree; 1 inf, Up a tree—not regarded as vulgar; 1 inf, Up a tree—usually restricted to unmarried women. **1957** *Sat. Eve. Post Letters* **MA,** She's up a tree—pregnant. **1966–69** *DARE* (Qu. AA28, *. . Joking or sly expressions . . women use to say that another is going to have a baby . . "She['s] _____.")* Infs **NJ**3, **NY**24, **ND**2, **RI**17, **WI**21, Up a tree.

tree wart   See **timber wart**

tree yelp   See **tree bark**

tree yucca n   chiefly **CA**

=**Joshua.**

1861 *Friends' Rev.* 14.221 **CA,** Skirting the Great Basin, . . we came suddenly on a peculiar vegetation of tall thick tree yuccas. **1897** Parsons *Wild Flowers CA* 44, The traveler crossing the Mojave Desert upon the railroad line has his curiosity violently aroused by certain fantastic tree forms that whirl by the car windows. These are the curious Joshuatrees . . , which are called in California tree-yucca. **1916** *Copeia* 32.52 **CA,** A specimen of . . the peculiar night lizard of the Mojave Desert. . . was found by splitting open a Tree Yucca. **1941** Jaeger *Wildflowers* 15 **Desert SW,** Tree yuccas are found only upon and about the bases of those high desert ranges which receive a rainfall of 8 to 10 in. a year. **1985** Dodge *Flowers SW Deserts* 25 **sCA,** Because the presence of this tree yucca marks, more effectively than any other plant, the limits and extent of the Mojave Desert, this species is worthy of special recognition. **2002** *DARE* File—Internet **CA,** The Mojave and Death Valley. . . Dramatic sunsets, eerie tree yucca forests, sand dunes, rugged mountains, . . coyotes, golden eagles, and abundant desert wildflowers are all found here.

trefoil n

1 also *trefoil clover:* Any of var often cultivated plants with compound trifoliate leaves, usu of the genera *Trifolium* and *Lotus,* but also occas of related genera. [*OED2* c1400 →]

scattered, but esp wNY, PA   See Map

[**1709** (1967) Lawson *New Voyage* 170, The Farmers . . should take with them some particular Seeds of Grass, as Trefoil, Clover-grass all sorts, Sanfoin, and Common Grass.] **1760** (1925) Washington *Diaries* 1.148 **VA,** Began to prepare a Small piece of Ground . . to put Trefoil in. **1786** in 1888 Cutler *Life* 2.264 **MA,** The two species of trefoil undoubtedly are native, for they abound in new settlements in the eastern, northern, and western parts of N. England. **1804** Roberts *PA Farmer* 26, I then sowed . . broad cast, at the rate of six pounds of clover, and four pounds of trefoil seed per acre. **1843** Torrey *Flora NY* 1.167, *Trifolium. . .* Clover. Trefoil. **1919** Sturtevant *Notes Edible Plants* 575, *T[rifolium] involucratum. . .* Trefoil. Western North America. This clover is eaten by the Digger tribes. **1925** *Book of Rural Life* 9.5603, *Trefoil,* the common name of the genus *Trifolium. . .* Several other plants of the legume family are also called *trefoil,* particularly plants belonging to the genus *Desmodium.* **1937** U.S. Forest Serv. *Range Plant Hdbk.* W110, Deervetches [=*Lotus* spp] are known by a variety of local names. . The "tree-leaved" . . species are frequently called trefoil, but historically that is a name which belongs to the clover genus *(Trifolium).* **1964** Kingsbury *Poisonous Plants U.S.* 341, *Medicago hispida* [=*M. polymorpha*]. . . Bur clover, trefoil. **1965–70** *DARE* (Qu. L9a, *. . Kinds of grass . . grown for hay*) Infs **NY**140, 148, 226, Trefoil; **NY**164, Bird's foot = trefoil—a clover; **PA**71, [trə'fɔɪl]; **PA**75, [tɚ'fɔɪl]; (Qu. L9b, *Hay from other kinds of plants [not grass];* not asked in early QRs) Infs **CA**136, **NY**102, 150, **PA**51, 174, Trefoil; (Qu. S26a, *Wildflowers. . . Roadside flowers*) Inf **NY**213, Trefoil—little, yellow, spreading out into fields; **NY**75, Trefoil [traɪˌfɔɪl] clover; (Qu. S26d, *Wildflowers that grow in meadows;* not asked in early QRs) Inf **CT**40, Trefoil—tiny, cloverlike yellow flower. **1968** *DARE* Wildfl QR Pl.107A Inf **NY**91, Probably a trefoil. **1990** *PA State Univ. Agronomy Guide* (Internet), Trefoil forage does not decrease rapidly in quality with maturity as do cool-season grasses, alfalfa, and red clover.

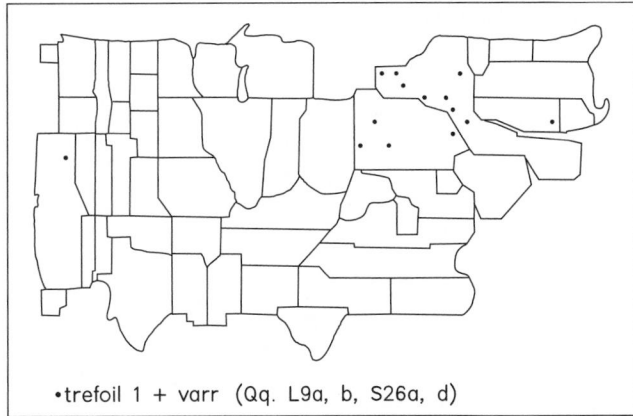

•trefoil 1 + varr (Qq. L9a, b, S26a, d)

2 Any of var other plants, either with three-parted leaves or three leaves; see quots.   Cf **marsh trefoil, shrubby ~**

1828 Rafinesque *Med. Flora* 1.238, *Hepatica triloba* [=*H. nobilis obtusa*]. . . Liverweed, Trefoil, Noble Liverwort. **1910** Graves *Flowering Plants* 189 **CT,** *Hepatica triloba.* . . Mayflower. Mouse-ears. Trefoil. . . The leaves are medicinal and still occasionally used in domestic practice. **1967–69** *DARE* (Qu. S2, *. . The flower that comes up in the woods early in spring, with three white petals that turn pink as the flower grows older*) Inf **NY**12, Trillium, trefoil; (Qu. S16, *A three-leaved plant that grows in woods and countryside and makes people's skin itch and swell*) Inf **NY**165, Poison ivy, trefoil.

trefoil clover   See **trefoil 1**

trembles n   Usu with *the*   Also *tremblings*   Pronc-sp *trimbles*   **scattered, but chiefly Sth, S Midl, TX**   See Map   Cf **delirium tremors, weak trembles**

A disease or condition characterized by involuntary shaking. Note: *Trembles* in ref to milk sickness is widespread and not treated here.

1845 *Amer. Penny Mag.* 1.387 **AL,** There he [=a bear] was ascending the tree, and we with the "trembles" so bad, that we couldn't keep the gun on his broad back at forty steps. **1850** Garrard *Wah-to-yah* 263 **NM,** I got almost to a streak of light, when thar was sich a rumpus back in the cave as give me the trembles. **1902** *DN* 2.247 **sIL,** *Tremblings* [trɪmlɪnz]. . . Tremblings, but used as singular for nervous prostration. **1906** Johnson *Highways Missip. Valley* 93 **TN** [Black], Dat man had caught her by de arm an' holp her up, an' no sooner did he do dat dan he fin' herse'f havin' de trembles. **1917** *DN* 4.418 **wNC,** *Trembles. . .* Tremor; palsy. **1952** *Reno Eve. Gaz.* (NV) 19 Feb 12/1, Wee Bobby, who a moment before had first money as good as banked, jumped and got the trembles and took four blows from the edge of the green to finish an exceedingly angry second. **1965–70** *DARE* (Qu. DD22, *. . Delirium tremens*) 16 Infs, **chiefly Sth, S Midl,** Trembles; **LA**12, Nervous trembles; (Qu. GG26, *A feeling of weakness from fear: "When she saw the dog coming at her she got _____."*) Infs **GA**82, **NY**205, **PA**11, **SC**26, **TN**56, **TX**43, **VA**73, **WV**18, (The) trembles; (Qu. P36, *When a hunter sees a deer or other game animal and gets so excited he can't shoot, he has _____.*) Inf **AR**41, The trembles. **1986** Pederson *LAGS Concordance,* 1 inf, **neLA,** Got the trembles.

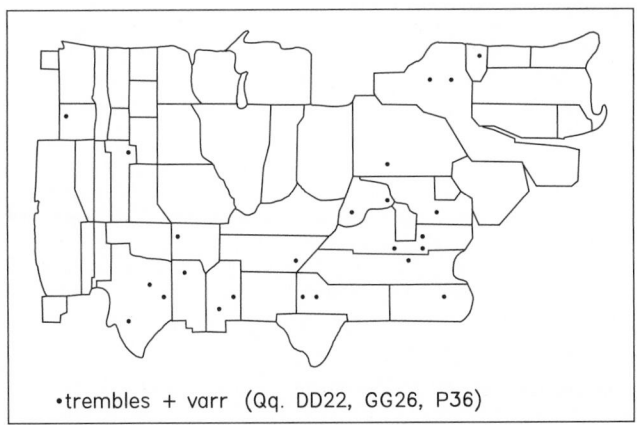

•trembles + varr (Qq. DD22, GG26, P36)

trembling asp(en) See **trembling poplar**

trembling earth n [Calque of Seminole *okefinokee*] **GA** =**trembling prairie.**

[**1876** GA Dept. Ag. *Hdbk. State GA* 55, Many small islands and clumps of trees dot these "prairies," as they are called; and these are generally surrounded by a floor of moss, which is sometimes firm enough to hold one's weight, and again forms a floating surface over the water; and while it does not break through beneath the feet, one can see it sink and rise for 10 or 20 feet around at every step; hence its name—Oke-fi-no-kee, or Trembling Earth.] [**1927** *Lima News* (OH) 27 Jan 13/8 **GA,** Okefeneokee [sic] swamp, known to the Indians as the land of trembling earth, has been encompassed by an industry of 400,000,000 tiny workers [=bees].] **1968–69** *DARE* Tape **GA**50, You have out there what they call trembling earth—it's rotten vegetation, a-floating. Now, you can walk on it, but you have to be particular because you could go through it. . . It's floating vegetation, and good-size brush grows on it; **GA**31, That's what trembling earth is, it's decay. **1981** Pederson *LAGS Basic Materials* **se**GA, 1 inf, The tremblin' earth—Okefenokee Swamp; 1 inf, Tremblin' earth—in the Okefenokee.

trembling marsh See **trembling prairie**

trembling poplar n Also *trembling asp(en)* =**quaking aspen.**

1861 Pratt *Flowering Plants* 5.117, (Aspen, or Trembling Poplar) . . is a middle-sized tree. **1897** Sudworth *Arborescent Flora* 128, *Populus tremuloides*. . . Trembling Poplar (Minn., Colo.) . . Trembling Aspen (Iowa). **1933** Small *Manual SE Flora* 411, *Trembling-poplar*. . . Woods and thickets, various provinces, Tenn. to Calif., Alas[ka]. **1968** *DARE* (Qu. T13, . . *Names . . for . . poplar*) Inf **MN**14, Quaking aspen or trembling aspen. **1971** Kieran *Nat. Hist. NYC* 170, The Quaking Aspen or Trembling Asp (*Populus tremuloides*) . . is common along roadsides, fences, the borders of woods, and in waste places with its roundish leaves so delicately balanced on stiff flattened petioles that they quiver and whisper with every passing breath of wind. **2002** *DARE* File—Internet, Quaking (Trembling) Aspen—*Populus tremuloides*.

trembling prairie n Also *trembling marsh* **sLA** Cf **prairie B1, trembling earth**

An area of wetland consisting of a layer of densely matted vegetation floating on water.

[**1807** Robin *Voyages Louisiane* 2.457, Sur les lieux marécageux, les massettes, les souchets se sèment de graines avec plus de profusion, . . et élèvent des touffes plus larges et plus fournies, jusqu'à former sur la surface de ces eaux marécageuses d'immenses plaines de verdures, nommées *prairies tremblantes*. [=In marshy areas [in contrast to dry prairies] cattails and rushes grow in greater profusion, . . and form larger and thicker clumps, until they form great plains of greenery on the surface of these marshy waters, called *trembling prairies*.]] **1831** (1832) Flint *Hist & Geog. Missip. Valley* 254 **LA,** Vast extents of marsh and trembling prairie interpose between the sea and the cultivable lands. **1868** *Putnam's Mag.* 11.591 **sLA,** The land that first attracts the attention of the voyager—if indeed a few "mud-lumps," a few almost floating islands, and a "trembling prairie," into which one would sink as into quicksand, can be called land—is scarcely raised above the surface of the water. **1871** Lockett *Second Rept. Topog. Surv. LA* 10 **seLA,** In the vicinity of the numerous lakes of the parish [=Lafourche] exist immense tracts called trembling prairies. These seem to be a surface composed of the matted roots and decayed stalks of the marsh vegetation, floating upon water in some instances, and upon very soft mud in others. Over these prairies it is practicable to walk, and cattle graze upon them, although they vibrate at every tread, and a cut of a few feet in depth will always discover a substratum of water. **1888** *Daily Picayune* (New Orleans LA) 30 Sept 9/6, I have often watched the floating islands of turf slowly sailing past me. . . In truth they are fragments wind-torn from the "trembling prairie." **1918** *Eve. State Jrl. Lincoln Daily News* (NE) 4 Feb 6/3 **sLA,** The trembling prairie . . was a myriad-voiced murmur when the dry cane rustled in the wind. **1941** Writers' Program *Guide LA* 583, These unsubstantial and treacherous flats, or marshes, are called "trembling prairies" after the old French term *prairie tremblante*. **1967** LeCompte *Word Atlas* 226 **seLA,** Soft prairie with water underneath. . . trembling marsh [1 of 21 infs]. **1981** Pederson *LAGS Basic Materials,* 1 inf, **seLA,** When that trembling prairie starts burning [it's] bad on people with asthma.

tremblings See **trembles**

trembly owl n Cf **quivering owl, shivering ~ 1**

A **screech owl 1** (here: *Megascops asio,* formerly *Otus a.*).

1975 Newell *If Nothin' Don't Happen* 65 **nwFL,** There's the little screech owls some folks call trembly owls. My Aunt Effie . . said when one hollers it's a sure sign of death and the only protection is to jump up and tie a knot in the sheet.

tremendous adj, adv Pronc-spp *termenjous, tremendeous, tremendious, tremengious, tremenj(i)ous, tremenju(ou)s, trimingeous* Cf **heinous, mischievous**

Std sense, var forms.

1692 in 1865 Fowler *Salem Witchcraft* xx **MA,** And we beholding continually the tremendious works of Divine Providence, not only every day but every hour. **1778** in 1873 Lee *Papers* 2.448 **PA,** A Most tremendious Cannonade Commenced on both Sides. **1803** (1965) Lewis *Jrls.* 70 **VA,** The highlands juts to the river and form a most tremendious Clift of rocks. **1806** (1905) Clark *Orig. Jrls. Lewis & Clark Exped.* 5.37, One of those tremendeous animals (the Bear). **1837** Sherwood *Gaz. GA* 72, *Provincialisms. . . Tremendeous,* for tremendous. **c1846** in 1981 *AmSp* 56.155 **swIL,** Wheat will soon need cutting and the quantity of work is *trimingeous.* **1851** Hooper *Widow Rugby's Husband* 95 **AL,** She was on [=under] a tremenjus strain. **1862** (1864) Browne *Artemus Ward Book* 60 **NEng,** A seleck assortment of the most tremenjious thunderbolts descended down onto me. **1871** Eggleston *Hoosier Schoolmaster* 105 **sIN,** They's a tremengious defference. **1904** Day *Kin o' Ktaadn* 137 **ME,** They do stir the air up suthin' termenjous! **1909** *DN* 3.385 **eAL, wGA,** *Tremendious, tremenjuous. . .* Common variants of *tremendous. Ibid* 405 **nwAR,** His success as a public speaker was something tremenjous. **1932** *Cullman Democrat* (AL) 29 Dec [4]/1 (newspaperarchive.com), The trunks and limbs of even the decidious [sic] trees were forced to sustain a tremendious weight of ice. **1969** *DARE* File **csPA,** *Tremendous* [ˌtrɪˈmɛnjəs].

trespass n, v, hence vbl n *trespassing* Usu |ˈtrɛsˌpæs, -pəs|; also |ˈtrʌsˌpæs| Pronc-spp *traspass, trus(s)pass;* by folk-etym, *trustpass*

Std sense, var forms.

1669 [see **tribble**]. **1923** *Star* (Kansas City MO) 5 Feb 20/6, Travelers on the road to Eldorado report this sign on a tract near the edge of town: "Keep Out—No Trust Passing." **1929** *Burlington Daily Times* (NC) 21 Nov [8]/3 (newspaperarchive.com), [Humorous column:] Mr. Brown has made a state case out of it for truss-passing. **1942** Hall *Smoky Mt. Speech* 20 **wNC, eTN,** Very often [ʌ] replaces [ɛ] in *steady,* . . and it usually appears in *trespass* [ˈtrʌspæs]. **1956** Hench *Coll.* **cVA,** George Barlow, Jr. (Charlottesville) told me today . . that he saw a sign in the mountains—No trust passing. **1985** Kuralt *On the Road* 65, We like the snappy rude signs. No Traspassing. You get the idea. No Trustpassing. Keep out. No Boats Aloud. **2004** *DARE* File—Internet **NE,** My mom called the cops and press charges aginst them with assault and trust passing and vandlism. **2005** *Ibid* **GA,** Forgive us our trust passes as we forgive those who trust pass against us. *Ibid* **MI,** Explain nicely that . . the cats are truspassing in you [sic] yard. **2006** *Ibid* **FL,** The kid will go [to jail] for trusspassing and maybe braking and entering. *Ibid* **OK,** The land owners often kill animals who truss pass on their land. *Ibid* **WI,** We got into a huge blow out she called the cops for trustpassing they laughed at her. *Ibid* **PA,** He's like 'I'm gunna kill u guys for trustpassing.'

tresses n

With modifiers: =**ladies' tresses.**

1907 *Amer. Botanist* 13.69, The maidens' tresses (*Spiranthes cernua*) fills the air with its delicate fragrance. **1938** Matschat *Suwannee R.* 292 **neFL, seGA,** Spring Tresses: *Ibidium cernuum* [=*Spiranthes c.*]; *Ibidium praecox* [=*Spiranthes p.*]; *Ibidium gracile* [=*Spiranthes lacera* var *gracilis*]. **1950** Correll *Native Orchids* 190, *Spiranthes cernua* var. *odorata*. . . Fragrant Tresses, Swamp Tresses. . . Tidal Tresses. *Ibid* 202, *Spiranthes Grayi* [=*S. lacera* var *gracilis*]. . . Beck's Tresses. *Ibid* 212, *Spiranthes ovalis*. . . Oval Tresses, Short Tresses. *Ibid* 218, *Spiranthes praecox*. . . Water-tresses. *Ibid* 227, *Spiranthes vernalis*. . . Spring Tresses. **1975** Duncan–Foote *Wildflowers SE* 274, Autumn-tresses. . . This species has several spirals forming a dense spike. **1987** Case *Orchids* 170, Autumn Tresses—*Spiranthes cernua.*

trestle n Pronc-spp *trussel, trussle, trustle;* for addit varr see **A** below

A Forms. [*OED2* attests spp with *u* from the 16th cent onward; see also *EDD* trustle.]

1794 Morse *Amer. Geog.* 342 **CT,** [A bridge] supported by two wooden trussels and two stone pillars. **1833** in 1847 *De Bow's Rev.* 4.354 **SC,** The foundation [for the railway], whether consisting of piles, sill, sleepers, or trussel work, is completed for the whole distance. **1853** *Scientific Amer.* 9.16, The cask should be placed on a bench or trussel, in a cool, dry cellar. **1856** in 1983 *PADS* 70.56 **ce,sePA,** We . . had a pleasant ride . . crossing the Gunpowder & Bush rivers . . on trussel Bridges a few feet above the water. **1893** Shands *MS Speech* 64, *Trussle.* . . Largely used by all classes for *trestle*. **1899** (1912) Green *VA Folk-Speech* 460, *Trussel*. **1905** *DN* 3.99 **nwAR,** How would you like to fall into the culvert from this trustle? **1950** *WELS (The bridge-like structure on which a train crosses a river or lake)* 1 Inf, **ceWI,** Trissel. **1956** Ker *Vocab. W. TX* 174, Trussel. [2 of 67 infs] **1965–70** *DARE* (Qu. L58, *An implement with an A-shaped frame . . that you put boards on to saw them*) 19 Infs, **esp Midl,** Trustle; **DE**1, 3, **MD**42, **NC**52, **TN**26, 62, Trustle bench; **DC**5, [ˈtrɑsl]; (Qu. L59, *An implement with an X-frame . . to hold firewood for sawing*) Infs **MD**40, **TN**30, Trustle; **NC**52, Trustle bench; (Qu. N19, . . *A structure that carries a road above railroad tracks, or above another road or a deep gully*) Infs **AL**39, **DC**8, **LA**12, **MI**36, **MS**47, **MO**35, **NY**75, 82, 198, **PA**107, Trustle. **1966** *DARE* Tape **AL**3, There's a big [ˈtrɑsl], railroad [ˈtrɑsl]. **1967** *DARE* FW Addit **csPA,** [trʌsl]. **1969** *Charleston Gaz.* (WV) 26 Sept 28/7, [Advt:] We are located. . . one block north of I-64 exit. Turn left under railroad trussel. **1973** Allen *LAUM* 1.222 **Upper MW** (as of c1950), *Trestle.* . . Pronounced with /ʌ/, not /ε/ [2 infs, **IA, ND**]. **1998** *Post–Std.* (Syracuse NY) 4 June sec C 11/2, [Advt:] *Ethan Allen* lite pine trustle style diningroom table.

B Sense.

Also *trestle bench, saw trestle:* A sawhorse or sawbuck. [*OED2 trestle* sb. 4.c 1823 →] **esp C Atl, Midl** See Map

1866 Morford *Utterly Wrecked* 36 **C Atl,** In the middle of the building stood two saw-benches or trestles with three or four unplaned boards laid over them. **1894** Riley *Armazindy* 152 **IN,** The Trestle and the Buck-Saw / Went out a-walking once. **1929** *Denton Jrl.* (MD) 31 Aug 6/6, 1 lot wire, 1 wheelbarrow wheel, 1 pair trestle benches [etc]. **1962** Atwood *Vocab. TX* 51, *Support used to saw boards.* . . Trestle (6[% of 273 infs]) is characteristic of the oldest informants. **1965–70** *DARE* (Qu. L58, *An implement with an A-shaped frame . . that you put boards on to saw them*) 52 Infs, **chiefly C Atl, Midl,** Trestle; 15 Infs, **esp Midl,** Trestle; 8 Infs, **S Midl,** Trestle bench; **DE**1, 3, **MD**42, **NC**52, **TN**26, 62, Trestle bench; (Qu. L59, *An implement with an X-frame . . to hold firewood for sawing*) 11 Infs, 7 **C Atl, Midl,** Trestle; **TN**30, Trustle; **OK**52, Saw trestle; **VA**49, Trestle bench. **1973** Allen *LAUM* 1.222 **Upper MW** (as of c1950), *Sawhorse.* . . *Trestle* appears sporadically in Iowa, North Dakota, and Nebraska for the total of 3.5%. *Ibid,* Trestle: Inf. heard this term used by a carpenter. . . [Another] Inf. says it is taller than a 'sawhorse,' about 6′ tall. **1982** *Barrick Coll.* **csPA,** Trestle— pron. trussel, esp. when referring to a saw horse.

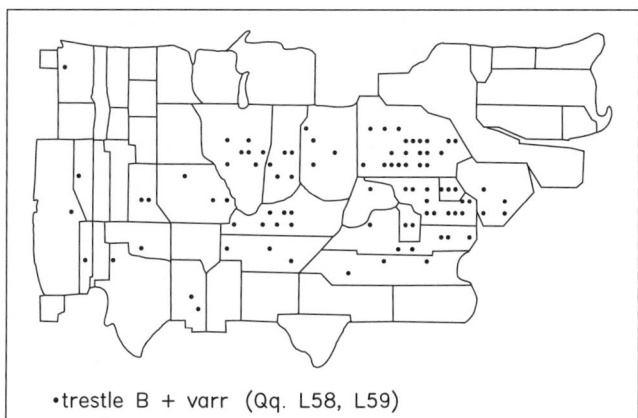

•trestle B + varr (Qq. L58, L59)

tret See **treat**

trew See **throw** A2

triangle fly See **three-cornered fly**

tribble adj, v Also sp *trible, tribil* [Old varr of *treble* (*OED2* at *treble* adj., adv. 1423 →), but prob also infl by *triple*] Cf **thribble, tripletree**

1669 in 1880 Groton MA *Early Rec.* 27, The shall pay . . for a third traspass a tribble damag. **1810** in 1835 NJ Supreme Court *Reports* 489, I . . gave judgment . . that . . the same [sum] be tribbled at $42 72.

1865 *Cultivator* 13.175 **NY,** The pasture was the last season double, if not tribble, to what it was when I commenced the practice. **1899** (1912) Green *VA Folk-Speech* 457, *Trebble, adj.* Tribil. **1908** Fox *Lonesome Pine* 282 **KY,** He made a 'investment' fer ye and tribbled the money. **1909** *DN* 3.381 **eAL, wGA,** *Thribble.* . . To treble. Also *tribble.* **1956** [see **tripletree**].

tribletree See **tripletree**

tribs See **trip(p)s**

trick v, hence vbl n *tricking* (pronc-sp *tricken*) **esp VA, MD** In **hoodoo** n 1a: to cast a spell on, bewitch.

1829 *VA Lit. Museum* 1.384 [Black], And, amongst the degraded and ignorant part of our own population, the notion of *"tricking"* or bewitching is universally and implicitly received, rendering the miserable victim of the fancied *"tricking"* wretched to himself and useless to his master. **1849** Bibb *Narrative* 25 **KY** [Black], There is much superstition among the slaves. Many of them believe in what they call "conjuration," *trick-ing, and witchcraft.* **1878** Burwell *Plantation* 64 **VA** [Black], They still have a strange belief in what they call "tricking," and often the most in-telligent, when sick, will say they have been "tricked," for which they have a regular treatment and "trick doctors" among themselves. **1893** Owen *Voodoo Tales* 174 **MO** [Black], Tow Head . . [repeated] the for-mula she had learned from Aunt Mymee for preparing a "tricken-bag." **1899** (1912) Green *VA Folk-Speech* 458, One who is effected [sic] by means of conjuration or witchcraft is said to be tricked. Hoodooed. **c1937** in 1976 *Weevils in the Wheat* 278 **VA** [Black], Uncle John still believes in tricking. When one negro became angry with another, he would bury in front of his enemy's house a bottle filled with pieces of snake, spiders, tadpoles, lizards and other curious substances, and the person expecting to be tricked would hang an old horseshoe outside of his door to break the spell. **c1938** in 1970 Hyatt *Hoodoo* 1.28 **cMD** [Black], He give her somepin to put under de runner where I walked when I come in de front doah—where dat I would walk over this, this would *trick* me. *Ibid* 2.1163 **seVA** [Black], But this garter must be *tricked.* **1968–70** *DARE* (Qu. CC14, . . *Where one person supposedly casts a spell over another*) Infs **KY**94, **MD**12, Tricked; **VA**37, He's been tricked—old-fashioned.

trick n

1 also attrib; In **hoodoo** n 1a: a spell or act of conjuration; an object used in such an act. **Sth, S Midl** Cf **trick bag, ~ doctor**

1871 [see **trick doctor**]. **1893** Owen *Voodoo Tales* 209 **MO** [Black], The aunties searched under every doorstone for "tricks." **1899** (1912) Green *VA Folk-Speech* 458, *Trick-roots.* . . Roots of plants used by con-jurers in their conjuration. **1926** (1968) Puckett *S. Negro* 207, One of the first things we conjure-doctors have to do is to diagnose the case . . and to find out who "layed de trick." The "trick" (charm) must be found and destroyed and the patient cured. If the patient wishes we must also be able to turn the trick back upon the one who set it. **c1938** in 1970 Hyatt *Hoodoo* 2.994 **Memphis TN** [Black], De sacrifice dat yo' offer up tuh Jesus removes de *trick,* fo' he is de *trick giver* an' de *trick taker.* **1941** Writers' Program *Guide AL* 368, Believing devoutly in conjure, ha'nts, and signs, many of the Cajans wear "tricks" to guard against dis-ease and bad fortune. **1962** *Jrl. Amer. Folkl.* 75.313 **NC,** Local syn-onyms for the spell are "curse," "trick," "fix," "conjure," "root," and "hoodoo." **1966** *DARE* Tape **GA**5, I went up to this nigger church yes-terday. . . You know . . the tricks they have? [They] conjured him. . . what they meant by tricks. . . And that nigger is dead in less than twenty-four hours. He just died, just from fear—I don't know what you'd call it, but he was dead.

2 usu pl: Small articles or personal belongings; toys, knick-knacks. **chiefly Sth, S Midl**

1869 *Overland Mth.* 3.131 **TX,** In Texas you never have *things* in your house, or *baggage* on your journey, but "tricks." **1886** *S. Bivouac* 4.343 **sAppalachians,** Tricks (little ornaments, etc.) **1886** *Amer. Philol. Assoc. Trans.* 17.46 **Sth,** List of common Southern expressions—many of them vulgarisms. . . little *tricks* (little ornaments). **1899** (1912) Green *VA Folk-Speech* 458, *Trick.* . . Any small article; a toy; a knicknack [sic]; a trifle; a mere nothing. **1902** *DN* 2.247 **sIL,** *Trick.* . . Personal property; equipment; part of a machine. Commonly used in the plural. Accoutrements; ornaments. A general term for things of value only to the owner, or miscellaneous objects of all sorts. **1903** *DN* 2.334 **seMO,** *Tricks.* . . Small articles. 'Pick up your tricks and get out of here.' **1907** *DN* 3.237 **nwAR,** "Buy your Christmas tricks at the Racket Store."—Newspaper adv. **1909** *DN* 3.384 **eAL, wGA,** *Tricks.* . . Small articles, trifles. "Get your tricks together." **1932** [see **3** below]. **1942** (1971) Campbell *Cloud-Walking* 30 **seKY,** She just said she reckoned the younguns needed learning more than they needs tricks and fixings to wear. **1950** *WELS (Other general words meaning "toy": "Here is a new _____ for the baby.")* 1 Inf, **csWI,** Trick. **1987** *DARE* File **sIL,** *Trick*—any little thing, edible or inedible; also *little trick.* "Do you want those tricks in a poke (=bag)?" **1999** Mason *Clear Springs* 244 **wKY,** I discovered that tricks were doodads and miscellaneous objects saved for no other reason than that they couldn't be thrown away. Conceivably, they might come in handy . . , but tricks could also include odd, broken pieces of machinery, rusted-out cans, swatches of moth-eaten cloth.

3 A small child; a woman, esp a small or attractive one. **esp S Midl** *joc*

1887 *Scribner's Mag.* 2.476 **AR,** If he was too busy to go to school himself, he never was too busy to drive "the little tricks" over to the school-house, and, every evening, Bulah, "the least little trick of all," used to teach him what she had learned. **1911** *DN* 3.540 **KY,** *Trick.* . . A small child. **1921** *Atlanta Constitution* (GA) 25 Feb 8/4 **NYC,** Mitzi, the actress. Cute little trick. **1932** *Hench Coll.* **seVA,** George Zehmer . . will call anything that interests him, even a person, a trick. Examples . . That child is certainly a cute trick. Mary Jones (a grown woman) is sure a good-looking trick. That's a pretty trick you've put on the mantelpiece. **1951** Giles *Harbin's Ridge* 7 **eKY,** She [=a woman] was a little trick of a person. **1967** *DARE* (Qu. Z12, *Nicknames and joking words meaning 'a small child': "He's a healthy little _____."*) Inf **NE8,** Trick.

trick bag n [Prob **trick** n 1] *orig esp among Black speakers, now more widespread*

In phr *in the (or a) trick bag:* In a disadvantageous or untenable position.

1962 Crump *Burn* 115 **Chicago IL,** I'm gonna try to put somebody in the trick bag, only I need time. **1970** *DARE* (Qu. V1, *When you suspect that somebody is trying to deceive you, or that something is going on behind your back*) Inf **NY249,** They're trying to put me in the trick bag. **1971** Roberts *Third Ear* np [Black], *Trick bag* . . an unfavorable position; an unfortunate predicament.] **1972** *Southtown Economist* (S. Beverly ed.) (Chicago IL) 30 Jan 1/5 [Black], We are in a trick bag. We inherit these things but we don't know what to do with them. **1996** *Chron.–Telegram* (Elyria OH) 25 Apr sec C 5/6 [Black], "I'm not getting put in the trick bag like I got put in the trick bag by Detective (Al) Lieby once before," Raymond Smith said of the Elyria police officer who investigated the case. **2005** *Frontline* (Television Program) **sLA,** Like so many other people [affected by Hurricane Katrina], I am now caught in the trick bag: what damage was caused by wind and what was caused by storm surge. **2006** *Chicago Sun–Times* (IL) 9 May (Internet), If you're wired or not wired that's your business. If you want to put me in the trick bag being wired, that's fine. The only thing, if I go to jail, you'd have to go under witness protection. **2006** *DARE* File—Internet [Black], If we work on the assumption that it isn't a demand problem but a supply problem . . we don't get in the trick bag of blaming black people, or somehow denigrating them. *Ibid,* Where I come from, we have a saying . . "put in the trick bag". It basically means that someone is made to look bad (often by a trusted person) because someone else created the conditions for it to happen, and finds a quick scapegoat.

trick doctor n [**trick** n 1] **Sth, S Midl** Cf **hoodoo** n 1b, **doctor** n 2, **goof doctor**

A practitioner of **hoodoo** n 1a.

1871 Med. Assoc. AL *Trans.* 157, When afflicted with any unusual or lingering disease they [=Negroes] imagine themselves "tricked" or conjured, and consult a "trick doctor." **1878** [see **trick** v]. **1879** *Decatur Daily Rev.* (IL) [21 Jan 3]/5 **DC,** Their colored friends persuaded them to send for the trick doctor, who goes by the name of "Minius Middleton," . . who is well known to the police as a sharp fellow, glib with his tongue and profuse in extraordinary adjectives and voodoo wisdom. **1889** Bruce *Plantation Negro* 115 **VA,** There are communities of negroes in the tobacco belt of Virginia to-day that so far resemble an African tribe as to have a professional trick doctor, a man whose only employment . . lies in the practice of the art of witchcraft. **1898** Page *Red Rock* 161 **Sth,** The trick-doctor . . bowed himself off. **1926** (1968) Puckett *S. Negro* 209, A slavery-time "trick-doctor" gave one of the slaves a "hand" (charm) that was supposed to enable him to "cuss out" the master without being harmed. **c1933** in 2006 *DARE* File—Internet, [Advt:] An old *Conjure Man or Trick Doctor* of the South used this Curio Charm consisting of a Red Flannel Bag filled with *Lodestone, Nails,* and Hair.

tricken, tricking See **trick** v

triddler n

1 =**pectoral sandpiper.**

1888 Trumbull *Names of Birds* 176 **NJ,** [Pectoral Sandpiper:] Known also to some Atlantic City gunners as *Triddler.*

2 See quot. [Cf *EDD* **triddling** "Trifling, talking nonsense"]

1936 *AmSp* 11.276 **eTN,** *Triddler.* A woman gossiper. 'The old triddler is busy.'

trifle on v phr [From euphem use of *trifle with* in ref to sexual misbehavior] **chiefly Sth, S Midl**

To be unfaithful to, "cheat on."

1923 in 1982 Rust *Jazz Rec.* 2.1108, [Title:] Triflin' Blues (Daddy Don't You Trifle On Me). **1947** (1964) Randolph *Ozark Superstitions* 170, A hillman whose wife is "triflin' on him" is sometimes persuaded that he can make everything right by going into the woods at midnight and boring a hole in the crotch of a pawpaw tree [etc]. **1970** *Max Hunter Folk Song Coll.* (Internet) *Ozarks, She'll Trifle on You.* . . Gonna trifle on you / She'll do it every time / When your baby starts to steppin'/ Lord, you nearly lose your mind. **1980** Banks *First-Person America* 186 **OK** (as of 1939), All this drinking led to looseness, and she started trifling on her old man [=husband]. . . It [=pregnancy] scared her so bad that she gave up drinking and trifling. **1982** in 2006 *DARE* File—Internet **MS,** After the [Civil] war, his son-in-law trifled on his daughter, and Gilbert determined to kill the son-in-law. **1995** *Brophy Coll.* 78 **swMO** (as of c1960), *Trifle.* [T]o philander, to "run around." "[S]he's been triflin' on her husband." **2001** in 2006 *DARE* File—Internet **TX,** I tired of her imprisonment in this marriage where her "dear boy" really loved another woman and trifled on her.

trifling adj

1 Lazy, shiftless, worthless; hence used as a vague term of abuse. **chiefly Sth, Midl** See Map

1832 Paulding *Westward Ho* 1.172 **KY,** I had to shoot the trifling creter [=a squirrel] after all. **1851** Hooper *Widow Rugby's Husband* 59 **AL,** Jim Sparks is a triflin' dog. **1866** Trowbridge *South* 107, The North Carolinians. . . are the triflin'est set of men! . . They ha'n't got no sense. They'll stoop to anything. They're more like savages than civilized men. **1871** Eggleston *Hoosier Schoolmaster* 118 **sIN,** These other triflin', good-fer-northin' ones. **c1885** in 1981 Woodward *Mary Chesnut's Civil War* 72 **SC** (as of 1861), The cow boy is very trifling and inefficient. **1899** Chesnutt *Conjure Woman* 66 **csNC,** He turned out to be very trifling, and I was much annoyed with his laziness, his carelessness, and his apparent lack of any sense of responsibility. **1899** (1912) Green *VA Folk-Speech* 458, *Trifling.* . . Good-for-nothing; worthless; mean. **1902** *DN* 2.248 **sIL,** *Tryflin* [sic]. . . Generally applied to persons of little account. **1903** *DN* 2.334 **seMO,** *Trifling* or *triflin.* . . Good for nothing; mean. **1906** *DN* 3.123 **sIN,** *Triflin.* . . Worthless. **1907** *DN* 3.237 **nwAR,** *Triflin', adj.* Worthless (person). **1909** *DN* 3.384 **eAL, wGA,** *Triflin(g).* . . Worthless, low-down, mean. **1936** in Lib. of Congress *Amer. Memory: WPA Life Hist.* (Internet) **SC,** Derrick too triflin tuh plant th' cleared land roun him. Plant uh tater patch en let th' grass eat hit up! **1938** *Ibid* **NC,** After that I married Jake Goslin. . . He was kind o' triflin' but I liked him. **1939** *Ibid* **FL,** You knows pufictly well we can't bide no triflin nigger lazy-bones! **1965–70** *DARE* (Qu. A18, *. . A very slow person: "What's keeping him? He certainly is _____!"*) Infs **FL51, IN79, NC5,** Trifling; (Qu. Y28, *A person who loiters about with nothing to do*) Infs **NC2, OK42,** Trifling; (Qu. HH18,

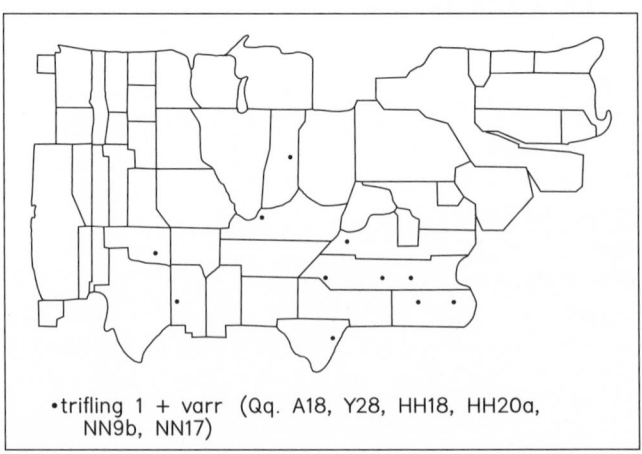

•trifling 1 + varr (Qq. A18, Y28, HH18, HH20a, NN9b, NN17)

Very insignificant or low-grade people) Infs **NC**55, **SC**39, Trifling; (Qu. HH20a, *An idle, worthless person: "He's a _____."*) Inf **VA**25, Trifling; **KY**78, Trifling person; (Qu. NN9b, *Exclamations showing great annoyance: "He's run off with my hammer again, _____!"*) Inf **SC**3, That trifling rascal; (Qu. NN17, *Something that keeps on annoying you—for example, a fly that keeps buzzing around you: "That _____ fly won't go away."*) Inf **LA**28, Trifling. [*DARE* Ed: Some of these resps may be intended as verbs rather than adjs.] **1966–67** *DARE* FW Addit **SC**, Trifling—no-good, undependable people. Any sort of (petty) nuisance; **TN**15, Not a triflin' person . . a person who "don't mind work." **1986** Pederson *LAGS Concordance* **Gulf Region**, 17 infs, Trifling; 1 inf, Trifling—lazy; 1 inf, Trifling—white trash; 1 inf, Trifling as a nigger; 1 inf, Trifling, good-for-nothing scoundrel; 1 inf, Sorry, trifling person— white; 1 inf, Trifling—"common"; 1 inf, Yonder's that trifling nigger; 1 inf, Trifling—of a lazy worker; 1 inf, Trifling people—good-for-nothing.

2 Of a person: tired, draggy, "under the weather"; of one's health: poor. **Sth, S Midl**

1887 *Century Illustr. Mag.* 34.112 **AR**, My health's mighty triflin' . . someway, I'm puny all the time; sorter mis'ry in my ches'; some days I feel pow'ful weak, caynt skeercely walk. **1892** *Ibid* 44.846 **sAppalachians**, She hev been sort o' puny 'n' triflin' o' late, but I reckon she 'll be all right ag'in in a day or two. **1929** *Davenport Democrat* (IA) 3 June 9/1 **TX**, [Advt:] I feel sort of thin and trifling like a fish worm to-day. **1954** *Harder Coll.* **cwTN**, *Trifling*. . . I jis' feel plumb triflin', ain't nar bit o' count fer nothin! **1967–69** *DARE* (Qu. BB39, *On a day when you don't feel just right, though not actually sick . . "I'll be all right to-morrow—I'm just feeling _____ today."*) Infs **AL**39, **SC**44, 46, Trifling; **KY**24, Plumb trifling and sorry; (Qu. BB5, *A general feeling of discomfort or illness that isn't any one place in particular*) Inf **TN**3, Trifling; (Qu. BB17, . . *Vomiting*) Inf **LA**8, Trifling; (Qu. KK30, *Feeling slowed up or without energy: "I certainly feel _____."*) Inf **LA**3, Trifling.

3 Sexually promiscuous. *esp freq among Black speakers*

1924 in 1983 Taft *Blues Lyric Poetry* 66 [Black], I hear these women raving : about their monkey-man / About their trifling husbands : and their no-good friends. *Ibid* 156 [Black], I can't understand / Why these trifling gals : run after a good gal's man. **1938** in Lib. of Congress *Amer. Memory: WPA Life Hist.* (Internet) **NC**, I'd give him my money to keep so we could save some and all the time he was a-spendin' it [on?] liquor and triflin' women. **1942** (1960) Robertson *Red Hills* 188 **SC** [Black], "Brer Rabbit," said Bill, "had trouble with his low-down, sorry, trifling tramp of a wife."

trig *n* [*OED2 trig* sb.¹ 1647 →, *trig* v.¹ 1591 →] **NEng, esp ME** Cf **chunk** *n* **1a, scotch** *n*

A chock used to keep something from rolling or shifting; any of var contrivances used to stop or slow a vehicle; see quots; hence v (phr) *trig (up)* to stop, steady, or slow by means of a trig; also fig.

1815 in 1947 *AmSp* 22.277 **NH**, To place a stone or block of wood to prevent a wheel from running back on a descent is called to trig a wheel, & the efficient the trig. **1845** Judd *Margaret* 455 **swME** (as of 18th cent), I remember when Hash was driving a cart up a hill, I used to trig the wheels, that is, put under a stone. **1871** in 2006 (acc) Lexis–Nexis Legal Research *State Case Law: MA* (Internet), There was evidence tending to show. . . that there were no blocks, chocks or trigs under any of the wheels of the truck; that the iron upon the truck was not blocked or trigged on either side. **1876** Knight *Amer. Mech. Dict.* 3.2627, *Trig*. A shoe for a wheel to ride on, in descending a hill. A form of brake. **1900** *New Engl. Mag.* 21.700, When they reached the Alleghany Mountains, the ascent was so steep that . . men walked behind with billets of wood to trig the wheels when they allowed the horses to stop and rest. **1907** *DN* 3.203 **seNH**, *Trig*. . . A stop (usually a stave or a block of wood) for a wheel or a cask. **1908** Day *King Spruce* 41 **ME**, "It will take a better man than you to trig talk that I'm makin'," he retorted. "This isn't a district school, where you are licked if you whisper!" *Ibid* 310, Put the swale hay to the rest of the pitches. It will trig better than gravel. *Ibid* 321, Twenty rods farther on they struck the hay, spread thickly for the trig—the checking of the runners. **1921** in 2006 (acc) Lexis–Nexis Legal Research *State Case Law: NH* (Internet), His attention was called to one [block of marble] that the truckman thought was likely to fall, and Marston trigged it up with a piece of wood. **1959** *VT Hist.* 27.166 **neVT**, *Trig the wheel*. . . To place a rock or block of wood behind the wheel to serve as a brake while at a stop. Common. Rural areas. **1975** Gould *ME Lingo* 299, *Trig*—A wedge or block to keep a wheel or barrel from rolling, and accordingly anything suggesting such a

device: "Town meetin' got trigged up on some foolish parliamentary question." A *trig* is also a pronged device hinged at the rear of a sled runner; when turned down it bites into the roadway and holds the load from sliding backwards while the team rests. When not needed, it is carried in a fold-back position. **1982** *Smithsonian Letters* **ME**, *Trig*, meaning to block a wheel so that the wagon won't run down hill. I had never thought of *trig* as a regional word, but when I say it to people from away, they never understand it. **2000** in 2006 (acc) Lexis–Nexis Legal Research *State Case Law: ME* (Internet), He testified that he believed the accident occurred because the mobile home had also not been properly trigged to prevent the trailer from moving side to side. . . Mr. Coffin testified that he placed one safety pier under the mobile home before he began his work, but did not place any trigs.

trig *adj* [*OED2 trig* a.¹ 3, 4 1513–1893] *somewhat old-fash* Pleasingly trim, tidy, neat.

1838 Gilman *Poetry* 338 **NEng**, The widow was a trig old lady. **1859** Smith *30 Yrs.* 170 **ME**, He had thrown me off twice and torn my coat pretty bad, so that I didn't look very trig to go through the city. **1886** *S. Bivouac* 4.343 **sAppalachians**, Trig (neat). **1902** Jewett in *Outlook* 4 Jan 59 **NEng**, A trig little brougham would tempt dozens of persons that pass him by. **1943** *Clearfield Progress* (PA) 8 Oct 1/5, [Advt:] A trig square toed Army Russet Calf Oxford. **1951** West *Witch Diggers* 138 **IN**, Ferris looked restrained and genteel; beside Christie, who was not very sprucy in her opinion, he looked trig and fashionable. **1995** *Brophy Coll.* 78 **swMO** (as of c1960), *Trig* . . trim, tidy.

trig *v*¹ See **trig** *n*

trig *v*²

1 with *out, up:* To dress up, adorn; hence ppl adj phrr *trigged out, ~ up*. [*OED2 trig* v.⁴ 1 1696 →]

1822 Garden *Anecdotes Revol. War* 237, At the moment, a *Negro*, trigged out in full *British* uniform, happened to pass. **1858** *Mt. Democrat* (Placerville CA) 26 June [2]/5 (newspaperarchive.com), The other day the idlers of Main street had the rare satisfaction of seeing a genuine native American belle trigged out in "georgeous [sic] array" of hoops. **1868** *Galveston Daily News* (TX) 8 Nov 1/4, He shortly afterwards appeared with the cock under his arm, fancifully decorated with stripes of yellow, red and blue flannel, and the three conchs trigged up pretty much in the same manner. **1882** Dayton *Last Days* 168 **NYC**, The much despised *thing* intruded itself . . in the presence of *Lize* trigged out in full regalia. **1899** (1912) Green *VA Folk-Speech* 458, *Trig*. . . To dress; trick. All trigged out. **1936** *Esquire* Sept 183 **KY**, Had the mule all trigged up. Had red tassels on the bridle. **1937** *Helena Independent* (MT) 12 Oct 4/2 **WA**, We who doubtless would have applauded you as a "panther woman" . . after Hollywood had dolled you up and trigged you out as such, like it better to think that you're back in Hackettstown. **1962** *Mt. Life* Spring 18 **sAppalachians**, His daughters rise early on Sunday to "trig" themselves up in "Sunday-go-to-meetin' duds." **1967** *DARE* (Qu. W30, *When a woman adds decorations to make something more attractive . . "It's too plain—I think I'll put on a few flowers to _____ it up."*) Inf **MA**5, Trig; (Qu. W37, *When a woman puts on her good clothes and tries to look her best . . she's _____*) Inf **IL**135, All trigged out; **CA**157, **KY**44, Trigged up. **1984** Doig *English Creek* 133 **nMT**, It was time we all had something else on our minds besides ruckus. Alec plainly already did, the way he intended to trig up on behalf of Leona and a calf. *Ibid* 162, He was trigged out in a black sateen shirt and nice gray gabardine pants and his dress stockman Stetson, so he looked like a million.

2 also with *up:* To adjust, tinker with; hence vbl n *trigging*. Cf **titrivate, trigger 1**

1920 Smith *Casting Tackle* 63, To the complaint sometimes made that there is too much "trigging" about the level winder, I would say that I have used them for a number of years and only once has a reel gotten out of order. **2005** *DARE* File **wMA** (as of early 1950s), One of the favorite expressions of my college buddy was to "trig" something up, such as a campfire or stove, meaning to get it going or to energize it. . . He was from Greenfield, MA.

Trigg (dog) See **Trigg hound**

trigged out (or up) See **trig** *v*² 1

trigger *v* [Prob by folk-etym from **trig** *v*²] **chiefly Midl**

1 To scheme, contrive; with *(a)round:* To putter, tinker; hence ppl adj *triggered*, vbl n *triggering*.

1888 *Century Illustr. Mag.* 36.777 **seTN**, All done tinkered up an' topped off,—primed an' triggered fer a-runnin' up hill ur down. **1898**

Lloyd *Country Life* 280 **AL,** My talents run to huntin and fishin and triggerin and trappin around free and promiscus like. **1898** Ellis *Poems* 119, Brudder Ivins / De opinion I mus' hold / Dat de debil am a triggerin' / Fer to keep you wid dat cold. **1902** *DN* 2.247 **sIL,** *Triggerin, n.* The minute and particular details of any work. Used as an adjective as in 'triggerin' work.' **1903** *DN* 2.334 **seMO,** *Trigger. . .* To lay plans. 'He's triggerin to get out of paying his just debts.' **1911** TN Court Civil Appeals *Leading Cases* 1.108, The proof is that he said, after using the word "bitch," "She is *'plotting'* or *'triggering,'* to get something to f_____." **1923** (1946) Greer-Petrie *Angeline Steppin'* 36 **csKY,** Now if thars one thing on 'arth that ketches Lum's eye, hit's walkin' sticks, and makin' 'em is the only thing I ever know'd him to work at stiddy. He's always a triggerin' round, a-fixin' sticks fur the neighbors.

2 with *out, up:* =**trig** v² **1.**
1938 in Lib. of Congress *Amer. Memory: WPA Life Hist.* (Internet) **cAL,** [I] get called for Sunday, right when me'n Joan are all triggered up to go down to the Baptist church to Sunday School. **1950** Stuart *Hie Hunters* 207 **eKY** (as of c1920), I jest want to see if I'd know old Sparkie all triggered-up in a new suit! **1953** Randolph–Wilson *Down in Holler* 294 **Ozarks,** *Trigger up. . .* To primp, to dress up. "Molly's back in the shed-room, a-triggerin' up for that town feller." The adjective form is common: "Lucy's all triggered up tonight; I reckon Bob's goin' to take her to the dance." **1953** *AmSp* 28.287 **Ozarks,** *All triggered out,* meaning 'ostentatiously dressed up.' **1954** *Harder Coll.* **cwTN,** *Trigger up . .* primp, dress up. **1958** *Pasadena Independent* (CA) 26 July 11/1, [Red Smith column:] He was triggered out like Mrs. Astor's famous horse, with red ribbons braided into his mane. **2000** Jayne *Home Grown Stories* 4 **Ozarks** (as of c1951), I once was teasing one of my sixth graders at a school party where a little girl was dressed up in her best. I said, "My, Mildred, are you getting all triggered up to get some boy to marry you?"

triggered See **trigger 1**

triggerfish n [See quots 1849, 1903] Cf **filefish**
A fish of the family Balistidae, usu of the genus *Balistes.* Also called **turbot 2.** For other names of *B. vetula* see **old wench, oldwife 1b, queen triggerfish** Cf **leatherjacket**
1814 in 1815 *Lit. & Philos. Soc. NY Trans.* 1.5 pl. 6, [Caption:] Trigger-fish. Balistes. [*Ibid* 467, Trigger file-fish (*Balistes sufflamen*).] **1849** Melville *Mardi* 1.177, The rank and file of the Trigger-fish—so called from their quaint dorsal fins being set in their backs with a comical curve, as if at half-cock. **1876** *U.S. Natl. Museum Bulletin* 6.13, *Fishes. . .* Useful products: . . Shagreen, (file-fish, trigger-fish.) **1884** Goode *Fisheries U.S.* 1.172, The Leather-jacket of Pensacola, *Balistes capriscus,* called "Trigger Fish" in the Carolinas, . . occasionally finds its way as far north as Massachusetts. **1903** NY State Museum & Sci. Serv. *Bulletin* 60.608, Balistidae *Triggerfishes. . .* First dorsal of three spines, the anterior of which is much the largest, the second acting as a trigger, locking the first when erected. **1966** *Carteret Co. News–Times* (Morehead City & Beaufort NC) 16 Aug 2/5, Mason Wren and Joe Ashkew . . made a fine catch of bass, and trigger fish. **2002** *DARE* File—Internet **NC,** These wrecks hold many black seabass, greater amberjack, grey triggerfish, Atlantic spadefish, and cobia.

triggering See **trigger 1**

trigger out See **trigger 2**

trigger round See **trigger 1**

trigger up See **trigger 2**

Trigg hound n Also *Trigg (dog), Trig hound* **esp S Midl** Cf **Plott hound**
A type of hound named for its original breeder, Colonel Hayden (or Haiden) Trigg of Kentucky.
1890 in 1895 Trigg *Amer. Fox-Hound* 5 **KY,** I have received . . many letters from parties who have come into possession of what has become known as the Trigg Dog, and . . have at last decided to write . . a brief history of my dogs and those of Messrs. Birdsong and Maupin from which the Trigg Dog originated. **1905** Williams *Horse & Hound* 96 **KY,** With probably the exception of the Walker strain the Trigg strain is the best known of the modern, up-to-date hounds. **1928** (1933) Thomas *Hounds & Hunting* 60 **VA,** The famous Trigg hounds of Kentucky descended from the Irish hounds [=a pack imported in 1830]. **1941** *Oakland Tribune* (CA) 22 Oct sec D 14/1, Ed Hale's dog 'Bill', a trig hound, is a new breed on the Coast. **1958** Humphrey *Home from the Hill* 48 **neTX,** He had Black and Tans, Redbones, Goodmans, Blueticks and

Redticks, Walkers, Triggs, a pair of Plott hounds. **1966–67** *DARE* Tape **DC9,** Night-hunters . . hunt hounds that are known . . as July hounds, and Trigg hounds, and different breeds; **LA3,** Trigg is very much like a Walker. He's a foxhound, more or less. . . He runs fast like a Walker, whereas the black-and-tan and bluetick and red bone, they're slower; **LA10,** Then there's two or three new kinds. The Trigg, . . they're a good deer dog. . . They're smaller than a . . Walker hound, but they . . all have long ears and they can move, too. **1967** *DARE* FW Addit **AR51,** *Trigg hound*—similar to the black-and-tan, but has a white chest and white stocking feet and a ring neck.

triggie n Also sp *triggy* [Perh dimin of **trig** n; cf **peggy** n¹]
=**cat** n **3a, b.**
1958 *Sat. Eve. Post Letters* **ceNY** (as of c1915), We use to play a game called *"triggie"* or *"triggy." . .* First you need a stick an inch or two in diameter and perhaps two feet long. Also a block of wood about four inches long and an inch square. One end of this is worked into a point with a jack knife and each side has a roman numeral cut in it from one through four. . . The batter . . hits the triggie a sharp rap on its nose . . which snaps the triggie . . into the air. While it is airborn [sic] the batter must hit it toward the [other] players. . . If the triggie is caught the batter is out but if he hits it in the clear he is scored by the number showing on the top side of the triggie where it landed. . . I never saw the game anywhere before and never after leaving Albany. **1963** *Yardmasters Jrl.* 15, How long is it since you saw kids playing marbles . . or spinning a top . . or playing triggy?

trigging See **trig** v² **2**

Trig hound See **Trigg hound**

trig out See **trig** v² **1**

trig up v phr¹ See **trig** n

trig up v phr² See **trig** v² **1, 2**

trilby duck n
=**pintail 1.**
1911 *Forest & Stream* 77.173 **seWI,** Pintail . . *Dafila* [=*Anas*] *acuta.* . . Trilby Duck, Delavan Lake, Wis.

trillium n
Std: a plant of the genus *Trillium.* Also called **three-leaved nightshade, three sisters, wake-robin 3, wood lily 3.** For other names of var spp see **bath flower, beefsteak** n **5, benjamin, bethroot, birthroot, birthwort 2, bloody nose, ~ butcher 2, bumblebee root, buttermilk-lily, corn ~ 3b, cowslip 4, crocus** n¹ **2e, daffadowndilly 2, daffodil 2, dishcloth 1, dogweed 3, dogwood 11, Easter lily 2, grandmother stinks, ground lily, headache flower 3, herb trinity, Indian balm, ~ pink 8, ~ shamrock, jack-in-the-pulpit 2c, Jew's harp B2, johnny-jump-up 2b, lamb's quarter(s) 2, lily 2d, mayflower 13, moose flower, much-hunger, niggerhead 3d, nightshade 2, nodding trillium, nosebleed 3, painted lady 3, ~ trillium, pig's eye 1, piss-a-bed 4, rattlesnake root 2f, Sarah, skunk cabbage 5, ~ flower 3, squawflower 1, squaw root 4, stinking benjamin, ~ willie 2, stinkpot 2, sweet Betsy 2, toadshade, trinity lily, wet-dog trillium, whippoorwill flower, white lily, wildcat piss**

trim v
1 also with *up, out:* To beat, thrash; to defeat (in a game); to scold; hence vbl nouns *trimming(-out).* [*OED2* a1518 →] **chiefly NEast, Gt Lakes** See Map
1888 *Semi-Weekly Age* (Coshocton OH) 22 June 1/6, The free trader got trimmed up [in a debate] worse than Dan Voorhees did in the U.S. Senate. **1894** *Eve. News* (Lincoln NE) 10 Mar [7]/3 (newspaperarchive.com), Everybody in the town got trimmed, and by way of a climax the minister attacked one of the town's most questionable resorts. **1899** (1912) Green *VA Folk-Speech* 458, *Trim. . .* To beat; thrash. *Ibid, Trimming . .* a sharp scolding; a drubbing or thrashing. **1913** *DN* 4.12 **MN,** *Trim up. . .* To defeat (in a game). "They trimmed up every team that came their way." **1932** Farrell *Young Lonigan* 112 **Chicago IL** (as of 1916), Well, anyway, he could trim a lot of guys who did shave. **1941** *LANE* Map 397 *(A whipping)* **scattered NEng,** 8 infs, Trimming; 1 inf, A regular trimming-out = a scolding; 1 inf, Your dad'll trim you out; 1 inf, You're going to get trimmed. **1945** Hamlin *9 Mile Bridge* 96 **nME,** We played cribbage until the sight of a cribbage board was sick-

ening—fifteen two, fifteen four and a pair is six, and nine times out of ten I was trimmed. **1965–70** *DARE* (Qu. Y16, *A thorough beating: "He gave the bully an awful _____."*) 15 Infs, **chiefly NEast, Gt Lakes,** Trimming; (Qu. Y15, *To beat somebody thoroughly: "John really _____ that fellow!"*) Infs **MI**2, **PA**57, **WV**2, Trimmed; **CT**1, Gave him a trimming; **MI**55, Really give him a bad trimming—or beating, for a parent with a child. He really gave him a good trimming; **NY**217, Give him a trimming; (Qu. II27, *If somebody gives you a very sharp scolding . . "I certainly got a _____ for that."*) Infs **CA**99, **MD**26, **NY**234, Trimming.

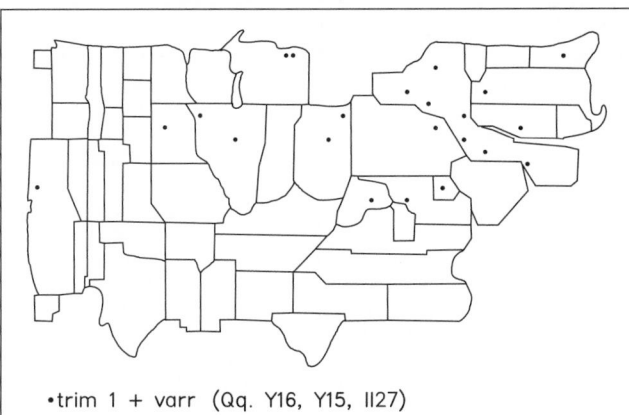

•trim 1 + varr (Qq. Y16, Y15, II27)

2 To castrate. **chiefly Midl, Mid Atl** See Map
1912 *DN* 3.592 **wIN,** Trim. . . To castrate. **1915** *DN* 4.192 **swVA,** Trim. . . To castrate. **1939** *LANE* Map 210 *(Castrate)* 1 inf, **cwNH,** Trim. **1944** *PADS* 2.50 **sVA,** Trim. . . To castrate. **1952** Brown *NC Folkl.* 1.602, Trim. . . To castrate.—Granville county. **1960** Criswell *Resp. to PADS 20* **Ozarks,** Trim was the common term for castrating pigs. **1965–70** *DARE* (Qu. K70, *Words used . . for castrating an animal*) 27 Infs, **chiefly Midl, Mid Atl,** Trim; (Qu. K58, *A castrated pig*) Inf **MD**38, Pig that's been trimmed; **VA**1, Trimmed. **1973** Allen *LAUM* 1.251 **Upper MW** (as of c1950), Castrate. . . trim [14 infs, 9 **IA, NE**]. . . trim up [1 inf, **IA**]. **1974** *AmSp* 49.16 **eTN,** [Phonetic transcription of "Barrow. . . he's a boar till he's trimmed."] **1982** Slone *How We Talked* 119 **eKY** (as of c1950), Hogs were "trimmed," also called "changed" (castrated).

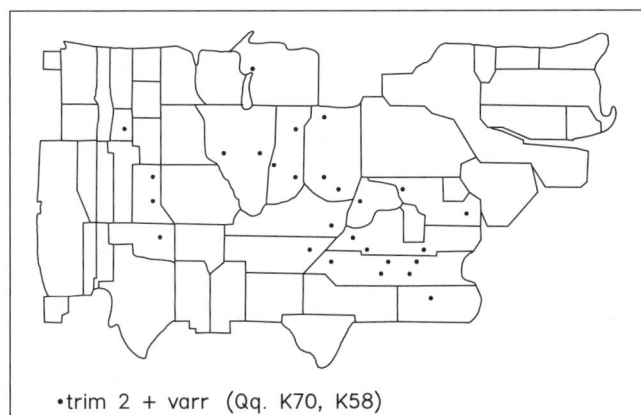

•trim 2 + varr (Qq. K70, K58)

trimble n [PaGer *drummbel* (Ger *Maultrommel*)]
A Jew's harp.
1967 *DARE* (Qu. FF8, . . *Small instrument that you hold between the teeth and pluck on*) Inf **PA**42, Jewish trimble.

trimbles See **trembles**

trimingeous See **tremendous**

trimming See **trim 1**

trimmings n
A surname.
1968 *DARE* File **seSC,** "Is your trimmings Simons?" Reported as having been said by a Low Country Negro.

trim out (or up) See **trim 1**

trinitas n
=**coffeeberry 2a(1).**
1898 *Jrl. Amer. Folkl.* 11.225 **CA,** *Rhamnus Californica, . . Trinitas,* coffee berry.

trinity lily n
A **trillium,** usu *Trillium grandiflorum.*
1892 *Jrl. Amer. Folkl.* 5.104 **WI,** *Trillium grandiflorum. . .* Trinity lily. **1949** Moldenke *Amer. Wild Flowers* 338, The *wakerobins, Trillium. . .* Because of this very conspicuous arrangement of all their organs in 3's or multiples thereof, these plants are often known as . . *trinitylilies.* **1966–67** *DARE* Wildfl QR Pl.23B Infs **TX**34, **WA**12, Trinity lily.

trink n
A **minnow B1;** see quot.
1927 *AmSp* 2.366 **cwWV,** *Trink . .* a small minnow used for bait. "Put on a fresh trink and maybe you will catch a good fish."

trinkle v, n [*OED2* 14 . . →]
To trickle; a trickle.
1835 *Adams Sentinel* (Gettysburg PA) 15 June [5]/4 (newspaper-archive.com), I . . discovered poor young Carter stretched on the floor, with the blood trinkling from his right eye. **1849** *Star & Banner* (Gettysburg PA) 9 Nov 1/7, He caught the handle of the pump, and . . caused a few drops of water to trinkle down from its spout. **1891** *Overland Mth.* (2d ser) 17.201 **CA,** The water of a ditch . . wooed us, with its musical tinkle, trinkle, on hot days, to the little beach. **1924** Raine *Land of Saddle-Bags* 114 **sAppalachians,** Don't you see my own heart's blood / Come trinkling down my knee? **1937** *NE Univ. Univ. Studies* 37.286 **TX, AR,** [Chorus of a song:] Children! don't get weary, [three times] / Love come a-trinklin' down. **1953** Randolph–Wilson *Down in Holler* 27 **Ozarks,** An *n* is often used in trickle and trickling, so that one hears "livin' water a-trinklin' over the rocks." **1968** *DARE* (Qu. B39, *A very light fall of snow*) Inf **LA**37, Trinkle of snow. **1968** *DARE* File **cWI,** Trinkling—the sound a deep well makes as water drains back into it. **c1974** Jones *Ozark Hill Boy* 36 **AR** (as of c1930), A built-up rock filled pen . . over which the sewage trinkled. **1976** Garber *Mountainese* 96 **sAppalachians,** I watched the water trinkle off the house when the snow melted. **1982** *Barrick Coll.* **csPA,** Trinkle.

trinkle root n
A **toothwort** (here: *Cardamine diphylla*).
1923 *Amer. Botanist* 29.155, *Dentaria diphylla* [=*Cardamine d.*] . . "Crinkle root," in allusion to the crinkly rootstock, is . . commonly used. Among the inattentive this becomes "trinkle root."

trip n **NEng** Cf **fare** n
The catch made on a commercial fishing voyage; a boatload of fish.
1872 *Overland Mth.* 8.59 **Gloucester MA,** They had come to get a trip of fish. **1896** *U.S. Bur. Fisheries Rept. for 1895* 117, The number of trips of fish brought into Boston in 1894 was 4,537. **1899** *Portsmouth Herald* (NH) 15 Sept [6]/5 (newspaperarchive.com), Suppose a fisherman brings in a trip of fish and takes them to a certain dealer. **1932** Wasson *Sailing Days* 114 **cME coast,** [His] wonderful skill in setting seines often resulted in "trips of fish" that filled the deck of his schooner, knee-deep, from rail to rail. **1939** Wolcott *Yankee Cook Book* 35, Quite often mackerel fishermen will leave Boston Fish Pier one day and return the next with a large trip of fish that have scarcely stopped wiggling. **1949** *Lowell Sun* (MA) 31 Aug 1/5, The vessel . . was last reported off Nantucket lightship . . , apparently heading back to New Bedford with a full trip of fish. **1952** (1973) Thomas *Fast & Able* 11 **neMA,** Just as the fish showed, the wind started up and blew north and northwest for a month, spoiling the chances of getting a trip. **1954** White *New Engl. Fishing* 30, Each sale is consummated when a vessel's captain accepts the prices bid by a given dealer for the species included in the captain's trip or boatload.

trip-hammer n
A **woodpecker B1.**
1968 *DARE* (Qu. Q18, *Joking names and nicknames for woodpeckers*) Inf **MN**38, Trip-hammer.

triple-awn, triple-awn(ed) grass See **three-awn**

triple-decker See **three-decker**

triple onion n
Perh a **scallion** such as *Allium cepa* var *cepa.*

1970 DARE (Qu. I5, . . *Kind of onions that keep coming up without replanting year after year*) Inf **IL**124, Triple onions—planted in the spring.

tripletail n

1 A widely distributed game fish *(Lobotes surinamensis)* esp common in coastal Atlantic and Gulf waters. [See quots 1803, 1884] Also called **black perch 2a, ~ grunt 1, dormeur 1, flasher 3, grouper 3, sea perch b, strawberry bass 2**

1803 Shaw *Genl. Zool.* 4.1.80, The tail . . appears as if composed of three distinct parts, . . hence the name of Triurus, or Triple-Tail, applied to this fish by Commerson. **1876** U.S. Natl. Museum *Bulletin* 6.62, Fishes, (eastern coast:) . . Triple-tail *(Lobotes surinamensis.)* **1884** Goode *Fisheries U.S.* 1.444, The Triple-tail of the New York market . . is also called by various authors the "Black Triple-tail." *Ibid* 445, The Triple-tail is a short, thick, heavily built fish. The dorsal and anal fins project backwards towards the base of the caudal so prominently as to give origin to the common name. **1933** LA Dept. of Conserv. *Fishes* 206, The Tripletails appear to be fond of lying on their sides at the surface of the sea, a behavior which the fishermen describe as "sunning themselves." **1968** DARE (Qu. P2, . . *Kinds of saltwater fish caught around here . . good to eat*) Inf **LA**26, Tripletail. **2000** DARE File **cLA,** Sea perch—black or dark gray, looks like a warmouth perch, weighs about eighteen pounds, good to eat. In this part of the country we call that a tripletail.

2 A **spadefish 2** (here: *Chaetodipterus faber*).

[**1842** DeKay *Zool. NY* 4.98, The popular names of *Three-tailed Sheepshead,* and *Three-tailed Porgee,* were given them [=*Chaetodipterus faber*] by the fishermen in allusion to their prolonged dorsal and anal fins.] **1903** NY State Museum & Sci. Serv. *Bulletin* 60.602, *Chaetodipterus faber.* . . Spadefish; Triple-tail.

triple-thorned acacia See **three-thorned acacia**

triplet lily n

A plant of the genus *Triteleia,* usu **Ithuriel's spear.**

1884 Miller *Dict. Engl. Names of Plants* 258, *Triteleia.* Triplet-lily. **1923** Abrams *Flora Pacific States* 1.402, *Triteleia laxa.* . . Common Triteleia or Triplet Lily. . . Open hillsides and valleys, especially in adobe soils. **1961** Peck *Manual OR* 215, Common Triplet Lily. Leaves folded, green at flowering time. **2002** DARE File—Internet **CA,** *Triteleia grandiflora . . ssp. howellii. . . Common names:* Howell's triplet-lily.

tripletree n Also *thrib(b)letree, thrippletree, trebletree, tribletree* Cf **evener 1, doubletree, singletree, thribble, tribble**

On a horse-drawn vehicle: a pivoting bar or set of bars used to equalize the force from three **singletrees;** sometimes the whole apparatus including the **singletrees.**

1849 (1850) Parke *Lectures* 327, If three horses of equal strength are to draw abreast at a plough, the triple tree at which they draw will be attached to the plough with the clevis at ⅓ its length from one end. **1865** *Scientific Amer.* 12.408 **IL,** I claim the combination of the adjustable lever, G, lever, J, and rod, K, with the treble tree, D, for equalizing the draft upon the horses of the team. **1872** (1876) Knight *Amer. Mech. Dict.* 1.813, *Evener.* A double or treble tree to 'even' or divide the work of pulling upon the respective horses. **1902** DN 2.248 **sIL,** *Tripple* [sic] *tree.* . . Draft-bar for three horses abreast, attached to the plow at one-third of its length from one end, and the leverage of the long end for the third horse. **1905** DN 3.99 **nwAR,** *Triple-tree.* . . A whiffletree, with two [sic] whiffletrees attached. Common. **1929** *Frederick Post* (MD) 26 Feb 5/5, [Advt:] Public Sale. . . 2 double trees, 1 triple tree [etc]. **1956** Ker *Vocab. W. TX* 179, For a bar to which three or four whippletrees are attached five informants report *tripletree, trebbletree* [sic], *tribletree, fobletree, fourbletree* and *evener.* **1966** Dakin *Dial. Vocab. Ohio R. Valley* 2.154, *Evener.* . . incidental . . names of devices for evening the load on three or more horses hitched abreast. . . *thribbletree, thrippletree.* **1967–70** DARE (Qu. L47, *The two movable bars behind a team of horses are fastened to a longer piece; this is a _____*) Inf **PA**21, Double singletree, tripletree, and four-horse tree; **TN**62, Thribbletree—tree for three horses. **1973** Allen *LAUM* 1.216 (as of c1950) 1 inf, **SD,** Thribbletree; 1 inf, **MN,** Tripletree.

tripodero n

An imaginary animal; see quots.

1910 Cox *Fearsome Creatures* 45 **CA,** The tripodero, an animal with two contractile or telescopic legs and a tail like a kangaroo's. . . its head

is nearly all snout. . . If it sights game within a range of ten rods it takes aim with its snout and tilts itself until the right elevation is obtained, then with astounding force blows a sun-dried quid of clay, knocking its victim senseless. . . The tripodero then contracts its legs and bores its way through the brush to its victim, where it stays until the last bone is cracked and eaten. **1929** *Nashua Reporter & Weekly Nashua Post* (IA) 13 Nov [9]/2 (newspaperarchive.com), The tripodero has never been known to miss a shot and as a result the mortality among tenderfeet in some parts of the West is said to be appalling. **1939** Tryon *Fearsome Critters* 57, The Tripodero. . . Usually seen around construction camps and engineering jobs. . . his extension legs (just like a transit) make it possible for him to prowl close to the ground.

trippe n Also sp *tripp* [Walloon *tripe* sausage] **chiefly ceWI**

Usu *Belgian trippe:* A kind of Belgian sausage usu made with pork and cabbage.

1969 *Sun. Post–Crescent* (Appleton WI) [21 Sept 117]/1 (newspaperarchive.com), *Belgian American Club.* . . The Belgians invite visitors to enjoy trippe, Belgian pie and coffee at the Folk Fest Booth. **1999** DARE File—Internet **ceWI,** *Tripp:* a sausage made with cabbage and pork that when cooked has the same odor as something you might scrape off of your shoe. **2000** DARE File **neWI,** They often ate many dishes with vegetables, like cabbage, in their meat called Belgian Trippe. **2002** DARE File—Internet **ceWI,** I know several Belgian families here. Have been invited to a number of dinners. . . the Trippe sausage, and Kolaches where [sic] a real treat. **2006** *Ibid* **ceWI,** Most Dairy State natives who relish the bratwurst have never heard of the local favorite sausage called trippe. **2007** Stuttgen–Allen *Cafe WI Cookbook* 142, Trippe packs a distinctly odorous punch because of its high cabbage content. Relatively unknown outside the lower Door County and Green Bay area, this Belgian-influenced specialty is beloved by descendents of Walloon Belgians who settled here. **2010** DARE File—Internet (Olsen's Sausage Shop) **ceWI,** *Belgium Tripp.* . . Fully cooked pork and cabbage sausage, stuffed in a natural casing, just heat and eat.

tripper n

One who transports illegal liquor from a still to a buyer, often in a specially modified car; similarly vbl n *tripping* the transporting of liquor in such a way.

1974 Dabney *Mountain Spirits* 149 **sAppalachians,** In the saga of corn whiskey in America's Appalachians, the "tripping" of the liquid contraband has left an indelible mark. *Ibid* 151 **wNC** (as of 1921), The usual method of the trippers, they'd come around a curve and see the road blocked, and they'd jump out and high-tail it and leave the car and the liquor. [*Ibid,* The 1929 Chevrolet touring car was modified into a liquor "trip" car.] *Ibid* 155, One night Carroll was barrelling down Atlanta's Northside Drive, chasing *two* '40 Ford coupes, each of them driven by well-known members of the liquor-tripping fraternity. **2005** *Old Huntsville Mag.* 3 Jan (Internet) **nAL,** The trippers, so called because they got paid per trip, were the men who hauled the whiskey from the stills to the customers.

trip(p)s exclam Also *tribs*

In marble play: used as a call to claim privileges when three marbles are involved.

1958 *Resp. to PADS 29* **cnOK,** Advantages could be gained by being the first to cry. . . trips—was the word applied to any place 3 was needed. **1963** *KY Folkl. Rec.* 9.3.63, *Demand for right to possess marbles when three . . are knocked off the square or out of the ring. . .* tribs: Boyd [County]—tripps: Perry, Greenup, Morgan [Counties]. [**1967** DARE Tape **LA**8, Sometime you knock out three, see, and you said "bent [*DARE* Ed: cf **vent** exclam, v²] your triples" or "dubs," you'd have to put two of 'em back in the ring and keep one, see. Well, if he said "triples" before you said that word, why, he kept all three of 'em. They were his if he shooting for keeps.]

triptoe n Cf **tangle-legs**

=**hobblebush.**

1894 *Jrl. Amer. Folkl.* 7.90 **NH,** *Viburnum lantanoides,* . . triptoe. . . From the fact that the branches often take root at the ends.

tritchet See **twitchet 1**

t'roat See **throat**

troft See **trough A1**

troke n [*SND troke* n. 4 "Any small piece of work or business, a task, errand, odd job"]

1959 *VT Hist.* 27.164 **nVT**, *Trokes*. . . Little chores. Occasional among the Scotch. Orleans.

troll v, hence vbl n *trolling* [*OED2 troll* v. 2 c1425–1841 "To move (a ball, bowl, round body) by or as by rolling; to roll, bowl, trundle"] **esp C Atl**
In marble play: to roll a marble (rather than toss it); hence nouns *troll(er), tom-troller* a shooter.

1864 *Amer. Boy's Book* 33, There are three ways of shooting a marble. 1, *Trolling,* which consists in projecting the marble so that it rolls along the ground, until it strikes the marble at which it is aimed [etc]. *Ibid* 40, The player may either hoist, troll, or knuckle down, as suits him. **1968–70** *DARE* (Qu. EE6a, . . *Different kinds of marbles—the big one that's used to knock others out of the ring*) Inf **NJ**33, Trollers, tom-trollers—big, used as shooters; **PA**148, Troller; **PA**247, Troll; **NJ**18, Tom-troller. **1968** *DARE* Tape **DE**3, You could what we called *troll.* You could roll your marble up . . at any speed that you want. . . The fellow that trolled, he might not hit a marble first time, but he was in a better position to hit it than the boy that plucked and missed one . . because his marble laid wherever it rolled . . and his next shot, he would be closer to the ring.

troll n **chiefly MI** Cf **Yooper**
A person who lives in or is from Michigan's Lower Peninsula.

1994 *MI Hist.* 78.40, Most Americans outside of Michigan remain unaware of this tasty pastry loved by Yoopers and Trolls alike. **1999** in 2006 *DARE* File—Internet **nMI**, Troll: Anyone born in or willingly residing in the area of Michigan located below the Mackinaw [sic] Bridge. **2000** *DARE* File **nwMI** [Pamphlet from restaurant], *Troll:* Loper, a person living below the Mackinac Bridge. **2001** *Ibid* **nMI**, She says Yooper speech peculiarities are declining because of the influx of people from the Lower Peninsula called *trolls* or *transplants.* **2005** *MI Today* July (Internet), It's hard to imagine trolls and Yoopers going mano a mano about which part of Michigan is flatter than the other. **2006** *DARE* File **nMI**, The people that live in the Upper Peninsula . . are called "Yoopers" and are proud of it. The people that live under the [Mackinac] bridge are called "trolls."

troller See **troll** v

trolley n Also *trolley car* **widespread, but esp freq NEast** See Map and Map Section Cf **streetcar**
A public conveyance for passengers that usu runs on tracks on city streets and is powered by an overhead wire.

1890 *Herald–Despatch* (Decatur IL) 1 Nov [2]/1 (newspaperarchive.com), The storage battery makes the car . . free to go . . around any obstruction which would impede travel on the cable or trolley car. **1896** *DN* 1.426 **CT, NJ, NY, nOH**, *Trolley:* an electric street car. **1926** *Bridgeport Telegram* (CT) 22 Oct 9/3, Busses will replace the trolleys. **1937** *News* (Frederick MD) 31 July 10/1, Three modern busses today replaced the trolleys as the mode of transportation throughout Frederick. **1939** *LANE* Map 184 (*Trolley car*) **widespread throughout NEng**, Trolley (car). **c1955** Reed–Person *Ling. Atlas Pacific NW* (*Streetcar*) 4 infs, Trolley; 2 infs, Trolley car. **1965–70** *DARE* (Qu. N34, *An electric car that runs on tracks in a city*) 220 Infs, **widespread, but esp freq NEast**, Trolley; 146 Infs, **widespread, but esp freq NEast**, Trolley car; **CA**86, Trolley car . . old-fashioned. . . Streetcar [is] common name; **KY**76, Trolley ['trɒli] car; **KY**77, Trolley ['trɔli] car; **PA**247, Trolley car [FW: Philadelphia has elevated subway, underground subway, subway trolley, and street trolley.]; **IL**137, **LA**45, **MO**27, **OH**99, Trolley bus; **MA**125, Trackless trolley; **CA**35, Trackless trolley—like a bus, but with

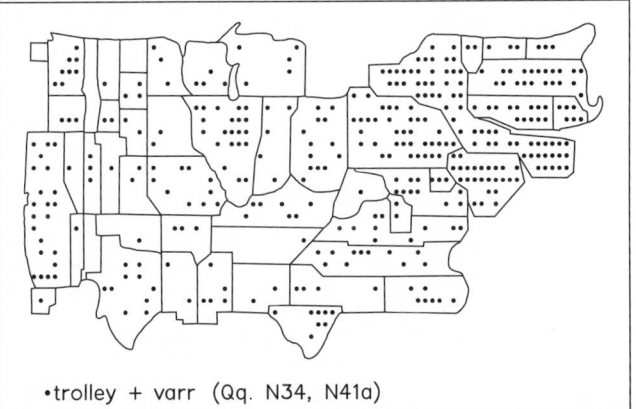

•trolley + varr (Qq. N34, N41a)

the trolley pole above; **DC**8, Electric trolley; (Qu. N41a, . . *Horse-drawn vehicles . . to carry people*) Infs **AL**26, **MO**14, **MA**122, Horse-drawn trolley; **MA**7, **NY**87, Trolley; **NY**63, Horse-drawn trolley car; **SC**66, Trolley car. **1967–70** *DARE* Tape **CA**184, The red trolley cars started in Los Angeles and ended up in Santa Monica, and Hollywood's gotten to be more or less on the way; **MA**8, Take a trolley, a trackless trolley that goes underground, into Park Street. **1973** Allen *LAUM* 1.382 **Upper MW** (as of c1950), 26 [of 437] infs, Trolley (car). [*DARE* Ed: 195 infs responded *streetcar.*] **1986** Pederson *LAGS Concordance* **Gulf Region,** 240 infs, Trolley(s); 130 infs, Trolley car(s); 3 infs, Trackless trolley(s); [2 infs, Trolley buses].

trolley bun n **NJ, PA**

1 A braided or twisted sweet roll.

1921 *Trenton Eve. Times* (NJ) 5 May 11/4, [Advt:] Those Famous Trolley Buns, Doz. . . 18c. **1931** *Clearfield Progress* (PA) 12 June 7/7, [Advt:] Trolley Buns—20c Doz. **1968** *DARE* FW Addit **Pennington NJ**, *Trolley buns*—long, plaited ['plætɪd] buns with sugar on top; in Perth Amboy [they] are called sugar buns. **2002** *DARE* File—Internet **sePA**, Although gone from the local business scene since the mid-1970's, the name . . still conjures up . . the smell and the taste of . . twisted trolley buns [etc]. **2005** *Ibid* **NJ**, Trolley buns. . . Anyone remember those? . . No trolley buns here in the Deep South. **2006** *Star–Ledger* (Newark NJ) 24 Feb (Internet), I really wanted to try the $4.99 fried dill pickles (dessert after the trolley buns and nachos?)

2 See quot.

1967 *DARE* (Qu. X3, *When a woman puts her hair up on her head in a bunch*) Inf **PA**53, Trolley bun.

trolley car See **trolley**

trolley park n **chiefly NEast, esp PA**
A park established at the end of a trolley line to attract weekend riders.

1900 *Fitchburg Daily Sentinel* (MA) 27 July 7/4, The two visited a trolley park near here [=New Bedford]. **1906** *Bucks Co. Gaz.* (Bristol PA) [28 June 3]/5 (newspaperarchive.com), The P., B. & T. "Electrics" will play the Algonquin Club again on Saturday at the trolley park above Tullytown. **1914** *Gettysburg Times* (PA) [18 July 3]/6 (newspaperarchive.com), [Advt:] *Western Maryland Railway*—Sunday Excursion *to Baltimore . . Visit Bay Shore . . The Beautiful Trolley Parks* [etc]. **1975** Gould *ME Lingo* 299, Present-day references to *trolley parks* are wholly reminiscent. **1981** *Valley Independent* (Monessen PA) 5 Aug 21/2, The property was renamed . . and turned into a trolley park. **2006** *DARE* File—Internet **CT**, [Headline:] Connecticut Theme Park is One of Only 11 Remaining Trolley Parks in the U.S. [*DARE* Ed: Of these 11, 5 are in Pennsylvania, 2 in New York, and 1 each in Connecticut, New Hampshire, Oregon, and West Virginia.]

trolling See **troll** v

trollock n Also *trollick* [*EDD trollock* "An old garment, esp. an old coat"] **eME**
Trash; worthless or unwanted material.

1901 Jewett in *Harper's Mth. Mag.* 104.45 **eME**, I ain't goin' to have . . [honey] full o' dry bark an' pine spills, dead bees, an' all them sorts o' trollick. **1927** *AmSp* 3.139 **eME**, "Old trollock" was applied to any trash or worthless stuff.

trollop v

1 also with *about, around;* To traipse around, gad about; hence ppl adj *trolloping.* Cf **strollop** v

1838 Campbell *Biog. Sketches* 141 **OH**, Another [woman] is always trolloping about, hunting a sweet-heart. **1856** Crippen *Green Peas* 101 **OH**, Ain't this a pretty time for young girls to be trolloping about on deck? **1859** Taliaferro *Fisher's R.* 52 **nwNC** (as of 1820s), Off I trolloped, and toddled about for some time. **1878** *Marion Daily Star* (OH) 18 Oct 1/3, Tickets be d—d! . . Get your ticket from the fellow you trolloped around with all day. **1879** *Daily Constitution* (Atlanta GA) 14 Jan [2]/4 (newspaperarchive.com), Instead of trolloping around with Ulysses, of Ulster, Noyes ought to be here to face Judge Cocke, of Florida. **1883** (1971) Harris *Nights with Remus* 52 **GA** [Black], He better be home lookin' atter de intruss er he fambly, 'stidder trapesin 'en trollopin' 'roun' ter all de frolics in de settlement. **1899** (1912) Green *VA Folk-Speech* 459, *Trollop*. . . To run hither and thither. **1909** *DN* 3.384 **eAL, wGA**, *Trollop*. . . To go romping about, go in a slovenly or slatternly way: chiefly used of women. **1926** *DN* 5.404 **Ozarks**, *Trollop*. . . I shore wouldn't let no gal o' mine go a-trollopin' 'round' that-a-way. **1932** *WI Rapids Daily Tribune* (WI) 25 Apr 4/6

Chicago IL, [Serial story:] Then Aunt Jessie began a tirade on . . those "trolloping girls you see on State street, all legs and lipstick." **1944** *PADS* 2.51 **cwNC,** *Trollop:* . . to go about a great deal. [**1952** Brown *NC Folkl.* 1.602 **c,eNC,** *Trollop.* . . To get around in a slovenly manner.]

2 To strike, beat; to outdo in a contest.

1842 Cooley *Amer. in Egypt* 147, [Caption:] Mrs. Wrinklebottom Trolloping the odious Pacha. [*DARE* Ed: Drawing shows a frowning woman writing a letter.] **1873** *Appletons' Jrl.* 9.410, He should be scathed in Maine, trolloped in Massachusetts, denounced in Connecticut, whipped in New York, pilloried in Philadelphia, and made to undergo everywhere else whatever punishment the ingenuity of men can devise. **1910** *Post-Std.* (Syracuse NY) 6 Apr 12/3, Flying Squirrel, the favorite [racehorse], trolloped his field home by many lengths. **1911** *DN* 3.548 **NE,** *Trollop.* . . Whip, strike. "He trolloped the horse good." Not common.

3 Of fabric: to draggle wetly; hence ppl adj *trolloped* sodden. [Scots dial]

1899 (1912) Green *VA Folk-Speech* 459, *Trollop.* . . To draggle, hang in a wet state. **1932** *Coshocton Tribune* (OH) 6 Sept 4/4 **NY,** I had to stagger for a mile thru a trolloped mush of wet earth.

trollop about (or around), trolloping See **trollop 1**

‡tromp n

1967 *DARE* FW Addit **seLA,** *Tromp* [trɑmp]—a white sweet potato raised for feeding stock, not raised for human consumption.

tromper n

One who compacts sheep fleece into a bag with the feet.

1940 Writers' Program *Guide NV* 78, During shearing season common terms are . . *wool tromper,* the man who presses the wool into sacks. **1941** Writers' Program *Guide WY* 241, The shearing crew, which travels from outfit to outfit, is composed of shearers, wranglers, herders, and a 'tromper.' *Ibid* 242, The tromper, his head usually below the rim of the sack, tromps five 9-pound fleeces into it at a time. **1992** Attebery *Sheep* 36 **swID, eOR,** The wool "tromper" is no longer employed here, although in Texas the tromper is still used, according to Phil Soulen.

trompetilla n [MexSpan for this and var other plants]

A low shrub *(Bouvardia ternifolia)* with clusters of long-tubed red flowers, native to Texas, New Mexico, and Arizona.

1935 Matschat *Mex. Plants* 219, *Bouvardia ternifolia, trompetilla,* is a handsome plant and often cultivated in North and South America. **1961** Wills–Irwin *Flowers TX* 214, *Bouvardia ternifolia.* . . Trompetilla flowers from July to September and is largely restricted to the mountains of the Trans-Pecos. **1967** *DARE* Wildfl QR (Wills–Irwin) Pl.49B Inf **TX44,** Trompetilla. **1970** Correll *Plants TX* 1486, *Bouvardia ternifolia.* . . Trompetilla. . . Corolla tube red. . . In dry soil, on rimrock or among boulders in mts. **2002** (acc) AZ State Univ. *Vascular Plant Herbarium* (Internet), *Bouvardia ternifolia* . . "Trompetilla or Clavillo".

trompillo n [MexSpan for this and var other plants; see quot 1892] **esp TX**

A **nightshade 1** (here: *Solanum elaeagnifolium*). Also called **bull nettle 2, Mexican nightshade, purple ~, silverleaf ~, nettle 2, poisonweed 3**

1886 Havard *Flora W. & S. TX for 1885* 512, *Solanum elaeagnifolium.* . . Trompillo. . . One of the most common of weeds in all valleys of Southern and Western Texas. **1892** *DN* 1.253 **TX,** *Trompillo:* a common weed. . . The berries . . are used for curdling milk. . . From the Spanish, a diminutive of *trompo,* a top. **1936** Whitehouse *TX Flowers* 128, *Purple Nightshade (Solanum elaeagnifolium)* is sometimes called . . "trompillo." **1967** *DARE* Wildfl QR (Wills–Irwin) Pl.37C Inf **TX44,** Trompillo. **c1979** TX Dept. Highways *Flowers* np, *Trompillo* displays silvery foliage, star-shaped lavender flowers and colorful berries. . . *Solanum elaeagnifolium.* **1999** Tull *Edible Plants TX* 275, Trompillo grows throughout the state and is particularly abundant in dry limestone and disturbed soils.

tronadora n [MexSpan, literally "thunderer," for *Tecoma stans* and var other plants]

1 A naturalized **tobacco B** (here: *Nicotiana glauca*).

1892 *DN* 1.247 **TX,** *Conetón:* an arborescent plant of the nightshade family, also called *tronadora. Nicotiana glauca.* **1931** U.S. Dept. Ag. *Misc. Pub.* 101.142, *Tree tobacco . . ,* known also as . . tronadora, is the only truly woody species of tobacco growing in the United States. **1961** Wills–Irwin *Flowers TX* 186, Mustard-tree, or Coneton, or Tronadora, as it is variously called, is presently known from three widely separated re-

gions in Texas, but undoubtedly is becoming quite general in the southern portion of the state. **2002** (acc) TX Univ.–El Paso *Chihuahuan Desert* (Internet), *Nicotiana glauca*—Tree Tobacco, Tronadora.

2 =**trumpet flower 1e.**

1970 Correll *Plants TX* 1444, *Tecoma stans.* . . Tronadora. . . Erect deciduous shrub. . . Flowers in terminal racemes or panicles; . . corolla bright-yellow. **2002** *DARE* File—Internet **SW,** Tecoma stans—Yellow bells/Tronadora.

troof See **truth**

troop duck n Cf **flock duck, raft ~ a, troopfowl** =**greater scaup.**

1895 Ridgway *Ornith. IL* 2.162, *Aythya marila nearctica.* . . *Popular synonyms.* . . Troop Duck. **1923** U.S. Dept. Ag. *Misc. Circular* 13.20 **MA,** *Greater Scaup Duck.* . . *Vernacular Names.* . . *In local use.* . . Troop duck, troop fowl.

troopfowl n Cf **flocking fowl, raft duck a, troop ~** The **greater scaup** or the **lesser scaup.**

1852 in 1876 *Forest & Stream* 7.212 **eMA,** *Fulix marila.* Troop fowl. **1955** MA Audubon Soc. *Bulletin* 39.315, *Greater Scaup Duck.* . . Troop Fowl (Mass. As a characteristically flocking species.) *Ibid* 316, *Lesser Scaup Duck.* . . Troop Fowl (Mass. Same reference.)

troot See **truth**

trophe See **throat**

trot n

1 =**dogtrot.**

c1937 in 2007 Fox *Country Houses* 268 **TX,** Entrance is not through a front door but an open-air "dogtrot" passage . . (in Staub's plans this passage is labeled a "trot"). **1944** Howard *Walkin' Preacher* 59 **Ozarks,** The chinked, hewn logs of the two original houses still showed: the ceiling and floor were wood and the two relatively new walls that enclosed the former "trot" had been covered with roll building paper of the kind that bears huge two-color flowers. **1990** Morgan *Log House* 31 **eTN,** An open passageway or "trot" was left between the two pens.

‡2 See quot.

1960 Williams *Walk Egypt* 18 **GA,** John Goforth supplied his customers with empty cans for spit-cups . . and Trot—soda crackers and peanuts parched together on the wood stove (and making for active use of the outhouse).

3 See **trotline n 1.**

4 See **trots.**

troth See **trough A2**

trotline n

1 also *trot:* A long fishing line to which a number of shorter lines with baited hooks are attached, the long line usually being anchored at each end and left unattended. [Though attested slightly earlier, presumably from Engl dial *trot* in same sense; see quot 1843] **chiefly Gulf States, W Midl, Cent, TX, SC** See Map Cf **outline, setline, throw line, troutline**

1825 *Amer. Jrl. Science* 10.325 **OH,** The greater quantity [of fish] . . are taken in the spring months, by setting a line, called a *"trot line,"* where the water is tolerably still and deep: this line is usually from forty to sixty yards in length, the middle supported by buoys, and the two ends kept at the bottom by stones; to this line are attached a large number of hooks, baited with crayfish or minnies. **1835** Audubon *Ornith. Biog.* 3.123 **nwKY,** A trot-line is one of considerable length and thickness . . varying according to the extent of water, and the size of the fish you expect to catch. **1841** in 1953 Lincoln *Coll. Wks.* 1.260 **IL,** The negroes were strung together precisely like so many fish upon a trot-line. [**1843** Bellamy *Housekeeper's Guide* 104 **swEngland,** *Spiller* or *Trot.*—This is a modification of the Bulter [*DARE* Ed: =a long line with many hooks].] **1884** U.S. Natl. Museum *Bulletin* 27.918 **Chesapeake Bay,** An India-ink drawing showing two Chesapeake negroes in an old-fashioned boat engaged in fishing a trot-line which has been set for crabs. One is hauling the line while the other uses the dip-net to secure the crab before it has let go of the bait. **1903** *DN* 2.335 **seMO,** *Trot-line.* . . A long fishing line to which short lines are attached. The lines are usually set over night and are sometimes called 'set-lines.' Hooks are attached to the short lines. **1907** *DN* 3.237 **nwAR,** *Trot-line.* **1909** *DN* 3.384 **eAL, wGA,** *Trot-line.* **1965–70** *DARE* (Qu. P13, . . *Ways of fishing . . besides the ordinary hook and line*) 195 Infs, **chiefly Gulf States, W Midl, Cent, TX, SC,** Trotline; **NC53,** Set trotline; **AL53,**

IL115, **NJ**21, Trot; (Qu. P17, . . *When . . people fish by lowering a line and sinker close to the bottom of the water*) Infs **CA**211, **IN**73, **MS**1, **VA**8, 22, Trotline(s); **TN**53, Trotline fishing.   **1966–70** *DARE* Tape **AR**36, [Inf:] I did most of my fishing at night. Was for catfish, a trotline. I'd sometimes put out three, four lines. Bait was live bait, perch, minnows. . . [FW:] How many hooks do these trotlines have? [Inf:] I generally put out about fifty-five, fifty to fifty-five, sometimes sixty if there's a wide place in the river. Generally about fifty hooks; **FL**16, Most of the fishing in this area is done by trotlines; **OH**58, Well, a trotline, . . when you fish 'em in the river, they generally put two weights, one on each end. The line'll be a hundred and fifty, two hundred foot long, and they'll stretch it out in the river, so they would drop the one at the shore first, then they row out in the river and put the other one, stretch the line and drop the other rock in; **IN**45, We . . put a trotline out, caught a gar about three feet long; **VA**47, There was a day and time round here when they used trotlines. That's a line with a lot of baits on it, maybe a mile of it in length.   **1986** Pederson *LAGS Concordance* **Gulf Region,** 15 infs, Trotline(s); 1 inf, Trotline fishing.   **1999** Haynes *Mother of Pearl* 177 **MS,** The teenager had been hooked in the ear by the last hook of the trot line set out two days earlier.   **2000** Shores *Tangier Is.* 113 **Chesapeake Bay,** The trotline and scrape, both relatively simple in technique and equipment, have been around since the last quarter of the nineteenth century.

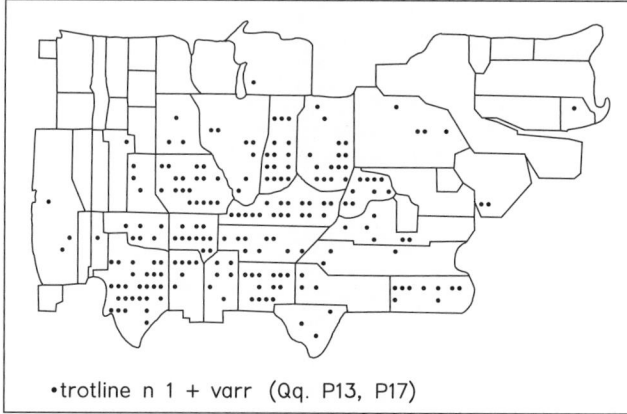

•trotline n 1 + varr (Qq. P13, P17)

2 Transf: see quots.

1941 Vestal *Short Grass Country* 290 **nTX,** In one of these towns where there was no jailhouse, prisoners were kept on a "trotline". . . A drill cable was strung between big timbers planted in the earth and the prisoners chained to the cable.   **1994** Hill *H.L. & Lyda* 75 **TX,** Being escorted away in chains to be brought to justice almost compared favorably to being kept on the trotline.

trotline v

To fish using a **trotline n 1;** hence n *trotliner;* vbl n *trotlining.*

1900 IN Comm. Fisheries & Game *Biennial Rept. 1899–1900* 10, Many members of the Legislature were pledged to introduce measures repealing all laws against seining and trot-lining.   **1903** U.S. Supreme Court *State MO vs. State IL & Sanitary Dist. Chicago* 4.3201 **cwIL,** This year I trot-lined.   **1936** *Eve. Tribune* (Albert Lea MN) 17 June 13/4, There is a ready market for these fish, caught mostly by rivermen who make their living by netting, jugging, and trotlining cats and other rough fish.   **1953** *Atchison Daily Globe* (KS) 16 Aug 5/1, The successful trotliner knows these habits and fishes accordingly.   **1968** *DARE* (Qu. P17, . . *When . . people fish by lowering a line and sinker close to the bottom of the water*) Inf **IN**13, Trotlining.   **1976** Warner *Beautiful Swimmers* 148 **Chesapeake Bay,** I was also eager to see trotlining, the classical method of taking Chesapeake crabs for over a century before the introduction of pots. *Ibid,* Eastern Bay and all its tributaries are . . the special province of trotliners.   **2004** *DARE* File—Internet **MD,** I've been trotlining since 1972.   **2006** *Ibid* **eVA** (as of c1920s), Everybody was trotlining then, because the crab pot hadn't been invented.

trots n pl   Rarely *trot*   [*OED2* 1808 →]   Cf **backdoor trot, mountain trots, runs**

Usu with *the:* An attack of diarrhea or frequent urination.

1900 *DN* 2.68 [College slang], *Trot.* . . In plural, diarrhœa.   **1909** *DN* 3.384 **eAL, wGA,** *Trots.* . . Diarrhea. Also *back-door trots.*   **1912** *DN* 3.592 **wIN,** *Trots.* . . Diarrhea.   **1937** Sandoz *Slogum* 85 **NE** (as of 1900–20), He said he had summer complaint. . . [but] Old Tit-Ear was scared into the trots by the Bullard business, filling his pants like a

damned tenderfoot.   **1945** *PADS* 3.9 **CT,** To have the trots. *Ibid* **SC,** *Trots* the only form I have heard here; common.   **1965–70** *DARE* (Qu. BB19, *Joking names for looseness of the bowels*) 227 Infs, **widespread,** Trots; **VA**18, Trots—when we lived in the country and had to use the garden house; **TX**11, 62, Trot; (Qu. BB20, *Joking names or expressions for overactive kidneys*) 21 Infs, **scattered,** Trots; **TX**62, Trot.   **1980** *Jrl. Amer. Folkl.* 93.44, [Boy Scout song:] Oh, it's pans and pots, that give us all the trots.   **1984** *MJLF* 10.159 **cnWI,** *Trots.* Diarrhea, of both animals or humans. Also called in Maine "backdoor trots", from "back house" or "privy".   **1990** Cavender *Folk Med. Lexicon* 33 **sAppalachians,** (The) *trots*—diarrhea.

trotter n

=**hermit thrush 1.**

1955 *Oriole* 20.1.11 **GA,** Hermit Thrush. . . Trotter.

trotting harness n   Also *trotting riggings*

One's good or best clothing.

1862 *Indiana Democrat* (PA) 17 July [5]/7 (newspaperarchive.com), [Comic sermon:] Did you come from the race track of the world to parade your "trotting harness" before the meek and lowly?   **1872** *Janesville Gaz.* (WI) 27 June [2]/2 (newspaperarchive.com), Frank Hatch took off his "Old Cushman" clothes, put on his trotting harness, and went back to the scene of his successful labors.   **1888** Herndon–Weik *Herndon's Lincoln* 477 **IL** (as of 1860), Mr. Lincoln . . returned with the report that "She will be down as soon as she has all her trotting harness on."   **1892** *KS Univ. Qrly.* 1.100 **KS,** *Trottin'-riggin's:* best suit of clothes.   **1968** *DARE* (Qu. W37, *When a woman puts on her good clothes and tries to look her best . . she's _____*) Inf **OH**49, Got on her trotting harness; (Qu. W43, . . *Joking words . . for clothes in general*) Inf **MD**17, Trotting harness.   **1984** Wilder *You All Spoken Here* 95 **Sth,** *She's got her trottin' harness on:* She's ready to go and ready for most anything.

troubling stick n

=**battling stick.**

1999 Morgan *Gap Creek* 60 **NC,** I dumped the dirty long handles in and stirred them with the troubling stick, then let them boil for a minute and lifted them out with the stick and dumped them smoking on the wash table.

trough n   Usu |trɔf, traf|; for varr see **A** below

A Forms.

1 |trɔft|; pronc-spp *troft, trawft, trough(f)t.*   **scattered, but esp Sth, Midl**   See Map on p. 720   Cf Intro "Language Changes" I.8, **cliff, skift** n[1], n[2]   Note: While the expected pl *trofts* does occur, it appears that many speakers have [t] only in the sg.

1655 in 1916 MA (Colony) Probate Court (Essex Co.) *Records* 1.204, Wood and a troft and pales, 3s.   **1836** in 1885 Strong *Hist. Terr. WI* 232, We have envited the gentlemen to come up to the troft, and argy the question on its merits.   **1847** in 1927 Jones *FL Plantation Rec.* 309 **nwFL,** 4 [hands] at the gin, 4 [hands] dig horse troughft.   **1893** Shands *MS Speech* 64, *Trawft* [trɔft]. Negro and illiterate white for trough.   **1903** *DN* 2.335 **seMO,** Troft.   **1907** *DN* 3.237 **nwAR,** I made a horse trought this morning.   **1909** *DN* 3.384 **eAL, wGA,** Troft.   **1915** *DN* 4.192 **swVA,** Troft.   **1917** *DN* 4.418 **wNC, KY,** Troft.   **1939** *LANE* Map 208 (*Trough; troughs*) 1 inf, **csNH,** [trɔft; trɔvz]; 1 inf, **swME,** [trɔft; trɔfs]; 1 inf, **swCT,** [trɔf; trɔfts].   **1944** *PADS* 2.26 **cwNC, cwOH,** *Troft* [trɔft]: A trough.   **1965–70** *DARE* (Qu. K59, *What do pigs eat out of?*) 53 Infs, **scattered, but esp Sth, Midl,** (Hog *or* slop) troft [proncs of the type [trɔft]]; 14 Infs, **scattered,** Troft [no pronc recorded]; **OH**80, **PA**71, [traft]; **VA**38, [trɔvt]; **KY**9, [trɔft], pl [trɔz]; **KY**39, Troft, pl [trɔfs]; **KY**76, [trɔft], pl [trɔfs]; **KY**90, [trɔft], pl [trɔvz]; **MN**3, Pl [trafts]; (Qu. D28, *What hangs below the edge of the roof to carry off rain-water?*) 30 Infs, **scattered,** (Eaves, eave, rain, cistern, etc) troft; **MO**19, **OK**1, Eaves (*or* cistern) trofts; (Qu. D29, *The pipe that takes the collected rain-water down to the ground or to a storage tank*) Inf **TN**49, Troft; (Qu. O2, *Nicknames . . for an old, clumsy boat*) Inf **KY**86, Cow troft.   **1966** *Wilson Coll.* **csKY,** Often trough is [trɔft], with [trɔvz] as plural.   **1968** *DARE* Tape **GA**48, He had. . . a tan troft. . . That's where he tanned the leather.   **1972** *Odessa Amer.* (TX) 22 June sec A 13/1, Everyone who wants can now feed at the public troft.   **1983** [see **B1** below].   **1989** Pederson *LAGS Tech. Index* 134 **Gulf Region,** [For the sg, 733 infs gave proncs of the type [trɔf] (or the minor variant [traf]); the next most frequent were proncs of the type [trɔft] (rarely [traft]), with 149 infs. Pl forms with [t], by contrast, were very rare; only 8 were recorded.]   **2006** *DARE* File—Internet **MO,** I have a Ideal Watering troft that I have been saving and I just don't have the room for it anymore.

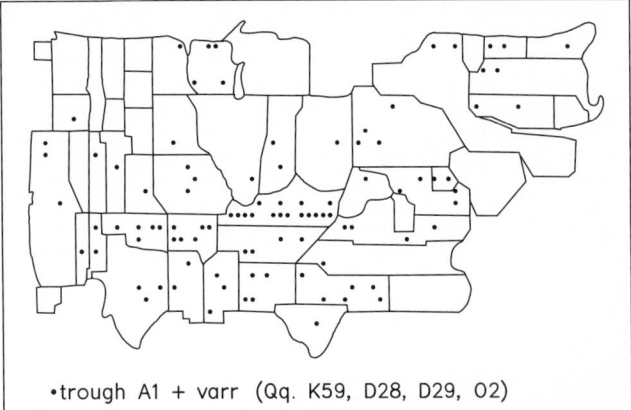

•trough A1 + varr (Qq. K59, D28, D29, O2)

2 |trɔθ|; pronc-spp *troth, trawth, trouth.* **scattered, but esp NEast** See Map Note: The corresponding plural is usu |trɔθs| or |trɔðz|, but other forms that may belong also with other singulars occur, esp |trɔz|.

1844 *Daily Picayune* (New Orleans LA) 16 Jan 1/6, She [=a woman from Massachusetts]'s got *every thing* that ever was perduced for sich pupposes. . . kittels, pots, a jonny-cake board, troth to mix rine-injin bread in. **1891** *DN* 1.166 **cNY**, [trɔθ]. **1903** *DN* 2.292 **Cape Cod MA** (as of 1850s), Consonantal changes appear in *trouth = trough.* **1916** *DN* 4.330 **KS**, *Trough.* . . Like *troth* and *trawth.* **1917** *DN* 4.402 **neOH**, *Troth* [trɔθ]. **1937** *AmSp* 12.126 **Upstate NY**, *Trough* occurs 53 times with [f], 51 times with [θ]. **1939** *LANE* Map 208 *(Trough; troughs),* [**Throughout NEng** the predominant pronc is of the type [trɔθ]; it occurs more than twice as frequently as [trɔf]. The corresponding plural is regularly [trɔðz] or, less than half as often, [trɔθs]. Other plurals that occasionally correspond to the singular form [trɔθ] are [trɔz] (10 infs, **wNEng**), [trɔs] (2 infs, **ceMA**), [trɔfs] (1 inf, **swCT**), [trɔvz] (1 inf, **swCT**), and [trɔð] (1 inf, **neMA**). [trɔvz] and [trɔfs] of course are also regularly the plurals corresponding to [trɔf]; [trɔz] also occurs occasionally as a plural to [trɔf]—as do a few instances of [trɔðz, trɔθs].] **1965–70** *DARE* (Qu. K59, *What do pigs eat out of?*) 142 Infs, **scattered, but esp NEast,** (Hog *or* pig) troth; **VA**10, [trɔð]; **VA**70, [trɒð]; **NY**102, 117, Troth, pl [trɔðz]; **VT**16, [trɔθ], pl [trɔːz]; **MO**15, 26, Pl [tɹɒθs]; (Qu. D28, *What hangs below the edge of the roof to carry off rain-water?*) 49 Infs, **chiefly sNEng, Upstate NY, MI,** (Eave, eaves, *or* rain) troth; **NY**107, Eave ~; **KY**52, Lead [trɔθs]; **MO**9, Leave [trɔθs]; (Qu. D29, *The pipe that takes the collected rain-water down to the ground or to a storage tank*) Inf **KY**52, Lead troths; **NY**215, Eaves [trat]; (Qu. O16, . . *The stirred-up water following a boat*) Inf **NY**117, Troth. **1968** *DARE* FW Addit **NY**88, *Troth or pig troth* [trɔθ], plural *troths* [trɔðz]. **1989** Pederson *LAGS Tech. Index* 134 **Gulf Region,** [18 infs gave proncs of the type [trɔθ], 1 of the type [traθ], for the singular; 13 infs gave plurals of the types [trɔθs, trɔðz], 1 of the type [trɔθ].] **2004** *DARE* File—Internet **CT,** Put heated water troths with automatic waterers in each pasture and paddock. **2006** *Ibid* **TX,** All three of these troths have been replaced. **2006** *DARE* File **nwMA** (as of 1960s–70s), When I was growing up we lived in a two story house, three stories in back because of the hill. It was so difficult to get up to the eaves troths [trɔθs] to clean them out that we hardly ever did it.

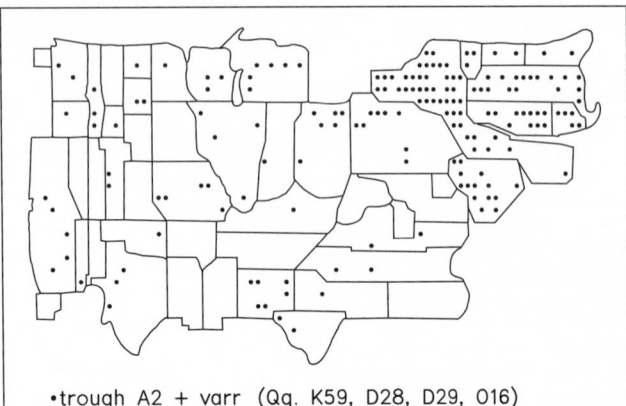

•trough A2 + varr (Qq. K59, D28, D29, O16)

3 |tro|; pronc-sp *trow.* Note: This pronc is largely confined to the sense "a vessel for holding bread dough." The sp *trow* is ambiguous, and the early quots given here may belong instead at **A4** below.

1678 in 1920 **MA** (Colony) Probate Court (Essex Co.) *Records* 3.228, Kneading Trow, 2 sives & 3 cheirs, 8s. 6d. **1683** in 1947 Hazen *Hazen Family* 22 **MA,** It: Six barrells. sydar press & trow & buckett. **1937** *AmSp* 12.107 **IA, NE, SD,** *Trough.* Walter Seiler of Grand Island, Nebraska, tells me that in the bakery in which he worked the word was always pronounced *tro,* rhyming with 'though' and 'dough.' His father, who has worked in bakeries in Nebraska, South Dakota, and Iowa for about thirty years, says that in all of them the word was pronounced with the long close vowel and no final consonant. Inquiry among others who have worked in bake shops brought testimony to the same effect. **1949** *Middletown Times Herald* (NY) 4 Feb 8/1, The conveyance is known as a dough trough, and the word trough is pronounced in the trade to rhyme with dough. **1995** *Brophy Coll.* 78 **swMO** (as of c1960), *Trough.* [O]ften rhymed with "dough." "[D]ough-trough."

4 |trau|. **scattered, but esp NEast**

1936 *AmSp* 11.309 **Upstate NY,** *Trough* usually occurs as [trɔf], [trɔθ], [trɒf], or [trɒθ], but occasionally, and in circumstances which make a spelling pronunciation unlikely, as [trau]. **1939** *LANE* Map 208 *(Trough; troughs)* 1 inf, **swME,** [træˇw], pl. [træˇwz] [inf has heard]. **1968** *DARE* (Qu. K59, *What do pigs eat out of?*) Inf **NY**80, [trau] *or* [trɔf]. **1979** *DARE* File **ceNY,** *Trough* [trau]. . . I would have used the word in combination with "eaves" . . and "watering" . . for the few horses still in town when I was a child. *Ibid* **wVT,** *Trough* [trau]—to rime with "plough." *Ibid* **CO,** *Trough* [trau]; context: feeding pigs. . . Until about 10 years ago he lived in New York City. **1989** Pederson *LAGS Tech. Index* 134 **Gulf Region,** [4 infs gave proncs of the type [trau] for the sg; 4 gave proncs of the type [trauz] for the pl.]

5 |trɔ|; pronc-sp *traw.* [Prob back-formation from [trɔz] as reduced form of [trɔvz] or [trɔðz]; see **A2** above]

1914 *DN* 4.114 **cKS,** *Trough* [trɔ·]. **1938** *AmSp* 13.238 **NE,** Ruth Odell reports that . . the pronunciation *traw* is sometimes heard, as recently in her presence from a farmhand. **1939** *LANE* Map 208 *(Trough; troughs)* 2 infs, **csMA,** [trɔ(·)]. **1968–69** *DARE* (Qu. K59, *What do pigs eat out of?*) Inf **NJ**45, [trɔ]; **KY**29, [trɔz] [*DARE* Ed: prob pl]. **1989** Pederson *LAGS Tech. Index* 134 **Gulf Region,** [5 infs gave proncs of the types [trɔ, trɑ] for the sg; 4 gave proncs of the type [trɔ] for the pl.]

6 Addit varr.

1939 *LANE* Map 208 *(Trough; troughs)* 1 inf, **swMA,** [tɹʌʊθ]. **1966–68** *DARE* (Qu. K59, *What do pigs eat out of?*) Inf **IA**32, [trauðz]; **NY**200, [traut]; **WI**71, [trɔs] [*DARE* Ed: prob pl]; **NC**30, Trofths [trɔfθs]; **MI**40, **OK**53, Truff. **1989** Pederson *LAGS Tech. Index* 134 **Gulf Region,** [7 infs gave proncs of the type [trauf] for the sg; 3 infs, [trauf(s), trauvz] for the pl; 6 infs gave proncs of the type [trof(s)]; 2 infs, [troθ]; 1 inf, [troft]; 1 inf, [trovž]; 1 inf, [trovš]; 1 inf, [trɔðz]; 4 infs gave proncs of the types [træv(z)] as pl; 2 infs, [trɔt]; 1 inf, [trɔfθ].]

B Senses.

1 =**eaves trough.** Cf **cistern trough, gutter** n[1] **1, lead trough, leave ~**

1955 *PADS* 23.42 **e,cSC, eNC, seGA,** *Troughs, water troughs—*'gutters.' **1965–70** *DARE* (Qu. D28, *What hangs below the edge of the roof to carry off rain-water?*) 27 Infs, **scattered, but esp west of Missip R,** Trough(s); **FL**31, **IN**12, **KY**40, **ME**1, **MS**72, **TX**35, **WI**58, Troft; **AL**1, **CT**39, **NY**31, 34, **VT**16, Troth; (Qu. D29, *The pipe that takes the collected rain-water down to the ground or to a storage tank*) Infs **AR**56, **LA**15, **NE**11, **TX**94, Trough; **TN**49, Troft. **1983** *MJLF* 9.1.59 **ceKY** (as of 1956), *Trought* . . a gutter.

2 In marble play: see quot. Cf **cow pathies**

c1970 Wiersma *Marbles Terms, Trough* /trɔf/—relates to a specific game in which three paths, or troughs, lead to the pot.

trough(f)t See **trough A1**

trout n

1 Any of var often anadromous fishes of the family Salmonidae, as:

a Std: an introduced freshwater fish *(Salmo trutta).* [*OED2* at *trout* sb.[1] 1.a c1050 →] For other names see **brown trout 1**

b Std: a fish of the genus *Salvelinus* or *Oncorhynchus.* For other names of var of these see **brook trout, cutthroat ~, Dolly Varden 1, Gila trout 2, lake ~ 1, rainbow ~, siscowet**

2 Any of var fishes that resemble **1** above in some way, as:

a =**black bass 1. Sth, S Midl**

[**1587** (1964) Laudonnière *Notable Hist.* (transl. Hakluyt) 5 **FL**, They loaded vs with troutes, greate mullets, plaise, turbuts and marueilous store of other sortes of fishes altogether different from ours.] **1772** in 1924 Phillips *Notes B. Romans* 123 **wFL**, The Rivers have in Common with those of Europe the Sturgeon, the Eel, the Pike, the Chab [sic] or Chevin, here Miscalled a Trout. **1842** DeKay *Zool. NY* 4.26, *Grystes salmoides* [=*Micropterus s.*] . . In Carolina, it attains a length of two feet, is considered as excellent food, and passes under the name of *Trout*. **1878** U.S. Natl. Museum *Bulletin* 12.15 **SE**, *Micropterus*. . . We collected none in the Saluda or Ennoree, but we were told that "Trout", as the species of *Micropterus* are universally called in the South, are frequently taken there. **1897** *Outing* 30.217, In the South, he [=the black bass] is commonly called "trout". **1929** *AmSp* 5.20 **Ozarks**, *Trout*. . . The small-mouth black bass. There are no true trout in the Ozarks, except a few rainbows which have been introduced in recent years. **1948** Hurston *Seraph* 2 **wFL**, They knew that there were plenty of black bass, locally known as trout, in the Suwanee. **1954** *Harder Coll.* **cwTN**, Trout. . . The smallmouth black bass (*Micropterus dolomieu*). **c1960** *Wilson Coll.* **csKY**, Trout. . . A bass, esp. the small-mouthed black bass. **1967–68** *DARE* Tape **GA**20, It's a regular black bass. . . We always called 'em trout; **LA**5, We call 'em trout around here and then further on north in Baton Rouge and all, they call 'em a bass. **1967** *DARE* FW Addit **LA**, "I caught German carp and some trout, but I gave 'em away 'cause I couldn't use 'em all." (Not many people use the term *bass*.)

b =**weakfish**, esp *Cynoscion nebulosus* or *C. regalis*. **chiefly Sth**

1873 in 1878 Smithsonian Inst. *Misc. Coll.* 14.2.26, *Cynoscion regalis*. . . Trout (*southern coast*). **1884** *Century Illustr. Mag.* 27.908 **Sth**, The name of "trout" is also applied in the South to a salt-water fish called "squeteague". **1907** NJ State Museum *Annual Rept. for 1906* 178, *Cynoscion nebulosus*. . . Reported to occur in the pounds occasionally at Barnegat Pier, and known as "trout." **1939** Natl. Geogr. Soc. *Fishes* 82, *Cynoscion regalis*. . . from Chesapeake Bay southward is known only as trout or gray trout. **1951** Taylor *Surv. Marine Fisheries NC* 127, *Cynoscion nebulosus*. . . has a wider distribution than the gray trout [=*C. regalis*]. . . Both species are . . important in North Carolina, where they are usually called trout, the names weakfish and squeteague being more common to the north. **1965–66** *DARE* Tape **FL**14, [FW:] What do they go out for? [Inf:] Mullet and trout and redfish; **FL**22, You get mullet, flounders, trout, croakers, redfish—all kinds of fish. **1986** Pederson *LAGS Concordance (Fish)* 18 infs, **Gulf Region**, Trout [infs indicate this is a saltwater fish]. **2004** in 2011 *DARE* File—Internet **FL**, We had some really good trout action on the flats with 2–4′ of water and landed quite a few 4–6lb fish. . . While targeting trout in these areas we also were rewarded with a nice bonus of Flounder.

c A chub of the genus *Gila*, usu **bonytail, roundtail 1a**, or *G. nigrescens*. **SW** Cf **Gila trout 1, Verde ~**

1846 in 1848 Emory *Notes Reconnoissance* 58 **sNM**, It [=the Mimbres River] is a rapid, dashing stream. . . filled with trout. **1889** (1971) Farmer *Americanisms* 541, *Trout*. . . In the Rio Azul of western New Mexico, and in many other pure streams where the real fish does not exist, the *trout* is a dace. **1996** in 2002 *DARE* File—Internet **SW**, Througout [sic] the southwest chubs are often referred to as "trout". The Chihuahua chub has been referred to as the "Gila trout" and "sucker".

d =**peamouth.**

1902 Jordan–Evermann *Amer. Fishes* 73, In the Snake River this minnow [=*Mylocheilus caurinus*] is one of the most abundant fishes, and is locally known by the misleading names "fresh-water herring" and "whitefish," and, at one place, they are even called trout.

trout bird n

=**golden plover.**

1888 Trumbull *Names of Birds* 196 **MA**, Mr. Henry P. Ives, of Salem, tells of its [=the golden plover's] being known as *trout-bird* at Hamilton, Mass.

trout-fish n [Redund for *trout;* cf Intro "Language Changes" I.4] **formerly widespread, now esp Sth, S Midl**

1763 in 1862 De Voe *Market Book* 1.144 **NYC**, For *trout fish*, or *tom cod, one shilling* by the dozen. **1809** *Balance & NY State Jrl.* (Albany) 8 Dec 3/5, [Advt:] 10 Bls. Pickled Trout Fish. **1855** *Suppl. Courant*

20.221 **NY**, Can any one tell me how long a trout fish will live? *Ibid*, One day he brought up a trout fish about the size of a man's little finger, in his whisky jug. **1918** Mulford *Man from Bar-20* 103 **West**, That was a spark what you saw, an' th' musical flop was a trout fish turnin' cartwheels on th' water. **1952** Brown *NC Folkl.* 1.602, *Trout-fish*. Trout.—West. **1974** *Post-Crescent* (Appleton WI) 17 Nov mag sec 6/3 (newspaperarchive.com) **KY**, Langlade County was settled at that time with Kentuckians. . . The "Kaintucks" wanted trout for Christmas. . . Mac . . reached into Jess's [=a Kentuckian's] bag and pulled out a trout. "I said Jus come home, huh, trying to get yourself some trout fish, huh?" **1986** Pederson *LAGS Concordance (Fish)* 9 infs, **Gulf Region**, Troutfish. **2006** (acc) College Sta. TX *City of College Sta.* (Internet), The Texas Parks and Wildlife Department will make four more stockings of trout fish at the small pond at Central Park.

trout flower See **trout lily**

trout fly n [*OED2* 1744–50 → for caddis fly]

1 A **mayfly 1** or similar insect.

1967 *DARE* (Qu. R4, *A large winged insect that hatches in summer in great numbers around lakes or rivers, crowds around lights, lives only a day or so, and is good fish bait*) Inf **CO**37, Trout flies.

2 A **midge 1**. Cf **lake fly 2**

1968 *DARE* (Qu. R10, *Very small flies that don't sting, often seen hovering in large groups or bunches outdoors in summer*) Inf **NY**92, Trout flies—hatch over streams.

trouth See **trough A2**

trout lily n Also *trout flower* [See quot 1964]

=**dogtooth violet.**

1893 Parsons *How Know Wild Flowers* 116, Mr. [John] Burroughs has suggested. . . "trout lily," which has a spring-like flavor not without charm. **1894** *Jrl. Amer. Folkl.* 7.101 **NY**, *Erythronium Americanum*, trout-flower (local). **1900** Lyons *Plant Names* 151, *E[rythronium] Americanum*. . . Trout Lily. **1933** Small *Manual SE Flora* 292, *Erythronium*. . . Trout-lilies. **1959** Barnes *Nat. Hist. Wasatch Winter* 96 **UT**, In a dense oak copse we unexpectedly come upon a bed of Easter bells, yellow dog tooth's violets, . . or trout lilies as they are variously called (*Erythronium grandiflorum parviflorum*). **1964** Campbell et al. *Gt. Smoky Wildflowers* 72, *Trout Lily—Erythronium americanum*. . . The mottling of the 6 to 8-inch leaves suggest [sic] the speckled trout of the mountain streams. . . Cherokee Indians regarded the flowering season of this lily as the time to fish for trout. **1965–70** *DARE* (Qu. S11, . . *Dogtooth violet*) 15 Infs, 14 **Nth**, Trout lily (*or* lilies); (Qu. S3, *A flower like a large violet with a yellow center and small ragged leaves—it comes up early in spring on open, stony hilltops*) Inf **PA**70, Trout lily. **1966–68** *DARE* Wildfl QR Pl.15A Infs **NH**4, **NY**91, **OR**12, **SC**41, **WA**12, **WI**35, 80, Trout lily. **1987** *Nature Conserv. News* 37.3.28 **MN**, This . . bottomland on the Zumbro River shelters the dwarf trout lily (*Erythronium propullans*). **2002** *DARE* File—Internet, One of the most noticeable and abundant eastern wildflowers of spring is the Trout Lily.

troutline n [Folk-etym for **trotline**] **chiefly Midl, Missip Valley** See Map

=**trotline** n **1.**

1857 WI State Hist. Soc. *Coll.* 3.240, He was once setting trout-lines under the ice on the border of Lake Michigan. **1876** *Appletons' Jrl.* 15.78, He took from his pocket a long piece of a "trout-line"—a heavy

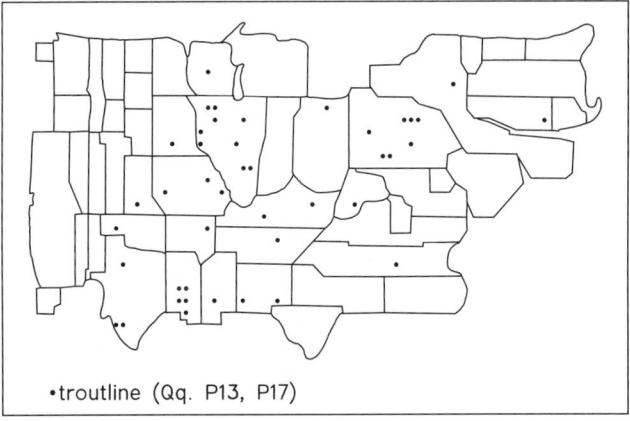

•troutline (Qq. P13, P17)

fishing-line made to hold forty or fifty hooks a yard apart. **1912** *DN* 3.592 **wIN**, *Trout-line. . . A trot-line. Trout-line* has grown from the belief that there was something incorrect about *trot-line.* The line, of course, is not used in catching trout. **1965–70** *DARE* (Qu. P13, . . *Ways of fishing . . besides the ordinary hook and line*) 41 Infs, **chiefly Midl, Missip Valley**, Troutline; (Qu. P17, . . *When . . people fish by lowering a line and sinker close to the bottom of the water*) Infs **IL29, 78**, Troutline. **1968** *DARE* Tape **IN36**, Close to the bridge, fellows will come and they'll put in throw lines and troutlines and fish all night; **WI75**, A troutline, you generally put a little weight on it and throw it out and then you have . . hooks on a kind of a trolley, like. . . That's mostly like for fishing off piers and that. **2005** *DARE* File—Internet **TX**, When I was a kid many years back, I used to callem troutlines. I used to wonder why as none ever seemd to catch any trout on them. **2007** *NY Times* (NY) 28 July sec A 8/4 **csIL**, Anyone can throw a trout line in the river and hang a perch on it.

trout-perch n

1 A **black bass 1.**

1820 *Western Rev.* 2.52, *Fishes of the River Ohio. . . Trout River-bass. Lepomis Salmonea* [=*Micropterus dolomieu*]. . . Vulgar names White Trout, Brown Trout, Trout Pearch [etc]. **1883** *Century Illustr. Mag.* 26.376, Indeed, the large-mouthed bass received its first scientific, specific name from a drawing and description of a Carolina bass sent to Lacépède under the local name of trout, or trout-perch, who accordingly named it *salmoides,* meaning trout-like. **1888** *Wildwood's Mag.* June 64, In southern Virginia the large-mouthed bass is known as "chub," as in North Carolina it is called "white salmon," "welchman," or "trout-perch." **1935** Caine *Game Fish* 7, *Small-mouthed Black Bass. . . Synonyms:* Bass . . Mountain Trout . . Trout Perch.

2 A fish of the genus *Percopsis,* usu *P. omiscomaycus.* [See quot 1956] Also called **sand roller;** for other names of *P. omiscomaycus* see **grounder minnow esp Gt Lakes**

1882 U.S. Natl. Museum *Bulletin* 16.322, *Percopsis. . . Trout Perch. . . P. guttatus* [=*P. omiscomaycus*]. . . Delaware River to Kansas and northward; abundant in the Great Lakes. **1908** Forbes–Richardson *Fishes of IL* 225, *Trout-Perch. . .* Atlantic slope and Great Lake region, in clear cold waters. **1943** Eddy–Surber *N. Fishes* 177, *Troutperch—Percopsis omiscomaycus. . .* Although this fish . . bears a general superficial resemblance to a perch or to a small walleye, it may be distinguished from these species by the presence of an adipose fin somewhat like that of a trout or whitefish. **1956** Harlan–Speaker *IA Fish* 158, *Trout-perch. . .* These fishes strongly resemble the young of the walleye and other perches, hence their name. **1966** *WI Acad. Trans.* 55.109, Troutperch—*Percopsis omiscomaycus. . .* Uncommon for the Mississippi River but . . "fairly large numbers" have been captured in the vicinity of La Crosse. **2002** (acc) *MN Univ. Fishes MN* (Internet), Trout-perch eat a variety of small aquatic animals including waterfleas, copepods, sideswimmers, fingernail clams, and midge larvae.

trout pickerel n

A **redfin pickerel** (here: *Esox americanus americanus*).

1858 *New Amer. Cyclop.* 13.323, The trout pickerel, or short-nosed pickerel (*E[sox] fasciatus* [=*E. americanus a.*] . .) is commonly somewhat smaller. **1887** Goode *Amer. Fishes* 277, *Esox americanus, . .* sometimes also called the . . "Trout Pickerel," . . is comparatively small. **1927** Weed *Pike* 42 **NEng, wPA**, *Esox americanus. . .* Trout Pickerel; New England States and western Pennsylvania.

trow n See **trough A3**

trow v See **throw A2, B1b, 2f**

t'row'd See **throw B2c**

trowed See **throw A2, B1a**

tru See **through** adv, prep **3**

truck n[1]

1 Garden vegetables grown for market; less freq, other farm products. Cf **bay truck, garden ~, sauce B1**

[**1784** *MD Jrl. & Baltimore Advt.* (MD) 14 Dec 3/3, [Advt:] *A large Room . . for his Customers to lodge in, and deposit their Market-Truck.*] **1805** Parkinson *Tour* 161 **MD** (as of 1799), I thought nothing in the farming-line likely to be profitable, except . . what in that country is called truck,—which is garden produce, fruits, &c. **1820** in 1822 Flint *Letters* 264 **IN, OH, KY** [Americanisms], Truck . . *Culinary vegetables; sometimes applied to baggage.* **1859** (1860) Creecy *Scenes South* 254, I often visited her and . . roamed over her little garden with her,

and asked numerous questions about her "truck," as she denominated everything she cultivated—amongst which was tobacco. **1862** Gilmore *Among the Pines* 247 **NC**, Wal, arter a while, . . I begun shipping my truck [=turpentine] to York and Bostin'. **1868** Clift *Tim Bunker* 37 **CT**, I suppose every man likes to know how the truck he sends to market suits his customers. At any rate that is the case at my house, where a good report of the butter . . is certain to keep my wife good-natured for a week. **1893** Frederic *Copperhead* 63 **nNY**, Marigolds and columbines . . had been allowed to usurp a lot of space where sweet-corn, potatoes and other table-truck used to be raised. **1903** *DN* 2.335 **seMO**, *Truck. . .* Produce; crops. . . The word includes grain, cotton, etc., instead of being applied only to garden stuff as at the North. **1905** *DN* 3.23 **cCT**, *Truck. . .* Produce, as garden *truck.* **1907** *DN* 3.237 **nwAR**, *Truck. . .* Produce; crops, including grain, cotton, etc. **1941** *LANE* Map 253 *(Garden vegetables)* **NEng**, [*Garden truck* is common throughout **NEng**; *truck* alone is very rare.] **1945** FWP *Lay My Burden Down* 71 **GA** (as of c1865) [Black], What they would give the field hands to eat would be the truck we had on the place, like greens, turnips, peas [etc]. **1966** *DARE* (Qu. I2, . . *General word . . for vegetables;* total Infs questioned, 75) Inf **NC14**, Truck—for early vegetables. **1969** *DARE* FW Addit **NJ**, Truck basket . . for all vegetables. **1986** Pederson *LAGS Concordance* **Gulf Region** *(Vegetables)* 2 infs, Truck; 1 inf, Home-grown truck; 1 inf, Truck—to sell.

2 By ext, food in general. **esp Sth, S Midl**

1838 Gilman *S. Matron* 133, Susy . . said, in a low tone—"Well, if that truck [=a dessert] an't gone mighty curious." **1867** Harris *Sut Lovingood Yarns* 93 **TN**, Taters, cabbige, meat, soup, beans, sop, dumplins, an' the truck what yu wallers 'em in . . were thar. **1878** Hart *Sazerac Lying Club* 195 **NV**, She tried to eat the cream with a knife and a fork, and because she did not succeed, said it was the most "unsatisfyin' truck" she "ever seed." **1885** Twain *Huck. Finn* 151 **MO** [Black], Dey brings me truck to eat every night. **1903** (1965) Adams *Log Cowboy* 282 **West**, Some of these fellows have n't had any of this kind of truck [=doughnuts] since they were little boys. **1939** FWP *Guide TN* 458 **nwTN**, "They" [=doctors] gin' her a 'bundance o' truck . . ; and none of 'em holp her at all. **1843** (1969) Lewis *Odd Leaves* 45 **LA**, No 'drap [of liquor],' 'cept in doctor's truck, should ever come on their plantation. **1856** Cartwright *Autobiog.* 49 **KY**, He had seen me take out a phial, in which I carried some truck that gave his sisters the jerks. **1880** (1881) Nye *Bill Nye & Boomerang* 26 **WY**, Just squeeze a little of your truck into a tumbler, and flavor it to suit the boys. **1883** (1971) Harris *Nights with Remus* 84 **GA** [Black], I aint tuck none er dat ar docter truck yit, ceppin' it's dish yer flas' er poke-root w'at ole Miss Favers fix up fer de stiffness in my j'ints. **1908** Lincoln *Cy Whittaker* 111 **MA**, Alpheus said you was thin and peaked and looked sick. Said you bought sass'p'rilla and all kind of truck. **1978** in 2003 (acc) *KY Univ. Oral Hist. Program Frontier Nursing Serv. Oral Hist. Project* (Internet) 8 **KY**, I grow all kinds of "worm truck" and worm medicine right around the house.

3 Medicine. **chiefly Sth, S Midl** *arch*

c1770 in 1833 Boucher *Glossary* 1 **MD**, Till now ne'er *crazy,* in my bones no pains,/ I *never took no truck,* nor doctor's *means.* **1827** (1939) Sherwood *Gaz. GA* 139, *Truck,* for medicine. **1835** Longstreet *GA Scenes* 210, Oh, they [=doctors] gin' her a 'bundance o' truck . . ; and none of 'em holp her at all. **1843** (1969) Lewis *Odd Leaves* 45 **LA**, No 'drap [of liquor],' 'cept in doctor's truck, should ever come on their plantation. **1856** Cartwright *Autobiog.* 49 **KY**, He had seen me take out a phial, in which I carried some truck that gave his sisters the jerks. **1880** (1881) Nye *Bill Nye & Boomerang* 26 **WY**, Just squeeze a little of your truck into a tumbler, and flavor it to suit the boys. **1883** (1971) Harris *Nights with Remus* 84 **GA** [Black], I aint tuck none er dat ar docter truck yit, ceppin' it's dish yer flas' er poke-root w'at ole Miss Favers fix up fer de stiffness in my j'ints. **1908** Lincoln *Cy Whittaker* 111 **MA**, Alpheus said you was thin and peaked and looked sick. Said you bought sass'p'rilla and all kind of truck. **1978** in 2003 (acc) *KY Univ. Oral Hist. Program Frontier Nursing Serv. Oral Hist. Project* (Internet) 8 **KY**, I grow all kinds of "worm truck" and worm medicine right around the house.

4 Personal possessions, goods, things. Cf **traps**

1827 (1939) Sherwood *Gaz. GA* 139, *Truck,* for produce, cloth, or almost any thing. **1840** *Huron Reflector* (Norwalk OH) [10 Mar 2]/1 (newspaperarchive.com), The antlers of the buck, bear skins, coon skins, blankets, guns, pouches, hunting shirts, &c. &c., in short all the truck of a pioneer. **1863** Alcott *Hospital Sketches* 41 **NH**, Burrowing under his pillow, he produced a little bundle of what he called "truck," and gallantly presented me with a pair of earrings. **1887** Kirkland *Zury* 538 **IL**, *Truck. . .* Personal property. **1899** (1912) Green *VA Folk-Speech* 459, *Truck. . .* Small wares; stuff; goods; gear; belongings. **1914** Dickinson *WI Plays* 32, She'd ought to have some clothes and some extry bedding. . . And you know what that means—attemptin' to get together truck like that. **1932** Randolph *Ozark Mt. Folks* 211, A gal got mad 'cause a feller give her sister a lot o' truck, an' so she tuck an' drownded her. **1942** McAtee *Dial. Grant Co. IN* 68 **IN, VA** (as of 1890s), *Truck . .* gear, belongings; "Load in your — an' let's go". **1976** Ryland *Richmond Co. VA* 378, *Truck*—small stuff, belongings. **1984** Wilder *You All Spoken Here* 31 **Sth**, *Truck, household truck:* Anything marauding Yankees could tote from Southern households in the Late Rebellion—silver, pots, pans, etc.

5 Worthless stuff of any sort, junk, trash; nonsense, foolishness.

1844 Thompson *Major Jones's Courtship* 31 **GA,** Thar's rich land, pore land what can be made tolerable good, and some bominable shaller, rollin truck what all the manure in creation wouldn't make grow cow peas. **1899** (1912) Green *VA Folk-Speech* 459, *Truck.* . . Trash. **1905** *DN* 3.23 **cCT,** *Truck.* . . worthless trumpery. **1907** *DN* 3.219 **nwAR,** *Truck.* . . Worthless trumpery. **1913** London *Valley of Moon* 403 **CA,** Talk about pluggin' away at a job in the city, an' goin' to movin' pictures and Sunday picnics for amusement! . . I can't see what was eatin' me that I ever put up with such truck. **c1937** in 1970 Yetman *Voices* 75 **MS** [Black], In dem days nobody but niggers and "shawl-strap" folks voted. Quality folks didn't have nothin' to do with such truck. **1941** *LANE* Map 346 **NEng,** The field workers asked for names applied to old, broken, useless things. . . [10 infs] truck. **1976** Ryland *Richmond Co. VA* 378, *Truck*—small stuff . . or trash. **c1980** *DARE* File **cnMA** (as of c1915), *Truck* = rubbish, trash, usually a collection a [sic] small things of no value. Junk. **2002** in 2006 *DARE* File—Internet **TN,** The same for electronic music—If you are expecting high-handled [sic] melodies and such truck, you aren't looking for the right things.

truck v, hence vbl n *trucking*

1 To stroll, walk, go. *orig chiefly among Black speakers*
Note: The popular phrr *keep on truckin'* and *truck on down* are not treated here.

1937 *AmSp* 12.183 [Jazz slang], *Truckin'.* . . The name came from the phrase 'I think I'll truck on home,' used by the negro porters and baggage carriers when leaving a group or place. The association was with the baggage trucks used in railroad stations, etc. **1937** in 1983 Taft *Blues Lyric Poetry* 149 **MS,** I got three legs to truck on : boys please don't block my road. **1942** *Amer. Mercury* 55.96 **Harlem NYC** [Black], *Trucking*—strolling. **1947** *True* 32.104 **New Orleans LA** [Black], These gals would come trucking into the joint one by one. **1970** *DARE* (Qu. Y20, *To run fast: "You should have seen him _____!"*) Inf **TN53,** Truck. [Inf Black] **1971** *Current Slang* 5.4.21 **VT,** *Truck around.* . . To go anywhere by foot or by vehicle. **1994** Smitherman *Black Talk* 228, *Truckin.* . . Going somewhere; moving forward with a purpose. . . Strolling.

2 To dance with a strolling or strutting gait; see quots; hence nouns *truck(ing)* a dance with such a step.

1935 *Washington Post* (DC) 19 July 19/2 **NYC** [Black], "Truckin'," in Harlem, is a description of a peculiar slouchy walk, and the new dance has the same contagion of rhythm that made an instantaneous hit of the Black Bottom. . . With one shoulder hoisted, the dancers do a spraddle-legged walk. **1935** *Chicago Defender* (IL) 14 Sept 8 *(Popik Coll.)* **NYC,** The history of the dance called "Trucking." The first revival of the dance was done on May 3, 1935 at the Harlem Opera House in the show called "Truck on Down." . . The title was given it . . almost two years ago in Philadelphia. **1935** *Sun* (Baltimore MD) 15 Nov 14/6 **NYC,** The truck, or truckin', that jerky yet rhythmic dance which combines a bend of the body, a tightening of the hand muscles and a slight strut with the legs, hit the theaters, sidewalks, gin taverns and dance floors of Harlem last summer. **1937** *AmSp* 12.183 [Jazz slang], *Truckin'.* Was first associated with the dance now so named about 1932. *Ibid,* Truckin' is a sort of dance solo. . . Only negroes can really truck, and the real artists are the pickaninnies in the streets. **1937** in 1983 Taft *Blues Lyric Poetry* 175 **MS** [Black], Now when you get you one of them faulty women : she won't do the truck / Get you a two-by-four : and I swear you can strut your stuff. **1938** [see **sugar foot 2**]. **1966–70** *DARE* (Qu. = FF5a, . . *Different steps and figures in dancing—in past years*) Infs **MO23, OK28,** Trucking; **CT42,** Trucking—just the opposite of Charleston—kicking legs in; **GA86,** Trucking—around 1940; **MD39,** Trucking—part of the Charleston step; **SC69,** Truck. [3 Infs Black] **1967** in 1993 Major *Calling the Wind* 280 **NYC** [Black], I began, with a dance called the Truck which was popular back then in the 1930s. My right forefinger waving, I trucked around the nearby trees and around Da-duh's awed and rigid form.

truck n[2] See **truck** v **2**

Truckee pine n [*Truckee* city in California]
=Jeffrey pine.

1871 *Gardener's Mth. & Horticult. Advt.* Oct 294, The timber from Truckee, so called Truckee Pine, belongs entirely to this species. **1897** Sudworth *Arborescent Flora* 22 **NV,** *Pinus jeffreyi.* . . Truckee Pine.

1908 Britton *N. Amer. Trees* 25, *Pinus Jeffreyi* . . , also known as . . Truckee pine, . . occurs on dry volcanic mountains from southern Oregon through California to Lower California, often forming pure forests.

Truckee trout n
=cutthroat trout.

1883 Robinson *Sinners & Saints* 284 **NV,** We supped heartily off "Truckee trout," one of the best fish that ever wagged a fin. **1896** U.S. Natl. Museum *Bulletin* 47.493, *Salmo mykiss henshawi* [=S. *clarkii h.*] . . Lake Tahoe Trout; Truckee Trout; Silver Trout. **1904** *Salmon & Trout* 210, The Lake Tahoe, Truckee, or "pogy" trout,—*Salmo clarkii henshawi.* **1938** Schrenkeisen *Field Book Fishes* 45, The Lake Tahoe Trout, known also as . . Truckee Trout, . . is found in most streams of the eastern slope of the Sierra Nevadas. Large round blackish spots are evenly scattered over the whole surface of the body above and below.

trucker n
A truck gardener.

1856 U.S. Patent Office *Annual Rept. for 1855: Ag.* 289 **DE,** I commenced market gardening, by procuring the services of an experienced "trucker," of Philadelphia county. **1865** *Atlantic Mth.* 16.54 **sePA,** These women are not producers of the fruits and vegetables they have to sell. Most of these are grown by truckers in the suburbs. **1881** *Scribner's Mth.* 22.347 **sePA,** A trucker's shanty, whitewashed, and with sashes filled with glass to force lettuce and the early radish, stands in the center of a rudely fenced patch of ground. **1899** (1912) Green *VA Folk-Speech* 459, *Trucker.* . . A truck-farmer; a market-gardener; one who sells garden stuff, especially at wholesale. **1939** Beck *Fare to Midlands* 35 **NJ,** I was a trucker from the first, growing my own vegetables and then taking them to Trenton to sell. **1965–70** *DARE* (Qu. U6, *Someone who sells vegetables or other articles from a wagon or truck, going from house to house*) 24 Infs, **scattered exc NEng, NW,** Trucker; **OH**78, Garden trucker; **CA**17, Vegetable trucker; (Qu. U7, *A man who goes from town to town selling things*) Infs **CO20, MO1,** Trucker; **MN29,** Produce trucker.

truck garden n [**truck** n[1] **1**] Cf **truck patch**
A vegetable garden.

1851 *Sartain's Union Mag.* 9.226, We find there the thousand thriving luxuries of the truck-garden, that renders the market of Philadelphia the best and cheapest in the world. **1859** *Davenport Daily Gaz.* (IA) 2 Apr 1/7, [Advt:] For rent.—A small truck garden of four acres or more. **1866** *N&Q* 3d ser 9.323 **Philadelphia PA,** A truck-garden, a truck-farm, is a market-garden or farm. **1866** Lossing *Hudson* 394 **NYC,** Numerous "truck" gardens, from which the city draws vegetable supplies. **1939** *LANE* Map 121 *(Garden)* 2 infs, **seNH, swCT,** Truck garden. **1965–70** *DARE* (Qu. I1, . . *The garden where you grow carrots, beans, and such things, to eat at home*) 50 Infs, **scattered,** Truck garden; **TX**105, Home truck garden; (Qu. L6a, . . *A piece of land under cultivation—less than an acre*) Infs **CA**11, **DC**5, **MN**2, **NY**200, **OH**47, Truck garden; (Qu. L6b, *A piece of land under cultivation—if it's several acres*) Infs **CA**91, **NC**36, **VT**16, Truck garden. **1986** Pederson *LAGS Concordance,* 9 infs, **Gulf Region,** Truck garden(s).

truck gardener n Cf **trucker**
One who grows garden produce for sale.

1844 *Pub. Ledger* (Philadelphia PA) 8 Feb 3/2, *Wanted* . . a Waiter and a Truck Gardener. **1869** Mombert *Authentic Hist. Lancaster Co.* 517 **PA,** Some of the land shells, have long been considered as destructive . . to the productions of the "Truck Gardener." **1874** *GA Weekly Telegraph & GA Jrl.* (Macon) 3 Feb 2/8, Southern farmers like too well the sound of the kingly title "planter," unmindful of the fact that truck gardeners rank them in these days of free labor. **1883** *Denton Jrl.* (MD) 25 Aug [6]/1 *(newspaperarchive.com),* It is only the depraved white youth from who the thrifty truck gardener needs to shield his melons. **1889** Bailey *The Horticulturist's Rule-Book: a Compendium of Useful Information for Fruit-Growers, Truck-Gardeners, Florists, and Others* [title]. **1911** *Elementary School Teacher* 11.413, The study of the source of food supply leads back to the farmer, the truck gardener [etc]. **1965–70** *DARE* (Qu. U6, *Someone who sells vegetables or other articles from a wagon or truck, going from house to house*) 16 Infs, **chiefly Upper MW, N Cent, PA,** Truck gardener; (Qu. U7, *A man who goes from town to town selling things*) Inf **CA**32, Truck gardener. **1986** Pederson *LAGS Concordance,* 1 inf, **cAR,** We were truck gardeners—raised things all year. **1992** *Daily Herald* (Arlington Heights IL) 5 June sec 5 2/4, He was also a farmer . . and a member of the board of directors of Cook County Truck Gardener's Association.

trucking vbl n See **truck** v

trucking n   See **truck** v **2**

truckle v   [Cf *SND troke* I.4 "to go hither and thither about a place, to trudge about"]

To proceed, go, esp in haste.

     1859 Taliaferro *Fisher's R.* 126 **nwNC** (as of 1820s), I seen a passel ov men com trucklin' to me, rockin' along, see-saw one side, then see-saw t'other side. *Ibid* 133, My old inimy were perfectly satisfied with me, and let me truckle off and save my bacon, so fur as he were consarned. **1953** Randolph–Wilson *Down in Holler* 294 **Ozarks,** *Truckle: v.i.* To hurry, to move rapidly under orders, with some criticism of the mover implied. A woman said to her grown son, "You truckle outdoors, an' wash them feet." Common usage among the old-timers in Stone and Taney counties, Mo. **1954** *Harder Coll.* **cwTN,** *Truckle. . .* hurry, move rapidly under orders. **1998** in 2004 Montgomery–Hall *Dict. Smoky Mt. Engl.* 619 **eTN,** He truckled off up the mountain to see if he could kill a squirrel.

truckle-bed trash   See **trundle-bed trash 2**

truck patch n   **chiefly Midl, Lower Missip Valley** See Map
=**truck garden.**

     1812 in 1944 *Thomas Jefferson's Garden Book* 483 **VA,** I am moving them into the truck patch, as I cannot afford them room enough in the garden. **1818** in 1819 *KY Almanac for 1820* 30, He had a fence round a bit of ground for a truck patch. **1836** (1861) Tucker *Partisan Leader* 2 **VA,** A sort of rude garden, denominated, in the ruder language of the country, a "truck-patch." **1849** *Ft. Wayne Times* (IN) 7 June 1/2, The same snake that fooled your mammy in Adam's truck patch. **1861** Owen *Fourth Rept. Geol. Surv. KY* 102, Soil from a garden . . badly cultivated as a 'truck patch,' or vegetable garden. **1911** *DN* 3.540 **eKY,** *Truck-patch. . .* Garden. **1925** Parrish *Perennial Bachelor* 97 **MD,** Out in the steaming heat of the "truck patch" Maggie was picking raspberries. **1948** Dick *Dixie Frontier* 289 **NE,** The little truck patch was often neglected. **1965–70** *DARE* (Qu. I1, . . *The garden where you grow carrots, beans, and such things, to eat at home*) 37 Infs, **chiefly Midl, Lower Missip Valley,** Truck patch; (Qu. L6a, . . *A piece of land under cultivation—less than an acre*) 36 Infs, **chiefly Sth, Midl,** Truck patch; [**MO4,** Truck patching;] (Qu. L6b, *A piece of land under cultivation—if it's several acres*) Infs **LA**18, **MD**34, **PA**29, Truck patch; (Qu. U6, *Someone who sells vegetables or other articles from a wagon or truck, going from house to house*) Inf **MO**34, Truck-patch man, truck-patch farmer. **1967–68** *DARE* Tape **IN**32, Any farmer, no matter how small his truck patch was or how large or what he chose to grow in them, he could sell it because these people needed food; **MD**30, All the flowers in the yard around the house, and then what was the old truck patch; **MO**11, In the last few years there's quite a few of 'em moved out of the city and moved onto small acreage where they just build a house and have a truck patch or garden; **TX**32, 'Course we move our garden about, you know. We plant peas and things in the field and have our truck patches mostly in the field. **1982** *Barrick Coll.* **csPA,** Truck patch—a large garden. **1986** Pederson *LAGS Concordance* **Gulf Region,** [59 infs responded *truck patch(es)*, adding remarks such as "if you sell the produce," "larger than garden—for market," "one-fourth to one-half acre," "3–4 acres."]

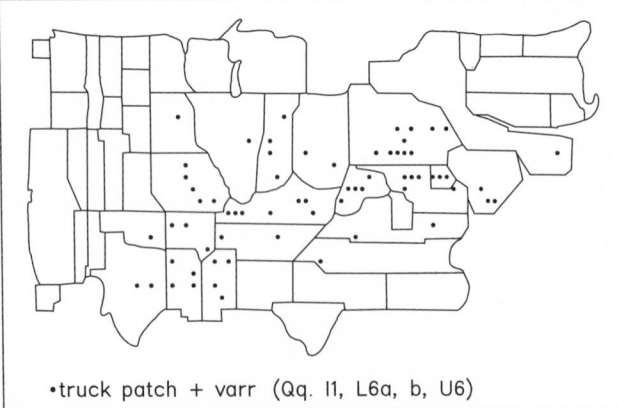

     •truck patch + varr (Qq. I1, L6a, b, U6)

truck to keelson, from   prep phr   Also *from main truck to keelson* [*truck* cap at the top of a ship's flagstaff + *keelson* structural piece in the hull of a ship] **chiefly NEng**

Fig: from top to bottom; thoroughly, in all respects.

     1849 Cooper *Sea Lions* 2.212 **Long Is. NY,** The heirs expectant, "a'ter reading the insterment . . fore and aft, and overhauling it from truck to keelson, give the matter up, as a bad job." **1877** Twain in *Atlantic Mth.* 40.445 **NEng,** And besides, he [=a sailor] was rigged out from main truck to keelson in the nobbiest clothes that ever saw a fo'castle. **1916** Lincoln *Mary-'Gusta* 32 **MA,** I know him from truck to keelson. He is honest and able and can handle any craft. **1920** Packard *Old Plymouth* 70 **seMA,** No doubt every old sea dog was his own architect, and the houses show it from main truck to keelson. **1921** O'Neill *Diff'rent* 271 **NEng,** He's a mean skunk from truck to keelson! **1936** in 1983 Truman *Dear Bess* 386 **MO,** Well after searching the desk from truck to keelson we found the pass. **1942** ME Univ. *Studies* 56.27, The extreme topmost point of the mast, however, was the truck. Hence *from truck to keelson . .* meant from top to bottom.

trudget n   Also *trudge(on)*   **NEast**
A small child.

     1814 in 1864 Irving *Life & Letters* 1.308 **NY,** I have allowed the little Major to take holiday and go to the country with his wife and little trudgeons. **1901** *DN* 2.149 **cwNY,** *Trudge. . .* A child. Orleans Co., N.Y. . . *Trudget. . .* A little child. Orleans Co., N.Y.; heard in St. Lawrence Co.; prob. rare. **1941** *LANE* Map 379 (*Kid, tot*) 1 inf, **cwCT,** [trʌdʒɪt], heard. **1980** *DARE* File **Tunbridge VT** (as of c1900), Trudget—small child, toddler.

true n   Cf **false** n **2**
The truth.

     1927 Kennedy *Gritny* 36 **sLA** [Black], You can't say I ain' correck, if you wan' leave yo'self tell de true. **2005** *DARE* File—Internet, We remember the horoscopes when they tell you the true for once, but not the gazillion times they were wrong.

true adv, prep   See **through** adv, prep **3**

true v   See **throw** A2

true blue n
A **spiderwort** (here: *Tradescantia virginiana*).

     1966 *DARE* Wildfl. QR Pl.7 [=*Tradescantia virginiana*] Inf **NC**28, True blue.

true unicorn root n   Cf **false unicorn root 2**
A **colicroot 2** (here: *Aletris farinosa*).

     1834 *Thomsonian Recorder* 2.352, *Aletris farinosa.* True Unicorn Root. **1882** *Med. Brief* 10.5 **NY,** Most druggists substitute in its place the aletris, or true unicorn root. **1930** Sievers *Amer. Med. Plants* 4, *Aletris farinosa. . . Common names.*—Stargrass, blazing star, . . true unicorn root. **1971** Krochmal *Appalachia Med. Plants* 40, *Aletris farinosa. . .* True unicorn root. . . Plant has a short thick root or rhizome.

truf(e)   See **truth**

truh   See **throw** A2

trumpery room n   Cf **lumber room, plunder** n **3**
A storage room, esp for unused or discarded items.

     1856 Holmes *Lena Rivers* 58 **MA,** "The *trumpery* room is plenty good enough for 'em," thought Corinda, retreating into the kitchen and cutting sundry flourishes in token of her contempt. **1900** *Eve. Herald* (Syracuse NY) [2 Feb] 10/2 (newspaperarchive.com), Three thousand dollars' worth of silk was too much, however, to be thrown into the trumpery room at once. **1949** Kurath *Word Geog.* 52, **neNC, seVA,** From Albemarle Sound to the lower Neuse *trumpery room* is current. **1985** *DARE* File **WV,** Trumpery room, catchall room, in West Virginia.

trumpet n

1 often pl; also *trumpet plant:* A **pitcher plant 1** with trumpet-shaped leaves, esp *Sarracenia flava.* **Sth** Cf **trumpet flower 2, trumpetleaf, trumpet root**

     1854 King *Amer. Eclectic Dispensatory* 854, In the yellow-flowered species [of *Sarracenia*] of the Southern States, the bottle is very long, resembling a trumpet, by which name it is often called. **1857** Gray *Manual of Botany* 24, *S[arracenia] flava. . . Trumpets. . . Leaves long . . and trumpet-shaped,* erect, with an open mouth. **1901** Lounsberry *S. Wild Flowers* 206, Trumpets, as without discrimination the members of this genus [=*Sarracenia*] are called in the south are among the characteristic flowers of the pine barren strip of country. **1927** Boston Soc. Nat. Hist. *Proc.* 38.236 **Okefenokee GA,** *Sarracenia minor* 'Trumpet' *Sarracenia psittacina* 'Trumpet'. **1936** Whitehouse *TX Flowers* 39, *Sarracenia sledgei* [=*S. alata*] . . is also called trumpets, water-cup, watches, and biscuits. **1938** FWP *Ocean Highway* 118 **NC,** Here grow the insectivorous plants including the pitcherplants, of which the trumpet is commonest. **1966–68** *DARE* (Qu. S1, . . *Jack-in-the-pulpit*) Inf **GA35**, Trumpet plant, flycatcher—two varieties of pitcher plant; **NC24**, Trumpets. **1979** Niering–Olmstead *Audubon Guide N. Amer. Wildflowers E. Region* 771, *Trumpets (Sarracenia flava).* . . A southern plant with hollow leaves that fill with water in which insects and other small organisms drown; their soft parts are then digested by the plant. **1986** Pederson *LAGS Concordance,* 1 inf, **nwFL,** Trumpets—hollow things, grow up, bees get inside. **2011** *DARE* File—Internet **NC,** *Sarracenia flava*—Trumpets—In the "pitcher plant" family; conspicuous flowers with maroon petals. . . *Call for availability.*

2 usu with adj: A **wild buckwheat 2** with inflated nodes, such as *Eriogonum inflatum, E. nudum,* or *E. trichopes.* Cf **desert trumpet**

1941 Jaeger *Wildflowers* 30 **Desert SW,** *Little Trumpet. Eriogonum trichopes.* . . Only the short basal node is inflated; this makes it easy to distinguish from . . *Eriogonum inflatum,* . . which shows large inflations in many of the upper nodes. *Ibid* 37, *Long Trumpet. Eriogonum nudum.* . . A distinguishing feature is the great length of the inflated lower joints. **1995** *Smithsonian* Mar 90 **SW,** Desert trumpets. . . the shape of them is odd and a little silly. Their stems are blue-gray and swollen and upright. . . Death Valley has been home to at least a trillion trumpets this year.

3 pl: A plant of the genus *Acleisanthes* with trumpet-shaped flowers, native to Texas and other parts of the Southwest. For other names of *A. longiflora* see **angel's-trumpet 2**

1970 Correll *Plants TX* 589, *Acleisanthes* . . *Trumpets.* . . Flowers axillary or terminal, . . perianth white, with a very much-elongated slender tube. *Ibid* 590, *Acleisanthes anisophylla.* . . Oblique-leaf trumpets. . . *Acleisanthes crassifolia.* . . Texas trumpets. **2003** (acc) TX A&M Univ. Ag. Research & Ext. Center Uvalde *Herbarium* (Internet), Berlandier Trumpets [=*Acleisanthes obtusa*]. . . grows in sandy and clay soils of the South Texas Plains and the Edwards Plateau. The fragrant white or light pink trumpet-shaped flowers bloom between April and December.

4 pl: A plant *(Ipomopsis longiflora)* with trumpet-shaped flowers native to much of the central US west of the Mississippi River.

1979 Spellenberg *Audubon Guide N. Amer. Wildflowers W. Region* 665, *Pale Trumpets (Ipomopsis longiflora).* . . Slender, *pale blue-violet, pale blue, or white, trumpet-shaped flowers* bloom singly or in pairs. . . Sandy deserts and arid grassland. . . Southern Utah to western Nebraska; south to western Texas, Arizona, and northern Mexico.

trumpet buffalo n
=**bigmouth buffalo.**

1983 Becker *Fishes WI* 615, *Ictiobus cyprinellus.* . . Trumpet buffalo. . . Snout bluntly rounded, often with a slight depression before the eyes, giving it a turned-up appearance.

trumpet bush See **trumpet flower 1e**

trumpet creeper n

1 A woody vine *(Campsis radicans)* with showy panicles of orange or red flowers, native in much of the eastern two-thirds of the US. Also called **cowitch 2, cow ivy, cross vine 2, devil's shoestring 3, foxglove 4, hell-vine 1, Indian creeper, jim climber, shoestring 1b, trumpet flower 1a, ~ honeysuckle 2, ~ vine 1** Cf **cow ivy**

1818 Barton *Compendium Florae Philadelphicae* 2.43 **PA,** *Trumpet Creeper.* . . Flowers red and orange. **1847** *Amer. Whig Rev.* 5.302, Very little ground will nourish a trumpet creeper, a monthly honey-suckle, a clustering flowered rose, or a jasmine. **1880** *Harper's New Mth. Mag.* 61.174 **VA,** The walls were overgrown with the red trumpet creeper. **1904** (1916) Porter *Freckles* 81 **MI,** The trumpet-creepers were flaunting their gorgeous horns of red and gold sweetness. **1937** Thornburgh *Gt. Smoky Mts.* 21, One finds in the lowlands the long red tubes of the trumpet creeper. **1967** *DARE* Wildfl QR (Wills–Irwin) Pl.46D Inf **TX44,** Trumpet creeper. **2009** *Paris News* (TX) 16 July 10/2, This time of year the big orange-red flowers of the trumpet creeper vine are a real hummer magnet!

2 also *tendriled trumpet creeper:* =**cross vine 1.** Note: This species was formerly often included in the same genus as **1** above.

1845 Gray *Bot. Text-Book* 47, Plants which climb by rootlets, like the Ivy, our own Poison Ivy . . , and the Bignonia or Trumpet-Creeper . .

in this way reach the summit of high trees. **1960** Vines *Trees SW* 924, *Bignonia capreolata.* . . Vernacular names are Tendriled Trumpet-creeper and Quarter-vine. **2003** *DARE* File—Internet **nwWA,** Our "Dragon Lady" Trumpet Creeper, or Crossvine, or Bignonia is a cultivar of *Bignonia capreolata.*

trumpet fireweed See **trumpet milkweed**

trumpet flower n

1 Any of several plants with trumpet-shaped flowers of the family Bignoniaceae or formerly included in this family, as:

a =**trumpet creeper 1.**

[**1706** London–Wise *Retir'd Gard'ner* 2.701, We have likewise had some of them from *Virginia,* by the Name of Trumpet-Flower, or Red Jessemin of Virginia, to distinguish it from an herbaceous Flower call'd likewise the Trumpet-Flower of *Virginia.* [*DARE* Ed: This quot may apply to another sense.]] **1731** Catesby *Nat. Hist. Carolina* 1.65, *Bignonia, Fraxini foliis, coccineo flore minore. The Trumpet-Flower.* . . In *May, June, July* and *August,* it produces Bunches of red Flowers, somewhat like the common Foxglove. **1800** (1803) Ellicott *Jrl.* 288 **FL,** Many of the trees in the low grounds are loaded with a variety of vines, the most conspicuous of which are the creeper, or trumpet flower, (begnonia [sic] radicans,) and common poison vine, (rhus radicans). **1847** Longfellow *Evangeline* 99 **LA,** Swinging from its [=a cedar's] great arms, the trumpet-flower and the grape-vine / Hung their ladder of ropes aloft like the ladder of Jacob. **1893** *Scribner's Mag.* 13.798 **TN,** Vines of wild grape and scarlet trumpet-flower swaying and blooming among them, tangled with the branches of sumach and sassafras. **1960** Vines *Trees SW* 925, *Bignonia radicans* [=*Campsis r.*] . . Some of its vernacular names are . . Trumpet-flower, Devil's-shoestring, . . and Cowitch.

b A **catalpa B1.**

1771 Forster *Flora* 27, Bignonia Catalpa—Trumpet flower. **1775** (1962) Romans *Nat. Hist. FL* 27, Bignonia, or trumpet flower, with single heart shaped leaves, flowers of a dirty white, through whose inside blue and purple spots are irregularly scattered, having a long and narrow seed pod (vulgo) catalpa. **1891** *Century Dict.* 6509, *Trumpet-flower.* . . One of various plants of other genera, as *Solandra, Brunfelsia, Catalpa* . . and *Datura.*

c =**Carolina jasmine.** Cf **evening trumpet flower**

1784 in 1785 *Amer. Acad. Arts & Sci. Memoirs* 1.465 **MA,** *Bignonia* [here: =*Gelsemium*]. . . *Trumpet-Flower. Yellow Jasmine.* . . On the borders of fields, and in open woods. **1891** *Century Dict.* 6509, *Trumpet-flower.* . . One of various plants . . as. . . *Evergreen trumpet-flower,* the yellow jasmine, *Gelsemium sempervirens.* **2003** (acc) N. Prairie Wildlife Research Center *S. Wetland Flora* (Internet), *Southern Wetland Flora.* . . Rankin's Trumpet-flower—*Gelsemium rankinii.* . . Woody vine climbing high on trees.

d =**cross vine 1.**

1831 Audubon *Ornith. Biog.* 1.334, The Ramping Trumpet-Flower. *Bignonia Capreolata.* **1869** Porcher *Resources* 500 **Sth,** *Trumpet Flower (Bignonia crucigera* [=*B. capreolata*]). . . The root and vine, in infusion or decoction, answer the purpose of sarsaparilla. . . This vine appears to be possessed of instinct; it shoots up to the highest tops of trees before sending out a branch. **1901** Lounsberry *S. Wild Flowers* 471, *Cross-vine. Tendrilled Trumpet-flower.* . . A woody vine, climbing sometimes fifty and sixty feet high. **1942** Tehon *Fieldbook IL Shrubs* 246, *Bignonia.* . . The trumpet-flowers are . . vines, which climb by means of tendrils. . . There is but a single species [=*B. capreolata*] in this genus. **1976** Bailey–Bailey *Hortus Third* 162, [*Bignonia*] *capreolata.* . . *Trumpet flower.* . . Fl[ower]s yellow-red, paler inside.

e also *trumpet bush, ~ flower shrub:* A shrub *(Tecoma stans)* native to the Southwest and Florida. Also called **tronodora 2, yellow bells 6**

1860 Chapman *Flora Southern U.S.* 285 **sFL,** *Tecoma* [spp]. . . Trumpet-flower. . . *T. stans.* **1892** Coulter *Botany W. TX* 318, *Trumpet-flower.* . . *T[ecoma] stans.* . . Erect shrub. . . The common species of southern and western Texas. **1908** NM Univ. *Biol. Ser.* 3.1.32, *Tecoma.* . . Trumpet-flower. **1933** Small *Manual SE Flora* 1240, *T[ecoma] stans.* . . *Yellow trumpet-flower.* . . Hammocks, woods, and thickets, Coastal Plain, Fla. to Tex. **1947** Carr *Desert Parade* 74 **SW,** The *Trumpet Flower* shrub, sometimes confused with the desert willow, is a smaller plant with trumpet-like yellow flowers and bright green leaves. **1971** Dodge *100 Desert Wildflowers* 78 **SW,** A glossy-leaved shrub with golden trumpet-shaped flowers, the trumpet-bush blooms from May to October on dry, rocky hillsides. **1979** Little *Checklist U.S. Trees*

284, *Other common names* [for *Tecoma stans*]—yellow trumpet-flower, hardy yellow-trumpet. **2002** *Jrl. Amer. Pharmaceutical Assoc.* 42.278 **Los Angeles CA,** In this community, "diabetina" typically refers to the tronadora plant, known in English as the trumpet flower.

2 A **pitcher plant 1.** *obs* Cf **trumpet 1**

1743 (1946) Gronovius *Flora Virginica* 164, Sarracena floribus flavis. . . Vulgo *Side saddle flower* / in Carolina Boreali *Trumpet flower* vocatur. [=Sarracena with yellow flowers. . . Vulgar *Side saddle flower* / in northern Carolina called *Trumpet flower.*]

3 Any of several other plants with similar flowers; see quots. [*EDD* 1878–86 for *Lonicera periclymenum*]

1966–67 *DARE* Wildfl QR Pl.214A [=*Lonicera sempervirens*] Inf **CO**7, Trumpet flower—wrong color; **MI**31, Trumpet flower. **1967** *DARE* (Qu. S5, . . *Wild morning glory*) Inf **AR**52, Trumpet flower—yellow; (Qu. S26a, . . *Wildflowers. . . Roadside flowers*) Inf **PA**22, Trumpet flower and trumpet vine.

trumpet flower shrub See **trumpet flower 1e**

trumpet gourd n   [*OED2* 1884]

A variety of **bottle gourd.**

1858 *Mag. Horticult.* 24.471, It [=the Chinese yam] resembles a very long trumpet gourd. **1889** *Century Dict.* 2583, *Gourd.* . . The fruit varies greatly in form, but is usually club-shaped, or enlarged toward the apex; its hard rind is used for bottles, dippers, etc. Different varieties are known as *bottle-, club-,* or *trumpet-gourd,* or *calabash.* **1901** Mohr *Plant Life AL* 831, *Lagenaria vulgaris clavata* [=*L. siceraria*]. . . *Trumpet Gourd.* Louisianian area. **1976** Bailey–Bailey *Hortus Third* 633, *[Lagenaria] siceraria.* . . Includes the *dipper, sugar-trough, Hercules'-club, bottle, knob-kerrie,* and *trumpet gourds.*

trumpet grass n   Cf **desert trumpet, trumpet 2**

Perh a **wild buckwheat 2.**

1968 *DARE* (Qu. S14, . . *Prickly seeds, small and flat, with two prongs at one end, that cling to clothing*) Inf **NV**8, Trumpet grass seeds.

trumpet honeysuckle n

1 A **honeysuckle 2,** usu *Lonicera sempervirens.* For other names of *L. sempervirens* see **coral honeysuckle, ~ vine 4, firecracker vine, scarlet trumpet**

[**1731** Miller *Gardeners Dict.* np, *Periclymenum;* . . Trumpet Honeysuckle. . . We have but one *Species* of this Plant at present, . . Virginian Scarlet Honey-suckle.] **a1782** (1788) Jefferson *Notes VA* 38, Trumpet honeysuckle. Lonicera sempervirens. **1843** Torrey *Flora NY* 1.296, *Lonicera sempervirens.* . . *Scarlet* or *Trumpet Honeysuckle.* . . Corolla trumpet-shaped, with short and broad nearly equal lobes. **1878** *Harper's New Mth. Mag.* 57.405, The "twiners" are represented in the veranda decorations by two varieties of the honeysuckle *(Lonicera)*—the yellow-flowered and the trumpet honeysuckle, . . the latter . . the most satisfactory. . . Its rich dark green leaf has a waxen surface, with which its scarlet flowers . . present a strong contrast. **1936** Whitehouse *TX Flowers* 145, *Trumpet Honeysuckle* . . is quite common in the woods of East Texas and other Southern States. **1968** *DARE* Wildfl QR Pl.214A [=*Lonicera sempervirens*] Inf **NY**91, Trumpet honeysuckle. **1973** Hitchcock–Cronquist *Flora Pacific NW* 452, Native twining vine; trumpet . . h[oneysuckle]. . . *L[onicera] ciliosa.* **2003** *DARE* File—Internet **KY,** The trumpet honeysuckle is actually native to western Kentucky. . . The long, slender trumpet-shaped orange to red flowers are found anywhere from May to October.

2 =**trumpet creeper 1.**

1902 Bailey *Cyclop. Horticult.* 4.1777, *[Tecoma]* [=*Campsis*] *radicans.* . . Trumpet Creeper. Trumpet Vine. Trumpet Honeysuckle. **1970** Correll *Plants TX* 1443, *Campsis radicans.* . . *Trumpet-honeysuckle, cow-itch vine.* Deciduous viny shrub climbing to 10 m. or more, with aerial rootlets.

trumpetleaf n   Also *trumpet-leaf pitcher plant*

Any of several **pitcher plants 1** with trumpet-shaped leaves, esp *Sarracenia flava.* **Sth** Cf **fiddler's trumpet, trumpet 1**

1812 *Med. & Phys. Jrl.* 27.392, The flowers of the *Sarracenia flava* (the yellow trumpet-leaf or side-saddle flower of the people of the United States) have a most offensive cadaverous or carrion-like odor. **1861** Wood *Class-Book* 222, *S[arracenia] Gronovii. Trumpet-leaf.* . . The largest species of the genus, in swampy pine woods, Va. to Fla. and La. **1869** Fuller *Uncle John* 187, Another species, very common in the Southern States, is the *Gronovii* or *Trumpet* Leaf, from the shape of the leaf, which is small at the base, swelling gradually toward the throat

like a trumpet. **1885** *Amer. Jrl. Pharmacy* 57.89 **Sth,** *Sarracenia variolaris,* . . Spotted Trumpetleaf, . . reported under the additional name of the "Hood-topped Fly-catcher." **1901** Lounsberry *S. Wild Flowers* 206, *S[arracenia] rubra,* red-flowered trumpet-leaf, has long and slim leaves. *Ibid* 207, *S. flava,* . . trumpet-leaf . . , is the largest and a most splendid representative of the family. . . *S. variolaris,* spotted trumpet-leaf, is found from Florida to North Carolina. **1936** Whitehouse *TX Flowers* 39, *Trumpet-Leaf (Sarracenia sledgei* [=*S. alata*]). . . Grows in swamps from East Texas to Alabama. **2006** *DARE* File—Internet **neFL,** Trumpet-leaf Pitcher Plant [*Sarracenia flava*].

trumpet milkweed n   Also *trumpet (fire)weed, trumpets* Cf **milkweed 4**

A **wild lettuce 1** (here: *Lactuca canadensis*).

1847 Wood *Class-Book* 359, *L[actuca] elongata* [=*L. canadensis*]. *Wild Lettuce. Trumpet Milkweed.* . . A common rank plant. **1892** (1974) Millspaugh *Amer. Med. Plants* 96–1, *Lactuca canadensis.* . . Trumpet-weed. **1897** IN Dept. Geol. & Nat. Resources *Rept. for 1896* 700, Trumpet Milk-weed. Borders of thickets and roadsides; frequent. **1900** Lyons *Plant Names* 212, *L[actuca] Canadensis.* . . Trumpets. **1925** Jepson *Manual Plants CA* 999, *L[actuca] canadensis.* . . *Trumpet Fireweed.* . . Flowers pale yellow. **1931** Harned *Wild Flowers Alleghanies* 491, *L[actuca] canadensis.* . . Also called Wild Opium and Trumpet Milkweed. **1973** Hitchcock–Cronquist *Flora Pacific NW* 534, Trumpet fireweed . . *L. canadensis.*

trumpet of death n   Also *death trumpet*

A **horn of plenty 2** (here: *Craterellus cornucopioides*).

1935 NY State Museum *Hdbk.* 11.29, Here is still another group, represented by this queer, trumpet-like specimen, the Trumpet of Death or Horn of Plenty. It has nothing whatever to do with death, as it is good to eat. **1980** Marteka *Mushrooms* 86, *Craterellus cornucopioides.* . . *Common Names*—Horn of plenty, trumpet of death, . . death trumpet.

trumpet phlox n

A **scarlet gilia.**

1967 Dodge *Roadside Wildflowers* 58, Skyrocket . . Scarlet gilia, Trumpet phlox.

trumpet plant See **trumpet 1**

trumpet root n   Cf **trumpet 1**

A **pitcher plant 1;** see quots.

1869 *Amer. Jrl. Pharmacy* 41.292, I prepared a tincture of the root according to the following formula. . . Trumpet root, . . four ounces. Diluted alcohol, . . two pints. **c1938** in 1970 Hyatt *Hoodoo* 2.985 **seGA** [Black], A *trumpet root* will grow dat high. An' a *trumpet root* have a figure on it like a man wit a cap stickin' from it—de *trumpet root,* an' it spreads out jest as wide as mah finger. **1968** *DARE* Tape **GA**30, The old-timers used that—what we called pitcher plant. They called it a trumpet root. They used that, boiled the roots of it, made tea out of it, and give it to children for whooping cough, things like that. **1974** Morton *Folk Remedies* 137 **SC,** "Trumpet Root;" Hooded Pitcher Plant—*Sarracenia minor.* . . *South Carolina (Current use):* Rootstock is boiled and the decoction kept in a jar, applied warm on skin rash or eruptions. People say the spots on the leaves are a sign that the plant is a good remedy for skin troubles.

trumpets n

1 See **trumpet 1.**

2 See **trumpet 4.**

3 See **trumpet 3.**

4 See **trumpet milkweed.**

trumpet vine n

1 =**trumpet creeper 1.**

1709 (1967) Lawson *New Voyage* 102 **NC, SC,** The Scarlet Trumpet-Vine bears a glorious red Flower, like a Bell, or Trumpet, and makes a Shade inferiour to none that I ever saw; yet it leaves us, when the Winter comes. **1716** Petiver *Petiveriana* 12, Scarlet *Trumpet-Vine.* Makes a fine *Arbour.* **1862** *Atlantic Mth.* 9.176 **Sth,** A huge trumpet-vine . . swung its pendant arms from one of the gables. **1883** *Peterson's Mag.* 83.460, The great porch in front . . [was] destitute of railing or ornament; but the creeping trumpet-vine that clung around it. **1901** Lounsberry *S. Wild Flowers* 471, *Campsis* or *Tecoma radicans,* trumpet-flower, vine, or creeper, is over the country one of the best known vines, for considerably further northward than its natural range it has become familiar through cultivation. **1937** Thornburgh *Gt. Smoky Mts.* 22, A few of the more common vines you may encounter . . are . . trumpet vine, crossvine, . . and greenbrier. **1965–70** *DARE* (Qu. S17, . . *Kinds of plants . . that . . cause itching and swelling*) Inf **AR**41, Trumpet vine; **VA**24, Trumpet vine—some people are allergic to it; (Qu. S21, . . *Weeds . . that are a trouble in gardens and fields*) Inf **GA**80, Trumpet vine; (Qu. S26a, . . *Wildflowers. . . Roadside flowers*) Infs **NJ**58, **PA**49, 136, **TX**33, Trumpet vine; (Qu. S26c, *Wildflowers that grow in woods*) Inf **DE**4, Trumpet vine; **SC**36, Trumpet vine—large, orange-yellow, trumpetlike flowers; (Qu. S26d, *Wildflowers that grow in meadows; not asked in early QRs*) Infs **KY**63, **PA**60, Trumpet vine; **AR**10, Wild trumpet vine—orange blossom, long blossom; (Qu. S26e, *Other wildflowers not yet mentioned; not asked in early QRs*) Inf **NC**21, Cowitch vine—has orange flowers (trumpet vine). [*DARE* Ed: Some of these Infs may refer instead to other senses below.] **1986** Pederson *LAGS Concordance,* 2 infs, **AR,** Trumpet vine; 1 inf, **neAL,** Trumpet vine—that's beautiful. **2006** *DARE* File—Internet **NC,** Hummingbird Trumpet vine—Campsis Radicans.

2 =cross vine 1. Cf **trumpet flower 1d**

1969 *DARE* FW Addit **KY,** Trumpet vine—cross vine or *Bignonia capreolata.*

3 A **morning glory 1,** such as **man-of-the-earth 1.**

1967–68 *DARE* (Qu. S5, . . *Wild morning glory*) Infs **IN**41, **MA**71, **WA**20, Trumpet vine. **1975** Hamel-Chiltoskey *Cherokee Plants* 51, Potato vine, wild; trumpet vine . . *Ipomoea pandurata.*

trumpet weed n

1 A **boneset 1,** usu *Eupatorium purpureum.*

1814 Bigelow *Florula Bostoniensis* 190, *Eupatorium purpureum. . . Trumpet weed. . .* A tall plant, growing about the borders of thickets in wet land. Stem five or six feet in height, straight, round, purplish, hollow throughout its whole length. **1849** (1911) Thoreau *Week on Concord* 27 **MA,** A tall dull red flower, *Eupatorium purpureum,* or trumpet-weed, formed the rear rank of the fluvial array. **1887** Eggleston *Graysons* 227 **IL,** Shaded by the broad-leaved horse and trumpet weeds in the fence-row. **1901** Mohr *Plant Life AL* 761, *Eupatorium purpureum. . .* Trumpet-weed. . . *Eupatorium maculatum. . .* Spotted Trumpet-weed. . . *Eupatorium amoenum* [=*E. purpureum* var purpureum]. . . Low Trumpet-weed. **1937** (1963) Hyatt *Kiverlid* 114 **KY,** When I wus a young-un, we called 'em [=bobbins made of Joe-Pye weed] trumpet weed. You could make a kind o' splittin' noise blowin' 'em like tootin' a dawg horn. **1970** GA Dept. Ag. *Farmers Market Bulletin* 12 Aug 8, Joe-Pye-Weed, sometimes called trumpet-weed or purple boneset, is the common name of Eupatorium maculatum. **1970** Correll *Plants TX* 1554, *Eupatorium fistulosum. . . Trumpet-weed. . .* At times confused with *E. purpureum . .* which has not been found in Tex. **2001** *Atlanta Jrl.–Constitution* (GA) 26 July Home & Garden sec 5/1, In Georgia, there is . . *pale joe-pye weed* (also known as *trumpet weed*).

2 See **trumpet milkweed.**

trun See **throw A4, B1e, 2d**

trundle-bed trash n

1 also attrib: A low-class, shiftless person or group.

1850 *Sheboygan Mercury* (WI) 26 Oct 1/3 **NEng,** 'I'm in for anything that's rich,' replied Strong, whose name contradicted itself—he being a little dried up, diminutive, weasel-faced man who would, in New England, have been termed 'trundle bed trash.' **1859** *Ft. Wayne Weekly Times* (IN) 4 May 2/1, And then, to complete the infinitesimal mean littleness, he resorts to downright mendacity on matters which none but trundle-bed trash could originate, or would use. **1879** *Daily Constitution* (Atlanta GA) 14 June 1/7, I never advised Mrs. Hill to get a nice friend. I told her that she ought to stay at home with her mother, father and husband, and leave trundle-bed trash alone. **1893** *Harper's New Mth. Mag.* 88.160 **VA** [Black], Dat's some lie o' dat black trundle-bed-trash nigger, Stable Dick . . I'll trick him if he fool wid me. **1929** *AmSp* 5.120 **ME,** "Trundle-bed trash" referred to very young, worthless people just married.

2 also *truckle-bed trash:* Small children. *joc* or *derog*

1853 Twain in 1912 *MLN* 44.258 **MO,** Of all the commodities, manu-factures—or whatever you please to call it—in New York, trundle-bed trash—children I mean—take the lead. Why, from Cliff street, up Frankfort to Nassau street . . I think I could count two hundred brats. **1883** Amer. Philol. Assoc. *Trans.* 14.54 **Sth,** Children are called *trundle-bed trash.* **1888** *Freeborn Co. Std.* (Albert Lea MN) [29 Feb 8]/4 (news-paperarchive.com), Quite a few of the trundle-bed trash went to the spelling school, and report a very fine time to the old maids. **1897** Livermore *Story* 177 **VA** (as of c1847), All united in a violent exorcism of the intruders [=the two youngest children], whom Dick styled

"mis'ble trundle bed trash." **1912** Green *VA Folk-Speech* 460, *Trundle-bed trash. . .* Applied to small children. **1941** *LANE* Map 379 *(Kid, tot)* 1 inf, **swCT,** Trucklebed trash. **1945** Bailey *Seaman Knapp* 10 neNY (as of 1840s), His fellow pupils ranged from timid youngsters of six and seven called unkindly by their older brothers and sisters "trucklebed trash," to fully grown, marriageable girls and strapping farm lads. **1972** *NYT Article Letters* c**NY,** My father's family always spoke of the smaller children in a family as the "trundlebed trash." This came also to me recently from relatives whose grandparents went from N.Y. to the Dakotas. **1984** Wilder *You All Spoken Here* 37 **Sth,** Trundlebed trash: Children, mildly censured.

trunk n

1 also *rice trunk:* A conduit penetrating the dike between a tidal river and a rice field and provided with hanging gates at each end that can be adjusted to flood or drain the field; now also used in the management of tidal wetlands; the gate itself; hence comb *trunk dock* the floodgate; comb *trunk-minder* one who controls the conduits. [*OED2 trunk* sb. 10.a "A box-like passage for light, air, water, or solid objects, usually made of boards"; 1610 →; *EDD trunk* sb.¹ 12 "An arched drain under a road; a culvert; a pipe or watercourse through an arch of masonry"] **SC**

1838 *Farmers' Reg.* 6.544 **SC,** I dug up my river trunks and replaced them at six inches above the low water mark. **1848** *Scientific Amer.* 3.282 **SC,** The inland planters, whose trunks have rotted away, and who are still trying to keep up this ancient practice in the culture of rice, are trying to mend up and sprout their seed. **1856** in 1910 Commons *Doc. Hist. Amer. Industrial Soc.* 1.120 **SC,** *Trunk-minders* undertake the whole care of the trunks. **1875** King *Gt. South* 435 **SC,** The trunks are opened in each section the day it is planted, and the fields are flooded. **1936** Smith-Sass *Carolina Rice* 24 **SC coast** (as of 1850s), There was necessary also a means of controlling the ingress and egress of water, keeping it on the land as long as needed and getting rid of it completely at other stages of the crop. This was accomplished by means of rectangular wooden culverts from twenty to thirty feet long, known as "trunks," placed in the main bank along the river, extending, of course, clear through the bank and equipped with a hanging door at each end. **1937** Heyward *Madagascar* 13 **sSC coast,** These sluice gates were known as "trunks," a name brought to the province by the early English settlers, who had seen them used in the freshwater marshes of England. **1966** *DARE* Tape **SC**9, [FW:] How do you flood the field? . . [Inf:] We call a trunk, but now they call 'em a gate. . . Trunk on nigh end of the field and a trunk on this end. **1966** *DARE* FW Addit **SC,** *Trunk*—a floodgate or lock used to control the level of water in the rice fields. *Ibid, Trunk dock*—doors, i.e., floodgates, used in rice planting; also *trunk,* generalized for any floodgate, whether or not concerned with rice. **1996** in 2006 *DARE* File—Internet **SC,** The next phase was to put trunk docks, also known as floodgates, in place to drain the [rice] fields. **2006** *Georgetown Times* (SC) 18 Aug (Internet), The humble rice trunk . . fits into the earthen dikes that made the borders of the rice fields. . . The gate on the river side of the dike would be set to open with the incoming tide to flood the fields. . . On the field side of the rice trunk another gate could be set to open with the incoming tide, but it would close as the tidal waters receded. When the time came to drain the water from the field, the gate on that side would be opened to allow the water to flow out. The other gate would allow water to leave the rice field on the out-going tide, but water pressure from the river would keep the gate closed on the incoming tide. . . Now, trunks made for some of the impound-ments and managed wetlands use 6 inch stainless steel nails.

2 also *trunk highway, trunk (line) road:* Used as a designa-tion for a main highway at the state or county level; hence combs *county trunk, state trunk.* [*OED2 trunk* sb. 4.a "the main line of a river, railway, telegraph or telephone, road or canal system"; 1817 →] **chiefly N Cent, Upper MW, esp WI** See Map on p. 728

1869 OH Laws *Genl. & Local Acts* 66.365. The county commissioners of Scioto County [may appoint persons to] . . survey and locate within their said county, one or more branch roads, beginning at and leading from any main trunk road. **1912** *Ft. Wayne Weekly Sentinel* (IN) 9 Oct [7]/7 (newspaperarchive.com), The plan is to improve county trunk line roads at the expense of the entire county. **1916** *Gazette* (Stevens Point WI) [29 Nov] 10/1 (newspaperarchive.com), We have . . distributed the state aid highway funds to the several trunk lines. **1916** *Van Nuys News* (CA) 30 June [4]/2 (newspaperarchive.com), Twelve million dollars will be used for the completion of the original system of trunk roads and county seat laterals. **1939** *IA City Press–Citizen* (IA) 21 Jan 2/1, There were 6.52 miles of county trunk and 11.59 miles of local county roads surfaced during the year. **1954** *Lincoln Eve. Jrl. & NE State Jrl.* (NE) 30 Apr 7/1, By the time the State Highway Commission has completed its work, every county in the state will have a trunk highway through it. **1965–70** *DARE* (Qu. N18, . . *Roads that have numbers or letters. For example, if someone asked directions . . "Take _____."*) Infs **WI**18, 19, 48, 51, 68, County trunk; **WI**12, 30, 43, County trunk + [letter]; **MN**1, 10, Trunk; **MI**105, Trunk line road; (Qu. N27a, *Names . . for different kinds of unpaved roads*) Inf **WI**62, Trunk road; (Qu. N29, . . *Names . . for a less important road running back from a main road*) Infs **IA**8, **WI**57, Trunk; **WI**5, County trunk. **1977** *Stevens Point Daily Jrl.* (WI) 20 Jan 11/2, Highways on the state trunk system are identified by numbers. **1994** *Daily Herald* (Arlington Heights IL) 7 Dec sec 1-A 46/3 **WI**, [Advt:] Located . . between Walworth County Trunk M & State Hwy 89.

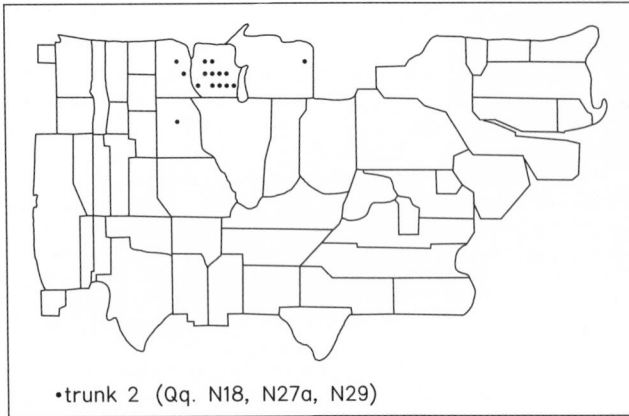

•trunk 2 (Qq. N18, N27a, N29)

3 also *trunk and tray:* One's best clothes—usu in phr *have on one's trunk.* among Black speakers

1966–70 *DARE* (Qu. W37, *When a woman puts on her good clothes and tries to look her best . . she's _____*) Inf **TN**53, She has on her trunk; (Qu. W38, *When a man dresses himself up in his best clothes . . he's _____*) Inf **TX**26, Got on his trunk; (Qu. W39, *Joking ways of referring to a person's best clothes*) Inf **VA**69, Has on his trunk; **TX**26, Smooth trunk; **MS**45, His trunk and tray. [All Infs Black]

trunkback n Also *trunk turtle* [*OED2* 1697 →]
=**leatherback 1.**

1738 Catesby in Royal Soc. London *Philos. Trans.* 39.117 **NC, SC**, *Testudo Arcuata:* The Trunk Turtle. . . [I]n the Repository of the Royal Society is a Turtle preserved entire, which [the author] takes to be of this Species. **1834** Audubon *Ornith. Biog.* 2.372, The Trunk Turtle, which is sometimes of an enormous size, and which has a pouch like a pelican, reaches the shores latest. **1883** Garman *Reptiles & Batrachians N. Amer.* vi, *Sea Turtles* are numerous off the coasts of Florida. "Trunk-backs" or "Leather-backs," *Sphargis,* are the largest. **1884** Goode *Fisheries U.S.* 1.147, Another species which may be mentioned is the so-called "Leather Turtle," or . . "Trunk Turtle." . . Occurs sparingly all along our Atlantic coast, from Massachusetts to Florida. **1935** Pratt *Manual Vertebrate Animals* 242, *D[ermochelys] coriacea.* . . Leather-turtle; trunk-back. . . Weight 700 lbs. and more: tropical seas; northward as far as Maine. **1966** *DARE* (Qu. P24, . . *Kinds of turtles*) Inf **FL**13, Trunkback—way out in Gulf, real big, not edible.

trunk dock See **trunk 1**

trunkfish n
Std: any of various fishes of the family Ostraciidae. For other names of these see **cowfish 1**

trunk highway, trunk line road See **trunk 2**

trunk-minder n See **trunk 1**

trunk peddler n Also *trunk pedler* **NEng** *obs* Cf **pack peddler**
An itinerant peddler who carries his stock in a trunk or trunks.

1827 in 2006 *DARE* File **NH**, Tonight we kept a trunk peddler, and paid us in pins and thread. **1828** *Ibid* **CT**, A trunk pedler calld. **1857** *Ibid* **CT**, Trunk peddler staied to dinner. How much longer he will stay no one knows. **1898** (1899) Earle *Home Life* 300 **NEng**, Chepa Rose

was one of those old-time chap-men known throughout New England as "trunk pedlers." Bearing on his back by means of a harness of stout hempen webbing two oblong trunks of thin metal,—probably tin,—for forty-eight years he had appeared at every considerable farmhouse.

trunk road See **trunk 2**

trunk turtle See **trunkback**

trupulo n
=**cupola B1.**

1987 *DARE* File **cMN**, On the top of the roof is a very small construction that is found on top of most older-model barns. It resembles a miniature barn with a tall roof. This "trupulo" [trupjʊloʊ] is made out of wood or metal and usually has a weathervane at the top on the crest.

trus'-me-Gawd See **trust-me-God**

truspass See **trespass**

trussel, trussle See **trestle**

trusspass See **trespass**

trustee n **IL, IA, OH, WI** Cf **pathmaster, surveyor**
Also in combs *trustee of roads, roads trustee:* A local official responsible for the upkeep of public roads.

1912 Weaver *Past and Pres.* 635 **IA**, He has acted as trustee of roads. **1968** *DARE* (Qu. N33, *A man whose job is to take care of roads in a certain locality*) Infs **OH**39, 48, 60, Trustee; **OH**61, Township trustee. **1985** *Daily Herald* (Arlington Heights IL) [1 Oct 36]/7 (newspaperarchive.com), Karl H. Schulz—Trustee of Roads. **2006** *DARE* File— Internet **seWI**, It was determined that the meeting with Wind Meadows Corp. should be scheduled with the incoming Roads Trustee. *Ibid* **neIL**, Village of McCullom Lake. . . Roads Trustee—Marilyn Shepit.

trust-God See **trust-me-God**

trustle See **trestle**

trust-me-God n Also *trust-God* Pronc-sp *trus'-me-Gawd* [See quot 1950] **seSC** *Gullah*
A small, unsteady boat, esp a **bateau B2.**

1922 Gonzales *Black Border* 335 **sSC, GA coasts** [Gullah glossary], *Trus'-me-Gawd*—a narrow dugout canoe, so cranky that one who ventures forth upon the waters must have faith in God to bring him through. **1937** Heyward *Madagascar* 244 **sSC coast**, I hurried to the landing on the Combahee, . . and crossed the angry river in a "trus'-me-Gawd." **1950** *PADS* 14.69 **eSC**, *Trus'-me-Gawd.* . . That is, *I trust my God*—a small canoe or small boat; a small dugout. Negro usage of S.C. coastal area. **1980** *Eve. Post* (Charleston SC) 12 Dec sec A 16/1, A fleet of little "trus' me gawds"—the leaky rowboats once so prevalent in the Lowcountry before there were such things as bridges. **1982** *McDavid Coll.* **seSC**, *Trust God*—Black name for the small flat-bottomed bateau. *Ibid* **Charleston SC**, *Trust-me-God*—homemade bateau.

trust one to See **to** prep **B14**

trust out v phr
To supply (goods) on credit; to give in credit, loan out (money).

[**1687** in 1849 *Doc. Hist. State of NY* 1.172, He was expressly forbid to trust out his Ma[jes]tys revenue notwithstanding I was forc't to take notes from him to the value of £800.] **1833** Smith *Life Jack Downing* 184 **ME**, That afternoon that Mr Clark spoke all day, I guess I sold nigh upon half a bushel [of apples] for cash, and trusted out most three pecks besides. **1843** in 2006 *DARE* File **seTX**, I . . must remain here as my money is all trusted out and I have considerable property. **1872** Griffin *Hist. Press ME* 84, Many young men . . miscalculated as to the available means of the place, trusted out their goods, and failed. **1876** *Harper's New Mth. Mag.* 52.790 **IN**, Supposing you . . had invested two or three thousand dollars in an enterprise which you designed to make an *exclusively cash* business; supposing . . you had trusted it out all over the country, from — to Jericho. **1878** *Ibid* 57.582 **CT**, You don't think I ever see a copper o' her cash, do ye? It's trusted out to a bank in Har'ford quick as lightnin'. **1895** *Fitchburg Daily Sentinel* (MA) 17 Dec 3/3, Nineteen years and over I have continued the credit [grocery] business and naturally have a large amount of money trusted out. **1929** *AmSp* 5.125 **ME**, Folk often spoke of someone who . . had "trusted out his money." **1965** *DARE* FW Addit **OK**, *Trusting out*—selling goods on credit—used by Cushing native.

trustpass See **trespass**

truth n Pronc-spp, *esp among Black speakers, troof, troot, truf(e), trute* **Sth** Cf Pronc Intro 3.I.17
Std sense, var forms.

1834 *Atl. Club-Book* 1.147 [Black], Yes, massa minister, me albays tell de troot to shame 'e debble. **1845** *Huron Reflector* (Norwalk OH) 13 May 1/5 **LA** [Black], Dat's de trute Sam, de trute, I know it is. **1860** *Harper's New Mth. Mag.* 21.571 **Sth** [Black], De fac is, ole massy, I tell you de troof. **1862** in 2006 *DARE* File—Internet **MD**, No honey I tell you the trute suh. No man here for long time. **1879** *Hagerstown Mail* (MD) 14 Mar 1/4 **GA** [Black], I'll tell yer de trufe, now honey! **1899** Chesnutt *Conjure Woman* 11 **csNC** [Black], De truf er de matter is dat dis yer ole vimya'd [=vineyard] is goophered. **1922** Gonzales *Black Border* 335 **sSC, GA coasts** [Gullah glossary], *Trute*—truth. **1936** Greene *Death Deep South* 209 [Black], Mr. Griffin done promise me I won't git in no trouble if I tell the trufe, the whole trufe and nothin' but the trufe.

truth-mouth n *Gullah* Cf **bad mouth** n 3, **hush-mouth** 1
One who speaks only the truth.

1922 Gonzales *Black Border* 335 **sSC, GA coasts** [Gullah glossary], *Trute-mouth'*—truth-mouth—one who will not lie. **1949** Turner *African-isms* 232 **sSC, GA coasts** [Gullah], [trut mʊut] 'truth'; 'a truthful person,' i.e., 'truth mouth.' Cf. the Twi expression *anokware* 'truth,' lit. 'the mouth true.' **2004** Belton *Beauty Basket* [2] **SC**, Nana gives me a big hug and tells me I'm beautiful. "A truth mouth, me," she says, and squeezes tight.

try v
1 To be about (to get sick or, rarely, to die). **chiefly Sth, S Midl**

1863 in 2006 *DARE* File—Internet **MS**, I feel much better today than usual. Add is also nearly well, and McNeill is trying to get sick. **1913** in 2007 *NADS Letters* **ceSC**, [Mother] has had a time lately with An-nie . . trying to have appendicitis but I believe A is all O.K. now. **1944** *PADS* 2.14 **AL**, *Try to:* . . To be on the point of, about to. Followed by infinitive auxiliary of near future without idea of intention. "Look at that girl's arms; she's trying to catch pneumonia." . . Popular colloquial. ((The Editor has heard the expression used in an ironical rebuking sense: Va., N.C., S.C., Tenn.)) **1957** *DE Folkl. Bulletin* 1.28, *Try* (be on the verge of—as in "She's trying to catch a cold.") **1967** *DARE* Tape **AL**20, We just tried to die when we missed him. **1995** in 2006 *DARE* File—Internet **sTX**, In South Texas the expression "trying to get sick" can be used for "about to get sick." **2003** *Ibid* **cOH**, Headache fading, dry mouth prevalent. I think I may be trying to catch a cold. **2005** *Ibid* **LA**, Usually, my great-aunt cooks them, but she's trying to catch a cold and didn't want to be coughing all over the food. *Ibid* **TN**, I'm really dragging today. I'm not sure, but I may be trying to get sick. **2006** *Ibid* **ceTX**, I think that Im trying to get sick. I havent had an earache in along time and now Im getting one. *Ibid* **FL**, Out of the eight needles, only one hurt me. . . She [=an acupuncturist] said, "You are probably trying to catch a cold, and that's why it hurt."

2 in phr *try oneself:* To behave in an unruly or extravagant manner; to misbehave, "act up."

1912 Green *VA Folk-Speech* 460, He tried himself yesterday; he was just as bad as he could be. **1942** McAtee *Dial. Grant Co. IN* 68 **MD, VA** (as of 1890s), *Try* . . go the limit, overdo; said of a wilful adult, but usually of children being naughty or showing off; "He's jest a'tryin' himself". **1946** *PADS* 6.31 **eNC** (as of 1900–10), *Try oneself.* . . To make a nuisance of oneself when company is around. Applied mainly to children. Pamlico. Common. **1947** *PADS* 8.15 **IN**, *Try oneself. Ibid* 21 **IA**, *Try oneself:* Also *to outdo oneself. Ibid* 29 **MO**, *Try oneself.* **1956** McAtee *Some Dialect NC* 48, *Try* . . go the limit, overdo; said usually of a persistently naughty child. "He's jest a-tryin' hisself." **2006** *DARE* File—Internet, As I had thought he [=a horse] might, he really tried himself—or should I say he really tested me.

3 with *for:* To perform beneficial magic for (a person) or against (an ailment). **PaGer area** Cf **brauche, powwow** n, v

1933 *Sun* (Baltimore MD) 29 Nov 12/3 **csPA**, Two "witch doctors". . . were credited with making plenty of money "trying" for afflicted persons. **1939** Aurand *Quaint Idioms* 18 [PaGer], Oh, my; that child has the *obnemma* (take-off; malnutrition); you must have her "tried for" (pow-wowed). **1940** Writers' Program *Guide MD* 8, Many curious words and expressions heard frequently in Maryland have been imported by German settlers. . . to 'try for' is the expression applied to running down a witch or hex. **1968** *DARE* (Qu. BB51b, . . 'Magical' cures for

corns or warts) Inf **MD**28, Trying for a wart—rub it with red thread three times, say words; person who knows what words to say is a pow-wow. **2003** *Jrl. Consumer Health* (Internet) 7.4.77 **sePA**, "To try for," is commonly employed when a healer agrees to see an ailing patient, e.g., to try for a rash.

4 Used to introduce imperatives; see quots. [Abbr for *try and* + imper; cf **and** conj B3] **HI**

1934 *AmSp* 9.123 [Engl dial of HI], *Try* has become an auxiliary of the imperative, a trifle less polite than *please: Mr. Reinecke, try read this page.* **1942** *AmSp* 17.18 **HI** [Engl of Hawaiian children], *Try.* . . Used with almost any imperative as in *Try come here.* **1972** Carr *Da Kine Talk* 155 **HI**, *Try* is sometimes heard . . as a polite form, replacing "if you please." **1981** *Pidgin To Da Max* np **HI**, *Try.* . . Halfway between *please* and nothing at all. **2006** *DARE* File—Internet **HI**, You like learn about Pidgin? Try go come den!

try for See **try 3**

try line n
=**taw C2a.**

1968 *DARE* (Qu. EE8, *The line toward which the players roll their marbles before beginning a game, to determine the order of shooting*) Inf **IN**14, Try line.

try oneself See **try 2**

trysting-out n

1952 Brown *NC Folkl.* 1.602, *Trysting-out: n.* . . A clandestine meeting between a married man and a married woman who are not married to each other.—Caldwell county.

T's exclam Cf **time out**
Time out; hence v phr *call T's.*

1967 *DARE* (Qu. EE17, *In a game of tag, if a player wants to rest, what does he call out so that he can't be tagged?*) Inf **MA**8, Times out or T.O. [FW: Inf's nine-year-old son responded with "T's."] **1996** *Focus USA* 79 **csWI** (as of 1994), In my son's 4th grade class . . there were nine responses of *T's* and 12 of *time out.* My daughter's 7th grade class . . answered with *T's* twice, *time out* ten times, and *times* three times.

tschawytscha n [Russ < Kamchatkan; see quot 1886] Also sp *chavitcha, chouicha, tchaviche, tshaviche*
=**chinook salmon.**

[**1870** Dall *Alaska* 201, Early in June the king salmon (*Kahthl'* of the Ingaliks, or *chowichee* of the Russians) begin to ascend the river.] **1882** U.S. Natl. Museum *Bulletin* 16.306, *O[ncorhynchus] chouicha.* . . *Quinnat Salmon; King Salmon; . . Saw-kwey; Chouicha.* Color dusky above. *Ibid* 307, *Salmo tshawytscha* Walbaum, 1792. [Footnote to *tshawytscha:*] A barbarous spelling of the word *"chouicha"* which we have thought proper to simplify. **1882** Petroff *Report on the Population, Industries, and Resources of Alaska* (1880 census) 26 (Tabbert *Dict. Alaskan Engl.*), The fishermen descend to tide-water only when king-salmon or "chavitcha", come up from the sea in dense masses. [**1884** Goode *Fisheries U.S.* 1.479, In Alaska and Kamtchatka . . this species is known as the 'King Salmon,' and as 'Choweecha' or 'Tchawy-tcha,' a name easier to pronounce than to spell, to the Russians.] [**1886** Turner *Contribs. AK* 107, The Russian-speaking people call this species [=*Oncorhynchus tschawytscha*] *Chavicha*, a word derived from the Kamchadale language and applied to this or kindred species.] **1896** U.S. Natl. Museum *Bulletin* 47.479, *Oncorhynchus tschawytscha.* . . *Chinook Salmon; Tyee Salmon; . . Tschawytscha. Ibid* 480, *Tschawy-tscha,* better spelled by earlier writers *Tshaviche,* the vernacular name in Alaska and Kamchatka. **1946** Dufresne *AK's Animals* 272, The King salmon. . . in various places . . is called Chinook, Spring, Tyee and Tschawytscha (Cha-wí-scha). **1976** Tryckare et al. *Lore of Sportfishing* 75, *Chinook Salmon.* . . Other common names: Columbia River salmon, tyee salmon, . . tchaviche, tschawytscha.

tsitterly See **zitterli**

T.T.I. See **two-toilet Irish**

(-)tu prep, adv See **to** prep, adv A2

tu v See **tew** v

tub n Cf **shell** n[1] 1, **snit**
See quots.

1936 Howard in *Cowboy Stories* June 120 **TX**, "Set down," said the big man, easing his bulk ponderously into a chair and sinking his mustaches into a tub of beer. **1945** *AmSp* 20.237, At the few taverns in Austin, Texas, where draught beer is sold, a large sixteen-ounce glass, regardless of shape, is quite generally called a *tub.* **1951** *Western Folkl.* 10.1.80 **NM,** *Barroom Slang from the Upper Rio Grande.* . . tub of beer (large stein).

tubercular n
Tuberculosis.

1943 *LANE* Map 510 *(Tuberculosis)* 1 inf, **sME coast,** [ðə tǔˇˈbɜˀˈkˑjulə], used as a name for the disease. **1968–70** *DARE* (Qu. K28, . . *Chief diseases that cows have*) Inf **PA**141, Tubercular; (Qu. BB49, . . *Other kinds of diseases*) Inf **NJ**67, Tubercular.

tuber root n   Also *tuber-root asclepias*
=butterfly weed 1.

1847 Wood *Class-Book* 460, *Tuber-root Asclepias. Butterfly Weed.* . . Root large, fleshy, sending up numerous stems. **1930** Sievers *Amer. Med. Plants* 18, *Asclepias tuberosa.* . . Pleurisy-root, . . orange-root, . . tuberroot, whiteroot. **1976** Bailey–Bailey *Hortus Third* 117, *[Asclepias] tuberosa.* . . Tuberroot. . . Rootstock woody. . . Dried root has medicinal properties.

tub mill n   esp sAppalachians
A simple grist mill operated by a horizontal waterwheel attached directly to the shaft that turns the stone.

[**1775** (1924) Cresswell *Jrl.* 66 [Engl traveler in **VA**], He has got a small tub mill.] **1803** *Boston Weekly Mag.* 1.191, *Died.* . . At Grafton, (N.H.) a child three years old. . . He fell into a mill pond while his father was grinding . . and was lodged upon the floats of the tub under the cylinder of a patent tub mill. **1818** Monroe *Message Congress* 79, There are three mills turned by the river Mapocho: they . . are what would be called, in the middle states of our union, tub mills. **1824** Doddridge *Notes Indian Wars* 143 **WV, PA,** Our first water mills were of that discription [sic] denominated tub mills. **1842** in 1959 *IN Mag. Hist.* 55.329 **wPA, neKY,** About the year 1768, Philip Shoot built a tub-mill on Dunbar's creek. **1851** Turner *Hist. Pioneer Settlement* 368 **cwNY** (as of 1789), They erected a crude "tub mill" on the small stream that puts into the river on the Markham farm. **1858** *Harper's New Mth. Mag.* 16.174 **wNC, eTN,** There was a tub-mill belonging to the mountaineer's establishment, and thither came the neighbors from far and near. **1913** Kephart *Highlanders* 132 **sAppalachians,** About every fourth or fifth farmer has a tiny tub-mill of his own. **1924** Raine *Land of Saddle-Bags* 80 **sAppalachians,** When a man lives on a branch or a prong of the creek, whar the water's lasty and thar's a right smart trickle all the time, he puts him in a tub mill, and lets the water grind fer him. . . Ye take a log and hew it till hit's kindly like a tub with a long spindle rising right out'n the midst of it. Run your water in a trough so it'll hit right in the tub and as fast as hit turns o' course the spindle turns too. Then ye fasten your grindin' stone on the top o' your spindle, and thar's your mill. **1973** *Foxfire 2* 158 **nGA,** Maude Shope . . had a little tub mill on her property. It was almost gone by the time we got there.

tub owl n
Perh a **screech owl 1;** see quot.

1966 *DARE* (Qu. Q2, . . *Kinds of owls*) Inf **NC**35, Tub owl—heard on knobs before bad weather—winter—live in hollow tree.

tub sugar n   NEast
Maple sugar of a soft, sticky consistency.

1834 *Hazard's Reg. PA* 13.207, We made one year, from 37 trees, 3 cwt. of tub sugar. **1863** *Scientific Amer.* 8.52 **NH,** If it [=maple syrup] is to be caked, it must be harder than for tub sugar. **1892** VT State Bd. Ag. *Report* 12.156, Nice tub sugar or cakes [sell] at eight to fifteen cents per pound. **1896** *DN* 1.426 **NYC,** *Tub-sugar:* coarse-grained sugar. **1967** *DARE* Tape **MA**5C, They had two kinds of sugar, . . cake sugar and a soft tub sugar. Soft tub sugar, you . . don't boil it so hard. . . You set that right on your table and you just take a spoon and dip this soft sugar out. **1978** (1990) Perrin *First Person* 27 **VT,** Vermonters have only four names for different degrees of hardness in maple candy: maple cream (which is too soft for a mold), soft tub sugar, hard tub sugar, and cakes.

tuck n   Cf tucks
In phr *take the tuck out of:* To deprive of toughness, courage, or strength.

1851 (1852) Lee *Summerfield Life* 23 **NY,** I thought Matthew was a gonner [sic], and the fright takes the tuck out o' my old knees. **1868** Holmes *Rose Mather* 92 **NY,** He'd take the tuck out of the Southern gen-

tlemen,—yes, he would. **1878** Twain in *Atlantic Mth.* 41.17, We had an iron-clad chicken that. . . ought to have been put through a quartz mill until the "tuck" was taken out of him, and then boiled till we came again. **1882** Peck *Peck's Sunshine* 296 **WI,** The incident seemed to take the tuck all out of him. **1914** *DN* 4.113 **cKS,** Take the tuck out of. . . To exhaust; dispirit. "So many lawyers on the other side took the tuck out of him." **1916** Baily *Homeward Trail* 121 **NC,** "That Salisbury prison kinder took the tuck out of me," he admitted. "I'm too darn' puny for any use." **1940** Fletcher *Raleigh's Eden* 69 **NC** [Black], He [=a horse] need more jumping to take the tuck out of he. **1988** Mieder *As Sweet* 16 **VT,** It took the tuck right out of me. **2004** *DARE* File—Internet, The way that the same tired old claims keep bouncing back no matter how thoroughly they've been debunked is enough to take the tuck out of just about anyone.

tuck v   See take v A2a, 3b

tuckahoe n   [See quot 1902 at 1 below]
1 also *tuckyhoe, tuckahoo:* Orig any of var plants with edible roots or the root of such a plant; more recently chiefly an **arrow arum** (here: *Peltandra virginica*) or **golden club 1;** see quots.   **chiefly C Atl**

[**1624** Smith *Genl. Hist. VA* 26, The chiefe root they haue for food is called *Tockawhoughe.* It groweth like a flagge in Marishes. In one day a Salvage will gather sufficient for a weeke. These roots are much of a greatnesse and taste of *Potatoes.*] **1662** in 1810 VA Laws *Statutes at Large* 2.140, The poore Indians whome the seating of the English hath forced from their wonted conveniencies of . . gathering tuckahoe, cuttyemnions, or other wild fruites. [**1705** Beverley *Hist. VA* 3.15, A Tuberous Root they call *Tuckahoe,* which while crude is of a very hot and virulent quality: but they can manage . . to make Bread of it.] **1748** in 1970 Kalm *Resejournal* 2.225, Mr. Bartram hade *Tubera terrae* . . dem han tagit uti sandig jord i Jersey, hvarest de växa ymnigt; dessa vste han åt mannen, som var från Carolina, och frågade honom, om de samma voro indianernes tuckahoo. . . Han svarade: nej. . . Men hvad tuckahoo angår, så växar den uti särskilta kärr och moraser, och det ofta ymnigt. [=Mr. Bartram had *tubera terrae* . . that he had collected from sandy soil in Jersey, where they grow abundantly; which he showed to a man who was from Carolina, and asked him if they were the same as the tuckahoo of the Indians. He said that they were not. . . But as for the tuckahoo, that it grew in certain swamps and marshes, and often abundantly.] [**1830** Rafinesque *Med. Flora* 2.270, All esculent roots called [by Amer Indians] *Tuckaho,* such as *Apios* and *Patatos.*] **1869** Porcher *Resources* 572 **Sth,** Wild Coontie; *Tuckahoe,* (*Zamia integrifolia*). . . The large succulent, fleshy roots, when properly treated, yield a large quantity of arrowroot. **1882** Torrey Bot. Club *Bulletin* 9.115 **NC,** The use of the word "crocus" for trailing arbutus is no more singular than the local employment of "tuckahoe" for *Orontium aquaticum.* **1902** *Jrl. Amer. Folkl.* 15.263, *Tuckahoe.* The name of several vegetable substances used for food by the Indians of the southern and middle Atlantic States,—the "Virginia wake-robin" . . , the "golden club" . . , etc. The name is also applied to a sort of fungus called also "Virginia truffle," "Indian bread," "Indian loaf,"—various species of *Pachyma, Lycoperdon,* etc. The Indian word seems to have had a generic meaning and to have been applied to a variety of bulbous roots. The origin of *tuckahoe* is seen in the Lenâpé *p'tuckqueu,* "something round, rounded." **1916** *Torreya* 16.237 **MD,** *Nymphaea advena* [=*Nuphar lutea* subsp *a.*] . . Tuckahoe. **1942** Footner *MD Main* 214 **seMD,** The cypress and tuckahoe fill its swamps. **1970** *DARE* (Qu. S26b, *Wildflowers that grow in water or wet places*) Inf **VA**52, Wild duck corn (arum) = tuckyhoe berry = whampy [sic for *wampee*] seed—large arrow-shaped leaf, wild duck eat seed, flower either nonexistent or inconspicuous. **1989** (1990) Baden *Maryland's E. Shore* 51, The shore seems to move in waves as a breeze sways the deep green tuckahoe marshes. **1995** *Amer. Jrl. Botany* 82.1230, [Title:] The Pollination Biology of Tuckahoe, *Peltandra virginica.*

2 also *tuckahoe truffle, tuckahoo:* An edible subterranean fungus (*Poria cocos*).   Cf **Indian bread 3**

1743 (1946) Gronovius *Flora Virginica* 205, Tubera Terræ maxima, externe pulla & scabra, intus candida. Ad panem conficiendum Indi utuntur, vulgo *Tuckahoo.* [=Tubera Terræ maxima, outside dark-colored & rough, inside white. Used in making bread by the Indians, commonly *Tuckahoo.*] **1809** Ramsay *Hist. SC* 2.194, Indian potatoe, suckahoe [sic] truffles, lycoperdon tuber is found in great abundance in old fields one or two feet beneath the surface of the earth, attached to the decayed roots of the hickory. This subterranean production afforded the indians wholesome bread. **1871** U.S. Dept. Ag. *Rept. of Secy. for 1870* 423,

Tuckahoe or Indian head, (Lycoperdon solidum.) . . These singular fungous growths are subterranean and parasitic on roots of large trees. **1882** Torrey Bot. Club *Bulletin* 9.125 **VA, MD,** *The Tuckahoe.*—In Virginia and in Maryland this name is applied exclusively to that curious subterranean tuber, *Pachyma cocos.* . . In Virginia and in Maryland, when large, they are frequently roasted and eaten with salt by the negroes. This use of them they learned from the Indians. **1902** [see **1** above]. **1902** McIlvaine–Macadam *1000 Amer. Fungi* 567, There is a well-known growth, found from New Jersey south to the Gulf and west to Kansas, called Tuckahoe (Pachyma cocos) . . , an Indian name meaning a round loaf or cake, and famed for its edible qualities.

3 usu cap; also *tuckyhoe, tucky hole:* Usu a person from Virginia, esp from east of the Blue Ridge, but occas with other local applications; the language of such a person; see quots. [Prob from a place name (in turn from sense **1** above). *Tuckahoe* occurs as the name of many watercourses and other geographic features, chiefly east of the Appalachians from southeastern New York through Georgia.] *often derog* Cf **cohee**

1815 in 1956 Eliason *Tarheel Talk* 302 **cn,cNC,** The low country people [of Virginia] are called Truhahoes [sic] from Truffles . . or from Tuckahou creek near Richmond. **1816** *OH Repository* (Canton) 12 Sept 1/2, The *Tuckahoes* and *Cohees* once the true blue Virginians, the former the low, and the latter the up country-men; but the name of Tuckahoes has sometimes been applied to all the low country people south of the Potomack; and it has again been limited, even in Virginia to the pale yellow skinned men, who wear copperas coloured hunting shirts, breakfast on pig soup and peas [etc]. . . [D]uring the revolutionary war it was considered a term of reproach.—The Cohees used to apply it, & their animosity to each other was little less than both to the British. **1851** *Ladies' Repository* 11.259 **nwOH** (as of 1813), The Yankees laughed at the tuckahoes; and they, in their turn, at the Yankees and their odd proverbialisms. **1855** Whitman *Leaves of Grass* 16, Kanuck, Tuckahoe, Congressman, Cuff, I give them the same, I receive them the same. **1887** *Atlantic Mth.* 60.334 **cVA** [Black], I jes' 'spicioned she come f'om over de mount'ins soon as I put my eyes on her. . . Ain't no po' white trash over yer kin tetch dat breed o' Tuckahoes. **1899** (1912) Green *VA Folk-Speech* 460, *Tuckahoe.* . . The name given to the eastern Virginians to distinguish them from the "*Quo'he's*" of the west. **1913** (1980) Hardy *OH Schoolmistress* 100, It was common in the neighborhood to speak of people who came from Kentucky as "Tuckahoes." **1930** *DN* 6.89 **cWV,** *Tuckyhoe,* a term applied to the dialect of people of Virginia. **1938** *Charleston Gaz.* (WV) 15 May 10/1, Asked if she is a West Virginian, she says "Go git the cows and milk 'em in a gourd. Bring home the buckets and cover 'em with a board; That's Tuckyhoe." **1950** *Zanesville Signal* (OH) 13 Mar 5/5, Tuckahoe was the name given by Putnam pioneers to Zanesville settlers who came from Virginia. . . By the end of the 19th century the word Tuckahoes was still used, but the origin had been forgotten and the form of the word had been corrupted to Tucky Holes. **1972** Cooper *NC Mt. Folkl.* 123, Tuckahoe. . . In the Carolina Mountains the appelation [sic] was given to a person who was lazy, shiftless and lacking sufficient ambition to improve his economic condition. **1984** Woods *WV Was Good* 223, Tuckahoe—in West Virginia this word referred to a person from Virginia who spoke with a Virginia accent more pronounced than in the speech of local people. **2006** *DARE* File—Internet **cVA,** Folks from over in the valley called us back here on this [=the east] side of the mountain, Tuckyhoes.

tuckahoe truffle See **tuckahoe 2**

tuck comb See **tucking comb**

tucked See **take** v A2e

tucken See **take** v A2f, 3d

tucker n, often cap   Cf **Dan Tucker**

A dancing game in which a lone player attempts to secure the partner of another; the partnerless player; hence n *Tucker party;* v phr *dance Tucker;* vbl n *dancing Tucker.*

1881 (1939) Mayne *Maud* 25 **sIL,** It was a tucker and I danced it with Mr. B. . . Just then the tucker swung me. **1891** *Harper's New Mth. Mag.* 82.215 **wNC, eTN,** The fun was waxing fast and furious with the added and unique diversion known as "Dancin' Tucker." *Ibid,* The forlorn "Tucker" himself, partnerless in the centre of the set, capered solemnly up and down. **1892** *Portsmouth Times* (OH) 3 Dec 6/1, The Iron Moulders' Union . . gave a ball. . . They . . danced "Tucker" for the close. **1943** Powell *I Can Go Home* 93 **swGA** (as of 1880s), We were not allowed to dance—that was against the rules of the churches—but we played "Tucker" and "twistification." The former was simply the

old fashioned square dance under another name. **1967** *DARE* Tape **MA**108, [**MA**108:] Used to have Tucker parties upstairs in the schoolhouse. . . [**MA**5:] That wasn't actually dancing. Some of those very strict people would let the young folks play Tucker because it was only marching and it wasn't dancing.

tuckernuck n [Prob from *Tuckernuck* small island near Nantucket, Massachusetts] Cf **squantum 1**

A picnic; hence adv *tuckernuck* in the fashion of a picnic.

1887 (1895) Robinson *Uncle Lisha* 157 **wVT,** We'll go tuckernuck, kerry aour own pervision; on'y mushrat an' fish we'll expeck you tu furnish. **1902** *Jrl. Amer. Folkl.* 15.264 **seMA,** *Tuckernuck.* In some parts of southeastern Massachusetts, etc., this word was used in the sense of "picnic." It is also the name of an island off Nantucket. **2005** *DARE* File—Internet **MO,** A tuckernuck is a picnic.

Tucker party See **tucker**

tucket corn n [Appar aphet form of *Nantucket,* Massachusetts] A variety of **Indian corn 1;** see quots. Note: The definition in quot 1872, which has been followed by many dictionaries, is not supported by other evidence.

1819 Butler *Farmer's Manual* 134, Plant early corn, such as the small tucket, sweet corn, Canada corn, and great tucket. [**1845** in 1899 *Provisional Govt. NE Terr.* 158, Set out twelve hills sweet potatoes, and [planted] fifteen [hills] Nantucket corn.] **1850** *People's Vade-Mecum* 39, *How to Pop Corn as it should be.*—Lard is to be heated . . and half a pint or such a matter, of the "eight row 'tucket corn" is to be thrown in and covered immediately. **1856** *MI State Ag. Soc. Trans. for 1855* 7.528, Wm. Knowles, bushel tucket corn. Good sample. **1858** *Harper's New Mth. Mag.* 16.763 **NEng,** He had made, during the day, frequent deposits of green corn, of the diminutive species called *tucket*—smuggled in from the garden, and designed for roasting and eating. [**1872** Schele de Vere *Americanisms* 39, The *tucket,* as the green ear is called as long as it is soft and milky, is quite a delicacy to some palates.] **1875** Barron *Foot Notes* 85 **CT,** I have a farm. . . It feeds a cow,/ . . and has / A cobbly patch for beans and tucket corn. **1881** in 2003 *DARE* File—Internet **KS,** [From the *Winfield Courier* of 4 Aug:] Andrew Hanney has the finest crop of corn on Silver Creek. He says that it is the Tucket corn, and he will have seed for sale. **1893** Roe *Rose Neighborhood* 308 **nwNY,** Mr Hickok has made a specialty of raising pop or tucket corn.

tuckey n[1]   See **tacky** n **1**

tuckey n[2]   See **turkey**

tuckil See **turtle**

tucking comb n   Also *tuck comb*   **chiefly S Midl**   Cf **redding comb**

A comb used to fasten the hair at the back of the head.

1822 in 1944 *DAE* **eNC,** Mr. Pettigrew Bot of D. McDowell one tucking Comb at $4.50. **1824** *Mo. Intelligencer* 8 May 3/3 (*DA*), Tortoise shell, tuck and side combs. **1853** *Daily Alton Telegraph* (IL) 20 Sept [2]/6 (newspaperarchive.com), On Thursday night last, there was stolen from my premises . . a silver Tucking Comb, and gold Pencil. **1871** Eggleston *Hoosier Schoolmaster* 50 **sIN,** Betsey Short giggled until her tuck-comb fell out. **1891** *Jrl. Amer. Folkl.* 4.317 **cTN,** The hair of the younger girls is "bobbed". . . The older girls wear theirs "roached" (combed back straight), and fastened in a loose knot at the back of the head with a "tucking comb"—a back comb without a top. **1899** (1912) Green *VA Folk-Speech* 461, *Tucking-comb.* **1903** *DN* 2.335 **seMO,** *Tuckin-comb.* . . Back comb; a large comb used for holding a woman's hair in place. **1907** *DN* 3.237 **nwAR,** *Tuckin'-comb.* **1909** *DN* 3.384 **eAL, wGA,** *Tuck(ing)-comb.* **1915** *DN* 4.192 **swVA,** *Tuckin' com'.* **1953** Randolph–Wilson *Down in Holler* 294 **Ozarks,** *Tuckin' comb.* . . A comb that old women wear at the back of their heads. . . In pioneer days, some long-haired men wore *tuckin' combs;* Major Elias Rector, of Fort Smith, Ark., was one of them. I saw an old man with a comb in his hair as recently as 1947, in Carroll County, Ark. **1966** *Wilson Coll.* **csKY,** *Tucking comb.* . . [T]he comb was fastened in the knot of hair, the "biscuit" or bun. **1983** *MJLF* 9.1.59 **ceKY** (as of 1956), *Tucking comb.* **2006** *DARE* File—Internet [Good Hair Days], 1 ½″ crystal tuck comb, 8-teeth.

tuckr(e)y See **turkey**

tucks n   Cf **tuck**

Stiffness—usu in phrr *take* (or *get*) *the tucks out of.*

1870 Duval *Advent. Big-Foot* 134 **TX,** Our author came down from his roost, and threw himself at full length upon the ground, for the purpose, as he said, of getting the tucks out of his legs. **1911** Porter *Harvester* 366 **IN,** I was all crippled up with the rheumatiz. . . 'Long comes David and says, 'I can fix you somethin',' and bless you, if the boy didn't take the tucks out of me, until here I am, and tickled to pieces that I can get here. [**1916** *DN* 4.341 **seOH,** *Tucks.* . . Rheumatism.] **1916** *England Pod Bender* 350 **PA,** We both need a brisk canter to take the tucks out. Let's hike.

tuckyhoe See **tuckahoe 1, 3**

tucky hole See **tuckahoe 3**

Tucson bed n   esp SW

See quots.

1923 Cook *50 Yrs.* 6 **West,** As some readers may not know what a "Tucson bed" is, I will explain that it is made by lying on your stomach and covering that with your back. **1932** Lockwood *Pioneer Days AZ* 328, There were no hotels, but the "Tucson bed" was famous all through the Southwest. The traveler made this bed by lying on his stomach and covering that with his back.

tudder, tudduh See **tother**

Tuesday n   **widespread, but esp Nth, N Midl** |ˈtuzˌde, -ˌdɪ|; **widespread, but more freq Sth, S Midl** |ˈtjuzˌde, -ˌdɪ|; **scattered, but esp NEng** |ˈtɪuzˌde, -ˌdɪ|; **chiefly Sth, S Midl** |ˈč(ɪ)uzˌde, -ˌdɪ| Cf Pronc Intro 3.I.10   Pronc-spp *Chewsday, Chus(e)day, Toosday;* for addit varr see quots

Std sense, var forms.

1814 Morgan *Elements Engl. Gram.* 5 **ME,** The most absurd [pronunciation] is that, which changes *t* before *u,* into *ch.* As . . chuesday. **1832** in 1927 *AmSp* 2.322 **NY,** [In an example of unsophisticated pronunciation:] She says she cannot abide a *dooelist,* although last *Toosday* she saw one in the street for the *fust* time. **1851** in 1956 Eliason *Tarheel Talk* 319 **NC,** Chusday. **1857** *Ibid,* Tussday. **1871** Eggleston *Hoosier Schoolmaster* 176 **sIN,** Have a spellin'-school a Chewsday night. **1902** *DN* 2.248 **sIL,** Tuesday. Pronounced chuzedy [čuzdɪ]. **1903** *DN* 2.335 **seMO,** *Tuesday.* . . Pronounced Chewsday [čɪuzde]. This is a very fashionable pronunciation. **1907** *DN* 3.227 **nwAR,** *Tuesday.* . . Pronounced [čuzdɪ]. *Ibid* 237 **nwAR,** *Tuesday.* . . Sometimes pronounced Chewsday [čɪuzde]. **1908** *DN* 3.298 **eAL, wGA,** Chewsday. **1922** Gonzales *Black Border* 293 **sSC, GA coasts** [Gullah glossary], Chuesday. **1928** *AmSp* 3.383 **NJ,** A Negro woman of Charlottesville, Virginia, who worked in Atlantic City for one season came back home pronouncing *Tuesday* and *newspaper* as if they were spelled *Toosday* and *noospaper.* **c1937** in 1972 *Amer. Slave* 2.2.88 **SC** [Black], On the plantation was a Meetin' house . . used to have meetin's every Chuseday night. **1952** Brown *NC Folkl.* 1.695, De old Kurnel lef' on Chusday. **1952** *AmSp* 27.188 **WA,** Words like . . *Tuesday* . . are frequently pronounced [. . tᴵuwzdij . .], sometimes with a centralized vowel, but are also commonly heard as [. . tuwzdij . .]. **1961** Kurath–McDavid *Pronc. Engl.* 174, The type of /nu, du, tiuzde/ is current throughout the North and the North Midland. . . [I]n the New England settlement area it is the predominant pronunciation, but not the only one. The type of /nju, dju, tjuzde/ has general currency in the South and the South Midland. . . The type of /niu, diu, tiuzde/ . . is largely confined to New England and the Yankee settlements to the west. It is especially common in folk speech. **1966** Wilson *Coll.* **csKY,** Tuesday is usually [tjuzdɪ]. **1989** Pederson *LAGS Tech. Index* 15 **Gulf Region,** [For *Tuesday,* 537 infs offered proncs of the types [ˈtɪuzdɪ, -de, -dɪ]; 219 of the types [ˈtuzdɪ, -de, -dɪ]; 9 of the types [ˈčɪuzdɪ, -de]; 6 infs, [ˈčuzdɪ].] **2000** Metcalf *How We Talk* 12 **Sth,** In the South, *news* is "nyews," *due* is "dyew," and *Tuesday* is "Tyewsday." **2003** *DARE* File—Internet **Sth,** And don't think one pronunciation of "Tuesday" is universal in the U.S.! I'm from the South originally where folks says "teeewesday".

Tuesday is longer than Monday See **Monday comes before Sunday**

tuffy n¹   See **toughy (minnow)**

tuffy n²

The tufted **titmouse** *(Baeolophus bicolor).*

1967 *Ozark Visitor* (Point Lookout MO) Feb 6, The "tuffies" whistled their own kind of cat-calls at the intrusion. **2006** *DARE* File—Internet **CO,** [Label for a painting of a tufted titmouse:] Little Tuffy. [*Ibid* **TX,** Tuffy was still immature when we found him plastered into a couple glue traps in my barn. It took us an hour and a half to get that poor bird out of the sticky contraption. . . My teacher . . told me she was informed the little fighter was a Tufted Titmouse.]

tuffy minnow See **toughy (minnow)**

tufted duck n

=**ring-necked duck.**

1814 Wilson *Amer. Ornith.* 8.60, *Tufted Duck. Anas Fuligula.* . . is a plump, short bodied Duck; its flesh generally tender, and well tasted. **1844** Giraud *Birds Long Is.* 324, *Ring-necked or Tufted Duck.* . . Head tufted; bill about two inches long. **1911** *Forest & Stream* 77.173 **NC,** *Ring-Necked Duck.* . . Wilson's name, Tufted Duck, is in use at Currituck Sound. **1999** in 2003 *DARE* File—Internet **NJ,** A female *tufted duck* was seen with a flock of scaup on Old Sam's Pond, Point Pleasant March 30.

tufted quail n   Also *(small-)tufted partridge*

Usu the **California quail 1;** rarely the **scaled quail;** see quots.

1839 (1919) Forbes *California* 178, The small-tufted partridges, peculiar to California, are most plentiful in the plains. They keep together in large flocks of three or four hundred, and are excellent eating. **1849** in 1850 U.S. Congress *Serial Set* 562 Doc 64 52 **TX,** Four different kinds of quails were killed: the common quail; the tufted quail [here: =**scaled quail**], slightly ash-colored; the California quail . . and another variety, with dark breast and black belly. **1849** (1850) Colton *3 Yrs.* 361 **CA,** The quail, or tufted partridge, abounds in California, and is a delicious bird. **1893** *Overland Mth.* (2d ser) 22.657 **CA,** In chaparral not hiding, seeking, running,/ My tufted quail went pertly strutting through,/ No thicket shunning. **1918** Grinnell et al. *Game Birds CA* 514, *Lophortyx californica vallicola.* . . Tufted Quail. . . *Adult male:* Head with black, forward-drooping topknot of six overlapping, broad-ended feathers. . . *Adult female:* Somewhat similar to male but . . topknot much shorter.

tug n

1 =**trace** n². [*OED2 tug* sb. 4 c1250 → in ref to var elements of harness; the earliest clear ref to traces is 1589.]   **chiefly Nth, N Midl, Missip Valley, West**   See Map and Map Section

1806 in 2006 *DARE* File—Internet **KY,** [Estate inventory:] 2 old sadles . . one mans sadle . . tuggs [etc]. **1850** *U.S. Mag. & Democratic Rev.* 26.325 **eKY, wWV,** From this circumstance [=starving men eating strips of buffalo hide], the south-east branch of Sandy was ever after called the "Tug Fork," from the resemblance these thongs bore to those used in that day for traces or tugs in harness, by the backwoodsmen. **1859** *Daily WI Patriot* (Madison) 20 July 1/2, In consequence of the tugs being left too short the cross bar of the wagon was brought in contact with the colt's hind legs. **1870** Magner *New System* 42, Put on harness, and tie the tugs into the rings of the breeching rather short. **1883** *Daily NE State Jrl.* (Lincoln) 8 Dec [6]/1 (newspaperarchive.com), Tie the straps to the end of the singletree that the horse is hitched to. Tie just long enough, so the horse can straighten his tugs. **1910** *DN* 3.455 **seVT,** *Tug.* . . The trace or drawing strap of a harness. **1917** *DN* 4.403 **neOH,** *Tug.* . . Trace. *Tug* and *tugs* are the natural words. *Trace* is used chiefly in the phrase *kick over the traces,* lit. and fig. **1937** Sandoz *Slogum* 285 **NE,** Ruedy was mending the tugs of his old harness, cutting the thick leather with a . . knife. **1950** *WELS* 53 Infs, **WI,** Tugs. [*DARE* Ed: 17 of these Infs offered both *tugs* and *traces.*] **1950** *WELS Suppl.* **cwWI,** *Tug* is almost entirely used in this community but the links at the end are always called *trace chains,* as I remember. **1958** *AmSp* 33.273 **eWA** [Ranching terms], *Tug.* One of the pair of long, heavy straps of a harness which connects the horse to the load. **1965–70** *DARE* (Qu. L49, *Leathers or ropes, fastened to the collar, that a horse or mule pulls by*) 354 Infs, **chiefly Nth, N Midl, Missip Valley, West,** Tugs; **NM13,**

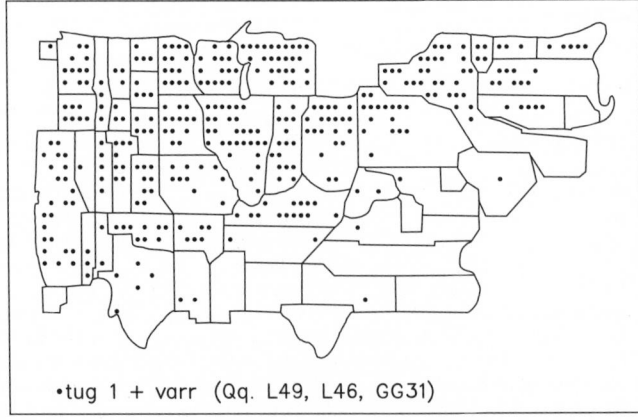

•tug 1 + varr (Qq. L49, L46, GG31)

OK18, Chain tug(s); **OK43**, Tugs—if made of leather; tug harness; **OK18**, Leather tugs; (Qu. L46) Infs **IL31**, **MA68**, Tug; **CA101**, Tugs—come from the collar, leather or chain, and hook onto singletree; **CA136**, Tug—runs from collar to singletree; (Qu. GG31, *To laugh very hard: "I thought I'd _____."*) Infs **NY223**, **PA234**, Bust a tug. **1972** *NYT Article Letters* **cNY**, Horses were attached to wagons by "tugs", not "traces". **2009** *DARE* File **csWI**, Stoney's harness was attached by tugs to the shafts of the cart.

2 Peat used for fuel; hence n *tugger* one who digs peat; n *tugging* the process of digging peat. [See quot 1877] **Block Is. RI**

1826 *Amer. Jrl. Sci. & Arts* 11.68, Those who may think it injudicious to apply the name wood, to that substance which has been called by the various names of peat, turf, tug, and firing, are reminded . . that Dr. M'Collock may be cited as a very respectable authority for so doing. **1840** Jackson *Rept. Geol. Surv. RI* 117 **Block Is. RI**, Nature has amply provided the inhabitants with a great . . supply of peat, or tug, as it is called. . . Attached to every dwelling we find a "tug-house," in which is stored up the winters fuel. . . I was informed . . that . . when several tug bogs were entirely dug out, . . the peat grew again in 40 years. **1877** (1961) Livermore *Hist. Block Is. RI* 29, *Tug* is its more common name among the Islanders, a name applied to it more than a century ago, and refers to the hard work of getting it from the bed. **1897** *New Engl. Mag.* 22.741 **Block Is. RI**, Owing to the hard work in getting the peat from its beds, it is generally known upon the island as "tug." . . So late as 1875, 544 cords were dug; and it is still used to a limited extent. **1941** *LANE* Map 330 *(Log)* 2 infs, **Block Is. RI**, [tʌg] = peat, used for fuel, dug in September and October. **1955** (1956) Ritchie *Block Is. Lore & Legends* 42 **sRI**, "Tugging" became one of the principal fall occupations of the eighteenth century Block Islanders. *Ibid*, Some "tuggers" even went further.

tugadoo n

The **great horned owl** or the barred owl *(Strix varia)*.

1955 *Oriole* 20.1.8 **GA**, Great Horned Owl. . . Tugadoo (apparently a sonic term). Barred Owl. . . Tugadoo.

tugboat n Cf **canal boat, canoe** n

A large foot or shoe.

1932 Dahlberg *From Flushing* 164, Hervey waddled along after her, his spouty tugboat shoes slipping across the wet sidewalk. **1935** *AmSp* 10.9, The resemblance of feet to various forms of water craft seems to prompt the currency of *tugboats, steamboats, gunboats, battleships, canal boats, sailboats, steamers, canoes,* and *submarines.* **1967–70** *DARE* (Qu. X38, *Joking names for unusually big or clumsy feet*) Infs **LA37**, **TN12**, **VA54**, Tugboats.

tug chain n Cf **trace chain**

A length of chain at the end of a leather tug used to secure it to the **singletree**.

1859 *Knickerbocker* 53.549 **NEng**, Did you never see a staid and sober old farm horse . . break into an awkward gallop for a rod or two, making the tug-chain rattle and the old cart fairly groan? **1910** *DN* 3.455 **seVT**, Tug-chain. . . A chain used to attach the tug to the whippletree; a trace chain. **1975** Logan *Land Remembers* 246 **swWI** (as of c1920), He flipped the lines . . and we glided out along the ridge to the west, . . the tug chains ringing like bells behind the trotting horses.

tugger, tugging See **tug 2**

(-)tuh See **to** prep, adv **A2**

tuhbackuh See **tobacco** n **A1**

tuhgedduh See **together**

tuh-mar, tuhmorrer See **tomorrow**

tu'ibly See **terrible**

tuk See **take** v **A2a, 3b**

tukr(e)y See **turkey**

tula See **tule 1**

tuladi n [*DCan* 1846 →; see quot 1896]

=**lake trout 1.**

1867 ME Dept. Ag. *Annual Rept.* 12.89, Besides the name of "lake trout" that of "tuladi" belongs to the same fish. **1884** Goode *Fisheries U.S.* 1.486, The "Namaycush" of the North, the "Togue" or "Tuladi" of the Maine and New Brunswick Indians and lumbermen, the "Siscowet" or "Siskawitz" of Lake Superior, . . have each been honored with a dis-

tinct binomial. [**1896** Chambers *Ouananiche* 270 **eCanada**, By the Montagnais Indians the Lake-trout is known as kokomesh, and by the Micmacs and Abenaquis as touladi.]

tulare n Also *tularosa* [AmSpan] **chiefly SW**

An area overgrown with **tules**.

1845 Frémont *Rept. Rocky Mts.* 251 **CA**, Over the bordering plain were interspersed spots of prairie among fields of *tulé* (bulrushes,) which in this country are called *tulares.* **1859** (1968) Bartlett *Americanisms* 490 **CA, TX**, Tulare. A marsh in which Tule abounds. **1903** (1950) Austin *Land of Little Rain* 87 **CA**, Last and inevitable resort of overflow waters is the tulares, great wastes of reeds *(Juncus)* in sickly, slow streams. **1933** *AmSp* 8.3.9 **SW**, If a pool or spring is well grown with reeds, it is called *carrizal* (place of reeds) from *carrizo,* a reed, or if with cattails, *tulare* or *tularosa.* **1970** *Daily Rev.* (Hayward CA) 27 Sept 31/1 (as of 1827), Naked "wild Indios" . . had guided the four to the Mission compound from their trapping-camp on the Stanislaus River, in the tulares.

tule n [MexSpan < Nahuatl *tollin, tullin*]

1 also sp *thulé, tool(e)y, t(o)ula, tuley, tullie:* Any of var bulrushes of the genera *Scirpus* and *Schoenoplectus,* but esp *Schoenoplectus acutus, S. californicus,* and *S. tabernaemontani;* occas another marsh plant such as a **cattail 1.** **chiefly Pacific (esp CA), SW**

1837 in 1932 Edwards *Diary* 20 July 26 **CA**, Driving her along the margin of a bulrush or tule pond she turned about. **1845** in 1847 Henry *Campaign Sketches* 24 **TX**, Their residences are . . nothing more than sheds . . thatched with a long grass which grows in the marshes, called "tula." **1850** M'Collum *CA Saw It* 37, The river . . winds like a tape worm, through low marshy ground, where the *tules,* (or bull rushes) grow to an enormous height. **1850** Ryan *Personal Advent.* 1.298 **CA**, Indians . . were despatched to hunt . . for toolies. **1850** (1955) Tyson *Diary* 66 **CA**, The shores [of the Sacramento River] were flat and marshy, being overgrown with thulé, a kind of light cane. **1854** (1932) Bell *Log TX–CA Trail* 35.304 **sCA**, Portions of the *Toula* roof, still in good preservation lie scattered on the ground. **1878** *Amer. Naturalist* 12.604, *Scirpus validus* (Tule plant). **1892** *Outing* 19.329 **OR**, Arriving at a small patch of tuleys about the middle of the lake, we decided to tie up there for the night. **1920** Hunter *Trail Drivers TX* 380, Meantime he . . erected a log cabin with a tullie roof, and began to live at home. **1920** *Torreya* 20.19 **UT**, *Scirpus occidentalis* [=*Schoenoplectus acutus*]. . . *Scirpus peludosus* [=*Schoenoplectus maritimus*]. . . Tule. **1935** Davis *Honey* 305 **OR**, Heavy pelicans . . flapped awkwardly . . at the edge of the tule-beds. **1967** *DARE* Wildfl QR (Wills–Irwin) Pl.1A [= *Typha latifolia*] Inf **TX44**, Tule—Spanish common name. **1968–70** *DARE* Tape **CA90**, And another thing about this pond water—when it got too hot, the cows wouldn't like to drink it, so we let tules, we call it, grow up into the pond and that shaded it, and so that gave . . cows cool water to drink; **CA209**, They take tules and go in all between them and fix it so it won't leak. . . [FW:] What's a tule, a reed? [Inf:] Yeah, . . they're green and then they turn brown, and they're tough. . . And those Indian women, they make those beautiful baskets. **1970** Correll *Plants TX* 85, *Typha domingensis.* . . Tule. . . In brackish or fresh marshes and pools throughout most of Tex.; . . from Fla. to Tex. and s. Calif. **1971** Brunvand *Guide Folkl. UT* 31, Hunters who have to tramp through rough country may say they are "brush busting" or "Tooley busting." **1984** Lesley *Winterkill* 28 **neOR**, Sitting cross-legged on tule mats, Danny ate the salmon, venison, roots, and berries.

2 also pl; also sp *toolies, tulies:* An area where such bulrushes grow thickly; a swamp; broadly, a remote area, "the sticks." **chiefly Pacific, esp CA** See Map on p. 734

1847 *Californian* (San Francisco) 15 Sept 3/1, Charley pointed out to me in the Tule an animal, which, he said was a bear. **1873** Harte *Mrs. Skaggs* 55 **CA**, The last mail had been abandoned in the *tules,* the rider swimming for his life. **1893** *Advance* (Chicago IL) 2 Feb 98/2 **CA**, Because of the tall rushes that grow there the land is called the *tule.* The tule is always low and level. **1929** Dobie *Vaquero* 295 **SW**, Meantime the suspects . . made for the tules. **1958** McCulloch *Woods Words* 128 **Pacific NW**, Out in the tules. . . In the back country. . . In the swamp; working on wet ground. **1964** *AmSp* 39.307 **SW**, In Arizona and California it is the *clods* who live, not in the *sticks,* but in the *tules.* **1967–70** *DARE* (Qu. C6, . . *A piece of land that's often wet, and has grass and weeds growing on it*) Inf **CA82**, Tules; **CA62**, Tules—water reeds and water grass area, not necessarily far away; (Qu. C33, . . *Joking names . . for an out-of-the-way place, or a very small or unimportant place*) Infs **CA184**, **WA19**, Tules; **CA177**, The tules, the boondocks; **WY2**, Out in the tules—meaning out in the wilderness; (Qu. HH1, *Names and nick-names for a rustic or countrified person*) Inf **NV4,** Lives in the boonies, lives in the tules. **1969** *DARE* Tape **CA**159, The part that they did dredge, the channel, through a tule cut there, . . they dredged that channel seven feet deep in order to accommodate that steamer. **1971** Bright *Word Geog. CA & NV* 162, Swamp . . inland . . *tules/tule land/tule swamp* 5% [of 300 infs]. **1973** *DARE* File **nwCO,** "Out in the too-lies"—wilderness—common in NW Colorado. **1979** in 1991 Tabbert *Dict. Alaskan Engl.* 48, We looked like the Senior Citizens club trekking through the toolies as we hobbled along. **1998** *DARE* File **ME,** All her relatives in Maine use the word toolies . . all the time. **2002** Perry *Population 485* 183 **WI,** Way out in the tules, lakeside. **2008** Guterson *Other* 237 **wWA** (as of 1960s), [We] got a handsome canoe and a pair of very nice paddles . . and off we went together. . . we identified plants. Out there in the tulies.

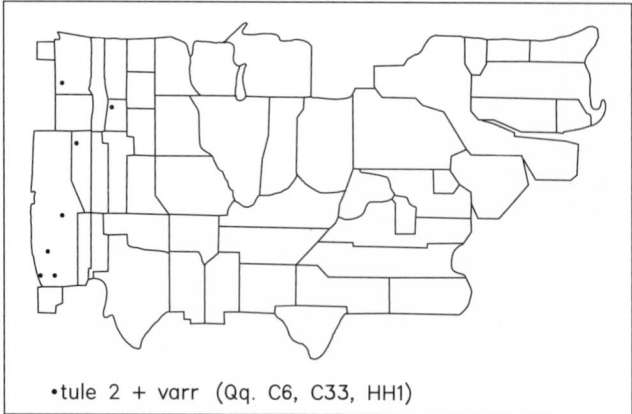

•tule 2 + varr (Qq. C6, C33, HH1)

3 A **yucca;** see quot.
1892 *DN* 1.195 **TX** [Span and Mex words used in TX], *Túle.* As with other plant names this applies to a variety of species that have nothing in common but the name. . . In Texas it is applied to several species of yucca, and to certain kinds of reeds not identified. From Mexican *tollin.*

4 See **tule fish.**
5 See **tule goose.**

tule beetle n Also *tule bug* [**tule 2**]
A ground beetle *(Agonum maculicolle)* native to California.
1923 CA Ag. Exper. Sta. *Circ.* 265.62, *Tule Bugs or Stink Bugs.—*These bugs cause great annoyance by entering houses often in great numbers. **1926** Essig *Insects N. Amer.* 377, The *tule beetle* . . is 10 mm. long. . . It breeds in the marsh lands along the rivers, and often appears in large swarms at dusk following rains, in the fall of the year. It freely enters houses and is very annoying because of the very offensive odor. It has been known as a nuisance in the Sacramento and San Joaquin Valleys in California since 1882. . . Other common names applied to it are *overflow bug, tule bug* [etc]. **2003** *DARE* File—Internet **CA,** In the central valleys of California, the tule beetle is the most troublesome carabid.

tule elk n [**tule 2**]
A small elk *(Cervus elaphus nannodes)* native to California.
1913 CA Fish & Game Comm. *Biennial Rept. for 1910–12* 18, In the San Joaquin Valley near Button Willow and in the Sequoia National Park range are all that are left of the thousands of "tule" elk that formerly were found throughout the San Joaquin and Sacramento valleys. **1942** U.S. Natl. Park Serv. *Fading Trails* 8 **CA,** The larger wild animals, such as the tule elk, pronghorn, bighorn sheep, and deer, were regarded as most important food supplies. **1947** Cahalane *Mammals* 23, The tule, dwarf, or California elk *(C[ervus] nannodes)* is a much smaller and paler animal than the wapiti of the Rockies. **1969–70** *DARE* (Qu. P32, . . *Other kinds of wild animals*) Infs **CA**114, 207, Tule elk. **2003** *DARE* File—Internet, This photo is . . fuzzy because it's taken through the tule fog, of the smallest of the elk family, the Tule Elk, in Kern County, California.

tule fish n Also *tule* [**tule 2**] **OR, WA**
A fall-run **chinook salmon** that spawns in the lower reaches of the Columbia River and is smaller, darker, and paler-fleshed than those spawning higher up.

1989 Lesley *River Song* 184 **cnOR,** Even though the tule fish caught nearby would bring low prices, Willis said some upriver brights followed the spawning tules, so it was still a good place. *Ibid* 188, If the buyer suspected one of the salmon of being an inferior tule, with the extended jaw and drab color of a spawner, he'd nod at the boy, and the kid would unsheath his hunting knife, first slitting the flesh just in front of the tail, then checking to see if the meat was red. **2002** in 2003 *DARE* File—Internet [WA–OR Game and Fish Mag.], There are two stocks of fall chinook that return to the Columbia. The tule stock is a darker, more mature fish that heads to lower river tributaries and the Spring Creek Hatchery at the Bonneville Pool. The upriver bright stock heads upriver to areas such as the Hanford Reach. Anglers target the bright stock more since the fish are brighter in color, larger in size and better tasting.

tule fog n Also *tule ground fog* [**tule 2**] **chiefly CA**
A typically shallow but very dense fog that forms over marshy areas.
1902 U.S. Weather Bur. *Bulletin* 31.32 **CA,** In winter . . tule fog forms in the great valleys and drifts slowly seaward. **1919** Kyne *Capt. Scraggs* 3 **CA,** I tell you she's a tule fog, Gib. She rises up in the marshes of the Sacramento and San Joaquin, drifts down to the bay and out the Golden Gate and just naturally blocks the wheels of commerce while she lasts. **1927** *AmSp* 2.278 **CA,** Tule (fog)—marsh fog. **1933** Crater L. Nat. Hist. Assoc. *Nature Notes* Apr (Internet) **csOR,** The Tule Fog Of The Klamath Basin. . . The fog is due to radiation of heat with the attendant ascending water vapor from the extensive water surfaces and adjacent tule swamp lands. The depth of this so-called Tule Fog mantle is a variable but usually it is quite shallow. **1934** White *Folded Hills* 340 **ceCA,** A *tule* fog hung thick over the bottomlands. **1971** Bright *Word Geog. CA & NV* 141 **CA,** Tule fog. . . A dense, low-lying fog. **1977** Didion *Book Common Prayer* 185 **CA,** After a while there were no more tule fogs at dawn. **2000** Ryan *Esperanza* 167 **CA,** A thick tule ground fog that hugged the earth settled in the valley. **2002** *San Francisco Chron.* (CA) 24 Oct sec C 1 (Internet), In December and January, dense tule fog often forms, reducing visibility to near zero.

tule goose n Also *tule (whitefront)* [**tule 2**]
A **white-fronted goose** (here: *Anser albifrons gambeli*) of the western US and Alaska.
1914 CA Fish & Game Comm. *Biennial Rept. for 1912–14* 21, [There is] a large gray goose resembling the gambel goose, but much larger, weighing as much as ten pounds or more; local name tule goose. **1917** CA Univ. (Berkeley) *Annual Rept. President* (Internet), Gifts to the Department of Zoology. . . 9 tule geese *(Anser albifrons gambeli).* **1969** *DARE* (Qu. Q6, . . *Kinds of wild geese*) Inf **CA**140, Tule geese. **1982** Elman *Hunter's Field Guide* 298, Tule Goose . . tule whitefront. . . The tule goose is a large localized subspecies of the whitefront. By the time a tule comes within gun range, it looks considerably bulkier than an ordinary specklebelly. **2002** in 2003 *DARE* File—Internet, The USGS is conducting its first research project with the . . transmitter on a vulnerable subspecies of greater white-fronted goose known as the tule goose *(Anser albifrons gambeli).*

tule ground fog See **tule fog**
tule lily n [**tule 2**]
A **spatterdock** (here: *Nuphar lutea* subsp *polysepala*).
1937 St. John *Flora SE WA & ID* 148, *Nuphar polysepalum* [=*N. lutea* subsp *p.*] . . Tule Lily, Wokas. . . In lakes and slow streams. . . The Klamath Indians roasted and ate the seeds.

tule mint n [**tule 2**] **CA**
A mint (here: *Mentha arvensis*).
1901 Jepson *Flora CA* 466, *M[entha] canadensis* [=*M. arvensis* L.] . . *Tule-mint.* . . Common in marshes: Lower Sacramento and Lower San Joaquin; San Francisco Bay. **1911** CA Ag. Exper. Sta. Berkeley *Bulletin* 217.1019, Tule Mint. . . Sacramento County. . . Honey from the flowers. **1995** in 2003 *DARE* File—Internet **CA,** A tiny, creeping, native mint that . . contains menthol is *Mentha arvensis,* or Tule Mint, and can be used in the same way that other mints are used, to flavor candies and sweets, calm upset stomachs, and aid digestion.

tule pea n [**tule 2**]
A **vetchling:** usu *Lathyrus jepsonii,* but also *L. bijugatus;* see quots.
1944 Abrams *Flora Pacific States* 2.623, *Lathyrus Jepsonii.* . . Tule Pea. . . Low marsh lands, . . the delta islands on the lower Sacramento and San Joaquin rivers, California. **2002** (acc) CA Dept. Transportation

Caltrans District 4 (Internet), The Delta Tule Pea *(Lathyrus jepsonii var. jepsonii)*. . . is a native perennial herb that is endemic in California. It is mostly found in the Delta region of the Central Valley, and in salt marshes and on tidal river banks of the San Francisco Bay Region. **2003** (acc) *MT Field Guide* (Internet), *Lathyrus bijugatus*. . . Latah Tule Pea is a perennial. . . The alternate leaves have . . a bristle instead of a tendril on the tip.

tule potato n CA

1 The edible root of **tule 1.**

[**1871** U.S. Dept. Ag. *Rept. of Secy. for 1870* 408, *Cattail flag, (Scirpus lacustris.)* . . In California it is called tule root, and is a great favorite, whether raw, or pounded and made into bread. . . The roots resemble artichokes, but are much longer.] **1873** *CA Acad. Sci. Proc.* 4.280, Specimens of the Tule potato (a species of artichoke), from the tule lands of the San Joaquin river. **1881** *Hist. Napa & Lake Counties CA* 2.23, The margin of the lakes afforded a large field for "tule potatoes," as the succulent and nutritive roots of that rush are called. **1914** *Sunset* 33.55 **CA,** Vegetables: Baked tule potatoes. . . Tules growing at the water-edge reminded me that a Chinaman had once taught me how to gather and how to prepare the potato-like roots.

2 An **arrowhead 1** (here: *Sagittaria cuneata* or *S. latifolia*) or its edible tuber. Cf **wapato**

1892 *Zoe* 3.201 **cCA,** A stone digging tool was found. . . It must have been very useful in digging the Tule potato *(Sagittaria)* which is now sometimes called "China potato." **1911** Jepson *Flora CA* 33, *S[agittaria] latifolia*. . . Tule Potato. . . The tubers of this species are edible and are made much use of by the Chinese of the lower Sacramento. **1914** *CA Fish & Game Comm. Biennial Rept. for 1912–14* 17, The most important of these duck foods are the two varieties of what is known locally as "tule potatoes," or bulbs and classified as *Sagittaria latifolia* and *Sagittaria arifolia*. **1959** Munz–Keck *CA Flora* 1313, *S[agittaria] latifolia*. . . Tule-Potato. . . Largely Freshwater Marsh; most of Calif. **2003** *DARE* File—Internet **CA,** Tubers of the Arrowhead or Tule Potato were dug up in the marshes and either roasted or boiled, some being preserved after roasting for winter use.

tule rooter n [tule 2]

1 =**razorback hog.** **CA**

1870 *CA State Ag. Soc. Trans. for 1868–69* 339, If our farmers would substitute the Berkshire, Suffolks or Chesterwhites, for the slab-sided, long nosed tule-rooter, so common in this State, . . he would not only get a much larger profit, but would be able to find his stock of swine when he needs them, without a week's ride on a worse animal, the bucking mustang, to hunt them up. **1915** Guilford *CA Hog Book* 107, Good hogs are better than ordinary ones, as much so as the ordinary ones are ahead of the scrubs, or 'tule rooters.' **1996** Cary *Hollywood Posse* 13 **swCA** (as of 1909), Wild Hogs. They call 'em tule rooters in these parts. They're mean, slippery descendants of some stray razorbacks that got loose from the Forty-niners back in Gold Rush days.

2 See quots.

1905 *Overland Mth.* (2d ser) 46.101 **swCA,** The inhabitants of the town of Santa Ana . . laughed genially at the "tenderfoot" who wanted to reclaim the bogs inhabited only by a few people living in miserable shanties and known as "tule rooters" or "swamp angels." **1964** Jackman–Long *OR Desert* 37, The old-established livestock men, with irrigated land, didn't believe in plowing up the desert and called this army of newcomers "sandlappers." . . [T]he drylanders retaliated by calling owners of grass meadows "tule rooters."

tule whitefront See tule goose

tule wren n [tule 2] Pacific

The long-billed **marsh wren** (here: *Cistothorus palustris* Paludicola Group).

1877 U.S. Army Corps Topog. Engineers *Rept. Explor. 40th Parallel* 4.425 **CA,** *Telmatodytes paludicola* [=*Cistothorus palustris* Paludicola Group]. . . Tule Wren. . . In all marshy localities where there existed even a limited growth of tules, the Long-billed Marsh Wren was more or less abundant. **1904** Wheelock *Birds CA* 290, To know the Tule Wren you must go to the tall reeds of a lowland marsh. **1940** Gabrielson *Birds OR* 458, The Tule Wren is not an abundant bird in Oregon due to a lack of suitable breeding sites. **1953** Jewett *Birds WA* 501, Tule Wren. . . Occurs both summer and winter in the marshes bordering Puget Sound and inlets and bays at intervals along the coast.

tuley See tule 1

tulies See tule 2

tulip n

1 A plant thought to resemble a tulip (*Tulipa* spp); see quots. Cf **blue tulip, globe ~, mountain ~, pine ~, star ~, tulip tree, wild tulip**

1897 *Jrl. Amer. Folkl.* 10.145 **swMO,** *Erythronium albidum,* tulip. **1898** *Ibid* 11.281 **sMT,** *Fritillaria pudica,* . . tulip.

2 See **tulip tree 1.**

tulip gum n

=**tulip tree 1.**

1928 *Gleanings Bee Culture* 56.510 **SC,** South of Columbia the main honey plants are the tulip gum and gallberry. **1968** *DARE* (Qu. T13, . . *Names . . for . . tulip tree*) Inf **GA20,** Tulip gum—what we call a pig squealer. **2003** *DARE* File—Internet **TN,** The bald cypress and tulip gum swamp was by far the experience that sticks out the most.

tulip magnolia n

A **magnolia 1,** esp *Magnolia* x *soulangiana* or **tulip tree 1.**

1917 *Nature-Study Rev.* 13.167 **DC,** All the top branches of the tulip magnolia try to grow as near vertical as possible. **1953** Hylander *Trees & Trails* 107, Another common name, tulip magnolia, is more appropriate since it [=the tulip tree] does belong to the magnolia family. **1986** Pederson *LAGS Concordance (Magnolia)* 1 inf, **ceTN,** Tulip magnolia. **1999** in 2003 *DARE* File—Internet **MD,** Even with all of the rain, the blossoms on . . the so-called tulip or saucer Magnolia (M. x soulangiana) have lasted and lasted and lasted. **2000** *Ibid* **sMD,** All products are made of tulip-magnolia hardwood (often erroneously called yellow poplar). **2002** *DARE* File **TN,** *Approved Plant Species for Airport Landscaping*. . . Magnolia quinquepeta—Tulip Magnolia. *Ibid* **TN,** *Liriodendron tulipifera*—Tulip Tree, Tulip Poplar, also called Tulip Magnolia.

tulip poplar n Also tulip popple chiefly Midl, Mid and C Atl See Map

=**tulip tree 1.**

1826 Darlington *Florula Cestrica* 59, *L[iriodendron] tulipifera*. . . *Vulgo*—Poplar. Tulip poplar, or Tulip tree. **1860** Mordecai *Virginia* 105 **VA,** A fine tulip poplar . . marks the corner where his house stood. **1897** Sudworth *Arborescent Flora* 198, *Liriodendron tulipifera*. . . Tulip Poplar (Del., Pa., S.C., Ill.) **1911** Porter *Harvester* 334 **IN,** The tulip poplar will bear you the loveliest flowers of all. **1931** Otis *MI Trees* 169, *Tulip Poplar*. . . Formerly common, but becoming rare. **1950** Moore *Trees AR* 72, *Liriodendron tulipifera*. . . Local Names: Yellow Poplar, Tulip Poplar. **1965–70** *DARE* (Qu. T13, . . *Names . . for . . tulip tree*) 81 Infs, **chiefly Midl, Mid and C Atl,** Tulip poplar; **OH4,** Yellow poplar is same as tulip poplar or whitewood; **OH33,** Tulip poplar—but that's brought in; **OH82,** Tulip poplar and yellow poplar are separate, but we call them either tulip poplar, yellow poplar, or cucumber tree; **PA29, 104,** Tulip popple; (Qu. T12, *The kind of poplar tree that has sticky, sweet-smelling buds*) 48 Infs, **chiefly Midl, Mid and C Atl,** Tulip poplar; **DE3,** Tulip poplar—occasional; tulip poplar and yellow poplar are synonyms; **IL96,** Tulip poplar, in late years; years ago, just poplar was all you heard; **IN69,** Tulip poplar, whitewood, yellow poplar—same tree; **NY227,** Yellow poplar is a tulip poplar; **TN14,** National Park people call it tulip poplar, but the local people have always said just poplar; **VA8,** Tulip poplar = mountain poplar; **OH33,** Yellow tulip poplar;

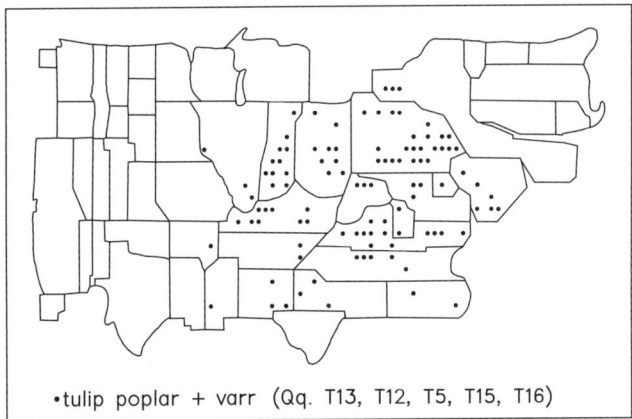

•tulip poplar + varr (Qq. T13, T12, T5, T15, T16)

PA29, Tulip popple; (Qu. T5, . . *Kinds of evergreens, other than pine*) Inf PA35, Tulip poplar; (Qu. T15, . . *Kinds of swamp trees*) Infs NY227, PA89, Tulip poplar; (Qu. T16, . . *Kinds of trees . . 'special'*) Inf IN27, Tulip poplar. **2003** *DARE* File—Internet, *Liriodendron tulipifera*. . . Tulip Poplar wood is considered a very valuable timber product.

tulip tree n

1 also *tulip;* Std: a tall timber tree *(Liriodendron tulipifera)* with flowers thought to resemble tulips, native to much of the eastern half of the US. Also called **basswood 2, blue poplar, canoewood, cucumber tree 2, flower ~, hickory poplar, linn 3, magnolia 2, old-wife's shirt tree, pig squealer, pillar poplar, poplar B2, popple** n¹**, saddleleaf, tulip gum, ~ magnolia, ~ poplar, white poplar 2, whitewood 1, yellow poplar 1, yellowwood 4**

2 A **magnolia 1** such as **southern magnolia** or *Magnolia* x *soulangiana;* see quots. Cf **tulip magnolia**

1709 (1967) Lawson *New Voyage* 102 **Carolinas,** The Bay-Tulip-Tree is a fine Ever-green which grows frequently here. **1785** Marshall *Arbustrum* 82, *Magnolia.* The Laurel-leaved Tulip-Tree. *Ibid* 84, *Magnolia grandiflora.* Ever-green Laurel-leaved Tulip-Tree. This grows naturally in Florida and South Carolina. **1966–69** *DARE* (Qu. S17, . . *Kinds of plants . . that . . cause itching and swelling*) Inf MA49, Tulip tree; (Qu. T13, . . *Names . . for . . tulip tree*) Inf CA150, Some call the Chinese magnolia a tulip tree, but it isn't the same thing; IL41, What he calls tulip trees, I call magnolia; IL45, I've always heard the magnolia tree called the tulip tree; LA33, Japanese magnolia, but most people call them tulip tree; MA6, Tulip tree = magnolia; WV17, Another "tulip" trees is magnolia; (Qu. T16, . . *Kinds of trees . . 'special'*) Inf IA8, Magnolia tree often called a tulip tree. **1986** Pederson *LAGS Concordance* *(Magnolia)* 1 inf, **neAL,** Tulip—probably same as magnolia; 1 inf, **ceGA,** Tulip trees. **2002** *DARE* File—Internet **AL** [Southern Gardening Forum], We planted a couple of tulip trees last spring. . . [Later message from same person:] Well, didn't mean to stir things up this much. The real name is star magnolia and/or jane magnolia.

3 A **rose of Sharon 1** or other bush with tulip-like flowers.

1966–70 *DARE* (Qu. T13) Inf CO20, Tulip tree—called by others rose of Sharon; FL49, Tulip tree? Not sure if it's native or not—yes, it's native, a bush, not a real tree, called wild tulip, purple; MD13, Tulip tree—a bush; OK32, Tulip tree—may be a few—I think they might call it rose of Sharon.

tull See **till A1**

tullibee n Also sp *telibee* [*DCan* 1789 →] **Gt Lakes, esp MN**

A **cisco,** usu *Coregonus artedi.*

1822 Morse *Rept. Indian Affairs* app 31 **MN,** A fish called . . by the English and French "Telibees," not equal to, but greatly resembling the white fish. **1882** U.S. Natl. Museum *Bulletin* 16.301, *C[oregonus] tullibee*. . . Tullibee; "Mongrel White Fish". . . Body short, deep, compressed, shad-like. . . Great Lakes and northward. **1908** Forbes–Richardson *Fishes of IL* 55, In addition to the common lake herring [= *Coregonus artedi*], four other species of the genus *Argyrosomus* [= *Coregonus*] . . , the mooneye cisco; . . the longjaw; . . the bluefin; and . . the tullibee . . are more or less commonly taken in Lake Michigan. **1938** FWP *Guide MN* 352 **nwMN,** Warroad's co-operative *Fish Meal Factory* converts tullibees, or whitefish, and burbots . . into chicken feed and fertilizer. **1967–68** *DARE* (Qu. P1, . . *Kinds of freshwater fish . . caught around here . . good to eat*) Inf MN35, Tullibee—like a whitefish, good smoked; (Qu. P14, . . *Commercial fishing . . what do the fishermen go out after?*) Inf MN5, Tullibees—used for mink feed; MN15, Tullibee—a fish a lot like a herring but bigger, runs to two feet long. **2003** *DARE* File—Internet **nMN,** Smoked tullibee and beer can't be beat! *Ibid* **nMN,** Mille Lacs muskies are known for their exceptional growth rates and chunkiness, thanks to the lake's tullibee population.

tullie See **tule 1**

tumbersault See **tumblesault**

tumberset See **tumbleset**

tumble v

1 freq with *up;* also with *about, around, together:* To mix up; to disarrange, throw into disorder; hence adjs *a-tumble, tumbled (up)* messy, disordered. [*OED2* 1562 →] **chiefly Sth, S Midl** See Map

1836 (1838) Farrar *Young Lady's Friend* 128, The practice of . . letting your boa sweep the floor, and the collar that is pinned to your cloak be all tumbled up with it [etc] . . will in three months greatly deface your clothes. **1857** *Putnam's Mag.* July 56 **Boston MA,** "How is my shirt collar?" "All tumbled up," said I. **1871** *Ladies' Repository* 7.452, Here I am in this soiled wrapper, my hair all tumbled up. **1887** *Sat. Rev.* (E. Liverpool OH) [30 July 7]/5 (newspaperarchive.com), The beds were all tumbled up. **1953** *News* (Frederick MD) 12 June 1/1, He found Cooley's room "all tumbled up" with blood stains on pillow, sheets, floor and wall. **1965–70** *DARE* (Qu. Y38, *Mixed together, confused: "The things in the drawer are all _____."*) 31 Infs, **chiefly Sth, S Midl,** Tumbled up; 10 Infs, **scattered,** Tumbled; CA87, Tumbled about; FL10, A-tumble; MO2, Tumbled together; SC26, Tumble up; TN23, Tumbled around; [VA26, In a tumble;] (Qu. E22, *If a house is untidy and everything is upset . . "It's a _____!" or "It looks like _____."*) Infs KY94, ME23, MS27, NC55, Tumbled-up mess; MS85, SC46, TX26, Tumbled up; AR55, Tumbled-up place; SC38, Tumbled-up house; (Qu. Y37, *To make a place untidy or disorderly: "I wish they wouldn't _____ the room so."*) Inf KY94, Tumble it up; SC3, Tumble; SC19, Tumble up. **1985** *DARE* File—Internet **NYC,** You're getting everything all tumbled up.

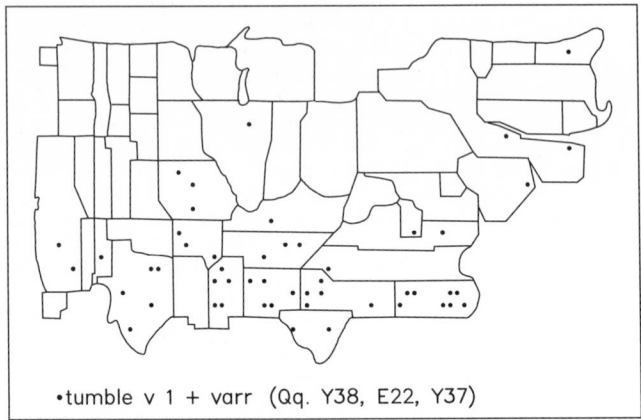

•tumble v 1 + varr (Qq. Y38, E22, Y37)

2 also with *up:* To gather (hay) into **tumbles;** with *up,* intr: to make **tumbles.** **chiefly nNEng**

1847 *Old Farmer's Almanac for 1848* 19 **NEng,** Tumble up the cocks, boys. **1850** in 2006 *DARE* File—Internet **nwMA,** Then we went to raking, and got it all raked, and most-all tumbled before supper. After supper we got four loads in. . . Loads averaged over 20 tumbles each. **1862** *Ibid* **csMA,** Raked the hay out from the pond & swale & tumbled up part of it. **1917** *DN* 4.402 **neOH, NEng,** Tumble up. . . Roll hay in the winrow into heaps suitable for pitching upon the wagon. . . "You go ahead and tumble it up and we'll follow with the wagon." "I'll tumble up while you rake." **1959** *VT Hist.* 27.165, Tumble the hay. . . To bunch the hay so that the pitchfork can pick it up easily. Common. Rural areas. **1966** *DARE* (Qu. L12) Inf NH5, Tumble up the hay—divide each windrow in two and roll up halves into a forkful. **1966–67** *DARE* Tape MA5, [The horse rake] rakes it [=hay] up into winrows, ready for them to tumble it up into stacks. Or hay tumbles, sometimes they said; VT1, [FW:] And after you went through it [=the hay] with the rake and tedder. . . what did you do? [Inf:] Then they tumbled it. Put it up in piles. [FW:] What did you call the piles called? [Inf:] Tumblers, tumbles. [FW:] Tumbles. How big was a tumble? [Inf:] Well, various sizes, usually—well, it would depend on how heavy the hay was. . . They were just . . humps of hay. . . They probably would be two or three pitchforks full. **2005** Williston Hist. Soc. *Bulletin* (Internet) **VT** (as of 1914–18), Grant and I did the raking with a horse dump rake and tumbled the hay so the men could pitch it onto the hay wagon. **2007** [see **tumble** n].

3 in phrr *tumble to* (or *in*) *pieces:* To give birth to a child. [Cf *OED2* *fall to pieces* (at *piece* sb. 1.e) "*dial.* and *Austral. slang*"]

1818 in 1824 Knight *Letters* 106 **KY,** Instead of saying of a promised mother, with Shakespearean delicacy, that she is "nigh fainting under the pleasing punishment, that women bear;" the hint is quite Shaker-like, that she is "about to tumble in pieces." **1899** (1912) Green *VA Folk-Speech* 44, To tumble to pieces. To give birth to a child.

tumble n Also *tumbler* [**tumble** v **2**] **chiefly nNEng, wMA** See Map Cf **cock** n², **doodle** n¹ **1**

A small pile of hay made in a field in preparation for pitching it onto a wagon.

1850 [see **tumble** v 2]. **1859** *Berkshire Co. Eagle* (Pittsfield MA) 11 Aug [3]/3 (newspaperarchive.com), A son of A.B. Fairfield, Esq., . . while spreading a tumble of hay, was whirled by a gust of wind and thrown upon the fork. **1883** *Overland Mth.* (2d ser) 1.222 **MA**, I had thrown myself down behind a tumble of hay. **1914** *DN* 4.154 **NH**, *Tumble of hay.* . . A part of a winrow rolled each way; when doubled up and dressed down it is called a *cock* of hay. **1934** *Hanley Disks* c**MA**, A large pile would be a stack but a small pile would be a tumble. **1949** Kurath *Word Geog.* 22 nN**Eng**, Other "Down East" expressions are . . *tumble* . . for the hay cock (in parts of upland New Hampshire and Maine, with relics in Worcester County, Massachusetts, and in the Berkshires). **1950** *WELS (The small piles of hay in the field)* 2 Infs, **WI**, Tumbles. **1953** *AmSp* 28.64 **NH, VT**, A *tumble* was a small heap of hay tossed together from the winrow (windrow), and the right size for pitching on. **1965–70** *DARE* (Qu. L12, . . *The small piles of hay standing in the field)* Infs **MA**6, 31, 58, **NH**5, **NY**32, **VT**12, Tumbles; **VT**2, Tumbles—just enough for one forkful; **ME**12, **MA**68, **NH**14, Tumbles of hay; **VT**16, Hay tumbles; (Qu. L14, *A large pile of hay stored outdoors: [Do names differ according to shape?])* Inf **MA**5, A tumble is a small haystack made up of windrows raked together. **1966–67** [see **tumble** v 2]. **1967** *DARE* Tape **MA**117, [FW:] Then after the hay was cut, what did you do with it? [Inf:] Rake it up and make it in winrows and then tumbles. [FW:] Is a tumble this small pile of hay? [Inf:] It's small and any size you want. . . they . . push it up into tumbles so to pitch it much easier. **2005** *DARE* File—Internet **VT**, He and a testy hired man were pitching hay from "tumbles" up to a third man who mowed it away on a horse-drawn wagon. **2007** *DARE* File w**MA** (as of early 20th cent), Dad says: Yes, they used to tumble up the hay. They would go down the windrows and with the pitchfork make small piles . . and then go along with the wagon and pick each tumble up with the pitchfork. This was different from "cocking" the hay. This you would do if it looked like rain. These piles were higher and would shed the rain so that underneath stayed dry.

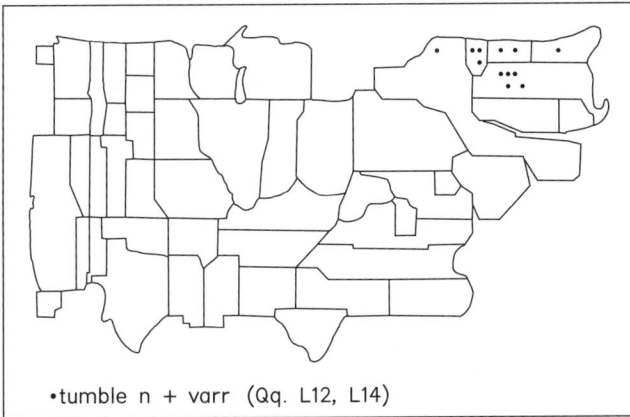

•tumble n + varr (Qq. L12, L14)

tumble about (or around)   See **tumble** v 1

tumblebug n

1 also *tumble beetle, tumbling beetle* (or *bug*): Any of var dung-rolling beetles of the family Scarabaeidae, esp those of the genera *Canthon, Copris, Deltochilum,* and *Phaneus.* **scattered, but esp Sth, Midl**   Also called **tumbledung, tumbler bug, tumbleturd 1, turd beetle, turd-roller 2**   Cf **camphor worm, dung beetle**

1803 Willich *Domestic Encycl.* 3.118 **DE**, Every body knows with what avidity ducks seize on the tumble bug, *(Scarabaeus carnifex).* **1805** Parkinson *Tour* 362 **C Atl**, There is a kind of beetle, called a tumblebug. **1845** Judd *Margaret* 86 sw**ME**, I am the fellow what see you running out of the store like a duck arter a tumble-bug. **1849** Howitt *Our Cousins in OH* 100, Nanny brought in a curious round ball from the farm-yard, about the size of a marble. . . This, their cousin told them, was formed by a little creature called the Tumble-bug. **1859** Jaeger *Life N. Amer. Insects* 16, When the Tumble-beetle in vain tries to roll its little ball up a hill, it runs for assistance, and brings back with it two or three other ones who roll up the ball in concert with it. **1862** (1863) Winthrop *Canoe & Saddle* 241 **NW**, Only such were left as had no more than power enough . . to pounce upon and bag every tumbling beetle of the plain. **1875** (1876) Twain *Tom Sawyer* 122 **MO**, A tumblebug

came next, heaving sturdily at its ball. **1899** (1912) Green *VA Folk-Speech* 461, Tumble-bug. . . One of several kinds of dung-beetles. **1909** *DN* 3.384 e**AL**, w**GA**, Tumble-bug. **1927** Adams *Congaree* 12 c**SC** [Black], Has you ever see a tumble bug roll he load? He ain't never satisfy wid it any way he got it. **1930** Dobie *Coronado* 132 **TX**, 'Huh, is this what you call money?' says the white man, stamping down on the tumblebugs. **1950** *WELS (Fat white worms often found in earth or rotting manure)* 1 Inf, **WI**, Adult [is] tumblebug. c**1960** *Wilson Coll.* cs**KY**, Tumblebug. **1965–70** *DARE* (Qu. R30, . . *Kinds of beetles;* not asked in early QRs) 37 Infs, **scattered, but chiefly Sth, Midl**, Tumblebug; **PA**70, 162, Tumbling beetle; **LA**15, **MO**27, Tumbling bug; (Qu. R2) Inf **MD**13, Tumbling bug; (Qu. R5, *A big brown beetle that comes out in large numbers in spring and early summer, and flies with a buzzing sound)* Inf **NC**80, Tumblebug; (Qu. R9b) Inf **MA**30, Tumblebug. **1988** Lincoln *Avenue* 259 w**NC** (as of c1940) [Black], When the eagle screams, . . the coo-koo knocks off from his foolishness and rolls hisself up like a tumblebug! **2003** *Times–Rec.* (Aledo IL) 16 Sept (Internet), We would pause and watch a couple of "tumbling bugs" roll a ball of manure.

2 See quot.

1939 Writers' Program *Guide KY* 100, A "tumble-bug" is a horse that likes to roll in his stall.

tumble cart   See **tumbler cart**

tumbled   See **tumble** v 1

tumbledung n
=**tumblebug 1.**

1763 Brookes *New System Nat. Hist.* 4.25, The *American ball Beetle,* called by the inhabitants Tumble-dung, is the most numerous and remarkable of the Beetle-kind of any in North-America. **1863** ME Scientific Surv. *Annual Rept. for 1862* 187, *Copris,* called Tumble Dungs, enclose their eggs in pellets of excrement. **1866** *Colman's Rural World* 18.4 **IL**, The common white "grub-worm" with a red head, is not . . the larva of the "tumble-dung" beetle. **1874** MO State Entomol. *Annual Rept.* 154, Such burrowing insects as the Tumble-dungs and Mole-crickets. **1880** Allan-Olney *New Virginians* 1.103 **VA**, Of diurnal beetles I only know a very beautiful small one, with wing-cases of blue and red, . . the flying green-and-bronze "June-bug," . . and the humble rusty-black "tumbledung." **1899** Bergen *Animal Lore* 63, Tumblebug, tumbledung, *Copris.*

tumbled up   See **tumble** v 1

tumble grass n   Also *tumbling grass*   Cf **tumbleweed**

1 Any of var grasses, some part of which breaks away at maturity and is blown about by the wind; see quots.   Note: Some of these quots may refer to spec senses below.

1899 MacMillan *MN Plant Life* 206, A great many different types of flower clusters are to be met with, varying from the solid spikes of the timothy or millet to the very loose and straggling clusters of the tumble-grasses and blue-grasses. *Ibid* 211, Tumbling grasses—after they have ripened their seeds—separate their flower-clusters, bring them together into balls and permit the wind to roll them over the plains or meadows. **1939** FWP *Guide KS* 11, Ubiquitous, but of little or no grazing value, are tumblegrass, green bristle, tickle and love grasses. **2003** (acc) MN Univ. *Cedar Creek Ecosystem* (Internet), *Leptoloma cognatum* [=*Digitaria cognata* var *cognata*] (False Witch Grass) became established in the 1980's, and this aggressive native tumble-grass is becoming increasingly abundant.

2 Spec:

a A grass *(Schedonnardus paniculatus)* native to much of the US west of the Mississippi Valley.   Also called **Texas crabgrass, wild crabgrass, wire grass 2l**

1950 Hitchcock–Chase *Manual Grasses* 508, *Schedonnardus paniculatus.* . . Tumblegrass. . . The axis of the inflorescence elongates after flowering, becoming 30 to 60 cm. long, curved in a loose spiral; the whole breaks away at maturity and rolls before the wind as a tumbleweed. **1968** Barkley *Plants KS* 60, Schedonnardus paniculatus. . . Tumblegrass. Prairies and plains especially in sandy soil. **1978** *Jrl. Range Management* 31.134 w**SD**, The two major grass species were threeawn (7%) and tumble grass *(Schedonnardus paniculatus)* (5%).

b A **panic grass**, usu *Panicum capillare.*   Cf **tumbleweed 2f**

1895 Gray *School & Field Book Botany* 472, *Panicum capillare.* . . Tumble Grass, Old Witch Grass. **1925** *Book of Rural Life* 9.5619, *Tumble grass,* an annual grass found commonly along roadsides, in waste places, pastures and among cultivated crops. It is called also *old witch* grass [=*Panicum capillare*]. **1936** Winter *Plants NE* 35, *Panicum* L. Panic-grass. Tickle-grass. Tumble-grass. Witch-grass.

c Any of var **love grasses**; see quots.

1895 KS Ag. Exper. Sta. Manhattan *Bulletin* 52.99, Tumble Grass (*Eragrostis pectinacea*). **1950** Gray–Fernald *Manual of Botany* 126, *E[ragrostis] spectabilis*. . . Tumble-grass. . . Dry sand, Fla. to Tex., n. on coastal sands to se. Mass. and inland n. to O., Mich. and Minn. **2004** Darke *Pocket Guide Grasses* 94, *Eragrostis spectabilis*—Purple lovegrass, tumble grass.

tumble in pieces See **tumble v 3**

tumble mustard n Also *tumbling mustard*

A **hedge mustard 1**, usu *Sisymbrium altissimum*.

1899 MacMillan *MN Plant Life* 21, Tumbling plants like the Russian thistle, the tumbling mustard and the tumbling grass, when their fruits are ripe separate all or the greater part of the stem from its attachment and curve their branches so that the whole takes the shape of a ball rolling freely for miles over the level prairies before the wind. **1923** Davidson–Moxley *Flora S. CA* 156, *N[orta] altissima*. . . Tumble mustard. Now widely distributed in cultivated fields and along waysides. **1937** U.S. Forest Serv. *Range Plant Hdbk.* W135, Tumblemustard, also known as . . tumbling mustard, is a rank, ungainly biennial with tumbleweed proclivities. **1953** Strausbaugh–Core *Flora WV* 430, *S[isymbrium] altissimum*. . . Tumble mustard. . . Waste places, occasional throughout the State. **1973** Hitchcock–Cronquist *Flora Pacific NW* 176, *Sisymbrium*. . . Tumblemustard. **2003** (acc) N. Prairie Wildlife Research Center *Biol. Resources* (Internet) seWA, Plant communities dominated by downy brome but containing substantial amounts of tumbling mustard (*Sisymbrium altissimum*), as well as other grass communities (e.g., wheatgrass [*Agropyron* spp.] communities), were not used for nesting [by long-billed curlews].

tumble pigweed See **tumbling pigweed**

tumbler n

1 See **tumbler bug.**

2 The pupa of a **mosquito** n[1] **B1.** [See quots] Cf **wiggler 1**

[**1841** Harris *Rept. Insects MA* 6, In the course of a few days these little water-tumblers are ready for another transformation.] **1859** *New Amer. Cyclop.* 8.317, They [=mosquito larvae] are changed into pupæ, called tumblers from the manner in which they roll over and over in the water by means of the fin-like paddles at the end of the tail. **1926** Essig *Insects N. Amer.* 533, The pupæ. . . are quite active and are called "tumblers" because of their quick, odd movements. **1949** Swain *Insect Guide* 189, The pupae, called "tumblers," are strange-looking creatures. **2003** *DARE* File—Internet **FL**, An even more active swimmer, the pupa is commonly called a "tumbler", describing the tumbling motion it uses to dive into deeper water.

3 See **tumbler cart.**

4 See **tumble n.**

tumbler bug n Also *tumbler*

=**tumblebug 1.**

1807 Irving *Salmagundi* 2.318, The aspiring politician, may be compared to that indefatigable insect, called the *Tumbler* . . which buries itself in filth, and works ignobly in the dirt until it forms a little ball, which it rolls laboriously along. **1896** *Amer. Jrl. Pharmacy* 68.658 **PA**, The beetles known as tumbler-bugs deposit eggs in the centre of balls made of animal droppings. **a1953** (1976) Guthrie *Seeds of Man* 144 **OK**, It took us a good half an hour to crawl like a tumbler bug up this sharp-rock, single-rut road. **1968** *DARE* (Qu. R30, . . Kinds of beetles; not asked in early QRs) Inf **LA15**, Tumbler or tumbling bug.

tumbler cart n Also *tumble cart, tumbler* [Folk-etym for *tumbrel*; *OED2* tumbler sb. 7 1673 →] **VA**

A two-wheeled cart, esp one with a tipping body.

1757 in 1889 Washington *Writings* 1.490 **VA**, Send them up by John who comes down with a Tumbler for that purpose. **1806** in 2006 *DARE* File—Internet **VA**, [Estate inventory:] 1 Tumbler Cart—7.00. **1847** McCallum *ME Letters* [7] **VA**, Imagine me sitting in the tumbler cart looking very sober. **1859** in 2006 *DARE* File—Internet **VA**, [Estate inventory:] Tumbler cart—10.00. **1863** *S. Lit. Messenger* 37.309 **VA**, He drove a tumbril or tumbler-cart. **1899** (1912) Green *VA Folk-Speech* 461, *Tumbler-cart*. . . The body of the cart is a separate box, and the load is thrown out by upsetting the body. **1938** FWP *Ocean Highway* 66 **VA**, The men load and carry the produce from the fields, using two-wheeled carts, locally called "tumble carts."

tumble ringwing n

=**winged pigweed.**

1942 Amer. Joint Comm. Horticult. Nomenclature *Std. Plant Names* 150, *Cycloloma* . . *atriplicifolium*. . . Tumble R[ingwing]. **1970** Correll *Plants TX* 529, *Cycloloma atriplicifolium*. . . Tumble ringwing, winged pigweed. **2003** (acc) N. Prairie Wildlife Research Center *Biol. Resources* (Internet) **West**, Lark Bunting. . . Nested in weedy areas beneath tumble ringwing (*Cycloloma atriplicifolium*).

tumblesault n, v Also *tumb(l)ersault, tummersault;* also, *esp freq among Black speakers, tumblesauce* [Blend of *tumble* + *somersault*] **chiefly NEast, C Atl; also Gulf States** See Map Cf **sumblesault, tumbleset**

A somersault; to turn a somersault.

1901 *Kappa Alpha Jrl.* 18.393 **VA**, Bro. Hart will not be able to turn any of his "patented mirth-creating tumble-saults" on account of a sprained muscle. **1943** *LANE* Map 578 (*Somersault*) 1 inf, **ceRI**, [tʌməsɒt]. **1965–70** *DARE* (Qu. EE9a, *The children's trick of turning over rapidly straight forward close to the ground*) 34 Infs, **chiefly NEast, C Atl; also Gulf States**, Tumblesault; **MA**8, **NY**250, **PA**239, Tumblesauce [all 3 Infs Black]; **IL**135, **MS**59, **NY**28, Tummersault; **WA**9, Tummersault, [corr to] tumbersault; **TX**13, Tumblersault; **AR**55, We always said ['tʌməsɛt], but ['tʌməsɒlt] is the name; (Qu. EE9b, *If children jump forward, land on the hands, and turn over*) Inf **NY**250, Tumblesault; **PA**239, Tumblesauce; (Qu. EE9c, . . *If children spread their arms and turn over sideways*) Inf **NY**250, Tumblesault; **PA**239, Tumblesauce. **1986** *AmSp* 61.379 **NYC**, An eleventh [variant of *somersault*] is *tumblesauce* (the last syllable is pronounced exactly like *sauce*), which I remember from my childhood in New York City (1945 →). **1986** Pederson *LAGS Concordance*, 40 infs, **Gulf Region**, Tumblesault(s). **2003** *DARE* File—Internet **Long Is. NY**, Crabs add to the surrealism of the undersea canvas as they tumblesault in the current. **2006** *Ibid* **csPA**, I could do a tumblesault and head stand.

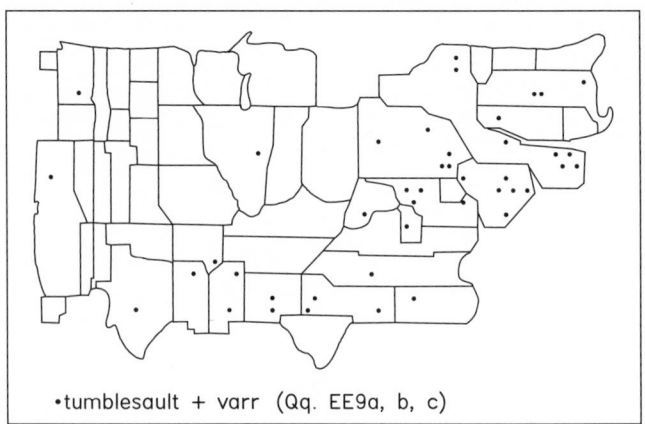

•tumblesault + varr (Qq. EE9a, b, c)

tumbleset n, v Also *tumberset, tummelset, tummerset* [Blend of *tumble* + **somerset**] **chiefly SE, Gulf States; also NEast** See Map Cf **sumbleset, tumblesault**

A somersault; to turn a somersault.

[**1864** in 1908 State Hist. Soc. ND *Coll.* 2.146 **NJ**, A horse tried to get up a bank and turned tumble set back into the water.] **1909** *DN* 3.384

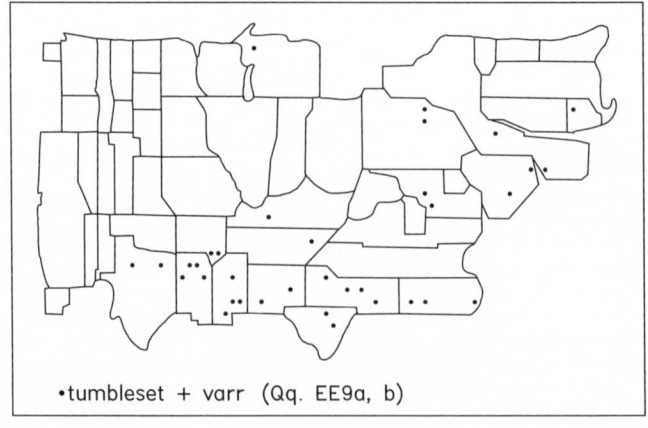

•tumbleset + varr (Qq. EE9a, b)

eAL, wGA, *Tumblesets. . .* Somersets. **1923** *DN* 5.244 **LA,** *Tumbleset. . .* Somersault. **1930s** in 1944 *ADD* **eWV,** *Tumbleset. . .* Commoner than *summerset.* **1940** *AmSp* 15.222 **cwTX,** They are certain to apprehend him if his horse 'turns a wildcat' (falls) or 'tumble-sets' (somersaults). **1965–70** *DARE* (Qu. EE9a, *The children's trick of turning over rapidly straight forward close to the ground*) 23 Infs, **chiefly SE, Gulf States; also NEast,** Tumbleset; **AR**52, I have heard "tumbleset," but they didn't know what they was saying; **AL**20, 26, **GA**72, **MI**44, **MS**6, 46, **NY**82, Tummerset; **AR**55, We always said ['tʌməsɛt], but ['tʌməsɔlt] is the name; **PA**81, Tumberset; **MD**20, Tummelset; (Qu. EE9b, *If children jump forward, land on the hands, and turn over*) Inf **LA**14, Tumbleset. **1972** *DARE* File **ceTX,** *Tumbleset*—somersault. **1986** Pederson *LAGS Concordance* **Gulf Region,** 67 infs, Tumbleset(s); 1 inf, Tumbleset—old term; 1 inf, Tumbleset—local term.

tumbletoad See **tumbleturd 1**

tumble together See **tumble** v 1

tumble to pieces See **tumble** v 3

tumbleturd n

1 also *Tom tumbleturd, tumbleturd bug;* pronc-sp *tumbletoad:* =**tumblebug 1;** also used as a term of abuse. **chiefly Sth, S Midl**

1687 in 1968 *VA Mag. Hist. & Biog.* 76.422, Another sort they call Tom Tumble Turds whose constant employ it is most of the Summer time to roll balls of horse dung up & down. **1737** (1911) Brickell *Nat. Hist. NC* 161, The *Tumble-turds,* are a Species of the *Beetles,* and so called, from their constant rowling the Horse-dung (whereon they feed) from one place to another, 'till it is no bigger than a small Bullet. **1748** Catesby *Nat. Hist. Carolina* app 11, *Scarobæus pilularis americanus. The Tumble-Turds.* This is the most numerous and remarkable of the Beetle kind of any in *North-America. . .* Their constant employ, in which they are indefatigable, is . . to provide proper nidi to deposite, their eggs; this they do by forming round pellets of human dung, or that of cattle, in the middle of which they lay an egg. **1863** in 1984 Whitman *Dear Brother Walt* 19 **NY,** And then the damnable conduct of those "big bugs" (I believe the biggest bugs are [ⁱ]tumble turds"). **1953** Randolph–Wilson *Down in Holler* 295 **Ozarks,** *Tumble-turd. . .* A dung beetle *(Coprini),* a scarab, a tumblebug. **1954** *Harder Coll.* **cwTN,** Tumbleturd. **c1960** *Wilson Coll.* **csKY,** Tumble-turd. **1965–70** *DARE* (Qu. P6, . . *Kinds of worms . . used for bait*) Inf **FL**48, Tumbleturd; (Qu. R5, *A big brown beetle that comes out in large numbers in spring and early summer, and flies with a buzzing sound*) Inf **NC**81, Tumbleturd; **MS**6, Tumbleturd bug; (Qu. R30, . . *Kinds of beetles;* not asked in early QRs) Infs **LA**2, **NJ**56, **SC**26, 40, 43, 57, Tumbleturd; **KY**86, Tumbletoads (tumblebugs). **1986** Pederson *LAGS Concordance,* 1 inf, **swTN,** Tumble-turd = tumblebug. **2001** *DARE* File—Internet **SC,** Why would I fear a tumble turd?

2 An infirm or clumsy creature.

1930 Shoemaker *1300 Words* 62 **cPA Mts** (as of c1900), *Tumble-t—d* —A weak, decrepit, and dying old horse. **1968** *DARE* (Qu. HH21, *A very awkward, clumsy person*) Inf **NH**14, Tumbleturd [laughter]. **2004** *DARE* File—Internet **VT,** Once, he [=a man with two artificial legs] landed in a brush pile as he was stepping off a horse-drawn sled to get wood. He refused assistance from his wife's brother, saying, " 'If I'm a big enough tumble turd to fall over, I'll get myself up.'"

tumbleturd bug See **tumbleturd 1**

tumble up See **tumble** v 1, 2

tumbleweed n Also *tumbling weed* **chiefly West** Cf **tumble grass**

1 Any of var plants, some part of which breaks away at maturity and is blown about by the wind; see quots. Note: Some of these quots may refer to specific senses below.

1885 *Atlantic Mth.* 56.107 **swKS,** Great tumble-weeds come rolling like hoops across the plain. **1888** *Century Illustr. Mag.* 35.453 **NE,** I secured a "tumble-weed" or "rolling-weed,"—one of those globular perennials of the plains that . . goes rolling around over the prairies at the mercy of the blast. **1897** IN Dept. Geol. & Nat. Resources *Rept. for 1896* 596, *P[anicum] capillare. . .* Old Witch Grass. . . Common. . . This species is a common tumble-weed. **1912** Baker *Book of Grasses* 119, The name Fly-away Grass [for *Agrostis hyemalis*] is more appropriate as the seeds ripen, for the light panicles are soon broken by the wind and drift over the fields as the earliest tumble-weed. **1914** Georgia *Manual Weeds* 368, *Buffalo Bur. . .* The plant frequently becomes a tumbleweed. **1941** Jaeger *Wildflowers* 51 **Desert SW,** *Redscale . . Atriplex rosea. . .*

When dried it is one of our common tumbleweeds. **1965–70** *DARE* (Qu. S21, . . *Weeds . . that are a trouble in gardens and fields*) 12 Infs, **chiefly West,** Tumbleweed; **TX**71, Tumbling weeds; (Qu. S9, . . *Kinds of grass that are hard to get rid of*) Inf **CA**165, Tumbleweed; (Qu. S15, . . *Weed seeds that cling to clothing*) Inf **CA**80, Tumbleweed thorns; **CA**181, Tumbleweed; (Qu. S26a, . . *Wildflowers. . . Roadside flowers*) Inf **KS**8, Tumbleweed. **1986** Pederson *LAGS Concordance,* 3 infs, **neAR, cMS, cTX,** Tumbleweed(s); 1 inf, **cTX,** Tumbleweeds = tumbling weeds. **2002** *DARE* File—Internet **NM,** We have found western harvest mice up in large, dry tumbleweeds, undoubtedly searching for seeds.

2 Spec:

a Any of several **amaranths,** esp *Amaranthus albus.* Cf **ghost plant 1**

1860 *Cultivator* 3d ser 8.345, White Amaranth. . . We call it the "tumble weed." When in motion it will scare a horse worse than a moving wheelbarrow. **1884** *Bot. Gaz.* 9.106 **MN,** A light wind will then cause the plant to break off and go rolling along in the same manner as happens with *Amaranthus albus . .* (commonly called "tumble-weed"), on the prairies of Minnesota. **1897** *Jrl. Amer. Folkl.* 10.53 **swMO,** *Amaranthus Albus. . .* Tumble weed. **1936** Winter *Plants NE* 194, *Amaranthus. . .* Pigweed. Tumble-weed. **1959** Barnes *Nat. Hist. Wasatch Winter* 53 **UT,** The tumbleweeds (*Amaranthus graecizans*) . . show more color, and are so stiff they readily roll over the snow. **1966** *DARE* (Qu. S21, . . *Weeds . . that are a trouble in gardens and fields*) Inf **ND**3, Pigweed—tumbling weed. **1966** *DARE* FW Addit **WA**10, *Amaranthus albus*—Tumbleweed; **WA**12, Pigweeds—all tumbleweeds—bloom doesn't amount to anything. **1987** Kindscher *Edible Wild Plants* 19, *Common names . .* [of] other species [of *Amaranthus*]—pigweed, . . redroot, tumbleweed.

b =**winged pigweed.**

1877 *Gardener's Mth. & Horticulturist* 19.180 **IL,** The "tumble weed" is not near so common in this neighborhood as formerly. It—the weed— appears to be . . one of the Chenopodiaceae, probably Cycloloma platyphyllum. **1898** *Jrl. Amer. Folkl.* 11.278 **West,** *Cycloloma platyphyllum,* . . tumble weed. **1915** (1926) Armstrong–Thornber *Western Wild Flowers* 98, *Tumbleweed—Cycloloma atriplicifolium. . .* Very curious round plants, six to twenty inches high, usually purple all over, sometimes green and rarely white. . . They are a mass of interlacing branches. . . When their seeds are ripe, and they are dry and brittle, the wind easily uproots them and starts them careening across the plain, their seeds flying out by the way. . . There are other Tumble-weeds, such as . . *Sisymbrium allissimum* [sic], and *Amaranthus álbus.* **1945** Wodehouse *Hayfever Plants* 101, The winged pigweed or tumbleweed . . is common along streams and river banks throughout the central part of the United States from the Mississippi River to the Rocky Mountains.

c A bugseed (here: *Corispermum americanum*).

1891 *Century Dict.* 6527, *Tumbleweed. . .* Species so called are *Amaranthus albus . .* and *A. blitoides, Psoralea lanceolata* (Dakota and Montana), the bug-seed, *Corispermum hyssopifolium* [=*C. americanum*], and the winged pigweed, *Cycloloma platyphylla.* **1936** Winter *Plants NE* 193, *C[orispermum] hyssopifolium. . .* Bug-seed. Tumbleweed. . . Occasional in sandy soil throughout the state.

d also *Russian tumbleweed:* =**Russian thistle.**

1894 U.S. Dept. Ag. Div. Botany *Bulletin* 15.7, This plant is generally called Russian thistle in South Dakota and Russian cactus in North Dakota. Russian tumbleweed and other appropriate names have been suggested. **1908** NM Univ. *Biol. Ser.* 3.1.83 **cNM,** [*Salsola*] *Kali,* var. *tragus.* The Russian Thistle, "*Tumble Weed.*" **1945** Wodehouse *Hayfever Plants* 102, Russian thistle . . , also known as tumbleweed . . , is an annual herb with dryish spine-tipped leaves. **1965–70** *DARE* (Qu. S21, . . *Weeds . . that are a trouble in gardens and fields*) Inf **AZ**9, Russian thistles = tumbleweeds; **CO**20, Russian thistle—more stickery— when dry, called tumbleweeds; **MT**3, Russian thistle—becomes tumbleweed in fall; **NM**6, Russian thistle—may be same as tumbleweed; **TX**5, Thistles—Russian thistle—tumbleweed; **TX**71, Thistles—tumbling weeds; **TX**78, Russian thistles—tumbleweeds; **WY**5, Tumbleweed—Russian thistle; (Qu. S15, . . *Weed seeds that cling to clothing*) Inf **CA**80, Tumbleweed thorns; (Qu. S17, . . *Kinds of plants . . that . . cause itching and swelling*) Inf **NM**9, Tumbleweed—affects those allergic to it; **TX**39, Tumbleweed; (Qu. S26e, *Other wildflowers not yet mentioned;* not asked in early QRs) Inf **ND**9, Russian thistle—small white flower—when dry are called tumbling weeds. **1968** Abbey *Desert Solitaire* 28 **seUT,** I can see . . the obnoxious Russian thistle, better known as tumbleweed, an exotic. **2003** *DARE* File—Internet **West,** Russian thistle. . . Tumbleweeds were first reported in the United States around

1877 in Bon Homme County, South Dakota, apparently transported in flax seed imported by Ukrainian farmers. Within two decades it had tumbled into a dozen states, and by 1900, it had reached the Pacific Coast.

e   A **scurf pea** (here: *Psoralidium* spp).

    [**1886** *Amer. Naturalist* 20.1053 **csNE,** Another "Tumble-weed". . . My attention was called to great masses of some much-branched, white-woolly plant which occupied the ditches by the side of the railway. . . Specimens . . proved to be *Psoralea tenuiflora* [=*Psoralidium t.*].] **1891** [see **2c** above]. **1936** Winter *Plants NE* 98, P[soralea] lanceolata. . . Tumble-weed. . . Common particularly in the sandy regions of western and central Nebr.

f   also *tumbleweed grass:* A **panic grass** (here: *Panicum capillare*).   Cf **tumble grass 2b**

    1912 Blatchley *IN Weed Book* 53, *Panicum capillare.* . . Tumbleweed. . The spreading tops, being very brittle, break off in autumn and are blown into fence corners or against some barrier where they form great piles. **1914** Georgia *Manual Weeds* 28, *Panicum capillare.* . . Tumbleweed Grass. **1952** Strausbaugh–Core *Flora WV* 84, *P[anicum] capillare.* . . Sometimes called tumbleweed because at maturity the panicles break away and are blown around by the wind.

g   A **hedge mustard 1** (here: *Sisymbrium altissimum*).   Cf **tumble mustard**

    [**1897** NV Ag. Exper. Sta. *Bulletin* 38.20, Tumbling Mustard, *Sisymbrium altissimum.* . . This is a veritable "tumble-weed," the stems breaking off near the ground, after which the plants are blown about by the wind, scattering their seeds far and near.] **1915** [see **2b** above]. **1952** Davis *Flora ID* 352, *S[isymbrium] altissimum.* . . *Jim Hill Mustard. Tumble-weed.* . . The mature plant breaks loose and is rolled for long distances by the wind. **2002** *DARE* File—Internet **CA,** Jim Hill Mustard, also refer[r]ed to as Tumbleweed.

h   =**bush morning-glory.**

    1967 *DARE* (Qu. S5, . . *Wild morning glory*) Inf **KS6,** Tumbleweeds—but they're not really tumbleweeds.

tumbleweed grass   See **tumbleweed 2f**

tumbling beetle (or bug)   See **tumblebug 1**

tumbling grass   See **tumble grass**

tumbling mustard   See **tumble mustard**

tumbling pigweed n   Also *tumble pigweed*   Cf **tumbleweed 2a**

An **amaranth,** usu *Amaranthus albus.*

    1909 IA State College Exper. Sta. *Bulletin* 104.291, One-half strength solution effectually destroyed leaves and tops of . . tumbling pigweed [etc]. **1914** Georgia *Manual Weeds* 122, *Amaranthus albus.* . . Tumbling Pigweed. . . When the plants mature . . , the stalk is uprooted or breaks off at the surface of the ground, and the weed rolls away to scatter the seeds wherever the wind wills. **1935** (1943) Muenscher *Weeds* 215, *Amaranthus graecizans* [=*A. albus*]. . . Tumble weed, tumbling pigweed. **1950** Stevens *ND Plants* 134, *Amaranthus albus.* . . *Tumbling Pigweed.* . . Common in dry soil, becoming a tumbleweed when dry. **2007** *Weed Sci.* 55.619, Tumble pigweed and barnyardgrass seeds were unaffected at 42 C and below. . . Tumble pigweed, *Amaranthus albus.*

tumbling weed   See **tumbleweed**

tumeric   See **turmeric 2**

tummelset   See **tumbleset**

tummersault   See **tumblesault**

tummerset   See **tumbleset**

tump v[1]   Cf **neck v 2**

To drag or carry using a **tumpline.**

    1848 Bartlett *Americanisms* 491 **ME,** *To Tump.* . . to draw a deer or other animal home through the woods, after he has been killed. "We tumped the deer to our cabin." [**1855** Haliburton *Nature* 1.268, One day, Sir, a man passed the north barrack gate, tumping, (as he said, which means in English, Sir, hauling,) an immense bull moose on a sled.] **1916** Miller *Boys' Book* 214, The pack should not weigh over twenty pounds all told, and you can tump it five or ten miles . . with ease. **2006** *DARE* File **NEast,** The traditional wanigan box was always portaged using just a tumpline. . . I have also heard the word *tump* used as a verb. We will tump our loads over the next portage.

tump n[1]   [*OED2 tump* sb. "1. A hillock, mound. . . *local.* . . 2. . .

a clump of grass, esp. one forming a dry spot in a bog or fen. *local.*"] **sDelmarva**

A hummock or clump (of vegetation) in a marsh; a small, marshy island.

    [**1754** in 1970 Mason *Papers* 1.33 **eVA,** Thence down the The [sic] Meanders of Occoquan Bay along the Bank. . . opposite to the Tump Island (from this Place Mr. Cock's Fish House bears N 31 E . .).] **1896** in 1897 VA Genl. Assembly House of Delegates *Jrl.* Doc 1 14 **Chesapeake Bay,** The tumps look to be about the same as when I first remember. . . Ques. What are tumps? Ans. They are little islands. **1902** *Natl. Geogr. Mag.* 13.29, Outward Tump; island, Chincoteague Bay, Worcester County, Maryland. **1935** *AmSp* 10.154 **eMD,** [In a list of "terms used for land adjacent to water":] *Tump.* Very rare; Eastern Shore. **1968–70** *DARE* (Qu. C7, . . *Land that usually has some standing water with trees or bushes growing in it*) Inf **VA**47, Tumps; tumps land; tumps of salt bushes—bunches of weeds or grass or bushes; (Qu. C17, . . *A small, rounded hill*) Inf **MD**36, Tump—a few feet in height and diameter. **1970** *DARE* Tape **VA**52, A man landed his boat on the northeast end of this tump. **1976** Warner *Beautiful Swimmers* 9 **Chesapeake Bay,** The larger islands are called hammocks. . . The smaller ones, with barely enough soil to nourish a single bush or tree, are dismissed as "tumps." **1996** Horton *Island Out of Time* 304 **Chesapeake Bay,** As for Smith Island, by the year 2100, it will be gone—perhaps a few marsh tumps still sticking up, and mudflats exposed on low tides. **2001** MD Ornith. Soc. *MD Yellowthroat* Mar–Apr 6 (Internet) **eVA, eMD,** All the old names, like Egg Harbor up in Jersey, Egg Marsh, Great Egging Island, and the like, that was cause they'd go out there to the tumps and other places and gather gull eggs. *Ibid* 7, Tump = small marshy island, used especially in the vicinity of the Maryland–Virginia boundary both in Chincoteague and Chesapeake Bays. **2006** *DARE* File—Internet **eVA,** [Advt:] $300,000 Tobacco Island. . . Land is all marsh with some tumps of trees.

tump n[2]   See **tumpline**

tump v[2]   **chiefly Sth, S Midl**

1   freq with *over:* To knock or tip (something, esp a container) over, usu by accident; hence ppl adj *tumped over.*

    1961 Maund *International* 284, She faced the ceiling like a tumped-over cemetery angel. **1973** *DARE* File **ceGA,** *Tump,* to overturn. Common usage in area of Savannah. **1975** *AmSp* 50.68 **AR** (as of c1970), *Tump over.* . . Tip or knock over—"Don't tump over that glass!" **1976** *DARE* File **AR** (as of c1945), "Tump" means to overturn, as in "Don't tump that bucket of berries." **1983** Allin *S. Legislative Dict.* 31 **Sth,** Judge Philpot tumped over his cheer [=chair]. **2000** *NADS Letters* **cnAL,** "Tump". . . Means to knock something over as in "He tumped his milk over." . . Was in use in the 1930's and still in use today. **2000** *DARE* File **TX,** As kids, we all hated the rambunctious little boys who got to swinging so high on the backyard swing set that they'd tump it over and scare the rest of us. **2001** *Ibid* **sIL,** "Tump": to knock over a pretty big container and have stuff spill out. I can "tump" over a tub of toys . . , or a tub of milk, but I can *never* "tump" over a glass of milk, that would have to be "spilled/t". **2004** *NADS Letters* **cnTX,** The first time I heard this was when I moved from Central Texas to North-central Texas to teach school. . . Students would exclaim, "Oh! Mrs. Williams, my desk tumped over!" Or, if a school box fell off and spilled, "I tumped over my school box." I've heard teachers say things such as, "Be careful not to tump the paint over, Susie." . . Usually, "over" comes after "tump" in the sentence, but not always as in, "Be careful! Don't tump it."

2   freq with *in, out:* To pour, dump.

    1967 *DARE* FW Addit **AR,** *Tump*—to pour something out. **2001** *DARE* File **cnKY,** I believe that when you are "tumping" some stuff out of a container that you must be prodding the movement along with a tap on the bottom. . . For me, therefore, it is a combination of "thump" and "dump." **2003** in 2006 *DARE* File—Internet **TX,** I got a tub that we can use to put him [=a snapping turtle] in then you could just carry him over and tump him out. **2004** *Ibid* **CO,** I just wait about 10 more minutes and then tump them upside down on the cookie rack and remove the pans. *Ibid* **cnKY,** Tump them into the pot. . . Don't cook your spinach yet. . . [T]ump it in at the very end. **2006** *Ibid* **OK,** He put a pitcher in the bathroom. We fill it and tump it in as we're flushing . . no more clogs.

3   freq with *over;* intr: To fall over abruptly, capsize.

    1952 Frank *Hold Back* 128 **MN,** The jeep tumped over, and the two men in the back were hit. **1976** *DARE* File **TX,** *Tump over*—Fall over. **1981** AR *Gaz.* (Little Rock) 25 June sec B 1/1, "Tump," . . means to turn over and spill out; or, to be turned over and spilled out; sometimes accidentally. As in, "when he brushed against the coffee table, his Coke tumped over." . . Constant Reader, from Little Rock, writes that "I have heard this word all my life." **1991** *DARE* File, My husband was putting a casserole on a warmer and it was in danger of sliding off the trivet. . . I hollered out—"Watch out, it's going to *tump* over!" [Inf grew up in the Panama Canal Zone, and now lives in Baltimore.] **1995** Karr *Liars' Club* 40 e**TX**, This might sound easy enough to do unless you're riding a two-wheeler, in which case slowing too far down makes you tump over. **1996** *DARE* File **LA**, Many of us remember the frequent admonitions of our elementary teachers, "Bobby, don't lean back in that chair— you'll *tump* over and crack your head." **1999** *Ibid*, Growing up in North Louisiana we used to warn each other that if we swang too high, the swingset would tump over. . . I have also lived in the Tulsa OK area, Arkansas Delta and Central MS, and everyone seemed to be familiar with this word. **2001** *Ibid* **AL**, She said the boat "almost tumped." **2004** [see **1** above]. **2006** *DARE* File—Internet **AR**, We tumped over in the canoe.

tumped over See **tump** v² 1

tump in See **tump** v² 2

tumpline n Also *tump (strap)* [Of Algonquian orig; cf Wampanoag (Mashpee) *tãˊmpãm* line to hold a back-basket] **chiefly Nth** Cf **tump** v¹ Cf *DCan*
A headstrap used to ease the weight of a load carried on the back or to draw a load along the ground.
  1758 in 1890 MA Hist. Soc. *Proc.* 2d ser 6.27, It[em] two pair of Stocking and Stocks and Napsack and tumpline at 1-0-0. **1796** Johnson *Narr. Captivity* 66 **nNH** (as of 1754), I was a novice at making canoes, bunks, and tumplines, which was the only occupation of the squaws. **1824** Hoyt *Antiq. Researches* 250, When one [Indian] falls, his nearest comrade crawls up, . . and fixing a *tump line* to the dead body, cautiously draggs it to the rear. **1897** *Outing* 30.531 **MN**, They consisted of a canvas bag with broad shoulder-straps . . and a still broader one to go across the forehead. . . This latter band, called the "tump-strap" in Minnesota, is mostly used to sustain the weight of the articles carried in the sack. **1911** *Atlanta Constitution* (GA) 2 Apr [17]/4 (newspaperarchive.com) **AK** [Story by Jack London], The toil of pick and shovel, the scars and mars of packstrap and tumpline. **1913** *Outing* 62.107, I have seen men carry 150 pounds with a tump and not seem to mind it. **1943** in 2006 *DARE* File—Internet, We developed a canvas bag with a tump strap for the head and packed the hospital supplies and personal equipment in this. **1958** McCulloch *Woods Words* 201 **Pacific NW**, *Tump line*—Back in the days when woodsmen were men and packed their gear in packsacks, the load on the back was eased by running an extra band from the sack around the forehead and back to the packsack. **1965** *Oshkosh Daily Northwestern* (WI) 26 Feb 24/4, A tumpline sewed onto a pack lets you take the strain off your shoulders from time to time and delays fatigue. **1965** Bowen *Alaskan Dict.* 33, *Tumpline.* . . The effect of the tumpline on an unseasoned human neckbone has to be experienced to be believed. **2005** *DARE* File—Internet, The operaters [sic] head will also be . . supported by an elastic tump strap. **2006** *DARE* File **NEast**, The original tumpline was simply a long leather strap, wider in the middle where it rested against the forehead.

tump out See **tump** v² 2

tump over See **tump** v² 1, 3

tump strap See **tumpline**

tuna n¹ [AmSpan; *OED2* 1555 →] **West, esp TX, CA** Cf **nopal, pad** n² 2
The edible fruit of any of several **prickly pears 1**; hence nouns *tuna (cactus)* any of several **prickly pears 1.**
  [**1722** in 1741 Coxe *Descr. Carolana* 74 **east of Missip R**, Tunas [are] a most delicious Fruit, especially in hot Weather.] **1842** in 1952 Green *Samuel Maverick* 184 **TX**, Thick forests. Villages at foot of mountains and tank. White tunas. **1846** (1848) Bryant *What I Saw in CA* 376, A juicy fruit is produced by the prickly-pear, named *tuna.* **1875** Bourke *Diary* 31 May **SD**, A plant, plentiful in this country [along the Cheyenne R.], called the nopal, or Tuna cactus, . . is employed with success to clarify the water for drinking purposes. **1889** *DN* 1.195 **TX**, *Túna:* the edible fruit of certain *Opuntiæ*. More specifically of *Opuntia tuna.* **1895** (1969) Graham *Stories of Foot-hills* 44 **CA**, You can go up the bank there and pick some tunas. **1914** Saunders *With Flowers in CA* 201, The cactus fruit, called tuna, . . [is] a really delicious morsel when divested of its prickly coat. **1929** Dobie *Vaquero* 35 **West**, They [=razor-

back hogs] desired no choicer diet than a mixture of *tunas* (prickly pear apples) and rattlesnakes. **1959** Munz–Keck *CA Flora* 310, The "prickly-pears" are those with flat joints and if they have edible fr[uit]s they are "tunas." **1967** *DARE* (Qu. I46, . . *Kinds of fruits that grow wild around here*) Inf **TX28**, Edible cacti—tuna, pitaya, anaqua. **2002** *DARE* File—Internet **TX**, Featured . . were recipes using the juice of the prickly pear cactus "tuna", or fruit.

tuna n² Cf **Grand River tuna, mackerel 1**
Std: any of several large saltwater food and game fishes of the family Scombridae, usu of the genera *Thunnus*, *Euthynnus*, *Katsuwonus*, and *Sarda.* For other names of var of these see **ahi, aku, bluefin 2, bonito 1, chicken of the sea 1, kawakawa, little tunny 1, 2, skipjack 1k, tunny**

tuna cactus See **tuna** n¹

tunament See **tournament**

tundish n [*OED2* 1389 → "now *local*"] *relic* Cf **tunjack**
A funnel.
  1941 *Language* 17.331 **WI** [*LANCS* fieldwork], *Tundish*—1 [of 50 infs]. . . Older than *funnel.*

tundra rose n **AK**
A **cinquefoil** (here: *Dasiphora floribunda*).
  1938 (1958) Sharples *AK Wild Flowers* 109, P[otentilla] fruticosa [= *Dasiphora floribunda*]. . . Known in some localities as the "Tundra Rose," as it has somewhat the appearance of a small, single, yellow rose. **1974** Welsh *Anderson's Flora AK* 384, Shrubby Cinquefoil, . . *Tundra Rose.* . . Through most of Alaska (except for southwestern and southeastern portions) and most of the Yukon. **2010** *DARE* File—Internet **AR**, After the first two weeks of being here the wild flowers started to bloom. The first ones to come out were the pink wild roses, then came the yellow tundra rose and then the blue bells.

tune n, v Usu |tun, tɪun, tjun|; also |čun, čɪun, čjun| Pronc-sp *chune*
Std senses, var forms.
  1805 *Weekly Visitor Ladies' Misc.* 3.317, I say of what service is all this to a man. . . whose most pleasing chune is the voice of the distressed widow? **1861** *Vanity Fair* 3.75 **NYC**, You kin excuse the words for the sake o' the chune. **1864** Taylor *John Godfrey's Fortunes* 142 **PA**, I believe it is a little out of chune. **1883** (1971) Harris *Nights with Remus* 51 **GA** [Black], Bless yo' soul, honey! dey wa'nt no chune gwine dat Brer Rabbit can't pat. **1893** Shands *MS Speech* 23, *Chune.* . . Negro for *tune.* **1903** *DN* 2.335 se**MO**, *Tune.* . . Pronounced chune [čɪun] [sic for [čɪun]]. **1907** *DN* 3.237 nw**AR**, *Tune.* . . Sometimes pronounced chune. **1909** *DN* 3.384 e**AL**, w**GA**, *Tune*, n. and v. Pronounced [čun]. **1922** Gonzales *Black Border* 293 s**SC, GA coasts** [Gullah glossary], *Chune*—(n. and v.) **1923** (1946) Greer-Petrie *Angeline Doin' Society* 8 cs**KY**, Sich quick and dev'lish chunes. **1940** *AmSp* 15.50 s**Appalachians, Ozarks**, [t] has a tendency to become [tʃ] before [ɪu], [ju], and [u] [sic for [ɪu], [ju], and [u]]: chune (tune), Chuseday (Tuesday) [etc.].

tune bow n Also *tuning bow*
=**mouth bow.**
  1978 in 2006 *DARE* File—Internet **Ozarks**, A related instrument found in limited white usage in the Ozarks is the tune bow. A hunting bow is held against the cheek and caused to sound by plucking the string. **1979** Irwin *Musical Instruments* 59 ne**TN**, I have found more people in Hancock County, Tennessee, than elsewhere who were familiar with the mouth bow—also called the music bow and the tuning bow. **1980** *Foxfire 6* 91 cw**NC**, In Madison County, North Carolina, they make a "tune bow" out of split hemlock tobacco-curing sticks and wire string.

tune up v phr Also *tune up one's pipes* **chiefly Sth, S Midl**
To get ready to cry; to begin crying.
  1857 Southworth *Vivia* 105 **MD**, "Oh! if she ain't agoing to cry," jeered one tall, coarse-looking girl. . . "See! see! she's tuning up her pipes now! . .," said another. **1899** (1912) Green *VA Folk-Speech* 461, *Tune up.* . . To get ready to cry, said of children. **1918** *Eve. State Jrl. Lincoln Daily News* (NE) 8 June 4/3, Delicate instruments were used to record whether or not a young baby breathed deeper or shallower or "tuned up to cry" yhen [sic] it heard another baby crying. **1929** (1954) Faulkner *Sound & Fury* 31 **MS** [Black], After a while even Jason was through eating, and he began to cry. "Now you got to tune up." Dilsey said. **1952** Brown *NC Folkl.*

1.603, *Tune up.* . . To cry. Also: *tune up and cry.* **1976** Ryland *Richmond Co. VA* 378, *Tune up*—get ready to cry, as of children. **1995** in 2006 *DARE* File—Internet **VA,** I saw Jessica's mom tuning up to cry. **2006** *Ibid* **KY,** The little boy was fixing to tune up and cry.

tuning bow See **tune bow**

‡tunjack n [Cf *EDD tun* 2 "To pour liquor into casks or bottles," *jack* sb. 23 "A drinking vessel"] Cf **tundish**
A funnel.
   1967 *DARE* (Qu. F9, *To get a liquid through a narrow opening—for example, the neck of a bottle—you'd pour it through a* _____) Inf **WY**4, Tunjack—one of [my] neighbors asked for this once.

tunk n[1]

1 A rap or blow. [Engl dial] **chiefly NEng, NY** Cf **belly-tunk**
   1843 Morleigh *Life in the West* 148 **NY,** In short, I had received a "tarnation tunk on the head," as one of the boatmen said. **a1856** Foster *NY Naked* 144 **NYC,** The other sputters, and . . hitting his friend a tunk in the ribs . . says "pretty well." **1858** *Harper's New Mth. Mag.* 16.768 **NEng,** I *did* give my head the all-firedest tunk! **1874** *Appletons' Jrl.* 12.494 **NEng,** Tunk—a light, sharp tap with the hammer. **1909** *DN* 3.417 **nME,** *Tunk.* . . A blow. **1918** *DN* 4.82 **ME, nNH,** *Tunk.* . . A blow. **1927** *AmSp* 3.141 **eME,** "He got an awful tunk" means blow or stroke. **1967** *Amer. Agric. & Rural New Yorker* 164.5.60, [In a list of old words not now commonly known:] A "tunk" was a sharp blow or thump.

2 also *tonk, tunket:* An informal party, usu one with dancing—usu in comb *kitchen tunk.* **chiefly VT, Upstate NY** Cf **junket, kitchen dance**
   1869 in 2006 *DARE* File—Internet **neNY,** Saturday. . . In the eve I carried Addie to M[orrisonville] Saw Walla and went to a "Tunk." **1894** *New Engl. Mag.* 15.753 **nVT,** There was a dance—a "kitchen tunk" the more piously inclined of the townspeople called it. **1900** *DN* 2.69 **cNY** [College slang], *Tunk.* . . An informal banquet [at Colgate Univ]. **1922** (1926) Cady *Rhymes VT* 220, Then there were spelling bouts and bees,/ And kitchen tunks and farmers' teas. **1930** *AmSp* 5.239 **cNY** [Univ slang], The author has collected the following expressions around the campus of Colgate University. . . *Tunk:* a smoker at which light refreshments are served, usually from 8.00–11.00, P.M. "Our fraternity is holding a tunk tonight." **1941** *LANE* Map 410 **VT** (*A dance*) 5 infs, *Kitchen tunk;* 1 inf, *Kitchen tunk,* now common among the French-Canadians; 1 inf, *Kitchen tunk,* usually but not necessarily in the kitchen; 1 inf, *Kitchen tunk,* a small neighborhood dance. **1951** *Post–Std.* (Syracuse NY) 27 May [mag sec 4] (newspaperarchive.com), Friday afternoons give the faculty [of Colgate Univ] a chance to get together outside of the classrooms in a more social atmosphere. These meetings, usually over coffee and doughnuts, are known locally as tunks, a word of undetermined origin and peculiar to Colgate. **1959** *VT Hist.* 27.146, *Kitchen hop* . . var. kitchen junket; kitchen tonk; kitchen tunket; kitchen tunket. A good time; a dance; a party. Formerly, a dance held in the kitchen of a private house, with music furnished by one fiddler who was usually seated in a chair placed on the top of the kitchen stove, in order to keep the floor clear for dancing. Common among older people; occasional among younger. **2000** *NADS Letters* **VT,** In Vermont I have heard people talk about old time "kitchen tunks or tonks" where people got together informally to make music.

3 also *tunkup:* Mashed potatoes. Cf **potato thump**
   1918 *DN* 4.83 **ME, nNH,** *Tunkup.* . . Mashed potato. **1966** *DARE* FW Addit **MA**6, Tater tunk—potatoes mashed and prepared on plate for individual serving.

tunk v [Engl dial] **chiefly NEng**
To strike, tap; hence nouns *tunker, tunking stick.*
   1892 Sullivan *Life & Reminiscences* 146, I pushed down those fists with my right, and with my left tunked Sheehan on the right side of his nose. **1903** *DN* 2.301 **Cape Cod MA** (as of a1857), *Tunk.* . . To thump with the finger and thumb. **1904** Day *Kin o' Ktaadn* 69 **ME,** He tunked with his hammer and he jabbed with his awl. **1913** *DN* 4.58 **seMA,** *Tunker.* . . Anything with which to pound. "Pass me a tunker to pound the earth in this post-hole with." **1918** *DN* 4.82 **ME, nNH,** *Tunk.* . . To strike. **1927** *DN* 5.478 **Ozarks,** *Tunk.* . . To thump, to rap. "Injuns haint no sense; allus a-tunkin' on drums, or somethin'." **1964** Gould *Parables of Peter* 169 **ME,** He tunked the spigot in firmly with a hammer. **1966** *DARE* Tape **ME**26, He said, "You better leave him alone, or I'll have to tunk you." **1967** *DARE* FW Addit **ME,** *Tunk him one*—hit him, sock him one. **1979** Lewis *How to Talk Yankee* [34] **nNEng,** I got to get me a new shotgun. Mine won't throw out the shell without I tunk it

every time. **2000** Chamberlain *River Stories* 94 **swWI,** Daddy always carried what he called his "tunkin-stick." The tunkin-stick was of good size and one of its uses was to test the strength of the ice. *Ibid* 95, The tunkin-stick had other uses as well. If an animal in a trap wasn't quite dead, Dad would 'tunk' it on the head and put it out of its misery.

tunk n[2] See **tonk** n[1]

tunkelhead See **tunklehead**

Tunker n[1] See **Dunker**

tunker n[2] See **tunk** v

tunket n[1]

1 Used as a euphem for *hell,* usu in interrog phrr *who* (or *where,* etc) *in tunket* or emphatic comparisons *cold* (or *hot,* etc) *as tunket.* **chiefly NEng**
   1847 (1853) Thompson *Locke Amsden* 69 **VT,** I found it as cold as tunket. **1905** Wasson *Green Shay* 37 **ME,** Who in tunket is it backs up the old creetur', anyways? **1916** Lincoln *Mary-'Gusta* 57 **MA,** Isaiah dropped the basket as if it was red hot. "What in tunket!" he exclaimed. **1918** *DN* 4.82 **ME, nNH,** *Tunket.* . . Hell. "Madder'n Tunket." **1943** *AN&Q* 3.78 **NEng,** *Tunket.* . . This mild expletive was formerly—and may well still be—in common use in rural New England. **1950** *WELS,* 2 Infs, **WI,** Tunket. [*DARE* Ed: One Inf had a parent from NY; the other had a parent from CT.] **1959** *VT Hist.* 27.165, *What in Tunket!* . . Occasional. **1968** Moody *Horse* 163 **nwKS** (as of c1920), Why in tunket would you put a shop in McCook or Oberlin? **1975** Gould *ME Lingo* 301, Where in tunket did you put my overhauls? **1978** *DARE* File **eMA** (as of c1915), My grandmother . . was the only one I ever heard use the word *tunket.* "Where in tunket did I put those gloves?" she might say. **1995** *DARE* File, My mother always said "Hot as tunket." But she never told us what tunket was, or how hot it was. . . She grew up in Freeport, Illinois, but she later lived in Old Greenwich, Connecticut.

2 See quot.
   1900 Day *Up in ME* 8, Didn't seem to care a tunket what she drunk or et.

tunket n[2] See **tunk** n[1] **2**

tunking stick See **tunk** v

tunklehead n Also sp *tunkelhead* [Varr of *EDD dunklehead* "A stupid, silly person"] **esp ME**
A fool; hence adj *tunkle-headed.*
   [**1852** Paul *Dashes Amer. Humour* 105 **ME,** If Deacon Dunklehead, or any of his daughters, were to come in neow, they'd think yeou'd gone stark mad.] **1903** McFaul *Ike Glidden* 190 **ME,** "That tunkle-headed thing [=a horse]! what's he good for 'ceptin' for an old woman ter drive?" **1941** *LANE* Map 465 (*Fool*) 1 inf, **neME,** [tʌŋkɬhɛᵊd]. **2006** in 2009 *DARE* File—Internet **ME,** Swift takes a poke at Peggy Noonan's crotch fruit who claims "Science is dead!" [oyg! what a tunkelhead. . .]

tunkup See **tunk** n[1] **3**

tunnel n Also *thunnel* [*OED2 tunnel* sb. 3 "*Obs.* exc. *dial.*"; a1529 →] **chiefly NEng, Upstate NY** See Map
A funnel.
   1729 in 2006 *DARE* File—Internet **nwMA,** [Inventory:] A tin tunnel. **1864** (1865) Parrish *Treatise Pharmacy* 51 **PA,** The *funnel,* sometimes called tunnel, is an article of every day use in the dispensing shop. **1899** (1912) Green *VA Folk-Speech* 461, *Tunnel.* . . A funnel. **1903** *DN* 2.301 **Cape Cod MA** (as of 1850s), *Tunnel.* . . Funnel. **1910** *DN* 3.450 **wNY,** *Tunnel.* . . Funnel for filling close vessels with liquids. **1941** *Language* 17.331 **WI** [*LANCS* fieldwork], *Tunnel*—7 [of 50 infs]. . . Primary to [1 inf] . . but 'not proper; *funnel* is right'. Considered old by [5 infs] . . [2 of the 5] . . laughed about it . . [1 of the 2] was 'cured of it in school' . . [the other of the 2] gave it up when his children made fun of him. . . *Tunnel* is a relic remembered or used almost wholly by the oldest, all American-derived; apparently unknown to foreign-derived. **1949** Kurath *Word Geog.* 16, *Tunnel* . . for the funnel, is another New England word that was carried westward into Upstate New York, but it is no longer common there. The Hudson Valley has only *funnel,* and this term has now wide currency in southern New England as well. **1965–70** *DARE* (Qu. F9, *To get a liquid through a narrow opening—for example, the neck of a bottle—you'd pour it through a* _____) 23 Infs, **chiefly NEng, Upstate NY,** Tunnel; **CA**79, **ME**16, **NH**15, **NY**75, Tunnel—old-fashioned; **CT**9, Tunnel is more often used by farmers; **CT**12, Tunnel [FW: Inf has heard it—uses it sometimes]; **NY**68, Thunnel. **1966** *DARE* FW Addit **NC,** *Tunnel*—funnel. **1967** *DARE*

Tape **MA**117, [FW:] When you want to get some liquid through a narrow opening, pouring it from one bottle to another, you pour it through what? [Inf:] Tunnel. Funnel. Either one. Tunnel or funnel. **1973** Allen *LAUM* 1.205 **sMN** (as of c1950), *Tunnel . .* survives as a remembered relic in southern Minnesota. **1980** *DARE* File **cnMA** (as of c1915), To the great disgust of some of the family my grandmother (born in Keene NH) sometimes called a funnel a tunnel. She probably learned it from her mother, who was born in Cornwall. **1985** Benes *Amer. Speech* 68 **ceMA**, The Concord [probate] inventories have 11 *funnel* citations, first appearing in the 1720s, and 73 *tunnel*, first appearing in the 1690s. Tunnels are listed as being made of tin, pewter, and wood.

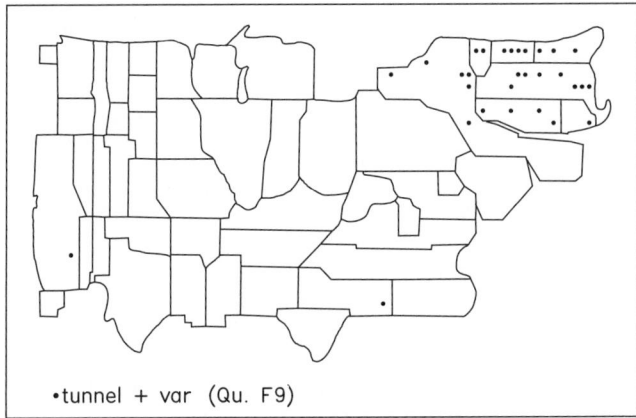

•tunnel + var (Qu. F9)

tunnel bed n   Also *tunnel*   [Folk-etym for *trundle (bed)*]   **esp S Midl**

1913 Gielow *Uncle Sam* 22 **sAppalachians**, Ef you keers fer the high bed me and maw will take the tunnel. *Ibid*, I 'lows to keep these here what's on this tunnel bed fer the twins. **1950** *PADS* 14.69 **SC**, *Tunnel bed.* . . A trundle bed. **1956** Ker *Vocab. W. TX* 137, *Bedding spread on floor.* . . tunnel bed. [1 of 67 infs] **1966** *Fresno Bee the Republican* (CA) 9 Dec sec C 10/6, *Maple* tunnel bed & chest, both $45. **1970** *DARE* FW Addit **KY**85, *Tunnel bed*—the little bed that was stored under a high bed during the day but pulled out for sleeping. Old-fashioned. **1977** Ginns *Rough Weather* 24 **NC**, The "tunnel bed," well, every day you'd make it up and push it under the big bed.

tunnel turtle n
=**gopher** n[1] **1a.**

1969 *DARE* (Qu. P29, . . '*Gophers*' . . *other name . . or what other animal are they most like*) Inf **GA**77, Gopher is an underground turtle, over twelve inches in diameter, shell is dark brown; live away from water, dig tunnels; in Tifton, Georgia, people call it a tunnel turtle.

tunny n   [*OED2* 1530 →]   Cf **little tunny**
A **tuna** n[2] of the genus *Thunnus,* esp *T. thynnus.*

1839 MA Zool. & Bot. Surv. *Fishes Reptiles* 47, *T. vulgaris* [= *Thunnus thynnus*]. . . The Common Tunny. . . On the coast of New England, this fish is called "*horse-mackerel*" and "*albicore.*" **1842** DeKay *Zool. NY* 4.105, The Common Tunny. *Thynnus vulgaris. Ibid* 106, The only American writer who has described the Tunny, as it appears on our coast, is Dr. Storer [=quot 1839 above]. . . I have met with this fish almost every season in the New-York market. . . The fishermen state that it is frequently taken off Block Island. **1902** Jordan–Evermann *Amer. Fishes* 279, On our Atlantic coast it [=*Thunnus thynnus*] is the "tunny," "horse mackerel," or "great albacore." **1926** Pan-Pacific Research Inst. *Jrl.* 1.1.8, Thunnus orientalis. . . Tuna; Tunny. **1947** Caine *Salt Water* 31, The *bluefin tuna* is. . . also known as horse mackerel, school tuna and tunny. **2001** in 2003 *DARE* File—Internet, Tuna are also known as "tunny," game and food fishes.

tupelo n   Pronc-spp *toopler, tupel(oo), tuplar, tupler, tupple, tupola*   **chiefly Sth**
A tree of the genus *Nyssa.*   Also called **gum tree 1, sour gum 1**; for other names of var spp see **black gum 1, gumberry 1, Ogeechee lime, swamp tupelo, tupelo-berry tree, tupelo gum**

1730 Catesby in Royal Soc. London *Philos. Trans.* 36.431, The Tupelo Tree. *Ibid* 434, The Water Tupelo. **1731** Catesby *Nat. Hist. Carolina* 1.41, *The Tupelo Tree.* . . They grow usually in moist Places, in *Virginia, Maryland,* and *Carolina.* **1765** (1942) Bartram *Diary of a Journey* 32

GA, A rare tupelo with large red acid fruite called limes. **1817** Darby *Geogr. Descr. LA* 130, The tupeloo is known in Louisiana by the popular name of olive. **1836** Simms *Mellichampe* 257 **SC**, It's a close place, and the tupolas and gums is mighty thick. **1854** *Putnam's Mag.* 3.473 **MA**, Woods were not wanting . . of pine, and oak, and maple, and the rarer tupelo with downward limbs. **1876** *Scribner's Mth.* 12.17 **TX**, He found as well tupelo leaves and bay leaves. **1927** Boston Soc. Nat. Hist. *Proc.* 38.7.326 **Okefenokee GA**, David Lee mentions . . tupelo berries, mistletoe, and perhaps sweet-bay berries [as the food of cat squirrels]. **1937** [see **tupelo gum**]. **1965–70** *DARE* (Qu. T15, . . *Kinds of swamp trees*) Infs **AL**17, **CA**15, **FL**27, **LA**26, **MA**100, **NC**24, **SC**4, Tupelo; **GA**7, Toopler; (Qu. H21, . . *The sweet stuff that's poured over these [pan]cakes*) Inf **GA**36, Tupelo honey; (Qu. T13, . . *Names . . for these trees:* . . *poplar*) Inf **MA**78, Tupelo. **1965–70** [see **tupelo gum**]. **1965** *DARE* Tape **FL**22, This is the only section in the United States that you get tupelo honey because it's the only ways where tupelo grows. **1986** Pederson *LAGS Concordance* (Common trees in the community) 3 infs, **nwFL, cwGA, nwTN**, Tupelo; 1 inf, **neMS**, Tupelo tree; (Poured over [pancakes]) 1 inf, **csGA**, Tupelo honey. **1986** [see **tupelo gum**]. **2000** *DARE* File—Internet **nwFL**, Along the Chipola and Apalachicola rivers of northwest Florida. . . during April and May they [=bees] fan out through the surrounding Tupelo-blossom-laden swamps. . . Real Tupelo honey is light amber in color, light golden with a greenish cast.

tupelo-berry tree n
A **tupelo.**

1970 *DARE* (Qu. T10, . . *Kinds of oak trees*) Inf **SC**67, Tupler-berry tree and blackjack are about the same. [FW: Blackjack is not an oak tree, Inf swears.]

tupelo gum n   **Sth, S Midl**
A **tupelo,** esp *Nyssa aquatica.*   For other names of this sp see **bay poplar 1, bottle-arsed tupelo, cotton gum, gum cottonwood, ~ tree 1, hornbeam 2, pawpaw gum, pepperidge, sap gum 2, sour ~ 1, swamp ~, swamp poplar 2, ~ tupelo, tupelo poplar, water tupelo, white gum 2, wild olive b**

1837 Croom *Catalogue Plants* 28 **NC**, Nyssa aquatica. . . Tupelo gum. **1847** De Bow's *Rev.* 4.506 **SC**, The trees forming the natural growth and dense cover of such lands are of great size and vigor—principally of tupelo gum, ash and cypress. **1871** *Appletons' Jrl.* 6.443 **AL**, A tree which . . sometimes attains quite a remarkable size and form. . . is the *Nyssa uniflora* [=*N. aquatica*] of the naturalists, the *Tupelo gum* of the natives. **1883** *Bot. Gaz.* 8.345 **IL**, The Tupelo Gum (*Nyssa uniflora*). . . is abundant in the cypress swamps of Johnson, Pulaski, and Massac counties. **1897** Sudworth *Arborescent Flora* 310, *Nyssa sylvatica.* . . Tupelo Gum (Fla.). *Ibid* 311, *Nyssa aquatica.* . . Tupelo Gum (Ala., Miss., La.) **1907** *DN* 3.238 **nwAR, seMO**, *Tupelo gum.* . . Swamp tupelo. **1927** Boston Soc. Nat. Hist. *Proc.* 38.7.377 **Okefenokee GA**, They [=deer] eat huckleberries, . . tupelo-gum [*Nyssa Ogeche*] berries, . . possum haws [*Viburnum nudum*]—nearly all the berries they can reach. **1937** in 1977 *Amer. Slave Suppl. 1* 1.39 **AL** [Black], Dem trays wuz made out ob "tuplar" gum trees. **1965–70** *DARE* (Qu. T15, . . *Kinds of swamp trees*) Infs **AL**38, **GA**25, 65, **IL**119, **LA**7, 40, **NC**10, **SC**43, Tupelo gum; **GA**3, Toopler gum; **MS**72, Tupler gum; **SC**10, Tupple gum. **1986** Pederson *LAGS Concordance* **Gulf Region**, 8 infs, Tupelo gum; 2 infs, Tupel gum. **2003** (acc) *MuseumLink IL* (Internet) **sIL**, Tupelo Gum (*Nyssa aquatica*). . . grows to between 80–100 feet tall, with a trunk diameter of up to 4 feet.

tupeloo   See **tupelo**

tupelo poplar n   Cf **bay poplar 1, swamp ~**
A **tupelo gum** (here: *Nyssa aquatica*).

1966 *DARE* (Qu. T13, . . *Names . . for . . poplar*) Inf **MS**38, Tupelo poplar.

tuplar, tupler   See **tupelo**

tup'mtime, tupntime, tupntine   See **turpentine** n, v

tupola   See **tupelo**

tuppentime, tuppentine   See **turpentine** n, v

tupple   See **tupelo**

tuque n   Usu |tuk|; for addit varr see quots   Also sp *took, toque* [CanFr *tuque* < Fr *toque; OED2* 1871 →, *DCan* 1882 →]   **Nth, esp Upstate NY, NEng**
A knitted stocking cap, orig a long, tapered one designed to be doubled inside itself for extra warmth; now also a short ski cap.

[1856 Kinzie *Wau-Bun* 44 **csWI,** The Judge and my husband were. . . prepared . . with a bright red cap (a *bonnet rouge,* or *tuque,* as the voyageurs call it).] **1919** Crowell *America's Munitions* 465 **OH,** An original article of equipment for the overseas troops had been a knitted woolen toque, which was a sort of stocking-cap. **1950** *WELS Suppl.* **Upstate NY,** Tuque [tuk]—used by Clintonville [WI] woman ([from] N.Y.; upper). **1959** *VT Hist.* 27.164, *Toque* [tuk] . . pronc. Also [twok]. A knitted hat, fitting closely on the head. Occasional. **1967** *DARE* FW Addit **Upstate NY,** [tuk]—a knitted cap. Sackets Harbor. **c1975** *DARE* File **Upstate NY,** She learned the word as an undergraduate at St. Lawrence U. [in Canton NY]. "All the girls were knitting tuques." **1976** *Progress* (Clearfield PA) 21 Oct 33/1, A warm and comfortable Ski-Doo knit tuque for only 99¢. **2000** Metcalf *How We Talk* 78 **VT,** A ski hat is a *toque.* **2000** *DARE* File—Internet **ME,** The "toque" (pronounced "took") is associated with the French Canadian Voyagers who travelled the rivers and lakes of the northcountry in the 1800's. **2005** *Ibid* **MN,** My parents said they used the term toque growing up (they grew up like ten miles from the Canadian border.) I adopted the term then. Plus it's easier to say than "stocking cap." **2006** *Ibid* **NY,** A distinctive folded brim style of sporting tuque, native to New York.

turable See **terrible**

turban See **turban squash**

turban cactus n   Cf **Turk's head 1**

A **barrel cactus** such as *Ferocactus viridescens.*

1886 *West Amer. Scientist* 3.168 **sCA,** A very variable cactus, commonly called the Turk's head or turban cactus, is Nuttall's Echinocactus viridescens. **1897** Parsons *Wild Flowers CA* 374, *Turban Cactus. Echinocactus viridescens.* **1920** Rice–Rice *Pop. Studies CA Wild Flowers* 66, In bloom, the Barrel Cactus (*Echinocactus*) is crowned with a circlet of pretty greenish yellow (or sometimes reddish green), cup-shaped flowers, which have found for them a common name of . . "Turban Cactus."

turban squash n   Also *turban*

Std: a hard-shelled **winter squash** (here: *Cucurbita maxima* var *turbaniformis*).   Also called **harlequin squash, Turk's-cap 2, Turk's turban 2**   Cf **hat squash**

tur'ble See **terrible**

turbot n   [*OED2* c1300 → for *Scophthalmus maximus;* 1555 → for other fish]

1 Any of several **flatfishes 1,** such as a **halibut B1** or a **windowpane,** or var fishes of the genera *Pleuronichthys* and *Reinhardtius;* see quots.

1616 Smith *Descr. New Engl.* 29, Whales, Grampus, Porkpisces, Turbut, Sturgion, . . and diuerse others. **1637** (1972) Morton *New English Canaan* 89 **MA,** There is a large sized fish called Hallibut, or Turbut: some are taken so bigg that two men have much a doe to hale them into the boate. **1772** in 1924 Phillips *Notes B. Romans* 125 **FL,** I lay by the side of a Spaniard . . who during Six Weeks made up a Cargo of Two Thousand Arobas of Red and Black Drum Fish . . , Besides Several hundred Turbots. **1842** DeKay *Zool. NY* 3.301, The Spotted Turbot. *Pleuronectes maculatus* [=*Scophthalmus aquosus*]. *Ibid* 302, On the coast of Massachusetts, it is sold as "the English Turbot;" from which, however, it is readily distinguished. **1882** U.S. Natl. Museum *Bulletin* 16.815, *Bothus* [spp]. . . *Turbots.* . . mostly of the Atlantic. *Ibid* 830, *Hypsopsetta guttulata* [=*Pleuronichthys g.*] . . *Diamond Flounder;* "*Turbot.*" . . Coast of California. **1884** Goode *Fisheries U.S.* 1.176, The common Flounder, *Paralichthys dentatus,* . . was in 1880 sold in Boston under the name "Turbot." *Ibid* 177, *Lophopsetta maculata* [= *Scophthalmus aquosus*], is sometimes called the Spotted Turbot. . . Another fish, *Platysomatichthys hippoglossoides* [=*Reinhardtius h.*] . . is often called the American . . Turbot. *Ibid* 185, *Hypsopsetta guttulata.* . . In the neighborhood of San Francisco . . is known as the "Turbot." *Ibid* 189, *Pleuronichthys verticalis.* . . *Pleuronichthys quadrituberculatus.* . . *Pleuronichthys cœnosus.* . . These three species have no distinctive popular names, the fishermen confounding them with various other species under the name [sic] of Turbot and Sole. **1953** Roedel *Common Fishes CA* 57, *Atheresthes stomias.* . . *Unauthorized Names:* Turbot, bastard halibut, French sole. *Ibid* 68, *Curlfin Turbot—Pleuronichthys decurrens.* . . The most desirable of the turbots; landed chiefly at San Francisco. *Ibid* 69, *Hornyhead Turbot—Pleuronichthys verticalis.* . . it ranks third among the turbots. . . *C-O Turbot—Pleuronichthys coenosus.* . . *Spotted Turbot—Pleuronichthys ritteri.* . . A very minor constituent of the turbot catch. **1959** Murie *Fauna Aleutian*

Is. 395 **AK,** *Atheresthes stomias,* one of the flounders, is called locally "turbot." It swims with its right side up. **2002** *DARE* File—Internet, Arrowtooth flounder, Atheresthes stomias, . . is found from California to Alaska. . . arrowtooth is usually sold on the West Coast as turbot, although it is not related to the true turbot (Psetta maxima) caught off Europe. . . Greenland turbot, Reinhardtius hippoglossoides, which is caught in both the North Atlantic and North Pacific oceans, is not really a turbot either, but instead is a member of the halibut family. . . To avoid marketing confusion with Pacific halibut, the halibut industry successfully lobbied to have the name of this flatfish changed to turbot.

2 A **triggerfish,** usu *Balistes carolinensis.*

[**1848** Schomburgk *Hist. Barbados* 676, Balistes maculatus. . . Ocean Turbot.] **1884** Goode *Fisheries U.S.* 1.172 **FL,** The Leather-jacket of Pensacola, *Balistes capriscus,* called "Trigger Fish" in the Carolinas, and at Key West and the Bermudas known as the "Turbot," occasionally finds its way as far north as Massachusetts. It is, however, of no importance, north of Florida. **1898** U.S. Natl. Museum *Bulletin* 47.1701, *Balistes carolinensis.* . . "*Turbot.*" . . Tropical parts of the Atlantic; occasional northward in the Gulf Stream. *Ibid* 1706, *Canthadermis maculatus.* . . Ocean Turbot. **2003** *DARE* File—Internet **Gulf Region,** Blistes [sic] capriscus . . *Other Names:* Common, Triggerfish, Common Turbot. . . Many consider Triggerfish fillets to be tasty. They are, however, more difficult to clean because of their tough skins.

turbul See **terrible**

turd beetle n

=**tumblebug 1;** also used as a term of abuse.

1901 Edgren–Burnet *French & Engl. Dict.* 310, *Fouille-merde* . . tumble-bug, turd-beetle. **1947** Sandoz *Tom-Walker* 334 **OH,** A turd-beetle letting wind of a hot day! **1969** *DARE* (Qu. R30, . . *Kinds of beetles; not asked in early QRs*) Inf **CT**26, Turd beetle—frequents barnyards. **1969** *DARE* FW Addit **ceCT,** Turd beetle—"I don't know as he does any hurt." Used occasionally. **2008** in 2009 *DARE* File—Internet **TX,** Don't bitch if you end up in jail for that red blanket killing a protected species of turd beetle though.

turd bird n

=**Canada jay.**

1968 *DARE* (Qu. Q16, . . *Kinds of jays*) Inf **NH**14, Gorby or turd bird or Canadian jay.

turd-brindle See **shit-brindle**

turd-eater n

1 =**jaeger** n[1].

1945 McAtee *Nomina Abitera* 36 **ME,** Names applied to jaegers in general . . turd-eater, Matinicus Island.

2 A **bullhead 1b** (here: *Ameirus* spp).

1954 McAtee *Suppl. to Nomina Abitera* [6] **sNJ,** Catfishes (*Ameirus spp.*)—Turd-eaters, from feeding about sewage outlets.

turd-floater n   esp **TX, OK**   Cf **trash mover 1**

A heavy rain.

1962 *McDavid Coll.* **cwOK,** Turd floater—sudden heavy rain. **1967–69** *DARE* (Qu. B25, . . *Joking names . . for a very heavy rain. . . "It's a regular _____."*) Infs **TX**22, 68, Turd-floater. **1984** Weaver *TX Crude* 99, Rain. . . "It was a turd floater." **1986** Pederson *LAGS Concordance (Heavy rain)* 1 inf, **csTX,** Turd floater. **2000** *NADS Letters* **neOK,** Another common (crude) term here for a very heavy rain is a turd floater. **2006** *DARE* File—Internet **cTX,** I can not see a situation where we actually play tonight. It is a real turd floater out there. **2007** in 2009 *Ibid* **seMS,** Looks like we got a turd floater fixin to hit—loud thunder out here. **2009** *Ibid* **nwMO,** A real turd floater. . . Smithville trails have just been *hammered* today with rain.

turd fly n

Prob a dung fly of the family Scatophagidae.

1967 *DARE* (Qu. R12, . . *Other kinds of flies*) Inf **OR**1, Turd fly, shit fly—hang around piles.

turd hearse n

A manure spreader.

1967 *DARE* File **csWI,** Turd hearse—manure spreader. **1969** *DARE* FW Addit **cwIL,** Turd hearse [laughter]. [FW: Farm implement dragged behind tractor, used for spreading manure.] **1981** *News* (Frederick MD) 20 May sec E 4/1, "Guess where I got the wood for this moulding?" "Got me." "Offa turd-hearse." "A what?" "A manure-spreader." **1989** Rhodes *Farm* 306 **MO,** Tom couldn't see wasting a feedlot full of free

745

fertilizer. Better to hook up the old turd hearse and spread it on the pasture. **2005** *DARE* File—Internet **MO**, My grandmother used to call the manure spreader a "turd hearse."

turd-rassler n
=shoveler.
1945 McAtee *Nomina Abitera* 31 **seLA**, Shoveller *(Spatula clypeata)* . . shit-digger, . . turd rassler.

turd-roller n
1 **=cowbird 1.**
1968 *DARE* (Qu. Q14, . . *Names* . . *for* . . *cowbird*) Inf **IL29**, Turd-rollers.
2 also *turd-roller bug:* **=tumblebug 1.** Cf **tumbleturd 1**
1969 *DARE* FW Addit **eNC**, Turd-rollers—bugs which roll up manure into big piles; also called doodlebug. **2003** *DARE* File—Internet **LA**, "Lets go look for snakes, or turd-roller bugs!" Bobby said.

turd-rustler n Cf **rustler 7**
=gaff-topsail catfish.
1945 McAtee *Nomina Abitera* 20 **sTX**, Gaff-topsail catfish *(Felichthys marinus)*—Turd rustler.

turdy See **thirty**

tureen dinner n Also *tureen, ~ party, ~ supper* **chiefly Upstate NY, wPA** See Map and Map Section
=potluck meal.
1909 *Olean Eve. Times* (NY) 2 Feb [5]/2 (newspaperarchive.com), Miss Sara Allen . . gave a tureen dinner yesterday. **1911** *Warren Eve. Mirror* (PA) 7 Dec 2/2, A tureen supper was served. **1916** *Everybody's Mag.* 34.630 **MI**, The paper says the Daughters of Rebecca are going to have a tureen supper in Alpena Hall. **1916** *Titusville Herald* (PA) 19 May 6/4, The Gleaners gave a farewell tureen party for their teacher. **1934** *Chron.–Telegram* (Elyria OH) 13 Dec 6/4, A children's Christmas party is scheduled for Thursday, . . begining [sic] with a tureen at 5:30. **1942** *AmSp* 13.129, General throughout the country is the custom among church organizations . . and like gatherings of bringing food for a company dinner or supper. . . In some communities the event is headlined as a *covered dish dinner,* or a *carry-in dinner.* In Western Pennsylvania it is a *tureen dinner.* **1965–70** *DARE* (Qu. H70, *When people bring baked dishes, salads, and so forth to a meeting-place and share them together, that's a _____ meal*) 9 Infs **NY, OH, PA,** Tureen supper; 9 Infs **NY, PA,** Tureen dinner; **PA234,** Tureen supper (or dinner); **NY109, 135, 146, PA131, 181, 200,** Tureen; (Qu. FF1, . . *A kind of group meeting called a 'social' or 'sociable'*) Infs **NY105, 115,** Tureen supper. **1985** *DARE* File **cnOH**, "Carry-in-dinner" (Pot luck) is a "Tureen" in our city. **2001** *Ibid* **nwPA**, Here in Erie the main phrases I've noticed are . . "tureen" meaning not just a soup dish but a potluck supper.

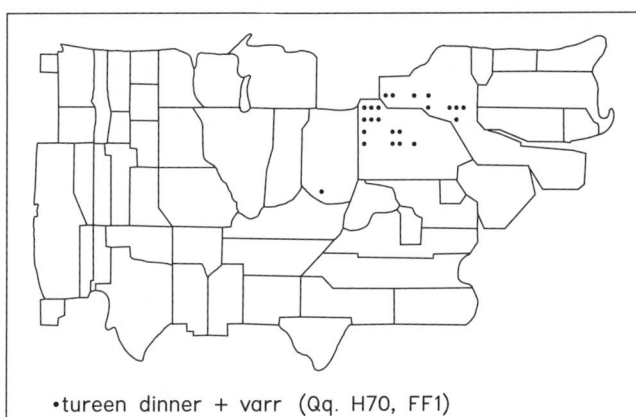

•tureen dinner + varr (Qq. H70, FF1)

turf v, hence vbl n *turfing,* ppl adj *turfed* Also sp *terf* [Appar var, by folk-etym, of *tuft*]
To form tufts in (a piece of fabric).
1882 U.S. Patent Office *Patent 269770* 1, Caspar W. Wood, of Bismarck, Illinois. *Machine for Turfing Fabrics.* . . My invention relates to a machine for producing on cloth . . a thick woolly surface by looping yarn or similar material through the cloth, leaving the ends free and protruding. This process, known as "turfing," has been employed . . in the making of mittens and similar articles of apparel . . ; but as heretofore accomplished by hand it is a very tedious operation. **1937** Eaton *Hand-*

icrafts 226 **nGA**, The tufted, or "turfed" as some of the old-timers call the operation, and the knotted spreads are not new to the Southern Highlands. **1968** Haun *Hawk's Done Gone* 149 **TN**, I bought meal from Arwoods. Turfed and pieced quilts to pay for it. **2005** Williams *Gratitude* 530 **wNC** (as of 1940s), *Terf* or *turf:* a method of quilting in which the layers of a quilt are tacked together wiith [sic] *terfin'* stitches. The stitches were separated and spaced a few inches apart, with the thread tied off and left a little long. **2006** *DARE* File—Internet **nGA**, The next step [in making a tufted bedspread], as explained by a practitioner of the craft, was to "turf" or tuft the sheets. Thick cotton yarn was needed for this. . . The yarn would then be threaded into a long, single or "double" needle.

turk n[1] See **turkey B2**
Turk n[2] **cSC** Cf **Moor**
A member of a racially mixed group of people living in Sumter County, South Carolina.
1934 *DN* 6.421 **SC**, There are many groups in the South which have been isolated for generations. . . A representative group of this sort are the "Turks" of Sumter County, South Carolina. **1945** *Amer. Jrl. Sociol.* 51.34 **cSC**, People . . who do not fit into the biracial caste system. . . These outcastes, whom I call "mestizos," are designated by a wide variety of names, none of them flattering. . . In Sumter they are called "Turks." **1956** *Univ. VA Cavalier Daily* 16 Oct 1/6 (Hench Coll.) **SC**, The Supreme Court today refused to hear the complaint of a group of dark-skinned "Turks" in South Carolina whose children were denied admission to white elementary schools. **1963** Berry *Almost White* 27, South Carolina abounds in groups who are "neither fish nor fowl." There are . . the Turks of Sumter. **2005** *Gamecock City Trading Post* (Sumter SC) 15 July (as of c1900), In the early part of the century when I was a boy growing up in Stateburg, there was a colony of Turks, consisting of probably several hundred men, women and children, living . . about eight miles northeast of Stateburg and near the small town of Dalzell. . . With their straight black hair and copper colored complexion, they looked like Turks. **2006** *DARE* File—Internet **cSC**, The most plausible theory as to where the "Turk" label originated was from "Turkey Town Indians" shortened over time to "Turkey Indians" to "Turks." These same family members who remained in Robeson, Warren, and Halifax counties NC are now known as "Lumbee" and "Haliwa-Saponi" Indians.

turkeldove See **turtledove**

turkemtime, turkentime See **turpentine** n, v

turkey n Pronc-sp *tuckey;* also *among Gullah speakers* by metath *tuckr(e)y, tukr(e)y*
A Forms.
1888 Jones *Negro Myths* 20 **GA coast** [Gullah], Buh Tukrey Buzzud, him yent [=didn't] hab no sense no how. **1899** (1912) Green *VA Folk-Speech* 461, *Tuckey.* . . A form of *turkey.* **1908** *S. Atl. Qrly.* 7.346 **sSC coast** [Gullah], Buh Tukrey Buzza'd duh sail 'roun een de element. **1922** Gonzales *Black Border* 115 **sSC, GA coasts** [Gullah], Mas' Rafe, you hu't me feelin's fuh talk 'bout bait dese tuckrey wid rice? **1923** Parsons *Folk-lore Sea Islands* 200 **csSC** [Gullah], Mary, have you seen my tukry? **1930** Stoney–Shelby *Black Genesis* 4 **seSC** [Gullah], He mek tuckry an' tuckry-buzzard. **1930** Woofter *Black Yeomanry* 129 **seSC** [Gullah], Someone had given her three "tuckrey aigs." **1949** *AmSp* 24.114 **seSC** [Gullah], *Tukry.* . . Turkey.
B Senses.
1 Esp among loggers: a bag used esp to carry clothes, bedding, and other personal possessions; a bedroll; a suitcase; hence phr *to hoist the turkey* to pack up one's belongings and leave. **chiefly Nth**
1888 (1889) Fitzmaurice *Shanty Boy* 35 **MI, WI**, Jes' get onto this 'turkey' (clothes bag) an' see all the socks, an' shirts, an' towels Daisy put in for me. **1893** *Scribner's Mag.* 13.715 **MI**, With his "time" in his pocket and his "turkey," a two-bushel bag in which he carries his belongings, strung over his shoulder, the shanty boy starts . . for town. **1905** U.S. Forest Serv. *Bulletin* 61.52 **NW, Gt Lakes** [Logging terms], *Turkey.* . . A bag containing a lumberjack's outfit. To "histe the turkey" is to take one's personal belongings and leave camp. **1911** (1913) Johnson *Highways Gt. Lakes* 245, Agencies don't care to hire a man who has only the clothes he wears. They insist that he shall have a 'turkey'—that is some baggage. **1913** *DN* 4.12 **MN**, *Turkey.* . . A lumberman's pack or kit. **1927** *AmSp* 2.386 [Vagabond argot], A bindle is sometimes called a *turkey,* but this word is also used to mean a suitcase. **1938** Stuart *Dark Hills* 316 **eKY**, He carried his little bag of belongings thrown

over his back in "turkey" fashion. **1950** *WELS Suppl.* **neWI,** *Turkey*—a tramp's bundle of belongings. Usually tied up in a turkey-red handkerchief. **1958** *AmSp* 33.273 **eWA** [Ranching terms], *Turkey.* A pack of bedding or clothes. **1959** *AmSp* 34.80 **nwCA** [Logger lingo], *Turkey. . .* An older term for a pack sack. **1966** *DARE* Tape **MI**10, A turkey was a sack for all your personal possessions. **1968** *DARE* FW Addit **WI**59, *Turkey*—a grain sack in which a "jack" brought all the possessions he had; carried on the back; a string encircled the shoulder and kept the turkey in place on the "jack's" back. **1969** *AmSp* 44.30 **Pacific NW** [Painter jargon], *Turkey. . .* A painter's soft-sided bag in which tools are carried. **1975** Gould *ME Lingo* 301, Usually *turkey* referred to something tied up in a grain bag and thrust under a bunk.

2 also *saltwater turkey, turk:* A person of Irish descent; a Catholic. [Perh from Ir *torc* pig, boar]

1911 *NY Eve. Jrl.* (NY) 28 Mar 13 (*Zwilling Coll.*), [Cartoon:] Just send him against some kaiser's lad / Or maybe a *wop* or two / There won't be much of that foreign bunch / When that turkey lad [=Jack McAuliffe] gets through. **1914** *Chicago Rec.-Herald* (IL) 21 Jan 9/2, You Italians have the votes, but it takes us Turks [=Irishmen] to run the government. **1932** Farrell *Young Lonigan* 31 **Chicago IL** (as of 1916), Dooley was one comical turkey, funnier than anything you'd find in real life. **1941** *LANE* Map 454 (*Nicknames for an Irishman*) 1 inf, **ceMA,** [tɜk]; 1 inf, **neMA,** [tɜ·kɪ]. **1945** Mencken *Amer. Lang. Suppl. 1* 603, Turk is used among Roman Catholic priests in the United States to designate a colleague of Irish birth: it is assumed that every such immigrant has a special talent for ecclesiastical politics, and hence gets on in the church. **1964** *PADS* 42.39 **Chicago IL,** Irish informants use *turkey* and *saltwater turkey* to designate a recent immigrant. *Ibid* 33, [Terms for *Catholic:*] 2 infs, Turk.

3 A teasing or scolding.

1982 *Barrick Coll.* **csPA,** *Turkey*—scolding; teasing. "Clair and I got a turkey yesterday." **1983** *Ibid,* Give someone a *turkey* = bawl out; criticize. "He always gives me a turkey for not using white brick." . . "They gave me a turkey about it" (caused me trouble). . . I've never found the phrase anywhere else, but practically everyone in western Cumberland Co., Pa., knows it.

4 also *turkey jerk,* ~ *trot:* **=wedgie 1.**

1989 *DARE* File **cCA,** The act of lifting a person (from behind) by the belt, belt buckles, top of the underwear, the seat of the pants: 1 inf, Turkey jerk. **1989–91** *Ibid* **UT,** The act of lifting a person (from behind) by the belt, belt buckles, top of the underwear, the seat of the pants: 8 infs, Turkey; 3 infs, Turkey trot.

turkey apple n   Also *turkey haw(thorn)*
A **hawthorn** (here: *Crataegus mollis*).

1911 *Century Dict. Suppl., Turkey-apple. . .* A small tree, *Crataegus induta* [=*C. mollis*], a native of Arkansas, sometimes 25 feet high, armed with stout spines, and bearing red or yellowish astringent sub-acid fruits. **1922** Sargent *Manual Trees* 476, *Crataegus induta. . .* Turkey Apple. **1960** Vines *Trees SW* 381, *Turkey Hawthorn—Crataegus invisa* [=*C. mollis*]. . . *Fruit.* Maturing in October, . . flesh yellow, scant, dry. . . *Range.* In woods of bottom lands; in Arkansas . . , Oklahoma . . , and Texas. **1973** Stephens *Woody Plants* 238, *Crataegus mollis. . .* Turkey haw. . . The fruits are large and edible. **2003** (acc) OK Univ. *OK Biol. Surv.* (Internet), *Crataegus mollis. . . Common names:* downy haw, summer haw, turkey apple. . . Alabama, west to Texas and Oklahoma, north to South Dakota and Minnesota, east to Ontario. . . The fruits are edible and are often made into preserves.

turkeyback n

1 also *winter turkeyback:* The greater **yellowlegs 1.**

1888 Trumbull *Names of Birds* 168 **MA,** At Salem, Mass., the larger birds of the species [=*Tringa melanoleuca*] have long been distinguished from the others under the name of *Turkey-back.* **1925** (1928) Forbush *Birds MA* 1.435, *Totanus melanoleucus. . . Winter turkey-back. . . Adults in breeding plumage (sexes alike):* . . spotted black and pale gray or whitish on upper back.

2 =golden plover.

1955 *Oriole* 20.1.7 **GA,** *Golden Plover—Turkey-back* (as being speckled).

turkey beard n

1 also *turkey's beard:* A plant of the genus *Xerophyllum.* [See quot 1976] **scattered, but esp NJ**   For other names of *X. tenax* see **squaw grass 1**

1847 Griffith *Med. Botany* 641, *Xerophyllum setifolium* [=*X. as-*

phodeloides], or Turkey's Beard, a native of sandy situations in many parts of the United States. **1866** *Friends' Intelligencer* 23.281 **NJ,** Lily pads and the turkey beard grow in the swamps. **1897** *Jrl. Amer. Folkl.* 10.146 **NJ,** *Xerophyllum setifolium* [=*X. asphodeloides*], . . turkeybeard. **1897** Parsons *Wild Flowers CA* 51, *Squaw-grass. Sour-grass. Turkey-beard. Xerophyllum tenax. . .* Often upon high ridges we notice large clumps of certain plants with long, slender, grasslike leaves, which . . resemble a small pampas-grass before it flowers. **1945** Beck *Jersey Genesis* 167 **NJ,** It began early in August, long after . . the turkey beard, goat's-rue, and wild indigo had flowered. **1968** *DARE* (Qu. S26b, *Wildflowers that grow in water or wet places*) Infs **NJ**39, 52, Turkey beard. **1976** Bruce *How to Grow Wildflowers* 173, As specialized in its own way as the Swamp-pink is the Turkey-beard, *Xerophyllum asphodeloides,* which grows only in acid pine barrens from New Jersey to Georgia. . . "Turkey-beard" is also purely descriptive. The cluster of leaves and the bracted stem, turned upside down, resemble the beard adorning a tom turkey's breast. **2002** *DARE* File—Internet **nwVA,** We saw some Turkey Beard in bloom and also some Rhododendron and Mountain Laurel in early bloom.

2 =flame azalea.

1975 Hamel–Chiltoskey *Cherokee Plants* 24, Turkey beard . . *Rhododendron calendulaceum. . .* Peel and boil a twig, rub on rheumatism.

turkeyberry n

1 A **partridgeberry 1** (here: *Mitchella repens*).   **Sth, S Midl**

1808 *Philadelphia Med. & Phys. Jrl.* 3.1.79, Mitchella. . . Partridge-berry. Turkey-berry [etc]. **1826** Darlington *Florula Cestrica* 19, M[itchella] repens. . . *Vulgo*—Partridge-berry. Turkey-berry. Checquerberry. **1909** *DN* 3.384 **eAL, wGA,** Turkey-berry. . . The twin-berry, or partridge-berry. **1926** *Torreya* 26.6 **MS,** *Mitchella repens. . .* Turkey berry. **1927** Boston Soc. Nat. Hist. *Proc.* 38.220 Okefenokee **GA,** *Mitchella repens*—Partridge berry; turkey berry. **1967** *DARE* (Qu. I44, *What kinds of berries grow wild around here?*) Inf **AR**52, Turkeyberries; **LA**12, Turkeyberries—grow low to the ground, they are bright red and pithy. **1967** *DARE* FW Addit **AR**44, *Mitchella repens*—we called it turkeyberry around Cale, Nevada County, Arkansas. **1986** Pederson *LAGS Concordance* (*Berries*) 1 inf, **cAL,** Turkeyberry—a red edible berry.

2 =coralberry 1.   Sth   Cf turkey bush

1900 Lyons *Plant Names* 361, S[ymphoricarpos] orbiculatus. . . Turkey-berry.

3 A **nightshade 1** (here: *Solanum torvum*).   **FL**

[**1756** Browne *Civil & Nat. Hist. Jamaica* 1.174, *Solanum 3. . .* Turky Berries. *Solanum 4. . .* The larger Turky Berries. Both these species are very common in the low lands of *Jamaica.*] **1933** Small *Manual SE Flora* 1115 **nFL,** S[olanum] torvum. . . *Turkey-berry. . .* Roadsides, waste-places, and swamps. **1966** *DARE* (Qu. S21, . . *Weeds . . that are a trouble in gardens and fields*) Inf **FL**4, Turkeyberries. **2002** *DARE* File—Internet **FL,** The insect's development and reproduction on . . turkeyberry, *Solanum torvum,* was comparable to its natural host silverleaf nightshade.

4 also *turkeyberry bush:* **=possum haw 2.**

1910 *Youth's Companion* 20 Jan 33, The great diamond-back rattlesnake lay under the green shade of the dense turkeyberry bushes that fringed the edge of the vast and lonely swamp. [*DARE* Ed: This quot may refer instead to another sense.] **1940** Clute *Amer. Plant Names* 261, *Ilex decidua.* Turkey-berry, winter-berry.

5 =French mulberry.

1862 in 1870 Tardy *Southland Writers* 2.711 **TN,** The long, green spears of the Kinnikinnick are peering out from their russet, mail-clad buds; the turkey-berry, its friendly comrade of the woods, . . is swelling in every branch with emulative sap. **1970** Correll *Plants TX* 1339, *Callicarpa americana. . . Turkeyberry.* Bush or shrub to 3 m. tall; . . fruit showy, rose-pink or lilac to violet or red-purple.

turkeyberry bush   See **turkeyberry 4**

turkey bird n   Cf **bird-on-the-wing, gaywings**
Perh **=fringed polygala.**

1969 *DARE* (Qu. S26c, *Wildflowers that grow in woods*) Inf **NJ**55, Turkey birds.

turkey bur n
A **burdock 1** (here: *Arctium lappa*).

1876 Hobbs *Bot. Hdbk.* 121, Turkey bur seed, Burdock seed, Arctium lappa.

turkey bush n Cf **turkeyberry 2**
=**coralberry 1.**

1960 Vines *Trees SW* 948, *Symphoricarpos orbiculatus.* . . is also known under the vernacular names of Coralberry, . . Waxberry, and Turkey-bush. . . It is known to be eaten by 12 species of birds, including the . . wild turkey. **2003** (acc) TX A&M Univ. *Aggie Horticult.* (Internet), Turkey-bush—*Symphoricarpos orbiculatus.* . . grows on clay and loam soils in Texas, east to Florida and New England and north to Colorado and South Dakota.

turkey buzzard n
=**turkey vulture.**

1615 Hamor *True Discourse* 21 **VA,** There are foule of diuers sorts, . . *Turckie Bussards, Partridge, Snipes* [etc]. **1672** Josselyn *New-England's Rarities* 12, The *Turkie Buzzard,* a kind of *Kite,* but as big as a *Turkie,* brown of colour, and very good meat. **1709** (1967) Lawson *New Voyage* 138 **NC, SC,** The Turkey-Buzzard of *Carolina* is a small Vulture, which lives on any dead Carcasses. **1796** in 1799 Weld *Travels* 112, In the lower parts of Virginia, and to the southward, are great numbers of large birds, called turkey buzzards. **1818** Palmer *Jrl.* 96 **sOH,** We saw several of a large species of vulture (called here turkey-buzzard) hovering over a dead carcase . . the people never kill these birds on account of their usefulness. **1899** Garland *Boy Life* 71 **nwIA,** (as of c1870s), One day as he went to the field he scared a great black bird. . . It was the prairie vulture or "turkey-buzzard." **1930** Stoney–Shelby [see **turkey A**]. **1938** Oberholser *Bird Life LA* 148, *Cathartes aura septentrionalis.* . . The almost universal name for this vulture is 'turkey buzzard'. [*Ibid* 149, Walking on the ground it has somewhat the bearing of a turkey, and this, together with its size and red head, have suggested the name.] **1965–70** *DARE* (Qu. Q13, *Names . . for the vulture*) 126 Infs, **widespread, but least freq NEng, NY, Missip-Ohio Valleys, NW, nCA,** Turkey buzzard. **2003** *DARE* File—Internet **csPA,** I have a blackameraucana shes so ugly. She looks exactly like a turkey buzzard.

turkey cactus n Cf **turkey pear**

A **prickly pear 1** (here: *Opuntia leptocaulis*).

1936 NM Univ. *Biol. Ser.* 4.5.55, The small, red fruits of the turkey or coyote cactus *(Opuntia leptocaulis)* . . are still used. . . They are reported as having such narcotic effects that the [Apache] Indians will not walk close to plants which bear them. **1942** TX Ag. Exper. Sta. College Sta. *Bulletin* 609.111 **wTX,** *Optunia* [sic] *leptocaulis.* Turkey Cactus or Tasahillo [sic]. A long stemmed, very spiny cactus that produces inconspicuous flowers and numerous small red fruits. **1964** U.S. Soil Conserv. Serv. *Grassland Restoration* 1.10, "Turkey cactus" [is so called] because turkeys are fond of the red, berry-like fruit.

turkey cheese n Also *turkey feed,* ~ *food* [Because it is sometimes fed to poultry]

Cottage cheese.

1931–33 *LANE* Worksheets **CT,** I've heard it [=cottage cheese] called turkey feed. We always started turkeys on it. **1968** *DARE* (Qu. H60, *The lumpy white cheese that is made from sour milk*) Inf **MO**4, When we were growing up, we called it turkey cheese; **PA**71, Turkey food—because they soured it on purpose to feed to the turkeys. [**1986** Pederson *LAGS Concordance,* 1 inf, **cnTX,** Clabber used for turkey feed and chicken feed.]

turkey corn n [See quot 1843]

Usu a **squirrel corn** (here: *Dicentra canadensis*), but also a related **bleeding heart 1** (here: *Dicentra eximia*) or **Dutchman's breeches 1.**

1834 *Western Jrl. Med. & Phys. Sci.* 31.339, Diclytra [=*Dicentra*] canadensis. . . Turkey corn. Squirrel corn. **1843** Torrey *Flora NY* 1.46, *Dicentra Canadensis. Squirrel Corn. Turkey Corn.* . . Rhizoma creeping, bearing at intervals roundish yellow tubers from a third to half an inch in diameter. . . rather common in the western and northern counties. **1872** [see **turkey pea 3a**]. **1900** Lyons *Plant Names* 62, Dicentra Canadensis. . . Turkey Corn. *Ibid* 63, Dicentra eximia. . . Turkey-corn. **1910** Graves *Flowering Plants* 198 **CT,** Squirrel or Turkey Corn. . . The tubers are medicinal. **1915** [see **turkey pea 3a**]. **1953** Greene–Blomquist *Flowers South* 40, Turkey-Corn. **1976** Bailey–Bailey *Hortus Third* 380, [*Dicentra*] *eximia.* . . *Turkey corn.* . . Mts., N.Y. to Ga.

turkey cress See **turkey mustard**

turkey egg n [Because turkey eggs are speckled]

A freckle; hence adj *turkey-egged* freckled, speckled.

[**1855** *Harper's New Mth. Mag.* 10.301, Your [sic] are getting as fat as

partridges. . . And as freckled as turkey eggs.] **1899** (1912) Green *VA Folk-Speech* 462, *Turkey-eggs.* . . Freckles. "His face is covered with turkey-eggs." **1912** CO Dept. Pub. Instruction *Biennial Rept. for 1911–12* 159, This building is constructed of stone and turkey-egged brick. **1950** *WELS* **WI** (*Brown spots that come on the skin from being in the sun*) 1 Inf, Turkey egg; 1 Inf, Turkey-egged—same as freckled.

turkey feed (or food) See **turkey cheese**

turkeyfoot n

1 also *turkeyfoot grass:* A **beardgrass:** usu either *Andropogon gerardii* or *A. hallii.* [See quot 1979] Cf **bluejoint turkeyfoot** (at **bluejoint 3**)

1894 *Jrl. Amer. Folkl.* 7.103 **wNE,** *Andropogon Hallii,* . . turkey-foot. **1910** Graves *Flowering Plants* 48 **CT,** *Andropogon furcatus* [=*A. gerardii*]. . . Big Blue-stem. Turkey-foot. . . It is of value for hay and pasturage in some localities in the United States. **1952** Strausbaugh–Core *Flora WV* 74, *A[ndropogon] gerardi.* . . Turkeyfoot. . . This is an extremely important forage grass in the prairie states, but . . it is generally too uncommon in West Virginia to be of great value. **1979** Niering–Olmstead *Audubon Guide N. Amer. Wildflowers E. Region* 686, Big Bluestem or Turkeyfoot *(A[ndropogon] gerardi)* has finger-like seed heads that somewhat resemble a turkey's foot. **2003** (acc) *MO Bot. Garden* (Internet), Big bluestem grass . . was the dominant grass of the tallgrass prairie . . of the Midwest. . . Flowering stems rise in late summer above the foliage clump bearing purplish 3-parted, finger-like flower clusters (to 4″ long) purportedly resembling turkey feet (hence the additional common name of turkeyfoot grass for this species).

2 Appar a **crabgrass 1** or similar grass. Cf **crowfoot 3, finger grass 1**

1950 *WELS* (*The kind of wild grass that throws out strong underground roots and is hard to get rid of*) 1 Inf, **cWI,** Turkeyfoot. **1966–67** *DARE* (Qu. S9, . . *Kinds of grass that are hard to get rid of*) Inf **IA**8, Crabgrass, wire grass, also turkey- or crow's-foot—four names for same grass; **WA**6, Turkeyfoot.

3 =**harbinger-of-spring.** Cf **turkey pea 2a**

1920 *Torreya* 20.24 **IN,** *Erigenia bulbosa.* . . Turkeyfoot.

4 also *turkey's foot:* A **toothwort** (here: *Cardamine concatenata*). Cf **turkey mustard**

1967 *DARE* Wildfl QR Pl.81A [=*Cardamine concatenata*] Inf **OH**14, Turkey's foot. **1973** *Foxfire 2* 80 **sAppalachians,** *Dentaria laciniata* [=*Cardamine concatenata*], crowfoot or turkeyfoot, has leaves divided into narrow segments. . . Peeled roots or young leaves add flavoring to salads, but a very little goes a long way.

5 See quot 1984.

1984 *DARE* File **csPA,** Turkeyfoot—an intersection of four roads other than a crossroads; often used as a proper noun: "We were workin' up at Turkeyfoot the other day." . . Common since at least 1940. [**2006** *DARE* File—Internet **sOH,** The improvement of the Turkeyfoot intersection has improved the safety tremendously.]

turkeyfoot grass See **turkeyfoot 1**

turkey foot mustard See **turkey mustard**

turkey frost n

A light frost.

1950 *WELS* (*A frost that does not kill plants*) 1 Inf, **seWI,** When I was a child it was always called turkey frost, but now the common name is light frost; [we] killed the young turkeys before Thanksgiving.

turkey gnat n

A **black fly,** usu *Simulium meridionale.*

1868 Swett *Trip to Honduras* 81 **MS,** In size it [=a bottle fly] is almost the same as the turkey gnat. **1891** *Century Dict.* 6536, *Turkey-gnat.* . . A small black fly, *Simulium meridionale,* which attacks poultry in the southern and western United States, particularly in the Mississippi Valley. **1895** Comstock–Comstock *Manual Insects* 453, *Simulium meridionale* . . closely resembles the preceding [=*Cnephia pecuarum*] . . ; but as it appears at the time that turkeys are setting and causes great injury to this fowl, it is commonly known as the Turkey-gnat. **1905** Kellogg *Amer. Insects* 313, Besides the mosquitoes and punkies a third kind of fly assails the rod-and-line fisherman. . . These are blackflies, buffalo-gnats or turkey-gnats, as they are variously called, composing the small family Simuliidae, distributed all over this country, but especially abundant in the southern states. **1926** Essig *Insects N. Amer.* 552, The turkey gnat, *S[imulium] meridionale* . . , is grayish or brownish black, . . and is often a great plague to man and domestic animals . . , and is often a pest to nesting turkeys. **1968–70** *DARE* (Qu. R10, *Very small flies that don't sting, often seen hovering in large groups or bunches outdoors in summer*) Inf **NC49**, Turkey gnats; (Qu. R11, *A very tiny fly that you can hardly see, but that stings*) Inf **TN24**, Turkey gnat—gets around turkeys; **VA75**, Turkey gnats. **2005** Garrett–Beck *TX Bug Book* 31, Buffalo Gnat—Common Names: Black Fly, . . Turkey Gnat. . . *Simulium meridionale.*

turkey grape n [See quot 1960]

A **summer grape** (here: *Vitis aestivalis* var *lincecumii*).

1868 (1869) Lucas *Wreath Eglantine* 13, Turkey-grape, and many a native vine,/ Along the banks their tangled garlands twine. **1914** Budd *Amer. Horticult. Manual* 1.230 **SW**, What are known as the Post-oak varieties are improved types of the Turkey grape of the Southwest, which is only a stocky variation of *Vitis æstivalis.* **1920** *Torreya* 20.23, *Vitis aestivalis* var. *lincecumi* Munson.—Postoak or turkey grape. **1938** Van Dersal *Native Woody Plants* 337, Grape, . . Turkey *(Vitis lincecumii).* **1960** Vines *Trees SW* 723, *Vitis lincecumii* [sic]. . . Vernacular names for the plant are Post-oak Grape, Turkey Grape, and Big Summer Grape. The green fruit is sometimes eaten by domestic turkey.

turkey grass n [*OED2* 1874]

A **cleavers** (here: *Galium aparine*).

1900 Lyons *Plant Names* 167, *G[alium] Aparine.* . . Goose-grass, . . Turkey-grass.

turkey gull n

=**great black-backed gull.**

1902 Job *Among Water-Fowl* 145, The Great Black-backed Gull . . is also known as Turkey Gull, Minister Gull [etc]. **1925** (1928) Forbush *Birds MA* 1.69, *Larus marinus.* . . Turkey gull. **1948** Pearson *Sea Flavor* 114 **NEng**, The big birds are called various names by the fishermen—minister gull, turkey gull, coffin bearer, and saddleback.

turkey haw(thorn) See **turkey apple**

turkey in the oven, have a See **oven 2**

turkey jerk See **turkey B4**

turkey lice n Cf **beggar's lice 3, Indian ~, turkey grass**

A **beggar ticks 1.**

1968 *DARE* (Qu. S14, . . *Prickly seeds, small and flat, with two prongs at one end, that cling to clothing*) Inf **NJ24**, Turkey lice.

turkey-mouth n, adj Cf **chop-mouth, wild goose mouth**

A hunting dog's voice or cry that resembles the call of a turkey; having such a voice.

1927 *Decatur Daily Rev.* (IL) [20 July 10]/3 (newspaperarchive.com) **csTX**, The unearthly sound is Dr. Jake, Flirt is turkey-mouth, and that wild-goose mouth is Jimmy Murphy's. **1951** Randolph *We Always Lie* 124 **Ozarks**, A long tenor bay is a *bugle-mouth*, a similar but deeper tone is a *horn-mouth*. So it goes with *long-mouth, turkey-mouth, squealin'-mouth, goose-mouth* [etc]. **1967** *DARE* Tape **LA3**, [Inf:] They [=dogs] have turkey-mouths. [FW:] What does a turkey-mouth sound like? [Inf:] Sort of like a turkey. **1976** *Bittersweet* 4.2.61 (Internet) **MO**, Hear old Maude? She's got a turkey mouth. It sounds like a turkey. **1999** *Capital* (Annapolis MD) 9 June sec A 11/3, ["Dog's World" column:] The treeing walker coonhound has "preferably a clear ringing bugle voice on a cold trail changing to a 'chop' or 'turkey mouth' on a running trail, and a deep, throaty loud chop at the tree."

turkey mullein n Also *turkey weed* [See quot 1902] **chiefly CA** Cf **mullein**

A croton (*Croton setigerus*) native to much of the western US. Also called **doveweed 2, fish locoweed, ~ poison 4, ginger leaf 2**

1885 CA State Ag. Soc. *Trans. 1884* 196, The drought-resisting turkey weed (*Eremocarpus setigerus* [=*Croton s.*]). **1894** *Jrl. Amer. Folkl.* 7.98 **CA**, *Eremocarpus setigerus*, . . turkey mullein. **1902** U.S. Natl. Museum *Contrib. Herbarium* 7.363, *Croton setigerus.* . . A very low, gray weed . . native to California, and popularly known as "turkey mullein." . . Turkeys feed on the seed also, and on this account, and on account of the wooly, mullein-like appearance of the leaf, the plant has been called turkey mullein. **1911** Jepson *Flora CA* 245, Turkey Mullein. . . The seeds are sought by turkeys and by turtle-doves. **1917** Abrams *Flora Los Angeles* 213 **sCA**, *P[iscaria]* [=*Croton*] *setigera.* . . A common autumnal weed in all our valleys. Known as turkey weed. **1939** Pickwell *Deserts* 13 **CA**, Turkey Mullein and many another plant

show leaves gray-woolly, hairy, or prickly to the blazing sun. **1952** Barrett *Material Pomo Culture* 150 **CA**, Some of my own informants stated that turkey mullein, or "turkey weed" as it is sometimes called, was fully as good as soaproot for securing fish. **1968** *DARE* (Qu. S20, *A common weed that grows on open hillsides: It has velvety green leaves close to the ground, and a tall stalk with small yellow flowers on a spike at the top*) Inf **CA60**, Turkey mullein. **2002** *DARE* File—Internet **cwCA**, I did notice turkey mullein, but by far the most common flowering plant was the invasive yellow star thistle.

turkey mustard n Also *turkey cress, ~ foot mustard, ~ salad* **sAppalachians** Cf **turkeyfoot 4**

A **toothwort** (here: *Cardamine diphylla*).

1962 Dargan *Innocent Bigamy* 31 **sAppalachians**, She took him to it. Rock-walled with heart-leaf and turkey mustard growing around it. **1972** *Foxfire* 6.161 **wNC**, I've hoed corn and picked turkey mustard greens and old field lettuce. **1981** *Our Smokies Heritage* May 4 **wNC, eTN**, Toothwort . . has more noticeable flowers growing above its edible leaves which settlers once called turkey foot mustard. **1991** Weals *Last Train* 15 **eTN** (as of 1920s), The cattle relished the first greens of spring—the ramps, bear lettuce, turkey mustard, lamb's tongue, and crow's foot.

turkey oak n **Sth**

Any of several **oaks**, as:

a A **post oak 1** (here: *Quercus stellata*). [Because the acorns are eaten by turkeys; see quots]

1709 (1967) Lawson *New Voyage* 99 **NC, SC**, Turkey-Oak is so call'd from a small Acorn it bears, which the wild Turkeys feed on. **1812** Michaux *Histoire des Arbres* 2.39, Les glands. . . sont très-doux; c'est ce qui les fait avidement rechercher par les écureuils et les dindons sauvages. C'est probablement aussi à cause de cela, que quelques habitans donnent encore à cet arbre le nom de *Turkey oak.* [=The acorns. . . are very sweet, which makes them much sought after by squirrels and wild turkeys. It is also probably for this reason that some inhabitants call this tree [=post oak] *Turkey oak.*] **1901** Lounsberry *S. Wild Flowers* 136, Along the lower slopes of the Alleghanies the country people call it [=*Quercus stellata*] by the same name as they do *Quercus digitata* [=*Q. falcata*], the turkey oak.

b Either of two **oaks** with leaves thought to resemble a turkey's foot in shape:

(1) =**red oak 2b.** [See quot 1860] Cf **cherrybark oak**

1860 Curtis *Cat. Plants NC* 39, Spanish Oak. (*Q[uercus] falcata* . .)—This is generally known in this State, I think, by the name of *Red Oak.* . . It is also, in some parts, denominated *Turkey Oak*, from a vague resemblance between the form of the leaf (when it has but three divisions,) and the track of a Turkey. **1901** *Plant World* 4.144 **KY**, The prevailing trees near are sweet gum, . . Spanish oak, called there "yellow-bottom oak," but in this county (Warren) called "turkey oak;" . . and . . spotted oak. **1901** Lounsberry *S. Wild Flowers* 125, Spanish Oak. Turkey Oak. *Quercus digitata* [=*Q. falcata*]. *Ibid* 127, In North Carolina where this oak [=*Q. falcata*] grows freely it is often and quite inappropriately called red oak, while by the mountaineers it is again one of the genus known as the turkey oak.

(2) A small, sometimes shrubby **oak** (here: *Quercus laevis*) of dry, sandy barrens that is native to the southeastern US. [See quot 1962] Also called **scrub oak**

1868 (1870) Gray *Field Botany* 304, *Q[uercus] Catesbaei* [=*Q. laevis*], *Turkey* or *Barrens Scrub-Oak.* Small tree in pine barrens S[outh]: leaves deeply pinnatifid or 3–5 cleft, the long and narrow or unequal lobes somewhat scythe-shaped and often nearly entire. **1897** Sudworth *Arborescent Flora* 170, *Quercus catesbæi* [=*Q. laevis*]. . . Turkey Oak (Ga., Ala., Fla., Miss., La., Tex.) **1901** Mohr *Plant Life AL* 96, The turkey or barren oak and the blue jack . . are frequent companions of the long-leaf pine of the dry-pine barrens. **1939** FWP *Guide FL* 378 **neFL**, Small rough-barked blackjack or turkey oak, smooth-barked water oak . . and the white-blossoming magnolia spread their foliage over the sandhills and ravines along the shore. **1958** Babcock *I Don't Want* 81 **eSC**, Out in the sandhills beyond our farm an endless sweep of turkey oaks, dwarfed and interlacing for companionship, were flaming scarlet against the setting sun. **1962** Kurz–Godfrey *Trees N. FL* 80, *Quercus laevis.* . . The turkey oak is a common, small tree of the deciduous oak scrub. . . Narrowly 3-lobed leaves suggest a turkey foot, hence the name turkey oak. **1965–70** *DARE* (Qu. T10, . . *Kinds of oak trees*) Infs **FL9, 27, GA5, 18, NJ39, 52, VA46**, Turkey oak; **NC49**, Turkey oak—a small oak. [*DARE* Ed: Some of these Infs may refer instead to other senses.] **1975** Newell *If Nothin' Don't Happen* 8 **nwFL,** Most of the trees was second-growth pine and scrub oaks—what we call black-jacks and turkey oaks. **1986** Pederson *LAGS Concordance (Trees)* 3 infs, **swGA,** 1 inf, **nwFL,** Turkey oak. [*DARE* Ed: Some of these infs may refer instead to other senses.]

c Another such **oak,** such as **bluejack 1,** a **water oak 2b** (here: *Quercus nigra*), **pin oak 1a,** a **bear oak** (here: *Q. ilicifolia*), or **red oak 2a;** see quots.

1793 in 1802 Priest *Travels U.S.A.* 11 **PA,** A settler. . . tells me they have ten species of oak; viz, . . spanish, turkey, chesnut, . . and live oak. [*DARE* Ed: This quot may refer instead to another sense above.] **1860** Curtis *Cat. Plants NC* 38, *Post Oak.* On the Roanoke I have heard this [=*Quercus nigra*] called *Turkey Oak,* a name also given to the *Spanish* and *Post Oaks* [=*Q. falcata* and *Q. stellata*]. **1882** U.S. Natl. Museum *Proc.* 5.83 **IL, IN,** *Quercus palustris.* "Water Oak"; "Turkey Oak." . . *Quercus rubra.* Red Oak; "Spanish Oak"; "Turkey Oak." **1897** Sudworth *Arborescent Flora* 176 **SC, GA,** *Quercus brevifolia* [=*Q. incana*]. . . Turkey Oak. **1938** Van Dersal *Native Woody Plants* 347, Turkey [oak] *(Quercus cinerea, Quercus ilicifolia, Quercus rubra).* **1940** Steyermark *Flora MO* 139, *Pin Oak, Turkey Oak, Water Oak (Quercus palustris . .).* Low or wet woods, sometimes on upland ridges near sinkhole ponds in the Ozarks where it is often called Turkey Oak. **1953** Strausbaugh–Core *Flora WV* 308, *Q[uercus] ilicifolia. . . Scrub oak. Bear oak. Turkey oak. . .* The acorns are eaten by black bears and wild turkeys. **1966–70** *DARE* (Qu. T10, . . *Kinds of oak trees*) Inf **FL**35, Turkey oak; **KY**80, Turkey oak—same as water oak; (Qu. T15, . . *Kinds of swamp trees*) Inf **FL**35, Turkey oak.

turkey pea n

1 Any of var fabaceous plants with pea-like flowers and pods, as:

a A **goat's rue,** usu *Tephrosia virginiana.*

1823 Hunter *Manners & Customs* 392 **Cent,** *Soo-ke-he-ah.*—Young turkies' feed. Turkey pea. **1830** Rafinesque *Med. Flora* 2.267, *Tephrosia. . . Turkey pea, Catgut, Devil's shoestrings, Suckehihaw* of Osages. 4 sp[ecies]. *T. virginica* most common, . . bad weed in fields. . . Seeds food of turkeys. **1863** Porcher *Resources* 187 **Sth,** *Tephrosia Virginiana. . .* Turkey pea; goat's-rue. . . The roots were used by Indians, and are now employed in popular practice as a vermifuge. **1892** (1974) Millspaugh *Amer. Med. Plants* 46–4, The roots of the North American Turkey Pea *(Tephrosia Virginiana . .)* are purgative and were greatly esteemed by the Aborigines as an anthelmintic. **1974** (1977) Coon *Useful Plants* 170, *Tephrosia virginiana. . .* turkey, rabbit, or hoary pea.

b A **black-eyed pea** such as **deer pea 3** or *Vigna sinensis* var; see quots.

1917 Burke–Lambert *Soil Surv. NC* 9, Laurel, rhododendron and turkey-pea vines formed a thick undergrowth throughout the uplands. **2001** in 2003 *DARE* File—Internet **AL, GA,** Wildlife pea or turkey pea is another of the cowpeas that benefits deer, turkey and quail.

c A **milk vetch** (here: *Astragalus nuttallianus*).

1936 Whitehouse *TX Flowers* 57, *Turkey Pea (Homosa nuttalliana* [= *Astragalus n.*]) is a low plant with few-flowered clusters of small flowers. **1961** Wills–Irwin *Flowers TX* 138, The most widely distributed Milk-vetch in Texas is the Turkey-pea, *A. nuttallianus . . ,* often lost to view among grasses but for the small lavender-to-purple flowers borne in spring. These are followed by curved pods. **2005** Holloway *Dict. Wildflowers TX* 21, *Astragalus nuttallianus. . .* Common Name: Turkey Pea, for the seeds, which are eaten by turkeys and other birds.

d A **false lupine 1** (here: *Thermopsis montana*).

1937 U.S. Forest Serv. *Range Plant Hdbk.* W186, *Thermopsis montana. . .* Mountain goldenpea, variously known as buffalo pea, . . turkeypea, . . etc., is a perennial herb with golden-yellow, pealike flowers and belongs to the legume family.

e =**butterfly pea a.**

1940 Steyermark *Flora MO* 312, *Butterfly Pea, Turkey Pea (Clitoria mariana . .).* Sometimes in age twining at the tips; . . flowers pale blue and lilac, delicately veined, very large, 2″ (5 cm.) long. . . Rocky open woods. Southern and east-central Mo.

2 Any of var apiaceous plants that grow from a rounded tuber:

a =**harbinger-of-spring. Cf turkeyfoot 3**

1834 *Western Jrl. Med. & Phys. Sci.* 31.333, Erigenia bulbosa. . . Turkey pea. **1892** *Jrl. Amer. Folkl.* 5.97, *Erigenia bulbosa,* turkey-pea.

1894 Ibid 7.89 **OH,** *Erigenia bulbosa,* . . turkey-pea, near Cincinnati, O., fifty years ago. **1896** Ibid 9.189 **IN,** *Erigenia bulbosa,* . . turkey pea, pepper and salt. . . Eaten by children and fowls. **1968** *DARE* (Qu. S26c, *Wildflowers that grow in woods*) Inf **IN**17, Turkey peas. [*DARE* Ed: This Inf may refer instead to another sense.]

b A **sanicle 1** (here: *Sanicula tuberosa*) native to California and Oregon.

1911 Jepson *Flora CA* 291, *S[anicula] tuberosa. . . Turkey-pea. . .* Fruit flattened laterally, tuberculate but not at all bristly. . . Rocky or gravelly slopes in the foothills and up to 5,000 ft. **1961** Peck *Manual OR* 555, *S[anicula] tuberosa. . .* Turkey Pea. **2003** *DARE* File—Internet **sCA,** *Sanicula tuberosa*—Common name: Turkey pea. . . Open to wooded places, gravelly meadows, chaparral, southern oak woodland, pine forests to 8000′.

c also pl: A plant of the genus *Orogenia,* native to much of the Rocky Mountain area and California. Also called **Indian potato i, pepper-and-salt 3, snowdrop 6**

1906 Rydberg *Flora CO* 254, *Orogenia. . . Turkey Pea. . .* On mountain ridges from Ida. and Wash. to Colo. and Ore. **1937** St. John *Flora SE WA & ID* 299, *Orogenia.* Turkey Peas. . . Fruit oblong, slightly flattened laterally. **1973** Hitchcock–Cronquist *Flora Pacific NW* 334, *Orogenia. . .* Turkey-peas. **1998** Couplan *Encycl. Edible Plants* 338, *Orogenia . .* Indian Potato, Turkey Pea. . . N.W. U.S.

3 Any of var other plants; see below.

a Usu a **squirrel corn** (here: *Dicentra canadensis*), but also **Dutchman's breeches 1.**

1872 (1874) Brown *Complete Herbalist* 56, I combine it [=*Buxus*] with corydalis [here: =*Dicentra*] (Turkey pea) and the compound syrup of stillingia, in such a manner that it will *surely* cure syphilis. *Ibid* 160, *Turkey Corn (Corydalis formosa* [=*Dicentra canadensis*])—*Common Names. Wild Turkey-pea, Stagger-weed, Choice Dielytra. . .* This indigenous perennial plant has a tuberous root. **1915** *Amer. Druggist & Pharmaceutical Rec.* Nov 23 **OH,** Two species of dicentra, very similar as concerns foliage and habits, are indiscriminately gathered by root diggers and sold under the name "turkey corn" or "turkey pea." *Ibid,* A recent lot of the green corms before me, brought by a responsible root digger, located near Cincinnati, as turkey pea, has the proportion of Dicentra cucullaria, 28 parts, to Dicentra canadensis, 1 part.

b A **spring beauty 1** (here: *Claytonia virginica*).

1876 IN Dept. Geol. & Nat. Resources *Rept. for 1875* 521, *C[laytonia] Virginica. . .* May or Turkey Pea. **1940** Clute *Amer. Plant Names* 256, *Claytonia Virginica.* Ground-nut, turkey pea.

c A **dogtooth violet** (here: *Erythronium americanum*).

1996 in 2003 *DARE* File—Internet **cNC,** Another wildflower I associate with spring of the year. . . is the trout lily *(Erythronium americanum).* We knew this plant as Turkey pea.

d Prob an anemone (here: *Anemone caroliniana*).

1953 Randolph–Wilson *Down in Holler* 295 **Ozarks,** *Turkey-pea. . .* A little flowering plant, probably *Anemone caroliniana.* Children eat the tuberous roots, which taste rather like young peas.

turkey pear n Cf **turkey cactus**

A **prickly pear 1** (here: *Opuntia leptocaulis*).

1956 Gipson *Old Yeller* 141 **TX,** I hid behind a turkey-pear bush on the far side of the wash. **1994** Davis–Schmidly *Mammals TX* 282, The 10 most favored foods [of white-tailed deer] as observed in the Edwards Plateau of Texas are grasses and weeds, Mexican persimmon, . . spike rush, *Foresteria* [sic] or elbow bush, and turkey pear.

turkey pen See **pen** n¹ **B1**

turkey pepper n [See quot] Cf **turkey-snout pepper** =**bird pepper.**

2003 *DARE* File—Internet **TX** [Redwood City Seed Co.], In Texas, where they call them [=bird peppers] Turkey Pepper, . . the wild birds intentionally eat a lot of peppers, which then flavors their flesh and makes the turkeys distasteful to carnivores.

turkey pine n

See quots.

1956 Rayford *Whistlin' Woman* 189 **swAL,** Well, this o' big tree, it was a turkey pine, and this farmer didn't want it cut down when he went off to the Civil War. **1969** SC Market Bulletin 11 Sept 4, [Advt:] *Hemlock pine, turkey pine,* red and yellow maple, . . white dogwood trees,

$1 each. **2006** Odenwald–Turner *Identification S. Plants* 484, *Pinus glabra*—Spruce Pine, Turkey Pine.

turkey plover n

=**upland plover.**

1923 U.S. Dept. Ag. *Misc. Circular* 13.64 **IL,** *Vernacular Names* [for *Bartramia longicauda*]. . . *In local use.* . . Turkey-plover.

turkey roost n   Cf **buzzard roost 2**

The upper balcony in a theater.

1969 *DARE* (Qu. D40, *Names and nicknames . . for the upper balcony in a theater*) Inf **PA**193, Turkey roost.

turkey run   See **turkey trot** n **3, 4**

turkey salad   See **turkey mustard**

turkey's beard   See **turkey beard 1**

turkey scratching   See **turkey tracks**

turkey's foot   See **turkeyfoot 4**

turkey snout n

A **shooting star** (here: *Dodecatheon meadea*).

1931 KS Acad. Sci. *Trans.* 34.258, Dodecatheon meadia [sic], Turkey snout, American cowslip.   **1942** Dorrance *Sundowners* 156 **MO,** It was edged with white-washed rock; and planted, to either side, with touch-me-not, turkey snout, and coxcomb.   **1968** *DARE* (Qu. S23, *Pale blue flowers with downy leaves and cups that come up on open, stony hill-sides in March or early April*) Inf **NC**49, Turkey snout—blue and tassely-like.

turkey-snout pepper n   Cf **turkey pepper**

A hot red pepper (*Capsicum annuum* var).

1968 *DARE* (Qu. I22b, . . *Peppers—large hot*) Inf **VA**24, Turkey-snout peppers—long red peppers.

turkey sparrow n

=**rufous-sided towhee.**

1889 Ridgway *Ornith. IL* 1.292, Pipilo erythrophthalmus. . . *Popular synonyms.* Jaree; . . Turkey Sparrow.   **1917** (1923) *Birds Amer.* 3.58, To-whee. . . *Other Names.*—Chewink; . . Turkey Sparrow.   [*Ibid* 59, This bird [=*Pipilo erythrophthalmus*] has. . . its way of scratching on the ground, an operation in which it uses its feet alternately, after the manner of the domesticated hen. Indeed, the bird gets much of its food by this ground-foraging, incidentally making a commotion among the dry leaves which suggests the efforts of a much larger bird.]

turkey-strip n

An **oat grass c** (here: *Danthonia spicata*).

1902 VT Dept. Educ. *Circulars Educ. Info.* 6.147, In addition to the common name "poverty grass", which we prefer, it is known as "white-top", "turkey-strip", "wire-grass" [etc].   **1914** Georgia *Manual Weeds* 50, *Danthonia spicata.* . . Turkey-strip.

turkey-tail v   Usu with *out*   **sAppalachians**

To fan out; to divide and head in various directions.

1913 Kephart *Highlanders* 282 **sAppalachians,** The creek away up thar turkey-tails out into numerous leetle forks.   **1920** Lundsford *Law Hemlock Mt.* 58 **KY,** We hev need ter split up an' turkey tail out along different routes.   **1967** Williams *Greenbones* 234 **GA** (as of c1910), He began paying more attention to his surroundings: . . and little roads that started from the big one, then turkey-tailed out among the springing hills.   **1972** Cooper *NC Mt. Folkl.* 96, Turkey tails out—spreads out.   **1975** *Appalachian Jrl.* 2.152 **wNC,** The pattern of shortening a phrase is evident. . . "The creek turkey-tails farther down the mountain."   **1996** *NY Times* (NY) 28 June sec A 14/2 **sAppalachians,** A creek "turkey-tails out in the bottom," in the dialect of my birthplace.

turkeytail n   [See quot 1997]   Cf **false turkeytail**

A **mushroom B1** (here: *Trametes versicolor*).

1981 Lincoff *Audubon Field Guide Mushrooms* 489, Turkey-tail—*Trametes versicolor.* . . May–December, sometimes reviving and persisting several seasons.   **1997** in 2003 *DARE* File—Internet **WI,** One of the most common fungi to be found in the woods is *Trametes versicolor,* the turkey tail fungus. The common name comes from the banding pattern on the fruiting bodies that resembles (in miniature, of course) the tail of a strutting turkey.   **2003** *DARE* File **csWI,** Turkey-tail: a brightly colored mushroom, formerly *Coriolis versicolor,* now *Trametes v.*

turkey-tail out   See **turkey-tail** v

turkey-tangle n

A **frogfruit** (here: *Phyla nodiflora*).

1970 Correll *Plants TX* 1333, *Phyla nodiflora.* . . *Turkey-tangle.* . . Stems prostrate, to 9 dm. long, mostly rooting at the nodes. . . Wet or moist soil, fields, clearings, hillsides, ditches, thickets and beaches.   **1980** *Jrl. Range Management* 33.128 **sTX,** Although lagunas made up only 3 to 5% of the total land area, the high use of burhead (*Echinodorus rostratus* . .), . . turkey-tangle (*Phyla nodiflora* . .), longtom, and sedges, which grow primarily on these sites, indicated the importance of these areas to feral pig diets during the fall and winter.   **2003** (acc) FL Univ. *Featured Creatures* (Internet), The common host [of *Phyciodes phaon*] throughout much of Florida is turkey tangle fogfruit, *Phyla nodiflora* (L.) Green also known as capeweed, mat plant, creeping charlie, and match heads.

turkey-tongue n

A **jack-in-the-pulpit 1.**

1968 *DARE* (Qu. S1, . . *Jack-in-the-pulpit*) Inf **IN**49, Turkey-tongue.

Turkey Town   See **turkey trot** n **3**

turkey tracks n pl   Also *turkey scratching, turkey-track handwriting*   Cf **crow tracks, hen scratching**

Illegible handwriting.

[**1857** (1858) Smith *Early IN Trials* 185, He scratched off some caricatures looking like Greek, or turkey tracks.]   **1870** *Our Boys & Girls* 699, They say he can't read his own writing after it gets cold. . . He expects me to make good sense out of turkey-tracks.   **1904** Davis *Hist. Doylestown* 86 **PA,** To read turkey tracks, which some correspondents call writing, to be dunned for ink, etc.—this is the unkindest cut of all.   **1955** *Ironwood Daily–Globe* (MI) 8 Oct 9/1, Printers who had to translate his [=Horace Greeley's] "turkey track" handwriting into type were said to turn it upside down to read it.   **1966–69** *DARE* (Qu. JJ11, *Joking names for handwriting that's hard to read: "I can't make anything out of his _____."*) Inf **MO**1, Turkey tracks; **MA**40, Turkey scratching.

turkey-troop n

A **smartweed** (here: *Polygonum punctatum*).

1892 *Jrl. Amer. Folkl.* 5.102 **Long Is. NY,** *Polygonum acre* [=*P. punctatum*], turkey-troop.

turkey trot n

1 A rapid walk or trot; hence adj *turkey-trotting.*   **esp Sth, S Midl**

1839 *S. Lit. Messenger* 5.377 **NC,** May-be I didn't set up a high turkey trot, and peeled it like thunder.   **1859** Taliaferro *Fisher's R.* 36 **nwNC** (as of 1820s), You're a purty set uv ill-begotten, turkey-trottin' pukes, to raise a quarrel with a peacebble man, and then run like a gang uv geese.   *Ibid* 71, I moseyed home in a turkey-trot.   **1878** *Galveston Daily News* (TX) [20 Dec 3]/3 (newspaperarchive.com), When called upon to halt he struck a turkey-trot.   **1887** *Ibid* 24 Sept 4/4 **San Antonio TX,** Briggs can call Jenkins, Lowe, et al. "everlasting, never-to-be-forgotten, flea-bitten, turkey-trotting, slew-footed, box ankled, knock-kneed, pigeon-toed, bean-eyed, bucket-headed cranks and liars" as much as he pleases.   **1895** Remington *Pony Tracks* 187, He would run me off the reservation at a turkey-trot if I did shoot.   **1907** *Chicago Tribune* (IL) 24 Nov sec B 2/5, [Advt:] You'd better *do a turkey trot* to the box office and exchange some of your soft money for *A Bunch of Geo. M. Cohan's Laughter.*   **1912** Green *VA Folk-Speech* 402, Turkey-trot. . . A fast walk, swaying from side to side: "He always goes at a turkey-trot."

2 A popular dance performed with the feet wide apart and a swaying up-and-down gait; hence v *turkey-trot* to perform the dance; vbl n *turkey-trotting.*   **chiefly Nth, N Midl**   See Map

1874 in 1962 Nathan *Dan Emmett* 88, De two best steps you hab forgot—/ De "long-jay-bow" an' "turkey trot."   [Footnote: Performed in 1855]   **1888** *Century Illustr. Mag.* 35.468 **Sth** [Black], A voice . . added words to the strains of the fiddle, the dancer adapting her steps to the hints given: "Shuffl', littl' Lou;/. . . / Forwood [sic] too;/. . . / Back step, Lou;/. . . / Turkey trot Lou."   **1908** Davenport *Butte & MT* 42, The light fantastic, the turkey trot and the pazamala were indulged in by all to a late hour.   **1910** *Washington Post* (DC) 1 Dec 6/6 **CA,** San Francisco has produced in the "Turkey Trot" dance a novelty in terpsichorean art.   **1913** *Current Opinion* 55.263 **csWI,** The University of Wisconsin proposes to expel any student guilty of "turkey-trotting," which it puts on the same plane as drunkenness.   **1965–70** *DARE* (Qu. FF5a, . . *Different steps and figures in dancing—in past years*) 36 Infs, **chiefly Nth, N Midl,** Turkey trot.   **1993** *NY Times* (NY) 13 July sec C 17/4, [Advt:] Non-stop stepping from a Fox-trot to a Turkey Trot.

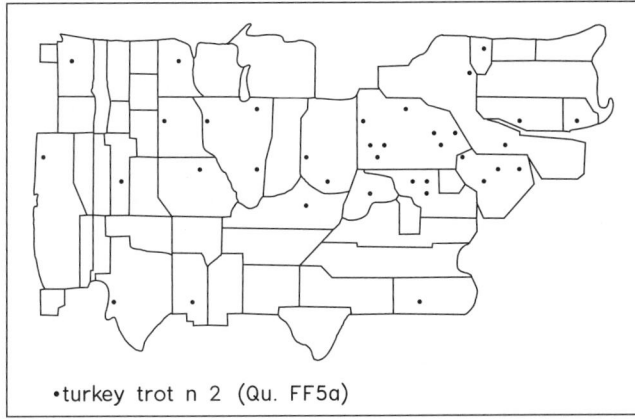

•turkey trot n 2 (Qu. FF5a)

3 also *Turkey Run,* ~ *Town:* A remote or insignificant place. Cf **possum** n **5**

1905 *Puck* 12 Apr 16, Cuck Uckleston came in from Turkey Trot, last Wednesday, and reported that everybody was fair to middling, out that way. **1906** *DN* 3.162 **nwAR,** *Turkey Run.* . . Name applied facetiously to an imaginary, remote, or insignificant hamlet or railroad station. **1910** *NY Observer* (NY) 9 June 739/2, The Turkey Trot Tribune useter be such a mild, conservative sort of paper. **1966** *DARE* (Qu. C33, . . *Joking names . . for an out-of-the-way place, or a very small or unimportant place*) Inf **FL6,** Turkey Town.

4 also *turkey run:* =**dogtrot.** **chiefly S Midl** Cf **possum trot 1**

1937 *MO Hist. Rev.* 31.442, The more pretentious homes consisted of two separate rooms connected by a roofed-over passage-way or hallway, which was left open and was used by the family in the summer. . . Different names seem to have been given to this entry or passage-way, a few of which are "dog trot," "turkey trot," and "turkey run." **1944** Howard *Walkin' Preacher* 56 **Ozarks,** The house . . was made largely of roughhewn logs. Originally it must have been two log houses with the traditional turkey trot between them, but now the center section or trot was closed with dressed-lumber boards. **1956** *AmSp* 31.310, Dog trot. . . turkey trot, wind-sweep, and *breezeway,* all meaning the same thing. **1970** *DARE* FW Addit **swKY,** *Turkey trot*—the space between two sections of a house. Function: to catch a breeze; also called dogtrot. **1975** McDonough *Garden Sass* 34 **AR,** More elaborate than these simple homes was the dog-trot style of house, which consisted of two separate log pens with a covered breezeway between them. This was also referred to as a possum trot, turkey run, wind-sweep, or But-and-Ben style. **1995–97** in 2004 Montgomery-Hall *Dict. Smoky Mt. Engl.* 621 **wNC, eTN,** Turkey trot.

5 See **turkey B4.**

turkey-trot v   See **turkey trot** n **2**

turkey-trotting adj   See **turkey trot** n **1**

turkey-trotting vbl n   See **turkey trot** n **2**

turkey-turd beer n **NEng**

A fertilizing mixture made of manure and water; hence adj phr *meaner than turkey-turd beer.*

1959 *Jrl. Amer. Folkl.* 72.76 **ME,** Cucumbers grow larger and more lush if they get about three good doses of "turkeyturd beer," a rich concoction of manure and water. **1967** *DARE* (Qu. HH22b, . . *A very mean person . . "He's meaner than _____."*) Inf **MA71,** Turkey-turd beer. **1975** Gould *ME Lingo* 302, *Turkey-turd beer*—Of all known beverages, this one is least liked by true Mainers; the expression is: "meaner than turkey-turd beer." **1994** MacLeod *Something* 30 **ME coast,** When it come to settling up for what he owed in honest wages or supplies, that was another and a sadder story. "Meaner than turkey-turd beer" was the general verdict on the so recently departed.

turkey vine n

See quots.

1969 *SC Market Bulletin* 11 Sept 4, [Advt:] Wayside lilies, lemon lilies, turkey vine, tr. periwinkle, . . 35c doz. **1987** Steitz *Grasses* 78, *Ampelopsis arborea*—Pepper Vine. . . Also called the turkey vine. **2001** Miller *TN Place-Names* 161, In settlement times, cattle here flourished on the wild turkey vine. . . Apparently, the vegetation was also known as peavine. **2004** Boughman-Oxendine *Herbal Remedies Lumbee* 61,

Partridge Berry (Mitchella repens); also known as Squaw Vine, Turkey Vine. **2006** *DARE* File—Internet **wTN,** Golden Turkey Vine (Lysimachia nummularia). . . Very low ⅛″ tall, but indefinate [sic] spread where happy.

turkey vulture n

Std: an American vulture *(Cathartes aura)* distinguished esp by the unfeathered reddish head.   Also called **bald-headed buzzard, carrion crow 1, Jersey glider, john crow, king buzzard 2, prairie vulture, redbill buzzard, red-headed vulture, red-necked buzzard, turkey** ~**, up-the-country-boys**

turkey weed n

1   See **turkey mullein.**

2   A **desert dandelion** (here: *Malacothrix saxatilis* var *tenuifolia*) native to California.

1898 Davidson *CA Plants* 46, One of the most hairy of California autumn plants is . . [*Malacothrix saxatilis* var *tenuifolia*]; children sometimes call it turkey-weed.

turkey wing n   Also *turkey-wing cradle (scythe), turkey-wing grain cradle*

A type of grain cradle.

1850 *Watertown Chron.* (WI) [14 Aug 4]/5 (newspaperarchive.com), [Advt:] *Cradles, Rakes, &c.* . . grape vine, Wisconsin clipper, turkey wing and other kinds grain cradles. **1884** *Canon City Mercury* (CO) 22 Aug 1/5 *(DA),* "Grapevine" and "Turky wing" cradles are the ones that cut most of the Hawes' grain. **1901** *Ft. Wayne Jrl.-Gaz.* (IN) 15 Mar 8/4, Mr. Blystone was the founder of the Bloomingdale flouring mills and the inventor of the Turkey-wing grain cradle. **1923** Adams *Pioneer Hist. Ingham Co.* 319 **MI,** Until I was seven years old the sickle cut all the grain in the neighborhood; then the turkey-wing cradle, the grapevine, the mully [etc]. **1978** Massey *Bittersweet Country* 57 **Ozarks,** Elvie's cradle, factory made and costing about five dollars, is called a "grapevine." The other cradle his father bought, a "turkey wing," was practically the same except that it was lighter. **1999** *Pif Mag.* 29 (Internet) **NY,** I recall gathering loose hay for an old man in Mt. Vision, New York. . . One of the last guys around who knew how to harvest grain crops with a turkey-wing cradle scythe.

Turkish rugging n   Also *Turk's rug* **CA**

A **spine-flower,** usu *Chorizanthe staticoides.*

1897 Parsons *Wild Flowers CA* 218, Turkish Rugging. *Chorizanthe staticoides.* . . In late spring the dry, open hills of the south are overrun with the soft lavender of the *Chorizanthe.* **1915** (1926) Armstrong-Thornber *Western Wild Flowers* 86 **CA,** Turkish Rugging—*Chorizanthe fimbriata.* . . An odd, dry-looking plant, making pretty patches of purplish color on dry mesas. **1923** in 1925 Jepson *Manual Plants CA* 297, *C[horizanthe] staticoides.* . . Turk's Rug. . . Dry sandy plains and foothills. **1974** Munz *Flora S. CA* 674, *C[horizanthe] staticoides.* . . Turkish Rugging. **2003** *DARE* File—Internet **sCA,** Turkish rugging is a low, much-branched annual with reddish-purple, pubescent stems . . from 4″ to 8″ tall.

Turkish turban squash   See **Turk's turban 2**

turkle   See **turtle**

turkledove   See **turtledove**

Turk's beard n   Cf **turkey beard 1**

=**squaw grass 1.**

1898 *Jrl. Amer. Folkl.* 11.282 **WA,** *Xerophyllum tenax,* . . Turk's beard.

Turk's-cap n

1   also *Turk's-cap lily:* Any of var **lilies 1** with nodding, often orange-red flowers and recurved tepals, such as the Canada lily *(Lilium canadense),* the Carolina lily *(L. michauxii),* or the Michigan lily *(L. michiganense),* but esp *Lilium superbum* native to much of the US east of the Mississippi River.   [*OED2* 1672 → for *Lilium martagon*]   For other names of *L. superbum* see **jack-in-the-pulpit 2d, nodding lily, swamp** ~ **b, tiger** ~**, Turk's head 2**

1826 Darlington *Florula Cestrica* 41, *L[ilium] superbum.* . . Turk's Cap. **1860** (1861) MI Geol. Surv. *First Biennial Rept.* 323, Of herbaceous plants attractive for the beauty of their flowers . . may be mentioned . . Turk's Cap Lily *(Lilium superbum).* **1909** Doubleday *Amer.*

Flower Garden 278, *Turk's Cap (Lilium superbum)*. . . Flowers turban-like, 2 inches across; numerous. **1933** Small *Manual SE Flora* 292, *L[ilium] carolinianum*. . . *Turk's-cap Lily*. . . Fla. to La. and N in the Appalachian provinces to S. Va. **1936** IL Nat. Hist. Surv. *Wildflowers* 54, *Turk's-cap Lily—Lilium michiganense*. . . The Turk's-cap Lily is the common species of the north central Mississippi valley. **1950** *WELS Suppl.* **WI,** Turk's-cap lily—tiger lily. **1966–68** *DARE* Wildfl QR Pl.14 [=*Lilium canadense*] Infs **NC**36, **OH**14, **WI**35, 80, Turk's-cap; **NY**91, Turk's-cap lily. **1968** Radford et al. *Manual Flora Carolinas* 311, *L[ilium] superbum*. . . Turk's-cap L[ily]. . . *L. michauxii* . . Turk's-cap L. **1968–70** *DARE* (Qu. S26b) Inf **GA**70, Turk's-cap—looks like day lily, petals turned back down; **RI**15, Turk's-cap lily; (Qu. S26c, *Wildflowers that grow in woods*) Inf **IA**8, Turk's-cap lily; (Qu. S26d, *Wildflowers that grow in meadows;* not asked in early QRs) Inf **VA**28, Turk's-cap; **MA**78, Turk's-cap lilies; (Qu. S26e, *Other wildflowers not yet mentioned;* not asked in early QRs) Inf **NY**106, Turk's-cap. **1979** Niering–Olmstead *Audubon Guide N. Amer. Wildflowers E. Region* 602, *Turk's-cap Lily (Lilium superbum)*. . . The largest and most spectacular of the native Lilies. **2003** *DARE* File—Internet **neWI,** Turk's Cap is used rather loosely for several different lily species. . . When responding to a request for information on this forum, I generally assume that people are talking about L. michiganense or L. superbum.

2 also *Turk's-cap gourd,* ~ *squash:* =**turban squash.**

[**1850** *Mag. Horticult.* 16.179, We would particularly mention the Turban, or Turk's Cap, and the Bottle Gourd, as these two varieties are considered hardier than the others.] **1863** Burr *Field & Garden* 222, *Turban*. . . Turk's-cap. Cucurbita piliformis. . . At the blossom-end, the fruit suddenly contracts to an irregular, cone-like point, or termination, of a greenish color, striped with white; and thus, in form and color, somewhat resembles a turban. **1988** Whealy *Garden Seed Inventory* (2d ed) 333, *Squash (Maxima)*. . . Turban, Turk's (Aladdin's Turban, Turk's Cap Gourd). **1994** FL Coop. Ext. Serv. *Fact Sheet HS 606* 1, A few of the edible squashes are quite ornamental when mature, such as the yellow crookneck squash and the turban (Turk's cap) squash.

3 also *Turk's-cap bush:* A **wax mallow,** usu *Malvaviscus arboreus* var *drummondii*. [See quots] **scattered, but esp TX**

1889 *San Francisco Municipal Rept. 1888–89* 820 **CA,** Achania Malvaviscus [=*Malvaviscus arboreus*]. . . Turk's cap. **1936** Whitehouse *TX Flowers* 71, *Turk's Cap (Malvaviscus drummondii* [=*M. arboreus* var *d.*]) . . The showy red flowers somewhat resemble a Turkish fez. . . It . . is hardier but not as showy, as the large-flowered Turk's cap (*Malvaviscus grandiflora* [=*M. penduliflorus*]). **1955** *S. Folkl. Qrly.* 19.233 **FL,** *Turks-Cup* [sic] (Malvaviscus drummondii) . . bears single, scarlet, showy, half-opened blossoms that look like small tasselled fezzes. **1964** *Clarke Co. Democrat* (Grove Hill AL) 6 Aug 4/2 (*Mathews Coll.*), Buster also informs me that the humming birds are again coming to the Turk's cap bush. **1967** *DARE* Wildfl QR (Wills–Irwin) Pl.25D [=*Malvaviscus drummondii*] Inf **TX**44, Turk's-cap. **2003** *DARE* File—Internet **TX,** Turk's Cap (Malvaviscus arboreus) is a shade-tolerant, deer-resistant Texas native that has blooms which hummingbirds love.

Turk's-cap gourd See **Turk's-cap 2**

Turk's-cap lily See **Turk's-cap 1**

Turk's-cap squash See **Turk's-cap 2**

Turk's head n

1 also *Turk's-head cactus:* A **barrel cactus:** any of var plants of the genus *Ferocactus,* but also *Echinocactus horizonthalonius*. [*OED2* 1725 for *Melocactus intortus*] **SW** Cf **turban cactus**

1849 in 1963 *San Diego Hist. Soc. Qrly.* 9.38 **CA,** I upset my flask and had no water. I cut open the Turk's-head cactus with my hatchet and ate the pulp, which reminded me of watermelon. **1854** in 1855 U.S. War Dept. *Rept. Explor. Railroad* (Final Rept.) 3.102, There are . . various kinds of Echino cactus, the most conspicuous being that named Wislizenus [=*Ferocactus wislizenii*], and sometimes called the "Turk's Head." **1886** Havard *Flora W. & S. TX for 1885* 479, *Cactaceæ* are never wanting on broken uplands; the most common species are . . *Echinocactus longehamatus* [=*E. horizonthalonius*] (Turk's Head), often a foot in diameter, yielding delicious fruit hardly inferior in size or quantity to that of *Cereus stramineus;* . . and several flat-jointed species. **1897** Parsons *Wild Flowers CA* 374, Turk's-head Cactus. . . *Echinocactus viridescens* [=*Ferocactus v.*]. **1920** Rice-Rice *Pop. Studies CA Wild Flowers* 66, In bloom, the Barrel Cactus (Echinocactus) is crowned with a circlet of pretty greenish yellow (or sometimes reddish green)

cup-shaped flowers, which have found for them a common name of "Turk's Head" or "Turban Cactus." **1940** Benson *Cacti AZ* 110, *Echinocactus horizonthalonius*. . . *Turk's head*. Small columnar or globular cactus not more than 1 foot high. **1970** Correll *Plants TX* 1103, *Ferocactus hamatacanthus*. . . *Turk's head*. . . Stems of mature plants ovoid or ovoid-cylindroid, . . fruit green, fleshy and juicy. *Ibid* 1104, *Echinocactus horizonthalonius*. . . *Turk's head*. . . Stem solitary, depressed-globose to ovoid or sometimes columnar, . . fruit at first juicy but drying at maturity. **2003** *DARE* File—Internet **NM,** Turk's head cactus (*Echinocactus horizonthalonius*) and robust hedgehog cactus (*Echinocereus fasciculatus*) also were common.

2 A **Turk's-cap 1** (here: *Lilium superbum*).

1892 *Jrl. Amer. Folkl.* 5.104 **MA,** Lilium superbum, . . Turk's head.

3 A bulrush (here: *Schoenoplectus robustus*).

1942 *Torreya* 42.158 **eSC,** Scirpus robustus [=*Schoenoplectus r.*] . . turks-head.

4 =**Turk's turban 1** (here: *Clerodendrum indicum*).

1970 Correll *Plants TX* 1341, *Clerodendrum indicum*. . . *Turk's head*. . . Virgate shrub or low tree. . . Naturalized in the Gulf States. **2003** (acc) TX A&M Univ. *TX Vascular Plant Checklist* (Internet), *Clerodendrum* . . *indicum* . . turk's head, turk's turban.

5 See **Turk's-head (cake) pan.**

Turk's-head cactus See **Turk's head 1**

Turk's-head (cake) pan n Also *Turk's head, Turk's-head (cake) mold* [From the resemblance of the cake made in it to a turban]

A roughly hemispherical cake mold with flutes, usu spiral, and usu a central tube; hence n *Turk's-head cake*.

1865 *Mrs. Goodfellow's Cookery* 299, A "Turk's head mould" has the best appearance on tables. **1880** *Bucks Co. Gaz.* (Bristol PA) [28 Oct 4]/1 (newspaperarchive.com), Sally Lunn Cake. . . When light, bake in a Turk's Head pan three-quarters of an hour. **1891** *Century Dict.* 6537, *Turk's-head*. . . A pan for baking cake, having a tin core in the center, thus bringing heat into the middle of the cake. **1897** (1968) Sears *Catalogue* 131, Turk's Head Pans, plain stamped tinware. 8 heads on frame, size, 3¼ x 1½ inches, each. **1903** *MA Ploughman & New Engl. Jrl. Ag.* 12 Dec 6/4 (Internet), Beat rapidly for a few moments and pour into a buttered Turk's head mould. **1941** *Chicago Tribune* (IL) 7 Dec 5/5, Grease a Turk's head cake pan generously (this kind of pan makes your cake look really Viennese). **1969** *DARE* File **seVA,** *Turk's-head cake*— A cake made in a round mold with a hole through the middle. **2006** *DARE* File—Internet, *Agate ware cake mold, 1880–1910*. . . This is called a "Turk's Head" cake mold because of its similarity to the shape of a turban. The spout in the middle helped to distribute the heat to the center of the cake.

Turk's rug See **Turkish rugging**

Turk's turban n

1 An introduced shrub or small tree (*Clerodendrum indicum*) naturalized in the Gulf States. Also called **Turk's head 4**

1906 Baerecke *Analytical Key* 115 **FL,** Clerodendron Siphonanthus [=*C. indicum*], Turk's Turban. **1933** Small *Manual SE Flora* 1144, *S[iphonanthus] indicus* [=*Clerodendrum i.*] . . Turk's-turban. . . Coastal Plain, Fla. to Tex. and S.C. **1970** Correll *Plants TX* 1341, *Clerodendrum indicum*. . . *Turk's-turban*. . . Naturalized in the Gulf States. **2003** *DARE* File—Internet **FL,** In [A]ugust the Turk's turban puts forth a huge spike of white tube-shaped flowers inspiring its other common name, "tubeflower".

2 also *Turkish turban squash, Turk's turban gourd:* =**turban squash.**

1854 IN State Bd. Ag. *Annual Rept. for 1853* 215, Among the curiosities exhibited at our Fair, I deem that special mention should be made of the Turkish turban squash. . . This vegetable is almost a perfect resemblance to the turbans worn by the Turks in shape, and is colored red and white. **1907** *MI Farmer & Livestock Jrl.* 51.520, The round Turk's turban gourd . . grows any size from 3 to 4 inches to a foot in diameter and is flat or depressed on the top and bottom. **1969** *DARE* (Qu. I23, . . *Kinds of squash*) Inf **IL**31, Turkish turban squash. **1988** [see **Turk's-cap 2**]. **2003** *DARE* File—Internet **ME,** In late August, stressed by a droughty season, our squash vines began to die back revealing party colored fruits. . . Wheel-shaped Cheese Pumpkins. Turk's Turban, actually a gourd, in clownish greens and oranges.

turmeric n [From the resemblance of their roots to that of the std *turmeric (Curcuma longa)*]

1 =**bloodroot 1.**

1803 A.F.M. Willich *Domestic Encycl.* (Amer. ed.) IV.442/1 (*OED2* at *Indian* A.4.b), Sanguinaria Canadensis, called commonly *Puccoon*, blood-wort, red-root, Indian paint, turmeric. **1837** Darlington *Flora Cestrica* 317 sePA, *Sanguinaria canadensis.* . . *Vulgo* . . Red-root. Turmeric. Indian Paint. **1892** (1974) Millspaugh *Amer. Med. Plants* 22-1, Bloodroot. . . Com[mon] Names. . . Turmeric. **1916** *Fur News Mag.* Oct 54, Bloodroot. . . Other Common Names,—Redroot, . . turmeric [etc].

2 also *turmeric root;* also sp *tumeric:* =**goldenseal 1.** Cf **Indian turmeric**

1814 Pursh *Flora Americae* 2.687, Hydrastis. *Yellow-root. Turmeric.* **1833** Eaton *Botany* 179, Hydrastis. . . *canadensis,* (orange-root, turmeric root . .). Root yellow. **1861** Wood *Class-Book* 212, Hydrastis. . . *Turmeric Root.* . . Rhizome thick, knotty, yellow, with long fibrous roots. **1863** Porcher *Resources* 18 Sth, *Hydrastis Canadensis.* . . Turmeric; golden seal. . . It has a narcotic smell; used in this country as a tonic. **1910** Graves *Flowering Plants* 193 CT, Turmeric-root. **1950** Gray-Fernald *Manual of Botany* 672, H[ydrastis] *canadensis.* . . *Golden-seal,* "Tumeric". . . Much sought for medicine and largely exterminated. **1971** Krochmal *Appalachia Med. Plants* 144, Hydrastis canadensis. . . Tumeric, wild turmeric.

turn v

A Gram form.

Past, past pple: usu *turned;* also **Sth, S Midl** *turnt.*

1880 (1881) Harris *Uncle Remus Songs* 55 **GA** [Black], Brer Rabbit he skint up de chimbly—dats w'at turnt de pot er greens over. **1889** *Overland Mth.* (2d ser) 13.631 **NC** [Black], He had n' got dis foot mo' d'n half turnt back befo' his strenk gin out. **1899** Chesnutt *Conjure Woman* 49 csNC [Black], De nex' time Sandy wuz turnt back. **1914** Furman *Sight* 68 **KY,** I let go all holts and turnt a-loose. **c1938** in 1970 Hyatt *Hoodoo* 2.1474 seGA [Black], When yo' go back the biggest majority of dat snail is turnt to water. **1957** Combs *Lang. S. Highlanders* sAppalachians, Turnt—pret. and p.p. of turn. **1975** Newell *If Nothin' Don't Happen* 99 nwFL, We turnt the dogs loose on the bear's trail. **2005** Williams *Gratitude* 533 wNC (as of 1940s), *Turnt:* turned.

B Senses.

1 To sour or curdle (milk); to become sour or curdled; hence ppl adjs *turned, turning;* adj phr *on the turn.* [*OED2* 1577 →] **widespread, but less freq Lower Missip Valley, nTX, OK, KY** See Map Cf **blinky 1a, off D2**

1828 (1970) Webster *Amer. Dict., Clabber.* . . Milk turned, become thick or inspissated. **1864** *Scientific Amer.* 11.4.56, Before the end of the day the pure milk had turned, while the mixture of milk and coffee remained in the same state. **1899** (1912) Green *VA Folk-Speech* 462, *Turn.* . . To curdle. To change from a fresh, sweet, or otherwise natural condition; cause to ferment, become sour, or the like: as, warm weather *turns* milk. **1929** *AmSp* 5.123 **ME,** Thick sour milk was "bonny clabber" but when lightly soured, it had "turned." **1950** *WELS* **WI** (*Milk that is just beginning to turn sour is* _____) 16 Infs, Turning; 7 Infs, Turned; 1 Inf, Beginning to turn. **1964** Wallace *Frontier Life* 73 **OK** (as of 1893–1906), Soured cream, which my mother spoke of as "turned." **1965–70** *DARE* (Qu. H58, *Milk that's just beginning to become sour*) 346 Infs, **widespread, but less freq Lower Missip Valley, nTX, OK, KY,** Turning; 33 Infs, **chiefly NEast, Gt Lakes,** Turned; **CT**5, Turned—no "turning," just sweet or sour; **CA**196, **MD**28, **MA**34, **NY**144, **WI**72, (Little) on the turn; **MD**21, Starting to turn;

MA98, **NY**39, (Just) beginning to turn. **1982** Slone *How We Talked* 7 eKY (as of c1950), *Turn*—For milk to turn, . . milk was put in a crock or churn and set before the fire or in the sun so the warmth would cause it to ferment, or become sour. **1986** Pederson *LAGS Concordance,* 1 inf, csAL, After hit's done turned—"clabber." **1991** Still *Wolfpen Notebooks* 163 sAppalachians, *Turning milk:* sour.

2 also with *off, out:* To pour (something). **esp NEng**

1773 in 1884 Drake *Tea Leaves* c ceMA, We'll turn the tea all in the sea,/ And all to keep our liberty. **1817** Riley *Authentic Narr.* 30 CT, My first care was to turn the water out of the boat, and haul her up out of the reach of the surf. **1830** Child *Frugal Housewife* 32 NEng, When they [=potatoes] are done turn the water off and let them steam. **1851** Webster *Improved Housewife* 207 CT, When perfectly clear, turn the water off carefully from the dregs. **1864** in 1918 Travers *Life of Jex-Blake* 170, [In America] they . . ask if they shall 'turn out the tea.' **1890** *AN&Q* 5.35 NEng, During a sojourn in New England, I often heard the word *turn* used for *pour,* especially at table. "Will you turn me a cup of coffee?" "Mr. Smith, will you please turn the water?" So far as I know, this is a strictly local use of the word. **1917** *DN* 4.402 neOH, VT, *Turn, turn out, v.t.* Pour, pour out. "Turn the tea." "Turn out some water." **1973** Allen *LAUM* 1.409 (as of c1950), 1 inf, NE, Turn. To pour. "[T]o turn a cup of tea." **1990** Hastings *Last Yankees* 65 VT, One day they turned out the tea into the cups, and a feather came out.

3 To drive (a squirrel) from one side of a tree so that another hunter can shoot it; hence vbl n *turning.* **esp S Midl** Cf **squirrel-turner**

1861 *S. Lit. Messenger* 32.50 wNC, As soon as Spank . . would tree a squirrel, daddy would say, 'Jim, run round and shake a bush, and turn it, and I'll give it bringer.' **1863** *Baily's Mag.* 6.348 **TX,** The wary little animals [=squirrels], although easily enough killed with a shot-gun, are not so easily brought to book with a rifle, unless you have some one to turn them for you—that is, when one runs up a tree he keeps the trunk of it between himself and his pursuer; and it is then necessary for some one else to walk round on the other side, which makes him take the opposite, and then the rifle does its work. **1921** Thompson *Jist Huntin'* 49 Ozarks, As an expert at turning squirrels for a gunner I never saw her equal. *Ibid* 50, "Hurry 'roun', City Feller!" cried Mizzoura. . . "He's on your side, turn him!" **1972** Parris *These Mountains* 116 wNC, I 'turned squirrels' for him. Huh? Turning squirrels? Why, that's getting the squirrels to move from one side of the tree to the other so the fellow that's got the gun can get a shot at 'em.

C Phrases.

1 *turn a hand (over)* (or rarely *turn a finger*) and varr: To do a stroke of work—usu in neg constrs. [Cf *turn one's hand to* to set to work on] **widespread, but less freq N Atl** See Map Cf **hand's turn 2, hit a lick 1**

1869 *Ladies' Repository* 4.391, Nobody's charity shall educate my boy while I can turn a hand. **1897** *Atlantic Mth.* 79.508 VA, Jane Ann Sims don't turn a hand ef Phemie's thar ter do it fur her. **1950** *WELS* **WI** (*To do no work at all, not even make any effort: "She hasn't* _____ *all day."*) 2 Infs, Turned a hand; 1 Inf, Turned her hand; 1 Inf, Turned over a hand; 1 Inf, Turned over her hand. **1965–70** *DARE* (Qu. LL18, *To do no work at all, not even make any effort: "She hasn't* _____ *all day."*) 125 Infs, **widespread, but less freq N Atl,** Turned a hand; 12 Infs, **esp KY, TN,** Turned her hand; **IL**143, **IN**80, **NE**8, **SC**2, 19, 40, **VA**103, Turned a finger; **KY**49, 60, **TN**6, (Ain't) turned her hand over; **KY**77, **MO**17, Turned her hands; **LA**40, Turned a hand over. [**1966** *DARE* Tape AR32, This year she'll receive seven thousand dollars, and doesn't

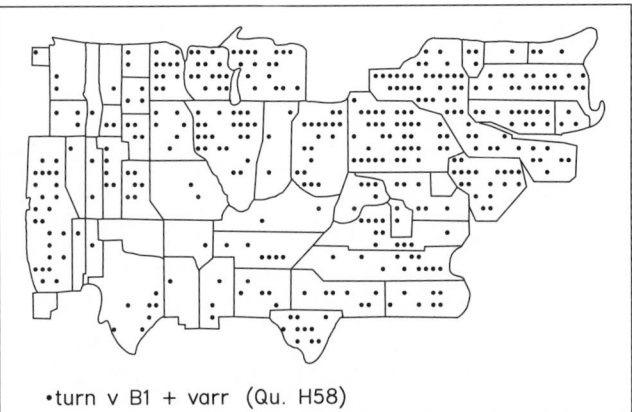

•turn v B1 + varr (Qu. H58)

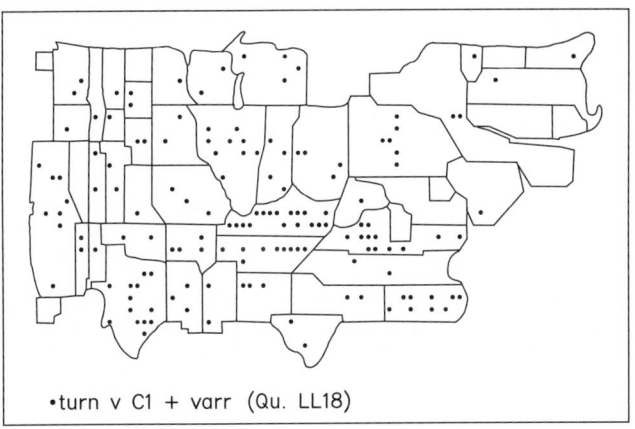

•turn v C1 + varr (Qu. LL18)

have to turn her hand on it to take her check.] **1989** Gibbons *Virtuous Woman* 1 **NC,** Used to I wouldn't turn my hand over for green peas.

2 *turn a wheel:* =**turn C1.**

1864 *NY Times* (NY) 19 Mar 1/1 **NC,** Your convention assembled can do nothing more toward realizing the end in view than your Legislature or your Governor can accomplish. It can't turn a wheel. **1880** *Portsmouth Times* (OH) 8 May [2]/3 (newspaperarchive.com), Chapman . . nor any one else could strike a lick or turn a wheel except by the consent of [the] Council of the city of Portsmouth. **1890** *Atlanta Constitution* (GA) 29 July 4/4 **TN,** Half the Southern manufacturers could not turn a wheel without East Tennessee coal. **1897** *KS Univ. Qrly.* (ser B) 6.93, *Turn a wheel:* usually negative; as, "They never turned a wheel." They didn't do a thing.—General. **1927** *McClure's Mag.* 52.29 **MO,** Some people write every day, rain or shine, but I have to work when the spirit is on or I can't turn a wheel. **1967** *DARE* Tape IA6, It started raining. We didn't turn a wheel for almost three weeks.

3 *turn dry:* To stop (a cow) from giving milk.

[**1801** Archer *Statist. Surv. Co. Dublin* 49, The best milch cows are the worst for fattening until turned dry.] **1840** *Amer. Farmer & Spirit* 2.234 **Sth,** One of them [=milch cows] was so nearly dried up that she was turned dry. **1859** *Cultivator* 7.193 **NH,** We came to the conclusion that I should have to turn her [=a cow] dry and fit her for the butcher. **1905** *S. Cultivator* 15 Feb 35, If this cow does not improve with the next calf, . . the best disposition you can make of her will be to turn her dry and fatten her for beef. **1943** *Star* (Kansas City MO) 13 Oct 8/3, By reducing her grain ration to nearly nothing I was able to turn her dry by the middle of the month. **1966–68** *DARE* (Qu. K3a, *When a cow stops giving milk*) Inf **MD**42, They turn her dry; **AR**40, You turn them dry. **2006** U.S. Dept. Ag. *Emergency Pub. Rulemaking Hearing* 12 Jan 181 **TN,** How would you produce milk only half the days of the year? . . You would freshen your cows, you'd milk them six months and you would turn them dry.

4 *turn go (of):* To let go (of), turn loose. [*EDD* (at *turn* v. 3.(6))] **chiefly Sth, S Midl**

1891 Whitely *Rural Life TX* 10, With a bath tub tied to his tail we turned him go—and go he did. **1902** in 2009 (acc) Lexis–Nexis Legal Research *State Case Law: TX* (Internet), The engineer seemed to pull it wide open and turn it 'go.' It appeared to me it was using all the steam it had. **1915** *DN* 4.192 **swVA,** *Turn (one) go.* . . To set free; to turn loose. **1930** in 2008 Hurston *Coll. Plays* 104 **NYC,** Turn go of me, fool! **1931** (1991) Hughes–Hurston *Mule Bone* 112 **cFL** [Black], Turn me go! **1937** (1977) Hurston *Their Eyes* 205 **csFL** [Black], "Turn go mah hands!" Janie seethed. But Tea Cake never let go. **1964** Miller *Siege Harlem* 128, And that hustler would not turn go of her. **1974** Wilson–Jacobs *Cajun Humor* 95 **LA,** He catch dat horseshoe in his han', look at it fas'er den you aver saw . . , an' turn it go.

5 *turn a (wild)cat, ~ one a cat, ~ the cat;* Of an animal: to fall, somersault; to trip up (an animal). [Scots, nIr dial *turn the wild cat, tumble the (wild) cat* to turn head over heels] **SW**

1909 *Pearson's Mag.* 22.307 **West,** Done broke his neck, that pore ol' hoss. Stuck his foot in a doghole an' turned a cat, he did. **1933** *SW Rev.* 18.136 **TX,** Rob Roy [=a dog] grabbed him by the hind leg and turned him a cat; then he had him by the throat before the coyote knew what was up. **1940** *AmSp* 15.222 **cwTX,** They are certain to apprehend him if his horse 'turns a wildcat' (falls) or 'tumble-sets' (somersaults). **1945** Thorp *Pardner* 99 **SW,** Tie Randolph had remarked more than once that if he ever got a good chance, he was going to pick up his [=a horse's] paws and turn him a cat, meaning, rope him by the forefeet while he was running and make him turn a somersault. **1954** *AZ Qrly.* 10.36 **TX,** A horse that stepped in a prairie-dog hole and fell was said to turn the cat. **1966** Hudson–Maxwell *Sunny Slopes* 47 **TX,** Further illustrative of this attitude is the incident . . when a bronc turned a cat on Cyclone Davis. **2006** Dearen *Saddling* 32 **TX** (as of 1960s), When his pony "turned a cat," the JA cowhand broke his collarbone and lost consciousness.

6 See **turn** n 3.

turn n

1a The quantity of anything that can be carried or brought in a single trip. [*OED2* 1792 →] **chiefly Mid and S Atl; also Gulf States** See Map

1800 in 1969 Herndon *Wm. Tatham Tobacco* 25 **VA,** A *turn* signifies such a quantity as each person . . can carry upon his shoulder or in his arms. **1842** *Spirit of Times* 12 Mar 20/3 **NC,** He can . . shell out "a turn of corn for mill" at night. **1856** in 1862 Colt *Went to KS* 99 **NY,** Have

just been to the spring for my turn of water. **1890** *DN* 1.70 **LA,** *Turn.* A turn of wood (for example) is an arm-load, a cart-load, or any other quantity that can be transported at one return. **1899** (1912) Green *VA Folk-Speech* 462, *Turn.* . . A load; a pack; as much as can be carried at one time by a man or an animal. "Bring in a turn or two of wood before night." **1909** *DN* 3.418 **nME,** *Turn.* . . Two pailfuls (of water). **1934** (1970) Wilson *Backwoods Amer.* 12 **AR, MO,** Uncle Homer proceeded to call . . to the Brentwood store, where his wife had gone for a turn of groceries. **1949** Kurath *Word Geog.* 43, The phrase *turn of wood* for an armful of wood has general currency in the Southern area, but *turn of corn* as a synonym of the Midland *grist of corn* is found only in the Piedmont of Virginia and in the part of the South Midland lying to the south of the Kanawha and the Roanoke. **1955** Ritchie *Singing Family* 7 **seKY,** You would most surely see . . Earl Engle on his mare taking a turn of corn to the mill. **1965–70** *DARE* (Qu. L56, *The amount of wood a person can carry in both arms:* "We're out of firewood—I'll just get in a _____.") 60 Infs, **chiefly Mid and S Atl; also Gulf States,** Turn; FL6, MD38, 43, Turn of wood; NC85, One turn, two turns. **1968–69** *DARE* Tape KY13, [FW:] What's a turn of corn? [Inf:] Well, it's the sack that they bring the corn to the mill in. . . It's the corn that they bring. They call that a turn. . . Whatever amount they wanted to bring, they call a turn of corn; VA2, She was on her way to the mill with a turn of corn. . . A turn of corn is a burlap sack, sometimes half-full, sometimes full. They call 'em small turns or large turns. That's just another way of speaking, you know, for a sack of corn. **1986** Pederson *LAGS Concordance* **Gulf Region** (A turn [of corn, meal, wood, etc]) 162 infs, Turn; 125 infs, Turn(s) of corn; 73 infs, Turn(s) of wood; 11 infs, Turn of meal; 4 infs, Turn of wheat; 1 inf, Turn or two of wood; 1 inf, Turn of vegetables; 1 inf, Turn of fodder; 1 inf, Turn of hay; 1 inf, Turn of water = barrel; [1 inf, Turn of pancakes—one preparation, no leftovers]. **2000** Shores *Tangier Is.* 201 **Chesapeake Bay,** The preferred term for an armful of wood was *turn of wood.*

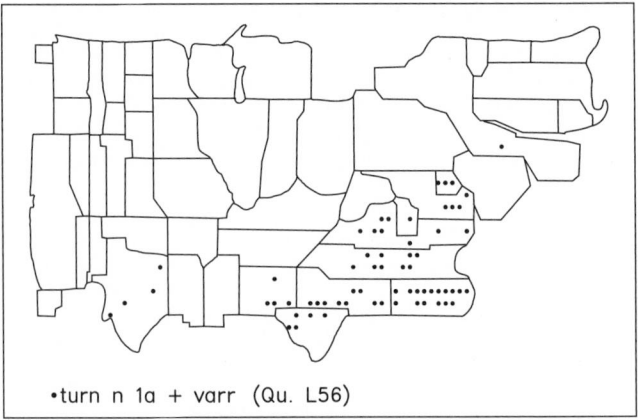

•turn n 1a + varr (Qu. L56)

b Spec; in logging: a number of logs bound or linked together for skidding. **esp Pacific NW**

1896 Munroe *Rick Dale* 257 **Pacific NW,** As this log rounded the bend and came directly towards them, another was seen to be chained to it, then another, and another, until the "turn" was seen to contain five of the woody monsters. **1905** U.S. Forest Serv. *Bulletin* 61.52 **Pacific NW** [Logging terms], *Turn.* . . Two or more logs coupled together end to end for hauling. **1938** (1939) Holbrook *Holy Mackinaw* 264 **Nth,** *Turn.* A unit of logs being yarded. **1950** *Western Folkl.* 9.123 **nwOR** [Team-logging terms], *Turn of logs.* Several logs lined up end to end on a skid road and dogged together. **1955** *Humboldt Std.* (Eureka CA) [8] Aug [17]/6 (newspaperarchive.com), When a catskinner is backing his tractor to where his choker setter stands ready to hook on a "turn" of logs, he holds a man's life in his hands. **1961** Labbe–Goe *Railroads* 260 **Pacific NW,** [Glossary:] *Turn:* The logs brought out of the woods in a single pull, whether it be the turn handled by a donkey, tractor, truck or train. **1968** *Coshocton Tribune* (OH) 27 Oct sec B 3/6, [Caption:] Crew member operating skidder with a turn of logs. **2006** *DARE* File—Internet **OR,** The crew was sending in a *turn* of four tree-length logs when the incident occurred.

2 Esp in logging: a round trip made in hauling.

1905 U.S. Forest Serv. *Bulletin* 61.52 **Nth** [Logging terms], *Turn.* . . A single trip and return made by one team in hauling logs—e.g., a four-turn road is a road the length of which will permit of only four round trips per day. **1916** *Fairbanks Sun. Times* (AK) 6 Aug [6]/5 (newspaperarchive.com), One of the eastern operators made three turns a day on a nine-mile road in hauling logs. **1942** ME Univ. *Studies* 57.134 [Logging terms], *Turn.* One round trip, as with a team, tractor, or truck. **1950** *Western Folkl.* 9.120 **nwOR** [Logger speech], *Turn.* A round trip; one round trip of butt rigging from donkey to woods and return with logs. *Oxen turn.* One round trip with team from landing to woods and return. **1956** *AmSp* 31.152 **nwCA** [Logger lingo], *Turn.* . . A task done by a cat, the size of which is measured by the elapsed time between the cat's leaving the landing to go into the brush for logs and its return to the landing with the logs. **1969** *AmSp* 44.209 [Trucker jargon], *Turn*—See *round.* [*Ibid* 208, *Round*—Round trip of a truck that leaves from and returns to the same terminal with a stop at a distant terminal.]

3 Personality, temperament, manner; hence v *turn* to show one's character.   **S Midl**   Cf **turned 1**

1902 *DN* 2.248 **sIL**, *Turn.* . . To act; conduct one's self. 'I don care so much about how a man looks as I do the way he turns.' **1923** (1946) Greer-Petrie *Angeline Doin' Society* 15 **KY,** That feller had a distant *turn* . . and jest play'd *shet mouth*. **1926** *AmSp* 1.419 **Okefenokee GA,** He 'uz a nice feller. I certainly liked 'is turn. [Footnote:] Manner, ways. **1927** *DN* 5.478 **Ozarks,** *Turn.* . . Inclination, disposition. 'Thet 'ar boy he tuk a turn jes' like his ol' pappy—allus a-fightin' an' a-jowerin'.' **1939** *Hall Coll.* **ceTN,** I don't like his turn. **1946** *AmSp* 21.191 **seKY,** *Turn* . . personality, nature. 'He's got a good turn' (i.e., a pleasing personality). **1952** Brown *NC Folkl.* 1.603 **c,eNC,** *Turn.* . . Manners. "She'll get along all right; she's got a good turn." **1953** Randolph–Wilson *Down in Holler* 295 **Ozarks,** My neighbor said of a politician, a good mixer with a pleasing manner, "I sure do like that feller's turn!" A woman once remarked to me: "Sallie Porter's always a-raisin' hell 'bout somethin'. That's her turn, an' she cain't help it." **1955** Ritchie *Singing Family* 247 **seKY,** She was a friendly and a nice-spoken woman, and she had a right good turn and people she'd meet up with would be talking away with her in no time. **1960** Criswell *Resp. to PADS 20* **Ozarks,** He is of a good turn, never loses his disposition. [Criswell: Always common, still so] **1969** *DARE* FW Addit **KY**31, Got a good turn—has a pleasant personality; **KY**39, Got a quare turn. . . Got a peculiar turn; **KY**44, So-and-so "has a queer turn"; **KY**52, They're just that turn. **1982** Slone *How We Talked* 7 **eKY** (as of c1950), *Turn*—personality; "He has a good turn." "She has a friendly turn."

4 in phr *on the turn:* See **turn** v **B1**.

turnabout (dance) n   Cf **tolo**

A dance to which girls invite boys.

1939 *Charleston Gaz.* (WV) 28 Nov 4/7, Chi Sigma Chi sorority will sponsor an informal "turnabout" dance. [**1965** *Oshkosh Daily Northwestern* (WI) 13 Feb 4/6, On Wednesday, Turnabout Day, girls will invite boys to the Code Week dance.] **1998** *DARE* File **cwCA** (as of c1960), When I was in high school, there were two dances a year to which the girls invited the boys. These were called *turnabouts*. **2008** *DARE* File **Chicago IL,** In Chicago, a dance where the girls asked the boys was called Turnabout.

turn a cat   See **turn** v **C5**

turn a finger, turn a hand (over)   See **turn** v **C1**

turn a wheel   See **turn** v **C2**

turn a wild cat   See **turn** v **C5**

turn down v phr   chiefly **S Midl**   Cf **cut down** v phr **2**

In a spelling or grammar contest: to displace (another) by spelling or parsing an item he or she has missed.

1875 (1876) Twain *Tom Sawyer* 71 **MO,** He took his place . . in the spelling class, and got "turned down," by a succession of mere baby words. **1893** *KS Univ. Qrly.* 1.142, *Turn down:* to pass above in the spelling-class. **1899** Woerner *Rebel's Daughter* 89 **Ozarks,** He [=the teacher of a class in grammar] . . proposed to enliven it by a parsing match, so that any one failing to answer properly should be "turned down" by the next one who gave a correct answer. **1903** Eggleston *First of Hoosiers* 45 **IN** (as of 1840s), The successful speller was said to have "turned down" all who had failed, and was entitled to take his place above them in the line. **1931** in 1996 *DARE* File—Internet **AR** (as of c1880), In the every day spelling classes, we stood in a single long row and 'turned down' those who stumbled over words that we could spell. **1941** in 1946 *PADS* 6.31 **cNC,** *Turn down.* . . To cut down in a spelling class. **1946** Stuart *Tales Plum Grove* 59 **neKY,** I wanted to outlearn the boys I was in class with. I wanted to turn them down in spelling and get the prize for the most headmarks. **1956** McAtee *Some Dialect NC* 48,

Turn down . . conquer in a spelling match. **2002** in 2006 *DARE* File—Internet **TN,** If the player misspells, the word goes to the next person in line. If he correctly spells the word, then the second speller gets to "turn down" the first by moving ahead on the bench toward the scorekeeper.

turn dry   See **turn** v **C3**

turned adj

1 Having a (specified) personality or nature.   [**turn** n **3** + *-ed*]   **chiefly S Midl, esp KY**

1867 Harris *Sut Lovingood Yarns* 73 **eTN,** I seed a-cummin, a ole widder, what wer a pow'ful pius turn'd pusson. **1910** *DN* 3.457 **KY,** *Turned.* . . To look like or to be like. "Mary is turned like her mother." "Don't you think Myrtle is turned a sight like John?" **1931** *AmSp* 7.94 **eKY,** *Quar-turned*, droll-natured. **1937** *Hall Coll.* **wNC, eTN,** He was very contrary and queer-turned. **1939** *Ibid, Mild-turned.* . . Possessing a good disposition; pleasing. "She's a mild-turned girl." **1946** *AmSp* 21.191 **seKY,** *Turned* is used as an adjective: 'Jim's better lookin' but John's better turned.' *Queer turned* (pronounced [kwær] or [kwar] near Pine Mountain), meaning odd or eccentric, has been noted by several authors. *Ibid* 272 **neKY,** He said I was the most hateful turned girl he ever met. **1966** *DARE* FW Addit **WA,** You're not turned like that—you're not that way, that's not your way. Southern. **1969** *DARE* (Qu. KK65, . . *'The same sort':* "If you like Bob, I'm sure you'll like his brother—they're _____.") Inf **KY**21, Turned alike. **1972** Thomas *Pop. Dict. Ozarks Talk* 88, *Timid-turned.* . . Bashful, often said of shy swains. **1972** *Atlanta Letters* **cnGA,** "Queer-turned." When a person is unusually peculiar or eccentric. **1979** Carpenter *Walton War* 150 **sAppalachians,** That girl is allright, but she allus was puny turned. **1981** *DARE* File **ceKY** (as of c1930), He was a sweet-turned boy, always laughing and smiling. **1982** *Smithsonian Letters* **cnWV,** Nice turned = possessing a pleasing personality.

2   See **turn** v **B1.**

turner n[1]   [Ger "gymnast" < *turnen* to do gymnastics < Fr *tourner*]   orig in German settlement areas, now widespread

A member of a **turnverein**—freq in comb *Turner Hall.*

1854 *Calif. Chronicle* (S.F.) 16 May 7/3 *(DA),* Yesterday we again paid a hasty visit to Russ' Gardens, where the Turners and their compatriots had resumed the sports of the previous day. **1872** Schele de Vere *Americanisms* 141, A *Turner* . . has become literally what Americans call an "institution." The word represents our "Gymnast," but being applied to members of clubs and societies who make gymnastics a subject of pleasure as well as of health, it is now universally admitted into our speech. **1880** *NY Times* (NY) 7 June 8/4, Three hundred and twenty Turners sailed yesterday . . to compete for the honors at the First International Turners Festival . . at Frankfort-on-the-Main. . . Most of the German-American Turners come from the West, but nearly all the States were represented. There were Turners from New-York, New-Jersey, Pennsylvania, Maryland, Kentucky, Georgia, Louisiana, Illinois, Iowa, Minnesota, Indiana, Kansas, Colorado, California, and Texas. **1894** Amer. Acad. Political & Social Sci. *Annals* Sept 84 **IL,** In Chicago . . many apprentices among stone cutters and other trades requiring drawing take lessons in a Turner hall from nine to twelve Sunday mornings. **1938** *Charleroi Mail* (PA) 26 Jan 1/7, *Local Turner Society Going To Flag Rites.* . . Few people know the part earliest German Turners' societies played in the Civil War; that it was Turners who nominated Abraham Lincoln for the presidency . . and that Lincoln's bodyguard, at his inauguration [sic] in 1861, comprised Turners of Washington, D.C. **1957** *Fitchburg Sentinel* (MA) 28 Oct 12/1, [Obituary:] Mr. Finneron was a member of the . . American Turners Society and a life member of the Painter and Decorators Local 175. **1968** *DARE* (Qu. FF22b, . . *Clubs and societies . . for men)* Inf **MN**36, Turners. **2005** Friends Max Kade Inst. *Friends Newsl.* Summer 7 **csWI,** The Turner Hall was not only a place for immigrants to . . preserve their Swiss traditions, it also became a center for community activities. **2006** *DARE* File—Internet **cTX,** *Turner Hall Established: 1871.* . . Fredericksburg, Texas. **2007** *Ibid,* American Turner Societies by District . . Central States . . Middle Atlantic . . New England . . New Jersey . . New York . . St. Louis . . Upper Mississippi . . W. Pennsylvania . . Western U.S.

turner n[2]   Rarely *turner (breaking) plow*   chiefly **Inland Sth, GA**   =**turning plow.**

1868 in 2006 *DARE* File—Internet **cwTN,** [Inventory:] 1 Turner plow. **1879** *Ibid* [*Weekly Constitution* (Atlanta GA) 21 Oct], [Advt:] Two Avery two Horse Turners. **1914** *Reno Eve. Gaz.* (NV) 24 June 6/3

ceAL, On the 7th of April I laid off the rows three feet apart and bedded the land with a one horse turner. **1943** *Limestone Democrat* (Athens AL) 2 Sept 4/3, [Advt:] One disc turner and cultivator attachment. **1953** *Middlesboro Daily News* (KY) 15 Aug 8/3, *Farm Sale. . .* No. 50 Lynchburg *Hillside Turners. . .* Ea. 21.98. **1966–69** *DARE* (Qu. L18, *Kinds of plows*) Infs **AL**11, **VA**7, Turner; **GA**72, **NC**48, Hillside turner; **KY**16, Level-land turners. **1986** Pederson *LAGS Concordance,* 10 infs, **chiefly nGA, AL, eTN, nMS,** Turner (plow); 2 infs, **nwGA, csTN,** Turner = turning plow; 3 infs, **nGA, eTN,** Hillside turner; 1 inf, **neMS,** Disc turner—a type of breaking plow; flat-bottom turners—a type of breaking plow; 1 inf, **cwGA,** Two-horse turner; 1 inf, **neGA,** Half-turner. **2005** *AL Farmers & Consumers Bulletin* Apr 5, 2-16″ flat bottom plow $225; 2 disc turner breaking plow $325. **2006** *DARE* File—Internet **cIN,** [Transcript of local TV show:] So I first go in with the turner plow, turn the soil over, day or two later go back and disc it up.

Turner Hall See **turner** n[1]

turner verein See **turnverein**

turn go (of) See **turn** v C4

turnhole n esp C and Mid Atl

A whirlpool in a river.

1830 *Reg. PA* 30 Jan 1, The *Broad Mountain* or fourth range from the Blue mountain . . crosses the Lehigh at *"The Turn Hole."* **1873** Coleman *Guidebook Lehigh Valley RR* 80 **PA,** At the Turnhole, a short distance above the town, formerly stood a famous bridge. **1879** *Eve. Gaz.* (Pt. Jervis NY) 23 Aug 1/1, The *turn-hole,* a provincialism now obsolete, was used to designate a sudden bend of a stream by which the water when deep was turned upon itself into an eddy or whirlpool. . . There is a "turn-hole" in the bend of the Delaware at the mouth of the Flat Brook. . . [D]uring great floods it becomes a powerful whirlpool, sucking in large pieces of timber and carrying them out of sight. **c1960** *Wilson Coll.* **csKY,** Turnhole. . . A whirlpool; hence Turnhole Bend, where a big whirlpool used to be before the lock at Brownsville was built. **1967–68** *DARE* (Qu. C8, . . *A place in a stream where water flows round and round and draws things in toward the center*) Infs **SC**43, **VA**8, Turnhole. **1969** *Sun. Gaz.-Mail* (Charleston WV) 25 May Showtime sec 10/5, The widely-known "turnhole" of Greenbrier River [is] within sight of the shaded, grassy park.

turn in v phr chiefly Midl

1 foll by *and:* To apply oneself to a task, set to work.

1822 Woods *2 Yrs. Residence* 293 **seIL,** I calculated to sell my creature there, and then when I got home, to turn in and earn some money to get me another. **1834** Crockett *Narrative* 93 **TN,** We killed that one [= a bear] also, which made three we had killed in less than half an hour. We turned in and butchered them, and then started to hunt for more. **1853** Kennedy *Blackwater Chron.* 52 **MD,** The hostler also was absent; and finding no representative of that very important individual, we turned in and groomed our own horses. **1864** in 1937 Hancock *South after Gettysburg* 86 **sNJ,** There was no food but hard tack to give the men so I turned in and dressed their wounds. It was all that could be done. **1909** *DN* 3.384 **eAL, wGA,** *Turn in.* . . To begin to work voluntarily: used with *and* and some other verb to indicate united action. "I turned in and helped him finish his job." **1914** Callison *Bill Jones* 26 **OK** (as of 1874), After the grasshoppers had eaten everything, we turned in and ate the grasshoppers. **1937** *Newark Advocate & Amer. Tribune* (OH) 1 Jan 8/4, After the schedule closed Newark turned in and won the state championship. **1954** *Julian Apple Day* [1] **csCA,** So they all turned in and built a good log house with a large fireplace. **1959** in 2004 Montgomery-Hall *Dict. Smoky Mt. Engl.* 622 **wNC,** They was just like one family. When one got sick, they all turned in and did his work. **1984** in 2006 *DARE* File—Internet **neFL,** Whenever the section crew was late with the depot housecleaning, Thelma . . turned in and worked to present the cleanest station on the division.

2 foll by *to* (also sp *turn into*) and vbl n (or rarely infin): To set about, begin.

1802 in 2006 *DARE* File—Internet **cNC,** We vewed the courious things that *Mr Culbeth & Powel* had till we ware satisfied than we turned in to froliceing till late in the Night. **1834** Crockett *Narrative* 38 **TN,** They had bows and arrows, and I turned in to shooting with their boys by a pine light. **1880** in 2006 *DARE* File—Internet **NE,** Borrowed a washing machine, and in a short time had the work done and out to dry; but it turned into raining and we can't get them dry. **1895** *DN* 1.395 **cwIN,** "*Turn in* to do a thing" = set about doing it. **1909** *DN* 3.405 **nwAR,** *Turn in.* . . To *turn in* to do is to set about doing. **1918** in 2006 *DARE* File—Internet **cIN,** But it finally got too smoky and, what

was worse, it turned in to raining. **1939** *Hall Coll.* **wNC, eTN,** We turned into shootin' at the limb under it . . and finally got it weak enough so the limb broke with the bear and fell down. *Ibid,* It turned into kind of sleetin'. *Ibid,* Rhody she got to laughin' and makin' fun of Nance. So Nance she turned into cryin'.

turn in and See **turn in** 1

turning See **turn** v B1, 3

turning plow n chiefly Sth, S Midl, TX See Map Cf **turner** n[2], **turnplow, turn shovel**

A plow that turns over the soil; usu a moldboard plow, but also (esp in comb *disc turning plow*) another type performing the same function.

1832 in 1833 *S. Agriculturist* 6.1.8 **VA,** I then commence giving it my last ploughing with a small turning-plough. **1848** *De Bow's Rev.* 5.178, Early in the spring bed to the plants with a good turning plow, to the width of four feet on each side. **1883** GA Dept. Ag. *Pub. Circular No. 29* 8.13, The land was well broken and the oats on bottom acre ploughed in with large turning plow. **1912** *Daily Northwestern* (Oshkosh WI) 25 Apr 11/1, [Assoc Farm Press article:] The turning plow turns the furrow slice over, leaving the hard upper soil at the bottom. **1942** *Limestone Democrat* (Athens AL) 7 May 8/5, [Advt:] Good used disc turning plow. **1965–70** *DARE* (Qu. L18, *Kinds of plows*) 99 Infs, **chiefly Sth, S Midl, TX,** Turning plow; **CA**181, Turning plow—turns soil over; horse-drawn or mechanical; **KY**6, Turning plows—disc and flat-bottomed; **LA**29, Turning plow—turned dirt over; **OK**33, Moldboard plow is also called turning plow; **TN**10, Turning plows—flat-bottomed, has shares and points, not disc type; **TX**13, Turning plow—moleboard [sic]; **TX**89, Horse-drawn turning plow—turns sod bottom side up; **KY**16, **NC**30, Hillside turning plow; **NC**49, **TX**105, One-horse turning plow; **LA**8, **OK**43, Walking turning plow; **TN**62, Steel turning plow; **GA**77, Straight-beam turning plow; **KY**86, Two-horse turning plow; [**CO**22, Turning share;] (Qu. L20, *The implement used in a field after it's been plowed to break up the lumps*) Infs **MS**58, **TX**57, Turning plow; (Qu. L25, *The implement used to clean out weeds and loosen the earth between rows of corn*) Inf **OK**14, Turning plow; **KY**90, Single turning plow. **1966–67** *DARE* Tape **LA**6, You mold this row on each side . . of that sweet potato. . . That leaves the middle in there. You take your turning plow and break the middle out; **NM**2, [FW:] What kind of plows did they use to turn the ground over with [in growing cotton]? [Inf:] Called turning plows; what we called breaking plows. **1983** *MJLF* 9.1.59 **ceKY** (as of 1956), *Turning plow* . . a plow with a big blade used for the first plowing in the Spring. **1986** Pederson *LAGS Concordance,* 336 infs, **Gulf Region, but esp AR, LA, MS, TN, nAL,** Turning plow(s). **2005** in 2006 *DARE* File—Internet **ceTN,** [Advt:] '48 Farmall Cub. . . Sickle bar mowing blade, belly mount disc turning plow [etc].

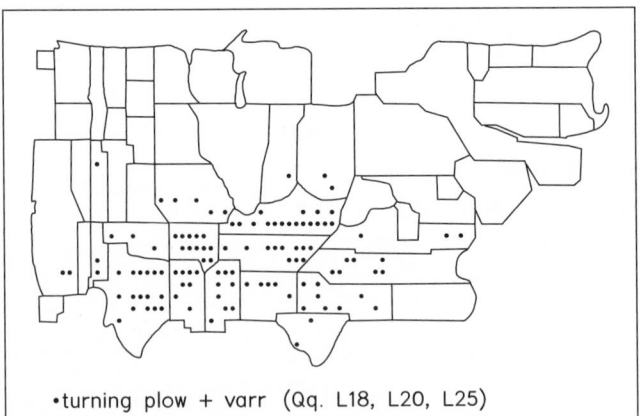

•turning plow + varr (Qq. L18, L20, L25)

turning row See **turnrow**

turning shovel See **turn shovel**

turn in to See **turn in** 2

turnip bank See **bank** n[1] 1

turnip grass n

A **panic grass** (here: *Panicum bulbosum*).

1901 U.S. Div. Agrostology *Bulletin* 25.46, [Caption:] Bulbous Panic-Grass or Turnip Grass, (Panicum bulbosum). Grown on Potomac Flats, Washington, D.C., from New Mexican Seed.

turnipweed n

A **boneset 1** (here: *Eupatorium purpureum*).

1920 Pellett *Amer. Honey Plants* 45, The Joe-Pye weed or turnip weed (*E[upatorium] purpureum*), is frequently reported as yielding honey.

turn off v phr

1 To produce, turn out (work). [*OED2* 1840 →]

1825 *Chr. Spectator* 7.578, It was surprising to see with what neatness and despatch they [=blind workers] would turn off work. **1842** *N. Amer. Rev.* 54.471 **MA,** They were paid according to the quantity of work turned off from their machines. **1897** *New Engl. Mag.* 22.22, There was a sublime faith that all work legislative could be turned off by tyros, provided only they were Know-nothings. **1913** London *Valley of Moon* 50 **cwCA,** Her grit, her ability to turn off work that was such an amazement to others, were her mother's. **1938** Stuart *Dark Hills* 197 **neKY,** You certainly can turn off the work. **c1950** *Halpert Coll.* 73 **wKY, nwTN,** I just can't turn off my work like I used to = housecleaning takes longer than it did when one was younger. **1956** McAtee *Some Dialect NC* 48, Then, I could turn off work as fast as anybody. **1966** *DARE* (Qu. JJ26, *If somebody has been doing poor work or not enough, the boss might say, "If he wants to keep his job he'd better _____."*) Inf **GA7,** Turn off some more work. **1984** Wilder *You All Spoken Here* 33 **Sth,** A productive worker who can prime, or crop, two rows of tobacco at a time can turn off work; he's a good hand.

2 Of weather: to become, change to being. **scattered, but esp Sth, Midl**

1848 *De Bow's Rev.* 5.226 **LA,** The weather should remain drizzly, misty, and warm, but if it should turn off cold, with a north wind, the deer resort to the thickets. **1863** in 2006 *DARE* File—Internet **MI,** Rain this morn. Turned off Quite Cold. **1901** *Janesville Daily Gaz.* (WI) 21 Oct 7/2, If . . the weather turned off cold and disagreeable, he manufactured a lot of sleds. . . If the weather turned off warm after each rain . . he would make but few sleds. **1953** *Reno Eve. Gaz.* (NV) 25 Nov 15/5, Tuesday's weather which turned off warmer and still in the afternoon seemingly accounted for the perfect and near perfect scores turned in by the field. **1975** Newell *If Nothin' Don't Happen* 96 **nwFL,** The weather had turned off warm, so the skeeters was really bad. **1986** Pederson *LAGS Concordance* **Gulf Region,** 6 infs, Turned off (dry, cool, pretty, etc); 2 infs, Going (to) turn off (bad, pretty). **2000** in 2006 *DARE* File—Internet **cME,** No fish last night. The weather turned off cool and windy. **2006** *Ibid* **cnAL,** One Saturday in April, the weather turned off really warm and we had spring fever really bad.

3 To throw (a rider).

1960 *McDavid Coll.* **OK,** Turned off = thrown (from a horse).

4 See **turn** v **B2.**

turn one a cat See **turn** v **C5**

turn one out of meeting See **meeting 2**

turn out v phr

1 To cease to cultivate (land), leave fallow. **chiefly Sth**

1813 Taylor *Arator* 117 **VA,** The phrase "the land is killed and must be turned out," has become common over a great portion of the United States. **1856** Olmsted *Journey Slave States* 373 **NC,** The greater part, even of these once rich low lands, that had been in cultivation, were now "turned out," and covered, either with pines, or broom-sedge and brushwood. **1879** (1880) Tourgée *Fool's Errand* 35 **Sth,** The overseer consequently reduced his cares . . by "turning out" from year to year portions of the plantation. **1903** *DN* 2.335 **seMO,** Turn out (ground).' . . To abandon worn out land. The opposite of 'taking in ground.' **1907** *DN* 3.238 **eME,** Turn out (ground). . . To abandon wornout land. **1909** *DN* 3.384 **eAL, wGA,** Turn out. . . To allow (land) to grow up in weeds, abandon from cultivation. **1915** *DN* 4.192 **swVA,** Turn out. . . Of land, to let (it) lie fallow.

2 To dismiss, let out (students, a school); to end a session of school; of a school (or rarely a church): to cease to be in session (for the day or for a vacation), "let out." **chiefly Sth, S Midl** Cf **take in, take out 2**

1866 *Old Guard* 4.350 **Sth,** Suddenly, slavery is abolished, and the negroes, like a parcel of school-boys unexpectedly turned out of school, rush off. **1887** *Century Illustr. Mag.* 34.550 **GA** [Black], Den atter school bin turn out, I is hide myse'f side de road. **1892** in 2006 *DARE* File—Internet **cwTN,** Prof. turned out his scholars and went to the funeral last Wednesday evening. **1893** Shands *MS Speech* 62, In Charleston, S.C., *take in* means to begin, and *take out,* to end, when school or church is spoken of. In Mississippi, *turn out* is used for this *take out.*

1893 in 2006 *DARE* File—Internet **cwTN,** Prof. Hess turned out school at noon yesterday. **1894** *Ibid,* Prof. Hess hurried through with his schoolwork, turned out at one o'clock. **1905** *DN* 3.99 **nwAR,** Turn out. . . To close, be dismissed. 'What time will school turn out?' **1941** Justus *Cabin on Kettle Creek* 30 **eTN,** It was customary for the school on Little Twin to turn out for two weeks during this season so that the children could help with the harvesting. **1944** Howard *Walkin' Preacher* 87 **Ozarks,** I had turned school out at early noon. **1946** *PADS* 5.42 **VA,** Turn out. . . Of school, be over; everywhere, but not common north of the James. **1976** Wolfram–Christian *Appalachian Speech* 178, When school turned out at four o'clock, you'd go home. **1986** Pederson *LAGS Concordance* **Gulf Region** (School _____) 110 infs, Turns out; 31 infs, Turned out; 11 infs, Turn out. **2006** Purcell *Reg.* (OK) 27 Apr (Internet), Officials want to address the need to provide a safe environment for the children of the community once school turns out at the end of the day. **2006** *DARE* File—Internet **cnTX,** I had just ordered lunch when church turned out and all 1444 residents of Maud [OK] arrived at the 30-seat restaurant at the same time.

3 See **turn** v **B2.**

turnover n[1] See **turnover plow**

turnover n[2] Cf **cake turner, egg turner**

A spatula.

1969–70 *DARE* (Qu. F3, *When you're frying things—for example, eggs—you turn them over with a _____*) Inf **MA14,** Turnover; spatula—new term; **MA69,** Turnover; spatula—word learned in school; **MA83,** Spatula, turnover, cake turner; **PA235,** Turner, turnover. **2000** Shores *Tangier Is.* 201 **Chesapeake Bay,** A small flat implement for turning eggs and other foods is called a *turnover.*

turnover, fruit basket See **fruit basket b**

turnover plow n Also *turnover (moldboard plow)*

A type of reversible plow.

1877 *OH Practical Farmer* 31 Mar 195, He had better have recommended a turnover mould-board plow and underdrains. **1901** Harben *Westerfelt* 59 **nGA,** He . . has been ploughin' a two-hoss turnover. **1954** *Greeley Daily Tribune & Greeley Republican* (CO) [27 Mar 8]/6 (newspaperarchive.com), [Advt:] Edwards 16 inch 2 bottom, two way turnover plow. **1967–69** *DARE* (Qu. L18, *Kinds of plows*) Inf **KY34,** Turnover plow; **PA218,** Turnover plow—flop 'em right over and you can go right back in the same furrow. **1986** Pederson *LAGS Concordance,* 1 inf, **cwGA,** Turnover plow. **2000** Baldacci *Wish You Well* 103 **VA,** "This here's a turnover blade," Louisa said, pointing to the oddly shaped disk of metal. "You run it down one row, turn mule and plow round, kick the blade over, go down the row again. Throws up some furrows of dirt on both sides. It kicks up big clods of earth too."] **2002** in 2006 *DARE* File—Internet **TX,** Dad decided that since I could reach the handles I was old enough to plow. He showed me how to start in the middle and work to each side with the turnover plow. **2006** *Ibid* **OH,** [Caption:] This is oliver turnover or hillside plow with *heavy* beam.

turnpike v Also with *up* **chiefly NEast, N Cent** Cf **pike** v[1]

To build (a road) after the manner of a turnpike; to grade (a road) so that its center is crowned; hence vbl n *turnpiking,* ppl adj *turnpiked.*

1791 (1893) Hiltzheimer *Extracts Diary* 172 **PA,** I took Mr. Francis . . to view the road, from Vine Street to Vanderen's Mill, six miles, which it is proposed to turnpike. **1816** in 1936 *OH Archeol. & Hist. Qrly.* 45.353 **MD,** The road is turnpiked throughout the whole distance. **1825** (1832) Pickering *Inquiries* 55 **Upstate NY,** In some of these new towns, the streets are as yet only ridged, or "turnpiked," in the centre; others are gravelled, but none, I believe, yet paved. **1861** *IL State Ag. Soc. Trans. for 1859–60* 4.202, There were worked streets, back-furrowed or turnpiked, . . traversing the fields. **1882** *Oshkosh Daily Northwestern* (WI) 23 Sept [4]/3 (newspaperarchive.com), A fine turnpiked and gravelled road well beaten down and solid has taken the place of sink holes and mud. **1906** *Daily Kennebec Jrl.* (Augusta ME) 24 Feb 7/3, Three hundred and forty-seven answers gave the time in years that turnpiking would last; this time ranging from 20 years to "until fall rains." **1915** *Stevens Point Jrl.* (WI) 30 Oct 1/2, The road winds between two slough holes, and is well turnpiked. **1926** *DN* 5.390 **ME,** Turn-pike (accent on turn). . . To rebuild a dirt road; an amateur process resorted to by farmers when working out their taxes on the highway. "They are turnpiking the roads; so they are pretty bad." **1939** *LANE* Map 42 **NEng,** The verb *turnpike (up)* is still used in the sense of 'crown (a road)', even by those to whom the corresponding noun is unfamiliar. **1949** *McDavid Coll.*

cNY, *Turnpike.* . . To grade a road so that it has a high crown. **1978** *Pioneer* (Bemidji MN) 6 Oct 3/4, All areas that were "turnpiked" or graded have been graveled.

turnpike (cake) n Also *turnpike emptins,* ~ *yeast* [See quot 1869] **chiefly NY** *old-fash* Cf **emptins 1**

A small cake of dried yeast dough used for leavening.

1834 *Genesee Farmer* 4.259 **cwNY,** Add two or three small yeast or turnpike cakes. **1844** Stephens *High Life in NY* 2.78 **CT,** Her face begun to swell and puff up, like a baking of bread wet up with turnpike emptins. **1847** (1852) Crowen *Amer. Cookery* 277 **NY,** Yeast Cakes, *called Turnpike Cakes.*—Put a quart of hops into two quarts of water, cover them, and let them boil, then strain it hot over a quart of fresh corn meal, stir it well together, when cooled . . , add a teacupful of good yeast, or one turnpike cake dissolved in warm water . . , make it in cakes . . , and set them in a dry, warm, but airy place, to rise and harden. . . These will remain good for months. **1852** *Graham's Mag.* 41.375, 'Well, wherever *was* you broughten up,' said my visitor, at length, 'to 'spose that turnpike-cakes was meant *to eat!*' **1869** in 2006 *DARE* File—Internet **ceNY,** When they were laying out the Windham Turnpike . . they were very much troubled to carry the soft yeast. . . One Mrs. Fowler, who cooked for them, contrived to dry it, so that she could carry it conveniently. This was done sixty years ago, and is what gave it the name of *Turnpike emptyings or Turnpike yeast.* **1914** *Trenton Eve. Times* (NJ) 5 Nov 11/4, *Buckwheat Griddle Cakes*—Put three pints of warm water into stone pot or jar[,] add gill of baker's yeast or an inch square of turnpike cake, dissolved into little warm water. **1991** *DARE* File **seNY,** Turnpike = yeast. Why? Who the hell knows. That's what my great-grandfather said.

turnpiked See **turnpike**

turnpike geranium n [See quot 1914]

A **Jerusalem oak 1** (here: *Chenopodium botrys*).

1900 Lyons *Plant Names* 95, *C[henopodium] Botrys.* . . Turnpike Geranium. **1914** Georgia *Manual Weeds* 110, *Chenopodium Botrys.* . . Its name of Turnpike Geranium indicates the fondness of this weed for the public road, where it is usually an unsightly object, with its glandular, hairy leaves and flowers overlaid with dust. **1933** Small *Manual SE Flora* 466, *B[otrydium] Botrys.* . . Jerusalem-oak. Turnpike-geranium. . . The foliage is aromatic.

turnpike up See **turnpike**

turnpike yeast See **turnpike (cake)**

turnpiking See **turnpike**

turnplow n **chiefly S Atl, Gulf States, WV** See Map =**turning plow.**

1842 in 1969 Turner *Cotton Planter's Manual* 54 **AL,** A *good plough-hand* follows with a turn-plough, which should run into the soil from *six to eight inches deep* at least, and turn well. **1854** in 1927 Jones *FL Plantation Rec.* 104 **nwFL,** I think you will nead about 10 turnplowes. **1856** Ibid 518, Received 12 turn plough points from Mr. George Jones. **1883** GA Dept. Ag. *Pub. Circular No. 35* 8.17, *Preparation.* . . Finished the beds with 6-inch turnplow. . . *Cultivation.*—May 25th, barred off with turnplow. **1939** *Morning News* (Florence SC) 23 Dec 3/1, With a two-horse turn plow . . throw one furrow down the slope. **1940** *Charleston Gaz.* (WV) 25 Feb 30/1, [Advt:] *One horse turn* plough, cheap. Like new. **1945** *Dothan Eagle* (AL) 24 Sept 8/2, When this strip is plowed out with a turn plow, the last furrow should be in the bottom

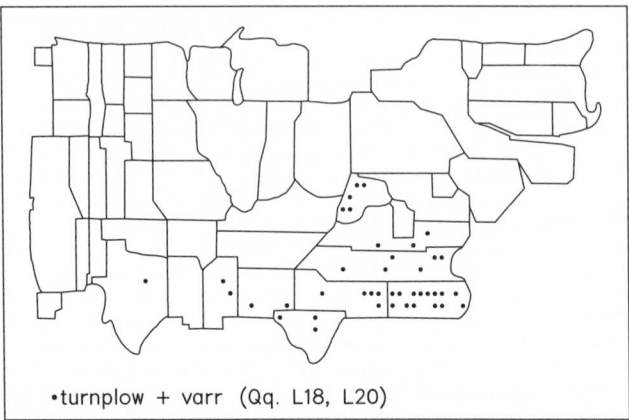

•turnplow + varr (Qq. L18, L20)

of the channel. **1952** *Charleston Gaz.* (WV) 3 Aug 29/6, [Advt:] A good one horse mowing machine, sled, disc turn plow. **1965–70** *DARE* (Qu. L18, *Kinds of plows*) 30 Infs, **chiefly S Atl, Gulf States, WV,** Turnplow; NC24, Turnplow—turns soil upside down; NC52, 81, Turnplow—turns the soil (up); SC32, Turnplow—one straight side and a wing to turn earth over; SC19, 23, Turnplow—to throw up a bed; SC26, Turnplow—to turn the soil to make beds; WV4, Turnplow—always plows downhill; [you] turn blade at end of each furrow; VA40, Single turnplow—one horse; double turnplow—two horse; NC12, Boy turnplow; SC30, Two-horse turnplow; (Qu. L20, *The implement used in a field after it's been plowed to break up the lumps*) Infs FL32, GA52, Turnplow. **1986** Pederson *LAGS Concordance,* 65 infs, **chiefly GA, FL, sAL, sMS,** Turn plow(s). **2003** *SC Market Bulletin* 3 Apr 6/3, [Advt:] 2 horse turn plow, w/metal beam, $50. **2006** *DARE* File—Internet **nwWV,** [Advt:] Rotary Mower, Scoop Pan, and Disc Turn Plow.

turnrow n Also *turning row* **chiefly Sth, S Midl** Cf **headland 1**

An unplanted strip of land at the edge of a field used for turning a plow or other implement.

1821 *Amer. Farmer* 3.16 **cnVA,** The first operation . . is to pull the blades . . and afterwards . . to carry them to the turning rows, or head lands, to be subsequently hauled to the fodder house. **1829** *S. Agriculturist* 2.317 **cSC,** The land which lay out, and that which was cultivated, were . . separated only by a turn row. **1842** in 1843 *S. Cultivator* 1.2.9 **SC,** I selected also and laid off separately four acres of cotton along the turn-row of the seventy-five acre cut of cotton. **1848** *De Bow's Rev.* 5.46, He used great ingenuity in so arranging his carriage . . as to enable him to turn it in a space not exceeding that usually reserved for turning-rows in the field. **1855** Douglass *My Bondage* 104 **MD,** Some [slaves] lie down on the "turning row," and go to sleep. **1890** *DN* 1.66 **KY,** *Turning-row:* a row unplanted in a corn or tobacco field, where the horses turn around in plowing. **1908** *Ft. Wayne Sentinel* (IN) [16 May 17]/4 (newspaperarchive.com), Leave a good wide turning row at each end of the garden, so that no plants will be tramped down in turning the horse. **1954** *Harder Coll.* **cwTN,** *Turning row.* . . The area at the end of rows or at the end of the field that is used for purposes of turning into other rows or for coming to and from the field. **1963** Owens *Look to River* 4 **TX,** Rows nearly a mile long . . ending in a brushy turnrow. **1967** *DARE* (Qu. KK12, *A meeting where there's a lot of talking: "They got together yesterday and had a real _____."*) Inf **LA**8, Turnrow talk—in a cornfield or somewhere. **2006** *DARE* File—Internet **MS** (as of c1956), The most private place for young amorous couples in the Delta back then was the turnrow. For the uninitiated, a turnrow is actually a small road at the end of a row of cotton or soy beans where a tractor turns around after having plowed a row.

turns, call the v phr Cf **call figures**

In dancing: to announce the figures or movements the dancers are to execute.

1915 *Mt. Democrat* (Placerville CA) 27 Mar 2/2, Hand . . still retains the lyric tones in which he was wont to 'call the turns' in harmony with the orchestral key. **1938** in Lib. of Congress *Amer. Memory: WPA Life Hist.* (Internet) **NE,** We used to go to dances a good deal and they would call the turns, such as 'Do-C-Do, Three in the Kitchen, Five in the hall, Do-C-Do- to your best partner and balance all!' **1940** Writers' Program *Guide GA* 127, To the accompaniment of fiddle, banjo, or guitar, the Georgia cracker sings old ballads, . . or "calls the turns" for spirited breakdowns at country dances.

turn shovel n Also *turning shovel* **chiefly Sth** Cf **turning plow, twister 1**

A plow shovel formed so as to throw the soil to one side; a **shovel plow** equipped with such a shovel; hence n *turn-shovel plow.*

1847 *S. Cultivator* 5.123 **Sth,** I have never used or wanted to use the turning-shovel since. . . Every body had them once. Since they have had an opportunity of comparing them with good turning-plows, I know of no one who uses them. **1849** Ibid 7.100 **AL,** I try to get back to give it [=corn] a second round [of cultivation] by running a small turn shovel. **1861** in 2006 *DARE* File—Internet **neMS,** 1 turning shovel plow, 1 hoe, and bull tongue. **1883** GA Dept. Ag. *Pub. Circular No. 35* 8.26, *Preparation.*—The land was turned over in January with a one-horse turn-shovel. **1906** *S. Cultivator* 64.3.2 **Sth,** [Advt:] Cut to the left shows turn shovel with slot and lugs as used on a single plowstock. **c1937** in 1977 *Amer. Slave Suppl. 1* 1.426 **AL,** Mules and oxen were used to cultivate the land. The plows that were used were called "turn-shovel plows".

1951 *Delta Democrat–Times* (Greenville MS) 7 June 8/2, [Advt:] All-Purpose Cultivator. . . Complete with turn shovel. **1964** *Ibid* 5 Apr 6/8, [Advt:] Right & Left Turn Shovel. **2006** *DARE* File—Internet **IL**, The Optional Turning Shovel Kit consists of the 3 turning shovels and mounting hardware. . . Turning Shovels act similar to a moldboard plow and turn the sod ribbon to the side. *Ibid* **NEng**, This Push Plow Turn Shovel is one of many top quality items.

turnt See **turn** v A

turn tag n
=**cross tag.**
1953 Brewster *Amer. Nonsinging Games* 66 **Sth**, *Cross Tag.* . . This is like the usual Tag, except that, if another player runs between the tagger and his intended quarry, the tagger must then try to tag the one who did the crossing. In the South the game is sometimes known as Turn Tag.

'turn thanks, 'turn thanks over (or to) the table See **return thanks**

turn the cat See **turn** v C5

turnverein n Also *turner verein* [Ger, literally "gymnastic society"] Cf **turner** n[1]
A club or society devoted primarily to fostering health and physical education, esp gymnastics, along with civic, educational, social, and cultural activities.
[**1850** *Milwaukee Sentinel & Gaz.* (WI) [27 Apr 2]/4 (newspaperarchive.com), In all parts of Germany, societies for gymnastical exercises are organized, so called "Turnverein." . . Mr. *Schultz*, a gentleman who took an active part in the last revolutionary movement in Southern Germany, . . has settled in our city, and made all arrangements . . to instruct in gymnastical exercises.] **1852** *Sun* (Baltimore MD) 5 Aug 1/6, The German Social Turnverein (Gymnastic Society) of Trenton, celebrate their anniversary on the 16th inst. **1859** (1931) DeLong *Jrls.* 10.44 **NY**, Went to a Turn Verein Ball in the evning and had a hell of a time dancing with the Dutch gal's. **1874** *Amer. Cyclop.* 8.352, In 1848 the political condition of Europe enabled the turnvereins to be reorganized, and the German emigration to the United States has brought these institutions with it. . . The organization, as first established, was confined to the practice of bodily exercises conducive to physical development; but it soon assumed a higher scope, without neglecting its original object; libraries were collected, schools were established, a newspaper . . was founded, and various arrangements were made for the diffusion of useful knowledge and for mental culture. **1875** King *Gt. South* 158 **TX**, There, too, the Turnverein takes its exercise; and in a long hall, dozens of children waltz. **1892** *Harper's New Mth. Mag.* 85.104 **MT**, There is a cricket club there, and a rod-and-gun club, and a strong Turnverein, or German athletic society. **1918** *Capital Times* (Madison WI) [18 June 8]/3 (newspaperarchive.com), About twenty men of the Madison Turnverein were honored at the Turner Hall when the service flag was dedicated. **1926** *Appleton Post–Crescent* (WI) 1 Sept 8/3 **ceWI** (as of c1900), The Appleton Turner Verein was at that time one of the most active in the state. **1938** *Oakland Tribune* (CA) 17 Feb 13/1, Oakland Turnverein To Give Masquerade. **1949** *MN Hist.* 1.26, The Cincinnati Turnverein built the first Turner Hall in the United States in 1850. **1973** Flach *Yankee German-America* 73 **csTX**, We found some gymnastic apparatus in a dark corner of the bowling alley, which had once been a Turnverein. . . In Chicago we had lived near the North Side Turnverein and we sometimes went there to watch those gorgeous Olympic gymnasts. **1997** *Daily Herald* (Arlington Heights IL) 1 Sept sec 5 3/5, The Elgin Turnverein (Turners), a German-American organization, holds the distinction of being Elgin's oldest club, having started in 1883. **2007** *DARE* File—Internet, *Denver Turnverein.* . . Join us for dancing or singing!

turpentine n, v Pronc-spp *tarpentine, teppentime, tup'mtime, tuppentime, tup(pe)ntine, turkemtime, turkentime, turpentime, turp'mtime*

A Std sense, var forms.
1840 *S. Lit. Messenger* 6.772 **Sth**, He larfs when I gives my chickins speerits of turpentime. **1843** (1916) Hall *New Purchase* 420 **IN**, Dipt in tarpentine—don't you smell it? **1869** *Coshocton Democrat* (OH) 3 Aug 1/7 **SC** [Black], De gemman . . talk like he swallud a pint ob tuppentine. **1880** (1881) Harris *Uncle Remus Songs* 7 **GA** [Black], Brer Fox . . got'im some tar en mix it wid some turkemtime. **1899** (1912) Green *VA Folk-Speech* 461, *Turkemtime.* . . Turpentine. *Turkentine.* **1899** Chesnutt *Conjure Woman* 49 **csNC** [Black], Fer ter let de tuppentime run. **1914** *DN* 4.82 **ME, nNH**, *Turpentime.* Var. of *turpen-*

tine. **1922** Gonzales *Black Border* 336 **sSC, GA coasts** [Gullah glossary], *Tup'mtime[b] tup'ntine*—turpentine. **1941** *Jrl. Amer. Folkl.* 54.69 **eTN**, The potion was "turkentime," as one fifteen year old boy pronounced it. **1948** Hurston *Seraph* 6 **FL** [Black], The dose of three "draps" of "teppentime on sugar." **1965–70** [see **B** below]. **1966–68** *DARE* Tape **FL**19, The only work they [=Black people] could get to make any money was . . dipping turpentine, they call it; **GA**22, I quit turp'mtiming in 1911.

B As noun.
=**pitch** n[1]. [*OED2* 1576 →] Note: This sense remains in technical use, but in popular use *turpentine* usu refers to the distillate formerly and still technically called *spirits* (or *oil*) *of turpentine.* **formerly widespread, now chiefly Sth, S Midl** See Map Cf **rosin B1a, tar** n B1
1634 Wood *New Engl. Prospect* 17, The Firre and Pine bee trees that . . doe afford good masts, good board, Rozin and Turpentine. **1694** in 1886 Sewall *Letter-Book* 1.142 **MA**, I have sent you . . five Barrels of Turpentine. **1743** *Amer. Mag. & Hist. Chron.* Sept 44 **SC**, *Prices of Goods* at Charlestown, South-Carolina. . . Pitch per Barrel 30 s. . . Turpentine 12 s. 6d. **1784** in 1785 Amer. Acad. Arts & Sci. *Memoirs* 1.394, The husbandmen of *New-Jersey* . . shave the bark from the pine trees in the latter part of winter, and in the spring, the turpentine running down over that part of the tree which has been barked, fills the pores. **1848** *Scientific Amer.* 3.218, The first turpentine which flows is called virgin turpentine. . . The sap is distilled like malt and the result is turpentine and rosin and tar. **1859** Perry *Turpentine Farming* 124 **NC**, Turpentine is a sort of sticky mucilage, partly composed of water: when it first comes to the air it looks as clear as a christal. **1965–70** *DARE* (Qu. T7, *The sticky stuff that comes out of pine trees*) 43 Infs, **chiefly Sth, S Midl**, Turpentine; **DE**5, ['tɝ.pm,taɪn]; **GA**46, ['tɝ.pɪntɪn]; **MD**36, ['tɝ.pm,taɪm]; (Qu. T8, *Joints of pine wood that burn easily and make good fuel*) Inf **MS**21, Turpentine knots. **1966** *DARE* Tape **GA**7, We have a small iron instrument; we call it a turpentine spoon. . . We take that cup off and put one end of it on a bucket and take that spoon and push it out. It's mighty thick; **SC**10, Turpentine still been right over there. . . that cooked the turpentine. **1986** Pederson *LAGS Concordance*, 1 inf, **csGA**, Best to start a fire with turpentine chips; 1 inf, **swGA**, Turpentine cutter—three-cornered file; 1 inf, **cwAL**, Fresh turpentine—put on a cut when in the woods.

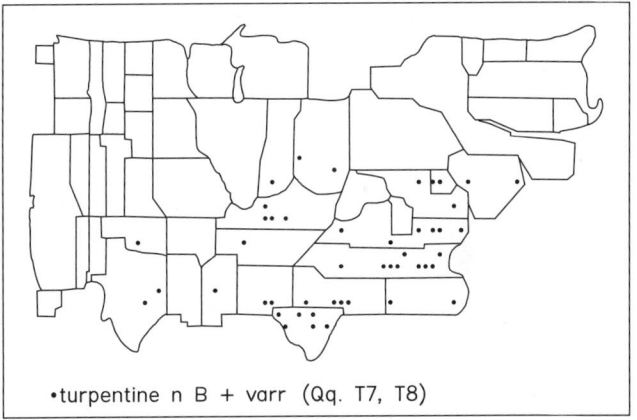

•turpentine n B + varr (Qq. T7, T8)

C As verb.
To collect or distill **turpentine** n **B**; to use (land or trees) for such purposes; hence vbl n *turpentining*; ppl adj *turpentined.* **chiefly Sth**
1862 Gilmore *Among the Pines* 247 **NC**, The young Cunnel backed my paper, and set me a runnin' at turpentining. **1891** *Sandusky Daily Reg.* (OH) 23 Mar [4]/6 (newspaperarchive.com) **FL**, The place was in the pine woods, which had been "logged," "turpentined" and then burnt over for grass. **1914** *Forest & Stream* 83.516 **SC**, [Advt:] During the closed season the lands could be farmed and the timber turpentined. **1933** Rawlings *South Moon* 140 **FL**, Zeke's figgerin' on turpentinin' if he cain't git nothin' else. **1966–68** [see **A** above]. **1968–69** *DARE* Tape **GA**25, We didn't know what flour bread was until the turpentining come through this section; **GA**50A, The thing about that and made that pine so much better . . in that swamp, it never had been turpentined. **1981** in 2006 (acc) U.S. Forest Serv. *S. Research Station* (Internet) **FL**, [Caption:] No more . . wasted timber as a result of turpentining. A turpentined tree . . is shown entering a German gang-saw. **2000**

Humphreys *Nowhere* 3 **seNC,** His daughter . . learned turpentining at his side.

turpentine adj
Of the backwoods; rustic.

1958 Humphrey *Home from the Hill* 124 **neTX,** A country man, emboldened by the sunshine, dared invade upper Main Street and disturb the quality's rest so early, his mule clop-clopping on the bois-d'arc bricks and he chanting in a nasal, backwoods, but not unmusical voice, a real turpentine twang.

turpentine broom n
A shrub or undershrub of the genus *Thamnosma,* esp *T. montana,* native to much of the southwestern US. Also called **desert-rue;** for other names of var spp see **Dutchman's breeches 3, turpentine bush b**

1925 Jepson *Manual Plants CA* 605, *T[hamnosma] montana. . . Turpentine Broom. . .* Stems freely branching broom-like, yellowish green, . . herbage heavily odorous. . . Dry or stony hills in the desert region. **1945** Benson–Darrow *Manual SW Trees* 210, *Thamnosma. Turpentine Broom.* Herbs or shrubs. . . *Thamnosma montana. . . Turpentine Broom.* **1960** Vines *Trees SW* 593, *Thamnosma texana. . .* is also known under the vernacular names of Turpentine Bloom [sic], because of the aromatic odor, or Dutchman's Breeches, for the oddly shaped fruit. **2003** *DARE* File—Internet **CA,** *Thamnosma montana* (turpentine broom) is a small desert shrub.

turpentine bush n SW
Any of several often similar composite plants or shrubs that are woody at the base and have resinous herbage, as:

a also *turpentine brush:* A **rabbit brush 1b** (here: *Ericameria laricifolia*).

1945 Benson–Darrow *Manual SW Trees* 323, *Haplopappus laricifolius* [=*Ericameria l.*] . . Turpentine bush is common on rocky mountain slopes. . . The plant is remarkably resinous, and the crushed foliage emits an odor similar to turpentine. **1959** Munz–Keck *CA Flora* 1183, *H[aplopappus] laricifolius. . . Turpentine-Brush.* **1960** Vines *Trees SW* 1006, *Haplopappus laricifolius. . .* A very handsome plant in bloom with its crown of yellow flowers. It is highly resinous with a turpentine-like odor which gives it the name of Turpentine Bush in some localities. **2006** Miller *Landscaping Native Plants TX* 111, *Ericameria laricifolia. . .* The aromatic leaves give the plant its other common name, turpentine bush.

b A **turpentine broom** (here: *Thamnosma montana*).

1937 Chicago Acad. Sci. *Program* 8.10 **AZ,** The dark blue blossoms of the turpentine bush (*Thamnosma montana*) were nearly all replaced by grayish-green fruit which . . gave off its aromatic odor. **1998** *Rangelands* 20.4.6 **Desert SW,** *Non-forage species* were turpentine bush (*thamnosma montana*), banana yucca [etc]. **1998** in 2003 *DARE* File—Internet **NV,** *Turpentine Bush (Thamnosma). . .* Extract from boiled stems and leaves were used [by the Paiute] as cold medicine. **1999** *Ibid* **CA,** *Astragalus jaegerianus* . . preferred. . . using its host shrub as a trellis to gain full exposure to sunlight while obtaining protection from predators by its host, usually a leafless species, such as turpentine bush (*Thamnosma montana*).

c A **goldenweed 1;** see quots.

2003 *DARE* File—Internet **AZ,** There are several woody shrubs that bloom in late fall. Most are composites such as turpentine bush (Isocoma tenuisecta) and desert broom (Baccharis sarothroides).

d =**snakeweed b(6).**

2003 *DARE* File—Internet **AZ,** Gutierrezia (Turpentine Bush).

turpentined See turpentine v C

turpentine pine n
=**longleaf pine 1.**

1811 *MD Gaz.* (Annapolis) 20 Mar [5]/4, [Advt:] The subscribers will contract for 1,000 feet *Wharf Logs,* to be hewed or sawed square . . of good yellow or turpentine pine, oak or poplar. **1856** in 1861 Olmsted *Cotton Kingdom* 177 **NC,** It was right cheerful to open the door . . into a large room, filled with blazing light from a great fire of turpentine pine. **1862** Gilmore *Among the Pines* 239 **NC,** Scattered over it [=a campground] were about forty small but neat log cottages, thatched with the long leaves of the turpentine pine, and chinked with branches of the same tree. **1896** Mohr–Roth *Timber Pines* 28 **NC,** *Pinus palustris. . . Local or Common Names. . .* Turpentine Pine. **1967** Jahoda *Other FL*

48, Fat pine, turpentine pine, southern and yellow and hard and heart and broom and pitch pine: all are the names people have given to the straight, bushy longleaf. **1970** *DARE* (Qu. T17, . . *Kinds of pine trees;* not asked in early QRs) Inf **PA234,** Turpentine pine. **2003** *DARE* File—Internet, Fat wood is available in small bags, or in boxes from Menards, Home Depot, fireplace shops, etc. It is pieces of turpentine pine.

turpentine weed n

1 also *turpentine plant:* A **rosinweed 1,** usu *Silphium laciniatum.* [From the resinous herbage]

1819 *Western Rev.* 1.95 **KY,** Among the most remarkable and singular [plants is]. . . *Silphium therebinthaceum,* Turpentine weed. **1877** *Galaxy* 23.562, *The Compass Plant. . .* is known scientifically as *silphium lacinatum* [sic], popularly as pilot weed, rosin weed, and turpentine weed. **1901** Lounsberry *S. Wild Flowers* 517, The whole genus [= *Silphium*] . . is possessed of a resinous juice, which especially of the species Silphium laciniatum, is obtained and considerably used by country people. *S[ilphium] laciniatum,* . . turpentine weed, . . is unusually rich in resin. **1914** Georgia *Manual Weeds* 447, Turpentine Weed. . . is a vigorous, grossly feeding weed, . . four to twelve feet tall, bristly-rough, and sticky with resinous juices. **1959** Carleton *Index Herb. Plants* 119, *Turpentine-plant. . .* Silphium laciniatum.

2 A **tickseed 1** (here: *Coreopsis gigantea*) native to California.

1898 *Jrl. Amer. Folkl.* 11.230 **CA,** *Leptosyne gigantea* [=*Coreopsis g.*] . . turpentine weed.

3 A **blue curls 1** (here: either *Trichostema lanceolatum* or *T. laxum*).

1890 CA Ag. Exper. Sta. *Rept. for 1888–89* 30, A weed commonly called "turpentine-weed" (*Trichostema*) [grows in Fresno County]. **1911** Jepson *Flora CA* 354, *T[richostema] laxum. . . Turpentine Weed. . .* Stream beds or low summer fields of the North Coast Ranges. **1920** Pellett *Amer. Honey Plants* 41, *Trichostema lanceolatum. . .* is a plant known by a great variety of names in California. . . as vinegar weed, . . turpentine weed [etc]. . . Both foliage and flowers have a pungent, penetrating odor. **1961** Peck *Manual OR* 671, *T[richostema] laxum. . . Turpentine Weed. . .* Open stony ground, Umpqua and Rogue River Valleys to Calif.

4 =**snakeweed b(6),** usu *Gutierrezia microcephala* or *G. sarothrae.*

1913 (1979) Barnes *Western Grazing* 236, There is a little green weed (Guttierrezia [sic]) known locally as snakeweed, fireweed, turpentine weed. **1937** U.S. Forest Serv. *Range Plant Hdbk.* B85, Broom snakeweed [=*Gutierrezia sarothrae*], often known as . . turpentine-weed and yellow-top, is a half-shrub with woody roots, crowns and stem bases. **1968** Schmutz et al. *Livestock-Poisoning Plants AZ* 40, Turpentineweed (*Gutierrezia microcephala*). . . Turpentineweed (*Gutierrezia sarothrae*). . . Snakeweeds are low, perennial half-shrubs growing 1 to 2 feet tall. They are many-branched and quite resinous. **1969** *DARE* (Qu. S21, . . *Weeds . . that are a trouble in gardens and fields*) Inf **TX66,** Turpentine weed—bushy plant, no stem. **2002** *DARE* File—Internet **NM,** Herders make inspiring companions commenting on the way the turpentine weed overruns the pasture land.

5 An umbelliferous plant (*Pteryxia terebinthinus*) native in much of the western US.

[**1973** Hitchcock–Cronquist *Flora Pacific NW* 324, Turpentine c[ymopterus]. . . *Cymopterus terebinthinus* [=*Pteryxia t.*].] **1997** *Oecologia* 111.211, *Lomatium* (biscuit root) and *Cymopterus* [= *Pteryxia*] (turpentine weed) are frequent hosts [of *P[apilio] zelicaon*] used throughout eastern Washington, eastern Oregon, Idaho, and scattered areas of California, Nevada, Utah, and Colorado.

turpentining See turpentine v C

turpin See terrapin

turp'mtime See turpentine

tur(rah) See tother

turrecly See directly

turrer See tother

turret n |ˈtɝɪt| [Var of *terret,* either continuing an older form (*OED2 toret, turret* sb. "*Obs.* or *dial.*") or by folk-etym]

1823 Cooper *Pioneers* 1.4 **NY,** Huge saddles . . supported four high, square-topped turrets, through which the stout reins led from the mouths of the horses to the hands of the driver. **1868** *Scientific Amer.* 18.11, M.A. Gates, Troy, Pa. I claim the combination of the check rein hook, B, strap, C, turret ring, A, [etc] . . with each other. **1917** *DN* 4.401 neOH, *Terret* ['tɜ·ɪt]. . . A supporting ring for a rein on a harness. I have not heard ['tɛrɪt]. Also N.Y., Kan. **1930** Shoemaker *1300 Words* 62 cPA Mts (as of c1900), *Turrets*—Rings through which reins are passed on the saddle of a harness: terrets. **2005** *DARE* File—Internet CA, [Advt:] *Driving Reins.* . . Swivel bolt snaps with rounded ends will go thru turrets and D rings as small as 1″. *Ibid* ME, [Advt:] *Deluxe Nylon Harness, $250.00.* . . Deep gullet, metal tree; Neck Strap Turrets; Padded Girth.

turret spider n

1 A burrowing **wolf spider** (here: *Geolycosa* spp). [See quot 1883]
    1884 *Acad. Nat. Sci. Philadelphia Proc. for 1883* 131, The Rev. Dr. H.C. McCook exhibited nests of *Tarentula arenicola* . . , a species of ground-spider, of the family Lycosidæ, popularly known as the Turret Spider. These nests . . are surmounted by structures which quite closely resemble miniature old-fashioned chimneys, composed of mud and crossed sticks. **1884** (1885) McCook *Tenants* 129 PA, I stooped . . and pointed out a little structure of straw that marked the cave of a turret spider, *Tarentula arenicola*. **1931** *Sun* (Baltimore MD) 2 May 10/6 (Hench Coll.), The turret or burrowing spider belongs to the family of hunters called *Lycosidae*, known as wolf spiders, and this branch of the family receives its name from the watch tower or turret constructed around the mouth of the burrow. **1947** Carr *Desert Parade* 59 SW, *Wolf spider, turret spider:* When walking over the desert in various types of localities, one frequently observes little turrets, or "raised holes," about the size of a five-cent piece or larger. . . Excavation with a shovel will reveal a large grayish-yellow spider. . . The excavator may well be a wolf, or turret-building, hunting spider, which pursues and captures insects in a "wolf-like" fashion.

2 A spider *(Atypoides riversi)* native to California. [See quot 1980]
    1957 *Amer. Mercury* 84.54, Another burrower is *Atypoides riversi*, the common turret spider, who camouflages her chimney or turret with vegetation. **1980** Milne–Milne *Audubon Field Guide Insects* 868, *Turret Spider (Atypoides riversi).* . . Spider constructs silk-lined burrow in soil and by elongating the silk lining builds a turretlike opening, which often incorporates debris. **2008** Haff et al. *Nat. Hist. UC Santa Cruz* 188 cCA, One of the most secretive invertebrates of the redwood forest—the California turret spider.

turrible See **terrible**

turruh See **tother**

tursh See **tush** n A1

turtle n   Usu |'tɜ·tl|; also **chiefly Sth, S Midl** |'tɜ(r)kl̩, 'tʌkl̩| Pronc-spp *torkle, tuckil, turkle*   Cf **turtledove, turtle witch**
A Forms.
    [**1629** in 1769 Hutchinson *Coll. Papers MA Bay* 40, This day we saw a fish called a turkle, a great and large shell fish, swimming above the water neere the ship.] **1770** in 1793 Edwards *Hist. Redemption* 467, Ojecketa, chief of the turkle tribe. **1834** Crockett *Narrative* 12 TN, I was certain his anger would hang on to him like a turkle does to a fisherman's toe. **1859** Taliaferro *Fisher's R.* 119 nwNC (as of 1820s), The preachin' didn't do me much good that day, sartin as a turkle fallin' off uv a log. **1867** Harris *Sut Lovingood Yarns* 243 TN, Wat wer es plum blind es ef his eyes wer two tuckil aigs. **1890** *AN&Q* 4.237 NEng, NJ, In New England, as well as in New Jersey, . . illiterate people often give the name *turkle* to the turtle or tortoise. **1893** Shands *MS Speech* 65, *Turkle.* . . Negro for *turtle*. **1903** *DN* 2.335 seMO, *Turkle*. **1907** *DN* 3.238 nwAR, seMO, *Turkle*. **1909** *DN* 3.384 eAL, wGA, *Turkle.* . . A negroism. **1911** *DN* 3.540 eKY, *Turkle*. **1938** FWP *Guide DE* 478, Watermen bring in snapping turtles . . speared with heavy barbed "turkle-progs." **1948** *WELS Suppl.* WI, Have you spotted the Kentuck settlement in Forest and Langlade counties? . . The old usages still hold with the older ones. *Torkle* for *turtle* [etc]. **1950** *WELS* WI, 9 Infs, Turkle [*DARE* Ed: second in frequency after *turtle*]; 1 Inf, Turkle—very small youngsters; 1 Inf, Turkle—occasional, jocular by some who may have heard this from people considered hicks. **1966–70** *DARE* (Qu. P24, . . *Kinds of turtles*) Inf KY44, Mud ['tɜ·kl̩]; TN22, Turtle is ['tɜ·kəl]; VA55, Sea turkle, green-fin turkle, diamond-backed turkle. **1966** *DARE* Tape SC15, See a sea turkle. . . That what sea turkle will do.

1969–70 *DARE* FW Addit MA68, Mud ['tʌkl̩]; VA47, Turkle Hole on Assateague where deer and ponies drink. **1991** Still *Wolfpen Notebooks* 66 sAppalachians, John M. went turkle hunting on Carr Creek yesterday.
B Sense.
Also *turtle-deck* (or *-hull, -shell*): The trunk or trunk lid of an automobile. **formerly widespread, now chiefly Lower Missip Valley, TX, OK**
    [**1906** *Atlanta Constitution* (GA) [18 Nov 26]/2 (newspaperarchive.com), It seems as if motor cars are to fall into two main classes, the full-fledged touring car . . and the fish-tail or turtle-back runabout.] **1907** *Trenton Eve. Times* (NJ) 18 May 9/1, [Advt:] Winton Model C, 1905, with tonneau and turtle deck, lamps, etc.; will sell for $550. **1928** *Appleton Post-Crescent* (WI) 24 May 20/1, [Advt:] 1926 Ford Roadsters in A-1 mechanical condition either with steel box or with turtle deck. **1950** *WELS Suppl.* WI, *Turtle*—The back of a one-seated car (esp Model T Ford). *Ibid, Turtle*—Trunk of a car. **1965–67** *DARE* FW Addit LA1, *Turtle-hull*—the trunk of a car. "He put that coon back there in the turtle-hull"; AR, TX, *Turtle-hull*—lid to the rear storage compartment of an automobile, a trunk lid—used by my wife, from Brinkley, AR; this is also used around my father's hometown of Gainesville, TX; OK, *Turtle-shell*—trunk lid of car. **1971** Green *Village Horse Doctor* 61 cwTX (as of 1940s), He drove up . . in my car, which had four new tires on the ground and a spare in the turtle. **1982** *Grit* (Williamsport PA) 4 July MS, [She] tells us in some parts of her region the trunk of a car is called a "turtle hull." **1995** *DARE* File MS, My 1950 Plymouth. . . had a huge very deep trunk (people sometimes referred to the trunks as "turtle shells") and no back seat. **2001** *Ibid* cTX, My grandmother (now deceased) always used turtle when referring to the trunk of a car and one of my aunts does as well. *Ibid* TX, During my years in Texas in the 1970's, I often heard "turtle" used for trunk in the Ft. Worth area. I will admit it was used among the Model T crowd mostly, but it was alive and well. **2004** Marler *Reflections on Life* 56 cLA (as of 1930s), *Turtle hull.* The trunk. **2006** *DARE* File—Internet OK, *Turtle hull*—The trunk of an automobile. *I travel with a first aid kit in my turtle hull.*

turtleback n [See quot 1979]
A plant of the genus *Psathyrotes*, esp *P. ramosissima*, native to desert regions of much of the southwestern US.
    1941 Jaeger *Wildflowers* 306 Desert SW, Velvet Rosette. *Psathyrotes ramosissima.* . . The rounded "cushions," suggesting the common name, "turtle back," are sometimes almost a foot across. **1979** Spellenberg *Audubon Guide N. Amer. Wildflowers W. Region* 383, *Turtleback; Desert Velvet (Psathyrotes ramosissima).* . . The plants form mounds resembling the shape of a turtle's shell, with the intermeshed leaves even fancied to represent its scales. **1995** *Smithsonian* Mar 80 Desert SW, [Caption:] At the top right is desert velvet, also known as turtleback. **2001** CA Native Plant Soc. Bristlecone Chapter *Newsletter* May 2 CA, Also blooming were *Nama demissum* (purple mat) . . and *Psathyrotes ramosissima* (turtleback) whose leaves always remind me of African violets.

turtlebloom See **turtlehead**

turtle-deck See **turtle** B

turtledove n   Also *turkeldove, turkledove* [*OED2 turtle* c1000 →, *turtle-dove* a1300 → for the European dove *Streptopelia turtur*] **now esp Missip Valley, Sth** See Map on p. 762
=mourning dove 1.
    1674 in 1889 Gt. Brit. Pub. Rec. Office *Calendar State Papers Colonial Ser. Amer. for 1669–1674* 7.581, [In] Maine. . . the islands and woods yield swarms of birds, . . pigeons, thrushes, turtle-doves, swans [etc]. **1709** (1967) Lawson *New Voyage* 146 NC, Turtle Doves are here very plentiful; they devour the Pease; for which Reason, People make Traps and catch them. **1791** Bartram *Travels* 11 GA, Moon-light nights, filled with the melody of the chearful mockbird . . and plaintive turtle dove. **1841** Catlin *Letters Indians* 1.158, The mourning or turtledove, . . being, as they call it, a *medicine-bird*, is not to be destroyed or harmed by any one. **1851** Hooper *Widow Rugby's Husband* 95 AL, My honey, my love / My turkle dove. **1893** Shands *MS Speech* 65, *Turkledove* is the common name given by negroes to the *turtle-dove*. **1934** Vines *Green Thicket* 61 cnAL, But Cindy loved the old *turkledove* best. **1954** *Harder Coll.* cwTN, Turtledove (turkel). . . Mourning dove. **c1960** *Wilson Coll.* csKY, Turtle dove. . . The Mourning Dove, undoubtedly influenced by the Bible. **1965–70** *DARE* (Qu. Q7, *Names and*

nicknames for . . game birds) 19 Infs, **scattered, but esp Missip Valley, Sth,** Turtledove; **GA**3, Turkledove; (Qu. Q8) Infs **IL**143, **OH**70, Turtle-dove; (Qu. Q14) Infs **IN**69, **KY**65, 76, **MD**36, **PA**198, **WA**18, Turtle-dove.

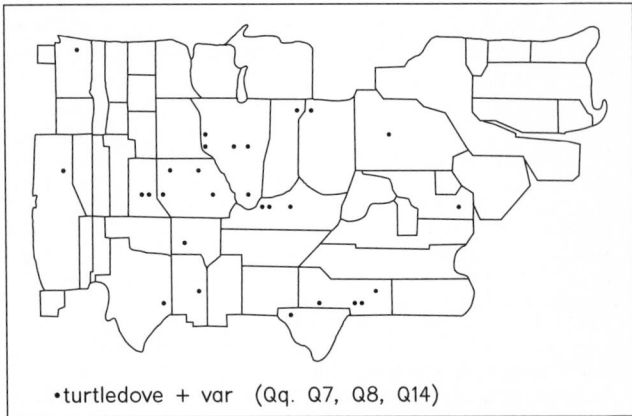

•turtledove + var   (Qq. Q7, Q8, Q14)

turtle grass n

A **pondweed** (here: *Potamogeton perfoliatus*).

1926 *Torreya* 26.4 **eVA,** *Potamogeton perfoliatus*. . . Turkle (turtle) grass.

turtlehead n   Also *turtle bloom*

Std: a plant of the genus *Chelone,* esp *C. glabra.*   Also called **fish head 1.**   For other names of var spp see **balmony 1, bitter herb, fishmouth, hummingbird weed, rheumatism root e, salt-rheum weed, shellflower 1, snakehead 1, snakemouth 2**   Cf **moccasin mouth**

turtle-hull (or -shell)   See **turtle B**

turtle witch n   Pronc sp *tarkle witch*

=**hermit thrush 1.**

1959 *Names* 7.112 **NC** [Black], Tarkle (i.e. turtle) witch, a negro name for the hermit thrush in North Carolina.

tush n   Usu |tʌš|; for addit pronc and sp varr see **A** below   Cf **tusk** n[1], **tusher 1**

A   Pronc forms.

1 |tɜ(r)š|; pronc-sp *tursh.*   **chiefly SE, sAppalachians**   See Map

1805 (1905) Lewis *Orig. Jrls. Lewis & Clark Exped.* 7.126 **KY,** Killed a panther on an Island. it . . was 7½ feet long, & of a redish coulour the turshes [tusks] long the tallants [talons] large.   **1940** in 1944 *ADD* swPA, nWV, [tɚʃ(ɪz)] tursh(es). Old illit. speaker.   **1965–70** *DARE* (Qu. K57) 17 Infs, **chiefly SE, sAppalachians,** Turshes; **AL**29, **IL**134, Tursh; (Qu. X12) Infs **IN**19, **OH**53, Turshes.   **1967** *Hall Coll.* eTN, He [=a hog] stuck a tursh right in this heel.   **1968** *DARE* FW Addit **VA**27, ['tɚšɪz]—rattlesnake fangs.   **1989** Pederson *LAGS Tech. Index* 134 **Gulf Region,** *Tusks* [Six infs gave [tɜ(r)š] for the sg; for the pl, 15 infs gave proncs of the types ['tɜ(r)šɪz] and 5 [tɜ(r)š].]   **1995** McCormack *Fields Pastures* 51 **cwAL** (as of 1960s) [Black], He better watch them tooth turshes. That hawg's liable to cut him bad!

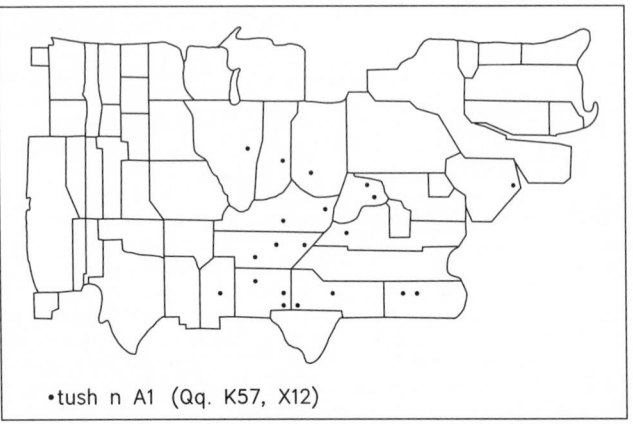

•tush n A1 (Qq. K57, X12)

2 |tɛš|; pronc-sp *tesh.*

1867 Lowell *Biglow* lxxi '**Upcountry' MA,** *U* changes in many words to *e*, always in *such, brush, tush,* [etc].   **1900** *Lincoln Eve. News* (NE) 4 Apr 6/7 **KS,** The handles wuz pure elephant teshes.   **1967** *DARE* (Qu. K57) Inf **MO**37, Teshes.   **1989** Pederson *LAGS Tech. Index* 134 **Gulf Region,** *Tusks* [Two infs gave proncs of the type [tɛšɪz].]

3 |tʌč|, |tɜ(r)č|; pronc-sp *tutch.*

1965–70 *DARE* (Qu. K57) Infs **DC**5, **FL**48, **LA**22, **MS**81, **MO**16, **SC**34, **VA**70, [Proncs of the type ['tʌči]]; **DC**8, [tʌč]; **MD**18, ['tɜčɪz]. [5 of 9 total Infs Black]   **1989** Pederson *LAGS Tech. Index* 134 **Gulf Region,** *Tusks* [Two infs gave [tʌč] and one [tɜč] for the sg; for the pl, 17 infs gave proncs of the type ['tʌčɪz], 2 [tʌč] and 1 [tɜčɪz].]   **1999** [see **B** below].

4 |tuš|; for addit varr see quots.

1966–70 *DARE* (Qu. K57) Infs **OK**52, **TX**66, ['tušɪz]; **NC**37, [tu⁀š] **IL**114, ['tušɪz]; **NC**68, [tʌš] or [taš]; **AL**2, ['tɑšəz].   **1989** Pederson *LAGS Tech. Index* 134 **Gulf Region,** *Tusks* [Four infs gave proncs of the types [tuš, tɤš] and 1 [tuš] for the sg; for the pl, 8 infs gave proncs of the types ['tušɪz, 'tɤšɪz], 2 ['tɑšɪz], and 1 [tɔš].]

5   pronc-sp *tosh.*

1957 Combs *Lang. S. Highlanders* **sAppalachians,** Tosh—var of *tusk.*

B   Gram forms.

Pl: usu *tushes* (and analogous forms for the varr recorded in **A** above); also *tush* (and analogous forms).

1965–70 *DARE* (Qu. K57, *The big teeth that stick out of a boar's mouth*) 59 Infs, **chiefly Sth, Midl,** Tush; **AL**29, **IL**134, Tursh; **DC**8, Tutch; **NC**37, [tu⁀š]; **NC**68, [taš]; (Qu. X12, . . *Large front teeth that stick out of the mouth*) Infs **AR**47, **FL**15, **IN**26, **LA**40, **NC**3, **VA**46, 48, Tush; **SC**70, Hog tush. [*DARE* Ed: Although both questions were phrased to elicit the pl, it is not certain that all these resps were in fact intended as pl.]   **1976** [see **C** below].   **1989** Pederson *LAGS Tech. Index* 134 **Gulf Region,** *Tusks* [The usual pl corresponding to sg *tush* was *tushes* (252 infs, proncs of the type ['tʌšɪz]); 37 infs used [tʌš] as the pl; 5 [tɜ⁀š, tɜš], 2 [tʌč], and 1 [tɔš].]   **1999** *Jrl. Engl. Ling.* 27.279 **neGA,** *Tusk. . . tushes . .* occurred six times [out of 32 resps]. . . The corpus contains in addition a single example of *tush* as plural. . . Two forms not recorded in *LAMSAS* are *tuft* [1 inf] . . and *tutch* [2 infs].   **2002** *DARE* File **AL,** "Tush"—A way of pronouncing "tusks". Used in the Tennessee Valley of North Alabama.

C   Senses.

1   A pointed or protruding tooth; a tusk, fang.   [From OE *tusc;* the more common metathesized OE *tux* is the ancestor of *tusk*]   **formerly widespread, now chiefly Sth, W Midl, Cent, TX; scattered NEast, Gt Lakes**   See Map

1781 Peters *Genl. Hist. CT* 251, The Cuba I suppose to be peculiar to New-England. The male is of the size of a large cat, has four long tushes sharp as a razor.   **1816** *Adams Centinel* (Gettysburg PA) 3 Jan [2]/1 (newspaperarchive.com), The head [of the sea serpent] being pointed . . , with upper and lower tushes or teeth . . like the tush of a hog.   **1867** Harris *Sut Lovingood Yarns* 212 **TN,** I . . cross-bar'd his upper lip wif white, ontil hit looked like boars' tushes.   **1899** (1912) Green *VA Folk-Speech* 463, *Tush.* . . A long pointed tooth; a tusk.   **1913** Johnson *Highways St. Lawrence to VA* 67, Rattlesnakes have tushes that are just like cat's claws.   **1923** *DN* 5.223 **swMO,** *Tush.* . . Tusk.   **1929** Sale *Tree Named John* 50 **MS,** Brer Li-yon . . showed Brer Rabbit his tushes.   **1932** Randolph *Ozark Mt. Folks* 84, If you was t' run onto a ol' sow with young-uns she'd . . rip your guts loose with them big tushes.   **1950** *WELS* (*The big teeth that stick out of a boar's mouth*) 4 Infs, **WI,** Tush(es).   **1956** *Hall Coll.* eTN, Bear tushes. . . A bear's teeth.   **1965–70** *DARE* (Qu. K57, *The big teeth that stick out of a boar's mouth*) 275 Infs, **chiefly Sth, W Midl, Cent, TX; scattered NEast, Gt Lakes,** Tush(es) (and varr, for which see **A** above); (Qu. X12, . . *Large front teeth that stick out of the mouth*) 38 Infs, **chiefly Sth, S Midl,** Tush(es) (and varr); **SC**70, Hog tush; **KY**85, Tushes like a hog—big teeth; **VA**39, Tush teeth—large eye teeth.   **1966–68** *DARE* Tape **NJ**53, They would kill you, them boars. . . They would tear you to pieces, certainly. . . [T]heir tushes stuck right up this way out of their mouth; **SC**15, We call him a boar hog, he get behind me . . that thing would cut me, cut me in half, got tush-hook that long.   **1976** Allen *LAUM* 3.314 **Upper MW** (as of c1950), Twelve percent in the U[pper] M[idwest] maintain an older cognate form, *tushes* /tʌšɪz/, which is not derived from *tusks. Tushes* rather clearly has strong Midland orientation . . and seems to be recessive. . . Two infs. apply a reduction rule to *tushes,* one . . having /tʌš/ and the other . . /tɜš/.   **1976** Garber *Mountain-ese* 97 **sAppalachians,** *Tush* . . protruding tooth—Jamie had to go to the dentist to have a tush removed. **2002** *DARE* File—Internet **GA, NC,** The operant image is of a boar hog rooting up the receptive earth with his phallic tusks. ("Tushes" is one local dialect version of word "tusks". . .)

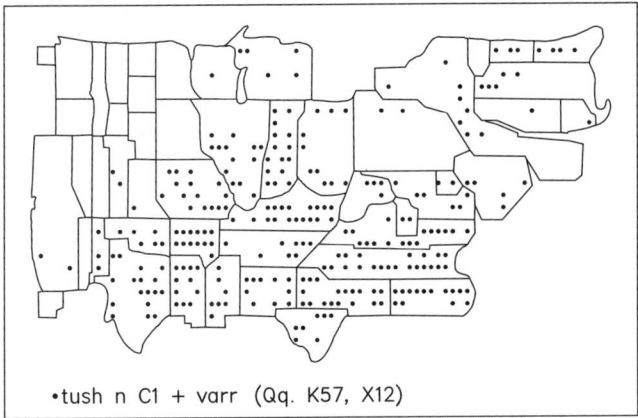

•tush n C1 + varr (Qq. K57, X12)

2 See quot. Cf **tush** adj **2, tush hog 3**
1960 Wentworth–Flexner *Slang* 557, *Tush.* . . A light complexioned Negro; a mulatto. *Negro use.* **1970** Major *Dict. Afro-Amer. Slang* 117, *Tush:* a wealthy, light-skinned society Negro.

tush adj [Prob by back-formation from **tush hog**]
1 See quot.
1934 *AmSp* 9.28 [Prison terms], *Tush* [Footnote: This word may be peculiar to the Negro.] Dangerous; belligerent.
2 See quot. Cf **tush** n **C2**
1960 Wentworth–Flexner *Slang* 557, *Tush.* . . Belonging to high society; wealthy, sophisticated and influential; ritzy. *Some Negro use.*

tusher n
1 =**tush** n **C1.** Cf **-er** affix **1**
1925 Benét *Tiger Joy* 52, There's a Pig in your garden,/ With silk bristles frizzy / And tushers of snow! **1966–70** *DARE* (Qu. K57, *The big teeth that stick out of a boar's mouth*) Infs **IL**108, 142, ['tʌšɚz]; **ME**22, ['tʌšə].
2 =**tush hog 1.** Cf **tusker**
1939 Clark *Rampaging Frontier* 210 **KY,** [John] Champion had a razorback sow which had mothered generation upon generation of long-snouted tushers. **1974** Farris *Sharp Practice* 190 **NC,** Big Plucky heard the tusher first as he rooted for mast beneath a lingonberry bush. **2007** *DARE* File—Internet **AL,** The thing to remember about a big boar hog is that he hasn't gotten big by being stupid. A big tusher is much like a buck that's 4-years old and scores 175 Boone & Crockett points. He's very elusive and hard to hunt. *Ibid* **MS,** The trophy boar trotted toward the young hog. . . But before I could get to a full-draw position, the big tusher had trotted behind the fallen tree.

tush hawk See **tush hog 3**

tush hog n [**tush** n **C1**]
1 A wild or feral hog with prominent tusks. **Sth, S Midl** Cf **razorback hog, tusher 2, tusker**
1934 Hurston *Jonah's Gourd Vine* 314 **AL,** *Tush hawg,* wild boar, very vicious, hence a tough character. The tusks of the wild boar curve out and are dangerous weapons. **1982** *Our Smokies Heritage Book 1* 67 **sAppalachians,** *Tush hog* . . a wild boar (because of its long, protruding tusks). **2001** TX Electric Cooperatives *TX Co-Op Power* Mar (Internet) **eTX,** Peacock had become increasingly active in the Big Thicket Association, formed in the 1950s to continue the long struggle to preserve some of the East Texas wilderness. . . [T]hose involved in the movement. . . nicknamed him "Tush Hog," a term usually reserved for the toughest ol' rooter in the woods. **2003** *DARE* File—Internet **AR,** [Caption:] Pro Staffer Bill Miller, Jr. with monster tush hog. *Ibid* **nwFL,** The fish camp is gone now, but then, there was . . a pen for dogs, Northwest Florida hog dogs, . . dogs that would charge a tush hog.
2 also attrib: A tough, aggressive person; a bully, rowdy. **Sth, S Midl** Cf **tush** adj **1**
1919 *Star* (Kansas City MO) 23 Oct 1/4 [Black], Williams said Mrs. McMullen was a "tush hog." . . Judge Porterfield inquired of Mrs. McMullen the definition of "tush hog." "Ah don' know, but Ah do

knows it means somethin' bad," she replied. **1925** in 1981 Lieb *Mother of the Blues* 111 **GA** [Black], Twenty years in the bottom, that ain't long to stay,/ If I can keep these tush-hog women from taking my man away. **1934** [see **1** above]. **1942** Perry *Texas* 134, In the sawmill communities a mean Negro is a "tush hog nigger." (Most long-tusked hogs are fighting hogs.) **1960** Weals *Hillbilly Dict.* 8 **sAppalachians,** *Tush hog.* . . A fighter, relentless, savage. Sometimes also applied to a man who is relentless in the pursuit and conquest of women. **1970** *DARE* FW Addit **TX,** He's a tush hog, meaning "he's mean or vicious." Inf—Timpson police officer, age 65, male, native of Timpson. **1978** *Wall St. Jrl.* (NY NY) 20 Jan 30/2 **AL,** "You've got some tush hogs in there," he says, using an old Southern term for vicious or tough characters. **1998** *Knoxville News–Sentinel* (TN) 17 Oct sec C 1 (Internet) **ceTN,** I'll just be glad when those 23 seniors they have graduate. Those tush-hog running backs they have . . run hard. **2006** *DARE* File—Internet **TX,** A tush-hog is. . . the person every Southern father has in mind when he tells his son, "Boy, there's some folks in this old world it just won't do to fart with."
3 also *tush hawk:* See quot. Cf **tush** adj **2, tush** n **C2**
1934 *AmSp* 9.289 **sePA** [Negro slang in Lincoln Univ.], *Tush hawk* (or *tush hawg*). A *city slicker;* a *big shot;* a sophisticated person with money, clothes, and a *line.*

tusk n¹ Usu |tʌsk|; for varr see **A** below Cf **tush** n
A Std sense, var forms.
1 |tʌs|. Note: For this as a plural form, see **Bb** below.
1920s in 1944 *ADD* **cNY,** [tʌs(k)], [tʌs(ks)] rather than tush(es). **1989** Pederson *LAGS Tech. Index* 134 **Gulf Region,** *Tusks* [For the sg, 68 infs gave [tʌsk] and 3 [tʌs]; for the pl, 4 infs gave proncs of the type ['tʌsɨz].]
2 |tus(k)|; for addit varr see quots.
1965–70 *DARE* (Qu. K57, *The big teeth that stick out of a boar's mouth*) Infs **CA**131, **MD**30, **MS**21, **NJ**6, 8, **PA**147, **RI**3, **WA**20, [Proncs of the type [tusks]]; **OH**4, [tusk]; **CA**99, 152, [tus]; **WI**14, 21, [tus]; **NY**155, [tæsks]. **1989** Pederson *LAGS Tech. Index* 134 **Gulf Region,** *Tusks* [For the pl, 3 infs gave proncs of the types [tʊsk(s)], 1 [tɜs], 1 ['tɜ·sɨz], and 1 [tɑs].]
3 |tʌks, tɜ·ks|. Cf Intro "Language Changes" I.1 Note: It is not clear whether these exx are sg or pl; perh the same form is used for both.
1965–70 *DARE* (Qu. K57, *The big teeth that stick out of a boar's mouth*) Infs **AL**7, **GA**93, **MS**46, [tʌks]; **MS**60, [tɜ·ks]. **1989** Pederson *LAGS Tech. Index* 134 **Gulf Region,** *Tusks* [Two infs, [tʌks].]
4 |tʌst|; pronc-sp *tust.* Cf Intro "Language Changes" IV.4
1966–68 *DARE* (Qu. K57, *The big teeth that stick out of a boar's mouth*) Infs **MI**27, **TX**4, 43, Tusts; **PA**137, Tust; [**MD**15, Tussets ['tʌsɨts]]. **1989** Pederson *LAGS Tech. Index* 134 **Gulf Region,** *Tusks* [For the pl, 6 infs gave [tʌst] and 1 [tʌsts].]
5 |tʌšk, tɜ·šk, tʌšt|. [Appar blend of **tusk** n¹ + **tush** n]
1966–68 *DARE* (Qu. K57, *The big teeth that stick out of a boar's mouth*) Infs **IN**49, **SC**1, [tʌšk]. **1989** Pederson *LAGS Tech. Index* 134 **Gulf Region,** *Tusks* [One inf gave [tʌšk], 1 [tɜ·šk], 1 [tʌštɨz].]
B Gram forms. Pl: usu *tusks* |tʌsks|; also: see below. Note: Only major forms are treated below; forms obviously corresponding to minor variant forms are included with them at **A** above.
a *tusk.*
1965–70 *DARE* (Qu. K57, *The big teeth that stick out of a boar's mouth*) 100 Infs, **scattered,** Tusk; (Qu. X12, . . *Large front teeth that stick out of the mouth*) Infs **MO**6, 35, **VA**2, Tusk. [*DARE* Ed: Although both questions were phrased to elicit the pl, it is not certain that all these resps were in fact intended as pl.] **1969** *DARE* Tape **TX**68, Jabalina is . . a small wild hog and they have great big teeth. . . And they've got these tusk. **1976** Allen *LAUM* 3.314 **Upper MW** (as of c1950), Tusks is pronounced with the full cluster by a large majority (71%). . . Seven percent reduce the cluster to /sk/, and 8%, mostly the least educated, reduce it to simple /s/, sometimes clearly lengthened. **1989** Pederson *LAGS Tech. Index* 134 **Gulf Region,** *Tusks* [For the pl, 112 infs offered proncs of the type [tʌsks], 155 of the type [tʌsk].] **1999** *Jrl. Engl. Ling.* 27.279 **neGA,** *Tusk* has six different plurals. As usual, the unmarked form occurs most commonly (sixteen of thirty-two . .). *Tusks* occurred six times . . in white upper-class and upper-middle-class usage. **2006** in 2007 *DARE* File—Internet **MS,** Those are some big tusk. **2007** *Ibid* **AL,** I arrowed a huge grey boar with Big tusk sticking out the sides of his mouth.

b |tʌs|.

1920s [see **A1** above]. **1965–70** *DARE* (Qu. K57, *The big teeth that stick out of a boar's mouth*) 59 Infs, **scattered,** [tʌs(·)]; [**NY24,** [trʌs]; **IN32,** ['tʌsɪs]; **OR4,** ['tʌsəs];] (Qu. X12, *. . Large front teeth that stick out of the mouth*) Infs **AR55, MI65, TN24,** [tʌs(·)]. **1976** [see **Ba** above]. **1989** Pederson *LAGS Tech. Index* 134 **Gulf Region,** Tusks [For the pl, 48 infs gave [tʌs].]

c |'tʌskɪz|.

1989 Pederson *LAGS Tech. Index* 134 **Gulf Region,** *Tusks* [For the pl, 5 infs gave ['tʌskɪz].]

tusk n² [*OED2* 1707 →] *obs*

=**cusk 1.**

1802 (1907) Bentley *Diary* 2.431 **MA,** Many tusk are taken, and an abundance of Cod, & particularly Haddock. **1814** in 1815 MA Hist. Soc. *Coll.* 2d ser 3.118 **NH,** The salmon trout, pickerel, eel, and cusk, . . or tusk, are the most plenty. **1867** De Voe *Market Asst.* 198, There is a large muscle-bank . . [which] abounds with sundry fish, such as . . tusk (cusk). **1884** Goode *Fisheries U.S.* 1.233, The name, "Tusk," used for this fish [=cusk] in Newfoundland, is now never used in the United States, although it seems to have been in use a century ago, a well-known fishing ground in the Gulf of Maine being known as the "Tusk Rock."

tusker n

=**tush hog 1.**

1891 *Outing* 19.119 **FL,** An enraged tusker utters a gruff cry, not unlike that of a grizzly bear. **1954** *Sportsman* 2.4.64, The big tuskers, those up to about 250 pounds classed as feral hogs, broadly speaking may be divided into three geographical classes. **2003** *DARE* File—Internet **TN,** [Caption:] Ken Moody with a big Tennessee Tusker.

tussel See **tassel**

tussick n¹ Also *tussock*

A pack or valise; see quots.

c1910 in 1944 *ADD* **MN,** *Tussick.* . . A satchel, valise, handbag, carpetbag. **1914** *DN* 4.82 **ME, nNH,** *Tussick.* . . Hand-bag, carpet-bag, valise. **1969** Sorden *Lumberjack Lingo* 133 **NEng, Gt Lakes,** *Tussock*— A packsack. Same as duffle bag, kennebecker, keister.

tussick n², **tussock** n¹ See **tussock liquor**

tussock n² See **tussick** n¹

tussock liquor n Also *tussick, tussock* [See quot 1940] **SC** Cf **stump liquor**

Illegally made whiskey.

1920 in 1993 Snowden–Bennett *Two Friends* 156 **SC,** James Fitz-James . . has not fed on "honey dew" or "the milk of Paradise"; his inspiration must have been the "tussick" of Newberry's back woods. **1940** McDavid *Coll.* **SC,** *Tussock* /tʌsɪk/—hummock in swamp. *Tussock, tussock liquor*—swamp-made moonshine. **1966–67** *DARE* (Qu. DD21c, *Nicknames for whiskey, especially illegally made whiskey*) Inf **SC26,** Tussock; **SC43,** Tussock, tussock liquor.

tust See **tusk** n¹ **A4**

tut See **toot** n²

tutch See **tush** n **A3**

tutchmonk, tutchmunk See **touchmonk**

tuther See **tother**

Tut (language) n Also *King Tut language* [From the name of the letter *t* in this "language"; later infl by the nickname *King Tut* given to the Pharaoh Tutankhamen soon after the discovery of his tomb in 1922] Cf **oodle-talk**

A disguised language formed by spelling words aloud using a special alphabet of letter names.

1893 Chrisman in *Science* 22.304 **TX,** One of the younger school-boys said to me: "I can talk so that you cannot understand me; I can talk Tut." *Ibid* 305, The name is usually given as Tut Language. . . The way to learn the language is to get the alphabet and then replace the letters of a word with those of the Tut alphabet. . . This young lady traced the origin of Tut Language as follows: She learned it from . . a negro girl, this girl learned it from a negro girl who got it at a female negro school at Austin, Texas, where it was brought by a negro girl from Galveston, Texas, who learned it from a negro girl who had come from Jamaica. . . Perhaps the most striking thing about this language is its close resemblance

to the alphabetic languages . . "Guitar Language," from Bonyhad, Hungary, "Bob Language," from Czernowitz, Austria, and "A-Bub-Cin-Dud Language," from Bergischen. **1898** Chrisman in *Century Illustr. Mag.* 56.54 **IL, TX,** These languages are found everywhere. . . A little Chicago girl playing on the beach at Galveston is delighted by her Texas friend saying to her in the Tut language: "Tuthushisus isus nunicuce susanundud" [=This is nice sand]. **1969** (1970) Angelou *Caged Bird* 138 **AR** [Black], We spent tedious hours teaching ourselves the Tut language. You (Yak oh you) know (kack nug oh wug) what (wack hash a tut). Since all the other children spoke Pig Latin, we were superior because Tut was hard to speak and even harder to understand. **1994** *AmSp* 69.111 **MA,** What they had been speaking was called Tut Language. She spoke the sounds /kʌtenʌndʌdyæk/. . . It spelled *candy*. She taught me to speak the sounds /hæšiskwerlʌlo/ 'hello' (the word *square* is said before a double letter). *Ibid* 112, My mother told me that she had learned Tut Language from her mother, who said it was a method devised by some African slaves in America to teach each other to spell—therefore, to read—at a time when reading by slaves was against the law. **2003** *DARE* File—Internet **nLA,** Barnes also demonstrated the "tut" language used by the black people of his home district when they did not want their activities known. **2005** *Ibid* **VA,** My grandmother spoke a made-up "King Tut language" with her school friends when she was young. . . Words are spoken by spelling them out.

tutor v Also with *up* [*EDD* tutor v 2. "To manage, handle; to humor, coax"] **esp sAppalachians, Ozarks**

1 To treat, manage.

1913 Kephart *Highlanders* 287 **sAppalachians,** I can make a hunderd pound o' pork outen that hog—tutor it jist right. **1931** *PMLA* 46.1304 **Appalachians,** Tutor hit up jist right, this old Ned (bacon) orter last a good span. **1995–97** in 2004 Montgomery-Hall *Dict. Smoky Mt. Engl.* 624 **eTN.**

2 To indulge, spoil (a child).

1927 *DN* 5.478 **Ozarks,** *Tutor.* . . To pamper, to indulge. "She jes' tutored up thet young-un till he aint wuth shucks fer nothin'." **1969** *DARE* (Qu. Z14a, *To give a child its own way or pay too much attention to it: "Everyone _____ that child."*) Inf **GA72,** Tutors; **IL135,** ['tučɚ] [FW: Inf has heard "she ['tučɚz] that child."]. **1983** *MJLF* 9.1.60 **ceKY** (as of 1956), *Tutor* . . to spoil (a child).

tutt See **toot** n²

tutter See **tother**

tutu n **HI**

A grandparent, esp a grandmother; rarely an aunt.

1938 Reinecke *Hawaiian Loanwords* 31, *Tutu.* . . Grandparent. (A children's word.) **1951** *AmSp* 26.23 **HI,** Other common Hawaiian words are . . *tutu* (grandparent). **1967** *DARE* (Qu. Z7, *Nicknames and affectionate words for any other relatives*) Inf **HI1,** Tutu ['tu,tu]—aunt or grandmother. **1969** *DARE* File **HI,** *Tutu* ['tutu]—grandmother. *Tutu muu*—a grandmother-type muumuu, a granny gown. **1972** McCormick *Vocab.* **HI** 71, Tutu—mother's or father's mother. **1984** Sunset *HI Guide* 85, *Tutu*—grandmother. **2004** [see **tapa 2**]. **2008** *NY Times* (NY) 25 Oct sec A 12/4 **HI,** A smile washed over his [=Barack Obama's] face . . as he spoke about the woman he calls "Toot," his own shorthand for "tutu," a Hawaiian term for "grandparent."

twan't v [Contr of *it was not*] **esp NEng, S Midl** Cf **be C2b, tain't** v²

1833 *Sketches D. Crockett* 59, 'Twan't long after my difficulty with M—l, before he got into a fight with a member of the senate. **1848** Bartlett *Americanisms* 367 **NEng,** *'Twa'n't,* for *it was not.* **1859** *Atlantic Mth.* 3.105 **MA,** She said she knew 'twa'n't anything. **1885** *Century Illustr. Mag.* 30.370 **OH,** 'Twa'n't a promise. **1913** Kephart *Highlanders* 130 **sAppalachians,** I wonder who *that* feller was! 'Twa'n't (so and so). **1926** *DN* 5.390 **ME,** *Twan't none o' me.* Negative expression. "I didn't do it, I am not responsible." Common. **1939** FWP *These are Our Lives* 22 **cNC** [Black], 'Twa'n't long 'fore here come Mr. Anderson orderin' us to move back. **1945** FWP *Lay My Burden Down* 34 **AL** (as of c1865) [Black], Old Mr. Buck Brasefield . . was so mean to his'n [= slaves] that 'twa'n't nothing for 'em to run away. **c1960** Wilson *Coll.* **csKY,** *'Twan't.* . . It wasn't. **1972** Cooper *NC Mt. Folkl.* 96, *'Twant nothing*—amounted to nothing.

twardge, twarg(e) See **toward A**

twayblade n [*OED2* 1578 → for *Listera* spp] Std: an orchid of the genus *Liparis.* For other names of var spp see **fen orchid**

tweeg n [See quot 1910]
=**hellbender 1.**

[**1824** *Amer. Jrl. Sci. & Arts* 7.63, The creature I mean, is that which the white fishermen have called by the vulgar name of *Hell-bender,* and the Indians *Tweeg.*] **1910** Hodge *Hdbk. Amer. Indians* 2.859, *Tweeg.* A large North American batrachian . . , called also hell-bender, mud-devil, . . etc. The name is from Lenape (Delaware) *twe'kw,* a radical word.

tweet n [Echoic]
=**goldfinch 1.**

1917 *Wilson Bulletin* 29.2.83 **swKY,** *Astragalinus tristis.*—Tweet.

tweezer n

The common **merganser** *(Mergus merganser).*

1888 Trumbull *Names of Birds* 65 **NY,** Another form of it [=*weaser*], or I should say a name that immediately suggests the other, is heard at Shinnecock Bay (designating same species [=*Mergus merganser*]), viz.: *tweezer.* I can hardly believe that this last is the original form, though the bird's beak is easily likened to a pair of tweezers. My idea is that early settlers on the Island associated our "fresh-water sheldrake" with the German river, and got to calling it in consequence the *Weser* sheldrake. **1910** Eaton *Birds NY* 1.178, This bird [=*Mergus merganser*] called also Goosander, . . and Wheezer or Tweezer, is fairly common and well known throughout the State.

tweezer-bird n [Echoic]

See quots.

1854 (1949) Thoreau *Jrl.* 6.369 **MA,** Examined, as well as I could with the glass, what I will call the *tweezer*-bird,—*tra-wee, shreea-shre,*—raspingly. . . Can it be the blue yellow-back warbler? **a1862** in 1906 Thoreau *Writings* 3.224 **MA,** I heard a night-warbler, wood thrush, kingfisher, tweezer-bird or parti-colored warbler, and a night-hawk. [**1965** *Amer. Lit.* 37.169, The incorrect definition of tweezer-bird as "the kingfisher" in both *DAE* and *DA* occurs because both cite the first edition of *The Maine Woods.* William Ellery Channing's careless editing of the third essay, "The Allegash and East Branch," two years after Thoreau's death, resulted in this textual corruption: I heard a Maryland yellow-throat's midnight strain, woodthrush, a kingfisher (tweezer bird), or parti-colored warbler, and a night-hawk.]

twel See **till A2**

twelfth month See **first month**

twell See **till A2**

twelve-o'clock n   Cf **four-o'clock**

1 =**apple (of) Peru 1.**

1891 AR State Geologist *Annual Rept. for 1888* 251, *Nicandra physaloides.* . . The name given to this flower is "twelve o'clock," from the fact that the corolla opens, for a little time only, about mid-day.

2 A **spiderwort** or closely related plant (here: *Tinantia anomala*).

1898 *Jrl. Amer. Folkl.* 11.282 **sKY,** *Tradescantia* (sp.), twelve o'clock. **1928** W. TX Hist. & Scientific Soc. *Pub.* 2.18, Commelinantia anomala [=*Tinantia a.*] . . Twelve O'Clock, Day Flower. . . They ordinarily close their flowers by noon.

twelves n pl
=**dozen** n **B1.**

1937 *Writer* 50.239 **neOH,** *Puttin' you in twelves*—swearing at you.

twenty-four-hour bug n   Also *twenty-four-hour fly*   **esp Gt Lakes**

A **mayfly 1.**

1960 Teale *Journey into Summer* 38 **nOH,** Other names [for mayflies] we encountered along the way were: lake flies, fish flies, June flies, Junebugs and twenty-four-hour bugs. **1967–69** *DARE* (Qu. R4, *A large winged insect that hatches in summer in great numbers around lakes or rivers, crowds around lights, lives only a day or so, and is good fish bait*) Infs **IL58, OH42,** Twenty-four-hour bug; **IL11, NY100,** Twenty-four-hour fly. **2004** *DARE* File—Internet **IA,** Dubuque is the best spot to dredge up the little devils. I know them as Mayflies or 24 hour bugs.

twice adv, adj   Usu |twaɪs|; also **chiefly Sth, S Midl** |twaɪst| Pronc-spp *twiced, twic(e)t, twist(e)* [Brit dial]   Cf **acrost, attackt** v, **cliff, once A, wish B**

Std sense, var forms.

1837 Sherwood *Gaz. GA* 72, *Twis't,* for twice. **1857** in 1956 Eliason *Tarheel Talk* 319 **cnNC,** Twist. **1867** Harris *Sut Lovingood Yarns* 237 **TN,** Yu hearn him call him *mammy twiste.* **1871** Eggleston *Hoosier Schoolmaster* 40 **sIN,** Had-n been slep on more'n wunst or twicet. **1883** (1971) Harris *Nights with Remus* 218 **GA** [Black], Remus 'ud be des twice-t ez ole ez w'at he is right now. **1893** Shands *MS Speech* 65, *Twiste* [twaɪst]. Negro and illiterate white for *twice.* This vulgarism is, I think, very common in many parts of the United States. **1902** Wister *Virginian* 302 **VA,** You've made that mistake twiced. **1902** *DN* 2.248 **sIL,** *Twict* [twaɪst]. . . Twice. **1907** White *AZ Nights* 225, Tusky and me used to feed them chickens twict a day. **1909** *DN* 3.385 **eAL, wGA,** *Twict.* . . Twice. **1911** *DN* 3.540 **eKY,** *Twict.* . . Twice. **1915** *DN* 4.192 **swVA,** *Twist* [twaɪst]. Variant of twice. **1940** (1941) Bell *Swamp Water* 192 **Okefenokee GA,** I ain't been up here more'n oncet er twicet. **1945** FWP *Lay My Burden Down* 79 **GA, TX** [Black], Twicet us gits burnt out, but builds it 'gain. **1955** Roberts *S. from Hell-fer-Sartin* 108 **seKY,** They went back twicet. **c1960** Wilson *Coll.* **csKY,** *Twice* is often /twaɪst/. **1961** Kurath–McDavid *Pronc. Engl.* 179, *Once, twice* . . An added /t/ occurs in *once* and *twice* throughout the Midland and the South, excepting only the Piedmont of Virginia. It is more frequent in *once* than in *twice.* Though most common in folk speech, it is widely used by middle-class speakers, especially in the South Midland. **1966** *DARE* Tape **AR15,** When the weather is favorable we like to go about [twaɪst] a week. **1968** *DARE* (Qu. KK40, . . *'Usually': "They come twice a month, _____."*) Inf **OH45,** Twicet a month always. **1989** Pederson *LAGS Tech. Index* 10 **Gulf Region,** *Twice* . . [twaɪs] (615 [of 914 infs]) . . [twaɪst] (166 [infs]). **2000** Kingsolver *Prodigal Summer* 150 **sAppalachians,** How many times a day you milk her, twiced? **2000** Shores *Tangier Is.* 188 **Chesapeake Bay,** The "t" appears in "onest," "twist."

twice out of sight adj phr   **sAppalachians**

Beyond visibility; somewhat remote.

1960 Allen *Asheville* 43 **wNC,** Other archaic words used by the mountain people are . . "Up yonder, the house is hidden twice out of sight" [etc]. **1976** Garber *Mountain-ese* 97 **sAppalachians,** *Twice-out-of-sight* . . twice as far as you can see—They's a store down the road jist twice out uv sight. **1982** Plowman *Twice* 120 **seKY** (as of 1930s), I want to remember these beautiful mountains and the people as we found them . . when we were "Twice Out of Sight."

twic(e)t See **twice**

‡**twid** n

1984 Woods *WV Was Good* 194, Several ads promised . . luxuriant hair to women who had never been able to grow more than a little "twid" of hair. [Footnote:] Twid is one of those West Virginia words seldom encountered anywhere else.

twig insect n   Also *twig bug*   [*OED2* 1882 for *twig insect*]
=**walkingstick 1.**

1882 (1883) Allen et al. *Nature Studies* 31, The so-called "stick insects," or "walking twigs," . . the *Phasmidæ* of the naturalist. . . The bodies of these "twig insects" . . are represented by mere lines. **1891** *Century Dict.* 6551, *Twig-insect.* . . Same as *stick-bug,* 1. Also *twig-bug.* **1905** Kellogg *Amer. Insects* 604, Another familiar and extreme case of special protective resemblance is that of the walking-stick, or twig-insect, *Diapheromera femorta* . . , a Phasmid wide-spread over the whole of our country. **1968** *DARE* (Qu. R9a, *An insect from two to four inches long that lives in bushes and looks like a dead twig*) Inf **WI54,** Twig bug. **2003** *DARE* File—Internet, Ron describes it [=the wit of Russell Hays] as "the sticklike quality of a twig-bug, developed to trap the unwary". *Ibid,* I saw a twig bug on a speed bump sign.

twilight n

1 See quots. [Joc var of Fr pronc of *toilet*]   Cf **toilet**

1914 *DN* 4.114 **cKS,** *Twilight.* . . Jocose for *toilet.* **1941** *LANE* Map 354 *(Privy)* 4 infs, **ME, MA, RI, VT,** Twilight. **1970** *DARE* (Qu. F37, . . *An indoor toilet*) Inf **NJ64,** Twilight.

2 A three-cornered scarf; see quots.

1967 *DARE* (Qu. W3, *A piece of cloth that a woman folds over her head and ties under her chin*) Inf **PA2,** Twilight—knitted tri-corner tied under chin. **1967** *DARE* Tape **PA4,** Elderly people wear a twilight. . . It's a knitted scarf, three-cornered.

twill See **till A2**

twill-do bird n   Cf **clew bird, clippo**

An imaginary bird; see quot.

1968 *DARE* Tape **GA**25, We have the twill-do bird. . . he flies backwards. He don't care where he's goin', he just wants to see where he's been.

twin band n Cf band n[2]

A flock of sheep in which most ewes have twins.

1937 *Billings Gaz.* (MT) 23 June 6/3, It has been a long time since an eastern Montana sheepman has been reported as running a twin band, but W.R. Woodson . . has so many twins that he is running a separate bunch for the twins until after shearing. **1952** *Natl. Wool Grower* 42.2.33 **MT,** The twin band is very loosely herded and left on a different bedground most every night. **1967** *DARE* Tape **OR**18, Ewe has one lamb or ewe has two lambs. . . If you have what they call a twin band, you generally have maybe seven, eight hundred ewes and just twice that many lambs. . . whereas with a, a single band you have just a lamb and a ewe for each one, and they're generally a little bigger.

twinberry n

1 A **honeysuckle 2:** in the eastern US usu a **fly honeysuckle** (here: *Lonicera canadensis*); in the western US usu **bearberry honeysuckle,** but also *Lonicera utahensis.*

1818 Eaton *Botany* 498, *Xylosteum. . . ciliatum* [=*Lonicera canadensis*] (fly-honeysuckle, twin-berry.) *Ibid, Xylosteum. . . solonis* [=*L. involucrata*] (swamp twin-berry.) **1839** in 1856 MI State Ag. Soc. *Trans. for 1855* 7.422, *Xylosteum ciilatum* [sic]. . . Twin-berry. **1870** Bolander *Catalogue Plants San Francisco* 14 **cwCA,** L[onicera] involucrata. . . Bank's Twinberry. . . Moist places. **1897** Parsons *Wild Flowers CA* 122, *Twin-Berry. Lonicera involucrata.* . . The yellow flowers of the twin-berry. . . are always borne in pairs at the summit of the stem. **1915** (1926) Armstrong–Thornber *Western Wild Flowers* 512, *Black Twinberry—Lonicera involucrata.* [*Ibid* 514, The involucre becomes dark-red, its lobes turn back and display a pair of berries, disagreeable to the taste, as large as peas, nearly black.] **1931** U.S. Dept. Ag. *Misc. Pub.* 101.147 **West,** *Utah honeysuckle,* . . known locally as . . red twinberry. **1942** Tehon *Fieldbook IL Shrubs* 271, *Lonicera canadensis* . . Twinberry. **1956** St. John *Flora SE WA* 393, *Lonicera involucrata.* . . Black Twinberry. . . *Lonicera utahensis.* . . Red Twinberry. **1967** *DARE* (Qu. S26e, *Other wildflowers not yet mentioned;* not asked in early QRs) Inf **CO**7, Twinberry. **1974** Welsh *Anderson's Flora AK* 72, *Lonicera involucrata.* . . Black Twinberry. **2001** in 2003 *DARE* File—Internet **OR,** Here on the north coast of Oregon, Rufous Hummingbirds continue to hit the Twinberry (Lonicera involucrata) pretty hard.

2 A **partridgeberry 1** (here: *Mitchella repens*). [*DCan* 1823 →]

1869 U.S. Dept. Ag. *Rept. of Secy. for 1868* 178 **AK,** Among them [= small fruits] may be noted red and black currants, . . twinberries [etc]. **1903** Porter *Flora PA* 290, *Mitchella repens.* . . *Partridge-berry. Twin-berry.* . . In woods. **1912** Mathews *Amer. Wild Flowers* 442, *Twinberry—Mitchella repens.* . . A little trailing vine with dark green evergreen leaves. **1933** Small *Manual SE Flora* 1261, *M[itchella] repens.* . . *Twin-berry.* . . Fla. to Tex., Minn., and N[ova] S[cotia] **1953** Greene–Blomquist *Flowers South* 122, *Twin-* or *Partridge-Berry (Mitchella repens).* . . Unique in that flowers are borne in pairs with partly joined ovaries which completely merge at maturity into a red berry-like fruit consisting of twin drupes. **1967** *DARE* Wildfl QR Pl.211B Infs **AR**44, **SC**41, Twinberry—edible. **2003** *DARE* File—Internet **VT,** Partridgeberry (Mitchella repens) is a very hardy, two-inch groundcover that is sometimes called Twinberry.

3 also *twinberry eugenia,* ~ *stopper:* =**stopper 1b.**

1940 U.S. Forest Serv. *Approved Changes* 98, *Naked Stopper (Eugenia dicrana)—Twinberry Eugenia.* . . The paired ("two-craniumed") berrylike fruits of this species are characteristic. **1971** Craighead *Trees S. FL* 203, Twinberry, *Eugenia dicrana.* **1979** Little *Checklist U.S. Trees* 174, *Myrcianthes fragrans* . . *twinberry stopper.* . . *Other common names*—twinberry eugenia, . . twinberry. **2002** *DARE* File—Internet **FL,** Simpson's stopper or twinberry (*Myrcianthes fragrans* (Swartz) McVaugh) is a beautiful small native tree ranging from Florida down through the Caribbean.

twin brothers n Cf Adam-and-Eve 1

Perh a **coralroot 1;** see quot.

c1938 in 1970 Hyatt *Hoodoo* 1.658 **seNC,** I . . got me some Adam-an'-Eve an' . . a root they call *twin brothers.*

twin day n

A day on which the moon is in the astrological sign Gemini.

1957 *Western Folkl.* 16.80 **NC,** Plant watermelons on a twin day in

April on the last quarter of the moon. **1982** Slone *How We Talked* 100 **eKY** (as of c1950), Plant vines on the 10th day of May. Watermelon, muskmelon, squash, cucumbers; also on "twin days" (Aquarius [sic]). **1986** Pederson *LAGS Concordance,* 1 inf, **ceLA,** Twin days—astrological sign used in planting. **1999** *DARE* File—Internet **TN,** Plant beans on twin days. . . My Pa *always* "planted by the signs". **2002** in 2006 *DARE* File—Internet [*Corsicana Daily Sun* (TX) 16 Apr], What got me going on the subject of twins was the fact that Twin Days are coming up on the calendar tomorrow and Thursday. My mother set a great store by planting on Twin Days.

twine n, also attrib NEast

As a mass noun: Netting, fishnet.

1893 in 1956 Ritchie *Block Is. Lore & Legends* 60 **RI,** The pound "heart" is made of spiles and twine as was the leader. It is 50 x 60 feet and its bottom is covered by twine, or netting, as is also its sides. **1930** *AmSp* 5.393 [Language of N Atl fishermen], *Twine.* . . Netting, especially that of which the otter trawl is made. *Twine-loft.* . . A place for making and mending trawls, seins [sic], etc. **1945** Hatcher *Lake Erie* 283, The fishermen "pay out the twine" (as they call the nets) in gangs over the fishing grounds, anchor them at the ends and mark them with flagpoles. **1957** Beck *Folkl. ME* 134, Thompson was given the delicate task of running "twine" (a seine) across the harbor mouth. **1975** Gould *ME Lingo* 303, *Twine*—A word of extremely general meaning in Maine fisheries; to some extent it is a synonym for cordage. *Twine* means fishing nets in the aggregate, so a man will tell how much *twine* he has out. **1988** Spinner 4.134 **seMA** (as of c1938) [Fishing industry jargon], *Twine Man:* Man who mends nets expertly.

twine plant n

A **bindweed 1.**

1968 *DARE* (Qu. S5, . . *Wild morning glory*) Inf **OH**82, Twine plant.

twine vine n

A plant of the genus *Funastrum.* Cf **vine milkweed**

1986 *Flora Gt. Plains* 636 **West,** *Sarcostemma cynanchoides* [= *Funastrum c.*] . . arroyo twine vine. Perennial twining or trailing vine. . . OK . . TX (w[estern] G[reat] P[lains] to NM & AZ; n Mex.) **1998** in 2004 *DARE* File—Internet **TX,** *Sarcostemma crispum* [=*Funastrum c.*]. Wavyleaf twine-vine. Native perennial herbaceous vine. **2003** [see **vine milkweed**]. **2004** *DARE* File—Internet, Jus kiss this girl an say I do when I say to / so you'll be twisted together fa-ever like a twine vine.

twinflower n

1 A widely distributed, low evergreen plant *(Linnaea borealis)* with pairs of usu pink flowers. Also called **deer vine, ground ~, twin sisters 3**

1818 Eaton *Botany* 304, *[Linnaea] borealis* (twin-flower). . . branches erect, each bearing 2 flowers. **1845** Judd *Margaret* 8 swME, She got running mosses, twin-flower vines, and mountain laurel blossoms. **1891** Victor *Atlantis Arisen* 225 **NW,** Side by side with the yerba buena is the twin-flower, *Linnaea borealis,* with a very similar leaf, vine, and flower, except that it supports . . a pair of blossoms instead of a single one. **1917** Eaton *Green Trails* 88 **nwMT,** Associated with the woods, too, is the fairy twin flower. **1944** Nute *Lake Superior* 293 **MI, WI, MN,** Everywhere in early July in this shore country may be found the twinflower trailing its vine under the evergreens. **1966–68** *DARE* Wildfl QR Pl.213A Infs **MI**7, 31, 57, **MN**14, **NH**4, **SC**41, **WA**10, 30, Twinflower(s). **1969** *DARE* (Qu. S26e, *Other wildflowers not yet mentioned;* not asked in early QRs) Inf **WI**78, Twinflower—pink and nice-smelling. **2003** *DARE* File—Internet **nMN,** *Twinflower*—Common name for the delicate, creeping shrublet of the northern forest floor, so named for its pairs of small, pink bell-like flowers hanging from shepherd's crook stems.

2 often *blue twinflower:* A **snake herb,** usu *Dyschoriste oblongifolia.* **esp FL**

1938 Baker *FL Wild Flowers* 204, *Blue Twinflower.* . . This small plant, which usually opens two flowers at a time, often grows in colonies in pinelands. . . *Dyschoriste oblongifolia.* . . Fla. to Va. **2003** *DARE* File—Internet **sGA,** *Dyschoriste oblongifolia—Twinflower* is a drought-tolerant perennial that does well in dry sand. It is a low-growing flower with small, five-lobed lavender flowers. **2005** in 2006 *Ibid* **FL,** *Dyschoriste oblongifolia*—Oblongleaf Twinflower . . Blue Twinflower. . . The common name derives from the trait of this plant to frequently have a pair of back to back flowers in bloom at the same time. **2006** *Ibid* **FL,** *Hernando County's Blue Flowers of Spring.* . . Wild Petunia (*Ruellia carolinensis*) and Blue Twinflower (*Dyschoriste oblongifolia*) are somewhat similar in appearance.

twinkle n
=**needle 1.**
  1913 Kephart *Highlanders* 295 **sAppalachians,** In some places pine needles are called twinkles.

twinleaf n [See quot 1916]
A white-flowered plant *(Jeffersonia diphylla)* distinguished by its two-lobed leaf. Also called **ground squirrel pea, helmet-pod, rheumatism root a, yellowroot 4**
  1818 Eaton *Botany* 287, *Jeffersonia. . . diphylla* (twin leaf). **1844** Lapham *Geogr. Descr. WI* 77, Some of the more useful or interesting plants of Wisconsin. . . [are] Clematis Virginiana, . . virgin's bower. . . Jeffersonia diphylla, . . twin leaf. **1897** IN *Dept. Geol. & Nat. Resources Rept. for 1896* 631, The leaflets are often five to seven-lobed. **1916** Keeler *Early Wildflowers* 89, *Jeffersonia diphylla. . .* Its common name, Twinleaf, is due to the fact that the leaf is parted into two similar leaflets. **1936** IL *Nat. Hist. Surv. Wildflowers* 116, *Twinleaf. . .* In rich woods of the central and northern parts of the state, as well as throughout the Great Lakes region and south to Tennessee. **1968** *DARE* (Qu. S26c, *Wildflowers that grow in woods*) Infs **IN**17, **PA**99, Twinleaf. **2003** *DARE* File—Internet **VA,** The *twinleaf (Jeffersonia)* and *bloodroot* were at their peak bloom on the 25th [of March].

twinpod n
=**double bladderpod.**
  1914 Frye–Rigg *Elementary Flora NW* 114, *Physaria* [spp] (Twin Pod). **1936** McDougall–Baggley *Plants of Yellowstone* 67, *Twinpod (Physaria didymocarpa).*—Most easily recognized by its fruits which consist of two inflated, papery-walled parts joined together. **1975** Zwinger *Run River* 178 **UT,** A short walk upstream still leads to a wall of Fremont drawings—a walk . . through garlands of . . gold parsleys and twinpod, starflowers and opulent drifts of pale blue chiming bells. **2003** *DARE* File—Internet **CO,** Rising dramatically from the valley floor . . , the 428-acre ranch. . . supports a high-quality occurrence of Bell's twinpod (Physaria bellii).

twin sisters n
1 A **honeysuckle 2** (here: *Lonicera tatarica*).
  1894 *Jrl. Amer. Folkl.* 7.90 **cwWI,** Lonicera Tatarica . . , "twin sisters."
2 =**fringed polygala.**
  1888 VT *State Bd. Ag. Rept. for 1887–88* 242, *[Polygala] paucifolia. . .* Twin Sisters. Fringed Polygala. Common. **1983** *DARE* File **cwMA,** Ruth Dickinson Ewell, [who] knows her flowers well, confirms "baby-toes" as MA usage. She adds another variant: "twin sisters."
3 =**twinflower 1.**
  1900 MI *State Horticult. Soc. Annual Rept. for 1899* 303, Linnaea borealis. . . Twin-flower. . . Twin-sisters. **1913** Britton–Brown *Illustr. Flora* 3.276, *Linnaea americana* [=*L. borealis*]. . . Twin-flower. . . Twin sisters. Two-eyed berries. **1948** Taylor *Encycl. Gardening* 632, *Linnaea. . . americana.* Twinflower of N.A. . . Also known as deer vine and twin sisters. **1960** Teale *Journey into Summer* 63 **MI,** Twin flowers . . nodded in pairs among the moldering logs. . . these "twin sisters" of the north-country woods. . . were. . . recorded in their scientific name, *Linnaea.*

twin-sled n esp wPA Cf bob n³ 1, double-runner, two-sled
One of a pair of short sleds designed to support one end of a load or vehicle; hence, usu pl, a vehicle consisting of two such sleds linked together and sometimes supporting a body.
  1874 *Indiana Progress* (PA) 15 Oct 1/3, List of Premiums. . . Best pair of twin sleds. . . $3.00. **1899** *Ft. Wayne News* (IN) [8 Feb 14]/4 (newspaperarchive.com) **cwPA,** In the winter they bundle up, mount the seat on the twin sleds to which is attached their favorite team and deliver hundreds of bushels of coal. **1905** [see **two-sled**]. **1913** Bryant *Logging* 159, The jumbo . . is used on a snow haul in the Lake States, . . where the conditions do not warrant the use of heavy sleds. It consists of twin-sleds, similar in construction to go-devils, joined together by cross-chains. *Ibid* [see **two-sled**]. **1922** *Indiana Weekly Messenger* (PA) 30 Nov 5/1, Twin sleds on which they were riding crashed into the side of an automobile . . on the East Mahoning street hill. **1967** *Derrick* (Oil City PA) 1 June 22/6, [Advt:] Wagon bed, pair of twin sleds, set of 15 ton scales.

twirlpool n
  1966 *DARE* (Qu. C8, . . *A place in a stream where water flows round and round and draws things in toward the center*) Infs **AL**6, **OK**52,

Twirlpool; (Qu. O18, *Different currents or actions of the water that are important when you're in a boat*) Inf **OK**52, Twirlpools—in rainy weather, they have currents called "suck pools," "whirlpools," and "twirlpools" on big creeks and rivers.

twirly bug n
=**whirligig beetle.**
  1960 Williams *Walk Egypt* 161 **GA,** Tom gon skate 'crost Jordan like a twirly-bug on the pond.

twirty adj [*EDD twirty* "Cross, easily put out; nervous, pert"]
  1850 *Sartain's Union Mag.* 7.63, Not young—he'd be sheepish or boorish or twirty;/ A man is no man till he's stepped over thirty. **1927** *AmSp* 3.135 **eME,** A "twirty" girl was a pert miss.

twist n
1 also *twist tobacco:* Tobacco twisted into a rope; a rope of tobacco; a piece of this—also in var combs. **scattered, but chiefly Midl, Sth, SW** See Map Cf **pigtail n 1**
  1748 in 1904 Thwaites *Early W. Travels* 1.32 **sePA,** I made a Present to the old Shawonese Chief . . [of] a large twist of Tobacco. **1830** in 1936 *KS Hist. Qrly.* 5.345 **PA,** A fire in the centre, near which I placed a few twists of tobacco for them all to smoke. **1900** *U.S. Dept. Ag. Yearbook for 1899* 430 **S Midl,** This leaf . . is particularly well adapted to plug fillers and plug and twist wrappers. **1911** in 1983 Truman *Dear Bess* 32 **MO,** She takes twist tobacco and steeps it in hot water as if you were making tea. **1944** *PADS* 2.72 **S Midl,** *Twist. . .* Leaves twisted into a roll for chewing. **1965–70** *DARE* (Qu. DD1, . . *Forms . . [of] chewing tobacco*) 193 Infs, **scattered, but chiefly Midl, Sth, SW,** Twist; **DE**1, **FL**22, **MD**20, 29, Picnic twist; **FL**35, **GA**3, **NC**80, Pig twist; **ID**4, Burley twist; **CA**114, Cable twist; **MO**19, Cut twist; **KY**49, Dry twist; **WI**44, Knobby twist; **AR**39, Long green in a twist; **IN**18, Natural leaf-twist; **KY**49, Wet twist; (Qu. DD2, *The portion or quantity of tobacco chewed at one time: "He's always got a big _____ in his cheek."*) Infs **MI**97, **MN**8, **PA**197, **VA**73, 96, Twist; **OK**42, Half a twist. **1986** Pederson *LAGS Concordance,* 1 inf, **cwGA,** Twist—roll of tobacco; 1 inf, **nwFL,** Twist tobacco.

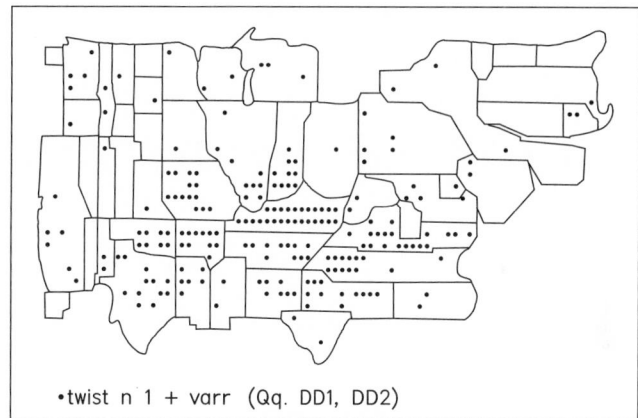

•twist n 1 + varr (Qq. DD1, DD2)

2 often in combs: =**cruller. scattered, but chiefly Inland Nth, N Midl, West** See Map Cf **twister 2**
  1887 Parloa *Miss Parloa's Kitchen Companion* 775, Raised Dough-

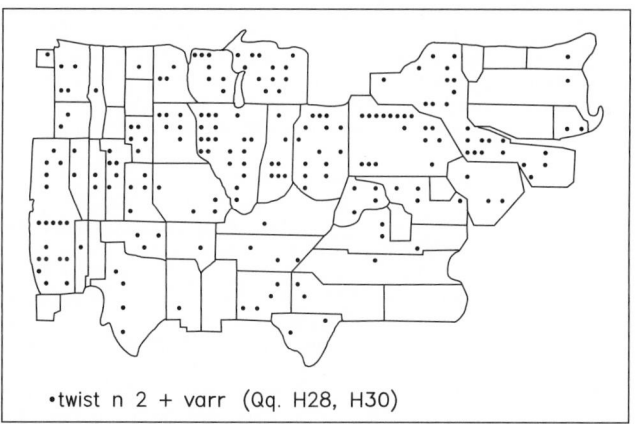

•twist n 2 + varr (Qq. H28, H30)

nuts. . . One of the best is what is called the twist; cut long narrow strips of the dough, double these, and twist loosely.   **1950** *WELS (Different names for different shapes or sizes of cakes like these [=cooked in deep fat])* 3 Infs, **WI,** Twists.   **1965–70** *DARE* (Qu. H28, *Different shapes or types of doughnuts*) 193 Infs, **scattered, but chiefly Inland Nth, N Midl, West,** Twist; **AK**8, **MA**27, **RI**14, Twist doughnut; **MO**14, 35, Twist roll; **MD**50, Doughnut twist; (Qu. H30, *An oblong cake, cooked in deep fat*) Inf **TX**58, Jelly twist; **NY**213, Twist.   **1989** Pederson *LAGS Tech. Index* 395 **Gulf Region,** Cruller . . [21 infs, Twist; 6 infs, Doughnut twist; 5 infs, Cinnamon twist; 2 infs, French twist; 1 inf, Sugar twist.]

twist adv, adj, **twiste**   See **twice**

twisted pine n
=**lodgepole pine.**

   1857 U.S. War Dept. *Rept. Explor. Railroad (Botany)* 6.34 **nCA,** *Pinus contorta.* . . The twisted pine. . . We first met with this pine on the banks of Canoe creek, a tributary of Pit river, in northern California.   **1863** Hittell *Resources CA* 95, The twisted pine *(Pinus contorta)* is found in the northern part of the state.   **1897** Sudworth *Arborescent Flora* 23 **MT, NV, ID,** *Pinus contorta.* . . Twisted Pine.   **1908** Britton *N. Amer. Trees* 28, It [=*Pinus contorta*] is variously known as Twisted pine, Scrub pine, . . and Tamarack.

twisted-stalk n

1 A plant of the genus *Streptopus.* [See quots 1901, 2003] For other names of var spp see **cucumber root 2, Jacob's ladder 6, liverberry, pagoda bells, rose mandarin, scootberry, Solomon's seal 4, white mandarin, wild cucumber 3**

   1843 Torrey *Flora NY* 2.322, Streptopus. . . Twisted-stalk.   **1890** *Harper's New Mth. Mag.* 80.709 **NY,** The twisted-stalk hangs its rosy cups.   **1901** Lounsberry *S. Wild Flowers* 59, *Twisted-stalk.* . . *Streptopus roseus.* [*Ibid* 60, It is a common error . . to think that its stalk is twisted; . . the popular name is altogether in allusion to the twist or bend which occurs about the middle of its fine peduncles.]   **1966–69** *DARE* (Qu. S26a, . . *Wildflowers.* . . *Roadside flowers*) Inf **MN**14, Rose twisted-stalk or liverberry; **MA**5, Twisted-stalk; (Qu. S26c, *Wildflowers that grow in woods*) Inf **ME**8, Twisted-stalk; (Qu. S26e, *Other wildflowers not yet mentioned;* not asked in early QRs) Inf **IL**37, Fairy bells or twisted-stalks.   **1987** Hughes–Blackwell *Wildflowers SE AK* 75, Twisted Stalk, White Mandarin. . . Flowers dangle on thin stalks which grow out of the leaf axils.   **2003** *DARE* File—Internet, Twisted-stalk takes its name from the fact that its tiny, bell-like flowers hang from short stems that display a distinctive bend along its length.

2 A ladies' tresses (here: *Spiranthes lacera*).

   1894 *Jrl. Amer. Folkl.* 7.101 **WV,** *Spiranthes gracilis,* . . twisted stalk.   **1936** Whitehouse *TX Flowers* 16, *Slender Ladies'-Tresses (Ibidium gracile* [=*Spiranthes lacera*]) is also called twisted-stalk or corkscrewplant because of the twisting of the flower-stalk.   **1979** *Greenfield Recorder* (MA) 24 Nov sec A 4/1, They . . grow in boggy places, and often have for companions those little sweet-scented green orchids, named "Ladies Tresses" or "Twisted Stalk." The greenish white blossoms grow in a spiral around the stalk.

twister n

1 =**turn shovel. Sth, S Midl** Cf **turning plow**

   a1857 in 1969 Turner *Cotton Planter's Manual* 44 **SC,** A substitute may be made by using a large twister, drawn by two horses, and passing up and down until the furrow is opened.   **1858** *De Bow's Rev.* 25.462 **SC,** Draw the [sweet potato] vines over the top of the bed and plow with a large twister and finish with a hoe.   **1883** GA Dept. Ag. *Pub. Circular No. 29* 8.13, Gossypium at rate of 400 lbs. to the acre, was ploughed in with a twister; ground was then thoroughly harrowed.   **1884** Smith *Bill Arp's Scrap Book* 66 **nwGA,** My farmer boy stripped the vines. . . Then ran a one-horse twister on each side.   **1899** Edwards *Defense* 14 **GA,** 'Look like any fool,' she said one day, 'look like any fool would know better'n ter lay off land with er twister. Whyn't yer git er roun' p'inted shovel?' My lan' was new, gentlemen, an' full of roots; that's why.   **1917** Taylor *Hdbk. for Rangers* 56 **MO,** Another suitable form of shovel for such a frame is known as a "twister." This is about 6 inches wide by 12 long and bears a 3- or 4-inch wing which serves the same purpose as the mould board on a turning plow. The wing may be either right or left turning.   **1923** Taylor in *DN* 5.223 **swMO,** Twister. . . A steel plow shovel equipped with a wing at one side.   **1966–67** *DARE* (Qu. L18, *Kinds of plows*) Inf **AL**2, Twister—Georgia stock with turning plow attached; **FL**7, Twister—brand name; **SC**19, Twister—for throwing up a bed; **SC**30, Twister—a one-horse turn plow—put on a plow

stock.   **1986** Pederson *LAGS Concordance (Plow)* 4 infs, **GA, MS, TN,** Twister; 1 inf, **cwAL,** Twisters—on Georgia stock—threw dirt one way.

2 also *doughnut-twister;* =**cruller.**   Cf **curler** n², **twist 2 chiefly NEast, N Cent**   See Map

   1886 *Good Housekeeping* 4.88, Do the water ices . . taste one half so good as . . the "twisters" (doughnuts) and the "sweet cake" they "passed 'round" at the play party?   **1908** *N.Y. Ev. Post* 31 Dec (1912 Thornton *Amer. Gloss.*), I had only time to . . seize a perfectly unmanageable thing called a "twister" . . and to spring aboard the train, twister in hand.   **1914** *DN* 4.82 **ME, nNH,** *Twister.* . . Cruller.   **1941** *LANE* Map 284 *(Doughnut)* 5 infs, **ME, MA, NH,** Twister.   **1947** Bowles–Towle *New Engl. Cooking* 202, In Maine, unsweetened doughnuts were twisters.   **c1955** Reed–Person *Ling. Atlas Pacific NW,* 1 inf, Twisters—sweet roll.   **1961** McDavid Coll. **OK,** Twisters = crullers.   **1965–70** *DARE* (Qu. H28, *Different shapes or types of doughnuts*) 19 Infs, **chiefly NEast, N Cent,** Twister; **NY**28, Twister; doughnut-twisters—old-fashioned; (Qu. H26, *A round cake of dough, cooked in deep fat, with a hole in the center*) Inf **NE**2, Twister; (Qu. H30, *An oblong cake, cooked in deep fat*) Inf **UT**3, Twister; (Qu. H32, . . *Fancy rolls and pastries*) Inf **PA**163, Twisters.   **1966** Dakin *Dial. Vocab. Ohio R. Valley* 2.322, Twister still . . [has] considerable currency. . . used for doughnuts of the long or looped and twisted variety (in contrast to the ring-shaped type). . . *Twister* is chiefly found scattered on the fringes of the *cruller* areas and seems possibly to be a new term developed by those who learned to make the cake but did not have an intimate enough contact with those who used the name *cruller* to borrow the name also.   **1973** Allen *LAUM* 1.281 **Upper MW** (as of c1950), *Doughnut.* . . the twisted variety. . . *Twister,* a minor variant for this kind in Maine and New Hampshire, survives in two occurrences, one in a Maine settled community [in Iowa]. It was reported twice in Wisconsin.   **1986** Pederson *LAGS Concordance (Cruller)* 5 infs, **AL, FL, TX,** Twister(s); 1 inf, **cTX,** Twister—two strips of dough wrapped together.

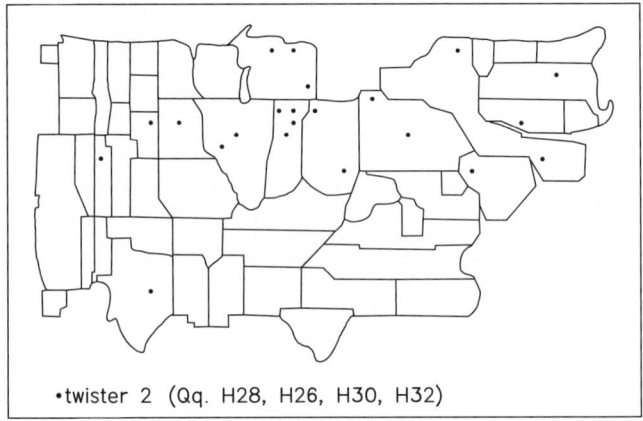

•twister 2 (Qq. H28, H26, H30, H32)

3 A twisting motion made by a bucking horse; a horse that makes such a motion.

   1903 *Wide World Mag.* Apr 548 **CO,** This movement unseated many a rider during the recent contest, however, and it was a broncho named "E.A." (who used a combination of "sun-fish" and "twister") that proved the hardest to ride.   **1929** *AmSp* 5.65 **NE** [Cattle country talk], If the "pony" turns completely around, "swaps ends" or does an "end for end," he is a "twister."   **1956** Moody *Home Ranch* 41 **CO** (as of 1911), Takes brains to make a good twister; that mav'rick's loco. *Ibid* 42, I'd ridden some pretty good bucking horses at the Y-B and the fair-grounds, though I'd never ridden any real twisters.

4 also *bronc(h)o-twister, bronc- ~:* =**bronco-buster. West**

   1904 Evans *Wylackie Jake* 46 **West,** He was . . a good bronco twister, a rattlin' first-rate buckaroo.   **1908** *Sat. Eve. Post* 4 July 22/2 **West,** Had they really appreciated Blackie they would never have permitted a Mexican "twister" to top him first, but only the professional buster of the range.   **1911** *DN* 3.550 **WY,** Broncho twister, same meaning as "broncho buster."   **1914** *Scribner's Mag.* 55.462, Only a small percentage of the cow-punchers are genuine "bronc' twisters." These few men at one time made a business of riding from ranch to ranch and breaking colts at five dollars per head.   **1920** *DN* 5.84 **eOR,** *Twister.* A man who rides a wild horse.   **1957** *Western Horseman* 22.4.67 **West,** If a twister knows his business, he should certainly know what methods and principles to apply in breaking a bronc.

5 =**mallard 1.**   Cf **Labrador twister**

1923 U.S. Dept. Ag. *Misc. Circular* 13.8 **IL,** *Mallard. . . Vernacular Names. . . In local use. . .* Twister. **1982** Elman *Hunter's Field Guide* 150, *Anas platyrhynchos . . twister. . .* Mallards . . will circle widely before cupping their wings over a decoy stand.

twist flower n

A plant of the genus *Streptanthus,* native to much of the western US.   For other names of var spp see **jewel flower 1**

1914 Frye–Rigg *Elementary Flora NW* 111, *Streptanthus* [spp] (Twist Flower). . . referring to the twisted petals. **1941** Jaeger *Wildflowers* 75 **Desert SW,** *Heart-leaved Twist-flower. Streptanthus cordatus.* **1954** Harrington *Manual Plants CO* 278, *Streptanthus. . . Twistflower.* Glabrous, perennial, herbaceous plants. **1970** Correll *Plants TX* 676, *Streptanthus. . . Twist-flower. . .* About 35 species in southwestern United States. **2002** in 2006 *DARE* File—Internet **TX,** [He] will . . make a presentation on *Streptanthus bracteatus,* the Bracted Twist Flower.

twistification n sAppalachians, GA, AL

A dance or quasi-dance with partners in facing columns; see quot 1909; a party at which this and similar dances are danced.

1864 (2000) Warren *Nellie Norton* 189 (Internet) **GA,** They [=slaves] were drawn up in two parallel lines, about ten feet apart. . . The movement consisted in locking arms, swinging round and moving to the foot of the line, all in time to the music. If the reader desires a better description, he can just witness the play called Twistification by our genteel ladies and gentlemen. **1904** (1913) Johnson *Highways South* 101 **nGA,** For Twistification we all gets in line, boys on one side, girls on the other, with room for a couple to march up between us in dancing step. At the end of the line they swing and we all promenade. Then we form the line and start again. **1909** *DN* 3.385 **eAL, wGA,** *Twistification. . .* A popular rural dance. The partners arrange themselves opposite each other in a "lane" or double column. The head couple join hands and promenade up and down the "lane," and then begin to "swing," or "circle," the players in turn. The girl begins at the head of the men's column, and the boy at the foot of the girl's column. The partners "swing" each other between times as they progress down the lines. In this way they are "twisting" or winding in and out continually: hence the name, *twistification.* The game is not called a dance, and so does not fall under the ban of church rules. **1913** Kephart *Highlanders* 263 **sAppalachians,** Wherever the church has not put its ban on "twistifications" the country dance is the chief amusement of young and old. **1932** Strong *Behind Gt. Smokies* 163 **wNC,** As for the gals, the most fun they have is a twistification in the schoolhouse fer them what's courtin'. . . Reckon ye'd call hit dancin'. **1938** Matschat *Suwannee R.* 134 **neFL, seGA,** Dancing was not allowed, in deference to the preacher, but Stealin' Partners, Fancy Four, and Twistification were almost as good. All these romping games were played to music. "Twistification," yelled Old Fiddler; and the lines began to form, the girls on one side and the boys on the other. **c1940** in 2004 Montgomery–Hall *Dict. Smoky Mt. Engl.* 625 **eTN,** *Twistification. . .* Oldtime dancing at arm's length from one's partner [was] not considered sinful—"that's just prancin' and cavortin'; the dancin's what's sinful, is where you go into the clinch and do the twistification." **1967** *DARE* (Qu. FF5a, . . *Different steps and figures in dancing—in past years*) Inf **AL32,** Twistification. **1972** Cooper *NC Mt. Folkl.* 96, *Twistification*—a dance. **1986** Pederson *LAGS Concordance,* 2 infs, **AL, GA,** Twistification—a dance; 1 inf, **csTN,** Twistification—a game; 1 inf, **csAL,** Twistification—primitive line game; swing partner.

twist-leaf vine n

=**snapdragon vine.**

1951 *PADS* 15.40 **TX,** *Antirrhinnum maurandioides* [=*Maurandella antirrhiniflora*] . . twist-leaf vine. . . pretty leaf-tendrils and . . lovely velvety flowers.

twist tobacco See twist 1

twit n [Prob echoic]

An **oyster-catcher.**

1969 *DARE* FW Addit **eNC,** *Twits*—type of bird—these are oyster catchers.

twitch v chiefly nNEng Cf snake v, twitch horse

In logging: =**skid** v 2a, also fig; hence vbl n, also attrib, *twitching;* ppl adj *twitched.*

1773 (1903) Patten *Diary* 299 **NH,** My bror Samuell and I and our boys and oxen went and Twitched in what logs we had at Major Goffes saw Mill. **1838** (1843) Haliburton *Clockmaker* (2d ser) 170 **NEng,** He is a giant . . and can twitch a mill-log as easy as a yoke of oxen. **1914** *DN* 4.82 **ME, nNH,** *Twitch. . .* To drag timber from the forest into a road, clearing or "yard." **1945** Hamlin *9 Mile Bridge* 46 **nME,** When the lumberjack is through with a log and it is ready to be taken away, a chain is looped around one end and tightened, and the log is hauled by a horse on the narrow "twitching" paths that lead to loading yards on the hauling road. **1952** *Badger Folkl.* 1.17 **WI** [Logging language], *Twitching chain*—Short chain having roundhook on one end and grabhook on the other, used in skidding logs. **1958** McCulloch *Woods Words* 202 **Pacific NW,** *Twitch. . .* To skid small logs with a horse. **1966–68** *DARE* (Qu. OO46a, *Talking about dragging something heavy: "We hitched the log on and _____ it out [of the woods]."*) Infs **ME**1, **NH**3, 14, Twitched; (Qu. OO46b, *Talking about dragging something heavy: "Half a mile or so we must have _____ [it]!"*) Infs **ME**1, **NH**14, Twitched. **1966** *DARE* Tape **ME**6, [FW:] What'd they call it . . when a horse pulls a log out of the woods out to a clearing? . . [Inf:] Twitching the logs. . . Twitching 'em out with a horse so you can get at 'em when they're in a bad place. **1970** *DARE* FW Addit **MA**75, *Twitchin'*—hauling or dragging logs out of the woods. **1975** Gould *ME Lingo* 303, The manner in which a *twitched* log bounces around on its way gives the word *twitch* great vividness when used in transferred situations: "Johnny sarssed teacher, and she twitched him right out'n his seat over the desk," or, "The dentist twitched a tooth." **1982** *Smithsonian Letters* **ME,** After I had felled the tree and limbed it, I put a chain around its butt and twitched it out with my tractor. **1985** McPhee *Table of Contents* 263 **ME,** The last time these woods were cut, the logs were twitched out by horse.

twitch n [twitch v 1]

In logging: see quots.

1946 Rich *Happy Land* 166 **ME,** A twitch is the distance an average twitch-horse can haul a tree without resting. It's the woods' equivalent of a city block. **1956** Sorden–Ebert *Logger's Words* 39 **Gt Lakes,** *Twitch,* A short chain. **1981** Blair & Ketchum's *Country Jrl.* June 7 **swNH,** I . . watched a logger guiding his team of horses hitched to a single crude sled (my father would have called it a "twitch") on which was chained a small load of logs. **2006** *DARE* File **w,nME** (as of 1970s), A bunch of logs that were bundled together and hauled out; that would be a twitch of logs. It could be three or four logs cabled together, or even a single log.

twitched See twitch v

twitchet n

1 also *twitchit,* rarely *tritchet:* The female genitals.   **chiefly Mid Atl, sAppalachians** Cf **tippet**

1899 (1912) Green *VA Folk-Speech* 464, *Twitchit. . .* Woman's generative organs. **1944** *PADS* 2.21 **sAppalachians,** *Twitchet. . .* Pudenda muliebria. *Ibid* 50 **sVA,** *Tritchet* ['trɪtʃet]. . . Pudenda muliebria. . . Rare. *Ibid* 51 **NC, SC, TN, VA,** *Twitchet* ['twɪtʃet]. . . Same as *tritchet.* **1977** Randolph *Pissing in the Snow* 51 **Ozarks** (as of c1895), She was scared pretty near to death, and her twitchet drawed up so tight he couldn't get his pecker out. **1983** *DARE* File **eVA, eNC,** Have you come across "twitchet" and "tippet" for the female genital organ? I heard these words on Tangier all the time in my younger days. . . A farmer friend of mine (about 60) said he heard it [=*twitchet*] in his youth in Moyock, North Carolina, not far from here. **2000** Jayne *Home Grown Stories* 4 **Ozarks** (as of c1951), She jist reached down and grabbed hold of her twitchet some way and kind of cocked her leg up and pissed plumb over three strands of bob wire fence.

2 =**spotted sandpiper.**

1923 U.S. Dept. Ag. *Misc. Circular* 13.64 **MA,** *Spotted Sandpiper. . . Vernacular Names. . . In local use. . .* Twitchet.

twitch grass n

1 =**quack grass 1. Nth, esp NEng**

1689 in 1911 *Proprietors' Records Waterbury CT* 28, Up the brooke above twich gras medow. **1790** Deane *New Engl. Farmer* 230, *Quitch-Grass,* called also *Witch-Grass, Twitch-Grass . . .*, a most obstinate and troublesome weed. **1862** Winthrop *John Brent* 243 **OR,** Daughters ought to stick closer 'n twitch-grass to their fathers, and sons to their mothers. **1880** *Scribner's Mth.* 19.688 **NY,** Turn over the sward, and up spring rag-weed and pig-weed and red-root; . . sweep the board of this trick, and down comes a bower in the shape of twitch-grass, or fox-tail, or some other pest. **1897** *Jrl. Amer. Folkl.* 10.147 **ME,** *Triticum repens* [=*Elymus repens*], twitch grass, dog grass. **1913** *DN* 4.6 **ME,** *Witch grass* or *twitch grass. . .* A grass common in gardens that spreads rapidly and is hard to kill. **1950** *WELS* (*The kind of wild grass that throws out strong underground roots and is hard to get rid of*) 1 Inf, **WI,** Twitch grass or quack grass. **1968–69** *DARE* (Qu. S8, *A common kind of wild* *grass that grows in fields: it spreads by sending out long underground roots, and it's hard to get rid of)* Inf **CT**2, Twitch grass . . you can't get rid of the stuff; **MA**57, We called it twitch grass; **WI**23, Twitch grass.

2 =**pearl millet 1.**

1910 Graves *Flowering Plants* 57 **CT**, *Setaria glauca* (L.) Beauv. [= *Pennisetum glaucum* (L.) R. Br.] . . Foxtail. Pigeon Grass. Twitch Grass. . . Naturalized from Europe. Often a troublesome weed in gardens.

twitch horse n Also *twitching horse* **ME**

In logging: a horse used for skidding logs.

1942 Rich *We Took to Woods* 95 **ME**, A yarding crew consists of three men and a twitch horse. **1946** [see **twitch** n]. **1948** *WELS Suppl.* **ME**, Single trees . . were twitched out by a twitch horse to where they could be sawed and piled for the sleds. **1975** Gould *ME Lingo* 304, *Twitchin' horse*—A carefully trained horse that *twitches* logs out of the woods by himself. Some regard this as the highest development of equine management. **2003** *DARE* File—Internet **ME**, We selective cut, using a big Belgian twitching horse and a homemade tractor.

twitching See **twitch** v

twitching horse See **twitch horse**

twitchit See **twitchet 1**

twitch road n Also *twitch trail* [**twitch** v] **chiefly ME** Cf **skid road 1**

A logging road; see quots.

1908 Day *King Spruce* 129 **ME**, The boys who were swampin' the twitch-roads yistiddy told me that deer kept traipsin' past all day. **1942** ME Univ. *Studies* 57.134, *Twitch Road*. A narrow road or trail for *twitching logs* or trees. **1969** Sorden *Lumberjack Lingo* 134 **NEng, Gt Lakes**, *Twitch road*—A narrow road or trail for twitching logs. **1995** Dobbs–Ober *N. Forest* 149 **ME**, That Bud horse, he'll just pull the log right down this twitch trail and out to the skid road. **2004** *DARE* File—Internet **ME**, We finally parked the truck and started walking down an old twitch road to a spot where we would head into the woods.

twitch-up n Also *twitch-up trap* Cf **yank-up**

A snare that uses a bent sapling or similar spring to lift the victim off the ground.

1841 *Pittsfield Sun* (MA) 4 Feb 1/3, Long before he had reached his ninth year, he had caught his father in a twitchup, blown up his grandmother with gunpowder [etc]. **1858** Hammett *Piney Woods Tavern* 173, The boys was dredful ignorant; didn't know nothin' about rabbit twitch-ups [sic], nor patridge snares. **1877** *Scribner's Mth.* 14.420, Master Barefoot finds a drumming-log, and at once whips out his jack-knife, and bending down a neighboring hickory sapling, sets a twitch-up, with a slip-noose at the end, made of a string pulled out of one of his capacious pockets. **1899** (1909) Earle *Child Life* 318 (as of c1750), Other methods of pigeon-killing were by snaring them in "twitch-ups." **1949** Sim *Pages from the Past* 57 **swNJ**, The . . "twitch-up" was a slipnoose of fine brass wire set in a runway and attached to an upright spring-pole. **1958** *Washington Post & Times Herald* (DC) 9 Sept sec A 23/1 *(Hench Coll.)*, Small animal "twitch up". . . the noose is attached to a sapling. It jerks the animal into the air, kills it promptly and keeps his carcass beyond reach of predators. **1972** *Fresno Bee the Republican* (CA) 18 June sec C 1/2, [Caption:] Tim McDaniel, 17, of Sacramento . . offers counseling to Dewayne Ditto, 13, . . on the construction of a twitch-up trap. **2006** *DARE* File—Internet, A twitch-up is a supple sapling, which, when bent over and secured with a triggering device, will provide power to a variety of snares.

t-witey See **tee-whitie**

twit sparrow n

=**chipping sparrow.**

1917 *Wilson Bulletin* 29.2.83 **eKY**, *Spizella passerina* . . twit-sparrow.

twitter bird n

=**goldfinch 1.**

1956 MA Audubon Soc. *Bulletin* 40.254, Goldfinch. . . Twitter Bird.

twix(t) See **betwixt**

'twixt-an'-'tweentimes See **betwixt and betweentimes**

twixt-hell-and-the-white-oak n [Echoic] Cf **chip-fell-out-of-a-white-oak, stick-far-the-red-oak**

=**chuck-will's-widow.**

[**1919** Pearson et al. *Birds NC* 197, There is a widespread impression that the Chuck-will's-widow is the male Whip-poor-will. Its note is frequently interpreted by negroes as "Chip-fell-out-o'-white-oak" and "Twixt-hell-and-white-oak."] **1949** Sprunt–Chamberlain *SC Bird Life* 315, *Chuck-will's-widow. . . Local Names . .* Twixt-hell-and-the-white-oak.

twizzle n [Engl dial]

A twist, tangle.

1915 (1916) Johnson *Highways New Engl.* 263, Every now and then the men would come across a snarl in their nets that they called a twizzle, and often a good deal of time and patience were required to pick and shake it out. **1944** Holton *Yankees Were Like This* 217 **Cape Cod MA** (as of c1890), Then the extra thickness of the pastry gave real scope to her talents and she worked out designs in squirls and twizzles of jagga crust.

two n, adj, pron Usu |tul|; also **chiefly NEast, Sth** |tju, tiu| Pronc-sp *tew* Cf Pronc Intro 3.I.10, **dew** n, **due** A, **new, to** A, **Tuesday**

Std senses, var forms.

1852 Paul *Dashes Amer. Humour* 22, [He] is so big around the kaff of the leg that it takes tew men to mezure him. **1861** Holmes *Venner* 1.41 **NEng**, 'T'll take tew on ye t' handle me. **1871** (1882) Stowe *Fireside Stories* 220 **MA**, Paint it over with tew coats o' paint. **1932** in 1944 *ADD* n**VA**, *Two*. . [tju]. 'About tew weeks ago.' **1939** *LANE* Map 53 **NEng**, [Scattered instances of proncs of the types [tiu, tɪu] occur in s**NEng**; 14 infs in n**NEng** describe "pronunciations of the type . . [tɪu] . . as older though still in use."] **1940** in 1944 *ADD* ne**PA**, *Two*. . . [tju]. **1969** *DARE* FW Addit ce**NC**, *Two*—[tju]. **c1970** Pederson *Dial. Surv. Rural GA* se**GA** *(Two)*, [Of 64 infs, 5 gave proncs of the type [t'ɪʉu]; 1 inf, [t'ɪʉ].] **1989** Pederson *LAGS Tech. Index* 1 **Gulf Region**, *Two* . . [trʉ] (164 [of 914 infs]).

two a cat (knocks) See **two old cat 1**

two-below n Also *two-below touch (football)* [See quots] esp **TX**

A form of touch football; see quots.

1957 *Sat. Eve. Post Letters* **TX**, *Two below*—A beginners game of football. The youngsters object to the violent tackles of the older children so the tackle is made by touching each leg below the knee; hence Two Below. **1977** *Sports Illustr.* 17 Jan (Internet) **TX**, They [=the Oakland Raiders] played throw-and-catch as if they were in a game of two-below touch. **2003** *DARE* File—Internet **TN**, When I was growing up (1960s) in Memphis we could play "football" . . , "two-below" (that is, two hands in contact with the ball carrier "below the belt"), and "touch." **2005** *Ibid* **TX**, *Saturday Afternoon Touch-Football League*— The Game: Two-below touch football. *Ibid* s**TX** (as of 1970), For you readers who are contact sports deprived, two-below is something like gladiators with rubber swords. . . You have to slap somebody twice on the backside, below the waist, in order to "tackle" them.

two-bit adj Cf **jackleg** adj, **two-by-four**

Of little value or significance; petty, small-time.

1870 Bragg *Tekel* 236, I've been a two-bit attorney, a ten-cent counselor [etc]. **1871** *Overland Mth.* 6.269 **CA**, Out of a light, alluvial sand, mixed with irregularly shaped gulch bowlders, Balty panned a "two-bit prospect." **1929** Burnett *Little Caesar* 274 **OH**, The desire to show these two-bit wops who they were yelling at would make him writhe in his chair. **1948** *Edwardsville Intelligencer* (IL) 3 June 4/2, Summoning Gen. Douglas MacArthur from Tokyo just to testify before a Senate Appropriations Committee, like some two-bit bureaucrat. **1950** *WELS Suppl.* cs**WI**, Two-bit town. **1962** Fox *Southern Fried* 127 **SC**, Either of us could handle that fountain and that two-bit sandwich board. **1966–69** *DARE* (Qu. C33, *. . Joking names . . for an out-of-the-way place, or a very small or unimportant place*) Inf **CA**97, Two-bit side of Main Street; (Qu. W36, *What . . people say . . about a woman who uses a lot of cosmetics*) Inf **TX**11, Painted like a two-bit whore; **MI**23, Two-bit whore; (Qu. AA7b, *. . A woman who is very fond of men and is always trying to know more—if she's not respectable about it*) Inf **TX**33, Two-bit whore; (Qu. HH37, *An immoral woman*) Infs **MO**27, **NM**4, **TX**33, Two-bit whore; **GA**83, Two-bit hole; (Qu. LL2, *. . Too small to be worth much: "I don't want that little _____ potato."*) Inf **CA**61, Two-bit. **1970** Tarpley *Blinky* 236 ne**TX**, *Local preacher—part time and not ordained* . . two-bit preacher [rare]. **1986** Pederson *LAGS Concordance*, 1 inf, cn**AR**, Two-bit carpenter; 1 inf, c**LA**, Two-bit lawyer; 1 inf, se**FL**, Two-bit whores. **1999** *Syracuse Herald-Jrl.* (NY)

7 Oct 47/2, I have got another simple and easy way to measure two-bit politicians.

two-boater n [Cf *DPEIE two-boater* "Also *Irish two-boater.* . . An immigrant who came to Prince Edward Island after an interim period elsewhere, usually in Newfoundland."] **esp eMA** *derog*

One who came, or one whose ancestors came, from Ireland to Boston by way of Canada.

1970 Sheehan *Governor* 191 **eMA,** As poor as she was she put on airs about his family, reviling them to Frank as "muckers" and "two-boaters" and warning her son to stay away from their house. **1974** O'Brien *No Final Victories* 48 **eMA** (as of 1950s), He would call an Irish-American who didn't impress him a "two boater," which meant that he or his parents hadn't had enough money to sail directly from Ireland to Boston, but had to stop off in Nova Scotia. **2003** *DARE* File **Boston MA,** [Query:] There was also another term suggesting a bit of smug superiority over those "Irish" who came from the Maritimes—they were referred to as "Two boaters." . . [Reply:] . . My Boston born and bred father (himself the grandson of a two boater) once told me about the expression. **2004** *DARE* File—Internet **Boston MA,** I learned a new insult from an Irish friend here: "Two-boater". It means someone who took a boat from Ireland to Canada and then moved down here.

two-by-four adj, also used absol **scattered, but esp Sth, S Midl**
=**two-bit.**

1887 Haddock *Life* 311 **Upstate NY,** I take no stock in a little two-by-four heaven. **1897** (1969) French *Missionary Sheriff* 13 **IA,** "That how she makes a living?" "Yes—little two-by-four bakery." **1900** *Congressional Record* 14 Feb 33.2.1804 **MO,** No small-bore, two-by-four, radical politicians can hurt that great court. **1916** *DN* 4.331 **KS,** Two by four. . . Small; in disparagement, perhaps in allusion to the dimensions, 2 x 4, of the smallest lumber used for framework. "A lot of little 2 x 4 politicians are yelling their heads off." Pa., W. Res. and southeast. **1917** McCutcheon *Green Fancy* 45 **NEng,** You'd be surprised to know how many great generals we have running two by four farms and choppin' wood for a livin' up here. **1927** *AmSp* 2.366 **cwWV,** *Two-by-four* . . small. "We don't want to buy any two-by-four car this time." **1941** Smith *Going to God's Country* 159 **MO** (as of 1900), So I told myself that we were going to build us a good house. I told H.H. that I was tired of living in a litel [sic] two by four. **1946** *PADS* 6.31 **eNC** (as of 1900–10), *Two-by-four.* . . A person of no importance. Used disparagingly. . . Occasional. **1947** *PADS* 8.23 **KY,** *Two-by-four:* Often *two bit.* *Ibid* 26 **wNY,** *Two-by-four.* **c1960** *Wilson Coll.* **csKY,** *Two-by-four.* . . A person you scorn, a whippersnapper, an upstart, one not dry behind the ears. **1961** Folk *Word Atlas N. LA* map 1312, A part-time preacher, in a local preacher . . [less freq responses include] two by four preacher. **1966–70** *DARE* (Qu. C33, . . *Joking names . . for an out-of-the-way place, or a very small or unimportant place*) Infs **LA**33, **TX**51, Two-by-four place; (Qu. BB53b, . . *A doctor who is not very capable or doesn't have a very good reputation*) Inf **TX**104, Two-by-four; (Qu. CC10, . . *An unprofessional, part-time lay preacher*) Inf **FL**7, Two-by-four preacher. **1986** Pederson *LAGS Concordance,* 1 inf, **ceTX,** Two-by-four carpenter— "botches up things"; 1 inf, **ceMS,** Two-by-four carpenters—laughing.

two-cornered cat n Also *two-corner cat* **esp Missip-Ohio Valleys**
=**two old cat 1.**

1884 *Sun. Herald* (Syracuse NY) 25 May 2/1, *Origin of Base-Ball.* . . I believe the old school game of two-corner cat was the original. **1889** *New Era* (Humeston IA) 26 June [5]/5 (newspaperarchive.com), Get a yarn ball and a knot-hole with a wide board around it and learn to play two-cornered cat. **1890** Howells *Boy's Town* 83 **sOH,** Two-cornered cat was played by four boys: two to bat, and two behind the batters to catch and pitch. **1940** Kennedy–Harlow *Schoolmaster* 228 **IN,** Two-cornered Cat could be played by four—two batters and two others who combined the duties of pitcher and catcher. **1966–69** *DARE* (Qu. EE11, *Bat-and-ball games for just a few players [when there aren't enough for a regular game]*) Inf **IN**5, Two-corner cat; **IL**96, Two-corner cat—you had to have four, two pitchers and two batters; **AR**39, Two-cornered cat.

two-dollar stove, smoke like a v phr **esp WV**

To smoke tobacco excessively.

1950 *WELS* (*A person who smokes a great deal:* . . *"He smokes like _____."*) 2 Infs, **WI,** Two-dollar stove. **1968–70** *DARE* (Qu. DD9b, *Of a person who smokes a great deal* . . *"He smokes like a _____."*) Infs **IN**18, **WV**8, 13, 16, 18, Two-dollar stove. [4 of 5 Infs old]

two-double adj [Engl dial; see *EDD two* num. adj. 10] Cf Intro "Language Changes" I.4
Double.

1899 (1912) Green *VA Folk-Speech* 464, *Two-double.* . . Double. "Make that string two-double, it will be stronger." **1972** Thomas *Pop. Dict. Ozarks Talk* 90, *Two-double.* . . Double, said of cloth or thread in sewing. Two-double in the Ozarks often meant two threads, or two thicknesses [sic] of cloth, not four.

two-eyed berry n Also *two-eye berry, two-eyed chequerberry,* ~ *plum* **esp NEng**
=**partridgeberry 1.**

1832 Williamson *Hist. ME* 1.128, Another [plant], called *Two-eyed berry,* is wild, and its fruit has two dimples, or eyes, and in other respects it resembles a chequerberry. **1849** Amer. Med. Assoc. *Trans.* 2.910, *Mitchella repens.* . . two-eyed chequer berry. **1892** *Jrl. Amer. Folkl.* 5.98 **MA,** *Mitchella repens.* . . Two-eye-berry. **1896** *Ibid* 9.190 **wME,** *Mitchella repens,* . . two-eyed plum. **1950** Gray–Fernald *Manual of Botany* 1327, *M[itchella] repens.* . . *Two-eyed-berry.* . . June, July. **1971** Krochmal *Appalachia Med. Plants* 175, *Mitchella repens.* . . Two-eyed berry, two-eyed chequer berry. . . The bright, orange-red berry and dark green leaves are very attractive.

two-eyed cat n **esp Sth, S Midl**
=**two old cat 1.**

1893 Shands *MS Speech* 22, *Cat.* . . A certain game of ball. In this sense there are two kinds of *cat,—one-eyed cat* and *two-eyed cat.* In the former there is only one batter, in the latter, two. This game is played also in Kentucky and District of Columbia. **1932** Randolph *Ozark Mt. Folks* 46, We played marbles an' blackman an' dare-base an' two-eyed-cat an' townball an' pig-in-a-hole. **1945** *Middlesboro Daily News* (KY) 20 Jan 2/6, Ball games back in those days: Quite different from our present baseball. . . like two-eyed cat. **1965–70** *DARE* (Qu. EE11, *Bat-and-ball games for just a few players [when there aren't enough for a regular game]*) 12 Infs, **scattered, but esp Sth, S Midl,** Two-eyed cat; **OK**42, Two-eyed cat—two bases—you hit ball, run to one base and back home if you can. [11 of 13 Infs old] **1966** *DARE* Tape **AL**4, Then two-eyed—one-eyed I've never seen—two-eyed cat, . . you take two people with the bats and two catchers. . . And of course, this man back here would pitch. And if he knocked this ball or if he got the ball and crossed you, threw it in front of you, you were out and he became the catcher and you became the batter. **1995** *OzarksWatch* 8.2.12 **MO** (as of 1920s), We played a ball game called "two-eyed cat." A batter stood at each end of the ball field with catchers behind them and a pitcher in the middle. Other players played the outfield. The pitcher took turns serving the ball to the batters. If either one hit a ball they would change bases. If they were tagged while running, or if either one struck out, that player went to the outfield and another player moved up. If someone caught a fly, they got to take the batter's place. **2000** *DARE* File—Internet **MS,** My brothers played marbles and "two eyed cat" in our yard. . . One person would get way up there, and another down here. They would have a bat apiece. Somebody was the pitcher, and somebody was the catcher behind.

two-eyed chequerberry (or plum) See **two-eyed berry**

twofer n Cf **fivefer**
In marble play: see quot.
1968 *DARE* (Qu. EE6c, *Cheap marbles*) Inf **IN**45, Twofers, threefers.

two-finger poi See **one-finger poi**

two-fours exclam Also *two-four*
Used to demand a pause or truce during a game or fight.
1949 *WELS Suppl.* **seWI,** "Two-fours" meant time out to catch breath, tie hair ribbon or generally pull self together. I have a faint memory of crossed fingers held up at same time. **1950** *WELS* (*In a game of tag, if you want to rest, what do you call out so that "it" can't catch you?*) 1 Inf, **seWI,** Two-fours. **1968** *DARE* (Qu. EE20, *When two boys are fighting, and the one who is losing wants to stop, he calls out, "_____."*) Inf **NY**113, Two-four.

twoge See **toward A**

two-head(ed) adj *among Black speakers*
=**double-head(ed).**
1927 *Amer. Mercury* 12.236 **AL, NC** [Black], "Some people calls 'em two-head doctors," she remarked next, and explained, "That's because they knows two kin's o' medicine. They can see both ways." **1931**

Hurston in *Jrl. Amer. Folkl.* 44.320 [Black], All of the hoodoo doctors have non-conjure cases. They prescribe folk medicine, "roots", and are for this reason called "two headed doctors". . . [A]ll hoodoo doctors also practice medicine. **1935** Cohn *God Shakes* 127 **MS** [Black], Ef hit wa'n't fer de fact dat you is a two-headed woman, you'd sho be dead. Dey is de strongest conjure on you an' yo' family what can be made. . . Dat same night she set down an' axed her secon' mind. **c1938** in 1970 Hyatt *Hoodoo* 1.265 **New Orleans LA** [Black], Well, you say, "I'm going to a doctor, a *medical doctor.*" Well, a *medical doctor* don't do you no good. "Well, I think I go to a *two-head doctor*"—[that] mean a *hoodoo.* *Ibid* 281 **cwMS** [Black], They never did take it to no *two-headed person* to find out what it was about; she went to a *medical doctor. Ibid* 916 **cnAL** [Black], Ah tell yo', son, you have to go to a *two-headed doctor.* **1945** FWP *Lay My Burden Down* 33 **Sth** (as of c1865) [Black], I says, "There ain't no use to send for Cain. Cain ain't coming up here because they say he is a 'two-head' nigger." (They called all them hoodoo men "two-head" niggers; I don't know why they called them two-head). **1970** *DARE* Tape **OH**102 [Black], What they call two-headed people, fortune tellers and things like this, I say it's a mental thing. **1978** *Culture Med. & Psychiatry* 2.91 [Black], They [=healers of magical illnesses] are often thought capable of doing evil as well as good; he or she may then be described as a 'two-headed' doctor, able to look both ways.

two-headed snake n [See quot 1974]
=**rubber boa.**

    1908 Ditmars *Reptile Book* 211, The Rubber Boa—Silver Snake—Two-headed Snake [etc]. . . The tail is almost as blunt as the head, hence one of the popular names. **1957** Barnes *Nat. Hist. Wasatch Summer* 71 **UT**, We have in the mountains hereabout a real boa constrictor. . . It is a rubber boa, silver snake, two-headed snake or worm snake . . , as it is variously called. **1974** Shaw–Campbell *Snakes West* 51, *Charina* is often called the two-headed snake. . . Its tail is shaped like a head, and when the snake is threatened, it may roll itself into a protective ball with its real head inside the coils and the tail sticking out.

two hole cat See **two old cat 1**

two-holer See **-holer**

two-in-a-hill n
A children's game; see quot.

    1967 Jacobs *Rejoicing* 130 **cIN** (as of c1930), Indoor games were played in the basement. . . Here, the most popular game was Two-in-a-Hill. Boys and girls paired off in a large circle, with each girl standing in front of a boy. One boy, however, was left without a girl, and he must get his girl by winking at the one of his choice. The girl ran to him the second she caught his wink, but if her former partner tagged her on the back before she got away, he could keep her.

two-inner See **inners** n pl[2]

two-knockers See **knocker 7c**

two-leaf pine n [**leaf** n[1] **B1**]

1 also *two-leafed pine, two-leaved Virginian ~, two-needle ~:* Either of two eastern pines: **shortleaf pine 1** or **Jersey pine.**

    1751 *Gentleman's Mag.* 21.561, A List of Seeds arrived this year from our North American Colonies—Dec. 1751. . . Mountain two-leafed pine [etc]. **1785** Marshall *Arbustrum* 102, Pinus virginiana. *Two-leaved Virginian, or Jersey Pine.* . . The leaves are broader and shorter than the other kinds, and of a deeper green colour; they are produced by twos in each sheath. **1908** NJ State Bd. Ag. *Annual Rept. 1907* 174, Near where I was raised there is a forest of old timber, in which there were quite a good many tall, large yellow, two-leaf pine. **1915** U.S. Dept. Ag. *Bulletin* 244.18, The extensive pineries near Lakewood, N.J., are mostly pure stands of shortleaf ("two-leaf") pine. **1968–69** *DARE* (Qu. T15, . . *Kinds of swamp trees*) Inf **NJ**56, Two-leaf pine; (Qu. T17, . . *Kinds of pine trees;* not asked in early QRs) Infs **NJ**52, 55, Two-leaf pine; **NJ**56, Two-needle pine.

2 A native western **pine 1:**

a =**lodgepole pine.**

    1911 Jepson *Flora CA* 20, *P[inus] murrayana* [=*P. contorta* var *m.*] . . is the Tamrac Pine, or Two-leaf Pine, of the high Sierra Nevada. **1915** Muir *Travels AK* 176, Birch and two-leaf pine were common.

b also *two-leaf pinyon, two-leaved (pinyon) pine, two-needle pinyon:* A **piñon 1** (here: *Pinus edulis*).

    1920 Saunders *Useful Wild Plants* 75, The most esteemed nut-pines

are the Two-leaved Pine *(Pinus edulis . .),* a low, round-topped tree . . common from Southern Colorado to Texas and westward to Arizona and Utah. **1962** Sweet *Plants of West* 9, Two-leaved Pinyon Pine, *P[inus] edulis,* and One-leaved Pinyon Pine, *P. monophylla,* are both desert mountain trees with short needles and small cones. **1979** Little *Checklist U.S. Trees* 192, *Pinus edulis.* . . Two-leaf pinyon, two-needle pinyon. **1980** Little *Audubon Guide N. Amer. Trees W. Region* 276, "Two-leaf Pinyon" . . *Pinus edulis.* . . Needles: *evergreen; 2 in bundle.* **2003** *DARE* File—Internet **NM**, Pinyon (two-leaf) Pine—*Pinus edulis.*

two-leaved Solomon's seal n [See quot 1975] esp **NEast**
A **false lily of the valley** (here: *Maianthemum canadense*).

    1807 *Med. Repository* 5.125, *Catalogue of Plants collected at Plandome, on Long-Island.* . . Convallaria bifolia, *Lin.* two-leaved Solomon's-seal. **1843** Torrey *Flora NY* 2.299, *Two-leaved Solomon's-seal.* . . Moist shady woods, particularly around the roots of trees: common. **1848** in 1850 Cooper *Rural Hours* 103 **NY**, The different varieties of Solomon's seal . . are now in bloom. . . [T]he flowers of the tribe are very numerous here, especially the false spikenard, the delicate two-leaved Solomon's seal, or bead-ruby, and the Clintonia. **1859** (1949) Thoreau *Jrl.* 12.290 **MA**, As for autumnal tints, the . . two-leaved Solomon's-seal is partly yellowed and withered. **1892** *Jrl. Amer. Folkl.* 5.104 **NH**, *Maianthemum Canadense,* . . two-leaved Solomon's seal. **1910** Graves *Flowering Plants* 123 **CT**, Two-leaved Solomon's Seal. **1946** Tatnall *Flora DE* 84, Two-leaved Solomon's Seal. Common in rich woodlands and occasional in swamps. **1975** Duncan–Foote *Wildflowers SE* 254, *Two-leaved Solomon's-seal.* . . The small white flowers and fruits are borne in a small raceme above the 2–3 (or rarely 1) leaves, suggestive of a diminutive False Solomon's-seal.

two-leaved Virginian pine See **two-leaf pine 1**

two-legged eel n [See quots] Cf **four-legged eel**
A **siren B.**

    1911 Acad. Sci. St. Louis *Trans.* 20.66, *Siren lacertina.* . . Two-legged Eel. Mud-Eel. . . The single pair of legs is placed close behind the head. **1928** Baylor Univ. Museum *Contrib.* 16.9 **TX**, *Siren lacertina.* . . *Two-legged Eel.* This name distinguishes the Siren from the four-legged Congo Snake. (In many east Texas and Louisiana localities all so-called eels are amphibians, the true (fish) eels being known by other names).

two-mule adj chiefly **Sth** Cf **one-horse 1**
In farming: requiring only two draft animals.

    1879 *Daily Constitution* (Atlanta GA) 3 Jan [3]/3 (newspaperarchive.com), Mr. J.R. Strother, of Dougherty, this year, on a two mule farm, made thirty-six bales of cotton, besides a good crop of general farm products. **1892** *Century Illustr. Mag.* 43.460 **GA**, He . . cultivated a two-mule farm on the Worthington lands with a pair of unfed steers. **1949** *Dothan Eagle* (AL) 30 Dec 12/7, [Advt:] *For Rent:* Small two mule crop the old way on halves. **1976** *Valley News & Green Sheet* (Van Nuys CA) 25 June 27/3, The last thing my mother wanted to remember was that 160-acre two-mule farm she came off of in Oklahoma. **1986** Pederson *LAGS Concordance,* 1 inf, **cAL**, Two-mule farming—farming with two mules. **1989** Flynt *Poor But Proud* 81 **ceAL** (as of 1910–30), Many farmers quantified farms not by how many acres they had but by how many horses or mules it took to cultivate them (hence such phrases as "a one-horse farm" or a "two-mule place"). **2002** *DARE* File—Internet **AL**, Everyday brings new lessons in "plowing a two mule crop with a shetland pony." **2006** *Ibid* **AL**, He and his sister grew up in a shack of a house in Bermuda, Alabama. His father was a two-mule farmer, his mother a part-time beautician.

two-needle pine See **two-leaf pine 1**

two-needle pinyon See **two-leaf pine 2b**

two o cat See **two old cat 1**

two o'clock (at the button factory), it's See **one o'clock, it's**

two old cat n

1 also *two a cat (knocks), ~ o cat, two hole cat:* A variation of the bat-and-ball game **one old cat 1. chiefly Nth** See Map Also called **two-cornered cat, two-eyed cat** Cf **four-cornered cat, four old cat, three old cat**

    1850 *Knickerbocker* 35.84 **NY**, [We] never indulged in a game of chance of any sort in the world, save the 'bassball,' 'one' and 'two-hole-cat,' and 'barn-ball' of our childhood. **1865** *Harper's New Mth. Mag.* 30.608 **CT** (as of c1815), On the very school-ground where I used to play ball are now visible the foot marks of the same old games: "one old cat," and "two old cat." **1883** Newell *Games & Songs* 185, We need only mention the game of "Old Cat." . . The game is . . named from the number of batters, "One Old Cat," or "Two Old Cat." **1894** *Century Illustr. Mag.* 47.854, There is a game of ball played with bats called simply "cat"—sometimes "two-hole cat," "three-hole cat," and so on; or, "two old cat," "three old cat," in the East, according to the number of holes, or bases. **1907** *DN* 3.195 **seNH,** Old cat. . . A simple game of ball with two . . players; hence called *two old cat.* **1908** *DN* 3.297 **eAL, wGA,** Cat, one (two, or three) ole. **1910** *DN* 3.446 **cwNY,** Old cat. . . If there are four players, two of them batters, the batters exchanging bases when one hits the ball, the game is called *two old cat.* **1965–70** *DARE* (Qu. EE11, *Bat-and-ball games for just a few players [when there aren't enough for a regular game]*) Infs **IL**14, 40, **MA**5, **NJ**6, 8, **NY**73, 75, 92, **SD**1, Two old cat; **MI**117, Two old cat—with more than three players; **PA**104, Two old cat—a couple of batters; **MA**58, **MI**45, **MT**3, **NY**68, Two o cat; **CT**9, Two o cat—two batters; **RI**17, Two o cat—two batters, catcher and fielder, two bases; **SC**32, Two o cat—one base—run from home to base without being put out . . , you had two batters and the second had to bat the first in from base if the first was unable (or unwilling) to make it home again on his own hit; **NY**78, **WY**5, Two a cat; **CA**166, Two a cat—one at bat and another waiting; **MI**24, Two a cat knocks.

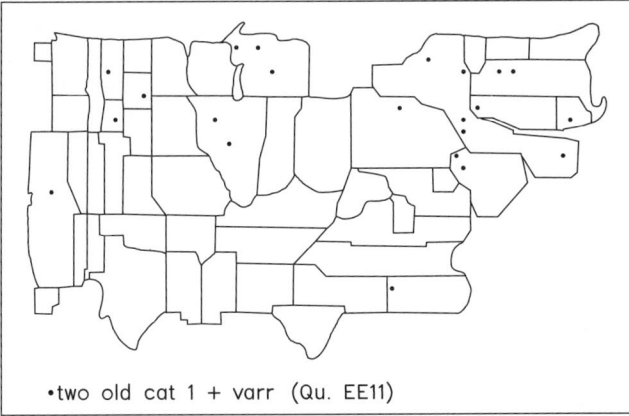

•two old cat 1 + varr (Qu. EE11)

2 See quot. Cf **cat** n **3a, one old cat 2**
1968 *DARE* (Qu. EE10, *A game in which a short stick lying on the ground is flipped into the air and then hit with a longer stick*) Inf **NY**57, Two old cat.

twoser n Also sp *tooser, toozer* **esp Boston MA**
A cheap clay playing-marble.
1854 Shillaber *Life Partington* 284 **Boston MA,** "And there's a twoser," continued Ike, still counting, "and a Chinese . . I mean marbles, aunt." **1890** *DN* 1.60 **cwMA,** Commy: a clay marble of the kind least valued by boys. . . [*DN* Ed: Tooser [tuzə] was used twenty years ago (and probably is still used) in Boston in this sense. It was supposed to be derived from *two.*] **1901** *Outing* 38.204 **NEng,** Beginning with the cheapest marble . . : The "peewee," small and made of potash, I believe; "commie," a clay marble of various colors; "doggie," a brown clay marble; "twoser" (two for a cent), similar to a doggie, but larger [etc]. **1933** *Hanley Disks* **Boston MA,** What did you call these little clays? . . Toozers.

twosie n
In marble play:
a A marble; see quot.
1957 *Sat. Eve. Post Letters* **GA,** Names of . . marbles. . . "Twosies" were by far the most popular, and cost more than "onesies". They were blue, tan or brown, highly glazed, with occasional white spots showing. Also known as "chinies", or "chinas".
b pl: A game played with or for two marbles.
c1970 Wiersma *Marbles Terms* **swMI** (as of c1965), Twosies . . same as definitions . . [below] except that two marbles are used. [*Ibid* **MI** (as of c1955), Foursies. . . A type of play in which four marbles are thrown out at once. *Ibid* **swMI** (as of c1967), Foursies. . . Playing for four marbles. . . Using only four marbles as shooters.] **1983** (1985) Fields–Fields *Lemon Swamp* 48 **SC,** They would play "onesies" and "twosies."

two-sled n Also *two-sleds* **esp ME** Cf **double sled, twin-sled, wagon sled**
A logging vehicle consisting of two short sleds linked to-

gether; hence comb *two-sled road* a road adapted for such vehicles.
1890 (1891) Heywood *Diary* 86 **ME,** We walked an hour and then hit the two-sled road. **1905** U.S. Forest Serv. *Bulletin* 61.42 [Logging terms], *Logging sled.* The heavy double sled used to haul logs from the skidway or yard to the landing. (N[orthern] F[orest]) Syn.: twin sleds, two sleds, wagon sled. **1913** Bryant *Logging* 160, The transportation of logs from the skidway to a landing on streams, to a railroad or to a mill is often effected by means of a heavy sled called the "two-sled," "twin-sled" or "wagon-sled." . . The front and rear sleds are often joined by two ½-inch or ⅞-inch chains attached to the back side of the forward bunk . . , then crossed and attached to the noses of the rear runners. *Ibid,* Two-sled roads should be built during the summer or early fall. **1945** Hamlin *9 Mile Bridge* 46 **nME,** The logs are piled on the side of the road to be loaded onto bobsleds—double sleds, two sleds or wagon sleds, as they are variously called—that carry them to the landing on the river. **1957** Beck *Folkl. ME* 230, There would be loaded onto "two-sleds," a double bob sled, and the whole hauled down to the river or driving stream. **1976** *Bennington Banner* (VT) 3 Feb 3/1 **ME,** Later still, . . roads were improved and the two-sled was put into use. A two-sled was made of two one-sleds. A two-sled road didn't mean a road wide enough for teams to meet and pass, but one over which logs were moved on two-sleds.

two-step n **esp N Cent, West** See Map Cf **squirts**
Usu in combs: Diarrhea.
1944 *Clinics* 2.1220, The Marines called this diarrhea epidemic "the green apple two-step." **1950** *WELS (Diarrhea or looseness of the bowels)* 2 Infs, **WI,** Green-apple two-step. **1953** Sherman *Aztec Two-Step* [title]. **1962** *Western Folkl.* 21.28 **swCA,** The North American in Mexico has coined a number of names for the inevitable dysentary [sic] and diarrhea: "Mexican two-step," . . "Aztec hop." **1965–70** *DARE* (Qu. BB19, *Joking names for looseness of the bowels*) Inf **IL**61, Apple-blossom two-step; **KS**2, Boot hill two-step; **OH**2, Crab-apple two-step; **CA**49, 59, **IA**47, **NE**2, **NY**1, **OH**15, 34, Green-apple two-step; **RI**15, Huckleberry two-step; **CA**7, Mexican two-step; **CA**170, Two-step; (Qu. BB28) Inf **IL**35, Green-apple two-step. **1987** *DARE* File, [Letter from 82-year-old woman:] I didn't go to church this morning did get partly dressed, but had the green apple two step, was keeping the bathroom busy, didn't want to take a chance.

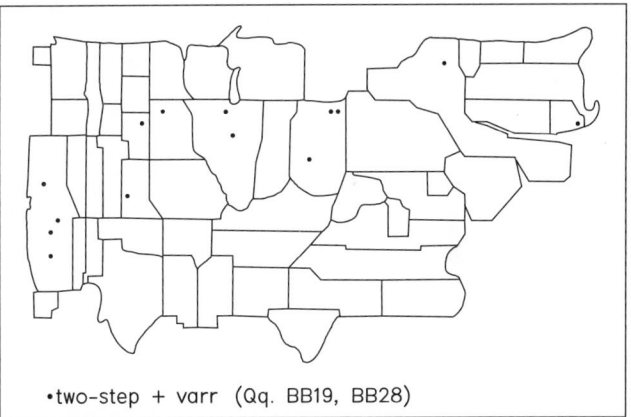

•two-step + varr (Qq. BB19, BB28)

two streaks of rust See **streak of rust**

two-striped skunk n Also *two-stripe*
A **skunk** n **1** (here: *Mephitis mephitis*).
1902 Biol. Soc. DC *Proc.* 15.2, If . . this is not one of the little spotted skunks, but the common two-striped skunk of the eastern United States, no further argument is required. **1959** in 2003 *DARE* File—Internet **IL, WI,** The two-striped skunk is about the size of a large cat. **1961** Jackson *Mammals WI* 374, *Mephitis mephitis hudsonica.* . . *Vernacular names.*—In Wisconsin, commonly called skunk. Other names include . . two-striped skunk. **1967** *DARE* (Qu. P26, *Names and nicknames . . for a skunk*) Inf **CO**4, Two-stripe.

two-tick-take n
In marble play: see quot.
c1970 Wiersma *Marbles Terms, Two-tick-take*—A convention whereby the opponents agree that a piece must be hit twice in succession before it is captured. *Ibid* **swMI** (as of 1960), *Two-tick-take*—Must hit the marble twice before you can keep it.

two-timer See **timer**

two-toilet Irish n pl Also *T.T.I.* **chiefly MA**

Middle-class descendants of lower-class Irish immigrants; hence adj *two-toilet Irish* characterized by such social mobility.

1973 Stroud *Viewpoints* 192 **MA,** "Two-toilet Irish," the deserters were called derisively by those who remained. **1975** *DARE* File **swMA,** T.T.I.—Two-Toilet-Irish: the Irish in America who have moved up in the world above *shanty, clay-pipe,* and *lace-curtain* Irish to having very comfortable homes—used in Boston and surrounding area to north and west, 1975 and before. **1976** *Times Herald Rec.* (Middletown NY) 3 Dec 83/1, I kept to my own career, aspiring to someday become two-toilet Irish. **1990** *Yankee* Mar 130 **swMA,** People in Hungry Hill describe themselves proudly as "shanty Irish." . . [T]hey refer to those of us who have moved on not as "lace curtain" Irish, a comforting sort of disparagement, but as "T.T." or "two-toilet Irish." **2005** *DARE* File—Internet **Boston MA,** The two-toilet Irish turned lace-curtain Irish have moved to Weston and Nantucket. **2006** *Boston Globe* (MA) 31 Jan (Internet) **MA,** Gamble . . grew up in Trumbull, Conn., and describes himself as the son "of a guy born and raised in Waltham, and a mom who was two-toilet Irish from Jamaica Plain."

t-wyty See **tee-whitie**

-ty See **to** prep, adv **A2**

tyee n [Chinook jargon *tyee* a chief]

1 also *tyhee;* also attrib; Among loggers: a boss; an important person. **Pacific NW**

1911 Clayson *Hist. Narr.* 45 **wWA** (as of c1880), Billy Jamieson's important position as a confidential "tyhee" of the mill company gave him a standing in the estimation of the community that the others did not enjoy. **1938** (1939) Holbrook *Holy Mackinaw* 265, Tyee. A chief or big shot. Hence, a tyee logger is head of a large logging operation. **1958** McCulloch *Woods Words* 202 **Pacific NW,** *Tyee*—Top man, the boss; from the Indian, meaning chief.

2 See **tyee salmon.**

tyee grouse n

=**spruce grouse.**

[**1860** U.S. War Dept. *Rept. Explor. Railroad* 12.3.221 **Pacific NW,** *Tetrao franklinii* [=*Falcipennis canadensis*]. . . *Franklin's Grouse; Tyee Grouse.* . . This bird, by the Indians, has the jargon name, "Tyee Kulla-Kulla" or the "chief bird." . . Mr. George Gibbs, in a letter to me, [says]. . . "It is a shorter bird than the sharp-tailed [grouse], but stout in proportion. The eyelids and wattles on the neck, *bright red.* . . Abundant and very tame. The Indians call them the *tyee* grouse."] **1917** (1923) *Birds Amer.* 2.16, *Canachites franklini* [=*Falcipennis canadensis*]. . . Mountain Grouse; Wood Grouse; Tyee Grouse. **1953** Jewett *Birds WA* 201, *Franklin Spruce Grouse.* . . Other names: Fool Hen; Tyee Grouse.

tyee salmon n Also *tyee* **esp WA, AK**

=**chinook salmon.**

[**1860** U.S. War Dept. *Rept. Explor. Railroad* 12.3.310 **WA,** I am convinced that should the business [of salting salmon for market] be undertaken properly by men *skilled in the business,* who, with ordinary care and a selection of none but the silvery spring salmon (*S[almo] quinnat, S. gairdneri,* and *S. paucidens*) on the Columbia, . . or those known to the Indians as *tyee* salmon, on Puget Sound, it will be found highly profitable.] [**1863** Gibbs *Chinook Jargon* 28 **Pacific NW,** Tyee salmon, *the spring salmon.*] **1881** *Amer. Naturalist* 15.177 **Pacific NW,** As vernacular names of definite application, the following are on record. . . Quinnat— . . Sacramento salmon. [T]yee salmon. **1904** *Salmon & Trout* 154, The quinnat salmon (*Oncorhynchus tschawytscha*) bears a number of other names in different regions, such as chinook salmon, tyee [etc]. **1940** Smith *Puyallup–Nisqually* 236 **WA,** Dried salmon was made from the tyee and the summer and early fall salmons. **1962** Salisbury *Quoth the Raven* 121 **seAK,** The *King* salmon, also called the *Tyee,* which means king in the Chinook jargon, and also the *Chinook,* are largely caught by trolling. **1968** *DARE* (Qu. P1, . . *Kinds of freshwater fish . . caught around here . . good to eat*) Inf **AK1,** Chinook = Columbia River and Puget Sound tyee [ˌtɑɪˈi]. **1979** *NYT Article Letters* **AK** [Fishing terms], King salmon: . . Tyee.

Tyewsday See **Tuesday**

tyhee See **tyee 1**

typa See **taba**

typewriter n

A queen (in a deck of playing cards).

1897 *KS Univ. Qrly.* (ser B) 6.93 **MO,** *Typewriter:* the queen in cards. **1918** *DN* 5.29 **NW,** *Typewriter.* . . Queen at cards. Rare.

ty-ty See **titi**

tzitterle See **zitterli**

u See **I** pron

ub See **of** prep

uddah, udder See **other**

udder fever n Cf **bag fever**
Bovine udder edema or a disease such as mastitis.

  1965–70 *DARE* (Qu. K7, *What sickness can a cow get in her udder—for example, if she's left unmilked too long?*) Infs **CA**31, 181, **IN**19, **OK**14, 53, **OR**13, Udder fever; **MI**40, Udder fever—usually caused by distended udder.

uff-da exclam, n |'uf də, 'uf͵dɑ| Pronc-spp *oofda, oof-dee, oofta, oof-tee, uff-dah* [Norw *uff da*] **orig in Norw settlement areas, esp MN, WI**
Used as an expression of surprise, aversion, disgust, or pain; something that evokes such a response; see quots.

  [**1941** Schlytter *Tall Brothers* 346 **WI**, Yes, we had quite a time—quite a time—oof da! I guess I[=a Swede]'ve had enough to eat.] **1950** *WELS (Exclamations caused by . . A slight burn)* 1 inf, **swWI**, Uff-da. **1966–68** *DARE* (Qu. NN21b, *Exclamations caused by sudden pain—a hard blow on the chest)* Inf **ND**2, Oofda; **AK**8, Uff-da ['ufta]; **ND**2, Uff-da ['ufdə]—Scandinavian expression; **SD**8, Uff-da. **1976** *Mt. Democrat & Placerville Times* (CA) 27 May sec A 7/3, *Uff da* reads the personalized license plate of Dave Hammero. . . Hammero says the expression was brought over by his Norwegian grandfather. Its rough translation is, "Oh my goodness" or "Oh no." "It's not a cuss word . . but it can be used when things go wrong or in disgust." **1977** *DARE* File **csWI**, *[Shoppers Window* (Madison WI) 21 June:] Uff da! Midsummer madness has hit Bord and Stol! **1980** *News* (Frederick MD) 31 Dec sec B 9/1 **MN**, Lutefisk lovers are made, not born. Even Nordics a few generations removed from the Old Country have to acquire a taste for the odoriferous codfish made flaky, and supposedly tasty, by being bathed in lye—"lute"—or caustic soda. Oofda! **1986** *NADS Letters* **ND**, Student from Parker, N.D., says a Norwegian-sounding term *uffda* or *oofta* is commonly used there in the way that *caramba* is used by Mexicans as an exclamation of wonder. **1991** *DARE* File **csWI**, A baker of Norwegian background said that the word *kling* was probably an uffda, meaning a mishearing or mistake. **1995** *Norw.-Amer. Studies & Rec.* 34.101, Uff da, but they were difficult times. We never knew when we would get paid, or how much money it would be when some checks did come. **1999** *DARE* File—Internet [Central Florida Green Bay Packer Backers] **WI**, *Uff-dah:* an expression of weariness or exertion. **2005** *DARE* File **csWI**, In Madison, Wisconsin one also hears *oof-dee* and *oof-tee* in addition to the usual *uff-da*. **2007** *DARE* File **neIA, seMN, csWI**, "Uff-da" ['uf͵dɑ] is an all-purpose exclamation of frustration ("The neighbor kids trampled my flower bed again—uff-da!"), disgust ("The sewer backed up—uff-da!"), or amazement ("Six inches of snow in May—uff-da!"). Its closest English translation seems to be "oh, for gosh sakes" (another conversational staple in Norwegian settlement areas). When a slightly more emphatic exclamation is warranted, some of the older folks still say "uff-da fyda" ['uf͵dɑ 'fi͵dɑ].

ugly adj, adv, n Pronc-sp *Gullah oagly* Cf *DBE* (at *ogly*), *DJE*
A Form.

  1922 Gonzales *Black Border* 316 **sSC, GA coasts** [Gullah glossary], *Oagly*—ugly. **1930** Stoney-Shelby *Black Genesis* 92 **seSC**, Do Lord! Dis is a oagly gang o' people. **1992** Geraty *Bittle* 10 **Charleston SC** [Gullah], Dey [=old roosters] stan' so oagly de hen nebbuh pay'um no min'.

B As adj.
1 Of a person: mean, bad-tempered, quarrelsome; unpleasant, offensive; hence adv *ugly* in such a manner. **chiefly NEast, Sth, S Midl** See Map on p. 776

  1814 in 1947 *AmSp* 22.275, *[Ugly]*—Ugly applied to the temper & disposition—never to the appearance. **1816** Pickering *Vocab.* 191, *Ugly.* Ill-tempered, bad. *(New England.)* Ex. He is an *ugly* fellow; that is, of a bad disposition, wicked. The compound *ugly-tempered* is sometimes used. They are both heard only among the illiterate. **1823** in 1839 Mathews *Memoirs* 3.386 **PA**, 'Ugly' means *ill-tempered.* 'It is a pity such a pretty woman should be so ugly.' **1842** Kirkland *Forest Life* 1.109 **MI**, He's got some grit, but he a'n't ugly. **1848** Lowell *Biglow* 146 '**Upcountry**' **MA**, Ugly, *ill-tempered, intractable.* **1854** in 1944 *AmSp* 19.228 **NEng**, R. Does Jeremi*ur* behave well now? S. No, he's very *ugly.* He tried to burn the barn. **1878** *Appletons' Jrl.* 5.415 **NEng**, An *ugly* person in New England is an *unamiable* person, and a person of simply unagreeable features is a *homely* person. **1886** *Education* 7.136, The writer well remembers her own surprise the first time she heard ugly used in the sense of ill-tempered. It was a boarding-house keeper, who remarked of her assistant that she was never ugly except on rainy Mondays. **1887** (1892) Hinman *Corporal Si Klegg* 110, 'Tain't a patchin' ter what they does ter them that's reel ugly; and there's some o' the soljers that's chuck full o' the old Nick. **1899** (1912) Green *VA Folk-Speech* 465, *Ugly.* . . Ill-natured; cross-grained; quarrelsome; ill-conditioned. **1905** *DN* 3.23 **cCT**, *Ugly.* . . Ill-tempered. **1907** *DN* 3.219 **nwAR**, *Ugly.* . . Ill-tempered. **1933** Rawlings *South Moon* 105 **nFL**, It made him ugly to find there was still much he did not know. **1965–70** *DARE* (Qu. GG35b, *[To sulk or pout:] "Because she couldn't go, she's been _____ all day."*) 9 Infs, 8 **NEast**, Ugly; (Qu. X10b, *To tell a person to stop talking—not very politely)* Inf **FL**6, Shut up; quit being so rude and ugly; (Qu. Y3, *To say uncomplimentary things about somebody)* Inf **NM**9, Being pretty ugly; **KS**2, To be catty; ugly [Inf queries]; (Qu. AA6b, . . *A man who is fond of being with women and tries to attract their attention—if he's rude or not respectful)* Inf **KY**80, Ugly; (Qu. AA7b, . . *A woman who is very fond of men and is always trying to know more—if she's not respectable about it)* Infs **MS**29, **NC**88, **SC**34, **VA**35, (She's) ugly; (Qu. AA8, *When people make too much of a show of affection in a public place . . "There they were at the church supper _____ [with each other]."*) Inf **MO**8, Acting ugly; (Qu. EE21b, *When boys were fighting very actively . . "For a while those fellows really _____."*) Inf **TN**62, Were really ugly; (Qu. GG4, *Stirred up, angry: "When he saw them coming he got _____."*) 8 Infs, 6 **Sth**, (Pretty) ugly; (Qu. GG16, . . *Finding fault, or complaining: "You just can't please him—he's always _____."*) Inf **MN**35, Ugly; (Qu. GG18, . . *'Obstinate': "Why does he have to be so _____."*) Infs **IN**49, **TN**37, **TX**74, Ugly; (Qu. GG35a, *To sulk or pout: "It won't do any good to _____ about it."*) Inf **MS**80, Act ugly; (Qu. GG38, *Somebody who is usually mean and bad tempered: "He's an awful _____."*) Infs **ME**19, **MN**3, **NM**9, Ugly (person); (Qu. GG41, *To lose patience easily: "You never did see such a _____ person."*) Inf **NY**22, Ugly; (Qu. HH22c, . . *A very mean person . . "He's mean enough to _____."*) Inf **MI**13, Ugly enough to stop a clock; (Qu. II21, *When somebody behaves unpleasantly or without manners: "The way he behaves, you'd think he was _____."*) Inf **LA**25, Ugly; (Qu. II36a, *Somebody who talks back or gives rude answers: "Did you ever see such a _____?"*) Inf **LA**3, Ugly person; (Qu. II36b, *Of somebody who talks back or gives rude answers . . "She certainly is _____!"*) Inf **GA**82, Ugly. [28 of 37 total Infs comm types 4, 5] **1969** *DARE* FW Addit **NC**, *Ugly*—bad or unmannerly, as in "I'm feeling ugly today."

1979 Lewis *How to Talk Yankee* [35] **nNEng,** *Ugly . . ill-tempered.* **2000** *NADS Letters* **AL, GA,** *Momma, she was bein' ugly to me.* **2005** Williams *Gratitude* 533 **wNC** (as of 1940s), *Act ugly: behave badly; be hateful, mean, or have a ugly temper.*

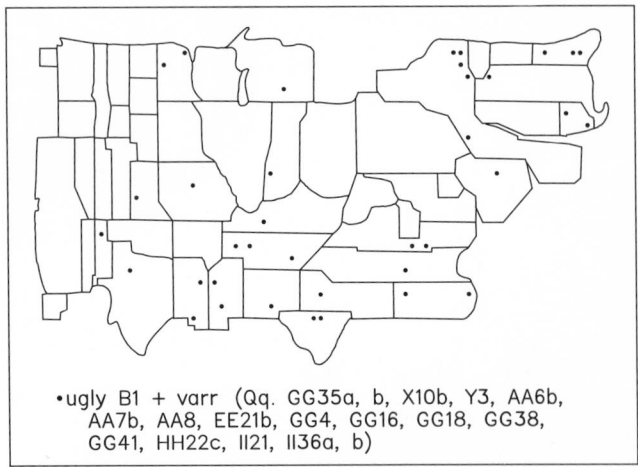

•ugly B1 + varr (Qq. GG35a, b, X10b, Y3, AA6b, AA7b, AA8, EE21b, GG4, GG16, GG18, GG38, GG41, HH22c, I121, I136a, b)

2 Of an animal: fractious, refractory.   **scattered, but chiefly NEast, N Cent, TN**   See Map

1845 *Evergreen* 2.78 **NY,** *What do you keep such an ugly dog for, George? He will be the death of me, I know.* **1876** MA *State Bd. Ag. Annual Rept. for 1875* 78, *It is a crime to breed an ugly dam either to an ugly horse, or a good-natured horse.* **1880** MI *State Bd. Ag. Annual Rept.* 168, *To break a heifer or subdue an ugly cow requires wisdom and patience.* **1898** *Recreation* 9.215 **csWI,** *A neighbor had an ugly cow he wished to butcher, but was afraid of her.* **1920** Barrus *John Burroughs* 294 **NY,** *He often says of himself, "I can look in the face of an ugly dog and win him, but with an ugly man I have less success, and with an ugly woman—I would turn and flee."* **1965–70** *DARE* (Qu. K16, *A cow with a bad temper*) 61 Infs, **scattered, but chiefly NEast, N Cent, TN,** *Ugly* (animal); **MN**12, **TN**31, 33, *Ugly cow;* **ME**19, *Kinda ugly;* **WI**14, *Ugly s.o.b.;* (Qu. K42, *A horse that is rough, wild, or dangerous*) Infs **ME**5, **MI**47, **MA**15, **NY**9, 72, 200, 233, **VT**9, *Ugly horse;* (Qu. K68, . . *A goat that habitually strikes people with its horns*) Infs **MI**47, 113, **NY**200, *Ugly goat.* **1966** *DARE* Tape **MI**2, *It [=a tame wolf] got so it was a little ugly with strangers.*

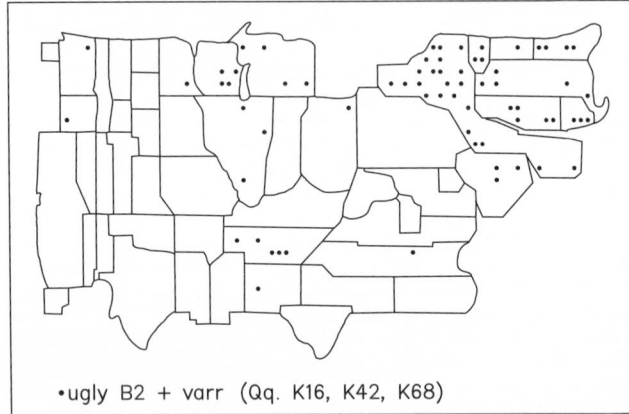

•ugly B2 + varr (Qq. K16, K42, K68)

3 Of speech: offensive, obscene; insulting, slanderous; hence adv *ugly* offensively, insultingly.   **formerly more widespread; now chiefly Sth**   See Map

1865 (1866) *Luke Darrell* 115, *"Be careful to read it quietly to yourself," said the lady, delivering to him the tract, "for fear some of those other boys may talk ugly to you about it, or even destroy it."* **1876** *Arthur's Illustr. Home Mag.* 44.372 **PA,** *He teased, and teased, until I had to let him go. . . Jane says that he talked ugly to her after he got there, and declared that he wasn't coming home any more.* **1889** *Galveston Daily News* (TX) 29 Aug 1/4, *Sheriff Garvey made some ugly talk about the jaybirds. . . He denounced the jaybirds as cowards and sons of _____.* **1892** Davis *Silhouettes* 126, *Though Jane knew nothing of clergymen or church doctrines, and had sometimes heard a good deal of ugly talk in the wings, she was a decent, pure girl, and had naturally a*

devout soul. **1893** *Overland Mth.* (2d ser) 22.257 **CA,** *The heavy stockholders in Sacramento were made to understand that the miners were talking ugly, and that possible mischief was brewing.* **1947** *Middletown Times Herald* (NY) [5 Aug] 6/3 (newspaperarchive.com), *Often I must read of the ugly things . . said by a child to his parents. . . I [often] hear from a mother who writes of a child cursing her.* **1965–70** *DARE* (Qu. Y4, . . *A very uncomplimentary remark*) Infs **FL**33, 35, **NC**2, 9, 22, 24, 47, **NJ**67, *Ugly remark;* **MI**55, **TN**24, **VA**31, *Ugly thing* (to say); **NC**82, *He said ugly things;* (Qu. Y3, *To say uncomplimentary things about somebody*) Infs **AL**8, **LA**23, **VA**5, *Talk ugly* (about); (Qu. NN16, *Swearing or using obscene language: "He's always _____.";* total Infs questioned, 75) Inf **FL**6, *Talking ugly; using ugly words.* **1966–67** *DARE* FW Addit **AL,** *"That was an ugly remark." . . It can refer to a statement that is catty or gossipy;* **GA**21, *"Ugly talk", or "talkin' ugly"—to use profanity and obscenities.* **1996** *Atlanta Jrl.–Constitution* (GA) 11 Feb sec M 3/1, *Bridle your tongue* (hush up talking ugly). **1999** *AmSp* 74.247 **ceSC,** *I don't be liking no ugly talk in the movies. I won't sit there and listen to it.* [female 50+ . .]. **2004** *DARE* File—Internet **DC,** *If you want to talk ugly take into account some tatics [sic] used by the pro-lottery folks.* **2005** *Ibid* **AL,** *Me Talk Ugly Some Days. . . [I]f you possess a delicate nature and are in the same room with me when I hit myself in the thumb with a hammer, allow me to suggest you plug your ears.* **2007** *Ibid* **TX,** *Don't you talk ugly to me.* *Ibid* **eMD,** *As a boat dealer, one of the faster ways to annoy your prospect is to talk ugly about his favorite engine.*

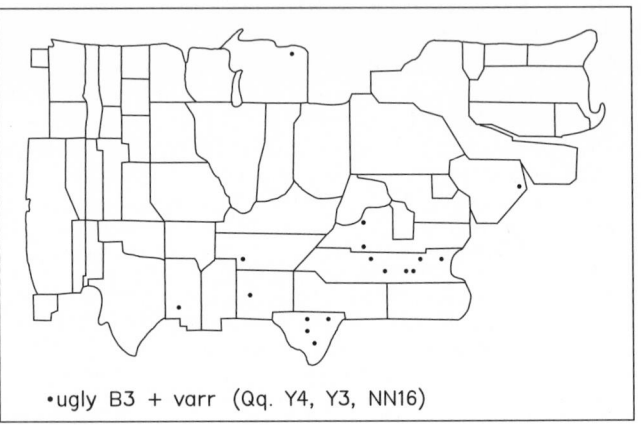

•ugly B3 + varr (Qq. Y4, Y3, NN16)

C As adv.

See **B1, 3** above.

D As noun.

1a Sin, wickedness—used in phr *God don't love ugly* and varr; see quots.   [This proverb appears to be widespread in the Caribbean: cf *DCEU, DJE* (1803 →).]   *chiefly among Black speakers*

1899 *Stevens Point Daily Jrl.* (WI) 1 Feb [3]/5 (newspaperarchive.com) **Chicago IL** [Black], *God don't love ugly, dat is de reason he's goin' ter destroy de white folks an' save only dose cullud people who flee de wrath ter come.* **1934** Hurston *Jonah's Gourd Vine* 205 **AL** [Black], *Youse in de majority now, but God sho don't love ugly.* **1939** in Lib. of Congress *Amer. Memory: WPA Life Hist.* (Internet) **NYC** [Black], *That's a lie an' you know it. An duh Lawd don't love ugly.* **1940** *Reader's Digest* July 59 **LA** [Black], *Hit was ugly, and God don't love ugly.* **1987** Kytle *Voices* 159 **NC** [Black], *They should mind out how they talk. Things come back to you, and God don't love ugly.* **1988** Naylor *Mama Day* 194 **GA, SC coast** [Black], *God don't like ugly, but He must have found something worth saving in her 'cause the child was gonna make it.* **1999** *News* (Frederick MD) 26 Oct sec B 1/5 **FL** [Black], *You take cheap shots, you claim to be a man of God, but God doesn't like ugly.* **2000** *Star–Herald* (Scottsbluff NE) 5 Oct sec A 5/1, *I once had a motherly little secretary who I heard commenting "God doesn't like ugly, Mr. West" when I was giving someone a deserved, but slightly profane piece of my mind.*

b Spec: fornication.   **esp Sth**

1938 *Atlantic Mth.* 62.407 **MS,** *He was in for thirty days for throwing bricks at a woman at a church social because she would n't do ugly for forty cents.* **1943** Cohn *Love in America* 42, *In the white vision they are always showing their ivory teeth in black laughter, . . or "doing ugly" with complaisant women.* **1980** King *Of Outlaws* 98 **TX,** *She did ugly to him for a bit, he permitting her to do the main work, while he drifted* toward sleep. **2006** Epstein *Friendship* 131 **NC,** The *New Yorker* writer Joseph Mitchell . . once, in a strong Carolinian accent, told me: "Joe. . . When I was a boy, if you did *ugly* with a girl, her brother might kill you."

2 in phr *like ugly on an ape* and varr: Tenaciously; incessantly; untiringly. **scattered, but esp freq TX** Cf **June bug 4; white on rice, like**

1968 *Coe Cosmos* (Cedar Rapids IA) 16 Feb 2/2, I intend to get on those people like ugly on an ape and whether I do it as chairman of United Students for Action or as an individual student, I am going to do it. **1968** *Ada Weekly News* (OK) 24 Oct 2/4, We get pretty narrow-minded when somebody takes your hard-earned money at the point of a gun. We'll stick to him like ugly on a baboon until we can take him. **1980** *Los Angeles Times* (CA) 30 Mar sec C 2/1 **AR,** [Leroy] Jones to Holmes: " . . I'm gonna be on your body and I'm gonna be on you like ugly on an ape." **1988** *Houston Chron.* (TX) 27 Nov sec H 7, *Like ugly on an ape. . .* "I first heard it spoken on the western classic series *Gunsmoke. . .* The phrase was *ugly on ape,* definitely not 'ugly on *an* ape.'" A dozen pioneer couch potatoes agree. . . *Frost:* Where did you get *like ugly on an ape?* [George H.W.] *Bush:* That's all over the oil fields. I got it in Odessa in 1948. **1993** Safire *Quoth the Maven* 151 **TX,** "Like ugly on an ape" is one of several zoological similes I remember from 25 or more years ago in high school in San Antonio. *Ibid* 153 **csOH,** I have heard this expression, sometimes as "ugly on the ape" all my life. **1995** Karr *Liars' Club* 277 **eTX,** They mess with you, you call me. . . I get on them like ugly on ape. **2005** in 2007 *DARE* File—Internet **TX,** As they say here in Texas, I'm on this story like ugly on a toad. **2006** *Ibid* **WA,** Food stuck to it like ugly on warthog. Now it's jet black and smooth and dull, just like Teflon.

ugly-nest caterpillar n [See quot 1998]
The larva of a tortricid moth *(Archips cerasivorana).*

[**1895** Comstock–Comstock *Manual Insects* 245, The Cherry-tree Ugly-nest Tortricid, *Cacaecia* [=*Archips*] *cerasivorana* . . lives upon the choke-cherry and sometimes upon the cultivated cherry.] **1901** Dickerson *Moths & Butterflies* 257, The Cherry-tree Ugly-nest caterpillar is of the latter kind [=living in large colonies in a nest made of many leaves]. **1938** U.S. Dept. Ag. States Rel. Serv. *Exper. Sta. Rec.* 78.223, A population study of nests of the ugly-nest caterpillar, collected near St. Paul, Minn. **1960** Hough *Silvical Characteristics* 16, Among the insect pests of the black cherry, the eastern tent caterpillar *(Malacosoma americana)* and the ugly-nest caterpillar *(Archips cerasivorana)* are the only defoliators of importance. **1997** MI State Univ. *Ext. Bulletin* 2633.4, Ugly nest caterpillars are well named. They construct dense webs of silk around shoots and leaves that become filled with bits of leaves and frass. **2003** (acc) WI Dept. Nat. Resources *Div. Forestry* (Internet), Ugly nest caterpillars web leaves together very tightly and feed within the protection of their web.

ugrook, ugrug, ugruk See **oogruk**

uh pron[1] See **I** pron

uh pron[2] See **her** pron

uh prep[1] See **of** prep

-uh prep[2], adv See **to** prep, adv **A2**

uhi n **HI**
1 A **wild yam** (here: *Dioscorea alata*).

[**1826** Ellis *Narrative HI* 10, The natives subsist principally on the roots of the *arum esculentum,* which they call *taro,* . . and *uhi,* or yam.] **1888** Hillebrand *Flora Hawaiian Is.* 314, The yam . . Polynesian . . "Uhi."] **1965** Neal *Gardens HI* 230, The yam commonly grown for food in the islands of the Pacific (uhi, *D[ioscorea] alata* . .), . . has square, more or less winged stems. *Ibid* 231, The uhi, hoi, and pi'a are distributed from tropical Asia eastward into Polynesia. **2004** *DARE* File—Internet **HI,** *Dioscorea alata*—'Uhi, or yam. . . an important dry land crop for the Hawaiians. . . Often trees . . were used as a support for 'uhi planted close by. 'Uhi are vines with heart-shaped leaves. . . *Dioscorea alata* [is] one of the more common species of 'uhi used by the Hawaiians, but they also had other yam species—*D. bulbifera* (pi'oi or hoi) and *D. pentaphylla* (pi'ia or pi'a).

2 also *ulehihi:* A **greenbrier** (here: *Smilax melastomifolia*) native to Hawaii.

[**1888** Hillebrand *Flora Hawaiian Is.* 441, *Pleiosmilax Sandwicensis* [=*Smilax melastomifolia*]. . . The "Uhi" and "Ulehihi" . . of the natives, who eat the tuberous rhizome in times of scarcity.] **1928** Pan-Pacific Research Inst. *Jrl.* 3.2.5 **HI,** Smilax, uhi or ulehihi, woody climber.

2004 (acc) HI Univ. Botany Dept. *Hawaiian Native Plant Genera* (Internet), *Smilax melastomifolia* . . uhi, ulehihi, catbrier, greenbrier.

uhu n [Haw *uhu*] **HI**
A parrot fish of the family Scaridae.

1905 U.S. Fish & Wildlife Serv. *Fishery Bulletin for 1903* 23.246, *Callyodon miniatus* [=*Scarus* sp?]. . . "Uhu." . . Color in life, body, head, and fins all dull red, becoming a lighter red on lower parts and darker to a dusky reddish brown on upper portions of body. **1960** Gosline–Brock *Hawaiian Fishes* 234, (Parrot Fishes or Uhus). . . The combination of beaklike jaw teeth and large scales on the body . . will immediately identify most of our uhus. **1967** *DARE* (Qu. P2, . . *Kinds of saltwater fish caught around here . . good to eat*) Inf **HI**14, Uhu [uʔhu]—parrot fish. **1975** Sunset *HI Guide* 144 [Game fish species], Uhu . . parrot fish. **2002** *DARE* File—Internet **HI,** I would say fish like the uhu (parrot fish), goatfishes (kumu, moana, moana kali, munu, malu), [etc] . . would be the "safer" fish to eat.

ujinctum n Also with *the*
Hell.

1919 Combs in *DN* 5.35 **seKY,** *Ujinctum, the*. . . Hell. **1944** Combs in *PADS* 2.21 **sAppalachians,** *Ujinctum* [juˈdʒɪŋktəm]. . . Hell (used with the definite article). "You ought to be in the ujinctum!" **2005** *VA Qrly. Rev.* 81.4.240, I hope to put this Brodie case behind me, if I have to posse up and send him and all the moonmen up there to Ujinctum.

uka n, adv [Haw] **HI** Cf **kai, mauka**
See quots.

1938 Reinecke *Hawaiian Loanwords* 31, *Uka* [û'-ka]. . . The shore; the country inland, as opposed to *kai,* the sea. **1954–1960** Hance et al. *Hawaiian Sugar* 4, Mauka—Toward the mountains. (Abbrev. *Uka*)

ukelele See **ukulele**

uker n See **euchre** n

uker v See **euchre** v

uki n Also *ukiuki* [Haw *'uki('uki)*] **HI**
Any of several plants with sedge-like leaves, esp such **sedges B1** as *Carex meyenii, Cladium mariscus,* and *Machaerina angustifolia,* or a liliaceous plant *(Dianella sandwicensis).*

[**1888** Hillebrand *Flora Hawaiian Is.* 445, *D[ianella] odorata* [=*D. sandwicensis*]. . . Common on the lower hills. . . Nat[ive] name: "Uki".] [**1930** Degener *Ferns of HI* 93, *Dianella* or *Ukiuki*. . . The collective Hawaiian name for many plants having sedge-like leaves was *ukiuki* or *uki.* The *uki* usually employed as an inner lining for the walls of the ancient Hawaiian grass house was the tall sedge *Vincentia angustifolia* [= *Machaerina a.*]] **1948** Neal *In Gardens HI* 159, The 'uki'uki *(Dianella)* has smooth, somewhat leathery leaves with close, longitudinally parallel veins 1 to 3 feet by 0.5 to 1 inch. **1965** Neal *Gardens HI* 89, 'Uki. . . Coarse sedges, three are natives of Hawaii. The commonest [*C[ladium] angustifolium* [=*Machaerina a.*] . .], often seen near Kilauea Volcano, has stems somewhat flattened, 3 to 4 feet high, which bear at and above their base long, smooth, leathery leaves 0.5 to 1 inch wide. . . A similar 'uki *(C[ladium] meyenii* [=*Carex m.*] . .) [has] slightly narrower leaves and a smaller . . inflorescence which is borne on a zigzag stem. . . Growing in damp places is a rarer, taller 'uki *(C[ladium] leptostachyum* [=*C. mariscus*] . .) with cylindrical stems and with many small round flower heads. *Ibid* 191, 'Uki'uki. *Dianella*. . . Around Kilauea Volcano. The erect or spreading, sword-shaped leaves are smooth and somewhat leathery. **1994** Stone–Pratt *Hawai'i's Plants* 202, 'Uki *(Machaerina angustifolia). Ibid* 203, Several native sedges are frequently seen in rain forests of Kilauea; the most abundant and conspicuous species in forests and woodlands near the Caldera is 'uki. . . 'Uki plants may be greatly reduced in pig-inhabited forests. 'Uki flowers are borne in elongate dense clusters on an erect stalk. **2003** *DARE* File—Internet **HI,** Just before emerging from the hanging valley onto the ridge, the Stairs pass through a bunch of uki [here: = *Machaerina angustifolia*] (not to be confused with uki uki), an endemic sedge. **2003** *Federal Reg.* 68.1224 **HI,** Associated native plant species include . . *Machaerina angustifolia* (uki). *Ibid, Bonamia menziesii* is found . . at elevations between 315 and 885 m. . . Associated species include . . *Dianella sandwicensis* (uki uki).

uku n [Haw] **HI**
A **snapper 1** (here: *Aprion virescens*).

1905 U.S. Fish & Wildlife Serv. *Fishery Bulletin for 1903* 23.239 **HI,** *Aprion virescens*. . . "Uku." **1960** Gosline–Brock *Hawaiian Fishes* 185, *Aprion virescens* (Uku). . . The fish is gray-blue in color. **1975**

Sunset *HI Guide* 144 [Game fish species], Uku—gray snapper. **2003** (acc) HI Dept. Business *HI Seafood* (Internet), Among the three most popular deepwater snapper species in Hawaii, uku occurs at the shallowest depths, usually no deeper than 60 fathoms.

ukulele n   Also sp *ukelele*   Cf **banjo 2**

A short-handled shovel.

1930 Williams *Logger-Talk* 30 **Pacific NW,** Ukulele: A short-handled shovel. **1942** Berrey–Van den Bark *Amer. Slang* 514.4, *Mining Equipment.* . . banjo, ukelele, *a short-handled shovel. Ibid* 773.4, *Railroad devices and supplies.* . . *Coal shovel.* . . ukelele, *a short-handled scoop shovel.* **1958** McCulloch *Woods Words* 203 **Pacific NW,** Ukulele—A short handle shovel. **1977** Adams *Lang. Railroader* 165, Ukelele: A short-handled scoop or shovel.

ula-ula n   [Haw redup *'ula* red]   **HI**

Any of several red **snappers 1,** esp *Etelis carbunculus* and *E. coruscans.*

1899 *Outing* 33.515 **HI,** This particular spot was the haunt of a famous fish called the "ulaula." **1905** U.S. Fish & Wildlife Serv. *Fishery Bulletin for 1903* 23.240 **HI,** *Etelis marshi* [=*E. carbunculus*]. . . "Ulaúla." *Ibid* 241, This species reaches a length of at least 2 feet, and is a common and important food-fish. **1926** Pan-Pacific Research Inst. *Jrl.* 1.1.7, Etelinus marshi [=*Etelis carbunculus*]. . . Ulaula. . . Etelis evurus [=*E. coruscans*]. . . Ulaula. **1967** *DARE* (Qu. P2, . . *Kinds of saltwater fish caught around here* . . *good to eat*) Inf **HI4,** Ula-ula niho—many colors, shiny. **1975** Sunset *HI Guide* 144 [Game fish species], 'Ula 'ula—red snapper. **2007** (acc) HI Dept. Business *HI Seafood* (Internet), Onaga (Etelis coruscans) is one of Hawaii's fish better known by its Japanese name than by its Hawaiian name, ula'ula.

ulehihi   See **uhi 2**

ulken   See **eulachon**

ulu n[1]   [Haw]   **HI**

The breadfruit *(Artocarpus altilis).*

[**1888** Hillebrand *Flora Hawaiian Is.* 408, The Breadfruit tree, called "Ulu" by the natives, has accompanied the Polynesians in all climates which allow the tree to live.] **1928** Pan-Pacific Research Inst. *Jrl.* 3.2.5 **HI,** Artocarpus, breadfruit, ulu. **1951** *AmSp* 26.22 **HI,** Other common Hawaiian words are . . *ulu* (breadfruit; a grove of trees). **2003** *DARE* File—Internet **HI,** Some loaves [of bread] have single flavors like *taro,* coconut, *ulu* (breadfruit) or passion fruit.

ulu n[2]   Also *oola, ooloo(k), ulun*   [Inupiaq *ulu;* other Alaskan Eskimo langs have cognate words; see 1991 Tabbert *Dict. Alaskan Engl.*]   **AK**

A traditional Eskimo knife with a crescent-shaped blade used primarily by women to dress and prepare game animals and fish, cut pelts, etc.

a1893 (1976) Thornton *Among Eskimos* 150, The *ulun* represents a very ancient type of cutlery. It has a semicircular blade, the straight edge of which is set in a handle of wood, bone, or ivory. . . The *ulun* is used exclusively by women, who are remarkably skillful with it in cutting up game and in cutting out clothes, boot soles, etc. **1936** *AK Sportsman* Dec 7, "Oolooks"—native knives, half-moon shaped blades of flint or metal, cut from the white man's saws and set in a bone handle—were being sharpened to keen edges. **1945** *Ibid* Sept 31, The old women cut chunks of meat with their sharp oolas. **1948** in 1957 Meyers *Eskimo Village* 109 **AK,** They are also very clever with the *ooloo,* or woman's knife. **1958** Carrighar *Moonlight* 42 **AK,** The cutting was done with a homemade knife shaped like a chopping knife—an *ulu,* as it is called. **1999** *Milwaukee Jrl. Sentinel* (WI) 5 Sept (Internet) **AK,** Eskimos . . still use the Ulu to skin seals, slice blubber, scrape beaver, fillet salmon, dress caribou and otherwise prepare or redeem anything that requires cleaning or cutting.

ulua n   [Haw]

Also with modifiers: a **crevalle a** or any of several other similar fish of the family Carangidae.   For other names of var of these see **paopao, pig ulua;** for other names of the young fish see **papio**

1891 Alexander *Brief Hist. Hawaiian* 57, If the fishermen failed to catch any *ulua* that night they killed a man in the village, and dragged his body to the heiau with a hook in his mouth, as a subsitute for the fish. **1898** *Haw. Almanac & Annual For 1899* 50, *Variety of fish supplying Honolulu market.* . . Ulua. **1905** U.S. Fish & Wildlife Serv. *Fishery Bulletin for 1903* 23.188 **HI,** Carangus. . . The Cavallas. . .

"Ulua," large size. *Ibid* 191, *Carangus marginatus* [=*Caranx sexfasciatus*]. . . "Ulua." **1926** Pan-Pacific Research Inst. *Jrl.* 1.1.8 **HI,** Carangidae. The Cavallas. Ulua. *Ibid* 9, Caranx melampygus. . . Ulua. **1951** *AmSp* 26.20 **HI,** Many terms for varieties of fish have been borrowed; among these are . . *ulua* (a large food fish). **1955** Day *HI People* 255, Hoping to hook a hundred-pound ulua (jack crevally) or a sixteen-pound *oio* (bonefish). **1960** Gosline–Brock *Hawaiian Fishes* 173, *Gnathanodon speciosus* . . Yellow ulua. *Ibid* 174, *Carangoides gymnostethoides* [=*C. gymnostethus*] (Ulua). *Ibid* 175, *Carangoides ferdau* [=*C. orthogrammus*] (Ulua). . . *Carangoides ajax* [=*Alectis ciliaris*] (White ulua). . . *Carangoides equula* (Ulua). *Ibid* 176, *Caranx helvolus* [=*Uraspis helvola*] (Black Ulua . .). . . *Caranx ignobilis* [=*Gnathanodon speciosus*] (Pa'u'u, Ulua . .). *Ibid* 177, *Caranx cheilio* [=*Pseudocaranx dentex*] (Thick-lipped ulua . .). *Ibid* 178, *Caranx melampygus.* . . *Caranx lugubris* (Ulua . .). *Ibid* 179, *Caranx sexfasciatus* (Ulua, Pake ulua, Mempachi ulua . .). **1967** *DARE* (Qu. P2, . . *Kinds of saltwater fish caught around here* . . *good to eat*) Inf **HI14,** Ulua—jack crevalle. **1967** *DARE* Tape **HI9,** Ulua is all kinds of size they have but it's kind of flat fish, and . . color is kind of white. . . The largest can be about . . 160 pound. . . [FW:] You can catch that? [Inf:] From the shore. **1975** Sunset *HI Guide* 144 [Game fish species], Ulua—jack crevally. **2002** *DARE* File—Internet **HI,** Which fish are good to eat? (ie- which reef and other small fish- I will not be equiped [sic] for a Ulua!)

ulun   See **ulu[2]**

um pron   See **him** pron

-um n   See **ma'am** n[1]

-um suff   [Cf *SND -um* suff "esp. in children's language"]   Cf **ies 2**

In the children's game of jacks: used after numbers (often with inserted -*s*-) to form names for moves involving a given number of jacks.

1966 *DARE* Tape **NC22,** But later on they began to play [jacks] with little balls. And let the ball bounce before they'd catch it. Then we'd have what we call one-um and twos-um and threes-um and fours-um and fives-um and six-um. If we were playing with ten bobjacks we'd go on up.

uman   See **woman A1**

umba   See **umbrella A2b**

umbarella   See **umbrella A1c**

umbel   See **umbil**

umber   See **hombre**

umberchute   See **umbershoot**

umberel(l)   See **umbrella A3**

umberella   See **umbrella A1c, 2b**

umbereller   See **umbrella A1c**

umberelly   See **umbrella A1c, 2b**

umberill   See **umbrella A3**

umberilla   See **umbrella A2b**

umberillo   See **umbrella A1c**

umbershoot n   Also sp *umberchute*   Cf **bumbershoot**

An umbrella.

1910 *Oakland Tribune* (CA) 16 Aug [Sports Page]/3, The magnate finally walloped Bauswine over the turret with an umbrella, spoiling the umbershoot. **1918** *Sun. Morning Decatur Rev.* (IL) 29 Dec 10/2, I thought if he was going as far as my house I would beg the shelter of his umbershoot. **1941** in 1944 *ADD* **eWV,** Umbrella. . . umbershoot. Said by a child. **1965–70** *DARE* (Qu. W1c, . . *Joking names . . for an umbrella*) 14 Infs, **scattered,** Umbershoot. [12 Infs old] **1972** *Indiana Eve. Gaz.* (PA) 18 Sept 1/6, *Chief Hunting Ol' Umbershoot.* . . He says it will be mostly cloudy with a chance of showers tonight. **2002** *DARE* File **AL,** "Umbershoot" or "umberchute" for umbrella.

umbersol n   Also *umbersoll*   [Prob blend of *umbrella* + *parasol*]   Cf **bumbersol**

An umbrella.

1879 *Cambridge Jeffersonian* (OH) 6 Feb [2]/5 (newspaperarchive.com), John Conner received the prize "umbersol" as the ugliest man. **1900** *NE State Jrl.* (Lincoln) 1 June 4/3, Would you submit to such abuse / And tamely say it is no use / To spoil an "umbersol" to hit / A fellow who has no more wit? **1913** *DN* 4.52, Humerous distortions . . *Bumberell* . . for umbrella. In common usage alongside the dialect blends *bumbershoot* . . *umbersoll.* **1941** *LANE* Map 367 (*Umbrella*) 1 inf, **cME,** Umbersol. **1950** *WELS* (What do you open up and hold over your head when it rains. . . *joking names*) 2 Infs, **WI,** Umbersol. **1967–69** *DARE* (Qu. W1c, . . *Joking names* . . *for an umbrella*) Infs **IA**8, **IL**74, **TN**23, **TX**65, 72, Umbersol. [4 of 5 Infs old] **1986** Pederson *LAGS Concordance* (*Umbrella*) 1 inf, **neMS,** Umbersol.

umbil n   Also *umbel, umbilroot, umble*

A **lady's slipper 1,** usu *Cypripedium pubescens.*

1828 Rafinesque *Med. Flora* 1.144, All the species of this fine genus being equally nervine, it will be well to notice them. . . *C[ypripedium] acaule* . . Dwarf Umbil. . . Best substitute [for valerian and opium]. *Ibid* 145, *C. candidum* . . White Umbil. **1854** King *Amer. Eclectic Dispensatory* 424, Cypripedium Pubescens is an indigenous plant, known by various names, as *American Valerian, Umbel, Nerve-Root, Yellow-Moccasin Flower, Noah's Ark,* etc. **1898** U.S. Dept. Ag. Div. Botany *Bulletin* 20.20, Cypripedium hirsutum [=*C. pubescens*]. . . Yellow umbil; nerve root; . . umble. . . A hairy or pubescent plant. . . It grows in bogs or low woods. **1950** Correll *Native Orchids* 20, *Cypripedium acaule.* . . Dwarf Umbil. *Ibid* 24, *Cypripedium Calceolus* L. var. *pubescens* [=*C. pubescens* var *pubescens*]. . . Umbil Root, Yellow Umbil.

umble adj, v   See **humble** adj, v

umble n   See **umbil**

umbrel(l)   See **umbrella A3**

umbrella n   Usu |ˌʌmˈbrɛlə|; for varr see below

A Forms.

1a |ˌʌmˈbrʌlə, -ˈbrɪlə|; also |ˌæmˈbrɛlə, -ˈbrɪlə|; for addit varr see quots.

1941 *LANE* Map 367 (*Umbrella*) **NEng,** [Proncs of the type [ʌmbrʌlə] are **scattered throughout western and southern NEng.** Those of the types [æmbrɪ⁽ə⁾lə, æ⁽ə⁾mbrɛlə] are **chiefly nNEng, esp ME;** 1 inf, **eME,** [æmbrɪloʊ]. Proncs with [æm-] are often regarded as older or old-fashioned.] **1965–70** *DARE* (Qu. W1a) Infs **AL**10, **MA**29, 40, **NH**1, 13, **NJ**18, **SC**46, Umbrella [ˌʌmˈbrʌlə]. **1989** Pederson *LAGS Tech. Index* 103 **Gulf Region,** *Umbrella.* [Of 914 infs, 12 infs, proncs of the type [ˌʌmˈbrʌlə]; 6 infs, [ˌɑmˈbrɛlə, -ˈbrʌlə]; 4 infs, [ˌʌmˈbrɪlə]; 1 inf, [ˌhʌmˈbrɛlə]; 1 inf, [ˌʌmˈbrɛloʊ]; 1 inf, [ˌʌmˈbrollə].]

b |ˌʌmˈbrɛlɚ|, rarely, |ˌæmˈbrɪlɚ|; pronc-sp *umbreller.* Cf Pronc Intro 3.I.12.d

1843 (1846) Haliburton *Attaché* (1st ser) 1.33 **NEng,** It jist clears up on purpose I do believe, to tempt you out without your umbreller. **1940** in 1944 *ADD* **wAR,** Umbrella. . . I want a umbreller. **1941** *LANE* Map 367 (*Umbrella*) **NEng,** 1 inf, **neMA,** [æəmbrɪlɚ]. **1966–69** *DARE* (Qu. W1a) Infs **GA**28, **MA**64, **RI**1, **SD**1, **TX**43, Umbreller [ˈʌmˈbrɛlɚ]. [All Infs old] **1989** Pederson *LAGS Tech. Index* 103 **Gulf Region,** *Umbrella.* [Of 914 infs, 6 infs, [ˌʌmˈbrɛlɾ].]

c |ˌʌmbəˈrɛlə, ˌʌmbɚˈɛlə, -ɚ|; for addit varr see quots; pronc-spp *umbarella, umberella, um(b)ereller, umberelly, umberillo. esp among speakers with little formal educ* Cf Intro "Language Changes" I.8

1837 Sherwood *Gaz. GA* 72, Umberillo, for umbrella. **1848** *MA Teacher* 1.334, A man of disciplined mind may be known by the way in which he . . manages an umberella [etc]. **1848** Thompson *Major Jones's Travel* 110 **GA,** Thar was old Pepperpod, with his old cotton umbereller. **1855** *Living Age* 44.144 **Boston MA,** Please don't crowd me to a jelly:/ Take away your umberelly. **1867** Harris *Sut Lovingood Yarns* 167 **TN,** A desirabil 'sortmint ove hyme books, fans, hanketchers, hats, caps, umerellers, walkin-sticks. **1890** *DN* 1.37 **csME,** Umbrella . . [əmbɚˈɛlə] . . *in New England is a vulgarism.* **1892** *Catholic World* 54.867 **cePA,** If it is [a hot day], ye'll put a wet rag in your hat an' carry an umbarella along. **1905** *DN* 3.58 **eNE,** Umbarella. **1941** *LANE* Map 367 (*Umbrella*) **NEng,** [Proncs with four syllables, of the types [ʌmbərɛlə, -rɪlə, ʌmbr̩lə], are **scattered throughout NEng, but least freq in ME.**] **1944** *PADS* 2.15 **NC, VA,** Umbrella. . . [In] low speech [ˌʌmbəˈrɪlə]. **1965–70** *DARE* (Qu. W1a, b, c) 44 Infs, **scattered,** Umberella [ˌʌmbəˈrɛlə, ˌʌmbɚˈɛlə]; **CA**178, Umberelly [ˌʌmbiˈrɛli]. [20 Infs gs educ or less] **1969** *PADS* 52.56 **seIL,** Umbrella [ˌʌmbəˈrɛlə]. **1976** Garber *Mountain-ese* 97 **sAppalachians,** I fergot and left my umbereller on the bus when I got off. **1989** Pederson *LAGS Tech. Index*

103 **Gulf Region,** *Umbrella.* [Of 914 infs, 29 infs, proncs of the types [ˌʌmbəˈrɛlə, -ˈrɛlɾ, ˌʌmbɾˈɛlə, ˌʌmbɨˈrɛlə]; 2 infs, [ˌɛmbəˈrɛlə, -ɾ]; 2 infs, [ˌʌmbəˈrʌlə]; 1 inf, [ˌɑmbəˈrɛlə].]

2a |ˈʌmˌbrɛlə, -ɚ|; for addit varr see quots; pronc-sp *umbreller.* Cf Intro "Language Changes" IV.2 **widespread, but esp Midl, Sth, SW**   See Map

1936 *AmSp* 11.153 **eTX,** In *umbrella,* the accent is sometimes shifted to the first syllable, [ˈʌmbrɛlə]. **1941** *LANE* Map 367 (*Umbrella*), The main stress generally falls on the second syllable (the third in pronunciations of the type of [ʌmbərɛlə]). . . Level stress was recorded in [19 instances, **chiefly CT, MA, RI**]. Initial stress with or without a secondary stress on the penultimate syllable was recorded in [11 instances, **chiefly CT**]. **1944** *PADS* 2.15 **AL, GA,** Umbrella [ˈʌmbrɛlə]: Frequent pronunciation of standard speakers, especially in black belt. **1965–70** *DARE* (Qq. W1a, b, c) 222 Infs, **widespread, but esp Midl, Sth, SW,** Umbrella [ˈʌmˌbrɛlə]; **CA**22, **GA**17, **KY**5, **SC**34, **TX**39, 45, Umbreller [ˈʌmˌbrɛlɚ]. **1989** Pederson *LAGS Tech. Index* 103 **Gulf Region,** *Umbrella.* [Of 914 infs, 310 infs, proncs of the types [ˈʌmˌbrɛlə, -ˌbrʌlə, -ˌbræʌlə, ˈʌmˌbrɛlə, -ˌbrʌlə]; 6 infs, [ˈʌmbrɛlɾ]; 3 infs, [ˈʌmˌbrɪlə].]

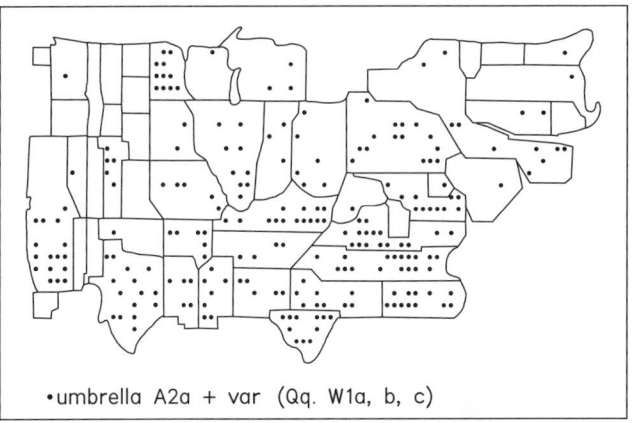

•umbrella A2a + var (Qq. W1a, b, c)

b |ˈʌmbəˌrɛlə, -ɚ, ˈʌmbɚˌɛlə|; for addit varr see quots; pronc-spp *umberella, umberelly, umberilla;* abbr *umba.* Cf Intro "Language Changes" I.8 **widespread, but less freq Nth, N Midl, West**   See Map   *esp among speakers with little formal educ*

1969–70 *DARE* (Qq. W1a, b, c) 117 Infs, **widespread, but less freq Nth, N Midl, West,** Umberella [ˈʌmbəˌrɛlə, ˈʌmbɚˌɛlə]; **IN**69, **NJ**20, 53, Umberella [ˈʌmbəˌrʌlə]; **IN**19, **NC**36, Umberelle [ˈʌmbɚˌɛlə]; **VA**73, Umberella [ˈʌmbəˌrʊlə]; **NC**50, Umberilla [ˈʌmbɚˌɪlə]; **MO**1, Umberelly [ˈʌmbɚˈɛlɪ]; **MS**25, Umba [ˈʌmˌbə]. [Of all Infs responding to Qq. W1a, b, c, 27%, 25%, and 23% respectively were gs educ or less; of all those giving the above responses, 45% were gs educ or less.] **1989** Pederson *LAGS Tech. Index* 103 **Gulf Region,** *Umbrella.* [Of 914 infs, 154 infs, proncs of the types [ˈʌmbəˈrɛlə, -ˌrɛlɾ, ˈʌmb(ə)rˌɛlə, ˈʌmbɨˌrɛlə]; 17 infs, proncs of the types [ˈ(h)ʌməˌrɛlə, ˈʌmrˌɛlə]; 6 infs, proncs of the types [ˈʌmbəˌrɪlə, ˈʌmbɨ-, ˈʌmbrʌlə]; 4 infs, proncs of the types [ˈ(h)ɑmbəˌrɛlə, ˈɑmbɨ-, ˈhɑmbəˌrɛlɾ].]

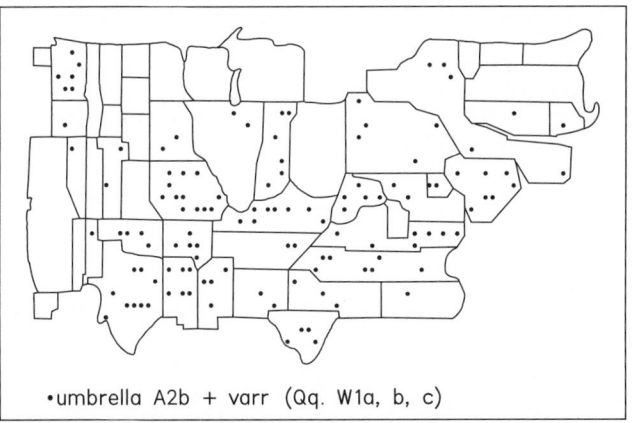

•umbrella A2b + varr (Qq. W1a, b, c)

3 |ˌʌmb(ə)ˈrɛl, ˈʌmb(ə)ˌrɛl|; also **chiefly nNEng, esp ME** |ˈæmbrɪl, æmbəˈrɪəl|; for addit varr see quots; pronc-spp *am-*

bril, umberel(l), umberill, umbrel(l), umbril. [*OED2 umbrel,
umberell* "dial. forms *umbrella*"]   *old-fash*

1806 (1970) Webster *Compendium Dict.* 321, *Umbrel, umbrella.*
[*DARE* Ed: This entry was carried over from Webster's English model.]
1816 in 1916 *MD Hist. Mag.* 11.151 **sePA,** [I] never was as wet in my
Clothing, through Great Coat umbrell & all. **1854** in 1983 *PADS* 70.56
ce,sePA, Papa went down to — [sic] in the morning in a sleigh had to
get an umberell. **1856** Holmes *Lena Rivers* 58 **NEng,** They'd break the
umberell. **1883** (1971) Harris *Nights with Remus* 57 **GA** [Black], I'll
des snatch down yo' pa buggy umbrell' fum up dar in de cornder. **1891**
DN 1.160 **cNY,** [ʌmbərˈɛl] for *umbrel,* shortened from '*umbrella.*'
1892 *DN* 1.212 **ceMA,** *Umbrella.* . . I heard last summer (1890) an aged
Cape Codder say [æmbɚˈɪl]. **1893** Shands *MS Speech* 65, Umbreel
[ʌmbərɛl]. Negro and illiterate white for *umbrella.* **1898** Westcott
Harum 19 **nNY,** I had my old umbrel'—though it didn't hender me f'm
gettin' more or less wet. **1906** Johnson *Highways Missip. Valley* 235
WI, "I'll lend you an umbrell," said he, in conclusion, "and that'll stop
the rain." **1907** *DN* 3.203 **seNH,** *Umbeˈrel, umˈbrel, umˈbril.* . . Umbrella. Used by the older generation. **1909** *DN* 3.385 **eAL, wGA,**
Umb(e)rell. . . Umbrella. **1911** in 1983 Truman *Dear Bess* 26 **MO,** I
am glad your "umbrell" is a useful as well as ornamental article. **1913**
Kephart *Highlanders* 217 **sAppalachians,** Umbrella . . "Umbrell".
1914 *DN* 4.68 **ME, nNH,** *Ambril.* . . Umbrella. **1917** in 1944 *ADD*
sWV, *Umbrella.* . . umbrell'. **1923** (1946) Greer-Petrie *Angeline Doin'
Society* 23 **csKY,** Some lamps a-settin' on hit [=a table] that look'd like
pink umberels. **1924–26** in 1944 *ADD* **cNY,** *Umbrella.* . . [ʌmˈbrɛl].
1940 *Ibid* **swPA, nWV,** *Umbrella.* . . umberell ['umbrˈɛl]. Old illit.
speaker. **1941** *LANE* Map 367 *(Umbrella)* **NEng,** [Proncs of the types
[ʌmbrɪl, -bərɪl, -b(ə)rɛl, -brəl] are infrequent and are considered older or
old-fashioned by 6 infs, **ME, NH, VT.** Those of the types [æˈ(ə)mbrɪl,
-brəl, æˈ(ə)mbrɪ(ə)l, æˈ(ə)mbərɪ(ə)l] are found **chiefly in ME, NH, neMA, esp
ME.** They are also often regarded as older or old-fashioned.] **1943**
in 1944 *ADD* **sVA,** *Umbrella.* . . ['ʌmbrˈɪl]. *Ibid* **cWV,** [ʌmˈbrɛl],
['ʌmbrˈɛl]. **1944** *PADS* 2.31 **eKY, cwNC,** *Umberel* ['ʌmbərɛl]. Umbrella. E. Ky. Rare. Wautauga Co., N.C. Common. **1965–70** *DARE*
(Qu. W1a, *What do you open up and hold over your head when it
rains?*) Infs **AR**23, **IN**13, **TN**27, Umberell ['ʌmbərɛl, 'ʌmbɚˌɛl]; (Qu.
W1b, *If you use an umbrella . . when the sun is too hot, you call it
a _____*) Infs **MO**37, 38, Umberell ['ʌmbæˌɛl]; **MT**5, Umberell
[ˌʌmbəˈrɛl]; (Qu. W1c, . . *Joking names . . for an umbrella*) Inf **SC**46,
Umberill; **NC**79, Umberill ['ʌmbɚˌɪl]. [7 of 8 Infs old] **1982** *Barrick
Coll.* **csPA,** Umbrella—pron. umbrél, umberél. **1983** *MJLF* 9.1.60
ceKY (as of 1956), *Umberel* . . umbrella. **1989** Pederson *LAGS
Tech. Index* 103 **Gulf Region,** Umbrella. [Of 914 infs, 7 infs, proncs of
the type ['ʌmˌbrɛl]; 2 infs, ['ʌmbəˌrɛl]; 2 infs, ['ʌməˌrɛl, -rʌl]; 1 inf,
['ʌmbrˌɛl]; 1 inf, [ˌʌmˈbrɛl].]

4 *pronc-spp* **brella, brelly.** [*Aphet* forms]

1914 *Pearson's Mag.* 31.720, "Here's your 'brella, Pa," shouted
Buddie. **1966–68** *DARE* (Qu. W1c, . . *Joking names . . for an umbrella*) Infs **AL**8, **SC**70, Brella; **OH**61, Brelly.

5 |ˌnʌmbɚˈɛl, 'nʌmˌbrɛlə|; *pronc-spp numb(e)rell.* [By met-
analysis]

1915 *DN* 4.186 **swVA,** Numbrell'. Variant of *umbrella.* Also *num-
berell.* **1941** *LANE* Map 367 *(Umbrella)* 1 inf, **ceMA,** [nʌmbərɛˈəl].
[*DARE* Ed: This pronc is marked obsolete.] [**1966** *DARE* (Qu. W1c, . .
Joking names . . for an umbrella) Inf **WA**33, Numberbelly [laughter].]
1989 Pederson *LAGS Tech. Index* 103 **Gulf Region,** Umbrella. [Of 914
infs, 2 infs, ['nʌmˌbrɛlə].]

6 |ˌʌnˈbrɛlə, -'brɪlə|.

1941 *LANE* Map 367 *(Umbrella)* **NEng,** 1 inf, **ceMA,** [ʌnbrɪᵛlə,
-brɛlə]. **1989** Pederson *LAGS Tech. Index* 103 **Gulf Region,** 1 inf,
[ˌʌnˈbrɛlə]; 1 inf, ['ʌnbrˌɛlə].

B Senses.

1 See **umbrella plant a, g, h.**

2 See **umbrella tree 1, 2.**

umbrella cactus n

=saguaro.

1895 *Jrl. Amer. Folkl.* 8.51 **SW,** The true Pitahaya is . . the Saguara
[sic] cactus of various writers; it has sometimes been called the umbrella
cactus.

umbrella caterpillar n

=tent caterpillar.

1969 *DARE* (Qu. R27, . . *Kinds of caterpillars or similar worms*) Inf
KY35, Umbrella caterpillars (tent caterpillars).

umbrella china (or chinaberry, china tree, Chinese)   See
umbrella tree 2

umbrella flower   See **umbrella plant a**

umbrella grass n

A **sedge B1** of the genus *Fuirena* native to the Southwest and
much of the eastern half of the US. Also called **umbrella
sedge 2**

1818 Eaton *Botany* 251, *Fuirena. . . squamosa* [sic] (umbrella grass).
1860 AR Geol. Surv. *Second Rept.* 394, *Fuirena.* . . Umbrella-grass.
F[uirena] squarrosa. **1894** Coulter *Botany W. TX* 472, *Fuirena.* . . Um-
brella-grass. . . In ours [=*Fuirena simplex* and *F. squarrosa*] the leaves
have well-developed blades. **1927** *Amer. Midland Naturalist* 10.258
nIL, *Fuirena squarrosa* . . , Umbrella-grass. **1968** Radford et al. *Manual Flora Carolinas* 201, *Fuirena.* . . Umbrella Grass. Tufted perennials
or annuals. **2004** (acc) Taylor Univ. *Wetland Comms. IN* (Internet), The
peculiar flora of this community [=sand/muck flat] includes many "minor" sedge genera: beaked sedge (*Rhynchospora macrostachya*), . . umbrella grass (*Fuirena pumila*) [etc].

umbrella leaf n

1 A plant (*Diphylleia cymosa*) with a peltate two-lobed leaf,
native in many parts of the southern Appalachians.

1857 Gray *Manual of Botany* 20, *Diphylleia.* . . Umbrella-leaf. . . A
perennial glabrous herb . . sending up each year either a huge, centrally
peltate and cut-lobed, rounded, umbrella-like radical leaf on a stout
stalk, or a flowering stem bearing two similar (but smaller and more 2-
cleft) alternate leaves which are peltate near one margin, and terminated
by a cyme of white flowers. **1901** Lounsberry *S. Wild Flowers* 189,
Through mountainous woods and along streams where the umbrella-leaf
grows its appearance is much too bold and striking to be easily overlooked. **1953** Greene–Blomquist *Flowers South* 39, The umbrella-leaf
has in common with may-apple (*Podophyllum peltatum*) and twin-leaf
(*Jeffersonia*) . . two large leaves between which the flowers are borne.
2004 (acc) Cornell Univ. *Cornell Plantations* (Internet), A member of
the barberry family, umbrella leaf offers the added ornamentation of attractive, blue, berry-like fruits that contrast markedly with the bright red
stems that hold them.

2 **=mayapple 1.**

1902 (1909) Mathews *Field Book Amer. Wild Flowers* 154, The May
Apple has also been called Umbrella Leaf. **1933** Small *Manual SE
Flora* 544, *P[odophyllum] peltatum.* . . Umbrella-leaf.

3 **=blue cohosh 1.**

1959 Carleton *Index Herb. Plants* 119, Umbrella-leaf: Caulophyllum
thalictroides; Petasites vulgarus [sic] (P. officinalis).

4 A **sweet coltsfoot 1** (here: *Petasites hybridus*).

1959 [see **3** above].

umbrella magnolia n   Cf **umbrella tree 1**

A **magnolia 1:** usu *Magnolia tripetala,* but also *M. fraseri.*

1762 in 1821 Smith *Selection Corresp. Linnaeus* 1.512 **SC,** [Letter of
Alexander Garden:] I must beg that you would endeavour to inform me
[of] . . the value of young plants of Loblolly Bay, Azalea, Umbrella-
Magnolia . . and such like. **1846** Browne *Trees* 10, *Magnolia umbrella,*
The Umbrella Magnolia. **1868** (1870) Gray *Field Botany* 43, *M[ag-
nolia] Umbrella,* Umbrella M[agnolia] (also called *M[agnolia] tripetala*). Wild in Penn. and southward. A low tree, with the leaves on the
end of the flowering branches crowded in an umbrella-like circle. . .
M[agnolia] Fraseri, Ear-leaved Umbrella M[agnolia]. Wild from Virginia S. **1935** *Amer. Midland Naturalist* 16.554, The understory contains in addition, dogwood, redbud, service berry, umbrella magnolia,
holly, and papaw. **1964** Batson *Wild Flowers SC* 47, Umbrella Magnolia: *M. tripetala.* . . Piedmont and Mountains. Pennsylvania to Georgia.
Ibid 48, Umbrella Magnolia: *Magnolia fraseri.* . . Leaves . . clustered at
the ends of twigs so as to form an umbrella-like appearance. . . Mountains. Virginia to Georgia. **1969** *DARE* (Qu. T16, . . *Kinds of trees . .
'special'*) Inf **KY**47, Umbrella magnolia—same as wahoo. **2006** in
2007 *DARE* File—Internet **cPA,** I have a 4 year old umbrella magnolia
that I started from seed growing in a good size pot.

umbrella mushroom   See **umbrella plant g**

umbrella plant n

Any of var plants that suggest an umbrella in some way, as:
a *also* *umbrella, umbrella flower, ~ root:* **=mayapple 1.**
chiefly N Cent, PA   See Map

c1800 in 1937 *Torreya* 37.97 **VA,** *Podophyllum peltatum.* . . Umbrella-root. [*DARE* Ed: Author of article states that this term was used for this plant in an unpublished journal of Dr. Benjamin Smith Barton (1766–1815).] **1895** *Atlantic Mth.* 75.463 **NEng,** "The umbrellas are out!" call country children in spring, when the peltate leaves of the May-apple spread their umbrella-shaped lobes, and the little girls gather them, and also the leaves of the wild sarsaparilla, for dolls' parasols. **1900** Lyons *Plant Names* 296, *P[odophyllum] peltatum.* . . Umbrella-plant. **1930** Sievers *Amer. Med. Plants* 41, *Mayapple.* . . *Other common names.* . . Umbrella plant. **1950** *WELS* **WI** *(Other names in your locality for the may-apple)* 2 Infs, Umbrella(s); 1 Inf, Umbrella flower; *(Small plants, shaped like an umbrella, that grow in woods and fields)* 1 Inf, Mayapple, wild lemons, umbrella plant. **1965–70** *DARE* (Qu. S4, . . *Mayapple: [Woodside plant, not a tree, with two large spreading leaves; they grow in patches and have a small yellow fruit late in summer])* 33 Infs, 30 **N Cent, PA,** Umbrella plant; **OH**5, **PA**167, Umbrella; **MI**114, Umbrella flower. **1972** *Names SC* 19.30, *Umbrella Plant* (Oconee County), Mayapple, *Podophyllum peltatum.* **1980** in 1982 *Barrick Coll.* **csPA,** *Umbrella plant*—May apple. **1998** in 2004 *DARE* File—Internet **IN,** *Podophyllum peltatum.* . . Any child who's ever walked through the woods or other undisturbed area knows the "Umbrella plant," named such for the large umbrella-like leaf atop a long stem.

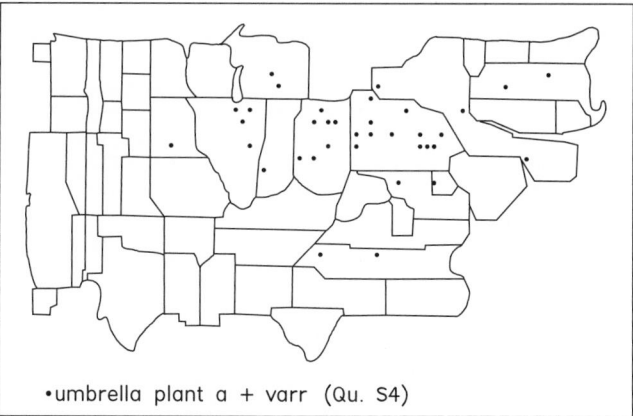

•umbrella plant a + varr (Qu. S4)

b =**Indian rhubarb 1.**

1866 Lindley–Moore *Treas. Botany* 1350, Umbrella-plant, *Saxifraga peltata* [=*Darmera peltata*]. **1897** Parsons *Wild Flowers CA* 242, *Indian Rhubarb. Umbrella-plant.* . . Upon the borders of our swift-flowing mountain streams . . may be seen the large lotus-like leaves of this great Saxifrage. **1934** Haskin *Wild Flowers Pacific Coast* 153, *Umbrella-plant—Peltiphyllum peltatum* [=*Darmera p.*] . . A big leaf—a very big umbrella-like leaf—is the most characteristic feature of this fine plant. **1973** Hitchcock–Cronquist *Flora Pacific NW* 192, Umbrella-plant. . . L[ea]v[e]s . . peltate, cupped in center; . . cold m[oun]t[ain] streams, where firmly anchored. **2004** (acc) Cornell Univ. *Cornell Plantations* (Internet), The umbrella plant *(Darmera peltata)* . . [is] a native of the northwestern United States.

c A **wild buckwheat 2;** see quots.

1903 (1904) Chittenden *Yellowstone* 251, The Sulphur Flower or Umbrella Plant *(Eriogonum,* five or six species) grows in great profusion through the mountain portions of the Park. **1936** Whitehouse *TX Flowers* 17, *Many-Flowered Buckwheat (Eriogonum multiflorum)* is also called umbrella-plant because of its spreading clusters at the top of the stem. **1958** Barnes *Nat. Hist. Wasatch Autumn* 48 **UT,** If an Indian had indigestion he ordinarily drank a tea made from . . the flowers of any of the umbrella plants *(Eriogonum).* **1973** Stephens *Woody Plants* 158 **Cent,** *Eriogonum effusum* . . Umbrella plant. . . A suffrutescent shrub . . , the old inflorescence persistent over winter. **2004** (acc) U.S. Forest Serv. *Fire Effects Info. System* (Internet) **NE,** Invaders of blowouts after blowout grass has stabilized the area include spiderwort (Tradescantia virginiana), annual umbrella plant (Eriogonum annuum), [etc].

d An introduced kalanchoe *(Kalanchoe delagoensis).*

1955 *S. Folkl. Qrly.* 19.235 **FL,** Kalanchoe verticilata [sic; =*Kalanchoe delagoensis*] . . the terminal cluster of branches from which the flower spike rises is responsible for the less popular epithet *Umbrella Plant.*

e A **biscuit root 1.**

1957 Barnes *Nat. Hist. Wasatch Spring* 64 **UT,** We stop to pick an umbrella plant *(Lomatium simplex),* now in full bloom. **1967** *DARE* (Qu.

S26a, . . *Wildflowers.* . . *Roadside flowers*) Inf **CA**1, Umbrella—purple flower, close to ground.

f A **hedge mustard 1** (here: *Sisymbrium altissimum*).

1966 Barnes–Jensen *Dict. UT Slang* 44, *Umbrella Plant* . . a name sometimes given to the coarse, introduced weed known as Tumbling Mustard *(Sisymbrium altissimum).*

g also *umbrella (mushroom):* A **mushroom B1.** Cf **devil's umbrella, fairy ~, parasol mushroom**

1966–68 *DARE* (Qu. I37, *Small plants shaped like an umbrella that grow in woods and fields—which are safe to eat*) Infs **PA**29, 102, Umbrella plant(s); (Qu. S18, *A kind of mushroom that grows like a globe* . . *sometimes gets as big as a man's head*) Inf **SC**32, Umbrella—top gets nearly the size of a plate; **MD**23, **MS**16, Umbrella mushroom.

h also *umbrella:* A **wild carrot 1** (here: *Daucus carota*).

1967–68 *DARE* (Qu. S6, . . *Queen Anne's lace: [Summertime roadside weed two feet high or so with a lacy white top]*) Inf **NY**37, Umbrella plant; **NY**35, Umbrellas.

umbrella root See **umbrella plant a**

umbrella sedge n

1 Any of several native **galingales 1;** see quots.

1885 *Med. & Surgical Reporter* 53.362, The umbrella sedge, *Cyperus alternifolius,* looks something like a miniature palm. **1948** *Ecological Monogr.* 18.453 **LA,** *Cyperus virens* . . Umbrella sedge. **1989** Torrey Bot. Club *Bulletin* 116.271 **NY,** *Cyperus filicinus* . . Umbrella-sedge. . . *Cyperus filiculmis* . . Umbrella-sedge. . . *Cyperus grayii.* . . *Cyperus odoratus.* . . *Cyperus retrorsus.* . . *Cyperus rivularis.* . . *Cyperus strigosus* . . Umbrella-sedge. . . Wet depressions on sandflats. . . Freshwater reed marshes. **1995** *Ecological Applications* 5.759 **West,** Umbrella sedge *(Cyperus schweinitzii).* **2000** in 2004 *DARE* File—Internet **OH,** Jim McCormac, Division Botanist for the Ohio Division of Natural Resources, discovered Pale Umbrella-sedge *(Cyperus acuminatus,* pictured at left) this summer, during a July trip to Gilmore Ponds.

2 =**umbrella grass.**

1963 Jones *Flora IL* 306, Fuirena [spp.] . . Umbrella Sedge. **2004** *DARE* File—Internet **NY,** The D[raft] E[nvironmental] I[mpact] S[tatement] also states that "no endangered or threatened plant species were observed on the project site," yet included Hairy Umbrella Sedge (Fuirena squarrosa) in its list of observed species which was believed, until now, to have been eradicated from the state of New York. **2004** *Ibid* **WI,** Umbrella sedge—*Fuirena pumila.*

umbrella tree n

1 also *umbrella:* Any of several **magnolias 1,** but usu *Magnolia tripetala, M. fraseri,* or *M. macrophylla.* [See quots] Cf **umbrella magnolia**

1738 Royal Soc. London *Philos. Trans.* 40.350 **Carolinas,** *Magnolia, amplissimo flore albo, fructu coccineo.* The *Umbrella-tree.* This much resembles that beautiful Plant the *Carolina Laurel-tree* . . but is not so high. **1785** Marshall *Arbustrum* 84, *Magnolia tripetala. The Umbrella Tree.* This grows pretty frequent in Carolina, and some parts of Pennsylvania. . . The leaves are very large and entire, . . narrowing to a point at each extremity, placed at the ends of the branches in a circular manner, somewhat resembling an umbrella. **1806** in 1808 Ashe *Travels America* 59, I confine myself to native plants. . . *Popular Name.* . . Umbrella. **1832** Browne *Sylva* 212, The large-leaved umbrella tree arrives at the height of 30 or 35 feet. **1860** Curtis *Cat. Plants NC* 67, Umbrella Tree (M[agnolia] Umbrella . .)—This is common in the Middle and Western States as well as in the Southern. . . *Large-leaved Umbrella Tree.* (M. macrophylla . .)—This and No. 6 [=*M. fraseri*] derive their names of *Umbrella Tree* from the mode in which their leaves spread from the ends of the branches. **1901** Lounsberry *S. Wild Flowers* 164, *Long or Ear-leaved Umbrella Tree. Magnolia Fraseri.* . . In the way in which its leaves grow at the ends of the branches this magnolia resembles the umbrella tree. In fact, the mountain people call it indiscriminately by that name. *Ibid* 165, *M. macrophylla,* great leaved magnolia or umbrella tree, is truly a remarkable sight. . . *M. tripetala,* umbrella-tree, . . bears also very large leaves. **1950** *Chicago Tribune* (IL) 18 May 6/2, When it is in full bloom, as it will be soon, the flowers of the umbrella tree fill the arboretum with their rich fragrance. **1968–70** *DARE* (Qu. T16, . . *Kinds of trees* . . *'special'*) Infs **MD**9, **NC**84, Umbrella tree; **MO**35, Umbrella tree, 'cause they always look like an umbrella. [*DARE* Ed: Some of these Infs may refer instead to other senses below.] **1976** Bruce *How to Grow Wildflowers* 153, A widespread species is *M[agnolia] tripetala,* called usually Umbrella Tree or Elkwood. *Ibid,* The remaining American magnolias. . . are usually called "Umbrella Trees" because of this effect. **1984** Wilder *You All Spoken Here* 177 **Sth,** Umbrella tree: Chinaberry; magnolia tripetela [sic]. **1999** in 2004 *AL Univ. N. AL Flora & Fauna TN R.* (Internet) **Inland Sth,** *Magnolia: Bigleaf Magnolia* "Silverleaf Magnolia" or "Umbrella-tree" *Magnolia macrophylla.* Broad rounded crown with wide spreading branches.

2 also *umbrella,* ~ *chinaberry,* ~ *china (tree),* ~ *Chinese:* = **Chinaberry 1,** esp of the variety *umbraculiformis.* Cf **Chinese umbrella, Texas umbrella (tree)**

1868 Swett *Trip to Honduras* 50, We found here the Umbrella China Tree growing in perfection, which we never saw in Mississippi, though it is planted in Texas for its shade. **1897** Sudworth *Arborescent Flora* 270, *Melia azedarach umbraculifera.* . . Umbrella China-tree. **1901** Lounsberry *S. Wild Flowers* 293, A connection of the mahogany . . is the China berry, umbrella tree, or pride-of-India, Melia azedarach. **1944** *AL Geol. Surv. Bulletin* 53.141, *M[elia] Azedarach.* . . The variety *umbraculifera,* known as umbrella china, is preferred for shade, but it seldom escapes, or if it does it must soon revert to the common form. **1958** Babcock *I Don't Want* 160 **eSC,** You had better seed the "umbrellas" in the park surreptitiously . . or you will find yourself hanged and quartered by the women's clubs. **1961** Folk *Word Atlas N. LA* map 215, Chinaberry tree 73% [of 275 infs] . . umbrella tree 12%. **1966–69** *DARE* (Qu. T16, . . *Kinds of trees* . . *'special'*) Inf **CA**42, Umbrella tree—deciduous, has a blossom and an umbrella-shaped foliage; **CA**53, Umbrella tree—a dense tree, has lavender blossom; **CA**79, Umbrella trees—Texas umbrella and Chinese umbrella; **CA**91, Elm and umbrella tree are the only ones that lose leaves completely here; **CA**113, Umbrella tree—used to be most common shade trees, round seed balls, waxy; **SC**11, Chinaberry—also called "umbrella tree." **c1977** in 2007 *DARE* File—Internet **cTX** (as of c1915), There was a very large umbrella China Tree in our front yard. **1979** Little *Checklist U.S. Trees* 172, *Chinaberry.* . . *Other common names*—umbrella chinaberry, . . umbrella-tree. **1984** [see **1** above]. **1986** Pederson *LAGS Concordance (Local trees)* 1 inf, **swGA,** Umbrella trees = chinaberry trees; 1 inf, **nwLA,** Umbrella china; 1 inf, **swLA,** Umbrella Chinese. **2007** *DARE* File—Internet **cwCA** (as of c1940), In the backyard under the three large umbrella (Chinaberry) trees, planted for shade, was an enormous woodpile.

3 A **dogwood 1** (here: *Cornus alternifolia*).

1897 Sudworth *Arborescent Flora* 310 **RI,** *Cornus alternifolia.* . . Umbrella-tree. **1908** Britton *N. Amer. Trees* 741, *Cornus alternifolia.* . . This small tree, or more often tall shrub, is also known as the . . Umbrella tree. [*Ibid* 742, The branches are . . nearly horizontal, forming a broad flat-topped bushy head.]

4 A **catalpa B1;** see quots.

1950 *WELS* (The tree with large heart-shaped leaves, clusters of white blossoms, and long slender seed pods) 1 Inf, **WI,** Indian cigar [in] Kentucky, umbrella tree [in] Arizona. **1966–70** *DARE* (Qu. T9, *The common shade tree with large heart-shaped leaves, clusters of white blossoms, and long thin seed pods or 'beans'*) Infs **AZ**9, **NE**11, **NY**68, **PA**134, **SD**2, **VA**15, Umbrella tree; **KY**75, Umbrella tree—top 'em and they just grow out; (Qu. T16, . . *Kinds of trees* . . *'special'*) Inf **IL**41, Umbrella tree—very straight, big umbrella-shaped top which is cut off every year. [*DARE* Ed: Some of these Infs may refer instead to other senses above.] [**1966** *DARE* Tape Inf **MA**6, They use 'em for umbrella trees, but the real name is. . . catalpa. . . They cut 'em back and they grow like the shape of an umbrella.] **1976** Bruce *How to Grow Wildflowers* 160, By far the most common form of catalpa seen in American gardens is the "Umbrella Tree," the so-called *Catalpa bungei* (of nurserymen, not the true species, which is a native of China), actually a dwarf form of the common species grafted on normal trunks at about shoulder height. **2004** (acc) Sandy City UT *Sandy City Online* (Internet), *Park Strip Trees.* . . Recommended. . . Umbrella Tree (Catalpa).

umbrellawort n [*OED2* 1829 →; see quot 2004]
=**four-o'clock 1;** also a plant of the closely related genus *Allionia.*

1806 McMahon *Amer. Gardener's Calendar* 611, *Oxybaphus viscosus* [=*Mirabilis v.*]—Viscid Umbrella-wort. **1890** *Century Dict.* 4216, *Oxybaphus.* . . A gardeners' name for plants of the genus is *umbrellawort.* **1899** MacMillan *MN Plant Life* 261, The four-o'clocks are represented by . . species known as umbrella-worts, and remarkable for the involucre which stands below the pink or reddish flowers. **1940** Steyermark *Flora MO* 172, Umbrella-wort, Wild Four-o'clock (*Mirabilis*). **1949** Moldenke *Amer. Wild Flowers* 97, Related [to the genus *Mirabilis*] are the *umbrellaworts* (*Allionia*), erect herbs with . . flowers

with enlarged basal involucres. **1970** Correll *Plants TX* 577, *Allionia incarnata.* . . Umbrella-wort, trailing allionia, hierba de la hormiga. . . *Allionia choisyi.* . . Smooth umbrella-wort. **2004** (acc) KS State Univ. *KS Wildflowers* (Internet), *Mirabilis nyctaginea.* . . "Umbrellawort" refers to the overhanging bracts that resemble an umbrella.

umbreller See **umbrella A1b, 2a**

umbril See **umbrella A3**

umbry See **hombre**

umereller See **umbrella A1c**

ummern See **woman A1**

ummie See **hommie**

umpire n Usu |'ʌmpaɪr|; also |'ɛmpaɪr| Pronc-sp *empire*
Std sense, var form.

1892 *DN* 1.210 **MA,** *Empire:* umpire. Almost universal among boys in Plymouth. **1909** *Eve. Times* (Cumberland MD) 23 Apr 5/4, Both teams have promised not to kill the empire. **1916** *DN* 4.341 **seOH,** Umpire [ɛmpaɪr]. **1939** in 1944 *ADD* **nWV,** *Empire.* . . Used by many children. **1942** *Time* 1 June 58 **NYC,** Dis team is filled with sissies wot . . never shoot an empire. **1946** *Times Recorder* (Zanesville OH) 8 Mar [6]/3 (newspaperarchive.com), [Cartoon caption:] Kill The Empire!

Umpke n [See quot 2007; cf **golumpki**]
A Polish person.

2005 Joseph et al. *Lang. Diversity MI & OH* 134 **Upper Peninsula MI,** Two sisters (born 1917 and 1919 respectively) of Finnish background list commonly known ethnic labels: . . the Italians were Dagos. The French were. . . Frogs. The Polish were umpkes. **2007** *DARE* File **Upper Peninsula MI,** Two of the M[ichigan] T[ech] U[niversity] archivists . . were familiar with "umpke." One is originally from Detroit: he said that he'd heard "umpke" and associated it with "galumpki," with a cabbage roll with meat and rice—which Polish eat, he said. . . The other archivist said that she was familiar with "umpke" but knew it from Wisconsin.

un- pref Usu |'ʌn, ˌən|; also |ən, ɔn| Pronc-sp *on-*
Std sense, var forms.

1835 Kennedy *Horse Shoe Robinson* 1.228 **SC,** It would be good news to hear that Sumpter was near their cruppers—which . . is not onlikely. **1841** (1952) Cooper *Deerslayer* 433 **cNY,** That's both oncommon and onreasonable. *Ibid* 439, Onequal matches, like onequal fri'indships, can't often tarminate kindly. **1854** *Harper's New Mth. Mag.* 10.5 **VA** [Black], Dis is onaccountable. **1858** [see **tax** v]. **1867** Harris *Sut Lovingood Yarns* 53 **TN,** Onbenowenst tu eny-body, I ontied my bag ove reptiles. **1867** Lowell *Biglow* lxxii '**Upcountry**' **MA,** *U* always becomes *o* in the prefix *un* (except *unto*). **1873** Eggleston *Mystery* 123 **IN,** He scrupulously pruned his conversation of profanity, so that he wouldn' be onfit to love her. **1877** Jewett *Deephaven* 87 **ME,** I spoke onpleasant of that swindling English fellow. **1888** Jones *Negro Myths* 54 **GA coast,** Buh Rabbit . . slip roun onbeknowinst ter Buh Wolf. **1903** *DN* 2.335 **seMO,** *Uneasy.* . . Pronounced oneasy, Also onpleasant; onwell. **1907** *DN* 3.238 **nwAR,** *Uneasy.* . . Pronounced oneasy. Also, onpleasant, onwell. **1909** *DN* 3.354 **eAL, wGA,** *On-.* . . Un-. Common in such words as *onnatural, onlucky, oncivil,* etc. **1914** *DN* 4.77 **ME, nNH,** *On-.* . . For "un," in words with that affix. "*On*load, *on*hitch," etc. *Ibid* 110 **cKS,** *On-.* . . Variant of *un-;* as, *onwilling* to *ontie* your shoe lace. **1930s** in 1944 *ADD* **eWV,** *Un-.* . . Rural. [O]nhitch, onhandy, ontie, onlock . . oneasy. **1934** *Language* 10.2 **cPA,** [ɔ] (as in *long*) is heard . . in the prefix *un-: unkind, unpleasant,* etc. **1942** Hall *Smoky Mt. Speech* 58 **wNC, eTN,** Typical forms are: *uncertain* [ˌʌnˈsɝtn̩], *unbeknownst* [ˌɔnbɪˈnoəns]. [Footnote:] Unkind is [ɔnˈka·n] in a recorded ballad sung by a woman in her thirties. **1959** *VT Hist.* 27.165, *Uneasy* [ˈɔnizɪ]. . . Rare. Rural areas. **c1960** *Wilson Coll.* **csKY,** *Un-* is often sounded as if spelled . . on-. **1989** Pederson *LAGS Tech. Index* 273 **Gulf Region,** *Un-* [prefix]. . . [Of 914 infs, 12 offered proncs of the type [ɑn], 9 of the type [ɔn].] **2007** *DARE* File **csWI,** Although I've lived here for more than thirty years, I'm still caught short whenever I hear Wisconsinites pronounce [ʌn] as [ɑn]. *Ibid* **csWI,** [Label on locally produced honey:] 2 lbs Red Clover Onheated.

un pron, adv, indef art See **one A**

-un suff See **-ing A**

una pron Often |'unə, 'hunə, 'wunə|; also |'hʌnə, 'jʌnə, 'jinə| Pronc-spp *honer, hoona(h), hoonuh, hunnah, hunnuh, o(o)na, oonuh, unu, yinnah, yinner, yuner, yunna(h), yunner, yunnuh*

[W Afr; cf Ibo *unu* you (pl); cf also *DJE unu, DBE ona*] *Gullah*

You (sg and pl).

1867 Allen et al. *Slave Songs* xxv **sSC coast** [Gullah], *Oona* or *ona,* "you" (both singular and plural, and used only for friends), as "Ona build a house in Paradise." **1883** (1971) Harris *Nights with Remus* 135 **GA** [Black], Oona bin know da' Tildy gal? **1888** Jones *Negro Myths* 90 **GA coast,** Mossa, hoona done head de ole coon dis time. **1892** (1969) Christensen *Afro-Amer. Folk Lore* 116 **seSC,** Greedy kill you daddy, an' ef honer [Footnote: You all] don' tek care, greedy da kill you. **1908** *S. Atl. Qrly.* 7.332 **sSC coast** [Gullah], Ona. [Footnote: *You,* familiar address between equals; *ona, oona;* down the coast, *hoonah.*] **1922** Gonzales *Black Border* 47 **sSC, GA coasts** [Gullah], Oonuh kin yeddy'um talk 'bout uh lazy man ent wut. [=You can hear him talk about a lazy man of no account.] *Ibid* 307, Hoonuh. . . Hunnuh—you, ye. **1928** Peterkin *Scarlet Sister Mary* 37 **SC** [Gullah], If you don' repent, yunnuh'll go to torment when you die too. **1930** Woofter *Black Yeomanry* 13 **seSC** [Gullah], Limus turned to the chattering group— "Yunna jump" [=You must hurry]. **c1937** in 1972 *Amer. Slave* 2.1.115 **SC,** Yinnah talk big storm hang people up on tree? **1949** Turner *Africanisms* 203 **sSC, GA coasts** [Gullah], [Words used in conversation:] 'unə ('hunə, 'wunə) 'you'. **1950** *PADS* 14.39 **SC,** Hunnah, hoonah. . . You, singular or plural. Same as *yunnah. Ibid* 73, Yinner, yunner, yunna ['jɪnə, 'jʌnə, 'jʌnə]. . . You all. Gullah. **1952** Brown *NC Folkl.* 1.610 **seNC,** Yuner ['jʌnə]: *pron.* You; you all.—Duplin county; also S.C. **1971** Cunningham *Syntactic Analysis Gullah* 16, [hənə] 'you' (pl). *Ibid* 21, Generally, S[ea] I[sland] Creole has retained the tendency of several West African languages (e.g., Ibo, Gã, Yoruba) of not distinguishing, by formal devices, case and gender. Specifically, *hEnE* [= [hənə]], 'you', the second person plural pronoun, parallels, in both form and function, Ibo, *unu.* **1987** Jones-Jackson *When Roots Die* 137 **sSC coast** [Gullah], *Unu,* "you."

uña de gato n [Span, literally "cat's claw"]

Any of var plants with usu recurved thorns or prickles resembling cat's claws, as:

a A **mimosa 1** such as *Mimosa aculeaticarpa* or *M. borealis.*

1886 Havard *Flora W. & S. TX for 1885* 500, *Mimosa biuncifera* [=*M. aculeaticarpa* var *b.*], . . and *M. borealis.* . . (Uña de Gato.) Common bushes west of the Pecos, on dry gravelly soil, noted for the abundance and stoutness of their prickles. **1892** *DN* 1.195 **TX,** *Uña de gáto: i.e.* cat's claw. Name of a shrub with sharp spines, of Western Texas (*Mimosa biuncifera*). **1932** Bentley *Spanish Terms* 211, *Uña de gato.* . . Shrubs (*Mimosa biuncifera* and *Acacia greggii*) with sharp spines found in western Texas and other parts of the Southwest. The leaves are similar to the mesquite leaves. **1960** Vines *Trees SW* 507, *Mimosa biuncifera.* . . Vernacular names are Uña de Gato, . . Wait-a-bit, and Wait-a-minute. **1975** Lamb *Woody Plants SW* 75, *Mimosa biuncifera* "Una [sic] de gato".

b A **cat's-claw** (here: *Acacia greggii*).

1897 Sudworth *Arborescent Flora* 250, *Acacia greggii.* . . Uña de gato. **1932** [see **a** above]. **1937** U.S. Forest Serv. *Range Plant Hdbk.* B2, Catclaw [=*Acacia greggii*], known also as . . uña de gato . . is a southwestern species ranging from western Texas to southern Nevada. **1951** *PADS* 15.33 **TX,** *Acacia greggii.* . . Una [sic] de gato, devil's-claw. **1970** Correll *Plants TX* 773, *Acacia Wrightii* [=*A. greggii* var *w.*] . . *Uña de gato.* **1975** Lamb *Woody Plants SW* 68, *Acacia greggii* "Una [sic] de gato". . . It will be easily recognized and not soon forgotten if a person gets too close to it, as the spines along the branches are curved back like the claws of a cat. **2004** *DARE* File—Internet, *Recommended Trees for the Lower Rio Grande Valley.* . . Wright's Catclaw or Una [sic] De Gato—Acacia wrightii.

c A **prickly ash 1** (here: *Zanthoxylum fagara*) native to Florida and Texas.

1970 Correll *Plants TX* 911, *Zanthoxylum Fagara.* . . *Uña de gato.* . . Shrub, rounded, very prickly.

uncle n

1a Used as a term of address or title for an elderly man unrelated to the speaker. **now chiefly Sth, S Midl** Cf **aunt B1**

1813 *Columbian Phenix Providence Patriot* (RI) 10 July 1/3, Bring your plots and intrigues, uncle *Tim,/* And let's all be tories together. **1855** Barnum *Life* 69 **CT,** [Footnote to *Uncle Phile:*] My father's name was Philo, but as it was the custom to call everybody in those parts uncle or aunt, deacon, colonel, captain, or squire, my father's general title was as above. **1899** (1912) Green *VA Folk-Speech* 465, *Uncle.* . . A term of

familiarity: *Uncle* Bob; *Uncle* Billy. **1902** *DN* 2.248 **sIL,** *Uncle.* . . Common designation of any old man. **1903** *DN* 2.335 **seMO,** *Uncle.* . . An elderly man; especially an aged negro. . . *Uncle Billy; Uncle Bob,* etc. An appellation used as a term of respect toward old men. *Uncle* prefixed to the full name is often applied to men of prominence, as 'Uncle Billy Norman,' etc. **1905** *DN* 3.99 **nwAR,** *Uncle.* . . Used with the given name to elderly men, whether white or black, as a token of affectionate esteem. 'Uncle Stephen, I'm glad to see you.' **1906** Casey *Parson's Boys* 139 **sIL** (as of c1860), On Friday we started back, an' about noon got to old Uncle Jacky Johnson's place. **1909** [see **1b** below]. **1986** Pederson *LAGS Concordance,* 1 inf, **csMS,** Uncle—used by whites to older whites or blacks; 1 inf, **cnAL,** Your aunt or your uncle—not relatives; 1 inf, **ceAR,** Uncle Bill—what Negroes called his father; 1 inf, **seMS,** Uncle Bill Clark—no kin; 1 inf, **seGA,** Uncles—old wore-out men; in respect, affection. **1991** Haynes *Haywood Home* 70 **wNC** (as of c1905), He was no kin to us that I know of. But the young of my time were taught to address older people as uncle or aunt whether they were any kin or not. It was respectful.

b Spec: used by a White person in reference to a Black man. **Sth, S Midl** Cf **aunt B2**

1830 Holbrook *Sketches* 111 **VA,** In many families . . the children are taught to address the older servant as *uncle* or *auntee.* **1859** (1968) Bartlett *Americanisms* 492, *Uncle.* Used in the Middle and Southern States in accosting an elderly colored man. **1893** Shands *MS Speech* 18 [Black], *Aunt* or *Aunty.* . . An appellation applied by all classes to old colored women, as *uncle* is applied to old colored men. **1909** *DN* 3.385 **eAL, wGA,** *Uncle.* . . Any elderly man, especially an elderly negro man. Also applied by children to any grown negro whose given name is not known. "Uncle, will you show me the way home?" A negro is never addressed as *Mr.* by a white person. **1937** *Natl. Geogr. Mag.* 71.278 **MS,** "Uncle, did you ever think of buying land of your own?" I asked a white-haired negro who was tinkering with his plough. **1961** Folk *Word Atlas N. LA* map 1414 B, Negro man . . uncle (elderly man) 33% [of 275 infs]. **1967** *DARE* Tape **AL20,** [FW:] I noticed you call some Negroes Aunt and Uncle. . . Was that a term of respect? [Inf:] Yes. [FW:] And . . would your parents not let you call an older Negro by their first name? Or was that just something everybody called 'em? [Inf:] No. It was kind of respectful. And we'd say it now like I say Aunt Lottie and Uncle Archie. . . In my time, growing up, nobody called anybody else by their first name like all of you do now. **1967** *DARE* FW Addit **SC,** Uncle Bill, Aunt Patsy—titles applied to *older* Negroes. Also without the name if you didn't know it—you were supposed "to put a handle to all elderly people." **1968–70** *DARE* (Qu. HH28, *Names and nicknames . . for people of foreign background: Negro*) Inf **SC59,** Uncle (name)—term of "deference" to elderly Negroes; (Qu. II10b, *Asking directions of somebody on the street when you don't know his name—what you'd say to a man: "Say, _____, how far is it to the next town?"*) Inf **FL48,** Uncle—Whites call Negroes "nigger" or "darky"; call older people "uncle" or "auntie"; **NC88,** Uncle—White man's expression is "Say, buddy," or "uncle" or "Say, John" (to Blacks). **1970** Tarpley *Blinky* 262 **neTX,** Your most polite word for black people . . auntie, uncle (for older Negroes) [rare]. **1986** Pederson *LAGS Concordance,* 20 infs, **Gulf Region,** Uncle [*DARE* Ed: These infs generally characterized their resp along the lines of "a term of respect for an elderly black man."]; 6 infs, Aunt and uncle (*or* uncle or aunt) [*DARE* Ed: generally characterized as "whites, deferentially, to older blacks"]; 1 inf, **ceAR,** Uncle Bob—black man worked for father; 1 inf, **cwTN,** Uncle Bob Wardlaw—a slave who visited them; 1 inf, **cnGA,** Uncle Pick—white folks called his grandfather; 1 inf, **cnMS,** Howdy, Uncle—to elderly black; respectful; 1 inf, **csTN,** Uncle John—old colored people called "Uncle." **1993** Delany-Delany *Having Our Say* 54 **cNC** [Black], He called Mama "auntie," which was one of the put-down ways white people referred to colored people. They'd call men "uncle" or "boy."

2 Used as an exclam to concede defeat in a fight or other contest. [Prob in allusion to the joke in quot 1891, which was widely reprinted (in var versions) in US newspapers from 1891–1908. As the joke appar first appeared in a London weekly, it clearly does not presuppose the sense of *uncle* treated here, which is unknown in England.] **widespread, but somewhat less freq Sth, S Midl** See Map on p. 784 Cf **calf-rope, holler**

[**1891** *IA Citizen* (IA City) [9 Oct] 16/3 (newspaperarchive.com), A gentleman was boasting that his parrot would repeat anything he told him. For example, he told him several times, before some friends, to say "Uncle," but the parrot would not repeat it. In anger he seized the bird, and half-twisting his neck, said: "Say 'uncle,' you beggar!" and threw him into the fowl pen, in which he had ten prize fowls. Shortly afterward, thinking he had killed the parrot, he went to the pen. To his surprise he found nine of the fowls dead on the floor with their necks wrung, and the parrot standing on the tenth twisting his neck and screaming: "Say 'uncle,' you beggar! say [']uncle.'"—Spare Moments.] **1912** *Modesto News* (CA) 11 May 4/2, [Advt:] *This Time* it is "Martie" Graves and Don Johns who made them say "Uncle." **1918** *Chicago Herald & Examiner* (IL) 1 Oct 11, [Cartoon:] Sic him Jenny Jinx— make him say "Uncle." **1932** *AmSp* 7.335 [Johns Hopkins jargon], To "*say uncle*"—to give in; to surrender. **1934** *AmSp* 9.313, I just happened to recall that North Texas says "Holler Calf Rope!" when New Jersey would say "Say Uncle!" **1939** *AmSp* 14.267 **IN,** 'He came to taw,' 'He hollered "calf rope," ' or 'He hollered "uncle," ' are publishments of his defeat. **1949** Hedgecock *Gone Are the Days* 59 **swMO,** He'd shoot bundles [of oats] at me like bullets out of a machine gun, but I can't remember that I ever said "uncle." **1965–70** *DARE* (Qu. EE20, *When two boys are fighting, and the one who is losing wants to stop, he calls out, "_____."*) 207 Infs, **widespread, but somewhat less freq Sth, S Midl,** Uncle; (Qu. Y17, *When two people agree to stop fighting and not be enemies any more . . "I hear they _____."*) Inf **LA35,** Called uncle; (Qu. EE17, *In a game of tag, if a player wants to rest, what does he call out so that he can't be tagged?*) Infs **OH89, 90,** Uncle; (Qu. JJ25, *To show somebody that you're the boss: "He thought he could take the place over, but I made him _____."*) Infs **IL11, 96, MA73, NY105,** Say uncle. **1984** *DARE* File **CA, CO, ID, Boston MA, MO, nNY, NW, SW, UT, WY** *When two boys are fighting, and the one who is losing wants to stop, he calls out, "_____":* uncle. **2004** *Chron.-Telegram* (Elyria OH) 25 Mar sec A 7/4, That explains why he has opted for . . "open war." It is the only way he can make the Palestinians cry uncle.

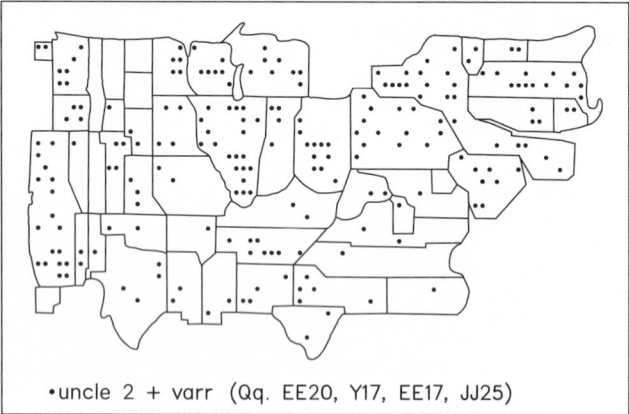

•uncle 2 + varr (Qq. EE20, Y17, EE17, JJ25)

3 A large ant. [By joc analogy with *aunt* [ænt]]
1960 in 2007 *DARE* File—Internet **IL,** Because they [=carpenter ants] are so big, some people call them uncles. **1966–69** *DARE* (Qu. R17, . . *Names . . for the big black ants that sting*) Infs **FL26, IN49, ME12, NC33, NY36, OH40, PA53,** Uncle.

Uncle Arthur n Cf **arthuritis, Old Arthur,** *DS* BB8
Arthritis personified.
1992 *DARE* File **seMD** (as of 1985) [Black], Asked how he was feeling, an old man replied, "Not so good. Uncle Arthur keeps comin' round." **2003** *DARE* File—Internet, We now know that Arthritis is a long-enduring virus which grows very slowly, until we wake up & "Uncle Arthur" (as this debilitating dis-ease is colloquially called by some) has knocked on our door. **2005** *Ibid,* I was diagnosed with uncle Arthur when I was 14. . . the problem is that where ever you have surgery, uncle Arthur has found a new home. *Ibid* **MO,** Whenever my dad would have trouble with his arthritis he would always say Uncle Arthur is visiting. *Ibid* **WV,** "Welcome to the club, the Uncle Arthur club." That's their affectionate name for arthritis.

Uncle Charlie's dead See **Charlie's dead**
Uncle Huldy n Cf **huldy**
=**old-squaw.**
[**1888** Trumbull *Names of Birds* 88 **CT,** I am told that in Stonington, Conn., the words "John Connolly" were popularly used, about fifty years ago, in imitation of this bird's [=the old-squaw's] gabble, and they can be so repeated as to produce a better imitation, I think, than the words

now in use at Stony Creek, same state, viz., "Uncle Huldy," and "my Aunt Huldy."] **1917** (1923) *Birds Amer.* 1.141, *Old-Squaw. . . Other Names. . .* Old Wife; . . Old Granny; Old Molly; Old Billy; . . Uncle Huldy.

Uncle Johnny-jump-up See **johnny-jump-up 1**
Uncle Melvin See **Melvin**
Uncle Sam coot n
=**white-winged scoter.**
1888 Trumbull *Names of Birds* 99 **CT,** At Stratford [the white-winged scoter is called] *Uncle-Sam coot.*

Uncle Sam's sheep n
=**government beef.**
[**1936** *Ironwood Daily–Globe* (MI) 28 Feb 3/4, Boatswain William Kincaide and his crew of 10 men. . . are doing their bit toward conservation by feeding many deer in that section. The deer have been affectionately dubbed, "Uncle Sam's sheep."] **1968** *DARE* (Qu. P35a, *Names or nicknames for any deer shot illegally*) Inf **WI**38A, Uncle Sam's sheep— they used to call them that in Adams County during the Depression. **1976** *DARE* File **nwWI** (as of 1930s), *Uncle Sam's sheep. . .* Illegally killed deer—commonly used.

Uncle Tom n [From the Black title character of Harriet Beecher Stowe's anti-slavery novel *Uncle Tom's Cabin* (1851–52)]
1 A Black man who is submissive toward White people or who adopts White culture; hence v *Uncle Tom* to behave like a servile Black person; vbl n *Uncle Tomming* behaving obsequiously toward White people; n *Uncle Tomism* a deferential phrase used when talking to White people. *esp freq among Black speakers; derog* Cf **Aunt Thomasina, oreo, tom** n[1] **2**
1922 in 1973 Dundes *Mother Wit* 400 **Sth** [Black], It does not occur to the Old South that there is a "New Negro"; that the "Uncle Toms" are passing. **1942** *Amer. Mercury* 55.223.95 [Harlem slang], *Handkerchiefhead*—sycophant type of Negro; also an *Uncle Tom.* **1944** Myrdal *Amer. Dilemma* 774 **Sth** [Among urban Blacks], They can afford to take it out on their leaders by defaming them for their . . "Uncle Tomming." **1965–70** *DARE* (Qu. HH28, *Names and nicknames . . for people of foreign background: Negro*) Inf **FL48,** Uncle Tom; **CA81,** Uncle Tom— not just by Black Power groups; (Qu. HH40, *Uncomplimentary words for an old man*) Inf **FL48,** Uncle Tom; (Qu. II20a, *A person who tries too hard to gain somebody else's favor: "He's an awful _____."*) Infs **FL48, 52, MI72, MS88, PA239, 247, TN50,** Uncle Tom [All Infs Black]; [(Qu. DD33b, *A person who is actively against drinking*) Inf **GA30,** Old Uncle Tom; **GA19,** Uncle Tom]. **1965** *Little Autobiog. Malcolm X* 48 [Black], The shoeshine customers, and any from the inside rest room who took a towel, you whiskbroomed a couple of licks. "A nickel or a dime tip, just give 'em that," Freddie said. "But for two bits, Uncle Tom a little—white cats especially like that." *Ibid* 76, The dining car waiters and Pullman porters knew it too, and they faked their Uncle Tomming to get bigger tips. **1968** *Current Slang* 3.2.50 [Watts slang; Black], *Uncle Tom. . .* Bourgeois Negro. One who has property and money. According to advocates of the new Black Nationalists, he is over solicitous to whites and is accused of pot-licking. **1968** *New Yorker* 17 Aug 21, [Cartoon; a White society matron is addressing her Black maid:] The guests will be arriving any minute now. Please, Amanda, try to Uncle Tom it a little just for tonight. **1972** Claerbaut *Black Jargon* 84, *Uncle Tom. . .* a black person who attempts to take on a white style of living. **1982** Walker *Color Purple* 82 **GA** [Black], This sound mighty much like some ole uncle Tomming to me. **1986** Pederson *LAGS Concordance,* 1 inf, **seFL,** Uncle Tom—less derogatory; 1 inf, **ceTN,** Uncle Tom—compromising Negro, sold out to whites; 1 inf, **csMS,** Uncle Tom—blacks use; insulting; 1 inf, **ceTX,** Uncle Tomisms—deferential phrases used by blacks [Note: preceding infs are White]; 1 inf, **nwMS,** Uncle Tom—insulting; 1 inf, **seMS,** Uncle Tom —some blacks called her father; 1 inf, **nwLA,** Uncle Tom—insulting— "plays up" to white people; 1 inf, **cwMS,** Uncle Tom—black; tells whites about blacks; 1 inf, **cwFL,** Oreo—Uncle Tom, "chocolate" outside, white inside [Note: preceding infs are Black].
2 A children's game; see quot. Cf **tin tin**
1972 Jones-Hawes *Step it Down* 157 **eGA** [Black], *Uncle Tom. . .* has a plot line and a bitter hilarity all its own. . . You come around to the children and then you knock to this one's door just like you were the door. . . They say, *Who is that?* You say, *Old Man Tom.* They say, *What*

you want? You say, *I want to sell some nails. How many pounds you want?* And they'll tell him . . one or two pounds or three. . . And then he goes to the next one and the same thing over. . . Then he'll go away. . . Make himself look real ugly and raggedy. Then he'll come back. . . They say, *Who is that?* And he say, *Old Man Tom.* They say, *What you want?* He say, *I want you to pay me for my nails please.* (He say it in a funny way). . . And they say, *I can't pay.* . . He say, like he's crying, *You ain't going to pay Uncle Tom?* And you're not supposed to laugh or not even smile, just be *hard* at him, and Uncle Tom have to do all kind of funny things to make you laugh. And if you laugh, then you got to give him the nails back.

Uncle Tom v, Uncle Tomism (or Tomming)   See Uncle Tom n 1

uncrunk(ed) adj   esp Sth

Of an engine: stalled, unable to start—usu in phrr *(be)come uncrunk(ed).*

1972 *Atlanta Letters* **nwGA,** Another funny expression which I have heard is for a car to become uncrunked, or it stopped running.   **1973** Mangum *Fargus Technique* 164 **MS,** He was just flyin' over and it come uncrunk on him . . cause I didn' hear nothin', when it come down. **2004** *FL Times–Union* (Jacksonville) 7 Dec (Internet) **seGA,** "I hooked up to one one night, and the truck came uncrunk," he said. As he was grinding on the starter and begging it to start, a bedroom light came on. **2005** in 2007 *DARE* File—Internet **AR** [Black], In the 70's when I first heard it Crunk was an ebonics version of Crank or Start. Especially in reference to starting a car or other motorized equipment. Crunk's counterpart then was Uncrunk. *He crunk up his car to let it warm up. But it come uncrunk when he went back in the house. Ibid* **SC,** *Uncrunk:* when a car's engine dies, as in "the car come uncrunk."

uncum n   Also *piuncum, (pi)unkum*
=golden ragwort.

[**1852** Beach *Amer. Practice Med.* 3.265, Life-root. *Indian Names.— Uncum, Nutqua-mequot,* &c.] **1854** King *Amer. Eclectic Dispensatory* 869, The *Senecio Gracilis, Unkum,* or *Female Regulator,* [is] a slender state of the species [=*Senecio aureus*], found on rocky shores. **1892** (1974) Millspaugh *Amer. Med. Plants* 91–1, *Senecio aureus. . . Unkum. . .* The Golden Ragwort is common everywhere.   **1940** Clute *Amer. Plant Names* 86, *S[enecio] aureus. . .* Piunkum.   *Ibid* 230, Piuncum.   **1974** (1977) Coon *Useful Plants* 115, *Senecio aureus . .* uncum.

under adj   chiefly Sth, S Midl, TX   See Map   Cf lower adj 1, over C

In comb with terms for var types of **earmark** n: Made in the lower edge of the ear; also transf.

1837 *Knickerbocker* 10.408 **NC,** The young bridegroom boasted that he had taken an 'under bit out of his left ear.' **1869** *Overland Mth.* 3.126 **SW,** He asked me if I had seen a red mulley cow, with a crop and an underbit in the right. **1890** in 1975 *Foxfire 3* 86 **nwGA,** His stock mark is as follows. A Smooth crop and an under bit in the right ear, and a [sic] under half crop in the left ear. **1899** (1912) Green *VA Folk-Speech* 465, *Undercut. . .* A piece cut out of the underpart of an animal's ear in marking. *Ibid* 466, *Underkeel, n.* Mark on the ear of an animal by cutting out a small piece on the underpart; *undercut.* **1903** *DN* 2.335 **seMO,** *Under-bit.* **1906** *DN* 3.162 **nwAR,** *Underbit.* . . Semicircular piece cut from the lower part of an animal's ear. A *right underbit* is taken from the right ear, a *left underbit* from the left ear. **1909** *DN* 3.385 **eAL, wGA,** *Under-crop. . .* An earmark. **1915** *DN* 4.185 **swVA,** *Under-bit,* a triangular cut from the lower side [of the ear of an animal]. **1923** (1946) Greer-Petrie *Angeline Steppin'* 31 **csKY,** Cuttin' his mark in thar years [=their ears] say a underbit in the left and a slit in the right. **1940** (1941) Bell *Swamp Water* 167 **Okefenokee GA,** "What's y'all's hog mark?" "Sometimes we use an under-bit, but mostly no mark a-tall." **1941** Writers' Program *Guide WY* 466, *Under-bit.* **1965–70** *DARE* (Qu. K18, . . *Kind of mark . . to identify a cow*) 14 Infs, **scattered, but esp Gulf States, TX,** Under-bit; **IA**8, Under-cut; **LA**7, Under-figure-seven; **TX**22, Underslope. **1967** *DARE* Tape **TX**24, Occasionally, maybe they'd mark a crop and an under-half-crop. Thataway, they'd cut . . a third of the ear off, the tip of the ear. And then, they'd cut down in there on the underside, and cut out . . another little piece, and it had to be a crop and under-half-crop. **1975** *Foxfire 3* 103 **nwGA,** They notched the ears of the sheep—something like a slit in the left ear and an undercrop, just a notch, cut out of the right ear. **1986** Pederson *LAGS Concordance,* 2 infs, **AR, TN,** Underbit(s).

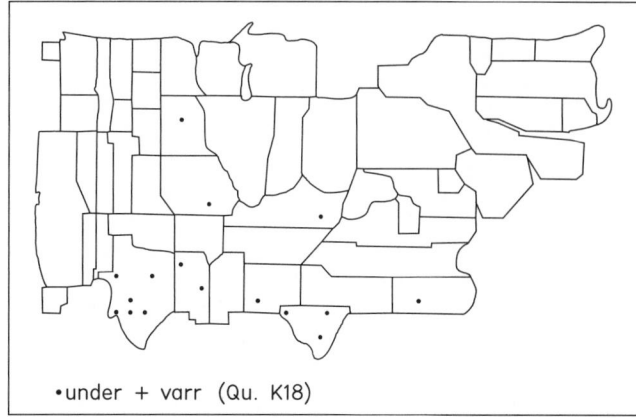

•under + varr (Qu. K18)

underbody n   Sth, S Midl

An undergarment for a woman or a child; see quots.

1863 *Frank Leslie's Mth.* 1.393, An underbody of fine muslin tucked, with full sleeves gathered into a band. **1873** in 1963 Albemarle Co. Hist. Soc. *Mag.* 20.57 **VA,** She gave me some mighty pretty nansook to make an underbody. **1906** *DN* 3.162 **nwAR,** *Underbody. . .* Corset cover. "I need a pretty underbody for this thin dress." **1909** *DN* 3.385 **eAL, wGA,** *Underbody. . .* A child's undershirt or bodice, used to support the trousers and worn underneath the blouse or shirt-waist. **1926** Roberts *Time of Man* 209 **KY,** This-here is Mrs. Prather's old petticoat, and here's her under-body, and here's her old blue dress. **1935** Glasgow *Vein of Iron* 7 **wVA,** She hoped the minister couldn't see the top of her red flannel underbody, which would poke up at the neck. **1949** Arnow *Hunter's Horn* 70 **KY,** Ruby with her dress falling down and her purple outing underbody showing. **1966–70** *DARE* (Qu. W15, *A shirt-length undergarment worn by women*) Infs **KY**94, **LA**25, **MD**41, **MS**72, **SC**26, Underbody; **AR**18, Underbody—very tight-fitting undergarment, down to the waist. [5 of 6 Infs old] **1993** Ison-Ison *Whole 'Nother Lang.* 72 **sAppalachians,** *Underbody*—Bra, usually homemade. **1997** in 2004 Montgomery-Hall *Dict. Smoky Mt. Engl.* 627 **wNC, eTN,** *Underbody. . .* a corset cover.

undercut n
=mangana.

1940 *Cattleman* May 22 **West,** This loop is often called an "undercut" although I believe the Mexicans call it a *mangana.* Whatever its name, it stands a big loop up in front of an animal and all he has to do is get in it.

under ditch adj phr, adv phr   chiefly West

Of land: within reach of an irrigation ditch, under irrigation.

[**1871** Union Colony CO *First Annual Rept.* 34, Of . . lands under Ditch No. 2 . . there are open to colonists . . the following. . . We desire to call the special attention of all who contemplate casting in their future lot with us, to the desirableness of the lands to be irrigated by this ditch.] **1872** Tice *Over Plains* 135 **CO,** Any one entering land 'under ditch,' . . that is, that can be irrigated from any completed canal, is required to pay the proprietors of the canal. **1892** *Harper's New Mth. Mag.* June 93 **MT,** The soil is of extraordinary fertility, and it is said that at least three-fifths of it can be laid under ditch. **1896** *N. Amer. Rev.* 163.714 **KS,** They want to have a large quantity of land under ditch. **1918** *Oakland Tribune* (CA) 3 Mar 60/3, [Advt:] *For Sale. . .* 20 acres of land . . gray silt soil and under ditch. **1938** *Helena Independent* (MT) 18 Mar 2/4, Nearly 10,000 acres of land now used only for pasturage will be put under ditch and in the tillable classification. **1956** *Reno Eve. Gaz.* (NV) 27 Apr 21/4, [Advt:] *Ranches, Farms. . .* Approx. 200 acres under ditch. **2005** *DARE* File—Internet **CO,** As the City [=Boulder] expanded . . the acreage "under ditch" gradually diminished.

underground bean   See underground pea

underground moon n   Nantucket MA   Cf south-moon-under

See quot 1916.

1905 *Boston Herald* (MA) 6 July 7/5, An "underground moon" is simply one which makes its change at "no hours"—between 12 and 1 o'clock—according to the traditions of Nantucket. The "underground moon" is a seafaring phrase. **1916** Macy-Hussey *Nantucket Scrap Basket* 156, The "underground moon." Here we have a strictly local phase of the orb of night. When the moon makes a change between the hours of

12 and 1 o'clock, she is classed as an "underground moon," and the claim is made that foul weather is sure to accompany. Careful notes indicate that such conditions do result, but that the rule is not infallible. The *real* "underground" moon is when that heavenly body makes its change between the time of setting and rising, and between the hours of 12 and 1 o'clock, being at the time below the horizon—or underground. **1938** *Hench Coll.* **Nantucket MA,** [As told to Hench by a Nantucket-born colleague:] If the moon changes quarter between 12 and 1 at night, it is called an "underground moon" and bad weather is coming—wind or rain or fog. **1964** *Newark Advocate* (OH) 3 Aug [4]/1 (newspaperarchive.com), Penned in quaint New England verse, the Almanac's weather outlook for August goes something like this. . . Aug. 22-31, Underground moon means cool bad weather soon.

underground pea n Also *underground bean*
=**peanut 1.**

[**1855** Johnston *Chem. Common Life* 188, Among these [=oily seeds and nuts] the earth-nut *(Arachis hypogaea),* a kind of oily underground pea, is roasted in South Carolina.] **1959** Carleton *Index Herb. Plants* 120, *Underground-bean:* Arachis hypogaea. **1966** *DARE* (Qu. I42, . . *Names or nicknames . . for peanuts)* Inf **MS**23, Pinders, underground peas.

underhold n Also *underholt* Cf *holt* (at **hold** n **A1, B1, 2**)
A Form. See also quots at **B** below

1875 *Scribner's Mth.* 10.240 **GA** [Black], Sence Jacob had dat wrastlin'-match, I, too, gwine do my bes';/ When Jacob got all underholt, de Lord He answered Yes! **1909** *DN* 3.385 **eAL, wGA,** *Underholt.* . . In wrestling, *all underholt* is the hold under both arms of an opponent. **1946** *PADS* 6.31 **eNC** (as of 1900–10), *Underholt.* . . Underhold—arm under opponent's arm in a side-by-side tussle. . . Common among schoolboys.
B Sense.

Fig: an advantage; the upper hand. **esp S Midl**

1874 in 2007 *DARE* File—Internet [*Winfield Courier* (KS) 5 June], Joy has gotten the underhold on the Neutral lands. **1879** *Daily Constitution* (Atlanta GA) 2 Dec 2/3, Bill Arp is unquestionably the favorite southern humorist. Joe [sic] Harris will please the critics better, but William takes an underholt on the masses. **1885** *Overland Mth.* (2d ser) 5.305 **MO,** I knowed yer feelin's had got the *underholt* of ye. **1899** Chesnutt *Conjure Woman* 32 **csNC** [Black], De goopher [=a spell] had got de under holt, en th'owed Henry. **1905** *DN* 3.99 **nwAR,** *Underholt.* . . Advantage. 'I've got the underholt on you there.' **1908** *Stevens Point Daily Jrl.* (WI) 30 Apr [4]/4 (newspaperarchive.com) **TN** [Black], Brethren, I thought fer a minute . . that old Satan had got the underholt on me. **1913** *Daily Northwestern* (Oshkosh WI) 18 Oct 11/1, All the people need is to see that it [=money] does not . . have a legislative "underholt." **1920** *Ft. Wayne Jrl.–Gaz.* (IN) 27 Aug 4/2, Governor Cox made the charge that the old predatory gang was preparing to buy an underhold on the government. **1933** *Charleston Gaz.* (WV) 14 Dec 6/2, It overlooks the great underhold it gives to the bootlegger. **1944** *Billboard* 17 June 21/2 **NC,** Robert L. Doughton . . declared that the "Senate took an underhold on the House."

underly adj
Underprivileged.

1991 Still *Wolfpen Notebooks* 47 **sAppalachians,** If you see some pore little underly children, give to'em, do for'em.

undermind v [Var of *undermine; OED2* 1694 →] Cf **drown, -ed** suff **1**

1788 in 1864 Hawks–Perry *Doc. Hist. Prot. Episc. Church* 2.322 **CT,** The members should be vigilant, lest the foundation should be underminded by clandestine enemies. **1807** *Centinel* (Gettysburg PA) 8 Apr 1/1, Whoever is acquainted with the Prussian states, will certainly see with vexation an edifice underminded, that once contained so much excellence. **1851** *Elyria Courier* (OH) 2 Apr 2/7, The track . . was underminded beyond the dam. **1899** (1912) Green *VA Folk-Speech* 466, *Underminded.* . . Undermined. "The place is all underminded with rats." **1903** *DN* 2.335 **seMO,** *Underminded.* **1907** *DN* 3.238 **nwAR,** *Underminded.* **1909** *DN* 3.385 **eAL, wGA,** *Underminded.* **1922** *Mexia Eve. News* (TX) 27 June 4/5, Those lands will be populated by those who fought for America . . and not by an . . undermining foreign element. **1951** *Chillicothe Constitution-Tribune* (MO) 17 Nov 1/8, Recent heavy rains . . had underminded the well curb. **1968–69** *DARE* (Qu. V1, *When you suspect that somebody is trying to deceive you, or that something is going on behind your back . . "There's _____."*) Infs **GA**19, 30, He's underminding me; (Qu. II33, *To get an advantage*

over somebody by tricky means: "I don't trust him, he's always trying to _____.") Inf **KY**21, Undermind. **1976** *Herald Times–Reporter* (Manitowoc WI) 15 Sept [28]/5 (newspaperarchive.com), Rain was light and fire was feeding on peat, underminding some trees. **2000** *Post-Std.* (Syracuse NY) 3 Nov 18/5, Entertaining, . . but underminded by cliches and distracting gags.

underminded ppl adj [Cf *EDD underminded* ppl. adj. "Underhand, mean, treacherous."]
Sly, deceptive.

1902 *DN* 2.248 **sIL,** *Underminded.* . . Double-faced or deceptive in character; hypocritical or tricky. **1968** *DARE* (Qu. KK37, *Words to describe a very sly person: "He's _____."*) Inf **GA**19, Underminded. **2001** in 2007 *DARE* File—Internet **AZ,** I think this dirty underminded thing of a man has already filed something. **2007** *Ibid* **WA,** A majority of those in Athletics simply do not want to change their rumored sneaky and underminded ways, "stealing from Peter to pay Paul" way of business.

underpend v, hence vbl n, n *underpending* [Varr of *underpin, underpinning*] **chiefly Sth, S Midl**

1957 *Beckley Post–Herald* (WV) 14 Aug 14/6, [Advt:] *Masonry,* underpending, block laying, . . free estimates. **1966** *Valley Independent* (Monessen PA) 17 Aug 15/3, [Advt:] Mobile home. . . Awning and underpending included. **1969** *Weakley Co. Press* (Martin TN) 2 Oct 15/4, [Advt:] I do underpending, fireplaces, chimney work, cisterns. **1973** *Daily Times–News* (Burlington NC) 23 May sec C 18/2, [Advt:] We underpend mobile home and do light repairs. **1999** *DARE* File—Internet **NC,** Mildew. . . Am having the same problem with my cabin in North Carolina. . . To-date I have put automatic vents in the underpending. **2002** *Ibid* **TX,** [Advt:] 2 used moblehomes [sic] joined . . homes need underpending. **2004** in 2007 *Ibid* **cAR,** *Problem:* Need new underpending at the end and back side of the building. (Repaint) *Solution:* Large section of the trailer was re-underpended with new wood and framing materials. **2005** *DARE* File—Internet **SC,** [Advt:] 1989 Fleetwood Double-wide with brick underpending. **2007** *Ibid* **cnNC,** The scarcity of development opportunities in Kernersville underpends the long-term success of Southside Square.

under-round See **round 2**

under the doctor prep phr **chiefly Sth, S Midl**
In the care of a physician.

1831 in 1914 Marshall *Political Doctrines* 136 **VA,** I have been under the doctor ever since my return in May from North Carolina and have been regularly growing worse. **1846** (1982) Magoffin *Down Santa Fé* 135 **KY,** He has been under the Dctor [sic] for some days past. **1854** *Ladies' Repository* 14.431, The editor has been . . in fact, "under" the doctor, for a week or two. **1931** in 2007 (acc) Lexis–Nexis Legal Research *State Case Law: VA* (Internet), I have been under the doctor practically ever since the accident. **1969** *DARE* FW Addit **ceNC,** *To be under the doctor*—under treatment by doctor—old-fashioned. **1972** *Atlanta Letters* **ceGA,** "Under the Doctor" (meaning ill). **1984** Wilder *You All Spoken Here* 205 **Sth,** *Under the doctor:* In the care of a physician.

under the hack See **hack** n¹ **1**

under through prep phr [Calque of PaGer or Du; see quots] **PaGer, Du settlement areas** Cf **in under**

Under and through; through (an underpass or the like).

1908 *German Amer. Annals* 10.49 **sePA,** *Under through.* Underneath, with idea of motion. "We went under through the fence." . . Pa. Ger. *unär dörch;* Ger. *unter durch.* **1950** *WELS Suppl.* **nwIA,** *Under through.* . . "The rabbit went under through the bridge." Tr. of Du.: 'onder duur.' *Ibid* **csWI,** *Under through.* . . Dutch people in Alto always say *under through* when referring to going under a viaduct or culvert. (Translation of *onder duur.* To say you go *under* means you stay there. To go under and come out on [the] other side is to go *under through.*)

unelse conj [Metath var of *unless*]
1 Unless.

1905 Sprague *Eddies* 16, Th' idee not t' jump unelse / You know jes' where t' light. **1909** *NV State Jrl.* (Reno) 23 Aug 5/5, Stock . . which remain[s] unpaid . . will be . . advertised for sale . . unelse payment is made. **1931** *Denton Jrl.* (MD) 31 Oct 2/6, He says he cant get married unelse he finds a garl by the Name of Emma. **1943** *LANE* Map 730 *(Unless)* 2 infs, **CT, ME,** Unelse. **1982** *Frederick Post* (MD) 15 Oct sec A 9/5 **PA,** More Malapropisms: From my copious notebooks I give you . . a high school principal who threatened dire punishment "unelse" we straightened up. **2005** *DARE* File—Internet **KS,** No one can even get a weekend off once a month unelse your one of the bosses favorties [sic]. *Ibid* **CA,** Don't weld the sucker—unelse you want a really big hole to look down.

‡**2** Otherwise. Cf **unless B**

2007 *DARE* File—Internet **seMI,** The only way I can think of is a straightener. If there's a serious health risk or something to using one, then don't. Unelse, just use the straightener.

unfinancial adj Also *non-financial* Pronc-spp *onfinancial, onfinanshul*

1 Of a member of an organization, esp a fraternal order: in arrears on dues, not paid up. [Cf *OED2 financial* a. 2 "Of a member in a society: That pays (his subscription)"; 1892; this sense is very common in Australia and New Zealand.] *formerly widespread, now esp freq among Black speakers*

1890 Brackett *Notes on Progress* 53 **MD,** It requires a membership of six months before benefits are given. . . After some weeks of non-payment, a member becomes unfinancial. **1900** in 2009 (acc) Lexis–Nexis Legal Research *State Case Law: MS* (Internet), Delia Murphy was not "nonfinancial" within the meaning of sec. 7, art. 5, and sec. 20 of same article. **1915** *Syracuse Herald* (NY) 21 Sept 17/1, The society [= Daughters of America] alleges that her dues were not paid and that she had been declared unfinancial. **1930** in 2007 (acc) Lexis–Nexis Legal Research *State Case Law: OK* (Internet), Defendant . . admitted that Alfred Aaron, the insured, was at one time a member of Excelsior Lodge No. 52 at Muskogee, Okla., but alleged that he was "unfinancial" at the date of his death in that he had not paid his dues for the quarter beginning January 1, 1925. [*DARE* Ed: This lodge was restricted to Blacks and Asians.] **1939** *Ibid: MA,* We think that upon that payment being made on August 16, 1937, she ceased to be "unfinancial" since she then owed dues for but two months and seventeen days, because . . an "unfinancial" member is one "owing three months' dues or an amount equal to three months' dues." **1957** *Ibid: LA* [Black], Throughout the record various witnesses used the very expressive and meaningful words 'financial' and 'unfinancial', and it appears that to be 'financial' a member must have met his monetary obligations to the church. A member who is 'unfinancial' is one who is in arrears. **2007** *DARE* File—Internet, *Dallas–Fort Worth Association of Black Communicators—*Organization Bylaws (Revised and emended: July 1989, July 1996, July 1997). . . Members not paying within 60 days will be unfinancial for the subsequent year until such dues and assessments are paid. *Ibid* **DC** [Black], As we approach the 3rd District Conference [of the Omega Psi Phi Fraternity], we need the support of every member financial and non-financial.

2 Insolvent, out of money. **chiefly Sth** Cf *AND, DNZE* (at *financial*)

1919 Means *More E.K. Means* 346 **LA** [Black], It cain't be did, niggers. . . Dis here chu'ch is a busted onfinancial institootion. **1923** *DN* 5.244 **LA,** *Onfinancial.* . . Without money. **1927** Kennedy *Gritny* 2 **sLA** [Black], Failing in this, he was declared "on-finanshul," and was denied the privilege of the house. **1933** *Landmark* (Statesville NC) 10 Feb 4/4, Proponents declared that it would put 100,000 cars on the road that are now in storage because the owners are "unfinancial" to the extent of the price of a license tag. **1942** Perry *Texas* 134, When the Negro's ordinarily precarious financial condition grows even worse, he's apt to . . say that he is "unfinancial." **1948** *Waterloo Daily Courier* (IA) 3 Mar 4/8 **MI,** I want to build a home, but I am unfinancial. Does the fact that I happen to be a World War II veteran give me any preference in getting a loan? **1955** in 1998 Foote–Percy *Correspondence* 101 **Sth,** I'm on tenterhooks right now, expecting to hear from the Guggenheim people whether I'll be financial or unfinancial this coming year.

unfitten adj Pronc-sp *onfitten* **esp sAppalachians** Cf **fitten**

Unfit, unqualified, unsuitable.

1889 *Current Lit.* 3.305 **Sth,** To "stand" for a couple may mean to help them to elope, or to simply ride for the preacher, lend the groom a dollar, or buy the bride a handkerchief. A couple that can get no one to stand for them are set down as "onfitten." **1894** *Freeborn Co. Std.* (Albert Lea MN) 28 Nov [3]/3 (newspaperarchive.com) **CO,** We're plumb unfitten ter be in ther house whar that innercent leetle gal is. **1899** (1912) Green *VA Folk-Speech* 466, *Unfitten.* . . Not fit. Improper; unsuitable; unbecoming. (2) Not suited or adapted. Wanting suitable qualifications, physical or moral; not competent. **1900** Harben *N. GA Sketches*

261, Ab Calihan is either fitten or unfitten. . . Brother Filmore, you've seed 'im the most, now what's he let fall that's undoctrinal? **c1940** in 2004 Montgomery-Hall *Dict. Smoky Mt. Engl.* 627 **wNC, eTN,** *Unfitten.* . . unfit. "He's just unfitten to do the work." **1996** *Ibid, Unfitten* . . Unfit, unqualified. . . (known to eight consultants).

unicorn n

1 See **unicorn plant 1.**

2 See **unicorn beetle.**

unicorn beetle n Also *unicorn*

Usu a **rhinoceros beetle 1;** occas also a similar horned beetle.

1891 *Century Dict.* 6615, *Unicorn.* . . A kind of beetle having a single long horn; a unicorn-beetle. Various large beetles literally answer to this definition, being unicornous, with a large single prothoracic horn. **1954** Borror–DeLong *Intro. Insects* 392, Subfamily *Dynastinae*—Rhinoceros Beetles, Unicorn Beetles, and Elephant Beetles. . . The most common Dynastinae in the East and Midwest belong to the genus *Dynastes.* The largest Eastern species is the unicorn beetle, *D[ynastes] tityus* . . , a Southern beetle 2.0 to 2.5 inches in length; . . the pronotal horn extends forward over the head. **2004** (acc) TX A&M Univ. *Discover Entomol.* (Internet), *Unicorn Beetle* . . *Dynastes* sp. . . The unicorn beetles, or Hercules beetles, are particularly striking insects.

unicorn fish n

1 also *unicorn filefish:* A **filefish,** usu *Aluterus* (formerly *Al[e]utera*) *monoceros, A. schoepfi,* or *A. scriptus.*

[**1734** Royal Soc. London *Philos. Trans.* 38.318, *Unicornis Piscis, Bahamensis* [=*Aluterus* spp]. The *Bahama Unicorn-Fish.* These *Fish* grow only to two or three *Feet* in length, and a little behind the *Eyes* have an *Horn* about nine *Inches* long, which they can move at pleasure. They are accounted poisonous.] **1842** DeKay *Zool. NY* 4.338, *The Long-Tailed Unicorn-fish. Aluteres cuspicauda* [=*Aluterus schoepfi*]. . . The dorsal spine stout, short, serrated. . . The *monoceros* of Storer is either very closely allied, or what is more probable, is the young of our Long-tailed Unicorn-fish. **1867** Storer *Hist. Fishes MA* 427, *Aluteres monoceros, Unicorn File-fish.* . . The dorsal spine is short and serrated. **1896** U.S. Bur. Fisheries *Rept. for 1895* 424, *Alutera scripta* [=*Aluterus scriptus*]. . . *Unicorn-fish.* . . West Indies; North Carolina [etc]. **1933** John G. Shedd Aquarium *Guide* 157, *Osbeckia scripta* [=*Aluterus scriptus*]—Unicornfish. . . American species. **1991** Amer. Fisheries Soc. *Common Names Fishes* 69, *Aluterus monoceros* . . unicorn filefish.

2 A **surgeonfish** of the genus *Naso,* usu *N. unicornis,* of Hawaiian waters. **HI**

1905 Jordan *Guide to Fishes* 2.409, *Acanthurus* [=*Naso*] *unicornis,* the unicorn-fish, is the commonest species and the one with the longest horn. **1933** Bryan *Hawaiian Nature* 240, The unicorn fish, or *kala* [here: =*Naso unicornis*] . . , is olive gray . . with blue spines, and blue on the fins. **1960** Gosline–Brock *Hawaiian Fishes* 251, *Naso unicornis* . . *Unicorn fish.* . . The horn, which first becomes evident (as a bony prominence) at a length of about 5 inches, originates at the level of the eye. **1967** *DARE* (Qu. P2, . . *Kinds of saltwater fish caught around here . . good to eat*) Inf **HI**4, Unicorn fish.

unicorn plant n Cf **unicorn root, unicorn's horn**

1 also *unicorn:* A **colicroot 2** (here: *Aletris farinosa*). Cf **false unicorn root 2, true unicorn root**

1784 in 1785 Amer. Acad. Arts & Sci. *Memoirs* 1.435 **CT,** Unicorn. . . is said to be useful in chronic rheumatisms. **1795** Winterbotham *Amer. U.S.* 3.397 **NEng,** Unicorn, Aletris farinosa. **1900** Lyons *Plant Names* 21, *A[letris] farinosa.* . . Unicorn-root, . . True Unicorn-root, Unicorn-plant, Unicorn's-horn. . . *Rhizome* bitter, tonic, stomachic. **1974** (1977) Coon *Useful Plants* 171, *Aletris farinosa* . . unicorn plant. . . This plant has long been held in esteem for its values.

2 =**blazing star 2.** Cf **false unicorn, ~ unicorn root 1**

1833 Beck *Botany N. & Middle States* 367, *H[elonias] dioica* [= *Chamaelirium luteum*]. . . N.J. to Geor. W. to Miss. . . *Unicorn Plant.* **1869** Fuller *Uncle John* 170 **sNEng,** The country people usually know it [=*Chamaelirium luteum*] as "The Blazing Star" or "Unicorn Plant." It grows in marshes, and the root is a popular tonic. **1892** (1974) Millspaugh *Amer. Med. Plants* 177-1, *Chamaelirium luteum.* . . Unicorn plant. [*Ibid* 177-2, On account more of the similarity of vulgarisms than aught else, this plant and Aletris are gathered as the same in various localities, or are interchanged.] **1921** *Amer. Botanist* 27.94, The names "Unicorn root" and "unicorn plant," doubtless refer to the root [of *Chamaelirium luteum*].

3 A plant of the genus *Proboscidea.* [See quot 1884] Also called **bullhorn, devil dog 1, devil's-claw 2, devil's-horns 1, double-claw, ram's horn 2;** for other names of var spp see **elephant's trunk 1, elephant tusks, pickled rats, toloache 2**

1818 Eaton *Botany* 315, *Martynia. . . proboscidea* [=*Proboscidea louisianica*] (unicorn plant. Western states). . . Fruit somewhat gourdlike, with one long horn. **1884** *Amer. Jrl. Pharmacy* 56.641 **SW,** The Martynia. . . is a native of the Southwestern States, . . and is commonly called Unicorn Plant. **1891** Herman *His Angel* 6 **NM,** Woodbine, unicorn plant, and wild currant surged all about it. **1947** Carr *Desert Parade* 80 **SW,** *Unicorn Plant . . :* The grotesque, long, curved, clawed seed pods of this plant lend themselves readily to the manufacture of odd little figures that are placed on sale in curio shops. . . *Martynia parviflora.* **1979** Spellenberg *Audubon Guide N. Amer. Wildflowers W. Region* 612, *Unicorn Plant (Proboscidea altheaefolia). . .* As the plump fruit matures, it divides into halves, the single "horn" forming two curved "devil's claws." **2006** (acc) *N. AZ Flora* (Internet), *Proboscidea althaeifolia. Desert Unicorn-Plant.* Perennial.

unicorn root n Cf **unicorn plant, unicorn's horn**

1 A **colicroot 2** (here: *Aletris farinosa*). Cf **false unicorn root 2, true ~**

1818 Eaton *Botany* 129 **MA,** *Aletris. . . farinosa. . .* unicorn-root. . . This plant grows plentifully in Brimfield. **1828** Rafinesque *Med. Flora* 1.37, *Aletris farinosa. . .* Unicorn Root. *Ibid* 39, Many vulgar names given to it [=*Aletris farinosa*] are common to other plants, dissimilar in properties if not in aspect. . . Unicorn-root is also a name of *Veratrum* [here: =*Chamaelirium luteum*] and of *Neottia.* . . Such is the confusion arising from vulgar names. **1869** Porcher *Resources* 611 **Sth,** *Unicorn root, . . Aletris farinosa . . .* The decoction of the root and leaves in liberal doses is much employed in popular practice in the lower portions of South Carolina. **1892** (1974) Millspaugh *Amer. Med. Plants* 172–1, *Aletris farinosa. . .* Unicorn root. **1950** Gray–Fernald *Manual of Botany* 447, *A[letris] farinosa. . .* Unicorn-root. . . Late May–Aug. **2007** *DARE* File—Internet, Unicorn root traditionally used by child-bearing aged women for support. . . Aletris Root (Unicorn Root) (Aletris Farinosa).

2 =**blazing star 2.** Cf **false unicorn root 1**

1824 Bigelow *Florula Bostoniensis* 141, *Helonias dioica* [=*Chamaelirium luteum*]. . . *Unicorn Root. . .* In various parts of Connecticut.—July.—Perennial. **1847** Wood *Class-Book* 559, *H[elonias] dioica. . . Unicorn Root. . .* In low grounds, Can. to Ga. and La. **1901** Lounsberry *S. Wild Flowers* 46, Unicorn-root. . . *Chamaelirium luteum.* **1949** Moldenke *Amer. Wild Flowers* 317, *Chamaelirium luteum. . .* Other names for this plant are . . *unicornroot . .* and *blazingstar.*

unicorn's horn n Cf **unicorn plant, ~ root**

1 =**blazing star 2.**

1762 Gronovius *Flora Virginica* 158 **VA,** *Veratrum racemo simplicissimo, foliis sessilibus. . .* nostratibus Unicorns-horn. **1840** MA Zool. & Bot. Surv. *Herb. Plants & Quadrupeds* 205, *H[elonias] dioica* [=*Chamaelirium luteum*]. . . Unicorn's Horn. . . Root premorse or bitten off at one end apparently, and very bitter. **1876** Hobbs *Bot. Hdbk.* 122, Unicorns' horn, False unicorn, Helonias dioica. **1930** Sievers *Amer. Med. Plants* 22, *Chamaelirium luteum. . .* Unicorn's-horn. This plant is frequently confused with *Aletris farinosa* L., not because it bears much resemblance to the latter but probably on account of a similarity in some of the common names by which they are sometimes designated.

2 A **colicroot 2** (here: *Aletris farinosa*).

1900 Lyons *Plant Names* 21, *A[letris] farinosa. . .* Unicorn's-horn. . . Rhizome bitter, tonic, stomachic. **1930** Sievers *Amer. Med. Plants* 4, *Aletris farinosa. . .* Unicorn's-horn. . . Some of the common names are also used in connection with . . *Chamaelirium luteum, . .* which causes much confusion. **1971** Krochmal *Appalachia Med. Plants* 40, *Aletris farinosa. . .* Unicorn's horns [sic], unicorn plant, unicorn root.

union See **unions 2**

unionalls n Also *unionhalls* Cf **unions**

1 rarely *unionall:* Overalls. [Orig trademarked by F.D. Lee 1916, renewed 1978, now dead]

1917 *Decatur Rev.* (IL) 20 Sept 7/3, The sudden smile of the two "boys," . . revealed to the interested Decatur man that the "boys" were young women dressed . . in khaki unionalls. **1940** (1968) Haun *Hawk's Done Gone* 121 **TN,** He had on new unionalls and they suited him. **c1960** *Wilson Coll.* **csKY,** Unionalls. . . Coveralls, overalls. **1965–70** *DARE* (Qu. W9, *A work garment, usually of blue cloth, covering the legs and sometimes the chest, worn by farmers*) **CT**23, **KS**3, 5, **KY**85, **ME**6,

NE8, **NY**107, **NC**55, Unionalls; **IN**13, Unionhalls. **1968** *DARE* Tape **NJ**41, We started to fill these bags up and 'round the grass, you know, getting the walnuts. . . and so I said, "Well, Jesus, there's so many out here, I guess I'll, I got a suit of unionalls in the car." So I said, "I'll get my unionall and I'll tie the legs to the arms and zip it up the front and I'll fill them up full." **1977** *Chillicothe Constitution–Tribune* (MO) 11 Jan 6/8, [Advt:] 50 Pr. Unionalls. $7.50. **1986** Pederson *LAGS Concordance (Overalls)* 3 infs, **AR, TN,** Unionalls; 1 inf, **neMS,** Unionall—trade name for overalls; 1 inf, **cwTN,** Unionalls = coveralls; 1 inf, **cnAR,** Wore little unionalls as a child. **1998** in 2004 Montgomery-Hall *Dict. Smoky Mt. Engl.* 627 **wNC, eTN,** *Unionalls. . .* (2 infs); *unionhalls* = overalls with black and white stripes having no suspenders over the shoulder.

2 Long underwear; a union suit.

1967–69 *DARE* (Qu. W14, *Names for underwear, including joking names*) Infs **GA**77, **MO**21, Unionalls; **GA**77, Unionhalls. **1998** in 2004 Montgomery-Hall *Dict. Smoky Mt. Engl.* 627 **wNC, eTN,** *Unionalls. . .* Long underwear. . . (1 inf); = even girls wore unionalls in the winter, which consisted of cotton knit with long sleeves and long legs with a "trap door" in the back (1 inf).

unions n pl

1 =**unionalls 1.**

1986 Pederson *LAGS Concordance (Overalls)* 1 inf, **cwTN,** Unions = coveralls.

2 also *union:* =**unionalls 2.** [Prob abbr for *union suit*] **chiefly Sth** See Map

1909 *World's Work* May advt sec np, Mentor Comfort Unions are knitted—not woven. **1965–70** *DARE* (Qu. W14, *Names for underwear, including joking names*) Inf **SC**26, Union—men's long; **MS**45, Unions—women's long; **GA**8, 42, **KY**81, **MS**45, 83, **SC**24, **TX**106, Unions—men's long. **1966** *DARE* Tape **SC**14, [Aux Inf:] How 'bout the clothes the old folks wear? [**SC**14:] . . Underwear and union come down . . under the stocking. **1986** Pederson *LAGS Concordance,* 1 inf, **cAL,** Unions—type of underwear.

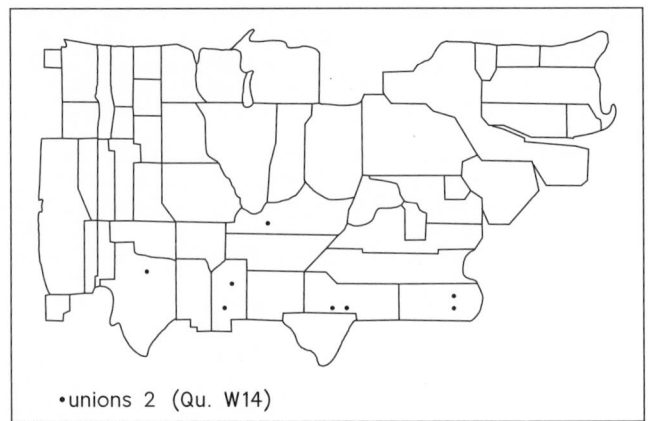

•unions 2 (Qu. W14)

united adj Pronc-sp *uninted* Cf Intro "Language Changes" I.8, **newnited**

Std senses, var form.

1905 *DN* 3.58 **NE,** Intrusive *n,* the "nasal infix," occurs in *Uni(n)ted States, migh(n)t, . . quie(n)t, a(n)ttic, . .* and perhaps a few words more; but it is rare except in the first two cases. **1940** *AmSp* 15.360, Intrusive *n* remains a recurrent phenomenon in oral and written speech. A college theme reader reported finding it [sic for *in*] one afternoon, *menance, prowness, fortunante, obstinancy, fanantic, Uninted States.* Perhaps commoner than any of these in both speech and writing is *grimance.* **1985** *Münchener Studien* 45.252 **TX,** An intrusive nasal . . is doubtless phonetically real, as in my (dialectal) pronunciation of the *Uninted States* (/yunayntid/).

universe vine n [See quot 1924]

A **bearberry 2** (here: *Arctostaphylos uva-ursi*).

1876 Hobbs *Bot. Hdbk.* 122, Universe vine, Bearberry, Arctostaphylos Uva Ursi. **1924** *Amer. Botanist* 30.12, "Bearberry". . . is . . conspicuous . . and has medicinal properties as well which insures a variety of common names made by the very common people. . . "Univese-vine" [sic] and "uversy" are attempts of the unlettered to pronounce the specific name. **1931** Clute *Common Plants* 52, Bearberry. . . Those who collect it for the market, knowing nothing of scientific terminology, call it universe vine. **1979** Erichsen-Brown *Med. N. Amer. Plants* 126, *Bearberry. . . Common names. . .* Yukon holly, universe vine.

unkept adj [Prob folk-etym for *unkempt*] Cf **ill-kept**

1858 Woodbury *Plain Words* 239 **NEng,** It is extremely difficult to discover the angel of courtship, in the unkept hair and the slatternly dress of the wife. **1882** *Stevens Point Jrl.* (WI) 28 Jan 1/1, He had the look of a ragman, . . with sunken eyes and unkept hair. **1913** *Atlanta Constitution* (GA) 28 May 6/6, If the mother is intelligent enough to know that their unkept bodies, their ragged clothes, will affect their characters through life, she has not the time to remedy it. **1953** *Eldora Herald–Ledger* (IA) 4 Aug 6/8, His mother was after him all the time about his unkept clothes. **1956** Ker *Vocab. W. TX* 352, *Slovenly; dressed in funny looking clothes or in bad taste. . . unkept* (variant of "unkempt"). [1 of 67 infs] **1966** *AmSp* 41.76, Ever since the late 1930s I have noticed examples like the following of the use of *unkept:* (1) "She has such unkept hair." (2) "Every week-end . . you can find him at home, unshaven, unkept, and holding a beer can in his hand." . . At last, I have a written example of it, in a letter . . : "Sept. 15, 1964. . . I'm unpressed, unkept (I need a permanent) and debilitated by the heat." . . The persons . . are . . literates, and they point the direction in which *unkempt* is probably going in Standard English. **1966–70** *DARE* (Qu. E22, *If a house is untidy*) Infs **DC**12, **MI**96, **NJ**67, **PA**234, **VA**8, (So) unkept; (Qu. W41, . . *Expressions. . . for someone whose clothes never look right or who always dresses carelessly*) Inf **OK**32, Unkept. **1970** *Atlanta Constitution* (GA) 9 July sec A 5, [Jack Anderson column:] The intense young man with the snarled hair, unkept clothes, and Harvard education, declared quietly that the United States is so rotten it must be cleansed by fire. **1989** *NADS Letters* c**NM,** I have heard people all over the country use "unkept" for "unkempt." **2007** *DARE* File, [It] is usually grown at the outer edges of the garden in the less desirable and unkept area.

unkum See **uncum**

unlegal adj **esp Gulf States** Cf **illegal**

Of a child: illegitimate.

1967 *DARE* (Qu. Z11b, . . *[A child whose parents were not married]*) Inf **LA**8, Unlegal. **1986** Pederson *LAGS Concordance (Bastard)* 4 infs, **GA, MS, TX,** Unlegal child; 1 inf, ne**LA,** Unlegal bastards.

unless conj, prep Pronc-spp *onless, onlest, unlest* Cf **unelse, unlessen** conj, prep

A Forms.

1678 in 1895 Sheldon *Hist. Deerfield* 1.189 **MA,** Unlest you will be pleased to take us . . , we are like Suddainly to breathe out o[u]r Last Breath. **1680** in 1866 NH Hist. Soc. Coll. 8.32, Ye goods . . shall not be Released . . onless ye Crr give under his hand yt he is satisfied. **1855** *Graham's Mag.* 47.209 **NY,** Onlest I'm a great sight more mistaken than I thinks to be. **1858** *S. Lit. Messenger* 26.188 **VA,** You doant know what you sea, unlest thar is sumbody thar to tell yew. **1872** *Atlantic Mth.* 29.355 **CA,** Don't take the lower road back onless you 're hard pushed for time. **1875** *Harper's New Mth. Mag.* 50.733 **CT,** She'll have to go to teachin' agin onless her aunt . . gives her a home. **1881** *Ibid* 62.885 **GA,** But I sha'n't move onlest you promise to keep your mouth shet. **1893** *Century Illustr. Mag.* 47.318 **SD,** Can't go anywhere,/ Ner do a trick, unlest the signs is right. **1899** (1912) Green *VA Folk-Speech* 306, *Onless, conj.* Form of *unless.* **1913** Kephart *Highlanders* 102 s**Appalachians,** A bear allers dies flat on his back, onless he's trapped. **1921** Lardner *Big Town* 217 **NYC,** I got a flop on my hands unlest I can get a couple of idears. **1994** in 2004 Montgomery-Hall *Dict. Smoky Mt. Engl.* 628 e**TN,** Onless. **2001** [see **B** below]. **2007** *DARE* File—Internet **CA,** They are open every weekend from 10:30 to 4:00 unlest some one rented it out for the day. *Ibid* w**NY,** Going to digout [sic] my tree books and have a look onless some one can help.

B As conj.

For fear that, in case.

1995 *AmSp* 70.441 ce,se**PA,** In Berks County, Pennsylvania, *unless* takes a special sense, sometimes substituting for 'in case': *Should I leave your fork here* unless *you want it later?* **2001** *DARE* File c**IN,** At a local family restaurant in a Central Indiana small town, the server, a local woman in her late 30s, asked if my chili was hot (spicy) enough. When I said it was, she replied, "I can't eat it like that unless I have heartburn all night." My wife and I disagreed on what she meant, so when she returned with more coffee I said, "So you like your chili hot." She responded, "Oh no! I can't eat it that way. It does awful things to my ulcer." *Ibid* c**PA,** [In response to the preceding:] I have heard people in Central PA use "unlest" in this context.

C As prep.

Except. [*OED2 unless* prep. 3.a 1531–32 →] Cf **lessen** prep, **unlessen** prep

1793 Morse *Amer. Universal Geog.* 2.30 **CT,** Unless the Swedish part, . . the Laplanders can be said to be under no regular government. **1841** (1952) Cooper *Deerslayer* 310 **NY,** When the feelin' begins, the young woman is thoughtful, and has no eyes or ears onless for the warrior that has taken her fancy. **1967** *DARE* Tape **TX**36, You see, we didn't have anybody to go with us unless Ma and Pa.

unlessen conj Also sp *unless'n* **chiefly Sth, S Midl** Cf **iffen, lessen** conj[1], **withouten** B

Unless.

1905 Wasson *Green Shay* 187 **ME,** That vessel is goin' to fetch up on the laidge . . unless'n this heavy out-wind shoves in the tide. **1914** *DN* 4.153 **ME,** *Unless'n. . .* Unless. "They won't go to the water unless'n they're obliged to." **1926** Roberts *Time of Man* 55 **KY,** I couldn't gorrentee to remember hit unlessen you write hit down. c**1938** in Lib. of Congress *Amer. Memory: WPA Life Hist.* (Internet) **AL,** Mandy cain't drink coffee unlessen she has sugar in it. **1942** Hurston *Dust Tracks* 49 **FL,** Don't you try to fight three kids at one time unlessen you just can't get around it. **1962** Faulkner *Reivers* 120 **MS,** But unlessen I done got rusty on my trading and made a mistake I dont know about, he dont disbelieve it. **1963** Owens *Look to River* 78 **TX,** Ain't nobody gonna run like that unless'n he's guilty. **1966** *DARE* Tape **GA**7, It usually stays soft unlessen it's cold weather; **MS**61, Horses. . . they ain't going to hurt you unlessen's just a real outlaw. **1969** Wilson *Stars* 49 **Ozarks,** I never yet before smacked nobody as old as you claim to be, but this here commences to feel like a first time. . . That's for shore unless'n maybe you'd like to squat down. **1989** Pederson *LAGS Tech. Index* 332 **Gulf Region,** *Unless* . . unlessen (25 [of 914 infs]). **2007** *DARE* File nw**MS,** *Unlessen*—for unless. I heard from a black woman from . . Marks, Mississippi. . . She was born in 1927 and has a third grade education.

unlessen prep Cf **lessen** prep, **unless** C

Except.

1997 in 2004 Montgomery-Hall *Dict. Smoky Mt. Engl.* 628 e**TN,** No one will come unlessen Paul.

unless'n See **unlessen** conj

unlest See **unless**

unlikely adj **chiefly VA**

Of the weather: threatening.

1885 McClelland *Oblivion* 8 **VA,** Dick increased his transgression by an inconsequent wonder as to what could have brought a woman abroad in such unlikely weather. **1912** Green *VA Folk-Speech* 467, *Unlikely. . .* Threatening, as applied to weather. "I'll not start if the weather is unlikely." **1914** *DN* 4.160 c**VA,** *Unlikely. . .* Threatening (of weather). "Hit's toleble unlikely." **1924** *Bee* (Danville VA) 12 Apr 3/5, Despite the unlikely weather of clouds and showers . . interested visitors made the number in attendance about two hundred and fifty. **1949** *Limestone Democrat* (Athens AL) 15 Dec 5/5, Attendance at last Sunday's services was slightly off due to the unlikely weather. **1957** *Hench Coll.* **VA,** A local congressman speaking before the Tobacco Jubilee meeting said: "The weather is unlikely—we may have falling weather." **1968–70** *DARE* (Qu. B2, *If the weather is very unpleasant . . it's a _____ day*) Inf **TN**30, Unlikely; (Qu. B5, *When the weather looks as if it will become bad . . it's _____*) Infs **IN**48, **VA**38, (Looks) unlikely; [(Qu. B8, *When clouds come and go all day . . it's _____*) Inf **VA**42, Unlikeable weather]. **1976** Ryland *Richmond Co. VA* 379, *Unlikely*— as of threatening weather. **1986** Pederson *LAGS Concordance (The weather is _____)* 1 inf, cw**TN,** Unlikely.

unlucky tree n

=**jack pine 1.**

1882 Essex Inst. *Bulletin* 13.187 ne**NY,** *Pinus banksiana. . .* This tree is known as the "unlucky tree" by the people in this part of the country. . . It is considered dangerous to pass within ten feet of its limbs and more so to women than to men.

unly See **only**

unpod See **pod** v 1

unsight and unseen See **unsight unseen**

unsighted adj

Unforeseen.

1903 *DN* 2.335 se**MO,** *Unsighted. . .* Unexpected; unforeseen. 'It was unsighted on my part.' **1907** *DN* 3.238 **nwAR**, *Unsighted. . .* Unexpected; unforeseen.

unsight unseen *adv phr, adj phr* Also *unsight and unseen;* perh by folk-etym *on sight (and) unseen* [*OED2* (at *unsight*) ?1622–1810; the now usu form *sight unseen* is a late 19th-cent US innovation] **chiefly Nth, West** See Map *old-fash*
Without examination, sight unseen; of a bargain: blind.
  1828 (1970) Webster *Amer. Dict., Unsight unseen,* a vulgar phrase, denoting *unseeing unseen,* or *unseen* repeated; as, to buy a thing *unsight unseen,* that is, without seeing it. **1846** in 2007 *DARE* File—Internet **IL**, He courted and engaged her by letter—"unsight, unseen",—as the pedlars say—last year. **1850** *U.S. Mag. & Democratic Rev.* 26.486, Of what value is the privilege of choosing a ruler, if it is to be done unsight, unseen? **1872** *Janesville Gaz.* (WI) 26 Mar [2]/2 (newspaperarchive.com) **MI**, *Unsight and Unseen*—Sales of Express Baggage—Good and Bad Bargains. **1892** *DN* 1.231, *Sight unseen. . . unsight unseen* in New England and Michigan. **1899** (1912) Green *VA Folk-Speech* 467, *Unsight. . .* Not seen. "Unsight, unseen," without inspection or examination: thus, to buy anything "unsight unseen" is to buy without seeing it. **1902** White *Blazed Trail* 134 **MI**, He knew that when he should embark on his attempt to enlist considerable capital in an "unsight unseen" investment, he would have to be well supplied with statistics. **1910** *DN* 3.451 **wNY**, *Unsight unseen. . .* Without seeing each other's knife or other article. Used by boys in swapping knives, marbles, etc. **1912** *DN* 3.569 **cNY**, *Sight unseen. . .* Varied often to *unsight unseen.* **1914** *DN* 4.114 **cKS**, *Unsight unseen . . sight unseen.* **1916** London *Little Lady* 142 **CA**, They know my standard so well that they'll buy unsight and unseen. **1923** *DN* 5.221 **swMO**, *Sight unseen. . .* Also, *Unsight, unseen.* **1953** *Holland Eve. Sentinel* (MI) 11 May 4/1, Congress virtually abdicated its constitutional functions, passing most of the bills almost unsight, unseen. **1965–70** *DARE* (Qu. U13, *When buying or exchanging something that you have not seen . . you're getting it* _____) 26 Infs, **chiefly Nth, West**, Unsight unseen; 11 Infs, **chiefly Nth, West**, Unsight and unseen; **IL**32, 46, **MO**9, On sight (and) unseen; [**MN**15, Unseen unsight;] (Qu. U14, *. . Exchanging with somebody when neither one has seen what the other has*) Infs **CA**197, **IL**25, **OR**13, **PA**234, Unsight unseen; **CA**145, **MI**76, Unsight and unseen trade; **IL**32, On sight and unseen trade; **UT**7, I'll trade you unsight and unseen; **MI**107, **NY**75, **OH**16, Trading unsight (and) unseen; **MI**82, Unsight-unseen swap. [43 of 46 total Infs old] **2007** *DARE* File—Internet **AR**, We do understand how difficult it can be to purchase vehicles unsight and unseen. *Ibid* **UT**, Bought straight unsight unseen from New York shipped direct.

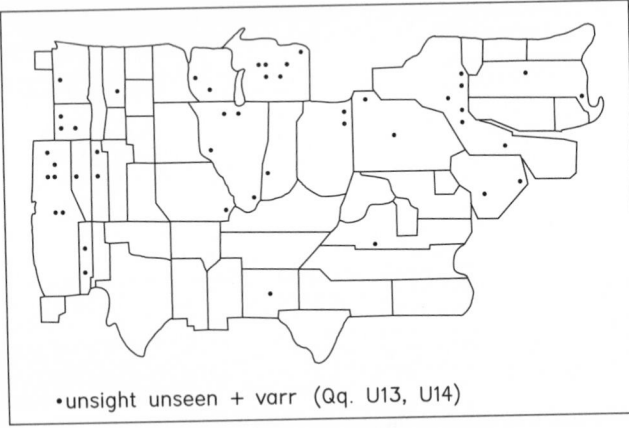

•unsight unseen + varr (Qq. U13, U14)

unsweet tea *n* Also *unsweet ice(d) tea* **Sth, S Midl** Cf **sweet tea**
Iced tea without sugar or other sweetener.
  1993 *Atlanta Constitution* (GA) 30 June sec F 1 (Internet), I didn't try the stew, but I did eat two chopped pork sandwiches with unsweet tea. **1993** White *Mama* 4 **sGA**, "One order of smoked mullet, and one unsweet iced tea, please," I said. **1993** *DARE* File **SC**, Here in South Carolina the common question when you're eating out is "Do you want sweet tea or unsweet tea?" Does the term "unsweet tea" without "-ened" occur elsewhere in the South? *Ibid* **GA**, It's very common in Georgia. Almost every waiter or waitress asks you if you want sweet or unsweet tea. *Ibid* **LA, TN, TX**, I've heard that phrase [=*unsweet tea*] all my life, in Texas, Louisiana, and now here in Tennessee. I love to hear diner waitresses say, "Sweet or unsweet, honey?" *Ibid* **MS**, Same

in Mississippi, but some do clearly add the -ed [sic] [to *unsweet tea*]. *Ibid* **AL**, Sweet tea & unsweet tea—that's the way we say it down here, too. **1999** *Ibid* **MS**, A sign at a fair advertised "Cold Ice Tea . . Sweet [or] Unsweet." **2003** *San Antonio Express–News* (TX) 1 Aug sec H 33 (Internet), The reason I don't bring in my own perfect jug of unsweet tea every day is that there usually isn't time. **2005** *Atlanta Jrl.–Constitution* (GA) 16 Aug sec E 1 (Internet), I ask the waitress for an iced tea. She brings unsweet tea and packets of sugar and Splenda.

untel(l) See **until**

untelling *ppl adj* Pronc-sp *ontelling* [Scots dial]
1 Beyond conjecture or expression. **chiefly sAppalachians**
  1916 *DN* 4.295 **sAppalachians**, *On(un)tellin'* (as in "there's a man says it's *ontellin'*"). **1936** *AmSp* 11.316 **Ozarks**, *Ontelling. . .* Unknown, untold. 'Hits plum ontellin' whut th' dang fool would of done if th' boys hadn't of stopped him.' **1940** (1978) Still *River of Earth* 131 **KY**, Alpha sets a store o' love for him that's ontelling. **1955** Ritchie *Singing Family* 36 **seKY**, Lordie mercy, why it's untelling what he'll do and him so franzy like that. **1979** Carpenter *Walton War* 158 **sAppalachians**, What I have seed in my time is untelling. **1991** Still *Wolfpen Notebooks* 145 **sAppalachians**, I say it's ontelling what a ton o' coal will sell for. . . I figure the price would double or treble. **1993** Gibbons *Charms* 72 **NC** (as of c1937), My thought was this: Oh, how she loves him is untelling. **1993** in 2004 Montgomery–Hall *Dict. Smoky Mt. Engl.* 628 **wNC, eTN**, It's untelling how many men and women I buried. **2001** in 2007 *DARE* File—Internet **nwTN**, Wiley & his group of associates raised untelling how much money. **2006** *Ibid* **swOH**, I know shes not stupid. But it's untelling what they said to her. **2007** *Ibid* **KY**, It is untelling what you will find in an old home that has been left for years! *Ibid* **seKY**, I killed a tom on public ground that was full of lead shot. . . He walked around for untelling how long with that in em.
2 also *superl ontellin'dest, ontellin'ist:* See quots.
  1926 (1930) MacKaye *Tall Tales KY* 91, Seecrets as usual! . . Whar ye ben dodgin' at all day, Sol? You's shore the ontellin'dest critter in your times and seasons. **1933** *AmSp* 8.1.51 **Ozarks**, *Ontelling,* adj. Erratic, unpredictable. *Sam is th' ontellin'ist feller I ever seen—nobody never knows whut he's a-goin' t' do next.*

unthoughted *adj* [*EDD unthoughtedly*] **chiefly Sth, S Midl** Cf **thoughty 1**
Thoughtless; hence *adv unthoughtedly* thoughtlessly, inadvertently; *n unthoughtedness;* rarely, by back-formation, *adj thoughted* thoughtful.
  1835 *Friend* 8.323, We unthoughtedly separated, and wandered far from each other. **a1845** in 1958 *Ethnohistory* 5.156 **AL**, Being an unthoughted selfish being he cared for only his own safety. **1858** *Harper's New Mth. Mag.* 16.422 **wTX** (as of c1840), I . . this morning unthoughtedly tied my office-key as a clapper into my cow's bell. **1861** *Macon Daily Telegraph* (GA) 12 Aug 1/2, Boys have no business riding on the cars. They are too heedless and unthoughted to be permitted such latitude. **1895** *DN* 1.394 **Sth**, *Unthoughtedly:* thoughtlessly. **1898** *Lima News* (OH) [16 Sept 8]/5 (newspaperarchive.com), While there he unthoughtedly exhibited a large sum of money, when he paid for a glass of beer. **1904** *DN* 2.422 **nwAR**, *Unthoughted. . .* Ill considered. 'That was an unthoughted remark you made yesterday.' **1909** *DN* 3.385 **eAL, wGA**, *Unthoughted. . .* Thoughtless, ill-considered. *Unthoughtedly. . .* Thoughtlessly. Practically universal. **1913** Kephart *Highlanders* 285 **sAppalachians**, If I'd a-been thoughted enough. **1915** *DN* 4.192 **swVA**, *Unthoughted. . .* Thoughtless.—*unthoughtedly.* **1915** *Ft. Wayne News* (IN) 13 Feb 20/1, The great majority of unhappy marriages are due to reckless carelessness, and unthoughtedness. **1927** *DN* 5.470 **Appalachians**, *Unthoughtedly. . .* Thoughtlessly; inadvertently. **1930** *VA Qrly. Rev.* 6.246 **S Midl**, If I'd a been thoughted enough I'd a brung along them onion sets. **1932** Randolph *Ozark Mt. Folks* 34, I rid into this hyar witch-ring unthoughted-like. **1949** *Cullman Democrat* (AL) 19 May 1/1, An unthoughted person took a flower [from a grave] for his button hole. **1968** *DARE* (Qu. GG42, *A reckless person, one who takes foolish chances*) Inf **VA**1, Non-thoughted [sic]. **1986** Pederson *LAGS Concordance,* 1 inf, **cnTN**, Unthoughtedly; 1 inf, **csTN**, Unthoughtedly = thoughtlessly. **2009** *DARE* File—Internet **cSC**, President Obama compared their results with his poor performance at bowling. . . What an unthoughted thing to do to these people.

unthoughtless *adj* [Cf *OED2 un-* prefix[1] 5.a "It is sometimes redundantly prefixed to adjs. ending in *-less.*"]
Thoughtless; unthinking; hence *n unthoughtlessness; adv unthoughtlessly.*

1909 *Hobart Daily Republican* (OK) 12 Apr 2/2, It . . should at once be brought to the attention of the publishers who have so unthought-lessly published a rank fabrication. [**1913** Kephart *Highlanders* 287 **sAppalachians,** I did it the unthoughtless of anything I ever done in my life. [*DARE* Ed: *Unthoughtless* presumably represents *unthoughtles-sest.*]] **1927** *AmSp* 2.366 **cwWV,** It was so unthoughtless of me to walk in on sister and her beau. **1995–97** in 2004 Montgomery-Hall *Dict. Smoky Mt. Engl.* 628 **wNC, eTN,** *Unthoughtless* . . Unthinking. . . [4 infs]. **2005** in 2007 *DARE* File—Internet **cnIN,** It's not just simple unthoughtlessness like walking right by an old lady who obviously needs some help. **2007** in 2009 *Ibid* **CT,** Being taught a very young age that food in tents is no-no, I unthoughtlessly tied the bread on my bike's handlebar, which was right next to the tent. **2009** *Ibid* **seVA,** The only absolutely unselfish, benevalant [*sic*] friend that women can have in this extremely ungratious [*sic*], unthoughtless, inconsiderate and egocentric world is . . *the one that never abandons . . you.*

unthoughty See **thoughty 1**

until prep, conj Usu |ʌnˈtɪl|; also |ʌnˈtɛl, ɔnˈtɪl|; for added varr see **A** below Pronc-spp *'ntwel, ontel(l), ontil, ontwel(l), untel(l), untwell* Cf **till**

A Forms.

1663 in 1897 CT Hist. Soc. *Coll.* 6.324, John keely . . shall liue With the sd Thomas Catlen an aprentes untell . . the agge of twenty:on years. **1756** in 1851 *Doc. Hist. State of NY* 4.284, We Laide there untell the Evening. **1840** in 1956 Eliason *Tarheel Talk* 319 **cnNC,** Untel. **1845** Hooper *Advent. Simon Suggs* 109 **AL,** I have to keep it here . . ontwell I git *my* orders. **1862** (1864) Browne *Artemus Ward Book* 91 **swPA,** I didn't observe the outrajus transacshuns ontil the next evening. **1875** *Scribner's Mth.* 10.131 **cwNY** (as of c1825), You must all be hanged untell your ded. **1876** Harte *Gabriel Conroy* 296 **CA,** Ye might hev stood thar ontel now. **1881** *Scribner's Mth.* 21.375 **GA** [Black], Coat arfter coat, breeches arfter breeches . . shirt arfter shirt ontwell he shucked hisself. **1883** *Century Illustr. Mag.* 26.189 **GA,** I traipse 'roun' this hill ontell I'm that wore out. **1884** *Anglia* 7.255 **Sth, S Midl** [Black], *Prepositions.* . . ontell, ontwell. **1892** *DN* 1.242 **cwMO,** *Until.* Popularly . . |ʌnˈtɛl|. **1903** *DN* 2.335 **seMO,** *Until.* . . Pronounced ontwell. **1906** *DN* 3.149 **nwAR,** *Ontil.* . . Until. **1909** *DN* 3.354 **eAL, wGA,** *Ontwel.* . . Until. *Ibid* 401 **nwAR,** *Ontil.* . . Until. Usually a negroism. *Ontwel.* . . Until. **1912** Green *VA Folk-Speech* 467, *Untell.* . . For *untill* [*sic*]. . . *Untwell.* . . For *untill.* **1922** Gonzales *Black Border* 316 **sSC, GA coasts** [Gullah glossary], *Ontel*—until. **1923** (1946) Greer-Petrie *Angeline Doin' Society* 22 **csKY,** Ontell I felt like I was about to bust! **1929** Sale *Tree Named John* 35 **MS** [Black], Brer Rabbit waited 'ntwel Brer Buzzu'd lef'. **1941** *AmSp* 16.4 **eTX** [Black], *Un-til* . . [ənˈtɛl]. **1942** Hall *Smoky Mt. Speech* 15 **wNC, eTN,** Laxer and lowered varieties of [ɪ], often reaching [ɛ], may frequently be heard in . . *until. Ibid* 59, *Until* [ɒnˈtɪl]. (*Until* may be heard also as [ˈʌntl], with shifted stress.) **c1960** Wilson *Coll.* **csKY,** *Until* /ˌɒnˈtɪl/ or /ˌɑnˈtɪl/ often /-ˈtɛl/.

B As prep.

1 To (a place of arrival). Cf **till B1**

1934 *AmSp* 9.127 [Engl dial of HI], The preposition may be . . con-fused in meaning with another preposition. . . *Till* and *until* for 'to' in space (possibly an imported Scotticism).

2 By; before. Cf **till B4**

1935 *AmSp* 10.169 **PA** [Engl of PA Germans], In a letter of application for a job a student wrote, 'I am a high school graduate and will have completed one year of college training until the end of this year.' **1949** in 1986 *DARE* File, Do you suppose it will rain until 1:30? (It was not then raining).

C As conj.

1 in phrr with *so* (rarely *enough, such*): So that—used to in-dicate a consequence or result. **Sth, S Midl** Cf **till C1a**

1934 *AmSp* 9.79 **nLA,** He was so angry until he didn't know what he was doing . . I was so hot until I nearly melted. **c1970** Pederson *Dial. Surv. Rural GA,* 1 inf, **seGA,** They have to go through so much [training to be a midwife] and a lot of people don't want to go through that. **1970** in 2004 Montgomery-Hall *Dict. Smoky Mt. Engl.* 629 **wNC, eTN,** *Until.* . . It made enough of noise until the snake went out . . the window. **1986** Pederson *LAGS Concordance,* 1 inf, **ceAL,** Tomatoes are so aw-fully high until he try to raise his tomatoes; so rich until they had slaves for everything; 1 inf, **csAR,** The mountain was so steep until the road just curved around it; 1 inf, **nwFL,** Hit was so green until it looked black-like; 1 inf, **seGA,** That boy was so dumb until he couldn't re-

peat behind you—repeat your words; 1 inf, **swGA,** So smart until they're just about dumb; 1 inf, **swLA,** The roof had such a slope until (= so that); 1 inf, **neMS,** It hurt him so bad until he cried; 1 inf, **ceTX,** They have pastures so big until they have roads built out to where their cattle are.

2 When; see quots. [Cf *OED2* till conj. B.1.c]

1940 in 1944 *ADD* **nWV,** *Until.* . . We had been here only a few hours until we began to hear such talk. **1942** *Ibid* **nWV,** *Until.* . . The Associ-ated Press wire had hardly opened this morning until a dispatch came over quoting Senator Wallgren of Washington . . Morgantown *Post J*[un]e 4.

3 By the time that. Cf **till C2**

1968 *Helen Adolf Festschrift* 38 [Engl of PA Germans], *Till* and *until* (Pennsylvania German *bis*) for 'by,' 'before,' or 'by the time that'; . . "Until I get home it will be 12 o'clock." **2004** [see **till C2**].

until the water gets hot See **water B3**

until who laid the chunk See **who laid the chunk 2**

until who laid the rail See **who laid the rail 3**

until yet See **yet** adv, conj **B2**

untwell See **until**

unu See **una**

unwell adj *euphem; old-fash* Cf **ill 2**
Menstruating.

1827 *NY Med. & Phys. Jrl.* 6.240, If a woman begins to be unwell on the first of May, she will be, if regular, again unwell on the 28th of that month. **1851** (1856) Dunglison *Med. Lexicon* 886, *Unwell,* see Men-struation. **1931** Randolph *Ozarks* 82, When the word *ill* is applied to a woman it usually means that she is bad-tempered, but sometimes it re-fers to menstruation, and *unwell* is always used in this sense—a man or boy could never be described as *unwell* in the Ozarks. **1948** *Word* 4.185 [Terms for a menstruating woman], Unwell. **1954** *AmSp* 29.298 **TX, OK, FL** [Vernacular of menstruation], *Unwell* (W[omen], passé). **1965–70** *DARE* (Qu. AA27, . . *A woman's menstruation*) 18 Infs, **scat-tered,** Unwell; **GA**19, Be unwell; **TN**52, I'm unwell; **CA**167, **LA**25, **UT**7, She's unwell; **CA**87, Unwell period; [**AL**10, The unwells]. [20 of 24 Infs old] **1995** *DARE* File **WI** (as of c1950), *Unwell* = menstruat-ing. Have heard *unwell* from Sheboygan, WI woman b. ca. 1890.

unwind v **West** Cf **sunfish** v
Of a horse: to buck violently, esp with a twisting motion.

1929 (1941) James *Sand* 68 **West,** Every time she seen a horse "un-wind" she found herself judging. . . She knowed bucking horses, she knowed good riding. **1931** (1986) Fletcher *Songs Sage* 12 **West,** An' then I piles on 'im [=a horse], an' raises the blind,/ I'm right in his mid-dle tuh see 'im unwind./ Well, he bows his old neck, an' I guess he un-wound,/ Fur he seems tuh quit livin' down on the ground. **1937** *DN* 6.619 **swTX,** When the bronco commences to buck, he *wrinkles his spine, unwinds, folds up,* or *boils over.* **1939** FWP *ID Lore* 244, The old bronc might crow hop (jump in a straight line) or unwind (twist and turn). **1940** Writers' Program *Guide NV* 76, The horse that bucks . . *un-winds.*

up adv, prep, adj, v
A As adv.

In var non-std v phrr: So as to improve; completely, success-fully, finally.

1747 (1901) Hempstead *Diary* 479 **seCT,** I went to mamacock & Crossman Lot & mended up fence. **1853** in 1928 OR Pioneer Assoc. *Trans.* 43 **MA,** Here, one of our hands, left up. **1871** (1882) Stowe *Fireside Stories* 21 **MA,** Cap'n Eb . . comforted him up, 'cause the crittur was in distress. **1902** *Centreville Press* (AL) 19 June [2]/2 (as of c1850), They [=the Presbyterians] always waits for us hard shells to . . settle up the wilderness. **1932** Wasson *Sailing Days* 133 **cME coast,** Old boats . . are constantly being "repaired-up" and converted into yachts. **1934** (1970) Wilson *Backwoods Amer.* 131 **Ozarks,** Now the whole family was feeling mighty good-for-nothing, so they all . . de-cided to travel in old Doc Abernathy's and get cured up. **1936** *AmSp* 11.63 **seWV,** I can do it good, but I ain't *skilled up* (thoroughly skilled). This last is farmer talk. **1939** Hall *Coll.* **wNC, eTN,** They've got [the town] renewed up. *Ibid,* She's improved up a bit. *Ibid,* Finally we traced him up. **1943** in 1944 *ADD* 506 **sPA,** *Repaired up.* . . They had the chair repaired up. **1947** Oakley *Restin'* 24 **eTN,** I was out trying to track up Rack coons and Oposams in the snow. **1960** Criswell *Resp. to*

PADS 20 **Ozarks,** He ought to go to Arizony and get himself cured up. **1966–69** *DARE* Tape **MA**62, They [=turkey hunters] take branches and build a little place where they can hide up; **MI**8, The boys as they grew up moved off and settled up their own farms. **1968** *DARE* (Qu. BB36, *When there's an open sore and this yellowish stuff is coming out of it . . it's* _____) Inf **NC**50, Curing up; (Qu. BB46, . . *Someone who has been very sick but now is getting better*) Inf **NC**79, After a while, that cure up [=cured up]. **1972** *Atlanta Letters* **cnGA,** Southernisms: "Ah stays Repented Up." **1986** Pederson *LAGS Concordance,* 1 inf, **cAL,** If it was flavored up just right; 1 inf, **cnMS,**We'd swap up—share; 1 inf, **neLA,** We going have to rush up—hurry.

B As prep.

Up to; up at or in—freq with omission of def art. See also **up attic** Cf **down** C

1862 Colt *Went to KS* 274 **NY,** My nephew is . . teaching among the Indians up Lake Superior. **1966** *DARE* (Qu. MM22, *If you are talking to a friend who lives in another place and you want to inquire about his neighborhood . . "How are things* _____?") Inf **ME**6, Up Springvale, etc. **1979** *NYT Article Letters* **Ocracoke Is. NC,** [Letters from school-children:] Some people call the road across the firehouse up trent[·] I live at a place called up pond. *Ibid,* Up pawn [sic] is where there are a little pond where I go swimming. **1986** Pederson *LAGS Concordance (I was [up in Knoxville])* 1 inf, **cTX,** Way up Illinois; 1 inf, **cwFL,** I was over here up my brother's; 1 inf, **ceGA,** Up North Georgia; 1 inf, **cAL,** Up Siluria. **1991** King *Needful Things* 193 **ME,** Keeton and Frazier had gone "up the city" (trips to Lewiston were always referred to in this way). **1991** *DARE* File **seNY,** Up/down ellipses, as in up lot, is a hallmark of north fork talk. **1997** *DARE* File—Internet **cePA** [Coal-Speak], *Up:* To. . . "I'm goin' up Joe's." **2000** in 2007 *DARE* Internet **NC,** Traditionally there are three unique sections of Ocracoke: "down point," " 'round creek" and "up trent."

C As adj.

Fig: pregnant. **chiefly NEng**

1941 *LANE* Map 392 *(Pregnant)* 1 inf, **neMA,** She's up. **1967–69** *DARE* (Qu. AA28, . . *Joking or sly expressions . . women use to say that another is going to have a baby . . "She['s]* _____.") Infs **CT**31, **MA**21, **PA**216, (She's) up; **CT**12, **MA**27, 33, (She's) up again.

D As verb.

To vomit. Cf **urp** v[1]

1967–70 *DARE* (Qu. BB17, . . *Vomiting*) Inf **CA**59, I have to go out and up; **LA**23, Up—"she upped"; **MA**122, Up; **AZ**2, Upped it; **IL**39, Upped his dinner.

up a flume See **flume, go up the**

up along adv phr [*OED2* "dial. . . Freq in Cornish speech"; a1552 →] **eMA** Cf **down-along**

See quots.

1913 *DN* 4.58 **seMA,** Up-along. . . Toward the eastern end of the town: noted at Provincetown. . . "Shall we walk up-along, or take the accommodation?" **1916** Macy–Hussey *Nantucket Scrap Basket* 130, "Up-along" is sometimes heard, but much less frequently [than *down-along*]. **1944** *AN&Q* 3.188 **neMA,** In Newburyport, Massachusetts, up-town is "up-along" and downtown is "down-along."

up and down, have it See **have** v[1] **D3a**

up and down the levee See **marching around the levee**

upapalu n [Haw]

A cardinal fish of the family Apogonidae, esp *Apogon taeniopterus* or *A. kallopterus.*

1864 in 1868 *CA Acad. Sci. Proc.* 3.105 **HI,** [*Apogon*] *maculiferus.* . . Vernacular, "Upapalu." **1898** *Haw. Almanac & Annual for 1899* 54, Upapalu. [**1905** *U.S. Fish & Wildlife Serv. Fishery Bulletin for 1903* 23.215 **HI,** *Amia menesema* [=*Apogon taeniopterus*]. . . "Upápalu." . . Color in life, coppery purple.] **1926** *Pan-Pacific Research Inst. Jrl.* 1.1.7 **HI,** Apogonidae. The Cardinal Fishes. Upapalu. . . *Pristiapogon menesemus* [=*Apogon taeniopterus*]. . . Upapalu. **1960** Gosline–Brock *Hawaiian Fishes* 161, Apogonidae (Cardinal fishes or 'Upapalus). The apogonids or cardinal fishes, of which the 'upapalu is perhaps the best known in Hawaii, are small- to moderate-size fishes with 2 completely separate dorsal fins. *Ibid* 164, *Apogon snyderi* [=*A. kallopterus*] ('Upapalu). This species and the very similar *Apogon menesemus* [=*A. taeniopterus*] are the most abundant and largest apogonids in the Hawaiian Islands. **2004** *DARE* File—Internet **HI** (as of 1940s), I remember the 1940s when a group of us boys would . . go to Kuhio Beach. . . If we

were lucky, we caught red squirrel fishes, known as menpachi, or 'upapalu.

up'ards See **upwards**

up a stump See **stump** n 6

up attic adv phr Also *up chamber, ~ garret* [**up B**] **chiefly NEast** Cf **down cellar**

Up in or up to an attic; upstairs.

1774 (1900) Fithian *Jrl.* 1.209 **NJ,** She then retired up chamber. **1805** (1904) White *Jrl.* 30 **MA,** I went up chamber and made up the beds on the floor. **1825** (2001) Grimes *Life* 44 (Internet) **CT,** I . . carried the whole that I found up garret. **1845** Kirkland *Western Clearings* 12 **MI,** [She] said there was no bed for him, unless he could sleep "up chamber" with the boys. **1854** in 1983 *PADS* 70.56 **ce,sePA,** Mary came at night did not sleep in the back room she wanted to go up garret so she went. **1885** *Century Illustr. Mag.* 29.559 **MO,** Up garret was a little cubby, with a pallet in it. **1891** *Ibid* 41.464 **RI,** She just sets up chamber and mopes. **1902** Day *Pine Tree Ballads* 206 **ME,** I've got a pair [of pants] up attic. **1904** *DN* 2.425 **Cape Cod MA** (as of a1857), *Garret.* . . Attic. 'He has gone up garret.' **1917** *DN* 4.403 **neOH,** *Up chamber.* . . Upstairs. "He has gone up chamber." . . Also Vt., N.H., Mass., Ia. **1922** in 1969 Frost *Poetry* 203 **nNH,** You wouldn't want to tell him what we have / Up attic, mother? **1941** *LANE* Map 345 *(Attic),* The adverbial expressions *up-attic* and *up-garret,* meaning 'up in the attic', were incidentally offered by a number of informants: *up-attic* [19 infs, 15 **MA**] . . *up garret* [25 infs, 9 **CT,** 8 **MA**]. **1959** *VT Hist.* 27.165, *Up attic.* . . In the attic. Common. Rural areas. *Ibid, Up chamber.* . . Up in the chamber; upstairs. Rare. **1967–70** *DARE* (Qu. D4, *The space up under the roof, usually used for storing things*) Infs **MA**83, 98, Up attic; (Qu. D19, *Referring to the part of the house below the ground floor . . "I'm going* _____.") Inf **MA**5, Up attic. [All Infs old] **1968** *DARE* FW Addit **swNJ,** Up garret = in the attic. Something is up garret. **1991** *DARE* File **seNY,** Up garret = up attic. Gone by the 20th C.

upcast v [nEngl, Scots, Ir dial]

1930 Shoemaker *1300 Words* 64 **cPA Mts** (as of c1900), *Upcast*—To taunt or reproach.

up chamber See **up attic**

upchuck v, hence vbl n *upchucking* Also *chuck (up), upchoke* esp freq among mid-aged and younger speakers, among coll educ speakers, and among women

To vomit, throw up; hence n *upchuck* an act or instance of vomiting—in phr *have an upchuck* to vomit; to throw up.

1930s in 1944 *ADD* **nWV,** *Upchuck.* . . To vomit. . . Common. **1943** *LANE* Map 504 *(Vomit)* 1 inf, **seMA,** Upchuck. **1943** *Sat. Eve. Post* 30 Oct 6, Adams and his mates lay over the gunwales and upchucked the stew. **c1960** *Wilson Coll.* **csKY,** *Have an upchuck.* . . Vomit. Very modern. . . *Upchuck.* . . A spell of vomiting; a very rare and recent word. **1960** Wentworth–Flexner *Slang* 104, *Chuck.* . . To vomit. *c1940; student use. Ibid* 561, *Up-chuck.* . . To vomit. Since *c1925. Orig. student use. Considered a smart and sophisticated term c1935, esp. when applied to sickness that had been induced by overdrinking.* **1965–70** *DARE* (Qu. BB17, . . *Vomiting*) 164 Infs, **widespread,** Upchuck; **DC**11, **KS**2, **MA**3, **MI**110, 122, **MO**29, **NC**31, **NY**55, Have an upchuck; **MO**17, **PA**205, **WY**4, Chuck (up); **MD**24, Really chucked up; **NC**4, Upchoke [Of all Infs responding to the question, 66% were old, 31% coll educ, 55% female; of those giving these responses, 51% were old, 46% coll educ, 68% female.]; (Qu. BB18, *To vomit a great deal at once*) 12 Infs, **scattered,** Upchuck; **CT**19, **GA**15, Upchucking [7 of 14 Infs old, 7 coll educ, 11 female]. **1985** Irving *Cider House* **eME** 302, The spout disgorged a pulp of seeds and skin and mashed apples, and even worms (if there were worms). It looked like what Nurse Angela calmly called upchuck. **1989** Pederson *LAGS Tech. Index* 295 **Gulf Region** (*Vomit [neutral]*) 70 infs, Upchuck; (*Vomit [crude]*) 51 infs, Upchuck; 1 inf, Upchoke.

up-country adv phr **esp NEng, Sth** Cf **up island**

In, to, or into the interior, upland, or remote part of a region.

1815 Humphreys *Yankey in England* 40 **CT,** Afore in was born, he moved up country, into the back parts. **1853** Hammett *Stray Yankee in TX* 54 **TX,** He was great upon speculation, usually spending one third of his time in expeditions "up country" in search of silver mines. **1892** (1893) Botume *First Days* 14 **seSC,** All the strong and able-bodied slaves had been carried "up country" by their masters. **1959** *VT Hist.* 27.165, *Up country.* . . In the northern part of the state. Common. Rural areas. **1965** Wolfe *Kandy-Kolored Baby* 141 **NC,** Junior uses certain older forms of English . . preserved up-country in his territory, Ingle Hollow. **1979** *DARE* File **wMA,** *Up country,* usually with stress [ˌəpˈkʌntrɨ], among old-timers is common [in phrases like] "I'm going up country" and "They live up country." **1986** Pederson *LAGS Concordance,* 1 inf, **swAL,** Upcountry—in middle Alabama.

updump v

To upset, overturn (something).

1908 *German Amer. Annals* 10.50 **sePA,** *Updump.* Upset. "Don't rock the boat or you'll updump it." **1998** *Newsweek* 1 June 78 **WA,** But we stopped laughing pretty fast when he did what he said he was going to—created enough turmoil to updump the shah. **2000** Arnold *Yr. of Full Moons* 336 **KY** (as of 1963), Trying to build up the gumption to updump the bucket. **2004** in 2009 *DARE* File—Internet **neGA,** I asked the manager, Brian, for some Tabasco. . . Absently, unthinkingly, . . I updumped the whole thing on the beans and rice. **2006** *Ibid* **PA,** My rain gauge overflowed at 5″, and I didn't bother to go outside to updump it.

up East adv phr   esp Sth, S Midl   Cf back East 1, out B9

In or to the northeastern part of the US.

1839 in 1866 Finley *Hoosier's Nest* 87, Now, some of us, away up East,/ Have worshiped long this mammoth beast. **1885** NJ State Bd. Ag. *Annual Rept. 1884–85* 393, The Carter pork went up East, where it was cut up into meats especially for the French and South American markets. **1943** Warren *At Heaven's Gate* 107 **KY,** We should never have sent her away to school. Up East. **1957** *New Yorker* 23 Feb 63/1 **TN,** The boys all knew that they would be going to college . . and the girls that they would be going off to finishing school, up East or in Virginia. **1965** U.S. Congress House *Contested Elections* 40 **MS,** But they were not satisfied after they got licked, they went up east and hired some lawyers. **2002** *Goizueta Mag.* Winter (Internet) **GA,** Coleman Budd . . "went up East" to get his MBA because Emory didn't offer one. . . He was hurt when Harvard classmates asked, "Where's Emory?" **2006** *DARE* File—Internet **TX,** I went up east for college after graduating from Austin High. **2007** *Ibid* **TX,** I love traveling, want to go up east to school.

up garret   See up attic

upheaded adj

1 also *uphead(y):* Holding the head high; hence nouns *upheader* one that holds the head high, *upheadedness.* [Cf *OED2 upheaded* a."*north. dial.* . . Of cattle: Having upright horns."]

1801 *Philadelphia Gaz. & Daily Advt.* (PA) 22 May 4/4, [Advt:] For Sale. An active upheaded Family *Horse.* **1843** in 1845 Green *Jrl. Texian Exped.* 224, They seemed to know that we were Texians. . . from our national *up-head* appearance. **1852** Bobo *Glimpses NYC* 53, Who's this with the "up-heady" grays? **1868** (1871) Woodruff *Trotting Horse* 234, He . . was a big horse, sixteen hands high, raw-boned and upheaded. **1883** *Forest & Stream* 21.91 **NY,** I mean the upheaded, up-standing, dignified-looking, muscular, lithe, graceful fellow [=a Great Dane] that we see a picture of. **1890** *Wallace's Mth.* 15.526, What may be called "style" in a road-horse sense, trappy, quick and short gait, with upheadedness and general gayety of carriage. **1892** *Fitchburg Daily Sentinel* (MA) 10 June 5/3, [Advt:] No. 10. Gray horse, 1100 lbs., 8 years. 15.2 hands. Upheaded and good knee actor. A fine, gentle family horse. Good style. **1894** *DN* 1.334 **NJ,** *Upheader:* horse that holds his head high. Applied figuratively to men. **1898** *Ft. Wayne News* (IN) 7 June [8]/2 (newspaperarchive.com), He was handsome, of the blonde type, . . upheaded, and evidently on a comfortable footing with the world. **1917** *DN* 4.418 **wNC,** *Upheaded.* . . Carrying the head erect. "A fine lookin', upheaded gal." **1927** *AmSp* 2.366 **cwWV,** Who owns that upheaded gray mare yonder? **1989** *Syracuse Herald–Jrl.* (NY) 28 June sec C 11/9, [Advt:] *Red Bay Morgan Gelding* 3 yr old . . flashy, upheaded, typey, excellent carriage driving prospect. **1994–97** in 2004 Montgomery–Hall *Dict. Smoky Mt. Engl.* 629 **wNC, eTN,** *Upheaded.* . . 1. Carrying the head erect. . . [3 infs]. **2006** *DARE* File—Internet **ND,** AMHA 2006 Featured Stallions. . . Gorgeous, proud, upheaded and all Morgan in looks.

2 Fig: alert, intelligent; self-confident, arrogant; hence nouns *upheadedness, upheadiness, upheadyness* self-confidence, arrogance.

1826 *Essex Reg.* (Salem MA) 25 May 2/1, In the one region he is all boldness, all invective, the up-headed, stiff necked patriot. . . In the other he was all suppleness. **1832** *Easton Gaz.* (MD) 28 Jan 3/2, It appeared to me that there was a certain forwardness and upheadedness of manner

in hese colored men which seemed to me somewhat strange and peculiar. **c1905** in 1993 Farwell–Nicholas *Smoky Mt. Voices* 175 **sAppalachians,** He's biggity and upheaded, and I'm glad to be shet o'him. **1919** *DN* 5.35 **seKY,** *Upheaded.* . . Shrewd, intelligent. **1942** Berrey–Van den Bark *Amer. Slang* 301.6, *Arrogant; haughty.* . . upheaded. **1944** *San Mateo Times* (CA) 26 Sept 6/1, No political action committee or any group or individual is going to tell me or any upheaded American how he is going to vote or what he is going to think. **1963** *Mt. Life* 39.2.53 **sAppalachians,** The mountain woman who, after moving to the county seat, achieves social standing and begins to "thank she's sumpin on a stick" loses the respect of her country cousins for her "upheadyness." **1992** Miller–Jones in Williams *S. Mt. Speech* 116 **sAppalachians,** *Upheadiness* . . conceit. **1995** in 2004 Montgomery–Hall *Dict. Smoky Mt. Engl.* 629 **eTN,** *Upheadiness.* . . Conceitness; arrogance. . . [1 inf]. **1997** *Ibid* **wNC, eTN,** *Upheaded.* . . 2. Shrewd, intelligent. . . [3 infs]. **2007** *DARE* File—Internet **NH** [Road's End Farm Horsemanship Camp for Girls], [Personnel advt:] Perhaps this invitation to caring and upheaded women has caught your eye and piqued your imagination.

upheader   See upheaded 1

upheadiness   See upheaded 2

upheady   See upheaded 1

upheadyness   See upheaded 2

up horse   See upland horse

up in prep phr   chiefly sAppalachians

In phrr *up in twenty* (or *thirty,* etc): In the twenties (or thirties, etc)—usu in ref to a person's age.

1938 Stuart *Dark Hills* 21 **eKY,** He must be up in 80. **1943** in 1944 *ADD* **VA,** *Up in.* Used with wds. denoting decades in giving a person's approx. age. . . 'He's a man up in thirty' = in his thirties, betw. 30 & 39 years of age. . . *Ibid* **WV,** *Up in.* . . Common. *Ibid* **MO,** He's up in 80. *Ibid* **VA,** I expect he's up in sixty. **1959** Roberts *Up Cutshin* 33 **eKY,** I've seen fifty eat at our house a many of a time, and up in fifty. **1981** in 2007 *DARE* File—Internet **WV,** It was a problem . . to keep him from trying to work when he was up in 80 years of age. **1995** *DARE* File **NC,** Up in 80 (or 70 or 90)—more polite than 84 (or 73 or 96) [in] guessing ages.

up in the air   See air, (up) in the

up island adv phr   Nth, esp NEast   Cf up-country

To or at a usu locally determined part of an island; hence adj *up-island* belonging to this part; infreq n *up island* this part of an island.

1885 *Zion's Herald* 62.266 **Martha's Vineyard MA,** If he will take a stage ride "up island," he may catch the tricky trout in the running Tisbury brooks. **1902** *Educ. Rev.* 23.304 **ME,** The place . . was then known as "The Up Island School" of Eastport, Me. **1933** *Fitchburg Sentinel* (MA) 17 June [9]/3 (newspaperarchive.com), In the [Vineyard] *Gazette* . . is a story of an up-island resident who . . was awakened every morning at 5 o'clock by a flock of crows. **1957** *Syracuse Herald–Jrl.* (NY) 8 Aug 22/1, I spent an hour, as I usually do, with George Graves at his up-island nursery. **1968** *Oakland Tribune* (CA) 9 Sept sec E 17/5 **Martha's Vineyard MA,** You living up-island or down-island? . . Even if you moved up-island, the people who live there all year round wouldn't have any use for you. **1999** *NY Times* (NY) 1 Aug (Internet), Most come from what Hamptons locals call "up Island"—from Nassau County and from farther west in Suffolk. **2000** *DARE* File **Long Is. NY,** UpIsland: toward New York City. **2005** in 2007 *DARE* File—Internet **Long Is. NY,** The Elegant John—East Hampton, NY Bed & Bath Accessories. . . They are a bit pricey. . . But location is important if you need to pick up some last minutes [sic] items locally and not go up island. **2006** *Ibid* **ME,** I plunked down on a bench and enjoyed the world famous view of Monhegan village below. . . After lunch I headed up-island past the Ice Pond and into Cathedral Woods. **2007** *Ibid* **Mackinac Is. MI,** A Grand Hotel Restaurant. . . Located up-island near the Inn at Stonecliffe.

up Jenkins n, exclam   Also *Jenk(in)s up, up-Jenks-down-Jenks* [*OED2 up Jenkins* 1889 →]

A guessing game played with a coin; also used as a call in the game.

[**1891** *Sun. Inter Ocean* (Chicago IL) 4 Jan 18/4, A very bright game which exercises both mind and muscles bears the odd name of "Jenkins Down, Jenkins Up." [*DARE* Ed: The author was a Canadian, but the article was widely reprinted in US papers.]] **1893** *Halcyon* 9.126 **sePA,**

Students may play "Jenkins up" in the parlor during social hour if the Dean be present, and they make not too much noise. **1899** *Bucks Co. Gaz.* (Bristol PA) 24 Aug [3]/1 (newspaperarchive.com), The evening was passed in playing Up-Jenkins and other amusing games. **1901** *DN* 2.150 **ME, NY,** *Up Jenkins.* . . Name of a game at matching coins. **1909** (1923) Bancroft *Games* 239, *Up, Jenkins!* . . It consists in the guessing by opposing parties of the hand under which a coin is hidden. **1957** *Sat. Eve. Post Letters* **swCA,** Jenks up is an indoor game with teams sitting on sides of a table, 3 to about 6 on a team. Each chooses a captain who flip [sic] coins to start the game. Team wins flip has a coin preferably a quarter that they pass around under the table—until opposing captain says "Jenks up" and other team all bring hands up fists closed and slam them down palms down on the table when other captain yells "Jenks down"—with the coin under someone's hand. Object is for captain of opponents to have hands lifted one at time and if get all hands up except the one with the coin, then coin goes to opponents. **1965** *Reading Times* (PA) 16 Sept 21/2 (*Mathews Coll.*), Our eventime pastimes were of the simplest. We'd play parchesi [sic] or dominoes or up-jenks-down-jenks or hide-the-button. **1968** *DARE* (Qu. EE33, . . *Outdoor games . . that children play*) Inf **PA**112, Jenkins up—like pass the button, but you use a quarter. **1969** *DARE* FW Addit **swNJ,** People sit around table with hands under table and pass coin. "It" says, "I say Jenkins up"—everyone puts up hands and person with coin is caught. If "it" says "Jenkins up" without [saying] "I say," whoever puts up his hands is "it." **2006** *DARE* File—Internet, *Up Jenkins.* . . Equipment: A coin. . . One of the teams has a small coin, which it must try and keep hidden from the other team. The members of the team pass it to each other beneath the table until the leader of the opposing team says "Up Jenkins". They must them [sic] put their clenched fists on the table and the other team have to guess who has the coin. . . They only have one guess and if they guess correctly, they then take the coin and the game starts again.

upland   See **upland plover 1**

upland cranberry n
=**bearberry 2.**

1822 Bigelow *Treatise Materia Medica* 385, *Uva Ursi.* . . With us it grows in beds . . which from their remote resemblance to those of the cranberry vine, frequently give to the plant the name of *upland cranberry.* **1859** (1880) Darlington *Amer. Weeds* 211, Upland Cranberry. . . The leaves . . are astringent and tonic. **1892** (1974) Millspaugh *Amer. Med. Plants* 100-1, *Upland Cranberry.* . . *Fruit* a glabrous, depressed-globose berry or drupe, about the size of a pea. **2004** *DARE* File—Internet **neMN,** *Upland Cranberry* (Arctostaphylos), also sometimes called Kinnikinnic or Bearberry.

upland crane n
=**sandhill crane 1.**

1917 (1923) *Birds Amer.* 1.200, *Sandhill Crane.* . . *Other Names.* . . Upland Crane. . . It is often found on the plains and prairies, sometimes in small flocks but oftener in pairs or singly.

upland cress n
A **winter cress:** usu *Barbarea verna,* but also *B. vulgaris.*

1886 *Amer. Agric.* 55.111, From these scanty materials, we judge that the plant now offered as "Upland Cress," is a form of the Winter Cress, *Barbarea vulgaris.* This is not rare. **1890** *Vick's Mag.* 13.221 **NY,** Under the name of Upland Cress two species of Barbarea are sometimes cultivated. These are B. vulgaris and B. præcox [=*B. verna*], the latter is considered the best. **1925** *Book of Rural Life* 1436, Upland cress, which tastes much like water cress . . , but is more pungent, is usually grown as an annual. **1962** Gibbons *Stalking Wild Asparagus* 228, *Barbarea* has many common names, being known as Winter Cress, Spring Cress, Upland Cress and Yellow Rocket. Many country people refer to it merely as Mustard Greens. **2003** *DARE* File—Internet, Last week, at the Durham Farmers' Market, . . there was a bright sprig called creasy salad, a country favorite that one old gent told me smoothes [sic] his mustard and turnips when he cooks them all together. N[orth] C[arolina] S[tate] U[niversity] calls it upland cress. **2007** *Ibid* **cwCA,** *Upland Cress.* . . Also called winter cress, or "Creasy Greens" in the South, this cut-and-come-again crop is similar to watercress but much easier to grow. *Ibid* **PA,** *Baby Upland Cress*—Spoony green leaves with a mild peppery flavor.

uplander   See **upland plover 1**

upland hickory n
A **shagbark hickory** (here: *Carya ovata*).

1858 Freedley *Philadelphia Manufactures* 202, There is commonly employed in the construction of wheels, and other parts requiring strength and lightness combined, a native wood (upland hickory), which is admirably adapted to the purpose. **1897** Sudworth *Arborescent Flora* 113 **IL,** *Hicoria ovata.* . . Upland Hickory. **1950** Grimm *Trees PA* 126, The Shagbark Hickory is also known as the . . Upland Hickory. . . While it occurs quite frequently in bottomlands, it is perhaps more common on the hill slopes. **1999** *Amer. Midland Naturalist* 141.73, We chose to examine the light responses of . . shagbark hickory (*Carya ovata* . .), also known as . . upland hickory.

upland horse n   Also *up horse*   Cf **hillside horse, land horse**
1968 *DARE* (Qu. K32a, *With a team of horses, . . the horse on the driver's right hand*) Inf **NJ**21, Furrow horse—opposite is upland horse or up horse; (Qu. K32b, *The horse on the left side in plowing or hauling*) Inf **NJ**21, Nigh horse or upland horse in plowing.

upland huckleberry n   Cf **swamp huckleberry**
Prob a **huckleberry 1.**

1903 (1965) Adams *Log Cowboy* 302 **West,** Along it grew endless quantities of a species of upland huckleberry. **1917** Weed *Butterflies* 79, The caterpillars are also known to feed upon the spice bush and upland huckleberry. **1968** *DARE* Tape **NJ**51, There's a swamp huckleberry that's wild, and there's an upland huckleberry that's wild. They grow on lower bushes.

upland moccasin n   Sth   Cf **highland moccasin**
=**copperhead snake 1.**

1828 Flint *Condensed Geog.* 1.113 **Missip Valley,** The upland moccasin has many aspects in common with the rattle snake, but is a serpent still more repulsive in appearance. **1854** Wailes *Rept. on Ag. & Geol. MS* 329, Toxicophis atrofuscus [=*Agkistrodon contortrix*] . . upland moccasin. **1904** Davis *Bits Gossip* 69 **AL,** The mile-long hedges of roses through which crawled rattlesnakes and the deadly upland moccasin . . made up for us children a strange, enchanted page of the past family history. **1969** *DARE* (Qu. P25, . . *Kinds of snakes*) Inf **GA**80, Upland moccasin—poisonous. **2003** *DARE* File—Internet **Sth,** They [= copperheads] are an upland moccasin and have the same temperament as a cottonmouth. **2005** in 2007 *Ibid* **GA,** Any of y'all ever heard of a copperhead referred to as a "High Land Moccasin"? That's what my uncle called them. [Resp:] I've also heard them referred to as an "Upland Moccasin."

upland plover n
1 also *upland sandpiper, upland(er):* A bird (*Bartramia longicauda*) of open grasslands, formerly much hunted. **chiefly NEng** Also called **cornfield plover, cotton-tree ~, field ~, flying horse 2, frostbird 1b, frost snipe 2, grass plover 1, gray ~ 2, gray whistler, highland plover, hillbird, humility 1, meadow plover 2, ~ sandpiper, Mexican plover, papabotte, pasture plover, plover, prairie chicken 5, ~ pigeon a, ~ plover 2, rainbird 1a, sandpiper, tattler, turkey plover, whistling ~, wild mare**

1832 Williamson *Hist. ME* 1.147, The upland Plover is larger than a robin. **1882** Godfrey *Is. Nantucket* 157 **MA,** In September, . . upland plover make their appearance on various parts of the island. **1888** Trumbull *Names of Birds* 172, *Bartramian Sandpiper.* . . In Maine at Bangor, Rockland, Bath, Portland, and Pine Point, at Portsmouth, N.H., in Massachusetts at Ipswich, Provincetown, and West Barnstable, *upland plover.* . . At Provincetown [MA], *uplander.* **1896** Robinson *In New Engl. Fields* 52, The upland plover wails his greeting. **1917** (1923) *Birds Amer.* 1.247, *Bartramia longicauda.* . . Upland Sandpiper; Uplander. *Ibid* 248, My early recollections of the Upland Plover, once a familiar game bird, are of open rolling grassy tracts on Cape Cod, Mass., . . and some very shy brown birds that, despite most of my attempts to stalk them, would rise wildly well out of gunshot and with shrill cries fly on to the next hillside. **1921** LA Dept. of Conserv. *Bulletin* 10.79, Their biennial visits to Louisiana have always been important stages in the migration of the upland plover. **1956** MA Audubon Soc. *Bulletin* 40.17, *Upland Plover.* . . Upland (Maine, Mass.); Uplander (Mass., Conn. Short versions of the standard name, Upland Plover, which is in rather general use.) **1966–69** *DARE* (Qu. Q7, *Names and nicknames for . . game birds*) Inf **NH**5, Upland sandpiper or plover; (Qu. Q10, . . *Water birds and marsh birds*) Inf **RI**4, Upland plover; (Qu. Q14) Inf **RI**4, Upland plover—little sassy things. **1977** Bull–Farrand *Audubon Field Guide Birds* 490, *Upland Sandpiper*—"*Upland Plover*" (*Bartramia longicauda*). . . Until recently this bird has been called the "Upland Plover." **2004** (acc) PA Dept. Conserv. *Wild Resource*

Conserv. Program (Internet), The upland sandpiper, formerly called the upland plover, is a large light brown shorebird that comes inland to nest. . . Upland sandpipers are birds of open country. They may be found in large fallow fields, pastures and grassy areas.

2 =mountain plover.

1911 Cumming–Dunn *CA Sportsman* 109, The Mountain or Upland Plover is familiar to very few sportsmen of the State. **1925** (1928) Forbush *Birds MA* 1.476 **Rocky Mts,** On its normal range, where it [= the mountain plover] is generally known as the "Upland Plover," it is regarded as a valuable game bird.

3 =killdeer 1.

1907 *Outing* 49.794, I want to make the most earnest of earnest appeals to sportsmen . . to let up for a while on the upland plover, or killdeer. **1962** Imhof *AL Birds* 225, *Killdeer. . . Other names . .* Upland Plover, Killdeer Plover. The Killdeer is a large plover.

upland sandpiper   See **upland plover 1**

upland sumac n

1 Usu **smooth sumac 1,** but also **dwarf sumac.**

1810 Barton *Coll. for an Essay* 53, The juice of the Upland-Sumac (Rhus glabrum) is said to be excellent for removing warts. **1876** Hobbs *Bot. Hdbk.* 122, Upland sumach, Rhus glabra. **1900** Lyons *Plant Names* 320, *R[hus] glabra. . .* Mountain or Upland Sumac. *. . R. copallina . .* of the eastern U.S. is called . . Upland or Mountain Sumac. **1960** Vines *Trees SW* 633, *Rhus copallina. . .* Vernacular names for this plant are Mountain Sumac, . . Upland Sumac, and Winged Sumac. *Ibid* 636, *Rhus glabra. . .* Vernacular names are Scarlet Sumac, . . Upland Sumac, and Sleek Sumac. **1968–69** DARE (Qu. T13, *. . Names . . for these trees: . . sumac*) Infs **IN**69, **NJ**31, Upland sumac.

2 A **poison sumac** (here: *Toxicodendron vernix*).

1941 LANE Map 250 *(Sumach),* The terms *swamp sumach . .* and *upland sumach . .* are applied in Rhode Island to the poison sumach according to the location in which it grows.

upland turtle n   Also *upland terrapin*   Cf **highland terrapin 1, land turtle**

A turtle such as a **box turtle** or a **gopher 1a.**

1967 DARE (Qu. P24, *. . Kinds of turtles*) Inf **SC**34, Upland terrapin—spotted, stays out of water; **NJ**1, Upland turtle. **2002** *Augusta Chron.* (GA) 10 July (Internet), *Gopher tortoises*—The rare upland turtle lives in coastal plains of Alabama, Florida and Georgia and is being restored to portions of South Carolina.

upland white oak   See **white oak 4**

upland willow n

Usu **=prairie willow,** but occas another **willow 1** such as *Salix commutata.*

1788 in 1873 May *Jrl.* 48 **PA,** To cure the rheumatism, take the bark of upland or red willow. **1924** Deam *Shrubs IN* 60, *Salix humilis. . . Prairie Willow. Upland Willow. Ibid, Salix tristis* [=*S. humilis* var *tristis*]. . . *Dwarf Upland Willow. . .* More or less dry and sandy uplands, roadsides, borders of thickets, etc. **1938** Mt. Rainier Natl. Park *Nature Notes* (Internet) **WA,** One of the most common willows in the Hudsonian meadows in moist situations. . . *Upland Willow (Salix commutata).* **1953** Strausbaugh–Core *Flora WV* 282, *S[alix] humilis. . . Upland Willow. . .* Common locally on dry uplands and roadside banks. **2000** WI Dept. Nat. Resources *Tech. Bulletin No. 191* 175, *Salix humilis. . . Upland* or *Prairie Willow.* A very wide-ranging North American species, from Labrador south to Florida and west to the northern Great Plains; in Wisconsin common in dry to *wet prairies. . .* Prairie Willow is the only one [=willow] that regularly occurs in dry upland sites.

upland willow oak n   =**bluejack 1.**

1765 (1942) Bartram *Diary of a Journey* 17 **NC,** Thay have ye upland willow oak with A hoary leafe; & ye swamp willow with A narrow leafe. **1812** Michaux *Histoire des Arbres* 2.81, Le *Quercus cinerea* appartient exclusivement à la partie méridionale et maritime des Etats du Sud, où il est connu sous le nom de *Upland Willow-oak.* [=*Quercus cinerea* belongs exclusively to the southern and coastal part of the Southern States, where it is known as Upland Willow Oak.] **1860** Curtis *Cat. Plants NC* 37, *Upland Willow Oak. . .* The bark affords a fine yellow dye. **1897** Sudworth *Arborescent Flora* 176 **NC, AL, TX,** *Quercus brevifolia* [=*Q. incana*]. . . Upland Willow Oak. **1954** *Amer. Midland Naturalist* 52.287, *Q. incana. . .* Upland willow oak, blue jack.—Very dry, sandy oak woods, oak barrens, and pinelands, common. **1980** Lit-

tle *Audubon Guide N. Amer. Trees E. Region* 392, "Upland Willow Oak"—*Quercus incana.*

upling block n   [Var of **upping block**]

1968 DARE FW Addit e**TN,** *Uplin'* ['ʌplɪn] *block*—block used to help women mount a horse (sidesaddle). Common, old-fashioned. **2006** DARE File—Internet s**Appalachians,** When I got older, they'd let me ride Lucy to the mill. I'd get on an upling block to make the saddle and Lucy would stand at an even walk.

uppards   See **upwards**

upper adj   Cf **lower** adj **1, under**

In combs with terms for var types of **earmarks:** See quots.

1773 in 1929 Summers *Annals* 607 **VA,** His Mark is ordered to be recorded a Swallow Fork in the right ear a Crop in the Left Ear and an Upper Keel. **1906** DN 3.157 nw**AR,** An *upper* (*right* or *left*) *slope* is taken from the upper part of the ear. **1936** Adams *Cowboy Lingo* 131 **West,** The 'upper half-crop' or 'over half-crop' was made by splitting the ear from the tip, midway about halfway back toward the head and cutting off the upper half. **1966–67** DARE (Qu. K18, *. . Kind of mark . . to identify a cow*) Inf **FL**20, Split and upper-cut; **FL**36, **SC**43, Upper-bit; **LA**2, Upper-figure-seven.

upping block n   Also *upping stock,* ~ *stone,* ~ *stump* [OED2 *upping-stock* a1691 →, *upping-block* 1796 →, *upping-stone* 1809] **chiefly Midl** Cf **upling block, upton block**

A mounting block.

1852 Nevin *Churches* 45 cs**PA,** Each log, each bench, each family upping-block,/ Some granddame held amidst her gathered brood. **1883** Amer. Philol. Assoc. *Trans.* 14.55 **WV,** *Upping-block,* 'a horse-block,' in common use in West Virginia. **1890** *Lima Daily Times* (OH) [14 Nov 3]/5 (newspaperarchive.com), How to mount the pillion? There must be an "upping stone." You will see these still standing at the gates of some of the churches and in front of some doors in the old towns of New York and Massachusetts. **1896** DN 1.426 sw**NC,** *Uppin'-block:* horse-block. **1914** Baldwin *In My Youth* 90 **IN** (as of c1850), Jonathon drove the farm wagon round to the "uppin' block" just inside the big gate. **1930** Shoemaker *1300 Words* 64 c**PA Mts** (as of c1900), *Upping-stock*—A horse mounting-block, or stone. **1930** *Athens Messenger* (OH) 7 Apr 4/2, Many "upping blocks" . . may be found in Athens, but . . they now serve as "No Parking" curb signs. **1932** *Dothan Eagle* (AL) 16 Nov 2/3, The upping block was a necessity for the lady riders to mount the side saddles. **1952** Brown *NC Folkl.* 1.603, *Upping-block. . .* A block used by ladies to mount a horse. **1970** *NC Folkl.* 18.122, Spit on the "uppin'" stump for love. (The "uppin'" stump is one used by ladies to mount side-saddle.) **1975** *Advocate* (Newark OH) 18 Feb 5/9, There is a market for everything the company has, even upping stones for getting on a horse. **2006** in 2007 DARE File—Internet, When I attempted to mount my horse, the saddle turned even though I was standing on an upping block.

uppitish adj   [Prob blend of *uppity* + *uppish*]

1968 DARE (Qu. HH35, *A woman who puts on a lot of airs: "She's too _____ for me."*) Infs **NY**50, **OH**66, Uppitish.

ups n, exclam   Cf **-s** suff², **upsies, upsy line**

In marble play: see quots.

1909 DN 3.385 e**AL,** w**GA,** Ups. . . Used in marbles for permission to move one's taw too behind one of the ring-men. **1955** PADS 23.33 cw**AL,** Ups. . . A call that allows the player to raise his hand from the ground in order to shoot. **1962** PADS 37.3 c**KS** [Marbles terms], Ups. . . The hand is held about six or eight inches off the ground.

upscuddle n   Also *upscuttle* [Cf EDD *scuttle* v. 3 "To take part in a street-feud"] **chiefly sAppalachians**

A noisy quarrel; a disturbance, tumult.

1904 *Outlook* 76.829 ce**OH,** I don't believe since Miss Gray whipped Billy at school we've been in sech an upscuttle at home as we was last evenin'. **1913** Kephart *Highlanders* 294 s**Appalachians,** If they quarrel, it is a ruction, a rippit, a jower, or an upscuddle—so be it there are no fatalities which would amount to a real fray. **1938** Matschat *Suwannee R.* 36 ne**FL,** se**GA,** Ye see, a Injun boy from this 'ere swamp was captured by some other Indians who had a upscuddle with 'em. **1941** Justus *Cabin on Kettle Creek* 51 e**TN,** "If I had any notion who took 'em—" he doubled up his fists and swung out his arms—"there'd be an upscuddle, all right!" **1952** Brown *NC Folkl.* 1.603, Upscuddle. . . A quarrel, a disturbance. **1975** in 1981 *NC Folkl. Jrl.* 29.40 w**NC,** They was a regular upscuddle at the schoolhouse. **1997** in 2004 Montgomery–Hall *Dict. Smoky Mt. Engl.* 630 **eTN,** *Upscuddle.* . . A quarrel. . . [1 inf]. **2003** KY Univ. College Arts & Sci. *Arts & Sci. Mag.* 3.1.28 **KY,** Oswald caused quite an upscuttle, primarily because of the sweeping organizational changes wrought in the university.

upset, fruit basket   See **fruit basket c**

upside prep

1 also *upside of:*

a Against, on (a vertical surface); close beside. **esp Sth** *esp freq among Black speakers*

1897 *Century Illustr. Mag.* 54.477 **Sth** [Black], Scritch-owl flewed in they house las' week, en it lit on Jim's hat hanging upside the wall. **1908** in 2007 (acc) Lexis–Nexis Legal Research *State Case Law: GA* (Internet), I first saw the fire up side of the railroad. **1924** *Ibid,* [He] picked up a piece of wood and hit him and knocked him up side of the door. **1928** *Ibid* [Black], The wife of the deceased testified that when her husband reached home he "had a big knot up side of his head." **1929** in 1983 Taft *Blues Lyric Poetry* 154 **TX** [Black], I'm going to buy me a pistol: hang it up side the wall. **c1938** in 1974 *Amer. Slave* 10.2.247 **TN** [Black], They had a bunk up side the wall and a trundle bed. **1986** Pederson *LAGS Concordance,* 5 infs, **AR, GA, LA, MS, TX,** Upside the wall; 1 inf, **cTX,** Butting your head upside a brick wall; 1 inf, **cwMS,** Hang them [=clothes] upside a wall; 1 inf, **neLA,** Upside that levee = next to the levee; 1 inf, **cAL,** He runned upside the driver; 2 infs, **neLA, cwLA,** Upside the fence; 1 inf, **cwTN,** Right upside the hearth; 2 infs, **LA, MS,** Hang(ing) them [=clothes] upside the house; 1 inf, **nwMS,** Gets right upside the stalk of cotton; 1 inf, **swGA,** They had that old clock hanging upside the wall; 2 infs, **TX,** Hanging upside the wall; 1 inf, **swGA,** A ladder upside the wall; 1 inf, **ceTX,** Mud upside the wall; 1 inf, **nwMS,** Run her [=a calf] upside the wall; 1 inf, **cwMS,** She had a mill upside the wall; 1 inf, **swGA,** Stand some of the boxes upside the wall; 1 inf, **seGA,** Right upside the house; 1 inf, **neMS,** Upside of that house; 1 inf, **swGA,** Throwed him upside the bank. [13 of 22 total infs Black] **1987** in 2007 *DARE* File—Internet **AR** [Black], In fact my dad played you know, he had a guitar hanging up side the wall. **2006** *Ibid* **nwFL,** We'd . . put them [=crabs] on what we call a cooling table that was a big old wire looking table upside the wall. **2006** *Chicago Reporter* Sept/Oct 9 [Black], "[The lobby] is like a bathroom. They stand right upside the wall," said Idella Ross. **2007** *DARE* File—Internet **cwNY** [Black], So I was propped up side the door, and all the sudden I happen to look across the street and I saw this little old man and this little old lady taking pictures.

b Spec: against the side of (one's head)—usu in phrr *hit one upside one's head, go* ~, *a whack* ~, and varr. **formerly Sth, now widespread**

1915 in 2007 (acc) Lexis–Nexis Legal Research *State Case Law: TX* (Internet), He hit my brother up side the head with his fist. **1964** *Ibid: AL,* He contended a red-headed policeman kicked him upside the head. **1969** *Panama City News–Herald* (FL) 22 June sec D 2/2, It isn't always that way, especially when one of those shoes goes up side his head . . while attached to a hoof. **1971** Roberts *Third Ear* np [Black], *Go upside one's head.* . . to hit; to give someone a hard blow. **1980** *NY Times* (NY) 12 Oct sec CN 28/4, Mean Jack smacked me upside the head for emphasis. **1983** *Los Angeles Times* (CA) 29 Sept sec D 7/1, There were no rude noises from an audience representing 158 nations while Ronald Reagan was . . whacking the Third World upside the head for "pseudo-nonalignment." **1985** *DARE* File **cwIN,** To threaten rascally children: "I'll slap you upside your face." **1986** Pederson *LAGS Concordance,* 1 inf, **cwFL,** Smack you upside of the head; 1 inf, **seLA,** Upside the head = hit someone in the head. **1992** Martone *Townships* 101 **WI,** His eyes . . rolled slighly in his head the way cartoon animals do when they've been whupped upside the head with a two-by-four. **2002** *Star-Herald* (Scottsbluff NE) 9 Oct neighbors sec 2/5, Somebody has to prove to me that Nebraska needs that kind of whack upside the head (that the new legislation mandates).

‡**2** Above. [Cf *OED2* upside sb. 2. "upside of, above, beyond"]

1967 *DARE* FW Addit **neNY,** Upside the door—above the door.

upside adv [**upside** prep **1a**]
Alongside.

1966 *DARE* Tape **SC9,** The mill right there . . and that's the creek, and the flat [=flatboat] come right upside.

upside-down bird n   Also *upside-down(er)* **esp Nth**
=**nuthatch,** usu the **red-breasted nuthatch** or the **white-breasted nuthatch.**

[**1889** (1900) Bailey *Birds* 101, White-bellied Nuthatch. . . A lady forgetting his name once aptly described him to me as "that little upside-down bird."] **1929** Forbush *Birds MA* 3.357, Nuthatches. . . are so often seen creeping head downward that some country people call them . . "Upside-down-birds." **1950** *WELS* (Insect-eating bird that goes head first down a tree) 2 Infs, **WI,** Upside-down bird. **1956** MA Audubon Soc. *Bulletin* 40.127, White-breasted Nuthatch. . . In clambering about trees, it seems as much at home head-downward as in any other position. . . Upside-down Bird (N.H., Mass. . .) Red-breasted Nuthatch. . . Upside-down Bird (Mass. . .) **1966–69** *DARE* (Qu. Q23, *The insect-eating bird that goes headfirst down a tree trunk*) Infs **IA3, PA**89, 188, 214, Upside-down bird(s); **MI**36, Nuthatch—the red-breasted and the white-breasted—the "upside-downer" we call them here; (Qu. Q18, *Joking names and nicknames for woodpeckers*) Inf **PA**89, Upside-down. **2004** *DARE* File—Internet **TN,** When I got around to mentioning the White-breasted Nuthatch, I got a chorus of "The Upside-Down Bird! The Upside-Down Bird!"

upside down, fruit basket   See **fruit basket d**

upside of   See **upside** prep **1**

upside right adv phr   Cf Intro "Language Changes" I.1
Rightside up.

1930 *Amer. Photography* 24.468, One customer was . . trying in vain to get the "darned film in up-side right." **1951** Phillips *Pagoda* 35 **TX,** The spindle-legged Ghurka took the yellow paper into the headlight glare and scrutinized it carefully, both sides, upside right and upside down. **1968** Amer. Microscopical Soc. *Trans.* 87.410, Figs. 9 and 10 . . were printed upside down; this caused the further error of mislocation of the figures. That is, Fig. 10, properly turned upside right, should really be Fig. 9. **1970** *Chicago Tribune* (IL) 22 Feb sec 10 3/1, A world of men at ease in a society still setting upside-right. **1977** *News* (Pt. Arthur TX) 21 Oct 17/4, [In syndicated cartoon *The Family Circus:*] Turn that book upside right, PJ, or you'll ruin your eyes. **1997** *DARE* File—Internet **WI** [Speak 'Scansin], Oops, hey, I dropped dis beer on da way, so turn it upside right for a while before you open it. **2006** in 2007 *Ibid* **NH,** The upside down bottle is kiind [sic] of silly, I prefer the normal upside right bottle, but the ketchup is the same. **2007** *Ibid* **TX,** Actually, I do make them upside right but store them upside down.

upsies exclam [**ups** + **-ies 2**]
Used as a call in marble games: see quot.

1982 Slone *How We Talked* 93 **eKY** (as of c1950), *Upsies*—allowed to place one fist on the ground to rest the other one on when shooting the marbles.

up-sitting n [Cf Ger *aufsitzen,* Du *opzitten*]
The custom of a man and woman sitting up together at night during courtship.

1930 Shoemaker *1300 Words* 64 **cPA Mts** (as of c1900), *Upsitting*—A lover sitting up at night with his sweetheart.

upsot v   Past, past pple, ppl adj *upsot* [Var of *upset*] **scattered, but esp S Midl, NEng**

1838 *Knickerbocker* 12.297 **Long Is. NY,** I b'lieve I'm upsot! **1840** *N. Amer. Rev.* 50.209 **MI,** Why, do tell if you 've been upsot in the mash. **1847** (1962) Robb *Squatter Life* 110 **MO,** This consomet animal had made up his mind to upsot that gal. **1867** Harris *Sut Lovingood Yarns* 92 **TN,** He upsot hit, smashin in the glass doors. **1878** *Scribner's Mth.* 17.39 **CA,** And Brown got down behind the stove allowin' he "was cold,"/ Till it upsot and down his legs the cinders freely rolled. **1887** Butterworth *Zigzag* 77 **MS,** Yo' don' go for to upsotting de chilluns dat ar way when yo' go for to see white pussons. **1887** (1892) Hinman *Corporal Si Klegg* 19, Si . . just upsot me an' driv all thoughts o' cookin' clean out o' my head. **1890** *Manford's Mag.* 34.203 **West,** I wus overcome . . an' musn't allow my feelins now to upsot me. **1899** (1912) Green *VA Folk-Speech* 468, *Upset, v.* Upsot. **1913** Kephart *Highlanders* 278 **sAppalachians,** Any . . vowel may serve in place of *e* . . upsot. **1916** Lincoln *Mary-'Gusta* 315 **MA,** I'm so upset ever since I looked into that kitchen and see the poor soul down on the floor. **1930** *VA Qrly. Rev.* 6.248 **S Midl,** The hill man . . may make . . internal vowel alterations like . . upsot. **1932** Wasson *Sailing Days* 48 **cME coast,** [It] had burnt one Bangor vessel a'ready and folks was all upsot. **1941** *LANE* Map 470, 1 inf, **seNH,** Easily upsot. **1997** in 2004 Montgomery–Hall *Dict. Smoky Mt. Engl.* 630 **wNC, eTN,** Upset . . variant form upsot . . [4 infs].

upstair adv [Var of *upstairs*]   Cf **downstair**
1894 Chittenden *Unknown Heroine* 69 **VA,** Early dis morning I steal in de house. I went upstair. **1937** in 1979 *Amer. Slave Suppl. 2* 7.2450

TX [Black], One 'r' d' boat boys say, 'Le's go upstair 'n' see.' **1950** *WELS Suppl.* *(When you go from the ground floor of a house to the floor above, you say, "I'm going _____.")* 1 Inf, **csWI,** Upstair. **1965** *DARE* (Qu. D5, . . *"I'm going _____";* total Infs questioned, 75) Inf **OK**13, Upstair. **1966** Phillips *Mojo Hand* 76 **NC** [Black], If you needs a room we gots plenty upstair for ten dollar. **1975** Gould *ME Lingo* 305, *Upstair*—Not so much in southern Maine, but in Aroostook *upstair* is heard for *upstairs:* "Now, you children get right upstair to bed!" **2002** Fickett *Nectar* 264 **ME,** When the girls had gone to school I went upstair and found some of Henry's old clothes.

upstreet adv   **formerly widespread, now esp NEast** Cf **downstreet**

Up the street; to or into the main or business section of a town; uptown.

1802 Martin *Mod. Gratitude* 62 **MD,** As . . [we] were coming up street yesterday, we met *Maria.* **1821** *Adams Centinel* (Gettysburg PA) [18 Apr 4]/3 (newspaperarchive.com), Thomas J. Cooper . . has *Removed his Store* a few doors further up street. **1855** *Harper's New Mth. Mag.* 10.292 **WV,** They marched up street in high good-humor. **1860** in 1938 *Colorado Mag.* 15.23 **PA,** A good deal of drinking and gambling tonight, and a dance in a dirty gambling shop up street. **1884** *Century Illustr. Mag.* 27.763 **LA,** He felt no greatness of emotion, . . as if he were here and emotion were yonder, down-street or up-street. **1912** *Mansfield News* (OH) 24 June 3/3, Everyone . . had remained up street to learn of the outcome. **1925** *Sheboygan Press* (WI) 18 June 3/3, I saw tears course down the cheeks of many as those old heroes of '61 slowly marched up street. **1959** *VT Hist.* 27.165, *Up street.* . . Up the street: to the shopping district of a town. Common. **1965** *Independent Press–Telegram* (Long Beach CA) 15 Aug Progress sec 1/2, Upstreet from the savings and loan building stretches a row of distinguished looking business structures. **1967** *Mebane Enterprise & Hillsborough Jrl.* (NC) 13 Apr sec B 6/1, Down street Cone Mills Granite Plant has moved so far up street, it practically takes up half the town. **1977** *Kennebec Jrl.* (Augusta ME) 13 Sept [4]/4 (newspaperarchive.com), I know from talk upstreet that these deer are publicized. **1982** *DARE* File **NH,** In N.H., people go "upstreet" or "upstreet" to visit a neighbor. **1985** *WI Alumnus Letters* **ceNY,** "Going upstreet"—they still use this in Berlin [NY]. To go into the village to shop. **1989** *DARE* File **cwMA,** People who use the term [=*downstreet*] invariably put the stress on *down.* Some use *up street* just as easily. **1997** *Syracuse Herald–Jrl.* (NY) 17 Sept sec C 2/3, "We'd get a call: 'He's upstreet. Come and get him.'" Marcellus people call the business district along Main Street "upstreet" or "downstreet," depending on if they live to the north, or south, of it. **2003** *NY Times* (NY) 22 Sept Long Island ed sec 14 14, Some other Bonac words and expressions: . . *To Go Upstreet*—To go downtown.

upstreeter n   [*EDD* (at *up* prep. 1.(80))]   **sNEng, NY**

One who lives **upstreet**—usu in contrast to members of one or more other locally defined sectional factions; see quots.

1827 *Lit. Cadet & RI Statesman* (Providence) 18 Apr 1/3, At the south western extremity of this town, there used to reside a distinct race of beings, 'yclept Blue Pointers; and isolated as they were, their habits, manners and customs, varied very materially from . . their neighbours, the up-streeters, the up-towners, the down-towners, Ship-streeters, and uphillers. **1879** *Springfield Sun. Republican* (MA) 7 Dec 4/6, Monson. . . On a recent occasion a down-streeter was speaking of the outlook for his vicinity, when the up-streeter replied as follows: "Well, there's one thing, you can't never get the depot moved, and, besides, we've got more burying-grounds than you have anyway." **1892** Brooklyn (NY) Fire Dept. *Our Firemen* 33 (as of 1827), The efforts of the two sides, each to elect its own candidate, made the election of Chief Wells quite an exciting event. The parties were the "Up-streeters," . . and the "Down-streeters." **1921** *Century Illustr. Mag.* 101.353 **Long Is. NY** (as of 1860s), The post-office, the two hotels, and two of the three churches were on Main Street. Most of the stores were there also . . sprinkled more or less regularly along its entire length. . . Locally, we spoke of one another as "upstreeters" and "downstreeters," with an undercurrent of rivalry in the designations. **1953** *NY Folkl. Qrly.* 9.197 **Long Island NY,** We met . . about two hundred others—summer people and year-'rounders. In the old days the latter would have been called Down-Neckers, Up-Streeters, Shadeyes, Turnip-Pullers, Hairleggers—depending on what part of the North Fork they came from. **1998** *East Hampton Star* (NY) 27 Aug (Internet), The village itself, said Mr. Kelsall, was divided into "territories." "Sometimes it was perilous to go 'below the bridge'" on North Main Street. "Being an upstreeter and being a below-the-bridger was a definite cutoff when I was a kid. I don't think I knew a real Bonacker until after the '38 hurricane." **2007** *NY Times* (NY) 7 July (Internet) **Long Is. NY,** For nearly four centuries they have lived in a section . .

now known as Springs or Bonac, north of the village that is the wealthy's playground. They are known as Bonackers, an insular group who fishes and farms and serves the grand homes and summer businesses of the fancy folk they call "upstreeters."

upstropolis, upstroppelous   See **obstropolous**

upstuck adj   [By metath; cf Intro "Language Changes" I.1]
Stuck up, arrogant, pretentious.

1904 *Reader* 5.25 **eIA,** "Well, if she ain't upstuck!" cried Hilma. **1930** Shoemaker *1300 Words* 64 **cPA Mts** (as of c1900), Upstuck—(Pennsylvania Dutch), Aristocratic, proud. **2005** in 2007 *DARE* File—Internet, It's a really nice way to attract people to the world of science by showing that we are not upstuck individuals. **2006** *Ibid* **cIN,** Instead of being rude and upstuck to the makers of DND i'm gonna respect their wishes and dreams. **2007** *Ibid* **swCA** [Black], I dont want to meet any upstuck people or boring ones! *Ibid* **VA,** I can laugh at sony for being a bunch of upstuck morons. *Ibid* **NYC,** Mary also falls in love with Alex Cheevy whom she thought was upstuck.

upsy line n   Cf **ups**

1967 *DARE* (Qu. EE8, *The line toward which the players roll their marbles before beginning a game, to determine the order of shooting*) Inf **MA**2, Upsy line.

up the country adv phr   Cf **down the country**

In or into the interior or rural part of a region.   Note: In recent years the phr has been popularized by musician Jimmy Buffett and the group Canned Heat.

c1680 in 1815 *MA Hist. Soc. Coll.* 2d ser 5.228, The eleventh [division], from the west side of Hudson's river, 30 miles up the country towards the 40th degree, where New England beginneth. **1834** *S. Lit. Messenger* 1.112 **VA,** He has been absent . . for some time, went up the country to his brother's, who I hear is lately dead. **1849** *Amer. Whig Rev.* 10.129, He went up the country a week ago to collect some money which was due me. . . That road passes over a dreary region. **1863** in 1890 U.S. War Dept. *War of Rebellion* 1st ser 31.3.192 **TN,** Wheeler's command went up the country last week, intending to cross the river somewhere above Loudon. **1879** *Indiana Progress* (PA) 23 May 1/2, Mr. Bird, on Monday, had gone up the country, and while gone, succeeded in shooting two tapirs. **1891** *Century Illustr. Mag.* 42.931 **CA,** While here the supercargo, both mates, and all the sailors but two ran off and went up the country. **1926** in 1983 Taft *Blues Lyric Poetry* 113 [Black], Say you can't quit me : no need of trying / I'm going up the country : don't you want to go. **1931** *AmSp* 7.120 **seID,** *Up the country* means somewhere in the vicinity [in rural southeastern Idaho]. **1939** in Lib. of Congress *Amer. Memory: WPA Life Hist.* (Internet) **neFL,** This has not been a good season for peas—drouth up the country, and they did not fill out. **1948** in 2009 (acc) Lexis-Nexis Legal Research *State Case Law: SC* (Internet), I wanted to see him (R.V.) about more insurance . . because we were bringing those cars from up the country, and I wanted them insured. **2004** *NY Times* (NY) 18 July (Internet), *Going Up the Country, But Keeping All the Toys.* . . [They] moved full-time from a walkup loft in Williamsburg, Brooklyn . . to their country house in Ghent, in Columbia County.

up the flume   See **flume, go up the**

up the hill adv phr   Cf **down the hill**

See quots.

1968 Adams *Western Words* 336, *Up the hill*—A riverman's reference to shore. When a riverman went ashore, he went up the hill, whether it be in a city, along a mountainside, or across a prairie. **1977** Jones *OR Folkl.* 19, Some traditional folk speech you might hear from fishermen off the Oregon Coast are the phrases *down the hill* to indicate heading south from port and *up the hill* to indicate going north along the coastline.

up the pole adv phr, adj phr   Cf *DS* DD11

Abstaining from alcoholic beverages; on the wagon.

1906 *NY Observer* (NY) 28 June 829, It came as a shock to the barracks to learn that "Bob" had gone "up the pole" (given up drink and started to live a better life). **1916** *Munsey's Mag.* 58.227, He made that stern, abstemious resolve known variously as going "on the wagon" or "up the pole." **1956** Sorden–Ebert *Logger's Words* 40 **NEng, Gt Lakes,** Up-the-pole, A logger on the water wagon; that is, one who does not drink. **1984** Smith *SW Vocab.* 137, *Up the pole:* A term to designate a trooper who had sworn off drinking, who had gone "on the wagon." The inference was that anyone who shinnied up a pole would not have access to booze. Back-sliders who took to the bottle again were said to be "down the pole." **2006** *DARE* File—Internet (as of c1940),

[Ref to Hollywood's "Irish Mafia":] [Frank] Morgan and [Pat] O'Brien were doing a little 'grog sampling,' as Lynne [Overman] was 'up the pole' [on the wagon].

‡up the pucker tree adj phr   Cf **pucker tree**

1982 *Smithsonian Letters* **cwWV** (as of 1926), Mrs. Adams has always used the expression "up the pucker tree" to mean that someone is angry or pouting. She heard this expression a great deal . . in Jackson County.

up the tree   See **tree, up a 1**

uptight adj   *chiefly among Black speakers*   Note: *Uptight* meaning "inhibited, anxious, angry" is widespread and not treated here.

1 All right, okay; superb—used as a term of approbation.

1962 *Down Beat* 2 Aug 20, *Jazz* Gene Ammons *Up Tight!* **1966** *Surfer* 7.4.11 **CA**, The waves are a perfection 10 to 15 feet and straight over. Really up tight and out of sight! **1966** in 2006 *DARE* File—Internet [Black], [Song lyric:] *Uptight (Everything's alright). . .* Baby, ev'rything is all right, uptight, out of sight. **1968** *Current Slang* 3.2.50 [Watts slang; Black], *Uptight. . .* Good; under control.—I think everything is uptight now that Ervine has arrived! (ironic). **1969** *Ibid* 3.4.10 [Univ of KY slang], *Up tight. . .* Sophisticated; "cool.". . Affectionate; intimate. **1970** Major *Dict. Afro-Amer. Slang* 118, *Uptight. . .* a good feeling. **1971** Roberts *Third Ear* np [Black], *Uptight . .* to be all right; OK. [**1986** Pederson *LAGS Concordance* 1 inf, **swGA**, Uptight [=a well dressed woman]. [Inf Black]]

2 Intimate; very friendly.

1969 [see **1** above]. **1970** *DARE* (Qu. II3, *Expressions to say that people are very friendly toward each other: "They're _____."*) Infs **FL48, TN50**, Uptight. [Infs Black] **1972** Claerbaut *Black Jargon* 85, *Uptight. . .* very friendly; intimate.

up till yet   See **yet** adv, conj **B2**

‡upton block n   [Var of **upping block**]

1933 Karns *Hist. Sketches* 25 **wPA**, There was usually a fence or stump to be used as an "upton block." In other days, when horseback riding was common, an "upton block" was in front of almost every home.

up to taw   See **taw C2b(1)**

up to the (last) notch   See **notch 2**

uptown adj   Also *uptownish, up-to-town*   Cf **intown B**

Stylish, sophisticated; prosperous—in phr *go uptown* to gain respectability.

1855 Willis *Rag-Bag* 340 **NEast**, Billings . . is a handsome man of a very up town address, with the finest teeth possible. **1930** *Reno Eve. Gaz.* (NV) 1 Oct 4/3 **NYC**, [McIntyre column:] A novelist describes the reputed break between a very uptown motion picture couple. **1943** *Monessen Daily Independent* (PA) 24 June 6/1 **NYC**, [Driscoll column:] Sheik Khalil also appeared occasionally at very uptown parties in the late evenings. **1966–68** *DARE* (Qu. GG19a, *When you can see from the way a person acts that he's feeling important or independent: "He surely is _____ these days."*) Inf **TX11**, Uptown; (Qu. HH2, *Names and nicknames for a citified person*) Infs **KS8, LA17, TX18**, 42, Uptown; **FL28**, Uptown boy; **TX11**, Uptownish. **1966** *DARE* FW Addit **OK24**, I can't do much with these up-to-town cars. [**1970** Major *Dict. Afro-Amer. Slang* 119, *Uptown:* stylishness; wealth.] **1970** *DARE* Tape **TN62**, Boy, when he had an agate marble, he was uptown with a derby hat on. It cost a nickel. **1976** Lynn–Vecsey *Loretta Lynn* xi **eKY**, Yeah, Madison Square Garden, that's right. So I've seen country music go uptown, like we say. **1979** *DARE* File **Madison WI**, Here, let me fix that so it looks real uptown. [Television crewman, adjusting microphone-tieclip.] **1986** Pederson *LAGS Concordance,* 1 inf, **cAL**, If a man had a corn sheller, he was uptown; 1 inf, **neAL**, Uptown = highfalutin. **1996** in 2006 *DARE* File—Internet, [He] was looking very uptown in a white suit and polka-dot shirt. **2004** in 2007 *Ibid* **csWI**, Java Potions Plus—a real uptown coffee shop in Wisconsin Dells. **2007** *Ibid* **csIL**, When I became a teenager I got to shop at Zwick's new Concept Two store & thought it was real uptown! *Ibid* **nwCA**, We also have food service right in the pits, real bathrooms & paved parking. . . *real uptown.*

uptrip v   [Cf *OED2 up-* prefix 4; but see also Intro "Language Changes" I.1]   **chiefly S Midl, esp KY**

To cause (someone) to make a mistake or commit a fault; to trip (someone) up.

1856 Montesano *Redstick* 20 **TN**, Mac, however, kept his twenty-five dollar pups with him, against the remonstrances of the old hunters who told him they would uptrip us. **1860** Kirk *Wooing & Warring* 254 **KY**, In the midst of their diversion, she uptripped the unsuspecting Indian woman, and in a trice had gagged and bound her. **1876** *Reno Eve. Gaz.* (NV) 12 June [2]/1 (newspaperarchive.com), The two great stumbling blocks which uptrip the majority of men are ignorance and conceit. **1878** *Harper's New Mth. Mag.* 52.129, No one could up-trip him or knock him down. **1936** *Esquire* Sept 183 **KY**, Devil can't uptrip that man. **1941** in 1944 *ADD* neKY, *Uptrip. . .* To trip (one) up. . . verified orally by author. **1980** *DARE* File **AR, wKY, wTN, eTX**, Up-trip instead of trip-up.

up until yet   See **yet** adv, conj **B2**

upwards adv   Pronc-spp *up'ards, uppards*   **scattered, but esp Sth, S Midl**   Cf **awkward, backward(s), inwards**

Std senses, var forms.

1797 in 1967 *PADS* 48.40 **NC**, *Uppards.* **1839** *Burton's Gentleman's Mag. & Amer. Mth. Rev.* 5.244, We . . seed the galley floating keep up'ards. **1867** Harris *Sut Lovingood Yarns* 19 **TN**, Look out, Laigs, if you aint ready tu go up'ards. **1870** Fowler *Wall St.* 438 **NYC**, The Erye Railroad Company has to pay up'ards of $20,000 for an ingyne. **1878** Hart *Sazerac Lying Club* 99 **NV**, There was up'ards of four hundred little trouts follerin' it around. **1894** Frederic *Marsena* 46 **nNY**, We must have took in up'ards of $11. **1895** *New Engl. Mag.* 17.696, We . . towed him behind the ship for up'ards of a week, feedin' him on orts. **1931** *PMLA* 46.1318 **sAppalachians**, *W*, is elided in several words: "awkard," . . "upards." **1940** *AmSp* 15.47 **sAppalachians, Ozarks**, Regularly [w] is lost in words compounded with -ward(s): back'ards . . for'ards . . up'ards. **1945** *Denton Jrl.* (MD) 3 Aug 6/2, Nute Crowley has finely had to give up his girl witch he has corted offen on for uppards of 8 yrs. **1954** Roberts *I Bought Dog* 12 **seKY**, I'll turn this bucket bottom uppards on the tater hill. [**2000** Shores *Tangier Is.* 77 **Chesapeake Bay**, Today, Canaan, now called Uppards, "Upper End," or "Up'ards," remains pretty much as Hall saw it in 1932.]

up yon   See **yon C1a**

ur   See **a** indef art

Urb   See **Arab** n

urf   See **earth**

uriah n   Cf **durgen** n **1**

See quot.

1953 Randolph–Wilson *Down in Holler* 295 **Ozarks**, *Uriah. . .* An ignorant, uncouth backwoodsman. I have seldom heard this myself, but Dean Virgil L. Jones, University of Arkansas, tells me that some of his students use it in the sense of *durgen.*

urinate n   Also *urinate water, urinine* ~ *among Black speakers*   Cf **menstruation B**

Urine.

c1938 in 1970 Hyatt *Hoodoo* 1.375 **seLA** [Black], You soak her feet in that saltpeter, red pepper and table salt and her *urinate*. *Ibid* 703 **swTN** [Black], Yo scrub it with *urinate*. *Ibid* 716 **ceVA** [Black], Then you take *urinate water* an' pepper or salt an' sweep. **1939** *Ibid* 2.1532 **ceSC** [Black], Yo' jes' mess aroun' an' take yore *urinate*. *Ibid* 1836 **ceSC** [Black], Den dey kin take yore *urinine watah* an' keep yo' home. . . Yo' put dem in it, jes' in de *urinine watah.*

urine n, v   Usu |ˈjʊrɪn|; also |ˈjuraɪn| Pronc-sp *you-reen, you-rine*

A Forms.

1939 in 1970 Hyatt *Hoodoo* 2.1118 **swTN** [Black], Yo' saturate dat little bow wit yore *you-reen.* **1974** Conrad *Club* 56 **AL** [Black], U-rine (he pronounced it you-rine). **2002** *DARE* File—Internet **Chicago IL**, How do you pronounce 'urine'? . . [When] I was in the US I remember some people in Chicago pronounce it /ˈjuraɪn/.

B As verb.   [*OED2* →1828]

To urinate.

c1938 in 1970 Hyatt *Hoodoo* 1.738 **swTN**, Ev'rytime they *ketch a trick*, they . . urine, they put 3 drops in this little vial. **2007** *DARE* File—Internet, My son was two when I potty trained him. . . I tracked how long it would take him to urine after liquid consumptions. . . I would sit him there until he urined. *Ibid,* How do I clean my couch my cat urined on it and its brandnew. *Ibid* **CA**, It smelled like someone had urined in the corner of the room.

urinine water   See **urinate**

urp v[1]   Also sp *e(a)rp*   Also *urpse*   **scattered, but chiefly Missip Valley, GA, SW**   See Map
To vomit.

1939 Faulkner *Wild Palms* 83 **MS,** It just spews you up somewhere to die. . . I had rather drown in the ocean than be urped up onto a strip of dead beach.   **1942** Berrey–Van den Bark *Amer. Slang* 130.32, Vomit. . . urp.   **1949** *PADS* 11.6 **wTX,** Earp [ɝp]. . . To vomit.   **1950** *WELS (Other words and expressions for vomiting)* 4 Infs, **WI,** Urp; [1 Inf, **csWI,** "Yurope."]   c**1955** Reed–Person *Ling. Atlas Pacific NW,* 1 inf, Urp.   **1965–70** *DARE* (Qu. BB17, . . *Vomiting*) 60 Infs, **chiefly Missip Valley, GA, SW,** Urp; (Qu. BB18, *To vomit a great deal at once*) 10 Infs, **scattered,** Urped up (his insides, his toenails, your insides); **TX45,** Urp up your socks; **IL110, LA1, 28,** Urped (and urped); **NY86,** Urped your insides out; (Qu. BB16b, *If something a person ate didn't agree with him, he might just feel a bit* _____) Inf **LA28,** He might want to urp.   **1966** Dakin *Dial. Vocab. Ohio R. Valley* 2.484, *Vomit. . .* Other expressions appear only once or twice: *urp.*   **1973** Allen *LAUM* 1.369 (as of c1950), *Vomit. . . Erp,* obviously onomatopoetic, is most informal and more likely to be found in the speech of a child or of a woman. . . [6 infs **NE,** 5 infs, **MN, IA, SD**].   **1974** *Gt. Bend Tribune* (KS) 13 Mar 7/3, A merchant . . was affected and during the most-miserable stage literally "urped up his toes" and unfortunately his dentures into the stool.   **1989** Pederson *LAGS Tech. Index* 295 **Gulf Region,** Vomit [neutral] . . urp (18 [infs]) . . urp it up (1) . . urp up (1). . . *Vomit* [crude] . . urp (13 [infs]) . . urp it up (3) . . urp (one's) toes up (1) . . urp up (1).   **2009** *DARE* File **seWI** (as of c1960), If one of the kids vomited, my mother would say he or she had "urpsed."

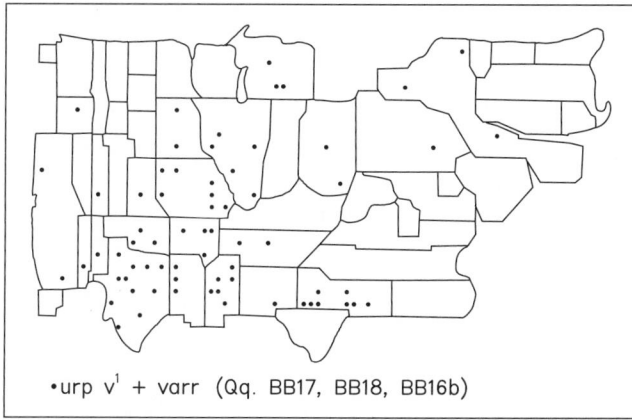

•urp v[1] + varr (Qq. BB17, BB18, BB16b)

urp v[2]   [Prob var of *irk*]
To annoy, bother, or irritate.

1967–69 *DARE* (Qu. Y7, *When one person never misses a chance to be mean to another or to annoy another: "I don't know why she keeps _____ me all the time!"*) Inf **IL26,** Urping; (Qu. GG13a, *When something keeps bothering a person and makes him nervous . . "It _____ me."*) Inf **TX71,** Urps; (Qu. II29b, . . *To explain the unpleasant effect that person has on you: "He just _____."*) Inf **AZ10,** Urps me.   **2003** in 2009 *DARE* File—Internet **CT,** What really urps me is that she forces the idea that her *music* is like this hard core punk rock.   **2007** *Ibid* **CA,** I don't know why but this just urps me. *Ibid* **nwGA,** And what even urps me even more—the people that send those things to me . . know how I feel and think this will change my mind.   **2009** *Ibid* **wTX,** Fishermen leavin jugs, and lines just urps me.

urpish adj   Also *erpish, urp(s)y*   [**urp** v[1]]
Nauseated, queasy; nauseating.

1949 in 1986 *DARE* File **cIA,** Urpy . . sick to the stomach. I've had a sick headache all day and I feel sort of urpy.   **1965** *Reno Eve. Gaz.* (NV) 30 Dec 9/1, [Ann Landers column:] Last week he wrote a couple poems for me that are urpy.   **1967–70** *DARE* (Qu. BB16b, *If something a person ate didn't agree with him, he might just feel a bit* _____) Inf **GA23,** Urpish on his stomach; **GA89, IL110, KS2, MI114,** Urpy; (Qu. BB39, *On a day when you don't feel just right, though not actually sick . . "I'll be all right tomorrow—I'm just feeling _____ today."*) Inf **VA11,** Urpish.   **1991** *Daily Herald* (Arlington Heights IL) 13 Dec sec 1 16/1, When you're sick, you don't feel like laughing. It's especially hard when you feel . . , well, urpy.   **2001** *DARE* File—Internet, That whole biker comment of *yours* still has me feeling a little "Urpish"

or is it "Erpish?" well it's a icky thought.   **2003** *DARE* File—Internet, I started to feel urpish at the register around 8:30. I got all hot and dizzy, and felt the strong desire to just collapse on the ground. I realized I wanted to throw up.   *Ibid,* When I start to feel urpy (even with the Bonine sometimes) I focus on the horizon.   **2009** *DARE* File **seWI** (as of c1960), My mom, who grew up in Milwaukee, would describe a queasy child as "a little urpsy."

urr   See **there** A4

urs   See **us** pron

urthe   See **other**

us pron   Usu |ʌs|; also rarely **Sth, S Midl** |ɝs| Pronc-sp *urs*
A Form.   Cf Intro "Language Changes" I.8

1911 *DN* 3.540 **eKY,** Us. Pronounced [ɝs].   **1931** *PMLA* 46.1318 **sAppalachians,** *R.* . . is frequently excrescent . . "urs" (us).   **1937** *AmSp* 12.268 **cVA,** That' what all urs (us) folks calls um.
B Senses.

1 We—used as a non-compound subject.   [*OED2 us* 5.a. 1607 →; "Now *dial.*"]   **Sth** *among Black speakers*   Note: The use of *us* rather than *we* in compound subjects (e.g. "Pa and us went home") or in close apposition in subject position ("Us kids went to school") is common and is not treated here.

1894 [see **whensomever**].   **1922** [see **us** adj].   **1923** (1951) Toomer *Cane* 56 **GA** [Black], Thats what us wants, sho, Louisa.   **1934** Hurston *Jonah's Gourd Vine* 9 **AL** [Black], When us lef' de field, you tole 'em.   **1937** in 1976 *Weevils in the Wheat* 179 **VA** [Black], When we got in Fort Hatton, us had to cross a bridge to git to de Yankees.   **1966** *DARE* Tape **GA4,** The bossman what us was stayin' with, was our neighbor; **MS75,** My stepsister said us was bad all that week. [Both Infs Black]   **1967** *DARE* FW Addit **LA6** [Black], Us had a good time.   **1981** Walker *You Can't* 9 **Sth** [Black], Us didn't come back home for two days.   **1986** Pederson *LAGS Concordance,* 1 inf, **cwMS,** Us didn't have nothing; 1 inf, **swGA,** Us didn't know no better; 1 inf, **swMS,** Us get happy; 1 inf, **swMS,** Us had a table made; 1 inf, **swMS,** That's all us had; 1 inf, **csGA,** Us had to get out; 1 inf, **cwGA,** Us is coming; 1 inf, **cwAL,** How in the world could us live?; 1 inf, **swMS,** Us cooked us some syrup. [All infs Black]

2 Ourselves, spec:

a Used as an indirect object or in place of std *for ourselves.*   [*OED2 us* 2.b "*Obs.* exc. *dial.*"]   Cf **me** pron **3a, her B1, him B1, them B2**

1833 *Sketches D. Crockett* 109, We made us a good fire.   **1861** in 1903 Norton *Army Letters* 35 **PA,** We . . made us good beds and slept well.   **1907** White *AZ Nights* 166, We got us timbers and made a scow.   **1939** in 2004 Montgomery–Hall *Dict. Smoky Mt. Engl.* 630 **wNC,** Us. . . We'd all just fix us up a sack of rations.   **1986** Pederson *LAGS Concordance,* 1 inf, **nwTN,** We got us a furnace that fall; 1 inf, **csTN,** We built us a little home; 1 inf, **swMS,** Us cooked us some syrup; 1 inf, **seMS,** Let's find us a place to sit down; 1 inf, **swAL,** We made us a living.

b Used redundantly to indicate that the speaker's advantage is concerned.   Cf **me** pron **3b**   Note: It is impossible to draw a sharp line between this and the previous sense.

1939 in 2004 Montgomery–Hall *Dict. Smoky Mt. Engl.* 630 **wNC, eTN,** Us. . . We had us a fence around the pasture between the barn and the house.   **1942** *Sat. Eve. Post* 22 Aug 42 **NC,** Le's go and wake us up a preacher.   **1985** Wilkinson *Moonshine* 76 **neNC,** Then he's going to turn around and grin at you and say, 'Aren't we having us a *time.*'   **1986** Pederson *LAGS Concordance,* 1 inf, **ceLA,** We had us a cow; 1 inf, **seAR,** We caught us a ferryboat; 1 inf, **neTN,** Eating us some strawberries.

us adj   [Engl dial; cf *EDD us* II.4]   *among Black speakers*   Cf **me** adj, **us's, usn** adj, **we** adj
Our.

1922 Gonzales *Black Border* 336 **sSC, GA coasts** [Gullah glossary], Us—we, our.   **1931** (1991) Hughes–Hurston *Mule Bone* 142 **cFL** [Black], Whut you gut to do wid us business?   **1934** Hurston *Jonah's Gourd Vine* 16 **AL** [Black], Us chillun is ourn.   c**1937** in 1976 *Weevils in the Wheat* 229 **VA** [Black], Den, us wuz us own boss.   **1938** in 1972 *Amer. Slave* 2.1.98 **SC** [Black], We chillun was 'fraid of dem en ran. Knew dey was dressed in a different direction from us white folks.   **1945** [see **we-uns** pron **1**].   **1967** *DARE* FW Addit **LA6,** Us—occas an attributive denoting possession. "Us telephone wires in the ground."   **1968** Moody *Coming of Age MS* 20 [Black], Us daddy ain't that color!

1986 Pederson *LAGS Concordance,* 1 inf, **swGA,** [It's] us book. [Inf Black]

-us suff   See **-es** suff[1] **3**

use v

A Forms.

1 pres (exc 3d pers sg): usu *use;* also *uses.* **chiefly Sth, S Midl**

1837 *Token & Atl. Souvenir* 272 **PA** [Black], The root is what we uses. **1839** Lester *Chains & Freedom* 120 **NJ** [Black], I uses the same words. **1861** Olmsted *Cotton Kingdom* 118 **Sth,** Two people uses a good deal of tobacco. **1864** Gilmore *Down in TN* 150, We uses them critters jest as ye does horses. **1895** [see **B** below]. **1899** Chesnutt *Conjure Woman* 127 **csNC** [Black], I can't make out w'at you means by some er dem wo'ds you uses. **1968–70** DARE Tape **IN**21, I don't like that word *slip* in the way that a lot of people uses it; **TN**51, I uses some kind of a aspirin, that's what they tells me to do. **1986** Pederson *LAGS Concordance,* 2 infs, **AR,** Some people uses (two lines); 1 inf, **TN,** Some people uses an egg like that against lice; 2 infs, **AL, AR,** Some uses (milk, and some doesn't use milk); 1 inf, **ceTN,** Me and my wife uses it all the time; 1 inf, **cAL,** Lots of people uses it; 1 inf, **neFL,** They uses it now; 1 inf, **csMS,** People that uses it; 1 inf, **seGA,** They uses it for appetite and blood; 1 inf, **swLA,** Lot of people uses; 1 inf, **cAL,** Some of us uses that; 1 inf, **swAL,** They still uses that; 1 inf, **swGA,** They uses that word; 1 inf, **csTN,** Lots of people uses two "G's".

2 past pple: usu *used;* also *useded, useted.* Cf **-ed** suff **1**

1871 (1892) Johnston *Dukesborough Tales* 58 **GA,** Between him and Sebe, that little innocent individiel is bent on bein' useded up bodaciously. **1902** DN 2.249 **sIL,** *Useted, . .* Accustomed; inured. 'The work ain't so hard when you get usted [sic] to it.

B Sense.

To go or stay habitually (in or about a place); of animals: to live or congregate, feed—usu with a prep phr or adv of place. [OED2 *use* v. 23 c1470 →; "Latterly *dial. . .* and *U.S.*"] **chiefly Sth, S Midl** Cf **using-ground**

1751 in 1912 NC Secy. of State *NC Wills* 113, I Give and Bequeath unto my well Beloved Wife . . all my Cattal that youses on trent. **1770** Washington in 1908 *OH Hist.* 17.466 **VA,** On this Creek many Buffaloes use according to the Indians Acct. **1833** Hall *Harpe's Head* 152 **KY,** Yes, I *use* about her some. **1837** Sherwood *Gaz. GA* 72, *Used,* for feed;—the sheep *used* in that field. **1854** (1932) Bell *Log TX–CA Trail* 36.49, I suppose it [?=a gila monster] uses in water and on trees. **1880** (1881) Harris *Uncle Remus Songs* 68 **GA** [Black], Ders er old gray rat w'at uses 'bout yer. **1883** Amer. Philol. Assoc. *Trans.* 14.54 **Sth,** *Use,* 'to frequent, to inhabit.' The word . . is still in daily use at the South. . . It is by no means a negroism, but common among almost all classes. "There's a cloud that uses around White Sides (mountain)," said a North Carolina mountaineer. **1885** Cable *Dr. Sevier* 440 **LA,** And if I sort o' use about this low country a little while for my health, . . why you ain't a-carin', is you? **1895** DN 1.375 **seKY, eTN, wNC,** *Uses:* lives, makes his home. "That's whar the bar uses." "These chickens uses round the place." **1902** DN 2.248 **sIL,** *Use. . .* To inhabit; to frequent or haunt, as animals. Always followed by the preposition. 'A foe [sic for *fox*] uses in this timber, or on this bluff.' **1903** DN 2.335 **seMO,** *Use around. . .* To frequent. 'His cattle use around my place all the time.' This peculiar phrase is very common. **1909** DN 3.386 **eAL, wGA,** *Use around. . .* To frequent, be accustomed to, graze, etc., around (a particular place). **1916** DN 4.302 **VA,** *Use. . .* To frequent, inhabit. "Watch where the squirrels use." "Bears do not use up here any more." **1923** DN 5.244 **VA, NC,** *Use. . .* To frequent: used by hunters. **1926** DN 5.404 **Ozarks,** *Use. . .* To frequent, to loiter. "You-all better gin up a-usin' 'roun' my still-house!" **1933** White *Dog Days* 123 **CA,** During the shooting season quail "used," not in coveys, but in astonishing packs counting literally into thousands. **1933** (1973) Sherman–Henry *Hollow Folk* 116 **cnVA,** These here children ain't a doin' what you told 'em. They is using around the house. **1944** PADS 2.21 **sAppalachians,** *Use. . .* To frequent (for food, forage, etc., of animals). "Squirrels are usin' in that tree." **1946** PADS 6.26 **eNC,** *Sand fiddler. . .* A small, crab-like crustacean that uses in the sands of the ocean, sounds, and creeks. **1967** DARE (Qu. CC17, *Imaginary animals or monsters*) Inf **TN**22, They's a whompus a-usin' around here. **1967** DARE FW Addit **GA**20, Gators use here in the summer; **TN**15, They's a bear a-usin' here. **1982** Powers *Cataloochee* 337 **cwNC,** One could see tracks in the dust of the dirt floor where deer and raccoon had been "usin'". **1996** Harrell *Fetch*

It 167 **eNC,** These signs were fairly fresh, meaning they [=bears] were "using" there at that time.

useded See **use** A2

used to v phr   Usu |'jus,tu, -,tʊ, -,tə| Pronc-spp *usetee, us(e)ta, us(e)ter, uset ter, uset to, use-tuh, ust to*   Note: The common sp *use to* is not illustr here.

A Pronc and sp varr.

1848 *Knickerbocker* 31.87 **KY,** My wyf useter af won oncet. **1858** *Harper's New Mth. Mag.* 17.45 **neNY,** Mr Hallard use'ter keep a kind o' tavern. **1884** *Anglia* 7.272 **Sth, S Midl** [Black], *Done useter* = to be used to. **1887** *Scribner's Mag.* 2.193 **NY,** Pritty ladies 'n' gentlemen he *use't* to travel with. **1890** DN 1.69 **KY, NEng,** *Uster* [justə]: used to. "When it rains and wets our old rooster,/ He don't look like he useter." **1894** *New Engl. Mag.* 16.733 **NEng,** I uset ter git awful hungry. **1894** Riley *Armazindy* 11 **IN,** Last, she called us back—in clear / Voice as man'll ever hear—/ Clear and stiddy, 'peared to me,/ As her old Pop's ust to be. **1909** DN 3.386 **eAL, wGA,** *Uster* [ustə] [sic]. The common colloquial pronunciation of *used to*. **1914** [see **C1** below]. **1928** AmSp 3.405 **Ozarks** (as of 1916–27), The *d* sound is frequently dropped from the word *used,* particularly in the combination *used to*—which is always pronounced *use ter*. [**1928** *Engl. Jrl.* 17.205, In the familiar locution "used to," as in "he used to go, he's used to going," the *d* of *used* assimilates to the *t* following and disappears, while the normal *z* heard in the verb sharpens to *s:* hiyōōstəgō, hizōōstəgōing. . . No one speaking freely, naturally, easily the speech of cultivated men says yōōztəgō.] **1937** NE Univ. *Univ. Studies* 37.114 [Terms from play-party songs], *Uster do. . .* Used to do; have done before. [**1944** Kenyon–Knott *Pronc. Dict.* 461, *Used to . .* 'accustomed to' . . 'was (were) accustomed to': before a pause ['justu], before vowels ['justu], before vowels or conss. ['justə].] **1997** *NY Times* (NY) 16 Nov sec 4 7/3 **UT,** Ustacould (Was once able to). **2000** Shores *Tangier Is.* 181 **Chesapeake Bay,** For forms like *kinda* (kind of), *wanta* (want to), and *useta* (used to), the Islanders regularly use a clearly pronounced variation of the vowel sound of seat: "kindee," "wantee," and "usetee" respectively.

B Gram form.

Contracted neg: *usen't (to);* pronc-sp *usen'ter.* [This form is much more common in Brit than Amer Engl (sometimes in the more analogical sp *usedn't*) and represents the regular contraction of ['just nɑt]; cf *mustn't* ['mʌsnt]. U.S. speakers generally do not use negative/interrogative inversion with *used to;* the usual negative is *didn't use(d) to.*]

1868 Nordhoff *Cape Cod* 16 **seMA,** He usen't to keep with the fleet. **1894** *Scribner's Mag.* 15.155 **LA,** I usen't to be so wicked when I was a little shaver. **1919** Kyne *Capt. Scraggs* 301 **CA,** You usen'ter be hard an' spiteful like that. **1953** Atwood *Survey of Verb Forms* 33, *Didn't use to. . .* is almost universal in all areas and among all types. . . The negative contraction *usen't* /jusənt/ occurs with regularity only in a very small area of w.c.Md. and in n.Va. . . There are six occurrences of this form, divided among Shenandoah and Loudoun counties in Va. and among Carroll, Frederick, and Montgomery counties in Md. Outside of this area there are only three occurrences in the East (Springfield, Mass., New York City, and Catawba Co., N.C.) **1960** AmSp 35.12, On Beaver Island (an Irish fishing colony in northern Lake Michigan) and in scattered communities of northern Wisconsin is found the negative form *usen't to,* not uncommon in British English but rare in the Atlantic states. **1964** De Vries *Reuben* 160, You usen't to be so uppity. **1966** Dakin *Dial. Vocab. Ohio R. Valley* 2.466, *Didn't use(d) to . .* is regular everywhere in the Ohio Valley. . . *Usen't to be . .* [is] quite rare and scattered. **1975** Allen *LAUM* 2.39 **Upper MW** (as of c1950), *Didn't use to. . .* One minor variant, *usen't to,* is sparsely spread with six instances . . in the Northern speech area (one in Canada). *Ibid* 40, Usen't to /jusənt tə/. . . Comment: . . [1 inf, **seMN:**] Inf. says this shows a lack of education. . . [1 inf, **swIA:**] Used by infs.'s uncle (born in Ireland). . . [1 inf, **seND:**] " 'Usen't' isn't a word." **1986** Pederson *LAGS Concordance* (. . *Didn't use to*) 1 inf, **nwLA,** [Trying to decide whether to use] Usen't; 1 inf, **cwMS,** Usen't to be. **2000** Shores *Tangier Is.* 247 **Chesapeake Bay,** It is interesting to find *he usen't do that* for "he didn't used to do that."

C Syntax.

1 in phrr *used to could* (or *would*): Was (or were) formerly able or accustomed to. [Cf *EDD use* II.1 (8, 10)] Cf **may** v **B**

1823 Cooper *Pioneers* 1.242 **cNY,** I can't shoot as I used to could. **1837** Sherwood *Gaz. GA* 72, *Use-to-could,* for could formerly;—I used-to-could do it. **1882** *Century Illustr. Mag.* 24.597 **ME,** I can't spin a yarn like I used to could. **1884** Smith *Bill Arp's Scrap Book* 66 **nwGA,** I used to could plow, but *it looks like I have lost the lick* [=skill]. **1891** *PMLA* 6.3.174 **TN,** "I can't play the fiddle now, but I used to could." *Would* is used in the same way, though probably less frequently. "He used to wouldn't dance." **1901** *DN* 2.150 **c,nNY,** *Used to could.* . . Common, but vulgar. **1902** *DN* 2.249 **sIL,** *Use to could.* **1905** *DN* 3.99 **nwAR,** Use to could, . . use to couldn't, . . use to would, . . use to wouldn't. **1908** *German Amer. Annals* 10.50 **sePA,** I used to could walk thirty miles a day. **1908** Johnson *Highways Pacific Coast* 92 **sCA,** I used to could say nobody could lose me in Los Angeles. **1909** *DN* 3.386 **eAL, wGA,** *Use(d) to could (would).* **1914** *DN* 4.164 **NW,** *Uster could.* **c1937** in 1972 *Amer. Slave* 2.1.181 **SC,** De peoples used to wouldn' tell dey chillun how old dey was. **1940** *AmSp* 15.214 **TX,** There is an appalling use of other double auxiliaries here. . . I cite the following . . examples: *I might can, I might could, I used to could* [etc]. **1966–69** *DARE* FW Addit **FL47,** I used to could imitate a bull alligator real good; **MD39,** We used to wouldn't wait; **seNC,** I use to could do that; **TN26,** Used to could. **1968** *DARE* Tape **GA30,** They used to would kill a lot of cattle and hogs. **1975** Allen *LAUM* 2.80 **Upper MW** (as of c1950), *Used to could* . . "I used to could remember a few words of Welsh"—[1 inf, **MN**]; "I used to could call them things"—[1 inf, **MN**]; "We used to could have fun"—[1 inf, **ND**]; "You used to could set your watch by it"—[1 inf, **SD**]. **1986** Pederson *LAGS Concordance* **scattered Gulf Region,** [84 infs, Used to could(n't); 36 infs, Used to would(n't).] **2002** *DARE* File—Internet **seKY,** Would you have listen to him[?] . . I use to would.

2 used adverbially to mark habitual past action: See below. **chiefly Sth, S Midl**

a followed by a past-tense verb: Formerly, earlier, once. [Cf *EDD use* II.1 (9)]

1827 Hilliard *Address* 46 **MA,** Times *isn't* as they used to *was,* Sirs. **1838** Kettell *Yankee Notions* 132, I don't feel as I used to did. **1861** *Harper's New Mth. Mag.* 23.765 **NJ,** Times ain't as they used to was. **1883** (1971) Harris *Nights with Remus* 308 **GA** [Black], Times is mighty diffunt fum w'at dey use ter wuz. **1894** *Amer. Missionary* 48.225 **LA** [Black], He don't go where he used to went and he don't do nothing he used to did. **1901** *DN* 2.150 **NY,** *Used to was.* . . For used to be. Ostego Co., N.Y.; very vulgar; occasional in Seneca Co., N.Y., where, however, it is always intentional. **1905** *DN* 3.99 **nwAR,** I use to didn't like to go to school. **1918** *DN* 5.21 **NC,** *Used to* . . *was.* **1940** Stuart *Trees of Heaven* 251 **eKY,** It ust to wasn't like this. **1950** Bissell *Stretch on River* 106, I use to had me a real nice guit-tar. **1950** *WELS Suppl.* **csWI,** I used to was. **1955** *PADS* 23.44 **e,sSC, eNC, seGA,** *Used to didn't.* **1966** Dakin *Dial. Vocab. Ohio R. Valley* 2.466 **eKY,** The regular usage of these speakers [=older, least educated] is *used to didn't.* . . When recorded in context with *be* the form is *used to wasn't.* **1966** *DARE* Tape **SC10,** One time it use to been so cold right first of the winter. **1986** Pederson *LAGS Concordance* **Gulf Region,** 127 infs, **widespread,** Used to did(n't); 13 infs, **scattered,** Used to was(n't); 1 inf, **csTX,** I used to went there. **2001** in 2004 Montgomery–Hall *Dict. Smoky Mt. Engl.* 631 **wNC, eTN,** It came out like it used to did. . . I thought I was going to get like I used to was. **2010** *DARE* File **csWI** (as of c1970), My mother would say, "Betty Nelson—Betty Peterson, used to was." This meant "Betty Nelson—her maiden name was Betty Peterson."

b parenthetically, esp at the beginning of a clause: Long ago, in the old days.

1931 Goodrich *Mt. Homespun* 72 **wNC,** Used to when we was little, we'd make us horses out of cornstalks. **1936** *AmSp* 11.353 **eTX,** Use to, say from about twelve o'clock on, I'd be typin' down the entries. **1942** (1971) Campbell *Cloud-Walking* 271 **seKY,** Used to, we never heared all these things. **1946** *PADS* 6.32 **eNC** (as of 1900–10), *Used to.* . . Formerly. "Used to, we had thick ice in winter." . . Common. **1956** McAtee *Some Dialect NC* 49, *Used to.* . . formerly; "Used to, we had skating in winter." **1966** *DARE* Tape **SC17,** Used to, our best cropping was our first; **NC4,** we made potato yeast. **1969** *DARE* FW Addit **swNC,** Used to you could—this use of "used to" at the beginning instead of "on" the verb phrase is very common. **c1970** Pederson *Dial. Surv. Rural GA,* 1 inf, **seGA,** Used to, you called it a pallet. **1970** *DARE* File **OK,** *Used to* =formerly, in past days. "I could go out, used to, and see them." **1972** in 1994 Thomas *Come Go with Me* 27 **S Midl** (as of c1900), Used to, Ma and Pa had a bed they put up on posts. **1976** Wolfram–Christian *Appalachian Speech* 175, And, used to, you took your money in your pocket and brought your groceries back in a shop-

ping bag. **1981** *New Yorker* 9 Feb 38 **KY,** Use to, if a storm was coming, people would put a bedpost on a child's dress tail, to keep him from blowing away. **1986** Pederson *LAGS Concordance* **Gulf Region,** *(Used to be)* 49 infs, **scattered,** Used to—sentence modifier; 1 inf, **cMS,** Used to, a bale of cottonseed wouldn't pay for the ginning; 1 inf, **swLA,** Used to, a cow couldn't hardly go in there; 1 inf, **cwAL,** Used to, a day was from sunup to sundown; 1 inf, **nwAL,** Used to, we called them kernels. **1995** Williams *Gt. Smoky Mts. Folklife* 118 **wNC, eTN,** They don't tell tales like they used to, but used to, they'd tell ghost tales. **1998** *DARE* File **OK,** Two informants from Purcell, Okla. prefix sentences with *Use to be*—"Use to be this was so well known." Both of them were born in 1958. One is a college grad. One is a high school dropout. The dropout also uses simple *use to* as in "Use to they'd kill 'em." So does a man with a 4th grade education born in 1907.

used to could (or would) See **used to C1**

uselves See **usself**

usen v [Engl dial: cf *EDD usen* v., past *usen(ed)* (at *use* v. I.1.(4), (5)), past pple *usen* (at *use* v. I.2.(5))] **chiefly Sth, S Midl** *old-fash*

1 To accustom (one to something); hence ppl adj *usen(ed), usent* used, accustomed (to something).

1845 Hooper *Advent. Simon Suggs* 167 **AL,** Throw a meal-bag, or somethin else over your head, twell my little 'squire gits sorter usen to the *big ugly!* **1851** Burke *Polly Peablossom* 49 **MO,** There's no countin' on them varmonts as I's been usened to. **1853** Simms *Sword & Distaff* 572 **SC,** What should give me, a strong man, usen to the city, the blasted Small Pox. **1861** *S. Lit. Messenger* 33.311 **NC,** Board and lodgin bettern we're usent to. **1886** Amer. Philol. Assoc. *Trans.* 17.45 **Sth,** *Usen,* 'accustomed.' A negro would say, "I ain't usen ter dat." It is vulgar, but not confined to the negroes. **1888** Johnston *Mr. Absalom Billingslea* 174 **GA,** I were never a person that were usened to dodgin'. **1890** *Scribner's Mag.* 8.440 **sAppalachians,** They's usen to it—an' born to it—an' likes it. **1900** Garland *Eagle's Heart* 99 **IA,** I'm usen to that, boys. **1940** Weygandt *Down Jersey* 58 **sNJ,** It ain't right to have the schools usening the children to soft jobs. **1952** Brown *NC Folkl.* 1.603 **wNC,** Pass me the beans; I want something to eat I'm usen to. **1994–97** in 2004 Montgomery–Hall *Dict. Smoky Mt. Engl.* 631, *Usen, usen to.* . . Used to. . . *usen* [1 inf, **eTN**]; *usen to* [1 inf, **wNC**].

2 past *usen(ed)* (neg *didn't usen*) foll by infin: Used, was (or were) accustomed.

1851 Burke *Polly Peablossom* 50 **MO,** 'Old Preach' (as them Cole boys usen to call me). **1872** *Atlantic Mth.* 29.539 **MS,** We did n't usen to have it, and had n't ought to now. **1885** *Century Illustr. Mag.* 29.854 **GA,** That were your name, or at leastways it usened to be. **1888** Jones *Negro Myths* 73 **GA coast,** Dem usen fuh tek ting outer um ebry now en den. [*DARE* Ed: For use of *for* as infin marker see **for** prep B2.] **1890** *Scribner's Mag.* 7.721 **sAppalachians,** Mammy usen to call me 'Miah.' **1924** Raine *Land of Saddle-Bags* 79 **sAppalachians,** Folks usen to burn out a sort of bowl in a tree stump. **1941** Hench Coll. **cVA,** [Heard:] We usen to go to town every Saturday. **1978** Hiser *Quare Appalachia* 180 **eKY** *(Montgomery Coll.),* My womarn Pop there usened to be a witch.

usen pron See **usn** pron[1]

usened See **usen** v 1, 2

usens See **us-uns**

usent v See **usen** v 1

usen't v phr, **usen'ter, usen't to** See **used to B**

uses See **us's**

useta, usetee See **used to**

useted See **use** A2

useter, uset ter (or to), use-tuh See **used to**

usher groomsman See **groomsman**

usin See **usn** pron[1]

using vbl n attrib [Cf *EDD using-things* "Domestic articles, such as crockery, &c."]

Fit for using or work; functional; working—freq in comb *using horse* a workhorse.

1869 in 1980 *Ho for CA* 221 **TX,** Travailed all day and had to make dry camp. We had a sufficiency of using water with us and they found enough for the horses. **1911** *Daily Kennebec Jrl.* (Augusta ME) 20 Apr 5/4, Two all-round, good using horses. **1941** Engle *Always Land* 283 **IA**, It's a good, using horse. What'll you give me to start? **1967** Green *Horse Tradin'* 93 **TX**, He was . . a big, stout, hard, using horse but not too trustworthy. **1985** Ehrlich *Solace* 98 **WY**, Compared to the arduous life of any "using horse" on a cattle or dude ranch, a bucking horse [in a rodeo] leads the life of Riley. **2006** *DARE* File—Internet **CA**, These oldtime saddles were designed and built from the ground up as a using saddle. *Ibid* **AL**, The category of using knives is intended to cover all blades that are designed for function first. *Ibid* **IL**, This colt has a good quiet disposition. Would make a good using horse. He is stocky built, and moves well. *Ibid*, The FR-8 is quite collectible in its own right but is equally valuable as a using carbine. [*Ibid* **Canada**, I wanted my best pup to go to a place where he could prove himself as a using dog on stock.]

using-ground n Also *using-place* [**use B**] **esp Sth, S Midl**
A place frequented by wild game of a particular type.

1888 *Frank Leslie's Pop. Mth.* 25.106 **KY**, We started for other ground, that had been recommended by a neighboring planter as "first-rate 'using' ground for partridges." **1893** *Harper's New Mth. Mag.* 87.681 **Sth**, The "using grounds" of the coveys are generally known or suspected by the farmer. **1913** *Oakland Tribune* (CA) 19 Sept [8]/2 (newspaperarchive.com), These flocks [of canvasback ducks]. . . were not protected in these watery "using grounds." They were harried by sneak-boxes and floating batteries. **1961** Ruark *Old Man's Boy* 234 **seNC**, Soon the bird [=quail] season would open, and I had spotted the using grounds of every covey in Brunswick County. **1975** *Appalachian Jrl.* 2.155 **wNC**, The place to which an animal or bird returns year after year is called his *usin' place.*

using horse See **using**

using-place See **using-ground**

usn pron[1] Also sp *usen, usin* *esp among Black speakers* Cf **us-uns**
1 Us.
1936 in 1976 *Weevils in the Wheat* 146 **VA** [Black], An' den dey tell usen dat we kain't cum no more tuh church school. **c1937** *Ibid* 227 **VA** [Black], Meat from de smoke house was gived usen every four week. **1972** *Atlanta Letters* **cnGA**, Efin youall get a chance drap in to see usin [etc]. **1986** Pederson *LAGS Concordance,* 1 inf, **nwTN**, Just like usn = just like us. [Inf Black]
2 We.
1949 Webber *Backwoods Teacher* 75 **Ozarks** [Black], Us'n don't like school.

usn pron[2] [Prob **us** adj + *-n* by analogy with *my/mine;* cf **hern, hisn, ourn**]
Ours.
1945 FWP *Lay My Burden Down* 34 **Sth** [Black], Old Mr. Buck Brasefield, what had a plantation 'jining us'n, was so mean to his'n [= slaves] that 'twa'n't nothing for 'em to run away. **1986** Pederson *LAGS Concordance,* 1 inf, **cnLA**, Usn [=ours]. [Inf Black]. **2001** *DARE* FIle **nwMS** [Black], I heard *us'n* for "ours" among Quitman County Miss. Blacks—but *not* "ourn."

usn adj Cf **usn** pron[1], **us** adj
Our.
1912 *Atlantic Mth.* 110.313 **Sth** [Black], Don't ax him to spile dat good tas'e in his mouf wid us'n po' truck! **1942** *Sat. Eve. Post* 14 Feb 52 **SC** [Black], I got us'n fishin' stuff loaded.

usns See **us-uns**

us's adj Also sp *uses* [Engl dial; cf *EDD* us's] **esp Sth** *esp among Black speakers* Cf **us** adj
Our; ours.
1905 Mertins *Storm Signal* 271 **sAL** [Black], Yassuh, us is done busted us's frawg-house. **1937** in 1977 *Amer. Slave Suppl. 1* 1.86 **AL**, Massa's house was a fine big white one. . . but uses houses was a one-room log cabin. **1945** FWP *Lay My Burden Down* 24 **Sth** [Black], They took all us's corn and didn't left us nothing to eat in the smoke-house. **1986** Pederson *LAGS Concordance,* 2 infs, **GA, LA**, Us's [= ours]; 1 inf, **seAL**, She was all of us's mamma. [2 of 3 infs Black]

usself pron Also *us(s)elves* [Engl dial; cf *EDD* ussels] **chiefly Sth** Cf **self B**
Ourselves.
1844 *Family Seisers* 1.138 **NYC**, Let's buy a penny 'orth to comfort usselves. **1885** Stroyer *My Life in the South* 52 **SC** [Black], I tinks us niggers need not trouble usselves about hell. **1920** Graham *Soul John* 170 **cGA**, Las' year we white people jus' had to pick the cotton usselves. **1937** in 1976 *Weevils in the Wheat* 78 **VA** [Black], Well now, we worked here an' we bought uselves a home an' paid fer it. *Ibid* 227 **VA** [Black], Dey was peach trees . . dat us could have fo usself. **1971** Grau *Condor Passes* 75 **LA**, "Make it usselves," Mama Landry told him, "best blackberry wine you find on the Lower Coast." **1998** Jones *Healing* 19 [Black], There's a lot of colored people that wouldn't want her to heal us usselves if she hadn't healed that famous Kong little girl, 'cause we's like that usselves.

ussens See **us-uns**

usta, uster, ust to See **used to**

us-uns pron Also sp *us(e)ns, ussens* [Scots, nIr dial; cf *SND us yins* (at *yin* pron. 3)] Cf **we-uns, you-uns** pron[1]
1 We.
1862 in 1872 Locke *Struggles Nasby* 48 **OH**, We are now . . the devoted friends uv the Union ez it used to be wen us uns and our breethrin uv the South run the masheen. **1863** *Atlantic Mth.* 11.13 **WV**, The Church thinks it is Christ's body an' us uns is outsiders. **1869** *Lippincott's Mag. Lit. Sci. Educ.* 3.316 **PA**, "Us'ens," for "us" or "we," is sometimes heard. **1922** Wood *Nigger* 1943 **AL** [Black], Us'n's don' need no preacher . . , do us, honey? [**1956** Ker *Vocab. W. TX* 342, With like irrelevance [to the plural of *you*], *us-uns* and *us* are offered by [1 inf].]
2 Us.
1863 *Atlantic Mth.* 11.589 **PA** [Black], An' pigs in June 's a disgrace ter Christians, let alone Presbyterians like us uns. **1869** [see **1** above]. **1875** *Harper's New Mth. Mag.* 50.20 **neFL**, To school? . . None of us-uns goes to school, my lady. **1890** (1891) Waterbury *Seven Yrs.* 71 **LA** [Black], Now de black 'uns is free, an' gwine tu de skule 'cept us 'uns. **1927** *AmSp* 3.6 **Ozarks**, First Person . . Plural . . Obj . . us, us-uns. **1928** *Crisis* (NY NY) 35.122 **GA**, Think you better dan ussens, doesn't you? **1941** *Catholic World* 153.142 **CA**, Each of usns contracted fo' fohty acres. **1961** TN Folk Lore Soc. *Bulletin* 27.36, None of usens is homesick right yit. **1996–97** in 2004 Montgomery–Hall *Dict. Smoky Mt. Engl.* 631 **wNC, eTN**, Us'uns. . . Us [6 infs].

Utah bugler n Cf **scarlet bugler**
A **beardtongue** (here: *Penstemon utahensis*).
1951 Abrams *Flora Pacific States* 3.756, *Penstemon utahensis*. . . Utah Bugler. **1957** *Plateau* 30.32 **AZ**, Firecracker flowers . . and the rare and lovely carmine-flowered Utah bugler *(Penstemon utahensis)*. . . added their color to the background of red sandstone and red sand.

Utah chub n
A chub (here: *Gila atraria*).
1889 U.S. Census Office *Census Bulletin* 2.5, *Suckers, carp, catfish, and eels* . . [include] the Utah chub. **1957** Blair et al. *Vertebrates U.S.* 100, *Gila atraria*. . . Utah chub. . . Colorado River system in Nevada, Utah, Wyoming, Colorado, California, Arizona, and New Mexico. **1963** Sigler–Miller *Fishes UT* 69, Utah chubs became established, probably by way of the bait bucket, in Fish Lake, since 1923, Strawberry Reservoir, 1933 or earlier, and Scofield Reservoir—all in the Colorado River system. **1971** Brown *Fishes MT* 87, Utah Chub. . . This chub is native to Utah in the Bonneville Basin and the upper Snake River drainage in Wyoming and Idaho. **2003** *Salt Lake Tribune* (UT) 11 Dec (Internet), A regulation change is producing larger cutthroat trout, which in turn may be controlling unwanted populations of Utah chub at the popular trout water.

Utah mile n
An indeterminate distance; also fig.
1941 Writers' Program *Guide UT* 295, This is the region of the "Utah mile," which, in the way of distance, may be anything from a half-hour to an all-day hike. **2006** *DARE* File—Internet, Greetings friends. Stacy O' Malley here, Lacy O' Malley's sister and a far better reporter by a Utah mile.

Utah oak n
=Gambel oak.
1904 U.S. Geol. Surv. *Professional Paper No. 22* 17 **CA**, Utah oak. . . Quercus utahensis [=*Q. gambelii*]. **1908** Britton *N. Amer. Trees* 339, *Utah Oak*. . . This small tree of the mountains of Utah, Colorado, Arizona, and New Mexico attains a maximum height of about 10 meters, al-

though a shrub. **1931** U.S. Dept. Ag. *Misc. Pub.* 101.21, *New Mexican oak* . . , *Vreeland oak* . . , and *Utah oak* . . are perhaps hardly more than forms, varieties, or subspecies of Gambel oak. **2004** *DARE* File—Internet **UT,** True to its name, the Gambel Oak trail climbs a hillside covered with gambel or Utah oak.

uth   See **earth**

'u'u n   [Haw]
A fish of the genus *Myripristis.*
   1905 U.S. Fish & Wildlife Serv. *Fishery Bulletin* 23.152 **HI,** *Myripristis murdjan.* . . "U'u." *Ibid* 153, This species is the common *U'u* of Hawaii, a food-fish always in the markets, taken in rocky places with the hook. **1960** Gosline–Brock *Hawaiian Fishes* 144, *Myripristis berndti* (*'U'u, Menpachi).* . . This and *Myripristis argyromus* [=*M. amaena*] are the two species most commonly speared and most abundant in the market. They are also the most difficult to separate. **1967** *DARE* (Qu. P2, . . *Kinds of saltwater fish caught around here . . good to eat*) Inf **HI**14, 'U'u [uʔu]. **1975** Sunset *HI Guide* 144, [Game fish species:] *U'u* . . squirrel fish. **2002** *DARE* File—Internet **HI,** Fish like the . . u'u (sol-

dier fish), aweoweo (glasseye), mu (emperor fish), aholehole (hawaiian flagtail) would be the "safer" fish to eat.

uv   See **of** prep

uver   See **ever** adv

uvursy n   Also *uversy*
   =**bearberry 2.**
   1899 *Plant World* 2.199 **csPA,** [Common names:] *Uversy* for *Arctostaphylos Uva-ursi.* . . An interesting survival of the old days when the plant used to be gathered in great quantities and shipped to manufacturing druggists in the cities, *uva-ursi* being the shop name for the plant. **1911** NJ State Museum *Annual Rept. for 1910* 621, *Arctostaphylos uva-ursi.* . . Bearberry, "Uvursy." . . The gathering of this plant . . employed in medicine, used to be a considerable industry in southern New Jersey. A reminiscence of this old-time trade still lingers in one of the common names of the plant down there, viz., *Uvursy.* **1924** [see **universe vine**].

uz conj, pron, prep, adv   See **as**

'uz v   See **be** A4

V n Also *Vee*

1 also *V-bill, ~-note, ~-spot:* A five-dollar bill; five dollars. **chiefly east of Missip R** See Map *old-fash* Cf **ex** n[2]

1837 *Knickerbocker* 9.96, My pocket-wallet. . . [was] distended with V's and X's to its utmost capacity. **1844** Cowell *30 Yrs.* 90 (as of 1829), By way of giving a business-like responsibility to our connexion, he became the borrower of a "V," as he called it, alias five dollars, which trifling obligation he soon increased to an "X." [*DARE* Ed: Both the author and the person spoken of here are English actors working in the US.] **1848** Lowell *Biglow* 103 **'Upcountry' MA,** My holl sheer o' the spiles would n't come nigh a V spot. *Ibid* 146, V spot, *a five-dollar bill.* **1864** *Atlantic Mth.* 14.647, A few Yankee phrases are pasted into Mr. Sludge's talk, such as "stiffish cock-tail," "V-notes," "sniggering." **1930** Williams *Logger-Talk* 30 **Pacific NW,** *Vee:* A five dollar bill. **1934** (1940) Weseen *Dict. Amer. Slang* 299, *V*—A five-dollar bill; five dollars. . . *V spot*—A five-dollar bill. **1945** O'Hara *Pipe Night* 185 **PA,** A guy is always looking out for himself. Like financially. One of these guys that they could hear a V-note dropping on the desert. **1950** *WELS* (*A five-dollar bill*) 5 Infs, **WI,** V. **1965–70** *DARE* (Qu. U28a, . . *A five-dollar bill*) 28 Infs, **chiefly east of Missip R,** V; **MA**15, V-bill; **DE**3, V-note; **NY**75, V-spot. [30 of 31 Infs old]

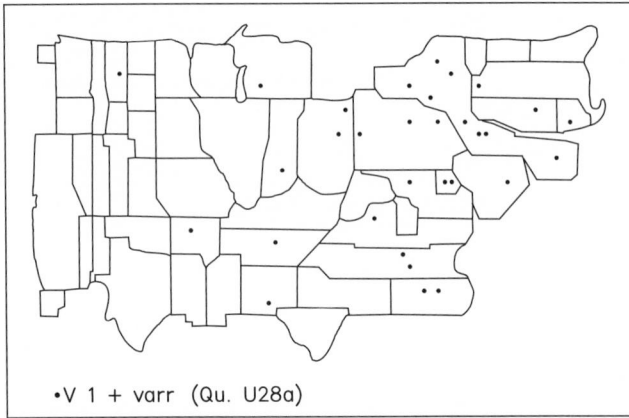

•V 1 + *varr* (Qu. U28a)

2 also *V-nickel:* A nickel. [US nickels minted from 1883–1912 were marked with a large V on the reverse] Cf **V and X (store)**

1966–69 *DARE* (Qu. U22, . . *A five-cent piece*) Infs **SC**26, 43, V; **SC**56, V [FW sugg]; **GA**77, V-nickel.

3 See **V and X (store).**

vaandoo See **vendue**

vacation n *esp freq among Black speakers*

Fig: a jail or prison sentence; hence n *vacation place* a jail or prison; phr *on vacation* serving a jail or prison sentence.

1930 Lavine *Third Degree* 223 **NYC,** One of the Italian boys . . won a twenty years' vacation in the Big House. **1970** *DARE* (Qu. V11, . . *Joking names . . for a county or city jail*) Inf **NY**249, Vacation; **MA**124, Vacation places. [Both Infs Black] **1971** Roberts *Third Ear* np [Black], *Vacation* . . time spent in jail. **1972** Claerbaut *Black Jargon* 85, *Vacation* . . a period spent in jail: *They gave the cat a vacation.* **1986** Pederson *LAGS Concordance* (*Jail*) 1 inf, **seFL,** On vacation—euphemism—over a week in jail [inf Black].

‡**vaccinate** n

A vaccination.

1976 Wolfram–Christian *Appalachian Speech* 173, Chicken pox, small pox, I had a vaccinate for small pox and they didn't take a good hold of me.

vaciero n Also *vacero* [MexSpan] **TX**

An overseer of shepherds; the tender of a sheepherding camp.

1826 in 1924 Austin *Papers* 1483 **TX,** Dn Luciano . . intended to collect his scattered flocks immediately. . . [He] rarely has communication with any one, except his Vaceros. **1892** *DN* 1.253 **TX,** *Vaciéro:* the name of the man who oversees the shepherds on a sheep ranch. **1908** Porter in *Everybody's Mag.* 19.20 **swTX,** Old man Ellison was his own *vaciero.* That means that he supplied his sheep camps with wood, water, and rations by his own labors instead of hiring a *vaciero.* **1930** Dobie *Coronado* 83 **TX,** Santos Cortez used to be *vaciero* on this ranch under the direction of Don Antonio Salinas. . . A *vaciero* is a kind of overseer and supply agent for sheep or goat camps. **1967** *DARE* Tape **TX**24, For every two herders, every two herds, they had what they called a vaciero [vɑˈseˌɾə], and he stayed at one of these camps and looked after 'em and helped this herder count 'em about once a week and picked up any of 'em that got lost.

vacuum, can of n Also *pail of vacuum*

A nonexistent item used as the basis of a practical joke.

1949 *Astounding Sci. Fiction* Dec 86, The first thing supply will send him for is a can of vacuum. **1967–69** *DARE* (Qu. HH14, *Ways of teasing a beginner or inexperienced person—for example, by sending him for a 'left-handed monkey wrench': "Go get me _____."*) Infs **CO**7, **MA**55, Can of vacuum; **MA**15, Pail of vacuum. **2006** *DARE* File—Internet, Auto Parts Sales. . . The new guy always has to find "A radiator hose for a Volkswagen Bug" or "A 12 ounce can of vacuum"—those mechanics think they are funny. *Ibid,* Check Your Tool Boxes! . . I just found an Un-opened pint can of Vacuum on the bottom of my tool box. Says on the can "replacement Vacuum for all L-79 engines." *Ibid* **AL** (as of 2003), Try this, it's fun: Call your local kiddy operated parts store and ask for a 5lb can of vacuum. Tell them your shop manual says you should have 14lbs of vacuum at an idle, and you are only indicating 12.

vagous adj |ˈveɡəs| Also sp *vagus* Cf **savagerous, vigrous**

Fierce; aggressive; important.

1944 *PADS* 2.51 **GA,** *Vagus* [ˈveɡəs]. . . Very important, powerful. "Judge Hankle is a vagus man."—A Negro woman. **1952** Hench Coll. **cVA,** Jr. Phillips told me today he knows a word I would be interested in: vagous [váy-gus] = fierce. Examples: That's a vagous dog. Don't be so vagous in your arguments.

vagrous See **vigrous**

vagus See **vagous**

valentine n Usu |ˈvælənˌtaɪn|; also |ˈvɔləntaɪn| and, by folk-etym, |ˈvælənˌtaɪm| Pronc-spp *valentime, volentine, volumtime, voluntine* [Spp with *o* for *a* are attested for the 14th and 15th cents (*OED2*) and also occur in 19th-cent Engl dial sources.] Std senses, var forms.

1768 in 2005 Monaghan *Learning to Read* 298 **RI,** A heart of gold a friend of mine / I chuse you for my volentine. **1803** *Alexandria Advt.* (VA) 22 July 1/2, [Advt:] *Books & Pamphlets* Just received for Sale. . . Art of Swimming; Book of Fate; the Union Volentine Writer [etc]. **1878** Hart *Sazerac Lying Club* 203 **NV,** I can lick the stuffin' out of the dog-goned, ornery, consarned critter what sent me this volumtime. **1899** Catherwood *Queen of Swamp* 36 **OH,** I've saw voluntines he's sent her. **1899** *Harper's New Mth. Mag.* 98.495 **Sth** [Black], When *I* sends a valentime, I sends de *quality* sort. **1912** Green *VA Folk-Speech* 471, *Volentine.* . . For *valentine.* "I got a volentine today.["] **1940** in 1944 *ADD* **nWV,** *Valentine.* . . ['vɔləntaɪn]. . . By 1 person. **1941** *Psychoanalytic Qrly.* 10.390, This sovereign use of words converted the meaningless 'valentine' to 'valen*time*'—like Christmas time. Such solutions temporarily settle problems for the child. **1942** Hall *Smoky Mt. Speech* 26 **wNC, eTN,** Substitution of [ɑ] or [ɒ] is usual [for [æ]] in . . *Valentine.* **1975** *Appalachian Jrl.* 2.151 **wNC,** A may become an *o: voluntine* (valentine). **2003** Garlock *Sisters* 269 **GA,** [Child:] Dad, can I make a Valentime for Mom?

valentine's flower n

A butterwort (here: *Pinguicula pumila*).

1893 *Atlantic Mth.* 72.788 **eFL,** I picked my first ones, which by chance were of the smaller purple species *(Pinguicula pumila).* . . At that moment a white man came up the road. "What do you call this flower?" said I. "Valentine's flower," he answered at once. . . "I could explain it better in Spanish," he continued, . . but he went on in perfectly good English: "If you put one of them under your pillow, and think of some one you would like very much to see,—some one who has been dead a long time,—you will be likely to dream of him. It is a very pretty flower," he added.

valerian n

1 Std: a plant of the genus *Valeriana.* For other names of var spp see **heliotrope 2, itchweed 2, quee, sweet anise 3, tobaccoroot 1**

2 =**lady's slipper 1.**

1841 Med. Convention OH *Proc.* 78, Cypripedium Pubescens. Lady's slipper. American valerian. **1876** Hobbs *Bot. Hdbk.* 123, Valerian, American, Cypripedium of many species. **1894** *Jrl. Amer. Folkl.* 7.100 **NH,** *Cypripedium acaule,* . . valerian. [Footnote to *valerian:*] Probably on account of its supposed efficacy as a cure for nervous disorders. The plant has a wide reputation as a remedy in such cases. **1897** *Ibid* 10.144 **ME,** *Cypripedium acaule,* . . valerian. **1950** Correll *Native Orchids* 20, *Cypripedium acaule.* . . Pink Moccasin-flower, . . Valerian, Whippoorwill-shoe. *Ibid* 24, *Cypripedium Calceolus* . . var. *pubescens* [=*C. pubescens* var *pubescens*]. . . Yellow Lady's-slipper, . . American Valerian, Monkey Flower. **1976** Bailey–Bailey *Hortus Third* 356, *C. pubescens.* . . American valerian.

valet See **ballad**

valie, valley See **value**

valley blue jay See **valley jay**

valley cottonwood n

A **cottonwood 1** (here: *Populus deltoides* subsp *wislizeni*) of the southwestern US.

1893 *Science* 22.313 **sNM,** Characteristic plants. . . Populus fremontii var. wislizeni [=*P. deltoides* subsp *w.*] (valley cottonwood). **1904** NM Ag. Exper. Station *Bulletin* 51.16, The Valley Cottonwood *(Populus Fremontii Wislizeni).* This is the common tree of the lower irrigable valleys of all the southwestern arid region from the Rio Grande to the Pacific, and forms much the greater part of the "bosques" of the Rio Grande, the Gila and the lower Pecos valleys. **1938** Van Dersal *Native Woody Plants* 198, *Populus wislizeni.* . . Valley cottonwood. **1960** Vines *Trees SW* 87, Valley Cottonwood . . is rapid-growing on moist sites. **2003** *Cochiti L. Sun Times* (NM) 15 July 4/2, For shade and flowering trees his favorites were . . Bur oak (Quercus macrocarpa), Western Catalpa (Catalpa speciosa), Valley Cottonwood (Populus fremonti "Wislizeni") [etc].

valley fever n Also *San Joaquin (valley) fever* [See quots] **SW, esp CA**

A fungal disease (coccidioidomycosis) usu affecting the lungs.

[**1877** *Daily NV State Jrl.* (Reno) 14 June 1/1, They [in the vicinity of Lovelock NV] have what they call the valley fever, which is something like dumb ague.] **1891** Carr *Pioneer Days* 30 **CA,** From 1850 to 1853 the most of the goods for the northern mines went through the [Sacramento] valley on pack-trains, and if a train made the trip without having fully one-half of the packers down with the "valley fever," they considered themselves in luck. **1937** Amer. Med. Assoc. *Jrl.* 109.66 **sCA,** The disease is often diagnosed as erythema nodosum and is popularly known in the valley as "San Joaquin Valley fever" or "desert fever." **1937** *Modesto Bee & News–Herald* (CA) 11 Nov 5/1, Twenty five thou-

sand dollars for the study of "valley fever" in the San Joaquin Valley is included in the list of cash gifts to Stanford University. **1955** *Science* 121.123 **CA,** Wild rodents are not an important reservoir for organisms that cause valley fever, or *coccidioidomycosis*—a respiratory disease found in the Southwest. **1969** *DARE* (Qu. BB13, . . *Chills and fever*) Inf **CA**134, Valley fever—had in Sacramento Valley, maybe same as malaria; (Qu. BB49, . . *Other kinds of diseases*) Inf **CA**113, The valley fever or San Joaquin fever—a lot of people have to move out of the valley. It's peculiar to here and has been studied a lot—a combination of lung trouble and great purple welts all over the body with pain like arthritis; not contagious, comes from something in the air. **1979** *Tucson Citizen* (AZ) 20 Sept sec D 1/3, He's already a full-fledged Arizonan because Homero is recovering from a bout with valley fever. **2000** Ryan *Esperanza* 260 **CA,** I worried that something dramatic had been found, until the doctor said, "You tested positive for Valley Fever."

valley foam n

A **meadow foam** (here: *Limnanthes douglasii* subsp *rosea*) native to California.

1925 Jepson *Manual Plants CA* 592, *L[imnanthes] rosea* [=*L. douglasii* subsp *r.*] . . *Valley Foam.* . . Petals white, the nerves rose-color, commonly aging or fading rosy or with a tinge of rose. **1949** Moldenke *Amer. Wild Flowers* 81, The . . *valleyfoam* . . has its many white flowers pink-veined, fading to rose color.

valley jay n Also *valley blue jay* **CA**

A **scrub jay** (here: *Aphelocoma californica*).

1867 in 1878 U.S. Army Corps Topog. Engineers *Rept. Explor. 40th Parallel* 332 **CA,** Among these [oak] trees sported . . an occasional screeching Valley Jay (Cyanocitta californica [=Aphelocoma c.]). *Ibid* 525, The common "Valley Jay" of California was observed in abundance only among the western foot-hills of the Sierra Nevada. **1910** Merriam *Dawn World* 223 **CA,** *The Northern Mewuk* . . say: Tim'-mel-le the Thunder is, or is like, *Ti'-e-te* the Valley Bluejay. **1968** *DARE* (Qu. Q16, . . *Kinds of jays*) Inf **CA**41, Not the tufted blue jay—the valley jay; **CA**99, Mountain jay and valley jay are types of blue jay; **CA**87, Valley blue jay and northern jay—the crested one.

valley oak n Also *valley white oak* [See quot 1902]

An **oak** (here: *Quercus lobata*) native to California. Also called **bottom oak 1, mush ~, roble, swamp oak 2c, white ~ 3**

[**1882** Rattan *Pop. CA Flora* 107, Quercus lobata . . The most common valley oak.] **1897** Sudworth *Arborescent Flora* 152 **CA,** *Quercus lobata.* . . Valley Oak. **1902** U.S. Natl. Museum *Contrib. Herbarium* 7.343 **CA,** The common valley white oak. . . grows in broad, fertile valleys throughout the district. **1948** *Economic Geog.* 24.138 **CA,** Several varieties of oak, including canyon live oak, blue oak, and valley oak, were intermingled with cottonwood and black walnut. **1967–70** *DARE* (Qu. T10, . . *Kinds of oak trees*) Infs **CA**4, 105, 150, 171, 185, Valley oak. **1999** *Ecological Applications* 9.165 **cCA,** Historical assessment of ecological similarity was based on the presence of coast live oak *(Quercus agrifolia),* valley oak *(Quercus lobata),* or blue oak *(Quercus douglasii)* trees >100 yr old.

valley quail n

1 also *valley partridge:* =**California quail 1.**

1857 U.S. War Dept. *Rept. Explor. Railroad* (Birds) 6.92 **CA,** Callipepla californica. . . in California . . is called the "valley quail," to distinguish it from *C. picta,* which, inhabiting the hills and highlands, has received the name of "mountain quail." **1867** in 1877 U.S. Army Corps Topog. Engineers *Rept. Explor. 40th Parallel* 333 **CA,** The . . "Valley Quail" (Lophortyx californicus) was common, and leading its young. **1887** Ridgway *N. Amer. Birds* 192, *C[allipepla] californica vallicola.* . . Valley Partridge. **1925** *Science* 61.622 **CA,** The Hungarian partridge, if . . it be once established in California, would . . eventually dominate our territory as against the less aggressive native valley quail and mountain quail. **1946** Peattie *Pacific Coast* 94, The California quail—the valley quail—is officially the State bird. **1967–70** *DARE* (Qu. Q7, *Names and nicknames for . . game birds*) Infs **CA**20, 78, 97, 130, 140, 150, 207, Valley quail; **CA**105, California valley quail; **CA**130, California valley quail—also called valley quail. **2004** *DARE* File—Internet, I have 24 valley quail eggs for sale to be delivered in early May for [$]36.00.

2 =**Gambel's quail.**

[**1917** (1923) *Birds Amer.* 2.9, Gambel's Quail. . . *Other Names.* . . Gambel's Valley Quail.] **1967** *DARE* (Qu. Q7, *Names and nicknames for . . game birds*) Inf **TX**5, Quail—valley and Mexican blues or scale quail.

valley sycamore n

A **sycamore B** (here: *Platanus racemosa*) native to California.

1967 *DARE* (Qu. T13, . . *Names* . . *for* . . *sycamore*) Inf **CA**7, Valley sycamore. **1974** L'Amour *Californios* 9 **CA,** Shading part of the dooryard was a valley sycamore, a huge old tree with mottled bark, and nearby stood several cottonwoods and another sycamore.

valley tassel(s) n

An **owl's clover** (here: *Castilleja attenuata*).

1925 Jepson *Manual Plants* CA 943, *O[rthocarpus] attenuatus* [= *Castilleja a.*] . . *Valley Tassels.* . . Spikes slender, loose below, slender above. . . Valleys and foothills. **1949** Moldenke *Amer. Wild Flowers* 275, The *valleytassels* . . differs in its more slender and elongate spikes. **2004** *DARE* File—Internet **CA,** A beautiful member of the snapdragon family, the valley tassel *(Castilleja attenuata)* looks like a big-nosed character from an animated Disney movie.

valley white oak See **valley oak**

vally, valoo See **value**

Valparaiso clover n

A clover (here: *Trifolium microdon*) native to California and the Pacific Northwest.

1944 Abrams *Flora Pacific States* 2.533, *Trifolium microdon.* . . Valparaiso Clover. . . Open hillsides and valleys. . . British Columbia to San Luis Obispo County, California; also Chile. **1961** Thomas *Flora Santa Cruz* 215 **cwCA,** Valparaiso Clover. Grassy slopes and open fields. . . March-July. **1973** Hitchcock–Cronquist *Flora Pacific NW* 275, Valparaiso c[lover], thimble c. . . *T[rifolium] microdon.* **2005** Kozloff *Plants Western OR WA* 226, *T[rifolium] microdon*—Valparaiso clover.

Valparaiso oak n

=**canyon oak 1.**

1884 Sargent *Forests of N. Amer.* 146, *Quercus chrysolepis.* . . *Live Oak. Maul Oak. Valparaiso Oak.* . . The most valuable oak of the Pacific forests. **1897** Sudworth *Arborescent Flora* 164 **CA,** *Quercus chrysolepis.* . . Valparaiso Oak. **1927** *Ecology* 8.36 **CA,** At middle altitudes on relatively stable northfacing slopes this type of [evergreen oak] forest may be seen at its best, with *Quercus chrysolepis* (canyon oak, Valparaiso oak) as the dominant tree. **1955** *Julian Apple Day* [4] **csCA** (as of c1887), Two bats, one of 'em made from native Valpariso [sic] oak. **1968–70** *DARE* (Qu. T10, . . *Kinds of oak trees*) Inf **CA**87, Valparaiso oak; **CA**200, Yellow-cup, or Valparaiso oak, or mountain live oak; (Qu. T5, . . *Kinds of evergreens, other than pine*) Inf **CA**87, Valparaiso oak— big acorns. **2004** *DARE* File—Internet **CA,** The dome of the observatory is . . hidden by tall stands of Valparaiso Oak, White Fir and Black Oak trees.

value n, v Usu |'vælju|, less freq |'væljə|; also *somewhat old-fash* |'vælə, 'vælɨ| Pronc-spp *valie, val(le)y, vally, valoo, vellew* Std senses, var forms.

1776 in 1926 VT Hist. Soc. *Proc.* 4.92, I have just thought that I wold Rite to Colo Peters By you as folows that I hear that T Paper money is of no valie their. **1781** in 1967 *PADS* 48.40 **NC,** *Valy*—'value.' **1795** Dearborn *Columbian Grammar* 139, *List of Improprieties.* . . Valley for Value. **1799** in 1956 Eliason *Tarheel Talk* 319 **ne,ceNC,** *Value*—vellew. **1845** Thompson *Pineville* 48 **cGA,** It aint the valley of the plunder, but it's the principle of the thing I looks at. **1848** Lowell *Biglow* 146 **'Up-country' MA,** Vally, *value.* **1853** Simms *Sword & Distaff* 563 **SC,** I *knows* what I've got, and knows its valley to you. **1859** in 1956 Eliason *Tarheel Talk* 319 **cNC,** *Value* . . valie. **1871** Eggleston *Hoosier Schoolmaster* 46 **sIN,** Work of inextricable valoo. **1933** *AmSp* 8.29 **eKY,** Jason don't valley no man. **1943** *LANE* Map 558 *(Value)* **NEng,** [Proncs of the type ['vælju] are widespread throughout the region. The 31 exx of proncs of the type ['vælɨ] are **chiefly nNEng,** with 24 infs describing it as obsolete or old-fashioned; 5 infs have proncs of the type ['vælə], with 2 calling it "older though still in use"; 1 inf, ceMA, [vælŭᵘ].] **1957** Combs *Lang. S. Highlanders* **sAppalachians,** Vallie—to value.

vamoose v Pronc-sp *bamoose* [**vamos;** for analogous exx of the shift from [o] to [u] in Fr and Span loans, cf **buckaroo,** *cahoo* (at **cahot**), *perloo* (at **pilau** n¹), and *pull-doo* (at **poule d'eau**).]

1 To make a hasty departure, disappear.

1848 *Farmers' Cabinet* (Amherst NH) 7 Sept 3/1,We vamoosed, and rejoined our friends. **1856** Fenner *Raising Veil* 185 **CA,** In the interim an Indian entered the tent, gathered up the tempting flap-jacks, . . and quietly vamoosed. **1893** Shands *MS Speech* 66, Vamoose [və'mus].

Bartlett gives *vamose* as colloquial in the United States, and as heard especially frequently in the Southwest. However, the common form of this word in Mississippi is *vamoose,* having exactly the same meaning as *vamose,* and being used by all classes. **1896** *DN* 1.426 **eMA, cNY,** *Vamoose:* for *vamose.* **1903** *DN* 2.335 **seMO,** *Vamose.* . . Pronounced vamoose. To disappear suddenly. **1907** Mulford *Bar-20* 117 **West,** "Yu are th' gents with th' hot-foot get-a-way that vamoosed when we got Tamale." **1907** *DN* 3.238 **nwAR,** *Vamoose.* . . To disappear suddenly. **1909** *DN* 3.386 **eAL, wGA,** *Vamoose.* . . To run away hurriedly, clean out. **1916** Lincoln *Mary-'Gusta* 184 **MA,** If you're busy you can send word for me to vamoose. **1920s** in 1944 *ADD* **cNY,** *Vamoose.* . . [vəmus]. Common. Not [vəmos]. **1926** *DN* 5.390 **ME,** *Vamoose.* (accented second syl.) . . To disappear. "He has vamoosed." "Git out o' here, vamoose!" Common. **1933** [see **vamos 1**]. **1939** Griswold *Sea Is. Lady* 80 **csSC** (as of 1868), Them soldiers vamoosed out of Bay Street double-quick. **1965–70** *DARE* (Qu. Y18, *To leave in a hurry:* "Before they find this out, we'd better _____!") 81 Infs, **scattered,** Vamoose; **ME**16, Vamoose out of here; [**GA**18, Vamboose;] (Qu. Y19, *To begin to go away from a place:* "It's about time for me to _____.") 20 Infs, **scattered,** Vamoose; (Qu. NN22b, *Expressions used to drive away children*) 10 Infs, **scattered,** Vamoose; (Qu. NN22c, *Expressions used to drive away a dog*) 10 Infs, **scattered,** Vamoose; (Qu. A19, *Other ways of saying* "I'll have to hurry": "I'm late, I'll have to _____.") Inf **OR**5, Vamoose; (Qu. Y20, *To run fast:* "You should have seen him _____!") Infs **IA**17, **TX**9, Vamoose; (Qu. Y26b, *To walk very quietly:* "The children filled their pockets and _____ out the back way.") Inf **WA**18, Vamoosed; [(Qu. II5b, *When you don't want to have anything to do with a certain person because you don't like him* . . "I'd certainly like to give him the _____.") Inf **IN**32, Vamoose;] (Qu. II22, *Expressions to tell somebody to keep to himself and mind his own business*) Infs **CT**42, **MA**51, **WI**51, Vamoose; [(Qu. LL17, . . *There's no more of something:* "The potatoes are _____.") Infs **DC**3, **ME**13, Vamoosed;] (Qu. NN22a, *Expressions used to drive away people or animals—for example, flies*) Inf **NH**14, Vamoose; (Qu. NN22d, . . *Expressions used to drive away people or animals*) Infs **IN**40, 76, **NJ**8, **NY**219, Vamoose. **1999** Mason *Clear Springs* 17 **wKY,** The idea of packing a valise fascinated me—the notion that we could stow our necessary belongings and then just vamoose.

2 To depart, steal away from (a place)—esp in phr *vamoose the ranch* to clear out; to make off. **West**

1847 in 1848 *Rough & Ready Annual* 245, They then stacked their arms and colors, and "vamoosed the ranch." **1903** (1965) Adams *Log Cowboy* 86 **TX,** Before you could say Jack Robinson, our dogies had vamoosed the ranch and were running in half a dozen different directions. **1905** *DN* 3.66 **eNE,** *Vamoose, vamose.* . . Leave, hurry away. "He vamoosed the country." **1939** Rollins *Gone Haywire* 126 **MT,** Vamoose th' kitchen an' find ef yer saddle fits. **1950** *Boston Globe* (MA) 8 Jan mag sec 11/2 **West,** That would have fixed us up so we could have vamoosed the camp.

vamos v Pronc-sp *vamose* [Span *vamos* let's go]

1 =**vamoose 1.** chiefly **West,** esp **TX**

1834 *Knickerbocker* 4.455, Be off, you good-for-nothing rascals— vamos. [*DARE* Ed: Speaker is an American in Chile.] **1847** *Yankee Doodle* 1.203 **NYC,** Nimrod took a tomahawk look at the tobacco man, and as the latter remarked, vomossed [sic] in the twinkling of a pigtail. **1848** Bartlett *Americanisms* 373, *To vamos.* A Spanish word signifying *let us go.* . . This and other Spanish expressions have lately become familiar to us through the letters of soldiers and officers from Mexico in the public prints. "I couldn't stand more than this stanza, coming from a street voice compared with which the notes of a hand-saw are positively dulcet, and I accordingly *vamosed.*"—*N.Y. Mirror,* May, 1848. **1849** [see **2** below]. **1850** Garrard *Wah-to-yah* 252 **NM,** He hollered somethin' I could n't make out. . . They *vamosed,* an' the old coon . . rared his head back. **1894** *DN* 1.325 **TX,** *Vámos, vamóse.* **1933** *AmSp* 8.1.32 **nwTX** [Ranch diction], *Vamos* (pronounced so, or *bamoose* or *vamoose*). To go away. Used with no respect for person, number, or mood of the Spanish. **1956** Ker *Vocab. W. TX* 395, Leave very fast. . . *Vamosed,* from a Spanish verb, is characteristic of the freedom the old-timer exercised in borrowing words. *Vamosed* is reported by three informants [of 67]. **1967** *DARE* (Qu. NN22b, *Expressions used to drive away children*) Inf **TX**41, Vamos ['bamoʊs]—used by English and Spanish speakers.

2 =**vamoose 2.**

1849 *Amer. Whig Rev.* 9.254, Our newly acquired State of Texas excels all others in additions and corruptions. . . When he wishes to leave, he does not say with the Yankee, "Well, we'd better be a goin'," but *"Let's vamos,"* or *"Let's vamos the ranche."* **1852** Baldwin *Southern & SW*

Sketches 141, The Camanches. . . came . . within one league of us, but *vamosed the ranch* when they learned that we were here. **1855** (1940) Chambers *Jrl.* 101 **MT**, Two Wolf Skin of Valles [=Valle's] Vamosed the Ranche. **1887** *Scribner's Mag.* 2.509 **West**, To *"vamos"* the ranch means to clear out. **1891** Sloan *Fogy Days* 134 **GA**, [I] soon had the pleasure of thinking I had paralyzed the whole party, and was now ready to vamose the ranche, cursing (in my mind) the unreliability of the entire fair sex. **1905** [see **vamoose 2**].

vamp v   Also with *it*   [*OED2 vamp* v.¹ II.4 "Now *dial.*"]   Cf **vap**

To walk; to leave.

   1914 in 1949 Handy *Treas. Blues* 78 **AL** [Black], Easy rider's got a stay away,/ So he had to vamp it—but the hike ain't far. [**1925** *DN* 5.345 **Nfld**, *Vamp it, to*. Walk.] **1970** *Current Slang* 5.2.14 [Black univ student slang], *Vamp*. . . To leave.

vamper n   [Cf *OED2 vamper* sb. 1 *"Obs."* Cited in an a1700 dict of cant; "Hence in later slang dicts."]

   1930 Shoemaker *1300 Words* 65 **cPA Mts** (as of c1900), *Vampers*—Women's stockings.

vamp it   See **vamp**

van v¹   Also *vanny*   **chiefly NEng**   *old-fash*   Cf **swan** v, **swanny** v, **vum**

To swear, declare; to swear to (someone); also used as an exclam in phr *by van*.

   1790 *Thomas' MA Spy or Worcester Gaz.* (MA) 30 Dec 1/1, In one village you will hear the phrase, "I snore"—In another, "I swowgar"—And in another, "I van you, I wunt do it." **1815** Humphreys *Yankey in England* 97 **CT**, I can hardly hold my hair on, I van. **1833** *Atkinson's Casket* 480, Oh, what a charming man you be,/ How fanciful I van you be. **a1852** in 1867 Whitcher *Widow Spriggins* 85 **cNY**, "I vanny she aint faint," says Missis Hawkins. **1889** in 1944 *ADD* **cNY**, *Van*. . . To vow, assert. **1903** (1984) Ayer *Autobiog.* 3 **NEng**, Older girls used words that I had been taught were wicked. I called them "swear words." They tried to get me to say them, "I swow, I van, I swanny, I vanny, good Lord," etc. **1959** *VT Hist.* 27.165, *By Van!* . . Obsolete. *Ibid* 166, *I Van!* . . Common. **1967** *DARE* (Qu. NN32, *Exclamations like 'I swear' or 'I vow'*) Inf **OR6**, Vanny.

van exclam, v²   See **vent** exclam, v²

van n, also attrib   [Prob < *van* a truck or dray for transporting goods]   **chiefly MI**   Cf **ark 3, wanigan 3**

A commissary in a logging camp; the camp office.

   1893 *Scribner's Mag.* 13.710 **MI**, There is the dealing out of tobacco and clothing to the men from the camp supply-chest, called the "Van." **1902** White *Blazed Trail* 62 **MI**, His wages were twenty-five dollars a month, which his van bill would reduce to the double eagle. *Ibid* 196, He would have to figure on blankets, harness . . blacksmith tools . . van-goods. *Ibid* 218, Thorpe looked through the ledger and van book, and . . handed the man his slip. **1905** *U.S. Forest Serv. Bulletin* 61.52 [Logging terms], *Van*. . . The small store in a logging camp in which clothing, tobacco, and medicine are kept to supply the crew. (N[orth] W[oods], L[ake] S[tates]). **1942** Beck *Songs MI Lumberjacks* 263, He staggered clear across the van—/ The van is the office, you know. **1942** *AmSp* 17.225 [Loggers' talk], *Van*. The camp store. A Lake states term. **1969** Sorden *Lumberjack Lingo* 137 **NEng, Gt Lakes**, *Van*—1. The small store in a logging camp in which clothing, tobacco, and medicine were kept to supply the crew. Same as wanigan. 2. A large iron chest banded with metal strips for reinforcement and used to store clothing, tobacco, and medicines in the early shanty days.

vance   See **vent** exclam, v²

vandoo, vandue   See **vendue**

V and X (store) n   Also *V*   [*V 2, ex* n²]   =**five-and-ten 1.**

   1942 *AmSp* 17.93 [Pitchmen's cant], *V and X*. Any five-and-ten-cent chain store. **1942** *Amer. Mercury* 55.223.96 **Harlem NYC** [Black], *V and X*—five-and-ten-cent store. **1965** *Tri-City Herald* (Pasco WA) 26 Sept *Family Weekly* 12/2, *Junior Treasure Chest*. . . Hi, Math Fans! When you say you go to a V and X store, where do you go? . . The five and ten. **1967** *DARE* (Qu. U43, . . *The kind of store where most articles cost . . only five or ten cents;* not asked in early QRs) Inf **NY34**, V and X store. **1971** *Suburbanite Economist* (Chicago IL) 22 Aug 4/3, In days gone by. . . The penny had value, also the nickle and dime—remember

the V and X? That was the five and dime store. **2006** *DARE* File—Internet **Chicago IL** (as of c1940), My father. . . worked for the Jones boys. . . They started the policy racket in Chicago, and they had the five and dime store. They used to call it the "V"—like the "V and X store," you know, for roman numerals.

vanella   See **vanilla**

vang vang oil   See **van van oil**

vanilla n   Usu |vəˈnɪlə|; also |vəˈnɛlə| Pronc-spp *fan ella, vanella, vinilla*   Cf **Illinois, milk, since**

A   Forms.

   1915–25 in 1944 *ADD* **NY**, Vanilla. . . [vəˈnɛlə]. Usual. **1930s** *Ibid* **eWV**, Vanilla. . . vanella. Very common. **1941** *Ibid* **nWV**, Vanilla. . . [vənɛlə]. **1943** *AmSp* 18.264 **VA**, The lowering of [ɪ] to [ɛ] is fairly common throughout the state in words like . . vanilla. . . [vənɛlə]. **1974** Gilbreth *Dictionary* 8 **seSC**, *Fan ella*: The flavor of white ice cream. **1985** *NYT Mag.* 3 Nov 15/3, I think the vast majority of American ice-cream lovers says *vin-El-la*, and a minority becoming minuscule says *vuh-Nil-uh*. **1986** *DARE* File, Vanilla [vənɛlə]. . . is usual in contemporary New York City and Philadelphia English (I have seen home-made signs for "vanella ice cream" in New York City). . . The [ɪ] pronunciation is probably more widespread. **1990** *Ibid* **cPA**, Vanilla [vəˈnɛlə]—"everyone says it."

B   Sense.

See **vanilla plant 1.**

vanilla bug n   [Appar from the odor of the fluid exuded]   =**whirligig beetle.**

   1940 Teale *Insects* 150, Elsewhere they [=whirligig beetles] have local names such as "Vanilla bugs" and "dishwashers."

vanilla grass n

1   A **holy grass**, esp *Hierochloe odorata* in the northeastern US and also *H. occidentalis* in California and the Pacific Northwest.

   1843 Torrey *Flora NY* 2.419, *Hierochloa borealis* [=*Hierochloe odorata*]. . . Seneca Grass. Vanilla Grass. **1887** *Atlantic Mth.* 60.425 **MA**, By this time the holy-grass is nodding its brown tassels in the meadow. . . Why should it also be called Seneca grass, or indeed vanilla grass, for the odor is not like that of vanilla? **1891** *Century Dict.* 6695, *Vanilla-grass*. . . A grass of the genus *Sevastana* [=*Hierochloe*], chiefly *S. odorata* [=*H. o.*] . . The large-leafed vanilla-grass is *S. macrophylla* [=*H. occidentalis*] of California. **1904** *Science* 19.72 **AK**, A fragrant grass, a species of *Hierochloe* called locally 'vanilla grass,' occurs. **1914** Georgia *Manual Weeds* 38, *Vanilla-grass*. . . has an odor much resembling the Vanilla bean. **1973** Hitchcock–Cronquist *Flora Pacific NW* 644, *Hierochloe*. . . Sweetgrass; Vanillagrass. **1992** *Ploughshares* Fall 85 **cNY**, The sweet scent of vanilla grass, *Hierochloe odorata*, fills the air.

2   A similarly sweet-smelling, naturalized vernal grass (*Anthoxanthum odoratum*).   Cf **sweet grass 1c**

   1888 *Stevens Point Jrl.* (WI) [28 Jan 3]/4 (newspaperarchive.com), There can not be a nicer gift for an invalid or delicate person than one of those decorated fans or hand screens of sweet vernal or vanilla grass which are so sweet that they make a whole room fragrant. **1930** *U.S. Natl. Park Serv. Glimpses Natl. Monuments* 40 **CA**, Sweet vernal, or vanilla grass, adds to the fragrance of the trails. **2004** *DARE* File—Internet, *Sweet Vernal Grass . . Anthoxanthum odoratum*. . . This grass has a very strong "freshly cut hay" scent. It is occasionally found in herb displays as "Vanilla Grass".

vanilla leaf n   [From the odor]

1   A plant (*Achlys triphylla*) native to the Pacific region of the US. Also called **angel leaves, butterflies 1, deer-foot 2, elkhorn 1, mayapple 6, new-mown hay, smell-leaves, sweet clover 3, sweetleaf 2, sweet-after-death, vanilla plant 2, wild vanilla 2**

   1896 *Mazama* 1.109 **NW**, *Achlys triphylla*. . . The sweet-smelling leaves of the plant have suggested the name "vanilla leaf." **1920** *DN* 5.84 **WA**, *Vanilla leaves*. Achlys leaves. **1949** Peattie *Cascades* 231 **Pacific NW**, The plant with three large, fan-shaped leaflets and a compact spike of small white flowers at the end of a long slender stalk is vanilla-leaf, so named for its odor. **1973** Hitchcock–Cronquist *Flora Pacific NW* 142, *A[chlys] triphylla*. . . Vanillaleaf, deerfoot. **1994** Guterson *Snow Falling* 153 **nwWA**, Everything was familiar and known to her here . . the upturned root wads hung with vine maple, the toadstools, the ivy, the salal, the vanilla leaf [etc]. **2004** *DARE* File—Internet **wWA**, The aromatic smell in these woods during October is mostly the leaves of the vanilla leaf 'dying back' for the winter dormant season.

2 =**vanilla plant 1.**

1830 Rafinesque *Med. Flora* 2.237, *Liatris*. . . The *L. odoratissima* [= *Carphephorus o.*] or *Vanilla leaf,* used . . to perfume Havana segars. **1876** Hobbs *Bot. Hdbk.* 123, Vanilla leaf, Carolina vanilla, Liatris odoratissima. **1938** Baker *FL Wild Flowers* 226, *Trilisa odoratissima.* . . Vanilla-leaf. Heads purple. . . Dried leaves vanilla-scented. **1971** Krochmal *Appalachia Med. Plants* 254, *Trilisa odoratissima.* . . Vanilla leaf, vanilla plant. . . It is used as a blend with tobacco, and because it is high in coumarin it has been used to flavor medicinal compounds. **2004** *DARE* File—Internet, *Trilisa odoratissima.* . . Common Names—Vanilla trilisa, deerstongue, dogtongue, vanilla leaf, vanilla plant.

vanilla plant n

1 also *vanilla:* A perennial plant *(Carphephorus odoratissimus)* with an odor of vanilla when drying, native to much of the southern US. Also called **buck tongue, Carolina vanilla, deer-tongue 1, dog's tongue 1, Florida vanilla, hound's tongue 2, Indian lettuce 4, vanilla leaf 2, wild vanilla**

1835 (1843) Simms *Yemassee* 2.58 **SC**, The dried leaves of the native and finely odorous vanella [sic] . . diffused a grateful perfume upon the gale. **1851** *De Bow's Rev.* 10.631 **TX**, The vanilla plant grows wild. It can be successfully cultivated, and will become a commercial commodity of inestimable value. **1875** (1973) Lanier *Florida* 32 **nFL**, You must know that in the low grounds of the Ocklawaha grows what is called the vanilla-plant—a plant with a leaf much like that of tobacco when dried. **1901** Lounsberry *S. Wild Flowers* 501, *Vanilla-plant. Trilisa odoratissima* [=*Carphephorus o.*] **1927** Boston Soc. Nat. Hist. *Proc.* 38.214 **Okefenokee GA**, *Trilisa odoratissima*—'Dog-tongue'; 'deer-tongue'; 'vanilla.' **1975** Duncan–Foote *Wildflowers SE* 198, *Vanilla-plant.* . . Tons of leaves are collected from the wild each year and sold for flavoring smoking tobacco. **1996** in 2007 *DARE* File—Internet **seLA**, Bloomed September 10–October 3, 1996: . . *Carphephorus odoratissima,* Vanilla plant—Perennial herb, 4–5′ tall, purplish flower clusters.

2 =**vanilla leaf 1.**

1920 *Torreya* 20.21 **WA**, *Achlys triphylla.* . . Vanilla plant.

vanny See **van** v[1]

vant See **vent** exclam, v[2]

'vantage See **advantage**

vants See **vent** exclam, v[2]

van van oil n Also *(essence of) van van, vang vang oil, van van holy oil* **orig New Orleans LA** *esp freq among Black speakers*

A perfume much used in **hoodoo** n **1a.**

1929 *Amer. Mercury* 17.299, Our Lucky Van Van Oil and Lucky Salts are used by many for good luck in their home and in winning in love, games and everything. **1931** *Jrl. Amer. Folkl.* 44.411 **LA** [Black], Essence of Van Van: Ten percent Oil of Lemon Grass in alcohol. . . used for luck and power of all kinds. It is the most popular conjure drug in Louisiana. **c1938** in 1974 *Amer. Slave* 9.4.113 **AR** [Black], I just got to git some High John the Conqueror root an' . . five finger grass, van van oil . . an' drawin' powder. Now, missy, the way I fixes that sure will ward off evil an' bring heaps of good luck. **c1938** in 1970 Hyatt *Hoodoo* 1.16 **New Orleans LA** [Black], Yo' doesn't light the candle with a match, yo' git *van-van.* . . Dat's whut ah use, *van-van,* an' put a little in de saucer an' light de *van-van* an' hold de candle to dat. *Ibid* 694 **swTN** [Black], If a *hustlin' womans* [=a prostitute] want tuh git out on de streets an' be lucky, make money, she'd use de *van-van holy oil. Ibid* 695 **swAL** [Black], Hit's whut chew call *van-van oil.* . . An' every time yo' see de law . . yo' sprinkle yo' place of business good wit dat water every morning. **c1940** in 2006 *DARE* File—Internet **Chicago IL**, [Catalog advt from a distributor of African-American hoodoo supplies:] Rabbits Foot—Free!—Van Van Oil. . . We sell only as a Curio and give a *Free* Bottle of *Van Van Oil.* **1940** Writers' Program *Guide TX* 233 **cTX**, From an establishment on Central Avenue come "wish-fulfillments" in ten-cent packages; . . and "van van oil" to shake the jinx. **1940** Writers' Program *Guide GA* 260 **ceGA** [Black], At small shops can be purchased such remedies as Vang-Vang Oil, Lucky Mojoe Drops of Love, or Mojoe Incense. **1988** Naylor *Mama Day* 90 **sSC, GA coasts** [Black], Walk naked in the moonlight stinking with Van-Van oil—and it won't do a bit of good. **2006** *DARE* File—Internet **MI**, Van

Van Oil—$8.75. . . Van Van—General all-purpose oil to change your luck for the good, feed any mojo or toby bag, consecrate your altar and do general spiritual cleansing.

vap v [Perh var of **vamp**]

To run quickly.

1941 *Sat. Eve. Post* 15 Feb 18 **AL** [Black], Ole Jake [=a dog] is sho vappin'!

vaquero n, also attrib [Span] **chiefly SW, esp TX** Cf **buckaroo**

A cowboy, esp one of Mexican nationality or ethnicity.

1844 (1954) Gregg *Commerce* 150 **NM**, The shanks of the *vaquero* spurs are three to five inches long. **1863** Hittell *Resources CA* 385, *Vaquero* . . a herdsman. **1887** *Scribner's Mag.* 2.509 **West**, Instead of herder, some say *vaquero* (Sp., cow-herd). **1892** *DN* 1.253 **TX**, *Vaquéro:* cowboy. From *vaca,* a cow. Occasionally heard on the border. **1929** Dobie *Vaquero* 1 **swTX**, In Southwest Texas, where sixty years ago and more I was "running cattle," cowboys were—and still are—generally referred to as "vaqueros". . . *Vaquero*—from *vaca* (cow)—was originally applied only to Spanish or Mexican cowboys. But from an early day, Texans, especially those near the border, have used the word without reference to race. **1934** White *Folded Hills* 136 **CA**, He could throw a knife, not by the blade, *vaquero* fashion, but from the flat of his hand. **1937** *DN* 6.620 **swTX**, The Texas cowboy is less frequently called . . *vaquero,* probably because of the connotation . . *vaquero* being a Mexican word for cowboy. **1940** Writers' Program *Guide TX* 670, *Vaquero:* A Mexican herdsman, cowboy. **c1940** in Lib. of Congress *Amer. Memory: WPA Life Hist.* (Internet) **TX**, I hunted and fished and ran races with the dashing vaqueros. **1969** *DARE* Tape **CA**113, We had more saloons per capita than any other town in the West, from the vaqueros, and from the ranchers, and from the people of the oil fields . . unmarried men particularly. **2004** *Intelligencer* (Doylestown PA) 13 Sept sec D 3/4, In 1873 . . Joseph F. Glidden changed the West forever with his patent on a new kind of fence: the barbed wire. "The Devil's Rope," as it was sometimes called, spelled the end of the traditional vaquero.

vara n [Span] **SW, esp NM, TX** *obs exc as a legal term*

A unit of length varying somewhat at different times and places, but usu between 33 and 34 inches; in Texas fixed early in the 19th cent by convention (and by law in 1919) at 33 ⅓ inches.

1831 in 1858 Dewees *Letters TX* 139, One labor shall be composed of one million square varas. **1854** (1932) Bell *Log TX–CA Trail* 35.296, Time, morning, place twenty five *varas* from the fifth wheel of the Ambulanche. **1869** Browne *Adventures* 259 **AZ**, This palatial edifice occupies a square of several hundred varas. **1892** *DN* 1.195 **TX**, *Vára:* a rod; a lineal land measure, 0.93118 American yards. . . Still the only measure in use in Texas. **1897** *New Engl. Mag.* 22.572 **AZ**, The building is described as "a large edifice . . with walls two varas thick." **1910** Hart *Vigilante Girl* 208 **nCA**, He had to take a hundred-vara lot for a legal fee—client could n't pay anything else. **1937** in Lib. of Congress *Amer. Memory: WPA Life Hist.* (Internet) **NM**, Some of the Americans called their grants "terrenas" but the correct name is Terreno. . . And a vara, by which the colonists measured the land, was not a yard of thirty-six inches, but thirty-three inches. **1940** Writers' Program *Guide TX* 670, *Vara:* Linear measure approximating 33 ⅜ inches. **1958** in 2006 (acc) Lexis–Nexis Legal Research *State Case Law: NM* (Internet), The appellee's title commenced with the Las Vegas Grant to the Pueblo of La Senora de Los Dolores de Las Vegas, by the Republic of Mexico, March 23, 1835, and an allotment of 200 varas of land, . . by the Constitutional Justice under the Mexican government. **1998** in 2007 *Ibid: TX*, The Tuckness defendants' expert . . testified that an "impossible" 388 varas call rendered the 1941 deed ambiguous as applied to the ground.

vara dulce n

1 A **bee brush** (here: *Aloysia* spp).

1929 Dobie *Vaquero* 202 **swTX**, Sweet scented white brush, and sweeter *vara dulce,* cousins, prickly without thorns, and fine for bees. **1940** Writers' Program *Guide TX* 450 **csTX**, Here also grows every type of thorny vegetation known to the Southwest: the catclaw, huajillo, agarita, *vara dulce* [etc]. **1960** Vines *Trees SW* 886, *Aloysia wrightii.* . . Vernacular names for the plant are . . Vara Dulce, and Wright's Lippia. *Ibid* 887, *Aloysia macrostachya.* . . This species is also commonly known as Vara Dulce. *Ibid* 888, *Lippia ligustrina* [=*Aloysia gratissima*]. . . Vernacular names are Bee-brush, White-brush, . . Vara Blanca, Vara Dulce [etc]. **2004** *Houston Chron.* (TX) 22 Apr (Internet), Past the screen of Spanish oaks . . and just the other side of the wall of *vara dulce* sat a seemingly empty and open patch of the Texas Hill Country.

2 A **kidneywood** (here: *Eysenhardtia texana*).

1922 U.S. Natl. Museum *Contrib. Herbarium* 22.2.444 **TX,** *Eysenhardtia texana. . .* "Vara dulce." **1970** Correll *Plants TX* 819, *Eysenhardtia texana. . . Vara dulce.* Shrub, usually 2–3 m. tall. **2004** *DARE* File—Internet **sTX,** *Texas Kidneywood,* Vara Dulce—Eysenhardtia texana. . . Much-branched, large shrub with small leaflets and many fragrant white flowers.

varebell(s) n

A **false hellebore 1.**

1933 Small *Manual SE Flora* 276, *Veratrum. . .* Varebells. False hellebores. *Ibid* 277, *V[eratrum] viride. . . Vernal-varebell. . .* Large quantities of roots are gathered in the Appalachians. **2004** *DARE* File—Internet, [Caption:] Varebell (Veratrum Parviflorum)—Blue Ridge Parkway—VA.

vargrous See **vigrous**

varied creeping warbler See **creeping warbler**

varied thrush n

Std: a thrush (*Ixoreus naevius*) native to coastal rain forests from central Alaska to northern California. Also called **Alaska robin, mountain ~, Oregon ~, painted ~, swamp ~ 1d, winter ~ 2**

variety shower n chiefly Nth Cf **greenback shower, pantry ~, stork ~**

A gift shower, usu for a bride, at which all sorts of household items are given.

1904 *Post-Std.* (Syracuse NY) 26 Aug 9/5, Mr. and Mrs. F.E. Goodjon gave a variety shower last evening at their home . . in honor of Miss Helen M. Draper. **1908** *Decatur Daily Rev.* (IL) 5 Oct 3/1, Young lady friends gave a variety shower . . for Miss Rosella Hoffner, whose marriage . . occurs on Tuesday. **1910** *NE State Jrl.* (Lincoln) 16 Jan sec B 2/2, Miss Emma Tyler entertained a company of young people at a variety shower for Miss Mabel McClanahan, whose marriage . . was to take place the following Saturday. **1920** *Hopewell Herald* (NJ) 2 June 8/4, A surprise variety shower was tendered Miss Beatrice Shepherd a few evenings ago in honor of her approaching marriage. . . [She] received many gifts of glass, silver, linen, pictures, money and books. **1941** *Warren Times–Mirror* (PA) 5 Aug 6/1, A variety shower was held for two newlywed couples. . . and they were presented many pretty and useful gifts for the new homes. **1968** *Catskill Mt. News* (Margaretville NY) 4 July 10/7, Mrs. Robert Delamarter gave Miss Patricia Ann Bolin a variety shower on June 17. The family, returning home that night, found the home decorated with streamers and balloons, with a guest of honor chair under an umbrella, showered with kitchen gadgets. **1968–69** *DARE* (Qu. FF3, . . '*Showers' or 'gift parties'*) Inf **NY**228, Variety shower; **NJ**6, Variety shower—a kind of wedding shower; **NJ**16, Variety shower—wedding coming—take small things bride can use, could be kitchen shower. **1972** *Lewiston Eve. Jrl.* (ME) 7 Aug 3/4, *Entertained At Variety Shower At Her Home*—Miss Jean Whittingham whose marriage takes place later this week was honored Friday evening. **2000** *Wellsboro Gaz.* (PA) 10 May 7/1, A variety shower is being held for Wayne and Elaine Strange who recently lost most of their possessions in a fire.

varmit n [Var of *varmint*]

1840 (1841) Thomas *Howard Pinckney* 30, Did the varmit bite or scratch you? **1856** *U.S. Democratic Rev.* 37.539 **NJ,** The cussed varmit rapped his teeth into Tom's leg. **1897** Byron-Curtiss *Life Nat Foster* 138 **Upstate NY,** With . . my faithful bitch dog Rose by my side, who could scent any kind of varmit a mile away, I started off. **1940** Stuart *Trees of Heaven* 266 **eKY,** Jest like varmits. **1966–70** *DARE* (Qu. J2, . . *Joking or uncomplimentary words . . for dogs*) Inf **VA**68, Varmit; (Qu. P29, . . '*Gophers' . . other name*) Inf **WA**20, Varmit; (Qu. Z12, *Nicknames and joking words meaning 'a small child': "He's a healthy little _____."*) Inf **SC**2, Varmit. [All Infs old] **1972** Thomas *Pop. Dict. Ozarks Talk* 91, Varmit, varmint. . . Any of the larger wild animals in the Ozarks. **1973** Allen *LAUM* 1.320 **Upper MW** (as of c1950), Varmints. . . varmits [6 infs, **MN, IA, ND, NE**]. **1989** Pederson *LAGS Tech. Index* 204 **Gulf Region,** Varmint. [Of 914 infs, 6 gave proncs of the type ['vɑmɪt(s)]; 1 inf, ['vɔrmɪts]; 1 inf, ['vɑrmɪts].] **2006** *DARE* File—Internet **SD,** Mid-Night goes varmit hunting for prairie dogs.

varnish See **varnished car**

varnish bush n

A **tar bush** (here: *Flourensia cernua*).

1913 *N. Amer. Fauna* 35.21 **NM,** *Flourensia cernua,* Varnish Bush. **1968** Schmutz et al. *Livestock-Poisoning Plants AZ* 138, Varnishbush. . . The fruits of this shrub, if eaten in large amounts, may cause poisoning of sheep and goats. **1985** Dodge *Flowers SW Deserts* 83, Varnishbush. . . *Flourensia cernua.* . . These resinous, much-branched shrubs are found on plains and mesas . . from western Texas to eastern Arizona.

varnished car n Also *varnish car, varnished box,* ~ *wagon* old-fash Cf **cushion B1**

A railroad passenger car; hence nouns *(string of) varnish, varnished job,* ~ *shot* a passenger train.

1885 *St. Joseph Traveler & Herald* (MI) 9 May [2]/3 (newspaperarchive.com), If you never rode in a varnished car before . . you will probably roam up and down . . meandering over the feet of the porter while he is making up the berths. **1891** *Star & Sentinel* (Gettysburg PA) 20 Jan 1/8, When a trainman prospers and gets a passenger train he speaks of his good fortune as running varnished cars and eating pie. **1926** *AmSp* 1.250 **PA** [Railroading terms], Locomotives are "mills" or "kettles" . . passenger car, "varnished car." **1927** *DN* 5.466 [Underworld jargon], *Varnish car.* . . A passenger car. **1931** *Writer's Digest* 11.64 [Railroad terms], *Varnished Wagons*—Passenger train equipment. **1938** Beebe *High Iron* 225 [Railroad terms], *Varnish:* Passenger-cars or train, dating from time when passenger equipment was highly lacquered. **1945** Hubbard *Railroad Ave.* 365, *Varnish*—Passenger train. Also called *varnished shot, varnished job, varnished boxes, string of varnish, varnished wagons,* etc. These nicknames are rarely applied to modern streamliners. **1946** in 1953 Botkin–Harlow *Treas. Railroad Folkl.* 350, The big shack was . . blowing smoke . . of the time he was a baby lifter on the varnish. Or, to say it another way: The brakeman was . . boasting . . of the time he was a brakeman on a passenger train.

varnish leaf n [See quot 1999] FL

An evergreen shrub or small tree (*Dodonaea viscosa*) native to southern Florida, Arizona, and Hawaii.

1923 *Jrl. NY Bot. Garden* 24.212 **sFL,** There are some species, both of woody and herbaceous plants, that occur only on the Keys. For example . . varnish-leaf (*Dodonaea Ehrenbergii* [=*D. viscosa*]). **1933** Small *Manual SE Flora* 821, *Dodonaea.* . . Erect shrubs or trees, with usually viscid foliage. . . *Varnish-leaves.* **1971** Craighead *Trees S. FL* 203, The more common trees in the pine lands are Dade County pine, rough leaf, bustic, varnish leaf [etc]. **1999** FL Coop. Ext. Serv. *Fact Sheet FPS 181* 1, *Dodonaea viscosa.* . . The shiny green leaves of this shrub have a varnished appearance that gives this plant its most widely used common name. . . Varnish-Leaf. **2004** *Miami Herald* (FL) 25 Apr (Internet) **sFL,** Here are some low-maintenance shrubs . . varnish leaf (colorful seed capsules) [etc].

varnishleaf ceanothus n

A **snowbrush 1** (here: *Ceanothus velutinus*).

1940 Jenkins *Population Study Mice* 66 **CA,** *Ceanothus velutinus.* Varnish-leaf Ceanothus. **1961** Thomas *Flora Santa Cruz* 235 **cwCA,** *C[eanothus] velutinus.* . . Sticky Laurel, Tobacco Bush. Varnishleaf Ceanothus. **1995** in 2004 *DARE* File—Internet **OR,** Varnish leaf ceanothus is locally plentiful in the early seal stage. **2002** MT Nat. Hist. Center *Field Notes Qrly.* Fall 4, In western Montana we know it as *Ceanothus velutinus,* a plant with more common names than zip codes in California. Varnish leaf ceanothus, slick leaf ceanothus, mountain balm, buckbrush, cinnamon bush and more.

varnish sumac n

=**dwarf sumac.**

1940 Clute *Amer. Plant Names* 126, *R[hus] copallina.* . . Varnish sumach. **1974** (1977) Coon *Useful Plants* 57, *Rhus copallina*—Shining sumac, varnish sumac, common sumac. . . It contains tannin. **2004** (acc) Forest Products Lab. Center for Wood Anatomy Research *Tech. Transf. Fact Sheet* (Internet), *Rhus copallina.* . . Upland Sumac, Varnish Sumac [etc].

varnish tree n Also *Japan varnish tree* [Appar by confusion with *Toxicodendron vernicifluum,* from which the lacquer of China and Japan is made; see quot 1916 at **b** below]

Any of var trees introduced from eastern Asia, as:

a also *Chinese varnish tree, Japanese* ~: The Chinese parasol tree (*Firmiana simplex*).

1802 in 1871 *Amer. Bibliopolist* 3.52 **Charleston SC,** [Letter from

Charles Cotesworth Pinckney:] As he may be desirous of having at his country seat on the Schuylkill some plants which grow well here, I in this enclosure transmit a few. Among them are some seeds of the Sterculia Platani Folia, or Varnish Tree of China. It does not produce the deleterious varnish of that country, but a different sort which is perfectly innocent. About fourteen years ago Mr. Michaux . . received some seeds of this plant. . . Only one of these vegetated, and the plant arising from it he gave to me. . . From the seeds it has produced many trees . . are now growing in the State. **1844** *S. Patriot* (Charleston SC) 15 Jan 2/2, The Varnish Tree. This tree may be seen . . at the corner of Bull and Coming streets. The bark . . is very green, smooth and strikingly beautiful. . . I have not sufficiently examined it to be able to express an opinion on its merits as a shade tree. **1855** *De Bow's Rev.* 19.718 **MS,** The Varnish tree (*Stericlua platynifolia* [sic]) is so called from its beautiful glossy bark, and large rich colored leaves, which seem all to have been recently coated with green varnish. **1886** [see **c** below]. **1913** Harper *Economic Botany AL* 268, *Firmiana platanifolia.* . . Japanese or Chinese Varnish Tree. **1941** Writers' Program *Guide LA* 22, Varnish tree, or Firmania [sic], is present in New Orleans as well as in Shreveport and other upland towns and cities. **1947** *Amer. Midland Naturalist* 37.735 **SC,** *F[irmiana] simplex.* . . Chinese Parasoltree; Japanese Varnishtree.—Occasionally escaped from cultivation. **1970** *Gt. Bend Tribune* (KS) 6 Sept 9/2, Another home had a beautiful smoke tree or as several call them a varnish tree. **2003** *DARE* File—Internet **TX,** The Chinese parasol tree (Firmiana simplex) has immense leaves measuring about a foot across. . . The seed pods open in an unusual petal-like formation with the seeds attached to the sides of each section, at the same time discharging a brown fluid that looks like varnish (hence another common name: varnish tree).

b =**tree of heaven. Cf false varnish tree**

1865 *3 Lect. MI State Ag. Soc.* 91 **MI,** Some recent developments, however, prove that the very best tree for binding dune sands, and one at the same time extremely tolerant of heat and cold, dryness and moisture, is the Japan Varnish Tree—*Ailanthus glandulosa.* The planting of this tree upon some of our dunes, in connection with the *Arundo arenana,* is an experiment well worth the trial. **1868** Cronise *Nat. Wealth CA* 374, The Japan varnish tree may be seen, in healthy growth, in the city gardens of San Francisco, and it would pay to cultivate. [**1916** Washington Acad. Sci. *Jrl.* 6.490, The seeds of the Tree of Heaven were first sent from China to the Royal Society of London in 1757 by Pierre d'Incarville. . . He sent the seeds under the impression that they were secured from the lacquer or varnish tree at Nanking.] **1976** Bailey–Bailey *Hortus Third* 42, [*Ailanthus*] *altissima.* . . *Varnish tree.* . . Naturalized in most of the U.S. except the extreme north.

c =**goldenrain tree.**

1886 *Gardener's Mth. & Horticulturist* 28.251, The Japan Varnish Tree.—Some years ago Northern nurserymen used this name for the Kolreuteria [sic] paniculata, but the late W.R. Prince protested so strongly against it, that the name was dropped. . . But in the South, at this time, Japan Varnish tree means the Sycamore Sterculia [=*Firmiana simplex*] . . which is one of the most popular large growing shade trees in that section. **1903** Peet *Trees* 151 **NYC,** Koelreuteria or Varnish Tree. *Koelreuteria paniculata.* **1931** Otis *MI Trees* 278, China-tree. . . Also, but incorrectly, called the *Varnish-tree* and *Pride of India.* **1955** *S. Folkl. Qrly.* 19.234, Golden Rain Tree. . . Varnish Tree. **2002** *DARE* File—Internet **WV,** The varnish tree, or Koelreuteria paniculata, . . is not only tough and pretty but pretty darn tough in handling any kind of environmental adversity thrown at it.

varnish weed n Cf **rosinweed 2**

A **gum plant 1.**

1914 *DN* 4.114 **cKS,** *Varnish-weed.* . . A weed that exudes, chiefly from the flowering heads, a resinous, pungent, aromatic gum.

vary See **very**

varying hare n

Std: a hare *(Lepus americanus)* native to the northern US and south into the Rocky Mountain regions and the Alleghenies. Also called **gray rabbit 2, jackrabbit 1, mountain hare, snowshoe rabbit, swamper 8, swamp hare 2, ~ rabbit 3, timber rabbit**

vasarator, vascinator See **fascinator**

vase flower See **vase vine**

vase-maker wasp n

A **potter wasp** (here: *Eumenes fraternus*).

1885 Hubbard *Insects* 187, The Vase-maker Wasp . *Eumenes fraterna.* . . The female of this wasp is solitary and makes single cells of mud and sand. . . [T]he structure resembles a globe-shaped flask, with a very short neck. **1892** Gibson *Sharp Eyes* 47 **CT,** These clay pots of the vase-maker wasp. . . [are] made of sand and yellow mud.

vase vine n Also *vase flower* [See quots 1949, 1979]

A **virgin's bower,** usu *Clematis viorna* in much of the eastern US and *C. hirsutissima* in much of the western US.

1903 Small *Flora SE U.S.* 439, *Viorna Viorna* [=*Clematis v.*] . . In woods, southern Pennsylvania to Ohio, West Virginia, Georgia and Alabama. . . *Leather-flower. Vase-vine.* **1949** Moldenke *Amer. Wild Flowers* 7, The *leatherflowers* or *vase-vines.* . . are all perennial herbs or vines, with . . handsome urn- or vaselike flowers somewhat like an individual hyacinth flower. Best known is *V[iorna] urnigera* [=*Clematis viorna*], the *common vasevine.* **1963** *Amer. Midland Naturalist* 69.353 **FL,** *C[lematis] glaucophylla.* . . Vase vine. Rocky woods, frequent. *C. reticulata.* . . Vase vine. Upland woods, frequent. **1973** Hitchcock–Cronquist *Flora Pacific NW* 129, Vasefl[ower]. . . *C[lematis] hirsutissima.* **2001** Porcher–Rayner *Guide Wildflowers SC* 93, Invariably some of the following herbaceous wildflowers occur in the community: . . vase-vine *(Clematis reticulata).*

vast See **avast**

vat n

1932 *DN* 6.234 **West,** *Vat.* This word is sometimes used in California and Arizona, generally in the plural, for a dried-up place around a water hole.

vaudoo, vaudoux See **voodoo** n

vault v

1933 *AmSp* 8.1.53 **Ozarks,** *Vault.* . . To conceal in a safe place. Used chiefly with reference to money or valuables. One hears of gold coin being *vaulted* under a fence post, or under a heavy hearth-stone.

vaunty adj [Scots, nIr dial]

Boastful; vain.

1867 Elliott *Carolina Sports* 189 **SC,** Then was it *my* turn to sound a "vaunty" peal! **1930** Shoemaker *1300 Words* 65 **cPA Mts** (as of c1900), *Vaunty*—Boastful. **1997** in 2004 Montgomery–Hall *Dict. Smoky Mt. Engl.* 632 **wNC, eTN,** *Vaunty* . . Boastful, vain. . . [2 infs]. **2005** *DARE* File—Internet, I flunked math . . not from lack of understanding, but from conceit, arrogance, and pride. . . [T]he Lord . . led me through many trials and tribulations to remove from me my vaunty (though little used) intellect.

vavite n Also *the vavites* [CanFr and LaFr < Fr *va vite* goes fast] Cf *DS* BB19

Diarrhea.

1969 Cagnon *Franco-Amer. Terms* 225 **RI,** *Vavite.* . . Diarrhea. "Peter had the vavite(s) last night." **1983** Reinecke *Coll.* 10 **LA,** *Va-Vite.* . . Diarrhea, the "runs." A comic or euphemistic form. [**2010** *DLF* 643, *Vavite* [vɑvit] . . diarrhea.]

vayeta See **bayeta**

vay-yay See **veiller**

V-bill See **V 1**

've See **have** v[2]

veal cod n

A young Atlantic cod *(Gadus morhua).*

1940 Brown *Amer. Cooks* 362 **MA,** In interesting local nomenclature, . . a young cod is called a "veal cod."

Vee See **V**

veeno See **vino**

veery n [Echoic]

Std: a thrush *(Catharus fuscescens)* noted for its distinctive call. Also called **nightingale b, scythe-whet, swamp robin 1e, wood thrush 2**

vega n [Span] **SW**

A grassy plain, meadow.

1850 (1968) Taylor *Eldorado* 1.67 **CA,** The grass on the vega before the house was still thick and green. **1855** U.S. War Dept. *Rept. Explor. Railroad* (Final Rept.) 3.62 **NM** [Final Rept.], The valley spreads out into a wide vega, covered with an abundance of grama. [Footnote to *vega:*] An open plain or valley. **1887** *Courier–Jrl.* (Louisville KY) 6 Feb 12/3 **CO,** We descended into wide grassy plains called "vegas." **1888** Wallace *Land of Pueblos* 80 **NM,** A plateau, the highest of equal area on the globe, varied with sterile *vegas* and dreary sierras . . had once been the home of wandering tribes. **1932** *DN* 6.234 **West,** *Vega.* This word may sometimes be heard in Spanish country with the meaning of *meadow,* but it is not nearly as common as several other such words. It remains as a place-name in Las Vegas, N.M. **1933** *AmSp* 8.3.9 **SW,** *Vega* is the word used for meadow (*Las Vegas,* the meadows). **1941** Cleaveland *No Life* 69 **cwNM,** We had fenced in a quarter-mile square of cañon *vega* land for an overnight horse pasture. **1949** *Sat. Eve. Post* 9 Apr 132 **NM,** There was loose horses and cattle in the *vegas.* **1967–69** *DARE* (Qu. C6, . . *A piece of land that's often wet, and has grass and weeds growing on it*) Inf **TX**66, Vega; (Qu. C19, . . *Low land running between hills [With and without water]*) Inf **CO**26, Vega—plain land between hills or from hills away.

vegetable antimony n [See quot 1828]

A **boneset 1** (here: *Eupatorium perfoliatum*).

1803 (1907) Downey *Investigation* [9] **MD,** The podophyllum peltatum . . and what has been emphatically called the vegetable antimony, the eupatorium perfoliatum, are medicines not inferior to any yet discovered. **1828** Rafinesque *Med. Flora* 1.174, *Eupatorium perfoliatum.* . . Vulgar Names—Thorough-wort, Boneset, Joe-pye, . . Vegetable Antimony. [*Ibid* 177, It acts somewhat like Antimony, without the danger attending the use of this mineral.] **1892** (1974) Millspaugh *Amer. Med. Plants* 79-1, *Eupatorium perfoliatum.* . . Com. Names.—Boneset, thoroughwort, ague-weed, vegetable antimony [etc]. **1974** (1977) Coon *Useful Plants* 108, Boneset, thoroughwort, Indian sage, ague weed, vegetable antimony, sweating plant.

vegetable calomel n Cf vegetable mercury

1 A medicinal extract of the root of **mayapple 1;** the plant itself.

1850 Davis *Gt. Harmonia* 1.255, The vegetable calomel is a lesser evil than the mineral calomel. **1898** Ellingwood–Lloyd *Systematic Treatise Materia Medica* 388, *Podophyllum peltatum.* . . John King isolated Podophyllin as a resinoid in 1833, and published a report . . on the remedy in 1844. . . Following King's suggestions, Lewis made an analysis of the drug in 1847 which was first quoted by the U.S. Dispensatory in 1854. . . It was called by the Eclectics of that time vegetable calomel because it was used to replace calomel in their therapeutics. **1915** *Newark Advocate* (OH) 1 June 7/1, [Advt:] Vegetable calomel, extract of the root of the old-fashioned may-apple plant, does not salivate. As a liver stimulator, it's great. It's a perfect substitute for ordinary calomel (mercury). **1930** *WI Rapids Daily Tribune* (WI) 27 Oct 10/7, [Advt:] Carter's Little Liver Pills, made of genuine vegetable calomel, is oldest liver remedy known. **1974** (1977) Coon *Useful Plants* 76, *Podophyllum peltatum*—May-apple, mandrake, . . vegetable mercury, vegetable calomel. . . Once a commonly dispensed drug, it disappeared from our pharmacopoeia in 1930.

2 A supposedly beneficial constituent thought to exist in the **tomato C.**

1892 *Beauty Attainment* 525, Tomatoes contain vegetable calomel and stimulate the secretions of the liver. **1911** *Sandusky Reg.* (OH) 10 Dec 1/6, Tomatoes are perhaps the best vegetable for the liver. They act directly upon that organ, for they contain large quantities of vegetable calomel. They should always be eaten raw when used medicinally. **1916** *Marion Daily Star* (OH) 25 July 9/6, Is it true that raw tomatoes contain vegetable calomel . . ? My grandmother says if one eats plenty of raw tomatoes, one will need no bilious medicine all summer long. **1918** Tuskegee Normal & Industrial Inst. Exper. Sta. *Bulletin No. 36* 3, Every normal person should make the tomato a very prominent part of the weekly diet. . . It contains distinct medicinal virtues (which are recognized by many authoritative books on household remedies), as "vegetable calomel."

vegetable cellar n scattered, but less freq S Atl, Gulf States, SW See Map

=**root cellar.**

1828 NY Inst. Deaf *Annual Rept. for 1827* 8, The other outhouses are two separate structures . . under one of which is a vegetable cellar for the institution. **1852** Morris *Lights & Shadows* 77, In some cases they [= aboriginal mounds] are selected as convenient sites for a *vegetable cellar* or *ice house.* **1881** *Scribner's Mth.* 22.618 **NEng,** He must be making himself a jimmy or a dark-lantern to break into our vegetable cellar with. **1900** *Stevens Point Jrl.* (WI) 24 Nov [4]/4 (newspaperarchive.com), The

plans contemplate an addition . . with a vegetable cellar under the whole. **1938** *Edwardsville Intelligencer* (IL) 17 Aug 1/6 **MO,** Max Brown, county sheriff, found her body in a vegetable cellar. **c1938** in Lib. of Congress *Amer. Memory: WPA Life Hist.* (Internet) **NE** (as of c1880), All hands rolled it [=a barrel] down into the vegetable cellar and set it in one corner by the door. **1960** *Progress* (Clearfield PA) 17 May 9/1, [Advt:] *Real Estate For Sale.* . . Double house with six rooms. . . fruit and vegetable cellar under house. . . and outside fruit and vegetable cave. **1965–70** *DARE* (Qu. M19, *A place for keeping carrots, turnips, potatoes, and so on over the winter*) 92 Infs, **scattered, but less freq S Atl, Gulf States, SW,** Vegetable cellar. **2002** *Post–Std.* (Syracuse NY) 7 July sec I 2/4, There is a walk-out basement with a wine and vegetable cellar.

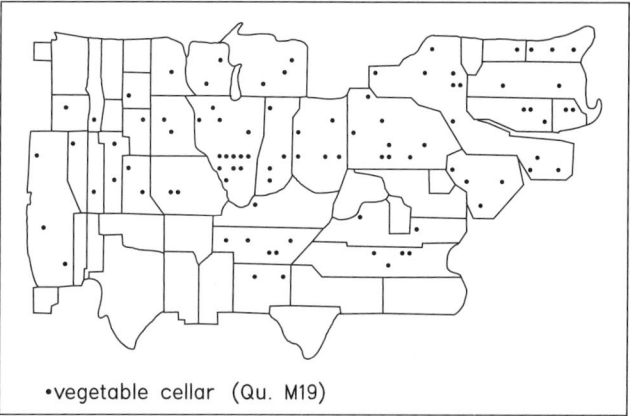

•vegetable cellar (Qu. M19)

vegetable egg n

The eggplant (*Solanum melogena*).

1859 MI State Ag. Soc. *Trans. for 1857* 9.443, The specimen [sic] of vegetable egg, exhibited by H. Seymour, are worthy of premium for their novelty. **1891** *Century Dict.* 6709, *Vegetable egg,* the egg-plant. **1981** *Waterloo Courier* (IA) 9 Apr garden sec 14/1, *The edible vegetable egg.* The eggplant is catching on. **1986** Pederson *LAGS Concordance (Vegetables)* 2 infs, **seAL,** Vegetable eggs = eggplants.

vegetable louse n

An aphid (family Aphidae).

1846 Bosson *Observations Potatoe* 49, The common aphis or vegetable louse. **1931** *Galveston Daily News* (TX) 22 Mar 4/1, The vegetable lice and keen competition of the Rio Grande Valley have just about paralyzed the vegetable shipping business in this county. **1965–69** *DARE* (Qu. R26, . . *The small greenish lice that come on plants*) Infs **GA**77, **LA**12, **OK**11, Vegetable lice.

vegetable marrow n [*OED2* 1822 →; "chiefly *Brit.*"] Cf marrow squash

Any of var cultivated **squashes** n[1] **B1,** esp *Cucurbita pepo* var.

1828 Fessenden *New Amer. Gardener* 309, Squash. Early bush summer. . . Vegetable marrow [etc]. **1847** (1861) Buist *Family Kitchen Gardener* 133, *Vegetable Marrow.* . . We have been frequently greatly amused by some of our friends kindly presenting us with seeds purporting to be the marrow of all the vegetables, or "Vegetable Marrow." It is a species of Gourd. . . This vegetable is characteristically situated between the Pumpkin and the Squash. **1849** Howitt *Our Cousins in OH* 131, Willie wrote down . . all the vegetable produce of their garden. . . It . . was as follows: . . salad, . . canteleup-melons, squashes, or vegetable marrow. **1854** Fox *Amer. Text Book Ag.* 255, It has been recommended to grow the Vegetable Marrow . . to feed hogs and other animals. **1906** *Decatur Daily Rev.* (IL) 21 Sept 12/3, Vegetable marrow, a kind of squash, is now on sale in Decatur. It is a good deal like the ordinary patty-pan squash. **1948** Beston *N. Farm* 140 **cME coast,** I like the Italian summer squash or vegetable marrow called the "Cocozelle." **1988** *Frederick Post* (MD) 20 July sec B 3/4, Summer squash varieties include crookneck and straightneck, scallop or patty pan, zucchini and vegetable marrow. **2004** (acc) TX A&M Univ. *Plantanswer Machine* (Internet), The [Cucurbita] pepo species is usually recognized as the true pumpkin. . . But the group also includes gourds, vegetable marrow, Pattypan summer squash [etc].

vegetable mercury n Cf mercury, vegetable calomel

Any of var plants or plant extracts thought to have medicinal effects similar to those of mercury.

1828 *OH Repository* (Canton) 30 May np/2 (newspaperarchive.com), *Stramonium. . . James Town Weed. . .* It may be termed to be the vegetable mercury, for its effects are very similar to those of mercury, without any of those bad ones produced by that powerful metallic preparation. The vegetable mercury, is certainly a great purifier of the blood. **1864** Hale *New Remedies* 273, *Iris versicolor. . .* It is used by eclectic physicians in bilious fevers, much as the allopath uses calomel; it is considered a sort of "vegetable mercury," causing copious bilious evacuations, salivation, etc. **1871** Millard *Guide* 120 **NY,** *Podophyllum.*—This acts upon the liver to such an extent, that it is often called the "vegetable mercury." **1900** King et al. *King's Amer. Dispensatory* 1078, This plant [=*Iris versicolor*] . . was also a highly popular domestic remedy when it was thought necessary to produce salivation without resorting to mercurials—hence it is sometimes called *"vegetable mercury."* **1958** Jacobs-Burlage *Index Plants NC* 24, *Podophyllum peltatum. . .* May-apple; . . vegetable mercury. . . The rhizome and roots are a slow but certain active cathartic similar to jalap. **1974** [see **vegetable calomel 1**].

vegetable oyster n [From the taste] Cf **oyster plant 1**

A naturalized and often cultivated **goatsbeard 1** (here: *Tragopogon porrifolius*).

1806 McMahon *Amer. Gardener's Calendar* 315, *Tragopogon porrifolium. . .* Some have carried their fondness for it so far, as to call it a vegetable oyster. **1829** *Republican Compiler* (Gettysburg PA) 4 Feb 1/5, *Salsafy* [sic], *or Vegetable Oyster.* This plant, *Tragopogon porrifolium,* is biennial, and the root is a good substitute for the real oyster. **1884** *Stevens Point Jrl.* (WI) [10 May 7/4] (newspaperarchive.com), Salsify. . . is often called "Oyster Plant" or ["]Vegetable Oyster." **1909** *DN* 3.355 **eAL, wGA,** *Oyster-plant. . .* Salsify. Also called *vegetable-oyster.* **1927** *Decatur Herald* (IL) 4 Oct 11/1, 'Vegetable Oyster' Is Now in Market Ready for Tables. **1950** *WELS* **WI** (*Other names in your neighborhood for . . salsify*) 12 Infs, Vegetable oyster; (*Kinds of soup favored in your neighborhood*) 1 Inf, Vegetable oyster (salsify) soup. **1965–70** *DARE* (Qu. I4, . . *Vegetables . . less commonly grown around here*) 32 Infs, **scattered,** Vegetable oyster; (Qu. I3, . . *The large yellowish root vegetable, similar to a turnip, with a strong taste*) Inf **OH**29, Vegetable oyster; (Qu. S21, . . *Weeds . . that are a trouble in gardens and fields*) Inf **NY**103, Vegetable oyster. **2004** (acc) IL Dept. Nat. Resources *Exotic Species* (Internet), *Salsify. . .* is sometimes called "vegetable oyster" because the boiled roots are said to taste like oysters.

vegetable peach n Cf **peach melon, vine lemon, ~ peach**
=**mango 3.**

1887 *Atlanta Constitution* (GA) 20 Nov 18/3, I would like to get some of that lady's vegetable peach seeds of North Carolina. **1894** MO Bot. Garden *Annual Rept.* 161 **Sth,** Related to the Dudaim [melon] . . is the other form of the musk melon . . which is likewise destitute of longitudinal grooves, and possesses a jelly-like pulp about the seeds. This appears to be cultivated more or less extensively under the names of mango and vegetable peach. **1903** *Daily Herald* (Delphos OH) 4 Nov 2/6, The latest thing in this line is a new early cucumber, cantaloupe, or vegetable peach. . . It grows on a vine, looks like a lime, and is of the size of a lemon. When cut in halves it resembles a muskmelon, the center being filled with seeds. It also has a muskmelon flavor. **1920** *Oakland Tribune* (CA) 29 Jan 17/7, [Advt:] The Egyptian Vegetable Peach— A new and wonderful Novelty Melon. . . Preserves made from it will equal any made from the choicest of fruit. **1966** *DARE* (Qu. I26, . . *Kinds of melons*) Inf **NC**5, Vegetable peach—look like a cantaloupe, but a little smaller, make preserves from them. **1988** Whealy *Garden Seed Inventory* (2d ed) 229, *Vine Peach* (Mango Melon, Vegetable Peach) . . native American annual, peach size and color, flavor & texture much like mango. **2003** *DARE* File—Internet, Cucumis melo. aka Vine Peach, Vegetable Peach, Plumgranny, Oueen [sic] Anne's Pocket Melon. . . Grown for its aroma and decorative qualities more so than for eating.

vegetable pear n
=**chayote.**

1847 *Mth. Jrl. Ag.* 2.412 (Internet) **AL,** You recollect, while we were traveling in Alabama last spring, you gave me a vegetable pear (or Militon). **1888** *Atlanta Constitution* (GA) 5 May 10/3, I would like to exchange some seeds of the vegetable pear for the peach seed. **1914** *Gettysburg Times* (PA) 18 Apr 23/6, Chayote. . . is a vegetable pear. . . The vegetable is grown on a queer vine. . . The product is white in color and pear shaped. One California farmer has succeeded in growing 250 of these vegetable pears on two vines. **1923** *DN* 5.244 **LA,** *Milleton. . .* Vegetable pears. **1924** *IA Recorder* (Greene) 22 Oct 4/6, The chayote has been grown for more than a generation in restricted areas of the South, where it has been known variously as vegetable pear, mirliton,

and mango squash. **1968** *DARE* (Qu. I23, . . *Kinds of squash*) Inf **LA**33, Vegetable pear—shaped like a pear, eaten like summer squash. **2004** (acc) TX A&M Univ. *Aggie Horticult.* (Internet), Or take chayote squash . . Floridians call it a vegetable pear.

vegetable porcupine n
=**blue palmetto 1.**

1933 Small *Manual SE Flora* 243, *R[hapidophyllum] Hystrix.* . . Shrub with . . leaf-sheaths persistent, the fibers fine, the rigid needle-like spines erect. . . *Needle-palm. Blue-palmetto. Vegetable-porcupine.* . . Fla. to Miss. and S.C.

vegetable spaghetti n

Spaghetti squash (*Cucurbita pepo* var).

1938 *Helena Independent* (MT) 17 Mar 4/7, Vegetable spaghetti is a type of squash which grows about eight inches long and four inches in diameter. It is cooked whole in boiling water and when cut open the interior resembles a mass of spaghetti. **1986** *Frederick Post* (MD) 19 Mar sec D 3/4, One is the vegetable spaghetti, oval, cream-colored turning yellow as they mature. Grow them as you would gourds. **1995** in 2004 (acc) GA Univ. Coop. Ext. Serv. *Fact Sheet* (Internet) **GA,** Other types of gourds may be sold as vegetable spaghetti, healing squash or possibly other names. **2004** *DARE* File—Internet, Vegetable spaghetti, vegetable marrow, spaghetti squash, noodle squash, and squaghetti. All are names for a variety of squash or marrow (*Cucurbita pepo*) that looks like a small yellow watermelon, with flesh composed of long thin spaghetti-like strings.

vegetable sponge n [See quots]

A cucurbit of the genus *Luffa*, usu *L. aegyptiaca.* Also called **bonnet squash, cassabanana 2, dishrag gourd, rag ~, vine okra**

1878 *Amer. Jrl. Pharmacy* 50.262, He described . . the *vegetable sponge* [Footnote: *Luffa* spec.], so called from the entangled fibres of the fruit, which is shaped like a cucumber, the fibres being a poor substitute for the sponge. **1893** *IA Citizen* (IA City) 13 Jan 4/4, A Vegetable Sponge. . . A correspondent in Kern county, Cal., sends to the San Francisco Chronicle specimens of a peculiar growth which . . may be called a vegetable sponge. . . When fully grown the interior of the gourd becomes a fibrous, spongy mass. **1911** *Trenton Eve. Times* (NJ) 21 Sept 11/1, *Loofahs. . .* The vegetable sponge, especially useful in the bath; holds water like a sponge, has a rough surface much desired for friction. **1965** *Oshkosh Daily Northwestern* (WI) 24 Sept 4/2, He and neighbor, Melvin Durant, hope to harvest the fruit, known variously as the dish cloth gourd, vegetable sponge, and California okra, and use its compact fibrous network for home grown sponges. **1986** *Frederick Post* (MD) 19 Mar sec D 3/4, In the same family is the luffa gourd, or vegetable sponge. **2003** *DARE* File—Internet, *Luffa (Sponge Gourd)*—Standard open pollinated sponge gourd also known as Vegetable Sponge and Dishcloth Gourd.

veil n [Engl dial] Cf **curtain B2, onion skin, skin cap**
A caul; hence adj *veiled* having a caul.

1815 *N. Amer. Rev.* 1.162 **NEng,** The philosopher with his wonderful stone is an unusual character. There exists . . a number of them in the country. They are distinguished at their birth by being born with a veil over their face. **1896** *DN* 1.426, *Veil:* "He was born with a veil over his head," said of one who was a fortune teller. O[ld] n[egro]. **1897** *Atlantic Mth.* 80.194, The Negro is a sort of seventh son, born with a veil, and gifted with second-sight in this American world. **1923** *Bee* (Danville VA) 26 Nov 10/1, [Advt:] *Palmist-Clairvoyant*—Madam Odell—Seventh daughter born with a veil, reads your past, present and future in all affairs of life. **c1938** in 1970 Hyatt *Hoodoo* 1.27 **wTN** [Black], If yo' evah had a child be bo'ned *veiled*—yo' know, yo' heard of 'em being *veiled.* **1945** Saxon *Gumbo Ya-Ya* 298 **LA,** Spirits is bad if you ain't a Christian, but if you is and you is borned with a veil over your face you ain't got nothin' to worry about. **1959** *Hall Coll.* **eTN,** *Born with a veil over her face.* Born with a caul. "Mother was born with a veil over her face, and she could tell you when somethin' was a-goin' to happen." **1966** *DARE* Tape **FL**19, When I was a child, there was an old colored man who . . said he could take off warts and that power was given to him . . by being born with a veil over his face. . . Several years later, my husband had an uncle and he said he was given the power by having been born with a veil over his face, but he . . would want to buy your warts. **1969** Emmons *Deep Rivers* 28 **eTX** [Black], "Why are these spirits seen by some and not by others?" The answer is simple. It is only that those born with the veil are so favored. **1982** *Barrick Coll.* **csPA,** *Veil—caul.* "He was born with a veil."

veillée n [LaFr < Fr *veillée* a vigil; a staying up late] **LA**
A visit, party.
  1968 *DARE* FW Addit **LA**32, *Veillée* ['veɪ‚jeɪ] = a visit. "We had a little veillée last night." **1981** Pederson *LAGS Basic Materials*, 1 inf, **cwLA**, Veillee [‚veˀˈjeˀ] (general post wedding party); 1 inf, **cwLA**, Veillee [‚vɪˀəlˈjeˀ] (a visit to a neighbor, party). **2001** *Times–Picayune* (New Orleans LA) 15 July 8 (Internet), Many customs that were quintessentially Cajun have all but died out, such as . . the veillee, a spontaneous trip to visit nearby family or friends in the evenings or on Sunday afternoons.

veiller v Also *go veiller* Pronc-sp *vay-yay* [LaFr < Fr *veiller* to sit up, keep awake] **LA**
To pay a visit.
  1967 LeCompte *Word Atlas* 279 **seLA**, *To go to see neighbors, friends, or relatives. . . veiller* [14 of 21 infs]. . . This word has come into the English of the area. **2006** *DARE* File—Internet **LA**, *Vay-yay*— spend time talking (French *veiller*)—he went *vay-yay* with his friends.

vellew See **value**

velvet n
1 =**frappe.** [Prob from the texture] **NEng**
  1952 in 2001 *W3* File **MA**, They're called Frappes—Velvets— Frosted—Cabinets. [Text accompanying illustration on a poster advertising Hood's Ice Cream (observed in Hancock Pharmacy . . Springfield, Mass., September 30, 1952).] **1954** *Los Angeles Times* (CA) 7 Jan 2/1, What do you call the soda-fountain drink made by dumping an order of ice cream in a milk shake? In different parts of the country it's called a frosted, a frappe, a velvet and a cabinet. **1965** *DARE* FW Addit **MA, RI,** A *velvet,* in Providence, RI and Fall River, MA means the same as a *frappe* or *cabinet:* an ice cream milk shake. **1975** Gould *ME Lingo* 307, *Velvet*—The *sody*-fountain delight otherwise called a frap *(frappe)* was always called a *velvet* in Maine, at least until summer people began asking for fraps. Why not? It's the milk and ice cream mixture whipped until it's smooth as *velvet.* **1983** Stern–Stern *Goodfood* 29 **ME,** Maine velvets, known also as frappes, are . . what the rest of us know as milk shakes. In Maine, if you order a chocolate milk shake, you will get chocolate milk.
2 See **velvet violet.**

velvet ant n
Std: any of var wasps of the family Mutillidae. For other names of var of these see **cow-killer ant, fuzzy ~, hot ~**

velvet ash n
Std: an ash *(Fraxinus velutina)* native to the southwestern US. Also called **desert ash, fresno, leatherleaf ash, mountain ~ 2**

velvet-back See **velvet-tail 1**

velvet bean n [See quot 1897]
=**cowitch 1,** native chiefly to the southeastern US.
  1896 FL Ag. Exper. Sta. *Bulletin* 35.340, In 1895, my attention was called to a "pea" which was reported to grow luxuriantly in poor soil. . . Afterwards, the same plant was found in Lake City and in other places in Florida, grown as an ornamental on trellises . . , under the name of the Velvet Bean. . . The bloom was followed by plump pods of rich, dark green, covered with a close down, like velvet. **1918** *NY Times* (NY) 4 Aug mag sec 7/3, The South is raising more velvet beans, peanuts, corn, sweet potatoes and Irish potatoes than it has ever grown. **1933** Small *Manual SE Flora* 717, *S[tizolobium] Deeringianum* [=*Mucuna puriens* var *utilis*]. . . *Velvet-bean. Florida-bean.* . . Pinelands, hammocks, citrus groves, and old fields, pen. Fla. . . Extensively grown as a ground cover. **1940** Writers' Program *Guide GA* 361 **ceGA,** The county produces large quantities of naval stores, sweet potatoes, corn, nuts, sugar cane, hay, and velvet beans. **1965–70** *DARE* (Qu. I20, . . *Kinds of beans*) Infs **AL**1, 6, **FL**17, 27, **GA**1, 8, 11, 16, 28, **LA**3, Velvet beans; (Qu. L9b, *Hay from other kinds of plants [not grass]; not asked in early QRs*) Inf **AL**20, Velvet beans; **LA**3, Velvet-bean hay; (Qu. L34, . . *Most important crops grown around here*) Inf **LA**22, Velvet beans; (Qu. S17, . . *Kinds of plants . . that . . cause itching and swelling*) Inf **SC**40, Velvet beans. **1986** Pederson *LAGS Concordance,* 10 infs, **GA**, 6 infs, **AL**, 2 infs, **FL**, 2 infs, **LA**, 1 inf, **AR**, Velvet bean(s)—feed for animals *(or cows, cattle)*. **1993** *St. Petersburg Times* (FL) 9 July sec F 1 (Internet), Cover crops shade out weeds and, when tilled back into the soil, improve and enrich Florida sand. Recommended crops include . . Velvet Beans (Victor and Osceola). **2002** *S. Cultures* 8.3.112 **SC,** We planted velvet beans. They would just climb up on the corn stalks, and that's what the cattle ate during the winter.

velvetbreast n
The common **merganser** *(Mergus merganser).*
  1888 Trumbull *Names of Birds* 65 **CT,** At Milford and Stratford, Conn., *Velvet-breast* [for common merganser]. **1955** MA Audubon Soc. *Bulletin* 39.379, Velvet-breast [for *Mergus merganser*] (Conn. The cream-to-salmon color of the breast of the male may suggest this name, but the plumage is no softer than in the other species.)

velvet bur n
A weedy perennial plant *(Priva lappulacea),* native to Florida and Texas, that produces a bristly and spiny fruit.
  [**1774** Long *Hist. Jamaica* 3.759, Stiptic, or Velvet-bur. . . This plant is applied to bleeding wounds.] **1866** Lindley–Moore *Treas. Botany* 1207, Velvet-bur. *Priva echinata* [=*P. lappulacea*]. **1913** Small *Flora FL Keys* 129, *P[riva] lappulacea.* . . Hammocks and cultivated grounds, Key West. . . *Velvet-bur.* **1970** Correll *Plants TX* 1337, *Priva lappulacea.* . . Common *velvet-bur.* . . Fields, thickets, resacas and roadsides, . . throughout year. **2004** (acc) TX A&M Univ. *TX Vascular Plant Checklist* (Internet), *Priva lappulacea* . . (velvet bur, . . burvervain, cat's-tongue [etc]).

velvet dock n [Engl dial]
1 A **mullein** (here: *Verbascum thapsus*).
  1900 Lyons *Plant Names* 389, *V[erbascum] Thapsus.* . . Nat. in U.S. and widely elsewhere. . . Velvet or Mullein Dock.
2 =**elecampane.**
  1900 Lyons *Plant Names* 202, *I[nula] Helenium.* . . Nat. in U.S. . . Velvet Dock.

velvet duck n [*DCan* 1823 for *Melanitta fusca* Deglandi Group]
=**black duck 1** (here: *Anas rubripes*).
  1923 U.S. Dept. Ag. *Misc. Circular* 13.9 **WI,** Black Duck *(Anas rubripes).* . . *Vernacular Names.* . . *In local use.* . . velvet duck.

velvet grass n
Std: a plant of the genus *Holcus,* usu the naturalized *H. lanatus.* For other names of this species see **feather grass 2, mesquite ~ 2b, salem ~**

velvetleaf n
Any of var plants with leaves having a soft surface resembling the nap of velvet, as:
a An **Indian mallow 1** (here: *Abutilon theophrasti*). Also called **butterprint, butterweed 3, buttonweed 2, cheese B1, cottonweed 3, elephant's ear 4, Indian hemp 5, mallow B, Mormon weed, old maid 3, piemarker, rabbitweed 5, rattletop 2, sheepweed 1, stinkweed 11, velvetweed 2, wild cotton 3b, ~ okra 1**
  1826 Darlington *Florula Cestrica* 77 **sePA,** *S[ida] abutilon* [=*Abutilon theophrasti*]. . . Indian Mallow. De Witt weed. Velvet-leaf. **1880** *Scribner's Mth.* 20.101 **NY,** In my section an annoying weed is *Abutilon,* or velvet-leaf. **1890** [see **b** below]. **1892** IN Dept. Geol. & Nat. Resources *Rept. for 1891* 269, *Abutilon avicenne* [=*A. theophrasti*]. . . The common name, velvet leaf, aptly describes the leaves of this plant. **1936** IL Nat. Hist. Surv. *Wildflowers* 193, The Velvet Leaf was introduced into this country from India and is now a common weed everywhere in waste places. **1968** Radford et al. *Manual Flora Carolinas* 703, *Velvet-leaf.* . . Leaves . . densely velvety stellate pubescent on both surfaces. **1991** Heat Moon *PrairyErth* 378 **ceKS,** We ride and he points out enemies—cheat grass . . mule tail . . velvet-leaf. **2000** *Evolution* 54.124 **IN,** Velvetleaf (*Abutilon theophrasti*) were raised in one of three environments.

b A **mullein** (here: *Verbascum thapsus*).
  1890 (1892) *Webster's Internatl. Dict.* 1599, *Velvetleaf.* . . A name given to several plants which have soft, velvety leaves, as the *Abutilon Avicennæ,* the *Cissampelos Pareira,* and the *Lavatera arborea,* and even the common mullein. **1965** Teale *Wandering Through Winter* 55, It [=*Verbascum thapsus*] is a plant of romantic history and many names— blanket leaf, hedge torch, velvet leaf, Adam's flannel. **1969** *DARE* (Qu. S20, *A common weed that grows on open hillsides: It has velvety green leaves close to the ground, and a tall stalk with small yellow flowers on a spike at the top*) Inf **NJ**58, Mullein, velvetleaf.

c also *velvetleaf gaura:* A **butterfly weed 2** (here: *Gaura mollis*).

1930 OK Univ. Biol. Surv. *Pub.* 2.73, *Gaura parviflora* [=*G. mollis*]. . . Velvet-leaf. Small-flowered Gaura. **1970** Correll *Plants TX* 1124, *Gaura parviflora.* . . Lizard-tail or velvet-leaf gaura. **2004** (acc) TX A&M Univ. *Plantanswer Machine* (Internet), *Gaura parviflora.* Velvet Leaf. This plant produces velvety lanceolate leaves and pink to rose-colored flowers.

d also *velvetleaf mallow:* A plant of the genus *Wissadula* or of the related genus *Allowissadula,* native to Texas and Louisiana.

1961 Wills–Irwin *Flowers TX* 152, *Velvet-leaf. Wissadula holosericea* [=*Allowissadula h.*] . . Velvet-leaf rather closely resembles the Indian Mallow [here: =*Abutilon incanum*], but may be distinguished by its larger size in nearly all respects. . . *W. amplisericea* . . of extreme south Texas . . is similar but more finely pubescent and bears yellow flowers. **2003** *DARE* File—Internet **TX,** A very different texture can be found on the velvetleaf mallow (*Wissadula holosericea* [=*Allowissadula h.*]). The leaves really do feel like velvet and are so soft that you almost don't feel them.

e =**satinleaf.**

1971 Craighead *Trees S. FL* 203, Velvetleaf (satinleaf), *Chrysophyllum olivaeforme.*

velvetleaf gaura See **velvetleaf c**

velvetleaf mallow See **velvetleaf d**

velvet mesquite n

A **mesquite B1** (here: *Prosopis velutina*).

1937 U.S. Forest Serv. *Range Plant Hdbk.* B112, Velvet mesquite, a multibranched tree sometimes attaining 50 feet in height and 2 feet in diameter, occurs in Arizona, Sonora, and Lower California. **1980** Little *Audubon Guide N. Amer. Trees W. Region* 502, The medium-sized tree mesquite of central and southern Arizona, Velvet Mesquite reaches larger size than related species. **2006** Kane *Herbal Med. Amer. SW* 131, Depending on soil and water conditions, Velvet mesquite can be a large shrub, or a small or large tree.

velvet plant n Also *velvet mullein*

A **mullein** (here: *Verbascum thapsus*).

[**1855** Beecher *Star Papers* 95, There is . . the mullein . . with broad-palmed, generous, velvet leaves. . . This fine plant is left, by most people, . . to a good-natured pity. But in other countries it is a *flower,* and called the "American velvet plant."] **1900** Lyons *Plant Names* 389, *V[erbascum] Thapsus.* . . Nat. in U.S. and widely elsewhere. . . Velvet-plant. **1933** Small *Manual SE Flora* 1199, *V[erbascum] Thapsus.* . . Great-mullen [sic]. *Wooly-mullen. Velvet-plant.* . . Old fields, roadsides and thickets. **1961** House *Wild Flowers* 246, The Common or Velvet Mullen [sic] . . has yellow flowers in very dense terminal spikes and is densely woolly or velvety all over. **1967** *DARE* (Qu. S21, . . *Weeds . . that are a trouble in gardens and fields*) Inf **IL**7, Velvet plant. [*DARE* Ed: This Inf may refer instead to another plant.]

velvet sumac n [See quot 1900]

=**staghorn sumac.**

1784 in 1785 Amer. Acad. Arts & Sci. *Memoirs* 1.427, Velvet Sumach. Blossoms greenish white. Fruit in large, ovate, close panicles; crimson. **1814** Bigelow *Florula Bostoniensis* 72, *Rhus typhinum* [=*R. hirta*]. . . Stag's horn or Velvet Sumach. . . its leafstalks and last years branches covered with thick bristly hair. Bunches of berries crowded, purple, velvet like. **1854** King *Amer. Eclectic Dispensatory* 808, *R. Typhinum,* Stag-horn or Velvet Sumach . . must be carefully distinguished from those which possess poisonous properties. **1900** (1927) Keeler *Our Native Trees* 90, The Velvet Sumach is well named, for its twigs and branches are really velvety to the eye and to the touch. **1948** Pearson *Sea Flavor* 133 **NH,** *Rhus hirta* is a distinctive fellow. . . often called velvet sumac because of the year-round dense growth of velvety hairs on the backs of young branches. **1980** Little *Audubon Guide N. Amer. Trees E. Region* 551, *Staghorn Sumac*—"Velvet Sumac."

velvet-tail n

1 also *velvet-back, velvet-tail(ed) rattler* (or *rattlesnake*): =**timber rattlesnake 1. esp Cent; also AL**

1905 *Lincoln Eve. News* (NE) 8 Feb 3/4, The Indian believes. . . he can cure any snake bite on earth, from a ground rattler to a velvet tail or diamond rattler. **1923** OK Geol. Surv. *Bulletin* 32.2.24, Others [=dangerous snakes] are the velvet-tail rattlesnake, the copperhead, and water-

moccasin (two species). **1952** Ditmars *N. Amer. Snakes* 259, In the region immediately west of the Mississippi, in Missouri, Arkansas, western Louisiana and coastal Texas, the form recognized as the *Canebrake Rattlesnake* or *Velvet-tail, Crotalus horridus atricaudatus* . . takes the place of the typical *horridus.* **1966–70** *DARE* (Qu. P25, . . *Kinds of snakes*) Inf **AL**2, Velvet-tail; **AR**56, **OK**52, Velvet-tail rattler. **1986** Pederson *LAGS Concordance (Snakes)* 1 inf, **cnAL,** Velvet-tail rattler. **1995** Brophy *Coll.* 81 swMO (as of c1960), *Velvetback, velvettail.* [A] timber-rattlesnake. **2000** McLeran *Cooper's Hawk* 272 **seKS,** Memories of my first encounter with the velvet-tail go back decades, when an uncle and I were camped along the Caney River. **2002** in 2007 *DARE* File—Internet **nwAR,** Would like information re: "velvet tailed" rattlesnake. It was killed by a workman on our property who identified it as such. It was a beautifully marked snake, similar to pictures of the blacktail, but the black part near the rattles looked "velvety", not scaley. **2004** *Ibid* **wAL,** Canebreak, Timber, or velvet tail as we call them up here in West Al[abama]. They are not as aggressive as the easterns but will put up a heck of a fight if cornered [sic]. **2007** *Ibid* **OK,** Out here where I live (Osage county) we have rattlesnakes, copperheads, chicken snakes, etc. Had never seen a velvet tailed rattler, or even heard of one until a coupla' summers ago and had a couple here at the house.

2 also *velvet-tail rattler:* The black-tailed **rattlesnake 1** (*Crotalus molossus molossus*).

2004 (acc) *Hdbk. TX Online* (Internet), The northern blacktail (*C[rotalus] molossus molossus*), the "green," "velvet-tail," or "dog-faced" rattler of the wooded canyons and mountains of West Texas, sometimes displays an olive cast but is more often brown or silvery gray. Besides its uniformly sooty tail (ahead of the rattle), the blacktail has a dark mask, and along the spine a wide, blackish-brown stripe encloses patches of pale scales. **2004** in 2007 *DARE* File—Internet **swAZ,** While living in Yuma, AZ noticed the locals there referred to a certain rattlesnake as a velvet tail. Believe they had dark area on last few inches of tail.

velvet-tailed rattler (or rattlesnake) See **velvet-tail 1**

velvet-tail rattler See **velvet-tail 1, 2**

velvet-tail rattlesnake See **velvet-tail 1**

velvet violet n Also *velvet*

=**bird's-foot violet 1.**

1878 *Bot. Gaz.* 3.51 **MO,** *Violet pedata.* . . Birds-foot violet or velvet violet. Rare in western Missouri, but common on dry ridges in Eastern Missouri. **1893** *Jrl. Amer. Folkl.* 6.138 **GA,** *Viola pedata,* var. *bicolor,* velvet violets, or (by children) velvets. **1966–70** *DARE* (Qu. S2) Inf **OK**22, Violet has five petals; velvet has three blue leaves [sic—for petals] and three velvet leaves; (Qu. S11, . . *Blue violet*) Inf **OK**22, Velvets for blue violet; (Qu. S26a, . . *Wildflowers*) Inf **VA**43, Velvet violet—three leaves, one plain and two velvet; (Qu. S26c, *Wildflowers that grow in woods*) Inf **GA**5, Velvet violet—rabbit violet.

velvetweed n

1 =**velvetleaf a. esp IL**

1856 OH State Bd. Ag. *Annual Rept. for 1855* 307, The most troublesome are the horse-weed, Spanish needle, . . velvet-weed and pusley. **1892** *Jrl. Amer. Folkl.* 5.93 **IL,** *Abutilon Avicennæ* [=*A. theophrasti*]. . . Velvet-weed. **1940** Gates *Flora KS* 144, Abutilon theophrasti . . Butterprint, Velvetweed. Waste places and fields. **1967–69** *DARE* (Qu. S21, . . *Weeds . . that are a trouble in gardens and fields*) Infs **IL**4, 11, Velvetweed; **IL**19, Cottonweed, buttonweed, piemarker, velvetweed—all same; **IL**44, Velvetweed, stinkweed, elephant's ears, buttonweed—all names for same plant—big leaves that look like elephant's ears and are velvety; small, button-like seeds; **IL**62, Velvetweed or butterprint—a great big leaf; the seed part is shaped like an old-fashioned butter mold; **WI**17, Velvetweed. **2007** in 2011 *DARE* File—Internet **IA,** It's velvet weed: you'll see it popping up everywhere; it's one of the things farmers are always spraying for. . . welcome to Iowa.

2 A **butterfly weed 2,** esp *Gaura mollis.* **West**

1897 AZ Ag. Exper. Sta. *Bulletin* 22.29, Velvet weed.—Gaura parviflora. **1925** Jepson *Manual Plants CA* 689, *G[aura] parviflora* [=*G. mollis*]. . . *Velvet Weed.* . . Herbage hirsute. **1937** St. John *Flora SE WA & ID* 276, *Velvet Weed.* . . Long white villous and densely glandular pilosulous throughout. **1966** *DARE* Wildfl QR Pl.148 Inf **WA**10, Velvetweed. **1967** Dodge *Roadside Wildflowers* 53, One or many species of gaura may be encountered at elevations from 2,000 feet to 8,000 feet from southern Canada to Mexico. . . One of the tall species is called "velvetweed." **2004** *DARE* File—Internet **CO,** Velvetweed, *Gaura mollis.*

3 A **mullein** (here: *Verbascum thapsus*).

1969–70 *DARE* (Qu. S20, *A common weed that grows on open hill-sides: It has velvety green leaves close to the ground, and a tall stalk with small yellow flowers on a spike at the top*) Infs **IL**33, 126, Velvetweed.

velvet willow n

1 The Sitka **willow 1** (*Salix sitchensis*).

1852 Nuttall *N. Amer. Sylva* 1.66 **nOR,** Velvet Willow. *Salix cuneata* [=*S. sitchensis*]. . . This beautiful willow we found growing in clumps near the rocky margin of the Oregon at its confluence with the Wahla-met. **1901** Jepson *Flora CA* 137, *S[alix] Sitchensis*. . . Velvet Willow. . . Staminate aments slender, white or silky with very long hairs which at first quite conceal the body of the ament. **1979** Little *Checklist U.S. Trees* 267, *Salix sessilifolia*. . . Northwest willow. . . Other common names—velvet willow. . . *Salix sitchensis*. . . Sitka willow. . . Other common names . . velvet willow. **2000** in 2004 *DARE* File—Internet, Salix sitchensis—Velvet Willow.

2 A **sandbar willow 2** (here: *Salix sessilifolia*).

1979 [see **1** above]. **1980** Little *Audubon Guide N. Amer. Trees W. Region* 364, "Velvet Willow" . . *Salix sessilifolia*. . . Handsome shrub or small tree with distinctive, soft, whitish, velvety-hairy twigs, foliage, and flowers. . . Extreme S. British Columbia, Washington, and W. Oregon; to 1000'. **2004** *DARE* File—Internet, *Salix sessilifolia*. . . Common name: velvet willow; soft-leaf willow. . . *Range:* s British Columbia to w Oregon.

‡velvet wine n

1941 Writers' Program *Guide SC* 154, The mountaineer has . . such drinks as cherry brandy, plum beer, scuppernong and elderberry wine, and velvet wine from dewberries.

ven(ce) See **vent** exclam, v[2]

venches See **vens**

vendue n Also sp *va(a)ndoo, vandue, vendoo* [Du *vendu,* earlier *vendue*] **chiefly NEast, esp NEng** *old-fash* Cf **sale** Note: The legal term *public vendue* is still current and not treated here.

An auction.

1680 in 1887 Huntington NY *Town Rec.* 1.262, [The] lot was . . sould to the above sd. finch at a vandue. **1726** in 1898 Smithtown NY *Records* 81, After 6 hours they are to be sold at a vandue. **1771** in 1915 *New Engl. Hist. & Geneal. Reg.* 69.14 **MA,** Their was a Vendue at Mr Ivorys to sel that hay of Butlers. **1774** (1957) Fithian *Jrl. & Letters* 177 **NJ,** What in New-Jersey we call a Vendue here [=in VA] they [call] a "Sale." **1806** (1904) Roe *Diary* 28 **NY,** This afternoon I have attended a vandue for John Tiler. **1816** Pickering *Vocab.* 192 **NEng,** *Vendue.* Auction. . . This word was formerly more common than *auction.* It is now chiefly used in *legal* proceedings, in conformity with the phraseology of ancient statutes of the different States. **1842** in 1959 *IN Mag. Hist.* 55.349 **wPA, neKY,** The plunder was all divided among the companies. . . It was sold at vendue on the spot. **1861** Holmes *Venner* 1.109 **NEng,** I don't mean to set *her* up at vaandoo. **1869** *Galaxy* 7.119 **SC** (as of 1842) [Black], I asked the meaning of the unusual crowd. "Vandoo, massa," was his reply. "Dese people hab jus' come down de riber from Massa Papineau's plantation, and goin' to be sold to-day." **1898** (1899) Earle *Home Life* 274 **NEng,** To this day at vendues or sales of old country households in New England, there will be handed out great rolls of woollen pieces. **1899** (1912) Green *VA Folk-Speech* 469, *Vendue*. . . Vandue. A public auction. **1907** *DN* 3.203 **seNH,** *Vendue*. . . Auction. A word remembered but no longer used by the oldest generation. **1929** *AmSp* 5.123 **ME,** Bought at a "vendoo" meant bought at auction. **1930** Shoemaker *1300 Words* 64 **cPA Mts** (as of c1900), *Vendue*—A country sale, or auction of household goods. **1932** *DN* 6.284 **swCT,** *Vandue.* An auction. **1943** *LANE* Map 564–65 **NEng,** The terms *auction, auction sale* and *vendue* . . were systematically asked for only during the second year of the investigation. The material is therefore incomplete, only 170 responses having been recorded. [26 infs gave the response *vendue;* of these, 15 indicated that it was obsolete, 2 that it was a book word, and 1 that he had heard it in NY.] **1945** Partridge *January Thaw* 232 **CT,** They began to feel the excitement of the vendue even before they had come near enough to see the long lines of cars. **1955** *DE Folkl. Bulletin* 1.20, Vendue (public sale). **1991** *DARE* File **seNY,** Vendue = auction.

vendue crier n **chiefly PA** Cf **cry** v **1**

An auctioneer.

1778 in 2000 Fox *Sweet Land* 132 **PA,** Before his departure from Philadelphia, Myler sold his watch "to one Ross, a vendue crier, for £13." **1799** *Aurora Genl. Advt.* (Philadelphia PA) 10 Apr 2/3, By profession [he] is a vendue crier. . . [and] said he would cry the vendue in spite of the Standing Army. **1801** Simmons *Simmons' Norfolk Directory* 29 **VA,** Spratly Richard, vendue crier 114 Main street. **1816** in 1996 Hagy *Charleston SC Directories* 11, Goldsmith, I M, Vendue Crier. **1877** *Hist. Northampton Co. PA* 81, He resumed his old occupation of vendue crier, and traversed the country as of old. . . [He] died in 1821. **1891** *Ligonier Echo* (PA) 4 Nov 1/7, Captain John was a very popular and active business man of that region . . and a vendue crier, as called in those days. [**1953** *PADS* 19.5 **PA,** The Pennsylvania German word *groier* occurs most commonly in the compound *fendue-groier* "auctioneer."]

venetian-blind Irish n Cf *lace-curtain Irish* (at **lace curtain 2**), **paper-shade Irish**

1947 Amory *Proper Bostonians* 15, The naturally democratic Irish . . have become known for graduating through Family stages from "Shanty" Irish to "Lace-curtain" Irish, and finally to "Venetian-blind" Irish. **1967** *DARE* File **ce,csMA** (as of c1945), *Venetian-blind Irish*—Middle class Irish. Sometimes called lace-curtain Irish. This is common in Boston and perhaps wherever there is an Irish population. I have heard variations on it, too.

venison n Usu |ˈvɛnəsn̩, ˈvɛnəzn̩|; also |ˈvɛnzən, ˈvɪnzən|; for addit varr see quot 1981 Pronc-spp *ven's'n, vensin, venson, venzen, venzon* [Proncs of the type [ˈvɛnzən] are old and are, or were until recently, std in Brit Engl.]

Std sense, var forms.

1823 Doddridge *Logan* 40 **wPA, WV,** Our vittals was venzon, bear meat [etc]. **1828** Webster *Amer. Dict., Venison, n. ven'izn,* or *ven'zn.* **1843** (1916) Hall *New Purchase* 147 **IN,** Many's the ven'sin and turkey they fotch'd as a sort of present. *Ibid* 469 **IN,** Turkeys, sang, coon-skins, ven's'n-hams, and even *cash* . . were offered. **1899** (1912) Green *VA Folk-Speech* 469, *Venson*. . . The flesh of animals of the deer tribe, used as food. **1942** Hall *Smoky Mt. Speech* 64 **wNC, eTN,** Venison [ˈvɛnzən]. **1942** McAtee *Dial. Grant Co. IN* 80 (as of 1890s), *Venzen* . . venison. **1967** *DARE* FW Addit **swAR,** Venison [ˈvɪnzən]. I have also heard [ˈvɪnzən] in rustic Florida speech. **1981** Pederson *LAGS Basic Materials,* 1 inf, **cwFL,** [ˈvɛ⌣nsn̩]; 1 inf, **cwLA,** [ˈvĩˑnzn̩].

venison bird n Also *venison hawk, ~ jay* **esp NY** =**Canada jay.**

1861 *Merry's Museum Parley's Mag.* 42.19, The other species of Jay, called the Canada Jay, Venison Hawk, or Whisky-Jack . . is found . . in the northern parts of the United States. **1869** Street *Ind. Pass* 133 **neNY,** "What a beautiful bird!" "The venison hawk," returned Merrill, picking up a stone. **1881** *Lippincott's Mag.* 28.404, Pshaw! it was only the cry of a venison-bird. **1885** *Outing* 7.75 **NY,** The venison birds fill the woods with their peculiar cry. **1889** *Internatl. Annual Anthony's Photographic Bulletin* 2.223 **Upstate NY,** About our door the venison hawks came flitting. **1961** *Jrl. Amer. Folk.* 74.1, The Canada Jay . . is more commonly called . . venison hawk . . or camp robber. Maine woodsmen usually call it either gorbey or moose-bird. **1967–70** *DARE* (Qu. Q16, . . *Kinds of jays*) Inf **NY**6, Venison hawk = Canadian jay; **NY**233, Canadian jay—whiskey jack—moose bird—venison jay—in Adirondacks.

vens n Also *venches* Cf **vent** exclam, v[2], **vince** v[1] =**dib** n[1] **2.**

1991 *DARE* File **eVA,** Playing marbles as a child we'd say we had "vens" on a marble we intended to knock out of the ring. Same as "dibs." **2000** Shores *Tangier Is.* 240 **Chesapeake Bay,** I got *venches* on that (during mustering, a claim on an item or portion of the shoreline).

vensin, ven's'n, venson See **venison**

vent n Also *vent brand* [Span *venta* a sale] **West** Cf **counterbrand**

A brand put on an already branded animal to indicate transfer of ownership.

1849 *Alta California* (S.F.) 18 Jan. 2/3 (*DA*), The Indian said he had bought the horse from a white man, and didn't like to give him up—showed the fresh '*vent*' &c. **1887** *Scribner's Mag.* 2.508 **West,** *Vent,* a brand announcing sale. **1897** Hough *Story Cowboy* 113 **West,** Here was the original of the bill of sale, and also of the counterbrand, or the "vent brand," as it is known on the upper ranges. **1922** Rollins *Cowboy* 236 **West,** The vent brand ordinarily was a facsimile of the seller's own-ership brand, though it might be reduced in size. **1967** in 2006 (acc)

Lexis–Nexis Legal Research *State Codes: CA* (Internet), Food and Agricultural Code Division 10 . . Section 20632. . . . A vent brand may be applied on the loin of an animal which corresponds to the side of the owner's registered brand.

vent v[1], hence vbl n *venting,* ppl adj *vented* **West** Cf **crossbrand**

To brand with a **vent;** to supersede (a previous brand) with a **vent.**

1844 Gregg *Commerce* 1.186 **NM,** It [is] impossible for persons not versed in this species of 'heraldry,' to determine whether the animal has been properly *vented* or not. **1846** *Californian* (Monterey) 19 Sept 1/1, The spaniards explained their laws and showed the animals not to be vented . . and told the Indians they must give them to the rightful owners. **1929** Dickson *Covered Wagon Days* 91 **WY** (as of 1860s), And furthermore the brand on this one had not been "vented," so that it could not have been a legal transfer anyway. **1936** McCarthy *Lang. Mosshorn* np **West** [Range term], *Vent.* . . To mark through a brand. **1939** FWP *ID Lore* 242, *Vent the brand*—change ownership. **1939** (1973) FWP *Guide MT* 416, *Vented brand*—Brand blotted out before witnesses, when the legal ownership of an animal is changed. **1946** Mora *Trail Dust* 191 **West,** When a branded cow changed ownership and the buyer wished to make a record of it, he would mark off the original brand with a running iron and then rebrand with his own. This, when legally done, was called "venting a brand." **1958** *AmSp* 33.273 **eWA** [Ranching terms], *Vented brand.* A duplicate of the animal's brand burned above the original, or the letter *v* burned above the brand, as a sign of transferred ownership. A vented brand must be authenticated by a bill of sale. **1967** in 2006 (acc) Lexis–Nexis Legal Research *State Codes: CA* (Internet), Food and Agricultural Code Division 10. . . Section 20631. . . Venting a brand consists of rebranding a branded animal, by the owner of the animal, for the purpose of voiding his prior brand.

vent exclam, v[2] Also *vents, vence, vant(s), vance, vints, vince, ven, van, venture, vincher, vonchers* [Prob varr of **fen** infl by *prevent,* with the addition in some cases of **-s** suff[2]; *venture* prob represents *vent your*] Cf **vens, vince** v[1]

Freq in combs: used as a call, esp in marble play, to disallow some action or prevent another player from claiming a privilege; to disallow (such a privilege).

1890 *DN* 1.24 **KY,** "Vent" or "vents" means (I) *prevent;* as in "vent(s) your every(s)." **1892** *DN* 1.220 **MO** [Marbles terms], *Evers* and *vent* are used as in Kentucky. [*DARE* Ed: = quot 1890] **1893** Shands *MS Speech* 66, *Venture.* In a game of marbles this word means *to forbid;* as, "venture roundance"; "venture dubs"; etc. . . *Venture* itself is most probably *(pre)vent you,* the first syllable of *prevent* being left off. **1899** (1912) Green *VA Folk-Speech* 469, *Vence.* . . A prohibitory exclamation used by boys in the games of marbles: as, *Vence!* Stop, I forbid you to play. **1905** *DN* 3.100 **nwAR,** *Vents.* . . Term used in playing marbles. **1909** *DN* 3.386 **eAL, wGA,** *Vence.* . . A term used in marbles, to prevent an opponent from an advantage, or to prevent oneself from suffering a disadvantage or penalty. **1917** *DN* 4.421 **LA,** *Ventz* [sic]. . . Case where a marble strikes a stick, rock, or the like. If the shooter cries "ventz", he may shoot from where the marble struck. [*DN* Ed: Connected with 'fen', defense?] **1922** *DN* 5.187 **KY,** If the opponent calls out "kicks," the "taw" must be placed where it presumably would have rolled. This is not necessary if the player first cries out, "Vence ye kicks." **1934** *AmSp* 9.75 **ND** [Marbles terms], *Van-burns.* . . *Van-dubbs* . . *Van-hand's length.* . . The term *van*–nullifies the word or phrase to which it is prefixed. **1935** *AmSp* 10.159 **seNE,** *Vants.* . . This is a general term of prohibition of any and all special privileges, or it may be limited in its scope by agreement among the players. The player cries *Vants* in an emphatic tone of voice at the instant he shoots, and the term becomes very nearly one of the reflexes attending the shot. My father tells me that in his boyhood the term was *Vents,* and a friend from Texas once informed me that he had said *Venture* in his playing. For example, 'Venture Crowpicks' meant that a player was not allowed to scoop up the dust about his *shooter* with his fingers. **1938** in 1944 *ADD* **seAR,** *Venture.* . . to forbid. . . 'Venture cutting my hair.' Used by A.&M. College students. **1950** *PADS* 14.70 **SC,** *Venture.* . . In playing marbles, used to prevent one's opponent from taking advantage of some rule of the game. *"Venture roundance!"* . . deprives the player from moving in an arc around his target for a better shot. **1950** *WELS* (Calls used in playing marbles: to stop another player from doing something) 1 Inf, **seWI,** Vant. Old-fashioned. **1956** *AmSp* 31.37, *Vance on your being first* . . from Big Horn, Wyoming, means 'You can't be first.' . . *Vents on histing!* ('Knucks down!'—in shooting marbles). **1958** *Resp. to PADS 29*

cnOK, Advantage could be gained by being the first to cry . . *Vints dubs (spelling?)*—The man who knocked two marbles from the ring was then allowed to keep only one. *Ibid,* I did not mean to imply that *rounds* was synonymous with *claning* [sic] up debris which might interfere with a shot. I meant that these were both privileges [sic] that the shooting player could take after claiming *Ventures.* **1966** *DARE* Tape **NM6,** The opponent would say "Ven fudge," meaning you weren't supposed to move your hand forward as you shot. **1967** *DARE* (Qu. EE17, *In a game of tag, if a player wants to rest, what does he call out so that he can't be tagged?*) Inf **CA15,** Vents; **TX9,** Vince; Vincher. **1976** *Philadelphia Mag.* Mar 125, A child would come out of his house with a ball that he or she didn't want to lose and call "chipsontheball." That meant if someone else "roofed" it, or knocked it down the sewer . . the responsible party had to reimburse the owner. Players could call out "venchips" *before* the owner called chips, meaning they were not responsible. **1976** *WI Acad. Rev.* June 20 (as of 1920s), While Bob and his friends shouted "fernanz" to halt a player's privilege, we yelled "vant." This usually was used to keep the opponent's knuckles on the ground. **1980** *NADS Letters* **Birmingham AL** (as of 1920s), After each shot [in marbles] any player may cry out "vance" or "vonchers." **1983** *MJLF* 9.1.60 **ceKY** (as of 1956), *Vent* . . : the call which prevents an opponent from taking an advantage; indistinguishable from *vence* or *ven* . . in such phrases as "vent ye pix," but clearly distinguishable in such phrases as the call often heard, "You can't vent averages." *Ibid* 30, *Averages* . . : A call which enables moving the taw to a better position but no closer to the marbles being shot at. In our games, "averages" was the only advantage which could not be "vented." **1994** *DARE* File **csWI** (as of 1930s), *Vence* had the variant [væ nt] in Cottage Grove, e.g., [væ nt haɪst] = no heisting (raising the hand for a gravity-assisted shot). I always thought it was related to *prevent.* **1998** *DARE* File **Portland OR** (as of 1950s), "Bites" was declared when one sibling saw another eating something coveted by the other. There was then the moral obligation to give that person a reasonable bite. This obligation, however, could be pre-empted if the possessor of the food declared "Van-bites" first.

vent brand See **vent** n

vent carême n [Fr *vent de carême*] **LA**
=Lent wind.

1968 *DARE* (Qu. B18, . . *Special kinds of wind*) [Inf **LA20,** Lent wind—a south wind that blows all the time in March;] **LA31,** Vent carême [ˌvɔnt ˌkɑˈræn]—Lent wind—this word used by French, but also by a lot of English speakers; **LA33,** March winds or vent carême [ˌvã ˌkɑˈræm].

vented See **vent** v[1]

venter See **venture** n, v[1]

venting See **vent** v[1]

vents See **vent** exclam, v[2]

venture n, v[1] Pronc-spp *venter, ventur* Cf **creature, nature, picture**

A Forms.

1799 in 1956 Eliason *Tarheel Talk* 319 **ce,seNC,** *Venture*—venter. **1841** *S. Lit. Messenger* 7.227 **nwVA** (as of c1775), He's got afeard to ventur his old red hide in this quarter, anymore. **1861** *Vanity Fair* 3.229 **NEng,** I was actooated . . to giv the peeple their moneys worth, by showin them . . Wax Statoots which I venter to say air onsurpast by any other statoots anywheres. **1867** Lowell *Biglow* xxix 'Upcountry' **MA,** The Yankee always shortens the *u* in the ending *ture,* making *ventur, natur, pictur,* and so on. This was common, also, among the educated of the last generation. I am inclined to think it may have been once universal, and I certainly think it more elegant than the vile *vencher, naychur, pickcher,* that have taken its place, sounding like the invention of a lexicographer with his mouth full of hot pudding. **1887** *Century Illustr. Mag.* 33.447 **GA,** I can but hope the good Lord'll send His blessin' on a poor sinner in the takin' *sech* a venter at this time of life. **1895** *New Engl. Mag.* 17.695 **NEng,** I ventur' to say he was half a mile long. **1924** Raine *Land of Saddle-Bags* 99 **sAppalachians,** The dialect writers pounce with derisive hilarity upon such awkward and slovenly slips as . . *ventur, natur.* **1930** *AmSp* 5.204 **Ozarks,** Shakespeare rhymed *venture* with *enter* on at least one occasion. . . The Ozark natives . . stand firm with Shakespeare . . in the pronunciation of *venture.* **1931** [see **B** below].

B As noun.

An adventure. [Aphet]

1843 (1916) Hall *New Purchase* 146 **IN,** We've time for that 'venture of yours. **1931** *AmSp* 7.91 **eKY,** *'Ventur,* adventure. "Davy's yearnin' fer some 'ventur o' his own." **1938** Matschat *Suwannee R.* 124 **seGA,** Plant Woman, iffen ye got a venture or a yarn to tell, we'd be pleased to hear it.

venture exclam, v² See **vent** exclam, v²

Venus'-cup See **Venus's-cup**

Venus flyplant (or flytrap) See **Venus's-flytrap 2**

Venus's-apron-strings n   Cf devil's-apron

A kelp (*Laminaria* spp).

1892 *Jrl. Amer. Folkl.* 5.106 **MA,** *Laminaria (saccharina?).* Venus's apron-strings.

Venus's-chariot n

A **monkshood 1** (here: *Aconitum napellus*).

1892 *Jrl. Amer. Folkl.* 5.91 **MA,** *Aconitum Napellus,* Venus' chariot. . . The swans are hidden in the hood.

Venus's-comb n

Std: an introduced plant *(Scandix pecten-veneris)* with finely dissected leaves.   Also called **crow needle, devil's darning needle 5**

Venus's-cup n   Also *Venus'-cup*   Cf dainty cups

A **lady's slipper 1:** either *Cypripedium parviflorum* or *C. pubescens.*

1880 (1881) Nickell *Bot. Ready Ref.* 52, *Cypripedium pubescens.* Yellow Ladies' Slipper. . . Venus Cup [etc]. **1898** U.S. Dept. Ag. Div. Botany *Bulletin* 20.20, *Cypripedium hirsutum* [here: =*C. pubescens*]. . . Venus's cup. . . A hairy or pubescent plant . . with large, inodorous yellow flowers. **1900** Lyons *Plant Names* 130, *C[ypripedium] hirsutum.* . . Venus'-cup. . . *C. parviflorum.* . . Synonyms and properties of (d) [=*C. hirsutum*], the two species being closely similar. **1950** Correll *Native Orchids* 24, *Cypripedium Calceolus* L. var. *pubescens* [=*C. pubescens*]. . . Venus' Cup.

Venus's-flytrap n

1 Std: an insectivorous plant *(Dionaea muscipula)* native chiefly to North and South Carolina.   Also called **flytrap 3, flycatcher 4c**

2 also *Venus flyplant, Venus flytrap:* A **sundew.**

1966 *DARE* Wildfl QR Pl.84 Inf **MI**57, Sundew—we have it in Michigan, called Venus flytrap here; **NH**4, Venus flytrap. **1968–69** *DARE* (Qu. S26b, *Wildflowers that grow in water or wet places*) Inf **NY**134, Venus flyplant; **CA**105, Venus flytrap. [**1973** *Herald* (Wheeling ed.) (Wheeling IL) 30 Aug sec 4 2/1, Lots of people confuse sundew with Venus fly trap.]

Venus's-looking-glass n

Std: a plant of the genus *Triodanis* with flowers resembling a mirror on a handle.   For other names of var spp see **hen and chickens 1d, mirrorweed, wild lettuce 5**

Venus's-paintbrush n   Cf devil's paintbrush 1

=**orange hawkweed.**

1891 *Amer. Gardening* 12.440 **NEng,** *Venus' Paint Brush (Hieraceum aurantiacum . .*) are the common and botanical names of an interesting little perennial . ., which has been introduced into cultivation in flower gardens from Europe. . . In many places it has escaped from gardens, and has already become a great trouble to farmers. . . A new name has been given to it, namely, Devil's Paint Brush. **1898** *Jrl. Amer. Folkl.* 11.230 **ME,** *Hieracium aurantiacum.* . . Venus's paint brush. **1905** MA Horticult. Soc. *Trans. for 1904* 15, Once in the field it [=orange hawkweed] made the most of its unrestrained liberty and soon spread so generally over large areas of Maine and other New England states as to undergo a change of its colloquial name from Venus' paint-brush to the Devil's paint-brush.

Venus's-pride n

A **bluet 2,** esp *Houstonia caerulea* and *H. purpurea.*

1784 in 1785 Amer. Acad. Arts & Sci. *Memoirs* 1.409, Venus Pride . . spreads over pastures and fields, in large beds, and gives them a white appearance. **1832** MA Hist. Soc. *Coll.* 2d ser 9.151 **cwVT,** Houstonia coerulea, Venus' pride. **1894** *Jrl. Amer. Folkl.* 7.90 **CT,** *Houstonia cærulea* . . Venus's pride. **1896** Ibid 9.190 **TX,** *Houstonia,* sp., Venus' pride. **1931** Harned *Wild Flowers Alleghanies* 460, *Houstonia caerulea.* . . Familiarly known also under the names of Innocence, Quaker La-

dies, Venus' Pride and Quaker Bonnets. . . This small perennial . . often forms dense tufts, which later cover large areas in old fields and meadows, and produce a veritable floral sea of pale blue or lilac flowers. **2009** LA Nat. Heritage Program *Nat. Comms. LA* 44, Some characteristic forbs include . . *Houstonia purpurea var. calycosa* (Venus' pride).

Venus's-slipper n   Cf fox slipper, lady's ~ 5
=**fairy slipper.**

1924 *Amer. Botanist* 30.32 **West,** Regarding the names of plants of western distribution . ., *Calypso bulbosa* is often referred to as "Venus' slipper." **1963** Craighead *Rocky Mt. Wildflowers* 36, *Calypso bulbosa.* . . Venus-slipper. . . The only pink or rose single-flowered orchid in the area.

Venus's-torch n

A **vervain;** see quot.

1938 FWP *Guide IA* 18, One of these "imported" weeds is the blue vervain (verbena, sometimes called Venus's torch) that colors many farmyards and pastures with its purple and blue masses.

venzen, venzon See **venison**

ver See **very**

verbena n   Pronc-spp *verbeen, verbenea, verbenia*   Cf berbenia

A Forms.

1886 *Semi-Weekly Age* (Coshocton OH) 26 Nov 2/6, [In list of awards for drawing and painting:] Verbenia . . Geo F Manning. **1909** *Oxnard Courier* (CA) 25 June 3/3, The dining room was decorated with . . lemon verbenia. **1923** *Decatur Daily Rev.* (IL) 22 July 18/1, Just now the verbenia beds are very pretty. **1943** *Sun. Jrl. & Star* (Lincoln NE) 30 May sec A 6/3, For Sale. . . Snapdragons, salvia, Oxford, verbenea. **1965–70** *DARE* (Qu. S26a, *. . Wildflowers. . . Roadside flowers*) Inf **IA**7, Verbeen ['vɝbɪn]—has a purple flower; (Qu. S26c, *Wildflowers that grow in woods*) Inf **MO**32, Verbenias; (Qu. S26e, *Other wildflowers not yet mentioned;* not asked in early QRs) Inf **CA**9, Desert verbenia; **MD**23, Verbenia [vɝˈbɪnjə]; **MD**24, Verbenia [vɝˈbɪnjə]—domestic, not wild; **PA**18, Verbenia [vɝˈbɪnjə]. **1977** *Valley News & Green Sheet* (Van Nuys CA) 28 Aug sec 3 7/3, He points out nearly every flowering plant, from the lowly ground verbenia to the towering Washingtonia palm. **2004** *DARE* File—Internet **TX,** I also bought two planter gardens with purple and pink verbenea and geraniums. *Ibid* **CA,** I will always remember David. . . talking to the verbenia, whos [sic] pretty purple flower only spans an eight [sic] of an inch.

B Senses.

1 Std: =**vervain.**

2 A **sand verbena 1.**

1947 Carr *Desert Parade* 76 **SW,** This verbena is an annual herb, but the leaves remain longer than upon some of the neighboring species. *(Abronia villosa.)* **1967** *DARE* Tape **CA**4, [FW:] What are your favorite desert flowers? [Inf:] I think the combination of verbena, primrose and coreopsis is most impressive. **1977** [see **A** above]. **2004** [see **A** above].

Verde trout n   [See quot 1881]   AZ
=**roundtail 1a.**

1881 Hamilton *Resources AZ* 20, What is known as the "Verde trout" is found in that stream [=Verde River] and its tributaries; it resembles the mountain trout, and were it not for the number of bones, would be a valuable food fish. **1902** *AZ Republican* (Phoenix) 5 Apr 4/1, Cat fish are biting we[l]l now, and carp suckers. Colorado river salmon and verde trout are plentiful. **1956** *Reno Eve. Gaz.* (NV) 29 June 18/2 **AZ,** A rainbow trout fillet looks just about the same as a Verde trout fillet, even to a game ranger. But there is a bag limit of 10 on a rainbow, none on a Verde, which is a trash fish. **1977** in 2004 (acc) *Tempe Hist. Museum* (Internet) **AZ** (as of c1920), The fish were not particularly what you wanted—they were boneytail, they called 'em, or Verde trout—but they'd hit a fly or spinner. **2007** *DARE* File—Internet **AZ,** The whole idea is that we anglers, at the grassroots level, help the native Verde trout recover *before* it becomes "officially" endangered.

verdigris n   Also *vordegrease*   Cf bardy grease

In moonshining: fusel oil.

[**1923** *Sheboygan Press-Telegram* (WI) 1 May 5/1, *State Chemist Points Out Moonshine Drinkers' Danger.* . . The acid in the mash acts on the copper of the still, forming verdigris, which is very poisonous.] **1939** FWP *Guide TN* 416, When aged, the deep red liquor was clear of verdigris (fusel oil) and held a bead the size of number five shot. **1956** in 2004 Montgomery–Hall *Dict. Smoky Mt. Engl.* 632 **eTN,** Vordegrease comes from the copper still. It comes from the pot ordinarily, which is very poisonous. . . You had a rag and put fire coals in there and strain it through them fire coals, take the vordegrease off.

verdin n [AmSpan]

A small bird *(Auriparus flaviceps)* native to low desert regions of the southwestern US. Also called **fat-eater, goldtit**

1865 (1869) Tenney *Nat. Hist.* 198, The Genus *Paroides* comprises the Verdin, *P. flaviceps,* . . of Texas, which is four and a half inches long, . . the color above cinereous, head yellow, under parts brownish white. **1937** *Scientific Mth.* 45.241, The related yellow-headed bird in Arizona gets the Spanish name *Verdin* in reference to its greenish-ashy dress. **1964** Phillips *Birds AZ* 113, The Verdin is another tiny gray bird, with a tail not as long as a Bushtit's. **1999** in 2004 *DARE* File—Internet **csAZ,** Verdins are small, industrious birds that build nests throughout the year.

verdolaga n [Span] chiefly SW

1 A **purslane 1** (here: *Portulaca oleracea*).

1935 NM Univ. *Biol. Ser.* 4.1.43, *Portulaca oleracea* . . Common purslane, verdolaga. This very important native plant is extensively used as a source of food in New Mexico. **1970** Correll *Plants TX* 607, *Portulaca oleracea.* . . Purslane, verdolaga. Glabrous fleshy annual. . . Throughout most of Tex. **2003** *Blackboard* (Bakersfield CA) Aug (Internet), Perhaps you recalled once seeing verdolaga mentioned in a recipe; or maybe the plant was part of your childhood. . . Verdolaga is a tender, trailing annual with meandering stems bearing dark green, shining and fleshy leaves. Common, wild verdolaga could be used in salad or as a potherb, but the cultivated variety Portulaca oleracea sativa (also known as Pusley) is the right choice for vegetable gardens because it's milder and tenderer. **2004** *San Francisco Chron.* (CA) 24 Apr sec F 7 (Internet), Common purslane (Portulaca oleracea) or verdolaga is starting to surface in yards and even in seedling pots in greenhouses. Considered a weed and notorious garden pest, verdolagas are revered by Latinos, Asians, Persians and some European cultures.

2 as *verdolaga blanca:* A low-growing plant *(Trianthema portulacastrum)* sometimes used similarly as "greens."

[**1949** Curtin *By the Prophet* 64 **AZ** [Among Spanish speakers], *Trianthema portulacastrum.* . . *Verdolagas,* locally called "pigweed," as are various other plants, is a common, low-growing, succulent annual found on irrigated land. . . This plant is gathered during the summer, cooked, and served as greens.] **1970** Correll *Plants TX* 603, *Trianthema portulacastrum.* . . Horse purslane, verdolaga blanca. Annual succulent herb. . . Mostly in s. and w. Tex.

verduque See belduque

verge n Cf DS N44

The strip of grass between the sidewalk and the curb or roadway.

1968 *DARE* File **RI,** Verge =the grass strip between the sidewalk and the curb. **1987** *DARE* File **nNJ, seNY, ceMA,** (In a town, the strip of grass and trees between the sidewalk and the curb) Verge. **2004** *DARE* File **cwFL,** We always called it [=the strip of grass and trees between the sidewalk and the curb] the verge—I am 48 years old, female and grew up in Florida to cracker parents. **2006** (acc) Vaux–Golder *Dial. Survey* (Internet), The area of grass between the sidewalk and the road [Of 10,589 infs, 2.56% responded with *verge;* scattered throughout the U.S., the heaviest concentration is to be found in the Boston-Philadelphia corridor, including the greater metropolitan NYC area.] **2006** *DARE* File **sePA,** My family has always called it [=the strip of grass between the sidewalk and the curb] a verge. We are of all Irish decent [sic], and although I have moved around a bit . . I was specifically raised in the Philadelphia western suburbs, or Main Line as it is called here. . . [I]n the Main Line the curb is a sometimes thing, most of the roads are curb less and the verge bleeds right up to the roadway. **2007** *Ibid* **seMN,** In South Minneapolis they call it a 'verge.' I had never heard it called that before I moved there in 1991.

verhuddelt See ferhoodle

verical vein See vertical vein

Vermont snakeroot See snakeroot b(3)

Vermont thaw n Cf silver thaw

See quots.

1891 *AN&Q* 7.204, "A Vermont thaw" . . used to be defined as "six

feet of snow and a hurricane." **1959** *VT Hist.* 27.163, Vermont thaw. . . Three feet of snow and a heck of a blow. Occasional.

versteh(en) See fersteh

vertical vein n Also *verical vein* [By folk-etym]

A varicose vein.

1966–68 *DARE* (Qu. AA29, . . *The blue, swollen veins that a woman often gets on her legs while expecting a baby)* Infs **GA**28, **MO**21, **NJ**52, Vertical veins; **MN**23, **NY**70, **OK**18, Verical veins. **2002** Karam *Into Breach* 127 **NJ,** Occasionally callers [to emergency medical dispatchers] describe pain in their "vertical veins" rather than "varicose veins."

vervain n

Std: a plant of the genus *Verbena.* Also called **verbena B1, burr vine.** For other names of var spp see **desert verbena, feverweed 3, horse nettle 2, Indian quinine, ~ tea weed, ironweed 3, moss verbena, sweet William e, thimbleweed 4, Venus's-torch**

very adj, adv Usu |ˈvɛrɪ|; for varr see quots Pronc-spp *ber(r)y, vary, ver, vey, vurry, werry*

A Forms.

1805 *Boston Weekly Mag.* 3.64, "Will they do?" "Bery well," quoth Cato. **1821** Cooper *Spy* 1.152 **seNY** [Black], Miss Fanny read . . to Dinah berry often. **1829** Tenney *Female Quixotism* 2.41 **Philadelphia PA** [Black], He begin bery well, spose he want to know how old you be first. **1840** in 1956 Eliason *Tarheel Talk* 319 **cnNC,** Ver well. **1851** *Ibid* **c,cnNC,** Vey. **1857** *Ibid* **cnNC,** Vurry. **1859** (1931) Tuttle *CA Diary* 15.77 **WI,** It was vary cold last night. **1891** *DN* 1.131 **cNY,** This [ɜ] is found regularly in closed syllables [before [r]], but occasionally in open ones, as [ˈvɜrɪ]. **1891** *PMLA* 6.166 **WV,** *W* is exchanged for *v* in *very* (wɛrɪ) and a few other words. **1896** Harris *Sister Jane* 132 **GA** [Black], Dat ve'y gal. She my young mistiss. **1922** Gonzales *Black Border* 337 **sSC, GA coasts** [Gullah glossary], *Werry*—very. **1937** in 1976 *Weevils in the Wheat* 149 **VA** [Black], My papa didn't stay wid us ve'y long. **1942** Hall *Smoky Mt. Speech* 21 **wNC, eTN,** Before r, [ɛ] is often retracted to [ɜ], as in: . . *very.* **1955** in 1958 Brewer *Dog Ghosts* 109 **TX** [Black], De haidless-hossman lib one time in de ver' house what mah gran'pa an' his fam'ly was libin' in. **1958** Humphrey *Home from the Hill* 51 **neTX,** Oh, ver' well. Git yoself settled. **1966** *DARE* Tape **DC**5, There's one [ˈwuːrɪ] particular thing you gotta do. **1981** Pederson *LAGS Basic Materials* **Gulf Region,** [Transcriptions of *very* (indicated in the *LAGS Concordance* by the spelling *ver(y)*) include eight exx of the types [vɛˑə, vɛˑɪ, və] before a consonant and two before a vowel; four exx of the types [vɛˑə, və, vɪˑə] before a consonant and three before a vowel.] **2000** Metcalf *How We Talk* 88 **Philadelphia PA,** In Philadelphia, the "short e" has an "uh" sound when followed by an "r." So Philadelphia *very* sounds like "vurry". **2010** *DARE* File **WV,** I have heard *very* pronounced [ˈvaˑə] by West Virginians.

B As adv.

Very much. **Gullah**

1888 Jones *Negro Myths* 76 **GA coast,** Dem soldier duh camp der street, an dem yent hab no fire. Dem berry lub rum. **1909** *S. Atl. Qrly.* 8.46 **seSC** [Gullah], Buh Mongkey kin talk, but 'im berry hate wuk [= work]. **1930** Stoney–Shelby *Black Genesis* 26 **seSC** [Gullah], Save dem for me, 'cause I is bery like apple myself.

very close vein n [By folk-etym]

A varicose vein.

1926 *Ruthven Free Press* (IA) 3 Mar [2]/1 (newspaperarchive.com) [Black], Ah goes to de doctah, an' he says mah veins am too close. Says Ah got very close veins. **1965–70** *DARE* (Qu. AA29, . . *The blue, swollen veins that a woman often gets on her legs while expecting a baby)* 36 Infs, **scattered,** Very close veins. **1979** Lewis *How to Talk Yankee* [36] **nNEng,** Very-close veins. Varicose—more common than you might think, esp. among older folk. **1989** Gurganus *Oldest Confederate Widow* 499 **Sth** (as of c1915), Now Ned tells twins . . "Look ya'll, poor Momma's got very-close veins." I laugh. What else can you do? **1990** *DARE* File **csWI,** My grandmother used to talk about very close veins. It wasn't until I went away from home that I learned the term *varicose veins.*

very coarse vein n [By folk-etym]

A varicose vein.

1854 Shillaber *Life Partington* 163 **MA,** "What is the matter with Mrs. Jewks, doctor?" . . "She is troubled with varicose veins, mem." . . "[W]ell, that accounts for her very coarse behavior, . . and if one has very coarse veins what can one expect?" **1897** *Harper's New Mth. Mag.* 96.123 **Sth** [Black], Most uv me ain't much 'count nohow, what with very coarse veins an' so fothe. **1907** *DN* 3.251 **eME,** *Very coarse veins. . .* Varicose veins. Common folk-etymology among the older generation. **1955** *Oakland Tribune* (CA) 3 Jan 9/8, We've all heard oldsters talk of "very coarse veins." **c1960** *Wilson Coll.* **csKY,** *Very coarse veins. . .* Folk pronunciation of varicose veins. . . Frequent. **1966–69** *DARE* (Qu. AA29, *. . The blue, swollen veins that a woman often gets on her legs while expecting a baby*) Infs **AR**37, **GA**57, **MA**25, **NC**52, Very coarse veins.

vesper n   Pronc-sp *fesper*   [Ger dial *vesper*]
An afternoon or evening meal or refreshment.

   1882 (1971) Gibbons *PA Dutch* 196, "The two o'clock vesper has generally fallen out of use, but if any one comes to town now that I want to invite, and it is not convenient to have them to dinner or supper, I say, 'Come to vesper.' Then we have coffee, and always sugar-cake." "It would not be a vesper without the sugar-cake," said Mrs. C.'s daughter. For a vesper-party for guests, Mrs. C. sets a table, and adds smoked beef, preserves, or anything that she chooses. **1944** *PADS* 2.42 **cnNC,** *Fesper* ['fɛspə]. *. .* The evening meal. *. .* Rare? Reported.

vesper sparrow n   Also *vesper (bird)*
Std: a streaked grayish sparrow *(Pooecetes gramineus)* common in grasslands.   Also called **bull sparrow, field ~ b, grass-bird 1a, grass sparrow a, ~ finch 1, gray bird b, ground ~ c, ground sparrow a, pasture bird 2, snakebird 3, song sparrow, summer ~**

vessel n   Also *bed vessel*   **chiefly NEast, Gt Lakes**   See Map *old-fash; euphem*   Cf **thunder mug**
A chamber pot.

   1930 Shoemaker *1300 Words* 65 **cPA Mts** (as of c1900), *Vessel*—A chamber pot. **1941** *LANE* Map 337, 1 inf, **nwVT,** Chamber = vessel = pot (vulgar). *Ibid* Map 339, 1 inf, **cnRI,** Commode, a wash stand with a vessel (i.e. a chamber pot in a bottom compartment). **1949** *McDavid Coll.* **cNY,** Vessel—(euph) = chamber pot. **1950** *WELS* (*Utensil kept under a bed for use at night: Give names and nicknames*) 5 Infs, **WI,** Vessel. **1957** *Sat. Eve. Post Letters* **MA,** A pot was a crockery affair used for the needs of nature and under the bed. My proper grandmother . . referred to this as "my vessel" or "my chamber." **1965–70** *DARE* (Qu. F38, *Utensil kept under the bed for use at night*) 28 Infs, **chiefly NEast, Gt Lakes,** Vessel; **CA**36, **NY**11, Bed vessel; **WI**19, Japanese vessels. [28 Infs old] **1975** *DARE* File **neMA,** Vessel—Euphemism for chamber pot. Used by grandmother (born near Salem MA 1862(?)). **1986** Pederson *LAGS Concordance* 1 inf, **ceAR,** Vessel— "genteel" name for slop jar. **2007** *DARE* File **nwMS** (as of 1964), *Vessel* for chamber pot—I heard this in 1964 from a black minister in Marks, Mississippi.

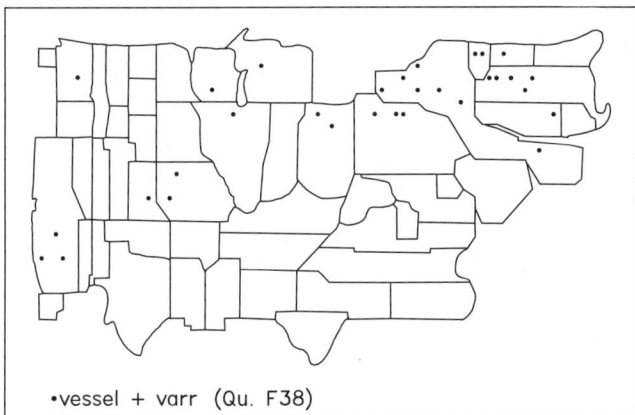

•vessel + varr (Qu. F38)

vest-pocket turtle n
Appar a **mud turtle 2b(1).**

   1966 *DARE* (Qu. P24, *. . Kinds of turtles*) Inf **FL**7, Vest-pocket turtle. **1977** *Nat. Hist.* 86.53 **IL,** Vest-pocket Turtle. . . *Kinosternon flavescens spooneri.*

vetbollen n pl   [Du *vetbol(len),* literally fat ball(s)]   **Upper MW, Gt Lakes in Du settlement areas**

=**oliebollen.**

   1941 Writers' Program *Guide WI* 337 **seWI,** Sunday dinners are prepared on Saturday by Dutch housewives who still cook the good things their mothers made— . . *oliebollen,* fried dumplings; *vetbollen,* coffee cake dough sugared and raisined and fried in deep fat. **1989** *Hist. Pella IA* 2.216 **csIA,** Dutch dumplings (with yeast), oilie koeken (with baking powder or soda) are also loosely called oilie bollen, vet bollen or fried cakes. Currants, raisins, apples, or citron are added. It is often an old year's evening treat. **2006** *DARE* File—Internet **ND, NE,** My father . . was the minister of the First Reformed Church [in Litchville ND]. Most of the members of that church were/are Dutch. . . When I was very young, we moved to a country church between Panama and Adams, Nebraska, the Pella Reformed Church. . . It was always a special treat to come home from school . . and discover that mom had just made Vet Bollen (Fat Balls). **2007** *DARE* File **cwMI,** Vetbollen: yes, they're the same as oliebollen. My grandma used to hand them to me with a phrase "Oliebollen zwart van krenten": oliebollen black with currants. But . . they're hardly cakes, more on the order of scones in shape; bollen, in fact.

vetch n   Cf **deervetch, joint vetch, milk ~, pointvetch, poison vetch, sweetvetch**

1 Std: a plant of the genus *Vicia.*   Also called **peavine 1b(5).** For other names of var spp see **broad bean 1, buffalo pea 2, Canada ~ 1, deer ~ 1, devil's shoestring 6, wild pea c**

2 usu with adj: =**vetchling.**

   1863 Burr *Field & Garden* 502, *Chickling Vetch. . .* Lathyrus sativus. **1896** *Perry Bulletin* (IA) 20 Feb [2]/3 (newspaperarchive.com), Their new [seed] catalogue. . . is brimfull of rare things. Of especial merit we name . . for the farmer, . . Germanica Vetch, the Lathyrus silvestris [sic]. **1911** NJ State Museum *Annual Rept. for 1910* 510, *Lathyrus myrtifolius. . . Myrtle-leaved Marsh Vetch. . .* Mid-June to mid-July, probably. **1922** *Amer. Botanist* 28.12 **ND,** This attractive flower [=*Lathyrus venosus*] has not received a distinctive common name. . . I have therefor [sic] proposd [sic] . . "bushy vetch." *Ibid,* The more slender wild vetch [= *Vicia Americana*] is somewhat overshadowed. **1940** Steyermark *Flora MO* 310, *Vetchling, Vetch (Lathyrus). . .* Flower-clusters . . with 1 to many purple or rose-purple flowers. *Ibid* 312, *Bushy Vetch (Lathyrus venosus . . var. venosus . .).* **1964** Kingsbury *Poisonous Plants U.S.* 326, Poisoning of human beings and livestock after ingestion of large quantities of the seeds of *Lathyrus sativus* L. (. . green vetch) . . and *L. clymenum* L. (Spanish vetch) . . has accounted for much disease and loss of life. **2001** *Nature* (London) 5 Apr 637, Even mistaken names—for instance, the North American beach vetch, *Lathyrus japonica*—are to be retained formally and technically.

vetchling n
Std: a plant of the genus *Lathyrus.*   Also called **pea 3, peavine 1b(7), vetch 2, wild pea b.**   For other names of var spp see **beach pea, marsh ~, redwood ~, sweet ~ 2, tule ~**

vettekost, vettikost   See **fetticus**

vey   See **very**

V-harrow n   esp **Sth, S Midl**
=**A-harrow.**

   1878 in 2006 *DARE* File—Internet [*Hickman Pioneer* (TN) 10 May], I took a large V harrow, hitched two horses to it, straddled a row, with it, . . put the ground in as nice fix as could be, and did not injure my corn. **1900** in 2007 *DARE* File—Internet **cwTN,** [Inventory:] ½ interest in V harrow. **1936** *Fresno Bee the Republican* (CA) 16 Feb sec B 6/3, [Advt:] *Auction. . .* 2 wagons, steel V harrow, plows, [etc.]. **1946** *Dixon Eve. Telegraph* (IL) 18 Feb 8/1, *Closing-Out Sale! . . Farm Machinery . .* V-harrow. **c1960** *Wilson Coll.* **csKY,** *A-harrow . .* a homemade harrow shaped like the capital A. Sometimes it is called a V-harrow, looked at from the other direction. **1965–68** *DARE* (Qu. L18) Inf **MS**28, V-harrow; (Qu. L20, *The implement used in a field after it's been plowed to break up the lumps*) Inf **AR**55, V-harrow; **LA**15, V-harrow— wooden frame with railroad spikes. **1966** *Press–Gaz.* (Hillsboro OH) 12 Aug 23/1, *Auction! . . Farm Equipment. . .* V harrow. **1966** Dakin *Dial. Vocab. Ohio R. Valley* 2.156, *Harrow. . .* The oldest form is an A-shaped wooden frame with metal (wooden in earlier times) "teeth" set in the bottom. Informants frequently call this an *A-harrow* or sometimes a *V-harrow.* **1986** Pederson *LAGS Concordance (Harrow)* 6 infs, **AL, LA, MS, TN,** V-harrow(s); 1 inf, **seTN,** V-harrow—with 28 teeth, 4″ X 4″.

viaduct n Pronc-spp *viadock, viadoct, vidock, vidoct, viduck, viduct, vy(e)dock*

Std sense, var forms.

1965–70 *DARE* (Qu. N19, . . *A structure that carries a road above railroad tracks, or above another road or a deep gully*) 20 Infs, **scattered,** Vidock; **CA**35, **KS**18, **MI**97, 108, Viadock; **FL**31, Viadock ['vɑɪjə,dɔk]; **GA**17, Viadock ['vajə,dɑk]; **MO**32, Viadock ['vɑˆɪə,dɑk]; **NY**84, Viadock ['vaɪə,dɑk]; **WI**30, Viadock ['vaɪə,dɑk]; **IL**26, Viadoct; **AR**15, Viduck. **1981** Pederson *LAGS Basic Materials,* 1 inf, neTN, ['vaˑᵗ,dɑˀks]—viaducts, expresses amusement with this pron, heard on local radio. **2004** Marler *Reflections on Life* 69 cLA (as of 1930s), *Vye dock.* = Railroad overpass. **2005** in 2007 *DARE* File—Internet cwIN, Its an old Railroad Vidoct. Legend has it that some guy hung himself over it and you can see the shadow of the guy at night. *Ibid* nwWI, About 2 blocks past the Vy-dock was our Grandma O's house. **2006** *Ibid* AR, People drive down a few blocks to another street where the railroad passes over on a little bridge. People call that "going under the vydock." . . I've only heard this expression once outside of Arkansas (in Tennessee). *Ibid* nwWA, I think something has to happen before the viduct falls down by itself. **2007** *Ibid* SW, I am from the South West New Mexico and Texas and this is where we use to gather, Under the vidocks. *Ibid* swOH, About me: Born downtown Cin[cinnati], but was raised across da Hopple st. viadoct on a st. called MooseWood ave.

viage See **voyage**

viburnum n

Std: a plant of the genus *Viburnum.* For other names of var spp see **arrowwood a, black haw 1, dockmackie, highbush cranberry, hobblebush, mealy tree, moosewood 3, nannyberry 1, possum berry, ~ haw 1, Shawnee haw, snowball 1, water elder, wild raisin, ~ snowball 2, withe rod**

v'ice See **voice**

victual n Usu |'vɪtl‖ Also sp *vittle;* rarely *vit(t)al* Pronc-sp, in *Gullah,* *bittle* [*OED2* 1303 →; < OF *vitail(l)e* < late Lat *victualia.* The etymological spelling, introduced in the 16th century, did not affect the colloquial pronunciation and never entirely superseded the sp *vittle.*] *old-fash* or *joc* Cf **meal of victuals, spoon victuals**

Usu pl: Food, esp as prepared for consumption.

1815 Humphreys *Yankey in England* 109, *Vittles,* victuals. **1828** Webster *Amer. Dict., Victuals, n. vit'lz.. .* This word is now never used in the singular. . . We . . apply it chiefly to food for men when cooked or prepared for the table. We do not now give this name to flesh, corn or flour, in a crude state; but we say, the *victuals* are well cooked. . . We say, a man eats his *victuals* with good relish. Such phrases as to buy *victuals* for the army or navy, to lay in *victuals* for the winter, &c. are now obsolete. We say, to buy *provisions.* **1858** Hammett *Piney Woods Tavern* 114, Vittles, cups, sassers. **1871** in 1983 *PADS* 70.56 ce,sePA, I would like to taste some strange victuals. [**1872** Holmes *Poet* 340 ceMA, You don't find fault with your vit—(Dr. Benjamin had schooled his parent on this point, and she altered the word) with your food.] **1887** (1967) Harris *Free Joe* 118 GA, Nobody 'roun' here don't begrudge him his vittles, I reckon. **1888** Jones *Negro Myths* 11 GA coast [Gullah], Eh cant git bittle fuh eat. **1899** (1912) Green *VA Folk-Speech* 470, *Vittles.. .* Provision of food; meat; provisions; signifying commonly food for human beings, prepared for eating. **1926** *DN* 5.390 ME, *Victuals* (vittles).. . Food. "Set up and eat your vittles." Obsol. **1937** in 1976 *Weevils in the Wheat* 37 VA [Black], She didn't give me no money but let me stay there an' work for vitals an' clothes. **1939** *LANE* Map 213, 1 inf, seMA, Warmed over vittles; 1 inf, swMA, Cold vittles; 1 inf, ceVT, Boiled vittles. **1941** *Ibid* Map 344, 1 inf, seRI, A neighbor keeps her vittles in her closet; 1 inf, cwVT, The old houses had two butteries, one for cold vittles, one for warm. **1950** *PADS* 14.14 SC [Gullah], *Bittle.. .* Victuals, food. **1959** *VT Hist.* 27.166, *Victuals.. .* Food. Occasional. Rural areas. **1961** Folk *Word Atlas N. LA* 263, *Vittles* (victuals) was used almost exclusively by the elderly. *Ibid* map 1611, I'll put the *food* on the table. . . vittles 19% [of 275 infs]. **1964** *Ferhoodled Engl.* [5] [PaGer], My Rufus is so sneaky (particular) about his vittals. **1965–70** *DARE* (Qu. H6, *Words for food in general: "He certainly enjoys his _____."*) 187 Infs, **widespread,** Vittles [*DARE* Ed: 29 of these Infs called the term old-fashioned; 15 Infs used it after FW sugg; 11 Infs said they had heard it.]; **AL**6, Vittles—heard from lower people esp Negro; **CA**126, Vittles—not used much now; **DC**7, Vittles—current—old folks

say; **IL**82, Vittles—not too common; **IL**97, Vittles—not unfamiliar but not frequent; **IN**97, Vittles—obsolete; **MI**1, Vittles—almost obsolete; **MI**100, Vittles—often heard formerly; **MS**54, Vittles—rarely used; **MA**122, Vittles—you hear this; **NC**84, Vittles—used to be common . . used by illiterates; **NC**88, Vittles—used to hear as a child; **NH**6, Vittles—not used anymore; **NY**194, Vittles—grandfather said this; **OH**98, Vittles—used but rare [FW sugg]; **SC**22, Vittles—grandmother used it [FW sugg]; **SC**29, Vittles—used a great deal [FW sugg]; **SC**51, Vittles—heard often [FW sugg]; **SC**70, Vittles—haven't used in *so* long; **TN**1, Vittles—old-timers; **UT**8, Vittles—that's what they used to say; **VA**72, Vittles—not heard today; **VT**3, Vittles—not used much now; **WI**41, Vittles—we wouldn't use it here, but it's a Yankee expression; folks from Maine would use it; (Qu. D10a, *The place to keep food cool, usually with ice, so that it won't spoil*) Inf **NY**230, Vittles cupboard; (Qu. G6, . . *Dishes that you might have on the table for a big dinner or special occasion—for example, Thanksgiving*) Inf **NC**5, Vittles; (Qu. H2, *The meal that people eat around the middle of the day*) Inf **MA**24, Vittles—grandmother used to say this; (Qu. H3, *The meal that people eat at the end of the day*) Inf **MA**24, Vittles—grandmother used to say this; (Qu. H15, *Bread made with wheat flour*) Inf **LA**24, Vittle; (Qu. H67, *Food that was not finished at one meal but saved for another*) Inf **GA**36, Warmed-over vittles; (Qu. U1b, . . *Buying groceries*) Inf **NY**75, Gotta get some vittles—old-fashioned; **SC**55, To buy vittles; (Qu. HH2c, *Of an idle, worthless person . . "He isn't worth _____."*) Inf **MD**31, Salt that goes in his vittles. **1986** Pederson *LAGS Concordance Gulf Region* (Food) 236 infs, **widespread,** Victuals. [*DARE* Ed: 19 infs described the term as old-fashioned, older, or still in use by the elderly; 13 said it was formerly common but is no longer; 9 had heard it; 7 described it as rural, "hillbilly," or country, 2 as ignorant, and 1 inf, cwGA, as very common]; 1 inf, cGA, Victual; 1 inf, nwAR, Victual—formerly common, now only joking. **1997** in 2004 Montgomery–Hall *Dict. Smoky Mt. Engl.* 633, *Victual. . .* [1 inf, eTN,] I come along for the vittles.

victual v, hence vbl n *victualing* Also sp *vittle,* vbl n *vittling* [*OED2* victual v. 2.a 1577 →]

To eat.

1885 (1886) Sanborn *Wit of Women* 72 **NH**, He fell to at the meal she had interrupted, hot potatoes, cold pork, dried venison, and blueberry pie vanishing down his throat with an alacrity and dispatch that augured well for the thorough "vittling" he intended. **1914** *DN* 4.83 **ME, nNH,** *Victual. . .* To eat. **1984** Wilder *You All Spoken Here* 83 Sth, That'll eat: That will make good vittling. **1994** in 2004 Montgomery–Hall *Dict. Smoky Mt. Engl.* 633, *Victual. . .* To eat a meal. . . [1 inf, eTN,] Have you already vittled?

victual the garrison v phr [*OED2* victual v. 1 13 . . →] Cf *DS* H9, H11a

Fig: see quot.

1916 *DN* 4.331 **KS**, *Victual the garrison. . .* To help one's self immoderately to food at table.

vidock, vidoct, viduck, viduct See **viaduct**

viewing n chiefly **PA, NJ, MD, DE**; also **UT** See Map =visitation.

1881 Perrin et al. *Hist. Medina Co. & OH* 497 **neOH,** After the viewing of the body, it was conveyed to the village cemetery. **1927** *Chester Times* (PA) 2 Feb 3/2, The funeral will be held on Saturday. The viewing will take place from his late residence. **1951** *Progress* (Clearfield PA) 5 Nov 9/4, A private viewing will be held from his late residence Tuesday until time of the services Wednesday. **1954** *Salisbury Times* (MD) 25 Sept 1/8, She said at the viewing prior to the funeral, Mrs. Banks came in and spoke to Mrs. Gray, the victim's mother. **1956** *Sun* (Baltimore MD) 10 Feb sec B 17/7 (Hench Coll.) **Philadelphia PA,** The viewing will be held tomorrow night at the Oliver H. Bair funeral home in downtown Philadelphia. . . Preliminary plans call for the general public to be admitted . . for tomorrow night's viewing unless the crush becomes too great. **1965–70** *DARE* (Qu. BB60, *When friends and relatives gather together at the place where the body is, usually the night before the funeral*) 77 Infs, **chiefly PA, NJ, MD, DE,** Viewing. **1968** *Co. Rec.* (Denton MD) 8 May 7/3, Viewing was held at the C.W. Hill Funeral Home. **1998** Millersville Univ. Center for PA Ger. Studies *Jrl.* Autumn 16, Many years later Chris Beiler came to pay respects at my father's viewing because he remembered us. **2003** *Intelligencer* (Doylestown PA) 18 Apr sec B 5/2, Services will be held . . at First Baptist Church . . where a viewing will be held from 9 until the time of service. **2008**

Irvine *Trespass* 229 **UT,** My mother shared my aversion, and my father was never present at a Mormon viewing.

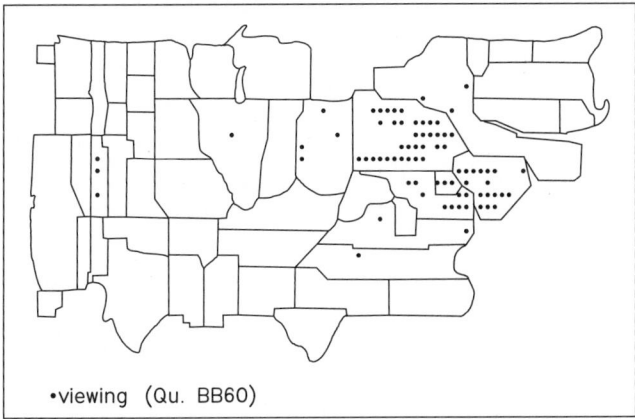

•viewing (Qu. BB60)

viga n [Span] **SW**

A roof-beam used in American Indian and Spanish colonial style architecture, typically consisting of a log that projects beyond the outer walls.

1844 (1954) Gregg *Commerce* 1.284 **NM,** Rooms . . [are] still covered with the *vigas* or joists, remaining nearly sound under the *azoteas* of earth. **1864** in 1893 U.S. War Dept. *War of Rebellion* 1st ser 41.2.812 **NM,** The shop. . . should not be too wide, on account of the difficulty of getting vigas of the proper length. You will furnish the vigas in case the Navajoes cannot get them. **1894** *Catholic World* 60.178 **sCA,** In this central building there is still soundness of *viga,* and resistance in roof and wall. . . the broken *vigas* whiten in the long sun of summer. **1948** *SW Rev.* 33.32 **NM,** Logs for *vigas* average six to ten inches in diameter and are sixteen or twenty feet long. **1968** Bradford *Red Sky* 106 **SW,** The big room has eighteen *vigas* across the ceiling. *Ibid* 138, Several cords of wood were neatly stacked under the *portal* near the front door, and strings of dried red chile hung from the *vigas.* **1984** in 2006 (acc) Lexis–Nexis Legal Research *State Case Law: NM* (Internet), Plaintiff started cutting off vigas which extended out from the north side of the building. . . Plaintiff reattached the cut vigas with nails and a rebar. **1997** *DARE* File swNM, Spanish loanwords that are in very common use among New Mexico Anglos. [V]iga—the rafter of a traditional New Mexico adobe house.

vige See **voyage**

vigrous adj Usu |ˈvaɪˌgrəs|; for addit varr see quots Pronc-spp *vagrous, vigous, vig(r)us, viguerous, vygrous, vyg(e)rus, vygorous* [Varr of *vigorous,* associated chiefly, but not exclusively, with non-std extended senses] **Sth, S Midl** Cf **servigrous, vagous**

Vigorous; fierce, dangerous, bad-tempered; also fig; hence superl *vigrousest,* advs *vigrous(ly).* Note: The spp *vigr(o)us* are ambiguous and may also represent the common colloquial pronc of *vigorous* [ˈvɪgrəs]. On the basis of sense and location it is likely, but not certain, that the early exx quoted here represent proncs of the type [ˈvaɪgrəs].

1798 (2004) Munford *Coll.* 101 (Internet) **VA,** By jing, he ran at me as vigue-rous as a lion, with a monstrous stick. **1836** *Amer. Mth. Mag.* 2.197 **KY,** She would . . come streaking it to me . . looking as fresh as if she was a new made dog. And then wan't she vig'rous? **1867** Harris *Sut Lovingood Yarns* 71 **wNC,** Every now an' then he'd gin his head a vishus, vigrus shake. **1883** (1971) Harris *Nights with Remus* 288 **GA** [Black], Ser-*vi*-gous; or ser-*vi*-gus. . . Aunt Tempy would have said "vigrous." **1888** *Century Illustr. Mag.* 36.775 **csTN,** They knowed 't he was might'ly out er kilter—a-blairin' straight ahead'n him ez vig'rous as a wild-cat. **1893** Shands *MS Speech* 61, *Suvigrous.* . . sometimes shortened to *vigrous* [vaɪgrəs], or *vigous* [vaɪgəs]. **1903** *DN* 2.335 **seMO,** *Vigrous* (pronounced [ˈvaɪgrəs]). . . Fierce; vicious. 'He keeps the vigrousest dog in town.' **1907** *DN* 3.238 **nwAR,** *Vigrous* [ˈvaɪgrəs]. . . Fierce, vicious. **1909** *DN* 3.386 **eAL, wGA,** *Vigrous* [ˈvaɪgrəs]. . . Fierce, vicious. **1915** *DN* 4.192 **swVA,** *Vigrus* [vaɪgrəs]. . . Angry; vicious:—of animals or humans. **1917** *DN* 4.419 **wNC,** *Vygorous.* . . Vigorously. "The pig squealed vygorous." **1921** *Harper's Mth. Mag.*

142.802, Oh, my land! he looked vigous. I'd be scared to death of him if I was Squire Lowe. **1927** Adams *Congaree* 18 **cSC** [Black], He so curious an' he so vigus he ain't never had no reason. **1928** in 1952 Mathes *Tall Tales* 79 **sAppalachians,** He's allus makin' out like he's a turrible vygrous feller, but he ain't. Why, he's jes' as saft-hearted as a gal! **1936** *AmSp* 11.318 **Ozarks,** *Vigrous.* . . Vicious, dangerous, likely to do some damage. It is pronounced with a long *i.* **1937** (1963) Hyatt *Kiverlid* 89 **KY,** Yer Gran'pap had the bear dawgs an' had fed 'em on hog hastlets an' gun powder to make 'em plumb fierce an' vygerus. **1942** Hall *Smoky Mt. Speech* 60 **wNC, eTN,** Hit [a rattlesnake] was intentioned to bite me; I never heard a snake sing so [ˈvaɪgrəs]! **1952** Brown *NC Folkl.* 1.604, *Vigrous* [ˈvaɪgrəs]. . . Angry, out of sorts. *Vigrously.* . . Angrily, testily. **1957** Combs *Lang. S. Highlanders* **sAppalachians,** Vargrous—var. of vigorous (of animals). **1958** *PADS* 29.18 **TN,** *Vigrous* [ˈvaɪgrəs]: Fierce, savage, vicious. **1966** *DARE* (Qu. K16, *A cow with a bad temper*) Inf SC1, Vigrous [ˈvæg(ʌ)rʌəs] [sic]. **1967** *Mt. Life* 43.1.15 **sAppalachians,** A high bull-weed, purple and vagrous, a-wavin thar amongst the rocks was plumb dry. **1975** Newell *If Nothin' Don't Happen* 201 **nwFL,** They was one of them great big old hammer-nose sharks. . . He were a vygrus-lookin' sump'n. **1981** Pederson *LAGS Basic Materials,* 1 inf, **ceAL,** [ˈvaˈgrɪs] dogs—mean dogs; 1 inf, **cnAR,** Bulldogs and boxers are [ˈvaˈˌɪgrəs] and they'll fight; 1 inf, **cwGA,** These bobcats look [ˈvaˌɪgrəs]; 1 inf, **cwMS,** [ˈvaˈgrɪs, ˈvaˈɪgrəs] [=angry]; 1 inf, **cwTN,** Red-headed scorpions—[ˈvaˈːɛgrəs ˌlukŋ]; wild hogs [are] [ˈvaˈˌɪgrəs]; 1 inf, **cnAR,** Mighty [ˈvaˈˌɪgrəsliˇ]. **1983** *DARE* File nwMS, Vigrus [ˈvaɪgrəs]—meaning garish, vivid, pungent, of a strong odor. One might say, "They really painted their house a vigrus green, didn't they?" or "Them collard greens sure smell vigrus, don't they?" **2001** *DARE* File nwMS [Black], Once in Marks, Mississippi I heard a Black woman use pronunciation [vaɪgrəs] for *vigorous.* [vaɪgrəs] means "in good health."

villain n Usu |ˈvɪlən|; also chiefly **Sth, S Midl** |ˈvɪljən| Pronc-spp *vil(l)ian, villion, vil(l)yun, vilyan* [*OED2 villian(e)* (at *villain*) 1598 →] Cf **melon, grievous**

Std sense, var forms.

1803 Davis *Travels* 318 **NYC,** He was a *Villian,* he must have been a *Villian,* or he would never impose upon a defenceless widow-woman. **1824** in 1956 Eliason *Tarheel Talk* 320 **csNC,** Vilian. **1837** Sherwood *Gaz. GA* 72, *Villian,* villain. **1850** Southworth *Deserted Wife* 65 **DC** [Black], Oh, he one gran' rascal, Missy, one gallows faced vilyun. **1888** *Harper's New Mth. Mag.* 76.708 **GA,** We heerd the villyun a-runnin'. **1899** (1912) Green *VA Folk-Speech* 470, *Vilyan.* . . Villain. **1909** *DN* 3.386 **eAL, wGA,** *Villyun.* . . Villain. **1942** Hall *Smoky Mt. Speech* 91 **wNC, eTN,** [ˈvɪljən] for *villain.* **1966** *DARE* FW Addit **AR43,** [Tape recording from 1958:] Oh, hold your tongues, you deceitful villians. **1997** in 2004 Montgomery–Hall *Dict. Smoky Mt. Engl.* 633 **wNC, eTN,** *Villain* . . variant form *vilyun* [6 infs].

-ville suff Usu |-vɪl|; also **Sth, S Midl** |-vəl, -vl̩| Pronc-sp *-vl*

Std sense, var forms.

1895 *DN* 1.375 **seKY, wNC,** *Bakervl̩* (=Bakerville; so *Knoxvl̩*). c**1940** Eliason *Word Lists FL* 4 **nwFL,** *Ville* [vʌl]. **1941** in 1944 *ADD* **nGA,** *-ville.* . . *-*[vl]. Knox*v'l,* Ashe*v'l.* **1942** Hall *Smoky Mt. Speech* 62 **wNC, eTN,** *Maryville* . . [ˈmærəvəl]. *Ibid* 69, *-ville:* Asheville [ˈæʃvəl]. **1943** in 1944 *ADD* **KY,** *-ville.* . . [luəvl̩]. Radio. *Ibid* **Sth,** [ˈʃɛlbɪvəl] Shelbyville, Tenn. **1989** Pederson *LAGS Tech. Index* 327 **Gulf Region,** *Asheville* . . [æʃvl̩] . . (248 [of 914 infs]) . . [æʃvɪl] . . (121). . . *Knoxville* . . [nɑksvl̩] . . (333) . . [nɑksvɪl] . . (152). *Ibid* 328, *Nashville* . . [næʃvl̩] . . (420) . . [næʃvɪl] . . (224).

villian, villion, villyun, vilyan, vilyun See **villain**

vinagron See **vinegarone**

vince v[1] Cf **vens, vent** exclam, v[2]

=**hosey.**

1922 *DN* 5.181 **NW,** *Vince,* verb, tr. To choose. "I vince the blue hat." Park City, Utah; Idaho.

vince exclam, v[2], **vincher** See **vent** exclam, v[2]

vine n *among Black speakers*

A suit of clothes, esp a stylish one, usu for a man; also n pl *vines* clothing, esp one's best clothes; hence adj *vined* dressed stylishly.

1932 *Sun* (Baltimore MD) 9 Dec [31/5] [Prison terms], *Vine*—a suit of clothes. **1947** *True* 32.102 **New Orleans LA** [Black], I taken my good hard earned money—bought Joe a couple of sharp *Vines* (Meaning suits) of clothes. **1954** Armstrong *Satchmo* 153 **LA,** I decided one afternoon to put on my sharpest vine. . . Just feel like putting on my Sunday-go-to-meeting suit. **1963** *Freedomways* 3.57 **Harlem NYC,** *Vine:* suit of clothes. **1970** *Current Slang* 5.2.14 [Black univ student slang], *Vines.* . . Stylish clothing. **1970** *DARE* (Qu. W37, *When a woman puts on her good clothes and tries to look her best . . she's* _____) Inf **NY240,** Vined to the gills; (Qu. W39, *Joking ways of referring to a person's best clothes*) Inf **PA248,** Vines; (Qu. W43, . . *Joking words . . for clothes in general*) Infs **DC11, NY237, 240A,** Vines. [All Infs Black] **1972** Claerbaut *Black Jargon* 85, *Vines* . . clothing; apparel. . . a suit; an outfit. **1972** *AmSp* 47.152 (as of 1970) [Black], Without your vines you're nothing but FBI [=Fat, Black, and Ignorant]. **1974** Baldwin *If Beale St. Could Talk* 20 **NYC** [Black], The men . . pass a bottle between them, walk to the corner to the bar, tease the girl behind the bar, fight with each other, and get very busy, later, with their vines.

vine cactus n
=ocotillo.

   1892 U.S. Dept. Ag. *Rept. of Secy. for 1891* 354 **Desert SW,** On the hillsides in the coarse gravel is found the vine cactus. This is not a cactus, but its appearance gives it its name. **1960** Vines *Trees SW* 762, Vernacular names for the plant [=*Fouquieria splendens*] are . . Vine-cactus, Slimwood [etc]. **1972** *Daily Tribune* (WI Rapids WI) 28 Dec 6/2, The ocotillo is a desert plant that grows in Mexico and southwestern United States. . . It is often called candlewood, coachwhip, vine cactus and Jacob's staff.

vined See vine

vine daisy n
A **fleabane** (here: *Erigeron flagellaris*).

   1937 U.S. Forest Serv. *Range Plant Hdbk.* W68, *Erigeron flagellaris.* . . Trailing wild-daisy, sometimes known as trailing fleabane and, most commonly, as vine daisy or trailing daisy, is a small biennial with prostrate creeping stems which root at the tips.

vinegar n Usu |'vɪnɪgɚ|; for addit varr see quots Pronc-spp *vinigger, winegar, wineguh*
Std sense, var forms.

   1821 in 1870 *Amer. Jrl. Educ.* 19.471 **Boston MA,** No one of the second class shall be advanced to the first class who has not learned perfectly by heart . . the catalogue of vulgarisms, such as chimney, not chimbly—vinegar, not winegar, &c. **1860** *Chr. Examiner* 69.14 **Boston MA,** Why does . . the old cockney of the North End in Boston say *winegar* for *vinegar,* . . though the "Bostoneer" of Salutation Alley never heard Bow Bells? **1894** *DN* 1.334 **sNJ,** *V* is often pronounced like *w* by the older people. . . A Gloucester County saying is, "Weal and winegar are good wittles to take aboard a wessel." **1919** *DN* 5.36 **seKY,** *Vinigger.* . . Vinegar. Stressed on the second syllable. **1922** Gonzales *Black Border* 338 **sSC, GA coasts** [Gullah glossary], *Wineguh*—vinegar. **1935** *AmSp* 10.165 **PA** [Engl of PA Germans], One of the most notable characteristics of the English of Pennsylvania Germans, and one which often persists even among the educated classes, is the confusion between *v* and *w*. . . Ordinarily the noticeable feature is the sounding of [w] instead of [v]—*winegar, weal, warnish,* and *wow*. **1976** *DARE* File **cTX,** Some people here pronounce vinegar ['vɪnɪkə]. **1982** *Barrick Coll.* **csPA,** *Vinegar*—pron. [və'nɪgər].

vinegar ant n
Prob a crater-nest ant (*Conomyrma* spp).

   1910 Wright *Black Bear* 95 **West,** Their [=black bears'] greatest feasts . . are obtained when they discover the huge low hills of what, in the West, are called Vinegar Ants. These are only moderate in size, but are extremely vicious. They get their name from a strong odor, resembling that of vinegar, that they exhale when aroused. They build large hills, sometimes several feet in diameter, made up for the most part of pine needles, bits of wood, pellets of earth, and such like stuff. They are red and black in color, have powerful jaws, and rush by the thousand to give battle to any intruder that disturbs their home.

vinegar bush n
A **sweet shrub** (here: *Calycanthus occidentalis*).

   1911 Jepson *Flora CA* 172, *C[alycanthus] occidentalis.* . . Called "Spice-wood" on Howell Mt. . . and "Vinegar bush" in the Kaweah region. **1967** *Fresno Bee the Republican* (CA) 7 May sec F 14/1, *Spice Bush.* . . Calycanthus occidentalis. . . The leaves. . . when crushed . . have a marked aromatic odor. . . This has led to many of the common

names which are: sweet-scented shrub, wine-flower, strawberry bush, vinegar bush and bubby bush.

vinegar fly n Also *vinegar gnat* chiefly NEast, N Cent, West See Map Cf sour fly, ~ gnat
A pomace fly (Drosophilidae family).

   1846 *OH Cultivator* 2.131 **seOH,** In the center of each speck, I found a perforation, the work, as I supposed, of the vinegar fly. **1872** CA State Ag. Soc. *Trans. 1870–71* 504, Rags on bungs should never be used. They . . sour in a short time. This will appear evident from the vinegar flies which collect around them. **1901** Howard *Insect Book* 185, They [=Drosophilidae] are also called "vinegar flies," from the fact that their white, slender larvae are frequently found in canned fruits and pickles which have been imperfectly sealed, . . but living without inconvenience in the briny or vinegary liquid. **1906** *Denton Jrl.* (MD) [20 Jan 8/3] (newspaperarchive.com), Animal products are attacked by larder beetles, etc., fruits by various fruit and vinegar flies. **1950** *WELS Suppl.* **neWI,** Vinegar flies—also called *fruit flies* and *beer flies*. **1953** Bradbury *Fahrenheit 451* 82 **IL,** I'll be with you the rest of the night, a vinegar gnat tickling your ear when you need me. **1960** *Salisbury Times* (MD) 14 June 26/1, One quart per acre of Diazinon should be used . . to give control of the vinegar gnat. **1965–70** *DARE* (Qu. R13, *Flies that come to meat or fruit*) 22 Infs, **chiefly NEast, N Cent, West,** Vinegar fly; **ME20,** Vinegar fly—small, brownish; **VT13,** Vinegar fly—same [as] fruit fly; **IL29, MO1, OH48, OR3,** Vinegar gnat; (Qu. R10, *Very small flies that don't sting, often seen hovering in large groups or bunches outdoors in summer*) Infs **CA65, OH28,** Vinegar flies; **OK3,** Vinegar gnats—get around anything sour; (Qu. R12, . . *Other kinds of flies*) Inf **CA114,** Vinegar fly. **1967** *DARE* FW Addit **CO30,** Vinegar gnats—gather around anything sour. **2000** *Gettysburg Times* (PA) 9 June sec C 3/4, The flies you sent with your letter are pomace flies, also known as fruit or vinegar flies. Usually they breed in decaying fruit or vegetables.

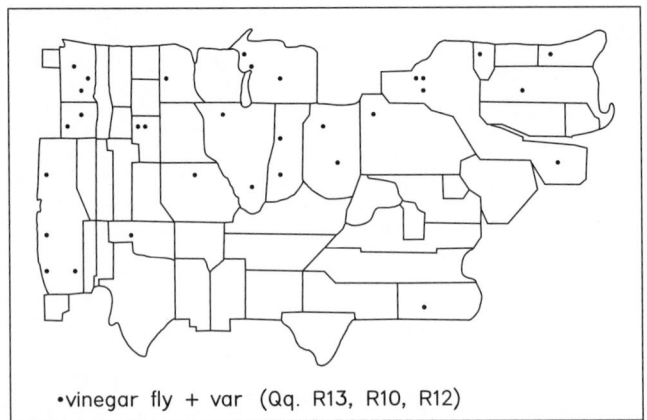

•vinegar fly + var (Qq. R13, R10, R12)

vinegarone n Also *vinagron, vineg(a)ron, vinegar(r)oon, vinegerone*
1 A **whip scorpion** (here: *Mastigoproctus giganteus*). Also called **grampus 2, mule killer 1, nigger ~ 2**

   [**1853** U.S. Army Corps Topog. Engineers *Rept. Sitgreaves* 34 **SW,** Frequently did I find in the road that disagreeable-looking object known to the Mexicans as the vinagron, (*Telephonis* [sic] *giganteus,*) and by them much dreaded.] **1884** *TX Courier–Rec. Med.* 2.265, In the frontier towns of Texas . . and especially in Mexico, another peculiar species of black scorpion occurs, known under the term: vinegaroon, (*thelyphonus caudatus*). **1891** *Century Dict.* 6758, *Vinegerone.* . . The whip-tailed scorpion. . . So called on account of the strong vinegar-like odor of an acid secretion noticeable when the creature is alarmed. . . [*Century* Ed: West Indies and Florida.] **1892** *DN* 1.253 **TX,** *Vineg(a)rón:* an insect of the family of *Arachnida,* said to be exceedingly poisonous, so much so that when a Mexican is bitten he does not send for the physician, but for the priest. **1894** *DN* 1.325 **TX,** Also *vinagrón.* **1948** *Pacific Discovery* Mar 8 **CO,** The vinegaroons, those queer, eight-legged devils of the desert night, raced at top speed in and out of the shadows to gather insect prey. **1966–67** *DARE* (Qu. R21, . . *Other kinds of stinging insects*) Inf **NM3,** Vinegaroon—may not sting, but I'm afraid of 'em; (Qu. R28, . . *Kinds of spiders*) Inf **CA1,** Vinegaroons. **1968** Abbey *Desert Solitaire* 31 **seUT,** Watch out for . . vinegaroons. **1984** Smith *SW Vocab.* 115, *Vinegarroon:* In Spanish, *vinagrón,* it is the large whip scorpion of the Southwest, *Thelyphonus Giganteus*. **2006** *DARE* File—Internet **NM**, There's a scorpion-looking thing there too called a vinegarone. We used to catch 'em and put 'em in a jar (for a little while). When you shake the jar or disturb them they would release a smell supposed to ward off enemies that was like vinegar. **2007** *Ibid*, What you saw in your Arizona driveway was a completely harmless, but intimidating looking, vinegaroon.

2 A wind scorpion. Cf **child of the earth 1**

1926 Essig *Insects N. Amer.* 13, *Solpugida*. . . In the western parts of America they are called "solpugids," "sun spiders," and "vinegarones." **1967** *DARE* (Qu. R28, . . *Kinds of spiders*) Inf **AZ**2, Vinegaroon is another name for child-of-the-earth spider. **2001** in **2007** *DARE* File—Internet **csCA**, Felt a tickle on my knee, looked down to see a vinegaroon the size of a quarter. Yikes! . . Ah, yes, for you not desert dwellers, a vinegaroon is an arachnid that looks like a scorpion without a tail. Ugly. Sometimes they are called sun spiders.

vinegar plant See **vinegar tree**

vinegarroon See **vinegarone**

vinegar stew n Cf **Quaker stew, stew**

A preparation of hot vinegar and honey or other sweetener, and sometimes other ingredients, used as a cold remedy.

c1845 in **1944** Dixon–Vann *Denny Geneal.* 1.202 **OH**, I washed and bathed myself . . and took a vinegar stew. I think it had a good effect. **1854** *NH Patriot & State Gaz.* (Concord) 16 Aug 2/5 (as of 1840), The very same men are organized into a coercive Temperance party, who . . in 1840, were organized to music, with choruses like this:—"Cold water may do for the Locos,/ Or a little vinegar stew;/ But give us *hard cider* and *whiskey* / To drink to 'Old Tippecanoe.' [ʳ] **1919** Hutton–Blake *Complete Angler* 261 **KY**, A vinegar stew, made of honey and vinegar, is fine for a severe cold. **1927** IL State Hist. Soc. *Jrl.* 19.176 (as of 1890), For colds, there was . . also the inhaling of hot fumes from a vinegar stew, a constituent element of which was honey or molasses. **1983** Burke *Plain Talk* 98 **IN**, When someone had a bad cold or flu, they used to make a vinegar stew. . . You take a pie tin . . and fill it with vinegar. . . you heat it, and you make it as hot as you can. Then you eat it.

vinegar tree n Also *vinegar plant*

Either **staghorn sumac** or **smooth sumac 1**.

[**1760** Jefferys *Nat. & Civil Hist. French Dominions* 1.41 **Canada**, *Le Vinagrier* or vinegar tree, is a shrub with a very large pith, which produces a sharp kind of fruit growing in clusters, of the colour of bullock's blood. These are infused in water, and make a sort of vinegar.] **1797** *Encycl. Brit.* (3d ed) 16.228, The . . Virginian sumach, or vinegar plant. **1874** Lindley–Moore *Treas. Botany* 1350, Vinegar-tree, *Rhus typhina*. **1900** Lyons *Plant Names* 320, *R[hus] glabra*. . . Vinegar tree. . . *R. hirta*. . . Vinegar tree. **1920** *Decatur Daily Rev.* (IL) 16 Aug 4/6, The poison ivy is a member of the sumac family, having as relatives the vinegar tree, the smooth sumac, and the *smoke-bush*. **1950** *WELS* (Other names used for . . sumac) 1 Inf, **WI**, Vinegar tree. **1974** (1977) Coon *Useful Plants* 57, *Rhus glabra* . . vinegar tree. *Ibid* 58, *Rhus typhina* . . vinegar tree.

vinegarweed n

1 A blue curls 1, usu *Trichostema lanceolatum* (native to California, Oregon, and Washington). [See quot 1962]

1898 CA Ag. Exper. Sta. *Rept. for 1895–97* 373, Reports on Plants Received for Identification. . . Vinegar-weed *(Trichostema lanceolatum)*. **1936** *Reno Eve. Gaz.* (NV) 2 Nov 2/7 **CA**, Blue curl or vinegar weed in the Sacramento and San Joaquin valleys failed to contribute a surplus of honey this year as they did last year. **1950** *Ibid* 20 June 26/7 **CA**, A remarkable bug is Heliothus Phloxiphaga—he likes. . . such plant outcasts as tarweed, vinegar weed, phlox, milkweed, dandelion, California poppy and plantain. **1962** Sweet *Plants of West* 29, Vinegar-weed . . *Trichostema* sp. . . The name of Vinegar Weed comes from the penetrating and acrid odor of the foliage of all species. **1973** Hitchcock–Cronquist *Flora Pacific NW* 409, W[ashingto]n to Baja Cal; vinegar weed . . *T[richostema] lanceolatum*. **2000** *DARE* File—Internet **CA**, [Caption:] Dolan Ridge below Eagle Rock, showing annual grassland and vinegar weed *(Trichostema lanceolatum)* on fire break.

2 A composite plant *(Lessingia lemmonii)* native to California, Nevada, and New Mexico.

1941 Jaeger *Wildflowers* 287 **Desert SW**, Autumn vinegar-weed. *Lessingia germanorum ramulosissima* [=*L. lemmonii* var *r.*] . . A short-statured, rounded annual, with marked sour-resinous odor. *Ibid* 290, Peirson vinegar-weed. *Lessingia germanorum Peirsonii* [=*L. lemmonii*

var *p.*] . . A low, pungent-odored annual. **2000** in **2004** *DARE* File—Internet **sCA**, *August observations. . . Plants in bloom* . . yellow vinegar weed (Lessingia lemmonii).

vinegerone See **vinegarone**

vine grass n Also *vine panic grass*

=**vine mesquite 1**.

1937 U.S. Forest Serv. *Range Plant Hdbk.* G91, Vine-mesquite. . . It is also known . . in the Southwest, as vine panic-grass. Other local names are ricegrass, vine grass, and wire grass.

vinegron See **vinegarone**

vine lemon n Cf **vegetable peach**

=**mango 3**.

1910 *Wellsboro Gaz.* (PA) 29 Sept 5/5, She saw advertised in a seed catalogue the "vine peach" and the "vine lemon" and bought a package of seed of each and planted them. While the flavor is not exactly that of a peach or lemon the fruit very much resembles both in shape and color and will ripen in this climate. **1956** Ker *Vocab. W. TX* 295, Vine lemons—used instead of fruit for pies, smaller than cantaloupe.

vinella See **vanilla**

vine maple n

1 also *vining maple;* Std: a **maple** (here: *Acer circinatum*) native to the Pacific Northwest and Alaska. [See quot 1908] Also called **green maple 1, mountain ~**

2 also *maple vine:* =**moonseed 1**.

1854 King *Amer. Eclectic Dispensatory* 630, *Menispermum canadense*. Yellow Parilla. . . This plant is also known by the names of *Sarsaparilla, Moonseed, Vine Maple*, etc. **1892** (1974) Millspaugh *Amer. Med. Plants* 14-1, *Menispermum canadense*. . . Canadian moonseed, . . maple vine. . . This perennial climber reaches a length of from 8 to 15 feet. **1971** Krochmal *Appalachia Med. Plants* 170, *Menispermum canadense*. . . Maple vine, . . vine maple. . . A woody, twining perennial vine that grows from a thick root.

vine mesquite n

1 also *vine mesquite grass:* A **panic grass** (here: *Panicum obtusum*) native chiefly to the Central and Southwestern states. [See quot 1937] Also called **grapevine mesquite, ricegrass 2, vine grass, wire ~ 2l**

1910 AZ Ag. Exp. Sta. *Bulletin* 65.275, Vine mesquite *(Panicum obtusum)* forms a turf under favorable conditions . . its distribution is limited . . to the alluvial soils of draws in the mesa-like mountain slopes between 3000 and 6000 feet. **1912** Wooton–Standley *Grasses NM* 47, *Panicum obtusum*. . . Vine Mesquite Grass. **1937** U.S. Forest Serv. *Range Plant Hdbk.* G91, Vine-mesquite is unusual among western range grasses in that it produces creeping stems, or stolons, which sometimes are 10 feet long. **1955** *Amer. Midland Naturalist* 54.471 **AZ**, Several composition estimates . . showed black grama to compose about 26 percent of the cover, the remaining 74 percent being variously divided among blue, sideoats and other gramas, . . vine mesquite *(Panicum obtusum)*, tobosa [etc]. **1997** *Ecology* 78.1223 **TX**, The dominant grass was *Stipa leucotricha* (Texas winter grass), . . with subdominant grasses including . . *Panicum obtusum* (vine mesquite). **2004** *DARE* File—Internet **AZ**, This mesquite bosque is composed of many large mesquite . . , forbs (like morning glories, amaranth, buffalo gourd), and grasses (like vine mesquite grass).

2 =**buffalo grass a.**

1941 *Torreya* 41.46 **TX**, *Buchloë dactyloides*. . . Vine mesquite.

vine mesquite grass See **vine mesquite 1**

vine milkweed n Also *viney milkweed*

Any of several related twining plants of the genera *Cynanchum, Funastrum,* and *Matelea*. Cf **sand vine, talayote a, b, twine vine**

1859 in **1942** Hafen *Overland Routes* 11.151 **VA**, Saw . . handsome flowers peculiar to these sand ridges . . a species of vine milk-weed, with clusters of white flowers. **1946** Reeves–Bain *Flora TX* 130, Cynanchum. . . Vine Milkweed. . . Twining perennial herbs. **2003** *TX Monarch Watch* 14 **TX**, One common vine milkweed, *Matelea reticulata* (pearl milkvine), is a food plant for the queen butterfly. **2004** *DARE* File—Internet, [Caption:] Above is the seed pod of the vine milkweed [here: =*Cynanchum laeve*] and a hungry cat[erpillar]. *Ibid, Monarch hostplants:* . . Cynanchum angustifolium . . (. . milkweed vine)[;]

C. laeve . . (. . vine milkweed). . . Matelea reticulata . . ([pearl, net-vein, netted] milkvine; milkvine, . . green milkweed vine). . . Sarcostemma clausum . . (. . white milkweed vine, viney milkweed, whitevine, narrow-leaf milkweed vine)[;] S. crispum TX (wavy-leaf milkweed vine, . . wavyleaf milkvine).

vine okra n   Also *vining okra*   **Sth**
=**vegetable sponge.**

    1969 *Daily Times–News* (Burlington NC) 9 Oct sec C 6/3, What is the proper name for what we locally call "vine" or "running okra"? . . This plant is not related to okra but the young fruit resemble okra and can be used as okra.   **1971** GA Dept. Ag. *Farmers Market Bulletin* 26 May 1/2, [Question:] I know vining okra is an edible gourd but do not know the botanical name. Can you help? [Response:] Luffa is the botanical name.   **1990** *Seed Savers Yearbook* 269, *Luffa Sponge (Vine Okra)* . . a.k.a. Running Okra, plant on fence or trellis, ready to eat when 8–10″ long, fry as any other okra.   **1995** in 2004 (acc) GA Univ. Coop. Ext. Serv. *Fact Sheet* (Internet) **GA**, The Luffa (dishrag gourd) has a number of possible uses. . . In the immature state it can be eaten and is often called vining or running okra.   **2004** *DARE* File—Internet **FL**, Ridged loofah (*Luffa acutangula*), or "vine okra", . . has white flowers and produces gourds that are ridged with ten angles.

vine orchid n

    A vanilla orchid (*Vanilla* spp) native to Florida.

    1971 Craighead *Trees S. FL* 128, Epiphytes are abundant, both bromeliads and orchids. The vine orchid occurs commonly. *Ibid* 203, Vine orchids, Vanilla spp.

vine panic grass   See **vine grass**

vine peach n   Cf **vegetable peach**
=**mango 3.**

    1895 Gray–Bailey *Field Botany* 192, *C[ùcumis] Mèlo*. . . Var. *Chito* is the *Vegetable Orange* or *Lemon* or *Apple,* also called *Vine Peach,* distinguished by slender vines and yellow sourish fruits the size of a goose egg.   **1910** [see **vine lemon**].   **1928** *Decatur Eve. Herald* (IL) 1 Sept 3/8, The vine peach is a vegetable, the fruit of a vine which in appearance and manner of growth is somewhat like the cucumber.   **1953** (1977) Hubbard *Shantyboat* 310 **Missip-Ohio Valleys**, The vine peach, or as Tom called it, "plumgranate," was another wild fruit new to us. It ripened late in the sandy fields, about the size and color of a small yellow tomato, and could be made into a thick preserve.   **1975** *News–Jrl.* (Mansfield OH) 10 Oct sec C 6/3, This summer he grew a plant called the vine peach or mango melon. It has the characteristics of both a vegetable and fruit.   **2004** *DARE* File—Internet, *Cantaloupes:* There are many varieties of these aromatic melons, including . . even a small, hardy indigenous North American sort called "mango melon" or "vine peach".

vines   See **vine**

vine snake n

1 A **green snake** (here: *Opheodrys aestivus*).

    1928 Baylor Univ. Museum *Contrib.* 16.14 **TX**, *Opheodrys aestivus*. . . is commonly known as the *Green Tree Snake* or *Vine Snake.*   **1958** Conant *Reptiles & Amphibians* 152, *Rough Green Snake*. . . The "vine snake." . . An excellent climber that, when foraging amid vines or shrubs, blends with the background so well as to be virtually invisible.   **2004** *DARE* File—Internet, *Opheodrys aestivus*. . . Common names include the Keeled Green Snake, . . the Vine Snake [etc]. . . Green Snakes are arboreal.

2 A very slender snake (*Oxybelis aeneus*) native to southern Arizona.

    1952 Ditmars *N. Amer. Snakes* 235, *Arizona Vine Snake, Oxybelis micropthalmus* [=*O. aeneus*]. . . Extremely slender. . . Resting in the foliage, in extended undulations they so resemble vines or twisted branches that they are extremely difficult to detect.   **1974** Shaw–Campbell *Snakes West* 167, More than slender, the vine snake is so thin it seems drawn out, as though a smaller, thicker snake had been stretched from both ends.   **2003** *DARE* File—Internet **AZ**, Brown Vine Snake—*Oxybelis aeneus*. . . A very thin (30″ to 60″) snake that closely resembles a vine.

vineweed n

    A **bindweed 1** or similar plant.

    1923 *Lincoln Star* (NE) 3 Jan 1/5, The vine weed, such as the morning glory, is especially bad in that it can shoot new plants from either the stem or root.   **1948** *Mansfield News–Jrl.* (OH) 24 June 8/3, She ex-

plained that the wild morning glory is often called hedge vine weed. . . It is found as far south as South Carolina and west to the Dakotas and Utah.   **1949** *Post–Std.* (Syracuse NY) 24 Apr 45/7, Kill or control vetch, yellow rocket, ragweed, vineweed, thistle, dock, buckhorn, wild carrot, etc., in your unseeded wheat.   **1966–67** *DARE* (Qu. S5, . . *Wild morning glory*) Inf **PA**18, Vineweed; (Qu. S21, . . *Weeds . . that are a trouble in gardens and fields*) Infs **NM**13, **OK**32, Vineweed.   **2002** *Star–Herald* (Scottsbluff NE) 10 July sec A 4/1, *Vine weed*—"The little white flowers all over town and in the county area are vine weed, which is a noxious weed."   **2002** in 2004 *DARE* File—Internet, A group at the University of Texas has looked at things such as vineweed.   *Ibid* **ND**, The raspberries have been slowly loosing [sic] the territory they previously held domain over to the vineweed that seems to be taking over our county.

vine-wicky n   [*vine* + **wicky**]

    An ericaceous vine (*Pieris phillyreifolia*).

    1966 Grimm *Recognizing Native Shrubs* 231, *Vine-wicky—Pieris phillyreifolia*. . . An evergreen vinelike shrub.   **1996** Nelson *Shrubs & Vines FL* 115, Climbing Heath, Climbing Pieris, Vine Wicky—*Pieris phillyreifolius*. . . The specimens growing . . in the Morman Branch Scenic area of the Ocala National Forest . . provide excellent examples of the climbing nature of this species.

viney milkweed   See **vine milkweed**

vinigger   See **vinegar**

vining maple   See **vine maple 1**

vining okra   See **vine okra**

vino n   Usu |ˈvino|; also |ˈvaino, ˈvino, ˈvinεo, ˈwino| Pronc-sp *veeno*   [Span, Ital]   **chiefly Nth, N Midl, West, esp CA**   See Map   Cf **dago red**
    Wine.

    1857 *Alta California* (San Francisco CA) 19 Oct (*AmSp* 16.265), *Spanish Words Frequently Used in English Conversation in Califoruia* [sic]. . . Vino, Wine.   **1927** *AmSp* 2.389 [Vagabond argot], *Veeno* means wine.   **1965–70** *DARE* (Qu. DD27, . . *Nicknames . . for wine*) 80 Infs, **chiefly Nth, N Midl, West, esp CA**, Vino; **IL**5, **OR**15, [ˈvaino]; **CA**17, [ˈvino]; **MD**11, [ˈvinεo]; **CO**4, [wino]; **LA**14, Da vino [FW: The "da" may be imitation of Italian pronc of *the.*]; **PA**245, Horky vino.   **1986** Pederson *LAGS Concordance (Wine)* 3 infs, **AL, TX**, Vino.

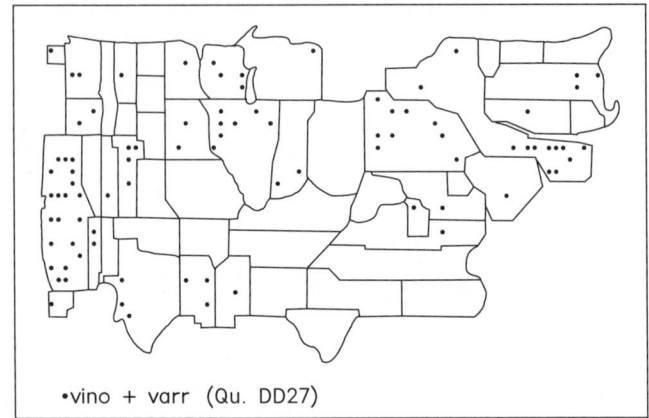

    •vino + varr (Qu. DD27)

vints   See **vent exclam, v²**

violean, violeen   See **violin**

violet n

    Std: a plant of the genus *Viola.*   Also called **johnny 3, johnny-jump-up 1, jump-up-johnny;** for other names of var spp see **bird's-foot violet, bright eyes 2, butterfly violet, Canadian wood ~, chicken fight 1, Confederate violet, dog's tongue 2, dog violet, forget-me-not 3, French violet, gallito 1, gray violet, heartsease 1, hen n¹ B2, hens and roosters, jack-in-the-pulpit 2i, jump-up 1, little johnny 2, marsh blue violet, marsh ~, meadow ~, mouse-ear ~, pansy, pansy violet, pine ~, pioneer ~, prairie ~ 1, rattlesnake ~ 1, rebel ~, redwood ~, rooster 2, rooster fight 1, ~ head 1, sagebrush violet, sand ~, swamp ~, wild okra 1, ~ pansy**

Cf **adder's violet, dogtooth** ~, **false** ~, **green** ~, **mad** ~, **mahukona** ~, **star** ~

violet bloom n
1 A **bittersweet** (here: *Solanum dulcamara*).
1830 Rafinesque *Med. Flora* 2.86, *Solanum Dulcamara* . . Violet bloom. . . Flowers on peduncles opposed to the leaves, bearing a loose cluster . . of many flowers, of a pretty violet color. **1854** King *Amer. Eclectic Dispensatory* 895, *Solanum Dulcamara*. Bittersweet. . . also known by the names of *Violet-bloom,* and *Scarlet-berry,* is common to both Europe and this country. **1898** U.S. Dept. Ag. Div. Botany *Bulletin* 20.53, *Solanum dulcamara* . . wolf grape; violet bloom. . . The flowers are purple, the fruit red. **1930** Sievers *Amer. Med. Plants* 11, *Solanum dulcamara* . . violet-bloom. . . The purplish flowers . . resemble those of the potato.
2 A **matrimony vine 1** (here: *Lycium barbarum*).
1940 Clute *Amer. Plant Names* 226, *Lycium halimifolium.* Fever-twig, morel, tether devil, violet bloom, wolf grape.

violet tail n   Also *violet dancer*   Cf **dancer 2**
A **damselfly** (here: *Argia violacea*).
1980 Milne–Milne *Audubon Field Guide Insects* 387, *Violet Tail—* "Violet Dancer" (*Argia violacea*). . . These striking damselflies are often seen flying in tandem over streams and ponds. **1987** *Providence Jrl.* (RI) 30 Aug sec M 21 (Internet), Though one name is now generally applied to dragonflies, the different varieties still have individual names— green clearwing, violet tail, black-faced skimmer, green darner. **2003** in 2006 *DARE* File—Internet **CA,** Got to love the paint job on the damselfly (probably a Violet Dancer, *Argia violacea*) at bottom—violet and metalic [sic] bronze. **2004** *Ibid,* The Violet Tail (Argia violacea) . . is found throughout the US and Canada.

violet tip n
=**question mark 1.**
1881 Scudder *Butterflies* 167, The most conspicuous case [of dimorphism] is in the largest, the Violet Tip (Polygonia interrogationis . .), where the two forms were once universally considered distinct species. **1909** *Atlanta Constitution* (GA) 17 Jan [44]/5 (newspaperarchive.com), Kitty thought the butterflies displayed much versatility in selecting places for enjoying long winter naps. Among these sleepers were . . the Violet Tip, lover of nettles [etc]. **1946** *Sci. News Letter* 49.103, [Caption:] The violet-tip butterfly . . spends the winter as an adult clinging to the stalk.

violin n   Usu |ˌvaɪəˈlɪn|; also |vaɪˈlin, ˈvaɪlɪn| Pronc-spp *violeen, violean*
Std sense, var forms.
1872 Eggleston *End of the World* 298 **IN,** Then we've got the paytent double whirlymagig hoss-violeen. **1936** *AmSp* 11.155 **eTX,** *Violin* (which in East Texas is stressed on the first syllable) . . [ˈvaɪlɪn]. **1940** Stuart *Trees of Heaven* 61 **eKY,** I love to hear a violean. **2001** *DARE* File **ceOK,** Have you heard of the pronunciation *violeen* [vaɪˈlin] for *violin?* I heard it from an informant in Tahlequah, Oklahoma, a Cherokee Indian woman born in 1902. She has six years school. She does not speak Cherokee.

violin case n   Also *violin*
=**fiddle case.**
1917 *Los Angeles Examiner* (CA) 12 Mar 8 (Zwilling Coll.), [Cartoon:] Dancing with a guy who wears a no 11 shoe [who] thinks himself the champion of the world. . . If those violin cases came down on my feet I'd declare war. **1925** *WI News* (Milwaukee) 4 Sept 14 (Zwilling Coll.), [Cartoon:] Did you get the pair of dogs on the twist and twirl who is to play Cinderella? If they're not violin cases I'm a riff. **1967** *DARE* (Qu. X38, *Joking names for unusually big or clumsy feet*) Inf **MI**67, Violin cases, violins.

violin spider n
A venomous spider (*Loxosceles reclusa*) distinguished by a violin-shaped mark on the dorsal side of the cephalothorax, native to much of the southern and midwestern US.   Also called **brown recluse spider, fiddle** ~ **1, recluse** ~
1963 *Tucson Daily Citizen* (AZ) 18 Sept 10/5, *Beware Of The 'Violin' Spider.* . . Beware of a common brown spider, which has a dark spot shaped like a violin on its head, the Veterans Administration said today. **1967** *Oakland Tribune* (CA) 6 Jan sec E 4/1, The spider, commonly called the Missouri Brown spider or violin spider, has an up to one inch leg spread and a purplish violin shaped spot on its back. **1968** *DARE* (Qu. R28, . . *Kinds of spiders*) Inf **IN**46, Violin spider = recluse spider.

1980 Milne–Milne *Audubon Field Guide Insects* 875, *Violin Spider—* "Brown Recluse Spider" (Loxosceles reclusa). . . Outdoors in sheltered corners among loose debris; indoors on the floor and behind furniture in houses and outbuildings. **2002** *Richmond Times–Dispatch* (VA) 4 Apr sec F 1 (Internet), Known as violin spiders because of the fiddle-shaped marking on their cephalothorax, recluse spiders are naturally abundant in the Mississippi River drainage.

viper n   Also *viper snake*   Cf **black viper, blowing** ~, **poison** ~, **sand** ~, **spreading** ~
=**hognose snake.**
[**1688** in 1694 Royal Soc. London *Philos. Trans.* 18.134 **VA,** The Blowing-Snake [is] an absolute Species of a Viper, but larger than any that I have seen in *Europe.*] **1851** *De Bow's Rev.* 11.54 **LA,** *Viper,* or *Spreading Adder*—A short, dark-colored snake; when irritated, enlarges the head and jaws. **1888** *Pop. Sci. Mth.* 33.660, The blow-snake of Illinois is variously known in other localities as hog-nose, flat-head, viper, and puff-adder. **1941** Stuart *Men of Mts.* 50 **eKY,** Pap used to tell us . . that when weeds got knee high in a corn patch, we ought to go through with a stick and shake the weeds and run the vipers, copperheads, rattlesnakes, and blacksnakes out. **1968–70** *DARE* (Qu. P25, . . *Kinds of snakes*) Infs **IN**45, 58, **NC**80, 82, **PA**235, Viper; **KY**49, Viper—swell its head; **MD**13, Viper—red or yellow, poisonous, land, one-inch diameter, 3–4 ft. long; **MD**15, Viper snake—small, poisonous. [*DARE* Ed: Some of these Infs may refer instead to another snake.]

viper's bugloss n
Std: a blue-flowered plant (*Echium vulgare*) naturalized throughout much of the US.   Also called **blue devil 4, blueweed 1, blue thistle, cattail 2d**

viper snake   See **viper**

vireo n
Std: any of var small birds of the family Vireonidae, esp those of the genus *Vireo.*   For other names see **greenlet, red-eyed vireo, white-eyed** ~

vire-vire n   [LaFr < Fr *virer* to turn]   **LA**
=**willet.**
1911 *Forest & Stream* 77.174 **LA,** *Catoptrophorus semipalmatus* [sic] . . Vive [sic] Vire. **1921** LA Dept. of Conserv. *Bulletin* 10.79 **LA,** The willet (*Catoptrophorus semipalmatus*) is known very well along the Louisiana coast. . . Its trait of circling, or "hanging around", the same place, has given it the Creole name of "vire-vire". **1937** *Galveston Daily News* (TX) 28 Sept 12/2 **LA,** Willet [sic], vire-vire, tell-tale, tattler, pill-willet. **1955** Lowery *LA Birds* 253, Local names of this large shore bird, *vire-vire* and "pill-will-willet." **1983** Reinecke *Coll.* 11 **LA,** *Virevire.* . . The willet, a good-sized, long-legged, long-beaked shore bird. La. Fr. from its turning flight. A common term to outdoorsmen.

Virginia n   Usu |və(r)ˈjɪnjə|; also **chiefly Sth** |və(r)ˈjɪni| Pronc-spp *Fe(r)ginny, Ferginyer, Virginny;* for addit pronc and sp varr see quots
Std sense, var forms.
1817 in 1830 Royall *Letters AL* 21, I will try to beguile the time in amusing myself with "mine host" and hostess, who I dare say, expect to make their Jack out of me—"Old Feginny begging!" **1825** Neal *Brother Jonathan* 2.179 **CT,** "Well done, Figinny! hourra for Fiqinny!" said Winslow. **1859** (1968) Bartlett *Americanisms* 497, *Virginny,* or *Old Virginny.* The common negro appellation of the State of Virginia. **1859** Taliaferro *Fisher's R.* 17 **nwNC,** It was honor enough for them that they came from "Fudginny." **1877** *Scribner's Mth.* 14.726 **Sth** [Black], When I was a boy in Ferginyer. **1884** Baldwin *Yankee School-Teacher* 35 **VA,** A woman's basque of dark "Virginny cloth" . . adorned the upper part of his person. **1887** (1967) Harris *Free Joe* 216 **cGA** [Black], My young marster w'at gwine ter college in Ferginny. **1899** Chesnutt *Conjure Woman* 137 **csNC** [Black], Becky's husban' wuz sol' [=sold] erway ter Fuhginny. **1909** *S. Atl. Qrly.* Jan 44 [Gullah], Ol' Mis' Preston lib een Fujinny. **1914** *DN* 4.154 **NH,** Virginny fence. **1916** *Scribner's Mag.* 59.358 **VA** [Black], De teeny-bitty nigger tetched up de Ole Ferginyeh Reel on his teeny-bitty fiddle. **1929** Sale *Tree Named John* 98 **MS** [Black], Now dis wuz back in ole Ferginny, Baby, way 'fo' de wah. **1939** *LANE* Map 12 (*Virginia*) **NEng,** [The pronunciations [vədʒɪnjə, -ɪə] are widespread, with scattered instances of the type [vədʒɪnɪ] throughout the region.] Pronunciations of the type of [vɑdʒɪnɪ] are regarded as older or old-fashioned though still in use by [23 infs]. **1942** Hall *Smoky Mt. Speech* 76 **wNC, eTN,** In the speech of most old people, of many middle-aged and young, . . -*a* and -*ia* . . appear as [ɪ]. . . Virginia [-nɪ]. **1950** Faulkner *Stories* 753 **MS** [Black], Dey tole us

back dar at Ferginny it was done wid. **1982** Slone *How We Talked* 34 **eKY** (as of c1950), *Old Fer'ginie*—Virginia. **1989** Pederson *LAGS Tech. Index* 316 **Gulf Region,** *Virginia.* [Of 689 infs who responded to the question, 508 offered proncs of the types [vǝ(r)'jɪnjǝ, -ɪǝ]; 44 infs, proncs of the types [vǝ(r)'jɪnjɪ]; 37 infs, proncs of the types [fǝ(r)'jɪnjǝ, -jɪ]; 33 infs, proncs of the types [vǝ(r)'jɛnjǝ, -jǝ]; 17 infs, proncs of the types [vǝ(r)'jɪnjɚ]; 15 infs, proncs of the types [vǝ(r)'jɪnjǝ, -ɪ, fǝ'jɪnjǝ]; 9 infs, proncs of the types [vǝ(r)'jɪnjǝ, -ɪǝ, -ɪ]; 3 infs, proncs of the types [vǝ(r)'jɪnɪ, -ǝ].]

Virginia bat n Cf bat n¹

A **whippoorwill B1** or other caprimulgid bird such as the **nighthawk 1.**

1688 in 1693 *Royal Soc. London Philos. Trans.* 17.991, The Night Raven, which some call the *Virginia* Bat, is about the bigness of a Cuckow, feather'd like them but very short, and short Leg'd, not discernable when it flies, which is only in the Evening scuding like our Night Raven. **1945** *AN&Q* 5.11 **VA,** Despite the dominance of *whippoorwill,* there are a number of local names for the bird: . . "Virginia bat" (Virginia, to distinguish it from the Carolina bat or chuck-will's-widow).

Virginia bluebell(s) n

Std: a **bluebell 1g** (here: *Mertensia virginica*) native to most of the eastern half of the US. Also called **brandywine cowslip, cowslip 3, gentleman's breeches, lungwort 1, pink and blue ladies, Virginia cowslip**

Virginia caviar n

Beans or peas.

1968 *DARE* FW Addit **GA46,** "Virginia caviar"—nickname for beans. **2006** *DARE* File—Internet **VA,** Virginia Caviar Salad combines black-eyed peas, sweet peppers, red onion, and diced tomatoes with a sweet and sour vinaigrette; finished with fresh cilantro.

Virginia corn cracker n Cf Virginia nightingale

=**cardinal 1.**

1984 in 1986 *Barrick Coll.* **csPA,** Virginia corn cracker—cardinal or redbird.

Virginia cowslip n Also Virginian cowslip

=**Virginia bluebell(s).**

1826 Darlington *Florula Cestrica* 23, *Pulmonaria. . . virginica. . .* Virginian Cowslip. **1843** Torrey *Flora NY* 2.85, *Pulmonaria Virginica* [= *Mertensia v.*] . . Virginian Cowslip. **1904** *Decatur Herald* (IL) 10 May 6/6, Virginia Cowslip, or Blue-bells, belongs to the Borage family. **1966–68** *DARE* Wildfl QR Pl.181 [=*Mertensia virginica*] Infs **MI**31, **NY**91, Virginia cowslip. **1994** *Pittsburgh Post-Gaz.* (PA) 10 Apr sec D 15 (Internet), Virginia cowslips (sometimes called bluebells) will burst into bloom any day.

Virginia creeper n

1 also *Virginian creeper;* Std: a climbing vine of the genus *Parthenocissus,* esp *P. quinquefolia.* Also called **creeper 1, ivy 2, woodbine 2.** For other names of *P. quinquefolia* see **false grape 1, five-fingered Joe, five-fingers 3, five-leaved ivy;** for other names of var spp see **thicket creeper**

2 =**hedge bindweed 1.**

1940 Clute *Amer. Plant Names* 92, *C[onvolvulus] sepium.* Hedge Bindweed. . . devil's vine, ladies' nightcap, hedge lily, harvest lily, lily-vine, (Virginia creeper.) **1967–70** *DARE* (Qu. S5, . . *Wild morning glory*) Infs **NY**21, 232, Virginia creeper.

Virginia fence n Also Virginia crooked fence, ~ rail ~, ~ worm ~ chiefly NEng, Sth Cf snake fence

1 =**worm fence.**

1671 in 1901 Portsmouth RI *Early Rec.* 160, For post and rayles it Shall be of the Same hight of the Virginia ffence. **1790** Deane *New Engl. Farmer* 92, A Virginia fence. . . is made by lapping the ends of rails or poles on each other, turning alternately to the right and left. **1809** in 1810 Cuming *Sketches* 34 **PA,** Two very beautiful red foxes playfully crossed the road . . leaping with ease a Virginia worm fence. **1851** *De Bow's Rev.* 11.59 **LA,** Our *fences* throughout the parish are mostly the old Virginia worm fence. **1875** Holland *Sevenoaks* 405 **N Atl,** They will be so much magnified as to present very much the appearance of a Virginia fence. **1881** *Decatur Daily Rev.* (IL) 13 Aug [2]/1 (newspaperarchive.com) **MO,** His meal . . was just about as digestible as a panel out of a Virginia worm fence. **1884** IL Superintendent Pub. Instruction *Biennial Rept. 1882–84* cxv (as of 1830s), He found the . . farmers busy, at great cost of labor, time and material, in fencing

their farms with split rails, laid in the Virginia crooked fence. **1949** Kurath *Word Geog.* 55, *Rail fence.* . . The old-fashioned rail fence built of overlapping rails laid zigzag fashion. . . In New England this type of fence is commonly known as a *Virginia rail fence* to distinguish it from the *post-and-rail fence* of New England. **1967–69** *DARE* (Qu. L62, *A fence made of split logs*) Inf **MA**68, Virginia fence; **MA**31, Virginia fence—used to be miles of them around here, mostly made of chestnut; **AL**14, Virginia rail fence; **CT**17, Virginia rail fence—zigzags; (Qu. L65, . . *Kinds of fences*) Inf **MA**37, Virginia rail fence—same as rail fence, only put up a different way, they zigzagged. **1975** *Daily Times-News* (Burlington NC) 1 Aug sec A 10/7, After extensive research, Sleepy Hollow installed. . . A field devoted to half an acre of fiber flax protected with a Virginia worm fence. **1984** Wilder *You All Spoken Here* 195 **Sth,** *Virginia fence:* Rail fence; worm fence; snake fence.

2 in phrr **make (a) Virginia fence** and varr: To walk unsteadily; to be drunk.

1737 *PA Gaz.* (Philadelphia) 13 Jan 2/2, He [being drunk] makes Virginia Fence. **1779** in 1789 Anburey *Travels* 2.324, The New-Englanders have a saying, when a man is in liquor, *he is making Virginia fences.* **1831** *Georgian* (Savannah) 22 Jan. 2/5 *(DAE),* I saw lots of fellers [in N.Y.] walking Virginia fence, and some at the corners holdin' up a post. **1867** Lowell *Biglow* lix **'Upcountry' MA,** *Virginia fence, to make a:* to walk like a drunken man. **1877** Bartlett *Americanisms* 734, The phrase "to walk like a Virginia fence" is applied to a drunken man. **1914** *DN* 4.154 **NH,** *Virginny fence.* . . "He is cutting a —," he is drunk.

Virginia mallow n Also Virginian mallow

A **mallow B** (here: *Sida hermaphrodita*).

[**1784** Abercrombie *Propagation Plants & Trees* 2.447, *Napæa*—Virginia Mallow— *[Napæa] hermaphrodita*—Hermaphrodite-flowered Virginia Mallow.] **1897** Britton–Brown *Illustr. Flora* 2.422, *Sida hermaphrodita.* . . Virginia Mallow. **1911** *Century Dict. Suppl.,* Virginia or Virginian mallow, *Sida hermaphrodita.* **1942** Hylander *Plant Life* 664, Virginia Mallow . . Sida hermaphrodita. **1987** *Amer. Antiq.* 52.365 **cKY,** Pokeweed *(Phytolacca americana),* Virginia (?) mallow *(Sida* sp.), and beggar's ticks *(Desmodium* sp.) were all present in low frequencies.

Virginia mullet n chiefly NC

=**kingfish 1.**

1892 Perry et al. *Amer. Game Fishes* 120, I have had them [=tarpon] take small catfish, and the variety termed "Virginia Mullet" by the coast fishermen. **1907** Smith *Fishes NC* 322, *Menticirrhus americanus.* . . Another name that is quite local is "Virginia mullet", which is heard from Beaufort to Wilmington. . . According to Mr. W.H. Yopp, this fish is supplied to the Wilmington market . . , being known there as "Virginia mullet." **1958** *Daily Times-News* (Burlington NC) 17 Sept sec D 3/2, The first consistent catches of spots, Virginia mullet and bluefish of the fall season were made this week. **1961** Ruark *Old Man's Boy* 58 **eNC,** There were mullet and shrimp and pan fish in the creek, and an occasional puppy drum or little blue or Virginia mullet in the sloughs. **1968** *DARE* (Qu. P2, . . *Kinds of saltwater fish caught around here . . good to eat*) Inf **NC**52, Virginia mullet. **1984** *DARE* File **Chesapeake Bay** [Watermen's vocab], Sand mullet / sea mullet / Virginia mullet. **2003** Humphries–Edgerton *North Carolina* 22, In Morehead City, we visit Ottis' Fish Market to buy fifteen or twenty Virginia mullet that we'll cut up and use for bait. **2006** *News & Observer* (Raleigh NC) 20 Apr sec C 9 (Internet), Sea mullet also are called Virginia mullet, tiger mullet, kingfish and whiting. There are three species common to the N.C. coast—the northern kingfish, southern kingfish and Gulf kingfish—but they are so similar that anglers seldom try to identify which species they are catching.

Virginian cowslip See Virginia cowslip

Virginian creeper See Virginia creeper 1

Virginia nightingale n Also Virginian nightingale [OED2 (at Virginian a.¹) 1668 →] obs Cf nightingale b

=**cardinal 1.**

1688 in 1693 *Royal Soc. London Philos. Trans.* 17.995, Of *Virginia* Nightingale, or red Bird, there are two sorts, the Cocks of both sorts of a pure Scarlet, the Hens of a Duskish red. **1729** *Ibid* 36.430 **NC,** *Cocothraustes rubra,* the red Bird, or *Virginia* Nightingal. **1806** (1905) Lewis *Orig. Jrls. Lewis & Clark Exped.* 5.111, The beak is reather more than half an inch in length, and is formed much like the virginia nitingale; it is thick and large for a bird of it's size; wide at the base, both chaps convex. [**1810** Wilson *Amer. Ornith.* 2.38, This is one of our most common cage birds; and is very generally known, . . even in Europe; numbers of them having been carried over both to France and England, in which last country they are usually called Virginia Nightingales.] **1895** (1896) Bruce *Economic Hist. VA* 1.119, Much more interesting was the cardinal or red bird, which was always described as the Virginian nightingale.

Virginian mallow   See **Virginia mallow**

Virginian nightingale   See **Virginia nightingale**

Virginian owl   See **Virginia owl**

Virginian pine   See **Virginia pine**

Virginian quail   See **Virginia quail**

Virginian rail   See **Virginia rail**

Virginian sumac   See **Virginia sumac**

Virginian swamp pine   See **Virginia pine 3**

Virginian thyme   See **Virginia thyme**

Virginia owl n   Also *Virginian owl*   Cf **screech owl 2c**
=**great horned owl.**

[**1806** Linné *Genl. System Nature* (transl. Turton) 1.166, [Bubo] Virginiana. . . Virginian Owl. Inhabits *America*. . . Feathers of the ears large; *bill* black; *irids* golden-yellow.] **1831** Audubon *Ornith. Biog.* 1.8, Of the numerous enemies of the Wild Turkey, the most formidable, excepting man, are the Lynx, the Snowy Owl, and the Virginian Owl. **1903** *WI State Jrl.* (Madison) 12 Sept 8/4, To the right and sitting on the top of a tall show case is a weird appearing, horned Virginia owl. **1939** *LANE* Map 230 (*Screech owl*) 1 inf, **cwMA**, Virginia owl = cat owl. **1946** Hausman *Eastern Birds* 355, *Great Horned Owl*. . Virginia Owl.

Virginia partridge n   Cf **Virginia quail**
=**bob-white.**

1783 Latham *Genl. Synopsis Birds* 2.777, Tetrao Virginianus. . . *Virginia P[artridge]*. . . *Smaller* than the *Common Partridge*. **1814** Wilson *Amer. Ornith.* 9.[index], Virginian Partridge. **1857** Lewis *Amer. Sportsman* 66, *Perdix virginianus* [=*Colinus v.*] . . The inhabitants of the Northern States call it quail; in the Middle or Southern States it is more familiarly known as the partridge, or Virginia partridge. **1883** *Century Illustr. Mag.* 26.484, If, however, many of our friends should persist—as they certainly will—in calling Bob White a quail, then they should call a brood of these birds a *bevy;* while a *covey* should designate a brood, if they call him a Virginia partridge. **1907** *Coshocton Weekly Times* (OH) 31 Oct 3/7, No person shall kill in any one day more than 18 Virginia partridge or quail—if he gets the chance. **1923** U.S. Dept. Ag. *Farmers' Bulletin* 1375.39 **WV**, Open seasons: . . Quail (Virginia partridge). . . Nov. 1–Nov. 30. **1968** *Times Recorder* (Zanesville OH) 14 Aug sec C 7/1, It is unlawful to catch, kill, injure or pursue with such intent any Virginia partridge or quail. **1982** Elman *Hunter's Field Guide* 84, *Colinus virginianus* . . Virginia partridge.

Virginia pine n   Also *Virginian pine*
1 =**longleaf pine 1.** *obs*

1760 in 1775 Burnaby *Travels* 80 **Sth**, It becomes beautifully covered with Virginian pines: the seeds of that tree . . are exceedingly small, and, when the cones open, are wafted through the air in great abundance. **1874** *Galveston Daily News* (TX) 27 Mar [2]/1 (newspaperarchive.com), Several hundred piles of Virginia pine, from forty to sixty feet long, have been driven for two of the four piers. **1890** *Century Dict.* 4496, *Virginian pine,* an old name of the long-leafed pine.

2 also *Virginia scrub pine:* =**Jersey pine.** esp **VA**   See Map

1785 Marshall *Arbustrum* 102, Pinus virginiana. Two-leaved Virginian, or Jersey Pine. This is generally of but low growth, but divided into many branches. **1854** *NY Daily Times* (NY) 23 June 7/3, Proposals will be received . . for furnishing the Schools . . with . . 200 cords of Virginia Pine. **1861** *Living Age* 68.505, The supply [of kindling for NYC] from Virginia is not in keeping with the demand; although the Virginia pine has a very rapid growth, shooting up from the brush to a size large enough for firewood in ten years. **1905** *Post–Std.* (Syracuse NY) 8 Nov 13/2, The Virginia pine, commonly known as scrub pine, is no longer regarded as worthless except for cordwood. **1943** Peattie *Great Smokies* 168 **sAppalachians**, The scrub or Virginia pine, a weed of a tree, . . slowly takes over from broom sedge. **1965–70** *DARE* (Qu. T17, . . *Kinds of pine trees;* not asked in early QRs) Infs **IN69, PA99, TN22, VA**15, 46, 57, 64, 89, **WV**2, Virginia pine; **NC**48, **VA**24, Virginia scrub pine; **VA**96, Old Virginia [pine]; (Qu. T16, . . *Kinds of trees . . 'special'*) Inf **VA**89, Virginia pine. **1972** *Winterthur Portfolio* 7.210, *Pinus virginiana.* . . Virginia Pine. A small, short-leaved pine . . widely distributed from Long Island to central Georgia. **2005** *Roanoke Times* (VA) 10 Dec 9 (Internet), The native Virginia pine (Pinus virginiana) also

called scrub pine or bull pine, has two slightly twisted needles. **2006** DE Center Inland Bays *Inland Bays Jrl.* 4 (Internet), At the edges of the maritime forest, where it opens to the high marsh, red cedars, black gum trees and Virginia scrub pine grow in the sunny border with the marsh.

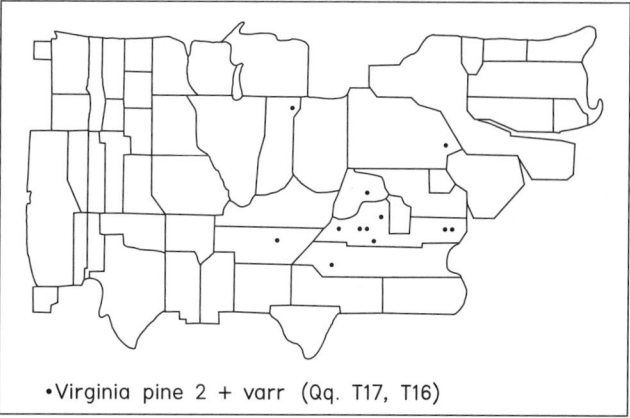

•Virginia pine 2 + varr (Qq. T17, T16)

3 also *Virginia sap pine, Virginian swamp* ~: =**loblolly pine 1.**

1785 Marshall *Arbustrum* 102, Pinus taeda. Virginian Swamp, or Frankincence Pine. This grows to a pretty large size. **1806** McMahon *Amer. Gardener's Calendar* 597, Pinus Taeda. . . v. rigida—Three-leaved Virginian [Pine]. **1896** Mohr–Roth *Timber Pines* 107, Pinus taeda . . Virginia Pine. . . Michaux states that three-fourths of the houses in lower Virginia were built of Loblolly Pine. **1916** *Torreya* 16.236 **VA**, Pinus taeda. . . Virginia pine, mainland near Wallops I[slan]d. **1972** *Winterthur Portfolio* 7.209, Pinus taeda. . . Common names . . three-leaved Virginian pine, . . Virginian swamp pine, Virginia pine, Virginia sap pine [etc].

Virginia quail n   Also *Virginian quail*   Cf **Virginia partridge**
=**bob-white.**

[**1803** in 1805 *Med. Repository* 2.125, The fowl which the Pennsylvanians call the partridge, and the New-Yorkers the quail, seems to me to be the Tetrao Virginianus of Linnaeus. He might be called the New-England or Virginian quail, to distinguish him from the partridge and quail of Old England.] **1844** *Amer. Jrl. Science* 46.270 **csPA**, Ortyx virginianus. . . Virginia Quail. Not abundant at present. Resident. **1846** *U.S. Mag. & Democratic Rev.* 18.131, Formerly, he . . was denominated *Coturnix Virginianus,* Virginia quail, owing to the fact, doubtless, that in Virginia he was found most abundantly, perhaps *only,* on the first landing of English settlers in America. **1886** *Bangor Daily Whig & Courier* (ME) 28 Oct [3]/5 (newspaperarchive.com), A pair of "Bob White" Virginia quail have been shot in the western part of the State. It is the first authenticated case of this species ever being found in Maine. **1916** *Adams Co. News* (Gettysburg PA) [15 July 5]/3 (newspaperarchive.com), While William Wolf . . was mowing a hayfield two weeks ago, the machine passed over the nest of a Virginia quail. **1950** *Lowell Sun* (MA) 29 Oct 50/6, Beginning the next year Crosby set out with local sportsmen to stock Virginia quail. **1996** *Virginian–Pilot* (Norfolk VA) 7 Apr sec F 1 (Internet), Washingtonian magazine said the Virginia quail at Windows justified the 2½-half-hour [sic] drive from D.C.

Virginia rail n   Also *Virginian rail*
Std: a small **rail** n[2] (here: *Rallus limicola*) with a long reddish bill.   Also called **bull 7, bull rail, didapper 4, freshwater marsh hen, long-billed rail, mammy coot 2, marsh hen 1a, meadow ~ 1, mud ~ 1a, queen sora, red-breasted rail 2, red ~ 1, water hen 1d**

Virginia rail fence   See **Virginia fence**

Virginia red fox   See **red fox 2**

Virginia sap pine   See **Virginia pine 3**

Virginia scrub pine   See **Virginia pine 2**

Virginia snakeroot n

1 also *Virginy snakeroot:* A **birthwort 1** (here: *Aristolochia serpentaria*) native to much of the eastern half of the US.

[**1633** Gerarde *Herball* 848, [Caption:] *Pistolochia Cretica sive Virginiana.* Virginian Snake-root.] **1739** (1946) Gronovius *Flora Virginica* 112, The Snake-root of Virginia. *Ibid,* [Index:] Virginy-Snake-root. **1804** *Philadelphia Med. & Phys. Jrl.* 1.1.23 **sePA**, In the treatment of this disease, Dr. De Normandie found nothing so beneficial as the Virginia Snake-root (Aristolochia Serpentaria of Linnaeus). **1859** (1880) Darlington *Amer. Weeds* 268, *[Aristolochia] Serpentaria.* . . Snake-root Aristolochia. Virginia Snake-root. **1915** *Middletown Times–Press* (NY) 8 Oct 3/2, Tincture of Virginia Snakeroot (Serpentaria)—61.0 [=percent by volume of alcohol]. **1970** *NC Folkl.* 18.25, Dose patient every two hours with Virginia snakeroot boiled in water. **2001** *Washington Post* (DC) 23 Jan sec T 7 (Internet), "Aristolochic acids are potent carcinogens" and kidney toxins, the FDA reported last year. . . There are still many U.S. vendors selling . . Virginia Snakeroot, Canada Snakeroot and Wild Ginger, all of which the FDA says are likely to contain aristolochic acid.

2 A **bugbane 1** (here: *Cimicifuga racemosa*).

1959 Carleton *Index Herb. Plants* 121, Virginia Snakeroot: . . Cimicifuga racemosa. **2006** *DARE* File—Internet, *Cimicifuga—Bugbane, Bugwort, Virginia Snakeroot, Black Cohosh*—To all persons who are familiar with the common wild or native woodland plants, the Snakeroot is well known. This Snakeroot (Cimicifuga racemosa) is a very tall, late blooming plant, growing from 4 feet to 8 feet tall and flowering from July or August on.

Virginia snakeweed See **snakeweed b(1)**

Virginia soldiers See **soldier B2**

Virginia sumac n Also *Virginian sumac*
=**staghorn sumac.**

[**1629** Parkinson *Paradisi* 611, *Rhus Virginiana.* The Virginia Sumach, or Buckes horne tree of Virginia.] [**1831** Davies *Man. Mat. Med.* 82 (*OED2*), The Narrow-leaved Sumach, *Rhus copallinum,* Willd.; the Pennsylvania Sumach, *R. glabrum,* Willd., and the Virginian Sumach, *R. typhinum,* Willd., are all native plants of North America.] **1880** *Marion Daily Star* (OH) [17 Sept 2]/3 (newspaperarchive.com), Years ago the virtue of Virginian sumac was very little known, . . but as soon as it was found to be among the best in the world, the demand for it has steadily increased. **1897** Sudworth *Arborescent Flora* 275 **TN**, *Rhus hirta.* . . Virginia Sumach. **1960** Vines *Trees SW* 635, Vernacular names are Hairy Sumac, Velvet Sumac, American Sumac, Virginia Sumac, and Vinegar-tree.

Virginia thyme n Also *Virginian thyme*
A **mountain mint 2:** either *Pycnanthemum flexuosum* or *P. virginianum*.

1814 Bigelow *Florula Bostoniensis* 146, Virginia thyme . . [has a] taste like pennyroyal. **1822** Eaton *Botany* 415, *Pycnanthemum linifolium* [= *P. flexuosum*], virginian thyme. . . *Pycnanthemum lanceolatum,* narrow-leaf virginian thyme. **1843** Torrey *Flora NY* 2.64, *Pycnanthemum linifolium.* Narrow-leaved Virginian Thyme. **1901** Mohr *Plant Life AL* 698, *Koellia flexuosa* [=*Pycnanthemum f.*] . . Virginian Thyme. . . The herb known as "mountain mint" or "Pycnanthemum" is used medicinally. **1940** Writers' Program *Guide VA* 20, Peculiar to the Alleghenies are . . mountain mint or Virginia thyme with its lavender-tipped white flowers; and trailing wolfsbane.

Virginia truffle n
=**Indian bread 3.**

1848 Bartlett *Americanisms* 366, Tuckahoe. . . The Virginia truffle. **1902** *Jrl. Amer. Folkl.* 15.263, *Túckahoe.* . . The name is also applied to a sort of fungus called also "Virginia truffle," "Indian bread," [etc.]. **1932** *Monessen Daily Independent* (PA) 14 Dec 6/5, "Tuckahoe". . . [T]he name also was applied to Virginia truffle, a curious fungus growth found under the soil in the southern states bordering the Atlantic. The Indians and early settlers were fond of these truffles and generally they located them by following hogs engaged in rooting.

Virginia wake-robin See **wake-robin 1**

Virginia willow n
Std: a shrub (*Itea virginica*) with racemes of small white flowers, native throughout the southeastern US from Pennsylvania west to Missouri, and south to Texas and Florida. Also called **Indian reed 1, sweet spire, tassel-white**

Virginia worm fence See **Virginia fence**

Virginia yellow pine n
=**shortleaf pine 1.**

1842 *Sun* (Baltimore MD) 31 Dec 3/2, [Advt:] 10,000 feet 5-4 Virginia yellow Pine *stepping,* at $29 per thousand. **1882** *Manufacturer & Builder* 14.215, Where could I obtain the most reliable information as to how to prepare for market the . . trees occurring in a tract of 1,800 acres

of Virginia yellow pine land?—E.O.F., Washington DC. **1895** *Marshfield Times* (WI) [22 Nov 7]/4 (newspaperarchive.com), Virginia yellow pine when freshly cut weighs 47.8 pounds per cubic foot. **1905** *Lincoln Eve. News* (NE) 26 Dec 5/6 **NJ**, There were 324 of them [=piles], of the best Virginia yellow pine, with the top fourteen inches or more in diameter. **1995** *Frederick Post* (MD) 22 Apr sec H 10/4, *Important Estate Auction.* . . Walnut step-back cupboard, . . Virginia yellow pine sideboard w/ punched tins, mahogany tilt-top tea table [etc]. **2006** *DARE* File—Internet **MD**, These tables are made by a local craftsman in Virginia. They are constructed from reclaimed Virginia yellow pine.

Virginny See **Virginia**

virgin's bower n
Std: a plant of the genus *Clematis,* such as *C. virginiana* of the eastern US and *C. ligusticifolia* of the western US. Also called **leather flower, old-man's-beard 3, vase vine.** For other names of var spp see **bluebell 1f, cinnamon vine 2, curly clematis, ~-heads, devil's darning needle 4, ~-hair 1, ~ thread 1, Dutchman's pipe 3, feather vine, gander grass 2, ~ vine, goatsbeard 4, granddaddy's pipe, grandfather's beard 2, graybeard 1, headache weed 2, Indian bluebells, ~ pipe 3, leatherweed 2, love vine 2, marsh clematis, mountain ~, old man 1e, old-man-of-the-mountain 4, old-man's-whiskers 3, pine hyacinth, pipestem b, pipe vine 2, red bluebell, Rocky Mountain clematis, satin curls, smoke vine 1, sugar bowl(s), sweet clematis, tassel-top, windflower d, woodbine 4;** for names of the fruit see **lion's beard 2**

Virginy snakeroot See **Virginia snakeroot 1**

visitation n scattered, but chiefly N Cent See Map Cf **viewing, visiting hours**
A scheduled occasion, freq at a funeral home, at which people can view the body before a funeral and condole with the relatives of the deceased.

1949 *Post–Std.* (Syracuse NY) 13 Apr 16/5, Services. . . Interment. . . Visitation. . . Monday 7–9 and Tuesday, 2–4 and 7–9 p.m. **1965–70** *DARE* (Qu. BB60, *When friends and relatives gather together at the place where the body is, usually the night before the funeral*) 31 Infs, **chiefly N Cent,** Visitation; **KY**54, Visitation night. **1969** *Richland Observer* (Richland Center WI) 22 May sec 1 5/2, Pastor G.E. Augustine will officiate and burial will be in the Richland Center cemetery. Visitation was at the Pratt Chapel. **1971** *AmSp* 46.70, Another interesting Boston area universal was the use, even among Protestants, of *wake* for what is elsewhere in the state often called a *visitation, calling hours,* or even a *viewing.* **1987** *Daily Herald* (Arlington Heights IL) 28 Dec sec 2 4/3, Visitation will be from 2 to 9 p.m. Tuesday at Martin Funeral Home. **1998** *Capital* (Annapolis MD) 6 Jan sec A 11/3, Visitation will be . . at John M Taylor Funeral Home. **2002** *Daily Plainsman* (Huron SD) 27 Dec 6/1, Visitation will be today beginning at 2 p.m. at Skroch Funeral Home in Flandreau. **2005** *Post–Std.* (Syracuse NY) 22 Dec sec B 4/1, Visitation is from 4 to 7 p.m. Thursday, at the funeral home in Oswego. **2009** Perry *Coop* 272 **nWI**, On visitation day. . . we pack up the family and drive north. . . We stand together just beside the casket and the line goes right out the door for hours.

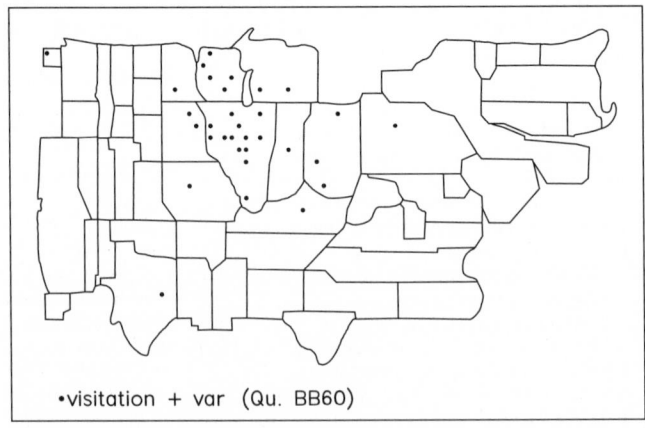

•visitation + var (Qu. BB60)

visiting hours n scattered, but chiefly NEast, OH See Map Cf **calling hours**
=**visitation.**

1949 *Fitchburg Sentinel* (MA) 17 Nov 10/3, Visiting hours will be observed at the funeral home today and tomorrow. **1954** *Portsmouth Herald* (NH) 27 Jan 3/2, Visiting hrs. at chapel, Thurs. 7–9 p.m. . . Visiting hours Weds. and Thurs. at the McIntyre Memorial Funeral Home. **1965–70** *DARE* (Qu. BB60, *When friends and relatives gather together at the place where the body is, usually the night before the funeral*) 35 Infs, **scattered, but chiefly NEast, OH,** Visiting hours. **1977** *Charleston Daily Mail* (WV) 25 Oct sec A 3/3, Visiting hours at the Barlow-Bonsall Funeral Home here will be Wednesday. **1991** *Post–Std.* (Syracuse NY) 7 Oct sec B 4/6, Visiting hours will be 10 to 11 a.m. Tuesday at the funeral home. **2005** *Marysville Jrl.–Tribune* (OH) 26 Apr 2/1, Visiting hours will be Wednesday . . at Evans Funeral Home, Columbus.

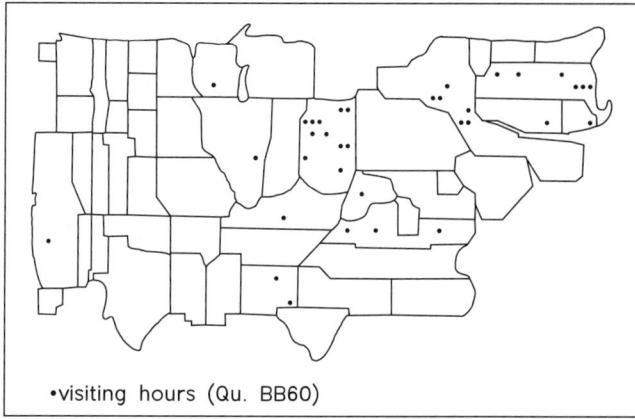

•visiting hours (Qu. BB60)

visitor n

1 A woman's menstrual period; pl: menstruation. Cf **friend 2**

1942 Berrey–Van den Bark *Amer. Slang* 123.1, *Menses*. . . visitors. **1948** *Word* 4.3.185, *List of Expressions* [for menstruation]. . . Have a visitor. **1968–69** *DARE* (Qu. AA27, . . *A woman's menstruation*) Infs **NY**67, **PA**90, 93, Visitor; **MD**9, Got a visitor; **IL**45, My visitor. **1984** *New Yorker* 29 Oct 45 **wKY,** Girls used to say they had the curse. Or they had a visitor. **2004** *Will & Grace* (Television Program), [Episode "Christmas Break" 9 Dec:] Rosario: Ms. Karen, we have a little visitor. Karen: Oh for God sakes, I'm not your mother. You know where the tampons are.

2 A **louse B1.**

1967 *DARE* (Qu. R25, *Joking names for a head louse, or body louse*) Inf **AZ**2, Visitor.

visnada, visnaga See **bisnaga**

vitae n [Abbr for *arborvitae*]
=**white cedar 2.**

1897 Sudworth *Arborescent Flora* 65 **DE,** *Thuja occidentalis*. . . *Common Names*. . . Vitae. **1950** Peattie *Nat. Hist. Trees* 65, Arbor-Vitae *Thuja occidentalis*. . . Vitae. **1967–69** *DARE* (Qu. T5, . . *Kinds of evergreens, other than pine*) Inf **AL**20, Vitae—cemetery plant; **NY**220, Vitae ['vaɪdə].

vit(t)al, vittle n See **victual** n

vittle v, vittling See **victual** v

viuva n [Port, literally "widow"] Cf **widow B1**
A **rockfish 3:** either *Sebastes ovalis* or *S. entomelas.*

1880 in 1882 Smithsonian Inst. *Misc. Coll.* 22.145, The following species of "rock-fish" were obtained by us in Monterey Bay. The names used by the fishermen of Monterey are appended. Most of these are evidently names in use for other species at the Azores, transferred to species of California waters: . . *S[ebastichthys] ovalis*—Vinva [sic] (Widow). **2002** Love et al. *Rockfishes NE Pacific* 12 **CA** (as of 1930s), Widow rockfish were beccafico and viuva, while speckled rockfish were not only viuva, but also zipola.

-vl See **-ville**

vly n Pronc-spp *fly(e)* [Du dial *vlaai, vlei* low-lying piece of land] **NY** Cf **flow** n[2]
A swamp or marshy pond—freq used in place names.

1645 in 1929 *AmSp* 5.161 **eNY,** Kieft's Patent 1645 to the town of Gravesend 'at ye head of a fly or marsh.' **1695** in 1849 *Doc. Hist. State*

of NY 1.630, A valley begginning att ye head of a flye or Marshe. **1737** in 1880 Brookhaven NY *Records* 1.139, The feftene aker lots . . which run from a place caled Squasacx pinte, to ye littel fly. **1877** Bartlett *Americanisms* 734 **NY,** *Vly*. . . In New York, a swamp, a marsh. **1929** *AmSp* 5.161 **eNY,** The Dutch word . . is used often enough in places on the edge of the Dutch districts to show that it too had a place in the common speech. Mosher Vly and Murphy Vly (Stoney Creek), Vly Lake (Lake Pleasant),[.] the Vly, a large swamp near Gloversville, the Vly, a pond now quite overgrown, near Rensselaerville . . may be cited as well as others further south. In these cases the word is clearly not a translation of a Dutch name for in these localities there never were any Dutch to give names to places. **1968** *DARE* (Qu. C6, . . *A piece of land that's often wet, and has grass and weeds growing on it*) Inf **NY**92, Vly [flaɪ], occasionally [vlaɪ]—a place where a lake or pond has silted up—usually a small shallow body of water surrounded by grass on firm ground—limited to Adirondacks. **2004** *DARE* File—Internet **Upstate NY,** A vly about a mile past McCanes which was supposed to be crossed on boardwalk and bridge had to be waded through.

V-nickel See **V 2**

V-note See **V 1**

vodoo See **voodoo** n

vog n [Blend of *volcanic* + *fog* or *smog*] **HI**
A mixture of volcanic ash, gasses, and other atmospheric pollutants.

1993 *USA Today* (Arlington VA) 2 Feb sec A 6, *Hawaii*. . . The state issued a burning ban due to excessive vog. . . Vog is a mixture of volcanic ash and other atmospheric pollutants. **1996** in 2006 (acc) Lexis-Nexis Legal Research *State Case Law: HI* (Internet), Dr. Shrader further stated that other factors on the Big Island (such as mold, dust, pollen, mites, vog, or other environmental factors) could play a role in Gap's asthma. **2005** *Honolulu Star–Bulletin* (HI) 1 Mar (Internet), *Big Island vog hazard*. . . Sulfur dioxide gas can eventually form a haze, commonly referred to as volcanic fog or "vog" in Hawaii. **2006** *DARE* File **HI,** Vog. I'm thinking I first heard it in the early-mid-80's, after the . . Kilauea eruption began . . but before I left for the mainland (Aug '85).

voice n Usu |vɔɪs|; also *esp among Gullah speakers* |wɔɪs|; for addit varr see quots Pronc-spp *v'ice, vyce, woice*
Std sense, var forms.

1841 (1952) Cooper *Deerslayer* 240 **cNY,** Canoe you shan't have, so long as the v'ice of fri'ndship and warning can count for anything. **1876** *Scribner's Mth.* 12.33 **CA,** I 'reckon ez you'll hear it from the same vyce ez I did. **1897** *Atlantic Mth.* 79.836 **sAppalachians,** Jes' let yer v'ice beat agin his ear till he can't keep the gospel out. **1901** *Ibid* 88.57 **ME,** Both on us heerd the v'ice right close aboard on us. **1909** *S. Atl. Qrly.* 8.45 **seSC** [Gullah], 'Im hab woice lak all dem Preston. **1922** Gonzales *Black Border* 338 **sSC, GA coasts** [Gullah glossary], *Woice*—voice. **1940** *AmSp* 15.374 **NYC,** In the second group [of words pronounced with [ɔɪ] in the standard dialects] is found a diphthong composed of a central vowel plus [ɪ], which . . I shall indicate by the transcription [əɪ]. The first element . . may vary between the limits of the [ʌ] in *cut* and a vowel which is considerably higher and farther forward. This group includes . . *voice*. . . [vəɪs]. **1942** *AmSp* 17.149 **seNY,** Occasionally it [=[ɔɪ]] shifts towards . . [əɪ]. . . *voice* [ɔɪ] 24 [infs], [əɪ] 2 [infs]. **1966** *DARE* FW Addit **SC**9 [Black], Pond chicken—a frog sought for its legs—not such a deep voice [wɔɪs].

volador n Pronc-sp *vollydo* [Span *volador* flyer]
=**flying jenny 1a.**

1916 *DN* 4.347 **New Orleans LA,** *Vollydo* ['vɑlɪˌdo]. . . A swing or merry-go-round. **1981** Pederson *LAGS Basic Materials* (Flying jenny) 1 inf, **nwFL,** [volador]—['vɐ͜ᵛli͜ᵛˌdoˡə, 'vɛl͡ɪˌdoɐ, 'voˑ͜ˡ͡ɪˌdoˌᵛᵊ]—Like a "merry go round", except that "the piece that went across was on top of a high pole, with seats hanging below it on a rope." Thinks term is of Scandinavian origin; 1 inf, **seLA,** [volador]—['vɔ͜ᵊˡ͡ˈdo͜ᵛᵊ]—Introduced in N[ew] O[rleans] by Mexicans. (Spanish *volador*). Tall upright pole, two crosspieces at top fixed with bolt. Ropes with loops at end suspended from each corner. Place hand in loop, run around and swing out. Can be dangerous; 1 inf, **seMS,** [volador]—['vɑ͜ᵊˡl͡ᶴ͜ˈ, dɐˈᵊʊ]—Goes round and round; it's not a seesaw.

volentine See **valentine**

vollydo See **volador**

vol'nterry See **voluntary**

volumtime See **valentine**

voluntary adj [*OED2* 1620–1718 "*Obs. rare.*"] Eye-dial sp *vol'nterry*

Growing as a **volunteer 1a.**

[**1834** *Farmers' Reg.* 1.524 **VA**, The most apparent injury is the destruction by cattle of the voluntary crop of grass and weeds, that land in tolerable condition will throw up after a wheat, oat, or other grain crop is severed.] **1858** Young in *Latter-Day Saints' Millennial Star* 20.718, At many times we have harvested three crops from one sowing, by what we call voluntary wheat springing up the second or third season. **1889** Edwards *Runaways* 20 **cGA** [Black], "Dis co'n," said Isam, shucking an ear, "es w'at dey calls 'vol'nterry co'n.' Hit es co'n w'at cum up fum las' year seed w'at de river en' de hog scatter." **1903** in 2007 *DARE* File—Internet **NE**, Julius Vahrankamp found 40 acres of voluntary wheat growing on an unoccupied piece of land which he thought worth cutting. **1942** Cox–Jackson *Field Crops* 148, Growers of rye, radishes, and sweet potatoes must destroy voluntary plants that may grow adjacent to seed fields. Seed-corn growers should cut or detassel voluntary corn plants that appear near seed-corn fields. **1968** *DARE* (Qu. L24, *A crop or part of a crop that springs up and grows by itself from old seed*) Inf **IN**40, Voluntary. **1971** GA Dept. Ag. *Farmers Market Bulletin* 28 July 1/2 **cGA**, [Letter:] What can I do to make my voluntary pecan tree bear? **2007** *DARE* File—Internet **KS**, We moved the cows home today. They were on cornstalks and voluntary wheat plus hubby was hauling feed to them each day to supplement what they could find on the cropland.

volunteer n

1a freq attrib: A plant (of a type usu deliberately planted) or crop that appears spontaneously; hence adv *volunteer* (in phr *come up volunteer*); v *volunteer* of a plant or crop: to appear spontaneously. [*OED2 volunteer* sb. A.4. 1657 →; adj B.2.b 1794 →] **widespread exc NEast** See Map Cf **self-sown**
1811 *Balance & State Jrl.* (Albany NY) 1.320/2 **cnVA**, They [= Hessian flies] may be found in the volunteer wheat from two to six in every stalk. **1838** (1930) W. Sewall *Diary* 190 **IL**, There is a considerable prospect for a second crop of rye (volunteer). **1858** *New Englander & Yale Rev.* 16.162 **CA**, Sixty or eighty bushels have been gathered for the volunteer crop of barley. This, in fact, is one of the evils to be encountered by California agriculture, that every crop perpetuates itself as a weed. **1882** *Century Illustr. Mag.* 24.869 **Pacific NW**, North of Snake River, the farmers . . harvest the volunteer crop of wheat which comes up on unplowed stubble fields. **1902** *DN* 2.248 **sIL**, Volunteer, n. and adj. Plants from self-sown seed as:—'Volunteer corn.' 'Volunteer oats.' **1903** *DN* 2.335 **seMO**, Volunteer (crop). . . Growth from seed accidentally distributed from former crop. **1906** *DN* 3.123 **sIN**, Volunteer. . . A plant from self-sown seed; or descriptive of such. *Ibid* 163 **nwAR**, Volunteer. . . Any plant, shrub, or tree which is self-sown. "This tulip-tree is a volunteer." **1909** *DN* 3.386 **eAL, wGA**, Volunteer. . . A plant that comes up from seed not regularly planted but distributed by natural processes. Also as *adj*. **1915** *DN* 4.192 **swVA**, Volunteer. . . A plant growing without being purposely sown. "The volunteer oats was good."—v.i. To grow as a 'volunteer.' "So much wheat volunteered that I let it stand." **1937** *AmSp* 12.107 **eNE** [Farm terms], After small grain has been removed, a field will become green soon with what is called *volunteer grain*. **1965–70** *DARE* (Qu. L24, *A crop or part of a crop that springs up and grows by itself from old seed*) 624 Infs, **widespread, but less freq NEast**, Volunteer; 10 Infs, **scattered**, Volunteer crop; **MO**20, Volunteer plant; **OK**43, **PA**166, Volunteered; **GA**22, Come up

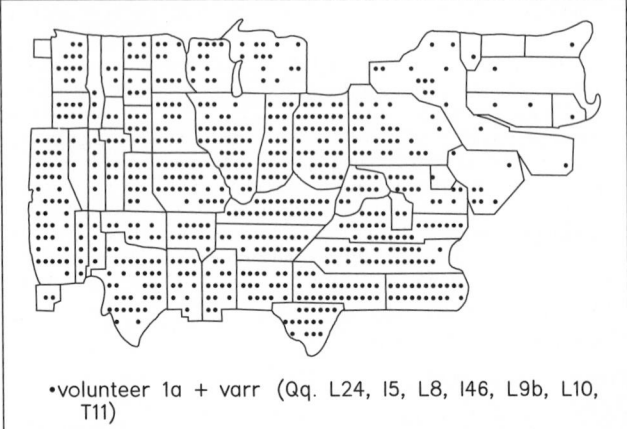

•volunteer 1a + varr (Qq. L24, I5, L8, I46, L9b, L10, T11)

volunteer; (Qu. I5, . . *Kind of onions that keep coming up without replanting year after year*) 19 Infs, **scattered**, Volunteer onions; **MO**7, 17, **NC**34, **OH**38, 47, 88, **TN**61, **WI**5, Volunteers; (Qu. L8, *Hay that grows naturally in damp places*) 17 Infs, **scattered**, Volunteer (hay); **CA**17, Volunteer grain; **MI**78, Volunteer wheat; (Qu. I46, . . *Kinds of fruits that grow wild around here*) Inf **GA**8, Volunteer peach; (Qu. L9b, *Hay from other kinds of plants [not grass]; not asked in early QRs*) Inf **CA**124, Volunteer hay; (Qu. L10, *After hay has been cut, then it grows back and you cut it again*) Infs **CA**63, 152, **FL**26, **HI**12, Volunteer; (Qu. T11, . . *Kinds of elm trees*) Inf **OH**56, Volunteer elm. **1966–67** *DARE* Tape **AZ**2, Every one of these larkspurs in my yard have come up volunteer from seeds that were scattered from their predecessors last year; [**NM**8, There wasn't any planted trees, you know, there was just old cottonwood trees . . that had come up by volunteer.] **1985** Clark *From Mailbox* 103 **ME**, Until this year I had not heard the term "volunteer" for plants which seed themselves. **1996** *DARE* File **TN**, I had a dogwood volunteer but it died last winter.

b attrib or as mass noun; Spec: rice that grows spontaneously, esp an inferior variety which, because of its greater tendency to reseed itself, threatens to overwhelm more desirable varieties.
1823 in 1945 Easterby *SC Rice Plantation* 248, 15 acker Betwen it an the River is hangin & is vary yallow & is Exelant Good Rice clear of voluntier. **1827** in 1829 *S. Agriculturist* 2.28 **SC**, Burning early in the winter . . exposes the volunteer rice, so that the birds destroy more of it. **1829** *Ibid* 2.193 **SC**, [He] selects his seed as free as possible from volunteer. **1846** *De Bow's Rev.* 1.331 **Sth**, Seed rice, having a greater proportion of red or volunteer rice than one per cent., is totally unfit for planting. **1930** (1972) Cate *Our Todays* 197 **seGA**, The great enemies of the rice-planter are volunteer and freshets; the first of these is the scattered seed of the rice, which becomes a very disagreeable weed, and is very difficult to eradicate. **2006** *Delta Farm Press* (MS) 13 Nov (Internet) **AR**, I got into a problem with one year of soybeans and one year of rice. That was before we had Roundup Ready soybeans. I could control 99 percent of the volunteer rice but still have heads of other varieties out there.

2 also attrib: An illegitimate child.
1938 *Atlantic Mth.* 162.369 **SC** [Black], To him [=the plantation Negro] an illegitimate child is a 'woods colt,' or a 'little volunteer.' **1970** *DARE* (Qu. Z11b, . . *[A child whose parents were not married]*) Inf **CA**201, Volunteer. **1986** Pederson *LAGS Concordance* (*Bastard*) 2 infs, **GA, TX**, A (little) volunteer; 1 inf, **neTN**, Volunteer babies.

volunteer onion See **volunteer 1a**

voluntine See **valentine**

vomit n, v Usu |ˈvɑmɪt|; also **chiefly Sth, S Midl** |ˈvɑmɪk| (See Map at **A** below) Pronc-spp *vomic(k)*, *vomik*, *vommix* For addit pronc and sp varr see quot 1965–70 Cf Intro "Language Changes" IV.4
A Forms.

1902 *DN* 2.248 **sIL**, Vomick. Pronunciation of vomit, when used, which is seldom. The phrase 'to *throw up*' is generally employed. **1906** *DN* 3.163 **nwAR**, Vomik. . . Vomit. "His vomik smelt like a drunk man's." **1909** *DN* 3.386 **eAL, wGA**, Vomik, n. and v. Vomit. Cf. *noxvomiky.* **1917** *DN* 4.419 **wNC**, Vomic. . . To vomit. Also Kan. (esp. a child's word), N.Y. **1928** *AmSp* 3.404 **Ozarks** (as of 1916–27), Occasionally the final *t* is replaced by a *k* sound, as when *vomit* is turned into *vomick.* **1930** Shoemaker *1300 Words* 64 **cPA Mts** (as of c1900), Vommix—To throw up, to vomit. **1939** Aurand *Quaint Idioms* 27 [PaGer], Don't vommix (vomit, throw-up) here; go home and vommix in your own house! **1965–70** *DARE* (Qu. BB17, . . *Vomiting*) Infs **GA**23, **NJ**67, 69, **VA**13, 52, Vomick [ˈvɑmɪk]; **TN**27, Vomick [ˈvɑmək]; **FL**49, Vomicking [ˈvɑmɪkɪn]; **NC**55, Vomicking [ˈvɔmɚˌkɪn]; **TX**52, Vomicupted [ˈvɑmɪkʌptɨd]; **SC**27, Wamick [ˈwɑmɪk]; (Qu. BB18, *To vomit a great deal at once*) Inf **LA**6, Vomick [vɑmɪk] all of your food up; **NC**77, Vomicking their head off. **1966** Dakin *Dial. Vocab. Ohio R. Valley* 2.483, Vomit. . . The variant *vomick* is scattered throughout Kentucky in the speech of the less educated simple folk of the oldest generation but is not common. This form does not appear in Illinois or Indiana, but it is used by the oldest informants in Darke and Clermont Counties in Ohio. **1983** *MJLF* 9.1.60 **ceKY** (as of 1956), Vomick . . : vomit. **1996** McDowell *Leaving Pipe Shop* 100 **AL** [Black] (as of 1950s), Reached for the orange wedge before I vomited it all back up. "Don't you vomick it up. If you vomick it up, I'll just have to give you some more." **2006** *DARE* File **MO** [Black], When I was a kid in St. Louis, the usual street phrase was "I fee' like I'm gon' vomic" . . since "vomit" was considered to be gross and nearly as taboo as any of the four-letter words.

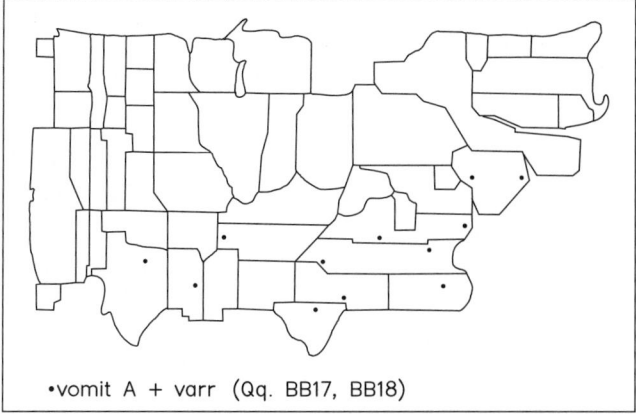

•vomit A + varr (Qq. BB17, BB18)

B　As verb.
To cause (one) to vomit.　[*OED2* 1662 →1843]

1841 Catlin *Letters Indians* 2.248 **PA**, He [=a Pawnee medicine-man] is vomiting and purging his patients with herbs. **1927** *AmSp* 2.366 **cwWV**, *Vommick* . . to vomit. "Run your finger down your throat and it will vommick you." **1938** Stuart *Dark Hills* 163 **eKY**, When one of them 'Weedmonkeys' smells she's enough to vomit a buzzard.

vomit like a dog　See **dog** n[1] **B17i**

vomit up one's heels　See **heels, throw up one's**

vomitwort　n　Cf **pukeweed**
=**Indian tobacco 1.**

1876 Hobbs *Bot. Hdbk.* 125, Vomit wort, Lobelia herb, Lobelia inflata. **1971** Krochmal *Appalachia Med. Plants* 164, *Lobelia inflata.* . . Vomitwort.

vommix　See **vomit**

vonchers　See **vent** exclam, v[2]

voodienne　See **voodoo** n 2

voodoo　n, freq attrib　[LaFr *voudou* of wAfr origin; cf Ewe, Fon *vodu* spirit, demon]　Also *vaudoo, vaudoux, vo(u)doo, voudou*　orig esp New Orleans LA; now scattered, but more freq Sth, S Midl　See Map at **1** below

1　=**hoodoo 1a;** a deity in this practice.

1820 *LA Gaz.* (New Orleans) 16 Aug 2/3, For some time past, a House in the suburb Tremé, has been used as a kind of temple for certain occult practices and the idolatrous worship of an African deity called *Vaudoo.* **1868** *De Bow's Rev.* 5.724 **LA**, Our Government . . has undertaken the task of obligating these people to sanctify their marriage unions by some outward solemnity or token; but may not the agent be met . . by some such valid objection, on the part of the *Vodoo* adorers . . that as long as polygamy is not prevented among the white race, (the Mormons,) so long may the African descendants be also allowed the rites of the . . *Vodoo* free love faith or interchanges? **1872** Schele de Vere *Americanisms* 108, *Vaudoux,* a French term, designating a certain form of worship and the object of this worship alike, introduced from the Island of Santo Domingo. . . *Vaudoux* . . has . . continued among the negroes of Louisiana, and an assembly was found engaged in it as late as the year 1862 in the State of North Carolina. **1886** *Century Illustr. Mag.* 31.815 **LA**, In Louisiana it is written Voudou and Voodoo, and is often changed on the negro's lips to Hoodoo. It is the name of an imaginary being of vast supernatural powers residing in the form of a harmless snake. **1929** in 1954 Porter *103 Lyrics* 183, Do do / That voodoo / That you do / So well. **1965–70** *DARE* (Qu. CC14, . . *Where one person supposedly casts a spell over another*) 38 Infs, **scattered, but more freq Sth, S Midl**, Voodoo; **AR**12, **FL**18, **TX**95, Voodoo—negroes; **GA**89, Voodoo—niggers say; **LA**35, Voodoo [ˌvuˈdu]; **NC**72, Voodoo—not here; **PA**66, Voodoo—heard, not used; (Qu. BB51a, . . *Cures for corns or warts*) Inf **LA**31, Voodoo. [Of 48 total Infs, 14 were Black] **1967** LeCompte *Word Atlas* 393 **seLA**, A negro religion of sorcery and the person who practices this religion. . . voo-doo [9 of 21 infs]. **1969** Wilson *Stars* 96 **Ozarks**, For it was said that the cave was a place of unholy magic which had served earlier as refuge for a spell caster from far south

in the voodoo country. **1986** Pederson *LAGS Concordance,* 1 inf, **ceTX**, Voodoo; 1 inf, **cLA**, Voodoo—still in practice among Blacks especially; 1 inf, **csLA**, Voodoo—not common; 1 inf, **csTX**, Voodoo—in Louisiana; 1 inf, **seLA**, It's voodoo—of local remedies; 1 inf, **cLA**, Voodoo medicine—draw circle around wound.

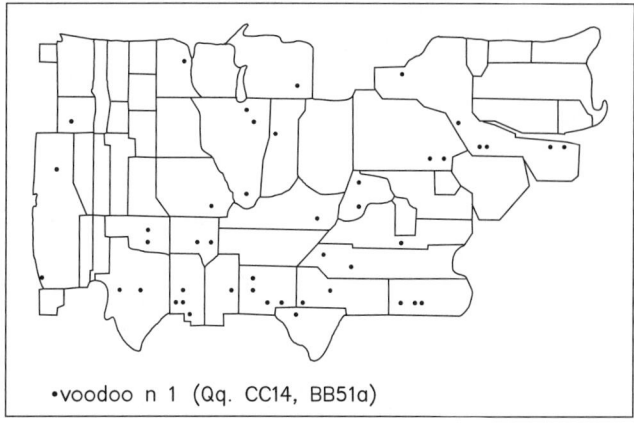

•voodoo n 1 (Qq. CC14, BB51a)

2　also *voodoo artist* (or *doctor, priestess, queen* etc), *voodooienne:* =**hoodoo 1b.**

1850 *N.O. Picayune* 3 July *(DA)* **New Orleans LA**, Marie Laveaux . . the head of the Voudou women, yesterday appeared before Recorder Suzeneau. **1870** *Ft. Wayne Daily Democrat* (IN) 19 July [2]/2 (newspaperarchive.com) **New Orleans LA**, The Voudou priestess . . may have purposely exaggerated her descriptions of the disgusting ceremonies . . which are said to be connected with the worship of the snake by superstitious Southern negroes. **1871** *N.O. Picayune* 10 May *(DA),* This woman is Marie Laveau, better known as priestess of the Voudous. **1875** in 1924 Hearn *Miscellanies* 1.128 **Cincinnati OH**, The Voudoo doctor who cured him gave him only native medicine. **1880** *Scribner's Mth.* 20.197 **New Orleans LA**, He had resort to a very familiar . . prescription—rum. He did not use it after the voudou fashion; the voudous pour it on the ground. **1889** Edwards *Runaways* 198 **cGA**, His mother was described as a sort of priestess—or, as we say, a Voodoo—in her native land, which was near the western coast of Africa. **1934** Carmer *Stars Fell on AL* 218, Well, there's Ella James down by Lafayette, they say she a voodoo and they's an old woman lives 'bout a mile up the pike I've heard tell about. **1946** Tallant *Voodoo* 199 **New Orleans LA**, But the most secure methods involve regular purchases from certain Voodooiennes of counter *gris-gris,* charms and amulets to be worn upon the person and kept within the home, involving the payment of small sums to these sinister merchants. **1976** Murray *Stomping the Blues* 10 **AL**, They think of them [=the blues] as coming . . from some specific. . . charm, or talisman, which can be counteracted only with the aid of a voodoo queen or madam (or somewhat less often, a voodoo king, doctor, witchdoctor, or snakedoctor). **1986** Pederson *LAGS Concordance,* 1 inf, **seGA**, Voodoo artist—practices witchcraft; 1 inf, **cLA**, Voodoo queen. **2011** *NY Times* (NY) 10 Apr sec A 26/1 **Brooklyn NYC**, Long misunderstood and maligned in Western popular culture, voodoo has become a spiritual anchor in New York City's vast Haitian community and in Haitian enclaves across the country. *Ibid* 26/2, Among younger Haitian-Americans, voodoo is a means to reconnect with their roots.

3　=**hoodoo 1c.**

1902 Eggleston *Dorothy South* 216 **VA** (as of 1860s) [Black], I'll put a Voodoo on anybody I ever heahs a callin' you a ole maid. **1966–70** *DARE* (Qu. CC14, . . *Where one person supposedly casts a spell over another*) Infs **DC**11, **VT**16, Put a voodoo on; **MS**45, Put the voodoo on.

voodoo　v　Also sp *voudou*　orig esp New Orleans LA; now esp Sth
=**hoodoo** v **1.**

1880 *New Orleans Picayune* 20 May *(OED2),* She flung this over into my yard to voudou me. **1880** *Scribner's Mth.* 19.855 **New Orleans LA**, It is true as he says, that he is voudoued. **1891** *Catholic World* 52.477 **LA** [Black], That ooman she voudou you shua. . . [White:] Aunt Martha thinks Miss Dawes has voudoued me. **1906** Bell *Carolina Lee* 199 **SC**, They think the baby is bewitched,—that he has been voodooed. **1965–70** *DARE* (Qu. CC14, . . *Where one person supposedly casts a spell over another*) Infs **GA**15, **TN**66, (Been) voodooed; (Qu. CC12b, . . *If a person has a lot of bad luck . . "He's been _____."*) Inf **NY**206,

Voodooed. **2007** *DARE* File—Internet **FL,** I voodooed my boss and the next day he got retarded. *Ibid* **TX,** I voodooed my ex-husband and 2 days later that flesh-eating bacteria ate one of his toes.

voodoo artist (or doctor), voodooienne, voodoo priestess (or queen) See **voodoo** n 2

vootie, voots(ie) See **wutz(ie)**

vordegrease See **verdigris**

vortex, cap the See **cap** v 1b

voudou n See **voodoo** n

voudou v See **voodoo** v

vowny v Cf **swanny,** *vanny* (at **van** v¹)
   1914 *DN* 4.82 **ME, nNH,** *Vowny. . . I.* Ejaculation . . equivalent of "I swear."

voyage n, v Usu |ˈvɔɪ-ɪ̆j|; also **chiefly NEng** |ˈvaɪ-ɪ̆j|; for addit var see quot 1940 at **A** below Pronc-spp *vi(a)ge, vy(a)ge*
A Forms.
   1815 Humphreys *Yankey in England* 109, *Viges,* voyages. **1818** Fessenden *Ladies Monitor* 172 **NEng,** Provincial words . . to be avoided. . . *Viage* for voyage. **1858** Hammett *Piney Woods Tavern* 133 **CT** writer in **TX,** It had been bottled up all the vyage. **1860** *Harper's New Mth. Mag.* 21.481 **NEng,** The fust time I ever sailed on any thing of a vy'ge, I went from Portland, Maine, daown to Savannah. **1890** *Century Illustr. Mag.* 39.548 **NEng,** We gave up the v'yage too soon. **1901** *Atlantic Mth.* 87.100 **ME** (as of c1776), 'T aint usual with me to have such feelin's in the outset of a v'y'ge. **1916** *DN* 4.267 **Cape Cod MA,** Make a good v'yage this year? **1929** *AmSp* 5.130 **ME,** The pronunciations "leftenant," . . "h'ist," . . "v'yge," were common. **1940** *AmSp* 15.375 **NYC,** *Voyage*—New York [ˈvɔɪɪj]—should seemingly have [ɔɪ] but the pronunciation [ˈvɔɪɪj] was common in the earlier period, and its normal development [ˈvaɪɪj] is frequently heard in the dialects today.
B As noun.
An expedition taken with the aim of acquisition or collection; the results of such an expedition; see quots. [By ext from naut usage] **Nantucket MA**
   [**1859** (1968) Bartlett *Americanisms* 497, *Voyage.* Among whalers, each man calls his share of the proceeds of the cruize, which he receives instead of wages, his *voyage.*] **1916** Macy–Hussey *Nantucket Scrap Basket* 149 **seMA,** "*Voyage*"—To the old-time resident every expedition is a voyage, and whatever results from the voyage is also a voyage. The term, so used, has come down from the whaling days, when the number of barrels of oil secured determined whether it had been a good or a poor voyage. So today, if one goes clamming, fishing, hunting or berrying, the result of his efforts is the "voyage", and on his return, he is asked, "What kind of a voyage have you had?" or "Did you have a good voyage?" **1929** Starbuck *My House* 147 **Nantucket MA,** This gunning-lunch receptacle . . was handy for holding berries, for instance, or later in the season, for wild grapes, if the birds failed. In any case one was expected to bring home a 'voyage.' *Ibid* 148, We came home in the clear gold sunset with a 'voyage,' consisting of a respectable bunch of yellow-legs, some late huckleberries, two wild roses, some bayberry and a few stalks of the beautiful liatris.

V-spot See **V** 1

vulture n
=**duck hawk.**
   1955 MA Audubon Soc. *Bulletin* 39.442 **VT,** *Peregrine Falcon. . .* Vulture (Vt. A predator.)

vum v Also *vummy* [Prob alter of *vow*] **chiefly NEng** See Map *old-fash* Cf **van** v¹
To declare, swear; also rarely used as an exclam in phr *by vum.*
   1785 *Thomas' MA Spy or Worcester Gaz.* (MA) 13 Oct 2/2, We all must dreadful mindful be / That we must fight for liberty / And vum we'll 'fend it if we die. **1806** in 1957 Old Farmer's Almanac *Sampler* 214 **NEng,** And Father's got a great bull calf,/ Which you shall have, I vum. **1815** Humphreys *Yankey in England* 109, *Vum. . .* [a species of asseveration.] **1890** *Harper's New Mth. Mag.* 80.808, Now and here I pack my little trunk. By vum! **1902** Day *Pine Tree Ballads* 127 **ME,** He had vummed that he could wallop any feller in the place. **1904** Day *Kin o' Ktaadn* 154 **ME,** Oh, Ezry vums 't was something fierce to see them. **1905** *DN* 3.23 **cCT,** *Vum. . .* To vow, in the expression I *vum!* **1907** *DN* 3.192 **seNH,** *I vum. . .* I vow. **1912** *DN* 3.575 **wIN,** *Do vum. . .* Used only in the expression of surprise, "Well, I do vum." It has much the force of "You don't say!" or sometimes, "Well, I should say so." **1914** *DN* 4.82 **ME, nNH,** *Vowny, vum, vummy! I.* Ejaculations, equivalent of "I swear." **1922** (1926) Cady *Rhymes VT* 139, "I vum!" said dad, "from now, I swear / I wouldn't lend a breath of air." **1926** Roberts *Time of Man* 127 **KY,** I vum, I'd soon put harness on myself as worry along with that lazy mule. **1939** in Lib. of Congress *Amer. Memory: WPA Life Hist.* (Internet) **MA,** I vum, I expect to live to see the day when babies is born with no legs at all, but wheels where their legs is supposed to be! **1941** Chase *Windswept* 60 **ME,** But I wouldn't take it on myself to say dig here or dig there on this land without his say so, I vum I wouldn't. **1951** *PADS* 15.68 **cwNH,** *Vum!, I:* exclamation of amazement. **1965–70** *DARE* (Qu. NN32, *Exclamations like 'I swear' or 'I vow'*) 12 Infs, **chiefly NEng,** Vum; **KS**13, Do vum; **MA**5, Vow and I vum; (Qu. NN7, *Exclamations of surprise: "They're getting married next week? Well, _____."*) Infs **MA**73, **VT**12, I vum. [All Infs old] **2007** *DARE* File **nwMA** (as of a1980), I can remember [great] Grandma Burrows using that phrase, but neither Grandma or Aunt used it, nor have I heard it that I can recall since Grandma B. When she used it, it meant: "I vow" or "I swear," as in "I vum I *shall* go t' that meetin', rain or no."

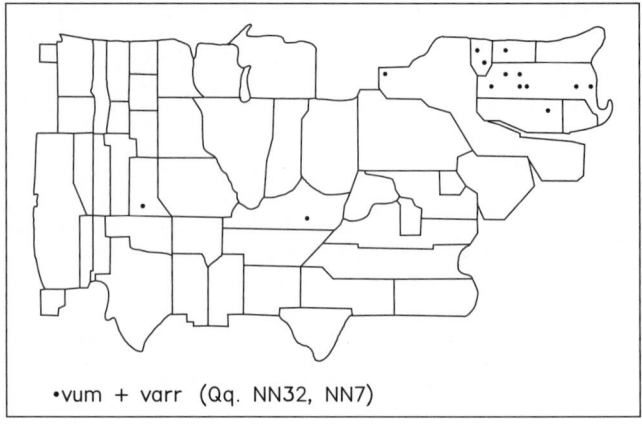

•vum + varr (Qq. NN32, NN7)

vurry See **very**

vyage See **voyage**

vyce See **voice**

vy(e)dock See **viaduct**

vyge See **voyage**

vygerus, vygorous, vygrous See **vigrous**

W n West
See quots.

1933 *AmSp* 8.1.29 **nwTX** [Ranch diction], *W.* A rope arrangement "W-shaped" used in taming a horse. By means of this anyone, with the minimum of strength and effort, could pull one or both forefeet from under the horse at will. Reserved for vicious horses. **1936** Adams *Cowboy Lingo* 58, In working wild horses, a throw line called a 'W' was sometimes used, being tied to a forefoot, then up through a ring in the belly-band, and back to the wagon. When the horse became unruly, he would be thrown to his knees, and by bruising them a few times he would desist. **1941** Writers' Program *Guide WY* 466, *W (to put W on a horse)*— A form of hobble on a bad horse.

waahoo n[1] See **wahoo** n[1]

waahoo n[2] See **wahoo** n[2]

waal See **well** intj

wab(bed up) See **wob**

wabble See **warble**

wabbled up See **wobbled up**

wabblegear adj Cf **wobble-jawed**, *DS* KK20a
   1959 *VT Hist.* 27.166 **nwVT**, *Wabblegear. . .* Rickety. Rare.

wabble-jawed See **wobble-jawed**

wackie v, n Also *wackers, wackies, whackie, whacky* [Cf *EDD whack* v.[1] 6 "To divide; to share"] **NEast** Cf **hosey**
To stake a claim or reserve a right to (something); the claim so made—often used as an exclam.

   1943 *AN&Q* 3.139, "Hosey". . . My wife remembers hearing a variation of this in Maplewood, New Jersey, a few years back—"I wackies!" (indicating that he who yelled that phrase first could share in the spoils). "No wackies!" was synonymous with "no dibs!" **1956** *AmSp* 31.36, Bill Burkhardt, of Concord, Massachusetts, said 'I've got dibs on that,' meaning 'That's mine.' Others said 'I finnie that,' 'I wackie that,' . . —all with the same meaning. *Ibid, No divvies, no dubs . .* for 'You can have no part of what I have,' . . *Fin whackie on my pie* means 'No whackie on my pie.' **1970** Lebofsky *Lexicon Philadelphia* 135, *Divvy up . . wackers . . wackie(s) . .* cry of have-not child to another who has something he would like a share of (e.g., candy). [**1970** *DARE* (Qu. II8, *When one person wants to share or divide something with another person . . "Let's _____ [on that]."*) Inf **NY**238, Wackie ['wæki].] **1981** *AmSp* 56.27 **NY**, For New Rochelle, New York, I have recorded the expression *I whacky it!* (1920s). **2003** *DARE* File **wPA**, Re "haggies" from a 2000 posting about the Bronx. . . Haggies or No Haggies. . . When someone bought a box of candy, you would yell haggies and he would have to share with you unless that person had shouted no haggies first[.] There are other forms, e.g., "wackies". . . maybe "haggies" and "wackies" are from "hack"/"whack" = "cut [into shares]".

wa-cup See **wake-up**

wad n Cf *polly-wad* (at **polly 1**) *old-fash*
A compact coil of hair at the top or back of a woman's head.

   1870 Alcott *Old-Fashioned Girl* 19 **MA**, "What is a wad?" asked Polly. . . "Somebody's hair on the top of her head in the place where it ought not to be." **1871** *Ladies' Repository* 7.310, For myself I should be thankful to return to the habits of our grandmothers; buy a bonnet which would do to wear ten years . . ; also twist up my hair in a plain wad at the back of my head. **1878** Hart *Sazerac Lying Club* 12 **NV**, The fact of the case is that she looked like the last rose of summer, and . .

had her hair done up in a wad on top of her head. **1967–68** *DARE* (Qu. X3, *When a woman puts her hair up on her head in a bunch*) Infs **MO**38, **NY**69, 73, Wad; **NY**75, Wad on top. [All Infs old, comm type 5, gs educ]

wadder See **water A1**

waddie See **waddy**

wadding n Also *pea-wadden, pee-wadden, ~-wadding, tar-wadding* [Cf the similar use of *stuffing*] Cf **willies 3**
In phrr to *beat* (or *scare*, etc) *the wadding out of:* To beat (or scare, etc) very thoroughly.

   1880 in 2006 *DARE* File—Internet **KS** [From the *Arkansas City Traveler* (KS) 8 Dec], There is a sense of justice and honor and a disposition to abide by the law characteristic of the American people that, when the test comes, will knock the wadding out of all such business. **1897** in 1996 Norris *Apprenticeship Writings* 2.31 **Chicago IL**, Oh, let's go and punch the wadding out of him, and be done with it! **1914** Flagg *I Should Say* 20 **MA**, The "Salena P. Peabody" hit the reef! It ripped the tar-wadding out of her. **1945** *Best from Yank* 192 **AK**, "I had never thrown a grenade in my life," Conrad admits. "Personally, they scare the wadding out of me." **1968** Kellner *Aunt Serena* 167 **IN**, A poor old tramp came to the door all give out, had the waddin' scared out of him. **1968** *DARE* Tape **IN**20, [Of a horse race:] They beat the wadding out of him the first heat. **1968** *DARE* FW Addit **IA**30, Scared the wadding out of us. **1984** *DARE* File **ceKS, cnWI**, Your recent letter astonished the pee-wadding (pronounced, pee-WADdin') out of me. This mildly disruptable [sic] term has been familiar to me since my childhood in Norton County, Kansas at the turn of the [20th] Century. **1996** *Ibid* **neTX** (as of 1920s–30s), You scared the waddin' out of me. **1997** *Ibid*, My wife uses an expression, common in her family, that something "scared the peawadden out of her." **1998** *DARE* File—Internet **OK**, The farmer . . will generally always have black cows that jump up and scare the wadding out of you. **2000** *NADS Letters* **TN**, Do you know what pee wadden means? I have heard it used (by a person in Memphis) as "I love the pee wadden" out of you. **2001** in 2007 *DARE* File—Internet **FL**, This happened just yesterday on a 5–600# blue [marlin] . . Karen . . had beaten the tarwaddin' out of fast and furious. **2002** *Ibid* **VA**, Another good one from Dad. "He got the Pee wadding knocked out of him", not good if you're the one missing the wadding.

waddy n Also *waddie* [Etym unknown]
1a also *cow-waddy:* A cowboy, ranch hand. **West** Cf **top waddy**

   1893 Griggs *Lyrics Lariat* 15 **NE**, When one began stealing / The cards they were dealing,/ And waddy objecting, was shot in the breast. *Ibid* 254, The Cowboy is the dauntless hero of a new chivalry. . . In speaking *to* a comrade, he calls him *waddy;* when talking *of* one, he refers to him as *puncher.* **1923** Cook *50 Yrs.* 39 **swTX** (as of 1870s), When Mr. Roberts informed me that I was to be one of his trail waddies, I immediately moved all my personal belongings over to his camp. **1928** French *Ranchman NM* 243 (as of 1880s), He said: 'Hell, fellows, we common cow-waddies ain't got but one vote nohow!' **1937** *DN* 6.620 **swTX**, Even for the cowboy there are different names. He is indifferently called *cow-hand, ranch-hand, cowpuncher, rawhide, waddie,* or *cow-waddie.* **c1938** in Lib. of Congress *Amer. Memory: WPA Life Hist.* (Internet) **TX** (as of c1883), Dad had dealings with a lotta ranches . . that I got to know all the waddies. . . Every waddy had six–eight hosses that really were cow hosses. **1941** Cleaveland *No Life* 111 **NM**, The ascending scale in open-range cattle business is from horse wrangler at the lowest rung to range boss at the highest. Between them lie cook, riders, fence-line riders (after there were fences), run-of-the-mill waddies. **1949** *PADS* 11.20 **CO,** *Cow waddy.* **1956** Almirall *From College* 76 **CO,** They don't come no better than them two waddies. **1964** Dobie *Cow People* 104 **TX,** I worked for the Stiles men as waddie, top-hand and then boss until the spring of 1876.

b spec: A **rustler 3,** cattle thief. *obs*

1897 Hough *Story Cowboy* 279 **WY, Plains, ND, SD,** The rustlers of the upper country rapidly joined their forces and arrived at an understanding with one another. . . They had in a way a creed and dialect of their own. A genuine rustler was called a "waddy," a name difficult to trace to its origin. **1907** Raine *WY Story* 231, Along with it went a recital of the crimes he had committed. How he was a noted "waddy," or cattle-rustler; how he and his gang had held up three trains in eighteen months. **1912** Raine *Brand Blotters* 45 **West,** I'm a waddy and a thief, but you're going to protect me for old times' sake. **1922** Rollins *Cowboy* 313 **eWY** (as of c1890), The movement had also militant apostles in the "waddies," men faithful to the illegal art of rustling.

2 in comb *hay-waddy:* A worker temporarily employed in haying. **NE**

1928 *AmSp* 4.128 **ncNE,** A "hay waddie" is a man who comes into the "hills" to work in the hay fields. **1929** *AmSp* 5.56 **NE** [Cattle country talk], During the "haying season," or "putting up hay," the rancher generally adds many "hay waddies," men temporarily employed to help cut and stack hay, to his "ranch hands." **1935** Sandoz *Jules* 126 **wNE,** He had spent the night at the Hippach hay camp with half a dozen hay waddies. **1947** *Prairie Schooner* 21.142 **nwNE** (as of c1910), Mother . . tied it up with a red ribbon from one of the candy boxes the hay waddies brought me. **1973** Allen *LAUM* 1.406 (as of c1950), In the Nebraska sandhill country [is] . . found *hay-waddy.* . . [5 infs, **NE**].

wadjit n [Cf *EDD wadjet* (at *wedget* sb. 1) "A small wad"] Cf *DS* LL6

A small amount, smidgeon.

1993 *Coast Watch* Sept/Oct 12 *Outer Banks NC,* Words like "begaumed," "benambered," "wadjit" and "jellywhopper" color coastal speech from Duck to Wilmington. **1994** NC Lang. & Life Project *Harkers Is. Vocab.* 11 **eNC,** *Wadjit.* . . Small amount of something. There's just a wadjit of mashed potatoes left.

wadn't See **be C2a**

waer See **water A3**

wafer ash n

A **hop tree** (here: *Ptelea trifoliata*); hence *wafer-ash tea* a tea made from the bark of this tree.

1855 *Eclectic Med. Jrl.* 14.198, Pteilin, or oil of Ptelea, (from wafer ash). **1872** Eggleston *End of the World* 140 **IN,** She should have a corn-sweat and some wafer-ash tea. . . The wafer-ash would cause a tendency of the blood to the head, and thus relieve the pressure on the juggler-vein. **1911** Porter *Harvester* 333 **IN,** Now here is wafer ash; it is for music as well as medicine. **1931** Clute *Common Plants* 61, The wafer ash *(Ptelea trifoliata)* is not an ash, but the fuits [sic] are like wafers. **1966** *Sun. Jrl. & Star* (Lincoln NE) 9 Jan sec D 17/4, Aguebark. . . is commonly known as pickaway anise or quininetree or wafer ash [etc]. **2006** *Cleveland Plain Dealer* (OH) 11 Oct sec B 4 (Internet), Bissell said the plants he has chosen, such as pawpaw, hackberry and wafer ash, will draw native and migrating birds and rarely seen butterflies.

wafer parsnip n

Any of var plants of the genus *Cymopterus.*

1967 Harrington *Edible Plants Rocky Mts.* 171, *Cymopterus* spp. . . Biscuit Root, Corkwing, Wafer Parsnip [etc]. **2006** *DARE* File—Internet NM, Wafer Parsnip *[Cymopterus bulbosus, C. montanus, C. purpureus, C. acaulis].*

waffle stomper n Cf **stomper 2**

A usu heavy boot or shoe with a corrugated sole.

1971 *Chicago Tribune* (IL) 25 Apr 8/4, [Advt:] *Hiking and Mountain Climbing* footwear. . . Dunham's are the importers of famous Waffle Stompers. **1972** *News-Jrl.* (Mansfield OH) 24 Aug 12/1, [Advt:] *Digger Boot* in genuine blue or brown suede, waffle stomper soles and heels. **1975** *AmSp* 50.68 **AR** (as of c1970), *Waffle stompers.* . . Shoes or boots with thick cleated soles. **1981** *Children's Folkl. Newsl.* Winter 4 **seMN** (as of 1977), *Waffle stomper*—Old tennis sneaker whose tread leaves a waffle-looking mark in the dirt; generally any old sneaker. **1982** Cleary *Ralph S. Mouse* 17 **neCA,** Never mind, thought Ralph

peeking out at two pair of boots, the kind known as waffle stompers, which had thick treads that held snow. **1985** McInerney *Ransom* 142 **NEng,** Their fellow passengers on the bus trip to the slopes were two student mountaineers in tweed knickers and waffle stompers. **1999** *DARE* File—Internet (Central Florida Green Bay Packer Backers) 6 **WI,** *Waffle Stompers:* heavy duty boots that leave a tire-like imprint when you walk through snow or mud.

wag v **Sth, S Midl**

1 To stagger along, esp under a heavy load.

1899 (1912) Green *VA Folk-Speech* 471, *Wag.* . . To move slowly, unevenly, as when one staggers along under a heavy load: as, "He had so much on his shoulder he just could wag." To move; to budge; to stir. **1939** in 1970 Hyatt *Hoodoo* 2.1043 **ceSC** [Black], Yo' know whut dey make whut Jesus *wagged* [Hyatt: waddled or staggered] wit . . when dey nail him tuh de cross jes' dat way. . . Say, "Now ah 'spect fo' yo' tuh *wag* wit dis cross . . ah make yo' *wag* wit de same cross whut Jesus Christ *wagged* wit." **1949** Turner *Africanisms* 277 **seSC** [Gullah], Somebody in the neighborhood will say, "Look here, where that had [sic for *hag*] at—[that] old lady wag around here so, keep abegging for something that way?" **1986** Pederson *LAGS Concordance* (I lugged) 1 inf, **cAL,** Had to wag with it.

2 To carry or transport with difficulty; to lug, tote, haul.

1931 *AmSp* 7.94 **eKY,** *Puny-lookin'.* . . Vicey's too puny-lookin' to wag that big young 'un aroun'. **1932** Stribling *Store* 63 **AL,** Jerry, don't allow him to wag a load like that! **1944** in 1953 Randolph–Wilson *Down in Holler* 296 **Ozarks,** A small child in Searcy County is often compelled to wag her baby brother around with her. **1952** Brown *NC Folkl.* 1.604 **wNC,** *Wag.* . . To carry about an object. "I got tired of wagging that young un on my hip."—West. **1954** *Harder Coll.* **cwTN,** *Wag.* . . To carry. I had to wag 'at baby 'roun' all day long. **1956** Ker *Vocab. W. TX* 429, To carry something heavy, as a bundle or sack of potatoes. . . The locution *wag* . . [was] reported by two older informants. **1966–67** *DARE* (Qu. Y30b, *To take something heavy up and move it from one place to another—for example, a bushel of apples*) Infs **MS6, TN13,** Wag. **1986** Pederson *LAGS Concordance* (I lugged) 2 infs, **TN, TX,** Wag (it); 1 inf, **ceTN,** Wag it—of a heavy suitcase up a hill; heavy load; 1 inf, **nwTN,** I had to wag it from here to yonder; 1 inf, **cAL,** Wagged. **2003** in 2007 *DARE* File—Internet **cwMO,** Easier to pull the whole pump, then wag it home and wrestle with the pulley privately. *Ibid* **KY,** I always see something that I can use sometime or another, and I can't resist buying. Then I have to wag it home and find a place to store it until that "sometime" comes around. **2004** *DARE* File **NC,** I could leave my car there and then "wag" my stuff via the trolley/subway to your house. *Ibid* **eTX** (as of c1950s) [Black], Among black . . women in East Texas, it [=*wag*] pretty much replaces "tote," which is guy-talk. A man *totes,* whereas a woman *wags* a load of groceries home, *wags* a child in her arms, *wags* a bag of laundry on her back, etc.

wag n

=**dogtail 3.**

1929 Needham–Heywood *Hdbk. Dragonflies* 178, Tetragoneuria. . . Dog-tails: Wags. . . Their flight is. . . a continual succession of dartings and dodgings from side to side.

wagalong n

A **tagalong.**

1965–66 *DARE* (Qu. Y9, *Somebody who always follows along behind others: "His little brother is an awful _____."*) Inf **MS63,** Wagalong; **SC19,** Wagalong [FW sugg].

wage n Usu |weǰ|; also |weǰ| Pronc-sp *wedge*

Std sense, var pronc.

1941 *AmSp* 16.6 **eTX** [Black], *Wages* ['wɛdʒɪ̜z]. **1965–66** *DARE* (Qu. L1, *A man who is employed to help with work on a farm*) Infs **MS46, 60,** Wedge hand. [Both Infs Black]

wage hand n Also *wages hand* **S Atl, Gulf States** See Map Cf **share hand**

A wage laborer, esp an agricultural worker; a hired hand.

1874 in 1927 Jones *FL Plantation Rec.* 201 **nwFL,** My only regret is that we had not planted 50 acres of cotton with wages hands. **1883** SC State Bd. Ag. *SC Resources* 84, In Barnwell, the laborer decides under which system he will work. Share hands and renters pick cleaner cotton than wage hands. **1892** in 2010 (acc) Lexis–Nexis Legal Research *State Case Law: GA* (Internet), He had plaintiff to assemble all the standing wages hands, croppers and tenants, and defendant asked each one of these what he was to receive under his contract with Zachry for that year. **1938–39** in Lib. of Congress *Amer. Memory: WPA Life Hist.* (Internet) **SC** [Black], Fer' years, I wuz' jes' a wages hand. *Ibid* **AL**, He had a wage hand to work his garden and to cultivate the patches around the home. *Ibid* **NC**, Bob was a wage hand then, gettin' twenty dollars a month. **1954** *PADS* 21.40 **SC**, *Wages hand.* . . A wage laborer. **1965–70** *DARE* (Qu. L1, *A man who is employed to help with work on a farm*) Infs **AL**55, **GA**7, 28, 45, 84, 87, **LA**12, 18, **MS**81, Wage hand; **AL**14, **SC**57, Wage hand [FW sugg]; **MS**63, Share hand, wage hand—depending on arrangement; **GA**9, 12, 16, Wages hand; **GA**1, Wages hand—paid by month; **MS**46, 60, Wedge hand; (Qu. HH42, *Names and nicknames for a common laborer;* total Infs questioned, 75) Inf **MS**21, Wage hand; **FL**7, **GA**9, Wages hand; **MS**60, Wedge hand. **1986** Pederson *LAGS Concordance,* 1 inf, **swTN**, Wage hand—paid daily wages; 1 inf, **csMS**, Wage hand—paid employee; 1 inf, **swGA**, Wages hand—hired help; 1 inf, **csGA**, Wages hands—hired laborers.

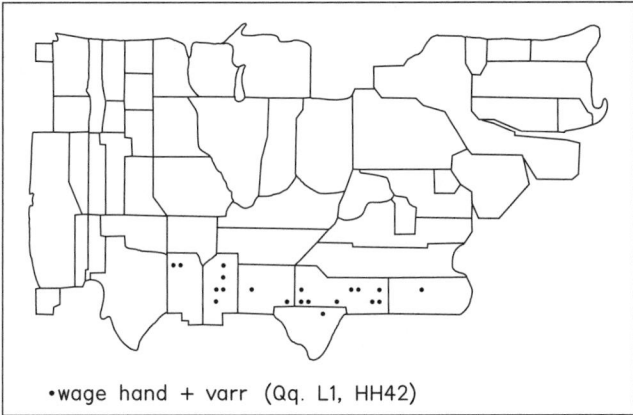

•wage hand + varr (Qq. L1, HH42)

wagged out adj phr Also *waggy* esp **MA, ME** Cf **wag** v
Tired out.

   [**1875** *Sat. Eve. Post* 1 May 2, *Facetiæ.* . . *Epitaph for a humorist.*—Wagged out.] **a1877** in 1950 *AmSp* 25.185 **MA**, *Wagged out.* Tired, worn out (as if finished wagging). **1898** *Brotherhood Locomotive Mth. Jrl.* 32.337 **cnMS**, After an all-night trip, we once more found ourselves at home tired and "wagged out." **1941** *LANE* Map 481 *(Tuckered out)* 1 inf, **neMA**, Wagged out. **1968** [see **streaked**].

wagin n [Perh echoic]
=**black-crowned night heron.**

   1925 (1928) Forbush *Birds* MA 1.336, Black-crowned Night Heron. *Other names* . . wagin.

wagon burner n derog Cf *DS* HH28
An American Indian.

   2000 *DARE* File—Internet **CA**, You don't want us to use the name Apache or Indian. Well wagon burner, I am with you. Take all your Indian names back to the reservation. **2001** *Ibid* **Pacific NW**, American Indian construction workers are pressing for a new committee to address racism and discrimination. . . "Every day I was either called 'Chief' or 'Wagon Burner.'" *Ibid* **ME** (as of c1985), Almost every day when I was a student in Old Town [High School], I was called a spear-chucker and wagon burner. **2002** *WI State Jrl.* (Madison) 6 July sec A 5/3 **sCA** (as of c1975), His grandfather told him, "Don't bring darkies home," and never to marry a "wagon-burner," a derogatory term for American Indians. **2005** *DARE* File—Internet **NV**, Her greatgrand [sic] mother was a full blooded wagon burner, and that's the only non-white blood she has.

wagon, fix one's See **fix** v B4b

wagon greasing n Also *wagon grease, wagon greasing distance* **chiefly Sth, S Midl**
The distance travelled between two greasings of a wagon's wheels—used as an indefinite measure of distance.

   1944 Buckmaster *Deep River* 32 **neGA** (as of 1859), "Don't get a wagon-greasin' away from the house very often," he said. **1953** Randolph–Wilson *Down in Holler* 213 **Ozarks**, Speaking of a journey undertaken in his youth, an aged hillman said: "I don't know how many miles it was. . . But we . . *greased the wagon four times.* That's how we measured distance in them days, by the *wagon-greasin's.*" **1953** *Time* 7 Dec 100 **CA**, When I started broadcasting seven years ago, there wasn't

a hillbilly disk jockey within wagon-greasing distance. **1968** *Grant Co. Herald* (Elbow Lake MN) 20 June 2/4, Lars, that was a long wagon-greasing past 65 was agreed with Joe. **1969** *DARE* (Qu. MM25, . . *A long distance: "Texas is a _____ [from here]."*) Inf **TX**70, Several wagon greasings. **c1975** in 2006 *DARE* File—Internet **swKY**, So on a beautiful Thanksgiving morning after a nine months stay, a covered wagon was greased and ready to roll . . with a four wagon greasings, or two hundred mi trip. . . He boarded the train at Mexico Ky for "White Sulphor [sic] Crossing" flagstation. A distance of about 12 or 15 mile, or about a wagon greasing that day from home. **1978** *New Yorker* 6 Feb 64 **GA**, Americus is only ten miles from Plains—"a wagon grease" away, in Georgia lingo. **1986** Pederson *LAGS Concordance,* 1 inf, **cwAR**, Three wagon greasings from town. **2000** Baylor Univ. Med. Center *Proc.* 13.52 (Internet) **MO**, Picture in your mind a good ole boy from my old hometown of Hardin, Missouri. . . Hardin is a suburb of Henrietta, out from Norborne, down the road from Carrollton, across the river from Lexington, one wagon greasing from Richmond—you get the picture.

wagon house See **wagon shed**

wagon mine n Also *mule-wagon mine* Cf **doghole 3**
A small coal mine.

   1920 Fay *Gloss. Mining* 728, *Wagon mine.* Same as Snowbird mine. [*Ibid* 629, *Snowbird mine.* . . A mine that produces or ships only small quantities of coal, and operates only when coal is high by reason of a scarcity or a shortage of cars for shipment.] **1934** *Sun* (Baltimore MD) 10 May 13/5 *(Hench Coll.)* **WV**, Several small "wagon mines" have been operating in Lewis county despite the shutdown. [**1939** *Ibid* 8 Apr 22/7 *(Hench Coll.)* **WV**, Of the so-called "wagon" type, the output is hauled away from the mines by wagons and trucks to tipples three to four miles away, and dumped into railroad cars.] **1973** *PADS* 59.60 **OH**, *Wagon mine* . . =*doghole mine.* *Ibid* 34, *Doghole mine* . . a very small *mine* operated by a few men, usually taking coal which lies very near the surface. **2003** *DARE* File—Internet **AL**, Down in Drummond Hollow . . Heman H. Drummond started a small mule wagon mine back in 1935. **2004** *Ibid* **NM**, Coal was produced from Wagon Mine No. 2 until the main Sugarite mine . . was opened in 1912. **2005** *Ibid* **WY**, The coal mine was originally opened as a "wagon" mine in 1921. **2006** *Ibid* **PA**, Wagon Mine depicts a scene of one of the last mines in Pennsylvania to employ mules for hauling coal carts.

wagon shed n Also *wagon house;* for addit varr see quot 1965–70 **scattered, but esp NEast, eN Midl** See Map on p. 836 Cf **machine shed**
A building where horse-drawn vehicles and farm equipment are stored.

   1773 (1900) Fithian *Jrl.* 1.39 **PA**, Whitehead has built a waggon house for his coach. **1851** *Scientific Amer.* 6.126 **NY**, They [=potatoes] were separated . . and spread on the floor of my wagon-house. **1855** MI State Ag. Soc. *Trans. for 1854* 6.161, My other buildings consist of an out house . . a common barn . . with a wagon shed and tool shop in connection, attached. **1860** *Harper's New Mth. Mag.* 22.82 **IN**, Its ragged wagon-shed . . neither wind-tight nor water-tight . . through whose board-sides several generations of idle horses had gnawed sundry holes. **1878** *Scribner's Mth.* 16.473 **PA**, We went to look for a ladder. We found one in the wagon-house. **1900** *Newark Daily Advocate* (OH) 7 June 7/6, For Sale—One of the best upland farms. . . one carriage house, one wagon shed and corn house. **1941** *LANE* Map 353 *(Shed)* 1 inf, **cMA**, Wagon shed, under the wood shed. **1965–70** *DARE* (Qu. M22, . . *Kinds of buildings . . on farms*) 51 Infs, **scattered, but esp NEast, eN Midl**, Wagon shed; **MD**24, Wagon shed—stores wagons, machines; **MD**31, Wagon shed—to store wagons and implements; **MA**42, **OH**10, Wagon shed—same as tool shed; **OH**77, Wagon shed—for tools; **VT**16, Wagon shed, tool shed—probably all the same thing; 10 Infs, **scattered, but esp NEast**, Wagon house; **NY**189, Wagon and tool barn; **GA**22, Wagon shelter; (Qu. M1, . . *Kinds of barns . . according to their use or the way they are built*) Infs **HI**2, **NJ**17, **PA**235, Wagon shed; **NY**70, Wagon barn; **NJ**20, Wagon house. **1967** *DARE* Tape **VT**1A, The shed chamber was over the woodshed and the—well, we called it garage in the later days, wagon house was the . . olden name for it. **1986** Pederson *LAGS Concordance (Shed)* 8 infs, **scattered Gulf Region**, (A) wagon shed; 1 inf, **nwTN**, Wagon sheds; 1 inf, **cwTN**, Wagon shed—wagons and farm implements; 1 inf, **cwLA**, Wagon shed—for tools and harnesses; *(Junk room)* 1 inf, **nwGA**, Wagon shed; *(Barn)* 1 inf, **ceAL**, Wagon shed; *(Stable)* 1 inf, **nwTN**, Wagon shed; *(Loft)* 1 inf, **ceAL**, Wagon house—where wagons kept inside; 1 inf, **cGA**, Wagon shed.

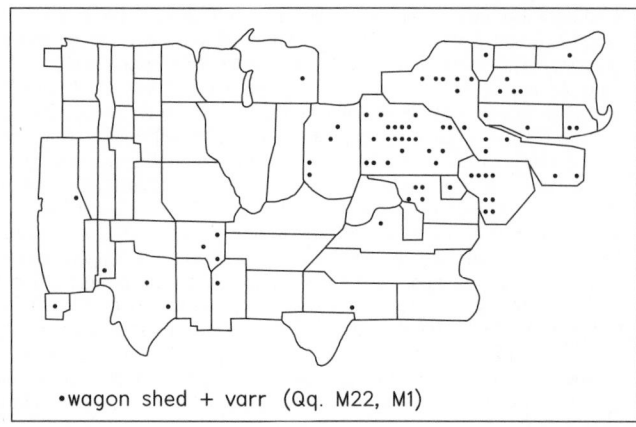

•wagon shed + varr (Qq. M22, M1)

wagon sled n esp ME Cf two-sled

A large sled, esp a logging sled, supported by two pairs of runners.

1902 *Daily Kennebec Jrl.* (Augusta ME) 3 Jan 6/4, [Advt:] One 2-horse wagon sled with high sideboards that will hold a cord or over. **1905** U.S. Forest Serv. *Bulletin* 61.52 [Logging terms], *Wagon sled. See* Logging sled. [*Ibid* 42, *Logging sled,* The heavy double sled used to haul logs from the skidway or yard to the landing.] **1918** *Daily Kennebec Jrl.* (Augusta ME) 13 Mar 7/3, [Advt:] For Sale. . . 1 Two-Horse Wagon Sled. 2 One-Horse Wagon Sled. **1945** Hamlin *9 Mile Bridge* 46 **nME,** The logs are piled on the side of the road to be loaded onto bobsleds—double sleds, two sleds or wagon sleds, as they are variously called—that carry them to the landing on the river. **1956** Sorden–Ebert *Logger's Words* 40 **NEng, Gt Lakes,** *Wagon-sled,* See sleigh. [*Ibid* 33, *Sleigh,* A logging sled for hauling logs on snow and ice.] **1966–69** *DARE* (Qu. N40a, . . *Sleighs . . for hauling loads*) Inf **IN**39, Wagon sled; **ME**19, Wagon sled—two runners; **CO**35, Big wagon with runners underneath; **IN**42, Wagon with sled runners on; (Qu. N40c, *Other kinds of sleighs*) Inf **ME**9, Wagon sled—for lumbering—wider than other sleds—as wide as a wagon. **1966** *DARE* Tape **ME**18, We used to have what you call a wagon sled. Two sleds, one hooked behind the other. You could turn 'em. They'd turn pretty easy. [FW:] Kinda like a double runner? [Inf:] Yup. . . Just same. **2006** *DARE* File—Internet **ME,** In 1996, the Rangeley Lakes Region Logging Museum acquired two miniature logging sleds. . . When the wagon sled gets under way, its two sets of runners twist and turn, as if following a road. . . Sticks of alder and yellow and silver birch fill up the rack sills of the wagon . . teaching how the pulpwood lays.

wagon wheel n

1 A silver dollar; a dollar. **scattered, but rare NEast** See Map Cf *cartwheel,* **wheel** n **2**

1909 *DN* 3.405 **nwAR,** *Wagon-wheel.* . . Silver dollar. **1936** Hench *Coll.,* [Prison slang:] Wagon wheel—a silver dollar. **1965–70** *DARE* (Qu. U27, . . *A silver dollar*) 56 Infs, **scattered, exc NEast,** Wagon wheel; (Qu. U20, . . *Dollars . . "It cost a hundred _____."*) Infs **MO**37, **OK**42, Wagon wheels.

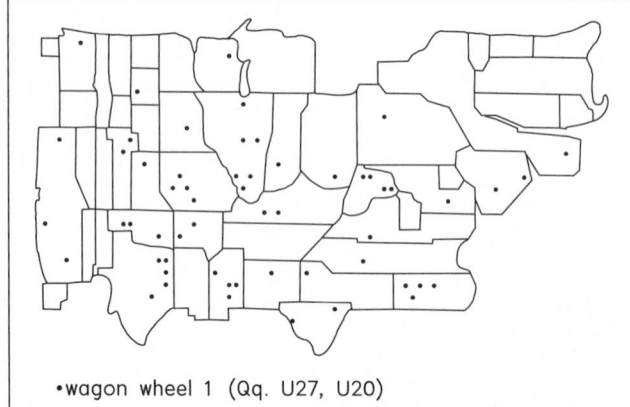

•wagon wheel 1 (Qq. U27, U20)

2 A cartwheel, handspring, or summersault. **chiefly Sth, S Midl, Missip-Ohio Valleys** See Map *esp among older speakers, rural speakers, and speakers with little formal educ*

1926 Sherwood *Here We Are* 77, He completed his act by turning wagon-wheels to the ring entrance, where he made his graceful bow. **1965–70** *DARE* (Qu. EE9c, . . *If children spread their arms and turn over sideways*) 30 Infs, **chiefly Sth, S Midl, Missip-Ohio Valleys,** Wagon wheel; (Qu. EE9a, *The children's trick of turning over rapidly straight forward close to the ground*) Infs **AR**28, **NC**7, Wagon wheels; (Qu. EE9b, *If children jump forward, land on the hands, and turn over*) Inf **MO**6, Wagon wheel. [Of 31 total Infs, 25 were comm types 4 and 5, 24 were old, 18 gs educ or less.] **1986** Pederson *LAGS Concordance,* 1 inf, **cAL,** Wagon wheel = cartwheel; 1 inf, **neAL,** Wagon wheels = cartwheels; turn on stretched arms. [**2006** *DARE* File—Internet **NC,** Gymnastics Assessment #3. . . Draw a line from what he names something we do or use in class to the correct name. [Column 1:] a. wagon wheel / b. candy bars / c. cinnamon roll—[Column 2:] a. forward roll / b. cartwheel / c. uneven bars.]

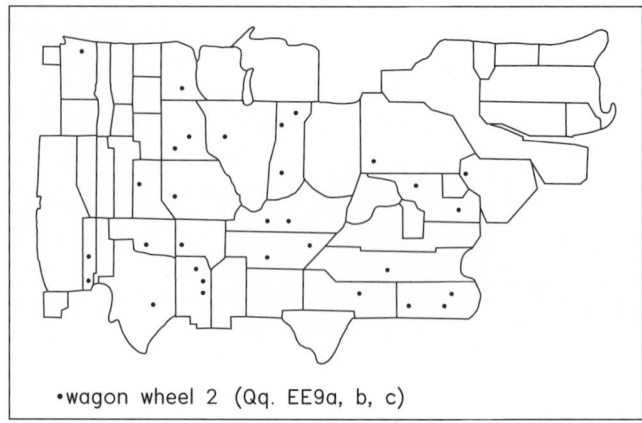

•wagon wheel 2 (Qq. EE9a, b, c)

wagtail n

1 A bird of the genus *Seiurus;* an **ovenbird** or **water thrush.**

1674 Josselyn *Two Voyages* 100 **NEng,** Other sorts of Birds there are, as the *Troculus, Wag-tail,* or *Dish-water,* which is here of a brown colour. **1848** (1851) Mather–Brockett *Geogr. Hist. NY* 40, New York water thrush, Oven bird, or Golden crowned wagtail. **1871** Burroughs *Wake-Robin* 223 **NY,** Of our small wood-birds we have three varieties, east of the Mississippi, closely related to each other, . . namely, the two species of water-thrush and wagtails, and the oven-bird, or wood-wagtail. **1891** Goss *Hist. Birds KS* 575, They move about with a graceful step, almost continually vibrating their tails, like the Pipits, and for this reason are usually known as the Wagtails. **1895** Minot *Land-Birds New Engl.* 83, *[Seiurus] aurocapillus.* "Ovenbird." "Wagtail." **1917** (1923) *Birds Amer.* 3.152, The tail-bobbing habit has given the birds [=water thrushes and the ovenbird] the popular name of "Wagtail". . . The Oven-bird is known as the Wood Wagtail. **1932** Howell *FL Bird Life* 412, Northern Water-thrush. . . Other names . . Wagtail.

2 A **pipit** (here: *Anthus rubescens*).

1872 Coues *Key to N. Amer. Birds* 90, *Anthus [ludovicianus].* . . Brown lark. Titlark. Wagtail. Pipit. **1932** Bennitt *Check-list* 50 **MO,** American pipit. . . Titlark; wagtail. **1954** Sprunt *FL Bird Life* 358, The warbler will hop, while the "wagtail" walks.

wah-cup See wake-up

wahine n |wɑˈhine, wɑˈhini| Also sp *waheenie, wahini* [Haw *wahine*] HI Cf kane

A female; spec: a woman; a wife.

1833 in 1934 Frear *Lowell & Abigail* 69 **HI,** They will send to Lahaina for my *wahine* (wife), etc. **1850** Cheever *Is. World Pacific* 165 **HI,** A company of natives attended us, one of whom waddled to my aid and held me by the arm, as a *haole* does his *wahine,* they said. **1870** *Overland Mth.* 4.218 **HI,** [The necklace] evidently belongs to the damsel beside him, who leans her head against an old *wahine's* back. **1919** Kyne *Capt. Scraggs* 260 **HI,** The sad, sweet falsetto singing of half a dozen *waheenies* fishing on the wharf. **1938** Reinecke *Hawaiian Loanwords* 32, *Wahine* ['wɑˈhiːne]. . . 1. A woman. 2. A female of any species, animal or plant. . . 3. Female in sex . . applied to any species. 4. A wife. **1951** *AmSp* 26.20 **HI,** *Kane* for 'man' or 'husband' and *wahine* for 'woman' or 'wife' are often heard, and seen as well on the doors of rest rooms. **1967** *DARE* (Qu. Z4, . . '*Grandmother'*) Inf **HI**6, Wahine; (Qu. HH34, *General words . . for a woman, not necessarily uncomplimentary*) Inf **HI**1, Wahine; **HI**6A, 13, Wahine [wɑˈhine]. **1967** Clark *All* *the Best HI* 55, *Wahine*—woman. The powder room is often so marked. **1969** *DARE* File **HI,** *Wahini* [ˌwɑˈhini]—woman. **1991** Saiki *From the Lanai* 101 **HI,** Every time Molly collected rent payments, a new *wahini* with or without the children greeted her.

wahloon See **walloon** n¹

wahoe See **wahoo** n¹ 4

wahoo n¹ Also *waahoo, warhew, whahoo* [Prob adaptation of one or more AmInd names; for suggestions see quot 1910 at **1** and **4** below]

Any of several shrubs or trees, as:

1 also *wahoo elm:* An elm, usu **winged elm.**

1770 in 1925 MS Hist. Soc. *Pub. Centenary Ser.* 5.62, The Trees which I remark'd to be the largest were Oaks of different Kinds, Wahoos, Button Wood [etc]. **1771** *Ibid* 79, Trees which I mostly found in this Part were The Elm or Wahoo [etc]. **1808** *Monitor* (DC) 20 Sept 4/2 **SC,** I rode down . . to view the screw-press for packing cotton, in poplar or wahoo bark. **1821** Elliott *Sketch* 1.334 **SC, GA,** [Ulmus] Alata. . . *Whahoo.* In our low country, however, the name *whahoo* is even now indiscriminately applied to every species of Elm. **1827** Williams *View W. FL* 54, Whahao [sic]. Ulmus alata. **1829** *Amer. Jrl. Med. Sci.* 5.262 **cwMS,** Bark of the Root of the Lynn or Wahoo, *(Ulmus alata . .)* as a Poultice. . . [H]e has . . been in the habit of using this application to all the varieties of phlegmonous inflammation, with remarkable success. **1855** *MO Geol. Surv. Report* 1.206, The alluvial bottoms . . sustain . . American, Slippery and Wahoo Elms. **1862** in 1863 Porcher *Resources* 311 **cAL,** Wahoo rope.—We have seen a specimen of rope made of wahoo bark. **1880** (1881) Harris *Uncle Remus Songs* 84 **GA,** All over the floor long strips of "wahoo" bark were spread, and these the old man was weaving into horse-collars. **1897** Sudworth *Arborescent Flora* 182, Ulmus racemosa. . . Wahoo (Ohio). . . Ulmus alata. . . Wahoo (W. Va., N.C., S.C., La., Tex., Ky., Mo.) . . Whahoo (S.C.) **1910** Hodge *Hdbk. Amer. Indians* 2.890, Wahoo. A Georgia and South Carolina name for *Ulmus alata,* the cork or winged elm, but for many years applied to the species of elm indiscriminately. . . The name is from *ûhawhu,* in the Creek language. **1950** Peattie *Nat. Hist. Trees* 250, In many a town in the lower Mississippi valley Wahoo makes a fine street tree. **1996** in 2007 *DARE* File—Internet **neLA,** Lately, two separate windstorms have provided me with much green wood, e.g., an entire Wahoo Elm tree. . . The Wahoo is a bit (understatement) tough to split.

2 A **linden** (here: *Tilia americana*).

1755 in 1821 Smith *Selection Corresp. Linnaeus* 1.355, [Letter from Alexander Garden:] I have sent some *Pavia* seeds, *Cassine* falsely so called here; it is a new genus; some Red Bay; some Wahoo, by the New York people, Linden tree; some Swamp *Palmetta* [etc]. **1846** Browne *Trees* 48, T[ilia] a[mericana] alba. . . *White-leaved Lime-tree, White Lime, Warhew* in the United States. **1874** *FL Comm. Lands & Immigration Annual Rept. for 1874* 147, The hammock lands in Marion . . are well timbered with . . wahoo (the basswood of the North), sugarberry, &c. **1884** Sargent *Forests N. Amer.* 28, Tilia heterophylla [=*T. americana heterophylla*]. . . White bass wood. Wahoo. **1897** Sudworth *Arborescent Flora* 302 **FL,** Tilia pubescens [=*T. americana pubescens*]. . . Wahoo. *Ibid* 303 **GA, FL,** Tilia heterophylla. . . Wahoo. **1948** Mathews *Some Southernisms* 79 **AL,** The tree that I was taught to call *wahoo* was neither of the preceding but . . a basswood.

3 A **magnolia 1** (here: **cucumber tree 1** or *Magnolia fraseri*). **NC, TN, KY, VA**

1842 *London Jrl. Botany* 1.226 **wNC,** Towards the summit of this ridge we first noticed the *Magnolia Fraseri.* . . This, as well as *M. acuminata* (the only other species of *Magnolia* that we observed), is occasionally termed *Cucumber-tree;* but the people of the country almost uniformly called the former *Wahoo,* a name which, in the lower part of the Southern States, is applied to *Ulmus alata,* or often to all the Elms indifferently. **1860** Curtis *Cat. Plants NC* 68, Long-leaved Cucumber Tree. . . Found only in ravines of the mountains where it is known by this name, and also as *Wahoo* and *Indian Physic.* **1883** Zeigler-Grosscup *Heart of Alleghanies* 49 **wNC,** A tree called the wahoo, grows here as well as on many of the ranges. It bears a white lily-shaped flower in the summer. **1897** Sudworth *Arborescent Flora* 197, Magnolia fraseri. . . Whahoo. **1968** *DARE* FW Addit **VA**15, [ˈwɑhu]—book term [is] Fraser's magnolia. **1969** *DARE* (Qu. T16, . . *Kinds of trees . . 'special'*) Infs **KY**39, 47, Wahoo—umbrella magnolia. **1969** *DARE* FW Addit **csKY,** Wahoo—old-fashioned, Inf's usage; cowcumber—later term, some say. A tree with leaves like a tobacco leaf. **1974–75** in 2004

Montgomery-Hall *Dict. Smoky Mt. Engl.* 634 **wNC, eTN,** They were one that was in here that we called him a wahoo. . . He was a big tree, and he had a small cucumber on him just about the size of your thumb. **1981** *High Coll.* **ceKY** (as of c1930), *Wahoo:* . . commonly used in the Gorge as a name for the cucumber magnolia *(Magnolia acuminata)* instead of as a term for the winged elm *(Ulmus alata),* though both trees grow in the area.

4 also *wahoe, wahoon, wahoo-wahoo tree:* A **burning bush 1,** usu *Euonymus atropurpurea.*

1828 Rafinesque *Med. Flora* 1.195, The leaves of . . *Evonymus atropurpureus* (the Wahoon or Arrow wood of the West and South) make a fine pectoral tea. **1829** *Transylvania Jrl. Med.* 2.446 **KY,** *Euonymus atropurpureus.* . . The Indian arrow-wood or Wahoo, by which names this shrub is here universally known. **1852** WI State Ag. Soc. *Trans.* 2.383, *Euonymus . . atropurpureus.* . . Here called Wahoo. **1857** MI State Ag. Soc. *Trans. for 1856* 8.419, Euonymus americanus. . . Whahoo. Burning bush. **1857** Gray *Manual of Botany* 81, E[uonymus] atropurpureus. . . Burning-Bush. Waahoo. . . New York to Wisconsin and southward. **1870** *Ladies' Repository* 30.407 **sIL,** In Summer the house was made cheerful by green branches, and in Winter by berries of the Wahoe. **1876** *Amer. Agric.* 35.27 **MO,** The fruit sent is that of the bush known in the western states as *Waahoo,* but in the east . . as Burning-bush and Spindle-tree. **1910** Hodge *Hdbk. Amer. Indians* 2.890, *Wahoo.* A name for *Euonymus purpureus.* . . *The word is from Dakota wanhu,* 'arrowwood' (fide the late Rev. J.O. Dorsey). **1937** Thornburgh *Gt. Smoky Mts.* 25, One of the showiest shrubs in the Great Smokies [is] the evonymus, wahoo or spindlebush. **1967** *DARE* FW Addit **AR**49, Cat's paw or wahoo [ˈwɒˌhu]—Kin to bittersweet. **1968** *DARE* (Qu. BB50d, *Favorite spring tonics*) Inf **WI**44, Wahoo, yellow perilla, and water. [*DARE* Ed: Inf may refer instead to n¹ **1** above.] **1988** *DARE* File **cwMA,** *Euonymus atropurpureus* is called the *wahoo bush* here. **1991** Heat Moon *PrairyErth* 231 **ceKS,** The wahoo tree is about ready to split open its four-cornered berry capsules. **2004** *DARE* File—Internet **MO,** I bought a small one [=*Euonymus*] from a lady at a swapmeet, . . but she called it a "Wahoo-Wahoo" tree.

5 A **hop tree** (here: *Ptelea trifoliata*).

1847 *Prairie Farmer* 7.369 **neIL,** Large quantities of the Ptelea trifoliata or "Whahoo" of this part of America, a very different plant from the true or Whahoo of the South. **1897** Sudworth *Arborescent Flora* 267, *Ptelea trifoliata.* . . Hoptree. Wafer Ash. Whahoo. **1918** *Amer. Jrl. Pharmacy* 90.160, The writer received four lots of a bark purchased as and labelled "Wahoo Bark." Upon examination, one of these was found to be entirely wafer ash bark, while the other three contained varying proportions of wahoo (euonymus) and wafer ash.

6 =**cascara 1.**

1891 *Century Dict.* 6802, *Wahoo.* . . The bearberry of the Pacific United States, *Rhamnus Purshiana,* the source of cascara sagrada. **1897** Parsons *Wild Flowers CA* 62 **OR,** In Oregon it [*Rhamnus purshiana*] is known as . . "wahoo" and "bear-wood."

7 Any of var other trees or shrubs; see quots.

1774 Bartram in 1944 *Amer. Philos. Soc. Trans.* 33.137 **GA,** The timber of this land is of an emence bulk; Chiefly Hicory[,] Ash, . . White & black Oak[,] Silver leaf't Maple[,] Hornbeam[,] Papaw, or Wahoo, Linden & Cane thickets. **1882** U.S. Natl. Museum *Proc.* 5.70 **IN,** Catalpa speciosa. Catalpa; "Patalpha"; "Wahoo." **1960** Vines *Trees SW* 505, *Leucaena retusa.* . . Mostly . . in central Texas and the Trans-Pecos area. . . It is apparently not abundant enough to warrant the application of other vernacular names except that of Mimosa and Wahoo-tree. **1986** Pederson *LAGS Concordance,* 1 inf, **seAL,** Wahoo = mock orange.

wahoo n² Also *waahoo*

A scombrid fish *(Acanthocybium solandri)* of warm oceans. Also called **kingfish 4, ono** n, **queenfish 2**

1884 U.S. Fish Comm. *Bulletin for 1884* 77 **sFL,** With these are occasionally found [at the market in Key West] the Spike-fish . . and the Wahoo *(Acanthocybium solandri).* **1911** *Century Dict. Suppl.,* Wahoo. . . A common name of *Acanthocybium solandri.* **1919** Grey *Tales Fishes* 136 **sFL,** Five or six years ago I heard the name "waahoo" mentioned at Long Key. The boatmen . . did not believe there was such a fish as a waahoo. . . Later I heard the particulars of a hard and spectacular fight Judge Shields had had with a strange fish which the Smithsonian declared to be a waahoo. **1966** *DARE* (Qu. P2, . . *Kinds of saltwater fish caught around here . . good to eat*) Inf **NC**12, [ˈwɔhuw]. **1975** Evanoff *Catch More Fish* 147, Another great fighter taken trolling offshore is the wahoo.

wahoo n³

1 In logging: =**meow**.

1958 McCulloch *Woods Words* 207 **Pacific NW**, *Wahoo*—a. A kink in a line or a choker. b. Anything out of line, same as meow.

2 =**nigger** n¹ **B10**.

1905 *DN* 3.101 **nwAR**, *Wa-h·oo*. . . A game also called 'nigger.'

3 =**yahoo**.

1882 *Amer. Church Rev.* July 81, Once relieve our hard-working presidents and professors from the exhausting wear and tear of faculty-meetings for the discipline of that wildest of "Wahoos" which a lazy but capable student can be, and you add incalculably to their efficiency. **1917** *ALC Pathfinder* April 8, I haven't read a book nor heard a bit of decent music since those wahoos descended upon us. **1950** Bissell *Stretch on River* 107 **Missip Valley**, Fer god's sake don't tell me you wahoos lapped up all that coffee awready. **1960** Wentworth–Flexner *Slang* 566, *Wahoo*. . . A yahoo; a rustic; a simp or yap. **1969–70** *DARE* (Qu. HH1, *Names and nicknames for a rustic or countrified person*) Inf **VT**16, Wahoo [FW: Yahoo was suggested, but the Inf changed it to wahoo.]; (Qu. HH3, *A dull and stupid person*) Inf **PA**245, Wahoo. **2006** in 2007 *DARE* File—Internet **NH**, I can't help wondering if these wahoos realize the damage they do to Christianity by sounding so far out. **2007** *Ibid* **cwOR**, Maybe there should be a private lake somewhere that all those wahoos can takes [sic] those machines [=jet skis]. *Ibid* **cTX**, Just as I would never watch a Jerry Springer Show, I dismiss the drivel these wahoos write. *Ibid* **IA**, Pappy always said: 'You may not always get what you pay for, but you damn sure always pay for what you get.' And he never knew these wahoos.

wahoo bush See **wahoo** n¹ **4**

wahoo elm See **wahoo** n¹ **1**

wahoon, wahoo-wahoo tree See **wahoo** n¹ **4**

wahr n See **wire**

wahr v See **be A5**

wahrn't See **be C2c**

wai n |wɑːi| [Haw] **HI** Cf **kai** n, adv
Fresh water.

1938 Reinecke *Hawaiian Loanwords* 32, *Wai* [wɑːi]. . . Fresh water. **1951** *AmSp* 26.23 **HI**, Other common Hawaiian words are . . *wai* (fresh water). **1967** Clark *All the Best HI* 55, *Wai*—fresh water, as opposed to kai, salt water. For example, Ala Wai Canal, behind Waikiki, means simply Fresh Water Canal (literally road). **1984** Sunset *HI Guide* 85, *Wai*—fresh water.

wain n Arch sp **wayne** [*OED2 wain* sb.¹; "As a colloquial word it survives only in dialects."] *old-fash*
A wagon. Note: *Wain* survived as a poetic and literary term long after falling out of general use: only clearly colloquial exx are given here.

1635 in 1916 MA (Colony) Probate Court (Essex Co.) *Records* 1.5, 2 wayne bodys, 16s. **1872** Schele de Vere *Americanisms* 565, *Wain,* the old and obsolete form of wagon, is still in daily use in some parts of the United States, e.g., in the peninsula east of the Chesapeake, one of the first parts of Virginia and of North America that were colonized, the earliest settlements made there dating back to a few years after the founding of Jamestown. **1894** *DN* 1.334 **sNJ**, *Wain:* wagon. . . Not much used. **1912** Green *VA Folk-Speech* 472, *Wain*. . . For *waggon.* On the Eastern shore. **1993** Norris *Dakota* 20 **SD**, Magnificent old words like farrow, common English five hundred years ago, are still in use on the Plains. I even heard an old man use wain for wagon. **2002** *DARE* File **AL**, "Wain" as in "he was born on a wain" or "I did not come to town on a hay wain"—A farm wagon with high wooden sides. Common when I was a child, but now rarely heard. Although I did hear a 50ish speaker use it recently in Tuscaloosa.

waist baby n Cf **apron child**
A baby that stands as high as one's waist.

1944 *PADS* 2.51 **SC**, *Waist-baby*. . . A baby tall enough when standing to reach one's waist. **1952** Brown *NC Folkl.* 1.604, *Waist baby*. . . A baby tall enough to reach one's waist.

waistline party n *among Black speakers* Cf **weight dance**
A party in which the price of admission is based on the size of one's waistline.

1967–70 *DARE* (Qu. FF2, . . *Kinds of parties*) Inf **LA**6, Waistline parties—if your waistline is 27 inches you get 27 cents; (Qu. FF4, . . *Kinds of dancing parties*) Inf **MO**30, Waistline parties. [Both Infs Black] **2003** *DARE* File—Internet **Chicago IL** (as of c1943) [Black], We'd give quarter parties. Everything was a quarter. A quarter to get in, a quarter for some wine or a quarter for some whiskey. . . Or a waistline party. It might be a nickel an inch. . . We had a tape measure and you'd pay according to how big your waist was.

wait-a-bit n [Cf *OED2 wait-a-bit* "A name given to various S. African plants and shrubs with humorous reference to their hooked and clinging thorns." 1785 →]
Any of several thorny shrubs or trees, as

a A **prickly ash 1** (here: usu *Zanthoxylum clava-herculis,* but also *Z. americanum*).

1898 Sudworth *Forest Trees* 84 **AR**, *Xanthoxylum clava-herculis.* . . Names in use. . . Wait-a-bit, Tear-blanket. **1950** Peattie *Nat. Hist. Trees* 427, *Zanthoxylum americanum.* . . Other Names: Prickly Ash. Wait-a-bit [etc]. **1960** Vines *Trees SW* 595, *Zanthoxylum clava-herculis.* . . Vernacular names are Toothache, . . Wait-a-bit.

b also *wait-a-while:* A **greenbrier** (here: *Smilax rotundifolia*).

1880 *Bot. Gaz.* 5.57 **eFL**, Occasionally rich hummock lands are met with. . . In such places trailing vines with ferns and mosses, fill up the back ground. The "Smilax" and "Wait a bit" bid you halt! **1884** Henshall *Camping in FL* 87, The trees and shrubs are draped with luxuriant vines and creepers, which retard one's progress materially—especially the "wait-a-while," which trips up one's feet, catches one under the chin, ties one's legs together, and takes other entwining and affectionate liberties with one's person. **1892** *Jrl. Amer. Folkl.* 5.104 **eMA**, *Smilax rotundifolia*. . . wait-a-bit. [Footnote:] On account of the difficulty of tearing loose clothing caught by its stout prickles. **1960** Vines *Trees SW* 75, *Smilax rotundifolia.* . . Vernacular names for the plant are Biscuit-leaves, wait-a-bit [etc].

c See **wait-a-minute (bush)**.

wait-a-minute (bush) n Also *wait-a-bit* Cf **cat's-claw**
A **mimosa 1** (here: *Mimosa aculeaticarpa*).

1877 Dodge *Plains Great West* 151 **TX**, He [=a wild bull] is probably . . ensconced in the darkest recesses of a dense thicket of 'wait-a-bit' thorns. This bush. . . stands . . about twelve feet high, the straight stems from the size of a pipe-stem to two inches in diameter. Lateral branches spring out from every stem so thickly as to make a jungle almost impenetrable even of themselves; and when each is armed with innumerable thorns bent like fish-hooks, sharp as needles, and strong and tough as steel, it will readily be understood that hunting in such a thicket is no sport. **1931** U.S. Dept. Ag. *Misc. Pub.* 101.79 **West**, Catclaw mimosa . . , often called wait-a-minute bush . . is a loose thorny bush. **1960** Vines *Trees SW* 507, Catclaw mimosa. . . Vernacular names . . [include] Wait-a-bit, and Wait-a-minute. **1975** Lamb *Woody Plants SW* 75, Catclaw mimosa or wait-a-minute bush occurs in the Lower Sonoran Zone in New Mexico and southeastern Arizona, thence northwest through central Arizona. **1981** Benson–Darrow *Trees SW Deserts* 233, Wait-a-minute bush, or cat claw, forms dense, nearly impenetrable thickets which offer food and shelter to wild life.

wait-a-while See **wait-a-bit b**

waiter n [*OED2 waiter* sb. III.6.b 1537 →; "*Obs.* exc *U.S. dial.*"] **chiefly Sth, S Midl** Cf **waitman, waitress**
An attendant on the bride or groom at a wedding.

1830 in 1956 Eliason *Tarheel Talk* 303 **seNC**, Says she hears you are to be married She wishes to know. . . when. . . as you promised she would be one of the waiters. **1842** (1934) Boynton *Jrl.* 43.351 **VA**, The waiters, as they are here called, i.e., the bridemen and bridesmaids, being 3 or 4 of each, waited on the table at supper and were the general waiters (according to their name) of the evening. **1871** in 1983 *PADS* 70.57 **ce,sePA**, The waiters were first John Atkinson & Aunt Deborah, second Willie Bond & Mary Walton. . . third Ellwood Walton & Carrie Atkinson. **1924** Raine *Land of Saddle-Bags* 111 **sAppalachians**, Our common usage at weddings alludes to a certain individual as "best man." Mountain usage calls him "waiter." **1928** Peterkin *Scarlet Sister Mary* 45 **SC** [Gullah], The "waiters" marched out next, a couple at a time, ten couples in all. **1937** (1963) Hyatt *Kiverlid* 104 **KY**, She was one o' my waiters when I married Jeems. **1949** Kurath *Word Geog.* 78, *Best man* . . The national term *best man* is current in all the Eastern States, but south of the Potomac it is not common among the simple folk or in rural areas. Here the usual folk word is *waiter,* which applies also to the bridesmaid. **1950** Klees *PA Dutch* 54, At the wedding there is the usual Amish order of service. . . The bride with her two bridesmaids, known as "waiters," and the groom with his attendants, also known as waiters. **1952** Brown *NC Folkl.* 1.604, *Waiter.* . . A man or woman attendant for the groom or bride at a wedding.   **1966** Dakin *Dial. Vocab. Ohio R. Valley* 2.499, *Best man.* . . older speakers in eastern and southwestern Kentucky still say *waiter.* . . for both male or female attendants.   **1966–70** *DARE* (Qu. AA17, . . *Other people beside the bride and groom* . . *in a wedding party*) Infs **MO8, NJ69, VA69,** Waiters; **SC46,** Waiter—old-fashioned; **SC26,** Waiters—held flowers, etc; walk ahead of the couple. [4 of 5 total Infs Black, 4 female]   **1989** Pederson *LAGS Tech. Index* 300 **Gulf Region** *(Best man)* 15 infs, Waiter [13 of 15 infs over 60, 12 Black, 10 male]; *(Bridesmaid)* 9 infs, Waiter [7 of 9 infs over 60, 8 Black, 7 male].   **2000** Shores *Tangier Is.* 203 **Chesapeake Bay,** Anyone in a wedding, the best man or a bridesmaid, was called a *waiter* years ago, a term generally not known on Tangier today.

waitman n   Also *waitsman*

=**waiter.**

   1966 Dakin *Dial. Vocab. Ohio R. Valley* 2.500, Figure 151 . . *Best Man* . . [In descending order of frequency excluding the regular term *best man* which was not included in the figure] waiter . . waitman . . groomsman . . witness . . bride(s) groom . . bridesman.   **1967–70** *DARE* (Qu. AA17, . . *Other people beside the bride and groom* . . *in a wedding party*) Inf **FL48,** Waitman—old word for bridesmaids; **LA8,** Waitsmen—the man have a waitsman and the woman have a waitsman. [Both Infs Black]

wait on v phr

1 also *wait upon:* To court (a woman).   **chiefly NEast, Sth**

   1877 Bartlett *Americanisms* 735, *To wait upon.* To pay attention to a lady with a view to matrimony.   **1880** *Harper's New Mth. Mag.* 61.690 **ME,** I heard he was waiting on that pretty Becket girl.   **1899** (1912) Green *VA Folk-Speech* 472, *Wait.* . . To wait on, to escort; accompany; attend: as, when a man is *waiting on* a woman with a view to marriage.   **1901** *DN* 2.150 **c,eNY,** *Wait on.* . . to court, pay attentions to.   **1907** *DN* 3.184 **seNH,** *Court.* . . synonymous expressions. . . go with . . wait on . . spark.   **1909** *DN* 3.386 **eAL, wGA,** *Wait on.* . . To pay court to.   **1923** *DN* 5.224 **swMO,** *Wait on.* . . To court. "Bill's a-waitin' on Mary."   **1941** *LANE* Map 404 *(Courting her)* 34 infs, **scattered NEng, but esp MA, CT,** Waiting on (her); 6 infs, **ME, MA, VT,** Waiting upon her.   **1946** *PADS* 6.32 **eNC, swVA,** *Wait on.* . . To pay court to. . . Obsolete.   **1952** Brown *NC Folkl.* 1.604, *Wait on.* . . To court. "He's been *waiting on* the widow now for nigh on four year."—Old people. Obsolescent.   **1966–70** *DARE* (Qu. AA1, *When a man goes to see a girl often and seems to want to marry her, he's* _____ *her*) Infs **AR15, MA38, NY234,** Waiting on; **PA126,** Waiting upon.   **1973** Allen *LAUM* 1.370 **Upper MW** (as of c1950), He is *courting* her. . . A few . . minor New England phrases very weakly survive, sometimes in isolated responses, such as . . *waiting on her.* . . [2 infs, **IA, MN**].   **1974** Fink *Mountain Speech* 29 **wNC, eTN,** *Wait on* . . court, woo. "John's waitin' on that new gal."   **1976** Ryland *Richmond Co. VA* 379, *Wait on* . . court.   **1986** Pederson *LAGS Concordance (Courting her)* 1 inf, **nwFL,** He's waiting on her—common.   **1996–97** in 2004 Montgomery–Hall *Dict. Smoky Mt. Engl.* 634 **wNC, eTN,** *Wait on.* . . To court (a woman). . . [5 infs].

2 To care for, attend (a pregnant or sick person).   **Sth, S Midl**

   1923 *DN* 5.224 **swMO,** *Wait on.* . . To take care of a sick person.   **1936** *AmSp* 11.352 **eTX,** *Wait on.* . . A doctor waits on his patients.   **1954** *Harder Coll.* **cwTN,** *Wait on.* . . To care for a sick person.   **c1960** *Wilson Coll.* **csKY,** *Wait on.* . . Attend, as a physician.   **1986** Pederson *LAGS Concordance,* 1 inf, **seGA,** Wait on—tend to a woman as a midwife; 1 inf, **cnLA,** Wait on a woman—tend to, nurse; 1 inf, **ceTX,** Wait on her—take care of a sick person; 1 inf, **csTN,** Wait on sick people; 1 inf, **csTN,** Wait on the sick; 1 inf, **cwAL,** Wait on them—to nurse or tend someone; 1 inf, **neMS,** They had doctors to wait on you in the clinic; 1 inf, **swMS,** Wait on you—take care of you after childbirth; 1 inf, **neTX,** My mother waited on her—attended as a midwife; 1 inf, **seGA,** The nurse that waited on her; 1 inf, **nwMS,** Waited on herself—delivered her own baby.

3 See **on** prep, adv **B3a.**

wait on the table v phr   sAppalachians   Cf read one's plate, talk 2

To say grace before a meal.

   1911 *DN* 3.540 **eKY,** *Wait on the table.* To "say grace."   **1936** *AmSp* 11.318 **Ozarks,** *Wait on the table.* . . To ask a blessing, to say a prayer before eating.   **1939** in 2004 Montgomery–Hall *Dict. Smoky Mt. Engl.* 634 **eTN, wNC,** *Wait on the table.* . . To say the blessing at a meal.   **1998** *Ibid* **eTN,** *Wait on the table* . . To say the blessing at a meal [1 inf].

waitress n   Cf waiter

A bridesmaid at a wedding.

   1966 Dakin *Dial. Vocab. Ohio R. Valley* 2.499, *Best man.* . . One Mountain speaker uses . . *waitress* for a female attendant.   **1970** *DARE* (Qu. AA17, . . *Other people beside the bride and groom* . . *in a wedding party*) Inf **VA69,** Waitress—the girl's sisters or cousins. [Inf Black]   **1986** Pederson *LAGS Concordance (Bridesmaid)* 2 infs, **MS, TN,** Waitress. [Both infs Black]

waitsman   See waitman

wait upon   See wait on 1

wake v

Std senses, var forms.   Note: Some speakers substitute forms of related verbs for some or all the forms of *wake;* for these see **awake, waken.** It is sometimes suggested that speakers choose, or should choose, different forms for transitive and intransitive uses; we have no systematic evidence on this point, but it should be noted that the *DARE* and Linguistic Atlas surveys elicited only the intransitive use. (The sense "to hold a wake (for)" is not treated here.)

1 past:

a *woke.*   Note: This form has been common in the US at least since the early 19th cent, but it appears only gradually to have achieved its present status as the overwhelmingly dominant form in all parts of the country and at all levels of usage.

   1821 *N. Amer. Rev.* 12.487, Not a New England mother . . woke but to fancy every wind . . burdened with a savage yell.   **1853** (1854) Baldwin *Flush Times* 158 **AL,** I thought he was dying, and after some trouble, woke him.   **1859** Taliaferro *Fisher's R.* 35 **wNC,** Some of them . . woke him up. . . He was so "slewed" . . that he had forgotten all his antecedents, and woke up, as he thought, in a "gin'ral row." *Ibid* 62, I . . nuver said a word to any on 'um, and waked up next mornin' ready fur breakfast. *Ibid* 130, In little ur no time it waked up the old hoss.   **1861** [see **1b** below].   **1865** (1868) Kerl *Common-School Gram.* 125, Wake, *[Past:]* waked, woke,* *[Perf. Participle:]* waked, woke.* *[Ibid* 121, * denotes that the form under it is seldom used, being either ancient, poetic, or of late introduction.]   **1871** Burroughs *Wake-Robin* 90 **NY,** I woke up to find myself the subject of discussion of a troop of chickadees.   **1885** [see **1b** below].   **1891** *Century Dict.* 6805, *Wake* . . pret. and pp. *waked* or *woke.*   **1953** Atwood *Survey of Verb Forms* 25, *Woke* /wok/ is by far the most common preterite form in all major areas. . . *Waked* /wekt/ occurs with fair frequency in e.N.Eng . . the heaviest concentration being in the northeast. It is evidently an older form. . . Seven cultured informants use this form. In w.N.Eng., N.Y., and the entire Midland (including N.J., Pa., e.O., w.Md., and n.W.Va.), *waked* is extremely rare. In s.W.Va. and the remainder of the South Midland and throughout the South, *waked* is somewhat more common, reaching its greatest frequency in N.C. . . There is a tendency in all areas where *waked* occurs toward the substitution of *woke.* . . Other preterite forms that occur in isolation are *woked* /wokt/, *woken* /wokən/, *wake* /wek/. . . Negro informants are not in much better agreement on this verb than cultured informants. *Waked* is most common among them, but *woke,* [and] *woked* . . also occur.   **1965–70** *DARE* (Qu. X42, . . *"I stopped sleeping at six o'clock."*) 754 Infs, **widespread,** Woke (up); (Qu. OO32a, *To wake: "Last night I* _____ *three times.";* total Infs questioned, 75) 60 Infs, **scattered,** Woke (up).   **1973** *PADS* 60.72 **seNC,** All of our Carteret County speakers said *woke* except one undecided lady who said, "Woke up; no, waked up; no, wakened."   **1981** *PADS* 67.47 **Mesabi Iron Range MN,** *Woke (up),* which is usual with the other Minnesota informants (42/54) is only frequent on the Iron Range (6/16). One-half of the Mesabi informants use *awoke,* the common Northern variant in the eastern states but infrequent with the other Minnesota group (7 occs.). Another Northern form, *awakened,* is frequent on the Range (4/16). This form is also infrequently used by other Minnesota informants (2 occs.)   **1989** [see **1b** below].

b *waked.*   **formerly widespread; now scattered, but chiefly Sth, S Midl, TX** See Map on p. 840   *esp among older speakers*

   1692 in 1914 Burr *Narr. Witchcraft* 224 **cMA,** He wak'd on a Night, and saw the Room where he lay full of Light.   [**1828** Webster *Amer. Dict., Wake.* [DARE Ed: Webster gives no principal parts, implying that he recognized only past, past ppl *waked.*]]   **1830** *Onondaga Std.* (Syracuse NY) 10 Nov 1/4, They both went to Mr. Loomis's, and waked him up.   **1844** *N. Amer. Rev.* 58.217 **NEng,** I waked up jist about the time when day ought to break.   **1846** Worcester *Universal Dict.* 811, *Wake* . . i[mperfect tense]* waked; *pp.* waking, waked.   **1859** [see **1a** above].

1861 Holmes *Venner* 2.176 **MA,** The village was waked up. The old
Doctor always waked easily. *Ibid* 258, When Elsie woke and lifted her
languid eyes upon her father's face, she saw in it a tenderness . . such as
she remembered. [*DARE* Ed: There are five exx of the past *waked* in this
book and 1 of *woke.*] **1885** Twain *Huck. Finn* 58 **MO,** When I woke up
I didn't know where I was. *Ibid* 66, Every time I waked I thought
somebody had me by the neck. *Ibid* 150, I waked him up. *Ibid* 235,
The duke . . woke me up. [*DARE* Ed: In Huck's narration and self-quo-
tation, there are 14 exx of the past *waked* and 4 of *woke.*] **1891** [see **1a**
above]. **1893** *DN* 1.278 **nwCT,** *Wake* . . [Preterite and past participle:]
waked. **1965–70** *DARE* (Qu. X42, . . *"I stopped sleeping at six
o'clock."*) 60 Infs, **scattered, but chiefly Sth, S Midl, TX,** Waked (up)
[Of all Infs responding to the question, 11% were young, 64% old; of
those giving these responses 2% were young, 80% old.]; (Qu. OO32a,
To wake: "Last night I _____ three times."; total Infs questioned, 75)
11 Infs, **Sth, S Midl,** Waked (up); (Qu. OO32b) Inf **CT**5, I waked up;
OK6, I waked him up. **1966** Dakin *Dial. Vocab. Ohio R. Valley* 2.527,
Woke up. . . Waked appears to be a more common older usage. . . most
common in eastern Kentucky . . in the Indiana hills, and in the Muskingum Valley. **1968** *PADS* 50.42 **swTN** [Black], In this study eighteen
of the twenty-two informants have /wok/. Three have /wekt/; one has
both forms. **1975** Allen *LAUM* 2.31 **Upper MW** (as of c1950), I *woke*
up early. . . *Waked (up),* described . . as an older Southern and South
Midland variant, consistently is used by Type I speakers [=old, with
little educ] in Iowa and Nebraska but once also in Minnesota. **1989**
Pederson *LAGS Tech. Index* **Gulf Region** 351, [Wake . . preterit . . 499
infs, proncs of the type [wok]; 77 infs, proncs of the type [wekt].] **2005**
DARE File—Internet **St Louis MO** (as of c1950) [Black], How about
this, then? Were others here taught a particular set of principle parts as
belonging to "wake" verbs? I had to learn the following: wake (up)—
waked (up)—waked (up).

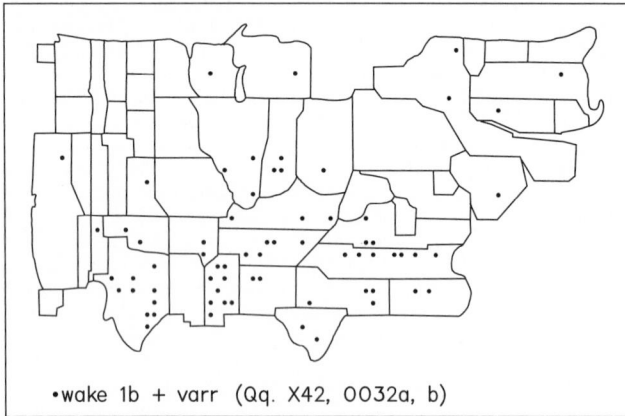

•wake 1b + varr (Qq. X42, OO32a, b)

c *woked.*   **esp Sth, S Midl**   Cf **-ed 1**
1864 Gilmore *Down in TN* 163, Whot d'ye s'pose it war thet woked
me? **1896** *Harper's New Mth. Mag.* 93.706 **AR** [Black], When Miss
Mary Ellen fust woked up dis mornin', she called out to Milly to fetch
de baby in to her. **1953** [see **1a** above]. **1966** *DARE* Tape **OK**25, I hit
the wall about three times before I woked up. **1986** Pederson *LAGS
Concordance (I woke up)* 2 infs, **LA,** Woked up.

d *wake.*
1885 Twain *Huck. Finn* 121 **MO** [Black], When I wake up en fine you
back agin', all safe en soun', de tears come en I could a got down on my
knees en kiss' yo' foot. **c1937** in 1976 *Weevils in the Wheat* 314 **VA**
[Black], Dey looked at it, an' wake it up. **1966–70** *DARE* (Qu. X42, . .
"I stopped sleeping at six o'clock.") Infs **CO**20, **GA**13, **NY**127, **SC**10,
26, Wake up (at). **1986** Pederson *LAGS Concordance,* 2 infs, **seGA,**
Wake up [=past]; 1 inf, **cGA,** Some noise wake me up; 1 inf, **ceGA,** I
wake Ronald [=past]. [All infs Black]

e *woken.*
1966–68 *DARE* (Qu. X42, . . *"I stopped sleeping at six o'clock."*) Inf
NC49, Woken; (Qu. OO32a, *To wake: "Last night I _____ three
times.";* total Infs questioned, 75) Inf **MS**1, Woken. **1986** Pederson
LAGS Concordance (I woke up) 3 infs, **AL, GA, MS,** Woken (up). [Infs
Black]

2 past pple:

a *woken.*   Note: This form is very rare in US texts at all levels of formality until after the middle of the 20th century,
though appar common in Brit use. It is now by far the most

common form in written use; a casual survey of informal
Internet usage suggests that it is now much more frequent in
spoken use than it was at the time of the *DARE* survey.

1848 (1850) Jenkins *Hist. War* 136, They . . were soon upon the Great
Prairie, . . for ages the pasture-ground of the elk and buffalo, and its solitary echoes woken but rarely by the sound of human voices. **1863**
Morford *Sprees* 134 **NY,** Of course he went to sleep in half an hour, and
the seven thunders would not have woken him. **1897** *Chicago Tribune*
(IL) 25 Feb 6/7 **WI,** "I think," said an Oshkosh damsel recently . . , "that
there is nothing more nicer than to be woken up at night with vocal singing." **1952** *Los Angeles Times* (CA) 3 Dec sec A 5, [Syndicated column
"Take My Word for It" by Frank Colby:] Woken. . . occurs in British usage, but in America it is archaic and dialectal. Better say I was waked; I
was waked up; I was wakened; I was awakened. **1965–70** *DARE* (Qu.
OO32b, *If a person can't sleep steadily but keeps on waking . . "Every
night this week I've _____ [several times]."*) 57 Infs, **scattered,**
Woken (up). [Of all Infs responding to the question, 6% were comm
type 1, 30% comm type 5, 11% young, 64% old; of those giving these
resps, 28% were comm type 1, 16% comm type 5, 32% young, and 42%
old.] **1989** *Webster's Dict. Engl. Usage* 945, We had a phone call not
long ago from a concerned grandmother who was disturbed by her
grandson's use of the past participle *woken.* She knew only *waked* and
was surprised to find that *woken* was recognized as legitimate in the dictionary. **2007** *Boston Globe* (MA) 5 Sept sec A 14 (Internet), [Letter:]
There are many Bostonians who go to bed every night only to be woken
up by gunshots. **2007** *Atlanta Jrl.–Constitution* (GA) 31 July sec B 1
(Internet), She had just woken up from a coma. **2007** *DARE* File—
Internet **MN,** My mother, an English major in college and former English teacher, is no doubt correct that 'waked' is the proper word . . but
even I, grammar queen though I also pride myself on being, find it
absolutely grates in my modern ears. So, now taking votes, should I use
woken, which sounds good to me, and brave my mother's wrath.

b *waked.*   **widespread, but esp Sth, S Midl, TX**   See Map
1800 *Adams Centinel* (Gettysburg PA) 3 Dec 6/2, An honest Irishman
was once waked from his slumbers. [**1828** see **1b** above.] **1830** in
1943 *William & Mary Qrly.* 23.288 **VA,** Was waked up by 3 oclock &
got in stage in a pet because I did not sleep enough. **1846** [see **1b**
above]. **1854** (1969) Thoreau *Walden* **ceMA,** My flute has waked the
echoes over that very water. **1865** [see **1a** above]. **1885** Twain *Huck.
Finn* 236 **MO,** They was hoping to slide out of the way of trouble . . if
they hadn't already waked you up. **1886** James *Bostonians* (Amer. ed.)
236 **MA,** I think I *have* waked it up a little. **1891** [see **1a** above]. **1920**
Lewis *Main Street* 354 **MN,** How long before he'll wake up to me? . .
I've waked up to myself. **1965–70** *DARE* (Qu. OO32b, *If a person
can't sleep steadily but keeps on waking . . "Every night this week I've
_____ [several times]."*) 104 Infs, **widespread, but esp Sth, S Midl,
TX,** Waked (up); **GA**59, Dozed off and waked up. [Of all Infs responding to the question, 6% were comm type 1, 30% comm type 5,
29% gs educ or less, 31% coll educ; of those giving these responses, 1%
were comm type 1, 23% comm type 5, 17% gs educ or less, and 48%
coll educ.] **1988** Lyon *Borrowed Children* 63 **KY** (as of 1930s), I'd
waked up that morning feeling jumbled. **2006** in 2007 *DARE* File—
Internet **VT,** Certainly Twoomey has waked up. **2007** *Ibid* **OR,** My
mind has waked up now. *Ibid* **MD,** Does this qualify as "shoegazer"
music??? If so, remarkable how it has waked me up. *Ibid* **ceTX,** I think
he has waked up to all of it now.

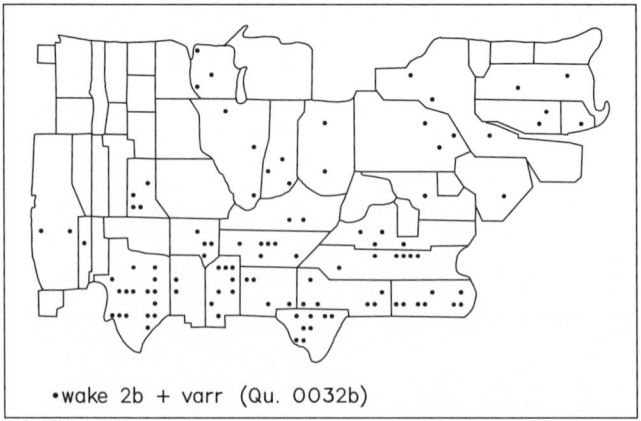

•wake 2b + varr (Qu. OO32b)

c *woke;* hence ppl adjs *woke (up).*   **widespread**
1814 *Adams Centinel* (Gettysburg PA) 12 Oct 1/3, I called for a fresh

pipe, and was woke out of a reverie.   **1823** (1825) Cooper *Pilot* 3.137, Jack has woke up the first lieutenant.   **1866** Trowbridge *South* 391 **AR,** If you had expressed abolition sentiments then, you'd have woke up some morning and found yourself hanging from some limb.   **1870** Duval *Advent. Big-Foot* 291 **TX,** It was enough to have woke up one of the Seven Sleepers.   **1891** [see **1a** above].   **1938** Rawlings *Yearling* 13 **nFL,** And him [=a bear] mebbe easier to ketch, not woke up good.   **1965–70** *DARE* (Qu. OO32b, *If a person can't sleep steadily but keeps on waking . . "Every night this week I've _____ [several times]."*) 501 Infs, **widespread,** Woke (up); **IL**131, Been woke up; **FL**48, Stayed woke.   **1971** in 1993 Major *Calling the Wind* 315 **LA** [Black], I don't move because I don't want them to know I'm woke.   **2003** in 2007 *DARE* File—Internet **TX,** I think I might have woke up from shear [sic] exhaustion.   *Ibid* **OH,** I wasn't suppose to have woke up and see it.   **2004** in 2007 *Ibid* **MN,** Somebody should've woke me up!   **2007** *Ibid* **FL,** There have been times he has woke me up.

d *wake.*

1966–68 *DARE* (Qu. OO32b, *If a person can't sleep steadily but keeps on waking . . "Every night this week I've _____ [several times]."*) Infs **MO**26, **SC**26, Wake up.

e *woked.*   Cf **-ed 3**

1966 *DARE* (Qu. OO32b, *If a person can't sleep steadily but keeps on waking . . "Every night this week I've _____ [several times]."*) Inf **SC**10, Woked up.

waked   See **wake 1b, 2b**

waken v   **scattered, but chiefly Nth, N Midl, West**   See Map *somewhat old-fash*

To wake up; to cause (one) to wake up; past pple usu *wakened,* also occas *waken.*   Note: Some speakers use *wakened* suppletively as the past ppl (less often past) of **wake.**

1834 *New Engl. Mag.* 6.338, These impressions on her senses had no power to waken her.   **1864** *Atlantic Mth.* 14.18 **NEng,** I had wakened up.   **1866** *Galaxy* 2.407 **NY,** Wake himself he will not. It is a pity to waken him now.   **1872** Twain *Roughing It* 60 **MO,** We tumbled out into the busy street feeling like meteoric people crumbled off the corner of some other world, and wakened up suddenly in this.   **1885** Howells *Rise Lapham* 444 **MA,** Lapham awoke confused. . . In that moment he wished that he had not wakened.   **1894** *Century Illustr. Mag.* 47.857 **ME,** Thought ye was fagged, or I'd 'a' wakened ye.   **1934** *AmSp* 9.124 [Engl dial of HI], Two verbs are confused in the conjugations: *lend, loaned, loaned* and *wake, wakened, wakened.*   **c1937** in 1976 *Weevils in the Wheat* 222 **VA** [Black], Den he say I waken up an' ax de chillun, "Who done been here?"   **1952** [see **wake 2a**].   **1953** Atwood *Survey of Verb Forms* 25, The preterite is recorded in the context "I (woke) up." . . *Wakened . .* is used by a scattering of informants in the North and the Midland (though not in the South). . . Five cultured informants use this form.   **1956** Ker *Vocab. W. TX* 422, I woke up. . . wakened (6 responses). . . preferred by four older informants and by two younger ones [out of 67 infs].   **1957** Carson *Drives My Green Age* 184 **Ozarks,** "You've woke her up now with your racket." "*Wakened* her, not woke her."   **1961** Folk *Word Atlas N. LA* map 1602 (I *woke up* early). . . [Other responses, comprising only 9% of total, in order of frequency] . . awakened . . wakened . . awoke.   **1965–70** *DARE* (Qu. OO32b, *If a person can't sleep steadily but keeps on waking . . "Every night this week I've _____ [several times]."*) 55 Infs, **scattered, but esp Nth, N Midl, West,** Wakened (up); **FL**22, **GA**3, **NJ**7, Waken (up); **FL**51, Waken up—what ordinary person would say [FW: Inf positive here, though it does sound funny]; **MI**33, Waken up, wakened up—with an awfully slurred "-ed" so you don't know quite what you have [Of all Infs responding to the question, 11% were young, 64% old, and 31% coll educ; of those giving these responses, 2% were young, 83% old, and 47% coll educ.]; (Qu. X42, . . "*I stopped sleeping at six o'clock.*") 16 Infs, **scattered,** Wakened (up); **FL**27, Wakened with a start [16 of 17 total Infs old]; (Qu. JJ16, *When there was something you didn't understand, then suddenly you do understand it . . "Oh, now I _____."*) Inf **MD**26, I've wakened up [Inf old]; (Qu. OO32a, *To wake: "Last night I _____ three times.";* total Infs questioned, 75) Infs **DC**8, **FL**2, 20, 30, **GA**13, **OH**29, **UT**3, Wakened [6 of 7 Infs old]; .   **1966** Dakin *Dial. Vocab. Ohio R. Valley* 2.528, *Woke up. . . Wakened* (two times) and *wakened up* (five times) are used only in Ohio.   **1975** Allen *LAUM* 2.31 **Upper MW** (as of c1950), I *woke* up early. . . *Wakened . .* [an] uncommon variant, is somewhat more frequent in Minnesota, North Dakota, and Canada than elsewhere, and it is typically a Type III [=mid-aged, with coll educ] form.   **1989** Pederson *LAGS Tech. Index* 351 **Gulf Region,** *Wake . .* [infinitive:] 7 infs, Waken; [preterit:] 4 infs, Waken; 2

infs, Wakened; [past participle:] 1 inf, Wakened. [*DARE* Ed: Only 12 total resps are recorded for the past participle.]

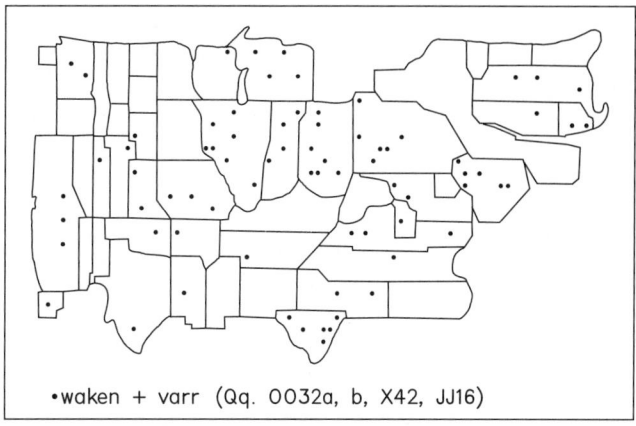

•waken + varr (Qq. OO32a, b, X42, JJ16)

wake-robin n   [*OED2* 1530 → for *Arum maculatum*]

1 also *Virginia wake-robin:* An **arrow arum** (here: *Peltandra virginica*).

1702 Petiver *Gazophylacii Naturae* 4, Gladiolus lacustris *Virginianus* cæruleus, Sagittariæ folio . . [=Lake-dwelling blue Virginian gladiolus with leaves like those of Sagittaria] . . I have received this from *Maryland* and *Virginia;* as also from *Mr. Edm. Bohun* who gathered it in *South Carolina,* where it *flowers in June and July,* and it is called by them *Wake-Robin.*   [**1770** Kalm *Travels N. Amer.* (transl. Forster) 1.125 **PA,** The Virginian Wake robin, or Arum Virginicum, grows in wet places.]   **1819** *Amer. Farmer* 1.109 **NY,** Our Indians also made use of the root of a vegetable which . . , Kalm says, is the *arum virginicum,* or wake robin.   **1883** U.S. Natl. Museum *Annual Rept. for 1881* 690, This name [=tuckahoe] . . belonged to all esculent bulbous roots used by the Indians, among which are these: *Orontium aquaticum,* Golden Club, and *Peltandra virginica,* Virginia Wake Robin.   **2004** *DARE* File—Internet, The Virginia wake-robin, arrow arum, or tuckahoe (*Peltandra virginica . .)* is a plant of still or slow moving waters.

2 A **jack-in-the-pulpit 1.**

1784 in 1785 Amer. Acad. Arts & Sci. *Memoirs* 1.487 **CT,** Arum. . . Cuckowpint. Dragon-root. Wake-Robin.   **1822** Eaton *Botany* 183, [*Arum*] *triphyllum* . . Indian turnip, wild turnip, wake-robin.   **1845** Judd *Margaret* 25 **swME** (as of 18th cent), It was a wake-robin, commonly known as dragon-root, devil's ear or Indian turnip. . . "Don't ye taste on't!" exclaimed Obed, "it's orful burnin."   **1896** Robinson *In New Engl. Fields* 134, A fiery wake-robin bulb.   **1950** *WELS (Other names for the jack-in-the-pulpit)* 1 Inf, **seWI,** Wake-robin.

3 =**trillium. chiefly NEast, N Cent, Mid Atl**   See Map

1832 MA Hist. Soc. *Coll.* 2d ser 9.157 **cwVT,** Trillium erectum. . . Wake-Robin.   **1840** MA Zool. & Bot. Surv. *Herb. Plants & Quadrupeds* 213, *Trillium. . . erectum.* . . Wake Robin. Very common in the woods in May.   *Ibid* 214, *T. cernuum.* . . Nodding Wake Robin.   *Ibid, T. pictum.* . . Painted or Variegated Wake Robin.   **1901** Lounsberry *S. Wild Flowers* 62, Ill-scented wake-robin, or nose bleed, is known by its handsome nodding flower, reddish in its gayest form, or sometimes pink, or white.   **1950** *WELS (A flower with three white petals that . . turns pink as the flower gets older)* 3 Infs, **WI,** Wake-robin.   **1951** Teale *North*

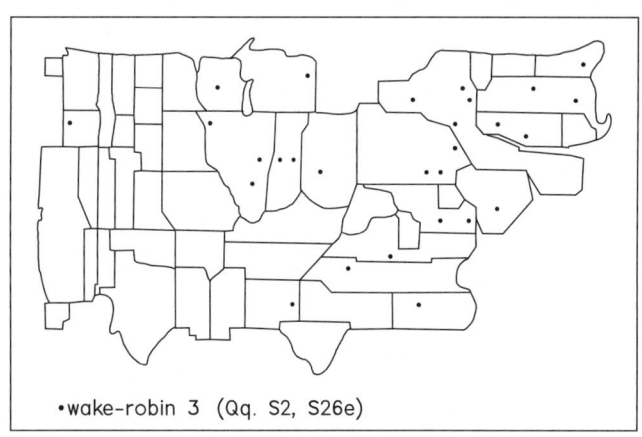

•wake-robin 3 (Qq. S2, S26e)

with Spring 169 **NC,** Changing color as they grow older, some wake-robins range from snowy white through pink to deep purple-pink before their petals wither.   **1965–70** *DARE* (Qu. S2, . . *The flower that comes up in the woods early in spring, with three white petals that turn pink as the flower grows older*) 26 Infs, **chiefly NEast, N Cent, Mid Atl,** Wake-robin; **NJ**58, Trillium—people call it wake-robin but their parents came from outside; (Qu. S26e) Inf **PA**49, Trillium—one of them is called a *wake-robin.*   **1972** GA Dept. Ag. *Farmers Market Bulletin* 26 Apr 8/1, Trilliums, poetically called Wake-robin, are a common sight in Georgia.

wake-up n   Also *wa(h)-cup, walk-up, way-(c)up, wick-up* [Echoic]
=flicker n² **1.**

   [**1840** Gosse *Can. Naturalist* 118 **sQuebec Canada,** I have obtained a specimen of a very beautiful bird, the Gold-winged Woodpecker. . . The common people here call it "Wickup;" its common cry consists of one note repeated very rapidly, many times, so as almost to resemble a shake in music.]   **1844** DeKay *Zool. NY* 2.192, This species [=*Picus auratus*] . . has . . received many popular names in different districts. It is called *High-hole, Yucker, Flicker, Wake-up,* and *Pigeon Woodpecker,* and usually *Clape* in this State.   **1869** (1911) Muir *First Summer* 233 **CA,** The waycup, or flicker, so familiar to every boy in the old Middle West States, is one of the most common of the woodpeckers hereabouts.   **1898** IN Dept. Geol. & Nat. Resources *Rept. for 1897* 844, *Colaptes auratus.* . . Flicker. Synonyms, *Golden-winged Woodpecker, High Hole, High Holder, Wickup.*   **1911** MI Pub. Instruction *Annual Rept. for 1910–11* 63, *Flicker.* . . Perhaps those [=variant names] most often heard in Michigan are High-hole, High-holder, Wake-up, Wick-up, Yellow Hammer, and Golden-winged Woodpecker.   **1956** MA Audubon Soc. *Bulletin* 40.82 **NH, MA, CT,** *Yellow-shafted flicker.* . . Wa-cup. . . Spelled also Wah-cup, Wake-up, Walk-up, Way-up, Wick-up. Sonic.

wal   See **well** intj

walink   See **wallink**

walk v

1a   To patrol, inspect (something) on foot.   Cf **ride** v¹ **B2a, b**
   1919 *Ft. Wayne News & Sentinel* (IN) 10 May [27]/4 (newspaper-archive.com), His work . . [was] to walk the fence lines to see that no posts gave way, that no wires were down and that no cattle strayed through his oversight.   **1925** in 1953 Botkin–Harlow *Treas. Railroad Folkl.* 302, While walking track one day, John found a broken rail and sent word to the foreman.   **1941** Percy *Lanterns* 246 **MS,** All of us who grew up in the Delta have had experience aplenty in guard duty, or "walking the levee," as we call it.   **1969** *AmSp* 44.262 [Railroad terms], *Walk the train*—Make a thorough inspection of the train line and brake equipment.   **1999** *Wall St. Jrl.* (NY NY) 28 June sec A 1/1 **nMI,** His father's friend . . let young John come along, walk his trap lines, learn about sets and scents.   **2006** *DARE* File—Internet **OH,** Periodically walk fence lines to see if Rover has been working on an escape route.

b   Spec: to go through (a field or crop, esp of soybeans) cutting or pulling weeds; hence vbl n phr *walking beans* (and varr).   **esp Upper MW**
   1963 *Malvern Leader* (IA) 18 July [11]/7 (newspaperarchive.com), Soy beans have been laid by, many are walking beans now to clean them of volunteer corn and weeds.   **1981** *Natl. Geogr. Mag.* May 621 **IA,** I'm out walking the beans. As any local teenager will tell you, that means going up and down the endless soybean rows hacking out the weeds.   **1983** *DARE* File **wIA,** We're going to walk the beans today.   **1984** *Ibid* **sMI,** To walk beans, corn, or sunflowers means to go between the rows pulling out weeds.   **1996** *Farm Boys* 12 **MN,** It was common for everyone in the family, regardless of gender, to be involved in certain seasonal tasks requiring a large number of hands, such as "walking beans."   *Ibid* 234 **cnIA,** Every summer, as a family, we walked all our beans and pulled out all the weeds and volunteer corn.   **1998** *Amer. Enterprise* Sept/Oct (Internet) **MO,** The Hursts were the only local farmers to use sharpened garden hoes to "walk beans." . . But hoes were what Grandpa used to walk corn in the 1920s.   **2005** *DARE* File—Internet, Jen hails from Carson, Iowa, a tiny town near Omaha, Nebraska. She grew up on a farm, and goes back every once in a while to walk beans for her dad.

2   in phr *walk (something) to (something)* and var: To apply (something) vigorously or copiously to (something); see quots.   **NEng**
   1965 *DARE* FW Addit **nME,** *Walk*—to apply liberally, as in: "Walk the gas (. . or torque) to a car or a truck." "Walk the lead to a horse that has been downed." "Walk the paint (oil, wax, etc) right to 'er."   **1979** Lewis *How to Talk Yankee* [37] **nNEng,** *Walk it to.* . . This denotes vari-

ous types of concentrated effort. "I see where Fred's put up his new page wire fence around that pasture. Said he did it in just two days." "Yup. He must have walked it right to her." Or: "Walk it to him." This is a common shouted encouragement at a pugilistic encounter, whether the participants are gloved or not. Or: "That new-seeded piece is coming right along. You ought to get a decent second cutting." "Ayuh, I walked the dressing right to it."

walk and hide v phr
=pack and back.
   1975 Gould *ME Lingo* 201, *Pack and back*—One of several woods terms to describe the carrying of two packsacks at once, which is done by alternating them on the trail. . . In prohibition days, this was the customary way to bring booze down from Canada. . . *Pack and back* is often called "walk and hide."

walk down v phr   **West**
To capture (wild horses) by keeping them moving until they become exhausted and docile; hence vbl n *walking down;* n *walk-down* the capture of wild horses by this method.
   1876 *Scribner's Mth.* 13.49, So great is the power of the man over the brute, that one man alone, and he on foot, can, in the end, walk down and take captive, even the mustang of the prairies.   **1883** Sweet–Knox *Mexican Mustang* 584 **TX,** Another mode of capturing them was called "walking them down." The hunters followed them for several days . . giving them no time to eat, drink, or rest. The result of this was, that the horses thus pursued became so fatigued that they were finally lassoed with comparative ease.   **1901** in 1961 Biggers *Chronicle* 66 **TX,** Much has been said about "walking down" a bunch of mustangs, but there was very little walk about the mustang until he became so thoroughly exhausted that he could not strike a trot even.   **1907** Cook *Border & Buffalo* 254 **KS,** I by previous arrangement joined in the walk-down.   **1929** Dobie *Vaquero* 243, In order to walk mustangs down two or more men relayed each other in riding after them. . . One man alone on one horse could walk a bunch of mustangs down if he hung on to them long enough.   **1945** Thorp *Pardner* 75 **SW,** One reasonably successful way of catching mustangs was to walk them down. Full moon was the time usually chosen, since the idea was to keep them going night and day.

Walker n¹   See **Walker hound**

walker n²   See **walking boss**

Walker hound n   Also *Walker (dog),* ~ *foxhound* [See quot 1948] **chiefly Sth, S Midl**
A type of foxhound, usu black, white, and tan.
   1904 Graham *Sporting Dog* 134, The Walkers are chiefly bred by men in Kentucky of that name, and have been shipped to nearly every part of America where foxes are found.   **1948** Camp *Hunter's Encycl.* 845 **KY,** The history of the Walker foxhound is an interesting one. The greatest portion of the credit for the development of the strain properly goes to two Kentucky sportsmen. . . George Washington Maupin . . and John W. Walker.   **1958** Humphrey *Home from the Hill* 48 **neTX,** He had Black and Tans, Redbones, Goodmans, Blueticks and Redticks, Walkers, Triggs, a pair of Plott hounds.   **1966–67** *DARE* Tape **AR**15, [FW:] Which dogs do you have for fox dogs? [Inf:] Well, there are different breeds, all right. The Walker dog, I reckon is about the best; **DC**10, [FW:] What makes a good hunting dog? [Inf:] Well, Walker dogs are as good as any. [FW:] Walker? [Inf:] That's a breed of 'em; **LA**2, She was part Walker and black-and-tan; **LA**10, [FW:] What different kinds of dogs do you use around here in deer hunting? [Inf:] Well, they used the Walker and the bloodhound and your beagle, beagle hounds.   **1991** Haynes *Haywood Home* 54 **wNC** (as of c1908), Most of the fox dogs were Walker Hounds that could be used to hunt all game.

walker pin   See **wankapin**

Walker's hack n   [Punning ref to common surname; cf *EDD Walker's-bus* (at *walker* sb.)]
=shank's mare.
   1918 *AK RR Rec.* 2.306, Finally, however, we could coax it [=a car] no farther and had to take to Walker's hack.   **a1923** (1976) Marshall *Memoirs* 22 **swPA,** "Walker's Hack" was the only certain transportation that we had, but no one else seemed to realize this.   **1967–68** *DARE* (Qu. Y24, . . *To walk, to go on foot:* "*I can't get a ride, so I'll just have to* _____.") Infs **AR**51, **PA**134, Go in (or on) Walker's hack; **DE**3, Take Walker's hack. [All Infs old, gs educ]   **1967** *Good Old Days* 3.9.9

nwAR (as of late 19th cent), Usually her mode of transportation was horseback or what was commonly called in those days—"Walker's-Hack".

walking ppl adj   **West**   Cf **flying, lazy**
Of a livestock brand: having foot-like extensions at its lower extremities.

   1936 Adams *Cowboy Lingo* 123 **West,** The 'walking brand' was one with lower designs like feet or legs, as 'Walking R.' **1939** *Sun* (Baltimore MD) 7 Mar 10/6 *(Hench Coll.),* For the "lion couchant," "fleur de lis," "griffon" and other chivalric emblems . . the West substituted the "hog eye," "the turkey track," "the walking A," and similar down-to-ear [sic] symbols. **2004** *DARE* File—Internet **UT,** On his shirt is the "walking X" brand of the Wilcox Ranch.

walking beans   See **walk 2**

walking boss n   Also *walker*   Cf **wandering boss**
A head foreman, superintendent; see quots.

   1868 *M'Kean Miner* (Smethport PA) 8 Aug 1/4, I was working for Mr. Collins, railroad contractor . . ; I was pit boss . . ; Patrick Gorman was walking boss. **1891** *Harper's New Mth. Mag.* 83.888, If a [railroad] contractor acts as "boss" himself, he stays upon the ground; but in this case the contractor had other undertakings in hand. Hence the presence of . . his walking boss or general foreman. **1902** White *Blazed Trail* 25 **eMI,** I think M. & D. is rather full up just now. . . I'm walkin'-boss there. **1915** Barnes *Longshoremen* 183 **NYC,** With the exception of the head foreman or "walking boss" the foremen are members of the union and engaged by the hour. **1927** Steiner–Brown *NC Chain Gang* 85, In 1925 a chain gang official, locally called the "walking boss," . . was dismissed by order of a Superior Court judge and indicted for murder. **1939** in Lib. of Congress *Amer. Memory: WPA Life Hist.* (Internet) **OR,** Once, I told the walking boss I wouldn't go into the tunnel because I could see death hangin' all around me. **1952** *Badger Folkl.* 1.17 **WI** [Logging language], *"He's the walker."*—Woods superintendent overseeing several camps, called walking boss. **1952** *Oakland Tribune* (CA) 9 Oct 1/4, Cargo work . . was delayed in San Francisco yesterday when longshoremen declined to work under a "walking boss" who was a witness against Harry Bridges at his perjury trial. **1957** *Traverse City Rec.–Eagle* (MI) 12 June 4/2, Dick . . is the walking boss for the Michigan Bell Telephone Company in this district. **1966** *DARE* Tape **MI**10, The camp foreman in the area . . was either the straw boss or the bull of the woods or the push. But over him, generally, there was a superintendent over two or more camps, and he was called a walking boss or a walker. **2002** *San Francisco Chron.* (CA) 9 Oct sec A 1 (Internet), The move enraged labor unions. . . "George Bush is the new walking boss on the waterfront," said Richard Mead, president of Local 10 of the ILWU.

walking boy n
In the practice of **hoodoo** n or conjuration: see quots.

   1899 *Jrl. Amer. Folkl.* 12.289, The 'walking boy' is a bottle with a string tied to its neck, deeply colored, that you may not see what the doctor puts in it—something alive, you may know, which enables it to move or even flutter briskly, and this makes you certain of whatever fact the doctor is trying to impress. **1937** in 1976 *Weevils in the Wheat* 263 **VA** [Black], When you sent for the conjure doctor he always brought a pack of cards and a bottle with a live bug in it, string tied around the neck of the bottle. He shuffles cards, you cut them, and he calls them off. All the time he is watching his bottle with the bug in it called "walking boy." Soon as the bug moved, that card he was holding told how to fix the conjure. With the string around the bottle he would pull the bottle around as the bug moved. The bug would tell the victim the direction of the enemy.

walking dandruff   See **galloping dandruff**

walking down   See **walk down**

walking horse n   Cf **walking toms**
See quots.

   1966 *DARE* (Qu. EE35, *Long wooden poles with a footpiece that children walk around on to make them tall*) Inf **NC**4, Tom walkers, walking horses. **1986** Pederson *LAGS Concordance,* 1 inf, **neLA,** Walking horse. [*LAGS* FW: Stilts? Hobbyhorse?]

walking onion n   [See quot 2006]
A **top onion** (here: *Allium cepa* Proliferum Group).

   1977 *Post-Std.* (Syracuse NY) 13 Apr sec B 15/1, Tree onion, also called Egyptian Onion, Walking Onion or Top Onion forms its clusters

on top of a long slender stem. **1988** [see **top onion**]. **2006** *DARE* File—Internet, As the weight of the bulbs increases the plant stalks fall to the ground, which may be as much as two feet from the parent plant. The bulbs waste no time in putting down roots. This is why these varieties are sometimes referred to as a walking onion.

walking plow n   For varr see quot 1965–70   **widespread, but less freq Sth**   See Map   Cf **riding plow**
A plow guided by an operator who walks behind it.

   1868 *IA State Ag. Soc. Rept. for 1867* 161, [The] ground [is] . . cultivated with riding and walking-plows. **1894** (1977) Montgomery Ward *Catalogue* 562, All Walking Plows set up, shipped first class. **1910** *NE State Jrl.* (Lincoln) 6 June [7]/7 (newspaperarchive.com), [Advt:] *For Sale* . . John Deere walking plow. **1927** (1970) Sears *Catalogue* 1060, David Bradley Garden City Clipper Walking Plows $14.85 and Up. **1959** Lahey–Hogan *As I Remember It* 8 **swKS,** They began . . breaking sod with their sod walking-plows. . . These were called "walking-plows" because the man walked behind the plow and guided the share through the virgin soil. **1965–70** *DARE* (Qu. L18, *Kinds of plows*) 281 Infs, **widespread, but less freq Sth,** Walking plow; **MD**29, **NC**49, Walking corn plow; **LA**8, **OK**43, Walking turning plow; **IL**83, Horse-drawn walking plow; **OH**70, Left-handed walking plow; **TN**35, One-man walking plow; **CT**26, One-way walking plow; **NC**49, Walking cotton plow; **LA**8, Walking double-shovel plow; **LA**8, Walking middle-buster plow. **1992** Phelps *Famous Last Words* 13 **NEng,** I learned to plow with a walking plow when I was thirteen. **2001** Millersville Univ. Center for PA Ger. Studies *Jrl.* Autumn 6 **eMT** (as of 1906), We did the plowing with a walking plow and two horses.

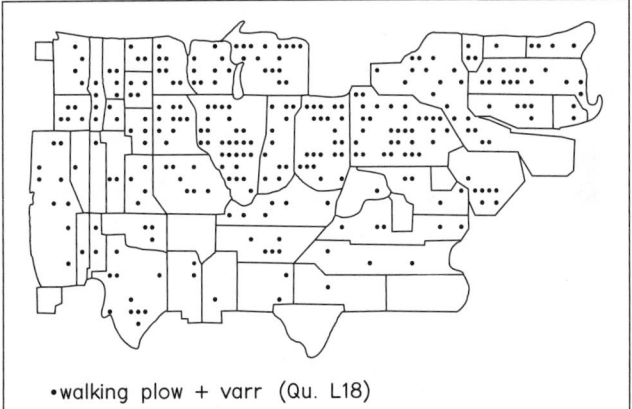

•walking plow + varr (Qu. L18)

walkingstick n
1   Std: an insect of the family Phasmidae, esp *Diapheromera femorata*.   For other names see **darning needle 2, devil's cane, ~ darning needle 2, ~ horse 4, ~ thorn-needle, ~ walkingstick 4, fence rail 3, flying mantis 2, fodder horse, granddaddy 4, ~ longlegs 2, grandmother's darning needle, hayrack 6, horse bug, jimmy longlegs, musk mare, needle 4, nightstick, prairie alligator, spitting devil, stick bug 1, ~ horse, toothpick bug, wooden horse**
2   also *devil's walkingstick, walkingstick insect, ~ mantis:* = **praying mantis B.**

   1938 Brimley *Insects NC* 18, B[runneria] borealis. . . Walking-stick Mantis. **1962** Atwood *Vocab. TX* 77, *Devil's horse, devil's walking stick.* A praying mantis. **1967** *DARE* File **MI,** *Walkingstick insect*—praying mantis. **1968** *AmSp* 43.53, Other names for 'praying mantis' . . included *walking stick,* 28 [of 1518 KS State Univ students]. **1968–70** *DARE* (Qu. R9b, *An insect that holds up its front feet as if saying a prayer; not asked in early QRs*) Inf **NY**59, Walkingstick; **AL**47, Praying mantis—same as walkingstick; [**IL**114, Walking mantis].

walkingstick cholla n   Also *walkingstick cactus*   Cf **cane cholla**
A **prickly pear 1** (here: *Opuntia imbricata*).

   1936 Whitehouse *TX Flowers* 77, "Cholla," or walking-stick cactus (*Opuntia imbricata*), with long slender stems . . is common on western plains. **1967** Dodge *Roadside Wildflowers* 47, *Walkingstick cholla*—Cane Cholla, Candelabrum Cactus.

walkingstick insect (or mantis)   See **walkingstick 2**

‡**walking toms** n pl   Cf **walking horse**
=**tom walkers.**

1966 *DARE* (Qu. EE35, *Long wooden poles with a footpiece that children walk around on to make them tall*) Inf **FL**33, Walking toms.

walk in high clover   See **high clover, be in**

walk jawbone   See **jawbone** n 2

walk off, ready to adj phr   Cf **ride out** v phr **1**

c1950 *Halpert Coll.* 52 **wKY, nwTN,** Ready to walk off = a table or desk cluttered and loaded till it looks like a pack animal.

walk out with v phr   Also *walk with*   [Cf *EDD* walk out (at *walk* v.[1] (3)) "of a lover: to take his lady out"]   Cf **ride out** v phr **2**

Of a man: to go out socially with, date, court (a woman).

1827 in 1956 Eliason *Tarheel Talk* 303 **c,csNC,** [He] has requested to let him have the supreme pleasure of walking out with her. **1940–41** Cassidy *WI Atlas* **swWI,** Walk out with. . . To court. [Used by White woman, 67 years old] **1941** *LANE* Map 405 *(Keeping company with)* 4 infs, **CT, ME, NH, RI,** Walking out with her; 1 inf, **csRI,** Walking out with her . . doesn't necessarily mean he's going to marry her. **1951** Graham *My Window* 38 **ME,** I never had anyone much to walk out with. **c1960** *Wilson Coll.* **csKY,** Walk with (or *walk out with*). . . To court, be one's steady company. **1969** *DARE* (Qu. AA1, *When a man goes to see a girl often and seems to want to marry her, he's _____ her*) Inf **IL**37, Walking out with. **1971** Wood *Vocab. Change* 38 **Sth,** *Social Life.* . . When a young man and woman show an attachment for each other. . . *walk out with* is not reported in Alabama and Florida. *Ibid* 278, *Walk out with* . . [15 infs, **AR, GA, LA, MS, OK, TN**]. **1984** Wilder *You All Spoken Here* 93 **Sth,** Walk out with.

walk (something) to (something)   See **walk 2**

walk Spanish, make one   See **Spanish, walk**

walk, strong enough to adj phr   **chiefly Sth, Midl, TX**   See Map

In varr phrr; Of food or drink, esp coffee: very strong-flavored.

1861 in 1988 Tapert *Brothers' War* 22 **NY,** Two of the soldiers have established a sort of boarding tent where we get . . butter strong enough to walk alone. **1889** *Chambers's Jrl.* 5th ser 6.118 **West,** The butter often was strong enough to walk alone. **1899** Cammann *Hist. Troop "A"* 160, The detail halted and interviewed a couple of Frenchmen . . whose sole offering in the way of refreshment on a hot day was some anisette strong enough to walk alone. **1915** Beach *Heart Sunset* 6, This coffee is strong enough to walk on its hands, and I reckon about two cups of it'll rastle you into shape. **1930** *Forest & Stream* 100.30 **ID,** After a good breakfast, washed down with coffee that was strong enough to walk alone, we packed our outfit. **1947** Baldwin *Give Love* 11 **NYC,** That coffee's strong enough to walk on. **1965–70** *DARE* (Qu. H74a, . . *Coffee* . . *very strong*) 143 Infs, **chiefly Sth, Midl,** Strong enough to walk; **AL**39, **FL**37, **IL**37, 61, **NC**63, **ND**5, **TX**21, Strong enough to walk (by) itself; **IA**7, **WA**31, Strong enough to walk alone; **IL**97, **TN**23, Strong enough to walk on; **NY**240, **WI**52, Strong enough to walk out of the cup (*or* pot); **FL**51, Strong enough to walk off; **FL**9, Strong enough to walk up hill; **AR**56, Strong enough to walk up a hill backwards. **1992** *Intelligencer* (Doylestown PA) 2 Oct sec A 10/1, Fresh-perked coffee strong enough to walk back to Colombia. **2008** Covey *Callye's Justice* 27, Cas always said he liked his coffee strong enough to walk and pay taxes.

walk the chalk (line) v phr   For varr see quots   [Prob orig as a test of sobriety]

To conform rigorously to a prescribed standard, behave oneself.

1845 Hooper *Advent. Simon Suggs* 89 **AL,** If any man or woman don't mind my orders, I'll have 'em shot right away. . . so let every body look out and walk the chalk! **1851** Arthur *Two Wives* 14 **NEast,** If I don't do just as she wants me to—If I don't walk her chalk line—*presto!* she goes off like a rocket. **1887** *Lantern* 8 Oct 3/3 *(AmSp 25.31)* **New Orleans LA,** The owners of those dives also knew they would have to . . walk the chalk-line once the police took the matter in hand. **1905** *DN* 3.23 **cCT,** Walk the chalk [mark]. . . To walk straight, to be strictly disciplined. **1907** *DN* 3.219 **nwAR,** *Walk the chalk (line).* . . To walk straight, to be strictly disciplined. **1909** *DN* 3.386 **eAL, wGA,** *Walk the chalk.* . . To obey implicitly, walk in the straight way, act rightly, mind one's manners. **1916** Lincoln *Mary-'Gusta* 45 **MA,** If she was to have the care of me, she said, she'd make me walk a chalk or know why. **1927** *AmSp* 2.366 **cwWV,** *Walk the chalk mark* . . to obey rules closely. "We have to walk the chalk mark this winter." **1930** Shoemaker *1300 Words* 65 **cPA Mts** (as of c1900), *Walk the chalk line*—To follow orders, to be careful. **1933** Williamson *Woods Colt* 181 **Ozarks,** "You see to it that you don't git tangled up with more'n one feller. . . D'ye hear me?" . . Clint lets go his grip. "You walk chalk," he grumbles. **1939** in Lib. of Congress *Amer. Memory: WPA Life Hist.* (Internet) **MA,** Parents was awful strict, girls 'specially had to walk the chalk line, I'm telling you I always did! **1946** *PADS* 6.32 **eNC,** *Walk a chalk line.* . . To behave circumspectly. . . Occasional. **1966–70** *DARE* (Qu. JJ25, *To show somebody that you're the boss:* "He thought he could take the place over, but I made him _____.") Infs **IA**22, **MD**22, **MO**9, **TN**43, Walk the chalk (line); **AL**6, **FL**14, Walk a chalk line; (Qu. JJ26, *If somebody has been doing poor work or not enough, the boss might say,* "If he wants to keep his job he'd better _____.") Inf **AL**46, Walk the chalk line. [6 of 7 Infs old, 5 gs educ]. **2007** *DARE* File—Internet **nwIN,** I had hoped after he was drafted Michael would walk the chalk.

walk-up adj, also used absol   **chiefly NEast exc NEng, N Cent**   See Map   Cf **elevator apartment**

Of an apartment or apartment building: not provided with an elevator.

1911 *Star* (Kansas City MO) 14 Oct 8/4 **NYC,** Formerly she has always insisted on an elevator but now thinks that a walk up apartment house will do providing it is first class. **1913** *NY Times* (NY) 23 Mar sec S 5/6, [Advt:] Bronx—For Sale or to Let. . . Bronx walk-up apartment: income $4000 year. **1914** *CO Springs Gaz.* (CO) 8 Jan [8]/4 (newspaperarchive.com), John and Mary married impecuniously on $30 a week and went to live in a "walk-up" apartment out south of Broadway. **1934** *AmSp* 9.152, *Walk-up* is a term used for flats or apartments in buildings without elevators in New York City and Chicago. **1965–70** *DARE* (Qu. D26, . . *Different kinds of apartments*) 18 Infs, **esp NEast exc NEng, N Cent,** Walk-up; **MI**122, Walk-up apartment; **WI**47, Walk-up flat. **1986** Pederson *LAGS Concordance (Apartment building)* 1 inf, **seFL,** Tenement housing or a walk-up. **1998** *NYT Mag.* 23 Aug 64 **NYC,** Like most of New York's old walk-ups, Lindy's building had a sociology divided by rent. **2011** *NY Times* (NY) 11 Apr Real Estate sec (Internet), 20 Units Walk-Up Apartment Building For Sale.

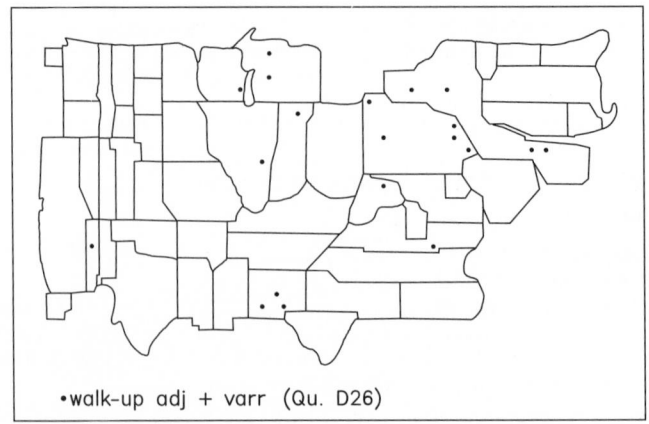

•walk-up adj + varr (Qu. D26)

walk-up n   See **wake-up**

walk uphill v phr   Cf *DS* AA28
To be pregnant.

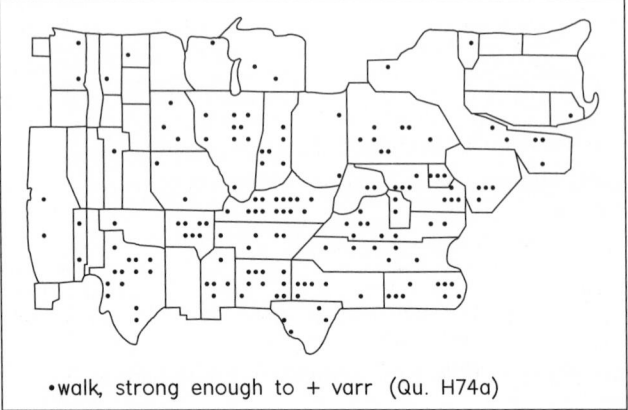

•walk, strong enough to + varr (Qu. H74a)

1944 *AN&Q* 4.41 **sIL,** I have heard . . *walkin' uphill* (pregnant), in southern Illinois.

walk-up-the-creek n   Cf **fly-up-the-creek**

Any of var wading birds; see quots.

  1881 *Atlantic Mth.* 48.694 **OH,** I occasionally saw a sandpiper (familiarly, "walk-up-the-creek") hunting a solitary meal along the margin. **1966–69** *DARE* (Qu. Q8, *A water bird that makes a booming sound before rain and often stands with its beak pointed almost straight up*) Inf **MI**10, Bittern—other nicknames—walk-up-the-creek; **NY**219, Walk-up-the-crick—them are them long-legged crane.

walk with   See **walk out with**

wall v, hence ppl adj phr *walled up* Also *waul* [*OED2 wall* v.[4] c1480 →; "Now only *U.S.*"]   **Sth, S Midl**

To roll (the eyes).

  1845 Hooper *Advent. Simon Suggs* 161 **AL,** Hit kept a *wallin'* its eyes and a moanin'.   **1875** (1876) Twain *Tom Sawyer* 55 **MO,** The ladies would lift up their hands . . and "wall" their eyes, and shake their heads. **1883** *Amer. Philol. Assoc. Trans.* 14.55 **Sth,** *Wall the eyes,* that is, 'to roll the eyes so as to show the white.'   **1907** Porter in *Everybody's Mag.* 17.597 **NC,** It walled its great eyes almost humanly toward Kearny and expired.   **1923** *DN* 5.244 **LA,** *Wall.* . . To roll. "They wall their eyes." **1935** Davis *Honey* 104 **OR,** He picked up the frying-pan and whacked himself across the head with it and keeled over with his eyes walled up. **1952** Brown *NC Folkl.* 1.604, *Wall, waul, the eyes.* . . To roll the eyes towards one without any or much movement of the head; generally indicative of dislike or contempt.   **1967** Green *Horse Tradin'* 6 **TX,** All of a sudden she [=a mare] swelled up like a toy balloon, walled her eyes, bawled, ran backward . . , fell over on her side, and started groaning. **1975** Newell *If Nothin' Don't Happen* 116 **nwFL,** Preacher Jones had the calf by the ears . . , and the calf was bracin' against him with its eyes walled up in its head. **2002** in 2007 *DARE* File—Internet **GA,** One day she [=a dog] was walling her eyes and crying at the door.

wall intj   See **well** intj

walled-off Astoria n   Also *walled-off hotel*   [Pun on the *Waldorf-Astoria* luxury hotel in New York City]

A jail.

  1966 *DARE* (Qu. V11, . . *Joking names . . for a county or city jail*) Inf **NC**36, Walled-off Astoria; **GA**3, Walled-off hotel.   **2004** in 2006 *DARE* File—Internet **VA,** After all this, better toss me in the Walled-Off Astoria, and I'll Sing-Sing for my supper.

walled up   See **wall**

waller   See **wallow**

wallet n

1a A bag or pouch for holding provisions and supplies when traveling; hence n *saddle wallet* a saddlebag.   **chiefly Sth, S Midl**

  c1738 (1929) Byrd *Histories* 288 **VA** (as of 1728), Before we marcht this Morning, every man took care to pack up some Buffalo Steaks in his Wallet.   **1819** *Republican Compiler* (Gettysburg PA) [28 Apr 2]/5 (newspaperarchive.com), Nineteen years ago, General Brown, with a wallet on his back containing 12 or 15 day's provisions, journeyed into the woods. **1823** Doddridge *Logan* 40 **neKY,** Our wallets were filled with cakes and good jirk. **1857** Long *Pictures Slavery* (2d ed) 16 **MD,** Over his left shoulder is suspended a wallet, with meal in one end and pork in the other. **1880** *Harper's New Mth. Mag.* 61.539 **GA,** Mr. Farjuice alone sat apart . . eating the corn-dodgers and bacon out of his wallet. **1899** (1912) Green *VA Folk-Speech* 472, *Wallet.* . . A long bag with a slit in the middle, and space for the contents at the two ends that are closed. **1903** *DN* 2.328 **seMO,** *Saddle-wallets.* . . Saddlebags. **1937** in Lib. of Congress *Amer. Memory: WPA Life Hist.* (Internet) **TX** (as of c1870), The equipment included a wallet which had one end sewed up, it was split in the middle, one end contained biscuit and the other raw bacon. . . The wallet was tied to the back of the saddle. **1945** FWP *Lay My Burden Down* 239 **TX** (as of c1865) [Black], He rid all the way on a mule, carrying a wallet what was thrown over the back of the mule like a pack saddle. **1949** *San Mateo Times & Daily News Leader* (CA) 31 Dec 14/2, Lost—Brown saddle wallet. [**1970** *DARE* (Qu. II3, *Expressions to say that people are very friendly toward each other: "They're _____."*) Inf **VA**41, Thick as forty black cats on a wallet.] **1978** Mayer *Beef Club* 6 **sSC,** For the trips on muleback, these sacks [of pieces of butchered beef] were placed into wallets and taken home. [Inf was 89 years old.]

b in fig phr *let the cat out of the wallet.*   [Var of phr *let the cat out of the bag*]   **Sth, S Midl**

  1804 *Balance & Columbian Repository* (Albany NY) 3.297/3 **KY,** They veered about, and shewed their cloven foot, threw off the cloak under which they wished to act, and let the cat out of the wallet. **1839** *Millennial Harbinger* new ser 3.454 **sOH,** He came very near letting the cat out of the wallet. **1864** (1999) Agnew *Diary* 221 (Internet) **NC,** That letter of Alice Boyd's has let the cat out of the wallet. **1884** *Galveston Daily News* (TX) 10 Aug 4/5, It [=the platform of a cattlemen's convention] "lets the cat out of the wallet." **1904** (1990) Le Guin *Home-Concealed Woman* 120 **cGA,** Fred found out that his Grand Pa had put it there and "let the cat out of the wallet." **1940** Hench Coll. **MS,** Cat out of the wallet—A student from Mississippi told me that he knows this version of the proverbial expression "cat out of the bag." **1966** *DARE* (Qu. JJ43, *To give away a secret or tell a piece of news too soon: "He wasn't supposed to know. Somebody must have _____."*) Infs **GA**1, 5, Let the cat out of the wallet.

2 A small, rectangular, flat or folding case with compartments for holding money, papers, cards, etc; a **billfold.**   **widespread, but more freq NEast, NCent; also Sth, West**   See Map

  1826 *Sandusky Clarion* (OH) [22 Apr 3]/3 (newspaperarchive.com), $20 Reward, For a small Morocco Wallet, containing between 90 and 100 dollars . . ; and some few papers. . . Said pocket book or wallet was lost on the 14th inst. **1834** Davis *Letters Downing* 39 **ME,** I out with my seal-skin wallet, and I showed him a mess on 'em [=bank notes]. **1871** *Daily Kennebec Jrl.* (Augusta ME) [25 Nov 3]/1 (newspaperarchive.com), Mr. Chas. H. Weeks of this city . . dropped his pocket book. . . He supposed he had put the wallet into his inside vest pocket. **1904** *Oakland Tribune* (CA) 20 July 10/7, The wallet contained a large number of greenbacks and an unlimited letter of credit issued by a San Francisco bank. **c1960** *Wilson Coll.* **csKY,** *Wallet.* . . A device to hold one's money. This term is known widely but used rarely. **1965–70** *DARE* (Qu. U30, *What . . you keep money in when you carry it around with you*) 495 Infs, **widespread, but more freq NEast, N Cent; also Sth, West,** Wallet; **CO**9, **LA**14, 18, **MI**18, 118, **OK**9, 28, 42, 47, **WI**12, Wallet—men; **FL**2, Wallet—men and women; **MS**6, **OK**9, Wallet—women; **PA**1, Folding wallet. **2006** in 2007 *DARE* File—Internet **Upstate NY,** For North Americans, the things on the left are wallets. If it's in a man's pocket, it's *wallet* in both dialects [=Brit and Amer]—but my dad (like others in his AmE-speaking generation) calls his a *billfold.* **2007** *DARE* File, 'Billfold' is still dotting the map in the Northern Plains. I regularly tease my wife (in her mid twenties, from central Minnesota) for calling my wallet a billfold. Tho I'm her elder (in my thirties) to me, 'billfold' sounds more antiquated and more indicative of a larger wallet.

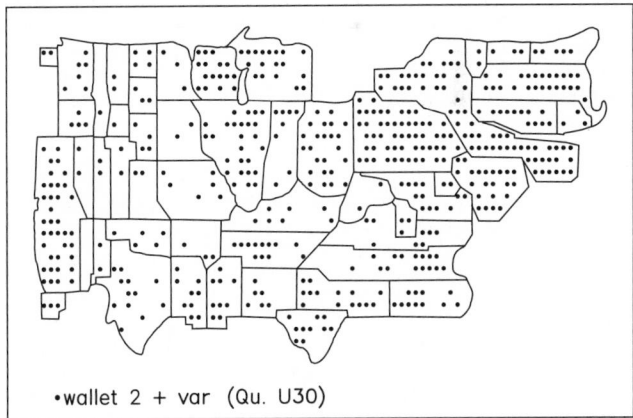

•wallet 2 + var (Qu. U30)

walleye n   Also *walleye(d) pike*

Std: a **pike perch** (here: *Stizostedion vitreum* and subspp). For other names see **blowfish 2, blue pike 1, dory** n[1] **1, glasseye** n[2]**, grass pike 2, gray ~ 2, green ~ 1, gum ~, hornfish 2a, jack** n[1] **24a(2), jackfish 1b, jack salmon 1, marble eye 2, Ohio pike, ~ salmon, pickerel 3, pickering, river trout, salmon B2a(1), sand pike, sauger** n[1]**, spike 1, spikenose, Susquehanna salmon, white-eye 3, white salmon 2, yellow pike**

wall-eyed pollack   See **walleye pollack**

walleye pike   See **walleye**

walleye pollack n Also *wall-eyed pollack*

A northern Pacific fish *(Theragra chalcogramma)* formerly included in the genus *Pollachius.* Also called **mackerel 4, pollack** n[1] **2, silver hake 2, tomcod 1b(2)**

1898 U.S. Natl. Museum *Bulletin* 47.2536, *Theragra fucensis.* . . (Wall-eyed Pollack). . . Pacific coast, from Vancouver Island to Monterey. **1955** U.S. Arctic Info. Center *Gloss.* 2, *Alaskan pollack.* A marine fish, *Theragra chalcogramma.* Also called the 'walleye pollack.' **1992** *Daily Herald* (Arlington Heights IL) 28 Apr sec 4 8/1, In 1991 the government . . announced it would stop Japanese boats . . from fishing for walleye pollack in the international waters of the Bering Sea.

wallflower n

Std: a plant of the genus *Erysimum.* For other names of var spp see **clump mustard, hedge ~ 2, Jim Hill ~ 1, orange ~, prairie rocket, ~ violet 2, wormseed mustard**

wallink n Also sp *walink, wall-link* [Scots, nEng, Ir dial *wellink, wallink* for *Veronica beccabunga*]

1 A **speedwell** (here: usu *Veronica americana*).

1824 Doddridge *Notes Indian Wars* 148 **wPA, WV,** The croup, or what was then called the "Bold hives" was a common disease among the children. . . For the cure of this, the juice of roasted onions or garlick was given in large doses. Wall-ink was also a favorite remedy with many of the old ladies. **1837** Darlington *Flora Cestrica* 4 **sePA,** *V[eronica] Beccabunga.* . . *Vulgò*—Brooklime. Wall-ink. . . This plant is somewhat variant from the European species of the same name. The late Mr. Schweinitz considered it a distinct species, and. . . in his Herbarium . . it is labelled *V. americana.* **1875** *Amer. Med. Jrl.* 3.543 **OH,** *Veronica Serpylifolia* (Wall-ink). . . A gentleman . . informed me that he gave an infusion of it to one of his children, and it brought away sixty worms. **1894** *Jrl. Amer. Folkl.* 7.96 **WV,** *Veronica Americana* . . wallink. **1940** Clute *Amer. Plant Names* 32, American Brooklime. Blue-bells, wall-link.

2 A **spleenwort** (here: *Asplenium rhizophyllum*). **S Midl, esp KY**

1893 *Garden and Forest* 6.99 **KY,** On the cliff above and below are masses of Ferns . . , the smaller ones growing in mats in the moss on the rocks. The latter were common Polypody . . , Walking-leaf Fern . . , called by the country people Wall-link [etc]. **1949** Arnow *Hunter's Horn* 237 **KY,** The three older ones were sent to the river bluff to hunt walink for tea to break out the hives on the baby. **1963** Arnow *Flowering Cumberland* 67 **TN,** Many of these teas—walink (walking leaf)[1] catnip, watermelon seed, rattleroot were some of the most common—are still used in the hills for babies. **1966** *KY Folkl. Rec.* 12.12 **KY,** Boil wallink leaves and make a tea so that a baby will break out with hives. Wallink grows in the woods, usually near cliffs. **1968** *S. Folkl. Qrly.* 32.326 **KY,** *Wallink. Camptosorus rhizophyllum.* The spores of this walking fern were dissolved in whiskey and used as a remedy for *jaundice, measles,* and *coughs.* **2003** Carter *My Little Mt. Home* 34 **seKY,** Daddy gathered the herb, wallink, from down by Granpas spring to make tea for the baby when she got colic. It was green leaves with speckles on the underside of them.

3 also *water wallink:* Either of two submersed plants: the American featherfoil *(Hottonia inflata)* or *Didiplis diandra.*

1901 PA Pharmaceutical Assoc. *Proc.* 24.178 **swPA,** Hottonis [sic for *Hottonia*] inflata.—Walink, Water. **1905** *IL Med. Jrl.* 8.163 **sIL,** The name of this plant as given to me by my father was Walink, or Water Purslane. It grows in great abundance in Southern Illinois. **1964** *Titusville Herald* (PA) 3 Dec 10/4 (as of c1880), J.J. was a great person to gather herbs and prepare them for medicines. . . During one winter night his youngest daughter . . became quite ill. He got the lantern and an axe and went out to the spring run, cut through the ice and reached into the cold water to jerk up a vine of wallink.

4 Prob a **wintergreen 2** (here: *Gaultheria procumbens*) or **partridgeberry 1.**

1917 (1972) *Child Care Rural Amer.* 78 **wNC,** The most commonly used [medicinal herbs] were . . partridge vine (also known as wallink, pheasant berry, one berry, and mouse ears) to break out the hives. **1937** *Hall Coll.* **eTN,** A tea made with 'ground ivy' was used by Aunt Rhoda Caton, 90, Catons Grove, Tenn., in the treatment of croup and phthisic. She also called this plant something which appears in phonetic transcription as [wɑlɪŋk].

wallio n Also *wal(l)yo, wally-o* [sItal dial *(g)uaglio* vocative of *(g)uaglione* boy, fellow] *often derog* Cf *DS* HH28

An Italian male—often used as a form of address.

1941 Algren in *S. Rev.* (Baton Rouge LA) 6.722 **Chicago IL,** We kep' right on goin' that way till we was doin' [=shaving the heads of] guys we never seen before even, Wallios 'n Greeks 'n a Flip from Clark Street. **1948** *Story* Summer 31 **NYC,** "Turn right here, *walyo*," said Pompey. "Speaking with respect, *caro* Pompeo," said Dominic, "I think you're drunk." **1956** Green *Last Angry Man* 369 **NYC,** One of the young Italians was reeling in a bouncing silvery fish. . . "Hey, *walyo!*" the doctor called to them, "porgies are good for stuffin'!" **1964** *PADS* 42.40 **Chicago IL,** Pejorative responses for Italian. . . [Unique responses include:] *wallio* ['wɑli,jo]. **1978** Kennedy *Billy Phelan's Game* 28 **Upstate NY** (as of 1938), Did you hear how the Wally-Os stole a ballot box in the Fifth Ward? **1997** *DARE* File **Chicago IL,** Italian-Americans when they speak of other "dagos" and "_____" (ah, the term escapes me now). [Response:] How about "wops" or "wallios" to fill in the blank? **2003** *DARE* File—Internet **Boston MA,** My father was born here but his Italian and French parents weren't. He hated the epithets thrown at his grandfather—wop, guinea, greaseball, wallyo—in the streets. **2007** *Ibid* **Brooklyn NYC,** Italian guy use to want to pay me to protect them from Irish Guys. . . But I didn't take their Money or protect their Walyo Asses.

wall-link See **wallink**

walloon n[1] Also *wahloon, warloon* [Echoic]

A **loon 1.**

1851 *De Bow's Rev.* 11.56, *Warloon,* or Walloon, a brown-colored water bird, making a noise which sounds like the name; feet partly webbed, with long, slender nails. **1873** Beadle *Undeveloped West* 771, [We] were soon surrounded by extensive flocks of ducks and wild geese, with occasionally a gull or walloon. **1912** Green *VA Folk-Speech* 473, *Warloon.* . . A loon. A waterfowl. His dismal cry at night foretells bad weather. **1962** Imhof *AL Birds* 59, Common Loon. . . Other Names: Diver, Helldiver, Loon, Wah-loon.

walloon n[2], also attrib Also *walloon mosaic* Cf **frenching**

An abnormal condition of tobacco, usu caused by the tobacco mosaic virus; tobacco mosaic disease.

1843 *S. Planter* 3.3, In land not completely drained, the [tobacco] plants are sometimes apt to take a diminutive growth, sending forth numerous long, narrow leaves, very thickly set on the stalk. This is called Walloon tobacco, and is good for nothing. **1877** TN Bur. Ag. Statistics & Mines *Rept. for 1876* 96, When grown upon soils having a very tenacious clay . . the plant, in wet weather more particularly, assumes an abnormal growth, the leaves becoming narrow, thick, stunted, and semi-transparent. In this condition it is said to be *"frenched."* . . Akin to this disease is *"Walloon,"* only the latter occurs in dry weather, and after the tobacco has been topped. . . *Walloon* tobacco is light, and of inferior size. **1895** *S. Planter* 56.56 **csVA,** Half of my crop last year became what we farmers in this section call "walloon" or a "frenchy" kind of stuff, growing about twenty leaves where there should be ten, and showing a diseased condition from that time on to curing. **1914** U.S. Bur. Plant Industry *Bulletin* 40.1 **KY, TN,** In the tobacco sections of Kentucky and Tennessee "walloon" is often used to denote mosaic or other abnormal appearances . . resembling symptoms of the mosaic disease. **1956** *Florence Morning News* (SC) 31 July 22/1, The plant bed is the breeding place for calico or walloon mosaic. **1957** *KY Folkl. Rec.* 3.64, In some parts of Western Kentucky it is called walloon; in other parts of the state, black french, dry weather french, frenching. **1967** Key *Tobacco Vocab.* 152, 1 inf, **TN,** Walloon. **2001** KY Univ. College Ag. *KY Pest News,* The few "old timers" still around . . may have called the disease by another name. TMV [=tobacco mosaic virus] was known by several names, including . . "mosaic", "walloon" [etc].

wallop v **Sth, S Midl** Cf **swoggle, wallow** B1

To sop (bread) in a liquid.

1875 King *Gt. South* 183 **TX,** Won't ye have a little bacon fat to wallop your corn dodgers in now? **1938** *AmSp* 13.237 **KY,** '*Wallop your dodger in the dope.*' The dodger was corn dodger and the dope was sowbelly gravy. **1976** *Harper's Weekly* 26 Jan 19 **MI,** "Walloping the dodger in the sop" was an expression used to describe how to get the last drop of gravy by wiping it off your plate with your cornbread. **2005** in 2007 *DARE* File—Internet **VA,** Does anyone else remember the phrase, "walloping your dodger" which refers to using your biscuit, bread or whatever to wipe around your plate to get up all the gravy? . . I remember my grandmother (who was born in Louisa Co., VA) using this phrase.

wallopa-willipus See **willipus-wallipus**

walloper n Also *whalloper* [*EDD* *walloper* (at *wallop* sb.[4]) "anything very large"] Cf **gee-whollicker**

=**lolloper.**

1912 Mulford–Clay *Buck Peters* 188 **West,** A loud splash in the nearby river brought his head around in the direction of the sound. . . "Walloper," commented Tex, immediately resolving to emulate that fish in the morning. **1913** Johnson *Highways St. Lawrence to VA* 19, The biggest pine I've seen lately was one the flood brought down on the meadow last spring. It was an old walloper, and sound as a nut. **1930** *Oakland Tribune* (CA) 23 Nov [95]/3 (newspaperarchive.com), [Comic strip:] Ah! Mr. Porky—you look so fat your Thanksgivin' dinner must have been a walloper. **1966–68** DARE (Qu. LL5, *Something impressively big: "That cabbage is really a _____."*) Infs **PA**35, **WA**18, Whalloper, **WI**70, Walloper; (Qu. R15b, . . *An extra-big mosquito*) Inf **MO**17, Wallopers. **2005** DARE File—Internet, That's some walloper of a sneeze you have there.

walloping adj, adv [EDD *walloping* (at *wallop* v.³) "large; powerful, strong"] Cf **larruping** adj **1**

Whopping, spectacular; exceptionally, extremely.

1922 *Galveston Daily News* (TX) 10 Aug 10/3, "The Referee," a Selznick picture starring Conway Tearle, . . is pronounced a walloping success. **c1938** in Lib. of Congress *Amer. Memory: WPA Life Hist.* (Internet) **TX,** Even if us cowpunchers was always broke we had a walloping good time. **1965–70** DARE (Qu. LL4, *Very large: "He took a _____ helping of potatoes."*) 10 Infs, **scattered,** Walloping. [8 Infs old, 5 gs educ] **1975** *Star–News* (Pasadena CA) 11 Apr sec B 4/3, When Dennis' dad took it over, there was a walloping collection of the antique art on the premises. **1994** *Waterloo–Cedar Falls Courier* (IA) 5 May sec C 2/2, A walloping 78 percent of the population said they feel sympathy toward smokers because they are addicted. **2007** DARE File—Internet **FL,** At its core is a seminal fuel injected, 955 cc, three-cylinder engine . . punching out a solid 104 bHP peak power output matched by a walloping 67 lbs. ft. torque.

wallopse v [Var of *wallop*] **NEng** Cf **wopse** v **3**

To thrash, beat; also fig.

1904 Day *Kin o' Ktaadn* 201 **ME,** The things that wallopse me / Are the pesky new contraptions that ye never, never see. **1914** DN 4.82 **ME, nNH,** *Wallopse.* . . To maul, handle. **1965** DARE File c**MA** (as of c1914–18), *Wallopse.* . . Two boys have had a fight. "Well, Tom wallopsed him good."

wallow n, v Usu |ˈwɑlo|; also **scattered, but more freq Sth, S Midl** |ˈwɑlə(r)| Pronc-spp *waller, woll* Cf Pronc Intro 3.I.12.d

A Forms. For addit exx, see **B** below

1843 (1916) Hall *New Purchase* 433 **IN,** You must keep down like . . till you strike B'ar Waller—(a creek). **1891** DN 1.164 c**NY,** [wɑlɚ] < wallow. **1894** Frederic *Marsena* 65 n**NY,** She'll have the whole male . . population . . down there wallerin' around in the Virginny swamps. **1899** Garland *Boy Life* 187 nw**IA** (as of c1870s), The men slit off great pink and green crescents [of a watermelon], and, disdaining knives, "wallered into it." **1905** DN 3.83 nw**AR,** Hog-wallow (*ow* as a final syllable is always pronounced ə). **1927** Kennedy *Gritny* 175 s**LA** [Black], You look like somebody bin wollin' in de ditch. **1941** *Esquire* May 132 **KY,** The boys got down and wallered on the grass. **1958** Humphrey *Home from the Hill* 54 ne**TX,** He couldn' find hisself no mud to waller in. **1960** Hall *Smoky Mt. Folks* 17 w**NC, eTN,** Ther's a bear waller in the swag under Spruce Mountain Tower. **1965–70** DARE (Qu. C34) Inf **SC**32, Hog waller; (Qu. N27b) Infs **MS**59, **TN**53, [Full of] hog wallers; (Qu. U37) Inf **AR**18, Wallerin' in the dough; (Qu. AA8) Inf **MS**16, Wallering all over each other; (Qu. DD17) Inf **OH**8, Wallers in it; (Qu. GG29) Inf **CA**117, Like two hogs in a waller. **1970** *Thompson Coll.* se**MI** (as of 1950s), *Waller.* **1982** Brooks *Quicksand* 59 sw**UT** (as of 1906), The log pigpen was also covered, that is, the "Waller-hole" was covered. **1983** MJLF 9.1.60 ce**KY** (as of 1956), *Waller* . . the pronunciation of wallow. **2000** Shores *Tangier Is.* 180 **Chesapeake Bay,** Tangier speakers generally use "-er," the sound of the vowel in *bird.* "Er," instead of "ow," will appear in *shadow, shallow, swallow, wallow, pillow, window,* and *follow.* **2005** Williams *Gratitude* 535 w**NC** (as of 1940s), Where hogs *waller* in the mud is called a *hog waller.*

B As verb.

1 also with *around:* To roll, tumble (someone or something on a surface or in some soft or sticky substance); to push or stir (something) about; fig, to turn (something) over (in one's mind). [OED2 *wallow* v.¹ 8 c1375–1673] **chiefly Sth, S Midl**

1833 in 1902 *Hist. Church of Latter-Day Saints* 1.325 **NY,** Our Heavenly Father hath blessed . . me, in enabling me to speak the praises of God . . in other tongues according to promise: and this without throwing me down or wallowing me on the ground. **1845** Thompson *Pineville* 49 **GA,** Boss wallowed it [=a cigar] in his mouth preparatory to smoking. **1854** Avery *Mrs. Partington's Carpet-Bag* 242, A Yankee wishing for some sauce for his dumplings, forgot the name of it, and said, "Here, waiter, fetch me some of that gravy that you wallow your dumplins in!" **1902** Gordon *Recollections* 50 **VA** [Black], De big ram rushed at 'im [=a dog] an' wallered 'im ove' an' over in de dus', leavin' 'im fuh daid. **1912** in 2007 (acc) Lexis–Nexis Legal Research *State Case Law: AR* (Internet), I did not get out my knife until they wallowed me on the floor and bit one of my fingers nearly off. **1921** Haswell *Daughter Ozarks* 30 (as of 1880s), Then I wallers them pills around in some powdered likkerish. **1939** in 2007 (acc) Lexis–Nexis Legal Research *State Case Law: KY* (Internet), The grandmother described the scratches and bruises on the body of prosecutrix, and said . . that "she looked like she had been wallowed in the mud." **1966** King *One-Eyed Man* 112 **TX,** Cullie Blanton returned the unblinking gaze, a dead cigar jutting from his mouth. He wallowed it on his tongue loosely. **1983** in 2007 DARE File—Internet **IN,** You have seen little children, and even many adults, fill a large plate with food, and then just sit with a fork, or a spoon, and wallow it around eating only a few bites. **2003** Ibid **TX,** I was always sent to the peach tree to get her a "toothbrush" twig which she carefully frayed on one end and wallowed it around in a can of Eli Garrett snuff until she had a ball clinging to the end. **2005** Williams *Gratitude* xiv w**NC** (as of 1940s), We dist take the time to *waller* a word around (or chaw on it) real good before we *turn aloose of it.* . . My other sister is named Juanita, and her name is wallered around and said as "Woineeder." **2005** in 2007 DARE File—Internet **KY,** Mary . . coaxed her into trying one small bite of mashed potatoes. She wallowed it around in her mouth for a time and then, cautiously swallowed. **2006** Ibid **OH,** I'm still wallering this thing around in my mind.

2 also with *around:* To handle roughly or inappropriately.

1995 Adams *Come Go Home* 53 w**NC,** Mama says if I keep on wallering them [=kittens] that they're gonna git sick and die. All I want to do is hold them. That oughten to kill them. **2007** DARE File—Internet s**Appalachians,** Sometimes I get a whiff of nicotine, especially when the GM comes in from sneaking one and decides to waller me around and call me his angel. . . I spotted one of my cousins over by the shopping carts, he saw me and came over, giving me a big ol' bear hug. The funny thing was, the Amazon didn't know who he was and thought I was being wallered by a long lost male suitor.

3 To throw (someone) down in a fight or wrestling match; to beat severely, wallop; also fig. **chiefly Sth, S Midl**

1886 *Harper's New Mth. Mag.* 72.305 **VA** [Black], He face wuz pale, an' he wuds tremble . . , but . . in a minute he was jes reshin. He voice soun' like a bell; and he jes wallered dat turr [=the other] man, and wared him out [in a debate]. **1897** *Scribner's Mag.* 23.689 **GA** [Black], Luck wuz runnin' his way, en she des run'd all over him. She got 'im down en wallered 'im, en den she sot on top un 'im. **1899** Garland *Prairie Folks* 192 **IA,** " 'N' ye wallered him good, did ye?" "I sho'ly did trounce him to my best capacities, sah," Eph said, in answer. **1903** DN 2.336 se**MO,** *Wallow* or *waller.* . . To throw in wrestling. 'I wallered him twict out of three times.' **1907** Wright *Shepherd* 289 **Ozarks,** That's the feller what wallered Wash Gibbs like I was a tellin' ye. Strongest man in the hills he is. **1907** DN 3.238 nw**AR,** *Wallow, waller.* . . To throw in wrestling. **1909** DN 3.387 e**AL,** w**GA,** *Wallow.* . . To roll (a person) in the dust, throw in wrestling. Pronounced *waller.* **2005** in 2007 DARE File—Internet **WV,** Waller—to be pummeled; only for use in west virginia! *kerie got wallered after a drunken fight.*

4 with *down:* To flatten (grass, crops, snow, etc) by or as if by rolling or trampling; to push (something) over by leaning on it; hence ppl adjs *wallowed (down)* crushed by or as if by being rolled on. **esp Sth, S Midl**

1888 Cox *Hist. Seward Co. NE* 29, He found the tall grass wallowed down. . . and following a slight trail further to the south, he found the old man dead and cold, in the midst of a large patch of wallowed grass. **1888** Riley *Pipes o' Pan* 95 **IN,** And yit the corn that's wallered down / May elbow up again! **1930** Sage *Last Rustler* 180 **UT,** Then they come to a big wallered-down place in the snow that showed many tracks. **1937** in 2007 (acc) Lexis–Nexis Legal Research *State Case Law: OK* (Internet), Right there where she was at, looked like it had been tromped down or wallowed down. **1964** Harris *S. Savory* 59 **NC,** The pigs rooted up unfenced gardens, wallowed down cotton. **1981** in 2007 (acc) Lexis–Nexis Legal Research *State Case Law: MO* (Internet), The fence failed to hold the cattle. . . He stated the fence was "wallered down."

5 as ppl adj *wallowed up;* Of a bed: rumpled.

1914 in 2007 (acc) Lexis–Nexis Legal Research *State Case Law: OK*

(Internet), He noticed mornings that only one bed was slept in, and that it would be "disarranged and wallered up."

6 with *out:* To make (a depression), make a depression in, by lying or rolling.

a1893 in 2000 Hentz *S. Practice* 538 **Sth,** I found the place where Mitchell had laid out the night before I found him—; There was a big bed wallowed out in the long wire grass.   **2000** Finch *Death Hornet* 245, The whale, apparently, had wallowed out a hollow in the sand a couple of feet deep.   **2000** in 2007 *DARE* File—Internet **TX,** The dogs were all penned up in one corner of the yard which they had wallered out and usually had several inches or [sic] water standing in it.   **2005** Williams *Gratitude* 148 **wNC** (as of 1940s), Them chickens liked to git up inunder the porch and fluff up and waller in th' dust, and they'd be big ol' round holes wallered out all over in the dry dirt 'nunder there.   **2006** in 2007 *DARE* File—Internet **TX,** Samson [=a boar] . . went directly to the acorn scent and rolled in it over and over covering both his sides with the acorn scent and totally wallering out a dent in the ground.

7a with *out:* To erode (a depression), enlarge (a hole) by repetitive action; esp, to cause a bearing or other machine part to become worn out of shape or fit; hence v phr *wallow off* to wear off; ppl adjs *wallowed off* (or *out*) worn out of shape or fit.   **chiefly Sth, S Midl**

1953 in 2007 (acc) Lexis–Nexis Legal Research *State Case Law: MS* (Internet), She said the openings, or holes, through which these bolts passed were "wallowed out" about twice their size, and the lug bolts had melted. . . Rosalee, servant of appellant and driver of the trailer-truck, testified, "I found the ten bolts that hold both sets of wheels on, about eight had been stripped off flush, and two were there, but the threads were all wallowed off, stripped—even with the brake drum."   **1966** *Ibid: MO,* These holes were "very deep" and as wide as the tires on a dual-wheeled truck. The holes had been "wallered out" by traffic.   **1989** Rhodes *Farm* 190 **MO,** In Osage Station . . Tom picked up a wooden bearing he needed to replace one that wear and tear had wallowed out.   **1990** in 1997 Lindahl et al. *Swapping Stories* 154 **LA,** He went out to the middle of the field, and he found a crawfish hole. He got the hoe handle, and he kind of wallowed it out.   **1990** Smith *Understanding Speaking S. Lang.* 9, *Waller*—To enlarge to an unusable size, as in *waller* out a bearing or a hole.   **2003** *DARE* File—Internet **OR,** I went the ghetto route and punched a hole in the fire wall with a screwdriver and a hammer, then wallowed it out enough for the fitting to fit through.   **2007** *Ibid* **NH,** If you're referring to the drum pulley that the belt wraps around, then there's trouble in doggie land, compadre—probably looking at wallowed out drum bearings.   *Ibid* **KS,** My old sled had an adjustable fence that had to be regularly replaced because the sawcut in the fence became so wallowed out from cutting various-angled segments that it would eventually become unsafe.

b with *out;* intr: To become hollowed or worn.

1969 in 2007 (acc) Lexis–Nexis Legal Research *State Case Law: MO* (Internet), "When it would wallow out [defendant] kept trying to fix it." But the trucks were "coming along there pretty frequently and it just wallowed out at the best they could do, and it was bad."   **1986** *Ibid: LA,* An inspection revealed that the stuffing box packing had wallered out caused by bent shafts.   **2006** in 2007 *DARE* File—Internet **CO,** I just redrilled mine and used a bunch of washers to keep the mount from wallowing out.

8a with *out:* To loosen (something) from the ground by working it back and forth.

2005 in 2007 *DARE* File—Internet **TX,** They took everything, even the concrete hunks the posts were in. There are now holes about three feet wide where they "wallered"[ˀ] the old posts out.   **2006** *Ibid* **MS,** We also have allot of oaks dying. Our forester feels that on many of them the wind from the hurricane "wallowed" out and broke allot of roots, stressing the trees.

b intr: To become loosened by rocking back and forth.

2007 *DARE* File—Internet **TX,** All fence panels had to be taken loose. All those metal posts had to be completely removed from their hard-digging, blister-making holes. The concrete had to be beaten off, as much as possible. Those posts had wallered in their holes until portions of that fence looked as if it had been doing the boogie.

wallow around See **wallow B1, 2**

wallow down, wallowed (down) See **wallow B4**

wallowed off (or out) See **wallow B7a**

wallowed up See **wallow B5**

wallow off See **wallow B7a**

wallow out See **wallow B6, 7a, b, 8a**

wall pepper n

Std: a **stonecrop 1** (here: *Sedum acre*).   Also called **creeping Charlie 1, ~ Jack, love-entangle 2, treasure of love**

wallweed n

A **goldenrod 1** (here: *Solidago rugosa*).

1910 Graves *Flowering Plants* 380 **CT,** *Solidago rugosa*. . . Goldenrod. Wallweed.

wally basket n [Scots *wallie* fine, beautiful + *basket*] =**Ithuriel's spear.**

1949 Moldenke *Amer. Wild Flowers* 355, In the grassnut, tripletlily, wallybasket, or Ithuriels-spear, *Triteleia laxa*, the funnel-form flowers are violet-purple.

wallyo See **wallio**

walnut n   Usu |ˈwɔlnət, ˈwalnət|; also **chiefly sNEng, Sth, S Midl** |ˈwɒnət|; **chiefly Sth, S Midl** |wɔrnət|; for addit varr see quots   Pronc-spp *wan(n)ut, warnet, warnit, warnut, wernet, wornut, wunnet*

A Forms.

1800 in 1967 *PADS* 48.40 **NC,** Warnets.   **1848** Lowell *Biglow* 147 'Upcountry' **MA,** Wannut, *walnut (hickory)*.   **1867** Harris *Sut Lovingood Yarns* 69 **TN,** A par ove iron hanvices, what his dad . . crac't warnuts wif.   **1890** *DN* 1.69 **KY,** Warnut [ˈwɔnət]: walnut. By children and negroes. [*DN* Ed: Also heard in New England.]   **1893** Shands *MS Speech* 67, Wa nut [ˈwɔnət]. Negro for *walnut*.   **1899** (1912) Green *VA Folk-Speech* 492, Wunnet. . . Warnut. The black walnut; and other nuts of the same family. Wornut.   **1903** *DN* 2.336 **seMO,** Warnut. . . Walnut.   **1909** *DN* 3.387 **eAL, wGA,** Wanut [ˈwɔnət]. . . Walnut.   *Ibid* 406 **nwAR,** Warnut. . . Walnut. By children and negroes, and grown-up whites too.   **1911** *DN* 3.540 **eKY,** Wärnet. . . Walnut.   **1915** *DN* 4.192 **swVA,** Warnet [ˈwɑrnɛt]. . . Walnut.   **1917** *DN* 4.419 **wNC,** Warnut. . . Walnut. Also Ky., Ill.   **1923** *DN* 5.224 **swMO,** Warnut. . . Walnut.   **1927** *DN* 5.470 **sAppalachians,** Walnut—warnet.   c**1940** in 2004 Montgomery–Hall *Dict. Smoky Mt. Engl.* 635, Walnuts are called "wernets" by the mountain people.   **1942** Hall *Smoky Mt. Speech* 32 **wNC, eTN,** An intrusive [ɚ] frequently appears in . . *walnut* [ˈwɔɚ·nət] (once [ˈwɑɚ·nət]).   **1955** *PADS* 23.42 **e,cSC, eNC, seGA,** /war–, wor–/ in *walnut* (also Delmarva and South Midland).   **1961** Kurath–McDavid *Pronc. Engl.* 179, Walnut. . . In two subareas of the Atlantic coast— Southern New England with Long Island, and Eastern Virginia with adjoining parts of Maryland and North Carolina—/l/ is often lost in *walnut.* Elsewhere this loss is rare, except perhaps in the Low Country of South Carolina. In two other areas—the Carolinas and Delmarva—the velarized /l/ is frequently replaced by /r ~ /. Both pronunciations are widely current in English folk speech of today, the former in the east, the latter in the west.   **1967–69** *DARE* (Qu. I43, *What kinds of nuts grow wild around here?*) Inf **KY34,** [ˈwɑɚ·nəts]—common pronunciation here; **KY42,** Warnuts—old-fashioned; **NC50,** [ˈwɔˑrnəts]; **VA69,** [ˈwɒnət]; (Qu. T16, . . *Kinds of trees . . 'special'*) Inf **KY34,** Warnuts.   **1967–68** *DARE* FW Addit **TN16,** Walnut pronounced [ˈwɔɚ·nət]; **VA15,** Walnut—old-fashioned pronunciation was *warnut* [ˈwæɚ·nət].   **1983** *MJLF* 9.1.60 **ceKY** (as of 1956), Warnit.   **1989** Pederson *LAGS Tech. Index* 181 **Gulf Region,** Walnut. [Of 914 infs, 501 gave proncs of the types [ˈwɔlnət, -nʌt, -nɪt]; 97 infs, proncs of the types [ˈwalnət, -nʌt, -nɪt]; 131 infs, proncs of the types [ˈwɔnət, -nʌt, -nɪt, ˈwɔʷnət, -nʌt, -nɪt]; 30 infs, proncs of the types [ˈwanət, -nʌt, -nɪt]; 3 infs, [ˈwɔɚ·nət, ˈwaɚ·nɪt]; 3 infs, [ˈwɑ(l)nək, wɔʷnʌk]; 3 infs, [ˈwɔlnut, ˈwɔʷnut]; 2 infs, [ˈwɔʷnɒč, ˈwalnɒč]; 1 each, [ˈwælnət, ˈhwɔlnət, ˈwʌlnʌt, ˈwalnə].]   **2000** Shores *Tangier Is.* 187 **Chesapeake Bay,** Sometimes, one hears . . "wa'nut," for *walnut.*

B Senses.

1 Std: a tree of the genus *Juglans;* also the fruit or wood of such a tree.   For other names of *J. cinerea* see **butternut 1;** for other names of var spp see **gunwood, Madeira nut, nogal**

2 A **hickory** n **B1,** esp **shagbark hickory.**   **scattered, but chiefly NEng**   Cf **bitter walnut, hog ~, pig ~,** *shagbark walnut* (at **shagbark hickory**), **sweet walnut, white ~ 2**

1588 (1903) Hariot *Briefe Rept. VA* sig D1ʳ, There are two kindes of Walnuts, and of the[m] infinit store. . . The one kind is of the same taste and forme or litle differing from ours of England, but that they are harder and thicker shelled: the other is greater and hath a verie ragged and harde shell: but the kernell great, verie oylie and sweete. Besides their eating of them after our ordinarie maner, they breake them with stones and pound them in morters with water to make a milk which they vse to put into some sorts of their spoonmeate . . which maketh them haue a farre more pleasant taste. **1793** *Amer. Philos. Soc. Trans.* 3.180, Walnut. . . [Iuglans] ovata, . . [Iuglans] glabra [=*Carya ovata, C. glabra*]. **1824** Bigelow *Florula Bostoniensis* 355, The wood of the three foregoing species of walnut [belonging to the "subgenus *Carya*" of the genus *Juglans*] possesses similar properties. **1850** Emerson *Rept. Trees & Shrubs* 194 **MA,** The Mockernut Hickory. . . This species is often called the walnut. **1869** *Scientific Amer.* 20.122 **cCT,** There are orchards of walnut or hickory trees, [bearing] a very superior nut, . . often more than three inches in circumference—with very thin shell, and meat of unusual sweetness. **1890** *DN* 1.76, In the east I only knew of 'walnut' for the hickory-nut tree, and 'black walnut' for the other. Here [= IN] 'walnut' distinctively means black walnut, and 'hickory' takes the place of the other. **1894** *Jrl. Amer. Folkl.* 7.98 **NEng, MN,** *Carya alba*. . . walnut. **1901** (1961) Greenough–Kittredge *Words* 340, In some parts of America the name *walnut* is given to the "shagbark," a kind of hickory nut, and the true walnut is known as the "English walnut." **1941** *LANE* Map 277 **NEng,** The walnut proper . . is not native to New England. The term *walnut* is most commonly used here to denote a *hickory nut,* either the *shagbark* or *shellbark* . . or the *pignut* or *hognut* . . *(Carya porcina).* Several informants explicitly state that a walnut is a hickory nut. **1966–68** *DARE* (Qu. I43, *What kinds of nuts grow wild around here?*) Inf **CT**11, Walnuts = pignuts; **CT**12, Shagbark nuts—type of walnut; **MA**6, Hickory nuts—same as walnuts. **1967** Borland *Hill Country* 308 **nwCT,** We went up the mountainside in October to gather nuts from the shagbark hickories there. To me they were hickory nuts, but to Barbara they were "walnuts." **1995** *DARE* File **cMA** (as of 1977), A friend in the Quabbin area called it [=the hickory nut] "walnut" as distinguished from "butternut." . . She corrected me when I said *hickory nut.* "Walnut," she said, firmly. **2004** *DARE* File—Internet **AL,** The small walnuts are hickory.

‡**walnut picker** n   Cf **cherry picker 5**
  1968 *DARE* (Qu. W42a, . . *Nicknames . . for men's sharp-pointed shoes*) Inf **DE**3, Walnut pickers.

walp See **well** intj

walyo See **wallio**

wamble-cropped adj   Also sp *wamble-cropt, wobble-cropped, womble-~, wumble-~;* for addit varr see quots [*OED2* (at *wamble* sb. 4) 1552 →; "now *U.S.*"] **chiefly NEng** *old-fash*
1   Queasy, tipsy; vaguely unwell, "under the weather."
  1736 *New Engl. Weekly Jrl.* 6 July 1, Sentences or Proverbs . . to express *Drunkenness.* . . He's . . Wamble Crop'd. **1844** Stephens *High Life in NY* 2.2 **CT,** As the spring come on I began to git peaked, and every morning felt sort of wamblecropped in my stomach when I woke up. **1932** *DN* 6.284 **swCT,** Wamblecropt. Poorly, drooping. "You kind of mince your victuals and you don't feel good." **1941** *LANE* Map 459 (*Emaciated; peaked*) 1 inf, **swCT,** Wobble crop; 1 inf, **cwCT,** Wamble-cropped—'The old New Englanders used it always.' Some local families still use this term; 1 inf, **nwCT,** Wamble-cropped, especially of a hypochondriac: 'If a man thinks he's sick but the doctor couldn't find nothing the matter of him [sic] you'd say, He must be wamble-cropped'; 1 inf, **cwCT,** Wobble-cropped, only of chickens. **1972** *NYT Article Letters* **cNY,** If grandmother felt weak after an illness, she was "wee-waw" or if ailing only a bit, she was "wumble-cropped".
2   Unhappy, discomfited, irritated.
  1798 *Thomas' MA Spy or Worcester Gaz.* (MA) 5 Sept 1/1, I feel a good deal womblecropped about dropping her acquaintance. **1836** (1838) Haliburton *Clockmaker* (1st ser) 216 **NEng,** It makes me so kinder wamblecropt when I think on it, that I'm afraid to venture on matrimony at all. **1844** Stephens *High Life in NY* 2.65 **CT,** At first I was mad enough to bite a tenpenny nail in tu without chawing; then I began to feel dreadful wamblecropped, and eenamost boo-hooed out a crying. *Ibid* 264, What makes you look so womblecroped? **1883** *Atlantic Mth.* 52.677 **ME,** I s'pose you 've been thinking you lost it. I thought you looked dreadful wamblecropped when I first saw you. **1898** Westcott *Harum* 260 **nNY,** I dunno 's I ever see the old man more kind o' womble-cropped over anythin'. Why, he wouldn't no more 'a' passed them bills 'n he'd 'a' cut his hand off. **1909** *DN* 3.418 **nME,** Wamble-cropped. . . Irritated, offended. **1941** *LANE* Map 459, 1 inf, **nwCT,** Wamble-cropped, common, = 'dissatisfied, complaining'; 1 inf, **nwCT,** Womble crock, ~ cock, sic, heard from very old peole [sic], = 'feeling kind of down in the mouth.'

wambus See **wamus**

wammikin See **wanigan**

wammus See **wamus**

wamp n[1]   Also *pied wamp* [Prob of Algonquian orig (cf Narragansett *wompi* white), in ref to the white back of the drake] **NEng**
=**eider duck.**
  1778 in 1903 NYC Pub. Lib. *Bulletin* 7.426 **RI,** The Cock-Wamp, a remarkable & beautiful species of Anas [and] the Hen Wamp, almost totally different from the other. . . have scarcely anything in common but the singular Cera, which somewhat answers to . . the Cera of the Eider Duck. **1888** Trumbull *Names of Birds* 94 **MA, CT,** *American Eider.* . . known also at New Bedford and Stony Creek as *wamp* (this being of Indian origin, probably; *wompi,* white). **1905** *Amer. Naturalist* 39.399 **RI,** Many of the vernacular names . . are still in use in the State as local cognomens of species; *e.g.,* wamp, for the Eider. **1923** U.S. Dept. Ag. *Misc. Circular* 13.26 **MA,** *Common Eider.* . . *In local use.* . . pied wamp.

wamp n[2]   See **wampus** n[2] **1**

wampapin See **wankapin**

wampa toole See **wapatuli**

wampee n [Prob of AmInd orig, but the suggested etymon Shawnee *wāpa* "white" does not explain the nasal of the Engl form. (The nasal appearing e.g. in Narragansett *wompi* "white" reflects an innovation confined to the eastern Algonquian langs of NEng and Quebec.)] **chiefly S Atl**
Any of several wetland plants, chiefly with arrow- or heart-shaped leaves, as:
a   A **jack-in-the-pulpit 1** (here: *Arisaema triphyllum*). *obs* Cf **cooter wampee 3**
  1802 Drayton *View of SC* 8, [Here grow] quantities of wampe (a species of arum). [*DARE* Ed: This quot may refer instead to another sense below.] **1806** Shecut *Flora Carolinæensis* 1.212, *Arum.* . . *Triphyllum* . . *Indian Turnip,* or *Wampee.* . . Wampee, is the Indian name. **1896** *Garden and Forest* 9.303 **SC,** *Wampee.*—A name of South Carolinian origin, assigned by Drayton (*View of S. Carol.,* 1802) and Shecut (*Flora Carolinæensis,* 1806) to Arisæma triphyllum; by Elliott (*Bot. S. Carol.,* 1817–24), Barton (*Flora Philad.,* 1818), Darby (*Bot. Southern States*) and others to Pontederia cordata, and by Rafinesque (*Med. Flora,* 1830) to Peltandra alba . . In the case of Arisæma and Peltandra, this [=the name meaning "it is white"] would refer to the color of the inside of the farinaceous root-stocks.
b   also *swamp wampee:* An **arrow arum** (here: usu *Peltandra virginica*). Cf **hog wampee**
  1830 Rafinesque *Med. Flora* 2.251, Five sp. blended in *Arum sagitifolium* [sic]. *Taroho, Tuckah, Wampee* of Indian tribes. Fresh roots and seeds acrid, pungent, stimulant, eq. to *Arum;* but mild and edible when roasted or boiled: seeds used like pepper. **1878** *Appletons' Jrl.* 4.502 **seSC,** A dense carpet, three feet deep, of ferns, dwarf-palms, young canes, and bright-leaved wampee. [*DARE* Ed: This quot may refer instead to another sense.] **1926** (1949) McQueen–Mizell *Hist. Okefenokee* 163 **seGA,** While the hogs seem to like this "wampee root" and thrive on it, a person who attempts to eat it will almost go into a spasm of pain, for it is as hot as fire and will not only burn the mouth and throat for hours, but will also cause a drawing sensation similar to a green persimmon. **1931** [see *below*]. **1972** *Amer. Midland Naturalist* 87.450 **Okefenokee GA,** Higher elevations may have . . a cover of maiden cane . . , wampee (Peltandra virginica and P. glauca) [etc]. **2002** *DARE* File—Internet **Okefenokee GA,** Swamp Wampee Root. For my Nature. My buddy swears by it. Supposed to be an old Indian cure. He said it would fix "trouble in the teepee", but it sure worked the opposite on me!
c   =**pickerelweed.** Cf **alligator wampee, cooter ~ 1, cow ~, dog-tongue ~ 1**
  1821 Elliott *Sketch* 1.382 **GA, SC,** *Pontederia.* . . *Cordata.* . . Grows in bogs and ditches. . . *Wampee.* **1870** in 1871 Featherman *Rept. Bot. Surv. LA* 111, Pontederia cordata, L., Wampee, Pickerel Weed, New Orleans, Orleans. **1896** *Garden and Forest* 9.303 **SC,** *Wampee.* . . Of the four languages formerly spoken in what is now the state of South Carolina, the name can be referred only to the Shawnee (Algonk.), in which the word would mean "it is white". . . As applied to the

Pontederia, it would refer to the color of the farinaceous seeds. **1926** (1949) McQueen–Mizell *Hist. Okefenokee* 163 **seGA,** There is a water plant in the Swamp, mostly on the prairies, called by the natives "wampee." **1945** Harper in 1951 *DA* **seGA, nFL,** [Letter to *DA* editor:] In Okefinokee Swamp, and perhaps also in northern Florida, the name 'wampee' is applied to certain aquatic plants with arrow-shaped leaves, perhaps mostly to *Pontederia cordata,* which is called 'pickerel weed' in northern books, but apparently not in the South. **1964** Batson *Wild Flowers SC* 29, Pickerel weed, Wampee. . . Swamps and pond margins. **1966–70** *DARE* (Qu. S26b, *Wildflowers that grow in water or wet places*) Inf **VA**52, ['tʌkiho] berry—same as [wæmpɨ] seed—large, arrow-shaped leaf, wild duck eat seed; (Qu. S26e, *Other wildflowers not yet mentioned;* not asked in early QRs) Inf **SC**10, Wampee roller [sic] [=*Pontederia cordata*]. **1969** *DARE* FW Addit **GA**51, Indian root— wampee [=*Pontederia cordata*]. **1981** Harper–Presley *Okefinokee* 20 **seGA,** Watery vistas between moss-hung prairie "heads" have an especially appealing beauty . . blue-flowered "wampee" *(Pontederia)* forming a border about every lake and 'gator-hole.

d =**water hyacinth.**

1903 Small *Flora SE U.S.* 244, *Piaropus crassipes* [=*Eichhornia c.*] . . In slow streams and lakes, Florida. . . Water Hyacinth. Wampee. **1936** Whitehouse *TX Flowers* 6, Water Hyacinth *(Eichhornia crassipes)* is also called wampee, river raft, and water orchid.

e An **arrowhead 1** (here: *Sagittaria latifolia*). Cf **dog-tongue wampee 2**

1931 Clute *Common Plants* 22, The arrow arum was also known as wampee and the name is still applied to the starchy tubers of the arrowleaf *(Sagittaria latifolia),* though they are now more frequently known as duck potatoes, in reference to the wild duck's fondness for them. **1964** Batson *Wild Flowers SC* 23, Swamp-potato, Wampee: S[*agittaria*] *latifolia.* . . Tubers have a high starch content and are edible. **1968** *DARE* (Qu. S26b, *Wildflowers that grow in water or wet places*) Inf **GA**35, [wɒmpɪ]—same as northern arrowhead.

f =**mud-baby.**

1937 *Torreya* 37.95 **SC,** *Echinodorus* sp.—Bean-leaved wampee, Combahee River.

wampus n[1] See **wamus**

wampus n[2] Also sp *w(h)ompus, wamputh* Also *wampus cat*
1 also *swamp wampus, tady-~, wamp, wampus kitty, whistling wampus:* =**catawampus n 1;** also occas identified with var wild animals; see quots. **scattered, but esp Sth, S Midl** See Map

1878 *Pomeroy's Illustr. Democrat* (Chicago IL) 16 Nov 1/6, An editor in Mazeppa, Minnesota, announces that he will suspend his paper two weeks, or till he can collect what is due him from subscribers. Unless he goes for them with the "wampus" or wild horse of Tartary, that two weeks will be so long that he will be too weak to dun a man, and his editoring will be done. **1899** *Ft. Worth Morning Reg.* (TX) 1 Oct 4/2, Ed Brown chased a wompus all night. It is now in order for Captain Paddock to capture a full grown nightmare. **1905** *Washington Post* (DC) 20 Jan 14/1 **CA,** Not expecting to find anything more dangerous than a wampus or a gruffini, he left his rifle in the scabbard and went to investigate. **1913** *Star* (Kansas City MO) 13 Nov sec B 6/7, The plan to put "teeth" in the new Anti-Trust Law is all right as far as it goes, but it will also need claws like a wampus-cat, and a stinger similar to that of the adder. **1913** *DN* 4.3 **ME,** *Wampus cat.* . . An unidentified imaginary animal. **1917** *Coshocton Tribune & Times-Age* (OH) 4 Nov 9/2, I thot that I would write and tell you about the night we spent in the woods hunting wampus cats [in Alabama]. **1934** *Jrl. Amer. Folkl.* 47.296 **cwNC,** He went out again and saw a wampus [a fictitious animal] sitting on the chimney top, with shiny eyes, sharp claws and teeth, and a long tail. **1950** *AR Hist. Qrly.* 9.70, The lumbermen down that way were always joking about the whistling wampus. **1950** *PADS* 14.70 **SC,** *Wampus.* . . An imaginary sea monster. "To catch a wampus." . . [W]ampus cat. . . A mythical green-eyed cat, having occult powers. **1951** Randolph *We Always Lie* 58 **Ozarks,** The old-timers up on Roark Creek say the valley is full of wampus-cats. . . "a blood-thirsty animal of some kind, found only in the wildest sections of the Ozarks." **1954** *PADS* 21.40 **seSC,** *Wampus kitty.* . . A variant of *wampus cat.* **1965–70** *DARE* (Qu. CC17, *Imaginary animals or monsters that people . . tell tales about—especially to tease greenhorns*) 13 Infs, **esp sAppalachians, SE,** Whompus (cat); **FL**26, Whompus—wild animal like a wolf; **NC**82, Whompus [FW: Inf thinks it was a bear]; **CT**27, **IN**45, **NC**72, **TX**104, **VA**1, **WV**13, Wampus cat; **IN**35, Wampus cat—related to tigers and such; **IN**41, Wampus cat—a bobcat; **WI**57, Swamp wampus;

GA13, Tady-wampus—descriptions vary widely, but it's either a cat or dog-wolf or something; (Qu. Q2, . . *Kinds of owls*) Inf **OK**11, Wampus cat—hoot owl or tree owl; (Qu. EE41, *A hobgoblin that is used to threaten children and make them behave*) Inf **VA**1, Wampus cat. **1969** Sorden *Lumberjack Lingo* 138 **NEng, Gt Lakes,** *Wampus cat*—An imaginary animal to which night noises were attributed. **1985** Madson *Up River* 245 **Upper Missip Valley,** "Wamp" is a River truncation of *wampus cat,* the legendary Kentucky varmint symbolizing pure, triple-distilled, uncorked mayhem. **1997** *DARE* File **TN,** Have you ever heard of the expression "wamputh cat"? In my area this refers in general to a wild cat, and the wilder the better. For example, what would be a normal house cat with proper domestication would be a "wamputh cat" if left to fend for itself in the wild. Of course the local panthers and mountain cats are the real "wamputh cats" of which I speak, but the term is not restricted soley [sic] to these larger and wilder vareities [sic] of cat.

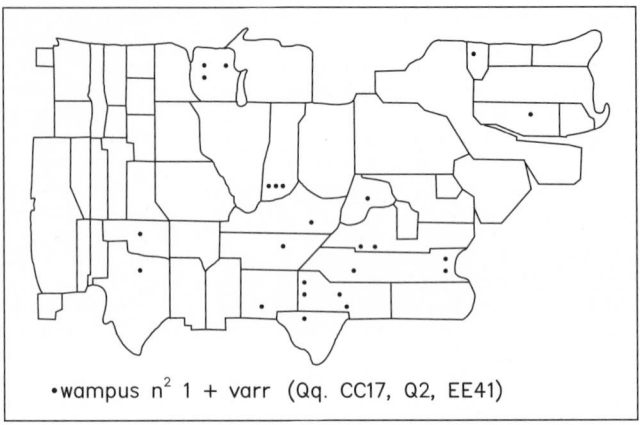

•wampus n[2] 1 + varr (Qq. CC17, Q2, EE41)

2 Transf: a mean, difficult, or objectionable person; see quots.

1912 *DN* 3.592 **wIN,** *Wampus.* . . Any offensive or loathsome person. . . Sometimes applied to a negro without regard to his personal qualities. **1915** *DN* 4.225 **TX,** *Catawampus* (or *wampus*) *cat.* . . A virago. **1928** (1964) Santee *Cowboy* 74 **AZ,** Boy! he's a wampus, what I mean. An' fight! It took all four of us to handle him. **1935** Davis *Honey* 100 **OR,** Grandma Simmons . . had been made by the artist to look like an iron-chinned old wampus. **1942** *AmSp* 17.88 **AZ,** *Button* is the term used frequently . . in referring to a child or baby. . . Tiny Lynn Aber was called not only a button but a *wampus cat.* **1967–68** *DARE* FW Addit **AR**47, *Wampus cat*—word for lively, mean, hard-to-deal-with person; **GA**30, *Wampus-cat*—a rough-looking negro. **1987** Doig *Dancing* 70 **MT** (as of c1890), You could rake hell from corner to corner and not find a nastier item than Warren Williamson. Or, as was supposedly replied to a traveler who innocently wondered what the cattle brand WW stood for, Wampus Cat Williamson.

3 An extraordinary example of its kind; see quots.

1907 *N&Q* 10th ser 7.447 **CT,** The third word [=wompus] has come into widespread use since my boyhood, no more in New England than otherwise. . . meaning a huge, shapeless, unmanageable mess. "He has got a wompus on his hands" will be said of a reformer tackling a social problem too heavy for his powers; "I had no idea my theme was going to grow into such a wompus," a student will say; and I have heard various Presidential messages indecorously, if accurately, referred to as "wompuses." . . I heard it first about forty years ago. **1958** Latham *Meskin Hound* 50 **cTX,** Sugar dropped the stub of pole [with which he was fishing] and wiped the water out of his face. "Be dog! I've hung Myrtle a regular wampus cat [=a catfish]!" **1994** NC Lang. & Life Project *Dial. Vocab. Ocracoke* 17 **eNC,** *Wampus cat*—A fictitious, wild cat. Used to refer to someone who is abnormal in some respect, possibly to someone especially silly or especially heavy. . . *Walt's a classic example of an off-island wampus cat.* **2000** Shores *Tangier Is.* 206 **Chesapeake Bay,** *Wampus* is used for some strange or imaginary animal or fish of great size.

wampus n[3] Also *wampus bread*
A kind of fried corn bread; see quots.

1938 FWP *U.S. One* xxvi **FL,** *Wampus or Hush Puppies:* corn meal scalded in milk, mixed with egg, baking powder, and onion, and cooked in the grease of frying fish. **2005** in 2007 *DARE* File—Internet **nwFL,** We don't know if grouper gets any better than how they prepare it. ([N]ot to mention the wampus bread and slaw.) **2007** *Ibid* **TX,** As far as fry-bread, my Choctaw relatives make a delicious fry bread they call wampus bread. It is mostly corn with a little wheat flour and spices. *Ibid* **OK** (as of 1907), *Wampus Bread* (Fry Bread) . . [Recipe includes cornmeal, flour, onion, potato, sugar, salt, baking powder, milk.] Drop by spoonsful into hot grease and cook until brown. Someone asked for a frybread recipe; this is a 1907 Oklahoma recipe and is Choctaw in origin.

wampus cat See **wampus** n[2]

wampus-jawed adj Also *whampus-jawed*

1 See quot. Cf **catawampus** adj

1967 *DARE* File **Tuscaloosa AL**, Antigodlin—out-of-plumb, skeewhonked, cut on the bias, whampus-jawed.

2 See quot. Cf *DS* X6

1950 *PADS* 14.70 **SC**, *Wampus-jawed*. . . Having a swollen jaw.

wampus kitty See **wampus** n[2] **1**

wamputh See **wampus** n[2]

wamus n Also *wambus, wammus, wampus, wappus, warmus, waumus, wawmus, wommis* [Du *wambuis, wammes,* dial Ger and PaGer *wammes* (Ger *Wams*)] **chiefly N Cent, PA** See Map *old-fash*

A man's work jacket.

[**1663** in 1869 Albany Co. NY *Early Rec.* 340, Inventory of the goods of Jan Gerritsen Van Marcken. . . 2 white roundabouts *(wambus).*] **1805** *Intelligencer & Weekly Advt.* (Lancaster PA) 12 Nov [2]/1, I got up, and found that my waumus was bloody. **1841** *S. Lit. Messenger* 7.525 **swPA**, His long, matted locks overhung the back of a red flannel *warm-us*, which constituted his principle [sic] outer garment. [Footnote to *warm-us:*] I am not sure that our narrator spells this word correctly. Its popular pronunciation is *wommis.* The garment is a long, loose roundabout, connecting in front with strings, and is much worn, even at the present time. **1846** *Independent Amer. & Genl. Advt.* (Platteville WI) 27 Nov [2]/4 (newspaperarchive.com), A coarse brown coat or wampus, with several kinds of buttons on it, . . was also found. **1861** Burton *City Saints* 29 **West**, The older hand prefers to buckskin a "wamba" [sic] or round-about, a red or rainbow-coloured flannel over a check cotton shirt. **1867** *Atlantic Mth.* 19.298 **NY**, Sim sat down, [and] pulled on the green wamus and the slippers. **1879** Tourgée *Figs & Thistles* 29 **OH**, The boy was . . permitted to wear . . a jacket or wampus made for his especial benefit. **1892** *KS Univ. Qrly.* 1.100 **IL, PA, OH, WI, NEng**, *Wamus, wampus, warmus;* a close, generally knit jacket. **1894** *Century Illustr. Mag.* 47.853, I have often heard a loose flannel or linsey-woolsey jacket called, on the Ohio River, a "wawmus," with a notion that it had something to do with "warm us." It is the German *wamms,* a doublet, without doubt. **1912** *DN* 3.592 **wIN**, *Wammus*. . . A coat-like jacket worn by men in such work as threshing wheat or oats and husking corn. Although *wammus* and *wampus* are the usual forms, one sometimes hears *wappus, warmus.* **1912** *Eve. Observer* (Dunkirk NY) 10 July 3/1, [Advt:] Boys' Indian Suits Consisting of Wampus, Long Trousers and Feathered Hats 98¢. **1913** (1980) Hardy *OH Schoolmistress* 99, *Wamus,* a garment generally made of red flannel worn as a blouse by farmers—the corners were usually tied in a knot in front of the waistline. **1917** *DN* 4.403 **neOH**, *Wamus* [woməs]. . . A kind of outer jacket made of overalls cloth, having buttoned wristbands, a buttoned, close collar, and a buttoned belt (attacht); worn by men at outdoor work. Also Pa., Ill., Ia. **1929** *AmSp* 4.303 **IA**, "Wammus" in *A Son of the Middle Border* called up a picture of the denim work jacket my father always wore on cool or rainy days. **1935** *AmSp* 10.172 **PA** [Engl of PA Germans], Other terms more rarely used include the following: . . *Wamus* for a knitted jacket worn with a belt. **1944** Howard *Walkin' Preacher* 123 **Ozarks**, A few of the men wore cotton-flannel-lined blue denim jackets which they called "wampuses." **1947** *WELS Suppl.* **csWI**, His jacket . . [my father] always called a "wamus." . . I never heard any one else say "wamus." c**1948** *Ibid* **cwWI**, Jim Blescoe . . uses the word *wamus* for the denim jacket that farmers wear to do chores in. **1965–70** *DARE* (Qu. W4, . . *Men's coats or jackets for work and outdoor wear*) Infs **IN**3, 28, 34, 66, 70, **KS**19, **MI**78, **WI**21, Wampus; **IN**35, Wampus—sheepskin-lined; **PA**139, Wampus—older term for any kind of coat; **NY**107, **OH**61, **PA**12, Wamus; **IL**29, Wamus—short one with band, comes to the waist; long ones have pockets and go below the waist; used to be made of blue denim; **MI**92, Wamus—blue jeans material, to waist; **PA**162, Wamus—any jacket is a wamus; **PA**42, Wambus; **WA**11, Warmus; [**OH**98, [womæk]—a work jacket of denim [Inf uncertain]]. **2000** Lewis *Redemption* 179 **sePA**, She smelled wood smoke on his heavy black *Wamus*-coat. **2000** *NADS Letters*, I . . remember a man

from NW NJ in the 1940s and 50s calling his jacket a "wamus". He was in his 50s at the time.

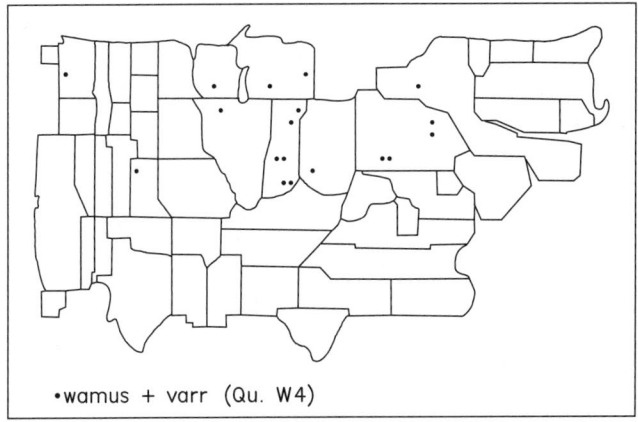

•wamus + varr (Qu. W4)

wan v See **want** v[1]

wan pron See **one**

wanagan See **wanigan**

wanagan camp (or man) See **wanigan 2**

wancet See **once**

wander v Usu |'wandə(r), 'wɔndə(r)|; also **chiefly Sth, S Midl** |'wʌndə(r)| Pronc-spp *wonder, wunder*

Std senses, var forms.

1894 Riley *Armazindy* 26 **IN**, When my little bare feet wundered down wher' the stream / In the Muskingum Valley flowed on like a dream. c**1938** in 1970 Hyatt *Hoodoo* 2.1493 **GA** [Black], Yes sir, he'll have tuh be 'bliged tuh go an' jes' keep goin'—too, dat's whut chew call a *wondering* [Hyatt: wandering] *mind.* **1939–44** in 1944 *ADD* **WV**, *Wander*. . . [wʌndɚ]. Not uncommon. . . [wɔ]-. Not uncommon. **1943** *AmSp* 18.267 **nwVA**, *Wander,* tested in close association with *wonder* (which always had [ʌ]), became [wʌndɚ], [wʌndə] in many cases. **1952** Brown *NC Folkl.* 1.609, *Wondering dew*. . . The *wandering Jew.* **1981** Pederson *LAGS Basic Materials,* 1 inf, **ceTX**, ['wʌ·ndə] . . wander [inf Black].

wandering boss n

=**walking boss.**

1959 *VT Hist.* 27.166, *Wandering boss*. . . A superintendent of several quarries or mills owned by one company. Common among quarry workers.

wandering dew See **wandering Jew**

wandering Jenny n Also *wandering sailor, ~ Sally*

=**moneywort 1.**

1936 *IL Nat. Hist. Surv. Wildflowers* 230, The Moneywort is sometimes called Wandering Jenny or Wandering Sally because of its habit of spreading by rooting at the nodes of its runners. **1940** Clute *Amer. Plant Names* 226, *Lysimachia nummularia.* Meadow runagates, string of sovereigns, wandering sailor.

wandering Jew n Also *wandering dew, wondering ~*

A **dayflower** (here: *Commelina communis*).

1952 Brown *NC Folkl.* 1.604 **seNC**, *Wandering dew*. . . The *wandering Jew.* Same as *wondering dew.* **1965–70** *DARE* (Qu. S9, . . *Kinds of grass that are hard to get rid of*) Inf **TX**101, Wandering Jew—small blue flowers; (Qu. S21, . . *Weeds . . that are a trouble in gardens and fields*) Infs **MO**2, **NY**34, **PA**89, Wandering Jew; (Qu. S26e, *Other wildflowers not yet mentioned;* not asked in early QRs) Inf **AL**42, Wandering Jew; **IL**135, Wandering Jew, baby blue-eyes—has a small blue flower. **1966–68** *DARE* Wildfl QR Pl.6B [=*Commelina communis*] Inf **AR**44, Wild wandering Jew; **NY**91, Wandering Jew; **NC**28, Wild wandering dew, wild wandering Jew.

wandering sailor (or Sally) See **wandering Jenny**

wandi(e) n [sItal dial < *guanti* pl of *guanto* a small pastry] **RI**

A deep-fried cookie dusted with confectioners' sugar.

2002 *DARE* File **RI**, Wandies are crispy fried doughs [sic]. They are very thin and usually shaped into a bow, after deep frying, they are taken out of the oil and sprinkled with sugar or powdered sugar. It is an Italian treat. . . Generally made for the holidays and weddings. **2002** *DARE* File—Internet **RI**, *Wandies:* Wandies by Pina, Cranston—We can't go to a party these days, it seems, without finding a package of wandies on the kitchen counter. **2006** *Ibid* **RI**, Wedding Dessert Menu—Rhode Island Convention Center. . . Italian Wandies ($16.00 per tray). *Ibid* **RI**, Corinna's Home Style Wandies . . Chepachet, RI. *Ibid* **RI**, Wandi are a flaky, deep-fried Italian pastry, sprinkled with powdered sugar.

wand lily n

A **death camas** (here: *Zigadenus elegans*).

1938 (1958) Sharples *AK Wild Flowers* 152, Zygadenus [spp]. . . "Wand Lily." **1953** Nelson *Plants Rocky Mt. Park* 49, Wandlily or mountain deathcamas, *Zygadenus elegans*. **1961** Douglas *My Wilderness* 19 **CO**, Waist-high is the wandlily (*Zygadénus elegans*) with creamy-white, saucer-shaped flowers growing along an upright stalk. **1966** *Charleston Gaz.* (WV) 27 July 5/1 (Internet) **CO**, There was wand lily, white and delicate on tall stems.

wang n¹   See **whang** n²

wang n²   See **whang** n³

wanga n   Also *ouanga, wang, wongah* [Haitian Creole, ult of Afr orig] **chiefly LA** Cf **gris-gris, mojo**

In the practice of **voodoo 1**: a magical charm or spell; a practitioner of **voodoo**.

1851 *Daily Picayune* (New Orleans LA) 20 July 2/6, The Voudous also threw "Wanga" or spells into the complainant's yard. **1886** *Century Illustr. Mag.* 31.820 **LA**, A planter once found a Voodoo charm, or *ouanga* (wongah) . . it was a bit of cotton cloth folded about three cowpeas and some breast feathers of a barn-yard fowl, and covered with a tight wrapping of thread. **c1938** in 1970 Hyatt *Hoodoo* 2.1255 **LA** [Black], If yo' happen tuh evah go dere, think if yo' kin, an' go to Monroe, Louisiana, tuh mah fren's house, *Doctor* Buzzard—red lips an' red eyes . . an' oh, he's a wang. **1941** Writers' Program *Guide LA* 692, *Wanga*—Of African origin. A spell. **1946** Tallant *Voodoo* 91 **New Orleans LA**, Another sort [of gris-gris] held gunpowder and red pepper; these were powerful *wangas* to be thrown into somebody's path to cause them to get into fights. **1949** Turner *Africanisms* 203 **sSC, GA coasts** [Gullah], [Words used in conversation:] ['waŋga] 'charm, witchcraft.' **2002** *DARE* File—Internet **New Orleans LA**, [Advt:] La Sirena Voodoo Fetish Wanga Dolls. . . Hand crafted with special mixtures of herbs, power objects and bits of sacred offerings . . , these old type fetish "Wanga" dolls unite the power of gris- gris and of voodoo dolls. . . Price: $35.00.

wangan   See **wanigan**

wangan bag   See **wanigan 4**

wangan boat   See **wanigan 1**

wangan box   See **wanigan 4**

wangan camp   See **wanigan 2, 3**

wangan chest   See **wanigan 4**

wangan man   See **wanigan 1, 2**

wangan store   See **wanigan 3**

wangin   See **wanigan**

wangish   See **whang** n³

wangun   See **wanigan**

wangun boat   See **wanigan 1**

wangy   See **whang** n³

wanigan n   Also sp *wannigan, wan(n)agan;* also **chiefly ME** *wangan, wangin, wangun, waungin;* rarely *wammikin* [Prob of Algonquian orig; etyma from var langs have been suggested, all implying that the orig sense was either "things carried around" or "storage place," but the precise source has not been determined.] Cf *DCan,* **yannigan**

1 also *wangan* (or *wangun*) *boat:* Orig a boat or raft that carried the cook and the commissary supplies for loggers on a river drive, and also often provided eating and sleeping accommodations; now usu a floating bunkhouse or houseboat; hence n *wangan man.* **chiefly ME, Gt Lakes; also AK** Cf **ark 3, chuck boat, shantyboat 2**

1848 Bartlett *Americanisms* 377, *Wangan.* (Indian.) In Maine, a boat for carrying provisions. **1851** (1856) Springer *Forest Life* 170 **ME**, The camping utensils for river-driving, with provisions, are moved along day by day. . . The boats appropriated for the removal of the whole company, apparatus, and provisions, when loaded, are called *"wanguns,"* an Indian word signifying bait, and, when thus appropriated, means bait or provision boats. Among the dangers to be incurred . . is that of "running the wangun" . . which . . means the act of taking these loaded bateaux down river from station to station, particularly down quick water. **1867** in 1907 Eckstorm *David Libbey* 71 **ME**, Ran wangun to chopping below Ham's. **1877** *Scribner's Mth.* 15.150 **Nth**, On the larger and wider streams where there are no rapids or dams, all is plain sailing; the drive is accompanied by what is called a *wammikin,* consisting of a raft of square timber, or long logs, on which is built a comfortable shanty, with complete cooking and sleeping facilities. **1888** Folsom *Fifty Yrs. NW* 704 **ceMN, nwWI** (as of 1845), The drivers are without tents, but a wangan, or small flat boat, containing bedding, provisions, and a cooking kit, is floated down the stream so as to be convenient at night. *Ibid* 706, The cook in the drive has . . a wangan man to assist in managing the boat. **1905** U.S. Forest Serv. *Bulletin* 61.52 [Logging terms], *Wanigan.* . . A houseboat used as sleeping quarters or as kitchen and dining room by river drivers. **1907** *DN* 3.251 **eME**, *Wangin* ['waŋgɪn] or ['wamgɪn]. . . A supply boat used in the woods on a stream. **1907** Eckstorm *David Libbey* 72 **ME**, One would suppose that a man who had been tumbled over a rolling dam . . would have taken a day off instead of hobbling back to run the wangun-boats. **1926** Rickaby *Ballads Shanty-Boy* 238 **MI, MN, WI** (as of a1920), Wanigan (also *wangan* and *wanagan*). . . A large, heavy boat or scow, generally enclosed, in charge of the cook and his helpers, which followed the drive down and was the base of provisions and supplies and the general headquarters on the drive. **1939** *AK Sportsman* Nov 10 (Tabbert *Dict. Alaskan Engl.*), In Southeastern Alaska, a wanigan is a bunkhouse built on a scow, and used to house the "outside crews" at canneries, the men working in isolated mines near the beach level of bays and inlets, or the logging crew of a lumber camp. **1940** in 2007 (acc) Lexis–Nexis Legal Research *State Case Law: AK* (Internet), For some time prior to 1936 he was employed as a watchman at a cannery . . , located on Gambier Bay, Alaska. He lived in a wanigan, a house built on a scow. **1955** Johnson *50 Yrs.* 188 **nMN** (as of early 20th cent), A floating building (having facilities for sleeping, cooking and eating) called a "wannagan" followed the flow of logs. **1966** *DARE* Tape **ME**26, They swamped their wangan. . . That's the boat that carries the grub and stuff like that. . . If it's a big drive, the wangan boat has stove in it. **1968** *DARE* (Qu. O2, *Nicknames . . for an old, clumsy boat*) Inf **MN**29, Wanigan—square front and rear—had a cover on it; carried supplies to feed river pigs (log drivers) on log drives; [(Qu. FF16, . . *Local contests or celebrations*) Inf **MN**19, Wanigan days—celebration of river history]. **1969** Sorden *Lumberjack Lingo* 113 **NEng, Gt Lakes**, *Sleeping wanigan*—A houseboat used solely for sleeping during the river drive. **1986** Rustad *I Married a Fisherman* 12 **AK**, The surveyors anchored their wanigan (bunkhouse on floating logs) on a flat, secluded beach . . and used it as their base camp. **2007** *DARE* File—Internet **AK**, The Wannigan is a very comfortable floating cabin anchored in the more remote arms of Prince William Sound and are occasionally moved to coincide with the different salmon runs.

2 also *wan(a)gan camp:* A temporary camp or shelter set up usu for feeding loggers on a river drive; a camp or rough building where loggers sleep during a drive; hence n *wan(a)gan man.* **chiefly ME, Gt Lakes**

1891 *New North* (Rhinelander WI) 21 May 1/5, Arriving at the wanagan Ben was apparently greatly surprised to learn that his cook was drunk. He apologized for inviting an old friend to supper at such a time, and swore around the camp until the water was blue. **1905** Stanton *Where the Sportsman* 112 **ME**, There are always pitched at convenient distances along the river during a log drive two tents—one a large "lean-to," for the men to sleep in, and the other a place to eat. In the latter, called a "wangan," are the cook's quarters. **1911** *Stevens Point Daily Jrl.* (WI) 22 Apr 1/2, The John Week Lumber Co.'s drive passed through here [=Mosinee] this week, and the wanagan and sleeping camps are at present located at the foot of the island near the power station. **1922** *Daily Kennebec Jrl.* (Augusta ME) 4 Oct 1/6, A Wangan camp has been set up, with cooks and food supplies to take care of the [forest-]firefighters. **1941** *AmSp* 16.234 **MT** [Lumberjack jargon], *Wangan* or *wannigan.* . . an overnight camp on the banks of a stream by log drivers riding logs to the mill or to the sea. **1942** Rich *We Took to Woods* 183 **ME**, I should explain "wangan." It is an Indian word, and can mean almost anything. . . It can mean a camp or building. . . Pondy wangan, as the drivers call it—is a long low shack . . where the Rapid River crew lives during the drive. **1942** ME Univ. *Studies* 57.135, *Wangan.* A camp (usually tents) where *river drivers* live. **1956** Sorden–Ebert *Logger's Words* 40 **Gt Lakes**, *Wanagan-man,* One who prepares camp for river-drivers. **1961** *Jrl. Amer. Folkl.* 74.2 **ME,** Well, he used to be wangan man up in the woods there, and he'd watch camp and tote-teams; he used to stay up there the year round. **1967** Pike *Tall Trees* 240 **NH,** In his younger days he had worked for the C.V.L. in the great north woods, and he too had "gone down the river." The river-drivers always put up their wangan on his meadow.

3 also *wangan camp, wanigan car:* The building or other shelter that houses the office of a logging or other work camp, where stores are kept and often sold to workers; (also *wangan store*) a company store in a logging or other camp. **chiefly ME, Gt Lakes** Cf **camp** n 1, **van** n

1902 *NY Times* (NY) 7 Dec 25/2 **ME,** There is nothing of which the men can rightfully complain unless it may be the excessive "wangan" charges. The "wangan" is a sort of general store, corresponding to the slop chest of the deep-water ship, from which the men can get tobacco, clothing, and other things in the woods camps. **1908** Day *King Spruce* 30 **ME,** Curiosity impelled him to ask what a "chaney man" was. "Why, a clerk—a camp clerk, time-keeper, wangan store overseer, supply accountant, and all that." *Ibid* 182, It [=a hand] was thrust out in welcome over the threshold of the wangan camp, and Britt hauled in his fellow-baron with boisterous greeting. *Ibid* 251, She led him away towards the office camp. . . In the wangan she faced him. **1910** Hodge *Hdbk. Amer. Indians* 2.910, *Wanigan.* . . A place in a lumber camp where accounts are kept and the men paid. **1914** [see **5** below]. **1924** in 2007 (acc) Lexis–Nexis Legal Research *State Case Law: MN* (Internet), Remer and his subcontractors maintained what are known as "Wanigans," from which the laborers were supplied with snuff, smoking tobacco, medicines, small articles of wearing apparel and the like. . . [I]t would be impracticable to run a [highway] construction camp without carrying tobacco and other articles such as were supplied to the men from the wanigans. **1926** Rickaby *Ballads Shanty-Boy* 238 **MI, MN, WI,** *Wanigan* (also *wangan* and *wanagan*). . . The store or canteen in the camp, maintained by the company, where the shanty boy obtained what he needed or wanted in the way of clothing, tobacco, etc. **1938** (1939) Holbrook *Holy Mackinaw* 265, *Wangan.* . . where the camp stores are kept; and the payroll charges for such goods. **1942** Rich *We Took to Woods* 184 **ME,** There is a sign in the bunk-house that reads, "Wangan open an hour after supper." That refers to the store where the cook sells candy, tobacco, snuff, and clothing. (It really is a big box in the kitchen, and the reason it isn't open all the time is that the cook doesn't want to be bothered in the middle of his baking to hand out and charge against wages a nickel's worth of makings.) [*DARE* Ed: Cf sense **5** below.] **1958** McCulloch *Woods Words* 207 **Pacific NW,** *Wanigan car*—A camp commissary and office car in a railroad car camp. **1965** Bowen *Alaskan Dict.* 34, *Wanigan.* . . the construction office on a job site or the wood's [sic] boss's shanty in lumbering.

4 as mass noun: Equipment and supplies for logging or camping; one's kit; also spec, stores kept for sale to loggers; the charges incurred for such stores; hence nouns *wangan bag, wangan box, wangan chest.* **scattered, but chiefly ME**

1889 in 1949 *Appalachia* 27.497 **ME,** Father found Reed stuck on the upper pitch having misjudged the water. He says that in the spring the driving boats run over after taking out the wangun. **1902** *Daily Kennebec Jrl.* (Augusta ME) 18 Feb 5/5, The logs had been driven under contract for so many years that there was very little wangan which belonged to the company, this necessitated the purchase of nearly everything. **1906** Hanks *Camp Kits* 25 **NEast,** Everything you take with you into the woods, except your guns and canoes, is known as the wangan. *Ibid* 36, The clothing and the things brought along for comfort will go into the two wangan bags. **1907** *Black Cat* June 19, Abe, limping about, bustled over to an ancient Wangan-chest, relic of his father's river-days. **1938** [see **3** above]. **1941** *AmSp* 16.234 **MI** [Lumberjack jargon], *Wangan* or *wannigan.* Debts incurred by lumberjacks at the cook shop. **1942** ME Univ. *Studies* 57.121, *Summary of Wangan Used at South Branch Operation During the Season of 1938*—Aspirin . . Atwoods bitters . . Blades, Gem razor . . Brushes, tooth . . Buttons, patent . . Candy [etc]. **1942** Rich *We Took to Woods* 183 **ME,** The cook may say, "I lost my wangan when the work boat swamped," and that means that his dishes are at the bottom of the lake. Or he may complain, "The wangan's runnin' low," meaning . . that he's short of food. Or a man may take his wangan and fly—leave the job with his little bundle of personal belongings. **1945** Hamlin *9 Mile Bridge* 40 **nME,** Cigarettes, plug tobacco, woolen socks, shirts and cotton work gloves are kept on

hand to sell to the men. Such supplies are part of the wangan—along with kitchen utensils, blankets and other office equipment. **1948** in 2007 (acc) Lexis–Nexis Legal Research *State Case Law: ME* (Internet), It was agreed that the decedent had been paid . . in full for his labor on logs delivered . . and that his wangan worth $263.25 and left in camp had been appropriated and used. . . [T]he plaintiff was entitled to recover. . . for the value of the supplies and equipment left in the camp. **1967** Pike *Tall Trees* 123 **NH,** A few dozen [horses] transported the C.V.L. rivermen's wangan (the tents, stores, blankets, and other impedimenta needed by the men) down on the drive. **1975** Gould *ME Lingo* 310, *Wangan.* . . The quickest definition of *wangan* is woods supplies; Maine canoeists have rope-handled wooden boxes for carrying their *wangan,* and these are *wangan* boxes.

5 A box or cupboard for stores or personal possessions, now esp a wood—or recently plastic—box for carrying supplies in a canoe. [Prob abbr for *wanigan box,* ~ *chest;* see **4** above] **chiefly NEast**

1910 Hodge *Hdbk. Amer. Indians* 2.910, *Wanigan.* . . A large chest in which the lumbermen of Maine and Minnesota keep their spare clothing, pipes, tobacco, etc. **1914** *DN* 4.82 **ME, nNH,** *Waungin.* . . The store or supply-room in a lumber-camp. Locker in a camp or "bateau." **1950** *Daily Messenger* (Canandaigua NY) 5 June 4/1, Today's camping family takes enough gear to fill the biggest wangan in the Maine woods. **2002** in 2007 *DARE* File—Internet, I just got a Wanigan the other day and I am currently stocking it. Does anyone here have experience with these boxes? **2005** *Ibid* **VT,** I owned a plastic Wanigin in the 90's that had removeable [sic] shelves and a wash basin and backpack straps. I loved it! **2007** *Ibid* **VA,** The Cedar Island Canoes "Wood Canvas Wanigan" provides rigid, spacious, water-resistant storage without sacrificing the traditional look of the wood canvas canoe. These wanigans are custom-built to fit the curvature of a canoe.

6 A small building on skids or sled runners that can be moved when necessary or even serve as a means of transport in arctic conditions; a temporary or makeshift cabin. **chiefly AK**

1938 *Anchorage Daily Times* (AK) 4 Nov 8/3, My outfit consisted of a Sjolseth drill, tractor and wanagan. Dut [sic] to the stormy weather . . I replaced the use of tents with a shack on skids. **1943** in 2007 *DARE* File—Internet **AK,** A wanigan is a small building on skids that may be moved anywhere. People in Fairbanks have them and when they buy a new lot they rent a tractor and move their "wanigan" to their new lot— thus their homes go with them. Also we use wanigans which are moved along as the job progresses—the fellows keep warm in them and also eat their dinner there during their shift—of course our wanigans are rough. **1949** *Survey* 85.302 **OR,** The industry is based no longer in isolated logging camps, with lonely men living in "wannigans" dragged through the forests on sled-like runners. **1953** *Jessen's Weekly* (Fairbanks AK) 11 June 10/1, [Advt:] *Wannigan* and *Lot*—Dandy little cabin on beautiful wooded 60 x 150 ft. lot. **1953** *Coshocton Tribune* (OH) 24 Dec 7/3, This is the Army's new all-purpose cold-climate sled-room, to be used for quarters and office space. Called the Wanigan, it . . can house four people and is designed to be pulled around on ski runners. **1953** *AK Sportsman* Dec 26, A wanigan on runners . . drawn by a tractor, now meets planes, and mail, freight and people go to town in the wanigan. **1958** *San Mateo Times* (CA) 6 Jan 5/4, The navy's first tractor train for Deepfreeze III, composed of nine 20-ton and three 10-ton sleds, . . three wanigan living quarters, spare parts and some fuel, traveled 645 miles from Little America to Byrd Station. **1965** Bowen *Alaskan Dict.* 34, *Wanigan.* . . A shack set up on timber skids so that it can be pulled by a tractor for relocation. **1988** *Fairbanks Daily News–Miner* (AK) 7 Sept 3, My father. . . moved his family from a beautiful home in Wisconsin with all the modern conveniences, to a one-room wanigan in Fairbanks with no conveniences, not even water. **2006** *DARE* File **AK,** When I lived in Fairbanks in the 70s and 80s a fishing shanty used in ice fishing was called a wanigan ['wɑnɪgɪn] as was a small enclosed shelter put up at the door of a trailer where you'd take off your jacket and boots before going inside.

7 An addition or entry porch, esp one attached to a mobile home. **AK**

1953 *Jessen's Weekly* (Fairbanks AK) 23 July 10/3, [Advt:] *For Sale*— 1948 24-ft. California Trailer with excellently-built 8x16 wanagin. **1973** *Valdez–Copper Basin News* (AK) 16 Aug 11/1, [Advt:] *For Sale or Lease With Option to Buy.* 3 bedroom 1971 Marlette Trailer with tipouts and wanigan. **1987** *Fairbanks Daily News–Miner* (AK) 21 June sec H 4, Trailers and wannigans are slowly giving way to frame homes and landscaped yards. **2000** *NADS Letters* **AK,** "Wannigan" . . meaning an enclosed porch/entry-way outside of the house as in "Take your boots off in the wannigan!" **2005** in 2007 *DARE* File—Internet **AK**, [Advt:] 1972 12x65 Broadmore mobile home with 8x20 addition. . . The well-built unfinished entry wannigan is ideal for storage, or maybe a workshop area. Who knows, even a 4th bedroom is a possibility! **2006** [see **6** above]. **2007** *DARE* File—Internet **AK**, Wannigan. . . "mud room" type addition to those dilapidated trailers and shacks. Often not built according to OSHA and hence develops crazy leans, floor sags, and is even subject to collapse!

wanigan car   See **wanigan 3**

wankapin n   Also *walker pin, wampapin, wankopin, waukapin, wanquapin, wonkapin;* for addit varr see quots [The geography of early attestations suggests a borrowing from an AmInd language of eastern Virginia; perh cognate with Ojibwa *wagipin* (see quots 1886, 1911).] **chiefly VA, DC** Cf **yonkapin** =**water chinquapin.** Note: In quot 1899 the term is applied to **spatterdock,** perh erroneously.

[**1767** in 1991 Lillard *Lillard Family* 2.B-39 **eVA,** This Deponent . . saith that . . he well remembers to have heard his Father say that the Wankapin branch was either the Beginning or ending of Alexander's Land.] **1832** Kennedy *Swallow Barn* 1.232 **seVA,** This fine garden of wankopins and snake-collards. **1878** Sunderland *Sketch William Gunton* 15 **DC** (as of c1810), Nearly the whole of the lower part of what is now called the Mall was then a piece of wet, marshy ground covered with weeds and wancopins. **1878** *Atlantic Mth.* 42.220 **nwTN,** From the tangle of curious forms the eye selects two noble flowers: our familiar Northern waterlily . . ; and another grander flower, the Wampapin Lily, the queen of American flowers. **1883** U.S. Natl. Museum *Bulletin* 26.17 **DC,** Along the edges of the river [=Anacostia] and of the "guts" . . grow the lily-pads *(Nuphar advena)* and wanquapins *(Nelumbium luteum).* [**1886** Cuoq *Lexique Algonquine* 417, Wagipin, *racine tortue qui pousse dans l'eau* [=*twisted root* that grows in water].] **1886** *Bot. Gaz.* 11.35 **neVA,** It [=*Nelumbium luteum*] is perfectly well known to the inhabitants of this part of the state by the name of *Wankapin* (if this is the correct spelling), the first vowel having the same sound as in *want.* **1896** *Jrl. Amer. Folkl.* 9.181 **sIN,** *Nelumbo lutea* . . wonkapin. **1898** *Military Surgeon* 1.506 **DC,** The swampy lowlands . . were covered with shrubby growths and bramble and waukapin bushes. **1899** *Forest & Stream* 53.293 **neVA,** This cove is deep, with great beds of wankapins. The great rhizomes of this lily are sometimes exposed on the streets of Washington as an insect destroyer, under the name of Walker Pin roots. The origin of the name Wankapin is obscure; probably to distinguish this little yellow water lily from the large white nelumbium, called the water chinquapin. [**1911** Blair *Ind. Tribes Gt. Lakes* 1.116, [Footnote:] This was the rhizome of *Nelumbo lutea,* called . . by the Ojibwa tribes *wâgipin* or *wargipin* ("crooked root"). . . —Wm. R. Gerard.] [**1928** Powell *Hist. Alexandria VA* 26, He passed the mouth of Waukapin Run nearly opposite the lower point of Analoston.] **1950** Gray–Fernald *Manual of Botany* 641, *N[elumbo] lutea.* . . Yellow Nelumbo, Water-Chinquapin, Pond-nuts, Wonkapin. . . Tubers farinaceous and edible. [**2010** *DARE* File—Internet **neVA,** Wankopin Branch, which crosses Route 50 just east of Middleburg . . was named by the Piscataway Indians. . . Most locals used to pronounce the stream "Walkerpen" or "Wankipin," with the accent on the first syllable.]

wannagan, wannigan   See **wanigan**

wannut   See **walnut**

wanquapin   See **wankapin**

want v[1]   Usu |wɑnt, wɔnt|; also **esp Sth, S Midl** |wɔnt|; also |(h)wʌnt| Pronc-spp *ont, wan, whant, whunt, wo(u)nt*
A Proncs.

1846 in 1956 Eliason *Tarheel Talk* 320 **cnNC,** Wount. **1885** *Century Illustr. Mag.* 29.681 **sAppalachians,** I don't whant ter hurt ye. **1892** *DN* 1.242 **cwMO,** Want. In Kansas City one often hears "what do you whunt (=[hwɔnt])?" **1938** in 1993 Major *Calling the Wind* 97 [Black], Ah just wan them white folks t try t make me tell *who* is *in* the party n who *ain!* **1943** *LANE* Map 699 *(I want to get off)* **NEng,** [Most proncs are of the types [wɒ⁽ᵊ⁾nt, wɔ⁽ᵊ⁾nt]; occas [wɑnt]; infreq [wʌnt, wɒnt, wɛnt].] **1957** *Sat. Eve. Post Letters* **sUT,** My grandmother. . . used to say, "I don't *whante* to." **1961** Kurath–McDavid *Pronc. Engl.* 163, The regional incidence of /ɔ/ and /ɑ/ after /w/ varies from word to word. The following table exhibits the predominant usage in selected subareas of the Eastern States along with the usage of substantial minorities. There seems to be no marked social cleavage anywhere. [For *want:* Upstate

N.Y. ɔ∼ɑ; Metropolitan N.Y. ɑ; Philadelphia area ɔ∼ɑ; W. Va. ɔ∼ɑ; Eastern Va. ɔ; Eastern S.C. ɔ.] **1962** Steinbeck *Travels* 202 **TX,** "Do you want a straight pin or a safety pin?" "Aont [=I want] a fountain pin," she said. **1972** Thomas *Pop. Dict. Ozarks Talk* 95, Wont: . . Want; wish. **1999** Proulx *Close Range* 67 **WY,** Never lived on a ranch. Never wont to. **2001** in 2007 *DARE* File—Internet, When i go to buy this cd and wount to lission first, you wount let me. **2007** *Ibid* **PA,** Hey bro just whunt to see whats up. *Ibid* **MS,** Every one has a cell phone and every one wount's to be a Cop. *Ibid* **TN,** Whant to grow your bussiness [sic]. *Ibid,* What we have in common . . is that we don't wont to talk or call people on the phone . . and we don't wont to talk about something that they don't wont to talk about. *Ibid,* My computer doesn't whant to read any other form of disc beside DVD's. . . [M]y computer has not been whanting to read audio cd's. **2007** *DARE* File **GA** (as of c1970), I remember being surprised to hear Southerners (and even people from as far north as southern Illinois) pronounce *want* as [wount]. **2008** in 2009 *DARE* File—Internet **csKY,** They wont to fill the prisons & jails with people that have drug problems.

B Gram forms.

1 pres (exc 3rd pers sg): usu *want;* also *wants.* **chiefly Sth, S Midl** *esp freq among Black speakers*

1843 (1916) Hall *New Purchase* 216 **IN,** I wants any how to go over to the post-office. **1894** *Scribner's Mag.* 16.248 **LA** [Black], You wants to know the secret o' my poweh? **1899** Chesnutt *Conjure Woman* 78 **csNC** [Black], I wants you ter run dis yer plantation. **1917** in 1993 Adero *Up South* 52 **New Orleans LA** [Black], [Letter in *Chicago Defender:*] We want more understanding about it for there is a great many wants to get ready for that day. **a1930** in 1991 Hughes–Hurston *Mule Bone* 31 **cFL** [Black], Mist' Clarke, Ah wants uh warrant took out fuh Jim Weston. **1945** FWP *Lay My Burden Down* 110 **LA** (as of c1865) [Black], I wants to hear him grumble like he used to. **1960** Lee *Mockingbird* 129 **sAL** [Black], I wants to know why you bringin' white chillun to nigger church. **1967** *DARE* Tape **AZ1,** For ones who wants to learn foreign languages. **1968** *PADS* 50.34 **swTN** [Black], Four type I [=old, with little educ] informants . . frequently use the uninflected form for the third singular. The inflected form is often used for the first and second person form, singular and plural. Such forms as *I wants, I carries, she do, you needs, we has* occur frequently in their recorded free conversation. **1970** *DARE* (Qu. U16, *If somebody was caught short of money and went to a friend to get some*) Inf **TX106,** I wants to borrows. [Inf Black] **1986** Pederson *LAGS Concordance,* 1 inf, **neTN,** People wants it; 1 inf, **nwFL,** I wants; 1 inf, **ceAR,** Mamma, I wants a apple; 1 inf, **cMS,** If I wants; 1 inf, **ceLA,** Some wants it black; 1 inf, **cTN,** Some just wants it black; 1 inf, **cwAR,** Some wants it both; 1 inf, **cnAR,** Lot of them wants it done; 1 inf, **cnAR,** The ones that wants it; 1 inf, **ceTX,** They wants me; 1 inf, **cnGA,** Some wants; 1 inf, **cnLA,** Peoples now wants the biggest; 1 inf, **cTN,** People wants them; 1 inf, **cnGA,** These . . people . . wants to bus these niggers; 1 inf, **ceAR,** People wants to do it; 1 inf, **nwFL,** I wants to find that out; 1 inf, **ceLA,** I wants to go; 1 inf, **csLA,** I wants to go to bed; 1 inf, **ceMS,** People who wants to go to school; 1 inf, **neTN,** Twins wants to stay close together. [8 of 20 infs Black; for addit exx see the *Concordance.*]

2 pres 3rd pers sg: usu *wants;* also *want. esp freq among Black speakers*

1986 Pederson *LAGS Concordance,* 1 inf, **cwTN,** She want me to do that; 1 inf, **seTN,** She want me to go; 1 inf, **csGA,** He want me to go; 1 inf, **cwMS,** She go where she want. [All infs Black]

3 past: usu *wanted;* also *want.*

1899 Chesnutt *Conjure Woman* 51 **csNC** [Black], One er Mars Marrabo's sons rid up . . en say his wife wuz monst'us sick, en he want his mammy ter len' 'im a 'oman fer ter nuss his wife. **1937** in 1976 *Weevils in the Wheat* 284 **VA** [Black], When Jeams was mustered out, he want to come to his home; so we came here. **1986** Pederson *LAGS Concordance,* 1 inf, **nwAR,** Nobody wouldn't give him what he want for her; 1 inf, **cwGA,** Want it = wanted it; 1 inf, **cnAL,** Want it; 1 inf, **cwGA,** Want to buy them; 1 inf, **cAR,** Want to get up = wanted to; 1 inf, **cwFL,** She want to go = she wanted to go; 1 inf, **cnLA,** She want to know from them did they think it was right; 1 inf, **ceFL,** If you want to plant it = if you wanted; 1 inf, **neMS,** Want to quit = wanted to quit; 1 inf, **csTX,** Want to talk = wanted to talk; 1 inf, **seMS,** I had some of the children that want to write. [*DARE* Ed: All of these are marked as exx of the "deleted preterite."]

C Syntax.

1 in phrr *want (that) one should:* To want one to. [Despite *OED2,* which labels this constr "*U.S.,*" it occurs in 18th-

and 19th- cent Brit Engl, chiefly among Scots and Anglo-Irish writers.] **formerly chiefly NEast, now more widespread**

1745 in 1822 Brainerd *Memoirs* 218 **CT,** They replied, "they wanted Christ should wipe their hearts quite clean." **1833** Neal *Down-Easters* 1.80 **NEng,** I want you should give me a letter o' recommend to Pheladelphy. **1840** in 1853 York *Memoir* 60 **ceMA,** I want that you should pray more in faith. **1853** in 1884 Thoreau *Summer* 164 **ceMA,** I wanted that he should straighten his back. **1856** in 1862 Colt *Went to KS* 117 **NY,** The men then wanted I should look out. **1860** in 1955 Lee *Mormon Chron.* 1.285 **IL,** He . . wantd I should come & help him out of Trouble. **1884** *Century Illustr. Mag.* 29.19 **OH,** I want you should put these in shape. **1917** *DN* 4.403 **neOH,** Want (I, he, *etc.*), should. . . Want that I (he, *etc.*) should, etc. . . Also N. Eng., N.Y. **1919** *DN* 5.76 **NH,** *Want . . should.* Quite common in rural New Hampshire. **1927** *AmSp* 2.366 **cwWV,** I want he should sell me his team. **1929** *AmSp* 5.128 **ME,** "I want you should," . . [was] characteristic of Maine speech. **1942** Rawlings *Cross Creek* 61 **nFL,** They don't want I should take it. **1956** Moody *Home Ranch* 124 **CO** (as of 1911), Want I should show you on Clay? **1962** Steinbeck *Travels* 92 **NY,** You want I should drive twenty miles because I got roots? **1975** Chalmers *Better* 59 **wNC, eTN,** Doc wants you should come and he'p him. **1980** *DARE* File **cnMA** (as of c1915), Some people of my grandmother's generation used *want* in rather an old-fashioned, perhaps countrified way: "Do you want I should pay now?" "I want you should remember what I'm going to tell you now." **2001** *DARE* File—Internet **NYC,** I want you should affix that red ball with some Krazy glue to the downtown local track at 42nd Street. **2007** *Ibid* **UT,** I think he wanted that I should read the Bible in Greek . . does that help?

2 foll by adv of place (esp *in, out*), with ellipsis of *to come, to go, to get,* or the like. [Scots, nIr dial, perh reinforced by parallel constrs in other Germanic langs] **widespread exc NEng** See Map Cf **like** v[1] **C2, need 3**

1843 (1916) Hall *New Purchase* 145 **IN,** "Maybe," says she to herself, "its some poor Injin wants in." **1853** in 1956 Eliason *Tarheel Talk* 145 **NC,** When the railroad is finished it will be a convenience . . especially to your children, for they will be of an age to want abroad. **1878** *Appletons' Jrl.* 5.413 **PA,** The Pennsylvanian. . . says "I want out" and "I want down" for "I want to get out" and "I want to get down." **1887** Kirkland *Zury* 157 **IL,** "What did you say?" "I want ou'doors." "You want out-doors." "That's wut I said! I want aout." At last she [=a teacher from Boston] understood this Westernism, new to her. To "want out" is to desire to go out. **1893** *KS Univ. Qrly.* 1.142 **KS,** 'He wants out,' 'I want in.' **1902** *DN* 2.249 **sIL,** *Want in, want out.* To want to go in or out, but never with the verb go. **1903** *DN* 2.336 **seMO,** *Want in, want out.* **1904** *DN* 2.422 **nwAR,** *Want in, want out, want up, want down, want here.* . . To wish to come (get, go) in, etc. 'Baby wants up.' **1905** *DN* 3.66 **eNE,** *Want in* (*out, up, down, off, on*). Very common. **1908** *German Amer. Annals* 10.51 **sePA,** "Open the door, I want out." . . "Want in," "want up," "want down," all used. fr. Pa. Ger. *will 'naus;* Ger. *will hinaus.* **1914** *DN* 4.164 **NW,** The dog wants in. **1921** *DN* 5.110 **CA,** *To want* in. **1925** *AmSp* 1.152, In Los Angeles, where not Far-Westernisms but Middle-Westernisms are prevalent, "I want out," and "The cat wants in" are as common as huge geraniums. **1931** [see **C3** below]. **1931** Jacobson *Milwaukee Dial.* 18 **WI,** *Want in.* . . common. *Ibid* 19 **WI,** *Want out.* **1937** in 1983 Truman *Dear Bess* 396 **MO,** So I'll have to tell Mr. Roosevelt he doesn't want on the Federal Reserve Board. **1949** Kurath *Word Geog.* 30, The records of the *Linguistic Atlas* show that *I want off* is in common use in nearly all of the Midland, except among the best educated, and that it is not current at all in the North and the South. **1954** Roberts *I Bought Dog* 7 **seKY,** Hurry up! I want in there. **c1955** Reed–Person *Ling. Atlas Pacific NW,* 10 infs, I want off; 1 inf, Wanted off. **1965–70** *DARE* (Qu. JJ31a, . . *To a bus driver:* "*Please stop at the next corner—I want _____.*") 186 Infs, **widespread exc NEng,** Off; 22 Infs, **scattered, but infreq NEast, NCent,** Out. **1975** Allen *LAUM* 2.71 **Upper MW, esp NE, IA** (as of c1950), I *want to get off* at the next corner. . . In the statement above, made to a streetcar conductor or bus operator, most infs. in the investigated areas use the full expression *want to get off.* . . But a significant proportion of U[pper] M[idwest] speakers, one-fifth, offer a simple variant *want off,* with the meaning of the verb of motion borne entirely by *off.* **1990** Pederson *LAGS Regional Matrix* 215, 112 infs, **chiefly AR, TN, nAL, nGA,** Want off. **2003** Benson *This Girl* 74, Only the results from *want by, want off, want out,* and possibly *want in* support the hypothesis of a stronger Midland distribution for the forms of W[ant] + P[repositional] A[dverb]. *Ibid* 131, The hypothesis that *want* + prepositional adverb is

used more in informal styles than more formal styles is supported, though not overwhelmingly.

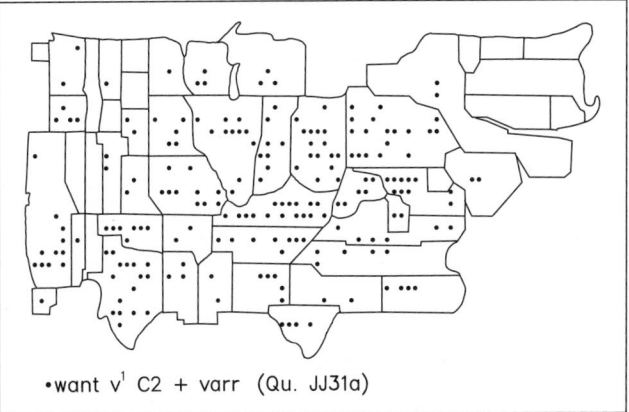

•want v[1] C2 + varr (Qu. JJ31a)

3 foll by past pple or ppl adj with ellipsis of *to be* or *to get.* [Prob of Scots, nIr orig; cf **need 2**] **chiefly Midl, esp wPA** Note: Ellipsis of the infinitive is a std option when the subj of the infinitive (or participial) phr is different from that of *want,* as in "He wants the dog (to be) fed," or "This is the page I want (to get) copied." Such exx are not included here.

1931 *AmSp* 7.20 **swPA,** *Want.* Used with certain prepositions to replace infinitive construction. "Conductor, I want out at Chestnut Street." "The cat wants in." More rarely used with past participles, as, "The dog wants freed." **1970** GA Dept. Ag. *Farmers Market Bulletin* 16 Sept 8/2 **TN,** To all those who want rid of something, . . may I plead with you to read Rachel Carson's *Silent Spring?* **1982** Heat Moon *Blue Highways* 33 **cTN,** I said to Thurmond, "Thurmond, unless you want shut of me, call the doctor." **1982** McCool *Sam McCool's Pittsburghese* 37 **PA,** The customer wants served. **1993** *DARE* File **ePA, wWV,** Just yesterday, when my husband called me to say he had finished teaching, I heard myself saying, "Do you want picked up?" *Ibid* **Pittsburgh PA,** Someone from Pittsburgh, b. 1947 . . said when he was growing up, he was frequently asked by his father, "You want spanked?" **1999** *AmSp* 74.145, *Want* + *V-en* shows clear regional patterning . . : of the 108 attestations, 65 (60%) occur in or just adjacent to the traditionally defined North Midland region, and 37 (34%) occur in the South Midlands, with the Appalachian area of West Virginia, western Virginia and western North Carolina, and eastern Kentucky and eastern Tennessee especially well represented. **2001** *DARE* File **PA,** Who Wants Dipped In Chocolate? [In the July issue of the trade magazine *Corporate & Incentive Travel,* p. 40.] **2002** *DARE* File—Internet **seKY,** If there was anything wrong with me, I wanted rid of it. **2004** *DARE* File **Pittsburgh PA,** The cat wants fed.

D Sense.

To forecast—in phr *the paper wants rain* and varr. [PaGer] **PA**

[**1924** Lambert *PA Ger. Dict.* 180, Di zeidung will schnee hawwe. [literally =The newspaper wants to have snow.]] **1934** *Language* 10.4 **cPA,** The paper wants rain. **1967** *DARE* FW Addit **sePA,** The paper wants rain = the paper calls for rain. **1982** Barrick *Coll.* **csPA,** *Want*—call for, predict. "The paper wants rain." **1987** *Jrl. Engl. Ling.* 20.2.176 **ePA,** *Want*—'to forecast' . . as in *The newspaper wants rain.* . . Despite the fact that twenty-one informants utilize this item, fifteen of them are 40 or older. The twenty-one informants represent various educational groups. **1997** in 1999 Millersville Univ. Center for PA Ger. Studies *Jrl.* Fall 22, To want rain. If you read in the paper that it will rain, you say the paper _____. 10% [of 40 infs], *wants rain;* 67.5%, *is predicting rain;* 30%, *is calling for rain.*

wan't v[2] See **be C2b**

want v[3] See **will v A**

want in See **want** v[1] **C2**

want (one) should See **want** v[1] **C1**

want out See **want** v[1] **C2**

want that (one) should See **want** v[1] **C1**

want to know(, I) See **know D1**

wanut   See **walnut**

wap n[1]   See **wop** n[1]

wap n[2]

A **mooneye 1** (here: *Hiodon alosoides*).

   1930 U.S. Bur. Fisheries *Bulletin 1929* 45.162, Gold-eyed Mooneye. *Hiodon alosoides.* . . "Toothed herring;" "wap."

wap n[3]   See **wapatuli**

wapaloosie n   Cf *DS* CC17

An imaginary animal.

   1910 Cox *Fearsome Creatures* 25, The wapaloosie . . is about the size of a sausage dog. . . The wapaloosie, according to lumber jacks, lives upon shelf fungus or conchs exclusively, and he is able to get them with ease. . . [He] has feet and toes like those of a woodpecker, and he humps himself along like a measuring worm. **1920** Lewis *Main Street* 319 MN, As long as I can . . tell whoppers to Olaf about his daddy's adventures in the woods, and how he snared a wapaloosie and knew Paul Bunyan, why, I don't mind being a bum.

wapato n   Also *wap(pa)to, whapto;* for addit varr see quots [Chinook Jargon *wappatoo,* perh of Algonquian orig] **Pacific NW**

An **arrowhead 1** (here: *Sagittaria cuneata* or *S. latifolia*).

   1805 (1905) Clark *Orig. Jrls. Lewis & Clark Exped.* 3.196, This root they call *Wap-pa-to* . . has an agreeable taste and answers verry well in place of bread. **1805** (1807) Gass *Jrl.* 230 wWA, We got some dogs and roots from the natives. The roots . . are called whapto; resemble a potatoe when cooked, and are about as big as a hen's egg. *Ibid* 246, We . . procured a few roots, called Wapto. **1830** Rafinesque *Med. Flora* 2.259 OR, Sagittaria . . *Wapatu* of Oregon tribes, . . valuable esculent roots. **1831** Cox *Advent. Columbia R.* 128 OR, We also got a quantity of excellent roots, called by the Indians *wappittoo:* in size they resemble a small potato, for which it is a good substitute when roasted or boiled. [**1863** Gibbs *Chinook Jargon* 28, *Wap'-pa-too.* . . Quære u[nde] d[erivatum] [=Query whence derived]. *The root of the Sagitaria* [sic] *sagittifolia . . ; the potato.* The word is neither Chinook nor Chihalis, but is everywhere in common use.] **1913** *Torreya* 13.227 NW, *Sagittaria latifolia.* . . This is the famous wapato, wappatoo, or duck potato of the Northwestern States. **1940** Writers' Program *Oregon* 21, Another root is the wappato, a marsh bulb growing in great quantity along the lowlands of the Columbia, on Chewaucan Marsh in Lake County, and in many other shallow lakes. **1967** *DARE* Tape WA19, They used . . wapato . . a sort of potato that grew . . in the swamp. . . Came to the top of the water. . . The potato . . was down in the mud and the Indian women used to . . stand in these swamps and would work the potatoes out of the mud. **1967** *DARE* Wildfl QR Pl.1 [=*Sagittaria latifolia*] Inf OR12, Arrowhead, ['wapəto]—Indians ate roots. **1976** Bruce *How to Grow Wildflowers* 278, Sagittaria—Arrowhead. . . Common names for various species include Swamp-potato, Duck-potato, and the Indian name "Wapato."

wapatuli n   Also sp *wampa toole, w(h)opatuli, whopatooli(e);* abbr *wap, w(h)op;* for addit varr see quots [Etym unknown] **orig chiefly WI, MN; now more widespread**

A homemade alcoholic drink consisting of any combination of hard liquors, with other beverages or fruit sometimes added; by ext, an occasion at which this is consumed.

   1980 *DARE* File **Madison WI** [Heard on UW campus], All the dental students could get alcohol from the labs. So when they had a wapatuli party, it was really something. **1981** *Ibid* **Madison WI**, Wampa toole party [caption on a photograph of people at a party]. [**1982** *Capital Times* (Madison WI) 11 Feb 21, Southern Wisconsin Area Tall Singles is planning a cross country ski outing. . . The evening will include wapatuli chili and hot wine.] **1991** *Ibid* 4 Apr sec A 3/5 **csWI**, The woman had consumed five beers and two cups of wapatulie, a mixture of numerous alcoholic beverages. **2003** *DARE* File—Internet, In Wisconsin, college students celebrate the transition to adulthood by throwing a "Wapatuli" party in which mass quantities of different varieties of hard liquor are poured willy-nilly into a garbage can. *Ibid* **seMN**, We are hosting a most debobalicious whopatoolie, and anybody is welcome. **2004** *Ibid* **WI**, I drank . . Kool-aide [sic], vodka, beer, coffee ground [sic], jungle juice, more vodka and some Jager. All in one 32oz cup. Ahhhh, college. . . [Comment:] In Waukesha, we used to call that Wapatuli. *Ibid*, Wopatuli. . . Who's had it? . . Alot of people haven't

had this. **2005** *Badger Herald* (Madison WI) 26 Oct (Internet) **csWI**, As individuals switch from kegs and half-barrels to . . tubs of whop, they put themselves at a far greater risk. **2005** *DARE* File—Internet, Question *wap, Wapatollie, Wop.* . . A wap. . . is a mixture of fruit, hard alcohol, and Juice. **2006** *Ibid* **WI**, [It] reminds me of a bad high school party, when everybody would pour all the alcoholic drinks into a punch bowl. [Comment:] Here in Wisconsin, that is known as a "wapatuli". *Ibid* **West**, Keg! Whopatooi! grilln! bonfire! *Ibid* **MN**, People would come from miles around . . to drink our wop with a brat and 'kraut. *Ibid*, In most of NY, it was always made with fresh fruit and Everclear, and ti [sic] was called Wapatuli. **2007** *Ibid* **ceWI**, [Ripon College website:] Kegs of beer and common containers (party balls, pony kegs, WOP containers, etc.) are prohibited in student rooms. *Ibid* **nID**, He came home [from World Campus Afloat in 1974] with a Wapatuli recipe. . . You get a garbage can, dump fifths of vodka, rum, whiskey, gin . . and mix in Seven-Up, fruit juices. *Ibid* **csWI**, Across the bar, . . [he] was settling into a private Wapatuli party of wine, gin, and scotch. *Ibid* **Minneapolis MN**, *Whopatooli. Ibid*, I am making whop or as some call it hunch punch. *Ibid* **nIL**, Alcoholic Drink? . . Whopatuli. **2007** *DARE* File **cMN** (as of 1976–80), One of my coworkers claims that she called it wapatuli back when she was going to college at Gustavus Adolfus.

wap-jawed   See **whopper-jawed**

wappato   See **wapato**

wappergee adj   Cf **gee-hawed,** *skew-gee* (at **skew- a**), **whopper-jawed 2**

   1959 *VT Hist.* 27.166 **nwVT**, *Wappergee.* . . Rickety. Rare.

wapper-jaw   See **whopper-jaw**

wapper-jawed   See **whopper-jawed**

‡**wapple-eyed** adj   [Cf *OED2 wapper-eyed* (at *wapper* v.[2] 3) "dial."; *EDD wapper-eyed*]

   1937 Sandoz *Slogum* 199 **NE** (as of 1900–20), That wapple-eyed Preacher Zug on Cedar Flats.

wapple-jawed   See **wobble-jawed**

wappus   See **wamus**

wappy-jawed   See **whopper-jawed**

waps   See **wasp 1c**

wapse   See **wopse**

wapsed down   See **wopse v 3**

wapsided   See **wopsided**

wapsy adj   See **wopsy** adj

wapsy n   See **wopsy** n

wapto   See **wapato**

war v[1]   See **be A5**

w'ar v[2]   See **wear** v

war n   See **wire**

war bag n   Also *war sack* [Transf from *war bag* (or *budget, bundle*) in ref to bag of amulets carried by an Indian war chief; sometimes applied to bag of supplies carried by warriors] **scattered, but chiefly West**

A drawstring bag or sack used for carrying one's personal effects; a duffel bag; a ditty bag; transf: the contents of such a bag or sack.

   1864 in 1956 *TN Hist. Qrly.* 15.167, We started back with good clothing and our war bags full of provisions. . . My new clothes, horse and last but not least, my war sack, being duly inspected and pronounced all right, I once more entered upon my duties. **1880** *Scribner's Mth.* 19.930 **Rocky Mts**, In place of trunks or valises, everything is stuffed into canvas cylinders each about the size of a section of stove-pipe, which close by means of puckering strings at the top. Nearly everything that each one carries must be inclosed in this one war-bag. **1887** (1888) Thayer *Marvels New West* 571 **CO**, On top of this the precious war-sack is fastened with especial care, and thus . . the cowboy sallies forth. **1903** (1965) Adams *Log Cowboy* 190 **West,** The . . guards . . ransacked their war bags, and donned their best toggery. **1908** Breck *Way of the Woods* 48 **NEng**, It [=extra duffle] is generally stored in an extra receptacle called the war-bag (duffle-bag, wangan-bag, dunnage-bag). **1910** Bronson *Reminiscences Ranchman* 32 **WY,** 'Bout two jumps an' a twist an' I allow he'll jes nachally fall t' pieces, 'n' we'll have t' bunch up th' *re*-mains in a war sack 'n' send 'em t' his ma. **1913** Beach *Iron Trail* 50 **AK,** He beheld a huge, loose-hung man of tremendous girth, with a war-bag in his hand and a wide black hat. [**1914** *DN* 4.165 **AZ,** *War-bag.* . . Roll of bedding, etc.] **1916** Kephart *Camping & Woodcraft* 1.164, *Dunnage Bag.*—A common sailor's bag or "war bag" (simple canvas sack closed by a puckering cord). **1933** *AmSp* 8.1.31 **nwTX** [Ranch diction], *War bag.* A receptacle for one's extra clothes, often a flour sack or pillow slip. **1956** Moody *Home Ranch* 202 **CO** (as of 1911), When you went to work on a ranch, nobody ever said, "This will be your bunk." You looked around till you found one without a blanket on it, then pushed your war sack underneath and moved in. **1981** *KS Qrly.* 13.2.71, *Warbag.* . . a cowboy's personal effects, kept in some kind of bag or sack, usually of canvas and handmade; word describes both bag and gear. **2005** in 2007 *DARE* File—Internet **Los Angeles CA,** The city . . only issues you your gun, sambrown and accessories, a flashlite, hat, raincoat, jacket, and 3 uniforms—you end up paying for the PT gear, tennis shoes, "war bag", dress shoes and boots, and add'l firearms ammo. **2007** *Ibid,* Terms used by Marines. . . *Ditty bag*—a caring [sic] bag for misc. items, also called a war bag. *Ibid* **TX,** I also carry a 30GB USB drive in my war bag which I use for backup when on the road, but it's getting a bit old and I'm starting to worry a bit about it.

War between the North and the South n   Also *War of the North and the South;* for addit varr see quots

The American Civil War.

  1865 *Old Guard* 3.553, Until the late war between the North and the South, America . . if we except its discovery by Columbus, had been distinguished by no great historical events. **1898** *N. Amer. Rev.* 166.231, They have . . established under the eyes of the people of this country almost as complete a system of slavery as that which existed here previous to the war between the North and the South. **1943** *LANE* Map 551 *(The Civil War)* 2 inf, **CT, NH,** War between the North and the South. **1966** Dakin *Dial. Vocab. Ohio R. Valley* 2.516, *The War between* (sometimes *of*) *the North and the South* is . . occasional in eastern Kentucky. These terms . . are much less common above the Ohio and limited almost entirely to the southernmost parts of the Northwest. **1969** *S. Speech Jrl.* 34.3.200, *The War Between the North and the South* has a peculiar distribution. Far less common than *War Between the States,* it occurs almost always in the speech of older and less-educated informants. It thus contrasts with *War Between the States,* which is used primarily by younger speakers. Geographically its principal concentration is in the lower Potomac Valley and upper Chesapeake Bay, where, as a territorial rather than an ideological designation, it expresses the neutrality that region sought in vain. **1989** Pederson *LAGS Tech. Index* 314 **Gulf Region,** 21 infs, War between (the) North (and) South.

War between the States n   chiefly Sth, S Midl

The American Civil War.

  1868 Stephens *Constitutional View of the Late War Between the States* [title]. **1934** *Sun* (Baltimore MD) 5 June 14/7 *(Hench Coll.),* There was a time when it was almost worth one's life in the city of Richmond to refer to the Civil War as the Civil War. The Richmonder who held the memories of the sixties close to his heart always called it the War Between the States. **1943** *LANE* Map 551 *(The Civil War)* 3 infs, **ME, MA,** War between the States; 1 inf, **cwCT,** If you talk to a Southerner and you want to please him, call it the War between the States. **c1960** *Wilson Coll.* **csKY,** *War Between the States* is a very rare usage; the regular term is Civil War. **1966** Dakin *Dial. Vocab. Ohio R. Valley* 2.516, *The Civil War.* . . The Southerner's traditional refusal to recognize the war as either civil war or rebellion is well known, and the Northerner's view that secession was little more than open rebellion is equally so. It is not surprising, then, that throughout Kentucky the neutral term *The War between the States* is still quite commonly used. **1969** *S. Speech Jrl.* 34.3.200, *The War Between the States* occurs only three times in New England. . . It is very rare in the Middle Atlantic states . . and in the border states of Delaware and Maryland. In the South, as an alternate to *Civil War,* it is second only to *Confederate War.* It is used somewhat more frequently by the younger and better-educated informants than by the oldest. This apparently supports an investigator's intuition (and [the author's] sense of indoctrination in school) that it is a term deliberately taught as representing southern attitudes. In contrast with *Confederate War,* which did not occur, there are several scattered examples of *War Between the States* in the North Central region. **1973** Allen *LAUM* 1.383 **Upper MW** (as of c1950), *Civil War.* . . In the U[pper] M[idwest]

nearly all speakers use simply *Civil War.* . . War between the States [3 infs, **IA**]. **1989** Pederson *LAGS Tech. Index* 314 **Gulf Region,** *Civil War.* . . Civil War (704 [of 914 infs]). . . War between the States (253 [infs]). [*DARE* Ed: The first and second most frequent responses respectively.]

warbird n *hist*

1 =**scarlet tanager.**

  [**1834** in 1836 Traill *Backwoods Canada* 289, I was a little amused by the appearance of one of these Indian Cupids, adorned with the wings of the American war-bird; a very beautiful creature, something like our British bullfinch, only far more lively in plumage: the breast and underfeathers of the wings being a tint of the most brilliant carmine, shaded with black and white. This bird has been called the "war-bird," from its having first made its appearance in this province during the late American war; a fact that I believe is well authenticated, or at any rate has obtained general credence.] **1893** *Scribner's Mag.* 13.769 **NEast,** The tanager . . , the Prometheus of Indian legends; the firebird, warbird, and blood-robin of the country folk.

2 See **war eagle.**

warble n Pronc-spp *wabble, wobble, warvel, worvel*

Std sense, var forms.

  1896 U.S. Dept. Ag. Div. Entomol. *Bulletin* 5.107 **Upstate NY,** A very large percentage [of fifty chipmunks] . . were infested with "wabbles." **1940** Stuart *Trees of Heaven* 82 **eKY,** Salt on a cow's back will kill the 'wobbles' that git into her back. **1966** *DARE* Tape **FL32,** [It] makes a kind of wobble ['wɑbl] wolf worm. **1967** *DARE* FW Addit **nwAR,** *Worvel* ['wɔrvəl] (perhaps *warvel*) = botfly grub. . . This name is common around my old home at Gateway, Arkansas. **2003** *DARE* File—Internet **TX,** We have a problem with warvels here. . . Warvels are some sort of weird flying insect larvae that burrow into the cheeks of infant cats.

warble fly n

Std: A fly of the family Oestridae whose larvae feed beneath the skin of cattle and other animals.   For other names of var spp see **bomb fly, heel ~, nose ~, Pontiac ~**

warbler n

Std: a bird of the family Parulidae.   For other names of var spp see **black-and-white warbler, Connecticut ~, golden ~, golden-winged ~, ground ~, hermit ~, jack-pine bird, magnolia warbler, mourning ~, myrtle ~, ovenbird, pine warbler, prothonotary ~, redpoll 2, tip-up warbler, yellow-crowned ~, yellow redpoll, yellowthroat 1, yellow tip-up, ~ warbler**

ward n, often attrib   in Mormon settlement areas

In the Mormon church: an administrative district and subdivision of a **stake,** presided over by a bishop.

  1859 *Mountaineer* (Salt Lake City) 27 Aug. 2/4 *(DA),* If the watermasters of our district or ward will see that we have a double portion of water during the ensuing week for our garden, we will now agree not to mention them again. **1870** Beadle *Life in UT* 178, The Tabernacle and Ward Assembly Rooms resounded with harangues in fierce denunciation of the Government. *Ibid* 387, Salt Lake City is divided into twenty-one wards, each of which has a bishop, and the entire Territory is in the same manner conveniently divided into wards with a bishop over each. *Ibid* 388, *Ward Teachers.* Their duty is to visit all the people in their ward, report all suspected persons, catechize every one as to personal feeling, belief, etc., to report all irregularities, heresies, false doctrine and schism, and generally to act as spies and informers. **1931** *AmSp* 7.119 **eID,** The *ward house* or *church house* is the building used by the Mormons for religious services and as a social center. The *ward* is the community, a unit of social organization. The *bishop* is the leader of the ward, who collects the tithes. **1966** Barnes–Jensen *Dict. UT Slang* 44, *Ward.* . . the basic working unit of the Mormon Church is called a "ward", under the head of a Bishop and Counsellors, with Sunday School and other divisions. There are hundreds of wards, to one about every 500 members. **1967** *Snowflake Herald* (AZ) 13 July 1/2, Each ward has a ward chairman to enlist registrations. **1983** *Salt Lake Tribune* (UT) 29 May sec B 19/5, [He] was chorister and organist in both stake and ward organizations. **1996** *Verbatim* Autumn 8 [Mormon English], The towns were organized politically in a way previous Mormon colonies in the eastern states (Kirtland, Ohio, and Nauvoo, Illinois) were, into *stakes* and *wards.* . .

The ward started out as a political subdivision, just like wards in most North American cities, but became the equivalent of a parish. . . and wards are headed by a *bishop.* **2003** Krakauer *Under Heaven* 143 **UT,** [Footnote:] Each LDS congregation (called a "ward") is headed by a bishop—a lay member, always male—who must be approved by the First Presidency and the Quorum of the Twelve Apostles.

war department n *joc*

A wife; rarely, a man's mother.

1942 Berrey–Van den Bark *Amer. Slang* 446.15, *Wife.* . . war department. **1950** *WELS (Joking names that a man may use to refer to his wife)* 2 Infs, **WI,** War department. **1958** McCulloch *Woods Words* 207 **Pacific NW,** *War department*—A wife. **1965–70** DARE (Qu. AA22, *Joking names that a man may use to refer to his wife: "I have to go down and pick up my _____."*) 24 Infs, **scattered,** War department; [**WI**27, War horse; **CO**37, My war secretary;] (Qu. Z2, . . *'Mother'*) Inf **OR**1, War department. **1968** DARE FW Addit **seLA,** *War department*—joking way of referring to a man's wife, especially when she calls him on the phone while he is in a bar. **1986** Pederson *LAGS Concordance (Wife)* 2 infs, **GA, TX,** War department; 1 inf, **nwLA,** My war department—facetious; 1 inf, **cnLA,** The war department—joking. **1987** Mohr *How Minnesotan* 175 **MN,** At every Minnesota poker party there will always be one guy we'll call Orv. . . He'll tell you he had to get permission from the War Department to play. The War Department is his wife.

wardrobe n [*OED2* wardrobe sb. 1a *"Obs."*]

A built-in storage place for clothing; a clothes closet. Note: The movable piece of furniture is widespread and is not treated here.

1912 *DN* 3.567 **cNY,** *Clothes-press.* . . Wardrobe is used for a closet that is built into one corner of a room. **1941** *LANE* Map 338 *(Clothes closet)* 1 inf, **swCT,** Some calls it wardrobe; but that's a thing setting up in the corner; 1 inf, **nwVT,** Wardrobe = closet. **1943** *AmSp* 18.17 **TN,** As indicating a separate room, *wardrobe* is supposedly obsolete. . . In Wilson County, Tennessee, however, it is used to describe any space in which clothes may be hung, whether it is a movable piece of furniture, a built-in wall closet, or a clothes closet. **1948** Davis *Word Atlas Gt. Lakes* app qu 9 (Small room for hanging clothes), 30 [of 233 infs], **IN, IL, MI,** Wardrobe. **1965–70** DARE (Qu. E2, *A built-in space in a room for hanging clothes*) 38 Infs, **scattered,** Wardrobe; [**NC**82, Built-in wardrobe;] (Qu. D7, *A small space anywhere in a house where you can hide things or get them out of the way*) Inf **IN**30, Closet, wardrobe; **PA**70, Cupboard, clothes press, clothes closet, wardrobe; (Qu. D11, *When you go into a house, the part just beyond the front door is the _____*) Inf **IA**31, Wardrobe—built in. **1966** Dakin *Dial. Vocab. Ohio R. Valley* 2.45, In the southern Mountain counties and the southern Knobs region, *wardrobe* is fairly common as the only word used or is used in addition to *closet. Wardrobe* is also used by some older speakers along the Tennessee and Cumberland Rivers in southwestern Kentucky, in the American Bottom and along the line of the Vincennes-St. Louis road in Illinois, and in southeastern Indiana. This term is scattered through Ohio, but occurs here only as an old term remembered and used in addition to *closet.* **1971** Bright *Word Geog. CA & NV* 146, *Clothes closet* /built in/. . . *wardrobe* / *wardrobe closet* 13% [of 300 infs]. **1973** Gawthrop *Dial. Calumet* 70 **nwIN,** *Small room for hanging clothes:* closet 103 [of 125 checklist infs] . . wardrobe 11 [infs]. **1986** Pederson *LAGS Concordance,* 1 inf, **nwFL,** Wardrobe—also built-in; curtain instead of a door; 1 inf, **neTN,** Wardrobes—built into the walls; 1 inf, **ceTN,** Wardrobes = closets; built-in; 1 inf, **neTN,** Wardrobes—built-in; 1 inf, **ceTN,** Wardrobes—closets; 1 inf, **nwFL,** Wardrobes—built into house.

Ward's ducks n [Etym unknown]

In phrr *go like Ward's ducks* and varr: To go to hell, destruction.

1856 *Jrl. of Discourses* 3.236 **UT,** I wish all the Saints to do right, and as for those who do not, my prayer is, "That they may all go hellwards, the way Ward's ducks went." **1863** *Daily Press* (Nashville TN) 8 July 2/4, Much of this salt has been bought for those who fled at the fall of Fort Donelson, and have gone as Ward's ducks went—hellward, and that is South. **1874** Evans *A la CA* 271, What became of him we never satisfactorily ascertained. The road to . . Prescott and Tucson was swarming with Apaches. Had he taken "the road which Ward's ducks went?" We shuddered at the thought, but he may have done so in sheer desperation. **1880** *Galveston Daily News* (TX) 30 Apr 1/5, A terrific storm of wind and rain struck our city at 12:40 A.M., leveling the handsome city hall,

completely demolishing the colored church, and most of the fencing has gone to hunt Ward's ducks. **1930** *Herald–Advt.* (Huntington WV) 30 Nov sec 3 6/8 **ceKY,** For things to be scattered to the four winds is for them to go like "Ward's ducks"—which, we are told, was perditionward.

ware n See **weir**

ware v See **be A5**

war eagle n Also *warbird* [Because the Plains Indians wore its feathers in their war headdress] *obs*

=golden eagle.

1819 (1821) Nuttall *Jrl.* 88 **AR,** The large feathers of the war-eagle . . are sometimes distributed throughout the nation, as sacred presents. **1832** in 1841 Catlin *Letters Indians* 1.68 **MT,** A war-eagle. This noble bird is the one which the Indians in these regions, value so highly for their tail feathers. **1855** in 1878 Longfellow *Poems* 161 **NEng,** Then began the greatest battle / That the sun had ever looked on,/ That the war-birds ever witnessed. **1916** Seton *Woodcraft Manual Girls* 305, The only other eagle found in the United States [beside the Bald Eagle] is the *Golden or War Eagle (Aquila chrysaëtos).* **1942** U.S. Natl. Park Serv. *Fading Trails* 260, The great American golden eagle, war eagle of the Indians, seems to be gone as a breeding bird from the western Great Plains.

War for Southern Independence n Also *second War for* (or *of*) *Independence; War of Southern Independence* **chiefly Sth, S Midl**

The American Civil War.

1861 *S. Lit. Messenger* 32.402, Sanguine men . . predict that the war of Southern Independence will be terminated by a few decisive engagements. **1861** *Alexandria* (Va.) *Gaz.* 2 May 3/1 *(DA),* This old flag, especially, can never serve again so good a purpose in this, our second War of Independence. [**1863** in 1880 *N. Amer. Rev.* 131.560 **GA,** We are fighting this war for Southern Independence, and for a government of Southern States recognizing African slavery as an institution ordained of God.] **1863** Cooke *Life Stonewall Jackson* 34 **VA,** You have already gained a proud position in the future history of this our second war of independence. **1929** IL State Hist. Soc. *Trans. for 1929* 36.125, From the crude and vast romanticism of that vigorous sovereignty emerged new philosophies to take the place of those which had gone down in the cataclysms of the War for Southern Independence. **1949** *FL Hist. Qrly.* 23.216, Bloxham enlisted first in the War for Southern Independence on April 2, 1861. **1963** *Eve. Capital* (Annapolis MD) 19 Apr 12/4, We can view it [=the South] historically in the context of the War of Southern Independence. **1973** *Daily Times–News* (Burlington NC) 15 Dec sec A 4/6 **GA,** Prior to the War for Southern Independence, as it still is termed in these parts, Savannah seemed destined for glory. **1984** Wilder *You All Spoken Here* 66 **Sth,** In the War for Southern Independence, Marse Robert gave Jeb Stuart too much slack. **1986** Pederson *LAGS Concordance (Civil War)* 2 infs, **LA, MS,** War for Southern Independence; 1 inf, **swTN,** Second War for Independence—joking.

warhew See **warhoo** n[1]

war hoop (or hoot) See **war whoop**

warloon See **walloon** n[1]

warm house n

A cellar.

1936 *Galveston Daily News* (TX) 1 Mar 14/8, A storm forces them to take shelter in a warmhouse where they aid in the birth of twins to a farm wife. **1969** DARE (Qu. D22, *Underground place to go to in case of a violent windstorm*) Inf **IL**134, Warm house. **1983** *MJLF* 9.1.60 **ceKY** (as of 1956), *Warm house* . . a root cellar. **1991** Still *Wolfpen Notebooks* 163 **sAppalachians,** *Warmhouse:* cellar.

warmouth n Also *warmouth bass, ~ bream, ~ perch, ~ sunfish*

Std: a **sunfish 1a** (here: *Chaenobryttus gulosus*) native to the Mississippi and Great Lakes basins and much of the southeastern US. Also called **bigmouth 1, bigmouthed sunfish, black perch 1b, ~ sunfish, bream B3, buffalo bass, goggle-eye 1a(2), Indianfish, jugmouth, mawmouth, molly** n[1] **7d, morgan, mud bass 3, ~ chub 1, ~ sunfish 3, open-mouth, perch** n[1] **B2, redeye 1b, red-eyed bream, rock bass 5, sacalait 2, shell-cracker, sun perch, widemouth sunfish, wood bass**

warm sugar n   **NEast, N Cent**   Cf **sugar on snow, sugar supper**

Maple syrup boiled to the point where it will crystallize, then poured out and eaten while still warm; hence nouns *warm sugar social* (or *party, supper*) a social gathering at which this confection is made and eaten.

1857 in 1862 Colt *Went to KS* 213 **NY,** My good niece . . myself and Mema, have been to Mr. Hinman's, visiting, and to eat warm sugar. **1864** *WI Chief* (Ft. Atkinson) 29 Feb [5]/1 (newspaperarchive.com), Sweet are the remembrances of Mr. & Mrs. Rockwell's "sugar party" in behalf of the Aid Society, for warm sugar was abundant. **1883** *Eve. Observer* (Dunkirk NY) 22 Mar 4/1, The warm sugar social was also a very enjoyable affair and reflects great credit upon the ladies. **1886** *New Engl. Mag.* 4.216 **VT,** As soon as the sugar begins to show signs of graining, all hands pass up their saucers to be filled. . . Not many . . can eat more than one, or at most two, saucerfuls of warm sugar. So, when the appetite is sated . . and the sugar is done a little harder, merry voices call for pans of snow. **1890** *Ledger* (Warren PA) 4 Apr [5]/2 (newspaperarchive.com), The ladies of the Presbyterian church held a warm sugar party . . last evening. **1902** *Wellsboro Agitator* (PA) 2 Apr 1/3, The proceeds of the warm sugar social at L.K. Gile's Tuesday evening were about $10. **1931** *Chron.-Telegram* (Elyria OH) 7 Mar [8]/3 (newspaperarchive.com), At the next meeting of the local chapter a warm sugar supper will be served. **1952** *Warren Times–Mirror* (PA) 23 Apr 6/2, Dorcas Society of Hessel Valley will sponsor a warm sugar social. **1963** *Oneonta Star* (NY) 16 Feb 8/5, Warm Sugar Social, 7 to 9 p.m. tonight, Methodist Church hall; benefit church. **1968** *DARE* (Qu. FF1, . . *A kind of group meeting called a 'social' or 'sociable'. . . [What goes on?]*) Inf **MI**96, Warm sugar social—old-fashioned.

warm-ups n pl

Leftover food.

1950 *WELS Suppl.* **ceWI,** Warm ups—Food left from previous meal. **1967–70** *DARE* (Qu. H68, *When food remains over from one meal and you heat it again for another meal*) Infs **IL**141, **PA**22, 136, 203, Warm-ups.

warmus See **wamus**

warn v

1 To give official notice of (a town meeting); hence vbl n *warning.* [*OED2 warn* v.[1] 7.b 1465–1792] **chiefly NEng** Cf **warning** n 1

1652 in 1926 Warwick RI *Early Rec.* 70, Ordred that all monthly meetinges bee warned three dayes before the Court. **1775** in 1894 Ostrander *Hist. Brooklyn* 1.208 **NYC,** At a general town meeting, regularly warned at Brooklyn . . the magistrates and freeholders met and voted Jer. Remsen, Esq., into the chair. **1846** Crawford *Hist. White Mts.* 15 **NH,** A neighboring town legally warned a meeting for the purpose of choosing military officers and to have a training. **1860** *Harper's New Mth. Mag.* 21.228 **CT** (as of 1749), A meeting was accordingly warned, and by a large vote . . it was resolved that the Squire was deserving of censure. **1972** *Transcript* (North Adams MA) 14 Feb 12/6, The meeting was warned November 29th which was between thirty and forty days as specified by Section 703. **1973** *Bennington Banner* (VT) 16 Apr 7/4, Selectmen 'perfectly legal' in warning special meeting. . . A warning for the Special Town Meeting . . was signed by Haynes and posted early Tuesday morning. **2007** *DARE* File—Internet **VT,** *Brattleboro Selectboard Meeting Warned.* . . The Brattleboro Selectboard will be holding a Special Meeting at 5:30pm on Friday, July 27, 2007.

2 To summon (one) to or notify (one) of a town meeting or referendum. [*OED2 warn* v.[1] 7.a "To summon (a person *to* a duty, place, etc.) . . To summon officially . . Now only *Mil.*"; a1250 →] **NEng** Cf **warning** n 1

1809 Kendall *Travels* 1.29 **CT,** The constables in the several towns are required to summon, or as it is said, to "*warn* all the freemen in their respective towns to meet together yearly." **1914** *Newport Daily News* (RI) 31 Mar 7/6, *Notice of Annual Town Meeting.* . . Therefore, the qualified electors of the Town of Middletown are hereby notified and warned, to assemble in Town Meeting . . on the first Wednesday of April next. **1965** *Bennington Banner* (VT) 9 Mar 11/2, *Warning*—The legal voters of the Village of Bennington are hereby *warned* to meet at the Elementary School . . to vote by ballot . . on Article 1 through Article 10 of the warning as follows.

3 freq with *out,* rarely *in*: To summon (one) to perform le-

gally required road work. [Cf **2** above] *hist* Cf **warning** n 2

[**1842** in 1956 Eliason *Tarheel Talk* 134 **cNC,** You are required to warn out your men when and where to meet; to patrol at least two nights and disperse all collections of *negroes* and white *boys* in the streets on Sundays.] **1862** in 2007 (acc) Lexis–Nexis Legal Research *State Case Law: NJ* (Internet), The plain and obvious purpose of the act was, to require all necessary expenditures on the highways to be defrayed from money kept in hand for that object, and in case the inhabitants neglect to furnish such money, to subject them to be warned out to work. **1869** *Ibid:* **WI,** I told him we were warned out to lay a road. He asked me who got up the petition, and I told him I did not know. **1879** *Ibid:* **AL,** The defendant . . warned out the hands, and worked the road four days and a half. **1905** *DN* 3.100 **nwAR,** *Warn out.* . . To warn to work on the public highway. 'The constable has him under arrest for refusing to work the roads after being warned out by the road overseer.' **1912** *Jrl. Amer. Folkl.* 25.142 **sAppalachians,** A group of men who, having been "warned" to work the road, were . . continually breaking into song. **1915** in 2007 (acc) Lexis–Nexis Legal Research *State Case Law: ND* (Internet), Complaint against defendant was made . . for failure to appear and work on the road of said district. . . I find the defendant . . liable to a fine of $ 12 for six days of failure to appear after being warned out. **1935** [see **warning** n 2]. **1977** Blackmun *Western NC* 177 (as of a1880), The highway was marked off into sections with one man assigned to oversee the construction and upkeep of each section. His crew consisted of "warned in" citizens, ordered by the county clerk to work a certain number of days. **1984** U.S. Natl. Park Serv. *At Home Smokies* 25 **wNC,** During the spring and fall, all able-bodied men were "warned out" for six days . . to keep up what had become the well-used Cataloochee Turnpike.

warnet See **walnut**

warn in See **warn 3**

warning n

1 An official notice of a town meeting or referendum; official notification of such a meeting; a **warrant** n. [**warn 1, 2**] **NEng**

1637 in 1827 Lincoln *Hist. Hingham MA* 51, Whosoever shall absent himself from any meeting appointed and shall have lawful warning of it [is to pay a fine]. **1784** CT *Acts & Laws* 179, A Copy of this Paragraph of this Act . . published on the Sign Post in said Town . . shall be a legal Warning of the Freemen of said City to attend said first Meeting. **1871** in 2007 (acc) Lexis–Nexis Legal Research *State Case Law: CT* (Internet), On the 14th day of October, 1871, the town of Chatham, in pursuance of a legal warning for that purpose, held a meeting and passed votes, which warning and votes were duly recorded in full in the records of the town. **1945** Webster *Town Meeting* 229 **NEng,** After the October assembly has been called to order by the first selectman, the town clerk reads the warning, or official notice. **1965** [see **warn 2**]. **1973** [see **warn B1**]. **1979** in 2007 (acc) Lexis–Nexis Legal Research *State Case Law: CT* (Internet), The legal warning to the voters called them to a "referendum to be held on May 31, 1978 to approve or disapprove an ordinance as set forth in a petition filed with the Town Clerk."

2 An official summons to perform legally required road work. [**warn 3**] *hist*

1649 in 1828 Bliss *Address* 65 **MA,** [It is ordered:] That they duly present to the select Tounsmen, all defects of persons, or teames, that, on lawful warning given, neglect to come to the worke appointed. **1651** in 1926 Warwick RI *Early Rec.* 58, Ord[ered]: that Mr Holiman & Mr Warner are chosen to bee surveyors about mendinge the highwayes . . and if any man after warninge refuse to come to worke that another be hired. **1888** in 2007 (acc) Lexis–Nexis Legal Research *State Case Law: AR* (Internet), Being subject to road duty, he neglected to attend at the time and place designated by the road overseer to work on a public road in obedience to the overseer's warning to do so. **1935** *Ibid:* **AL,** The person giving the warning to this defendant to work the road, and who signed himself "Overseer," had no commission as required by section 21 of the ordinance. . . The evidence discloses that the work which the defendant was warned to do was to dig gravel in a gravel pit.

3 also *warning paper:* A notification of a death and forthcoming funeral. [Cf *EDD warning* sb. 5 "the verbal invitation to attend a funeral."]

1807 (1935) Janson *Stranger in Amer.* 429, What they call "warnings," is the day before, or early in the morning, given of the funeral. This is a notice or warning of the event in writing, which is regularly carried from house to house, and shewn or read to some of the family. **1950** *PADS* 14.70 **SC,** *Warning paper.* . . A paper with black ribbon attached, bearing the names of friends and neighbors to whom it is carried, announcing a death and the time and place of the funeral.

warning vbl n   See **warn 1**

warning paper   See **warning n 3**

warnit   See **walnut**

warn out   See **warn 3**

warnut   See **walnut**

War of Rebellion   See **Rebellion**

War of Southern Independence   See **War for Southern Independence**

War of the North and the South   See **War between the North and the South**

War of the Rebellion   See **Rebellion**

War of the Revolution   See **Revolution**

warp v   Also *wharp* [Prob pronc var of *whop;* cf Intro "Language Changes" I.8]   Cf **swarp** v
To hit or beat (someone)—also in phr *warp it to (someone)* to strike a blow at (someone); also fig.
    1861 in 2006 *DARE* File—Internet **TN,** Col. Savage . . took a turnip out of a fellows hand and warped him over the head with it.   **1876** *Harper's New Mth. Mag.* 52.629, She wants some [cards] with marked backs, so she can deal lone hands and warp it to dad.   **1905** *DN* 3.100 **nwAR,** *Warp.* . . To hit. 'I warped him over the head.' Common.   **1915** *DN* 4.235 **neOH** [College slang], *Warp.* . . To beat decisively.   **1917** *DN* 4.403 **neOH, KS,** *Warp it to* (him, *etc.*) . . Strike, beat (him) violently. "Warp it to him, Jim."   **1940** *Middlesboro Daily News* (KY) 6 Dec 2/4, The Widder ast Bud iffen he dident think she wuz purtty as a picture, and he sed well, som pitchers I've saw, and she warped him over the her [sic] with a battlin stick.   **1954** *Harder Coll.* **cwTN,** *Warp.* . . to hit. "I'll warp ye over ye head with a plank."   **1958** McCulloch *Woods Words* 208 **Pacific NW,** *Warp it to him*—To make it very tough for a man.   **1981** *High Coll.* **ceKY** (as of c1930), She warped him on the head with her umbrella.   **2005** Williams *Gratitude* 527 **wNC** (as of 1940s), He wharped his hat against his pants leg.

war-paint shiner n   [See quot 1983]
A **shiner 1** (here: *Luxilus coccogenis*).
    1957 Blair et al. *Vertebrates U.S.* 126, *Notropis coccogenis.* . . Warpaint shiner. . . Tennessee uplands from Virginia and Kentucky south to Georgia and Alabama.   **1983** *Audubon Field Guide N. Amer. Fishes* 435, *Notropis coccogenis.* . . The common name Warpaint Shiner . . calls attention to the bright red coloration.   **2003** *DARE* File—Internet **ceTN,** Virginia Harrison . . looked with admiration at the war paint shiner, which is marked by colorful patterns at the upper end of its body.

warp it to (someone)   See **warp**

warrant n   **NEng**   Cf **warning n 1**
An official document calling a town meeting and listing the articles of business to be considered.
    1646 in 1901 Portsmouth RI *Early Rec.* 32, It is further ordered that the businesse of such metinge dayes shalbe specified in the warant of warninge to the metinge.   **1720** in 1883 Boston Registry Dept. *Records* 8.147, The Town will proceed to the choyce of a Comittee . . as is exprest in the warr[an]t for the calling of this meeting.   **1775** in 1870 VT Hist. Soc. *Coll.* 1.11, There has been several warrants or notifications sent up the country for a general meeting.   **1875** Holland *Sevenoaks* 23 **NEng,** At this moment, there arose in his memory a single sentence he had read in the warrant for the meeting tomorrow.   **1909** *Fitchburg Daily Sentinel* (MA) 3 Aug 5/5, The warrant was posted, today, for a town meeting. . . There are three articles in the warrant.   **1914** McLaughlin–Hart *Cyclop. Amer. Govt.* 3.542 **NEng,** A warrant . . is posted in a public place, or mailed to the voters before the meeting; and no business can be transacted which is not mentioned in the warrant.   **1966** *Lowell Sun* (MA) 15 Dec 28/1, Concord—The warrant has closed for the regular 1967 town meeting. . . Some 13 articles have been submitted to the board. . . The first chance for citizens to preview the March 6 town meeting will be when the warrant is distributed on Jan. 9.   **2002**

Sentinel & Enterprise (Fitchburg MA) 26 Feb sec A 3/6, She would . . assist in preparing documentation to place an article on the annual town meeting warrant to allow voters to decide how the building should be used.

warrant v   **chiefly Sth, S Midl**
To procure a warrant against, serve with a warrant; to arrest or indict (someone) on a warrant.
    1720 in 1883 Boston Registry Dept. *Records* 8.147, The Town will proceed to the choyce of a Comittee to Consider ab[ou]t promoting of a Spinning School . . as is exprest in the warr[an]t for the calling of this meeting.   **1818** *Niles' Weekly Reg.* 13.406, You would be warranted or sued one hundred times every day.   **1836** in 1892 MA Hist. Soc. *Proc.* 2d ser 7.286 **VA,** Three other passengers, of whom he had extorted an excessive sum, warranted him for the excess and recovered it.   **1911** *DN* 3.540 **eKY,** *Warrant.* . . To indict; e.g., "The grand jury warranted him for stealing."   **1924** Raine *Land of Saddle-Bags* 103 **sAppalachians,** "I raised five sons, and none of 'em war ever *warranted*" (arrested on a warrant).   **1942** (1971) Campbell *Cloud-Walking* 179 **seKY,** But won't nobody hardly warrant nobody for being feared they won't get lected. . . The jail houses are nigh empty these times, from nobody not getting warranted.   **1996–97** in 2004 Montgomery–Hall *Dict. Smoky Mt. Engl.* 637, *Warrant* . . To be arrested on a warrant. [5 infs]   **2000** Shores *Tangier Is.* 235 **Chesapeake Bay,** The sheriff warranted him yesterday (arrested).

war sack   See **war bag**

warsaw n   [Alter of AmSpan *guasa* jewfish]
1 also *warsaw grouper:* A **grouper 1a** (here: *Epinephelus nigritus*).   Also called **black grouper 2, ~ jewfish, jewfish 1b**
    1884 Goode *Fisheries U.S.* 1.411 **nwFL,** The Black Grouper, . . called in Florida and Texas the "Jew-fish," is at Pensacola known by the name "Warsaw," evidently a corruption of the Spanish name "Guasa."   **1955** Zim–Shoemaker *Fishes* 109, The Warsaw or Black jewfish does not occur north of the Carolinas.   **1975** Evanoff *Catch More Fish* 106, The groupers . . also run big in size, with some members such as the Warsaw grouper and Jewfish.
2 =**jewfish 1a.**
    1884 Goode *Fisheries U.S.* 1.412, There is another fish which is also called "Jew-fish," or "Warsaw," and "Black Grouper," of which only enormously large specimens have been obtained, and which is entered upon our catalogues under the name *Promicrops guasa* [=*Epinephelus itajara*].   **1908** *Forest & Stream* 70.500 **FL,** The jewfish (*Promicrops itaiara*) is better known as black grouper or warsaw.   **1947** Caine *Salt Water* 20, The jewfish. . . is also known as black grouper, giant sea bass . . and warsaw.
3 =**black grouper 1.**
    1935 Caine *Game Fish* 71 **Sth,** Black Grouper. . . Warsaw. . . found from slightly north of Florida . . and is abundant around the Florida Keys.   **1946** La Monte *N. Amer. Game Fishes* 49, Black Grouper—*Mycteroperca bonaci.* . . Names: Warsaw, Jewfish, Black Rockfish [etc.]

warsaw grouper   See **warsaw 1**

warsh   See **wash**

warsper   See **wasper**

wart   See **worrit** v **1**

warter   See **water** A2

wart frog n
1 A **toad** n **1.**
    c**1950** *LANCS Checklists,* 1 inf, **WV,** Wart frog.   **1965–70** *DARE* (Qu. P23, *Names for the animal similar to the frog that lives away from water*) Infs **AL**14, 59, **MI**32, 109, **MA**2, **NC**63, **OK**52, **OR**4, **WI**61, Wart frog.   **1973** Allen *LAUM* 1.325 **IA** (as of c1950), *Wart-frog* likewise persists in the speech of one Iowan, and warty-toad in the speech of five infs., three of whom are in Iowa.   **1986** Pederson *LAGS Concordance,* 2 infs, **swAL, seLA,** Wart frog.
2 =**bullfrog 1.**
    1969 *DARE* (Qu. P22, *Names or nicknames for a very large frog that makes a deep, loud sound*) Inf **IL**97, Wart frog.

wart toad, warty   See **warty toad**

wartyback n   chiefly Upper Missip Valley

Often with modifier: Any of several **freshwater clams,** esp *Quadrula nodulata;* see quots.

1938 FWP *Guide IA* 327, The fisherman's haul usually contained a wide assortment of shells . . the warty black [sic], yellow back, mucket, washboard [etc]. **1941** *AmSp* 16.156 **Missip R,** Common names as applied by the cutter and fisher of shells. . . purple and . . three horned warty-back. **1966** *WI Conserv. Bulletin* 31.3.27 **WI,** Other less important species are the warty-back, mapleleaf, and pigtoe. These names, which have evolved over the years among local fishermen, are fairly descriptive of the clam itself—if you use a little imagination. **1982** U.S. Fish & Wildlife Serv. *Fresh-Water Mussels* [Wall chart] 1.4, Wartyback. . . *Quadrula nodulata.* **1985** Madson *Up River* 59 **Upper Missip Valley,** Wartyback. **1992** Cummings–Mayer *Field Guide Freshwater Mussels MW* 48, Purple wartyback—*Cyclonaias tuberculata.* *Ibid* 52, White wartyback—*Plethobasus cicatricosus.* *Ibid* 100, Threehorn wartyback—*Obliquaria reflexa.* *Ibid* 102, Fanshell. . . *Other common names* . . ringed wartyback.

warty toad n   Also *wart toad, warty*   chiefly NEast, N Cent
See Map
A **toad** n **1.**

1939 *LANE* Map 232 *(Toad)* 4 infs, **wNEng,** Warty toad; 1 inf, **wCT,** Wart toad. **1948** Davis *Word Atlas Gt. Lakes* app qu 74, 16 [of 233] infs, **IL, IN, MI, OH,** Warty-toad. **1965–70** *DARE* (Qu. P23, *Names for the animal similar to the frog that lives away from water)* 10 Infs, **NEast, N Cent,** Warty toad; **IL**144, **NY**52, 71, 74, **PA**245, **WI**50, Wart toad; **MI**65, There's tree toads and ordinary "warty toad," we call 'im; **MI**67, I saw a warty. **1973** [see **wart-frog 1**].

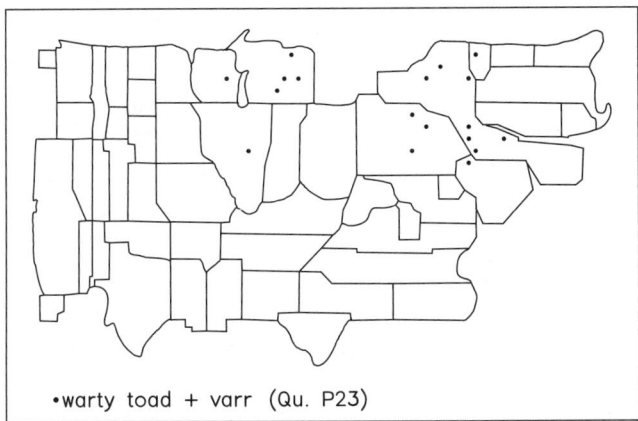

•warty toad + varr (Qu. P23)

warvel   See **warble**

war whoop n   Also *hoop, war hoop, ~ hoot* [Transf from *war whoop* the war cry of the Native American]   chiefly West
An American Indian or one of partial American Indian ancestry.

1930 Williams *Logger-Talk* 16 **Pacific NW,** War-whoop: An Indian. **1958** McCulloch *Woods Words* 207 **Pacific NW,** War whoops—Indians. **1967–69** *DARE* (Qu. HH28, *Names and nicknames . . for people of foreign background: Indian)* Infs **CA**145, **NE**4, **VT**12, War whoop; **CA**136, War hoot; (Qu. HH29a, *. . People of mixed blood—part Indian)* Inf **UT**11, War hoop. **1967** *DARE* Tape **WA**30, We decided what them . . war whoops could do, we could do. **2000** Launspach *ID Dial. Project* 6 **seID,** Terms for Indians—3 infs, (War)hoop.

was   See **wasp 1a**

wase   See **waste** v **1**

wash n, v   Usu |waš, wɔš|; also **widespread but esp freq Midl** |warš, wɔrš|; for addit varr see quots   Pronc-spp *warsh, wersh, woish, worsh*   Cf Intro "Language Changes" I.8, **squash** n¹
A **Forms.**

1897 *Century Illustr. Mag.* 55.109 **IN,** [He] warshed his hands. **1905** *DN* 3.57 **eNE,** Intrusive *r* is very common: wa(r)sh. **1928** *AmSp* 3.404 **Ozarks** (as of 1916–27), The verb *wash* nearly always sounds like *woish.* **1933** *AmSp* 8.1.25 **sAppalachians,** In certain words "r" is added where it does not belong. Among these are *wash, hush* and *mush,* which

become *warsh, hursh* and *mursh.* These are particularly noticeable in southern West Virginia and eastern Kentucky. *Ibid* 32 **wTX,** I warshed this mornin' and arned this evenin'. **1949** in 1986 *DARE* File **MI,** Wash—[wɔrʃ]. **1952** *AmSp* 27.187 **WA,** A number of speakers pronounce words like *wash* and *Washington* with an 'r-colored' vowel, so that extreme examples sound like 'worsh' and 'Worshington.' . . [M]ost of the speakers thus involved were . . in the vicinity of the largest cities. If there is any chance that urban people will influence vernacular of near-by areas, the 'worsh' type of pronunciation would seem to stand a good possibility of further expansion. Besides 'worsh' there is, of course, another type of pronunciation that is found wherever Southern mountaineers have settled, namely, 'woish.' **1966–69** *DARE* Tape **CA**163, Fed them and fattened them and got them gentle, and worshed [waršt] 'em; **DC**9, We paint it [=fox blood] on their face and they're not s'posed to worsh [wɔəš] this off; **IN**3, There's soap to scrub with and to wash [waəš] clothes; **TX**24, The warsh [waəš] is over next to the bluff. **1968–69** *DARE* (Qu. B27, *A sudden rush of water coming from heavy rain)* Inf **MO**37, Warshing rain; (Qu. C21, *A deep place cut in sloping ground by running water)* Inf **IA**22, Warsh [warš]. **1969** *DARE* FW Addit **MA**14, [worš] = wash. **1982** McCool *Sam McCool's Pittsburghese* 38 **PA,** Worsh: wash. **1982** *Barrick Coll.* **csPA,** Wash—pron. warsh. **1989** Pederson *LAGS Tech. Index* 70 **Gulf Region,** Wash. [Of 914 infs, 656 offered proncs of the type [waš]; 150 infs, proncs of the type [wɔš]; 66 infs, proncs of the type [warš]; 54 infs, proncs of the type [worš]; 2 infs, proncs of the type [wærš]; 1 inf, [worš].] **1995** *Brophy Coll.* 82 **swMO** (as of c1960), Wash. [P]ronounced with diphthong: "wo-ish"; I have heard "warsh" only among Kansans. **1999** *DARE* File—Internet (Central Florida Green Bay Packer Backers) **WI,** Warsh: what one does to dirty dishes or laundry. **2000** Shores *Tangier Is.* 176 **Chesapeake Bay,** When the "ah" occurs before "-sh," however, as in *gosh* and *wash,* it has a changing sound (or two sounds) as in *die,* giving us "guy-ee-sh" and "why-ee-sh." **2000** Metcalf *How We Talk* 39 **Midl,** If you "warsh" your hands or your clothes . . , you're likely from the Midlands. **2003** *DARE* File—Internet **IA,** My sister-in-law says "I'm going to do the '*wersh*' " (wash as in laundry).

B   **As verb.**

To bathe, swim, esp as an amusement—usu in phr *go in washing.*   **Sth, S Midl**   Cf **wash-hole**

1861 (1969) Berry *Slavery & Abolitionism* 26 **GA** [Black], The Slave children and their young masters and mistresses, are all raised up together. They . . go a hunting together, go a fishing together, go in washing together, and . . every other kind of amusement. **1892** *DN* 1.233 **KY,** Washin'. To go in washin' = to go in bathing. **1897** Page *Social Life in VA* 25, They [=children] were all over the place; in the orchard robbing birds' nests . . ; in spring and summer fishing or "washing" in the creek. **1898** *Galveston Daily News* (TX) 15 Aug 8/5, The visitors spent most of the day at the beach and "went in washing." **1899** (1912) Green *VA Folk-Speech* 474, Washing. . . Boys' term for bathing in the rivers and streams. "He went in washing at 9 o'clock and didn't come out untill 12." **1903** *DN* 2.336 **seMO,** All the boys in school went in washing. **1909** *DN* 3.386 **eAL, wGA,** Washing. . . Bathing, swimming. **1926** Roberts *Time of Man* 61 **KY,** Did you ever go a-washen in the ocean? **1950** *PADS* 14.70 **SC,** Washing: n. Bathing; swimming. "To go in washing, or awashing." **1986** Pederson *LAGS Concordance,* 1 inf, **ceAL,** Going in washing (=swimming). **1991** Still *Wolfpen Notebooks* 13 **sAppalachians,** I seemed not to be doing anything that summer except picking blackberries and going in "washing," as we called it. Swimming.

wash-ashore n   **Cape Cod, Nantucket, Martha's Vineyard MA**

A visitor or non-native resident.

1983 Beyle *How Talk Cape Cod* 15 **seMA,** Year-round residents and others who aren't natives (you *must* be born here) are frequently referred to as "wash-ashores" by Cape Codders. **1998** *Sun. Capital* (Annapolis MD) 20 Sept sec E 7/3 **Cape Cod MA,** If You Go To Martha's Vineyard. . . People who were not born there are called "washashores." **1998** *DARE* File **Cape Cod MA,** Natives of the Cape refer to persons who have come from elsewhere to live on the Cape as "wash-ashores," which is pronounced as if it were one word. **2006** *Nantucket Independent* (MA) 25 Jan (Internet), I'm surprised that there aren't two sets of water fountains in town one labeled "native," the other labeled "wash-ashore." **2006** in 2007 *DARE* File—Internet **Cape Cod MA,** I think the situation will worsen as the old timers on Cape Cod move own [sic] and are replaced by "wash ashores" who don't care for the traditions of the past.

washateria n Also sp *washeteria; rarely washiteria*

1 A self-service laundry. **scattered, but chiefly Sth, S Midl, West, esp TX, LA** Cf **washhouse**

1940 *Dallas Morning News* (TX) 27 Oct sec 2 7 *(Popik Coll.),* For Sale . . Washateria, all new equipment. **1946** *Galveston Daily News* (TX) 21 Apr 19/2, Washateria, 10 Maytags. . . 16 miles from Fort Worth. **1947** *Mexia Weekly Herald* (TX) 7 Feb 1/3, Her husband has been manager and owner of the Mexia Washateria and agent for Maytag in this area. **1948** *Middlesboro Daily News* (KY) 10 Jan 7/2 **TN,** Available immediately. . . self-service laundry equipment sufficient for one medium-sized washateria. . . Chattanooga, Tennessee. **1948** *Walla Walla Union–Bulletin* (WA) 19 Nov 12/5, Expert ironing. . . College Place, across from Washateria. **1950** *Santa Fe New Mexican* (NM) 16 Nov sec A 12/3, *Maytag Washateria*. . . open Wednesday nights. . . 12 Maytag machines available. **1959** *Daily Times-News* (Burlington NC) 2 Oct sec A 9/5, *City Laundry And Cleaners* . . Announces The Purchase Of The DeLuxe Laundry, Cleaners & Washateria. **1965** *Silver City Daily Press* (Frontier Recreation ed.) (NM) July np, Washateria and dry cleaning. **1967** *Playground Daily News* (Ft. Walton Beach FL) 27 Feb 14/7, *Commercial Waterfront Property*. . . Ideal for trailer park[·] Frozen food lockers and washateria. **1967** *DARE* FW Addit **MI,** On sign, outskirts Sault Ste. Marie, Mich. Washeteria; and on another sign, outskirts same city, laundro-mat; **seTX,** Washeteria—most common term (for what is usually called a laundromat in Idaho, Montana). **1968** *ID Daily Statesman* (Boise) 25 Feb sec D 6/2, Washateria—In near-by town, shows good return, selling price $12,000. **1996** *DARE* File **TX,** In Texas they go to the washateria rather than the laundromat. **2005** *DARE* File—Internet [The *Writer's Almanac* from American Public Media], Monday, 18 April. . . In 1934 on this day, the first laundromat opened in America. J.F. Cantrell opened the Washateria in Fort Worth, Texas with four electric washing machines. **2007** *Ibid* **LA,** [Advt:] *Unique Washiteria* . . Monroe, LA. *Ibid* **TX,** *Sun Washiteria* . . Pasadena, TX. *Ibid* **TX,** *U Do Washiteria* . . Houston, TX.

2 A community building housing laundry and bathing facilities and serving as a source of treated drinking water. **AK**

1982 *Tundra Times* (Fairbanks AK) 22 Sept 20/1, There is a washeteria here in Gambell and it really is popular. . . It is so good to have, not only for washing clothes, but for showers and bath tub baths too. **1987** *AK Geographic* 14.3.65, A centrally located washeteria provides shower and laundry facilities [on St. Lawrence Island]. **2001** U.S. Environmental Protection Agency *Drinking Water Infrastructure Surv.* **AK,** The only drinking water available to many Alaska Natives is from the community washeteria, particularly during cold weather. . . A washeteria is a single building with showers, toilets, and washing machines. The washeteria often doubles as a water treatment plant with heated water storage. **2007** *DARE* File—Internet **wAK,** The Shageluk Washeteria was built in 1994. Public Health Services built it because we needed a new building.

wash bear n Also *washing bear* [Cf Ger *Waschbär*] =**raccoon.**

[**1866** *Amer. Agric.* 25.348, The Raccoon has a curious habit, which gives it its specific name, *lotor,* or washer. The Germans call it *waschbär,* or washing bear, from this peculiarity.] **1900** *Century Illustr. Mag.* 60.5, The scientific name of the Coon means "washer," and one of his popular names is "wash-bear." **1938** FWP *Guide* CT 487 **nw,cnCT,** Coon hunting has been a traditional sport since the dog of some early settler first treed a raccoon and the farmer's son discovered the excitement of shaking the 'washing bear' to the ground. **1963** North *Rascal* 139 **WI** (as of 1918), "Does this raccoon remind you of any other animal?" Miss Whalen asked. "He looks like a little bear," Bud Babcock said. "You are right, Bud," the teacher agreed. "He is a cousin of the bear and is sometimes called a 'wash bear' because he washes all his food." **1966–69** *DARE* (Qu. P31, . . *Names or nicknames . . for the . . raccoon)* Infs **FL**7, **MI**93, **NJ**56, **NY**103, Wash bear.

washboard n

1 A baseboard. **scattered, but esp C Atl** See Map *esp freq among rural speakers, older speakers, and those with little formal educ* Cf **mopboard, scrubboard 2**

1806 (1970) Webster *Compendious Dict.* 347, *Washboard*. . . a board on a wall next the floor. [*DARE* Ed: This entry does not appear in Webster's English model.] **1847** in 2007 *DARE* File—Internet **sePA,** Room No. 1 on the right of entry . . with a fireplace, a neat white marble mantel and fire grate, 3 windows and wash boards. **1876** Knight *Amer.*

Mech. Dict. 3.2726, *Washboard.* . . (Carpentry.) A skirting around the lower part of the wall of an apartment. **1965–70** *DARE* (Qu. D37, *The strip of wood about eight inches high along the bottom of the wall [inside a room] joining to the floor)* 23 Infs, **scattered, but esp C Atl,** Washboard(s). [19 Infs comm types 4 and 5, 21 old, 13 gs educ or less]

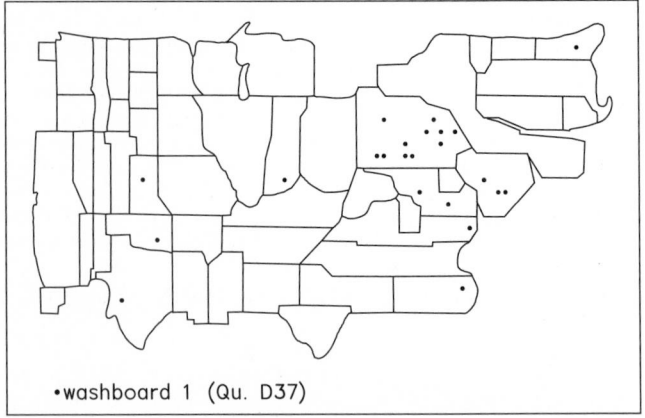

•washboard 1 (Qu. D37)

2 A **freshwater clam** (here: *Megalonaias gigantea* or *M. nervosa*).

1938 [see **wartyback**]. **1953** (1977) Hubbard *Shantyboat* 211 **Missip-Ohio Valleys,** We learned that there are many classes of shells, of different value. . . washboards, river run, blues and culls [etc]. **1979** *WI Week-End* 6 Apr 6, Such clams as maple leaf, washboard, and three-ridged varieties were harvested for the overseas market. **1991** IL Nat. Hist. Surv. *Biol. Notes* 137.13, *Megalonaias nervosa* . . washboard.

washers n Also *pitching washers* **Sth, S Midl**
A game in which washers are tossed at a distance into a hole or holes.

[**1953** *Life* 9 Nov 37, [Caption:] Ironworkers on strike pass the time pitching washers in impromptu quoits game.] **1967–70** *DARE* (Qu. EE37, *The game where you try to throw metal rings or something similar over a stake in the ground)* Infs **GA**23, **IL**116, **KY**74A, **TX**4, Washers; **TX**99, Washers—washers are thrown into holes. **1970** *DARE* Tape **KY**75, Washers is pretty good game. . . It's called pitching dollars or pitching washers. 'Course we never had the dollars to pitch. We had to substitute washers. . . You dig holes in the ground . . maybe fifteen foot apart. And you stand just in front of the hole at one end, and you pitch this washer to the other end at that hole. . . Two can play. Or you can play four and have partners. And the one that's the closest to the hole, he gets the point. And if you pitch one that goes in the hole, you get five points. And uh, about twenty-five points was the game. **1986** Pederson *LAGS Concordance (Quoits)* 1 inf, **swTN,** We played washers; 1 inf, **seTX,** Pitching washers—never horseshoes; 1 inf, **neTX,** Pitching washers—at a hole; 1 inf, **seMS,** Pitching washers; [4 infs, **AL, TN,** Pitch washers]. **1998** *NADS Letters* **TX,** Rolle bolle—I have seen a similar game called "washers" in which large washers are tossed, horseshoe style, into holes marked with point values. **2002** *DARE* File—Internet [*Yale Herald* 27 Sept], Weissler points to many exciting experiences pitching washers in Springfield, the Queen City of the Ozarks. . . According to Weissler, pitching washers is originally a St. Louis tradition that migrated south in the last century. **2006** *DARE* File—Internet **TX,** Bombat Washer Games. . . This site is dedicated to the game of washers. . . Officially Licensed Collegiate Products [in **AR, KS, LA, OK**].

washeteria See **washateria**

wash-foot Baptist n [Cf Intro "Language Changes" I.1] **chiefly S Atl** See Map
=**foot-washing Baptist.**

1889 Deland *FL Days* 135 [Black], The Wash-foot Baptists worship in a single room which is made of rough planks put together so carelessly that one can look out between the boards. **1890** *Harper's New Mth. Mag.* 80.894 **AL,** I take you to be a wash-foot Baptist. **1965–70** *DARE* (Qu. CC4, . . *Nicknames . . for various religions or religious groups)* Infs **FL**48, **GA**31, **NC**4, 23, **SC**2, 44, 68, **VA**58, Wash-foot Baptists; **SC**24, Wash-foot Babtists.

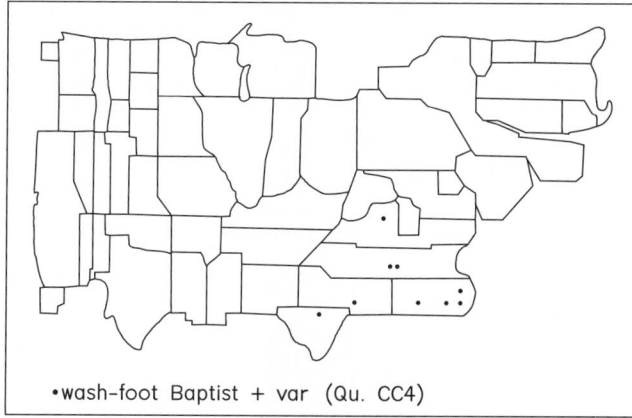

•wash-foot Baptist + var (Qu. CC4)

wash-hole n Also *washing hole* [**wash** v B] **Sth, S Midl** Cf **hole** n **1c, washup**

An area of comparatively deep water in a stream, used for bathing or swimming.

1872 (1967) Kellogg *TX Jrl.* 119, I had been searching . . on the banks of the muddy, steep ditch for a chance to get my feet in some pool . . and I made for Tim's wash hole & found a seat at its muddy edge. **1883** (1971) Harris *Nights with Remus* 269 **GA** [Black], Dey all 'gree dat dem en Brer Rabbit can't drink out er de same branch, . . ner go in washin' in de same wash-hole. **1894** *Scribner's Mag.* 16.286 **VA,** Their children now and then met down on the river fishing, or at "the Washing Hole," as the deep place in the little stream below . . was called. **1909** *DN* 3.386 **eAL, wGA,** Wash-hole. . . A swimming hole. **1934** *Kingsport Times* (TN) 10 Jan 4/1, The problem was . . how to get more free days; more time at the old "wash hole" in the creek and less time over arithmetic. **1945** Wilson *Passing Institutions* 142 **KY** (as of c1900), Other parts of the world may call a hole in the creek a "swimming hole," but our name for it was "washing hole." Swimming was not necessarily part of the Saturday-afternoon dip in the creek. **1950** *PADS* 14.70 **SC,** Washhole. . . Swimming hole, especially a broad, deep place in a stream used for swimming. **1954** *Harder Coll.* **cwTN,** Wash hole. . . Swimming hole. **1959** Sanders *Echoes* 19 **swAR,** The other boys who had gathered there would go swimming down at the wash-hole. **1978** [see **washup**]. **1986** Pederson *LAGS Concordance,* 1 inf, **cwGA,** Wash hole—swimming hole created by washout; 1 inf, **swGA,** Wash hole—swimming hole; 1 inf, **swAL,** Wash hole—for swimming; 1 inf, **seMS,** Wash hole—in the creek, for swimming. **2005** *DARE* File—Internet **SC,** Daddy and [a] few friends went out to the wash hole (a place in a creek that is big enough for swimming). **2006** *Ibid* **eTX,** I was baptized when I was twelve. I was baptized in what we call the "wash hole". It was a water hole where we all went swimming down in the creek.

washhouse n
=**washateria 1.**

1967 in 2007 (acc) Lexis–Nexis Legal Research *State Case Law: KS* (Internet), A pay-telephone was stolen from a commercial washhouse (laundromat) in Wichita. **1970** *Las Cruces Sun–News* (NM) 14 July 3/1, You can learn a lot in a laundromat. . . A conversation between three ladies who were strangers but for the hour they were in the public wash house together . . led me to this conclusion: There is an umbilical cord tying the male creature to his car. **1986** *DARE* File **csOK,** An elderly rural man near Wynnewood, Oklahoma uses *warsh house* to mean a laundromat. **1991** *Houston Post* (TX) 18 July sec A 2 **FL,** A "wishy-washy" in Nashville is a "washhouse" in Miami. Or maybe you call it a "washateria." **2002** *Univ. Chicago Mag.* Oct (Internet) **neIL** (as of 1940s), Just north of the cross drive were two "wash houses" with coin-operated washers and centrifugal dryers. **2007** *DARE* File—Internet **csPA,** Welcome to Dolly's Wash House. Dolly's is a coin laundry conveniently located in Carlisle. *Ibid* **seFL,** [Advt:] *Laundromat for sale (Wash House).* . . It's the neighbourhood wash house. Minimum attendant needed, machines are card operated.

washing bear See **wash bear**

washing hole See **wash-hole**

washing paddle n Cf **battling stick**

c1960 *Wilson Coll.* **csKY,** *Battling stick.* . . A stick or paddle to beat clothes or remove dirt. . . Also washing paddle.

Washington canvasback n
=**redhead 1a(1).**

1883 Coues & Prentiss in U.S. Natl. Museum *Bulletin* 26.105 **DC,** *Fuligula ferina americana.* . . "Washington Canvas-back". . . One of the commonest market Ducks, passing about half the time for the Canvas-back, and equally available for promoting Congressional legislation. **1903** Coues *Key to N. Amer. Birds* 2.926, The name "Washington Canvas-back," which Mr. Gordon Trumbull quotes with relish from Coues and Prentiss' Avifauna Columbiana [=quot 1883 above], is simply a political witticism of the latter authors.

Washington clam n

1 A Pacific clam *(Tresus nuttallii).* Also called **gaper 1, geoduck 2**

1911 Keep *West Coast Shells* 108, *Schizothaerus nuttallii* [=*Tresus n.*] . . the Washington Clam. **1921** CA Fish & Game Comm. *Fish Bulletin* 4.35 **CA,** The name "Washington clam" is also applied to the gaper, *Schizothaerus* [=*Tresus nuttallii*]. **1947** Morris *Field Guide Shells Atl.* 57, Washington Clam. . . This is probably the largest bivalve found along the west coast.

2 A Pacific clam: usu *Saxidomus nuttalli,* but also *S. gigantea.* For other names see **butter clam, gaper 2, money shell**

1921 CA Fish & Game Comm. *Fish Bulletin* 4.35, The name "Washington clam" . . for *Saxidomus* is said to have come from its resemblance to *Venus mercenaria* of the Atlantic coast, as noted by Indian chiefs at the time certain of them were in Washington, D.C. **1954** Abbott *Amer. Seashells* 417, *Saxidomus nuttalli* . . Common Washington Clam. *Ibid, Saxidomus gigantea* . . Smooth Washington Clam. **2001** *California's Marine Resources* 447, Two principal species of Washington clam are harvested in California. The Washington clam *(Saxidomus nuttalli)* is the principal species sought. . . The second popular Washington clam, the butter clam *(Saxidomus giganteus),* . . is seldom taken south of Humboldt Bay.

Washington eagle n Also *bird of Washington* arch
The immature **bald eagle 1,** formerly thought to be a distinct species.

1831 Audubon *Ornith. Biog.* 1.60, The name which I have chosen for this new species of Eagle, "The Bird of Washington," may, by some, be considered as preposterous and unfit; but as it is indisputably the noblest bird of its genus that has yet been discovered in the United States, I trust I shall be allowed to honour it with the name of one yet nobler. **1839** MA Zool. & Bot. Surv. *Fishes Reptiles* 262, The *Washington Eagle, Falco Washingtonianus.* . . sometimes wanders into New England. **1870** *Amer. Naturalist* 4.525, The opinion long since advanced by some writers that the "Washington Eagle" is but a very large immature Bald Eagle, is hence gaining ground. **1917** (1923) *Birds Amer.* 2.80, Bald Eagle. . . Black Eagle; Gray Eagle; Washington Eagle. The last three names refer to the immature Bald Eagle.

Washington fan palm See **Washington palm**

Washington haw(thorn) See **Washington thorn**

Washingtonian palm See **Washington palm**

Washington lily n Also *Lady Washington lily*
A large, white-flowered **lily 1** (here: *Lilium washingtonianum*) native to Oregon and California.

1859 in 1863 CA Acad. Nat. Sci. *Proc.* 2.13, Dr. Kellogg also exhibited a drawing and growing specimens of a new species of lily from the Sierra Nevada. . . *L. washingtonianum,* (Kellogg) *Lady Washington Lily.* **1889** *Century Dict.* 784, Among the eight species of the Pacific slope [is] the Washington lily. **1915** (1926) Armstrong–Thornber *Western Wild Flowers* 34, Washington Lily. . . This is never found in the Coast Range and is the only pure white American Lily. **1950** *Nature Mag.* 43.40, Probably the most spectacular of all western wild flowers is the Washington lily. **1979** Spellenberg *Audubon Guide N. Amer. Wildflowers W. Region* 586, Cascade Lily; Washington Lily.

Washington palm n Also *Washington fan palm, Washingtonian palm*
=**fan palm.**

1885 *Marion Weekly Star* (OH) 27 June 4/4, The Washington palm (Washingtonian [sic] filifera) from southern California is also curious. **1897** Sudworth *Arborescent Flora* 105 **CA,** *Neowashingtonia filamentosa* [=*Washingtonia filifera*]. . . Washington Palm. **1955** *S. Folkl. Qrly.*

19.232, The *Washington Palm* (*Washingtonia filamentosa*) is just as often called the *Colonial Palm,* from the historical period in which Washington lived, or *Pantaloon Palm,* from the supposed resemblance of the drooping dead foliage just beneath the green fronds to pantaloons, that were commonly worn with colonial costumes. **1968** *DARE* (Qu. T16, . . *Kinds of trees . . 'special'*) Inf **CA9,** Washingtonian palm; **CA42,** Washington palm. **2006** *DARE* File—Internet, Washington Fan palm trees also are lined along interstate highways and at metropolitan boulevard parks.

Washington poke n   Also *Washington punch,* ~ *(poke) tag* **chiefly MN, WI**
=**tap the icebox.**

 1917 St. Paul (MN) Surv. Comm. *Report* 220, We play Washington poke tag, and hide an go seek. **1925** Weeks *Psych. Child Training* 287 **ND,** Preferred games . . for the different periods [=ages] are reported by five young women. . . *Youth* . . Stump the leader—Washington punch— Run sheep run. **1930** *Child Development* 1.251 **Minneapolis MN,** Tag . . is listed among the five most popular games for each sex and every age [from 7 to 11]. Washington poke (a form of tag) appears in seven of the ten lists. **1938** *WI Rapids Daily Tribune* (WI) 23 Sept 8/1, This particular night we were playing "Washington Poke." **1945** Boyd *Hdbk. Games* 67, *Washington Tag*—One player . . blinds while the others stand close behind him. One of them touches him, whereupon he quickly turns around and says, "Go to the corner and kiss the post"; . . or anything he chooses. He then guesses who touched him. If his guess is correct, the one who touched him must carry out his order and then become *It.* If he does not guess correctly, he must himself carry out the order and continue to be *It.* While the victim performs the task, the other players run and hide. From this point the game is the same as *Hide and Seek.* **1950** *WELS* (*Games in which one player's eyes are covered and he has to catch the others and guess who they are*) 1 Inf, **cwWI,** Washington punch. **1957** *Sat. Eve. Post Letters* **ceWI** (as of c1915), In the event that you do not have Washington poke . . I can give you the rules. **1966** *DARE* File **swIN,** Washington punch. . . Hide and seek type [of children's game]. Players form circle around "It" who hides eyes. One player gives "It" a poke in the back and "It" must guess who. All scatter and hide.

Washington punch   See **Washington poke**

Washington's bower n

 A **matrimony vine 1** (here: *Lycium barbarum*).

 1849 Howitt *Our Cousins in OH* 53, The piazzas were wreathed and clustered about with roses and jessamines,—here called Washington's bower,—and other beautiful creepers. **1897** *Jrl. Amer. Folkl.* 10.51 **swMO,** *Lycium vulgare* [=*L. barbarum*] . . Washington's bower.

Washington tag   See **Washington poke**

Washington thorn n   Also *Washington haw,* ~ *hawthorn*

 A **hawthorn** (here: *Crataegus phaenopyrum*).

 1837 Darlington *Flora Cestrica* 293 **sePA,** Cordate Crataegus. Vulgò—*Washington Thorn.* [*Ibid,* This species was introduced into this [=Chester] County, from the neighborhood of Washington City, about the commencement of the present century,—and is now extensively used in hedging.] **1897** Sudworth *Arborescent Flora* 231, *Crataegus cordata.* . . Washington Haw. *Ibid* 232 **NJ, PA, DE, NC, SC, IL,** Washington Thorn. **1950** Peattie *Nat. Hist. Trees* 358, Washington Thorn. . . Of all the Hawthorns of America, . . this is by all means the daintiest. **2006** (acc) U.S. Dept. Ag. *Plants Database* (Internet), *Crataegus phaenopyrum* . . Washington hawthorn.

washiteria   See **washateria**

wash one's (or the) head   See **head** n **B1**

washup n
=**wash-hole.**

 1978 in 2006 *DARE* File—Internet **nFL** [*Baker Co. Press* (Macclenny FL) 9 Mar], A large pool area in a large stream is a washup or wash hole and there are several by the name of Stokes', Vaughn's[,] Bennett's, etc.

wasiper   See **wasper**

wasp n   Cf **post** n, **wasper**
 Std sense, var forms.

 1 sg: usu |wasp, wɔsp|; rarely |wæsp|; also:

 a |was, wɔs|; rarely |wæs|; pronc-sp *was.* **chiefly Sth, S Midl**

 1883 (1971) Harris *Nights with Remus* 89 **GA** [Black], Dem ar grapes all so fine wuz needer mo' ner less dan a great big was'-nes', en dem bugs wuz deze yer red wassies. **1892** *DN* 1.234 **KY,** Wasp nest [wɔs nɛs]. **1893** Shands *MS Speech* 14, *P.* . . is left out in [wɔs nɛs] for *wasp-nest.* **1909** *DN* 3.386 **eAL, wGA,** *Was* [wɔs]. . . Wasp. **1939** *LANE* Map 239 (*Wasp*) 2 infs, **swCT, seMA,** [wɔ⁽ə⁾s]; 1 inf, **seMA,** [wɒs]. [**1942** Hall *Smoky Mt. Speech* 90 **wNC, eTN,** *-sps* was reduced to [s] in the reported pronunciation [wɔs nɛs] for *wasp's nest.*] **1950** [see **wasp nest 2**]. **1989** Pederson *LAGS Tech. Index* 214 **Gulf Region,** *Wasp* [24 infs, [wɔs]; 7 infs, [was]; 3 infs, [wɑs]; 1 inf, [wæs]].

 b |wɑst, wɔst|; rarely |wæst|; pronc-sp *wast.* **chiefly Sth** Cf Pronc Intro 3.1.14

 1893 Shands *MS Speech* 67, *Wast* [wɔst]. Negro for *wasp.* **1909** *DN* 3.386 **eAL, wGA,** *Was* [wɔs]. . . Wasp. Also occasionally *wast.* **1939** *LANE* Map 239 (*Wasp*) 1 inf, **swMA,** [wast]. **c1940** Eliason *Word Lists FL* 11 **wFL,** *Wast.* . . Wasp. **1945** Saxon *Gumbo Ya-Ya* 560 **LA,** *Wast*—wasp. **1968–69** *DARE* (Qu. H13, *Bread that is not made at home*) Inf **MS46,** Wast nest; (Qu. R21, . . *Other kinds of stinging insects*) Inf **GA35,** Red wast [wɑst]. **1989** Pederson *LAGS Tech. Index* 214 **Gulf Region,** *Wasp* [35 infs, [wɔst]; 6 infs, [wast]; 6 infs, [wɑst]; 1 inf, [wæst]].

 c |waps, wɔps|; pronc-spp *waps, wops.* [By metath; cf *EDD wasp* sb. I.1 and Intro "Language Changes" I.1]

 1905 *DN* 3.58 **eNE,** Metathesis . . is very frequent. . . Several reported *brefkast (breakfast)* and *waps.* **1909** *S. Atl. Qrly.* 8.51 **seSC,** The transposition of *sp* to *ps,* in such words as *wasp, waps* . . are all characteristics of Gullah. **1967** LeCompte *Word Atlas* 201 **seLA,** *Insects that build mud nests.* . . waps [1 of 21 infs]. **1989** Pederson *LAGS Tech. Index* 214 **Gulf Region,** *Wasps* [4 infs, [waps]; 2 infs, [wɔps]]. **1995** Brophy *Coll.* 82 **swMO** (as of c1960), *Waps, wops.* [A] wasp.

 d pronc-spp *waspie, wassup, wassy.*

 1883 [see **1a** above]. **1929** *AmSp* 5.20 **Ozarks,** *Waspie.* . . Wasp. **1933** *AmSp* 8.1.53 **Ozarks,** *Wassy.* . . Wasp. The plural is *wassies,* and such compounds as *wassy nests,* wasp nests, are not uncommon. **1955** McAtee *Dial. Grant Co. IN Suppl.* 6 [2], *Wassup* (jocular for wasp).

 2 pl: usu |wasps, wɔsps| (rarely |wæsps|); also, see below. Note: It is not always possible to correlate a pl form with a particular sg form.

 a |wasp, wɔsp|; rarely |wæsp|. **chiefly Sth**

 c1970 Pederson *Dial. Surv. Rural GA* **seGA** (*Insects that build big nests and that sting are* _____), [Proncs of the types [wɑ(ə)sp, wɒ(ə)sp, wɔ(ə)sp] were recorded from 20 of 64 infs.] **1989** Pederson *LAGS Tech. Index* 214 **Gulf Region,** *Wasps* [102 infs, [wasp]; 100 infs, [wɔsp]; 24 infs, [wasp]; 3 infs, [wæsp]].

 b |was, wɔs|; rarely |wæs|. **chiefly Sth, S Midl**

 1867 Harris *Sut Lovingood Yarns* 118 **TN,** Hit jis' rain'd rotten wood, nails, mud-daubers' nests, . . black bugs, was' nests, an' ole dust. **1936** *AmSp* 11.333 **eTX,** [An . . owl came . . to pick the young wasps [was] out of the wasp [was] nest.] **1939** *LANE* Map 239 (*Wasp*) 10 infs, **CT, MA,** [Proncs of the types [wass, wɔss, wasz̧, wɔsz̧]]. **1942** [see **2d** below]. **c1970** Pederson *Dial. Surv. Rural GA* **seGA** (*Insects that build big nests and that sting are* _____), [Proncs of the types [wɑ(ə)s, wɔ(ə)s] were recorded from 19 of 64 infs.] **1989** Pederson *LAGS Tech. Index* 214 **Gulf Region,** *Wasps* [64 infs, [wɔs]; 23 infs, [was]; 11 infs, [wɑs]; 3 infs, [wæs]].

 c |wɑst, wɔst|; rarely |wæst|. **esp Sth**

 c1970 Pederson *Dial. Surv. Rural GA* **seGA** (*Insects that build big nests and that sting are* _____), [Proncs of the types [wɑɑst, wɔɑst] were recorded from 2 of 64 infs.] **1989** Pederson *LAGS Tech. Index* 214 **Gulf Region,** *Wasps* [35 infs, [wɔst]; 14 infs, [wast]; 4 infs, [wɑst]; 1 inf, [wæst]].

 d |'waspɪz, 'wɔsp-|; pronc-sp *waspes.* **esp Sth, S Midl** Cf **-es** suff[1] **1a**

 1917 in 1944 *ADD* **sWV,** Waspes. **1942** Hall *Smoky Mt. Speech* 82 **wNC, eTN,** *Wasps* ['wɔspəs] [sic]. . . but now usually [wɔs:]. **c1970** Pederson *Dial. Surv. Rural GA* **seGA** (*Insects that build big nests and that sting are* _____) 1 inf, ['waspɪz]. **1974** Fink *Mountain Speech* 29 **wNC, eTN,** *Waspes or waspers* . . wasps. **1989** Pederson *LAGS Tech. Index* 214 **Gulf Region,** *Wasps* [5 infs, [waspɪz]; 1 inf, [wɔspɪz]].

 e |'wastɪz, 'wɔst-|; pronc-sp *wastes.*

 1909 *DN* 3.406 **nwAR,** *Wastes* [wastɪz]. . . Wasps. "We seed the wastes' nests." **1989** Pederson *LAGS Tech. Index* 214 **Gulf Region,** *Wasps* [25 infs, ['wɔstɪz]; 4 infs, ['wastɪz]; 1 inf, [wastɪz]].

 f |'wɔsɪz|.

 1950 *WELS Suppl.* **csWI,** *Wasp.* . . [wɔsp] plural [wɔsəz].

wasper n Pronc-spp *warsper, wasiper, wausper* [**wasp** + **-er** affix 1] **chiefly S Midl** See Map Cf **billfolder, musicianer, rattler 6**

A wasp.

1942 Hall *Smoky Mt. Speech* 79 **wNC, eTN,** In the speech of children and some grown-ups, *wasp* frequently occurs as ['wɔ̜spɚ], ['wɔspɚ], with inorganic [ɚ]. 1944 *PADS* 2.51 **NC,** *Wasper:* . . Wasp. "These ain't no crickets; they's damned waspers." 1949 Arnow *Hunter's Horn* 146 **KY,** The youngens had left the lid off the biggest crock and the yellow jackets and waspers got in it. 1965–70 *DARE* (Qu. R20, *Wasps that build their nests of mud*) Inf **NJ31,** Waspers; (Qu. R21, . . *Other kinds of stinging insects*) Infs **KY9, 16, 34, 47, 76, TN22, VA7, 15,** Wasper. 1968 *DARE* Tape **NC53,** We use waspers. . . over thar where I work at the folk school, we get wasper bait over there and Tom fell over a fence, running from 'em, he 'bout got stung. 1974 [see **wasp 2d**]. 1982 Barrick *Coll.* **csPA,** *Wasipers*—wasps. 1983 *MJLF* 9.1.60 **ceKY** (as of 1956), *Wasper* . . a wasp. 1989 Pederson *LAGS Tech. Index* 214 **Gulf Region,** *Wasps* [8 infs, ['wɔspɚ(z)]; 2 infs, ['wæspɚ(z)]; 1 inf, ['wɔspɚz]; 1 inf, ['wɔ̌špɚz]]. 1993 Mason *Feather Crowns* 192 **KY** (as of c1900), Them waspers will get in here after the babies. 2002 Morgan *Mt. Born* 163 **wNC,** Wausper. 2005 *Joplin Globe* (MO) 10 July (Internet), Wasps are also known as "waspers." That's what my cousins and I called them when we were young. 2005 Williams *Gratitude* 535 **wNC** (as of 1940s), *Wasper, warsper:* a wasp. 2005 *DARE* File—Internet **FL,** Waspers don't like the cold. *Ibid* **TX,** Got chased out by waspers or something. *Ibid* **VA,** Be observant for "waspers" in the trees you are sizing up.

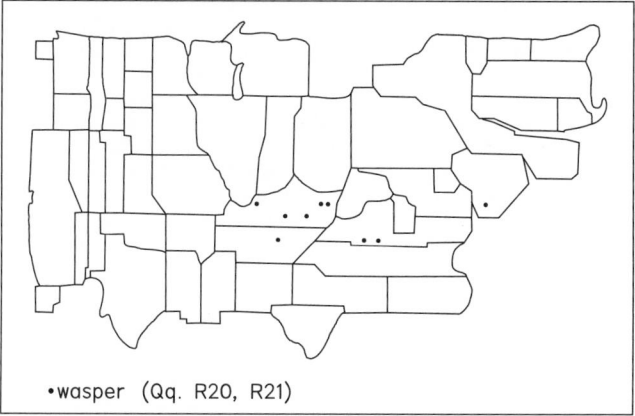

•wasper (Qq. R20, R21)

waspes See **wasp 2d**

waspie See **wasp 1d**

wasp nest n Also *wasp's nest*

1 also *wasp('s) nest bread:* Yeast-leavened wheat bread, **light bread;** a poor grade of such bread. **Sth, S Midl** *freq derog* Cf **gun-wadding**

1861 in 2006 *DARE* File—Internet **GA,** After a hearty repast of irish potatoes boiled collards and dry light bread. (called by the boys waspnest . . bread) we strolled down to the river. 1905 *Atlanta Constitution* (GA) 27 Apr 7/2, *Menu*— . . Egg Bread—Old Homestead Wheat Wasp Nest Bread. 1906 *DN* 3.163 **nwAR,** *Was's nest.* . . White bread, light bread. Name applied to white bread because its texture suggests the cells made by wasps. Rare. 1909 *DN* 3.386 **eAL, wGA,** *Was(p)-nes(t) bread.* . . A poor grade of light (white) bread, being tough and porous: often used in the expression, 'drink branch water and eat wasp-nest bread.' c1937 in 1970 Yetman *Voices* 220 **MS** [Black], After de War was over slaves was worse off dan when dey had marsters. . . Dey fed 'em wasp-nest bread, 'stead o' corn pone and hoecake, and all such like. 1942 Rawlings *Cross Creek* 208 **nFL,** Bread as I once knew it [=baked wheat loaf, white or whole grain] is called "light bread," and healthy appetites despise it for "wasp's-nest bread," with contempt for its texture and its filling qualities. 1950 [see **2** below]. 1958 *PADS* 29.18 **TN,** *Wasp's nest.* . . Bread made from wheat. It is "dry, tasteless, sponge-like baker's bread." 1966–69 *DARE* (Qu. H13, *Bread that is not made at home*) Inf **FL15,** Wasp nest; **GA11,** Wasp's nest; **MS46,** Wast nest. 1975 Newell *If Nothin' Don't Happen* 176 **nwFL,** One of the fellers had brought in a few loaves of storebought white bread, but we called it "wasp nest" and didn't like it much. It were half air bubbles. 1986 Pederson *LAGS Concordance,* 1 inf, **cAL,** Wasp nest bread—light

bread; 1 inf, **seAL,** Wasp nest bread—coarse light bread. 1996 *Verbatim* Autumn 2 **Sth,** The earlier generation of males wanted hot biscuits for breakfast and spoke disparagingly of baker's bread as *wasps' nests.* 2004 in 2007 *DARE* File—Internet **AR,** In my childhood there were three kinds of bread—cornbread or bi[s]cuits, . . or light bread which you bought by the loaf from the grocery store . . (mostly white—you could get it with caramel coloring which they called 'wheat' bread, but it wasn't the same). My daddy called it 'waspnest bread.'

2 A small loaf of bread, perforated and filled with molasses; similarly n *wasp's nest biscuit.* Cf **molasses biscuit**

1950 *PADS* 14.70 **SC,** *Wasp nest, was'nes'.* . . Ordinary baker's bread, so called because of its insubstantial, porous structure. . . A small loaf, pierced with finger thrusts, with molasses poured into the openings. Florence. From Charleston: A small loaf with a pointed end scooped out and filled with molasses. Another prescription is to take the end of a loaf, scoop out the crumb, pour the molasses in and replace the crumb. 1967 *DARE* FW Addit **SC,** *Wasp's nest biscuit*—punch a hole in the biscuit and pour syrup in it. Common.

‡3 See quot.

1938 *AmSp* 13.7 **seAR,** *Wasp-nest.* . . Corn bread.

wassup, wassy See **wasp 1d**

wast See **wasp 1b**

waste v

1 also pronc-sp *wase:* Of the moon: to wane. [Engl dial] **esp Sth** Cf **waste** n

1864 *Harper's New Mth. Mag.* 29.731, Over that man only he paused . . till in the light of the dying fire and the wasting moon he should see and know the gaunt demon glaring above him. 1894 *Scribner's Mag.* 15.468 **Sth,** On their right a wasted moon rose and stared at them over the mountain's shoulder. 1931 *Jrl. Amer. Folkl.* 44.377 **seLA** [Black], *To Run a Person.* . . Take a toad when the moon is wasting. Roll those names up in a small ball and give it to the toad. c1938 in 1970 Hyatt *Hoodoo* 1.359 **New Orleans LA** [Black], They say you do it on the waste of the moon—an' as de moon wases away, you wases away until that's all of you. 1975 *Western Folkl.* 34.50 **MS,** "When the moon is 'wasting away' [in the last quarter], this is the time to [kill hogs and] cook the fat because it will make more Lard and less crackling" (DeSoto County, Mississippi).

2 To use up, consume. [*OED2 waste* v. 3 c1230 → "*Obs.*"]

1924 Raine *Land of Saddle-Bags* 100 **sAppalachians,** "I've wasted it." Which means used or spent, not squandered. 1931 *AmSp* 7.91 **eKY,** *Waste,* to spend, or use up. "Whar's that last load of coal gone? I've wasted hit."

3 also *wasten:* To spill. **chiefly Sth** See Map *esp freq among Black speakers*

1937 in 1976 *Weevils in the Wheat* 316 **VA** [Black], Dancin' wid a glass o' water on my head. . . I hada grea' big reaf roun' my head an' a big ribbon bow on each side an' didn't wase a drap o' water on neider. 1938 Rawlings *Yearling* 11 **nFL,** Carry in the milk and don't trip and waste it outen the gourd. 1965–70 *DARE* (Qu. Y36, *To spill something over the sides of a container: "See if you can carry that water without _____ [it all over]."*) 33 Infs, **chiefly Sth,** Wasting (it); **DC13,** Wastening; (Qu. Y45, *Talking of a liquid—to scatter in all directions: "When he opened the can, the beer _____ [all over the kitchen]."*) Inf **MO8,** It wasted it over the kitchen; **AL61,** Wasted. [21 of 34 total Infs Black] 1966 *DARE* FW Addit **SC,** *Waste*—to spill—"Don't waste

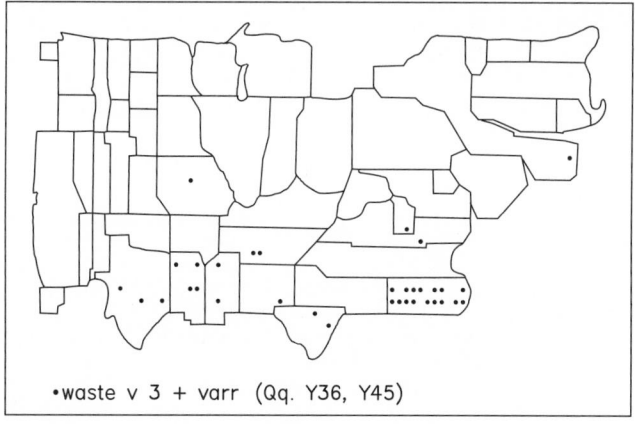

•waste v 3 + varr (Qq. Y36, Y45)

water on my clean floor!" **1973** *DARE* File **Chicago IL** (as of 1960s) [Black], Spill. . . "You wasted the marbles all over the floor", "Look out, someone wasted some water there!" **1976** *Ibid* **seLA** [Black], Don't waste that milk. **1986** Pederson *LAGS Concordance*, 1 inf, **seLA**, Waste it = spill something, among Blacks.

4 also with *away:* To hemorrhage, esp from the uterus.

c1938 [see **waste** n]. **1942** (1971) Campbell *Cloud-Walking* 50 **seKY**, But come night time, Marthy was wasting so bad [following childbirth] Sary couldn't noways leave her. **1946** *AmSp* 21.192 **seKY**, *Waste* . . to have a hemorrhage, especially from the uterus. 'Go git the doctor quick, an' tell him Maw's a-wastin'.' **1954** *PADS* 21.40 **SC**, *Wastin'*. . . Having uterine bleeding. Negro usage.

waste n [**waste** v 1] **Sth, S Midl** Cf **dark of the moon, shrink of the moon**

The period of the waning moon—usu in phr *on the waste of the moon.*

1899 *Jrl. Amer. Folkl.* 12.265 **cGA**, If you kill a hog in the waste of the moon and cook the meat, it will go away in grease. **1923** Parsons *Folk-lore Sea Islands* 209 **csSC** [Black], Kill on de waste o' de moon, de meat will sh'ink to not'in'. **c1937** in Lib. of Congress *Amer. Memory: Born in Slavery* (Internet) **GA** [Black], Always plant corn on the waste of the moon in order for it to yield a good crop. *Ibid* **GA** [Black], Plant yo' crap on de waste ov de moon an' dat crap sho' gwine ter waste er way. **c1938** in 1970 Hyatt *Hoodoo* 1.359 **TN** [Black], On the waste of the moon that person will jest waste away, they'll jest *ministrate* too much, jest flood to death. *Ibid* 2.1825 **LA** [Black], You ketch 'em on the dark of the moon or when the moon's on the waste. **1939** Harris *Purslane* 208 **NC**, She had learned from experience that to attempt soap on the waste of the moon was to have soap shrink and dry up. **1970** *DARE* Tape **VA38**, The old people usually kill by the moon, certain moon now, that they kills hogs on. . . It usually on the waste of the moon. **1984** Wilder *You All Spoken Here* 61 **Sth**, *Dark of the moon, waste of the moon, down side of the moon, shrink of the moon:* When the moon is waning, or decreasing.

wasten See **waste** v 3

wastes See **wasp** 2e

waste up v phr **chiefly Sth** *chiefly among Black speakers*
To consume wastefully.

1919 Austrian *We Need Business* 7 **NYC**, You must learn to *keep away from accounts rated K4* and in that neighborhood. It only wastes up your time and makes unnecessary expenses. **1937** (1977) Hurston *Their Eyes* 17 **FL** [Black], People like dem wastes up too much time puttin' they mouf on things they don't know nothin' about. **1981** Mebane *Mary* 32 **cnNC** [Black], They wouldn't do anything with it but waste it up. **1991** in 1994 *Art Jrl.* Spring 22 **neGA** [Black], I say, "Mama, you gonna have to get me some more crayons." Mama said, "You better quit wasting up that crayon." **2005** Due *Joplin's Ghost* 53 **FL** [Black], Tell her to stop wasting up our money, hear? **2007** *DARE* File—Internet **TX**, So you acknowledge it's stupid? If so, then just stop . . not hard bro. You're wasting up space on the internet.

wasty adj Also sp *wastey* [*W3* wasty adj 1 "archaic"]
Wasteful.

1823 Cooper *Pioneers* 2.45 **cNY** (as of 1790s), It's wicked to be shooting into flocks in this wastey manner. *Ibid* 72, I call it sinful and wasty to catch more than can be eat. **1942** (1971) Campbell *Cloud-Walking* 31 **seKY**, Mort Collins got all riled up and said learning never had no call to be so wasty of house room. **2007** *DARE* File—Internet **OR**, Taxpaers money are going to b spent on burying a piece of meat that can't be sold—*wasty!*

watches n [From the disc-shaped style of the flower] Cf **dumb watches**

A **pitcher plant 1:** usu *Sarracenia flava,* but also *S. purpurea.*

1893 *Jrl. Amer. Folkl.* 6.137 **NJ**, *Sarracenia purpurea,* watches. Atlantic City. **1901** Lounsberry *S. Wild Flowers* 207, *S[arracenia] flava* . . or watches . . is the largest . . representative of the family. Its great lemon-yellow flowers . . are often five inches in diameter. **1936** Whitehouse *TX Flowers* 39, Yellow Pitcher-Plant. . . is also called . . watches, and biscuits. The last two names are suggestive of the broad, umbrella-shaped structure bearing the stigmas and occupying the center of the flower. **1968** Radford et al. *Manual Flora Carolinas* 511, *S[arracenia] flava.* . . Trumpets, Watches, Biscuit-Flower.

watch eye n

A walleye; an animal with a walleye; hence adj *watch-eye(d)*.

1880 *Warren Ledger* (PA) 10 Dec [3]/1 (newspaperarchive.com), *Lost.*—A pointer bitch, watch eyed, color seal brown and white, three white legs and one brown. **1885** *Catholic World* 41.773, In a stall a little to one side of the shrine is a watch-eyed, milk-white pony. **1891** *Outing* 19.183 **WY**, He brought with him for my special use a watch-eyed pinto, a compact, wiry little beast. **1930** Shoemaker *1300 Words* 65 **cPA Mts** (as of c1900), *Watch-eye*—A horse with one blue eye, "wall-eyed." **2006** *DARE* File—Internet, Gallant Fox was a big bay colt with a blaze, a watch eye, and four white coronets. *Ibid*, My breeder . . said all of her watch eye pups tended to be sillier and goofier than the rest. **2007** *DARE* File **csWI** (as of c1960), "Watch eye"—a term used to describe a permanent, unusual, milky appearance of an eye—I've only heard it used in conjunction with horses and dogs. As used in: [⁺]"The horse that I want you to look at is the one with the watch eye."

watchman n Also *watchie*

1965–69 *DARE* (Qu. EE13b, *In games in which all the others hide, the one who must try to find them, he's _____*) Infs **NC72, SC19, 32,** Watchman [FW sugg]; **MS46,** Watchman; **AL3,** Watchie; **OK1,** Watchie [FW sugg].

water n, v

A Forms.

1 usu |ˈwɔtə(r), ˈwɑtə(r)| (see quot 1961); also **chiefly C Atl** |ˈwʌtər, ˈwʊtər|; for addit varr see quots. Pronc-spp *wadder, watter, woe'ter, wooder*

1841 in 1934 *AmSp* 9.263 **eTN**, *Watter.* [*AmSp* author: Evidence for the current Southern pronunciation of [wætə(r)].]] **1961** Kurath-McDavid *Pronc. Engl.* 163, *Water.* . . A rounded back vowel . . is current in all areas, except the greater part of the South Midland. . . Except for Eastern New England and Western Pennsylvania, which lack the /ɔ : ɑ/ contrast, these phones clearly belong to the /ɔ/ phoneme. . . An unrounded low-back vowel [ɑ] . . , clearly the /ɑ/ phoneme . . , is nearly universal in West Virginia, in eastern Ohio . . , and in the westernmost section of North Carolina. In adjoining parts of the South Midland, /ɑ/ stands beside /ɔ/. . . A slightly rounded [ɒ] sound . . has some currency in Western New England and Upstate New York, which can safely be taken as a positional allophone of /ɑ/ following the /w/. [ɒ] phones occur also in Eastern New England and in Western Pennsylvania, where /ɑ/ and /ɔ/ have been merged in the phoneme /ɒ/. In large parts of New Jersey, a subarea of Western Pennsylvania, and on the Eastern Shore of Maryland, *water* often has the /ʌ/ phoneme. **1967** *DARE* FW Addit **LA**14, *Water* [ˈwɔtə]. [Inf] commented on a waitress's pronunciation of the word—[ˈwɑtə]—as odd. . . He characterized the pronunciation as hillbilly. **c1970** Pederson *Dial. Surv. Rural GA* **seGA**, [Among 64 infs, proncs of *water* included 36 of the types [ˈwɔtə, ˈwɑtə, ˈwɒtə]; 20 of the types [ˈwɔtɚ, ˈwɑtɚ, ˈwɒtɚ]; 4 of the types [ˈwɛrə, -ɚ, ˈwʌtɚ]; 2 [ˈwɑtɚ]; 1 [ˈwoʊtɨ].] **1982** Slone *How We Talked* 30 **eKY** (as of c1950), *Woe'ter*—water. **1989** Pederson *LAGS Tech. Index* 166 **Gulf Region**, *Water.* [Of 914 infs, 538 offered proncs of the types [ˈwɔtə(r), ˈwɔdə(r)]; 403 infs, proncs of the types [ˈwɑtə(r)]; 11 infs, proncs of the types [ˈwɒtə(r)]; 2 infs, proncs of the type [ˈwoʊtə].] **1998** *DARE* File—Internet [Language of the Hayna Valley] **cePA**, *Wadder*—Comes out of the *fosset.* **1999** *DARE* File **NJ**, Growing up in suburban New Jersey. . . water sounded more like "wooder." **2004** *News Jrl.* (Wilmington DE) 27 Feb sec E 1/2, *Deltalk* [=Delaware Talk]—"The pitcher of the woman warshing dishes in crick wooder in the zinc was on the wall next to the chimley." **2007** *DARE* File **Philadelphia PA** (as of c1950), Could I have a glass of [ˈwʌtɚ]? *Ibid* **sNJ**, I listened to the whistling of the [ˈwʌtɚ]. **2009** *AmSp* 84.443 **NJ**, Principal Pronunciations of *water.* . . 1. The high-back rounded vowel of *wood* is found mainly in South Jersey. . . It is rare in the north. 2. The vowel of *what* is very common in all counties of the state. . . . 3. The vowel of *awe* is the most common form in the area influenced by New York City and is rarer in the southernmost counties. . . . 4. The vowel of *ah* appears throughout the state, but only rarely in the northeast. There are also some cases of a rhotic vowel in the first syllable, making it equivalent to *wore.*

2 |ˈwɔrtə(r)|; pronc-spp *warter, worter.* **chiefly S Midl** [Cf Intro "Language Changes" I.8]

1777 in 1906 Essex Inst. *Coll.* 42.315 **MA**, He was then order'd . . to Stillwarter, then ordered from Stillwarter to Benington. **1796** in 1956 Eliason *Tarheel Talk* 320 **nw,cnNC**, Warters. **1820** *Ibid* **nw,cnNC**, Worter. **1888** *Century Illustr. Mag.* 35.547 **IN**, Which air / Most destructive element,/ Fire er worter? **1890** *Ibid* 40.640 **Sth** [Black], Some day de warters fall 'n, leab ole Jasper high an' dry. **1899** Garland *Boy Life* 47, And the waters tricklin' round / Makes the barn-yard like a puddle,/ An' softens up the ground,/ Till y'r ankle-deep in worter. **1927** *DN* 5.470 **sAppalachians,** *Water*—warter. **c1960** *Wilson Coll.* **csKY,** Water. . . /'wɔrtə/—rare. **1961** *Mt. Life* 37.1.6 **sAppalachians,** Frequently *r* is inserted in other words: *bursh, pursh,* . . *warter.* **1976** Garber *Mountain-ese* 103 **sAppalachians,** *Worter* . . water—Fetch me a pail uv worter. **2006** *DARE* File **St. Louis MO** [Black], *Water* rhymes with *barter;* it's ['wɔətə].

3 See quots. Pronc-spp *waer, wore* [Cf Intro "Language Changes" I.9]

1910 *Univ. NC Mag.* 40.3.8 **Hatteras Is. NC,** The pronunciation of words with the omission of certain letters; as, . . waer (water). **c1970** Pederson *Dial. Surv. Rural GA* **seGA,** *Water.* . . 1 inf, [wɔ^ɘɛ]. **1989** Pederson *LAGS Tech. Index* 166 **Gulf Region,** 1 inf, ['wɔɚɝ]. **2009** [see **A1** above].

B As noun.

1 in phr *take water:* To retreat (literally or figuratively), back down; to take refuge. [Cf *take water* enter a body of water, in ref to the evasive action of a hunted animal] **chiefly Midl** See Map Cf **backwater** n 1

1853 (1854) Baldwin *Flush Times* 275 **AL,** "Why," said K., "if it please your honor, I believe *I will take water*" (a common expression, signifying that the person using it would take a nonsuit). **1859** (1968) Bartlett *Americanisms* 470, *To Take Water.* To run away, make off. A Western expression, doubtless borrowed from sportsmen. ["]He quitted the wheel [of the steam-boat] and made for his state-room, where he stayed till the boat reached Natchez, when he *took water,* and they do say moved to the North.["]—*Maj. Bunkum, N.Y. Sp. Times.* **1878** *Scribner's Mth.* 17.139, When anything unanswerable or inexplicable is offered to them they take water in serene remarks about the "presumption of human reason." **1887** *NY Times* (NY) 10 Jan 1/1 **neNY,** Congressman Burleigh seemed more elated than ever. "I made him take water on several men," he chuckled, "and I guess I swelled his doubtful list considerably." **1913** London *Valley of Moon* 54 **CA,** Well, you know, any other man to take water the way he did from Butch—why, everybody'd despise him. **1914** *DN* 4.113 **cKS,** *Take water* . . =*back water,* retract, recede. **1923** *DN* 5.223 **swMO,** *Take water.* . . To retreat, to retract a statement. **1930** *Herald–Advt.* (Huntington WV) 30 Nov sec 3 6/6 **KY, WV,** [Fights occur] usually when both sides refuse, in hill-country parlance, to "take water," which means to withdraw boasts made or recent words spoken. **1966–70** *DARE* (Qu. II31, *In an argument between two people, when one of them claims too much and the other shows him up: "He saw that he was wrong, so he started to _____."*) Infs **CO**27, **IL**14, **NC**33, **NJ**2, **PA**104, **VA**31, 91, Take water; (Qu. JJ25, *To show somebody that you're the boss: "He thought he could take the place over, but I made him _____."*) Infs **IL**115, **IN**5, **MD**17, **NJ**53, **VA**31, Take water; **VA**31, Back down and take water. [10 of 11 total Infs comm type 4 or 5] **1968** *DARE* FW Addit **NJ**18, "First man I ever took water from." Backed down, avoided a fight with. **1969** Sorden *Lumberjack Lingo* 131 **NEng, Gt Lakes,** *Took water*—The camp bully who "bit off more than he could chew" and then chose to quit fighting was said to have took water.

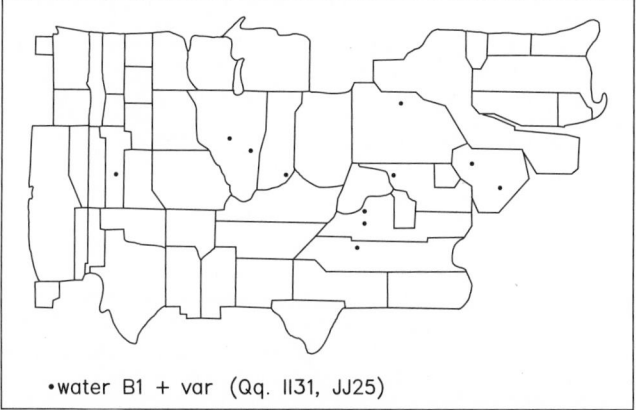

•water B1 + var (Qq. II31, JJ25)

2 in phr *not to get one's water hot* and varr: To exercise patience, refrain from making a hasty judgment. **chiefly Nth**

1935 (1938) De Jong *Old Haven* 377, 'Don't get your water hot,' Klaas said calmly, staring at him unwaveringly, with a faint smile of contempt. 'Don't get yourself in a fit.' [*DARE* Ed: novel set in Netherlands by a Dutch-born American author] **1948** Manfred *Chokecherry* 134 **nwIA,** "For catsake, do something then." "I am," he said, "and don't get your water hot." **1959** Williams *Town Burning* 86 **NH,** Bruce could not win in an exchange of sarcasm, and yet like a compulsive gambler played at it until John, forgetting, said the stupid, unanswerable words, "Don't get your water hot, Brucie." **1965–70** *DARE* (Qu. A21, *When someone is in too much of a hurry* . . *"Now just slow down! Don't _____."*) Infs **CA**35, **CT**32, **MN**42, Get your water hot (*or* boiling); [(Qu. GG23a, *If you speak sharply to somebody to make him be patient* . . *"Now just keep your _____."*) Inf **CT**13, Water from boiling;] (Qu. GG23c, . . *Expressions [to tell someone to be patient]*) Infs **MN**42, **NH**15, **PA**223, Don't get your water hot; **WA**6, Don't let your water get hot. **2006** *DARE* File—Internet, I think the entire idea of littering the ocean to provide wildlife with an artificial reef is just another way of them trying to put their trash into the ocean. [Response:] Don't get your water hot. This is a fitting end for one of our warships.

3 in phrr *until* (or *till*) *the water gets hot* and varr, foll a neg: Even a short time, any time at all. **chiefly Sth, S Midl**

[**1915** *Dog Fancier* 24.5.46 **MO,** [Advt:] *Topsy.* . . winner two good battles for large amounts. I guarantee this bitch to stay till the water gets hot.] **1936** *Pt. Arthur News* (TX) 4 June 8/2, This three-run lead didn't last until the water got hot. The Buffs came back in the sixth to score three runs on four hits. **1938** *Amer. Mercury* 45.56, Unless you can turn out such pieces [=magazine articles] quickly, accurately, and readably . . , you won't last until the water gets hot. **1943** *Eve. Std.* (Uniontown PA) 3 Feb 4/6, The first consignment of the belated dog license tags didn't last till the water got hot. [**1960** *Panola Watchman* (Carthage TX) 14 Jan 7/1, Syracuse scored two touchdowns before the water got hot. Then scored another, also without fuss or sweat scored the extra points.] **1966–67** *DARE* (Qu. V2b, *About a deceiving person, or somebody that you can't trust* . . *"I wouldn't trust him _____.";* not asked in early QRs) Infs **AL**19, **MS**1, **NC**31, 33, **TX**40, Till the water gets hot. **1971** *Baytown Sun* (TX) 22 Sept 23/3, [Advt:] *Eddie Cox Realty*—This One Won't Last Till The Water Gets Hot. **2006** in 2007 *DARE* File—Internet **AR,** They told us the Patriot Act would only be used to fight "the War on Terror." I told you that wouldn't last until the water got hot and I was right, it didn't. **2007** *Ibid* **TX,** Do you consistently have a problem with DVD-Rs . . not lasting until the water gets hot?

water adder n

An aquatic snake such as a **water snake 1.**

1842 DeKay *Zool. NY* 3.42, *Tropidonotus* [=*Nerodia*] *sipedon.* . . It is called indifferently the *Water Snake* or *Water Adder,* and is erroneously said to be poisonous. **1877** Smith *Genl. Hist. Duchess Co.* 39 **NY,** The Brown Water Snake or Water Adder—a snake with its tail tipped with a horn, and frequently regarded with terror, but without cause. **1901** (2005) Pierson *Among Pond People* 122 (Internet) **MI,** The Water-Adders were certainly the cleverest people in the pond. **1921** *Van Wert Daily Bulletin* (OH) 6/1 **NJ,** Onct when I was up at Bear Mountain park I saw a water adder with a catfish as long as that in his mouth. **1966** *DARE* (Qu. P25, . . *Kinds of snakes*) Inf **GA**16, Water adder.

water agrimony n [*OED2* 1597]

=**beggar ticks 1.**

1900 Lyons *Plant Names* 63, *B*[*idens*] *cernua.* . . Water Agrimony. *Ibid,* *B*[*idens*] *tripartita.* . . Water Agrimony. [*DARE* Ed: This may have been based on a British source.] **1914** Georgia *Manual Weeds* 476, Nodding Bur Marigold. . . Water Agrimony.

water apple-blossom n

A **floating heart 1** (here: *Nymphoides aquatica*).

1951 *PADS* 15.37 **TX,** *Nymphoides lacunosum.* . . Water gentian; water apple-blossom [etc] . . are localized names for the plant which crowds out everything else but "water hyacinths," where it gets a good start.

water ash n

1 Any of several North American ashes, as:

a =**Carolina ash.**

1709 (1967) Lawson *New Voyage* 100, The Water-Ash is brittle. The Bark is Food for the Bevers. **1860** Curtis *Cat. Plants NC* 53, Water Ash. . . This is a Southern species, peculiar to the marshy borders of creeks and rivers in the Lower Districts. **1901** Lounsberry *S. Wild Flowers* 422, *F[raxinus] Caroliniana*, water ash . . a beautiful although small tree of deep river-swamps. **1979** Little *Checklist U.S. Trees* 135, *Fraxinus caroliniana*. . . water ash, Florida ash, pop ash, swamp ash.

b =**black ash 1.**

1810 Michaux *Histoire des Arbres* 1.33, *Black ash.* . . dénomination la plus générale dans les Etats du nord et du milieu. *Water ash*, nom secondaire dans cette même partie des Etats-Unis. [=*Black ash.* . . the most common name in the northern and middle states. *Water ash*, a secondary name in this same part of the United States.] **1832** MA Hist. Soc. *Coll.* 2d ser 9.150 cwVT, [*Fraxinus*] Sambucifolia [=*F. nigra*], Water ash. **1837** Darlington *Flora Cestrica* 8 sePA, Sambucus-leaved Fraxinus. *Vulgò*—Black Ash. Water Ash. **1916** Seton *Woodcraft Manual Girls* 295, Black Ash, Hoop Ash, or Water Ash (*Fraxinus nigra*). **2005** Pijut *Native Hardwood Trees* 11, *Fraxinus nigra*. . . Black ash, swamp ash, . . water ash.

c =**green ash.**

1897 Sudworth *Arborescent Flora* 330 IA, *Fraxinus lanceolata* [=*F. pennsylvanica*]. . . Water Ash. **1960** Vines *Trees SW* 864, Vernacular names [for the green ash] are Water Ash, River Ash, Red Ash [etc]. **2005** Pijut *Native Hardwood Trees* 11, *Fraxinus pennsylvanica*. . . Green ash, swamp ash, red ash, water ash. Wet sites along streambanks, bottomland.

d The Oregon ash *(Fraxinus latifolia).*

1966 *Fresno Bee the Republican* (CA) 28 Aug sec F 10/1, The Oregon Ash, or, as it is sometimes called, Broadleaved Ash, Water Ash or Black Ash.

2 A **hop tree** (here: *Ptelea trifoliata*).

1852 Owen *Rept. Geol. Surv. WI IA MN* 610, Ptelea trifoliata. . . Dry river-banks. Called "water-ash," from the singular appearance of its fruit. **1906** Rydberg *Flora CO* 221, *Ptelea* [spp] . . Hop-tree, Water Ash. **1958** Jacobs–Burlage *Index Plants NC* 195, *Ptelea trifoliata*. . . Water ash . . grows from New York to Florida and west to Minnesota and Texas.

3 =**box elder.**

1897 Sudworth *Arborescent Flora* 291 **ND, SD,** *Acer negundo*. . . Common Names. . . Water Ash. **1936** Winter *Plants NE* 179, Box Elder. Ash-leaved Maple. Water Ash. **2006** (acc) FL Univ. Herbarium *Coll. Catalog* (Internet), *Acer negundo*—ash-leaved maple; box-elder; water-ash.

water avens n

Std: an avens (here: *Geum rivale*). Also called **chocolate root, cure-all 1, evans'-root, Indian chocolate, maidenhair 2, throatroot**

water bandit (snake) n [Prob folk-etym for *banded water snake*] **FL**

A **water snake 1** (here: *Nerodia fasciata pictiventris*).

1966 DARE (Qu. P25, . . *Kinds of snakes*) Inf **FL4**, Water bandit. **2004** DARE File—Internet **FL**, My father told me and allot of other people agreed it was a Florida water bandit but that is just a given local name I beleive the accurite one is the Florida banded water snake. **2007** *Ibid* **FL**, [Caption:] A Water Bandit snake relaxes in the rocks.

water bar n Also *bar* **NEng**

=**water break.**

1850 NH Hist. Soc. *Coll.* 6.220, In passing a water bar, he was thrown from his carriage and killed. **1869** U.S. Dept. Ag. *Rept. of Secy. for 1868* 362, *Water Bars.* The purpse [sic] of the bar is to cast the surface water from the road to the side or sides before it has accumulated in such amount as to cut the ruts into gullies. **1874** VT State Bd. Ag. *Report* 2.657, It is a common custom in many places to construct what are called "water-bars" on hill-roads. **1878** *Fitchburg Daily Sentinel* (MA) 19 June [2]/2, There was only a slight water bar in the road. **1899** *Atlantic Mth.* 83.57 **MA**, The horses pausing for breath as one water-bar after another is surmounted . . we are at the height of land. **1940** Gilbert *Country Preacher* 65 **VT**, It had rained and the road was rough, with sandy spots and water bars. **1963** Haywood *Yankee Dict.* 192, *Water Bar.* . . A low, gently graded gravel ridge or mound extending across a North Country hill road at a downward angle to carry rain water that collects at one side to the drainage ditch at the other. **1966–69** DARE (Qu. N30, . . *A sudden short dip in a road*) Inf **CT**14, Hump—old road had bars across on hills to keep water from running all the way down; **VT**7, Water bar; **MA**58, Water bar—on back roads (water conduits under road to ditch); **NH**5, Water bar—in dirt road—put these on purpose

to divert water into ditch, a small dam. **1967** *DARE* Tape **VT**1A, A little hump? Yeah, water bars, water bars they used to call them. . . They turned the water so it wouldn't wash the whole way—length of the road. **2000** in 2006 (acc) Lexis–Nexis Legal Research *State Case Law: ME* (Internet), Sugarloaf constructed the water bar to channel water across the trail. . . When there is no snow, the water bar appears as a ditch lined with rocks. **2007** *DARE* File **NEng,** A water bar is a poor man's culvert and they are in widespread use on hiking trails and woods roads all over New England.

water beater n

A **dragonfly.**

1968 *DARE* (Qu. R2, . . *The dragonfly*) Inf **PA**68, Water beater.

water beech n

1 A **sycamore B** (here: *Platanus occidentalis*).

1748 in 1970 Kalm *Resejournal* 2.138 **Philadelphia PA,** *Platanus.* . . Af de engelska här kallades den dels *button-wood*, dels och mäst *water-beech*. [=*Platanus.* . . called *button-wood* by some of the English here, and by most *water-beech*.] **1814** Pursh *Flora Americae* 2.635, *[Platanus] occidentalis.* . . On the banks of rivers. . . This tree is known by the name of *Button-wood, Water Beech, Sycamore* and *Plane Tree.* **1860** Curtis *Cat. Plants NC* 76, Sycamore. . . In some sections it is called *Water Beech* and *Plane Tree.* **1897** Sudworth *Arborescent Flora* 206 **DE,** Sycamore. . . Common Names. . . Water Beech. **1950** Peattie *Nat. Hist. Trees* 315, Sycamore. . . Water Beech. **1968–70** DARE (Qu. T15, . . *Kinds of swamp trees*) Infs **IN**11, 32, 35, **NY**233, Water beech. [DARE Ed: Some of these Infs may refer instead to **2** below.]

2 =**hornbeam 1.**

1837 Darlington *Flora Cestrica* 541 sePA, American Carpinus. *Vulgò*—Hornbeam. Water Beech. . . Margins of rivulets: frequent. **1894** Coulter *Botany W. TX* 413, *C[arpinus] Caroliniana*. . . American hornbeam. Blue or water beech. **1916** Seton *Woodcraft Manual Girls* 280, *Blue Beech, Water Beech,* or *American Hornbeam (Carpinus caroliniana)*—A small tree 10 to 25, rarely 40, feet high; bark smooth. Wood hard, close-grained, very strong; much like Ironwood. **1979** Little *Checklist U.S. Trees* 71, *Carpinus caroliniana*. . . Blue-beech, water-beech, "ironwood."

waterbelly n

A **kiyi** (here: *Coregonus kiyi*).

1983 Becker *Fishes WI* 361, Kiyi. . . Other common names: bigeye, paperbelly, waterbelly [etc]. **2007** U.S. Food & Drug Admin. *Seafood List* (Internet), Common name—Kiyi[·] Vernacular name(s)—Waterbelly[·] Mooneye.

water bewitched n [Engl dial; *OED2* (at *water* sb. 2.c) 1678 →]

Fig: an excessively diluted drink such as weak tea or coffee—usu in phrr *water bewitched and coffee* (or *tea*) *begrudged* and varr; similarly phr *water bewitched and meal begrudged* thin porridge.

1840 (1841) Dana *2 Yrs.* 387, Our common beverage—'water bewitched, and tea begrudged,' as it was. [Footnote:] The proportions of the ingredients of the tea that was made for us . . were, a pint of tea, and a pint and a half of molasses, to about three gallons of water. **1905** *Fresno Morning Republican* (CA) 27 Oct 9/3, If these proportions are used one will not be accused of being sparing with her tea or have a guest consider the cheering cup no more than water bewitched. **1909** *DN* 3.419 Cape Cod MA (as of a1857), Begretched. . . Begrudged. "It was said of thin porridge that it was *water bewitched and meal begretched*." **1951** Johnson *Resp. to PADS 20* **DE** (*Weak coffee*) Water bewitched and coffee begrudged. **1952** *DE Folkl. Bulletin* 1.11, "Water bewitched and coffee begrudged"—said of weak coffee. **1975** *Syracuse Herald–Amer.* (NY) 31 Aug mag sec 14/1, It is shocking to see the weak-colored brew, with a taste that my mother used to call "water bewitched," that one is served. It's no more a good cup of coffee than is cold dishwater.

water birch n

Either a **river birch** (here: *Betula nigra*) or **western birch.**

1859 *S. Lit. Messenger* 28.143, Yisterday, I was . . fishin in the deep hole thar for peerch, an had two lines out for cat, hitched to water-birch limbs. **1897** Sudworth *Arborescent Flora* 141 **KS, WV,** *Betula nigra*, River Birch. . . Water Birch. **1954** Roberts *I Bought Dog* 18 seKY, A great big flock of wild geese . . flew up in a water-birch. **1961** Douglas *My Wilderness* 63 sUT, The water birch—greatly loved in our western country—lines the banks. . . Unlike the other birches, this one has bark that does not peel. **1969** *DARE* (Qu. T15, . . *Kinds of swamp trees*) Infs **KY**16, 29, Water birch. **2006** (acc) U.S. Dept. Ag. *Plants Database* (Internet), *Betula occidentalis . .* water birch.

water biscuit n cwNY

A disk-shaped concretion of lime secreted by fresh-water algae.

1915 *Amer. Philos. Soc. Proc.* 54.250, The concretions of the Little Conestoga are very similar to the "Lake Balls" from Lake Canandaigua, New York, so vividly described by Dr. Clarke, under the name of "Water Biscuits." **1952** *Daily Messenger* (Canandaigua NY) 8 Apr 3/2, Through a continuous process the "water biscuit" is developed. The biscuits are round and are composed of a soft, light-colored substance which crumbles easily as a cracker. **1972** *NYT Article Letters* **cwNY**, *Water Biscuit.* They are *not* a generic name for "flat pebbles"! They are formed by lime-secreting, fresh-water algae; and I think that in Canandaigua Lake, they are found only on Squaw Island. **2006** *DARE* File—Internet **cwNY**, Squaw Island. . . is one of the unique and few places on earth that makes water biscuits.

water bitternut n [See quot 1810] Cf bitter waternut

=water hickory.

1810 Michaux *Histoire des Arbres* 1.20, J[uglans] [=*Carya*] aqua-tica—*Water bitter nut hickery. . . Water bitter nut,* nom donné par moi à cette espèce qui n'en a aucun dans les Etats méridionaux où elle croît. [=*Water bitter nut,* a name given by me to this species which has none in the southern states where it grows.] **1908** Britton *N. Amer. Trees* 227, Water hickory. . . It is also called the Bitter pecan, Swamp hickory, and Water bitternut. **1939** Tharp *Vegetation TX* 37, Hickories range from Buckley's hickory on the uplands to the water bitternut in the bottoms along sloughs.

water bonnet n [From the shape of the rosette] Cf bonnet B1c

=water lettuce.

1933 Small *Manual SE Flora* 247, *P[istia] Stratiotes. . . Water-lettuce. Water-bonnets. . .* Frequently forming a complete, often extensive gray-green carpet. The hairy ribbed myriad leaf-surfaces produce an iri-descent effect. **1938** Neely *Tales S. IL* 45, The pond was all growed up in water bonnets, and they was a thicket all around it. **1965** Will *Okeechobee Boats* 14 **FL**, Dead rivers a-ziggin and a-zagging among the water bonnets and flags and reeds. **2005** *FL Times–Union* (Jacksonville) 21 Oct (Internet), Climbing fall aster, moonflower vine, water bonnets, . . and the red leaves of Florida maple trees appeared along the banks of the various streams.

water-bonnet worm See bonnet worm

water bread n

=hot-water corn bread.

1958 *PADS* 29.18 **TN**, *Water bread. . .* Corn bread. "Corn bread mixed with water." **1986** Pederson *LAGS Concordance (Bread and cakes made with cornmeal)* 1 inf, **neMS**, Water bread—cornmeal, salt, water, top of stove; 1 inf, **nwAL**, Water bread.

water break n Cf breaker 2, 4, thank-you-ma'am 1, water bar, ~ butt

A diagonal ridge made on a hill road to divert water and prevent erosion.

1846 OH *Documents Genl. Assembly* 10.2.47, The Resident Engineer required bidders for putting on stone to take into consideration . . the removal of all water-breaks. **1889** in 2007 (acc) Lexis–Nexis Legal Research *State Case Law: MI* (Internet), There was a water-break, being a slight elevation crossing the road to turn the water which might flow down through the cutting to the sides of the embankment. **1912** *Gettysburg Comp.* (PA) 17 July [2]/3 (newspaperarchive.com), The Court held that time did not sanction unlawful obstructions and that water breaks were not considered necessary by modern road builders. **1968** *DARE* (Qu. N30, . . *A sudden short dip in a road*) Inf **MN**23, Water break—put there on purpose to keep road from washing out [FW illustr: a ridge or hump]; **VA**27, Water break—where water runs over the road; **VA**30, Water break—where the water runs partway down the road, hits the hump of dirt, and goes into the side ditches. **1982** Ginns *Snowbird Gravy* 134 **nwNC**, And there was an old water break there where we had cut it to keep from washing the old road away. **1994** in 2006 (acc) Lexis–Nexis Legal Research *State Case Law: NC* (Internet), We had somebody go check the road . . if there was any erosion, and we kept putting water breaks on it as the years went by, so that you could drive over it. **1994** *Mt. Democrat & Placerville Times* (CA) 24 Oct 24/5,

[Advt:] Snow removal, bar ditches, fire breaks, water breaks, drainage, road & driveway grading.

water brush See water bush 1

water bug n [Because it prefers water pipes and moist places in houses] Cf water roach

A cockroach, esp a large one, or a similar insect.

1875 *Sedalia Daily Democrat* (MO) 9 July 1/3, If you are troubled with ants, water-bugs, cockroaches, or insects of any description, powdered borax laid in their haunts will dismiss them to a new ranging ground. **1897** *Century Illustr. Mag.* 54.452, No trouble with refrigerators and plumbers, no water-bugs, no cockroaches. **1933** Smiley *Gloss. New Paltz* se**NY**, In calling my attention to some roaches Mrs. Decker used the expression "water bugs". I think this may be rather general. **1950** *WELS (Other names for the cockroach)* 4 Infs, **WI**, Water bug. **1965–70** *DARE* (Qu. R30, . . *Kinds of beetles;* not asked in early QRs) Infs **KS**8, **KY**60, **TX**22, 26, **VT**16, Water bug; **DC**11, Water bug—this is a big black bug found in basements; **IN**7, Water bugs, roaches; **NC**87, Water bugs—black, about the shape of a roach, but much bigger; hangs around plumbing; **NJ**67, Water bug, roach bug; **NY**36, Cockaroaches [sic], water bugs; **VA**73, Water bug—looks like a three-inch cockroach [FW: I saw some; description fits]. **1970** GA Dept. Ag. *Farmers Market Bulletin* 28 Oct 8/2, They do look like the legs of those famous Florida waterbugs or ugly roaches. **1995** *DARE* File **Sth**, Terms like *water bug, croton bug, steam fly,* and *palmetto bug* are easier to talk about than admitting you have "roaches." **2007** *DARE* File—Internet s**FL**, The Roach you saw flying across your living room is the *American roach,* most often called the *palmetto* in the south, or *water bug* in the north. The *palmetto* is a water roach that normally feeds on decaying organic matter.

water bush n

1 also *water brush:* Any of several bushes that grow in bogs or swampy areas, such as **leatherleaf 1, buttonbush 1,** or bog rosemary *(Andromeda polifolia).* **eMA, sNH** *?obs*

1793 Whitney *Hist. Co. Worcester* 141 c**MA**, The sixth [island] is another Grass Island, having upon it willows and waterbushes. **1829** *NH Patriot & State Gaz.* (Concord) 2 Nov 2/2, cs**NH**, Capt. Coffin has about twelve acres of meadow land, five of which has [sic] been redeemed from a sunken situation, producing nothing but flags and water bushes. **1841** *Amer. Farmer* 8.227 **NEng**, *Those Bushes in the Swamp.*—Might it not be well for you . . to wage war upon the alders, blueberry bushes, water bushes, &c. which skirt your mowing lands? **1846** *Cultivator* new ser 3.378 ce**MA**, [He] was another claimant for the premium on bog-meadows. His land was formerly occupied, he says, with "water-grass, or cotton-head, water-brush, and blue-vengeance." **1854** NH State Ag. Soc. *Trans. for 1853* 285 se**NH**, My first object was to drain the water off, . . which gave me an opportunity to commence cutting the water-bushes, (which were from three to eight feet high.) **1856** NH State Ag. Soc. *Trans. for 1855* 298 sw**NH**, The more moist portions of them seem obstinately determined to grow moss, boxberry, blue-berry, hard-hack, water brush, spruce, pines, birches, etc. **1857** (1949) Thoreau *Jrl.* 9.467 ce**MA**, He stepped on to some "water-brush" (probably water andromeda), and suddenly sank very deep. **1859** in 1861 Boston Soc. Nat. Hist. *Proc.* 7.159 ce**MA**, It [=the trout pickerel] is generally found either in what is called "water-bushes," *(Cephalanthus occidentalis,)* or in pickerel-weed. **1860** (1949) Thoreau *Jrl.* 13.255 ce**MA**, *April 22. . .* The cassandra (water-brush) is well out. **1899** Boston Soc. Nat. Hist. *Proc.* 28.183, They . . were busily engaged in making large nests in the water bushes, Cephalanthus.

2 A **groundsel tree** (here: *Baccharis halimifolia*). **chiefly C Atl**

1911 U.S. Coast & Geodetic Surv. *Oyster Bars* 39 **MD**, Point on which station is located has a sugar-berry tree, several small locust trees and water bushes. **1920** *Torreya* 20.25 **VA**, *Baccharis halimifolia . .* Waterbush, water-gall, Horn Point. **1938** Torrey Bot. Club *Bulletin* 65.489 **NC**, The most resistant woody plant is the water bush *(Baccharis halimifolia).* **1969** *DARE* (Qu. S15, . . *Weed seeds that cling to clothing*) Inf **NC**76, Your water bush does, going through the marsh. **1973** *Copeia* 499 e**NC**, As elsewhere on the Banks, *Ammophila* (beach grass), *Baccharis* (water bush) and *Rhus radicans* (poison ivy) hold the dunes in their early seral stages. **1973** *NY Folkl. Qrly.* 29.24 s**MD**, It was an old Indian custom to break water-bushes off, we call them. I don't know the proper name of the bush. But they grow in this brackish water area around the marsh edges and on the banks of the creeks. **2000** Shores *Tangier Is.* 220 **Chesapeake Bay,** Before refrigerated trucks, they shipped hard crabs in a basket with the limbs and leaves of a bush, a kind of myrtle, that grew near the water, which they call *gall bushes* and *water bushes*.

water-buster n   Cf **belly-buster 2**

=**belly-flop 2.**

    1969 *DARE* (Qu. EE29, *When swimmers are diving and one comes down flat onto the water, that's a* _____) Inf **GA**77, Belly-buster, water-buster.

water butt n   [Perh *OED2 butt* sb.⁶ 1 "One of the parallel divisions of a ploughed field contained between two parallel furrows, called also a 'ridge'."] *?obs*

=**water break.**

    1876 CT State Bd. Ag. *Annual Rept. 1875–76* 299, We favor the plan of making a narrow road best, the highest in the middle, and as few water butts as possible. **1895** *DN* 1.385, *Breaker:* ridge of earth in hilly part of country road, to throw surface water into side ditches. . . [*DN* Ed: In Conn. *"water-butt"* is the usual word; *"thank-you-ma'am"* is known.]

water buzzard n   chiefly **Sth, S Midl**

=**double-crested cormorant.**

    1876 *Daily Constitution* (Atlanta GA) 17 Dec [2]/6 (newspaperarchive.com) **FL,** And then I gazed at that oblong head . . , and wondered what it profited after all, when it didn't enable its owner to tell a water-buzzard from a spoon-bill drake. **1917** A.H. Howell in *Wilson Bulletin* 29.2.76 **AL,** Phalacrocorax auritus.—Water buzzard, Autagaville. **1918** *Janesville Daily Gaz.* (WI) 19 Oct 6/1 **nwTN,** The owls and heavy-winged "water-buzzards" have never left. **1947** Bedichek *Advent. TX Naturalist* 189, The cormorant is also called a black swan, in derision; a water buzzard—he eats no carrion; and a water turkey, an obvious mistake in identification. **1980** *Chicago Tribune* (IL) 8 June sec I 6/4, Until you see the water buzzards swimming completely submerged except for their snakelike neck and bill, you will never quite understand how birds can be descended from reptiles. **2005** in 2007 *DARE* File—Internet **IA,** I've heard those water buzzards can eat 6–10 lbs of fish a day! Keep them away from your smaller farm ponds. . . Cormerants [sic] are evil little bastages!

water cabbage n

1 A **white water lily** (here: usu *Nymphaea odorata*).

    1830 Rafinesque *Med. Flora* 2.44, *Nymphea odorata. Names. . . Vulgar.* White Pond Lily, Toad Lily, Cow Cabbage, Water Cabbage. **1900** Lyons *Plant Names* 85, *C[astalia] odorata.* . . Water Cabbage, Toad Lily. [The same names . . are given to the very similar but larger and scentless . . *C. tuberosa* . . , northern U.S. to Nebraska.] **1974** (1977) Coon *Useful Plants* 193, *Nymphaea odorata*—Fragrant waterlily, pondlily, bonnets, water cabbage.

2 =**water lettuce.**

    1894 *San Antonio Daily Light* (TX) 27 Sept 3/2, The boat glides easily across the surface, past floating water cabbage, with their velvet leaves. **1897** *Oölogist* 14.75 **LA,** I have seen one [=a least bittern] standing on the floating water-cabbages, (a curious aquatic plant which carpets many southern bayous). **1938** *Ecological Monogr.* 8.15 **LA,** The open water of the fresh water habitat is often coated with duckweeds and the water fern and in some ponds with introduced water cabbage *(Pistia stratiotes).* **2006** *DARE* File—Internet **nwFL,** There was water cabbage and water "parsley" on the surface.

water camp n   **West**   Cf **dry camp**

A camping place with access to water.

    1862 *Harper's New Mth. Mag.* 25.459 **West,** At our "Water Camp" . . we were doomed to spend the two succeeding days. **1898** King *Warrior Gap* 177 **West,** Ordinarily when making summer marches over the range, the first "water camp" on the Sweetwater trail was here at Cañon Springs.

water carpet n   Also *water mat*

=**golden saxifrage.**

    1822 Eaton *Botany* 237, *Chrysosplenium . . oppositifolium* (golden saxifrage, water-carpet). . . In rivulets, springs, &c. **1832** MA Hist. Soc. *Coll.* 2d ser 9.148 **cwVT,** Chrysosplenium oppositifolium, . . Water carpet. **1837** Darlington *Flora Cestrica* 270 **sePA,** American Chrysosplenium. *Vulgò*—Golden Saxifrage. Water carpet. **1950** Gray–Fernald *Manual of Botany* 744, *C. americanum.* . . Water-mat, Water-carpet. **1953** Strausbaugh–Core *Flora WV* 452, *C[hrysosplenium] americanum.* . . Golden saxifrage. Water carpet.

water cedar   See **cedar moss**

water celery n

1 =**tape grass.**   esp Chesapeake Bay

    1885 *Lake Shore Observer* (Dunkirk NY) 12 Oct [2]/3 (newspaperarchive.com) **Chesapeake Bay,** Like the canvasback duck, the terrapin feeds chiefly on water celery or watercress. **1891** *Century Dict.* 6690 **Chesapeake Bay,** *V[allisneria] spiralis.* . . In streams flowing into Chesapeake Bay, where it grows in great masses, it is known as *water-celery* or *wild celery.* **1952** Strausbaugh–Core *Flora WV* 64, *V[allisneria] americana.* . . Eelgrass. Tapegrass. Water Celery. . . Much eaten by ducks. **1970** Correll *Plants TX* 102, *Vallisneria americana* Michx. Water-celery. **2001** *Congressional Record* 27 Nov 147.H8393 [Speaker from **MD**], Some 300,000 diving ducks stop in the Lower Detroit River on their fall migration from Canada . . to rest and feed in beds of water celery found in the region.

2 A **buttercup 1** (here: *Ranunculus sceleratus*).

    1940 Clute *Amer. Plant Names* 5, *R[anunculus] sceleratus.* . . water celery. **1979** Erichsen-Brown *Med. N. Amer. Plants* 272, The Cursed Crowfoot. . . Common Names. Celery leaved crowfoot, . . water celery.

water chicken n

1 A frog, considered as food.

    1859 *Berkshire Co. Eagle* (Pittsfield MA) 20 Oct 1/5 **MN,** A traveler stopping at one of the hotels in Minnesota, recently saw the phrase "Fried Water Chickens" on the dinner bill of fare. . . After a hearty dinner, he found he had dined on frogs. **1860** *Vanity Fair* 2.258 **Boston MA,** As the visitor . . approaches this miniature lake and its water-chickens, he beholds conspicuously affixed to the surrounding trees this mandate: "Dogs not allowed in the Frog Pond on Sundays." **1862** *Continental Mth.* 2.246, That exquisite process of nature, tadpoles turning into spring water-chickens, as they call frogs on hotel bill of fares. **1885** *Oshkosh Daily Northwestern* (WI) 20 Mar [3]/5 (newspaperarchive.com) **Chicago IL,** The large green bullfrogs is [sic] the chief kind sold in this market. In Chicago they are called water chickens, because their flesh is white as that of a chicken when dressed properly. **2006** *DARE* File—Internet **FL,** As for eating things, I'll eat anything that doesn't eat me first. . . Speaking of which, think I'll go pull some water chicken out the freeze [sic] for tomorrow. [*DARE* Ed: This quot may refer instead to other senses below.]

2 =**Florida gallinule.**   Cf **poule d'eau 2, swamp chicken 2, water hen 1a**

    1881 *NY Evangelist* (NY) 17 Feb 7/2, It adds to the list of birds not to be shot between May 1 and September 1, except on Long Island . . coots, rail, snipe, plover, and water chickens. **1886** in 1888 Trumbull *Names of Birds* 122 **NY,** In a list of the birds of Oneida Co. and its vicinity, New York . . this species [=*Gallinula galeata*] is mentioned as . . locally known as *water-chicken.* **2010** *DARE* File—Internet **cnFL,** Nearby were two birds locally known as 'water chickens' that had bright orange duck-like bills but chicken-like feet.

3 A **coot** n¹ **1** (here: *Fulica americana*).   Cf **poule d'eau 1, water hen 1c**

    1867 Dorsey *Lucia Dare* 63 **sLA,** She looked out on the white gulls . . ; at the flocks of water-chickens ducking and rising with the roll of the sea. **1910** *Hunter-Trader-Trapper* 21.154, A coot is commonly called a mud hen or water chicken. **1918** *CA Fish & Game* 4.36, There is nothing new about the use of mudhens on this coast. Leading hotels have served them as "water chickens" in San Diego for years. **1954** *Harder Coll.* **cwTN,** Water chicken. . . A type of duck. **1967–69** *DARE* (Qu. Q9, *The bird that looks like a small, dull-colored duck and is commonly found on ponds and lakes*) Inf **KY**65, Water chicken; (Qu. Q10, . . *Water birds and marsh birds*) Inf **MO**38, Water chicken. **2009** in 2010 *DARE* File—Internet **cNC,** The only time this happens when you have a gun is when you look up to find blue feet. . . daggum water chickens (coots). **2010** *Ibid,* You may get teased mercilessly by your friends if you add water chickens to your spread, but coot decoys are good confidence decoys.

water chickweed n   [*OED2* 1760]

A **miner's lettuce** (here: *Montia fontana*).

    1853 NY State Museum *Catalogue Cabinet Nat. Hist.* 36, Callitriche verna, *Common Water Chickweed.* **1923** in 1925 Jepson *Manual Plants CA* 346, *M[ontia] fontana* . . Water Chickweed. . . In water on margins of small surface streams or in muddy places. **1987** Hughes–Blackwell *Wildflowers SE AK* 90, Blinks, water chickweed. . . Wet places, shallow water.

water chinquapin n [water + **chinquapin**]

An American lotus (Nelumbo lutea) or its edible nutlike seed. Also called **alligator buttons, ~ corn, bonnet B1b, chinquapin B4, duck acorn, ~ potato 2, graine à voler, Indian potato p, knock-knock 2, lily nut, monaca ~, pond ~, wankapin, yonkanut, yonkapin, yonker pad, yorky nut**

1822 Barton Flora 2.79 **sePA,** Capsule very large . . having embedded in it from seventeen to twenty ovate seeds. . . They are esculent in the green state, and are collected eagerly by boys who eat and sell them under the name of water chinquapins. **1836** Lincoln Famil. Lectures app 119, Water chinquepin, sacred bean. . . Flowers larger than those of any other plant in North America, except one species of magnolia. **1878** Chester Daily Times (PA) 24 Aug 4/1 **MA,** A pale yellow blossom—the nelumbium luteum, or Water Chinquapin. **1885** Thompson By-Ways 103, From Florida to Michigan one may run the gamut of nuts, beginning with the lily-nuts, or water chinquepins. **1906** DN 3.163 **nwAR,** Water-chinkapin. . . Yoncopin. **1945** Saxon Gumbo Ya-Ya 562 **LA,** Water chinquapins: seeds of the yellow lotus. **1998** News (Frederick MD) 16 July 12/5, Nelumbo Lutea (sometimes called American Lotus) . . is native to North America. You may also hear it referred to as the Water Chinquapin, an American Indian name.

water crab See **crab** n 1

water crow n

=**anhinga.**

1838 Audubon Ornith. Biog. 4.138 **seLA,** At the mouths of the [Mississippi] river it bears the name of "Water Crow." **1931** Read LA French 5, American Snakebird . . commonly known as the "water turkey"—sometimes as the "negro goose" or "water crow."

water crowfoot n [OED2 c1550 →]

A **buttercup 1,** esp Ranunculus aquatilis.

1876 Hobbs Bot. Hdbk. 125, Water crowfoot, Ranunculus aquatica. **1910** Graves Flowering Plants 185 **CT,** Ranunculus aquatilis. . . Common White Water Crowfoot. . . Ponds and slow streams. **1968** Barkley Plants KS 151, Ranunculus longirostris . . White Water Crowfoot.

watercup n

A **pitcher plant 1,** esp Sarracenia purpurea.

1892 (1974) Millspaugh Amer. Med. Plants 19-1, Pitcher-plant. . . Com[mon] Names. . . huntsman's cup, water-cup, Eve's cups [etc]. **1936** Whitehouse TX Flowers 39, Trumpet-Leaf (Sarracenia sledgei) is also called trumpets, water-cup [etc]. . . The . . names refer to the tubular, ribbed, trumpet-shaped leaves. **2006** WI Flora May 3, Northern Pitcher Plant. . . Other Names: Virgin Mary's Socks . . Water-Cup [etc].

‡**water daisy** n

A **pipewort** (here: Eriocaulon decangulare).

1951 PADS 15.27 **TX,** Eriocaulon decangulare. . . Water daisy.

water dipper n

A **dragonfly.**

1968–70 DARE (Qu. R2, . . The dragonfly) Infs **CA**199, **NJ**21, **TN**33, Water dipper; **PA**128, Water dipper [FW sugg]; **WI**61, Water dipper—not too often.

water dock n

=**golden club 1.**

1900 Lyons Plant Names 269, [Orontium] aquaticum. . . Massachusetts to Louisiana, mostly near the coast. Golden-club, . . Water Dock. **1940** Clute Amer. Plant Names 152, Oronticum [sic] . . aquaticum. Golden Club . . water dock.

water dog n

1 Any of var **salamanders 1,** but esp Necturus spp. Also called **water puppy** For other names of Necturus spp see **ground puppy 1c, hog-nosed water dog, man-eater 2, mud puppy b, thunder dog**

1832 Edinburgh New Philos. Jrl. 12.298, I believe that the animal [= Siren lacertina] occurs also in creeks of the Mississippi and Ohio; for M. Audubon . . happening to be in Edinburgh in the spring of 1830 . . recognized the siren as an old acquaintance, occasionally taken in trawl-nets, and called by the fishermen water-dog and water-puppy. **1859** (1968) Bartlett Americanisms 502, Water-dogs. The Western name for various species of salamanders, or lizard-shaped animals with smooth, shiny, naked skins; sometimes called Water-puppies and Ground-pup-

pies. **1883** Chicago Acad. Sci. Trans. 1.26 **IL,** Necturus lateralis. . . Mud-puppy or Water-dog. Exceedingly abundant in Lake Michigan; found also in Mississippi and other rivers throughout the State. **1899** Marine Biol. Lab. Biol. Lect. 1898 295, Our large fresh-water salamander, popularly called mud-puppy, water-dog, hellbender, etc., is another animal that may be profitably studied. **1906** DN 3.163 **nwAR,** Water-dog. . . A kind of newt with a doglike face. **1912** Science 36.594 **CO,** When the writer was a boy residing at Colorado Springs, he confined some "water-dogs" (Amblystoma) . . in an artificial pool of water. **1958** Conant Reptiles & Amphibians 198, Necturus maculosus. . . This salamander is a Mudpuppy in the North, but Southerners, not to be outdone in coining colorful names, refer to it and all its relatives as Waterdogs. **1966–69** DARE (Qu. P3, Freshwater fish that are not good to eat) Infs **IL**16, **NC**33, **PA**199, Water dog(s); (Qu. P6, . . Kinds of worms . . used for bait) Inf **PA**168, Water dogs, salamanders; (Qu. P7, Small fish used as bait for bigger fish) Infs **CA**95, **PA**168, Water dogs; (Qu. P13, . . Ways of fishing . . besides the ordinary hook and line) Inf **PA**168, Other bait . . water dogs; (Qu. P19) Inf **NM**3, They have water dogs—like a catfish with four legs, brown with black and white spots; (Qu. P23, Names for the animal similar to the frog that lives away from water) Inf **CO**4, Water dog; (Qu. P32, . . Other kinds of wild animals) Inf **OK**25, Water dog—another lizard; **WY**1, Water dog—salamander. **1968** DARE Tape **NC**53, Its real name is hellbinder, but . . around here it's a water dog or a mud puppy. . . You catch 'em usually at the Brasstown creeks. **1969** DARE FW Addits **KY**44, 60, 68, Water dog—salamander—common. **1982** Slone How We Talked 111 **eKY** (as of c1950), Water dogs or thunder dogs—A small, worm-like animal that lives in the water. We were told that if one bites you, it would not let go until it thundered or a cow bawled. I don't think they bit at all. **1991** Still Wolfpen Notebooks 163 **sAppalachians,** Water dog: spring lizard.

2 See quot. [Engl dial] Cf **rain dog**

2004 DARE File **NM,** Water Dog: low lying cloud at treetop level. Usually appears after a storm.

3 =**sun dog.**

1954 PADS 21.40 **SC,** Water-dog. . . A small patch, a short strip of rainbow. **c1960** Wilson Coll. **csKY,** Water-dog. . . A sundog or broken bit of rainbow formation, at some distance from the sun; a partial halo.

water dragon n

1 A **marsh marigold** (here: Caltha palustris). [Perh by confusion with Calla palustris, also called water dragon (OED2 1578)]

1876 Hobbs Bot. Hdbk. 125, Water dragon, Marsh marigold, Caltha palustris. **1892** (1974) Millspaugh Amer. Med. Plants 7-1, Caltha palustris. . . Com[mon] Names.—Marsh marigold, . . water dragon. **1900** Lyons Plant Names 77, C[altha] palustris. . . Water-dragon.

2 =**lizard's tail 1.**

1950 Gray–Fernald Manual of Botany 487, Lizard's-tail. . . Water-dragon, Swamp-lily.—Extensively creeping. . . Swamps and shallow water. **1976** Bruce How to Grow Wildflowers 281, Lizard's-tail for dense shade. . . It is also called Water-dragon and Swamp-lily.

waterdrop n

A **downspout.**

1970 DARE (Qu. D29, The pipe that takes the collected rain-water down to the ground or to a storage tank) Inf **MA**124, Waterdrop or rain spout.

water-dropwort n [OED2 (at dropwort sb. 2) 1597 for spp of Oenanthe, to which these plants were originally assigned]

A **cowbane 2.**

1897 Britton–Brown Illustr. Flora 2.513, Oxypolis rigidus. . . Hemlock, or Water Dropwort. . . In swamps, New York to Florida, west to Wisconsin, Minnesota. **1933** Small Manual SE Flora 986, O[xypolis] filiformis. . . Water-dropwort. . . Coastal Plain, Fla. to La. and S.C. . . O. rigidior. . . Water-dropwort. . . Wet woods, swamps, and cliffs. . . Fla. to La., Minn., and N.Y. **2004** Austin FL Ethnobotany 475, Oxypolis filiformis . . water dropwort (Florida, Bahamas)—Thomas Walter described Oenanthe filiformis in 1788 based on specimens from South Carolina. It was not until 1894 that N.L. Britton moved the species to Oxypolis.

water elder n [OED2 1597 →]

A **viburnum** (here: V. opulus var americanum).

1900 Lyons Plant Names 392, V[iburnum] Opulus. . . Marsh or Water Elder. [DARE Ed: This may have been based on a British source.] **1940**

Clute *Amer. Plant Names* 56, *V[iburnum] opulus var Americana*. . . marsh elder, water elder.　**1960** Teale *Journey into Summer* 10, A cranberry tree spread its broad, three-pointed leaves. This north-country viburnum, *Viburnum opulus,* is variously known as the squaw bush, the water elder, the high-bush cranberry and the pincushion tree.

water elm n

Any of several trees of the family Ulmaceae, as:

a　=**planer tree.**

　1820 Gilleland *Ohio & Missip. Pilot* 257, *U[lmus] aquatica* (water elm) in marshes, generally in the rear of rich bottoms.　**1894** U.S. Natl. Museum *Proc.* 17.415 **sIL, sIN,** *Planera aquatica*. . . Water Elm.　**1937** Stemen–Myers *OK Flora* 96 **eOK,** Water Elm. . . Swamps. Eastern parts of the State.　**1950** Moore *Trees AR* 63, Planertree. . . Local Name: Water Elm. . . difficult to grow except in very wet situations.　**1979** Ajilvsgi *Wild Flowers* 14 **eTX, wLA,** Some of the understory plants of these quiet, watery places are water elm *(Planera aquatica)* [etc].

b　A **white elm** (here: *Ulmus americana*).

　1832 *Amer. Almanac & Repository* 265 **IL,** The kinds of timber most abundant are cotton-wood, . . red and water elm [etc].　**1857** MI State Ag. Soc. *Trans. for 1856* 395, The American water elm . . does not always indicate a wet soil.　**1870** *Grand Traverse Herald* (Traverse City MI) 20 Oct [7]/1 (newspaperarchive.com), There is on the farm of Mr. E. Woodard . . a water elm tree 28 feet in circumference.　**1897** Sudworth *Arborescent Flora* 181, Water Elm (Miss., Tex., Ark., Mo., Ill., Iowa, Mich., Ohio, Minn., Nebr.)　**1950** *WELS* 3 Infs, **WI,** Water Elm.　**1965–70** *DARE* (Qu. T11, . . *Kinds of elm trees*) 18 Infs, 8 **Missip. Valley,** 5 **TX,** Water elm; **IL**13, White elm or water elm. [*DARE* Ed: Some of these Infs may refer instead to other senses.]

c　=**winged elm.**

　1897 Sudworth *Arborescent Flora* 182 **AL,** *Ulmus alata*. . . Common Names. . . Water Elm.　**1933** Small *Manual SE Flora* 441, *U[lmus] alata*. . . Water-elm. . . River banks, swamps and woods.　**1960** Vines *Trees SW* 211, Winged Elm. . . Water Elm.

d　=**slippery elm 1.**

　1914 *DN* 4.106 **KS,** Piss-elm. . . A water elm. When burnt green, the sap steams out and hisses.　**1965–68** *DARE* (Qu. T11, . . *Kinds of elm trees*) Infs **AR**5, **IA**8, **OK**1, Water elm, piss elm—same; **LA**15, Water elm—don't make any size; has red leaves in fall.

water feather n

=**water milfoil.**

　1927 *Youth's Companion* 101.717, Good aquatic plants [to furnish an aquarium] . . are . . water feather, and pipewort.　**1933** Small *Manual SE Flora* 955, *[Myriophyllum] proserpinacoides*. . . Water-feather. . . Pools, and ditches, Coastal Plain, Fla. to Tex.　**1944** AL Geol. Surv. *Bulletin* 53.168, *M[yriophyllum] proserpinacoides* . . often cultivated in ornamental pools, and called parrot's feather or water-feather.　**1970** Correll *Plants TX* 1138, *Myriophyllum brasiliense*. . . Parrot's-feather, water-feather.　**2005** (acc) MA Invasive Plant Advisory Group *Evaluation Non-Native Plant Species* (Internet), *Myriophyllum aquaticum* . . (Parrot-feather; water-feather). . . commonly used in the water-garden trade.

water fern n

=**mosquito fern.**

　1870 in 1871 Featherman *Rept. Bot. Surv. LA* 118, Hydropterides— *Water Fern Family.* Azolla Caroliniana.　**1976** Bailey–Bailey *Hortus Third* 132, *Azolla* [spp] . . Mosquito fern, water f[ern].

water flaxseed n　[See quot 1822]

A **duckweed 1** (here: *Spirodela polyrrhiza*).

　1818 Eaton *Botany* 299, *Lemna*. . .*polyrhiza* . . water flaxseed. . . The leaves of this species become purplish and greatly resemble flaxseed, scattered on the surface of the stagnant waters.　**1832** MA Hist. Soc. *Coll.* 2d ser 9.152 **cwVT,** Lemna polyrhiza, Water flax-seed.　**1863** Porcher *Resources* 548 **SC,** *Spirodelia* [sic] *polyrrhiza* . . Water flaxseed. . . Santee canal.　**1950** Gray–Fernald *Manual of Botany* 385, *S[pirodela] polyrrhiza*. . . Water-flaxseed. . . Pools and pond- and stream-margins.　**2005** *DARE* File—Internet **NC,** [Caption:] *Spirodela polyrrhiza* (Common water-flaxseed, Big duckweed).

water fly n

A **dragonfly.**

　1970 *DARE* (Qu. R2, . . *The dragonfly*) Inf **PA**247, Water fly.　**2000** Launspach *ID Dial. Project* 7 **seID,** (*What do you call an insect with a long slender body and flimsy wings often seen around water*) 1 inf, Waterfly.

water fountain　See **fountain B**

water-fringe　See **fringe** n 1

water frog n　esp **Sth**　Cf **land frog**

=**bullfrog 1** or **tree frog 1.**

　1966–70 *DARE* (Qu. P21, *Small frogs that sing or chirp loudly in spring*) Infs **GA**1, **MS**81, Water frogs; **TX**40, Water frogs—make good fish bait if you can get 'em.　**1986** Pederson *LAGS Concordance* **Gulf Region** *(Bullfrog)* 3 infs, Water frog(s); *(Spring frog)* 1 inf, Water frogs; 1 inf, Water frogs—when you hear them, it will rain; 1 inf, Water frogs—small, green . . "tree frogs."

water frost n　[Cf *EDD* water-frost (at *water* sb. 1.(48)) "hoar-frost" and *watery-rime* (at *watery* adj. 1.(7)) "a heavy dew when the thermometer is only just above freezing point"]　Cf **dry frost**

A light frost.

　1950 *WELS* (*A frost that does not kill plants*) 1 Inf, **swWI,** Water frost.　**1967–70** *DARE* (Qu. B29) Infs **NY**227, **PA**63, 141, 146, Water frost; **PA**239, Water frost [FW: Inf has heard, but doesn't use].

water gall n

A **groundsel tree** (here: *Baccharis halimifolia*).

　1920 *Torreya* 20.25 **ceVA,** *Baccharis halimifolia*. . . Waterbush, water-gall.

water gap n

1　The point at which a fence crosses a watercourse; esp, any of various contrivances designed to prevent the passage of livestock while being able to withstand floodwaters or break away without damage to the rest of the fence.　[Brit dial. Cf *EDD* water-gate (at *water* sb. 1.(52) (c)) "a flood-gate; a water-gap in a fence; a rail hung across a stream to serve as a fence; the place where such a rail is hung"; *water-gap* is not documented in *OED2* or *EDD,* but exx can be found from the 16th cent onward.]　**chiefly Sth, S Midl, esp KY**　Cf **gap** n[1] 2

　1829 in 1909 Phillips *Plantation & Frontier Documents* 232 **MS,** Women & three men finished fence on the line by Mackeys and mended the water gap.　**1843** *S. Cultivator* 1.97 **cGA,** All farmers should keep their fencing in good order; see that the holes and water-gaps are well stopped.　**1851** in 1852 KY Laws *Acts Genl. Assembly* 494, All persons are prohibited from building fences or water gaps on main Quicksand creek, . . on any part of said creek which may be navigable.　**1859** in 1992 Murray-Wooley *Rock Fences* 58 **KY,** The best water gaps are pillars made of stone, with stone wall wings. . . A good shutter is a common horse rack, suspended by hinges or wooden hooks upon a pole resting on the pillars.　**1901** *Galveston Daily News* (TX) 10 Sept 8/2, If a . . farmer's fence at a low place was to wash down he would then put in what he calls a "water gap."　**1903** *DN* 2.336 **seMO,** Water-gap. . . Water gate. A swinging gate hung over a stream which rises with the water and closes when the water goes down.　**1916** Dreiser *Hoosier Holiday* 432 **sIN,** Out here on the farms, . . hanging around the old watergaps along the creeks, are boys just like we used to be.　**1926** Roberts *Time of Man* 31 **KY,** She crawled down to the branch and went secretly over the watergap.　**1948** Wentworth *America's Sheep Trails* 408 **West,** In crossing dips or sloughs the wire is usually run straight across, and the space below filled with more mesh fencing. Across draws that carry flood water, a separate section is usually built so that when the water pressure becomes great the fence automatically opens. It can then be repaired after the waters subside, avoiding the extensive damage done to fences not provided with water gaps.　**1949** (1958) Stuart *Thread* 175 **eKY,** A water-gap fence spanned the creek.　**1954** *PADS* 21.40 **SC,** Water gap. . . A structure of posts or stakes across a stream, joining with a fence on either side to prevent cattle from getting out of the pasture by walking in the channel.　**c1960** Wilson *Coll.* **csKY,** Water gap or gate. . . A swinging panel of fence across a stream, which can rise or fall with the water and thus keep the stock out.　**1964** *Press–Gaz.* (Hillsboro OH) 21 Jan 1/2, The hogs got through a water gap in fencing.　**1969** *DARE* FW Addit **KY**64, Water gaps—a log structure built in a stream under a fence to prevent livestock from escaping.　**1986** Pederson *LAGS Concordance,* 1 inf, **nwTN,** Water gaps—part of wire fence across creek; 1 inf, **nwLA,** Water gaps = water gates.　**2007** *DARE* File—Internet **swKS,** Our creek has flooded twice and taken out all the water gaps. Water gaps are the portion of the fence built across a waterway. . . If a water gap is built right, usually it will just break away and allow the trash to flow on down the creek to the next gap. Sometimes, however, a large tree will wash down the creek and tear out the water gap, the corner posts and several yards of fence.

2 A narrow pass or gorge through which water flows. **orig chiefly NY, NJ, PA; now more widespread in technical language** Cf **gap** n[1] **1, wind gap**
  1756 in 1897 *Documents Colonial & Post-Revol. Hist. NJ* 19.577, They are now building a Fort One Mile West of Broadhead's, Six from my House, and Four from the Water Gap. **1834** Gordon *Gaz. NJ* 17 (as of 1811), Water Gap, from the Morris and Sussex turnpike . . through Milton and Hope, to the Delaware, near the Water Gap. **1835** *New Engl. Mag.* 9.277 **cwNY,** One of the pleasantest excursions is to a spot about nine miles from the village of Geneseo, called the 'high banks,' where the Genessee bursts through the western range of hills and finds its way to the valley. . . Next to Niagara I think this water gap the most majestic scene in the western land. **1863** *Harper's New Mth. Mag.* 27.455 **cePA, nwNJ,** At New Hampton we change cars, taking the Delaware, Lackawanna and Western Railroad across Warren County to the Delaware Water Gap—one of those abrupt miracles of nature which it is impossible to appreciate at a glance. *Ibid* 464 **cePA,** Tier above tier of mountains arise in the distance; and far above . . tower up the cleft sides which form the Lehigh Water Gap. **1910** *Orange Co. Times–Press* (Middletown NY) 19 Aug 4/6 **seNY,** Central Valley Mens Outing—Drive to Culver Lake Via the Water Gap, Today. **1925** Campbell et al. *Valley Coal Fields VA* 167, The most notable water gap in Brushy Mountain is that of Poverty Gap. **1975** *Progress* (Clearfield PA) 4 June 3/1, "I believe this to be one of the most spectacular water gaps in the eastern United States," says Paul Wiegman, naturalist-at-large for the Western Pennsylvania Conservancy. **2004** *DARE* File—Internet [IA State Univ. Dept. of Geol. & Atmospheric Sci. *Illustr. Gloss. of Geologic Terms*], *Water gap*—A gap in a ridge or mountain through which a stream flows.

3 A fenced corridor giving livestock access to a limited stretch of a stream bank. **Sth, West**
  1933 *NM Recreational Mag.* Apr 30, It is planned to fence off many of the river bottoms, leaving water gaps at proper intervals for stock, permitting revegetation along the banks . . now so badly over-grazed. **1939** in 2007 (acc) Lexis–Nexis Legal Research *State Case Law: FL* (Internet), Q. Did you fence down to the Creek? A. Yes, sir, made a water gap down just to the edge of the creek, where my stock could get water. **1982** *N. Amer. Jrl. Fisheries Management* 2.54 **ID,** The riparian area was fenced in 1975 to exclude livestock grazing. . . Three water gaps were constructed to provide livestock watering areas. **1985** in 2007 (acc) Lexis–Nexis Legal Research *State Case Law: LA* (Internet), In 1938 defendant constructed a water gap extending from his undisputed property to the edge of a side stream near the main creek and has maintained this water gap constantly since that date. **1998** *Ibid: OR,* In the spring of 1988, defendant met . . Willie Noll, a representative of the Oregon Department of Fish and Wildlife . . to discuss construction of the riparian fence. Noll had staked out the fence, as well as a water gap in the fence, to allow limited access to the creek. **2000** *Ibid: WY,* The location of the disputed fence was never changed except in the 1980s when Frank built a water gap for his cattle to reach water. **2004** McKinstry et al. *Wetland & Riparian Areas* 246 **WY,** Water gaps can be included to allow livestock access to water. . . The fence should extend far enough into the water to prevent livestock from wading around the end.

water garter snake See **water snake 2**

water gentian n
  A **floating heart 1** (here: *Nymphoides aquatica*).
  1951 [see **water apple-blossom**].

water gladiole n [*OED2* (at *water* sb. 31) 1597]
  A **lobelia B1** (here: *Lobelia dortmanna*).
  1893 *Bot. Gaz.* 19.433 **NY,** *Lobelia Dortmanna* . . water gladiole. **1949** Moldenke *Amer. Wild Flowers* 243, In the Far North, from Newfoundland and Nova Scotia west to British Columbia and south to New Jersey, Pennsylvania, Wisconsin, and Washington, is the water lobelia or watergladiole, *L. dortmanna*. **1973** Hitchcock–Cronquist *Flora Pacific NW* 461.

water glider n
  A **water strider.**
  1942 (1960) Robertson *Red Hills* 137 **SC,** We had tornadoes and rattlesnakes and buzzards and whippoorwills—screech owls, snake doctors, water gliders so light they could walk on the top of water. **1996** Alberts *Price of Land* 61 **NEng,** Jamie trailed a finger in the warm river; water gliders sped away on their skinny pontoons. **2007** *DARE* File—Internet

WA, Add a tiny fresh-water clam, some tiny snails, damselfly nymphs, waterboatmen, water gliders, a picnic lunch, smelly pond gunk, and sunshine. It was superb. *Ibid* **NY,** If the water is calm, it is almost black and glasslike in apperance [*sic*] and you can see a multitude of water gliders skimming the surface. *Ibid* **AZ,** [Caption:] Water Gliders.

water grampus See **grampus 3**

water grass n

1 Any of var grasses or grasslike plants that thrive in water or wet places.
  1838 *S. Lit. Messenger* 4.494, Yon old and sentimental trout, who lies so softly in the water-grass. . . wags his pliant tail in all the luxury of piscatory contentment. **1855** Hammond–Mansfield *Country Margins* 291 **NY,** Farther off, still, are two small Islands. . . No brush, no water-grass, no sandy shore surround them. **1912** Wooton–Standley *Grasses NM* 79, *Alopecurus fulvus* [=*A. aequalis*]. . . A not uncommon grass found growing in wet places. . . It is sometimes called "water grass" but this is purely a local name. **1965–70** *DARE* (Qu. S9, . . *Kinds of grass that are hard to get rid of*) 25 Infs, 14 **IL, IA, MO,** Water grass; **LA6,** Water grass—just sits up like old ditch grass, grows in a clump; **LA28,** Water grass—comes with a big flood; comes up and looks like oats; (Qu. L8, *Hay that grows naturally in damp places*) 10 Infs, **scattered,** Water grass; (Qu. C6, . . *A piece of land that's often wet, and has grass and weeds growing on it*) Inf **CA62,** Tules—water reeds and water grass area; (Qu. S8, *A common kind of wild grass that grows in fields: it spreads by sending out long underground roots, and it's hard to get rid of*) Infs **IL63,** 80, 104, **MS16, MO**1, 2, **OK**58, Water grass; (Qu. S15, . . *Weed seeds that cling to clothing*) Inf **CO4,** Water grass; (Qu. S21, . . *Weeds . . that are a trouble in gardens and fields*) Infs **AL30, FL7, IL6, MN16, MS47, NC8,** Water grass. [*DARE* Ed: Some of these Infs may refer instead to other senses below.] **1986** Pederson *LAGS Concordance* (*Undesirable grass in a cotton field*) 16 infs, **Gulf Region,** Water grass.

2 Spec:
a =**barnyard grass.**
  1923 in 1925 Jepson *Manual Plants CA* 140, *E[chinochloa] crusgalli.* . . Water Grass. . . Fields and cultivated soil, especially along irrigating ditches; serious pest in the Sacramento Valley rice-fields. **1930** OK Univ. Biol. Surv. *Pub.* 2.50, Barnyard-grass. Water-grass. **1973** Hitchcock–Cronquist *Flora Pacific NW* 636, Watergrass. . . *E[chinochloa] crusgalli.*

b A **bullgrass 1** such as *Paspalum boscianum* or **Dallis grass.**
  1933 *Torreya* 33.82 **swGA, nwFL,** *Paspalum boscianum.* . . Bull grass, water grass. **1945** Wodehouse *Hayfever Plants* 56, Dallis grass . . , also called water grass and tall bull grass. **1986** Pederson *LAGS Concordance* (*Undesirable grass in a cotton field*) 1 inf, **cnAL,** Inch-a-night—formerly "water grass"—grows fast.

water gravy n **esp Sth, S Midl** Cf **cream gravy, red-eye ~**
  Gravy made from the drippings of ham or other cured meat and water.
  1895 *Decatur Daily Rev.* (IL) 17 Nov 1/2, On Monday we get for breakfast some bad bacon and stale bread, and water gravy, and something they call coffee. **1912** MI Hist. Comm. *MI Hist. Coll.* 38.300 **nMI** (as of c1875), Mother could only spare one slice of pork for a meal using the drippings to season the water gravy for the potatoes and corn bread. **c1938** in Lib. of Congress *Amer. Memory: WPA Life Hist.* (Internet) **TX** (as of 1890s), Boiled beef and Arbuckle coffee was our standby. The boys used to say . . if it wasn't for . . water gravy and Arbuckle coffee we would starve to death. **1949** *Independent* (Long Beach CA) 17 Mar 24/4 **IN,** The drippings from this [=ham] make for an exceedingly fine and rich water gravy. **1955** McAtee *Dial. Grant Co. IN Suppl. 6* [2], *Water gravy:* . . made from the melted fat of sausage, bacon, or the like, cooked in a frying pan, with water only added; used on bread and pancakes. In contrast to milk gravy. **1966–70** *DARE* (Qu. H37, . . *Gravy*) Infs **AR56, KY79, MI**1, **TX**51, Water gravy; **NC8,** Water gravy—from water and the grease of fried ham, served on grits or on biscuits; **KY85,** Brown—water gravy. **1982** Slone *How We Talked* 55 **eKY** (as of c1950), Water gravy was only used when there was no milk available.

water guider See **guiding rod**

water guinea (hen) n Also *guinea hen* **Inland Sth, esp KY**
  =**coot** n[1] **1.**
  1917 *Wilson Bulletin* 29.2.79 **AL, KY,** *Fulica americana.* . . water

guinea, Leighton, Ala. . . water guinea hen, . . Hickman, Ky. **c1960** *Wilson Coll.* **csKY,** *Coot:* . . Known locally as water guinea. . . It is usually classed as a duck with queer feet. **1962** Imhof *AL Birds* 215, American Coot. . . Other names . . Water Guinea. **1966–70** *DARE* (Qu. Q9, *The bird that looks like a small, dull-colored duck and is commonly found on ponds and lakes*) Inf **KY**21, Guinea hen; **KY**86, Water guinea; (Qu. Q10, . . *Water birds and marsh birds*) Inf **MS**6, Water guinea.

water haul n Also sp *water hall* [Cf *EDD watery-haul* (at *watery* adj. 1.(1)) "Jesting phrase of fishermen when an amateur . . hauls in the line and finds he is deceived" (Cornwall)] **scattered, but chiefly Midl, Sth, TX** See Map

A haul of a fishnet in which no fish are caught; fig: a fruitless effort of any kind.

1823 in 1931 Sweet *Relig. Amer. Frontier* 130 **VA,** The whole of this tour, disagreeable as it was, I considered an entire water hall. **1859** Taliaferro *Fisher's R.* 74 **nwNC** (as of 1820s), I'd made a water haul [= useless trip] that time. **1886** *New Era* (Humeston IA) 20 May [8]/2 (newspaperarchive.com), At Funk's they [=thieves] got about eight dollars in change, and at Horn's they made a water-haul, or if anything was taken it was a few cigars. **1895** Wright *Lewis & Dryden's Marine Hist.* 442 **Pacific NW,** Her owners were too cautious to be captured, and when she was intercepted the custom-house officers invariably found that they had made a "water haul." **1903** *DN* 2.336 **seMO,** *Water-haul.* . . We thought we had them surrounded, but when we closed in it proved to be a water-haul. **1907** *DN* 3.238 **nwAR,** *Water-haul.* . . A fruitless effort. **1909** *DN* 3.386 **eAL, wGA,** *Water-haul.* . . A haul of a fish-net or a seine in which no fish are caught; hence a fruitless effort. **1912** Green *VA Folk-Speech* 475, *Water-haul.* . . A piece of work without good end, as when a seine has been hauled and no fish caught. **1927** in 2007 (acc) Lexis–Nexis Legal Research *State Case Law: PA* (Internet), When there is no property in his keeping at the time of service, the writ is a water haul and service on the empty handed garnishee amounts to nothing. **1949** Faulkner *Knight's Gambit* 67 **MS,** [Of someone who went on a fruitless errand:] Looks like you made a water haul. **1965–70** *DARE* (Qu. P9, *When you're fishing but not catching any*) 21 Infs, **chiefly Midl, Sth, TX,** (Made a) water haul; **CA**145, **IL**6, 115, **IN**42, **KS**12, **LA**8, **TX**29, Made a water haul [FW sugg]; **AL**1, Made a water haul—adopted from seiners; **NJ**21, Made a water haul—this is commercial fishing with a net, a trawl; **MO**3, Had a water haul; **SC**63, Making a water haul; **VA**47, Nothing but a water haul. **1985** *DARE* File **nwMS,** "That really was a water haul—neither you nor I got what we went to the store for." . . She said, "Oh, you mean a burnt run." **1997** Junger *Perfect Storm* 25 **MA,** Sometimes the school escaped before the net was tightened and the crew drew up what was called a "water haul." **2005** in 2007 *DARE* File—Internet **MS,** I made a water haul to town trying to do errands and meeting with frustration at every turn.

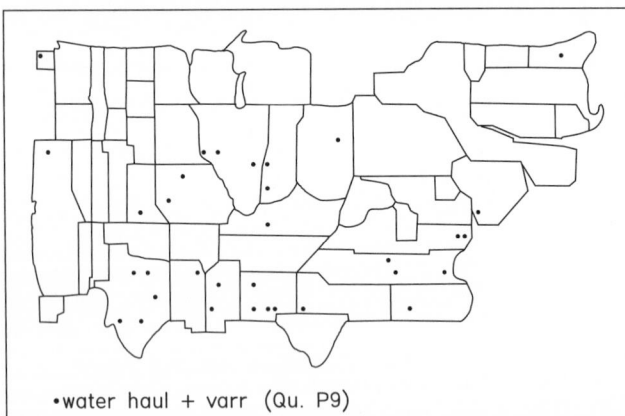

•water haul + varr (Qu. P9)

water hemlock n

Std: a plant of the genus *Cicuta,* esp *C. maculata.* Also called **cowbane 1, poison hemlock 2, mock-eel root, wild parsnip 2a.** For other names of *C. maculata* see **spotted cowbane 1;** for other names of var spp see **poison parsnip, muskrat weed 1, wild carrot 2, ~ parsley 2a** Cf **feverroot 2**

water hemp n

Std: any of several **amaranths,** but esp *Amaranthus cannabinus* and *A. tuberculatus.* For other names of the former see **marsh poke**

water hen n

1 A bird of the family Rallidae:

a The **Florida gallinule** or the **purple gallinule.** Cf **water chicken 2**

[**1709** (1967) Lawson *New Voyage* 154 **NC,** *Blue-Peters.* The same as you call Water-Hens in *England,* are here very numerous, and not regarded for eating.] **1778** Carver *Travels N. Amer.* 466 **MI, WI, MN,** The Water-Hen. **1833** Bonaparte *Amer. Ornith.* 4.132, The Florida Gallinule, or Water Hen, . . is common in Florida and Jamaica on the streams and pools, and extends over a great portion of the southern continent of America. **1953** *AmSp* 28.283 **GA, TX,** Water hen—Purple gallinule. *Ibid* **NY,** Water hen (blue). . . Water hen (Virginia)—Common gallinule. *Ibid* **WI,** Water hen (red-billed)—Common gallinule.

b =**sora.**

1824 Latham *Genl. Hist. Birds* 9.421 **GA,** In Georgia it [=the soree gallinule] is seen frequently in the marshes, and . . is known there by the name of Water-Hen, or Sedge-Hen, also the Water-Rail. **1832** *New Engl. Farmer* (Fessenden) 10.240 **NY,** The *Rallus Virginianus,* a small bird of 9 inches in length, is in Virginia called the Sora, in Pennsylvania the Rail, in New York the Water Hen. **1888** Trumbull *Names of Birds* 131, Little American Water-hen . . Sora Rail. **1953** *AmSp* 28.283 **GA,** Water hen—Sora. **1966** *DARE* (Qu. Q9, *The bird that looks like a small, dull-colored duck and is commonly found on ponds and lakes*) Inf **AR**42, Water hen—dominicker color.

c =**coot** n[1] **1.** Cf **swamp hen, water chicken 3**

1841 *S. Lit. Messenger* 7.77 **LA,** There are to be found . . the Pouille-d'eau [sic], or Water-hen [etc]. **1891** *Century Dict.* 6843 **MA,** *Water-hen.* . . The American coot, *Fulica americana.* **1924** [see **swamp hen**]. **1953** *AmSp* 28.283, Water hen—American coot. **1966–70** *DARE* (Qu. Q9, *The bird that looks like a small, dull-colored duck and is commonly found on ponds and lakes*) Infs **AR**5, **IN**45, **KY**60, 65, 75, Water hen; **TX**62, Summer duck or water hen or mud hen.

d Any of three **rails** n[2]: **clapper rail, king rail 1,** or **Virginia rail.**

1918 Grinnell et al. *Game Birds CA* 283, *California Clapper Rail.* . . Other names—San Mateo Rail; Water-hen [etc]. **1923** U.S. Dept. Ag. *Misc. Circular* 13.40 **IA,** King Rail. . . *Vernacular Names.* . . *In local use.* . . water-hen. *Ibid* 41, *California Clapper Rail (Rallus obsoletus [=R. longirostris]).* . . In view of the very limited distribution of this species the following local names may be considered to be in both general and local use: Marsh-hen, . . water-hen. **1953** *AmSp* 28.282 **MA,** Water hen—Slender-billed rail [=**Virginia rail**].

2 A **puffin** (here: *Fratercula arctica*). *obs*

1792 Belknap *Hist. NH* 3.168, Water Hen, or Water Witch—*Alea arctica?* **1794** Williams *Nat. & Civil Hist. VT* 119, Waterhen. *Alea artica.*

3 Any of var other marsh birds; see quot.

1953 *AmSp* 28.282 **MO,** Water hen—Least bittern. *Ibid* **AK,** Water hen—Red-breasted merganser. *Ibid* 283 **MO,** Water hen (big)—Black-crowned night heron. . . Water hen (big)—American bittern.

water hickory n

Std: a **hickory** n B1 (here: *Carya aquatica*). Also called **bitter pecan, ~ water hickory, pignut 1, swamp hickory c, water bitternut, wild pecan**

water hog n Cf *mudhog* (at **mudfish h**)

The common carp *(Cyprinus carpio).*

1949 Caine *N. Amer. Sport Fish* 154, Carp. . . *Colloquial Names.* . . Hogfish. . . Mudhog. . . Waterhog. **1975** Evanoff *Catch More Fish* 96, The carp *(Cyprinus carpio)* is also called . . mudhog, waterhog, river hog [etc]. **2002** *DARE* File—Internet **CA,** [Caption:] Water Hog Monster. . . This is one huge carp.

water horehound n

1 Std: a plant of the genus *Lycopus.* For other names of var spp see **archangel 2, bugleweed, rattlesnake weed 1f**

‡2 =**horehound 1.**

1975 Hamel–Chiltoskey *Cherokee Plants* 39, Horehound—water, white—*Marrubium vulgare.* . . For hoarseness; coughs; colds.

water hyacinth n

Std: a plant of the genus *Eichhornia,* esp *E. crassipes.* Also called **hyacinth 3, million-dollar weed, pitcher plant 3, wampee d, water lily 6**

water ice n Also *Italian water ice* now esp sePA, sNJ
=**Italian ice.**

1853 *S. Qrly. Rev.* 7.412 **seSC,** Ethereal young ladies think it gross to
eat before men—unless it be a little water-ice. **1895** (1900) Arnold
Century Cook Book 508, Water-ices are made of fruit-juice sweetened
with sugar syrup. . . A good way of preparing it is to make a syrup of
32° and add enough fruit juice to dilute it to 20°. Freeze the same as ice-
cream. . . The ices will not get so hard as creams. **1900** in 1995
Millersville Univ. Center for PA Ger. Studies *Jrl.* Fall 14, August 10,
1900—Friday—Minnie made water-ice flavored with lemon. Our folks
never ate it before. **1997** *Chr. Sci. Monitor* (Boston MA) 20 Aug 15/1
eNJ, [They] each work 77 hours a week—making sandwiches by day
and scooping water ice by night. But these are no ordinary Jersey Shore
summer workers. **2007** *DARE* File—Internet, We are not from Philadelphia, and even though we have loved calling it home the past four
years or so, we still don't really understand water ice. *Ibid* **Philadelphia PA,** Philadelphia Water Ice is the leader in the Italian Ice market.
2008 *Ibid* **Philadelphia PA,** Water-Ice a.k.a. Italian Water-Ice or Italian
Ice is a legendary summertime treat in Philadelphia. It is a water-based
product made with real fruit blended in fine ice to form a soft, velvety
smooth texture. *Ibid* **NYC,** [Advt:] *Worksman Ice Cream/Water Ice
Carts*—Built sturdy and tough, . . [they] have been the industry standard
since the beginning of the 20th century. **2009** *AmSp* 84.421 **NJ,** *Italian
ice/water ice.* . . responses provided the cleanest north-south [NJ] division line in the survey. . . Terms for this product, flavored soft ice, separate north *(Italian ice)* from south *(water ice)* quite clearly with Atlantic
County . . and Mercer County . . on the dividing line.

water jack n esp Sth, S Midl
A water boy.

1930 *DN* 6.89 **cWV,** *Water jack,* water boy. **c1939** in 1984 Lambert–
Franks *Voices* 72 **OK,** I tried to get a job as a water jack on every job I
could walk out to, but it took a man to haul water for that bunch of whis-
key-heads. **1949** *NE State Jrl.* (Lincoln) 7 Aug feature sec [1]/2 (news-
paperarchive.com), On a hot afternoon do you pause and listen almost
sure you heard those three frantic blasts of the steam whistle with which
an angry engineer [of a threshing machine] used to urge to haste a loitering water jack who had paused to watch the fish in the creek from which
he had just pumped a tank full of water? **1952** Brown *NC Folkl.* 1.605,
Water-jack. . . A man or boy who brings water to workmen.—General.
1969 *NC Folkl.* 17.29 **wNC,** Moving behind the *dropper,* the setter put
the plant into the earth . . , making a hole in the soil and slipping the
plant into a standing position. . . Behind the setter came the *waterjack* or
waterboy with bucket and long-handled dipper or gourd, watering the
plants. **1970** *Thompson Coll.* **cnAL** (as of 1920s), Water jack, water
jack, you ought to be here and half way back. **a1975** Lunsford *It Used
to Be* 164 **sAppalachians,** "Waterjack" is a boy who carries water to the
field. **1995** in 2006 *DARE* File—Internet **FL** (as of 1920s), The old
saying, 'Water Jack, you ought'er been there and half way back' was a
common adage.

water lead See **lead 2**

waterleaf n
Std: a plant of the genus *Hydrophyllum.* For other names of
var spp see **brookflower, burr flower, cat's-breeches, Indian
salad, John's cabbage, linsey britches, rule-of-five, Shawnee, squaw lettuce 2, woolen breeches 1**

water lentil n [*OED2* 1548 →]
A **duckweed 1** (here: *Lemna* spp).

1856 *Putnam's Mag.* 7.362, The common water-lentil rises to the surface, at the time of blooming, and descends when its purpose is fulfilled.
1970 Correll *Plants TX* 346, *Lemna minor.* . . Water lentil. . . In quiet
waters of sloughs, lakes, canals and ponds, mostly in the w. half of Tex.

water lettuce n [See quot 1901]
The tropical duckweed (*Pistia stratiotes*). Also called **lettuce 1,
water bonnet, ~ cabbage 2**

[**1866** Lindley–Moore *Treas. Botany* 897, *Pistia Stratiotes.* . . It is
sometimes called Tropical Duckweed, but is very different in appearance; indeed, its common West Indian name, Water Lettuce, is much
more expressive of its general resemblance.] **1883** *Century Illustr.
Mag.* 26.383 **FL,** The saw-grass, water-lettuce, bonnets, or other aquatic
plants which border the fresh-water streams and lakes of Florida. **1901**
Lounsberry *S. Wild Flowers* 36, Water lettuce. . . This little plant of
tender green floats freely in the rivers and ponds of many tropical regions, and appears like a young, unsophisticated head of lettuce. **1933**

Rawlings *South Moon* 164 **nFL,** The water lettuce whirled slowly
around and around, like dancers waltzing in their sleep. **1969** *DARE*
(Qu. S26b, *Wildflowers that grow in water or wet places*) Inf **IL110,**
Water lettuce. **1975** Natl. Audubon Soc. *Corkscrew* 20 **FL,** Here and
there among the large cypresses are deeper lakes, most of which
are covered with water lettuce *(Pistia stratiotes)* which floats freely on
the surface. **2007** (acc) U.S. Dept. Ag. *Plants Database* (Internet),
Pistia stratiotes L.—water lettuce.

water lily n

1 Std: a plant of the order Nymphaeales, esp *Nymphaea* spp.
Also called **swamp lily c.** For other names of *Nymphaea* spp
see **alligator blankets, banana waterlily, duckpond lily, sun
lotus, white water lily,** and cf **lily pad 1;** for other names of
Nelumbo lutea and its fruit see **water chinquapin;** for other
names of *Nuphar lutea* and subspp see **spatterdock**

2 =**lizard's tail 1.** *obs*

1837 Darlington *Flora Cestrica* 237 **sePA,** Nodding Saururus.
Vulgò. . . Water lilies. . . This plant is found along the Schuylkill—also
in the Great Valley, and at the forks of Brandywine.

3 A **death camas** (here: *Zigadenus fremontii* or *Z. venenosus*).

1897 Parsons *Wild Flowers CA* 6, *Zygadenus Fremonti.* . . The fact
that it grows in boggy places has given rise to the name of "water-lily"
in certain localities. **1934** Haskin *Wild Flowers Pacific Coast* 35, As a
stock poisoning plant death camas is one of the worst. . . Other names
locally applied to this plant are lobelia, poison sego, poison grass, alkali
grass, water lily, and soap-root.

4 An **arrowhead 1** (here: *Sagittaria latifolia*).

1897 *Jrl. Amer. Folkl.* 10.146 **swMO,** *Sagittaria variabilis* [=*S. latifolia*] . . water lily. **1967** *DARE* FW Addit **AR44,** Water lily—broad-
leaved arrowhead.

5 =**water shield.**

1900 Lyons *Plant Names* 68, *B[rasenia] purpurea.* . . Little Lily-pad,
Little Water-lily. **1910** Graves *Flowering Plants* 184 **CT,** *Brasenia
purpurea.* . . Little Water Lily. . . Frequent along the coast in New London
County. **1977** *Brainerd Daily Dispatch* (MN) 14 Aug 15/6, If you pick
a stem of the water-shield . . you will notice a slimy coating on the outside of the plant. This slime acts as a barrier that keeps too much water
from entering the water lily.

6 =**water hyacinth.**

1913 *Torreya* 13.229 **LA,** *Piaropus crassipes* [=*Eichhornia c.*] . .
Waterlilies. **1968** *DARE* (Qu. S26b, *Wildflowers that grow in water or
wet places*) Inf **LA33,** Water lily—they are water hyacinths, really.

7 A **floating heart 1** (here: *Nymphoides aquatica* or *N.
peltata*) Cf **fringed waterlily**

1926 *Gettysburg Times* (PA) 21 July 4/4, Right there on the water
floated a mottled olive and bronze leaf shaped like a heart. . . "Why, it's
a water lily," exclaimed the disappointed bunny. **1940** Clute *Amer.
Plant Names* 58, *N[ymphoides] peltatum.* Floating Heart. (water-lily).
Ibid 227, *Nymphoides peltatum.* . . dwarf water-lily.

water lizard n Cf **lizard n 2**
Any of var aquatic **salamanders 1.**

1842 DeKay *Zool. NY* 3.87, The Menobranchus, or Big Water-lizard
as it is occasionally called in this State, feeds on fluviatile shells,
crustacea, and the smaller fishes. **1854** Wailes *Rept. on Ag. & Geol. MS*
328, Siren lacertina—Water lizard. *Ibid,* Menobranchus lateralis—Water lizard. **1892** IN Dept. Geol. & Nat. Resources *Rept. for 1891* 417,
Mud-eel. Siren. . . Where it abounds it is, according to Barton, called
"Alligator" and "Water-lizard." **1906** *DN* 3.163 **nwAR,** *Water-lizard.* . .
A newt. **1909** *DN* 3.386 **eAL, wGA,** *Water-lizard.* . . A newt. **1926**
Frederick Post (MD) 20 Feb 4/1, A Swiss scientist has removed the eyes
from a water lizard, substituting other eyes which eventually established
nerve connections with the salamander's brain. **1928** Baylor Univ. Museum *Contrib.* 16.8 **neLA,** Louisiana Newt. . . In the extreme northeastern corner of the state, this species of water salamander is frequently
known as the *Water Lizard.* . . Poor whites and negroes, who know all
lizards as "Scorpions," classify all salamanders as lizards.

water lobelia n
A **lobelia B1** (here: *Lobelia dortmanna*).

1818 in 1826 MA Hist. Soc. *Coll.* 2d ser 8.170, In August the eye is
gratified with . . the inflated, pale and water lobelias. **1847** Wood
Class-Book 364, *Dortmann's or Water Lobelia.* . . A curious aquatic,

growing in ponds, N. States to Ga., the flowers only rising above the water. **1912** Mathews *Amer. Wild Flowers* 464, *Water Lobelia—Lobelia Dortmanna.* . . N. Eng. to Pa., and northwestward. **1927** *Torreya* 27.35 **NY, NJ,** Water lobelia. . . A water plant with . . blue unsymmetrical flowers in an erect spike that grows out of the water. **1948** Wherry *Wild Flower Guide* 128, *Water lobelia* . . in northern ponds. **1973** Hitchcock–Cronquist *Flora Pacific NW* 461, Water l[obelia], water gladiole. . . *L. dortmanna.*

water locust n

Std: a **honey locust 1** (here: *Gleditsia aquatica*).   Also called **swamp locust**

waterman n   [*OED2 waterman* sb. 2 "A man working on a boat or among boats"; 1458 →]   **Chesapeake Bay**

One who makes a living on the water, esp by fishing, crabbing, or oystering.

1854 Drayton *Personal Memoir* 22 **Chesapeake Bay,** There is not a waterman who ever sailed in Chesapeake Bay who will not tell you that . . the difficulty is . . to make them [=runaway slaves seeking assistance] take no for an answer. **1872** *Scribner's Mth.* 3.514 **Chesapeake Bay MD,** [Caption:] A Chesapeake Waterman. **1884** *Harper's New Mth. Mag.* 68.809 **Chesapeake Bay VA,** He has produced a series of life-like pictures of Virginia life . . so that we are enabled . . to study the men of every class . . the Dissenting preacher . . the rough waterman of the Chesapeake . . the African slave. **1932** *Sun* (Baltimore MD) 22 Aug 4/4 *(Hench Coll.),* Former Well Known Waterman . . Survived By Widow And Daughter. **1968** *DARE* Tape **MD**36, The rule was, up until a couple years ago, a waterman depended on the wind to eat. No wind, no eat; **MD**41, He was quite a waterman. And he loved the water. He was a very hard worker. He was up four o'clock in the morning getting ready to go to work. . . They go out in their boats and they have these oyster rakes on their boats. **1968–70** *DARE* FW Addit **MD**43, 45, Waterman—catches crabs and oysters; **VA**47, [The Inf] is currently a waterman; **VA**52, Waterman, clammer, oysterman; **VA**55, Inf was a retired waterman. **1976** Warner *Beautiful Swimmers* 62 **Chesapeake Bay,** There also came some called watermen. . . Why the word took firm root on this continent only along the shores of the Chesapeake is a matter of speculation. . . [T]he word . . came to be used . . in the Chesapeake country to separate those who had the resources to acquire land and those who didn't and went out on the waters for subsistence. That it has endured so strongly suggests the distinction is still sharp. **1996** Horton *Island Out of Time* 160 **Chesapeake Bay MD,** Watermen is a good name for us because we aren't just oystermen, or fishermen, or crabbers. We follow the water; we say we're in the water business. We catch whatever we can make a livin' on. **2000** Shores *Tangier Is.* 11 **Chesapeake Bay,** I was born into a waterman family on Tangier Island.

water maple n

Any of several **maples** that grow in wet places, as:

a **=big-leaf maple.**

1872 *Ballou's Mth. Mag.* 35.286, The Water Maple is a native of southern Oregon, and grows only immediately on the water courses. **1925** Jepson *Manual Plants CA* 611, Big-leaf Maple. . . Also called Water Maple, White Maple and Oregon Maple.

b A **red maple** (here: *Acer rubrum*).

1884 Sargent *Forests of N. Amer.* 50, *Acer rubrum.* . . Red maple. . . Water maple. **1908** Britton *N. Amer. Trees* 647, Red Maple. . . Among the local names for this tree are Swamp maple, . . Water maple, and White maple. **1967** *DARE* (Qu. T14, . . *Kinds of maples*) Inf **DC**2, Water maple—likes to grow in swampy area—rich red coloring in fall, some gold. **1974** (1977) Coon *Useful Plants* 48, *Acer rubrum*—Swamp maple, red, scarlet, or water maple. Usually found in the East growing in low or swampy ground.

c **=silver maple. esp KY, WV**

1896 Robinson *In New Engl. Fields* 66, The meshed shadows of the water-maples are full of the reflections of the green and silver of young leaves. **1897** Sudworth *Arborescent Flora* 287 **PA, WV,** *Acer saccharinum.* . . Common Names. . . Water Maple [etc]. **1950** Peattie *Nat. Hist. Trees* 462, Silver Maple. . . Other Names: Soft, . . Water, Creek, or Swamp Maple. **1968–70** *DARE* (Qu. T14, . . *Kinds of maples*) Inf **KY**80, Water maple—same as silver maple; **KY**94, Water maples grow very large and are not very strong; **WV**4, Swamp maple—same as water maple—grow quickly and well; used for shade trees. **1973** Wharton–Barbour *Trees KY* 544, *Acer saccharinum.* . . Silver Maple, Water Maple. . . Growing large in its native habitat of river banks and floodplains . . the silver maple is a graceful and beautiful tree.

d A **mountain maple** (here: *Acer spicatum*).

1897 Sudworth *Arborescent Flora* 282 **KY,** *Acer spicatum.* . . Common Names. . . Water Maple. **1950** Peattie *Nat. Hist. Trees* 470, Mountain Maple. . . Other Names: Moose, Low, or Water Maple.

e A **sugar maple** (here: *Acer saccharum*).

c1960 *Wilson Coll.* **csKY,** The other common maple is the gray maple or water maple (*Acer saccharinum* [here: =*A. saccharum*]). **1979** Little *Checklist U.S. Trees* 42, *Acer saccharinum* [here: =*A. saccharum*]. . . Other common names—soft maple, . . water maple [etc].

f Used generically or in ref to specific plants not identifiable from the context.

1834 *Western Jrl. Med. & Phys. Sci.* July–Sept 248, Our forests present a number [of shade trees]. . . Among these may be enumerated the elm . . and water maple. **1875** *Forest & Stream* 4.365 **NJ,** A full-grown cock arose and skirted off around a big water-maple. **1908** Fox *Lonesome Pine* 45 **KY,** Above and below him the stream was arched with beech, poplar and water maple. **1965–70** *DARE* (Qu. T14, . . *Kinds of maples*) 24 Infs, **chiefly S Midl,** Water maple; (Qu. T15, . . *Kinds of swamp trees*) Infs **FL**7, **IL**25, Water maple.

watermaster n   **West** Cf **majordomo 2** **=ditch rider.**

1859 *Mountaineer* (Great Salt Lake City UT) 27 Aug 2/4, If the watermasters of our district or ward will see that we have a double portion of water during this ensuing week for our garden, we will now agree not to mention them again. **1897** *ID Daily Statesman* (Boise) 7 Dec 1/2, This was an action for wages, Wood having been in the service of the company as watermaster. **1902** Newell *Irrigation* 107 **SW,** The person charged with the management of the canal . . is usually known as the "watermaster" or "ditch-rider." **1925** *Fresno Bee* (CA) 5 June 3/3, Failure of the conference . . brought a statement from Watermaster Charles L. Kaupke that he would permit the leakage to continue. **1942** *Albuquerque Jrl.* (NM) 10 Mar 5/7, Gov. Miles ordered State Police to break locks placed by the water master upon ditches supplying Southwestern New Mexico farmers. **1949** Sierra Club *Bulletin* June 75 **ceCA,** The Water Master for the Pacific Gas and Electric Company who controlled the level of the lake, was contentedly weathering the storm. **1968** *ID Sun. Statesman* (Boise) 25 Feb 1/1, Is it illegal to shut the water off at Lucky Peak so no water can run in the river at all?—Name withheld. It's not only legal, but it's done from time to time, the Boise River watermaster reports. **1999** *Pinedale Roundup* (WY) 20 May 17/2, *Applications are now being* accepted for the position of Watermaster for the Fox Creek Canal Co. **2006** *DARE* File—Internet **TX,** Rio Grande Watermaster . . Harlingen, TX.

water mat See **water carpet**

watermeal n

A **duckweed 1** (here: *Wolffia* spp).

1925 *Ecology* 6.289, The bulk of this sample was made up of thousands of plants of star duckweed *Lemna trisulca* and hundreds of thousands of those of water meal, *Wolffia brasiliensis*. **1949** Palmer *Nat. Hist.* 125, *Watermeal—Wolffia* sp. . . *Wolffia* is interesting to biologists because it is probably the smallest of all flowering plants; although it may be abundant, it may never be noticed. **1952** Strausbaugh–Core *Flora WV* 208, *W[olffia] punctata.* . . Watermeal. **1971** *Ecology* 52.507, The water was about 70 cm deep, lacked measurable current, and received effluent from organically enriched Hoenig's slough. . . Duckweed (*Lemna* spp.), watermeal (*Wolffia* sp.), and mosquito fern (*Azolla* sp.) sometimes blanketed the water's surface. **2007** *DARE* File—Internet, [Advt:] Lake Cleanser Special gets rid of scum on ponds, will reduce and control duckweed and watermeal, reduces ponds filamentous algae, and naturally controls blue green algae and pond weeds.

watermelon n

Std: the vine *Citrullus lanatus* or its fruit.   For other names of the latter see **apple melon, August ham, black watermelon, cymling 2, guinea melon, icebox ~, ice-cream ~, Irish gray watermelon, letter from home, poor man's apple, rattlesnake melon, sugar ~**

watermelon cutting n   **Sth, S Midl**

A social event at which watermelons are cut and eaten.

1898 *San Antonio Daily Light* (TX) 25 July [2]/3 (newspaperarchive.com), *Birthday Party.* . . Watermelon cutting was called at 10 o'clock. **1909** *DN* 3.387 **eAL, wGA,** *Watermelon-cuttin(g).* . . An entertainment at which watermelons are cut for the guests. "Miss Drake gave a watermelon-cutting in honor of her guest, Miss Myrick." **1912** *Jrl. Amer. Folkl.* 25.143 **sAppalachians,** At "Square" Murray's . . there is pretty sure to be . . a "watermelon-cuttin'," a "candy-pullin'," or a "pea-hullin'." **1919** *Ada Eve. News* (OK) 25 July 4/3, The social was in the nature of a watermelon cutting. **1936** *Morning News* (Florence SC) 15 Aug 6/7, At the close of the tour the entire group enjoyed a water-melon cutting with iced lemonade. **1940** *Kingsport Times* (TN) 11 Aug 2/1, Around 100 are expected to attend the watermelon cutting and out-ing at Silver Lake. **1958** *Middlesboro Daily News* (KY) 17 July 11/3, There is talk of a watermelon cutting . . when Orgill comes to speak at the courthouse in Tazewell. **1969–70** DARE (Qu. FF2, . . *Kinds of parties*) Inf **GA**89, Watermelon cuttings—for young people; **TX**80, Wa-termelon cuttings—everybody brings watermelon, cut and eat. **1986** Pederson *LAGS Concordance (A dance)* 2 infs, **MS,** (A) watermelon cutting; 1 inf, **swGA,** Watermelon cuttings—social affairs.

water milfoil n

Std: a freshwater aquatic plant of the genus *Myriophyllum*. For other names of var spp see **coontail 2, green parrot('s) feather, parrot's ~, water ~**

watermillion, watermillyum, watermilyun   See **melon**

water mint n

Std: a mint (here: *Mentha aquatica*). Also called **brook mint, fish ~**

water moats   See **water motie**

water moccasin n   Cf **dry-land moccasin**

1 also rarely *water-mouth moccasin:* =**cottonmouth.**

1819 (1821) Nuttall *Jrl.* 154 **AR,** The other [snake] frequents waters, and is called the water-mokasin, and poisonous black-snake. **1828** *Sat. Eve. Post* 23 Aug 2/4 **TN,** Woe betide any unfortunate water Moccasin (no matter how great his size or how terrific his appearance,) who was found lurking below. **1849** *Adams Sentinel* (Gettysburg PA) 11 June [8]/3 (newspaperarchive.com) **New Orleans LA,** The water moccasin has come forth from his swampy lair, and now swims unconcernedly through [the] streets. [DARE Ed: This may be the yellow-bellied water snake.] **1851** *De Bow's Rev.* 10.635 **TX,** Land and water moccasins, coach-whip and copperhead, are the only venomous snakes beside the rattle found in Texas. **1884** Twain in *Century Illustr. Mag.* 29.276, He oughter know a body don't love water-moccasins enough to go around hunting for them. **1928** Baylor Univ. Museum *Contrib.* 16.19 **TX,** The venomous Cottonmouth is the *Water Moccasin* and *Black Moccasin.* **1965–70** DARE (Qu. P25, . . *Kinds of snakes*) [Of 213 Infs who offered the term *water moccasin,* 15, **chiefly Sth, S Midl,** described it as ven-omous.] **1976** Brown *Gloss. Faulkner* 131 **MS,** The general tendency among people who know snakes in Faulkner's country is to reserve the name *moccasin* (or *water moccasin* . .) for the venomous snake and to call the others water snakes. **1986** Pederson *LAGS Concordance,* 67 infs, **Gulf Region,** Water moccasin(s); 1 inf, Water-mouth moccasin.

2 A **water snake 1,** esp *Nerodia sipedon.* For other names see **black watersnake, gray moccasin, moccasin 1b, salt-marsh snake, water pilot, ~ rattle 1** Cf **brown adder, salt-water moccasin**

1891 *Century Dict.* 6845, *Water-moccasin.* . . A name applied with lit-tle discrimination in the United States to several species of aquatic snakes; properly the venomous *Toxicophis* or *Ancistrodon piscivorus,* with which the harmless *Tropidonotus* (or *Nerodia*) *sipedon* is some-times confounded. **1892** IN Dept. Geol. & Nat. Resources *Rept. for 1891* 508, *Natrix sipedon,* known as the "Water-snake," "Water Mocca-sin," is extremely abundant in all our streams. Under the impression that it is poisonous it is greatly feared by many people who suppose it to be the same as the poisonous moccasin of the Southern rivers. **1916** Acad. Nat. Sci. Philadelphia *Proc. for 1915* 67.173 **Okefenokee GA,** The pied water snakes [=*Nerodia taxispilota*] are very large and in general very shy and elusive. . . The natives call them "water moccasin" and consider them as poisonous as rattlesnakes or true moccasins. *Ibid* 177, This species [=*Nerodia fasciata*] was not so common as the pied watersnake. Like it, however, this snake is called "water moccasin" by the natives who fear it. **1949** *Scientific Mth.* Jan 57, The dreaded water moccasin of our Northern states all too often turns out to be the banded water snake *(Natrix sipedon),* erroneously called the "water rattle" and "water pilot" in certain localities. **1954** *Harder Coll.* **cwTN,** Water mocca-sin. . . Usually applied to any water snake and never poisonous. **1965–70** DARE (Qu. P25, . . *Kinds of snakes*) [Of 213 Infs who offered the term *water moccasin,* 23, **chiefly Midl,** described it as not venomous.]

2001 (acc) IN Dept. Nat. Resources *Snakes* (Internet), It's a Water Moc-casin! I *know* it is! Well, probably not—not in Indiana. . . The color patterns are easily confused with those of the northern or midland water snake.

water mosquito n

1 =**midge 1.**

1966 DARE (Qu. R10, *Very small flies that don't sting, often seen hov-ering in large groups or bunches outdoors in summer*) Inf **MI**37, Water mosquitoes—built just like a mosquito, don't sting.

‡**2** =**dragonfly.**

1969 DARE (Qu. R2, . . *The dragonfly*) Inf **GA**77, Water mosquito.

water motie n   Also *water moats, ~ mote* [Partial folk-etym for MexSpan *guatamote, batamote* seepwillow] =**seepwillow.**

1879 *Gleanings Bee Culture* 7.341 **swCA,** The bushes are willow, wa-ter mote, alder, and California sumach. **1904** U.S. Dept. Interior *Deci-sions* 32.181 **sCA,** The vegetation which subsists on the surface flow in the San Gabriel canyon is composed almost exclusively of alders, water moties, and willows. **1909** *Condor* 11.49 **AZ,** Along its banks are a few cotton-woods, many willows, and much water-mote (*Baccharis glutinosa*). **1931** U.S. Dept. Ag. *Misc. Pub.* 101.158, Seepwillow . . , locally named false, Gila, or water willow, groundsel tree, water motie, and water-wally . . has an enormous distribution from western Texas to Colorado and southern California and south. *Ibid,* Emory baccharis . . , locally known as water moats. **1967** DARE (Qu. T15, . . *Kinds of swamp trees*) Inf **CA**7, Water moties (willow) along river. **1976** Elmore *Shrubs & Trees SW* 77, Seep-willow. . . water-motie, batamote. **2001** Adkison *Utah's Natl. Parks* 149, Shrubs in this canyon reach atypical proportions. Squawbush . . ; serviceberry; . . singleleaf ash; and water-motie, or seep-willow, are much larger than their counterparts growing on adjacent ledges and slopes.

water-mouth moccasin   See **water moccasin 1**

water oak n   Cf **swamp oak**

1 Any of var unidentified **oaks.** **chiefly Sth, S Midl**

1687 in 1940 *AmSp* 15.156 **VA,** To a Water Oake Standing by ye side of ye black Swamp. **1716** Petiver *Petiveriana* 11, *Water Oak.* Is an Ev-ergreen, growing in *Swamps, Fresh-water Ponds,* and by *River Sides.* **1765** (1942) Bartram *Diary of a Journey* 36, [He] walked with us about his land, on which grew very large evergreen and water oaks. **1793** in 1802 Priest *Travels U.S.A.* 12 **swNJ,** Water and barren oak are small and bushy, and only used for firing. **1834** (1847) Lundy *Life & Travels* 121 **TX,** The water-oak is a species intermediate between the live-oak and the other kinds. **1901** *Forest & Stream* 57.222 **VA,** [There] are live oak, pine, holly, dogwood, sassafras, water oak, and cherry trees. **1917** Kephart *Camping & Woodcraft* 2.205 **sAppalachians,** Our first choice for clapboards is "mountain oak," when we can find one that splits well. . . Otherwise we take white, black, red, or water oak. **1934** Carmer *Stars Fell on AL* 24, The singers concealed by dark water oaks and white sycamores. **1965–70** DARE (Qu. T10, . . *Kinds of oak trees*) 168 Infs, **chiefly Sth, S Midl,** Water oak; **AL**2, Live—in southern part of state; water—in the northern part—same thing; (Qu. T15, . . *Kinds of swamp trees*) 17 Infs, **chiefly Sth, S Midl,** Water oak; (Qu. T16, . . *Kinds of trees . . 'special'*) Infs **FL**34, **MS**1, 21, Water oak; (Qu. T5, . . *Kinds of evergreens, other than pine*) Infs **GA**11, 20, 65, **SC**24, 26, 46, **TX**9, 99, Water oak; **SC**40, Live oak, water oak—same—one that stays live year round. **1966–68** DARE Tape **FL**5, There are two . . kinds of oaks in our yard: live oak and water oak; **GA**18, Along the coast we have the live oak, but we do have the water oaks here . . these are decid-uous. **1975** Newell *If Nothin' Don't Happen* 43 **nwFL,** A young shoat fattened on water-oak acorns ain't bad to take.

2 Spec:

a =**willow oak 2.**

[**1709** (1967) Lawson *New Voyage* 100 **NC, SC,** Willow-Oak is a sort of Water-Oak. It grows in Ponds and Branches, and is useful for many things.] **1851** *De Bow's Rev.* 11.46 **LA,** Oak, *Quercus,* of five different varieties, viz., the white, black, water or willow, over-cup, basket, Span-ish and red oaks. **1897** Sudworth *Arborescent Flora* 178 **SC,** *Quercus phellos.* . . Water Oak. **1947** Collingwood–Brush *Knowing Trees* 198, *Quercus phellos.* . . is so frequently found along wet margins of streams and swamps as to be erroneously known as swamp oak, or water oak. **1956** McAtee *Some Dialect NC* 49, *Water Oak.* . . The willow oak (*Quercus phellos*). **1999** DARE File—Internet **VA,** Black cherry . . and sweetgum . . were affected more than water oak (*Quercus phellos* L.)

b *Quercus nigra* (formerly *Q. aquatica*). Also called **bastard oak 3, blackjack ~, bluejack ~ 2, duck ~, pin ~ 2d, possum ~, spotted ~, turkey ~ c** Cf **pond oak**

1801 Michaux *Histoire* 7, Chêne aquatique. *Water oak.* **1810** Michaux *Histoire des Arbres* 1.24 Sth, Q[*uercus*] *aquatica.* . . *Water oak* . . , dénomination générale en Virginie et dans les Etats plus au sud. [=*Q*[*uercus*] *aquatica.* . . *Water oak* . . , the name common in Virginia and States further south.] **1822** Eaton *Botany* 419, [*Quercus*] *aquatica.* . . water oak. . . Leaves very variable. **1860** Curtis *Cat. Plants NC* 37, Water Oak. . . The leaves are pear-shaped, as in the *Black Jack.* **1897** Sudworth *Arborescent Flora* 175 **AL, AR, DE, FL, LA, MS, MO, NC, SC, TX,** *Quercus nigra.* . . Water Oak. **1934** *Natl. Geogr. Mag.* 65.604 **Okefenokee GA,** On some of the islands there are "hammocks". . . The trees are mainly live oaks and water oaks. **1967–70** *DARE* (Qu. T10, . . *Kinds of oak trees*) Inf **KY**80, Water oak, turkey oak—same; **LA**3, Water oak [FW illustr: drawing of leaf]. **1973** Wharton–Barbour *Trees KY* 515, The water oak grows in swamps and alluvial bottomlands in western Kentucky but is rare.

c =**pin oak 1a.**

1834 Peck *Gaz. IL* 23, Of oaks there are several species, as . . swamp or water oak, white oak, red or spanish oak [etc]. **1897** Sudworth *Arborescent Flora* 172 **RI, IL,** *Quercus palustris.* . . Common Names. . . Water Oak. **1950** Moore *Trees AR* 52, Pin Oak. . . Local Names: Swamp Spanish, Water, Swamp, and Water Red Oak. **1969** *DARE* (Qu. T10, . . *Kinds of oak trees*) Inf **NC**72, Water oak, pin oak—same. **1979** Little *Checklist U.S. Trees* 238.

d =**shingle oak.**

1860 Curtis *Cat. Plants NC* 36, Shingle Oak. . . In those parts of our State where it occurs, I have heard it called only *Water Oak.* **1897** Sudworth *Arborescent Flora* 176 **NC,** *Quercus imbricaria.* . . Water Oak. **1921** Deam *Trees IN* 119, *Quercus imbricaria.* . . Shingle Oak. . . It is also called black oak, peach oak, jack oak and water oak. **1950** Grimm *Trees PA* 175, The Shingle Oak is also known as the Laurel Oak and as Water Oak, but the latter two names are properly applied to two other species of oaks which are common in the South.

e =**laurel oak 2.**

1897 Sudworth *Arborescent Flora* 175 **GA,** *Quercus laurifolia.* . . Water Oak. **1913** *Torreya* 13.229 **LA,** *Quercus laurifolia.* . . Red, pin or water oak, Abbeville, La. **1979** Little *Checklist U.S. Trees* 235, *Quercus laurifolia.* . . Other common names—Darlington oak, . . water oak [etc].

f also *Spanish water oak:* =**red oak 2b.**

1897 Sudworth *Arborescent Flora* 171 **LA,** *Quercus digitata* [=*Q. falcata*]. . . Common names. . . Spanish Water Oak. **1937** Stemen–Myers *OK Flora* 90, *Quercus triloba* Michx. [=*Q. falcata*]—Spanish or Water Oak. . . In dry soil. **1947** Collingwood–Brush *Knowing Trees* 194, Southern Red Oak. . . Locally called Spanish oak, Spanish water oak [etc].

g also *Arkansas water oak:* *Quercus arkansana.*

1938 Van Dersal *Native Woody Plants* 347, Water [oak] (*Quercus arkansana*). **1960** Vines *Trees SW* 196, Arkansas Oak. . . Also known locally as Water Oak and Arkansas Water Oak.

h also *white water oak:* =**overcup oak 1.**

1938 Van Dersal *Native Woody Plants* 347, White water [oak] (*Quercus lyrata*). **1966** *DARE* (Qu. T10, . . *Kinds of oak trees*) Inf **MS**21, Water oak, overcup oak—same.

water oats n

A **wild rice 1** (here: *Zizania aquatica*).

1822 Eaton *Botany* 519, *Zizania clavulosa.* . . water-oats, wild-rice. **1830** Rafinesque *Med. Flora* 2.276, Zizania . . *Wild Rice, Water Oats.* . . Seeds like oats and like rice when cleaned. **1851** *De Bow's Rev.* 11.510 **PA,** Any one who will take a walk to the nearest river bank of the Delaware and Schuylkill, . . will have a perfect idea of what wild rice is; these same reeds, or water oats, as they are often called, being exactly the same plant as the wild rice of Minnesota. **1903** Small *Flora SE U.S.* 112, *Zizania aquatica.* . . Indian Rice. . . Water Oats. Marsh Rice. **1939** *Daily Courier* (Connellsville PA) 3 Mar 1/2, [The carp's] food consists mostly of vegetation, seeds of waterlilies, and wild rice and water oats. **1972** *Pioneer* (Bemidji MN) 8 Sept 3/5, Minnesota's economy could be boosted considerably by a . . purplish-black grain sometimes called Indian rice or water oats, but most commonly known as wild rice.

water out v phr

1 To put out (a fire) with water. **esp S Midl** See Map
1809 (2007) M'Harry *Practical Distiller* (Internet) **sePA,** Shut up your

furnace door and put in your damper; . . this plan I deem preferable to watering out the fire. **1900** Carter *NC Sketches* 106 **wNC,** Before we went we watered out the fire . . ; so it weren't *that* as sot the fire. **1912** *Daily Democrat* (Greenville MS) 14 Feb 5/5, As the cottage was already burned to the ground . . , the department did not attempt to water out the fire. **1966–69** *DARE* (Qu. Y43a) Inf **LA**2, Water it out; (Qu. Y43b, . . *To put out a fire*) Infs **GA**77, **NC**37, 55, Water out (the fire); **SC**34, Water it out; **AR**51, Water the fire out. [5 of 6 infs comm type 5, 4 gs educ or less] **1976** Browne *Night with Hants* 77 **AL,** Took a bucket of water and watered out the fire after they'd all gone in. **2004** *DARE* File **TX** [Black], Have this fire that's fueling inside, just wanting me to die / Niggaz try to water it out, but they get burned when they try.

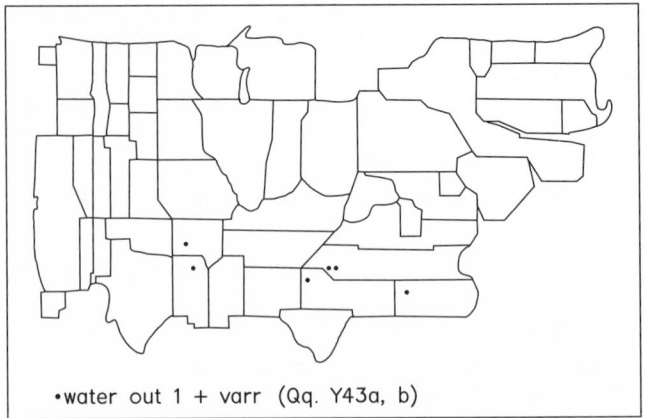

•water out 1 + varr (Qq. Y43a, b)

2 See quots. [Prob calque of Norw *utvanne*] **Norw settlement areas**

1970 Drache *Challenge of Prairie* 121 **wND** (as of a1914), "Lutefisk," another Norwegian dish, was often on hand at Christmas, even though it came all the way from Norway in a "dry form and had to be watered out by the consumer." **1984** *MJLF* 10.159 **cnWI,** Water out. To de-salt meat by soaking it in fresh water. **1989** in 2007 *DARE* File—Internet **ND,** [*Hannaford Area Hist.:*] Mrs. Johnny Haugen and Mrs. Marcus Bakken have "soaked and watered out" the lutefisk so as to get rid of the lye taste. Many wash tubs full of the lutefisk is used at these suppers.

water ouzel n

Std: an aquatic passerine bird of western North America (*Cinclus cinclus* or *C. mexicanus unicolor*). Also called **dipper 4, teeter** n **2, water turkey 3**

water parsley n

1 =**water parsnip.** [*OED2* 1562 →]

1940 Gates *Flora KS* 228 **ceKS,** *Sium suave.* . . Water Parsley. Water Parsnip. . . In water or very wet places. **1963** Craighead *Rocky Mt. Wildflowers* 131, Water-parsnip. . . Other names: Water-parsley. . . Look for this in low swampy ground, along streams and borders of lakes and ponds.

2 A **marsh pennywort** (here: *Hydrocotyle ranunculoides*).

1942 *Torreya* 42.163 **LA,** *Hydrocotyle ranunculoides.* . . Water parsley, parasol.

water parsnip n [*OED2* 1597 →] Cf **parsnip B**

Std: an umbelliferous aquatic plant (*Sium suave*). Also called **false hemlock, pepperweed 4, water parsley 1**

water partridge n

1 =**ruddy duck. MD**

1874 *Forest & Stream* 1.411 **Baltimore MD,** Here they call . . the ruddy duck a coot and water partridge. **1888** Trumbull *Names of Birds* 112 **MD,** A well known Washington gunner . . tells of hearing it [=the ruddy duck] called *water-partridge,* and *steel-head,* on the Patuxent River, Md. **1923** U.S. Dept. Ag. *Misc. Circular* 13.31 **MD,** Ruddy Duck. . . Vernacular names. . . *In local use.* . . water-partridge (Potomac River).

2 =**green-winged teal.** Cf **sea partridge**

1982 Elman *Hunter's Field Guide* 178, Green-winged Teal. . . Common & Regional Names. . . *partridge duck, water-partridge* [etc].

water pepper n [*OED2* 1538 →]

Std: a **smartweed:** usu *Polygonum hydropiper* or *P. hydropiperoides,* but also *P. punctatum.* For other names see **ass-**

smart, bite-tongue, biting knotweed, heartweed 2, marsh-pepper smartweed, water ~   Cf **hell-pepper**

water pewee n   Also *water pewit*

A **phoebe** (here: *Sayornis phoebe*).

1884 Coues *Key to N. Amer. Birds* 437, S*[ayiornis] fusca* [=*Sayornis phoebe*]. . . Pewit Flycatcher. Water Pewee. Pewit. Phœbe. **1890** *Century Dict.* 4431, The common pewit. . . Also called *water-pewit* and *phoebe-bird* or *phoebe*. **1895** (1907) Wright *Birdcraft* 185, Phoebe: *Sayornis phoebe. Water Pewee*. . . In its native woods the nest is of moss, mud, and grass bracketed on a rock, near or over running water. **1946** Hausman *Eastern Birds* 401, Eastern Phoebe. . . Other Names—Bridge Bird, . . Water Pewee, . . Water Pewit [etc.].

water pheasant n

1 Either the **hooded merganser** or the common **merganser** (*Mergus merganser*).

a**1782** (1788) Jefferson *Notes VA* 77, Besides these, we have. . . Water-pheasant. **1814** Wilson *Amer. Ornith.* 8.68, The Goosander [is] called by some the Water Pheasant, and by others the Sheldrake, Fisherman, Diver, &c. **1844** DeKay *Zool. NY* 2.320, The Hooded Sheldrake. . . The *Hairy-head*, or *Whistler*, or *Water Pheasant*, as this species is called in this State. **1910** Eaton *Birds NY* 1.181, The Hooded merganser, Swamp sheldrake, Hairy-head, or Water pheasant is generally distributed in New York State, occurring in many places where the other mergansers are unknown, because of its habit of frequenting swamps and ponds which are too small to attract the other species. **1923** U.S. Dept. Ag. *Misc. Circular* 13.7, Hooded Merganser. . . *Vernacular Names*. . . *In local use.* . . water-pheasant (N.Y. to S.C.) **1955** MA Audubon Soc. *Bulletin* 39.379 **MA**, Water Pheasant (Mass. As a conspicuous aquatic bird.) **1968** *DARE* (Qu. Q7, *Names and nicknames for . . game birds*) Inf **MD**36, Water pheasant or merganser—sharp bill, webbed feet, stays on water.

2 =**pintail 1.**

1888 Trumbull *Names of Birds* 38 **CT**, To the older gunners about Milford, this is the *pheasant duck* or *pheasant;* and similar names by which the species has been known are *sea pheasant* and *water pheasant.* **1955** MA Audubon Soc. *Bulletin* 39.314 **CT**, Pintail. . . Water Pheasant.

water pilot n   [See quot c1981]

A **water snake 1** (here: *Nerodia taxispilota* or *N. sipedon*).

1884 *NY Times* (NY) 3 Aug 2/4 **NY**, The writer, hidden behind a tree along the Beaver Mill Creek, in Sullivan County, saw a mink, a king-fisher, and a water pilot all watching for trout within a distance of 100 feet. **1929** *Copeia* 172.76 **cSC**, Brown Water Snake; a name not open to obvious objections as are the better known terms Water Pilot and Water Rattle. **1937** Pope *Snakes Alive* 202, Water pilot. . . Eastern Virginia southward through Florida, thence westward to Louisiana. **1949** [see **water moccasin 2**]. **1967** *DARE* (Qu. P25, . . *Kinds of snakes*) Inf **NJ**1, Water pilot. c**1981** Linzey–Clifford *Snakes VA* 41, Brown water snakes are also called "water pilots" in the belief that they guide other snakes to safety. **2005** Lovell et al. *Snakes GA* (Internet), The Brown Water Snake. Often called the "Water Pilot" or the "Water Rattle."

water pipit n

A **pipit** (here: *Anthus spinoletta* [but see quot 2007]).

[**1831** Audubon *Ornith. Biog.* 1.50, I am inclined to consider the Brown Titlark identical with the Water Pipit of Europe.] [**1891** *Century Dict.* 6845, *Water-pipit*. . . One of several species of *Anthus* which are common in various parts of Europe, especially that usually called *A. aquaticus,* also *A. spinoletta,* and more correctly *A. spipoletta*.] **1955** Lowery *LA Birds* 408, The Water Pipit is one of our commonest winter birds. **1963** Murie *Birds Mt. McKinley* 75, The water pipit. . . walks rather than hops, and has a habit of moving its tail up and down. **2007** (acc) Cornell Univ. Lab. Ornith. *Birds N. Amer.* (Internet), The American Pipit was long known as the Water Pipit (*Anthus spinoletta*), a wide ranging species with seven subspecies occurring from the shores of Great Britain and Scandinavia, and the high mountains of Europe and central Asia, to North America. Recent taxonomic studies, however, have shown that the three North American subspecies and the most eastern asiatic subspecies are best regarded as a distinct species, now referred to as the American Pipit (*A. rubescens*).

water plantain n

1 Std: a plant of the genus *Alisma*.   For other names of var spp see **devil's spoons, mad-dog weed 2, mud plantain 2**

2 as *creeping* (or *dwarf*) *water plantain:* =**mud-baby.**

1933 Small *Manual SE Flora* 21, *Echinodorus* [spp]. . . Mud-babies. Creeping Water-plantains. **1937** Stemen–Myers *OK Flora* 31, Dwarf Water-plantain. . . *Echinodorus tenellus.*

waterpod n

=**Aunt Lucy 1.**

1917 *Amer. Midland Naturalist* 5.112 **KS**, *Macrocalyx Nyctelea.* . . Water Pod. . . This common name was first used by the writer in an earlier publication. **1950** Stevens *ND Plants* 234, *Ellisia nyctelea.* . . Waterpod. . . Common weed in fields in Red River Valley. **2007** (acc) Bell Museum Nat. Hist. *Annotated Checklist Flora MN* (Internet), *Ellisia nyctelea.* . . waterpod; aunt lucy.

water poplar n

=**Carolina poplar 1.**

1749 in 1985 Kalm *Resejournal* 3.136 **ceNY**, Folcket här på orten kallade detta träd *Water-poplar;* det växte ömsom med Waterbeech vid sidan af floden. [=The people in this part of the country call this tree *Water-poplar;* it grows sometimes with Waterbeech on the river banks.] **1822** Eaton *Botany* 404, *Populus angulata* [=*P. deltoides*], balm-of-gilead, water poplar, cotton wood. **1847** Wood *Class-Book* 507, P*[opulus] angulata.* Water Poplar. . . A tree of noble dimensions, growing along the rivers of the Southern and Western States. **1883** *Forest & Stream* 20.25 **sFL**, The cocoa-plum . . grows in endless profusion amid the swamp maple, . . water poplar [etc.]. **1968** *DARE* (Qu. T12, *The kind of poplar tree that has sticky, sweet-smelling buds*) Inf **NJ**8, Water poplar—grows in wet places; (Qu. T15, . . *Kinds of swamp trees*) Inf **WV**8, Water poplar. **1974** *Bennington Banner* (VT) 6 July 6/5, [Caption:] Ray Allen stands beside a mammoth water poplar.

water primrose n

A **false loosestrife.**

1942 *Jrl. Wildlife Management* 6.303 **eTX**, Where the water is shallower and drought first occurs the plants are cutgrass . . , maiden cane . . , water primrose (*Jussiaea* sp.), pickerelweed . . , white water-lily . . , and square-stem spikerush. **1948** Stevens *KS Wild Flowers* 306, [Caption:] Floating Water-primrose (*Jussiaea diffusa*). **1961** Douglas *My Wilderness* 132 **sFL**, And in the shade I found a small yellow flower . . —the lovely water primrose. **1996** *Frederick Post* (MD) 9 May sec C 2/1, [Advt:] Receive a *Free* Water Primrose . . when you bring this ad. **2001** *Jrl. Wildlife Management* 65.740, Emergent and floating vegetation [consisted] of water primrose (*Ludwigia uruguayensis, L. palustris),* water hyacinth . . , and duckweeds.

water pump n   Cf **pumper, slough-pumper, thunder pumper 1**

=**bittern.**

[**1952** *San Antonio Express–News* (TX) 27 Apr [32]/3 (newspaperarchive.com), Sometimes the note [of the bittern] has the sound of an axe driving a stake and again like the creaking thump of a water pump.] **1968** *DARE* (Qu. Q8, *A water bird that makes a booming sound before rain and often stands with its beak pointed almost straight up*) Inf **MN**15, Water pump or slough pump.

water puppy n   Also *water pup*   **chiefly Missip–Ohio Valleys**

=**water dog 1.**

1832 [see **water dog 1**]. **1843** Trego *Geog. PA* 78, The most remarkable animals of this family [=the salamanders] are the Water puppy, young alligator, *(Necturus lateralis,)* of the Ohio, Lake Erie, &c. two feet in length; and the Hellbender. **1859** [see **water dog 1**]. **1862** IN State Geologist *Rept. Geol. Reconnoissance IN* 148, This county has numerous fine springs and water privileges; from one of which a boy was fishing had just drawn a Menopoma (water-puppy) twenty-two inches long. **1899** *Waterloo Daily Reporter* (IA) 14 Jan 1/2, The animal was about ten inches in length and the general form of the body was like that of a catfish, except that it . . had four legs similar to those of a lizard. . . On the upper part of the head were a couple of ears, lopping down on either side, which gave the object an amusingly puppy-like appearance. One of the parties who inspected it and who had seen such creatures before said it was called a water puppy. **1906** *Lake Co. Times* (Hammond IN) 19 Nov 2/4, [Headline:] Salamander, otherwise water puppy, finds home. **1928** Baylor Univ. Museum *Contrib.* 16.7 **eTX**, Mud-puppy. Ground-puppy. Water-puppy. Ground-dog. In Texas, these four names refer to three species of land salamanders which inhabit the eastern part of the State. In one locality, all four names may commonly apply to one species of salamander, while in another, one of the names may be used indiscriminately for all three of the amphibians. The three species . . are the Spotted (Ambystoma maculatum) . . , Marbed [sic] (A. opacum) . . , and Texan (A. texanum) . . salamanders. **1935** Sandoz *Jules* 399 **wNE** (as of 1880–1930), Almost every Kinkaider with a mud hole briny enough for water puppies (the sandhill salamander) carried a bottle of the gray water with him. **1940** Stong *Hawkeyes* 251 **IA**, We caught a water-pup one day, that belonged down in the Gulf of Mexico.

1952 *NW AR Times* (Fayetteville) 13 Feb 9/3, A "water puppy," taken on a hook from Clear Creek . . was displayed at the *Times* office yesterday afternoon. About 15 inches long, it had gills with red-feathery tips, four legs with four toes on each, and was brown with black spots on its back. **1968** *DARE* (Qu. P3, *Freshwater fish that are not good to eat*) Inf **IA**22, Water puppy; (Qu. P13, . . *Ways of fishing . . besides the ordinary hook and line*) Inf **IA**29, Water puppy—as bait for catfish. **2007** *DARE* File—Internet [Pet store chain in **OH, IN, KY**], *Tiger Salamander (Water Puppy). . .* Water Puppies will do well on bloodworms, small feeder fish [etc].

water purslane n

A **false loosestrife** (here: *Ludwigia palustris*).

1822 Eaton *Botany* 320, *Isnardia* [=*Ludwigia*] . . *palustris . .* water purslane. **1840** MA Zool. & Bot. Surv. *Herb. Plants & Quadrupeds* 47, *Isnardia. . . palustris. . .* Water Purslane. . . grows in wet places and pools. . . Has a slight resemblance to common Purslane. **1896** *Jrl. Amer. Folkl.* 9.188, *Ludwigia palustris. . .* water purslane, West. **1930** OK Univ. Biol. Surv. *Pub.* 2.74, *Ludvigia palustris. . .* Water Purslane. **1967** Gilkey–Dennis *Hdbk. NW Plants* 267, *Water purslane. . .* Rather common along margins of ponds, forming broad mats.

water rat n

1 =**muskrat 1.**

[**1694** Clayton in Royal Soc. London *Philos. Trans.* 18.123 **VA**, *Musk-Rats*, in all things shaped like our Water-Rats, only something larger, and is an absolute Species of Water-Rats, only having a curious Musky scent.] **1835** Whittier in *New Engl. Mag.* Mar 163, Hush, let the Sachem's voice be weak—/ The water-rat shall hear him speak. **1941** *Daily Times–News* (Burlington NC) 18 Feb 2/5, Neighbors stood around tentatively calling it a "black possum," or a water rat. . . It is a musk-rat. **1950** *WELS (Muskrat)* 1 inf, **WI**, Water rat. **1951** Teale *North with Spring* 103 **LA**, Dominating the scene below, strange in infinite numbers, was the multitude of muskrat houses. . . Some years, Maurice shouted above the roar of the engine, the water rats "almost eat up the earth." **1967–70** *DARE* (Qu. P31, . . *Names or nicknames . . for the . . muskrat*) Infs **KY**72, **MA**4, **NC**85, **NJ**3, **NY**87, 198, **VA**32, Water rat.

2 =**round-tailed muskrat.** Cf **Florida water rat**

1927 Boston Soc. Nat. Hist. *Proc.* 38.360 **Okefenokee GA**, *Neofiber alleni nigrescens. . .* This unique little animal goes for the most part by the local names of 'Prairie-rat' and 'Water-rat.' The former term seems to be in more general use on Billy's Island, and the latter on the eastern side of the swamp. **1934** *Natl. Geogr. Mag.* 65.621 **Okefenokee GA**, [Caption:] Hiding in a water rat's nest, these timid rodents were snapped . . when the top was lifted.

water rattle n Also *water rattler*, ~ *rattlesnake* **chiefly Sth**

1 =**water moccasin 2.**

1736 Catesby in Royal Soc. London *Philos. Trans.* 39.254 **NC, SC**, The Water Viper. . . This Sort is commonly called in *Carolina*, the Water Rattle-Snake, not that it hath a Rattle, but from the Likeness of its Colour. . . Its Tail terminates in a sharp pointed Horn. **1882** *Ft. Wayne Daily Gaz.* (IN) [5]/6 **GA** (newspaperarchive.com), A trout thirteen inches long was found the other day in a water rattle snake, 5 1–2 feet long and 13 inches around, at Reid's Station, Ga. **1929** [see **water pilot**]. **1949** [see **water moccasin 2**]. **1952** Ditmars *N. Amer. Snakes* 113, "Water Rattle," . . *Natrix taxispilota*. . . Maryland to central Florida and westward to Louisiana. Particularly common in swampy waterways of South Carolina, Georgia and Florida. *Ibid* 114, These snakes. . . [have] a trait of lying in circular coil, half hidden in matted swamp grass, and striking like a flash. . . [I]n such places there is always the thought of the dangerous Canebrake Rattler, which coils in similar fashion and in color of dark individuals is not much different; hence a common name, among the Negroes, of this water snake—the "Water Rattle." **1966–70** *DARE* (Qu. P25, . . *Kinds of snakes*) Infs **NC**13, 21, 24, 49, **SC**26, Water rattler; **NC**85, Water rattle—brown, speckled, not a rattlesnake; **AR**56, Water rattlesnake. [*DARE* Ed: Some of these Infs may refer instead to **2** below.] **1986** Pederson *LAGS Concordance (Snakes)* 1 inf, **csAL**, Ground rattle, water rattle—in water, has lost its rattle. **2005** [see **water pilot**].

2 =**diamondback rattlesnake.**

1810 Lambert *Travels* 3.60 **nGA, sSC**, The shores abounded with a species of *water rattle-snake*, whose bite was also of a deadly nature. **1839** *Anti-Slavery Examiner* 6.18 **GA** (as of 1817–24), The moccasin snakes, so called, and water rattle-snakes—the bites of both of which are as poisonous as our upland rattle-snakes at the north,—are found in myriads about the stagnant waters and swamps of the South. **1861** *New Amer. Cyclop.* 23.773 **S Atl**, The diamond or water rattlesnake . . dark

brown or dusky above, with a series of large rhomboidal spots continuous from head to tail. **1923** *Youth's Companion* 5 Apr 212, The great diamond-back of the far South, which lives among slow streams, ponds and bayous, is commonly known as the "water rattler." **1926** (1949) McQueen–Mizell *Hist. Okefenokee* 61 **seGA**, The deadly water rattler . . the most deadly thing to be encountered in the swamp.

water red oak See **red oak 2d**

water roach n [Because it prefers water pipes and moist places in houses] Cf **water bug**

A cockroach, esp a large one.

1864 *Scientific Amer.* 10.239, [Advt:] Jaques Pure Extract of Tobacco. . . Kills Bed-bugs and Water-roaches. **1930** *Charleston Gaz.* (WV) 25 May 5/4, The scourge of water roaches and other insects that has descended on Charleston is a problem for individual householders to solve, Dr. Hugh Robias, city health commissioner, said yesterday. **1950** *WELS (Other names for the cockroach)* 1 Inf, **WI**, Water roach. **2005** *DARE* File—Internet **TX**, I found a water roach the size of a '59 Cadillac in the shower. I valiantly squashed it with one of my wife's shoes. **2007** [see **water bug**].

water scooter n Cf **water skeeter**

A **water strider.**

1943 *Tucson Daily Citizen* (AZ) 25 Aug 4/2 **CA**, Lean "water scooters" skating on their silvery bulbs of air. **1965** Snyder *Velvet Room* 88 **CA**, In the calm eddies, water scooters zipped away to hide and dragonflies hovered on tinsel wings. **1994** Homer *Drownt Boy* 67 **MO**, Water scooters come close to living in a two-dimensional world, but we'd have to be reflections on the water's surface to be two-dimensional. **2002** *DARE* File—Internet **CA**, Alas, no pup fish. Wrong season, I suppose. Just plenty of pickleweed, water scooters, dragonflies, and tiny brown birds. **2007** *Ibid* **MI**, Here are some water scooters that we saw yesterday at Ludington State Park.

water shamrock n

=**buckbean 1.**

1830 Rafinesque *Med. Flora* 2.33, *Menyanthes verna . . Vulgar.* Marsh Trefoil, Water Shamrock, Bitter Root. **1854** King *Amer. Eclectic Dispensatory* 633, *Menyanthes trifoliata.* Buckbean. . . This plant is also known by the names of *Bog-bean, Marsh-trefoil, Water-shamrock*, etc. **1910** Graves *Flowering Plants* 320 **CT**, *Menyanthes trifoliata. . .* Water Shamrock. Bogs, borders of ponds and in wet meadows. **1974** (1977) Coon *Useful Plants* 144, Water shamrock. . . with its tri-foliate leaves, easily acquired the name of trefoil.

water shelf n Sth, S Midl

A shelf or bench on which a bucket of water and other utensils are kept for drinking and washing.

1853 Ramsey *Annals TN* 716, The whole furniture, of the one apartment, answering in these primitive times, the purpose of the kitchen, the dining-room, the nursery and the dormitory, were a plain home-made bedstead or two, . . a water shelf and a bucket . . , and sometimes a loom. **1895** (2001) Anderson *Anderson Surpriser* 33 (Internet) **GA**, One day she was setting out some flowers under the water shelf; they were beneath the place where they would wash their faces and hands. **1897** *Harper's New Mth. Mag.* 95.644 **AR**, Just then Enoch came in and approached the water-shelf. "Don't keer how you polish it, a brass lantern an' coal ile is like murder on a man's hands. It will out." **1928** Peterkin *Scarlet Sister Mary* 32 **SC**, She tried hard to get one more paper to fix a cover . . for the water shelf. **1933** Rawlings *South Moon* 42 **nFL**, Lantry watched Piety as she washed the dishes at the water-shelf. **1941** Justus *Cabin on Kettle Creek* 5 **eTN**, Matt was sent to the dog-trot to slick up his hair . . , and for several minutes they heard him sloshing about at the water shelf. **1986** Pederson *LAGS Concordance*, 1 inf, **csGA**, Water shelf; 1 inf, **swGA**, Water shelf—a table outside, on porch, for washing; 1 inf, **cnFL**, Water shelf—outside house; washed hands; 1 inf, **nwFL**, Water shelf—for washing hands and face; 1 inf, **swMS**, Water shelf—separate from house; 1 inf, **swMS**, Water shelf—at end of porch; a wash box; 1 inf, **ceAR**, Water shelf—outside for drinking, cooking; 1 inf, **nwLA**, Water shelf—on porch; held bucket, bath equipment; 1 inf, **ceTX**, Water shelf—where you kept drinking water; 1 inf, **csMS**, The water shelf—on porch with bowl for cleaning; 1 inf, **neMS**, Water shelves—without mirrors. **2000** *DARE* File—Internet **seGA**, You are very Wiregrass if . . you know what a water shelf is.

water shield n

Std: an American aquatic plant (*Brasenia schreberi*) with large ovate leaves. Also called **bonnet B1d, coltsfoot 7, cooter** grass 1, deer-foot 1, egg bonnet, fanwort, fish grass, frog leaf, purple bonnet, water lily 5

water shrew n   Also *water shrewmouse*

A North American aquatic **shrew** (here: usu *Sorex palustris,* but also *S. bendirii*).   For other names see **marsh shrew, muskrat mouse**

   1842 *Parley's Mag.* 10.198, He was a *water-shrewmouse,* and very much like the common shrewmouse; but he was larger . . and altogether a much handsomer animal. **1857** U.S. War Dept. *Rept. Explor. Railroad* 8.xxxii swWA, *Neosorex navigator* [=*Sorex palustris*]. . . Water Shrew.—Fort Vancouver. **1906** Stephens *CA Mammals* 254, Water Shrews are found in the Rocky Mountains. . . They frequent the swifter mountain streams. **1952** Burt *Field Guide Mammals* 13, Pacific Water Shrew. *Sorex bendirei* [sic]. . . Along the humid Pacific Coast, near and in *streams,* lives this *large, dark-brown* shrew. **1961** Jackson *Mammals WI* 36, *Sorex palustris hydrobadistes*. . . In Wisconsin, when recognized, usually called water shrew. **2004** *Valley Independent* (Monessen PA) 3 Jan sec B 4/2, Portions of Forbes State Forest . . are home to the West Virginia water shrew.

watersilk n   [See quot 2002]

A **frog spit 1** (here: *Spirogyra* spp).

   1863 *OH Educ. Mth.* 12.161, A great number of them [=algae] grow in our creeks, streams and ponds; as, for instance, the beautiful green water-silk, which you have often seen. **1950** *PADS* 14.71 SC, *Water-silk*. . . Same as *frog spittle* and *froggum.* **2002** (acc) U.S. Army Corps Engineers *PMIS* (Internet), *Spirogyra* or water silk is a common green alga found in shallow warm water where it can form extensive floating mats. One can detect the "silky" quality of the filaments by trying to lift the alga from the water.

water skeeter n   [**skeet** v **1, 2;** cf **skater, water scooter**] **chiefly West**

A **water strider.**

   1897 *Los Angeles Times* (CA) 15 Jan 12/2, A tiny canoe angled across the stream an elusive water 'skeeter. **1929** *Ecology* 10.324 **MO,** *Rhagovelia obesa* Uhler, the small water skeeter, congregates on the surface near the shore in the vicinity of rapid water. **1932** *Middletown Times Herald* (NY) 16 Dec 4/7 **CA,** You know what water skeeters are. They have long legs, tiny bodies and they skim so lightly across the water that they never break through and get their feet wet. **1968** *DARE* (Qu. R28, . . *Kinds of spiders*) Inf NC54, Water skeeters—brown bugs that live on surface of water; some calls 'em water spider. **1969** *Lowell Sun* (MA) 28 July 27/2, The water skeeters were the most fun. They float on top of the water, and seem to skid across the surface in short bursts. **2007** *DARE* File—Internet **WA,** We watched as the sun warmed the water, rousing the last of the dragonflies and water skeeters. *Ibid* **UT,** I grew up in Provo. . . Down the road a ¼ block was a dirt road that ran alongside a ditch that we played at. We would catch water skeeters. *Ibid* **TX,** It is amazing how fast a small eco system has developed. There are numerous water skeeters and water beetles.

water skipper n

1   See **skipper 2.**

2   See **skipper 3.**

‡**3**   =**dragonfly.**

   1967 *DARE* (Qu. R2, . . *The dragonfly*) Inf **NE**11, Water skipper.

water smartweed n

Any of several **smartweeds:** either a **water pepper** (usu *Polygonum punctatum*) or *P. amphibium.*

   1868 (1870) Gray *Field Botany* 288, [*Polygonum*] *acre* [=*P. punctatum*], Water Smartweed. **1911** Porter *Harvester* 250 **IN,** Water smartweed spread a glowing pink background. **1941** *Sheboygan Press* (WI) 22 May 26/4, *1941 Marsh Planting Program.* . . 1,000 true water smartweed. **1966** *DARE* (Qu. S26b, *Wildflowers that grow in water or wet places*) Inf **MI**31, Water smartweed. **1970** U.S. Ag. Research Serv. *Selected Weeds* 114, *Polygonum amphibium.* . . Water smartweed. . . Throughout all the northern half of the United States excepting parts of States in the West.

water smeller n   Also *water sniffer* [Calques of Ger *Wasserschmecker, Wasserriecher*]   **chiefly PA**

=**water witch** n **3, 4.**

   1810 in 1877 Linn *Annals Buffalo Valley PA* 388, T. Clingan had a water-smeller, to find where he should put the well on his place. **1886** *Hist. Susquehanna* 673, Some odd occupations are named: Charles Hoyt (Hite), of Milford, in 1830, is said to be a "water-smeller." **1954**

Charleston Gaz. (WV) 31 Mar [61]/2 (newspaperarchive.com), All the old folks on this mountain ridge know that Willie could use a water smeller better than anyone else. . . "A forked limb of a peach tree makes the best smeller." . . Willie . . began to smell for water. **1966** *Sun. Post-Crescent* (Appleton WI) 17 Apr sec A 15/2 **PA,** Amish "Water Smeller" David Mast King . . uses a pair of pliers to locate an underground water source for Lititz, Pa. **1967–69** *DARE* (Qu. CC13a, . . *A forked stick that's used to show where there's water underground*) Inf **PA**29, Water smeller; [**PA**11, Smelling for water;] (Qu. CC13b, . . *The person who knows how to use a forked stick to find water*) Infs **PA**27, 29, Water smeller; **PA**205, Water sniffer. **1972** *Progress* (Clearfield PA) 17 Nov 16/7, The little town of Mountville . . continues to rely on a "water smeller" to find its water. . . To do so, Keck has but to carry a pair of chrome plated pliers.

water snake n

1   Std: a snake of the genus *Nerodia.*   For other names of var spp see **black watersnake, copper-belly 2, diamondback water snake, gray moccasin, moccasin 1b, pearl-finder, pink flamingo snake, red-bellied water ~, salt-marsh ~, saltwater moccasin, striped ~, striped water snake, water adder, ~ bandit (snake), ~ pilot, ~ moccasin 2, ~ rattle 1** Cf **copper-back snake**

2   also *water garter snake*: =**garter snake 1.**

   1847 Mather–Brockett *Geog. NY* 42, Of the harmless species, we have . . the striped water, green water, or water garter snake. **1915** *Copeia* 15.[4] sCA, Pacific Garter Snake, or "Water-snake," *Thamnophis hammondi. Ibid* 19.10 sCA, Now and then . . a "Water" Snake (*Thamnophis hammondi*) will wander in search of food. **1958** Conant *Reptiles & Amphibians* 130 *West,* Garter snakes are closely related to the Water Snakes (*Natrix*). . . Toward the west, members of the group are often found near water, with the inevitable result of being called "water snakes."

3   A snake of the genus *Regina.*   For other names of var spp see **queen snake, striped moccasin, ~ water snake, swamp snake c**

   1892 IN Dept. Geol. & Nat. Resources *Rept. for 1891* 589, *Natrix grahamii.* . . Graham's Water Snake. **1928** Baylor Univ. Museum *Contrib.* 16.17 **TX,** Graham's Water Snake. . . In eastern and central Texas this species is commonly known as the *Striped Moccasin.* **1958** Conant *Reptiles & Amphibians* 123, Glossy Water Snake—*Natrix rigida* [=*Regina rigida*]. c**1981** Linzey-Clifford *Snakes VA* 48, Queen Snake (*Regina septemvittata*). . . Other Common Names: Garter snake, willow snake, . . water snake.

water sniffer   See **water smeller**

water-sob(bed)   See **sob** v

water-sog(ged)   See **sog** v **1**

water spider n   [*OED2* 1552 →; "In early use applied loosely to insects that move swiftly on the surface of the water"]

A **water strider.**   Note: Some of these quots may refer instead (or also) to a true spider of the genus *Dolomedes,* but specific references to these spiders are not included here.

   1813 Allston *Sylphs* 24, In circling dance they gaily skim;/ And now upon its surface swim,/ And water-spiders chase. **1860** Street *Woods & Waters* 178 **NY,** There was the emerald flash of the dragon-fly, and around the brown water-spider skated. **1886** *Overland Mth.* (2d ser) 8.348 cwCA, Occasionally, a *Ploteres,* one of the so-called "water spiders," that spend life in an eternal skate on top of the water, comes up in my dredger. **1891** *Ibid* 17.202 cwCA, We whiled away many a morning, watching the blithe and active water spiders, commonly called skaters, as they skimmed the water. **1898** Smith *Caleb West* 25 **NJ,** Its glassy surface [was] rippled now and then . . by the quick water-spider strokes of some lobster-fisherman. **1965–70** *DARE* (Qu. R28, . . *Kinds of spiders*) 93 Infs, **scattered, but esp freq PA,** Water spider; DC2, Water spider walked on water; MA42, Water spider—big legs go to diameter of a half-dollar; MI42, Water spider—some call 'em skaters; NC54, Water skeeters—brown bugs that live on surface of water; some calls 'em water spider; PA6, Water spider—skipper; PA49, Skaters = water spiders; WY5, Water spider—or skater.

water-spider orchid n

A **fringed orchid** (here: *Habenaria repens*).

   1950 Correll *Native Orchids* 103, The Water-spider Orchid grows in very wet places, even at times forming floating islands, usually in the midst of coarse grasses. **1972** Brown *Wildflowers LA* 39, Water-spider

Orchid. . . Very abundant in southern Louisiana in canals and water bodies which are infested with water hyacinth. Also Texas and Mississippi.

waterspout n

1 A terrestrial tornado, esp one accompanied by torrential rain; broadly, a violent downpour of rain. [Transf from *waterspout* a tornado that forms over a body of water] **scattered, but esp freq Missip Valley** See Map

[**1774** Franklin in *Royal Amer. Mag.* 1.343, But, if that which appears a water-spout at sea, does some times . . pass over land, and there produce all the phænomena and effects of a whirlwind, it should thence seem still more evident, that a whirlwind and a spout are the same.] **1822** *Amer. Jrl. Sci. & Arts* 4.137 **ceNY,** The configuration of the ground is in each instance such, as to forbid the supposition, that the water might have accumulated from the adjoining ground. Did a cloud highly surcharged with water, rest upon each of these places . . ? Did waterspouts discharge themselves here? **1859** *Knickerbocker* 54.86 **VT,** The windows of heaven were opened, and out of a summer sky there broke loose an instantaneous flood, a visitation hitherto unknown to the inhabitants . . —a *water-spout,* like that which sometimes rests upon the surface of the ocean, columnar, or as a hollow cone. **1871** *Overland Mth.* 7.458 **SW,** The old man, wife, two girls . . , and a boy . . , were coming through this dry wash, when a water-spout burst over them, and they were lost. **1877** *Galaxy* 24.705 **CO,** A heavy dark cloud in the northwest set up a rapid rotary motion, and a rapid whirl began in the air, resting on the earth to the west of it. . . A waterspout formed suddenly in the centre and swept across the prairie in a track about five hundred yards wide. **1879** *Waterloo Courier* (IA) 13 Aug 1/2, The clouds looked to be of a peculiar formation and the column of water came down in a funnel shape. . . The symmetry of the water spout seemed almost perfect. **1881** *Chicago Times* 11 June *(OED2)* **MO,** The village . . was nearly annihilated last night by a water-spout or a cloud-burst. **1890** **VA RR** *Comm. Annual Rept. for 1889–90* xxxvi, That night I heard several loud claps of thunder, followed afterwards by a roaring noise. I got up and remarked to my wife that it must be a water spout. **1898** Lloyd *Country Life* 39 **AL,** I knew in a minit that there had been a water-spout or cloudburst somewhere in the up-country. **1912** *Oelwein Daily Reg.* (IA) 6 May 1/7 **KS,** A terrific water spout accompanied the twister. **1939** *Hall Coll.* **wNC, eTN,** They'd been a water spout, a cloud burst, up there. **1954** *Harder Coll.* **cwTN,** Waterspout. . . A heavy rain that keeps on falling. **1965–70** *DARE* (Qu. B24, . . *A sudden, very heavy rain*) Infs **KY**86, **MO**3, **SD**8, Waterspout; **TX**2, Regular waterspout; [**TX**17, Waterspout—funnel like tornado, but composed of rain—over the bay;] (Qu. B25, . . *Joking names . . for a very heavy rain.* . . "*It's a regular _____.*") Infs **AR**34, 53, **LA**12, **MO**3, **OK**1, **TN**26, **TX**2, 37, Waterspout; (Qu. B27, *A sudden rush of water coming from heavy rain*) Infs **KY**15, **MS**48, **TX**2, Waterspout; **OR**14, Waterspout—up the foothills; **WA**8, Waterspout—a cloudburst, all in one place; **KY**12, Waterspat [sic]. **1986** Pederson *LAGS Concordance,* 1 inf, **neTN,** Waterspout—a heavy rain; 1 inf, **cTN,** Waterspout—cloudburst; 1 inf, **cwTN,** Waterspout—could drown a goose; 1 inf, **cnAR,** Waterspout—it all falls out at once; 1 inf, **swAR,** Waterspout—heavy rain; 1 inf, **cwLA,** Waterspout—heavy, quick rain, just pours down; 1 inf, **ceTX,** Waterspout—figurative for hard rain.

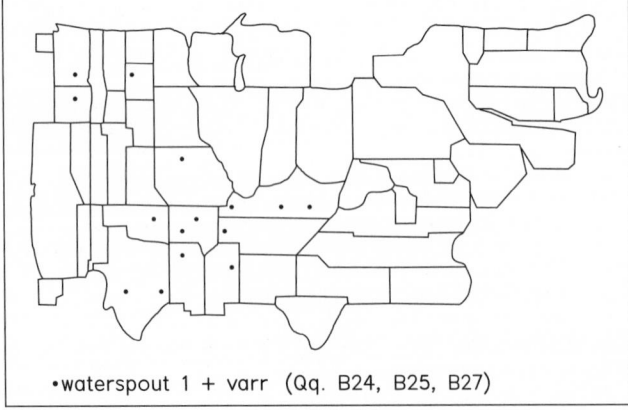

•waterspout 1 + varr (Qq. B24, B25, B27)

2 See **spout.**

water star-grass n

A **mud plantain 1** (here: *Heteranthera dubia*).

1832 *MA Hist. Soc. Coll.* 2d ser 9.152 **cwVT,** Leptanthus graminea [= *Heteranthera dubia*] . . Water star-grass. **1895** Gray–Bailey *Field Bot-*

any 452, *[Heteranthera] graminea* [=*H. dubia*]. . . Water Star Grass. . . the flower with a slender, pale yellow perianth, of 6 narrow, equal divisions. **1937** St. John *Flora SE WA & ID* 78, *Heteranthera dubia.* . . Water Stargrass. . . Rare, aquatic. **1961** Peck *Manual OR* 190, Water Star-grass. . . to Wash., Calif., Mexico, and the eastern states.

water strider n

Std: an insect of the family Gerridae or Veliidae. For other names see **crazy bug, four-oarsman, Jesus bug, riffle ~, skater, skipper 2, topwater 2, water glider, ~ scooter, ~ skeeter, ~ spider**

water thrush n

Std: either of two closely related birds: *Seiurus motacilla* or *S. noveboracensis.* Also called **wagtail 1, water ~**

water thyme n

1 =**ditch moss.**

[**1854** *Scientific Amer.* 10.54, A new water plant, named water thyme by the people, and *Aanacharis* [sic] *alsinastrum* by the discoverer, has appeared in some of the English rivers and canals, within a few years, in such abundance and strength as to threaten obstruction to navigation.] **1873** *Appletons' Jrl.* 10.534, There are certain plants which, in addition to beauty of structure and vigorous growth, are of great service as oxygen-producers: such are . . water-thyme *(Anacharis alsinastrum)* [etc]. **1920** *Forest & Stream* 90.439 **MI,** Much quaint learning and fanciful discourse have been had anent him [=the Michigan grayling]. That he fed on gold and grains of it were found on [sic] his belly; that he loves the water Thyme (hence *thymallus*) and smells of it. **1950** Gray–Fernald *Manual of Botany* 93, *Elodea.* . . Waterweed. Water-thyme. Ditch-moss.

2 An invasive introduced water plant *(Hydrilla verticillata).*

1997 *NY Times* (NY) 7 Sept sec 1 40/3, Hydrilla, also known as water thyme, is a native of South America that reached Florida several decades ago and has since spread throughout the United States. **2007** (acc) GA Dept. Nat. Resources *Fishing* (Internet), Hydrilla, *Hydrilla verticillata,* is an aquatic plant species . . believed to have been first introduced to the US in the 1960s. It is also known as Florida elodea, water thyme, water-thyme, and waterthyme.

water tiger n

A **diving beetle** or its larva.

1863 ME *Scientific Surv. Annual Rept. for 1862* 184, *Dysticidæ,* or Diving beetles, are, by their carnivorous habits closely allied to the Carabidae. . . Their larvae are ferocious looking objects, and from their long curved jaws, and agile and stealthy habits, called Water Tigers. **1904** *Forest & Stream* 62.88, The predaceous insects which are ever on the alert to seize the helpless fry are almost numberless; among these the larvae of the dragon fly, [and] . . ditiscus beetle, or water tiger, are most destructive. **1954** Borror–DeLong *Intro. Insects* 338, The larvae [of diving beetles] . . are often called water tigers. . . These larvae are very active and will not hesitate to attack an animal much larger than themselves. **1998** *NE Naturalist* 5.8, After the eggs hatch the water tigers grow through three larval instars.

water tupelo n

Usu a **tupelo gum** (here: *Nyssa aquatica*), but also a **swamp tupelo** (here: *N. biflora*).

1730 Catesby in Royal Soc. London *Philos. Trans.* 36.434 **NC, SC,** The Water Tupelo. **1785** Marshall *Arbustrum* 96, Nyssa aquatica, *Virginian Water Tupelo-Tree.* This grows naturally in wet swamps, or near large rivers, in Carolina and Florida. **1810** Michaux *Histoire des Arbres* 1.29, Nyssa grandidentata [=*Nyssa aquatica*]. . . *Water tupelo . . ,* nom secondaire dans les mêmes Etats. [=*Water tupelo . . ,* secondary name in the same [=southern] states.] *Ibid* 30, N. biflora. . . *Water tupelo . . ,* nom secondaire dans les mêmes Etats. [=*Water tupelo . . ,* secondary name in the same [=southern] states.] **1908** Britton *N. Amer. Trees* 737, The Water gum, also called the Black gum, and Water tupelo, inhabits swamps and the margins of ponds from New Jersey to Florida and Louisiana. **1975** *Bucks Co. Courier Times* (Levittown PA) 19 June sec B 29/2 **SC,** The swamp is thick with giant loblolly pines, bald cypress, water tupelo and other trees with no match for their size. **2005** [see **swamp gum**].

water turkey n

1 =**anhinga.** [See quot 1841]

1836 (1935) Holley *Texas* 100, King-fishers and water-turkies . . are found in great abundance. **1837** (1962) Williams *Territory FL* 73, The water turkey, ichthyophagus, is less than the wild turkey, and usually of a darker color... These birds usually sit over the water on some pendant limb, from which they suddenly drop, when disturbed, and sink to the bottom, where they may be seen walking, if the water be clear. **1841** S. Lit. Messenger 1.77 **swLA**, The Water-Turkey, similar to the common wild-turkey, but web-footed. **1879** Forest & Stream 13.763 **eFL**, The scene is enlivened by the numerous water-fowl, egrets, herons, pelicans, gallinules, water-turkies, cormorants and fish-crows. **1926** (1949) McQueen–Mizell Hist. Okefenokee 133 **seGA**, The water turkey is a well-known bird in the Okefenokee Swamp. While very much like the wild turkey in size and shape it differs a little in color. The water turkey is black and differs from the wild turkey in that it has webbed feet. **1946** Kopman Wild Acres 19 **LA**, A fastness in the remoter swamps of the Atchafalaya River is... the home of water-turkeys. **1965–70** DARE (Qu. Q10, .. Water birds and marsh birds) Infs **FL**4, 32, 35, 39, **GA**35, **SC**40, 43, 62, **TX**1, 37, Water turkey; **FL**27, Water turkey or anhinga; **GA**3, Water turkey—two-feet-high standing; swims with entire body underwater; **LA**31, Water turkey or nigger goose; **OK**18, Water turkey—small body, large wingspread, colored like turkey, built similar to shitepoke. [DARE Ed: Some of these Infs may refer instead to other senses below.] **2007** Orlando Sentinel (FL) 10 Mar (Internet), On the Central Ave. (South side) of the park near where the new building is rising, water turkeys are once again pooping all over the azaleas, sidewalks and street... Now, I've heard all the b.s... about so called laws protecting water turkeys (Anhingas) and about the species of Oaks they are nesting annually in.

2 =**double-crested cormorant.**

1867 in 1903 Dawson Birds OH 2.625, On the south side of the Reservoir, about seven miles from Celina, was the Water Turkey's rookery. **1911** Howell Birds AR 16, Many persons call this species [=Phalacrocorax auritus] "water turkey" as well as the species properly so named. **1939** FWP Guide TN 428 **nwTN**, More than 250 species of birds stop off here on their annual migrations. Among them are ducks, geese, water turkeys or cormorants ("nigger geese"), coots, and white herons. **1947** [see **water buzzard**]. **1986** Houston Chron. (TX) 29 Nov 26 (Internet), "There were 20 or 30 pelicans with about a hundred or so water turkeys," or cormorants, Blankenship said. "A water turkey would surface with a fish, and four or five pelicans would grab him." **2003** in 2007 DARE File—Internet **sAR**, I need some suggestions about taking care of business with the blue herons and water turkeys as we call them in South Arkansas. I hate to kill the wildlife, but I will not let them distory [sic] my catfish pond.

3 Any of var other birds; see quots.

1874 Coues Birds NW 229, The Dipper [=**water ouzel**] is called "Water Turkey" by the miners and mountaineers. Ibid 513, Wood Ibis... on the Colorado it is known as the Water Turkey. **1953** Randolph–Wilson Down in Holler 297 **swMO**, Water turkey... The coot, or mud hen (Fulica americana). This term is common in southwest Missouri. The real water turkey or snakebird (Anhinga anhinga) seems to be unknown to the Missouri hillfolk. **1965–69** DARE (Qu. Q8) Infs **FL**35, **IL**89, Water turkey; (Qu. Q10, .. Water birds and marsh birds) Inf **UT**3, Water turkey—hell-diver. **1978** [see **storm bird 1**].

water velvet n
=**mosquito fern.**

1942 Torreya 42.156 **LA**, Azolla caroliniana... Water-velvet. **2006** (acc) MN Dept. Nat. Resources Invasive Aquatic Plants (Internet), Water Velvet (Azolla pinnata).

water wagtail n [OED2 1611 → for Motacilla spp; see quot 1917]
=**water thrush.**

a1782 (1788) Jefferson Notes VA 77, Besides these, we have The Royston crow, .. Water wagtail [etc]. **1791** Bartram Travels 184, M[otacilla] fluviatilis, the water wagtail. **1874** NY Acad. Sci. Annals Lyceum Nat. Hist. 10.369 **IL**, S[eiurus] Noveboracensis... Small-billed Water Thrush, or "Water Wagtail." .. S[eiurus] Ludovicianus... Large-billed Water Thrush, or "Water Wagtail." **1917** (1923) Birds Amer. 3.153, The Louisiana Water-Thrush is one of the comparatively few birds that walk. Like the Oven-bird it also bobs its tail as it proceeds, a peculiarity from which it derives its popular name of Water Wagtail, the "water" being in recognition of its fondness for the banks of running streams. **1951** Teale North with Spring 257 **NC**, Water thrushes pump their tails so regularly that they are popularly known as water wagtails.

water wallink See **wallink 3**

water wally n
=**seepwillow.**

1925 Jepson Manual Plants CA 1060, B[accharis] glutinosa [=B.

salicifolia]... Water-Wally... Along streams and in moist ground. **1937** U.S. Forest Serv. Range Plant Hdbk. B33, Seepwillow, known locally as .. water-wally, is a graceful, willowy shrub.

waterweed n
1 =**ditch moss.**

1852 WI State Ag. Soc. Trans. 2.409, Udora... Canadensis... Water Weed. **1891** Century Dict. 6848, Water-weed... The choke-pondweed or water-thyme, Elodia Canadensis. **1950** Gray–Fernald Manual of Botany 93, Elodea [spp]... Waterweed. Water-thyme. **2007** (acc) U.S. Dept. Ag. Plants Database (Internet), Elodea [spp]... waterweed.

2 =**jewelweed 1.**

1955 Monessen Daily Independent (PA) 18 June 4/7, The touch-me-not or jewelweed bears the more common title of water weed. It has earned this name, for it not only likes to stand about on the loamy banks of woodland waterways, but it maintains a constant moisture in its hollow stems, and after a shower each leaf impounds jewel-like drops which sparkle and gleam. **1967** DARE FW Addit **KY**34, Waterweed = touch-me-nots—some are orange, .. some are yellow. **1982** Slone How We Talked 49 **eKY** (as of c1950), Water Weed (also called "Jewelweed").

3 =**hogweed 1.**

1969 DARE (Qu. S21, .. Weeds .. that are a trouble in gardens and fields) Inf **KY**28, Waterweed—same as hogweed.

water white oak n
=**overcup oak 1.**

1801 Michaux Histoire 5, Chêne blanc aquatique... Water white oak. **1811** Michaux Histoire des Arbres 2.42, Le Quercus Lyrata n'est pas très-multiplié dans le Basse-Caroline et la Basse-Géorgie, ce qui fait que, jusqu'à présent, il n'a été remarqué que des habitans qui demeurent à proximité des lieux où il croît. Ils le connoissent sous les noms d'Over cup oak . . ; de Swamp post oak . . , et plus rarement sous celui de Water white oak. [=The Quercus lyrata is not widespread in the lowlands of the Carolinas and Georgia, so that hitherto it has not been noticed except by those who live near the places it grows. They know it as Over cup oak . . ; as Swamp post oak . . , and more rarely as Water white oak.] **1908** Britton N. Amer. Trees 336, It [=the overcup oak] is also called .. Swamp white oak, and Water white oak.

water willow n
1 Std: a plant of the genus Justicia, esp J. americana.

2 =**swamp loosestrife 1.**

1910 Graves Flowering Plants 289 **CT**, Water Willow. Swamp Loosestrife... Shallow water of swamps or edges of ponds and streams, sometimes plentifully bordering such places. **1936** IL Nat. Hist. Surv. Wildflowers 205, Swamp Loosestrife. Water Willow... The willowlike leaves are sometimes opposite and sometimes whorled. **1976** Bruce How to Grow Wildflowers 279, Decodon verticillatus—Water-willow or Swamp-loosestrife. A relative of Purple Loosestrife (Lythrum) with similar lavender flowers in summer.

3 =**seepwillow** or a **groundsel tree** (here: Baccharis emoryi).

1931 U.S. Dept. Ag. Misc. Pub. 101.158, Emory baccharis . . , locally known as water moats and water willow, is a shrub, 3 to 12 feet high, ranging from Colorado to California and New Mexico, usually along washes and in coastal or inland flood plains. **1966–68** DARE (Qu. T15, .. Kinds of swamp trees) Infs **NM**13, **UT**7, Water willow. **1976** Elmore Shrubs & Trees SW 77, Seep-willow .. sticky or broom baccharis; water-willow [etc]... Baccharis glutinosa [=B. salicifolia].

water witch n
1 also witch(-diver): A **grebe,** esp the **pied-bill(ed) grebe.** [From its uncanny ability to elude hunters] **chiefly Atlantic, esp Mid Atl** Cf **pigwick**

1709 (1967) Lawson New Voyage 155 **NC, SC**, Water-Witch, or Ware-Coots, are a Fowl with Down and no Feathers; they dive incomparably, so that no Fowler can hit them. **1785** Pennant Arctic Zool. 2.497 **NY**, Pied-bill grebe... Columbus podiceps... Inhabits from New York to South Carolina; is called in the first, the Hen-beaked Wigeon, or Water Witch. **1824** Latham Genl. Hist. Birds 10.35 **GA**, Pied-billed Grebe... Columbus Podiceps... is common in the rivers and ponds about Savannah, in Georgia .. [and] called Didapper, or Water Witch. **1852** in 1876 Forest & Stream 7.212 **eMA**, [In a list of gunners' names for birds:] Podiceps. All varieties. Water-witch. **1899** (1912) Green VA Folk-Speech 475, Water-witch... One of several water-birds noted for their quickness in diving, as a kind of duck. **1917** (1923) Birds Amer. 1.8, The Pied-billed Grebe... is at home in the water to an astonishing degree, in fact "Water-witch" is one of the favorite local names by which it is known... I have seen it dive at the flash of discharge and be safely beneath the surface before the death-seeking shot came over the water. **1959** *Names* 7.110 **SC, MD,** The pied-billed grebe... is termed witch-diver also in South Carolina. *Ibid* 111, The horned grebe is known as water-witch in various localities... and as witch, simply, in Maryland. **1966–68** *DARE* (Qu. Q5, . . *Kinds of wild ducks*) Inf **MD**45, Water witch—stay in deep water, eat minners, about six inches long, odd-looking; (Qu. Q7, *Names and nicknames for . . game birds*) Inf **MD**36, Water witch—size of pigeon, sharp bill, not very good to eat, waterfowl; (Qu. Q9, *The bird that looks like a small, dull-colored duck and is commonly found on ponds and lakes*) Inf **NC**12, Didapper—also called hell-diver and water witch. **1970** *DARE* Tape **VA**112, [FW:] What are the kinds of diving ducks you have around here? [Inf:] We've got a southerly and we got a water witch. That's a little sharp duck, a little small duck, very small... He dives all the time, and if you ever catch one, his eyes is blood red from the water. **2005** in 2007 *Canyon Courier* (Evergreen CO) 12 Mar (Internet), When frightened, they [=grebes] do not take flight but instead sink quietly out of sight... or dive, swimming underwater to some distant location before they emerge. These habits have earned them the common name of "water witch."

2 =merganser.

1959 *Names* 7.111 **MD,** Some Marylanders extend usage of the name water-witch to the mergansers or fish-ducks, and in British Columbia the term refers locally to the water ouzel.

3 One who dowses for water. **widespread, but less freq Atlantic** See Map Cf **dowser, water smeller, witch n 1**

1817 Brown *Western Gaz.* 96 **seKY,** This discovery was made by a *water-witch*. **1848** *OH Cultivator* 4.154, More than twenty-five years ago I witnessed the performance, in Mansfield in this State, by a professed Water Witch, as he was called in those days. **1883** *Harper's New Mth. Mag.* 67.708, Utah . . abounds in "water-witches" of varying degree of local celebrity, but all held more or less in popular repute. **1906** *DN* 3.163 **nwAR,** *Water-witch*. . . A man who uses a forked stick of witch-hazel or peach to find the place where a well should be dug. Common. **1929** Dobie *Vaquero* 275 **West,** The numerous "water witches" with their "gift" of locating water by holding a forked stick a certain way in their hands and walking over the country until the stick "pulls" down have not done a great deal towards watering the land. **1957** [see **witch n 1**]. **1965–70** *DARE* (Qu. CC13b, . . *The person who knows how to use a forked stick to find water*) 235 Infs, **widespread, but less freq Atlantic,** Water witch; (Qu. CC13a, . . *A forked stick that's used to show where there's water underground*) Infs **KY**11, **TX**33, Water witch's stick. **1968** Kellner *Aunt Serena* 132 **IN,** But we had our own Well Diviner—Lawnie. (Or Water Witch, as some folks said.) **1976** Garber *Mountain-ese* 99 **sAppalachians,** *Water-witch* . . diviner of water. **1977** in 1994 Thomas *Come Go with Me* 7 **S Midl** (as of 1890s), My daddy, he wouldn't have a well dug without he knowed where the water was. He'd want a water witch. He wouldn't do it hisself. **1991** in 2006 *DARE* File—Internet **AZ,** The waters, the waters, the waters,/ I see them in memory yet,/ Like the pull on a water-witch's stick / They're always calling me back.

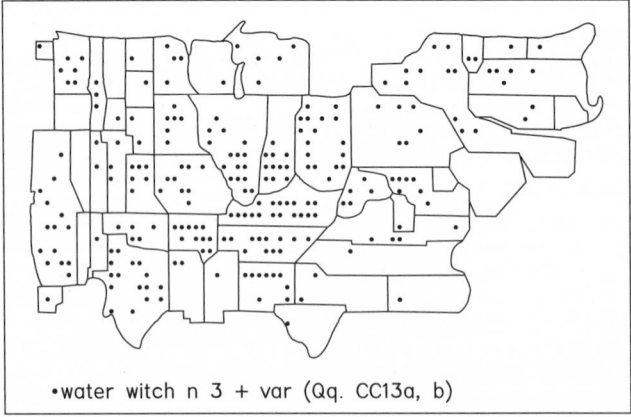

•water witch n 3 + var (Qq. CC13a, b)

4 also *water witch stick:* A divining rod used in dowsing for water. **scattered, but chiefly Missip-Ohio Valleys, West** See Map Cf **dowsing rod, water smeller, witch n 2, witching stick**

1832 *Boston Eve. Transcript* (MA) 3 Feb 1/2, The subscriber offers for sale, at his Store . . the following articles. . . Wooden Shoes, Water Witches, &c. **1937** Sandoz *Slogum* 46 **NE,** With a willow water witch she went carefully over the yard . . until the crotched end of the stick jerked and pulled downward just southwest of the house. **1938** *Geophysics* 3.2.154, Consider the forked water witch stick which is so commonly used to find hidden water streams. **1939** in Lib. of Congress *Amer. Memory: WPA Life Hist.* (Internet) **NE,** A forked stick of witch hazel, about 16 inches long is used, as a "water witch", or "divining rod", to ascertain the ideal spot for diggin [sic] a well. **1965–70** *DARE* (Qu. CC13a, . . *A forked stick that's used to show where there's water underground. . . [What kind of wood?]*) 59 Infs, **chiefly Missip-Ohio Valleys, Rocky Mts, Pacific; scattered NEast,** Water witch; 10 Infs, **chiefly Missip-Ohio Valleys,** Water witch stick; **OK**51, Water witch stick, peach limb.

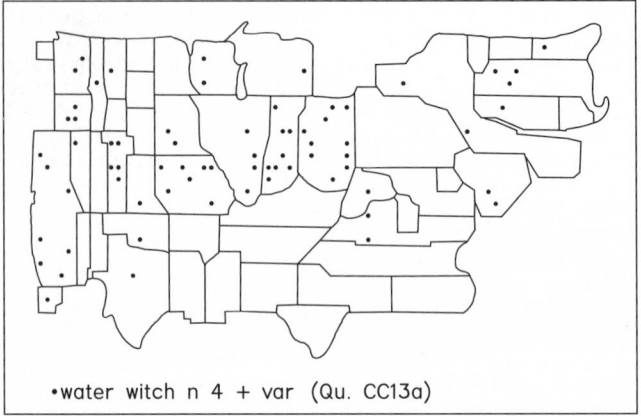

•water witch n 4 + var (Qu. CC13a)

water witch v phr, hence vbl n *water witching* **scattered, but chiefly Missip-Ohio Valleys, West** See Map Cf **witch v**

To dowse for water; hence n *water witcher* =**water witch** n **3**.

1850 *OH Cultivator* 6.6, Do the facts presented tend to prove that the practice of water-witching is not all pretence? **1871** *Prairie Farmer* 42.272 **cwIL,** Some are "water-witching" with but little success. **1877** in 1937 Ruede *Sod-House* 196 **KS,** He told me about one new neighbor . . who has a firm faith in water witching. **1939** in Lib. of Congress *Amer. Memory: WPA Life Hist.* (Internet) **NE,** While we were "water-witchin'", our neighbor . . came by. . . He laughed at our "water-witching". **1952** *NW AR Times* (Fayetteville) 17 May 6/6, There's them what can and them what can't, and no water witcher can make one out of those not psychic or whatever you have to be. **1958** *Jrl. Amer. Folkl.* 71.524, We knew that water divining was often called "water witching" in some parts of the United States . . , but we were astonished to discover how overwhelming this usage is in almost all regions. Of the 258 counties reporting the certain presence of water diviners, over seventy-eight percent reported that the most common name is "water witching." **1965–70** *DARE* (Qu. CC13b, . . *The person who knows how to use a forked stick to find water*) 70 Infs, **scattered, but chiefly Missip-Ohio Valleys, West,** Water witcher; (Qu. CC13a, . . *A forked stick that's used to show where there's water underground*) Inf **CA**141, Water witching; **KY**19, 21, **MO**11, Water-witching stick; **KS**20, Water-witching rod; **KS**15, Water-witching wand. **1972** *Daily Tribune* (WI Rapids WI) 25 Aug 1/8, Another well known water witcher found two wells for the Dairy State Cheese Co. in Rudolph. **1978** *Bittersweet* 6.1.5 (Internet)

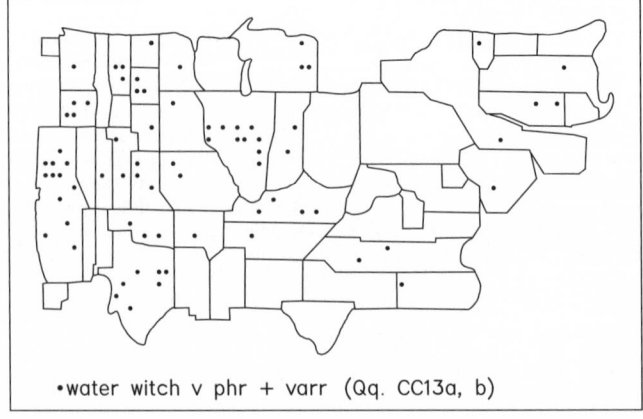

•water witch v phr + varr (Qq. CC13a, b)

Ozarks, The art of water witching has been recorded far back in history. . . [T]he best time to water witch is in the spring when the sap is in the limbs, making them limber. . . He hasn't checked for the accuracy of his witching yet. "I've never water witched for wells but my dad used to." . . "There was a man up in Michigan who witched a well for me." **2003** *DARE* File—Internet **sOR,** The drilling contractor may recommend having a Water Witcher . . help locate a drilling site. **2007** *Ibid* **TN,** Back in the 70's we were taught how to water witch at Girl Scout camp in northeast Tennessee.

water witch stick See **water witch** n 4

watter See **water** A1

wattle n[1] [Scots, nEngl, nIr dial] Cf *DS* K27

1949 Kurath *Word Geog.* 56, *Ox goad.* . . *wattle* in southern Pennsylvania from the Susquehanna to the Monongahela.

wattle n[2] **West, esp Rocky Mts** See Map

=**dewlap** n.

1880 in 1958 *AmSp* 33.142, Beside the brand there must be a distinctive ear-mark or a "wattle" (i.e., flesh-mark) cut elsewhere than in the ear. **1936** Adams *Cowboy Lingo* 132, The 'wattle' was made on the neck or jaw of an animal by pinching up a quantity of skin, and cutting it all, but not entirely off. When healed, it left a hanging flap of skin. **1941** Writers' Program *Guide WY* 466, *Wattle*—A dewlap which forms a bunch instead of a string. Made for identification. **1958** *AmSp* 33.273 **eWA** [Ranching terms], *Wattle.* A piece of the skin of the jaw cut and allowed to hang, providing a mark of identification. **1965–70** *DARE* (Qu. K18, . . *Kind of mark . . to identify a cow*) Infs **CA**136, **WY**4, Wattle(s); **CA**31, Wattle—cuts on the throat of the animal, hang down; **CO**4, Wattle—jaw; **CO**33, Wattle—cut on chin or throat, drops down, makes a bell wattle; **MT**5, Wattle—cut loose a piece of skin under neck; **UT**15, Wattle [wɑːdl]—a chunk of hide cut from the neck or nose; **WY**1, Wattle—cut piece of skin loose under neck so it hangs down; **WY**5, Wattle—used to use. **1981** *KS Qrly.* 13.2.71, *Wattle* . . a special cut of the fatty portion of a cow's hide under the neck made with the pocket knife at the time of branding and ear marking that serves as one of the identification marks for cattle; the cut hide heals and hangs down in a certain position; each rancher has a special wattle style.

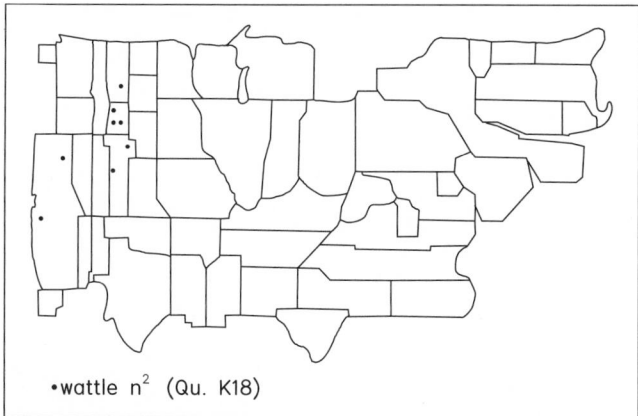

•wattle n[2] (Qu. K18)

waukapin See **wankapin**

Waukegan juniper n

=**creeping juniper.**

1942 Tehon *Fieldbook IL Shrubs* 28, *Juniperus horizontalis.* . . On the Waukegan moorland it has developed . . as a low, trailing shrub with bright steel-blue foliage which, in autumn, turns pale purple and becomes glaucous. These distinctive characteristics, valuable when this shrub is used as an ornamental, have given rise to a common name, Waukegan Juniper, and to technical recognition as forma *Douglasii.* **2005** *Chicago Wilderness Mag.* Winter (Internet), Roughly a century ago, Douglas Nurseries of Waukegan . . earned fame far and wide when they cut and propagated the "Waukegan juniper," a handsome steel-blue variety of trailing juniper found there.

waul See **wall**

waumus See **wamus**

waun See **one**

waungin See **wanigan**

waupajawed See **whopper-jawed**

wausper See **wasper**

wave v Cf **waver**

Std sense, var forms.

Past, past pple: usu *waved,* also *wove.*

1896 *DN* 1.427 **cNY,** *Wave* (pret.): *wove* sometimes heard. "He wove the flag." **1908** Wasson *Home from Sea* 159 **sME coast,** Any one would nach'ally think she'd ought to wove her hand at ye, or else signalized ye someways. **a1944** in 2000 Bell *Brag Dog* 34 **GA,** I swear I never seen you, Clem, er I'd a-shore retched out and wove to you. **1955** FWP *NC Guide* 13, If I'd a-knowed it was you I'd a-flang out my arm and wove to you. **1996** in 2004 Montgomery–Hall *Dict. Smoky Mt. Engl.* 638 **eTN,** *Wave.* . . He retch out and wove at me. **1999** *Ibid* **wNC, eTN,** *Wave.* . . I poked my hand out the window and wove at you. **2000** *DARE* File **AR,** I seed I knowed ya when ya driv up, so I retched out and wove at ya.

wave n Cf **beckon, sheep in my pen**

In combs *give me a wave, piggy wants a wave, wave wanted*: A children's hiding game in which a captured player may escape upon seeing another player wave if the captured player is not seen by the seeker.

1949 Webber *Backwoods Teacher* 56 **Ozarks,** It was too hot to play running games so we played "give me a wave," a form of hide and seek but less strenuous. **1965** *Ada Weekly News* (OK) 29 July 4/1, There was a time when youngsters rushed outdoors . . and played . . piggy wants a wave and king of the mountain. **1966–69** *DARE* (Qu. EE13a, *Games in which every player hides except one, and that one must try to find the others*) Inf **OK**31, Wave wanted—same as [hide-and-seek] except player who is caught can escape and hide again if another player waves at him and he can escape without being seen by the hunter; (Qu. EE16, *Hiding games that start with a special, elaborate method of sending the players out to hide*) Inf **TN**35, Piggy wants a wave. **2006** *DARE* File—Internet **WA,** Remember how you taught us that game, "piggy wants a wave?"

wave chaser n

=**sanderling.**

1946 Hausman *Eastern Birds* 291, Sanderling. . . Other Names. . . Wave Chaser, Surf Snipe [etc]. **2006** *DARE* File—Internet **NEng,** The Sanderlings were still in breeding plumage; instead of the light gray and white wave-chaser usually seen during the Fall and Winter, these birds had a dark back and head.

waver v **esp Mid Atl** Cf **-er** affix 2

To wave, brandish (something); to wave one's hand.

1938 FWP *Guide DE* 500, He never seen me till I wavered at him, then he struck a-runnin'. **1939** in 1941 *Amer. Poet* Dec 20 **wNC,** He pulled out his wide sword and wavered hit round. **1956** McAtee *Some Dialect NC* 58, *Waver.* . . To wave. *Obs.* A friend confused by the traffic circles in Washington, D.C., said that he "driv around one of them so many times that the general on the [statue] started to waver at me." Knott's Island, Upper Currituck Sound. **2000** Shores *Tangier Is.* 172 **Chesapeake Bay,** The Islanders use . . "wavering" for *waving.*

wave the (red) flag See **flag** n[2] 2

wave wanted See **wave** n

wavey n Also sp *wavy* [See quot 1910] Cf **gray wavey,** *DCan*

1 =**blue goose** n **1.**

[**1792** (1934) Hearne *Jrls. Hearne & Turner* 329 **Canada,** The birds feet and bills made choice of on such occasions are generally those of the laughing goose, wavey, (or white goose,) gulls [etc]. *Ibid* 442, *Horned Wavey.* . . I have seen them in as large flocks as the Common Wavey, or Snow Goose.] [**1910** Hodge *Hdbk. Amer. Indians* 2.923, *Wavey.* A Canadian French corruption of *wehwew,* the Cree (onomatopoetic) name of the snow goose, *Chen hyperboreus* [=*C. caerulescens*], called by the Chippewa *wewe.*] **1949** Kitchin *Birds Olympic Peninsula* 33 **cwWA,** Lesser Snow Goose. . . Other common names: Wavy, white brant.

2 =**white-fronted goose.**

1949 Kitchin *Birds Olympic Peninsula* 33, White-fronted Goose. . . Other common names . . Speckle-belly, Wavy [etc].

waving butterfly n

A **butterfly weed 2** (here: *Gaura coccinea*).

1950 Stevens *ND Plants* 216, Gaura coccinea. . . "Waving Butterfly." **2006** (acc) N. Prairie Wildlife Research Center *Native Wildflowers ND* (Internet), Scarlet gaura is sometimes called "waving butterfly" because the four white-to-red petals are twisted and move like wings in the slightest breeze.

wavy See **wavey**

wawaron n [LaFr *ouaouaron* < CanFr] **LA** =**bullfrog 1.**

[**1844** Tixier *Voyage* 50 **LA,** Pour la première fois j'entendis, au milieu de leurs voix, le mugissement de la grenouille-taureau (bull-frog), que les créoles ont nommée *ouararong.* [=For the first time I heard among their voices the roaring of the bull-frog, which the Creoles call *ouararong.*]] **1917** *DN* 4.420 **LA,** Wawaron. . . A frog. [**1931** Read *LA French* 98, Ouaouaron is pronounced as a French word—usually *wawarō,* but sometimes *warwarō* (Ouararon)—with the stress in each case on the open nasal "o" of the final syllable.]

wawmus See **wamus**

wax n

1 also *maple sugar wax:* =**jack wax 1**—often in phr *wax on snow;* hence v *wax* to make or form **jack wax 1. NEast**

1845 Judd *Margaret* 185 swME (as of 18th cent), The "wax" is freely distributed to be cooled on lumps of snow, or the axehead. **1892** *Outing* 19.462 **nNY,** When the proprietor, who has been boiling a portion of the syrup in a kettle over brushwood fire . . invites us to partake of wax on snow, I gladly accept. **1900** *Post–Std.* (Syracuse NY) 3 Mar 5/1, Let's have maple sugar wax on snow after the playing is over. **1952** *Berkshire Eve. Eagle* (Pittsfield MA) 25 Mar 12/4, The menu includes pancakes and syrup, "wax" on snow, maple sundaes and coffee and doughnuts. . . Cecil E. Alderman will boil down the syrup for the wax. **1954** White *Adirondack Country* 305 **NY,** Now and then "snow parties" do take place these days, with singing and dancing in the kitchen by the stove and the chief point of the party, eating "wax on snow." **1967** *DARE* Tape **VT**1A, We didn't . . boil it down hard enough . . for waxing on snow at the sugar house. . . It was made into syrup there, but wasn't . . thick enough so it would wax on the snow. **1967** *DARE* FW Addit **cnNY,** Maple syrup on snow not known as *jack wax,* but *wax* alone. **1970** *DARE* (Qu. H80, *Kinds of candy . . made at home*) Inf **NY**230, Wax—boiled maple sugar poured on snow. **1982** *Post–Std.* (Syracuse NY) 26 Mar sec B(N) 2/4, Wax on snow will also be served.

2 A plant resin or gum, esp one used for chewing. **esp Midl** See Map Cf **gum wax**

1943 Weslager *DE Forgotten Folk* 160, Pine Wax. . . Chewed by children for enjoyment. **1949** *PADS* 11.8 **wTX,** Mesquite wax. . . Rosin from the mesquite tree. **1950** *WELS (Other names for chewing gum)* 1 Inf, **ceWI,** Spruce wax. **1965–70** *DARE* (Qu. T7, *The sticky stuff that comes out of pine trees*) 11 Infs, **scattered, but esp Midl,** Wax; **AL**38, **DE**3, **IN**31, **KY**21, **MD**18, 42, **NM**2, Pine wax. [16 of 18 Infs comm type 4 or 5, 15 old, 13 gs educ]

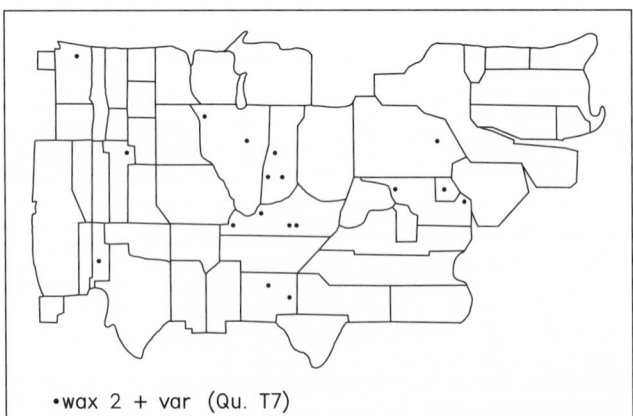

•wax 2 + var (Qu. T7)

3 Chewing gum. **esp S Midl** Cf **chewing wax**

1903 *DN* 2.336 **seMO,** Wax. . . Chewing gum. **1906** *DN* 3.163 **nwAR,** Wax. . . Gum. "Let me chew your wax till recess." **1915** *DN* 4.230 **wTX,** Wax. . . Always used for *chewing gum.* **1923** *DN* 5.224 **swMO,** Wax. . . Chewing gum. **1931** Randolph *Ozarks* 70 **nwAR,**

swMO, The word *gum* means a beehive or a rabbit-trap—when the hillman wants chewing-gum he calls for *wax!* **c1960** *Wilson Coll.* **csKY,** Wax. . . The former name for chewing gum. **1972** Claerbaut *Black Jargon* 86, Wax . . chewing gum. **1983** *MJLF* 9.1.60 **ceKY** (as of 1956), Wax . . chewing gum. **2001** *DARE* File **OH,** I am 90 and my Grandma called chewing gum "wax." The term was so common that a small boy hearing that Baby Jesus, in a Christmas Display, was made of wax he took a large bite.

waxberry n

1 The **wax myrtle** or its fruit.

c1695 in 1847 Hist. Soc. PA *Proc.* 1.163, Here are waxberries growing in these parts,/ Whose virtues are best known to men of arts;/ This argument of them I'll only handle,/ They make a pleasant, sweet, and lasting candle. [**1812** *Select Revs. Lit.* 7.180 **Nova Scotia,** He informed me that in the uncleared woods there grow abundance of the *Myrica Cerifera,* wax-bearing myrica, or, vulgarly, the candle-berry myrtle. With these wax-berries, he says, they make excellent wax candles.] **1830** Rafinesque *Med. Flora* 2.244, Myrica [spp]. . . Waxberry, Wax-myrtle. . . The berries are covered with a peculiar wax. **1897** Sudworth *Arborescent Flora* 117 **RI, PA, SC,** *Myrica cerifera.* . . Waxberry. **1930** Sievers *Amer. Med. Plants* 10, Bayberry. . . Other common names. . . Southern waxmyrtle, waxberry, tallow berry, candleberry [etc]. **1957** *Independent Star–News* (Pasadena CA) 2 June Scene sec 18/2, Every year I have my pitch pine kindling sent from the Fort Bragg area. They come along with sprays of western waxberry. **1974** Morton *Folk Remedies* 99 **SC,** Wax Myrtle . . Waxberry; Candleberry; Tallow Berry [etc].

2 A **snowberry 1** or its fruit.

1836 *Amer. Mth. Mag.* 8.114, It had . . pure white flowers, which . . had given place to beautiful white drops, like the wax berries of our country. **1845** *IN Farmer & Gardener* 1.226, Waxberry or snowberry (*Symphora racemosa*) [=*Symphoricarpos albus*] introduced by Lewis and Clark to the public attention. **1874** *Horticulturist & Jrl. Rural Art* 29.7, Symphoricarpus Racemosus, more commonly known under the names of Waxberry and Snowberry; the flowers are insignificant, but the berries are rather pretty in the fall. **1891** Victor *Atlantis Arisen* 222 **NW,** The wax-berry, with its tiny pink flowers and delicate leaves, is found in bottom-lands and on river-banks. **1942** Hylander *Plant Life* 465, The Waxberry of California and states adjacent to New Mexico, has pink flowers in small clusters, and white berries. **1960** Vines *Trees SW* 948, It [=*Symphoricarpos orbiculatus*] is also known under the vernacular names of Coralberry, . . Waxberry, and Turkey-bush.

waxberry cornel n *obs*
=**red osier.**

1828 Rafinesque *Med. Flora* 1.135, C[ornus] alba [=*C. sericea*] or Wax-berry Cornel, is also a shrub, growing from New England to Siberia in Asia, with . . berries round, white like wax. **1876** Hobbs *Bot. Hdbk.* 127, Waxberry cornel. . . Cornus alba.

wax bird n
=**cedar waxwing.**

1832 Lockwood *Geog. SC* 131, There are also others to be named, some of which are seldom seen, and many that visit us only at certain seasons of the year. . . Night-hawk, perroquet, . . wax-bird [etc]. **1836** *Amer. Jrl. Sci. & Arts* 30.86 **SC,** Other families of birds, such as feed on ripe berries, that abound in the winter also remain with us; these are . . the wax bird, (*Bombycilla Americana,*) [etc]. **1838** Gilman *Poetry* 218 **SC,** The Goldfinch, Wax-bird, and like forms of grace. **1851** *Living Age* 30.523 **CT,** Any person who shall shoot . . [a] spider-bird or wax-bird . . shall be punished by a fine not exceeding five dollars. **1936** Smith–Sass *Carolina Rice* 85 **SC coast** (as of 1850s), The wax-birds escaped us, because they fed on the cedar and other berries, and the mocking birds did not fear us. **1955** *Oriole* 20.1.11, Cedar Waxwing.—Wax Bird (the shafts of the secondary wing feathers look as if tipped with red sealing-wax).

waxbush n
=**wax myrtle.**

1937 *Fresno Bee the Republican* (CA) 12 Sept sec D 6/1, The waxbush, whose berries are pearly white, [contrasts] with the ordinary chaparal [sic]. **1968** *DARE* (Qu. T5, . . *Kinds of evergreens, other than pine*) Inf **LA**33, Waxbush. **1973** *Sun* (Lowell MA) 1 Dec [4]/2 **ME** (newspaperarchive.com), The bayberry is flourishing in many part [sic] of the country, and is a laurel sometimes called the waxbush.

waxen kernel See **kernel 4**

waxflower n

1 =**pipsissewa.**

1897 *Jrl. Amer. Folkl.* 10.49 **Long Is. NY,** *Chimaphila maculata* . . wax flower, Southold. **1963** Craighead *Rocky Mt. Wildflowers* 134, *Chimaphila umbellata.* . . Waxflower. . . standing 6–14 in. tall, with a cluster of waxy white to pink flowers well above the leaves. **1974** (1977) Coon *Useful Plants* 217, *Chimaphila umbellata.* . . rheumatism weed, waxflower, etc.

2 An **arrowhead 1** (here: *Sagittaria latifolia*).

1898 *Jrl. Amer. Folkl.* 11.282 **ME,** *Sagittaria variabilis* [=*S. latifolia*] . . wax flower, South Berwick. **1929** *Torreya* 29.149 **ME,** The *Sagittaria* in the brook (variabilis in those days), was never called anything but "*Waxflower.*"

3 A **wintergreen 1** (here: *Moneses uniflora* or *Pyrola elliptica*).

1952 Williams *AK Wildfl. Glimpses* 45, Wax Flower or Single Delight. . . This plant is found in the woods, growing from two to six inches tall, with one single wax white, nodding flower to a stem. **1968** *DARE* (Qu. S26c, *Wildflowers that grow in woods*) Inf **AK**1, Waxflowers—four [sic] white petals, drop of wax in center—very fragrant, small. **1972** Courtenay–Zimmerman *Wild Flowers* 79, Wax Flower, *Pyrola elliptica*. . . dry to medium woods and forests. **1987** Hughes–Blackwell *Wildflowers SE AK* 109, Single Delight, Wax-flower. . . *Moneses uniflora.*

waxing kernel See **kernel 4**

waxmallow n

Std: a **mallow B** (here: *Malvaviscus* spp). For other names of these plants see **cigarette flower, fire dart, Indian apple 3, manzanilla 2, mayapple 5, Mexican apple, sleeping hibiscus, Texas mallow, Turk's cap 3**

wax milkweed n

A southwestern **milkweed 1** (here: *Asclepias albicans*).

1945 Benson–Darrow *Manual SW Trees* 270, Wax milkweed. . . Similar to *Asclepias subulata* . . covered with white wax. **1998** Rea *Folk Mammalogy* xx **AZ,** One day while climbing a desert range, I brought down . . a specimen of Wax Milkweed, *Asclepias albicans.*

wax myrtle n Cf **flea myrtle, michael tea**

Std: a small tree or shrub of the genus *Morella*, esp *M. cerifera*. For other names of these see **bayberry 1, candleberry myrtle, candle tree 2, candlewood 4, dwarf myrtle, mickleberry, myrtle n[1] B2, myrtleberry 1, spice bush 6, swamp myrtle, sweet bay 7, ~ myrtle 1, ~ oak 2, tallowberry 1, tallow shrub, tea bark, waxberry 1, waxbush, wax tree**

wax on snow See **wax 1**

wax plant n

1 =**Indian pipe 1.**

1851 *Horticulturist & Jrl. Rural Art* 5.211, The wax plant, with no green leaves, but the whole stem, as well as flower, of a frosty whiteness, makes us doubt whether it is natural or artificial. **1859** (1968) Bartlett *Americanisms* 503, Wax-Plant. (*Monotropa uniflora.*) A perfectly white, fleshy plant, looking as if made of wax. **2007** *DARE* File—Internet, But to return to the weird little Ghost Flower: Because it seems to be fashioned from snow or carved from ice, & oozes (or "melts") if picked or bruised, it is sometimes called the American Ice Plant, or the Wax Plant.

2 =**garden catchfly.**

1892 *Jrl. Amer. Folkl.* 5.93 **OH,** *Silene Armeria*, wax plant. Mansfield.

3 A **spurge** (here: *Euphorbia antisyphilitica*). **TX**

1928 Quillin *TX Wild Flowers* 199, *Euphorbia antisyphilitica*. . . Common Names: Wax Plant, "Candelilla". . . The plant is of commercial importance because of the wax which accumulates on the stems in the form of white powder. **1940** Writers' Program *Guide TX* 24 **wTX,** The guayule, or rubber plant, is found in the western part of the State, and the candelilla, or wax plant, in the Big Bend. **1957** Jaeger *N. Amer. Deserts* 266, *Candelilla*. . . Also called waxplant because it yields a wax used in candle making. . . To obtain the wax the stems are boiled in water, and the wax is allowed to rise to the surface. **1967** *Austin Statesman* (TX) 22 Jan sec A 3/1, Last week's article on Texas' commercially-valuable native wax plant, Candelilla, produced a most interesting letter.

wax tree n

=**wax myrtle.**

[**1791** Bartram *Travels* 405, A species of Myrica (Myrica inodora) this very beautiful evergreen shrub, which the French inhabitants call the Wax tree, grows in wet sandy ground about the edges of swamps.] **1804** *Lit. Mag. & Amer. Reg.* 1.272, The tree which furnishes this matter [=wax] in the greatest abundance . . is the *Myrica ceriferat* [sic] or wax-tree. **1841** in 1906 Thwaites *Early W. Travels* 2.257, On the plains we find . . now and then the willow, the alder, the wax tree [etc]. **1960** Vines *Trees SW* 119, Odorless Wax-myrtle. . . Also known under the vernacular names of Waxberry, Candleberry, and Wax-tree. **1971** Krochmal *Appalachia Med. Plants* 180, *Myrica cerifera*. . . Common Names . . bayberry waxtree [etc].

waxweed n

1 Std: a plant of the genus *Cuphea*, esp *C. viscosissima*. For other names see **firefly 3, tarweed 2**

2 =**golden ragwort.**

1971 Krochmal *Appalachia Med. Plants* 234, *Senecio aureus* [= *Packera aurea*]. . . Common Names: Golden ragwort, . . waxweed [etc].

waxwork n [From the waxy aril of the fruit] Cf **Roxbury waxwork**

A **bittersweet** (here: *Celastrus scandens*).

1814 Bigelow *Florula Bostoniensis* 57, *Celastrus scandens*. . . Climbing staff tree. Wax work. **1893** *Harper's New Mth. Mag.* 87.432, Every one knows the climbing-bittersweet or "waxwork" (*Celastrus scandens*), with its bright berries hanging in clusters in the autumn copses. **1924** *Mansfield News* (OH) 8 Nov [8]/5 (newspaper-archive.com), Bittersweet or waxwork is a climbing vine . . commonly gathered in the fall and . . used for decorating the house or schoolroom. **1975** *Greeley Tribune & Greeley Republican* (CO) 9 June 15/1, Another plant commonly known as waxwork, prized for its colorful fruits, has sometimes been called bittersweet.

waxy adj Cf **black wax, gumbo 6a, b, jack wax 2**

Of soil: smooth and sticky.

1790 *Amer. Museum* 7.64 **eMD,** Those who have a proper waxy earth, which becomes glossy by treading wheat on it . . will have no more dirt in their wheat, than the thresher, who beats it out on a plank. **1847** *ME Farmer* (Augusta) 14 Jan 1/1, The most waxy clay-lands, well dressed over with well-burnt clay, not only become lighter and milder . . but so they continue for several years. **1873** Hilgard *Suppl. Rept. Geol. Reconnoissance LA* 27, *Waxy Soil.* . . an exceedingly heavy, close, intractable clay, mostly in low ground. **1874** *Out West Mag.* 13.349, A great portion of the valley consists of sloping volcanic *mesas*, . . there being little good farm-land. This last lies in narrow margins along the river, of a dense, black, waxy soil, yielding a species of tough tule-grass. **1925** *Book of Rural Life* 1.193, Very fine-grained bottom-land clay soil . . is a rich, black, waxy soil, usually poorly drained and difficult to work. It is often called "gumbo." **1967** *DARE* (Qu. C31, . . *Heavy, sticky soil*) Inf **TX**22, Waxy—black soil. **1986** Pederson *LAGS Concordance*, 1 inf, **ceMS,** Gumbo land is kind of a waxy land; sticky; 1 inf, **cTX,** Waxy soil—like gumbo.

way adv See **where A3**

way exclam See **whay**

way-cup See **wake-up**

wayfaring tree n Also *wayfarer's tree* [*OED2* 1597 → for the similar European sp *Viburnum lantana,* now widely naturalized in the US]

=**hobblebush.**

[**1785** Marshall *Arbustrum* 159, *Viburnum* [spp]. Pliant Mealy, or Way-faring Tree.] **1814** Pursh *Flora Americae* 2.711, Way-faring-tree. . . *Viburnum lantanoides*. **1860** Curtis *Cat. Plants NC* 91, The branches spread upon the ground, and, taking root at their ends, form well secured loops for tripping the feet of inexperienced way-farers; a habit which has been revenged upon by the unlucky, in the names imposed upon it of *American Way-fairer's* [sic] *Tree* and the *Devil's Shoe-strings*. **1901** Lounsberry *S. Wild Flowers* 478, American Way-faring Tree. . . *Viburnum alnifolium* [=*V. lantanoides*]. **1967** *WI Conserv. Bulletin* 32.1.21 **seWI,** The planting includes as wide a variety of native trees and shrubs as were available. . . The shrubs include . . wayfaring tree, honeysuckle, and hazel.

wayne See **wain**

way-up See **wake-up**

way yonder See **yonder B4**

we pron [Cf *EDD* *we* pers. pron. II.1; *OED2* *we* pron. 3 "now only by the uneducated"] **chiefly SC, GA coasts** *chiefly among Gullah speakers*

Us—used as the object of a verb or preposition. Note: The use of *we* with appositives, as in "What makes we women happy," is widespread in colloquial speech and is not illustrated here.

1853 Simms *Sword & Distaff* 76 **SC,** He hab big, rawbone, coal black hoss, same time he catch we, and carry we to town. **1888** Jones *Negro Myths* 156 **GA coast,** Dem walk up tarrur side de fire an look at we, but dem yent bin crack eh teet ter we. **1922** [see **we** adj]. **1928** Peterkin *Scarlet Sister Mary* 29 **SC** [Gullah], Satan is de one sent dat rat here to kill we joy an' make we have sin today. **1932** in 1944 *ADD* **nVA,** We. . . 2. Us. . . 'No, hit didn' barn [burn] innythin' to we.' **1945** FWP *Lay My Burden Down* 149 **Sth** (as of c1865) [Black], Old Missus . . tell we children to get back to the chimney corner. **1949** Turner *Africanisms* 281 **seSC** [Gullah], We'll have the drum and the bass, and all play for we. **1966** *DARE* (Qu. II14, *To pay a short visit: "Last night our new neighbors _____."*) Inf **ME**1, Called in on we. [Inf old, no formal educ] **1966** *DARE* Tape **SC**15, He get behind we. **1966** *DARE* FW Addit **MA**5, Now, let's sit we down to tea. **1971** [see **we** adj]. **2002** *Sun. News Jrl.* (Wilmington DE) 7 July sec A 6/4, Wilson, a lifelong Sussex County resident, said he notices the biggest changes in language when he visits Rehoboth Beach. "They're mostly all imports," he said. "They don't talk like we."

we adj [Cf *EDD* *we* pers. pron. II.2] **SC, GA coasts** *chiefly among Gullah speakers* Cf **me** adj **a, us** adj

Our; hence pron *we's* ours.

1853 Simms *Sword & Distaff* 460 **SC** [Black], Lawd ha' massy; we does we bes'. **1909** *S. Atl. Qrly.* 8.50 **sSC coast** [Gullah], We hat. **1922** Gonzales *Black Border* 337 **sSC, GA coasts** [Gullah glossary], *We*—our, us. **1928** [see **we** pron]. **1939** Griswold *Sea Is. Lady* 518 **csSC** (as of c1893) [Gullah], A delegation of women . . presented themselves . . to beg newspapers "fuh dress-up we house fuh Yeastuh." **1959** Ruark *Poor No More* 509 **Sth** [Black], Any friend of Mistah Craig . . friends of we's. **1966** *DARE* Tape **SC**15, One time I went in the wood. In we days, you go hunt hog, wild hog with stick, carry a stick. **1971** Cunningham *Syntactic Analysis Gullah* 116, *We* 'we, us, our'.

weak See **wick** n[1]

weak as pond water See **pond water 2**

weaked, weakedness See **wicked** adj

weakfish n

Std: a Gulf or Atlantic food fish of the genus *Cynoscion,* esp *C. nebulosus* or *C. regalis.* For other names of *C. nebulosus* see **drummer 1, gator trout, gray ~ 1, gulf ~, salmon B2b, ~ trout 2, saltwater trout, sea ~ a, shad ~, silverfish 5, speck** n[1] **5, speckled trout 2, spike 1, spotted seatrout, ~ squeteague, ~ weakfish, squeteague, summer trout, trout 2b;** for other names of *C. regalis* see **chickwit, deepwater trout, drummer 1, gray trout 1, saltwater ~, sea ~ a, shad ~, silverfish 5, squeteague, summer trout, sun ~ 1, tide runner 1, trout 2b;** for other names of var spp see **bluefish 2, chickrod, corvina b, sand trout, sea bass 2, ~ trout a, silver ~ 4, trout 2b, white ~ 1**

weak trembles n Also with *the* Also *weak jerks, ~ tremblings* Pronc-spp *weak trim'les, ~ trimmels, ~ trimlins* **chiefly S Midl** See Map Cf **trembles**

A feeling of faintness and shakiness or palpitations, often as a result of hunger, fear, or anxiety.

1889 Morgan *Hist. Wheel* 619 **AR,** The wrangling of the committee on platform at the St. Louis convention, had given them the "weak trembles." **1902** *DN* 2.248 **sIL,** *Weak trimlins* (i.e. tremblings). . . Nervous prostration; palpitation of the heart; excessive fear or terror. A common expression. **1905** *Ft. Wayne News* (IN) 8 May 9/4, [Advt:] *Doctor Tucker's Scientific and Certain Cure* For . . Melancholia, Weak Trembles, Lack of Strength [etc]. **1906** *DN* 3.163 **nwAR,** *Weak trim'les.* . . Trembling caused by physical weakness. **1913** Kephart *Highlanders* 228 **sAppalachians,** Uncle Neddy Cyarter went to jump one of his teeth

out . . and missed the nail and mashed his nose with the hammer. He had the weak trembles. **1938** Rawlings *Yearling* 285 **nFL,** I git the weak jerks, thinkin' about 'em [=wolves]. **1950** Stuart *Hie Hunters* 157 **eKY,** That shadow skeered me till I have the weak trembles! **1952** Brown *NC Folk.* 1.605, *Weak trembles, to have the.* . . To be worried. **1954** *Harder Coll.* **cwTN,** *Weak trimmels.* **1958** *PADS* 29.18 **TN,** *Weak trembles:* "Weak trembles is getting weak and shaky because of an empty stomach." **c1960** *Wilson Coll.* **csKY,** *Weak trembles* (or *tremblings*). **1968–70** *DARE* (Qu. BB6, *A sudden feeling of weakness, when sometimes the person loses consciousness*) Infs **IN**32, **KY**11, **MO**17, **TX**104, Weak trembles; (Qu. GG26, *A feeling of weakness from fear: "When she saw the dog coming at her she got _____."*) Infs **AL**5, **OH**49, **OK**18, **TX**104, Weak trembles; **GA**26, Weak tremblings. **a1978** (1983) Carpenter *Aunt Arie* 79, It scared me s'bad it give me th'weak jerks. **1994–97** in 2004 Montgomery–Hall *Dict. Smoky Mt. Engl.* 638 **wNC, eTN,** *Weak trembles.* . . Tremor, general weakness of the body; anxiety. [10 infs] **2000** in 2007 *DARE* File—Internet **TN,** I wonder why the doctors don't explain to the families of diabetics what these 'weak-trembles' really are. When Mom was here she would get weak-trembles and had to have food like she was starving to death. **2005** *Ibid,* I have anxiety really bad . . and sometimes I get what I call the (shakes or weak trembles).

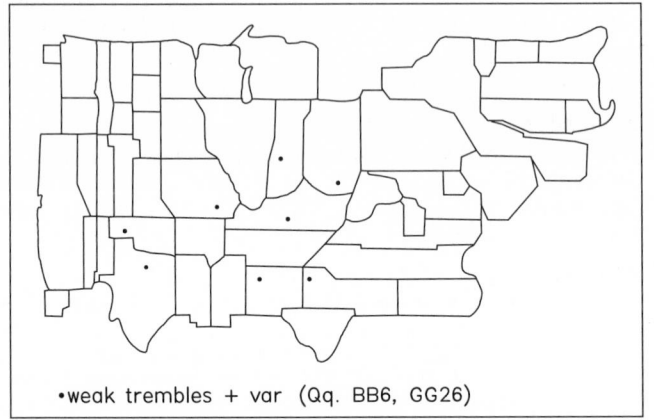

•weak trembles + var (Qq. BB6, GG26)

we-all pron Also *we-alls* Cf **we-all** adj, **we-uns, you-all**

1 We. **chiefly Sth, S Midl**

1856 Pickard *Kidnapped & Ransomed* 116 **KY** [Black], Bless my life! if dar aint Mass'r! Hi! we all's so glad see Missus, we done forget Mass'r gwine come too! **1862** Bagby *Letters of Mozis Addums* 26 **VA,** This elustraits the diffrents between Nothun and Sothun peepil, havin white mades heer . . , while we all has cullud mades. **1865** Clemens *Tobias Wilson* 309, When the colonel gits in one of his tantrums and sets up for honest . . , the captain . . reports to him that there ain't nothin' been taken, and that we all's been slandered. **1875** in 1917 Twain *Letters* 1.268 **MO,** We-all send love to you-all. **1886** *S. Bivouac* 4.345 **sAppalachians,** You-all and we-all (just a little better than *you-uns* and *we-uns,* and the same thing in effect). **1887** (1967) Harris *Free Joe* 81 **GA** [Black], We-all des pick 'im up, suh. **1890** Goss *Recoll. of a Private* 305 **VA** (as of 1864), If we alls hadn't hankered to go to war with the Yanks, durned if I believe you alls would care enough about fighting to come down here to fight we alls. **1897** Lewis *Wolfville* 81 **AZ,** First we-alls knows, these yere Britons would be runnin' cimmaron in the hills. **1899** [see **we-all's** adj]. **1909** *DN* 3.390 **eAL, wGA,** Y'all. . . The regular possessive is *yall's.* *We all* is also used, but the words have not yet coalesced, and there is no possessive. **1923** *DN* 5.224 **swMO,** *We-all.* . . We. Also *We-alls.* **1932** Randolph *Ozark Mt. Folks* 122, I reckon we-all better go t' th' sale. **1964** *NYT Mag.* 23 Aug 62, Soul brother . . *we-all* . . the people. **1986** Pederson *LAGS Concordance* (He and I) 1 inf, **neFL,** We all. **2008** *DARE* File [Black], Heard on The Judges— Judge: "What were you-all doing?" Twelve-year-old black male speaker: "We-all was playin' an' havin' fun." *Ibid* **sMD,** I don't use they-all, but i certainly do use we-all (though only after i've been constantly hanging out with family and friends i grew up with for several days). It's an exclusive we.

2 Us—used as the object of a verb or preposition. **Sth, S Midl** *esp freq among Black speakers*

1877 *Scribner's Mth.* 14.543 **Sth** [Black], De Yankee soldiers . . mawched we alls off. **1883** (1971) Harris *Nights with Remus* 232 **GA** [Black], I hope dey aint gwine ter be no famishin' 'roun' yer 'mungs we all. **1884** Morgan *Yazoo* 70 **cwMS** (as of 1865), Paw says the Yankees wor' always meddling in ouah affairs, after they sold their nigros to we all. **1890** [see **1** above]. **1927** [see **we-all** adj]. **1931** (1991) Hughes–Hurston *Mule Bone* 85 **cFL** [Black], Glad to be round home with we-all again, ain't you Daisy? **c1937** in 1976 *Weevils in the Wheat* 189 **VA** [Black], He nebber sold mammy or us chilluns; he kept we alls tergether.

we-all adj
Our.

1887 (1967) Harris *Free Joe* 83 **nwGA** [Black], He ain' b'long ter we-all folks, no furder dan he my young mistiss ole man, but dee ain' no finer w'ite man dan him. **1927** Kennedy *Gritny* 60 **sLA** [Black], Take yo' tex' from somh'n cuncernin' we-all color. Maggie ain' nothin' to we-all, no way.

we-alls pron[1]   See **we-all** pron

we-all's adj, pron[2]   **chiefly Sth**   *esp freq among Black speakers*
Our; ours.

1857 Terhune *Moss-Side* 241 **VA** [Black], You and Miss Annie stans pretty nigh together in we-all's hearts—don't dey, Sultan? **1884** *Century Illustr. Mag.* 27.934 **VA** [Black], I use' to go 'long wid him an' tote he books an' we all's snacks. **1893** Shands *MS Speech* 67, *We all's. A possessive form of we all used by negroes and illiterate whites. You all's also is heard. "That house is we all's" means that the house belongs to all of us.* **1899** (1912) Green *VA Folk-Speech* 476, *We-all's. . . Our.* "We-all's Miss Mary." *We all*, we. **[1909** see **we-all** pron **1.] 1913** Pickett *Heart* 105 **VA** (as of 1863), I heard one of the men . . say . . "I'm blamed ef I wouldn't be . . willin' to go right through it all . . to hear Marse Robert . . say over again as how he grieved bout'n we-all's losses and honored us for we-all's bravery!" **1927** *AmSp* 3.6 **Ozarks,** [First pers pl poss:] Ourn, we-all's, we uns'. **1939** Harris *Purslane* 235 **cNC** [Black], She brought a pa'cel o' papers and stuff dat tell how to take keer o' we-alls' bodies, she say, and I never told how we can't read.

weaner house n   Also *weaner, ~ cabin, weaning cabin, ~ house*   **chiefly S Midl**
A small house, usu on a family farm, provided as a temporary first home for newlyweds by the parents or other relatives of one of the couple.

1929 Parker *Grand Mt. School* 43 **nwAR** (as of 1890s), The first two years together were spent in the "Weaner" house a short distance from the Parker home. **1965** *TN Hist. Qrly.* 24.106 **eTN,** Later [the house] was used as a "weaner" by the Shields family. When one of the boys married, he occupied the house until he could get his own dwelling built. **1973** *Pennington Pedigrees* 5.1.66 **KY,** Grandfather had a tenant house in which the young people lived until they could build their own house. He called it his "weaning house." **1977** *San Jacinto News–Times* (Shepherd TX) 14 Apr 5/8, It was built in 1868 for the Nikolas Crane family and used as a "weaning cabin." **1979** *Our Smokies Heritage* Sept 308 **eTN,** When the eldest son (about 18 yrs) decided to get married they built him a smaller log cabin and barn at the back of the Flats about a half mile away—This cabin was called the Weaner cabin or Honeymoon house. **1981** Kennedy *Our Baldridge Forebears* 4 **AR,** As Wiley's and Tennie's children married, different ones of them lived in the old house so that it became known as the "weaning house". **1982** Slone *How We Talked* 5 **eKY** (as of c1950), Some parents had a small, one-room house close by where the newlyweds first lived, while waiting to build a house of their own. This house was called "a weaning house." **1990** in 2007 *DARE* File—Internet **nwLA** (as of 1930s), We still lived in the little "weaning house" almost three years later when baby Chris was born. **2006** *Ibid,* My country relatives have employed something called a "Weaner House" or "Brooder House" for at least three generations to help start off new couples. **2007** *Ibid* **ceKY,** Bascom inherited a portion of the original May Farm, and for many years he and his wife Annie lived in the Weaning House.

weapon n   Usu |'wɛpən|; also **chiefly S Midl** |'wipən, -pɪn|
Pronc-spp *weep(i)n, weepon, weepun*
Std sense, var forms.

1851 Burke *Polly Peablossom* 111 **OR,** I hadn't a weepun about me. **1861** Holmes *Venner* 2.140 **wMA,** I shouldn't like to have him raoun' me, 'f there wa'n't a . . weep'n within reach. **1872** Twain *Roughing It* 225 **AR,** Draw your weepon! **1890** *DN* 1.69 **KY,** *Weepuns* [wipn̩z]: weapons. **1893** Shands *MS Speech* 67, *Weepons* [wipənz]. Negro and illiterate white for *weapons.* **1899** (1912) Green *VA Folk-Speech* 478, *Weepon. . . For weapon.* **1903** *DN* 2.336 **seMO,** *Weapon. . .* I never have carried weepons since the war. **1907** *DN* 3.238 **nwAR,**

Weapon. . . Pronounced [wipən]. **1909** *DN* 3.406 **nwAR,** *Weepuns.* **1915** *DN* 4.192 **swVA,** *Weepin'* ['wipɪn]. **a1930** in 1991 Hughes–Hurston *Mule Bone* 36 **cFL** [Black], They says you got tuh have a weepon befo' you kin commit uh 'ssault. **1932** Randolph *Ozark Mt. Folks* 28, I reckon my 'ponents is a-comin' atter me jest like Samson, an' 'pears like they're a-usin' th' same weepons, too! **1942** Hall *Smoky Mt. Speech* 21 **wNC, eTN,** *Weapons* ['wipənz] (once; said to be obsolescent). **c1960** Wilson *Coll.* **csKY,** *Weapon. . .* /'wipən/ rare.

wear n   See **weir**

wear v   Usu |wɛ(ə)r, wɛə, wæ(ə)r, wæə| Pronc-sp *w'ar*   Cf **bear** n[1] **A**

A   Pronc forms.

1899 (1967) Chesnutt *Wife of Youth* 144 **NC** [Black], We 'll hafter . . nuss 'im tel de fevuh w'ars off. **1913** Kephart *Highlanders* 260 **sAppalachians,** I'll w'ar ye out with a hick'ry!

B   Gram forms.

1   pres (exc 3rd pers sg): usu *wear;* also **esp Sth, S Midl** *wears.*

1853 Simms *Sword & Distaff* 372 **SC** [Black], Ef you wears de buffs, maussa, you hab for wear de shirt. **1862** *Continental Mth.* 1.189 **SC** [Black], I wears 'em out mighty fass. **1875** Southworth *Mystery of Dark Hollow* 167 **Sth,** I wears my own hair, and I don't change the color, neither. **1986** Pederson *LAGS Concordance,* 1 inf, **nwLA,** Lots of them wears aprons; 1 inf, **csTN,** Lots of them wears a tie; 1 inf, **swGA,** Most women wears aprons; 1 inf, **nwMS,** Biggest part of them wears beads; 1 inf, **swGA,** They wears bracelets; 1 inf, **swGA,** We just . . wears out; 1 inf, **cnGA,** Most all farmers wears overalls; 1 inf, **cwGA,** Some people wears T-shirts; 1 inf, **ceLA,** Niggers that wears the name of Watts; 1 inf, **neAR,** Lots of people wears them.

2   past: usu *wore;* also rarely *weared.*   Cf **-ed 2**

1864 Sargent *Peculiar* 91 **Sth,** He was . . so short-sighted he weared specs. **1986** Pederson *LAGS Concordance,* 1 inf, **ceMS,** We weared = we wore. **2000** Shores *Tangier Is.* 248 **Chesapeake Bay,** Nonstandard forms showing past times are common . . *weared.* **2006** *DARE* File—Internet **AR,** He took me to the batting cages where we weared it out! **2007** *Ibid,* [The keyboard] weared out in less than 1 year.

3   past pple, ppl adj: usu *worn;* also:
a   *weared.*   Cf **-ed 2**

1859 Lasselle *Hope Marshall* 38 **KY** [Black], If you had weared that, you would be 'stinguished from all the other ladies,—sartin. **1986** Pederson *LAGS Concordance,* 1 inf, **cnGA,** Weared out = worn out. **1989** Pederson *LAGS Tech. Index* 278 **Gulf Region,** *Wear* [past pple: 3 infs, proncs of the types [wæ(r)d].] **2005** in 2007 *DARE* File—Internet **nCA,** Cutting mats will wear out (not that I've weared one out yet . .).

b   *wore.*   **scattered, but esp Sth, S Midl, Cent**   See Map   *esp freq among rural speakers and those with little formal educ*

1744 (1907) Hamilton *Itinerarium* 100 **NYC,** These gloves . . were fit for nothing but to be wore by itchified persons. **1848** *Scientific Amer.* 3.412, They are apt to be wore flat in some places. **1893** *DN* 1.278 **nwCT,** *Wear* [past and past participle]—wore. **1899** (1912) Green *VA Folk-Speech* 489, Yes, he's old and wore out now. **1911** (1913) Johnson *Highways Gt. Lakes* 166, Many of the whites wore moccasins in winter, and I've wore 'em myself. **1938** Rawlings *Yearling* 42 **nFL,** I'm wore out. **1953** Atwood *Survey of Verb Forms* 25, *Wear. . .* The past participle is recorded in the context "He is (worn) out." The standard *worn* . . predominates on all levels in s. N. Eng., N.Y., and the northern two thirds of N.J. Elsewhere, except in cultivated speech, it is considerably limited by the variant *wore. Wore . .* is used in n.e. N. Eng. by about three fourths of the Type IA [=old, with little educ] informants and by about half the other noncultured informants. In s. N. Eng., e. N.Y., and n. N.J. *wore* is given by less than one third of the Type I [= with little educ] informants; elsewhere in the M[iddle] A[tlantic] S[tates] and the S[outh] A[tlantic] S[tates] its frequency in this group varies from about two thirds (Pa.) to more than nine tenths (N.C.). *Wore* is given by a negligible number of Type II [=with moderate educ] informants in s. N. Eng. and e. N.Y.; elsewhere by from one fourth (Va.) to two thirds (Md. and W. Va.) of this group. Three cultured informants in N. Eng., three in the M.A.S., and one in the S.A.S. use *wore.* **1965–70** *DARE* (Qu. X47, *. . "I'm very tired, at the end of my strength"*) 57 Infs, **scattered, but esp Sth, S Midl, Cent,** Wore out; NY73, All wore out; IA11, Completely wore out; SC10, Wore down; GA77, Wore to a frazzle; (Qu. KK20b, *Something that looks as if it might collapse any minute: "Our old washing machine is _____."*) 27 Infs, **scattered, but Sth, S Midl,**

Cent, Wore out; **ME**19, All wore out; **SC**8, Plumb wore out; **OK**6, Wore plumb out; (Qu. FF21a, *A joke that is so old it doesn't seem funny any more: "His jokes are all _____."*) 26 Infs, **scattered, but esp Sth, S Midl,** Wore out; (Qu. OO36b, *To wear: "His new shoes were no good. He has _____ a hole in them already.";* total Infs questioned, 75) 18 Infs, **esp Sth,** Wore; (Qu. O2, *Nicknames . . for an old, clumsy boat*) Inf **LA**12, Wore-out boat; (Qu. W26, *When a piece of clothing has been used until it gets thin and breaks . . it was _____;* total Infs questioned, 75) Infs **AR**23, **FL**39, **GA**3, **ME**6, **MS**7, 72, **OK**9, Wore out; (Qu. X48b, *. . If a person is not so young any more . . "He's _____."*) Infs **IN**13, **LA**6, (Getting about) wore out; (Qu. Y35, *To spoil something so that it can't be used . . "My new coffee pot—it's completely _____."*) Infs **AL**61, **MO**8, 34, Wore; (Qu. BB5, *A general feeling of discomfort or illness that isn't any one place in particular*) Inf **OH**43, Wore out; **NY**209, Wore down; (Qu. BB38, *When a person doesn't look healthy, or looks as if he hadn't been well for some time . . "He looks _____."*) Inf **OH**43, Wore out; (Qu. BB39, *On a day when you don't feel just right, though not actually sick . . "I'll be all right tomorrow—I'm just feeling _____ today."*) Inf **OH**43, Wore out; (Qu. KK19, *If a machine or appliance is temporarily out of order: "My sewing machine _____."*) Infs **AZ**1, **AR**22, (Is) wore out; (Qu. KK23, *Weak or unsteady: "I think the footbridge will hold but it is a bit _____."*) Inf **CA**120, Wore out; (Qu. KK30, *Feeling slowed up or without energy: "I certainly feel _____."*) Infs **AR**3, **ID**2, **KY**47, **MO**30, **TX**81, Wore out. [Of all Infs giving these responses, 82% were comm type 4 or 5, 57% gs educ or less.] **1991** Pederson *LAGS Social Matrix* 195 **Gulf Region,** [*Wear*—Of 914 infs, 50% had a 10th-grade educ or less; of the 197 who gave *wore* as the past participle of *wear,* 136, or approx 70%, had a 10th-grade educ or less.] **1999** Morgan *Gap Creek* 32 **NC,** Papa died, and it seemed to leave her wore out. **2007** *DARE* File—Internet **TN,** I've wore them while staying outside in 20 degrees for 2–3 hours.

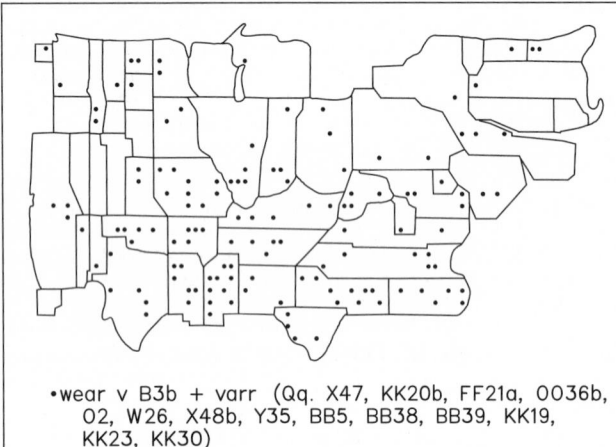

•wear v B3b + varr (Qq. X47, KK20b, FF21a, OO36b, O2, W26, X48b, Y35, BB5, BB38, BB39, KK19, KK23, KK30)

c *wored;* pronc-sp *wo'de.* Cf **-ed 3**

1862 *Continental Mth.* 1.189 **SC** [Black], 'Jake,' he said, 'where are your shoes?' 'Wored out, massa.' **1899** *Atlantic Mth.* 83.381 **VA** [Black], De wuz all wored out en ragged. **1947** Ballowe *The Lawd* 61 **LA** [Black], She . . was so wo'de down when she got to town that she actually dragged herself to the Bat Woman's house. **1989** Pederson *LAGS Tech. Index* 278 **Gulf Region,** Wear [past pple: 4 infs, proncs of the types [wo(r)d]].

C Phrases.

1 in phr *wear (someone) out:* To beat or whip (someone) severely—esp a child as a means of punishment. **chiefly Sth, S Midl**

1851 Hooper *Widow Rugby's Husband* 75 **AL,** I'd come over thar and wear you out, afore a cat could lick her tail. **1893** Shands *MS Speech* 76, *Wear out. . .* A word used by all classes as synonymous with *whip thoroughly.* **1895** *DN* 1.395 **wFL,** *Wear out:* to chastise. A father says of his son, "If he doesn't come home soon I'll wear him out with a strap when he does come." **1905** *DN* 3.101 **nwAR,** *Wear out. . .* To whip unmercifully. 'I'll wear you out, if you don't quit running away.' Common. **1937** *Hall Coll.* **wNC, eTN,** *Wear out. .* To whip, or lick badly. . . I wore him out. **1941** Faulkner *Men Working* 142 **MS,** "I'm gonna tell maw." . . "That's right, little girl. You go tell her and I hope she wears

him out." **1941** *AmSp* 16.25 **sIN, MO,** *Wear out.* Whip. 'I'll wear you out if you don't behave.' **1942** McAtee *Dial. Grant Co. IN* 70 (as of 1890s), *Wear out . .* chastise, beat thoroughly: "I'll wear you out for that". **1949** *PADS* 11.12 **wTX** (as of 1911–29), *Wear out. . .* To whip thoroughly. "I'll wear you out if you do that again." **1950** *PADS* 14.71 **SC,** *Wear. . .* Followed by . . *out.* To beat, to thrash, to whip, but only of children by way of correction. "If you don't bring in that stove-wood, I'm going to wear you out!" **c1960** *Wilson Coll.* **csKY,** *Wear out. . .* Whip soundly; one of the exaggerated expressions that are so common. **1960** Lee *Mockingbird* 82 **sAL,** Atticus had promised me he would wear me out if he ever heard of me fighting any more. **1967** *DARE* Tape **TX**46, She got a shillelagh and she went after him and really wore him out. **1989** Pederson *LAGS Tech. Index* 234 **Gulf Region,** Whipping . . wear you out (7 [infs]). **2000** *DARE* File **seKY** (as of c1960), If you don't be good I'll wear you out.

2 in phr *wear (a garment) on (one):* To dress (one) in (a garment). **PA**

1882 (1971) Gibbons *PA Dutch* 390, A neighbor told me of her daughter's being invited to a picnic, and added, "I don't know what I'll wear on her." **1931** *AmSp* 7.20 **swPA,** I wear white shoes on my baby. **1957** *Sat. Eve. Post Letters* **csPA,** An acquaintance here spoke of clothing she "wore on" her children. Since then I've heard the same expression many times. **1968** *DARE* FW Addit **nwPA,** "I wore yellow socks on my little girl today."—Overheard in beanery from a middle-aged mother. **1973** *DARE* File **swPA,** I don't wear diapers on him any more; his mother won't wear his braces on him; her mother wears the prettiest dresses on her.

weared See **wear** v B2, 3a

wear-hen n [*wear* var of *weir*]
=**red-necked grebe.**

1917 *Wilson Bulletin* 29.2.74 **cME coast,** *Columbus holboelli* [= *Podiceps grisegna*].—Bobtail, Shitepoke, Wear hen (so called because they perch on projecting parts of fish-wears).

wear (someone) out See **wear** v C1

weary See **worry** A1

weary dismals See **dismals** 1

weasely See **weasly**

weaser n Also *weaser sheldrake, wheezer, woozer* **NY**
The common **merganser** (*Mergus merganser*).

1844 DeKay *Zool. NY* 2.318, The female is thought by our sportsmen to be a distinct species, and is called *Weaser,* or *Swamp Sheldrake.* **1888** Trumbull *Names of Birds* 65, On Long Island at Moriches, [*Merganser americanus* [=*M. merganser*] is called] *weaser sheldrake;* at Bellport and Seaford (Hempstead), *weaser. . .* Another form of it, or I should say a name that immediately suggests the other, is heard at Shinnecock Bay (designating same species), viz.: *tweezer.* **1923** U.S. Dept. Ag. *Misc. Circular* 13.5 **Long Is. NY,** American Merganser. . . weaser, weaser sheldrake, wheezer . . woozer (this name, tweezer, and the variations of weaser, are forms of the same name.)

weasle v Also with *up* Also sp *weasel, weazle* **esp NEast** See Map Cf **weasly, wizzle**
Of a person: to shrink, shrivel; hence ppl adjs *weasled (up).*

1856 Olcott *Torchlight* 180 **CT,** The widow seemed to have weasled

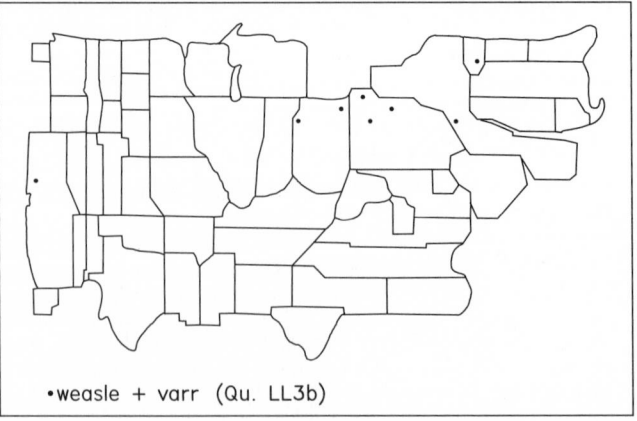

•weasle + varr (Qu. LL3b)

up into smaller dimensions. *Ibid* 337, The Selden family have given up all hopes of catching Mr. Miller for poor weasled up Jane. **1936** Chamberlain *Call of Gold* 167 **West,** Some day, a little, weasled old man would come walking up the trail and buy the mine. **1945** in 1947 Blankfort *Big Yankee* 345 **VT,** Do you remember . . Studer, the small, weaseled, bald-headed guy? **1967–70** *DARE* (Qu. LL3b, *Shrunk, dried up: "He's a little _____ old man."*) Infs **CA**99, **NY**94, **OH**16, 89, **PA**122, 175, Weasled; **PA**234, **VT**6, Weasled up. **a1969** (1971) Kerouac *Pic* 106 **NC,** He was a funny old man, was short and thin, all weazled up . . looked so shrunk and wan under his hat. **2007** *DARE* File—Internet **sMD,** You are bigoted against weaseled up old men?

weasly adj *Also weasely, weasley, weezly* **chiefly Sth, S Midl** See Map and Map Section Cf **weasle, weezledy**
Shriveled, stunted; contemptibly small or worthless.

1856 (1857) Browne *Autobiog.* 288 **KY,** She clasped to her breast a weasly suckling, that every now and then gave a sickly cry. **1902** Harris *Gabriel Tolliver* 411 **GA,** He would have said that he was a weasly looking creature, half gristle and half ghost. His hands were small and thin, and the skin of his face had the appearance of parchment. **1908** Shinn *Pioneers AR* 164, A little weasley, shrunken, half-starved body was never designed to carry anything but a weasly, shrunken and half-starved mind. **1931** (1991) Hughes–Hurston *Mule Bone* 49 **cFL** [Black], I don't want yo' lil ole weasley turnip greens. **1933** *Amer. Mercury* 28.155 **neKY,** It would be fun to see the A's come rolling in to take the place of my weasly C's and D's. **1965–70** *DARE* (Qu. LL2, . . *Too small to be worth much: "I don't want that little _____ potato."*) 10 Infs, **Sth, S Midl,** Weasly; **MS**30, Weasly [wɪzlɪ]; [**TN**6, Old weasy [wɪzɪ];] (Qu. K55, *A pig that doesn't grow well and is not worth keeping*) Inf **OK**43, Weasly [wɪzəlɪ]; **MS**72, Weasly pig; (Qu. X52, . . *A person . . who had been sick was looking*) Inf **GA**77, Weasly; (Qu. BB38, *When a person doesn't look healthy, or looks as if he hadn't been well for some time . . "He looks _____."*) Infs **GA**72, 77, **LA**6, Weasly; (Qu. LL3a, *Shrunk, dried up: "These apples are all _____."*) Inf **NJ**70, Weasely [wɪzəlɪ]; (Qu. LL3b, *Shrunk, dried up: "He's a little _____ old man."*) Inf **IL**96, Weasely [wɪzəlɪ]; **NY**150, Weasely [wɪzɛlɪ]; **AR**31, **FL**48, Weasly; **AL**6, Weasly [wɪzlɪ]; [**TN**6, Weasy [wɪzɪ]]. [20 of 22 total Infs comm type 4 or 5, 13 gs educ or less] **1970** *Thompson Coll.* **cnAL, seMI,** Measly, as in "weren't nothing but a weezly little rat dog, about two beer cans high." Birmingham 1920's; southerners in Detroit 1946–60. **1974** Fink *Mountain Speech* 29 **wNC, eTN,** *Weasley . . wizened. "Looks sorter weasley, don't he?"* **1986** Helton *Around Home* 377 **eTN,** Aged and wrinkled—weasly. **1995–96** in 2004 Montgomery–Hall *Dict. Smoky Mt. Engl.* 639 **wNC, eTN,** *Weasely. . . Esp of a person's appearance: wizened, shriveled up. . .* [6 infs].

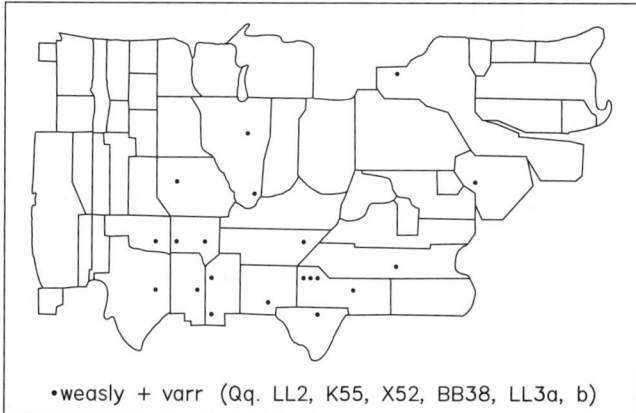

•weasly + varr (Qq. LL2, K55, X52, BB38, LL3a, b)

weasy adj |ˈwizi| [Var of *queasy*; cf *EDG* 241 "Initial *kw* has gen. remained. . . But it has often become . . *w*."] **scattered esc Sth** See Map
See quots.

1965–70 *DARE* (Qu. BB16b, *If something a person ate didn't agree with him, he might just feel a bit _____*) 11 Infs, **scattered,** Weasy; **CA**140, **MD**37, **MA**73, **NY**18, **TX**53, Weasy [wizi]; **IL**75, Weasy, [corr to] queasy; [**AL**43, Weavy]. **2005** *DARE* File—Internet, By that point my lack of sleep had me feeling weasy. *Ibid,* "I need to go home." "I'm feeling really weasy. . . " "I'm feeling kind of weasy can you come pick me up?"

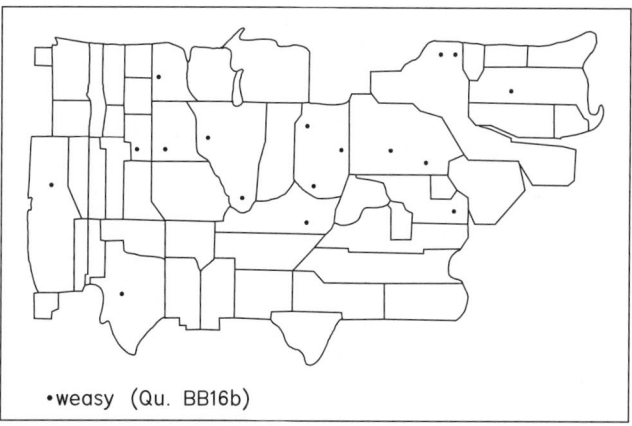

•weasy (Qu. BB16b)

weather v *Also with up* Pronc-sp *wedduh* **Sth, S Midl**
To rain, storm.

1896 *DN* 1.427 **TX,** *Weather. . . to rain.* **1922** Gonzales *Black Border* 337 **sSC, GA coasts** [Gullah glossary], *Wedduh*—weather, . . to rain or storm, in such phrases as: " 'E gwine tuh wedduh"—it is going to or looks like rain or storm. **1923** *DN* 5.224 **swMO,** *Weather. . . To storm.* "Hit'll prob'ly weather ag'in mornin'." **1926** *DN* 5.404 **Ozarks,** *Weather. . . To storm.* " 'Pears like hits a-goin' t' weather some t'night." **1940** (1978) Still *River of Earth* 44 **KY,** "When it 'gins to blow around the north points of a morning," Father said, "sign it's going to weather." **1941** Skidmore *Hawk's Nest* 16 **WV,** I don't hardly reckon it'll weather up. **1946** *PADS* 5.42 **VA,** *(To) weather:* To storm; not common. **1949** Webber *Backwoods Teacher* 269 **Ozarks,** When it "weathers up" or "fixes to weather up" . . it refers to wetness or snow or something unpleasant. **c1960** *Wilson Coll.* **csKY,** *Weather. . . to rain or storm more than usual.* **1965–70** *DARE* (Qu. B5, *When the weather looks as if it will become bad . . it's _____*) Infs **IL**114, **KY**12, 67, 84, 88, **OK**47, **VA**39, 42, Going to weather; (Qu. B6, *When clouds begin to increase . . it's _____*) Inf **KY**67, Going to weather. **1966** Dykeman *Far Family* 181 **sAppalachians,** When it snows or rains or weathers up any way a-tall, I'll just build me the biggest blaze I can. **1983** *MJLF* 9.1.60 **ceKY, NC** (as of 1956), *Weather . . to precipitate, any form.*

weather n See **weather bundle**

weather bird n *Also weather-prophet bird, weather vane* Cf **rainbird 1c**
A cuckoo.

1951 *AmSp* 26.269, Names of the cuckoos, not embodying the terms *rain* or *wet* but having about the same significance, include *weather bird* and *weather vane* (Ky.) and *weather-prophet bird* (Miss.) . . The idea of foretelling seems to underlie these names.

weatherboard n **chiefly Sth, Midl** See Map on p. 892
=**clapboard B;** hence collectively n *weatherboarding;* v *weatherboard* to cover with such boards; vbl n *weatherboarding;* ppl adj *weatherboarded.*

1684 (1977) Mather *Essay Providences* 143 **MA,** A burnt Brick, and a piece of weather-board were thrown in at the Window. **1768** in 1906 VA House of Burgesses *Jrls.* 162, [Soldiers] ripped off the Weather boards of the dwelling House and Stable. **1838** *S. Lit. Messenger* 4.232, The dwelling-house is usually built of logs: after the lapse of some years, perhaps it is plastered within and weather-boarded without. **1844** (1927) Rodman *Diary* 257 **MA,** The fire had reached the garret by ascending between the weather boards and the ceiling. **1849** *Scientific Amer.* 4.247, This machine . . is peculiarly adapted to plane and joint clapboards or weather boarding. **1899** (1912) Green *VA Folk-Speech* 477, *Weather-boarding. . . A facing of thin boards, having usually a feather-edge, and nailed lapping one over the other, used as an outside covering for the walls of a wooden building.* **1906** *DN* 3.163 **nwAR,** *Weatherboard. . . Clapboard. . . To clapboard.* "Mrs. Avis Lee has her house weather boarded and covered and improved in every way until it looks like a new house." Universal. *Siding* is not much used. **1963** Allen *Legends & Lore S. IL* 261 **csIL,** The original cabin, sixteen feet square, is of logs and has a stone chimney at the north end. . . The entire house is now covered by weatherboarding. **1965–70** *DARE* (Qu. D27, *Strips of wood used to cover the outside of a frame house*) 202 Infs, **chiefly Sth, Midl,** Weatherboarding; 75 Infs, **chiefly Sth, Midl,**

Weatherboard(s); (Qu. D28, *What hangs below the edge of the roof to carry off rain-water?*) Inf **IL**93, Weatherboard; (Qu. D37) Inf **TX**2, Weatherboard; (Qu. K15, *A thin, bony, or poor-looking cow*) Inf **IN**3, Needs weatherboarding; (Qu. K44, *A bony or poor-looking horse*) Inf **IN**30, Needs weatherboarding; (Qu. M1, . . *Kinds of barns . . according to their use or the way they are built*) Inf **GA**80, Weatherboard barn. **1968** *PADS* 49.16 **Upper MW**, Another reason for vocabulary change is the widespread use of commercial terms. . . examples are . . *siding* (field informants, 80%) for *clapboards* (field informants, 11%) and *weatherboards* (field informants, 26%). **1969** *AmSp* 44.31 **Pacific NW** [Painter jargon], *Weatherboard*. . . The siding or surface on the outside of wood-frame homes. **1971** in 1994 Thomas *Come Go with Me* 12 **S Midl** (as of c1900), Part of it is the o-o-old original logs. Course, it's been weatherboarded. **1972** *PADS* 58.14 **cwAL**, *Siding*. Midland and Southern *weatherboarding* . . is more frequent than the trade term *siding*. . . Northern *clapboards* does not occur. **1995** (1998) *Brophy Coll.* 82 **swMO** (as of c1960), *Weatherboarding*. . . for clapboards. **1998** Millersville Univ. Center for PA Ger. Studies *Jrl.* Autumn 11, The houses were typical of mining patches throughout the coal region. . . The only protection from the elements were the rickety weatherboards. **2000** Shores *Tangier Is.* 69 **Chesapeake Bay**, The weatherboarded houses . . are spaced tightly together.

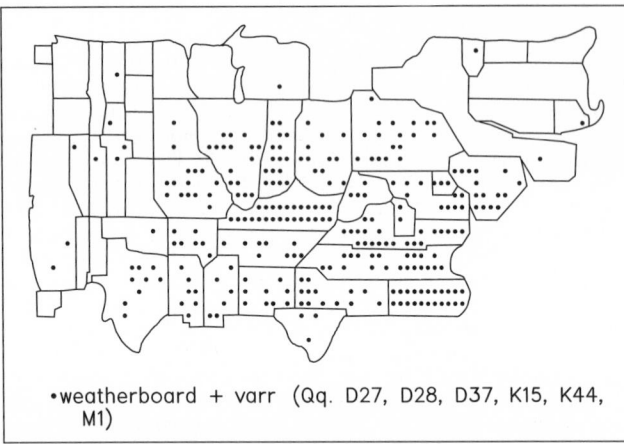

•weatherboard + varr (Qq. D27, D28, D37, K15, K44, M1)

weather breeder n   Also *breeder*   [*OED2 weather-breeder* 1655 →]

Any of var meteorological phenomena, esp an unseasonably or unusually fine day, regarded as presaging bad weather.

1780 (1821) Smith *Extracts Jrls.* 147 **ME**, *January*. . . 29. A most delightful day; a weather breeder. **1824** (1922) Anthony *New Bedford* 75 **MA**, Weather fine. A "weather breeder", as grandmother would say. **1899** (1912) Green *VA Folk-Speech* 477, *Weather-breeder*. . . A fine serene day which precedes and prepares a storm. **1903** *DN* 2.336 **seMO**, Hit's mighty fair to-day, but I'm afraid its only a weather-breeder. **1904** *DN* 2.429 **Cape Cod MA** (as of a1857), *Weather-breeder*. . . An unusually still, fine day is often said to breed a storm. **1923** in 2002 *DARE* File **cMA**, [Jrl entry for 11 Jan:] Good day. A regular *weather breeder*. [12 Jan:] Snowy morning. **1944** *PADS* 2.62 **MO**, *Weather-breeder*. . . An unusually fine day. **1952** Brown *NC Folkl.* 1.605, *Weather-breeder*. . . Good weather which is supposed to presage bad weather. **1954** [see **weather gall**]. **1957** *Hand Coll.* **cOH**, Sun dogs, ends of rainbows in the morning, are "weather breeders," i.e., storms are coming. **1965–70** *DARE* (Qu. B5, *When the weather looks as if it will become bad . . it's _____*) 12 Infs, **scattered,** Weather breeder; **CT**13, Weather breeder—it's gonna breed a storm; **MA**36, Weather breeder—especially when ponds are calm; **NC**31, Weather breeder—a good day before bad spell; **WI**75, Weather breeder—a day (in winter particularly) when there are sun dogs in the morning and generally a southeast or northeast wind; bad weather coming; [**IA**17, Weather breather;] **NY**34, Breeder; (Qu. B32, *A period of warm weather late in the fall*) 9 Infs, **scattered,** Weather breeder; **CT**26, Weather breeder—not Indian summer; four or five days of nice weather leads to a change in weather; **NY**194, Weather breeder—also used for any hot, threatening day; **PA**126, Weather breeder [FW sugg]—any unusual weather—a very beautiful day is one; (Qu. B1, *If a day is very pleasant . . it's a _____ day*) Inf **NY**233, Weather breeder—if it's real clear—you're gonna get it; **VA**47, Weather breeder—next few days, look out for hell; (Qu. B4, *A day when the air is very still, moist, and warm—it's _____*) Infs **CA**30, 203, **MN**38, **NE**7, Weather breeder;

(Qu. B6, *When clouds begin to increase . . it's _____*) Inf **NY**52, Weather breeder; (Qu. B8, *When clouds come and go all day . . it's _____*) Inf **NE**11, Weather breeder; (Qu. B10, . . *Long trailing clouds high in the sky*) Infs **GA**80, **IL**81, Weather breeders; (Qu. B18, . . *Special kinds of wind*) Inf **CO**7, Weather breeder—warm, balmy wind. **1975** *Appalachian Jrl.* 2.158 **wNC**, An unseasonably warm day in winter is called a *weather breeder* because it is invariably followed by bad weather. **1975** Gould *ME Lingo* 22, A *breeder* is a salubrious day that is making up a storm. **1986** Pederson *LAGS Concordance,* 1 inf, **nwTN**, Weather breeder—pretty day; 1 inf, **neMS**, Weather breeder—the time before a bad storm. **2008** *DARE* File **NH**, Weather breeder? Certainly! I picked it up from my wife, Jane. . . She must have got it . . in her hometown of New Boston, NH. That would have been in the late 1940s or early 1950s. . . [I]t refers to a warm day with clear, deep blue sky that often precedes a storm, especially in the winter.

weather bundle n   Also *weather (cap)*, ~ *hat*, ~ *shock* **esp Gt Lakes, N Midl**   See Map   Cf **cap bundle**

=**cap** n¹ **1**

1965–70 *DARE* (Qu. L31, . . *The top bundle of a shock*) Infs **IL**29, **KS**7, **MD**15, **MS**66, **NY**140, **OH**15, **WV**16, **WI**61, 68, Weather bundle; **NJ**8, Weather—because sheds water from stack; **NJ**53, Weather hat; **OH**90, Weather shock. **2006** *DARE* File—Internet **seWI** (as of early 1940s), A grain shock was made up of approximately 15–20 bundles of grain stood up on their butts with several bundles laid across the top to form a weather cap.

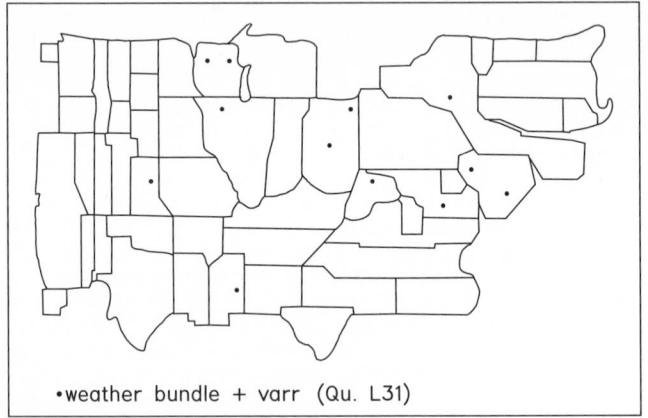

•weather bundle + varr (Qu. L31)

weather cap v phr   Cf *DS* L31

To put a **cap** n¹ **1** on a shock of grain.

1965 Guthrie *Blue Hen's Chick* 61 **MT**, So they shocked and weather-capped the bundles.

weathercock n

1 =**jewelweed 1.**

1830 Rafinesque *Med. Flora* 2.231, Impatiens. . . Touchmenot, Jewel weed, . . Weathercocks. **1876** Hobbs *Bot. Hdbk.* 127, Weathercock, Wild celandine, Impatiens pallida. **1940** Clute *Amer. Plant Names* 130, *Impatiens*. . . *biflora*. . . weather-cock. *Ibid* 225, *Impatiens pallida*. . . weather-cock.

2 Prob either the **pileated woodpecker B** or the **ivory-billed woodpecker.**

1981 Pederson *LAGS Basic Materials (Woodpecker)* 1 inf, **cwAR**, Weathercock—large black bird with red tips on wings, big beak. [*DARE* Ed: No American woodpecker has red wingtips.]

‡**weather fall** n

A period of **falling weather 1.**

1965 *DARE* (Qu. B5, *When the weather looks as if it will become bad . . it's _____*) Inf **OK**1, [We] might get a weather fall of some kind.

weather gall n   [nEngl, Scots, nIr dial]   Cf **windgall**

=**sun dog.**

1785 in 1931 *PA Mag. Hist. & Biog.* 55.254, This Morning at 7 O Clock see a large white rain Bow & at the same Time a white weather gall, appear'd in the Horison, about 1 Hour after, came on a gale of Wind. **1899** (1912) Green *VA Folk-Speech* 477, *Weather-gall*. . . A faint indication of a double rainbow. **1934** in 1947 Botkin *Treas. New Engl. Folkl.* 369, In the afternoon a weathergall (rainbow) shone over the ocean, like a handle to a great blue basket. The weathergall was taken as a "sign." **1941** *Salamanca Republican-Press* (NY) 14 July 7/3, Although the large, rainbow-like halo which surrounded the overhead sun shortly before noon today was not, scientifically speaking, a sundog, . . it was quite similar to that mock sun, also called a weather gall and parhelion, which seems to be an image of the sun on the horizon. **1954** *Newport Daily News* (RI) 12 Mar 8/7, Thursday morning saw a very bright sun dog, with a halo, in the eastern sky. Such a phenomenon is also called a weather gall, or weather breeder, and presages bad weather. **1964** *Daily Courier* (Connellsville PA) 6 Aug 24/7, The "rainbow" around the sun seen shortly after noon Saturday was a sun-dog, otherwise known as a parhelion. . . It is also called dog and weather gall.

weather grass n [See quot 1861]
A **needlegrass 1** (here: *Hesperostipa spartea*).
    1861 Wood *Class-Book* 780, *Stipa*. . . Weather Grass. . . The long awns are delicately hygrometic [sic], twisting or untwisting according to the state of the atmosphere. **1914** Georgia *Manual Weeds* 39, Porcupine-grass—*Stipa spartea*. . . *Other English names:* Weather Grass. **1935** (1943) Muenscher *Weeds* 172, Porcupine-grass, Needle-grass, Weather-grass.

weather hat See **weather bundle**

weather hen n
=**flicker** n² **1.**
    1900 *Wilson Bulletin* 12.2.10 **VT,** Weather hen. Vermont. Doubtless so called because it [=the flicker] becomes, in common with many other species of birds, particularly vociferous before or after a storm.

weather hog n Also *weather swine*
A **woodchuck 1,** esp one designated to predict the weather on Groundhog Day.
    1886 *Herald & Torch-Light* (Hagerstown MD) 4 Feb [3]/1 (newspaperarchive.com), *The Weather Swine.* Ground Hog day passed off quietly. No demonstration of any kind in honor of the weather king was noticed in Hagerstown. **1970** *DARE* (Qu. P31, . . *Names or nicknames . . for the groundhog*) Inf **TN53,** Weather hog. **1994** *San Francisco Chron.* (CA) 3 Feb sec A 3 (Internet), [Caption:] Handler William Deely pulled Phil, the famous weather hog of Punxsutawney, Pa., from his den yesterday. **2004** *DARE* File—Internet, If Georgia's most famous groundhog, General Beauregard Lee is any indication, a good weather-hog can really live large.

weather house n **SC, GA, AL**
A structure built as a shelter from inclement weather.
    1822 SC Constitutional Court of Appeals *Rept. of Cases* 1.440, The witness was standing near the weather house on the cause-way and behind the carriage when it entered the flat. **c1840** in 1976 Rose *Doc. Hist. Slavery* 351 **SC,** At 11 ½ M. the plow hands repair to the nearest weather house. **1877** U.S. Congress House *Recent Election SC* 2.200, On the left . . was an old weather-house, with a wide opening, without doors, in the north and south ends, intended as a protection for carriages and teams in rough weather. **1899** in 2010 (acc) Lexis–Nexis Legal Research *State Case Law: SC* (Internet), The indictment . . [charged] the defendant with feloniously breaking and entering . . the weather house of one Eli Kinard. **1930** (1972) Cate *Our Todays* 35 **seGA,** The older inhabitants of St. Simons say it was built as a weather house for the Couper slaves who might be working in the fields nearby and who would need some sort of shelter from rain and storm. **1945** AL Educ. Surv. Comm. *Pub. Educ. AL* 425, On rainy days the boys who are doing farm work spend their time in "the weather house," a small building with no glass in the windows and with many cracks in the weatherboarded walls. . . In bad weather, 50 or 60—occasionally as many as 200—boys have been corralled in this building. **1953** in 2010 (acc) Lexis–Nexis Legal Research *State Case Law: AL* (Internet), He bought the property . . in 1937, . . and built a small weather house on it to protect his workers in rain storms. **1957** Newton *Why Baptist* 28 **GA** (as of 1902), We ran to the nearest weather house in the field, which was used for various purposes—storing commercial fertilizer in the spring, cotton in the fall, and always a haven of shelter in time of storm.

weather light n [Cf *DNE* weather light "gleam or flicker of light at sea thought to presage a storm"; *EDD* weather gleam (at *weather* 7.(23)) "clear sky near a dark horizon"] **esp S Midl**
See quots.
    1837 (1955) *Crockett Almanacks* 85 **wTN,** The singular glare seen on the eastern horizon, and called by the settlers "weather light," portends either terrible weather or continued dry weather. **1873** *Scientific Amer.*

28.373 **cnTN,** Recently . . during a stormy evening, when more than one weather light could be seen, one seemed to be approaching from the southwest. It came nearer and nearer, and increased in brightness. . . Suddenly a violent whirlwind passed over the town and went toward the northeast accompanied by the light. **1884** *Mth. Weather Rev.* 12.85 **AR,** A phenomenon known locally as "weather lights" was the precursor of a violent snow storm. . . The appearance is that of rosy red to white light appearing above the horizon, 5°, 10°, and even 30°, and all the way from northeast around to southwest—sometimes only in the northwest. . . These lights invariably precede a change in weather—either rain or snow. **1966–70** *DARE* (Qu. CC16, *A small light that seems to dance or flicker over a marsh or swamp at night*) Inf **OK42,** There's a weather light too that older people used to speak of—I don't know what it is—seen in [the] sky like a glow; **TX89,** Weather light. **1981** Brehm–Curtis *Narrows Harpeth* [24] **TN,** It has been stated by some that this is only a weather light, jack-o-lantern, or will-o'-the-wisp, a phosphorescent light that moves about at night.

weather plant See **weather vine**

weather-prophet bird See **weather bird**

weather shock See **weather bundle**

weather swine See **weather hog**

weather up See **weather** v

weather vane See **weather bird**

weather vine n Also *weather plant* [See quot 1929]
=**crab's eye.**
    1929 Neal *Honolulu Gardens* 156, Weather plant, crab's-eye vine (*Abrus precatorius*). . . At one time it was believed that the plant prophesied the weather. **1933** Small *Manual SE Flora* 743 **FL,** Rosary-pea, Weather-vine. . . Woods, thickets and roadsides, pen[insular] Fla. **1976** Bailey–Bailey *Hortus Third* 3, *Abrus*. . . *precatorius*. . . weather plant, weather vine.

weather worm n
=**woolly bear 1.**
    1968 *DARE* (Qu. R27, . . *Kinds of caterpillars or similar worms*) Inf **MN19,** Weather worm—a caterpillar; it's brown and black; the length of the black designates the length of the winter. **2005** *DARE* File—Internet **MO,** The banded woollybear caterpillar is often called the "weather worm" because in folklore the width of its black bands indicates the severity of the coming winter.

weave v
A Gram forms.
Past pple, ppl adj: usu *woven, weaved;* also:
1 *wove.* esp **Sth, S Midl**
    1793 Morse *Amer. Universal Geog.* 1.93 **CT,** On their heads they wore a cap of the same kind, but commonly wove double, the better to secure them against a mortal blow from the death-mall. **1801** in 1996 *E. TN Roots* 8.3, There was thirty two pieces of Cloth wove in Double Heads Town within 14 months past. **1828** Webster *Amer. Dict.,* Weave, v.t. pret. *wove;* pp. *woven, wove.* The regular form, *weaved,* is rarely or never used. **1893** *DN* 1.278 **nwCT,** Weave [preterite and past participle]—wove. **1937** *Hall Coll.* **wNC,** I've spun many a thread and wove many a cloth. **1968–70** *DARE* (Qu. L63, *Kinds of fences made with wire*) Infs **KY46, LA29, NC68, VA57,** Wove wire fence. **1969** *DARE* Tape **KY5,** It was wove thicker. **1986** Pederson *LAGS Concordance,* 9 infs, **AL, GA, TN,** Wove wire.
2 *woved.*
    1880 *Scribner's Mth.* 19.666 [Black], Dis figure woved into de carpet hyar is Daniel. **1884** *Anglia* 7.253 **Sth, S Midl,** [Black], To the regular forms of the Irregular verbs as used by the whites, the Negro adds the following forms of his own. . . [Past pple:] weaved, woved, weefed. **2007** *DARE* File—Internet, [It] has elements of the original Dragonheart theme seamlessly woved into the sometimes majestic, sometimes impish new score. *Ibid,* [Advt:] One tube color coded, blood pressure cuff, woved nylon.
3 *weaven.* Cf **-en** suff⁵
    1986 Pederson *LAGS Concordance,* 1 inf, **csTX,** It's weaven—of tow sacks. **2006** *DARE* File—Internet, Hand weaven seed beads.
B Sense.
Orig to shave (split shingles), later to pack (sawn shingles) in bundles; hence n *weaver* one who performs such tasks. Cf **shingle weaver**

1860 Street *Woods & Waters* 161 **NY,** A single light like a star told where the woodman was weaving his shingles by his pine-knot torch. **1877** *Madison & Surrounding Towns* 562, When Pinneo, the shingle weaver, was in want of a drink, he was accustomed to go to Squire Seymour . . and run his credit until the shingles he had wove were sold. **1909** *DN* 3.418 **nME,** *Weave.* . . To shave shingles. **1922** Janes *Amer. Trade Unionism* 26, The question naturally arises why a worker in a shingle mill is called a weaver. . . Weaving shingles is the process of dovetailing them together, after they are cut, so as to form the standard commercial bundle of shingles. Shingle makers are called weavers because the work of shingle packers in a measure has the appearance of weaving.

weaven See **weave A3**

weaver n

1 See **weave B.**

2 =**crane fly.**
 1921 U.S. Natl. Museum *Proc.* 58.385 **Sth,** In parts of the Southern States the large dancing crane-flies pass by the name of "weavers."

3 A weasel.
 1966–70 *DARE* (Qu. P32, . . *Other kinds of wild animals*) Inf **MS**11, Weasel—weaver; **MS**81, Foxes, weavers. [Both Infs Black]

weaver v, hence vbl n *weavering* [Prob blend of *weave + waver*]

To move from side to side; to waver; hence v phr *weaver one's way* to follow an irregular course; adj *weavery* unsteady.
 a**1953** (1976) Guthrie *Seeds of Man* 221 **OK,** We moved on along the road in the dark, sort of by side steps, and by long pushes, rocking, swaying, weavering, and shuffling our feet. **1968–69** *DARE* (Qu. KK23, *Weak or unsteady: "I think the footbridge will hold but it is a bit _____."*) Infs **GA**77, **MO**34, Weavery. **2006** in 2007 *DARE* File—Internet **VA,** We weavered our way through the apple orchard. *Ibid* **TX,** Corso picked Texas right after the OSU game. Stuck with them all year. Kinda weavered just a little bit when Bush ran for 5000 yards against Fresno St. but eventually came back to his original position. **2007** *Ibid* **neOH,** If this is what you do then this is *going to be your punishment.* No weavering, no side baring on plea bargining, no choise of sentences.

weaver bird n
=**Baltimore oriole.**
 1913 Bailey *Birds VA* 209, *Baltimore Oriole.* . . [Local names:] Weaver Bird. Basket Bird. Golden Robin. **2007** *DARE* File—Internet **IN,** [Lecture title:] The Weaver Bird: A Look into the Life of the Baltimore Oriole.

weavering, weaver one's way, weavery See **weaver** v

weave the thimble See **thimble 1**

weazle See **weasle**

web n esp **West** Cf **snowshoe 1**
A snowshoe; hence v *web* to travel, make (one's way) on snowshoes.
 1902 Long *School Woods* 258 **NEast,** I saw him [=a moose] charge a little wiry guide, who went up a spruce tree with his snowshoes on . . spite of the four-foot webs in which his feet were tangled. **1911** *Forestry Qrly.* 9.558 **CA,** Only a few times . . was the snow hard enough to make walking without webs possible. **1948** Lavender *Big Divide* 287 **CO** (as of c1878), Early skis (. . were called "snowshoes," and what we term snowshoes were known as webs). **1956** Almirall *From College* 145 **CO,** The winter snows were so deep the mail carrier had to use "webs." **1959** Martin *Gunbarrel* 16 **WY,** We had another reason for webbing our way to Gunbarrel Creek that winter morning. **1965** Bowen *Alaskan Dict.* 34, *Webs*—Snowshoes. **1969** Backus *Tomboy Bride* 60 **CO** (as of 1906), George took off his snowshoes (webs, as we called them). **1976** Sublette Co. Artist Guild *More Tales* 71 **WY** (as of c1900), In winter, there were skiis, webs, or horse-drawn toboggans or sleds. *Ibid* 300, Then out came the snowshoes. Whenever there was a dance at a neighbors, everybody "webbed" over, danced all night and then "webbed" back home. **2002** in 2007 *DARE* File—Internet, *Do* wear your webs! Snowshoes are among your best friends while snow camping.

webbing n Pronc-sp *webbin* chiefly **ME, NH** Cf **line** n[1] **1,** DS L51
A line for driving a horse; see quot 1939.
 1900 Day *Up in ME* 168, And you'd think to see the sawin' and the

jerkin' and the h'ists,/ The boys they was a-usin' partent webbin's made of j'ists. **1911** *Century Dict. Suppl., Webbing.* . . pl. Reins. [*Century* Ed: Slang.] **1911** Shute *Plupy* 232 **NH,** Pewt electrified an old farm horse into coltlike activity while its astonished owner frantically pulled on the "webbins" and "whoaed" and "hawed" with astonishment and indignation. **1939** *LANE* Map 177 **ME, NH,** *Webbings* are sometimes distinguished from reins or lines (which are made of leather) in their manner of construction. They are said to be woven . . made 'partly of webbing' . . of cloth . . of hemp . . of fibre or cotton . . or 'padded inside'. . . They are described as a piece added to lengthen short reins . . or as a short pair of lines buckled on to the reins . . or to the splices used in driving one horse. . . [or] the rear half of the reins . . or that they extend from the back of the horse to the driver. . . In other cases, *webbings* appears to denote a different part of the harness, namely the cross-straps which connect the two pairs of reins used in driving two horses abreast. [Of the 30 infs who responded with *webbing(s)* to the question about reins—14 **NH,** 13 **ME,** 3 **VT**—8 described the term as older or old-fashioned, and 2 as rare.]

web-footed peep n
Either the **northern phalarope** or the **red phalarope.**
 1956 MA Audubon Soc. *Bulletin* 40.21 **MA,** *Red Phalarope.* . . Web-footed Peep (Mass. The toes are lobate, not webbed.) *Ibid, Northern Phalarope.* . . Web-footed Peep.

web wire n, also attrib esp **Sth, S Midl** Cf **net wire**
A stout wire mesh used for fencing.
 1885 *Indiana Progress* (PA) 17 Sept [3]/4 (newspaperarchive.com), The U.P. church has recently been enclosed with a neat and tasty web-wire fence, which is a model of neatness and good taste. **1909** *Eve. News* (Ada OK) 2 Mar 1/1, The openings near the ground shall be not less than four inches provided that where twenty-four inches of web fencing wire is used there shall be three barb wires above the web wire. **1947** *Fresno Bee the Republican* (CA) 8 Jan 15/3, [Advt:] Diversified farm, good improvements, well watered, web wire cross fences. **1966–68** *DARE* (Qu. L63, *Kinds of fences made with wire*) Infs **AL**38, **AR**4, 21, **MO**17, Web-wire fence; [**MO**35, Web fence]. **1986** Pederson *LAGS Concordance* (Wire fences) 8 infs, **AL, AR, FL, GA,** Web wire (fence); 1 inf, **cAR,** Web wire—around hogpen; 1 inf, **cnAR,** Web wire—at bottom of fence, barb wire above it; 1 inf, **seAR,** Web wire = hog wire; 1 inf, **cLA,** Web wire—woven-wire fence; 1 inf, **neAL,** Web wire—for hogs. **2001** in 2006 (acc) Lexis-Nexis Legal Research *State Case Law: AR* (Internet), When he and his wife moved onto their property in 1971, there was a web-wire fence covered with vines and honeysuckle. **2005** *DARE* File—Internet **GA,** [Effingham County Commissioners' meeting minutes:] The fencing that we had discussed was the four foot web wire fence with two strands of barb wire along the top of the fence and it would be more of a farm type fence.

weck, beef on See **beef on weck**

wed See **weed** v

weddinger n Pronc-spp *weddener, weddiner, wedner* [Brit dial] Cf **meetinger, musicianer**
A member of a wedding party; rarely, spec a bride or groom, newlywed.
 1774 (2007) Ashley *Romance Remedies & Revol.* 148 **nwMA,** I went with Poy up to the wedding, found the wedners all there. **1823** Doddridge *Logan* 44 **wPA, WV,** Your wedners are as still as mice—I dont like it; marriage commonly comes but once in a body's life and there ought to be some fun about it. **1834** Sedgwick *Allen Prescott* 2.212 **NEng,** Love and Allen, attended by their relatives and friends, . . set off as gay and happy a party of "weddingers" as ever crossed the border. **1843** (1916) Hall *New Purchase* 144 **IN,** They, amid no small uproar of laughter from the whole assembled "weddeners," waded to the bank. **1872** *Appletons' Jrl.* 8.701 **S Midl,** After a young couple have been married, or the day or so after, the wedding-guests—"weddingers," as they are styled—accompany the newly-made bride and groom to their future residence. **1872** Schele de Vere *Americanisms* 565 **VA,** *Weddiner* . . designates in Virginia the persons in attendance on the bridegroom. **1887** in 1985 Davenport-Davenport *George Says* 35 **IL,** Some weddens seal the fate of the weddeners while others do not. For some times the warmth from the domestic circle is so warm as to melt the seal. **1892** Sanborn *People at Pisgah* 164 **VT,** They're weddiners—jest married this mornin'. **1895** *DN* 1.375 **seKY, eTN, wNC,** *Weddiners:* the bride and groom, with the wedding party. **1913** (1980) Hardy *OH Schoolmistress* 146, Such wedding processions as our four carriages were not uncommon. People would say . . "Oh, there go some

weddiners!" **1913** *DN* 4.6 **ME,** *Weddingers.* . . A newly married couple. Pronounced *weddeners.* **1926** *DN* 5.404 **Ozarks,** *Weddiners.* . . Members of a wedding party. **1952** Brown *NC Folkl.* 1.605, *Weddinger.* . . Member of a wedding party.

wedduh See **weather**

wedge n[1]

1 in phr *float an iron wedge* and varr: Used hyperbolically in reference to strong coffee.   **scattered, but chiefly Sth, S Midl** See Map   Cf **egg** n **B3**

1859 *Harper's New Mth. Mag.* 20.136, Coffee is the greatest luxury an old Texan can think of . . but he wants it strong enough to float an iron wedge! **1916** Howells *Daughter* 142, She filled me up with coffee that would float an iron wedge. [**1933** *AmSp* 8.1.53 **Ozarks,** *Wedge floating.* . . Concentrated, strong. There is an old saying to the effect that one tests coffee by dropping an iron wedge into it—if the wedge floats, the coffee is too strong!] **1939** FWP *ID Lore* 243, An Idaho native was heard to say: "Damn it, this coffee is strong enough to float an iron wedge around Cape Horn!" **1946** *PADS* 6.42 **swVA,** Strong enough to bounce . . an iron wedge. **1965–70** *DARE* (Qu. H74a, . . *Coffee* . . *very strong*) 26 Infs, **scattered, but esp Sth, S Midl,** (Strong enough to) float (or hold up) an iron wedge; 9 Infs, **scattered, but esp Sth, Midl,** (Strong enough to) float a wedge; **IN3, 30, KY40, NY52, 220,** (Strong enough to) bear up an iron wedge; **AL34, GA70, MS55, NC31, TN13,** Swim a(n) iron wedge; **NJ56,** Bear a wedge; **PA13,** Carry an iron wedge; **MD30,** Strong enough to carry a wedge; **MO19,** Strong enough to hold up a iron wedge; **NJ5,** Would bear up an iron wedge. [45 of 50 total Infs comm type 4 or 5, 23 gs educ or less] **1986** Pederson *LAGS Concordance,* 1 inf, **csTN,** Strong as an iron wedge—of coffee.

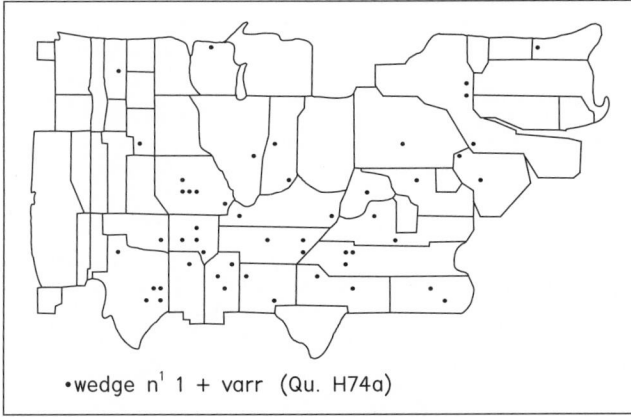

•wedge n[1] 1 + varr (Qu. H74a)

2 also *wedgie:* A large sandwich.   **chiefly seNY** Cf **submarine sandwich**

1958 in 2002 *Popik Coll.* **seNY** [Yellow Pages], *Gaito's Inn*—Specializes in Hot Wedges. **1967** *DARE* FW Addit **seNY,** *Wedge*—hero sandwich. **1968–70** *DARE* (Qu. H42, . . *[A sandwich]* . . *in a much larger, longer bun, that's a meal in itself*) [Inf **VA**88, Wedge [FW sugg];] **NY**58, Wedgie. **1977** *Washington Post* (DC) 4 Aug sec E 10/2 **seNY,** Submarine . . is the most popular name for the sandwich. . . Other names . . wedgie in Westchester County, N.Y. **1999** *DARE* File **seNY** (as of 1970s), When I was a boy, my favorite sandwich was either a steak & pepper wedge or a meatball wedge. **2000** *Ibid* **seNY,** In our town, Rye Brook/Port Chester NY (in southern Westchester County) we have always referred to a large sandwich as a *"wedge".* **2003** *NY Times* (NY) 4 June sec F 1/6 **seNY,** I have lived in Yonkers all of my life, and we refer to the hero/hoagie/grinder/submarine as a wedge. When I went to a coffee shop in Brooklyn, they had a sign listing meatballs as a sandwich special of the day, and I ordered a meatball wedge and they hadn't a clue as to what I was talking about! **2010** *DARE* File—Internet **swCT,** I must have had a roast beef wedge every other day in high school in Greenwich.

3 See **wedgie 1.**

wedge n[2] See **wage**

wedge-ass n
=**ruddy duck.**

1945 McAtee *Nomina Abitera* 32 **NW,** Ruddy Duck. . . The ruddy duck has a number of epithets based on peculiarities of its tail. . . [including] wedge-ass.

wedgie n

1 also *wedge, wedgy:* A prank involving the abrupt and rough yanking upwards of someone's belt loop, belt buckle, underwear top, or seat of the pants so that the victim's underwear becomes wedged between the buttocks.   Also called **Melvin, turkey B4, Wilma**

1986 *Capital Times* (Madison WI) 8 Oct 42/2 **CA,** [*Bloom County* comic strip:] Do you have any idea what happens when you hike up a pair of shorts and your legs are only two inches long? . . The expression is called "getting a wedgie," but I shan't elaborate. **1986** *NADS Letters* **wWA** (as of 1970s), When I was growing up . . the term 'wedgie' was used by elementary and junior high school students to refer to a *prank* . . [which] involved pulling up abruptly on another child's rear belt loop. . . The usual expression was, "to give someone a wedgie," but taunts and jeers of "Wedgie!" alone also rang in the halls. **1989–91** *DARE* File, The act of reaching into another person's belt, and either grabbing the underwear or the belt and lifting the person off the ground. . . Wedgie; wedge [reported by 47 people from 24 states]. **1990** *AmSp* 65.247, *Wedgy, wedgie*—Pulling of the cloth of one's underpants tightly between the buttocks, usu in the collocation *give someone a wedgy.* **1993** *Capital Times* (Madison WI) 28 May sec D 6/6 **RI,** If . . any of my friends had walked in, I'd have been an outcast: "Did y'hear Patinkin has his barber shampoo him? What a geek. Next time we see him, let's give him some head nouggies and a wedgie."

2 See **wedge 2.**

wedgy See **wedgie 1**

wedner See **weddinger**

weed n [Scots, Ir dial]   **now chiefly sAppalachians**
Any of var diseases affecting nursing mothers, but esp mastitis; bovine mastitis.

1850 Meigs *Observations Diseases* 19, I touched the breast. The answer was an outcry; she had a lump in her breast; she had a *weed* in her breast, and did not know it. **1868** (1874) Bedford *Principles Obstetrics* 428, *Weed or Ephemeral Fever.* . . The three principal phenomena, which mark this disease are—chill, fever, and perspiration. **1885** Ostrom *Treatise Breast* 150, A variety of inflammation of the breast called "weed" is occasionally met with about the tenth day of lactation. **1893** Coplin–Bevan *Manual Practical Hygiene* 142, The udders of cows are often the site of tubercular disease and many cases supposed to be garget or weed (simple mammitis) are in reality tuberculosis. **1896** *Med. & Surgical Reporter* 75.615 **DE,** The pain was referred to the left breast, and the patient, a young married woman, was convinced that it was a case of mammitis or "weed," as she termed it. [**1935** Hyatt *Folkl. Adams Co. IL* 128, If a woman has "weed breasts" or caked breasts, they can be cured by letting a puppy suck them.] **1953** Harder in *AmSp* 28.236 **cwTN,** The expressions, 'She has a weed in her breast and the baby can't suck' and 'A weed growed in her breast' are quite common descriptions for the inflamed mammary glands. **1954** *Harder Coll.* **cwTN,** A weed's right after calf is born if not milked soon. That is a *caked sack* that throws a fever, *milk fever.* Pump up sack, take air out. Milk all day 'fore she's cured. **1958** Browne *Pop. Beliefs AL* 12, For weed in women's breasts: Get four or five nice collard leaves, roll with a rolling pin on the table until the leaves are thoroughly bruised, put in a tin plate on a rack in a warm stove. When they are hot enough to handle, place on the breast, cover with a thick folded towel, and let the patient sleep an hour. **1982** Slone *How We Talked* 103 **eKY** (as of c1950), *Weed in the breast*—Mastitis. **1990** Cavender *Folk Med. Lexicon* 34 **csAppalachians,** *Weed*—an abscess in the breast acquired during breastfeeding that causes the breast to become hard and sore. **2000** in 2004 Montgomery–Hall *Dict. Smoky Mt. Engl.* 640, *Weed.* . . mastitis, esp during the time a newborn is nursed.

weed v
Std sense, var forms.
Past and past pple: usu *weeded;* also *wed.*

1805 (1904) White *Jrl.* 19 **MA,** I went into the garden and wed out one parsnip bed. **1807** in 1944 *Thomas Jefferson's Garden Book* 348 **VA,** Keep the thorns constantly clean wed. **1828** (1938) Bolling *Diary* 46.327 **VA,** But a small portion of corn wed. **1860** *Harper's New Mth. Mag.* 20.767 **NEng,** He . . wed out its weeds. **1896** *DN* 1.427 **c,w,swNY,** He wed the garden. **1899** (1912) Green *VA Folk-Speech* 477, He wed all of his corn before the drought. **1908** Wasson *Home from Sea* 49 **sME coast,** He started in with a garden-patch that spring, and they all said kept her wed out nice as a pin for a spell. **1936** *AmSp*

11.192 **seWY,** I wed three rows this morning. **1946** *PADS* 6.32 **eNC** (as of 1900–10), *Wed. . .* Past tense of *weed. . .* Common among farmers. **1952** Brown *NC Folkl.* 1.605, "I wed my tobacco last week."—General. Common even among educated. **1959** *VT Hist.* 27.166, *Wed . .* past tense of To *weed. . .* Rare. **1982** *Barrick Coll.* **csPA,** *Wed*—p.t. and p.p. *weed*—"I wed out my onion patch yesterday."

weed-bender n   Also *weed-monkey*   Cf **weed-sucker**
See quots.

   1933 *AmSp* 8.1.53 **Ozarks,** *Weed-bender. . .* A derisive name for the unprogressive hillman. **1945** Hubbard *Railroad Ave.* 366, *Weed bender*—Railroaders' derisive term for cowboy. **1955** in 1991 Rexroth–Laughlin *Selected Letters* 208, I was highly amused the way Marshall seemed to think he was really out in the sticks c̄ the weed monkeys. **1967** *DARE* (Qu. HH1, *Names and nicknames for a rustic or countrified person*) Inf **IL20,** Weed-bender.

weed duck n
=**mallard 1.**

   1946 Goodrich *Birds in KS* 315, Duck, . . weed—mallard, common.

weedily n, intj   Also sp *weedely*   [Cf *EDD widdle* sb[2] "A very young duck"]   Cf **wheedle, widdie** n, intj
A young chicken; used as a call to a chick.

   1966 *DARE* (Qu. K79, *How do you call the chickens to you at feeding time?*) Inf **AL34,** Weedily, weedily ['widɪlɪ] repeated. **1984** Woods *WV Was Good* 221, Little weedelies—chickens newly hatched.

weed monkey n
1 A dissolute woman; a slut; hence n *weedmonkeying* seeking the company of such women.

   1938 Stuart *Dark Hills* 163 **eKY,** You know I messed around with nearly every 'Weedmonkey' in this town. . . I got tired of going around by myself and I asked Foreman Sheff out with me. We got to 'Weedmonkeying' together. **1973** *DARE* File **Ozarks,** *Weed-monkey . .* a girl of easy virtue. Current. **2006** in 2007 *DARE* File—Internet **WV,** *Weed monkey*—this term is used in some parts of rural Appalachia to refer to a woman with whom a married man is having clandestine sexual liaisons. I once asked my West Virginia native mother "Why 'weed monkey'?" To which my mother replied, "because they do it in the weeds and he cain't bring her in the house, out of respect for his wife." **2007** *Ibid* **swWV,** I certainly don't want to be abrasive or nasty, . . but I can remember the terms "weed monkeys" and "jazzebells" normally being associated with "beer gardens!"

2 also *weed mule;* In moonshining: see quot.

   1949 *AmSp* 24.13 **KY, TN,** *Weed monkey. . .* The old car or truck used to haul supplies and to transport liquor. Also *weed mule.* Mostly Tennessee usage. 'Take that old weed monkey and go get the meal.'

3 See **weed-bender.**

weedmonkeying   See **weed monkey 1**

weed mule   See **weed monkey 2**

weed one's own row v phr   chiefly **Sth, S Midl**   Cf *hoe one's (own) row* (at **row 2**)
To take care of oneself; to mind one's own business.

   1856 in 1964 Autry *Louis DeShong Revol. Soldier* 95 **TN,** I am a boy who must weed his own row. **1859** Taliaferro *Fisher's R.* 28 **nwNC** (as of 1820s), He "axed nobody no boot, and could weed his own row, and keep it clean too—that's sartin." **1883** Macon *Uncle Gabe Tucker* 42 **AL** [Black], *Cabin Reflections*—Don't 'pen' 'pon nobody; weed your own row; paddle your own skiff. **1884** *Anglia* 7.262 **Sth, S Midl** [Black], To weed yo' own row = to mind your own business. **1885** *Disciple of Christ* 2.367 **KY,** A feller is jist about as well off to weed his own row, an' let the hull set on 'em alone. **1887** in 2003 *DARE* File—Internet **GA** [An obit in the *Middle Ga Argus*], At a very early period of his life he exhibited an ability to "weed his own row" should he ever be thrown upon his resources. **1902** Culp *Twentieth Cent. Negro Lit.* 69 **eTN,** There is to be no more special legislation in his [=the Negro's] direct interest; he will be expected more than ever "to weed his own row," and by self-endeavor continue to prove his right to be. **1963** Edwards *Gravel* 61 **eTN,** Every man must weed his own row; he must face and master his fate.

weed shiner n
A **shiner 1** (here: *Notropis texanus*).

   1943 Eddy–Surber *N. Fishes* 143, The northern weed shiner ranges through southern Minnesota, Wisconsin, northern Iowa and Illinois, and

western Michigan. **1951** Harlan–Speaker *IA Fish* 80, Northern Weed Shiner. . . As its name implies, it prefers quiet, weedy areas. **2005** *WI Nat. Resources* Aug (Internet), Weed shiners like many Wisconsin River fishes reach their northern limit of distribution in Wisconsin. **2007** *DARE* File—Internet **neMS,** Bob looks suitably guilty after losing the weed shiners and gilt darter.

weed sling n   Also *weed slinger*   **Sth, S Midl**
=**sling blade.**

   1966 *Daily Times–News* (Burlington NC) [20 May 24]/6 (newspaper-archive.com), [Advt:] Long Handle—Grass Or Weed Sling—$1.99. **1966–68** *DARE* (Qu. L37, *A hand tool used for cutting weeds and grass*) Inf **AL15,** Weed sling—sharp on both sides; **AR51,** Weed sling; **OK33, TX54,** Weed slinger; **AR52,** Weed slinger or swinging blade. **2004** *DARE* File—Internet **TX,** As punishment one time, my mother made me go clear out our garden using a weed sling. If you don't know, a weed sling is like a scythe . . basically a sharp metal edge attached to a wooden handle that you swing.

weed-sucker n   Cf **weed-bender,** *DS* HH1
See quots.

   2002 Offutt *No Heroes* 18, You won't hear these words spoken anymore: redneck, hillbilly, cracker, stump-jumper, weed-sucker, ridge-runner. **2005** *Ploughshares* Fall 87 **WY,** The chicken bones gave me enough purchase to propel myself just high and far enough . . to hit the little weed sucker right in the Adam's apple.

weedy adj   [*OED2 weedy* a.[1] 3 "Having a taste or tang of weeds"; 1867 →]   chiefly **Sth, S Midl, West**   See Map   Cf **garlicky, grassy**
Of milk: tainted by a cow's feed.

   1903 *CA Ag. Exper. Sta. Rept. for 1901–03* 121, *Weedy Flavors in Butter. . .* We spent several days . . endeavoring . . to get rid of flavors in butter which seemed traceable to weeds which the cows found in the pastures. **1950** *WELS* (*Milk that has a taste from something the cow ate in the pasture*) 1 Inf, **swWI,** Weedy. **1954** *Harder Coll.* **cwTN,** *Weedy. . .* of milk that has a taste from something the cow ate in the pasture. **1956** Ker *Vocab. W. TX* 267, *Milk that is beginning to sour. . .* weedy—abounding with weeds. [1 of 67 infs] **1958** Browne *Pop. Beliefs AL* 236, Weedy milk comes from the cow's teats rubbing against weeds. **c1960** *Wilson Coll.* **csKY,** *Weedy. . .* Taste of milk from cows that have eaten some plants not normally on their diet. **1965–70** *DARE* (Qu. K14, *Milk that has a taste from something the cow ate in the pasture . . "That milk is _____."*) 53 Infs, chiefly **Sth, S Midl, West,** Weedy; **MO37, TN24,** (Has a) weedy taste; **SC39,** Tastes weedy. **1998** in 2004 Montgomery–Hall *Dict. Smoky Mt. Engl.* 640, *Weedy. . .* Of milk: tasting of a plant a cow has eaten. . . [1 inf, **eTN**].

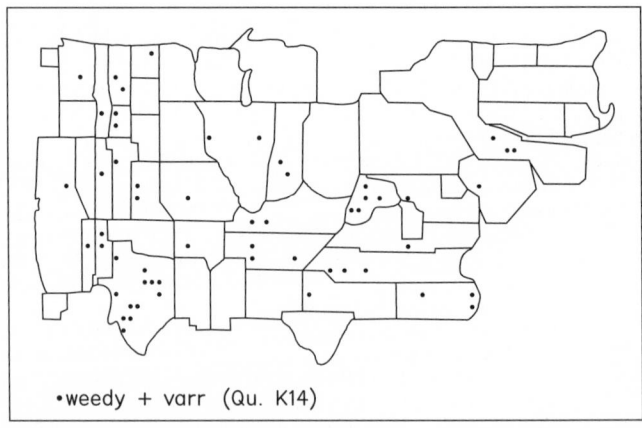

•weedy + varr (Qu. K14)

weehaw   See **weewaw A1**

wee house n   [*wee* small, perh with pun on *wee* to urinate]   Cf *DS* M21a, b
=**little house 1.**

   1981 *PADS* 67.21 **Mesabi Iron Range MN,** *Privy. . . Chick sale, little house,* and *wee house* are three infrequent Iron Range terms (1 occ. each) not recorded for other Minnesota informants.

week n[1]
A Gram form.

Pl: usu *weeks;* also, when preceded by a number, *week.* [Cf Intro "Language Changes" II.7] **esp Sth, S Midl** Cf **month B**
  1968 *DARE* FW Addit **Chesapeake Bay,** *Week*—no *s* in plural—"He's six week old." **1986** Pederson *LAGS Concordance,* 2 infs, **LA,** Three week ago; 1 inf, **seAL,** Couple of week; 1 inf, **swAL,** Two week from now; 1 inf, **nwLA,** Nearly two week; 2 infs, **FL, LA,** Six week; 1 inf, **cnAR,** Six or seven week; 2 infs, **GA, LA,** Three week; 2 infs, **AR, LA,** Two week.

B In var phrr serving to fix a date, as:

a *Sunday (a) week, today* ~, etc: A week before or after the day specified. [*OED2* at *week* sb. 5.b 1810 →] **chiefly Sth, S Midl**
  1784 in 1956 Eliason *Tarheel Talk* 304 **ce,seNC,** I shall . . leave this Detested place . . this day week. **1801** *Ibid* 304 **cnNC,** She had a son born this night week. **1831** (1940) Motte *Charleston to Harvard* 57 **SC,** My last latin recitation was to-day week. **1848** (1927) Rodman *Diary* 286 **MA,** Learned that she had not left her bed since this day week. **1874** in 1994 *TN Ancestors* 10.165 **seTN,** Our School . . will repoen [sic] Sunday week. **1930s** in 1944 *ADD* **eWV,** *Week.* . . In 'today a . . week,' 'yesterday a week,' 'tomorrow a week,' 'Monday a week,' . . a week from today, a week from yesterday . . from the coming Monday, &c. **1933** Rawlings *South Moon* 149 **nFL,** Monday-week the sign's the Two Fishes. **1934** Carmer *Stars Fell on AL* 77, Miz Nabors an' her husband are comin' over Sunday week. **1944** *PADS* 2.14 **Sth,** *(Tuesday) (a) week:* A week from the following (Tuesday). Over much of the South. Standard. **1950** *WELS* (*If you are talking about something that happened on Friday of the previous week, you might say: "She came to see me _____."*) 2 Infs, **WI,** Friday a week; 1 Inf, **csWI,** Last Friday week—occasional; 1 Inf, **cnWI,** On Friday week—occasional. **1958** Humphrey *Home from the Hill* 80 **neTX,** Hit uz Monday a week when I uz runnin' mah line. **c1960** Wilson *Coll.* **csKY,** *Friday week* (usually past but may be future). **1965** *DARE* File **cwMA** (as of c1917), Sunday a week, Thursday a week—I remember our minister's using this in making church announcement[s]. It sounded very strange. **1967–68** *DARE* FW Addit **DE2,** We're going to have a horse show here Sunday week; **cnLA,** Today week = a week from today. **1970** Tarpley *Blinky* 117 **neTX,** Northeast Texans have a variety of ways to express *a week from next Sunday,* but the most frequent choice is *Sunday week.* Among the remaining phrases, . . *next Sunday week* is used most often by rural males. *Ibid* 119, To specify *a week from last Sunday.* . . *Last Sunday week* occurs most often among rural males in the two lower educational groups. **1989** Pederson *LAGS Tech. Index* 18 **Gulf Region,** *Sunday a week [past].* . . 28 infs, Sunday week; 13 infs, Sunday a week; 3 infs, Last Sunday week. *Ibid* 19, *Sunday a week [future].* . . 301 infs, Sunday week; 17 infs, Sunday a week; 7 infs, Next Sunday week; 1 inf, Next Sunday a week; 1 inf, The Sunday week; 1 inf, This coming Sunday week; 4 infs, Tomorrow week. **1995** *Brophy Coll.* 65 **swMO** (as of c1960), *Saturday week, Saturday a week.* [A] week ago Saturday; a week from now on Saturday.

b *Sunday was* (rarely *is, 's, were*) *a week (ago),* etc: A week prior to the day specified. [*OED2* at *week* sb. 5.b 1700 →] **Sth, S Midl**
  1849 Lanman *Letters Alleghany Mts.* 22, I saw one, Monday was a week. **1887** (1967) Harris *Free Joe* 157 **cGA,** I was down in 'Zalia Monday was a week. **1921** Haswell *Daughter Ozarks* 28 (as of 1880s), Now only yesterday were a week ago I were called up in the middle of the night. **1944** *PADS* 2.14 **AL, GA, SC,** *(Tuesday) was a week ago.* . . "The first time I came to see you, Tuesday was a week ago, you were away." . . Popular. **1970** Tarpley *Blinky* 119 **neTX,** The three most frequently used phrases to specify *a week from last Sunday* are *Sunday before last, Sunday a week ago,* or *Sunday's a week ago.* . . The last of these responses is concentrated in the northeast corner of the region and in communities outside the cities. **1989** Pederson *LAGS Tech. Index* 18 **Gulf Region,** *Sunday a week [past].* . . 33 infs, Sunday was a week ago; 7 infs, Sunday's a week ago; 4 infs, Last Sunday was a week ago; 1 inf, Sunday is a week ago.

week n² See **wick** n¹

week-a-day See **weeky-day**

weeked(ness), weekid See **wicked** adj

weeky-day n Also *week-a-day* [Varr of *weekday,* prob by analogy with *workaday;* cf *EDD week* sb. 2.(1)] **chiefly SE, esp GA**
  1837 Sherwood *Gaz. GA* 72, *Provincialisms.* . . *Weeky-day,* week day. **1868** Cook *Ante Bellum* 40 **GA** [Black], Thar's no time weeky days, but

when Sunday comes . . she takes her little book. **1888** Johnston *Mr. Absalom Billingslea* 21 **GA,** You ought not have went there all dressed up and perfumed up on a weeky-day. **1899** (1912) Green *VA Folk-Speech* 478, *Week-day.* . . Weeky-day. **1922** Gonzales *Black Border* 337 **sSC, GA coasts** [Gullah glossary], *Weeky-day*—a week day. **1946** in 1958 Brewer *Dog Ghosts* 85 **TX** [Black], Wuck durin' de week-a-days an' go to chu'ch on a Sundays. **1967** *DARE* FW Addit **swAL,** *Weeky-day*—a week day or Monday through Saturday.

weelbar See **wheelbarrow 2**

weeman, weemen, weemin See **woman B1**

‡**ween** v [Cf *EDD ween* v.¹ "To whine, whimper, cry fretfully"; but perh pronc var of *weaken*]
  1926 *DN* 5.404 **Ozarks,** *Ween.* . . To exhibit fear, to weaken. "Hank he talks mighty brash, but he'll mostly ween when th' shootin' sets in."

weenie See **wienie**

we'ens See **we-uns** pron

weensy adj Also *weentsy, weenzy* [Perh *wee* infl by **teensy;** cf also Ger *winzig* tiny] Cf *eensy-weensy* (at **eentsy**), *teensy-weensy* (at **teensy**)
  Tiny—also used as a nickname.
  1889 *Good Housekeeping* 8.107, When I said I wanted dollie, in a little, weensy tone,/ He was near enough to hear me, 'less he hears by telephone. **1905** *WI Valley Leader* (Grand Rapids) 28 Sept [4]/1 (newspaperarchive.com) **LA,** I jus' turned my head a weensy bit over my shoulder. **1916** *DN* 4.331 **KS, NE, PA,** *Weensy.* . . Very small; tiny. Also *weentsy.* **1951** West *Witch Diggers* 340 **IN,** It's a picture to see him lift her up now. She's so weensy and Ferris so powerful. **1958** *Oneonta Star* (NY) 27 May [4]/2 (newspaperarchive.com), Her souvenirs from the jungle included . . Crocodile her weentsy Chihuahua. **1967–70** *DARE* (Qu. LL1, *Something very small: "I only took a _____ one."*) Infs **CA39, CT9, DC1, PA234,** Weensy; (Qu. LL2, . . *Too small to be worth much: "I don't want that little _____ potato."*) Inf **VA58,** Weensy. [4 of 5 Infs old] **1995** Karr *Liars' Club* 85 **eTX,** Grandma . . was tatting those weensy stitches. **1995** *Brophy Coll.* 82 **swMO** (as of c1960), *Weensy, weenzy.* "[T]eensy," tiny; often as a name.

weenty adj Cf **teenty**
  Tiny.
  1861 *Ladies' Repository* 21.529, You will not be very much pleased when you see this 'weenty' sheet; but it is all I have time to fill. **1892** *Century Illustr. Mag.* 45.318 **IN,** An' nen he showed us little holes / All bored there in the ground,/ An' little weenty heaps o' dust / 'At's piled there all around. **1912** (1914) Sinclair *Flying U Ranch* 16 **MT,** They stretch 'em out with two ropes—*calves,* remember! Little, weenty fellers you could pack under one arm. **1917** Ferber *Fanny Herself* 48 **WI,** "Come now! Not another minute." . . "Just to the end of this chapter! Just this weenty bit!"

weeny adj [Var of *waney* < *ween,* Engl dial var of *wane* (*EDD wane* sb.¹)]
  1895 *DN* 1.395 **CT,** *Weeny:* of boards or timbers, not of full width throughout because the saw in cutting ran out into the bark.

weenzy See **weensy**

weepin See **weapon**

weeping juniper n Also *weeping cedar*
  A **juniper 1** (here: *Juniperus flaccida*).
  1936 *Mansfield News-Jrl.* (OH) 27 Mar 27/1, The area [=west Texas]. . . includes . . the weeping cedar that occurs in few parts of the United States. **1940** Writers' Program *Guide TX* 628 **cwTX,** At 6 *m.* is a botanical rarity, a weeping juniper. . . The Chisos Mountains are said to be the only place on the North American Continent where this particular variety is known to grow. **1960** Vines *Trees SW* 35, Mexican Drooping Juniper—*Juniperus flaccida.* . . Also known under the vernacular names of Weeping Cedar, Weeping Juniper [etc]. **2006** *DARE* File—Internet, I have a beautiful four year old weeping juniper that has just had three of its main lower branches snapped by a 1000 pound steer that got loose.

weeping palm n
  A **fan palm** (here: *Washingtonia filifera*).
  1891 *Youth's Companion* 64.108, [Advt:] This King of Ornamental Plants, the Weeping or Filifera Palm, is stately and beautiful beyond description. **1929** Neal *Honolulu Gardens* 42, Washington palm, hula

palm, California fan palm, weeping palm [etc]. **1960** *NV State Jrl.* (Reno) 14 Feb Family Weekly sec 12/1, [Advt:] Weeping Palm—A fine Showy Window Palm.

weeping spruce n

1 A **hemlock 2** (here: usu *Tsuga canadensis*).

1862 *Friends' Intelligencer* 19.461 **PA,** The weeping spruce with its long arms bending mournfully down and wailing with every passing breeze. **1878** *Forest & Stream* 11.24 **NY,** Weeping Spruce, most picturesque and characteristic, with pendent branches hugging the stem in grotesque forms. **1897** Sudworth *Arborescent Flora* 45 **CA,** *Tsuga pattonia* [=*T. mertensiana*]. . . Weeping Spruce. **1930** Sievers *Amer. Med. Plants* 33, *Tsuga canadensis*. . . Other common names.—Hemlock spruce, weeping spruce [etc]. **1971** Krochmal *Appalachia Med. Plants* 258, *Tsuga canadensis*. . . Common Names: Eastern hemlock, . . weeping spruce.

2 A **spruce 1** (here: *Picea breweriana*).

1897 Sudworth *Arborescent Flora* 41, *Picea breweriana*. . . Weeping Spruce. **1912** *Oakland Tribune* (CA) 17 Mar 26/1, John McLaren, superintendent of Golden Gate Park, . . has finally found on the slopes of Mt. Shasta a tree he has been seeking for a long time. It is the weeping spruce and it is considered a fine botanical product for decorative or ornamental purposes. **1967** *Times–Std.* (Eureka CA) 12 July 15/1 **swOR,** This region is home of the pre-ice age tree, the Brewer, or weeping spruce.

weepn, weepon, weepun See **weapon**

we-erunses pron [Prob by analogy with **yourns's**] Cf **we-uns's**

1931 *PMLA* 46.1320 **sAppalachians,** Look at these forms!: "we-erunses" and "you-erunses."

weesh See **wish A3**

weevil n esp **TX, OK**
=**boll weevil.**

c**1939** in 1984 Lambert-Franks *Voices* 235 **OK,** Another thing that'll knock a weevil [a new, inexperienced worker] is the difference in the gas that comes off the oil. **1966** *DARE* Tape **OK**29, Now, you don't call a new hand a roughneck. . . Well, you call him a worm or you call him a weevil. Now, years ago, we called 'em weevils because the boll weevils in east Texas used to eat up the cotton down there, so we called 'em boll weevils. . . Now they call 'em worms. **1969** *DARE* (Qu. HH3, *A dull and stupid person*) Inf **TX**72, Weevil—especially a greenhorn in the oil fields; (Qu. HH15, *A very inexperienced person, one who is just learning how to do a new thing*) Inf **TX**72, Weevil—on ranch or in oil fields. **2002** Proulx *That Old Ace* 116 **TX,** Buckskin Bill reminded them of oil, the boom-and-bust days when a ranch kid could hire on as a weevil or roustabout, work his way up to tool dresser and eventually driller.

weevily wheat n

A children's ring game similar to **needle's eye;** a refrain in the game.

1916 *DN* 4.331 **KS,** *Weevily wheat*. . . Used in a game played by boys and girls who promenade in circles, by couples, singing: "Your weevily wheat aint fit to eat / And neither is your barley;/ With many a beau that I let go / Because I wanted you." **1937** Wilder *On Plum Creek* 236 **MN** (as of c1875), Pa tuned the fiddle and . . filled the house with "Oh, Charley he's a fine young man /. . . / I don't want none of your weevily wheat,/ I don't want none of your barley,/ I want fine flour in half an hour,/ To bake a cake for Charley!" . . Laura's feet were dancing. **1937** NE Univ. *Univ. Studies* 37.114 [Terms from play-party songs], Weevily Wheat. **1959** *Western Folkl.* 18.238 **WY** (as of c1898), *Play-Party Song:* "*Weevily Wheat*". . . Come down this way with your weevily wheat,/ Come down this way with your barley,/ Come down this way with your weevily wheat / To make a cake for Charley. *Ibid* **CO** (as of c1900), I don't want none of your weevily wheat,/ I don't want none of your barley./ Take some flour in the course of an hour / To bake a cake for Charley. **2008** *DARE* File—Internet **TX,** If I could choose my very favorite game to teach—it would be "Weevily Wheat"! This is such a fun game, and useful for reinforcing the math facts!

weewaw adj, adv, v [Engl dial; cf *EDD* wee-wow]

A As adj.

1 also *weehaw, weewary, weewoppy, wheejaw, wheewhaw;* for addit varr see quots: Askew, crooked, uneven; shaky, unstable; rarely adv *weewaw* crookedly, unevenly. **scattered, but esp NEng**

1894 (1934) Robinson *Danvis Folks* 98 **VT,** The chair gave a creak

ominous of collapse, and he carefully readjusted it to its complete if precarious support of his weight. "Seems 's 'ough this 'ere chair was a leetle mite more weewaw 'an it useter be." **1895** *DN* 1.395 **seMA,** *Weewary:* "When calico is torn, the torn edge is called weewary." **1909** *DN* 3.418 **nME,** *Wee waw*. . Crooked, out of plumb. **1911** *DN* 3.548 **NE,** *Wheejaw*. . Askew, awry. "That stove is set wheejaw." **1913** *DN* 4.6 **ME,** *Weewaw*. . Askew. **1914** [see **B** below]. **1916** *DN* 4.331 **KS,** *Weehaw*. . Askew, awry. "He had the shed made all weehaw." **1954** Forbes *Rainbow* 315 **NEng,** All those wagons and rigs that came late were hitched all wee-waw over the place, no order to it. **1959** *VT Hist.* 27.166 **nwVT,** *Wee waw*. . Rickety; unstable; Rare. **1968–69** *DARE* (Qu. KK70, *Something that has got out of proper shape:* "*That house is all* _____.") Inf **IN**45, Wheewhaw; (Qu. MM13, *The table was nice and straight until he came along and knocked it* _____) Inf **IL**30, Weewaw. **1975** Gould *ME Lingo* 312, *Weewaw*—Aslant and askew, not plumb or vertical. **1982** *Smithsonian Letters* **neVA** (as of 1957), Wee-woppy means shaky, unstable, or rickety, like a table with one short leg, or sloppy construction where the parts are inadequately joined. **1995** *Brophy Coll.* 83 **swMO** (as of c1960), *Wheewhaugh*. [C]rooked, out of plumb.

2 also *wee-waw-y;* Of a person: somewhat unwell, "under the weather." **NEast**

1932 *DN* 6.284 **swCT,** *Wee-waw-y*. Sick at one's stomach. **1941** *LANE* Map 459 (*Emaciated, peaked*) 1 inf, **ceMA,** Weewaw [wiwɔ]. **1965** *DARE* File **cMA** (as of c1914), *Weewaw*. . . Pale, unsteady. Of a person who had just recovered from an illness: "She still looks pretty weewaw." You could *feel* weewaw, too. **1967** *Ibid* **csMA,** *Wee-waw,* adj. Pale and listless, suggesting the onset of an illness. 'He looks a little wee-waw today.' It's an expression used by my parents in Southbridge, Mass., and more usually applied to children than to adults. **1972** *NYT Article Letters* **cNY,** If grandmother felt weak after an illness, she was "wee-waw".

B As verb.

Also *weewow, wheehaw:* To set askew; to proceed unsteadily; fig, to vacillate; to perplex or distract; hence ppl adj *weewawed* askew, crooked. **esp NEast** Cf **gee-haw v 3, gee-hawed, yew-yaw**

1890 Whitney *Ascutney St.* 42 **NEng,** I—can—*not*—bear being—wee-wawed! Pulled—first one way—and then the other,—you know, in my work—or in my—feelings! **1898** Westcott *Harum* 276 **cNY,** We run slap onto one o' them dum'd road-engines that had got wee-wawed putty near square across the track. **1914** *DN* 4.82 **ME, nNH,** *Wee-waw, adj.* Shaky, loose, rickety. "The ole waggin was weewawin' all over the road." **1921** *Harper's Mth. Mag.* May 802 **Sth,** He [=a lawyer] said, with exasperation: "Old Mrs. Emerson was in again today, wee-wawing about her will. Can't make up her mind to cut off her daughter-in-law, and can't make up her mind to leave her anything." **1927** *AmSp* 2.366 **cwWV,** *Wheehawed* . . crooked. "That picture hangs all wheehawed." *Ibid* 3.135 **eME,** A man or woman who vacillated or was perennially undecided was called "whiffle minded," whiffle meaning to shift, turn, change from one course to another. "Wee-waw" or "wee-wow," to be shaky or wobbly, was used in the same way. **1967–69** *DARE* (Qu. KK70, *Something that has got out of proper shape: "That house is all* _____.") Infs **NY**88, 219, Weewawed; **OR**3, Wheehawed.

wee-waw-y See **weewaw A2**

weewoppy See **weewaw A1**

weewow See **weewaw B**

weezledy adj [Prob *weasled* (at **weasle**) + *-y;* cf **fadedy** and Intro "Language Changes" III.1]
=**weasly.**

1943 Chase *Jack Tales* 98 **wNC** (as of 1880s), Jack sat down under that oak tree and had just reached in his little poke for the ash cake when there stood that weezledy old man.

weezly See **weasly**

weh See **where A3**

weigh dance n Also *pay-your-weigh dance* Cf **waistline party, weight social**

A public dance, usu a fundraiser for an organization, to which one pays an admission in proportion to one's (or one's partner's) weight.

1923 *Ogden Std.–Examiner* (UT) 2 Jan [12]/3 (newspaperarchive.com), For the benefit of the missionaries in the Samoa Islands, a "weigh dance" will be given. . . Each lady will be weighed at the door as she enters and later in the evening the men [sic] will draw for his lady. He pays his ticket according to the number of pounds the lady he draws weighs. **1939** *Monessen Daily Independent* (PA) 15 June 4/6, A Penny-a-Pound or Pay-Your-Weigh dance is to be held Wednesday. **1966** *DARE* (Qu. FF1, . . *A kind of group meeting called a 'social' or 'sociable'. . . [What goes on?]*) Inf **NM9**, Weigh dances—boy pays for pounds you weigh.

weight v

Intr: To have (a specified weight).

c1938 in 1970 Hyatt *Hoodoo* 2.1812 **GA** [Black], A man dat *weights* about 150 pounds prob'bly may be able to use his *nature* fo' 1500 times in life. **1941** Stuart *Men of Mts.* 313 **eKY,** I don't weight but one hundred and twenty pounds now.

weight social n Cf weigh dance

A social gathering, usu a fundraiser for an organization, to which one pays an admission in proportion to one's weight.

1888 *Van Wert Republican* (OH) 1/6, A grand weight social will be given . . by the Woman's Baptist Aid Society. Proceeds to be used to help the building of the new church. **1906** *DN* 3.163 **nwAR,** *Weight social. . .* A party to which one pays an admission fee proportioned to one's weight. **1908** *Syracuse Herald* (NY) 23 Jan 2/4, Weight Social To-night. . . A musical and literary programme will be given. **1939** *Centralia Daily Chron.* (WA) 13 Mar 3/4, Plans were made for a weight social to be held . . at the . . school-house.

weiner See wiener

weinie See wienie

we-ins See we-uns pron

weir n Usu |wɪr, 'wɪə(r)|; also chiefly Atlantic |wɛr, 'wɛə(r), 'wæə(r)|; rarely |'waɪɚ, wɝ| Also sp ware, wear, wyre [Both the [wɪr] and [wɛr] types appear to be old; the latter was the dominant form in the 18th cent as indicated in the dictionaries of Johnson (implicitly), Sheridan, and Walker. *OED2* has exx of the sp wire a1722 →, but remarks that this variant is "difficult to account for."] Cf wear-hen

Std senses, var forms. Note: As the sp *wear* is ambiguous and was once std, only exx that indicate (implicitly or explicitly) a non-std pronc are given here.

1634 in 1904 Ipswich Hist. Soc. *Pub.* 13.24 **MA,** Mr. Nicholas Easton shall have libertye to build a Mill and Ware upon the Town River. **1768** in 1946 *Archives of MD* 63.143, [An act] for preventing the Erecting of Fish Wares. **1800** in 1848 Bolton *Hist. Co. Westchester* 2.398 **NY,** Here we find 18 obstructions, such as small rapids, fish wares, stony, &c. **1828** Webster *Amer. Dict., Wēar, n.* . . often written *wier* [sic]. [*DARE* Ed: The pronc indicated is the same as that for the verb *wear.*] **1899** (1912) Green *VA Folk-Speech* 478, Weir. . . Pronounced *ware.* **1906** Rideout *Beached Keels* 69 **NEng,** They was forty in that wyre if they was a fish. **1913** *DN* 4.58 **seMA,** Weir [waɪr]. **1924** *DN* 5.288 Cape Cod **MA,** 'Weir' [is pronounced] as tho it were 'wire'. **1940** in 1942 White *One Man's Meat* 237 **ME,** Fish weir is pronounced fish ware. **1945** *AmSp* 20.76, *The Pronunciation of 'Weir'*—This spelling . . is given preference by dictionaries, but I have not heard the assigned pronunciations except from the book-learned. My attention was first drawn to the colloquial pronunciation at Matinicus Island, Maine (1915), through the term 'wear-hen' applied to Holboell's grebe because it frequented fish-wears. . . I have heard the V's of stones, used so commonly in the Susquehanna River of Pennsylvania as the wings of eel-traps, also called wears. Thus for a considerable distance through the Atlantic states, a pronunciation is, or has been, in use, the prevalence of which would scarcely be imagined from comment in the dictionaries. **1966–69** *DARE* (Qu. O3, *A small platform sticking out into the water where boats can tie up, and people can get into them*) Inf **MA30**, Weirs [waɪjəz]; (Qu. P13, . . *Ways of fishing . . besides the ordinary hook and line*) Inf **ME22**, Weirs [wɝz]; [**MA56**, Weirs [wijəz]—we call 'em traps around here; **NJ39**, Nets used are fyke, weir [wɪr]]. **1975** Gould *ME Lingo* 312, Weir—Pronounced ware. **1981** Pederson *LAGS Basic Materials,* 1 inf, **cMS,** Weir [wæ^ɛɚ]. **2002** in 2007 *DARE* File—Internet **NC** [*Washington Daily News* (NC) 7 June], He stood on shore and pointed out a line where there are fish wares and stuff like that.

weke n HI

A goatfish 1; see quots.

1926 Pan-Pacific Research Inst. *Jrl.* 1.1.10, Mullidae. The Surmullets. Weke. *Ibid,* Mulloides pflugeri [=*Mulloidichthys pfluegeri*]. . . Weke Ula-Ula. *Ibid,* Mulloides samoensis [=*Mulloidichthys flavolineatus*]. . . Weke A'a. *Ibid,* Upeneoides arge [*Upeneus a.*] . . Weke Pueo; Weke

Pahulu. **1975** Sunset *HI Guide* 144 [Game fish species], Weke . . goat fish. **1978** Tinker *Fishes HI* 230, *The Band-tailed Goat Fish*—Also known as We-ke pu-e-o, We-ke pa-hu-lu, and We-ke a-hu-lu. *Ibid, The Golden-banded Goat Fish*—Also known as We-ke and We-ke 'u-la. *Ibid* 231, *Pfluger's Goat Fish*—Also known as We-ke 'u-la. *Ibid, The Samoan Goat Fish*—Also known as We-ke, We-ke-'a, and We-ke-'a-'a. **1979** Bushnell *Stone of Kannon* 394 **HI,** Five minutes later, . . he hooked a weke. **1996** *Honolulu Star-Bulletin* (HI) 19 Aug (Internet), Weke have one or more stripes running the entire length of the fish's body. Four of Hawaii's nine native species of goatfish are called weke, some with variations such as weke'a, weke-ula, or weke pueo.

Welch drake See Welsh drake

Welchman See Welshman

well n Also *hay well, well hole* esp NEast See Map Cf hay hole 1, pitch hole 2, *scuttle hole* (at scuttle) =hay chute.

1851 *Genesee Farmer* 12.42 **NY,** At B is a hay-well, or hole in the floor, with a curb round it, through which the hay is thrown into the feeding passage in the cow stable below. . . This well-hole acts also as a ventilator. **1965–70** *DARE* (Qu. M5, . . *The hole for throwing hay down below*) Infs **MS66**, **NJ16**, 20, 56, 67, **NY62**, **OH66**, **WI58**, Well; **CT7**, **DE3**, Well [FW sugg]; **NY20**, Hay well [FW sugg]; **RI12**, Hay well; **VA40**, Well hole. [12 of 13 Infs old]

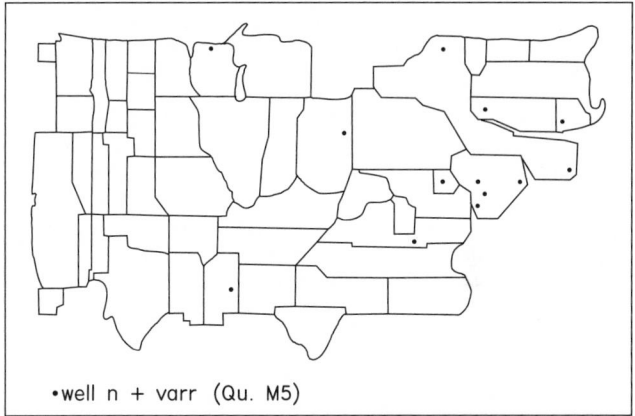

•well n + varr (Qu. M5)

well intj Usu |wɛ(ə)l|; also esp NEng, Sth, S Midl |wɑl| Pronc-spp waal, wael, wal(l), walp, welp

Std senses, var forms.

1844 *Yale Lit. Mag.* 9.16 **sNEng,** Two rifles! wal! I never heerd the like in all my born days. **1848** Lowell *Biglow* 147 **'Upcountry' MA,** Wal, *well;* spoken with great deliberation, and sometimes with the *a* very much flattened, sometimes (but more seldom) very much broad-ened. **1878** *Appletons' Jrl.* 5.415 **NEng,** Wal, I s'pose you don't come from West Brookfield? **1887** (1892) Hinman *Corporal Si Klegg* 188, "Wall," said Si, with an air of resignation. **1907** in 1953 Botkin-Harlow *Treas. Railroad Folkl.* 156 **TX,** Waal, then he's got to go on to Victoria to get it, I reckon. **1921** Haswell *Daughter Ozarks* 22 (as of 1880s), Wal no, I don't reckin' ye do have to ask no permit. **1931** *PMLA* 46.1304 **sAppalachians,** Wall (well), that exceeds the measure. **1935** Sandoz *Jules* 67 **wNE** (as of 1880–1930), Wall, I ain't stayin' to stir dirt hard as dobe bricks. **1945** Taylor *Proof* 39 **eMA,** "Wa-el," Asey drawled, "I don't know just what you *would* call it, now." **1946** *AmSp* 21.90, If the speaker is American, and will observe himself when he utters *well* . . (as in 'Well'—pause—'what do we do next?'), he will often discover that he has used *welp,* with unfinished *p.* **1959** *VT Hist.* 27.166, *Well* [wɑl]: interj. Occasional. Rural areas. **1977** *UpCountry* July 7 **Martha's Vineyard MA,** Walp, goin' over to America Thursday to get my damn teeth fixed agin'.

well bucket See bucket 2b

well hole See well n

wellup, welp n See whelp

welp intj See well intj

Welsh drake n Also *Welch drake, Welsh duck* =gadwall.

1844 Giraud *Birds Long Is.* 304 **seNJ,** At Egg Harbor a few [gadwall] are seen almost every spring and autumn, and are there known by the name of "Welsh Drake[1] or "German Duck." **1844** DeKay *Zool. NY*

2.343 **NJ,** In New Jersey it is called the *Welsh* or *German Duck.* **1898** Elliot *Wild Fowl* 113, In North America it [=the gadwall] is known by various names, those most commonly employed being, Creek Duck, . . Welch Drake, German Duck [etc].

Welshman n   Also *Welchman*

Any of three closely related fishes: usu the **largemouth bass,** but also the **smallmouth bass** or a **spotted bass 1** (here: *Micropterus punctulatus*).

1709 (1967) Lawson *New Voyage* 162 **NC, SC,** The brown Pearch, which some call *Welch-men,* are the largest sort of Pearches that we have, and very firm, white and sweet Fish. These grow to be larger than any Carp, and are very frequent in every Creek and Pond. **1884** Goode *Fisheries U.S.* 1.401 **NC,** On the Tar River of North Carolina it [=the largemouth bass] is called "Chub," and on the Neuse "Welshman." **1935** Caine *Game Fish* 10, Southern Small-mouthed Black Bass or Spotted Small-mouthed Black Bass—*Micropterus pseudoplites* [=*M. punctulatus*]. . . Welshman. **1978** *Outdoor Life* Sept 56, Scientists call the large-mouth bass Micropterus salmoides. . . But there are many lesser-known names too. Some of them are . . welchman, chub [etc].

Welsh onion n

An **onion** n B (here: *Allium fistulosum*).

1839 *Bangor Daily Whig & Courier* (ME) 31 July [2]/1 (newspaperarchive.com), Mr Beacroft, the talented gardener on the estate of Mr E French in this city, has what he calls the Welsh Onion, a hardy plant that endures our winters in the open ground. **1863** Burr *Field & Garden* 147, The Welsh Onion is a hardy perennial from Siberia. **1910** *Indiana Democrat* (PA) [20 July] 3/2 (newspaperarchive.com), The Welsh onion is much better for an extra early green onion than the old Egyptian or winter onion. **1968** *DARE* (Qu. I5, . . *Kind of onions that keep coming up without replanting year after year*) Inf **CT**4, Welsh onion. **1986** *Seed Savers Exchange* Harvest ed 98, *Allium fistulosum*—bunching, Japanese bunching or Welsh onion.

wemes pron   [The *-m-* almost certainly represents *am,* which at one time was the form of *be* used regularly on Cape Cod for all personal pronouns except those of the 3rd pers sing (see **be** v **B2a(1)** and cf *EDG* §435); for a similar absorption of *am,* cf *I'm am, I'm is* (at **be** v **B2c**).]

We.

1924 *DN* 5.286 **Cape Cod MA,** In the village of Wellfleet it is possible to hear "Youmes goin' the wrong way, mister, wemes'l show you the road." [**1925** *DN* 5.342 **Nfld,** We'm 'll be out a smack yet.] [**1931** *AmSp* 6.291 **nLabrador,** We'ms got to have old trained dogs, isn't us Bert?]

wen n   Usu |wɛn|; also |wɪn|, rarely |wen| Pronc-spp *win(d)* [*OED2* c1000 → (marked as obs in general application to swellings on the human body, but not in ref to a sebaceous cyst or a goiter). The forms *win(d)* may be infl by *windgall* a soft swelling on a horse's leg.] **chiefly Nth, N Midl, esp nOH**   See Map   Cf **bone felon**

A lump or swelling under the skin.

1845 Judd *Margaret* 445 **swME** (as of 18th cent), Alas for the persons of quality who have wens on their necks! **1904** *Black Cat* 10.40, On her left elbow was a wen which made that arm look nearly twice as large as the other. **1909** *DN* 3.389 **eAL, wGA,** *Win.* . . A wen. Sometimes *wind.* **1929** Sale *Specialist* 7 **IL,** Just ripples on / 'Bout the home fokes, or doggone / Barnyard scene, some ginny hens / Hair-lipped fokes an' family wens. **1965–70** *DARE* (Qu. BB30, . . *A hard, painful swelling [often on a finger] that seems to come from deep under the skin*) 24 Infs, **chiefly NEast, Gt Lakes,** Wen; **CT**11, Wen—calcium deposits; **MD**32, Wen [wɛn]; **MA**6, Wen—hard formation under skin; **SC**19, Wen [wɪn]; **WA**28, Wen—movable ball under skin; (Qu. X59, . . *The small infected pimples that form usually on the face*) Infs **MN**15, **NY**179, Wens; (Qu. BB33a, . . *A swelling under the skin, bigger than a pimple, that comes to a head*) Infs **IL**126, **OH**95, Wen; **NY**73, Wen—don't come to a head—a little bunch under the skin; **PA**4, Wen [wɪn]; (Qu. BB33b, . . *A swelling under the skin—if it is very big or serious*) Infs **IL**126, **MI**13, **WA**1, Wen; **MI**89A, Wen—a lycoma [*DARE* Ed: sic for *lipoma*]; **MO**29, Wen—a large hickey. [29 of 38 total Infs old] **1987** Grafton *D Is for Deadbeat* 23 **CA,** She had a wen on the side of her nose about the size of a kernel of popcorn. **1995** McCormack *Fields Pastures* 90 **cwAL** (as of 1960s), "It's gotta be a wind, I'm tellin' ye!" declared another. Everyone there except the new vet knew that a "wind" (as in "a cold northwest wind") was just a colloquialism refer-

ring to a swollen place somewhere on an animal. It might be an abscess, a tumor, or a cyst.

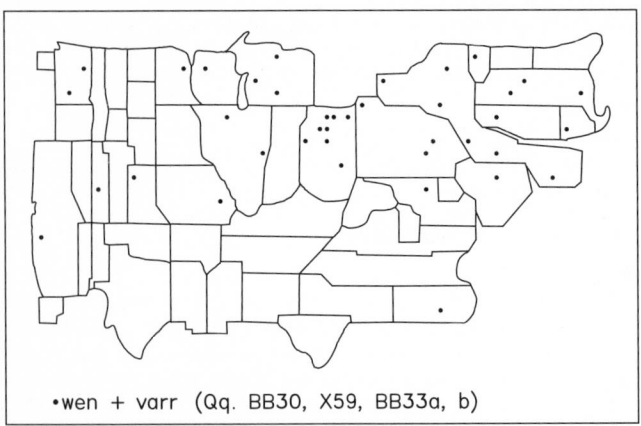

•wen + varr (Qq. BB30, X59, BB33a, b)

we'ns pron   See **we-uns** pron

we'ns' adj   See **we-uns'** adj

we'nses   See **we-uns's** adj

were   See **be A5**

werman   See **woman A3**

wernet   See **walnut**

werrit   See **worrit** v **2**

werry adv   See **very**

werry v, n   See **worry A2**

wersh   See **wash**

we's   See **we** adj

Wesaw   See **Wesort**

weself pron   Also *weselves, wesels*   **Gullah**   Cf **self B**

Ourself, ourselves.

1853 Simms *Sword & Distaff* 76 **SC** [Black], Better we bury wese'f up to de neck in de swamp. **1892** (1893) Botume *First Days* 54 **seSC** (as of 1864) [Gullah], Us all larn to do leetle tings for wesels. **1922** Gonzales *Black Border* 338 **sSC, GA coasts** [Gullah], We'self—ourselves. **1949** Turner *Africanisms* 281 **seSC** [Gullah], This is the way we enjoys weselves in the summer time.

Wesort n   Also *Wesaw*   Cf **brass ankle, Croatan, dominicker 7, Melungeon**

A member of a racially mixed group of people centered in southern Maryland.

1908 *Catholic Missions* 2.10 **MD,** In the missions of Charles County there is a peculiar race called "We Sorts," who are classed as colored but who claim to be of Indian origin. **1928** Clements *Origins Clements-Spalding Families* 14 **swMD,** Here and there a dilapidated cottage mostly occupied by that mongrel race known, I was told, by the name of "We-Sorts." This mixture of Piscataway Indian, negro and . . whites, is descended from twenty families of Proctors and Swanns recorded in the Census of 1790 as free mulattoes. They cannot associate socially with the whites and will not associate with the negroes, but keep in a little world of their own and having no distinguishing name, refer to themselves as We-Sorts, hence the cant name. **1940** Writers' Program *Guide MD* 21, The Jesuit missionaries . . made a fair number of converts among the natives, a few of whose descendants, somewhat mixed in blood, still survive in Charles and Prince Georges counties under the name of We-Sorts. **1963** Berry *Almost White* 36, Tradition has it that the Wesorts of Maryland got their name from one of their own number, "Aunt" Sallie Thompson, who, around 1880, began using the expression "we sort of people" in order to set her group off from the recently freed Negroes. **1970** *DARE* (Qu. HH29a, . . *People of mixed blood—part Indian*) Inf **DC**11, Wesaw—in reference to families around Brandywine, Maryland, who married within the family to keep the skin coloring fair and the hair straight; they could be part Negro, or part Indian; (Qu. HH29b, . . *People of mixed blood—part Negro*) Inf **DC**11, Wesaw. **1979** *Eve. Capital* (Annapolis MD) 29 Dec 11/1, He is one of the Brandywine People. . . also called Wesorts. . . A budding Indian awareness movement in the area has attracted many Wesorts, especially to their roots in the Piscataway tribe. **2003** in 2007 *DARE* File—Internet **sMD,** I grew up with the Wesorts of Southern Maryland. They were of mixed race: black, American Indian and white. One of them was the principal of a local, public elementary school. He wouldn't let his daughter date a black man from D.C.! **2004** Randers-Pehrson *For My Father* 309 **sMD,** (as of 1940s), The Proctors were a minority group in the region: sometimes they were known as Newmans. Proctor and Newman were their most frequently occurring family names. They looked Portuguese to me, with their bright skin and shiny black hair. . . Their name for themselves as a group was *We-Sorts,* and they tended to describe themselves a[s] "a separate nation."

western   See **western sandwich**

western birch n

Std: a birch (here: *Betula occidentalis*).   Also called **gray birch c, mountain ~ 1, paper ~, red ~ 3, river ~, swamp ~ 3, water ~**

western chinquapin   See **chinquapin B3**

western coffee n

=**cascara 1.**

1897 Sudworth *Arborescent Flora* 299 **CA, OR,** *Rhamnus purshiana* [=*Frangula p.*] . . Common Names. . . Western Coffee.

western daisy n

A plant of the genus *Astranthium* (usu *A. integrifolium*) native chiefly to the South Midland.   Also called **daisy 2d**

1891 *Century Dict.* 6881, Western daisy, a plant, *Bellis integrifolia* [= *Astranthium integrifolium*], found from Kentucky southwestward, the only species of the true daisy genus native in the United States. **1950** *Daily Oklahoman* (Oklahoma City OK) 2 Apr sec A 11/5, Western daisy, wild mint, wild onion, and other weeds . . were fed to the cows. **2007** (acc) U.S. Dept. Ag. *Plants Database* (Internet), *Astranthium integrifolium* . . entireleaf western daisy.

western omelet n

=**Denver omelet.**

[**1927** *Decatur Herald* (IL) 10 Nov 17/8, [Vaudeville act:] *Joe & Pete Michon* in "A Western Omelette."] **1931** *Chron.–Telegram* (Elyria OH) 27 Nov 6/7, [Local restaurant menu item:] Western Omelet. **1967** *DARE* FW Addit **cnNY,** A western omelet or sandwich (egg, ham, pepper, onion) is called a Denver sandwich or omelet in the west. **2006** *DARE* File—Internet, Southern U.S. Cuisine— Western Omelet. . . Make this omelet in smaller portions for Western sandwiches. [Recipe includes eggs, green bell pepper, chopped onion, ham.]

western sandwich n   Also *western*

A sandwich consisting of a **western omelet** between slices of bread.

1908 *San Antonio Light* (TX) 5 Aug 3/7, *Western Sandwiches.* Chop fine uncooked bacon, green peppers and onions; . . season with salt and a little pepper. Fry until bacon is done, then scramble in two eggs. Place between white or rye bread. This makes a delicious sandwich. **1911** *Syracuse Herald* (NY) 12 Sept 5/3, *Western Sandwich.* Blend 1 c. of chopped . . ham with 1 well beaten egg, season with a very little grated onion; saute in hot dripping made from the fat of the ham; place between toasted bread that has been dipped in a little hot milk, then butter and set in a hot oven for a few minutes to dry out. **1930** *Havre Daily News* (MT) 18 Oct 3/5, *Sandwiches Men Like.* . . *Western Sandwich.* . . onion . . ham . . eggs. . . Cook . . to get firm. . . Spread between slices of buttered bread. **1967** [see **western omelet**]. **1968** *DARE* (Qu. H42, . . [A sandwich] . . in a much larger, longer bun, that's a meal in itself) Inf **NY**72, Western—they're eggs and onion, and beef and a lot of everything. **1985** *DARE* File **Denver CO,** The chef at the Brown Palace Hotel . . says that out here a "Denver" is an omelet made with ham, green peppers and onions. A "Western" is a sandwich: it has the same ingredients as the "Denver," but is prepared in such a way that it can be eaten between two pieces of toast. **2006** [see **western omelet**].

western wheatgrass   See **wheatgrass 4, 5**

western white pine   See **white pine 3, 4, 9**

western yellow pine n

Usu the **ponderosa pine 1,** but also **Jeffrey pine.**

1857 U.S. War Dept. *Rept. Explor. Railroad* (Botany) 6.36, *Pinus ponderosa.* . . The western yellow pine. **1903** *Reno Eve. Gaz.* (NV) 25 Feb [4]/2 (newspaperarchive.com), Nearly 600 pounds of seed, principally western yellow pine, red cedar, and jack pine, has been collected for

planting in the spring. **1924** Hawkins *Trees & Shrubs* 15 **nwWY,** Western Yellow Pine (Pinus ponderosa and Pinus scopulorum). **1952** Peattie *Black Hills* 23 **SD,** Rock pine, bull pine, western yellow pine—but ponderosa is their right name, according to the scientific folk who should know. **1999** *Mt. Democrat* (Placerville CA) 30 Sept sec A 7/5, The Ponderosa Pine (also known as the Western Yellow Pine).

wet adj

1 Of livestock: stolen.   **SW, esp TX**   Cf **wetback**

1888 in 2006 (acc) Lexis–Nexis Legal Research *State Case Law: TX* (Internet), The conviction in this case was for the theft of a horse. . . Defendant then said: "We have got two wet horses, and we want you to run them off for us; we will give you one of them if you will run them off." **1922** in 2007 (acc) *Ibid: OK,* A. First I asked him if he wanted to buy some cattle of my own, and the next time I saw him I decided to keep mine, and I said I had some stuff in view— . . Q. What do you mean by stuff? A. Wet stuff; stolen property. **1929** Dobie *Vaquero* 81 **TX,** The code of these ranchers . . forbade stealing from a neighbor, but it generally permitted trading in "wet" horses—horses stolen in Mexico and smuggled across the Rio Grande. **1940** *AmSp* 15.222 **cwTX,** At all events, if cattle 'stray' from Chihuahua or Coahuila into Texas, these cattle are pronounced 'wet.' **1956** *AmSp* 31.100 **SW** [Smuggler's argot], The *chili chasers,* border patrolmen, ride horses when chasing *wet* cattle across arroyos or *biyookies* (a distortion of *bayous*).

2 Of a cow: lactating, fresh.   **chiefly Sth, West**   See Map

1904 *Galveston Daily News* (TX) 24 Aug 8/3, *Exports—Foreign.* . . Per steamship Carmelina: 650 wet cows . . ; 650 calves . . ; 650 dry cows. **1915** Beach *Heart Sunset* 170 **TX,** The bulls were quarrelsome, the steers were stubborn, and the wet cows were distracted. **1935** *AmSp* 10.272 [Stockyard language], *Wet.* Having milk in the udder. The price of *wet* stock is usually cut. **1953** in 2007 (acc) Lexis–Nexis Legal Research *State Case Law: NM* (Internet), The discovery . . of some wet cows with enlarged bags . . , two of which cows . . mothered the two calves caught in the roundup. **1965–70** *DARE* (Qu. K1, *A cow that is giving milk is a _____*) 19 Infs, **chiefly Sth, West,** Wet cow; **GA**80, Wet cattle; (Qu. K10, *Words used about a cow that is going to have a calf*) Inf **CO**33, Going to be wet; (Qu. K11, *When a cow has a calf . . she _____*) Inf **CO**33, Is a wet cow. **1968** Adams *Western Words* 344, *Wet stuff*—A cowboy's name for cows that are giving milk. **1995** McCormack *Fields Pastures* 41 **cwAL** (as of 1960s), The wet cows, those nursing calves, were being cut into one pen.

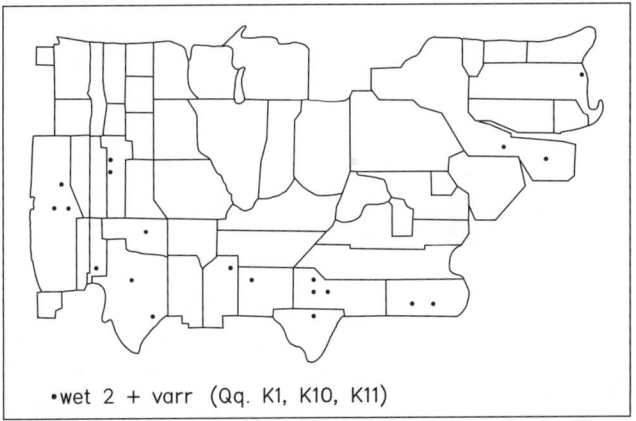

•wet 2 + varr (Qq. K1, K10, K11)

wetback n   Rarely *wet*   **orig chiefly TX, SW; now more widespread**   Cf **wet 1**

An illegal immigrant to the US, orig and esp a Mexican who crosses the Rio Grande; see quots.

1920 *Galveston Daily News* (TX) 15 Feb 12/5, Congress was introduced to a brand new term when a witness before the house immigration committee . . told how the Texas land owners secured "wet backs." These are Mexicans brought across the border at points where there are no immigration inspectors. . . They are supposed to have swam the Rio Grande, and their backs are still wet when they reach the plantation. **1948** Cain *Moth* 204 **CA,** To me, an American's as good as a wetback, who is a Mexican that we don't know how he got here . . but if he happened accidentally on purpose to do it by swimming the Rio Grande River, his hindside would be a little wet. **1948** *Rotarian* Jan 39, In Texan slang, a "wetback" is a Mexican laborer who has entered the United States without due recourse to the immigration authorities. *Ibid,* It is a meaning which is by no means limited to Texas. There are "wetbacks" of one kind or another in almost every part of the United States. **1965–70** *DARE* (Qu. HH28, *Names and nicknames . . for people of foreign background: Mexican*) 52 Infs, **widespread, but more freq TX, CA,** Wetback; **TX**4, 10, Wetback, wet; [**MO**21, Waterbacks]. **1984** *TX Mth.* Apr 157, Alfonso. . . evidently had "wetback" written all over him. They must have nailed him about twice a month. **2005** *DARE* File—Internet, Wetback, a quietly commanding documentary, follows in the footsteps of immigrants traveling from Nicaragua to the United States.

wet Baptist n   Also *wetback, wet-wash Baptist*   Cf **wet-foot Baptist**
=**deep-water Baptist.**
   1852 Sullivan *Rambles N. & S. Amer.* 182, If I was astonished at the violence of religious sects in the Eastern States, I was doubly struck with it in the West. Every sort of Baptist and Unitarian, Wet Baptists, and Dry Baptists, and Every-day Baptists, and Holy-day Baptists, &c., flourish in great numbers. **1921** Speek *Stake Land* 24, There are in the Western states about a thousand families . . of Russian peasant sectarians—Molokans, Holy Jumpers, Wet and Dry Baptists, and others. **1966–70** *DARE* (Qu. CC4, . . *Nicknames . . for various religions or religious groups*) Inf **CA**7, Wet and dry Baptists; **IN**32, Wetbacks—Baptists; **SC**69, Dry-clean Methodist baptizes by sprinkling; wet-wash Baptist immerses. **2008** *DARE* File—Internet, I used to be a wet baptist. But I went dry when I learned the truth about it [=water baptism].

wet-dog trillium n   Also *wet-dog willie* [From the odor]
A **trillium** (here: *Trillium erectum*).
   1948 Wherry *Wild Flower Guide* 4, Wet-dog Trillium. . . the deeper-colored forms exhaling a rank odor to which the common name refers. **1968** *DARE* (Qu. S2, . . *The flower that comes up in the woods early in spring, with three white petals that turn pink as the flower grows older*) Inf **PA**99, Stinking-dog willie, wet-dog willie. **1972** *Sun. Dominion-Post* (Morgantown WV) 14 May Panorama sec 1/3, Along with its meat-red color goes an unpleasant odor suggesting a wet dog or rotten meat. . . The odor has given the plant a number of names: raw meat, wet dog trillium, stinking Benjamin [etc]. **1976** Bruce *How to Grow Wildflowers* 69, Other names for it are "Birthroot," "Stinking Benjamin," and "Wet-dog Trillium."

wet-foot Baptist n   Cf **wet Baptist**
=**foot-washing Baptist.**
   1966 *DARE* (Qu. CC4, . . *Nicknames . . for various religions or religious groups*) Inf **SC**26, Wet-foot Baptist. **1968** in 2008 Terrell et al. *Forest Park* 53 **cnGA,** Finally, the 'Wet Foot' Baptist walked out and the 'Dry Foot' Baptist put new locks on the doors. **1974** in 2008 *DARE* File—Internet [*Waycross Journal Herald* (GA) 22 Apr], Having been a "Wet foot" Baptist church . . , Millwood Baptist in 1924 became affiliated with the Piedmont Baptist Association.

wet moon n   Cf **dry moon, wet-weather horn**
A crescent (usu new) moon sometimes believed—on the basis of its orientation (that is, whether the horns appear able to "hold water")—to prognosticate wet weather.
   1856 *Harper's New Mth. Mag.* 12.273, "Is that a wet or a dry moon?" inquired the teacher. The boy had never heard those terms applied to the moon as a weather-sign. **1883** *Century Illustr. Mag.* 25.5, Every new moon is either a dry moon or a wet moon—dry if a powderhorn would hang upon the lower limb, wet if it would not. **1923** TX Folkl. Soc. *Pub.* 2.96 **sTX,** The sign of the "wet moon" is in dispute. Some claim that if the new moon comes in tipped up, a wet quarter may be expected; just as many . . hold that the tipped moon is "drained" and that unless the new moon is on its back the probability of rain is slight. **1926** *AmSp* 2.80 **ME,** Much faith is expressed in a "wet moon" or a "dry" one, as determined by the position of the "horn." If curved upwards it is said to "hold water;" if reversed it rejects it, and hence warrants preparation for a "rainy spell." **1932** Stribling *Store* 132 **AL,** The thin crescent was tipped far over. It was a wet moon. **1937** in 1976 *Weevils in the Wheat* 247 **VA** [Black], You know what wet moon is? Well when de points of de moon is down to de earth, de moon is wet an' you kin look fo' rain till de moon change, ef de points is up, you kin speck dry weather. **1944** *AmSp* 19.121 **neMA,** 'Dry moon' and 'wet moon,' designating the position of the crescent in the sky, [are] regarded as a prognostic of the weather. . . My father's account was that the superstition originated from the Indians: when the Indian saw the new moon in such position that he could hang his powder-horn on it, he expected fair weather; when the horn could not be hung on the moon without sliding off, rain. I think a

more familiar way of formulating the same belief is that if the saucer of the moon stands so that it will hold water, the water will not come down; but if it is so tipped as to let the water all spill out, then down comes the rain. **1970** *NC Folkl.* 18.52, When it [=the moon] is tipped up so water will run out, it is known as wet moon. **2004** *Post–Std.* (Syracuse NY) 13 Sept sec D 8/1, Season of year and observer's latitude determine the angle a line joining the crescent Moon's cusps makes with the horizon. Currently this line is more nearly horizontal, making the pre-sunrise crescent look more like a cup that might hold water—call this the "wet Moon" if you want to follow tradition.

wet-the-bed   See **piss-a-bed 2, 3**

wet-wash Baptist   See **wet Baptist**

wet-weather horn n   Cf **wet moon**
   1927 *DN* 5.478 **Ozarks,** *Wet-weather horn.* . . A horn which turns upward. "Th' ol' brindle 'ith th' wet-weather horns she up an' died on me."

we-uns pron   Also *we-ins, we'(e)ns* [*we* + pronc-spp for *ones*] **chiefly S Midl**   Cf **us-uns, we-all** pron, **we-unses, you-uns** pron[1]
1 We.
   1863 in 1865 Post *Soldiers' Letters* 301 **eTN,** The country people in East Tennessee all say *weuns* and *youans,* for *we* and *you.* For instance, I heard one of them say to another: "Waal, if youans can stand it, weuns can." **1864** [see **we-uns'** adj]. **1865** (1922) Jackson *Col.'s Diary* 208 **NC,** A common interrogatory . . was, "If we'uns were to go down to Goldsboro or Raleigh, do you think we'uns could get ary old creetur, a horse or a mule?" **1869** *Lippincott's Mag. Lit. Sci. Educ.* [see **you-uns** pron[1] 1]. **1888** *Century Illustr. Mag.* 36.799, [Letter:] I notice an article from . . L.C. Catlett of Virginia, denying that the people of his State ever made use of the expressions "we-uns" or "you-uns." During the years 1862 and 1865 I heard these expressions used in almost every section. . . [O]ur regiment . . was detailed to act as provost-guard in Appomattox Court-House. As we were passing one of the houses on the outskirts of the town, a woman who was standing at the gate made use of the following expression: "It is no wonder you-uns whipped we-uns. I have been yer three days, and you-uns ain't all gone yet." *Ibid,* [Letter:] If Mr. Catlett will come to Georgia and go among the "po' whites" and "piney-wood tackeys," he will hear the terms "we-uns" and "you-uns" in every-day use. I have heard them, too, in the Cumberland Valley and other parts of Tennessee, and, unless my memory fails me, in South Carolina. **1893** Shands *MS Speech* 67, *We uns.* . . Illiterate white for *we.* **1907** Wright *Shepherd* 105 **Ozarks,** He sure talks so we'uns can understand. **1913** Kephart *Highlanders* 119 **sAppalachians,** We-uns hain't no call to be ashamed of ourselves. **1923** *DN* 5.223 **swMO,** *We-uns.* . . We. **1924** Raine *Land of Saddle-Bags* 130 **sAppalachians,** The only farm produce we-uns can sell is corn. **1930** *VA Qrly. Rev.* 6.247 **S Midl,** The Tennesseean usage, we'uns and you'uns. An habitual user of these superfluities myself, I am convinced that primarily at least the purpose of the usage is to bestow an emphatically inclusive plural. **1945** FWP *Lay My Burden Down* 160 **TX** [Black], On Sunday we-uns do us washing. **1946** *AmSp* 21.98 **sIL,** We-uns, we. **1952** Brown *NC Folkl.* 1.606, *We-uns.* . . *We ones.* . . Illiterate. **1963** Owens *Look to River* 52 **TX,** We'uns been good to you, Jed. **1976** Garber *Mountain-ese* 100 **sAppalachians,** We'uns will be over to visit you next week. **1996–97** in 2004 Montgomery–Hall *Dict. Smoky Mt. Engl.* 641 **wNC, eTN,** *We'uns.* . . Both of us, all of us. [5 infs] **2006** in 2007 *DARE* File—Internet **ceIN,** I have heard "you-ins, we-ins and they-ins" for a long time in this area. I've been told that you-ins is two more than Ya'll. I'm used to hearing these slang terms but it is "you guysez" that rakes me the wrong way. **2007** *Ibid* **cnTN,** In addition to you-uns, I've also heard we-uns, like if you-uns is gonna be there, we-uns is going too!
2 Us.
   1862 *Janesville Daily Gaz.* (WI) 9 June 2/4 **NC,** A returned prisoner. . . says that an inquiry was put to the prisoners in the following vernacular: "What have you'uns come down here to fight we'uns fur?" **1865** Fleharty *Our Regiment* 69 **nwGA,** You'ns don't fight we'ns fair. **1865** (1866) *Cotton Stealing* 26 **AR,** He killed two of we'uns. **1888** *Overland Mth.* (2d ser) 12.140 **Sth** [Black], Look lak dey gwine ter gobble we uns up. **1888** [see **1** above]. **1907** Wright *Shepherd* 105 **Ozarks,** You can get out o' these hills an' be somebody like we'uns. **1913** [see **yourns's**]. **1916** [see **we-unses**]. **1928** *AmSp* 4.97 **FL, GA,** They left we-uns to home. **1968** Hosch *Nevah Come Back* 147 **nGA** (as of 1890s), Dey's fo' of yo', en only two of we'uns! **1999** *Red Ink* 7.2.87 **OK,** Usually [they talk] 'bout how we'ins is a-losin' our language. Now they match that up with we'ins completely disappearin'.

we-uns' adj   Also *we'ns'*   Cf **you-uns'** adj, pron[2]
Our.

   1864 in 1904 Northrop *Chron. from War Prisoner* 137 **SC,** We'ns poor. . . You'ns sees we'ns' mens had to fight for 'em what has to save the South.   **1865** (1870) Glazier *Capture & Escape* 41 **VA,** What did you'uns want to come down here to run off we'uns niggers and burn we'uns houses for?   **1876** *Arthur's Illustr. Home Mag.* 44.203 **MO,** We reckoned it mought fall to'uds we uns house and mought squash thet house all tew kindlin' wood.   **1927** *AmSp* 3.6 **Ozarks,** [First pers pl poss:] Ourn, we-all's, we-uns'.

we-unses pron   Cf **-es** suff[1] **2, you-unses**
We, us.

   1916 *Gleanings Bee Culture* 44.471 **cTX,** *Weunses* have produced a crop of over 35,000 pounds of bulk comb honey.   **1916** *Editor* 44.520, A Few South-West Virginia Expressions. . . "You'uns (or you'unses) must come over and see we'uns (or we'unses).["]   **c1930** in 2006 Hashaw *Children of Perdition* 64 **wLA** (as of 1881), We unses don't want you here no how.   **1941** Writers' Program *Guide MO* 132, We'unses shore air dauncey.   **1966** *DARE* Tape **AR41,** [Inf:] He always said "you-unses" and "we-unses." Instead of saying "you-all" or "you" and "we," he'd say "you-unses" and "we-unses." [FW:] And this is what area of Arkansas? [Inf:] That's west of Lincoln.

we-uns's adj   Also *we(u)nses*   Cf **you-uns's**
Our.

   1864 in 1904 Northrop *Chron. from War Prisoner* 136 **SC,** Had a talk with a group of women with poor vegetables to exchange, or sell. To my question, they said, sadly: "We'nses mens all in Fedrit army."   **1898** Dromgoole *Cinch* 37 **seTN,** It ain't been locked sence Bragg busted of it open . . ter git we-uns's meat out fur the rebels ter feed on.   **1911** Miller *Red Swan's Neck* 93 **wNC,** But w'en tha keep a-huntin' us like coons an' foxes, an' shootin' us an' burnin' weunses houses, tha's jes' gotter look out.

Wewoka switch n   [See quot 2008]   **esp OK**
In phr *caught in the Wewoka switch* (and varr): Utterly lost; in an untenable or disadvantageous position; see quots.

   1951 *Daily Oklahoman* (Oklahoma City OK) 6 Nov [37/3] (news-paperarchive.com), "I wasn't as surprised as you'd think," the former Sooner and professional [football] star reported. "We just caught them in a Wewoka switch."   **1960** in 1963 *Chron. OK* 41.455 (as of c1923), Wewoka Switch was the name applied to the railroad station in Wewoka during the boom days. Often mounds of misguided freight would sit near the tracks for months before being found by their owners.   **1963** *Ibid* 456, The expression, 'I'm in the Wewoka Switch' has grown to mean that one suddenly finds himself in a dangerous or trying situation. In later years oil men . . carried this expression to all parts of the world.   **1992** Wallis *Pretty Boy* 185 **MO,** It [="Happy Days Are Here Again"] was a sunny tune for a nation that was doomed to spend a long, long time "caught in a Wewoka switch" [=the Great Depression].   **1995** Owens *OK Justice* 105, Now came into play an old Oklahoma tradition known as "getting caught in the Wewoka switch", i.e. the rules some-times change on very short notice and not to your advantage.   **1999** *DARE* File **OK,** I have heard this only in Oklahoma, and [it] would be used as follows: "I don't want to get caught in a Wewoka Switch." It can mean 1) getting caught in a lie, or more specifically, 2) getting caught cheating on your wife. I have also heard it used in the same way that the phrase "caught coming and going" is used.   **2008** *DARE* File—Internet **OK,** [OK travel website:] Wewoka gained further recognition as the switching station of the Santa Fe, Rock Island and MKT Railroads. "Wewoka Switch" was known all along the railroad lines; if shipments were lost or delayed, they were reportedly "caught in the Wewoka Switch."

wey   See **where A3**

wezzen   See **wizzen**

wha   See **where A1**

whack n

1   A deal; a bargain; an agreement—freq in phrr *it's* (or *that's*) *a whack.*

   1860 *Johnson's Orig. Comic Songs* (ed. 2) 45 *(OED2),* I axed her for to marry me, she said it was a whack.   **1875** (1876) Twain *Tom Sawyer* 70 **MO,** "I'll stay if you will." "Good,—that's a whack."   **1887** Kirkland *Zury* 538 **IL,** *Whack.* . . A bargain struck.   **1911** *DN* 3.540 **eKY,** *Whăck.* . . An agreement, a "go;" e.g., "That's a whack!"   **1919** Kyne

Capt. Scraggs 55 **CA,** "It's a whack," yelled McGuffey joyfully.   **1929** *AmSp* 5.21 **Ozarks,** *Whack.* . . A bargain, an agreement.   **1944** *PADS* 2.62 **Ozarks,** *Whack.* . . A bargain, an agreement. "John and I made a whack."

2   A lie; also v *whack* to lie, exaggerate.   [Cf *OED2 whacker* sb. 2 "Anything abnormally large of its kind; . . a 'thumping' lie"]   **Sth, S Midl**

   1906 Casey *Parson's Boys* 64 **sIL** (as of c1860), Dern'd old stick-in-the-mud; to tell us sich a lot of whacks as that, jist to git us to work!   **1906** *DN* 3.163 **nwAR,** *Whack.* . . Lie. "Jeeminy Christmas, that's a whack." *Whack.* . . To lie. "He's a-whacking all right."   **1944** *PADS* 2.62 **MO,** *Whack.* . . A lie. . . Also Va., N.C.   **1945** *PADS* 3.12 **SC,** *Whack.* . . Familiar to me in the sense of "a lie."   **1953** Randolph–Wilson *Down in Holler* 297 **Ozarks,** *Whack.* . . To exaggerate, to tell a tall tale. May Kennedy McCord, of Springfield, Mo., was accused of *whackin'* when she spoke of a sow nursing sixteen pigs.   **1956** McAtee *Some Dialect NC* 50, *Whack.* . . A lie. "He told some of the biggest whacks."   **1960** Carpenter *Tales Manchaca* 196 **cTX,** I pushed Mae into the position of having to tell a whack just to relieve me of an un-comfortable situation.   **1983** *NADS Letters* **MO,** Do you have the word "whack" meaning a fib or a lie? This is common in Missouri.   **1983** *MJLF* 9.1.60 **ceKY** (as of 1956), *Whack . .* a lie.

whacker n   [Abbr for **bullwhacker** (or *mulewhacker*)]   **esp West**
An ox or mule driver.

   1827 C. Bryant *Letter* 1 Jan. (MS) *(DA),* If our doors were closed, the country whackers who bring in cotton, corn and other produce for sale, would never find the way in.   **1880** *Harper's New Mth. Mag.* 60.679 **NM,** The whacker's long whip [cracks] . . as he lashes his unwieldy beasts into position.   **1886** KS State Hist. Soc. *Coll.* 3.544, One distin-guished freighter . . went so far as to furnish his "whackers" with Bibles, but the effort was a religious and financial failure.   **1943** Hamner *Short Grass* 163 **nTX,** Long, snakelike whips carried by the whackers . . sang out across the backs of the animals.

whackie, whacky   See **wackie**

whafler n   [Echoic]   *obs*   Cf **yaffle**
A **flicker** n[2] **1** (here: *Colaptes auratus*).

   1807 in 1846 MA Hist. Soc. *Coll.* 2d ser 3.54 **seMA,** The birds, which frequent this and the adjacent islands, are the crow; . . the wood-pecker, two species, the red-headed, and the speckled or whafler.

whah   See **where A1**

whahoo n   See **wahoo** n[1]

whale   See **whale crab**

whaleback n

1   also *whaleback ridge, whalesback:* =**hogback 2b.**   Cf **horseback**

   [**1869** Twain *Innocents* 441 **MO,** We can see the long, whale-backed ridge of Mt. Hermon projecting above the eastern hills.]   **1879** *Appala-chia* 2.247 (as of 1877), From most points in the valley it is seen as a long, high, whaleback ridge, thrust up above many subordinate hills.   **1890** *Century Illustr. Mag.* 40.491, In general views the Yosemite Creek basin seems to be paved with domes and smooth whaleback masses of granite in every stage of development.   **1893** *Scribner's Mag.* 13.471, A mile to the south . . a whaleback ridge noses the uncanny valley.   **1941** Writers' Program *Guide UT* 509, The tops of plateaus, mesas, and mountains in the area around Rainbow Bridge are rounded; natives call them whalebacks and baldheads.   **1946** Attwood *Length ME* 17 [Geo-graphical terms], *Whaleback, whalesback*—A horseback. . . because of its shape.

2   also *whaleback barge, ~ steamer:* A cargo steamship or barge with a largely smooth, cigar-shaped hull, used esp in Great Lakes shipping.   *hist*   Cf **pig** n[1] **B5**

   1891 *Newark Advocate* (OH) 13 Aug [2]/1 (newspaperarchive.com), This whaleback steamer, the Charles W. Wetmore, sailed direct from Duluth, Minn., to Liverpool, carrying a cargo of 95,000 bushels of grain. One advantage of the whaleback is that it costs not nearly so much to build as the ordinary vessel. . . There are two kinds of whaleback ves-sels, steam propellers and steel barges for towing. . . When the whale-back vessel first appeared in the lake waters the seamen christened it the "pig," a name by which it is still known there. But undoubtedly it will be known in commerce as the whaleback, from its shape.   **1892** *Mt. Demo-crat* (Placerville CA) [3 Dec 6]/4 (newspaperarchive.com), A new 4000-

ton whaleback barge has been ordered built by the American Steel Barge Company at Tacoma for the Northern Pacific steamship lines between Puget Sound and China. **1929** *Pt. Arthur News* (TX) 17 Jan 1/5, Death sealed the friendship of two comrades in the gas-filled hold of a whaleback barge at Smith's Bluff on the Neches river. **1937** *New Castle News* (PA) 4 Mar 13/4, Here we see the whaleback steamer South Park arriving at Cleveland breakwater from Detroit with the first cargo of automobiles for the season. **1940** in Lib. of Congress *Amer. Memory: WPA Life Hist.* (Internet) **IL,** For errors of judgement in navigation he may lose his pilot's license, but if he is too cautious he may lose his job. The end of the "Colgate", a "pig" or "whaleback" as they are called, illustrates the point. **1944** *Sheboygan Press* (WI) 22 Nov 22/2, The last of the famous whaleback fleet of the Great Lakes, the Alex McDougall, is scheduled for the scrap heap.

whaleback ridge   See **whaleback 1**

whaleback steamer   See **whaleback 2**

whalebird n

‡1 =**ruddy turnstone.** *obs*

[**1795** Hearne *Journey* 427 (as of 1769–72), *Hebridal Sandpipers,* but more commonly known in Hudson's Bay by the Name of Whale Birds, on account of their feeding on the carcases of those animals which frequently lie on the shores.] **1923** U.S. Dept. Ag. *Misc. Circular* 13.72, Ruddy Turnstone *(Arenaria interpres).* . . Book Names. . . whale-bird.

2 Either the **sooty shearwater** or the short-tailed **shearwater 1** *(Puffinus tenuirostris).*

1853 *S. Lit. Messenger* 19.140, We have had for two or three days past, Cape pigeons, *(Procellaria,)* and "whale birds," *(Puffinus obscurus,)* about the ship. **1901** *Hayward Rev.* (CA) 8 Nov 1/6 **NW,** They [=Amer Indians and early settlers] base their [weather] predictions on the flight southward of unnumbered thousands of whale birds from Alaska and probably Siberia. **1923** Dawson *Birds CA* 3.2001, Dark-bodied Shearwater. . . Sooty Shearwater. Whale-bird. **1940** Gabrielson *Birds OR* 82, The graceful *Sooty Shearwater,* known to the fishermen on the coast as the "Whale Bird," is the most abundant seafowl present. **1966** Dufresne *My Way* 7 **AK,** In the bird guides I'd fetched from New Hampshire I had known them as Slender Shearwaters, but the doctor used the sea-farer's name, "whale-birds." **1986** [see **sooty shearwater**]. **1991** Tabbert *Dict. Alaskan Engl.* 171, *Whale bird.* . . In Alaskan waters the name is used for *Puffinus tenuirostris* . . and for *Puffinus griseus.*

3 also *right whale bird:* A **phalarope;** see quots.

1867 Hunt *Shenandoah* 147, Thousands of right whale birds, as they are known among whalers, from being always found in the vicinity of the marine monster bearing that cognomen. **1917** (1923) *Birds Amer.* 1.217, Red Phalarope. . . In the North it feeds on the animal-life which forms the food of the right whale—hence its name of Whale-bird. *Ibid* 218, Northern Phalarope. . . Other Names. . . Whale-bird [etc]. **1956** MA Audubon Soc. *Bulletin* 40.21 **MA,** Wilson's Phalarope. . . Whale Bird. *Ibid* **ME, MA,** Northern Phalarope. . . Whale Bird. **2003** *DARE* File—Internet **CA,** We whale- and bird watchers call phalaropes "whale birds" because we would invariably see blue whales if we found phalaropes as they feed on the same krill.

whale crab n   Also *whale*   **chiefly Chesapeake Bay**

A very large crab, esp a **soft-shell crab 1.**

1965 *San Mateo Times* (CA) 30 Dec 2/8, [Advt:] *Alaska King Crab*—Fresh from the icy waters of Alaska. Whale Crab weighing from 5–7 pounds. Delivered to your door. $9 each. **1981** *Seventeen Letters* **MD,** A few of the expressions used around the harbor. Our whales are jumbo crabs. **2000** Shores *Tangier Is.* 223 **Chesapeake Bay,** With regard to mixture and meaning, there are many instances, of course, of words for the same thing: . . jumbo, whale, and slab for the large softcrab. **2006** *DARE* File—Internet **DC,** In the spring the Whale Crabs first come up to us from Florida, and as temperatures warm up, our supply is provided from Maryland waters. . . Crab connoisseurs eagerly await their appearance each spring and these Whales are not easy to find.

whalesback   See **whaleback 1**

whaley n   Rarely *whalley*   [Etym unknown]

1 in phr *play whaley:* To blunder, fail; to play havoc (with something).   **chiefly Cent, S Midl**

1897 *KS Univ. Qrly.* (ser B) 6.58 **KS,** *Whaley, to play:* to play hob; to fail (in doing something.) **1905** *DN* 3.67 **eNE,** *Whaley.* . . Used in phrase "*play whaley* with," meaning spoil, or ruin. **1906** *DN* 3.151 **nwAR,** *Play whaley.* . . To make a mistake, do the wrong thing. **1909** *DN* 3.358 **eAL, wGA,** *Play whaley.* . . To upset one's plans completely,

do the wrong thing, ruin everything. "Now you've played whaley!" *Ibid* 387 **eAL, wGA,** *Whaley.* . . Mischief: in the expression 'play whaley (with),' i.e., spoil, ruin. **1912** *DN* 3.585 **wIN,** *Play whaley.* . . The same as *play hob.* **1916** *DN* 4.327 **KS, NE,** *Play whaley.* . . To attempt what is beyond one's capabilities. "He thought he knew how to set that ladder, but he played whaley; he fell and broke the window." **1921** Haswell *Daughter Ozarks* 38 (as of 1880s), You'd play whalley wouldn't ye now, a' ridin' to heaven a' straddle of a calf! **1923** *DN* 5.217 **swMO,** *Play whaley.* . . To make a failure. "He played whaley a-farmin'." **1927** *AmSp* 2.362 **cwWV,** *Play whaley* . . , to attempt what one has not the ability to accomplish. "He will play whaley when he tries to pull the hill with one pair of horses." **1944** *PADS* 2.37 **NC, sVA,** *Whaley, to play.* . . To bungle. "You played whaley and didn't know the tune." **c1960** *Wilson Coll.* **csKY,** *Play whaley.* . . To mess things up, to blunder. **1991** Heat Moon *PrairyErth* 314 **ceKS,** The dang highway boys got that triple-archer [=a stone bridge] over to Bazaar, but they're going to play whaley getting this one. **2008** *DARE* File—Internet **GA,** I sure would like to try it just once, even if it does play Whaley with my sugar levels.

‡2 See quot.

1935 Davis *Honey* 215 **OR,** The water was colder than whaley.

whalloper   See **walloper**

whang n[1]   [Brit, esp Scots, nIr, dial var of *thong*]

1 A leather thong or lace.

1824 Doddridge *Notes Indian Wars* 114 **WV, wPA** (as of a1783), [Moccasins] were sewed together and patched with deer skin thongs, or whangs as they were commonly called. **1836** *Amer. Mth. Mag.* 1.302 **AR,** A *thong* is called a "whang." **1848** (1855) Ruxton *Life Far West* 124 **Rocky Mts,** Scattered fringes down the outside of the leg . . had been pretty well thinned to supply "whangs" for mending moccasins or pack-saddles. **1859** Taliaferro *Fisher's R.* 169 **nwNC** (as of 1854), There were leggins of tanned buckskin . . laced up with "whangs." **1895** (1969) Montgomery Ward *Catalogue* 336, Stirrup straps, 3 inches wide to fasten with whangs. **1902** *DN* 2.249 **sIL,** *Whang.* . . Thong. **1916** OR Pioneer Assoc. *Trans.* 58, The saddle tree was covered with rawhide, sewed tightly with whangs. **1917** [see **whang leather**]. **1958** *AmSp* 33.273 **eWA** [Ranching terms], *Whang; whang leather.* . . A long, narrow strip of leather, usually rawhide, used for many purposes. **1991** [see **2** below].

2 also attrib: =**whang leather;** hence phrr *tough as* (or *tougher than*) *whang.*

1923 *DN* 5.224 **swMO,** *Whang.* . . Lace leather. **1938** *AmSp* 13.74 **OH,** 'Tougher than whale bone' (or 'whang'). **1942** McAtee *Dial. Grant Co. IN* 70 (as of 1890s), *Whang* . . rawhide; . . of rawhide; as "a — string". **1956** Almirall *From College* 105 **CO,** We met Bill, that thin old-timer, tough as whang. *Ibid* 142, Rather slender, of medium height, his frame looked like it might be of the whang variety. **1984** Woods *WV Was Good* 229, A *whang-string* meant a stout leather string cut from a groundhog hide or tanned cowhide. **1991** Haynes *Haywood Home* 37 **wNC** (as of c1920), New strings were cut from tanned groundhog hides. We called these strings "whang" strings. These groundhog whangs caused problems because they stretched when they got wet.

whang v   With *together, up,* rarely *out* [Orig from **whang** n[1] **1** meaning spec to sew with thongs, but now freq assoc with *whang* to strike, bang]   **chiefly Midl**   See Map

To sew up quickly or roughly; to make or mend in a makeshift way.

1855 Smith *Legends of War* 330 **KY,** He "whanged," together some pieces of deer skin, with the hair outside and wore it for a covering to his head in very cold or snowy weather. **1859** in 1959 *Colorado Mag.* 102 **MO,** Stopped at noon two hours and whanged up my moccasins—pretty near barefooted. **1892** Smith *On Wheels* 138 **cwIL,** I . . was encumbered with my heavy boots, which at Meridian I had so badly burned while drying them that the soles and uppers had to be "whanged" together with strings. **1909** *Pioneer Days SW* 179, He then killed an antelope, took the hide and made the girls some moccasins, that is he whanged up something for their feet. **1939** *AmSp* 14.92 **eTN,** *To whang up.* To sew up roughly. 'She whanged up the ripped place.' **1946** *PADS* 6.32 **swVA,** *Whang up.* . . To patch or repair a garment hurriedly. . . Occasional. **1950** *WELS* (When a woman wants to sew up a torn place quickly, she says, "I'll just _____.") 1 Inf, **csWI,** Whang it up. **1954** Harder *Coll.* **cwTN,** *Whang it together.* . . Whoop it up. **1965–70** *DARE* (Qu. W28, *When a woman is in a hurry and has to sew up a torn place quickly . . "I'll just _____."*) Infs **AR40, IL74, KY37, 84,**

MD17, **MS**59, **MO**4, **OK**1, 47, Whang it up; **OH**53, 87, **OK**47, Whang it together; (Qu. W29, . . *Expressions* . . *for things that are sewn carelessly* . . "They're _____.") Infs **AR**40, **KY**84, (Just) whanged up; **MD**17, Just whanged out; **OH**53, Whanged together. [10 of 11 total Infs comm type 4 or 5, 9 old, 8 gs educ or less] **2005** in 2008 *DARE* File—Internet **MD**, Maybe I should whang together one of those PVC trebuchets I saw on the web a while back, and bombard her with water balloons. **2008** *Ibid* **OH**, I just whanged up a couple of elisp modules to support fontified editing of Java source code.

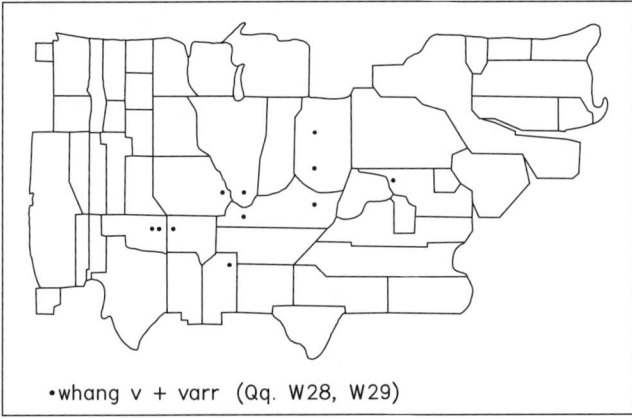

•whang v + varr (Qq. W28, W29)

whang n[2]   Also *wang* [Alter of *twang,* perh infl by **whang** n[3]]
A distinctive manner of pronunciation or speech, esp one assoc with a particular region; hence adj *whangy.*

1876 Twain *Old Times* 68 **MO**, An agonized voice, with the backwoods "whang" to it, would wail out. **1886** *Kansas City Med. Index* 7.131, There is constantly a feeling of stuffiness and fullness in the parts [of the nose], while the voice has the characteristic nasal whang. **1888** Twain in *Century Illustr. Mag.* 35.461, It's got a business whang to it that's almost American. **1941** Ward *Holding Hills* 128 **IA** (as of early 20th cent), His words are short, his voice whangy. **1967** *DARE* FW Addit **TN**17, You've got a whang [hwæŋ] to your talkin'. **1969** *DARE* Tape **IL**78, You couldn't hardly understand 'em. . . They got a Yankee whang to their talk. **1971** *Today Show Letters* **MO**, This western dialect is *not* Texan, *not* Missouri "wang," but distinctly western, with an accent all it's [sic] own. . . Also Missouri, Arkansas have a "wang" all their own which is *not* Southern. **1995** *Brophy Coll.* 82 **swMO** (as of c1960), *Whang.* [T]wang (voice inflection).

whang n[3]   Also *wang* [nIr dial (1996 *Concise Ulster Dict. whang* n.[2] 1 "a 'tang': a rancid taste in milk or butter"); prob < *twang,* perh infl by *whang* sharp blow] **chiefly Sth, S Midl**
An unpleasant or sharp taste; a "bite"; hence adjs *w(h)angy, w(h)angish.*

1905 *DN* 3.78 **nwAR**, *Farewell whang.* . . After-taste. 'That medicine had a farewell whang to it.' Rare. [*DARE* Ed: cf **farewell 1**] **1935** Davis *Honey* 86 **OR**, Clay . . spat to clear his mouth of the ammoniacal whang the barn had planted in it. **1942** McAtee *Dial. Grant Co. IN* 70 (as of 1890s), *Whang* . . flavor, aftertaste; of twang, tang of the dictionary. **1957** *Sat. Eve. Post Letters* **sIN** (as of 1910–20), It's got a whang to it (a sour, brassy or fruity taste; applied to any food, such as gravy, which is beginning to spoil). **1968** *Foxfire* 2.3.107 **nGA**, It makes "pretty" whiskey which holds a good bead, but has a funny "whang" flavor. **1970** *Thompson Coll.* **cwGA**, Syrup made from the cane, . . and having a whang ("bite") that is definitely different from the . . dead sweet taste of . . sorghum syrup. **1970** *DARE* (QR, near Qu. I46) Inf **KY**75, Mayapple—kind of a sour whang [hweɪŋ]. **1984** Weaver *TX Crude* 64, *A whang.* A slightly bitter taste, redolent of skunk. A musky smell, in beer. **1986** Pederson *LAGS Concordance,* 1 inf, **cnMS**, Whang = taste; (The butter . .) 1 inf, **swAR**, Has a whang to it. **1991** Still *Wolfpen Notebooks* 102 **sAppalachians**, Reach me one more little horn o' that likker. Hit's got a whang to it I like. **2006** in 2008 *DARE* File—Internet **AL**, You better like it [=potato salad] with a whang. It's really whangy. [Comment:] But what does whangy mean? [Response:] It means vinegary and spicy. The opposite of sweet. *Ibid* **MS**, I killed a doe last Saturday and have had it on ice in a cooler since then. . . Last night . . it had a smell to it. Not a rotten smell but sorta like a wangish smell. [Comment:] Wangish has different meaning for different folks. If you have kept it iced well all of the time, that is probably just aging. Aged beef has a wang to its raw aroma. **2007** *Ibid* **KY**, I used the distilled white

vinegar and it didn't have a bitter wangy taste. **2008** *Ibid* **TX** (as of 1969), Some of us nervously watched as the first bites were sampled hoping that nobody caught on to the suspiciously whangish aftertaste of the alleged Alcapulco [sic] Gold ingredient.

whang n[4] **NEng**
A party; see quots.

1888 *NY Times* (NY) 27 Apr 5/4 **ME**, A good housewife in a suburb of Lewiston, whose reputation is of thrift, and whose wits are as keen as the razor's edge, issued cards not long ago, it is said, for an afternoon party at her home, terming it a "whang." A "whang" is an unknown term in that vicinity, although they had heard it employed in a metaphoric or symbolic or hyperbolic sense many times to the country jubilee of various kinds. . . A "whang" is a housecleaning party, and some of the ladies are sorry that they didn't dress accordingly. **1891** *Century Dict.* 6885, *Whang.* . . Formerly, in Maine and some other parts of New England, a house-cleaning party; a gathering of neighbors to aid one of their number in cleaning house. **1898** (1899) Earle *Home Life* 417 **NEng**, Even those evil days of New England households, the annual house-cleaning, were robbed of some of their dismal terrors by what was known as a "whang," a gathering of a few friendly women neighbors to assist one another in that dire time, and thus speed and shorten the hours of misery. **1902** Day *Pine Tree Ballads* 218 **ME**, At the Old Folks' Whang [title]. . . Old Branscomb plays the fiddle at the old folks' whang.

whangish   See **whang** n[3]

whang leather n, also attrib [**whang** n[1] 1]
Tough leather, usu rawhide, suitable for making thongs or laces; also fig; hence phr *tough as whang leather.*

1837 Wetmore *Gaz. MO* 313, He never would be content to make his moccasins like any other white man, with a good piece of tanned deer-skin, and whang leather to sew them with. **1855** *Weekly Hawk-Eye & Telegraph* (Burlington IA) 14 Nov [2]/7 (newspaperarchive.com), [Advt:] Vulcanized Gum Belting and Packing, Whang Leather and dressed Deer Skins. **1893** *KS Univ. Qrly.* 1.142, *Whang leather:* coarse undressed leather used for cord. **1902** *DN* 2.249 **sIL**, *Whang-leather.* . . Leather from which to make thongs. **1907** *DN* 3.228 **nwAR**, *Whang-leather.* **1917** Kephart *Camping & Woodcraft* 2.315, *Whang leather.*— Woodchuck skins are proverbially tough, and are good for whangs or shoe strings. . . Whang-leather is prepared just like rawhide, but the thongs are cut out before softening. **1937** Sandoz *Slogum* 251 **NE**, These boys raised out here in the West—they're tough as whang leather. **1952** Brown *NC Folkl.* 1.606, *Whang-leather.* . . Tough rawhide cut into strips and used to sew shoes or belting. **1958** [see **whang** n[1] 1]. **1965** Will *Okeechobee Boats* 97 **FL**, She [=a boat] was tough as old whang leather. **1984** Lesley *Winterkill* 25 **neOR**, Red Shirt was over forty then, but still honking bulls and tough as whang leather. **1993** Doig *Heart Earth* 11 **MT**, But this ulcer deal. . . how could a gastric squall put my whangleather father on the couch, sick as a poisoned pup?

whang out (or together, up)   See **whang** v

whangy adj[1]   See **whang** n[2]

whangy adj[2]   See **whang** n[3]

whanker-jawed adj
=**whopper-jawed 1.**

1966–69 *DARE* (Qu. X6, *If a person's lower jaw sticks out prominently* . . *he's* _____) Infs **FL**26, **IL**86, **TX**36, 42, **WA**17, Whankerjawed. [All Infs old]

whant   See **want** v[1]

whap over   See **whop over**

whapper-jaw   See **whopper-jaw**

whapper-jawed   See **whopper-jawed**

whapple-jawed   See **wobble-jawed**

whapto   See **wapato**

whar adv, conj[1], pron   See **where A1**

whar conj[2]   See **whether 2**

wharfing n   Pronc-sp *wuff-in* **NEng**
An earthen bank (on dry land) supported by a retaining wall; now esp the bank or ramp that gives access to the mow of a barn; sometimes applied also, or esp, to the wooden bridge that is sometimes interposed between the bank and the barn.

1823 Peirce *Conversations Arithmetic* 136 **MA,** The eaves of a house are 18 feet high; there is a wharfing in front of the house 12 feet wide; what is the length of a ladder that will just reach from the edge of the wharfing to the eaves of the house? **1852** *Plough Loom & Anvil* 4.555 **nwVT,** The entrance into the second story is on the east end of the barn, from a wharfing twelve feet distant. **1860** in 2008 (acc) Lexis–Nexis Legal Research *State Case Law: VT* (Internet), The auditors reported . . that some of the wharfings or back walls of the road were not so substantially laid, and the track in other places not graded so low, as the contract required. **1881** NH Bd. Ag. *NH Ag.* 138, A small platform is built . . to put a fodder-cutter on, and a wharfing made just high enough for convenience in unloading at the side of the platform. **1916** Miniter *Our Natupski Neighbors* 229 **MA,** The girls thought of other dangerous places and examined the rickety cellar stairs, the ell room with the missing floor boards, the teetery barnyard wharfing. **1928** Weygandt *Tuesdays at Ten* 814 **NH,** So regular is the bat in dropping down from his resting place under the gable . . that it seems my step on the wharfing must be the signal for his departure. [**1968** *DARE* (Qu. O3, *A small platform sticking out into the water where boats can tie up, and people can get into them*) Inf **NH**14, Wharfing; (Qu. O4, *A much larger and solider structure where ships can come to land*) Inf **NH**14, Wharfing.] **1999** *DARE* File **nwMA,** What do you call the wooden ramp that goes up into a barn? . . Well, you know after the house was built they would come and serenade. The fellows ran and hid under the wharfin'. Dad crept out and rattled a chain on top of it and scared them half to death. **2005** *Greenfield Recorder* (MA) 18 July 1/2, In this most practical of Yankee structures, a horse-drawn wagon could back a load of hay from the . . bridge entrance onto the top floor. . . [T]he massive stone "wharfing" tower . . supports the top-floor bridge. **2005** *DARE* File **MA,** I wonder if you have been collecting terms for the earthen ramp which some barns have as an access way to the haymow? My neighbors here in Heath, Massachusetts, whose family has lived here for more than 200 years, call this structure a "wuff-in." They are aware that it is not standard English, and have no idea how it should be spelled. *Ibid* **cVT,** A wharfin' [ˈhwɔɚfɪn] is an entrance to the first floor of a barn, built up with stone. People my age (about eighty) still remember the term.

wharf rat n
=**Norway rat.**

1824 Cooper *Pilot* 2.13 **NY,** To burrow like a rabbit, or jump from hole to hole, like a wharf-rat! **1849** Foster *NY in Slices* 85, Overrun from basement to garret with cockroaches, fleas, bedbugs, wharf-rats, and every other sort of vermin indigenous or possible to the climate. **1874** *NY Times* (NY) 26 July 3/6 **cMA,** Messrs. Clark, Sawyer & Co., of this city [=Worcester], are much annoyed by the depredations of a colony of large gray wharf rats, which were probably imported in crates of crockery. **1938** *Clearfield Progress* (PA) 7 Jan 6/3 **VA,** The cat caught a baby wharf rat and gave it to her three kittens to play with. **1974** *Fresno Bee the Republican* (CA) 15 Feb sec A 3/2 **MS,** Amendments to make the black widow the state spider . . and the wharf rat the state rodent were defeated. **2003** *Gettysburg Times* (PA) 12 May sec A 4/3, I had never seen a squirrel like this . . sort of a cross between a wharf rat and H. Ross Perot.

wharsomever, wharsumevuh See **wheresomever**

what pron

1 pronc-sp *hwa:* Used as a relative pron with all types of antecedents; that, who, which. [*OED2 what* pron C.7.a (with pron antecedent) c1200 →, C.7.b (with noun antecedent) a1568 →; "Now *dial.* or *vulgar*"]

1844 Thompson *Major Jones's Courtship* 28 **GA,** Squire Pettybone was a little short fat man, what had rode afore, and knowed how to talk to the boys. **1848** McCallum *ME Letters* [11], It is rather a noisy place to write, especially [for] those what don't write. **1852** in 1958 Dickinson *Letters* 1.176 **MA,** Susie, forgive me, forget all what I say. **1863** in 1873 Smith *Bill Arp's Peace Papers* 36 **nwGA,** The big mud cat gobble up the yearth worms what chanse to fall into its waters. **1871** Eggleston *Hoosier Schoolmaster* 99 **sIN,** I hated Bill Jones what keeps the poorhouse. **1878** Hart *Sazerac Lying Club* 50 **NV,** He was one of them fellers what aint afraid of nothin'. **1917** *Jrl. Amer. Folkl.* 30.175 **NC** [Black], Fox . . would "take all what grows on top of de groun' an' I take all what grows under de groun'." **1934** *AmSp* 9.125 [Engl dial of HI], *What* is a relative pronoun, generally substituted for *that: Anything what you want.* **1944** *PADS* 2.44 **NC, VA,** *Hwa* [hwa]: rel pron. Who. The interrogative pronoun *who* is pronounced in the current standard way. . . Rural. Mainly uneducated. **1952** in 1958 Brewer *Dog Ghosts*

27 **TX** [Black], Fryin'-size chickens, what his wife, Aunt Hetty, done tol' 'im to git shed of. **1953** Brewer *Word Brazos* 9 **eTX** [Black], You kin fin' . . a brothuh or a sistuh what ain't nevuh set foot in de chu'ch ez long ez dey live. **1963** Wright *Lawd Today* 60 **Chicago IL** [Black], He's the only one what can guide you through such tough days as that. **1966–68** *DARE* Tape **GA**4, We didn't have the opportunity what children got now; **GA**25, Alum was good for anythin' what ailed you. **1967–68** *DARE* FW Addit **LA**6, So she fixed the little article what they use; **LA**18, These people what live down there were overflowed. **1976** [see **something A5**]. **2001** *DARE* File **ceOK, cCA,** An informant in Tahlequah, Oklahoma, a Cherokee Indian woman born in 1902. . . uses relative *what* [as in] "winter grapes what gets white[.]." The youngest person I have found who uses relative *what* is a male high school graduate from Sacramento, California born 1973.

2 The one(s) who; whoever.

1967 Fetterman *Stinking Creek* 33 **seKY,** What don't work is drawin'. . . . They draw welfare checks or commodities or both. **1967** *DARE* FW Addit **sNJ,** What—instead of who—"He's what brought me to the hospital." **2001** *DARE* File **swNM,** Here is a use of *what* meaning "the one who" from a white male from Lordsburg, New Mexico born 1922. "This lady is what gave me the picture."

3 Of an item for sale: offered at what price? [nIr dial]

1920 *DN* 5.86 **NC,** *What is this?* What is the price of this article (I am pointing to)? **1926** *DN* 5.395 **KS,** *What is that?* Is constantly interpreted, in a shop, as meaning "What is the price of the article?"

what adv [*OED2 what* pron. C.6 1818 →; "*dial.* or *vulgar*"]
Used as a redundant relative after comparative conjs *than, as.*

1883 (1971) Harris *Nights with Remus* 218 **GA** [Black], Remus 'ud be des twice-t ez ole ez w'at he is right now. **1885** Twain *Huck. Finn* 30 **MO,** I couldn't make out how he was agoing to be any better off then than what he was before. **1914** *DN* 4.81 **ME, nNH,** *Than what.* Redundant for "than." **1916** Howells *Leatherwood God* 161 **OH** (as of 1830s), Then it's as much ourn as what it's yourn. **1980** *DARE* File **cMA, cwWI,** *Than what*—"She's no better than what she has to be." Common. **1986** Pederson *LAGS Concordance,* 1 inf, **swAL,** Younger than what I was; 1 inf, **seTX,** Younger than what I am; 1 inf, **seMS,** Your left eye is trained more than what the right eye; That's somebody that's a little different than what I am; 1 inf, **cMS,** Better than what it is now; 1 inf, **nwLA,** Longer than what it normally would; 1 inf, **cnLA,** Way bigger than what it was; 1 inf, **cnAL,** Colder than what it were; 1 inf, **neTN,** But they were still bigger than what them was; 1 inf, **ceFL,** More here than what there were; 1 inf, **csLA,** Than what I can [FW:= than I can]. [6 of 10 infs Black]

what-all pron

1a Used as a direct or indirect interrogative in place of *what* to emphasize the comprehensive scope of the question. [Scots, nIr dial] Cf **what-all** adj, **what and all, where-all, who-all** pron

1843 *Weekly Messenger* (Chambersburg PA) 20 Dec 1722/1, I find it stated with at least sufficient clearness what all is intended under these general terms. **1859** *Youth's Companion* 33.147 **NY,** She said she could take the whole charge of the boys' wardrobe . . , and see to the chambers and cellars so her mother need not run up and down stairs—and, mother I'm sure I don't know what all she isn't going to do. **1868** Moos *Hannah* 270 **OH,** Now he related to her how he had met the man who had taken him about town, and what all had transpired. **1882** Howells *Modern Instance* 455, I don't know what all she expects of you. **1905** (1975) Miles *Spirit of Mts.* 106 **seTN,** If the moon knowed what all you-uns hold hit reponsible fur hit'd git scared and fall down out o' the sky. **1913** U.S. Congress *Proc. Impeachment Robert W. Archbald* 1.310 **AL,** Q. What all did he say and what all did you say?—A. I do not know as I could repeat it all. **1933** Rawlings *South Moon* 6 **nFL,** What-all you reckon's here in the scrub? *Ibid* 89, If you was to say what-all you wants o' Zeke . . I could find him and tell him. **1944** in 1946 *AmSp* 21.52 **nwMN,** We always said, as the town still does, 'Who-all was there?' and 'What-all did you do?' Many of the Irish also use 'who-all' and 'what-all.' **1963** Mencken–McDavid *Amer. Lang.* 548, The Linguistic Atlas finds the interrogative *who-all* fairly widespread in the South and adjacent territory. The interrogative *what-all* is even more widespread, and may be considered national. **1975** Allen *LAUM* 2.54 **Upper MW** (as of c1950), For the plural or inclusive meaning of the neuter interrogative pronoun . . more than one-third [of infs] . . use the phrase *what-all.* [T]he somewhat higher frequency in North Dakota does not accord with the inference, clearly implied by the more than two-thirds majority in Nebraska, that *what-all* may be Midland oriented. **2008** *DARE* File—Internet **seOH**, My son is going to college in Aug and I don't know what all I am supposed to send him away with.

b Used elliptically in phrr meaning "and many more things of the same sort; and so forth, et cetera"; as:

(1) *and I don't know what-all, and God knows what-all* and varr. [*OED2 what* pron. A.8.b 1702 →]

1701 in 1879 MA Hist. Soc. Coll. 5th ser 6.44 **ME**, [He] Charg'd the Council with Lying, Hypocrisy, Tricks, and I know not what all. **1824** Child *Hobomok* 159 **NEng**, A pretty piece of business it would be of a truth, to have a parcel of tawny grandchildren at your heels, squeaking *powaw*, and *sheshikwee*, and the devil know-eth what all. **1832** Kennedy *Swallow Barn* 2.185 **VA**, There were Oreads and Dryads and Hamadryads, Napeæ, Nereids, Naiads, and—the devil knows what all! **1872** *Harper's New Mth. Mag.* 44.446 **NEng**, Tea-service, dish-covers, coffee-urn, spoons, . . —and Heaven knows what and all—everything vanished. **1884** Twain *Huck. Finn* 148 **MO**, They all . . had such a powerful lot to say about faith, and good works, and free grace, and preforeordestination, and I don't know what all. **1889** *Harper's New Mth. Mag.* 79.701 **CT**, He talked reel fluent 'bout the saints, an' purg't'ry, an' Fridays, . . an' penances, an' I d' know whatall. **1912** Green *VA Folk-Speech* 480, And I don't know what all. **1920** Lewis *Main Street* 50 **MN**, I simply can't understand all these complications and hoop-te-doodles and government reports and wage-scales and God knows what all that these fellows are balling up the labor situation with. **1954** Foote *Trip to Bountiful* 20 **TX**, They've got servants and I don't know what all. **2004** in 2008 *DARE* File—Internet **eTN**, It's got lots of critters like tiny shrimps and a few small snails and god only knows what all else growing in it.

(2) *and what-all.* [*OED2 what* pron. A.8.b 1901 →]

1854 Haliburton *Americans at Home* 3.343 **MS**, He . . went an' got him er jug er ball-face whiskey, an' some red pepper, an' dogwood bark, an' snake root, an' Injun turnip, an jimston weed, an' what all. **1895** Brown *Meadow-Grass* 266 **NH**, An' as for that money, I guess it went for doctor's stuff an' what all. **1919** Kyne *Capt. Scraggs* 5 **CA**, By the time we've taken on coal an' water an' what-all, it'll be eight or nine o'clock. **1952** *Post–Std.* (Syracuse NY) 17 July sec 2 15/2, The mules and elephants and whatall might as well be brought in to take down the big top. **2002** *DARE* File—Internet, I've . . appeared as an "expert witness," have been involved in trials and lots of depositions and whatall these last three-four years. **2006** *Ibid*, So, I'm not even saying, oh, effort and self-discipline and whatall can solve all your problems.

2 Used as a rel pron: all that, everything that.

1955 in 1971 O'Connor *Complete Stories* 131 **cGA**, I can't make what all I done wrong fit what all I gone through in punishment. **1971** *Appalachian Oral Hist. Project* 160 **eKY, cAppalachians** (*Montgomery Coll.*), We growed the most of what all we was living on on the farm. **1975** in 2004 Montgomery–Hall *Dict. Smoky Mt. Engl.* 642, What all. . . He'd take something on his plate of what all they was on the table and put it in his plate and mix it up. **1981** *Ibid*, What all. . . That's just about what all I've done.

what-all adj Cf **what-all** pron **1a**
Used as a pl interrogative.

1973 *Appalachian Oral Hist. Project* 111 **eKY, cAppalachians** (*Montgomery Coll.*), Well, what all jobs have you worked at during your life? **2001** *DARE* File **swNM**, The informant . . is a half Anglo/half Hispanic, born 1982, dropped out after sixth grade. . . he says "*What-all* rides?" meaning "what kinds of rides?" at an amusement park. **2007** in 2008 *DARE* File—Internet **Pacific NW**, Who knows what all kinds of good seedlings could arise from this mating?

what and all pron [Brit dial] Note: The use of *what and all* in formal writing in the sense "that, and all that, which" is not treated here.

1a **=what-all** pron **1a. chiefly Sth, S Midl**
1939 Harris *Purslane* 260 **cNC**, Mary, what and all did Miss Jennie have in that funny box last night? **1940** Schauffler *Days* 21 **NJ**, Well, young fellow, what and all have you got here? **1946** *PADS* 6.32 **eNC** (as of 1900–10), *What and (in) all. . .* What. "What and (in) all did you do?" . . Common. **1948** Chase *Grandfather* 147 **sAppalachians**, So fin'lly they stopped and sent one rogue back to find out what'n-all had happened. **1959** Roberts *Up Cutshin* 104 **KY**, She . . started walking down the road to see where it went to and what all she could see down there. **2002** Ellis *If I Live* 225 **sAL** [Black], She could cook up I

don't know what'n'all and have it ready for you. **2005** Flood *Sometimey Friend* 94 **SC** [Black], Well, what 'n all did they do?

b **=what-all** pron **1b(1).**
1859 *Godey's Lady's Book* 59.219 **NH**, Silks, and satins, . . and loose gowns, and basques, and the Lordy knows what'n all! **1878** *Harper's New Mth. Mag.* 58.138 **NY**, I . . saw there the broken fishing rods, the old rabbit-hutches, the bird-traps, kites, marbles, and Heaven knows what and all! **1897** Spofford *Stepping-Stones* 148 **NEng**, A lawyer came, and we signed our names to papers, and I don't know what and all. c**1975** in 1991 Thomas *S. Appalachia* 215 **NC**, An' I don't know what 'n all.

2 **=what-all** pron **2.**
1948 Chase *Grandfather Tales* 192 **sAppalachians**, And out of what'n-all we gathered, we sold the other half. **1962** *Prairie Schooner* 36.5 **wNC**, That ain't the half what'n all we gonna get.

what for adv phr

1 Why, for what reason? [nEngl, Scots dial] **chiefly Sth, S Midl** Note: Sentences such as "What did he do it for?" and stand-alone elliptical "What for?" are widespread in colloq use and are not illustr here.

1830 Sedgwick *Clarence* 1.113 **NYC**, What for did you ask me? **1861** *Harper's New Mth. Mag.* 23.656 **NEng**, I don't know what for you want to quarrel. **1875** in 1884 Lanier *Poems* 179 **GA** [Black], And what for waste de vittles. **1909** *DN* 3.387 **eAL, wGA**, *What for.* . . Why. "What for did you do that?" Rare. **1922** Gonzales *Black Border* 281 **sSC, GA coasts** [Gullah], Wuffuh you duh do dat? **1931** Goodrich *Mt. Homespun* 45 **sAppalachians**, What for did you tell me Paw warn't at home? **1937** Thornburgh *Gt. Smoky Mts.* 134 **eTN**, I . . couldn't think what fur he'd be talkin' to me about grasshoppers.

2 foll by ppl adj: How, like what?—freq in phr *what for (a) looking* having what appearance? Cf **what for (a)** adj phr
1859 Victor *Miss Slimmens' Window* 146 **NEast**, [They are] dying this blessed minit . . to see how the bride is dressed, and what for a looking person . . the bridegroom . . is. **1871** *Atlantic Mth.* 27.42 **NEng**, "What for a looking fellow was he?" said the policeman. **1887** Eggleston *Graysons* 218 **cIL**, "Un [=and] what fer sized man?" asked Bijy. **1910** Glass *Potash & Perlmutter* 335 **NYC**, "I wouldn't do nothing rash, Gans," Abe advised. "What for a looking feller is this salesman of yours?" **1921** U.S. Congress House *Contested Election Campbell vs. Doughton* 1124, This man Crayton you spoke of, what for looking man is he? **1931** Runyon *Guys* 64 **NYC**, Do you say a doll from St. Pierre? What-for looking kind of a doll, Bob? **1952** [see **what for (a)** adj phr].

what for (a) adj phr [In some areas obviously a calque of Ger *was für (ein)*, but in others perh from the same idiom in Scots and Engl (Kentish) dial (*SND what* pron. V.6; *EDD for* prep. 1.(32)).]
What kind of (a); which, what?

1853 (1854) Baldwin *Flush Times* 149 **AL, MS**, He asked about you . . and what for a lawyer you was. **1859** (1968) Bartlett *Americanisms* 506, *What for a*, is frequently used by Pennsylvanians, instead of "What kind of a," in asking questions. **1872** *Scribner's Mth.* 3.522 **eMD**, "What for a sort of a man" is hardly indigenous, but sounds suspiciously like an imitation of "Fildelfy" or "Baltmer" business talk. **1877** Wright *Big Bonanza* 55 **NV**, They . . wanted to know what for critter it war. **1890** *DN* 1.70 **LA**, *Whatfer.* "Whatfer man is he?" = what sort of man is he? Prevalent where Germans are numerous, and evidently their "was für." Very common in Red River parish, and perhaps in Webster, where there are many German-Jewish merchants. **1895** *DN* 1.375 **eTN**, "What fer of country is it?"—a question to one returning from the Far West. [*DN* Ed: *Of* here may be simply *a*. The pronunciation is likely to be [hwɑt fɚə] in both cases.] **1897** Lewis *Wolfville* 152 **AZ**, What for a hoss is she? **1908** *German Amer. Annals* 10.51 **sePA**, What for book is that? **1927** *AmSp* 2.366 **cwWV**, What for man is he? . . "Did you want to know what for man he is?" **1942** Warnick *Garrett Co. MD* 16 **nwMD** (as of 1900–18), *What-fer* . . what kind, what particular one, which. "What-fer horse was Joe riding?" **1946** *PADS* 6.32 **eNC** (as of 1900–10), "What for time did you have?" . . Still somewhat common in parts of Va. and N.C. **1952** Brown *NC Folkl.* 1.606, *What for.* . . What kind. "What for man is your new boss?" "What for looking book is it?" c**1960** Wilson *Coll.* **csKY**, What for time did you have at the party? **1966** *DARE* (Qu. KK69, . . 'Sort' or 'kind'? "What _____ rifle is that?"; total Infs questioned, 75) Inf **GA1**, For a. **1969** *DARE* FW

Addit **csPA,** What fer [fər] kind of car is that? **2006** *DARE* File **Madison WI,** What for a beer do you want?

what for (a) looking   See **what for** adv phr **2**

what make (so) adv phr   Pronc-spp *wuh make, ~ mekso, w'ymekso*   Gullah   Cf *DJE wa mek, DCEU wha[t]¹* 2.8
How comes it that, why?

    1867 Allen et al. *Slave Songs* xxxi **eSC,** What make you leff we? **1922** Gonzales *Black Border* 146 **sSC, GA coasts** [Gullah], Wuh mekso you ent tek anodduh lady fuh wife? *Ibid* 339, *W'ymekso*—what makes it so, why. **1927** Adams *Congaree* 12 **cSC** [Gullah], *Jube:* They must be ain't no white folks dere. *Sam:* Wuh make? *Ibid* 13, What make he fine ole man Hall fi' dollahs? *Ibid* 18, If I wants to talk wid Mensa, wuh make I ain't can talk to him? **1977** Dillard *Lexicon* 62 **LA** (as of c1960) [Black], An occasional basilect form . . turns up, as in John Henry Jackson's "What make I love you so" in a blues lyric.

whatness, of a adj phr   **esp Sth**
Of the same quality, "of a muchness."

    1864 in 2006 *DARE* File—Internet **AL** [*Mobile Register and Advertiser* (AL) 11 Nov 1/7], It were useless to attempt a description of my daily life in durance vile. It's all of a whatness. **1881** Clark *Baby Rue* 202 **Sth,** It's most like they would be together: they're much of a whatness for pride and hatin' pale-faces. **1909** *DN* 3.387 **eAL, wGA,** *Whatness. . .* Equal value, size, importance, or the like. "Them two pigs are about of a whatness." **1916** *DN* 4.348 **KS** (as of 1896), *Whatness, of a. . .* Similar. "They are of a whatness." **1999** Proulx *Close Range* 51 **WY,** They leaned under the hood. "Shoot, I hate pawin around in these goddamn greasy guts, all of a whatness to me."

what side adv phr   *Gullah*   Cf *DBE, DJE* (at *what side*), *DCEU* (at *wisside*)
Where?

    1867 Allen et al. *Slave Songs* xxx **seSC,** "What side you stayin', sir?" was one of the first questions put to me. **1923** Parsons *Folk-lore Sea Islands* 200 **csSC,** Leader. Mary, have you seen my tukry? Ring. Mam? Leader. What side did it go? Ring. So [=in that direction (pointing)].

whatsomever pron   Pronc-sp *whatsomevuh* [*OED2* c1400 →; "*Obs.* exc. *dial.*"]   **now esp Sth**   *esp freq among Black speakers*   Cf **howsomever, whatsomever** adj, adv, **whensomever, wheresomever, whosomever**
Anything that, whatever.

    1858 Hammett *Piney Woods Tavern* 301 **CT,** Whatsumever they hed to trade. **1875** Holland *Sevenoaks* 40 **nNEng,** "Look 'ere, boy; can you keep right 'ere," tapping him on his breast, "whatsomever I tell ye?" **1895** Johnston in *Century Illustr. Mag.* 49.468 **GA,** It hurt one of 'em when the tother turned him down at whatsomever they went at. **1945** FWP *Lay My Burden Down* 25 **Sth** (as of c1865) [Black], Do whatsomever your master tells you to do. **1952** in 1958 Brewer *Dog Ghosts* 26 **TX** [Black], Whatsomevuh come to pass am awright wid him. **1993** Mason *Feather Crowns* 96 **KY** (as of c1900), Claude does just whatsomever he pleases. **2008** *DARE* File—Internet **cnGA** [Black], When them songs come to me they already written. Whatsomever I be speakin' is already written on my tongue.

whatsomever adj   [*OED2* 1429 →1894; "Now *obs.* or *dial.*"]
Of any sort, what(so)ever.

    1843 Thompson *Major Jones' Courtship* 28 **GA,** I am posed . . to all manner of shecoonery whatsumever! **1843** (1916) Hall *New Purchase* 172 **IN,** I don't pretend to no larnin whatsomever. **1870** *Punchinello* 2.155 **VT,** His son-in-law had no sorter hesitation, whatsomever, in planten his muddy feet into my wife's work basket. **1890** Holley *Samantha among Brethren* 26 **NY,** She had . . insisted that wedlock wuz a state of perfect serenity, never broken in upon by any cares or vexations whatsomever. **1969** Wilson *Stars* 151 **Ozarks,** He was natural-born muleheaded enough to argy about anything a-tall or nothing whatsomever. **2008** *DARE* File—Internet **wMA,** I have a Savage Model 10 also but mine has no flash suppressor or hider whatsomever. *Ibid* **cwCA,** If anyone knows how I could lobby publishers to reprint the book, without any modification whatsomever, drop me a line.

‡**whatsomever** adv
To any extent, at all.

    2005 *DARE* File—Internet **TX,** And as a side note not relevant to FD whatsomever, but definitely relevant to the topic of bootlegs—you're not a good citizen if you don't buy a legit . . version.

whatsomevuh   See **whatsomever** pron

what takes one   See **take** v **B7**

‡**what time** conj phr   [Cf arch *what time* at the time when, when(ever)]
As long as.

    1963 *Mt. Life* 39.2.53 **sAppalachians,** He might declare his willingness to "cross hell on a rotten log fer a chanch fer to give 'er a piece o' the workin's o' his mind, er aither nuver speak to the slankin' thang agin what time breath's in his old cyarcass, one."

whay exclam   Also *way*   [Perh var of **hey** exclam **2;** but cf *EDD way* int. 1 "A call to a horse to stop."]   **esp nNEng, Upstate NY** See Map   *old-fash*   Cf **whee**
Go, go on—used as a command to a cow, rarely to a horse.

    1854 (1949) Thoreau *Jrl.* 6.484 **ceMA,** Cattle are driven down from up-country. Hear the drovers' *whoa whoa whoa* or *whay whay whay.* **1881** Hall *Lyrics of Home-land* 47 **NH,** With sparklin' eyes, an' cheeks aglow,/ Returned the maiden gay,/ Who waved her arms an' shouted low:/ "*Whay boss! whay boss! o whay!*" **1891** Garland *Main-Travelled Roads* 42 **IA,** An old man was driving the cows, crying out: "St—boy, here! Go on there! Whay, boss!" **1903** *DN* 2.336, In the North cattle are driven with shouts of 'Whay! Whay!' **1945** *AmSp* 20.117 **VT,** In my boyhood, when the horse got into the wrong place we used to drive it out by shouting *whay.* . . I heard from my father that in his farm boyhood (Western Vermont, about 1850) they used to drive a horse away with *whay.* . . As far as I now remember, we chivied a cow as well as a horse with *whay.* **1965–70** *DARE* (Qu. NN22d, . . *Expressions used to drive away . . animals . . [for a cow]*) Infs **NH5, NY22,** 68, 73, 96, 163, **VT7, WI21,** Whay [hweɪ]; **NY108,** Whay; **NY75,** Whay cow; **NY68,** Whay out of here; **NY200,** Way [we]. [All Infs old]

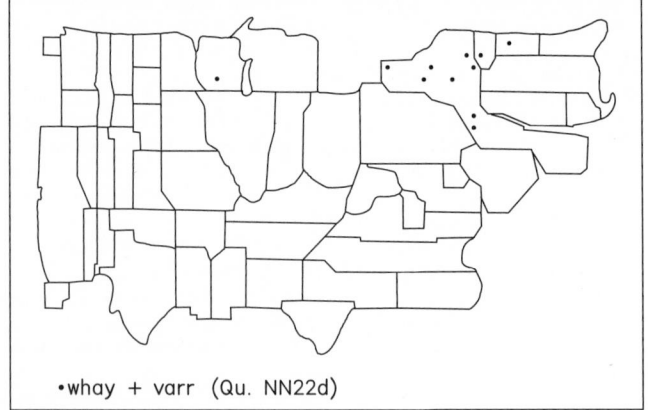

•whay + varr (Qu. NN22d)

whe   See **where** **A3**

wheat   See **wheat cake**

wheat bird n
1 =**bobolink B.**

    [**1747** Catesby in Royal Soc. London *Philos. Trans.* 44.444 **VA,** These exotic Birds. . . arrive annually at the time that Wheat . . is at a certain Degree of Maturity; and have constantly every Year from their first Appearance arrived about the same time in numerous Flights. They have attain'd the Name of *Wheat-Birds.* [*DARE* Ed: This quot may refer instead to another sense.]] **1857** *Porter's Spirit of Times* 16 May 162 **MD,** The merry song of the wheat-bird of Maryland, *alias* reed-bird of Pennsylvania, *alias* rice-bird of South Carolina. **1887** *Forest & Stream* 28.412 **FL,** Here, at least, little Robert o'Lincoln is not persecuted. He is here known by the name of "wheat bird." Why he should be called that I don't know. Surely if he depended on wheat for a living in Florida he would not live long. **1967** *DARE* (Qu. Q14, . . *Names . . for . . bobolink*) Inf **TX43,** Wheat bird [FW: Inf queries]. [*DARE* Ed: Cf sense **3** below.]

2 =**dickcissel.**

    1851 *S. Planter* 11.340 **NC,** This [wheat] the Col. drilled, and it yielded, after suffering greatly from the depredations of the little yellow bird, (called here the "wheat bird,") about three quarts. [*DARE* Ed: This quot may refer instead to another sense.] **1901** Moore *Summer Hymnal* 94 **TN,** A yellow-breasted wheat-bird, almost a miniature field lark, swung on a tall wheat-stalk and eyed me as he sang his monotonous chee-chee-che-e-e. **1901** *Galveston Daily News* (TX) 7 July [16]/3 (newspaperarchive.com), Another bird seen in that part of the State [= cTX] is the black-throat bunting or wheat bird. They are good songsters and sing during the nesting season. A person can not help from recognizing them from their habit of sitting on a weed singing their song, which is like this: "Chit! Chit, Chee! Chee! Chee!" **1918** *Wilson Bulletin* 30.58 **cOK,** Dickcissels, known locally as "field canaries" or "wheat birds," bred abundantly around Minco. **1956** *Daily Jrl.* (Commerce TX) 17 May 1/1, Mr. Smith has reported in detail the commuter's life of a [""]Wheatbird," known also as a Dickcissel, who chose the lower section of a tractor seat for a low cost bird-housing project.

3 =**horned lark. esp TX**

1858 *TX Almanac 1859* 70, The ravages of the *Wheat-Bird* are sometimes formidable. This is a small bird, about the size of a snow-bird or sparrow, somewhat resembling the former. In 1849 they appeared for the first time in countless myriads, when the wheat was in the dough, and destroyed nearly the entire crop. **1859** *NY Observer* (NY) 27 Jan 32/3 **TX,** We saw on the prairies myriads of the wheat birds, sometimes so destructive to the wheat crops in this region. We have heretofore contended . . that these destroyers were migratory in their habits, and did not winter in the country. We are now convinced to the contrary. **1882** *Galveston Daily News* (TX) [18 Aug 4]/4 (newspaperarchive.com), The wheat bird, a tiny and insignificant-looking little feathered biped, is going for the boll worm as eagerly as the boll worm is going for the cotton. **1892** *Forest & Stream* 38.124 **TX,** Some call him here the "wheatbird," but he is not the wheat-bird that I have known before—which has not the black markings that this bird has. Some call him the "prairie bird," but I find him both on the prairie and in the woods. . . [*Forest & Stream* Ed: The bird is a shore lark *(Otocoris alpestris)* [=*Eremophila a.*]] **1893** *Death Valley Exped.* 2.68, He found it [=Mexican horned lark] excessively abundant on the San Joaquin Plain, where it is locally known as the 'wheat bird' in the grain districts, owing to its habit of following the farmer and eating the newly-sown wheat. **1895** *IA Ornith.* 1.34 **nwIA,** They [=horned larks] bear in Buena Vista Co. the names of "snowbird", "ground bird", and "wheat bird[·]" The last name is well deserved, for they are very fond of wheat. **1917** (1923) *Birds Amer.* 2.212, Horned Lark. . . Other Names. . . Road Trotter; Wheat Bird [etc]. **1934** *Amarillo Sun. News–Globe* (TX) 11 Feb [7]/2 (newspaper-archive.com), I estimated that two common Panhandle birds, the horned lark or "wheat bird" and the western lark sparrow eat 12,500,000 pounds of week [sic] seeds a year. **1975** *Sun. Post-Crescent* (Appleton WI) 30 Mar sec A 8/4, Some of their nicknames, including road trotter, wheat bird, and prairie bird indicate the strictly terrestrial nature of these larks.

4 =**white-throated sparrow.** [See quot 1951]

1864 Coffin *Forest Arcadia NY* 125, The fine and silver-sweet pipe of the wheat-bird . . repeated its gay song of "Sow your wheat,—wheat, wheat." **1865** U.S. Dept. Ag. *Rept. of Secy. for 1864* 422 **MA,** White-throated Sparrow—Peabody Bird—Wheat Bird. . . This beautiful sparrow arrives in Massachusetts by the first week in April. **1951** *AmSp* 26.277 **MA,** The wood thrush is called *cornfield bird* in southern Indiana and *corn-planting bird* in Kentucky, because its song is especially noted by farmers when sowing corn. For like reason . . the white-throated sparrow is named *sow-wheat* (Pa.), *sow-your-wheat-bird* (Maine), and *wheat bird* (Mass.) **1967** *DARE* (Qu. Q21, . . Kinds of sparrows) Inf **TX**42, Wheat bird.

5 =**meadowlark 1.**

1903 Natl. Assoc. Audubon Soc. *Educ. Leaflet* 3.[4] **GA,** In some of the Southern states, notably in Georgia, the meadowlark is called the wheatbird, as it is claimed it destroys wheat.

6 Either of two similar birds: the blue **grosbeak** *(Passerina caerulea)* or the **indigo bunting.**

1884 *Young Oologist* 1.44 **NC,** There are two birds called "wheatbird," one the blue grosbeak . . and the other the Indigo bunting. **1917** *Wilson Bulletin* 29.2.83 **KY,** *Guiraca caerulea.*—Wheat-bird, Hickman, Ky.

wheat cake n   **chiefly N Cent, NEast (exc NEng)**   See Map

A pancake made with wheat flour; *occas* a **buckwheat cake;** also abbr *wheat,* usu in phr *stack of wheats.*

1772 (1903) Patten *Diary* 293 **NH,** Robt Forsith gave me about 1¼ bushell of Wheat and his wife baked a parcel of Wheat Cakes for me when I went up to Cockermouth. **1865** (1889) Whitney *Gayworthys* 218 **NEng,** There are wheat-cakes and maple syrup for your breakfast. **1903** *Cedar Rapids Eve. Gaz.* (IA) 19 Dec 8/1, *Refrigerators Robbed; No Butter For Buckwheats.* . . The head of the house . . wended his way to the ice box to procure the butter for his stack of wheats. **1918** IL State Bee-keepers' Assoc. *Annual Rept.* 17.25, There is no better break-

fast than wheat cakes or buckwheat cakes and honey. **1941** *Language* 17.335 **WI** [*LANCS* fieldwork], *Wheat cakes*—1 [of 50 infs] . . *o[ld].* **1965–70** *DARE* (Qu. H20b, . . Names . . for pancakes) 41 Infs, **chiefly N Cent, NEast (exc NEng),** Wheat cakes; **CT**2, Wheat cakes—made with wheat; **IL**27, Wheat cakes—made with buckwheat; **IL**49, Wheat cakes—"a stack of wheats" is what you'd probably order if you stopped to eat in a trucker's diner; **IL**99, Wheat cakes—restaurant name; **MD**17, Wheat cakes—standard wheat pancake; **MD**50, Wheat cakes—regular flour pancakes; **MI**52, Wheat cakes—local restaurant menu; **MI**102, Wheatcakes—used in restaurants; **NY**194, Wheat cakes—with buckwheat flour; **PA**131, Wheat cakes—made with white flour; **SD**3, Wheat cakes—restaurants. **1966** Dakin *Dial. Vocab. Ohio R. Valley* 2.327, *Griddle cakes.* . . *Wheat-cake* is scattered and rare in Ohio and Indiana, but is fairly common in Illinois west of the Little Wabash from the Shawnee Hills northward. It is mentioned by only one speaker in Kentucky. . . For this businessman . . *wheat-cake* may quite possibly be a restaurant term. For Illinois informants and other scattered speakers north of the river it seems to be a familiar name used to distinguish between wheat pancakes and griddle cakes made of corn meal. **1969** *DARE* FW Addit **cIL,** [Restaurant menu:] Wheat cakes—short stack 30¢—Wheat cakes—full stack 35¢. **1973** Gawthrop *Dial. Calumet* 72 **nwIN,** *Fried round, flat cakes made with white flour:* . . pancakes 120 [of 125 checklist infs] . . wheat cakes 4 [infs]. **1986** Pederson *LAGS Concordance* (Pancakes / of wheat) 9 infs, **scattered Gulf Region,** Wheat cakes. **2005** *DARE* File—Internet **Chicago IL** ["Chi" Slang Glossary], Wheats, as in "a stack of wheats": Pancakes.

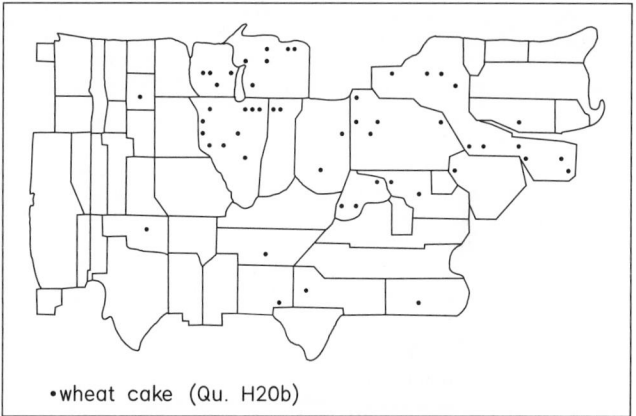

• wheat cake (Qu. H20b)

wheat duck n   **OR**

Either of two related ducks: the **baldpate 1** or the **gadwall.**

1882 Nash *2 Yrs. OR* 95, First come the mallard and his mate . . ; next follow the whistling and the common teal . . ; then the pintail . . ; following these, the wheat-duck, or gadwall *(Chaulelasmus streperus),* in multitudes. **1888** Trumbull *Names of Birds* 21 **OR** (as of 1885), He found this species [=the American widgeon] in enormous flocks on the wheat-fields, and . . it was there called the wheat-duck. **1940** (2000) *WPA Interview Morgan* (Internet) **nwOR,** When the settlers began to break up the sod and plant wheat the ducks would come in great flocks and strip whole fields in a night. We called them "wheat ducks" and had to guard the fields to save the crop.

wheatgrass n

1 =**quack grass 1** or a closely related grass of the genus *Elymus.*

1822 Eaton *Botany* 494, *Triticum* [=*Elymus*] . . *repens,* (wheat-grass, couch-grass, quack-grass . .) . . Very troublesome in fertile soil, and useful in barren sand. **1843** Torrey *Flora NY* 2.475, *Triticum caninum* [= *Elymus caninus*]. . . Fibrous-rooted Wheat-grass. **1903** Porter *Flora PA* 40, *Agropyron Novæ-Angliæ* [=*Elymus trachycaulus*]. . . New England Wheat-grass. Mountains of northeastern North America. **1937** U.S. Forest Serv. *Range Plant Hdbk.* G3, Thickspike wheatgrass, known also as downy, fuzzyhead, northern, small, thickstalk, and Yukon wheatgrass. **1966** *DARE* (Qu. L9a, . . Kinds of grass . . grown for hay) Inf **WA**1, Slender wheatgrass. **2007** [see **2** below].

2 A grass of the genus *Agropyron* native to the central and western US and commonly grown for hay and forage.

1891 *Century Dict.* 6889, *Wheat-grass.* . . any wild grass of the genus *Agropyron* or *Triticum.* **1937** U.S. Forest Serv. *Range Plant Hdbk.* G1, For many years botanists considered the wheatgrasses and wheat *(Tri-*

ticum) as belonging to the same genus, and the older species of *Agropyron* were originally placed under *Triticum.* No doubt the common name, wheatgrass, was applied because of the resemblance of many of the agropyrons to wheat. **1965–70** *DARE* (Qu. L9a, . . *Kinds of grass . . grown for hay)* Infs **ID1, MT2, 3, ND5, SD5, WY4,** Wheatgrass; **ID1, ND1, 9,** Crested wheatgrass; **SD8,** Native wheatgrass; (Qu. S9, . . *Kinds of grass that are hard to get rid of*) Inf **ID1,** Wheatgrass. [*DARE* Ed: Some of these Infs may refer instead to other senses below.] **2007** (acc) U.S. Dept. Ag. *Plants Database* (Internet), *Agropyron* [spp]. . . wheatgrass. . . *Elymus caninus.* . . bearded wheatgrass. . . *Pascopyrum* [spp]. . . wheatgrass. . . *Pseudoroegneria* [spp]. . . wheatgrass. . . *Thinopyrum* [spp]. . . wheatgrass.

3 A grass of the genus *Thinopyrum* native to the western, central, and northeastern US.

    1894 *Jrl. Amer. Folkl.* 7.103 **cNE,** *Agropyrum glaucum* [=*Thinopyrum intermedium*] . . wheat-grass. **1924** *Jrl. Ecology* 12.220 **CO,** Wheatgrass *(Agropyrum glaucum)* at Burlington . . occurs most abundantly in areas where the short-grass sod has been broken. **2007** [see **2** above].

4 also *western wheatgrass:* A grass *(Pascopyrum smithii)* native to the US except for the Gulf and Atlantic coasts. Also called **bluejoint 2, bluestem 2, pondgrass 1, slough grass 2c.**

    1911 *Century Dict. Suppl.,* Western wheat-grass. . . *Agropyron occidentale* [=*Pascopyrum smithii*], distinguished by its bluish tinge throughout and known as *(Colorado) blue-stem* and *gumbo-grass.* **1937** U.S. Forest Serv. *Range Plant Hdbk.* G5, Bluestem, . . sometimes called Colorado bluestem, Smith bluejoint, and western wheatgrass, is one of the commonest and most abundant of the western wheatgrasses. **1967** Harrington *Edible Plants Rocky Mts.* 301, Any species of *Agropyron* could surely be utlized [for food], particularly western wheatgrass *(A. smithii),* which is a common native grass. **2007** [see **2** above].

5 also *(blue)bunch wheatgrass, western ~:* A grass *(Pseudoroegneria spicata)* native to the western US.

    1911 *Century Dict. Suppl.,* Bunch wheatgrass, *Agropyron spicatum* [= *Pseudoroegneria s.*], a densely tufted species, one of the most valuable bunch-grasses of Washington and Oregon. **1937** U.S. Forest Serv. *Range Plant Hdbk.* G6, Bluebunch wheatgrass, also known as . . western wheatgrass, and spiked wheatgrass. **1950** Hitchcock–Chase *Manual Grasses* 241, *Agropyron spicatum.* . . Bluebunch wheatgrass. **2007** [see **2** above].

wheat mow   See **mow** n[1] **2**

whee exclam   **chiefly Nth**   Cf **whay**

Used as a call to animals, esp for driving away pigs.

    1889 *Jrl. Amer. Folkl.* 2.162 **NH,** We had different terms for frightening or driving away different animals. . . [A]lways "whee! whee! whee!" to drive the pigs and hogs. **1894** MI Pioneer & Hist. Soc. *Hist. Coll.* 22.541, I thought of sending a deacon, to drive them [=hogs] out but knew that if I did I should soon hear him under there crying out "whee, whee." **1945** *AmSp* 20.118 **VT,** I heard from my father that in his boyhood (Western Vermont, about 1850) they used to drive a horse away with *whay* and a pig with *whee.* **1966** Dakin *Dial. Vocab. Ohio R. Valley* 2.288, *Calls to chickens.* . . miscellaneous calls . . *whee!* **1967–69** *DARE* (Qu. NN22d, . . *Expressions used to drive away . . animals . . [for a hog]*) Infs **NY163, 219,** Whee [hwi]; **MN41, MI66,** (Whee,) whee; **MI63,** Whee [huɪ].

wheedle n   Also *whiddle*   [Cf *EDD* *widdle* sb.[2] "A very young duck."]   Cf **weedily, widdie** n

A baby chick.

    1968 *DARE* FW Addit **VA15,** *Wheedles* or *whiddles*—baby chicks. Old-fashioned.

wheedle-dee n   **KY**

=**wood thrush 1.**

    1940 (1978) Still *River of Earth* 37 **KY,** I caught a wheedle-dee throwing his voice once, him setting in one tree, making out he was in another'n, and me looking my eyeballs out trying to see him. **1968** *DARE* FW Addit **KY,** Wheedle-dee—wood thrush *(Hylocichla mustelina).* **2007** *DARE* File—Internet **KY,** It was a wheedle-dee he'd heard. He could recollect the last time he'd heard one—wood thrush, she called it.

whee-haw(ed)   See **weewaw B**

wheejaw   See **weewaw A1**

wheel n

1 used attrib in combs *wheel dog, ~ horse, ~ mule, ~ ox, ~ steer, ~ team;* In a team of two or more pairs of draft animals or two or more animals harnessed in tandem: rearmost.   Cf **swing** n **1, wheeler** n[1]

    1760 (1925) Washington *Diaries* 1.136 **VA,** With much difficulty made my Chariot wheel horses plow. **1860** in 1938 *Colorado Mag.* 15.25 **PA,** Traded our wheel mules . . for a span of horses. **1869** *Overland Mth.* 3.127 **TX,** The Texan driver . . has his "wheel steers," his "swing steers," and his "lead steers." **1875** *Atlantic Mth.* 35.556 **West,** The wheel team is under the immediate control of the driver, who rides on the back of the near mule, holding his line in his left hand. **1903** (1965) Adams *Log Cowboy* 6 **TX,** One of the wheel oxen . . could be ridden. **1965** Bowen *Alaskan Dict.* 34, *Wheel dog*—The dog nearest the sled in a sled dog team. **1965–70** *DARE* (Qu. K32a, *With a team of horses, . . the horse on the driver's right hand*) 13 Infs, **scattered,** Wheel horse; **DC8, MD20, 26, 30, 48, TN24,** Off-wheel horse; (Qu. K32b, *The horse on the left side in plowing or hauling*) 13 Infs, **scattered,** Wheel horse. **1967** *DARE* FW Addit **seOR,** *Wheel team*—the team behind the lead team, when you have 2 teams; **CO,** *Wheel horses*—in four-horse team, two next to wheels. **1986** Pederson *LAGS Concordance* **Gulf Region,** 21 infs, Wheelhorse(s); 1 inf, **cnAL,** Wheelhorse—in back; 1 inf, **cnMS,** Wheelhorse—with four, one in front of wheel; 1 inf, **cLA,** Wheelhorse—the one in back when four horses used; 1 inf, **cLA,** Wheelhorse—in back; 1 inf, **ceAL,** Wheelhorses—two next to wagon if driving four; 1 inf, **nwMS,** Wheelhorses—the back horses; 5 infs, Wheel mule(s); 1 inf, **cwTN,** Wheel mule—on left—the one you ride; 1 inf, **nwMS,** Wheel mules—immediately in front of wagon; 2 infs, **AR,** Wheel team; 1 inf, **cnAR,** Wheel team—in back hooked to tongue; 1 inf, **cnAR,** Wheel team—back team of two teams; 1 inf, **ceAR,** Wheel team—the two in back.

2 also *iron wheel, silver ~:* A dollar, esp a silver dollar. **scattered, but esp W Midl, SW** See Map   *old-fash* Cf **wagon wheel 1**

    1807 (1930) Tufts *Autobiog. of a Criminal* 293 **NH,** Wheel—a dollar. **1857** *Spirit of Times* 10 Oct 91/2 **seIA,** We have looked in vain for the man who had the pluck and "wheels" (cash) to come amongst us. **1900** *DN* 2.69 [College slang], *Wheel.* . . A dollar. **1905** *DN* 3.100 **nwAR,** *Wheel.* . . Dollar. 'They paid two silver wheels for the paper.' Rare. **1907** Mulford *Bar-20* 60 **SW,** I paid twenty wheels for that eight years ago. **1909** *DN* 3.387 **eAL, wGA,** *Wheel.* . . A dollar: referring to the silver dollar which is in common use, a dollar bill being almost an object of curiosity in rural districts. **1965–70** *DARE* (Qu. U27, . . *A silver dollar*) 13 Infs, **scattered, but esp W Midl, SW,** Wheel; **IL7,** Iron wheel; **MS23,** Silver wheel; (Qu. U20, . . *Dollars* . . *"It cost a hundred _____."*) Infs **SC10, TX37, 42, 83,** Wheels. [17 of 19 Infs old] **1972** Cooper *NC Mt. Folkl.* 89, A wheel—a silver dollar.

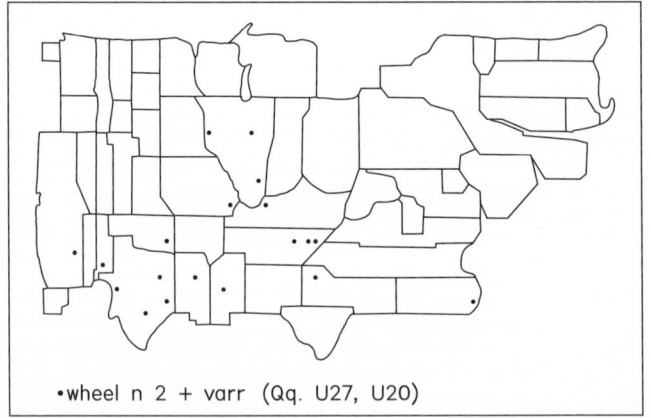

•wheel n 2 + varr (Qq. U27, U20)

wheel v, hence vbl n *wheeling* [*OED2* *wheel* v. II.8.a "To convey in a wheeled vehicle"]   **chiefly Nth, N Midl**   Cf **ride** v[1] **B13b, roll 1**

To push (a baby) in its carriage.

    1884 *Daily News* (Frederick MD) 16 Dec [4]/3 (newspaperarchive.com), When a fellow is asked to wheel the baby while his wife gets supper it always happens on the day he's been fishing and he feels like leaving the Prohibition party. **1923** in 2008 (acc) Lexis–Nexis Legal Research *State Case Law: NY* (Internet), The mother. . . left plaintiff and a baby temporarily in charge of Evelyn Kaye, about thirteen years old. The latter wheeled the baby and was looking after plaintiff. **1949** Kurath *Word Geog.* 77, *Wheel the baby* is in universal use in the North and the North Midland, including the Shenandoah Valley and the northern half of West Virginia. It is also the usual expression in the southern half of that state, and in all of Maryland west of the Bay except around St. Mary's. **1972** *PADS* 57.41 **Marietta OH** [Older native speakers], *Wheel the baby*—The Northern and North Midland form, *wheel the baby,* was given only by [1 inf]. **1989** Pederson *LAGS Tech. Index* 228 **Gulf Region,** *(Wheel [the baby])* 21 [of 914] infs, Wheel; 7 infs, Wheeling; 1 inf, Wheel (the baby) out. **2006** in 2008 *DARE* File—Internet **NYC,** She looks eternally tired wheeling the baby around and around the block.

wheelbar   See **wheelbarrow 2**

wheelbarrel n   [Folk-etym for **wheelbarrow**]

[**1849** *Chr. Reg.* (Boston MA) 24 Mar 48/2 **NEast,** [They have] no more skill than is sufficient to wheel a barrel or use a shovel.] **1870** *Riverside Mag.* 4.269, Charlie might run with his little "wheelbarrel" loaded with chips and weeds. **1894** *Newark Daily Advocate* (OH) 19 Dec 8/3, *Dear Santa Clause* [sic].—I wish you would bring me a wheel barrel, a horn, an express wagon a foot ball, and a train of cars, please don't forget good night. **1922** *Oakland Tribune* (CA) 16 Sept 1/3, A man stooping over may push a wheelbarrel full of muck. **1939** *LANE* Map 163 *(Wheelbarrow)* 6 infs, **MA, RI,** [(h)wil bærl, -l]; 2 infs, **MA, RI,** [(h)wilbærəl]. **1966** *Good Old Days* Feb 26 **ceKS,** One year he had a flat-bed wheel barrel with buggy wheels. **1967–69** *DARE* (Qu. L41, *A device for moving dirt and other loads, with one wheel in front and handles to lift and push it behind*) Infs **KS4, MO26, 36, MA2, PA67, 147,** Wheelbarrel. **1971** Bright *Word Geog. CA & NV* 158, *Wheelbarrow* . . wheelbarrel 3% [of 300 infs] P[attern] xiv [=the city] . . One in San Francisco noted "not *wheelbarrel.*" **1974** *DARE* File **csWI** (as of 1950), Wanted to buy: 2 wheel-barrels (rubber-tired). **1986** Pederson *LAGS Concordance (Wheelbarrow)* 11 infs, **scattered Gulf Region,** Wheelbarrel(s). **2005** in 2008 *DARE* File—Internet **sCA,** My point here is that they were selling wheelbarrows. In all my 31 years on this blue planet I have thought it was called a wheelbarrel. Makes sense. You have ½ tub on a squeaky single wheel. **2006** *DARE* File, We discussed wheelbarrel (which my wife, born in NYC and raised in Old Greenwich, CT, uses) vs. wheelbarrow.

wheelbarrel race   See **wheelbarrow race**

wheelbarrow n   Usu |'(h)wi(ə)l bæro, -ə, -ˌbɛro, -ə|; for addit varr see below   Note: *DARE* evidence at Qu. L41 shows aspirated |hwil-| forms to be slightly more common in the **Sth** than elsewhere, and least common in **NYC, NJ.** Cf **wheelbarrel** Std senses, var forms.

1 |-ˌbɑro, -ˌbɔro, -ə|; for addit varr see quots; pronc-sp *wheelborrow.*

1835 *Lit. Jrl.* 1.78 **sePA,** If I must go, it must be on the Yankee principle of rotation—bring a wheel-borrow. **1844** Hall *Primary Reader* 47, When your wheel-borrow is broken, mend it. **1883** Harris *Nights with Remus* 68 **GA** [Black], Dey ketch up Brer Rabbit en put 'im in a wheelborrow. **1893** Shands *MS Speech* 67, *Wheel-borrow* [hwil-bɔrə]. Illiterate white and negro for *wheel barrow.* **1935** *AmSp* 10.166 **PA** [Engl of PA Germans], There is the type of pronunciation, not general among the Pennsylvania Germans but heard now and again among both educated and illiterate speakers, in which [ar] is heard in such words as . . *wheelbarrow.* **1961** Kurath–McDavid *Pronc. Engl.* 125, In *wheelbarrow,* a farm word, the vowel /ɑ/, varying regionally from [a ~ ɑ] to [ɒ]. . . In folk speech . . is rather generally used in all parts of the Eastern States, except southeastern New England, the rather densely populated area extending from the lower Hudson Valley to the lower Potomac (including New York City, Philadelphia, Baltimore, and Washington), parts of the Virginia Piedmont (Richmond and vicinity), and the Low Country of South Carolina with the lower Savannah Valley (Charleston, Savannah, Augusta). In an area extending from western Pennsylvania southward to western North Carolina, even middle-class speakers predominantly use /ɑ/ in this word, and not all cultured speakers avoid it. **1965–70** *DARE* (Qu. L41, *A device for moving dirt and other loads, with one wheel in front and handles to lift and push it behind*) 121 Infs, **widespread, but less freq NEng,** Wheelbarrow ['(h)wi(ə)l barɔ, -ə]; **GA74, IN35, 45, 63, PA132, SC32, 69,** ['(h)wi(ə)l bɔro, -ə]; **MS81, OK14, PA163, 166,** ['(h)wil barɔ, -ə]; **OK43, TX43, 45,** ['(h)wil bɔrɔ];

AK8, CA57, KS6, MN9, ['(h)wil boro, -ə]. **1969** *DARE* FW Addit **cCA,** Wheelbarrow ['wil barə]. [**1989** Pederson *LAGS Tech. Index* 88 **Gulf Region,** *Wheelbarrow* . . 126 [of 914] infs offered proncs of the types ['(h)wil baro]; 3 infs, ['(h)wil bɔro].] **2003** in 2008 *DARE* File—Internet **MD,** Took my wheel borrow and put 100 pounds in it. **2008** *Ibid* **swNY,** This is a production type wheeel [sic] borrow for the contractor, commercial grade quality.

2 |-ˌbɑ(r), -ˌbær, -ˌbɛr, -ˌbɔ(r)|; pronc-spp *w(h)eelbar;* for addit pronc varr see quots.   **scattered, but chiefly Sth, Midl** See Map   *esp freq among rural speakers and those with little formal educ*

1898 Dunbar *Folks from Dixie* 197 **OH** [Black], Ain't he the one that made you haul him in the wheelbar'? **1917** *Jrl. Amer. Folkl.* 30.192 **cnNC,** He . . seed a little boy runnin' through the house with a wheelbar'. **1930s** *ADD* **eWV,** Wheelbarrow. . . wheelbar. **1941** *AmSp* 16.10 **eTX** [Black], *Wheelbarrow* . . usually. -ə . . ['wiəl bɑ:]. **1965–70** *DARE* (Qu. L41, *A device for moving dirt and other loads, with one wheel in front and handles to lift and push it behind*) 107 Infs, **scattered, but chiefly Sth, Midl,** W(h)eelbar ['(h)wi(ə)l bar, -ˌbar, -ˌbær, -ˌbɛr, -ˌbɔɚ]; **NC68, VA75,** Wheelbaw ['wi(ə)l baə]; **LA8,** Wheelbaw ['hwil bɑ:]; **VA68,** Wheelbaw ['hwil bau] [*DARE* Ed: Perh an r-less var of [-ˌbɛro].] [Of all Infs responding to the question, 46% were comm type 5, 38% gs educ or less; of those giving these responses, 58% were comm type 5, 60% gs educ or less.] **1974** *TX Mth.* Aug 60, By day we . . mixed cement and pushed it in iron wheelbarrows ("wheelbars"), [etc]. **1976** Garber *Mountain-ese* 100 **sAppalachians,** I need a wheelbar to haul away all my trash. **1982** *Barrick Coll.* **csPA,** *Wheelbarrow*—pron. ['wil baɚ]. **1989** Pederson *LAGS Tech. Index* 88 **Gulf Region,** *Wheelbarrow* [161 of 914] infs offered proncs of the types ['(h)wil baɚ]; 27 infs, proncs of the types ['(h)wil bæɚ, -bɔɚ, -bʌɚ]; 2 infs, ['hwil bɔ]; 1 inf, ['hwil bæ].] **1990** Smith *Understanding Speaking S. Lang.* 9, *Weelbar*—A one-wheeled cart. **2004** Marler *Reflections on Life* 42 **cLA** (as of 1930s), We always had a wheelbarrow (which we called a wheelbar). **2008** *DARE* File—Internet **NC,** Sherry said I told them you would say wheelbar. . . I do call it a wheelbar. All us southerners do, or used to.

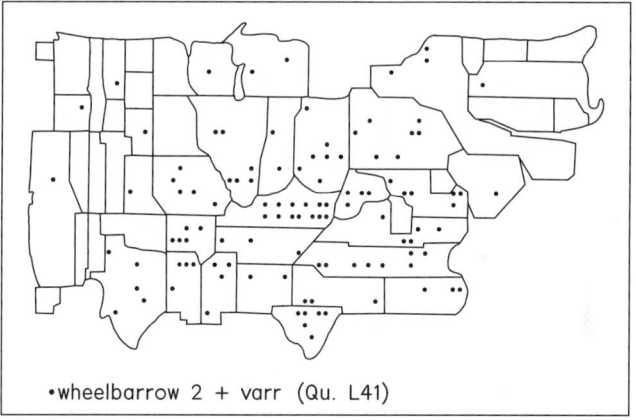

•wheelbarrow 2 + varr (Qu. L41)

3 |-ˌbærər, -ˌbɑrər|; for addit varr see quots.   Cf Intro "Language Changes" IV.1.c

[**1908** *DN* 3.289 **eAL, wGA,** *Barrow.* . . ['bɑrə].] **c1940** Eliason *Word Lists FL* 14 **wFL,** *Wheelbarrow* [hwilbɔrɪə]: Common in rural sections. **1959** *VT Hist.* 27.166 **cs,seVT,** *Wheelbarrow* ['hwil barlɚ] . . pronc. Rare. Windham. **1969** *DARE* (Qu. L41, *A device for moving dirt and other loads, with one wheel in front and handles to lift and push it behind*) Inf **IL93,** Wheelbarrow ['hwil bærɚ]. **1989** Pederson *LAGS Tech. Index* 88 **Gulf Region,** *Wheelbarrow* . . 2 infs [of 914], ['hwil bærɚ, -ˌbɛrɚ].

4 |-ˌbærɪ, -ˌbarɪ, -ˌbɛri|; pronc-sp *wheelborry.*

1894 Riley *Armazindy* 137 **IN,** Wunst he et his dinner, spread / In our ole wheel-borry-bed. **1939** *LANE* Map 163 *(Wheelbarrow)* 1 inf, **csCT,** ['hwilbɛri], heard from a native of New York State. **1940** in 1944 *ADD* **swPA, nWV,** *Wheelbarrow.* . . [hwil'bæri]. Old illit. speaker. **1989** Pederson *LAGS Tech. Index* 88 **Gulf Region,** *Wheelbarrow* . . 3 infs, ['(h)wil bæɚɪ, -ˌbɑɚɪ].

wheelbarrow race n   Also *human wheelbarrow race, wheelbarrel race*   Cf **elephant walk**

A race between two-person teams, one member of which holds the ankles of the other, who walks on his or her hands.

[**1890** *DN* 1.63 **swOH,** *Wheelbarrow.* A "Dutch wheelbarrow" is made by taking a boy by the ankles and holding his legs up in the air, and letting him walk on his hands.] **1896** *Hawaiian Gaz.* (Honolulu) 7 July 2/3, Wheelbarrow race—En Chang and W.H. Cummings, first; J. Fernandes and Dyde, second. **1899** *Racine Daily Jrl.* (WI) 24 July 1/5, Human wheel barrow race, for a two-bladed knife, Cummings and Olson. **1917** *Syracuse Herald* (NY) 16 Sept 25/1, In the wheelbarrow race one man held another by the feet while the latter walked on his hands. **1923** Acker *400 Games* 251, Wheelbarrow Race. **1948** *Limestone Democrat* (Athens AL) 17 June 1/7, Wheelbarrow race—Winner, DuPuy and Woodroof. **1969** *DARE* (Qu. EE33, . . *Outdoor games . . that children play*) Infs **IN**73, **MA**58, Wheelbarrow race. **2000** *News* (Frederick MD) 27 June sec A 7/5, [Caption:] Jamie Hill, left, and Suzanne Perdue cooperate to maneuver their way through the wheelbarrow race during the barnyard olympics. **2006** *DARE* File—Internet, *How to Hold Wheelbarrow Races.* . . this game is called the wheelbarrow race because the team looks like a person pushing a wheelbarrow. . . This game, which is for old and young alike, is fun at family reunions and church picnics.

wheelbarrow seed n esp **Sth, S Midl** See Map

A non-existent item used as the basis for a practical joke; see quots.

1898 in 2006 *DARE* File—Internet [*Ft. Gibson Post* (OK) 13 Oct 5/3], Allen Bros, the mammoth mercantile firm is here to stay and they have everything from wheelbarrow seed to an icicle from the North start [sic]. **1966–70** *DARE* (Qu. HH14, *Ways of teasing a beginner or inexperienced person—for example, by sending him for a 'left-handed monkey wrench'*: "Go get me _____.") Infs **AL**16, **GA**3, 12, **KY**30, 50, **VA**42, Wheelbarrow seed. **1999** *DARE* File—Internet, Got to run to Ace's and git some of them wheelbarrow seed before they all git gone. It'll soon be time to plant em.

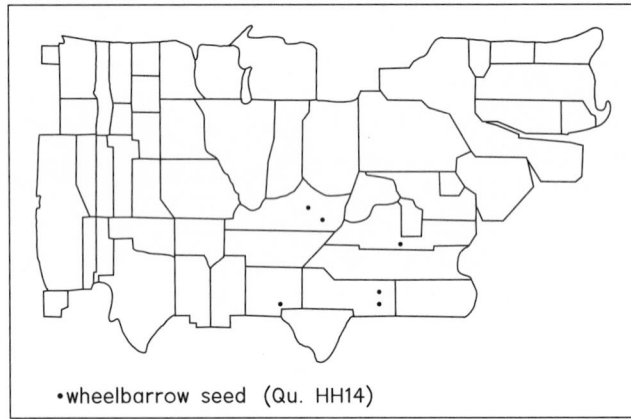

•wheelbarrow seed (Qu. HH14)

wheelborrow See **wheelbarrow 1**

wheelborry See **wheelbarrow 4**

wheel bug n [See quot 1905]

An **assassin bug** (here: *Arilus cristatus*).

[**1815** Kirby–Spence *Intro. Entomology* 1.112, *Reduvius serratus,* [= *Arilus cristatus*], . . commonly known in the West Indies by the name of the *wheel-bug.*] **1869** U.S. Dept. Ag. *Rept. of Secy. for 1868* 316, The *Reduvius,* or wheel-bug, is found in gardens, feeding voraciously upon caterpillars. **1905** Kellogg *Amer. Insects* 204, Another fairly well-known member of this family is the wheel-bug, *Prionidus cristatus,* especially common in the South. The full-grown bug is about an inch long, black, and has on its thorax a thin convex crest with nine teeth. This is the "wheel." **1954** Borror–DeLong *Intro. Insects* 228, One of the most curious species . . is the wheel bug, *Arilus cristatus.* **1997** *Syracuse Herald–Jrl.* (NY) 1 Dec sec D 4/4, The wheel bug and the ambush bug suck the innards out of other bugs.

wheel dog See **wheel** n **1**

wheeler n[1] [*OED2* 1813 →] Cf **lead horse, pointer 1, wheel** n **1**

In a draft team of at least two pairs, one of the animals closest to the front wheels—hence *near-wheeler* and varr, the animal

closest to the left wheel; *off-wheeler* and varr, the animal closest to the right wheel; also fig.

1852 Bristed *Upper Ten Thousand* 223 **NY,** In the next quarter the wheeler instead of the leader was alongside the other team. **1887** (1892) Hinman *Corporal Si Klegg* 225, The motive power of an army wagon usually consisted of six mules. Two large animals, called the "wheelers," one of which the charioteer bestrode, were "hooked" to the wagon. **1897** *Outing* 30.254, This . . leaves the right hand free to use the whip on off-wheeler. **1898** (1899) Warman *Story RR* 274 **West,** Station hands, one writer tells us, began to make trouble for the Mormons by marrying "off wheelers," "nigh leaders," and "swing girls" out of the handcart teams. **1935** Davis *Honey* 311 **OR,** The freighter sat in his saddle on the near-wheeler. **1965–70** *DARE* (Qu. K32a, *With a team of horses, . . the horse on the driver's right hand*) Infs **AR**51, **CA**23, 199, Off-wheeler; **CA**79, **GA**1, Right-wheeler; **CA**11, 31, 101, Wheeler; (Qu. K32b, *The horse on the left side in plowing or hauling*) Infs **CA**31, 79, **GA**1, Left-wheeler; **CA**23, 199, Near-wheeler. **1967** *DARE* Tape **NV**2, If you were driving six on one of those Concords there was a wheeler, then the swing team, and the leaders, that made six. **1986** Pederson *LAGS Concordance,* 1 inf, **cnLA,** Off-wheeler—the horse on the right; 1 inf, **ceAR,** Off-wheeler—the one on the other side; 1 inf, **neGA,** Wheelers—the wheelhorses; 1 inf, **ceAR,** Wheelers—horses in the back on a four-horse team; 1 inf, **csAR,** Wheelers—the mules in back; 1 inf, **seAR,** Wheelers—biggest mules; 1 inf, **cnLA,** Wheelers—closest to logging wagon.

wheeler n[2] Also *yellow wheeler* [Echoic] **MD, VA**
=**flicker** n[2] **1.**

1900 *Wilson Bulletin* 12.2.10 **sMD,** *Wheeler.* Somerset county, Maryland. Probably of onomatopoetic origin. **1917** *Ibid* 29.2.82 **seVA,** Burns records the name "wheeler" as being used in Maryland; with the prefix "yellow," this name is used on Wallops I[slan]d, Va., where we hear also "yellow whicker."

wheelhorse n

1 See **wheel** n **1.**

2 Fig: one who does the hard work in some enterprise or cause; a trusted assistant; a hardworking or powerful person.
chiefly **S Midl, TX** See Map

1843 *Niles' Natl. Reg.* 73.352 **NC,** We were greatly pleased with the homely remarks of Mr. Dobson, a western farmer, and the wheel horse of "democracy" in that quarter. **1845** Hooper *Advent. Simon Suggs* 129 **AL,** I'm jist a hunderd and forty sev*ing* pound, *neat* weight, and I'm a wheel-horse! **1848** Bartlett *Americanisms* 380, *Wheel horse.* . . one's right hand man. Western. **1899** (1912) Green *VA Folk-Speech* 481, *Wheel-horse.* . . A person who bears the brunt, or on whom the burden mostly rests. **1906** Lynde *Quickening* 213 **eTN,** His first care was to assure the "wheel-horse" member of the municipal purchasing board that he was ready to talk business. **1959** *VT Hist.* 27.166, *Wheel horse.* . . [A] good worker. Rare. **1965–70** *DARE* (Qu. HH27a, *A very able and energetic person who gets things done*) 10 Infs, **S Midl, TX,** Wheelhorse; (Qu. GG19b, *When you can see from the way a person acts that he's feeling important or independent*: "He seems to think he's _____.") Inf **TX**98, Wheelhorse; (Qu. HH17, *A person who tries to appear important, or who tries to lay down the law in his community*: "He'd like to be the _____ around here.") Infs **TX**5, **VA**15, Wheelhorse. **1969** Wilson *Stars* 112 **Ozarks,** Like my Pa used to say to me, "Myrtle," he'd say, "if you'd work as much as you talk you'd shore be a wheelhoss for labor." **1973** McCarthy *Child of God* 165 **TN,** One

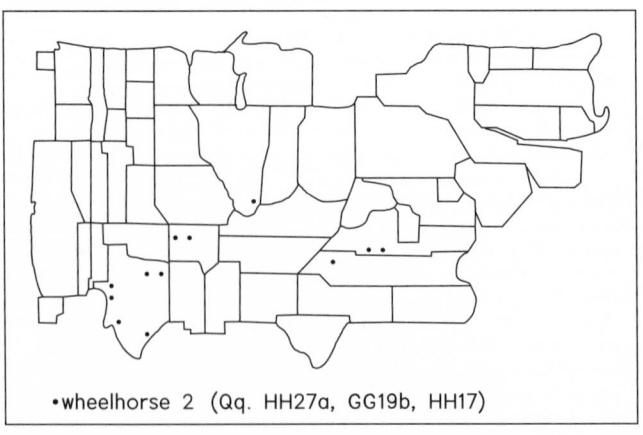

•wheelhorse 2 (Qq. HH27a, GG19b, HH17)

man with a little guts stood up to em and that was Tom Davis. He was a wheelhorse. **1976** Garber *Mountain-ese* 100 **sAppalachians,** Ask Charlie about that, he's the boss' wheel-horse. **1986** Pederson *LAGS Concordance,* 1 inf, **cnAL,** The wheelhorse—one who thinks he's important.

wheeling See **wheel** v

wheeling time n
Spring.

1914 *DN* 4.72 **ME, nNH,** *'Fore wheelin' time . . .* Before spring. **1989** *DARE* File, *Wheeling time,* meaning spring, is used in opposition to *sledding time,* for winter.

wheel mule (or ox, steer, team) See **wheel** n 1

wheep n [Echoic]
A **crested flycatcher** (here: *Myiarchus crinitus*).

[**1899** *Independent* 51.1426, A great-crested flycatcher went before me from tree to tree crying "whip" or "wheep" in a clear, high treble.] **1927** Forbush *Birds MA* 2.336, Crested Flycatcher. Other names: Great Crested Flycatcher; Wheep.

whe'er See **whether 2**

wheewhaw See **weewaw 1**

wheezer See **weaser**

whelk n [*OED2* c1000 →; infl in sense by *welt*] **Sth, S Midl** Cf **whelp, whelt**
A pustule, pimple; a welt, bruise; hence rarely v *whelk* to raise a welt on.

1848 Bartlett *Americanisms* 380, *Whelk.* An old name for a pustule, a pimple. The word is not much used in America. **1856** (1875) Jones *Wild Western* 250 **nwMO,** They [=rattlesnakes] hurt like fury, but their tails ain't pisen. Look what a whelk they've made on the hoss. **1934** [see **whelp**]. **1939** Hench Coll. **VA,** [Two men] told me that they know "whelk" in Richmond and Petersburg as the name for this kind of bruise. **c1950** Halpert Coll. 9 **wKY, nwTN,** Bump = a place [on one's body] raised when struck by a rock. Variants: Frog, . . Whelk, Whelp[ɪ] Welt. **c1960** Wilson Coll. **csKY,** *Whelk. . .* A welt or bump on the skin. **1969** *DARE* FW Addit **KY6,** Referring to dog fennel, Inf said, "They'll whelk you." **1976** Garber *Mountain-ese* 100 **sAppalachians,** He has big whelks where his pa whupped him with a hickory. **2007** *Winston-Salem Jrl.* (NC) 14 Apr (Internet), A welt is a ridge or lump raised on the body, as by a blow or allergic reaction. A whelk is a small, usually conical elevation of the skin, sometimes inflamed.

whelp n, v Also sp *wel(lu)p* [Varr of *welt*] **chiefly Sth, S Midl** Cf **whelk, whelt**
A bump or ridge on the surface of the skin; a bruise; hence v phr *whelp up* to break out, cause to break out (in such bumps or ridges).

1895 in 2007 (acc) Lexis-Nexis Legal Research *State Case Law: NC* (Internet), His leg was swollen and had three whelps on the calf. In one of them the skin was broken and it appeared to be irritated—had a bluish, reddish look. **1909** *Ibid* **GA,** One witness testified that she [=a mule] had "whelps all over her body," and a bruised place on her head. **1912** *DN* 3.593 **wIN,** *Whelp. . .* Welt. "She whipped the horse till she raised great whelps on him." **1912** Green *VA Folk-Speech* 481, *Whelp. . .* For *welt.* Caused by a blow by a whip. **1916** *DN* 4.270 **New Orleans LA,** *Whelp.* *Ibid* 302 **VA,** *Whelp.* **1934** *AmSp* 9.71 **TX,** What is the word for the swelling caused by a mosquito or chigger bite? I heard one of my students complain, "Chiggers raise great whelps on me." "Not whelps—" objected her friend. "You mean welts." . . I found that among my Texas informants the *whelp* group predominates, and the *welt* group feels slightly superior. Both are wrong. The proper word, I should think, is *whelk. . .* Today it is rare in American speech. **c1937** in 1972 *Amer. Slave* 2.1.170 **SC** [Black], You couldn't put a hand on her shoulder and back widout touching a whelp. **1939** Hench Coll. **VA,** She always said "whelp" for a bruise. "That bump raised a whelp on my arm." **1946** *PADS* 6.32 **eNC** (as of 1900–10), *Whelp. . .* A welt, wale. . . Common. **1952** *PADS* 17.34 **SC,** Time was in the upcountry when the teacher would, with a *hickory,* raise *whelps* on the legs of a recalcitrant pupil. **1962** Fox *Southern Fried* 119 **SC,** He had a razor welp that looked like someone had laid a ruler from the tip of his left ear to the edge of his chin and carefully followed it. **1963** in 2007 (acc) Lexis-Nexis Legal Research *State Case Law: MI* (Internet), When she saw him he bore evidence of manifest physical abuse, broken skin,

"welps." **1966–68** *DARE* (Qu. X39, *A mark on the skin where somebody has sucked it hard and brought the blood to the surface*) Inf **SC46,** Whelp; (Qu. BB24, . . *A rash that comes out suddenly—from hives or something else: "He's got some kind of _____ all over his chest."*) Infs **GA9,** 12, **LA14, MS73,** Whelps; (Qu. BB33a, . . *A swelling under the skin, bigger than a pimple, that comes to a head*) Inf **GA28,** Whelp; (Qu. BB33b, . . *A swelling under the skin—if it is very big or serious*) Inf **GA28,** Whelp. **1969** *DARE* FW Addit **KY60,** Allergies to certain weeds can raise whelps or swollen lumps on the skin. **1985** *Amer. Jrl. Med.* Feb 184 **eTN,** *Wellup . .* localized swelling of subcutaneous tissue. **1986** Pederson *LAGS Concordance,* 1 inf, **seAL,** Whelp—a little white spot; 1 inf, **csTN,** Your skin would whelp up in bevels; 1 inf, **cnMS,** Insect bites will whelp you up. **2006** in 2007 *DARE* File—Internet **IN,** [She] left her child in the daycare, returning only to find her daughter with a big welp on the side of her head.

whelt n, v [Var of *welt; EDD* "Also written *whelt* Cum. e.Lan. War."] **chiefly Sth, S Midl** Cf **whelk, whelp**

1895 *DN* 1.375 **seKY, eTN, wNC,** *Whelts* (welts). **1928** *AmSp* 3.405 **Ozarks,** *Welt* is often pronounced *whelt.* **1949** *PADS* 11.37 **ME,** *Whelted. . .* See *browsed. Ibid* 30, *Browsed. . .* bruised. **1983** *MJLF* 9.1.60 **ceKY** (as of 1956), *Whelt . .* a welt. **2006** *DARE* File—Internet **TX,** My daughter had had an outbreak of hives and whelts everyday for 10 days straight. **2007** *Ibid* **GA** (as of c1965), [He] let a broadhead "kiss" his bow string while climbing a tree top [sic] hunt. I remember the whelt it gave him. *Ibid* **OH,** Try saying *whelt* on the side of someone's head.

when chickens have teeth See **chicken** n C1

whenever conj Cf **whenevern, wherever**
Used in contexts where *when* would be expected, as:

a in ref to a single punctual event: At the time that, as soon as. [*OED2 whenever* adv. 2. "At the very time or moment when; as soon as. (Now only in *Sc.* and *Irish* use.)"; *SND* (at *whan*); for further discussion see 2001 *Jrl. Engl. Ling.* 29.234–39] **Sth, S Midl, wPA** Note: The emphatic sense "at *any* time that, no matter when" in ref to future events is std and is not illustrated here.

1878 *Appletons' Jrl.* 5.413 **PA,** The Pennsylvanians use the word *whenever* to signify "as soon as." Thus it will be said that, "whenever the carriage came, the lady got in." **1912** Green *VA Folk-Speech* 481, *Whenever. . .* As soon as; "He will go whenever he gets ready." **1939** Hall Coll. **wNC, eTN,** *Whenever. . .* When. "What did they do with you whenever you killed that man some two or three years ago?" **1952** Brown *NC Folkl.* 1.606, *Whenever. . .* When; as soon as. **1968** *DARE* Tape **GA21A,** What was that . . you said the other night whenever we was, whenever Jean and them was here and you wanted to go with them?; **GA25,** I told a good joke on my daughter . . whenever she got married. **1978** in 2001 *Jrl. Engl. Ling.* 29.235 **TN,** My mother, whenever she passed away, she had pneumonia. **1978** Massey *Bittersweet Country* 207 **Ozarks,** *Whenever* (when): Whenever you leave, come get me. **1982** McCool *Sam McCool's Pittsburghese* 38 **PA,** Whenever: an indefinite time, literally "when"—"Whenever I finish the car, I'll take you for a ride." **1983** *DARE* File **swIN,** South of Terre Haute, *whenever* is used commonly for *when* in such a phrase as "Whenever we finished, we went back." (No implication of repeated action.) **2001** *Ibid* **TX,** I left school whenever I was 14 years old. *Ibid* **wPA,** My boyfriend recently pointed out that I say "whenever" in place of "when". For instance: "You wore your green sweater whenever David and Emma came for dinner." . . I grew up in Pittsburgh which I know is a hot bed for strange colloquialisms.

b in ref to an extended period of time: During or within the time that. [**1996** *Concise Ulster Dict.* 384 "Whenever I was young I could do it"; see also 2006 Montgomery *From Ulster* 170] **Sth, S Midl**

1926 *DN* 5.404 **Ozarks,** *Whenever. . .* When. "Whenever I was a gal, folks kep' ther' clo'es on, an' th' men-folks allus wore th' britches." Sometimes a final *n* is added, and the word sounds like *whenever'n.* **1943** in 1944 *ADD* **nWV,** *Whenever. . .* 'My growth was stunted whenever I was small.' **1944** *AmSp* 19.156 **sIN,** *Whenever* (for 'when'). 'That must have been whenever Jerry was a baby.' **1968** *Foxfire* Fall–Winter 23 **neGA, cwNC,** "Whenever" for "when" as in "I was in the seventh grade whenever I went to that school." **1969** *DARE* Tape **IL69,** Whenever I was a boy just a-farming with . . mules, well that didn't raise over about seventy bushel to the eighty. **1998** *DARE* File **TX,** Whenever I was a young girl. **1999** *Ibid* **LA,** I have in-laws from Louisiana who say "whenever" where I, and most people I know, would say "when." Example: Whenever I was a kid, we went fishing with my grandpa. **2001** *Ibid* **AL**, I worked for a while (1971) with a guy from Bay Minette, Alabama . . and I was very interested in and amused by the fact that the word "when" was not in his vocabulary. He always used "whenever" whenever I would have used "when." I have seldom heard "whenever" used this way in Virginia.

c in ref to a predictable repeated event: Every time that.

1919 *DN* 5.36 **KY**, *Whenever*. . . Often used for *when.* " 'Possums gits fat whenever pawpaws gits black and ripe."

whenevern conj **S Midl** Cf **evern, iffen**

1 On any or all occasions that, whenever.

1882 *Eau Claire News* (WI) [16 Dec 4]/2 (newspaperarchive.com) **S Midl**, Hit used to smoke so whenever'n the wind got in the east, hit's been shut up so long, folks has forgot it's there. **1931** *Folk-Say* 5.220 **eTX**, Whenevern the other git-tar couldn't handle one of them runs, he'd just leave it go and let Barly have it. **1978** Hiser *Quare Appalachia* 176 **eKY**, The log house soon became a favorite hangout with us younguns whenevern we could manage to get away from the ever-night gin work of ginning cotton.

2 =**whenever a.**

1923 *DN* 5.198 **swMO**, Hit shore did seem like Spike was right whenever 'n he said we-alls had a language of our own. **c1970** in 2001 *Jrl. Engl. Ling.* 29.244 **eTN**, Whenevern we got married, we went on back to Marks Cove. **1983** in 2004 Montgomery–Hall *Dict. Smoky Mt. Engl.* 643 **wNC, eTN**, I . . run plumb out of the shack . . with that hose up my britches leg, and whenevern I seen what it was, why I went back to the shack. **1978** Hiser *Quare Appalachia* 180 **eKY**, I never knowed it whenevern we was married back yander nigh onto forty-five year ago.

3 =**whenever b.**

1926 [see **whenever b**].

whensomever conj Also sp *whensumever* [*OED2* a1425 →; "Now *dial.* or *vulgar*"] esp **Sth, S Midl** Cf **howsomever, whatsomever** pron, adj, adv, **wheresomever, whosomever** Whenever.

1828 *Philadelphia Mth. Mag.* 2.106, I have no conceit of drowning, whensomever I think of crabs. **1837** *Knickerbocker* 10.443 **NY**, Whensumever I threw out the mail-bags at a stoppin' place, I replenished the inner individual. **1853** Bennett *Ella Barnwell* 9 **KY**, I always do it, whensomever I get a chance. **1882** *Marion Daily Star* (OH) [21 July 2]/2 (newspaperarchive.com) **NEng**, Whensomever they fetched a man before him that had been took up for a misdeed . . he always asked 'Who is she?' **1894** *Scribner's Mag.* 15.61 **GA** [Black], Whensomever she happy, us happy. **c1938** in 1970 Hyatt *Hoodoo* 1.12 **seGA** [Black], Whensomever ah git out . . ah may go back to mah business agin. *Ibid* 2.1643 **New Orleans** [Black], Now, whensomever he comes, he come with a chain. **1964** Will *Hist. Okeechobee* 128 **FL**, Raulerson delivered the babies when somever they arrived. **1982** *Hush Child* 74 **GA** (as of 1930s–40s) [Black], Whensomever the good spirit is with you, he drives that evil one out.

wher See **whether 2**

where adv, conj, pron Usu |(h)wɛr, (h)wɛə(r), (h)wær, (h)wæə(r)|; for varr see **A** below

A Forms.

1 |(h)wɑ(r)|; pronc-spp *wha(r), whah.* **chiefly Sth, S Midl**
1834 in 1956 Eliason *Tarheel Talk* 320 **nw,cwNC**, Whar. **1843** (1916) Hall *New Purchase* 325 **IN**, Thar's whar the grammur man lives. **1851** Hooper *Widow Rugby's Husband* 28 **AL**, What is it to you whar I come from, or whar my connexion lived? **1852** *Yankee Notions* 1.354, Whar on airth, Eb, have you been? **1867** (1969) Lanier *Tiger-Lilies* 128 **GA** [Black], Dey done hung old Marster up to a tree-limb to make him tell whah he put de las' year's brandy. **1893** Shands *MS Speech* 67, *Whar* [hwɑr]. Is used by illiterate whites to mean . . *where.* **1901** *DN* 2.184 **neKY** [Black], *Where* wha'. **1901** Harben *Westerfelt* 2 **nGA**, "Whar's Sally?" asked Mrs. Slogan. **1908** Fox *Lonesome Pine* 17 **KY**, I'll show ye whar you can ketch a mess. **1909** *DN* 3.387 **eAL, wGA**, *Whar*. . . *Where. Whur* is also heard. **1917** Torrence *Granny Maumee* 66 [Black], Whah you bin? **1936** in 1976 *Weevils in the Wheat* 266 **VA** [Black], We got rid of de water whar we don scald him by puttin' hit in de river. **1941** *AmSp* 16.5 **eTX** [Black], *Where* . . [hwɑ]. **1942** [see **A2** below]. **1976** Garber *Mountain-ese* 100 **sAppalachians**, *Whar* . . where.

2 |hwɜ˞, hwʌr|; pronc-sp *whur(r).* **chiefly Sth, S Midl**

1852 Byrn *Rattlehead's Chron.* 160, He axed me a heap ov questions—such as "Whur ar you frum, what mite your name be, whar are ye gowin?" **1862** Bagby *Letters of Mozis Addums* 63 **VA**, She . . come heer, whur she's bin goin on 2 ears. **1866** Trowbridge *South* 303 **swTN**, You may stop at a house now whur they 'll steal your horse. **1894** Chopin *Bayou Folk* 94 **LA**, Whur 's my wife an' that Frenchman? **1909** [see **A1** above]. **1909** *DN* 3.406 **nwAR**, *Whur*. . . Where. **1910** *DN* 3.451 **cwNY**, *Where, adv.* Often [hwɜ˞]. **1923** *DN* 5.224 **swMO**, *Whur*. . . Where. **1942** Hall *Smoky Mt. Speech* 25 **wNC, eTN**, [ɑ] was observed also in . . *where*. . . In the speech of most people, the retroflex central vowels [ɜ˞], [ʌ˞], [ɝ] (unstressed) are by far more common than any others in *where, anywhere, everywhere, nowhere, somewhere. Ibid* 105, You can see where [hwɝ] it was. **1946** *AmSp* 21.98 **sIL**, Pronunciations such as . . *whur* . . are common among uneducated natives. **1949** Webber *Backwoods Teacher* 92 **Ozarks**, He seen whur if you send in a dime you get big mail. **1981** in 2000 Shores *Tangier Is.* 155 **Chesapeake Bay**, The boy looked up at us and asked, "Whur you frum?" **1981** Pederson *LAGS Basic Materials*, 1 inf, **csLA**, *Where* [hwɝ] are your coats? **2010** *DARE* File **St Louis MO** [Black], Two black couples from Saint Louis were on one of the shows. Sure enough, the . . sound . . in *here*, . . *there, air*, etc., was uniformly pronounced [ʌr], "hurr, thurr, and urrwhurr," as the song says.

3 |wɛ|; pronc-spp *way, weh, wey, whe.* **sSC, GA coast** *Gullah*

1888 Jones *Negro Myths* 12 **GA coast**, Eh set on de tree-limb right ober way Buh Rooster duh sleep. **1922** Gonzales *Black Border* 187 **sSC, GA coasts** [Gullah], "*Duh plat-eye! Uh shum! uh shum!* [=I see him]." "*Weh-weh 'e dey?*" **1927** Adams *Congaree* 1 **cSC** [Black], Down wey de wild turkey gobbles, way down on de Congaree. **1928** Peterkin *Scarlet Sister Mary* 80 **seSC** [Gullah], Come set down whe de air is cool here by de window. **1949** Turner *Africanisms* 268 **seSC** [Gullah], [wɛ dɪ də ste dɛ nɒʊ.] *Ibid* 269, Where I am staying there now.

B As pron.

Who, whom, that. **sAppalachians** Cf **what** pron **1** Note: The exx from Page may indicate an r-less pronc [hwə] that should instead be interpreted as *what.*

1886 Page in *Harper's New Mth. Mag.* 74.40 **VA** [Black], Didn't none on 'em hol' a candle to his young mistis, whar wuz de ve'y pink an' flow'r on 'em all. **1890** *Ibid* 82.112 **VA** [Black], I name him arter Mr. P'laski Greener, whar Lucindy use to b'longst to. *Ibid* 113 **VA** [Black], We done see hoss-races whar wuz hoss-races. **1917** in 1944 *ADD* **sWV**, *Where* [as relative pronoun]. **1918** *DN* 5.19 **NC**, *Ware* (and *where*), who, whom as relatives. "The man ware I saw is gone." **1941** in 1944 *ADD* **eWV**, *Where*. . . 'The book where I bought . . ' = the book that I bought.

C As conj.

1 also *to where:* In order that, so that. **esp Sth, S Midl** Note: Both *where* and *to where* meaning "that" (as in "I read in the paper where he got married" and "You are big enough to where it will fit you") or "(to or at) the point at which" (as in "It got (or was) (to) where I couldn't stand it") are widespread in informal use and are not treated here.

1967 Green *Horse Tradin'* 179 **TX**, He would sell them to me to where they would make money. **1970** *Thompson Coll.* **AL, MI**, You gotta write it [=an order] where I kin read it. He's got him a bicycle where he kin ride to work if it comes a strike. I'm fixed up where I won't hafta werry [=worry] none. (Birmingham AL 1920's, Detroit 1946–60 from southerners) **1986** Pederson *LAGS Concordance*, 1 inf, **swAR**, It was made to where you could pour that coal out; 1 inf, **cwLA**, To hold the plate down to where that the hot tamales wouldn't rise to the top. **1994** *DARE* File **LA**, I'd weld a gusset between the legs of that table to where it wouldn't wobble. *Ibid* **AL**, We piggybacked on a telephone survey, to where we were able to get a random sample without having to set up the sample ourselves. *Ibid* **LA**, The one [thread]'s regular and th'other's reverse, to where it won't come off with the vibration. *Ibid* **AL**, I like to read books about native Americans, to where I can, you know, understand their culture better. *Ibid* **TN**, You can shop around, and write for lists and so forth, to where you won't get ripped off on the price.

2 foll *the kind of (something):* A (something) of such a kind that, such a (something) that.

2001 *DARE* File **ceIA**, While talking about a management training workshop he had attended, my cousin said, "I want to be the kind of supervisor where everyone respects me." **2002** *Ibid* **swFL**, Have you ever heard of *where* used as a relative pronoun? Example—"Jeff was the kind of person *where* he wanted to be a clean-cut businessman." The speaker was a white male from Fort Meyers [sic] Beach, Florida, being interviewed on a TV documentary. From what he said about himself, he was apparently born around 1950 and had at least some college.

3 See **whether 2.**

where-all adv [Prob (like **what-all** pron) Scots, nIr dial; widespread Brit colloq in phrr like "and I don't know where-all." Cf **who-all** pron]   **scattered, but more freq Sth, S Midl**
To or at what places, where?—used as a direct or indirect interrogative.

1853 Stowe *Uncle Sam's Emancipation* 32 **sOH,** A meddlesome, canting, Quaker rascal, that all these black hounds run to, to be helped into Canada, and nobody knows where all.   **1879** U.S. Congress House *Contested Election Curtin vs. Yocum* 3826 **PA,** Where all have you lived since you have been in the United States?   **1912** in 2008 (acc) Lexis–Nexis Legal Research *State Case Law: MT* (Internet), I think I had been up in town, I couldn't say where all I had been—around town.   **1920** Lewis *Main Street* 406 **MN,** Where-all did you go?   **1941** Faherty *Big Old Sun* 31 **sFL,** It's time Sylla come back, Mis' Penny. Where-all is she?   **1941** Smith *Going to God's Country* 53 **MO** (as of 1890), We traveld miles and God only knows where all we were travling.   **1946** McCullers *Member* 64 **AL,** You would be mighty surprised if you knew whereall I've been today. I was all over this whole town.   **1953** Salinger *Nine Stories* 281 **NEast,** Where all did you go?   **1973** in 2004 Montgomery–Hall *Dict. Smoky Mt. Engl.* 643 **wNC, eTN,** Where all. . . I don't know where all he sold it [=honey] at.   **1986** Pederson *LAGS Concordance,* 1 inf, **cnLA,** I couldn't tell you where-all I stayed; 1 inf, **ceAL,** I don't know where-all he went; 1 inf, **nwGA,** I don't know where-all they sold them to.   **2001** DARE File **OK,** I have heard *where-all* as "*where-all* did you go?" meaning "to which places?"   **2006** in 2010 DARE File—Internet **nwMI,** "Where all did you take the car?" My dad asked.

where at adv phr   Cf **at** prep **4**
Where—used at the beginning of an interrog sentence or clause.

1896 *DN* 1.411 **NYC,** Where at you goin'?   **1921** Wiley *Lady Luck* 147 [Black], Where at's de five dollahs?   **1926** Nason *Chevrons* 14, Hey, guy, where at's the division P.C.?   **1934** in 2005 Howard *Riot Bucksnort* 37 **TX,** If you're the sheriff, where at's your star?   **1940** *Sat. Eve. Post* 20 July 25 **AL** [Black], Where at is the nearest place us can sit down?   **1941** O'Donnell *Great Big Doorstep* 118 **sLA,** I meet Cake on his pony, I say, "Well, where at's the mule, Cake?"   **2004** in 2008 DARE File—Internet **sePA,** Where at are your seats my family has seats in the center grandstand.   **2005** *Ibid* **swIN,** Where at are you in Indiana? I'm in the Evansville area.

where in tunket See **tunket 1**

where it doesn't snow n   Also *where it don't rain,* ~ *snow, where the wind don't blow*   **esp Sth, TX**   See Map
Hell.

1905 (1911) Reed *Jumbles* 36, If I should die to-night / And go / From Here to There / (Or where / It doesn't snow)—/ And, looking back from there / To here,/ Behold / Those six large beers,/ So large, and oh!—/ So cold / . . 'Twould be so sad,/ For I would need them—/ Then.   **1949** Nordyke *Cattle Empire* 151 **TX,** Campbell's self-control dissolved in a

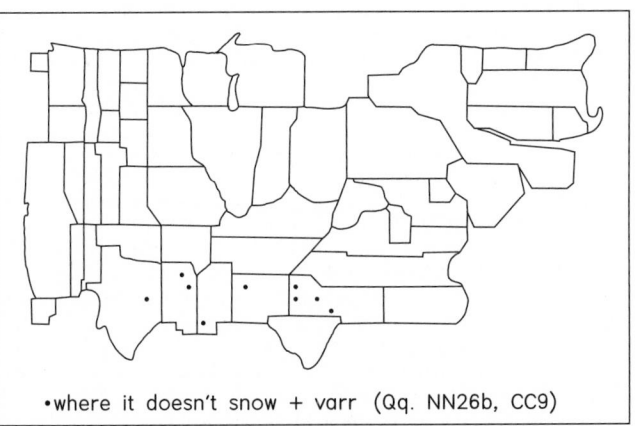

•where it doesn't snow + varr (Qq. NN26b, CC9)

desperate urge to tell everybody to go where "it don't snow."   **1965–70** DARE (Qu. NN26b, *Weakened substitutes for 'hell':* "Go to _____!") Infs **GA**7, 54, 84, **LA**2, 3, **MS**71, **TX**32, Where it don't (*or* doesn't) snow; **AL**3, Where it don't rain; **GA**77, Where the wind don't blow; (Qu. CC9, . . *Words or expressions for hell:* "That man is headed straight for _____.") Inf **GA**54, Where it doesn't snow.   **2007** in 2008 DARE File—Internet **TX,** Why don't you go where it don't snow. we don't need people like you on here.

wheresomever adv   Pronc-spp *wharsomever, wharsumevuh* [OED2 "*Obs.* exc *dial.*"]   **esp Sth, S Midl**   Cf **howsomever, whatsomever** pron, adj, adv, **whensomever, whosomever**
Wherever.

1837 Bird *Nick of Woods* 1.64 **KY,** He kills 'em [=Indians] wheresomever he catches 'em.   **1861** *Harper's New Mth. Mag.* 23.763 **NJ coast,** Oliver had a deal o' money with him wheresomever he mout be.   **1871** (1892) Johnston *Dukesborough Tales* 83 **GA,** He wouldn't let you rest wheresomever he mout see you for talkin' about old North Calliner.   **1886** *Century Illustr. Mag.* 32.281 **GA,** I shall talk up for the house whensomever and wharsomever I go or stay.   c**1937** in 1972 *Amer. Slave* 2.1.35 **SC** [Black], But wheresomever I go, I kept a thinkin' 'bout Rosa.   **1937** in 1958 Brewer *Dog Ghosts* 98 **TX** [Black], He hab to tag 'long wid de fiddler wharsumevuh he kin latch on to a job playin' de fiddle.   **1938** Rawlings *Yearling* 144 **nFL,** "Well, son, we're obliged to follow." "Clare to the Forresters?" "Clare to wheresomever the hogs be."

where the goose bit one n   Also *where the chicken* (or *hen*) *pecked one,* ~ *goose pecked*   Cf *where the Indian(s) shot one* (at **Indian** n **B6**)
1968–70 DARE (Qu. X34, . . *Names and nicknames for the navel*) Infs **IL**96, 143, **MO**20, Where the goose bit you; **GA**75, **NC**6, Where the chicken (*or* hen) pecked you; **GA**59, Where the goose pecked.

where the Indian(s) shot one See **Indian** n **B6**

where the wind don't blow See **where it doesn't snow**

wherever conj   Cf **whenever a**
At the particular place in which; see quot.

2001 *Jrl. Engl. Ling.* 29.244 **Sth,** *Wherever* we parked this afternoon, the car was covered with pedals [sic] when we came out of the store. . . In [this example] the speaker knew exactly where the car was parked, and this occurred in only one location.

wherrer See **whether 2**

whet n   Also *whit* [OED2 *whet* sb. 1 "the interval between two sharpenings of a scythe, etc.; also *fig.* an occasion, turn, 'go'. Now *dial.*" The form *whit* prob reflects infl of *whit* bit.]   **Sth, S Midl**
A turn, try, spell of activity; an indefinite interval of time.

1834 Caruthers *Kentuckian* 1.21, That was jist the corner of an Injin's hatchet. Bob Wiley jist knocked up his arm in time to save me for another whet at the varmints.   *Ibid* 30, They asked us all to sit down to dinner! Well, things went on smooth enough for a while, till we had got through one whet at it.   **1859** Taliaferro *Fisher's R.* 84 **wNC** (as of 1820s), I piked fur home with my pigeons, and we made uvry pan and pot stink with 'um fur one whet.   **1868** Beggs *Pages from Early Hist.* 298 **VA,** What! . . Another Methodist preacher! I left Virginia to get out of reach of them, went to a new settlement in Georgia, and thought to have a long whet, but they got my daughter into the Church.   **1892** Harris *On Plantation* 139 **GA,** Arter they'er been in [the army] a right smart whet, they gits words that their wives an' children is lookin' starvation in the face.   **1896** in 1950 *PADS* 13.11 **AL,** Whet. . . You have lived a long whet.   **1899** (1912) Green *VA Folk-Speech* 481, Whet. . . A turn; a bout. A long space of time: as, "He staid such a whet." "He has been such a whet doing that."   **1909** *DN* 3.387 **eAL, wGA,** Whet. . . A time, a while, a turn. "They talked quite a whet." "I'll try it a whet." Common.   **1915** *DN* 4.192 **swVA,** Whet. . . Turn or 'spell' of work.   **1922** Cowan *Sergeant & People* 86 **cnTN,** I asked a white-haired mountaineer how long the place had been known as Pall Mall. With a memory-reviving shake of his head that ended in a convinced nod, his answer was, "quite a-whit."   **1956** McAtee *Some Dialect NC* 50, Whet: . . a considerable period of time; "She's staying away quite a whet."   **1963** Owens *Look to River* 54 **TX,** It'll be a long whet till he comes agin.   **1968** Haun *Hawk's Done Gone* 34 **eTN,** I set there till it was a right smart whet after dark.   **1994** NC Lang. & Life Project *Dial. Vocab. Ocracoke* 17 **eNC,** Whit. . . A considerable period of time, a bit of time. . . *He's been gone a whit now.*

whet a banter See **banter** n **3**

whether conj Usu |'(h)wɛðə(r)|; for addit varr see below · Std sense, var forms.

1 |'(h)wʌðɚ|; rarely |'hwuðɚ|; pronc-spp *w(h)uther, whurther.*

1865 *Atlantic Mth.* 16.404 **NEast,** I did n't know whuther to believe Taddy or not. **1899** Chesnutt *Conjure Woman* 74 **csNC** [Black], Whuther his own co'tin' made 'im kin' er easy on de co'tin' in de qua'ters, dey ain' no tellin'. **1917** *DN* 4.404 **neOH, MA,** Wuther [wʌðɚ]. . . Whether. **1923** *DN* 5.224 **swMO,** Whuther, conj. Whether. Also *Whe'r.* **1936** in 1944 *ADD* **sePA,** Whether. . . to think [wʌðɚ] he should. **c1938** in 1970 Hyatt *Hoodoo* 1.579 **seGA,** I don't know whurther to fade dis dollar and a half or whurther to wait and shoot it. **1942** in 1944 *ADD* **wNY,** Whether. . . whuther [hwuðɚ]. **1942** Hall *Smoky Mt. Speech* 20 **wNC, eTN,** Very often [ʌ] replaces [ɛ] in . . whether ['hwʌðɚ].

2 |hwɛr, hwɝ, hwɑr|; for addit varr see quots; pronc-spp *whar, whe'er, wher(e), wherrer, whur.* [*OED2 wher. . .* "obs. or dial. contr. f. *whether.*"] **Sth, S Midl**

1795 Dearborn *Columbian Grammar* 139, *List of Improprieties. . . Where* for Whether. **1880** Tourgée *Bricks* 54 **NC** [Black], They all 'llowed I got ter have two names whe'er or no. **1883** (1971) Harris *Nights with Remus* 216 **GA** [Black], Hit aint skacely make no diffunce whe'er Brer Wolf dead er whe'er he 's a high-primin' 'roun' bodder'n 'longer de yuther creeturs. **1887** (1967) Harris *Free Joe* 171 **cGA,** I ain't never year um say wherrer I wuz name Willum, er wherrer I wuz des name Bill. **1893** Shands *MS Speech* 67, *Whar* [hwɑr]. Is used by illiterate whites to mean both *where* and *whether.* They say: "I don't know whar he went or whar he has come back or not." **1899** Chesnutt *Conjure Woman* 11 **csNC** [Black], Well, I dunno whe'r you b'lieves in cunj'in' er not. **1915** *DN* 4.192 **swVA,** Whar [hwɑr . . hwur]. . . short for *whether.* **1923** [see **1** above]. **1940** (1941) Bell *Swamp Water* 31 **Okefenokee GA,** I don't care where I git back er no. **1943** Chase *Jack Tales* 14 **wNC,** We'll have to test him out a little, and see whe'er he's as bad as he claims he is. **1944** *PADS* 2.22 **sAppalachians,** Wher [hwɝ]. . . Whether. **1952** Brown *NC Folkl.* 1.606, Where. . . Whether. . . Granville county and west. **1958** Humphrey *Home from the Hill* 129 **neTX,** The truth don't much seem to care wh'er it's believed in or not. **c1960** *Wilson Coll.* **csKY,** Whether is often /hwɝ/. **1969** *DARE* Tape **GA**51, Now wh'er [hwɔɚ] the 'gator killed 'im or wh'er he—I wouldn't know what killed the otter. **1974** Fink *Mountain Speech* 29 **wNC, eTN,** I don't know whur to go or not. **1981** Pederson *LAGS Basic Materials,* 1 inf, **cnTX,** ['hwɝˤɚ] = whether.

whet owl n Pronc-sp *whit owl*
=saw-whet owl.

1966–69 *DARE* (Qu. Q2, . . *Kinds of owls*) Inf **MI**36, Whet owl—lives on mice and squirrels; a small bird; **NY**227, Whit-owl—smallest owl he's ever seen.

whetrock See **rock** n¹ **4b**

whets and grindstones See **chips and whetstones**

whet-saw See **saw-whet owl**

whew v Also with *around* [*OED2 whew* v.² 1684 →; *whew* sb.² 1905 →] **chiefly NEng**
To hurry, bustle about; hence n *whew* a hurry, rush.

1847 *Expounder* 4.308 **nwOH,** He accompanied me to the depot, from which place I soon set off with a *whew.* **1855** (1856) Holmes *Homestead Hillside* 159 **MA,** The dinner dishes were washed with a whew. **1873** Whitney *Other Girls* 112 **MA,** Nothing ever got ahead of her; she "whewed round;" when she was "whewing," she neither wanted Bell to hinder nor help. **1878** (1887) Cooke *Happy Dodd* 151 **NEng,** Don't whew into everything as though there wan't no more days in the week. **1913** Aplington *Pilgrims* 173 **West,** I scrub my face, and twist my hair up in any kind of a knot, slip into my double-gown, tie on my nightcap—"all with a whew," as sister Martha would say,—and I am ready to jump into bed! **1927** *AmSp* 3.138 **eME,** A child who did not respond instantly when told to do something, might be told . . "come with a whew." **1967** *DARE* (Qu. A21, *When someone is in too much of a hurry*) Inf **MA**5, Whewing around.

whey v [Perh pronc var of *wale, whale* to beat, flog; poss infl by *whey* in the phr *beat the whey out of (someone)*]
To beat severely; hence n *wheying* a beating.

1936 *AmSp* 11.318 **Ozarks,** Whey. . . To beat severely. 'If he was my

boy, I'd jest cut me a hick'ry an' whey him good!' **1967** *DARE* (Qu. Y16, *A thorough beating:* "He gave the bully an awful _____.") Inf **IL**25, Wheying.

which pron

1 used as a relative pron: Who. [*OED2 which* pron. 9. "Now only *dial.*"] **Sth, S Midl**

1870 in 1884 Lanier *Poems* 175 **GA,** That air same Jones, which lived in Jones,/ He had this pint about him. **1916** *DN* 4.285 **sAppalachians,** Which for *who.* **1931** *AmSp* 6.171 **eVA** [Black], My name is W.T. Parker, son of Ellet Parker, which . . [was] born in James City County. . . I'm . . one of the grandsons of the grandsons. . . *which* used to belong to. . . the Egglestons, Travises family. **1969** in 2004 Montgomery–Hall *Dict. Smoky Mt. Engl.* 644 **wNC, eTN,** His other son Giles, which was a-working at it at that time, got caught in the mill. **2002** *DARE* File—Internet **seKY,** [Caption:] Bro. Lay, one of Bro. Terrells ministers, which later became my husband. **2004** *Jrl. Appalachian* 10.136 **wNC** [Black], Miss M—'s son, which done made it big.

2 What? Pardon me?—used to request the repetition or explanation of something improperly heard or understood. [*Concise Ulster Dict. which* 2 "What? pardon?"] **Sth, S Midl**
Cf *do which* (at **do what**), **say which**

1835 Parker *Trip to TX* 88 **Sth,** Ask a question, and if they do not understand you, they reply *"which?"* **1886** *Amer. Philol. Assoc. Trans.* 17.46 **Sth,** Which (among common people, a polite way of saying, "I don't understand"). **1902** *DN* 2.249 **sIL,** Which. . . Always used instead of what, interrogatively. **1903** *DN* 2.336 **seMO,** Which. . . What? Used when one fails to hear distinctly. **1906** *DN* 3.164 **nwAR,** Which. . . What? [**1910** Joyce *English* 348 **Ireland,** 'What's that you say?' Our people often express this query by the single word 'which?' I knew a highly educated and highly placed Dublin official who always so used the word.] **1918** *DN* 5.19 **NC,** Which . . in asking for a statement to be repeated. **1923** *DN* 5.224 **swMO,** Which. . . What did you say? **1925** Kroll *Compar. Study S. Folk Speech* 82 **AL,** Which. . . What did you say. **1936** *AmSp* 11.351 **eTX,** Instead of 'I beg your pardon?' or 'I'm sorry; I didn't understand you' people often say simply 'Which?' **1968–70** *DARE* (Qu. X18, . . *When one person doesn't quite hear what another person said, what does he say?*) Inf **NC**49, Which. **1986** Pederson *LAGS Concordance* (*What's that?—failing to hear someone's utterance*) 11 infs, **Gulf Region,** Which?

which conj

1 Used with a following anaphoric pronoun or pronominal adj or adv to form the equivalent of a non-restrictive relative pronoun or adv. [*OED2 which* pron. 14.a c1374 →] **chiefly Sth, S Midl** Cf *that* **C1**

1851 Burke *Polly Peablossom* 100 **GA,** You know how I *fit* for you, in that last run you had 'long er Jim Smith, what like to a beat you for sheriff, which he would a done it, if it hadn't been for yer Uncle Josey's influence. **1858** *S. Lit. Messenger* 27.203 **VA,** And thar he set, Billy, the Cheef Majistrait uv the Yunitid Staits, which I thought his har ware gray, but twuz blac, died, Oans sed, fer an evenin party. **1866** (1867) Locke *Swingin Round* 246 **KY,** President Johnson, who hez bin likened to Androo Jaxon, and wich, since my appintment I conseed him to be . . his sooperior, requested me . . to draw up . . an address. **1871** (1892) Johnston *Dukesborough Tales* 83 **GA,** If my father was here, which now he is dead and goned, he wouldn't let you rest wheresomever he mout see you. **1891** Johnston *Primes & Neighbors* 36 **GA,** If I have anybody to git mad with, it were Dock Lewis, which it were him that saved my life. **1892** Harris *On Plantation* 75 **GA,** Miss Chicken Hawk she coyspon' wid Mr. Eagle, which he was de big buckra er all de birds. **1897** Lewis *Wolfville* 29 **AZ,** So the girl . . , which her name is Susan, puts on her shaker an' goes stampedin' off. **1898** Lloyd *Country Life* 24 **AL,** I had saw the girl mount her wheel and go spinnin and flyin around the picnic grounds . —which I didn't have no better sense than to think it was as easy as it looked. **1922** Gonzales *Black Border* 231 **sSC, GA coasts** [Gullah], My niece Hacklus, w'ich dat nigguh nebbuh did hab a Gawd' piece uh sense, him paddle de boat 'puntop de snag. **c1938** in 1970 Hyatt *Hoodoo* 2.1244 **cwFL** [Black], Yo' face de jedge—which he may be overbearin' an' a hard unailin' . . jedge. **1976** Wolfram–Christian *Appalachian Speech* 121 **sWV,** I went to Cleveland which my cousin lives there. **1982** Ginns *Snowbird Gravy* 26 **nwNC,** They'd save the [coffee] grounds. . . Then they'd go back and make it again. Which it got very weak toward the last of it. **2001** *DARE* File **nwTX,** Singin' exactly like on the radio, *which* it sucks. **2002** *DARE* File—Internet **seKY,** She attended one of R.A. West's meetings at Renfro Valley. Which he has the devine spirit of Christ in him. **2003** *DARE* File swNC [Black], Most people—Which I guess they was much healthier than we are now, . . they would walk.

2 Used without an anaphoric pronoun as a connective particle to introduce a parenthetical, usu explanatory remark. [*OED2* *which* pron. 14.b 1723 →]

1845 Hooper *Advent. Simon Suggs* 147 **AL,** I rolled up my shirt sleeves—which it was a tollude warm day and my koat was off—and ses I, you see that hoss yonder? **1859** Taliaferro *Fisher's R.* 59 **nwNC** (as of 1820s), I 'riv on the spot in the cool uv the evening', which it were mighty hot weather. **1870** in 1884 Lanier *Poems* 169 **GA,** I was drivin' my two-mule wagon,/. . . / Towards Macon, to git some baggin'/ (Which my cotton was ready to bale). **c1937** in Lib. of Congress *Amer. Memory: WPA Life Hist.* (Internet) **GA** [Black], Seem like he spirit jes' wouldn' 'low 'im t' take er lickin' fum *nobody. Which he were* whipped quite er few times. **1975** *Foxfire 3* 38 **nGA,** This one time I was gonna lay down there and wait till daylight 'cause I was going over in a pretty rough place (which I didn't care for the rough woods nor nothing). **1976** Wolfram–Christian *Appalachian Speech* 121, I remember the doctor comin' and deliverin' the baby which we were in the other room. **2001** *DARE* File **NM,** When I lived over on A street last winter which I can see the house from here. **2009** *Ibid,* Water was running down the side of the truck, which we had rain prior.

3 also *and which, but which;* Used without an anaphoric pronoun to mark the connection of a clause or sentence to what precedes: and; and so, as to that.

1858 *Zion Minutes* 43 (*Montgomery Coll.*), Also the door of the church was opened for the reception of members & which Valentine Tipton joined by experience. **1891** Johnston *Primes & Neighbors* 12 **GA,** They isn't any telling what would happen after the perfect *ocean* of physic he seems like it's his bounden duty to take for fears of giving up his final ghost. . . But which I've tried . . to tell him in vain that, if so be in his angzieties, he better mind how he expose hisself to every night a'r that is. *Ibid* 114 **GA,** "And which, Susan Ann," she said in conclusion, "no longer than last Sunday evening . . I think I see his eyes water." **1897** Lewis *Wolfville* 129 **AZ,** "I challenges that vote. Mexicans is barred." "Which Mexicans is not barred," replies Ormsby. *Ibid* 330, What's air-tights? Which you Eastern shorthorns is shore ignorant. **2001** *DARE* File **swNM,** Have you heard *which* as sort of a subordinator of all work—as in "I'd sleep all day *which* I'd wake up" meaning "and then I'd wake up." The informant who provided this example is a Hispanic woman from Silver City, New Mexico, born in 1961, one year college. **2002** *DARE* File—Internet **seKY,** His son drowned when he was thirteen years old . . , and he blamed God for it, and he lost all faith. Which I felt sorry for him and began to love him and his family.

which adv
For which.

1889 *Harper's New Mth. Mag.* 80.120, Thet thar rock house o' his'n, which he hev quayried the rock an' put up hisse'f, I 'low it's the beatenes' house in creation. **1970** *DARE* Tape **PA242,** Schnitz and knepp is a Lancaster County dish, which you take ham and dried apple snits . . and then these are boiled with the . . ham. **2003** in 2004 *DARE* File—Internet **KS,** After my French presentation (which my prof emailed me my grade, I got an A, yay), I went home and packed.

which and tother n, adj phr, adv phr   **chiefly NEast**   Cf **which from tother**

One thing or the other; a close thing; touch-and-go; slapdash; from all angles.

1825 Jones *Refugee* 1.103 **NY,** They've got it, them red-coats—gad, they've got it which and tother. **1868** Pinckney et al. *Reminiscences Catskill* 60 **NY,** He fell sick—very sick—indeed, it was about "which and t'other" with the darkey, who believed and averred that he *would* die. **1889** *New Engl. Mag.* 7.14 **MA,** A good many drew off, and some were between which and t'other what to do; for . . both sides were set as the east wind. **1902** *DN* 2.249 **sIL,** Which and *tother.* Of indeterminate preferableness. 'It's which and tother I reckon,' as to two sides of a question. **1915** *Middletown Times–Press* (NY) 16 Aug 4/3, It certainly was an up-hill job, and was 'which and tother' with us for a long time. **1945** *Berkshire Eve. Eagle* (Pittsfield MA) 28 Dec 10/3 (as of 1920), He says he was taken suddenly ill December 10, and for a time it was "which and tother" with him. **1968–69** *DARE* (Qu. W29, . . *Expressions . . for things that are sewn carelessly . . "They're _____."*) Inf **NY220,** Which and tother; (Qu. KK54, *Just about equal, very close: "They were both fast runners and it was _____ all the way.")* Infs **NY75, 96,** Which and tother.

which and way, every adv phr   Also *every which and where* [Varr, prob by folk-etym, of *every whichaway* (at **whichaway(s)**)] **esp Sth**

In every way, in or from all directions.

a1894 in 1898 King *Ben King's Verse* 171, Dey war hitched to a monsus lookin' alligatah sleigh,/ An' filled wid gifts fo' de chillun, piled ebery which un way. **1934** Hurston *Jonah's Gourd Vine* 35 **AL** [Black], "Whar hit gwine?" "Oh eve'y which and whar," the other Negro answered. **1949** Turner *Africanisms* 288 **seSC** [Gullah], Five hundred head of man from all about—Virginia, Georgia, and every which and way. **2004** in 2008 *DARE* File—Internet **cnAL,** I hope things turn out for the best. Every which and way I mean. **2007** *Ibid* **NC** [Black], I feel like my school life is just about to come back together but my friendships are falling every which and way. **2008** *Ibid* **UT,** I turned every which and way to dodge him. . . but he was determined.

whichaway adj
Askew, awry, crooked.

1967–69 *DARE* (Qu. KK70, *Something that has got out of proper shape: "That house is all _____."*) Infs **LA14, MI108,** Whichaway.

whichaway(s) adv   Often in phr *every whichaway* and varr [Varr of *which way, (every) whichway(s);* cf **-s** suff[1], **thataway** adv, **thisaway**]   **scattered, but more freq Sth, Midl, TX, N Cent**   See Map

1883 *Century Illustr. Mag.* 26.778 **GA** [Black], No diffunce which-a-way he creep, dar wuz ole Sis Cow hawns p'intin' right straight at 'im. **1886** *Ibid* 32.201 **GA** [Black], He ax whichaways, an' I show him de pahf. **1896** Twain *Tom Sawyer Abroad; Detective* 188 **AR,** He got that big di'mond . . and held it up and let it flash and blaze and squirt sunlight everwhichaway. **1899** (1912) Green *VA Folk-Speech* 481, *Whichaway.* . . *Everywhichaway,* everywhere. **1906** *DN* 3.135 **nwAR,** Everwhich a way I turn I meet him. **1908** *DN* 3.309 **eAL, wGA,** *Ever(y) which a way.* . . In all directions. **1923** *DN* 5.225 **swMO,** *Which-away.* . . Which way? How? In what direction? **1933** Miller *Lamb in His Bosom* 96 **GA,** Mixing the colors every whichaway. **1935** Hurston *Mules & Men* 142 **FL** [Black], But every which a way he run de fire meet him. **1940** *AmSp* 15.52 **sAppalachians, Ozarks,** Adverbial *-s* survives in: nowheres, anywheres, ever'-which-aways. **1946** in 1958 Brewer *Dog Ghosts* 53 **TX** [Black], He heahs a lots of stampedin' an' sees de cattle runnin' evuhwhichawhar. **1956** McAtee *Some Dialect NC* 50, *Whichaway.* . . In what manner or direction. "I don't know whichaway would be best." **1965–70** *DARE* (Qu. MM12a, . . *'In all directions'* . . *"He shot into a flock of birds and they went _____."*) 135 Infs, **scattered, but more freq Sth, Midl, TX, N Cent,** Ever(y) (*or* all) whichaway; **TX92,** Such every whichaway; (Qu. MM12b, . . *'In all directions'* . . *"When she was out on the dance floor, she broke her beads and they went _____."*) 21 Infs, **esp S Atl, TX,** Every whichaway; **FL26, TX29, 39, 42,** Ever whichaway. **1986** Pederson *LAGS Concordance* **Gulf Region** (*Do it _____*) 22 infs, (Every) whichaway; (*Kitty-cornered*) 3 infs, Every whichaway; 8 infs, (Every) whichaway.

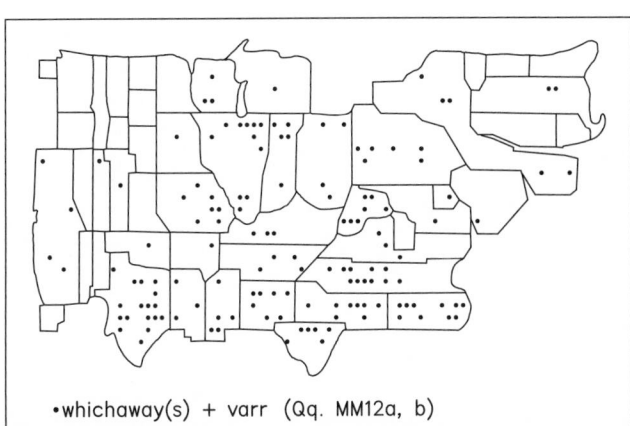

•whichaway(s) + varr (Qq. MM12a, b)

which from tother pron phr   Also *tother from which* [Cf *EDD which was tother* (at *which* pron. 2(2)) "one from another"] **chiefly Sth, S Midl**   Cf **which and tother**
One from the other.

1843 Marion *Marion's Men* 34 **SC,** The English . . not know tother from which when they fire at the hogshead instead of me. **1847** *Scientific Amer.* 27 Feb 178, The nurses placed both babies in the same cradle, and were afterwards unable to tell "which from t'other." **1856** *Harper's New Mth. Mag.* 13.282, Two sisters in Newark, New Jersey, are so much alike you can't tell t'other from which. **1865** Byrn *Advent. Fudge Fumble* 55 **TN,** When he went to eat his dinner he swallowed the schoolmaster's day book and afterwards said his lesson to a piece of corn-bread, without knowing which from t'other. **1893** Shands *MS Speech* 67, *Which from tother.* . . Illiterate white for *one from another.* It is frequently said of twins that one can't tell "which from tother." **1909** *DN* 3.383 **eAL, wGA,** Tother from which. . . "They both so 'zackly like, you wouldn't know tother from which." **1912** *DN* 3.593 **wIN,** *Which from tother.* . . Sometimes *tother from which.* Used only in the comparison of things that are very much alike. "Have you seen the Jones twins? You can't tell which from tother." **1915** *DN* 4.192 **swVA,** Them twins 'so much alike, you can't tell tother from t'other. **1965** Randolph *Hot Springs* 115 **Ozarks,** He was so drunk he didn't know which from t'other. **1976** Garber *Mountain-ese* 92 **sAppalachians,** Them two twins favor so much I kaint tell tother from which.

whicker n[1], v   Pronc-sp *wicker;* also rarely *whinker, whitiker,* and, by lambdacism, *whickle*   **chiefly SE, Mid Atl**   See Map
=**nicker** n[1], v; hence n, ppl adj *whickering.*

1850 *S. Lit. Messenger* 16.43 **VA,** He [=a horse] . . would bear such a rider as I thirty leagues between sunrise and sunset, and whicker for his food when the task was over. **1859** Taliaferro *Fisher's R.* 83 **nwNC** (as of 1820s), The way he [=a horse] whickered were a fact. **1887** (1967) Harris *Free Joe* 224 **GA** [Black], Bimeby I year hoss whicker. **1899** (1912) Green *VA Folk-Speech* 481, *Whicker.* . . The cry of a horse. *Whicker.* . . To make the sound of a horse's voice; to neigh. **1902** *DN* 2.249 **sIL,** *Whicker.* . . To whinny. **1906** *DN* 3.123 **sIN,** *Whicker.* . . To whinny. **1907** *DN* 3.228 **nwAR,** *Whicker.* . . To whinny. **1909** *DN* 3.388 **eAL, wGA,** *Whicker.* . . To neigh, whinny. Common. **1918** *DN* 5.20 **NC,** *Whicker,* whinny. **1923** *DN* 5.224 **swMO,** *Whicker.* . . To neigh softly. **1946** *PADS* 5.43 **VA,** *Whicker* . . : Noise made by a horse at feeding time; on the Tidewater and Eastern Shore. **1946** *PADS* 6.32 **eNC** (as of 1900–10), *Whicker.* . . Whinny; to whinny. **1949** Kurath *Word Geog.* 63, *Whicker* is now used in four separate areas: (1) in southeastern New England . . (2) in Maine, which derived part of its population from the Plymouth and Cape Cod areas; (3) on the lower Susquehanna; and (4) in the southern two thirds of Delamarvia, in the Virginia Tidewater . . and in the Carolinas. **1963** North *Rascal* 119 **WI** (as of 1918), The black stallion immediately became gentle, changing his shrill whinny to a soft whicker. **1965–70** *DARE* (Qu. K40, *The sound that a horse makes*) 63 Infs, **chiefly SE, Mid Atl,** Whicker; **GA**16, 87, Wicker; **MS**74, Whinker; **SC**26, Whickle; **GA**3, Whitiker. **1973** Allen *LAUM* 1.254 **Upper MW** (as of c1950), *Whinny.* . . *Whinker* is the term of an inf. in se. Iowa. **1989** Pederson *LAGS Tech. Index* 136 **Gulf Region,** *Whinny* [of horse] . . whicker [v.] (75 [infs]) . . whicker [n.] (2 [infs]) . . whickering [n.] (1 [inf]) . . whickering noise (1 [inf]) . . whickering sound (1 [inf]) . . whinker (14 [infs]).

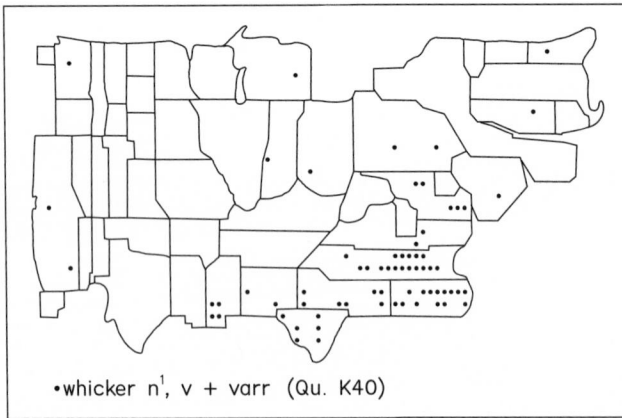

•whicker n[1], v + varr (Qu. K40)

whicker n[2]   Also *yellow whicker*   **Sth, S Midl**   Cf **billy whicker**

A woodpecker such as the **flicker** n[2] **1** or **pileated woodpecker B.**

[**1891** *Auk* 8.127 **sGA, nFL,** On one occasion two birds on coming together gave utterance to the *whicker* calls so characteristic of *Colaptes.*]
1906 Johnson *Highways Missip. Valley* 118 **AR,** With these domestic

sounds was mingled . . the tapping of the "whickers" or yellow hammers, and the clatter and songs of many other birds. **1917** [see **wheeler** n[2]]. **1968–70** *DARE* (Qu. Q17, . . *Kinds of woodpeckers*) Inf **MD**45, Flicker—also called yellow whicker ['jælə ˌwɪkɚ]; **VA**43, Ivory-billed whicker; (Qu. Q18, *Joking names and nicknames for woodpeckers*) **VA**43, Whicker, billy-whicker [FW: prob pileated woodpecker]; **VA**75, Whicker—nickname for logcock or pileated woodpecker.

whickerbill n   Also *wickerbill*

1 A **red-neck 2**—also used as a vaguely derog (rarely affectionate) term.   **chiefly Sth, S Midl**

1921 Knibbs *Partners* 80 **SW,** He was a young, long, spindlin' hombre from Texas—a reg'lar Whicker-bill, with that drawlin' kind of a voice that hosses and folks listen to. **1925** Kroll *Compar. Study S. Folk Speech* 82 **MS,** *Whicker bill*—A rustic, servant, poor white trash. **1932** *Santa Fe Mag.* Jan 34, A new brakeman, or a beginner, is a *sizzer* or a *whicker bill.* **1937** Kroll *I Was a Share-Cropper* 244 **seMO,** And you sit here talking about marrying the leavings of those two whickerbills! You make me sick! **1958** Latham *Meskin Hound* 46 **cTX,** Seems like the minute word gits out that a convict's loose, every whickerbill in the country grabs his gun and starts looking on hisself as a man hunter. **1967** Johnson *House Corbett St.* 40 **IN** [Black], You kain't pick up nothin worthwhile in this ole whickerbill town. **1971** Murray *S. to a Place* 11 **AL** [Black], Because, after all, like it or not, or concede it or not, long before it became your boy-blue stamping ground the old country had already been old man whicker-bill's buckskin camping ground, back when it was still Indian territory. **1984** Weaver *TX Crude* 136, *Wickerbill.* . . Term of endearment. "Lay down, you little wickerbill; I think I love you."

2 The mouth; the snout, proboscis.

1923 *DN* 5.224 **swMO,** *Whicker bill.* . . Mouth. "Shet y'r whicker bill." **1972** *Mission Messenger* 34.137 **MO,** Let the rest of us respect congregational autonomy enough to keep our "whickerbills" out of their business. **2008** *DARE* File—Internet **FL,** When 'skeeter' season gets here I don't want any voids that'll let them little ladies gettin' thier [sic] wickerbill in me and mine.

3 A contraption, gadget; a **doohickey 1.**   Note: In reference to the Gurney flap this is now widespread, esp in auto racing (see quot 2005).

1951 in 2008 *DARE* File—Internet [*Warsaw Times Union* (IN) 2 July] (as of c1900), Many people remember the car John Bond built for himself. He called it his "Whickerbill." Shaped in front like a buckboard wagon, its wheels were cut down from steel cultivator wheels. **2004** *Ibid* **IN,** My computer had like some catastrophic whickerbill thingamajigger and wouldn't let me get on the internet but I got it fixed! **2005** *Ibid* **swCA,** About the "Gurney Flap." . . I heard Gurney call the little lip or fence at the rear edge of a major wing [of a race car], a "whickerbill." Never found it in a dictionary, nor in any other source I've tried. **2007** *Ibid* **TX,** The Glock has a longer pull, a stiffer release, a thicker (wider) trigger guard, and the little "safe action" whickerbill in the trigger face. **2008** *Ibid* **nCA,** OK for a 72 what cha call it the wickerbill that covers the post? Stupid question guys but the interior trim piece that covers the post on the passengers side between the passenger door window and the quarter window it essentially is just the plastic piece that covers the post.

4 The foreskin; the penis.   Cf **whip-cracker 2**

1939 in 1977 Randolph *Pissing in the Snow* 154 **Ozarks,** They got to talking about which one had the longest tool. . . "Does whickerbills count?" . . The boys argued awhile, but there ain't no denying that a whickerbill is part of a man's prick. **c1960** Wilson *Coll.* **csKY,** *Whickerbill.* . . The prepuce. **2002** in 2005 *Double-Tongued Dict.* (Internet) **GA,** *Whickerbill.* . . He and my father's nickname for penis was "wickerbill." **2008** *DARE* File—Internet **Sth,** My MIL had the most idiotic names for them, the penis was wickerbill and the vagina was cooter. . . gotta love old southern nick names.

whickering   See **whicker** n[1], v

whickering owl   See **whinnering owl**

whickety   See **wicket**

whickle   See **whicker** n[1], v

whiddle   See **wheedle**

whiff n[1]   [Engl dial; cf *EDD whiff* sb. 2]

A short space of time; a jiffy—used in phr *in a whiff.*

1823 (1825) Cooper *Pilot* 3.188 **NY,** There goes my commission of captain of this craft, in a whiff. **1874** *Appletons' Jrl.* 11.301, Had this writing received the briefest examination, its importance would have evaporated in a whiff. **1888** *Lippincott's Mth. Mag.* Apr 454 **VA,** All this passed through his mind in a whiff. **1902** Janvier *Christmas Kalends* 167 **sePA,** All in a whiff our feast ended; and in another whiff we were up and off. **1943** *St. Nicholas* 70.824, Billy had to leave school, all in a whiff, most of us were mighty sorry to have him go. **1965** Barbour *Proverbs IL* 197, *To be off in a whiff* (To leave in a hurry.) **1968** *DARE* (Qu. KK42b, *Expressions about a person who does something very easily: "He could do that _____."*) Inf **MD**14, In a whiff.

whiff n[2] [*OED2* 1713 →]

A **flounder B** of the genus *Citharichthys* or the closely related *Etropus microstomus.*

1873 in 1878 Smithsonian Inst. *Misc. Coll.* 14.2.17, *Citharichthys* [= *Etropus*] *microstomus.* . . Whiff. New Jersey to Cape Hatteras. **1898** U.S. Natl. Museum *Bulletin* 47.2678, *Citharichthys* [spp]. . . Whiffs. **1955** Carr–Goin *Guide Reptiles* 115 **FL,** *Citharichthys spilopterus.* . . Whiff. . . A very flat fish with both eyes and all its color on the left side. **1961** *Odessa Amer.* (TX) 21 Mar 19/1, *The flounder* is one of the favorite fish along the Texas Gulf coast. . . The fish has many aliases such as flatfish, fluke, whiff and sole. **1966** WI Acad. *Trans.* 55.128 **LA,** *Citharichthys spilopterus.* . . bay whiff.

whiffenpoof n Also *whiffenpuff, wiffenpoof* [Introduced in the 1908 Victor Herbert musical comedy "Little Nemo" in which the *whiffenpoof* was a fish] Cf **wampus** n[2] 1

An imaginary animal; see quots.

1922 *DN* 5.188, *Whiffenpuff.* A strange animal that ranges at night. 1932 *Hench Coll.* **cVA,** Whiffenpoof—imaginary comic animal of vague description. Heard orally often. One student said it has no mouth. Usually the name is used for some animal that cannot be better named. "What's that noise?" "Must be a whiffenpoof." **1939** Tryon *Fearsome Critters* 63, *The Wiffenpoof.* . . A tasty fish, found only in perfectly round lakes. . . To catch him . . bore a square hole in the water. Bait . . with a bit of cheese. . . When he emerges, spit tobacco-juice in his eye. This will make him so swell with rage that he won't be able to withdraw into the hole. **1968** *DARE* (Qu. CC17, *Imaginary animals or monsters that people . . tell tales about—especially to tease greenhorns*) Inf **NY**84, Whiffenpoof.

whiffer n [Cf *EDD whiffler* (at *whiffle* v.[2] 4(2)) 'an inconstant person; a turncoat']

1952 Brown *NC Folkl.* 1.607, *Whiffer.* . . A tattletale.—Chapel Hill.

whiffet n Also sp *whiffit* [Pronc var of *whippet*]

1 freq attrib: A small, often noisy, dog; see quots. **chiefly NEast, esp PA**

1767 *Boston Eve.–Post* (MA) 30 Nov 4/1, The most pampered of them will rend a bone from the most hungry whiffet with all the rage imaginable. **1801** in 1912 Thornton *Amer. Gloss.* 2.938 **PA,** Who heed's the Whiffit's bark, when tempests howl?/ Or, if you please, when noble mastiffs growl. **1839** U.S. Congress *Jrl. House of Repr.* 627 **OH,** Edward Stanly. . . assumed all the pertness of a whiffet, hissed on, puppy-like, to do that which a bigger dog had not the courage to attempt. **1848** *Ladies' Repository* 8.315 **PA,** The best protection to a house, with a family in it . . is, a little, barking, noisy, cowardly, whiffet dog. **1877** Holley *Josiah Allen's Wife* 309 **cnNY,** "Whiffet pups!" says Delila in angry tones, "they are poodles." "Well," says I calmly, "whiffet poodle pups, if that suits you any better." **1878** *Scribner's Mth.* 16.466 **NY,** The king-bird will worry the hawk as a whiffet dog will worry a bear. **1916** *Wellsboro Agitator* (PA) 16 Nov 2/2, An old she bear . . was streaking it up the trail to get out of the way of a whiffet dog at her heels. **1930** Shoemaker *1300 Words* 65 **cPA Mts** (as of c1900), *Whiffet*—A small, nervous, twitchy dog.

2 Transf: a small or contemptible person.

1767 *NY Gaz. Weekly Post–Boy* (NY) 26 Mar 4/1, Go on . . like a couple of generous *Mastiffs,* in your combat, and never mind a little *Whiffet* who cries *bew, wew, wew,* to interrupt you. **1805** *True Amer.* (Trenton NJ) 16 Sept 2/4, Why is the Connecticut whiffet always barking at *Persons?* Why does he not employ genius in discussion *principles?* **1848** *U.S. Mag. & Democratic Rev.* 23.86, In particular are we ready . . to admit or promise anything which will prevent our . . being assured by some whiffet whom our freedom of the press permits to spoil paper . . that he was "the first to nail to his masthead . . the names of *Taylor & Fillmore.*" **1860** Claiborne *Life Dale* 195 **MS,** Yet this little whiffet of a man . . was the Atlas that bore upon his shoulders the weight of Jackson's administration. **1879** Fitzgerald *CA Sketches* 100, I did n't throw the contemptible little whiffet who commanded the lake steamer over-

board for his unbearable insolence. **1882–83** Whitman *Specimen Days* 89 **seNY,** This gusty-temper'd little whiffet, man, that runs indoors at a mite of rain or snow. **1927** *AmSp* 3.135 **eME,** A "whiffet" was an insignificant looking person. **1950** *WELS Suppl.* **cwWI,** *Whiffet*—A lazy or do-nothing boy. "You can't get any work out of that young whiffet." **1952** *NY Times* (NY) 9 Oct 24/3, Representative Charles A. Halleck, Republican of Indiana struck back today by denouncing Mr. Truman as . . a "whiffet". . . A whiffet, the dictionary says, is a "small, insignificant person."

whiffle n[1] See **whiffletree**

whiffle n[2], also attrib Also *whiffler, whipple* **chiefly eMA** See Map

A crew cut.

1942 *Lowell Sun & Citizen–Leader* (MA) 16 July 21/1, But what New England newspapermen will see . . is . . a kid with a "whiffle" haircut. **1943** *Portsmouth Herald* (NH) 15 July 8/1, Wherever the tall red-head with the whiffle haircut goes all of us . . know that he will make good as well as make a lot of friends. **1965–70** *DARE* (Qu. X5, . . *Different kinds of men's haircuts*) Infs **MA**3, 4, 7, 8, 44, 50, Whiffle; **DC**8, Whiffle—a puff in front, otherwise like crew cut; **MA**13, Whiffle—slightly longer than a crew; **MA**27, Whiffle; flattop—shorter than a whiffle; **MA**33, Whiffle—a short haircut—same as a crew cut; **MA**72, Whiffle—same as a crew; **MA**9, Whiffler; **NH**16, Whipple. [10 of 13 Infs were comm types 1 or 2] c**1975** *DARE* File c**MA** (as of c1945), My brother remembers them [=whiffle haircuts], and he says you could buy *w(h)iffle sticks* from a barber to grease your w(h)iffle cut so it would stand up. (They were a type of crew cut.) **1979** *NYT Article Letters* ce**MA,** A crew cut haircut is a "whiffle." **1988** *Syracuse Herald–Amer.* (NY) 11 Sept sec AA 2/2 ce**MA,** One summer it was the shimmel shirt that was all the rage; during another, it was the whiffle haircut. **2005** Fletcher *Marshfield Dreams* 14 e**MA,** Mom gave me a whiffle haircut so short I could see my scalp when I looked in the mirror. **2006** *Boston Globe* (MA) 12 Feb (Internet), The player with muscular dystrophy was Jake Currie, an eight grader with a whiffle haircut.

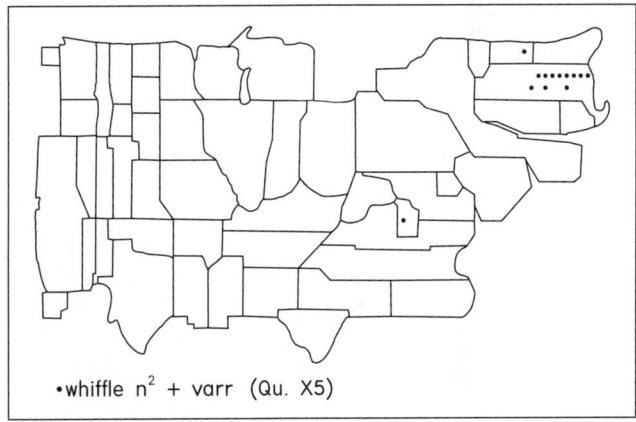

•whiffle n[2] + varr (Qu. X5)

whiffle-minded adj [Engl dial] **NEast, esp ME**

Fickle; vacillating.

1844 in 2007 *DARE* File—Internet **NH,** Put no confidence in John C. Philbrick he is whiffle-minded. **1863** *Godey's Lady's Book* 66.251 e**PA,** I ain't one of your whiffle-minded ones. Besides, a bargain is a bargain; when I make one, I al'ays calc'late to stick to it. **1902** Day *Pine Tree Ballads* 47 **ME,** Hate to act so whiffle-minded, but my father used to say,/ 'Men would sometimes change opinions; mules would stick the same old way.' **1927** *AmSp* 3.135 e**ME,** A man or woman who vacillated or was perennially undecided was called "whiffle minded," whiffle meaning to shift, turn, change from one course to another. **1935** *Time* 29 Apr 70 **ME,** The Bragdons had never been whiffle-minded. **1949** Carroll *West Hill* 61 **ME,** "Changeable," Molly nodded. "Whiffle-minded. Costly kind of womenfolks for a man to have."

whiffler n[1] [Because its wings make a whistling sound] **chiefly MD, VA**

A **goldeneye 1** (here: *Bucephala clangula*).

1888 Trumbull *Names of Birds* 79 **MD,** At Baltimore and on the Patapsco River, *Whiffler* [is a name for the goldeneye]. **1923** U.S. Dept. Ag. *Misc. Circular* 13.22 **MD, NC, VA,** Goldeneye. . . Vernacular Names. . . *In local use.* . . whiffler. **1947** *Eve. Capital* (Annapolis MD) 26 Dec 2/3 **MD,** If the hunter goes to the proper section, he will find plenty of canvasbacks, blackheads, blue bills, whifflers [etc]. **1958** *Ibid* 12 Dec 8/3, Local names for waterfowl are quite confusing for beginners. It seems, a plain "Whiffler" is a Whistler, Golden-eye or Bufflehead. **2001** *MD Ornith. Soc. MD Yellowthroat* Mar–Apr 6 (Internet) **eVA, eMD,** Ducks was commoner then but there's still lots of . . Clubheads (also called Whifflers or Whistlers).

whiffler n[2]   See **whiffle** n[2]

whiffletree n [Var of **whippletree**; appar of US origin, but cf *EDD whiffles* "The whipple-tree of a plough"] **scattered, but chiefly NEast, Gt Lakes** See Map   Cf **double whiffletree** =**whippletree.**

    1805 *Repertory* (Boston MA) 3 Sept 4/3, [Advt:] Set of elegant brass mounted tandem or whiffletree Harness. **1820** Nicholson *Farmer's Asst.* 377 **cNY,** Where two animals draw against each other, the weaker one should have the longer end of the ox-bow, or whiffletree, by which they draw. **1849** (1934) Boynton *Jrl.* 43.370 **VT,** I broke the whiffletree of my carriage. **1862** *Horticulturist & Jrl. Rural Art* 17.149 **wNY,** An orchard should be so planted as to be cultivated . . using but one horse, with so short a whiffletree as to drive within one foot of the tree. **1887** *Century Illustr. Mag.* 34.700 **NJ,** I yanked the string that slips the hook in the whiffletree, set free the mules, and got 'em all out. **1949** Kurath *Word Geog.* 12, Characteristic Northern expressions . . current in all of New England and the New England settlement area in New York State and northern Pennsylvania, as well as in the Hudson Valley, on Long Island, and in East Jersey are . . *whiffletree* or *whippletree. Ibid* 58, *Whiffletree* is the usual form of the Northern expression; *whippletree* is not uncommon in Western New England, in Upstate New York, and in northwestern Pennsylvania and the Western Reserve of Ohio, but there is a trend to *whiffletree* here too. **1956** *PADS* 25.7 **WA,** Percentage frequency of eastern words in Washington check sheets. . . Whiffletree 2[%] . . Whipple tree 6[%]. **1962** Atwood *Vocab. TX* 52, Wooden bar to which a single horse is attached. . . The Northern . . *whiffletree* (4[% of 273 infs]) and *whippletree* (2.9[%]) are confined to the oldest informants in Texas. **1965–70** *DARE* (Qu. L46, *Behind each horse there's a movable bar [the leathers or ropes from the collar are fastened to it]*) 145 Infs, **scattered, but chiefly NEast, N Cent,** Whiffletree; (Qu. L44, *On a buggy, two long pieces of wood stick out in front and the horse goes between them. You call them the _____*) Inf **NY105,** Whiffletrees; (Qu. L45, *The long piece of wood that sticks out in front of a wagon, and you put a horse on each side*) Infs **GA60, KS5,** Whiffletree; (Qu. L47, *The two movable bars behind a team of horses are fastened to a longer piece; this is a _____*) Infs **MO1, NJ50, NY205, TX63,** Whiffletree; [**NY206,** Double whiffle]. [*DARE* Ed: The apparent confusion at Qq. L44 and 45 probably reflects unfamiliarity with the implement.] **1973** Allen *LAUM* 1.215 **Upper MW** (as of c1950), Northern *whiffletree* and *whippletree* were clearly retreating even before farm mechanization. They dominate only Minnesota and occur elsewhere only in conservative Northern speech areas. . . The *whippletree* variant is largely restricted to an inner core of the *whiffletree* region, specifically southern and eastern Minnesota and Iowa. **1975** Gould *ME Lingo* 315, Whiffletree. . . Mainers never say whippletree. Sometimes, of course, they specify singletree or doubletree. **1981** *PADS* 67.26 **neMN,** Northern *whiffletree* or *whippletree* is usual on the Iron Range. **1988** Palmer *Lang. W. Cent. MA* 32, ['wɪfltri]—That's the part of a wagon that's hitched to the horse. I never heard it called 'whippletree.'

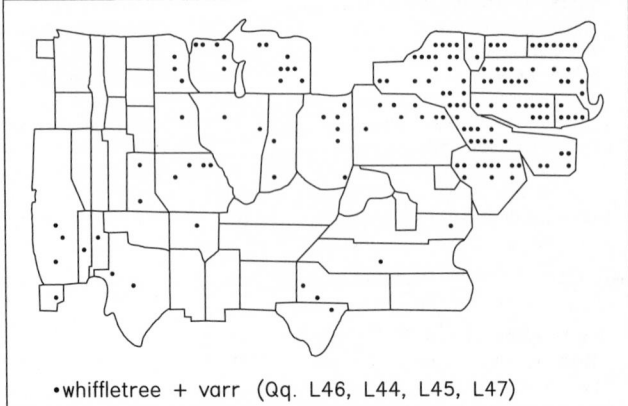

•whiffletree + varr (Qq. L46, L44, L45, L47)

whiggered adj [Cf *EDD whiggered whey*. . . *"Obs."* . . "A beverage made by infusing herbs in fermented whey."]

1958 *PADS* 29.18 **cTN,** *Whiggered:* A condition of milk. "Sour milk is sometimes called whiggered when it is going to whey."

whiles conj   Also *w'iles* [*OED2* "*Obs.* or *arch.*"]   **esp Sth, S Midl**   Cf **whilst** While.

    1732 in 1852 *PA Archives* 1st ser 1.316, Isaac Smally Saith . . was . . oblieged to leap into ye River . . whiles a young man there present ran above a mile to call help. **1901** *Atlantic Mth.* 87.786 **NE,** A man that can set still an' grin whiles another feller 's callin' him a liar, he 's dif'rent from me. **1905** Chesnutt *Col.'s Dream* 149 **GA** [Black], W'iles he sot dere wond'rin' whar de hole wuz dat dat ole cat come in at, fus' thing he knowed, de ole cat wuz settin' right up 'side of 'im. **1909** *DN* 3.388 **eAL, wGA,** *Whiles, conj.* While. **1943** *LANE* Map 727, *While*—The map shows the adverbial conjunctions *while* [etc] . . recorded in the context *while I was talking to him.* . . 1 inf, **sME coast,** Whiles [wɛˑɪlz]. **1945** FWP *Lay My Burden Down* 180 **Sth** (as of c1865) [Black], They put Uncle Isom (my steppappy) in jail, and whiles he was in there he killed a white guardman. **2001** *DARE* File **nwMS,** From Black speakers in Marks, Mississippi, . . *whiles* for *while* not (whilst) (hwaɛlz) "Whiles I was asleep[ɹ]." . . . [T]hese usages are certainly common among Blacks in Marks, Mississippi, born befor [sic] 1930 and maybe among those younger.

whiles n [*OED2 whiles* sb. I.1 *"Obs."*] A time, while.

    1857 Gladstone *Englishman* 50 **KS,** I reckon they won't be a tryin' on this game again a little whiles. **1901** *Atlantic Mth.* 87.786 **NE,** They had to stop their talkin' every little whiles till somebody 'd go poke him to wake him up. **1938** Rawlings *Yearling* 27 **nFL,** We got meat to eat for a whiles now. **1986** Pederson *LAGS Concordance,* 1 inf, **swTN,** A little whiles to go. [Inf Black]

whilst conj   Also sp *whilest, whilse* [*W3* "*chiefly Brit.*"] Note: The sp *whilse* is here assumed to represent the reduction of the [st] consonant cluster; it is possible, however, that some exx belong instead at **whiles** conj. While.

    1860 Street *Woods & Waters* 15 **neNY,** Allen, whilse the b'ys was a goin' one way inter the fort, went t'other. **1872** *Atlantic Mth.* 29.351 **CA,** Ye'd better hold on a second out yer, whilst I go in and see thet things is all right. **1891** (1967) Freeman *New Engl. Nun* 137, I would ha' done as much for *him* if I'd had any need to whilst he was alive. **1894** Riley *Armazindy* 5 **IN,** [She] couldn't rag out stylisher—/ Like some *neighber*-girls . . /. . . / Whilse their pore old mothers sloshed / Round the old back-porch and washed / Their clothes fer 'em. **1894** *Scribner's Mag.* 15.467 **Sth** [Black], It neveh will whilse I'm there to *pre*ventuate. **1926** Roberts *Time of Man* 36 **KY,** Get the water hot whilst I see what's to do. **1930** *AmSp* 5.269 [Ozark dialect], The old form *whilst* . . is still used regularly in the Ozarks, although not much heard in other parts of the United States. **c1937** in 1970 Yetman *Voices* 314 **AL** [Black], De lights was . . moved from place to place whilst we picked. **1943** *LANE* Map 727 **NEng,** [In the context "While I was talking to him," *whilst* is scattered throughout the region, but esp along the east coast. It is described as common by 2 infs [**MA, ME**], as rarely used or heard by 11, as older or old-fashioned though still in use by 18, and as obsolete by 18.] **1947** Ballowe *The Lawd* 81 **LA** [Black], Gwineter sen' Duppy to 'n'int the soles whilest she resses. **1966** *DARE* Tape **FL37,** We killed fifty-two [=rattlesnakes] whilst we was there. **1969** Wilson *Stars* 81 **Ozarks,** You'll wait here whilst I go fetch and hitch up my team wagon. **1986** Pederson *LAGS Concordance,* 1 inf, **cnLA,** It snowed whilest we were up there; 1 inf, **cwMS,** Whilst you's milking. [Both infs Black]

whimmer   See **whimper**

whimmy-diddle n   Also *wimmy-diddle*   **chiefly sAppalachians**
1 also *whimmy-doodle, whimpadiddle:* A thingamajig, contraption; a non-existent object.

    1934 *Jrl. Amer. Assoc. Univ. Women* 27.19, The Bureau of Home Economics. . . has been established to help the poor consumer thread his way through the. . . hickidoos, and whimmydiddles that suave salesmen have palmed off upon the credulous. **1941** in 1944 *ADD* **eWV,** *Whimmy-diddle.* . . =thingamajig. **1946** *PADS* 6.43 **eNC** (as of 1900–10), *Whimmydoodle* to wind up the moon with. (An evasive, flippant reply given to inquisitive children or grown-ups.) . . Probably obsolete. **1968** *DARE* (Qu. HH14, *Ways of teasing a beginner or inexperienced person—for example, by sending him for a 'left-handed monkey wrench': "Go get me _____."*) Inf **VA15,** Wimmy-diddle to a smoke-grinder; (Qu. NN12b, *Things that people say to put off a child when he asks, "What are you making?"*) Inf **WV**12, Whimpadiddle to grind smoke with; **VA**11, Wimmy-diddle to grind smoke. **1985** *DARE* File **neIN,** Do you know what a *"Whimmy-diddle"* is? My mother often used this term referring to something she didn't know the name of. After visiting our local reconstructed Army Fort, I learned the early settlers made home made toys carved from wood. One such toy was called a "Whimmy-diddle." **1995** in **2008** *DARE* File—Internet **WV,** Are you perhaps confusing the common blurfl with the whimmydiddle? **2006** *News & Observer* (Raleigh NC) 21 Dec (Internet), Well, we're building a this-'n'-that turbine, and putting it into a whimmydiddle combustion whatsit, mounting it on some cylindrical thingamajigs. **2007** in **2008** *DARE* File—Internet **cwCA,** I prefer to use more customized language that approaches each sitution [sic] on its own terms. "If the whatzit does not synchronize with the whimmydiddle within specs, then:" takes more effort to write, but it is usually more useful. **2008** *Ibid* **seNC,** You catch spottail bass with spottail lures—they are sorta shaped like a whimmy-diddle to a goats bridle. *Ibid* **NM,** Doodad's [sic] by definition have to be able to fit in a pocket[.] A gew-gaw has to be bigger than a whimmy-diddle.

2 Applied spec to:

a A type of wagon; see quot.

1888 Smith *Life of George Foster Pierce* 304 **Sth,** The *stage* was a carriage of the sort that is known in different places by different names. By some it is called 'Jersey wagon;' by others, 'pedler's wagon,' 'dearborn,' 'whimmy-diddle,' 'go-cart.'

b also *whimmy-doodle:* A type of wooden folk-toy; see quot 1967 Daily Times–News. Cf **gee-haw whimm(e)y-diddle**

1963 *Chr. Sci. Monitor* (Boston MA) 26 Apr 6/6 **nwNC,** The whimmy-diddle . . was used in China and Sweden . . Cherokee Indians knew the whimmydiddle as the hoodoo stick. **1967** *Daily Times–News* (Burlington NC) 21 Sept [21]/6 (newspaperarchive.com), A whimmy diddle is an old fashioned wooden toy consisting of a notched stick with a small propeller attached to one end. . . when the notches are vigorously rubbed by another stick the vibrations cause the propeller to revolve. **1967** *DARE* Tape **MI**40, The mountain folks of Tennessee . . as well as Kentucky and North Carolina, . . are making a similar type . . which has the same principle involved in it and they call it a whimmy doodle. **1968** *Daily Progress* (Charlottesville VA) 27 June sec A 2/1 **WV,** The whimmy diddle. . . This mountain toy—which turns a propeller when one stick is rubbed against the other—is in one of the more than 200 booths at the fair. **1980** *Foxfire 6* 252 **neGA,** [Caption:] Mr. Davis shows us how he rubs the stick across the grooves of the whimmy-diddle to make the propeller turn. **1985** [see **1** above].

whimmy-doodle See **whimmy-diddle 1, 2b**

whimpadiddle See **whimmy-diddle 1**

whimper n, v Also *whimmer*
=**nicker** n[1], v.

1939 *LANE* Map 198 *(Whinny)* 3 infs, **MA,** Whimper; 1 inf, **csCT,** Whimmer. **1941** *Language* 17.337 **WI** [*LANCS* fieldwork], Nicker. . . *whimmer*—1 [of 50 infs]. **1949** in 1980 Welty *Coll. Stories* 454 **MS,** A horse stamped and whimpered from the dark road. **1966** Dakin *Dial. Vocab. Ohio R. Valley* 2.255, Whinny. . . Whimper appears once in the Virginia Military District. **1966–69** *DARE* (Qu. K40, *The sound that a horse makes*) Infs **CA**131, **MS**19, Whimper. [Both Infs old] **1986** Pederson *LAGS Concordance* *(Whinny)* 6 infs, **GA,** 2 infs, **MS, TN,** Whimper(ing).

whimpus See **whirling whimpus**

whim-wham for a goose('s) bridle n Also *wim-wam for a goose's bridle* [Scots, nIr dial; cf *EDD* whim-wham 9.(3)] Cf **wing-wong for a duck's bridle**

A non-existent object; see quots.

1928 Harlow *Making a Sailor* 92 **ceMA** (as of 1875), "What's a tinker's damn, Mr. Burris?" asked Alonzo. "It's a wim-wam for a goose's bridle, damn you! and don't you put your head in it," said the mate. **1944** *Sat. Rev. Lit.* 27.14.31, When I was a child and we asked our mother what anything was, any gadget, or a part of the sewing machine or such-like, she always answered: "Oh, that's a whimwham for a goose's bridle and a waylay for meddlers!" **1955** Giddens *Std. Oil Co.* 12 (as of c1890), Upon being questioned as to what he was going to do with so much land, Towle said: "I'm going to build a whim-wham for a goose's bridle." **1968–69** *DARE* (Qu. NN12b, *Things that people say to put off a child when he asks, "What are you making?"*) Inf **MI**103, Whim-wham for a goose bridle; **OH**49, Whim-wham for a goose's bri-

dle—grandfather said that. [**2007** *DARE* File—Internet **NC,** *Making crutches for lame ducks and a whim-wham for a goose's bridle*—My grandfather from Northern Ireland would give this answer to anyone who asked him "what are you doing?" when it was obvious what he was doing.]

whim-whams n Also *wim-wams* Cf **jimjams 1**
=**all overs** n pl **1, 2.**

1931 *Times Recorder* (Zanesville OH) 24 June 11/4, [*Little Annie Rooney* comic strip:] Honest, Zero—I got the wim-wams! **1950** *WELS* (*When something is upsetting, or makes a person nervous:* "It gives me the _____.") 1 Inf, **ceWI,** Whim-whams. **1966–70** *DARE* (Qu. BB28, *Joking names . . for imaginary diseases:* "He must have the _____.") Inf **MI**55, Wim-wams; (Qu. GG13b, *When something keeps bothering a person and makes him nervous . .* "It gives me the _____.") Infs **IL**113, **MI**28, 55, **WA**28, Wim-wams; (Qu. GG34a, *To feel depressed or in a gloomy mood:* "He has the _____ today.") Inf **NY**105, Whim-whams. **1977** *Time* 29 Aug 76, She played the runaway child prostitute in *Taxi Driver* and now, in *The Little Girl Who Lives Down the Lane,* she appears as a possibly homicidal rebel . . both characterizations calculated to give any parent the whim-whams. **2005** *DARE* File—Internet [DallasNews.com 23 June], In a hall filled with pastels and bright lights, this booth was defiantly Army drab. The first time I walked by, I must admit it gave me the whim-whams.

whindging See **whinge**

whindig n [Perh blend of *whindging + shindig*]
A party, esp a lavish or boisterous one.

1930 *Kendallabrum* (Internet) **OK,** Friday, Sept. 20, the Phi Delts opened the fraternity social year with a big whindig in the gym. **1954** *AZ Highways* Aug 37 **West,** Only a short time later there was another whindig [=makeshift rodeo] at the ball park. *Ibid* 38, Word went out that they were to put on a "big one" in town; nor was this a ball park affair, it was to be at the new rodeo grounds. . . Furthermore, a movie outfit was coming . . to take pictures of the whindig. **1966–68** *DARE* (Qu. FF4, *Names and joking names for different kinds of dancing parties*) Inf **NC**36, Whindig; (Qu. FF18, *Joking words . . about a noisy or boisterous celebration or party:* "They certainly _____ last night.") Inf **MN**28, Had a whindig. **2002** *DARE* File—Internet, I'm on my way to a big Apple whindig . . this morning. **2008** *Ibid* **CA,** Today was Senior Awareness Day for the county, and they put on a huge whindig at Micke Grove Park.

whindle v, hence vbl n *whindling* Also *whinnel, whin(n)le* [Engl dial] **Sth, S Midl**
To whimper, whine.

1770 (1965) Carter *Diary* 1.347 **VA,** Tony goes on with his scheme of old age creeping and whindling about often pretending to be sick when nothing ails him. **1840** in 1938 Frost–Frost *Peffley Families* 92 **VA,** [Republicans] are crying and whindling continually to get into office what a keen apetite the feds have for the public pap. **1886** Amer. Philol. Assoc. *Trans.* 17.34 **sOH,** A gentleman from Ohio . . has attempted to indicate for me the words that were imported during or after the war from the South into Southern Ohio. . . So *whindle* (to whine) is coming into use. *Ibid* 45 **eTN,** To *whindle* or *whinnel,* 'to cry peevishly, to whimper' (used of a child), is very common in East Tennessee. **1899** (1912) Green *VA Folk-Speech* 482, Whindle. . . To whimper or whine; to cry peevishly; to whimper, used of a child. **1917** *DN* 4.419 **wNC, KY,** Whinnle. . . To whine. "I never did cry but wunst; I whinnled a little endurin' the war." **1944** *PADS* 2.52 **wNC,** Whin(d)le. . . To whine, to fret. **1949** Arnow *Hunter's Horn* 54 **KY,** The talk and laughter and whindling of the babies was like a blanket between her and her troubles. **1951** *Middlesboro Daily News* (KY) 20 Jan 7/6 **VA,** The children tugged at her skirts, whindling their disappointment at not being permitted to go with daddy. **1957** Neel *Word-Book* 48 **swVA,** Whindle: . . To whine or fret (said of children).

whing See **wing** n

whinge v [Scots, nEngl dial]
To whine; to complain; hence vbl n *whingeing* (pronc-sp *whindging*).

1930 Shoemaker *1300 Words* 68 **cPA Mts** (as of c1900), *Whingeing*—Whining. **1991** *DARE* File **Bronx NYC,** I happened to think of a word from my childhood that parents used when children were unhappy with their lot and showed it with a half-hearted crying sound that apparently was annoying. It was a cross between whining, crying and a low moan. Parents, in desperation, would shout[,] "Stop your whindging (sic)"[.] That's about as close as I can come to the pronunciation. The "whin" as in "win" plus "dging," as in "edging"; accent on the first syllable. **2000** *DARE* File **wPA**, I haven't heard much whingeing about this from Japan. *Ibid* **seNY**, I've always heard *whinge* as rhyming with *hinge*. And come to think about it as "w" not "hw." **2000** *Columbus Dispatch* (OH) 6 Sept sec A 9/2, You'd think after the risible rift between Dan Quayle and Murphy Brown, that Republicans would know better than to whinge about fictional characters. [*DARE* Ed: From a nationally syndicated column by Maureen Dowd.]

whinker See **whicker** n¹, v

whinle, whinnel See **whindle**

whinner See **whinny 1**

whinnering owl n   Also *whickering owl, whinnying ~, winnering ~*   **esp NY, NJ, CT**

A **screech owl 1** (here: *Otus asio*).

1932 *DN* 6.284 **swCT**, *Whickering owls.* Little screech owls. **1939** *LANE* Map 230 (*Screech owl*), 1 inf, **eCT**, [hwɪnɾɪn] owl, makes a noise like a horse; 1 inf, **eCT**, The [hwɪkərɪn] owl makes a kind of tremolo noise; 1 inf, **eCT**, [hwɪnərɪn ɛuɫ]. **1939** FWP *Guide TN* 140, The cur-dog slouching across the road, the whickering owl that perches in your yard, a cat, a snake, a fish, or even a stone may be a witch in disguise. **c1940** *LAMSAS Materials*, 1 inf, **NY**, [huɪnərɪ⁺vn ɛuɫ]; 4 infs, **NJ**, [proncs of the type [wɪnəˑn æuɫ]]; 1 inf, **NJ**, [wɪnowɪŋ æˑʊɫ]. **1967** Faries *Word Geog. MO* 137, 1 inf, *Winnering owl.* **2007** (acc) AL Dept. Conserv. *Outdoor AL* (Internet), Eastern Screech Owl. . . whickering owl, whinnying owl.

whinnle See **whindle**

whinnow See **whinny 2**

whinny n, v

Std senses, var forms.

1 *w(h)inner.* [Brit dial] **chiefly Nth, sNJ, WV** See Map *esp among older, rural speakers with little formal educ*

1855 (1949) Thoreau *Jrl.* 7.457 **MA**, I hear . . a loud, piercing scream, much like the whinner of a colt. **1875** *Scribner's Mth.* 10.433 **NEng**, I'd jest walk up to the pastur'-bars like a hoss, an' whinner to git in. **1910** (1913) White *Book Daniel Drew* 345 **NY**, Another stallion had been whinnering around Fisk's mare. **1939** (1962) Thompson *Body & Britches* 99 **NY**, I said, "Hello, old pard," and rubbed my hand along his [=a horse's] back. I noticed he did not whinner as he always had before. **1941** *Language* 17.337 **WI** [*LANCS* fieldwork], *Whinner*—26 [of 50 infs]. . . Throughout state. . . The most common term is *whinner,* though *whinny* is also widely known, especially among informants of the middle generation and the better educated. **1965–70** *DARE* (Qu. K40, *The sound that a horse makes*) 64 Infs, **chiefly Nth, sNJ, WV**, Whinner; (Qu. K82) Inf **CT**2, Whinner; **IN**54, **ND**5, Winner. [Of all Infs responding to Qu. K40, 76% were comm types 4 and 5, 73% were old; of those giving these responses, 87% were comm types 4 and 5, 86% were old.] **1973** Allen *LAUM* 1.253 **Upper MW** (as of c1950), *Whinny,* the most common term, co-exists with its old-fashioned variant, *whinner.* . . *Whinner,* the popularity of which drops from 39% for Type I [=elderly, locally-born lifelong resident with little education] to 20% for Type II [=a generation younger, locally-born lifelong resident with a high school education] and to only 6% for Type III [=between 40 and 50 years of age, locally-born lifelong resident with a college or university education], is clearly losing ground to *whinny* and perhaps *neigh.*

2 *w(h)innow.* **esp N and C Atl**

1833 *N. Amer. Rev.* 36.523 **MD**, Sometimes a clownish colt . . bounds off towards the brook, . . gallops away, with a hideous whinnowing, to the fields. **1843** (1916) Hall *New Purchase* 202 **sePA**, The whole intended field . . was resounding with . . the snorting and winnowing of horses. **1862** in 2007 *DARE* File—Internet **NY**, He [=a horse] fell bleeding profusely & I left him for dead but after the Battle I found him standing up & whinnowing for me. **1939** *LANE* Map 198 (*Whinny*) 8 infs, **ME, MA, CT**, Whinnow. **1941** *Language* 17.337 **WI** [*LANCS* fieldwork], *Whinnow*—1 [of 50 infs] . . *o[ld].* **1968** *DARE* (Qu. K40, *The sound that a horse makes*) Infs **NJ**40, **NY**62, **PA**147, Whinnow; **IN**54, Winnow. [All Infs old]

3 *whinter.* **esp Nth**

1939 *LANE* Map 198 (*Whinny*) 1 inf, **nwVT**, Whinter. **1941** *Language* 17.337 **WI**, [*LANCS* fieldwork] *Whinter*—1 [of 50 infs]. . . Says this was used before *whinny* came in. **1966–70** *DARE* (Qu. K40, *The sound that a horse makes*) Infs **CA**105, **ID**1, **MI**47, 98, **NJ**69, **NY**196, **OR**2, Whinter. [All Infs old] **1973** Allen *LAUM* 1.253 **Upper MW** (as of c1950), *Whinny.* . . *Whinter* is used by two Iowa and Nebraska infs., both with Midland ancestry.

whinnying owl See **whinnering owl**

whinter See **whinny 3**

whip v, n   Usu |(h)wɪp|; for varr see **A** below

A Forms.

1 |(h)wʌp, (h)wup|; pronc-spp *whoop, whup, woop* [Scots dial *whup*] **chiefly Sth, S Midl** See Map

1845 Thompson *Pineville* 28 **GA**, Unloose me, I say! and I'll whoop the whole belin' of ye! **1864** Wilson *Confederate Private* 74 **VA** (*Montgomery Coll.*), Our sharp shuters whuped them back & kild several yanks & a good meny horses. **1890** *DN* 1.69 **KY**, *Whip.* Often pronounced [hwup]. **1893** Shands *MS Speech* 68, *Whup* [hwup]. Negro for *whip.* **1902** *DN* 2.249 **sIL**, *Whip.* . . Pronounced . . [hwʌp]. **1906** *DN* 3.164 **nwAR**, *Whup* [hwup]. . . To vanquish, to punish, to tire. "That whups me." **1908** Fox *Lonesome Pine* 84 **KY**, I reckon you ain't goin' to whoop me no more, pap. **1909** *DN* 3.388 **eAL, wGA**, *Whoop* [hwup], v. and n. Whip. **1915** *DN* 4.192 **swVA**, *Whup.* **1917** *DN* 4.419 **wNC**, *Whup.* **1923** *DN* 5.224 **swMO**, *Whup.* **1936** *AmSp* 11.13 **eTX**, *Whip* is habitually [ʌup], [ʌʌp] in the speech of the more illiterate. **1937** in 1976 *Weevils in the Wheat* 43 **VA** [Black], Lawd, chile, dere ain't nowheres else fo' him to whup you. **1942** Hall *Smoky Mt. Speech* 17 **wNC, eTN**, *Whip* [hwup]. **1942** Faulkner *Go Down* 147 **MS**, Ah gots something hyar now dat kin whup you. **1965–70** *DARE* (Qu. Y15, *To beat somebody thoroughly: "John really _____ that fellow!"*) Infs **CA**65, **IL**17, **KY**85, 94, **MS**80, **MO**29, **NJ**15, **TN**31, **VA**2, Whupped [hwʌp]; **KY**19, Give him a good whupping ['hwʌpɪn]; **MS**60, Whupped; **CA**140, **PA**244, **TX**12, **VA**24, **WA**26, Whupped [wʌp]; **AL**24, 43, **OH**57, Whooped [hwup]; **GA**77, Whooped [hwup] the tar out of; **AL**39, **CT**43, **TX**16, Wooped [wup] (up); (Qu. L32a, *In early days, how was the grain separated from the straw?*) Inf **MS**87, Whupped off; (Qu. W28, *When a woman is in a hurry and has to sew up a torn place quickly . . "I'll just _____."*) Infs **NY**48, **TX**106, Whoop it up; **MS**63, Whup [hwup] it over; (Qu. X47, *"I'm very tired, at the end of my strength"*) Inf **NC**45, Whupped; (Qu. EE21a, *When somebody goes into a fight very actively: "You should have seen Jack _____ Bob.";* total Infs questioned, 75) Inf **MS**60, Whup; (Qu. II27, *If somebody gives you a very sharp scolding . . "I certainly got a*

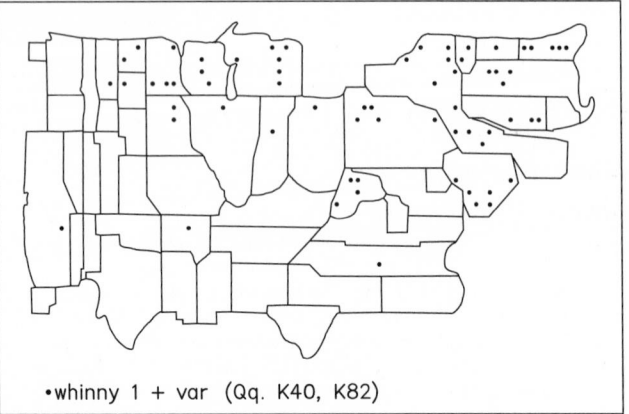

•whinny 1 + var (Qq. K40, K82)

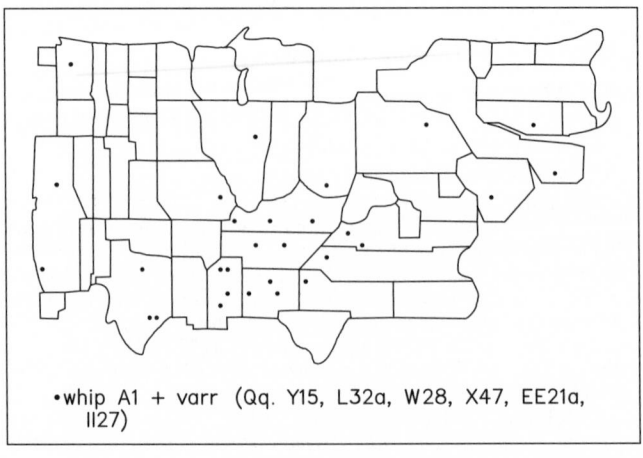

•whip A1 + varr (Qq. Y15, L32a, W28, X47, EE21a, II27)

_____ for that.") Inf **TN**15, Whupping-out. **1966** _DARE_ Tape **AL**1, Mama was gonna whip [hwʊp] me. . . We both got a whipping ['hwɪpɪn]; **MS**75, So she grabbed the brush broom and she whipped [hwʊpt] little Roberta. **1972** Claerbaut _Black Jargon_ 87, _Woop._ . . See _whup._ **1976** Garber _Mountain-ese_ 101 **sAppalachians,** That kid's pa is gonna whup him when he sees his torn overalls. **1989** Pederson _LAGS Tech. Index_ 73 **Gulf Region,** _Whip_ [for driving horses]. [594 infs, [hwɪp(s), 'hwɪpn̩]; 136 infs [wɪp(s), 'wɪpn̩]; 57 infs, [hwʊp(s), hwʊpt]; 15 infs, [hwʌp(s)].] **1992** Martone _Townships_ 101 **ceWI,** His eyes . . rolled slightly in his head the way cartoon animals do when they've been whupped upside the head.

2 |hwʊrp, hwʌrp|; pronc-spp _whirp, whoorp, whurp._ **esp Sth** Cf Intro "Language Changes" I.8

1894 Riley _Armazindy_ 52 **IN,** Flick ye wid er buggy-whirp. **1933** _AmSp_ 8.1.24 **sAppalachians,** _Whip_ is _whoop_ or _whoorp_ to the south; in Kentucky, Virginia and West Virginia it may be either of these, or _whirp_ and _whurp_ with the vowel of _pull._ **1946** _PADS_ 6.32 **eNC, sVA,** _Whirp: n._ and _vb._ Whip. . . Rare. **1989** Pederson _LAGS Tech. Index_ 73 **Gulf Region,** _Whip_ [for driving horses] . . 2 infs, [hwuɚp, hwʌɚp].

3 pronc-sp _hoop._

1905 _DN_ 3.62 **NE,** _Hoop, v._ Whip. "He hooped up his horse, and away he went." **1908** _DN_ 3.321 **eAL, wGA,** _Hoop, v._ and _n._ Whip: especially common among the negroes.

4 |(h)wip|. [Scots dial]

1989 Pederson _LAGS Tech. Index_ 73 **Gulf Region,** [2 infs, [hwip]; 1 inf, [wip].]

B As verb.

1 also with _off, out:_ To thresh out (grain), shell (beans), or clean (cotton) by beating. **chiefly Sth, S Midl** See Map

1854 _De Bow's Rev._ 17.483, Two men then go in with a bundle of long smooth rods . . and they both set to work to whip the cotton with their rods. **1903** in 1961 Pringle _Woman Rice Planter_ 44 **SC,** The hands are now whipping out the seed rice, which is a tedious business. **1927** Jones _FL Plantation Rec._ 590 **nwFL** (as of 1850s–60s), [Glossary:] _Whipping cotton:_ beating, to free it from dirt and bits of dead leaves. **1965–70** _DARE_ (Qu. I13, _When you take dry beans out of the cover you are _____ them_) Inf **GA**46, Whipping; **OR**3, Whipping out; (Qu. L32a, _In early days, how was the grain separated from the straw?_) Inf **TX**32, Spread on the floor and whipped; **FL**17, Whip; **KY**86, Whipped it out with sticks; **TN**62, Whipped it over a rail on a windy day in March; **MS**74, Whipped off on a blanket over a log; **IA**39, Whipping it with your hands; **MS**87, Whupped off; (Qu. L32b, _In early days, how was the grain separated from the chaff?_) Inf **AL**43, Whipped it. [8 of 10 total Infs comm types 4, 5; 7 Infs old] **1986** Pederson _LAGS Concordance,_ 1 inf, **ceLA,** Whip it—of rice; 1 inf, **nwFL,** Whip it out—you whip the oats out; 1 inf, **cMS,** Whip the oats in a barrel; 1 inf, **nwLA,** Whip those things—thrash oats.

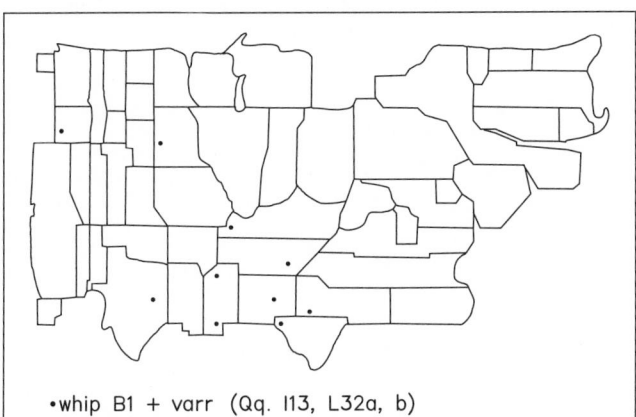

•whip B1 + varr (Qq. I13, L32a, b)

2 ppl adj _whipped;_ also with _down, out:_ Fatigued, exhausted. **chiefly Sth, S Midl** See Map

1906 _DN_ 3.164 **nwAR,** _Whup_ . . to tire. . . "I'm clean whupped out." **1935** Sheppard _Cabins_ 284 **wNC,** She panted as she climbed the steep steps to the porch and admitted that she was "fair whipped down." **1942** (1971) Campbell _Cloud-Walking_ 251 **seKY,** Marthy was like to get plumb whipped down waiting on her all the time. **1956** Ker _Vocab. W. TX_ 358, _Tired, exhausted._ . . whipped. [1 of 67 infs] **1965–70** _DARE_ (Qu. X47, . . _"I'm very tired, at the end of my strength"_) Infs **AR**3,

CT34, **FL**5, **IL**25, **NY**84, 111, 161, **TX**9, **VA**65, Whipped; **NC**52, Absolutely whipped; **FL**22, Whipped down; **LA**11, 18, **SC**7, 26, 44, Whipped out; **NC**45, Whupped; (Qu. KK30, _Feeling slowed up or without energy: "I certainly feel _____."_) Inf **KY**60, Whipped. **1968** _DARE_ FW Addit **LA**18A, _Whipped out_—extremely tired. **1973** Allen _LAUM_ 1.362 (as of c1950), _Tired._ . . whipped [2 infs, **IA, NE**]. **1975** Chalmers _Better_ 66 **wNC, eTN,** He is merely tired and whupped out. **1984** Wilder _You All Spoken Here_ 206 **Sth,** _Fair whipped down:_ Debilitated. **1984** Ehle _Last One Home_ 30 **NC** (as of c1900), "The boy's about whooped . . ," she complained, but on he went striding forward. **1986** Pederson _LAGS Concordance (Tired; exhausted)_ 6 infs, **AR, FL, GA, LA, MS,** Whipped; _(He is worn-out)_ 5 infs, **AL, GA, MS,** (All) whipped; 4 infs, **FL, GA,** Whipped out. **1990** Cavender _Folk Med. Lexicon_ 34 **sAppalachians,** _Whipped out_—tired, fatigued.

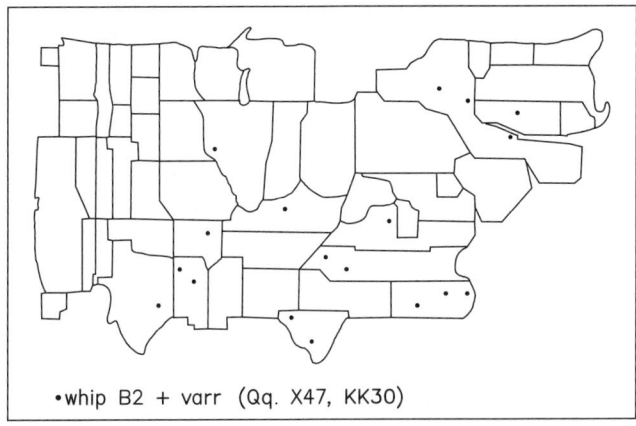

•whip B2 + varr (Qq. X47, KK30)

C As noun.

A **rush** n¹ **B.**

1942 _Torreya_ 42.158 **LA,** _Juncus roemerianus_ . . Jonc negre, jonc piquant, fouet, whip.

whipcoach See **coachwhip snake**

whip-cracker n

1 also _whip-crack(ing):_ The game of crack-the-whip. **chiefly S Midl** See Map Cf **snap-the-whip, whip-popper**

1879 (1880) Bender _Hoosier's Experience_ 73 **IN,** The coaches flew, and when passing over a curve it reminded me of the old game of whip-cracker when I was on the tail-end of the line. **1892** _Belford's Mth._ 9.744, I played. . . "whip cracker" . . in the school yard. **1905** _DN_ 3.100 **nwAR,** _Whip-crack(er)._ . . The game of 'Snap the whip.' **1906** Casey _Parson's Boys_ 251 **sIL** (as of c1860), Some of the big boys already mentioned were in the habit of playing "whip-cracker." Once, during recess, they formed a long line for the sport, and just as it started, the end man, who was nearly twice as big as William, seized him by the wrist in passing, and when the final sweeping crack came, let him go. **1946** _TN Folk Lore Soc. Bulletin_ 12.1.17, "Whip-crack," "Rooster Fighting," and other games were played. **1957** _Sat. Eve. Post Letters_ **IL,** Games we played . . about the years 1885 to 1891 or '92 . . Whip Crack. **1963** Allen _Legends & Lore S. IL_ viii **csIL,** The boys played bull pen, move up, hat ball, old sow, sling dutch, whip cracker, wolf-on-the-ridge, stink base, and anti-over. **1967** Jacobs _Rejoicing_ 121 **cIN** (as of c1930),

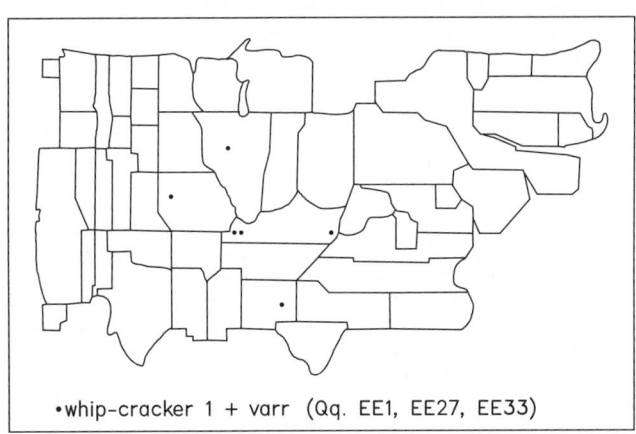

•whip-cracker 1 + varr (Qq. EE1, EE27, EE33)

Have you ever played whipcracker? . . Everybody line up—Jacobs is pigtail. **1967–70** *DARE* (Qu. EE1, . . *Games . . children play . . in which they form a ring, and either sing or recite a rhyme*) Inf **AL26,** Whip-cracking—not in a ring, on skates; (Qu. EE27, *Games played on the ice*) Inf **MO13,** Whip-crack; **KY85,** Whip-cracker; (Qu. EE33, . . *Outdoor games . . that children play*) Infs **IL63, KY40,** 89, Whip-cracker; **KY85,** Whip-cracker—old-fashioned. [5 of 6 total Infs old]

2 See quot. Cf **whickerbill 4**

c1960 *Wilson Coll.* **csKY,** Whipcracker. . . The prepuce.

whip-cracking See **whip-cracker 1**

whip grass n

A **nut rush 1** (here: *Scleria triglomerata*).

1822 Eaton *Botany* 454, *Scleria. . . triglomerata* (whip-grass). **1876** Hobbs *Bot. Hdbk.* 48, Grass[s] Whip . . *Scleria triglomerata*. **1970** Correll *Plants TX* 314, *Scleria triglomerata* . . Whip-grass.

whip her well See **whippoorwill**

whiplash daisy n

A **fleabane** (here: *Erigeron flagellaris*).

1953 Nelson *Plants Rocky Mt. Park* 163, Whiplash daisy or trailing fleabane, *Erigeron flagellaris.* **2007** *DARE* File—Internet **CO,** *Erigeron flagellaris.* . . The runners, sometimes called "whips", give rise to another common name, "Whiplash Daisy".

whip off (or out) See **whip B1**

whipped See **whip B2**

whipped-cream n attrib Cf **ice-cream 1**

See quots.

1955 *Kingsport Times–News* (TN) 18 Sept sec B 4/2 **NY,** The great man [=Mark Twain] with his Niagara of white hair, whipped cream suit . . and rich, fascinating drawl made a profound impression upon me. **1968** *DARE* File **swIN,** *Whipped cream pants*—riding or other breeches made out of cloth "the color of whipped cream" (off-white)—"dress-up" clothes—to go to the store.

whipped down (or out) See **whip B2**

whipper-ca-loo See **whippoorwill**

whipper-jawed adj

=**whopper-jawed 2.**

1951 in 1958 Selekman et al. *Problems Labor Relations* 210 **Chicago IL,** Because you have got the thing around there so that the rates are cockeyed and whipper-jawed. **1994** *NC Lang. & Life Project Harkers Is. Vocab.* 11 **eNC,** Whipper jawed. . . Crooked, out of line. *That tree is whipper jawed.* **1997** Ammons *Glare* 193 **NC,** Well, it's Easter / morning right now, with a nor'easter,/ out-of-whack, whipper-jawed, eight-inch dump / load of snow on the ground. **2007** in 2008 *DARE* File—Internet **VA,** Unless you're expecting it to take the place of a 2K watt pa sub . . I suspect your cab might be whipperjawed. *Ibid* **MT,** Whatever was going on before a guy wanders on here, it gets all whipperjawed, and he starts doin things a little "differnt".

whipper-will(er) See **whippoorwill**

whipple n[1] See **whippletree**

whipple n[2] See **whiffle** n[2]

whippletree n [*OED2* 1733 →] **chiefly Nth** See Map Cf **double whiffletree, swingletree, whiffletree**

A **singletree, doubletree,** or **evener.**

1801 MA Soc. Promoting Ag. *Papers* 23 **ceMA,** I use a short whippletree, with a steady horse and a careful man to lead, while ploughing near the trees. **1819** *Plough Boy* 1.226 **cNY,** It [=a canal boat] was drawn by one horse, by means of a rope eighty feet long, of which one end was connected to the whippletree. **1825** in 1988 Palmer *Lang. W. Cent. MA* 33, [Owed to] Lyman Brainard [for] a Whippletree—.25. **1851** NY Ag. Soc. *Trans. for 1850* 644, When three horses are worked abreast, the two horses placed together should have only half the length of arm of the main whipple-tree as the single horse. **1863** *Continental Mth.* 4.145 **ME,** At length I was aroused by a sudden stop. The 'whippletree' had broken. **1905** *DN* 3.100 **nwAR,** Whipple-tree. . . Whiffle-tree. 'The badge will be a purple ribbon surmounted by a *whipple-tree* bearing the word 'Delegate.'—Arkansas *Daily Sentinel*, Dec. 17, 1904. Rare, 'single-tree' being the universal word. **1945** FWP *Lay My Burden Down* 172 **TX** (as of c1865) [Black], The wheel hits a stump, and the team

jerks, and that breaks the whippletree. **1949** [see **whiffletree**]. **1956** [see **whiffletree**]. **1962** [see **whiffletree**]. **1965–70** *DARE* (Qu. L46, *Behind each horse there's a movable bar [the leathers or ropes from the collar are fastened to it]*) 114 Infs, **chiefly Nth,** Whippletree; **NJ1,** Single whippletree; (Qu. L45, *The long piece of wood that sticks out in front of a wagon, and you put a horse on each side*) Inf **NY2,** Whippletree; (Qu. L47, *The two movable bars behind a team of horses are fastened to a longer piece; this is a* _____) Infs **CO33, NY24,** 230, **WI17,** (Big) whippletree; [**NY206,** Double whipple; **NY213,** Double whippletree;] **NY219,** Set of whippletrees. **1968** *DARE* FW Addit **Upstate NY,** Jump over the whippletrees = leave unexpectedly. **1973** [see **whiffletree**]. **1981** [see **whiffletree**]. **1988** Palmer *Lang. W. Cent. MA* 33, The whippletree is part of the wagon.

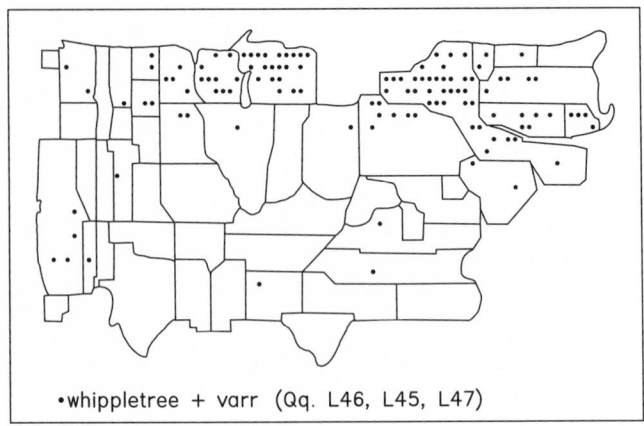

•whippletree + varr (Qq. L46, L45, L47)

whippoorwill n Also *whip her well, whipper-ca-loo, whipper-willer, whip'will, whip-willow-the-wish, wippervill* Also sp *w(h)ipperwill, whipporwill, whippowil(l)*

A Forms.

1709 (1967) Lawson *New Voyage* 150 **NC, SC,** *Whippo-Will,* so nam'd, because it makes those Words exactly. **1778** Carver *Travels N. Amer.* 468 **MI, WI, MN,** The *Whipperwill,* or as it is termed by the Indians, the Muckawiss. . . acquires its name by the noise it makes. **1788** *Hist. Rev. & Directory* 1.239 **NJ,** Here is also a bird called, the *Whip Her Well, or, Whip Poor Will.* Its name is taken from its note. **1809** (1910) Ayer *Diary* 102 **MA,** We were at length roused from meditations, by the sweet notes of the *Wip-per-will.* **1822** Woods *2 Yrs. Residence* 197 **IL,** Wipperwill, or whip-poor-will, or wippervill,—a brown bird . . is generally heard of an evening in spring and summer. **1828** Webster *Amer. Dict., Whippowil* . . The popular name of an American bird. . . [Webster: Not *whip-poor-will.*] **1869** *S. Rev.* (Baltimore MD) 6.36, In changing the name of the bird whip-poor-will (which everybody calls whipperwill) into 'whippowil,' he [=Noah Webster] forgot that such words are intended to be adaptations rather than exact imitations of the original sound. **1885** Twain *Huck. Finn* 20 **MO,** I heard . . a whippo-will and a dog crying about somebody that was going to die. **1896** Harris *Sister Jane* 132 **GA** [Black], Whip'will say 'he comin'.' **1907** Anderson *Birds IA* 280, The Whipporwill is a common summer resident in all wooded portions of the state. **1909** *DN* 3.388 **eAL,** Whipper-willer. . . Same as the preceding [=chuck-will's-widow]. **1919** Burns *Ornith. Chester Co. PA* 62, *Anstromus vociferus vociferus* Whip-poor-will, "whipper-will," "whipper-ca-loo." **1967** *DARE* (Qu. Q3, . . *Birds that come out only after dark*) Inf **SC62,** Whipwillow-the-wish = whippoorwill.

B Senses.

1 Std: a nocturnal bird (*Caprimulgus vociferus*) found chiefly in the eastern half of the US. Also called **bullbat 2, chilly-lou, dustbird, katydid B3, nighthawk** n **2, nightingale b, nightjar 2, night owl 2, poorwill 2, rainbird 1e, rain crow 1g, Virginia bat, woodchuck 3**

2 =**chuck-will's-widow.** Cf German **whippoorwill, poorwill,** Spanish **whippoorwill**

1909 [see **A** above]. **1913** *Auk* 30.497 **Okefenokee GA,** Chuck-will's-widow; 'Whip-poor-will.' **1924** Howell *Birds AL* 176, The chuck-will's-widow . . , universally but incorrectly called "whip-poor-will" in the South, is a common and generally distributed summer resident. **1938** Rawlings *Yearling* 397 **nFL,** When the first whip-poor-will

calls, the corn had ought to be in the ground.   **1955** Lowery *LA Birds*
326, Throughout the state the Chuck-will's-widow is confused with the
Whip-poor-will.   **2001** MD Ornith. Soc. *MD Yellowthroat* Mar–Apr 6
(Internet) **eVA, eMD,** In the summer when the light's about gone in the
piney woods you hear what we call the Whip-poor-will. *Ibid* 7, Whip-
poor-will = Chuck-will's-widow.

3   See **whippoorwill flower.**

4   See **whippoorwill's shoes 2.**

5   See **whippoorwill pea.**

whippoorwill flower n   Also *whippoorwill*

A **trillium** (here: *Trillium cernuum* or *T. cuneatum*).

   1933 Small *Manual SE Flora* 307, T[rillium] Hugeri [=*T. cuneatum*]. . . Whippoorwill-flower.   **1949** (1958) Stuart *Thread* 289 **eKY,**
From the soft loamy soil beneath these trees grew blue and pink Agera-
tum, whippoorwill flowers, May apple, and blue beggar's-lice.   **1969**
DARE (Qu. S2, . . *The flower that comes up in the woods early in spring,
with three white petals that turn pink as the flower grows older*) Inf
GA70, We call it whippoorwill because it comes with them—same as
trillium.   **2007** (acc) U.S. Dept. Ag. *Plants Database* (Internet), *Trillium
cernuum* . . whip-poor-will flower.

whippoorwill pea n   Also *whippoorwill* [See quot 1953]
chiefly Sth, S Midl   See Map

A cultivated **black-eyed pea** (here: *Vigna unguiculata* subsp
unguiculata) with speckled seeds.

   1864 in 2008 *DARE* File—Internet [*Mobile Register and Advertiser* 8
Nov 2/2] **nwMS,** I paid a neighbor ten dollars for four bushels of very
prolific peas known in my neighborhood as the Whippoorwill Pea.
1878 Killebrew *Grasses TN* 440, Select peas which run least. . . They
are the black bunch pea, and the speckle or whippoorwill pea.   **1889** *S.
Cultivator* 47.240, The speckled, or whippoorwill pea, does better on
poor land unmanured.   **1941** Justus *Cabin on Kettle Creek* 98 **eTN,** The
dried corn, the shucky beans, the whippoorwill peas . . had all been put
in.   **1953** Randolph–Wilson *Down in Holler* 298 **Ozarks,** *Whippoorwill
peas*. . . A variety of peas or beans, mottled exactly like the whippoorwill's eggs.   **1964** *PADS* 42.24 **csKY,** Whippoorwill peas. A variety
with many spots on the seeds.   **1965–70** *DARE* (Qu. I20, . . *Kinds of
beans*) 9 Infs, 8 **Sth, S Midl,** Whippoorwill peas; (Qu. I4, . . *Vegetables . . less commonly grown around here*) Inf **GA**13, Whippoorwill
pea; **AR**47, Whippoorwill peas—purple-splotched hulls.   **c1974** Jones
Ozark Hill Boy 23 **AR** (as of c1920), In the fall, we had picked whippoorwill peas on the halves for a farmer and had stored them in the attic.
2004 in 2008 *DARE* File—Internet **eOK,** My father has been growing
several varieties of cowpeas and at least three types of whippoorwill
peas in his garden in eastern Oklahoma for over fifty years. Some of
these came originally from Arkansas through family members; others
were purchased at country feed stores.   **2006** *Ibid* **TN, VA,** I gave my
grandma a call and she advised to sow whippoorwill peas on "the poorest soil you've got, or they'll go all to vines." . . [She] noted that no one
grew whippoorwills anymore—they've all switched to purple-hulled.

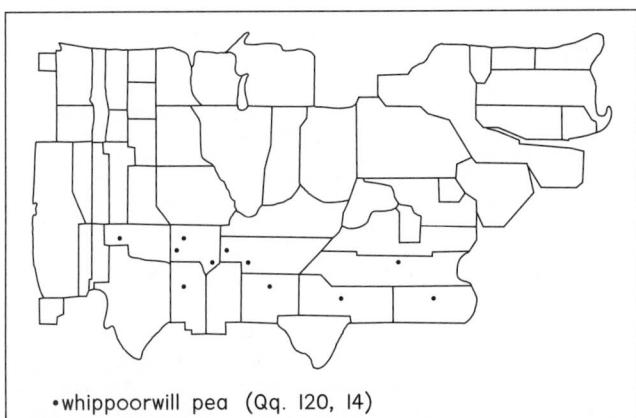

•whippoorwill pea (Qq. I20, I4)

whippoorwill's boots   See **whippoorwill's shoes 1**

whippoorwill shoes   See **whippoorwill's shoes 2**

whippoorwill squall   See **whippoorwill winter**

whippoorwill's shoe   See **whippoorwill's shoes 2**

whippoorwill's shoes n

1   also *whippoorwill's boots:* A **pitcher plant 1** (here: *Sarracenia purpurea*).

   1832 Williamson *Hist. ME* 1.126, *Meadow-cup,* called forefathers'
pitcher, or Whippoorwill's shoes.   **1867** *Flag of Our Union* (Boston
MA) 22.48, Dorel always had a fancy for whippoorwill's shoes, they
made the wood so bright with their tall, nodding heads.   **1896** *Jrl. Amer.
Folkl.* 9.181 **Philadelphia PA,** *Sarracenia purpurea*. . . whippoorwill's
boots.   **1940** Clute *Amer. Plant Names* 145, Pitcher-plant. . . whip-poor-
will's boots, whip-poor-will's shoes.

2   also *whippoorwill (shoes), whippoorwill's shoe:* =**lady's
slipper 1.**

   1876 Hobbs *Bot. Hdbk.* 127, Whip-poor-will's shoe. . . Cypripedium
acaule.   **1886** *New Princeton Rev.* 1.404 **seCT,** I was pleased with Bay's
name for it [=pink lady's slipper] of Whippoorwill's Shoes. He gathered
the whole plant, giving me the flower . . , but keeping the fibrous root
among his choicest treasures as "good for narves and high strikes."
1892 *Jrl. Amer. Folkl.* 5.103 **MA,** *Cypripedium acaule* . . whip-poor-
will. Boston.   *Ibid* **CT,** *Cypripedium spectabile* [=*C. reginae*] . . whip-
poor-will shoes.   **1924** *Amer. Botanist* 30.153, *Cypripedium parvulum*
[=*C. parviflorum*] is the "yellow-" or "downy yellow Lady's slipper,"
"yellow moccasin flower," "whip-poor-will's shoes" [etc] . . all ringing
the changes on the sh[a]pe of the lower lip. *Cypripedium hirsutum* [=*C.
pubescens*] is also known as "whip-poor-will's shoe."   **1938** FWP *Guide
CT* 468 **nwCT,** Mountain laurel, the rare 'whippoorwill-shoe' or moccasin flower, trailing arbutus, and a variety of ferns furnish coverage for
the forest floor.   **1960** Teale *Journey into Summer* 100 **eWI,** The memory that lingers most vividly in our minds is coming suddenly upon almost half a hundred "whip-poor-will's shoes"—showy lady's-slippers—
all in bloom in an area no larger than a city lot.   **1968** McPhee *Pine
Barrens* 59 **NJ,** They even have a better name than lady's slipper. This
small and exquisite orchid grows in the pines, where the natives call it a
whippoorwill shoe.   **1979** *Greenfield Recorder* (MA) 2 June np, Lady's
slippers sometimes were called "whippoorwill shoes."

whippoorwill winter n   **Sth, S Midl**   Cf **blackberry winter**

A period of cold weather in the spring; similarly *whippoorwill
squall,* ~ *storm* a spring storm; see quots.

   1933 *AmSp* 8.1.80 **OK,** A *whippoor-will storm* is a cold rain attended
by a driving wind and considerable bluster; it occurs in the spring of the
year after the season is well advanced; and it is so called, presumably,
from the fact that one often hears the call of the whippoor-will after the
storm subsides.   **1934** Vines *Green Thicket* 182 **cnAL,** Everybody
talked about the whippoorwill winter and knew that the birds would be
on the ground the next morning.   **1936** *AmSp* 11.315 **Ozarks,** *Frog
storm*. . . The first bad weather in the spring, after a warm period. The
term *whip-poor-will storm* is synonymous.   **1945** *Middlesboro Daily
News* (KY) 14 May 2/6, John Estep, of Cumberland Gap, keeps up week
by week the kind of winter through which we have been passing. The
latest was "whippoorwill winter."   **c1960** *Wilson Coll.* **csKY,** *Whippoorwill squall* (or *storm*). . . One of the early-spring cold spells.   **1962**
Dykeman *Tall Woman* 14 **NC** (as of 1860), After the cold spell, when
dogwoods bloomed, there would be whippoorwill winter and blackberry
winter.   **1963** *Clarke Co. Democrat* (Grove Hill AL) 4 April 4/2
(*Mathews Coll.*), One turkey hunter remarked last week that it was about
time we were having a "whippoorwill storm."   **1971** *Advocate* (Newark
OH) 27 May 23/2, According to the old-timers, when there is hot
weather in the middle of May, at least two cold snaps are bound to follow. In Licking County [OH], I never have heard these spells of chilly
weather called by any special name, but in the environs of Atlanta,
Ga., . . one was called . . whippoorwill winter, which always came when
the whippoorwills began calling—about the last week in May, if I remember correctly.   **1995** *Brophy Coll.* 83 **swMO** (as of c1960), *Whippoorwill winter*. [I]nfrequent for "blackberry winter."   **2006** *DARE*
File—Internet **TN,** If you listen to the old folks we will have . . Dogwood Winter, Whippoorwill Winter and Blackberry winter, three more
cold spells.

whip-popper n   esp **Sth, S Midl**   See Map on p. 926   Cf **popper** n[1], **pop-the-whip, whip-cracker 1**

The game of crack-the-whip.

   1965–70 *DARE* (Qu. EE1, . . *Games . . children play . . in which they
form a ring, and either sing or recite a rhyme*) Infs **AL**6, 15, 20, **CA**99,
MD20, **OK**1, **TN**46, Whip-popper.   **1966** *DARE* Tape **AL**6A, Whip-

popper, that's the one when everybody makes a long line and then you run and the one in the front kind of jerks it that way and tries to whip off the one on the end. . . Pop-the-whip is what we call it.

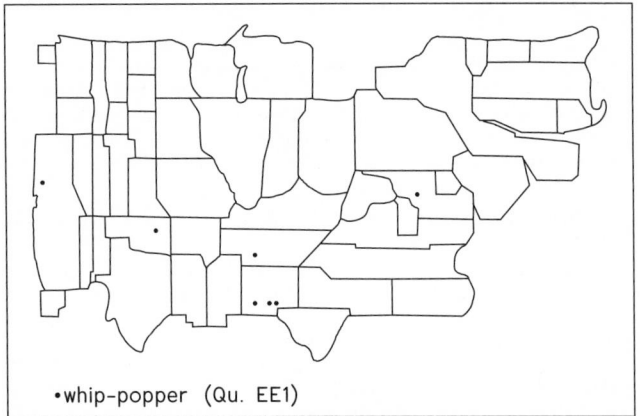

•whip-popper (Qu. EE1)

whipporwill, whippowil(l) See **whippoorwill**

whip scorpion n Also *whiptail scorpion*
A nonvenomous **scorpion B1** of the order Uropygi or Amblypygi. For other names see **vinegarone 1**

  1878 *Harper's New Mth. Mag.* 57.472, The whip-tail scorpion *(Thelyphonus giganteus)* of Mexico and adjoining parts of the United States . . is offensively odorous, apparently emitting the smell from its tail, which is long and filiform. **1913** Comstock *Spider Book* 18, Whip-scorpions [=family Thelyphonidae] are greatly feared on account of their supposed venomous powers. *Ibid* 19, Family Phrynidae. . . *The Tailless Whip-scorpions.* **1947** Dodge *Poisonous Dwellers* 41, Since people coming from Arkansas, Oklahoma, and Texas bring the majority of tales regarding the deadly characteristics of the little vinegarone or whip-tail scorpion, fear of it is apparently more widespread over the cotton belt as a whole than within the desert regions of the Southwest. **1992** *Frederick Post* (MD) 14 Dec sec B 4/1, Among the insects crawling up the arms of visitors were . . a vinegaroon, a brown 4-inch-long whip scorpion.

whip snake n Also *whiptail snake*
Std: a slender nonvenomous southern snake of the genus *Masticophis,* esp *M. flagellum* or *M. taeniatus.* For other names see **cedar racer, coachwhip snake, green racer 2, racer 1d**

whipstick n esp Sth, Midl See Map Cf **flip-stick**
=**cricket** n[2].

  1950 *WELS (Game in which you flip a short stick into the air and try to hit it with a longer stick)* 2 Infs, **WI,** Whipstick. **1965–70** *DARE* (Qu. EE10) Infs **IL**78, 85, **TN**33, 34, **TX**54, **VA**69, **WA**9, **WV**14, 16, Whipstick; **GA**77, Whipstick—same as jumpstick, sky rocket—sometimes you light the little stick, do it at night; **AR**47, **CA**182, **IN**30, **MS**6, **TX**37, **WI**64, Whipstick [FW sugg].

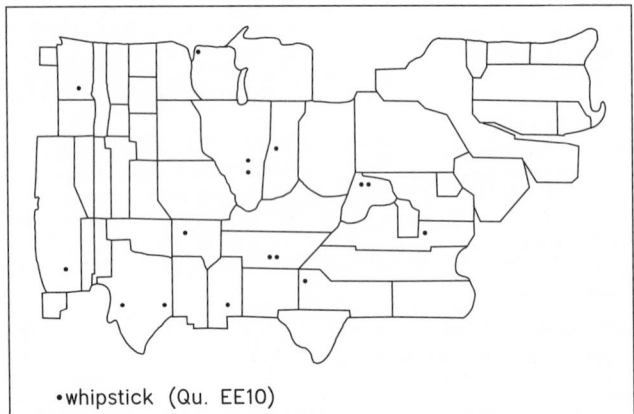

•whipstick (Qu. EE10)

whipstitch n
1 A brief interval of time, moment—freq used in phr *(at) ev-*

ery whipstitch frequently; continuously; from time to time. [Engl dial *(EDD* at whip v. 1.(14) (c))] **scattered, but chiefly Sth, S Midl**

  1809 (1814) Weems *F. Marion* 3, What can one do when one's friends are eternally teazing him, . . calling out at every whipstitch and corner of the streets, "Well, but, sir, where's Marion?" **1827** *Adams Sentinel* (Gettysburg PA) 28 Mar [2]/1 (newspaperarchive.com), Imagine . . a crowd of men . . all pressing forward, and making up their lips ready for a smack, and then . . poking their snout into my very face—and me wiping my face, every whipstitch, to appear a little decent. **1854** in 1875 Palmer *Life Thornwell* 378 **SC,** I see Palmer every whip-stitch; he is really beginning to look down-right *well.* **1859** Taliaferro *Fisher's R.* 136 **wNC** (as of 1820s), I hearn suthin' . . snortin' uvry whip-stitch like he smelt suthin' he didn't adzackly like. **1870** *Overland Mth.* 4.143 **CA,** Laborers are off every whip-stitch. **1899** (1912) Green *VA Folk-Speech* 482, Whipstitch. . . A short space of time; a thing repeated often: as, he went in and out at every *whipstitch.* **1903** Malone *Sons Vengeance* 137 **eKY,** She knows a heap sight more o' th' Bible than I does, an' kin fin' all th' places in a whipstich [sic]. **1906** *DN* 3.164 **nwAR,** She's coming over here every whipstitch. **1944** *PADS* 2.52 **NC, VA,** *Whip-stitch, every.* . . All the time. "I've been working every whip-stitch since you left." **1953** Randolph-Wilson *Down in Holler* 298 **Ozarks,** Bob's folks are a-sendin' him money every whip-stitch, but he won't even pay his store-bill. **1954** Welty *Ponder Heart* 22 **MS,** He'd go back to the Fair every whipstitch—morning, noon, or night. **1957** in 2008 (acc) Lexis–Nexis Legal Research *State Case Law: FL* (Internet), That was just a whip-stitch of time before the collision and the school bus was not stopped. **1978** Massey *Bittersweet Country* 207 **Ozarks,** Whip stitch (brief interval): My cousin visits me every whip stitch. **1994** NC Lang. & Life Project *Dial. Vocab. Ocracoke* 17 **eNC,** Whipstitch. . . Every now and then, sporadically. . . Used now mostly by older speakers. **1999** in 2004 Montgomery-Hall *Dict. Smoky Mt. Engl.* 645, Whipstitch . . A brief interval of time. . . "I'll be there in a whipstitch. [1 inf, **eTN**] **2003** in 2008 *DARE* File—Internet **IA,** It is outpatient surgery so I should be back to normal in a whipstitch. **2008** *Ibid* **cwNC,** Way back then, we didn't run to the doctor every whipstitch.

2 The least bit—also in phr *every whipstitch (thing)* every last thing.

  1888 *Century Illustr. Mag.* 35.623, Every whip-stitch of his bag and baggage shall be trundled after him as soon as I kin git it away. **1929** *AmSp* 5.127 **ME,** Women might have to "do every whipstich [sic]" (Eng. Dial. Col. U.S.) if there were inefficient help in the family. **1950** *PADS* 14.72 **SC,** Whipstitch. . . "He took advantage of every whipstitch to win." **1951** *AmSp* 26.74 **sIL,** 'I don't care a whipstitch!' or 'I wouldn't give a whipstitch for it.' **1967** *DARE* Tape **PA**65, It didn't make a whipstitch of business [sic, prob for *difference*] that you went across the middle or not. **1968** Kellner *Aunt Serena* 148 **IN,** She had never learned to read and write, and didn't care a whipstitch. **2003** U.S. Congress House *U.S. Leadership HIV/AIDS, Mr. Smith of Michigan.* Mr. Chairman, I would respectfully request that everybody consider that there is not a whip stitch of difference between these two amendments. **2006** in 2008 *DARE* File—Internet **IN,** My son is a reporter to his dad on everything, every whipstitch thing any of us do.

whiptail n
1 =**long-tailed jaeger.**

  1884 U.S. Bur. Fisheries *Rept. for 1882* 325, There are several varieties of jaegers, of the genus *Stercorarius* that frequent the fishing-banks, and which are known to the fishermen by the names of "Marlingspikes," "Whiptails," etc. The former term being generally applied to the larger species, and the latter name to those that are smaller, both appellations having a special reference to the two long central tail feathers which is a distinguishing feature of birds of these species. **1956** MA Audubon Soc. *Bulletin* 40.21 **MA,** Long-tailed Jaeger . . Whiptail.

2 also *whiptail lizard:* A **lizard n 1** (here: *Cnemidophorus* spp). For other names of *C. sexlineatus* see **race nag, racer 3, sandlapper 4, sand runner 2, scuttler, streakfield, swift 2, swift-jack;** for other names of var spp see **race runner 1, roadrunner 2, sand flirt, sandlapper 4, sand lizard, ~ swift 1, tiger lizard**

  1893 *Death Valley Exped.* 2.199 **seCA,** The whip-tail lizard *(Cnemidophorus tigris)* is nearly as common as the gridiron-tail in much of the area. **1915** *Nature & Sci.* 111 **CA,** The fleet-footed leopard lizards and whip-tails are among the first to attract the attention of a rider across the desert. **1928** Baylor Univ. Museum *Contrib.* 16.13, The handsome Tesselated Lizard is sometimes called *Whip-tail Lizard* on account of the extreme length of its tail. **1969** *Arcadia Tribune* (CA) 28 May 34/5, Snakes, lizards, iguanas, whiptails, geckos 50 cents. **2006** *Post–Std.* (Syracuse NY) 5 Jan 26/4, The new western whiptail lizards have joined the communal Lizard Exhibit in the . . Zoo. . . . Whiptails rely on burrows for shelter from predators and the desert heat.

whiptail scorpion See **whip scorpion**

whiptail snake See **whip snake**

whip the devil round the bush (or stump) See **devil** n B2

whip the fire out of someone See **fire** B2b

whip-tongue n [A Brit folk-name for this plant]
A **bedstraw** (here: *Galium mollugo*).

1876 Hobbs *Bot. Hdbk.* 127, Whip-tongue, Galium mollugo. **1890** Billings *Natl. Med. Dict.* 1.559, *G[alium] Mollugo.* . . Whip-tongue, a European plant, sparingly naturalized in the U.S. **1935** (1943) Muenscher *Weeds* 436, *Galium Mollugo.* . . Cleavers, Wild madder, . . Whip-tongue.

whip-will(ow-the-wish) See **whippoorwill**

whip-will's-widow n
A **chuck-will's-widow** or, perh less freq, **whippoorwill B1.**

c1742 in 1849 Darlington *Mem. John Bartram* 323, There is a bird in Virginia and Carolina and I suppose in Pennsylvania, that at night calls *Whipper Will,* and sometimes, *Whip Will's widow,* by which names it is called (as the bird clinketh, the fool thinketh). **1876** Eggleston *Capt. Sam* 158 **sAL,** When I want you, I'll come down here to the water's edge and whistle like a Whip-Will's Widow. **1894** Cable *John March* 492, Suddenly the cry of the whip-Will's-widow filled the grove— "whip-Will's-widow! whip-Will's-widow! whip-Will's-widow!"—in headlong importunity until the whole air sobbed and quivered with the overcharge of its melancholy passion. [**1933** *Landmark* (Statesville NC) 1 Dec 6/2 (as of 1862), My beat ran along . . a thicket full of whip-poor-wills, singing whip-will's-widow.] **1948** Hurston *Seraph* 206 **FL,** Arvay heard the first whip-wills-widow of the year from somewhere outside in the dark. [**1959** *Western Folkl.* 18.88 **TX,** Whippoorwill: "Whíp poŏr Wíll!" Variant: "Whip Wǐll's wǐdŏw!" Variant: "Chúck Wǐll's wǐdŏw!" East Texas variant: "Chíp fěll oūt ŏf thĕ white oăk!"]

whirlicue n Also sp *whirlycue* [Blend of *whirl* + *curlicue*] Cf **curlimacue**
1 also *whirlimacue:* A curlicue.
1942 Berrey–Van den Bark *Amer. Slang* 37.3, *Decoration; ornament.* . . whirly-cue. *Ibid* 43.2, *Something curved.* . . whirlycue. **1968–70** *DARE* (Qu. JJ12, *Little flourishes that some people put on their handwriting or signature to make it look fancy*) Inf **VA38,** Whirlicues; **IN8,** Whirlimacues. **2008** *DARE* File—Internet, Devoid of any gimmicks or crazy whirly-cues, the interior seems restrained and yet contemporary.
2 A merry-go-round, also fig.
1968 *DARE* (Qu. EE32, *A homemade merry-go-round*) Inf **MI75,** Whirlicue. **2006** in 2008 *DARE* File—Internet **IL,** Lou is just the latest horse we are riding on that nightmarish baseball whirly-cue which leads ever in a circle, right back where we have always been: the bottom.

whirligig n
1 also *whirlijig:* A curlicue.
1967–70 *DARE* (Qu. JJ12, *Little flourishes that some people put on their handwriting or signature to make it look fancy*) Infs **KY90, MA14,** 79, **MO19, RI1, TN4,** Whirligigs; **OH89,** Fancy whirlijigs. [6 Infs old]
2 =**key** n **2.** Cf **whirlybird**
1995 *DARE* File, I've heard both 'helicopter' and 'whirligig' for maple seeds in the New York and Connecticut areas. *Ibid,* I seem to remember calling them [=maple seeds] whirligigs as a kid in the Chicago area.

whirligig beetle n
Std: an aquatic insect of the family Gyrinidae. Also called **apple bug, coffee bean 4, dishwasher 3, dollar bug, eel ~, lackey ~, lucky ~, mellow ~, scuttle ~, sugar ~, twirly ~, vanilla ~, whirlybug**

whirligust See **whirlygust**

whirlijig See **whirligig 1**

whirlimacue See **whirlicue 1**

whirlimagig n Also *whirlimajig, whirlimygig, whirlimyjig,*

whirlymagig, whirlymajig [Varr of *whirligig*] Cf **-ma-** infix, *whirlimacue* (at **whirlicue 1**)
1909 *DN* 3.388 **eAL, wGA,** Whirlimyjig, whirlimygig. . . A pin wheel, a whirligig. **1931** *Galveston Daily News* (TX) 15 Jan 4/3, [Title of a crossword puzzle:] Whirlimagig. **1986** Pederson *LAGS Concordance,* 1 inf, **cGA,** Whirlimajig. **2002** *DARE* File—Internet, I often notice front yards as I walk by. . . The carefully placed stone rabbit . . a rainbow-colored whirlimajig blowing in the wind. **2006** *Ibid* **OH,** I love the little whirlymagig [=a pinwheel] in the middle of the photos. **2007** *Ibid* **nwOR,** A wind-driven kinetic sculpture . . installed . . [in] 1999. . . . The Whirlymajig, an altered water pump windmill with a five-foot diameter fan wheel atop a thirty-foot steel flag pool [sic].

whirling jenny n Also *whirl jenny* esp Sth Cf **flying jenny 1a**
A homemade merry-go-round.
1902 *Mansfield News* (OH) 26 Feb sec 2 1/7 **IN,** A whirling jenny is made by sawing off a sapling about four feet from the ground. The core of the tree is left sticking up to form a peg and a hole to fit the peg is bored in the middle of a long and heavy plank. This plank is placed across the stump, a boy running at each end of the plank and away they go. **1967–68** *DARE* (Qu. EE32, *A homemade merry-go-round*) Inf **VA27,** Whirling jenny; **SC40,** Whirl jenny. **1971** Wood *Vocab. Change* 368 **MS,** Volunteered [for a homemade merry-go-round] . . whirling jenny. **1986** Pederson *LAGS Concordance (Flying jenny)* 2 infs, **csAL, nwGA,** Whirling jenny; 1 inf, **neLA,** Wing [sic] jenny.

whirling whimpus n Also *whimpus* Cf **wampus** n[2] **1,** *DS* CC17
A fictitious animal; see quots.
1910 Cox *Fearsome Creatures* 33 **eTN,** According to woodsmen who have been "looking" timber in eastern Tennessee, the whimpus . . has a gorilla-shaped head and body and enormous front feet. Its unique method of obtaining food is to station itself upon a trail . . where it stands on its diminutive hind legs and whirls. The speed is increased until the animal is invisible. . . . Any creature coming along the trail . . is almost certain to walk into the danger zone and become instantly deposited in the form of syrup or varnish upon the huge paws of the whimpus. **1949** *Jrl. Amer. Folkl.* 62.419, The phantoms and monsters which daunted the lad of Brittany [=Bon Jean, a folkloric source of Paul Bunyan] became the Ring-tailed Bavalorus, the Whirling Whimpus, and, perhaps already, the Blue Ox.

whirl jenny See **whirling jenny**

whirlybird n [From *whirlybird* helicopter] Cf **whirligig 2** =**key** n **2.**
1995 *NADS* **GA,** I've never heard the word 'key' for maple and similar seeds. We called them as children 'whirlybirds' and I guess I would still call them that today, if pressed for a term. So-called because when you drop one from as high as you can reach, it spins around like the propeller of a helicopter. **2003** *Chron.–Telegram* (Elyria OH) 29 May 1/1, [Headline:] *Flocks of 'whirlybirds' covering the state.* . . The state's silver and red maple trees have produced a bumper crop of seeds this spring. **2006** *DARE* File—Internet **neIL,** Around here we call them whirlybirds. *Ibid* **KS,** I used to love the helicopter seeds when I was a kid. (Actually, in Kansas, we called them whirlybirds.) **2007** *DARE* File **seWI** (as of c1960), When we were kids we called the spinning maple seeds "whirlybirds," maybe from the TV show of the same name which featured helicopter pilots.

whirlybug n Also *whirly-whirly bug* =**whirligig beetle.**
1960 Williams *Walk Egypt* 133 **GA,** Rose Crawford took no more notice of the cold than one of the whirlybugs that skittered across the surface of the water. **1969** *DARE* FW Addit **ceNC,** Whirly-whirly bug—It is described as sort of like a crayfish. **2006** *DARE* File—Internet **LA,** After returning to class, we put all our data together. . . Mostly, all the groups found the same kind of organisms. . . [including] Whirly Bugs.

whirlycue See **whirlicue**

whirlygust n Also *whirligust* esp NC, TN
A whirlwind; freq fig.
1859 Taliaferro *Fisher's R.* 138 **nwNC** (as of 1820s), Away went the bar like a whirlygust uv woodpeckers were arter it. *Ibid* 190, De Lord he raise a mighty whirlygust, and de ship he rock to and fro like a drunkard man. **1864** Gilmore *Down in TN* 93, All Secesh wull be arter us in no time. We must ter take ter the woods . . till the whirlygust ar over.

Ibid 151, She piked out quicker'n a whirlygust chasin' a streak o' lightnin'. **1916** in 2006 *DARE* File—Internet **TN,** [From a letter to the *Alamo Weekly Guide* of 25 Aug:] The preacher denounced playing marbles as being a worldly, and, therefore, evil activity and . . concluded about the players that, "The whole copudle will go to hell like a whirlygust of woodpeckers". **1970** *NC Folkl.* 18.55, When whirligusts, called devil dancers and little whirlwinds, are seen along roads, it is a sure sign of rain. **2006** *DARE* File—Internet **IA,** Like a whirlygust in a teacup.

whirlymagig, whirlymajig See **whirlimagig**

whirly-whirly bug See **whirlybug**

whirly wind n Cf **whirlygust,** *AND*

A **dust devil 1** or tornado.

  1967 *DARE* FW Addit **CO,** *Whirly wind* ['wɚli wɪnd]—a very small (1–3 inches) cyclone. A dust devil. **2003** in 2008 *DARE* File—Internet **KS,** Jeff if your part of Alabammy is in the alley: consider the purchase of a whirlywind box. . . One of those above ground cement FEMA approved tornado box shelters. **2006** *Ibid* **OK,** Yeah, them there whirlywinds can be a bit disturbing to the neighborhood, can't they?

whirp See **whip A2**

whis broom See **whisk broom A3**

whis-capalian See **whiskey-palian**

whish broom See **whisk broom A4**

whisk See **whist 1**

whisk broom n Cf **swish broom**

A Forms.

1 *w(h)isp broom.* [Prob infl by *wisp*]

  1848 *Knickerbocker* 32.80 **seNY,** It [=a horse's tail] looked like a barber's wisp-broom. **1851** *Ibid* 37.340 **PA,** If you dress in black from head to foot, (and have in your trunk a black glazed cap, and small whisp-broom . .) [you will be taken for] an American. **1879** *OH Democrat* (New Philadelphia) 26 June [4]/2 (newspaperarchive.com), The water may be sprinkled upon the leaves and stems by means of a whisp-broom or watering-pot. **1883** (1885) *Dixie Cook-Book* 612, It is an excellent plan . . to brush it carefully all over with a small . . wisp broom. **1899** (1912) Green *VA Folk-Speech* 483, *Whisp-broom.* . . A handfull of straw gathered and tied at the butt-ends and used as a broom for brushing clothes. **1910** London *Burning Daylight* 2 **CA,** Taking the wisp broom from its nail . . , the newcomer brushed the snow from his moccasins. **1911** *New Engl. Mag.* 44.366 **NEng,** The woman explained that she was going to have it painted or guilded . . to hold a "whisp" broom in. **1950** *WELS (Different kinds of brooms used around the house)* 1 Inf, **ceWI,** Whisp broom. **1963** *Corpus Christi Times* (TX) [16 Sept 23]/2 (newspaperarchive.com), [Advt:] Genuine Wee Wisp Broom. **1965–70** *DARE* (Qu. F35, *A small broom that you hold in one hand, and use . . in places that are hard to get at*) 21 Infs, **esp Midl,** W(h)isp (broom). **2002** in 2008 *DARE* File—Internet **MA,** Knock off the small remnants with a hand whisp broom. **2008** *Ibid* **cCA,** Take a small wisp broom to sweep off the soot on the fire ring and firebox.

2 *w(h)ist broom.* **scattered, but chiefly Nth**

  1853 *Philadelphia Gas Wks. Annual Rept.* 49 **sePA,** T.J. Dohen, for Whist Broom, . . 10. **1855** New York (NY) *Office Alms House Annual Rept. for 1854* 152 **seNY,** 8 Wist Brooms. . . 1 25. **1885** in 1984 Maynard *Hist. & Geneal.* 1.116 **NY,** Julia gave him a whist broom and a necktie. **1887** in 2002 Poppenheim *S. Women Vassar* 157 **SC,** Can you send us wist-broom? **1897** *Woman's Med. Jrl.* 6.311 **NYC,** The electrode is made up . . of a bundle of very fine steel wires . . arranged in the form of a small whist broom. **1920** *Daily Northwestern* (Oshkosh WI) 20 Feb 15/7, [Advt:] We are going to . . give you a Whist Broom absolutely free. **c1938** in 1970 Hyatt *Hoodoo* 1.10 **seNC** [Black], And he went out there and he took a wist [Hyatt: whisk] broom and brushed papa off. **1939** *LANE* Map 155, 1 inf, **swCT,** Whist broom. **1948** *Walla Walla Union–Bulletin* (WA) 18 Apr [4]/7 (newspaperarchive.com), [Advt:] Close-outs. . . Whist broom. **1950** *WELS (Games in which you hide an object and look for it)* 1 Inf, **ceWI,** Pass the whist broom. **1965–70** *DARE* (Qu. F35, *A small broom that you hold in one hand, and use . . in places that are hard to get at*) 11 Infs, **scattered, but esp Midl,** W(h)ist broom. **1967** *Lowell Sun* (MA) 18 Sept 13/6, It is well to use a whist broom first. **2003** in 2008 *DARE* File—Internet **neOH,** I think a wist broom would be a smart investment. **2007** *Ibid* **OR,** You would be better off with a wist-broom.

3 *whis(s) broom, wiss (broom).* Cf Pronc Intro 3.I.22

  1912 Lippmann *Martha* 27 **NYC,** I heard the knockin' o' your whis'-broom. You was brushin' down the stairs. **1939** *LANE* Map 155, 4 infs, **MA, CT,** Whiss broom. **1966–69** *DARE* (Qu. F35, *A small broom that you hold in one hand, and use . . in places that are hard to get at*) 13 Infs, **scattered,** Whis broom; **AR**17, **DE**3, **NY**130, **OH**89, Wiss broom; **NY**233, Wiss.

4 *w(h)ish broom.*

  1917 in 1944 *ADD* **sWV,** Whiskbroom. . . whishbroom. **1950** *WELS (Different kinds of brooms used around the house)* 1 Inf, **ceWI,** Whish broom. **1965–70** *DARE* (Qu. F35, *A small broom that you hold in one hand, and use . . in places that are hard to get at*) 11 Infs, **scattered, but esp Gulf States,** W(h)ish broom; **WA**13, Whish brush. [11 Infs comm type 4 or 5, 10 Infs old, 6 Infs gs educ or less] **2006** *DARE* File—Internet **Philadelphia PA,** The living room will get a base coat of a cheery yellow and then another coat of a golden color over top, which I will run a new wish broom over top of to make lines through. **2008** *Ibid,* You may need to use a paintbrush, stippling brush, sponge, whish broom or other household item to achieve the texture you want.

B Sense.

Also *whiskbroom buckwheat:* A **wild buckwheat 2** (here: *Eriogonum nidularium*).

  1941 Jaeger *Wildflowers* 40 **Desert SW,** Whisk broom. *Eriogonum nidularium.* . . A pleasing little annual, 3–8 in. high, having parts covered with cobwebby hairs. **2007** *DARE* File—Internet **seNV,** Species Common Name—Whisk broom buckwheat[.] Species Scientific Name—Eriogonum nidularium.

whiskbroom parsley n [See quot 1915] Cf **parsley B1**

A **biscuit root 1.**

  1915 (1926) Armstrong–Thornber *Western Wild Flowers* 334, Whiskbroom Parsley—*Cogswellia platycarpa* [=*Lomatium simplex*]. . . An odd-looking plant, for the foliage looks like pieces of a whisk-broom stuck in the ground. **1923** Pellett *Amer. Honey Plants* 90, *Cogswellia* [=*Lomatium* spp]. . . The plants belong to the parsley family and are locally known as whisk-broom parsley, biscuit root, or cous. **1940** Gates *Flora KS* 227, Lomatium daucifolium [=*L. foeniculaceum* subsp *daucifolium*]. . . Whiskbroom Parsley. *Ibid,* Lomatium orientale. . . Whiskbroom Parsley. **1957** Barnes *Nat. Hist. Wasatch Summer* 91 **UT,** We notice . . whiskbroom parsley (*Lomatium bicolor*).

whisker n

In logging: =**jagger** n[1] **c.**

  1919 *DN* 5.59 **NW,** Whisker. . . Loose end of wire. . . A *whisker* on a line. **1958** McCulloch *Woods Words* 210 **Pacific NW,** Whiskers. . . Ends of cables sticking out at splices, or broken wires on a cable, same as jaggers. **1969** Sorden *Lumberjack Lingo* 140 **NEng, Gt Lakes,** Whiskers—Jaggers on worn wire chokers or cable.

whisker brush n

A **gilia** (here: *Leptosiphon* [formerly *Linanthus*] *ciliatus*).

  1961 Thomas *Flora Santa Cruz* 279 **cwCA,** L[*inanthus*] *ciliatus.* . . Whisker Brush, Bristly-leaved Linanthus. **2007** *DARE* File **CA,** Easy to overlook due to its small size, Whisker Brush (Linanthus Ciliatus) can be seen in the meadow hidden among the grasses.

whisker cactus n [See quot 1985]

=**senita.**

  1941 *Oakland Tribune* (CA) 18 July [44]/2 (newspaperarchive.com) **sAZ,** Miles filled with long-armed organ pipe cactus, the torch-like clumps of senita or whisker cactus. **1985** Dodge *Flowers SW Deserts* 51, Senita or "whisker cactus." The name refers to the long, gray, hairlike spines covering the upper ends of the senita stems.

whiskered owl n Also *whiskered screech owl*

A **screech owl 1** (here: *Megascops* [formerly *Otus*] *trichopsis*). Also called **mountain owl**

  1957 Pough *Audubon W. Bird Guide* 137, Whiskered Owl—*Otus trichopsis.* . . can be distinguished neither by its whiskers nor its coarse streaking from the local gray race of the screech owl. **1986** *Frederick Post* (MD) 24 Jan sec B 8/1 **AZ,** I've whistled at a whiskered owl in Ramsey Canyon. **2007** *DARE* File—Internet, Whiskered Screech-Owl. . . Other Common Names: Arizona Whiskered Owl; Spotted Screech-Owl; Whiskered Owl. [*Ibid,* Its facial "whiskers" give rise to the owl's name.]

whiskey bean n [From the narcotic properties of the seeds]
=frijolillo 1.
   1951 *PADS* 15.34 **TX,** *Sophora secundiflora* Lagasca.—Mountain laurel; frijolillo; whiskey bean; mescal bean.

whiskey cherry n Also *whisky cherry* [See quot 1898] Cf
rum cherry
=black cherry.
   1897 Sudworth *Arborescent Flora* 245 **MN,** *Prunus serotina.* . .
Whisky Cherry. **1898** U.S. Dept. Ag. Div. Botany *Bulletin* 20.26,
Whisky cherry. . . The fruit is rather agreeable, being but slightly bitter
and astringent in taste. In some localities it is much used to flavor liquors. **1950** Peattie *Nat. Hist. Trees* 385, Wild Black Cherry. . . Other
Names: Rum, or Whiskey, Cherry. **1973** *NW AR Times* (Fayetteville)
19 Sept 40/2, To make the Longrifle and Hawken replicas . . he uses
walnut and whiskey cherry ("For those hunters who like to chew on their
gun stocks," Sloan jokes). **1999** *Frederick Post* (MD) [9 Oct] USA
Weekend sec 25/1 (newspaperarchive.com), Handmade computers in 14
woods, including exotic Mexican *cocobolo,* teak, mahogany and whiskey cherry.

whiskey house n Also *corn whiskey house* **chiefly Sth, S
Midl**
   A low-class or illegal bar or saloon; a honky-tonk; see quots.
   1828 in 1936 *KS Hist. Qrly.* 5.239 **PA,** The last were the drunkards
who had stopped at a whiskey house 4 miles from ours. **1829** in 2007
(acc) Lexis–Nexis Legal Research *State Case Law: TN* (Internet), There
is not in the history of man, a more disgusting scene than the filthy whiskey house, filled with a horde of gamblers. **1927** *Charleston Gaz.*
(WV) 18 Mar 5/1, The troopers . . search[ed] a home . . which was purported to be a "wide open whiskey house." **1939** in 1972 *Amer. Slave*
8.2.188 **AR,** That man across the street runs a whiskey house where they
dance. **1948** *Delta Democrat-Times* (Greenville MS) 23 Aug 1/6, A
"good" citizen, has publicly complained about the whiskey house and
the gambling house. **1985** in 2007 (acc) Lexis–Nexis Legal Research
State Case Law: NC (Internet), The Defendant is an excessive user of alcoholic beverages, having frequented illegal "whiskey houses." **2003**
DARE File **nwMS** (as of 1960s–70s) [Black], *Whiskey house.* . . apparently originally referred to a rather crude illegal saloon when Mississippi
was a dry state—before about 1968. In 1970 I heard a Black minister in
Quitman County, Mississippi—born 1900, with a sixth-grade education—use *whiskey house* apparently meaning liquor stores that opened in
Mississippi after liquor became legal. **2003** *DARE* File—Internet **OK,**
D.C., who was born on January 28, 1935, was raised by his grandmother
in Rentiesville, Oklahoma. His granny ran a corn whiskey house; there
he saw many entertainers.

whiskey jack n Also *whiskey jay,* ~ *john, whisky jack* [See
quot 1902; cf *DCan*] **Nth** See Map
=Canada jay.
   [**1772** Royal Soc. London *Philos. Trans.* 62.386, These birds are called
Whiskijohn and *Whiskijack* at the Hudson's Bay.] **1842** Thompson *Hist.
VT* 1.73, This jay, which is called in some places the *Whiskey Jack.* . . is
found in the state of Maine, and in the north parts of New Hampshire,
Vermont and New York. **1902** *Jrl. Amer. Folkl.* 15.266, *Whiskey-Jack.*
A name in western Canada and parts of the United States for the blue
jay. . . The word is a corruption, by folk-etymology, as the form *Whiskey-John* also in use indicates, from *wisketjân,* the Cree name of the jay.

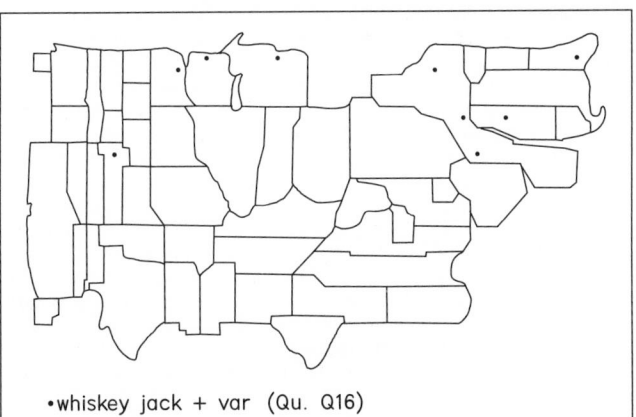

•whiskey jack + var (Qu. Q16)

1941 Writers' Program *Guide WY* 35, Unpopular for his insolence and
thievery, the Canada jay, known also as Whiskey Jack, moose bird, meat
hawk, and grease bird, is a native of the evergreen forests. **1945** Hamlin
9 Mile Bridge 223 **nME,** We spread bread crumbs for the gorbies—
"Whisky Jack," "Woodsman's Ghost" or "Canada Jay"—a dirty-gray,
noisy bird that hangs around camps in the woods. **1958** McCulloch
Woods Words 210 **Pacific NW,** *Whiskey jack*—A jay bird which follows
loggers around in the woods to get any scraps thrown away at lunch
time. **1965–70** *DARE* (Qu. Q16, . . *Kinds of jays*) Infs **CO**7, **ME**8,
NY207, 219, 233, Whiskey jack; **WI**58, Whiskey jack; **MI**10, I believe I've also heard
the Canada jay called a whiskey jack; **MN**14, Canada jay or whiskey
jack—moose bird or camp robber; **CT**13, Whiskey jay. **1966** *DARE*
Tape **MI**36, The Canadian jay or Whiskey jack. . . They're really nice
pets. **1975** Gould *ME Lingo* 113, The handsome Canada jay of Audubon, also called moosebird and whiskeyjack.

whiskey-palian n Also *whis-capalian, whisky-palian* [Joc
varr of *Episcopalian*] **chiefly Sth, S Midl** See Map
   1868 *Decatur Republican* (IL) 6 Aug 4/6, The religious opinions of
Seymour and Blair are being canvassed. We know nothing about Seymour, but Blair is a whiskypalian. **1944** Albemarle Co. Hist. Soc. *Papers* 4.30 **VA** (as of 1880s), Rev. Robb White's somewhat scandalous
Whiskey-palians . . sometimes played six-handed euchre and in extreme
instances countenanced "round dancing." **1965–70** *DARE* (Qu. CC4, . .
Nicknames . . for various religions or religious groups) 13 Infs, **Sth, S
Midl,** Whiskey-palians; **FL**5, Whis-capalians. **1993** *DARE* File **NC,**
Episcopalians—down here they're sometimes called "Whiskeypalians"
by the run of teetotaling Baptists. *Ibid,* One of the most remarkable
sentences was uttered in a church meeting, by a visiting Baptist, of
course, *not* by one of us Whiskeypalians. **2002** *DARE* File—Internet
TX, I'm a white male, age 39. I was churched mostly as an Episcopalian
("Whiskey-palian" to my foot-washin' Primitive Baptist great Granny).
2006 *Ibid* **MS,** I'm Catholic, and my husband's a cradle "Whiskey-palian", so we're biased. . . but I'll tell you what, we're friends with
some true-blue Baptists, and they love a good high-ball regularly themselves!

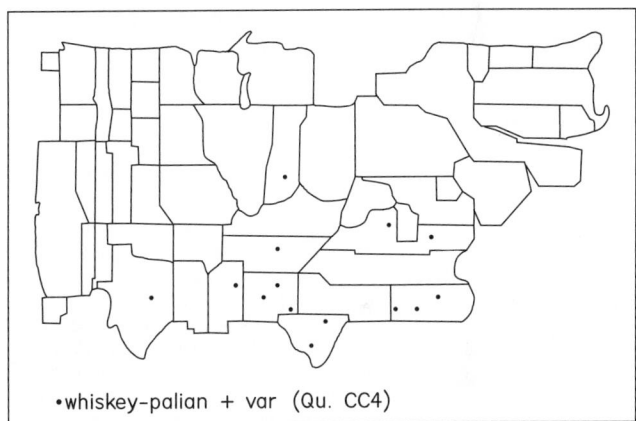

•whiskey-palian + var (Qu. CC4)

whiskey plant n Also *whiskey root* *obs*
=peyote.
   1859 (1968) Bartlett *Americanisms* 509, *Whiskey-root.* A plant of the
Cactus species possessing intoxicating properties . . "It is what the Indians call Pie-o-ke. . . The Indians eat it for its exhilarating effect on the
system, it producing precisely the same as alcoholic drinks." **1872**
Schele de Vere *Americanisms* 399, [Quotation from an unidentified
source:] Our men had found some *Whiskey Plants,* and Jack, having
long been with the Indians, taught them at once how to use the delightful
treasure: in a few hours they were not only merry, but wild as devils, and
we had to guard the corral ourselves all night, for they were utterly unconscious of what they were doing.

whiskey-soak See **soak** n[1]

whiskey stew See **stew**

whiskey tree n
   1 **=hard maple.** [See quot 1991]
   1958 *Fresno Bee* (CA) 18 Nov sec B 7/6, [Advt for Jack Daniel's
whiskey:] Only a few whiskey makers with long memories might know
what we mean by a "Tennessee Whiskey Tree." It's a *hard maple* growing on *high* ground. And when its charcoal is employed in an old-fash-

ioned Tennessee way, it has a most unusual virtue. It can smooth out a whiskey like nothing else in all the world. **1991** Still *Wolfpen Notebooks* 86 **sAppalachians,** We call these hard maples either 'whiskey trees' or 'sugar trees,' depending on what you need them for. . . Whiskey trees to make charcoal to use at the 'still. Charcoal don't make all that smoke for the law to spot you at your business.

2 as *whisky tree:* See quot. *joc*

1939 FWP *Guide NC* 518, Right on State 24, paralleling the north shore of Bogue Sound and traversing forests of maritime pine and scrub oaks, are occasional fields of corn locally called "whisky trees."

whisky cherry See **whiskey cherry**

whisky jack See **whiskey jack**

whisky-palian See **whiskey-palian**

whisky stew See **stew**

whisky tree See **whiskey tree 2**

whisp broom See **whisk broom A1**

whispering bells n [See quot 1897]
A plant of the Desert Southwest (*Emmenanthe penduliflora*). Also called **yellow bells 5**

1897 Parsons *Wild Flowers CA* 130, Whispering Bells. . . In midspring . . our attention is often attracted by a certain delicate, rustling sound, which we find emanates from the little papery bells of the dried blossoms of the *Emmenanthe,* which retain the semblance of their first freshness for many weeks. **1922** *Independent* 108.510 **CA,** There the chapel stands to this day, with its exquisite campanile, its graveyard where bushes of whispering bells keep the little Indian children happy in their long sleep. **1947** *Atlantic Mth.* 180.110 **sCA,** You mean my Whispering Bells are dead? **2007** (acc) U.S. Dept. Ag. *Plants Database* (Internet), *Emmenanthe penduliflora* . . whisperingbells.

whispering owl n
A **screech owl 1** (here: *Otus asio*).

1950 *WELS,* 1 Inf, **ceWI,** Pigeon owl—shivering, whispering owl.

whiss broom See **whisk broom A3**

whist n Cf **bid whist**
Std sense, var forms.

1 *whisk.* [This is actually the earlier name of the game: *OED2 whisk* sb.² 1621 →; "*Obs.* or *dial.*"] *now chiefly among Black speakers*

1894 in 2008 *DARE* File—Internet **VA,** I have been out to several Whisk parties lately. Can you plat [sic] Whisk? **1913** (1919) Foote *Blister Jones* 284 **OH,** He's goin' to take her out High Street to a whisk party at Mrs. Rucker's. **1966–70** *DARE* (Qu. DD35, . . *Card games*) Infs **NY**55, **TX**26, Whisk; (Qu. FF2, . . *Kinds of parties*) Inf **MA**128, Whisk party or card party. [All Infs Black] **2003** Ramsey *Race Music* 262 **Chicago IL** [Black], The big pot on the stove . . the bid whisk, and hearty laughter all remind me why I love being a Ramsey from the Windy City. **2004** *DARE* File—Internet **WI,** While parents play chess or a game of whisk at the pub tables, children enjoy watching or joining in a puppet show. **2007** in 2008 *Ibid* **NYC,** We met playing bid whisk together up at a club on Columbus Avenue in New York City, a disco, but they had bid whisk tables along a back wall and it was a prominently black club and blacks love bid whisk, a kind of a wild form of pinochle. **2008** *Ibid* **MI** [Black], I really enjoy good music, cards (bid whisk, tunk, spades and even a little poker).

2 *whiz. chiefly among Black speakers*

1970 *DARE* (Qu. DD35, . . *Card games*) Infs **IL**138, **OK**55, Whiz. [Both Infs Black] **1973** Andrews–Owens *Black Lang.* 77, Bid Whiz—A Black man's card game. Played mostly in college—on their way out. **2002** in 2008 *DARE* File—Internet **Chicago IL** [Black], I spent many a Friday night with the babysitter when I was a kid and I *know* my parents weren't playing Bid Whiz (that's the black version of Bridge). **2005** *Los Angeles Wave* (CA) 10 Aug (Internet) [Black], Forty years ago today . . Jacquette was hanging out with the other "young bloods" of the block playing Bid Whiz and drinking beer. **2007** in 2008 *DARE* File—Internet **cnKY,** Newburg Festival will feature a bid whiz tournament. **2008** *Ibid,* For all you Bid Whist (Whiz as we typically call it) pros, Get ready for the first annual Bid Whist tournament.

3 *whitz.*

1991 *Durham Morning Herald* (NC) 14 July np (as of 1960s–70s) [Black], Almost anything you might want could be had at Minnie's [=a liquor house], from a chitterling sandwich to a soul-rousing whitz game. **2008** *DARE* File—Internet **NYC** [Black], Matching Interests: cards, parties, video games, *spades, bid whitz, dominoes.*

whist broom See **whisk broom A2**

‡**whistle-bicky** n
=**woodcock 1.**

1968 *DARE* (Qu. Q7, *Names and nicknames for . . game birds*) Inf **NY**97, Woodcock or timberdoodle or whistle-bicky.

whistle britches n Also *whistle trousers* [From the noise the fabric makes when the legs brush together]
Corduroy pants; also used as a nickname for one who wears such pants, or broadly as a teasing or derog nickname, esp for a self-important person; see quots.

[**1883** in 1895 Lillie *Madame Blavatsky* 102, Tell Damodar please, the "Holy" whistle breeches, and St. Poultice that they do not perfume enough with incense the *inner* shrine. [*DARE* Ed: Madame Blavatsky lived in the US from 1873–1879.]] [**1900** *Eve. Herald* (Syracuse NY) 2 Nov 14/1, The games in the Harvard scrub football series yesterday resulted as follows: Pigskins, 0; Inanes, 2; Walloweers, 0; Whistle Breeches, 0. What names?] **1904** *McKean Democrat* (Smethport PA) 21 Jan 1/4, "Don't you think you're smart, Whistle Breeches?" he whispered. "Whist—whist," said the breeches in reply, as Willie moved. . . Who'd want whistle breeches? **1910** *Galveston Daily News* (TX) 20 Feb mag sec 4/6, *"Whistle Britches".* . . I have a pair of corduroys,/ That neither sing nor talk,/ But they are cheerful breeches, though—/ They whistle as I walk. . . They call me "Whistle Breeches" now,/ A name I don't admire. **1952** Brown *NC Folkl.* 1.607, *Whistle-breeches.* . . A small boy who has put on his first trousers and is quite proud of them.—Alamance county. **1959** *VT Hist.* 27.167, *Whistle breeches.* . . Corduroy breeches. Rare. **1962** Faulkner *Reivers* 163 **MS,** "Whistle-britches," Ned said. "That money-mouthed runt boy that was with us last night." **1966** *DARE* (Qu. NN12a, *Things that people say to put a child off when he asks too many questions: "What's that for?"*) Inf **NC**45, Cat's fur to make whistle britches. **1984** *MJLF* 10.159 **cnWI,** *Whistle trousers.* Corduroy knickers. Made a noise as the wearer walked. **2000** in 2008 *DARE* File—Internet **ceFL,** I'll tell you all the real reason I hated cords. At the risk of public ridicule . . whenever I wore them my pop would call me, "Willie Whistle Britches." **2003** *DARE* File—Internet **TX,** I recall hearing the term "whistle britches" in Texas, usually referring to a lout or self-important, egotistical liar. **2008** *Ibid* **cnMS,** Whistle-Britches was probably the most frequently used nickname in Dad's arsenal. You see, it was his name for *every boy* who ever showed any interest in dating any one of Dad's daughters.

whistle duck n [From the whistling sound of its wings]
A **goldeneye 1** (here: *Bucephala clangula*).

1857 NJ Geol. Surv. *Geol. Cape May* 145 **seNJ,** Anas clangula, *Golden-eye,* or *Whistle Duck.* **1888** Trumbull *Names of Birds* 78 **seNJ,** At Cape May [the golden-eye is called] *whistle duck.*

whistle pig n

1 also *whistle hog, whistling pig:* A **marmot a,** esp the **woodchuck 1. chiefly Appalachians** See Map Cf **whistling marmot**

1901 U.S. Dept. Ag. Bur. Biol. Surv. *N. Amer. Fauna* 21.63 **AK,** *Arctomys caligatus.* . . Hoary Marmot. Abundant in the mountains about Turnagain Arm they are known to the miners as 'whistling pigs.' **1904** (1913) Johnson *Highways South* 141 **eTN,** The doctor amplified the list of game by adding "turkle doves, 'possums, and whistlepigs." The whistlepigs, or woodchucks as we would call them in the North, get very fat in the autumn feeding on chestnuts. **1909** *Indiana Progress* (PA) 22 Sept 5/3, Quite a number of men who are not employed are putting in their time catching "whistle pigs." **1917** *DN* 4.419 **wNC,** *Whistlepig.* . . Groundhog. **1927** *AmSp* 2.366 **cwWV,** *Whistle-pig* . . groundhog. "The whistle-pigs have ruined the corn on the hill." **1942** Warnick *Garrett Co. MD* 16 **nwMD** (as of 1900–18), *Whistle-pig* . . woodchuck. **1944** *PADS* 2.52 **wNC,** *Whistle-pig.* . . A groundhog. . . Common. **1961** Douglas *My Wilderness* 22 **CO,** These animals—locally known as woodchucks, rock chucks, and whistle-pigs—are fat, saucy, and inquisitive. **1965–70** *DARE* (Qu. P31, . . *Names or nicknames . . for the groundhog*) 40 Infs, **chiefly Appalachians,** Whistle pig; **CO**47, **KY**11, **PA**168, **WA**12, Whistling pig; **IL**119, **OH**82, Whistle pig—same as woodchuck; [**NY**71, Whistling rufus—old-fashioned;] (Qu. P29, . . *'Gophers' . . other name . . or what other animal are they most like*) Inf **NC**44, Whistle hog—groundhog; **GA**72, Whistle pig—same as groundhog. **1967** *DARE* FW Addit **CO**31, *Whistle pig*—a groundhog. **1982** Slone *How We Talked* 45 **eKY** (as of c1950), *"Groundhog"* (also called a "whistle pig")—woodchuck. **1983** Glimm *Flatlanders* 166 **cnPA**, All through the summer months we lived on whistle pigs. That's what we called woodchucks. **2002** *DARE* File **nAL**, "Whistle pig"—Another name for a ground hog. Tennessee Valley.

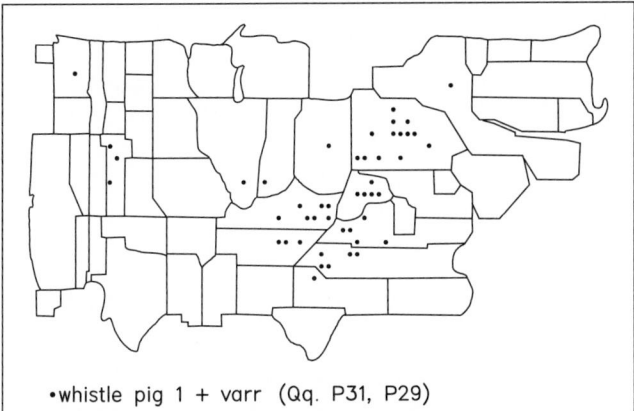

•whistle pig 1 + varr (Qq. P31, P29)

2 =ground squirrel n b. chiefly ID

2004 *Jrl. Star* (Peoria IL) 27 Feb sec C 5 (Internet), The Franklin's ground squirrel is on its way to being a state threatened species. . . That may lead to additional research about the "whistle pig," a nickname referring to the squirrel's distinct trilling call. **2005** *Airman* Feb 47 **ID**, [Caption:] *The high desert is.* . . home to a cannibalistic ground squirrel the locals call a "whistle pig." **2008** *DARE* File—Internet **ID**, Never heard that term [=potgut] before but, Sounds like the same critter called "whistle pigs" here in Idaho, IE Townsends ground squirrel. *Ibid* **ID**, I went over to Kuna, which is in Idaho. . . The whistle pigs are out in force. I did not know what a whistle pig was either until we moved up here. They look like miniature prairie dogs that are not much bigger than a roll of quarters but are actually a ground squirrel and they give an alarm whistle, hence the name. . . It's a funny, very faint whistle they have and as you walk along you constantly hear this far off sounding whistle. *Ibid* **ID**, Its a purpose-built whistle pig gun. (Whistle pig = Columbian ground squirrel. Think of a 1/4 scale prairie dog.) *Ibid* **ID**, I live out here in Idaho, and we have these damn little things called "whistle pigs". I'm not sure what they are exactly, but they look just like prairie dogs, but about a quarter of the size. . . They live in there little wholes and have towns just like prairie dogs.

3 =prairie dog. chiefly ID

2004 in **2008** *DARE* File—Internet **ID**, We call them [=prairie dogs] rock chucks, picket pens, whistle pigs. **2007** *DARE* File **ID**, [Caption:] *Whistle pig.* . . [Response:] Ummmm. . . that is a prarie [sic] dog, a whistle pig is a ground hog or wood chuck. **2008** *Ibid* **ID**, [He] told us a story of living in Idaho and passing the time by sitting on his back porch, cocktail and shotgun in hand, and shooting at the prairie dogs that were sticking their heads out of their holes, whistling at one another. Since prairie dogs are also known as whistle pigs, and we thought this was a funny story, we named the band Whistle Pigs.

whistle punk n Also *punk* chiefly Pacific NW

In logging: a worker, formerly often a boy, who signals the operation of log-hauling machinery by controlling the whistle of the *donkey engine* (at **donkey 1**).

1909 *Outlook* 92.613 **OR**, Their ages ran from that of the nine-year-old "whistle punk," who gave the signals for log-hauling, up to forty-five and fifty. **1914** *Overland Mth.* (2d ser) 63.440 **CA**, The "donkey tender," who controls the power, acts upon signals given by the "whistle-punk," who is no other than some youngster receiving a salary of perhaps $35 per month. **1918** *Oxnard Daily Courier* (CA) 17 Oct [4]/3 (newspaperarchive.com) **WA**, First Woman Logger Holds Down "Whistle Punk" Job. **1920** *DN* 5.84 **NW**, *Whistle punk.* Boy who blows the whistle on a donkey engine. **1938** FWP *Guide MN* 169 **csMN**, Most of the jobs offered were seasonal, and back again came "whistlepunks," "shovel stiffs," and harvest hands by the hundreds. **1938** (1939) Holbrook *Holy Mackinaw* 263, *Punk.* Any young man, but specifically a *whistle punk.* **1940** Writers' Program *Oregon* 369, Out in the timber a chokerman places a heavy wire slip-loop, or choker, around a log and a rigging-slinger attaches this loop to the main cable, when the hooker yells "Hi", then the whistle-punk presses an electric grip and the donkey

1,500 feet away whistles a short, sharp blast. **1956** *AmSp* 31.151 **nwCA** [Logger lingo], *Punk.* . . A signalman for a logging crew. **1966** *DARE* Tape **MT**4, The engineer . . gave orders to . . what they called a whistle punk. They blew whistles as a signal for the engineer to . . stop the drag of logs or to speed up. **1982** *Smithsonian Letters* **swWA** (as of c1900), The crew in the woods the Hooktender (who was the head of the crew) and the choker setters (who put the cable around the logs) and the whistle punk who signaled the donkey puncher (operator) when to go and when to stop by means of a wire which reached from the logging area to the whistle on the donkey.

whistler n

1 A marmot a, usu *Marmota caligata.* Cf **whistling marmot**

[**1703** Lahontan *New Voyages* (transl. Anon.) 1.62, I was likewise entertain'd upon this occasion, with the killing of certain little Beasts, call'd *Siffleurs,* or Whistlers, with allusion to their wonted way of whistling or whizzing at the Mouth of their Holes in fair Weather.] [**1820** Harmon *Jrl. Voyages N. Amer* 427, There is a small animal, found only on the Rocky Mountain, denominated, by the Natives, Quis-qui-su, or whistlers, from the noise which they frequently make, and always when surprised, strongly resembling the noise made by a person in whistling.] **1880** Murphy *Sporting Advent.* 389 **NW**, After toiling all day, we came back to camp with only one poor marmot, known as the "whistler," from the quaint noises it makes. **1890** *Century Dict.* 3636, *Marmot.* . . North America has at least three species [including] . . the large hoary marmot or whistler of northwestern America, *A[rctomys] pruinosus* [=*Marmota caligata*]. **1939** FWP *Guide AK* 286, Hoary marmots are often called whistlers from their habit of announcing any enemy's presence with a loud "traffic cop" whistle. **1945** Atwood *Rocky Mts.* 293, Among the smaller mammals found are the . . pike, and hoary marmot, or "whistler." **1968** *DARE* (Qu. P31, . . *Names or nicknames* . . *for the groundhog*) Inf **AK**1, Hoary marmot—whistler.

2 Transf: =mountain beaver.

1930 *CA Fish & Game* 16.65, The mountain beaver, a rodent inhabiting the Pacific Northwest. . . also variously termed sewellel, boomer, or whistler, did not materially affect man's interests. **1947** Cahalane *Mammals* 550, The mountain beaver is not a beaver. . . Neither does it whistle, although "whistler" is what some people call it.

3 also *whistler duck*: =goldeneye 1. [See quot 1844] **scattered, but esp Atlantic** See Map Cf **pied whistler**

1709 (1967) Lawson *New Voyage* 153 **NC, SC**, These are called Whistlers, from the whistling Noise they make, as they fly. **1792** Belknap *Hist. NH* 3.168, Whistler, *Anas clangula?* **1844** Giraud *Birds Long Is.* 334, Golden-eye. . . This species is better known to our gunners by the name of "Whistler." **1877** *Hagerstown Mail* (MD) 22 June 1/8, My eyes chanced to fall on a whistler duck. **1928** Beston *Outermost House* 116 **Cape Cod MA**, The sound of a pair of "whistler" ducks on the wing is a lovely, mysterious sound. . . made with wings, a clear, sibilant note which increases as the birds draw near, and dies away in the distance like a faint and whistling sigh. **1965–70** *DARE* (Qu. Q5, . . *Kinds of wild ducks*) 10 Infs, 8 **Atlantic**, Whistler; **MI**53, Whistler or whistlewing—that is, the "goldeneye"; **WY**1, Golden-eyed whistler; (Qu. Q7, *Names and nicknames for . . game birds*) Inf **NY**52, Whistler; (Qu. Q10, . . *Water birds and marsh birds*) Inf **MA**98, Whistler. **2001** MD Ornith. Soc. *MD Yellowthroat* Mar–Apr 6 (Internet) **eVA, eMD**, Ducks was commoner then but there's still lots of . . Clubheads (also called Whifflers or Whistlers). **2006** *Post-Std.* (Syracuse NY) 27 Apr 7/3,

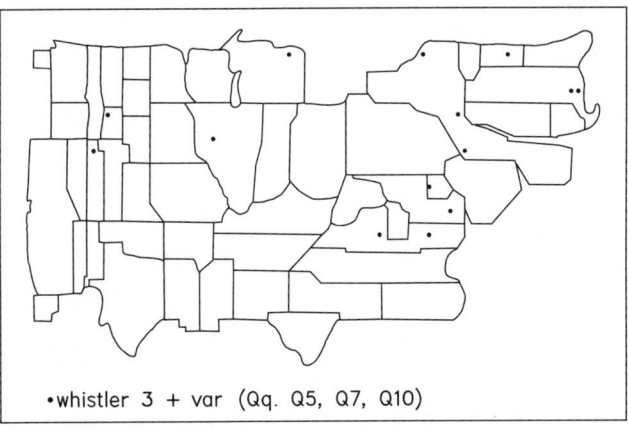

•whistler 3 + var (Qq. Q5, Q7, Q10)

[Auction advt:] Coll. of approx. 40 decoys . . hen whistler, . . drake whistler, plus much more.

4 Either the **hooded merganser** or **red-breasted merganser.**

1844 DeKay *Zool. NY* 2.319, The Red-breasted Sheldrake. . . This species is also called the *Sawbill, Whistler,* and *Pied Sheldrake* in this state. *Ibid* 320, The Hooded Sheldrake. . . The *Hairy-head,* or *Whistler,* or *Water Pheasant,* as this species is called in this state . . is more confined to the interior. **1923** U.S. Dept. Ag. *Misc. Circular* 13.6 **NY,** Red-breasted Merganser. . . whistler. *Ibid* 7 **NY, TN,** Hooded Merganser. . . whistler.

5 =**woodcock 1.** [See quot 1955]

1880 *Forest & Stream* 14.132 **NY,** If summer shooting is not prohibited we will soon find woodcock a "scarce commodity." Any true sportsman would rather stop one rapid flying whistler in the fall than half a dozen in July. **1888** Trumbull *Names of Birds* 154 **wMA, CT,** Some old gunners believe that these "whistlers" or "little whistlers," as they are called in western Massachusetts and portions of Connecticut, are late birds from the far North. **1955** MA Audubon Soc. *Bulletin* 39.446 **MA, CT,** American Woodcock. . . Whistler. . . Some of the courtship sounds suggest whistling.

6 =**European widgeon.**

1891 *Century Dict.* 6908, *Whistler.* . . The widgeon, *Mareca penelope* [=*Anas p.*] **1917** (1923) *Birds Amer.* 1.119, European Widgeon. . . Other Names.—Widgeon; Whistler; Whewer, Whew, Whim. [**1923** U.S. Dept. Ag. *Misc. Circular* 13.11, European Widgeon. . . Some of the British names for the species are . . whew duck, whewer, whim, whistler [etc.].]

7 also *whistler swan:* =**whistling swan.**

1903 Dawson *Birds OH* 2.573, The names, "Whistler" and "Trumpeter" are not meant to express a difference in kind in the notes of the two birds [=the whistling swan and the trumpeter swan], so much as a difference in volume. **1936** Roberts *MN Birds* 1.201, Whistlers still pass to and fro through the state in considerable numbers and occasionally alight to rest and feed. **1966** DARE (Qu. Q6, . . *Kinds of wild geese*) Inf **WA**15, Whistler swan or wild swan—Spokane.

8 =**baldpate 1.**

1923 U.S. Dept. Ag. *Misc. Circular* 13.12, Baldpate. . . whistler (Fla.); whistling-dick; whistling duck (La.) **1932** Howell *FL Bird Life* 136, Baldpate. . . Other Names: American Widgeon; . . Whistler [etc.]. [*Ibid,* Baldpates fly in small flocks of irregular formation, usually at no great height, often uttering a sweet, mellow whistle as they go.]

9 =**white-throated sparrow.**

1956 MA Audubon Soc. *Bulletin* 40.255 **ME,** White-throated Sparrow. . . Whistler.

10 =**old-squaw.**

1970 DARE (Qu. Q5, . . *Kinds of wild ducks*) Inf **VA**79, Whistler—wings whistle when bird flies (old squaw).

whistler duck See **whistler 3**

whistler swan See **whistler 7**

whistle sneak n

A **ground squirrel** n b (here: *Spermophilus tridecemlineatus*).

1961 Jackson *Mammals WI* 130, Striped Ground Squirrel. . . In Wisconsin commonly called gopher or striped gopher. Other names include . . streaked gopher, and whistle sneak.

whistle trousers See **whistle britches**

whistle willow n Cf **whistlewood**

Any of var **willows 1;** see quots.

1890 *Daily Independent* (Monroe WI) [16 May 2]/5 (newspaperarchive.com), Then the lads sought the meadow where the whistle willows grew,/ And over the fields you could hear the music flow / From the boys' willow whistles—forty years ago. **1894** *Herald & Torch-Light* (Hagerstown MD) 6 Sept [7]/3 (newspaperarchive.com), Over these two fishermen falls the shade of the "whistle" willows. **1935** Davis *Honey* 1 **OR,** Around the springs were thickets of whistle-willow and wild crabapple.

whistlewing n

1 also *whistlewing duck, whistlewings:* =**goldeneye 1.**

[**1852** Traill *Can. Crusoes* 234, The silence of the forest was unbroken save by . . the whirring sound of the large white and grey duck (called by the frequenters of these lonely waters the whistle-wing).] **1855** in 1860 *Prairie Farmer* 5.346, I helped to prepare a "whistle-wing" duck that O. killed, for supper. **1857** U.S. War Dept. *Rept. Explor. Railroad*

(Beckwith's Exped.) 10.16, *Bucephala americana.* . . Golden Eye; Whistle Wing. **1877** *Forest & Stream* 8.21 **DC,** Canvas backs, red necks, shufflers, mallard, teal, whistle wings and butter balls are among the varieties killed by the members. **1902** *Outing* 39.456 **Pacific NW,** With the mallards will most likely come . . the American golden-eye, called in that section whistle-wing. **1912** *Sheboygan Press* (WI) [23 Jan 2]/3 (newspaperarchive.com), The golden eye, or whistle wing, frequents the cold waters of Lake Michigan all through the winter. **1962** *Lancaster Eagle–Gaz.* (OH) 10 Mar 4/2, With whistling wings, it flew toward the other ducks and settled in their midst. That's why duck hunters have named this duck [=the goldeneye] the whistler or whistle-wings. **1967** DARE (Qu. Q5, . . *Kinds of wild ducks*) Inf **MI**53, Whistlewing—that is, the "goldeneye." **2004** in 2008 DARE File—Internet **ceWI,** Our good friend of past years . . always called them "whistle-wings," clearly reflected in its scientific name of clangula.

2 =**ring-necked duck.**

1955 *Oriole* 20.1.4 **GA,** Ring-necked Duck. . . Whistle-wing (from the winnowing sound made by the wings in flight).

whistlewing duck, whistlewings See **whistlewing 1**

whistlewood n [Scots, nIr dial]

1 A tree or section of a tree branch suitable for making whistles because of its easily removable bark; any of var spec trees of this sort.

1840 (1857) Abbott *Jonas Judge* 34 **NEng,** Oliver had some whistle wood. . . Some pieces of willow that he was going to make whistles of. **1878** (1977) Stowe *Poganuc People* 170 **NEng,** There was the elderbush, growing whistle-wood by the yard; and then the gigantic whistles that could be manufactured from willow, and poplar, and black alder were mysteries distressing to contemplate. **1891** [see **2** below]. **1892** Johnson *End Rainbow* 14 **wNY,** Whistle-wood was any kind of wood the bark of which could be taken off whole, so as to make a whistle. Fred found a young chestnut-tree, declared that was the very best kind of whistle-wood . ., and soon produced three whistles. **1918** *Hunter-Trader-Trapper* May 72, Look very carefully for bush-like trees with green bark. Note: These trees are known as whistle-wood or willow and are best for flute making. If there are no whistle-wood trees about, maple answers well for the purpose.

2 Esp: =**striped maple.**

1847 Wood *Class-Book* 213, *A[cer] Pennsylvanicum.* . . The smaller branches are straight and smooth, easily separated from the bark in spring, and are often manufactured by the boys into certain wind instruments. Hence it is called whistle-wood. **1868** *New Engl. Farmer* 2.54 **neMA,** He then applies, while warm, a wash made by boiling one hour, wormwood and the bark of whistlewood in urine. **1891** *Century Dict.* 6908, *Whistle-wood.* . . The striped maple, *Acer Pennsylvanicum,* thus named because used by boys to make whistles, the bark easily separating from a section of the stem in spring. The name is also given to the basswood, *Tilia Americana,* having the same property. **1965** Needham-Mussey *Country Things* 83 **VT,** Striped maple is what the boys call whistlewood—a little tree never much beyond the size of a shrub. It has very smooth bright green bark with white stripes. It's not used for anything except whistles. **1968–69** DARE (Qu. T14, . . *Kinds of maples*) Inf **PA**223, Striped or moose maple; also called whistlewood; [(Qu. T16, . . *Kinds of trees* . . *'special'*) Inf **PA**93, Whistlewood—this used to be used for making kids' whistles].

whistling coot n [See quot 1955]

The American **scoter** (*Melanitta nigra*).

1888 Trumbull *Names of Birds* 107 **CT,** At Stony Creek, Conn., whistling-coot [is a name for the American scoter]. **1895** Nye *Scientific Shooting* 20 **MA,** They flew at such a great height that we could not determine for a surety whether they were whistling coots or white-wings. **1898** Elliot *Wild Fowl* 208, This Duck has many names, the best known being, Black Coot, Whistling Coot, Butter-billed, and Hollow-billed Coot. **1955** MA Audubon Soc. *Bulletin* 39.377, American Scoter. . . Whistling Coot. . . From the sound made by the wings in flight; the bird also has a whistling note.

whistling dick n

=**baldpate 1.**

1918 LA Dept. of Conserv. *Bulletin* 5.22, Baldpate. . . Zin zin; Whistling duck; American widgeon; Whistling Dick.

whistling diver n [See quot 1955]

=**surf scoter.**

1813 Spafford *Gaz. State NY* 251 **NYC,** This market is abundantly supplied with almost every thing in its season, which the land and water affords. . . [including] whistling-diver. **1955** MA Audubon Soc. *Bulletin* 39.377 **RI,** Surf Scoter. . . Whistling Diver. . . A note, and the sound made by the wings in flight, both may be described as whistling.

whistling duck n

1 The American **scoter** *(Melanitta nigra).* Cf *DCan*

   [**1831** Richardson *Fauna Boreali-Amer.* 2.450, Oidemia Americana. *American Scoter*. . . Whistling duck. Hudson's Bay Residents.] **1876** *Forest & Stream* 6.99 **MA,** Salem harbor is open, and whistling ducks and other wild fowl are abundant. [*DARE* Ed: This quot may refer instead to other senses below.] **1889** *Century Dict.* 1789, *Whistling duck* or *coot,* the American black scoter.

2 =**goldeneye 1.**

   1709 (1967) Lawson *New Voyage* 152 **NC,** *Whistling duck.* Towards the Mountains in the hilly Country on the West-Branch of *Cape-Fair* Inlet, we saw great Flocks of pretty pied Ducks, that whistled as they flew, or as they fed. **1880** *Harper's New Mth. Mag.* 61.674, The golden-eyed or whistling duck. **1942** *Daily Courier* (Connellsville PA) 28 Feb 7/5, The golden-eye or "Whistling" duck usually lays from about eight to 12 eggs.

3 =**baldpate 1.**

   1897 *Auk* 14.285 **LA,** Anas americana. Baldpate.—Commonly known as *Zan-zan,* from the noise it makes; also as Widgeon and Whistling duck. **1918** [see **whistling dick**].

whistling field plover n   [See quots]

=**black-bellied plover.**

   1813 (1824) Wilson *Amer. Ornith.* 7.42, Black-Bellied Plover. . . is known in some parts of the country by the name of the large Whistling Field Plover. **1842** Audubon *Birds Amer.* 5.200 **PA,** This species is known in Pennsylvania by the name of Whistling Field Plover, suggested by the loud and modulated cries which it emits during the love-season. **1854** *Graham's Mag.* 44.538, The black-bellied plover . . is the least strictly littoral of the tribe, frequenting inland marshes, and even upland meadows, pastures and ploughed fields . . whence she has her name, inland, of "large whistling field plover."

whistling hare n   Cf **piping hare**

=**pika.**

   1901 *Youth's Companion* 31 Oct 573 **NV,** She has thus secured excellent photographs, at close range, of pine-hens, sage-grouse, whistling hares and other mountain birds and animals. **1937** *Albuquerque Jrl.* (NM) 28 Mar [12]/6 (newspaperarchive.com), There is the Whistling hare of Colorado. **2007** *DARE* File—Internet, The pika. . . sometimes is known as "whistling hare" because when it dives into its burrow, it emits a high-pitched warning cry.

whistling marmot n   Cf **whistle pig 1, whistler 1**

A **marmot a** (here usu: *Marmota caligata*).

   [**1868** Sproat *Scenes* 233 **Vancouver Is. Canada,** I may record that I have seen a whistling marmot, and only one, on the West Coast.] **1874** Essex Inst. *Bulletin* 6.57 **CO,** *Arctomys flaviventer*. . . Their sharp call, in character somewhat between a clear whistle and a short, sharp bark, well entitle them to the name of "whistling marmot." **1900** *Mazama* 2.224 **OR,** Even at meal-time the horn that sounds for the gathering of the clans . . always finds a score of . . exultant wanderers . . poised on a dizzy ledge of rocks studying the strange ways of the whistling marmot. **1908** Smithsonian Inst. *Misc. Coll.* 50.89 **WA,** *Marmota caligata*. . . It is commonly called "whistling marmot," or simply "whistler," in distinction to "marmot," a term popularly applied to the mountain beavers, *Aplodontia.* **1941** Writers' Program *Guide WY* 34, The whistling marmot is the largest and most handsome of American marmots. Similar in appearance to the woodchuck, the marmot is about twice as heavy. **2006** in 2008 *DARE* File—Internet **WA,** All the other whistling marmots steered well clear of us once the "whistle-alarm" went out that people were approaching, but this one marmot hung around to check us out.

whistling pig See **whistle pig 1**

whistling plover n   [*OED2* 1668 → (for the European golden plover)]

Any of three closely related birds: the **black-bellied plover,** the **golden plover,** or the **upland plover 1.**

   1682 Wilson *Acct. of Carolina* 12 **NC, SC, GA, nFL,** On the grassy plaines the whistling *Plover* and *Cranes* and divers sorts of Birds unknowne in *England.* **1709** (1967) Lawson *New Voyage* 145 **NC, SC,** The gray or whistling Plover, are very scarce amongst us. . . They differ

very little from those in *Europe,* as far as I could discern. **a1782** (1788) Jefferson *Notes VA* 197, Besides these [birds], we have . . Whistling plover. **1844** DeKay *Zool. NY* 2.215, The large *Whistling Plover,* or *Bull* and *Beetle-head Plover* as it is called in its autumnal dress, appears with us from the south in May. **1857** Lewis *Amer. Sportsman* 248, They [= black-bellied plovers] then retire to the high upland districts to breed. . . At this time more particularly they are known as old field-plover, or whistling plover. . . Plovers generally fly high, and keep up an incessant whistling. **1874** Bogardus *Field Shooting* 162, We now come to the upland or highland, grass, gray, or whistling plover, which, according to scientific naturalists, is no plover at all, strictly speaking, but a bird of similar habits and appearance, called Bartram's tatler. **1888** Trumbull *Names of Birds* 190, Black-bellied plover: swiss plover: whistling plover . . : [etc]. *Ibid* 195, American golden plover: common plover: whistling plover . . : [etc]. **1903** Dawson *Birds OH* 2.529, Probably the bird is better known throughout the state as the Upland Plover, or . . the Whistling Plover. **1917** (1923) *Birds Amer.* 1.256, Black-bellied Plover. . . *Other Names*. . . Whistling Plover [etc]. *Ibid* 257, Golden Plover. . . *Other Names*. . . Whistling Plover [etc].

whistling snipe n

=**woodcock 1.**

   1888 Trumbull *Names of Birds* 152 **NH,** Dr. William Jarvis writes of hearing it [=the American woodcock] termed whistling snipe and mud hen some ten years ago at Cornish, N.H. **1893** *Forest & Stream* 40.385 **nwIA,** Very few jack or whistling snipe have arrived yet, although past time. **1946** Hall *Woodcock Ways* 19 **NY,** Our 'whistling snipe' sometimes assume domestic cares when the field music of the hylas first thrills through the spring marshes.

whistling swan n

Std: a swan *(Cygnus columbianus)* native to North America. Also called **hooper 1, whistler 7**   Note: In 1982 the whistling swan and the Bewick's swan were jointly reclassified as the tundra swan.

whistling wampus   See **wampus** n² **1**

whit   See **whet**

white acre pea n   **Sth**

A variety of **black-eyed pea.**

   1950 *Panama City News–Herald* (FL) 29 June 8/1, [Advt:] In Our Fresh Vegetable Department. . . white acre peas. . . blackeye peas. **1976** *DARE* File **GA,** [Label:] Margaret Holmes White Acre Peas . . small variety Field Peas. **1977** *Ibid* **cnFL,** He . . spoke of *white acre peas* but said they are not the same as cowpeas. He insisted that *white* was always used. **2005** *DARE* File—Internet **wNC,** I'm not sure if white acre peas are local or not, some of the smaller markets have 'em here in cans. . . They're small and sorta white/yellowy.

white alder n

1 =**sweet pepperbush.**

   1837 Darlington *Flora Cestrica* 264 **sePA,** Alder-leaved Clethra. Vulgò—Sweet Pepper-bush. White Alder. **1860** Curtis *Cat. Plants NC* 100, White Alder. Sweet Pepper-Bush. . . The leaves are a little like those of the common *Alder,* but are smaller and narrower. **1885** Alley *Beekeeper's Book* 167 **MA,** The white alder *(Clethra alnifolia)* is another fine and valuable honey plant. **1913** *Torreya* 13.32 **seNY,** Late in July the swamps and woods are made most attractive by the beautiful and fragrant white alder *(Clethra alnifolia).* **1929** *Appleton Post–Crescent* (WI) 19 July 16/6, These [species] are now called Clethra, although formerly they were known as White Alder. **1984** Schenk *Complete Gardener* 92, *Clethra acuminata* (White Alder). . . a small tree or large shrub with unremarkable full foliage and fragrant white flowers.

2 A **winterberry 1** (here: *Ilex verticillata).*   **esp ME**

   1896 *Jrl. Amer. Folkl.* 9.184 **cME,** *Ilex verticillata* . . white alder, Oxford County. **1916** *Torreya* 16.238 **ME,** *Ilex verticillata.* . . white alder, Matinicus I[slan]d. **1966** *DARE* (Qu. T15, . . *Kinds of swamp trees*) Inf **ME12,** White alder—small.

3 A **maleberry** (here: *Lyonia ligustrina).*

   1900 Lyons *Plant Names* 400, X[olisma] ligustrina [=Lyonia l.] . . White Alder, White-bush, White Pepper.

white apple n   Cf **pomme blanche**

1 An **Indian breadroot** (here: *Pediomelum* [formerly *Psoralea*] *esculentum).*   Note: Some of these quots may refer instead to **2** below.

1805 in 1904 Lewis *Orig. Jrls. Lewis & Clark Exped.* 2.10 **MT,** The white apple is found in great abundance in this neighbourhood... This root forms a considerable article of food with the Indians of the Missouri. [**1843** in 1930 *Society CA Pioneers Qrly.* 7.150 **KS,** They [= Kansa squaws] gave me to eat a root growing in the prairie which is about the size and shape of a hen's egg. It is both palatable and nutritious and serves the Indians as an excellent substitute for bread. It is very white and is called by the French, "le pomme blanc" or white apple.] **1881** *Bismarck Tribune* (ND) 5 Aug 1/4, A detachment was then sent out to hunt an aged squaw, who had wandered away to dig pomme blanc, or white apple, and got lost.

2 A **groundnut B1** (here: *Apios americana*).

1830 Rafinesque *Med. Flora* 2.193 **OR,** *Apios tuberosa* [=*A. americana*]... *Hanke* or White apple of the Oregon tribes... The roots are white, tender, very good boiled or roasted. **1876** Hobbs *Bot. Hdbk.* 127, White apple, Apios tuberosa.

white-arsed hornet   See **white-tailed hornet**

white ash n

1 Std: an ash (*Fraxinus americana*).   Also called **cane ash, gray ~, fresno 1**

2 =**fringe tree.**   esp sAppalachians

1821 Elliott *Sketch* 1.6, Chionanthus.. Virginica... *Fringe Tree. Virginian Chionanthus. White Ash. Old Man's Beard.* **1874** *Godey's Lady's Book* 89.355 **cnVA,** Among those [flowers] I have seen are the "fringe tree," or white ash. **1897** Sudworth *Arborescent Flora* 332 **WV,** *Chionanthus virginica...* White Ash. **1966** *Sun. Gaz.–Mail* (Charleston WV) 19 June mag sec 17/1, On the hills above Hinton there is another showy southern shrub, the fringe tree, or "white-fringe," also known, unfortunately, as "white ash." **1971** *Charleston Daily Mail* (WV) 15 Sept 45/1, Is the fringe tree that is listed in nursery ads from Tennessee, the native white ash as grown on lawns for ornamental shrubs?

3 =**green ash.**

1897 Sudworth *Arborescent Flora* 330 **KS, NE,** *Fraxinus lanceolata* [=*F. pennsylvanica*]... White Ash. **1921** Deam *Trees IN* 272, *Fraxinus lanceolata...* White Ash. Green Ash. *Ibid* 274, *Fraxinus pennsylvanica...* Red Ash. White Ash. **1969** *DARE* (Qu. T16,.. *Kinds of trees.. 'special'*) Inf **NY227,** White ash, black ash—same.

white-ash breeze   See **ash breeze**

white-ass n

=**red-headed woodpecker 1.**

1954 McAtee *Suppl. to Nomina Abitera* [9] **TN,** Red-headed Woodpecker (*Melanerpes erythrocephalus*)... White-ass (the lower back and rump are white), Clinch River Valley, Tennessee.

white-ass(ed) hornet   See **white-tailed hornet**

white bachelor's button n

A **milkwort** (here: *Polygala baldwinii*).

1933 Small *Manual SE Flora* 774, *P[ilostaxis]* [=*Polygala*] *Baldwinii...* White Bachelor's-button... Low pinelands and swamps, Coastal Plain, Fla. to Miss. and Ga.

whiteback n   **DC, MD, VA**

=**canvasback duck.**

1814 Wilson *Amer. Ornith.* 8.104 **MD, DC, nVA,** At the Susquehannah they are called *Canvas-backs*, on the Potowmac *White-backs*. **1888** Trumbull *Names of Birds* 47 **DC, VA,** The name "White-back" is still a familiar one to duckers on the Potomac, at least to those about Washington and Alexandria. **1897** *Century Illustr. Mag.* 53.804 **DC,** In the late fall and winter myriads of canvasback ducks, then [=1826] commonly called "whitebacks," came to feed on the small white celery that grew so abundantly in the swamps and flats of the Potomac and the Susquehanna.

white-backed skunk n

=**hognose skunk.**

1862 *New Amer. Cyclop.* 14.690, There are several other species [of skunk] in the United States, among them the white-backed skunk (*M. mesoleuca ..*), with broad uninterrupted white dorsal band and entirely white tail. **1879** U.S. Natl. Museum *Bulletin* 14.4 **SW,** *Conepatus mapurito...* White-backed Skunk. **1928** Anthony *N. Amer. Mammals* 133, Swamp Hog-nosed Skunk; White-backed Skunk.—*Conepatus mesoleucus telmalestes...* Whole upperparts and tail white. **1959** *TX Jrl. Sci.* 11.419, A commercial fisherman on the Trinity River just west

of Romayor described to me a "white backed skunk" which was killed on the highway... His description of this animal fitted that of *Conepatus mesoleucus.* **2001** *DARE* File—Internet, There's that cute little white-backed skunk.

white bacon n   chiefly **FL, GA**   See Map   Cf **bacon B, white meat, ~ side meat**
=**salt pork.**

1849 *S. Cultivator* 7.5, My friends say that boiled corn and slops make the meat soft; and that it will not make firm white bacon. **1884** Henshall *Camping in FL* 23, Frank's ducks.. were now cut up, and, with the addition of some white bacon, and an onion, were soon simmering away and exhaling the odor of a "hunter's stew." **1913** *Atlanta Constitution* (GA) 29 Dec 2/7, [Advt:] Fancy White Bacon, pound—12 1/2c. **c1938** in Lib. of Congress *Amer. Memory: WPA Life Hist.* (Internet) **TX,** Our main chuck was white beans and white bacon. **1938** Rawlings *Yearling* 56 **nFL,** There were dried cow-peas boiled with white bacon. **1939** FWP *Guide FL* 432 **cnFL,** The workers carry lunch buckets filled usually with corn bread, blackeyed peas boiled with white bacon (salt pork), and a jar of cane syrup. **1939** in Lib. of Congress *Amer. Memory: WPA Life Hist.* (Internet) **FL,** She brought out a palatable looking section of white bacon to show me; this came from one of Frank's uncles in Georgia. **c1955** Reed–Person *Ling. Atlas Pacific NW,* 1 inf, White bacon [=salt pork]. **1965–70** *DARE* (Qu. H38,.. *Words for bacon*) Infs **FL1, 3, 11, 30, 31, 33, 36, GA19,** White bacon; **FL19,** White bacon—for salt pork; **FL51,** White bacon—all white, from the side of the hog; **GA32,** White bacon—fatback; (Qu. BB34b, *What is a poultice made with?*; total Infs questioned, 75) Inf **FL10,** Soap and sugar plaster, white bacon, leaves. **1966** *DARE* Tape **FL31,** I have used it [=hog jowl] lots of times for putting it in these different kind of greens... If I don't have the white bacon, well, I put the smoke bacon right in that; **FL37,** Put it [=swamp cabbage] in a pot, and put your piece of white bacon, I always use.. the salt pork, and put it in it to season it. **1986** Pederson *LAGS Concordance (Salt pork)* 22 infs, 17 **FL, GA,** White bacon; *(Middling)* 2 infs, **FL, LA,** White bacon; *(Smoked meat)* 4 infs, **FL, GA, AL,** White bacon. **1998** in 2007 *DARE* File—Internet [*Herald–Tribune* (Sarasota FL) 30 July food sec], *Okra and Tomatoes*—This is a Southern standby and a summer favorite when growing up on a Florida farm... 1/4 pound salt (white) bacon.

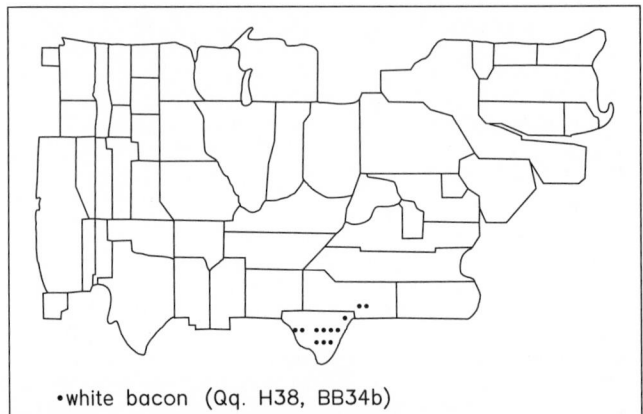

• white bacon (Qq. H38, BB34b)

whitebait n   [*OED2* 1758 →]
The fry of var fish, considered a delicacy; see quots.

1878 *Galveston Daily News* (TX) 19 June [7]/3 (newspaperarchive.com) **NY,** When it was announced that whitebait were to be found in the waters about New York, a considerable commotion occurred among gourmets... Prof. Baird.. declared.. [that] those procured in New York are the young of the alewife and the sea shad. **1878** *Forest & Stream* 10.328 **NY,** Fish in Market—Retail Prices.—Bass 18 cents; blue fish, 12;.. white bait, per pound, $1. **1887** Goode *Amer. Fishes* 394 **NY,** The young of one or both species [=*Alosa aestivalis* and *A. vernalis* [=*A. pseudoharengus*]] are sold in the Boston markets under the name "Sprats," and in New York they make up a large proportion of the so-called "Whitebait." **1892** *Harper's New Mth. Mag.* 85.342 **NYC,** "And how is my future sister-in-law?" asked Wayne Morris, while the waiter was gone, for a Delmonico's magical moment, to fetch the whitebait. **1903** Goode–Gill *Amer. Fishes* 408, Our Anchovy has recently been sold in considerable numbers in New York under the name "Whitebait," although the fishermen distinguish it from the true "Whitebait," the young of the herring, calling it "Spearing." **1935** CA Fish & Game

Comm. *Fish Bulletin* 44.45, Whitebait—Allosmerus attenuatus[ₜ] Spirinchus starksi[ₜ] Young of several species of fishes. **1955** *Humboldt Std.* (Eureka CA) 12 Oct 5/5, Other August landings follow: . . whitebait, 500 pounds. **2003** *Charlotte Sun Herald* (Charlotte Harbor FL) 27 Feb [61]/3 (newspaperarchive.com), Anglers will be pleased to know that whitebait is showing up in the harbor.

white balsam n

1 also *fragrant white balsam, sweet ~:* A **cudweed 1** (here: *Pseudognaphalium obtusifolium*).

1833 Beach *Amer. Practice Med.* 3.262, *Life Everlasting.* Common Names—Sweet Balsam, White Balsam, Cudweed, Live-for-ever, &c. **1848** Bolton *Hist. Co. Westchester* 2.338 **seNY**, White Plains . . derived its name from the *White Balsam,* (Gnaphalium Polycephalum of Linnæus,) which still grows in great abundance in and around the plains. **1876** Hobbs *Bot. Hdbk.* 57, Indian posey, White balsam, Gnaphalium polycephalum. **1914** Georgia *Manual Weeds* 443, Sweet, or Common, Everlasting. . . *Other English names.* . . Sweet White Balsam, Balsam Posy [etc]. **1930** OK Univ. Biol. Surv. *Pub.* 2.85, *Gnaphalium polycephalum* . . Fragrant White Balsam. **1974** Morton *Folk Remedies* 65 **SC**, White Balsam. . . *Gnaphalium obtusifolium.*

2 also *white balsam fir:* Either the **alpine fir** or a **white fir 1** (here: *Abies concolor*).

1876 U.S. Dept. Ag. *Rept. of Secy. for 1875* 182 **UT**, *Abies subalpina.* . . Rocky Mountains. . . It is known among the lumbermen of the Wasatch Mountains as White Balsam, or Pumpkin-tree. . . It has often been collected, and generally referred to *A. grandis,* the incorrectness of which has been but lately pointed out by Dr. Engelmann. **1897** Sudworth *Arborescent Flora* 53 **CA**, *Abies lasiocarpa.* . . White Balsam. *Ibid* 55 **UT**, *Abies concolor.* . . White Balsam. **1908** Britton *N. Amer. Trees* 77, This Fir, variously called White balsam fir, Oregon balsam fir [etc] . . , has probably a greater range than any other American fir. **1941** Writers' Program *Guide UT* 20, The alpine fir, known as "white balsam," is a native of mountain highlands. **1965** *Arcadia Tribune* (CA) 19 Dec 14/1, White Fir—Also called Silver Fir and White Balsam. **1967** *DARE* (Qu. T5, . . *Kinds of evergreens, other than pine*) Inf **CO**37, White balsam.

white baneberry n

Std: a **baneberry 1** (here: *Actaea pachypoda* [formerly *A. alba*]) or its fruit. Also called **black snakeroot 4, blue cohosh 2, bugbane 3, doll's-eyes, necklaceweed 1, Noah's ark 2, sang-sign, snakeroot b(10), white beads, ~ cohosh**

whitebark maple n [Transl of the scientific name]
=chalk maple.

[**1895** Torrey Bot. Club *Bulletin* 22.367, *Acer leucoderme* n[ew] sp[ecies]. . . A very handsome maple, characteristic on account of its habit of branching near the base . . , and the white bark.] **1897** Sudworth *Arborescent Flora* 285, *Acer saccharum leucoderme.* . . Whitebark Maple. **1955** *Post-Std.* (Syracuse NY) 12 June 37/5, The maple spindle gall mite . . causes the spindle-shaped galls on the upper surface of the leaves of silver maple, sugar maple, and white bark maple. **1979** Little *Checklist U.S. Trees* 41, *Acer leucoderme.* . . Other common name—white-bark maple.

whitebark pine n

Std: a **pine 1** (here: *Pinus albicaulis*) native to California, Nevada, and the northwestern US. Also called **pitch pine c(2), rubber ~, scrub ~, white ~ 6**

white bass n

1 Std: a bass *(Morone chrysops)* formerly native chiefly to the Great Lakes and upper Mississippi River, but now widely introduced. Also called **barfish 3, golden bass, gray ~ 2, sand ~ 3, silver ~ 3, silverfish 2, silversides 5, streaked bass, striped ~ 1, striped lake ~**

2 =**largemouth bass** or **smallmouth bass.**

1869 (1873) Scott *Fishing Amer. Waters* 284, *The Oswego Bass.* . . In some places it is known as the yellow bass, and at others as the white bass. **1887** Goode *Amer. Fishes* 56, "Marsh Bass," "River Bass," . . "White Bass" [etc] are other names applied to both species [=largemouth and smallmouth bass]. **1933** LA Dept. of Conserv. *Fishes* 313, White Bass; White Salmon; White Trout [are names of the large-mouthed black bass]. **1935** Caine *Game Fish* 8, Small-mouthed Black Bass. . . *Synonyms.* . . White Bass. **1976** Tryckare et al. *Lore of*

Sportfishing 101, Largemouth Black Bass. . . Other common names . . white bass, grey bass [etc].

3 The white **crappie** *(Pomoxis annularis).*

1946 La Monte *N. Amer. Game Fishes* 143, White Crappie. . . Names: Sac-à-lait, Crappie, White Bass [etc].

white basswood n

A **linden** (here: *Tilia americana* var *heterophylla*) native to the eastern half of the US.

1848 Gray *Manual of Botany* 72, T[ilia] heterophylla. . . (White Basswood). . . Mountains of Penn. and southward. **1898** Sudworth *Forest Trees* 97 **AL, IN**, *Tilia heterophylla.* . . White Basswood. **1908** Rogers *Tree Book* 396, The White Basswood, or Bee Tree of the South *(Tilia heterophylla . .)* is an exceptionally handsome tree, for its bright leaves are pale beneath, often lined with a fine, silvery down. **1955** Forest Products Lab. *Wood Hdbk.* 12, American basswood *(Tilia americana)* is the most important of the several native basswood species; next in importance is white basswood *(T. heterophylla).* . . Because of the uniformity of the wood of the different species, no attempt is made to distinguish between them in lumber form. . . In commercial usage, the term "white basswood" is used to specify white wood or sapwood of either species. **1998** *Ecology* 79.1769, Dominant species included . . white basswood *(Tilia heterophylla).*

white bay n

1 =**sweet bay 2.**

1810 Michaux *Histoire des Arbres* 1.27 **Sth**, M[agnolia] glauca. . . *Sweet bay, White bay et swamp's laurel, noms plus en usage dans la partie maritime des Etats méridionaux.* [=M[agnolia] glauca. . . *Sweet bay, White bay* and *swamp's laurel,* names used mostly in the coastal parts of the southern States.] **1849** *Milwaukee Sentinel & Gaz.* (WI) 20 July 2/4 **MA**, With us it is generally called simply the Magnolia although it has various other names elsewhere such as Swamp Magnolia, Small Magnolia, White Bay tree, Swamp Sassafras, Berry Tree, etc. **1878** Bishop *Voyage Paper Canoe* 335 **seGA**, The red and white bay-tree, a few red-cedars [etc] . . made up a rich wall of verdure on either side. **1890** *San Antonio Daily Light* (TX) 2 Apr 6/2, The following is given as a sample of what one county proposes to exhibit at the Texas spring palace. . . White oak, post oak, . . white bay, sweet bay [etc]. **1927** Boston Soc. Nat. Hist. *Proc.* 38.239 **Okefenokee GA**, Near the borders are still smaller 'white bays' *(Magnolia).* **1966–70** *DARE* (Qu. T15, . . *Kinds of swamp trees*) Infs **FL**26, **SC**7, 26, White bay; **FL**49, Bay tree, red and white—wood like iron. **2004** *DARE* File—Internet **FL**, The leaf backs are covered with white hairs. When the wind blows, they flip up and are very attractive. Some people call them [=*Magnolia virginiana*] "silver or white bay."

2 =**red bay 1.**

1894 *Jrl. Amer. Folkl.* 7.97 **NC**, *Persea Carolinensis* [=*P. borbonia*]. . . white bay. **1968** *DARE* (Qu. T5, . . *Kinds of evergreens, other than pine*) Inf **GA**35, White bay. **1984** *Applied & Environmental Microbiology* 47.686 **Okefenokee GA**, Grand Cypress is a forested swamp . . with an understory of white bay *(Persea borbonia).*

white beads n

=**white baneberry.** Cf **necklaceweed 1**

1822 Eaton *Botany* 155, [*Actaea*] alba. . . necklace weed, white beads. . . Berries white. **1876** Hobbs *Bot. Hdbk.* 127, White beads, White cohosh, Actaea alba. **1979** Erichsen-Brown *Med. N. Amer. Plants* 348, White Baneberry. . . *Common names.* White cohosh, doll's eyes, necklace weed, white beads [etc].

white beech n

The American beech *(Fagus grandifolia)* or its wood—used esp (in contrast to **red beech**) to distinguish specimens in which the light-colored sapwood predominates.

1637 (1972) Morton *New English Canaan* 183, Beech there is of two sorts, redd and white. **1792** Belknap *Hist. NH* 3.102, Beech. . . Of this there are three varieties. The white and the red are used as fewel. **1812** Michaux *Histoire des Arbres* 2.170, [Les] habitans des Etats les plus septentrionaux. . . donnent à l'espèce que je décris le nom de *White Beech,* Hêtre blanc, et à l'autre, celui de *Red Beech,* Hêtre rouge, distinction faite d'après la couleur du bois et non d'après celle du feuillage. [=The inhabitants of the northernmost States. . . give to the species which I describe the name of *White Beech,* and to the other that of *Red Beech,* a distinction based on the color of the wood, and not on that of the foliage.] **1842** Thompson *Hist. VT* 1.212, In the White Beech the greater part of the tree is sap-wood and very perishable, while in the Red

Beech the sap wood is thin, and the heart, or perfect wood exceedingly compact and durable. **1894** *Jrl. Amer. Folkl.* 7.99 **NY,** *Fagus sylvatica* . . white beech, red beech. **1897** *Ibid* 10.144 **West,** *Fagus ferruginea* . . white beech, red beech, black beech. **1964** Stupka *Trees* 43 **Smoky Mts,** At lowest elevations . . the 'white' beech, of primarily southern distribution, may be recognized.

white bee sage　See **bee sage 2**

white-bellied brant　n

The American **brant** (here: *Branta bernicla* var *hrota*).

1897 *Auk* 14.207, There are three recognizable forms, two of which occur in North America, though neither of these is the ordinary Brant of Europe. We have the two extremes of the White-bellied and Black-bellied, between which typical *B. bernicla* is intermediate. **1921** *Ibid* 38.584 **CT,** *Branta bernicla glaucogastra.* White-bellied Brant.—A young male was shot . . on the Sound at West Haven. **1963** Gromme *Birds WI* 213, Brant, . . White-bellied. **1997** in 2008 *DARE* File—Internet **OR,** The only Brant that we observed were all white-bellied Brant, and no dark-bellied Brant.

white-bellied grouse　See **whitebelly 1**

white-bellied martin　See **white-breasted martin**

white-bellied nuthatch　See **white-breasted nuthatch**

white-bellied swallow　n　Also *white-breasted swallow*
=**tree swallow.**

1812 Wilson *Amer. Ornith.* 5.44 **NEast,** The White-Bellied Swallow. . . often takes possession of an apartment in the boxes appropriated to the Purple Martin. **1835** Frost *Youth's Book* 65, The second in order of arrival is the white-breasted swallow, which constructs its nest of clay under the eaves of houses or in the corners of windows, or in hollow trees, or even in the habitations prepared for martins; this is the most numerous species, and is known by its white breast and black back. **1842** Thompson *Hist. VT* 1.98, *White-Bellied Swallow.* . . Color above light glossy greenish blue; . . belly white. **1866** *Harper's New Mth. Mag.* 33.242, Take the hardy "white-bellied swallow" (*Hirundo bicolor*) for an example. **1892** Torrey *Foot-Path Way* 180 **neMA,** I saw the white-breasted swallows congregated in the Ipswich dunes,—a sight never to be forgotten. **1895** Minot *Land-Birds New Engl.* 147, *Tachycineta . . bicolor.* White-breasted swallow. White-bellied swallow. A common summer resident nearly throughout New England. **1938** Oberholser *Bird Life LA* 402, Tree Swallow. . . sometimes called 'White-bellied Swallow.' **1956** MA Audubon Soc. *Bulletin* 40.84 **NEng,** Tree Swallow. . . White-bellied Swallow (N.H., Mass.) . . White-breasted Swallow (Mass., R.I.) **2004** *DARE* File **OR,** "White-bellied" Swallow . . Jan 21.

whitebelly　n

1 also *white-bellied grouse, white-breasted* ~: =**sharp-tailed grouse.**

1874 Coues *Birds NW* 410 **seSD,** Suddenly one of the "White-bellies" whirs up from the roadside. **1878** *Forest & Stream* 9.457, Pinnated grouse lie closer to a dog, and are not as swift flyers as the sharp-tails or white-breasted grouse. **1888** Trumbull *Names of Birds* 139, *Sharp-tailed grouse.* . . Popularly known also as *white-belly,* and in some locations as *white grouse.* **1923** U.S. Dept. Ag. *Farmers' Bulletin* 1375.23 **MN,** *Open seasons:* . . white-breasted or sharp-tailed grouse. . . Sept. 16–Oct. 1. **1942** Briggs *Dakota Morning* 237 **SD,** Fat and juicy, these young prairie chickens had been hatched out last Spring, feeding in the ripening fields of grain. Bub, these is pintails, sometimes called white-bellies. **1955** Forbush–May *Birds* 145, Prairie Sharp-tailed Grouse—*Pedioecetes phasianellus campestris.* . . Other names: Pintail Grouse; . . White-belly; . . White-breasted Grouse. **1982** Elman *Hunter's Field Guide* 26, Sharp-tailed Grouse. . . Common & Regional Names. . . white-breasted grouse.

2 also *whitebelly duck:* =**baldpate 1.**

1888 Trumbull *Names of Birds* 20 **MA, CT,** In the vicinity of Edgertown [the American widgeon is known] as *white-belly.* This latter name is a familiar one also to the older gunners of Milford, Conn. **1955** MA Audubon Soc. *Bulletin* 39.314 **MA,** Baldpate. . . white-belly, white-belly duck.

3 A recently molted crab. **Chesapeake Bay** Cf *snow-belly* (at **snowball 4**)

1976 Warner *Beautiful Swimmers* 161 **Chesapeake Bay,** The crabs in the Number Three basket showed the telltale grayish cast on their topsides and the lustrous white on their abdomens that are the marks of a recently moulted adult crab. Post-buckrams, you might say. Lester calls

them "whiteys." In other parts of the Bay they are known as "snowballs" or "white bellies" and not taken by crabbers. **2000** *Shores Tangier Is.* 220 **Chesapeake Bay,** When the crab first becomes hard, it is not of great market value because it is not *fat,* meaning, if cooked, its body cavity would not be solidly packed. *White-belly, snowball,* and *snow-belly* are names for this crab; Tangiermen say that such a crab is *bucky.*

whitebelly duck　See **whitebelly 2**

whitebill　n
=**coot** n[1] **1.**

1844 Giraud *Birds Long Is.* 200 **Long Is. NY, NJ,** In the middle Atlantic districts, the Coot is not plentiful, though its occurrence on the sea coast of New Jersey, as with us, is sufficiently frequent to be known to the gunners, by whom the more familiar appellation of "Mud Hen"—or, . . as at Egg Harbor, "White" or "Henbill," is applied. **1874** Coues *Birds NW* 543, They are generally, however, called Mud Hens—a name shared by some Grebes—as well as *Poules-d'eau,* White-bills, and other local designations. **1945** *Daily Times–News* (Burlington NC) 4 May 7/4, Come next fall hunters will begin bagging the whitebill, little wotting that they're actually knocking down the former pariah, coot or mudhen. **1970** *Daily Rev.* (Hayward CA) 18 Jan 30/6, All you have to do to skin a whitebill is to give the wings and legs a real strong jerk.

white-billed mud hen　n　Cf **red-billed mud hen**
=**coot** n[1] **1.**

1874 NY Acad. Sci. *Annals Lyceum Nat. Hist.* 10.387 **IL,** *F[ulica] Americana.* . . "White-billed Mud Hen." Summer sojourner. **1895** (1907) Wright *Birdcraft* 249, American Coot. . . *White-billed Mud Hen.* A bird of like appearance to the Florida Gallinule.

white-billed woodpecker　n
=**ivory-billed woodpecker.**

1730 Catesby in Royal Soc. London *Philos. Trans.* 36.427 **NC, SC,** *Picus maximus rostro albo,* the large white Bill'd Wood-pecker. **1782** Latham *Genl. Synopsis Birds* 1.553, White-billed Woodpecker. . . This bird inhabits *Carolina, Virginia, New Spain.* **1889** Ridgway *Ornith. IL* 1.374, Ivory-billed Woodpecker. *Popular synonyms.* White-billed Woodpecker; White-billed Logcock. **1932** Bennitt *Check-list* 42 **MO,** Ivory-billed woodpecker. . . White-billed woodpecker. . . According to reports received from several observers, a few members of this rare species are still to be found in the deep woods of southern Missouri.

white birch　n

Any of var birches with white bark: a **paper birch** (here: *Betula papyrifera*) of the northern US, **gray birch a** of the northeastern US, or *Betula neoalaskana* of Alaska.

1789 Morse *Amer. Geog.* 197 **ME,** The white birch in this part of the country, is unlike that which grows in other parts. It is a large sightly tree, fit for many uses. Its bark, which is composed of a great number of thicknesses, is, when separated, smoother and softer than any paper. **1792** Belknap *Hist. NH* 3.98, *Birch.* Of this we have four species. I. *White (betula alba.)* The bark of this tree is a substance of a singular kind, and is perhaps the only bark which is less liable to rot than the wood which it incloses. **1810** Michaux *Histoire des Arbres* 1.26, *Betula papyracea.* . . *White birch* (Bouleau blanc), également employée dans les mêmes contrées. [=Betula populifolia. . . *White birch,* [a name] likewise used in the same areas [=NH, VT, ME]. *Ibid,* Betula populifolia. . . *White birch* (Bouleau blanc), dénomination générale dans les Etats du nord et du milieu. [=Betula populifolia. . . *White birch,* a common designation in the northern and middle States.] **1824** Bigelow *Florula Bostoniensis* 355, Betula populifolia. . . *Common White Birch.* . . The name of white birch is indiscriminately applied to this species and to Betula papyracea. **1844** Lapham *Geogr. Descr. WI* 82, Betula papyracea . . paper, canoe, or white birch. **1884** Sargent *Forests of N. Amer.* 160, Canoe Birch. White Birch. Paper Birch. . . The very tough, durable bark easily separated into thin layers. **1900** (1927) Keeler *Our Native Trees* 297, White Birch. Gray Birch. Aspen-leaved Birch. . . Least common of the birches. *Ibid* 302, Paper Birch. Canoe Birch. White Birch. . . Widely distributed over a northern range. **1908** Sudworth *Forest Trees Pacific* 258 **AK,** White Birch. Betula alaskana [=B. neoalaskana]. . . White birch is a little-known Alaskan species. **1922** Sargent *Manual Trees* 217 **AK,** Betula alaskana. . . White Birch. . . the common Birch-tree of the Yukon basin. **1965–70** *DARE* (Qu. T16, . . *Kinds of trees* . . *'special'*) 25 Infs, 20 **NEast, N Cent,** White birch; (Qu. T13) Inf **NY97,** White birch; (Qu. T15, . . *Kinds of swamp trees*) Infs **CT31, KY75, MI36, NY52, UT3, WI37,** White birch. **c1980** in 2005 *DARE* File—Internet **NH** (as of c1905), There is a difference between gray birch and white birch. Gray birch never grows big.

white bird n

1 A **chickweed 1a** (here: *Stellaria holostea* or *S. media*).

1900 Lyons *Plant Names* 25, *[Alsine] Holostea* [=*Stellaria h.*] . . White-bird. . . *A. media.* . . White-bird.

2 =**sanderling.**

1908 Lynn MA Park Comms. *Gt. Woods & Pub. Parks* 47 **MA,** *Tringa arenaria.* . . White Bird—Sanderling. **1956** MA Audubon Soc. *Bulletin* 40.21 **MA,** Sanderling. . . White Beach-bird, White Bird, White Snipe, Whitey. . . In winter plumage it is the whitest of shore birds, except the Piping Plover.

white blossom n

A **deer brush 1** (here: *Ceanothus integerrimus*).

1968 DARE (Qu. T16, . . *Kinds of trees* . . *'special'*) Inf **CA**105, White blossom—in Sierras, like blueblossom of coast.

whitebone porgy n   Also *white-boned porgy*

A **porgy** n[1] **1b(4)** (here: *Calamus leucosteus*).

1887 Goode *Amer. Fishes* 100 **SC,** There are other species . . , such as *Calamus bajonado,* common also at Charleston, where it is called the "White-boned Porgy." **1902** Jordan–Evermann *Amer. Fishes* 440, The white-boned porgy *(Calamus leucosteus)* is a rather deep-water species known only from off the Carolina coast. **1974** McClane *McClane's New Std. Fishing Encycl.* 1090, *Whitebone Porgy.* . . found in the Atlantic waters off the Carolinas, Georgia, and Florida. **2005** in 2008 DARE File—Internet **seGA,** Several nice flounder, white boned porgy, red porgy and a few vermilion snapper in the box as well. **2008** *Ibid* **TX,** Species taken on those stops included kingfish, red snapper, vermilion snapper, triggerfish, whitebone porgy, mangrove snapper, etc.

white bottle n   [Brit folk name]

A **bladder campion** (here: *Silene vulgaris*).

1914 Georgia *Manual Weeds* 148, Bladder Campion. . . *Other English names:* White Bottle [etc]. **1935** (1943) Muenscher *Weeds* 232, *Silene latifolia.* . . Bladder campion. White bottle [etc].

white-breasted grouse   See **whitebelly 1**

white-breasted martin n   Also *white-bellied martin*   **chiefly NEng**

=**tree swallow.**

1840 Audubon *Birds Amer.* 1.186, They probably here breed in trees, as I observed the White-bellied Martin do. **1889** *Independent* 7 Nov 5 **seNY,** We heard the faint wash of the bay beyond, and thousands of white-breasted martins were flying before our approach. **1892** Torrey *Foot-Path Way* 182 **neMA,** Our Ipswich birds were all tree swallows,— white-breasted martins. **1894** (1904) Thaxter *Is. Garden* 49 **sME coast,** The barn swallows do not visit my small inclosure as often as do my nearer neighbors, the white-breasted Martins. **1956** MA Audubon Soc. *Bulletin* 40.84 **ME, MA,** Tree swallow. . . White-bellied Martin. *Ibid* **MA,** White-breasted Martin.

white-breasted nuthatch n   Also *white-bellied nuthatch*

Std: a North American **nuthatch** *(Sitta carolinensis)* with a white face and breast and bluish-gray back.   Also called **black-capped nuthatch, Carolina ~, clown, devil-down-head 1, Florida nuthatch, head-down bird, tomtit b, tree creeper, upside-down bird, yank** n[1]

white-breasted swallow   See **white-bellied swallow**

white-breasted woodpecker n

=**hairy woodpecker** (here: usu *Picoides villosus leucotho-rectis*).

1912 *Auk* 29.332 **SW,** *Dryobates villosus leucothorectis.* White-breasted Woodpecker. **1918** *Condor* 20.86 **CA,** *Dryobates villosus leucothorectis.* . . White-breasted Woodpecker. **1923** Dawson *Birds CA* 2.989, White-breasted Woodpecker. . . Southwestern Hairy Woodpecker. Arizona Hairy Woodpecker. **1944** Hausman *Amer. Birds* 453, White-breasted Woodpecker. . . Quite similar to the Rocky Mountain Hairy Woodpecker. **1964** Phillips *Birds AZ* 74, Hairy Woodpecker; White-breasted Woodpecker; Chihuahua Woodpecker—*Dendrocopos* [=*Picoides*] *villosus.* **2002** in 2008 DARE File—Internet **PA,** White-breasted woodpeckers.

whitebrush n

1 A **bee brush** (here: *Aloysia gratissima*).   Cf **white bush 4, ~ chaparral**

1898 *Progr. Bee-Keeper* 8.110 **TX,** White brush blooms about two weeks after the first good rain in the spring, and also after *every* good rain throughout the entire summer and fall. **1938** Van Dersal *Native Woody Plants* 156, *Lippia ligustrina.* . . Whitebrush. . . A large, sometimes spinescent shrub. . . Palatable to livestock, and a good honey plant. **1940** Writers' Program *Guide TX* 448 **csTX,** During winters and extended droughts, cattle fed on the leaves and beans of the huajillo, the soft brittle stems of the white brush. **1967–69** DARE (Qu. C28, *A place where underbrush, weeds, vines and small trees grow together so that it's nearly impossible to get through*) Inf **TX**66, Whitebrush thicket; (Qu. T5, . . *Kinds of evergreens, other than pine*) Inf **TX**43, Whitebrush. **2006** DARE File—Internet **TX,** *Vara Dulce, Sweet-stem* . . *Aloysia macrostachya.* . . Its leaves are larger and more hairy than those of whitebrush (*A. gratissima*).

2 A **deer brush 1** (here: *Ceanothus integerrimus*).

1931 U.S. Dept. Ag. *Misc. Pub.* 101.105, Bluebrush (*Ceanothus integerrimus,* syn *C. nevadensis*) . . is often known locally as sweet birch. . . White-flowered forms give rise to the name whitebrush.

white buffalo n

=**bigmouth buffalo** or **smallmouth buffalo.**

1878 U.S. Natl. Museum *Bulletin* 12.72 **TN,** *List of Fishes of Nashville, as given by a Fisherman.* . . White Buffalo. Blue Buffalo. **1899** U.S. Bur. Fisheries *Report* 303 **MS, LA, TX,** The more abundant fishes seen by us or reported by the fishermen . . [include] white buffalo, reaching a weight of 35 pounds. *Ibid* 307, *Ictiobus bubalus.* . . Small-mouthed Buffalo; "White Buffalo"; "Rooter." **1903** NE State Bd. Ag. *Annual Rept. for 1902* 189, In waters where white buffalo, suckers, gar fish . . abound the commissioner may in his discretion issue to any responsible person a permit to take such fish. **1933** LA Dept. of Conserv. *Fishes* 434, Smallmouth Buffalo, Razorback Buffalo or White Buffalo— *Ictiobus bubalus. Ibid* 441, The Common Buffalo—*Megastomatobus cyprinella* [=*Ictiobus cyprinellus*]. . . has come to be known under many popular names. . . [such as] Mud Buffalo and White Buffalo. **1983** Becker *Fishes WI* 615, Bigmouth buffalo. . . Other common names: redmouth buffalo, . . white buffalo [etc]. **2008** McClelland *Third Coast* 302 **ceMI,** Everybody wants whitefish. We ship a lot to Chicago. . . We're shipping a lot of white buffalo, too. Normally, I don't want those, because they're carp and they're bony. But they use 'em as filler for gefilte fish. **2008** DARE File—Internet **TX,** In my day grandma still went bonkers over what she called white buffalo. For those who may not know a buffalo fish looks much like a carp. . . I remember it as being not as flaky as catfish. More like a drum.

white bush n

1 A **maleberry** (here: *Lyonia ligustrina*).

1818 Eaton *Botany* 135, *[Andromeda] paniculata* [=*Lyonia ligustrina*] . . white bush. . . A shrub running into several varieties—flowers small. **1873** CT State Bd. Ag. *Annual Rept. 1872–73* 115, The other [weed] he calls White-Bush, and says it is bad for sheep. It is the *Andromeda ligustrina* of botanists. A different shrub is usually known as white-bush in other localities.

2 A **sweet pepperbush** (here: *Clethra alnifolia*).

1847 Darby *Manual Botany* 2.111, *Clethra* . . *alnifolia.* . . Spiked Alder. White Bush. **1873** [see **1** above]. **1913** Britton–Brown *Illustr. Flora* 667, *Clethra alnifolia.* . . White bush.

3 A **brittlebush** (here: *Encelia farinosa*).

1931 U.S. Dept. Ag. *Misc. Pub.* 101.164 **West,** White brittlebush (*E[ncelia] farinosa*). . . Other vernacular names include brittlebrush . . and whitebush.

4 A **bee brush** (here: *Aloysia gratissima*).   Cf **whitebrush 1**

1967 DARE (Qu. T16, . . *Kinds of trees* . . *'special'*) Inf **TX**13, White bush. **1970** Correll *Plants TX* 1335, *Aloysia gratissima.* . . Common bee-brush, white bush, white brush [etc]. **1984** Nelson *Last Campfire* 74 **wTX,** Some of them lived in whitebush thickets that were matted together and hard to get through horseback. **2008** DARE File—Internet **AZ,** This Flame Skimmer used the hummingbird feeder stand as a perch to catch the many insects pollinating my Whitebush, Aloyisa [sic] gratissima.

white butterfly orchid n

=**palm-polly.**

1933 Small *Manual SE Flora* 398, *[Polyrrhiza]* [=*Dendrophylax*] *Lindenii.* . . White butterfly-orchid. Palm-polly. . . Restricted mostly to the Big Cypress Swamp. **1950** Correll *Native Orchids* 375, *Polyrrhiza Lindenii.* . . Common names: Palm-polly, . . White Butterfly-orchid. . . When one looks up into the gloom of a thickly leaved tree and sees the extraordinary flowers of this little orchid for the first time, one is instantly impressed with its likeness to a thin flat snow-white frog suspended in mid-air.

white buttons n   Also *white shoe buttons*
=pipewort.

[**1860** MS State Geologist *Rept. Geol. & Ag. MS* 369, For the rest, the Pitcher-plants, long-leaved Sundew, bright-colored *Orchideae,* and the Cord-rushes crowned with their white buttons, with the never failing Gallberry, form the bulk of the vegetation.] **1940** Clute *Amer. Plant Names* 222, *Eriocaulon decangulare.* Hatpins, white shoe buttons. **1976** Bruce *How to Grow Wildflowers* 206, Here other bog plants may also grow . . Pipeworts (*Eriocaulon*) more descriptively called "White Buttons," and various species of the tiny insect-catching sundews. **2007** (acc) WI State Herbarium *WI Bot. Info. System* (Internet), *Eriocaulon aquaticum.* . . Common name—seven-angle pipewort, white buttons.

white buttonwood   See **buttonwood 4**

white camas n   Also sp *white camass*
=death camas.

1897 U.S. Natl. Museum *Contrib. Herbarium* 5.93 **OR,** *Zygadenus venenosus.* . . well known locally under the name "poison camas," "white camas," and "lobelia," and common in the natural meadows. **1911** *Century Dict. Suppl., Camass.* . . White camass, the death camass. **1920** Saunders *Useful Wild Plants* 245, On the Pacific slope . . is a plant of the Lily tribe in general appearance resembling Camas but with a bulb that is poisonous. It is realistically known as Death Camas, and also as White Camas. **1970** Correll *Plants TX* 381, *White camas, alkali-grass.* . . On wet ledges and seepage in canyons.

white campion n   [*OED2* 1578 →]
Std: a **catchfly 1** (here: *Silene latifolia*).   Also called **bull rattle, cow ~, white cockle**

white carp n
1 A carpsucker (*Carpiodes* spp).

1819 Warden *Statist. Political Hist. U.S.* 1.63, The other fish [of Lake Superior] are sturgeon, pike, pickerel, red and white carp, black bass [etc]. **1914** Acad. Nat. Sci. Philadelphia *Proc. for 1913* 65.46 **MD,** *Carpiodes cyprinus.* . . It is known to the fisherman . . along the Susquehanna in Maryland, usually as "white carp" or "Susquehanna carp." **1920** U.S. Bur. Fisheries *Rept. for 1918* 78, Quillback or white carp, sunfish, and various other species were taken in smaller quantities. **1922** *Scientific Mth.* 14.193 **cwWI,** There was also a good number of sheepshead, river carp (which the Lake Pepin fishermen call "white carp") [etc]. **1951** Harlan–Speaker *IA Fish* 61, Quillback—*Carpiodes cyprinus.* . . Other Names—White carp . . and white sucker. *Ibid* 62, Northern River Carpsucker—*Carpiodes carpio carpio.* . . Other names—Carpsucker, white carp [etc]. **1953** (1977) Hubbard *Shantyboat* 210 **wKY,** Ike called them white carp. **1969** *DARE* (Qu. P3, *Freshwater fish that are not good to eat*) Inf **KY**6, White carp. **1995** Lund *Flatheads & Spooneys* 55 **KY,** You go on a mud bottom, throw a little cottonseed in them [=nets], you catch a fill of white carp [Lund: highfin] or carp.

2 **=smallmouth buffalo.**

1983 Becker *Fishes WI* 625, Smallmouth Buffalo. . . Other common names: razorback buffalo, . . white carp [etc].

white catfish n   Also *white cat*
1 **=blue catfish 1.**

1804 (1904) Clark *Orig. Jrls. Lewis & Clark Exped.* 1.90 **seNE,** This evening Guthrege Cought a *White Catfish,* its eyes Small & tale much like that of a *Dolfin.* [*DARE* Ed: Dolphin prob =*Coryphaena hippurus,* a fish with a deeply forked tail.] **1957** Trautman *Fishes* 414, In Ohio, the species [=*Ictalurus furcatus*] is called "Mississippi" or "White Cat," the latter a most appropriate name, for all specimens I have seen were whitish or milk-white, not predominantly bluish as is the Channel Catfish. **1967** Cross *Hdbk. Fishes KS* 210, The blue catfish, which is more often called the "fulton," "white fulton," or "white cat" in the Kansas region, occurs fairly commonly in the Missouri River but only rarely in the lower Kansas River. **1967–70** *DARE* (Qu. P1, . . *Kinds of freshwater fish . . caught around here . . good to eat*) Infs **LA**8, 10, 20, **MO**3, White cat; **IN**13, White catfish; (Qu. P14, . . *Commercial fishing . . what do the fishermen go out after?*) Inf **LA**8, White cat. [*DARE* Ed: Some of these Infs may refer instead to **2** below.] **1986** *Syracuse Herald–Jrl.* (NY) 27 July sec BB 7/4, The channel cat and the white catfish are the only two catfish which have deeply forked caudal fins, or tails.

2 A **channel catfish** (here: *Ictalurus punctatus*).

1818 Rafinesque in *Amer. Monthly Mag. & Crit. Rev.* 3.447, Silurus pallodus. . . White catfish. **1877** U.S. Natl. Museum *Bulletin* 10.76, *Ichthælurus punctatus.* . . Blue Cat—White Cat—Silver Cat—Channel Cat. . . It would seem as if every naturalist who had obtained a Channel Cat was sure that such a Cat-fish, so slender, so clean, and so white, must surely be unknown to science, or else he would have heard of it before. **1903** NY State Museum & Sci. Serv. *Bulletin* 60.80, *Ictalurus punctatus.* . . This species is variously styled the channel cat, white cat, silver cat, blue cat and spotted cat. **1923** *Eve. State Jrl. Lincoln Daily News* (NE) 7 Aug 1/2, What is said to be the biggest fish caught in the Missouri river here this season . . was taken on a common trout line. . . It was the white catfish variety, and tipped the scales at fifty pounds and two ounces. **1933** LA Dept. of Conserv. *Fishes* 422, Widest ranging of our big Cats, the Channel Cat or White Cat is to be found over the continent from the Great Lakes to the Gulf Coast. **1983** Becker *Fishes WI* 712, Channel Catfish. . . Other common names . . white cat, blue cat, lady cat [etc].

3 A freshwater or tidewater catfish (here: *Ameiurus catus*) native to the East Coast and eastern Gulf States, but widely introduced elsewhere.   Also called **channel catfish, forktail ~ 2, horned pout 3, pout, river cat, Schuylkill ~**   Cf **rock cat**

1839 Randolph *VA Housewife* 19, Catfish Soup. . . Take two large or four small white catfish that have been caught in deep water, . . put them in a pot. **1859** *Friends' Intelligencer* 16.651 **PA,** The delicate white catfish, peculiar to the Schuylkill, and famous . . has almost wholly disappeared. **1866** *Athletic Sports* 146, There is a variety, called the white catfish, which comes from the sea in the east, to spawn yearly, . . that is game, and rather handsome. He is more slender than the others, semitransparent when held to the light, has a forked tail like a herring, and weighs from four ounces up to four pounds. **1868** Cook *Geol. NJ* 826, *Amiurus albidus.* White Catfish. This, as an article of food, is the finest of our catfish species. They are very abundant in tide-water streams. **1884** Goode *Fisheries U.S.* 1.628, *Ictalurus albidus.* The White Catfish of the tributaries of the Chesapeake Bay is very abundant in the Susquehanna and Potomac Rivers, and forms an important part of the fish supply of the Washington market. **1946** La Monte *N. Amer. Game Fishes* 163, White Catfish—*Ictalurus catus.* . . Confusion has been caused because this fish has also been called the Channel Catfish. **1970** *DARE* (Qu. P1, . . *Kinds of freshwater fish . . caught around here . . good to eat*) Inf **VA**79, White cat. **1994** *Frederick Post* (MD) 11 June sec A 8/1 **DE,** The Delaware Department of Natural Resources and Environmental control issued a fish consumption advisory for channel catfish, white catfish, rockfish and white perch.

white cedar n
1 A coniferous tree of the genus *Chamaecyparis:* in the Atlantic states, *C. thyoides;* on the West Coast, *C. lawsoniana.* For other names of *C. thyoides* see **juniper 2b, post cedar 2, swamp ~ 1, swamp juniper, ~ white cedar;** for other names of *C. lawsoniana* see **ginger pine, Oregon cedar, Port Orford cedar**

1674 Josselyn *Two Voyages* 67 **NEng,** The white Cedar is a stately Tree. **1709** (1967) Lawson *New Voyage* 97 **Carolinas,** Ever-Greens are here plentifully found, of a very quick Growth, and pleasant Shade: Cypress, or white Cedar, the Pitch Pine, the yellow Pine [etc]. **1775** (1962) Romans *Nat. Hist. FL* 5, On account of the abundance of that species of cypress [Footnote: Cupressus thyoides] vulgarly called white cedar . . [it] is called cedar river. **a1782** (1788) Jefferson *Notes VA* 39, White cedar. *Cupressus Thyoides.* **1792** [see **2** below]. **1810** Michaux *Histoire des Arbres* 1.31, Cupressus thyoides. . . *White cedar* (Cèdre blanc), seule dénomination dans les Etats de New-York, du New-Jersey, de la Delaware et de la Pensylvanie. [=Cupressus thyoides. . . *White cedar,* the only name in the States of New-York, New Jersey, Delaware and Pennsylvania.] **1853** in 1928 OR Pioneer Assoc. *Trans.* 52 **OR,** These mountains are a dense forest of pines, fir, white cedar or redwood. **1856** Olmsted *Journey Slave States* 151, The main production [of the Great Dismal Swamp] . . has been of cypress and juniper; (the latter commonly known as white cedar, at the North). **1894** *Jrl. Amer. Folkl.* 7.99 **OR, nCA,** Chamaecyparis Lawsoniana. . . Oregon cedar, white cedar, ginger-pine. **1910** Jepson *Silva CA* 152, Some woodsmen use the names "Oregon Cedar" and "White Cedar" [for *Chamaecyparis lawsoniana*]. **1968** *DARE* (Qu. T15, . . *Kinds of swamp trees*) Inf **NC**81, Juniper or white cedar—they're the same. **2005** [see **swamp cedar 1**].

2 An arborvitae (here: *Thuja occidentalis*). Also called **cedar 2, hackmatack 1d, swamp cedar 3, vitae**

1792 Belknap *Hist. NH* 3.111, White cedar *(thuja occidentalis.)* . . The white cedar of the southern States *(cupressus thyoides)* is a very different tree from the white cedar of the northern States. **1805** (1905) Clark *Orig. Jrls. Lewis & Clark Exped.* 3.154, A certain number of Spars which are Covered with the Bark of the white Ceadar, or *Arber Vitea.* **1810** Michaux *Histoire des Arbres* 1.31, Thuya occidentalis. *Arbor vitae. . . White cedar,* nom plus en usage dans le district de Maine, l'Etat du Vermont, et la partie la plus reculée du New-Hampshire. [=Thuya occidentalis. *Arbor vitae. . . White cedar,* the name most used in the district of Maine, the State of Vermont, and the remotest part of New Hampshire.] **1832** *NY Farmer & Horticult. Repository* 5.227 **NJ,** Here I could not avoid noticing the great number of the stumps of the white cedar, . . the Thuja occidentalis. **1897** Sudworth *Arborescent Flora* 65, *Thuja occidentalis. . .* Common Names. . . White Cedar (Me., N.H., Vt., R.I., Mass., N.Y., N.J., Va., N.C., Wis., Mich., Minn., Ont.) **1942** Peattie *Friendly Mts.* 151 **nNH, nVT,** Anyone who drives across northern New Hampshire and Vermont will be impressed by the way in which the white cedar *(Thuja occidentalis)* appears as soon as the limestone region is entered. **1979** Little *Checklist U.S. Trees* 285, *Thuja occidentalis. . .* northern white-cedar. . . Other common names—white-cedar, eastern white-cedar [etc.].

3 =**incense cedar.**

1863 Hittell *Resources CA* 97, The Californian white cedar *(Libocedrus decurrens)* grows one hundred feet high, and seven feet thick in the trunk. **1884** Sargent *Forests of N. Amer.* 176, Libocedrus decurrens. . . White cedar. . . A large tree 30 to 45 meters in height. **1897** Sudworth *Arborescent Flora* 64 **CA, OR,** *Libocedrus decurrens. . .* Common Names. White Cedar. **1910** Jepson *Silva CA* 149, Incense Cedar. . . by woodsmen . . is variously called Red Cedar, White Cedar, Bastard Cedar, and Post Cedar.

4 A **juniper 1** such as *Juniperus californica;* see quots.

1897 Sudworth *Arborescent Flora* 98, *Juniperus californica. . .* Common Names. White Cedar. **1910** Jepson *Silva CA* 162, The California Juniper, known also locally as "White Cedar," . . lives on dry hills and mountain slopes. **1931** *CA Ag. Exper. Sta. Berkeley Bulletin* 517.43, White cedar honey is of light color, granulates snow white, and enjoys a good local demand. **1940** Steyermark *Flora MO* 39, White Cedar . . *Juniperus mexicana* [=*J. ashei*]. . . Limestone glades and bluffs of the White River. **1950** Moore *Trees AR* 22, Ashe Juniper. . . Local Names: Ozark White Cedar, Yellow Cedar.

white chaparral n TX Cf white bush 4

A **bee brush** (here: *Aloysia gratissima*).

1904 Adams *TX Matchmaker* 133, We entered some chalky hills, interspersed with white chaparral thickets which were just bursting into bloom, with a fragrance that was almost intoxicating. **1910** *Daily Express* (San Antonio TX) 24 July 9/4, The land . . is open mesquite with a heavy growth of white brush or white chaparral. **1916** *U.S. Geol. Surv. Water-Supply Papers* 375.144 **TX,** The soil is sparse, but the familiar, thickly set brush, collectively designated by the name chaparral, including black chaparral or "black brush," white chaparral or "white brush," cat's claw, guallacón . . , and guajillo, is everywhere present. **1939** *TX Geogr. Mag.* 3.2.42, The so-called Caliche Plateau . . is characterized particularly by prickly pear, huajillo, white chaparral.

white-cheeked goose n Also white-cheeked Canada goose

A **Canada goose** (here: usu *Branta canadensis occidentalis;* rarely, *B. c. canadensis* or *B. c. leucopareia*).

1858 U.S. War Dept. *Rept. Explor. Railroad* 9.xlix, *Bernicla . . leucopareia. . .* White-cheeked Goose. West coast of America. **1884** U.S. Natl. Museum *Bulletin* 27.158, *Bernicla* [=*Branta*] *canadensis leucoparia* [sic]. . . White-cheeked Goose. . . south in winter along Pacific coast to California, and occasionally straggling eastward. *Ibid, Bernicla* [=*Branta*] *canadensis occidentalis. . .* Larger White-cheeked Goose. . . south to California in winter. **1918** Grinnell et al. *Game Birds CA* 225, The true White-cheeked Goose *(Branta canadensis occidentalis)* does not occur in California. The many references in literature to this goose really apply to the Canada goose *(Branta canadensis canadensis).* **1937** *Ironwood Daily–Globe* (MI) 28 July 4/8 **seAK,** An unusual race of wild geese is said to exist in British Columbia and southeastern Alaska. They are known locally as white-cheeked geese and resemble the well-known Canada goose in many respects, being approximately the same size but much darker in plumage. **1953** Jewett *Birds WA* 104, White-cheeked Canada Goose. *Branta canadensis occidentalis.*

1989 *Frederick Post* (MD) 9 Nov sec B 1/4, The Western Canada or the white-cheeked goose is about the same size as the common species.

white chestnut oak n

=**swamp chestnut oak 1.**

1858 *Dispensatory U.S.A.* 633, Several other species afford barks equally useful. . . Such are . . *Q[uercus] prinus* or white chestnut-oak [etc]. **1876** Hobbs *Bot. Hdbk.* 205, Quercus prinus, White chestnut oak. **1940** Clute *Amer. Plant Names* 163, *Q[uercus] prinus. . .* Rock chestnut oak, white chestnut oak [etc]. **2006** *DARE* File—Internet **MD,** Chestnut Oak. . . Their large size and woody nature make them ideal for logging in a similar manner to the white chestnut oak.

white chin n Also white-chin tautog

=**tautog,** esp a large one.

1941 Camp *Fishing* 82 **NEng,** The blackfish, known also as tautog, oyster-fish and white-chin, is strictly a cold-water inhabitant. **1953** Bigelow–Schroeder *Fishes Gulf ME* 478, *Tautoga onitis . . White chin. . .* The tautog is a rather dark fish. . . but the chin is usually white on large ones. **2007** *Providence Jrl.* (RI) 4 May (Internet), Divers have been spotting large, white-chin tautog off Ocean Drive in Newport.

white coal-black See white lampblack

white cockle n

=**white campion.**

[**1897** U.S. Dept. Ag. States Rel. Serv. *Exper. Sta. Rec. for 1895–96* 7.689 **Canada,** Of the 60 samples examined, 53 contained grass seed; 27, seeds of white cockle (*Lychnis vespertina* [=*Silene latifolia*]).] **1913** IA Geol. Surv. *Bulletin* 4.126, White Campion (*Lychnis alba* Mill. [=*Silene latifolia*]). . . A freely branching biennial, with a slightly pleasant odor. **1914** Georgia *Manual Weeds* 145, White cockle—*Lychnis alba. . .* Eastern and middle United States and Canada. **1935** (1943) Muenscher *Weeds* 227, *Lychnis alba. . .* White cockle, White campion. . . Introduced from Europe. **1970** U.S. Ag. Research Serv. *Selected Weeds* 160, *Lychnis alba. . .* White cockle. . . Throughout approximately the northern half of the United States. **2007** *WI Crop Manager* 2 May, White cockle's name is officially white campion, but you will most likely still see it as white cockle on some herbicide labels.

white cod n

=**lingcod 1.**

1941 Camp *Fishing* 152 **Pacific NW,** The cultus, also known as greenling, ling cod, cod, blue cod, white cod [etc] . . is another deep-water species. **1953** Roedel *Common Fishes CA* 139, Lingcod. . . Unauthorized Names . . blue cod, white cod, . . green cod [etc]. **2007** (acc) Monterey Bay Aquarium *Seafood Watch* (Internet) **cwCA,** *Lingcod—Common Market Names*—Blue cod, Bluefish, Buffalo cod, Green cod, White cod.

white cohosh n

=**white baneberry.**

1814 Pursh *Flora Americae* 2.367, *Actaea. . . alba. . .* Known by the name of *Red* and *White Cohosh,* and considered by the natives as a valuable medicine. **1843** Torrey *Flora NY* 1.22, White Cohosh. . . Rocky woods; . . common . . in the southern counties. . . A mild astringent and tonic. **1869** Porcher *Resources* 20, Baneberry; White Cohosh. . . Rocky Woods, Mts. of South Carolina; North Carolina. **1896** *Jrl. Amer. Folkl.* 9.179 **ME,** Actæa alba . . white cohosh, blue cohosh, Paris, Me. **1903** Small *Flora SE U.S.* 432, Actaea alba. . . White Baneberry. White Cohosh. **1960** Seymour *Flora Lincoln Co. WI* 16, Red and White Cohosh, *Actaea.* **1979** Erichsen-Brown *Med. N. Amer. Plants* 348, White Baneberry. . . Common names. White cohosh, . . white beads [etc].

white-collared pigeon n

=**band-tailed pigeon.**

1884 Coues *Key to N. Amer. Birds* 565, *C[olumba] fasciata* [=*Patagioenas f.*] . . White-collared Pigeon. **1899** *Forest & Stream* 53.305, The bird here described is probably the band-tailed pigeon, or white-collared pigeon, which ranges from the Rocky Mountains to the Pacific. **1953** Jewett *Birds WA* 334, Pacific Band-tailed Pigeon. *Columba fasciata monilis. . .* Other names: Wild Pigeon; White-collared Pigeon.

white crane n

1 =**whooping crane 1.**

[**1768** in 2008 *DARE* File—Internet **Canada,** The white crane is a fine bold bird. The white are the largest. . . From the talons to the end of the beak ten and a half feet. . . The legs, beak, and pinion feathers are black, all the other parts milk white.] **1805** (1904) Lewis *Orig. Jrls. Lewis & Clark Exped.* 1.295, Saw some large white cranes pass up the river—these are the largest bird of that genus common to the country through which the Missouri and Mississippi pass. they are perfectly white except the large feathers of the two first joints of the wing which are black. **1854** *Putnam's Mag.* 4.79 **West,** Besides the great difference in size [between the whooping crane and the sandhill crane], the white crane standing near a foot taller, the color of the naked skin of the head, and of the bill, is sufficiently different to mark them as distinct species. **1858** U.S. War Dept. *Rept. Explor. Railroad* 9.654, *Grus Americanus.* . . White Crane; Whooping Crane. **1872** Coues *Key to N. Amer. Birds* 271, *White or Whooping Crane.* . . Adult plumage pure white, with black primaries, primary coverts and alula. **1903** Dawson *Birds OH* 2.459, Whooping Crane. . . Synonym.—White Crane. **1955** *Oriole* 20.1.6, *Whooping Crane.*—Great White Crane; White Crane (general).

2 =white heron.

1851 *De Bow's Rev.* 11.55 **LA,** *White Crane, Ardea Alba*—Two kinds, large and small; seen very often in large gangs, particularly during highwater or the subsidence. **1874** NY Acad. Sci. *Annals Lyceum Nat. Hist.* 10.386 **IL,** *[Herodias] alba* . . var *egretta.* . . White Heron; American Egret; White "Crane." **1886** *Forest & Stream* 26.348 **IL,** The white herons . . are here universally known as "white cranes." **1940** Todd *Birds W. PA* 706, Crane, . . White, *see* . . Heron, Little Blue. **1954** Sprunt *FL Bird Life* 23, Great White Heron. . . Local Names: White Crane. **1955** MA Audubon Soc. *Bulletin* 39.312, *Little Blue Heron.* Blue Crane. . . Little White Crane, White Crane (general). *Ibid, American Egret.* White Crane (General. . .) *Ibid, Snowy Egret.* White Crane (General. Herons are frequently miscalled cranes.) **1962** Imhof *AL Birds* 85, Little Blue Heron. . . Other Names: Blue Crane, White Crane. **1968** *DARE* (Qu. Q10, . . *Water birds and marsh birds*) Inf LA8, White crane [FW: names for great white and blue herons]. **2001** MD Ornith. Soc. *MD Yellowthroat* Mar–Apr 6 (Internet) **eVA, eMD,** Of course you know the White Crane. *Ibid* 7, White crane = Great or other egrets.

white crappie See **crappie**

white croaker n

Either of two closely related fishes of the Pacific coast: the **queenfish 1** or the **little roncador.**

1896 U.S. Bur. Fisheries *Rept. for 1895* 393 **sCA,** *Seriphus politus.* . . *Queenfish. White Croaker.* Coast of southern California. **1928** S. CA Acad. Sci. *Bulletin* 27.34, *Seriphus politus.* . . Queen fish, (White croaker). **1946** La Monte *N. Amer. Game Fishes* 74, Queenfish. . . Names: White Croaker, Herring. . . Bluish-silvery on back and upper sides; rest of body silvery. *Ibid* 82, Kingfish. . . Names: White Croaker [etc]. . . Silvered brownish above, shading into silvery white below. **1966** *Independent* (Long Beach CA) 28 Aug sec C 5/1, The croaker family consists of the queenfish, white croaker (also called a kingfish) [etc]. **1970** *DARE* (Qu. P2, . . *Kinds of saltwater fish caught around here . . good to eat*) Inf **CA**177, White croaker—same as tomcod. **2007** *Los Angeles Times* (CA) 28 Jan sec B 1 (Internet), Some highly contaminated white croaker is still showing up in a handful of Asian markets in Los Angeles and Orange counties.

white-crowned sparrow n

Std: a widely distributed American sparrow *(Zonotrichia leucophrys).* Also called **Gambel's sparrow, quailhead**

white curlew n

1 =white ibis. esp FL

1731 Catesby *Nat. Hist. Carolina* 1.82, Numenius albus. The White Curlew. **1789** Morse *Amer. Geog.* 59, Upwards of one hundred and thirty American Birds have been enumerated [including]. . . White Curlew. **1858** U.S. War Dept. *Rept. Explor. Railroad* 9.684, Ibis alba. . . White Curlew; White Ibis; Spanish Curlew. **1885** *Harper's New Mth. Mag.* 70.228 **FL,** Of the beautiful white curlew, with the tender rose legs and bill, whose snowy wings are tipped with green bronze, . . we killed many a one. **1903** *Outing* 43.167 **sFL,** They [=white ibises] are locally called "white curlews," and are esteemed one of the best food-birds of the region. **1917** (1923) *Birds Amer.* 1.177, The young birds before they assume the adult plumage are called "Stone Curlews" by the fishermen, and the old birds, which are popularly supposed to be of a different species, are usually referred to as "Spanish Curlews" or "White Curlews." **1938** *Charleston Gaz.* (WV) 1 Apr 12/2 **FL,** There is a true ibis in Florida, known as the white curlew. **2006** *DARE* File—Internet **sFL,** [Caption:] White Curlew (White Ibis).

2 =bluestocking 2.

1868 Cronise *Nat. Wealth CA* 471, The Avocet . . is nearly all white, with black patches on the back. It is sometimes called the White Curlew, but its bill turns up, instead of downwards. **1918** Grinnell et al. *Game Birds CA* 337, Avocet. . . Other names. . . White Curlew.

white cypress n

1 A **bald cypress** (here: *Taxodium distichum*), esp one with light-colored heartwood.

1810 Michaux *Histoire des Arbres* 1.30, Cupressus disticha. . . *Black and White cypress* (Cyprès noir *et* Cyprès blanc), eu égard à la qualité et à la couleur du bois. [=Cupressus disticha. . . *Black and White cypress* (Black cypress *and* White cypress), depending upon the quality and color of the wood.] **1843** *Niles' Natl. Reg.* 26 Aug 408, The *Randolph* had all her old wood work of beams, decks, &c. about the hull, removed, and the yellow pine replaced with white cypress. **1860** Curtis *Cat. Plants NC* 29, There are three varieties of this tree recognized by those who deal in its timber—The *Red, Black* and *White* Cypress, characterized by the different color of their heart-wood. **1897** Sudworth *Arborescent Flora* 59 **NC, SC, FL, MS,** Bald Cypress. . . Common Names. . . White Cypress. **1920** *Amer. Architect* 8 Dec 765, Southern bald cypress is about the most variable in color of any of our native woods, and in different localities is known as red cypress, yellow cypress, white cypress and black cypress. **1960** Vines *Trees SW* 14, Common Bald Cypress. . . Other vernacular names are White Cypress, Gulf Cypress [etc]. **1967–68** *DARE* (Qu. T15, . . *Kinds of swamp trees*) Inf **LA**15, Scrub or white cypress; **SC**43, Cypress—white, yellow, black.

2 =white cedar 1.

1842 *Mirror of Lit.* 1.35, Case XIII contains some baskets, mats, &c., made in various parts of the west coast of North America. Here is some of the inner bark of the white cedar or white cypress *(Cupressus thyoides)* in its different stages of preparation. **1846** Gardner *Farmer's Dict.* 141, The *white cypress, C[upressus] thyoides,* . . is abundant in New-Jersey, Maryland, and Virginia. **1960** Vines *Trees SW* 9, *Chamaecyparis thyoides.* . . Other vernacular names are Northern White Cedar, . . and White Cypress.

white daisy n   **scattered, but chiefly Nth, esp NEast**   See Map

=oxeye daisy 1.

1848 Gray *Manual of Botany* 234, Leucanthemum. . . vulgare. . . Oxeye or White Daisy. Whiteweed. . . A pernicious weed with large and showy heads. **1912** Blatchley *IN Weed Book* 180, Ox-eye Daisy. White Daisy. . . One of the most handsome and popular of our Compositæ yet, where it gets a good start, one of the worst of weeds. **1933** Small *Manual SE Flora* 1470, L[eucanthemum] Leucanthemum. . . White-Daisy. . . Widely distributed in the Southern States in the Civil War. **1965–70** *DARE* (Qu. S26a, . . *Wildflowers. . . Roadside flowers*) 11 Infs, **esp NEast,** White daisy (*or* daisies); **KY**18, White daisies—oxeye daisy; (Qu. S7) Infs **CA**60, **ME**7, White daisy; (Qu. S21, . . *Weeds . . that are a trouble in gardens and fields*) Inf **MI**106, White daisy; **OH**65, Wild white daisy; (Qu. S26d, *Wildflowers that grow in meadows;* not asked in early QRs) 8 Infs, **esp NEast,** White daisy (*or* daisies); (Qu. S26e, *Other wildflowers not yet mentioned;* not asked in early QRs) Inf **PA**122, White daisy; **MD**30, Lee Master's clover—local term for white daisy; (Qu. DD28b, . . *Fermented drinks . . made at home*) Inf **MA**6, White daisy wine. **1969** *DARE* FW Addit **KY**17, White daisy—oxeye daisy.

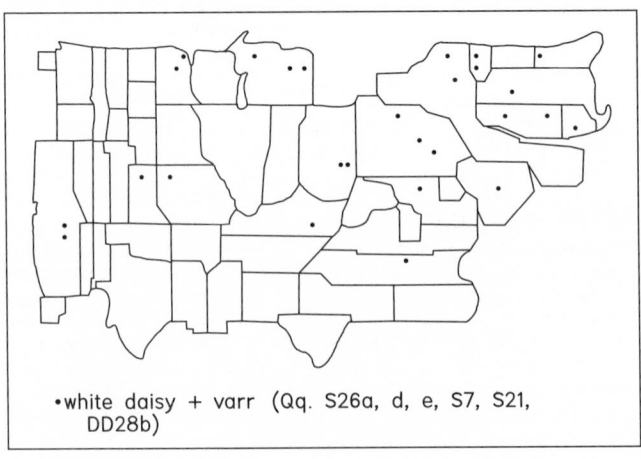

•white daisy + varr (Qq. S26a, d, e, S7, S21, DD28b)

white dock n

A **dock** n[1] (here: usu *Rumex salicifolius,* but also *R. pallidus*).

1824 Bigelow *Florula Bostoniensis* 143, *Rumex pallidus.* White Dock. . . Salt marshes.—June.—Perennial. **1868** (1870) Gray *Field Botany* 290, *R[umex] salicifolius.* . . White D[ock]. . . root white. **1935** (1943) Muenscher *Weeds* 200, *Rumex mexicanus* [=*R. salicifolius* var *m.*] . . Pale dock, Willow-leaved dock, White dock. **1973** Foxfire 2 61, Dock (*Rumex crispa* [=*R. crispus*]) . . (pike plant, curled dock, yellow dock, white dock).

white Dutch clover n Cf **dana clover**

Std: a clover (here: *Trifolium repens*). Also called **Dutch clover a, honeysuckle 1, ladino (clover)**

white dynamite See **dynamite**

white egret n Cf **little white egret**

Either the **snowy egret** or the great egret (*Ardea alba*).

1835 Audubon *Ornith. Biog.* 3.137, [The Louisiana Heron] is at all seasons a social bird, moving about in company with the Blue Heron or the White Egret. *Ibid* 417, The White Egret. *Ardea candidissima* [= *Egretta thula*]. **1898** (1910) Willoughby *Across Everglades* 111 **sFL,** We saw the white egret (plume birds) in every direction. **1968** *DARE* (Qu. Q10, . . *Water birds and marsh birds*) Inf **GA25,** White egret, snowy egret [etc]. **1969** *DARE* FW Addit **Okefenokee GA,** Pond scoggin—the white egret of Okefenokee Swamp. So called formerly by grandmother (from this area). **1994** *Waterloo–Cedar Falls Courier* (IA) 6 June sec B 1/5, Herons and white egrets prowl for fish in the shallows.

white elm n

Std: the American elm, *Ulmus americana.* Also called **feathered elm, red ~ 2, river ~, rock ~ 2, swamp ~, water ~ b, wineglass ~** Cf **buckhorn elm, hard ~**

white-eye n

1 Any of var distilled liquors; see quots. **esp NEng** Cf **white liquor**

1827 *Western Mth. Rev.* 1.320 **Sth,** They found by experience that [whiskey] made them . . more frisky than 'white eye,' as they called New England rum. **1828** *Yankee* (Portland ME) July 227 **swME,** The boy who bears the invitation sometimes carries the empty jugs about with him, as a sort of *bait,* or to let them know that white-eye [New-Rum] will be there. **1830** Ames *Mariner's Sketches* 253 **MA,** In a merchantman, where no liquor is allowed or at farthest, half a gill of 'white-eye,' the great inferiority of the provisions reduces the value of the ration to about thirteen cents. **1872** Burnham *Memoirs U.S. Secret Service* 98, He was well aware that New England "white-eye," like "good wine, will loosen the tongue" wonderfully, at times! **1907** *DN* 3.251 **eME,** *White-eye.* . . A beverage consisting of alcohol and water. **1944** *PADS* 2.14 **NC, VA,** *White-eye,* strong whisky.

2 =**white-eyed vireo.**

1872 Coues *Key to N. Amer. Birds* 119, In the quaint and curious ditty of the white-eye, . . he is insensible who does not hear the echo of thoughts he never clothes in words. **1884** Torrey in *Atlantic Mth.* 54.496 **NEng,** Even at that time . . this white-eye was nearly the only one who was still in song. **1890** Warren *Birds PA* 266, In different sections of Pennsylvania where green briers and blackberry bushes abound, there you will generally find the White-eye. **1895** Minot *Land-Birds New Engl.* 165, I observed a "White-eye" . . on the 18th of October, traveling with many other birds in a "wave." **1903** Dawson *Birds OH* 1.304, Mimicry is the White-eye's specialty.

3 A **walleye** (here: *Stizostedion vitreum vitreum*).

1896 U.S. Natl. Museum *Bulletin* 47.1021, *Stizostedion vitreum.* . . Wall-eyed Pike . . White-eye. **1933** *Woodland Daily Democrat* (CA) 18 Dec 2/6 **Gt Lakes,** Names for Wall-eyed Pike—On the Great Lakes, the wall-eyed pike, white-eye, Jack-salmon [etc].

4 See **white-eyed coot.**

5 See **white-eyed mooneye.**

white-eye v Cf **white-eyed**

1 To be overcome by heat or exhaustion while working; to quit working, quit (on one); hence vbl n *white-eyeing.* **chiefly sAppalachians, esp eKY**

1911 *DN* 3.540 **eKY,** *White-eye on.* To desert, to abandon; e.g., "He white-eyed on us." **1918** Whitaker *Hist. Corporal Fess Whitaker* 31 **KY,** After working one day and a half I white-eyed on account of the

dust. **1928** in 1952 Mathes *Tall Tales* 76 **sAppalachians,** Ye ain't no dawg o' mine if ye go an' white-eye on me now! **1931** *AmSp* 7.94 **eKY,** *White-eye,* to quit work. "Jake'll white-eye on you afore noon if you don't watch him." **1936** *AmSp* 11.373 **TN,** *White-eye,* used as a verb, is, I suspect, a rather recent coinage. It means to be overcome, usually by heat: as, 'I nearly white-eyed, digging in that ditch.' **1944** *PADS* 2.14 **AL,** *White-eye.* . . To become exhausted, to faint from exhaustion. "I almost white-eyed." . . Rural. Sometimes used by standard speakers jocularly. Reported. **1946** Nixon *Lower Piedmont* 138 **neAL,** Seasoned workers sometimes gave out, or "white-eyed," when the sun got hot in summer time. . . He just had to lay down the shovel at times and seek the shade, even if fellow workers embarrassed him by kidding him for "white-eyeing." **1946** *AmSp* 21.192 **seKY,** *White-eye* . . to quit. 'What you studyin' to do? White-eye on me?' **1959** Roberts *Up Cutshin* 14 **seKY,** You talk about white-eying on the job—I come in a pea a-doing it on my first job in the mines. **1976** Garber *Mountain-ese* 101 **sAppalachians,** *White-eyed* . . gave out, quit—Ned white-eyed on me before the job was finished.

2 To knock (one) unconscious.

1991 Norman *Fielder's Choice* 184 **AR,** Bubba had that look like he wouldn't mind getting even for the melon that white-eyed him such a long time ago. **1999** *DARE* File, I'm familiar with this [=*white-eye*] as 'knock unconscious,' as in, "He plumb white-eyed me!"

white-eyed adj

1 pronc-sp *white-eye:* Exhausted, worn out. **chiefly sAppalachians** Cf **white-eye** v 1

1944 *PADS* 2.14 **AL,** *White-eyed.* . . Greatly fatigued, utterly worn out. "I came out just white-eyed." [*PADS* Ed: Also, reported from upper S.C.] **1968** *DARE* File **seKY,** *White-eyed*—worn out. "Ma's white-eyed from hoein'." **1971** Wood *Vocab. Change* 316 **GA, TN,** White eyed . . [Fatigue]. **1972** *Atlanta Letters* **nwGA,** White eyed . . extremely tired and white around the eyes. **1990** Cavender *Folk Med. Lexicon* 34 **sAppalachians,** He's white eye from working in the fields. **1998** in 2004 Montgomery–Hall *Dict. Smoky Mt. Engl.* 646 **TN,** *White eye.* . . "White eyed" is one [word that's not heard much anymore]. I believe it began as a description of one who became faint from fieldwork in the sun and gets pale around the eyes and mouth.

2 Unconscious. Cf **white-eye** v 2

1979 Portis *Dog* 70 **LA,** He'll knock you white-eyed on the least provocation.

white-eyed coot n Also *white-eye*
=**white-winged scoter.**

1903 Huntington *Our Feathered Game* 200, The white-winged scoter. . . This bird is also known as the white-eye and white-winged coot. **1911** *Forest & Stream* 77.173 **MA,** White-Winged Scoter. . . White-Eyed Coot, Manomet, Mass. **1955** MA Audubon Soc. *Bulletin* 39.376 **MA,** White-eye, White-eyed Coot. . . A spot including the eye and the iris of the male are white.

white-eyed mooneye n Also *white-eye*
=**mooneye 1.**

1946 La Monte *N. Amer. Game Fishes* 102, Mooneye—*Hiodon tergisus.* . . Names: White Shad, . . White-eyed Mooneye. **1976** *DARE* File **Isle Royale MI,** Some people call them [=mooneyes] white-eyes.

white-eyed shad n

A **gizzard shad 1** (here: *Dorosoma cepedianum*).

1884 Goode *Fisheries U.S.* 1.610 **eFL,** In the Chesapeake region it is known as the "mud-shad," . . in the Saint John's River as the "Gizzard Shad," "Stink Shad," or "White-eyed Shad."

white-eyed towhee n

A **rufous-sided towhee** (here: *Pipilo erythrophthalmus alleni*).

1874 Coues *Field Ornith.* 41, *Pipilo erythrophthalmus.* . . White-eyed Towhee. **1898** (1900) Davie *Nests N. Amer. Birds* 396, The Florida or White-eyed Towhee has been found breeding as far north as Beaufort county, South Carolina. **1938** Matschat *Suwannee R.* 219 **neFL, seGA,** They crossed a pine bluff where white-eyed towhees and yellowthroats were plentiful among the palmetto scrub. **1954** *Post-Std.* (Syracuse NY) 16 May 6/1 **FL,** White-eyed towhees called and flashed about in the sun. **2001** *DARE* File—Internet **FL,** The White-eyed Towhee. There is a Florida race . . that has a distinct white eye. I have seen it.

white-eyed vireo n

Std: an eastern **vireo** (*Vireo griseus*) whose eyes have a distinctive white iris. Also called **hanging bird 2, hangnest bird, white-eye** n **2**

white-eyeing See **white-eye** v phr **1**

whiteface n
=**baldpate 1.**
 1709 (1967) Lawson *New Voyage* 155 **NC, SC,** The bald, or white Faces are a good Fowl. They cannot dive, and are easily shotten. **1923** U.S. Dept. Ag. *Misc. Circular* 13.12 **NY, NC,** Baldpate. . . Vernacular Names. . . whiteface.

white-face black hornet See **white-faced hornet**

white-faced calf n Cf **government beef**
 1965–70 DARE (Qu. P35a, *Names or nicknames for any deer shot illegally*) Infs **MO**32, **NY**227, White-faced calf; **KS**15, **NC**85, **WI**62, White-faced calf [FW sugg]; **NY**35, 89, White-faced calf [FW: Infs have heard]; **OK**52, I got a white-faced calf the other day; **SC**69, White-faced calf—what hunters tell the game warden they thought they saw.

white-faced hornet n Also *white-face (black) hornet* **chiefly NEast** See Map Cf **striped-ass (hornet), white-tailed hornet**
=**bald-faced hornet.**
 1881 Torrey Bot. Club *Bulletin* 8.68 **cNY,** After a while I succeeded in detecting a white-faced hornet *(Vespa maculata)* in the act of cutting these holes with its mandibles. **1882** *Century Illustr. Mag.* 24.211, A white-faced hornet hurtles by. **1924** *Kingston Daily Freeman* (NY) 18 Mar 2/1, Now there is Mr. White-Faced Hornet and his family. **1939** LANE Map 240–41 *(Hornet)* **esp wCT,** [Of 26 infs responding *white-face(d) hornet,* 20 were in Connecticut; of these, 17 were west of the Connecticut River.] **1965–70** DARE (Qu. R21, . . *Other kinds of stinging insects*) 13 Infs, 12 **NEast,** White-face(d) hornet; **NY**233, White-faced hornet—when he hits you, you raise right up; **VT**13, White-face black hornet. **2007** DARE File—Internet, The Bald faced hornet (Dolichovespula maculata) is sometimes called the white-faced hornet, but is actually a yellowjacket.

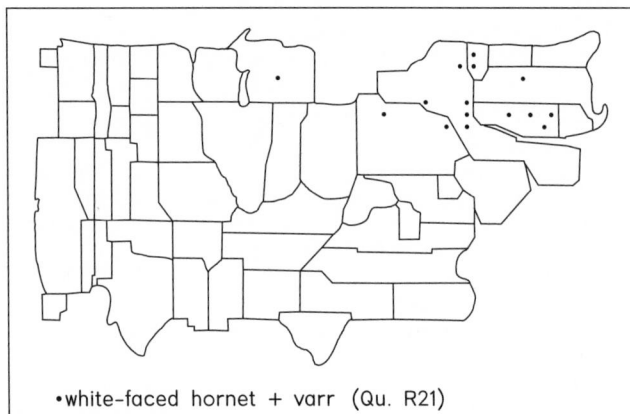

•white-faced hornet + varr (Qu. R21)

white-faced ibis n
 Std: an American ibis *(Plegadis chihi)* found chiefly in the Gulf States and California; in breeding plumage it exhibits white feathers surrounding the lores and eyes. Also called **black bec-croche, ~ curlew, bronze curlew, glossy ibis 2, Mexican curlew**

white-faced owl n Also *white-headed owl*
=**barn owl 1.**
 1911 Houghton *Exped. Donner Party* 274, It was the old white-faced owl leaving the hollow in the live oak for the night's hunt. **1967–69** DARE (Qu. Q2, . . *Kinds of owls*) Inf **PA**26, White-faced owl; **IL**48, White-headed owl. **1969** *Mt. Democrat & Placerville Times* (CA) 27 Mar sec B 5/8 **FL,** Coons, possums and a big, white-faced owl were hunting the frogs.

white-face hornet See **white-faced hornet**

white fir n
 1 Std: a fir tree *(Abies concolor)* of the western US. Also called **balsam 5, ~ fir, ~ tree c, bastard pine 2, black bal-**

sam 2, ~ gum 2, Colorado fir, piss ~, silver ~ 2c, white balsam 2
 2 Any of var other chiefly western firs, as:
a =**grand fir.**
 1857 U.S. War Dept. *Rept. Explor. Railroad* (Botany) 6.49 **OR,** We first met with *P[inus] grandis* near McCumber's. . . On the Columbia and Willamette it is known as the "white fir," to distinguish it from the "red fir" *(Abies Douglasii).* **1863** Hittell *Resources CA* 96, The Western balsam-fir *(Picea grandis),* or white fir, attains a height of one hundred and fifty feet. **1881** Muir in *Scribner's Mth.* 22.921 **CA,** Grand silver-fir. White-fir. *(Picea grandis).* . . In its younger days, *Picea grandis* is a strikingly symmetrical tree . . with its branches regularly whorled in level collars around the whitish-gray axis. **1897** Sudworth *Arborescent Flora* 54 **CA, OR, ID,** *Abies grandis.* . . Common Names. . . White Fir (Cal., Oreg., Idaho). *Ibid,* Oregon White Fir (Cal.). Western White Fir. Grand or Oregon White Fir (Cal. lit.) **1908** Rogers *Tree Book* 81, The White Fir . . earns its name by the silvery lining of its leaves. **1938** Van Dersal *Native Woody Plants* 36, *Abies grandis.* . . Lowland white fir. **1950** *San Antonio Sun. Light* (TX) 10 Sept sec E 2/3, More than 90 per cent of white fir in the western pine region is abies amabilis, abies concolor, abies grandis or abies magnifica.
b =**alpine fir.**
 1897 Sudworth *Arborescent Flora* 53 **ID, MT,** *Abies lasiocarpa.* . . Common Names. . . White Fir. **1908** Britton *N. Amer. Trees* 77, White Fir—*Abies lasiocarpa.* . . This Fir, variously called White balsam fir, Oregon balsam fir [etc] . . has probably a greater range than any other American Fir. **1972** Viereck–Little *AK Trees* 62, Subalpine Fir. . . Other names: alpine fir, white fir (lumber). **1976** Elmore *Shrubs & Trees SW* 175, Subalpine Fir—Alpine fir, "balsam" fir, "white" fir, . . blanco de las sierras [mountain white (fir)].
c =**silver fir 2a.**
 1908 Sudworth *Forest Trees Pacific* 125, Amabilis fir is known by woodsmen as "white" fir or "silver" fir, from the white, smooth bark. Woodsmen distinguished it from the grand fir *(Abies grandis),* also called white fir, as "another variety." **1922** Sargent *Manual Trees* 56, *Abies amabilis.* . . White Fir. Leaves deeply grooved, very dark green and lustrous on the upper surface, silvery white on the lower. **1950** [see **2a** above].
d =**noble fir.**
 1910 OR State Bd. Forestry *Official Proc.* Feb 42, Noble fir. . . Like all the white firs, it is variously called fir, white fir, balsam [etc]. **1973** Hitchcock–Cronquist *Flora Pacific NW* 61, Noble, red, or white f[ir]. . . *A[bies] procera.* **1980** Little *Audubon Guide N. Amer. Trees W. Region* 36, Noble Fir. . . "White Fir". . . The largest native true fir.
e =**red fir b.**
 1950 [see **2a** above].

whitefish n
 1 A salmonid fish of the subfamily Coregoninae, as:
a A **cisco,** usu *Coregonus clupeaformis.* For other names of the latter see **gizzard fish 1, humpback whitefish b, lake ~, Otsego (Lake) bass, shad 3**
 [**1748** Ellis *Voyage* 185 *(OED2)* **Canada,** Called by the *French,* White Fish, but by the *Indians* and *English,* Titymagg.] **1791** Long *Voyages & Travels* 43 **nMI,** At this place [=Sault Ste. Marie] there is abundance of fine fish, particularly pickerill, trout, and white fish. **1814** in 1815 *Lit. & Philos. Soc. NY Trans.* 1.495, At the head of the western fishes, may be placed the *white fish,* which is universally admitted to be the most delicious. . . I am induced to believe, that it belongs to the salmo genus. **1842** DeKay *Zool. NY* 4.247, *Coregonus albus.* . . is the celebrated *White-fish* of the lakes, which is most abundant in Lake Huron, but is occasionally found in Lake Erie. **1902** Jordan–Evermann *Amer. Fishes* 23, Common Whitefish. . . This important and delicious food-fish is known also as humpback, bowback and highback whitefish (Lake Superior). **1903** NY State Museum & Sci. Serv. *Bulletin* 60.225, *Coregonus clupeiformis.* . . The name whitefish is thoroughly identified with this species and is seldom varied except by means of the prefix "common" or "lake." **1947** Hubbs–Lagler *Fishes Gt. Lakes* 43, Great Lakes whitefish—*Coregonus clupeaformis clupeaformis.* **1965–70** DARE (Qu. P1, . . *Kinds of freshwater fish . . caught around here . . good to eat*) 35 Infs, 32 **Gt Lakes,** Whitefish; (Qu. P14, . . *Commercial fishing . . what do the fishermen go out after*) 25 Infs, 24 **Gt Lakes,** Whitefish; **NY**132, Lake Erie whitefish; (Qu. H45, *Dishes made with meat, fish, or poultry that everybody around here would know, but that people in other places might not*) Inf **NY**119, Boiled whitefish; **WI**72, Whitefish livers;

(Qu. H49, *Dishes made by boiling potatoes with other foods*) Inf **NY**119, Boiled whitefish; (Qu. P3, *Freshwater fish that are not good to eat*) Inf **PA**155, Whitefish. [*DARE* Ed: Some of these Infs may refer instead to other senses below.] **1966–69** *DARE* Tape **MI**21, Whitefish is a fish that's got a tendency to lead, and if you got a shallow net, you haven't got much of a lead for it; **MI**29, We had quite a few walleyes and a few whitefish, too; **MI**109, There haven't been too many whitefish last few years. **1974** WI Univ. *Fish Lake MI* 12, The whitefish has always been a prime commercial target, prized for the delectable quality of its meat. **1991** Amer. Fisheries Soc. *Common Names Fishes* 27, *Coregonus huntsmani.* . . Atlantic whitefish.

b =**inconnu.**

[**1870** Dall *Alaska* 579, Fresh-water Fishes of the Yukon. . . *Luciotrutta leucichthys* [=*Stenodus l.*] . . Great Whitefish.] **1909** (1910) W.T. Lopp in *Report on Education in Alaska* app li (Tabbert *Dict. Alaskan Engl.*), In the fall they [of "Pinokameet" above Bethel] get a large quantity of whitefish, known at Kotzebue as "sheah," and considered by some to be the best fish in Alaska. **1952** Giddings *Arctic Woodland* 3, The Arctic shee, a variety of whitefish, sometimes reaches a weight of over sixty pounds. **1968** *DARE* (Qu. P1, . . *Kinds of freshwater fish . . caught around here . . good to eat*) Inf **AK**9, Whitefish—delicacy; (Qu. P17, . . *When . . people fish by lowering a line and sinker close to the bottom of the water*) Inf **AK**9, Whitefish set.

c A fish of the genus *Prosopium,* esp *P. williamsoni.* For other names of the latter see **freshwater herring 1, mountain ~, mountain whitefish, Rocky Mountain ~ 1;** for other names of *P. cylindraceum* see **round whitefish**

1881 *Forest & Stream* 16.456, Of the "Winnepesaukee whitefish," or "shad-waiter" (*Prosopium quadrilateralis* [=*P. cylindraceum*]), 60,000 eggs were taken and evenly divided with Massachusetts. **1884** Goode *Fisheries U.S.* 1.542, Rocky Mountain White-fish—Coregonus Williamsoni. This species is usually known as the White-fish. **1949** Caine *N. Amer. Sport Fish* 163, The Rocky Mountain whitefish is considered by many to be the most gamy member of the whitefish family. **1963** Sigler–Miller *Fishes UT* 59, Whitefish are caught most readily during the winter months. **1972** Sparano *Outdoors Encycl.* 358, Montana whitefish. . . *Prosopium williamsoni.*

2 A **menhaden 1** (here: *Brevoortia tyrannus*). **NEast**

1806 Webster *Elements Useful Knowledge* 2.84, Alewives are caught in vast numbers for foreign markets, and menhaden or white fish, for manuring land. **a1817** (1821) Dwight *Travels* 2.343 **NEng,** Fields, manured with the white fish, have yielded wheat, universally, in great abundance. . . The white-fish is a species of herring, very fat and oily, and remarkably favourable to vegetation of every kind. **1848** (1851) Mather–Brockett *Geogr. Hist. NY* 165, There are large tracts [in Suffolk County], however, of highly fertile land, which, manured with ashes, seaweed, and the fertilizing mossbonker, or whitefish, yield ample crops. **1878** *Amer. Naturalist* 12.735, From the eastern boundary of Connecticut to the mouth of the Connecticut river the name "bony-fish" predominates, while in the western part of the State the species is usually known as the "white-fish." **1967–68** *DARE* (Qu. P4, *Saltwater fish that are not good to eat*) Inf **CT**14, Whitefish—used for fertilizer; (Qu. P2, . . *Kinds of saltwater fish caught around here . . good to eat*) Infs **MD**36, **NY**34, Whitefish. [*DARE* Ed: Some of these Infs may refer instead to other senses.]

3 The beluga or white whale (*Delphinapterus leucas*). [*OED2* 1743 →]

1859 *New Amer. Cyclop.* 6.556, The whitefish, or white whale (*B[eluga] borealis,* Less.), is a very swift dolphin, of a beautiful cream-white color. **1869** Acad. Nat. Sci. Philadelphia *Proc. for 1869* 57, The Whitefish.—Beluga sp.? My opportunities for observing the habits of the Whitefish, as termed by the American whalemen, have been as follows. **1879** U.S. Natl. Museum *Bulletin* 14.10, *Delphinapterus catodon* [=*D. leucas*]. . . White-fish or White Whale.—Arctic and Subarctic Seas. **1911** U.S. Bur. Census *Fisheries 1908* 307, Beluga. . . It is also called "white whale," "whitefish" [etc]. [**1955** U.S. Arctic Info. Center *Gloss.* 88, *Whitefish.* . . A Canadian name for the white whale.]

4 =**bluefish 1.**

1873 Baird *Rept. Condition Sea Fisheries* 235, *Pomatomus saltatrix.* . . The young bear the name of skip-mackerel about New York, and white-fish higher up the Hudson River.

5 =**squawfish 2.**

1884 U.S. Natl. Museum *Bulletin* 27.487, *Ptychochilus oregonensis.* . . "whitefish." Rivers of the Pacific slope, chiefly west of the Sierra Nevada. **1963** Sigler–Miller *Fishes UT* 78, Colorado Squawfish. . . Common Names . . Colorado salmon, whitefish [etc]. **1969** *DARE* (Qu. P3, *Freshwater fish that are not good to eat*) Infs **CA**114, 120, 136, 147, 163, Whitefish; **CA**130, Whitefish—actually a member of the pike family; all bone, very little meat. [*DARE* Ed: Some of these Infs may refer instead to other senses.] **1976** Tryckare et al. *Lore of Sportfishing* 82, Northern Squawfish. . . Other common names . . whitefish, chub [etc]. **1998** Frankenberger–Engberg *Environmental Chem.* 299 **CO,** Many noted how good Colorado "whitefish" (Colorado squawfish) tasted.

6 =**peamouth.**

1893 U.S. Fish Comm. *Bulletin for 1891* 43 **MT,** *Mylocheilus caurinus.* . . Curiously enough, at Flathead Lake it is called "whitefish" and is served at the hotels as such. **1902** Jordan–Evermann *Amer. Fishes* 73 **ID, MT, OR, WA,** The name "whitefish" for this minnow [=*Mylocheilus caurinus*] . . is used not only on Snake River, but at Flathead Lake and perhaps elsewhere. **1965–70** *DARE* (Qu. P1, . . *Kinds of freshwater fish . . caught around here . . good to eat*) 9 Infs, 7 **NW,** Whitefish; (Qu. P3, *Freshwater fish that are not good to eat*) Infs **OR**1, **WA**20, 30, Whitefish. [*DARE* Ed: Some of these Infs may refer instead to other senses above.]

7 A mushroom; see quot. **Ozarks** Cf **dry-land fish 1**

1933 *AmSp* 8.1.53 **Ozarks,** *Whitefish.* . . Mushrooms. Most hillfolk do not eat mushrooms at all, but those who do usually call them whitefish—perhaps because they roll them in cornmeal and fry in deep grease, like fish.

white-flowered milkweed n

A **milkweed 1** (here: *Asclepias variegata*).

1919 Dunn *Indiana* 80, They [=the Miamis] do not eat the shoots . . of the white-flowered milkweed, which they . . pronounce poisonous. **1970** Correll *Plants TX* 1228, White-flowered milkweed. . . One of the most beautiful of all milkweeds. **1979** Ajilvsgi *Wild Flowers* 233, White-flowered milkweed. . . herbaceous perennial to 3 ½ feet tall.

white-flowering raspberry n

A **thimbleberry** (here: *Rubus parviflorus*).

1848 Gray *Manual of Botany* 125, *R[ubus] Nutkanus* [=*R. parviflorus*]. . . (White Flowering Raspberry). . . Upper Michigan, and northwestward along the Lakes. **1875** *Amer. Cyclop.* 14.209, The white-flowering raspberry, *R. Nutkanus,* was first discovered at Nootka on the N.W. coast. **1936** McDougall–Baggley *Plants of Yellowstone* 73, Whiteflowering raspberry *(Rubus parviflorus).*—This is a shrub with stems 3 to 6 feet high. **1995** Epple *Field Guide Plants AZ* 101, Thimbleberry. . . white-flowering raspberry.

white-footed mouse n

Std: a mouse of the genus *Peromyscus,* esp *P. leucopus.* Also called **deer mouse.** For other names of *P. leucopus* see **buck mouse, jumping ~ 2;** for other names of var spp see **cotton mouse, country ~, gopher ~ 1, piñon ~, scorpion ~ 2, wood ~ 1**

white forget-me-not See forget-me-not 1d, f, 7

white fox n

A **bonefish 1** (here: *Albula vulpes*).

[**1964** *Time* 31 Jan 50, There is one little fish found in the world's warm waters that sends salt-water anglers into shivering ecstasy and rates up with the monster marlin and tuna. The name is bonefish (*Albula vulpes,* literally white fox).] **1975** Evanoff *Catch More Fish* 216, The bonefish, (*Albula vulpes*) is also known as the white ghost, gray ghost, white fox [etc].

white fringe (tree) n

A **fringe tree:** usu *Chionanthus virginicus,* but also *C. pygmaeus.*

1822 Prince *Catalogue Linnaean Botanic Garden* 36 **NY,** Snowdrop, or white fringe tree, with flowers resembling cut paper. . . Chionanthus virginica. **1828** Prince *Short Treatise Horticult.* 92, Snowdrop, or *White Fringe Tree.*—Of this there are two species, both natives of the United States. **1837** (1962) Williams *Territory FL* 83, White Fringe tree. *Chionanthus virginica.* **1878** *Scribner's Mth.* 17.151, *Chionanthus Virginica,* the white fringe, old, well-known and choice, is not usually spoken of for its autumnal beauty. **1897** Sudworth *Arborescent Flora* 332 **MA, PA, RI,** *Chionanthus virginica.* . . Common Names. . . White Fringe [etc]. **c1979** TX Dept. Highways *Flowers* 31, White Fringe-tree, named for the small white flowers hanging like fringe, is found in the humid woodlands of Southeast Texas.

white frog n

A southeastern **gopher frog** (here: *Rana capito*).

1958 Conant *Reptiles & Amphibians* 305, Florida gopher frog. . . The light ground color has earned this species the name of "white frog." The coloration varies from creamy white to brown through various shades of yellow or purplish. **2003** (acc) *Jacksonville Zoo* (Internet) **FL,** One of the nicknames for this frog [=the Florida gopher frog] is "White Frog."

white-fronted goose n   Also *American white-fronted goose*

Std: a large gray-brown goose (*Anser albifrons* and subspp) that in North America breeds in Alaska and northern Canada and winters in Mexico and along the Gulf and Pacific coasts of the US. Also called **checkerbelly, Chinese goose, gray brant 1, ~ goose 2, ~ wavey 1, laughing goose, marblebelly, Mexican brant, ~ goose 1c, mottled brant, pied ~, specklebelly 1, Texas goose 2, tiger ~, timber ~, tule ~, yellowlegs 3, wavey 2**

white-fronted owl n

=**saw-whet owl.**

1811 Wilson *Amer. Ornith.* 4.67, Turton describes a species called the White-fronted Owl, *(S. albifrons).* **1859** Goodrich *Illustr. Nat. Hist.* 75, The White-fronted Owl or Kirtland's Owl, *N[yctala] albifrons,* resembles the Acadian Owl, and has been regarded by some as identical with it. **1874** Coues *Birds NW* 315, The so-called "White-fronted Owl," *Strix albifrons, S. frontalis,* and *N. kirtlandii,* of various authors, was simply the young of the present species [=the Acadian or saw-whet owl].

white fulton n   Cf **blue fulton**

=**blue catfish 1** or **channel catfish.**

1888 IL Bd. Fish Comms. *Report* 80, Willow Cat, Channel Cat, White Fulton (*Ictalurus punctatus,* Raf.) **1908** Forbes–Richardson *Fishes of IL* 179, It [=*Ictalurus furcatus*] is called "White Fulton" by those who apply to the smaller species *(I. punctatus)* the name "blue Fulton." **1967** [see **white catfish 1**].

white gale n

A windstorm on the water with rough seas, a clear sky, and no precipitation.

[**1834** Howison *European Colonies* 2.347, The North Atlantic is remarkable for a peculiar kind of tempest which occurs nowhere else in so marked and distinct a form. This is called by mariners a white gale, because it is unaccompanied with that obscurity of the atmosphere, and that showery weather, which in general attend violent winds in all parts of the ocean.] **1986** MA Univ.–Amherst *Campus Chron.* 5 Sept 6, *White Gale Strands Campus Crew in Edgartown Harbor.* . . The captain blamed the mishap on "a white gale" which caused whitecaps and 8-foot swells in Nantucket Sound, and wind gusts to 40 miles per hour, but which left the skies blue, and the town comfortable. **1986** *DARE* File seMA, *White gale*—Strong winds, usually in advance of a storm center, producing high seas and whitecaps, but leaving the sky relatively clear and free of precipitation.

white gannet n

=**gannet 1.**

1862 in 1894 U.S. Navy Dept. *Official Records Union & Confederate Navies* 815, The north islet seems to be divided between the white gannet (with lower edges of its wings black) and the black warrior. **1898** (1900) Davie *Nests N. Amer. Birds* 63, The White Gannet, or Solan Goose, is widely distributed throughout the Northern Atlantic Ocean. **1955** MA Audubon Soc. *Bulletin* 39.311 **MA,** White Gannet.

white gentian n   Cf **white ginseng**

A **horse gentian** (here: *Triosteum perfoliatum*).

1787 Schöpf *Materia Medica Amer.* 23, *Triosteum perfoliatum.* . . White Gentian. **1817** Barton *Vegetable Materia Medica* 1.59, Feverroot. . . White Gentian. . . Triosteum Perfoliatum. **1848** [see **white ginseng**]. **1867** *Scientific Amer.* 16.340, The alkaline properties are got rid of by soaking the skins in an infusion of white gentian in fresh water for twenty-four hours. **1948** Stevens *KS Wild Flowers* 357, Various vernacular names have been given to this species: horse gentian, . . white gentian, genson, and feverwort.

white ghost n

A **bonefish 1** (here: *Albula vulpes*).

1975 [see **white fox**].

white ginseng n   Cf **white gentian**

A **horse gentian** (here: *Triosteum perfoliatum*).

1830 Rafinesque *Med. Flora* 2.269, Triosteum perfoliatum. . . *Wild Coffee, White Ginseng.* **1848** Dunglison *Med. Lexicon* 858, T[riosteum] Perfoliatum. . . White Ginseng, . . White Gentian. **1892** (1974) Millspaugh *Amer. Med. Plants* 74-1, *Fever-wort.* . . Com. Names. . . Horse-gentian, or Ginseng; White Ginseng [etc].

white goat n

=**mountain goat.**

1857 U.S. War Dept. *Rept. Explor. Railroad* 8.671, The white goat of the Rocky Mountains is, in all its essential features and affinities, a true antelope. **1877** Hallock *Sportsman's Gaz.* 40, The White Goat is confined to the loftiest peaks of the Rocky Mountains. **1917** Anthony *Mammals Amer.* 58, From the color of its fleece, it is sometimes called the White Goat. **1982** Elman *Hunter's Field Guide* 518, Mountain Goat. . . Common & Regional Names: *Rocky Mountain goat, white goat.*

white goldenrod n   chiefly **NEast**

A **goldenrod 1** (here: *Solidago bicolor*).

1814 Bigelow *Florula Bostoniensis* 195 **eMA,** Solidago bicolor. . . *White Golden rod.* . . Dry woods. **1832** MA Hist. Soc. *Coll.* 2d ser 9.156 **cwVT,** [Solidago] bicolor, White golden-rod. **1853** NY State Museum *Catalogue Cabinet Nat. Hist.* 21, Solidago bicolor, White Goldenrod. **1898** *Jrl. Amer. Folkl.* 11.230 **ME,** White goldenrod, silver rod, South Berwick. **1947** *Gaz. & Bulletin* (Williamsport PA) 22 Oct 6/7, Solidago bicolor or white goldenrod.

white grama n

1 A **muhly grass** (here: *Muhlenbergia porteri* or *M. torreyi*).

1872 Bourke *Diary* 15 Dec **AZ,** Hills to-day well grassed with blue & white grama. **1941** *Torreya* 41.46 **AZ,** *Muhlenbergia porteri.* . . Bush grama, . . white grama, Tucson, Ariz.

2 A **grama grass 1** (here: *Bouteloua gracilis,* formerly *B. oligostachya*).

1890 Soc. Promotion Ag. Sci. *Proc.* 110, Bouteloua oligostachya. . . White Grama. **1912** Wooton–Standley *Grasses NM* 97, Probably over one third of the total area of range land in New Mexico is more or less completely occupied by the best known Grama Grass (*Bouteloua oligostachya*) which goes under the names "Blue Grama," "White Grama" or more rarely "Crowfoot Grama." . . Why the adjective blue is applied to this grass is not apparent, . . and white is . . unexplainable unless it be in contrast to "Black Grama."

white grass n

A grass of the genus *Leersia,* usu *L. virginica.*

1818 Eaton *Botany* 298, Leersia. . . *lenticularis* (white grass). **1856** MI State Ag. Soc. *Trans. for 1855* 7.411, Leersia . . virginica. . . White-grass. **1889** *Century Dict.* 3398, Three species occur in the United States, and are known as *white-grass,* especially *L[eersia] Virginica. L. oryzoides* is the rice cut-grass, and *L. lenticularis* the fly catch grass. **1892** *AN&Q* 9.18, "Rice's Cousin" is in some parts of this country a popular name for a kind of grass, *Leersia oryzoides,* which resembles the true rice. It is also called white grass, cut grass, etc. It has no special value. **1940** Gates *Flora KS* 130, Leersia virginica. . . Cutgrass, Whitegrass. Moist or wet ground along streams and in woods. **1950** Stevens *ND Plants* 79, Leersia virginica. . . Whitegrass.

white gravy n   chiefly **Sth, S Midl**   See Map   Cf **cream gravy, flour ~, white sop**

Light-colored gravy, now usu consisting mainly of grease, unbrowned flour, and often milk.

1832 Lee *Cook's Own Book* 215, Stock, for gravy soup or gravy. . . When thus prepared it will serve either for soup, or brown or white gravy. **1851** Webster *Improved Housewife* 76, *Virginia Chicken Pudding.* . . White gravy for sauce. **1876** *Atlantic Mth.* 38.514 **WA,** The . . melting biscuits, and broiled chicken, with rich, white gravy, heightened the effect of her words. **1879** (1965) Tyree *Housekeeping in Old VA* 161, *Roast Veal.* . . Thicken the gravy with brown flour, if brown gravy is wanted, but always with mashed Irish potato if white gravy is desired. **1884** Roosevelt *Superior Fishing* 341 **NY,** White gravy is made as already directed for fish. For brown gravy, a little flour is heated in a frying-pan, and stirred till it is brown. *Ibid* 343, Make a white gravy of flour and butter. **1932** (1946) Hibben *Amer. Regional Cookery* 64 **TX,** Tomatoes and Eggs with White Gravy. . . Without washing the skillet in which the bacon has been fried, put in 2 teaspoons of butter . . add flour and cook over low heat. . . Pour in the milk gradually. **1959** Faulkner

Mansion 65 **MS,** You could eat . . twice as much fried sowbelly and white gravy. **1965–70** *DARE* (Qu. H37, . . *Words . . for gravy. Any joking ones?*) Infs **KY37, TN49,** White gravy; **KY22,** White gravy—grease in the skillet, add flour, brown, then add milk or milk and water; **KY28,** White gravy—don't brown flour; **KY84,** White gravy—same as milk gravy, flour gravy; **LA33,** White gravy—a little grease, water, and whatever you use with it—potatoes, etc. **TN30,** White gravy (or thickened gravy) is made by lightly browning slightly some flour in this fat in pan and adding milk; **TN37,** White gravy is the same [as cream gravy—made with bacon fat . . flour . . and cream] except that plain milk or half water and half milk is used; **VA13,** White gravy—meat juice and water, no thickening. **1977** *Albuquerque Jrl.* (NM) 17 Sept sec C 5/6, The Mississippi boys like bland food, white gravy. If you're from Louisiana, everything has to be highly spiced. **2007** in 2008 *DARE* File—Internet, I grew up in Michigan, and never encountered white gravy. . . I went to grad school in southern Indiana, where I first encountered white gravy. It wasn't used extensively, but could be found. . . I moved to Oklahoma about 13 years ago. It's mostly white gravy down here. Sausage gravy on biscuits, cream gravy on chicken-fried steak . . , on mashed potatoes, or pretty much anything. You'll occasionally see brown gravy, but not often. *Ibid* **Sth,** For me, white gravy has always been a staple in our home. There were many times as a child when all we had was white gravy. . . and *lots* of times it was made with water, not milk.

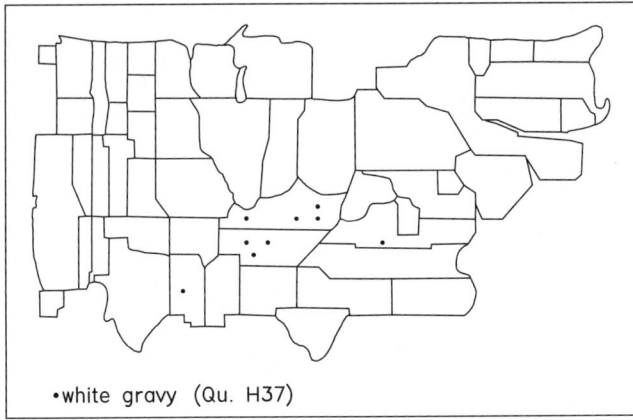

•white gravy (Qu. H37)

white grouper n

A **grouper 1a** (here: *Epinephelus striatus*).

1903 Holder *Big Game Fishes* 221 **FL,** I never saw a black grouper, a "white grouper," or a red grouper in the market at Key West. **1935** Caine *Game Fish* 72, Nassau Grouper—*Epinephilus strialus* [sic]. . . *Synonyms*. . . White Grouper [etc]. **1989** *N. Hills News Rec.* (Allison Park PA) [15 July 4/2] (newspaperarchive.com), [Advt:] Boneless White Grouper lb. $2.69.

white grouse n

1 =**ptarmigan.** [*OED2* 1797 →]

1840 Goodrich *Peter Parley's Animal Kingdom* 99, The White Grouse or Ptarmigan is found in Europe, . . but in America it is confined to the Arctic regions. [**1873** *Atlantic Mth.* 31.676 **Canada,** Several years ago the districts lying along the southern bank of the St. Lawrence, far away below Quebec, were visited by vast numbers of ptarmigans, or white grouse.] **1917** (1923) *Birds Amer.* 2.20, Willow Ptarmigan. . . Other Names.—Ptarmigan; . . white grouse; Snow Grouse.

2 =**sharp-tailed grouse.**

1884 *Forest & Stream* 24.344 **MN,** This was the "sharptailed grouse," though generally called the "white grouse." **1888** Trumbull *Names of Birds* 139, Sharp-tailed Grouse. . . Popularly known also as *white-belly,* and in some localities as *white grouse,* the latter name immediately suggesting the ptarmigans . . , but to people familiar with our live sharptails, the word "white" seems rather appropriately applied, as the birds display so much of their white while flying. **1953** Jewett *Birds WA* 212, Columbian Sharp-tailed Grouse. . . Other names: Prairie Chicken, . . White Grouse.

white grub n esp Nth See Map

The larva of a **June bug 1.**

a1817 (1821) Dwight *Travels* 1.77 **NEng,** The *white-grub* has . . extensively injured meadows, and pastures. **1823** *Amer. Farmer* 5.190 **PA,** Last year my [strawberry] plants were attacked by the White Grub. **1871** IL Dept. Ag. *Trans.* 8.172, The manure is . . instrumental in breed-

ing the white-grub (May-beetle), which often ruins our meadows and strawberry beds. **1882** (1903) Treat *Injurious Insects* 73, Comparatively few are aware that the frequent White Grub and the familiar May-bug, or June-bug, or Dor-bug, are different forms of the same insect. **1954** Borror-DeLong *Intro. Insects* 388, [Caption:] White grubs (*Phyllophaga* sp.) **1966–69** *DARE* (Qu. P6, . . *Kinds of worms . . used for bait*) Infs **MI2, PA192, VA33, VT16,** White grub; **MI47,** White grubs—1¼–1½" long; I don't like 'em; (Qu. R27, . . *Kinds of caterpillars or similar worms*) Inf **MA74,** White grubs—get into potatoes.

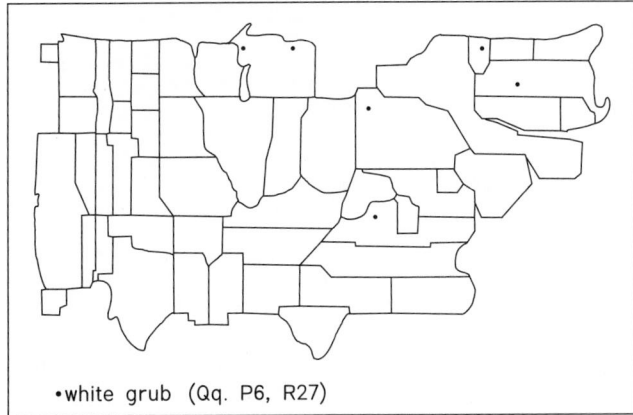

•white grub (Qq. P6, R27)

white grunt n

A **grunt n 1;** see quots.

1877 *Amer. Jrl. Science* 3d ser 14.292, Haemylum capeuna [=*Haemulon striatum*]. . . White Grunt. **1904** *Outing* 43.616 **seFL,** The most distinguishing mark on the common grunts is a series of narrow, irregular lines on the head, and sometimes on other parts of the body, of different colors—hence the name of yellow grunt, white grunt, black grunt, etc. **1933** John G. Shedd Aquarium *Guide* 109, *Bathystoma striatum* [= *Haemulon s.*] . . White Grunt. A small grunt of the West Indies and the Florida Keys, this fish is often mistaken for the young of other similar species. **1946** La Monte *N. Amer. Game Fishes* 66, White Grunt. . . Names: Boca Colorado, . . Squirrelfish [etc]. **2002** *DARE* File—Internet **wFL,** They [=*Haemulon aurolineatum*] look very similar to the white grunt that we all call "grey snapper" (it sounds better for the tourists than grunt), but they have a spot on the tail.

white gull n

Usu =**herring gull,** but also =**ring-billed gull.**

1792 Belknap *Hist. NH* 3.169, White Gull, *Larus canus.* **1852** in 1876 *Forest & Stream* 7.212, L[arus] argentatus. Adult, white; young, gray gull. **1932** Bennitt *Check-list* 33 **MO,** Herring gull. . . White gull; gray gull. C[ommon] W[inter] R[esident] throughout the state. *Ibid,* Ring-billed gull. . . White gull; gray gull. **1956** MA Audubon Soc. *Bulletin* 40.22 **NH, MA,** Herring Gull . . ; White Gull . . Adults, except for the mantle and wings, are white.

white gum n

1 also *white sweet gum:* =**sweet gum** or its wood—used esp (in contrast to **red gum**) to distinguish specimens in which the whitish sapwood predominates.

1739 (1946) Gronovius *Flora Virginica* 41, Sweet-gum. White-gum. **1851** *De Bow's Rev.* 11.45 **LA,** Pre-eminent among the forest trees stands the *gum*. . . There are three kinds known here, viz. the *white* and *red* sweet gum, and the *black gum, nyssa sylvatica.* **1876** Hobbs *Bot. Hdbk.* 128, White gum, Sweet gum, Liquidambar styraciflua. **1919** Besley-Dorrance *Wood-Using MD* 52, The marked difference between the sapwood and the heartwood . . has led many manufacturers to distinguish two species—the white sapwood being called white gum, while the dark red heart is called red gum. **1968–69** *DARE* (Qu. T15, . . *Kinds of swamp trees*) Infs **KY11, MD36,** White gum. [*DARE* Ed: These Infs may refer instead to **2** below.] **1985** *Capital* (Annapolis MD) 29 Mar 33/8, Thence to a maple tree; thence to a marked white gum tree.

2 A **tupelo gum** (here: *Nyssa aquatica*).

1909 U.S. Bur. Census *Forest Products U.S. 1908* 10.42, Included under tupelo is also some lumber cut from other species of the genus *Nyssa* and known locally as pepperidge, black gum, white gum, etc. **1911** U.S. Forest Serv. *Bulletin* 103.14 **NC,** Cotton Gum. *Nyssa aquatica.* . . *Common names in use.* . . White gum [etc]. **1940** *Gleanings Bee Cul-*

ture 68.147 **nFL,** There are two varieties of tupelo tree, white or cotton gum . . , and black or sour gum. . . White gum . . [makes] the lighter and better product of the two. **1967** *DARE* (Qu. T15, . . *Kinds of swamp trees*) Inf **LA**7, Red gum grows bigger than white gum. [*DARE* Ed: This Inf may refer instead to **1** above.]

white-haired boy n [Ir dial < Ir *bán* white, fair, beloved] Cf **fair-haired, red-headed stepchild**

A favorite child; a pet, favorite.

1869 Fitzgerald *Caseine* 28 **cnNY,** The silent, quiet boy, the white-haired boy, mamma's pet, the spoiled favorite of the school-master, too often develops the most dangerous qualities in mature years. **1900** *San Antonio Daily Light* (TX) 16 Feb [2]/2 (newspaperarchive.com), Petti-grew is patted on the head as the white haired boy of the anti-expansion-ists. **1920** *Mansfield News* (OH) 29 Aug 9/3, [Syndicated short story:] How'd they get on to him? Thought he was the white-haired boy with the old man. **1940** *Helena Independent* (MT) 3 May 8/1, [Syndicated short story:] Thought you were the white-haired boy in steeplechasing. **1958** McCulloch *Woods Words* 210 **Pacific NW,** *White-haired boy*—Favorite of the boss. **1968** *DARE* (Qu. HH17, *A person who tries to appear important, or who tries to lay down the law in his community: "He'd like to be the _____ around here."*) Inf **OH**57, White-haired boy. **1982** *Daily Intelligencer* (Doylestown PA) 20 Jan 42/5, [Syndicated column:] He was her white-haired boy.

white hake n

1 A **hake 2** (here: *Urophycis tenuis*).

1858 *Amer. Acad. Arts & Sci. Memoirs* new ser 6.365 **MA,** *Phycis Americanus* [=*Urophycis tenuis*]. . . The White Hake. **1884** Goode *Fisheries U.S.* 1.234, *Phycis tenuis,* the Squirrel Hake or White Hake. **1939** *Natl. Geogr. Soc. Fishes* 51, The white hake (*Urophycis tenuis*) reaches a length of 42 inches. **1983** *Audubon Field Guide N. Amer. Fishes* 498, White Hake (*Urophycis tenuis*). . . from Nova Scotia to Cape Hatteras. **2006** *Boston Globe* (MA) 5 Nov 1 (Internet), The plan seeks to reduce the mortality of seven groundfish species [including] . . white hake.

2 =**hake 1a.**

1930 *AmSp* 5.390 [Language of N Atl fishermen], Hake. . . (Sometimes called *white hake*). The whiting.

white half-runner (bean) See **half-runner bean**

whitehead n

1 in phr *like a whitehead:* Very fast or vigorously. [Etym unknown]

[**1821** Martin *Life* 77, I mounted my horse, and *cleared out like a white head.* [*DARE* Ed: Martin was an Irish highwayman who emigrated to NEng in 1819; the *Life* was written by a Boston lawyer on the basis of jailhouse interviews.]] **1826** *Salem Gaz.* (MA) 20 Jan 1/5, In the twinkling of an eye, he was as bald as when he came into this wicked world. The clumsy attempts of the barber to get hold of his nose . . awoke him, and he—"cleared out like a *white-head.*" **1830** *MA Spy & Worcester Co. Advt.* (Worcester MA) 28 July 4, *Southerner.* Well, away with you—clear out like a white-head. **1860** Kirk *Wooing & Warring* 259 **KY,** Why, mammy, I was so skeered that I dropped the pail and run like a white-head. **1882** Peck *Peck's Sunshine* 179 **WI,** If a boy knows that there will be no school on the afternoon of circus day, he will study like a white-head all the forenoon. **1887** *Daily Northwestern* (Oshkosh WI) 27 May [4]/3 (newspaperarchive.com), The boy jumped up and run off like a whitehead. **1895** *Atlantic Mth.* 76.688 **VT,** Naow clipper like a whitehead, an' I'll just wait. **1901** *DN* 2.150 **c,n,wNY,** 'To run like a *white-head'* = very fast. **1925** in 1953 Botkin–Harlow *Treas. Railroad Folkl.* 228, The train hit a curve so fast I had to fight like a whitehead to keep her from pitchin' me out. **1930** Shoemaker *1300 Words* 67 **cPA Mts** (as of c1900), *White-head*—To "run like a whitehead." **1941** *LANE* Map 474 (*He ran like a house afire*) 2 infs, **CT, NH,** Whitehead. **1976** *Hillsboro Press Gaz.* (OH) 22 June 3/1, My father used a phrase that has long troubled me, "run like a whitehead." What is a whitehead, and why did he run? V.B., Alexandria, Va.

2 See **white-headed goose.**

3 also *whitehead coot:* =**surf scoter.**

1888 Trumbull *Names of Birds* 103 **Long Is. NY,** Surf Scoter. . . At Bellport, L.I., [called] *Morocco-jaw* and *White-head.* **1955** MA Audubon Soc. *Bulletin* 39.377 **NH,** Surf Scoter. . . White-head Coot. . . there are two white spots on the upper surface of the head of the adult male.

white-headed goose n Also *whitehead, white-headed brant* =**blue goose 1.**

1858 U.S. War Dept. *Rept. Explor. Railroad* 9.xlix, *Anser (Chen)* *caerulescens.* . . White-headed Goose. **1888** Trumbull *Names of Birds* 9, Names of *Chen cærulescens,* as follows: . . White-headed Goose or White-head [etc]. **1923** U.S. Dept. Ag. *Misc. Circular* 13.34 **AL, MO,** Blue Goose. . . Vernacular Names. . . *In local use.* . . whitehead, white-headed goose. **1943** Musgrove–Musgrove *Waterfowl IA* 14, Whitehead, white-headed goose, . . white-headed brant. . . Head and neck white, usually stained rusty.

white-headed gull n

Heermann's **gull** (*Larus heermanni*).

1853 *Lit. World* 12.309, The first number contains finely colored figures of the . . white-headed Gull [etc]. **1858** U.S. War Dept. *Rept. Explor. Railroad* 9.848, *Blasipus Heermanni* [=*Larus h.*]. . The White-headed Gull. **1872** Coues *Key to N. Amer. Birds* 314, *White-headed Gull.* Adult with the head white, gradually merging on the neck and under parts into pale ash. **1898** (1900) Davie *Nests N. Amer. Birds* 35, Heerman's [sic] Gull. . . This is said to be one of the handsomest birds of the family to which it belongs, and is commonly called the White-headed Gull.

white-headed jay n

A **Canada jay** (here: *Perisoreus canadensis capitalis*).

1881 U.S. Natl. Museum *Bulletin* 21.30, *Perisoreus canadensis capitalis.* . . White-headed jay. **1898** (1900) Davie *Nests N. Amer. Birds* 328, Rocky Mountain Jay. . . This bird is called the White-headed Jay or Rocky Mountain Whisky Jack—a race of the Canada Jay, but very much different. It is peculiar to the Rocky Mountain region, and is especially common in Northern New Mexico and Colorado. **1917** (1923) *Birds Amer.* 2.226 **West,** In the West, in the Rocky Mountain region, . . is the White-headed or Rocky Mountain Jay.

white-headed owl See **white-faced owl**

whiteheart hickory n Also *whiteheart* Cf **redheart hickory** =**mockernut hickory.**

1810 Michaux *Histoire des Arbres* 1.20 **NJ, NY,** *White heart hickery,* [nom] secondairement usité dans ces deux Etats. [=*White heart hickery,* the name used secondarily in these two States.] *Ibid* 189, Pour cet usage on choisit les arbres qui ont de 16 à 20 centimètres . . de diamètre, . . et comme le coeur qui est de couleur rougeâtre n'est pas encore développé, on donne alors fréquemment à cette espèce le nom de *White heart hickery.* [=For this use [=as fuel] trees are chosen which are from 16 to 20 centimeters . . in diameter, . . and since the heartwood which is of a reddish color has not yet developed, this species is frequently given the name *White heart hickery.*] **1850** Emerson *Rept. Trees & Shrubs* 194 **MA,** The Mockernut Hickory. . . It is also called the white heart, though, in old trees, the heart is of the same dark red as in the other hickories. **1867** De Voe *Market Asst.* 398, *Mocker-nuts,* or *thick-shelled hickories.*—These are usually a larger and rounder nut, but with a very thick shell, while the kernel is small but sweet. There is also a smaller thick-shelled nut, which some call the *white-heart hickories.* **1896** NC State Bd. Ag. *NC Resources* 51, H[icoria] alba . . [Footnote: Carya tomentosa, Nutt.], the white-heart hickory. . . The wood of this species is largely white; of all the others brownish. It is preferred to the others, particularly for buggy spokes and rims, tool handles and hoops. The other kinds are . . used for these purposes when the white-heart cannot be obtained. **1907** *Wilson Bulletin* 19.2.43, In the center of this woodland are . . thickets of . . White-heart Hickory, *Carya tomentosa.* **1935** *Amer. Midland Naturalist* 16.526, The forest composition is: . . white-heart hickory—3[%].

white hearts n pl, but sg or pl in constr =**Dutchman's breeches 1.**

1887 John Burroughs in *Century Illustr. Mag.* 34.325 **NEast,** I have an eye out for the white-hearts (related to the bleeding-hearts of the gardens, and absurdly called "Dutchman's breeches"). **1901** Lounsberry *S. Wild Flowers* 196, [*Dicentra] Cucullaria,* Dutchman's breeches, soldier's cap or white hearts, sends out its exquisite, elfish little flowers in earliest spring. **1949** Moldenke *Amer. Wild Flowers* 29, Rich leaf mold . . is the favorite habitat of that popular spring flower inelegantly known as dutchmans-breeches or, more esthetically, whitehearts, *Dicentra cucullaria.*

white heather n

1 A **mountain heather 3** (here: *Cassiope mertensiana*).

1896 *Mazama* 1.268 **WA,** On the hillsides are patches of . . the white heather (*Cassiope Mertensiana*). **1924** *Jrl. Mammalogy* 5.15 **Pacific NW,** Much of the foreground is covered with white heather (*Cassiope*). **1953** Jewett *Birds WA* 212, The food of the ptarmigan is largely vegetable in nature, including . . leaves and flowers of red and white heather

(*Phyllodoce empetriformis* and *Cassiope mertensiana*). **1979** Spellenberg *Audubon Guide N. Amer. Wildflowers W. Region* 479, White Heather; Mountain Heather *(Cassiope mertensiana)*. **2005** *DARE* File—Internet, [Caption:] White heather *(Cassiope mertensiana)*.

2 A **mountain heather 2**; see quots.

1901 in 2007 (acc) *Smithsonian Amer. Art Museum* (Internet), [Title of painting by Mary Vaux Walcott:] White heather *(Phyllodoce grandiflora* [sic]). **1911** *Century Dict. Suppl.* (at *heather*), White heather, *Phyllodoce empetriformis*, of the same region [=northwestern America] as the red heather. **1973** Franklin–Dyrness *Nat. Vegetation OR & WA* 368, *Phyllodoce glanduliflora*. . . cream mountainheath or white heather.

white hellebore n   [*OED2* 1398 →]

A **false hellebore 1**, esp **Indian poke 1**.

1687 (1878) S. Sewall *Diary* 1.179 **MA**, Mr. Cook scrapes white Hellebore which he snuffs up. **1737** (1911) Brickell *Nat. Hist. NC* 22, *Sarsaparilla, White Hellebor*, several sorts of *Thistles* [etc grow here]. **1784** in 1785 *Amer. Acad. Arts & Sci. Memoirs* 1.409, In collecting the roots, particular care ought to be taken that the *white hellebore*, or *poke root*, which some people call scunk [sic] weed, be not mistaken for this plant [=skunk cabbage]. **1837** *OH Repository* (Canton) 5 Jan [4]/6 (newspaperarchive.com), [Advt:] *New Drug Store*. . . The following articles constitute a part of the stock. . . White Hellebore, White Bar Soap [etc]. **1875** *Janesville Gaz.* (WI) 28 Sept 1/5, For the residue of insects which infest my vegetable garden, I find that . . white hellebore and cayenne pepper are of the most utility. **1907** Hodge *Hdbk. Amer. Indians* 1.606, *Indian poke*. . . American white hellebore *(Veratrum viride)*. **1967** *DARE* FW Addit **ceNY**, Indian poke, poke root, white (or) false hellebore—all are the root of *Veratrum viride*. **2007** (acc) AK Univ. *eInfo* (Internet), White Hellebore. *(Veratrum album* L.) Venomously Poisonous.

white heron n

A heron with white plumage, as an immature **little blue heron**, a **snowy egret**, a great egret *(Ardea alba)*, or a **great white heron**. Also called **white crane 2, ~ poke**

1792 Belknap *Hist. NH* 3.169, White heron, *Ardea alba*. **1804** (1905) Lewis *Orig. Jrls. Lewis & Clark Exped.* 6.123, This day one of our Hunters brought me a *white Heron*. . . this bird as [is] an inhabitant of ponds and Marasses, and feeds upon tadpoles, frogs, small fish &c. they are common to the Missisippi and the lower part of the *ohio*. River. **1843** Audubon *Birds Amer.* 6.144, The White Heron. *Ardea Egretta*. Resident in the Floridas. **1874** [see **white crane 2**]. **1926** (1949) McQueen–Mizell *Hist. Okefenokee* 131 **seGA**, The white heron is almost like the blue species, with the exception that he has a plume during certain seasons of the year. **1939** FWP *Guide TN* 428 **nwTN**, More than 250 species of birds stop off here on their annual migrations. Among them are . . white herons. **1946** Hausman *Eastern Birds* 106, Little Blue Heron. . . Other Names—Blue Egret, White Heron (young) [etc]. . . Young: white plumage, gray wing tips, and dull greenish-yellow legs and feet. **1965–70** *DARE* (Qu. Q10, . . *Water birds and marsh birds*) Infs **CA**115, **FL**4, 29, 39, **IL**104, **NC**1, **NJ**22, **PA**10, White heron; (Qu. Q8, *A water bird that makes a booming sound before rain and often stands with its beak pointed almost straight up*) Inf **NC**60, White heron. **1974** *Naples Daily News* (FL) 5 May sec A 9/2, The saga of a huge Great White Heron named George. . . [Caption:] George the white heron.

white hickory n   Note: Early quots for *white hickory* reflect the fact that fewer species of hickory were then discriminated than is now the case. Some quots may apply to other senses.

A **hickory** n **B1**, spec:

a =**bitternut 1**.

1785 Marshall *Arbustrum* 68, *Juglans alba minima. White, or Pig-nut Hickory*. **1810** Michaux *Histoire des Arbres* 1.177 **PA**, Bitter Nut, Hickory. . . Cette espèce est généralement connue dans l'État de New-Jersey, sous le nom de *Bitter nut* . . ; tandis que dans la Pensylvanie, et notamment dans le Comté de Lancaster, elle est désignée par celui de *White Hickery*. [=Bitter Nut, Hickory. . . This species is generally known in the State of New Jersey, as *Bitter nut* . . ; while in Pennsylvania, and especially in Lancaster County, it is designated as *White Hickery*.] **1897** Sudworth *Arborescent Flora* 111 **TX**, *Hicoria minima* [=*Carya cordiformis*]. . . Common Names. . . White Hickory. **1930** OK Univ. Biol. Surv. *Pub.* 2.57, *Carya cordiformis*. . . Bitter-nut. Swamp or White Hickory.

b A **shagbark hickory** (here: *Carya ovata*).

1897 Sudworth *Arborescent Flora* 113 **AR, IA**, *Hicoria ovata* [=*Carya o.*] . . Common Names. . . White Hickory. **1933** Small *Manual*

SE Flora 406, *H[icoria] ovata*. . . White-hickory. . . Rich soil and woods, various provinces, Fla. to Tex., Minn., and Que. **2007** *DARE* File—Internet, Any hickory I have bought, especially from local mills, is shagbark and is white, and is referred to as white hickory by local sawyers.

c =**mockernut hickory**.

1792 Belknap *Hist. NH* 3.100, *Walnut*. The American species of this genus, have been confounded by botanical writers. There are at least three in New-Hampshire. 1. *White* or *Round nut hiccory. (juglans alba.)* . . Its wood is smooth and tough, and is much used for gun-stocks, axe-handles and walking-sticks. **1842** Thompson *Hist. VT* 1.174 **NEng**, The Forest Trees of New England not found in Vermont are . . White Hickory, *Carya alba*. **1860** Curtis *Cat. Plants NC* 44, Common Hickory. (C. *tomentosa* [=*C. alba*]). . . This species is white to the heart, for which reason, probably, it is called *White Hickory* in some parts of the State. The other species have their wood more or less reddish. **1897** Sudworth *Arborescent Flora* 114 **PA, SC**, *Hicoria alba* [=*Carya a.*] . . Common Names. . . White Hickory. **1897** *Jrl. Amer. Folkl.* 10.144 **swMO**, *Carya tomentosa* . . white hickory. **1953** Strausbaugh–Core *Flora WV* 290, Mockernut. . . its white color suggests the common name White Hickory.

d A **pignut 1** (here: *Carya glabra*).

1848 in 1870 Drake *Pioneer Life* 73 **KY**, Of the whole forest the red or slippery elm was the best; next to that the white elm, and then the pignut or white hickory. **1897** Sudworth *Arborescent Flora* 115 **IA, NH**, *Hicoria glabra* [=*Carya g.*] . . Common Names. . . White Hickory. **1937** *Chillicothe Constitution–Tribune* (MO) 13 Sept 2/4, Next a white hickory or pignut tree, in the top of which a raven has alighted.

white hoarhound   See **white horehound**

white holly n

A common **holly** n[1] **1** (here: *Ilex opaca*) or its wood.

1830 *Archer's Manual* 19 **PA**, The United Bowmen prefer the white holly, which is rather more dense, and permits the arrow to be made thinner. **1838** Goodrich *Peter Parley's Cyclop. Botany* 133, *I[lex] opaca*. . . The wood is fine-grained, heavy and compact; the alburnum very white, from which it is sometimes called white holly. **1850** Wise *System Aeronautics* 279 **PA**, As bird-lime is an article rarely found in this country, it will be proper to state how it is made: Take the middle bark of the white holly in any quantity; boil it for seven or eight hours in water [etc]. **1895** GA Dept. Ag. *GA Resources* 245, The pine timber on Floyd's Island is poor, but as soon as you reach the hammock land commences the red bay, the magnolia, the white bay, the white holly, etc. . . The white holly is there known as Henderson wood, and from this wood of the piano keys in this country are made. **1932** *Ecological Monogr.* 2.144 **Okefenokee GA**, Shrubs: . . *Ilex Cassine*. . . "Hendersonwood," White holly. **1960** Vines *Trees SW* 649, *Ilex* . . *opaca*. . . Vernacular names are Yule Holly, Christmas Holly, and White Holly. The foliage and fruit are often used for holiday decorations. **1968** *DARE* (Qu. T5, . . *Kinds of evergreens, other than pine*) Inf **GA**25, White holly.

white horehound n   Also sp *white hoarhound* [*OED2* 1794 →]

=**horehound 1**.

1801 Stearns *Amer. Herbal* 180, *Marrubium Vulgare*. . . White Horehound. **1903** Porter *Flora PA* 266, *Marrubium vulgare*. . . White Hoarhound. . . In waste places. **1961** Thomas *Flora Santa Cruz* 297 **cwCA**, Common or White Hoarhound. Widely distributed in disturbed areas. **1975** Hamel–Chiltoskey *Cherokee Plants* 39, Horehound—water, white. . . For hoarseness; coughs; colds [etc].

white horse n

1 also *white-horse sucker*: A catostomid fish such as the **white sucker 1b** or a **redhorse 1** (here: *Moxostoma anisurum*).

1855 IL State Ag. Soc. *Trans. for 1853–54* 1.594, *Catostomus anisurus* [=*Moxostoma a.*]. River Sucker, White Horse. **1951** Harlan–Speaker *IA Fish* 67, Common White Sucker. . . Other Names—Sucker, . . mullet, and whitehorse. **1966** *DARE* (Qu. P1, . . *Kinds of freshwater fish . . caught around here . . good to eat*) Inf **MI**32, White-horse sucker. **1983** Becker *Fishes WI* 682, White Sucker. . . Other common names. . . June sucker, whitehorse, carp.

2 An **oat grass c** (here: *Danthonia spicata*).

1935 (1943) Muenscher *Weeds* 149, *Danthonia spicata*. . . Wild oat-grass, Poverty-grass, Bonnet-grass, White horse [etc].

3 =**white liquor**.

1914 *DN* 4.114 **cKS**, *White horse* or *mule*. . . Diluted alcohol used as a beverage. **1968** *DARE* (Qu. DD21c, *Nicknames for whiskey, especially illegally made whiskey*) Infs **DE**1, **MD**18, White horse.

white-horse sucker See **white horse 1**

White House n Cf **federal building, government house, Roosevelt**

An outhouse.

1967–70 *DARE* (Qu. M21b, *Joking names for an outside toilet building*) Infs **IL**16, **MD**29, White House [laughter]; **VA**40, White House; **TX**63, White House, Post Office; **WY**4, White House; going to see the President's wife. **2004** in 2008 *DARE* File—Internet **cPA**, Bush was making his big push for the White House. Me, I was contemplating another kind of run to the White House—only my White House was an outhouse at Echo Hollow Lodge. **2005** Bollinger *Outhouses* 41, *The White House* (American). . . Whether it was called Aunt Sue, Uncle John, or the White House, this outhouse was used by many a miner.

white ibis n

Std: a grallatorial bird *(Eudocimus albus)* of the southern Atlantic and Gulf coasts. Also called **bec-croche, black-pied curlew, curlew 2, gannet 5, pieded curlew, pond guinea 3, Spanish curlew 1, stone ~ 2, white ~ 1**

white Indian hemp See **Indian hemp 3**

white ironwood n Cf **ironwood**

1 A small tree of Florida and the West Indies *(Hypelate trifoliata)*. Also called **inkwood 2**

1884 Sargent *Forests of N. Amer.* 45, *Hypelate trifoliata*. . . White Iron Wood. . . Wood very heavy, hard, close grained, compact. **1933** Small *Manual SE Flora* 829, White-ironwood. . . The largest trees in our range occur on Umbrella Key. **2007** (acc) *Fairchild Tropical Botanic Garden* (Internet), *Hypelate trifoliata,* white ironwood, is an evergreen shrub to small tree. . . It is quite rare in Florida where it grows in hammocks in the Everglades and the Florida Keys.

2 =**Florida boxwood 1.**

1971 Craighead *Trees S. FL* 199, Boxwood (white ironwood), *Schaefferia frutescens.*

white juniper n

A **juniper 1**; see quots.

1910 Jepson *Silva CA* 164, *Juniperus occidentalis*. . . "White Juniper," "Yellow Cedar," and "Red Cedar" are names in local use. **1937** Stemen–Myers *OK Flora* 25, *Juniperus monosperma*. . . White Juniper. **2007** (acc) Tarleton State Univ. *Range Types N. Amer.* (Internet), *Juniperus ashei*—This species is commonly known . . as Ashe, post, . . rock, or white juniper or cedar.

white lace cactus See **lace cactus**

white lake perch See **white perch 1**

white lampblack n Also *white coal-black, ~ stove-blacking* chiefly **Nth, N Midl** See Map

A nonexistent item used as the basis of a practical joke.

1846 *Yale Lit. Mag.* 11.172, Invention was racked to find him business. White lamp black, soft soap moulds, strap oil and dove's milk, fresh salt, pocket saw mills, salamander caps, and leather jewsharps, were among the various articles which he inquired for from house to house. **1890** *San Antonio Daily Light* (TX) 17 Dec [3]/2 (newspaperarchive.com), It has been the custom among shop and counting house employes [sic] from time immemorial to play practical jokes upon newcomers, such as sending them after white lampblack or a round square. **1921** *DN* 5.95, *White lamp-black.* From store selling paints and oils. Used also at soldier's camp, Montgomery, Ala. **1946** *CA Folkl. Qrly.* 5.165 **MT**, Every young miner at one time or another has been on a fool's errand in quest of . . red oil for a red lantern, a bucket of white lampblack, . . and the like. **1965–70** *DARE* (Qu. HH14, *Ways of teasing a beginner or inexperienced person—for example, by sending him for a 'left-handed monkey wrench': "Go get me _____."*) 15 Infs, chiefly **Nth, N Midl**, (Bottle of or pound of) white lampblack; **PA**142, A nickel's worth of white lampblack; **CO**23, Some white coal-black; **WA**20, White stove-blacking. **1972** *Oneonta Star* (NY) 31 Mar [4]/6 (newspaperarchive.com), Let someone else go for the white lampblack, the left-handed monkey wrench, the strap oil and the sky hook. **2007** *DARE* File—Internet, How about a pinion seal for a '68 Toronado? Board stretcher from the wood shop? Jar of white lampblack? Radiator cap for a '66 Corvair?

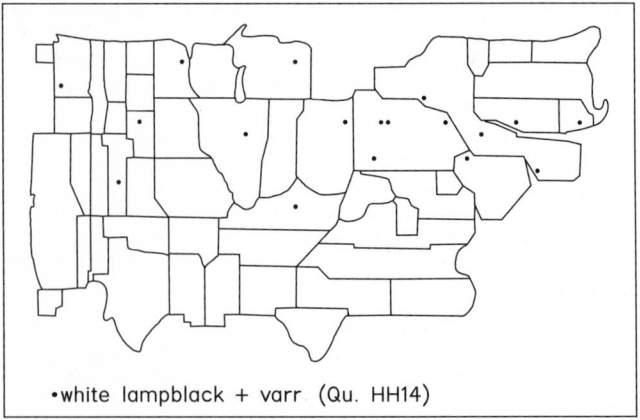

•white lampblack + varr. (Qu. HH14)

whiteleaf oak

Std: an **oak** (here: *Quercus hypoleucoides*). Also called **silverleaf oak**

whiteleaf sage See **white sage 3**

white lettuce n

=**rattlesnake root 2b.**

1813 Muhlenberg *Catalogus Plantarum* 69, Prenanthes—white lettuce, ivy leaf. **1832** *MA Hist. Soc. Coll.* 2d ser 9.154 **cwVT**, Prenanthes alba. . . White-lettuce. **1848** Gray *Manual of Botany* 248, *N[abalus]* [=*Prenanthes*] *albus*. . . White Lettuce. Rattlesnake-root. **1914** Georgia *Manual Weeds* 551, Smooth White Lettuce—*Prenanthes racemosa*. *Ibid* 552, Rough White Lettuce—*Prenanthes aspera*. **1931** Harned *Wild Flowers Alleghanies* 494, Tall White Lettuce (*Prenanthes altissima*). . . Common in woods throughout the mountains. **2007** (acc) WI Dept. Nat. Resources *Endangered Species Factsheets* (Internet), Nodding Rattlesnake-root (Great White Lettuce) (*Prenanthes crepidinea*).

white lightning n scattered, but chiefly **Sth, Midl, SW** See Map

=**white liquor.**

1904 *Daily Oklahoman* (Oklahoma City OK) 22 Jan 9/6, Distillers are captured every day, and when they are sent to prison others take their places, and thus the perpetual flow of "white lightning." **1929** *AmSp* 4.386 **KS** [Wet words], Such terms as *rookus juice, third-rail, giggle water, nose paint, whoopee, joy water, red eye, white lightning, popskull,* and *bust-head* are evidently references to the potency or the effect of the liquor designated. **1959** Lomax *Rainbow Sign* 78 **AL** [Black], We just stayed at our table and had some of this stuff you call "white lightnin." **1965–70** *DARE* (Qu. DD21c, *Nicknames for whiskey, especially illegally made whiskey*) 151 Infs, scattered, but chiefly **Sth, Midl, SW**, White lightning; (Qu. DD21b, *General words . . for bad liquor*) 14 Infs, chiefly **Sth, S Midl**, White lightning; (Qu. DD31, *Joking names for homemade hard liquor;* total Infs questioned, 75) 13 Infs, **Sth, SW**, White lightning; (Qu. DD21a, *General words . . for any kind of liquor*) Infs **FL**28, **GA**19, 30, 72, **IL**115, **NC**33, 35, 80, **SC**10, White lightning; (Qu. DD28b, . . *Fermented drinks . . made at home*) Infs

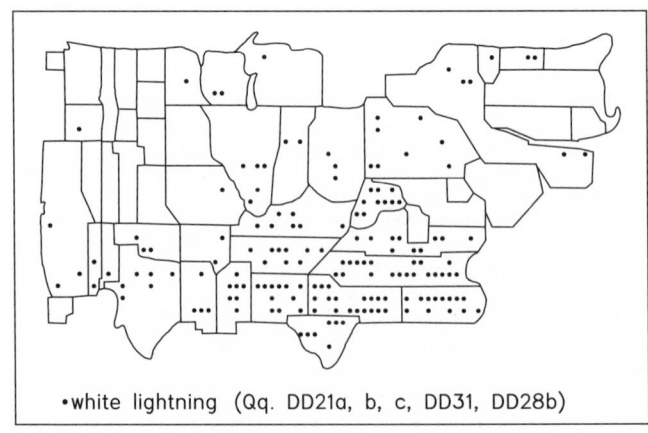

•white lightning (Qq. DD21a, b, c, DD31, DD28b)

IL118, 123, White lightning. **1972** *Atlanta Letters* **cGA**, *White Lightning*—In rural sections of Georgia in the Good Ole Days a good quality of brandy or whiskey, distilled, illegally, for home use or sale in the bootlegging trade. . . This liquid was clear and colorless. **1989** Pederson *LAGS Tech. Index* 172 **Gulf Region**, *Moonshine* . . white lightning (298 [of 914 infs]). **2006** *Chron.–Telegram* (Elyria OH) 26 Feb sec H 3/3, [Syndicated column:] Buckshot victim Harry Whittington is recovering. . . The Democrats' probe of Cheney's possible consumption of white lightning, peach brandy and rubbing alcohol at lunch that day is still ongoing.

white lily n Also *whitelilies* **esp Nth**
A **trillium** (here: usu *Trillium grandiflorum*).
  1886 Dudley *Cayuga Flora* 99 **NY**, *T[rillium] grandiflorum*. . . White Trillium. "White Lily," (local). **1892** *Jrl. Amer. Folkl.* 5.104 **MD, OH**, *Trillium grandiflorum*, white lilies. No. Ohio; Chestertown, Md. **1949** Moldenke *Amer. Wild Flowers* 338, The large-flowered or white wakerobin, *T[rillium] grandiflorum*, also referred to as whitelilies. **1966–70** *DARE* (Qu. S2, . . *The flower that comes up in the woods early in spring, with three white petals that turn pink as the flower grows older*) Infs **FL16, MI9, 120, NY134, PA235, WA1**, White lily.

white line crab See **white sign (crab)**

white liquor n **chiefly Sth, S Midl** Also called **white horse, ~ lightning, ~ mule, ~ whiskey** Cf **red liquor, white-eye 1**
Colorless whiskey, moonshine.
  1871 *Defiance Democrat* (OH) 7 Oct 1/6, Whisky adulteration has become a profession, and is known among the trade as "grading it." To ten barrels of white liquor at 95 cents a gallon one barrel of common whisky is added. **1896** *Decatur Daily Rev.* (IL) 21 Jan [7]/3 (newspaperarchive.com) **AR**, The lank . . back-woodsman who was running the store had brought out a bottle of whiteliquor, better known as moonshine whisky. **1903** *DN* 2.336 **seMO**, *White-liquor*. . . The raw product of distillation. Moonshine whiskey. **1929** *AmSp* 4.386 **KS** [Wet words], *White liquor* . . any colorless whiskey or alcohol. **1968** *DARE* FW Addit **VA15**, Spearmint, peppermint . . both used to flavor white liquor. **1985** Wilkinson *Moonshine* 18 **neNC**, White liquor is privately made whiskey, and occasionally brandy, on which no taxes have been, or are likely to be, paid. **1986** Pederson *LAGS Concordance (Moonshine)* 3 infs, **GA, TN**, White liquor. **1990** Simpson *Gt. Dismal* 99 **nNC, sVA**, It was the largest moonshine still ever seized in the Great Dismal Swamp, and the biggest white-liquor bust, period, in North Carolina in ten years. **1997** *Syracuse Herald–Jrl.* (NY) 11 Dec sec A 7/2 **NC**, The local specialties are white liquor, a crystal-clear grain spirit made from corn, wheat, rye or oats, and fruit brandies. **2009** Hicks *Beech Mt. Man* 109 **wNC**, I knowed all these guys was goin' up 'ere buying white liquor off the sheriff.

white live oak n
=**canyon oak 1.**
  1886 Van Dyke *Southern CA* 87, The broad arms of the black live-oak full of glistening leaves, may take the place of the silver-fir, and the white live-oak may guard the passes instead of the lofty pine. **1908** Britton *N. Amer. Trees* 310, White Live Oak. . . This evergreen oak occurs from southern Oregon south along the mountains to Lower California. **1947** Collingwood-Brush *Knowing Trees* 205, The canyon live oak is often known locally as white live oak, California live oak [etc]. **1969** *DARE* (Qu. T10, . . *Kinds of oak trees*) Inf **CA130**, White live oak—stays green all year; leaf looks like bay leaf—special to the 2000–3000 ft. altitude.

white liver n [Cf *EDD white liver(ed)* (at *white* adj. 1.54.(b) and 55.(a)) and *SND white liver* (at *white* adj. I.(39)); also cf Fr *foie blanc*, Ital *fegato bianco*, Ger *weisse Leber*, all associated with hypersexuality and danger to sexual partners] **esp Sth, S Midl**
A presumed condition of the liver characterized by an abnormally powerful sexual drive and the death of sexual partners; hence adj phr *white-livered* sexually insatiable; lethal to one's sexual partners.
  [**1871** (1872) De Forest *Kate Beaumont* 147 **Sth**, You are stark crazy about that pale-faced, white-eyed, white-livered creature. . . I don't care if he is a clergyman. I don't like him. I don't like his looks. He has a white liver. He's just that kind of a man that the niggers call a white-livered man.] **1893** *Overland Mth.* (2d ser) 22.273, 'Is your mother a mur-

deress?' 'No, . . but if you marry her your hat will be on that fourteenth peg in less than a year.' 'What is it?' I gasped. 'My mother has,—' she replied in a stage whisper, 'she has a white liver!' **1930** Shoemaker *1300 Words* 67 **cPA Mts** (as of c1900), *White-livered*—A peculiar type of pale faced man, who buries many wives and noted for amorous propensities. **1946** *Jrl. Amer. Folkl.* 59.323, *White Liver:*—In Salt Lake City several years ago a middle-aged Dutchman, newly married to a countrywoman, passed away quite suddenly. Superstitious Dutch women in the community laid the death to the fact that his wife must have a white liver, as witnessed by the fact that she had been married a few times before and had curiously lost each of her husbands not long after marriage. **1947** (1964) Randolph *Ozark Superstitions* 172, In the Ozarks . . white-livered generally means oversexed. When a lively, buxom, good-looking woman loses several husbands by death, it is often said that her inordinate sexual passion has killed 'em off, and she is referred to as a white-livered widder. **1947** Ballowe *The Lawd* 95 **LA** [Black], By this time [=after two husbands had suddenly died] the hands in the quarters knew: *Patsy was a white-livered woman*. **1949** Webber *Backwoods Teacher* 227 **Ozarks**, Voice atremble, she exclaimed, "The old sow! The old white-livered sow!" In the hills, a boar is supposed to have white spots on his liver, and "white-livered," rather than being only a term of cowardice, in proper context meant an oversexed and probably immoral person. **1968** *DARE* (Qu. AA7b, . . *A woman who is very fond of men and is always trying to know more—if she's not respectable about it*) Inf **LA46**, White-livered woman. **1968** *DARE* FW Addit **seLA**, *White-livered woman* = nymphomaniac. **1983** Jones *For Ancestors* 10 **GA** [Black], He killed off all those women, but after the doctor examined him they said the reason why most of his wives died was he had a white liver. **1983** *DARE* File **Chicago IL**, A neighboring [Black] woman, age 62 . . was known to have had intercourse with five other men, . . now all dead. The neighboring woman was referred to as having "white liver" and these men referred to as having died of "white liver." . . I polled our [hospital] employees, black & white, and found around 15 (black) who knew the meaning & no whites (equal number) who did. **1986** Pederson *LAGS Concordance*, 1 inf, **csGA**, White-livered—you kill everyone you marry; 1 inf, **swAL**, White-livered—means she can't get enough. **2008** *DARE* File—Internet **cwNY**, Sayings from Grandpa Norm. . . She has a white liver (outlived three husbands).

white loco n Also *white locoweed, ~ point loco*
A **locoweed** (here: *Oxytropis lambertii* or *O. sericea*).
  1901 U.S. Dept. Ag. Div. Botany *Bulletin* 26.86 **MT**, White Loco Weed. (*Aragallus spicatus* [=*Oxytropis sericea*]). **1913** (1979) Barnes *Western Grazing* 257, [Caption:] White Loco or Rattle Weed in Flower (*Aragallus lamberti*). **1935** (1943) Muenscher *Weeds* 312, The commonest kinds of loco weeds are *Astragalus mollissimus* . . Purple loco, *Astragalus diphysus* . . Blue loco, and *Oxytropis Lamberti* . . White loco. **1964** Kingsbury *Poisonous Plants U.S.* 307, *Oxytropis lambertii*. . . (White loco, white point loco).

white locust n
A **black locust** (here: *Robinia pseudoacacia*).
  1813 Michaux *Histoire des Arbres* 3.249 **PA**, Ainsi, dans les environs de Lancaster, et à Harrisburgh . . on préfère d'abord ceux qui proviennent d'arbres dont le coeur est rouge, ensuite ceux dont il est jauneverdâtre et enfin ceux chez lesquels il est blanc; et c'est cette différence dans la couleur du bois, qui, très-probablement, est un effet de la nature du terrein dans lequel les arbres ont végété, qui lui a fait donner les noms de *Red, Green,* et *White locust.* [=Thus, in the vicinity of Lancaster and Harrisburg . . the most desirable is that which comes from trees in which the heart is red, next those in which it is greenish-yellow, and last those in which it is white; and it is this difference in the color of the wood, which, very probably, is an effect of the nature of the soil in which these trees have grown, which has given them the names of *Red, Green,* and *White locust.*] **1893** *Jrl. Amer. Folkl.* 6.140 **NY**, *Robinia pseudacacia*, white locust; yellow locust. **1913** *Torreya* 13.30 **seNY**, There is a superstition among country people that lightning will not strike a house near which grows either a white locust or a mountain ash. **1968–69** *DARE* (Qu. T16, . . *Kinds of trees* . . *'special'*) Infs **KY62, WV8**, White locust; **GA80**, White locust, yellow locust, black locust—colors from wood or bark. **2007** *DARE* File—Internet **MI**, There was about a thousand of bees in the white locust trees.

white mahogany n
Lumber from a **catalpa B1** (here: *Catalpa speciosa*).
  1907 *Amer. Botanist* 14.85, The catalpa . . is known in the furniture trade as white mahogany.

white mandarin n Cf **mandarin**

A **twisted stalk 1** (here: *Streptopus amplexifolius*).

1949 Moldenke *Amer. Wild Flowers* 336, The pagodabells, white-mandarin, or liverberry, *Tortipes* [=*Streptopus*] *amplexifolius,* . . has greenish white flowers and its leaves are green on both surfaces. **1975** Hamel–Chiltoskey *Cherokee Plants* 59, Twisted stalk, white mandarin—*Streptopus amplexifolius*. **1987** Hughes–Blackwell *Wildflowers SE AK* 75, Twisted-stalk, White Mandarin. . . moist woods and meadows.

white mangrove n

1 A tree or shrub *(Laguncularia racemosa)* of Florida swamps and tidewaters. Also called **button tree 2, buttonwood 4, mangle** n[1] **2e, mangrove 2e**

1804 McMahon *Catalogue Amer. Seeds* 4, Conocarpus [=*Laguncularia*] racemosa. . . White Mangrove. **1823** Vignoles *Observations Floridas* 52 **FL,** At Cape Sable . . are fresh water wells: these wells are distinguished by a tuft of button trees or white mangroves, being the only trees on the point. **1837** (1962) Williams *Territory FL* 98, The White Mangrove grows to the size of a forest tree. . . It grows in profound swamps, unmixed with any other timber. Trees are connected together by large hooplike roots, that rise high above the ground. **1884** Sargent *Forests of N. Amer.* 87, White Button Wood. White Mangrove. Semi-tropical Florida, cape Canaveral to the southern keys. **1907** Amer. Geogr. Soc. NY *Bulletin* 39.262, If he has not seen them in Florida, the mangrove trees, growing out of the very ocean on the coral reefs, may attract his attention. Here he finds the black mangrove *(Avicennia nitida),* the white mangrove *(Laguncularia racemosa)* [etc]. **1934** *Torreya* 34.138, The White Mangrove or White Button-wood. . . is not a true mangrove and belongs to quite a different family. **1961** Douglas *My Wilderness* 130 **Everglades FL,** Within the first twelve inches of the sea, there are four zones where four species grow—the red mangrove at salt water's edge, next the black mangrove, then the white mangrove, and, highest of all, the buttonwood, long sought after for charcoal. **1979** Little *Checklist U.S. Trees* 158, *White-mangrove. . . Other common names*—white buttonwood, buttonwood.

2 In Florida and on the Gulf coast, =**black mangrove;** in California, the related *Avicennia marina* var *resinifera.*

1880 Sargent *Catalogue Trees N. Amer.* 36, *Avicennia nitida* [=*A. germinans*]. . . White Mangrove. Southern Florida, Louisiana, at the mouth of the Mississippi River. **1914** Bailey *Std. Cyclop. Horticult.* 436, *Avicennia. . . nitida. . .* Black Mangrove. White Mangrove. **1960** Vines *Trees SW* 890, Black Mangrove. . . Also known as White Mangrove or Mangle Blanco. **2007** (acc) CA Univ.–Berkeley *CalPhotos* (Internet), [Caption:] *Avicennia marina var. resinifera*—White Mangrove.

white man's fire n Cf **squaw fire**

A campfire that is larger than necessary.

[**1910** McClintock *Old N. Trail* 44 **Pacific NW,** The Indian invariably builds a small fire. He will tell you that it is more convenient for cooking and better for warmth, and will speak with derision of the white man's fire as too large and wasteful.] **c1980** *DARE* File **csWI,** Campers are advised to keep their campfires small—only large enough to cook a meal and ward off cold. Large, ostentatious fires are denigrated as "White man's fires." **2005** *DARE* File—Internet **TX,** Kay stood by the big, loud-popping white man's fire.

white man's foot n *hist*

A **plantain;** see quots.

[**1672** Josselyn *New-Englands Rarities* 86, *Plantain,* which the *Indians* call *English-Mans Foot,* as though produced through their treading.] **1826** Darlington *Florula Cestrica* 21, Common, or Great Plantain. . . It is said our native Indians call this plant *"The white man's foot,"*—from the circumstance of its delighting to grow in traveled pathways, and advancing into the country *pari passu* with the whites. **1840** MA Zool. & Bot. Surv. *Herb. Plants & Quadrupeds* 114, Common Plantain. . . The Indians called it the *White Man's Foot.* **1948** Coatsworth *South Shore* 82 **MA,** Her garden must have been a wild one where various medicinal woodland plants were transplanted along with certain European herbs and weeds, like plantain—"the white man's foot"—which the Indians were quick to adopt from the colonists. **2000** *Marysville Jrl.–Tribune* (OH) 17 May 6/1, Plantain. . . acquired the nickname "white man's foot" by the native Americans as it spread through the countryside.

White man's out of jail See **Mr. White is out of jail**

white maple n

1 =**silver maple.**

1810 Michaux *Histoire des Arbres* 1.28, Acer eriocarpum [=*A. saccharinum*]. . . *White maple . . ,* seule dénomination sur les bords de l'Ohio et des rivières qui viennent s'y rendre. [=Acer eriocarpum [=*A. saccharinum*]. . . *White maple . .*, the only name on the banks of the Ohio and of the rivers which flow into it.] **1839** *Freeman & Messenger* (Lodi NY) 28 Mar 1/1, Experience, however, shows, particularly in New Hampshire and Maine, that the soft or white maple, (Acer eriocarpum) is as rich in sweets, or nearly so, as the common sugar maple. **1878** *Indiana Progress* (PA) 18 Apr [7]/1 (newspaperarchive.com), The bulk of these [=street trees] are made up of twelve varieties, . . [including] White maple *(acer dasycarpum)* [etc]. **1897** Sudworth *Arborescent Flora* 287 **Atlantic, Missip-Ohio Valleys,** Silver Maple . . White Maple. **1939** Medsger *Edible Wild Plants* 231, Silver Maple, or Soft or White Maple. . . a large forest tree with light gray, flaky bark. **1965–70** *DARE* (Qu. T14, . . *Kinds of maples*) 46 Infs, **chiefly NEng, S Midl,** White maple; **NC**30, Soft white maple; (Qu. T3, *The tree that produces syrup and sugar*) Inf **MD**22, White maple; (Qu. T13) Inf **NC**49, White maple; (Qu. T15, . . *Kinds of swamp trees*) Inf **KY**6, White maple. [*DARE* Ed: Some of these Infs may refer instead to other senses below.]

2 A **red maple** (here: *Acer rubrum*).

1850 Emerson *Rept. Trees & Shrubs* 483 **MA,** The Red Maple, called also the White, the Swamp, the Scarlet, and the Soft Maple, is a tree of middling size, growing abundantly in the swamps and low grounds, in most parts of the state. **1896** *Jrl. Amer. Folkl.* 9.184 **ME,** *Acer rubrum* . . white maple, Paris, Me. **1897** Sudworth *Arborescent Flora* 290 **ME, NH,** Red Maple. . . White Maple. **1913** *Torreya* 13.232 **LA,** *Acer drummondii.* . . White maple, Lake Pearl. **1950** [see **3** below]. **1969** *DARE* (Qu. T14, . . *Kinds of maples*) Inf **MA**58, White maple (red and white same here)—red buds in spring.

3 Any of var other **maples,** as **big-leaf maple, dwarf ~, striped ~,** or **sugar ~.**

1805 (1904) Lewis *Orig. Jrls. Lewis & Clark Exped.* 2.337, I saw near the creek some bushes of the white maple. **1897** Sudworth *Arborescent Flora* 283 **OR, WA,** Oregon Maple. . . White Maple. **1950** Moore *Trees AR* 92, Sugar Maple. . . Local Names: Hard Rock, Black, and White Maple. *Ibid* 93, Red Maple. . . Local Names: Swamp, Soft, Water, and White Maple. **1966–68** *DARE* (Qu. T3, *The tree that produces syrup and sugar*) Inf **CT**6, White maple = sugar maple; (Qu. T14, . . *Kinds of maples*) Inf **ME**8, Mountain maple (white maple)—a shrub. **1975** Hamel–Chiltoskey *Cherokee Plants* 44, Maple—green, striped, white. . . *Acer pennsylvanicum.* **1981** *PADS* 67.37 **Mesabi Iron Range MN,** *Sugar maple.* . . On the Mesabi single instances of *soft maple, sugar maple,* and *white maple* are recorded.

white marrow(fat) See **marrowfat (bean)**

white marsh marigold n

A western **marsh marigold** (here: *Caltha leptosepala*).

1907 Clements *Plant Physiology* 166, [Caption:] An amphibious plant, the white marsh-marigold, *Caltha leptosepala*. **1933** *Chron.–Telegram* (Elyria OH) 1 Apr 8/7, White marsh marigold is another April bloomer, having a handsome pure white flower the size of a silver dollar. **1967** Gilkey–Dennis *Hdbk. NW Plants* 141, *Caltha biflora.* . . White Marsh marigold. . . flowers 2.5–4 cm. broad, showy, white. **2005** *DARE* File—Internet **WA,** White Marsh-marigold: *Caltha leptosepala* ssp. *howellii*—Found along Crofton Creek.

white meat n **chiefly Sth, esp AL** Cf **meat** n 2, **white bacon, ~ side meat**

=**salt pork.**

1913 Johnson *Highways St. Lawrence to VA* 285 **ceVA** [Black], Why, jus' the common white meat—I mean hog—what we call fat back, that you never see no lean in—costs fifteen cents a pound! **1927** U.S. Pub. Health Serv. *Pub. Health Rept.* 42.2721 **Sth,** The components of a typical pellagra-producing diet may be the following: Corn meal . . , white wheat flour . . , white rice, dried beans, "white meat" (salt pork), sorghum, or cane molasses, collards, or "greens." **c1938** in Lib. of Congress *Amer. Memory: WPA Life Hist.* (Internet) **AL,** A bowl of lima beans, fresh garden lettuce, homemade jelly, fried white meat, and buttermilk . . what we have to eat. **1940** *Ibid* **GA,** When the crash came. . . White meat that was bought for 32 and 35 ¢ was sold for as low as 12 ¢ and some of it for 4 and 5 ¢ per pound. **1941** *LANE* Map 301 *(Salt pork)* 1 inf, **ceMA,** White meat, a Southern term. **1944** *PADS* 2.14 **AL,** *White meat. . .* Fat salt pork, the best of "sow belly." . . Negro and white.

Up to standard use. **1949** Kurath *Word Geog.* 70 **Sth, S Midl,** *Salt pork.* . . Less common terms are . . *white-meat,* and *fat-meat.* **1966–70** *DARE* (Qu. H38, . . *Words for bacon*) Infs **AL**6, 25, **MS**65, White meat; **AR**14, White meat—very fat; **VA**39, White meat—same as fatback. **1966** *DARE* Tape **AL**1, We called it white meat, sowbelly . . that's some real good meat; **AL**14, Just some plain old . . white meat . . didn't have any lean meat in it at all. Just solid white . . old fatback. **1971** *Today Show Letters* **cnAL** (as of a1940), White meat wasn't breast of chicken or other fowl but was fat, unsalted, pork used to season butter (ripe lima) beans. **1972** *PADS* 58.20 **cwAL,** *Salt pork.* . . *white meat* (4 [of 27 infs]). **1990** Pederson *LAGS Regional Matrix* 122, 54 [of 914] infs, **chiefly coastal Gulf Region, esp AL,** *Salt pork* . . white meat.

white milkweed n

A **milkweed 1** (here: *Asclepias variegata*).

[**1895** *Atlantic Mth.* 75.610, Another recollection of this path is of a snow-white milkweed *(Asclepias variegata),*—white with the merest touch of purple to set it off.] **1901** Lounsberry *S. Wild Flowers* 435, White Milkweed. . . *Asclepias variegata.* **1949** Moldenke *Amer. Wild Flowers* 167, The white milkweed, *Biventraria* [=*Asclepias*] *variegata,* with its corolla segments white, or purple, near the base. . . may be met locally in dry woods and thickets from Connecticut, southern New York, and Illinois to Florida, Arkansas, and Texas. **1999** *DARE* File—Internet **NC,** [Caption:] This photo of White Milkweed, Asclepias variegata was taken in May of 1999 along my driveway in Orange County, NC.

white milkwort n

A **milkwort** (here: *Polygala alba*).

1930 *OK Univ. Biol. Surv. Pub.* 2.69, *Polygala alba.* . . White Milkwort. **1947** *Abilene Reporter–News* (TX) 4 May [6]/4 (newspaperarchive.com), The wild flowers included almost every species ever seen on West Texas prairies. Among them were bluebonnets, . . white milkwort [etc]. **1961** Wills–Irwin *Flowers TX* 146, In Texas, the most widely distributed species is the White Milkwort, which occurs in fields and open woods.

white minister n Cf minister 2, black minister

=**glaucous gull.**

1909 Allen *Fauna New Engl.* 11, *Larus hyperboreus.* . . Glaucous gull; Burgomaster; Owl gull; White minister.

white moss n

A **moss 1** (here: *Leucobryum* spp). Also called **pincushion moss**

1871 *LA State Univ. Annual Rept. for 1870* 119, Leucobryum glaucum, Pale-green White Moss. **1907** Marshall *Mosses* 34, Some mosses, as the . . white-mosses *(Leucobryum* . .*)* appear light gray when dry and green when wet. **1947** Grout–Howe *Mosses & Liverworts* 90, *L[euco-bryum] glaucum* . . the White Moss, Cushion Moss. Any one accustomed to walk in the woods must have noticed the grayish-white tufts of the White Moss, looking like giant pincushions. **2007** (acc) WI Univ. Freckmann Herbarium *Plants WI* (Internet), *Leucobryum glaucum.* . . cushion moss, white moss, white cushion moss [etc].

white mossycup See mossycup oak

white mountainweed n

A western **gilia** (here: *Leptosiphon nuttallii*).

1931 *U.S. Dept. Ag. Misc. Pub.* 101.139, Nuttall gilia, locally known as stickerbush, stinkweed, white gilia, white mountainweed, and whorl phlox, is sometimes woody throughout, but usually is semiherbaceous.

white mouse n

1967–69 *DARE* (Qu. E20, *Soft rolls of dust that collect on the floor under beds or other furniture*) Infs **KY**41, **MO**21, **PA**131, White mice. [All Infs old]

white mouth n

1 Oral thrush. [Engl dial]

1990 Cavender *Folk Med. Lexicon* 34 **sAppalachians,** *White mouth—*thrush.

2 See quots. Cf **ashy 2**

1931 (1991) Hughes–Hurston *Mule Bone* 95 **cFL** [Black], You was so hungry you had the white mouth. **1935** Hurston *Mules & Men* 159 **FL** [Black], Well, de hongry times caught 'em. . . De white folks all got faces look lak blue-John and de niggers had de white mouf. **2008** *DARE* File—Internet [Black], [Of a woman on a restrictive diet:] She

needs to be drinking water. Why does she have the *white* mouth? [*Ibid,* She look ashy as hell!]

white mule n Also *white mule whiskey* [From its lack of color and powerful kick] **scattered, but esp freq Midl, West** See Map

=**white liquor.**

1888 (1889) McConnell *Five Yrs.* 60 **TX** (as of 1860s), About this time I first became acquainted with a . . drink, known as "pine-top" or "white-mule" whiskey. **1904** *DN* 2.422 **nwAR,** *White mule.* . . . New whiskey, illicitly distilled. "Now white mule is new moonshine whiskey." **1914** [see **white horse**]. **1923** *DN* 5.224 **swMO,** *White mule.* . . 'Moonshine' liquor, or illegally manufactured whiskey. **1927** *AmSp* 3.25 **eTX** [Sawmill talk], The liquor on tap at these dances is called "pine-top," "Shinny," "white mule," or "corn." **1929** in 1952 Mathes *Tall Tales* 145 **sAppalachians,** Hit's what a heap o' people calls white mule. Hit's made out o' corn. **1929** *AmSp* 4.386 **KS** [Wet words], *White mule* may mean any colorless whiskey or alcohol. **1931** *AmSp* 7.50 **Sth, SW** [Lumberjack lingo], There are plenty of native liquors "on tap" for the refreshment of the men. The "drinks" are "pine-top," "white mule," "mountain dew," "honey dip," and "red eye." **1942** Faulkner *Go Down* 60 **MS,** Haven't I told and told every man woman and child on this place what I would do the first drop of white mule whisky I found on my land? **1965–70** *DARE* (Qu. DD21c, *Nicknames for whiskey, especially illegally made whiskey*) 54 Infs, **scattered, but esp freq Midl, West,** White mule; **MI**67, White mule—haven't heard that in quite a while; **NJ**3, White mule—not common anymore; **OK**18, White mule—made from corn; **TN**30, White mule—colorless, fresh corn whiskey, usually illegally made; **TN**37, White mule—made in woods, not aged, therefore colorless; (Qu. DD21a, *General words* . . *for any kind of liquor*) Inf **IL**128, White mule; (Qu. DD21b, *General words* . . *for bad liquor*) Infs **CO**27, **MO**13, **NJ**2, **NY**150, White mule; **RI**17, White mule—pure alcohol and supposed to have quite a kick; (Qu. DD28b, . . *Fermented drinks* . . *made at home*) Infs **IL**118, **WI**44, White mule; (Qu. DD31, *Joking names for homemade hard liquor;* total Infs questioned, 75) Infs **MS**53, **OK**18, White mule. **1974** Dabney *Mountain Spirits* 24 **sAppalachians,** It [=corn whiskey] is called "white mule" in areas of Kentucky and Tennessee, apparently due to its kick. **1989** Pederson *LAGS Tech. Index* 172 **Gulf Region,** *Moonshine* . . white mule (whiskey) (12 [of 914 infs]).

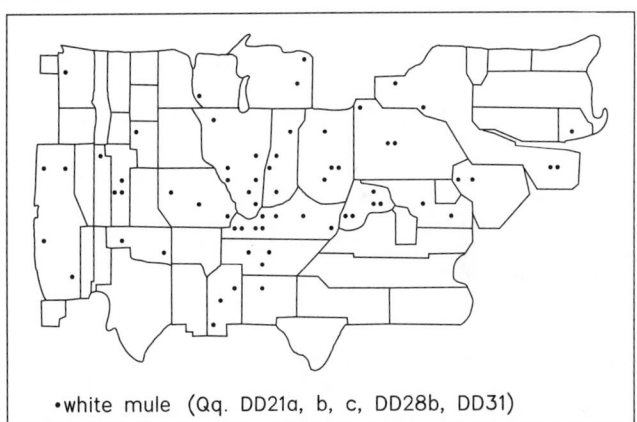

•white mule (Qq. DD21a, b, c, DD28b, DD31)

white mullein n [*OED2* 1578 (at *mullein* sb. 1)]

A **mullein** (here: *Verbascum lychnitis*).

1843 Torrey *Flora NY* 2.30, *Verbascum lychnitis.* . . White Mullein. . . Old sandy fields near Oneida lake. **1903** Porter *Flora PA* 278, *Verbascum Lychnitis.* . . White Mullen. . . In fields and waste places, Ont. to N.J. and Pa. **1942** Hylander *Plant Life* 461, White Mullen is . . a woolly species, with white or cream colored flowers. **2007** (acc) U.S. Dept. Ag. *Plants Database* (Internet), *Verbascum lychnitis.* . . white mullein.

white mullet n

1 A **redhorse 1,** usu *Moxostoma pappillosum*.

1839 (1863) Kemble *Jrl. Georgian* 53, Had I been the ingenious man who wrote a poem upon fish, the white mullet of the Altamaha should have been at least my heroine's cousin. **1869** *Amer. Philos. Soc. Proc.* 11.472 **NC,** *Ptychostomus albus* [=*Moxostoma pappillosum*]. . . It is much valued by the people living in the neighborhood of the Catawba

River, North Carolina, as an article of food. They call it the "White Mullet." **1928** *Copeia* 167.29, *Moxostoma cervinum*, White mullet. Restricted range in Carolinas and Virginia. **1938** Schrenkeisen *Field Book Fishes* 93, *Moxostoma album* (Cope), The White Mullet.

2 A **mullet** n¹ **1**, usu *Mugil curema*. For other names of the latter see **liza** n² **1**, **silversides 6**

1835 Hitchcock *Rept. Geol. MA* 537, *Mugil albula* [=*M. curema*]. White Mullet. **1842** DeKay *Zool. NY* 4.146, *The White Mullet. Mugil Albula.* . . is in high repute among epicures. It is a plump firm fish, and appears in our markets in July and August. **1857** *NJ Geol. Surv. Geol. Cape May* 147, *Mugil albula* . . . *The White Mullet.* **1879** *U.S. Natl. Museum Proc.* 1.381 **SC**, *Mugil brasiliensis* [=*M. curema*]. . . White Mullet. Very common in the harbor [=Beaufort Harbor]. **1906** *NJ State Museum Annual Rept. for 1905* 219, *Mugil curema.* . . Mullet. White Mullet. . . Side and lower surface pure silver-white. **1951** Taylor *Surv. Marine Fisheries NC* 114, Two species of mullet are caught and marketed under this name in North Carolina, namely, the striped or jumping mullet . . and the white or silverside mullet. **2007** *DARE* File—Internet **FL**, *White Mullet.* . . Hard to tell apart from the Black Mullet, especially if comparable in size.

whitening n **Sth, S Midl**

Face powder.

1905 *DN* 3.100 **nwAR**, *Whitening.* . . Face powder. 'She uses too much whitening.' Common. **1909** *DN* 3.388 **eAL, wGA**, *Whitenin(g).* . . Face powder. **1929** *AmSp* 5.21 **Ozarks**, *Whitening.* . . Face powder. "Molly she puts on too dam' much whitenin', hit makes her look kinder puny like." **1936** *AmSp* 11.276 **eTN**, *Whitening.* Face powder. 'She uses too much whitening.' **1954** *Harder Coll.* **cwTN**. **c1960** *Wilson Coll.* **csKY**. [**1966** *PADS* 46.30 **cnAR** (as of 1952), *Whiten.* . . To use face powder.—"They was whitening their face."] **1980** *DARE* File **neTX** (as of c1930), Face powder = whitening. **1983** *MJLF* 9.1.60 **ceKY** (as of 1956), *Whitening* . . women's face powder.

white northern bean See **northern bean**

white-nose(d) sucker n Also *whitenose (redhorse)*

A **redhorse 1** (here: *Moxostoma anisurum*).

1875 Jordan in *IN Geol. Surv. Annual Rept. for 1874* 221, *Moxostoma.* . . Chub Sucker, White-nosed Sucker, Creek Fish, (Wis). . . *M. oblongum* and others (if there are any others). **1908** Forbes–Richardson *Fishes of IL* 90, *Moxostoma anisurum.* . . This is the so-called whitenosed sucker of the Great Lakes. **1938** Schrenkeisen *Field Book Fishes* 93, The White-nosed Sucker, or Whitenose, *Moxostoma anisurum* . . has a large dorsal fin with some 15 rays or more. **1943** Eddy–Surber *N. Fishes* 116, Silver Redhorse (Whitenose Sucker, Silver Mullet). **1983** Becker *Fishes WI* 661, Silver Redhorse. . . Other common names: silver mullet, whitenose redhorse, white sucker [etc].

white oak n

1 Std: an **oak** (*Quercus alba*) native from the eastern US westward to the Mississippi Valley. Also called **fork-leaf white oak** Cf **pine oak 1** Note: *White oak* is also std in generic ref to the group of oaks characterized by pale bark, round-lobed leaves, acorns that mature in one season, and brownish-tan wood that is comparatively impervious to water.

2 also *Oregon white oak:* =**Oregon oak**.

1805 (1905) Clark *Orig. Jrls. Lewis & Clark Exped.* 3.143 **sWA**, We got from those people a fiew pounded roo[t]s fish and *Acorns* of white oake, those *Acorns* they make use of as food. **1860** *U.S. War Dept. Rept. Explor. Railroad* 12.3.183, They [=Louisiana tanagers] are generally seen during the middle of the day sunning themselves in the firs, occasionally darting from one of these trees to another, or to some of the neighboring white oaks (*Q[uercus] Garryana*) on the prairie. **1923** *Modesto Eve. News* (CA) 11 Sept 4/7, The White oak of British Columbia and Washington, the largest and most frequent oak of Oregon—indeed called the Oregon oak up there—is our Garry oak. **1991** *Mt. Democrat & Placerville Times* (CA) 28 Feb sec A 12/1, The species of oaks designated in the ordinance [include] . . Canyon Live Oak and Garry Oak/Oregon White Oak. **1993** (2006) Ocean *Acorns* np, Mountain White Oak or Pacific Post Oak or Oregon Oak and also called White Oak—*Quercus garryana.* . . This oak . . resembles the Valley White Oak, except the Valley White grows in the valleys and this grows in the lower hills.

3 usu as *California white oak:* =**valley oak**.

1868 Cronise *Nat. Wealth CA* 513, *Q[uercus] hindsii* [=*Q. lobata*], . .

California White Oak. . . the characteristic oak of California. **1884** Sargent *Forests of N. Amer.* 138, *Quercus lobata.* . . White oak. Weeping oak. . . The largest of the Pacific oaks. **1910** Jepson *Silva CA* 204, The Valley Oak, known also as California White Oak. . . is . . strictly Californian and all but confined to the Sacramento and San Joaquin valleys and the valleys of the Sierra foothills and Coast Ranges. **1961** Thomas *Flora Santa Cruz* 137 **cwCA**, *Q. lobata.* . . California White or Valley Oak, Roble. Mainly in the valleys and on low, rolling foothills. **1993** (2006) Ocean *Acorns* np, Valley White Oak or . . White Oak or Roble. . . The leaves are dark green with pale green undersides.

4 also *upland white oak, Rocky Mountain ~:* =**Gambel oak**.

1875 *CA Acad. Sci. Proc.* 5.289, *Quercus Gambelii.* . . Upland White Oak. **1897** Sudworth *Arborescent Flora* 153, Gambel Oak. . . Common Names. . . White Oak. **1909** *Amer. Geogr. Soc. NY Bulletin* 41.259 **AZ**, White Oak. *Quercus ganbelii* [sic]. . . Fringes all the mesas—and turns a beautiful yellow the middle of October. **1931** *U.S. Dept. Ag. Misc. Pub.* 101.21, New Mexican oak . . , Vreeland oak . . , and Utah oak . . the latter known as Rocky Mountain white oak . . are perhaps hardly more than forms, varieties, or subspecies of Gambel oak. **1993** (2006) Ocean *Acorns* np, Scrub Oak also called White Oak—*Quercus gambelii.* . . grows in the Southern Rocky Mountains from Colorado to Nevada and also from the Rockies to Mexico.

5 =**blue oak 3**. Cf **evergreen white oak**

1880 Sargent *Catalogue Trees N. Amer.* 50, *Quercus oblongifolia.* . . Evergreen White Oak. Live Oak. Mountains of Southwestern California, from San Diego to Los Angeles. **1908** Britton *N. Amer. Trees* 320, Blue Oak. . . A native of western Texas, southern New Mexico, Arizona, and adjacent Mexico. . . It is often called White oak. **1938** Van Dersal *Native Woody Plants* 347, White [oak] . . *Quercus oblongifolia*.

6 =**gray oak 2**.

1884 Sargent *Forests of N. Amer.* 144, *Quercus grisea.* . . White Oak. Mountains of southern Colorado and western Texas . . , southern New Mexico and Arizona . . west to the Colorado desert of California.

7 also *Texas white oak, Texan ~:* =**Durand oak**.

1897 Sudworth *Arborescent Flora* 159 **AL, TX**, Durand Oak. . . Common Names. White Oak (Tex.). Texas White Oak (Ala.) **1908** Britton *N. Amer. Trees* 318, Texan white oak—*Quercus breviloba* [=*Q. sinuata* var *breviloba*]. . . It is also called white oak [etc]. **1938** Van Dersal *Native Woody Plants* 347, White [oak] . . (*Quercus . . durandii*). **2003** Stein et al. *Field Guide Native Oak* 94, *Quercus sinuata.* . . bastard white oak, . . Durand white oak, white shin oak, . . white oak.

8 A **post oak 1a** (here: *Quercus stellata*). Cf *box white oak* (at **box oak**), *rough white oak* (at **rough oak**)

[**1812** Michaux *Histoire des Arbres* 2.36, Post oak. . . *Q. Stellata.* . . Dans la partie du New-Jersey, qui avoisine la mer, ainsi que dans les environs de Philadelphie, cette espèce de Chêne . . paroît y avoir été considérée jusqu'ici comme une variété du Chêne blanc; par suite elle n'y est connue sons aucun nom particulier. [=Along the sea coast of New Jersey, as in the neighborhood of Philadelphia, this species of oak . . seems to be regarded as a variety of white oak, and so has no special name.]] **1897** Sudworth *Arborescent Flora* 154 **IN, KY**, *Quercus minor* [=*Q. stellata*]. . . Common Names. . . White Oak.

9 =**blue oak 2**.

1897 Sudworth *Arborescent Flora* 160 **CA**, *Quercus douglasii.* . . White Oak. **1908** Sudworth *Forest Trees Pacific* 285, Blue Oak. . . Appropriately called blue oak on account of the blue-green color of its foliage, but known locally also as "white oak," from its light, ashy-gray bark. Trunks exposed to the sun are especially light colored. **1910** Jepson *Silva CA* 216, Blue Oak has many common names. . . In many localities it is simply called White Oak.

10 also *Arizona white oak:* A southwestern **oak** (here: *Quercus arizonica*). Also called **live oak 2, roble**

1897 Sudworth *Arborescent Flora* 161, *Quercus arizonica.* . . Common Name. White Oak. **1931** *U.S. Dept. Ag. Misc. Pub.* 101.22, Arizona white oak (*Q. arizonica*), or Arizona oak, a medium-sized tree, is . . the commonest live oak in southern New Mexico and Arizona. **1987** *Daily Intelligencer* (Doylestown PA) 4 Jan [35]/2 (newspaperarchive.com) **AZ**, The new habitat represents the desert's highest elevation, and it features . . 200-year-old Arizona white oak trees.

11 =**basket oak 1**.

[**1883** *Bot. Gaz.* 8.348 **IN**, *Quercus Michauxii*. In the spring of 1883, I found this species very abundant, in fact, the prevailing "white" oak in certian [sic] portions of the bottom lands near Wheatland, Indiana.]

1901 *Plant World* 4.144 **KY,** The prevailing trees near are . . basket oak, called white oak [etc]. **1921** Deam *Trees IN* 109, *Quercus michauxii.* . . In the flats of southeastern Indiana it is generally called white oak.

12 =**burr oak.**

1940 Clute *Amer. Plant Names* 269, *Quercus macrocarpa.* White oak.

13 =**overcup oak 1.** Cf **swamp white oak 2, water ~**

1960 Vines *Trees SW* 148, Overcup Oak. . . Other vernacular names are Water White Oak, Swamp White Oak, . . and White Oak.

white oak racer n

A white-spotted color phase of a **blue racer 1** (here: *Coluber constrictor flaviventris*).

1930 *Copeia* 3.85 **LA,** This phase [of *Coluber constrictor flaviventris*] is known locally as the ash snake and the white oak racer. The first name refers to its appearance, the second to its favored habitat. The markings may consist of white scales sparsely and irregularly interspersed among the normally colored scales . . ; or white scales may be very numerous and intermixed with variously mottled scales intermediate between these and the normal, dark, steel-blue ones.

white oak snake n chiefly S Atl See Map

A **rat snake 1** such as *Elaphe obsoleta.*

1895 *Daily Northwestern* (Oshkosh WI) 12 Aug 3/3 **FL,** The boy ran into the house, screaming with pain and fright, and found a monster "white oak" snake wrapped about his arm. **1955** Carr–Goin *Guide Reptiles* 276 **FL,** *Elaphe obsoleta spiloides* . . Whiteoak Snake. . . A medium-sized, blotched, grayish or whitish snake. **1966–70** *DARE* (Qu. P25, . . *Kinds of snakes*) Infs **FL**7, 26, 48, **GA**41, White oak; **NC**10, White oak or copperhead; **NC**3, 12, White oak snake; **GA**25, White oak snake—same as chicken snake. [*DARE* Ed: "Copperhead" and "chicken snake" are used for some *Elaphe* spp.] **1986** *Daily Intelligencer* (Doylestown PA) 23 Feb sec C 17/1 **LA,** Picking up a gray rat snake, he said, "In Louisiana, they call it the white oak snake."

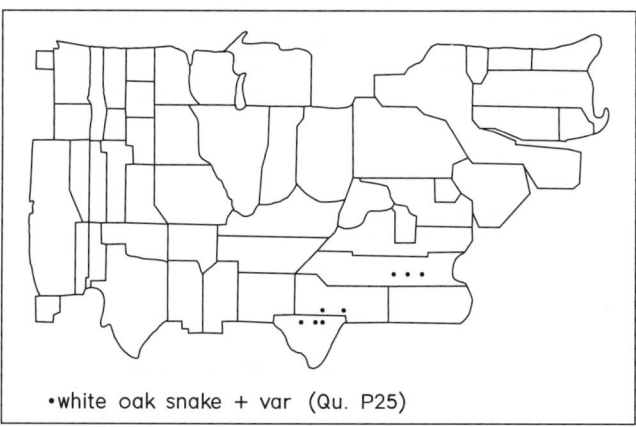

•white oak snake + var (Qu. P25)

white old-hand n Cf old hand

An **egret** (here: *Ardea alba*).

1955 MA Audubon Soc. *Bulletin* 39.312 **MA,** American Egret. White Crane . . ; White Old-hand.

white on rice n *orig among Black speakers; now more widely known* Cf *like ugly on an ape* (at **ugly D2**)

Used in comparisons as an example of very close contact or intimacy—often used in phrr *be (down) on one* (or *on one's back, all over one, after one*) *like white on rice* referring to literal or fig attack or pursuit.

1938 *AmSp* 13.4 **seAR,** 'He got all over me, like the white on rice,' that is, he scolded me as thoroughly as the color of white covers rice. *Ibid* 317 **NE** [Black], *Stick like white on rice.* **1943** Ottley *New World* 258 **NYC** [Black], Although temperamentally, sharply vivid differences exist among them, as to objectives they are as close as white on rice. **1963** Wright *Lawd Today* 182 **Chicago IL** [Black] (as of 1940s), Old Ben Kitty was on you like white on rice. **1968** Baldwin *Tell Me* 178 **NY** [Black], Sometime that man get on my back like white on rice. **1970** *DARE* (Qu. II3, *Expressions to say that people are very friendly toward each other: "They're _____."*) Infs **NC**88, **SC**68, **VA**69, Like white on rice; **FL**52, Like white on rice—can also be used between two enemies: "He won't get away from me; I'm gonna stick to him like

white on rice"; (Qu. II11b, *If two people can't bear each other at all . . "Those two are _____."*) Inf **NC**84, Stick to each other like white on rice—two people who are spoiling for a fight. [All Infs Black] **1971** Roberts *Third Ear* np [Black], *White-on-rice,* on top of. **1981** Walker *You Can't* 9 [Black], But even in the army the womens was on him like white on rice. **1981** *Capital Times* (Madison WI) 19 Oct 3/3, "Reagan is after us like white on rice and must face the consequences!" shouted the black welfare rights activist from Chicago. **1992** *NYT Mag.* 20 Dec 19 **swWA,** By now I couldn't see the trail. . . I stuck to him like white on rice and did what he did and somehow made it to the bottom without sailing off a cliff. **1999** *Appalachian Jrl.* 26.416 **wNC,** I have to make sure I use expressions that people here would say rather than eastern Carolina expressions, which come more naturally to me. For example, . . I'd never heard the expression "as tight as white on rice." **2002** *Intelligencer* (Doylestown PA) 23 May sec D 4/4, Forget that the ACLU would be down on this town like white on rice.

white osier n

A **fetterbush 3** (here: *Eubotrys racemosa,* formerly *Leucothoe r.*).

1830 Rafinesque *Med. Flora* 2.192, The *A[ndromeda] racemosa* or *White Pepperbush, White Osier,* is used for baskets and fish flakes.

white owl n

1 also *great white owl:* =**snowy owl 1.**

[**1772** *Royal Soc. London Philos. Trans.* 62.385 **Canada,** Snowy Owl. . . Churchill River. . . White Owl. It seems to be in its winter dress, as it is intirely white.] **1792** Belknap *Hist. NH* 3.165, Of birds we have a great variety . . [including] white owl, *Strix nyctea.* **1832** *N. Amer. Rev.* 34.372, Some, like the great white owl, delight in the prospect of moonlight gleaming on the snowy plains of the north, where all is still as death. **1838** [see **snowy owl 1**]. **1858** U.S. War Dept. *Rept. Explor. Railroad* 9.63, The Snowy Owl; The White Owl. . . In the winter it . . is frequently to be met with in the Northern and Middle United States. **1890** Warren *Birds PA* 143, Some persons, not versed in ornithological matters, name both the Snowy Owl . . and Barn Owl . . "White" or "Snowy" Owls. **1965–70** *DARE* (Qu. Q2, . . *Kinds of owls*) Inf **ME**6, White owl—also called an arctic owl; **MI**2, White owl—snow owl—arctic owl; **MA**42, White owl—further north; **ND**9, White owl—snow owl; **NY**97, Arctic owls or white owls; **PA**192, White owl—he comes down winters from Canada; **PA**242, White owl—same as snowy owl; **RI**4, White owl—driven out from north because their feed is gone; **WI**32, White owl—rare—from the north; **WI**58, White owl—snowy owl; **WI**78, White owl—arctic owl—used to see them, not anymore. [*DARE* Ed: 50 other Infs who gave the response *white owl* did not describe the bird and are not included either here or at **2** below.]

2 =**barn owl 1.** Cf **white-faced owl** [*OED2* 1770 → (at *owl sb.* 1.b)]

1812 Wilson *Amer. Ornith.* 6.57, White, or Barn Owl, *Strix Flammea.* . . is said to make a blowing noise resembling the snoring of a man. **1832** Nuttall *Manual Ornith.* 1.139, White or Barn Owl. . . it is perhaps no where more rare than in this part of the United States, and is only met with in Pennsylvania and New Jersey in cold and severe winters. **1856** in 1859 Smithsonian Inst. *Smithsonian Contrib.* 11.2.62, *Strix pratincola.* . . The American Barn Owl. The White Owl. **1890** [see **1** above]. **1970** *DARE* (Qu. Q2, . . *Kinds of owls*) Inf **TN**65, White owl—same as barn owl. **1971** *ID State Jrl.* (Pocatello) 15 Oct sec C 2/1, Money-faced [sic] owl, they call it [=the barn owl], and golden owl and white owl and monkey owl [etc].

3 A chamber pot. Cf **thunder mug**

1909 *DN* 3.388 **eAL, wGA,** White-owl. . . A chamber pot. **1950** *WELS* (*Utensil kept under a bed for use at night: Give names and nicknames*) 4 Infs, **WI,** White owl. **1966–69** *DARE* (Qu. F38) Infs **IN**23, 30, **OH**87, **VA**28, White owl; **FL**19, **GA**75, White owl [laughter]; **CO**3, White owl—old-fashioned; white—made of china; **MI**104, White owl—heard this years ago. **2005** *DARE* File—Internet **LA,** *Pot-du-chambre:* . . A chamber pot. A white owl. You know. **2007** Kalish *Little Heathens* 164 **IA** (as of 1930s), There was a heavy ceramic chamber pot in the oak chest at the head of the stairs. The older folks called it the "white owl." . . It was to be used only in emergencies.

white paintbrush n Cf paintbrush

An **Indian paintbrush 1**; see quots.

1938 *Amer. Midland Naturalist* 19.334 **CA,** *Castilleja pilosa.* . . White Paintbrush. Usually in sagebrush. **2000** *Jrl. Range Management* 53.578, Herbaceous species characterizing this association were . . white paintbrush *(Castilleja pilosa)* [etc]. **2006** *DARE* File—Internet **ID,** Though its [sic] bright yellow this is white paintbrush or *Castilleja longispica.*

white partridge n   [*OED2* 1674 →]   Cf **white quail**
=willow ptarmigan.

[**1748** Ellis *Voyage* 37 **Canada,** The *white Partridge* is of a middle Size, between our common Partridge and the Pheasant.] [**1859** *Scientific Amer.* 14.213, White partridges have appeared in considerable numbers, about Quebec, this winter.] **1899** Howe–Sturtevant *Birds RI* 90, *Lagopus lagopus.* . . Willow Ptarmigan. *White Partridge.*—It is reported that several White Partridges, supposedly Ptarmigans, were seen during the winter of 1887.

white pepper   See **pepperbush 1, 2**

white pepperbush   See **pepperbush 2**

white perch n

1   also *white lake perch;* Std: a small sea bass *(Morone americana)* formerly native to the Atlantic tidal region and now found in the Great Lakes as well.   Also called **black perch 2d, perch** n[1] **B7, sea perch c, silver bass 3, ~ perch 4, stiffback perch, yellow ~ 3**

2   A **pike perch.**   *obs*

1792 Belknap *Hist. NH* 3.178, White Perch, *Perca* [=*Sander*] *lucioperca?* **1842** Thompson *Hist. VT* 1.130, American Pike-perch. . . This fish is called by Dr. Williams, in his History of Vermont, the *White Perch,* but is generally known in Vermont simply by the name of *Pike.*

3   **=mademoiselle.**

1814 in 1815 *Lit. & Philos. Soc. NY Trans.* 1.420, White Perch. (Bodianus pallidus [=*Bairdiella chrysoura*]). **1862** *Acad. Nat. Sci. Philadelphia Proc. for 1861* 33, *Bairdiella argyroleuca* [=*B. chrysoura*]. . . "White Perch." **1902** Gregg–Gardner *Where When & How* 97 **FL,** Yellow-tail; Mademoiselle; White Perch. . . Bairdiella chrysura. **1953** MD Dept. Educ. *Our Underwater Farm* 15, On the Western Shore the common white perch is called a black perch, and the sand perch is a white perch.

4   **=freshwater drum.**

1818 Rafinesque in *Amer. Monthly Mag. & Crit. Rev.* 3.354, Sciena grunniens. . . White-Perch. **1820** Rafinesque *Ohio R. Fishes* 24, *Aplodinotus grunniens.* . . The vulgar names of this fish are White-perch, White-pearch, Buffaloe-perch [etc]. . . It is one of the largest and best found in the Ohio, reaching sometimes to the length of three feet and the weight of thirty pounds, and affording a delicate food. **1850** Lanman *Haw-ho-noo* 147 **Cincinnati OH,** We found it [="white perch"] at a fish market] to be not a legitimate white perch, but simply the fish known on Lake Erie as the fresh water sheeps-head. **1881** *Forest & Stream* 16.12 **MI, WI,** Sheepshead; white perch; grunter; drum, *Haploidonotus grunniens.* **1908** Forbes–Richardson *Fishes of IL* 323, *Aplodinotus grunniens.* . . In the Ohio Valley, in the South, and to some extent on the Illinois River, it is known and marketed as the white perch. **1969** *DARE* (Qu. P1, . . *Kinds of freshwater fish . . caught around here . . good to eat*) Inf **KY**16, Drum. [FW: White perch is book name, according to Inf.] **2007** *DARE* File—Internet **IN,** White perch here are *freshwater drum.*

5   The white **crappie** *(Pomoxis annularis).*   **chiefly Gulf States, esp LA**   See Map

1851 *Spirit of Times* 21.254 **AL,** The White-perch, or Goggle-eye, somewhat resembles both the trout and the bream. **1941** Writers' Program *Guide LA* 673, Right on this road to *Jeems* (or *James*) Bayou . . an excellent fishing spot for . . warmouth bass (locally called goggle-eye), and crappie, or "white perch." **1966–68** *DARE* (Qu. P1, . . *Kinds of freshwater fish . . caught around here . . good to eat*) Infs **LA**14, 18, 31, **OK**23, **SC**3, **TX**19, White perch—same as crappie; **LA**3, White perch or sacalait; **LA**10, White perch—white crappie. **1968** *DARE* FW Addit **sLA,** White perch—alternate term for "crappie." [FW: These answers must be considered general for southern Louisiana; the man who gave them was well-traveled in the Cajun country.] **2007** *DARE* File—Internet **LA,** I think 'white perch' is a solid indicator you are from north louisiana. *Ibid,* When I lived in Cenla [=central Louisiana] it was mostly speck, but sometimes white perch. *Ibid* **MS,** I grew up n [sic] Wayne County and the whole time I was growing up, we called them white perch. Then later when I moved to Jackson, then the Delta, everybody called them Crappie. **2008** *Ibid* **eTX,** I can not think of a finer tasting fresh water fish than Crappie. Most of us in East Texas tend to call them

White Perch. *Ibid* **MS,** Here's my rule of thumb: Below I-20 they're White Perch. Above I-20, they're Crappy.

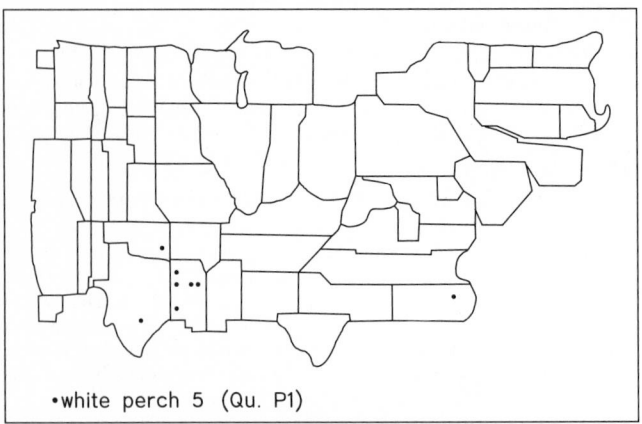

•white perch 5 (Qu. P1)

6   A **surfperch;** see quots.   **CA**

1882 U.S. Natl. Museum *Bulletin* 16.591 **wCA,** *A[mphistichus] arcuatus* [=*Hyperprosopon argenteum*]. . . Wall-eyed Perch; White Perch. *Ibid* 597, *D[amalichthys] argyrosomus* [=*Rhacochilus vacca*]. . . White Perch; Porgee. **1884** Goode *Fisheries U.S.* 1.277 **CA,** White Perch (*Ditrema furcatum* [=*Phanerodon furcatus*]). . . ranges from Cape Mendocino to the Mexican line. *Ibid* 278 **CA,** Silver Surf-fish *(Amphistichus argenteus).* . . This species is known as "Surf-fish" and "White Perch." **2005** *DARE* File—Internet **swCA,** Swimming out to depth, underwater, I saw large schools of white perch.

white pine n

1   Std: an eastern **pine 1** (here: *Pinus strobus*).   Also called **cork pine 1, king's ~, mast ~, Michigan ~, northern ~, pumpkin ~, sapling ~, spruce ~ 2h**

2   **=loblolly pine 1.**

1810 Michaux *Histoire des Arbres* 1.97 **eVA,** *Pinus taeda.* . . Cette espèce de Pin est connue, dans toute la partie basse des Etats méridionaux, sous le nom de *Loblolly pine;* et quelquefois sous celui de *White pine,* aux environs de Richemond et de Petersburgh en Virginie. [=*Pinus taeda.* . . This species of Pine is known, in all the lower part of the Southern states, as *Loblolly pine;* and sometimes as *White pine* in the environs of Richmond and Petersburg in Virginia.] **1968–70** *DARE* (Qu. T17, . . *Kinds of pine trees;* not asked in early QRs) Inf **VA**15, White pine—same as Virginia pine; [**CA**185, White [ˈlaləbi] pine].

3   also *western white pine:* A **pine 1** (here: *Pinus monticola*) native chiefly to the area west of the Rocky Mountains.   Also called **cork pine 2, finger-cone ~, little sugar ~, mountain ~, silver ~**   Cf **glacier pine**

[**1860** U.S. War Dept. *Rept. Explor. Railroad* 12.2.27 **WA,** A "white pine" is said to grow abundantly on the Olympia range and along the west side of Hood's Canal, where, I believe, it is sawed into lumber. I could never ascertain whether it was the species found on the Cascade mountains *(P. Monticola)* or some other.] **1869** *Amer. Naturalist* 3.410 **MT,** *Western White Pine (Pinus monticola).* I found scattered trees of this beautiful species on the highest parts of the Rocky Mountains. **1897** Sudworth *Arborescent Flora* 15 **CA, NV, OR,** *Pinus monticola.* . . White Pine. **1979** Little *Checklist U.S. Trees* 195, *Pinus monticola.* . . Other common names—mountain white pine, Idaho white pine, white pine [etc]. **2007** (acc) [see **8** below].

4   also *Rocky Mountain white pine, western ~:* **=limber pine 1.**

1868 *Eclectic Mag.* 7.373 **NM,** Lastly, the *Pinus flexilis,* or white pine of the Rocky Mountains. **1879** Sargent in *Amer. Jrl. Sci. & Arts* 17.420 **cNV,** *Pinus flexilis,* the Nevada representative of the Eastern White and the California Sugar Pine, is the largest and the most valuable timber tree of the central portion of the "Great Basin". . . it gives their names to "White Pine" District, "White Pine" Range, etc. **1881** Muir in *Scribner's Mth.* 22.930, White-pine. *(Pinus flexilis).* . . This species has long been confounded with the *Pinus albicaulis* of Engelmann, though quite distinct. **1885** Torrey Bot. Club *Bulletin* 12.24 **CA,** The black pine . . often ascends to the timber-line along the dryer ridges where it is frequently found with the western white pine *(Pinus flexilis).* **1897** Sudworth *Arborescent Flora* 16 **CA, NV, UT, CO, NM,** *Pinus flexilis.* . .

White Pine. **1913** [see **9** below]. **1938** Van Dersal *Native Woody Plants* 349, White [pine] . . *Pinus flexilis.* **1985** *Chron.-Telegram* (Elyria OH) 6 Jan sec B 7/2 **Pacific,** Pinus flexilis. . . is widely spread over the mountains of the Pacific Coast area where it is known as Rocky Mountain White Pine.

5 A **spruce 1** (here: *Picea engelmanni*).

1873 U.S. Geol. Surv. Terr. *Annual Rept. for 1872* 782, Abies Engelmanni. . . White Pine. **1897** Sudworth *Arborescent Flora* 39 **ID,** *Picea engelmanni.* . . White Pine. **1938** Van Dersal *Native Woody Plants* 349, Pine, White *(Picea engelmanni).*

6 =**whitebark pine.**

[**1881** see **4** above.] **1922** Sargent *Manual Trees* 6, *Pinus albicaulis.* . . White Pine. . . Bark thin, . . broken by narrow fissures into thin narrow brown or creamy white plate-like scales.

7 =**spruce pine 2b.**

1884 Sargent *Forests of N. Amer.* 201, *Pinus glabra.* . . Cedar Pine. Spruce Pine. White Pine. **1896** Mohr–Roth *Timber Pines* 127 **FL,** The Spruce Pine. *(Pinus glabra).* . . Common or Local Names. . . White pine. **1938** Van Dersal *Native Woody Plants* 349, Pine, White. . . *Pinus glabra.*

8 =**lodgepole pine.**

1882 U.S. Geol. & Geog. Surv. *Bulletin* 6.12, *Pinus contorta.* . . The wood is white and light so that the tree is sometimes called Spruce or White Pine. **1897** Sudworth *Arborescent Flora* 23 **MT,** Lodgepole Pine. . . White Pine. **1905** *Daily Rev.* (Decatur IL) 27 Apr 12/4 **CO, MT,** The lodgepole pine . . in Colorado and Montana is sometimes called white pine. **1969** *DARE* (Qu. T17, . . *Kinds of pine trees;* not asked in early QRs) Inf **CA**130, White pine—same as lodgepole. **2007** (acc) CA Univ.-Riverside *Plants Economic* (Internet), Other species with similar wood and uses that have been called white pine in the lumber trade are Western White Pine, *Pinus monticola,* Sugar Pine, *P. lambertiana,* . . and Lodgepole Pine, *P. contorta.* **2007** *DARE* File—Internet **eOR,** Lodgepole pine is also known as white pine in eastern Oregon.

9 also *Arizona white pine, (south)western ~*: A **pine 1** (here: *Pinus strobiformis*).   Also called **limber pine 2, Mexican white ~**

1883 Amer. Acad. Arts & Sci. *Proc.* 18.158, *Pinus Ayacahuite* . . *P. strobiformis.* . . "White Pine"; "Acanita." **1897** Sudworth *Arborescent Flora* 17 **AZ,** *Pinus strobiformis.* . . White Pine. **1908** Britton *N. Amer. Trees* 11, Mexican White Pine—*Pinus strobiformis.* . . It is also called Arizona White Pine. **1913** Wooton *Trees NM* 17, The Western White Pine or Limber Pine *(Pinus flexilis)* and its nearly related congener *Pinus strobiformis,* to which both of the foregoing common names are also applied, occur in the higher mountains. **2007** *DARE* File—Internet **AZ,** [Caption:] This picture shows a cross section of a southwestern white pine tree *(Pinus strobiformis)* collected in the Pinaleño Mountains of southeastern Arizona.

10 also *ponderosa white pine*: =**ponderosa pine 1.**

1892 *Littell's Living Age* 192.472 **CA,** Higher up occurs the large white pine *(Pinus ponderosa).* **1953** Peattie *Nat. Hist. W. Trees* 79, Western Yellow Pine. . . Other Names: . . Ponderosa White Pine [etc.].

white pizza n **chiefly NY**

A pizza that contains cheese but no tomatoes.

[**1973** *Coshocton Tribune* (OH) 8 Apr 3/1, A baker chops off a slice of white pizza, surprisingly tasty plain baked pizza dough.] **1977** Rice-Wolf *Where to Eat* 415 **DC,** The city's closest approach to New York's Little Italy type of restaurant is this run-down but still very much alive place located between midtown and Union Station. What to eat? "White" pizza. **1980** *Eve. Capital* (Annapolis MD) 20 Dec 23/4 **NY,** If you ever get to Utica, N.Y., try white pizza. Delicious, no tomatoes. **1982** *Frederick Post* (MD) 11 Nov sec E 2/1 **PA,** It was worth noting, however, that a unique pizza variation exists in Scranton, Pa., an otherwise obscure city. Called white pizza, it's a two-crust affair filled with cheese and onion and spiced with rosemary. **1982** *NY Mag.* 1 Mar 113 **NYC,** [Advt:] Marco of Lexington. . . Regional Italian Spcls: white pizza, zuppa de pesce [etc.]. **1985** *Post-Std.* (Syracuse NY) 20 Feb sec P 1/5, *White Pizza.* [Recipe includes pizza dough, vegetable oil, ground walnuts, oregano, grated Parmesan cheese.] **1997** Emmons *Vegetarian Planet* 447 **NYC,** I'll never forget my first white pizza. . . soft, white ricotta cheese, laced with garlic and herbs and dotted with droplets of olive oil, on a tender crust. **2009** *DARE* File **Newburgh NY,** My best from the land of "white pizza," "flokati," and the "growler" of beer.

white plantain n

1 A **pussytoes,** usu *Antennaria plantaginifolia.*

1696 (1769) Plukenet *Almagestum* 171, Gnaphalium Plantaginis folio, *Virginianum, White Plantain* (i.e.) Plantago candida *Nostratibus,* vulgò. [=Plantain-leaved Gnaphalium of Virginia, called by our people in the common tongue "White Plantain."] **1796** André Michaux in 1888 Amer. Philos. Soc. *Proc.* 26.134 **KY,** Le Gnaphalium dioicum y croit assai abondamment. Il est nommé par les Am. White Plantain. [=*Gnaphalium dioicum* grows quite abundantly there. It is called by the Americans White Plantain.] **1830** Rafinesque *Med. Flora* 2.224, Gnaphalium. . . The *Gn. plantagineum* and *dioicum,* belonging to S[ub] G[enus] *Antennaria,* have many names, *White plantain, Poor robin* or *Rattle snake plantain* [etc.]. . . used in coughs, fevers, bruises, inflammations, debility. **1837** Darlington *Flora Cestrica* 495 **sePA,** Antennaria plantaginea. . . Vulgò—White Plantain. **1843** (1844) Johnson *Farmer's Encycl.* 373, *Dioicous Gnaphalium,* commonly called *Mouse-ear Cudweed.* . . The *White Plantain,* or *Plantain-head cudweed,* is a variety of this last species. **1876** Hobbs *Bot. Hdbk.* 96, Rattlesnakes' plantain, White plantain, Antennaria plantagineum. **1935** (1943) Muenscher *Weeds* 450, Antennaria plantaginifolia. . . White plantain, Pussy-toes [etc.]. **1975** Hamel-Chiltoskey *Cherokee Plants* 50, Plantain, white—*Antennaria plantaginifolia.* . . For bowel complaint (especially children) use tea of entire plant; tea for excessive discharge in monthly period.

2 A **rattlesnake plantain 1** (here: *Goodyera repens*).

1823 Hunter *Memoirs Captivity* 426, Se-in-ja-shu.—*A little squirrel's ear. White plantain.*—This is a small ever-green plant, growing abundantly on the southern exposures of gravelly hills, and on poor lands. **1869** (1970) Jones *Wild Western* 253, Sneak . . desired to know the name of the plant that was used by the Indians with universal success when wounded by the fangs of the rattlesnake. The girl told him it was the *white plantain* that grew in the prairies. **1894** *Herald & Torch-Light* (Hagerstown MD) 20 Dec [3]/2 (newspaperarchive.com), Different varieties of this plant have commonly been called rattlesnake plantain, squirrel ear, poor robin and white plantain. **1924** *Amer. Botanist* 30.151, *Epipactis repens* [=*Goodyera r.*] is the "lesser rattlesnake plantain," "white plantain" and "squirrel's ear," all of which are suggested by the leaves. **1975** *Raleigh Reg. Beckley Post–Herald* (WV) 10 May 4/3, White plantain was of value, it was figured, when boiled in sweet milk and used in case of snake bite.

white plover n

=**sanderling.**

1923 U.S. Dept. Ag. *Misc. Circular* 13.57 **WA,** Sanderling. . . Vernacular Names. . . *In local use.* . . white-plover.

white poinsettia n   Cf **poinsettia B1**

A **snow-on-the-mountain 1** (here: *Euphorbia marginata*).

1950 *PADS* 15.35 **TX,** Lepedena marginata . . White poinsettia.

white point loco   See **white loco**

white poison n

A **poison sumac** (here: *Toxicodendron vernix*).

1941 *LANE* Map 250 *(Sumach)* 1 inf, **csCT,** White poison.

white poke n   chiefly **NEast**   Cf **poke** n⁴ **1, shitepoke B1**

A **white heron,** esp a **snowy egret** or immature **little blue heron.**

[**a1783** (1969) Williams *Mr. Penrose* 192, Here we landed again and Godart shott a White Poke or large kind of White Crane.] **1844** DeKay *Zool. NY* 2.221, The white-crested heron. . . This southern species. . . is often seen on our coast, where it is familiarly known as the *White Poke.* **1853** in 1949 Megquier *Apron* 70 [**ME** author in **cwCA**], Late in the fall, wild game is very plenty, a few miles from the City, the creeks & low lands are literally lined with them, they are shot by the dozens, & brought to this market, so are ducks, plovers, snipes, quales, cranes, white pokes, & I think I have seen in the market every kind of birds that ever flew, or swam. **1867** De Voe *Market Asst.* 171 **NEast,** White poke, snowy heron, or white-crested heron. **1937** (1965) Stone *Bird Studies* 116 **NJ,** There are two kinds [of white herons], the Little Blue which is white in its first summer and autumn, and the larger, less abundant, American Egret. To the local gunners and baymen the former is the "white poke."

white pollom n

A **wintergreen 2** (here: *Gaultheria hispidula*).

1880 (1881) Nickell *Bot. Ready Ref.* 98, *Oxycoccos hispidula* [= *Gaultheria h.*]. White Cranberry. Sweet Berry. White Pollom.

whitepoll warbler n
=black-and-white warbler.

1783 Latham *Genl. Synopsis Birds* 2.488, *Motacilla varia*. . . Whitepoll Warbler. **1799** *Med. Repository* 3.180 **PA,** White-poll warbler *(motacilla varia).*

white popinac See **popinac 2**

white poplar n

1 also *white-wood poplar;* Std: a tree of the genus *Populus,* usu *Populus alba,* but also *P. balsamifera, P. tremuloides,* or *P. grandidentata.* For other names of *P. alba* see **silver poplar, silverleaf ~** Cf **popple** n[1]

2 **=tulip tree 1,** esp one in which the white sapwood predominates; the sapwood of this tree. **chiefly S Midl, esp KY** See Map Cf **poplar B2, yellow poplar 1**

1810 Michaux *Histoire des Arbres* 1.37, Liriodendron tulipifera. . . *Yellow* or *white poplar* . . eu égard à la couleur du bois de cet arbre. [= Liriodendron tulipifera. . . *Yellow* or *white poplar* . . in reference to the color of the wood of this tree.] **1876** Maury-Fontaine *Resources WV* 134, *The Poplar,—* (Liriodendron tulipifera). . . The nature of the soil on which it grows has a striking effect on the color and quality of the wood. Mechanics distinguish three kinds, "White," "Blue," and "Yellow." . . In general, the White Poplar grows on dry, gravelly, elevated ground, and has a branchy summit, with a small amount of heartwood. **1893** *Jrl. Amer. Folkl.* 6.136 **WV,** *Liriodendron tulipifera,* white, yellow, or hickory poplar. **1908** *Cedar Rapids Eve. Gaz.* (IA) 8 Aug 6/2 **IN,** The tulip poplar is. . . white poplar in Indiana, blue poplar in Delaware [etc]. **1912** Simmons *Wood-Using Industries* 21, *Yellow Poplar.* . . The light colored wood of the tree is often sold on the markets as white poplar and the darker as yellow poplar. **1921** *Ft. Wayne News & Sentinel* (IN) 23 Feb 4/5, The Liriodendron is known under the common names of white poplar, yellow poplar, hickory poplar and the white-wood. **1965–70** *DARE* (Qu. T13, . . *Names . . for . . tulip tree*) 17 Infs, **chiefly S Midl, esp KY,** White poplar; (Qu. T12) Inf **VA2,** White poplar [FW: Inf described tulip tree].

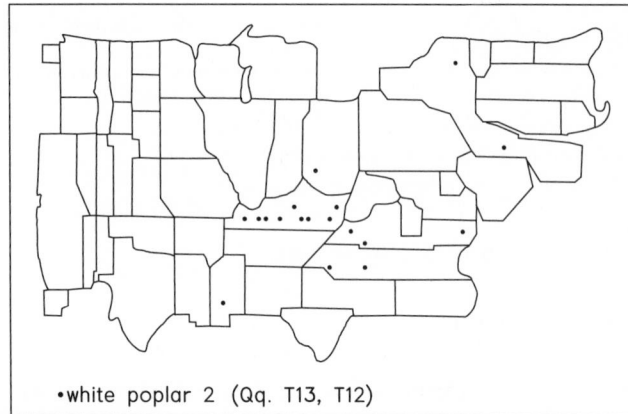

•white poplar 2 (Qq. T13, T12)

white potato n

1 The edible tuber of *Solanum tuberosum,* esp as contrasted with that of the **sweet potato 1;** the plant itself. **chiefly Sth, S Midl** See Map Also called **baker** n[1] **3, bluenose 2, cobbler** n[2], **goober** n[1] **3, ground apple 2, ice potato, Irish apple, ~ potato, Mick 3, murphy, pig potato 3, potato B1, pratie, round potato** Cf **potato B2**

1820 *Amer. Farmer* 2.259, It is a fine climate and soil, for every description of melons, and for the sweet and white potato [etc]. **1831** *Hagerstown Mail* (MD) [22 July 4]/3 (newspaperarchive.com), [Advt:] 20 bushels of fine large White Potatoes, at 75 cents per bushel. **1857** *MI State Ag. Soc. Trans. for 1856* 8.84, [In a list of competitive entries:] Moses Hunter. . . 1 peck white potatoes. **1905** *Elementary School Teacher* 5.504, Sometimes we call it the white potato, that we may know it from the sweet potato. **1939** in Lib. of Congress *Amer. Memory: WPA Life Hist.* (Internet) **FL,** He cultivated truck, selling quantities of vegetables—carots [sic], cabbage, tomatoes, sweet potatoes, white potatoes [etc]. **1953** (1977) Hubbard *Shantyboat* 321 **Missip-Ohio Valleys,** Plenty of storage space in the hold was available since there were no

white potatoes to stow away. **1965–70** *DARE* (Qu. H36, *Kinds of soup*) Inf **VA39,** White potato soup; (Qu. H47, *Kinds of fried potatoes*) Inf **FL36,** Fried white potatoes; **KY62,** White potatoes; (Qu. H49, *Dishes made by boiling potatoes with other foods*) Inf **LA33,** White potato stew; **GA17,** White potatoes in snap beans and garden peas and add soup; (Qu. H63, *Kinds of desserts*) Infs **MD35, VA39,** White potato pie; (Qu. I4, . . *Vegetables . . less commonly grown around here*) Inf **NJ17,** White potato; (Qu. I9, . . *Names [including nicknames] for potatoes*) Infs **GA6, MS54, NJ69, SC26,** White potatoes; **DC3,** They call Irish potatoes white potatoes; **NJ67,** White potato; in [the] South it's an Irish potato; **SC4,** White potato, Irish potato—potato means "yam" here—the white kinds must be designated specifically; (Qu. L34, . . *Most important crops grown around here*) Infs **FL1, NC80, NJ2, SC4,** White potatoes. **1966** *DARE* Tape **FL41,** We grew turnips and nice carrots and white potatoes and also sweet potatoes. **1986** Pederson *LAGS Concordance,* 90 infs, **Gulf Region,** White potato(es). [10 infs add comment "Irish (potato[es])."]

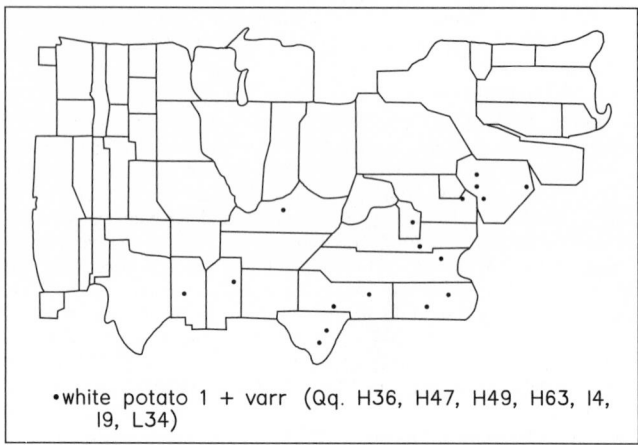

•white potato 1 + varr (Qq. H36, H47, H49, H63, I4, I9, L34)

2 An **arrowhead 1** (here: *Sagittaria platyphylla*).

1913 *Torreya* 13.227 **LA,** *Sagittaria platyphylla.* . . white potato, Venice, La.

white puccoon n Cf **red puccoon**
=bloodroot 1.

1844 *MA Ploughman* 20 Jan 4/6 **OH,** The doctor looked wise, as doctors will, and then commenced his directions as follows: "Take of white puccoon root and red puccoon root equal quantities." **1893** *Jrl. Amer. Folkl.* 6.137 **NY,** *Sanguinaria Canadensis.* . . white puccoon. **1930** Sievers *Amer. Med. Plants* 14, Bloodroot. . . Other common names. . . red puccoon, . . white puccoon.

white quail n Cf **white partridge**
=white-tailed ptarmigan.

1874 *Forest & Stream* 1.390 **CO,** They [=*Lagopus leucurus*] are generally known in Colorado as White and Mountain Quails by the hunters, miners and ranchmen. **1920** (1921) Mills *Waiting* 8 **Rocky Mts,** Farther up the slope I came upon a flock of ptarmigan—"white quail."

white ratany n
A **ratany** (here: *Krameria grayi*).

1931 U.S. Dept. Ag. *Misc. Pub.* 101.82 **AZ,** White ratany . . is browsed, sometimes almost to the point of extinction, by all classes of livestock in spring and early summer on Arizona foothill ranges. **1941** Jaeger *Wildflowers* 110 **Desert SW,** White ratany. . . In May the rigid branches are almost buried in masses of fragrant flowers. **1970** Correll *Plants TX* 890, White ratany. . . Frequent in desertic scrub in the trans-Pecos. **2007** (acc) U.S. Dept. Ag. *Plants Database* (Internet), *Krameria grayi* . . white ratany.

white rattlesnake n
=speckled rattlesnake.

1889 *West Amer. Scientist* 6.166, His specimens are in fact referred to as the 'white rattlesnake.' In all of them the ground color is a slightly buffy white, more or less sprinkled with black dots, giving it a kind of 'pepper and salt' appearance. **1911** *Century Dict. Suppl.,* White rattlesnake, *Crotalus mitchelli,* a pale desert species found from the Colorado Desert to Cape St. Lucas. **1952** Ditmars *N. Amer. Snakes* 257, White Rattlesnake. . . *Crotalus mitchellii mitchellii.* . . The author has seen specimens of this desert snake so pale that they could quite properly be called "white rattlesnakes."

white rim See **white sign (crab)**

white robin snipe n

The **knot** n[2] in fall plumage.

1844 DeKay *Zool. NY* 2.244, *The Red-breasted Sandpiper.* . . On its return southwardly, . . the red plumage beneath disappears, giving place to a white plumage spotted with dusky, ash-colored above; when it is called *White Robin Snipe,* and *Grey-back.* **1850** *Graham's Mag.* 37.127 **NY,** The Red-breasted Sandpiper . . known on the Long Island waters . . as the "Robin Snipe," by which name it is generally called, owing to the resemblance of its lower plumage to that of the Red-breasted Thrush, or Robin. . . In autumn this bird assumes a dusky gray upper, and white under, plumage, and is then termed the "White Robin Snipe." **1897** Samuels *With Rod & Gun* 117 **NEng,** "Yes," added the Doctor, "but that must have been in the spring, for in the autumn the under plumage is white or grayish-white, hence its familiar name of white-robin snipe."

white root n

1 An **angelica 1a** (here: *Angelica lucida*).

1791 Bartram *Travels* 45, I observed . . the carminative Angelica lucida. [Bartram: Called Nondo in Virginia: by the Creek and Cherokee traders, White Root.] **1830** Rafinesque *Med. Flora* 2.192, *Angelica lucida.* . . *Nendo* of the Virginian Indians. *White root* of the Southern tribes.

2 =**butterfly weed 1.**

1817 Barton *Vegetable Materia Medica* 1.239, *Asclepias tuberosa.* . . White-root. **1828** Rafinesque *Med. Flora* 1.74, *Asclepias tuberosa.* . . Vulgar Names . . Wind root, White root [etc]. **1856** MI State Ag. Soc. *Trans. for 1855* 400, Asclepias tuberosa. . . Pleurisy-root. White-root. **1876** Hobbs *Bot. Hdbk.* 128, White root, Pleurisy root, Asclepias tuberosa. **1974** Morton *Folk Remedies* 33 **SC,** White root; silkweed; pleurisy root. . . *Asclepias tuberosa.*

3 A **fleabane** (here: *Erigeron philadelphicus*).

1873 in 1976 Miller *Shaker Herbs* 252 **PA,** White Root—*Erigeron philadelphicus.*

4 A **spikenard** (here: *Aralia racemosa* or **Hercules'-club 1**). Cf **quiet root**

1886 Dudley *Cayuga Flora* 41 **NY,** A[ralia] racemosa. . . Spikenard. White-root. . . In ravines and shaded hollows. **1974** Morton *Folk Remedies* 29 **SC,** "White root" [etc]. . . *Aralia spinosa.* . . (Current use): "Tea" of root is taken to relieve arthritis, rheumatism and backache; also drunk by some men for "courage" (potency).

white round squash See **round squash**

whiterump n

1 =**Hudsonian godwit.**

1888 Trumbull *Names of Birds* 209 **MA,** In Massachusetts . . at West Barnstable [the Hudsonian Godwit is called] *white-rump.*

2 See **white-rumped sandpiper.**

white-rumped hawk n

=**marsh hawk 1.**

1912 Barrows *MI Bird Life* 262, Marsh Harrier, Mouse Hawk, White-rumped Hawk. . . Circus cyaneus var. hudsonius.

white-rumped kite n

=**everglade kite.**

1946 Hausman *Eastern Birds* 182, Everglade Kite. . . Other Names— Black Kite, Snail Kite, Hook-bill Hawk, White-rumped Kite.

white-rumped peep n

=**white-rumped sandpiper.**

1884 *Forest & Stream* 22.483 **eMA,** The white-rumped "peep" . . is given as "abundant."

white-rumped petrel n

=**fork-tailed petrel.**

1884 Coues *Key to N. Amer. Birds* 781, C[ymochorea] [=Oceanodroma] leucorrhoa. . . White-rumped Petrel. . . Abundant on our N. Atlantic coast. **1891** *Century Dict.* 6912, *White-rumped petrel,* Leach's petrel, *Cymochorea leucorrhoa,* of a fuliginous color with white upper tail-coverts: found on both east and west coasts of the United States. **1917** (1923) *Birds Amer.* 1.85, Leach's Petrel. . . Other Names. . . White-rumped Petrel [etc]. **1923** Dawson *Birds CA* 4.2013, Leach's Petrel. . . Synonyms. . . Pacific White-rumped Petrel [etc].

white-rumped sandpiper n   Also *whiterump*

Std: a **sandpiper** (here: *Calidris fuscicollis*).   Also called **bull peep 1, grass-bird 2c, oxeye 1a, peep** n **2, pin snipe, sand bird 1, sea chicken, white-rumped peep, white-tailed stib**

white-rumped shrike n

A **loggerhead shrike** (here: *Lanius ludovicianus excubitorides*).

1858 U.S. War Dept. *Rept. Explor. Railroad* 9.327, *Collyrio excubitoroides.* . . White-rumped Shrike. . . Head and body above ashy blue, . . the lower part of rump and upper tail coverts, with the outer scapulars, almost white. **1881** *Amer. Naturalist* 15.210 **CA,** One of the earliest birds to nest in the vicinity of Los Angeles, was the white-rumped shrike. **1900** *NE State Jrl.* (Lincoln) 23 July 3/5, A network of twigs and vines in one of the small willows afforded a site for the nest of a pair of white-rumped shrikes. **1917** (1923) *Birds Amer.* 3.101, The White-rumped Shrike, or Mouse-bird *(Lanius ludovicianus excubitorides)* is similar to the Migrant Shrike, but the gray of the upper parts is decidedly paler and changes abruptly to white on the upper tail-coverts. **1961** Ligon *NM Birds* 241, The Loggerhead—or White-rumped, as the common Shrike is often called—is for the most part resident and state-wide in distribution. **2007** *DARE* File—Internet **AZ,** I usually throw in a real name or two as sucker's bait, maybe a white-winged dove or a white-rumped shrike.

white sage n

1 A **winter fat** (here: *Krascheninnikovia lanata*).

1870 U.S. Genl. Land Office *Annual Rept. for 1869* 333, There grows in the valleys a grayish-white shrub, called "white sage." . . It has been aptly called "winter-fat" by stock growers and herders. **1877** Wright *Big Bonanza* 208 **West,** The white sage differs from the common sagebrush of the country, which few animals can eat, owing to its extreme bitterness. It sends up a great number of white shoots, which become quite tender and nutritious after the fall frosts, when cattle greedily feed and rapidly fatten upon them. **1878** Havard *Bot. Outlines* 1685 **ND, MT,** *Eurotia lanata* [=*Krascheninnikovia l.*] . . (White Sage). **1937** U.S. Forest Serv. *Range Plant Hdbk.* B76-2, Winterfat, a shrubby perennial, is largely known to western stockmen under the name "white sage", because it resembles many of the herbaceous sagebrushes, or "sages." **2007** (acc) Tarleton State Univ. *Range Types N. Amer.* (Internet), Winterfat or, sometimes, white sage (*Eurotia lanata* = *Ceratoides lanata*) [= *Krascheninnikovia l.*] . . another major (frequently dominant) shrub of the Great Basin Desertscrub.

2 also *white sagebrush:* A **sagebrush 1;** see quots.

1873 Lester *Atl. to Pacific* 346, Artemisia Canadensis . . (Wormwood, white sage). **1931** U.S. Dept. Ag. *Misc. Pub.* 101.167, Big sagebrush (Artemisia tridentata). . . Other vernacular names include . . white sage(brush) referring to the pale leaves. **1933** Small *Manual SE Flora* 1473, A[rtemisia] vulgaris. . . Mugwort. White-sage. . . Roadsides, stream-banks, cult. grounds, and waste-places. **1960** Vines *Trees SW* 966, Silver Sage-brush—Artemisia cana. . . Also known under the name of White Sage-brush. **1970** Correll *Plants TX* 1706, Artemisia ludoviciana. . . Western mugwort, white sage. . . all the herbage grayish or whitish-pubescent except in some plants the upper surface of the leaves nearly glabrous. **2007** (acc) U.S. Dept. Ag. *Plants Database* (Internet), Artemisia ludoviciana . . white sagebrush.

3 also *whiteleaf sage:* A **sage 1,** usu the California species *Salvia apiana.* Cf **bee sage 2, greasewood 2c**

1874 *Amer. Bee Jrl.* 10.272, Apiarists, who have kept bees east of the Rocky Mountains, and in California, give the palm to the white sage honey, above the white clover. **1876** *Prairie Farmer* 47.184 **CA,** The whole country is covered with white sage—the best bee food in the world. **1911** CA Ag. Exper. Sta. Berkeley *Bulletin* 217.1019, Salvia apiana. . . White Sage. . . Common from Santa Barbara County southward. **1920** Pellett *Amer. Honey Plants* 57 **CA,** Up to an elevation of 7,000 feet he found white sage in abundance, and all alive with bees. **1931** U.S. Dept. Ag. *Misc. Pub.* 101.141 **West,** White sage *(S. apiana . .),* known also as bee sage, greasewood, and white bee sage, is a white-leaved, white-flowered shrub 3 to 10 feet high. *Ibid,* Whiteleaf sage *(S. leucophylla . .)* is the common white sage of the apiarists. **1946** Peattie *Pacific Coast* 53, White sage, black sage, and purple sage all yield fine honeys. **1967–68** *DARE* (Qu. S26a, . . *Wildflowers.* . . *Roadside flowers)* Inf **CA4,** White sage; (Qu. S26e, *Other wildflowers not yet mentioned;* not asked in early QRs) Infs **CA60, 79,** White sage. **2007** (acc) U.S. Dept. Ag. *Plants Database* (Internet), *Salvia apiana* Jepson—white sage.

4 A **saltbush 1**; see quots.

1880 Torrey Bot. Club *Bulletin* 7.76, *Atriplex confertifolia* . . has an oil which the Mormons use for the hair. The plant goes by the name of "white sage." **1898** *Jrl. Amer. Folkl.* 11.277 **CO,** *Atriplex canescens* . . white sage, salty sage.

5 also *white sagebrush:* A **rabbit brush 1b** (here: *Ericameria nauseosa*).

1931 U.S. Dept. Ag. *Misc. Pub.* 101.161, Rubber rabbit brush . . , known also as . . white sage (brush), is a linear-leaved shrub . . with the older branches permanently white cottony woolly.

6 A **wild buckwheat 2** (here: *Eriogonum wrightii*).

1937 U.S. Forest Serv. *Range Plant Hdbk.* B75-2, Wright buckwheatbrush, known locally as bastard sage, white sage [etc] . . is a low, white-woolly-hairy shrub usually less than 2 feet high.

white sagebrush See **white sage 2, 5**

white salmon n

1 also *white salmon trout:* =**coho salmon.** Cf **silver salmon**

1806 in 1905 Lewis *Orig. Jrls. Lewis & Clark Exped.* 4.175 **nwOR,** The *White Salmon Trout* which we had previously seen only at the Great Falls of the Columbia . . has now made its appearance in the creeks near this place. **1887** Goode *Amer. Fishes* 483, On the Columbia it [= *Oncorhynchus kisutch*] is called "Silver Salmon" or "White Salmon." **1912** U.S. Congress Senate *AK Fisheries* 349 **AK,** Each man to receive 2 cents for each good red salmon caught . . , and 5 cents for each king salmon . . , and $5 for each 1,000 white salmon caught with a seine. **1949** Caine *N. Amer. Sport Fish* 53, Silver Salmon. . . This salmon is also known as the Coho Salmon, . . White Salmon and Arctic Trout.

2 =**walleye.**

1809 in 1810 Cuming *Sketches* 20 **PA,** The Susquehannah . . abounds with rock-fish, . . cat-fish and white salmon. **1820** Rafinesque *Ohio R. Fishes* 21, Salmon Perch. *Perca Salmonea.* . . A fine fish, from one to three feet long; . . its flesh is esteemed a delicacy, being white, tender, and well flavoured, whence the name of Salmon was given to it, and its shape, which is nearly cylindrical and slightly compressed, with the head and jaws somewhat similar to those of the Salmons, has induced many to consider it a real Salmon. . . It has received the vulgar names of *Salmon, White Salmon,* and *Ohio Salmon.* **1873** *Forest & Stream* 1.107, White salmon weigh from twelve to eighteen pounds. These fish are the same that are called wall eyed pike on the great lakes, from lake Ontario to lake Superior. **1887** Goode *Amer. Fishes* 14, "White Salmon" is a local name at the Falls of the Ohio; "Jack Salmon" is another bad name [for the walleye]. **1952** *Charleston Daily Mail* (WV) 18 May 18/2, Barnett caught a 39-inch fish, very slim, and was believed to be a walleye, and a man at the boat dock said was a "white salmon." In the old days wall-eye pike were called "white Salmon." **1957** Trautman *Fishes* 523, Early writers considered the Sauger and the Walleye to be a single species, usually considering the more distinctly marked Saugers to be the male ("Jack-Salmon" of the Ohio River fishermen) and the more plainly colored Walleyes to be the female ("White-Salmon" of Ohio River fishermen).

3 =**largemouth bass.** Cf **white trout 3**

1855 *Putnam's Mag.* 6.149, In the Susquehanna and rivers still further south, . . the first discoverers . . gave the name of white salmon to a fish which, . . though belonging to a totally distinct family, being a percoid fish, *gristes salmocides,* or in the vernacular, the growler, retains the honors of its unduly-applied title. **1880** *Lib. Universal Knowledge* 2.281 **Sth,** The growler, *grystes salmonus,* is the white salmon of the southern states. **1888** [see **trout-perch 1**].

4 =**California yellowtail.**

1882 U.S. Natl. Museum *Proc.* 27.46, Seriola lalandi. . . *Yellow Tail; White Salmon.* **1895** *Forest & Stream* 44.370 **CA,** In shape it somewhat resembled the salmon, hence one of its names—the white salmon. . . The median line is a yellow, while the tail is also brilliantly yellow. **1897** *Overland Mth.* (2d ser) 30.487 **CA,** I . . turn to my friend the yellow tail, sometimes called the white salmon.

5 A **squawfish 2** (here: *Ptychocheilus lucius*).

1896 Jordan–Evermann *Check List Fishes* 225, *Ptychocheilus lucius.* . . "White Salmon" of the Colorado. **1935** Pratt *Manual Vertebrate Animals* 69, *P[tychocheilus] lucius.* . . White salmon. . . Colorado basin; very common. **1950** *Mt. Democrat* (Placerville CA) 13 Apr [4]/4 (newspaperarchive.com), There are only two minnows that are bigger; the carp and the so-called "white salmon" of the Colorado River, which reaches a maximum weight of 80 pounds. **1974** *Long Beach Independent* (CA) sec C 8/7, At one time this particular squawfish was important

food for the Indians. Early settlers called it "white salmon" because of its great size and upstream migration.

white salmon trout See **white salmon 1**

white salt n Cf **red salt, salt grass a(1)**

A **cordgrass** (here: *Spartina patens*).

1912 Baker *Book of Grasses* 155, [Caption:] Fox-grass *(Spartina patens).* . . Locally called "White Salt."

white sanicle n Also *white sanicle root*

A **boneset 1** (here: *Ageratina altissima*).

1852 Beach *Amer. Practice Med.* 3.245, White Sanicle. . . *E[upatorium] ageratoides* [=*Ageratina altissima*]. **1872** Rudolphy *Pharmaceutical Directory* 43, Eupatorium ageratoides. White sanicle root. **1935** (1943) Muenscher *Weeds* 487, *Eupatorium urticaefolium* [= *Ageratina altissima*]. . . White sanicle [etc]. **1958** Jacobs–Burlage *Index Plants NC* 53, White sanicle. . . This species grows on mountain sides and in rich woodlands in Canada and most parts of the United States.

white sea bass n

A sciaenid fish of the California coast *(Atractoscion nobilis).* Also called **corvina b, croaker** n[1] **1a(2), Santa Catalina salmon, sea bass 2, ~ trout c(1)**

1881 CA *App. Jrls. Legislature* 2.45, Cynoscion nobilis *(Atractoscion nobilis),* Sea Bass, White Sea Bass—Very abundant in spring and summer from San Francisco southward. **1890** *Forest & Stream* 34.312 **CA,** In the books he figures as *Cynoscion nobile.* . . To the fishermen and anglers he is the sea bass, white sea bass, corvina or caravina. **1946** La Monte *N. Amer. Game Fishes* 78, *California White Sea Bass.* . . Names . . Santa Catalina Salmon. . . Reaches 80 pounds. Said to grow much larger. **1968–70** *DARE* (Qu. P2, . . *Kinds of saltwater fish caught around here . . good to eat)* Infs **CA**36, 176, 181, 191, White sea bass; (Qu. P14, . . *Commercial fishing . . what do the fishermen go out after?)* Inf **CA**191, White sea bass. **2007** *DARE* File—Internet **sCA,** I sure wish the weather would let me see a white sea bass instead of just talking about it.

white sea-chicken n

=**sanderling.**

1923 U.S. Dept. Ag. *Misc. Circular* 13.57 **NC,** Sanderling. . . white sea-chicken.

white shad n

1 =**gizzard shad 1.**

1820 Rafinesque *Ohio R. Fishes* 40, Spotted Gizzard. . . Vulgar nomes [sic] Gizzard, Hickory Shad, White Shad, &c. **2005** *DARE* File—Internet, I live on the lower susquehanna. . . our local boards always get a post where some dude says everyone was snagging white shad (you out of towners might call them american shad;) . . this post is always early in the season, and of course the species in question is a big, fat, stinky mud shad or gizzard shad if you prefer.

2 =**shad 1.** esp S Atl

1819 Warden *Statist. Political Hist. U.S.* 191, The mean weight of each, as communicated by Mr. Blodget, is. . . white shad, taylor shad, 3 lb. [etc]. **1843** *Brother Jonathan* (NY NY) 4.475 **eVA,** The men were discovered busily setting seines of a novel construction, the success of which soon developed itself by the transmition [sic] of large numbers of our finest white shad to the Northern markets. **1878** *Forest & Stream* 10.82 **Sth,** In the Southern States this fish [=*Alosa sapidissima*] is sometimes called "white shad," to distinguish it from the *Dorosoma cepedianum,* there known as the "mud-shad" or "gizzard shad." **1887** Goode *Amer. Fishes* 405 **GA,** In the Altamaha river, Georgia, the catch of "Hickory" Shad is equal to that of "Common" or "White Shad," and in the markets they sell for more than one-half as much. **1903** NY State Museum & Sci. Serv. *Bulletin* 60.205, The shad is known also as the white shad. **1966–67** *DARE* (Qu. P1, . . *Kinds of freshwater fish . . caught around here . . good to eat)* Inf **SC**43, Shadfish; white shad—eat up with bones—very bony; (Qu. P14, . . *Commercial fishing . . what do the fishermen go out after?)* **NC**13, White shad. **1966** *DARE* Tape **NC**1, White shad . . they're a very bony fish, but they are a delicious fish.

3 A **mooneye 1** (here: *Hiodon tergisus*).

1902 U.S. Bur. Fisheries *Rept. for 1901* 223, Hiodon tergisus. . . Moon-eye; "White Shad." **1946** La Monte *N. Amer. Game Fishes* 102, Mooneye—*Hiodon tergisus.* . . Names: White Shad, Toothed Herring [etc].

whiteshank n Also *white shank grass* **SC**
=barnyard grass.

1828 *S. Agriculturist* 1.168 **SC,** There is much grass that flourishes in water. . . The red and white shank for instance, with other water grasses. **1829** *Ibid* 2.252 **SC,** In this hoeing also, there should be great care taken to take all the grass from the Rice rows, . . and particularly the white shank grass, which is the most injurious grass we have to a Rice crop, . . and which will grow as well in the water as on dry land. **1920** *Torreya* 20.18 **SC,** *Echinochloa crus-galli.* . . Whiteshank, red-shank, Brunswick Co.

white shirt n [See quot 2003] **FL, GA, SC** Cf **shirttail n 2**
=red-headed woodpecker.

1913 *Auk* 30.497 **Okefenokee GA,** Red-headed woodpecker; 'White Shirt'; 'Jerry Coat'; 'Shirt-tail.' **1938** Matschat *Suwannee R.* 26 **neFL, seGA,** Two other woodpeckers, called "white-shirts" and "cham-chacks" work with a continuous *r-r-r-rat-a-tat-tat-tat.* **1956** *AmSp* 31.184 **GA, SC,** The redheaded woodpecker . . is called *shirttail* throughout the Southeast, as well as *shirttailer* (Del.), *half shirt* (S.C.), and *white shirt* (S.C., Ga.) **2003** *DARE* File—Internet **sGA,** To end on a "Georgia Cracker Trivial Pursuit" note, answer the following: What do local South Georgian's call the Red-headed Woodpecker & why? . . "White Shirt"—because of the large amounts of white plumage.

white shitepoke n Also *white shypoke*
An **egret** (here: *Ardea alba*) or similar bird.

1930 Spier *Klamath* 109 **OR,** The grass-stuffed skins of various animals and birds . . are hung under the slanting roof beams; mink, skunk, . . white shitepoke [etc]. **1945** McAtee *Nomina Abitera* 26 **WI,** American Egret . . White shypoke.

white shoe buttons See **white buttons**

white shypoke See **white shitepoke**

white side meat n Also *white side (bacon)* **Sth, S Midl** Cf **white bacon, ~ meat**
=side meat.

1898 *Gunton's Mag.* 15.20 **SE,** At noon he eats his dinner alone, which is made up of corn bread and white side meat. **1907** *Eve. Times* (Cumberland MD) 7 Nov 3/4, *White Side Meat,* lb—12c. **1927** *Bee* (Danville VA) 18 Nov 11/1, Good white side meat, per lb—19½c. **1948** *Dothan Eagle* (AL) 22 Apr 8/1, White Side Meat lb. 39c. **1950** *PADS* 14.72 **SC,** *White side meat.* . . Salt pork sides with one or more streaks of lean meat. **1966–69** *DARE* (Qu. H38, . . *Words for bacon [including joking ones]*) Inf **KY**28, White side; **NC**11, Bacon for breakfast; white side for cooking. **1971** Wood *Vocab. Change* 316 **FL, GA,** Volunteered Word List. . . white side . . [Meat from sides of hog, salted but not smoked]. **1973** *DARE* File **Ozarks** (as of c1910), Cured fat of swine without lean was white side or fatback. **1986** Pederson *LAGS Concordance (Salt pork)* 4 infs, **FL,** 4 infs, **GA,** 1 inf, **AL,** White side (meat *or* bacon).

white sign (crab) n Also *white line crab, white rim* Cf **pink sign, snot 1**
=fat crab.

[1905 U.S. Bur. Fisheries *Rept. for 1904* 411, As the crab approaches the shedding period it begins to show its condition by various external "signs." . . The first indication is a narrow white line which appears just within the thin margin of the last two joints of the posterior pair of legs.] **1970** *DARE* Tape **VA**112, [If there's a green crab . . and he will one day turn around and make a soft shell, he'll have a white sign. . . Where a rainbow is pink, he'll have a white rim streak crawling around that back fin that he paddles with.] *Ibid,* If they put the white sign in with the pink rim, or the red rim, . . the white sign will go to that . . pink rim and red rim and eat him. **1976** Warner *Beautiful Swimmers* 27 **Chesapeake Bay,** In time-honored Chesapeake practice, Mike reads these crabs by examining the translucent next-to-last segment of their swimming legs. Some will be "white sign" crabs, also known as "snots" or "greens," which have about two weeks or less to moult. **1984** *DARE* File **Chesapeake Bay** [Watermen's vocab], White sign crab, white line crab, white rim. **2001** [see **snot 1**].

white snakeroot n Also *white snakewort* Cf **snakeroot b(5)**
A **boneset 1:** usu *Ageratina altissima*, but also *A. aromatica.*

1843 Torrey *Flora NY* 1.329, *Eupatorium ageratoides* [=*Ageratina altissima*]. . . White Snakeroot. **1854** King *Amer. Eclectic Dispensatory* 455, *Eupatorium aromaticum* [=*Ageratina a.*]. White Snakeroot. . . In hysteria, hypochondria, nervous irritability and flatulence, it is very

beneficial. **1914** Georgia *Manual Weeds* 418, White Snakeroot. . . Other English names: White Sanicle, Indian Sanicle [etc]. **1945** Pickard–Buley *Midwest Pioneer* 21 (as of c1820), Among the chief offenders were white snakeroot and jimmyweed or rayless goldenrod. **1976** Bruce *How to Grow Wildflowers* 259, White Snakewort, *E. rugosum.* **1981** [see **staggerweed 4**]. **1998** (acc) Purdue Univ. Coop. Ext. Serv. *IN Plants* (Internet), White Snakeroot, White Sanicle, Richweed.

white snipe n

1 =sanderling.

1895 Ridgway *Ornith. IL* 2.55, Sanderling. Popular synonyms. Skinner . . ; White Snipe. **1948** Pearson *Sea Flavor* 143 **NEng,** Lobstermen have given *Crocethia* [=*Calidris*] a roster of nicknames—beach bird, whitey (in the fall he's the whitest of all shore birds), whiting, stib, white snipe, and beach snipe.

2 =bluestocking 2.

1845 *Albion* (NY NY) 4.339 **sTX,** Through this [tall grass] I struck, startling at every step a gray or white snipe. [*DARE* Ed: This quot may refer instead to **1** above.] **1872** *Amer. Naturalist* 6.400 **UT,** The avocet, and the black-necked stilt. . . are called "white snipes!" **1874** *Jackson Sentinel* (Maquoketa IA) 26 Nov [23]/2 (newspaperarchive.com), Game in Colorado is abundant. . . White snipe, geese, duck and plover are numerous. [*DARE* Ed: This quot may refer instead to **3** below.]

3 =black-necked stilt.

1872 [see **2** above]. **1904** Doubleday *Birds* 199, Black-necked Stilt *(Himantopus mexicanus)*—Called also: Lawyer; Longshanks; Tilt; Tildillo; White Snipe.

white sock(s) n Also *sock* [See quot 1965] **AK**
=black fly.

1942 *Bulletin Garden Club Amer.* May 19 **AK,** The most dangerous are the "white socks," a minute black fly with tiny white legs and a venom-ladened [sic] proboscis. **1965** Bowen *Alaskan Dict.* 35, *Whitesocks*—A tiny mosquito with a terrific authority. The whitesocks is a worse pest than the *no-see-um*. Under a magnifying glass its white feet are visible—if anyone cares to look. **1977** *Fairbanks Daily News-Miner* (AK) 7 Oct 17/4, Mosquitoes and no seeums & white socks have given up the battle for the season. **2000** *Anchorage Daily News* (AK) 23 July Lifestyles sec (Internet), *Black flies (aka white socks, buffalo gnats).* . . Most common are "white socks," so-called because of the white stripes on their legs. Females bite and can be extremely annoying in forested areas. **2007** *DARE* File—Internet **AK,** Which is worse, 'skeeters in [sic] masse or white socks? . . Much as I dread skeeters, I *really* abhor a cloud of them bitin' socks.

white sop n Cf **black sop, sop 1**
=white gravy.

1852 Paul *Dashes Amer. Humour* 58, Miserable Muss, the fat cowboy, was standing at the dresser . . industriously engaged in licking a platter unobserved, which had contained a compound of cream and bacon, recognized in Yankee land as "white sop." **1884** *Weekly NV State Jrl.* (Reno) 16 Aug [3]/2 (newspaperarchive.com), I eat nothing now but broiled snipe and yellow-legged chickens with big white sop. **1920** *Oakland Tribune* (CA) 10 Oct [46]/2 (newspaperarchive.com), What was more exhilarating than a spin out to Tony's place, where a dinner in which "white sop and chicken fixin's" . . could be counted on. **1960** Hall *Smoky Mt. Folks* 60 **wNC, eTN,** *White sop:* chicken gravy or other white gravy made with unbrowned flour. **1969** *DARE* (Qu. H37, . . *Words . . for gravy. Any joking ones?*) Inf **IL**76, White sop. **1978** *AP Letters* **FL,** In North West Fla. they call cream gravy "white sop." **1986** Pederson *LAGS Concordance,* 1 inf, **neTN,** White sop—gravy made of white meat; fat.

white spruce n

Std: a **spruce 1:** usu *Picea glauca,* but also **black spruce 1, blue spruce,** or **red spruce.** For other names of *P. glauca* see **Black Hills spruce, black ~ 2, cat pine, ~ spruce, double spruce 1, highland ~, single ~ 1, skunk ~**

white spurge n
=flowering spurge.

1891 Chicago Acad. Sci. *Bulletin* 2.102, *E[uphorbia] corollata.* . . White Spurge. In dry soil; everywhere common. **1941** *Capital Times* (Madison WI) 2 July 20/2, Among the things which the Scout group will remember are . . the white spurge and the yellow daisies [etc]. **1948** Wherry *Wild Flower Guide* 71, White Spurge. . . flower lobes conspicuous, white. **2002** [see **tramp's spurge**].

white squash n   For varr see quot 1965–70   **chiefly Sth, S Midl, TX**   See Map   Cf **pattypan squash**
A **summer squash**, esp **pattypan squash.**

1874 *NY Evangelist* (NY) 30 July 8/7, Long Island white squash, per basket, 25c. **1942** *San Mateo Times* (CA) 15 July 8/5, White squash, flat and scalloped-edged, . . generally known as pattypan. **1965–70** *DARE* (Qu. I23, . . *Kinds of squash*) 86 Infs, **chiefly Sth, S Midl, TX,** White squash; **GA**3, VA74, White round squash [illustr shows scalloped edge]; **AL**34, White squashes; **FL**51, White squash—not a cymling— has indentations, however; **IL**117, White dish squash—shaped like a dish; **LA**40, White scalloped squash; **MS**72, White bush squash; **MO**34, Little white squash; **NC**3, White—round, white squash; **OK**43, White squash—round and flat and white plumb through; **SC**57, White bunch squash; **TN**49, Yellow—long; white—round; **TX**21, White summer squash; **VA**46, White cymling squash. **2007** *DARE* File—Internet **sLA,** The white squash is similar to the pattypan squash found throughout America. It is grown in abundance here in the bayous and is normally the only squash seen on tables in South Louisiana.

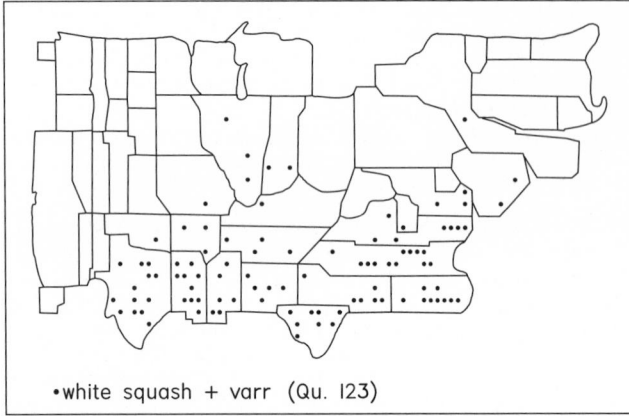

•white squash + varr (Qu. I23)

white squawk n   Cf **squawk**
=**snowy egret.**

1914 *Condor* 16.246 **cnUT,** The next morning we went by team to the outskirts of the marshes, where Mr. Knudson secured for us a specimen of the "White Squawk" which proved to be the Snowy Heron *(Ardea candidissima).*

white star n   Also *white star Ipomoea*
A **morning glory 1** (here: *Ipomoea lacunosa*).

1881 U.S. Natl. Museum *Bulletin* 22.100 **DC,** *Ipomoea lacunosa,* . . White-Star Ipomoea. First half of September. **1901** Mohr *Plant Life AL* 680, *Ipomoea lacunosa.* . . White Star Ipomoea. **1949** Moldenke *Amer. Wild Flowers* 268, Extending northward in moist soil to Pennsylvania and Illinois, is found the whitestar, *I. lacunosa,* whose pure white (or white and purple) flowers are less than an inch long. **2007** (acc) U.S. Dept. Ag. *Plants Database* (Internet), *Ipomoea lacunosa* . . whitestar.

‡**whitestone** n
=**madstone.**

1970 Anderson *TX Folk Med.* 58 **ceTX,** Use the whitestone [mad-stone] of an albino deer for any poisonous bites or the bites of a rabid animal.

white stopper n   Also *white-stopper eugenia* Cf **red stopper**
A **stopper 1a** (here: *Eugenia axillaris*).

1837 (1962) Williams *Territory FL* 99, [In a list of "vegetable productions":] White Stopper. Red Stopper. **1884** Sargent *Forests of N. Amer.* 89 **FL,** *Eugenia monticola* [=*E. axillaris*]. . . Stopper. White Stopper. Florida, Saint John's river to Umbrella Key. **1946** West–Arnold *Native Trees FL* 155, *Eugenia axillaris* . . , white-stopper eugenia, is a small tree occurring in coastal hammocks. **1982** *Miami Herald* (FL) 24 Oct sec H 11/3, *E. axillaris* has bigger, elongated leaves. . . This one, white stopper, is a fuller-growing stopper. The name comes from the grayish white bark. **2007** (acc) U.S. Dept. Ag. *Plants Database* (Internet), Eugenia axillaris . . white stopper.

white stove-blacking   See **white lampblack**

white sucker n

1   A **sucker 1,** as:

a   A **redhorse 1;** see quots.

1820 Rafinesque *Ohio R. Fishes* 60, Pittsburgh Sucker. *Catostomus duquesne* [=*Moxostoma duquesnii*]. . . found in the Ohio as far as Pitts-burgh: vulgar name White Sucker. **1842** DeKay *Zool. NY* 4.203, C[atostomus] duquesnii, The White Sucker. **1876** NY Acad. Sci. *Annals Lyceum Nat. Hist.* 11.350 **nGA,** They [=*Myxostoma* [=*Moxostoma*] *duquesnii*] are locally known as White Sucker. *Ibid* 366 **nGA,** *Myxostoma papillosum.* . . This marked and handsome species abounds in the Ocmulgee River, where it is known as the White Sucker. **1917** *Jrl. Elisha Mitchell Scientific Soc.* 32.156 **wNC,** *Moxostoma aureolum* [=*M. pisolabrum*]. . . It is found principally in . . Madison County. It is used locally as a food fish in that section, where it is known as the white sucker. **1983** Becker *Fishes WI* 657, Golden Redhorse—*Moxostoma erythurum.* . . Other common names . . white sucker [etc]. *Ibid* 661, Silver Redhorse—*Moxostoma anisurum.* . . Other common names . . white sucker [etc].

b   Std: the common white sucker, *Catostomus commersoni.* Also called **black sucker 3, family whitefish 2, gaspergou 3a, Grand River tuna, gray sucker, June ~ 1, mud ~ 1b, mullet n[1] 2, rainbow sucker, sewer bass, whitehorse 1**

2   A carpsucker (*Carpiodes cyprinus*).
1951 Harlan–Speaker *IA Fish* 61, Quillback—*Carpiodes cyprinus.* . . Other Names—White carp, carpsucker, silver carp and white sucker.

white sumac n

1   A **poison sumac** (here: *Toxicodendron vernix*).   **esp NEast**
1798 Horsfield *Exper. Diss.* 3 **PA,** The *Rhus Vernix.* This tree is distin-guished in Pennsylvania by the different names of: Poison tree, Poison wood, Varnish tree, Poison ash, Swamp Sumach and white Sumach. **1838** Holmes *Boylston Diss.* 114 **cnMA** (as of 1760), He owned a rich tract of intervale land covered with a poisonous shrub called dogwood, or white sumach (the Linnæan name I do not recollect). The proprietor being subject to eruptions, from working among ivy or dogwood, built a dam across the river, in order to flow this intervale. **1911** *News* (Freder-ick MD) 13 Feb 7/2 **PA,** *White Sumac Cane Poisons.* . . The cane was cut by a young son, who failed to distinguish between the harmless red-berried and the very poisonous white or green-berried sumac. **1941** *LANE* Map 250 (*Sumach*) 1 inf, **seCT,** White sumach, poisonous. **1966–69** *DARE* (Qu. S17, . . *Kinds of plants* . . *that* . . *cause itching and swelling*) Infs **ME**7, **VA**11, White sumac; **NY**71, White sumac—called this because of white berries; (Qu. T13, . . *Names* . . *for* . . *sumac*) Inf **CT**6, White sumac; **CT**23, White sumac—poison. **1970** *S. Illinoisan* (Carbondale) 5 Aug 6/2, For Indian lemonade, pick red staghorn su-mac. . . Then crush the berries for juice. . . As white sumac is poisonous, people should take special care, that they pick the red staghorn sumac. **1975** Hamel–Chiltoskey *Cherokee Plants* 57, Sumach, white . . *Rhus vernix* . . *Poison*—For clap; asthma; phthisic; ague and fever [etc]. **1986** Pederson *LAGS Concordance,* 1 inf, **cwGA,** White sumac—poi-sonous.

2   A **sumac B:** usu **smooth sumac 1,** but occas **staghorn su-mac.**   **esp Sth, S Midl**
1804 in 1963 Amer. Philos. Soc. *Trans.* 53.2.28 **neGA,** A decoction of the root of Chionanthus virginicus called in the southern states white ash/in an equal proportion with Ceanothus erythrorhiza/Red root/and Rhus glabrum/white Sumack/ is said to cure effectually the venerial dis-ease. **1846** *S. Lit. Messenger* 12.693, She proved herself conversant in indigo, coperas, walnut, black and white sumac dyes. **1884** Hilgard *Rept. Cotton MS* 63 **MS,** *Rhus typhina,* here called "white sumach", a name elsewhere given to *Rhus venenata,* or varnish tree. **1891** AR State Geologist *Annual Rept.* 251, The fruit of the . . white sumac (*Rhus glabra*) produces on its surface a slippery whitish transparent coating, which is composed largely of malic acid. **1898** in 1905 S. Hist. Soc. *Papers* 33.169 **Sth,** White sumac, red elm, prickly ash, and poke, will in connection with my black wash cure recent cases of syphilis. **1907** *Harper's Bazaar* 41.1128, The only innocent member of the genus [is] the white, or staghorn sumac. **1930** OK Univ. Biol. Surv. *Pub.* 2.70, *Rhus glabra.* . . White Sumac. **1976** Elmore *Shrubs & Trees SW* 28, Smooth Sumac—scarlet, red or white sumac. **1979** *Kerrville Mt. Sun* (TX) 16 June 7/3, The wild chinaberry and white sumac along the coun-try roads also have bountiful crops.

white sweet clover n
Std: a **sweet clover 1** (here: *Melilotus albus*).   Also called **bee clover, ~ weed 2d, galygumber, honey clover**

white sweet gum   See **white gum 1**

whitetail   See **white-tailed ptarmigan**

whitetail deer See **white-tailed deer**

whitetail dowitcher See **white-tailed dowitcher**

white-tailed deer n Also *whitetail deer*

Std: a North American deer (*Odocoileus virginianus* and races). Also called **cottontail deer, flagtail ~, red ~, tideland ~**

white-tailed dowitcher n Also *whitetail dowitcher*

A **dowitcher** (here: *Limnodromus scolopaceus*).

1880 Nuttall *Ornith. Club Bulletin* 5.156 **Long Is. NY,** The gunners in the vicinity of Rockaway, L.I., make a distinction between the two birds, calling *M. scolopaceus* [=*Limnodromus s.*] the *White-tail Dowitcher.* **1923** U.S. Dept. Ag. *Misc. Circular* 13.52 **Long Is. NY,** White-tailed dowitcher (this is a distinctive term for the western subspecies).

white-tailed grouse n *obs*
=**white-tailed ptarmigan.**

[**1831** Richardson *Fauna Boreali-Amer.* 2.356, Tetrao (Lagopus) leucurus. . . *White-tailed Grouse.* . . It is said to have the habits of the Ptarmigan, and to inhabit the snowy peaks near the mouth of the Columbia as well as the snowy ridges of the Rocky Mountains.] **1839** Audubon *Ornith. Biog.* 5.200, [The] *White-tailed Grous* [sic], *Tetrao Leucurus.* . . is an inhabitant of the Rocky Mountains. **1854** Capron *Hist. CA* 119, Grouse of various kinds, such as the great cock of the plains, dusky grouse, rock grouse, ruffed grouse, white-tailed grouse, and pin-tailed grouse, inhabit the plains and mountains.

white-tailed hawk See **white-tailed kite**

white-tailed hornet n Also *white-arsed hornet, white-ass(ed) ~, whitetail ~* **chiefly NEast, esp NEng** Cf **striped-ass (hornet), white-faced hornet, yellow-tailed hornet**
=**bald-faced hornet.**

1840 *TX in 1840* 204, Many stories have been told of the . . venom of this insect [=a spider], but from no person could any direct evidence be found . . that the wound he inflicts is either dangerous or more painful than the sting of the large white tailed hornet. **1878** *Forest & Stream* 11.378, The common brown wasp, the "white tailed hornet" and "yellow jacket" are good examples [of social wasps]. **1902** Manchester *Inst. Arts & Sci. Proc.* 3.139 **seNH,** Vespa maculata (White-tailed Hornet). **1936** in 1969 Frost *Poetry* 277 **NEng,** The white-tailed hornet lives in a balloon / That floats against the ceiling of the woodshed. **1939** *LANE* Map 240–41 *(Hornet)* 10 infs, **chiefly sNH, sME, neMA,** White-ass(ed) *(or* white-arsed) hornet; 5 infs, **chiefly sNEast, eMA,** White-tail(ed) hornet. **1958** Mayo *Forever Strangers* 236 **ME,** Once you get a woman stirred up, you might just as well try to cope with a nest of white-tailed hornets. **1968–69** *DARE* (Qu. R21, . . *Other kinds of stinging insects)* Infs **CT9, PA**180, White-assed hornet; **MA**15, White-assed hornet—different from regular hornet, which is called yellow jacket here; **NH**14, White-assed hornet—similar [to ground hornet or yellow-assed hornet]. **2004** *DARE* File—Internet **ME,** White ass hornets. . . I got stung by one last year. **2005** in 2008 *Ibid* **Upstate NY,** I have been stung alot of times but never on my chest. Feels like someone has a match on it. At least they where [sic] not white ass hornets. **2007** *Ibid* **MA,** These spambots were attacking my site like a bunch of ticked off white-tailed hornets! *Ibid* **VT,** Often referred to as white tail hornets by vermonters and tree surgeons, these buggers swing a sledgehammer when they sting, and seem to have a "grumpy, don't even look at me" attitude.

white-tailed kite n Also *white-tailed hawk*

Std: a kite *(Elanus leucurus)* native to southernmost Florida, southeastern Texas, and parts of the West Coast. Also called **nighthawk** n 2

white-tailed ptarmigan n Also *whitetail*

A **ptarmigan** (here: *Lagopus leucura*). Also called **snowbird 4, snow partridge, white quail, ~-tailed grouse**

1834 Jardine *Nat. Hist. Game-Birds* 152, An American species [of ptarmigan] . . has been termed by Dr Richardson *Lagopus leucurus,* or White-tailed Ptarmigan. **1842** Audubon *Birds Amer.* 5.125, *White-Tailed Ptarmigan.* . . This pretty little Grouse is an inhabitant of the Rocky Mountains. . . It is said to extend as far as the Columbia river. **1932** U.S. Natl. Museum *Bulletin* 162.234 **AK,** *Lagopus leucurus peninsularis.* . . Kenai White-tailed Ptarmigan. **1963** Murie *Birds Mt. McKinley* 40 **AK,** The white-tail is extremely tame in summer. *Ibid,* Sometime in late summer, a change in the psychology of the white-tailed ptarmigan takes place, and they become wild spirits, alert and restless.

1989 Mickelson *Nat. Hist.* 124 **AK,** Generally white-tailed ptarmigan occur on the rockiest crags.

white-tailed sparrow n

A **junco** n[1] (here: *Junco hyemalis* Hyemalis Group).

1904 *Oölogist* 21.155 **ceNY,** This bird Mr. Robinson [=a local farmer] called the white tailed Sparrow, but he described the bird so ably that there is no doubt as to its identification [as the slate-colored junco]. **1914** *Auk* 31.228 **AL,** *Junco Hyemalis hyemalis.* Slate-colored Junco. [Local names:] 'Snowbird.' 'White-tailed Sparrow.'—Common winter resident.

white-tailed stib n Cf **stib 1**
=**white-rumped sandpiper.**

[**1852** in 1876 *Forest & Stream* 7.212 **Plymouth MA,** *T[ringa] alpina.* Stile. *T[ringa] Bonapartei.* White-tailed Stile.] **1876** *Ibid* 7.245, In looking over the "List of Gunner's Names," printed from my manuscript, I notice two errors, or rather one repeated, which should be corrected. Against the two trinqas [sic]—*Alpina* and *Bonapartei*—for "stile," as you have it, read "stib." Why stib, I can't make out.

whitetail hornet See **white-tailed hornet**

white tea-tree n [See quot 1976] Cf **mountain tea-tree**

A **deer brush 1** (here: *Ceanothus integerrimus*).

1897 Parsons *Wild Flowers CA* 84, Mountain Birch. White Tea-tree. . . It often covers great mountain-sides with its white bloom as with drifted snow. **1915** (1926) Armstrong–Thornber *Western Wild Flowers* 284, *Ceanothus integerrimus.* . . It is often called White Tea-tree, because the bark is used medicinally. **1976** Elmore *Shrubs & Trees SW* 120, White tea-tree. . . The bark of the root of this shrub is used as a remedy for numerous ailments, including colds, liver disorder and malaria.

white thistle n

A **saltbush 1** (here: *Atriplex lentiformis*).

1949 Curtin *By the Prophet* 66 **AZ,** *Atriplex lentiformis.* . . Common name . . White-thistle. **1976** Bailey–Bailey *Hortus Third* 129, *Atriplex. . . lentiformis.* . . white thistle. **2001** Armitage *Armitage's Manual* 85, White thistle *(A[triplex] lentiformis)* may be found in southwestern United States.

whitethorn n

1 Std: =**hawthorn.**

2 also *whitethorn chaparral*: A **ceanothus;** see quots.

1911 Jepson *Flora CA* 255, *C[eanothus] incanus.* . . Called "White Thorn" in southwestern Humboldt. **1931** U.S. Dept. Ag. *Misc. Pub.* 101.108, Whitethorn *(C. cordulatus)* . . occurs abundantly in parts of the Sierra Nevada, northern California, and southwestern Oregon. **1937** U.S. Forest Serv. *Range Plant Hdbk.* B39-1, Many species of *Ceanothus* have individual names as, . . whitethorn, deerbrush, bluebrush, or sweet birch *(C. integerrimus).* **1946** Peattie *Pacific Coast* 55, The most characteristic chaparral plants are the gnarled tree-shrubs, numberless in species and variously called wild or California lilac or blue blossom when their flowers are blue or lavender, and whitethorn or snowbush when they are white. **1958** *Fresno Bee the Republican* (CA) 25 May sec D 14/1, White thorn chaparral and wedge leaf ceanothus are two of the better non sprouting types [of browse]. **1968** *DARE* (Qu. C28, *A place where underbrush, weeds, vines and small trees grow together so that it's nearly impossible to get through)* Inf **CA**105, Whitethorn. [*DARE* Ed: This quot may refer instead to another sense.]

3 A **lotebush** (here: *Ziziphus obtusifolia*).

1931 U.S. Dept. Ag. *Misc. Pub.* 101.113, Southwestern jujube . . , known locally as whitethorn and by a variety of Mexican names including . . paloblanco, is the most widely distributed and best known of these native species.

4 An acacia (here: usu *Acacia constricta*).

1938 Van Dersal *Native Woody Plants* 343, Mendocino whitethorn *(Ceanothus incanus).* **1945** Benson–Darrow *Manual SW Trees* 153, As a forage plant, white thorn has negligible value, due partly at least to its spiny character. **1949** *Brownsville Herald* (TX) 20 June 9/6 **OR,** Mrs. Inga Danielson, 78, who was forced to spend 48 hours in a rain-swept Rogue riverside thicket of white thorn after her hair had become entangled, was home safe again today. **1975** Lamb *Woody Plants SW* 68, Mescat acacia or whitethorn is. . . a shrub, usually 6 to 8 feet tall, that may reach heights of up to 18 feet. **1991** *AZ Daily Star* (Tucson) 16 May sec C 1 (Internet), Mesquites and palo verdes are the most cooperative, followed by cat claw and white thorn acacia with ironwood being the most difficult and fragile to transplant. **2007** (acc) U.S. Dept. Ag. *Plants Database* (Internet), *Acacia constricta* . . whitethorn acacia.

whitethorn chaparral See **whitethorn 2**

White thrash See **White trash**

white-throated sparrow n

Std: a crown sparrow *(Zonotrichia albicollis)* with a white patch at the throat. Also called **Canada bird, ~ sparrow, fiddler bird, mountain lark, nightingale b, peabody bird, sow-your-wheat bird, wheat ~ 4, whistler 9**

white-throated swift n

Std: a swift *(Aeronautes saxatalis). Also called* **night flyer**

white thunder n

See quots.

1968 Coatsworth *ME Memories* 155 **eME,** Thunder at a distance is "white thunder." **1987** DuFresne *Glacier Bay* 119 **AK,** White Thunder Ridge . . picked up its name at a time when it overlooked three glaciers . . that were almost continuously calving (hence white thunder).

white titi n Cf **black titi 2, red ~, titi 1b** =**he-huckleberry 1.**

1897 Sudworth *Arborescent Flora* 277, *Cyrilla racemiflora.* . . Common Names. . . White Titi. **1946** West–Arnold *Native Trees FL* 116, White Titi. . . grows in damp, sour, sandy peat-soil in the shady bayheads of western Florida. **2004** Austin *FL Ethnobotany* 259, In the United States this name [=*titi*] has been given . . to leatherwood, red titit [sic] or white titi, *Cyrilla racemiflora.*

whitetop n

1 A **redtop 1a** (here: *Agrostis gigantea,* formerly *A. alba).*

1818 Eaton *Botany* 127, *Agrostis.* . . *alba* (white top). **1832** MA Hist. Soc. *Coll.* 2d ser 9.146 **cwVT,** Agrostis alba. . . White-top. **1857** Flint *Practical Treatise* 111, *Field or Pasture Grasses.* . . Whitetop, *(agrostis alba.)* **1881** Phares *Farmer's Book of Grasses* 40, *A[grostis] alba.* White top, dew grass, bonnet grass, has become naturalized in some of our southern swamps. **1945** Wodehouse *Hayfever Plants* 51, Redtop or Herd's grass *(Agrostis alba* . . *),* also called whitetop or creeping bent grass.

2 also *whitetop grass:* An **oatgrass c** (here: *Danthonia spicata).*

1857 Flint *Practical Treatise* 65, Wild Oat Grass, White Top, *(danthonia spicata,)* is common in dry, sunny pastures. **1877** VT State Bd. Ag. *Report* 4.169, White-top Grass, *(Danthonia spicata,)* makes unwholesome hay. **1922** Boston Soc. Nat. Hist. *Proc.* 36.212 **MA,** *D[anthonia] spicata.* . . White Top. . . common, especially on the upland.

3 also *whitetop weed:* A **fleabane** (here: *Erigeron* spp).

1878 Killebrew *Grasses TN* 286, There are several plants exceedingly troublesome to the meadows in Tennessee. Among them is the White Top *(Erigeron Philadelphicum),* or Fleabane. **1896** *Jrl. Amer. Folkl.* 9.192 **OH,** *Erigeron annus* . . white-top weed, Sulphur Grove. **1912** Blatchley *IN Weed Book* 178, Associated with it [=*Erigeron annuus*] is the slender daisy fleabane *(E. ramosus).* . . Both are commonly known as "white-top" and are not separated by the average farmer. **1929** *Van Wert Daily Bulletin* (OH) 22 June 2/3, This salt spray is effective against . . whitetop or fleabane. **1966** *DARE* [see **6** below]. **1969** *DARE* FW Addit **KY11,** Whitetop or chiggerweed—book name: robin's plantain *(Erigeron pulchellus).* **1970** Correll *Plants TX* 1605, *Erigeron strigosus.* . . White-top. **1993** Mason *Feather Crowns* 312 **KY** (as of c1900), Outside the barn . . was a bank of whitetop, the weed farmers hated. . . It was a tiny daisy, hundreds of blooms on a single stalk.

4 also *whitetop quail:* =**scaled quail.**

1928 Bailey *Birds NM* 217, So well do its pale colors and scale-like markings conceal it . . that the white tip of its crest, which gives it the local name of White-top or Cotton-top, is often all that catches one's eye. **1966** *DARE* (Qu. Q7, *Names and nicknames for . . game birds)* Inf **NM13,** Whitetop quail.

5 also *whitetop rivergrass:* The common river grass *Scolochloa festucacea.* Also called **hoary grass, hollow stem, sprangletop 2, wild rice 3**

1933 *Torreya* 33.82 **MT,** *Scolochloa festucacea.* . . Whitetop, Homestead, Montana. **1968** *Mackay Miner* (ID) 25 Jan 4/3, The Board of County Commissioners of Custer County, Idaho, does hereby formulate and declare: that weeds known as Canadian Thistle, Wild Morning Glory, Russian Knapweed, White Top or Hoary Grass, . . are nox-

ious weeds. **1972** *DARE* File—Internet **ND,** [Caption:] Shallow-marsh emergent vegetation . . with . . scattered *Scolochloa festucacea* (whitetop). **2007** (acc) Cornell Univ. Lab. Ornith. *Birds N. Amer.* (Internet), *Canvasback.* . . Prefers wetlands bordered by dense emergent vegetation, including . . whitetop rivergrass *(Scolochloa festucacea).*

6 also *whitetop peppergrass:* The hoary cress *(Lepidium draba);* rarely, *L. chalapensis* or *L. appelianum.* Cf **white-weed 5**

1935 (1943) Muenscher *Weeds* 271, *Lepidium Draba.* . . Hoary cress, . . White-top [etc]. **1948** Stevens *KS Wild Flowers* 129, Lepidium draba—Whitetop Peppergrass. **1964** *Fresno Bee the Republican* (CA) 21 June sec F 4/1, Russian knapweed . . and hoary cress (whitetop) are the most serious broadleafed weeds spreading in Kern County. **1966** Barnes–Jensen *Dict. UT Slang* 45, White Top . . a name given locally to the introduced Hoary Cress *(Lepidium draba).* **1966** *DARE* FW Addit **WA10,** *Cardaria* [=*Lepidium*] . . whitetop—often applied to daisy fleabane. **1971** *Daily News* (Red Bluff CA) 8 May 3/5, Whitetop or hoary cress, another serious weed pest of range and croplands, was found at a new location. **2007** *DARE* File—Internet **MT,** The three species of whitetop differ in the shape of their seed pods. *C. draba* has the heart-shaped seed pods and is most common in Montana. *C. pubescens* [=*L. appelianum*] has purplish, globe-shaped seed pods, and *C. chalapa* [=*L. chalapensis*] has lens-shaped seed pods.

7 A **boneset 1** (here: *Ageratina altissima).*

1917 *Jrl. Ag. Research* 11.700, Other names which have been applied to it [=*Ageratina altissima*] are white sanicle, . . squawweed, whitetop [etc]. **1958** Jacobs–Burlage *Index Plants NC* 53, *Eupatorium urticaefolium* [=*Ageratina altissima*]. . . White snakeroot; . . white top [etc].

whitetop grass See **whitetop 2**

whitetop peppergrass See **whitetop 6**

whitetop quail See **whitetop 4**

whitetop rivergrass See **whitetop 5**

whitetop weed See **whitetop 3**

White trash n Also rarely sp *White thrash* Cf *poor White trash* (at **poor White 2a**) orig Sth, S Midl; now widely known

A **poor White 1** or such people as a group; hence adj *White-trashy;* see quots.

1824 Smith *Winter in Washington* 1.281 **DC,** Do you think because I bemean'd myself to marry such a neger as you, I'll be beholden to them white trash, that with their hard hearted ways forced me to do the like? **1831** Finn *Amer. Comic Annual* 88 **Philadelphia PA** [Black], What fur he go more 'mong niggers den de white *trash?* **1856** *Harper's New Mth. Mag.* 12.343, Some . . acquire loose notions and bad principles from associating with the independent whites and vagabonds—the white trash, as a Southerner would say. **1886** *Atlantic Mth.* 58.653 **NC,** Along with these there was a lawless population of "white trash." **1922** *Hopewell Herald* (NJ) 26 July 4/3, Jenny was as obsequious now as she had been curt when she imagined herself dealing with "white trash" instead of "quality." **1942** (1960) Robertson *Red Hills* 87 **SC,** Once . . I called a colored boy a nigger, and the colored boy called me poor buckra and white trash. **1965–70** *DARE* (Qu. HH18, *Very insignificant or low-grade people)* 47 Infs, **scattered,** White trash; **AK8,** Dirty White trash; **MS73,** Low White trash; **KY59,** White thrash; (Qu. HH19, *Other words or nicknames for a tramp)* Inf **NC76,** White trash; (Qu. HH28, *Names and nicknames . . for people of foreign background)* Inf **LA11,** White trash. **1971** O'Connor *Complete Stories* 490 **cGA,** She could tell by the way they sat—kind of vacant and white-trashy, as if they would sit there until Doomsday if nobody called and told them to get up. **1989** Pederson *LAGS Tech. Index* 254 **Gulf Region,** *Poor whites* [white usage] . . common white trash (1 [inf]) . . (lazy), low-down white trash (2) . . poor white trash (120) . . pure white trash (1) . . sorry white trash (3) . . white trash (162). . . *Poor whites* [black usage] . . old white trash (2) . . poor white trash (59) . . sorry white trash (1) . . white trash (71). **2005** *Chron.-Telegram* (Elyria OH) 8 Apr 5/4, Swank is a waitress from a white-trash background.

white trout n

1 A **weakfish** (here: *Cynoscion arenarius* or *C. nothus).* **chiefly Gulf States, S Atl**

1737 (1911) Brickell *Nat. Hist. NC* 234, The *Salt-Water Trouts,* commonly called the *White Trouts,* are exactly shaped like the *Trouts* with us, only these have blackish and not Red Spots. They are in great plenty in the Sounds, near the Inlets, and Salt Waters; but they are not red within like some Trouts. **1889** *Amer. Angler* 15.174, Another species, *C[ynoscion] nothum*—"white trout" . . is also found along our Atlantic and Gulf coasts. **1931** *Copeia* 144, In Louisiana, Mississippi, and Alabama, they [=*Cynoscion arenarius* and *C. nothus*] are collectively known as "white trout" while in Texas they are called "sand trout." The fishermen are unable to distinguish the two species. **1967–68** *DARE* (Qu. P1, . . *Kinds of freshwater fish . . caught around here . . good to eat*) Inf **GA65**, White trout; (Qu. P2, . . *Kinds of saltwater fish caught around here . . good to eat*) Infs **AL37**, White trout; **LA26**, White trout [FW: =weakfish]. **1996** Hein et al. *Fisherman's Guide LA* 34, Sand Seatrout (White Trout, Sand Trout)—*Cynoscion arenarius*. . . Normally confused with silver seatrout [=*C. nothus*] and both referred to as white trout. **2000** *DARE* File—Internet **sLA**, Anglers on the bridge connecting Grand Isle to the mainland cast for croakers, white trout, Spanish mackerel, sea perch and sheepshead. **2007** *Ibid* **MS**, As summer progresses, white trout and ground mullet will work their way up coastal bays, bayous and rivers.

2 Any of several salmonid fish, but esp the **lake trout 1**; see quots.

1788 *New-Haven Gaz. & CT Mag.* 30 Oct 2/1 **NY**, All the lakes, rivers and creeks, teem with fish, namely the Salmon Trout with yellow flesh, and common spotted white trout of a large size [etc]. **1817** *Amer. Monthly Mag. & Crit. Rev.* 2.120, *Salmo Pallidus*. . . vulgar names Salmon-trout, White-trout, Lake-trout, &c. Length from two to four feet, it affords a delicious food, the flesh is redish [sic]. In Lake George, Lake Champlain, and other lakes: it does not ascend the brooks. **1852** *Spirit of Times* 22.195 **NY**, The White Trout—*Salmo confinis*—is taken at Buffalo during the winter and spring, and in some parts of the lake the entire year. **1861** Burton *City Saints* 334 **UT**, The white trout weigh thirty pounds. **1875** Scott *Fishing Amer. Waters* 258 **ME**, *The White Trout*. . . This trout inhabits Schoodic and Grand Lakes in the State of Maine. Although it is eminently a lake fish, yet it is found in the tributaries and outlets near the lakes named. **1879** *Scribner's Mth.* 19.17 **MI**, Hunters . . began to talk of a white-meated fish with all the game qualities of the trout. . . It was known to them as the "white trout." **1883** *Forest & Stream* 21.282, There are two varieties of trout in the Rocky Mountain streams, the yellow and the white trout. The former attain considerable size, . . but they are sluggish. . . On the other hand, the white trout fights vigorously and viciously until exhausted. **1890** *Appleton's Annual Cyclop. 1889* 792, *Sunapee Lake Trout*. . . In 1881, a strange trout appeared in Sunapee Lake, N.H., and was at once recognized by the native fishermen as distinct from the brook trout. . . In summer the fish is silvery, and hence it is known as the white trout. **1991** *DARE* File—Internet **ME** (as of c1947), He knew where all the various people came to fish and caught their fish. Brown trout seemed to be the most popular, and the white trout,—togue.

3 =**largemouth bass** or **smallmouth bass**. Cf **white salmon 3**

1820 *Western Rev.* 2.52, *Fishes of the River Ohio*. . . Trout River-bass. *Lepomis Salmonea* [=*Micropterus dolomieui*]. . . Vulgar names White Trout, Brown Trout, Trout Pearch [etc]. **1878** *Forest & Stream* 10.318 **TN**, The fish that are to be found here are two varieties of bass, called here black and white trout [etc]. **1878** U.S. Natl. Museum *Bulletin* 12.75 **KY, TN**, *Micropterus pallidus* [=*M. salmoides*]. . . The "White Trout", as this species is often called, is common in the Cumberland. **1897** U.S. Bur. Fisheries *Report* 185, The conspicuous development of the under jaw in the males led to the local names of 'hawk-bill' and 'hook-bill'; the silvery sides of the fish [=largemouth bass] in summer gave rise to that of 'white trout.' **1933** [see **white bass 2**].

white tupelo n, also attrib Also *white tupelo gum*
=**Ogeechee lime.**

1900 *Gleanings Bee Culture* 28.478 **FL**, The flow first started from ti-ti, followed by black tupelo, black gum, holly, haw, red bay, and yet to come are white tupelo, gall-berry, . . and several others of less importance. However, the white tupelo is the main source from which the great flow is obtained. **1920** Pellett *Amer. Honey Plants* 263, The ogeche plum or wild lime-tree . . , called white tupelo, is much smaller than the other gum-trees. . . It is common to the swamps of Georgia, Florida and South Carolina. **1928** *Dixie Beekeeper* 10.188, Almost the only fruit we had for more than fifty years is the Ogeechee Lime, commonly called White Tupelo gum. **1947** *Gleanings Bee Culture* 75.493, [Advt:] *Tupelo Honey:* packed in steel drums; from our apiaries in the heart of the white tupelo belt in Florida. **2007** *DARE* File **nwFL**, Good White Tupelo, unmixed with other honeys, will not granulate.

white walnut n
1 =**butternut 1.**

1731 Catesby *Nat. Hist. Carolina* 1.38, Another Walnut remains to be observed, which I never saw but in *Virginia* and is there called the white Walnut. The Tree is usually small; the Bark and Grain of the Wood very White; The Nut is about the size or rater [sic] less than the black Walnut, of an oval form, the outermost shell being rough. **1785** Marshall *Arbustrum* 67, *Juglans oblonga alba*. *Butter-nut, or White Walnut*. This often grows to the height of twenty or thirty feet . . , with a smooth light colored bark. **1810** Michaux *Histoire des Arbres* 1.165, *The Butter Nut*. . . Dans la Pensylvanie, le Maryland et sur les bords de l'Ohio, elle est plus connue sous . . [le nom] de *White Walnut*. [=*The Butter Nut*. . . In Pennsylvania, Maryland, and on the banks of the Ohio, it is more often called *White Walnut*.] **1849** Howitt *Our Cousins in OH* 13, In the autumn, hickory nuts, beech nuts, white walnuts, or butter-nuts, attracted our cousins to its precincts. **1860** Curtis *Cat. Plants NC* 45, White walnut. . . This is the common name of the tree in the section of State where it grows, though that of *Butternut*, applied to it in the Northern States, is not unknown. **1903** *DN* 2.336 **seMO**, *White-walnut*. . . Butternut. **1907** *DN* 3.238 **nwAR**, *White-walnut*. . . Butternut (tree). **1908** in 1995 Millersville Univ. Center for PA Ger. Studies *Jrl.* Winter 4, Some of it [=yarn] was colored with the bark of the white walnut-tree, also called butternut by reason of its rich nuts. **1965–70** *DARE* (Qu. I43, *What kinds of nuts grow wild around here?*) Infs **IN30**, **KY37, 40, 84**, **VA19, 24**, White walnut(s); **KY44**, White walnuts = butter walnuts; (Qu. T16, . . *Kinds of trees . . 'special'*) Infs **IL104**, **KY80**, **NC36**, **WI43**, **WV4, 14**, White walnut; (Qu. BB22, . . *Home remedies . . for constipation*) Inf **KY84**, White-walnut bark tea—a purge. [*DARE* Ed: Some of these Infs may refer instead to **2** below.] **1975** *Vidette–Messenger* (Valparaiso IN) 17 Oct 14/1, A close relative of the black walnut, often called the white walnut, is the butternut.

2 =**mockernut hickory** or a **shagbark hickory** (here: *Carya ovata*); the fruit of these trees.

1814 Bigelow *Florula Bostoniensis* 228, *Juglans alba*. . . *White walnut. Common hickory*. . . The buds in winter are large, hard, and of a greyish white. **1847** Wood *Class-Book* 491, *C. tomentosa*. . . White Walnut. Mockernut Hickory. **1877** Smith *Genl. Hist. Duchess Co.* 32 **NY**, Shell Bark Hickory *(Carya Alba)* bears the common white walnut, so pleasant to crack by the Winter fireside. **1897** Sudworth *Arborescent Flora* 113 **NJ**, *Hicoria ovata*. . . White Walnut. **1939** Medsger *Edible Wild Plants* 100, Shagbark or Shellbark Hickory—*Carya ovata*. . . Because of their color, the nuts are known in some parts of the country as white walnuts. **1959** *VT Hist.* 27.167, *White walnuts*. . . Hickory nuts. Common. Rutland. **1979** Erichsen-Brown *Med. N. Amer. Plants* 70, White Walnut—Small tree to 30 m with ash-gray bark.

white water lily n Cf **lily pad 1**
Std: a **water lily 1** (here: usu *Nymphaea odorata*). For other names of this species see **alligator bonnet(s) 1, bonnet B1c, fairy-boats, pond lily, star lotus, toad lily 2, water cabbage 1**

white water oak See **water oak 2h**

whiteweed n
1 =**oxeye daisy 1.** chiefly **NEng**

1784 in 1785 Amer. Acad. Arts & Sci. *Memoirs* 1.483, *Chrysanthemum foliis amplexicaulibus oblongis*. . . White Weed. Goldens. Daisie. **1814** *MA Ag. Jrl.* 3.115, Of weeds, the yellow and the white weed are the most troublesome. **1824** Bigelow *Florula Bostoniensis* 301, *Chrysanthemum leucanthemum* . . *White Weed*. . . exceedingly frequent and troublesome in pastures and mowing land. **1838** *MA Ag. Surv. Rept. for 1837* 69, The principal weeds which infest the fields, and are considered pernicious to agriculture, are the ox-eyed daisy or white weed [etc]. **1863** Porcher *Resources* 426 **Sth**, *Leucanthemum vulgare*. . . Ox-eyed daisy; white weed. **1874** *Tyrone Herald* (PA) [23 May 9]/1 (newspaperarchive.com) **ME**, A Maine farmer says of whiteweed for fodder: I have fed white weed . . with satisfactory results. **1929** *Torreya* 29.151 **ME**, Chrysanthemum Leucanthemum was "*White-weed*." **1966** *DARE* (Qu. S7, *A kind of daisy, bright yellow with a dark center, that grows along roadsides in late summer*) Inf **ME7**, Whiteweed; (Qu. S26a, . . *Wildflowers. . . Roadside flowers*) Inf **ME20**, Whiteweed. **1996** Silverthorne *Legends TX Wildflowers* 42, The oxeye daisy . . immigrated along with early settlers from Europe to North America, where it took over crop fields to the dismay of farmers, who called it whiteweed.

2 A **fleabane** of the genus *Erigeron*; see quots.

1847 Wood *Class-Book* 326, E[rigeron] heterophyllum [=*E. an-*

nuus]. . . Common Fleabane. White-weed. Ibid, E. strigosum [=*E. strigosus*]. *Fleabane. White-weed. Daisy.* **1873** in 1976 Miller *Shaker Herbs* 252, White Root—*Erigeron philadelphicus*—White Weed. Ox Eye Daisy. White Daisy. **1897** OH Ag. Exper. Sta. *Bulletin* 83.351, White-top, Whiteweed, Daisy-fleabane. . . *Erigeron annuus.*

3 A **mallow B** (here: *Malvella leprosa*).

1911 Jepson *Flora CA* 262, *S[ida] hederacea* [=*Malvella leprosa*]. . . Abundant in subsaline soils throughout the Sacramento, San Joaquin, and South Coast Range valleys. . . called "White Weed" at Elmira. **2003** Beidleman–Kozloff *Plants San Francisco Bay* 254 **cwCA,** *Malvella leprosa.* . . Alkali Mallow, Whiteweed.

4 A **heliotrope 1** (here: *Heliotropium curassavicum*).

1935 (1943) Muenscher *Weeds* 382, *Heliotropium curassavicum.* . . White-weed, Devil-weed. . . Fields, pastures and waste places; especially on alkaline soils in the West.

5 The hoary cress *(Lepidium draba).* Cf **whitetop 6**

1935 (1943) Muenscher *Weeds* 271, *Lepidium Draba.* . . Hoary cress, . . White-top, . . Whiteweed. . . most troublesome in the Rocky Mountain region. **2004** Guennel *Guide CO Wildflowers* 143, White-top (Whiteweed, Hoary Cress, Pepperweed)—*Cardaria draba* [=*Lepidium d.*]

6 A **ragweed 2** (here: *Ambrosia tomentosa*).

1995 Brako et al. *Scientific & Common Names Plants* 7, *Ambrosia.* . . *tomentosa.* . . bur ragweed, . . white-weed.

white whiskey n Also sp *white whisky* **Sth, S Midl** =**white liquor.**

1848 *Ft. Wayne Times & People's Press* (IN) 17 Feb [2]/1 (newspaperarchive.com), Every body knows that wine, as well as white whiskey, is a great inflamer of *patriotism.* **1888** *Scribner's Mag.* 4.170 **Sth** [Black], I kin remember when . . the store didn't sell nuthin' much 'cept white whiskey. **1924** Raine *Land of Saddle-Bags* 142 **sAppalachians,** When he thinks it over . . and drinks it over in white whiskey, he concludes that you will be sure to waylay him, therefore he had better kill you also to be safe. **1957** Faulkner *Town* 357 **MS,** Ratliff . . took a pint of white whiskey from inside his shirt. **1962** Fox *Southern Fried* 9 **SC,** A small skinny colored boy called Grit. . . would appear at the door for another spider webbed pint of white whisky. **1969** Lyons *My Florida* 41, Occasionally he would trade some fish for a fruit jar of white whiskey. **1969–70** *DARE* (Qu. DD21c, *Nicknames for whiskey, especially illegally made whiskey*) Infs **GA**77, **TN**53, White (whiskey). **1986** Pederson *LAGS Concordance* (*Cheap whiskey* . . *home-brewed* . . *whiskey*) 5 infs, **TN,** 2 infs, **AL,** White whiskey. **1995** McCormack *Fields Pastures* 131 **cwAL** (as of 1960s), Immediately another hunter produced a quart fruit jar which was about a third full of a clear liquid. I assumed this was "white" whiskey, or genuine, homemade Choctaw County moonshine liquor. **2000** in 2011 (acc) NC Univ.–Chapel Hill *S. Oral Hist. Program* (Internet) **nwNC** (as of 1970s), "I understand that white whiskey is still made in this county." Bard said, "Would you like some?" And I said, "Well, I don't want to be poisoned."

white willow n

1 Std: the widely naturalized European **willow 1,** *Salix alba.* Also called **gray willow**

2 Any of several other willows with light-colored bark or foliage, as:

a also *bog white willow:* The northern sageleaf or hoary **willow 1,** *Salix candida.*

1822 Eaton *Botany* 441 **NY,** *[Salix] candida,* . . white willow. . . Catskill Mt. **1847** Wood *Class-Book* 501, *S. candida.* . . White Willow. . . A beautiful species in shady woods. **1883** *Gardener's Mth. & Horticulturist* 25.338, The white willow, Salix Candida, is often used for coarse work. **1929** *Annals IA* (3d ser) 17.428, One of the most interesting plants in the bog is the bog white willow, also known as the sage or hoary willow *(Salix candida).*

b =**sandbar willow 1.**

1897 Sudworth *Arborescent Flora* 122 **MO,** *Salix fluviatilis* [=*S. exigua*]. . . Common Names. . . White Willow.

c The western arroyo **willow 1,** *Salix lasiolepis.*

1908 Sudworth *Forest Trees Pacific* 226, The white willow, so called on account of the smooth ashy gray bark (with brownish tinge) of young trunks and limbs of older trees. **1980** Little *Audubon Guide N. Amer. Trees W. Region* 360, *Salix lasiolepis.* . . The name "White Willow" may come from the light-colored bark and leaves with whitish lower surfaces. **2000** Barbour–Billings *N. Amer. Vegetation* 488, White willow or arroyo

willow *(Salix lasiolepis)* is found along perennial streams at low elevations.

whitewing n

1 also *white-winged woodpecker:* =**red-headed woodpecker.**

[**1800** in 1876 Wilson *Poems & Lit. Prose* 2.344, The white-wing'd Woodpecker, with crimson crest,/ Who digs from solid trunks his curious nest.] **1916** Morton *Hist. Monroe Co. WV* 14, Of smaller birds are the following kinds: whippoorwill, . . white-winged woodpecker [etc]. **1924** Howell *Birds AL* 170, Red-headed Woodpecker; Redhead; Whitewing. **1955** *Oriole* 20.1.10 **GA,** Red-headed Woodpecker. . . White-wing (the secondary wing-feathers are white). **1969** Longstreet *Birds FL* 90, Red-headed Woodpecker—*Other names:* Redhead; Whitewing. **1995** (1998) Dorsey *Wildfowler's Season* 72, White-winged Scoter. . . Other Names: sea coot, velvet scoter, whitewing.

2 also *white-wing(ed) curlew, white-winged plover:* =**willet.**

1840 Lee *Delusion* 60 **NEng,** The white-winged curlew was wheeling around in perfect security. **1923** U.S. Dept. Ag. *Misc. Circular* 13.62, Willet. . . whitewing (N.S., Mass.); whitewing curlew (Fla.); white-winged plover (Calif.) **1969** Longstreet *Birds FL* 63, Willet—*Other names:* White-wing Curlew [etc].

3 also *eastern whitewing, white-winger:* =**white-winged scoter;** hence n *black whitewing* the adult male of this species.

1852 in 1876 *Forest & Stream* 7.212 **eMA,** Gunner's Names for Birds and Wild Fowl obtained in Plymouth Bay, Mass. . . *Melanetta velvetina* [=*Melanitta fusca*]. White-wing. **1888** Trumbull *Names of Birds* 98, White-winged Scoter. . . From New Brunswick to Chesapeake region (in localities far too numerous to mention) *white-winged coot* or *white-wing.* In Massachusetts at Pigeon Cove and North Scituate, *black white-wing* for adult drake. **1892** *Forest & Stream* 38.517 **MA,** While at Seaconnett Point . . waiting for the flight of whitewings, which occurs . . about May 17 . . I was called on to identify a bird which had been killed near Westport. **1895** [see **whistling coot**]. **1923** U.S. Dept. Ag. *Misc. Circular* 13.29 **MA, RI,** White-winged Scoter. . . Vernacular Names. . . *Mass.,* black whitewing, bull whitewing, eastern whitewing, gray whitewing, May whitewing. . . *R.I.,* May whitewing. **2006** in 2008 *DARE* File—Internet **seVA,** If for some reason you detour down this way I can get you your surf. . . and an old squaw and maybe a white wing to boot. *Ibid* **wWA,** I am in washington and get more surfs that [sic] you can imagine, surfs whitewingers squaws harlis. **2007** *Ibid* **sME,** I am heading out next week—southern maine—anybody seen anything of the whitewings—or skunkheads[?] **2008** *Ibid* **ceWI,** We get blacks and whitewings on the great lakes but no surfs.

4 also *whitewing dove:* The white-winged dove *(Zenaida asiatica)* of the southernmost US.

1914 *Outing* 64.760, *Game Laws for 1914.* . . Arizona. . . 35 doves or whitewings per day. **1940** *Jrl. Wildlife Management* 4.119, Deputy state wardens in southern Arizona report small numbers of whitewings spending the entire summer and apparently nesting successfully. **1967–69** *DARE* (Qu. Q7, *Names and nicknames for . . game birds*) Inf **TX**31, Whitewing; **AZ**11, Whitewing—a kind of dove; **TX**26, Whitewing—further down south; **TX**11, 23, 28, Whitewing dove. **1968** Fulbright *Cow-Country Counselor* 110 **AZ,** They had been hunting white wings. **2005** in 2008 *DARE* File—Internet **cTX,** A gathering of whitewings—This morning I went out and found a small conclave of whitewing doves at the birdbath. **2008** *Ibid* **cTX,** The whitewings are just now moving into the Brenham area.

5 See **white-winged blackbird 1.**

whitewing blackbird See **white-winged blackbird**

whitewing coot See **white-winged coot**

whitewing curlew See **whitewing 2**

whitewing dove See **whitewing 4**

white-winged blackbird n Also *whitewing blackbird*

1 also *whitewing(s):* =**lark bunting.**

1858 U.S. War Dept. *Rept. Explor. Railroad* 9.492, *Calamospiza bicolor.* . . Lark Bunting; White-winged Blackbird. **1876** U.S. Army Corps Topog. Engineers *Rept. Reconnaissance Yellowstone* 85, Calamospiza bicolor. . . Lark Bunting; White-winged Blackbird. . . It becomes very numerous soon after leaving that stream [=the Missouri River], and continues to be found in large numbers until we reach the Black Hills. **1917** (1923) *Birds Amer.* 3.76, Lark Bunting. . . Sometimes out on the plains it is called the White-winged Blackbird. **1927**

Forbush *Birds MA* 3.125, Lark Bunting. *Other names:* White-winged Blackbird; White-wings. **1936** Roberts *MN Birds* 2.384 **sND** (as of 1883), The Lark Bunting, or White-winged Blackbird as it was then called, was abundant. **1944** Hausman *Amer. Birds* 27, Lark Bunting. . . The common name for this bird is White-wing. **1966–68** *DARE* (Qu. Q11, . . *Kinds of blackbirds*) Infs **CO**31, **KS**15, White-winged blackbird; **ND**9, Whitewing blackbird. [*DARE* Ed: Some of these Infs may refer instead to **2** below.]

2   =bobolink B.   Cf redwing bobolink
   1891 *IN Horticult. Soc. Trans. for 1890* 65, Bobolink; White-winged Blackbird. **1937** *Ironwood Daily–Globe* (MI) 31 May 4/5, The blackbirds . . that are native to Michigan include . . the bobolink, frequently referred to as the white-winged blackbird.

white-winged coot n   Also *whitewing coot*   **chiefly NEng, esp MA**
=white-winged scoter.
   1807 in 1815 *MA Hist. Soc. Coll.* 2d ser 3.54, The birds, which frequent this and the adjacent islands, are the crow, . . the white winged coot [etc]. **1844** DeKay *Zool. NY* 2.337, This duck, which is described in the books under the name of *Velvet Duck,* is better known here as the *White-winged Coot.* It is much prized for the quantity and quality of its down. **1864** Samuels *Descr. Catalogue Birds MA* 13, *Velvet Duck,* White-wing Coot, *Melanetta velvetina.* . . Common in migrations. **1876** *Forest & Stream* 6.417 **eMA,** Saw a white-winged coot off Gray's Rock this morning. **1888** [see **whitewing 3**]. **1903** Dawson *Birds OH* 2.616, Although the White-winged Coot is occasionally seen upon inland waters . . , it is difficult to recall it as anything but a sea-bird. **1928** Beston *Outermost House* 101 **Cape Cod MA,** I have for neighbours the three varieties of "scoters," or more familiarly and wrongly "coots," . . the white-winged coot *Oidemia deglandi* . . and others. **1966** *DARE* Tape **ME**10, We call [it] a whitewing coot—when they're flying, the tips of the wings are white. [**2005** in 2008 *DARE* File—Internet **Nova Scotia Canada,** We call all the scooters [sic] we get coots don't ask I don't know why. we have gray coots patch poll coots and white wing coots and butter bill coots.]

white-winged curlew   See **whitewing 2**

white-winged gull n   Also *white-winged winter gull*
Either of two similar gulls: the Iceland gull *(Larus glaucoides)* or **glaucous gull.**
   [**1818** O'Reilly *Greenland* 121, *Larus Maximus,* (burgomaster, or the white-winged gull.) Bill, pale yellow, with a blackish band across near the tip.] [**1835** Audubon *Ornith. Biog.* 3.553, The White-Winged Silvery Gull, *Larus leucopterus* [=*L. glaucoides*].] **1843** Thompson *Hist. Long Is.* 2.267 **seNY,** White winged Winter Gull, *Leucopterus* [=*Larus glaucoides*]. **1858** U.S. War Dept. *Rept. Explor. Railroad* 9.843, *Larus leucopterus.* . . The White-winged Gull. . . Back and wings pale bluish gray; the terminal part of the quills and their shafts, as well as the rest of the plumage pure white. **1898** (1900) Davie *Nests N. Amer. Birds* 29, Iceland Gull. . . Another common name for it is White-winged Gull. **1951** Pough *Audubon Water Bird* 351, White-winged gull. *See* Glaucous, Iceland . . gulls. **1971** Kieran *Nat. Hist. NYC* 225, Those who have the patience . . will be rewarded now and then by finding a "white-winged gull" that will be either the Glaucous Gull *(Larus hyperboreus)* . . or the Iceland Gull *(Larus glaucoides).*

white-winged plover   See **whitewing 2**

white-winged scoter n
Std: a large common scoter *(Melanitta fusca)* distinguished by white patches on the wings. Also called **African goose, assemblyman, bell-tongue coot, booby** n[1] **3, brant 2, brant coot, bull ~, bull whitewing, Canadian duck, coot** n[1] **2a, deaf duck 2, fish ~ 3, French ~ 2, frost ~, gray whitewing, half-moon eye, horse coot, ice duck 1, Indian ~, iron pot, May whitewing, muscovy, nigger duck 2, pied-winged coot, scooter** n[3]**, scoter, sea coot 1, snuff-taker, Uncle Sam coot, white-eyed coot, whitewing 3, white-winged coot**

white-winged winter gull   See **white-winged gull**

white-winged woodpecker   See **whitewing 1**

white-winger   See **whitewing 3**

whitewings   See **white-winged blackbird 1**

whitewood n

1   =tulip tree 1.   chiefly NEast   See Map
   1663 in 1889 Plymouth MA *Records* 1.66, Lott . . bounded with . . a great white wood tree. [*DARE* Ed: This quot may refer instead to **2** below.] **1798** Barton *Coll. for an Essay* 1.15, The Liriodendron Tulipifera, well known in the United-States, by the names of Tulip-Tree, Poplar, White-Wood, &c. **1813** Michaux *Histoire des Arbres* 3.202, Dans la plus grande partie des Etats-Unis, et partout où il est le plus abondant, cet arbre est désigné par le nom de *Poplar,* Peuplier; et secondairement dans les Etats de New-York et de New-Jersey, par ceux de *White wood* et de *Canoe wood,* Bois blanc et Bois à canot. [=In most of the United States and everywhere it is most abundant, this tree is called *Poplar* . . and secondarily in the States of New York and New Jersey, *White wood* and *Canoe wood.*] **1832** *N. Amer. Rev.* 35.425, Michaux speaks of its most common name as Poplar, but we must confess that we have never heard that name applied to it. . . Whitewood is its most general name at present, but this is giving way to Tulip-tree. **1867** *Prairie Farmer* 19.302, Tulip Tree, or Poplar of the West (Whitewood of the Eastern States). **1901** Lounsberry *S. Wild Flowers* 167, Tulip Tree. Whitewood. . . Those through the South . . usually refer to it as the "yaller poplar." **1917** *DN* 4.403 **neOH, NY,** *White-wood.* . . Tulip tree, or its timber. The regular term. Poplar, so used elsewhere, is here applied to other trees only. **1950** Peattie *Nat. Hist. Trees* 267, Tuliptree. . . In pioneer days it was called Whitewood, and architects in New England sometimes specify it by this name for interior finish. **1965–70** *DARE* (Qu. T13, . . *Names . . for . . tulip tree*) 9 Infs, 7 **NEast,** Whitewood; **CT**9, Whitewood tree; (Qu. T9) Inf **CT**6, Whitewood or tulip tree. **1997** [see **10** below].

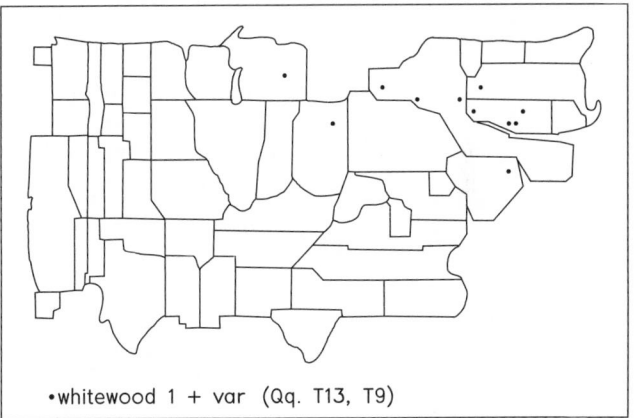

•whitewood 1 + var (Qq. T13, T9)

2   =linden, esp *Tilia americana.*
   1778 Carver *Travels N. Amer.* 499 **MI, WI, MN,** The *Bass* or *White Wood* is a tree of a middling size, and the whitest and softest wood that grows. **1860** Curtis *Cat. Plants NC* 78, Linn or Lime Trees. . . They are known in the Northern States by the names of *Lime Tree* and *White Wood,* but more generally by that of *Bass Wood.* **1901** Lounsberry *S. Wild Flowers* 333, *T[ilia] Americana,* American linden, basswood or white wood, grows along river bottoms and in rich, moist woods from Georgia and Texas northward. **1967–68** *DARE* (Qu. T13, . . *Names . . for . . linden*) Inf **NY**113, Whitewood tree; **TN**11, Whitewood.

3   also attrib: White cinnamon *(Canella winteriana,* formerly *C. alba).*
   1852 Beach *Amer. Practice Med.* 3.19, The leading tonics are American century, . . whitewood-bark [etc]. **1861** *Chambers's Encycl.* 2.562, The bark of the young branches is the *C[anella] Bark* of apothecaries, also known in commerce as *White-wood Bark,* and sometimes called *White Cinnamon.* **1897** Sudworth *Arborescent Flora* 273, *Canella winteriana.* . . Common Names. . . Whitewood. Wild Cinnamon.

4   A sycamore B (here: *Platanus occidentalis*).
   1873 *Reedsburg Free Press* (WI) 28 Nov [2]/4 (newspaperarchive.com) **IN,** The names of many of the trees were changed. Rock maple was sugar tree, basswood was linn, butternut was white walnut, whitewood was sycamore [etc]. **1941** *LANE* Map 244 *(Sycamore)* 1 inf, **csCT,** Basswood—almost the same as the tulip tree and the whitewood tree; 1 inf, **cMA,** Plane tree, whitewood. **1950** Peattie *Nat. Hist. Trees* 315, Sycamore. . . Other Names: Buttonwood . . Whitewood [etc].

5   =Carolina poplar 1.
   [**1876** Vasey *Catalogue Trees* 29, *Populus monilifera* [=*P. deltoides*]. . . The wood is light and soft, much employed in some of the

Western States for building purposes, and for inside work of houses, under the name of Whitewood and Cottonwood.] **1897** Sudworth *Arborescent Flora* 47 **IA,** *Populus deltoides.* . . Whitewood.

6 A Guiana plum (*Drypetes* spp) such as **milkbark.**

1884 Sargent *Forests of N. Amer.* 121, *Drypetes crocea* [=*D. lateriflora*]. . . Guiana Plum. White Wood. Semi-tropical Florida. **1897** Sudworth *Arborescent Flora* 271 **FL,** *Drypetes lateriflora.* . . Common Names. . . Whitewood. *Ibid, Drypetes keyensis* [=*D. diversifolia*]. . . Whitewood. **1946** FL Dept. Ag. *Qrly. Bulletin* 77.35, *Drypetes diversifolia*—Whitewood—South Florida and West Indies.

7 A **maleberry** (here: *Lyonia ligustrina*).

1924 *Amer. Botanist* 30.61, I am at a loss to know why *Lyonia ligustrina* should be called "male-berry". Among its other names is . . "white wood".

8 =**gray twig.**

1933 Small *Manual SE Flora* 1250, *S[choepfia] chrysophylloides* [=*S. schreberei*]. . . Whitewood. . . Coastal and inland hammocks, pen. Fla. and the Keys. **1962** Harrar–Harrar *Guide S. Trees* 266, Gulf Gray-twig—Whitewood.

9 A **forestiera** (here: *Forestiera acuminata*).

1953 Little *Native Trees U.S.* 186, Texas forestiera . . , common adelia, Texas adelia, whitewood. **1972** Brown *Wildflowers LA* 135, Swamp-privet, Whitewood. . . Abundant on the Mississippi River floodplain and along small streams and swamps.

10 A **hemlock 2** (here: *Tsuga heterophylla*).

1997 *DARE* File—Internet **WA,** Whereas I've heard of this wood [= tulip tree] being sold as whitewood, around here whitewood almost invariably refers to Western Hemlock.

white-wood poplar See **white poplar 1**

whitey n

1 usu cap; also sp *Whitie*: A White person; White people collectively. *chiefly among Black speakers; usu derog* Cf **Charlie 2, honky 1, Mister Charlie, ofay, paddy** n[1] **4,** *poor Whitey* (at **poor White**)

1921 *Jrl. Amer. Folkl.* 34.34 **SC,** Whitey in a whitey,/ Whitey told a whitey / To go drive whitey / Out of whitey. *Ans[wer:]* A white lady told a white dog to drive the white cow out of the white house. **1942** Berrey–Van den Bark *Amer. Slang* 385.2, White person. . . whitie. **1964** *Time* 31 July 12 **NYC** [Black], Harlem. . . is where the white man is no longer the "ofay" . . but "Mr. Charlie" or "the man," and mostly "whitey," derived from the Black Nationalist talk of "the blue-eyed white devil." **1965** *Oakland Tribune* (CA) 22 Aug 6/3 [Black], "We did it to get Whitey," said one. Whitey means the white man. **1968** *DARE* (Qu. HH28, *Names and nicknames . . for people of foreign background*) Inf **CA**81, Whitey—Whites are called by Negroes; **MI**88, Whitey—White people. **1970** *DARE* Tape **IL**140, People doesn't care. In other words, Whitey doesn't care whether we succeed or not. **1972** Claerbaut *Black Jargon* 86, *Whitey* . . a Caucasian; white person. **1980** *AmSp* 55.211, It [=bop/bebop] encompassed a protest of whitey's "theft" of yet another style of jazz—swing. **1989** Pederson *LAGS Tech. Index* 251 **Gulf Region,** Caucasian . . Whitey (41 [infs]). [*DARE* Ed: In the *Concordance,* virtually every inf characterized *Whitey* as Black usage and/or derogatory.]

2 =**sanderling. esp NEng**

1904 Hoffmann *Guide Birds New Engl.* 266, The gunners' name, "Whitey," well describes the Sanderling, especially in late summer and fall, when no trace of the rusty brown remains. **1905** Townsend *Birds Essex Co. MA* 179, Sanderling; "Beach-bird"; "Whitey"; "Beach Plover." **1948** [see **white snipe 1**]. **1969** Longstreet *Birds FL* 66, Sanderling. . . Their bodies . . give a general effect of white at all seasons and for this reason [they] are commonly referred to as "whities."

3 See **whiting 1.**

4 A recently molted crab that is almost completely hard; see quot. Cf **snowball 4**

1976 Warner *Beautiful Swimmers* 161 **Chesapeake Bay,** The crabs in the Number Three basket showed the telltale grayish cast on their topsides and the lustrous white on their abdomens that are the marks of a recently moulted adult crab. Post-buckrams, you might say. Lester calls them "whiteys." In other parts of the Bay they are known as "snowballs" or "white bellies" and not taken by crabbers.

whitey-ganzer n

=**hooded merganser.**

1933 *AmSp* 8.1.53 **Ozarks,** *Whitey-ganzer.* . . The hooded merganser, a kind of fish duck, not common in the Ozark country.

white yolk See **yolk B**

Whitey's out of jail See **Mr. White is out of jail**

Whitie See **Whitey 1**

whitiker See **whicker** n[1], v

whiting n

1 often in combs; also *whitey:* =**kingfish 1.** Cf **Carolina whiting, sand ~**

1743 Catesby *Nat. Hist. Carolina* 2.12 **SC,** *Alburnus Americanus*—The Carolina Whiting. . . The Market at *Charlestown* in *Carolina* is plentifully supplied with these Fish, and are accounted tolerable good Meat. **1787** Gesellschaft Naturforschender Freunde *Schriften* 8.162, *Perca Alburnus.* . . Der *Whiting* ist ungleich häufiger an den südlichen Küsten von Carolina und Florida, als nordlich. [=The *whiting* is much more common along the southern coasts of Carolina and Florida than further north.] **1867** De Voe *Market Asst.* 239 **S Atl,** King-fish (called *barb* along the Jersey shore, and *whiting* on the coast of Florida, Carolina, etc.) **1884** Goode *Fisheries U.S.* 1.376, The Whitings—*Menticirrus alburnus* [=*M. americanus*] and M. littoralis. *Ibid* 377 **SC,** Many [of *M. littoralis*] are captured with the seine and are sold in the market under the name 'Surf Whiting,' in contradistinction to the other species, which is called the 'Deep-water Whiting.' *Ibid* **FL,** About New Smyrna, Florida . . it is called "Whiting" . . and "Bull-head Whiting." **1939** Natl. Geogr. Soc. *Fishes* 93, Besides kingfish they [=*Menticirrhus saxatilis, M. americanus,* and *M. littoralis*] are called whiting, king whiting, surf whiting, shore whiting, silver whiting [etc]. **1965–70** *DARE* (Qu. P2, . . *Kinds of saltwater fish caught around here . . good to eat*) 22 Infs, **chiefly Atlantic,** Whiting(s); **DE**3, Kingfish—book name is king whiting; **PA**66, Whities; (Qu. P3, *Freshwater fish that are not good to eat*) Inf **MA**35, Whiting; (Qu. P7, *Small fish used as bait for bigger fish*) Inf **NY**58, Whiting; (Qu. P14, . . *Commercial fishing . . what do the fishermen go out after?*) Infs **MA**97, **SC**4, 66, 69, Whiting. [*DARE* Ed: Some of these Infs may refer instead to other senses below.] **1967** *DARE* FW Addit **TX,** Whiting—kind of fish caught in surf in Texas. **2007** *DARE* File—Internet **swAL,** The Southern Kingfish . . or Gulf Kingfish . . are known on the Alabama coast as Whiting.

2 A **hake 1a,** usu *Merluccius bilinearis.* **esp NEast**

1839 MA Zool. & Bot. Surv. *Fishes Reptiles* 132, The Hake. . . is generally known by the fishermen of Massachusetts as the *"Whiting."* **1842** DeKay *Zool. NY* 4.282, The American Hake. . . The specimen described above, was taken in November, off Sandy Hook. The fisherman from whom I procured it, called it the *Whiting.* **1873** in 1878 Smithsonian Inst. *Misc. Coll.* 14.2.18 **MA,** *Merluccius bilinearis.* . . whiting. **1946** La Monte *N. Amer. Game Fishes* 92, Silver Hake. . . Names: New England Hake, Whiting. **2007** *Sun* (Baltimore MD) 9 Aug (Internet), South of Maryland, fishermen call kingfish "whiting;" north of it, they call silver hake "whiting."

3 A **pigfish c** (here: *Orthopristis chrysoptera*).

1884 U.S. Fish Comm. *Bulletin for 1884* 80 **FL,** At Jacksonville, Fla., the Sailor's Choice is *Pomadasys chrysopterus,* known at Key West as "Whiting."

4 A **menhaden 1** (here: *Brevoortia tyrannus*).

1890 *Century Dict.* 3707, Menhaden. . . This fish has at least 30 different popular names in the United States . . [including] *whiting* or *whitefish.*

5 Either of two closely related birds:

a The immature **knot** n[2].

1893 *Auk* 10.31 **Cape Cod MA,** The plumage of the young birds [= knots] (sometimes called 'Whitings' on Cape Cod, and which are usually smaller than the adults) is of a general slate gray for the upper parts, and white underneath.

b =**sanderling.**

1923 U.S. Dept. Ag. *Misc. Circular* 13.57 **MA,** Sanderling. . . whitey, whiting. **1948** [see **white snipe 1**].

6 A **butterfish 1** (here: *Peprilus paru*).

1902 Jordan–Evermann *Amer. Fishes* 329 **VA,** Harvest-fish—*Peprilus paru.* . . At Norfolk, where it is called whiting, it is a fish of considerable commercial importance.

whitleather n [*OED2 whitleather* sb. 1.a "Leather . . prepared by tawing" 1366–7 →; 1.b "In comparisons, or as a type of toughness, elasticity, softness, etc." 1605 →]

1 in phr *tough as whitleather* and varr: Very tough. **chiefly Sth, S Midl**

1786 Franklin in *Amer. Philos. Soc. Trans.* 2.321, As they [=fowl] are generally treated at present in ships, they are for the most part sick, and their flesh tough and hard as whitleather. **1854** Kane *Grinnell Exped.* 97 **sePA,** A fourth [variety of ice] was as finely granulated as loaf-sugar, yet as tough as whitleather. **1859** Taliaferro *Fisher's R.* 184 **nwNC,** Some on 'um [=dumplings] which the seasonin' hadn't toch, was tough as whitleather. **1909** *DN* 3.383 **eAL, wGA,** *Tough as whit leather.* . . Exceedingly tough. *Whit-leather* is used only in this or similar expressions indicating toughness. **1923** *DN* 5.239 **swWI,** *Whit leather, tougher than.* . . Tougher than rawhide. **1949** *PADS* 11.15 **wTX** (as of 1911–29), As tough as whitleather. **1955** *AmSp* 30.234 **ceIN,** *Whit-leather.* Heard only in the simile *tough as whit-leather.* **1959** Ruark *Poor No More* 257 **Sth,** She's as tough as whitleather. **1972** *Delta Democrat–Times* (Greenville MS) 20 Sept 3/1, The boy, the mother, and the girl are all tough as whitleather in their own ways. **1976** Garber *Mountain-ese* 95 **sAppalachians,** I jist kaint chew this steak, it's as tough as whitleather. **1979** Bowden *Always Rivers Flow* 129 **nwFL** (as of 1930s–40s), They were *real* men, tough as whitleather.

2 in combs *whitleather age, ~ stage, ~ state:* See quots.

1830 *Methodist Mag. & Qrly. Rev.* 12.127, If we passed this period [= the age of 63], we advanced to what he called the *whitleather* state, and perhaps after this glide down to a good old or advanced stage of life. **1876** Southworth *Ishmael* 425 **VA,** She was fooling herself worse than she was deceiving her old beau, who had got into the whit-leather age, and would be sartin' sure to live twenty-five or thirty years longer. **1899** (1912) Green *VA Folk-Speech* 483, *Whitleather.* . . People old and tough, are said to be in the "*whitleather* state." **1952** Brown *NC Folkl.* 1.607, *Whitleather stage, at the:* . . At the stage (age) of an old maid— tough and unmarriageable.—West.

3 The ligament or tendon of an animal; gristle. [*OED2* 1692, 1713 (at *paxwax*), 1712 (at *whitleather* sb. 2)] **chiefly Sth** Cf **packwack**

1875 Terhune *Breakfast Luncheon* 144 **VA,** All gristly portions, soft bones, and the cartilage known as "whitleather" should be removed. **1899** (1912) Green *VA Folk-Speech* 483, *Whitleather.* . . The nuchal ligament of grazing animals, as the ox, supporting the head. **1949** *PADS* 11.13 **wTX** (as of 1911–29), *Whitleather.* . . The white tendons in meat. **1952** Brown *NC Folkl.* 1.607, *Whitleather.* . . The cartilage of an animal. **1955** *AmSp* 30.234, *Whitleather.* . . In North Carolina, I find it is the tough ligaments found in a beef carcass, especially in the neck. **1958** *AmSp* 33.273 **eWA** [Ranching terms], *Whit leather.* . . The gristle in a piece of beef. **1967** *DARE* FW Addit **SC,** *Whitleather* = beef tendon.

whitleather age (or stage, state) See **whitleather 2**

whitlow-wort n [*OED2* 1650]
Std: a plant of the genus *Paronychia.* Also called **chick-weed 1c**

whit owl See **whet owl**

whittle v [*OED2 whittle* v.[2] 4 "To worry or fret. . . *dial.*"; 1880 →]
See quot 1916.

1834 Smith *Life Jack Downing* 39 **ME,** Do you think I am going to pay you for the biscuit and let you keep 'em tu? Aint they there now on your shelf, what more do you want? I guess sir, you don't whittle me in that way. So I turned about and marched off. . . Howsomever, I did n't want to cheat him, only jest to show 'em it want so easy a matter to pull my eye teeth out. **1916** Macy–Hussey *Nantucket Scrap Basket* 166 **seMA,** "Whittle" . . meaning to fuss, to get uneasy; also, sometimes, to tease, to pester. One says, "Well, it's time to go. Mother'll be whittling." What child of a Nantucket mother hasn't been told, when he had exhausted her patience to the point of exasperation by teasing for something, "Oh, stop your whittling!"

whittle-ding n Cf **kittledee 2**
=**wood thrush 1.**

1955 Ritchie *Singing Family* 100 **seKY,** Marthe was singing a high part-like, just sweet and cler as a whittle-ding. **2008** *DARE* File—Internet **KY,** I knew elderly people who would get all excited with the first sounds of the wood thrush, what they called the "whittleding," because of the sound of its song. . . they would get all excited because it was nature's sure sign that winter weather was over.

whittledy cut See **whittlety whet**

whittle-ee-cut n
A situation in which a choice must be made between alternatives.

1943 *Hench Coll.* **cVA,** This evening [she] said of the way the children

were playing that a child in a game had to do one thing or another, he couldn't do nothing. "With them," she said, "it's whittle-ee-cut." When I asked what she meant, she said it was the way children said "whittle or cut."

whittlety whet adj, n Also *whittledy cut* Cf **tit for tat**
Even, neck and neck; a close thing.

1890 *DN* 1.66 **KY,** *Whittlety-whet.* When two are running a race, we say, "It is whittlety-whet who will get there first." **1909** White *Certain Rich Man* 420 **KS,** He grinned as he added: "But I found it was nearly whittlety whet. A lot of fellows had been doing me up, while I had been doing others up." **1938** *WI Rapids Daily Tribune* (WI) 31 Oct 4/2 **KS,** Mussolini . . and the tyrant of Turkey are about whittlety-whet in the contest for the tail piece in the race for autocrats. . . Emporia Gazette. **1954** *Time* 5 July 13 **KY,** For many a Kentucky voter the choice will be difficult. In the words of a Penny-royalist, "It'll be 'whittledycut'"— which in Kentucky means a real fine horse race. [**1958** *Gettysburg Times* (PA) 30 July 5/6, Whittledy Cut ($7) won the feature at Monmouth Park.] **1968** *DARE* (Qu. KK54, *Just about equal, very close: "They were both fast runners and it was _____ all the way."*) Inf **TN26,** Whittledy cut [ˈhwɪtl̩dɪkət].

whitz See **whist 3**

whiz n[1] Also *whizz* **chiefly S Midl** Cf **whizzing**
Used in var intensive comparisons, esp *cold as whiz, mad as whiz.*

1874 in 2007 *DARE* File—Internet **OH,** Cold as whiz. Snowed and rained all day. **1889** *Ibid* **MO,** Cold as whizz 20 above zero. Clear this evening getting warm fast. **1909** (1910) Powell *Trailing & Camping AK* 246, You eat a double handful of them [=currants], make a wry face, and decide them to be about as sour as whiz. **1960** Hall *Smoky Mt. Folks* 63 **wNC, eTN,** As mad as whiz. **1962** *Daily Times–News* (Burlington NC) 21 Apr sec B 2/3, It was cold as whiz, and the game went on and on. **1982** [see **whizzing**]. **2001** Karon *Common Life* 180 **NC,** He didn't have nothin' to say, seem like he was mad as whiz. **2005** Marin *Motherland* 94 **neIL,** Dad was just as mad as whiz. **2005** *DARE* File—Internet **seTN,** Storms and rain here for two days, then it turned cold as whizz. **2006** *Ibid,* Hi there! Its cold as whiz here in IL. . . I am originally from the South so I am not going to let the cold get me down. **2006** in 2008 *Ibid* **cTN,** It gets cold as whiz up here on the Cumberland Plateau.

whiz n[2] See **whist 2**

whiz oak n [Perh *whiz* to urinate; cf **piss oak**] **NC**
A kind of oak.

1966 *DARE* (Qu. T10, . . *Kinds of oak trees*) Infs **NC**30, 35, Whiz oak. **2007** Hardy *Remembering Avery Co.* 16 **nwNC,** It don't pay to be stingy with wood on a morning like this, specially if your [sic] burning whiz oak or sourwood.

whizz See **whiz** n[1]

whizzing adv Also *gee-whizzing* **chiefly Sth, S Midl** Cf **whiz** n[1]
Extremely—usu in phr *whizzing cold.*

1879 *Decatur Daily Rev.* (IL) [12 July 3]/2 (newspaperarchive.com) **IA,** The one I picked up was not so everlastingly gee-whizzing cold, and I did not investigate any further. **1887** *Landmark* (Statesville NC) 1 Dec [3]/2 (newspaperarchive.com), It was whizzing cold up there last Saturday. **1893** *Galveston Daily News* (TX) 27 May 1/4, It was whizzing cold the first two days of our stay. **1909** *DN* 3.406 **nwAR,** *Whizzing.* . . Extremely, unusually. "The matron gave him a whizzing big dose of salts." **1913** Hornaday *Our Wild Life* 57, One whizzing cold day in winter he called upon me. **1982** Powers *Cataloochee* 417 **cwNC,** Mark still writes of winters in Maggie Valley . . as 'whizzin' cold' or 'cold as whiz'. **2006** *DARE* File—Internet **NC,** Last time I was there was back in April and it was whizzing cold. **2008** *Ibid* **GA,** It's getting whizzing cold here in Ga. *Ibid* **swVA,** We basically ditched the house about halfway through the tour (whizzing cold inside) and spent the afternoon in the winery. ▪

who pron Usu |hu|; also rarely |hɪu, hiu|
A Forms.
1939 in 1944 *ADD* **WV,** *Who.* . . [ˈhɪu], [ˈhiu].
B Sense.
Whose. *esp freq among Black speakers* Cf **he** pron **2, it** pron **B, she** pron **2**
1927 Adams *Congaree* 4 **cSC** [Black], Scip: I been to de trial. Voice:

Who trial? **1971** in 1993 Major *Calling the Wind* 340 **LA** [Black], "Who field this is [=is this]?" Daddy asks. "Mr. Roger Bedlow," the man says. **2006** *DARE* File—Internet, This book is . . *a must read for every woman who husband is* . . dealing with sexual sin. **2008** *Ibid* [Black], Who House is this? *Ibid* **cnIN**, I just want to say best wishes to this family who house cough [sic] on fire. *Ibid,* What rights have a person who car is impounded?

who-all pron Cf **what-all** pron, **what and all, where-all**

1a also rarely *who and all:* Used as an interrogative in place of *who(m)* (rarely *whose*), usu to emphasize the comprehensive scope of the question, but occas with emphatic force where a singular response is expected. **scattered, but chiefly Sth, S Midl**

1863 in 1888 *Old Guard* 3.5 **Sth**, Tel me who all is flying round the girls if there is any body to fly round there. **1872** U.S. Congress *Serial Set* 1486.1579 **SC**, We were in another man's house, and his wife and he were lying on the floor; and he says, "Who all have you got here, God damn you?" **1883** *Harper's New Mth. Mag.* 68.114 **VA**, Who all are at the Eyrie, Uncle Brutus? **1899** (1912) Green *VA Folk-Speech* 483, *Who-all, interrog.* . . "Who all were there." **1903** *Atlantic Mth.* 92.225 **MO**, Who-all is he anyway, this new man, I wish you'd say. **1927** [see **who-all's**]. **1936** *AmSp* 11.353 **eTX**, Who all are going? Who all is going? **1938** Rawlings *Yearling* 67 **nFL**, Who-all's your sweetheart? **1944** in 1946 *AmSp* 21.52 **nwMN**, We always said, as the town still does, 'Who-all was there?' and 'What-all did you do?' Many of the Irish also use 'who-all' and 'what-all.' **1946** *PADS* 6.33 **eNC**, *Who and (in) all.* . . Who. "Who and (in) all was at the party?" Pamlico. Common. **1952** [see **who-all's**]. **1963** Mencken–McDavid *Amer. Lang.* 548, The Linguistic Atlas finds the interrogative *who-all* fairly widespread in the South and adjacent territory. The interrogative *what-all* is even more widespread. **1965** Carmony *Speech Terre Haute* 144 **sIN**, *Who-all* . . is used by a majority of informants of every class. . . Even among the younger informants the generous form is holding its own. **1971** Bright *Word Geog. CA & NV* 176, *Who-all* (was there? . . *who* 66% [of 300 infs] . . *who-all* 30%. Several who gave this response used the plural *were* with it; others said they would use it but "not in the Southern sense." **1975** Allen *LAUM* 2.53 **Upper MW** (as of c1950), *Who-all was/were there?* For the plural of the interrogative pronoun more than one-half of the U[pper] M[idwest] infs. use the phrase *who-all.* . . Despite the frequency of *who-all* in North Dakota, the drop in the proportion between Iowa and Minnesota, and between Nebraska and South Dakota, strongly suggests that this form has Midland orientation. **1989** Pederson *LAGS Tech. Index* 150 **Gulf Region**, *Who-all* . . who (265 [infs]) . . who-all (307) . . who and all (1). . . *Who-all's* . . who-all (11) . . who-all's (61) . . whose (192). **1989** Smith *Flyin' Bullets* 58 **eTN** (as of c1930), Who alls been a'teachin' you to dance?

b in elliptical phrr *and I don't know who-all, and God knows who-all:* And various other people.

1844 Haliburton *Attaché* (2d ser) 2.17 **NEng**, He'd go over a whole string—Mason, Mickle, Burns, and I don't know who all. **1847** in 1953 Lincoln *Coll. Wks.* 1.394 **IL**, It reminds me to write you the result of your two cases of Moore vs. Brown, & God knows who all. **1854** in 1869 Irving *Life & Letters* 3.276, It was to meet Mr Lawrence . . who has come out with letters from Thackeray, and I don't know who all. **1921** Tarkington *Alice Adams* 270 **IN**, It'd have to go through a clerk and that secretary of his, and I don't know who all. **1938** Lewis *Prodigal Parents* 29 **NY**, I certainly don't want you here, filling this place up with a lot of your fancy college friends, Guy Staybridge and God knows who all else. **1987** *NY Times* (NY) 24 July sec A 8/3, I feel that Admiral Poindexter was certainly on the other side of it. I felt that Director Casey was on the other side of it. And I don't know who all else, but they were the principals.

2 Whoever, all those who—used as an indefinite relative.

1967 *DARE* (Qu. EE15, *When he has caught the first of those that were hiding what does the player who is 'it' call out to the others?*) Inf **MO**18, Who-all's out's in free.

who-all's pron

Whose?—used as the possessive of interrog **who-all 1a.**

1927 *AmSp* 3.6 **Ozarks**, The hyphenated pronouns *who-all* and *what-all* are common, particularly in interrogative sentences, as *who-all was at th' frolic?* . . The possessive form of *who-all* is also frequently heard—*who-all's is this hyar choppin'-axe?* **1952** Brown *NC Folkl.* 1.607, *Who all.* . . Who. The use of *all* in this phrase is an attempt to make an indefinite pronoun. It means "who in the world?" "Who in general?" It may be used in the possessive: "Who all's horse is that?" **1975** Allen *LAUM* 2.55 **Upper MW** (as of c1950), Attempts to elicit a geni-

tive for the compound plurals in *-all* proved fruitless except for *who-all's.* Four infs., three of them in the Midland speech zone, have this genitive. **1989** Pederson [see **who-all 1a**].

who and all See **who-all 1a**

whoap See **whope 1**

whocker-jawed See **whonker-jawed**

whoig See **hoog**

who in tunket See **tunket** n¹ 1

who laid the chunk phr **chiefly TX, Cent**

1 in adj phrr *from who laid the chunk(s):* =**who laid the rail 1.**

1896 *Dallas Morning News* (TX) 3 Mar 4/4, He is a hell-bender from who laid the chunk. **1906** *San Antonio Daily Light* (TX) 8 Nov 11/2, They don't know a note from a hoss-fly if they'd see it on a music sheet, but they are fiddlers from who laid the chunk. **1932** Randolph *Ozark Mt. Folks* 146, Gran'pap Paisley was a bee-hunter from who laid th' chunk, an' he was jest obleeged t' find out whar all them bees was a-goin'. **1952** *AmSp* 27.290 **cIL**, 'He is a hawnyock *from who laid the chunk*' meant a yokel 'from way back.' **1960** Criswell *Resp. to PADS* 20 **Ozarks**, Through and through, from head to toe, . . from who laid the chunks. **1977** *Amer. West* 14.6.5, Lee and Gililland were sons of Confederates, Texas-born, and raised there. . . [They] were "cowmen from who laid the chunk." **1995** Brophy *Coll.* 27 **swMO** (as of c1960), *From who laid the chunk.* . . "from way back."

2 in adv phrr *for* (or *from, like, till, to, until*) *who laid the chunk, from where you laid the chunk,* and varr: =**who laid the rail 2.**

1893 Collins *Chapters Unwritten Hist.* 243 **TX**, You can bet your high ocean wave that it poured the shot and shell into us "from who laid the chunk." **1893** James *Cow-Boy Life in TX* 167, If one horse beat another very badly in a race he beat him "from where you laid the chunk." **1905** *Washington Post* (DC) 21 Sept [2]/2 (newspaperarchive.com) **MO**, On the steamers there was beer and most anything you would want. Music and waltzing to who laid the chunk. **1905** *Galveston Daily News* (TX) 7 Nov 1/2, The average public man in Texas . . is of and for the people from who laid the chunk. **1915** *DN* 4.226 **TX**, *From who laid the chunk.* . . Phrase expressing great approval. "She can sing from who laid the chunk." **1941** Street *In My Father's House* 73 **seMS**, They could raise hogs to who-laid-a-chunk, but they couldn't raise children. **1942** Perry *Texas* 137, For a superlative action as, say, in the case of playing a violin, we remark, "He sawed that fiddle to a who laid the chunk." **1944** Wellman *Bowl* 103 **KS**, He's got the money bags—an' he'll play the game with us from who laid the chunk. **1952** Giles *40 Acres* 151 **KY**, Uncle Marion is a fisherman for who-laid-the-chunk. It is said . . that he never fails to catch fish. **1966–68** *DARE* (Qu. LL9b, . . *All you need or more*) Inf **OH**49, Till who laid the chunk; (Qu. LL27, . . *'Thoroughly':* "The boss bawled him out _____."; total Infs questioned, 75) Inf **OK**45, To who laid the chunk. **1991** Heat Moon *PrairyErth* 225 **ceKS**, One countian said, *They intermarried until who-laid-the-chunk.* **2007** in 2008 *DARE* File—Internet **IA**, Somehow the topic of alternative energy was broached and the following phrase was used about wind energy: *When the wind is blowing like who laid the chunk.*

who laid the rail phr Cf **who laid the chunk**

1 in adj phr *from who laid the rail:* Of the most thoroughgoing or experienced sort; through and through, "dyed-in-the-wool."

1889 *Daily Eve. Bulletin* (San Francisco CA) 10 Dec 4/5 **GA**, The Democrats of Montana are fighters from who laid the rail. **1905** *Everybody's Mag.* 13.610 **OH**, I'd want him to work out the story of the Mediterranean stocks [of barnyard fowls], trim, neat of figure, flyers from who laid the rail, poor sitters, but prodigal layers. **1911** Adams *Wells Brothers* 208 **West**, These boys of mine are cowmen from who laid the rail. **1945** Buckingham *Game Bag* 151 **TN**, He was . . a retriever from Who-Laid-the-Rail.

2 in adv phrr *for* (or *from, like, till, to*) *who laid the rail(s):* Very thoroughly, vigorously, or well; to an extreme degree. **chiefly Sth, S Midl**

1881 *Macon Telegraph & Messenger* (GA) 15 Oct 4/2, The city fathers, mothers, sisters, cousins and aunts were abused from who laid the rail. **1889** Folsom *Scraps* 193 **GA**, The Deacon settled himself for a regular snooze. He had got down to business and was sawing gourds for who laid the rails, when my attention was attracted by a big brindled grasshopper. **1893** Shands *MS Speech* 68, *Who laid the rails.* An expression used by negroes. . . It generally occurs in such constructions as the following: "Dat man kin speak fum who laid the rails"; "He gimme a beatin' fum who laid the rails." **1901** *ID Daily Statesman* (Boise) 23 Dec 6/2, The animal struck out on a dead run. . . My friend followed and it was a race for who laid the rail, as they say in the country. **1936** *Syracuse Herald* (NY) 27 Nov 29/1 **TN,** They had open betting . . and the rich cotton planters would bet you from who laid the rail. **1946** *PADS* 6.39 **swVA,** He lit out down the road for who laid the rail. (Used in horse-and-buggy days of a person who got off at full speed.) **1951** Babcock *Tales* 80 **VA,** Mosey up to the hole, drop it in, and run like who-laid-the-rail. **1952** Willson *Who Did What* 22 **IA,** Before mornin' it'll be snowin' till 'who laid the rails.' **1953** *Charleston Gaz.* (WV) 1 Sept 12/7, The man screamed like he had been bitten by a rattlesnake and threw paint for who laid the rails. **1979** *DARE* File **KY,** My mother always used to say "to who laid the rail," meaning something that was extreme. For example, "It's hot to who laid the rail!" **1982** *Smithsonian Letters* **VA,** They were working on that, (whatever project) for (or like) "who laid the rail," meaning with fierce and energetic activity. **2006** *San Diego Union–Tribune* (CA) 17 Dec (Internet) **KY,** From that point on it was Katie bar the door, or, as my native Kentuckian mother would put it, it was language books to who laid the rail. **2007** in 2008 *DARE* File—Internet **cnIA,** Sure we have a huge tax base to buy all the equipment to fill fire stations to who laid the rail.

3 in adv phrr *since* (or *till, until*) *who laid the rail(s):* Since (or until) a remote point in the past (or future).

1910 *Daily Rev.* (Decatur IL) 1 Nov 9/2, He praised the Republican party and declared that it was the only progressive party from the time of George Washington until who laid the rail. **1958** Babcock *I Don't Want* 10 **eSC,** He can outhunt, outfight, and outlast any dog you've seen since who-laid-the-rail. **1958** Willson *Music Man* 60 **IA,** Now you stay away from my oldest girl or you'll hear from me till who laid the rails!

whole *adj, n* Usu |ho(ʊ)l|; also **chiefly NEng, Sth, S Midl** |hʌl|; **esp NEng** |həl|; infreq |hɔl| Pronc-spp *holl, hull, whull* Cf **home** A, **road** n¹ A
Std senses, var forms.

1815 Humphreys *Yankey in England* 105, *Hull,* whole. **a1824** (1937) Guild *Jrl.* 3.288 **VT,** I beat the hull number. **1843** (1916) Hall *New Purchase* 227 **IN,** The hull settlement over thare was a sort a sker'd. **1848** Bartlett *Americanisms* 184, *Hull.* A vulgar pronunciation of the word *whole* very common in New England. **1848** Cooper *Oak-Openings* 1.51 **NY,** The whull lake country don't contain Blossom's equal. **1848** Lowell *Biglow* 66 **'Upcountry' MA,** "I should like to shoot / The holl gang, by the gret horn spoon!" sez he. **1890** *DN* 1.39 **csME,** *Whole.* . . [The author's pronc] *originally and still sometimes* [həl]; *now also* [hoʊl]. **1905** *DN* 3.12 **CT,** *Hull.* . . Whole. **1907** *DN* 3.213 **nwAR,** *Hull.* . . Whole. **1914** *DN* 4.76 **ME, nNH,** Him an' her was lollygaggin' the hull 'tarnal time. **1917** *DN* 4.408 **wNC,** The hull kit an' bilin' of 'em. **1923** *DN* 5.211 **swMO,** *Hull.* . . Whole. **1929** (1951) Faulkner *Sartoris* 223 **nMS,** The hull country's overrun with bears. **1931** Hannum *Thursday April* 29 **wNC,** The hull family would die of doctor's bills starvation! **1932** Randolph *Ozark Mt. Folks* 45, They fixed up a reg'lar contract, giner'ly for th' hull three months. **1933** Rawlings *South Moon* 12 **nFL,** A hull mess o' deer! **1939** Writers' Program *Guide* KY 89, The hull kit and bilin' can go to the devil. **1961** Kurath–McDavid *Pronc. Engl.* 111, *The Vowel in . . whole . .* /həl/. . . does not occur outside the New England settlement area, i.e., the Northern dialect area. . . It is preserved most extensively in northeastern New England (from the Green Mountains in Vermont eastward), less so in the southeast. In the lower Connecticut Valley and westward it is now rather uncommon, except among the older generation, and in the New England settlements of Upstate New York, northern Pennsylvania, and east-central New Jersey it survives only as a rare relic. . . Occasionally the /ə/ is replaced by /ʌ/, especially in the word *whole* /hʌl/, which survives in this pronunciation in the New England settlements of Upstate New York, northern Pennsylvania, and the Western Reserve of Ohio. **1966** *DARE* (Qu. GG22a, *When you have come to the end of your patience . . "Well that's the _____."*) Inf **MO**1, Whole ['hɔɬ] of it. **1989** Pederson *LAGS Tech. Index* 302 **Gulf Region,** *Whole.* [1 inf offered a pronc of the type [hɔl].]

whole caboodle See **caboodle**

whole enduring day, the See **enduring** *adj*

whole kit and (ca)boodle See **kit** n **2b**

whompa-sided See **whomper-sided**

whomper See **womper**

whomper-jawed *adj* Also *w(h)ompy-jawed, womper-~, wompey-jaw*

1 =**whopper-jawed 1. Midl, Sth, TX** See Map
1927 *DN* 5.478 **Ozarks,** *Whomper-jawed.* . . Distorted, misshapen. "Anse's oldes' boy is kinder whomper-jawed." The term is sometimes applied to inanimate objects—crooked cabins, vehicles and articles of furniture. **1958** Humphrey *Home from the Hill* 51 **neTX,** 'At's my ole whomper-jawed Rip hound! Lissen to im go! **1965–70** *DARE* (Qu. X6, *If a person's lower jaw sticks out prominently . . he's _____*) 28 Infs, **Midl, Sth, TX,** Womper-jawed; **FL**19, Whomper-jawed; **TX**98, Wompy-jawed. **1998** *State Jrl.–Reg.* (Springfield IL) 14 June 17 (Internet) **TX,** [Molly Ivins column:] I'm shocked and appalled. . . Goggle-eyed, whomper-jawed, the whole nine yards. **2002** in 2008 *DARE* File—Internet **AR,** The huge tin was full of candy / like the kind you suck, not chew. . . / 'Cause one bite could make you womper-jawed / or break your teeth in two!

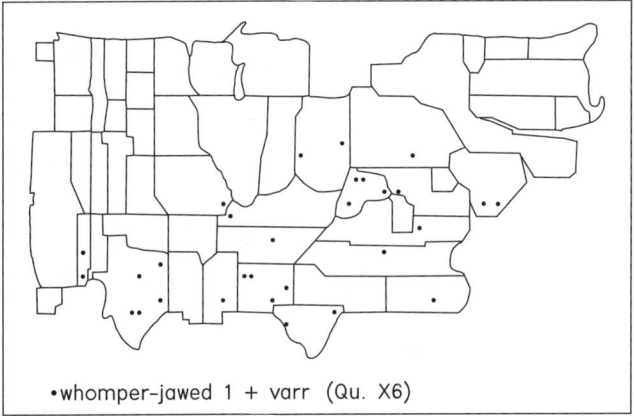

•whomper-jawed 1 + varr (Qu. X6)

2 =**whopper-jawed 2;** hence adv *whomper-jawed* diagonally. **chiefly Midl, Sth, TX** See Map
1905 *DN* 3.100 **nwAR,** *Womper-jawed.* . . Crooked. More common than 'wopper-jawed.' **1927** [see **1** above]. **1944** *PADS* 2.62 **MO,** *Whomper-jawed* ['hwɑmpɚˌdʒɔd]. . . Irregular, uneven, lopsided. "This pattern is whomper-jawed." "Your barn is a bit whomper-jawed." . . Common. **1956** Ker *Vocab. W. TX* 416, *He walked diagonally across a field.* . . whomperjawed. [1 of 67 infs] **1965–70** *DARE* (Qu. KK70, *Something that has got out of proper shape: "That house is all _____."*) 34 Infs, **chiefly Midl, Sth, TX,** Whomper-jawed; **AL**12, **TX**90, W(h)ompy-jawed; (Qu. W23, *When a collar or other clothing works itself up out of place . . "It's _____.";* total Infs questioned, 75) Inf **FL**28, Womper-jawed; (Qu. KK20a, *Something that looks as if it might collapse any minute: "That old shed is certainly _____."*) Inf **IN**7, Whomper-jawed; (Qu. MM3, *When someone does something the wrong way round . . "This is the front, you've got the whole thing turned _____."*) Inf **OH**84, Whomper-jawed; (Qu. MM13, *The table was nice and straight until he came along and knocked it _____*) Infs **AR**52, **TX**5, 52, 104, W(h)omper-jawed. **1985** Ladwig *How to Talk Dirty* 9 **Ozarks,** *Whomperjawed . .* askew. **1986** Pederson *LAGS Concordance (Kitty-cornered)* 1 inf, **ceTX,** Whompy-jawed. **2003** in 2008 *DARE* File—Internet **ceTX,** I've never heard of that one [=*wonky*] but I do occasionally use wompey-jaw, which of course means "out of whack." **2006** *DARE* File—Internet **ceTX,** I upgraded my software to

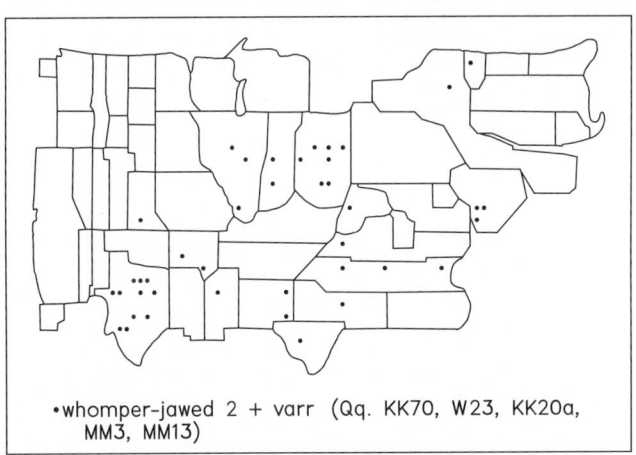

•whomper-jawed 2 + varr (Qq. KK70, W23, KK20a, MM3, MM13)

Wordpress 2.0 last night, so if anything is wompyjawed, let me know. **2006** in 2008 *Ibid* **seMN**, MPlayer's splash screen is all womper-jawed (sorry for those who may try a translator the [sic] that one) gives me a fatal error. **2007** *Ibid* **TX**, Either our compass went womper jawed on us or our South at 25 the day before was now North at 20.

whomper-sided adj　Also *whompa-sided, womper-~*　Cf **wop-sided**
=**whopper-jawed 2.**

　1967 *DARE* (Qu. KK70, *Something that has got out of proper shape: "That house is all _____."*) Inf **AL**16, Whomper-sided. **1996** Wells *Divine Secrets* 176 **LA**, Baylor and Lulu were still half asleep, rubbing their eyes, their . . pajamas all whompa-sided. **2008** *DARE* File—Internet **sGA**, Ken's greatest joy is to ensure that your window package does not end up "womper-sided", as his friends from South Georgia would say.

whompny-jawed adj　Also *whompsey-jawed, whopsy-~, wompny-~*
1 =**whopper-jawed 1.**

　1967 *DARE* (Qu. X6, *If a person's lower jaw sticks out prominently . . he's _____*) Inf **SC**34, Wompny-jawed—reported used by a few others.
2 =**whopper-jawed 2.**

　1966–67 *DARE* (Qu. KK70, *Something that has got out of proper shape: "That house is all _____."*) Inf **MS**71, Whopsy-jawed; (Qu. MM13, *The table was nice and straight until he came along and knocked it _____*) Inf **SC**34, Whompny-jawed. **2000** *NADS Letters* **MS**, "Whompsey-jawed" (sp??), a term I've heard all of my life but have never seen written and don't know how to spell. It definitely means "askew."

whompus　See **wampus** n²

whompy-jawed　See **whomper-jawed**

whonker-jawed adj　Also *whocker-jawed, w(h)onky-~*　esp **TX, S Midl**
=**whopper-jawed 2.**

　1905 *DN* 3.67 **eNE**, Whocker-jawed. . . Askew, awry. "A whocker-jawed skirt." **1966–67** *DARE* (Qu. KK70, *Something that has got out of proper shape: "That house is all _____."*) Infs **NM**4, **TX**3, 36, Whonker-jawed; (Qu. MM13, *The table was nice and straight until he came along and knocked it _____*) Inf **NM**4, Whonker-jawed. **1969** *DARE* File **Dallas TX**, Whonky-jawed—catty cornered, off center. **2002** in 2008 *DARE* File—Internet **TX**, Lost the back mounting bolt for the A/C compressor . . it is a little whonky-jawed (as we say in Texas). **2003** *Ibid* **cAL**, I use "wonky-jawed," meaning "out of whack" or "crooked." **2007** *DARE* File—Internet **KY**, The lid sets just a tad whonker-jawed, which I think can be adjusted by almost anyone handier than I am. **2007** in 2008 *Ibid* **MO**, When young my Dad would use the term "wonky jawed" to describe something uneven or not kind of right. Then, I just thought he made it up and never used it in public for that reason.

whoo exclam　Usu |(h)wu, hu|; for addit varr see quot 1965–70　Also sp *hoo, woo*　chiefly **Sth, S Midl**　See Map
Also in combs: Used as a call to animals; see quots.

　1882 [see **whoop** D]. **1949** Kurath *Word Geog.* 63, Calls to Cows. . . [A] number of more local calls have survived: . . *woo!* . . in the Pennsylvania German settlements on the Lower Susquehanna and from there southward to the head of the Shenandoah, as well as in northern West Virginia . . , with scattered instances in the Ohio Valley. **1965–70** *DARE* (Qu. K84, *The call used . . to get the pigs in at feeding time*) Infs **AL**43, **GA**33, 68, **MS**60, Whoo [hwu(:)] pig (*or* piggy, pig pig); **MS**74, Pig whoo [hwu:]; **SC**3, Whee-whoo [hwii hwu:] pig; **AR**55, Whoo [hwu:] pig; **AR**56, **FL**4, **OK**20, Whoo-pig (pig); **GA**39, **MS**21, **NC**3, **SC**40, Hoo [hu(:)] pig; **SC**63, Wee-hoo [wi hu]; **FL**6, Hoo-pig; **IL**93, **KY**80, **NM**3, **SC**47, **TN**58, Woo [wu(:)] pig (*or* piggies, piggoo); **IL**73, Piggy piggy piggy woo-hoo; **MD**29, Woo-hoo-hoo ['wu 'hu 'hu] for adult pigs; **TN**17, Pig woo [wu:]; **GA**28, **OK**52, 53, **SC**12, Woo-hoo (pig pig pig); **KY**86, **NC**87, **SC**69, Woo-pig (*or* piggy piggy piggy); (Qu. K80, *The call that's used . . to get the cows in from the pasture*) Infs **AR**4, **MS**74, Whoo [hwu(:)]; **NC**36, Whoo whoo [hwu: hwu:]; **FL**4, **KY**35, Whoo cow (*or* sook sook sook); **TX**37, 102, Hoo-hoo; **OK**27, **PA**33, **TX**8, Woo [wu:]; **CA**136, Woo-oo [wu:u]; **MO**35, Woo [wu^:]; **KY**46, Woo [wu] or hoo [hu] to cow; **NJ**2, **OK**43, Woo-woo(-woo); **OK**8, Woo-hoo; (Qu. K82, *The call used . . to get horses in from the pasture*) Inf **NY**24, Woo [wu]; (Qu. K83, *To call a calf to you at feeding time*) Inf **PA**21, Whoo-whoo [hwu hwu]; **FL**4, Whoo cow; (Qu. K85, *The call to sheep*

to come in from the pasture) Inf **VA**89, Whoo [hwu] sheep; **IL**16, Hoo sheep; **LA**8, Woo come on, come on. **1966** Dakin *Dial. Vocab. Ohio R. Valley* 2.270, Whoo!, hoo!, are used [as calls to cows] in the Bluegrass. . . Whoo sook! and hoo sook! in the Bluegrass seem to be blends which developed from the Pennsylvania German calls. *Ibid* 273, Calls [to calves] with *whoo! (whoo sook! whoo calf!)* are very rare. *Ibid* 282, A second call [to pigs] . . *whoo(p)-pig(gie)!* . . seems to be southern in origin. *Ibid* 285, Other variations [of pig calls include] . . *whoo!, woo!* **1967** Faries *Word Geog. MO* 92, Calls to cows. . . The informants write in . . *woo!* [1 inf]. *Ibid* 93, Call to pigs. . . Expressions used by the informants but not listed by Kurath . . [include] *whoo-pig!* [1 inf]. **1973** Allen *LAUM* 1.258 **Upper MW** (as of c1950), Calls to cows. . . West Virginia *woo* somehow was acquired in southeastern Nebraska by a farmer of Czech ancestry.

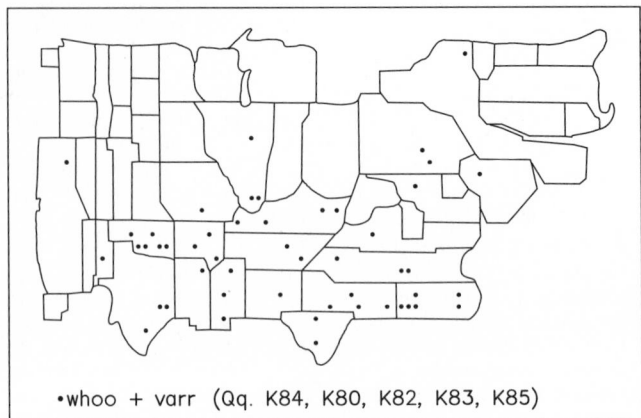

•whoo + varr (Qq. K84, K80, K82, K83, K85)

whooee exclam　Usu |'wu(w)i, 'hu(w)i|; less freq |'hwu:-i|　Also sp *hooee, hooie, hoowie, whooey, whooie, wooee, woo(w)ie;* for addit pronc and sp varr see quots

1　Used as a call to attract attention or to express surprise, joy, pain, etc.　chiefly **Sth, S Midl**　See Map　Cf **oo-wee**

　1874 *Overland Mth.* 13.530 **SW**, Jest as I was about to give a desperate howl, I heerd 'Hoo-ee-ah!' I answered, 'Hoo-ee!' **1882** *Harper's New Mth. Mag.* 65.806 **Sth** [Black], Hain't he [=a fish] a whopper, dough! Hoo-wee! **1888** *Amer. Mag.* 7.571 **nwIA**, One Joe Gilman— "Shouting Joe"—mounts one of the tall stacks, and . . lifts up his voice in the old familiar way. On a still morning like this, his "Chippeway war-whoop" can be heard three miles. . . "Whoo-ee whooee-oo-oo-oop!" **1892** Harris *On Plantation* 112 **GA** [Black], Whoo-ee! . . I'm dat tired dat I can't skacely drag one foot 'fo' de yuther. **1900** Harben *N. GA Sketches* 129 [Black], Dem boys done made up, en I fotch twenty thousand dollars! Whooee! **1910** Harben *Dixie Hart* 329 **GA**, He heard little Joe calling to Dixie from the kitchen door, and from the cow-lot her clear answering "Whooee!" **1924** *DN* 5.279 [Exclams], *Whoo-ee* or *whooie* (surp[rise], com[ic papers]). **1932** King *Memories S. Woman* 20 **seLA**, We all joined in, following Mamma's example. "Whoo! Whooee! Whooeee!" went our cry of distress. **1965–69** *DARE* (Qu. NN6a, *Exclamations of joy . . when somebody gets a pleasant surprise, he might shout "_____."*) Inf **KY**49, Hoo-wee ['huwi:ˇ]; **LA**25, Hoo-wee [ˌhu'wi]; **NC**7, Hoo-hee ['huw 'hij]; **TN**46, Whoo-wee; **TN**36, Woo-ee; (Qu. NN6b, *Expressions of joy used mostly by children*) Inf **OK**1, Hoo-ee; **TN**46, Whoo-wee; (Qu. NN23, *Exclamations when people smell a very bad odor*) Inf **DC**8, Whoo-ee [hwu: i:]; **NM**11, Hoo-ee.

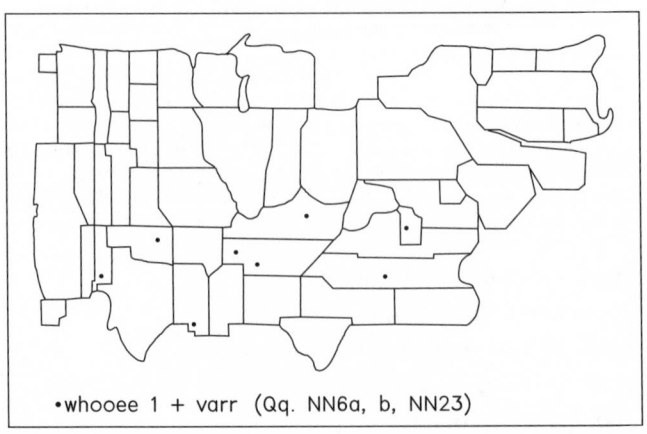

•whooee 1 + varr (Qq. NN6a, b, NN23)

2 Used as a call to animals; see quots. **widespread exc NEast; most freq Midl, esp IA, IL, IN** See Map

1886 in 1932 *AmSp* 7.455 **IN,** It is amusing to note the different ways people call their pigs. If your neighbor [is] . . a Hoosier, he yells Who-ee, who-ee, who-ee. **1892** *St. Nicholas* 19.398 **VA,** Every night Dick . . comes to the gate of the deer-park, and calls, "Who-e-e! who-e-e!" and the deer . . come bounding up to him. **1941** Ward *Holding Hills* 128 **IA** (as of early 20th cent), He shouts "Whu-u-ey! Whu-u-ey!" and as the drove comes 'loping through the dust to him, he has a friendly word: "Pig! Pig! Pig!" **1946** *PADS* 6.33 **eNC,** Woooooooy ['wuːˑɪ]. . . A hog call used for calling hogs a quarter of a mile or more away. **1948** Davis *Word Atlas Gt. Lakes* app qu 70, 17 [of 233] infs, **IL, IN, MI, OH,** Woo-ee! [as a call to pigs]. **1949** Kurath *Word Geog.* 65, Other calls [to pigs] . . *hoo-ie!,* . . *woo-ie!* in northern Delaware and on the lower Susquehanna. . . also in common use in a well-defined area centering on Wheeling, West Virginia. **1949** Webber *Backwoods Teacher* 181 **Ozarks,** Sister Viny raised her voice: "Whoo-o-oooooooooo-ee-e-ee! Soo-ooo-ooook, now! Cooooooooooo-eeeeeee!" And then, to my surprise, she put her head back, hands to mouth, and gave a startling imitation of a cow bellowing. **1951** Johnson *Resp. to PADS 20* **DE** *(Call to cows to come in from the pasture)* Whooey, whooey! **1965–70** *DARE* (Qu. K84, *The call used . . to get the pigs in at feeding time*) 23 Infs, **scattered, exc NEast; esp IA, IL, IN,** Wooee (pig *or* piggy) [proncs of the types ['wu-ɪ, wuː(w)iː]]; **MD29,** Wooee [wu-i]—for baby pigs; **IL114, IN77,** Wooee (pig pig); 19 Infs, **scattered, but esp Midl,** Hooee (hooee *or* pig) [proncs of the types ['hu(w)i]]; **CO44,** Hooee [hui:]—a Kansas call; **IL4,** Hooee ['huwi]; **FL15, IA33, OH58,** Hooee (hooee); **AZ10, IA8, IL142, IN40, 67, MS19, TN53,** Whooee [proncs of the types ['hwuːi, 'hwuːi]]; **IN80,** Whooee; (Qu. K80, *The call that's used . . to get the cows in from the pasture*) Infs **AZ10, TX13,** Hooee (hooee hooee) [hui]; **AL26,** Hooee hooee cow cow; (Qu. K82, *The call used . . to get horses in from the pasture*) Inf **OH31,** Hooee ['hui]; **MS19,** Whooee ['hwui]; (Qu. K85, *The call to sheep to come in from the pasture*) Inf **VA43,** Hooee [hu:wi:]. **1966** Dakin *Dial. Vocab. Ohio R. Valley* 2.284, [Calls to pigs:] *Hoo-(w)ie!* . . *woo-(w)ie!,* and, from the Miami River westward, *whoo-(w)ie!* are distributed over a wider area [than *pooie!*]. **1967** Faries *Word Geog. MO* 93, Call to pigs. . . *woo-ie!* (125 occurrences) and *hoo-ie!* (121 occurrences). . . *whooie!* (9 occurrences). **1971** Wood *Vocab. Change* 46 **Sth, S Midl,** Customary calls for pigs at feeding time [include] . . *hoo-ee.* Ibid 303, [Call to hogs:] Woo-ee [43 of 1,000 infs]. **1973** Gawthrop *Dial. Calumet* 77 **nwIN,** *Calls to hogs at feeding time* . . woo-ee 3 [of 125 checklist infs]. **1973** Allen *LAUM* 1.259 **Upper MW** (as of c1950), Calls to cows. . . wooie [1 inf, **NE**]. Ibid 265, Calls to pigs at feeding time. . . *Hooie* has been brought west from Delaware and the lower Susquehanna Valley to be a still viable call in southern Iowa, southeastern South Dakota, and Nebraska. *Wooie,* a south Midland call found in Virginia and North Carolina, has a solitary echo in the South Midland speech area of southeastern Iowa and another in northwestern Nebraska. **1983** *MJLF* 9.1.60 **ceKY** (as of 1956), *Whoooie pig, pig, pig, pig!* . . a call to make the pigs come.

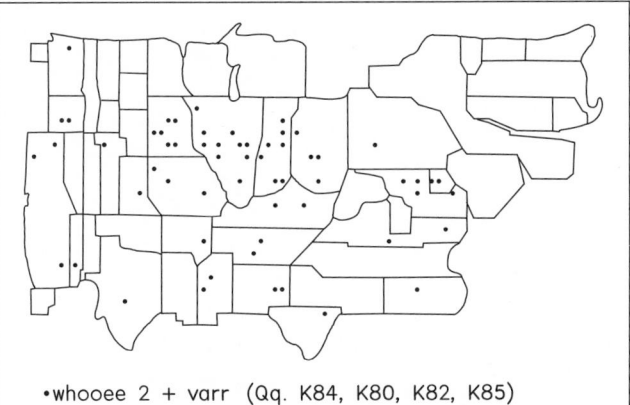

•whooee 2 + varr (Qq. K84, K80, K82, K85)

3 usu as *hooee:* Used as a call to drive away animals; see quots. **esp Sth, S Midl** See Map

1811 *Lady's Misc.* 13.45, Happening to go by there . . , I was half deafened with the cry of—'Who-ee—who-ee—stu-boy—stu-boy.' A drove of hogs had come along, and while my neighbour was taking a nap, they had crawled through the broken fence. **1965–70** *DARE* (Qu. NN22d, . . *Expressions used to drive away people or animals*) Infs

IN42, KY24, 84, LA28, 35, Hooee [proncs of the types [hui, huɪ, 'hʌwi]]; **IN32,** Hooee; **NJ16,** Hooey—for a dog; **OK20,** Hooey ['huwi]—for cattle; **SC32,** Hooey ['hʌ- i]—for cattle; **TX26,** Hooey—for a cow; **VA69,** Hooey—for hogs.

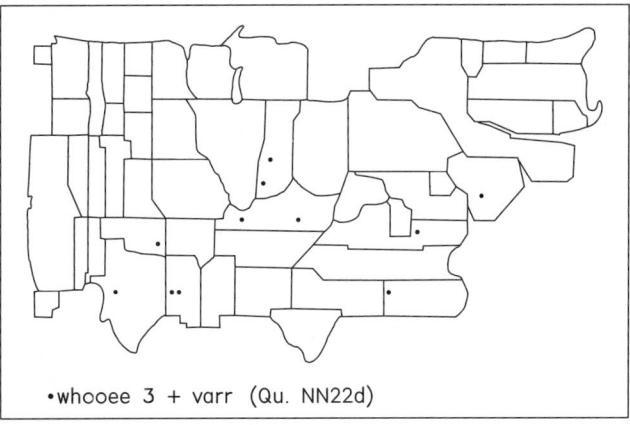

•whooee 3 + varr (Qu. NN22d)

whooee stick n Also *whooie stick*
=gee-haw whimm(e)y-diddle.

1970 *DARE* FW Addit **KY,** *Whooee stick . .* (so called because the person operating it shouts "whoo-ee!" as he does so) = gee-haw whimmy-diddle. Said to be "the Texas term." **2005** *DARE* File—Internet **TX,** My adopted Dad, bein' a Yankee, made a wooden kind of windwheel for me when I was very young, but he called it a whooie stick. . . Everytime he would say: Whooie, the thing would spin back the opposite direction. Ibid **AR,** Here Elder Anderson . . and Elder Porter . . are being taught . . how to run a whooie stick—a propeller equipped toy that requires no battery or motor. This was . . near *Mena Arkansas.*

whooey, whooie See **whooee.**

whooie stick See **whooee stick**

whook exclam Also *hookey, (w)hookie, woak, wook(ey), wookie* **esp Mid Atl** See Map
Used as a call to animals; see quots.

1897 *Amer. Anthropologist* 10.104 **AL,** List of words used in calling swine. . . Whook—Alabama. **1949** Kurath *Word Geog.* 65, Calls to Pigs. . . On the Eastern Shore [of Maryland] and between the lower James and the Neuse *wook!, wookie!, woak!* predominates. Ibid 63, Calls to Cows in the Pasture. . . *wookie! (whookie!, hookie!)* in the Pennsylvania German settlements on the Lower Susquehanna and from there southward to the head of the Shenandoah, as well as in northern West Virginia . . , with scattered instances in the Ohio Valley. **1966** Dakin *Dial. Vocab. Ohio R. Valley* 2.270, The northern Seven Ranges and the river counties downriver from Marietta have *whook!* . . *Wook!* appears in the Muskingum Valley. **1967** Faries *Word Geog. MO* 91, *Calls to cows.* . . There are a few occurrences of . . *wookie!* . . and *whookie!* (Pennsylvania German settlement areas). **1968–70** *DARE* (Qu. K80, *The call that's used . . to get the cows in from the pasture*) Inf **IN77,** Wook; **WV8,** Wook [wuːwk]; **KY46,** Wook-cow; **MD20,** Wookey ['wuki]; **MD29,** Wookey ['wuki]; **VA27,** Hookey ['huki] repeated; (Qu. K84, *The call used . . to get the pigs in at feeding time*) Inf **VA40,** Wook-wook-wook ['wuk 'wuk 'wuk]; **VA57,** Woak [wouk].

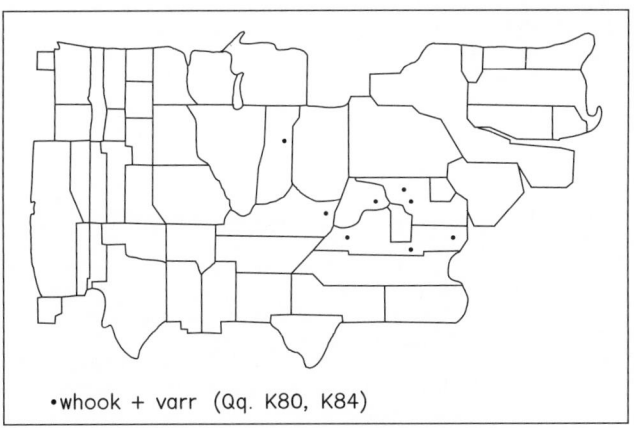

•whook + varr (Qq. K80, K84)

whoop v[1], n, exclam   Usu |hup| (and in form *whooping* often |hup|); infreq |hwup, hwʌp|; rarely |wup, wʌp|; for addit varr see quot 1965–70 at **A**   Pronc-sp *hoop*

A Forms.

1817 *Analectic Mag.* 9.143, Men, women, and children hooped and yelled. **1845** Hering *Domestic Physician* 201, When hooping cough prevails, . . give immediately of the above described medicines. **1847** *De Bow's Rev.* 3.369, [Life Insurance at the South:] *Causes of Death.* . . Hooping Cough . . Influenza . . Measles. **1856** *Knickerbocker* 48.431, All have the hooping-cough together. **1859** Atson *Heart Whispers* 65 **TN,** Hill and the Captain hooped and halloed. [**1892** U.S. Bur. Amer. Ethnology *Annual Rept. for 1887–88* 459, While the "hoop-me-koff" was raging among the Mohave the fathers of families afflicted with it were forbidden to touch coffee or salt.] **1931** *AmSp* 6.347, An *m* for the *-ing* of the present participle appears in *whoopmcough* or *hoopmcough.* **1965–70** *DARE* (Qu. BB49, . . *Other kinds of diseases*) 111 Infs, **widespread,** Whooping cough [no transcr]; 45 Infs, **scattered, but more freq Sth, Midl,** Proncs of the types ['hupɪŋ, -ɪn, -n̩]; 19 Infs, **chiefly Nth, Midl,** Proncs of the types ['hupɪŋ, -ɪn, -n̩]; CT6, MI62, PA228, WA6, [hʌpɪŋ, -ɪn]; 13 Infs, **scattered,** [FW indicated pronc with initial [h]]; AR51, CA87, MI65, 69, NY186, PA182, ['hwupɪŋ, -ɪn]; IA7, ['hwupɪŋ]; CT12, MA43, ['wupɪŋ, -ɪn]; IL97, RI10, ['wupən, -ɪn]; (Qu. BB11, *Speaking of a deep cough that you can't seem to get rid of:* "*Listen to him _____.*") 49 Infs, **scattered,** Whoop (*or* whooping cough) [no transcr]; 21 Infs, **scattered, but more freq Sth, Midl,** Proncs of the type [hup]; CO33, GA8, 33, SC46, Proncs of the types ['hupɪŋ, -ɪn]; MO11, NY96, [hup] it (*or* her) up; MO5, ['hupn̩] cough; 8 Infs, **scattered,** [FW indicated pronc with initial [h]]; AL50, [hwup]; (Qu. BB9, *A sickness in which you have a severe cough and difficult breathing—it often starts with a cold, and lasts a week or two*) Infs GA23, 42, MI93, MN15, Whooping cough; NJ54, ['hupɪŋ] cough; MO29, Whooping cough [FW indicated pronc with initial [h]]; (Qu. BB12, *The kind of cough that comes with bronchitis:* "*He has a _____ cough.*") Infs FL51, GA23, NC77, Whooping (cough); MA9, PA195, ['hupɪŋ]; MA43, ['hwupɪŋ]; (Qu. BB50a, . . *Favorite remedies . . for a cough*) Inf NJ39, Whooping cough—hold a frog to mouth when you whoop. **1967–69** *DARE* Tape CA136, They'd whoop [hu^p] and holler and sing all night; GA30, The sandhill crane is brown, but he whoops [hups] just like the whoopin ['hupɪn] crane; MI42, I let a whoop [hu^u^p] out of me, and Chris hollered, "What's the matter?" **2007** *DARE* File—Internet, [Audio:] What about whooping ['hwupɪŋ] cough?

B As verb.

1 also with *up*: To vomit.

1912 *DN* 3.593 **wIN,** Whoop her up. . . To vomit. "He helped to eat a green watermelon, and the first thing he knew he was whooping her up in grand style." **1968** *DARE* (Qu. BB18, *To vomit a great deal at once*) Inf MN15, Whooped it up. **1999** Moore *I Will Survive* 172 **NYC,** I nearly whooped my Oreos.

2 To use non-singing vocal effects in musical or spiritual contexts; hence vbl n *whooping.*   Cf **eephing, hoodling, whoop** v **C3**

1978 Wolfe *I'm On My Journey Home* 1 **KY,** This body of vocal effects is characterized by the use of the voice in diverse musical ways, but to ends other than formal song. It includes utilitarian functions such as auctioneering, dance calls, educational or mnemonic devices, and some forms of hollering; it includes examples of sheer entertainment such as imitations, whooping, nonsense songs, and recreational hollers. **1994** Smitherman *Black Talk* 204, Shout . . To express religious/spiritual ecstasy . . ; may be in the form of hollering, whooping, moaning. **2003** Ramsey *Race Music* 44 **Chicago IL** [Black], *Race, Entertainment, and the Blues Muse.* . . Washington delivers the song with classy, matter-of-fact understatement and reserve. She doesn't whoop, holler, or bray the lyrics but sings with a quiet sass.

C As noun.

1 Fig: an indefinite, esp short, distance—used esp in phrr *a whoop and (a) holler* and varr.   **chiefly Sth, S Midl** Cf **holler** v **C3**

1898 *Daily Rev.* (Decatur IL) [17 Aug 2]/1 (newspaperarchive.com), If you ask a typical southerner how far it is to East Lake from Chattanooga he may reply, 'About two whoops and a holler.' **1919** *DN* 5.36 **KY,** *Whoops and a holler, two.* . . A short distance. As far as the combined sounds of "two whoops and a holler" would carry? **1920s** in 1944 *ADD* **cNY,** *Whoop and a holler.* . . He lives a whoop and a holler down the road. **1951** Craig *Singing Hills* 22 **sAppalachians,** "Let's go," said Cleve. "It's no more than a whoop away." *Ibid* 155, They

lived in a cabin which Miriam said was three whoops and two hollers away. **1952** *DE Folkl. Bulletin* 1.11, It's only a whoop and a holler from here. **1955** *Julian Apple Day* [32] **csCA,** A whoop and a holler farther away. **1957** *Daily Progress* (Charlottesville VA) 5 Feb 8/1 *(Hench Coll.),* He lives about two whoops and an extra-loud holler from my place. **1967–70** *DARE* (Qu. MM4, . . *A short distance past* . . "*The mail box is just _____ the pine tree.*") Inf **GA31,** So many whoops and a holler; (Qu. MM6, . . '*Very close' or 'only a short distance away':* "*The house is _____ the park.*") Inf **CT6,** Whoop and a holler from; (Qu. MM24, . . '*A short distance':* "*The river is just a _____ from the house.*") Infs **DC1, GA31, SC39, VA5, 34, WV16,** (Scant) whoop and a holler. **1976** Garber *Mountain-ese* 101 **sAppalachians,** *Whoop-and-a-holler* . . short way. The Jones boys live just a whoop and a holler up the road from me. **1982** *Barrick Coll.* **csPA,** He jist lives a whoop and holler down the road. **1986** Pederson *LAGS Concordance,* 1 inf, **neFL,** A whoop and a holler and a mile away; 1 inf, **ceGA,** A whoop and holler—a short distance.

2 Fig: something of negligible value—usu in neg phrr *not to give a whoop, not worth a whoop,* and varr.   **scattered, but esp S Atl, Gulf States, Gt Lakes, Upper MW, Pacific**   See Map

1877 *Salt Lake Daily Tribune* (UT) 11 Nov [4]/2 (newspaperarchive.com), And they say this here outfit don't pay hired girls worth a whoop in purgatory no how, and take tithing out of their wages besides. **1884** *Weekly NV State Jrl.* (Reno) 12 Apr [2]/7 (newspaperarchive.com), Prichard and Eagle Creeks, about which so much has been said and written, are not worth a whoop in Halifax. **1893** *Cedar Rapids Eve. Gaz.* (IA) 13 Oct 8/2, One stage manager . . didn't care a whoop for Davis. **1914** *Gaz. & Bulletin* (Williamsport PA) 16 Nov 4/4, We people don't care a hoop which side wins. **1919** Kyne *Capt. Scraggs* 146 **CA,** And are they worth a whoop after you get them? **1925** *Bridgeport Telegram* (CT) 18 Aug [7]/5 (newspaperarchive.com), There must be something doing every minute of the day or her life isn't worth a hoop. **1940** Faulkner *Hamlet* 53 **MS,** The separator. . . sounded strong as ever, like it . . didn't give a whoop whether that milk had been separated once or a hundred times. **1946** *PADS* 6.43 **eNC** (as of 1900–10), *Not worth two whoops in hell.* . . Occasional. **1946** McAtee *Dial. Grant Co. IN Suppl.* 3 7 (as of 1890s), *Not worth a [w]hoop in hell.* . . worthless. **1956** *Tri-City Herald* (Pasco WA) 26 Oct 3/7, The farmer was told that the unit he wanted to farm was "not worth a hoop". **1965–70** *DARE* (Qu. GG21b, *If you don't care what a person does* . . "*Go ahead—I don't give a _____.*") 31 Infs, **scattered, but esp S Atl, Gulf States, Gt Lakes, Upper MW, Pacific,** (W)hoop; (Qu. HH20c, *Of an idle, worthless person* . . "*He isn't worth _____.*") Infs **IL4, MI10, 94, MN33, SD3,** Two hoops (in hell); **CA158, VA42, WA11,** Hoop in hell; **LA40, TX62,** Whoop; **GA19,** Two whoops in Hades. **1966** Barnes–Jensen *Dict. UT Slang* 23, *He's not worth a whoop in hell:* saying, worthless. **1973** *Oakland Tribune* (CA) 23 Jan [79]/1 (newspaperarchive.com), These are . . guys who just don't give a hoop. **1976** Garber *Mountain-ese* 34 **sAppalachians,** Sally don't give a whoop about any uv the boys in the neighborhood.

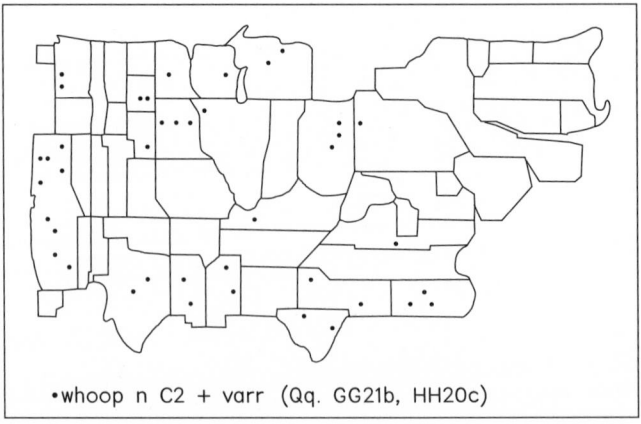

•whoop n C2 + varr (Qq. GG21b, HH20c)

3 =holler C2.

1955 *Phylon* 16.16 **Sth** [Black], Cries which are articulate from the standpoint of music, but not from the standpoint of words. . . Famous among those yet surviving names are "corn field holler," "nigger squall," "piney-woods whoop," "roustabout drunk-yell," and "loud-mouthing." **1978** Wolfe *I'm On My Journey Home* 1 **KY,** The Kentucky whoop by

"Red" Buck Estes . . is a more recent and a more complex example of hollering. Here there is even more integration of melody into the holler, and, after a statement of a descending melodic motif, Estes even uses words. . . These common-property blues lines, and the fact that Estes privately referred to his holler as a "nigger whoop," suggest that it might have been derived at least in part from black sources. **2005** *Music Cultures U.S.* 194 **Sth** [Black], *Field cry (corn field whoop):* a brief statement frequently heard in silent, open country; signifies a loneliness of spirit . . or merely as a bit of self-indulgence.

D As exclam.

Also *hoopie, w(h)oopie:* Used to call (or rarely drive away) animals. **esp S Atl, Gulf States** See Map

1882 *Century Illustr. Mag.* 24.160 **GA** [Black], *Hog-feeder's song.* Oh, rise up, my ladies! Lissen unter me!/ *Gwoop!—Gwoop! Gee-woop!—Goo-whee!/* I'm a-gwine dis night fer ter knock along er you!/ *Gwoop!—Gwoop! Gee-woop!—Goo-whoo!/ Pig-goo! pig-gee! Gee-o-whee!* **1893** Shands *MS Speech* 37, *Hoop-hooee* (hûp-hûî). This represents as nearly as I can represent it, the sound made by farmers in calling hogs. The accent is equally emphatic on each syllable of the word. **1897** *Amer. Anthropologist* 10.104 **GA,** List of words used in calling swine . . Whoop. **1931** *AmSp* 6.394, "Whoop". . . [as a] call to animals found its chief home in the Southwest. **1949** Kurath *Word Geog.* 65, [Calls to pigs] In North Carolina south of the Neuse, in South Carolina, and in Georgia . . *woop!, woopie!* [are in regular use]. **1961** *Folk Word Atlas N. LA* map 807, *Calls to cows.* . . [Other responses] whoop. **1965–70** *DARE* (Qu. K84, *The call used . . to get the pigs in at feeding time*) Infs **GA**11, **IN**44, (Pig) whoop [hwup]; **LA**2, Whoop [hwuːp]— for large hogs; **SC**9, Piggy piggy piggy hoop [huːp]; **FL**26, 32, Hoop (hoop) [no transcr]; **AL**11, Woop [wuˑɪp]; **AR**51, Woo piggy woop ['wuː ˌpɪgɪ 'wuːp]; **SC**43, Woop [wup] (Qu. K82, *The call used . . to get horses in from the pasture*) Inf **LA**3, Woop, woop [wuˣp wuˣp]; (Qu. NN22d, . . *Expressions used to drive away people or animals*) Inf **AZ**1, Hoopie—to a cow. **1966** Dakin *Dial. Vocab. Ohio R. Valley* 2.276, [Calls to horses] *Hoop!* plus a whistle . . [is] used in . . Marion Count[y], Indiana. *Ibid* 282, A second call [to pigs], most commonly occurring as *whoo(p)-pig(gie)!* (also *woop!, hoop!* and *whoo-pie!),* also seems to be southern in origin. *Ibid* 283, *Whoo(p)-pig(gie)!* is common in the western Pennyroyal, the Purchase, and the southern Illinois counties across the Ohio. [**1967** LeCompte *Word Atlas* 188 **seLA,** *Calls to cows.* . . whooo-ip [1 of 21 infs].]

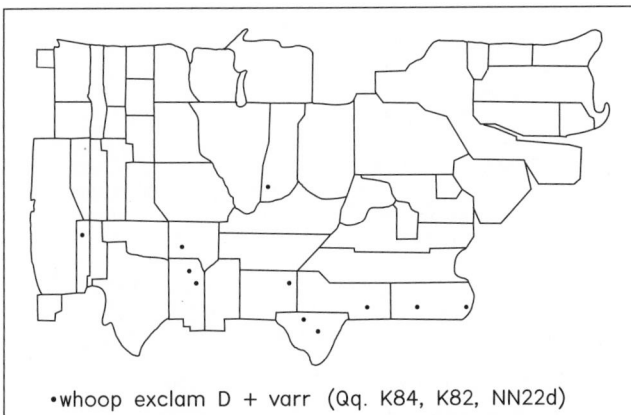

•whoop exclam D + varr (Qq. K84, K82, NN22d)

whoop v² See **whip A1**

whoop and a holler, a See **whoop n C1**

whoop-and-hide n Also *hoop(-and)-hide, hoot-and-hide, whoopee hide, whoopie ~, whoopin' ~, (w)hoopy ~* Cf **hide-and-whoop**

1 =**hide-and-seek A.** [*OED2 hoop and hide* (at *hoop* v.² 1.b) 1710–11] **chiefly S Midl, S Atl** See Map

1822 Holmes *Recreations* 43 **seSC,** On the right of my aunt, sat her maiden sister, to whom . . the children would run to refer the decision of some controversy respecting the precise manner in which "hot beans," or "whoop and hide," should be played. **1874** Gilman–Jervey *Young Fortune Teller* 15, *Whoop and hide* is a very nice play,/ Out in the yard or under the hay. **1904** *DN* 2.418 **nwAR,** *Hoop* [hup] *and hide.* . . Hide and seek. 'The kids are playing hoop and hide.' **1915** *DN* 4.192 **swVA,** *Whoopin' hide.* Variant of *whoop and hide,* a children's game. **1940** *Qrly. Jrl. Speech* 26.266 **VA,** "Hoopy hide" *(hide and go seek).* **1946**

PADS 6.33 **eNC** (as of 1900–10), *Whoop and hide.* . . Hide and seek. . . The usual term among children. **1946** TN Folk Lore Soc. *Bulletin* Mar 18, Some of the mixed games required a good deal of running, as. . . "Whoop and Hide." [*DARE* Ed: This quot may refer instead to sense **2** below.] **1954** *Harder Coll.* **cwTN,** *Whoop and hide.* . . A game in which children hide. **c1960** *Wilson Coll.* **csKY,** *Hide and go seek*—a child's game; also called . . Whoop and Hide, Whoopy Hide. **1965–70** *DARE* (Qu. EE13a, *Games in which every player hides except one, and that one must try to find the others*) Infs **GA**72, **KY**34, **NC**33, **TN**8, 12, 14, 16, **VA**1, (W)hoopy-hide; **NC**79, **SC**19, Hoop-and-hide; **KY**41, Hoop-hide—old-fashioned; **KY**23, Hoot-and-hide; (Qu. EE16, *Hiding games that start with a special, elaborate method of sending the players out to hide*) Inf **NC**1, Whoop-and-hide—everyone whooped when he got hid to confuse the looker; (Qu. EE33, . . *Outdoor games . . that children play*) Inf **KY**34, Hoopy-hide. **1982** Powers *Cataloochee* 178 **cwNC** (as of a1940), Another game we played in the barn that was filled with hay was . . 'Whoopie Hide'. . . We would start this game by selecting one to hide her eyes, or blind them with a handkerchief, (or) maybe (with) her hands, while all the others hid themselves in the hay loft. **1983** *MJLF* 9.1.61 **ceKY** (as of 1956), *Whoopy hide* . . hide 'n seek. **1986** Pederson *LAGS Concordance,* 1 inf, **neFL,** Whoop and hide. **1996** in 2004 Montgomery–Hall *Dict. Smoky Mt. Engl.* 649 **wNC, eTN,** *Whoopy hide.* . . The children's game hide and seek [5 infs]. **2005** Williams *Gratitude* 169 **wNC** (as of 1940s), Some of the outdoor games I remember us a-playin' was *Whoopee Hide,* which the *town doods* at school called "Hide And Seek."

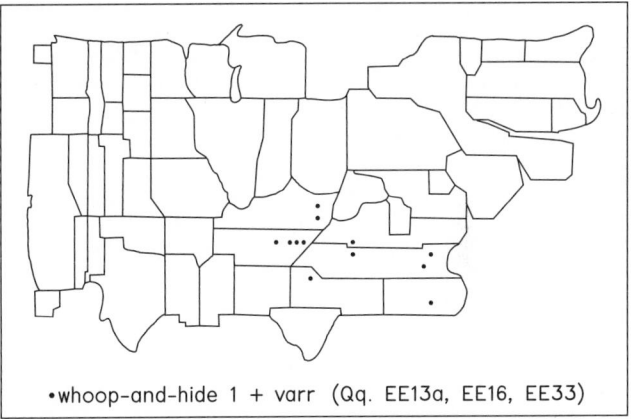

•whoop-and-hide 1 + varr (Qq. EE13a, EE16, EE33)

‡2 The game **run sheep run.** Cf **hide-and-seek B2**

1966 *DARE* (Qu. EE12, *Games in which one captain hides his team and the other team tries to find it*) Inf **SC**10, Hoop-and-hide.

whoop and holler, a See **whoop n C1**

whoop-de-do(o) n Also *whoopdiedo, whoop-te-doo* Cf *DS* N27b, 30

=**thank-you-ma'am 1.**

1972 *Times–Std.* (Eureka CA) 21 Feb 10/6, *Muddy Track, Sun For Cycle Races.* . . Richter then went down on the "whoop-de-doo". **1974** *Bucks Co. Courier Times* (Levittown PA) 10 Feb mag sec 6/3, The epitome of danger is the . . motorsport park outside of Reading. . . The constant up-and-down, whoop-de-doo laden hills are just short of suicide when taken with 30 or so over-anxious amatuers [sic] at breakneck speed. **1980** *Dirt Bike* Oct 15 **NJ,** Very soon we were all lying beside the road, for even though the road looked good at first, it was plagued with whoopdiedoos, and we came into them a little hot. **1985** *DARE* File **MO,** In Missouri (Carthage) circa 1918 according to my Grandfather . . it was a dip in the road, paved tho [sic] the road was gravel, which we took at a slightly accelerated speed, so that it made us catch our breath. Sometimes we called it a "Whoop-te-do" as we went down and up again. These Missouri Thank-you-Ma'ams were built thus to permit rain water to run off, rather than wash out roadways. **1999** *DARE* File—Internet, *Whoop-de-do's*—Consecutive small jumps or bumps on a straightaway [=in a motocross course].

whoopee See **whoopy**

whoopee hide See **whoop-and-hide**

whoopee pie See **whoopie pie**

whoopensocker n Also *hoopensocker, whoopensacker, whoopensoccer, whop and soccer* **chiefly WI**

1 Something extraordinary of its kind; see quots.

1934 *WI State Jrl.* (Madison) 23 Jan 14/3, That old colored guy Wallace Heath put on a buck and wing dance that was a whoopensocker. That guy was good. **1934** *Greeley Daily Tribune & Greeley Republican* (CO) 15 June 10/5, [Advt:] *"It's A Whoopensocker"* If the Greeks had a name for a music-splashed fun show like "Hollywood Party". . . they kept it a secret! . . 2000 in the cast headed by Laurel and Hardy, Jimmie Durante [etc]. **2006** *DARE* File—Internet **WI,** Whoopensocker is a word an old, deceased friend of mine used to describe something even bigger than gigantic, or immense. **2007** in 2008 *Ibid* **WI,** First, though let me show you my baby brother. He is, as my godmother says, a whoopensocker. He's 6′5″ and built like a linebacker. **2008** *Ibid* **WI,** If it combines with the cold temperatures . . we might have quite a whoopen-socker of a snowstorm.

2 Spec: a large or strong drink; liquor.

1926 *Appleton Post–Crescent* (WI) 1 Sept 8/4, Even though we didn't have prohibition at that time, you didn't see as many drunkards then as you do now. . . We takes our whoopensocker or two and an eye opener or so and goes home to bed. **1933** *WI State Jrl.* (Madison) 12 July 8/7, Madison's approval of Bert's special "Hoopensocker" beer stein has been evidenced by the crowds which thronged the tavern at the old location. **1950** *WELS (A little drink)* 1 Inf, **csWI,** Whop and soccer shot; *(Names and nicknames for liquor in general)* 1 Inf, **csWI,** Whoopen-soccer. [*DARE* Ed: Same Inf responded to both qq.] **1966** *DARE* File **csWI,** *Whoopensacker.* . . in phrase "to have a whoopensacker," i.e. "a cup of red-eye." The expression is widely used around Portage currently. Heard from an elderly woman. **2002** *DARE* File—Internet **csWI,** She enjoyed singing and telling jokes. She also liked the occasional hoopensocker with her friends at the Avenue Bar. **2006** *Ibid* **WI,** Dang! almost forgot about the breakfast club! a Hoopensocker to get the day started. (that's a shot of Whiskey, or in my case Scotch).

whooper n

1 also *hooper:* =**whooping crane 1.**

1860 *S. Cultivator* 18.324 **FL,** Here is found every grade, kind, size and color . . from the beautiful little mourning Dove . . to the tall Whooper, of 5 or 6 feet high. **1886** *Forest & Stream* 26.348, Sandhill Crane. . . They always were much more plenty than the whoopers. **1939** *MT Std.* (Butte) 16 Feb 4/7, The cranes, tall as a man, were named "whoopers" because of the whooping-cough sound they make in flight. **1967** *DARE* (Qu. Q8, *A water bird that makes a booming sound before rain and often stands with its beak pointed almost straight up*) Inf **MO18,** It must be a hooper, but we don't have 'im. **1979** *Time* 2 Apr 91, Whatever he felt about the whooper, Carter appreciated the award, which recognized his support for environmental protection. **2006** *Star–Herald* (Scottsbluff NE) 19 Feb sec A 5/4, Wildlife experts believe the whoopers and the sandhill cranes that migrate through south-central Nebraska roost in the Platte shallows.

2 also *gray whooper, sandhill* ~ =**sandhill crane.**

1932 Howell *FL Bird Life* 197, Florida Crane. . . Other Names: Sandhill Crane; Sandhill Whooper; Whooper; Whooping Crane. **1938** Matschat *Suwannee R.* 286 **neFL, seGA,** It is a favorite haunt of the gray whoopers. **1955** *Oriole* 20.1.6 **GA,** Sandhill Crane.—Gray Crane, Gray Whooper, Sandhill Whooper, Whooping Crane (the cries are sonorous and far-carrying).

whooper snipe See **snipe hunt**

whoopie See **whoop** exclam **D**

whoopie hide See **whoop-and-hide**

whoopie pie n Also *whoopee pie* **chiefly NEast**
A confection consisting of two circular usu chocolate cakes with a sweet, creamy filling between them.

1931 *Syracuse Herald* (NY) 6 June 5/8, [Advt:] Distributors for *Berwick Whoopee Pie* The Largest Selling 5c Cake. . . Very Profitable Offer—Berwick Cake Co. 24 Palmer St. Roxbury, Mass. **1932** *Bedford Gaz.* (PA) [27 May 6]/4 (newspaperarchive.com), [Advt:] Stop At Ross Spriggs For A *Whoopee Pie* Fresh Every Day. **1950** *Fitchburg Sentinel* (MA) 26 Jan [28]/4 (newspaperarchive.com), [Advt:] Enter the Berwick *"All Prizes No Blanks" Contest.* . . The object of this contest is to obtain the greatest possible number of Berwick Whoopie Pie labels. . . Distributors. . . Lancaster, Mass. . . Keene, New Hampshire. **c1965** Randle *Cookbooks* (Ask Neighbor) 3.63, *Chocolate Whoopie Pies.* . . Sandwich cookie style. *Filling for Whoopie Pies.* . . Madison, Ohio. **1965** *Edwardsville Intelligencer* (IL) 28 Oct 8/1, Mrs. Robert Dennis . . has a dessert recipe for Whoopie Pie which she acquired from a young Amish

girl whom she met, while residing in Sullivan. The sandwich-like pies have a powdered sugar filling. **1977** *Portsmouth Herald* (NH) 4 Mar 13/1, School Menu. . . Choc. Whoopie Pie, Milk. **1998** King Arthur Flour *Baker's Catalogue* Sept 33, *Kyle's Whoopie Pies*—OK, we understand if you're not from northern New England, you probably don't know what a Whoopie Pie is. Well, read on. . . *Chocolate Cakes* [thin, about 3″ diameter]. . . *Filling* [of shortening, sugar, marshmallow creme, salt, vanilla]. **2011** *DARE* File—Internet [What's Cooking America], Whoopie pies are considered a New England phenomenon and a Pennsylvania Amish tradition. . . They are one of Maine's best known and most loved comfort foods. . . In Maine, these treats are more like a cake than a pie or a cookie, as they are very generously sized (about hamburger size). . . [I]n Lancaster county, Pennsylvania, it is not uncommon to find roadside farm stands offering these desserts.

whooping See **whoop** v[1] **B2**

whooping crane n

1 also sp *hooping crane;* Std: a large white North American crane *(Grus americana),* once nearly extinct. Also called **garoo, gourdhead 2, great white crane 1, hooping ~, sky bugler, stork, white crane 1, whooper 1**

2 =**sandhill crane.**

1838 Geol. Surv. OH *Second Annual Rept.* 184, *G[rus] Americana.* The sand-hill or whooping crane . . occasionally visits Ohio. **1857** U.S. Patent Office *Annual Rept. for 1856: Ag.* 157, The whooping crane, or sand-hill crane, breeds from upper California northward to the Arctic regions. **1913** *Auk* 30.493 **Okefenokee GA,** *Grus mexicana* [=*Grus canadensis*]. Sandhill Crane; 'Whooping Crane.' . . Unfortunately, the natives have a decided penchant for the 'Whooping Crane,' and never lose an opportunity to secure the 'fine eating' it affords them. **1932** [see **whooper 2**]. **1955** [see **whooper 2**]. **1966–68** *DARE* Tape **FL45,** I went up to the little general store and here the kids were playing with a big whooping ['hupɪn] crane that stood about five feet high; **GA30,** And then we have the whooping ['hupɪn] cranes in there. . . It's a sandhill crane, but all of the old-timers around the swamp known them, call them whooping cranes. **1968** *DARE* (Qu. Q10, . . *Water birds and marsh birds*) Inf **GA25,** Sandhill crane—same as whooping crane (old-timey name); **GA35,** ['hupɪn] crane—old-timers' name for sandhill crane.

whooping owl n Also *hooping owl, whoop owl* **esp NEng, S Atl, Ozarks** Cf **hoot owl 1, screech owl**
Any of var owls; see quots.

1781 Peters *Genl. Hist.* CT 261, The tree-frogs, whipperwills, and hooping-owls, serenade the inhabitants every night with music. **1837** (1962) Williams *Territory FL* 73, Whooping Owl. S[trix] acclamator. **1875** Thompson *Hoosier Mosaics* 118 **GA,** What a yowl something did give right over me in a tree! . . It was one o' them whooping owls they have down there. **1939** *LANE* Map 230 **NEng,** [4 infs, proncs of the type [hup æul]; 1 inf, [hupɪn aol].] **1953** Randolph–Wilson *Down in Holler* 299 **Ozarks,** Whoop owl. . . Hoot owl, also called *whoopin' owl.* Any large owl that makes a lot of noise. Usually it is the great horned owl *(Bubo virginianus),* sometimes the barred owl *(Strix varia)* common along many of the Ozark streams. **1968–70** *DARE* (Qu. Q1, . . *Kind of owl that makes a shrill, trembling cry*) Infs **NC64, 85, VA70,** Hooping owl; (Qu. Q2, . . *Kinds of owls*) Inf **GA28,** Hoopin' ['hupɪn] owl; **NC64, 85,** Hoopin' owl; **VA73,** Hooping owl—same as tree owl. **1995** Brophy Coll. 83 **swMO** (as of c1960), *Whoop-owl.* [A] hoot-owl.

whoopin' hide See **whoop-and-hide**

whoopity scoot adv phr
=**lickety-split.**

1923 *DN* 5.224 **swMO,** *Whoopity scoot,* adv. See *Likkety whoop.* [*Ibid* 213, *Likkety whoop.* . . Rapidly and more or less at random.]

whoop owl See **whooping owl**

whoop-te-doo See **whoop-de-do(o)**

whoopty See **whoopy** B

whoop up See **whoop** v[1] **B1**

whoopy exclam, n Usu |'(h)wupi, '(h)wʊpi|; for addit varr see **A** below Also sp *hoop-ee, whoopee*
A Forms.

1845 Hooper *Advent. Simon Suggs* 31 **AL,** I think I see him now, with his shirt tail a-flyin'! Hoop-ee! **1924** *DN* 5.270, *Hoopee* (joy). **1965–70** *DARE* (Qq. DD34, FF18, NN6a, b) 35 Infs, **scattered,** Whoopee [no transcr]; 45 Infs, **scattered,** ['(h)wupi]; 19 Infs, **scattered,** ['(h)wʊpi];

18 Infs, **scattered**, ['hupi]; 9 Infs, **scattered**, [(h)wu'pi]; **GA**84, **IL**17, **IN**1, **LA**7, **TX**20, **WA**18, **WV**16, [hu'pi]; **TX**76, **WV**5, 10, ['(h)wu'pi]; **FL**48, **TX**42, ['hu'pi]; **TN**26, **NY**200, ['hupi]; **LA**40, **TN**39, [hu'pi]; **NY**92, ['wupɪ]; **VT**16, [wu'pi]; **MI**51, ['hupɪ]; **CT**27, ['wɪpi].

B As noun.

Also *hoopy, (w)hoopty:* A car, esp one that is dilapidated or modified; see quots. **scattered, but esp freq TX** See Map

1922 *Atlantic Mth.* 129.641 **OK,** He left his 'Whoopy,' as he called his Ford, out along the roadside. **1943** *AmSp* 18.75 **WI** [Apple-picking terms], *Whoopee* . . a wondrous contraption made by taking the body off an old Ford or Chevrolet, and substituting a flat wooden platform directly on the chassis. The whoopee holds about twenty crates, and, with the aid of chains, makes its way up hill and down, throughout the orchard, without the benefit of roads. **1966–70** *DARE* (Qu. N5, *Nicknames for an automobile, especially an old or broken-down car*) Infs **OR**3, **SD**5, **TX**5, 32, 35, 36, 37, 102, **LA**2, Hoopy—common; **WA**12, Hoopy—especially an old pickup; [**IL**48, Hupmobile—laughter]. [All Infs comm type 4 or 5] **1968** *Current Slang* 3.2.30 **sCA** [Watts slang; Black], *Hoopty, whoopty*. . . A car.—I don't think I'll get the hoopty tonight. *Hoopy, whoopty*. . . A car. **c1974** Jones *Ozark Hill Boy* 12 **AR** (as of c1920), Ira's brother-in-law, driving a model "T" Ford strip-down (a whoopee) came to the picnic. **1988** Fulghum *All I Really Need* 178 **TX,** Ever come out after work to find your . . battery's dead but you're parked on a hill and you let your old hoopy roll and it fires the first time you pop the clutch? **2007** *DARE* File—Internet, *My Whoopty:* If you have a nice car that is really beat up, just put it back into your garage, when you open the garage door the car will be in perfect condition!

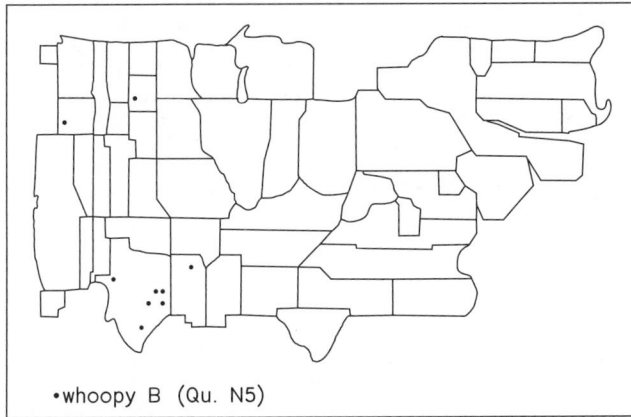

•whoopy B (Qu. N5)

whoopy hide See **whoop-and-hide**

whoor See **whore**

whoorp See **whip A2**

whop See **wapatuli**

whop and soccer See **whoopensocker**

whopatooli(e), whopatuli See **wapatuli**

whope exclam Also *wope* Cf **wup**

1 also *w(h)oap:* Whoa! Stop!—also used to express surprise or incredulity.

1851 Springer *Forest Life* 109 **ME,** He varies the whole exercise by constant addresses to the oxen, individually and collectively: "Haw, Bright!" "Ge, Duke!" "Whoap! whoap!" **1896** in 2008 (acc) Lexis-Nexis Legal Research *State Case Law: NE* (Internet), He came to the express car door and said: 'Hold on, Hoops, I've got some express to put off here.' I was then standing on the station platform and the train had already started. I said 'whoap.' Someone pulled the cord. **1898** *Overland Mth.* (2d ser) 32.512, Now just give me a big kiss, and we will jest unharness. That's the girl! Woap-ah! **1907** *Brotherhood Enginemen's Mag.* 42.42, "Whope! Whope! Wo-o-o-ah!" from a dozen throats; the engineer has given her the emergency at the instant of receiving the signal to stop. **1942** Warnick *Garrett Co. MD* 16 **nwMD** (as of 1900–18), *Wope,* or *wup* . . an exclamation, probably a modification of "whoa." **1942** McAtee *Dial. Grant Co. IN* 71 (as of 1890s), *Wope* . . used to halt any talk that was a strain on credulity; "Wope there, you're a'fibbin' now". **1953** Randolph-Wilson *Down in Holler* 300 **Ozarks,** *Wope.* . . A mild exclamation indicating surprise. Perhaps it means *whoa!* or *stop!* **1954** *Harder Coll.* **cwTN,** *Wo* . . referring to a horse or mule. Stop. Also . . *wope.*

2 Used as a call to animals.

1900 *Colored Amer. Mag.* 1.325 **MA,** Whope sir! Who-ope! Come up, sir! Been shut up too long a spell; feel your oats. **1966** Dakin *Dial. Vocab. Ohio R. Valley* 2.276, [Calls to horses] In Kentucky variants of the types *kwoop!* . . *kwurp! wope!, whope!* are used. **1966–70** *DARE* (Qu. K80, *The call that's used . . to get the cows in from the pasture*) Inf **FL**12, Whope; (Qu. K82, *The call used . . to get horses in from the pasture*) Inf **FL**12, Whope and whistle; **IN**63, Wope [woəp] (repeated); **MO**18, Whope [hwo:p]; (Qu. K84, *The call used . . to get the pigs in at feeding time*) Inf **GA**7, Whope [hwop].

whop over v phr Also *whap over* **NEng**

To collapse, tumble, flop.

1841 Paige *Short Patent Sermons* 121 **NEast,** Sleigh suddenly runs on a snow-bank, whops over, and spills all its live stock. **1843** *Brother Jonathan* (NY NY) 5.202 **ME,** Here the poor man . . drew a long breath and whapped over on his pillow. *Ibid* 447, Not he!—wide awake as you are . . ; had but just whopped over, when we heerd your foot on the stairs. **1851** Natl. Temperance Convention *Proc.* 19 **MA,** The oxen started; soon it [=a harrow] struck a stump, and whapped over. **1871** *Ballou's Mth. Mag.* 34.189 **NEng,** My strange bedfellow whopped over, and in less than half a minute was snoring. **1900** *New Engl. Mag.* 21.711, He would sit upright, letting his head hang down until his nose almost reached his hind feet, and then whop over on one side, rolled up into a perfect ball.

whopper-jaw n Also *w(h)apper-jaw* [EDD *wapper-jaws*. . . a crooked jaw] Cf **wobble-jaw**

A protruding or misshapen lower jaw—also used as a nickname for someone having such a jaw.

1850 in 1864 Ticknor *Life William Hickling Prescott* 301 **MA,** The glass was of the time of Charles the Fifth, and I soon recognized his familiar face, the *whapper-jaw* of the Austrian line. **1874** *Warren Ledger* (PA) 3 Dec 1/7, His whapper-jaw was more whappered than ever. **1877** Bartlett *Americanisms* 746, *Whapper-Jaw*. A protruding under-jaw. **1886** *Century Illustr. Mag.* 33.44 **OH,** "What's become o' them art-students you used to have 't the St. Albans?" she began, her whopper-jaw twitching with excitement. **1899** (1912) Green *VA Folk-Speech* 473, *Wapper-jaw.* . . A projecting under-jaw. **1903** *NY Times* (NY) 15 Nov 28/5, His profile with its whopper-jaw and thin, mean nose is repeated on a white pilaster between two pictures. **1915** *IL Med. Jrl.* 28.128, The lower jaw is drawn downward and forward by muscular action . . and we have the type known as "wapper jaw."

whopper-jawed adj Also *wap(per)-jawed, wappy-~, whapper-~, w(h)opper-jaw, w(h)oppy-jawed, wopper-jawed;* for addit varr see quots

1 Of a person; having a protruding or otherwise misshapen lower jaw; by ext: slack-jawed. **chiefly C and Mid Atl, SE, N Cent** See Map Cf **slew-jawed, whanker-~, whomper-~ 1, whompny-~ 1, wobble-~ 1**

1836 Dunlap *30 Yrs. Ago* 1.65 **NYC,** His chin with the parts adjacent, assumed the appearance vulgarly called wapper-jaw'd. **1899** (1912) Green *VA Folk-Speech* 480, *Whapper-jawed.* . . Having one jaw bigger than the other. **1905** *DN* 3.67 **eNE,** *Whopper-jawed.* . . (1) With underhung or projecting jaw; (2) askew, awry. **1909** *DN* 3.388 **eAL, wGA,** *Whopper-jawed.* . . Having large, fleshy, or distorted jaws. **1915** *DN* 4.192 **swVA,** *Whopper-jawed.* . . Having very large (usually distorted) jaws. **1930** in 1952 Mathes *Tall Tales* 167 **sAppalachians,** Ye're sorty

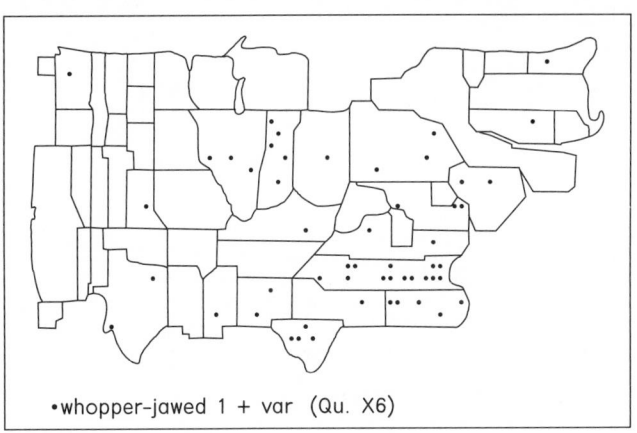

•whopper-jawed 1 + var (Qu. X6)

wopper-jawed anyway, an' a beard would set right well on ye till ye git fleshed up some. **1942** McAtee *Dial. Grant Co. IN* 71 (as of 1890s), *Whopper-jawed . .* with a crooked set to the face. **1965–70** *DARE* (Qu. X6, *If a person's lower jaw sticks out prominently . . he's _____*) 53 Infs, **chiefly C and Mid Atl, SE, N Cent,** W(h)opper-jawed. **1972** *Atlanta Letters* nwGA, Wapper-jawed—mostly used by farmers to designate crooked rows—also used to describe under shot jaws. **1983** *MJLF* 9.1.61 ceKY (as of 1956), *Whopper jawed . .* lantern jawed. **2008** *Tulsa World* (OK) 16 Oct sec A 19 (Internet), In a move that leaves me whopper-jawed, George W.'s secretary of Veterans Affairs issued an edict in May banning voter-registration drives inside VA facilities.

2 Transf: crooked, askew, out of shape; out of whack, messed up. **chiefly Midl** See Map Cf **wappergee, whipper-jawed, whomper-~ 2, whomper-sided, whompny-jawed 2, wobble-~ 2**

1856 *WI Farmer & NW Cultivator* 8.210, The fact that inexperienced, ignorant men have often been induced . . to undertake this kind of building, resulting . . in ungainly, crooked, whopper-jawed, and cracked walls, is no evidence whatever against the system. **1884** Nye *Baled Hay* 60 **WI,** Old traditions . . are forked over to posterity like a wappy-jawed teapot or a long-time mortgage. **1890** *DN* 1.63 swOH, *Wapper-jawed* (pronounced [wɔpɚ]): crooked. "The curtain is wapper-jawed." Western Ohio. [DN Ed: In Massachusetts and New Hampshire with an *h* [hwɔpəjɔd], in this sense.] **1905** [see **1** above]. **1905** *DN* 3.100 nwAR, *Wopper-jawed. . .* Crooked. **1911** *DN* 3.548 NE, *Wap-jawed. . .* Askew, awry. **1912** in 1983 Truman *Dear Bess* 101 MO, Don't suppose I have used it [=a fountain pen] more than twice and the bloomin' thing is plumb whopperjawed. **1912** *DN* 3.593 wIN, *Whopperjawed. . .* Askew; out of symmetry. **1916** *DN* 4.331 **KS,** *Whopperjawed. . .* Awry; askew. In W[estern] Res[erve], *wopperjawed.* **1930** *VA Qrly. Rev.* 6.249 **S Midl,** The gentleman of the backwoods . . may affirm . . that the line of his barn roof is . . waupajawed. **1934** (1970) Wilson *Backwoods Amer.* 196 **AR, MO,** Alfred lives and works over at . . that little house yonder with the wopajawed roof. **1944** *PADS* 2.62 **MO,** *Whopper-jawed* [ˈhwɑpɚˌdʒɔd]. . . Crooked, uneven. **1965–70** *DARE* (Qu. KK70, *Something that has got out of proper shape: "That house is all _____."*) 18 Infs, **scattered, but esp Midl,** Whopper-jawed; **IN**1, **KY**60, **NC**82, **OH**56, 90, Wopper-jawed; **CA**105, **OH**8, **KY**84, **TX**38, W(h)oppy-jawed; **VA**46, Wop-jawed; (Qu. MM13, *The table was nice and straight until he came along and knocked it _____*) Infs **IA**27, **KY**60, **NC**76, 82, **NJ**39, **OH**66, Whopper-jawed; **NC**7, Whoppy-jawed; **NJ**57, **OH**45, Wopper-jawed; **OH**63, **TN**20, W(h)opper-jaw; (Qu. MM3, *When someone does something the wrong way round . . "This is the front, you've got the whole thing turned _____."*) Infs **IL**126, **OH**52, Whopper-jawed. **1972** [see **1** above]. **1978** *AP Letters* swMI, Whopper-jawed, meaning askew . . was a word I grew up on. . . My mother came from Owensborough, Kentucky. **1992** *DARE* File KS, OK, Whopperjawed = askew. **1995** *Brophy Coll.* 82 swMO (as of c1960), *Whapperjawed, wapperjawed.* [C]rooked, cattycorner. **2008** *DARE* File—Internet **MT,** One of my small rugs got so "whopper-jawed" that I had to remove the whole thing and start again. *Ibid* **TX,** The gas gauge was all whopper-jawed (it showed empty all the time when there was fuel still left in it).

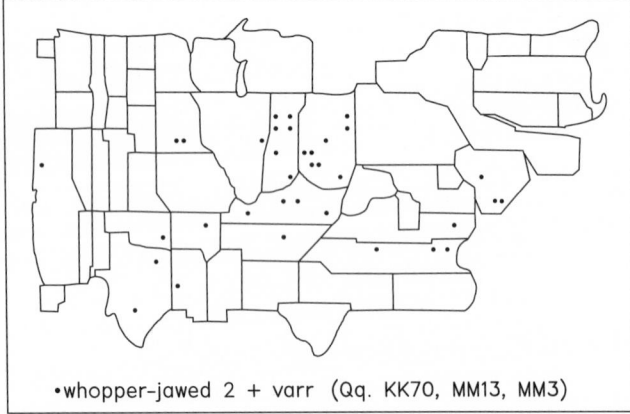

•whopper-jawed 2 + varr (Qq. KK70, MM13, MM3)

whopple-jaw See **wobble-jaw**

whopple-jawed See **wobble-jawed**

whoppy-jawed See **whopper-jawed**

whopsy-jawed See **whompny-jawed**

whore n Usu |hor, hɔr, hoə(r), hɔə(r)|; also |ho, hu(ə)r, huə|; sp-proncs |hwor, hwɔr| Pronc-spp *ho(ah), hoor(e), huwa, whoor;* for addit pronc and sp varr see quots [*OED2 whore* sb. "The pronunciation [hʊə(r)], now dialectal, . . was widespread in the 17th and 18th centuries, and continued into the 19th century."] Std senses, var forms.

1935 (1937) Steinbeck *Tortilla Flat* i **CA,** We called her, with a great deal of respect, a hoor-lady. **1965–70** *DARE* (Qu. Y29b, . . *About a man [who doesn't stay home much]: "He's always _____."*) Inf **GA**84, Whore [hoʊ]-hopping; (Qu. AA7b, . . *A woman who is very fond of men and is always trying to know more—if she's not respectable about it*) Inf **GA**37, Ho-har [ˈho͵hɑr]—it's what the Bible would put it; **MI**42, [hur]; **NY**29, [ˈwɔr]; **VA**109, [hɔ]; (Qu. AA19, . . *A man and woman who are not married but live together as if they were*) Inf **SC**7, Whoremongery [ˈho͵mɔŋgorɪ]; (Qu. HH34, *General words . . for a woman, not necessarily uncomplimentary*) Inf **PA**236, Fine ho; (Qu. HH37, *An immoral woman*) Inf **CA**4, [ˈhwor]; **GA**67, [hwɔr]; **LA**8, Whore [ˈhoʊ]-chasers; **MD**9, [huə˞]; **MA**71, [ˈhowə]; **PA**185, [hur]; **SC**40, [horə]. **1969** *DARE* File **PA,** *Whore* [ˈhuə˞]. **1971** Jennings *Cowboys* 208 **MT, WY** (as of 1877), It's one thing to be a whoor and something else again to act like one. **1979** Lewis *How to Talk Yankee* [15] **nNEng,** Ho-ah, son of a . . (sp. "whore, son of a"). (Can also be prounounced [sic] "hoore," depending on locality . .) **1982** *DARE* File eME, Son of a ho-ah: also son of a hoor: not necessarily vulgar: a 12 lb. lobster I snagged while fishing for cod was so identified by Cap'n Ames. **1997** Silverberg *Reflections* 335 **NYC,** I've always regarded "whore" as rather a tony sort of word. In the schoolyards of Brooklyn when I was a boy we pronounced the word "hooer." **2000** *DARE* File **NYC,** Living in NYC, around 1963–65, I was puzzled by a graffito on a wall on 104th St. just west of Broadway: *Your mother is a huwa.* It took me a long time (years?) to figure it out. **2007** *WI State Jrl.* (Madison) 10 Apr 1/1, Radio host Don Imus has been in a pile of trouble in the past week because he called members of the Rutgers women's basketball team "nappy-headed hos."

whore bath See **whore's bath**

whore boil n Also *whore pimple* Cf **jack bump**
A skin eruption; see quots.

1949 McDavid *Coll.* cNY, *Whore pimple* = adolescent acne. **1967–69** *DARE* (Qu. X59, . . *The small infected pimples that form usually on the face*) Infs **MA**15, **VT**12, 16, Whore boils; (Qu. BB33b, . . *A swelling under the skin—if it is very big or serious*) Inf **MN**10, Whore boil. **1968** Exley *Fan's Notes* 370 **nNY,** Their countenances were being assailed by pubescent acne ("whore boils," we had called it).

whore-hop v phr, hence vbl n *whore-hopping* **esp Sth, S Midl**
Of a man: to pursue women indiscriminately, usu with sexual intent; hence n *whore-hopper.*

1935 in 1947 Anderson *Sherwood Anderson Reader* 425 **OH,** He . . hadn't gone off, after pay-day, drinking or whore-hopping like most of the young fellows in the camps. **1947** Willingham *End as Man* 112 **Sth,** This kid wasn't any whore-hopper. . . He'd never had a piece of tail. **1954** *Harder Coll.* cwTN, *Whore hopper.* . . A predatory male, locally notorious for woman-chasing without discrimination. **1966–70** *DARE* (Qu. Y29b, . . *About a man [who doesn't stay home much]: "He's always _____."*) Inf **GA**84, Whore-hopping; (Qu. AA6b, . . *A man who is fond of being with women and tries to attract their attention—if he's rude or not respectful*) Infs **GA**13, 84, **TN**27, **VA**42, Whore-hopper; (Qu. HH38, *A womanish man*) Inf **NC**55, Whore-hopper. **1967** in 1968 Haun *Hawk's Done Gone* 305 eTN, Pa didn't know that he was going to get kilt by old Esco Jarnigan. That old whore-hopper was mad because he couldn't find out where Pa got his lead. **1986** Pederson *LAGS Concordance* (Sexually overactive male) 4 infs, **AL, FL, TN,** (A) whore hopper. **2007** *DARE* File—Internet sCA, Arnold's level of language may be appropriate for a Hollywood Whore-Hopper bragging about his latest conquests in the locker room.

whorehouse tea n
=**Mormon tea 1,** esp *Ephedra antisyphilitica;* see quots.

1878 U.S. Army Corps Engineers *Rept. U.S. Geogr. Surv.* 6.50, *Ephedra antisyphilitica. . .* "Whorehouse Tea."—The names, scientific and popular, might be regarded as sufficiently indicative of the alleged properties of the plant. **1909** King et al. *King's Amer. Dispensatory*

1.309, *Mormon tea, Mountain rush, Whore-house tea, Brigham weed.* Nevada. Used in *gonorrhea* in doses of 1 to 2 fluid drachms of the fluid extract.

whore pimple   See **whore boil**

whore's bath n   Also *whore bath*   Cf **bitch bath**
See quots.

  1944 Liebling *Road to Paris* 242, The army helmet. . . may also serve on occasion as a bathtub. The bather fills it with water, removes one article of clothing at a time, rubs the water hastily over the surface thus exposed, and replaces the garment before taking off another one. This is called taking a whore's bath. **1953** *AmSp* 28.145, A *bitch bath* requires talcum powder, deodorant, and perfume. In general usage *whore bath* is the same as *bitch bath;* however, in the services it means a bath *with water* out of one's helmet and is usually heard in its possessive form, *whore's bath.* **1995** in 2007 *DARE* File—Internet (as of 1944), In our [prisoner of war] compound we had no showers as such but I did try to take a whore bath at the washstands once a week. **2007** *DARE* File—Internet (as of 1942), Proper hygiene—the 'whore's bath' accomplished with helmet shell filled to capacity with rainwater. *Ibid,* [Urban Dictionary:] *Whore bath* . . instead of taking a bath or shower, you spray yourself down with cologne or perfume. . . To wash up the stinkiest parts with a small washcloth and hot water in the sink. . . Quickly trying to make yourself presentable by straightening your clothes, running your fingers through your hair. . . *Whore's bath* . . quickly washing the crotch and underarms as a quick way to get ready for sex. . . A bit of talcum powder in the armpits; fingers run through the hair.

whore's egg n   **ME**   Cf *DNE, DPEIE*
A sea urchin.

  1674 Josselyn *Two Voyages* 110 **NEng,** The *Whore* is a shell-fish, the shells are called whores-eggs, being fine round white shells, in shape like a *Mexico* pompion, but no bigger than a good large Hens-egg; they are wrought down the sides with little knobs and holes very prettily, but are but thin and brittle. **1832** Williamson *Hist. ME* 1.168, The *Sea-urchin* resembles a chestnut burr, its back is covered with bony prickles. [Footnote to *Sea-urchin:* Erinaceus marinus, or *whore's egg.*] **1875** Drake *Nooks & Corners New Engl.* 128 **ME,** Now and then I picked up a sea-chestnut, or "whore's egg," as they are called by the fishermen. **1930** *AmSp* 5.393 [Language of N Atl fishermen], *Whore's egg.* . . A small spiny crustacean esteemed by the Italians as a delicacy. **1947** *Atlantic Mth.* 179.2.81 **ME,** "They do grow on you," Bill Thompson said, cutting a whore's-egg thorn from his finger and reaffirming the outside world's opinion. **1966** *DARE* Tape **ME**24, Whore's eggs [ˈɔrz ɛgz] . . there are all kind of thorns on 'em, they're all alive. You stick one your finger, why you start aching that minute. . . People've been known to eat those sea-eggs, those whore's eggs. **1983** *Nat. Hist.* Mar 91 **ME,** Maine's urchin industry is minute. Locals apparently call them "whores' eggs." **1998** (2004) Graves *Dead Cat* 73 **ME,** "That's what they call the sea urchins," she explained. "Whore's eggs."

whore's wool n   Cf *DS* E20
=**dust bunny.**

  1955 Roberts *S. from Hell-fer-Sartin* 181 **seKY,** Nothing under it but a rug and a lot o' whore's wool—or whatever you call it. **1982** Johnson *Oxherding* 163 **SC** (as of 1860s), Wife and I stood to one side, watching her pull out the sofa, pointing triumphantly at lint and whore's wool in the corners. **2005** *DARE* File—Internet **ME,** Do you know what a dust bunny is? Yes, indeedy! My paternal grandmother preferred the term "whore's wool" to dust bunny, but she would never explain why.

whorled milkweed n
A **milkweed 1** (here: usu *Asclepias verticillata* or *A. subverticillata*).

  1848 Gray *Manual of Botany* 369, *A[sclepias] verticillata.* . . Whorled Milkweed. . . Leaves 2′-3′ long, scarcely 1″ wide, 3–6 in a whorl. **1920** *Bedford Gaz.* (PA) 6 Aug 4/2 **SW,** Stockmen should learn to recognize and avoid the whorled milkweed. **1935** (1943) Muenscher *Weeds* 366, *Asclepias galioides* [=*A. subverticillata*]. . . Poison milkweed or Whorled milkweed, a native perennial of the ranges and dry hillsides from Colorado and Utah southward into Mexico.

whorl phlox n
A **gilia** (here: *Leptosiphon nuttallii*).

  1931 U.S. Dept. Ag. *Misc. Pub.* 101.139, Nuttall gilia, locally known as stickerbush, stinkweed, white gilia, white mountainweed, and whorl phlox, is sometimes woody throughout, but usually is semiherbaceous.

whorlywort n
=**culver's root 1.**

  1830 Rafinesque *Med. Flora* 2.20, *Leptandra purpurea* [=*Veronicastrum virginicum*]. Names. . . *Vulgar.* . . Whorlywort, Culvert-root [etc]. **1892** (1974) Millspaugh *Amer. Med. Plants* 114-1, Culver's Physic. . . Com. Names. . . Whorly Wort, Quintel [etc]. **1971** Krochmal *Appalachia Med. Plants* 268, Culver's root, physic root, tall speedwell, whorlywort.

whortleberry n

1 A **blueberry 1** or **huckleberry 1;** see quots.
  1702 (1972) Mather *Magnalia* 6.11 **NEng,** Sometimes we liv'd on *Wortle berries,* sometimes on a kind of *Wild Cherry.* **1804** in 1930 Dunbar *Life* 250 **MS,** We also found some of the larger Wrotle[sic]-berry in fruit. **1814** *Amer. Med. & Philos. Reg.* 4.549, The blue huckleberry or whortleberry (Vaccinium) gives a blue superior to the mazarine. **1838** in 1944 Nute *Lake Superior* 96 **MI, WI, MN,** We had only to look under our blankets & eat whortleberries [blueberries] the ground being blue with them. **1867** De Voe *Market Asst.* 393, *Whortleberries, huckleberries,* or *blueberries.*—There are several varieties of this prolific fruit known, among which those growing on the high bushes are usually preferred. **1900** Lyons *Plant Names* 386, *V[accinium] corymbosum.* . . Giant Whortleberry or Huckleberry. *Ibid, V. Myrtillus.* . . Whortleberry (of Europe). *Ibid, V. Pennsylvanicum.* . . Dwarf, Low-bush or Sugar Blueberry, Whortleberry [etc]. *Ibid, V. stamineum.* . . Deerberry, Dangleberry . . or Whortleberry. *Ibid, V. Vitis-Idaea.* . . Red Whortleberry. **1939** Medsger *Edible Wild Plants* 68, Black Huckleberry, or Whortleberry. . . Gaylussacia baccata. **1953** Randolph–Wilson *Down in Holler* 247 **Ozarks,** The names *buck berry, hog berry, whortleberry, goose berry,* and *he-huckleberry* are applied rather loosely to several species of *Vaccinium.* **1968** *DARE* (Qu. I44, *What kinds of berries grow wild around here?*) Inf **CA**57, Whortleberries—same as huckleberries; **VA**13, Whortleberries.

2 A **bearberry 2** (here: *Arctostaphylos uva-ursi*).
  1827 Ewell *Med. Companion* 642, Bearberry, *Arbutas Uva Ursi*—Bears whortleberry—wild cranberry. Is a low evergreen shrub somewhat resembling the myrtle. **1892** (1974) Millspaugh *Amer. Med. Plants* 100-1, Uva-ursi. . . Com. Names.—Bearberry, . . Whortleberry [etc].

who's got the button   See **button B2b**

who's got the thimble   See **thimble 1**

who-shot-John n   Cf *DS* DD21a, c
Intoxicating liquor, esp illegally made.

  1930 *Outlook & Independent* 154.488 **VA,** All night parties are notorious for their drinks—wines . . home brews . . and hard liquor, of which the most poisonous is known as "Who Shot John?" **1963** *Mt. Life* Summer 52 **sAppalachians,** He'd take and go off to the woods some'eres and make hisself a little run o' who-shot-John. **1972** (1978) Carr *Second Oldest Profession* 166 **Sth,** Regional names by which the illicit distillate is recognized. . . [include] "who shot John" (drink that brings instant unconsciousness). **2002** *DARE* File—Internet **MO,** No redeye or who-shot-John served here.

whosomever pron   [*OED2* "*Obs.* or *?dial.*"]   Cf **howsomever, whatsomever** pron, adj, adv, **whensomever, wheresomever** Who(m)ever.

  1833 Greene *Life Dr. Dodimus* 1.214 **NEng,** Help! help! whosomever you are. **1881** *Scribner's Mth.* 22.109 **VA** [Black], But whosomever dey is . . dey aint agwine to keer for a piece of yo' mind. **1903** *Atlanta Constitution* (GA) [1 Mar mag sec] 5/2 (newspaperarchive.com) **sAppalachians,** Rocks an' things keeps a fallin' down fum th' clifts, an' genully kills whosomever be below 'em. **1974** *Daily Times–News* (Burlington NC) [3 Jan sec B 3]/1 (newspaperarchive.com), *Mismatch of the year No. 1:* Ragsdale's football team against whosomever it was playing in the Mid-State Conference. **1982** *NY Times* (NY) 10 June sec A 30/2 **AL** [Black], Let whosomever wishes sit around recollecting. I'm looking up the line. **2000** in 2008 *DARE* File—Internet **sePA,** My wife and her viola will join me and my cello along with whosomever they dragged in. **2006** *Ibid* **ND,** I wuz merely making a gift suggestion. . . whosomever wants to utilize that listing is welcome to do so.

whull   See **whole**

whunt   See **want** v[1]

whup v[1], n   See **whip A1**

whup v² See **hup e**

whur adv, conj¹ See **where A2**

whur conj² See **whether 2**

whurp See **whip A2**

whurr See **where A2**

whu(r)ther See **whether 1**

why-all adv
Why, why ever.
1928 Chapman *Happy Mt.* 303 **seTN,** Why-all so serious solemn? **1955** Ritchie *Singing Family* 101 **seKY,** Don't know for shore why-*all* I do it, but child when you get to be eighty-nine year old you'll set fore the fire and rub your old eyes out, too, and you won't know why. **2004** *DARE* File—Internet **Sth,** If that pokeweed has bad luck why all did you bring it here in the first place? **2007** *Ibid,* Why all did they use testers [of snowboards] with all the same foot size, and weight!

why come adv phr **esp Sth**
How does (or did) it come about (that); how come.
1938 Steele *Sound Rowlocks* 89 **MD,** Why-come he looked razor blades at me when I told the officers about them two dollars? **1944–45** (1970) *Negro Story* Dec-Jan 10, Why come he got to stop in the middle of the day? **1962** Fox *Southern Fried* 44 **SC,** Dammit, Frog. Why come you do that? . . Always low-rating my stories. **1984** Burns *Cold Sassy* 241 **nGA** (as of 1906), Why come you hate Hosie, Will? **1986** Pederson *LAGS Concordance,* 1 inf, **csTX,** Why come = how come. [Inf Black] **2001** *Afr. Amer. Rev.* 35.49 [Black], So why come you start beating on her, Granpa? **2006** *DARE* File—Internet **MD** [Black], Why come its only monday. . . why come i gotta leave frostburg to have that much fun?

why for adv Also sp *whyfore* [Orig swEngl, Scots dial; more widely used after the mid-19th cent, perh infl by *wherefore*] Cf **for why, what for**
Why; for what purpose.
1850 *N. Lancet* 1.130 **neNY,** Whyfore should all this energy and intelligence have been thrown away upon this "creature" of imagination? **1870** (1871) Shaw *Josh Billings' Farmer's Allminax for 1871* np, The cat hath been called a domestick animile but i never could tell whyfore. **1872** *Atlantic Mth.* 30.328 **Sth,** "It's a horrid thing to say about God, and *I* don't believe it!" "Don't you, chile? Whyfor now?" **1884** *Chronicle* 16.11, Whyfore such a dearth of good umpires in the University? **1894** Robinson in *Forest & Stream* 42.310 **VT,** Be we so tu onderstan' it, an' ef so wherefore an' whyfore? **1908** in 1981 Marcus *Amer. Jewish Woman* 242, When the choir began to sing, the tears rolled down my cheeks and I did not know whyfore. **1910** Raine *Bucky O'Connor* 24 **West,** Whyfor do they let a sick man like you travel all by his lone? **1922** Cobb *J. Poindexter* 82 **KY** [Black], "Whyfore you can't go?" . . "I jes' this minute remembers 'at I got to ketch the 'leven-forty-two fur Hartford, . . tha's whyfore." **1954** *Harder Coll.* **cwTN,** Why for. . . what for. "He done 'er anyways. I don't know why for." **1956** Almirall *From College* 89 **CO,** I always pack a gun on such trips. A feller can never tell whyfor it might come in handy.

wi See **with A2**

wick n¹ Usu |wɪk|; also |wik| Pronc-spp *weak, week*
Std sense, var forms.
1795 Dearborn *Columbian Grammar* 139, *List of Improprieties. . . Week* for Wick *(of a candle).* **1899** (1912) Green *VA Folk-Speech* 478, *Week. . .* The *wick* of a candle. **1912** *Ibid* 476, *Weak. . .* For *wick.* **1942** Hall *Smoky Mt. Speech* 15 **wNC, eTN,** There is a tendency in some speakers to use . . [i] in *fish, itch . . wick.*

wick n² [Cf *OED2 wick* a.²; *EDG* §241 "Initial *kw . .* has often become *hw, w, . .* especially in Sh.I. Sc. and n.Cy."]
2000 Shores *Tangier Is.* 240 **Chesapeake Bay,** He was cut right down to the *wick* (quick, the raw exposed flesh).

wickakee n Also *wickapee* [See quot 1910]
An **Indian paintbrush 1** (here: *Castilleja coccinea*).
1844 Fuller *Summer Lakes* 33 **IL,** The flame-like flower I was taught afterwards, by an Indian girl, to call "Wickapee." **1892** *Jrl. Amer. Folkl.* 5.101 **MA,** *Castilleia coccinea. . .* Wickakee. . . An Indian name. **1910** Hodge *Hdbk. Amer. Indians* 2.950, *Wickakee.* One of the names of the scarlet painted-cup *(Castilleia coccinea) . .* probably derived from one of the Algonquian dialects.

wickape(e) n¹ See **wicopy 1**

wickapee n² See **wickakee**

wickapy See **wicopy 1**

wicke See **wicky**

wicked adj Pronc-spp **esp NEast, Sth** *weaked, weeked, weekid*
Similarly nouns *weakedness, weekedness*
Std sense, var forms.
1863 in 1956 *GA Hist. Qrly.* 40.184, Do you Ever pray that god may bless our cause & soon close this weaked war. **1864** *Rubina* 228 **NEng,** That ain't weekid, is it? **1868** *Godey's Lady's Book* 77.44 **NY,** I jest told him to shet up his weekedness, and he shet up. **1876** *Harper's New Mth. Mag.* 52.190 **seMS** [Black], De bell was de cap'n's bell, an' he war a mighty weeked man. **1904** *Jrl. Amer. Folkl.* 17.39 **MD** [Black], He wuz a mighty weeked man, an' treat he wife an' chil'en like a dawg. **1904** *Atlantic Mth.* 94.220 **ME,** Ezry Bowse was allus counted a master weeked old creatur'. **1927** Adams *Congaree* 7 **cSC** [Black], Is you hear 'bout dat Congaree nigger wuh . . have so much weeked ways an' how he dead? **1936** Robinson *Sam Lovel's Boy with Fables* 211 **VT,** An' she commit a weeked sin—/ She kicked him with her pooty foot. **1940** Stuart *Trees of Heaven* 209 **eKY,** Anse, you air a weaked man. **1941** Stuart *Men of Mts.* 21 **eKY,** Effie and she says there's so much weakedness in the world she hates to die and leave her. **1946** *Natl. Geogr. Mag.* 89.770 **Cape Cod MA,** There were Good Walter, Bad Walter, and "Weeked" Walter, I was told.

wicked adv Pronc-sp *wikkit* [Cf *EDD wicked* adj.¹, adv. 5 "*Obs.* Very, exceedingly; used as an intensitive."] **NEng, chiefly ME, MA**
Very; extremely; really—esp in adj phr *wicked good;* also rarely adj, very great.
1960 Wilson *Let's Barter* 66 **NEng,** Justin Persons never spent time or brawn drilling into that wicked hard granite mountain. **1974** *Bennington Banner* (VT) 28 Mar 12/7 **ME,** They were wicked good. **1979** Lewis *How to Talk Yankee* [39] **nNEng,** "How was the horsepulling?" "Wicked good. Seth took top money with his new team." **1981** *Seventeen Letters* **MA,** The word "wicked" when used by teens in New England, particularly the Massachusetts, Greater Boston area, does not mean evil or bad, but "very" or extra in such phrases as "wicked cute" . . or "wicked hard." **1981** *DARE* File **ceMA,** In my town, instead of saying "very", we say "wicked." It is used in sentences like "I would like to see her a wicked lot," or "I'm wicked sorry." **1982** Chaika *Speaking RI* [9], *Wicked* = extremely, as in "wicked good" aw [=or] "wicked depressed." **1999** *DARE* File **ME,** Now that was a "wicked" quick reply. The use of the word *wicked* for 'very' always amuses me. I think it is a Maine thing. **1999** *DARE* File—Internet [Boston Online *Wicked Good Guide to Boston English*], *Wicked*—A general intensifier: "He's wicked nuts!" **2006** *DARE* File—Internet **RI,** *Wikkit*—An intensifier that's interchangeable with "very," as in, "We was drivin' wikkit fast."

wicker See **whicker** n¹, v

wickerbill See **whickerbill**

wickerby See **wicopy 1**

wicket n Also *w(h)ickety, wicki(e)* **esp PA, NJ** See Map Cf **cat n 3a, b, kick the can, kick the stick, sticky-wicky, throw the stick**
A stick or other small object used in var children's games; hence nouns *whickety, wicket, hit the wicket, kick ~, wicket's out* any of var games that involve such an object; see quots.
1891 *Jrl. Amer. Folkl.* 4.230 **Brooklyn NY,** Kick the wicket. A lamppost or a tree is chosen as "home," and several bases are agreed upon, usually four, around which the players run. The boy who is "it" places the wicket, which is sometimes made of wood, and sometimes of a piece of old rubber hose, against the tree or post chosen as home, and then stations himself at some distance from it, ready to catch it when it is kicked by the other players. They take turns in kicking the wicket. If it is caught by the boy who is "it," the kicker becomes "it." If the boy who is "it" does not catch the wicket, he runs after it and puts it in place, and any boy whom he catches running between the bases, when the wicket is up, becomes "it." **1907** *DN* 3.251 **eME,** Wicket. . . An outdoor game played by boys. **1927** *Bridgeport Telegram* (CT) 23 June 12/5, The boy with companions was playing kick the wicket when he darted into the path of an automobile. **1932** *Hamburg Reporter* (IA) 24 Mar [5]/2 (newspaperarchive.com), The game was "kick the wicket" and one of

the children threw a stick, hitting her in the mouth. **1957** *Sat. Eve. Post Letters* (as of c1908), "Kick the Wicket"—the wicket was a broom stick about 18″ long. The game was played at the intersection of two streets. The wicket was placed against the curb, and the "kicker" would push his instep under the wicket and lift it rather than kick it. . . One man would be "it." . . He would stand near the center of the intersection and try and get the wicket back across the curb line before the "kicker" could reach one of the four corners—if he caught a player, that player would be "it." *Ibid* **csPA** (as of c1930), Kick-the-Wicki—This consisted of four street corners being used as bases. The person who was "it" would stand in the middle of the street. Players would prop a stick against a light pole and kick it and then try to reach first base without being tagged. The "It" person had to retrieve the stick and tag the runner with it. **1965–70** *DARE* (Qu. EE10, *A game in which a short stick lying on the ground is flipped into the air and then hit with a longer stick*) Infs **NJ**33, 39, **PA**148, Wicket; **NJ**21, Hit the wicket; **PA**245, Hit the wickie; (Qu. EE13a, *Games in which every player hides except one, and that one must try to find the others*) Inf **WA**13, Wicket's out—all but one hide, caught are in circle and uncaught hider comes in and kicks stick (wicket) out of prison ring—all are free—he calls "Wicket's out"; (Qu. EE18, *Games in which the players set up a stone, a tin can, or something similar, and then try to knock it down*) Infs **NJ**55, **PA**72, Kick the wicket; **MD**34, Kick the wicket—played with tin cans, players run and kick cans to a certain point; **PA**126, Kick the wicket—put a stick against the stone, kick stick, the "it" must retrieve the stick and stone—same as kick the can; (Qu. EE27, *Games played on the ice*) Inf **NJ**33, Whickety—set up a block of ice; then like duck on davy; (Qu. EE33, *. . Outdoor games . . that children play*) Inf **NY**44, Kick the wicket—two teams, kick the stick and advance to bases while other team returns stick to base; **PA**72, Kick the wicket. [9 of 11 total Infs old, 9 male] **1979** Lewis *Family Reunion* 211 **ePA,** Kick the Wickety. . . A stick was used as the "wickety" and it was laid against the curb at one corner. Someone would kick it and run clockwise around the corners, while the one who was "it" would recover the wickety and replace it. As soon as it was in place, the "runner" had to stop. Then the next player would kick it and the players would run again. . . if the person who was "it" caught someone running with the wickety in place, he would point him out and then he was "it." **2004** *DARE* File—Internet **PA** (as of 1930s), In those days we only needed sticks, cans, pebbles and dirt. . . I'm sure you remember Kick the Can and Hit the Wicket.

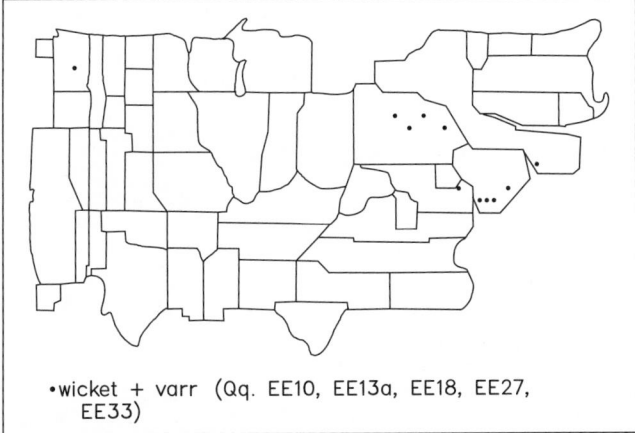

•wicket + varr (Qq. EE10, EE13a, EE18, EE27, EE33)

wickeyup See **wickiup**

wicki See **wicket**

wickie n See **wicket**

wickiup n Also *wickeyup, wickie-up, wicky-up* [In var AmInd langs, e.g., Sac, Fox, and Kickapoo, *wikiyap* a temporary dwelling or hut consisting of a frame covered with brushwood or grass mats and assoc primarily with Amer Indians in the West] **chiefly West**

Transf: any of var shelters or dwellings not assoc with Amer Indians; hence v *wickie-up* to improvise a temporary shelter; see quots.

1876 *Sun* (NY NY) 10 May 2/6 (sic *DAE*—quot not found), Come up and see me at my wickiup in Montana. **1897** Lewis *Wolfville* 28 **AZ,** This Wilkins lives in a wickeyup out on the aige of the town. **1907** White *AZ Nights* 34, With one of the prettiest twenty-foot flip throws I

ever see done he snaked old Texas Pete right out of his wicky-up, gun and all. **1910** Raine *Bucky O'Connor* 209 **West,** "I reckon we'll begin by taking a preliminary survey of this wickiup." Wickiup was distinctly good, since the word is used to apply to a frail Indian hut, and this cell was nothing less than a tomb built in the solid rock. **1918** *DN* 5.29 **NW,** *Wickiup*. . . Any meagre shelter, improvised of brush, boughs, etc. Woodsmen. **1944** Adams *Western Words* 177, *Wickiup*. . . Sometimes used colloquially by cowmen in referring to their own houses. **1958** McCulloch *Woods Words* 210 **Pacific NW,** *Wickiup*—A shelter, sometimes used to mean a shack or a bunkhouse (from the Indian). **1975** Gould *ME Lingo* 317, *Wickie-up*—A temporary and usually one-night bedding down on a wilderness trail. It suggests a man overtaken by night, and a make-do shelter which, while primitive, becomes comfortable through his woods wisdom. It also suggests the experienced and competent woodsman. . . A man who makes such a camp *wickie-ups,* and is said to have *wickie-upped.* Maine use derives from Abnaki Indian.

wickopee See **wicopy 1**

wickopick See **wickup** n[1]

wickopy See **wicopy 1**

wickup n[1] Also *wickopick, wickupp* [From an Algonquian lang; see quots 1830 and 1910 below and quot 1902 at **wicopy 1**]

A **linden** (here: *Tilia americana*). Note: the identification of the trees in quots 1704 and 1778 is not certain.

1704 in 1894 Providence RI Rec. Comm. *Early Rec.* 5.244, Two trees growing out of one Roote called Wickupp trees. [**1778** Carver *Travels N. Amer.* 499 **MI, WI, MN,** The *Wickopick* or *Suckwick* appears to be a species of the white wood, . . distinguished . . by a peculiar quality in the bark, which when pounded and moistened . . becomes . . of the consistence . . of size.] [**1830** Rafinesque *Med. Flora* 2.268, *Tilia. . . Linden, Basswood, Whitewood, Spoonwood, Sucumug* or *Sugamuck* of Mohegans, *Sucuy* or *Wuckopy* of Algic tribes.] **1897** Sudworth *Arborescent Flora* 302 **MA,** *Tilia americana*. . . Wickup. **1910** Hodge *Hdbk. Amer. Indians* 2.950, *Wickup.* A New England name particularly in Massachusetts, of the American linden or basswood *(Tilia americana),* from *wikop,* the name of this tree in Massachuset, Chippewa, and closely related dialects of the Algonquian stock.

wickup n[2] See **wake-up**

wickup n[3] See **wicopy 2**

wickupp See **wickup** n[1]

wicky n Also *wicke, wicky laurel* [Perh transf from Engl dial *wick(e)y* (<*wicken* < **quicken tree**) *Sorbus aucuparia*] **S Atl** Cf **vine-wicky**

A **mountain laurel 1,** esp **sheep laurel** (here: *Kalmia angustifolia*); rarely a **staggerbush** (here: *Lyonia lucida*).

1798 Barton *Coll. for an Essay* 47, Besides the Andromeda Mariana . . , a decoction of the leaves of the Kalmia latifolia is used for the cure of this complaint [=toe itch]. The decoction of the leaves of both these plants is used. They are both called "Wicke" to the southward. **1834** in 1837 *Boston Jrl. Nat. Hist.* 1.100 **NC,** Kalmia angustifolia, *Wicky.* **1860** Chapman *Flora Southern U.S.* 264 **FL, GA,** *K. hirsuta*. . . (Wicky.) . . Flat pine barrens. **1901** Lounsberry *S. Wild Flowers* 386, Wicky. . . *Kalmia cuneata. Ibid,* 389, *K. angustifolia,* lambkill, wicky or sheep-laurel, a charming one of the laurels, is known by its oblong, blunt leaves and deep crimson . . flowers. **1901** NC State Bd. Ag. *Bulletin* 22.9.10, *Kalmia angustifolia.* The wicky laurel is found in all parts of the state. **1902** Hodge *Nature Study* 115, Narrow-Leaf Laurel, *Kalmia angustifolia.* . . dwarf laurel, wicky. **1932** *Country Life* 62.65, Mountain-laurel . . more familiarly called by the Carolinians Calicobush, Spoonwort, Wicky, or Bush-ivy. **1966** *DARE* Wildfl QR Pl.160A [= *Kalmia angustifolia*] Inf **NC**28, Wicky. **2006** *DARE* File—Internet **FL,** *Kalmia hirsuta. . . Common name:* Wicky; hairy laurel.

wicky-up n See **wickiup**

wicopy n [See quot 1902 at **1**] **esp NEng**

1 also *wickape(e), wickapy, wickerby, wickopee, wickopy:* A **leatherwood 1** (here: *Dirca palustris*). Cf **Indian wicopy 1**

1823 *New Engl. Farmer* (Fessenden) 1.232, Your limbs will be lithe as a wickapy wand,/ And your sinews be soften'd, like wax in the sun. [Footnote to *wickapy:*] Wickapy is the popular name for a shrub, which is remarkably flexible. **1832** Williamson *Hist. ME* 1.112, Wickape, or Leather wood. *Leatherwood* or *Indian Wickape* is a small tree [Footnote:

Dirca palustris] which grows on the best hardwood land and none other. **1849** Hanson *Hist. Norridgewock & Canaan* 110 **ME,** The indigenous trees and shrubs [include] . . wickapee or leather-wood. **1870** *Amer. Naturalist* 4.217, Leather-wood *(Dirca palustris),* also called Wicopy, with pale yellowish flowers is a curious shrub, its wood soft and brittle, its bark so tough that it can be used for thongs, requiring a strong man to break even its slenderest twigs. **1891** *Atlantic Mth.* 68.466 **NEng,** Sam saw a sprawling moosewood or wicopy close at hand, and presently fitted the old man out with a thong of its tough bark. **1897** *Jrl. Amer. Folkl.* 10.143 **ME,** *Dirca palustris,* . . wickopy. **1901** *Forest & Stream* 57.262 **VT,** "Will you be good enough to give me a strip of wickopee bark?" **1902** *Jrl. Amer. Folkl.* 15.266, *Wicopy (wickopy).* A New England name of the "leatherwood" *(Dirca palustris).* . . But the name *wicopy* does not properly belong to the "leatherwood," but to the basswood of Canada, the "whitewood" *(Tilia Americana)* of the eastern United States. Lenâpé *wikbi,* Abnaki *wigbi,* signify the stringy bark of the basswood; the basswood itself is called in Ojibwa *wikop* (or *wekopimish* (*-mish* ="tree")[)], which properly signifies the "inner bark" of the basswood,—the radical *kop* ="inner bark." **1907** *DN* 3.251 **eME,** *Wickerby.* . . A shrub, the bark of which is used for thongs; moosewood. *Direa* [sic] *palustris.*

2 also *wic(k)up:* A **willow herb 1** (here: *Chamerion angustifolium).* [Perh a different word] Cf **Indian wicopy 2**

[**1837** in 1890 Gosse *Life Philip Henry Gosse* 106 **sQuebec Canada,** We had to climb over the fallen trees . . ; and to make it worse, these were concealed by the tall wickup plants with which the ground was absolutely covered. [*DARE* Ed: E. Gosse's identification of this as *Dirca palustris* is erroneous.]] **1876** Hobbs *Bot. Hdbk.* 129, Wickup, Willow herb, Epilobium angustifolium and other species. . . Wicopy herb, [wicopy,] Indian, [wicopy] root, Wickopy, Epilobium spicatum [=*Chamerion angustifolium*] and other spec. **1891** *Jrl. Amer. Folkl.* 4.148 **MA,** Epilobium angustifolium we only knew by the name our grandmother taught us, *Wickup.* **1896** *Ibid* 9.188 **ME,** Epilobium angustifolium [= *Chamerion a.*], . . wickup. **1896** *Garden and Forest* 9.303, *Wickup, or Wicup* (Epilobium angustifolium). An alteration of the foregoing word [=*wickopy*].

wicup See **wicopy 2**

wid See **with A3**

widdah, widder See **widow**

wid(d)erer See **widower**

widdie n Also sp *widdy* [Cf *EDD* *widdy* (at *wid* int) "a young duckling".] Cf **biddy** n³, **weedily, wheedle**

A baby chick; rarely, a hen.

1936 Morehouse *Rain on Just* 20 **NC,** His young bitch Drum had been . . sucking eggs from under Aunt Largey Drake's setting hen, and the little widdies all but pecking through their shells. **1939** Rawson *Forever Farm* 340, Hens were biddies and the newly hatched chickens were widdies, when I was a little shaver. **1940** *AL Hist. Qrly.* 2.426 **sLA,** To the Cajan . . a chicken hen is a "widdie", and all little chicks "little widdies." So general is the use of these terms that the writer has known numbers of school children to write "hen" and to pronounce the word "widdie." **1968** *DARE* FW Addit **swVA,** Widdy ['wɪdɪ]—baby chick. **2003** *DARE* File—Internet **VA,** I'm trying to find any information on a word heard in Carroll County, Virginia. The spelling of the word is unclear; it sounds like "widdie" and refers to a pre-pubescent chicken, just before becoming a "pullet"—an adolescent chicken. This was (or still is) a common term among farmers in the area.

widdie intj Also sp *widdy* [Cf *EDD* *wheetie* 1. "A call to poultry, esp ducks"; *widdy* (at *wid,* int) "A word used to call ducks."] **chiefly S Midl, esp NC**

Used as a call to chickens or other domestic fowl.

1902 McCulloch-Williams *Next to the Ground* 356 **S Midl,** The guinea call: "Widdie! Widdie! Wi-iddie! Widdie!" Young guineas are so small, so shy, . . they look much more like game birds than . . domestic fowl. **c1920** in 1993 Farwell–Nicholas *Smoky Mt. Voices* 180 **sAppalachians,** *(Come) widdy, widdy:* call for ducks and geese. **1949** Kurath *Word Geog.* 44, The chicken call *biddie!, widdie!* . . though used in New England and on Delmarvia, is nevertheless characteristic of North Carolina, since it is not used across the state line in Virginia or south of the Peedee in South Carolina. **1966** Dakin *Dial. Vocab. Ohio R. Valley* 2.288, *Calls to chickens. . . Widdie!* . . also used in the South, appear[s] once. **1966–67** *DARE* (Qu. K79, *How do you call the chickens to you at feeding time?*) Inf **NC26,** Widdie widdie widdie. **1967** Faries *Word Geog. MO* 94, *Calls to chickens. . .* scattered instances of *widdie!* **1971**

Wood *Vocab. Change* 299 **Sth,** A call to chickens. . . *widdie.* [Offered by 5 of 1000 infs] **1975** Purkey *Home in Madison Co.* 75 **wNC,** Mama mixed a little cornmeal dough and ran out into the back yard calling: "Widdie, Widdie." And when all the chickens flocked around her, picking up the dough, she nabbed the fattest one in the bunch and wrung its neck off. **1997** in 2004 Montgomery–Hall *Dict. Smoky Mt. Engl.* 649 **wNC,** *Widdy* . . Come! (a call to chickens or ducks). . . [1 inf].

widduh, widdy n¹ See **widow**

widdy n² See **widdie** n

widdy intj See **widdie** intj

wide-awake n

The sooty **tern** *(Sterna fuscata).*

[**1869** *Zoologist* 2d ser 4.1867, On Ascension Island, the sooty tern nests regularly in great numbers. . . The bird is there known to the sailors as the "wide-awake" tern.] **1917** (1923) *Birds Amer.* 1.68, Sooty Tern, *Sterna fuscata.* . . [Also called] Egg Bird; Wide-awake. **1947** *Natl. Geogr. Mag.* Feb 230 **sFL,** And there they [=terns] remain . . voicing their age-old tumult across the sands. No wonder they are known as "wide-awakes"! **1962** Imhof *AL Birds* 279, Sooty Tern, *Sterna fuscata* . . [Also called:] Wideawake. [**2006** *DARE* File—Internet, *Sooty Tern.* . . Loud night "wide-awake" call from nesting colony.]

wide eye n Cf **white-eye** v 1

1990 Cavender *Folk Med. Lexicon* 34 **sAppalachians,** *Wide eye*—a. severe exhaustion. b. insomnia.

wide-gape n [*OED2* 1808 →]

=**goosefish.**

1911 U.S. Bur. Census *Fisheries 1908* 310, Goosefish. . . A large sluggish fish found on the north Atlantic coast from Nova Scotia to Cape Lookout. Local names are "angler" . . "all-mouth," "wide-gape" [etc].

widemouth bass n Also *wide-mouthed bass*

=**largemouth bass.**

1845 *Knickerbocker* 26.281 **swMI,** We will . . bait for you a hook, which . . will enable you to transfer a spotted pickerel or wide-mouthed bass from the element in which he has so long preyed upon his species. **1875** (1876) Hallock *Camp Life* 162, Under the bonnets are voracious wide-mouthed bass, called trout by the natives [of FL]. **1908** DuBois *Fun & Pathos* 108, Every community has men who resemble fish. The boastful are the wide-mouth bass. **1965** *Valley News & Valley Green Sheet* (Van Nuys CA) 18 Mar sec B 24/3, He caught a six pound, widemouthed bass, 20 inches long from the shores of Lake Sherwood. **1968–70** *DARE* (Qu. P1, . . *Kinds of freshwater fish . . caught around here . . good to eat*) Infs **KS15, PA176, TX89, WI68,** Widemouth bass. **1977** *Independent Press–Telegram* (Long Beach CA) 9 Oct [47]/1 (newspaperarchive.com), There used to be a couple huge widemouth bass in this pond. **1986** Pederson *LAGS Concordance,* 1 inf, **neFL,** Widemouth bass. **1999** *Sun* (Baltimore MD) 30 Sept sec B 3 (Internet), Class starts at Piney Run Park Nature Center with a food web game. . . that starts with tiny plants and insects and ends with herons, otters and widemouth bass.

widemouth sunfish n Also *wide-mouthed sunfish*

=**warmouth.**

1875 IN Geol. Surv. *Annual Rept. 1874* 215, Chænobryttus. . . Wide-mouthed Sun-fish. . . Southern and Western streams. I have seen none from this region. **1885** IL Bd. Fish Comms. *Report* 2 sec K 110, *Chænobryttus gulosus.* . . Wide-Mouthed Sunfish. This fine species is among the commonest of the family in . . Southern Illinois, where it is commonly known as the "Goggle Eye." **1933** LA Dept. of Conserv. *Fishes* 342, Chaenobryttus gulosus. . . Wide-mouthed Sunfish. **1935** Caine *Game Fish* 33, Chaenobryttus gulosus. . . Wide-mouth Sunfish.

wide place in the road n Also *wide spot in the road;* for addit varr see quots **chiefly Midl, Sth, West** See Map Cf **four corners 2**

Fig: a very small town.

1879 *Daily Constitution* (Atlanta GA) 3 July [4]/6 (newspaperarchive.com), The village of to-day is only a wide place in the road, where the city of yore used to stand. **1890** *Harper's New Mth. Mag.* 80.888 **AL,** We were standing outside the door of the only thing in Booker City that could be called a building—Booker City, that might have been described as a "wide place in the road." **1906** *DN* 3.164 **nwAR,** *Wide place in the road.* . . A hamlet. "It's not a town; it's just a wide place in the road." **1909** *Indianapolis Star* (IN) 26 Dec 4/1,

Weiser is a jumping off station in the wilds of Idaho, where Johnson began his career. He came directly from that wide spot in the road to one of the fastest leagues in the country. **1909** *DN* 3.387 **eAL, wGA,** *Wide place in the road.* . . A small village. Facetious. **1929** Dobie *Vaquero* 130 **TX,** It would go . . on north to Beaver Lake (near the present wide place in the road called Juno, Val Verde County). **1937** *AmSp* 12.239, New additions to the names for 'hick towns' are Alfalfa Junction, Alfalfa Center, Pruneville, a Dump, a One Horse Town, and 'a wide (variant, narrow) place in the road.' **1950** *WELS Suppl., Wide spot in the middle of the road.* . . Hamlet, small town. **1965–70** DARE (Qu. C33, . . *Joking names* . . *for an out-of-the-way place, or a very small or unimportant place*) 149 Infs, **chiefly Midl, Sth, West,** Wide place (*or* spot) in the road; **AL**43, Wide place; **KS**19, **MI**76, Wide space in the road; **MO**26, Wide hole in the road; **MO**5, Wide path in the road; (Qu. C34, *Nicknames for nearby settlements, villages, or districts*) Infs **IL**68, **TN**66, Wide places in the road. **1967–70** DARE Tape **CA**181, Little towns like Garden Grove, which is now around 150,000, I believe now, was just merely a wide spot in the road back at those times; **TX**3, [FW:] Langtry must have been a whole lot more of a town then than it is now. [Inf:] Oh, no, it was always just a wide place in the road. **1986** Pederson *LAGS Concordance,* 1 inf, **nwFL,** Wide place in road—her small community. **2005** *Mt. Democrat* (Placerville CA) 17 Mar sec A 6/1, The county seat needs four things to be something more than a wide spot in the road.

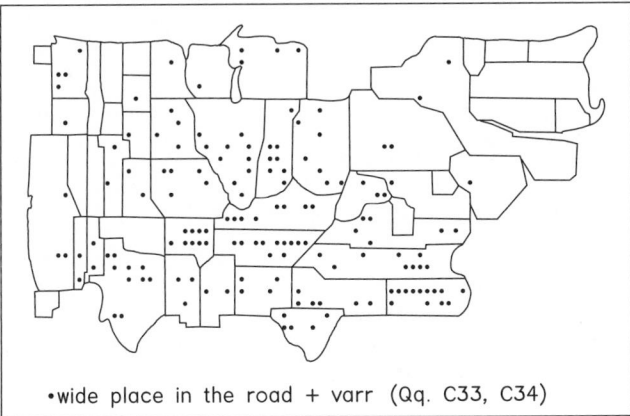

•wide place in the road + varr (Qq. C33, C34)

wider See **widow**

widerer See **widower**

wide spot in the road See **wide place in the road**

widgeon n

1 Std: any of var ducks of the genus *Anas,* as **baldpate 1, European widgeon, gadwall,** and **pintail 1.** Cf **bald widgeon, brown ~, gray ~ 2, green-headed ~, kite-tailed ~, marsh ~, Norwegian ~, pied ~, red-headed ~, sea ~ 1, swamp ~**

2 Any of var wild ducks of other genera, as:

a =**wood duck.** Cf **wood widgeon**

1832 Williamson *Hist. ME* 1.142, The *Widgeon* is supposed to be the same as a wood duck; the female lays her eggs in some hollow tree. **1888** Trumbull *Names of Birds* 34 **CT,** *Aix sponsa* . . At East Haddam, Conn., it is the Widgeon. "A good many here call it Wood Duck," said a local gunner, "because it builds its nests in trees, but most of us know that its real name is Widgeon." Farther down the Connecticut River, we hear Wood Widgeon. **1955** MA Audubon Soc. *Bulletin* 39.315, *Wood Duck.* Widgeon (Maine, Conn. A general purpose name for the smaller ducks.)

b Usu the **greater scaup,** but also the **lesser scaup.**

1888 Trumbull *Names of Birds* 54 **MA, RI,** *Aythya marila nearctica.* . . at Falmouth, Mass., and to native duckers at Newport, R.I., Widgeon. **1911** *Forest & Stream* 77.173 **MA,** Big Black head or Bluebill. . . *Marila* [=*Aythya*] *marila* . . Widgeon, Ponkapog, Mass. *Ibid,* Little Blackhead or Bluebill. . . *Marila* [=*Aythya*] *affinis* . . Widgeon, Ponkapog, Mass. **1925** (1986) Phillips *Nat. Hist. Ducks* 3.248, *Aythya marila* . . Scaup Duck, Greater Scaup, Common Scaup . . Widgeon.

c also *goose widgeon, stiff-tailed ~, widgeon coot:* =**ruddy duck.**

1888 Trumbull *Names of Birds* 111, In the vicinity of Plymouth, Mass., [the ruddy duck is called] *goose widgeon;* at West Barnstable,

same state, *widgeon coot* or *widgeon* simply. **1912** Forbush *Hist. Game Birds* 166, *Ruddy Duck.* . . Common or local names: Toughhead; Stiff-tailed Widgeon; Dipper [etc].

d =**goldeneye 1.** [*EDD* 1893]

1955 MA Audubon Soc. *Bulletin* 39.316 **MA,** *American Goldeneye.* . . Widgeon, Winter Duck.

widgeon coot See **widgeon 2c**

widgeon grass n

1 A **ditch grass 2,** usu *Ruppia maritima.*

1876 in 1895 Minot *Private Letters* 99 **NC,** The Atlantic has heaped up a sand beach some ten miles distant from the mainland, the interval being marshes interlaced by intricate, shallow waters in which grow the wild celery and widgeon grass, the choice food of the canvas-back and other wild fowl. **1895** *Forest & Stream* 45.493 **nwOR,** You know that the carp have eaten up all our wapatoos, widgeon grass and other duck food. **1912** [see **2** below]. **1913** *Torreya* 13.226 **SC,** *Ruppia maritima.* . . Widgeon grass. **1918** *Bridgeport Telegram* (CT) 11 July 18/3, Where one [sic] widgeon grass, joint grass and eel grass grew in luxuriance, furnishing food for thousands of wild fowl, the flats are now covered with an oily, tarry silt in which nothing can live. **1921** LA Dept. of Conserv. *Bulletin* 10.47, Widgeon-grass (*Ruppia maritima*), or niggerwool, . . is eaten by gadwalls, widgeons and other ducks. **1938** FWP *Guide DE* 410, Ducks and geese feed on the heavy growth of widgeon grass. **1946** MA Audubon Soc. *Bulletin* 30.6, Widgeon grass (*Ruppia maritima*), which is the principal pondweed found in the numerous potholes on the Essex marshes, is also utilized to some extent by black ducks. **1975** *Oakland Tribune* (CA) 10 Aug sec C 3/2, Widgeon grass (*Ruppia maritima*) is a flowering grass that roots on the bottom. . . In Lake Merritt much of the grass is eight feet long. **2006** *Capital* (Annapolis MD) 1 June 1 (Internet), Underwater grasses such as eelgrass, widgeon grass and sago pondweed are a vital link in the bay's [= Chesapeake Bay's] ecosystem.

2 A **pondweed** (here: *Potamogeton epihydrus*).

1912 Forbush *Hist. Game Birds* 578 **MA,** The seed of a plant called widgeon grass by Cape Cod gunners has been identified for me by Mr. W.L. McAtee of the Biological Survey as that of *Potamogeton epihydrus.* Wood Ducks and Black Ducks are fond of this pondweed and it grows commonly in some of the ponds of Massachusetts. The widgeon grass of the south Atlantic coast of the United States is quite a different plant,—the ditch grass (*Ruppia maritima*).

widout See **without A2**

widow n   Usu |'wɪdo(ʊ)|; also |'wɪdə, 'wɪd(ʊ)u|; **chiefly Sth, S Midl** |'wɪdɚ|; for addit varr see quots Pronc-spp *widdah, wid(d)er, widduh, widdy*

A Forms.

1795 Dearborn *Columbian Grammar* 140, *List of Improprieties.* . . Widder for Widow. **1819** in 1956 Eliason *Tarheel Talk* 320 **c,cwNC,** Wider. **1843** (1916) Hall *New Purchase* 213 **IN,** Missus Widder Dolly Johnsin. **1854** in 1855 Holbrook *Ten Yrs.* 361 **wNY,** The wider stacy and her to girls they are poor and haf to work for their living. **1869** Stowe *Oldtown Folks* 31 **MA,** Must visit the widdahs in their affliction. **1891** *DN* 1.132 **cNY,** [wɪdə] (also [wɪdɚ]) . . widow. **1915** *DN* 4.192 **swVA,** *Widder.* Variant of *widow,* and used also in the sense 'widower.' **1922** Gonzales *Black Border* 338 **sSC, GA coasts** [Gullah glossary], *Widduh*—widow, widows. **1923** *DN* 5.224 **swMO,** *Widder:* . . Widow. **1928** *AmSp* 3.403 **Ozarks** (as of 1916–27), The final *o* sound represented by *ow* is very often replaced by *er* in an unaccented final syllable, giving us such words as *holler, beller, feller, swaller, widder, winder.* **1936** *AmSp* 11.159 **eTX,** The vowel in the final syllable of . . the words listed below is usually [ə]. . . banjo . . widow . . yellow. *Ibid* 161, In addition to the usual sound of [ə] in the final syllable, some . . words . . have [ɚ] in less literate speech. . . *mosquito* . . *widow* . . *yellow.* **1941** *LANE* Map 389 *(Widow),* [Proncs of the types ['wɪdo(ʊ)] are most freq; those of the type ['wɪdə] are also very common; those of the types ['wɪd(ʊ)u] are occasional; ['wɪdɚ] was offered by only a single inf who characterized it as joc.] **1942** Hall *Smoky Mt. Speech* 80 **wNC, eTN,** A considerable degree of education or subjection to modernizing influences is required before speakers regularly avoid [ɚ] for general American [o]. Examples: Banjo . . widow. **1961** Kurath–McDavid *Pronc. Engl.* 170, Widow, meadow, yellow. . . These words end in /o/, /ə/, or /ɚ/. In cultivated speech, the /o/ of *ago* predominates in the North and the North Midland, the final /ə/ of *Martha* in the South Midland and the Lower South; in Virginia the two vowels are rather evenly matched. . . [The] /ɚ/ . . pronunciation is common in the mountains of the South . . , in eastern North Carolina, and on the Delmarva Peninsula, being most frequent among the folk. Relics of /ɜ/ survive in the folk speech of the North. Cultured speakers avoid it altogether. **1965–70** *DARE* (Qu. R28, . . *Kinds of spiders*) Infs **NM**6, **OK**1, 11, 23, 25, 42, 46, Black widder spider; **OK**11, Brown widder; **OK**11, Fly widder; **OK**46, Merry widder spider; **ME**20, **OK**46, Widder spider; (Qu. R21, . . *Other kinds of stinging insects*) Infs **OK**13, 23, Black widder (spider); (Qu. AA24, *A man whose wife is dead*) Infs **GA**23, 37, **MO**16, 34, Widder; (Qu. AA25, *A woman whose husband is dead*) Infs **GA**37, **KY**19, **MI**64, **MN**29, **VA**24, Widder; **KY**19, Widder-woman; **VA**5, Widdy; (Qu. HH22c, . . *A very mean person* . . *"He's mean enough to _____."*) Inf **TX**43, Push a widder woman's dog in the well. **1967** *DARE* File **MI**, [ˈwɪdɚ]. **1976** Allen *LAUM* 3.294 **Upper MW** (as of c1950), *Widow*. . . The few examples with final /ə/ give little hint of Northern/Midland contrast, and final /o/ is actually stronger in Midland Iowa and Nebraska. The shift is apparently occasioned by the strength of the /u/ variant in Northern speech. Manifested as [ʊᶜ], [ʊᵊ], [ʊᵚ], and even [u], it is reported the choice of 20% of the infs. in . . Wisconsin, 31% . . in Minnesota, and 60% . . in North Dakota. . . /u/ in *widow* is less favored by educated speakers than is /o/. . . One Iowa inf. . . has . . /ˈwɪdɚ/. **1989** Pederson *LAGS Tech. Index* 224 **Gulf Region**, *Widow* . . [Of 914 primary infs, 479 offered proncs of the types [ˈwɪdə(z), ˈwɪddə, ˈhwɪdə, ˈwɪtə(z)]; 101 infs, [ˈwɪdɚ(z), ˈwɪddɚ, ˈwɪtɚ]; 25 infs, [ˈwɪdu, ˈwɪtu]].

B Senses.

1 also *widow fish*, ~ *rockfish*, ~ *rock cod:* Any of several **rockfish 3** of the Pacific coast; orig esp *Sebastes ovalis*, but now (esp as *widow rockfish*) usu *S. entomelas*. [Transl of **viuva**]

[**1880** see **viuva**.] **1881** *CA App. Jrls. Legislature* 2.12.37, *S[ebastichthys] ovalis*, Viuda [sic], Widow—A southern species, taken with hook and line in very deep water. **1896** Jordan–Evermann *Check List Fishes* 429, *Sebastodes ovalis*. . . *Viuva; Widow-fish.* **1939** *CA Fish & Game* 25.216 **cwCA**, *Widow Rock Cod* denotes *S[ebastodes] entomelas*, primarily, but some of the markets may include *S. ovalis* and *S. hopkinsi* here. **1953** Cannon *How to Fish* 164 **nCA**, Along the northern California coast alone, the *black rockfish, Sebastodes melanops*, is variously called *"blue fish," "widow fish," "cherna,"* [etc]. **1953** Roedel *Common Fishes CA* 128, Widow Rockfish, *Sebastodes entomelas*. **1975** *Daily Rev.* (Hayward CA) 10 Aug 5/1, We pulled in a number of yellowish-colored rockfish, called widow fish, ranging from 2 to 5 pounds. **2005** *Nature Conserv. CA Program CA Update* Fall 3, The catch they [= trawlers' nets] produce . . puts pressure on several rockfish populations, like boccacio, canary and widow fish. **2006** *DARE* File—Internet **CA**, *Sebastes entomelas*. . . *Range:* Widow rockfish occur from Todos Santos Bay, Baja California, to Kodiak Island, Alaska. . . *Other Common Names:* widow, widowfish, red snapper.

2 A widower. [*OED2 widow* sb.[2] *"Obs. exc dial."*] **scattered, but esp Sth, S Midl** See Map *esp among rural speakers and among those with little formal educ* Cf **widowman**

1915 [see **A** above]. **1965–70** *DARE* (Qu. AA24, *A man whose wife is dead*) 36 Infs, **scattered, but esp Sth, S Midl**, Widow. [31 Infs comm types 4, 5; 19 Infs gs educ or less] **1982** Slone *How We Talked* 36 **eKY** (as of c1950), *Widder*—widow; both men and women were called "widders." **1986** Pederson *LAGS Concordance*, 2 infs, **GA**, **MS**, Widow—man or woman; 1 inf, **seGA**, Widow—of a man; 1 inf, **csGA**, Widow—man whose wife has died.

3 also with *the;* also *widow Jones (house):* An outhouse or toilet—also used in var allusive phrr. Cf **Mrs. Jones**

1900 *DN* 2.69 **MA** [College slang], *Widow, Widow Jones*. . . Water-closet. **1941** *LANE* Map 354 *(Privy)*, Jocular euphemisms . . are here summarized. . . *The widow* (*going out to see the widow,* etc.) [8 infs, **sNEng**]; *to see if the widow is up or has a fire going* [3 infs, **VT**]; *Widow Jones* [8 infs, **CT, MA, VT**]. **1969** *DARE* (Qu. M21b, *Joking names for an outside toilet building*) Inf **PA**191, The widow; **NY**224, Widow Jones house.

4 in phr *a game for the widow:* =**cat's game**.

1968 *DARE* (Qu. EE38b, *If the game of tick-tack-toe . . comes out so that neither X nor O wins, you call that _____*) Inf **DE**3, A game for the widow. **1978** *NADS Letters* **swAR** (as of 1950s), I seem to recall that my mother used the term *a game for the widow* when she taught us how to play tic-tac-toe. [**1978** *AP Letters,* A game for the widow . . My grandfather . . who was born in Chateaugay, New York in the 1850's explained that if you neither win nor lose, the contest is a draw—so get rid of it by saying "give it to a widow."]

5 also *widow skimmer:* A **skimmer 3** (here: *Libellula luctuosa*). [Prob because of the dark coloration]

1929 Needham–Heywood *Hdbk. Dragonflies* 221, *Libellula luctuosa*. . . The Widow. . . A blackish species of moderate size. **1938** *TN Acad. Sci. Jrl.* 13.105, *Libellula luctuosa*. . . This observer collected and saw specimens of the "widow." **1980** Milne–Milne *Audubon Field Guide Insects* 372, Widow (*Libellula luctuosa*). . . Body dark brown. . . *Fore and hind wings blackish brown up to halfway toward tip;* wing tips clear or smoky brown, especially in female. . . Range: Ontario and Atlantic Coast to Georgia and Gulf Coast, west to Texas and . . north to South Dakota. **1987** *Providence Jrl.* (RI) 30 Aug sec M 21 (Internet), Though one name is now generally applied to dragonflies, the different varieties still have individual names . . My favorite name is the widow. The widow is dark, with gaudy yellow stripes down its sides—a bit garish, actually, for widow's weeds. **2006** *DARE* File—Internet, *Libellula luctuosa*. . . The Widow Skimmer is a fairly common dragonfly, and is present in most of North America, spring thru [sic] summer. . . The male leaves the female to lay her eggs alone.

6 See **mourning bride**.

widow bird n Also *widow-maker* Cf **loggerhead shrike, northern ~, southern ~**
A shrike (*Lanius* spp).

1968 *DARE* (Qu. Q14, . . *Names . . for . . shrike*) Inf **IL**27, Widow bird, widow-maker.

widower n Usu |ˈwɪdəwɚ|; also esp **Sth, S Midl** (See Map at **A** below) |ˈwɪdərə(r)|; for addit varr see quots Pronc-spp *wid(d)erer* Cf **widow A**
A Forms.

1844 *Sandusky Clarion* (OH) [19 Oct 4]/4 **IL** (newspaperarchive.com), Wun of my sparks . . is a widderer and wants to marry me next week. **1882** *Harper's New Mth. Mag.* 64.244 **GA**, Not a-wishin' and a-desirin' of a-bein' of a widderer. **1911** Day *Skipper* 183 **ME**, You're a nice widderer, you are! **1965–70** *DARE* (Qu. AA24, *A man whose wife is dead*) 11 Infs, **scattered, but esp Sth, S Midl**, Widderer [ˈwɪdɚˌɚ]; **GA**81, **LA**3, 20, **SC**3, Widderer [ˈwɪdərə]; **NC**61, **VA**69, Widderer [ˈwɪdəˌə]; **AL**26, Widderer; **AR**56, Widderer [ˈwɪdɚˌo]; **AZ**6, Widderer [ˈwɪdəˌɚ]; **TX**103, Widderer [ˈwɪdəˌɚ]. [12 of 21 total Infs gs educ or less] **2000** Shores *Tangier Is.* 203 **Chesapeake Bay**, A woman who

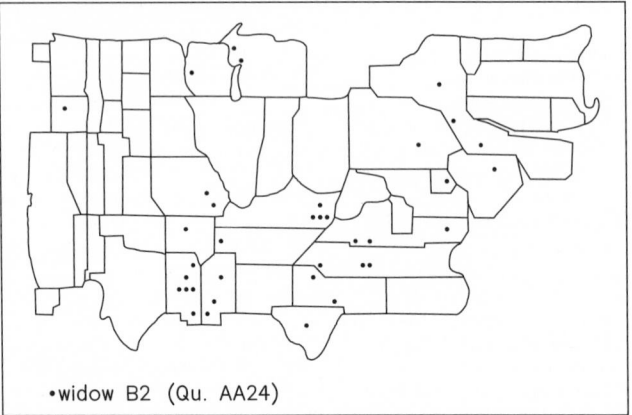

•widow B2 (Qu. AA24)

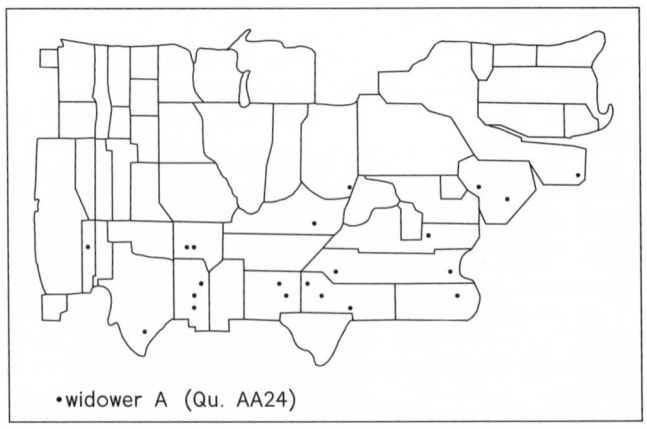

•widower A (Qu. AA24)

loses her husband is called a *wider,* and the man who loses his wife, a *widerer.*

B Sense.

A widow; a woman abandoned by, or separated from, her husband.

1965–70 *DARE* (Qu. AA25, *A woman whose husband is dead*) Infs **LA**33, **MI**27, **MO**25, **NC**41, **PA**70, **WI**66, Widower; **DC**13, Widow, [wɪdowə]—same thing, isn't it? (Qu. AA26, *A divorced woman*) Inf **ME**19, Widower [Inf queries]. **1986** Pederson *LAGS Concordance,* 3 infs, **GA, TN, TX,** Widower—woman; 1 inf, **cwMS,** Widower—husband has left her but is still alive; 1 inf, **cwAR,** Widower—husband has left her; heard all his life; 1 inf, **cnTX,** Widower = widow. [*DARE* Ed: Only those responses where the referent is explicitly identified as a woman are recorded here.]

widow fish See **widow B1**

widow gentleman See **widowman**

widow Jones (house) See **widow B3**

widow lady See **widow woman 1**

widow-maker n Cf **foolkiller 2**

1 In logging: a tree or branch that has fallen on or is likely to fall on or snap back at the logger. **chiefly Nth, esp NW** Cf **sidewinder 2**

1899 Whipple *Lights & Shadows* 246 **MN,** I wish I could describe . . the shout "Look out for the widow-makers," as the tree falls, leaving broken limbs (the widow-makers) suspended from the next tree. **1905** U.S. Forest Serv. *Bulletin* 61.52 **Nth** [Logging terms], *Widow maker.* A broken limb hanging loose in the top of a tree, which in its fall may injure a man below . . , or a breaking cable. **1939** FWP *ID Lore* 244, Lumberjack jargon in the St. Maries area and elsewhere: . . *Widow-maker*—a falling tree top or branch. **1949** Powers *Redwood Country* 118, "Widow-makers," the bull buck explained, indicating precariously hanging limbs liable to fall at any moment. **1950** *Western Folkl.* 9.121 **nwOR** [Logger speech], *Widow-maker.* A loose limb hanging in a tree; a leaning snag. **1952** *Badger Folkl.* 1.17 **WI** [Logging language], *Widowmaker*—Green pole bent over by a falling tree, sometimes called a springpole. **1953** Randolph–Wilson *Down in Holler* 299 **Ozarks,** Widow-maker. . . The woodsman's name for a big dead limb that falls unexpectedly. **1956** *AmSp* 31.152 **nwCA** [Logger lingo], *Widow maker.* . . A limb from a fallen tree which belatedly falls after being snagged in the boughs of another tree. **1966** *DARE* Tape **MI**10, And if, when you were felling timber, you looked up and happened to see a big limb hanging in the top of the tree, you knew that you were standing under a widowmaker. I have . . known . . three men . . who were killed by such hanging portions of trees. **1975** Gould *ME Lingo* 317, *Widow maker*—A tree with a broken top or loose limbs that can drop when the tree is felled and kill a man. **1982** *Smithsonian Letters* **ID,** A widow-maker . . is a tree with a crotch and the cutter has to be very careful when falling it or his wife will become a widow in a hurry as the tree has a tendency to split in all directions. *Ibid* **swWA** (as of c1900), When a tree was about to fall the faller yelled . . "look out for widow makers" . . If the falling tree fell close to another tree the other tree would bend over and then snap back and if there was any loose limbs on it they were thrown back. My uncle was killed this way. **1995** Lesley *Sky Fisherman* 287 **OR,** "Seeing those trees come straight at you makes you a little more sympathetic towards the loggers, doesn't it?" Jake said. "You know how some poor fella feels when a widow maker splits wrong and falls right toward him." **2005** *Down East* Feb 16 **ME,** *Widow Maker:* A leaning, half-toppled tree that might come crashing down and kill a man. As in, "After that ice storm I couldn't cross my woodlot for all the widow makers."

2 By ext: any of var other potentially deadly machines, creatures, or commodities; see quots. **scattered, but esp West**

1929 *AmSp* 5.146 **CO** [Mining expressions], *The stoping machine, . .* when adapted to the drilling of holes for blasting, is called *wiggle-tail;* if run without water, it is a *duster;* and in some cases, a *widow-maker.* **1949** Emrich *Wild West Custom* 165 **West,** *Window* [sic] *makers* were the early compressed-air drills creating silicosis. **1968** Adams *Western Words* 347, *Widow-maker*—A cowman's name for an extra-bad horse. **1969** *DARE* FW Addit **nwCA,** *Widowmaker*—Burley air drill—mining term. **1970** *DARE* (Qu. DD6b, *Nicknames for cigarettes*) Inf **NY**234, Widow-maker. **1971** Brunvand *Guide Folkl.* UT 32, *Widowmaker:* This is the name given to the jackhammer because the man lies on it with his stomach to hold it down and it shakes him to pieces. A lot of men were

really killed that way. **1974** Dabney *Mountain Spirits* 25 **sAppalachians,** The names [=for corn whiskey] go on . . "widow makers." **1997** *DARE* File **csMA** [Truck driver lingo], "Widow makers" were a special type of sleeper [=sleeping compartment] that could only be accessed through small doors on the outside of the cab.

3 See **widow bird.**

widowman n Rarely *widow gentleman* [Engl, Scots, nIr dial] **scattered, but chiefly Sth, S Midl** See Map Cf **widow woman**

A widower.

1688 in 1876 *Boston Registry Dept. Records* 1.142, Robbert Nokes, widow man. **1877** Holley *Josiah Allen's Wife* 471 **NY,** When a Widder woman or a Widder man embarks in a new sea of matrimony, they ort to burn the ship behind 'em that they sailed round with in them other waters. **1892** *DN* 1.233 **KY,** *Widow-man:* widower. **1909** *DN* 3.406 **nwAR,** *Widow-man.* . . A widower. **1923** *DN* 5.224 **swMO,** *Widder. . . -man.* Widower. **1930** *AmSp* 5.393 [Language of N Atl fishermen], *Widow man.* . . A widower. **1931** *AmSp* 7.94 **eKY,** *Widow-man,* a widower. **1946** McCullers *Member* 43 **AL,** He was a widowman, for her mother had died the very day that she was born. **1952** Brown *NC Folkl.* 1.607, *Widow man.* . . A widower. **1955** Ritchie *Singing Family* 127 **seKY,** He at that time had been a widder-man for about two year. **c1960** *Wilson Coll.* **csKY,** Widower (rarely *widow-man*). **1961** (1962) Griffin *Black Like Me* 30 **TX,** I'll just tell her you're a widow man. **1965–70** *DARE* (Qu. AA24, *A man whose wife is dead*) 20 Infs, **chiefly Sth, S Midl,** Widowman; **IL**25, Widow gentleman. **1966** Dakin *Dial. Vocab. Ohio R. Valley* 2.418, For some of the most old-fashioned, *widow-woman* is a necessary contrast with *widow-man = widower,* but the latter usage is apparently quite rare. **1974** Fink *Mountain Speech* 29 **wNC, eTN,** *Widder-man* . . widower.

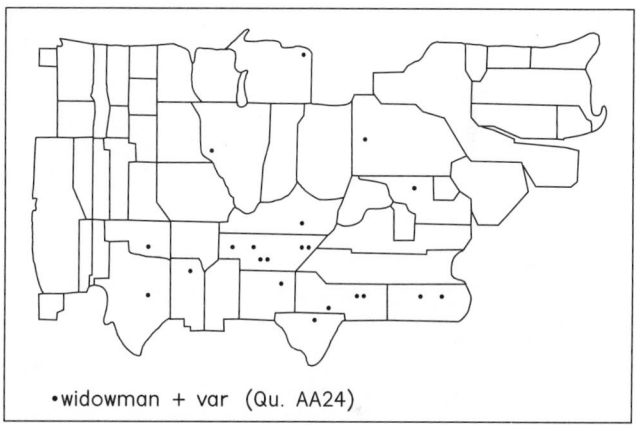

•widowman + var (Qu. AA24)

widow rock cod, widow rockfish See **widow B1**

widow's cross n

A **stonecrop 1** (here: *Sedum pulchellum*) native to much of the central and southern US.

1875 *Amer. Cyclop.* 14.751, *S[edum] pulchellum, . .* one of the handsomest of the genus, is a more southern plant; its stems . . are crowded with linear cylindrical leaves, and at the top bear a broad cyme, the spikes of which are arranged in a very regular manner, and bear a profusion of rose-purple flowers; it is now and then cultivated, and in some localities is known as the widow's cross. **1917** *Gaz. & Bulletin* (Williamsport PA) 28 Apr 5/1, Get acquainted with that pretty little sedum, "The Widow's Cross" (Pulchellim) [sic]. **1953** *Traverse City Rec.-Eagle* (MI) 20 June 7/5, Widow's Cross. . . is a handsome but little known native evergreen which grows about one foot high and looks like a bright little spruce tree. **2006** *DARE* File—Internet **MO,** This particular glade is special because upon it grows widow's cross sedum (Sedum pulchellum).

widow's frill n

=**starry campion.**

1933 Small *Manual SE Flora* 506, *S[ilene] stellata.* . . (Starry-campion. Widow's-frill.)—Rich or dry woods, various provinces. **1961** Smith *MI Wildflowers* 115, Starry Campion, Widow's-frill. **2006** (acc) *Lady Bird Johnson Wildfl. Center* (Internet), *Silene stellata.* . . Widow's-frill.

widow skimmer See **widow B5**

widow spider n

Std: a venomous spider of the genus *Latrodectus.* For other names of var of these see **brown widow, fly ~, hourglass spider, merry widow 1, privy spider**

widow's tears n

1 =**spiderwort.** [See quots 1949, 2004]

1886 *Amer. Naturalist* 20.551, *Tradescantia virginica,* or spiderwort, also called, in quaint allusion to the ephemeral nature of its petals, "widow's tears." **1949** Moldenke *Amer. Wild Flowers* 307, All these spiderworts are often called *jobstears* or *widowstears* because the handsome flowers early in the afternoon transform themselves into "tears"— about noon the petals begin to contract in size, shrivel up, and deliquesce into a fluid jelly, which trickles away like a tear if touched. **1966** *DARE* Wildfl QR Pl.7 [=*Tradescantia virginiana*] Infs **TX**34, 44, Widow's tears. **2004** *News & Rec.* (Greensboro NC) 20 June 3 (Internet), Tradescantias. . . are called "widow's tears" because each morning, tiny drops of water are noted along the straplike leaves.

2 A **dayflower** or a related plant *(Tinantia anomala)* formerly included in the genus *Commelina.* [See quot 2000] **TX**

1936 Whitehouse *TX Flowers* 5, Widow's Tears (Commelina crispa) has two large blue petals and a third, minute, white, and inconspicuous. **1965** Teale *Wandering Through Winter* 150, All across Texas, a host of . . picturesque names have been bestowed on the wild plants of the state. They run from angel's trumpet, . . [to] tiny Tim . . and widow's tears. **1989** *Austin Amer.-Statesman* (TX) 17 Mar sec B 1 (Internet), In spring. . . The Hedyotis crassifolia becomes a for-get-me-not, the Commelina angustifolia a widow's tear [sic]. **2000** in 2007 (acc) TX A&M Univ. Ag. Research & Ext. Center Uvalde *Herbarium* (Internet) **TX,** *Widow's Tears, Day Flower. Commelina erecta* L. var. *erecta.* . . When the spathe of this plant is squeezed it produces a drop of liquid, hence the name Widow's Tears.

3 A perennial plant of the genus *Achimenes,* often grown as a house plant or in hanging baskets.

1962 *Chron.-Telegram* (Elyria OH) 14 Dec 22/5, Achimenes. . . Many indoor gardeners in this country either don't know them at all, or else know them by such names as nut-orchid, monkey-face, or widow's-tears. **1972** *Sun. Gaz.-Mail* (Charleston WV) 16 Jan sec E 10/4, An achimenes is a waxy, long-keeping flower sometimes called widow's tears or nut orchid.

widow's walk n **orig NEng; now more widespread** Cf **captain's walk, widow's watch**

An observation platform built on the roof of a house.

1920 *Green Book Mag.* 24.3.45 **Nantucket MA,** Reaching the little white cottage with its characteristic "widow's walk" on the roof, we entered the living-room. **1924** Mumford *Sticks & Stones* 61 **NEng,** Under McIntire's . . hands, the low-lying traditional farmhouse was converted into the bulky square house with its hipped roof, its classical pilasters, its frequently ill-proportioned cupola, its "captain's walk," or "widow's walk." **1943** *Sheboygan Press* (WI) 23 Sept 21/3, What is a "widow's walk"? . . Along the coast, especially in New England, in the days of the sailing ships, many of the houses were built with a balcony near the roof line, which wives of men missing at sea were apt to walk while they watched for a message from the missing ship. **1967** *DARE* Tape **MA**71, A captain's walk. . . it's sometimes called a widow's walk. [**1968** *DARE* (Qu. M2, . . *The small wooden construction on top of a barn with slats for ventilation*) Inf **OH**78, Widow's walk—but it's not large enough to be a real walk.] **1970** *Sun. Dominion-Post* (Morgantown WV) 8 Mar sec B 3/2, One of the Boughners was a river boat captain, who plied his trade on the Monongahela and at one time there was a "widow's walk" on the house. **1986** Pederson *LAGS Concordance,* 1 inf, **neFL,** Widow's walk—overlooking the sea; 1 inf, **csFL,** Widow's walk—small porch on top of the house; 1 inf, **seAL,** Widow's walk— second story porch; 1 inf, **ceTX,** Widow's walk—on roof; metal deck and weather vane. **1997** *Columbus Dispatch* (OH) 27 July advertising sec 91/2, Situated high on a promontory overlooking Buckeye Lake, this 1997 . . [home] offers unparalleled views. . . From its main deck, to the cozy second floor porch, to the widow's walk high atop the roof.

widow's watch n **chiefly NEast**

A cupola or turret on a house, serving as a lookout; less freq, a **widow's walk.**

1922 Holland *Peter Cotterell's Treasure* 10 **NH,** Tom Hallett's house had the cupola on top of its roof that told of the old sailing days, the "widow's watch," as it was commonly called, for from there the wives of sailors used to watch for the first sign of homebound sails. **1947**

Ironwood Daily–Globe (MI) 26 Aug 8/5 **seMA,** What is a widow's watch? . . It is a small plaza [sic for *piazza*] enclosed by a railing at the top of many homes on Martha's Vineyard. The outlook faces the sea and there wives of the old whalers waited and watched for the return of the ships. **1969** *Yankee* July 68 **NEng,** [Caption:] Note the "widow's watch" or large cupola on the house in the foreground. **1986** Pederson *LAGS Concordance,* 1 inf, **cAL,** Widow's watch—tower on roof; 1 inf, **swFL,** Widow's watch—upstairs porch? **1999** Barnes *Hustling* 175 **seNY,** On Long Island, where I grew up, there are still some old Victorian homes that were built during the times its beach communities were supported by the whaling industry. Many of these homes have a very small room that sits on the top of the roof called the "widow's watch." **2000** *Capital* (Annapolis MD) 13 Oct entertainment sec 30/2, *Waterfront Properties.* . . 2 story 4 BR, 4 BA Contemporary with sweeping waterviews. . . "Widow's Watch" and private dock at West River Yacht Harbor.

widow woman n Cf Intro "Language Changes" I.4

1 also *widow lady:* A widow. [Engl, Scots, nIr dial] **formerly widespread, now esp Midl, Sth** See Map

1739 *Boston Weekly Post Boy* (MA) 2 Apr 4/2, [Advt:] Taken up and brought to *Salem* Goal [sic], a likely young Negro Man . . who . . belongs to a Widow Woman in *Boston.* **1784** *Freeman's Jrl. N. Amer. Intelligencer* (Philadelphia PA) 24 Nov 1/3, [Advt:] *Stolen,* out of the house of an aged widow woman, . . one dark striped callico gown. **1877** *Sun* (Baltimore MD) 9 Feb 4/4, The boy who it is said did the stabbing is the son of Mrs Mason, a widow woman. **1803** Davis *Travels* 318 **NYC,** He was a *Villian* . . or he would never impose upon a defenceless widow-woman. **1892** *DN* 1.233 **KY,** *Widow-woman:* widow. [*DN* Ed: Also New England and Michigan.] **1893** Shands *MS Speech* 68, Negroes and illiterate whites almost never say simply *widow,* but in nearly every instance add either *woman* or *lady* to this word. Cultivated white people very frequently use this redundancy also. **1899** (1912) Green *VA Folk-Speech* 484, *Widow-woman.* **1909** *DN* 3.388 **eAL, wGA,** *Widow (w)oman.* Ibid 406 **nwAR,** *Widow-woman.* **1911** *DN* 3.549 **NE,** Some stock pleonastic expressions [include] . . *widow woman.* **1912** *DN* 3.593 **wIN,** *Widow lady.* **1915** *DN* 4.230 **wTX,** *Widder-woman.* **1929** *MT Std.* (Butte) 31 Mar 31/1, [Advt:] *Lost— Twenty-five dollars in currency* by widow woman. **1938** Rawlings *Yearling* 168 **nFL,** I got a widder-woman at Fort Gates, knows how to be faithful. **1941** *LANE* Map 389 *(Widow),* [*Widow woman* is found throughout the region, especially in **nNEng;** *widow lady* is less common. Some infs characterize *widow woman* as "impolite" or "not proper."] **1952** Brown *NC Folkl.* 1.607, Widow lady. Ibid, Widow woman. **1965–70** *DARE* (Qu. AA25, *A woman whose husband is dead*) 49 Infs, **chiefly Midl, Sth,** Widow woman; **AL**24, 34, **OK**58, **SC**3, 7, 26, 40, Widow lady; **KY**19, Widder-woman; (Qu. HH22c, . . *A very mean person* . . *"He's mean enough to _____."*) Inf **TX**43, Push a widder woman's dog in the well. **1968** *PADS* 49.14 **Upper MW,** The schools tend to establish literary terms in place of or alongside indigenous folk terms. This influence is also evident in . . the decline of *widow woman.* **1970** *DARE* Tape **CA**181, I married a widow woman with three children. **1970** *DARE* FW Addit **MA,** *Widow woman—*old-fashioned. **1982** *Barrick Coll.* **csPA,** *Widow-woman.* **1989** Pederson *LAGS Tech. Index* 224 **Gulf Region,** *Widow* . . widow (724 [of 924 infs]) . . widow lady (5 [infs]) . . widow woman (60 [infs]). **1991** Still *Wolfpen Notebooks* 74 **sAppalachians,** One of the pleasures of my life is to bring together the men and women who are dying to marry. I mean the widow-women and the widow-men.

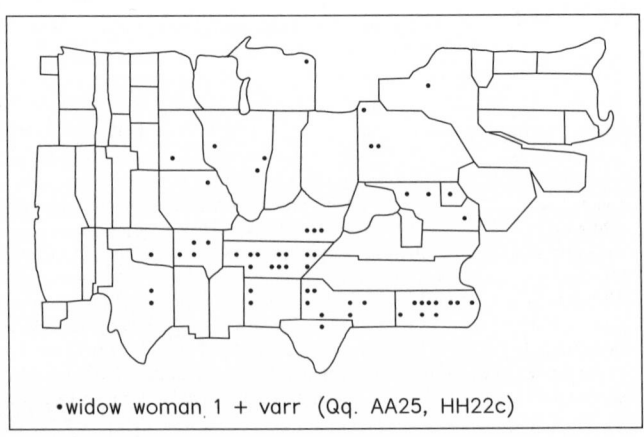

•widow woman 1 + varr (Qq. AA25, HH22c)

2 A divorced woman.

1941 Stuart *Men of Mts.* 255 **eKY,** Being with a widder woman who hadn't been divorced from her man very long.   **1969** *DARE* (Qu. AA26, *A divorced woman*) Inf **KY**28, Widow woman.

wiener n   Also sp *weiner* [Abbr for *wienerwurst*] **widespread, but less freq Atlantic, West**   See Map   Cf **frankfurt, wienie, winny**

A frankfurter; hence *wiener roast* a social gathering at which frankfurters are roasted and eaten.

1889 *Current Lit.* 3.175 **wNY,** Give me instead my mug of Weyand's,/ Two wieners mustard-coated, rare!/ Away with all your dainty viands!/ Give me the homely German fare.   **1899** Peck *Peck's Uncle Ike* 166 **WI,** When they had come out of the last side show . . he had bought a mess of hot wiener sausages for them. . . the boys grabbed their wieners and run across the fair grounds.   **1905** *Decatur Daily Rev.* (IL) 25 Oct 10/3, The Epworth league of the First Methodist church will give a wiener roast at Riverside park this evening.   **1965–70** *DARE* (Qu. H40, *A small sausage that is put into a long roll or bun to make a sandwich*) 278 Infs, **widespread, but less freq Atlantic, West,** Wiener; **CT**12, Hot wiener; (Qu. H41, . . *Kinds of roll or bun sandwiches . . in a round bun or roll*) Inf **MO**1, Wiener roll; (Qu. H43, *Foods made from parts of the head and inner organs of an animal*) Inf **CO**7, Wieners; (Qu. H50, *Dishes made with beans, peas, or corn that everybody around here knows, but people in other places might not*) Inf **MI**96, Sauerkraut and wieners; (Qu. H65, *Foreign foods favored by people around here*) Infs **NM**5, **NY**109, **PA**131, Sauerkraut and (pork and) wieners; **IL**131, **WA**13, Wieners (and sauerkraut); (Qu. FF1, . . *A kind of group meeting*) Infs **CO**17, **KS**20, **MI**45, 51, **WV**10, Wiener roast; (Qu. FF2, . . *Kinds of parties*) Inf **MO**18, Wiener roasts; (Qu. HH30, *Things that are nick-named for different nationalities—for example, a 'Dutch treat'*) Inf **NY**80, Texas hot wiener.   **1989** Pederson *LAGS Tech. Index* 393 **Gulf Region,** *Sausage . .* wiener (42 [infs]).   **2004** *Gettysburg Times* (PA) 1 Sept sec A 6/3, Take advantage of their carry-out special of 5 weiners, burgers, or a mix for only $8.25.

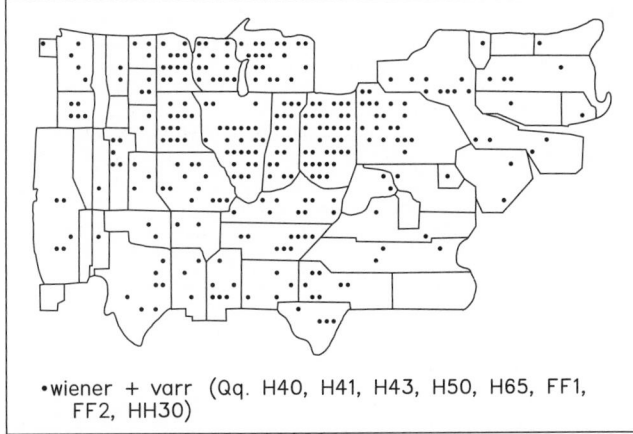

•wiener + varr (Qq. H40, H41, H43, H50, H65, FF1, FF2, HH30)

wienie n   Also sp *weenie, weinie* **widespread, but chiefly Sth, S Midl, N Cent, West**   See Map

=**wiener.**

1891 *Tacoma Daily News* (WA) 19 Mar 5/1, Just as they were struggling fiercely a wiener wurst peddler came along. . . and all three fell in a heap. When they got up again . . a string of weenies was round the officer's neck.   **1902** *Daily IA State Press* (IA City) 17 Jan 1/5, Toy steins were favors and "wienies" were refreshments.   **1905** *Duluth News Tribune* (MN) 12 Aug 6/1, [Advt:] Weinies. . . 10¢—Bologna. . . 8¢.   **1907** *Cedar Rapids Eve. Gaz.* (IA) 28 June 1/6, All of the diseased meat . . was . . destroyed, together with a large quantity of bologna, weenies and sausage.   **1916** *Morning Oregonian* (Portland OR) 16 July sec 3 10/6, A bonfire each Friday night . . with a menu of campfire edibles such as toasted weinies, sandwiches and coffee.   **1925** *AmSp* 1.151 **West,** There is something characteristic in the names given to different varieties of food. . . There are "weenies," from "wieners," from "wienerwurst," the Eastern Frankfurters and the universal "hot dogs."   **1965–70** *DARE* (Qu. H40, *A small sausage that is put into a long roll or bun to make a sandwich*) 222 Infs, **widespread, but chiefly Sth, S Midl, N Cent, West,** Wienie; **LA**6, **SC**34, Wienie-sausage; (Qu. FF1, . . *A kind of group meeting called a 'social' or 'sociable'. . . [What goes on?]*) 40 Infs, **scattered, but infreq West,** Wienie roast; (Qu. H41, . . *Kinds of roll or bun sandwiches . . in a round bun or roll*) Inf **OK**1, Wienie and

chili; **CA**32, Wienie roast; (Qu. H42, . . *[A sandwich] . . in a much larger, longer bun, that's a meal in itself*) Infs **OK**32, **TN**24, Wienie; (Qu. H65, *Foreign foods favored by people around here*) Inf **OK**9, Sauerkraut and wienies; (Qu. FF2, . . *Kinds of parties*) Infs **CO**9, **OK**6, **TX**38, Wienie roasts.   **1989** Pederson *LAGS Tech. Index* 393 **Gulf Region,** *Sausage . .* (roast) wienie (29 [infs]).   **2007** *DARE* File—Internet **MI,** The club organizes the Minard Mills Bicycle Tour and Wienie Roast.

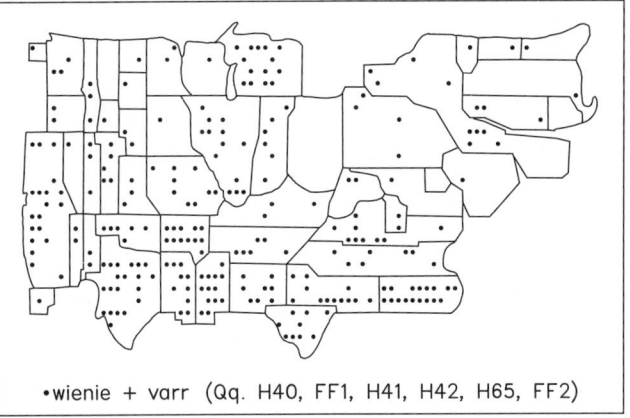

•wienie + varr (Qq. H40, FF1, H41, H42, H65, FF2)

wif   See **with** A4

wiffenpoof   See **whiffenpoof**

wifout   See **without** A2

wiggertail   See **wiggletail 1**

wiggle n

=**wiggler 1.**

1831 Buttrick *Voyages* 49 **OH** (as of 1817), The water was very bad. . . After straining it would still exhibit live insects, which they call wiggles.   **1968** *DARE* (Qu. R14, *Small worm-like things [seen in rain barrels or standing water] that hatch into mosquitoes*) Inf **PA**135, Wiggles.

wiggler n

1 The larva of a **mosquito** n[1] **B1.** **widespread, but less freq Lower Missip Valley**   See Map   Also called **crawler** n[1] **4, jigger** n[2] **3, pollywog 2, rainworm 2, snapper 6, tadpole 2, wiggle, wiggletail 1, wiggle-woggle 2, wiggleworm 2, wriggler 1, wriggletail**   Cf **tumbler 2**

1854 *Horticult. Rev. & Bot. Mag.* 4.517, The larva of musketoes consume myriads of infusoria that grow in stagnant water. The millions of "wigglers" that may be seen in reservoirs of rain water, grow and wax fat on something more substantial than air or pure water.   **1859** (1968) Bartlett *Americanisms* 498, Waggletail. The larva of the mosquito, etc.; also called a wiggler.   **1863** *Scientific Amer.* 8.356, The young trout, when first hatched, is about half an inch long, and looks and acts more like a wiggler you often see in rain-water.   **1900** *Daily Northwestern* (Oshkosh WI) 8 Jan 3/1, They are the wigglers that used to infest the rainwater barrel at the corner of the house "in the early days."   **1907** *DN* 3.204 **NH,** The water in the hogshead is full of wigglers.   **1909** *DN* 3.422, Wiggler. . . Small rapidly moving animals in standing rain water, supposed to be young mosquitoes.   **1914** *DN* 4.114 **KS,** Wiggle-wag-

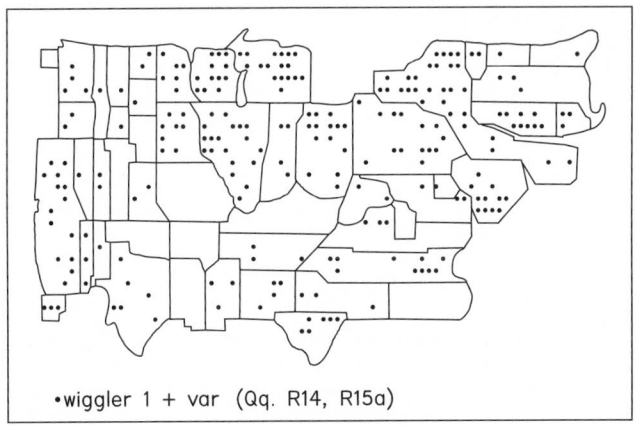

•wiggler 1 + var (Qq. R14, R15a)

gle. . . =*wiggler,* a larval mosquito. **1938** Steinbeck *Long Valley* 182 **CA,** Jim could see the mosquito wigglers, tumbling up and down, end over end, in the water. **1950** *WELS* **WI** *(Small worm-like things [seen in rain barrels or standing water] that hatch into mosquitoes)* 24 Infs, Wigglers; 11 Infs, Wrigglers. **1965–70** *DARE* (Qu. R14, *Small worm-like things [seen in rain barrels or standing water] that hatch into mosquitoes)* 233 Infs, **widespread, but less freq Lower Missip Valley,** Wiggler(s); **CA**150, Mosquito wigglers; (Qu. R15a, . . *Names or nicknames . . for mosquitoes)* Inf **FL**27, Wiggler. **2006** *Star Tribune* (Minneapolis MN) 21 July sec C 8 (Internet), Adults of the dragonflies are enemies of mosquitoes. They gobble them down as mosquito wigglers when they are nymphs, and they snatch them out of the air as flying mosquitoes when they are adult dragonflies.

2 also *silver wiggler:* Another insect larva, as:

a The larva of the **mayfly 1.** **Gt Lakes**

1966–67 *DARE* (Qu. P6, . . *Kinds of worms . . used for bait)* Inf **MI**27, Wigglers—a Green Bay fly before it gets its wings; **MI**54, Wiggler— that's the June fly, before it has wings. **1967** *DARE* Tape **MI**53, [FW:] Does the larva of the mayfly have a name in the area? [Inf:] Yes, wiggler. . . They're the important bait for fishing through the ice for panfish, perch. . . You are required to have a minnow and wiggler license to sell wigglers. **2002** in 2006 *DARE* File—Internet **MN,** Occasionally, panfish that won't touch a wad of maggots will embrace a solitary one. Desperate times call for desperate measures. If locally available, present nitpickers a freshwater shrimp or mayfly larva (silver wiggler). **2006** *Buffalo News* (NY) 22 Jan sec D 13 (Internet), Randy had just received a fresh shipment of Michigan wigglers, a delicate water bug that often can be deadly perch bait. . . Perch rode the same cycles this day, starting with a preference for live minnows, then wigglers, then wax worms and back to minnows.

b =**rat-tailed maggot.**

1982 Sternberg *Fishing* 88, Silver wigglers, or *spikes,* are the larvae of flies such as the housefly and blowfly. About ½ inch long, they have an unpleasant smell. *Ibid* 89, Fly larvae . . are most popular among ice fishermen. Favorites are silver wigglers [etc].

3 An **earthworm.** **chiefly S Atl, Gulf States** See Map Cf **African wiggler, banana ~, Georgia ~, night ~, red ~, swamp ~** (at **swamp worm**), **wriggler 2**

1871 Eggleston *Book of Stories* 58 **IN,** Catching wigglers [said the bass, is] . . not easy. **1895** *Outing* 26.375 **RI,** We . . took . . a box of worms, . . for without one squirming wiggler the Madame would not have secured her bass. *Ibid* 376, I baited with wigglers and cast astern. **c1940** Eliason *Word Lists FL* 12 **wFL,** Wiggler: The common name of a worm used for fish bait. It is found in low damp ground, in leaf mold and muck. **1965–70** *DARE* (Qu. P6, . . *Kinds of worms . . used for bait)* 29 Infs, **chiefly S Atl, Gulf States,** Wiggler; (Qu. P5, . . *The common worm used as bait)* 21 Infs, **chiefly S Atl, Gulf States,** Wiggler; **LA**10, Wiggler—a commercial worm that wiggles all the time; **OK**42, Wigglers—a small redworm. **1971** Wood *Vocab. Change* 36 **Sth,** For a large worm used in fishing. . . *Georgia wiggler* or *wiggler* is the first choice [of terms] in Georgia, Alabama, and Florida; it is the second choice in the other states. **2006** *AL Game & Fish* (Internet), The old timers ask, 'Have you ever dug up the wiggler to catch the bream to catch the flathead?'

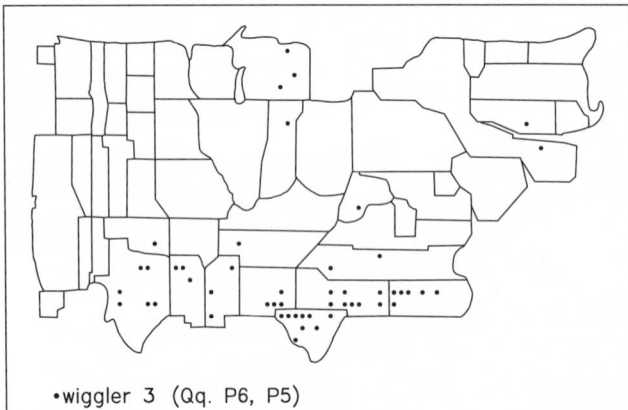

•wiggler 3 (Qq. P6, P5)

4 The larva of a frog or toad. Cf **tadpole 1, wiggletail 2**

1884 *New Englander & Yale Rev.* 43.160, When everything was ready, some fittest surviving wiggler . . was in turn advanced to the statelier

tadpole. And this elevating process . . went with increasing momentum, until our favorite, the *frog,* leaped forth. **1969** *DARE* (Qu. P20, *Very young frogs—when they still have tails but no legs)* Inf **IN**73, Wigglers. **2006** *DARE* File—Internet, After the frog is fully developed, students will illustrate the life cycle of a frog. They will need to include the four stages: eggs, polliwog/tadpole, tiny wiggler and frog.

5 An eel *(Anguilla rostrata);* see quots.

1891 *San Antonio Daily Light* (TX) 18 Apr [3]/2 (newspaperarchive.com), An eel spear is built like Neptune's trident. . . The spear is jabbed in the mud gently; if it meets resistance when pulled out the fisherman yanks it out like lightning and shakes the wiggler off on the ice. Sometimes three or four come out at once. **2006** *DARE* File— Internet **Delmarva,** Put the hook in through the eel's lower jaw and out through the upper jaw just forward of the eyes, then drop it down and let that wiggler drag across the bottom.

6 =**pope's nose 1.**

1966 *DARE* (Qu. K73, . . *Names . . for the rump of a cooked chicken)* Inf **NC**6, Wiggler.

wiggletail n

1 also *wig(ger)tail, wigglertail:* =**wiggler 1.** **chiefly Sth, S Midl, TX, OK** See Map

1848 *Spirit of Times* 18.308 **neNY,** I could easily distinguish with the naked eye the unmistakable form of the musquito embryo, as well and euphoneously known as the "wiggle-tail." **1855** *Ft. Wayne Times* (IN) 26 July [2]/5 (newspaperarchive.com), The mosquitoe proceeds from the animalculae commonly termed the 'wiggle-tail.' **1872** *Defiance Democrat* (OH) 20 Jan [4]/1 (newspaperarchive.com), The water of many wells is often nothing but stagnant water-pools in which "green scum" and "wiggle-tails" form the larger half. **1883** (1971) Harris *Nights with Remus* 220 **GA** [Black], Some say it too full er wiggletails, Brer Rabbit. [Footnote:] Is it necessary to say that the wiggletail is the embryo mosquito? **1899** (1912) Green *VA Folk-Speech* 484, *Wiggletail.* . . One of the active larvæ, as of mosquitoes, seen in stagnant water. **1906** *DN* 3.164 **nwAR,** *Wiggletail.* . . Young mosquito. . . Tadpole. **1941** Percy *Lanterns* 310 **MS,** My drinking-water had come from the cistern in the back gallery and sometimes it suffered attacks of wiggle-tails. **1950** *WELS (Small worm-like things [seen in rain barrels or standing water] that hatch into mosquitoes)* 2 Infs, **WI,** Wiggletails. **c1960** Wilson *Coll.* **csKY,** Wiggletail—larvae of mosquitoes. **1965–70** *DARE* (Qu. R14, *Small worm-like things [seen in rain barrels or standing water] that hatch into mosquitoes)* 249 Infs, **chiefly Sth, S Midl, TX, OK,** Wiggletail(s); **FL**22, 26, Wiggertails; **AR**52, Wigglertails; **AR**55, Wigtail. **1966** *DARE* Tape **SC**12, I'd heard people say they [=shallow wells] had wiggletails in 'em. Some kind of old wiggly thing. . . You wouldn't drink the water. **2004** in 2006 *DARE* File—Internet **MS,** Wiggletails are mosquito larvae.

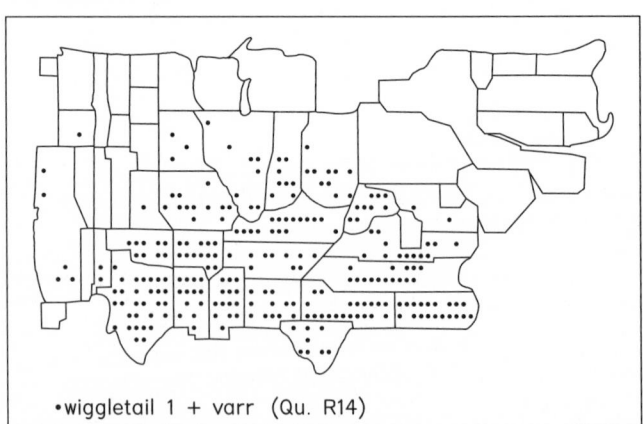

•wiggletail 1 + varr (Qu. R14)

2 The larva of a frog or toad. **esp Sth, S Midl** Cf **tadpole 1, wiggler 4**

1887 *Semi-Weekly Age* (Coshocton OH) 7 Jan 1/6, The Immortal John . . says "Meek has a corps of wiggle-tails (tadpoles) throughout the country for correspondents"; and he nows [sic] offers a fair price to any man who will bring him a live tadpole in a bottle, which he wishes to put on exhibition in his store, and which is to represent "Meek's correspondents." **1906** [see **1** above]. **1965–70** *DARE* (Qu. P20, *Very young frogs—when they still have tails but no legs)* Infs **MS**63, **MO**24, 36, **NC**85, **SC**9, **TX**9, 26, Wiggletails; [(Qu. P23, *Names for the animal similar to the frog that lives away from water)* Inf **IL**135, Wiggletail].

3 as *wigglytail:* An **earthworm.** Cf **wiggler 3, wiggle-worm 1**

1970 *DARE* (Qu. P5, . . *The common worm used as bait*) Inf **TN**46, Wigglytails.

wiggle-waggle See **wiggle-woggle 2**

wiggle-woggle n

1 The larva of a frog or toad. Cf **tadpole 1, wiggler 4, wiggletail 2**

1880 *Decatur Daily Rev.* (IL) 13 Nov 2/1, For the benefit of wiggle-woggle or tadpole editors, . . we beg to say that the life of the latter [= the Democratic party] is co-equal with that of constitutional government. [**1941** Justin–Rust *Home & Family* 160, Little children watching his mad motion call, "Wiggle-woggle polliwog, pretty soon you will be a frog."]

2 also *wiggle-waggle:* =**wiggler 1.**

1892 *News* (Frederick MD) 22 Sept [6]/1 (newspaperarchive.com), Now that it is assured that ice water is prolific of wiggle-waggles, the beer industry ought to thrive. **1914** *DN* 4.114 **KS,** *Wiggle-waggle . . wiggler,* a larval mosquito. **1968** *DARE* (Qu. R14, *Small worm-like things [seen in rain barrels or standing water] that hatch into mosquitoes*) Inf **MN**12, Wiggle-woggle.

wiggleworm n

1 An **earthworm.** Cf **wiggler 3**

1896 Hussey *River Bend* 80, A wiggle-worm came,/ And said, as he wiggled about,/ "This brother of mine, when a tight place was found,/ Always wiggled so carefully out!" **1907** *Daily Independent* (Monessen PA) 4 May 1/1, Mrs. Mitchell, after looking on the flowing bowl until it moved itself like a wiggle-worm, discovered that she had a grudge against Mr. Lewis Webster. **1923** *IA City Press–Citizen* (IA) 5 Oct [10]/1 (newspaperarchive.com), Right now Wiggle Worm is over in your field, . . loosening up the dirt around your grain so that when the rain does come, the grain will get all it needs. **1948** *Daily Reg.* (Harrisburg IL) 7 June 5/4, Then they run out into the back yard and fork up the soil until they find a fishing worm, or wiggle worm, as we used to call 'em back in Illinois. **1954** *Chillicothe Constitution–Tribune* (MO) 1 Apr 3/5, These are called hybrid worms, a cross between the orchid worm and the wiggle worm. **1966** *Frederick Post* (MD) 20 July 8/2, Even before I could get Robbie's rod ready, Jimmy had hooked a wiggleworm to his line and dropped it into the current. **1966** *DARE* (Qu. P5, . . *The common worm used as bait*) Infs **MS**6, 72, Wiggleworm. **1988** *Mt. Democrat* (Placerville CA) 23 Nov sec A 11/1, I suspect that I found one of my dad's snelled hooks and managed to impale a wiggle worm on it.

2 also *wigglyworm:* =**wiggler 1.** **chiefly Midl** See Map

1965–70 *DARE* (Qu. R14, *Small worm-like things [seen in rain barrels or standing water] that hatch into mosquitoes*) 25 Infs, **chiefly Midl,** Wiggleworm(s); **IN**35, **OH**90, Wigglyworms. **1983** *MJLF* 9.1.61 **ceKY** (as of 1956), *Wiggle worm . . a mosquito larva.*

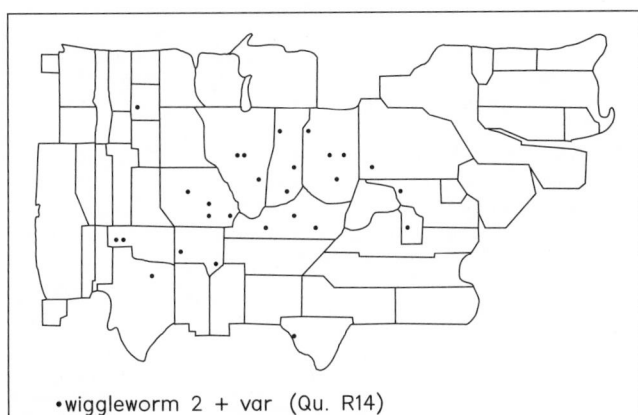

•wiggleworm 2 + var (Qu. R14)

wigglytail See **wiggletail 3**

wigglyworm See **wiggleworm 2**

wigtail See **wiggletail 1**

wigwam n

In logging: see quots; hence n *wigwam-maker.*

1905 *U.S. Forest Serv. Bulletin* 61.53 [Logging terms], *Wigwam, to*

make a. In felling trees, to lodge several in such a way that they support each other. (N[orthern] F[orest]) **1958** McCulloch *Woods Words* 211 **Pacific NW,** *Wigwam*—Two or more trees lodged together when falling timber. *Wigwam-maker*—A faller who has got himself into a jackpot with several cut trees wedged together.

wikiwiki adj, adv, exclam [Haw] **HI**

Quick; quickly.

1917 *Sunset* 38.23 **HI,** Wikiwiki! It's time I go to bed. **1932** *Oakland Tribune* (CA) 18 Jan mag sec 2/6 **HI,** I say dinnah on table now; boss he come wikiwiki or boss he get new cook heah. **1938** Reinecke *Hawaiian Loanwords* 32 **HI,** *Wikiwiki. . .* Quickly; in haste; right away. **1951** *AmSp* 26.21 **HI,** Handy phrases include *wikiwiki* (hurry up). **1967** Clark *All the Best HI* 55, *Wikiwiki*—hurry up; "step on it." **1969** *DARE* FW Addit **HI,** *Wikiwiki* ['wiki 'wiki] . . fast, speedy. **1972** Carr *Da Kine Talk* 118 **HI,** *Wikiwiki burger* (Hawaiian + English). A hamburger put together in a hurry and sold at drive-in restaurants. *Wikiwiki* is the popular reduplicated form of *wiki* 'to hurry', 'to hasten'. **1984** Sunset *HI Guide* 85, *Wikiwiki*—fast, hurry.

wikkit See **wicked** adv

wild alfalfa n

1 =**deerweed 1.** **CA**

1881 Van Dyke *Flirtation Camp* 109 **CA,** The golden blossoms of the wild alfalfa begin to glow on every hand. **1887** *Fresno Weekly Republican* (CA) 22 July [1]/4 (newspaperarchive.com), *Wild Alfalfa. . .* grows on the margin, and in the bottom of Huero . . Creek, as the water recedes. It is eaten by stock as readily as tame alfalfa is. The specimen in our office is about four feet long. It grows very thick and if left to itself, when it is two or three feet high it falls down as heavy grain does. **1911** Jepson *Flora CA* 232, *L[otus] glaber. . . Deer-weed. . .* Esteemed as a bee-plant in the southern part of the State and also called Deer-clover, Wild Broom and Wild Alfalfa. **1926** *Van Nuys News* (CA) 18 June 4/3, The bees of San Fernando Valley have plenty of feed to keep them working. After the orange blossoms become a thing of the past there follows wild alfalfa, sage and other wild flowers. **1967** *DARE* (Qu. S21, . . *Weeds . . that are a trouble in gardens and fields*) Inf **CA**7, Wild alfalfa. **1997** *Los Angeles Times* (CA) 24 Aug 17 (Internet), Prime, lush, organic, honey-producing sage, wild California buckwheat, hollyberry, wild alfalfa, . . and other nectar-producing acres are at least four years from recovering [from a fire].

2 A **scurf pea,** esp *Psoralidium tenuiflorum.* **chiefly Cent, Upper MW**

1918 Visher *Geog. SD* 81, The Legume family . . includes some of the more abundant plants of these plains, notably . . buffalo-bean, loco, lupine, and wild alfalfas. **1934** *Ecological Monogr.* 4.223 **West,** *Psoralea floribunda* [=*Psoralidium tenuiflorum*]. . . is sometimes called "wild alfalfa" and indeed where the stand is thickest the prairie appears at a distance like an old, partially deteriorated field of alfalfa. **1954** *Amer. Midland Naturalist* 51.328 **eNE,** Before the drought the most abundant forbs . . were lead plant (*Amorpha canescens*) . . and the many-flowered psoralea or wild alfalfa (*Psoralea floribunda*). **1961** Wills–Irwin *Flowers TX* 136, The Wild-alfalfas, *P[soralea] simplex* . . and *P. psoralioides . . var. glandulosa* [=*Psoralidium tenuiflorum*] . . are erect plants to 3 ft. in height with alfalfalike flowers. **1973** Lommasson *NE Wild Flowers* 49, In the past a common name of this plant was wild alfalfa, and fields of this scurf-pea have been mistaken for alfalfa. **2006** *DARE* File—Internet **KS** (as of 1998), [He] identified the walkingsticks' prairie host as a plant Kansans call wild alfalfa or scurf pea (depending on the part of the state).

3 =**lupine.**

1917 NV Ag. Exper. Sta. *Bulletin* 88.16, The lupines in Nevada are known by various common names, being improperly called blue bean, wild bean, wild alfalfa, blue pea. **1937** U.S. Forest Serv. *Range Plant Hdbk.* W112, These plants have many common names, including blue-bean, bluebonnet, blue-pea, quakerbonn[e]ts, wild-alfalfa, wildbean and wolf plant, although lupine . . is . . the name in most popular use.

wild allspice n

=**spicebush 1,** usu *Lindera benzoin.*

1762 Gronovius *Flora Virginica* 63, *Laurus foliis enervibus obverse ovatis utrinque acutis integris annuis. . . Nostratibus* Wild all Spice, vel Wild Pimento. **1789** in 1801 Crèvecoeur *Voyage* 3.208 **wPA,** Presque toutes les plantes et les fleurs qu'on cultive chez vous avec tant de soin, croissent ici spontanément; le buisson à épice *(wild all spice),* le ginseng [etc.]. [=Nearly all the plants and flowers which are cultivated so carefully where you are [=NJ] grow here spontaneously; the spice bush *(wild all spice)*, ginseng [etc].] **1837** Darlington *Flora Cestrica* 253 **sePA,** L[aurus] pseudo-benzoin. . . *Vulgò*—Spice-wood. Wild All-spice. **1860** Curtis *Cat. Plants NC* 91, *Wild Allspice.* . . An infusion of the twigs is sometimes used in country fevers, and for sickly cattle in the Spring. **1920** Saunders *Useful Wild Plants* 145, The common Spice-wood, Wild Allspice, or Feverbush. . . The whole bush is spicily fragrant, and a decoction of the twigs makes another pleasant substitute for tea. **1982** *Chron.–Telegram* (Elyria OH) 10 Jan sec E 8/2, Near the upper pond is a specimen of Wild Allspice, Benzoin aestivale.

wild almond n Cf **desert almond**

A tree or shrub of the genus *Prunus,* usu the western *P. fasciculata.*

1841 Audubon *Birds Amer.* 3.203, *Prunus caroliniana.* . . The *wild almond* is altogether a southern tree. **1875** *Amer. Naturalist* 9.17 **sUT,** *Prunus . . fasciculata.* . . By the inhabitants of the country it is known under the appropriate name of *"wild almond",* its small fruit, though bitter, being occasionally eaten. **1893** *Jrl. Amer. Folkl.* 6.140 **sUT,** *Prunus fasciculata,* wild almond. **1913** *Jrl. Ag. Research* 1.147, Small downy fruits with thin dry flesh which have won for them the local names "wild almond" in the Great Basin region, "wild peach" or "desert almond" for another form in the Mohave Desert. **1931** U.S. Dept. Ag. *Misc. Pub.* 101.69, Peachbrush (*Emplectocladus* spp). . . is known also as wild peach (brush) and wild almond. [*DARE* Ed: Species in *Emplectocladus* have been reassigned to *Prunus.*] **1976** *Fresno Bee* (CA) 3 Mar [15]/3 (newspaperarchive.com), California live oak trees surround the house. A few thin but white-blossoming wild almond trees have sprouted in between some of the spindly oaks.

wild alum n

1 A cranesbill 1; see quots. Cf **alumroot 2**

1891 U.S. Bur. Amer. Ethnology *Annual Rept. for 1885–86* 326, Geranium maculatum—Wild Alum, Cranesbill. . . One of our best indigenous astringents. **1910** *Amer. Botanist* 16.9 **ceKY,** The wild geranium I only knew as "wild alum" so called, probably, on account of the astringency of its roots. **1911** Porter *Harvester* 99 **IN,** He harvested the wild alum by hand, and heaped large stacks of roots around the edges of the bed. **1968** *DARE* FW Addit **VA,** Wild alum = cranesbill, wild geranium. Common, woods. **2005** *Charleston Gaz.* (WV) 30 Apr sec B 2 (Internet), Pure white trilliums are scattered over the forest floor, and wild geraniums (we always called these wild alum) add their pink hues.

2 An alumroot 1 such as *Heuchera villosa.*

1928 CA Dept. Ag. *Mth. Bulletin* 17.367, I have taken many specimens from wild alum root *(Heuchera)* and dogwood *(Cornus)* in the woods at La Honda, California. **1939** *Hall Coll.* **eTN,** Wild alum, that's the best thing I ever saw used for cholera marvus and diarrhea. **1969** *DARE* FW Addit **KY,** Wild alum—hairy alumroot *(Heuchera villosa)*. The roots are boiled down for diarrhea and stomachache. **2006** *DARE* File—Internet **TN,** Alumroot *(Heuchera americana) Wild Alum.*

wild angelica See **angelica 2**

wild anise n

1 A yampah. CA

1868 Amer. Acad. Arts & Sci. *Proc.* 7.344, *Carum kelloggii* [= *Perideridia k.*] . . According to Dr. Kellogg the plant is known as "Wild Anise," and the fruit yields a pleasant anisate odor. **1889** *Bot. Gaz.* 14.283 **CA,** *Carum Kelloggii.* . . The recorded range of this supposed rare species has been increased by its discovery in abundance in Tuolumne county, California, August, 1889 . . , thus extending it throughout the central part of the state, where it is known as "wild anise." **1925** *Oakland Tribune* (CA) 21 Sept 8/1, I feed the caterpillers [sic] on wild anise and dahlia leaves. **2006** *DARE* File—Internet **CA,** The common name Anise Swallowtail comes from a California hostplant, a *Perideridia* species, also named "wild anise" or "Yampah".

2 =sweet fennel. Cf **sweet anise 2**

1927 Comstock *Butterflies CA* 20, The Anise Swallowtail. . . is most abundant in the lowlands, about townsites, where an introduced wild anise or fennel now furnishes its favorite food-plant. **1950** *Oxnard Press–Courier* (CA) 20 May 8/4, Weed killers, such as 2,4-D are successful on broad-leafed weeds, such as plantain and wild anise. **1973** *Austin Statesman* (TX) 14 May [5]/3 (newspaperarchive.com) **CA,** The entree was clams stuffed with breadcrumbs, cheese, wild anise and dock. **1979** Spellenberg *Audubon Guide N. Amer. Wildflowers W. Region* 329, Sweet Fennel. . . is sometimes called Wild Anise, although true Anise is of the genus *Pimpinella.*

3 A sweet cicely, usu *Osmorhiza longistylis.* Cf **anise root, sweet anise 1**

1931 *Decatur Herald* (IL) 26 Apr 10/2, Scattered thickly over the floor of the valley there grows also sweet Cicely or wild anise. **1963** Cook Co. IL Forest Preserve *Nature Bulletin* 7 Dec (Internet), A wild anise, called Sweet Cicely, is one of the most common plants in our forest preserve woodlands. **2006** *DARE* File—Internet, *Osmorhiza claytoni.* . . Also named: wild anise, sweet Jarvil, woolly sweet-cicely. . . The plant. . . is anise or licorice scented.

wild apple n

=squaw apple.

1931 U.S. Dept. Ag. *Misc. Pub.* 101.66, *Peraphyllum ramosissimum.* . . is of an almost innumerable series of western shrubs called buckbrush, and is often known locally as wild apple or wild peach, and in Oregon as Oregon apple. **1938** Van Dersal *Native Woody Plants* 323, Apple. . . Wild *(Peraphyllum ramosissimum).*

wild apricot See **apricot B**

wild arsenic n VA, S Atl

=spotted wintergreen.

1825 *Amer. Farmer* 6.381 **csVA,** *Pipsisaway—Cure For Rheumatism.* . . It is here called wild arsenic, or wild ratsbane, and the most poisonous qualities are ascribed to it. **1869** *S. Cultivator* 27.256 **cSC,** Goslings are generally poisoned by the "milk weed" or "Wild arsenic." **1877** *Atlanta Med. & Surgical Jrl.* 15.525 **neGA,** The *chimaphila maculata* . . grows quite abundantly in . . eastern counties, where it is popularly called wild arsenic. It is also found in Fulton county, where it passes under the name of wild ratsbane. **1892** *Jrl. Amer. Folkl.* 5.100 **swVA,** *Chimaphila maculata,* ratsbane; wild arsenic. Blue Ridge, Va.

wild artichoke n

1 A sunflower 1, usu **Jerusalem artichoke.**

1845 *Merry's Museum* 10.340, We had collected fourteen sprigs of bayberry, half a dozen handfuls of pennyroyal, seven huge dandelions, and one wild artichoke. These . . were carefully laid by on shelves to dry, to be taken down and administered in the various forms of infusion, decoction, and potion, as occasion might require. **1851** *Davenport Gaz.* (IA) 13 Mar [2]/4 (newspaperarchive.com), Hogs . . also eat a great many wild artichoke roots. **1860** U.S. Congress Senate *Statist. Rept. Sickness* 40 **seSD,** After the potatoes gave out . . the disease [=scurvy] showed a strong disposition to return. I then commenced with the wild artichoke—a most excellent antiscorbutic and substitute for the potato. **1885** *Amer. Naturalist* 19.114 **seIN,** A large quantity of the tuberous roots of the plant commonly called "wild artichoke" (*Helianthus doronicoides* . .) were found in one of the store-houses of a colony of these mice. **1908** *Stevens Point Jrl.* (WI) 5 Sept [7]/2 (newspaperarchive.com), The wild artichoke has taken possession of many fields during the summer where small grains were sowed last spring. **1966–70** *DARE* (Qu. S7, *A kind of daisy, bright yellow with a dark center, that grows along roadsides in late summer*) Inf **OH95,** Wild artichoke; (Qu. S21, . . *Weeds . . that are a trouble in gardens and fields*) Inf **NJ29,** Wild artichoke; (Qu. S26a, . . *Wildflowers. . . Roadside flowers*) Infs **NC36, VA24,** Wild artichoke(s). **1966** *DARE* Wildfl QR Pl.256 [= *Helianthus giganteus*] Inf **AR46,** Wild artichokes. **2006** *DARE* File—Internet, *Helianthus resinosus.* . . Resindot Sunflower is also known as Wild Artichoke and Woodland Sunflower.

2 An introduced invasive plant *(Cynara cardunculus)* common throughout most of California.

[**1843** (1844) Johnson *Farmer's Encycl.* 264, Cardoon, or Chardon . . *Cynara cardunculus.* . . A kind of wild artichoke, which is principally confined to garden culture, as it has not yet been employed as an article of food for any sort of live stock.] **1915** *San Jose Mercury Herald* (CA) 16 May 15/5, *Extermination of Wild Artichoke Means Hundreds of Acres for Cultivation.* . . In no other county has the thistle—which is nothing more nor less than artichoke run wild—attained such a stronghold. **1931** *Woodland Daily Democrat* (CA) 3 Apr [8]/4 (newspaperarchive.com), Dr. Robbins and Walter S. Ball of the State Department of Agriculture . . are making a study of certain grazing lands which are infested with wild artichoke. **1969** *DARE* (Qu. S26a, . . *Wildflowers. . . Roadside flowers*) Inf **CA107,** Wild artichokes. **1987** *Los Angeles Times* (CA) 4 Oct 1 (Internet), Tidwell said he has seen some field mice and small birds eat some of the wild artichoke seeds, but cattle won't touch them. **2006** *Orange Co. Reg.* (Santa Ana CA) 29 June 1 (Internet), As you clear the green canopy and ride along the Lone Pine Ridge Trail, you can see the bright purple from the wild artichokes.

3 =**jack-in-the-pulpit 1.**

1968 *DARE* (Qu. S1, . . *Jack-in-the-pulpit*) Inf **MN**19, Wild artichoke.

4 A **hedgenettle** (here: *Stachys floridana*) native to the southern US.   Cf **Chinese artichoke, Japanese ~**

1966 *DARE* (Qu. S21, . . *Weeds . . that are a trouble in gardens and fields*) Inf **FL**16, Wild artichoke.   **1969** *Florence Morning News* (SC) 1 Dec sec A 5/4, *Skull Cap*. . . is a perennial broad leaf weed that resembles the mint plant that is a real pest in beds of azaleas and camellias. . . The plant is sometimes called wild artichoke because of the underground white finger-sized tubers that look like artichokes.   **1996** *FL Times-Union* (Jacksonville) 3 Feb sec D 2 (Internet), Rattlesnake weed, also known as Florida betony and wild artichoke, is one of the common weeds that cannot be effectively pulled. It has a tuber that resembles a grubworm and it will regrow rapidly from that tuber.

wild asparagus n

1   The young shoots of a **greenbrier**, esp **China brier.**

[**1869** Porcher *Resources* 616, The young shoots of the China-briar are eaten as asparagus, with which they are closely allied.]   **1889** *Good Housekeeping* 8.202 **SE**, I went to a colored vendor for information as to the time the "wild asparagus" would be in market. . . This pseudo asparagus is nothing more than the young suckers of the China-briar.   **1901** MT Ag. Exper. Sta. *Bulletin* 30.46, *Lygodesmia juncea*. . . Wild asparagus; Skeleton-weed.   **1910** Graves *Flowering Plants* 125 **CT**, *Smilax herbacea*. . . The young shoots are sometimes used as a pot-herb and are called Wild Asparagus.   **1954** *PADS* 21.41 **seSC**, *Wild asparagus*. . . The tender shoots of the bull briar, purveyed in season in bunches and used as a vegetable.   **1967** *DARE* FW Addit, [From a Charleston SC cookbook:] *Chainey Briar* = wild asparagus.   **2007** *DARE* File—Internet **FL**, *Smilax laurifolia*. . . Wild asparagus is the term for the young shoots that are a favorite in salads (or sautéed).

2 =**skeletonweed 3.**

1917 Rydberg *Flora Rocky Mts.* 1023, *Lygodesmia* . . Wild Asparagus, Skeleton-weed, Prairie Pink.   **1938** *Helena Independent* (MT) 20 Apr 6/6, Skeleton weed, known as rush pink or wild asparagus, appears almost leafless.

3   A **milkweed 1** (here: *Asclepias syriaca*).

1997 in **2007** *DARE* File—Internet **KS**, *Milkweed (Common)*. . . *Asclepias syriaca*. . . Also called Milk plant, Wild asparagus, Silkweed, and Wild cotton. . . In the spring, many Native American tribes cooked the young shoots and ate them as an asparagus-like food. . . The shoots were throughly [sic] boiled with a change of water before being eaten.

wild ax-handle   See **ax-handle 2**

wild bachelor's button n

1 =**chicory 1.**

1896 *Jrl. Amer. Folkl.* 9.191 **MA**, *Cichorium Intybus*, . . wild bachelors' buttons.   **1906** (1918) Parsons *Wild Flowers CA* 306, Whole fields may often be seen covered with its [=*Cichorium intybus*'s] lovely bright-blue blossoms, which are known as "ragged sailors," and "wild bachelor's-buttons."   **1968** *DARE* (Qu. S11, . . *Bachelor's button*) Inf **PA**99, Chicory, wild bachelor button.

2   A **milkwort:** either **orange milkwort** or *Polygala nana.* Cf **bachelor wort**

1897 Britton–Brown *Illustr. Flora* 2.356, *Polygala lutea*. . . Orange Milkwort. Wild Bachelor's Button.   **1949** Moldenke *Amer. Wild Flowers* 51, On the coastal plain . . one may commonly find the spectacularly beautiful *wildbachelorsbutton*, *candyweed* or *orangemilkwort*, *Pilostaxis lutea* [=*Polygala lutea*].   **2006** *DARE* File—Internet **FL**, *Polygala*. . . *Wild bachelor's button*. . . This small plant is common in wet flatwoods, bogs and coastal swales throughout [sic] most of Florida, with locations becoming more scattered towards the northern part of the range which extends into Tennessee and North Carolina.   **2007** *Ibid, Polygala nana*. . . Wild bachelor's button, also known as candy root or dwarf milkwort, can be found in moist pinelands, often growing up between dead pine needles. This herb is most easily recognizable by its fuzzy yellow ball shaped flowers that bloom from March to October.

3   A **star thistle;** see quots.

1927 *Sheboygan Press* (WI) 20 Aug 10/6, Brown-eyed Susans and wild bachelor buttons mingled their gold and sapphire along the road.   **1995** *Grand Rapids Press* (MI) 20 Apr sec D 12 (Internet), A new wildflower is the knapweed, or wild bachelor button. It resembles a thistle, with its purple blossom, but the leaves are soft not prickly. It is an immigrant from Canada. It was introduced there by settlers from Russia,

who brought it along accidentally with their wheat seed from the vast steppes.   **2007** *DARE* File—Internet, *Centaurea cyanus*—cornflower; blue-bottle; wild bachelor's button.

wild balsam n

1   See **balsam 2.**

2   A **yerba santa** (here: *Eriodictyon californicum*).   Cf **mountain balsam 3**

1902 U.S. Natl. Museum *Contrib. Herbarium* 7.381 **nCA**, *Eriodictyon californicum*. . . The well-known yerba santa . . of California, a dark-green resinous shrub, . . is known under the names . . mountain balm, wild balsam, gum leaves, tar weed. . . No plant is more highly valued as a medicine by all the tribes of Mendocino County.

3   also *wild balsam apple, ~ gourd:* A cucurbitaceous vine of the genus *Ibervillea*, native to Arizona, New Mexico, Oklahoma, and Texas.   esp **TX**   Also called **balsam gourd, globe-berry**

1936 Whitehouse *TX Flowers* 148, Wild balsam gourd (*Ibervillea lindheimeri*) has bright scarlet balls about an inch in diameter and makes conspicuous spots of color on fences in the fall.   **1937** TX Ag. Exper. Sta. College Sta. *Bulletin* 551.134, *Ibervillea Lindheimeri*. . . Wild Balsam Apple. A little known beautiful ornamental. . . produces . . fruits one inch in length . . [that] turn bright red and . . hang in clusters.   **1966** *DARE* Wildfl QR Pl.51A (Wills–Irwin) [=*Ibervillea lindheimeri*] Inf **TX**44, Wild balsam.   **c1979** TX Dept. Highways *Flowers* 54, *Wild Balsam* flowers in early summer . . throughout Central Texas. . . The fruit of this climbing gourd is red when mature, and clings to the plant through fall. *Ibervillea lindheimeri*.   **2005** in **2007** *DARE* File—Internet **sTX**, *Ibervillea tenella* . . (Wild Balsam, Yerba-de-vibrona, Snake Eggs).   **2007** (acc) TX A&M Univ. *Plantanswer Machine* (Internet), *Ibervillea Lindheimeri*. Wild Balsam Apple. This heavy underground native tuber produces . . fruits having the appearance of tiny green watermelons, until they turn bright red in late summer.

wild balsam apple n

1   also *balsam apple:* A **wild cucumber 1a** (here: *Echinocystis lobata*).

1840 MA Zool. & Bot. Surv. *Herb. Plants & Quadrupeds* 113, *M[omordica] echinata* [=*Echinocystis lobata*]. . . Balsam Apple. Wild Cucumber.   **1870** *Amer. Naturalist* 4.584 **IA**, **nIL**, Other climbers are frequent, including the singular wild cucumber, or balsam apple (*Echinocystis lobata* . .), here and there abundantly enveloping the trees.   **1881** *Atlantic Mth.* 48.695, Nor had she any eyes for the roving intricacies of the greenbrier and wild-balsam apple.   **1906** *Daily Northwestern* (Oshkosh WI) 4 Dec [13]/7 (newspaperarchive.com), In the brooks of autumn . . little lacelike bags may be seen drifting along. . . They are the inner coats or bodies of the wild balsam apples (Echinocystis lobata) which have dropped from the vines overhanging the stream.   **1954** *Monessen Daily Independent* (PA) 19 Nov 4/7, Here and there in the underbrush the empty husks of wild balsam apple hung across the bushes which this cousin to the cucumber had chosen to clamber over.   **1967** *DARE* FW Addit **AR**44, Wild balsam apple—*Micrampelis* [= *Echinocystis*] *lobata*.   **2006** *DARE* File—Internet **MA**, *Wild Cucumber or Wild Balsam Apple, Echinocystis lobata*—Some of the tiny white flowers on this climbing vine will develop into large (walnut sized) spiny two-chambered capsules containing two large seeds.

2   A **balsam pear,** usu *Momordica charantia.*   [*OED2 balsam apple* (at *balsam* sb. 10) 1578 →]

1933 Small *Manual SE Flora* 1285, *M[omordica] Charantia*. . . (*Wild balsam-apple*.)—Hammocks, thickets, and waste-places, outer Coastal Plain, Fla. to Tex.   **1953** Greene–Blomquist *Flowers South* 124, Wild Balsam-Apple (*Momordica Charantia*).   **1970** Correll *Plants TX* 1508, *Momordica Charantia* . . Wild balsam-apple. . . Naturalized in thickets and waste places in s.e. Tex.   **2006** *DARE* File—Internet **swFL**, *Powell Creek Preserve*. . . Problem plants include air potato (*Dioscorea bulbifera*), wild balsam apple (*Momordica charantia*), Java plum (*Syzgium cumini*), woman's tongue (*Albizia auriculiformis*) [etc].

3   See **wild balsam 3.**

wild balsam gourd   See **wild balsam 3**

wild bamboo n

1   also *wild bamboo vine:* A **greenbrier** (here: *Smilax auriculata*).   Cf **bamboo, bamboo vine**

1876 Andrews *Family Secret* 70 **GA**, Here, the wild bamboo and scarlet trumpet-vine might be seen interlacing their tendrils with the rarest of creeping roses. **1896** *Amer. Missionary* 50.279 **GA,** On Wednesday, palms, magnolias, cape jasmine, and wild bamboo-vine have lent their charm to render the chapel a fragrant abode of beauty. **1933** Small *Manual SE Flora* 313, *S[milax auriculata]*. . . Wild-bamboo. **1940** *Panama City News–Herald* (FL) 13 Dec 6/1, The windows were outlined with wild bamboo vines, smilax, holly and cedar. . . for the Christmas program. **1956** *Charleston Gaz.* (WV) 16 Nov 25/2, Some of the materials used by the women and which came from this area are milkweed pods, . . pine needles, wild bamboo, . . magnolia leaves [etc]. **2003** in 2007 *DARE* File—Internet **NC,** Past the beds / of the dead camellias, each shrub threaded through / with a rusted snarl of wild bamboo.

2 A small cane *(Lasiacis divaricata)* native to southern Florida.

1965 Kimball *Lepidoptera FL* 336, *Lasiacis divaricata*. . . (wild bamboo). **1996** Nelson *Shrubs & Vines FL* 8, Wild Bamboo, Small Cane, Florida Tibisee—*Lasiacis divaricata*. . . The bamboolike appearance, rigid stem, and shiny black seeds set this species apart from most other south Florida plants.

wild bamboo vine See **wild bamboo 1**

wild banana See **banana B1**

wild barley n

Std: a wild plant of the genus *Hordeum,* usu *H. jubatum.* For other names of this sp see **flickertail grass, foxtail 1, squirreltail (grass) 1, tickle grass e**

wild basil n

Any of var aromatic plants of the mint family, as:

a A native plant of the genus *Clinopodium,* usu *C. vulgare.* For other names of the latter see **dog mint**

1698 Royal Soc. London *Philos. Trans.* 20.402 **MD,** Satureia Virginiana [=*Clinopodium vulgare*]. . . *Dr. Herman's* Virginiana *Wild Basil* with yellow Flowers. **1840** MA Zool. & Bot. Surv. *Herb. Plants & Quadrupeds* 178, *C. vulgare* . . Wild Basil. Field Thyme. Found in rocky woods, and doubtless indigenous to this country. **1900** IN Dept. Geol. & Nat. Resources *Rept. for 1899* 909, *C[linopodium] vulgare*. . . Wild Basil. Basil-weed. . . Confined to the counties fronting the Ohio River, and there found but sparingly. **1947** *Amer. Midland Naturalist* 38.56 **MD,** *Satureja vulgaris* [=*Clinopodium v.*] (Wild-basil). **1995** *Torrey Bot. Club Bulletin* 122.71 **NY,** Blooming along roadsides and trail margins were Wild Basil *(Satureja vulgaris)* [etc].

b =**dittany.**

1787 Schöpf *Materia Medica Amer.* 5, Cunila mariana. . . *Wild Basil; Dittany*. . . *Loc.* Pensylvaniae, Marylandiae, Virginiae sicca [=dry places in Pennsylvania, Maryland, and Virginia]. **1828** Rafinesque *Med. Flora* 1.136, *Cunila Mariana.* . . Mountain Dittany, Stone Mint, Wild Basil, Sweet Horsemint. **1900** Lyons *Plant Names* 125, C[unila] origanoides. . . New York to Ohio and south to Florida. . . Wild Basil. . . *Herb* diaphoretic. **2007** *DARE* File—Internet **VA,** Dittany (Maryland cunila, stone mint, wild basil). Cunila origanoides.

c =**mountain mint 2,** esp *Pycnanthemum incanum* or *P. virginianum.*

1814 Bigelow *Florula Bostoniensis* 147 **MA,** Pycnanthemum incanum. . . Wild Basil. **1830** Rafinesque *Med. Flora* 2.254, *Pycnanthemum*. . . *Mountain mint, Wild Basil.* Aromatic plants. **1854** King *Amer. Eclectic Dispensatory* 785, There are several species of this genus [=*Pycnanthemum*] which possess similar medicinal properties, as. . . the *P[ycnanthemum] Aristatum,* or *Wild Basil.* **1910** *OH Naturalist* 10.81, *Pycnanthemum incanum.* . . Wild Basil. . . *Leaves and tops.* **2007** *DARE* File—Internet **VA,** Pycnanthemum virginianum is typically used as a flavoring. Virginia mountain mint (sometimes called wild basil and prairie hyssop) is most commonly used cooked.

wild bean n

1 Any of var legumes, spec:

a =**hog peanut 1.**

1844 Lapham *Geogr. Descr. WI* 78, Amphicarpæa monoica [=*A. bracteata*] . . Wild Bean. **1892** Gibson *Sharp Eyes* 165, It is the delicate "wild bean;" and if the threefold leaf and long raceme of pale drooping blossoms do not at once suggest the name, a little further search will disclose the telltale cluster of flat pods, like tiny Limas hanging among the leaves. [**1921** *Annals IA* (3d ser) 12.606, There is a native wild bean found growing over an area of wide distribution in North America. The botanical name of this bean is *Falcata comosa* [=*Amphi-*

carpaea bracteata].] **1967** *DARE* Wildfl QR Pl.118A [=*Amphicarpaea bracteata*] Inf **WA30,** Wild bean.

b A **groundnut B1** (here: *Apios americana*).

1832 MA Hist. Soc. *Coll.* 2d ser 9.150 **VT,** Plants, which are indigenous in the township of Middlebury . . Glycine. . . apios [=*Apios americana*], Slender wild bean. **1843** (1844) Johnson *Farmer's Encycl.* 594, *Ground-nut (Apios tuberosa. . .)* sometimes called wild bean. **1882** *Defiance Democrat* (OH) 6 July 1/6, The ground nut or wild bean, *apios tuberosa,* is the modo, or wild potato, of the Sioux Indians. . . It is said that when properly boiled it is by no means unpalatable, but should not be confounded with the ground nut of the south. **1908** *Ft. Wayne Jrl.–Gaz.* (IN) 24 May 5/2, A-pe-kon-it is what we know as the "ground nut," or "wild bean" (apios tuberosa), which grows in low ground. **1934** *Charleston Daily Mail* (WV) 7 Dec 10/3, Among the better wild foods he mentioned . . the wild bean, whose tubers are starchy and when cooked taste somewhat like a white potato. **1972** *Sun. Gaz.–Mail* (Charleston WV) 8 Oct [84]/4 (newspaperarchive.com), We call it wild bean or ground nut (Apios americana). **2005** in 2007 *DARE* File—Internet **CT,** *Ground Nut (Wild Bean)—Apios americana.* . . Vine up to 10 feet long. . . Native.

c A plant of the genus *Phaseolus,* esp *P. polystachios,* which is native to most of the eastern and southern US.

1848 Gray *Manual of Botany* 95, P[haseolus] perennis [=*P. polystachios*]. . . Perennial Wild Bean. . . Copses, Connecticut to Penn. and southward. **1859** (1968) Bartlett *Americanisms* 512, Wild Bean. (*Phaseolus diversifolius* [=*P. polystachios*].) A plant common in the alluvial bottoms of the West, the Wild Potato of the Sioux Indians, much used as food. **1896** *Bot. Gaz.* 21.233, Our common northern wild bean, *P[haseolus] polystachyus* [sic]. **1933** *Ecology* 14.178, *Phaseolus polystachyus* [sic] . . Wild bean. **1954** *Amer. Midland Naturalist* 52.298 **GA,** *Phaseolus polystachios*. . . Wild bean. . . *P. sinuatus*. . . Wild bean. **2007** *DARE* File—Internet **GA,** *Phaseolus polystachios* (wild bean).

d A plant of the genus *Strophostyles,* which is native to much of the eastern two-thirds of the US.

1872 Schele de Vere *Americanisms* 410, The *Wild-bean* (Phaseolus diversifolius [=*Strophostyles helvula*]) is also known as the *Wild Potato* of several Indian tribes. **1898** *Jrl. Amer. Folkl.* 11.225 **KS,** *Strophostyles angulosa* [=*S. helvola*] . . wild bean. . . *Strophostyles pauciflorus* [=*S. leiosperma*] . . wild bean. **1932** *Ecological Monogr.* 2.227, *Strophostyles helvola* . . Wild Bean. **1977** *Atlas Flora Gt. Plains* 183, *Strophostyles helvola.* . . Wild Bean. *Ibid* 184, *Strophostyles leiosperma.* . . Smoothseed Wild Bean. **2005** *Torrey Bot. Soc. Jrl.* 132.372 **seNY,** We walked to the far southwest corner of the parcel to examine the wild-bean . . in flower, and determined that it was not *S[trophostyles]* umbellata, but the more common *S. helvola,* which itself is rare in New York City.

e A **snoutbean,** which is native to the southern and southwestern US; see quots.

1889 KS Acad. Sci. *Trans.* 12.63 **TX,** Rhynchosia volubilis [=*R. difformis*]. . . Wild bean. **1944** *Condor* 46.207 **AZ,** Seeds of unidentified species of sweet clover *(Melilotus),* trefoil *(Lotus),* and wild bean *(Rhynchosia)* were found in Arizona specimens [of white-winged dove]. **2007** (acc) LA State Univ. *Herbarium* (Internet), *Rhynchosia minima.* . . *Common Name:* Wild bean.

f =**lupine.** West, esp MT

1901 U.S. Dept. Ag. Div. Entomol. *Bulletin* 26.100 **MT,** *Lupinus* spp. . . Other names: Blue pea, . . Pea vine. . . A number of stockmen call these plants lupines, but perhaps the names wild bean, blue bean, and blue pea are more generally applied to them in Montana. **1906** *Anaconda Std.* (MT) 11 Mar 22/6, The lupine, or as it is commonly known, the wild bean, poisoned 3,000 sheep, of which 1,900 died. **1929** *Helena Independent* (MT) 19 Jan 3/3, Poisonous plants include the hemlock, the wild bean, poisonous to sheep, and the locoweed, which gives animals a habit similar to the drug habit. **1953** *Soda Springs Sun* (ID) 31 Dec 5/3, Wild bean or lupine is the most abundant poisonous plant in Caribou county.

2 Usu =**black bindweed;** occas another **smartweed. esp NEng**

1784 in 1785 *Amer. Acad. Arts & Sci. Memoirs* 1.440 **sePA,** *Black bindweed. Wild bean.* Blossoms greenish white. About barns and in corn fields. **1851** (1993) Thoreau *Yr. Jrl.* 187 **eMA,** I suspect that the common wild bean vine of the gardens must be the Polygonum Convolvulus or Black bindweed. **1891** *Jrl. Amer. Folkl.* 4.148 **swNH,** Several vines of the same genus [=*Polygonum*] we knew only as *Wild Bean,* evidently from the form of the leaves. **1897** *Ibid* 10.54 **ME,** *Polygonum convol-*

vulus, . . wild bean. **1929** *Torreya* 29.150 **ME,** Polygonum Convolvulus we knew as *"Wild Bean."*

wild beet n

Any of var plants used as greens, as:

a An **evening primrose a:** usu *Oenothera fruticosa,* but also *O. biennis.*

1892 WV Ag. Exper. Sta. *Bulletin* 23.237, Sun-drops. "Wild Beet." . . *(Oenothera fruticosa).* . . This plant when young is used with the last [= *O. biennis*] as a pot herb . . , and in domestic practice meets with the same medicinal use. It is also used for croup . . , and as a vulnerary for recent wounds. **1940** Clute *Amer. Plant Names* 93, *O[enothera] fruticosa.* Sundrops. Wild beet, scabish. *Ibid* 265, *Oenothera biennis.* Cradle weed, wild beet, wild coffeeweed. **2002** in 2007 *DARE* File—Internet, Oenothera Biennis. Other Names: Common Evening Primrose, . . Wild beet. . . The leaves are cooked and eaten as greens and the roots are said to be sweet succulent and delicious when boiled like potatoes.

b An **amaranth,** usu *Amaranthus hybridus* or *A. retroflexus.*

1897 *Jrl. Amer. Folkl.* 10.53 **ME,** *Amaranthus retroflexus,* . . wild beet. . . Said to taste like beets when cooked for "greens." **1934** *Newark Advocate* (OH) 16 May 9/3, Some of the greens used in the [cooking] demonstration were: Plantain, . . wild lettuce, nettles and wild beet. **1955** *Charleston Gaz.* (WV) 1 May [75]/1 (newspaperarchive.com), Weed hunters are on the prowl. . . snipping off tender shoots of mouse ear, wild beet, rock lettuce or a dozen other varieties of Spring plants. **1966–69** *DARE* (Qu. S21, . . *Weeds . . that are a trouble in gardens and fields*) Infs **AR**24, **MO**19, Wild beets. **1968** *DARE* Tape **IN**32, I get mountain sprouts, sourdock, wild beets, shawnee, crow foot, deer tongue, hen pepper, and oh so many others. **1986** Pederson *LAGS Concordance,* 1 inf, **cLA,** Wild beet. **2007** *DARE* File—Internet **ID,** *Amaranthus hybridus.* . . Green amaranth; Pigweed; Smooth Pigweed; Wild beet. . . *Amaranthus retroflexus*—Green amaranth; Pigweed; Redroot; Rough Pigweed; Wild beet.

c A **saxifrage** n² (here: *Saxifraga pensylvanica*). **esp NEast** Cf **swamp beet**

1898 *Jrl. Amer. Folkl.* 11.226 **ME,** *Saxifraga Pennsylvanica,* . . wild beet, swamp beet. **1929** *Torreya* 29.150 **ME,** Saxifraga pennsylvanica was used as greens, and never called anything but *"Wild Beet."* **1966** *DARE* (Qu. S26a, . . *Wildflowers . . Roadside flowers*) Inf **ME**7, Wild beet. **2007** *DARE* File—Internet **NJ,** *Saxifraga pensylvanica*—Swamp Saxifrage, Pennsylvania Saxifrage, Wild Beet. . . Native Plant List.

d A **wintergreen 1** (here: *Pyrola asarifolia* subsp *bracteata*).

1937 St. John *Flora SE WA & ID* 307, *Pyrola bracteata* [=*P. asarifolia* subsp *bracteata*]. . . Wild Beet.

wild begonia n [See quot 2003]

A **dock** n¹ (here: usu *Rumex venosus*).

1899 Knapp *In Christmas Woods* 13 **CA,** But by what long process of evolution has come from that common ancestor . . the wild begonia here at my feet. **1917** Rydberg *Flora Rocky Mts.* 231, *R[umex] venosus.* . . Wild Begonia, Sour Greens, Wild Hydrangea. **1931** *Fayetteville Daily Democrat* (AR) 16 May 4/3, There are lady's-slippers, bloodroot, . . wild begonia, wild ginger—all found and brought in from our own Ozark hills of Arkansas. **1938** *Helena Independent* (MT) 30 July 7/6, Canadian thistles, white top, bindweed, . . and wild begonia have increased. **1968** *DARE* (Qu. S26c, *Wildflowers that grow in woods*) Inf **VA**24, Wild begonia. **2003** in 2007 *DARE* File—Internet, *Rumex venosus.* . . Wild Begonia. . . The reddish-orange flower clusters are conspicuous in the late spring. Although their pale translucence and shape are reminiscent of clusters of begonias (hence one of the common names), this plant is not closely related to begonias.

wild bergamot n

1 A **horsemint 1,** esp *Monarda fistulosa.* For other names of this sp see **Oswego tea**

1833 Eaton *Botany* 228, *Monarda.* . . *oblongata* [=*M. fistulosa*]. . . wild burgamot. **1848** in 1850 Cooper *Rural Hours* 117 **NY,** Hummingbirds. . . are partial, to the bee larkspur also, with the wild bergamot or Oswego tea. **1892** Torrey Bot. Club *Bulletin* 19.45, The verbenas . . and the mountain mint . . and wild bergamot (*Monarda fistulosa*) do not prevail in waste land in New Jersey. **1945** *Copeia* 2.63 **OH,** In a shallow prairie swale. . . the characteristic plants growing there are . . wild bergamot (*Monarda fistulosa*), scattered saplings of *Crataegus* [etc]. **1967** *DARE* Wildfl QR Pl.190A [=*Monarda fistulosa*] Inf **OH**14, Wild bergamont. **1968** *DARE* (Qu. S26e, *Other wildflowers not yet mentioned;* not asked in early QRs) Inf **OH**61, Wild bergamot, a mint.

2006 *Pittsburgh Tribune–Rev.* (PA) 9 July (Internet), One species of the group is Monarda fistulosa, wild bergamot. . . Wild bergamot is native to North America and found nowhere else in the world, a homegrown wildflower.

2 A mint (here: *Mentha arvensis*).

1897 *Jrl. Amer. Folkl.* 10.53 **ME,** *Mentha Canadensis* [=*M. arvensis*], . . wild bergamot or bergamont.

wild black cherry See **black cherry**

wild boar n Cf **wild hog** n, **~ pig**

=**jabalina.** Note: The feral *Sus scrofa* is not treated here.

1892 *DN* 1.191 **TX,** Wild boar, peccary. **1894** *Scribner's Mag.* 15.603 **csTX,** Lucky indeed will be the guest who shall be invited to partake of . . stewed "jabalin," or wild boar. **1924** Freeman *Down Grand Canyon* 36, As it was a hulking wild boar that I wanted above all other specimens for my trophy room, these signs of the presence and plenitude of the festive *javelina* were more than welcome. **1997** in 2007 *DARE* File—Internet **TX,** [Inside Hudson's kitchen, the snarling javelina (a wild boar common to South Texas scrubland) becomes a chile-infused explosion of flavor.] **2007** *Ibid* **sTX,** If you are looking for a challenge, come take on one of the most wily animals in South Texas hunting! . . Whether you are wild boar hunting from a blind or stalking the wild boar, your trophy will round out any . . collection. . . Our 27,000 acres of South Texas brushland and river bottom provide the perfect habitat for javelina hunting.

wild bouvardia n

A **gilia** (here: *Collomia grandiflora*).

1897 Parsons *Wild Flowers CA* 178, From the resemblance of its showy buff or salmon-colored flowers to the *Bouvardias* of our gardens, these plants [=*Collomia grandiflora*] are popularly known as "wild Bouvardia." The blossoms are found in early summer, and grow usually in dry places, exposed to the sun. **1915** (1926) Armstrong–Thornber *Western Wild Flowers* 400, *Collomia grandiflora.* . . This is quite common in Yosemite. . . It is sometimes called Wild Bouvardia, but this is a poor name, as it is that of a plant belonging to an entirely different family. **2006** in 2007 *DARE* File—Internet **CA,** *Collomia grandiflora.* . . Wild Bouvardia. . . Buff Gilia.

wild bridal-wreath See **bridal-wreath 2**

wild broom n

=**deerweed 1.**

1897 Parsons *Wild Flowers CA* 152, Deer-weed. Wild Broom. . . This graceful, willowy plant . . is as ornamental as any of the small-flowered foreign . . brooms, we grow in our gardens. **1936** *Fresno Bee the Republican* (CA) 24 May sec D 3/3, The low bush covered with sprays of tiny yellow flowers tipped with red is the wild broom. **1954** *Ibid* 31 May sec B 2/3, Underneath those . . are masses of azure beard tongue, . . wild broom, brass buttons, . . and lanterns of the fairies.

wild broom corn n

A **reed 1** (here: *Phragmites australis*).

[**1896** Britton–Brown *Illustr. Flora* 1.184, *Phragmites.* . . Tall perennial reed-like grasses, with broad flat leaves and ample panicles.] **1898** *Ibid* 3.559, Broom . . Corn, Wild. **1910** Graves *Flowering Plants* 70 **CT,** *Phragmites communis.* . . Wild Broom Corn. Borders of marshes, either salt or fresh. Apparently rare inland. **1939** Medsger *Edible Wild Plants* 227, From the large panicle and the size of the stalk, the plant is sometimes called Wild Broomcorn.

wild buckwheat n

1 Any of several plants of the genus *Polygonum,* but esp **black bindweed** or **climbing false buckwheat;** see quots. [Cf *OED2 running buckwheat* (at *buckwheat* sb. 2) 1548 → for *Polygonum convolvulus*] **chiefly Nth** Cf **buckwheat 4**

1793 Amer. Philos. Soc. *Trans.* 3.259 **NY,** A variety of plants . . are agreeable to the bees, such as the Polygonum *scandens,* or *Wild-buckwheat,* and many others. **1837** Darlington *Flora Cestrica* 252 **sePA,** *P[olygonum] Convolvulus.* . . Wild Buckwheat. Black Bindweed. **1850** *Janesville Gaz.* (WI) 26 Dec [4]/8 (newspaperarchive.com), I had a large harvest, much of it in bad condition to cut, being full of grass and wild buckwheat. **1897** *Jrl. Amer. Folkl.* 10.54 **SD,** *Polygonum dumetorum,* . . var. *scandens,* . . wild buckwheat. **1938** KS Acad. Sci. *Trans.* 41.184 **KS,** The . . sawfly. . . feeds on plants belonging to the buckwheat family, including . . wild buckwheat (*Polygonum*). **1966** *DARE* Wildfl QR Pl.15B [=*Polygonum scandens*] Infs **MI**7, **MN**14, Wild buckwheat. **1967–70** *DARE* (Qu. S5, . . *Wild morning glory*) Infs **CT**2, **IA**13,

MN16, **NY**155, **PA**163, **WA**30, Wild buckwheat; (Qu. S21, . . *Weeds . . that are a trouble in gardens and fields*) Infs **MI**45, 116, **MN**23, **WI**78, Wild buckwheat; **MD**23, Wild buckweed [sic]. **2004** *Bismarck Tribune* (ND) 17 June 8 (Internet), Japan stopped buying durum from the United States after wild buckwheat mixed in with the durum caused specks in pasta.

2 A plant of the genus *Eriogonum.* **chiefly Sth, SW** Also called **buckwheat 2;** for other names of var spp see **antelope brush 2, bee feed, butterball 4, desert trumpet, dog's tongue 3, flattop 2, graleweed, ground chaparral, Indian tobacco 8, napkin-ring buckwheat, redroot j, skeletonweed 2, sour grass f, sulfur flower, trumpet 2, umbrella plant c, whiskbroom, white sage 6, yellow turban(s)**

1868 Cronise *Nat. Wealth CA* 373, The wild buckwheat affords good autumn bee pasture. **1882** *Harper's New Mth. Mag.* 66.63 **sCA,** A number of varieties of wild sage, with wild buckwheat and sumac, furnish bees an exceptionally good support. **1929** *Jrl. Mammalogy* 10.56 **sCA,** On the same date No. 8 [=a wood rat's nest] was in wild buckwheat *(Eriogonum fasciculatum).* **1950** *Amer. Midland Naturalist* 43.274 **TX,** Wild buckwheat *(Eriogonum tenellum).* **1954** *Ibid* 52.289 **GA,** *Eriogonum tomentosum.* . . Wild-buckwheat. . . Common. **1967** *DARE* (Qu. S26e, *Other wildflowers not yet mentioned;* not asked in early QRs) Inf **CA**4, Wild buckwheat—grows in valleys and desert. **1967** *DARE* Wildfl QR Pl.6D (Wills–Irwin) [=*Eriogonum annuum*] Inf **TX**44, Wild buckwheat. **1992** *Amer. Midland Naturalist* 127.60 **FL,** Herbs included wild buckwheat, *Eriogonum tomentosum.* **2006** *Santa Fe New Mexican* (NM) 12 Feb sec E 8 (Internet), If they could, the Pecos sunflower, Holy Ghost ipomopsis . . , gypsum wild buckwheat [= *Eriogonum gypsophilum*] and Zuni fleabane would praise [Bob] Sivinski as a "prime example of dedication."

3 A **butterflyweed 2** (here: *Gaura coccinea*).

1937 TX Ag. Exper. Sta. College Sta. *Bulletin* 551.87, *Gaura coccinea.* . . Wild Buckwheat. . . will thrive anywhere in Texas west of Houston.

wild cabbage n

1 Std: a plant of the genus *Caulanthus.* For other names of var spp see **desert candle 4, Paiute cabbage, squaw ~ 2**

2 A plant of any of var related genera; see quots. Cf **skunk cabbage, swamp ~ 1**

1805 *Med. Repository* 3.306, The party proceeded no further than the Hot-Springs. . . Here they discovered a kind of wild cabbage, which they cooked, and found to be mild and good for food. **1830** Rafinesque *Med. Flora* 2.202, *C[acalia] reniformis* [=*Arnoglossum r.*] (called *Wild Cabbage!*) used like beet leaves. **1920** Saunders *Useful Wild Plants* 126, Two large cruciferous plants of the arid regions of the Far West . . go by the name of Wild Cabbage among the whites who know them. Their tender stems and leaves have a cabbage-like taste and have at times gone into the pioneer's cooking pots. One is *Stanleya pinnatifida* . . , found in dry, even desert soil, from South Dakota to New Mexico and westward to California. . . The other is *Caulanthus crassicaulis.* **1969** *DARE* (Qu. S26e, *Other wildflowers not yet mentioned;* not asked in early QRs) Inf **WI**78, Wild cabbage = skunk cabbage. **2003** *Charleston Gaz.* (WV) 25 Apr sec C 2 (Internet), The waxy-white trilliums are in bloom. Some folks call these flowers "wild cabbage" and cook them for greens. **2004** *Milwaukee Jrl. Sentinel* (WI) 18 Apr sec H 10 (Internet), Chequamegon Bay offers. . . ubiquitous wild rice, wild celery and wild cabbage beds. **2007** *DARE* File—Internet **CA,** Scientific Name: *Guillenia lasiophylla.* . . Common Synonym: *Thelypodium utahense.* . . Common Name: *Coast Wild Cabbage.*

wild calla n Also *wild calla lily*

1 The water arum *(Calla palustris),* native chiefly to the Northeast, Great Lakes, and Upper Midwest. Also called **false jack-in-the-pulpit, iris B2, jack-in-the-pulpit 2a, swamp robin 3**

1854 (1857) Green–Congdon *Analytical Botany* 200, *C[alla] palustris.* Wild Calla. **1862** *Atlantic Mth.* 10.652 **NEast,** The same rich creamy hue and texture show themselves in the Wild Calla, which . . sometimes well rivals, in all but size, . . the Ethiopic Calla of the conservatory. **1934** *Sheboygan Press* (WI) 29 Sept 9/4, Water arum or wild calla is a relative of the jack and also has red berries. **1951** *New Castle News* (PA) 7 June 9/2, We found this waterway choked by the plants of the wild calla lily, with apparently every plant showing off the oddly beautiful pure white blossom. **1966–68** *DARE* (Qu. S26b, *Wildflowers that grow in water or wet places*) Infs **MI**31, **PA**99, Wild calla (lily). **1966**

DARE Wildfl QR Pl.4 [=*Calla palustris*] Infs **MI**7, 31, Wild calla; **NH**4, **WA**15, Wild calla lily. **2000** *Arctic Antarctic & Alpine Research* 32.312 **AK,** Buckbean and swamp horsetail then invade the wild calla mats, producing a thick . . fibrous floating mat of peat, rhizomes, and fine rootlets.

2 An **arrow arum** (here: *Peltandra sagittifolia*).

1886 *Harper's New Mth. Mag.* 72.420 **FL,** Wild calla-lilies flourished on the margin of the river, the bud greener without than on the cultivated lily, but white within, and with its golden rod. **1938** Matschat *Suwannee R.* 291 **neFL, seGA,** Calla, Wild: *Peltandra sagittaefolia.* **1977** MS Geol. Economic & Topog. Surv. *Bulletin* 17.107, *Peltandra sagittæfolia.* . . Wild Calla Lily. Boggy borders of pine barren streams; Gulf Coast.

wild camomile See **wild chamomile**

wild canary n

1 **=goldfinch 1.** [See quot 1918] **widespread, but less freq Sth** See Map

[**1860** Traill *Can. Settlers' Guide* 57, In the orchard and gardens, the blue-bird and the wild canary, or American goldfinch, dart to-and-fro in the sunshine.] **1876** CA Acad. Sci. *Proc.* 6.194, *Chrysomitris tristis—* American Goldfinch. . . This and the two next [=*C. psaltria* and *C. Lawrencii*] are called here, "Wild Canaries." **1918** (1927) Chapman *Our Winter Birds* 69, The males are now changing the olive winter plumage for their gold and black wedding dress and will soon be true Goldfinches. It is this costume, together with their canary-like song, that has won them the name of "Wild Canary." **1933** *Amer. Midland Naturalist* 14.568 **KY,** The pretty wild canary, or yellowbird, as the goldfinch is often called, although his yellow body is set off by black cap, wings, and tail, is one of the common birds of Kentucky in summer. **1944** *Migrant* 15.28 **TN,** The following list of vernacular or nick-names of birds are those that have been found . . to be used locally for the better known Tennessee birds. . . Yellow Warbler; Wild Canary. . . Prothonotary Warbler; Wild Canary. . . Goldfinch; Wild Canary. **1950** *WELS (Other names for . . goldfinch)* 23 Infs, **WI,** Wild canary. **1965–70** *DARE* (Qu. Q14, . . *Names . . for . . goldfinch*) 324 Infs, **widespread, but less freq Sth,** Wild canary; (Qu. Q21, . . *Kinds of sparrows*) Inf **UT**3, Wild canary. **1985** *Morning Call* (Allentown PA) 31 Mar sec C 16 (Internet), American goldfinch—There's seldom much time for the wild canary to have more than one family as it's the bird world's chief procrastinator.

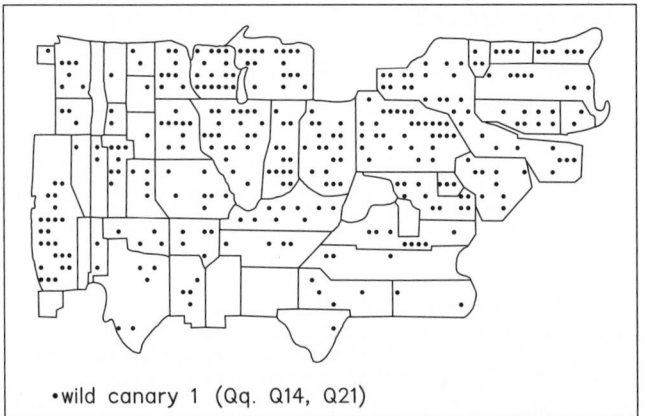

•wild canary 1 (Qq. Q14, Q21)

2 **=yellow warbler.**

1866 *Our Young Folks* 2.425, Variously known as the "Yellow-Bird," and by some confounded with our American Goldfinch, which it very little resembles, as the "Blue-eyed Yellow Warbler," the "Wild Canary," the "Yellow Poll," these birds are found in great abundance all over the continent. **1876** IL State Lab. Nat. Hist. *Bulletin* 1.4.174, *[Dendroeca] aestiva* [=*D. petechia*]. . . Familiarly known, in many sections, as the "Wild Canary." **1897** *Daily Times* (Portsmouth OH) 5 Mar 3/4, *Wood Warblers.* . . Summer Yellow bird or Wild Canary. **1909** MO Bot. Garden *Annual Rept.* 68, Yellow Warbler. *Dendroica aestiva.* This is the wild canary of the boys. . . The Yellow Warbler, also known as Summer Yellowbird, has nothing in common with the Canary except that it is entirely yellow and is of about the same size. **1944** [see **1** above]. **1950** *PADS* 14.72 **SC,** *Wild canary.* . . The yellow warbler; the eastern goldfinch. **c1960** *Wilson Coll.* **csKY,** Wild canary. . . Any wild, small, yellow bird: the American Goldfinch, the Yellow Warbler, the Prothonotary Warbler.

3 =**prothonotary warbler.**

1944 [see **1** above]. **c1960** [see **2** above].

wild candytuft n

1 =**pennycress. West**

1886 *Vick's Mag.* 9.102, We find on sandy knolls the little white flower which is called often the Wild Candytuft, which it does somewhat resemble. **1915** (1926) Armstrong–Thornber *Western Wild Flowers* 178, *Wild Candytuft, Pennycress. Thlaspi glaucum* [=*Noccaea montana* var *montana*]. . . A rather pretty little plant . . ; the flowers small, slightly fragrant, forming clusters. **1945** *Deming Headlight* (NM) 15 June 1/7, Ivy and wild candytuft banked the mantles of the fireplaces throughout the house and bouquets of garden flowers were used. **1977** *Arctic & Alpine Research* 9.211 **CO,** *Thlaspi alpestre* [=*Noccaea montana* var *montana*] . . , wild candytuft, is a perennial plant with one or more short stems. **2005** *Houston Chron.* (TX) 27 Mar 1 (Internet), Desert marigolds, pale-pink wild candytuft and wild geraniums dotted the rocky terrain.

2 Rock cress (*Arabis* spp).

1917 Rydberg *Flora Rocky Mts.* 356, *Arabis* [spp]. . . Rock Cress, Wild Candytuft. **1943** Elmore *Ethnobotany Navajo* 48, *Arabis communis.* . . Common Rockcress, Wild Candytuft.

wild Canterbury bell n   Cf **California bluebell 2**

A **scorpionweed 2** (here: *Phacelia minor*).

1897 Parsons *Wild Flowers CA* 288, *Wild Canterbury-Bell. Phacelia Whitlavia* [=*P. minor*]. . . The wild Canterbury-bell is one of the most charming flowers to be found anywhere. **1935** *Fresno Bee the Republican* (CA) 10 Mar [27]/1 (newspaperarchive.com), The wild Canterbury Bell, known as the Phacelia whitlavia, bears purple blossoms. **1959** Munz–Keck *CA Flora* 541, *P[hacelia] minor.* . . *Wild Canterbury-bell.* . . Common in dry disturbed places like burns. **2007** *DARE* File—Internet **CA,** Wild canterbury-bell (*Phacelia minor*). . . The seeds . . often germinate during the rainy months of winter and early spring, following brush fires of the previous year.

wild caraway n

1 =**Indian plantain.** Note: The spp formerly in *Cacalia* are now distributed among nine genera; all the individual spp mentioned in the quots are now in *Arnoglossum*, except *C. suaveolens*, now *Hasteola s.*

1822 Eaton *Botany* 213, [*Cacalia*] *suaveolens.* . . wild caraway. **1861** Wood *Class-Book* 462, *Cacalia.* . . *Wild Caraway. Tassel Flower.* . . Flowers all tubular. **1901** Lounsberry *S. Wild Flowers* 532, *Mesadenia atriplicifolia,* pale Indian plantain, wild caraway, grows through woods in inland places from Florida to North Carolina and westward. **1940** Clute *Amer. Plant Names* 78, *C[acalia] atriplicifolia. Pale Indian Plantain.* Wild caraway. *Ibid, C[acalia] suaveolens. Sweet-scented Indian Plantain.* Wild caraway.

2 A **yampah.**

1901 U.S. Dept. Ag. Div. Botany *Bulletin* 26.145, Wild Caraway . . *Carum gairdneri* [=*Perideridia g.*] . . This species of wild caraway has been suspected of being poisonous to stock, but this is undoubtedly a mistake, for, . . the roots . . are . . frequently eaten in the raw state by boys, . . and . . it is an article of food among the Indians. **1937** U.S. Forest Serv. *Range Plant Hdbk.* W48, Yampa, a smooth, slender, erect perennial plant of the carrot or parsnip family (Umbelliferae), is also known as squawroot, wildcaraway, breadroot, [etc.] **1987** Elliott *Hist. NV* 28, The edible roots of plants like the wild carrot, wild onion, bitterroot, trail potato, sego lily, wild caraway, camas, and white sage were used extensively.

wild carrot n

1 Std: a plant of the genus *Daucus*, esp *D. carota*. Also called **bee's nest plant, bee weed 2c, beggar's basket, ~ lice 7, beggar ticks 6, bird's nest 4, carrot weed 1, chiggerweed 4, crow's nest 1, devil-in-the-bush 4, devil's-plague, ~-weed 6, dindle, Jacob's ladder 11, Indian carrot, lace flower 1, lady's lace, powder puff 3, Queen Anne's lace 1, parsnip B, ragged robin 4, tobacco flower, umbrella plant h;** for other names of *D. pusillus* see **rattlesnake-bite cure, rattlesnake weed 1g, seed tick 3**

2 A **water hemlock;** see quots.

1790 in 1793 *Amer. Philos. Soc. Trans.* 3.234 **sVA,** I have heard this poisonous herb, called by the names of Wild-Carrot, Wild-Parsnep, Fever-Root, and Mock-Eel-Root. . . It does not resemble a carrot or parsnep, in the stalks, leaves, or flowers; though the root has some resemblance to a parsnep, in colour and smell; and the seeds have also a great likeness. . . *Cicuta Venenosa.* **1869** *NY Times* (NY) 24 Apr 3/5 **KY,** On Sunday last five children . . were poisoned by eating wild carrot. **1900** *Stevens Point Jrl.* (WI) [2 June 6]/7 (newspaperarchive.com), Henry Darling, aged seven . . died from the effects of having eaten a root of wild carrot. **1952** Williams *AK Wildfl. Glimpses* 10, Interior Alaska has . . two different species of poison water hemlock. They are all deadly if eaten, especially the root, which has been mistakenly called "wild carrot" and cooked in early spring by prospectors and settlers or eaten raw by children, with usually fatal results.

3 =**biscuit root 1.** Cf **carrotleaf**

1937 U.S. Forest Serv. *Range Plant Hdbk.* W55, Biscuitroots. . . *Lomatium* spp., . . The plants are also known locally as hogfennel, . . wildcarrot, wildparsley, and by the generic name, *Cogswellia. Ibid* W56, *Nineleaf Biscuitroot.* . . *Lomatium simplex.* . . [I]t has been locally called wildcarrot, [etc]. **1960** Kearney–Peebles *AZ Flora* 622, *Lomatium dissectum.* . . The plant is sometimes known as carrot-leaf and wild-carrot. It is reported that it is palatable to livestock and that the Indians roasted and ate the large roots. **1999** (2005) Campbell *Survival Skills* 139, Wild carrot *(Lomatium macrocarpum):* The Kashaya Pomo ate the young leaves of this plant.

4 A **yampah.**

1877 *Contrib. N. Amer. Ethnology* 1.343, Edible plants: . . *wild carrot,* sha'-gak. [**1934** Haskin *Wild Flowers Pacific Coast* 238, The yampah is common throughout Western Washington, and both species [=*Perideridia gairdneri* and *P. oregana*] are found in Oregon. . . Their white blossoms are often confused with those of the wild carrot, but the leaves are quite different.] **2006** Snell *Taste of Heritage* 12 **csMT,** Wild carrot: split root, we call it. Others call it yampa or squaw root.

wildcat n

Std: any of several wild felines of North America, including the bobcat, **lynx 1,** and **mountain lion.** For other names of the bobcat, see **bay lynx, link** n, **lucivee, mail carrier, mountain cat 1**

wildcat adj [Cf *W3* ²*wildcat* 1.b "operating or being produced . . outside the bounds of standard, recognized, . . or legitimate business practices"] **chiefly S Midl, AL, OK** See Map

Of a still or its products: illicit; hence n *wildcat* illicit liquor; n *wildcatter* one who makes or distributes illicit liquor.

1881 Hughes *Rugby TN* 64, They are sadly weak when wild-cat whisky—or "moonshine," as the favorite illicit beverage of the mountains is called—crosses their path. **1883** (1972) McDowell *Dialect Tales* 143 **eTN,** You're up the Cumberland spyin' for wild-cat stills. **1886** *S. Bivouac* 4.348 **sAppalachians,** There are no "wild-cat stills" now, and consequently little drunkenness. **1886** *Atlantic Mth.* 58.850 **TN,** Ef he had a leetle wild-cat whiskey now 't would save his life. **1909** *DN* 3.388 **eAL, wGA,** Wil(d)cat whisky. . . Illicit whisky, 'moonshine.' **1938** Matschat *Suwannee R.* 135 **neFL, seGA,** Cane beer, with a sweet-sour taste, would be made from the fermented skimmings and, later, would form excellent "buck" for a wildcat still. **1965–70** *DARE* (Qu. DD21c, *Nicknames for whiskey, especially illegally made whiskey*) 13 Infs, **chiefly S Midl, AL, OK,** Wildcat; TN62, Wildcat liquor; (Qu. DD21a, *General words . . for any kind of liquor*) Inf NC54, Wildcat; (Qu. DD21b, *General words . . for bad liquor*) Infs **AL32, KY**84, **MS**59, **OK**11, 20, Wildcat; [(Qu. DD30, *Joking names for a place*

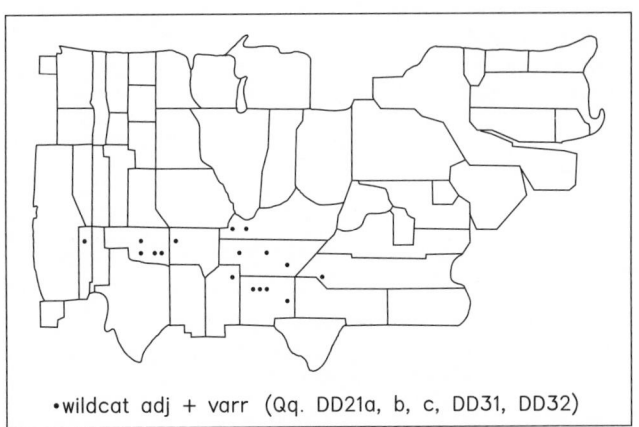

•wildcat adj + varr (Qq. DD21a, b, c, DD31, DD32)

where liquor is [or was] sold and consumed illegally) Inf **GA**77, Wildcat house;] (Qu. DD31, *Joking names for homemade hard liquor;* total Infs questioned, 75) Infs **OK**11, 42, 52, Wildcat; (Qu. DD32, *A person who sells illegal liquor)* Infs **AL**28, 39, **AR**39, Wildcatter. **1972** Thomas *Pop. Dict. Ozarks Talk* 94, Wildcatters. . . Unlicensed whiskey-makers. **1975** McDonough *Garden Sass* 128 **AR,** Most of the whiskey in the saloons came from the local "wildcatter" and the wise man never located the source of his liquor. **1985** Wilkinson *Moonshine* 28 **neNC,** "After that they'd serve you North Carolina Corn." It is called . . wildcat. **1989** Pederson *LAGS Tech. Index* 172 **Gulf Region,** *Moonshine* . . wildcat (19 [of 914 infs]) . . wildcat liquor (1) . . wildcat piss (1) . . wildcat stuff (1) . . wildcat whiskey (10).

wildcat grass n [Appar calque of LaFr *paille (à) chat-tigre*] **sLA**

Either of two marsh plants: **A** a **rush** n[1] **B** (here: *Juncus roemerianus*) or a **cordgrass** (here: *Spartina patens*).

1926 LA Dept. Conserv. *Biennial Rept.* 103 **sLA,** [Caption:] A clump of paille chat tigre or "wild cat grass," (Juncus roemerianus), showing the manner in which muskrats feed on the root systems of this marsh plant. **1933** *Torreya* 33.83 **swLA,** *Juncus roemerianus.* . . Wildcat grass. **1942** *Ibid* 42.158 **sLA,** *Spartina patens.* . . Wildcat grass, paille chat-tigre, wire grass, coastal Louisiana, Lynch. [**1942** *Geogr. Rev.* 32.81 **sLA,** The vegetation is likely to consist wholly of the dominant species [=*Spartina patens*], which is known locally as *paille à chat tigre.*]

wildcat gravy n
=**red-eye gravy.**

1970 *DARE* (Qu. H37, . . *Words . . for gravy. Any joking ones?*) Inf **KY**74, Red gravy, red-eye gravy, wildcat gravy [are the same]; from country man.

wildcat piss n
A **trillium.**

1945 McAtee *Nomina Abitera* 9 **NW,** Wake-Robins (*Trillium* spp.)—Wildcat piss.

wildcatter See **wildcat** adj

wild cauliflower n **TX** Cf **old plainsman**

A **woolly-white** (here: *Hymenopappus scabiosaeus* or *H. artemisiifolius*).

1931 *San Antonio Express* (TX) 11 Apr 3/2, Barkley grade school was featuring another Texas flag, composed of wine cups, blue bonnets, wild cauliflower and daisies. **1938** *Ibid* 22 Aug 4/2, The intensive "drive" . . is intended primarily to relieve hay-fever sufferers plagued by pollen-dust from ragweed, bloodweed, wild cauliflower and other species. **1946** Reeves–Bain *Flora TX* 267, H[ymenopappus] scabiosaeus. . . (Wild Cauliflower.) **1956** *San Antonio Light* (TX) 19 May [2]/3 (newspaperarchive.com), Amazing assortment of native plants the San Antonio Audubon society had for a centerpiece. . . Everything from pink beefsteak begonia to white wild cauliflower. **2007** *DARE* File—Internet **TX,** *Wooly-White—Scientific Name:* (Hymenopappus artemisiaefolius). . . The head of the stem is stalked, with 30 to 60 flower heads per stem. The top of the Wooly-white forms a large, showy cluster. The plant prefers sandy soils and is often called "wild cauliflower". **2009** *Ibid* **csTX,** Plants of Webb County, Texas and surrounding area. . . Hymenopappus scabiosaeus L'Her. var. corymbosus (T. & G.) Turner (Wild Cauliflower).

wild celandine n esp **NEng**
=**jewelweed 1.**

1826 Jewett *New-Engl. Farrier* 67 **neMA,** To take a Film off the Eye. Drop in the juice of wild celandine. **1848** *Voices from Kenduskeag* 269 **ME,** The breeze stirred the shrubbery and a branch near bent and touched a wild celandine; the pods flew open and the seeds were scattered round. **1876** Hobbs *Bot. Hdbk.* 107, Slippers, Celandine, Wild, Impatiens pallida. **1896** Bergen *Current Superstitions* 102 **NH,** The juice of "wild celandine" (*Impatiens fulva*) is used as a wart cure. **1924** *Infantry Jrl.* 25.85 **MD,** For mild attacks [of poison ivy] it suffices to rub with the bruised leaves of the jewel weed, which is also known as lady slipper and wild celandine. The botanical name is *Impatiens flavus* [sic].

wild celery n Cf **wild parsley, ~ parsnip**

1 Any of var plants of the family Apiaceae, as:

a A **cow parsnip 1** (here: *Heracleum maximum*) or an **angelica 1a** (here: *Angelica lucida*). **AK**

[**1805** in 1814 Langsdorff *Voyages & Travels* (transl. Anon.) 2.25 **swAK,** Of eatable vegetables I saw . . *rumex,* or sorrel, wild celery [etc].] **1869** Hartwig *Polar World* 428 **AK,** These heaps [of old shells] can be distinguished at a distance by the bright green color of certain plants, such as the wild celery and scurvy grass, which invariably grow on them. **1897** Thompson *Rept. Behring Sea* 5 **swAK,** On the front of the green hill-side, two thick patches of wild celery *(angelica)* form a conspicuous land-mark. **1918** IA Acad. Sci. Proc. 25.443 **seAK,** *Heracleum lanatum.* . . Cow Parsnip. . . Locally called wild celery. **1962** Salisbury *Quoth the Raven* 131 **seAK,** The wild celery, which grows on every side and which looks like a squash vine trying to be a bush, is peeled and eaten raw, much as we eat rhubarb or sugar cane; but it also is pressed in cakes with fish eggs and preserved for winter use. **1980** *AK Geographic* 7.3.65, [Caption:] Locally, this abundant weed is called wild celery and parts of it are edible at certain times of the year. The field guide calls it cow parsnip *(Heracleum lanatum)*—Aleuts call it *putske.* **1998** *Anchorage Daily News* (AK) 19 July sec H 3 (Internet), The botany books call it *Heracleum lanatum,* but it was Indian celery in Wrangell. When I got to Anchorage, people called it wild celery, or cow parsnip. When we moved to the Aleutians, it was called by its Russian name, putchki. **2004** Miller *Explor. Kenai* 278 **sAK,** Wild Celery (*Angelica lucida*).

b The common water parsley (*Oenanthe sarmentosa*) native to the Pacific Northwest and California.

1898 U.S. Dept. Ag. Div. Botany *Bulletin* 20.42, The Oregon water hemlock has often been mistaken for. . . the so-called "wild celery" *(Oenanthe sarmentosa).* **1967** Gilkey–Dennis *Hdbk. NW Plants* 284, *Oenanthe sarmentosa.* . . Wild celery. Wild parsley.

c =**lovage.**

1915 *Jrl. Ag. Research* 3.97, Wild celery (*Ligusticum oreganum*). **1934** MacDonald *Big Game* 76, Ligusticum sp.—Wild celery. **1937** U.S. Forest Serv. *Range Plant Hdbk.* W106, The loveroots, known commonly as wildcelery, lovage, osha, wildparsley, and ligusticum, are smooth perennial herbs of the carrot . . family. *Ibid* W107, Fernleaf Loveroot . . *Ligusticum filicinum.* . . wildcelery. . . is highly prized as a forage plant. **1984** *Qrly. Rev. Biol.* 59.72, Missing are the abundant, staple Indian and pioneer foods and beverages of Alaska, such as Eskimo potato (*Hedysarum alpinum*), cloudberry (*Rubus chamaemorus*), and wild celery (*Ligusticum hultenii*).

d Spring-parsley (*Cymopterus* spp). Cf **Indian parsnip, wild parsley 2d, ~ parsnip 1**

1940 Writers' Program *Guide NM* 15, Chimajá (wild celery) . . a plant whose leaves and root both cooked and raw are edible. **1943** Elmore *Ethnobotany Navajo* 32, They [=onion bulbs] are soaked with or without wild celery (*Phellopterus montanus* [=*Cymopterus m.*]) before eating. **1967** Harrington *Edible Plants Rocky Mts.* 171, *Cymopterus* spp. . . Biscuit Root, Corkwing, Wafer Parsnip, Wild Celery. [*Ibid* 173, The upper part of the plant in the early stages has been used raw as a salad, like celery, or it has been cooked as a potherb.] **2007** *DARE* File—Internet **NM,** Wild Celery [*Cymopterus fendleri* [=*C. acaulis* var *f.*]] Chimajá. A small early-spring perennial herb one to two inches high, found in the sandy soil among the stones, with glossy deep green dissected leaves. . . Both the leaves and the crunchy root taste like celery.

e A low-growing apiaceous plant *(Apiastrum angustifolium)* native to Arizona and California.

1951 Abrams *Flora Pacific States* 3.222, *Apiastrum.* . . [Name Latin, meaning wild celery.] A monotypic Californian genus. . . *Apiastrum angustifolium* . . Wild Celery. **2005** in 2007 *DARE* File—Internet **sCA,** *Apiastrum angustifolium* . . Common name: Wild celery. . . Habitat: Dry sandy flats and slopes to 3000', coastal sage scrub, chaparral, common after fires.

2 Any of var submerged aquatic plants, but esp **tape grass.** Cf **celery grass, water celery**

1834 *Counsel for Emigrants* 100 **VA,** Its [=the canvasback duck's] flavour is owing to the root of the Vallisneria Americana, or wild celery, on which it feeds. **1900** *Auk* 17.339 **csTX,** *Aythya americana.* . . The abundance of these Ducks and *A. vallisneria* is governed by the quantity of wild celery growing in the bays, upon which they feed. **1905** *Galveston Daily News* (TX) 13 Aug 13/3, The canvasback . . ranks as a delicacy only at certain seasons, and only when he has been able to get the particular kind of food which . . is the plant called Vallisneria spiralis [=*V. americana*], . . wild celery. **1913** *Torreya* 13.226 **TX,** *Potamogeton pectinatus.* . . Wild celery, Lake Surprise, Texas, Winnipeg, Manitoba. **1958** *Daily Progress* (Charlottesville VA) 21 Oct 10/3 (Hench Coll.), *Zostera Marina* is variously known as eelgrass, tape grass, barnacle grass, wild celery, and water celery. It flowers underwater. **1963** *Ecology* 44.360 **MI,** Wild celery (*Vallisneria americana* Michx.) . . is generally recognized as a valuable waterfowl food. **1967** *DARE* (Qu. S26b, *Wildflowers that grow in water or wet places*) Inf **WA20,** Wild celery. **1993** *Jrl. Wildlife Management* 57.763 **Delmarva,** Because of a decline in preferred foods, such as wild celery *(Vallisneria americana) . . ,* canvasbacks have shifted to a diet of primarily Baltic clams. **2007** *Sun* (Baltimore MD) 19 Mar sec B 1 (Internet), Thousands of those birds flocked to the Susquehanna Flats near Havre de Grace, where they dined on the plentiful wild celery grasses.

wild chamomile n   Also sp *wild camomile*

Any of var similar plants of the family Asteraceae, some of which have been used medicinally; spec:

a A **dog fennel 1,** usu *Anthemis cotula.*

   1828 Rafinesque *Med. Flora* 1.44, *Anthemis cotula.* . . Wild camomile. **1868** *Davenport Daily Gaz.* (IA) 8 Aug 1/1 **swIL,** Every vacant lot or untrodden spot in East St. Louis is densely overgrown with the wild camomile (or "dog fennel"). **1882** *Torrey Bot. Club Bulletin* 9.114 **SC,** Not many years ago. . . *Maruta Cotula* (wild camomile) was also very common. **1950** *WELS Suppl.* **csWI,** Stinkweeds, stink daisies—wild camomile. **1952** *Chicago Heights Star* (IL) 13 June 10/6, Dog fennel or wild chamomile and the tall coarse Jimson or Jamestown weed . . are two plants which smell and taste so bad that neither hogs nor chickens will eat them.

b A plant of the genus *Matricaria* or *Tripleurospermum* (formerly included in *Matricaria*).   Also called **mayweed 2;** for other names of var spp see **little snowball 2, pineapple weed**

   1818 Eaton *Botany* 315, *Matricaria.* . . *chamomilla.* . . wild chamomile. **1861** *Weekly Std.* (Raleigh NC) 2 Oct 1/6, We are told that the wild camomile is an excellent remedy for chills. **1925** *Charleroi Mail* (PA) [27 Mar 8]/4 (newspaperarchive.com) **LA,** The fragrance of the rich golden-hued wild camomile flowers pervaded these humble streets as the scent of roses and jasmine the streets of the rich. **1942** Bent *Life Histories N. Amer. Flycatchers* 357, And here it [=a nest] is nearly always placed alongside of . . wild chamomile *(Matricaria coronata)* growing close to the road. **1977** *Atlas Flora Gt. Plains* 392, *Matricaria maritima.* . . Wild Chamomile. **1995** *Ecological Applications* 5.570, Grazing [by geese] effectively selected for unpalatable weed species (including pineapple weed, *Matricaria matricarioides,* . . and wild chamomile, *Tripleurospermum phaeocephalum* [=*T. maritima* subsp *phaeocephala*]). **2006** *Newsday* (Hempstead NY) 7 June sec B 14 (Internet), I remember grabbing fistfuls of wild chamomile that grew beside the strawberry plants and taking it home to dry.

wild cherry n

Std: a usu wild-growing tree of the genus *Prunus.*   For other names of var of these see **black cherry, chokecherry 1, islay 1, pin cherry 1, red ~ 1**

wild chervil n

=**honewort.**

   1943 Fernald–Kinsey *Edible Wild Plants E. N. Amer.* 287, Honewort, Wild Chervil, *Cryptotaenia . . canadensis.* . . Late spring and early summer, while young and tender. *Uses:* soup, potherb, salad, root-vegetable, seasoning. **2004** Choukas-Bradley *Illustr. Guide E. Wildflowers & Trees* 169 **MD,** Honewort (Wild Chervil) *Cryptotaenia canadensis.* . . Native to the eastern United States and Canada, honewort is a common early summer wildflower.

wild Chickasaw   See **Chickasaw rose**

wild chicken n   Cf **chicken B1**

1 =**prairie chicken 1.** Cf **wild hen 1**

   [**1865** *Elyria Independent Democrat* (OH) 5 Apr [2]/4 (newspaperarchive.com), It shall be unlawful . . in any place to catch, kill, or injure, or pursue with such intent any quail or Virginia patridge [sic], ruffed grouse, or pheasant, pinnated grouse or prairie chicken, or any wild chicken.] **1881** *Cambridge Jeffersonian* (OH) 27 Oct 1/9 **IA,** This little village, being situated on a high prairie . . , affords great pleasure for sportsmen who come here to hunt ducks, geese, wild chickens and other game. **1917** Garland *Son Middle Border* 147 **IA,** I loved to go out into the fairy forest of it [=growing wheat], and lying there, . . hear the wild chickens peep. **1939** *WI Rapids Daily Tribune* (WI) 28 Mar 7/4 **nWI,** I have not tasted a wild chicken in 15 years. **1953** *AmSp* 28.279 **CT,** Wild chicken—Heath hen. **2007** *Cleveland Plain Dealer* (OH) 29 Mar sec F 13 (Internet), The greater prairie chicken was once one of the most

abundant birds of the Great Plains, but its population plummeted as the nation's prairies were plowed under. Remnant flocks of this fascinating fowl remain, however, including in Illinois' Prairie Ridge State Natural Area—the easternmost location the wild chickens can be found.

2 =**sage grouse.**

   1877 in 1900 MT Hist. Soc. *Contrib.* 3.154, At noon, went through Gallatin Canyon; some very pretty scenery, shot two wild chickens. **1888** *ID Daily Statesman* (Boise) 6 Nov [3]/1 (newspaperarchive.com), Quite a bunch of wild chickens were brought in yesterday. **1919** *Ogden Std.* (UT) 1 Sept 6/1, *Good Hunting.*—Although precipitation resembling cloudbursts interrupted the shooting yesterday afternoon . . , evidence in the form of full game bags . . proved that there is still an abundance of wild chicken in the hills. **1972** *Caribou Co. Sun* (Soda Springs ID) 12 Oct 10/1, Mr. and Mrs. Farrell Fowler . . were guests . . over the weekend. They came for the opening of the wild chicken season.

wild China (tree)   See **China tree 2**

wild chrysanthemum n

1 A yellow-flowered asteraceous plant *(Bahia dissecta)* native to much of the western US.

   1897 *Bucks Co. Gaz.* (Bristol PA) 8 July 1/6 **CA,** There before me was the wild poppy, the lupine, the cammas [sic], the wild chrysanthemum, the sand lily and baby blue eyes, . . a wealth of blue and red and yellow and purple as far as the eye could discern. **1933** Nelson *Plants Rocky Mt. Park* 127 **CO,** Wild chrysanthemum . . *Bahia dissecta.* . . Plants 1 to 2 feet tall, branching, with golden yellow heads, the disk darker than the short, broad rays. **1970** Zwinger *Beyond Aspen Grove* 299 **CO,** Through this nest of stolons and roots and rhizomes grow cinquefoils, wild strawberry, . . wild chrysanthemum, [etc]. *Ibid* 297, Wild Chrysanthemum *(Bahia dissecta).* **2000** *DARE* File—Internet **NM,** Other yellow patches are created by yellow puccoon (Lithospermum multiflorum), pingue bitterweed (Hymenoxys richardsonii), gumweed (Grindelia aphanactis), wild chrysanthemum (Bahia dissecta), [etc]. **2007** *Ibid* **NM,** Wild Chrysanthemum *(Bahia dissecta)*—Blooms in late summer. Found in most areas of the park except high elevation.

2 also *wild chrysis,* ~ *mum:* A **mugwort** (here: *Artemisia vulgaris).*   [See quots]

   1953 *Daily Progress* (Charlottesville VA) 10 Dec sec 1 1/4 *(Hench Coll.),* Another weed that is spreading rapidly in the Fredericksburg and Charlottesville areas is wormwood or wild chrysanthemum. **1966–70** *DARE* (Qu. S21, . . *Weeds . . that are a trouble in gardens and fields*) Inf **NC36,** Wild chrysanthemum; (Qu. S25, . . *The small wild chrysanthemum-like flowers . . that bloom in fields late in the fall*) Infs **IA12, IL69, IN54, KS1, TN13,** Wild chrysanthemum(s); **DC8, MO20,** Wild mum(s); **OK58,** Wild chrysis; (Qu. S26a, . . *Wildflowers . . . Roadside flowers*) Inf **NY66,** Wild mums. [*DARE* Ed: Some of these Infs may refer instead to other plants of the family Asteraceae.] **1989** *NY Times* (NY) 16 July sec A 47 (Internet) **CT,** Questions/Answers "Wild 'Mums" Q[uestion]. The ground under our new azaleas is thick with a weed growth that our neighbors call wild chrysanthemums. . . How can we get rid of it? A[nswer]. This weed is one of nature's look alikes. Although the plant resembles the cultivated perennial, it is not and it is one of the most difficult weeds to get rid of. **2007** *DARE* File—Internet **NJ,** Mugwort is also called wild chrysanthemum because of the shape of the lower leaves. The plant is a perennial that spreads rapidly by rhizomes. It is one of the most severe weeds of the nursery and landscape plantings.

wild chufa n

=**salt-marsh bulrush.**

   1926 *Torreya* 26.4 **SC,** *Scirpus robustus* [=*Schoenoplectus r.*] . . Wild chufa, McClellanville, S.C.

wild cinnamon vine n

A **greenbrier** (here: *Smilax pseudochina).*

   1903 KS Acad. Sci. *Trans.* 18.205, S[milax] pseudochina, wild cinnamon vine. Eastern Kansas. Alterative, aperient, emetic.

wild citron n   Cf **wild lemon**

=**mayapple 1.**

   [**1795** in 1967 *Dict. Canadianisms* 469, Baron La Hontan says the root of the May apple (or, as the French call them *citrons sauvages*) is poisonous.] **1883** (1884) Hamlin *Legends* 242 **seMI,** The poison . . was probably the distilled juice from the roots of the wild citron plant. . . The fruit of this plant is not poisonous; it is used for preserving. [**1910** *OH Hist.* 19.47, [Translation from German ms written by David Zeisberger c1780:] Wild citrons or May apples grow on a stalk not over a foot high. The Indians enjoy eating the fruit, which has a sour but pleasant taste. The roots are a powerful poison.] **1950** *WELS (Other names in your locality for the may-apple)* 1 Inf, **seWI**, Wild citron. **1966–69** *DARE* (Qu. S4, . . *Mayapple: [Woodside plant, not a tree, with two large spreading leaves; they grow in patches and have a small yellow fruit late in summer]*) Infs **GA**7, **PA**78, Wild citron; **IL**110, Wild citron [FW sugg; Inf doubtful].

wild coffee n

1 A **horse gentian**, usu *Triosteum perfoliatum*.

1817 Barton *Vegetable Materia Medica* 1.59, *Triosteum perfoliatum*. . . Wild-Coffee. **1830** Rafinesque *Med. Flora* 2.269 **PA**, *Triosteum perfoliatum*. . . *Wild Coffee*. . . seeds used as coffee by the Germans near Lancaster. **1861** *De Bow's Rev.* 31.124, *Wild Coffee* . . *Triosteum perfoliatum*. . . It is stated by Dr. Muhlenberg that the hard seeds, properly prepared, are a good substitute for coffee. The T. angustifolium, also growing in South Carolina, is said to possess similar properties. **1929** *Torreya* 29.169 **NY**, Triosteum, the Wild Coffee, or Tinker's Weed, . . [had] plentiful orange fruit which some of the party gathered to take home to try out as a beverage. **1979** Niering–Olmstead *Audubon Guide N. Amer. Wildflowers E. Region* 449, *Wild Coffee; Feverwort; Tinker's-weed (Triosteum perfoliatum).* [*Ibid* 450, The fruits can be dried, roasted, ground, and used as a coffee substitute.]

2 also *wild coffeeweed:* A **senna B1**: usu *Senna occidentalis*, but occas also another sp such as *S. obtusifolia* or *S. marilandica*. Cf **coffeeweed 1b, magdad coffee, Negro ~**

1837 *Adams Sentinel* (Gettysburg PA) [9 Jan 3]/1 (newspaperarchive.com) **LA**, The wild coffee is also abundant here; that announced sometime since as being found in Florida, and as being equal to the coffee of Cuba. But this latter is erroneous; and it is questionable whether both are even species of the same genus. **1850** *De Bow's Rev.* 9.289 **LA**, The wild sarsaparilla, the malo grass, the cuirage, the wild coffee, [etc] . . are all indigenous to the country. **1854** Wailes *Rept. on Ag. & Geol. MS* 345, Wild coffee weed, Cassia occidentalis [=*Senna o.*] **1862** in 2007 *DARE* File—Internet **AL** [*Mobile Advt. & Reg.* (AL) 27 Sept], Please warn persons who might try to gather wild coffee without knowing it, not to mistake for the same the wild indigo, or Cassia Tora [=*Senna obtusifolia*], which has the active properties of senna, and in large doses might prove poisonous. The Cassia Occidentalis [=*Senna o.*], or wild coffee, has a lance-shaped leaf, ending in a sharp point, its pods are wide and flat, and its seeds flat and small. **1901** *Atlanta Constitution* (GA) 10 Nov [18]/2 (newspaperarchive.com), Many kinds of weeds, notably cockle bur, wild coffee (cassia), etc. continue to come up and mature seeds after a corn crop is laid by. **1976** *DARE* Wildfl QR Pl.104 [=*Senna marilandica*] Inf **TX**44, Wild coffee—(doesn't grow *here*). **1986** Pederson *LAGS Concordance*, 1 inf, **swLA**, Wild coffeeweed.

3 also *wild coffee bean shrub, wild coffee plant:* A **rattlebox 1h**, esp **Colorado River hemp**. Cf **coffeeweed 1a**

1869 *Galveston Daily News* (TX) 3 Oct [6]/1 (newspaperarchive.com), This view is diversified by an occasional fractured tin kettle, the fragment of an old boiler, a few wild coffee bean shrubs, and occasionally a dead cat. **1881** Hamilton *Resources AZ* 19, The wild coffee plant is found on the plateau of the central portion of the Territory [of Arizona]; the berry looks like the coffee of commerce and the flavor bears a slight resemblance to the domestic article. **1882** *Ft. Wayne Daily Gaz.* (IN) [20 June] 3/3 (newspaperarchive.com) **Sth**, It appears there is a weed in the South known as the wild coffee plant. . . It has recently been discovered that rope produced from this weed is equal to the best of hemp. **1999** *Jrl. Wildlife Management* 63.141 **LA**, Common plants invading the dredge deposits were panic grass (*Panicum* spp.), . . and wild coffee (*Sesbania* spp.)

4 also *wild coffee bean, ~ bush, ~ shrub, ~ tree:* Either the **coffeeberry 2a(1)** or the related **cascara 1**. Cf **coffee tree 2**

1874 *Overland Mth.* 13.380 **CA**, The so-called "wild coffee," . . turns out to be no other than the seeds of a plant growing in abundance around San Francisco. . . It . . is known to botanists as *Frangula Californica.* Its properties are astringent and cathartic, and, though coffee, by dexterous manipulation, may be and probably is made from horse-beans, the unpleasant effects likely to ensue from an extended use of the berries of the *Frangula* would soon settle the question of its usefulness as a substitute for the favorite beverage. **1874** *Mt. Democrat* (Placerville CA) 25 July 2/1, The so called wild coffee shrub . . grows abundantly in some of the more mountainous altitudes of this State. **1874** *Ladies' Repository* 14.65 **CA**, Wild coffee-trees have been discovered growing in California. **1893** *Jrl. Amer. Folkl.* 6.139 **CA**, *Rhamnus Californica*, wild cof-

fee. . . S. Barbara Co. **1897** Sudworth *Arborescent Flora* 299, *Rhamnus purshana*. . . Coffee-berry (Cal.). Wild Coffee-bush (Cal.). Western Coffee (Oreg., Cal.) . . Wild Coffee (Cal.). California Coffee (Cal.) **1923** *Landmark* (Statesville NC) 20 Aug 7/3 **West**, Cascara. . . Obtained from a Pacific coast tree or shrub. . . it . . is often called wahoo, bitter-bark, wild coffee, pigeon berry, etc. Correctly named Rhamnus purshjana. **1957** *Mt. Democrat* (Placerville CA) 15 Aug 8/6, Their fair exhibit is almost finished. . . The addition of mountain misery, California-holly, and wild coffee bean should be the finishing touch.

5 A tree or shrub of the genus *Psychotria*, esp *P. nervosa*.

[**1804** M'Kinnen *Tour Brit. W. Indies* 154, I beheld some extensive fields . . covered with a luxuriant growth of indigenous shrubs and plants . . [including] here and there the wild coffee *(Psychotria).*] **1901** Entomol. Soc. Washington *Proc.* 4.482 **sFL**, The larva mines the leaves of the "wild coffee" *(Psychotria undata)*. **1961** Douglas *My Wilderness* 148 **Everglades FL**, Wild coffee, whose leaves are dried and used as coffee was everywhere. So was the poisonwood tree. **2003** Torrey Bot. Soc. *Jrl.* 130.140 **FL**, *Psychotria nervosa* . . Wild Coffee. . . *Psychotria sulzneri* . . Shortleaf Wild Coffee.

6 A **nakedwood 1** (here: *Colubrina arborescens*).

[**1905** Shattuck *Bahama Is.* 234, *Colubrina colubrina* . . (Wild coffee) . . was also rather abundant.] **1933** Small *Manual SE Flora* 834 **FL**, *C[olubrina] Colubrina* [=*C. arborescens*]. . . *(Wild-coffee.)*—Hammocks, Everglade Keys, Fla. and Florida Keys. **1971** Craighead *Trees S. FL* 177, On the rim hammocks the important trees include live oak, marlberry, . . two species of wild coffee [etc]. *Ibid* 203, Wild coffee tree, *Colubrina arborescens*. **2007** *DARE* File—Internet **sFL**, *Wild Coffee or Coffee Colubrina*. . . The star-shaped flowers are yellow and the ripe fruits are purple to black. They sometimes open explosively and scatter three black seeds.

7 A vinelike shrub *(Morinda umbellata)* native to Florida. Cf **redroot g**

1943 *Mycologia* 35.482 **FL**, There is a shrub on the Keys and on the west shore of Bay of Biscayne called "Wild Coffee" but it is neither coffee nor (what I predicted) Glottidium, but a . . shrub . . named Morinda Roioc [=*M. umbellata*]. . . Although the people of that region call it Wild Coffee, yet the decoction of the leaves which they use they call tea.

8 A **mullein** (here: *Verbascum thapsus*). Cf **coffee plant 3, coffeeweed 2c**

1950 *WELS Suppl.*, Wild coffee—wild mullein, because the dried seeds on their stalks looked like coffee beans—from a distance. **1966–70** *DARE* (Qu. S20, *A common weed that grows on open hillsides: It has velvety green leaves close to the ground, and a tall stalk with small yellow flowers on a spike at the top*) Infs **AL**62, **NH**10, **SC**41, Wild coffee; **MN**28, Wild coffee [FW sugg]; **MA**13, Wild coffee [FW sugg; Inf uncertain]; (Qu. S21) Inf **WA**28, Wild coffee; (Qu. S15, . . *Weed seeds that cling to clothing*) Inf **NY**165, Wild coffee.

wild coffee bean See **wild coffee 4**

wild coffee bean shrub See **wild coffee 3**

wild coffee bush See **wild coffee 4**

wild coffee plant See **wild coffee 3**

wild coffee shrub (or tree) See **wild coffee 4**

wild coffeeweed n

1 See **wild coffee 2.**

2 An **evening primrose a** (here: *Oenothera biennis*). Cf **coffee plant 2**

1940 Clute *Amer. Plant Names* 265, *Oenothera biennis.* Cradle weed, wild beet, wild coffeeweed.

wild collard n

An **Indian plantain** (here: *Arnoglossum reniforme*).

1867 Curtis *Botany* 33, *Cacalia . . reniformis* [=*Arnoglossum r.*] . . (Wild Collard.)—Mountain sides. **1940** Clute *Amer. Plant Names* 78, *C[acalia] reniformis* [=*Arnoglossum reniforme*] Great Indian plantain. Wild collard.

wild colt n

=**woods colt 2.**

1950 *WELS (Words for a child whose parents were not married . . Joking)* 1 Inf, **csWI**, Wild colt. **1965–69** *DARE* (Qu. Z11b, . . *[A child* *whose parents were not married]*) Infs **FL**17, **IL**68, Wild colt. **1970** Tarpley *Blinky* 220 **neTX,** *Child of an unwed mother* . . other responses . . wild colt.

wild columbine n

Std: a red or mostly red-flowered columbine: usu *Aquilegia canadensis* native in much of the eastern two-thirds of the US, but also *A. formosa* of the western US. For other names of the former see **firecracker flower 3, five crimson doves, honey horns, honeysucker 4, honeysuckle 4, jacket-and-breeches, Jack-in-trousers, lady's slipper 6, meeting-house 2, red bell 2, rock bells, rock lily 1, tinkerbell**

wild comfrey n

A **hound's-tongue 1** (here: *Cynoglossum virginianum*). Cf **comfrey**

1826 Darlington *Florula Cestrica* 23, *Cynoglossum. . . amplexicaule* [=*C. virginianum*]. . . *Vulgo*—Wild Comfrey. Virginian Hounds-tongue. **1854** King *Amer. Eclectic Dispensatory* 365, The *C[ynoglossum] Amplexicaule* [=*C. virginianum*], or Wild Comfrey, affords a root which may be substituted for the officinal Comfrey. **1891** Jesup *Plants Hanover NH* 28, *C[ynoglossum] Virginicum* [sic]. . . Wild Comfrey. **1912** Blatchley *IN Weed Book* 113, *The Borage Family*. . . [is] represented in Indiana by 20 or more species, among them . . the wild comfrey. **1963** *AmSp* 38.36, *Dog bur*. . . The wild comfrey, *Cynoglossum virginianum*. **2001** Torrey Bot. Soc. *Jrl.* 129.383 **NJ,** In bloom in this area were . . *Cynoglossum virginianum* (wild comfrey) and *Helianthemum canadense* (frostweed).

wild coral n

A **glasswort** (here: *Salicornia depressa*).

[**1920** Britton–Millspaugh *Bahama Flora* 122, *Salicornia perennis*. . . Woody Glasswort. Wild Coral.] **1974** Morton *Folk Remedies* 131 **SC,** *Wild coral—Salicornia virginica* [=*S. depressa*]. . . Plant decoction is taken as a cold remedy and given to children to stop whooping cough.

wild coreopsis n

A **tarweed 1b(2)** (here: *Madia elegans*).

1897 Parsons *Wild Flowers CA* 182, Tarweed. Wild Coreopsis. Madia elegans. **1934** Haskin *Wild Flowers Pacific Coast* 375, Wild coreopsis.—*Madia elegans*. [*Ibid* 377, Each petal-like ray [flower] is deeply three-lobed, bright yellow at the summit, with a velvety brown base. The whole effect is very pleasing, and much like the garden coreopsis after which it is called.]

wild corn n

1 A **bead lily:** *Clintonia borealis* or *C. umbellulata*. Cf **bear corn 1, calf ~, corn lily 3c**

1893 *Jrl. Amer. Folkl.* 7.101 **ME,** *Clintonia borealis*, . . wild corn. **1940** Clute *Amer. Plant Names* 11, *C[lintonia] umbellulata*. White Clintonia. Dog-plum, wild corn. **1968** *DARE* Tape **IN**14, [In discussion of wildflowers:] Indian corn, as it is called, or wild corn.

2 also *wild corn lily:* A **false hellebore 1** (here: *Veratrum californicum*). Cf **corn lily 3a**

1905 *Condor* 7.16 **CA,** This nest was placed in a slight hollow on the ground in a patch of broad-leaved plants called locally "wild corn" (*Veratrum* [sic] *californicum*). **1964** NY Acad. Sci. *Annals* 111.571, *Veratrum californicum*. . . commonly called western hellebore, false hellebore, wild corn, or skunk cabbage. **2000** in 2007 *DARE* File—Internet, Pregnant sheep left to pasture had eaten wild corn lilies, high in cyclopamine. **2007** (acc) U.S. Ag. Research Serv. *Poisonous Plant Research* (Internet) **West,** *False Hellebore (Veratrum californicum)*—False hellebore, or veratrum (sometimes called wild corn or cow cabbage), is a range plant that causes severe poisoning in sheep.

3 =**chicken corn 1, 2.**

1923 IN Acad. Sci. *Proc. for 1922* 295, The young wild corn plants resemble corn seedlings so closely that recognition is difficult and they become large plants before they can be identified. **1935** (1943) Muenscher *Weeds* 158, *Holcus Sorghum* L. var. *Drummondii* [=*Sorghum bicolor*]. . . Wild corn, Chicken corn. Reported as a serious weed in corn fields in the overflow lands of the Ohio River in Indiana and Kentucky and also in the lower Mississippi Valley.

wild corn lily   See **wild corn 2**

wild cosmos n

A **woolly-white** (here: *Hymenopappus newberryi*).

1915 Wooton–Standley *Flora NM* 723, Wild cosmos. . . *Leucampyx newberryi* [=*Hymenopappus n.*] . . Colorado to Arizona and New Mexico. **2003** in 2007 *DARE* File—Internet **swCO,** *Hymenopappus newberryi* (Wild Cosmos). . . enjoys open, sunny hillsides, even, as in this case, hot, south-facing hillsides.

wild cotton n   Cf **cottonweed**

1 A **milkweed 1,** usu *Asclepias syriaca*. Cf **silkweed 1**

1803 in 1809 Amer. Philos. Soc. *Trans.* 6.80, Having collected some branches, in flower, of the Asclepias syriaca, . . well known in the United States by the names of Wild-cotton, cotton-plant, &c; . . I was not a little surprized to find, in the course of a few hours, a number of the common houseflies strongly attached to the flowers. **1816** *Niles' Weekly Reg.* 9.189, A young school girl effecting a cure of one by rubbing it every day . . with the juice of *Milk or Wild Cotton Weeds* which finally destroyed the wen. **1853** Gray *Bot. Text-Book* 464, Seeds usually with a silky coma.—*Ex[ample]*. Asclepias (Milkweed, Wild Cotton). **1868** Davis *Dallas Galbraith* 81 **NJ,** Gerty Rattin was going through the garden-walks cutting crimson seed vessels from the roses, and wild cotton-pods for a berry-pot. **1877** Powers *Tribes CA* 336, These are pierced in the center, and strung on strings made of the inner bark of the wild cotton or milkweed (*Asclepias*). **1894** *Jrl. Amer. Folkl.* 7.94 **WV,** *Asclepias cornuti* [=*A. syriaca*], . . wild cotton. **1901** *Torreya* 1.117 **GA,** *Asclepias humistrata*. . . Wild cotton. [Name heard in] Bulloch [County]. **1997** (acc) KS State Univ. *KS Wildflowers* (Internet), *Milkweed (Common)*. . . *Asclepias syriaca*. . . Also called Milk plant, Wild asparagus, Silkweed, and Wild cotton.

2 =**Indian hemp 1.**

1891 WV Ag. Exper. Sta. *Bulletin* 13.406, *Apocynum*. . . *cannabinum*. . . Indian Hemp. "Wild Cotton." **1913** Cather *O Pioneers* 247 **NE,** She walked slowly down through the orchard, where the evening air was heavy with the smell of wild cotton. **1930** Sievers *Amer. Med. Plants* 34, *Apocynum cannabinum*. . . wild cotton. . . Hemp dogbane is a native of this country and may be found in thickets and along the borders of old fields throughout the United States.

3 A plant of the family Malvaceae, as:

a A **hibiscus,** esp *Hibiscus moscheutos*. **chiefly Sth** Cf **cotton rose 1, swamp cotton 2**

1896 Clendenin *Prelim. Rept.* 253, Hibiscus Moscheutos, Wild cotton. Hibiscus incanus, Wild cotton. **1901** U.S. Natl. Museum *Contrib. Herbarium* 5.364 **seVA, neNC,** No less beautiful is *Hibiscus moscheutos* (locally, "wild cotton") with its large whitish or deep rose-colored flowers, a species very characteristic of the marsh borders. **1913** *Torreya* 13.232 **LA,** *Hibiscus lasiocarpus*. . . Wild cotton, [name used in] Marksville, La. **1946** *PADS* 6.33 **NC** (as of 1900–10), Wild cotton. . . A salt-marsh weed that produces blossoms resembling cotton blossoms. . . Occasional among old people. **1966–68** *DARE* (Qu. S2, . . *The flower that comes up in the woods early in spring, with three white petals that turn pink as the flower grows older*) Inf **GA**3, Wild cotton flower; (Qu. S26a, . . *Wildflowers*. . . *Roadside flowers*) Inf **NC**1, Wild cotton; (Qu. S26b, *Wildflowers that grow in water or wet places*) Inf **LA**15, Wild cotton. **1973** *News* (Pt. Arthur TX) 22 Apr sec E 1/3, The wild cotton or rose mallow is one of the best known [wildflowers]. **1998** *Virginian–Pilot* (Norfolk VA) 9 Aug 2 (Internet), Rose mallows have bright red centers and sometimes bloom in such profusion, that they have been called wild cotton.

b =**velvetleaf a.**

1888 TN Univ. Ag. Exper. Sta. *Bulletin* 1.35, Velvet-leaf. Wild Cotton. . . *Abutilon Avicennae*. . . stem and large heartshaped leaves densely clothed with soft hairs. **1937** *Torreya* 37.98 **VA** (as of a1815), *Abutilon Theophrasti*. . . Wild-cotton.

wild cowpea n   esp **LA**

=**deer pea 3.**

1911 Wing *Meadows & Pastures* 196, There is also a wild cowpea growing in Louisiana that perpetuates itself from year to year and makes much forage. **1913** U.S. Bur. Plant Industry *Circulars* 124.31, *Vigna triloba* . . differs from the wild cowpea mainly in its leaflets being almost always three lobed. **1938** *Ecological Monogr.* 8.19 **seLA,** *Vigna repens* [=*V. luteola*]. . . Wild cowpea. **1942** *Geogr. Rev.* 32.80 **LA,** Black willow (*Salix nigra*) . . and wild cowpea (*Vigna repens*) appear wherever slight advantages in drainage are created by higher altitude. **1972** Brown *Wildflowers LA* 94, Deer pea, Wild Cowpea (*Vigna luteola*). . . Related to cultivated cowpea. **2006** in 2007 *DARE* File—Internet **LA,** [Caption:] Deer Pea/Wild Cowpea *Vigna luteola*.

wild crabgrass n
=**tumblegrass 2a.**

1894 SD Ag. Exper. Sta. *Bulletin* 40.96, Wild Crab Grass. Schedonnardus paniculatus. . . Readily distinguished from common crab grass by its curved, spreading panicles, its general habit of growth and the structure of its flowers. **1912** Wooton–Standley *Grasses NM* 108, *Schedonnardus.* . . Wild crab grass. **1944** KS Acad. Sci. *Trans.* 47.198 **KS,** A few short lived perennial grasses such as wild crab grass *(Schedonnardus paniculatus)* and windmill grass *(Chloris verticillata)* were beginning to make their appearance. **1969** *DARE* (Qu. S8, *A common kind of wild grass that grows in fields: it spreads by sending out long underground roots, and it's hard to get rid of*) Inf **IL**110, Wild crab grass.

wild cranberry n

1 A **bearberry 2** (here: *Arctostaphylos uva-ursi*).

[**1823** Paris–Ives *Pharmacologia* 2.363, Uva Ursi, Bear-berry, . . Wild Cranberry, &c.] **1876** Hobbs *Bot. Hdbk.* 130, Wild cranberry, Bearberry. **1975** Hamel–Chiltoskey *Cherokee Plants* 25, Bear-berry, wild cranberry. *Arctostaphylos uva-ursi.*

2 A **wolfberry 2** (here: *Lycium carolinianum*). **esp TX**

1932 *Corpus Christi Times* (TX) 16 Dec 7/8, There are some wild cranberry in that section and the fresh water and this feed attract mallard. **1943** *Brownsville Herald* (TX) 31 Oct 10/3, Today it is a commonplace matter to see or hear the lordly honkers in their V shape flight seeking some favored rendezvous where choice bits of vegetation can be found, the wild cranberry being favored. **1950** Writers' Round Table *Padre Is.* 135 **csTX,** Wild cranberries grow along the marshes on the laguna side of the Island and are eaten raw or preserved. Indians gathered and dried these berries for out-of-season food. Botanists list the plant as *Lycium carolinianum* var. *quadrifidum.*

wild crape myrtle n Cf **manzanita 4, Mexican myrtle**
A Barbados cherry *(Malpighia glabra).*

1938 Van Dersal *Native Woody Plants* 165, *Malpighia glabra.* . . Wild crapemyrtle. . . A small to large shrub. **1960** Vines *Trees SW* 603, *Malpighia glabra.* . . is sometimes known in cultivation under the name of Wild Crape-myrtle because of its superficial resemblance to Crapemyrtle.

wild crocus n

1 See **crocus** n[1] **2a.**

2 A **spiderwort** (here: *Tradescantia longipes*) native to Arkansas and Missouri.

1940 Steyermark *Flora MO* 63, Spiderwort, Wild Crocus *(Tradescantia longipes* . .). Eastern and south-central Ozark region. **2002** Hemmerly *Ozark Wildflowers* 158, *Wild Crocus—Tradescantia longipes.* . . This rare spiderwort. . . occurs in woodlands with acidic soils, especially in the St. Francois Mountains of e. MO; it has also been reported from several counties of AR; Apr., May.

wild cucumber n

1 Any of var plants of the family Cucurbitaceae thought to resemble *Cucumis sativus* in some way, as:

a Std: a climbing vine *(Echinocystis lobata)* that produces an inedible cucumber-like fruit covered with spines, native throughout much of the US. Also called **creeping Jennie 3, cucumber B2, mock apple 1, ~ orange 2c, ~ cucumber, wild balsam apple 1**

b =**bigroot 1.**

1854 in c1855 U.S. War Dept. *Rept. Explor. Railroad* (Stevens' Exped.) 1.469 **WA,** A plant fully capable of producing the result is the wild cucumber vine, whose root, sometimes reaching the size of a flour-barrel, would constitute no small nucleus of itself. **1873** Amer. Geogr. Soc. NY *Jrl.* 4.307 **NW,** They [=hillocks] have been attributed to the pushing up of the soil by the roots of the wild cucumber vine (Megarrhiza Oregona [=*Marah o.*]), which frequently reach the size of a half barrel, and are very commonly found in them. **1897** Parsons *Wild Flowers CA* 26, Wild Cucumber. Big-Root. Chilicothe. . . *Megarrhiza Californica* [=*Marah fabaceus*]. **1953** *Chillicothe Constitution–Tribune* (MO) 8 Oct 3/4 **sCA,** The Chilicothe. . . the official name of which is Enchinocystis [sic] macrocarpa or wild cucumber, is abundant. . . The Chilicothe develops a spiny, lemon-shaped fruit which grows bigger than a fist. It has sharp, thickly set spines. **1966** *DARE* FW Addit **WA**10, A Washington variety of wild cucumber is manroot, with root three feet long and perhaps four inches in diameter. **1968** *DARE* (Qu. S26e,

Other wildflowers not yet mentioned; not asked in early QRs) Inf **CA**87, Wild cucumber. **2007** *DARE* File—Internet *AZ, Wild Cucumber—Marah gilensis.* . . A perennial vine, the star-shaped flowers are about 3/8 inches wide and are followed by round, spiny, green goards [sic] about 2 inches in diameter. This plant has a very large underground tuber.

c Oneseed burr cucumber *(Sicyos angulatus).*

1857 in 1862 Essex Inst. *Proc.* 2.241 **MA,** Sicyos angulatus; Wild Cucumber. **1896** *Jrl. Amer. Folkl.* 9.188 **cIL, OH,** Sicyos angulatus, . . wild cucumber. **1942** *Amer. Midland Naturalist* 27.599 **MO,** A single specimen [of *Leptoglossus gonagra*] . . was found feeding on the under side of a stem of wild cucumber, Sicyos. **1966–67** *DARE* (Qu. S13, . . *A common wild bush with bunches of round, prickly seeds; when they get dry they stick to your clothing*) Inf **IL**50, Wild cucumber—a vine; (Qu. S15, . . *Weed seeds that cling to clothing*) Inf **NY**28, Wild cucumbers—look like egg-size puffball, "pickers" are soft, but grip clothing. **1966–67** *DARE* Wildfl QR Pl.216 [=*Sicyos angulatus*] Infs **MI**31, 57, **OH**14, **WA**10, 15, 30, Wild cucumber. **2003** *Scientific Amer.* Sept 109, You can see shattered glass under a leaf of a type of wild cucumber called Nimble Kate *(Sicyos angulatus).*

d A **calabacilla** (here: *Cucurbita foetidissima*).

1972 *SW Naturalist* 17.47 **CO,** Often herbs are present, such as . . wild cucumber *(Cucurbita foetidissima)* . . and others.

2 An **anemone** (here: *Anemone nemorosa*).

1892 *Jrl. Amer. Folkl.* 5.91 **NH,** *Anemone nemorosa,* wild cucumber.

3 A **twisted stalk 1** (here: *Streptopus amplexifolius*). [See quot 1991] Cf **cucumber root 2**

[**1971** *Lily Yr. Book* 34.135, We begin with Kunashiri Island, where we found growing the Wild Cucumber, *Streptopus amplexifolius.*] **1991** Tabbert *Dict. Alaskan Engl.* 174, Streptopus amplexifolius. . . Various common names are reported for this plant. *Wild cucumber* and *cucumber root* reflect the cucumberlike odor and taste of its parts. **2007** *DARE* File—Internet *MT, Streptopus amplexifolius.* . . Wild cucumber. . . Fruits: berries, dark yellowish to red, many-seeded, oval-oblong, 10–12 mm long.

4 See **cucumber tree 1.**

5 as *wild cucumber tree:* See **cucumber tree 2.**

wild curcuma n
=**goldenseal 1.**

1843 Torrey *Flora NY* 1.26, Hydrastis Canadensis. . . This plant has received various names, such as *Wild Curcuma, Golden Seal* [etc]. **1892** (1974) Millspaugh *Amer. Med. Plants* 9–1, Hydrastis. . . Com. Names. . . ground-raspberry, wild curcuma.

wild cypress n
=**scarlet gilia.**

1884 *Wide Awake* R.51 **SW,** Too tangled for trail lay the storm-felled trees, and no man's foot but his own ever trod the gramma grass or brushed the wild cypress bending by the stream. **1901** Eastwood *Bergen's Botany* 132, Scarlet Gilia, Wild Cypress. . . grows in the mountains or near streams on the plains. **1915** (1926) Armstrong–Thornber *Western Wild Flowers* 394, This [=scarlet gilia] has several common names which are very misleading, such as Wild Cypress and Wild Honeysuckle. **1939** *Abilene Reporter–News* (TX) 15 Jan 5/7, Again there have been Indian paintbrush in all its bright coloring, wild cypress, purple thistle, yellow daisies, Indian blanket, . . and coral berries. **1966** *DARE* FW Addit **WA**12, Scarlet gilia or wild cypress—finely-cut leaves, almost like ferns, star-shaped petals, bright scarlet blooms. **1977** Wetherill *Wetherills of Mesa Verde* 273 **CO** (as of 1902), The gilia, often called shooting stars or wild cypress, is the most noticeable.

wild daisy n

1 Std: either of two introduced plants: esp the **oxeye daisy 1,** widely distributed throughout the US, but also the English daisy *(Bellis perennis),* found chiefly in the northern and western US. Cf **daisy 2a**

2 A wild plant thought to resemble the above in some way, as:

a A white-, pink-, lavender-, or purple-flowered plant of the family Asteraceae, as:

(1) =**fleabane. chiefly West** Cf **daisy 2b**

1895 NE Ag. Exper. Sta. *Bulletin* No. 40.151, Fleabane, or Wild Daisy *(Erigeron strigosus).* **1911** Garrett *Spring Flora Wasatch* 102 **UT,** E[rigeron] pumilus. . . "Wild Daisy." **1935** Davis *Honey* 1 **sOR,** The creek-meadow in season was full of flowers—wild daisies, lamb-tongues, cat-ears, big patches of camas. **1937** U.S. Forest Serv. *Range Plant Hdbk.* W67, Annual wild-daisy (*E[rigeron] annuus*) and Philadelphia wild-daisy, misnamed sweet scabious (*E. philadelphicus*) . . are other wild-daisies with similar properties. **1961** Thomas *Flora Santa Cruz* 352 **cwCA,** *Erigeron* . . Wild Daisy, Fleabane. **2006** in 2007 *DARE* File—Internet **AZ,** I identify this as an Aspen Fleabane (Erigeron macranthus). . . Also known as a wild daisy.

(2) An aster (*Aster* spp). Cf **daisy 2c**

1966 *DARE* Wildfl QR Plates 240, 241 [=*Aster macrophyllus, A. puniceus*] Inf **WA**15, Wild daisy. **1968** *DARE* (Qu. S25, . . *The small wild chrysanthemum-like flowers . . that bloom in fields late in the fall*) Inf **GA**18, Wild daisy [Inf uncertain]. **2007** *DARE* File—Internet **CA,** *Weeds.* . . Wild Daisy—Aster subulatus.

b Any of var yellow-flowered plants of the family Asteraceae, esp of such genera as *Coreopsis, Helianthus, Rudbeckia,* and *Tetraneuris;* see quots. Cf **daisy 2e**

1841 Amer. Philos. Soc. *Trans.* 7.382 **CA,** *Ptilomeris aristata* [here: = *Tetraneuris acaulis*]. . . Near St. Diego, Upper California. . . Flowers bright yellow, a little smaller than those of the common wild daisy. **1965–70** *DARE* (Qu. S7, *A kind of daisy, bright yellow with a dark center, that grows along roadsides in late summer*) 16 Infs, **chiefly Midl, Sth,** Wild daisy; (Qu. S22, . . *The bright yellow flowers that bloom in clusters in marshes in early springtime*) Inf **UT**13, Wild daisies; **CA**137, Wild daisy. **1966–68** *DARE* Wildfl QR Pl.249A [=*Helianthus angustifolius*] Infs **MN**30, **WA**30, **WI**79, Wild daisy; Pl.250 [=*Inula helenium*] Inf **WA**30, Wild daisy; Pl.252 [=*Heliopsis helianthoides*] Inf **WA**30, Wild daisy; Pl.253 [=*Rudbeckia triloba*] Inf **WA**30, Wild daisy; Pl.254 [=*R. hirta*] Inf **WA**30, Wild daisy; Pl.255 [=*R. laciniata*] Inf **WA**30, Wild daisy; Pl.256 [=*Helianthus giganteus*] Inf **WA**30, Wild daisy; Pl.257 [=*H. divaricatus*] Inf **WA**30, Wild daisy; Pl.258 [=*H. mollis*] Inf **WA**30, Wild daisy; Pl.259 [=*H. strumosus*] Inf **WA**30, Wild daisy; Pl.260A [=*Coreopsis lanceolata*] Inf **WA**30, Wild daisy. **1991** *Washington Post* (DC) 25 Apr sec T 22 (Internet), Among the flowers that attract beneficials are Queen Anne's lace or wild carrot, . . Joe-Pye weed, . . black-eyed Susan and other wild daisies. **2005** in 2007 *DARE* File—Internet **IA,** The Wild Daisy is a yellow flowering plant with a sandy yellow center. The petals are thicker and longer than those of the prairie daisy.

wild date n

1 A **yucca:** the **banana yucca,** *Yucca schidigera, Y.* x *schotti,* or *Y. glauca.* Cf **datil**

1886 *West Amer. Scientist* 2.58, The wild date or 'datiles' a giant yucca some thirty feet in height . . here makes its most northern appearance [in Baja California]. **1887** *Daily Era* (Bradford PA) 11 Aug [4]/4 (newspaperarchive.com) **CA,** Between these plants the first place belongs to the wild date or datilillo tree (Yucca Scottii [=*Y.* x *schottii*]), a tall tree, occasionally forty and fifty feet high. **1906** (1918) Parsons *Wild Flowers CA* 22, Yucca Mohavensis [=*Y. schidigera*], commonly called "wild date," or "Spanish bayonet," is more widely distributed within our borders than either of our other species. . . The fruit, which ripens in August and September, turns from green to a tawny yellow, afterward becoming brownish purple, and eventually almost black. This has a sweet, succulent flesh. **1920** Saunders *Useful Wild Plants* facing 270 **SW,** [Caption:] Wild Date *(Yucca glauca).* The root furnishes a satisfactory substitute for soap. **1993** in 2007 *DARE* File—Internet **SW,** Y[ucca] schidigera—Spanish dagger, Wild date. Young stems are chopped and cooked or baked like a sweet potato. Fruits and flowers are eaten raw or in jellies.

2 =**fan palm.**

1897 Sudworth *Arborescent Flora* 105 **CA,** *Neowashingtonia filamentosa* [=*Washingtonia filifera*]. . . Wild Date. **1953** Peattie *Nat. Hist. W. Trees* 295, *Desert Palm—Washingtonia filifera.* . . California Fan Palm. . . Overcoat Palm. Wild Date. . . *Berry* ⅓ inch long, the skin black, the flesh thin and dry; seed ¼ inch long, ⅛ inch thick, russet.

wild dill n

1 The eastern **yampah** (*Perideridia americana*).

1968 *DARE* (Qu. S6, . . *Queen Anne's lace: [Summertime roadside weed two feet high or so with a lacy white top]*) Inf **IN**41, Wild dill. **2007** *DARE* File—Internet **IL,** Wild Dill—Perideridia americana. . . This perennial native plant is 2–3½' tall, branching sparingly. . . Wild Dill occurs occasionally in NE and central Illinois.

2 A prairie parsley (here: *Polytaenia nuttallii*).

1984 Loughmiller-Loughmiller *TX Wildflowers* 232, *Polytaenia nut-*

talli—Wild Dill (Prairie Parsley, Prairie Parsnip) Wild dill has stiff, stout stems, usually 2 feet high, which become dry and brown and remain standing through the winter months. The leaves are 1–3 inches long and nearly as broad, deeply cut, and lobed. . . The flowers are small, ¼ inch across, greenish-yellow, and grow in umbel-like clusters, 2 inches across. **2007** *DARE* File—Internet **TX,** *Parsley.* . . Polytaenia nuttallii. . . Also called "wild dill", the plant can easily be used in much the same way.

wild dove n

=**mourning dove 1.**

1873 *Overland Mth.* 11.536 **West,** I hear the wild dove's note forlorn,/ The piping quail beneath the thorn. **1911** *Le Grand Reporter* (IA) [24 Mar 34]/1 (newspaperarchive.com), It invariably has been found that the discoverers [of the wild pigeon] had seen nothing more nor less than the common wild dove (venaidura macroura), or mourning dove, which is so familiar a bird . . of the countryside. **1925** *Science* new ser 61.444, When later I did see them [=tumbler pigeons] their behavior impressed me as similar to that of the wild dove. **1967–69** *DARE* (Qu. Q7, *Names and nicknames for . . game birds*) Infs **DC**2, **GA**84, **MN**34, Wild dove; (Qu. Q14) Inf **NY**205, Wild dove. **2001** *Columbus Dispatch* (OH) 21 July sec F 8 (Internet), Other names for the mourning dove include Carolina dove, moaning dove, turtle dove, wild dove and wood dove.

wild elder n

A **spikenard:** usu *Aralia hispida,* but occas *A. racemosa.*

1814 Pursh *Flora Americae* 1.209, [*Aralia*] *hispida.* . . In stony woods: Canada, New England, &c. On high mountains: Pennsylvania, Virginia. . . Called *Wild Elder.* **1840** MA Zool. & Bot. Surv. *Herb. Plants & Quadrupeds* 14, *A. hispida.* . . Wild Elder. **1874** NH Geol. Surv. *Geol. NH* 1.400, *A. hispida.* Wild Elder. **1901** Lounsberry *S. Wild Flowers* 363, *A. hispida,* bristly sarsaparilla, or wild elder, frequently occurs through the mountainous parts of North Carolina and from there northward. **1916** *Torreya* 16.239 **nWI,** *Aralia racemosa.* . . Wild elder, false sarsaparilla. **1950** *Chron.-Telegram* (Elyria OH) 29 Apr 9/1, A plant in the park is the Wild Sarsaparilla or Wild Elder. There is also the Bristly Sarsaparilla or Wild Spikenard.

wild endive See **endive 2**

wild-eyed Susan n

Appar a **black-eyed Susan 2;** see quots.

1967 *DARE* (Qu. S7, *A kind of daisy, bright yellow with a dark center, that grows along roadsides in late summer*) Inf **PA**26, Wild-eyed Susan. **2006** in 2007 *DARE* File—Internet, Both are flowers, one a wild eyed susan and another a zinnia. . . What gives with pink zinnias and wild eyed susans?

wildfire n [*OED2 wild-fire* 4.a c1000 →, but here a calque of PaGer *wildfeier* (Ger *Wildfeuer*)] **PA**

Erysipelas.

1930 Shoemaker *1300 Words* 68 **cPA Mts** (as of c1900), Wildfire—Erysipelas. **1940** Yoder *Rosanna* 142 **PA,** Many of our people can powwow to stop pain and bleeding and *Roth Lafe,* (billious [sic] chills), the take-off in children, and wildfire (erysipelas) and *Püscht Bloder* (inflamed eyeball). **1964** Smith *PA Germans* 160, In the old days, erysipelas was referred to as *wild fire,* and a wide variety of rituals associated with it were known. **1970** *DARE* Tape **PA**249, My mother had what they called wildfire. . . That's an old disease. . . Today, they'd call it erysipelas.

wild flax n [*OED2* (at *flax* sb. 2.a) c1387 →]

=**butter-and-eggs 1.**

1892 *Science* 19.356, Wild Flax, Toad Flax, Linaria vulgaris. **1894** *Jrl. Amer. Folkl.* 7.96 **WV,** Linaria vulgaris, . . wild flax. **1936** Winter *Plants NE* 128, [*Linaria*] *linaria.* . . Butter-and-eggs. Wild Flax. Snapdragon. **1966–68** *DARE* (Qu. S11, . . *Wild snapdragon*) Inf **MN**33, Wild flax; (Qu. S26c, *Wildflowers that grow in woods*) Inf **MN**42, Wild flax.

wild forget-me-not See **forget-me-not 1a, b, h, 2**

wild four-o'clock See **four-o'clock 2**

wild geese n

=**fox and geese 2.**

1969 *DARE* (Qu. EE26, . . *Games . . children play in the snow*) Inf **IN**56, Wild geese—any number of children can play; played in a big circular path made in the snow. One child is "it" and must tag all the other children; none of them can get outside of the path until they're caught; then they're eliminated. The last person caught is the winner.

wild gentian n
=**pickerelweed.**

  1916 *Torreya* 16.237 **ceSC**, *Pontederia cordata* . . wild gentian, Cat Id., S.C.

wild geranium n

  1 An **alum root 1;** see quots.

  1898 *Jrl. Amer. Folkl.* 11.226 **CA**, *Heuchera micrantha,* . . wild geranium. **1921** Burbank *How Plants Are Trained* 6.197, The plant in question is a species of "wild geranium" known as *Heuchera micrantha,* a native of the western coast. **1967** *DARE* Wildfl QR Pl.89 [=*Heuchera americana*] Inf **AR**46A, Wild geranium. **1988** Weatherford *Ind. Givers* 185, The Indians made an astringent called alumroot from the wild geranium, *Heuchera americana.*

  2 A **globe mallow 1:** either *Sphaeralcea ambigua* or *S. coccinea.*

  1950 Stevens *ND Plants* 206, *Sphaeralcea coccinea.* . . Often called "wild geranium", suggested by both leaf and flower. **2007** *DARE* File—Internet, Wild Geranium (Sphaeralcea Ambigua)—Used with Desert Mallow by Shoshone women after birth to become infertile for one year.

wild ginger n

  1 Std: a plant either of the genus *Asarum,* native chiefly to the eastern half and northern parts of the US, or of the closely related genus *Hexastylis,* native to much of the south and midland areas of the US. For other names of var spp of both genera see **asarabacca, ginger 5, heartleaf 3, heart snakeroot, jug 1, jug plant, little brown jug, monkey jugs, pig n[1] B15, snakeroot b(3);** for other names of *A. canadense* see **black snakeroot, catfoot 1, colicroot 5, coltsfoot 2, coltsfoot snakeroot, false coltsfoot, gingerroot 2, hazelwort, Indian ginger, sweet coltsfoot 2.** For other names of var spp of *Hexastylis* see **colicroot 5, heartsease 4, Sampson's snakeroot 4**

  2 A **birthwort 1** (here: *Aristolochia macrophylla*).

  1900 Lyons *Plant Names* 45, *A[ristolochia] macrophylla.* . . Wild Ginger.

  3 A **toothache grass** (here: *Ctenium aromaticum*).

  1901 *Torreya* 1.115 **swGA**, *Campulosus aromaticus.* . . Wild ginger. Sumter [Co.]. **1913** Britton–Brown *Illustr. Flora* 1.225, Campulosus aromaticus. . . Lemon-grass, Wild Ginger.

wild goldenglow n

  A **beggar ticks 1** (here: *Bidens laevis*).

  1933 Small *Manual SE Flora* 1453, *B[idens] laevis.* . . (Wild-goldenglow.) **1975** Duncan–Foote *Wildflowers SE* 220, Wild-goldenglow. . . *Bidens laevis.* **2005** in 2007 *DARE* File—Internet **TX**, *Smooth Bidens.* . . is also known as: wild-goldenglow and bur-marigold. The fruit of this plant has barbs that will attach to you. Plant is found in wet areas.

wild goose bean See **goose bean**

wild goose mouth n   Cf **turkey mouth**

  A hunting dog's voice or cry that resembles the call of a wild goose.

  1927 [see **turkey mouth**]. **1977** Kilpatrick *Foxes' Union* 92 **VA**, She had what hunters call a wild goose mouth. A great hound, and no doubt about it.

wild goose plum n   [See quot 1888]   Cf **goose plum**

  A **wild plum 1:** usu *Prunus hortulana* or *P. munsoniana,* native to much of the central and south-central US, but occas *P. americana.*

  1868 *Amer. Entomologist* 1.93, The Miner plum, . . distinguished by botanists as the Chickasaw or wild-goose plum (*Prunus chicasa* [here:=*P. hortulana*]. **1873** *Indiana Progress* (PA) 13 Mar [7]/1 (newspaperarchive.com), The *cultivation of plums* is assuming considerable commercial importance, especially in Southern Ohio, where the yield . . is so great as to stimulate more extensive planting, for which purpose the Wild Goose plum, from Tennessee, is the favorite. **1888** *Denton Jrl.* (MD) 14 July 4/5, The wild goose plum is nothing more than the wild Chicasau plum refined and perfected by cultivation. It was

given its name by a Tennessee farmer named McCane, who, having killed a wild goose, found a peculiar seed in the bird's stomach, which he planted and from which grew the first wild goose plum. This was forty years ago. **1892** *Jrl. Amer. Folkl.* 5.95 **MD**, *Prunus Americana,* wild goose plum. *Ibid, Prunus hortulana,* wild goose plum. Markets of Boston and elsewhere. **1906** *DN* 3.164 **nwAR**, Wild goose plum. . . A small, sour, salmon-colored plum, extremely common in Arkansas. **1935** MO Bot. Garden *Annals* 22.572 **MO**, *Prunus Munsoniana.* . . Wild Goose Plum. Thickets, prairies, borders of streams, and waste ground. **1967–69** *DARE* (Qu. 146, . . *Kinds of fruits that grow wild around here*) Inf **SC**34, Wild goose plum—blueish; (Qu. T15, . . *Kinds of swamp trees*) Inf **KY**16, Wild goose plum. **2001** Zickefoose *Nat. Gardening Birds* 198 **CA**, I like the native holly-leaved cherry and the hardy wild goose plum for their reliability and lovely pinkish white flowers.

wild hay n   **widespread, but more freq Upper MW, West** See Map   Cf **marsh hay, slough grass 1, swale grass, swamp hay**

  Hay made from any of var grasses, such as **bluejoint 1,** and used for forage or pasturage; see quots.

  1819 *OH Repository* (Canton) 22 Oct 3/4, [Advt:] The subscriber . . will offer for sale on Saturday the 23d of October inst. . . *Wheat & Rye,* by the bushel, *one barrel of Salt, three tons of Wild Hay, and a quantity of Tobacco.* **1835** Hoffman *Winter in West* 1.193 **MI**, Settlers . . , for the sake of the wild hay, locate themselves near the great marshes. **1869** *Harper's New Mth. Mag.* 39.469 **West**, The emigrant . . might be able to secure [sustenance] by cutting and preparing wild hay for the use of the great mining companies which dot those sections of the Rocky Mountains. **1884** Vasey *Ag. Grasses* 61, *Muhlenbergia glomerata.* (Spiked Muhlenbergia.) . . In the Eastern States it is utilized as one of the native products of wet meadows in the making of what is called wild hay. **1917** *Scientific Mth.* 4.459, The farmers who cut wild hay from the meadows and marshes of New England and the prairies of the west also have similar problems on a smaller scale. **1965–70** *DARE* (Qu. L8, *Hay that grows naturally in damp places*) 108 Infs, **widespread, but more freq Upper MW, West,** Wild hay; (Qu. L9a, . . *Kinds of grass . . grown for hay*) Inf **NV**9, Wild hay; (Qu. L9b, *Hay from other kinds of plants [not grass]; not asked in early QRs*) Inf **WV**2, Wild hay. **1986** *Los Angeles Times* (CA) 2 Nov 16 (Internet) **MT**, But at least this year the summer rains had been generous across Montana, producing good crops of alfalfa and wild hay for winter feed. **2005** *Star–Herald* (Scottsbluff NE) 23 June 18/3, *Wild Hay.* 2004. 50 bales tarped since August.

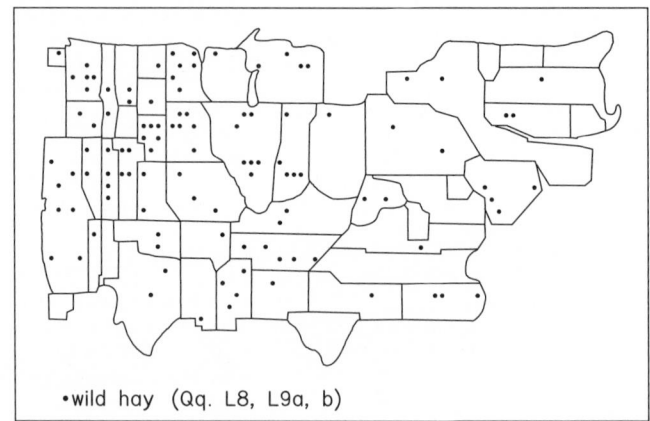

•wild hay (Qq. L8, L9a, b)

wild hazel n
=**jojoba.**

  1920 Saunders *Useful Wild Plants* 78 **West**, Possessing a fascination all its own is the so-called Wild Hazel, Goat-nut or Sheep-nut, the fruit of a non-deciduous, grayish-green shrub, *Simmondsia Californica* [=*S. chinensis*]. **1936** *Denton Rec.–Chron.* (TX) 3 Dec 6/1, Department of Agriculture scientists report that a vegetable oil equal to sperm oil can be made cheaply from the wild hazel nut which grows in arid sections of Arizona and Northern Mexico.

wild heliotrope n

  A **scorpionweed 2** with blue or purple flowers.

  1897 Parsons *Wild Flowers CA* 282, Wild heliotrope. . . *Phacelia tanacetifolia.* . . Among the Spanish-Californians it is known as "vervenia." **1932** *Van Nuys News* (CA) 28 Apr 6/3, Among the flowers were the wild heliotrope with its fairy like blue flowers. **1953** *Tucson Daily Citizen* (AZ) 4 Apr 16/6, Phacelia or Scorpionweed: A rich lavender wild heliotrope, often fragrant. **1968** *DARE* (Qu. S26e, *Other wildflowers not yet mentioned;* not asked in early QRs) Inf **CA**60, Wild heliotrope—a type of phacelia—grows around the creosote bushes. **2007** *DARE* File—Internet **sCA**, People who walk into a field of desert wildflowers in Spring are likely to come across clumps of blue flowers. Quite possibly this is a group of wild-heliotropes, or *Phacelia distans.*

wild hemlock n

1 =**spotted cowbane 1.**

1767 *Boston News–Letter* (MA) 21 May 3/1, Persons (especially Children) would do well to beware of this Weed: It is called wild Hemlock by some, and Musquash weed by others: It grows in low Lands, especially by running Water. **1828** Rafinesque *Med. Flora* 1.107, *Cicuta maculata.* . . *Vulgar Names*—Snakeweed, Death of man, Water Parsley, Poison root, Wild hemlock, Children's bane. **1898** U.S. Dept. Ag. Div. Botany *Bulletin* 20.40, *Cicuta maculata.* . . *Other names:* . . wild hemlock. **1912** *Indiana Eve. Gaz.* (PA) 9 May 1/6, Water hemlock . . is known by a variety of names: wild hemlock, . . cow bane and children's bane. It is widely distributed over the eastern portion of the United States being found most frequently in marshy places. **2002** Greenberg *Nat. Hist. Chicago* 296, *[Papaipemas] Birdi* feeds only on wild hemlock, *Cicuta maculata,* but we had never previously caught it either.

2 =**poison hemlock 1.**

1876 Hobbs *Bot. Hdbk.* 52, Hemlock, . . Wild, . . Conium maculatum. **1898** U.S. Dept. Ag. Div. Botany *Bulletin* 20.43, *Conium maculatum.* . . *Other names:* . . wild hemlock. **1964** *Gastonia Gaz.* (NC) 1 Sept sec B 5/3, One of the most dangerous plants is the tall wild hemlock, topped with flat circles of fluffy leaves. Its frothy leaves have been mistaken for parsley, its roots have been mistaken for wild turnips and its seeds have been mistaken for anise.

wild hemp n

1 =**giant ragweed.**

1830 Rafinesque *Med. Flora* 2.190, *A[mbrosia] trifida* is called Horseweed and Wild Hemp, . . sometimes 10 feet high. **1851** (1856) Dunglison *Med. Lexicon* 64, *Ambrosia trifida.* . . *Great Ragweed, Wild Hemp.* This indigenous plant is found in low grounds and along streams, from Canada to Georgia, and west to Louisiana and Arkansas. **1898** *Jrl. Amer. Folkl.* 11.229 **KS**, *Ambrosia trifida,* . . wild hemp. **1956** Teale *Autumn across Amer.* 80, *Ambrosia trifida.* . . Known variously as bitterweed, richweed, horse cane, buffalo weed and wild hemp, the giant ragweed usually occupies lower land. **1974** (1977) Coon *Useful Plants* 101, *Ambrosia trifida* . . wild hemp.

2 =**hemp nettle.** [*OED2* (at *hemp* sb. 5) 1597 →]

1835 Audubon *Ornith. Biog.* 3.56 **KY**, Locusts . . were gathered by boys from the trunks of trees and the "iron weeds," a species of wild hemp very abundant in that portion of the country. **1914** Georgia *Manual Weeds* 354, *Galeopsis Tetrahit.* . . *Other English names:* . . Wild Hemp. **1935** (1943) Muenscher *Weeds* 391, *Galeopsis Tetrahit.* . . Hemp nettle . . Wild hemp . . Ironweed. . . Locally common in Canada and the northeastern United States. **2003** in 2007 *DARE* File—Internet, *Galeopsis tetrahit* . . is common around barns and in rich damp soils. . . *Common Names* . . wild hemp, ironweed, brittle-stem hemp nettle [etc.].

wild hen n

1 =**prairie chicken 1.** Note: The extinct eastern population called **heath hen 1** is included in this definition. Cf **wild chicken**

1830 (1833) Dow *Dealings of God* 338 **IL**, About three fifths of this state [=IL] is savannas, or natural meadows, called Prairie. There are to be found . . wild hens, snakes and wolves, peculiar to these natural openings. **a1862** (1865) Thoreau *Cape Cod* 82 **eMA**, He also described the killing of what he called "wild hens" here . . when he was a boy. Perhaps they were "Prairie hens" (pinnated grouse). **1864** (1868) Trowbridge *3 Scouts* 162, He was a good shot, having had practice on the Illinois prairies . . bringing down wild hens on the wing. **1953** *AmSp* 28.279, The title *wild hen* is given for the usual reasons of size and sufficient resemblance to the heath hen (Mass.), [and] prairie chicken (N.Dak.)

2 =**flicker** n[2] **1.**

1882 Ingersoll *Birds'-Nesting* 70 **ME**, Its [=the flicker's] practice of laying additional eggs when the first set is removed gives the bird the name of "wild hen" among the people of Maine.

3 =**Florida gallinule.**

1919 Burns *Ornith. Chester Co.* PA 43, *Gallinula galeata*—Florida

Gallinule, "blue rail," "wild hen." **1923** U.S. Dept. Ag. *Misc. Circular* 13.44 **NJ, PA**, *Gallinula chloropus.* . . *Vernacular names* . . wild-hen. **1966** *DARE* (Qu. Q7, *Names and nicknames for . . game birds*) Inf **GA**6, Wild hen—like a chicken but with a long neck.

wild hippo n   Cf **hippo** n[2], **wild ipecac 1**

=**flowering spurge.**

1849 Amer. Med. Assoc. *Trans.* 2.726, *Euphorbia corollata,* . . Wild hippo. . . It is emetic, diaphoretic, and cathartic. **1863** Porcher *Resources* 126, *Euphorbia corollata.* . . Wild hippo; wild ipecac. **1892** (1974) Millspaugh *Amer. Med. Plants* 38-4, *Euphorbia corollata.* . . Com. names . . wild hippo. **2007** *DARE* File—Internet **MA**, *Euphorbia corollata* . . Wild Hippo.

wild hog n   Cf **wild boar, ~ pig**

=**jabalina.**

1805 in 1852 U.S. Congress *Debates & Proc.* 9th Cong 2d Sess app 1082 **TX**, Wild hogs are likewise plenty in their country. **1854** in 1856 Parker *Notes Exped.* 37 **TX**, The hogs . . met with, were a long-nosed, long-legged, slab-sided species, black in color, and evidently descendants of the wild hog, or peccary. **1861** U.S. Army Corps Topog. Engineers *Rept. Colorado R.* 55 **TX**, *Dicotyles torquatus* [=*D. tajassu*]. . . This animal, known in Texas as the wild hog, is found on the Canadian river, in the Indian territory, and from there south becomes quite abundant in Texas. **1900** *Portsmouth Herald* (NH) [12 Sept 3]/3 (newspaperarchive.com) **TX**, One of the men had shot a peccary. Another had a small package of salt in a pocket of his saddle. We roasted and ate the wild hog without bread. **1962** *Amer. Anthropologist* 64.953, The association of peyote with the "wild hog" (javalina, peccary), which ranges primarily in southern Texas, may reflect . . cultural ties with . . groups to the south.

wild-hog v phr, hence vbl n *wild-hogging*   **sAppalachians**

=**tomcat.**

1939 *Hall Coll.* **wNC, eTN**, *Wild-hog.* . . When they get on one of these big drunks and go to these honky-tonks; it's the same as tom-cattin'; both wild-hoggin' and tom-cattin' mean to look for a woman especially. *Ibid,* They must have been out wild-hogging around last night. **1952** Brown *NC Folkl.* 1.608 **wNC**, *Wild-hog.* . . To live a life of debauchery; to be wild. **1967** *DARE* (Qu. DD34, *A party at which there is considerable drinking*) Inf **TN**14, Wild-hogging. **a1975** Lunsford *It Used to Be* 176 **sAppalachians**, "Wildhoggin'" is similar to "Tomcattin'", but perhaps it is a rougher life of debauchery as the song goes: . . "And drinkin' of a few drinks of liquor,/ and fightin' some,/ And wildhoggin' and just romancin' around." **1994** in 2004 Montgomery–Hall *Dict. Smoky Mt. Engl.* 650, *Wild hog.* . . We used to go into Gatlinburg and wild hog on the weekends.

wild holly n

=**toyon.**

1919 *Fresno Morning Republican* (CA) 2 Dec 9/1, *To Save Wild Holly Bushes.* . . Vigorous efforts are being put forth to secure protection for the toyon or Christmas berry, California's wild holly. **1920** *Oakland Tribune* (CA) 19 Dec 8/8, Toyon trees have been almost obliterated in places. . . Vendors of wild holly and greenery are having shipped to them daily, and in immense quantities, such material from various parts of the state. **2001** *News from Native CA* 14.9 (Internet), Toyon . . is also known as California Holly, Wild Holly, Christmas Berry, Hollyberry, Toyon Berry, Redberry. . . The common name, "California Holly," refers more to the berries than to the leaves, which are unlike those of holly.

wild hollyhock n

1 Any of var native **mallows B**, esp a **globe mallow 1** or **2**, a **poppy mallow**, or a plant of the genus *Sidalcea*.

1778 Carver *Travels N. Amer.* 346, Wild Hollyhock, Wild Pinks [etc.]. **1897** Parsons *Wild Flowers CA* 198, *Sidalcea malvæflora.* . . In early spring the graceful sprays . . bend over our meadows everywhere, making them bright with their pink blossoms, which the children call "wild hollyhocks." **1917** Rydberg *Flora Rocky Mts.* 561, Wild Hollyhock, Maple-leaved Mallow. . . *Iliamna.* **1917** Eaton *Green Trails* 92 **nwMT**, Later it [=wild hollyhock] was identified as the *Sidalcea neo-mexicana.* **1919** Chase *CA Desert* 378, Sphæralcea ambigua. Wild Hollyhock. **1923** Clute *Dict. Amer. Plant Names* 169, Wild hollyhock.—*Callirhoe digitata.* **1937** *San Mateo Times* (CA) 24 Apr 4/5, Checkerbloom or wild hollyhock is fairly common. **1967** Dodge *Roadside Wildflowers* 41, Soft globemallow—false mallow, wild hollyhock, rose-of-Sharon. **1967–68** *DARE* (Qu. S2, . . *The flower that comes up in the woods early in spring, with three white petals that turn pink as the flower grows* *older*) Inf **TX**40, Maybe a wild hollyhock; (Qu. S11, . . *Bachelor's button, blue violet, bluets, dandelion, dog-tooth violet, peony, wild snapdragon, zinnia*) Inf **CA**20, Wild hollyhocks; (Qu. S26b, *Wildflowers that grow in water or wet places*) Inf **NJ**16, Wild hollyhock—in meadows, wet areas. **1967** *DARE* Wildfl QR Pl.128 [=*Malva moschata*] Inf **OR**12, Wild hollyhock; Pl.129 [=*Hibiscus moscheutos*] Inf **CA**24, Wild hollyhock or mallow flower. **2003** *NW Native Plant Jrl.* 1.3.17 (Internet) **OR**, *Iliamna latibracteata*. . . This species is one of the more showy of Oregon's rare wildflowers, resembling closely the hollyhock and in the same plant family. Sometimes referred to as a wild hollyhock. **2005** *Trinity Forks Native Plant Press* April 5 **TX**, Winecups (*Callirhoe involucrata*) have been my favorite wildflower since I was a child. . . I first knew it as the wild hollyhock. **2007** *DARE* File—Internet **CA**, *Sidalcea* spp. (*Sidalcea hickmanii—Rare & S. malvaeflora*)—*Checkerbloom/Wild Hollyhock*. These plants were eaten as greens by the tribes.

2 A **bindweed 1** (here: *Calystegia spithamaea*).

1898 *Jrl. Amer. Folkl.* 11.275 **ME**, *Convolvulus spithamaeus*, . . wild hollyhock.

wild honeysuckle n

1 =**rhododendron**, esp a **pinkster 2** (here: *Rhododendron periclymenoides*). **chiefly Sth, S Midl** Cf **honeysuckle 3**

1761 Kalm *Resa* III.109 *(DAE)*, Af Ängelsmännerna heta de wild Honeysuckle, emedan de äro på långt håll mycket like Periclymenum eller Caprifolium. [=It [=*Rhododendron periclymenoides*] is called "wild honeysuckle" by the English, because from a distance it looks much like *Periclymenum* or *Caprifolium*.] **1830** Rafinesque *Med. Flora* 2.198, *Azalea*. . . Beautiful ornamental genus of shrubs, with fragrant splendid blossoms, often called *Swamp Pink, Wild Honey-suckle, Springbloom*. **1843** Torrey *Flora NY* 2.1.438, *Rhododendron nudiflorum*. . . Upright Wild Honeysuckle. *Ibid* 439, *Rhododendron viscosum*. . . White Wild Honeysuckle. **1894** *Jrl. Amer. Folkl.* 7.93 **GA, WV**, *Rhododendron nudiflorum*, . . wild honeysuckle. **1902** *Piqua Daily Call* (OH) 22 Oct [150]/3 (newspaperarchive.com) **TN**, The pink flush that mantles the side of yonder mountain is shed by myriads of blossoms of azalea, or wild honeysuckle, the mountain folk call it. **1934** *San Antonio Express–News* (TX) 8 July sec C 8/3, Wild honeysuckle is a strange name for our Eastern wild azalea, but that is the name it commonly goes by. **1967** *DARE* Wildfl QR Pl.154 [=*Rhododendron periclymenoides*] Inf **AR**44, Wild azalea, some say wild honeysuckle. **1969** *DARE* (Qu. S26c, *Wildflowers that grow in woods*) Inf **GA**80, Wild honeysuckle, azalea—same. **2006** *Charleston Gaz.* (WV) 27 May sec B 2 (Internet), Lacy ferns grew underfoot, and the pink and orange wild honeysuckle (azalea) bloomed in clumps close by.

2 =**butterflyweed 2. chiefly TX** Cf **honeysuckle 5h**

1896 *Jrl. Amer. Folkl.* 9.188 **TX**, *Gaura*, sp., wild honeysuckle. **1936** Whitehouse *TX Flowers* 84, *Lindheimer's Gaura* . . is, like other members of this group, called kisses and wild honeysuckle because of its sweet fragrance. **1967** *DARE* Wildfl QR (Wills–Irwin) Pl.30B [= *Gaura suffulta*] Inf **TX**44, Wild honeysuckle, bee-blossom. **2007** *DARE* File—Internet **TX**, *Gaura suffulta*. . . Bee blossom, Kisses, Wild Honeysuckle.

3 =**scarlet gilia.** Cf **honeysuckle 5i**

1911 Garrett *Spring Flora Wasatch* 75 **UT**, Scarlet Gilia. . . Locally known as "Wild Honeysuckle." Often characterized by an offensive odor. **1915** (1926) Armstrong–Thornber *Western Wild Flowers* 394, This [=*Ipomopsis aggregata*] has several common names which are very misleading, such as Wild Cypress and Wild Honeysuckle. **1950** Douglas *Of Men & Mts.* 86, At various elevations bloom the scarlet gilia or wild honeysuckle, delicate as a hothouse orchid.

wild hop n Pronc-sp *wild op*

A **jack bean 1** (here: *Canavalia rosea*).

1896 *Jrl. Amer. Folkl.* 9.185 **sFL**, *Canavalia obtusifolia* [=*C. rosea*], . . wild hop or " 'op."

wild hyacinth n

1 =**camas 1.**

1828 *Transylvania Jrl. Med.* 1.420 **KY**, Genus *Phalangium* [=*Camassia*]. . . Wild Hyacinth. **1878** *Amer. Naturalist* 12.601, *Camassia esculenta*.—Wild hyacinth, a very common plant in the upper Mississippi valley. Indians and Whites eat this root and find it very nutritious, with an agreeable, mucilaginous taste. **1897** *Jrl. Amer. Folkl.* 10.145 **CA**, *Camassia esculenta*, wild hyacinth. **1939** *KS Acad. Sci. Trans.* 42.165, A prairie meadow . . delighted us with the beauty and opulence of bloom of . . *Camassia esculenta*, often not inaptly called wild hya-

cinth. **1946** *Maryville Daily Forum* (MO) 14 May 3/6, Camassia. . . is an early American native of Missouri where it has often been called the wild hyacinth. It has a resemblance of hyacinths. **1966–70** *DARE* (Qu. S26d, *Wildflowers that grow in meadows;* not asked in early QRs) Infs **KY**77, **OH**57, **VA**21, Wild hyacinth(s); (Qu. S23, *Pale blue flowers with downy leaves and cups that come up on open, stony hillsides in March or early April*) Inf **GA**28, Wild hyacinth; (Qu. S24, *A wild flower that grows in swamps and marshes and looks like a small blue iris*) Inf **OK**28, Wild hyacinth; (Qu. S26a, . . *Wildflowers. . . Roadside flowers*) Inf **WA**12, Wild hyacinth; (Qu. S26c, *Wildflowers that grow in woods*) Inf **KY**60, Wild hyacinths. [*DARE* Ed: Some of these Infs may refer instead to other senses below.] **2002** Hemmerly *Ozark Wildflowers* 160, Wild Hyacinth—*Camassia scilloides*. . . A less common species, *C. angusta* . . , also called Wild Hyacinth, has more numerous (50–100) lavender to light purple flowers.

2 Any of a group of similar western liliaceous plants (formerly composing the genus *Brodiaea*) of the genera *Brodiaea, Dichelostemma,* and *Triteleia;* esp a **blue dicks** (here: *D. capitatum*).

1897 Parsons *Wild Flowers CA* 262, Wild hyacinth. *Brodiaea capitata* [=*Dichelostemma capitatum*]. **1915** (1926) Armstrong–Thornber *Western Wild Flowers* 16, Blue Dicks. . . There are several other names, such as Cluster Lily and Hog-onion. The name Wild Hyacinth is poor, as it does not resemble a hyacinth in character. **1916** *Muhlenbergia* 2.375 **OR**, *Hookera* [=*Brodiaea*] . . Wild hyacinth. **1924** *Amer. Botanist* 30.2 **CA**, In the early spring the brodiaea or wild hyacinth, takes the lead with its clusters of purplish blue blossoms, a very magnificent flower, lasting for weeks. **1937** St. John *Flora SE WA & ID* 86, Wild Hyacinth. . . *B. grandiflora*. **1940** *Amer. Midland Naturalist* 24.468 **CA**, The inflated perianth-tube and rotate segments give to the flowers of *D[ichelostemma] multiflorum* an appearance strongly suggesting miniature hyacinths, so that the common name "Wild Hyacinth," often applied to various members of the genus, is rather appropriate for this species. **1961** Thomas *Flora Santa Cruz* 126 **cwCA**, Wild Hyacinth. . . *Triteleia hyacinthina*. **1977** *San Mateo Times* (CA) 15 Apr 10/4, Brodiaea . . is also a native of our Western United States. B. puchella [sic; =*Dichelostemma capitatum*], is commonly called wild hyacinth because of its lovely violet blue flowers. **2009** *DARE* File—Internet, Californica Brodiaea 'Wild Hyacinth' should be planted roughly 4″ deep. *Ibid* **CA**, The Wild Hyacinth (also known as the Blue Dicks) member of the Lily family, grows in the surrounding foothills March–April.

3 A **fringed orchid;** see quots. **NEng, AK**

1896 *Jrl. Amer. Folkl.* 9.144 **ME**, *Habenaria psycodes* [=*Platanthera p.*] . . and *Habenaria fimbriata* [=*P. grandiflora*], . . wild hyacinth. **1897** *Overland Mth.* (2d ser) 30.520 **AK**, Right in the pass and within ten feet of a snow bank . . , I gathered . . a wild hyacinth. **1945** *IA State College Jrl. Sci.* 19.189 **AK**, *P[latanthera] dilitata* [sic]. . . Var. *leucostachys*. . . This is the form known as Wild Hyacinth. **1961** *Bryologist* 64.8 **AK**, Forbs occur only rarely, mostly as individual plants—notably, the very fragrant "wild hyacinth" (*Platanthera dilatata* . .).

4 =**sand lily 2.**

1901 U.S. Dept. Ag. Div. Botany *Bulletin* 26.143, Wild hyacinth. (*Leucocrinum montanum*.) **1929** Stuhr *Native Drug Plants NE* 4, *Leucocrinum montanum*. . . Sand-lily, Mountain Lily, Wild Hyacinth.

5 A **death camas.**

1903 KS Acad. Sci. *Trans.* 18.207, Zygadenus elegans, Z. nuttallii. Wild hyacinth. . . Cathartic, emetic, narcotic. **1951** *PADS* 15.28 **TX**, *Toxicoscordion nuttalli*. . . wild hyacinth, poison hyacinth.

wild hydrangea n

1 A **dock** n[1] (here: *Rumex venosus*).

1917 Rydberg *Flora Rocky Mts.* 231, *R[umex] venosus*. . . Wild Hydrangea. **1940** Gates *Flora KS* 172, Rumex venosus. . . Wild Hydrangea.

2 =**hobblebush.**

[**1848** Catlow *Pop. Field Botany* 213, *Viburnum lantana*. . . It has been called the Wild Hydrangea, from its general resemblance to that garden plant.] **1940** Clute *Amer. Plant Names* 56, *Viburnum*. . . *alnifolium*. . . wild hydrangea.

wild ilima n Cf **ilima**

A **mallow B** (here: *Abutilon grandifolium*).

1929 Pope *Plants HI* 145, *Wild ilima—Abutilon molle* [=*A. grandifolium*]. . . Flowers orange. . . common . . throughout the Hawaiian Islands. The species is said to be of rather recent introduction, probably from some other tropical country.

wild indigo n

1 Std: a plant of the genus *Baptisia*. Also called **false indigo 2, horse devil, indigo 2a;** for other names of var spp see **deer grass 3, false lupine 2, gopher grass, hen and chickens 1b, honesty-weed, horsefly weed, indigo broom, ~ weed 2, rattlebush 1, rattleweed e, scareweed, shoofly 5, yellow broom 1, ~ wisteria**

2 =**false indigo 1.**

[1788 Schöpf *Reise Staaten* 2.252, Eine dritte Sorte wird *wilder Indigo* (*Amorpha fruticosa* L.), genannt. [=A third kind is called wild indigo (*Amorpha fruticosa*).]] **1814** Pursh *Flora Americae* 2.466, *Amorpha* . . *fruticosa*. . . On the banks of rivers: Carolina and Florida. . . It is generally known by the name of *Wild Indigo*. **1828** Flint *Condensed Geog.* 2.509 **LA,** *Amorpha, Angustifolia*. Wild Indigo; inhabits borders of swamps and lakes. **1950** Stevens *ND Plants* 188, *Amorpha nana*. . . Dwarf wild indigo. **1960** Vines *Trees SW* 520, *Amorpha*. . . *paniculata*. . . Another name is False Indigo or Wild Indigo. **2002** Perrow-Davy *Hdbk. Ecological Restoration* 10, The ground cover consisted of bluegrasses (*Poa* spp.), sedges (*Carex* spp.), dwarf wild indigo (*Amorpha nana*) [etc].

3 A **senna** n[1] **B1** such as *Cassia marilandica* or *C. obtusifolia*; see quots.

1851 De Bow's Rev. 11.49 **LA,** *Wild Coffee, or Wild Indigo*, grows abundantly, and is indigenous. There seems to be two kinds of it. It infests our lanes, and nothing feeds upon it. **1862** in 2007 *DARE* File—Internet **AL** [*Mobile Advt. & Reg.* (AL) 27 Sept], Messrs. Editors: Will you please warn persons who might try to gather wild coffee without knowing it, not to mistake for the same the wild indigo, or Cassia Tora, which has the active properties of senna, and in large doses might prove poisonous. **1898** *Jrl. Amer. Folkl.* 11.225 **KS,** *Cassia Marilandica*, . . wild indigo.

wild ipecac n

1 also *wild ipecacuanha:* A **spurge,** usu *Euphorbia ipecacuanhae.* Cf **milk ipecac, wild hippo**

1815 Drake *Natural View Cincinnati* 87, *Emetics*. . . Euphorbia ipecacuanha—wild ipecac, *the root.* **1853** NY State Museum *Catalogue Cabinet Nat. Hist.* 36, *Euphorbia ipecacuanha*, Wild Ipecac. **1854** Griffith *Universal Formulary* 226, *Euphorbia ipecacuanha. Wild Ipecacuanha*. . . The root, the part used, is large, white, almost inodorous, and has a somewhat sweet taste. **1863** [see **wild hippo**]. **1882** *Helena Independent* (MT) 3 Dec 1/6 **Sth,** As we tramped along through woods of ash, elm and water oak, we saw wild ipecac and sweet william growing at the sides of the odd pathway. **1924** *Ecology* 5.248 **NJ,** The interesting wild ipecac, *Euphorbia ipecacuanhae*, is also very conspicuous at this season. **1977** Torrey Bot. Club *Bulletin* 104.67 **NY,** After considerable searching, the group found *Euphorbia ipecacuanhae* (wild ipecac) growing in the same location as it had the previous summer. **1988** *Morning Call* (Allentown PA) 19 Dec sec B 1 (Internet), They [= plants in danger of extinction] range from the wild ipecac to the forked rush to the spotted pondweed.

2 also *false ipecac:* A **horse gentian** (here: *Triosteum perfoliatum*).

1817 Bigelow *Amer. Med. Botany* 1.90, *Triosteum perfoliatum*. . . Its common names are *Fever root* and *Wild ipecac.* **1832** Williamson *Hist. ME* 1.123, The *Fever-root*, or *wild Ipecac*, occurs in limestone soils. . . It may be used for an emetic or cathartic. **1853** Esrey–Hering *Materia Medica* 249, *Triosteum perfoliatum*. . . Dr. Tinker's weed, Wild Coffee, . . Wild Ipecac [etc]. **1896** *Jrl. Amer. Folkl.* 9.190 **West,** *Triosteum perfoliatum*, . . wild ipecac. **1920** *Sheboygan Press* (WI) 11 Sept 3/4, The plant called "tinker's weed" is wild ipecac, known also as feverwort. **1940** Clute *Amer. Plant Names* 274, *Triosteum perfoliatum*. False ipecac. **1948** Stevens *KS Wild Flowers* 357, *Triosteum perfoliatum*. . . Various vernacular names have been given to this species: . . wild or wood ipecac because a decoction of the plant was found to have the well-known emetic effect of ipecac.

3 =**spreading dogbane.**

1900 Lyons *Plant Names* 40, *A[pocynum] androsaemifolium*. . . Wild Ipecac. **1971** Krochmal *Appalachia Med. Plants* 50, *Apocynum androsaemifolium*. . . Common names: . . wild ipecac.

wild ipecacuanha See **wild ipecac 1**

wild Isaac n

A **boneset 1** (here: *Eupatorium perfoliatum*).

1902 U.S. Dept. Ag. *Farmers' Bulletin* 150.31, Boneset. . . Other common names.—Thoroughwort, . . wild Isaac. **1930** Sievers *Amer. Med. Plants* 16, *Eupatorium perfoliatum*. . . wild isaac. **1971** Krochmal *Appalachia Med. Plants* 118, *Eupatorium perfoliatum*. . . *Common names:* . . wild Isaac.

wild jalap n Cf **jalap**

1 =**man-of-the-earth 1.**

[**1775** (1962) Romans *Nat. Hist. FL* 155, Jalap. . . I accidentally found it growing wild near *Pensacola;* being led to think, that a certain tuberous root made use of by the savages as a purgative might be it.] **1828** Rafinesque *Med. Flora* 1.123, *Convolvulus panduratus* [=*Ipomoea p.*] . . Wild Jalap. [*Ibid* 125, The true jalap of commerce has been ascribed to several plants. . . This plant is one of the false jalaps.] **1854** King *Amer. Eclectic Dispensatory* 391, *Convolvulus panduratus*. . . This plant, likewise known as *Wild Jalap, Man in the Ground, Mechameck, Man of the Earth*, etc., has a perennial, very large, cylindrical or fusiform *root.* **1881** (1882) Maisch *Manual Organic Materia Medica* 74, *Ipomœa panadurata*.—Wild Jalap, Manroot. . . United States, in sandy fields. **1954** *GA Hist. Qrly.* 38.20 (as of 1860s), Plants like wild jalap (*Ipomoea pandurata*) . . served their purposes fairly well.

2 =**mayapple 1.**

1849 Amer. Med. Assoc. *Trans.* 2.687, *Podophyllum peltatum*. . . Wild jalap; May apple; wild lemon; duck weed. . . Bigelow says it is a sure and active cathartic. **1861** De Bow's Rev. 31.111 **Sth,** Various species of *Euphorbia* . . are found growing in the South, and with the wild Jalap (*Podophyllum peltatum*) may be used as substitutes for emetics and purgatives. **1974** (1977) Coon *Useful Plants* 76, *Podophyllum peltatum*. . . At times called wild jalap because it causes cathartic action.

wild Job's tears n [From the resemblance to **Job's tears 1**]

A **false gromwell** (here: *Onosmodium virginianum*).

1854 King *Amer. Eclectic Dispensatory* 691, *Onosmodium Virginianum*. . . This plant . . is also known by the common names of *Gravel-weed*, and *Wild Job's Tears*. **1886** *Homoeopathic News* 15.36, "False Gromwell," or "Wild Job's Tears,"—*Onosmodium Virginianum*—sprang up over the new-made grave. **1910** Graves *Flowering Plants* 330 **CT,** *Onosmodium virginianum*. . . Gravel-weed. Pearl-plant. Wild Job's Tears. False Gromwell. **2009** *DARE* File—Internet **FL** [Wild Florida Photo], *Onosmodium virginianum*—False Gromwell, Wild Job's Tears.

wild lavender n

1 =**chaste tree.**

1955 *Phytologia* 5.172 **FL,** Common names for [*Vitex trifolia*] are very numerous and include . . "wild lavender". . . Of these names . . "wild lavender" and "wild-pepper" [are used] in Florida. **1960** Vines *Trees SW* 899, *Vitex* . . *agnus-castus*. . . Vernacular names are . . Wild Lavender, Common Chaste-tree, True Chaste-tree [etc].

2 A **cudweed 1** such as *Pseudognaphalium obtusifolium;* see quot.

1840 MA Zool. & Bot. Surv. *Herb. Plants & Quadrupeds* 125, *G[naphalium] polycephalum* [=*Pseudognaphalium obtusifolium*]. . . Wild Lavender.

wild lemon n Cf **wild citron**

=**mayapple 1.**

1818 Barton *Vegetable Materia Medica* 2.9, May-apple. Mandrake. Wild Lemon [etc]. **1879** *Eve. Gaz.* (Pt. Jervis NY) 5 July [2]/2 (newspaperarchive.com), *Podophyllum peltatum* . . the writer once heard a lively dispute as to whether the fruit of this plant ought to be called May-apple or wild lemon. **1907** *Mansfield News* (OH) 28 Oct 6/5, Black Cherry Root, Wild Lemon and Nux Vomica are splendid medicines for Bad Blood, Dyspepsia, Nervousness and Insomnia. **1939** Medsger *Edible Wild Plants* 13, *May Apple, or Mandrake, or Wild Lemon*. . . This beautiful but ill-smelling plant of the Barberry family grows in dense patches along fences, roadsides, and in open woods. . . The edible fruit . . is about two inches long, egg-shaped, yellow, with a many-seeded pulp within a rather tough skin. **1950** *WELS* ce**WI** (*Small plants, shaped like an umbrella, that grow in woods and fields: Those safe to eat*) 1 Inf, Wild lemon; (*Other names in your locality for the may-apple*) 1 Inf, Wild lemons—we believed that we would die if we ate more than one of these wild lemons when we were small. **1969** *DARE* (Qu. S4, . . *Mayapple:* [*Woodside plant, not a tree, with two large spreading leaves; they grow in patches and have a small yellow fruit late in summer*]) Inf **NY**183, Wild lemon. **1981** Howell *Surv. Folklife* 66 ne**TN,** se**KY,** *Podophyllum peltatum*—May-apple; wild lemon—Fruit which ripens in July or August can be eaten in small quantities.

wild lettuce n

1 Std: any of var native wild plants of the genus *Lactuca.* [*OED2* c1290 →] Also called **milkweed 4.** For other names of var spp see **butterweed 4, compass plant 4, devil's ironweed, devil's-weed 2a, false lettuce, fireweed b, gall of the earth 3, gopher plant 2, horseweed 5, larkspur lettuce, oldfield ~, prickly ~, trumpet milkweed, wild opium** Cf **China lettuce 1, groundhog's ear**

2 =**rattlesnake root 2b.**

1752 Miller *Gardeners Dict.* np, *Prenanthes,* Wild Lettuce. **1793** *Amer. Philos. Soc. Trans.* 3.176, *Prenanthes,* Wild-Lettuce, Ivy-leaf. **1925** *Natl. Geogr. Mag.* 48.46, *Prenanthes alba.* . . Joy-leaf, cancerweed, lion's-foot, and wild lettuce are some of its local names. **2007** *DARE* File—Internet **NY,** *Prenanthes sp.* wild lettuce.

3 Usu a **wintergreen 1** but also *Moneses uniflora.*

1830 Rafinesque *Med. Flora* 2.72, *P[yrola] rotundifolia, P. elliptica,* and *P.* [=*Moneses*] *uniflora,* are called vulgarly *Wild Lettuce, Roundleaf,* and *Consumption Weed.* **1850** (1859) Comfort *Practice Med.* 305, *Wild Lettuce (Pyrola Rotundifolia)* is recommended by Samuel Thomson as a good remedy in mild cases of dropsy. **1924** *Amer. Botanist* 30.55, *P[yrola] rotundifolia* . . has the most common names. . . The names "wild lettuce", "Indian lettuce", and "liverwort lettuce" seem to indicate the use of the plants as food though they may refer to the shape . . of the leaves.

4 A **miner's lettuce** (here: *Claytonia perfoliata*). **CA**

1875 CA Acad. Sci. *Proc.* 5.377, The wild lettuce, *(Claytonia perfoliata* . . *).* **1893** *Jrl. Amer. Folkl.* 6.138 **CA,** *Claytonia perfoliata,* wild lettuce. [Footnote:] Sometimes eaten by children as they would eat lettuce. [**2003** in 2007 *DARE* File—Internet, Miner's lettuce is of the species Claytonia perfoliata and grows wild . . in California's Sacramento and northern San Joaquin valleys. . . Because this wild lettuce provided valuable nutrition to the early miners of the Northwest, it was appropriately named "miner's lettuce".]

5 A **Venus's-looking-glass** (here: *Triodanis perfoliata*).

1944 AL Geol. Surv. *Bulletin* 53.215, [*Specularia* [=*Triodanis*] *perfoliata*] is sometimes cooked and eaten for greens in the spring, and called "wild lettuce." **1966** *DARE* Wildfl QR Pl.219B [=*Specularia perfoliata*] Inf **AR44,** Wild lettuce; **AR46,** Wild lettuce—picked for greens.

6 A **monkey flower 1** (here: *Mimulus guttatus*). **West**

1963 Craighead *Rocky Mt. Wildflowers* 172, *Yellow monkeyflower—Mimulus guttatus.* . . *Other names:* Wild Lettuce. **1970** Kirk *Wild Edible Plants W. U.S.* 75, *Mimulus guttatus.* . . Yellow Monkey-flower, . . Wild Lettuce. **2007** *DARE* File—Internet, *Mimulus guttatus*—Monkey Flower, Wild Lettuce. . . Native to north-western North America. A lush, loose, mat-forming (stoloniferous) plant with mid green leaves and bright-yellow flowers with red spotted throats. . . Young leaves are used in salad.

wild licorice n   Also sp *wild liquorice*

1 =**crab's eye.** Cf **Indian licorice, licorice vine**

1876 Hobbs *Bot. Hdbk.* 139, Abrus precatorius . . Love pea, Wild liquorice. **1915** *DN* 4.240, *Black-eyed Susans.* . . The seeds of the wild licorice *(Abrus precatorius)* indigenous to India, the West Indies, and Brazil.

2 A **spikenard:** usu **wild sarsaparilla 1,** but also *Aralia racemosa.*

1787 Schöpf *Materia Medica Amer.* 42, *Aralia racemosa.* . . *Spikenard, Wild Liquorice.* Loc. *Noveboracum* [=NY], Pensylvania. **1828** Rafinesque *Med. Flora* 1.53, *Aralia nudicaulis.* . . *Vulgar names—*Spiknard, . . Wild Liquorice, Sweet-root. **1876** Hobbs *Bot. Hdbk.* 64, Liquorice, . . Wild . . Aralia nudicaulis. **1947** (1964) Randolph *Ozark Superstitions* 199 **AR,** People near Paris tell me that spikenard is also known as wild licorice; it may be *Aralia racemosa,* but I'm not sure about this.

3 A **licorice B1** (here: *Glycyrrhiza lepidota*).

1806 (1905) Lewis *Orig. Jrls. Lewis & Clark Exped.* 5.211, The wild liquorice and sunflower are very abundant in the plains and river bottoms. **1830** Albany Inst. *Trans.* 1.19 **West,** *Glycyrrhiza lepidota, Nutt.* (wild liquorice). **1895** Torrey Bot. Club *Bulletin* 22.108 **West,** Another member of the Leguminous family is our Wild Liquorice (*Glycyrrhiza lepidota* . . *),* mostly noteworthy as a very bad weed in the west, everywhere too prevalent. **1926** *Amer. Anthropologist* new ser 28.571 **ND, SD,** Also attached all round the edge of the disk were the burrs of wild licorice (*Glycyrrhiza lepidota*). **1961** *Jrl. Wildlife Management*

25.48 **MT,** Wild licorice (*Glycyrrhiza lepidota*). **2006** *Daily Herald* (Arlington Heights IL) 4 June [135]/2 (newspaperarchive.com), [*Mark Trail* comic strip:] Blackfoot Indians used wild licorice to treat many ailments, including earaches, colds, sore throats, asthma, and certain types of wounds.

4 =**bedstraw,** usu *Galium circaezans, G. lanceolatum,* or *G. kamtschaticum.*

1822 Eaton *Botany* 286, [*Galium*] *circaezans* . . wild liquorice. [**1840** MA Zool. & Bot. Surv. *Herb. Plants & Quadrupeds* 144, *G[alium] circaezans.* . . Liquorice. So called from its taste. *Ibid, G. lanceolatum.* . . Popularly called *liquorice,* from the sweet taste of its stem and leaves.] **1891** Jesup *Plants Hanover NH* 20, G[alium] circaezans. . . (Wild Liquorice). Woods; not rare. G. lanceolatum. . . (Wild Liquorice.) **1925** *Amer. Midland Naturalist* 9.430, *Galium circaezans.* . . Wild Liquorice. **1954** Sharpe *101 Wildflowers* 9 **AK,** The northern wildlicorice (G[alium] kamtschaticum), has 4 broad, 3-veined leaves in a whorl, and greenish yellow flowers. **1967** *DARE* (Qu. S13, . . *A common wild bush with bunches of round, prickly seeds; when they get dry they stick to your clothing*) Inf **IA13,** Wild licorice. [*DARE* Ed: This Inf may refer instead to **3** above.] **1997** Torrey Bot. Soc. *Jrl.* 124.340 **NJ,** Wild licorice (*Galium circaezans*), lance-leaved wild licorice (*G. lanceolatum*).

wild lilac n

1 =**ceanothus.** **CA**   See Map

1854 *Horticult. Rev. & Bot. Mag.* 4.85 **CA,** Our California tea-tree is the *Ceanothus Thyrsiflorus.* Called also here, *Wild Lilac.* **1857** U.S. War Dept. *Rept. Explor. Railroad* (Botany) 6.12 **CA,** Near San Francisco the shrubby undergrowth is made up, in a great degree, of the "wild lilac," (*Ceanothus thyrsiflorus,*) *Ceanothus rigidus,* and the bush lupine, (*Lupinus macrocarpus.*) **1883** *Elyria Republican* (OH) 27 Sept 2/3 **sCA,** From whatever side one approaches Santa Anita in May, he will drive through a wild garden—asters, . . alder, wild lilac, white sage—all in riotous flowering. **1904** *Condor* 6.25 **CA,** The ridges are covered for the most part with . . considerable underbrush such as wild lilac (*Ceanothus thrysifloris* [sic]). **1947** Peattie *Sierra Nevada* 142 **CA,** Buckbrush and other ceanothus (wild lilac, to use its common though mistaken name). **1967–70** *DARE* (Qu. S6, . . *Queen Anne's lace: [Summertime roadside weed two feet high or so with a lacy white top]*) Inf **CA165,** Wild lilac; (Qu. S26a, . . *Wildflowers. . . Roadside flowers*) Infs **CA4, 53, 126,** Wild lilac(s); (Qu. S26c, *Wildflowers that grow in woods*) Inf **CA79,** Wild lilacs; (Qu. S26e, *Other wildflowers not yet mentioned; not asked in early QRs*) Inf **CA65,** Wild lilac or ceanothus; **CA140,** ['sɪən,ɔufəs] or wild lilac; **CA144,** Wild lilac. **1982** *Mod. Maturity* 25.50 **cwCA,** When you reach the coastal bluffs, take in the heady aroma of sage and wild lilacs floating in the salty sea air. **2007** *Modesto Bee* (CA) 11 Apr sec G 3/2, [Caption:] Heuchera rosada, above, and Ceanothus (California wild lilacs) put on a show in Davis.

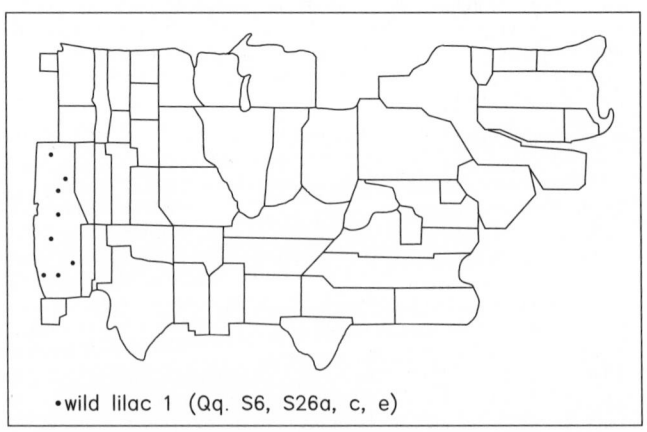

•wild lilac 1 (Qq. S6, S26a, c, e)

2 A **silverleaf 8** (here: *Leucophyllum frutescens*). **TX**

1952 McCampbell *TX Seaport* 239, [*Leucophyllum frutescens*] is also called wild lilac and ash plant. **1960** Vines *Trees SW* 921, The Spanish vernacular name, Cenizo, is much used in the Southwest. . . Other vernacular names are Ash-bush, Wild Lilac, Purple Sage [etc]. **1985** Dodge *Flowers SW Deserts* 111, *Silverleaf*—Ceniza, . . Wild-Lilac. . . *Leucophyllum frutescens.* Texas desert.

wild lily of the valley n   Cf **lily of the valley**

1 A **bead lily** (here: *Clintonia borealis*).

1822 Eaton *Botany* 269, *Dracaena [b]orealis* . . wild lily of the valley, or dragoness plant. **1847** Wood *Class-Book* 553, *C[lintonia] bore-*

alis. . . Wild Lily of the Valley. . . Berries of a rich amethystine blue. **1894** *Jrl. Amer. Folkl.* 7.101 **MA,** *Clintonia borealis. . .* wild lily-of-the-valley. **1929** *Torreya* 29.149 **ME,** Clintonia borealis was *"Wild Lily of the Valley,"* as were Pyrola elliptica and rotundifolia, and Dwarf Solomon's Seal [=*Maianthemum canadense*] and Spiranthes cernua. **1960** *Appleton Post–Crescent* (WI) 17 June sec A 14/7, *Clintonia in Bloom*—One family of plants which is blooming lushly now is the wild lily of the valley. In moist shady woods you can find the clintonia, which most resembles the garden variety of lily of the valley. **1972** *Sun. Post–Crescent* (Appleton WI) 6 Aug sec E 2/3, The large blue berries of the wildflower Clintonia (wild lily of the valley) is said to be poisonous.

2 A **wintergreen 1,** esp *Pyrola elliptica.* **chiefly NEast**
1869 *Putnam's Mag.* 4.671 **neNY,** Great spikes of the sweet heavy bells of the pyrola, or wild lily of the valley, appear along the trail. **1894** *Jrl. Amer. Folkl.* 7.93 **MA,** *Pyrola elliptica, . .* wild lily-of-the-valley. **1898** *Ibid* 11.274, *Pyrola elliptica . .* wild lily-of-the-valley, South Berwick, Me. *Pyrola rotundifolia* [=*P. americana*] *. .* wild lily-of-the-valley, Auburndale, Mass. **1929** [see **1** above]. **1966** Heller *Wild Flowers AK* 61, Wild lily-of-the-valley—*Pyrola grandiflora Radius (wintergreen family.)* **2007** Rhoads–Block *Plants PA* 735, *Pyrola americana. . .* Wild lily-of-the-valley—Leaves firm and glossy, blades elliptic to nearly circular. *Ibid, Pyrola elliptica. . .* Shinleaf, wild lily-of-the-valley—Leaves thin and dull, blades oblong to elliptic.

3 =**false lily of the valley.**
1875 *Essex Inst. Bulletin* 7.109 **neMA,** *List of Plants Found in Flower at Essex,* June 3, 1875. . . *Smilacina bifolia* [=*Maianthemum dilatatum*], Ker. Wild lily of the valley. **1881** Henderson *Henderson's Hdbk. Plants* 211 **NEng,** *S[milacina] bifolia . .* is . . popularly known in the New England States as Wild Lily of the Valley. **1894** *Jrl. Amer. Folkl.* 7.102 **ME,** *Maianthemum Canadense . .* wild lily-of-the-valley. **1915** Torrey Bot. Club *Bulletin* 42.358 **MI,** *Vagnera trifolia* [=*Maianthemum t.*] *. .* This species and *Unifolium bifolium* [=*Maianthemum dilatatum*] are locally known as wild lily-of-the-valley. **1929** [see **1** above]. **1941** *Amer. Midland Naturalist* 25.290 **Pacific NW,** Wild lily-of-the-valley (*Mianthemum* [sic] *dilatatum*). **1963** Craighead *Rocky Mt. Wildflowers* 27, *Smilacina racemosa. . .* Other names: . . Wild Spikenard, Wild Lily-of-the-Valley. *Ibid* 28, *Wild Lily-of-the-valley . . Smilacina stellata. . .* [F]lowers in a raceme . . distinguish this plant from other species of *Smilacina.* **1966** *DARE* Wildfl QR Pl.19 [=*Maianthemum canadense*] Infs **MI**57, **NY**91, Wild lily of the valley. **1967–68** *DARE* (Qu. S26c, *Wildflowers that grow in woods*) Infs **CT**12, 15, **PA**176, **WA**20, Wild lily of the valley; **MA**50, Canadian mayflower—we call it wild lily of the valley; (Qu. S26b, *Wildflowers that grow in water or wet places*) Inf **VT**4, Wild lily of the valley. [*DARE* Ed: Some of these Infs may refer instead to another sense above.] **1967** *DARE* Wildfl QR (Craighead) Pl.1.9 [=*Maianthemum stellata*] Infs **CO**15, 29, Wild lily of the valley. **2002** *Providence Jrl.* (RI) 25 May sec B 7 (Internet), The Canada mayflowers . . we prefer to call wild lilies-of-the-valley.

wild lime n
1 =**hog plum 1.**
1765 (1942) Bartram *Diary of a Journey* 37 **FL,** Found a pretty evergreen, which produces nuts or stones as big as acorns, and good to eat. . . it bears plentifully, grows 8 or 10 foot high, the people call them wild limes, for this shrub much resembles that tree. **1791** Bartram *Travels* 94 **FL,** These shelly ridges have a vegetable surface [that] . . naturally produces Orange groves, Live Oak, . . Tallow-nut, or Wild Lime, and many others. **1884** Sargent *Forests of N. Amer.* 34, *Ximenia Americana. . .* Wild lime.

2 also *wild lime tree:* =**Ogeechee lime.** Cf **lime tree** n²
1812 Michaux *Histoire des Arbres* 2.257, Cette espèce de Nyssa est connue en Géorgie, sous les noms de *Sour Tupelo . .* et de *wild limes. . .* J'ai préféré la premièr de ces deux dénominations, quoique la moins usitée. [=This species of Nyssa is known in Georgia by the names of *Sour Tupelo . .* and *wild limes. . .* I have preferred the first of these two designations, although it is less used.] **1849** (1852) Downing *Treatise on Landscape Gardening* 247 **Sth,** The sour Tupelo (*N[yssa] capitata*), with long, smooth, laurel-like leaves, and light red, oval fruit, called the Wild Lime, from its abounding in a strong acid, resembling that of the latter fruit. **1897** Sudworth *Arborescent Flora* 311, *Nyssa ogeche. . .* Sour Tupelo. . . Wild Limetree. **1965** Fowells *Silvics Forest Trees* 281, *Ogeechee Tupelo. . .* Other common names: Ogeechee gum, Ogeechee-lime, wild lime tree, gopher plum, Ogeechee plum.

3 also *wild lime tree:* A **prickly ash 1** (here: *Zanthoxylum fagara*) native to Florida and Texas.
1884 Sargent *Forests of N. Amer.* 31, *Xanthoxylum Pterota. . .* Wild lime. **1911** (1932) Blatchley *In Days Agone* 136 **sFL,** Growing with

---

this "potato tree" along the margins of the hammock was the "wild lime," a species of prickly ash, Zanthoxylum pterota. **1959** *Ecology* 40.7 **swFL,** Mulberry *(Morus rubra)* and wild-lime *(Zanthoxylum fagara)* are often present. **1996** *Audubon Mag.* Nov-Dec 58, Emmel's research team placed 760 pupae near torchwood and wild lime trees (the Schaus swallowtail's food plants). **2001** *FL Entomol.* 84.255, Wild lime, *Zanthoxylum fagara. . .* Young torchwood and wild lime leaves are the primary food of most Schaus caterpillars.

wild lime tree See **wild lime 2, 3**
wild liquorice See **wild licorice**
wild madder n Cf **madder**
A **bedstraw,** usu either *Galium mollugo* or *G. tinctorium.*
[**1789** Pilkington *View of Derbyshire* 1.342, *Galium mollugo. White Ladies bed straw. Wild Madder. Great bastard Madder.* Hedges, frequent.] **1814** Bancroft *Exper. Researches* 2.229 **MA,** Galium mollugo; or great ladies' bedstraw, commonly called wild madder, and great bastard madder. Its roots . . produce, by dyeing, a red colour equally bright and lasting. **1837** Darlington *Flora Cestrica* 100 **sePA,** *G[alium] tinctorium. . .* Dyer's Goose grass. Wild Madder. . . The early travellers among our Aborigines inform us, that the roots of *G. tinctorium* are used for dyeing porcupine quills, and other savage ornaments, of a red color. **1903** Porter *Flora PA* 291, *Galium Mollugo. . .* Wild madder. **1921** *Waterloo Eve. Courier & Waterloo Daily Reporter* (IA) 1 Sept 6/8, Alder bark gave yellowish brown and orange [dyes], . . bloodroot, flowering dogwood and wild madder, red. **1952** *Amer. Midland Naturalist* 48.761 **neIL,** Galium obtusum—wild madder. **2007** *Bangor Daily News* (ME) 6 Aug 6 (Internet), A tangle of wild madder, with tiny white stars for flowers and green whorls for leaves, is crowding around a post of the porch.

wild mandrake See **mandrake**
wild man-of-the-earth See **man-of-the-earth 1**
wild mare n Cf **flying horse 2**
=**upland plover.**
1919 Pearson et al. *Birds NC* 141, *Bartramia longicauda. . .* The negroes give the names "Wild Mare" and "Flying Colt" to this bird, from the fancied "whinnying" notes that may be clearly heard falling from aloft.

wild mare's milk n Cf **cougar milk**
Distilled liquor.
1937 *DN* 6.621 **swTX,** One of the most pungent phrases used by the cowboy is *wild mare's milk* for hard liquor. **1948** Manfred *Chokecherry* 105 **nwIA,** "Give him some a that wild mare's milk. . . " "What the hell's that?" Elof asked. "Whisky." [**1950** *WELS* (Nicknames for whiskey) 1 Inf, **cWI,** Milk of wild cows.]

wild marigold n
1 =**pineapple weed.**
1887 *Overland Mth.* (2d ser) 636 **CO,** Wild marigold, Mexican poppies, coreopsis, cone flowers, and asters tangled themselves in riotous profusion by the wayside. [*DARE* Ed: This quot may refer instead to **2** below.] **1894** *Jrl. Amer. Folkl.* 7.92 **CA,** *Matricaria discoidea, . .* wild marigold. **1931** *Amer. Botanist* 37.107, The "wild marigold" is *M[atricaria] suaveolens* [=*M. discoidea*]. The specific name means fragrant, which makes "pineapple weed" appropriate.

2 =**desert marigold.**
1901 *Galveston Daily News* (TX) 1 July 6/2, The flaming sword of the "pink root" glows in the forests of pine and oak that cover the hills, and the ruddy wild marigold nods in the valleys between. **1928** *Abilene Reporter-News* (TX) 20 May sec B 20/2, This grass carpet is profusely decorated with blue bonnets (buffalo clover) with wild marigold, blue bells, poppies, wild holly hock and many other flowers. **2006** Massey *Backcountry Advent. AZ* 126, Also called wild marigold, paperdaisy, and desert baileya, desert marigolds are attractive spring annuals of the sunflower family.

wild mercury See **mercury weed**
wild millet n
Any of var grasses, spec:
a A **barnyard grass,** usu *Echinochloa crus-galli.*
[**1845** *Cultivator* new ser 2.62, Foxtail, or barn grass, is a wild millet, and the seed should be saved and used.] **1858** *Athens Messenger & Hocking Valley Gaz.* (OH) 10 Dec [4]/1 (newspaperarchive.com), We suppose the 'barn grass' alluded to by our cotemporary [sic] is a species closely allied to the Hungarian grass and sometimes called wild millet.

1900 *Marble Rock Weekly* (IA) 24 May [5]/4 (newspaperarchive.com), The number of acres and tons of wild millet and Hungarian grasses, clover, and other tame and cultivated grasses and grains cut green for hay. **1940** *Jrl. Wildlife Management* 4.364 **TX,** *Echinochloa crus-galli*—wild millet. **1969** *SW Naturalist* 14.178 **TX,** Vegetation on the remaining shore was a complex of wild millet, *Echinochloa crusgalli,* carelessweed, kochia, and occasional patches of smartweeds. **2007** *DARE* File—Internet **TX,** Rough Barnyardgrass (Wild Millet)—*Echinochloa muricata.*

b A **bristlegrass 1,** esp *Setaria viridis* or the closely related **pearl millet 1.** Cf **foxtail 1**

　1884 WI State Ag. Soc. *Trans.* 21.332, I buy mill screenings mostly and what is called pigeon grass or wild millet. **1902** *Weekly Chron.* (Elyria OH) 15 Mar 8/6, One [weed] that is getting quite thick is called by some wild millet, but what we used to call "fox tail" is a great drain on the soil and is not seen until after the crop is cut. **1914** Georgia *Manual Weeds* 31, Yellow foxtail grass—*Setaria glauca* [=*Pennisetum glaucum*]. . . *Other English names:* Pigeon Grass, . . Wild Millet. **1935** (1943) Muenscher *Weeds* 168, *Setaria lutescens* [=*Pennisetum glaucum*]. . . Yellow foxtail, Summer-grass, Golden foxtail, Wild millet. *Ibid* 169, *Setaria viridis.* . . Green foxtail, Bottle-grass, Pigeon-grass, Wild millet. **1937** *Sioux Co. Capital* (Orange City IA) 4/4, The shocks that looked golden at a distance were wild millet or pigeon grass or foxtail and not golden at all when we got near. **1951** *Dixon Eve. Telegraph* (IL) 2 Oct 3/1, Giant foxtail, commonly called wild millet, has become the most serious hazard to cultivated crops on some farms in east-central Illinois. **1967** *DARE* (Qu. S8, *A common kind of wild grass that grows in fields: it spreads by sending out long underground roots, and it's hard to get rid of*) Inf **MO5,** Wild millet; (Qu. S9, . . *Kinds of grass that are hard to get rid of*) Inf **IL104,** Wild millet; **MO38,** Wild millet grass. [*DARE* Ed: Some of these Infs may refer instead to another sense.] **1970** *Holland Eve. Sentinel* (MI) 30 July 4/6, Foxtail. . . is known in different localities by different names such as Wild Millet, Golden Foxtail, Pigeon Grass and Yellow Foxtail.

c A **wild rice 1** (here: *Zizania aquatica*).

　1913 *Torreya* 13.227 **FL,** *Zizania aquatica.* . . wild millet.

wild morning glory n　Cf **morning glory**
Any of numerous plants of the family Convolvulaceae, esp of the genera *Calystegia, Convolvulus,* and *Ipomoea.*

　1829 *Hist. Co. Berkshire MA* 61, *Convolvulus. . . sepium* [=*Calystegia s.*]. Wild morning-glory. **1856** MI State Ag. Soc. *Trans. for 1855* 7.405, *Convolvulus Sepium.* . . Wild morning glory. **1923** *Scientific Mth.* 17.81, *Plants eaten by desert mammals.* . . Wild morning glory *(Evolvulus),* young leaves 70 per cent. [water] (approximately). **1933** Pan-Pacific Research Inst. *Jrl.* 8.11 **HI,** The wild morning-glory, or convolvulus, . . grows from sea level . . up to the foot-hills. **1939** Medsger *Edible Wild Plants* 194, *Ipomoea Jalapa,* another wild morning-glory native of the south Atlantic states, is reported to have a root that weighs from forty to fifty pounds. **1951** *PADS* 15.38 **TX,** *Convolvulaceae.* . . Wild morning-glories; bind-weeds; devil's shoe strings; tie-vines. **1965–70** *DARE* (Qu. S21, . . *Weeds . . that are a trouble in gardens and fields*) Infs **AZ10, CA97, IL40, MD23, NC87, SC31, VA15,** Wild morning glory; (Qu. S26a, . . *Wildflowers. . . Roadside flowers*) Inf **CA53,** Wild morning glories; **CA80,** Wild morning glory; (Qu. S26d, *Wildflowers that grow in meadows;* not asked in early QRs) Infs **CO31, MI49,** Wild morning glory; (Qu. S9, . . *Kinds of grass that are hard to get rid of*) Inf **MD23,** Wild morning glory. **2003** *Seattle Post–Intelligencer* (WA) 29 May sec E 8 (Internet), Annual morning glory vine (Ipomoea) is nothing like the horribly invasive, impossible to eradicate wild morning glory (Convolvulus arvensis) aka bindweed. **2005** *Post-Std.* (Syracuse NY) 18 Sept 28 (Internet), There are a couple of species around here, field bindweed (Convolvulus arvensis) and hedge bindweed (Calystegia sepium). They are perennial vines in the morning glory family, and the white or pinkish flowers are typical funnel shapes, so they are often called wild morning glory.

wild mum　See **wild chrysanthemum 2**

wild oat n

1　See **wild oats.**

2　A child born out of wedlock.　**esp S Midl**

　1929 Larsen *Passing* 38 **NYC** [Black], They were Bob Kendry's aunts. He had been a son of their brother's, on the left hand. A wild oat. **1966–69** *DARE* (Qu. Z11b, . . *[A child whose parents were not married]*) Infs **DC6, KY10, SD1, WV7, 10,** Wild oat. **1997** in 2004 Montgomery–Hall *Dict. Smoky Mt. Engl.* 651 **eTN,** *Wild oat.* . . an illegitimate child [1 inf].

wild oat grass n　Cf **wild oats**

1　also *wild oats grass:* =**oat grass c.**　Cf **wild oats 2b**

　1853 Darlington *Flora Cestrica* 376 **sePA,** *D[anthonia] spicata.* . . Wild Oat-grass. **1887** KS Acad. Sci. *Trans.* 11.96, *Danthonia spicata . . ;* Spiked Wild Oat grass. **1912** Wooton–Standley *Grasses NM* 89, A fourth genus *(Danthonia)* [is] sometimes called *Wild Oats Grass* (though this name is not in use in this region). **1925** *Amer. Midland Naturalist* 9.389, *Danthania* [sic] *spicata.* . . Common Wild Oat-grass. **1964** *Ibid* 71.191 **OR,** Western wild oat grass *(Danthonia californica).* **2001** Torrey Bot. Soc. *Jrl.* 128.153, Wild oat grass—*Danthonia compressa* Aust.

2　=**oat grass b.**

　1933 Small *Manual SE Flora* 109, Wild oat-grasses. . . *T[risetum] spicatum.* . . *T. flavescens.* . . *T. pennsylvanicum.*

3　See **wild oats 2d, e, f.**

wild oat lily　See **wild oats 3**

wild oats n　Also *wild oat*　Cf **wild oat grass**

1　Std: any of var grasses of the genus *Avena* naturalized in the US, esp the widespread *A. fatua.*

2　Any of var other grasses that resemble oats, or whose grain is used for food, spec:

a　A **wild rice 1** or **2:** usu *Zizania aquatica,* rarely *Zizaniopsis milacea;* see quots.

　[**1705** Beverley *Hist. VA* 3.14, They make their Bread of the *Indian* Corn, Wild Oats, or the Seed of the Sunflower.] [**1744** in 2002 Collinson *Forget Not My Garden* 111 **VA,** I writt to him [=John Mitchell] to know the Reason for his Name Elymus [=*Zizania*] for a Species of Wild Oats.] **1762** Gronovius *Flora Virginica* 148, *Zizania panicula effusa.* . . Elymus, Wild-Oats.] **a1782** (1788) Jefferson *Notes VA* 36, Wild oat. *Zizania aquatica.* **1819** Warden *Statist. Political Hist. U.S.* 75 **MI,** Around the numerous lakes which give rise to the rivers, and near the mouth of Raisin and of Huron, there are thousands of acres covered with the wild oats, *Zizania aquatica.* **1848** Owen *Rept. Geol. Reconnoissance Chippewa District WI* 118 **nWI,** Those [lakes] . . are filled with aquatic plants, many of them containing large fields of the *zizania aquatica,* the wild oat or northern rice plant. **1874** Long *Amer. Wild-Fowl* 135, The entire surface [of a 300-acre pond] is covered with the dense growth of the wild oats or rice. **1906** *Auk* 23.231 **SC,** I determined to explore Bulls Island, which is covered along almost the entire length (ten miles) with wild oats (*Zizania miliacea* [=*Zizaniopsis m.*])

b　An **oat grass c** (here: *Danthonia spicata*).　**chiefly NEng** Cf **wild oat grass 1**

　1822 Eaton *Botany* 262, *Danthonia. . . spicata . .* wild oats. . . leaves subulate, short. **1856** *New Engl. Farmer* 8.211, This mean grass. . . is the *Danthonia spicata* of the botanists, and in some books is called wild oats. **1911** Aiken *Catalogue Ferns* 10 **OH,** *Danthonia spicata.* Wild oats. Common. **1995** in 2007 *DARE* File—Internet **NY,** *Danthonia spicata*—Wild Oats.

c　A **reed grass a** (here: *Calamagrostis coarctata*).

　1841 *Farmers' Reg.* 9.691 **NC,** *Calamagrostis coarctata. Wild oats.* So called in the mountains of North Carolina. Not a common grass, and seldom noticed. **1867** Curtis *Botany* 63, *Calamagrostis* coarctata. . . Reed Bent Grass. Wild Oats. . . Common.

d　also *wild oat grass:* A **spike-grass 3,** usu *Chasmanthium latifolium.*

　1862 *New Amer. Cyclop.* 15.721, *Uniola,* wild oats or union grass, 4 species of which are natives of the southern states, and the *U. nitida* is highly prized. **1881** Phares *Farmer's Book of Grasses* 68 **MS,** *U[niola] latifolia.* . . A local name for it in Mississippi is, I believe, 'wild oats.' **1960** *Castanea* 25.14 **VA,** *Uniola latifolia.* . . Wild-oats. Along New River. **2000** *Ibid* 65.255, *Chasmanthium latifolium . . ,* wild oats. **2006** *Spokesman–Rev.* (Spokane WA) 23 May sec Z 8 (Internet), These are a few of the grasses that members of the Independent Landscape Design Association recommend. . . Chasmanthium latifolium, wild oat grass [etc]. **2006** *DARE* File—Internet **MD,** Wild Oat (*Chasmanthium latifolium*).

e　also *wild oat grass:* An **Indian grass 1a:** either *Sorghastrum nutans* or *S. secundum.*

　1889 Vasey *Ag. Grasses* 36, *Chrysopogon nutans (Sorghum nutans* [=*Sorghastrum n.*]) (Wild Oats). . . It grows rather sparsely and forms a thin bed of grass. **1911** *Century Dict. Suppl.,* Oat-grass. . . *Wild oatgrass.* . . The *Indian grass, Sorghastrum avenaceum* [=*S. nutans*]. **1932** *Ecological Monogr.* 2.208, This area of dead "lighter" trees had saw palmetto, dwarf oak, dwarf myrica, gallberry, wild oats *(Sorghas-*

trum secundum) and "huckleberries" *(Vaccinium Myrsinites).* **1997** MacCubbin–Tasker *FL Gardener's Guide* 178, *Sorghastrum secundum.* . . This is a native clump-forming grass that ranchers refer to as "wild oats."

f also *wild oat grass:* A **needlegrass 1** such as *Nassella viridula* or *Hesperostipa* spp; see quots.

1887 Beal *Grasses N. Amer.* 1.89 **MT,** Both this [=*Stipa comata*] and the *Stipa viridula* are sometimes called wild-oat grass. **1889** U.S. Dept. Ag. *Rept. of Secy. for 1888* 318, *Stipa viridula* [=*Nassella v.*], Trin. (Feather-Grass, Bunch-Grass, "Wild Oats"). **1906** Rydberg *Flora CO* 23, *Stipa.* . . Porcupine-grass, Oat-grass, Wild oats. **1914** Georgia *Manual Weeds* 39, In South Dakota it [=*Stipa* [=*Hesperostipa*] *spartea*] is called Wild Oats.

g =**bromegrass.**

1908 NM Ag. Exper. Station *Bulletin* 66.13, The brome grasses *(Bromus* spp.),—the "wild oats" of the stockman—and the spear grasses *(Poa* spp.)—relatives of the Kentucky blue grass. **1912** Wooton–Standley *Grasses NM* 124, *The brome grasses (Bromus* spp.) are common in the mountains. . . where they are generally known by the name of Wild Oats. **1918** U.S. Dept. Ag. *Bulletin* 675.19 **UT,** Native bromegrass, locally called wild oats *(Bromus marginatus* . . *).* **2000** *SW Naturalist* 45.47 **cnKS,** In between and at the edges of plum thickets, herbaceous vegetation often included wild oats *(Bromus* sp.)

h A **wild rye** (here: *Elymus virginicus).*

1916 *Torreya* 16.237 **ME,** *Elymus virginicus.* . . Wild oats, Matinicus Id.

i A grass of the genus *Helictotrichon.*

1969 Barrell *Flora Gunnison Basin* 228 **CO,** *Helictotrichon* . . , The Wild Oats.

3 also *wild oat lily:* =**bellwort. esp NEng**

1847 Wood *Class-Book* 554, *U[vularia] sessilifolia.* . . Wild Oats. . . A common species, found in woods and grasslands. **1892** *Jrl. Amer. Folkl.* 5.104 **NH,** *Oakesia sessilifolia* [=*Uvularia s.*], wild oats. **1894** *Ibid* 7.102 **ME,** *Oakesia sessilifolia,* . . wild oats. **1939** Medsger *Edible Wild Plants* 162, Perfoliate Bellwort, or Wild Oat, *Uvularia perfoliata.* **1966–69** *DARE* (Qu. S26a, . . *Wildflowers.* . . *Roadside flowers)* Inf **RI**15, Wild oat, bellwort—similar; **CA**4, Wild oats; **ME**7, Wild oats have a small yellow flower; (Qu. S26c, *Wildflowers that grow in woods)* Inf **FL**31, Wild oats. **1966** *DARE* Wildfl QR Pl.20A [=*Uvularia sessilifolia*] Inf **NH**4, Wild oats. **1972** GA Dept. Ag. *Farmers Market Bulletin* 10 May 8/1, Merrybells, Wild Oats, or Bellwort are all common names for this lovely member of the Liliaceae family. **2005** in 2007 *DARE* File—Internet **MA,** *Uvularia perfoliata* (strawbell) and *Uvularia sessifolia* 'Variegata' (wild oat lily) are both easy to grow, even though their nodding yellow flowers give such a delicate appearance.

wild oats grass See **wild oat grass 1**

wild okra n

1 A **violet,** usu *Viola* x *palmata.* **esp Sth**

1821 Elliott *Sketch* 1.300, *[Viola] Palmata.* . . Wild Okra. This Violet is very mucilaginous and much used by negroes in their soups. **1954** Land *LA Cookery* 11, Early Blue Violet—This is the wild okra, and is used for stews and soups. **1974** Morton *Folk Remedies* 140 **SC,** Young sassafras leaves are cooked with "wild okra" *(Viola palmata* . . *)* and "dog's tongue" . . to make soup.

2 =**velvetleaf a.**

1916 *Torreya* 16.239 **ceSC,** *Abutilon abutilon* [=*A. theophrasti*]. . . Wild okra, Cat Id., S.C.

wild olive n Cf **California olive**

Any of several plants or their fruits thought to resemble the olive tree *(Olea europaea),* as:

a =**devilwood.**

1741 in 1895 *William & Mary Qrly.* 3.229 **VA,** I have sent yr Ldp some Ginseng seed & Black gum berries with a box contg some Indigo roots, Chincapin bushes & wild Olive bushes which I wish may be acceptable. [**1785** Marshall *Arbustrum* 98, *Olea americana* [= *Osmanthus a.*]. American Olive Tree. This grows naturally in Carolina and Florida.] **1825** *Amer. Farmer* 7.186 **GA, SC,** We have discovered . . a species of the wild olive, abundant along the sandy shores of our coasts. **1897** Sudworth *Arborescent Flora* 332 **FL,** *Osmanthus americanus.* . . Wild Olive. **1947** *Amer. Midland Naturalist* 37.746 **SC,** *Osmanthus.* Wild-olive. American-olive. **1976** *Castanea* 41.318 **swFL,** *Osmanthus americana.* . . Wild Olive. Big scrub; moist or dry hammocks. **2007** *DARE* File—Internet **FL,** *Osmanthus americanus.* . . Wild olive, or devilwood, is an evergreen small tree or large shrub with

shiny opposite leaves and tiny fragrant flowers. . . The fruits are drupes or "stone fruits", dark bluish purple when mature and almost spherical, about 0.5 in (1.3 cm) in diameter.

b A **tupelo gum** (here: *Nyssa aquatica)* or its fruit.

1812 Michaux *Histoire des Arbres* 2.252 **LA,** *Nyssa grandidentata. The Large Tupelo.* . . On m'a assuré qu'il étoit aussi fort commun dans la Basse-Louisiane, sur les bords du Mississippi, où il est appelé *Olivier sauvage, wild olive.* [=I was told that it is also very common in lower Louisiana, on the banks of the Mississippi, where it is called *wild olive.*] **1890** *Bot. Gaz.* 15.93, The fruit [of *Nyssa uniflora*] is commonly called "wild olive." **1897** Sudworth *Arborescent Flora* 312 **LA,** *Nyssa aquatica.* . . Wild Olivetree (La.) . . Olivetree (Miss.) **1939** Medsger *Edible Wild Plants* 90, Large Tupelo, or Wild Olive, Nyssa aquatica, *Nyssa uniflora.* The Large Tupelo grows in swampy regions from Virginia to Missouri, south to Florida and Texas. The dark blue fruits when ripe are about an inch long.

c =**Carolina cherry.**

1819 in 1918 Ruffin *Papers* 1.213 **DC,** I have inclosed you six seed of the wild Olive. It is a beautiful evergreen that grows rapidly and to the hight of 40 feet. **1858** *S. Cultivator* 16.56 **Sth,** If an evergreen hedge . . is needed, we have . . the Wild Olive (Cerasus Carolinianus) or "Mock Orange." **1904** *Auk* 21.460 **FL,** They feed extensively on the berries of mistletoe, wild olive *(Prunus)* and China tree. **1926** *Torreya* 26.5 **GA,** *Laurocerasus caroliniana* [=*Prunus c.*] . . Wild olive. **2003** Cothran *Gardens Antebellum South* 245, *Prunus caroliniana* . . Cherry Laurel, Carolina Bird Cherry, Lauri Mundi, Wild Olive/Orange, Mock Orange. . . Native shrub or small tree that ranges from North Carolina to Florida and westward to Texas.

d A **silver bell 1,** usu *Halesia carolina* or *H. tetraptera.*

1831 Audubon *Ornith. Biog.* 1.122 **LA,** The Wild Olive . . is small, brittle and useless. *Ibid* 123, The Snow-drop Tree, Silver-bell Tree, or Wild Olive. *Halesia tetraptera.* **1897** Sudworth *Arborescent Flora* 323 **TN,** *Mohrodendron carolinum* [=*Halesia c.*] . . Wild Olive Tree. **1919** Sturtevant *Notes Edible Plants* 297, *Halesia tetraptera.* . . *Silver-Bell Tree. Wild Olive.* North Carolina to Texas. The ripe fruit is eaten by some people and when green is sometimes made into a pickle. **1953** Greene–Blomquist *Flowers South* 95, Silver-bell trees, Bell-trees (Halesia). . . The most common species is *H. carolina* which is variously called, "Wild-Olive," "Possum-Wood," [etc]. **2001** Cope *Muenscher's Woody Plants* 263, *H[alesia] tetraptera* . . silverbell, wild-olive, shittimwood, oppossumwood [sic].

e =**hog plum 1.**

1890 *Century Dict.* 4103, Wild olive. . . *Ximenia Americana.* **1908** Britton *N. Amer. Trees* 377, *Ximenia americana.* . . It is also called Seaside plum, . . False sandalwood, and Wild olive.

f A **buffalo berry** (here: *Shepherdia canadensis).*

1900 Lyons *Plant Names* 220, *L[epargyrea] Canadensis* [=*Shepherdia c.*] . . Wild Oleaster- or Olive-tree. **1931** U.S. Dept. Ag. *Misc. Pub.* 101.119, *Buffaloberries (Lepargyrea* spp., syn. *Shepherdia* spp.) . . Russet buffaloberry *(L. canadensis)* . . known locally as . . wild oleaster, and wild olive.

wild onion n

1 Std: any of numerous wild-growing **onions B,** esp such widely distributed spp as *Allium canadense, A. cernuum, A. drummondii,* and *A. vineale.* For other names of var of these see **grassnut 3, graveyard onion, horse ~, Indian ~ 3, lady's leek, paper-flowered onion, prairie ~, ramp** n[2], **rock onion**

2 Any of several related plants thought to resemble **1** above, as:

a A **brodiaea. CA** Cf **grassnut 2, Indian onion 2**

1894 *Land of Sunshine* June 5, In quick succession come the brodiaea, or wild onion, a rich lavender cluster of blossoms, delicately poised. **1914** Saunders *With Flowers in CA* 94, Country children have a way of calling it wild onion, which is more accurate than some common names, for its bulbous root is edible and the plant is really related to the garden onion. **1920** *Torreya* 20.19 **CA,** *Brodiaea* sp.—Wild onion, groundnut. **1936** Prior *Lota of the Little Trees* 89 **sCA,** They were roots of the blue *brodiaea,* or wild onion, prized alike by the Indians and *Californio* children.

b =**death camas. West**

1901 U.S. Dept. Ag. Div. Botany *Bulletin* 26.51 **MT,** *Death Camas.* . . Other names: Poison camas, lobelia, squirrel food, wild onion. [Footnote to *death camas:*] Under the name death camas we mean to include those Montana forms which for many years have been known as *Zyga-*

denus venenosus. **1913** (1979) Barnes *Western Grazing* 267, It [=death camas] is often called "wild onion," and at certain periods of its growth resembles a young onion plant. **1957** Smith–Jones *Vet. Pathology* 569, *Zygadenus gramineus, Z. nuttallii* and other closely related species are known by the name of death camas or by the descriptive synonym of wild onion.

c An **arrowhead 1** (here: *Sagittaria platyphylla*).

1913 *Torreya* 13.227 **LA,** *Sagittaria platyphylla.* . . wild onion, Vermilion Bay, La.

d =**mariposa lily.**

1920 Rice–Rice *Pop. Studies CA Wild Flowers* 30, The Digger Indians of California received their name because the first white men saw them digging about in search of lily [=*Calochortus*] corms and roots of different sorts—"Indian Potatoes" or "Wild Onions," the early settlers called them.

wild op　See **wild hop**

wild opium　n　Also *wild opium lettuce*

A **wild lettuce 1:** either *Lactuca canadensis* or **prickly lettuce.**

1876 Hobbs *Bot. Hdbk.* 184, *[Lactuca] elongata,* Wild opium lettuce. **1880** (1881) Nickell *Bot. Ready Ref.* 78, *Lactuca Elongata.* Wild Lettuce. Wild Opium Lettuce. Snake Weed. Trumpet Weed. Snake Bite. **1901** Lounsberry *S. Wild Flowers* 490, *L[actuca] Canadensis,* tall wild lettuce or wild opium, is a common thing along roadsides. **1964** *Bennington Banner* (VT) 26 Aug 7/5, The tall wild lettuce . . , sometimes called wild opium, grows three to 10 feet high. **2007** *DARE* File—Internet IL, *Prickly Lettuce—Lactuca serriola.* . . Prickly Lettuce is a common plant that occurs in every county of Illinois. . . Another common name for this plant is Wild Opium because the latex contains compounds that are mildly sedating and analgesic.

wild orange　n

1　=**Carolina cherry.　Cf mock orange 1a, wild peach 1**

1802 Drayton *View of SC* 8, Small rising grounds sometimes present themselves; on which grow . . wild orange. **1810** Michaux *Histoire des Arbres* 1.36, Cerasus caroliniana. . . *Wild orange* . . seul nom donné à cet arbre dans la partie maritime des Etats méridionaux. [=Cerasus caroliniana [=*Prunus c.*] . . *Wild orange* . . the only name given to this tree in the coastal part of the southern States.] **1835** *N. Amer. Archives Med. & Surgical Sci.* 2.31, We are inclined to believe, however, that the prunus Caroliniana, or, as it is commonly called, *"wild orange,"* which grows extensively in the Southern states, possesses the same virtues. **1869** *Amer. Naturalist* 3.463 **FL,** In the vicinity may be seen the *Cerasus Caroliniana* or Wild Orange. **1893** *Jrl. Amer. Folkl.* 6.140 **Sth,** *Prunus Caroliniana,* cherry laurel; wild orange; mock-orange; wild peach. **1936** Smith–Sass *Carolina Rice* 61 **SC coast** (as of 1850s), Beyond the circle was the fence with a wild-orange screen or hedge which separated the garden from the "stable-lot." **1962** Harrar–Harrar *Guide S. Trees* 354, *Wild Orange—Prunus caroliniana.* . . A tree, 30′ to 40′ in height. . . From North Carolina to Florida and west to Louisiana and Texas. **2007** Williams *Identifying Trees* 180 **Sth,** *Prunus caroliniana* . . Wild Orange.

2　=**Osage orange.**

1857 Gerhard *IL as It Is* 355, The Maclura hedges which have been planted four years or more, have become a fixed, tangible, and well established reality. . . This wild orange, of which the hedges are made, is very similar in appearance to the orange of the tropics. **1894** *Jrl. Amer. Folkl.* 7.98 **NJ,** *Maclura aurantiaca,* . . wild orange. **1936** NE Univ. Conserv. & Surv. Div. *Bulletin* 13.178, Osage Orange or Wild Orange. Native to Kan. and Mo. Planted, especially for hedges, by early settlers. **1968** *DARE* (Qu. T13, . . *Names . . for . . osage orange*) Inf **NC**49, I've seed wild orange.

3　A **prickly ash 1** (here: *Zanthoxylum clava-herculis*).

1884 Sargent *Forests of N. Amer.* 30, *Xanthoxylum Clava-Herculis.* . . Wild Orange. **1897** Sudworth *Arborescent Flora* 265, *Xanthoxylum clava-herculis.* . . Wild Orange. **1974** (1977) Coon *Useful Plants* 240, *Zanthoxylum clava-herculis.* . . Hercules club, toothache tree, wild orange, prickly ash. **1984** Vines *Trees Cent. TX* 230, *Zanthoxylum* . . *clava-herculis.* . . Vernacular names are Toothache, . . Wild Orange, . . and Wait-a-bit. . . A number of species of birds eat the fruit.

4　=**Hercules'-club 1.**

1891 *Century Dict.* 6382, *Toothache-tree.* . . The somewhat similar *Aralia spinosa,* or angelica-tree, sometimes called *wild orange.* **1940** Clute *Amer. Plant Names* 97, *A[ralia] spinosa.* . . toothache-tree, wild orange [etc].

5　A **hackberry** (here: *Celtis laevigata* var *reticulata*).

1920 *Torreya* 20.20 **WA,** *Celtis douglasii* [=*C. laevigata* var *reticulata*]. . . Wild orange.

wild orange-red lily　See **red lily a**

wild pansy　n　Cf **johnny-jump-up 1, pansy**

Any of several **violets,** esp the introduced *Viola arvensis* and *V. tricolor,* as well as the native *V. bicolor* and *V. pedunculata.*

1869 Porcher *Resources* 80 **Sth,** *Wild pansy, heartsease,* (*Viola tricolor,* Linn.) Cultivated in gardens. **1905** *DN* 3.84, *Johnny-jumper.* . . *Johnny-jump-up.* . . Wild violet, wild pansy. Common. **1940** Steyermark *Flora MO* 368, *Johnny-jump-up, wild pansy* (*Viola Kitaibeliana* Roem. & Schultes var. *Rafinesquii* [=*V. bicolor*] . .). *Ibid,* Wild pansy (*Viola arvensis* . .). Resembling the preceding but with smaller petals. **1965–70** *DARE* (Qu. S11, . . *Blue violet*) 30 Infs, **scattered exc Upper MW, wGt Lakes,** Wild pansy; **CA**20, Wild pansy—violet-shaped but yellow; **IN**1, Wild pansy = wood violet; **MD**17, Wild pansy—same as blue violet, wood violet; (Qu. S3, *A flower like a large violet with a yellow center and small ragged leaves—it comes up early in spring on open, stony hilltops*) Infs **CA**20, **KY**24, 47, **MA**50, 74, **TN**65, Wild pansy; [**CA**41, Wild yellow pansy or johnny-jump-up;] **CA**87, Wild pansy or johnny-jump-up; **VT**17, Johnny-jump-up—that's a little wild pansy; (Qu. S26a, . . *Wildflowers. . . Roadside flowers*) Infs **CA**127, **NJ**67, Wild pansies; (Qu. S26c, *Wildflowers that grow in woods*) Inf **MO**12, Wild pansies; (Qu. S26d, *Wildflowers that grow in meadows;* not asked in early QRs) Inf **GA**18, Wild pansy; (Qu. S26e, *Other wildflowers not yet mentioned;* not asked in early QRs) Infs **CA**70, 195, **MD**30, **OR**10, Wild pansy. **1966** *DARE* FW Addit **MA**6, *Lady's delight*—wild pansy—often come in grass seed. **2008** *DARE* File—Internet **CA,** *Viola pedunculata* . . *Wild pansy.* . . Unusually large, yellow-orange flowers with brown-purple nectar guides on the lower petals occur on stems much exceeding the leaves in height.

wild parsley　n　Cf **parsley B, wild celery 1, ~ parsnip**

1　Used generically or specifically for any of var plants of the family Apiaceae, esp those resembling in some way the garden parsley *(Petroselinum crispum);* see quots.

1785 (1903) Cutler *Account* 426, *Sium.* . . *Wild parsley.* Water parsnip. Blossoms white. In watery places. **1905** *Morning World–Herald* (Omaha NE) 29 May 4/4, Cattle . . are being poisoned by feeding on what is supposed to be a species of wild parsley. **1946** *Jrl. Wildlife Management* 10.327 **TX,** Wild parsley (*Cynosciadum* [sic]). **1967–70** *DARE* (Qu. S6, . . *Queen Anne's lace:* [*Summertime roadside weed two feet high or so with a lacy white top*]) Infs **CA**24, **IL**55, **NC**87, Wild parsley; (Qu. S17, . . *Kinds of plants . . that . . cause itching and swelling*) Inf **NJ**45, Wild parsley; (Qu. S21, . . *Weeds . . that are a trouble in gardens and fields*) Inf **PA**176, Wild parsley; (Qu. S26b, *Wildflowers that grow in water or wet places*) Inf **CT**11, Wild parsley. **1976** *Jrl. Range Management* 29.345 **CO,** Wild parsley (*Pseudocymopterus montanus*). **1999** Johnson *CRC Ethnobotany Desk Ref.* 547, *Musineon divaricatum* . . *Leafy wild parsley.* . . *Musineon tenuifolium* . . *Slender wild parsley.* . . *Musineon vaginatum* . . *Sheathed wild parsley.* **2004** *Fresno Bee* (CA) 10 July sec E 3 (Internet), The weed is wild celery (*Apium leptophyllum* [=*Cyclospermum l.*]), also known as marsh parsley or wild parsley, and it has become a serious problem for many lawns.

2　Spec:

a　Either **poison hemlock** or **water hemlock.**

1784 *Gentleman & Lady's Town & Country Mag.* June 66 **eMA,** In many gardens and fields in and adjacent to this metropolis [=Boston] grows a species of *wild parsley* [prob =*Conium maculatum*]; it is very poisonous. . . The herb resembles common garden-parsley; . . it may be distinguished by rubbing between the hands, when it will have rather a disagreeable smell. . . The root is no less dangerous than the herb; when full grown, may be easily taken for horse-reddish. **1866** *Daily Columbus Enquirer* (GA) 13 May 1/3, Near the bodies were found considerable quantities of wild parsley (conium maculatum). . . There is evidence that the men suffered terribly in their dying moments. [*DARE* Ed: This description suggests that the plant was in fact *Cicuta maculata.*] **1876** *Jackson Sentinel* (Maquoketa IA) [4 May 9]/3 (newspaperarchive.com), Four boys . . were poisoned at Muscatine . . by eating wild parsley or hemlock. **1889** *Marshfield Times* (WI) [21 June 2]/8 (newspaperarchive.com), Seymour Mills . . was taken, as was supposed, with fits, and before he could be brought to the city was dead. . . His stomach was found to contain a quantity of roots of the wild parsley. **1953** *Iola Reg.* (KS) 7 Apr 1/1, Millard Cress . . has lost one cow . . from eating wild parsley or parsnip as it is sometimes called. . . It is a member of the Hemlock family and very poisonous, particularly in the spring.

b =**lovage.**

1864 in 1955 *Ethnohistory* 2.171 **OR,** All but the largest [of the springs] are thoroughly shaded by manges [sic] of the wild parsley. **1899** *Century Illustr. Mag.* 58.314 **CO,** The spring was sunk so deep in the ground that we could not reach it when lying down. . . A long stalk of wild parsley was cut, and through its hollow stem we sucked up our mountain julep. **1937** U.S. Forest Serv. *Range Plant Hdbk.* W106, *Ligusticum spp.* The loveroots, known commonly as . . wildparsley, . . grow in scattered stands in . . marshes, meadows, along stream banks. . . The stems are hollow, generally slender and smooth, and quite variable in size. **1961** *AK Sportsman* Nov 29, Wild plants have been gathered in Alaska for many years to supplement the diet. There is the wild parsley, *petrushki,* which I think far excels the parsley from our gardens. **1968** *DARE* (Qu. I28a, . . *Kinds of things . . you call 'greens' . . [Those that are eaten raw]*) Inf **AK**3, Wild parsley—near salt water, tastes like but not looks like parsley, late in season puts up stalk of minute flowers. **1991** Tabbert *Dict. Alaskan Engl.* 173, A traditional source of dietary greens in coastal areas is *Ligusticum scoticum,* named "officially" *beach lovage,* but also called popularly *wild parsley, sea parsley, Scotch lovage,* etc.

c A **golden alexanders 1** (here: *Zizia aurea*).

1876 Hobbs *Bot. Hdbk.* 131, Wild parsley, Meadow parsnip, Zizia aurea. **1950** *Jrl. Elisha Mitchell Scientific Soc.* 66.241 **NC,** *Zizia aurea* . . Golden Meadow Parsnip, Golden Alexander, Early Meadow Parsnip, Wild Parsley.

d Spring-parsley (*Cymopterus* spp). Cf **wild celery 1d**

1911 NE State Horticult. Soc. *Annual Rept. for 1911* 265, Low, smooth plants, with very small whitish flowers, Wild Parsley *(Cymopterus).* **1950** Stevens *ND Plants* 219, *Cymopterus acaulis.* . . *Wild parsley.* . . leaves and flower stalks from a thick root. . . the plant closely resembles No. 14 [=*Lomatium orientale*]. **1989** Smith *Wild Plants Amer.* 224 **AZ,** Still another low-growing plant is Wild Parsley (*Cymopterus* sp.), with crinkly bluish compound leaves and umbels of an unusual dark yellow hue.

e =**biscuit root 1.**

1905 Blankinship–Henshall *Common MT Plants* 128, *Wild parsley;* Lomatium montanum. **1937** U.S. Forest Serv. *Range Plant Hdbk.* W55, *Biscuitroots.* . . *Lomatium spp.* . . The plants are also known locally as . . wildparsley. . . In many species the leaves are cut up into very fine divisions and in general resemble parsley leaves. *Ibid* W56, *Nineleaf biscuitroot.* . . has been locally called wildcarrot, wildparsley, wildparsnip, and hogfennel. **2008** *DARE* File—Internet **AZ,** *Lomatium nevadense* . . wild parsley. . . Sagebrush, woodland, desert scrub.

wild parsnip n

1 Any of var plants of the family Apiaceae thought to resemble the garden parsnip (*Pastinaca sativa*) in some way; see quots. Cf **Indian parsnip, parsnip B, Queen Anne's lace 4, wild celery 1, ~ parsley**

1877 *Yr.-Book Pharmacy 1876–77* 174, *Sium latifolium,* an umbelliferous plant, growing in California and along the Pacific coast, in damp and marshy places, commonly known as wild parsnip. **1890** Wells–Kelly *Engl.-Eskimo Vocab.* 56 **nwAK,** *Musho*—Wild parsnip. **1901** [see **2b** below]. **1901** U.S. Dept. Ag. Div. Botany *Bulletin* 26.126, *Cymopterus acaulis.* . . has been suspected by some stockmen in Montana, being included by them in the general term "wild parsnip." *Ibid* 145, *Carum gairdneri* [=*Perideridia g.*] . . the roots under the erroneous name of wild parsnip are very frequently eaten in the raw state by boys. **1903** KS Acad. Sci. *Trans.* 18.204, Polytænia nuttallii. Wild parsnip. . . Poisonous to cows. **1921** *Jrl. Dental Research* 3.288, Orogenia linearifolia (wild parsnip). **1937** U.S. Forest Serv. *Range Plant Hdbk.* W15, The angelicas, also commonly but loosely called wildparsnips, are perennial herbs of the carrot family. **1974** Smith *Est. Nat. Areas AZ* 132, *Pseudocymopterus montanus* . . wild parsnip. **2008** *DARE* File—Internet **MT,** Wild Parsnip—Berula erecta.

2 Spec:

a =**water hemlock,** esp **spotted cowbane 1.** Cf **poison parsnip**

1775 *CT Courant & Hartford Weekly Intelligencer* 14 Aug 3/2, A few days since three children . . pulled up the hemlock, or wild parsnip root, and eat of it, and in about five hours they all expired. **1807** *Thomas' MA Spy or Worcester Gaz.* (MA) 22 July [3]/4 **cNY,** Five children were lately poisoned in Scipio (Newyork) by eating *Wild Parsnip,* or *Musquash Root.* **1893** Torrey Bot. Club *Bulletin* 20.442 **IA,** I was permitted last spring to examine some roots in a case in which three children had consumed "Wild Parsnip." . . The specimens sent me . .

proved to be *Cicuta maculata.* **1901** *Science* 13.833 **MT,** Water hemlock [here: =*Cicuta douglasii*] is usually known as 'wild parsnip' and is commonly supposed to be the garden parsnip run wild, an error, of course. The roots and foliage are poisonous, and cases of poisoning of cattle, sheep and even human beings are reported. **1967** *Wasmann Jrl. Biol.* 25.296 **CA,** *Cicuta Douglasii.* . . Water hemlock; locally, erroneously, and somewhat dangerously, wild parsnip. **1968** *DARE* (Qu. S6, . . *Queen Anne's lace: [Summertime roadside weed two feet high or so with a lacy white top]*) Inf **CA**53, Wild parsnip—Indians eat that to commit suicide; **NV**6, Wild parsnip—kills the stock; **NV**8, Wild parsnip—dangerous to cattle. **1984** *Rangelands* 6.128, The *Cicuta* spp. are known by several common names: cowbane, wild parsnip, . . water hemlock, and others. . . They are toxic to all species of livestock and also to man.

b =**biscuit root 1.** Cf **lace parsnip**

1879 KS Acad. Sci. *Trans.* 7.48 **swKS,** One is a little wild parsnip, three inches high, with umbels of very small, white, fragrant flowers. It is said to be Peucedanum nudicaule [=*Lomatium n.*] **1901** U.S. Dept. Ag. Div. Botany *Bulletin* 26.81, Not only water hemlock [here: =*Cicuta douglasii*], but a number of other plants belonging to the parsnip family are often called by the name of wild parsnip, as if they all belonged to the same species. Among the plants whose identity is thus mistaken may be mentioned the cow parsnip (*Heracleum lanatum*) and species of Lomatium, Phellopterus, and Leptotaenia. **1937** U.S. Forest Serv. *Range Plant Hdbk.* W56, *Nineleaf biscuitroot.* . . has been locally called wildcarrot, wildparsley, wildparsnip, and hogfennel. These names are undesirable, however, because they are loosely used for a large number of other umbelliferous plants. **2006** Rakel–Faass *Complementary Med.* 423, Those plants containing natural psoralens include . . *Lomatium* species (wild parsnip).

c A **cow parsnip 1** (here: *Heracleum lanatum*).

1856 Reinhold *Farmer's Promotion Book* 43, The Low or Wild parsnip (H. lanatum . .)—Grows from three to six feet high. **1901** U.S. Dept. Ag. Div. Botany *Bulletin* 26.143, *Heracleum lanatum.* . . This plant is sometimes called wild parsnip, but may be readily distinguished from that plant by its much greater size and coarser character. **1966** *Jrl. Wildlife Management* 30.821 **OH,** Plants common in the pens were wild parsnip (*Heracleum maximum*) [etc.].

d =**lovage.**

1907 *Amer. Anthropologist* 9.273 **swOR,** The only musical instrument known to them . . seems to have been a rude flute or fife . . made out of a dry reed of the wild parsnip. **1917** Sampson *Important Range Plants* 44, *Ligusticum oreganum,* sometimes called wild parsnip. . . has the characteristic parsnip aroma, and resembles the parsnip somewhat. **1937** U.S. Forest Serv. *Range Plant Hdbk.* W107, Fernleaf loveroot, also called fernleaf lovage, osha, wildcelery, and wildparsnip, is one of the most abundant of the western loveroots. **1960** *Jrl. Range Management* 13.89 **West,** Some believe that plants other than lupine such as wild parsnip (*Ligusticum gravi*), are responsible [for causing deformities in cattle].

wild pea n

Any of var legumes, spec:

a =**lupine.**

[**1797** Deane *New Engl. Farmer* 194, *Lupines,* a species of wild pea, cultivated principally for a green dressing.] **1870** *Amer. Naturalist* 4.30 **NV,** The meadows are bounded . . by the Pea-vine mountains (so-called from the frequency with which the lupines or wild peas are met with on its sides). **1892** *Jrl. Amer. Folkl.* 5.94 **MA,** *Lupinus perennis,* wild pea. **1913** (1979) Barnes *Western Grazing* 265, *Lupines.* . . The common name among stockmen is wild pea, blue pea, blue bean and peavine. **1939** Medsger *Edible Wild Plants* 129, Wild Lupine, or Wild Pea, Lupinus perennis, ranges from Maine to Minnesota, south to Florida and Louisiana.

b =**vetchling,** esp **marsh pea.**

1840 MA Zool. & Bot. Surv. *Herb. Plants & Quadrupeds* 64 **ceMA,** *L[athyrus] palustris.* . . Marsh Wild Pea. . . Blossoms in June, in wet meadows or low grounds. [**1893** *Science* 21.304, Of the vegetable matter, I found the seed of a wild pea (Lathysus ochrolencus [sic]), growing abundantly all over the Northwest.] **1934** *Amer. Midland Naturalist* 15.335 **MI,** *Lathyrus palustris.* . . Marsh Vetchling. Wild Pea. **1966–68** *DARE* Wildfl QR Pl.115 [=*Lathyrus japonicus* var *maritimus*] Infs **AR**46, **MN**30, 37, **OH**82, **WA**15, 30, Wild pea(s). *Ibid* Pl.116 [=*L. palustris*] Infs **AR**46, **OH**82, **WA**10, 15, Wild pea(s). **1967** *DARE* (Qu. S26c, *Wildflowers that grow in woods*) Inf **CA**22, Wild sweet peas—wherever it's brushy—also called wild peas. **2000** Rhoads–Block *Plants PA* 410, *Lathyrus ochroleucus.* . . Wild pea.

c =**vetch 1.**

1889 KS Acad. Sci. Trans. 12.63 **TX,** Vicia micantha . . Wild pea. **1923** Thone Trees & Flowers Yellowstone 42 **nwWY,** Wild Pea (Vicia). There are many kinds of wild pea, but in general appearance they are all alike. **1956** Darling Pelican 112 **UT,** There was a small patch of wild pea, Vicia, at the top of the bank. **2005** in 2008 DARE File—Internet **CA,** On the Ridge trail there are a lot of Spring vetch (a lady I talked to was calling it wild pea).

d A **rattlebox 1a** (here: Crotalaria sagittalis).

1884 Vet. Jrl. 19.458, It is stated that in the valley of the Missouri grows a weed known as wild pea, or rattle-box. **1893** Jrl. Amer. Folkl. 6.140 **IA,** Crotalaria sagittalis, wild pea. **1990** Green Paul Green's Wordbook 2.930 **NC,** Rattlebox weed. The common wild pea. . . We children used to pluck the dry pods and shake them close to our ears and listen with delight at the little seeds rattling within. **2006** Sandbeck Organic Housekeeping 375, Canary bird bush and wild pea, Crotalaria species.

e A **goat's rue** (here: Tephrosia virginiana).

[**1890** MI State Horticult. Soc. Annual Rept. for 1889 45, Tephrosia Virginiana is a wild pea with beautifully shaded blossoms.] **1896** Jrl. Amer. Folkl. 9.186 **swMO,** Tephrosia Virginiana, . . wild pea. **1921** Albertson Nantucket Wild Flowers 160 **seMA,** Tephrosia virginiana. . . Wild Pea. . . The preferred habitat: dry, sandy soil of the Commons. **1941** Amer. Midland Naturalist 26.564 **VA,** The wild pea (Tephrosia virginiana . .). **1967–68** DARE Wildfl QR Pl.108B [=Tephrosia virginiana] Infs **MN**37, **WA**30, Wild pea.

wild peach n

1 =**Carolina cherry. wGulf States, esp eTX** Cf **wild orange 1**

1801 (1976) Hall Brief Hist. MS Terr. 27, Mount Washington is. . . generally covered with holly, wild peach-tree and magnolio [sic]. **1819** in 1826 Flint Recollections 253 **AR,** The . . willows in full foliage . . so nearly resembled the leaves of the peach tree, that I asked one of the boatmen . . what kind of tree it was, who answered with much solemnity, that it was the wild peach. **1831** in 1833 Holley Texas 50, A species of laurel, the leaves of which taste like the kernel of the peach stone. . . The leaves resemble those of the peach tree. Hence it is called by the colonists, wild peach. **1849** (1850) Allen Amer. Farm Book 288 **MS,** The wild peach . . furnishes one of the most beautiful hedges when tastefully managed. **1853** Mag. Horticult. 19.562, We allude to the C[erasus] Caroliniana, or "Wild Peach," as it is called in the Southwestern States, (owing to the strong peach-kernel odor . .). **1877** McDanield–Taylor Coming Empire 81 **eTX,** The Texans have a saying: "Where the wild peach grows, buy and grow rich." . . This tree is a beautiful evergreen, closely resembling the orange, but with the smell of the peach. **1897** Sudworth Arborescent Flora 246, Prunus caroliniana. . . Wild Peach (Miss., La., Tex.) **1932** San Antonio Express (TX) 10 Jan sec D 2/2, Small evergreen trees . . : wild peach (Laurocerasus caroliniana), 20 to 30 feet, best when trimmed to a cone shape. **1967** DARE (Qu. I46, . . Kinds of fruits that grow wild around here) Inf **TX**33, Wild peach; (Qu. T5, . . Kinds of evergreens, other than pine) Inf **TX**35, Wild peach. **2003** Watson Reflections Neches 194 **ceTX,** Arriving there [= Peach Tree Ridge], I saw that it was crowned with a dense growth of Carolina laurel cherry, locally called wild peach.

2 Any of var other plants of the genus Prunus that are native to the Southwest and have downy fruit, as:

a =**desert almond.**

1881 Amer. Naturalist 15.230 **UT,** M.E. Jones in an article on the wild fruits of Utah, in Case's Botanical Index, mentions fourteen species; among these is a curious wild peach which grows in the sand and on lava beds. **1913** Jrl. Ag. Research 1.170, The desert almond, also called the "wild peach" and "wild almond," occupies a range much farther south and east than that of the Nevada wild almond, Prunus andersonii. **1976** Bailey–Bailey Hortus Third 919, [Prunus] fasciculata. . . Wild peach.

b also **wild peachbrush, ~ peach bush:** =**desert peach.**

1911 Bot. Gaz. 51.286 **NV,** Emplectocladus Andersoni [=Prunus a.] (wild peach). **1931** U.S. Dept. Ag. Misc. Pub. 101.70 **West,** Anderson peachbrush (. . Prunus andersonii), called also . . wild peach(brush), is probably the nearest of the peachbrush species to the cultivated peach. **1944** Amer. Midland Naturalist 32.417 **CA,** Wild Peach (Prunus andersoni). Ibid 427, Nest 6, built one and one-half feet from the ground in a small Wild peach, was exposed to almost any animal. **1967–68** DARE (Qu. I46, . . Kinds of fruits that grow wild around here) Inf **CA**15, Wild peach tree; (Qu. T16, . . Kinds of trees . . 'special') Inf **NV**8, Wild

peach—a brush, thorny, with pink flowers, very pungent smell. **2002** in 2008 DARE File—Internet **CA,** Be on the look out for the wild peach bush. A pink, very beautiful bush. It's just starting to bloom in that area [=Yosemite].

c A **wild plum 1** (here: Prunus texana).

1880 in 1982 TX Jrl. Sci. 34.111 **TX,** The Americans call it [=wild plum] "Wild Peach" because like the peach, its skin is thickly covered with fuzz. The fruit is small, becomes yellow when ripe, is sweet. **1913** Jrl. Ag. Research 1.150, The Texas "wild peach," Prunus texana, occurs in scattered localities over a region of eastern Texas . . lying wholly in the lower Sonoran or lower Austral zones. **1938** Van Dersal Native Woody Plants 207, Prunus texana. . . Wild peach.

wild peachbrush (or peach bush) See **wild peach 2b**

wild peanut n

=**hog peanut 1.**

1899 MacMillan MN Plant Life 304, The wild peanut forms two kinds of flowers, small purple or white, ordinary butterfly-shaped flowers on lateral racemes, and peculiar little flowers without petals, on certain slender prostrate stems. **1922** Amer. Botanist 28.74, Amphicarpa monoica is "hog peanut", "wild pea-vine" and "wild peanut" which names refer to the underground pods produced by the cleistogamous flowers of this plant. **1939** Natl. Geogr. Mag. 76.222, The wild peanut . . ripens some of its fruits underground, as does its namesake.

wild pear n **chiefly NEast, esp ME** See Map

=**serviceberry.**

[**1802** in 1954 Assoc. Amer. Geogrs. Annals 44.309 **Nova Scotia Canada,** Wild or Indian Pear—Mespilus.] **1810** Michaux Histoire des Arbres 1.32, Mespilus arborea—June berry, nom donné à cet arbre dans tous les Etats du milieu. Wild pear . . , dans le district de Maine. [= Mespilus arborea—June berry, name given to that tree in all the States of the region. Wild pear . . , in the district of Maine.] **1896** Jrl. Amer. Folkl. 9.186 **West,** Amelanchier Canadensis, . . wild pear. **1926** Torreya 26.5 **ME,** Amelanchier spp.—Wild pear. **1965–70** DARE (Qu. I46, . . Kinds of fruits that grow wild around here) 9 Infs, **esp NEast,** Wild pear(s); **OH**8, Wild pears—not edible; (Qu. T13) Inf **ME**5, Sugarberry—might be wild pear; (Qu. T16, . . Kinds of trees . . 'special') Inf **ME**24, Wild pear. **2005** Martha's Vineyard Times (MA) 12 May (Internet), The current show is composed of . . the delicate beauty of the wild pear or shadbush.

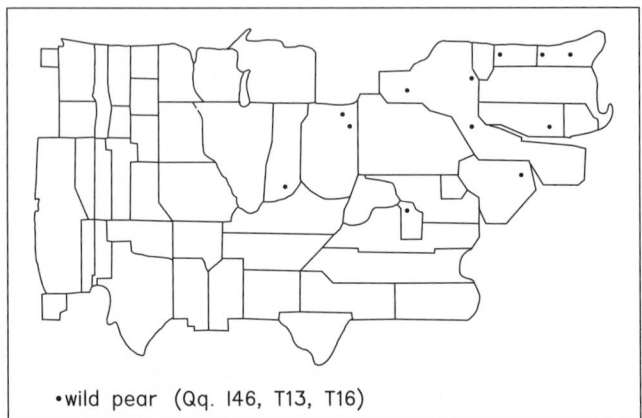

•wild pear (Qq. I46, T13, T16)

wild pecan n

=**water hickory.**

1920 in 1922 Jrl. NY Bot. Garden 23.155 **FL,** A "wild pecan" had been reported as growing along the North Fork; it proved to be the water-hickory. **1947** Clarke Co. Democrat (Grove Hill AL) 2 Oct 4/1 (DA), Our so-called lakes, or river sloughs, are lined with the water-hickory, pignut or wild pecan, as it is variously called. **1979** Little Checklist U.S. Trees 72, Carya aquatica. . . bitter pecan, swamp hickory, bitter water hickory, wild pecan. **2005** in 2008 DARE File—Internet, Carya aquatica. . . is also known as Bitter Hickory, . . Water Hickory or Wild Pecan; . . the bitter nuts are flatter than those of C[arya] illinoinensis [sic].

wild pepper n

1 =**New Jersey tea.**

1896 Jrl. Amer. Folkl. 9.184 **MO,** Ceanothus Americanus, . . wild pepper. **1960** Vines Trees SW 689, Ceanothus. . . americanus. . . is also

known under the names of . . Wild-pepper [etc]. . . The leaves were considered . . the best substitute for tea during the American Revolution.
2 =**jack-in-the-pulpit 1.**
   1900 Lyons *Plant Names* 45, *A[risaema] triphyllum.* . . Wild Pepper. **1930** Sievers *Amer. Med. Plants* 37, *Arisaema triphyllum.* . . Indian-turnip, wakerobin, wild pepper. . . It has an extremely burning taste.

wild petunia n   Also *wild prairie petunia*
A plant of the genus *Ruellia.*   Also called **pasture petunia**
   1893 *Garden and Forest* 6.242 **TX, KS,** There are several species of Ruellia growing in the vicinity of Austin. Of these, R. strepens and R. ciliosa extend northward into Kansas. These species, especially R. ciliosa, are known everywhere within their range as wild Petunia. **1902** Mackenzie *Manual Flora Jackson Co.* 176 **MO,** *Ruellia.* . . Wild Petunia. **1935** MO Bot. Garden *Annals* 22.646, *Ruellia caroliniensis.* . . Wild Petunia. **1951** *PADS* 15.40 **TX,** *Ruellia* spp.—Wild, wild prairie, or pasture, petunias. **1967** *DARE* Wildfl QR (Wills–Irwin) Pl.46B [= *Ruellia occidentalis*] Inf **TX**44, Wild petunia. *Ibid* Pl.46C [= *Ruellia caroliniensis* var *semicalva*] Infs **TX**34, 44, Wild petunia. **2006** [see **twinflower 2**].

wild pieplant n   Cf **pieplant, wild rhubarb**
=**canaigre.**
   1852 in 1986 Holmes *Covered Wagon Women* 281 [**cNY** writer in **ID**], Thurs traveled on till noon and then stoped to repare our wagon. . . find wild flax red yellow and black currnts Narrow dock and cranesbill and wild pie plant. **1897** Parsons *Wild Flowers CA* 378, The wild pie-plant is closely related to the garden rhubarb, and also to the dock and the sorrel. In early days in both Utah and Southern California housewives used its stems as a substitute for the cultivated pie-plant. **1920** Saunders *Useful Wild Plants* 121, These stalks, stripped off before the toughness of age has come upon them, and cooked like rhubarb, are hardly distinguishable from it. Westerners know it [= *Rumex hymenosepalus*] as Wild Rhubarb, Wild Pie Plant [etc]. **1975** Sweet *Common Edible & Useful Plants* 41, Wild Pieplant, *Rumex hymenosepalus.* **1999** Garcia *Brujas Tales* 179 **nNM,** People used to treat the evil eye with remedies. For example, you treated it by spitting wild pie plant with *cachana,* a root.

wild pig n   Cf **wild boar, ~ hog**
=**jabalina.**
   1870 Duval *Advent. Big-Foot* 133 **TX,** Can't you see that I am trying to keep my legs out of the reach of these outrageous wild pigs. **1878** in 1990 Silverthorne *Christmas TX* 83, We had killed a wild pig, and had intended to have boar's head for Christmas dinner. . . but unfortunately a dog ran off with the head. **1922** *NY Times* (NY) 8 Jan 33 **sTX,** This will be a refuge for the collared peccary, known as the wild pig, though it is not precisely a pig. It is like a cross between an antelope and a wild boar. **1951** *Jrl. Parasitology* 37.328 **TX,** The following Texas records of the flea . . which normally parasitizes the javelina or wild pig, are of interest. **1967** *DARE* (QR, near Qu. K27) Inf **CO**22, [ˈhævəlinəz]—wild pigs—terrible tusks. **2008** *DARE* File—Internet **wTX,** The animals here are mostly nocturnal but deer, coyotes, javelinas (wild pig), skunks and jackrabbits can sometimes be seen.

wild pigeon n
=**band-tailed pigeon.**
   [**1863** Hittell *Resources CA* 136, The band-tailed pigeon . . [is] the only wild pigeon found on the Pacific coast.] **1899** Cooper *Ornith. Club Bulletin* 1.57 **cwCA,** During the last four years I have found two nests of the Band-tailed Pigeon. . . Although the Wild Pigeon has never been recorded as nesting in the valleys of California, there seems to be no doubt of the above record being true. **1953** Jewett *Birds WA* 334, The wild or band-tailed pigeon fills a place in the Far West corresponding to that formerly occupied in the East by the now extinct passenger pigeon. **1967–69** *DARE* (Qu. Q7, *Names and nicknames for . . game birds*) Infs **CA**31, 97, 136, 160, Wild pigeon. **2009** *DARE* File—Internet **cnCA,** The wooded shoreline [of Shasta Lake] offers good hunting for bear, squirrels, quail, wild pigeon, turkey, deer and doves.

wild pimento n   Cf **pimento**
A **spicebush 1** (here: *Lindera benzoin*).
   1762 [see **wild allspice**]. **1771** Forster *Flora* 19 **LA,** Benzoin. . . wild pimento. **1803** in 1904 Thwaites *Early W. Travels* 3.359 **OH,** There is but little underwood; but on the sides of the creeks and near the river, the papaw . . , the spicebush, or wild pimento *(Laurus benzoin)* and the dogberry . . , grow in the greatest abundance. **1839** *Farmers' Reg.* 7.416 **neVA,** In this region the sassafras and wild pimento, *(laurus benzoin,)* . . have occasionally been killed, and the ground freezes to the depth of

fifteen inches. **1886** *Stoddart's Encycl. Americana* 3.36, *Lindera Benzoin,* also called spice-bush. . . is our wild allspice and wild pimento **1937** *Torreya* 37.97 **MO,** *Benzoin aestivale* [= *Lindera benzoin*]. . . Poivrier, wild pimento.

wild pine n   [*DJE* 1696 →; see quot 1828]   **FL**   Cf **pine** n **2, Spanish moss**
Any of several bromeliads of the genus *Tillandsia* with leaves somewhat resembling those of pineapple.
   1791 Bartram *Travels* 61 **eFL,** Wild Pine . . is a very large flourishing plant, greatly resembling . . a well grown plant of the Bromelia Ananas. **1828** NY Acad. Sci. *Annals Lyceum Nat. Hist.* 2.130 **neFL,** *Tillandsia utriculata.* . . is the plant mentioned by Bartram in his travels. . . It is vulgarly called Wild Pine. The first English settlers . . probably intended by this appellation Wild Pine Apple, as it very much resembles some species of Bromelia. **1933** Small *Manual SE Flora* 269, *Tillandsia.* . . Wild-pines. **1938** Baker *FL Wild Flowers* 36, Air plants. Wild Pines. Genus *Tillandsia.* . . Air plants crowd their leaves in the characteristic manner of pineapples, to which they are related, as the local name of wild pine indicates. **1975** Natl. Audubon Soc. *Corkscrew* 7 **FL,** *Stiff-leaved wild pine (Tillandsia fasciculata)*—This plant . . is the commonest of the pineapple air plants in Florida. **1994** Lantz–Hale *Young Naturalist's FL* 15, The giant Wildpine, growing on the sturdy limbs of Live Oak and other hammock trees, is another well-known Everglades bromeliad.

wild pink n
1 =**catchfly 1,** esp **Carolina pink 2.**   Cf **mountain pink 6, peat ~**
   1814 Bigelow *Florula Bostoniensis* 110, *Silene Pennsylvanica* [= *S. caroliniana*]. . . Sometimes called *wild pink,* from its similarity in habit to some of that genus. **1830** Rafinesque *Med. Flora* 2.263, *Silene.* . . Wild Pink. **1893** *Jrl. Amer. Folkl.* 6.138 **CA,** *Silene laciniata,* wild pink. **1913** *Torreya* 13.254 **NY,** In the woods about the clay pits the wild pink, *Silene caroliniana* . . , grew sparingly. **1929** Weygandt *Red Hills* 200 **sePA,** On the woods' floor . . we find always the wild pink *(silene Pennsylvanica)* in blossom. **1966–69** *DARE* (Qu. S26c, *Wildflowers that grow in woods*) Inf **MI**69, Wild pinks; **MA**13, Wild pinks—like a carnation; (Qu. S26e, *Other wildflowers not yet mentioned;* not asked in early QRs) Inf **MD**24, Wild pink—small pink flower, five pointed petals, grows in dry places; (Qu. S2) Inf **CA**165, Wild pink. **1967** *DARE* Wildfl QR Pl.53 [= *Silene caroliniana*] Infs **CO**11, 29, Wild pinks. **2001** Porcher–Rayner *Guide Wildflowers SC* 279, *Wild pink; Carolina pink.* . . Petals vary from pink to white. . . Common.
2 A **phlox,** usu =**moss pink 1.**
   1828 *Transylvania Jrl. Med.* 1.415 **KY,** *Phlox.* . . Wild Pink. **1837** *Boston Jrl. Nat. Hist.* 1.105 **NC,** Phlox . . subulàta. *Wild pink.* **1951** *PADS* 15.38 **TX,** *Phlox.* . . Wild, prairie, or woods, pinks. **1967** *DARE* Wildfl QR Pl.178 [= *Phlox subulata*] Inf **OH**14, Wild pink.
3 =**swamp pink 2.**
   1894 *Jrl. Amer. Folkl.* 7.100 **NJ,** *Arethusa bulbosa,* . . wild pink. **1964** *Castanea* 29.78 **DE,** *Arethusa bulbosa.* . . Arethusa, Bog-rose, Wild Pink. **1987** Case *Orchids* 157, Wild pink—*Arethusa bulbosa.* **2005** [see **swamp rose orchid**].

wild plum n   Cf **desert wild plum, plum** n
1 Std: any of var uncultivated or wild-growing plants of the genus *Prunus;* also the fruit of such a plant.   For other names of var spp see **beach plum, Canada ~, Cherokee ~, Chickasaw ~, creek ~, dwarf ~, flatwoods ~, goose ~, hog ~ 2, horse ~, inch ~, Indian ~ 1, May ~, penepne, pomegranate B1, possum plum 2, prairie ~, red ~, sand cherry 2, sandhill plum, sand ~ 2, sloe 1, thorn ~ 2, wild goose ~, wild peach 2c, yellow plum**   Cf **shinnery plum**
2 A **lotebush** (here: *Ziziphus parryi*) native to California.
   1941 Jaeger *Wildflowers* 138 **Desert SW,** *Condalia Parryi* [= *Ziziphus p.*] . . The desert people call it "wild plum" and prize it much for fuel. The fruits ripen in mid-August, turning golden yellow. . . The fruit pulp is very bitter. **1999** Campbell *Survival Skills* 155, *Crucillo* or wild plum *(Condalia parryi):* Pulp of this red desert drupe was eaten fresh or dried and ground to flour for mush.

wild poinsettia n   chiefly Sth, Midl
Any of var **spurges** that resemble **poinsettia B1,** such as **fire-on-the-mountain.**

1928 Quillin *TX Wild Flowers* 202, *Scientific Name: Euphorbia havanensis. . . Common Name:* Wild Poinsettia. **1965–70** *DARE* (Qu. S26c, *Wildflowers that grow in woods*) 15 Infs, 12 **Sth, Midl,** Wild poinsetta; **AL**20, Wild poinsetta—a hypocrite (I call it)—imitates our Christmas poinsetta; **TN**22, Wild poinsetta—small ones, not "Floridy" poinsettas. **2002** in 2008 *DARE* File—Internet **TX,** *Euphorbia dentata* is called toothed spurge, wild poinsettia, and tooth-leaf poinsettia. It is not often included in wildflower books, but grows profusely in our yard. **2007** *DARE* File—Internet **FL,** Wild Poinsettia is a Florida native plant, it's pretty, it doesn't get too tall, it's colorful, and *butterflies* taste it once in a while.

wild poppy n
1 =**prickly poppy.**
1902 NE State Bd. Ag. *Annual Rept. for 1901* 104, We have a species of Wild Poppy (Argemone intermedia) which grows throughout the greater part of the state. **1951** *PADS* 15.32, *Argemone. . .* Our prickle-guarded silken wild poppies . . are all known also as wild hollyhocks. **1966–69** *DARE* (Qu. S15, . . *Weed seeds that cling to clothing*) Inf **NM**13, Seeds of wild poppy (has white blossoms and large petals)—stickers are just on stems & leaves; (Qu. S21, . . *Weeds . . that are a trouble in gardens and fields*) Infs **GA**11, **TX**12, Wild poppies; (Qu. S26c, *Wildflowers that grow in woods*) Inf **MO**19, Wild poppies; (Qu. S26e, *Other wildflowers not yet mentioned;* not asked in early QRs) Inf **TX**19, Wild poppy—white poppy-like flower—thistle-like plant. **1992** Kirkpatrick *Wildflowers W. Plains* 181, *Argemone polyanthemos. . .* The white petals of this wild poppy are some of the purest white and most delicate and fragile-looking . . of all white wildflowers.
2 A **sweet shrub** (here: *Calycanthus occidentalis*) native to California and Washington.
1911 Jepson *Flora CA* 172 **cnCA,** *Calycanthus. . .* Flowers livid red. . . "Wild Poppy" in Trinity Co., where it is reputed poisonous to cattle. **1939** McMinn *Illustr. Manual CA Shrubs* 118, *Calycanthus occidentalis. . . Spice Bush. . .* This shrub has been given a variety of common names because of the interesting flowers, fruits, and aromatic odor of the leaves. Wine-flower, Wild-poppy, California Calycanth, [etc.].

wild portulaca n
=**red maids** (here: *Calandrinia ciliata*).
1897 Parsons *Wild Flowers CA* 212, *Wild Portulaca. Calandrinia caulescens. . .* The wild portulaca is very abundant, and in seasons favorable to its development is a very noticeable little plant. **1934** Haskin *Wild Flowers Pacific Coast* 87, *Wild portulaca—Calandrinia caulescens. . .* This plant is a close relative of our showy garden portulaca. **1965** Neitzel *Flora Solano Co.* 29 **cwCA,** Wild Portulaca . . *Calandrinia ciliata var. menziesii. . .* Appears everywhere in Solano County.

wild potato n
1 Any of var plants of the family Convolvulaceae, esp **man-of-the-earth 1,** a **bindweed 1** (here: *Convolvulus arvensis*), or **hedge bindweed 1.** Cf **wild potato vine, wild sweet potato**
1772 in 1924 Phillips *Notes B. Romans* 124 **FL,** The Savages are not so Well Provided with Bread as the Spaniards. . . But both . . [use] a Species of Convolvulus known by the Name of Wild Potatoe. **1798** [see **wild rhubarb 2**]. **1849** Amer. Med. Assoc. *Trans.* 2.899 **MA,** *Convolvulus arvensis.* Field bind-weed; wild potato. **1870** in 1871 Featherman *Rept. Bot. Surv. LA* 101, *Batatas littoralis* [=*Ipomoea imperati*], . . Seacoast Wild Potato. **1897** *Jrl. Amer. Folkl.* 10.51 **swMO,** *Ipomoea pandurata,* . . and *Convolvulus sepium,* . . wild potato. *Ibid* **AL,** *Ipomoea pandurata,* . . wild potato. **1956** McAtee *Some Dialect NC* 50, *Wild potato* . . the bindweed, *Convolvulus arvensis.* **1966** *DARE* Wildfl QR Pl.176 [=*Calystegia sepium*] Inf **NC**28, Wild potato. **1990** Castanea 55.168 **FL,** *Ipomoea pandurata. . .* Morning-glory, wild potato, man-of-the-earth. Open mesic pine-oak woods, wet hammocks; occasional.
2 A plant of the family Fabaceae, as:
a =**groundnut B1.**
1737 (1911) Brickell *Nat. Hist. NC* 289, *Ground-Nuts,* or *Wild Potatoes.* **1791** in 1799 Barton *Fragments Nat. Hist. PA* 6, *Progress of Vegetation. . .* July. . . 30. . . Eupatorium perfoliatum, and Glycine Apios [=*Apios americana*] (Wild Potato), in flower. **1814** in 1815 Lit. & Philos. Soc. NY *Trans.* 1.163, The glycine apios, or wild potato, which is nearly as good as the common, and which was, when boiled, a favourite food of the Indians. **1851** Audubon–Bachman *Quadru\[Quadrupeds\]* 2.136, Towards spring, he [=the fox squirrel] feeds on . . several kinds of roots, especially the wild potato, (*Apios tuberosa.*) **1882** *Defiance Democrat*

(OH) 6 July 1/6, The ground nut or wild bean, *apios tuberosa* [=*A. americana*], is the mode, or wild potato, of the Sioux Indians. **1897** *Morning World–Herald* (Omaha NE) 13 Nov 5/3 **ME,** Occasionally he would bring to light a string of the wild potato or ground nuts. **1920** Evermann–Clark *Lake Maxinkuckee* 2.344 **IN,** Ground-nut; "Wild potato" *Glycine apios L.* Rather common in low rich black ground along the bank of the lake.
b An **Indian breadroot** (here: *Pediomelum esculentum*).
1943 Fernald–Kinsey *Edible Wild Plants E. N. Amer.* 246, Wild potato, Indian bread-root . . *Psoralea esculenta* [=*Pediomelum e.*]. **1974** Angier *Field Guide Edible Plants* 174, *Prairie turnip. . . Other names*—Breadroot, Wild Potato, . . Prairie Potato, Indian Breadroot. . . It is a perennial whose large root, or sometimes group of roots, resembling sweet potato roots and having an agreeable odor, lies entirely beneath the ground.
c A **sweetvetch** (here: *Hedysarum alpinum*). **AK** Cf **Eskimo potato, Indian ~ m**
1953 *AK Sportsman* Feb 17 **AK,** They [=Little Diomeders] find greens too—sourdock leaves, Eskimo or wild potatoes, salmonberries and willow greens. **1989** [see **wild rhubarb 3**]. **1996** Krakauer *Into the Wild* 191 **AK,** Above ground the wild potato grows as a bushy herb, two feet tall, with stalks of delicate pink flowers reminiscent of miniature sweet-pea blossoms.
3 Any of several **nightshades 1;** see quots.
1848 Emory *Notes Reconnoissance* 48 **NM,** The plains and river bottoms were covered with . . a solanum, a kind of wild potato, with narrow leaves, which Dr. Torrey says is different from any in the United States. **1869** MO State Entomol. *Annual Rept. for 1868* 108, The bogus and the true Colorado Potato-beetles [feed] respectively . . upon very closely allied species of wild potato (*Solanum rostratum* and *S. carolinense.*) **1897** *Amer. Anthropologist* 10.38 **AZ,** Solanum Jamesii. . . The wild potato. The tubers are gathered [by the Hopi], mixed with clay, and eaten. **1937** *Ecology* 18.432 **CO,** *Solanum jamesii. . .* Wild potatoes planted in three different localities in the vicinity of Boulder, Colorado, varied considerably not only in yield but also in color. **1970** Kirk *Wild Edible Plants W. U.S.* 241, *S. fendleri* (Wild Potato) is found in rich soil in open pine forests in New Mexico and Arizona. **1985** Dodge *Flowers SW Deserts* 119, *Nightshade*—Groundcherry, Wild Potato, Trompillo, Horsenettle. **2008** *DARE* File—Internet **CO,** *Solanum jamesii* . . wild potato.
4 Any of var plants of other families, as:
a =**stretchberry 1.**
1875 *Appletons' Jrl.* 14.173 **FL,** This was the . . China brier, by some called the wild-potato. **1940** Writers' Program *Food FL Indians* 6, This food consists of flour from the roots of the China briar, or wild potato.
b =**spring beauty 1.**
1892 *Jrl. Amer. Folkl.* 5.93 **PA,** *Claytonia Virginica,* . . wild potatoes. **1910** Amer. Museum Nat. Hist. *Anthro. Papers* 5.20 **ID, MT,** Wild potato, *Claytonia lanceolata.* **2006** Vizgirdas *Wild Plants* 155 **CA,** Spring Beauty *(Claytonia). . .* Often called Indian potato, wild potato, or mountain potato, the small corms can be eaten raw, boiled, or roasted.
c A **soap plant 1** (here: *Chlorogalum pomeridianum*).
1895 Torrey Bot. Club *Bulletin* 22.114 **CA,** *Chlorogalum pomeridianum* . . of California, is better known as a soap and a fiber plant than as a food plant, but it is also sometimes called . . "Wild Potato." . . Cooking eliminates all acrid and injurious substances, rendering the bulb good, wholesome food. **1939** Medsger *Edible Wild Plants* 197 **CA,** Amole, or Wild Potato, or Soap Plant, *Chlorogalum pomeridianum.*
d An **arrowhead 1** (here: *Sagittaria platyphylla*).
1913 *Torreya* 13.227 **LA,** *Sagittaria platyphylla. . .* Wild potato, Venice, La., Mississippi Delta, La. **1917** U.S. Dept. Ag. *Bulletin* 465.21, The attraction was found to be a tuberous species *(Sagittaria platyphylla),* known to the hunters of this and other parts of Louisiana as wild potato or wild onion. *Ibid* 23, A glance at . . the tubers . . of this species shows the aptness of the name "wild potato." **1976** Smith *Wonderful Wappato* 1 **OR,** Wappato, or wild potato, is an edible water plant. It is called arrowhead which describes the foliage.
e =**chickweed wintergreen.**
1937 St. John *Flora SE WA & ID* 313, *Trientalis latifolia. . .* Wild Potato. Tubers 4–20 mm. long, white, more or less fusiform, warty, and horizontal, forming filiform rhizomes.
f =**rue anemone.**
1939 Medsger *Edible Wild Plants* 198 **PA,** Rue Anemone. . . The starchy tuberous roots are edible when cooked. I know of mountainous

districts in Pennsylvania where these roots are collected and eaten under the name of "wild potato."

g =**sand food.**

1960 in 1962 *Ethnology* 1.188 **AZ,** During the ethnographic present they [=the Pima and the Papago] used such foods as . . roots and bulbs of the sandroot (wild potato), covenas and others.

h =**cowbane 2.** Cf **pig potato 2**

1975 Hamel–Chiltoskey *Cherokee Plants* 51, Potato, wild; cowbane . . *Oxypolis rigidior* . . Root is baked and eaten.

i A **wild yam** (here: *Dioscorea bulbifera*). Cf **air potato**

1978 *Castanea* 43.39 **FL,** *Dioscorea bulbifera*. . . Wild Potato. Edges of wet to mesic hardwoods; occasional.

wild potato vine n Cf **wild potato 1**

1 =**man-of-the-earth 1.**

1810 Barton *Coll. for an Essay* 1.30 **DE,** It is . . *Convolvulus panduratus*. This plant is called, in the state of Delaware, Wild-Potatoe-Vine. **1860** (1861) MI Geol. Surv. *First Biennial Rept.* 286, Wild Potato-vine, Man-of-the-earth. Ipomoea pandurata. **1912** *Star* (Kansas City MO) 21 Apr sec D 7/3, Later in the spring we will find the lamb's quarters and the wild potato vine. **1938** FWP *Guide IA* 15, The wild potato vine may be recognized by patches of moonflower-like bloom. **1966–70** DARE (Qu. S5, . . *Wild morning glory*) Infs **KY**77, **NC**1, Wild potato vine; (Qu. S26e, *Other wildflowers not yet mentioned;* not asked in early QRs) Inf **SC**32, Wild potato vine. **2005** Wiggins *VA Native Plants* 30, Local representatives of the Morning Glory Family in our flora include . . Wild Potato Vine *(Ipomoea pandurata).*

2 =**bush morning-glory.**

1871 U.S. Dept. Ag. *Rept. of Secy. for 1870* 407, *Wild potato vine, (Ipomoea leptophylla.)*—This showy plant of the dry deserts of the West is commonly called man root, or man of the earth. . . The Cheyennes, Arapahoes, and Kiowas roast it for food when pressed by hunger. **1897** *Jrl. Amer. Folkl.* 10.51 **CA,** *Ipomoea leptophylla,* . . wild potato vine. **1970** Kirk *Wild Edible Plants W. U.S.* 288, *Ipomoea leptophylla* . . Wild Potato Vine [etc].

wild prairie petunia See **wild petunia**

wild quinine n Cf **Florida bark**

1 =**feverfew 3.** Cf **quinine weed 2, Saint-Jacob's-quinine**

1890 *IA State Reporter* (Waterloo) 16 Jan 1/3, Geo. Stine, of Mt. Vernon twp., has a remedy for la grippe. He gathers an herb that he calls wild quinine, steeps the leaves and gives freely to the patient. **1894** *Jrl. Amer. Folkl.* 7.92 **wIN,** *Parthenium integrifolium,* . . wild quinine. **1932** *San Antonio Express* (TX) 31 July sec D 9/4, The reception suite was adorned with ferns and wild quinine blossoms brought by the host from the Medina hills. **1960** *Castanea* 25.50 **VA,** *Parthenium integrifolium.* . . Wild-quinine. Dry woods. **1982** *Sci. News* 122.251 **nIL,** Among the Indian grass and bluestem, he points out the forb species: . . wild quinine *[Parthenium integrifolium].* **2002** *Castanea* 67.6 **cVA,** *Parthenium integrifolium* . . var. *auriculatum* . . wild quinine. . *Parthenium integrifolium* . . var. *integrifolium*—wild quinine.

2 A **centaury** (here: *Centaurium venustum*). Cf **canchalagua, quinine weed 1**

1920 Saunders *Useful Wild Plants* 207, Among Spanish Californians an herb of the Pacific Coast believed useful in fevers is Canchalagua, or as the Americans call it Wild Quinine (*Erythraea venusta* [=*Centaurium v.*] . .).

wild raisin n [See quot 1945]

A **viburnum:** usu a **nannyberry 1** (here: *Viburnum lentago*) or a **withe rod** (here: *V. nudum* var *cassinoides*), but also a **black haw 1** (here: *V. rufidulum*); see quots.

1894 *Jrl. Amer. Folkl.* 7.90 **ME,** *Viburnum lentago,* . . wild raisin. **1901** *Des Moines Daily Leader* (IA) 19 Dec 5/4 **ME,** The coral-red berry of the wild raisin, which grows by fence sides and on waste land all over Maine, is not so imposing in its festive appearance, or as renowned as the English holly. **1934** *Ecology* 15.163 **NY,** Only two shrubs, wild raisin, *Viburnum cassinoides* [=*V. nudum* var. *cassinoides*] . . and dwarf raspberry, are able to maintain normal growth. **1945** *MI Hist. Mag.* 29.233, Viburnum Lentago goes by the name of nannyberry or wild raisin. Its fruit is black and when ripe or dried has an agreeable taste similar to that of a raisin. **1949** *Jrl. Wildlife Management* 13.257 **WV,** Wild raisin (*Viburnum* sp.) **1968** *Traverse City Rec.-Eagle* (MI) 14 Sept 12/8, Other places of high use [by ruffed grouse] for this year could be among the wild raisin or wild cherries under the oaks. **1973** Stephens *Woody Plants* 486, *Viburnum rufidulum.* . . Southern

black haw, wild raisin, rusty nannyberry. **2007** *NY Times* (NY) 6 May sec 14 7 (Internet), "The violets have been coming up early," he said. . . "The wild raisins are already budding. And the dandelions were flowering in February. They wouldn't have dared to do that back in the 70s."

wild ratsbane See **ratsbane 1**

wild red cherry See **red cherry 1**

wild red lily See **red lily a, c**

wild red plum See **red plum**

wild redtop n Cf **redtop 1**

1 =**switch grass 1.**

1862 IN State Geologist *Rept. Geol. Reconnoissance IN* 206, From these low lands of rich, black soil, and some bowlders and gravel, with the wild indigo, ferns, wild red-top, &c., . . we rose gradually to rolling prairies of Flutter-dock and Rosin weed. **1869** Goddard *Where to Emigrate* 265 **IA,** Wild prairie grasses, blue-joint, white clover, wild red-top, marsh and slough grass, sedge, wild pea or vetch, and buffalo grass, are the principal natural grasses. **1897** *Jrl. Amer. Folkl.* 10.147 **cNE,** *Panicum virgatum,* . . Also called "wild red-top" by the farmers. **1925** *Amer. Midland Naturalist* 9.391 **NY,** *Panicum virgatum.* . . Wild Red-Top. **1980** Smith–Smith *Prairie Garden* 185, *Panicum virgatum.* . . Switchgrass; Panicgrass; Wild Redtop. . . This aggressive grass grows in large clumps and needs strong competition.

2 A **bentgrass 1;** see quots. Cf **redtop 1a**

1877 *Bot. Gaz.* 2.126 **OR,** *Agrostis microphylla.* . . This is called Wild Red-top, grows on bottom lands, and averages 4 feet in height. **1910** Johnson *Highways Rocky Mts.* 267 **seND,** For hay we depend a good deal on the wild red top that grows on the bottoms. I've seen it waist high and so heavy that the rains would lodge it down. **1969** Barrell *Flora Gunnison Basin* 26 **CO,** Two minor grasses were wild redtop (*Agrostis scabra*) and squirreltail (*Hordeum brachyantherum*).

3 A **reed grass a** (here: *Calamagrostis stricta*). **chiefly AK**

1896 *Denver Republican* (CO) 2 Oct 7/8 **AK,** [Headline:] *Alaska as a Cattle Country*—There Are Enormous Areas of Wild Redtop Growing. **1913** AK Ag. Exper. Stations *Annual Rept. for 1912* 52, Wild red top, white top, and blue stem all come up along the slopes both north and south where the timber has been cut off or killed by forest fires. **1920** *Torreya* 20.18 **CA,** *Calamagrostis inexpansa* [=*C. stricta*]. . . Wild redtop. **1923** Carpenter *AK Wonderland* facing 228, Glacier-scoured and snow-capped mountains tower above Resurrection Bay, while close to the shore are dense spruce forests and wild red-top grass.

wild rhubarb n

1 Any of several **docks** n¹, but esp **canaigre** which is native chiefly to the Southwest. Cf **wild pieplant**

1709 (1967) Lawson *New Voyage* 83 **NC, SC,** *Of The Herbs of Carolina.* . . Samphire in the Marshes excellent, so is the Dock or Wild-Rhubarb. **1821** Cobbett *Amer. Gardener* [150], The *Dock* (which is the wild *Rhubarb*) puts forth its leaves very quickly after the Dandelion. *Ibid* [173], The *Dock* is the wild Rhubarb, and if you look at, and *taste,* the *root,* you will see the proof of it. **1861** *Janesville Daily Gaz.* (WI) 30 Aug [3]/6 (newspaperarchive.com) **cCO,** The inhabitants were congratulating themselves on finding in large quantities, wild rhubarb or pieplant. I saw several lots of it which would measure from twelve to fifteen inches in length, and about the size of the forefinger. It looks as good as that we raise in our gardens. **1891** *Santa Fe Daily New Mexican* (NM) 15 Oct 1/5, A company [formed] for the purpose of tanning leather. . . will use the canaigre plant, or more commonly known as wild rhubarb, or pie plant, which grows so abundantly on the mesas in this county. **1937** *Jrl. Amer. Folkl.* 50.322 **WY,** The young [Crow] men and women go together to gather wild rhubarb. **1972** *AZ Daily Sun* (Flagstaff) 13 June 6/3, We also ate narrow-leaf dock or sheep sorrel (Rumex crispus), sometimes called wild rhubarb. **1996** Andersen–Holmgren *Mt. Plants UT* 20, (Rumex venosus). . . Wild rhubarb or wild begonia is an erect perennial 12 to 24 inches high that grows in sandy soil. . . *Rumex hymenosepalus* is similar but has smaller seeds. It was called *wild rhubarb* by early settlers who used it for food. **2006** Kane *Herbal Med. Amer. SW* 88, *Rumex hymenosepalus*—Wild rhubarb, Tanner's dock, Canaigre. . . can be found from western Texas to stretches of the Mohave Desert in California, south from Wyoming, Utah, and Colorado, to Arizona and New Mexico.

2 Usu =**man-of-the-earth 1,** rarely =**bush morning-glory;** see quots.

1798 Barton *Coll. for an Essay* 1.30, I know nothing, from experience, of the *Mechameck,* or Wild-Rhubarb, of some of our Indians. It is, certainly, a species of Convolvulus, or Bind-weed, and I believe the Convolvulus panduratus, which in Virginia is called "wild potatoe." **1828** Rafinesque *Med. Flora* 1.123, *Convolvulus panduratus. . . Vulgar names*—Wild Potatoe, Wild Rhubarb, [etc]. [*Ibid* 125, Our *C. panduratus* has also been mistaken for Scamony, Rhubarb, and Mechoacan.] **1851** (1856) Dunglison *Med. Lexicon* 235, *Convolvulus panduratus. . . Wild Rhubarb. . .* In Virginia, and some other parts of the United States, the root of this plant has been much recommended in cases of gravel.

3 A **knotweed 1** (here: *Polygonum alpinum*).

1868 Whymper *Travel AK* 214, I had previously seen a quantity of wild rhubarb, which the Indians gather in quantities, and it really was very little inferior in flavour. **1947** *Western Folkl.* 6.125 **Aleutians** (as of 1868–70), The only indigenous vegetable used is a sort of wild rhubarb, which is boiled with fish or spawn for soup. **1970** *Fairbanks Daily News-Miner* (AK) 18 May 5/5, Wild rhubarb (Polygonum alpinum) grows everywhere in Alaska. . . The young, red stems are edible and taste like cultivated rhubarb. **1989** *Arctic & Alpine Research* 21.335 **AK**, Vegetable foods harvested included blueberries, cranberries, cloudberries, wild rhubarb *(Polygonum alaskanum),* wild potato *(Hedysarum alpinum),* and more than one species of willow leaves.

4 =cow parsnip 1. Cf **Indian celery, ~ rhubarb 2**

1910 McClintock *Old N. Trail* 294 **nwMT** (as of c1890), Bending towards the west, was a single stalk of wild rhubarb (cow parsnip), with an eagle plume fastened to the top. *Ibid* 529, Wild Rhubarb.—Cow Parsnip. *Heracleum lanatum.* **1952** Williams *AK Wildfl. Glimpses* 12, A very large member of this tribe [=Carrot family] which starts to bloom in June or July, is the *cow parsnip* or *wild rhubarb,* as it is sometimes called in Southeastern Alaska. **1968** *DARE* (Qu. S6) Inf **AK1**, Wild rhubarb—Indian rhubarb—Indian celery—(palmated leaf). **2006** Hungrywolf *Blackfoot Papers* 1.131 **MT**, (Heracleum lanatum) . . Wild Rhubarb. . . The roots of wild rhubarb were also split, then cut up and dried for winter use.

wild rice n

1 A plant of the genus *Zizania,* usu *Z. aquatica* or *Z. palustris.* **widespread, but esp Nth** For other names of var spp see **duck oats, ~ rice 1, Indian rice 1, oats 3, reed 2, rice B1, water oats, wild millet c, ~ oats 2a**

[**1748** Ellis *Voyage* 79 **Canada**, By the Sides of Lakes and Rivers there is abundance of wild Rice.] **1775** (1962) Romans *Nat. Hist. FL* 180, At *Ilionois,* in latitude 40, snow seldom lays three days, and cattle are out all winter; in . . latitude 45 and 46, . . snow rarely exceeds three inches in depth, and the wild rice is found spontaneous in amazing tracts. **1795** *Argus Greenleaf's New Daily Advt.* (NY NY) 27 June [2]/1, For the first peck of American wild rice, growing on the sides of lakes Michigan, Superior, or any of the upper lakes, in a condition fit for sowing—*a premium of twenty dollars.* **1816** *Reporter* (Brattleboro VT) 29 Oct [1]/4 **neWI**, Camp on Fox River, Green Bay. . . In the spring and fall, myriads of water fowl, attracted by the wild rice, darken the air. This plant springs up in water six or seven feet deep. **1851** *De Bow's Rev.* 11.510 **PA**, Any one who will take a walk to the nearest river bank of the Delaware and Schuylkill, . . will have a perfect idea of what wild rice is; these same reeds, or water oats, as they are often called, being exactly the same plant as the wild rice of Minnesota. **1864** *Daily Eve. Bulletin* (San Francisco CA) 12 Mar 5/3, *California Rice.*—A correspondent of the *Bulletin* says that last fall wild rice [here: =Zizania palustris] was found extremely abundant in some parts of the Tulare country. . . Wild rice is also found in the Klamath lakes. **1911** Porter *Harvester* 94 **IN**, Above all arose wild rice he had planted for the birds. **1965** *Bee* (Phillips WI) 19 Aug [3]/2, A sure sign of approaching fall came . . last week when the first wild rice season opening for 1965 was announced. **1969** *DARE* FW Addit **NC**, Wild rice—plant common on Hatteras Island, NC. **2004** *Milwaukee Jrl. Sentinel* (WI) 18 Apr sec H 10 (Internet), Lake Superior's Chequamegon Bay offers. . . [u]biquitous wild rice, wild celery and wild cabbage beds . . for great [smallmouth] bass cover and structure. **2008** *Oregonian* (Portland OR) 8 Jan sec FD 2 (Internet), With its rich color, wonderfully chewy texture and deliciously nutty flavor, wild rice is certainly an upscale grain—and it has the price tag to go with it.

2 also *southern wild rice:* A very large, thick-stemmed, tall grass *(Zizaniopsis miliacea)* native chiefly to the southern US. Also called **cut-grass 3, wild oats 2a**

1896 Beal *Grasses N. Amer.* 2.176, Wild rice. Zizania [=Zizaniopsis] miliacea Michx. **1920** *Sun.* Oregonian (Portland OR) 19 Dec sec 6 5/5 **LA**, There are about 4000 square miles of thick-grown wild rice straw

going to waste every year on the Louisiana marshes. Technically, the cereal in question is not a rice at all, but a form of wild barley. . . The straw is three to four to five feet in height, topped with heads similar to those of rice, whence the common name. **1942** Reelfoot L. Biol. Sta. *Report* 6.8 **TN**, Along the muddy banks dense growths of *Zizaniopsis* (cut-grass or wild rice) are found in stretches where the sunlight is not shut out. **1980** *Jrl. Wildlife Management* 44.508 **eSC**, Grasses, including wild rice *(Zizania aquatica),* southern wild rice *(Zizaniopsis maliacea* [sic]), and panic grasses *(Panicum* spp.) were consumed [by feral hogs] more than any other type of herbage. **2004** in 2008 *DARE* File—Internet **TX**, Given the size of the wetlands and that the dominant plant was Zizaniopsis miliacea (Giant Cutgrass, Wild Rice), I'm sure there must be dozens [of Broad-winged Skippers].

3 Var other grasses used like or thought to resemble **1** above, as **rice cut-grass, mountain rice,** a **spike-grass 3** (here: *Chasmantheum latifolium*), **barnyard grass, whitetop 5,** or a **cordgrass** (here: *Spartina alterniflora*); see quots.

1847 Darlington *Ag. Botany* 205, *Leersia. . . Oryza*—or Rice-like *Leersia. Vulgò*—Cut-Grass. Wild Rice. . . is not only worthless, but rather a nuisance. **1906** *Amer. Geogr. Soc. NY Bulletin* 38.11, Nearer the Gulf [of California] are found great sloughs, in which are extensive fields of the "wild rice" (Uniola Palmeri [=Chasmanthium latifolium]). **1913** *Torreya* 13.227 **LA**, Echinochloa crus-galli. . . Wild rice . . this name is in use throughout lower Louisiana. *Ibid* **LA**, *Spartina glabra* [=*S. alterniflora*]. . . Wild rice, Cameron, La. **1920** *Ibid* 20.18 **ND**, Scolochloa festucacea. . . Wild Rice. **1932** Rydberg *Flora Prairies* 86, *Wild rice,* . . *E[riocoma] hymenoides* [=*Achnatherum h.*] **1938** Palacio 44.42 **NM**, It [=*Achnatherum hymenoides*] is known by several other vernacular names, such as Indian Ricegrass, Mountain Rice, Wild Rice, Sand Grass and Sand Bunch-Grass. **1996** Reitz et al. *Case Studies Environmental Archeol.* 342, The Ojibwa along the northern shore of Lake Superior used wild rice *(Oryzopsis hymenoides)* and cranberries *(Vacinium* sp.), which were not prevalent to the south.

wild rooter See **rooter 1**

wild rose n

Std: any uncultivated or wild-growing plant of the genus *Rosa.* For other names of var of these see **cabbage rose, Cherokee ~, Chickasaw ~, Illinois ~, meadow ~, pasture ~, prairie ~, primrose 4, swamp rose, wood ~**

wild rosemary n

1 A **Labrador tea,** usu *Ledum palustre.*

[**1768** *NY Gaz. & Weekly Mercury* (NY) 25 Apr [2]/2, A Sample of the Labrador tea has been sent from *Boston.* It is something like wild rosemary.] **1785** Marshall *Arbustrum* 75, *Ledum. Marsh cistus,* or *wild rosemary. . . The* Species *with us, but one,* viz. *Ledum thymifolium* [= *Leiophyllum buxifolium*]. . . It is a small ever-green shrub, scarcely rising above eighteen inches or two feet in height and divided into several branches. **1850** Laurie *Elements Homoeopathic Practice* xix, *Ledum palustre. . .* Wild Rosemary, Marsh Tea. **1897** Britton–Brown *Illustr. Flora* 2.557, *Ledum palustre. . .* Narrow-leaved Labrador Tea. . . In bogs, Newfoundland to Alaska. . . Called also Marsh Tea, Wild Rosemary. **1952** Blackburn *Trees* 175, *Ledum palustre. . .* Wild rosemary. **2008** *DARE* File—Internet, *Ledum palustre* (Wild Rosemary)—Ledum palustre is a bushy evergreen shrub. . . Very pretty plant for cool, boggy areas.

2 A small aromatic shrub *(Conradina canescens)* native to Florida, Alabama, and Mississippi.

1870 Gray in 1873 *Amer. Acad. Arts & Sci. Proc.* 8.295 **wFL, swAL**, From Appalachicola [sic] to Pensacola and Mobile: called "Wild Rosemary."—A well-marked genus in habit and character. **1894** *Jrl. Amer. Folkl.* 7.96 **FL**, *Conradina canescens,* . . wild rosemary. **1980** Collins-Aird *Collins Family* 3.142 **wFL**, One species in this genus is Conradina Canescens, . . known as "Wild Rosemary". **2006** Harrison *Groundcovers* 69, *Conradina canescens*—Wild Rosemary. . . Plants are reminiscent of very fine and lax or soft rosemary.

wild rye n Also *wild ryegrass*

Any of var grasses of the genus *Elymus* or of the related genus *Leymus.* Also called **ryegrass 2;** for other names relating to *Elymus* spp see **squirreltail (grass) 2, wild oats 2h;** for other names relating to *Leymus* spp see **dune grass, rancheria ~, sea lyme ~, squaw ~ 2** Cf **Indian rye**

1751 (1893) Gist *Jrls.* 43 **VA**, The wild Rye appeared very green and flourishing. **1832** MA Hist. Soc. *Coll.* 2d ser 9.149 **cwVT,** Elymus striatus, . . Wild rye. **1865** Crockett *Life* 97 **TN,** We came to a large prairie. . . and the low grounds were all set over with wild rye, looking as green as a wheat field. **1882** U.S. Dept. Ag. *Rept. of Secy. for 1881–82* 235 **OR, WA,** But little native grass is cut for hay, some little wild red top, wild-rye grass, salt marsh grass upon tide-water, and east of the Cascades a little bunch grass is cut. **1923** Carrier *Beginnings of Ag.* 27, *Wild Rye Grasses.* . . The common grass along the Atlantic Coast from Virginia northward was wild rye (*Elymus* sp.) **1961** Thomas *Flora Santa Cruz* 87 **cwCA,** *[Elymus] glaucus* . . Western Rye Grass, Blue Wild Rye. **1967–68** *DARE* (Qu. S8, *A common kind of wild grass that grows in fields: it spreads by sending out long underground roots, and it's hard to get rid of*) Inf **AK**1, Wild rye, beach grass . . along seashores; (Qu. S14, . . *Prickly seeds, small and flat, with two prongs at one end, that cling to clothing*) Inf **MO**18, Wild rye; (Qu. S15, . . *Weed seeds that cling to clothing*) Inf **MO**38, Wild rye. **2008** *DARE* File—Internet, *Leymus cinereus—Great Basin wild rye.* . . [T]his large, bold bunchgrass can grow 3–5 ft. tall in a dense, slowly spreading clump.

wild sage n
1 also *wild sagebrush:* **=sagebrush 1.**
  1805 (1807) Gass *Jrl.* 127 **WA,** A kind of wild sage . . as high as a man's head . . grows in these bottoms. **1826** in 1827 *Boston Weekly Messenger* (MA) 31 May [3]/3 **Rocky Mts,** The country on the S. W. and N. W. is very barren, bearing but little more than wild sage and short grass. **1874** *Amer. Naturalist* 8.209 **WY,** There are straggling bushes of "wild sage" (*Artemisia tridentata* . .) growing on all the hilly portions of the land. **1891** *Amer. Anthropologist* 4.337 **ND, SD,** They load them [=popguns] with bark which they have chewed, or else with wild sage (*Artemisia*). **1925** Stuart *40 Yrs.* 1.20 **MT,** Now I see fields of alfalfa and waving grain where were once the bunch grass and the wild sage. **1968** *DARE* FW Addit **CO**7A, Wild sagebrush—horses and cattle eat and go crazy. . . The sagebrush is the same you are thinking of; when pastures are poor, horses eat too much and they become more or less crazy. **1990** *Gt. Plains Qrly.* 10.25, Wild sage (*Artemisia ludoviciana* . .) has also been consistently used at religious ceremonies. **2007** *San Francisco Chron.* (CA) 21 Feb (Internet), She'd graced her Thanksgiving turkey with "wild sage," a native sagebrush, Artemisia pycnocephala, not at all a good substitute for culinary sage and not related to it, either.
2 A **boneset 1** (here: *Eupatorium perfoliatum*).
  1867 Curtis *Botany* 27, *Eupatorium* . . perfoliatum. . . Wild Sage. Boneset. Thoroughwort. **1930** Sievers *Amer. Med. Plants* 16, *Eupatorium perfoliatum.* . . *Other common names.* . . Indian sage, wild sage, [etc]. **1970** *DARE* (Qu. BB50a, . . *Favorite remedies* . . *for a cough*) Inf **KY**81, Wild sage tea.
3 **=self-heal.**
  1897 *Jrl. Amer. Folkl.* 10.53 **ME,** *Brunella* [sic] *vulgaris,* . . wild sage.

wild sagebrush See **wild sage 1**

wild sago n
=coontie.
  1817 in 1843 Baldwin *Reliquiae* 225 **FL,** Here, in a thin sandy hammock . . I had the gratification to find the "Wild Sago" or *Coontia,* of the Seminoles. *Ibid* 230, I now find that my *Coontia,* or "Wild Sago," is nothing more nor less than *Zamia pumila.* **1849** *Amer. Agric.* 8.303 **FL,** A similar substance is also obtained from the wild sago, (*Zamia pumila,*) of Florida. **1911** *Amer. Botanist* 17.48, In many of the waste places of Florida there grows an humble little plant known as the coontie, koonti, or wild sago (*Zamia pumila*). **1934** *Jrl. NY Bot. Garden* 35.180, Florida can boast of four species of the cycad *Zamia,* the commercial name for which is Florida-arrowroot. The popular names are coontie, conti, comptie, comfort-root, and wild sago. **2003** Coile–Garland *Notes FL Endangered Plants* 87, All native species of *Zamia* [=*Zamia pumila* L.] . . coontie[,] wild sago[,] FL-arrowroot. . . Dade, Monroe, north to Dixie, Suwannee and St. Johns co[untie]s.

wild salvia n
=sage 1.
  1851 (1856) Dunglison *Med. Lexicon* 812, *Sage, Wild,* Salvia Africana, S. Lyrata. **1941** O'Donnell *Great Big Doorstep* 28 **LA,** There were humming-birds working around a wild salvia bush in the grove. **1951** *PADS* 15.40 **TX,** *Salvia* spp.—Horse mints and wild salvias are the usual folk names for the taller and more conspicuously flowered mints. **2006** in 2008 *DARE* File—Internet **CA,** The hills are loaded

with some late flowers due to the late rains, and I suspect my birds are using wild Salvia and Mimulus.

wild sarsaparilla n   Cf **false sarsaparilla, sarsaparilla B**
1 Std: a **spikenard** (here: *Aralia nudicaulis*).   Also called **rabbit's foot 1, rabbit's-root, shotbush, sweet root 2, wild licorice 2**
2 **=bay star vine.**
  1841 Audubon *Birds Amer.* 3.98, They [=birds] are placed on a plant usually called the *wild sarsaparilla.* It grows in Louisiana, on the skirts of the forests, in low damp places. *Ibid* 100, The Wild Sarsaparilla. Schisandra coccinea. **1901** Mohr *Plant Life AL* 507, Schizandra coccinea. . . Wild Sarsaparilla. **1933** Small *Manual SE Flora* 534, *S[chizandra] coccinea.* . . (Wild-sarsaparilla. Bay star-vine.) **1960** Vines *Trees SW* 287, *Carolina magnolia-vine.* . . Also known under the vernacular names of Bay Star-vine and Wild Sarsaparilla. **2005** Samuels *GA Native Plant Guide* 18, Schisandra glabra (Bay Starvine, Climbing Magnolia, Wild Sarsaparilla).
3 A **greenbrier** such as *Smilax glauca;* see quots.   Cf **sarsaparilla B1, false sarsaparilla 2**
  1869 Porcher *Resources* 617, *Wild sarsaparilla.* . . Smilax glauca. . . Rich soils. **1901** Lounsberry *S. Wild Flowers* 64, *S[milax] bona-nox,* bristly green brier, or wild sarsaparilla. **1960** Vines *Trees SW* 72, *Smilax pumila.* . . Vernacular names are Hairy Greenbrier . . Ground-brier, and Wild Sarsaparilla. *Ibid* 74, *S[milax] tamnoides.* . . Hagbrier, Devil Greenbrier, Hellfetter, and Wild Sarsaparilla. **1998** Robertson et al. *Management Peatland Comms.* 25 **Sth,** Blaspheme vine and wild sarsaparilla (*Smilax glauca*) may be common.
4 **=moonseed 2.**
  1928 Quillin *TX Wild Flowers* 95, *Cocculus carolinus.* . . *Common Names:* Coral-bead, Wild Sarsaparilla, Margil, Coral-vine. **1960** Vines *Trees SW* 275, *Cocculus carolinus.* . . Vernacular names are Coral-bead, . . Red Moonseed, Wild-sarsaparilla, Margil, and Hierba del Ojo. **2003** in 2008 *DARE* File—Internet **TX,** *Cocculus carolinus—*I call this vine "Wild Sarsaparilla" and my Spanish speaking friends call it "Hierba del Ojo". It produces beautiful shiny red drupes in late summer and fall.
5 A **pepper vine** (here: *Ampelopsis arborea*).
  1960 Vines *Trees SW* 708, *Ampelopsis arborea.* . . Vernacular names . . [include] Cow Vine, and Wild-sarsaparilla.

wild scammony (root) See **scammony**

wild senna n
A **senna** n[1] **B1,** usu *S. hebecarpa* and *S. marilandica.*
  1735 (1849) Darlington *Mem. John Bartram* 61, [Letter from Peter Collinson:] Your wild Senna, with yellow flowers, is a pretty plant. Send seeds. **1818** *Eclectic Repertory & Analytical Rev.* 8.234, *Cassia Marilandica* [=*Senna m.*], or *Wild Senna.* This plant is found very abundantly in New York, and in the States south as far as Carolina. . . It is but little inferior to the Senna of the shops; and . . we think that the indigenous plant ought to be brought into general use, as a substitute for the imported Senna. **1822** Eaton *Botany* 226, *Cassia.* . . *marilandica* (wild senna . .). An excellent mild cathartic. **1863** Porcher *Resources* 195, *Cassia Marylandica.* . . Wild Senna. Grows along the banks of rivers; vicinity of Charleston. **1910** *Amer. Midland Naturalist* 1.179 **IN,** The food plants are cassia, wild senna and clover. **1931** Harned *Wild Flowers Alleghanies* 250, *Wild Senna* (Cassia marilandica L.) . . Flower bright yellow. . . Swamps and wet lands. **2007** Scherr–McNeely *Farming with Nature* 75, Wild senna (*Senna marilandica* and *Senna hebecarpa*) is a wild perennial herbaceous legume native to the United States that produces abundant seed yields.

wild sensitive plant n   Cf **sensitive plant 2**
A **partridge pea** (here: *Chamaecrista nictitans*).
  1818 Barton *Compendium Florae Philadelphicae* 1.206, *[Cassia] nictitans* [=*Chamaecrista n.*] . . Wild Sensitive-plant. **1884** *Chicago Med. Jrl. & Examiner* 49.219, C[assia] nictitans (Wild Sensitive Plant). . . Cathartic, anthelmintic, diuretic, antisyphilitic. **1901** Lounsberry *S. Wild Flowers* 261, Wild sensitive plant, or sensitive pea, is known by its small flowers . . and its numerous and also small leaflets. **1964** Batson *Wild Flowers SC* 61, Wild sensitive plant: C[assia] nictitans. **2002** Hemmerly *Ozark Wildflowers* 90, Also common, Wild Sensitive-plant, C[hamaecrista] nictitans . . , is a smaller plant . . that produces smaller flowers and has leaves that fold when touched.

wild shoestring See **shoestring weed 1**

wild snakeroot n
=ground ivy 1.

1872 Sewall *Condensed Botany* 102, *Examples of Leaf-forms, as to the Margin. . . Dentate:* Wild Snakeroot, Groundsel. **1892** *Jrl. Amer. Folkl.* 5.102 **MA,** *Nepeta Glechoma* [=*Glechoma hederacea*], . . wild snake-root.

wild snapdragon n
1 also *wild snap:* **=butter-and-eggs 1.**

1889 NJ State Geologist *Final Rept.* 2.1.184, *L[inaria] vulgaris*. . . Butter-and-Eggs. Wild Snapdragon. Ranstead Weed. Rancid. In old fields and along roadsides, etc.; very common. **1898** *Jrl. Amer. Folkl.* 11.276 **sKY,** *Linaria vulgaris* . . , wild snapdragon. **1921** *Kansas City Times* (MO) 27 July 12/1, Butter-and-eggs, as the wild snapdragon is called, is now in blossom. **1949** *WELS Suppl.* seWI, "Wild snapdragon" = sometimes called "lion's mouth." **1965–70** DARE (Qu. S11, . . *Wild snapdragon*) 182 Infs, **widespread,** Wild snapdragon(s); **CA**150, **MI**80, Wild snap; [**CA**157, **MI**69, Dragon's-mouth—wild snapdragon; **MA**25, Hens and chickens—wild snapdragon [FW: Inf heard]; **NJ**31, Allmouth—wild snapdragon;] (Qu. S26c, *Wildflowers that grow in woods*) Inf **KY**35, Wild snapdragon; (Qu. S26d, *Wildflowers that grow in meadows;* not asked in early QRs) Inf **MI**34, Wild snapdragon. [*DARE* Ed: Some of these Infs may refer instead to other senses below.] **2003** Eastman *Book Field & Roadside* 79, *Linaria vulgaris*. . . *Other names:* Yellow toadflax, eggs-and-bacon, . . wild snapdragon.

2 **=monkey flower 1.** **esp AK**

1938 (1958) Sharples *AK Wild Flowers* 88, *Mimulus*. . . Vigorous herbs with showy flowers, shaped somewhat like those of the snapdragon. Sometimes called "Wild Snapdragon," "Monkey Flower." **2002** in 2008 *DARE* File—Internet **AK,** [Caption:] Yellow Monkey Flower or Wild Snapdragon.

3 **=beardtongue.**

1969 DARE (Qu. S26e, *Other wildflowers not yet mentioned;* not asked in early QRs) Inf **CA**140, Chinese house [sic]—comes up on spikelet, light purple with white throat, sort of like wild snapdragon. **1982** *Plants SW* (Catalog) 23, *Penstemon* also known as *Beardtongue,* or *Wild Snapdragon.* *Ibid* 24, *Pink Wild Snapdragon—P[enstemon] palmeri*. . . Blooms in summer. California, east to Utah and Arizona. **1995** Epple *Field Guide Plants AZ* 233, *Palmer's Penstemon* . . Pink wild snapdragon. . . Roadsides, washes, and mountain slopes.

wild snowball n
1 **=New Jersey tea.**

1849 *New Engl. Botanic Med. & Surgical Jrl.* 3.19, Ceanothus Americanus. *Common names—Red Root, New Jersey Tea, Wild Snowball,* [etc]. **1948** *Field & Stream Game Bag* 206, New Jersey tea. . . is easily identified by its other name, wild snowball. The small white flowers growing in clusters resemble a snowball from a distance. **1974** (1977) Coon *Useful Plants* 234, *Ceanothus americanus* . . wild snowball.

2 A wild-growing **viburnum.** Cf **snowball 1**

1847 *W. Med. Reformer* 1.18, *Ceanothus Americanus, (Common names)—Red Root, New Jersey Tea, Wild Snowball, Bohea,* etc. **1881** IA State Horticult. Soc. *Trans. for 1880* 231, We like the Bush cranberry, or, as we call it, wild snowball. Its fruit is ornamental and we find it specially valuable for jelly. **1916** Bailey *Std. Cyclop. Horticult.* 5.2656, In the wild snowball . . the large marginal flowers are . . sterile, while the small inconspicuous central flowers are fertile. **1950** Stuart *Hie Hunters* 78 **eKY,** They . . tied their mules to clumps of wild snowball bushes. *Ibid* 104, He killed a weasel by hitting it over the head with a wild snowball stick.

wild sorrel n
A **dock** n¹, usu *Rumex acetosa, R. acetosella,* or *R. hastatulus.*

1860 *Bulletin* (San Francisco CA) 1 Aug 1/2 **OR,** It requires very heavy labor to overcome the forests, scrub-oaks, hazel brush, fern and wild sorrel, so prevalent throughout this State. **1895** *Star* (Kansas City MO) 16 Apr 6/2, The wild sorrel is equally good; but, being very small, requires considerable time to gather and prepare. **1968** Barkley *Plants KS* 127, *Rumex acetosa*. . Wild Sorrel. . . *Rumex hastatulus*. . Wild Sorrel. **1987** Kafka *Microwave Gourmet* 541, I prefer the small wild sorrel to the larger leaves of French sorrel, a garden perennial. **2002** McNab *Living Land* 57, Wild Sorrel (*Rumex acetosa*). . . Eat while young. Leaves can be eaten raw but boiling makes them more palatable.

wild spikenard n
=false Solomon's seal.

1826 Darlington *Florula Cestrica* 41 **sePA,** *S[milacina] racemosa* [= *Maianthemum r.*] . . Wild Spikenard. . . The berries are handsomely speckled with red, when ripe. **1903** Small *Flora SE U.S.* 269, *Vagnera*. . . [*Smilacina* Desf.] *Wild Spikenard.* **1910** MacGowan *Sword* 10 **seTN,** A huge bouquet of the month's flowers—fringed orchids from the spring branch, black-eyed Susan, ironweed, the blue-dusky berries of Solomon's-seal, and red clustered ones of wild spikenard. **1924** *Torreya* 24.2, Well buried, two to six inches deep, one may find the horizontal rootstocks of the False Solomon's Seal or Wild Spikenard, *(Smilacina racemosa).* **1967** DARE Wildfl QR Pl.18 [=*Maianthemum racemosum*] Inf **MI**57, Wild spikenard or false Solomon's seal.

wild spinach n
1 A **goosefoot,** usu *Chenopodium album* or *C. bonus-henricus.* [*OED2* c1710 →]

1900 Lyons *Plant Names* 95, *C[henopodium] album*. . . Nat. in U.S. . . Wild Spinach. . . *C. Bonus-Henricus*. . . Wild Spinach. **1939** Medsger *Edible Wild Plants* 140, *Lamb's Quarter, or Wild Spinach* Chenopodium album. . . When small, . . the plants are succulent and tender.

2 **=pokeweed 1a.**

1974 Morton *Folk Remedies* 109 **SC,** Wild Spinach. *Phytolacca americana*. . . Tender young leaves are cooked like spinach. **1989** *SE Wildlife Cookbook* 172 **SC,** Pokeweed. . . Also known as poke, . . wild spinach. . . Pokeweed, prepared like a potherb or asparagus, is one of the most commonly eaten wild plants.

3 A **greenbrier** such as *Smilax laurifolia.*

1974 Morton *Folk Remedies* 145 **SC,** Wild Spinach. *Smilax laurifolia*. . . Tender shoots of this rampant vine, as well as those of the broad-leaved *China Brier* . . (*S. bona-nox* L.) . . are much eaten cooked as a vegetable or made into soup.

wild spiraea n Also sp *wild spirea*
A **goatsbeard 2** (here: *Aruncus dioicus*).

1951 Voss–Eifert *IL Wild Flowers* 136, The wild spiraea, the goat's beard, blossoms. **1968** DARE (Qu. S21, . . *Weeds . . that are a trouble in gardens and fields*) Inf **AK**1, Wild spiraea/goatsbeard. **2008** DARE File—Internet, Goat's beard, or wild spirea, is an enormous and showy perennial that can grow as high as six feet and look like a bush. . . In early autumn, the plants come into bloom, producing many dramatic plumes composed of tiny, white flowers. . . *Aruncus dioicus.*

wild sunflower See **sunflower 2, 3, 4, 5, 6, 10**

wild sweet alyssum n
A **pennycress** of the genus *Noccaea.*

1917 Rydberg *Flora Rocky Mts.* 328, *Thláspi*. . . Penny Cress, Penny-grass. Wild Sweet Alyssum. [*DARE* Ed: *Noccaea* was formerly included in *Thlaspi*.] **1937** U.S. Forest Serv. *Range Plant Hdbk.* W187, The genus *Thlaspi*, usually called pennycress, but also known locally as candytuft, pennygrass, and wild sweet-alyssum, is a member of the crucifer, or mustard family. **1956** St. John *Flora SE WA* 179, *Thlaspi glaucum* [= *Noccaea montana* var *montana*]. . . Wild Sweet Alyssum. **2008** DARE File—Internet **TX,** *Wild Sweet Alyssum*—this stretched for miles along the highway.

wild sweet pea n
A **goat's rue** (here: *Tephrosia virginiana*).

1891 *Century Dict.* 6238, *T[ephrosia] Virginiana* is locally known as *wild sweet-pea* from its flowers. **1914** Georgia *Manual Weeds* 238, *Hoary Pea*. . . *Other English names:* Wild Sweet Pea, [etc]. **1967** DARE Wildfl QR Pl.108B [=*Tephrosia virginiana*] Infs **OH**14, 37, Wild sweet pea. **1968–69** DARE (Qu. S26a, . . *Wildflowers . . Roadside flowers*) Infs **CT**40, **OH**72, Wild sweet pea(s); (Qu. S26e, *Other wildflowers not yet mentioned;* not asked in early QRs) Infs **KS**19, **NY**28, **OH**65, Wild sweet pea(s). [Some of these Infs may refer instead to some other plant.]

wild sweet potato n Also *wild sweet potato vine* Cf **wild potato 1**
=man-of-the-earth 1.

1862 Smith *Hist. Delaware Co. PA* 425 **sePA,** *Ipomoea* . . pandurata. . . *(Wild Sweet Potato.)* **1890** *Wheeling Reg.* (WV) 29 Sept [3]/5 (newspaperarchive.com), A wild sweet potato found growing near Paulsboro, N.J., measured twenty inches in circumference. **1894** *Jrl. Amer. Folkl.* 7.95 **WV,** *Ipomoea pandurata*, . . wild sweet potato. **1897**

Ibid 10.51 **OH,** *Ipomoea pandurata,* . . wild sweet potato. **1941** Walker *Lookout* 57 **TN,** Wild sweet-potato rambles over the ground adding a singular beauty to the semi-shaded woodlands with its large white flowers. **1949** Arnow *Hunter's Horn* 194 **KY,** She gathered wild sweet-potato vine . . and wilted it in hot grease and vinegar. **1966–70** *DARE* (Qu. S5, . . *Wild morning glory)* Infs **IL**143, **KY**56, **VA**15, Wild sweet potato; (Qu. S21, . . *Weeds . . that are a trouble in gardens and fields)* Infs **IN**32, 41, **KY**53, Wild sweet potatoe(s); **KY**71, Wild sweet potato vine; **VA**7, Wild sweet potato weed; (Qu. S26e, *Other wildflowers not yet mentioned;* not asked in early QRs) Inf **DC**5, Wild sweet potato. **1996** Silverthorne *Legends TX Wildflowers* 104, A useful member of the family is the wild sweet potato, which has morning glory type blossoms and large tuberous roots.

wild sweet potato vine n

1 =**sand vine.**

1914 in 1916 Tichenor *Farm Contracts* 102 **OH,** The lessee agrees . . to destroy all wild sweet potato vines in the corn fields, and to mow the meadows and stubble fields to destroy the weeds. **1920** Pellett *Amer. Honey Plants* 43, *Gonolobus laevis* [=*Cynanchum l.*] . . This plant is also known as devil's shoestring, climbing milkweed, sand vine, wild sweet potato vine and anglepod. . . It is especially troublesome in the corn fields, where it may be found climbing the stalks.

2 See **wild sweet potato.**

wild sweet William n

1 =**phlox,** esp *Phlox maculata* or *P. divaricata.*

1826 Darlington *Florula Cestrica* 26 **sePA,** *P[hlox] maculata.* . . *Vulgo*—Wild Sweet-William. **1890** *Albuquerque Morning Democrat* (NM) 14 Nov [3]/1 (newspaperarchive.com) **UT,** The Wasatch mountain range is rich in a delicate pink species of phlox. The people here call it wild sweet William, just as the people of Nebraska do the purple species, although the real sweet William is a dianthus or pink. **1906** WI *State Horticult. Soc. Annual Rept.* 36.35, *P[hlox] divaricata.* . . This species has generally been called the Wild Sweet William, although Gray gives this common name to the *P. maculata.* **1918** *Star* (Kansas City MO) 5 May 6/2, The wild Sweet William and the fire or Indian pink secrets [sic] a sticky juice in their stems, which prevents ants from crawling up. **1966–70** *DARE* (Qu. S26c, *Wildflowers that grow in woods)* Infs **KY**82, **MO**32, Wild sweet William(s); (Qu. S26e, *Other wildflowers not yet mentioned;* not asked in early QRs) Inf **AR**41, Wild sweet Williams. [*DARE* Ed: Some of these Infs may refer instead to **2** below.] **2008** Jackson *Going after Cows* 113 **nwMO,** In the spring a large patch of wild Sweet William (blue phlox) and purple violets bloomed in the woods.

2 =**bouncing Bet 1.**

1900 Lyons *Plant Names* 334, *S[aponaria] officinalis.* . . Europe to middle Asia, nat. in U.S. . . Wild Sweet William. **1935** (1943) Muenscher *Weeds* 230, *Saponaria officinalis.* . . Wild sweet William. . . Common throughout eastern North America, local on the Pacific Coast.

wild thrift See **thrift 2**

wild tiger lily See **tiger lily**

wild timothy n

1 A native wild grass *(Phleum alpinum)* closely related to **timothy.**

1804 (1904) Clark *Orig. Jrls. Lewis & Clark Exped.* 1.79, In those small Praries or Glades I saw wild Timothy, lambs-quarter, Cuckle burs, & rich weed. [*DARE* Ed: This quot may refer instead to another sense below.] **1872** Tice *Over Plains* 137 **CO,** There is a wild timothy in the mountain parks, . . which is said to yield heavily and to make a better hay than the tame on the plains below. It may prove identical with the *Phleum alpinum,* found on the White Mountains in New Hampshire, and on the mountains of Europe. **1922** U.S. Dept. Ag. *Bulletin* 1089.70 **AK,** Phleum alpinum (wild timothy). **2003** Stubbendieck et al. *N. Amer. Wildland Plants* 67, *Phleum alpinum.* . . Wild timothy. . . Native. . . Mountain meadows, bogs, and moist woods . . ; generally above 1,250 m elevation.

2 A **bristlegrass 1** (here: *Setaria viridis).*

1824 Torrey *Flora N. & Mid. U.S.* 1.152, *S[etaria] viridis.* . . Wild Timothy, Bottle Grass. **1890** FL Ag. Exper. Sta. Gainesville *Bulletin* 8.12, Setaria viridis. . . Wild Timothy.

3 A **muhly grass,** usu *Muhlenbergia glomerata* or *M. racemosa.*

1887 Beal *Grasses N. Amer.* 1.181, *M[uhlenbergia] glomerata.* . .

Satin Grass, Wild Timothy. . . Common northward in bogs, or at the west on dryer land. **1899** KS Ag. Exper. Sta. Manhattan *Bulletin* 87.14, *Wild Timothy (Muhlenbergia glomerata . .)* Altho it is not closely related to Timothy, its general appearance has suggested the name of Wild Timothy. **1902** U.S. Bur. Plant Industry *Bulletin* 12.53 **TX,** *Wild Timothy (Muhlenbergia racemosa).* This is not, in fact, a timothy grass, but in general appearance resembles it, and is known locally as wild timothy. **1923** Abrams *Flora Pacific States* 1.139, *Muhlenbergia racemosa.* . . Wild Timothy, Satin-grass. . . Moist meadows and low ground. **1937** U.S. Forest Serv. *Range Plant Hdbk.* G85, The common names [for *Muhlenbergia wrightii*] spike muhly, timothy-like muhly, black-timothy, and wild-timothy have originated from the characteristic flower head. **1998** Rabeler *Gleason's Plants MI* 104, Marsh Wild-timothy, *Muhlenbergia glomerata.*

4 Any of var other grasses; see quots.

1887 CA Univ. College Ag. *Suppl. Biennial Rept.* 96 **nwCA,** *Hordeum jubatum.* . . "Wild timothy." It grows from three to four feet high and stands next to "bunch grass" in quantity in the upland hay. **1902** Griffiths *Forage Conditions* 53 **nNV, sOR,** *Reed canary grass (Phalaris arundinacea).*—A tall, handsome, lowland species, often called wild timothy. It is . . of little importance as a hay grass. **1912** SD Geol. Surv. *Bulletin* 5.86, *Alopecurus aristulatus* [=*A. aequalis*]. . . Foxtail Grass, Wild Timothy. Common in meadows along valleys. *Ibid* 4.87, *Sphenopholis (Eatonia) obtusata.* . . "Wild Timothy." Frequent in moist ravines.

wild tobacco n

1 =**Indian tobacco 1.**

1818 Eaton *Botany* 306, *Lobelia.* . . *inflata* (wild tobacco . .). **1830** Rafinesque *Med. Flora* 2.22, *Lobelia inflata. Names.*—*Vulgar.* Indian Tobacco, Wild Tobacco, Emetic Weed, Puke Weed. **1872** (1874) Brown *Complete Herbalist* 116, *Lobelia Inflata.* . . *Common Names.* Indian Tobacco, Wild Tobacco. **1949** Moldenke *Amer. Wild Flowers* 244, Of interest because of its narcotic-poisonous juice is the *indian-tobacco,* . . also known as *gagroot, eyebright,* and *wild-tobacco.* **2005** Kozloff *Plants Western OR WA* 178, *Lobelia inflata—Wild tobacco* (central and E United States).

2 A **monkey flower 1** (here: *Mimulus bolanderi).* Cf **tobacco monkey flower**

1885 CA Acad. Sci. *Bulletin* 1.105, *Mimulus Bolanderi.* . . Mrs. Curran . . informs me that the plant has the odor of *Nicotiana* and is commonly called "wild tobacco." **1911** Jepson *Flora CA* 377, *M[imulus] bolanderi.* . . in some localities called "Wild Tobacco."

3 also *wild tobacco plant:* A **mullein** (here: *Verbascum thapsus).* Cf **tobacco plant 1**

1891 NJ Ag. Exper. Stations *Annual Rept. for 1890* 380, [List of serious weeds:] Wild Tobacco, or Mullein. **1965–70** *DARE* (Qu. S20, *A common weed that grows on open hillsides: It has velvety green leaves close to the ground, and a tall stalk with small yellow flowers on a spike at the top)* 12 Infs, **scattered,** Wild tobacco; **FL**20, Wild tobacco plant; **LA**6, Wild tobacco—has leaves just like tame tobacco; (Qu. S26a, . . *Wildflowers. . . Roadside flowers)* Inf **CA**4, Wild tobacco; (Qu. S26e, *Other wildflowers not yet mentioned;* not asked in early QRs) Inf **VA**46, Wild tobacco. [*DARE* Ed: Some of these Infs may refer instead to other senses.] **2008** *DARE* File—Internet **nMI,** Mullein (Verbascum thapsus). . . Back in my early teens . . in those areas where man had cut roads or clear cut a big chunk of forest I would often find a broad leaved plant that I called "wild tobacco". Being rather fond of my little corn cob pipe and seldom having anything to put in it . . , I would pick the dry leaves around the base of the plant and smoke them.

4 =**butter-and-eggs 1.**

1894 *Jrl. Amer. Folkl.* 7.96 **WV,** *Linaria vulgaris,* . . wild tobacco.

wild tobacco plant See **wild tobacco 3**

wild tomato n

1 A **ground-cherry;** see quots.

1857 IL State Ag. Soc. *Trans. for 1856–57* 2.297, W.R. Fairburn also exhibited a new variety of tomato or ground cherry, produced from the common wild tomato found in many parts of our county, covered with a husk. **1873** Beadle *Undeveloped West* 708 **MN** (as of 1859), After strawberries and wild tomatoes came in the whole family usually took to the prairie on Sunday and "browsed." **1890** *AN&Q* 6.4, I suppose . . [your correspondent's] *wild tomato* to be some species of *Physalis;* I have found them growing wild with edible smooth fruits. The marketmen call them *strawberry tomatoes.* They are often cultivated. **1894**

Scribner's Mag. May 603 **sTX,** 'Cabrito', or goat meat, is made into a stew with frijoles and wild tomato. **1894** *Jrl. Amer. Folkl.* 7.95 **nMN,** *Physalis grandiflora,* . . wild tomato. **1967–70** *DARE* (Qu. I44, *What kinds of berries grow wild around here?*) Inf **HI**1, Wild tomato; (Qu. I46, . . *Kinds of fruits that grow wild around here*) Inf **CA**190, Wild tomatoes; (Qu. S13, . . *A common wild bush with bunches of round, prickly seeds; when they get dry they stick to your clothing*) Inf **NY**99, Wild tomato. [*DARE* Ed: Some of these Infs may refer instead to other senses below.]

2 A **nightshade 1,** esp *Solanum triflorum.*

1898 *Jrl. Amer. Folkl.* 11.276 **WY,** *Solanum triflorum,* . . wild tomato. **1923** *Amer. Nature-Study Soc. Nature-Study Rev.* 19.178 **NY,** One day we found around a rock the poison Nightshade, Solanum Dulcamara. The little wild tomato berries were very suggestive of our garden beauties. **1935** (1943) Muenscher *Weeds* 414, *Solanum triflorum.* . . Wild tomato. . . Originally limited to native prairies. . . The berries of *Solanum triflorum* are poisonous. **2007** Jones *Tomato Plant* 5, Wild tomato species have tiny fruits, with only the red ones being edible.

3 =**Aunt Lucy 1.**

1951 Voss–Eifert *IL Wild Flowers* 92, The double green fruit. . . is the little "wild tomato" which gives the Ellisia its commonest name. The whole plant, perhaps, might be compared with the appearance of a weak tomato seedling in despair of its life. **1981** IA Acad. Sci. *Proc.* 88.165, *Ellisia nyctelea* L. (Wild Tomato). **2002** in 2008 *DARE* File—Internet **IA,** Wild tomato—*Ellisia nyctelea.*

wild tuberose n

1 =**ladies' tresses.**

1890 *Century Dict.* 5839, *Spiranthes.* . . They are known as *lady's-tresses, S. cernua* also locally as *wild tuberose.*

2 =**sand lily 2.**

1905 Blankinship–Henshall *Common MT Plants* 129, *Wild Tuberose:* Leucocrinum montanum. **1917** Rydberg *Flora Rocky Mts.* 163, *Leucocrinum* [spp]. . . Wild Tuberose. **1973** Hitchcock–Cronquist *Flora Pacific NW* 691, *L[eucocrinum] montanum.* . . Sand lily, . . wild tuberose [etc].

3 An **agave** (here: *Manfreda maculosa*).

1928 Quillin *TX Wild Flowers* 55, *Manfreda maculosa.* . . Common Names: Wild Tuberose, Amole Plant, Spice Lily, Soap Plant. **1941** *Brownsville Herald* (TX) 13 Feb 2/3, Indian maidens are said to have crushed the roots of the amole, called the wild tuberose, spice lily or soap plant. **1952** Williams *Blind Bull* 210 **eTX,** She made soap by steeping the chopped-up roots of the *amole,* or wild tuberose, in water for a few days.

wild tulip n
=**mariposa lily.**

1846 in 1993 Morgan *Overland in 1846* 563 **West,** We have found the wild tulip, the primrose, the lupine, the ear-drop, the larkspur, and creeping hollyhock. **1882** *Daily Eve. Bulletin* (San Francisco CA) 3 July 1/1, We have also the wild tulip, that is ocasionally [sic] found in the vicinity of the Yosemite Valley. **1900** OR Hist. Soc. *Hist. Qrly.* 1.325, Wild tulip, or brown lily—Clatsop, *Eck-ut-le-pat-le.* **1967–68** *DARE* (Qu. S26c, *Wildflowers that grow in woods*) Inf **CA**65, Wild tulips; (Qu. S26d, *Wildflowers that grow in meadows; not asked in early QRs*) Inf **WY**5, Wild tulip. **2007** Tawrell *Wilderness Camping* 179, All bulbs are high in starch content. . . Examples are the wild onion, and wild tulip.

wild turnip n

1 A **jack-in-the-pulpit 1** (here: *Arisaema triphyllum*). **chiefly NEast** See Map

1772 *Burlington Almanack for 1773* [33] **NJ,** For a violent Cough or Cold. . . Take . . the flour of dry'd wild turnip mix'd with milk. **1792** *Amer. Mercury* (Hartford CT) 23 Apr 4/1, For the throat distemper in a horse. Take devils bit, wild turnip, and wake robbin, as people differently call it, when it is green—shreed [sic] it fine, take about half of one about the bigness of a small turnip, mix it with wet brand or oats. **1837** *Boston Jrl. Nat. Hist.* 1.112 **seNC,** Arum triphyllum. *Wild turnip.* **1887** (1895) Robinson *Uncle Lisha* 134 **wVT,** He seen a wild turnip an' pulled it, an' kerried it 'long, thinkin' mebbe 't he'd dry it agin he had a cough in the fall. **1892** *Jrl. Amer. Folkl.* 5.104 **VT,** *Arisæma triphyllum,* . . wild turnip. **1965** Needham–Mussey *Country Things* 139 **VT,** The herb I know best about is wild turnip or jack-in-the-pulpit. **1965–70** *DARE* (Qu. S1, . . *Jack-in-the-pulpit*) Infs **IL**143, **IN**67, **MA**58, **NY**21, 92, 103, 219, **PA**70, **VT**4, Wild turnip; (Qu. S26a, . . *Wild-*

flowers. . . *Roadside flowers*) Inf **MA**42, Wild turnip; (Qu. S26e, *Other wildflowers not yet mentioned; not asked in early QRs*) Inf **NY**21, Wild turnip or jack-in-the-pulpit.

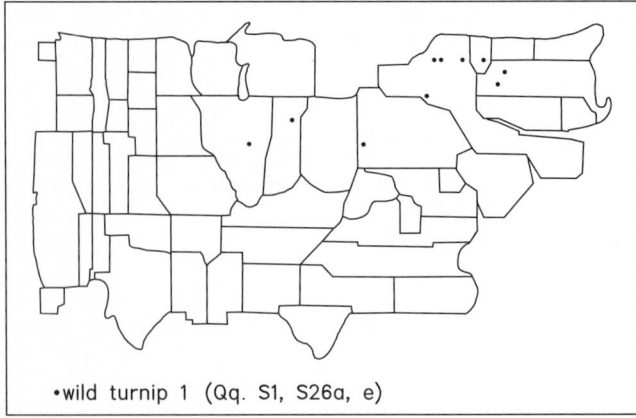

•wild turnip 1 (Qq. S1, S26a, e)

2 Any of var plants of the genus *Brassica,* but esp **rutabaga** n **B.**

1807 *Mt. Hope Eagle* (Bristol RI) 30 May 3/3, Botanical observations on pig weed and wild turnip, with directions for procuring the largest possible crops of both. **1860** Harbison *Bees & Bee-Keeping* 135 **PA,** We have also a species of kale, or wild turnip, which if sowed very early in the spring will commence to bloom toward the latter part of May, and is very valuable. **1908** *Sun. Mercury & Herald* (San Jose CA) 26 July 20/7, It is believed that kale crosses with wild mustard and wild turnip; hence none of these plants should be allowed to grow near kale that is intended for seed. **1949** Moldenke *Amer. Wild Flowers* 39, Common weeds in cultivated ground . . are *Brassica nigra,* the *black mustard,* and *B. campestris* [=*B. rapa*], the *wild turnip* or *common yellow mustard* (of California). **1967–70** *DARE* (Qu. I3, . . *The large yellowish root vegetable, similar to a turnip, with a strong taste*) Inf **NY**5, Wild turnips; (Qu. I28a, . . *Kinds of things* . . *you call 'greens'* . . *[Those that are eaten raw]*) Inf **GA**23, Wild turnips; (Qu. I37, *Small plants shaped like an umbrella that grow in woods and fields—which are safe to eat*) Inf **NY**72, Wild turnip—this has a long root, no bulb; (Qu. S21, . . *Weeds* . . *that are a trouble in gardens and fields*) Inf **LA**15, Wild turnip—a funny-looking weed with a lot of root to it; made it mean to get rid of; (Qu. S26d, *Wildflowers that grow in meadows; not asked in early QRs*) Inf **KY**77, Wild turnip—yellow bloom. **2003** Beidleman–Kozloff *Plants San Francisco Bay* 162, *Brassica rapa* . . Field Mustard, Wild Turnip. **2007** in 2009 *DARE* File—Internet **MS,** I planted several acres of clover in places that I knew were infested with wild turnips.

3 An **Indian breadroot** (here: *Pediomelum esculentum*).

1835 *S. Lit. Messenger* 1.394 **West,** I learned that eight of our women who were gathering wild turnip in the prairies, had been captured and carried away by the *Flat-heads.* **1839** Wied *Reise Innere Nord-America* 1.321 **SD,** In dem Grunde der engen Schlucht befand sich . . auch die sogenannte Wild-Turnip oder Pomme-Blanche der Franzosen (*Psoralea esculenta*), mit knollig dicker Wurzel von der Grösse eines Hühnereies, welche von Indianern und Weissen aufgesucht und gegessen wird. [=In the bottom of the narrow gorge there was . . also the so-called Wild Turnip or Pomme-Blanche of the French (*Psoralea esculenta*), with a tuberous thick root the size of a hen's egg which is sought after and eaten by Indians and whites.] **1854** in c1855 U.S. War Dept. *Rept. Explor. Railroad* (Stevens' Exped.) 1.162 **West,** The wild turnip is . . probably the only vegetable food of the wandering Indians, by whom it is regularly gathered. **1891** *Sun* (Baltimore MD) 25 July suppl 1/7 **ND, SD,** Many [Sioux] have returned to their old ways of digging wild turnips, a few get a little game and furs, and an occasional pony is sold. **1926** *Amer. Anthropologist* 28.573, This same article, tipsin, is . . miscalled "wild turnip." **2006** Snell *Taste of Heritage* 4, *Wild Turnip.* . . The scientists used to call it *Psoralea esculenta,* but now they tell me the Latin name is *Pediomelum esculentum.* . . Some say wild turnips taste like raw green beans or unroasted peanuts.

wild valerian n
A **golden ragwort** (here: *Packera aureus*).

1850 *Amer. Med. Assoc. Trans.* 3.311, *Senecio aureus.* . . Wild valerian. . . A cough arising from an affection of the liver has been removed speedily and permanently by the use of the *Senecio aureus.*

1864 Hale *New Remedies* 391, *Senecio gracilis*. . . it has a great reputation among the country people, who, under the name of "Unkum" . . and "Wild Valerian," use it extensively for nervousness, hysteria, lowness of spirits, and sleeplessness [sic]. **1971** Krochmal *Appalachia Med. Plants* 234, *Senecio aureus*. . . wild valerian.

wild vanilla n

1 =vanilla plant 1.

1861 *De Bow's Rev.* 31.111 **Sth,** *Wild Vanilla, hound's tongue* (*Liatris odoratissima* . .). Florida to North Carolina. Possessing very aromatic properties, used as a substitute for vanilla in seasoning, and "in Florida for scenting segars." (Croom.) **1877** *U.S. Dept. Ag. Rept. of Secy. for 1876* 69, Assertions have been made that the vanilla-plant grows wild in Florida. In answer to requests for specimens, leaves of *Liatris odoratissima* have been received. This plant has aromatic foliage, and . . is locally known as wild vanilla. **1939** Snell-Snell *Chemicals of Commerce* 362, *Deertongue leaves* or *deer's tongue leaves* are obtained from a plant, *Trilisa odoratissima*, which grows in the southeastern part of the United States. It is also known as *wild vanilla*. **2007** Allen *Herbalist Kitchen* 89, *Carphephorus odoratissimus—Other common . . names. . .* wild vanilla. . . Southeastern United States to middle of Florida. . . Dried leaves have a vanilla-like scent and have been used to flavor tobacco.

2 =vanilla leaf 1.

1908 *Amer. Pharmaceutical Assoc. Proc.* 56.223, *Achlys Triphylla*. . . More frequently called "wild vanilla" on account of its odor. **1966** *DARE* FW Addit **WA**12, Wild vanilla—leaves divided into three sections, spike with white flowers.

wild wisteria n

A groundnut B1 (here: *Apios americana*).

1922 *Amer. Botanist* 28.75, Owing to the resemblance of *Apios tuberosa* to the *Wisteria*, it is often called "wild wisteria." It is however, more frequently known as "ground-nut."

wild yam n Also *wild yam root*

Std: any of var usu uncult plants of the genus *Dioscorea*. For other names of var of these see **air potato, Chinese yam, uhi 1, wild potato 4i;** for other names of *D. villosa* see **Atlantic yam, Chinaroot 2, colicroot 3, devil's-bones, rattlebox 1g, rheumatism root b**

wild yellow lily n esp NEast

A lily n 1 (here: *Lilium canadense*).

1842 Thompson *Hist. VT* 1.200, *Lilium . . canadense.* . . Wild Yellow Lily, Moist meadows. **a1862** (1864) Thoreau *ME Woods* 270, Elms and ash trees made their appearance; also the wild yellow lily *(Lilium Canadense),* some of whose bulbs I collected for a soup. **1908** WI *State Horticult. Soc. Annual Rept.* 38.64, Lilium Canadense—Wild yellow lily. **1957** *Torrey Bot. Club Bulletin* 84.54 **NY,** *Lilium canadense.* . . Wild Yellow Lily. **1979** Niering-Olmstead *Audubon Guide N. Amer. Wildflowers E. Region* 600, *Canada Lily; Meadow Lily; Wild Yellow Lily (Lilium canadense).* . . *Nodding flowers,* . . ranging in color from yellow to orange-red with dark spots. **2001** *Torrey Bot. Soc. Jrl.* 128.183 **NJ,** The highlight in the fields surrounding Cushetunk Mountain was *Lilium canadense* (wild yellow lily).

wild yellow plum   See **yellow plum**

w'iles   See **whiles** conj

wiliwili n   HI

A coral tree (here: *Erythrina sandwicensis*).

1850 Cheever *Is. World Pacific* 255 **HI,** The way . . was . . through a dense growth of the *wiliwili* and *ohi* trees. The one is a wood almost as light as cork, of which the natives make the outriggers to their canoes. **1886** *All the Year Round* new ser 38.224 **HI,** To be able to . . build a canoe, making the outrigger of the cork-like wood of the wiliwili (Erythrina) . . is better still. **1929** Neal *Honolulu Gardens* 160, *Wiliwili (Erythrina monosperma* . .).—A native Hawaiian *wiliwili* is common from near sea level to 2,000 feet elevation on . . all the large islands. **1970** Carlquist *Hawaii* 105, The wiliwili *(Erythrina sandwicensis)* might be another example—the only relative in the Pacific is located on Tahiti, although one would expect a tree readily carried by seawater would become established on many Pacific islands. **2007** Kampion *Greg Noll Surfboard* [34] **HI,** There were only three kinds of trees known to be used for making boards for surfriding, viz.: the wiliwili *(Erythrina monosperma),* ulu or breadfruit *(Artocarpus incisa),* and koa *(Acacia koa).*

wilkrissen   See **will crisson**

will v

A Forms.

Contracted neg *won't:* usu |wont|; also |wʌnt, wunt, wʊnt, wɔnt|; pronc-spp *want, woont, w(o)unt.* Cf **want**

1825 Neal *Brother Jonathan* 1.200 **CT,** I wun't be bullied, by anybody. **1846** Worcester *Universal Dict.* 827, *Wont.* . . used for *will not.* In New England, commonly pronounced *wŭnt* [=[wʌnt]]. **1848** Lowell *Biglow* 147 **'Upcountry' MA,** Wunt, *will not.* **1853** Simms *Sword & Distaff* 349 **SC** [Black], I wunt le' you go! **1885** (1897) Phyfe *How I Pronounce* 281, Won't—wŏnt (Web[ster]), wōnt [=[wont]] or wŭnt [= [wʌnt]] (Wor[cester]). This last pronunciation, together with wōont [= [wʊnt]] is common in New England. **1887** *Scribner's Mag.* 2.478 **AR,** You wunt never dance at *my* weddin'. **1889** (1890) Howells *Hazard* 167, [PaGer speaker:] I woon't put any more money in it; but what I've put in a'ready, can stay. **1906** *Everybody's Mag.* 14.425 **sAppalachians,** "I see I had better be going . . " . . "You woon't do no such a thing!" **1913** Kephart *Highlanders* 122 **sAppalachians,** The law wunt let us have liquor shipped to us from anywhars in the State. **1919** *Boys' Life* 9.6 **KY,** They woun't be no moonshine whiskey flowin', neither. **1936** Mitchell *Gone* 136 **seSC,** She thought if she ever again heard voices that said . . "woon't" for "won't" . . she would scream. . . Better to be tormented with memories of Ashley than Charleston accents. **1961** Kurath-McDavid *Pronc. Engl.* 158, Won't. . . The /o/ of *stone* occurs in all parts of the Eastern States. . . It is nearly universal (1) in the Midland, from Pennsylvania to northern Georgia; (2) in the Upper South . . ; and (3) in Georgia and adjoining parts of South Carolina. . . *Won't* with the vowel /ʌ/ . . predominates in New England and in the New England settlements along the Great Lakes and in the northern counties of Pennsylvania. . . *Won't* with the vowel /u/ . . is a striking feature of the speech (1) of Metropolitan New York and vicinity and (2) the Carolina coast. . . On the Southern coast, the /u/ of *moon* occurs . . from Albemarle Sound southward to Florida. In South Carolina, free /u/ competes with the checked /ʊ/ of *bull,* which is nearly as frequent here, and with the /o/ of *stone* (in Charleston, as in Savannah, /u/ is preferred by cultured speakers). . . Relics of /u/ and /ʊ/ occur on Chesapeake Bay . . , in central Pennsylvania, in New York State, and in south-eastern New England. . . In parts of North Carolina, chiefly in the valleys of the Neuse and the Yadkin, *won't* often rhymes with *want,* the /ɔ/ being pronounced as an upgliding diphthong [ɒɔ]. **1976** Allen *LAUM* 3.256 **Upper MW** (as of c1950), The U[pper] M[idwest] is dominated throughout by /wont/. . . Twenty UM infs., however, mostly in Minnesota and northern Iowa, have Northern /wʌnt/. . . The UM provides no examples of New York City /u/, but the lax /ʊ/ is reflected in three isolated examples. The low rounded /ɔ/ also occurs, but only in Nebraska and there perhaps as a result of foreign-language background. **2002** *DARE* File—Internet **seKY,** If he is rebellous [sic] like Saul, it want make me stop serving God. . . I want support him. **2010** *Ibid* **seTN,** The police hasnt done anything . . he had his cousin steal the child an run up north and the police want help the mothers family do anything.

B Syntax.

1 also *would:* Used as the first member of a multiple modal; see quots. Cf **may v B1**

1906 *McClure's Mag.* 28.93 **sePA,** He won't can home hisself [=make himself comfortable] in here. **1930s** in **1944** *ADD* **eWV,** Can. . . 2. . . Known to be awkward or ungrammatical by users. 'He'll not kin go.' Occas. Always in combination *'ll not kin* or *'ll never kin.* 'She'll never kin catch a mouse now.' Said when a pet cat became crippled. **1931** in **1944** *ADD* **swPA,** Can. . . 2. . . I don't think I will can go. **1932** Smiley *Gloss. New Paltz* **seNY,** "Wouldn't could," "won't can" meaning respectively couldn't and Can't. Father says he has heard these many times, but I do not recall them. **1950** *WELS Suppl.* **csWI,** *Won't can*—If you simply refuse, you say, "I can't." If you really want to go, but you can't, you say "I won't can go." **1986** Pederson *LAGS Concordance,* 1 inf, **cnTN,** You would might have ask me [inf Black]. **1994** *AmSp* 69.10 **SC,** We would might run maybe ten hams a week.

2 *would* foll by pres infin (esp *be*): Used in place of past (or past subjunctive *were*) in a contrary-to-fact condition. **esp PaGer area** Note: The parallel use of *would have* + past pple in past contrary-to-fact conditions is widespread in informal speech.

1926 Roberts *Time of Man* 291 **KY,** If it would be light I could see a far piece. **1931** *AmSp* 7.20 **swPA,** *Would.* Were. "If you would be me." (If you were I.) **1935** *AmSp* 10.168 **PA** [Engl of PA Germans], Another feature of Pennsylvania-German English: the almost universal use of *would* in a conditional clause. . . 'If he would be here, you wouldn't say that,' 'If I would be you, I would never listen to him,' and 'If I would go, I would have to let the baby with John,' are examples of what may be heard daily from pulpit and teacher's desk. **1968** *Helen Adolf Festschrift* 40 **sePA,** The form *would* is used almost exclusively in contrary-to-fact conditional clauses; for example, "If I would be you, I wouldn't do that." "If he would be here, we'd go to Sunbury." **1968** *DARE* FW Addit **LA35,** *Would be* = subjunctive—"If she would be on the payroll now, she would make her work tomorrow." **1997** in 1999 Millersville Univ. Center for PA Ger. Studies *Jrl.* Fall 23, *Would be. If he _____ here, he would do that for us.* 42.5% [of 40 Old Order Mennonite infs], *would be;* 50%, *were;* 12.5% *was.*

3 See quot. [*SND will* v.[1] 4 "With the verb *be* followed by . . *to* with the *inf.*"]

1944 *PADS* 2.37 **NC,** *Won't be* + an infinitive. . . Used as a future negative. "I won't be to go to church tonight." . . Uneducated.

willapus-wallapus (or -wampus) See **willipus-wallipus**

willawaw See **williwaw**

will crisson n Also *wilkrissen*
=**flicker** n[2] **1.**

1887 Colburn in *Forest & Stream* 28.248 **Sth,** I send you . . the names . . applied to this bird [=*Colaptes auratus*]. . . Will-Crisson. **1900** *Wilson Bulletin* 12.2.10 **NC,** *Will Crisson.* Dismal Swamp Region, North Carolina. Given me by a gentleman who visited and hunted in that section and heard it applied . . —W.W. Colburn. **1917** (1919) Pearson *Bird Study* 108 **eNC,** The people of Cape Hatteras know it as Wilkrissen. . . Naturalists call it *Colaptes auratus.*

willet n

Std: a large native sandpiper *(Tringa semipalmata)* with distinct subspecies: *T. s. semipalmata* in the eastern US and *T. s. inornatus* (formerly *Catoptrophorus s. i.*) in the west. For other names of these see **candlestick plover, Christmas ~, frost snipe 3, goose bird 2, gray plover 4, humility 1, pant-ass, pied-winged curlew, pill-willet 1, Spanish curlew 3, stone ~ 1, tattler, telltale 2, vire-vire, whitewing 2**

willey wags See **willywags**

William n Also *Willy* [Pun on *bill*] **scattered, but more freq Sth, S Midl** *joc*
A piece of paper currency; rarely spec a hundred-dollar bill.

1850 in 1853 *Pen & Pencil* 1.414, This is the last five dollar *William,* of an estate of $20,000, left me three years ago by my father. **1865** *Republican Banner* (Nashville TN) 5 Oct 3/1, Will had to remember the Workhouse in his will to the tune of a "ten dollar William." **1869** *Overland Mth.* 3.128 **TX,** In Texas. . . $100 bills were there called "Williams," . . a Texan once told me . . that "he had $100,000 in 'Williams' laid up." **1887** in 1950 *AmSp* 25.38 **New Orleans LA,** That poor printer lost his five dollar William. **1909** *DN* 3.388 **eAL, wGA,** *William.* . . A bank-note, a bill. "I'd give a ten-dollar william to see that." Facetious. **1927** Siringo *Riata* 10 **TX** (as of 1871), Mr. Myers wrote me . . to buy a suit of clothes with the twenty-dollar 'william.' **1950** *WELS (Joking names and nicknames for: A five-dollar bill: A ten-dollar bill: A twenty-dollar bill)* 1 Inf, **csWI,** William. **1965–70** *DARE* (Qu. U26, *Names or nicknames . . for a paper dollar*) Inf **IL39,** Dollar Willy; **TX32,** Long, green Williams; (Qu. U28a, . . *A five-dollar bill*) Infs **GA77, IN9, OK1, PA63, TN30, TX35,** Five-dollar William; **IL39,** Five-dollar Willy; **GA77,** Five William; [**NJ56,** Sweet William;] (Qu. U28b, . . *A ten-dollar bill*) Infs **GA77, IL117, NJ56,** (Ten-dollar) William. **1986** Pederson *LAGS Concordance (Money)* 1 inf, **swTN,** William—a ten-dollar bill.

willies n pl Usu with *the* Also *willy-nillies* Cf **woolies** n pl[2]
1 Feelings of uneasiness, apprehension, depression, or nervousness—freq in phr *give (someone) the willies.* Cf **jimmies** n pl[1] **1**

1896 *DN* 1.427 **cNY,** Willies: "To have the willies," to be nervous. **1900** Bonner *Hard-Pan* 99 **San Francisco CA,** It just gives me the willies to think of your being down on your luck. **1938** in Lib. of Congress *Amer. Memory: WPA Life Hist.* (Internet) **NYC,** Those chickens kept screeching their heads off it gave me the willies. **1954** *Harder Coll.* **cwTN,** Willies. . . Name of a feeling engendered by a person who is dis-

liked. **1965–70** *DARE* (Qu. GG13b, *When something keeps bothering a person and makes him nervous . . "It gives me the _____."*) 363 Infs, **widespread,** Willies; **NY235,** Willy-nillies; (Qu. GG34a, *To feel depressed or in a gloomy mood: "He has the _____ today."*) 22 Infs, **scattered,** Willies; (Qu. II29b, . . *To explain the unpleasant effect that person has on you: "He just _____."*) 14 Infs, **scattered,** Gives me the willies; (Qu. GG34b, *To feel depressed or in a gloomy mood: "She's feeling _____ today."*) Inf **CT23,** Willies. **1988** Kingsolver *Bean Trees* 41 **KY,** The sound of the air hose alone gave me the willies.

2 General feelings of physical discomfort or illness, esp delirium tremens—also used in var combs; see quots. Cf **jimmies** n pl[1] **2**

1905 (1906) Green *At the Actors' Boarding House* 360, He's got it bad. The Willies, I guess. . . I see it all now. It ain't licker ails him at all. It's hop! **1921** *Everybody's Mag.* Feb 40, Another [letter], [to] Jackson Vogleman, that place up in Michigan where they cure you of the willies. **1933** *Hench Coll.,* Willies—The expression means upset stomach or dizziness (physical or imaginary). Going around a curve fast gives her the willies. **1950** *WELS (Delirium tremens)* 3 Infs, **WI,** (The) willies. **1965–70** *DARE* (Qu. BB28, *Joking names . . for imaginary diseases: "He must have the _____."*) Infs **AL30, IL14, 57, MD20, MS68, SC4, WA3,** Willies; **MA2, MN2,** Willy-nillies; (Qu. BB5, *A general feeling of discomfort or illness that isn't any one place in particular*) Inf **MD50,** Weary willies; **NY14, WI30,** Willies; (Qu. BB20, *Joking names or expressions for overactive kidneys*) Inf **NC30,** Piss willies; (Qu. DD22, . . *Delirium tremens*) Infs **CT13, IL99, NM11, OH41, PA118, TX11, WA6, WI19,** Willies. **1995** Tyler *Ladder of Yrs.* 269 **eMD,** There's this place there we buy our barley in bulk, to make Grandma's gripe water recipe. . . It's for babies. Soothes the colic and the afternoon frets and the nighttime willies.

3 in phrr *scare (or pound) the willies* (or *pee-willy*) *out of:* To scare (or beat) severely. Cf *pee-wadding* (at **wadding**)

1963 Bier *Trial Bannock* 314 **WY,** Beautiful. It scares the willies out of me. **1976** *Current Biog.* 37.262 **AL,** Mathews told one reporter that the Administration's "overly high expectations" occasionally "[scared] the willies out of [him]." **1994** *WI State Jrl.* (Madison) 24 Sept sec D 22/2, While working with the scout team last year, Smith, according to [Indiana football] coach Bill Mallory, "pounded the pee-willy out of our defense." **2000** Inman *Coming Home* 156 **AL,** It must have scared the willies out of my mother. **2005** *DARE* File—Internet **NY,** The news just said the UN is thinking about coming out with a brief resolution condemning the bombings in London. Now that ought to scare the pee-willy out of those guys. **2007** *Ibid,* In the process, I scared the pee-willy out of myself several times.

willipus-wallipus n Also *wallopa-willipus, willapus-wallapus, willapus-wampus;* for addit varr see quots

1 A fictitious animal; a bogeyman. **chiefly Sth, S Midl** Cf **DS CC17**

[**1867** *Leavenworth Eve. Bulletin* (KS) 29 Aug 4/1, John and Mary . . were among the number dressed for the occasion—that of welcoming the renowned quadruped, the "Egyptian Wallapus," traveling with Yankee Robinson's great show.] **1892** *Daily Inter Ocean* (Chicago IL) 21 May 4/3, The *Atlanta Constitution* . . reached the climax of its chosen method of assault when it called the ex-President the "willipus wallapus." . . It is claimed for this euphonious name that it originated some ten years ago. . . It seems to have been invented by an ingenious editor in Tennessee to apply to the mysterious monster which he declared haunted his watermelon patch about picking time. **1896** *Harper's New Mth. Mag.* 92.927, And still cheerful? Cheerful, gentlemen, as a durned red-headed willipus-wallipus—or more so. **1921** *Macon Daily Telegraph* (GA) 11 Aug 2/4, After keeping married men home at nights . . , breaking up a colored revival service and causing a state of terror to prevail among the negro population generally, Thomasville's willapus wampus has turned out to be a bull calf. **1953** Randolph–Wilson *Down in Holler* 299 **Ozarks,** *Willipus-wallipus.* . . A vague legendary monster, according to the old-timers. **1957** in 2007 *DARE* File—Internet [*AR Democrat* (Little Rock) 13 Sept], He is witty, the amateur cartoonist who created the friendly "willipus wallipus," a legendary Arkansas beast with eight legs. . . Under great pressure, Hays admitted it did not exist. **2007** *Ibid* **TN,** Hope the kitties don't run afoul of the Wallopa Willipus—or whatever it is—and become dinner.

2 A steamroller or similar large machine; also fig. **Sth, S Midl** *obs*

1885 *TX Siftings* 1 Aug 4 **GA,** Sam Jones, the revivalist, says that "when the great willipus-wallapus of Christianity passes over humanity it levels all alike." **1891** *Knoxville Jrl.* (TN) 8 Jan 3/4, By motion it was allowed that the North Knoxville "willopus wallopus" be secured to do the mashing act on the Third creek road. **1897** in 2007 *DARE* File—Internet **MO** [1998 *Mornin' Mail* (Carthage MO) 23 Jan], As will be remembered the "Willipus Wallipus" is the name applied to the road roller tested here a year ago last fall. **1909** *Independent* 66.625, The curtain . . rises upon something new and strange in Tennessee politics—the willipus-wallipus. This is a political steam roller designed to crush the old "machine." **1912** *Lexington Herald* (KY) 27 Mar 4/2, The fact that the Taft willipus-wallapus came near being ditched . . by the Colonel's friends, leads up to the suspicion that the Hon. Samuel Judson Roberts, master mechanic of the Federal machine, had temporarily lost control of the throttle. **1950** *AR Hist. Qrly.* 9.69, In Springfield, Missouri, the name [=*willipus-wallipus*] was applied to a large road-building machine, a sort of roller propelled by a powerful steam engine. An old resident of Springfield assured me that this machine was always known as the willipus-wallipus, and that he had never heard it called by any other name. May Kennedy McCord says that the contraption was listed in official documents of the time as the willipus-wallipus. **1959** *Daily Progress* (Charlottesville VA) 16 Dec 24/3 *(Hench Coll.)*, City officials scratched their heads when they uncovered a 50-year-old ordinance directing the mayor to authorize repairs "upon the willapus-wallapus at a cost not to exceed $85." . . A willapus-wallapus is an outmoded name for a steamroller. **1982** *Smithsonian Letters* **KY,** My mother taught me to call a steam roller a "willa-pus-wallapus" . . in Georgetown, Kentucky, about 1912 or 13. . . My aunt used the term, until her death [in 1977] at age 99, for any large piece of road equipment. **1995** *Brophy Coll.* 83 swMO (as of c1960), *Willipus-wallopus.* [A] self-propelled steam-engine used in threshing; any monstrous thing.

williwacks, williwags   See **willywags**

williwaw n   Also *willawaw* [Orig a violent squall assoc with the Straits of Magellan; *OED2* 1842 →]   chiefly **AK**   Cf **chinook** n B2, **woolly** n[2]

A sudden violent wind or windstorm.

1896 Scidmore *Appleton's Guide-Book* **AK** 80, Taku Inlet is the cradle of squalls. . . In winter, fierce *willawaws* or "woolies" sweep from the heights, beat the waters to foam, and drive the spray in dense, blinding sheets. **1944** Williamson *Far North* 8 **AK,** There was a wind to be known in later ages as the williwaws: a fierce gust that comes swinging down mountain slopes and onto the sea in a sudden tempest, changing course without warning. **1948** *AK Sportsman* Oct 16, While we were anchored in Vere Cove I heard the word "williwaw" for the first time. **1958** Carrighar *Moonlight* 247 **AK,** The winds called the williwaws can come up so fast and can be so devastating that a dory going ashore from the mail boat has set out in calm, sunny weather and before it had made the short run to the beach has capsized in gigantic waves. **1966** Keithahn *AK Curious* 143, Of late, the gales in the Aleutians and at Kodiak are called williwaws, a term that came in with the war. **1966–70** *DARE* (Qu. B14, *When the wind is blowing unevenly, sometimes strong and sometimes weak, . . it's _____*) Inf **AK**2, Williwaw ['wɪli,wɔ]—gusty wind along coast; (Qu. B18, . . *Special kinds of wind*) Inf **ME**16, Williwaw ['wɪlɪ,wɔw]—puff of strong wind often seen on water; (Qu. O12, *A disturbance caused by wind which seems to run and spread quickly along the surface of water*) Inf **ME**16, Williwaw; (Qu. O19, . . *Kinds or degrees of wind that are important when you're in a boat*) Inf **CA**191, Changeable wind—a ['wɪli,wɔ]; **AK**1, Williwaw ['wɪlə,wɔ]—gust coming down off mountains—term from Aleutians, coming into Juneau area. **2006** DuFresne–Spitzer *Alaska* 423, In Anchorage and throughout the Interior, these sudden rushes of air over or through mountain gaps are called 'williwaws.'

will-o'-the-wisp n

1 Std: a phosphorescent light that appears to flit or hover over marshy ground.   Also called **devil's lantern, fairy light, fireball 2, fool's light, fox fire 2, ~ glow, ghost light, graveyard ~, jack-o-lantern 1, Jacob's lantern, marsh light, mineral ~, money ~, spook ~, witch ~**

2   =**nighthawk 1.**

1889 Ridgway *Ornith. IL* 1.369 **CT,** Nighthawk. *Popular synonyms.* Whip-poor-will; Bull Bat; Will-o'the-wisp.

3   =**firefly 1.**

1939 *LANE* Map 238 *(Lightning bug)* 1 inf, **eMA,** Will-o'-the-wisp.

1968 *DARE* (Qu. R1, . . *The small insect that flies at night and flashes a light at its tail*) Inf **PA**104, Sometimes called will-o'-the-wisp.

willow n

1   Std: a shrub or tree of the genus *Salix;* also its wood.   For other names of var of these see **ball willow, bog ~, corkscrew ~, crack ~, diamond ~, ditch ~, dog ~, dune ~, feltleaf ~, frog ~, globe ~, gray ~, heartleaf ~, meadow ~, mountain ~, peachleaf ~, piss ~, planeleaf ~, possum bush, prairie willow, pussy ~** n[1]**, red ~ 1, sage ~, sandbar ~ 1, 2, Scouler ~, silverleaf ~, silver ~, swamp ~ 1, upland ~, velvet ~ 1, whistle ~, white ~**

2   in phrr *keep* (or *hold*) *close to the willows:* To act cautiously and conservatively.

1913 Natl. Lumber Manufacturers *Official Rept.* 55 **MO,** The thought to be developed will not permit of oratorical attempts or rhetorical flourishes. We will have to hold close to the willows and examine the situation with care and caution. **1936** *AmSp* 11.315 **Ozarks,** *Keep close to the willows.* . . To be conventional, conservative, modest. Nude boys, swimming in the willow-bordered creeks, keep close to the trees to avoid being seen by passing tourists. **1953** Randolph–Wilson *Down in Holler* 258 **Ozarks,** Jim's woman used to be kinder wild, but she keeps close to the willers now that the children's a-growin' up.

willow britches   See **woolen breeches 1**

willow bug   See **willow fly 1**

willow cat n

Any of var fishes of the family Ictaluridae, as:

a   A **channel catfish** (here: *Ictalurus punctatus*), freq the so-called **eel catfish.   chiefly SE, Lower Missip Valley**   Note: The latter was thought to be a separate sp until the 1940s.

1877 *Forest & Stream* 7.403 swTN, The water was muddy enough for us to catch quite a number of perch, bream and suckers. Only one willow cat raised his whiskers above the surface. **1890** *IL State Lab. Nat. Hist. Bulletin* 3.146, Willow Cat, Channel Cat, White Fulton *(Ictalurus punctatus . .)*. **1898** U.S. Natl. Museum *Bulletin* 47.2788 **LA,** *Ictalurus anguilla. . .* Eel Cat; Willow Cat. *Ibid* 2789, [Footnote:] This species is well known to the fishermen of the Atchafalaya River, by whom it is usually called the "eel cat," though the name "willow cat" is sometimes applied to it. It was explained by the fishermen that the name "eel cat" was given on account of the long feelers (i.e., barbels) and the name "willow cat" because it is most frequently found about the roots of willow trees. **1909** *DN* 3.389 eAL, Willow cat. . . A kind of catfish of a yellowish color. **1940** *NW AR Times* (Fayetteville) 22 June 6/6, The two fish, one a yellow cat, weighing 24 ½ pounds and the other a willow cat weighing 33 ½ pounds were only part of the night's catch. **1966–70** *DARE* (Qu. P1, . . *Kinds of freshwater fish . . caught around here . . good to eat*) Infs **GA**84, **MS**1, Willow cat; **KY**86, Willow cat—near willow trees; **SC**40, Willow cat—same as blue cat. **2005** in 2008 *DARE* File—Internet **IA,** Have heard channels called willow cats before, not sure if same thing or not, fish get different names different places. *Ibid* **AR,** We call channel cats that are really yellow and dont have any spots willow cats. Most of the time we do catch them in and around willow trees, but this is probably just coincidental.

b   A **bullhead 1b** (here: *Ameiurus* spp); see quots.

1941 *Jrl. Wildlife Management* 5.39 **TN,** [Footnote:] Bullhead: Locally called willow cat, includes three species of *Ameiurus; melas catulus, natalis natalis,* and *nebulosus marmoratus.* **1989** Grooms *Channel Catfish Fever* 30, Bullheads—Horned pout, pout, chucklehead, butterball, yellow belly, wogger, paper skin, polly, wally, wooly[,] willow cat, mud cat. A bullhead by any other name is still a bullhead. **2004** *Jrl. Star* (Peoria IL) 13 June sec D 12 (Internet), This has been a particularly good spring at Rice Lake, as anglers have caught numbers of willow cats, or brown bullheads.

c   =**flathead catfish 1.**

1945 *Ada Eve. News* (OK) 17 Oct 5/2, The fish, known to many as flathead, to others as the willow cat and to the more scientific fishermen as Appalutian [sic], was weighed on a pair of cotton scales. **1966** *DARE* (Qu. P1, . . *Kinds of freshwater fish . . caught around here . . good to eat*) Inf **OK**52, Willow cat—same as shovelbill—nose like a duck. **2005** in 2008 *DARE* File—Internet **AL,** Most of my mom's side of the family calls flatheads "willow" cats. They sure aren't the smallest members though. **2008** *Longview News-Jrl.* (TX) 7 June (Internet), There are three main species of catfish . . that inhabit our area waterways. The channel cat, blue cat and the flathead are the proper names and, as usual, all have local monikers. Flatheads are often called "Ops," short for Opelousas, or willow cats.

d =**stone catfish 1**, esp *Noturus gyrinus*. **Upper Missip Valley**

1955 *Cedar Rapids Gaz.* (IA) 6 Feb sec 4 4/3, The best bait [for walleyes] seems to be a small catfish called the willow cat. **1968** *Waterloo Daily Courier* (IA) 14 July 44/3, The hot bait for walleyes is the willow cat, and bait shops are having a hard time keeping them. **1974** *Winona Daily News* (MN) 28 June [14]/1 (newspaperarchive.com), Fishing near Fountain City earlier this week he used a willow cat to take this eight-pound walleye. **1985** Madson *Up River* 147 **Upper Missip Valley,** Scuba divers might have done that more effectively, but the plant beds held many little mad toms or "willow cats," and Worth and his divers "didn't relish contact with them." **2007** in 2008 *DARE* File—Internet **nwWI,** The willow cat, also known as Tadpole Mad tom (*Noturus gyrinus*) in our area, is a small bullhead-looking fish that is related to the catfish family. They usually are about 2 or 3 inches long. There are actually quite a few different species of willow cats.

willow fly n [*OED2* (at *willow* sb. 6) "any insect of the family *Perlidae*" 1787]

1 also *willow bug*: =**mayfly 1. chiefly Inland Sth, IL** See Map

1888 (1939) Mayne *Maud* 411 **csIL,** Dr. Bower . . brushed a willow-fly from my belt. **1892** *ID Daily Statesman* (Boise) 14 Sept 5/3 **sIL,** An army of willow flies last night covered the city in swarms of millions. . . They could be shoveled up or swept off by the bushel, and handfuls could be gathered in the air. **1960** Teale *Journey into Summer* 38, Other names [for mayflies] we encountered along the way were: lake flies, fish flies, June flies, Junebugs, and twenty-four-hour bugs. . . and on the Mississippi they are referred to as willow bugs. **1965–70** *DARE* (Qu. R4, *A large winged insect that hatches in summer in great numbers around lakes or rivers, crowds around lights, lives only a day or so, and is good fish bait*) 18 Infs, **chiefly Inland Sth, IL,** Willow fly; **AL**47, **MO**38, **TN**6, 42, 44, Willow bug; (Qu. P6, . . *Kinds of worms . . used for bait*) Inf **AL**28, Willow flies. **1969** *DARE* FW Addit **KY**60, Willow fly—a small green fly that comes in huge swarms in summer, then all at once are gone. One-quarter inch long, small lacy wings. **1994** *Knoxville News–Sentinel* (TN) 14 Aug sec C 14 (Internet), Willow flies—a large type of mayfly—hatch on the mainstem reservoirs every summer, usually starting in mid-July. . . Willow flies—their scientific name is Hexiagenia [sic] bilineata—are such a boon to fishing that the Tennessee Wildlife Resources Agency has actually stocked them. **2007** *DARE* File—Internet **KY,** My dad called it a "willow fly" as did all the local fishermen. Biologically speaking it was a "mayfly" but it seemed we always found them hatching in late June and throughout July.

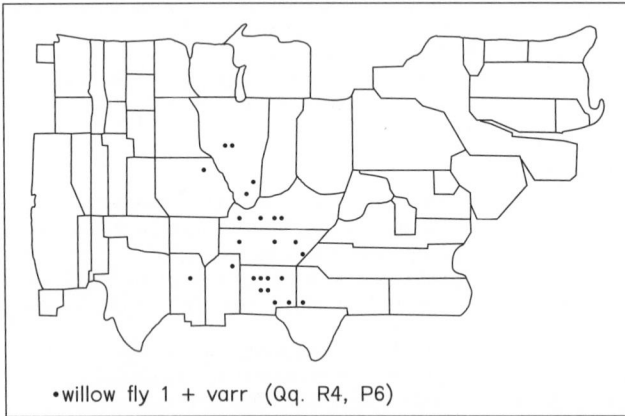

•willow fly 1 + varr (Qq. R4, P6)

2 Any of several stoneflies (family Plecoptera). **West, esp CO** Cf **salmonfly**

1891 *New North* (Rhinelander WI) 16 July [8]/2 (newspaperarchive.com) **wNE,** He states that the helgramite [sic] is extremely common in the north fork of the Platte, and by its fly form, which is there known as the willow fly, is one of the best natural foods for trout. **1917** *Pueblo Chieftain* (CO) 14 July 5/2, Willow flies plentiful this week. **1967** *DARE* (Qu. R4, *A large winged insect that hatches in summer in great numbers around lakes or rivers, crowds around lights, lives only a day or so, and is good fish bait*) Infs **CO**31, **WY**5, Willow fly. **1968**

Reclamation Era 54.100 **CO,** Large stone fly nymphs, commonly and erroneously called hellgrammites, drift into the lake from the river. These nymphs are immature forms which give rise to the famous Gunnison River willow fly. **1981** Vandenbusche–Smith *Land Alone* 255 **CO,** When the willow-fly hatch occurred on the Gunnison River around June 1 to June 10 every year before dams were built, fishermen from all over Colorado flocked into Gunnison and nearby resorts for some of the finest fishing anywhere. **1995** *DARE* File, Stonefly—called willow fly in the West and salmonfly in Montana. **2006** *Rocky Mt. News* (Denver CO) 9 June sec C 24 (Internet), State of the stonefly—Salmonflies, willow flies, whatever you call them, tend to turn up at the most inconvenient times, namely peak runoff.

willow grouse n

1 =**willow ptarmigan.** [*DCan* 1823 →] **chiefly AK**

1833 Bonaparte *Amer. Ornith.* 4.327, The willow grouse inhabits the fur countries . . breeding in the valleys of the Rocky Mountains. **1844** Lapham *Geogr. Descr. WI* 70 [Footnote:] Tetrao. . . saliceti [=*Lagopus lagopus*], . . willow grouse, or white partridge. **1881** in 1883 U.S. Revenue Cutter Serv. *Cruise Corwin* 80 **AK,** The White Ptarmigan, or Willow Grouse, occurs in greater numbers in Northern Alaska than all the other species of grouse combined. **1917** Dixon *Human Side Birds* 240 **AK,** The willow grouse ptarmigan is commonly found over all the tundras and open barrens of Alaska. **1999** Marsh *Breakfast at Trout's* 15 **AK,** This is more a season for hunting ptarmigan, the white willow grouse stalked on snowshoes over hard-packed drifts.

2 =**sharp-tailed grouse.**

1877 Dodge *Plains Great West* 228, Sharp-tailed grouse. . . This bird is commonly and erroneously called the 'willow grouse.' **1899** *Helena Independent* (MT) 14 Aug 8/2, The big blue grouse may be a dunce in his youth . . , but he learns quickly. . . His less pretty cousin, the willow grouse, of the low lands—too often called a "prairie chicken"—has his same characteristics. **1917** *ID Daily Statesman* (Boise) 20 Feb 4/5, A bag limit of six on blue grouse, willow grouse (commonly known as prairie chickens), fool hens and ducks. **1940** Writers' Program *Guide NV* 18, The big blue grouse and the smaller willow grouse are fairly plentiful in the big timber of Elko County. **1960** U.S. Natl. Museum *Bulletin* 217.137 **AK,** Sharp-tailed grouse (often called "willow grouse" in Alaska and Yukon). **1967** *DARE* (Qu. Q7, *Names and nicknames for . . game birds*) Infs **CO**37, **WY**1, Willow grouse.

3 =**dusky grouse.**

1893 *Dallas Morning News* (TX) 1 Oct 11/6 **Rocky Mts,** In the mountains the willow grouse and sage hen are sought at this season. As the name suggests, this kind of grouse is found along the willows of the small mountain streams, and in the openings of the gulches, where they widen out into the valleys. The cock is bluish and is sometimes known as the blue grouse. The hen is grayish in color. **1950** Carhart *Fishing West* 89, Willow grouse, the summer and early autumn phase of the dusky grouse, may scare up out of patches of berry bushes.

4 =**ruffed grouse.** [*DCan* 1907 →]

1975 Johnsgard *N. Amer. Game Birds* 47, Ruffed Grouse. . . Other vernacular names . . pheasant, tippet, white-flesher, willow grouse, wood grouse [etc]. **1988** *Fairbanks Daily News–Miner* (AK) 1 Dec 13 (Tabbert *Dict. Alaskan Engl.*), Various species of willows bear buds during the autumn and hold them in a dormant state till spring. As a result of their reliance upon this phenomenon, the ruffed grouse is often referred to as willow grouse.

willow herb n Cf **milk willow herb, night ~**

1 Std: a plant of the genus *Epilobium* or the closely related genus *Chamerion* (formerly included in *Epilobium*), esp *C. angustifolium*. Also called **cottonweed 4, fireweed e, Indian wicopy 2, wicopy 2.** For other names of *C. angustifolium* see **blooming sally, burntweed, firetop, flowering willow 2, moose tongue, slinkweed c**

2 =**swamp loosestrife 1.**

1901 Acad. Nat. Sci. Philadelphia Entomol. Sec. *Entomol. News & Proc.* 12.76, The most remarkable specimens to be collected on Staten Island occur on the swamp loosestrife or willow-herb *(Decodon verticillatus)*. **1930** Pellett *Amer. Honey Plants* 349, Swamp Loosestrife *(Decodon verticillatus)*. . . Also known as water-willow, grass-poly, wild oleander, peat-weed, stinkweed, willow-herb. **2002** MacKenzie *Perennial Ground Covers* 124, *Decodon verticillatus*. . . Willow-herb. . . A robust North American native . . , willow-herb is clearly not a ground cover for every landscape.

willow-leaved catalpa n Also *willowleaf catalpa*
=**desert willow.**
   1873 *Gardener's Mth. & Horticult. Advt.* 15.339 **TX,** A Dallas, Texas, correspondent says: "I have Chilopsis linearis (Don.) growing". . . and [it] is called Willow Leaved Catalpa, from shape and color of flowers. **1951** *PADS* 15.41 **TX,** *Chilopsis linearis.* . . Flowering willow; willow-leaved, or desert, catalpa; mimbre. **1998** Taylor *Plants for Dry Gardens* 40, *Chilopsis linearis . . ,* the desert willow or willowleaf catalpa, grows along dry washes in the south-western United States and Mexico.

willowlegs n [In ref to the greenish color of the legs; *willow* is commonly used in this sense in ref to poultry.]
The young of the American **scoter** *(Melanitta nigra).*
   1955 *MA Audubon Soc. Bulletin* 39.377 **MA,** *American scoter.* . . Willow-legs (Mass. The young.)

willow oak n Cf **high-ground willow oak, upland ~**
1 Any of var unidentified **oaks;** see quots.
   1709 (1967) Lawson *New Voyage* 100 **NC, SC,** Willow-Oak is a sort of Water-Oak. **1899** (1912) Green *VA Folk-Speech* 485, *Willow-oak.* . . An oak the leaves of which are large and entire, like those of a willow. **1961** Douglas *My Wilderness* 189 **MD,** A cardinal hopped from limb to limb in a willow oak, whose nuts are bitter to our taste but liked by squirrels and some birds. **1965–70** *DARE* (Qu. T10, . . *Kinds of oak trees*) 38 Infs, **scattered,** Willow oak; (Qu. T15, . . *Kinds of swamp trees*) Infs **VA**38, 79, Willow oak.
2 Std: an **oak** (here: *Quercus phellos*) native from New York across much of the Midland and through the South to Texas. Also called **laurel oak 4, peach ~ 1, pin ~ 2b, red ~ 2i, sand jack 2, swamp oak 2b(2), water ~ 2a**
3 also *evergreen willow oak, swamp ~:* =**laurel oak 2.**
   1801 Michaux *Histoire* np, Chêne laurier à feuilles aiguës [=Laurel oak with pointed leaves]. Swamp's [sic] willow oak. **1803** *Med. Repository* 6.69, Q[uercus] Laurifolia—swamp willow-oak. **1897** Sudworth *Arborescent Flora* 175 **FL, SC,** *Quercus laurifolia.* . . *Laurel Oak.* . . *Common names.* . . Willow Oak. **1914** FL Geol. Surv. *Annual Rept.* 6.196, Quercus laurifolia—(Evergreen willow oak)—rich woods. **2004** Austin *FL Ethnobotany* 207, The Seminoles used coco-plum in a medicine. . . Logs are cut a specific size from live oak . . , willow oak *(Q. laurifolia),* mastic . . and wax myrtle. . . The logs are burned and the ashes boiled.

willow partridge n
=**willow ptarmigan.**
   [**1795** Hearne *Journey* 411 **Canada** (as of a1772), The *Willow Partridges.* . . proceed . . to the woods and brush-willows, where they hord together.] [**1862** Acad. Nat. Sci. Philadelphia *Proc. 1861* 227 **Labrador Canada,** *Lagopus albus.* . . Ptarmigan. "Willow Partridge." . . Great confusion prevails among the North American Ptarmigan.] **1901** French *Nome Nuggets* 93 **AK,** Ptarmigan, or willow partridge, being so numerous as to be easily dispatched with a stick. **1927** Forbush *Birds MA* 2.37, *Lagopus lagopus lagopus.* . . Willow Ptarmigan. Other names: willow grouse; willow partridge.

willow ptarmigan n
Std: a **ptarmigan** (here: *Lagopus lagopus*) native in North America primarily to Arctic, subarctic, and subalpine tundra. Also called **chicken B1, partridge B4, willow grouse 1, ~ partridge, white partridge**

willow snake n
=**queen snake.**
   1905 MI Acad. Sci. *Report* 7.116, *Natrix leberis.* . . Willow Snake. Yellow-bellied or Leather Snake. United States east of the Mississippi. Not uncommon in Michigan. **1914** *Jrl. Elisha Mitchell Scientific Soc.* 30.202, *Natrix leberis* (Willow Snake, Queen Snake). . . Raleigh, Chapel Hill, Kinston, Waynesville, Blantyre, Cane River. Not common. **1950** *Herpetologica* 6.154, Willow snake . . *N[atrix] septemvittata.*

willow wacks See **willywags**

willow warbler n
=**prothonotary warbler.**
   1889 Ridgway *Ornith. IL* 1.119, *Protonotaria citrea.* . . Golden Swamp Warbler; Willow Warbler. . . Wherever there are swamps surrounded by woods and bordered by willow trees, and especially if the growth of the latter be extensive, this beautiful bird is almost sure to occur. **1917** (1923) *Birds Amer.* 3.113, *Prothonotary warbler—Protonotaria citrea.* . . It must have its home by running water and generally in the willows. . . This has given it the names of the Golden Swamp Warbler and Willow Warbler. **1992** *Aiken Std.* (SC) 12 Apr mag sec 8/3, Measuring 5 ½ inches from tip of dark bill to tip of blue-gray tail, this colorful warbler is called swamp warbler, golden swamp warbler, or willow warbler because of his fondness for the swamp willow.

willow witch n Cf **witch** n 3, 4
1 =**dowsing rod** (whether made of willow or not). **esp MT**
   1930 Lee *Powder R.* 21 **MT,** I dug these out of a canyon side,/ Frum a lead thet wuz fourteen inches wide,/ Whether twuz luck 'er a willow witch,/ I tied the pack with a diamond hitch. **1936** *Helena Independent* (MT) 18 Nov 4/5, A willow witch cut in the shape of a wishbone is generally the type used. Mountain maple works faster than any other wood, . . but almost any wood with a pethy heart is all right for witching. **1966–67** *DARE* (Qu. CC13a, . . *A forked stick that's used to show where there's water underground.* . . *[What kind of wood?]*) Inf **MI**47, He uses a willow witch; **SD**2, Willow witch—forked willow stick or copper wire; **MT**2, Willow witch.
2 =**dowser.**
   1977 *Sun. Sun* (Lowell MA) 14 Aug 6/2 **nWI,** The mayor of Rhinelander is not only a woman, but also the town's resident "willow witch." . . "I've been willow witching for over 30 years," said the 59-year-old grandmother. Though it's called willow witching, Mrs. Prosser uses hazel bush instead of willow because hazel is tougher wood.

willow witching vbl n Cf **willow witch, witch** v
Dowsing; hence n *willow witcher* =**dowser.**
   1929 *Eve. Huronite* (Huron SD) 26 Dec 2/2, The days of the willow-witching method of locating water under the surface of the ground are not past. **1970** *DARE* (Qu. CC13b, . . *The person who knows how to use a forked stick to find water*) Inf **CA**196, Willow witcher. **1977** [see **willow witch 2**]. **2007** in 2009 *DARE* File—Internet **MD,** He'd bring his metal detector . . a magical device to me, like the water divining rod, or 'willow witching' as we sometimes referred to it.

will-willet See **pill-willet**

‡**willy** n[1] Cf *DS* E20
See quot.
   1970 *DARE* File **NE,** *Willies.* . . the rolls of dust that gather under beds, furniture, etc.

Willy n[2] See **William**

willy britches See **woolen breeches 1**

willy-nillies See **willies**

willywags n pl With *the* Also *williwags, willey wags, willyw(h)acks, williwacks, willow wacks* **chiefly nNEng, esp ME** Cf **puckerbrush**
Tangled underbrush; an area covered with such underbrush; a remote, sparsely inhabited area.
   1965 ME Univ. Outdoor Recreation Study Team *Outdoor Recreation ME* 40, Most of Maine's better brooks and streams . . provide excellent fishing for the angler who still likes to rub elbows with alders and "willy-wags." **1972** *Daily Kennebec Jrl.* (Augusta ME) 29 May 5/7, Richard Cook . . spent . . a weekend at a camp way up in the willy wacks near Spencer Bay. **1983** King *Different Seasons* 40 **ME,** Somewhere out in the willywags . . they were having a regular May holiday in the sun. **1985** McPhee *Table of Contents* 256 **ME,** He does indeed seem most in his element when he is out in the big woods . . "out in the williwags," as he refers to the backcountry. **1988** *DARE* File **nME,** Words I have as part of my upbringing in the willey wags of northern Maine. **2002** in 2008 *DARE* File—Internet **cME,** She loved trees, loved living out in the 'willow wacks' as she called it. **2003** Gilpatrick *Allagash* 131 **ME,** A jill-poke was a log caught crossways or otherwise out of the mainstream of moving logs. A jill-poke in the willywags was a log out of the mainstream. **2004** in 2007 *DARE* File—Internet **ME** [*Bangor Daily News* 2 Aug], Roughly 60,000 fans . . flocked to the willywags of northern Maine. **2004** in 2008 *Ibid* **ME,** I went to work for a very small firm in the willywacks of Maine (most of the state is the willywacks by the way). **2005** in 2008 *Ibid* **nNH,** Then the trail finally decided to open up for us, and after one more quick, steep scramble through the willywags (which had even the most hardy souls second-guessing Pete), we made it to our base camp. *Ibid* **VT,** Is it allowed to

rig up a net or diverter behind the target to catch the balls? Otherwise we will be chasing them into the willy-wags. **2006** Wormser *Road in Spring* 145 **ME,** How are you doin' out there in the williwacks? Seen any moose lately? **2007** *DARE* File—Internet **UT,** FFBC Camp Ministry. . . Teen camps in the willywags of the Great Rocky Mountains. *Ibid* **NJ,** I suppose you are so far out in the willywags that you can't get anything but AOL? **2008** *Ibid* **ME,** I live in Benton with my dog. . . I love it out here in the willywhacks!

willy worm See **wooly worm**

Wilma n
=**wedgie 1.**
 1989 *DARE* File **UT,** The act of lifting a person (from behind) by the belt, belt buckles, top of the underwear, the seat of the pants: Wilma—3 infs.

Wilson's phalarope n
Std: a **phalarope** (here: *Phalaropus tricolor*) native to much of the western half of the US. Also called **harbor goose, sea ~ 1, sewing-machine bird, whale ~**

Wilson's plover n
Std: a **plover** (here: *Charadrius wilsonia*) native chiefly along the Atlantic and Gulf coasts from southern New Jersey to Florida and Texas. Also called **collier** n[2], **ringneck 3**

Wilson's snipe n
Std: a **snipe 1** (here: *Gallinago delicata*) common throughout most of the US. Also called **alewife bird, butter ~, drill face, English snipe 1, guttersnipe 1, hagaloo bird, jack** n[1] **23e, jacksnipe 3, longbill 2, marsh snipe, meadow ~ 1, mud ~ 2, robin ~ 5, shadbird 1, shad spirit, squatting snipe** Cf **brown snipe 3**

wimmens See **woman B2**

wimmern See **woman B4**

wimmins See **woman B2**

wimmy-diddle See **whimmy-diddle**

wim-wam for a goose's bridle See **whim-wham for a goose('s) bridle**

wim-wams See **whim-whams**

win v
Std sense, var forms.

1 past: usu *won;* also **esp Sth, S Midl** *winned;* rarely *wint, wunt.*
 1857 *Harper's New Mth. Mag.* 14.754 **NC,** That spangle winned his fight last year. **1884** *Anglia* 7.253 **Sth, S Midl,** [Black], To the regular forms of the Irregular verbs as used by the whites, the Negro adds the following forms of his own. . . *Pres.* win—*Past.* winned, wint, wunt— *Pass. Part.*—. **1885** in 2009 (acc) Lexis–Nexis Legal Research *State Case Law: TX* (Internet), Witness did not . . say: "I winned this pistol and another pistol and $280." **1891** *Century Illustr. Mag.* 42.799 **Sth** [Black], He winned . . de race. **1930** in 2009 (acc) Lexis–Nexis Legal Research *State Case Law: GA* (Internet), After Wright returned from court . . he said: "I think we winned the case." **1938** *Esquire* May 160 **KY,** Pa winned th' suit. **1947** (1997) Herman–Herman *Amer. Dials.* 13, *Win.* . . "Winned" is also heard, especially in rural areas, as in "We winned everything." **1962** [see **2** below]. **1986** Pederson *LAGS Concordance,* 1 inf, **ceMS,** Winned [inf Black].

2 past pple: usu *won;* also *winned.*
 1839 (1841) Hoffman *Viator* 35 **MD,** The child had winned greatly upon my sympathies. **1946** Stuart *Tales Plum Grove* 121 **eKY,** Tell about fights you've winned. **1962** *Mt. Life* 38.1.17 **sAppalachians,** Certain persistent perversities in the use of verbs are also widespread. Strong verbs are often weakened, irregular verbs made regular. The past and past participle of . . win [become] winned.

win n See **wen**

winch v [*W3* "archaic var of *[1]wince*"] Cf **quinch** v, n[2], **squinch** v[2] **3**
To wince.
 1941 in 1944 *ADD* **MS,** Wince. . . Hohman, winching from the pain of a badly bruised head. **1947** in 1965 *DARE* File, *Wince,* vb.—pron. [wɪntʃ], by . . [a man who] has lived in Wis., Ind., Ill., Cal., Tex.—no-

where for more than 2 yrs. . . Doesn't know where he acquired this pron. **1967** *DARE* (Qu. X24, *When a person opens and closes his eyes quickly, he* _____) Inf **MA33,** Winches. **2008** in 2009 *DARE* File—Internet **cwCA,** I am amazed when I . . realize I had not winched in pain once.

wind v |wɪnd| [Engl dial; *OED2* a1500 →] **scattered, but esp Mid and S Atl** See Map
To winnow; hence vbl n *winding.*
 1820 Mason *Gentleman's Farrier* 35 **VA,** His [=a horse's] homony (Indian corn ground coarse) should be first winded, then thrown into clean water, so as to separate the part that is nutritious from the husk and chaff. **1918** Bates *Hist. Denton Co.* 301 **TX** (as of c1850), He cleaned off a spot of ground and circled the wheat with wooden pitchforks and then winded out the chaff. **1933** Freeman–Olds *Hist. Marshall Co. KY* app 6, The grain and chaff were taken up and poured out so the wind could blow the chaff away. This was called "winding the wheat." **1954** *Harder Coll.* **cwTN,** *Winding.* . . Separating grain from the chaff: "Winding's blowing the hulls away, fan it out with a fan. Hold it up in a pan, pour it out, let the wind blow the thrash out." **1966** *Abilene Reporter–News* (TX) 15 June 1/1 (as of 1889), We beat the wheat with a 'frailing' stick and 'winded' the chaff out by dipping the grain and pouring it slowly back onto a wagonsheet. **1966–70** *DARE* (Qu. L32b, *In early days, how was the grain separated from the chaff?*) 9 Infs, **esp S Atl,** Winding; **NC1, 12, 81, SC57, VA57, 75,** Wind it (out); **AR52, CA138, SC63,** Winded (it); **MN7, NC24, OK27,** Winding it; **KY23, MI27,** Winding the grain; (Qu. L32a, *In early days, how was the grain separated from the straw?*) Infs **MT5, TN14, WA11,** Winding; (Qu. L33, *How is the grain separated from the straw nowadays?*) Inf **TN14,** Thrashing machine and winding; **GA28,** Winding. [25 of 26 Infs comm type 4, 5; 13 gs educ or less] **1966** *DARE* Tape **MI23,** The . . process . . known as winding ['wɪndɪŋ]. The grain was . . winded. You'd have a large sheet, such as a tarpaulin . . and you went outdoors and spread it down on the ground. And then, took the flailed grain and chaff and passed it through a sieve up about four to five feet above the ground and sifted it through the sieve, allowing the wind to pass through and blow the chaff and other material from the grain . . and that was . . what they termed as winding. **1986** Pederson *LAGS Concordance (Oats is thrashed)* 1 inf, **nwFL,** Wind them—of oats; 1 inf, **nwFL,** Wind them— not sure.

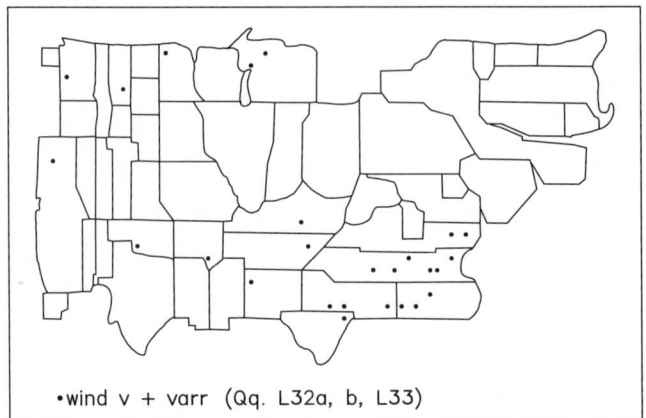

•wind v + varr (Qq. L32a, b, L33)

wind n See **wen**

windbags n
A **duckweed 1** (here: *Lemna gibba*).
 1957 Mason *Flora Marshes CA* 331, *Lemna gibba.* . . Inflated duckweed, wind bags. **1973** Hitchcock–Cronquist *Flora Pacific NW* 677, Wind bags—*L[emna] gibba.* **1990** Wasmann *Jrl. Biol.* 48.94 **CA,** *Lemna gibba.* . . Windbags; Inflated Duckweed. Our collections found mostly inland at mid-elevations, sea level to 1524 m elevation.

wind-busted adj Also *busted* **esp S Atl** See Map
Wind-broken.
 1892 Mitchell *Chickamauga* 65 **TN,** "Say, boy, did you see a woman with a striped dress and goggles go by?" " 'N a long-legged wind-busted critter?" **1908** (1910) Flandrau *Viva Mex.* 221, The occasional traveling opera company, with one wind-busted, middle-aged star . . is a torture. **1912** in 1950 Clark *Papers* 2.146 **NC,** It may be that they will "bellows" themselves, or in other words become "wind-busted," and thereby lose the race. **1965–70** *DARE* (Qu. K48, *When a horse is short of breath*)

Infs **FL**32, **GA**72, **NC**37, **SC**32, **TN**44, Wind-busted; **NC**53, **TN**44, Busted; [**GA**74, Wind is busted].

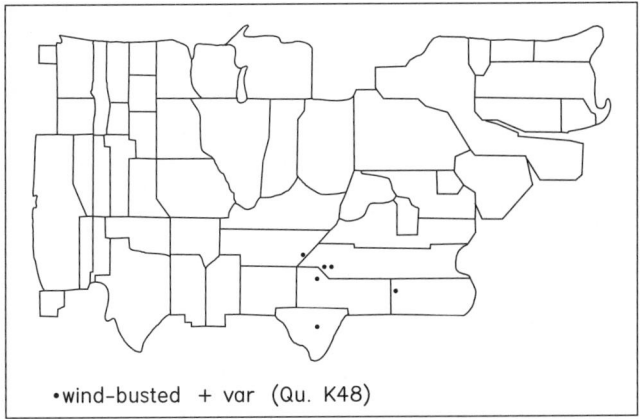

•wind-busted + var (Qu. K48)

wind devil n   Cf **dust devil 1**

A whirlwind; see quots.

1905 *McClure's Mag.* 24.175 **AZ,** The sun mounted; the desert went silently through its changes. Wind devils raised straight, true columns of dust six, eight hundred, even a thousand feet into the air. **1928** Beston *Outermost House* 14 **Cape Cod MA,** While a high, gusty westerly was blowing, I saw a little "wind devil," a miniature tornado six feet high, rush at full speed out of a cut, whirl itself full of sand upon the beach, and spin off breakerward. **1953** *Tucson Daily Citizen* (AZ) [17 June 2]/1 (newspaperarchive.com), Only last week . . a wind devil ripped one of the small craft from its moorings, causing some damage to the plane. **1957** *Hand Coll.* **IA,** Wind devils mean dry weather is coming. (Heard from grandmother on Iowa farm in 1940. Wind devils is name for twisters.) **1970** *Reno Eve. Gaz.* (NV) 1 Sept 11/7, The fire storm was comparable to a desert wind devil which lifts dust high off the ground. **1971** *Sun* (Lowell MA) 12 May 15/4, A "baby tornado" or a mighty powerful "wind devil" hit the home of the Hayden family . . , lifting the porch roof and carrying light aluminum porch furniture onto the lawn and up into a nearby tree. **1983** *News* (Frederick MD) 12 Sept sec B 5/1 **AZ,** When a wind devil dances toward us, I hold tight to the wheel. . . The whirlwind flings sage brush and pebbles around us and shrieks off into the desert.

windfish n

1 A **fallfish** (here: *Semotilus corporalis*). [See quot 1817]

1817 *Amer. Monthly Mag. & Crit. Rev.* 2.120, *Cyprinus bullaris.* . . [V]ulgar name Wind-fish, because it produces a bubble whenever it comes near the surface of the water. **1867** U.S. Dept. Ag. *Rept. of Secy. for 1866* 415, Of the eastern species [of cyprinids], those of *Semotilus,* generally known under the names of "wind-fish," "chub," &c., attain a goodly size, and furnish much sport to the angler. **1939** *LANE* Map 234 (*Minnow*) 1 inf, **wCT,** Shiners, the young of the windfish (silver chub).

2 =**golden shiner.** [See quot 1842]

1842 DeKay *Zool. NY* 4.192, The Variegated Bream. *Abramis versicolor* [=*Notemigonus crysoleucas*]. . . The name of *Wind-fish* is derived from one of its habits. Whenever a light flaw of wind ruffles the water, thousands of these fish may be seen darting to the surface, and as suddenly disappearing. **1906** NJ State Museum *Annual Rept. for 1905* 135, *Brama crysoleacus* [=*Notemigonus c.*]. . . Shiner. . . Dace. Wind Fish. **1933** LA Dept. of Conserv. *Fishes* 445, Known by a wide variety of popular names, such as Bitterhead, . . and Windfish, the Golden Shiner can be successfully reared.

windflower n   [*OED2* 1551 → as a transl of the Gk *anemone*]

Any of var plants of the family Ranunculaceae resembling those of the genus *Anemone*, as: see below.   Note: Most of these plants have at one time been regarded as species of *Anemone*.

a The roundlobe **hepatica** (*Hepatica nobilis* var *obtusa*).

1822 Bryant in *Idle Man* 1.4.64, Lodged in sunny cleft,/ Where the cold breezes come not, blooms alone / The little wind-flower, whose just-opened eye / Is blue as the spring heaven it gazes at. **1891** *Jrl. Amer. Folkl.* 4.147 **NEng,** You will remember that Bryant, who came from Cummington [MA], calls the Hepatica triloba [=*H. nobilis* var *obtusa*] the Wind Flower. So we [in Gilsum NH] called it, but also Liverwort.

b =**rue anemone.**

1892 *Jrl. Amer. Folkl.* 5.91 **OH,** *Anemonella thalictroides,* windflower. **1933** Small *Manual SE Flora* 518, *Anemonella thalictroides*. . . Wind-flower.

c =**pasqueflower.**

1884 *Kansas City Rev. Sci. & Industry* 7.190, Here is the downy Wind-Flower *Anemone patens,* var. *Pulsatilliana,* "little gosling" the prairie children call it. **1891** *Century Dict.* 6935, *Wind-flower.* . . The American pasque-flower, *A[nemone] patens,* var. *Nuttalliana* [=*Pulsatilla patens*], bears the name specifically in the western United States. **1896** *Jrl. Amer. Folkl.* 9.179 **cWI,** *Anemone patens,* var. *Nuttalliana* . . wind-flower, rock-lily, wild crocus. **1937** U.S. Forest Serv. *Range Plant Hdbk.* W159-2, Although pasqueflower is the common name most widely used, such other appellations as April-fools, Easter-flower, hartshorn, headache-plant, Mayflower, rocklily, wild-crocus, and windflower have variously designated this species. **1950** *WELS* (*Pale blue flowers with downy leaves and petals that bloom on hillsides in March or early April*) 9 Infs, **WI,** Windflowers. [*DARE* Ed: Some of these Infs may refer instead to other senses.] **1968** *DARE* (Qu. S23) Inf **IA**18, Windflowers, anemone, Easter flowers [are] all the same thing—lavender, shaped like little tulips. **2004** Guennel *Guide CO Wildflowers* 1.327, American Pasqueflower, . . Windflower . . *Pulsatilla patens hirsutissima.* . . Life Zones: Plains to Alpine.

d A **virgin's bower** (here: *Clematis ligusticifolia* var *californica*).

1896 *Jrl. Amer. Folkl.* 9.179 **CA,** *Clematis ligusticifolia,* . . var. *Californica,* . . wind-flower.

windgall n   [*OED2* →1860]   Cf **weather gall**
=**sun dog.**

1823 Cooper *Pilot* 1.19, There be streaked wind-galls in the offing, that speak . . plainly . . to shorten sail. **1899** (1912) Green *VA Folk-Speech* 485, *Wind-gall.* . . Fragments of rainbows seen on detached clouds.

wind gap n   Cf **gap** n¹ **1, water gap 2**

A notch or valley in a mountain ridge that is not occupied by a watercourse—often used as the name of such a feature.

1769 (1906) Smith *Tour Great Rivers* 78 **wPA,** Leaving Otters at 7 oCloc we passed thro the Wind Gap and stopt at Easton. **a1782** (1788) Jefferson *Notes VA* 215, The place where the Delaware now flows through the Kittatinny mountain . . was not its original course, but . . it passed through what is now called the 'Wind-gap,' a place several miles to the westward, and above an hundred feet higher than the present bed of the river. **1836** O'Bryan *Narr. Travels U.S.* 98 **ePA,** We passed through what is called the *wind gap,* a chasm in the same ridge of mountains. **1865** Baxley *What I Saw* 406 **CA,** San Francisco . . sporting in the gale that rushed through the wind-gap of the coast range. **1908** *Racine Daily Jrl.* (WI) 7 Feb 8/3, [Syndicated fiction:] There's a trail up here that goes over the ridge and down through a wind gap to a settlement about five miles south of Lamar. **1932** *DN* 6.234 **West,** Windgap. A slight gap in a mountain line, not deep enough for a watercourse. Not common, however. **1960** *Bridgeport Sun. Post* (CT) 21 Feb sec B 9/4, There is some open acreage between the northern boundary of the school land . . and more than 10 open acres between the southern boundary and "Windgap." **2004** *DARE* File—Internet **PA,** Wind Gap—The Wind Gap of the Lehigh Valley is a great display of natural forces. A wind gap is a water gap in where the water source did not "survive" the complete erosion of the mountain.

wind goggle   See **goggle** n

winding adv   Rarely sp *wynding*   **Sth, S Midl**   Cf **sky-winding**

Askew, cockeyed; often used hyperbolically in phr *knock (someone) winding* and varr: to deal (someone) a staggering blow.

1903 *DN* 2.336 **seMO,** *Winding, to knock.* . . To give a staggering blow. 'He knocked the fellow winding' [wɪndɪŋ]. **1907** *DN* 3.238 **nwAR,** *Winding, to knock.* . . To give a staggering blow. **1908** *DN* 3.327 **eAL, wGA,** *Knock winding.* . . To give a staggering or knockout blow to. **1924** (1946) Greer-Petrie *Angeline Gits an Eyeful* 3 **csKY,** They'd haul away and *knock 'em a-wynding* ag'in. **1933** Miller *Lamb in His Bosom* 90 **GA,** Lias's hand slapped her a-windin', and the fried fish were scattered all over the floor. **1963** Edwards *Gravel* 154 **eTN** (as of 1920s), Willis would . . raise one of his big feet . . and kick Fido winding and yell, "Get away from here dog; I'll kick your damn brains out." **1965–70** *DARE* (Qu. Y11, . . *A very hard blow: "You should have seen Bill go down. Joe really hit him a _____."*) Inf **VA**11, Winding; (Qu. MM13, *The table was nice and straight until he came along and knocked it _____*) Infs **AR**33, **KY**10, 84, **MS**64, **VA**11, Winding. **1981** Pederson *LAGS Basic Materials,* 1 inf, **cnLA**, Cow would kick you winding [waɪnɪn] summersets. **1983** *MJLF* 9.1.46 **ceKY** (as of 1956), *Knock winding* . . to give a staggering blow to. **2001** Karon *Common Life* 83 **NC**, Moses Marshall flashed a smile that nearly knocked her winding.

winding vbl n   See **wind** v

winding blades n pl, but occas sing in constr   Also *pair of winding blades* [*OED2* (at *blade* sb. 10.c) 1530]   **chiefly Sth, Midl** *old-fash*   Cf **quill wheel**

A reel, usu consisting of four arms with pegs at the outer ends, used to wind or unwind a skein of yarn; hence adv phrr *like (a pair of) winding blades* with a rapid spinning or flailing motion.

   1654 in 1911 MA Essex Co. Court *Records* 1.354, A pcell of linnen, yearne & winding blads, 4s. 6d. **1771** in 1890 *PA Mag. Hist. & Biog.* 14.216, Real & Winding Blades. **1835** *Farmers' Reg.* 2.559 **VA**, The implement . . resembles in shape, a common pair of winding blades [or reel]. **1861** Wiggs *Hal's Travels* 73 **cnAL**, [There] stood the blue-shirted individual, with his arms going like winding-blades. **1888** in 1919 Dunn *Indiana* 2.1169, He [=a pioneer] could make . . a loom, a reel, a winding blades, [etc]. **1895** Hallum *Diary Old Lawyer* 121 **TN**, The poor, tortured animal jumped twenty feet and knocked one of the gentry like a pair of winding blades. **1899** (1912) Green *VA Folk-Speech* 485, *Winding-blades.* . . Four arms on which a skein of cotton or yarn is put to be wound into balls. **1903** *DN* 2.336 **seMO**, I had just got my yarn offen my winding-blades. **1942** in 1991 Barden *VA Folk Legends* 99, Hit wasn't long 'till she was back to borrow grandma's windin' blades. **1952** Brown *NC Folkl.* 1.608, *Winding-blades.* . . When he fell, he went down that there mountain side like winding-blades. **1970** Green *Home Valley* 46 **NC**, He was walking the floor, pacing unafraid about the coffin, his eyes flashing, his long plowhandle arms weaving like winding blades.

windjammer n   Cf **airjammer**

A big talker; a boaster, "bloviator"; hence, by back-formation, v *windjam*.

   1887 *Athens Messenger* (OH) 25 Aug 4/4, Democrats. . . are going to have all the illustrious wind jammers of the country stumping the Buckeye State. **1896** *Century Illustr. Mag.* 51.430 **West**, There was a howl of derision from the assembled troop. "Come off, you young windjammer!" this from the first sergeant. "I suppose he really gave you a good dressing down, did n't he?" **1911** (1913) Johnson *Highways Gt. Lakes* 254, I knew he was a wind-jammer, and that he was much more likely to tell what he'd do to you if you were two or three miles away than right to your face. **1912** *DN* 3.593 **wIN**, *Wind-jammer.* . . A braggart. **1915** *DN* 4.230 **wTX**, *Windjammer.* . . One who "windjams," or talks "hot air." **1916** *DN* 4.331 **KS**, *Windjammer.* . . A talkative or boastful person. **1919** *DN* 5.64 **NM** [Among hs students], *Windjammer,* a talkative person. **1927** *AmSp* 2.366 **cwWV**, *Windjammer* . . a boaster. **1933** *AmSp* 8.1.32 **nwTX** [Ranch diction], *Windjammer.* A teller of windies. **1953** Randolph–Wilson *Down in Holler* 299 **Ozarks**, *Wind-jammer.* . . A teller of tall tales, a windy-spinner, a blanket-stretcher. **1965–70** *DARE* (Qu. HH7a, *Someone who talks too much, or too loud: "He's an awful _____."*) 21 Infs, **scattered**, Windjammer; (Qu. HH8, *A person who likes to brag*) Infs **ID**5, **IL**80, **MN**33, **MS**6, **PA**199, **TN**53, **TX**40, **VA**21, Windjammer; (Qu. HH16, *Uncomplimentary words with no definite meaning—just used when you want to show that you don't think much of a person: "Don't invite him. He's a _____."*) Inf **MI**47, One of them windjammers; [(Qu. X9, *Joking or uncomplimentary words for a person's mouth* . . *"I wish he'd shut his _____."*) Inf **AL**3, Windjammer; (Qu. KK12, *A meeting where there's a lot of talking: "They got together yesterday and had a real _____."*) Inf **KS**18, Windjammer.] **1967** *DARE* FW Addit **TN**22, A "windjammer" is somebody who's "always a-braggin'." **1995** Brophy *Coll.* 83 **swMO** (as of c1960), *Windjammer.* [O]ne who talks too much, one who blarneys.

windmill grass n   [*OED2* 1889 for *Chloris truncata*]   **esp Plains States, TX**
=**finger grass 2.**

   1900 NE Univ. Ag. Exper. Sta. *Annual Rept.* 1900 147, Chloris verticillata. . . Windmill grass. Prairies Kansas to Texas. May to Septem-

ber. **1912** KS Acad. Sci. *Trans.* 25.69, Chloris. Windmill-grass. *Ibid* 94, Chloris verticillata. . . Prairie Windmill-grass. . . middle and southwestern Kansas; common. . . Chloris elegans. . . White Windmill-grass. . . Extreme S[outh] W[est] K[ansas]. **1938** *Abilene Reporter-News* (TX) 6 Oct 5/2 **wTX**, Thirty-three varieties of grass—the main range types found in Taylor county are shown. . . Varieties exhibited are turkey foot sage, . . windmill grass, . . and brown top millet. **1967** *DARE* (Qu. S9, . . *Kinds of grass that are hard to get rid of*) Inf **IA**13, Windmill grass. **1973** *Kerrville Mt. Sun* (TX) 18 Oct sec 2 8/4, The Johnson grass with its tall heads makes lovely dried arrangements—the bluestems—the unusual "windmill" grass, with seed pods arranged like a parasol. **2007** Rhoads–Block *Plants PA* 361, *Chloris verticillata.* . . Windmill-grass. . . native to midwestern U.S.

windmill pink n   [See quot 1915]   **esp CA**

A naturalized **catchfly 1** (here: *Silene gallica*).

   1911 Jepson *Flora CA* 152, *S[ilene] gallica.* . . Windmill pink. **1915** (1926) Armstrong–Thornber *Western Wild Flowers* 114, *Windmill Pink* . . *(S[ilene] Gallica).* . . The small flowers . . have . . white or pinkish petals, with a small "crown," each petal twisted to one side like the sails of a windmill. **1968** *Fresno Bee the Republican* (CA) 12 May sec A 17/1, Another [catchfly] with twisted petals, is called "Windmill Pink." **2003** Beidleman–Kozloff *Plants San Francisco Bay* 177 **cwCA**, *Silene gallica* . . Windmill Pink.

wind my icebox   See **tap the icebox**

windowpane n   Also *windowlight, windowpane flounder* [See quot 1884]

A **flatfish 1** (here: *Scophthalmus aquosus*) of Atlantic coastal waters.   Also called **daylight 2, sand dab 1a, ~ flounder 1, turbot 1**

   1873 in 1878 Smithsonian Inst. *Misc. Coll.* 14.2.17 **NJ**, *Lophopsetta maculata* [=*Scophthalmus aquosus*]. . . windowpane *(New Jersey);* sand flounder *(New York).* **1884** Goode *Fisheries U.S.* 1.177, The Spotted Turbot . . in New Jersey is called Window-pane, or Daylight, because it is so thin that when held to the light the sun can be seen through its translucent flesh. **1889** U.S. Fish Comm. *Bulletin for 1887* 135 **seNJ**, *Bothus maculatus.* . . A single small example of the "window-light" was seined by Capt. Thomas Steelman of the menhaden steamer *Nellie Rawson.* **1904** *Outing* 44.507, The most delicate of all is the one known simply as the "window pane," which is caught in the warm months from Boston to the mouth of the Mississippi River. **1955** Richardson *House on Nauset Marsh* 60 **MA**, In the inside channel between the Cedar Bank Channel and First Hummock, I saw a "windowpane" flounder, or sand dab, lying still, heading upstream. **1982** Heat Moon *Blue Highways* 350 **ME**, Flats [=flatfish] that are too small to take to market—the ones we call 'windowpanes'—those fish end up on the pier as lobster bait at six dollars a box. **1986** *Providence Jrl.* (RI) 13 Feb sec A 4 (Internet), A fishery management plan that aims to conserve dwindling species of bottom-dwelling fish in New England waters. . . proposes to regulate the taking of . . cod, yellowtail flounder, haddock, winter flounder, American plaice, pollock, redfish, witch flounder, white hake and windowpane flounder. **2001** in 2009 *DARE* File—Internet **neMA**, A lot of the other flounders, especially windowpanes and sand dabs, get mistaken for fluke.

wind poppy n   [See quot 1965]

A wild poppy *(Stylomecon heterophylla)* native to California.   Also called **blooddrops, flaming poppy**

   1897 Parsons *Wild Flowers CA* 129, The wind-poppy is an exceedingly variable flower. . . in the south it is usually very small, making tiny flecks of red in the grass. **1928** Clements *Flowers Coast & Sierra* 14 **CA**, The vermilion-red disks of the wind poppy glow here and there like bright flecks of flame in the shelter of the chaparral. **1965** Sharsmith *Spring Wildflowers* 76 **cwCA**, The Wind Poppy is so-named because its 4, delicate, red-orange petals are very ephemeral, falling when the wind or an unwary hand disturbs them. **2007** Huber *60 Hikes San Francisco* 156 **CA**, This little stretch features . . spring wildflowers including wind poppy, Chinese houses, . . and elegant clarkia.

wind root n   Also *windweed* [See quot 1869]
=**butterflyweed 1.**

   1828 Rafinesque *Med. Flora* 1.74, *Asclepias tuberosa.* . . *Vulgar names*—Pleurisy root, . . Wind root [etc]. **1869** Porcher *Resources* 562 **Sth**, Pleurisy root; Butterfly-weed, *(Asclepias tuberosa* . . *).* It is sometimes called wind root, on account of the relief it gives in flatulence. **1892** (1974) Millspaugh *Amer. Med. Plants* 135-1, *Asclepias tube-*

rosa. . . Com. Names.—Pleurisy-root, . . wind root, wind weed [etc]. **1974** Morton *Folk Remedies* 33 **SC,** Wind root. . . *Asclepias tuberosa.*

wind scorpion n

Std: an arachnid of the order Solifugae.   For other names see **child of the earth 1, scorpion B1, sun spider, vinegarone 2**

Windsor bean n   Also *Windsor*   [*OED2* 1712]
=**broad bean 1.**

1737 in 1909 Wesley *Jrl.* 1.402 **eGA,** Sewee-beans, about the size of our scarlet, but to be shelled and eaten like Windsor beans.   **1790** Deane *New Engl. Farmer* 19 **MA,** The English bean, to which the name windsor is applied.   **1842** *Sentinel & Farmer* (Milwaukee WI) 26 Mar 1/3, The Windsor bean shrank under the influence of the hot sun of this country [=the US] for some years, and produced little or nothing. The plant now is acclimated, and it produces almost as well as it did in England.   **1900** *Homestead* 29 Nov 10/2, The ash gray blister beetle is particularly fond of the English Windsor bean and also of the early snapped beans.   **1922** *Daily Northwestern* (Oshkosh WI) 3 July 6/3, The Windsor bean may be planted earlier than the Limas, in fact, with the earliest string beans.   **1978** *Wanigan Catalog* 5, *Broad* . . Not the Broad or Windsor bean . . , but a flat wide green snap, with white kidney seeds.   **2007** in 2008 *DARE* File—Internet **OR,** *You say horsebean,* I say tickbean. You say broad bean, I say Windsor bean. You say faba, I say fava.

wind splitter n   Cf hazel splitter 1
=**razorback hog.**

1854 in 1856 IN State Bd. Ag. *Annual Rept. for 1854–55* 61, They (the rain-bowed, long-legged, long-eared, slab-sided wind-splitters . .) must soon give way for . . the more civilized hog.   **1869** *Colman's Rural World* 23.179 **MO,** Why, Sir! if we have a fine sow, the first thing we know there is a wind-splitter in with her.   **1884** Pioneer Soc. MI *Pioneer Coll.* 5.253 (as of 1837), We gave thirteen dollars . . for a shoat of the wind-splitter breed, weighing probably sixty pounds, dressed. It was so lean it would not fry itself.   **1893** Owen *Voodoo Tales* 28 **VA** [Black], I seed dem ole win'-splittehs (wind-splitter)—the name in the vernacular of a species of long, lean hog that ranges half-wild.   **1910** *Ft. Worth Star–Telegram* (TX) 10 Apr 22/2, East Texas is awakening to the importance of the hog as a money maker, and the pure-blooded kind is fast displacing the "razorback" and "wind-splitter."   **1942** Kennedy *Palmetto Country* 237 **FL** (as of 1870s), The razorback, or long-nosed wind splitter . . rustles the marshes for wampee, a root similar to the arrow.   **1953** Johnston *Legendary Mizners* 269 **FL** (as of 1925), Wild hogs. . . have been running wild since the old Spanish days. . . They are locally called "wind-splitters" and "the Devil's right bowers," because of their speed and savageness.   **1969** Wall *Hist. Davie Co.* 39 **wNC,** Chickens were kept, and hogs, "razor-back" or "wind splitter" species, were raised in large numbers.

wind sucker n   Cf cribber
=**stump sucker 1;** also transf; see quots.

1845 *Amer. Agric.* 4.299, When once the habit of eating the manger is established, the horse may and often does become a confirmed crib-biter, or wind-sucker.   **1850** *New Engl. Farmer* 2.55 **OH,** How to Cure a "Wind Sucker."   **1912** Green *VA Folk-Speech* 486, *Wind-sucker.* . . A crib-biter. A horse that bites his trough and sucks wind into his lungs.   **1932** *Sun* (Baltimore MD) 10 Oct 10/6 *(Hench Coll.),* After three dismal races Trainer Hildreth claimed he was a wind sucker, and Sinclair asked Johnson to return the "100 grand."   **1939** *Hall Coll.* wNC, My daddy . . he was an awful horse trader. He had an old wind sucker.   **1940** *AmSp* 15.376 **NE,** The sleek looking gray turned out to be a 'wind-sucker,' who clamped his jaws on a wooden pole or fence and sucked in air until he bloated. When his 'wind-pressure' went down he looked like a walking skeleton.   **1952** Brown *NC Folkl.* 1.608, *Wind-sucker.* . . A lean, runty pig that is supposed to stand in a corner and suck wind; by transference, a thin weak person, generally a child.

wind sweep n   Cf breezeway, windway
=**dogtrot.**

1936 *AmSp* 11.315 **Ozarks,** *Dog run.* . . The covered porch between the two parts of a double log cabin. The term *dog trot* is also common. If the *dog run* is open at both ends, as it usually is, it is sometimes called a *wind sweep.*   **1956** *AmSp* 31.310 **swKY,** It is unfortunate that too little data has been collected to place in proper historical perspective these two terms [=*dog run, dog trot*] and also such terms as *turkey trot, wind-sweep,* and *breezeway,* all meaning the same thing.   **1975** McDonough *Garden Sass* 34 **AR,** More elaborate than these simple homes was the

dog-trot style of house, which consisted of two separate log pens with a covered breezeway between them. This was also referred to as a possum trot, turkey run, wind-sweep, or But-and-Ben style.

wind tumor n   [Cf *wind gall, wind puff* a soft swelling on a horse's leg]

A soft swelling on the body.

1870 *Med. Rec.* 4.522 **NY,** A tumor was found in the left ileo-lumbar region . . [which] was suspected to be malignant. . . He afterwards consulted a notorious homœopath, who told him it was nothing but a "wind tumor."   **1990** Cavender *Folk Med. Lexicon* 34 **sAppalachians,** *Wind tumor*—hernia in the groin area near the small bowel.

windway n   Cf wind sweep

1940 Writers' Program *Guide TX* 378 **ceTX,** Pioneer customs prevail in the "back country," where, in houses with wide, open halls called windways or dog-runs, Saturday night gatherings locally called play parties are given.

windweed   See wind root

wind witch n   Cf tumbleweed 2d

A **Russian thistle** (here: *Salsola tragus*).

[**1842** *Museum Foreign Lit. Sci. & Art* 16.388, Another description of weed that stands in very bad odour in the steppe [of Russia], has been aptly denominated wind-witch by the German colonists.]   [**1905** *Woodland Daily Democrat* (CA) 1 Aug 1/5, The Russian thistle. . . is a new weed in this state and is classed as noxious. . . In its native land it is called the "wind witch".]   **1952** *Walla Walla Union–Bulletin* (WA) 14 Sept 3/2, He explained that Russian thistle, sometimes called wind witch, tumble weed and less complimentary names, is not a true thistle.   **1970** *Reno Eve. Gaz.* (NV) 30 Nov 7/2, Russian thistle, better known here as tumbleweed or wind witch, arrived in the United States with a group of Russian immigrants in the 1870s.   **2006** Ingham *You Know TX* 93, The tumbleweed, also called a Russian thistle or wind witch, does go drifting along like a rolling skeleton across prairies and highways in west Texas.

windy n   esp West

An extravagantly exaggerated or boastful story; a tall tale, lie.

[**1901** *Dallas Morning News* (TX) 5 Apr 6/4, The Populists are not in it with the Democrats as "windies." . . Didn't the Democrats claim that if Bryan was defeated this country would become a monarchy and the fourth of July would never be celebrated again?]   **1911** *Wellington Leader* (TX) [31 Mar] 6/2 (newspaperarchive.com), We aim to give a truthful, accurate account of the things that actually exist and no boom "windies" are indulged in by the Leader.   **1925** Hunter *Trail Drivers TX* 333, "Telling a windy" means telling a boastful story.   **1933** *AmSp* 8.1.53 **Ozarks,** *Windy.* . . A tall tale, a wildly unreasonable story.   **1935** Davis *Honey* 23 **OR,** He could invent windies about his stand-in with the girls faster than a turkey could gobble grasshoppers.   **1956** Almirall *From College* 393 **CO,** Kind o' sounds like a windy to me.   **1956** Gipson *Old Yeller* 44 **TX,** He told the biggest windy I ever heard about how he'd dived 'way down into a deep hole under the rocks and dragged that fish out.   **1964** *AmSp* 39.235 **KS,** *Windy.* . . A tall story.   **1969** Emmons *Deep Rivers* 33 **eTX** [Black], Now Jack. You've told lots o' big windies, but this one's just too big.   **1974** Fink *Mountain Speech* 29 **wNC, eTN,** *Windy.* . . Look out or them fellers'll tell you a windy.   **1987** Childress *Out of the Ozarks* 124, My neighbor Dick . . began what we call a "windy."   **2003** *DARE* File **TX,** *Windy*—a tall story or untruth. My grandfather would often say "That's a windy!" when I told him something he didn't believe. He was born in Gainesville, Texas in 1892 and grew up on a farm on the outskirts of Oklahoma City.   **2005** *DARE* File seIA (as of c1970), "Windy" was the term on my father's side of the family for a fib or a tall tale. "You wouldn't be telling me a windy, now, would you?" Dad would invariably ask if I tried to convince him I had no homework to do.

wineberry n

1 also *wine raspberry:* A naturalized **raspberry B** (here: *Rubus phoenicolasius*).   **scattered, but esp NEast, PA**

1892 *S. Cultivator* 50.559 **LA,** It is strange that some old and well known Japanese fruits are again coming before the public under new and growing names, as for instance . . Rubus Phenicolasius the famous Wineberry of John Lewis Childs which was figured in the Botanical Magazine in 1877, and which was known in Holland for a generation before and cultivated simply as a curiosity . . , the fruit being devoid of any value.   **1893** Cornell Univ. Ag. Exper. Sta. *Bulletin* 51.61, Although I find no fruit with commercial value in our wineberry plants, I am nevertheless ready to believe that the species may eventually give us fruit of considerable value. **1925** *Amer. Midland Naturalist* 9.411 **NY,** *Rubus phoeniculasius* [sic]. . . Wineberry. Escaped from cultivation. **1931–33** *LANE Worksheets* **RI**56, Wineberry—type of berry, has a flat taste. **1965–70** *DARE* (Qu. I44, *What kinds of berries grow wild around here?*) Infs **NC**15, **PA**9, 26, 49, 136, 242, **RI**9, Wineberries; **CT**37, Wineberry—like raspberries, but fall apart if you pick it; **MD**50, Wineberries—sour, red, grow on prickly bush; **PA**29, Wineberries—look like a raspberry, but larger with hairs; **VA**28, Wineberries—grow in a burr, used to make jelly. **1982** Gupton–Swope *Wildflowers Tidewater VA* 19, *Wineberry—Rubus phoenicolasius*. . . The foliage, reddish purple bristles, and tart fruits, cited for preserving and eating, make this an attractive plant. It is also named Wine Raspberry. **2007** *Berkshire Eagle* (Pittsfield MA) 14 Aug (Internet), The other pretty raspberry is wineberry, a native to Japan and China that has naturalized in America.

2 =**nagoonberry. AK**

[**1889** *Overland Mth.* (2d ser) 14.262 **British Columbia Canada,** Back among the trees a thick undergrowth of wild raspberries, salmon berries, huckleberries, and wineberries, is interspersed with giant brakes.] **1898** Bailey *Sketch Native Fruits* 389, Some of the berries are utilized to a considerable extent in making wine, the wineberry of Kadiak [sic] being largely used in that way. **1949** *AK Sportsman* Apr 7, We have an abundance of wild berries—high and low bush cranberries, blueberries, wine berries and strawberries, besides the salmonberries. **1979** *Theata* 3 (1991 Tabbert) **AK,** One is wine berries that taste and look like raspberries. They are on a plant which grows along the ground. They are dark red colored and are about half the size of a marble. **1992** *NY Times* (NY) 9 Aug (Internet) **AK,** We also found a smaller, purplish relative of the raspberry, the nagoonberry or wineberry, more time-consuming and harder to pluck out of the brambles but ever so rewarding to consume with their sweet, slightly tart, taste. **2008** *DARE* File—Internet **AK,** Nagoonberry—Also called dewberry and wineberry, this dainty member of the rose family favors forest clearings with acidic soil.

3 A **gooseberry 1;** as *wine gooseberry, Ribes inerme.* [*OED2* 1703]

1923 Amer. Joint Comm. Horticult. Nomenclature *Std. Plant Names* 400, *[Ribes] inerme.* . . Wine Gooseberry. **1931** U.S. Dept. Ag. *Misc. Pub.* 101.40, *Whitestem gooseberry* . . , known also as smooth, wine, or common wild gooseberry, . . is probably as common and well known as any western gooseberry. **1938** Smithsonian Inst. Bur. Ethnology *Bulletin* 120.16, Wine gooseberry, Grossularia inermis. **1940** Clute *Amer. Plant Names* 60, *R[ibes] grossularia.* . . Garden gooseberry, wine-berry [etc]. *Ibid* 229, *Ribes vulgare.* . . wine-berry.

wine blossom See **wine weed**

wine-cup n esp **TX**
=**poppy mallow.**

1924 *Amer. Botanist* 30.108, The "fringed poppy mallow" *(Callirhoe digitata)* is also known as "wine-cup" and "wild hollyhock," both names being self-explanatory. **1934** Dormon *Wild Flowers LA* 70, *Poppy Mallow; Callirhoe* . . The showy, wine-red, poppy-like flowers have been given many local names, such as "Indian poppy." In Texas it is called "wine-cup." **1967** *DARE* Wildfl QR (Wills–Irwin) Plates 25C.1 [=*Callirhoe involucrata*], 25C.2 [=*C. leiocarpa*], 25C.3 [=*C. digitata*] Inf **TX**44, Wine-cups. **1968** *DARE* FW Addit **LA**21, *Wine-cup* = a purple cup-shaped flower the color of wine. It comes in spring and gets no more than a foot high. **2002** Proulx *That Old Ace* 66 **TX,** And Cowboy Rose is named after a flar. The wine cup. That's the other name for the cowboy rose. You couldn't have a town called "wine cup." **2004** *Rocky Mt. News* (Denver CO) 7 May sec L 3 (Internet), The plains and foothills offer a wealth of beautiful flowers that include . . wine cup (Callirhoe involucrata).

winegar See **vinegar**

wineglass elm n esp **NEng**

A **white elm** having a graceful, gradually spreading form.

1884 Howells in *Century Illustr. Mag.* 29.18 **NEng,** There aint any man enjoys a sightly bit of nature—a smooth piece of interval with half a dozen good-sized wine-glass elms in it—more than *I* do. **1893** *Hist. Hingham MA* 1.150, The White Elm *(Ulmus Americana* . .) is one of our noblest trees. . . The variety of growth in trees standing alone on wet meadows, leading to their being called "wine-glass elms," is extremely beautiful and graceful. **1913** *Aberdeen Daily News* (SD) 25 Jan 5/1 **VT,** The weathercock above the clustered barns,/ The lilac hedges, and the wineglass elm,/ And gable windows looking toward the sea. **1930** *Kokomo Tribune Kokomo Dispatch* (IN) 29 Aug 2/3, It is older than any

tree in its dooryard, save the wineglass elm that shades its front. **1937** *FWP Guide MA* 607, South of the junction with State 122, . . State 32 passes a cemetery at the edge of which . . stands a *Wineglass Elm,* so called from its shape. **1942** Hale *Prodigal Women* 123 **MA,** She took a subway to Cambridge, sometimes, and walked down Brattle Street between the wineglass elms. **1978** *UpCountry* Jan 38 **MA,** Through the dormer window I can see only the top of a wine glass elm . . and the Holyoke Range beyond.

wineguh See **vinegar**

wine plant n esp **NEast, N Cent** Cf **pie plant**
=**rhubarb B.**

1863 *Daily Palladium* (New Haven CT) 3 Feb 4/7, This Wine is manufactured by me from the Strawberry variety of the Rhubarb Wine Plant. **1865** *Pittsfield Sun* (MA) 21 Sept 2/7, Mr. H.D. Rood of Sheffield has made this season . . 45 barrels of wine from the wine plant. **1887** *Harper's New Mth. Mag.* Jan 303, There is . . rhubarb, sold in some instances under the name of "wine-plant." **1897** *Jrl. Amer. Folkl.* 10.54 **OH,** *Rheum Rhaponticum,* . . wine plant. **1917** *Grand Forks Herald* (ND) 15 Apr 9/3, Select wine plant or strawberry rhubarb and if it is young and tender, it is much richer not to be peeled. **1950** *WELS* (*Other names for rhubarb*) 5 Infs, **WI,** Wine plant. **1965–70** *DARE* (Qu. I30, *Other names for rhubarb*) Infs **IL**69, 134, **MA**6, **NJ**46, **NY**181, 233, **PA**67, 119, **VA**24, Wine plant; [**MA**15, Wine stripe]. **1966** *DARE* FW Addit **MA**6, Wine plant—rhubarb—green stuff is rhubarb. **1999** *Washington Post* (DC) 25 Feb sec T 19 (Internet), Sometimes referred to as the "wine" plant for its tart flavor, rhubarb is finding a niche in contemporary American cuisine.

wine raspberry See **wineberry 1**

wine shed n

A bar or tavern, esp one that features entertainment.

1972 *Arcadia Tribune* (CA) 28 Dec 7/2, Santa Anita Wine Shed To Have Entertainment. **1984** Weaver *TX Crude* 58, *Wine shed.* A tavern, bar, or beer joint. Any establishment other than a liquor store that sells alcoholic beverages. "He spends so much time in that wine shed, I thought maybe he was renting a barstool." **2001** *DARE* File—Internet **OK,** I've been in the beer joint business for over 30 years with 2 years in gulf shores. . . there is no wine shed in the world more fun than the bama. **2006** *Ibid* **TX,** Sure beats pickin' guitar in some wine shed somewhere. . . for tips.

wine tree n

1 =**mountain ash 1.**

1860 Curtis *Cat. Plants NC* 70, *Mountain Ash.* . . It is not rare on our higher Mountains, from Ashe to Macon, where it is called *Wine Tree,* (from a kind of liquor said to be made from it,) and *Mountain Sumach.* **1897** Sudworth *Arborescent Flora* 211 **NC,** *Pyrus americana* [=*Sorbus a.*] . . Wine Tree. **1913** Britton–Brown *Illustr. Flora* 2.287, *Sorbus americana.* . . Round- or wine-tree.

‡**2** =**butterfly weed 1.**

1971 Krochmal *Appalachia Med. Plants* 70, *Asclepias tuberosa.* . . *Common names:* . . wine tree.

wine weed n Also *wine blossom*
=**dandelion 1.**

1969–70 *DARE* (Qu. S11, . . *Dandelion*) Inf **MA**78, Wine blossom; **MO**19, Wine weed.

wing n Usu |wɪŋ|; also esp **NC** |hwɪŋ, (h)weŋ, wɛŋ| Pronc-sp *whing*
Std senses, var forms.

1893 Shands *MS Speech* 68, *Whing* [hweŋ]—Used by illiterate white immigrants from North Carolina for *wing.* **1918** *DN* 5.20 **NC,** *Whing,* a wing. **1934** in 1944 *ADD* **NC,** *Wing.* . . [wɛŋ]. **1941** *AmSp* 16.4 e**TX** [Black], Before *ng* . . [ɪ] becomes [ẽ], [eĩ] . . *wing.* **1942** Hall *Smoky Mt. Speech* 16 w**NC,** e**TN,** [ɛ] often occurs in . . *wing.* **1946** *PADS* 6.32 e**NC** (as of 1900–10), *Whing.* . . *Wing.* . . Used by a few families. **1952** Brown *NC Folkl.* 1.607, *Whing* [hwɪŋ]. . . The wing of a plow.

wing v, hence ppl adj *winged* Also with *out* [*OED2* 1669 →] **NEng**
To brush, esp using a bird's wing.

1865 (1866) Whittier *Snow-Bound* 18 **MA,** We sat the clean-winged hearth about. **1914** *DN* 4.82 **ME, nNH,** *Wing.* . . To sweep or brush. **1959** *VT Hist.* 27.167, *Wing out.* . . To cover a turkey wing with a cloth and use it to dust with. Obsolete. **1975** Gould *ME Lingo* 131, A bird plucked for Sunday dinner would yield two wing tips that made excellent household brushes on the old farms. In certain expressions *wing* is equivalent to brush: "Wing the crumbs off the table while I'm bringing the pie."

‡**wing bone** n Cf *DS* K74

c1970 Pederson *Dial. Surv. Rural GA,* 1 Inf, **seGA,** Wing bone. [Inf had not heard of a *wish bone.*]

winged See **wing** v

winged elm n

Std: an elm *(Ulmus alata)* distinguished by irregular winglike growths along the branchlets, which is native throughout the South and Midwest. Also called **cork elm 2, mountain ~ 1, red ~ 2, wahoo** n[1] **1, water elm c, witch ~ 1**

winged pigweed n [From the continuous membranous wing surrounding the fruit]

Std: a weedy plant *(Cycloloma atriplicifolium)* common in the central US from the Mississippi River to the Rockies. Also called **tumble ringwing, tumbleweed 2b**

winged sumac n Also *wing sumac* [From the wide "wings" on the midribs]

=**dwarf sumac.**

1916 *Jrl. Elisha Mitchell Scientific Soc.* 22.73, *Rhus copallina.* . . Winged Sumach. 1935 *Ecology* 16.555 **wIN,** The shining or winged sumac, is very common especially in old abandoned fields, along borders of woodlands, and along fences and roadsides. 1970 *DARE* (Qu. T13, . . *Names* . . *for* . . *sumac)* Inf **IL**119, Winged sumac. 2002 O'Connell *Stabilizing Dunes* 26 **MA,** We call it wing sumac because of the little wings, if you will, between the leaflets.

wingfish n

A **sea robin 1a** such as *Prionotus carolinus;* see quots.

1882 U.S. Fish Comm. *Bulletin for 1881* 48 **RI** (as of c1850), The first fish that usually came along would be the herring and shad, next tautog and flounders, and, in a few days, striped bass and sea-robins or wingfish. 1884 Goode *Fisheries U.S.* 1.255 **CT,** They [=*Prionotus palmipes* and *P. evolans*] have excellent food qualities, but are eaten . . only in the vicinity of Hartford, Connecticut, where they are known as "Wing-fish." 1912 *Cosmopolitan* 52.785 **NY,** He could no more have told you than I can how many tarpon, sharks, or wing-fish he had caught.

wing-footed adj esp Sth

Having feet that turn out or are otherwise misshapen; hence adv *wing-footed* with turned-out feet.

1913 *Harper's Mth. Mag.* 127.345 **nGA,** The man who was approaching walked wing-footed, reared back, with his coattails flapping behind him in the wind. 1946 *PADS* 6.33 **eNC** (as of 1900–10), *Wing-footed.* . . Slue-footed. . . Common. 1966–68 *DARE* (Qu. X37, . . *Words* . . *to describe people's legs if they're noticeably bent, or uneven, or not right)* Inf **DE**2, Wing-footed—feet point out; **GA**6, Wing-footed—toes pointed outward; **MD**31, Wing-footed—toes point out; **NC**2, Wing-footed—feet turn out; (Qu. X38, *Joking names for unusually big or clumsy feet)* Inf **NC**49, Wing-footed—toes apart. [All Infs comm types 4, 5; 4 of 5 Infs gs educ or less] 1971 Evans *Tommy Johnson* 87 **MS,** Only one picture of Tommy Johnson is known to exist. . . He is remembered as being of medium height, somewhat wing-footed, and quite lean.

wingle v [*SND wingle* v. 1 "To walk unsteadily," 2 "To twist, wriggle; to meander"] esp sAppalachians

See quots.

1913 Kephart *Highlanders* 30 **sAppalachians,** All roads and trails "wiggled and wingled around" so that some families were several miles from a neighbor. *Ibid* 100, I girded myself and ran, "wiggling and wingling" along the main divide. 1917 Kephart in *DN* 4.419 **wNC,** *Wingle.* . . To wind in and out. "Kinder wingle around." 1994 in 2004 Montgomery–Hall *Dict. Smoky Mt. Engl.* 652 **wTN,** *Wingle* . . To wind and twist, meander. [1 inf; "unknown to other consultants"]

wing out See **wing** v

wingscale n [See quot 1941]

A **saltbush 1** (here: *Atriplex canescens*).

1923 Hall–Clements *Phylogenetic Taxonomy* 19, Wingscale for *A[triplex] canescens,* lenscale for *A. lentiformis,* allscale for *A. polycarpa.* 1941 Jaeger *Wildflowers* 53 **Desert SW,** *Wingscale.* . . *Atriplex canes-*

cens. . . The fruiting bracts have conspicuous wings arising from the middle of the exposed face of the seed and from this the English name "wingscale" is derived. . . Alkaline and sandy soils from western Tex. to the Colorado and southern Mohave deserts. 1976 Elmore *Shrubs & Trees SW* 37, Wingscale . . *Atriplex canescens.* 2006 Lindsay–Lindsay *Anza-Borrego Desert* 290 **sCA,** *[Genus/species].* . . *Atriplex canescens.* . . *[Common Name].* . . Wingscale.

wingseed n [See quot 1875]

A **hop tree** (here: *Ptelea trifoliata*).

1830 Rafinesque *Med. Flora* 2.254, *Ptelea.* . . Wingseed, . . 3 sp. 1875 Hale *Materia Medica* 1.526, *Ptelea trifoliata.* . . This plant is also known as *Wingseed, Shrubby trefoil,* and *Swamp Dogwood.* . . fruit a two-celled samara, nearly an inch in diameter, winged all around, nearly orbicular. It is common to this country, growing mostly west of the Alleghanies. 1897 Britton–Brown *Illustr. Flora* 2.354, *Ptelea trifoliata.* . . Three-leaved Hop-tree. Shrubby Trefoil. . . Called also Wafer-ash, Swamp-Dogwood, Wingseed. 1960 Vines *Trees SW* 593, *Ptelea.* . . *trifoliata.* . . Vernacular names are . . Pickaway-anise . . and Wingseed. All parts of the plant emit a disagreeable odor.

wingstem n [See quot 2007]

A **crownbeard,** usu *Verbesina alternifolia.*

1892 *Science* 19.356, Wing-Stem, *Actinomeris alternifolia* [=*Verbesina a.*] 1894 *Jrl. Amer. Folkl.* 7.90 **WV,** *Actinomeris squarrosa* [= *Verbesina alternifolia*], . . wing-stem. 1968 Barkley *Plants KS* 363, Verbesina alternifolia. . . Wingstem. Lowland woods and thickets. 2007 *Pittsburgh Tribune-Rev.* (PA) 19 Aug (Internet), Wingstem has disk flowers that also are yellow. . . The common name comes from the stems of the plant. Up and down the tall stalk are distinctive paper-thin "wings."

wing sumac See **winged sumac**

wing-wong for a duck's bridle n Also *wing-wong for a mustard mill* [Cf *EDD* whim-wham 9] Cf **whim-wham for a goose('s) bridle**

See quot.

1967–69 *DARE* (Qu. NN12b, *Things that people say to put off a child when he asks, "What are you making?")* Inf **NH**18, Wing-wong for a duck's bridle [FW: Old-fashioned—Inf heard from a Maine farmer in answer to "What are you planting?"]; **OR**15, Wing-wong for a mustard mill.

wink n Also *(bloody) winkum, snap and wink 'em, wink 'em (slyly), wink on the sly;* for addit varr see quots Also called **squint-eye 3**

A game of changing places; see quots.

1858 Sikes *Book Fireside* 56 **wNY,** Mrs. Bradley (fat old soul!) toddled around after friend Bower in *"Wink 'em slily,"* . . ; while Bower . . pulled the circle hither and thither in his frantic efforts to elude the dame. 1873 Holley *My Opinions* 47 **NY,** I should love to see you and Deecon Gowdey or old Bobbet, playin' wink 'em slyly. 1886 Heverly *Hist. Towandas* 228 **PA,** The affair [=a spinning bee] generally wound up in the evening by a dance, or with "snap-and-wink-em" and other games. 1901 *DN* 2.150 **nNY,** Wink 'em. . . A parlor game. 1909 (1923) Bancroft *Games* 207, Wink. . . [C]hairs are placed in a circle to allow one chair to each two players and one for the odd player. . . A player sits in each chair . . facing inward. Behind each chair stands a second player, who acts as guard. There should be one empty chair with a guard behind it. This odd player winks at some one sitting in the circle, who at once tries to slip out of his chair without being tagged by his guard and take his place in the empty chair. . . The object of the guards should be to avoid being the keeper of an empty chair, and therefore the one who has to wink. 1922 La Porte *Hdbk. Games* 15, Where "Clap In, Clap Out" and "Winkum" continue to hold sovereign sway, it is not surprising that young folks go to the dance hall rather than the church social. 1932 Farrell *Young Lonigan* 92 **Chicago IL** (as of 1916), Everybody wondered what they would do. Lucy set them at ease, by boldly suggesting wink. 1938 FWP *Guide IA* 123, Forty years ago the young people entertained themselves indoors with parlor games—post office, wink-on-the-sly, and spin the platter. 1965–70 *DARE* (Qu. EE1, . . *Games* . . *children play* . . *in which they form a ring, and either sing or recite a rhyme)* Inf **NY**75, Wink 'em—one empty seat, a ring of chairs with people standing behind them; when you winked at somebody they sat in your chair; (Qu. EE2, *Games that have one extra player—when a signal is given, the players change places, and the extra one tries to get a place)* Infs **CA**8, **MN**16, **WA**22, **WI**18, Wink 'em; **OR**6, Wink 'em—

you wink at someone and he changes chairs with you; **FL**18, **MI**2, Wink; **CT**5, Wink—played in high school—girls in chairs—boy behind each—one boy has empty chair—he winks at a girl who must get to his chair without being grabbed by boy behind her. Success—a kiss; **OK**31, Wink—form a circle, girls in chair, boys standing behind. One boy does not have a girl in chair before him. When he winks at a girl, she tries to get to his chair before boy behind can touch her on head; (Qu. EE33, . . *Outdoor games . . that children play*) Inf **VA**26, Wink; **VT**5, Wink 'em—child sits in a chair, another stands behind him (several pairs are in a row); another child stands before the row and winks at certain seated children; the child standing tries to hold the seated child down; **TX**79, Wink 'em—one stands in center of room and tries to catch someone winking; if he does, he changes places with the winker. **1966** *DARE* Tape **AL**3, [FW:] How do you play wink? . . [Aux Inf:] They're seated in a circle, and the boys are behind the girls' chairs. And . . one boy over here 'll wink at . . what girl he wants, and that boy that the girl is sittin' in his chair tries to keep her. If he doesn't . . hold her back, she gets away from him. . . This boy that has the empty chair has to wink at . . whatever girl he wants. **c2004** in 2009 *DARE* File—Internet, *Wink!* . . I have only ever heard of this game as played by Quakers. Quakers in Britain, where they call it "Screwdriver"; New England and Maryland, where they call it "Bloody Winkum"; Pennsylvania. . . [H]ave them all choose a partner, except for one person, and have them decide upon who sits in the front and who sits in the back. . . The person left over . . is known as the "Winker". . . The Winker then chooses three sets of partners. . . The front partners in these three sets must try to get to the Winker and kiss them. . . The back partners must try to stop the front partners from doing this. When the Winker is finally kissed, the kisser becomes his/her partner, and the kisser's old partner becomes the new Winker. . . [Comment:] Wink is also quite popular at my Jewish camp in rural PA! . . [Comment:] I'm a Unitarian Universalist kid, and i just wanted to let you know that my [sic] and my friends . . have been playing wink since forever. **2009** *Ibid* **WA**, Current Age: 18—Current Residence: Seattle, WA— . . Favourite game: Bloody Wink'em.

winker n

1 =**eyewink(er)**. [Orig nEngl, Scots dial; cf *EDD winker sb.* 1]

1845 Thompson *Pineville* 57 **cGA**, Feeling for their eye-brows and winkers in the dark. **1899** (1912) Green *VA Folk-Speech* 486, *Winker. . .* An eyelash. **1951** Morgan *Skid Road* 124 **WA**, With powdered wigs, with faces rouged and powdered, eyebrows with winkers smutted up and blackened, there stood the female contingency.

‡2 See quot.

1950 *WELS Suppl.*, Winkers—Granules in the corners of eyes.

winkle-hawk n Also *winkle-haw*; prob by folk-etym *(w)rinkle-hawk*, and by rhotacism *rinkerhawk* [Du *winkelhaak* a carpenter's square, a right-angled tear in clothing] **chiefly Hudson River Valley** See Map *old-fash*

A three-cornered tear in cloth; a rip or cut.

1848 Bartlett *Americanisms* 386 **NY**, Winkle-hawk. (Dutch *winkelhaak*.) A rent in the shape of the letter L, frequently made in cloth. . . A New York term. **1872** *Galaxy* 13.460 **ceNY**, You ain't afeared to come to me when you hev a wrinkle hawk in your trousers. **1895** *DN* 1.383 **NJ**, *Winklehawk*: triangular tear in cloth. [**1896** *Forest & Stream* 47.25 **ceNY**, Reuben's humor was manifested in the use of strange words which he probably manufactured, as I never heard them from any other person. A bad knot in a fish line was a "wrinkle-hawk."] **1950** Hench *Coll.* **NJ**, *Winklehawk*—Mrs. Rose, who uses this word to mean a right-angle tear in cloth, grew up in Middlebush, near New Brunswick, N.J. Her husband tells me that Middlebush is an island of Dutch people. **1950** *WELS* (*A three-cornered tear in a piece of clothing from catching it on something sharp*) 1 Inf, **swWI**, Wrinkle-hawk. **1951** *NY Folkl. Qrly.* 7.183 **NY**, Winklehawk, rinklehawk, for a tear in one's clothes. **1957** *Sat. Eve. Post Letters* **Staten Is. NY**, Rinkerhawk, meaning an angled, or three-cornered tear. As children, running wild over our 15 acres in Tottenville, we often got rinkerhawks in our clothes. **1965–70** *DARE* (Qu. W27, . . *A three-cornered tear in a piece of clothing from catching it on something sharp*) 12 Infs, **chiefly NY**, Winkle-hawk; **MS**37, Winkle-hawk—this is learned; **NY**52, Winkle-haw—you might say it for a regular rip, too, but it would be especially fitting for the three-cornered tear; **NY**83, Wrinkle-hawk. [13 Infs old] **1968** *DARE* FW Addit **NY**71, He couldn't use that blade without cuttin' a winkle-haw in his cheek. **1983** *Lutz Coll.* **neNJ** (as of 1910–25), When I was a child . . the usual word among schoolmates for a three-cornered tear, such as one made by

a nail catching one's coat, was winklehawk. **1990** *DARE* File **ceNY**, I once described to a puzzled friend the corner cut that you get in your pants while trying to climb over a barbed-wire fence as a "winklehawk." **2002** in 2009 *DARE* File—Internet **ceNY**, Does anyone know the origin and correct spelling of the term "wrinklehawk"? Elder relatives tell me it is an old word referring to a 3-corner tear in one's clothing. I . . have since found other unrelated seniors who also remember using the term.

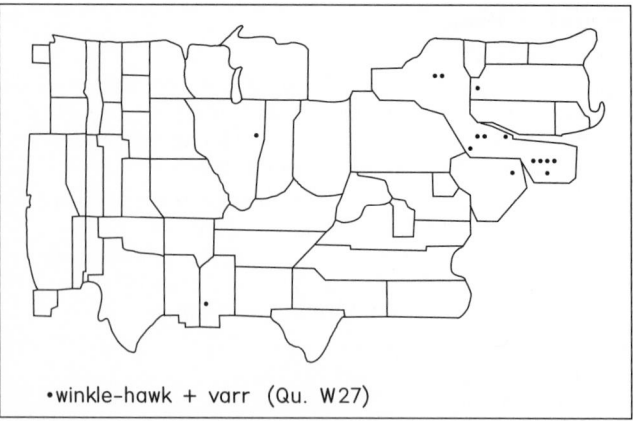

•winkle-hawk + varr (Qu. W27)

wink on the sly, winkum See **wink**

winned See **win** v **1, 2**

winner See **whinny 1**

winnering owl See **whinnering owl**

winnie See **winny**

Winnipeg goldeye n [*DCan* 1954 →]

A **goldeye**, esp when prepared by smoking.

1983 Becker *Fishes WI* 283, There seems to be general agreement . . that smoked goldeye is a gourmet delicacy. This product, whether it comes from Canada or the border states, is known as "Winnipeg goldeye," and since 1930 the demand has regularly exceeded the supply. **1983** *NY Times* (NY) 23 Jan sec A 49 (Internet), Handwritten cards at each plate set forth the menu, beginning with smoked Winnipeg goldeye. . . The goldeye, he explained, is an increasingly rare Canadian whitefish, and for this dish it had been put into a brine and smoked with oak chips.

winnow See **whinny 2**

winny n Also sp *winnie* **esp Sth**

=**wiener**.

1896 *Chicago Tribune* (IL) 24 Nov 12/1, For a week longer he served at his usual business, which was that of peddling "winnies," mostly among the saloons. **1917** *Ft. Wayne Jrl.–Gaz.* (IN) 4 Apr 3/7, Refreshments consisted of candy, buns, winnies, beans, pickles and toasted marshmallows. **1929** Wolfe *Look Homeward* 333 **NC**, Mr. Eugene Gant was the host last night at a hot winnie roast. **1935** *Morning News* (Florence SC) 3 Aug 3/1, Small or Big Winnies, lb—20c. **1945** Saxon *Gumbo Ya-Ya* 449 **LA**, In New Orleans 'weiner wurst' has become 'winny wish' among children. **1967** *DARE* (Qu. H40, *A small sausage that is put into a long roll or bun to make a sandwich*) Inf **NC**48, Winny. **2007** *DARE* File—Internet **NC**, We are ganna be eaten beans and winnies after we move in!

wint See **win** v **1**

winter bed onion See **winter onion**

winterberry n

1 Std: any of several **hollies** n[1] **1** with persistent, usu red, berries, esp *Ilex verticillata* and *I. laevigata;* also the fruit of such a plant. For other names of these see **black alder 2, dogberry h, false alder, feverbush 2, hoopwood 2b, inkberry 1, Michigan holly, pigeonberry 9, possum haw 2, swamp holly 1, white alder 2**

2 also *creeping winterberry*: A **wintergreen 2** (here: *Gaultheria procumbens*).

[**1898** *Jrl. Amer. Folkl.* 11.273 **eCanada**, Gaultheria procumbens, . . winter berry.] **1933** Small *Manual SE Flora* 1006, G[aultheria] pro-

cumbens. . . Winter-berry. Teaberry.   **1979** Erichsen-Brown *Med. N. Amer. Plants* 309, *Gaultheria procumbens.* . . *Common names.* Tea berry, winterberry, partridge berry, mountain tea.   **2007** *DARE* File— Internet **ME,** Creeping Winterberry (Gaultheria procumbens)—3–5″ groundcover, full sun to shade.

winter bird n

1 See **winter snipe.**
2 See **winter gull c.**
3 See **winter rockbird.**

winter black duck n   Cf **old winter duck, winter ~ 4**

A **black duck 1** (here: *Anas rubripes*).

   1905 Townsend *Birds Essex Co. MA* 126, "Winter black duck." Abundant transient and winter visitor.   **1923** U.S. Dept. Ag. *Misc. Circular* 13.9 **MA, NC,** The red-legged black duck *(Anas rubripes rubripes).* . . is locally known as . . winter black duck.

winter cherry n

1 **=ground-cherry,** esp *Physalis alkekengi.* [*OED2* 1548 →]

   1793 *Amer. Philos. Soc. Trans.* 3.164 **PA,** Physalis, Winter-cherry.   **1817** *Natl. Reg.* 3.316 **neOH,** Among the numerous plants are the . . Winter cherry—Physalis.   **1822** Eaton *Botany* 390, [*Physalis*] *alkekengi* (common winter cherry . .).   **1860** *Sun* (Baltimore MD) 30 Oct 1/5, One tumbler preserved winter cherry—by Mrs. C.V. Tarman.   **1878** *Richwood Gaz.* (OH) 23 May [4]/4 (newspaperarchive.com), Winter Cherry. . . The fruit is the size of a small cherry, half an inch or more in diameter, bright yellow and inclined to transparency when well ripened. . . [S]tewed, . . or canned or preserved . . , this Physalis is well worth the little trouble required in its cultivation. Alkekenzi is really a distinct species that bears scarlet berries, and ought not to be applied as a familiar name for the species of which we have written, which is Peruviana.   **1933** *Amer. Pharmaceutical Assoc. Yr. Book* 22.247, The pigments . . at various stages of ripening were identified and estimated in *Physalis* (the winter cherry).   **1972** *Names SC* 19.30, *Red Flowered Jap Lantern* (Saluda County), Chinese Lantern or Winter Cherry, *Physalis.*

2 **=balloon vine.** [*OED2* 1597 →]

   1892 *Chambers's Encycl.* 10.689, Winter-cherry. . . The name is given too in the United States to the *Cardiospermum halicacabum,* also called Balloon Vine.   **1913** Britton–Brown *Illustr. Flora* 2.501, Heart-pea. Winter-cherry. Puff-ball.

winter chickweed   See **winterweed**

winter chippy n   Also *winter chipbird*   **chiefly NEast, Gt Lakes**   Cf **chipping sparrow**

Usu **=tree sparrow 1,** rarely another sparrow such as **Harris's sparrow;** see quots.

   1884 Coues *Key to N. Amer. Birds* 379, *S[pizella] monticola* [=*S. arborea*]. . . *Tree Sparrow. Winter Chip-bird.* . . Abundant in the U.S. in winter.   **1889** Ridgway *Ornith. IL* 1.271, *Spizella monticola.* . . Canadian Sparrow; Winter Chippy. . . This pretty little sparrow is one of our most common and familiar winter residents, occurring everywhere throughout the State.   **1922** *Auk* 39.263 **MA,** *Spizella monticola monticola.* . . I am well acquainted with the "winter chippy," a dozen or two of whom spend part of each winter in our garden or vicinity.   **1951** *AmSp* 26.274, Winter chipbird—Canadian sparrow—Mass., Ontario, Ohio, Ky., Wis., Minn. *Ibid,* Winter chippy—Canadian sparrow—Maine, Mass., N.Y., Pa., N.J., Md., Ontario, Mich. Ill., Minn.[;] Harris's sparrow—Kans.   **1962** *Winona Sun. News* (MN) 14 Jan mag sec 2/1, In one day they counted 1,100 sparrows—but no winter chippies (you'll recognize one by his rust-colored cap and spot on the breast that looks like a stick pin).   **1966** *DARE* (Qu. Q21, . . *Kinds of sparrows*) Inf **NH5,** Winter chippy.   **1991** *Star Tribune* (Minneapolis MN) 15 Jan sec E 3 (Internet), The tree sparrow is nicknamed the "winter chippy" and looks remarkably like the familiar chipping sparrow of our summers.   **2006** *Mt. Desert Islander* (Ellsworth ME) 3 Nov (Internet), I believe the birds being seen are Tree Sparrows on migration. Some people also call them "Winter Chippies."

winter clover n   **=partridgeberry 1.**

   1837 *S. Botanic Jrl.* 1.192, *Gaultheria procumbens* [*DARE* Ed: Error for *Mitchella repens*]. This is the *Partridge Berry*—called also squaw vine, winter clover, one berry. . . The leaves are small, round and green, resembling clover and [it] bears one red berry in a place.   **1846** Sage *Scenes Rocky Mts.* 232, The larb-berry. . . grows upon a small ground-vine of evergreen, with a leaf assimilating the winter-clover in shape, and is found only in mountainous regions.

winter cress n   [*OED2* 1548 →]   **esp N and C Atl**

Any of var cresses of the genus *Barbarea,* esp *B. vulgaris.* Also called **cress.** For other names of var spp see **dry-land cress, poor man's cabbage, scurvy grass 2, upland cress**

   1810 *Independent Amer.* (Georgetown DC) 1 Mar 1/3, The Subscriber informs the inhabitants of Georgetown and the City of Washington, he has . . an assortment of Seeds of the following kind: Early Charleston Peas, . . Windsor Beans, . . Winter Cress, Borecole [etc].   **1819** *Boston Intelligencer & Eve. Gaz.* (MA) 24 July 1/3, *Winter Cresses.*—The winter cress is sown and treated, as the corn sallad.   **1852** *Semi-Weekly Eagle* (Brattleboro VT) 29 Apr 2/6, *Catalogue of Native Plants in Brattleboro.* . . Barbarea vulgaris. *Winter Cress.*   **1896** *Eve. Bulletin* (Decatur IL) 7 Dec [5]/7 (newspaperarchive.com) **NY,** "Winter cress," or Barbarea proecox, which is cultivated from this city [=New York] southward and is sold in large quantities in the Washington [DC] markets, is planted in late summer or early fall and needs very little cultivation.   **1922** *Lexington Herald* (KY) 8 May [9]/1, A supposedly new weed, said to resemble wild mustard . . , probably is . . either the common Barbarea vulgaris or Barbarea verna, both of which are common weeds in Kentucky. . . Both are known by the common name of winter cress.   **1936** *Sun* (Baltimore MD) 16 Mar 7/4 **MD,** The "winter cress" is a native uncultivated weed. The women and children gather it from the fields while the farmer father visits his muskrat traps on the marshes.   **1968–69** *DARE* (Qu. I28a, . . *Kinds of things . . you call 'greens'* . . *[Those that are eaten raw]*) Inf **MD**37, Winter crease; **PA**163, Winter cress; (Qu. I28b, *Kinds of greens that are cooked*) Inf **DE**1, Winter cress; **DE**3, Winter cress or wild mustard; [**MD**39, Winter cress—local name for watercress;] (Qu. S21, . . *Weeds . . that are a trouble in gardens and fields*) Inf **PA**191, Winter cress.   **1980** *Tyrone Daily Herald* (PA) 30 Apr 3/1, April is the time for wild greens, first the winter cress, which the family hurries to harvest before the shiny, dark leaves become bitter.   **2005** Irvin *Seasons Heart* 96 **Upper MW,** And I found Winter cress and Shepherd's Purse and even some berries to make rosehip tea.

winter duck n

1 **=pintail 1.** [*OED2* 1804 →]

   1834 Nuttall *Manual Ornith.* 2.386, *Pintail,* or *winter duck.*   **1849** Herbert *Frank Forester's Field Sports* 1.128, Pintail duck. . . The Winter Duck, Sprigtail, Pigeontail, vulgo.   **1867** De Voe *Market Asst.* 154, *Pintail duck, winter duck, sprig-tail duck.*—This duck is found more plentifully at the West than here [=NY], although we have them some seasons in large numbers in the fall months, and scattering in the first winter months.   **1951** *AmSp* 26.274, Winter duck—Pintail—Mass., N.Y.[;] Common goldeneye—Ontario, Mich., Wis., Iowa[;] Old squaw—Mich., Ill., Alaska.

2 **=old-squaw.** [From the scientific name *hyemalis* of winter]   **esp Gt Lakes**

   1888 Trumbull *Names of Birds* 89 **Gt Lakes,** To some at Lake St. Clair and Chicago this is the *Winter-duck . .* , while others at Chicago are more familiar with the New England title Old Squaw.   **1912** Barrows *MI Bird Life* 102, *Old-squaw. Harelda hyemalis.* . . Cockawee, Squealing Duck, Winter Duck. . . This duck is by no means uncommon during cold weather on the Great Lakes. . . The fact that it winters regularly wherever open water can be found has given it the name of Winter Duck.   **1951** [see **1** above].

3 **=goldeneye 1.**

   1925 (1986) Phillips *Nat. Hist. Ducks* 3.298, *Golden-eye.* . . *Vernacular names.* . . Whistler, Whistle-wing, . . Winter Duck [etc].   **1951** [see **1** above].

4 A **black duck 1** (here: *Anas rubripes*).   Cf **old winter duck, winter black ~**

   1955 MA Audubon Soc. *Bulletin* 39.314 **MA,** *Black duck.* . . Winter Duck.

5 **=bufflehead 2.**

   1955 MA Audubon Soc. *Bulletin* 39.316, *Buffle-head.* . . Winter Duck.

6 **=greater scaup.**

   1982 Elman *Hunter's Field Guide* 206, Greater Scaup . . Common & regional names. . . winter duck.

winter falcon   See **winter hawk**

winter fat n

A shrubby forage plant *(Krascheninnikovia lanata)* native to the western US.   Also called **sweet sage 2**

1874 *U.S. Geol. & Geogr. Surv. Misc. Pub.* 4.118 **CO,** Known both as "White Sage" and "Winter Fat." **1898** *Racine Jrl.* (WI) 29 Dec 11/5 **West,** There is a great variety of plants called "sage" on the range, which form an important part of the annual supply of stock food—as, for example, the bitter sages or "sagebrush," the green sages or "rabbit brush," salt sage, sweet sage or winter fat. **1913** (1979) Barnes *Western Grazing* 57, The forage is greatly augmented by the great sage family, especially the sweet sage or "winter fat" *(Eurotia lanata),* which furnishes an unequaled feed for stock, especially sheep and horses. **1938** Amer. Forestry Assoc. *Conserv. Digest* 4.20, Sage, bitter weeds and Russian thistles were plentiful, but where was the grass, the "winter-fat", the salt brush? **1961** *Billings Gaz.* (MT) 5 Nov 7/1, Quantities of edible shrubs, such as winter fat and salt bush, would approach minimum protein requirements now, but provide far too little phosphorus and vitamin A is definitely lacking. **2007** *Albuquerque Jrl.* (NM) 8 Dec sec B 1 (Internet), Rejuvenation pruning is recommended for shrubs such as Russian sage, chamisa, native sage, four-wing saltbush and winterfat.

winter flounder n

Std: a common **flounder B** (here: *Pseudopleuronectes americanus*) native to Atlantic coastal waters.   Also called **blackback flounder, flatfish 2, gray sole, lemon ~ 2, mud dab 1, niggerfish 2**

winter gannet n

A **gannet 1** (here: *Morus bassanus*).

1917 *Wilson Bulletin* 29.2.76 **eVA,** *Sula bassana* [=*Morus b.*].—Winter gannet.

winter goose n

1 =**Hutchins's goose.** *obs* Note: This bird is now regarded as a subsp of the cackling goose *(Branta hutchinsii).*

1835 Audubon *Ornith. Biog.* 3.526 **ME,** I had occasion to allude to a small species called by the gunners of Maine the Winter or Flight Goose. **1839** MA Zool. & Bot. Surv. *Fishes Reptiles* 385, Hutchins' Goose, *Anser Hutchinsii.* . . They [=gunners on the coast] call it the Flight, or Winter Goose. It resembles the common wild goose, except that it is less in size.

2 =**purple sandpiper.**

1923 U.S. Dept. Ag. *Misc. Circular* 13.53, Purple-back . . ; wintergeese (Mass.); winter rock-bird. . . All these names . . apply to the . . common purple sandpiper.

winter grape n

1 A **frost grape** (here: *Vitis vulpina*).

1692 in 1970 Ewan–Ewan *John Banister VA* 253, Fox grapes Black & White, and many other Kinds sweet and sowre, or as we call them Summer and Winter grapes. **1769** in 1789 Amer. Philos. Soc. *Trans.* 2d ed 1.261 **NJ,** The frost or winter grape is known to every body, both the bunches and berries are small, and yield but little juice. **1804** Bartram in Willich *Domestic Encycl.* 5.291, Winter-grape, *Vitis serotina.* . . The fruit bunches branched, but the berries small and black . . : the fruit not ripe till late in the autumn, and the juice extremely sour and ill-tasted, so that even birds will not eat them till winter frosts have meliorated them. **1859** *Weekly GA Telegraph* (Macon) 22 Feb 3/3, I made some wine of the Winter Grape, the sourest of the grape tribe, without adding anything to the must or juice, and it was pretty good. **1896** *Jrl. Amer. Folkl.* 9.184 **MO,** *Vitis cordifolia,* . . winter grape. **1969** *DARE* (Qu. I46, . . *Kinds of fruits that grow wild around here*) Inf **KY50,** Winter grape—small and sour, edible after frost. **2003** in 2008 *DARE* File—Internet, At least four North American native grapes share the name "Winter Grape"—*Vitis berlandieri* [=*V. cinerea* var *helleri*], *V. bicolor* [=*V. aestivalis* var *b.*], *V. cordifolia* (properly, *V. vulpina*), and *V. cinerea*—but only *Vitis berlandieri* owns the name "Fall Grape." *V. cordifolia/vulpina* rightfully owns the "Winter Grape" name.

2 A **riverbank grape** (here: *Vitis riparia*).

1824 Elliott *Sketch* 2.688 **GA, SC,** [*Vitis*] *riparia.* . . Flowers very fragrant. . . To this species probably belongs the winter grape of our upper districts. . . It is said to surpass in flavor all of our native grapes. **1842** NY Univ. Bd. Regents *Annual Rept.* 279, Vitis. . . riparia, *Michx.* Winter Grape. Thickets. **1888** AR State Geologist *Annual Rept.* 4.244, The box elder *(Negundo aceroides),* redbud, winter grape *(Vitis riparia),* . . are abundant in these places [=prairie regions]. **1891** MN State Horti-

cult. Soc. *Annual Rept. for 1891* 161 **nMN,** *Vitis ripens* [sic], the winter grape. . . bears good clusters of small black berries with a rich foxy and very acid flavor, which is mellowed by the first autumnal frosts.

3 A **grape** (here: *Vitis cinerea*) native to much of the eastern half of the US except for New England, the Great Lakes states, and the Upper Midwest.   Also called **mountain grape 1, pigeon ~, possum ~ 1, raccoon ~ 1, sweet winter ~**

1856 *New Orleans Daily Creole* (LA) 16 Oct 3/1 **MS,** There is also another grape known as the winter grape, which is very delicious to the taste and highly flavored. These grapes are eagerly sought for by bears, which become very fat upon them. [*DARE* Ed: This quot may refer instead to another species.] **1920** *Torreya* 20.23, *Vitis berlandieri.* . . Fall or winter grape. **1938** KS Acad. Sci. *Trans.* 41.105, Vitis cinerea. . . Winter grape. **1977** *Condor* 79.192 **IL,** Poison-ivy *(Rhus radicans),* . . winter grape *(Vitis cinerea),* and hawthorn *(Crataegus mollis)* were the most prevalent woody, understory species. **2001** *DARE* File **ceOK,** The two Cherokee Indian informants from Tahlequah, Oklahoma, who told me about *possum grapes* also called them *winter grapes.* **2003** [see **1** above]. **2007** in 2008 *DARE* File—Internet **IL,** *Vitis cinerea.* . . The fruits of Winter Grape are sweet-tart when mature and edible. . . Winter Grape occurs occasionally in southern and central Illinois; it is uncommon or absent in the northern portion of the state.

4 A **summer grape.**

1898 NC Ag. Exper. Sta. *Bulletin* 150.350, *Vitis bicolor* [=*Vitis aestivalis* var *b.*] . . *Winter Grape.* . . The fruit is acid, antiscorbutic, nutritious and refrigerant. **1937** Wagner *Wine Grapes* 187, *Vitis aestivalis.* . . Summer Grape (in the south). Winter Grape (in the north). This species, valuable for wine, inhabits a considerable region. **1949** *Amer. Photography* Apr 244, The blue, or winter grape *(Vitis bicolor)* is one of our commonest species from northern New York to Michigan and North Carolina. **2003** [see **1** above].

winter grass n   Cf **Texas winter grass**

A grass that grows well in winter; applied locally to var specific usu forage grasses; see quots.

1790 *Daily Advt.* (NY NY) 6 Nov 2/3 **nNH,** As you ascend [the mountain], . . you meet with . . a sort of grass called winter grass mixed with moss. **1797** in 1916 Hawkins *Letters* 107 **NC,** We saw some fine grass in bloom, the small winter grass common on the hills in bloom. **1819** *Amer. Farmer* 1.109 **NY,** In the western parts of this state there are several native grasses worthy of attention. One kind, called the winter grass, resists the effects of frost; and when the snow leaves the ground in the spring, furnishes nourishing pasture. **1850** U.S. Patent Office *Annual Rept. for 1849: Ag.* 157 **MS,** The 'winter-grass' of this region, the nearly universal *Poa annua* . . [reaches] a height from four to eight inches. **1912** Baker *Book of Grasses* 100, White-grained Mountain Rice. Winter-grass. *Oryzopsis asperifolia.* **1945** Wodehouse *Hayfever Plants* 45, Italian ryegrass *(L[olium] multiflorum* . . *L. italicum* . . *)* also called rye grass or wintergrass, is similar in most respects to perennial ryegrass. **1967** *DARE* Tape **TX8,** 'Bout the only type of winter grass that I plant is the red rolled common ryegrass, or winter grass. **1968** *DARE* (Qu. L9a, . . *Kinds of grass . . grown for hay*) Inf **LA20,** Winter grass. **2008** *DARE* File—Internet **AZ,** When the nights start cooling down, sow winter grass (annual rye grass) if you want your lawn to stay green.

wintergreen n   Cf **flowering wintergreen**

1 Std: a plant of the genus *Pyrola,* esp *P. minor,* but also plants formerly included in *Pyrola* such as *Moneses uniflora* and *Orthilia secunda.*   [*OED2* 1548 →]   For other names of var spp see **bog wintergreen, canker lettuce, consumption weed 1, dollarleaf 1, false wintergreen 1, Indian lettuce 2, lettuce 3, liverwort 4, moosemise 2, shinleaf, snowdrop 4, waxflower 3, wild beet d, ~ lettuce 3, ~ lily of the valley 2, wood nymph**

2 Std: a plant of the genus *Gaultheria,* esp *G. procumbens.* For other names of var spp see **boxberry 1, Canadian tea, checkerberry 1, chickenberry 1, chinks 1, clink, creeping snowberry, ~ wintergreen 1, deerberry b, drunkard 2, ginger leaf 1, groundberry 1, ground holly 1, ~ ivy 2a, ~ tea, grouseberry 1, hillberry 1, Indian tea b, ivory n[2], ivory leaf, ~ plum, ivy 6, ivyberry, ivyleaf, jinks n[2], maidenhair-berry, moxie 1, mountain berry, ~ partridgeberry, ~ tea 1, oneberry 4, partridgeberry 3, pigeonberry 13, redberry d, red**

pollom, running birch, ~ tea, salal, snowberry 3, spiceberry 1, sugarberry 3, sugar plum 2, teaberry 1, wallink 4, white pollom, winterberry 2; for other names of the leaf or shoot of such a plant see **little johnny 1, pippin** Cf **chink vine, penny berry, piss-a-bed 6**

3 A **chickweed wintergreen** (here: *Trientalis borealis*).

[**1760** Lee *Intro. Botany* 320, Winter Green, with Chick-weed Flowers.] **1784** in 1785 Amer. Acad. Arts & Sci. *Memoirs* 1.437, *Trientalis. . . Trientalis foliis lanceolatis integerrimis. . . Wintergreen*. Blossoms white. Common in wood land. May. **1848** Beck *Botany U.S. North of VA* 290, *Trientalis*. . . Wintergreen. **1903** Porter *Flora PA* 244, *Trientalis Americana*. . . Star-flower chickweed. Wintergreen. **1931** Harned *Wild Flowers Alleghanies* 381, Star-flower. Chickweed. Wintergreen *(Trientalis borealis . .)*.

4 =**pipsissewa.** Cf **bitter wintergreen, false ~ 2, fragrant ~, spotted ~**

1814 Pursh *Flora Americae* 1.300, *Chimaphila maculata*. . . *C. corymbosa*. . . Both species are handsome evergreens, and known by the name of *Winter-green*. I have ventured to form a new genus of these two species of *Pyrola*, so very distinct in habit as well as character. **a1862** (1864) Thoreau *ME Woods* 280, The wintergreen *(Chimaphila umbellata)* was still in bloom here, and *Clintonia* berries were abundant and ripe. **1894** *Jrl. Amer. Folkl.* 7.93 **ME,** *Chimaphila umbellata,* . . wintergreen. **1950** Gray–Fernald *Manual of Botany* 1109, *Chimaphila*. . Pipsissewa. Wintergreen. Waxflower. **1973** Stephens *Woody Plants* 424, *Chimaphila umbellata*. . . var. *occidentalis*. . . Prince's pine, wintergreen, wax flower, pipsissewa. **2006** Mohlenbrock *This Land* 148, In dry sandy areas are stands of jack pine with an understory that may include rattlesnake plantain orchid, wintergreen, and even an occasional lady's-slipper orchid. *Ibid* 387, Wintergreen *(Chimaphila maculata)*.

5 A **periwinkle** n¹ (here: *Vinca minor*).

1879 Smith *List Medicines* 141, *Vinca minor*. . . *Vulg.,* Common periwinkle, Lesser periwinkle, Small periwinkle, Wintergreen. **1897** *Jrl. Amer. Folkl.* 10.50 **OH,** *Vinca minor,* . . wintergreen.

wintergreen chickweed See **chickweed wintergreen**

winter gull n   [*OED2* at *winter* sb.¹ 5.b 1804 for *Larus canus*] Any of several birds of the family Laridae, as:

a also *brown winter gull:* =**ring-billed gull.**

1843 Thompson *Hist. Long Is.* 2.267 **seNY,** Gulls, Terns, &c. . . Winter Gull, Zonorhyncus. **1844** DeKay *Zool. NY* 2.309, The common gull above described, although called the *Ring-billed Gull* in the books, has received no other popular name than *Brown Winter Gull;* although, as we have seen above, the adult has a white plumage. This would lead us to infer that the young, or at least the immature birds, are most numerous. **1857** NJ Geol. Surv. *Geol. Cape May* 145, *Larus zonorhynchus,* American Winter Gull. **1951** *AmSp* 26.274, Winter gull—Ring-billed gull—N.Y., N.J., Texas.

b also *gray winter gull:* =**herring gull.**

1844 Giraud *Birds Long Is.* 357 **seNY,** *Larus argentatus*. . . Winter dress, the head and neck all round mottled and streaked with grayish-brown. Young in winter, bill brownish-black; head and lower plumage grayish-brown. . . In this plumage it is the "Gray Winter Gull" of our gunners. **1899** Howe–Sturtevant *Birds RI* 28, *Larus argentatus smithsonianus*. . . *Sea Gull. Winter Gull.*—An abundant winter resident along the coast, and in Narragansett Bay and rivers. **1917** *Wilson Bulletin* 29.2.75 **eVA,** *Larus argentatus*. . . winter gull. **1951** *AmSp* 26.274, Winter gull—Herring gull—R.I., N.Y., Pa., N.J., Va., Wis., La., Texas. **1968–70** *DARE* (Qu. Q10, . . *Water birds and marsh birds*) Inf **MD**36, Winter gull; **VA**47, Winter gull—herring gull—here only in winter.

c also *winter bird:* The black-legged **kittiwake** (*Rissa tridactyla*).

1884 U.S. Bur. Fisheries *Rept. for 1882* 330, *Larus tridactylus* [=*Rissa t.*]. Of all the birds which visit the fishing-banks the kittiwake gull ("winter gull," "pinyole," etc. of the fishermen) is beyond question the most abundant. **1905** Townsend *Birds Essex Co. MA* 89, When one has become accustomed to the two species [=kittiwake and herring gull] they are easily distinguished. This I found to be the case when sailing off Rockport in winter, and the fishermen who have taken me out, rarely made a mistake in pointing out "Winter Gulls," as they called the Kittiwakes. **1917** *Wilson Bulletin* 29.2.75 **eVA,** *Rissa tridactyla*. . . winter gull. **1951** *AmSp* 26.274, Winter bird—Common kittiwake—George's Bank. *Ibid,* Winter gull—Common kittiwake—Northeastern Banks, Mass., Va.

d =**great black-backed gull.**

1917 *Wilson Bulletin* 29.2.75 **eVA,** *Larus Marinus*. . . winter gull.

winter hawk n   Also *winter falcon*
=**red-shouldered hawk,** esp when immature.

1811 Wilson *Amer. Ornith.* 4.73, *Winter falcon. Falco hyemalis*. . . He visits us from the north early in November, and leaves us late in March. **1831** Audubon *Ornith. Biog.* 1.364, *Falco hyemalis* [=*Buteo lineatus*]. . . The Winter Hawk is not a constant resident in the United States, but merely visits them, making its first appearance there at the approach of winter. **1837** *Boston Jrl. Nat. Hist.* 1.435, *Falco lineatus*. . . This bird has been the cause of some dispute among our naturalists, owing to its supposed identity with the winter-hawk (*Falco hyemalis* . .). **1855** in 1860 U.S. War Dept. *Rept. Explor. Railroad* 12.3.147, I have lately seen a hawk which . . has the loud scream and high-sailing habit of the winter hawk at midday. **1868** Cook *Geol. NJ* 762, *Buteo lineatus*. Red-shouldered Hawk. . . Young.—Breast and belly yellowish-white, with longitudinal bands and spots of brown. Tail brown with numerous bands of rufus white. Thus plumaged it is known as "Winter Falcon." **1897** Silloway *Sketches Birds* 259, In the east the red-shouldered hawk is commonly called the "winter hawk." **1898** (1900) Davie *Nests N. Amer. Birds* 209, *Red-shouldered hawk*. . . This large species is one of the commonest hawks in the United States, and it is especially abundant in winter, from which it receives the name of Winter Falcon.

winter huckleberry n

1 =**farkleberry.**

1877 *St. Nicholas* 4.29 **TN,** A 'possum waddled on its short legs up a winter huckleberry-tree, whose bright little berries sparkled in the sunshine like points of jet. **1901** *Dallas Morning News* (TX) 24 Feb 16/3, The timber consists of hickory, sycamore, postoak, blackjack and cottonwood, while on the mountains are pine, cedar and winter huckleberries. **1912** *Gleanings Bee Culture* 40.638 **nwGA,** Even our very fine sourwood honey gets more body by blending with honey from winter huckleberry. **1941** Walker *Lookout* 60 **TN,** Farkleberry, or winter huckleberry, is a common shrub whose . . fruit which ripens in autumn may remain on the trees throughout the winter. **1967** *DARE* (Qu. I44, *What kinds of berries grow wild around here?*) Inf **LA**12, Winter huckleberries grow on a taller tree or bush than regular huckleberry. **1972** Brown *Wildflowers LA* 133, Tree Huckleberry, Winter Huckleberry. . . A small tree with variable evergreen, usually glossy leaves. . . Fruit black, . . dry, poor flavor.

2 A **huckleberry 1** (here: *Gaylussacia dumosa*).

1967 *DARE* Wildfl QR Pl.157B [=*Gaylussacia dumosa*] Inf **AR**44, Winter huckleberry.

winter lark n   Cf **snowbird 6, snow lark**
=**horned lark.**

1853 Krider *Krider's Sporting Anecdotes* 115 **AL,** The shore or winter-lark was also more common than usual in this section of the country. They fly in flocks of from twenty to a hundred, and have a shrill, pitiful note. **1951** *AmSp* 26.274 **PA,** Winter lark—Horned lark.

winter mushroom n

A **mushroom B1** (here: *Flammulina velutipes*).

[**1896** NY State Botanist *Annual Rept.* 305, The velvet-stemmed Collybia is one of the few mushrooms that appear very late in the season. . . It has even been called a winter mushroom because it is possible to find it in prolonged mild thawing weather in winter.] [**1919** KS Acad. Sci. *Trans.* 30.176, What may well be called our winter mushroom is known scientifically as *Collybia velutipes* [=*Flammulina v.*]] **1972** Miller *Mushrooms* 91, *Flammulina velutipes* . . "Winter Mushroom." **2006** Miller *N. Amer. Mushrooms* 158, *Flammulina velutipes*. . . Also known as *Collybia velutipes* . . , the "Winter Mushroom" or "Velvet Foot" often fruits in late winter after warm spells.

winter onion n   Also *winter bed onion*   **chiefly Inland Nth, Midl**   See Map on p. 1034   Cf **green onion 1**
An **onion B,** often a **top onion.**

1784 *Providence Gaz. & Country Jrl.* (RI) 20 Mar [4]/1, Garden Seeds. . . Hyssop and Lavender, Shalots and Winter Onion. **1893** *Topeka Daily Capital* (KS) 26 Jan 10/3 **nwKS,** We want to speak a word for the old winter onion that is always ready for use from the time frost leaves the ground until they get too strong along about June. **1917** *Boston Jrl.* (MA) 27 Apr 11/4, Winter onions are grown from sets, but must be well cultivated and free from weeds. **1950** *WELS* (The kind of onions that last from year to year) 28 Infs, **WI,** Winter onions. **1965–**

70 *DARE* (Qu. I5, . . *Kind of onions that keep coming up without re-planting year after year*) 216 Infs, **chiefly Inland Nth, Midl,** Winter onions; **NY**9, Winter bed onion; (Qu. I6, *The kind of onions that come up fresh early in the year, and you eat them raw*) 37 Infs, **chiefly Inland Nth, Midl,** Winter onions. **1966** Dakin *Dial. Vocab. Ohio R. Valley* 2.367, The names *potato onion* (apparently from the cluster of new bulbs which grow around the set—several informants say *hill onion*), . . *winter onion* all clearly refer to the latter type [="spring onions"]. **1997** *Omaha World–Herald* (NE) 21 Sept sec F 2 (Internet), *Hearty Walking Onions Produce Spring Bounty.* . . Beginning in early spring, we harvest our fill of the green onions produced by these bulbs (also known as winter, tree or top onions).

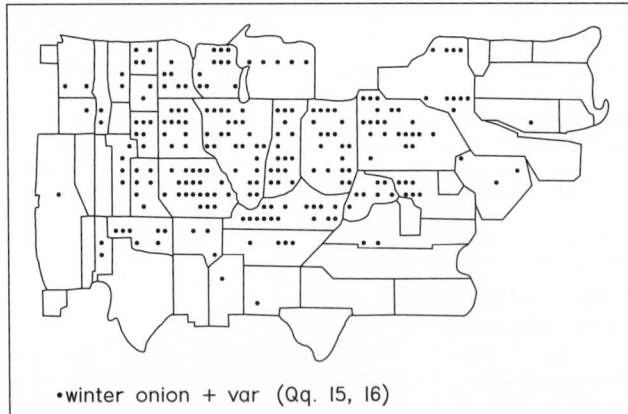

•winter onion + var (Qq. I5, I6)

winter oxeye n   Cf oxeye 1a
=red-backed sandpiper.

1897 Murdoch in *Chautauquan* 16.152, These [=dunlins] are the small sandpipers that appear on the Atlantic coast in autumn . . , when they are known as "fall snipes" or "winter ox-eyes." **1917** *Wilson Bulletin* 29.2.79 **eMA,** *Pelinda alpina sakhalina.* . . winter ox-eye, Cape Cod, Mass. (Murdoch).

winter peep n
=purple sandpiper.

1908 Knight *Birds ME* 162, Purple Sandpiper; Winter Peep; Rock Snipe; Winter Snipe. . . This species occurs along the coast in winter. **1925** (1928) Forbush *Birds MA* 1.404, *Purple Sandpiper.* . . *Other names* . . Winter snipe; winter peep.

winter pink n   Cf mountain pink 2
=arbutus.

1854 King *Amer. Eclectic Dispensatory* 447, *Epigea repens.* Trailing Arbutus. . . This plant has several names, as *Winter-pink, Gravel-weed, Mountain-pink, Ground Laurel, May-flower,* etc. **1924** *Amer. Botanist* 30.57, *Epigea repens.* . . "Winter pink" is a poetic name. **1961** *WI Archeologist* 42.122, *Trailing Arbutus (Epigaea repens)*—Known as mayflower, ground laurel, winter pink and gravel plant, this herb has astringent and tonic qualities.

winter plum n
A **persimmon B** (here: *Diospyros virginiana*).

1828 Rafinesque *Med. Flora* 1.153, *Diospyros Virginiana.* . . Persimons, . . Winter Plums [etc]. **1960** Vines *Trees SW* 838, Vernacular names [for *Diospyros virginiana*] are Jove's-fruit, Winter-plum, and Possum-wood.

winter potato n   WI   joc
A stone that is heaved to the surface of a field by freezing and thawing of the ground.

1972 WI Statist. Reporting Serv. *Report* 15 May 2, Lots of "winter potato picking" (stones). **2000** *DARE* File **neWI,** The rationale behind picking stones each spring is to save the "wear and tear" on all of the equipment and my grandma therefore called stones, "winter potatoes". **2001** Leary *So Ole Says* 252 **ceWI,** Some southern Door County farmers facetiously referred to the rocks heaved from frozen earth as "winter potatoes." **2006** in 2009 *DARE* File—Internet **WI,** Re: *Rocks!!* Here in Wisconsin most of them are winter potatoes. . . self germinating. **2008** *DARE* File **nWI** (as of c1940s), Farm people in northern WI labeled the little round stones as winter potatoes. . . One could pick up the stones from a field, [then] plant, cultivate and harvest a crop; then over winter the stones would freeze and thaw to the surface and lay across the field.

winter redbird n   Cf redbird, summer ~
=cardinal 1.

1886 *Pop. Sci. Mth.* 28.641 **NJ,** Of the cardinal-grossbeak, or winter redbird, it is said: "The redbird lies, without regret:/ However dry, it whistles 'wet!'" **1889** *Hardwicke's Science-Gossip* 25.146 **NJ,** Our lively cardinal grosbeak. . . is known as the "winter red bird," because . . [it is] more of a songster in December than in June. **1928** *Titusville Herald* (PA) 9 Feb [7]/2 (newspaperarchive.com), The strange bird mentioned by the Porkey correspondent last Tuesday was no doubt the Cardinal or Winter Redbird. **1951** *AmSp* 26.274, Winter redbird—Cardinal—Pa., N.J., N.C., Mich. **1974** *Robesonian* (Lumberton NC) 2 June sec B 11/6, This bird [=the cardinal] is sometimes called the Winter Redbird because it is most conspicuous in the winter and is the only "redbird" present at that season. **1996** *Aiken Std.* (SC) 5 May sec C 6/2, To distinguish the summer tanager from the cardinal, a year-round resident, and often called the winter redbird, the summer is a smaller, more slender bird with protruding black eyes.

winter robin n
1 =pine grosbeak.

1887 *Swiss Cross* 1.95 **cNY,** The pine-grosbeak, known often as the winter-robin, is a mischievous visitor, especially among plantations of European larch. **1956** MA Audubon Soc. *Bulletin* 40.254 **VT,** Pine Grosbeak. . . Winter Robin.

2 =varied thrush.

1917 *Wilson Bulletin* 29.2.85 **OR, wWA,** *Ixoreus naevius.*—Winter robin. **1923** Dawson *Birds CA* 2.771, The Varied Thrush is known by a variety of names, none more persistent or fitting than . . "Winter Robin." It is a Robin in size, . . color, and general make-up; and it appears in the lowlands . . only in the winter time, when the deep snows have driven it out of the hills. **1967** *DARE* (Qu. Q14, . . *Names* . . *for these birds:* . . *thrush*) Inf WA20, Winter robin. [**2001** in 2008 *DARE* File—Internet **Canada,** Most of us have seen the Varied thrush early in the year. Its nickname is the Winter Robin and it vies with the Robin for the title of being the first bird back in spring.]

winter rockbird n   Also *winter bird*
=purple sandpiper.

1888 Trumbull *Names of Birds* 182 **ME,** [Footnote:] I have heard it [= the purple sandpiper] called Winter Rock-bird at Ash Point, Me. **1951** *AmSp* 26.274 **MA,** Winter bird—Purple sandpiper.

winter rush n   Also *winter scouring rush*
A **horsetail 1** (here: *Equisetum hyemale*).

1905 Clute *Fern Allies* 24, "Winter rush" alludes to the fact that this [=*Equisetum hyemale*] is our commonest evergreen species. **1952** *Amer. Fern Jrl.* 42.144, [*Equisetum*] *prealtum* [=*E. hyemale* var *affine*] . . American Scouring-rush, . . Winter Rush, Winter Scouring-rush.

winter salmon n
1 also *silvery winter salmon:* **=rainbow trout.**

1860 U.S. War Dept. *Rept. Explor. Railroad* 12.3.316, *List of salmon and trout found in the waters of Washington Territory and Oregon.* . . *Salmo truncatus* [=*Oncorhynchus mykiss*]. . . Vernacular. . . Silvery winter salmon. **1904** *Salmon & Trout* 165, The steelhead *(Salmo gairdneri),* while in reality a trout, is popularly regarded as a salmon, and on the west coast is known as winter salmon, hardhead, salmon-trout, and square-tailed trout. **1942** *Daily Chron.* (Centralia WA) 29 Jan 1/2, Sharp-eyed firemen spotted the steelhead in China creek, and said they were spawning. . . The powerful winter salmon were not of the small variety, either.

2 Usu **chinook salmon,** but also **coho salmon** or **chum salmon;** see quots.

1863 Gibbs *Chinook Jargon* 15 **OR,** Lekye salmon, *the spotted or winter salmon (salmo canis,* Suckley [=*Oncorhynchus keta*]). **1881** *Amer. Naturalist* 15.177 **Pacific,** Vernacular names of definite application. . . Silver salmon [here: **=coho salmon**]—kisutch, winter salmon [etc]. **1882** U.S. Natl. Museum *Bulletin* 16.306, O[ncorhynchus] chouicha. . . *Chinook Salmon;* . . *Winter Salmon* [etc]. **2001** Teeny *Teeny Technique* 51, Chinook salmon . . , like migratory steel-head, are known simply as spring, summer, fall, and winter salmon, with the summer and fall runs being crossovers.

winter scouring rush   See winter rush

winter shad n
A **gizzard shad 1** (here: *Dorosoma cepedianum*).

1793 *Diary Loudon's Reg.* (NY NY) 12 Feb 3/1, A correspondent participates in the felicity of those *Philadelphians* who had it in their power, owing to the mildness of the season, to dine on an *extra* winter *Shad, the 24th January.* **1826** Royall *Sketches* 109 **VA,** Besides the cat-fish, . . they have the rock, winter shad, mackerel, and perch, shad and herring. The winter shad is very fine indeed. **1859** *DE State Reporter* (Dover) 25 Feb 1/6, Large numbers of winter shad are now caught at various places on the Potomac River. This is regarded as indicating an excellent spring fishery. **1911** *News* (Frederick MD) 26 June 8/1, Shad are sometimes called menhaden in North Carolina, and menhaden are called "hardhead shad" at Cape Ann. . . Then there are "mud shad," "gizzard shad," "winter shad," "stink shad," which are names applied to a different species [=*Dorosoma cepedianum*]. **1967** *Bridgeport Sun. Post* (CT) 18 June sec E 8/1, If you're going out just for the fun and exercise and not for a fish bag, cast for winter shad on light tackle in the Housatonic river.

winter sheldrake n

The common **merganser** *(Mergus merganser).*

1888 Trumbull *Names of Birds* 64 **ME, NH,** *American merganser.* . . At Bath and Kennebunk, Me., and Portsmouth, N.H., *Winter sheldrake.* **1955** MA Audubon Soc. *Bulletin* 39.379 **ME, MA, NH,** *American merganser.* . . Winter Sheldrake.

winter shrike n

=**northern shrike.**

[**1897** Silloway *Sketches Birds* 93, I learned by examination of the birds that our winter shrike differs in important details from the summer resident. The great northern shrike visits us only in winter, and is not known to nest in Illinois.] **1901** Eckstorm *Bird Book* 240, We have two kinds of shrikes,—the great northern, or winter shrike, and the loggerhead, or summer shrike.

winter snipe n Also *winter bird*

Either the **purple sandpiper** or the **red-backed sandpiper;** see quots.

1850 *Graham's Mag.* 37.127, In October it [=the red-backed sandpiper] is usually very fat. . . In its autumnal plumage it is generally known to fowlers as the "Winter Snipe." **1897** Crawford *Summer Days* 256, From the bed of fading grasses on the far side the winter snipe comes, and its startled "Scaip" contrasts with the wild scream of the summer snipe. **1906** *Springfield Daily Republican* (MA) 12 Sept 6/7, **seNY,** Long Island's open season. . . began this year on July 16 . . for the following birds: English snipe, jacksnipe, . . winter snipe, sandpiper [etc]. **1951** *AmSp* 26.274, Winter bird—Dunlin—Mass. *Ibid,* Winter snipe—Dunlin—Mass., R.I., N.Y., N.J., Va., N.C.[;] Purple sandpiper—New Brunswick, Nova Scotia, Maine, Mass., Conn., N.Y.

winter squash n scattered, but esp NEast, N Cent See Map Cf summer squash

Any of var, often late-maturing, edible **squashes n[1] B1** such as *Cucurbita maxima, C. mixta, C. moschata,* or *C. pepo.* For other names of var of these see **butterball squash, hubbard ~, marblehead 2, potato squash, Seminole pumpkin, sweet-potato squash, turban ~, vegetable spaghetti** Cf **hardshell squash, peanut ~**

1771 *Boston Eve.-Post* (MA) 8 Apr [4]/2, [Advt:] *To be sold by Susanna Renken at her Shop . . Boston,* . . Lavender, Sage, summer & winter Squash, Musmellon, Hemp [etc]. **1806** *CT Centinel* (Norwich) 11 Nov [4]/4, A Winter Squash, last season, we learn was taken from the garden of Asa Johnson, Esq. of Leominster, which weighed 35 pounds. **1841** *WI Enquirer* (Madison) 9 Jan 1/2, The sweet potato has not yet been cultivated [in WI]; but there is a mode of preparing the winter squash for the table, by baking it, after being cut into pieces in the same way with potatoes, which renders it undistinguishable from the best varieties of the sweet potato. **1886** *Cherokee Advocate* (Tahlequah OK) 5 Mar [1]/7 **OH,** About June I plant not less than 1,000 late cabbage and next, winter squash, Hubbard, Marblehead, etc. **1925** *Book of Rural Life* 9.5251, Winter squashes produce long vines. . . Their flesh is thicker and of richer flavor than that of the summer squashes. **1965–70** *DARE* (Qu. I23, . . *Kinds of squash*) 65 Infs, **chiefly NEast, N Cent,** Winter squash; **NJ**21, Beechnut winter squash. **1982** *Sci. News* 121.422, Fruits and vegetables high in vitamins A and C. . . include . . winter squash. **2008** *Anchorage Daily News* (AK) 20 Aug sec D 1 (Internet), Mark Rempel, who farms out by the Butte, said he's getting several kinds of winter squash: spaghetti, stripetti and a few red kuri, buttercup and sugar pumpkin.

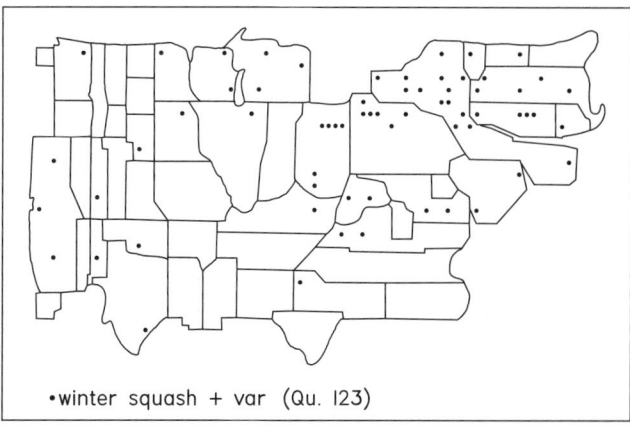

•winter squash + var (Qu. I23)

winter teal n Cf spring teal 1

=**green-winged teal.**

1888 Trumbull *Names of Birds* 28 **seNY,** *Green-winged Teal.* . . At Moriches, Long Island, *Winter Teal.* **1930** *CA Fish & Game* 16.61, To the old-time gunners, the green-wing teal was known as the winter teal, the bluewing as the summer teal. **1951** *AmSp* 26.274, Winter teal—Green-winged teal—Mass., N.Y., N.C., Ala., La., Texas. **2001** Tucci *On Waterfowl TX* 14, *Green-winged Teal* (Red-headed Teal or Winter Teal)—This is one of the earliest birds to migrate in spring.

winter turkeyback See turkeyback 1

winter waxwing n

=**Bohemian waxwing.**

[**1955** Griscom–Snyder *Birds MA* 184, Inexperienced observers at one time thought any winter Waxwing was a Bohemian.] **1956** MA Audubon Soc. *Bulletin* 40.129 **ME,** *Bohemian Waxwing.* Waxwing, Winter Waxwing. (. . The shafts of the secondary wing feathers look as if tipped with red sealing wax.)

winterweed n Also *winter chickweed*

A **chickweed 1a,** usu *Stellaria media.*

1843 (1844) Johnson *Farmer's Encycl.* 1149, *Winter chickweed.* See *Chickweed, European.* **1900** Lyons *Plant Names* 25, *A[lsine] media* . . (Stellaria media . .) . . Common Chickweed, . . Winter-weed. **1936** IL Nat. Hist. Surv. *Wildflowers* 82, *Common Chickweed.* Winterweed—*Stellaria media.* . . It is sometimes called Winterweed because it blooms nearly the whole year round. **1973** *Foxfire 2* 70, Chickweed *(Stellaria media)* . . (birdseed, . . winterweed [etc]). **2007** LaRoche *Wild Fare* 46, Another common name for it [=chickweed] is winterweed since it grows year round unless the Winter is severe.

winter wren n

Std: a widely distributed, very small wren *(Troglodytes troglodytes).* Also called **change bird, elephant ~, fiddling ~, flycatch, mouse wren**

wipe the clock (or gauge) See clean the clock

wippervill, wipperwill See whippoorwill

wire n Usu |ˈwaɪə(r), waɪr|; also esp Midl |war|; also esp sAppalachians, Delmarva |wɔr|; for addit varr see quots Pronc-spp *wa(h)r, wor* Cf **fire A, hire A, tire v, n**

Std senses, var forms.

1924 (1946) Greer-Petrie *Angeline Gits an Eyeful* 14 **csKY,** A whole passle of little bitty wors. **1928** *AmSp* 3.403 **Ozarks** (as of 1916–27), Such words as *fire, iron, wire,* and *hire* have a vowel much like the *a* in *far.* **1942** Hall *Smoky Mt. Speech* 44 **wNC, eTN,** In the speech of those who have been little exposed to classroom influences . . wire [wɔɚ]. **1949** Webber *Backwoods Teacher* 62 **Ozarks,** In the final analysis it is surely as correct to say "wahr" for "wire." **c1960** Wilson Coll. **csKY,** Wire is often /war/. **1961** Kurath–McDavid *Pronc. Engl.* 122, Three different vowel phonemes are current in *wire, tired, fire.* . . The phoneme /ai/ . . (1) has general currency in the North, in the Hudson Valley with Metropolitan New York, and in East Jersey, (2) is nearly universal in the South, except for Delmarva, and well established in the Valley of Virginia, (3) predominates decidedly in Pennsylvania east of the Susquehanna . . , and (4) is rare in the South Midland, from West Virginia to the South Carolina line, though apparently preferred by cultured speakers. In Eastern New England, Metropolitan New York, and the Upper South—

areas in which postvocalic /r/ does not occur—*wire* . . [is] disyllabic /waiə/ . . ; wherever the /r/ is preserved, these words are predominantly monosyllabic /wair/ . . , as in Western New England, Upstate New York, and Pennsylvania. In the piedmont of South Carolina and adjoining parts of Georgia, . . *wire* . . [is] often . . /wai/. . . It is important to note that in this area *wire* . . [does] not rime with *car*. . . The phoneme /ɑ/ . . occurs in *wire* . . /wɑr/ . . throughout the Midland. . . In the South Midland . . it is nearly universal. . . The dialect of the Delmarva Peninsula and southern New Jersey is unique in that . . /air, ɑr, ɔr/, as in *wire* . . , coalesce in /ɔr/. **1965** Carmony *Speech Terre Haute* 114 **sIN,** In the pronunciation of *wire,* /a/ frequently occurs in folk and common speech. **1968** *DARE* (Qu. L63) Inf **NJ50,** American steel wire [wɑr]. **2000** Shores *Tangier Is.* 176 **Chesapeake Bay,** Words typically ending in "r" or "l" . . , such as *wire* and *file,* have the "ah" sound of *father* resulting in "tar" for *tire,* . . "war" for *wire.* **2002** Proulx *That Old Ace* 87 **TX,** The freight wagon . . was supposed a drop off four spools a war every quarter mile.

wire ball n   esp sePA, MD
An urban street game in which a ball is thrown at an overhead utility wire; see quots.

   1957 *Sat. Eve. Post Letters* **Philadelphia PA** (as of 1937–47), Games I played as a child. . . Wire Ball. **1970** Lebofsky *Lexicon Philadelphia* 202, *Wireball*—game in which the object is to hit a telephone wire with a rubber ball. **1975** Ferretti *Gt. Amer. Book Sidewalk Games* 236, *Wire Ball* involves throwing a spaldeen against the triple strands of telephone wires. . . The object of the game is to throw the ball into the wires, skimming through them, so that it travels on through and is not caught by the player standing underneath the wires. **1996** in 2007 *DARE* File—Internet **New Orleans LA,** Wire ball. . . One or two guys on a team were enough. . . The batting team would throw a ball (tennis, baseball, golf) up at the electric wire. If it hit the wire it was a "Home Run", providing the other team didn't catch it in the air. In that case it was an "out". A thrown ball that didn't hit the wire became a potential "Single" if not caught in the air. . . We usually played seven to nine innings per game. . . A single would advance the "runners" one base. A "Home Run" would clear the bases. There were no doubles or triples. **1998** *DARE* File **Baltimore MD** (as of 1967), Wireball is a game that is played on the street with a tennis ball and 3 telephone wires. Two people usually play at a time. One person stands on each side of the wires. The person on offense throws the ball at the wires and if he hits the first one it is a single, the 2nd wire is a double, and the top wire is a home run. However, the hit is only recorded if the 2nd person does not catch the ball after it hits the wire. If the ball is caught, it is an out. The game is played for 9 innings. **2006** *DARE* File—Internet **Philadelphia PA** (as of 1950s), If we had a whole ball, we'd play. . . *Wire ball* which consisted of . . throwing the ball straight up, hitting the electric wires and if you didn't catch it, the amount of bounces moved the "runner" forward.

wire birch n   [*DCan* 1917 →]
=**gray birch a.**
   1950 Peattie *Nat. Hist. Trees* 168, Gray Birch—*Betula populifolia* . . *Other Names:* Poplar-leaved, Poverty, Wire or Small White Birch.

wirecrown n
=**hooded merganser.**
   1923 U.S. Dept. Ag. *Misc. Circular* 13.7 **MA,** *In local use.* . . wirecrown [for hooded merganser]. **1955** MA Audubon Soc. *Bulletin* 39.378 **MA,** Hooded Merganser. . . Wirecrown (. . In allusion to the rays of the ample crest of the male, which can be opened and closed like a fan.)

wire grama n
Either a **grama grass 1** (here: *Bouteloua eriopoda*) or a **muhly (grass)** (here: *Muhlenbergia porteri*).
   1898 U.S. Div. Agrostology *Bulletin* 14.48 **SW,** *Muhlenbergia porteri.* . . Wire grama. This grass is a native of New Mexico and Arizona, growing on the dry mesas and table-lands. It has a straggling habit of growth. **1910** AZ Ag. Exper. Sta. *Bulletin* 65.313, The principal grasses used were . . woolly foot or wire grama [etc]. **1916** U.S. Dept. Ag. *Bulletin* 367.13, The wire grama (*Bouteloua eriopoda*) also contributes considerable [sic] to the forage crop.

wire grass n   Cf **iron grass 1**
1 Any of var coarse, wiry grasses or grasslike plants.   Note: Some of these quots may refer to specific senses below.
   1775 (1962) Romans *Nat. Hist. FL* 16, The most natural grass on this soil is of a very harsh nature, and . . is known by the name of wire grass;

and they [=cattle] only eat it while young. **1869** *Amer. Naturalist* 3.233 **MA,** The Willet breeds in the sandy marshes of Nantucket and its neighboring islands, constructing a well-made nest of woven wire-grass. **1915** *Daily Herald* (Biloxi MS) 8 Jan 4/3, While fishing he met with an accident by having a piece of wire grass pierce his eye. **1930** MD Ag. Exper. Sta. *Bulletin* 323.275, *Agropyron repens,* quack grass, couch grass, is the most common wire grass in the State, especially northward. **1950** *WELS* **WI** (*The kind of wild grass that throws out strong underground roots and is hard to get rid of*) 1 Inf, Wire grass; (*Other kinds of grass that are hard to get rid of*) 6 Infs, Wire grass. **1965–70** *DARE* (Qu. S9, . . *Kinds of grass that are hard to get rid of*) 128 Infs, **widespread, but least freq NEng, NW,** Wire grass; **NC80,** Low-ground wire grass; (Qu. S8, *A common kind of wild grass that grows in fields: it spreads by sending out long underground roots, and it's hard to get rid of*) 27 Infs, **chiefly S Atl,** Wire grass; (Qu. S15, . . *Weed seeds that cling to clothing*) 24 Infs, **scattered, chiefly east of Missip R,** Wire grass; (Qu. C34, *Nicknames for nearby settlements, villages, or districts*) Inf **NC49,** Wire grass road; (Qu. L8, *Hay that grows naturally in damp places*) Infs **CO38, GA17, 72, NV2, WY4,** Wire grass; **GA77,** Wild wire grass; (Qu. L9a, . . *Kinds of grass . . grown for hay*) Infs **GA77, LA3,** Wire grass; (Qu. S21, . . *Weeds . . that are a trouble in gardens and fields*) Infs **HI2, NY10, 34, VA38,** Wire grass; (Qu. S26a, . . *Wildflowers. . . Roadside flowers*) Inf **NV8,** Wire grass. **1985** *Mt. Democrat & Placerville Times* (CA) 28 June sec B 11/6, [Advt:] *Wire grass* stock hay for sale—$2 bale. **2000** Shores *Tangier Is.* 202 **Chesapeake Bay,** For any wiry grass such as Bermuda, the Islanders still use *wire grass.*

2 Spec:
a A **bluegrass 1,** usu *Poa compressa.*   Cf **swamp wire grass**
   1751 in 1934 Eliot *Field Husbandry* 65 **CT,** The Land that you would improve this way, must be intirely free from Blue Grass, called by some *Dutch Grass, or Wire Grass.* **1793** (1888) Cutler *Life* 2.294 **neMA,** Wire-grass, which is Poa compressa. **1841** *Farmers' Reg.* 9.454 **PA,** Our blue grass *(poa compressa . .)* is often called *"wire grass"* in this district. **1892** *ID Daily Statesman* (Boise) 5 May [7]/1, Poa compressa. . . is next to worthless for lawns and has little or no value as fodder, being so hard that animals do not relish it, hence its other common name, wire grass. **1913** *Ft. Worth Star–Telegram* (TX) 19 Oct 30/2, Texas blue grass—Poa arachnifera. . . If allowed to grow too long before it is grazed . . becomes hard and wiry, and this accounts for the name of wire grass given it in some sections. **1927** *Lima News* (OH) 8 Sept 16/5, Canada bluegrass. . . is known as wire grass in northeastern Ohio, and fully deserves the name. **1976** Bailey–Bailey *Hortus Third* 889, *[Poa] compressa . .* Wire Grass.

b =**goose grass 2b,** usu *Eleusine indica.*
   1814 Pursh *Flora Americae* 1.87, E*[leusine] indica. . .* In Virginia it is known by the name of *Wire-grass,* as a weed very noxious to the cultivator. **1854** WI State Ag. Soc. *Trans.* 3.440, *Eleusine Indica. . .* Dog's-tail or wire-grass, yard-grass. Called crow's-foot at the South. **1894** *Jrl. Amer. Folkl.* 7.104 **WV,** *Eleusine Indica,* . . dog's tail-grass, wire-grass. **1907** *IA State Reg. & Farmer* (Des Moines) 18 Oct 4/2, Mr. Y. of Council Bluffs sends a specimen of wire grass, or dog's cress, (eleusine Indica,) . . It is a coarse annual. **1929** Pope *Plants HI* 25, Wire-grass—*Eleusine indica. . .* The term Wire-grass is very suitable in Hawaii as the stems become very hard and tough with age, particularly in dry weather. **1957** (1974) Spencer *All About Weeds* 52, Some people call Goose grass [here: =*Eleusine indica*] Wire grass, and others call it Yard grass. Any tough grass is likely to be called wire grass, and any grass that frequents a back yard is just as likely to be called yard grass; but so few grasses deserve these names that one can be sure, within a range of two or three grasses, what is meant when either name is used. **1967** *DARE* (Qu. S9, . . *Kinds of grass that are hard to get rid of*) Inf **IA8,** Crabgrass, wire grass, also turkey or crow's-foot—four names for same grass.

c(1) =**needlegrass 2,** esp *Aristida stricta.*
   1797 in 1916 Hawkins *Letters* 85 **GA,** The whole country was a pine barron [sic], with wiregrass and saw palmetto. **1837** *Boston Jrl. Nat. Hist.* 1.134 **NC,** *Aristida stricta. . .* Well known under the name of *wire grass.* **1841** [see **2f** below]. **1869** Porcher *Resources* 678 **Sth,** *Wire Grass,* (*Aristida,* or *Sporobolus.*) Mr. Simms writes me that bonnets are made of this grass, 1863. **1910** Torrey Bot. Club *Bulletin* 37.601 **S Atl,** *Aristida stricta. . .* After leaving Georgia I saw this very characteristic grass of dry pine-barrens (from which the "wire-grass country" of Georgia, Alabama, etc. takes its name) only between Hamlet and Plymouth, North Carolina. **1925** Assoc. Amer. Geogrs. *Annals* 15.80 **seWY,** On hillsides especially, the less valuable three-awn-grass, Aristida (locally

called "wire grass") is common. **1957** (1974) Spencer *All About Weeds* 42, *Aristida oligantha*. . . The grass has the following common names: Prairie three awn grass, . . and wire grass. The last name is the only one except needle grass that has come from the people. **1997** Manning *Orange Blossom Trails* 197 **FL**, Wire grass *(Aristida stricta)* has fine, wire-like leaves. It grows in dense tussocks. **2008** [see **2c(2)** below].

(2) freq attrib: An area (comprising parts of southern Georgia, southeast Alabama, and northwest Florida) characterized by the growth of this grass.

1832 *NY Farmer & Horticult. Repository* 1 Sept 317 **GA**, Like the goat, all it [=the sheep] requires are salt and a shelter, especially in the wire-grass region. **1845** Thompson *Pineville* 41 **GA**, Then might be seen the cadaverous looking wiregrass boy in his glory. **1874** *Atlantic Mth.* 33.543 **FL**, He was a lively little fellow, fond of a joke, and spirited as a wire-grass pony. **1890** *Current Lit.* 4.125, Down in the wiregrass, where the stately Georgia pine mingles with the spreading Florida magnolia, lies the great Okeefeenokee [sic] Swamp. **1905** *Torreya* 5.113, The wire-grass country takes its name from the wire-grass, *Aristida stricta,* which is common all over it. In a broad sense, the wire-grass country coincides with the pine-barrens, which constitute about two thirds of the coastal plains of Georgia, but for the present purposes the term is restricted to the Altamaha Grit region. **1910** [see **2c(1)** above]. **1941** Writers' Program *Guide AL* 6, Peanuts, corn, watermelons, dairying and hog raising are now the agricultural mainstays of the Wiregrass. **1951** *Panama City News–Herald* (FL) 13 May 5/4, Shown are three sample jars of roasted and salted . . peanuts, now being produced in the Wiregrass area of Northwest Florida and Southeast Alabama. **2008** in 2009 *DARE* File—Internet, True wiregrass—aristida spicata—is actually quite an attractive plant. I live in the Wiregrass region, and finding a remnant spot of longleaf pine/wiregrass is now rare—but beautiful if you can find one.

d =quack grass **1.**
[**1838** Ruffin in *Farmers' Reg.* 6.407 **VA**, [Footnote:] The "wire-grass" of lower Virginia is the "couch" or "twitch-grass" of England. [*DARE* Ed: Ruffin misidentified this grass; see quot 1841 at **2f** below.]] **1848** *Farmers' Cabinet* (Amherst NH) 24 Aug 1/4, Yet wire grass (witch grass) may be put to death by a proper course of tillage. . . It should not be buried, like common weeds, for its long pointed roots shoots [sic] through the soil very soon. **1901** Massey *Crop Growing & Feeding* 134, The farmers of this section know this [=*Cynodon dactylon*] under the name of wire grass, and in Northern Maryland it meets and mingles with the Northern quack (or couch) grass, and both go under the common name of "wire grass." **1968** *DARE* (Qu. S8, *A common kind of wild grass that grows in fields: it spreads by sending out long underground roots, and it's hard to get rid of*) Inf **MD23**, Wire grass, quack grass—same thing; **WI43**, Wire grass = quack grass.

e =dropseed **3.** chiefly **Sth, SW**
1867 Curtis *Botany* 63 **NC**, *Sporobolus* junceus. . . (Wire Grass.) **1869** [see **2c(1)** above]. **1890** FL Ag. Exper. Sta. *Bulletin* 8.10, Sporobolus junceus. . . Sporobolus Floridanus. . . Sporobolus Indicus. . . Wire grass. Dropseed grass. **1906** Rydberg *Flora CO* 29, *Sporobolus.* . . Dropseed, Poverty-grass, Wire-grass. **1981** *Paris News* (TX) 8 May 5/1, We note an increase in switch and gamma [sic] grasses, and meadow dropseed or wire grass due to the burning in 1980. **2006** White *Prairie Time* 25 **TX**, After this sedge stops blooming, Silveus's dropseed—called wire grass by pioneers—takes its place. . . Its name comes from the stout baling wire-like stalks that bear the seed heads two or three feet into the air.

f Bermuda grass *(Cynodon dactilis).*
1832 Ruffin *Essay* 162 **VA**, Some other plants less welcome than clover, are. . . blue grass, wire grass, and partridge pea. **1841** *Farmers' Reg.* 9.568 **eVA**, The grass you [=Ruffin] pointed out to me as the *"wire grass"* of lower Virginia is not the *Triticum repens* of the botanists, but the *Cynodon dactylon* of Persoon. **1876** *Galveston Daily News* (TX) 25 May [7]/3 (newspaperarchive.com), In many places you will see the Burmuda [sic] or wire grass growing green. **1895** *Biloxi Herald* (MS) 22 June [3]/2, Cynodon dactylon. . . When the corn was about four or five feet high, we began to think the wire grass would have a hard time of it. **1922** *Grand Forks Herald* (ND) 24 Sept 4/5, Bermuda grass. . . In Virginia and Maryland where it is more troublesome as a weed . . it is commonly called wire grass. **1968–70** *DARE* (Qu. S8, *A common kind of wild grass that grows in fields: it spreads by sending out long underground roots, and it's hard to get rid of*) Inf **NC81**, Wire grass—properly Bermuda grass; **VA24**, Wire grass = common Bermuda grass; **VA96**, Wire grass = Bermuda grass; (Qu. S9, . . *Kinds of grass that are*

hard to get rid of) Inf **NC87**, I think wire grass and Bermuda grass are the same thing. **2008** *Capital* (Annapolis MD) 28 Aug sec B 2 (Internet), Bermuda grass, or wire grass, is extremely hardy. You pull it, and think you've got it all, but its roots are extremely long and deep.

g A muhly (grass) (here: *Muhlenbergia schreberi*). Cf **wire grama, wirestem muhly**
1881 Phares *Farmer's Book of Grasses* 38, *M[uhlenbergia] diffusa,* Wire Grass [etc]. **1936** Winter *Plants NE* 32, *M[uhlenbergia] schreberi*. . . Wire-grass. **1957** (1974) Spencer *All About Weeds* 43, *Muhlenbergia Schreberi.* . . The long, slender stems . . help to identify the plant. These slender, wiry stems, often from two to three feet in length, recline more or less. . . The weed is also called . . Wire grass.

h =rush n[1] **B.**
1870 *Amer. Entomologist* 2.319 **MO**, The common Rush-grass *(Juncus . .*), very well characterized as "Wire-grass," and of little practical value. **1894** *Jrl. Amer. Folkl.* 7.103 **IA**, *Juncus tenuis,* . . wire-grass. **1898** U.S. Forest Serv. *Bulletin* 15.26 **OR**, Wire grass *(Juncus balticus* [=*J. arcticus* subsp *littoralis*]).—This plant, which grows in meadows, is eaten by sheep, but not with much relish. **1921** Hitchcock *Manual Farm Grasses* 140, A notable case of this kind is the so-called wire grass of the Rocky Mountain region. This is a species of rush *(Juncus balticus . .*) and not a true grass. **1961** Douglas *My Wilderness* 29 **CO**, Wire grass (wire rush). . . serves a special protective role in high basins, because its roots make a matlike layer, safeguarding the soil against erosion. **2006** Vizgirdas *Wild Plants* 241 **sCA**, Rush, Wire grass (Juncus).

i A spike rush, usu *Eleocharis palustris;* see quots.
1898 *Erythea* 9 **West**, Next in abundance is the Wire Grass, a species of Eleocharis near *E. Acicularis,* which is said to "put flesh on a beef wonderful quick," in spite of its appearing to contain little or no nutriment. **1912** KS Acad. Sci. *Trans.* 25.102, Eleocharis acicularis. . . Needle Wire-grass. . . Eleocharis tenuis. . . Slender Wire-grass. . . Eleocharis acuminata. . . Flattish Wire-grass. **1928** U.S. Dept. Ag. *Dept. Bulletin* 1151.47, The worst weeds in the California rice fields are . . scale-grass *(Leptochloa fascicularis),* locally known as ray-grass; . . spike rush *(Eleocharis palustris),* locally known as wire-grass; sedges [etc]. **1982** *Ecology* 63.482, Spike rush or wire grass *(Eleocharis macrostyla).*

j A knotweed **1** (here: *Polygonum aviculare*).
1892 *Jrl. Amer. Folkl.* 5.102 **nOH**, *Polygonum aviculare,* wire-grass. **1925** *CA Hist. Soc. Qrly.* 4.365, Wire grass—*Polygonum aviculare.* **2003** Heiser *Weeds* 182 **IN**, *Polygonum aviculare.* . . In southern Indiana the plant is sometimes called wire grass because of the wire-like nature of the stems, and one who has tried to hoe out the plants knows that the name is an appropriate one.

k A cordgrass (here: *Spartina patens*). **LA**
1928 LA Dept. of Conserv. *Bulletin* 18.338, Couch Grass *(Spartina patens* [sic] *var. juncea).* Paille fine, "Payfeen," "Hay grass," "Marsh grass," "Salt meadow grass," "Wire grass," "Needle grass" [etc]. **1947** *Jrl. Wildlife Management* 11.53 **LA**, About 80 per cent of the annual muskrat catch . . is produced on two types of brackish marsh, . . "three-cornered grass marsh" . . and cordgrass or "wiregrass" *(Spartina patens).* **1975** Walker *Coastal Resources* 92 **LA**, The marsh, dominated by couch or wire grass *(Spartina patens),* is essentially land. **2008** Hood *Rivertime* 167 **Gulf coast**, The biologist rattled off the names of the plants like an auctioneer: . . brackish water wire grass or salt meadow cord grass *(S. patens)* [etc].

l Any of var other grasses or grasslike plants, including a **bullgrass 1,** a **crabgrass 1,** a **galleta, little bluestem,** an **oat grass b, c, salt grass a(2), tumble grass 2a,** and **vine mesquite 1.**
1819 *Amer. Farmer* 1.280 **CT**, The grass. . . is known, generally among our farmers, by the name of *"tickle mouth"*—although some call it *"wire grass."* It is found on the low grounds: it grows from one foot and a half to two feet and a half high; cattle refuse to eat it. **1885** Fernald *Grasses ME* 52, *Danthonia spicata.* . . Common Names. Wild Oat-Grass, Wire Grass, . . White Top, Old Fog. **1886** Havard *Flora W. & S. TX for 1885* 529, The most common grass on bottoms and low prairies is *Hilaria mutica* [=*Pleuraphis m.*], sometimes called Wire-Grass. **1890** NE State Bd. Ag. *Annual Rept. for 1889* 155, Wire grass *(Schedonnardus texanus* [=*S. paniculatus*] . .). **1892** *Science* 19.356 **NY**, Wire-grass, *Eatonia Pennsylvanica* [=*Sphenopholis pensylvanica*]. **1896** U.S. Div. Agrostology *Bulletin* 3.68 **NM**, *Panicum obtusum.* . . Vine Mesquit. . . A stoloniferous grass. . . In New Mexico this species is called "Wire-grass." **1910** Graves *Flowering Plants* 48 **CT**, *Andropogon scoparius.* . . Broom Beard Grass. Wire Grass. Bunch Grass.

Blue-stem. **1913** *Torreya* 13.228 **SC,** *Distichlis spicata.* . . Wire grass. **1913** Britton–Brown *Illustr. Flora* 1.122, *Syntherisma filiforme.* . . *Digitaria filiformis.* . . Wire-grass. **1935** (1943) Muenscher *Weeds* 36, Paspalum distichum—Wire-grass—Texas. **1964** *Amer. Midland Naturalist* 72.167 **nwWI,** A big change . . began in 1912 with the purchase of the entire wetlands by the Crex Carpet Company. . . With the purchase the harvesting of "wire grass" *(Carex stricta)* for the manufacture of mats, rugs, and carpets began. **1968** *DARE* (Qu. S8, *A common kind of wild grass that grows in fields: it spreads by sending out long underground roots, and it's hard to get rid of*) Inf **VA**15, Johnson grass = wire grass; (Qu. S15, . . *Weed seeds that cling to clothing*) Inf **VA**15, Wire grass = Johnson grass.

wire lettuce n

A plant of the genus *Stephanomeria.* Also called **flowering straw 1, skeletonweed 4;** for other names of var spp see **desert pink, ~ straw, rock pink 3**

1936 McDougall–Baggley *Plants of Yellowstone* 136, *Wirelettuce (Stephanomeria tenuifolia)* is a smooth, perennial herb with several slender stems. . . The leaves are almost grasslike, and the heads are terminal. **1960** Kearney–Peebles *AZ Flora* 960, *Stephanomeria.* . . The names "stick-weed" and "wire-lettuce" have been applied to these plants. **2004** *Jrl. Range Management* 57.146 **CO,** Species such as pale comandra . . , wire lettuce *(Stephanomeria pauciflora . .),* and lavenderleaf primrose . . are a significant component of the little bluestem community near the bluffs.

wire moss n
=**ball moss.**

1951 *PADS* 15.28 **TX,** *Diaphoranthema recurvata.* . . Bunch, wire, or fence, moss. It grows on wires of various electric services, and on wire fences. **1961** *Kenyon Rev.* 23.238 **LA,** He rose slowly—into a beard of wire moss.

wire netting See **netting (wire)**

wire road n **Sth, S Midl**

A road along which telegraph wires or, later, telephone wires, were strung.

1862 in 1885 U.S. War Dept. *War of Rebellion* 1st ser 13.334 **Sth,** General Rains moved on to Holcomb's on the wire road. **1889** Prentis *KS Misc.* 12, The "Wire road" was in the beginning a military road . . from Springfield, Missouri, to Fort Smith. Along it was built, according to tradition, the first telegraph line west of the Mississippi river. The people past whose fields it ran. . . called the highway it followed the "Wire road." **1905** *DN* 3.100 **nwAR,** J.J. Hutcherson is hauling lumber to build a residence on the east bank of Horsehead on the wire-road. **1939** in Lib. of Congress *Amer. Memory: WPA Life Hist.* (Internet) **GA** (as of c1875), The traveling wasn't bad from Georgia. We come by way of the "wire road." . . [T]he road followed the telegraph line. **1952** Brown *NC Folkl.* 1.608, *Wire road.* . . A road along which telephone or telegraph wires are strung. **1969** Wilson *Stars* 7 **Ozarks,** The Ozarks began acquiring their first interstate, in time transcontinental, stage-coach lines, and presently a first bold show of telegraph lines along the "wire roads." [**1986** Pederson *LAGS Concordance,* 1 inf, **ceAR,** Wire road—a path in a field [*DARE* Ed: Perh what was once a wire road].] **1995** Brophy *Coll.* 83 **swMO** (as of c1960), Wire Road, the. [A] road following a telegraph line; especially the stagecoach road from St. Louis to Rolla (the railroad), Springfield, Carthage, and Ft. Smith, Ark., in the Civil War period.

wirestem muhly n **Cf wire grass 2g**

A **muhly (grass)** (here: either *Muhlenbergia frondosa* or *M. mexicana*).

1935 Hitchcock *Manual Grasses* 373, *Muhlenbergia mexicana.* . . Wirestem muhly. **1947** *Amer. Midland Naturalist* 38.30 **MD,** *Muhlenbergia frondosa* (Wirestem Muhly). . . bottomland forest and fallow field. **1968** Barkley *Plants KS* 52, Muhlenbergia frondosa. . . Satin Grass, Wirestem Muhly. *Ibid,* Muhlenbergia mexicana. . . Bearded Wirestem Muhly. **2001** *WI State Jrl.* (Madison) 17 Jan sec B 3 (Internet), A UW-Madison agronomist . . said weeds like comfrey, wirestem muhly, henbit and dogbane are likely to invade fields and cause trouble this planting season.

wiretail n [See quot 1918] **West**
=**ruddy duck.**

1909 *Forest & Stream* 73.936 **swCA,** On one of our ponds . . is a sort of convention hall for wiretails, as the ruddies are commonly known on [sic] the clubs. **1912** *Western Field* 18.130, Ruddy duck. . . Better op-

portunity to judge of the work of gun and ammunition than this wiretail drive seldom presents itself. **1918** Grinnell et al. *Game Birds CA* 205, *Ruddy Duck.* . . Other Names—Wiretail. . . short, exposed, "wire-like" tail, carried almost perpendicularly to back. **1928** Bailey *Birds NM* 144, Few birds are more worth watching than the individual Ruddy, or Wiretail, especially during his days of courtship.

wireweed n

1 A **tea weed 2;** see quots.

1916 *Torreya* 16.239 **SC,** *Sida spinosa.* . . Wire-weed, Waccamaw Plantation, S.C. **1967** *DARE* (Qu. S21, . . *Weeds . . that are a trouble in gardens and fields*) Inf **MI**73, Wireweeds—I think that's a family term. Flat leaf that spreads out on the ground, and then one spike that comes up, small ball at the top, *extremely* hard to cut; **NE**4, Wireweed. **1974** Morton *Folk Remedies* 143 **SC,** Ironweed; . . Tea Weed; Wire Weed; . . *Sida rhombifolia.* **2002** Hammer *Everglades* 129 **FL,** *Wireweed Sida acuta.* . . An ubiquitous plant of pinelands and hammock margins as well as a weed of lawns and other disturbed sites.

2 =**jointweed 1.**

1933 Small *Manual SE Flora* 450, *Delopyrum* [=*Polygonella*]. . . Jointweeds. Wireweeds. **1954** *Amer. Midland Naturalist* 52.289 **GA,** *Polygonella gracilis.* . . Jointweed, wireweed.—Dry, sandy oak barrens and pinelands. **2003** *Castanea* 68.170 **FL,** *Polygonella basiramia.* . . Tufted Wireweed.

wish v, n Usu |wɪš|; for varr see **A** below
A Forms.

1 |wuš|; pronc-spp *woosh, wush.* **chiefly Sth**

1890 *Catholic World* 52.257 **Sth** [Black], I did sho wush I wuz er white lady dat day. **1893** Shands *MS Speech* 68, *Wush* [wuš]. Negroes and illiterate whites use . . this form . . for *wish.* **1899** (1912) Green *VA Folk-Speech* 492, *Wush.* . . A wish. **1899** in 1993 Major *Calling the Wind* 4 **NC** [Black], Den de scuppernon' make you smack yo' lip en roll yo' eye en wush fer mo'. **1927** Shewmake *Engl. Pronc. VA* 34, All but careful speakers in Virginia, and probably throughout the South, pronounce *wish* so that it rimes perfectly with *push* and *bush.* **1936** *AmSp* 11.13 **eTX,** *Wish* is [wuʃ]. **1942** Hall *Smoky Mt. Speech* 17 **wNC, eTN,** *Wish* [wuʃ]. **1956** McAtee *Some Dialect NC* 51, *Wush* . . wish. Dial. **1965** West *Time Was* 279 **nwNC,** We're bound to go along with what he wanted. That was all he had left in creation, that woosh and his few cabinet tools. **2005** *DARE* File **St. Louis MO** (as of 1958), In a line that the lyrics pages [for Chuck Berry's song "Carol"] all transcribe as "You can't dance,/ I know you wish you could," Chuck distinctly sings: ". . . you wush /wuš/ you could."

2 pronc-sp *wursh.* Cf Intro "Language Changes" I.8

1905 *DN* 3.57 **eNE,** Intrusive *r* is very common. . . wu(r)sh (=wish). **1909** *DN* 3.390 **eAL, wGA,** *Wursh, v.* and *n.* Wish.

3 |wiš|; pronc-sp *weesh.*

1930s in 1944 *ADD* **eWV,** *Wish.* . . weesh, v. & n. **1936** *AmSp* 11.63 **seWV,** The pronunciation of words like *condition, position, wish,* with the sound of *ee* in *feet* (condeetion, poseetion, weesh). **1939** in 1944 *ADD* **wWV,** *Wish.* . . [wiš] weesh.

B Gram form.

Pres (exc 3rd pers sg): usu *wish;* also *wisht, wished.* [Perh *wish* + excrescent *t:* see Pronc Intro 3.I.23] Cf **acrost, attackt** v, *clift* (at **cliff**), *onc(e)t* (at **once A**), *twic(e)t* (at **twice**)

1840 *S. Lit. Messenger* 6.508 **seGA,** Well, I *wisht* you well of it, Miss Lid. **1843** *Knickerbocker* 21.257 **NY,** Why can't you go out to Tinnecum with me . . ? . . Can't you, Mister? I wisht you would. **1878** *Harper's New Mth. Mag.* 57.578 **CT,** "I'll think on't." "Well, I wisht you would." **1885** Twain *Huck. Finn* 314 **MO** [Black], If I didn't b'lieve I see most a million dogs . . , I wisht I may die right heah in dese tracks. **1887** *Century Illustr. Mag.* 34.231 **eMA,** And he says, 'Teen, I wished I was a better man.' And I says 'Jack, I wished you was.' **1891** *DN* 1.165 **cNY,** *T* is excrescent in . . [wišt], present, 'wish'. **1893** Shands *MS Speech* 68, Even educated people frequently say *wisht* for *wish.* **1897** Lummis *King of Broncos* 162 **NM,** An' ef they don't, I'll make yo' wisht they hed! **1909** *Out West Mag.* 30.70 **AZ,** Aw, Mary! Don't you *wisht* you knew? **1909** *DN* 3.389 **eAL, wGA,** *Wisht.* . . To wish: used as a present. "I wisht he would come." *Ibid* 406 **nwAR,** *Wish't.* . . Wish that. . . "I wish't I could go but I can't." **1910** *DN* 3.451 **cwNY,** *Wished,* pres. of wish. **1920** Martin *Schoolmaster* 184 **sePA,** I'd think . . your hard luck would near make you wisht you'd never got married. **1926** *DN* 5.404 **Ozarks,** *Wisht, v.* Wish. **1934** Carmer *Stars Fell on AL* 37, Wisht I might could go, too. **1943** *LANE* Map 703 **NEng,** The map shows the phrase *I wish* . . referring to present time, usually recorded in the sentence *I wish you could come tonight.* . . [The form [wɪʃt] is found throughout the region.] **1957** Faulkner *Town* 243 **MS**, I just wisht she would. . . Her or anybody else, I don't care who, to bring a court suit. **1968–69** *DARE* FW Addit **NY**75, Wisht [wɪʃt]—this pronunc. used in present tense; **eNC**, Wisht—present tense form. "I wisht he'd come back." **1981** Pederson *LAGS Basic Materials,* 1 inf, **cnGA**, wɪˑ·ʃt—excrescent /t/; 1 inf, **nwAL**, à·ˑwíʃt ʰi wʌz—"I wish he was". NB Present tense; 1 inf, **cAL**, I wɪˑˑʃt I had one. **1982** Barrick Coll. **csPA**, Wisht—first pers. pres. of *wish* when I is postpositional: "I wisht I had one." **2000** Shores *Tangier Is.* 188 **Chesapeake Bay**, The "t" appears in . . "wisht." **2008** in 2009 *DARE* File—Internet **OK**, *What I Wished I Had Known*—I recently asked Pastor Herbert Cooper what he knows now that he wished he had known when he began *Peoples Church.*

wishbone bush n [See quot 1957] **esp CA**

A **four o'clock 1** (here: *Mirabilis laevis*).

  1923 in 1925 Jepson *Manual Plants CA* 340, M[irabilis] laevis. . . Wishbone bush. **1957** Jaeger *N. Amer. Deserts* 242, Wishbone Bush. *Mirabilis bigelovii retrorsa* [=M. laevis var r.] . . Called "wishbone bush" because of its manner of branching. Gravelly flats and rocky surfaces of Colorado and Mohave deserts. **2001** *SW Naturalist* 46.4 **sCA**, Creosotebush (*Larrea divaricata*), . . wishbone bush (*Mirabilis*), and *Encelia californica* also are common. **2006** McKinney *California's Parks* 86, If all desert bushes look more or less the same to you, interpretive signs at the site positively identify indigo bush, wishbone bush, cheese bush, thorn bush, burro bush, and creosote bush.

wish book n Also *wishing book*

A mail-order catalog.

  1931 *AmSp* 7.121 **eID**, A *wish book* is the catalog of Montgomery Ward or other mail order house. **1933** *AmSp* 8.1.32 **nwTX** [Ranch diction], *Wishbook.* A mail-order catalogue. **1933** Rawlings *South Moon* 150 **nFL**, She reached up to the mantel for the mail-order catalogue. . . Kezzy called it "the wish book." **1938** FWP *Guide MN* 5, The trade catalogs of the mail-order houses are still read diligently. . . In some localities they are spoken of as "wish books." **1941** Writers' Program *Guide AL* 6, The mountaineer['s] . . clothes are plain and cheap, and the mail order catalogue is usually just a "wishin' book." **1941** Justus *Cabin on Kettle Creek* 146 **eTN**, Glory sat down before the fire to feast her eyes on the wish book. . . What a sight of fanciful things there were . . girls' frocks, boys' suits, fine hats and shiny shoes. **1967** *DARE* FW Addit **cnLA**, Wish-book—joking name for Sears Roebuck or Montgomery Ward catalog. **1975** Gould *ME Lingo* 319, *Wishing book*—This name for the big mail-order catalog originated in the Maritime Provinces for the T. Eaton publication, but Mainers picked it up for Sears, Monkey-Ward, etc. **1982** Barrick Coll. **csPA**, Wishbook—mail order catalog.

wish broom See **whisk broom A4**

wished See **wish B**

wished together ppl adj phr Also *witched together*

Put together insecurely, cobbled up.

  1918 in 1999 Farwell *Over There* 139, The show was out of doors—the stage two tables 'wished' together. **1929** *AmSp* 5.125 **ME**, A slovenly woman was a "draggle-tail." . . Her sewing if badly done was just "witched together." **1967** *DARE* (Qu. W29, . . *Expressions . . for things that are sewn carelessly* . . "They're _____.") Inf **DC**1, Wished together. **2006** in 2009 *DARE* File—Internet **neIL**, The end user didn't see it but I dreaded going to work everyday because I knew how much everything was ducked taped and wished together.

wishing book See **wish book**

wisht See **wish B**

wisp broom See **whisk broom A1**

wiss (broom) See **whisk broom A3**

wist broom See **whisk broom A2**

wit See **with A3**

witch n [Cf **witching stick**]

1 also *witch doctor:* =**dowser 1.** Cf **water witch** n **3**, **willow witch 2**

  1843 (1916) Hall *New Purchase* 427 **IN**, Bringing Mr. Hum, the wizard (or witch, there so called) to me, the two prevailed on me to go only four feet lower [in digging a well]. **1850** *OH Cultivator* 6.99, Then to test his skill—for he staked his reputation as a witch doctor on the result—he traced the vein to a spring some fifteen or twenty rods distant.

1857 Owen *Second Rept. Geol. Surv. KY* 329, There may be all that the mineral witches declare there is, of lead and silver, but the Mineralogical and Geological signs do not accompany them here. **1872** *Prairie Farmer* 43.50 **IL**, I once called on a "witch" to locate a well. . . The man instructed me how to hold the stick, and I went at it. In a few weeks I knew as much about it as any one,—that is, I knew it was all "bosh." **1957** *Julian Apple Day* [9] **csCA**, There are several witches—water witches—in the Julian area who will find water for you. **1965–70** *DARE* (Qu. CC13b, . . *The person who knows how to use a forked stick to find water*) 10 Infs, scattered, Witch; **AR**47, Witch, water witch; **CA**97, Dowser, witch, water wizard; **NC**23, Water finder, witch; **OH**37, Diviner, witch; [**OK**20, Some kind of witch; **CA**158, Belongs to the witch crew; **MT**1, Man witch;] (Qu. CC13a, . . *A forked stick that's used to show where there's water underground. . . [What kind of wood?]*) Infs **NC**13, 61, **WA**6, Witch's stick. **1975** Gould *ME Lingo* 319, Witch remains the favored Maine word for a water dowser, and it is applied to both men and women who divine underground water. Usually Mainers say in full, *water-witch,* and the divining is called *water-witchin'.* Although Mainers have about the same percentage of belief and disbelief as other people, there has never been any black-magic nuance in this use of *witch.*

2 =**dowsing rod;** hence n *witch wiggler* =**dowser 1.** Cf **water smeller, ~ witch 4, willow witch 1**

  1914 [see **v.**]. **1931** Randolph *Ozarks* 121, In every mountain settlement there is at least one water-witch, or "witch-wiggler"—a person who walks about with a forked twig, which is supposed to move in the hands when he walks over a hidden stream of water. **1967–69** *DARE* (Qu. CC13a, . . *A forked stick that's used to show where there's water underground. . . [What kind of wood?]*) Inf **CO**10, Witch—y shaped, willow; **CO**17, Witch—made of willow, -y shaped; **IL**21, Witch—made of wire or a willow branch; **IN**82, Witch—should be peach tree.

3 See **old witch 1.**

4 See **water witch** n **1.**

witch v, hence vbl n *witching* [Cf **witching stick**] **chiefly N Cent, Cent, nCA** See Map on p. 1040 Cf **water witch** v phr, **willow witching**

Occas with *around:* To dowse, search with a **dowsing rod** (for water, ore, buried treasure, etc); to search (an area), locate (water, a well) in this way; hence n *witcher* =**dowser 1; dowsing rod.**

  1848 *OH Cultivator* 4.124, I know that some people laugh at the idea of *witching* for water, as it is called. **1872** *Prairie Farmer* 43.50 **seMN**, I know of several wells around here which were "witched;" in every case water was found as stated. **1897** in 2009 (acc) Lexis–Nexis Legal Research *State Case Law: MO* (Internet), Wilson "witched" around and told Jesse that there was a weak vein of water there. **1903** Garland *Hesper* 136 **West**, Once they passed a couple of men "witching" for their vein [of ore]. One of them, with a forked willow in his outstretched palms, was ambling to and fro. **1907** *Outing* 49.516 **ND**, I picked it up when I was a boy of thirteen by watching an old, blind negro 'witch' for water on my father's farm. **1914** IL Farmers' Inst. *Annual Rept. for 1913* 18.345, There was a water witch who would witch for water for $15.00 and guarantee to find water. I shall never forget that gaunt, cadaverous fellow who took a bit of hazel with two prongs called a witch. **1915** *Sun. News Tribune* (Duluth MN) 28 Nov sec 3 1/1, This very day a great railroad corporation has a remarkable water witch on its pay rolls. . . His magic witcher is a hazelwood branch. **1929** *Atlantic Mth.* 144.243, There are treasure finders who witch for buried gold and silver by slipping a silver dime or a piece of gold into the fork of their twig. **1947** (1964) Randolph *Ozark Superstitions* 84, Dr. St. John told me about a chap named Patterson . . who was rated as the best "witcher" in all that region. . . One of Patterson's aunts "follered the witchin' trade." *Ibid* 86, My mother-in-law witched all the country around Bolivar, and *always* found water. [**1963** Thomson *Crocus Country* xi.74 (OED2) **Alberta Canada**, The term to "witch for water" is said to come from the fact that it was usually done with a witch-hazel wand.] **1966–70** *DARE* (Qu. CC13b, . . *The person who knows how to use a forked stick to find water*) 13 Infs, **esp N Cent, Cent, nCA**, Witcher; **CA**154, **IL**102, **MI**67, **MN**10, **MO**18, **OH**47, 56, Well witcher; **MO**20, **TN**59, Man (or person) who witches for water; **MO**12, Witching for water; (Qu. CC13a) Infs **AR**27, **IL**145, Witch(ing) for water; **MO**34, Witch water; **WI**5, Witcher—it is a verb too, you witch it; **CA**32, Witcher stick. **1968** *DARE* Tape **CA**99, We would have had one of these three men come and witch it [=a piece of land] and see whether there was water here or not; **WI**7, There's an old fellah out here that witches wells

and he'll get you water every time.   **1978** [see **water witch** v phr].
1986 Pederson *LAGS Concordance*, 1 inf, **cnAR**, We witch it for water.
1993 Luther *Cottonwood Roots* 82 **NE**, I know a genealogist who brings
her husband to graveyards to witch for buried stones.   **2005** Tingle–
Moore *Spooky TX Tales* 20, She could witch for water.

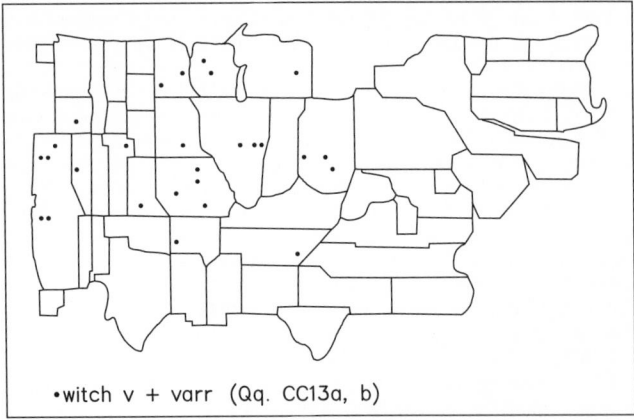

•witch v + varr (Qq. CC13a, b)

witch alder n

A woody southeastern plant of the genus *Fothergilla*.   Also
called **dwarf alder 2**

   1822 Eaton *Botany* 282 **Sth**, *Fothergilla. . . alnifolia*, . . witch alder.
1836 (1840) Phelps *Lectures on Botany* App. 98, *Fothergilla. . . alni-*
folia, (witch-alder . .).   **1900** Lyons *Plant Names* 163, *Fothergilla. . .*
Witch Alder.   **1947** *Amer. Midland Naturalist* 37.721 **SC**, *Fothergilla.*
Witch-alder.   **2005** *Chron.–Telegram* (Elyria OH) 8 May sec E 6/6, Another less common woody native also in its glory in mid-May is the
Witch Alder (*Fothergilla gardenii*). Though the foliage of this small
multi-stemmed member of the Witch-hazel family is similar to that of
the Vernal Witchhazel, its flowers are distinctly different.

witch around   See **witch** v

witch-cat n

A mischievous, high-spirited person, esp a child.

   1844 *Rural Life New Engl.* 62, Any one might know . . that Mr.
Howard would n't marry such a witch-cat as Jane.   **1851** Hentz *Rena*
26, "Why, Rena! you little witch-cat—you naughty child!" cried he,
hugging her so tightly as almost to squeeze the breath out of her body.
1860 Holland *Miss Gilbert* 354 **CT**, Aunt Catharine . . finally acknowledged . . that he was an excellent fellow, though a "perfect witch-cat."
1888 Randall-Diehl *2000 Words* 220, *Witchcat*, A frolicsome, mischievous girl.   **1903** *DN* 2.301 **Cape Cod MA** (as of a1857), *Witch-cat.* . .
A roguish boy.   **1985** Rattray *Advent. Dimon* 243 **Long Is. NY**, He must
have been reading my mind without even looking at me, witchcat that he
was, for he turned and smiled.

witch chicken n   Cf **chicken owl**
=great horned owl.

   1947 (1964) Randolph *Ozark Superstitions* 277, The great horned owl
is often called a witch chicken, perhaps because of the belief that owls
can charm a chicken off its roost.   **1949** Webber *Backwoods Teacher*
136 **Ozarks**, Some hillmen call the horned—or hoot—owls "witch-
chickens" because of their hellish ability to come into a tree where
chickens are roosting without disturbing the fowls.   **1958** *VA Qrly. Rev.*
34.258 **KY**, "Tell me, what's a witch chicken, Mester Tolliver?" "What
say? Why that's a mean hoot owl. They got a way of coming soft into a
tree."

witchcraft v, hence vbl n *witchcrafting* Past, past ppl, ppl
adj usu *witchcrafted;* pronc-spp *witchcraf(t)* esp among *Black*
speakers Cf *root-work* v (at **root work**)

To cast a spell on; to work magic; hence nouns *witchcraft(er)*.

   1898 *Century Illustr. Mag.* 55.743 **sePA**, Funny, Sam, ain't it—how
t'ey air haexed an' witchcrafted?   **1905** (1913) Pringle *Woman Rice*
Planter 357 **SC** [Black], De whole plantashun stir up. Some say dem
g'wine 'way, say dis is a witchcraf' place.   **1927** *Amer. Mercury* 12.238
VA [Black], Where she was witchcrafted she was covered with scales
jus' like a fish.   **c1938** in 1970 Hyatt *Hoodoo* 1.6 **seMD** [Black], Aunt
Zippy Tull . . in those days were looked upon as a great *witchcraft* and
fortune teller.   *Ibid* 57 **cwFL** [Black], Mah ole parents said that she was

witchcraf' once by a buzzard. . . They had *witchcraf'* 'er so that buzzard
follow 'er.   *Ibid* 79 **ceVA** [Black], If you kin stand fer whut you
see, you'll be able to *witchcraft* in anything you want to.   *Ibid* 177
seNC [Black], I've been *hurted* with this here *witchcrafter* twicet in my
life.   *Ibid* 180 **swFL**, Mah husband was *witchcrafted*.   *Ibid* 198 **seNC**
[Black], Mah husband, he was *witchcraft* heah a little before Christmas.
Ibid 2.1543 **ceGA** [Black], If anybody wanta *rootwork* yo' or *witchcraft*
yo', if yo' wear a dime aroun' your laig, . . dat dime will turn black.
1954 *Western Folkl.* 13.79 **MI** [Black], In Benton Harbor, John himself had had an experience with a witchcrafter.   **1970** Shepardson–
Hammond *Navajo Mt. Comm.* 150 **seUT**, A third Singer suspected of
"witchcrafting" was a man who had married in from outside.

witch-diver   See **water witch** n 1

witch doctor n

1   See **witch** n **1**.

2   =**dragonfly**.   esp **S Midl**   Cf **snake doctor 2**

   1965 *MO Conservationist* 26.7, Along the streams the dragon fly or
witch doctor maintains a vigil over water loving insects.   **1968** *DARE*
(Qu. R2, . . *The dragonfly*) Inf **WV** 12, Witch doctor.   **1968** *AmSp* 43.53
KS, Answers written in for 'dragonfly' . . included . . *witch doctor*, 1
[inf].   [**1973** Rabe *Rass* 48 **seMO**, The little striped kitten chased a
dragonfly, and he called to it "Better come back here. That old dragonfly
is a witch doctor and could cast a spell."]   **2003** White *Tadpole* 143 **KY**
(as of c1950), The blue dragonflies we called witch doctors flitted and
skimmed the surface of the creek water.

witched together   See **wished together**

witch elm n

1   =**winged elm**.

   1897 Sudworth *Arborescent Flora* 182 **WV**, *Ulmus alata*. . . Witch
Elm.   **1900** (1972) Goldsborough *Ole Mars* 53 **eMD** [Black], Now I
ondastan' why dis branch so full ub *witch-elm* an' *witch-hazel* trees.
1947 (1964) Randolph *Ozark Superstitions* 85, Some fellows prefer the
wahoo, which used to be called 'witch elm,' but a good hazel fork works
better for me [in water-witching].

2   =**witch hazel**.

   1837 Hoffman *NY Book Poetry* 55, Beaded with dew the witch-elm's
tassels shiver;/ The timid rabbit from the furze is peeping.   **1903** Small
Flora SE U.S. 510, [*Hamamelis*]—Witch hazel. Witch elm.   **1960** Vines
Trees SW 324, *Hamamelis*. . . Vernacular names are Winter Bloom, . .
Witch-elm.

witcher   See **witch** v

witches' bridle   See **witches' stirrup**

witches' broom n   Also *witch's broom*

An abnormal growth of clustered twigs and branches from a
common point caused by var sources such as mites, viruses,
fungi, and insects.   Also called **hurrah's nest 4, porcupine**
nest

   1879 *Mt. Democrat* (Placerville CA) 7 June 1/5, More curious than the
mistletoe is the parasite that grows on pines. For some time I thought
this must be the monstrosity called "witches' broom," . . The latter is
caused by the sting of insects producing unnatural activity in the branch,
causing it to send out clumps of twigs or cones on the injured spot.
1893 *Bot. Gaz.* 18.334, Professor MacMillan mentioned an unusual case
of hypertrophy . . observed in Minnesota, in which trees twenty to thirty
years old only attained the height of a man, the whole tree becoming a
kind of witch's broom.   **1916** *Torreya* 16.235, On this island [=Matini-
cus Island ME] I heard the fungoid malformation of trees, known as
witches' broom, called hoorah's-nest.   **1950** *WELS* (*Trees that are found*
in your neighborhood) 1 Inf, **WI**, Witch's broom.   **1960** Teale *Journey*
into Summer 100, Witch's-brooms, those still mysterious spurtings of
tree growth that produce tangled masses of twigs—known in the west as
"porcupine nests"—appeared in many of the higher junipers.   **1979**
Wellman *Old Gods* 2 **sAppalachians**, The branches of a gum showed
shaggy with the close bunches of witches'-broom. Folks said that grew
where someone had been murdered.   **2007** *Providence Jrl.* (RI) 24 Nov
sec F 3 (Internet), Dozens of American robins, cedar waxwings and European starlings filled the witches-broom branches of a tall honey locust
tree.

witches' butter n

1   also *witch's butter:* Any of var fungi of the order Tremellales, esp a **jelly fungus** of the genus *Tremella,* but also the dark-colored *Exidia glandulosa* and the similar orange jelly *Dacrymyces palmatus;* see quots. [*OED2* (at *witch* n.² 5.c) 1836 →] For other names of *Dacrymyces* see **fairy butter**

1899 Herbst *Fungal Flora Lehigh Valley* 186 **PA,** *E[xidia] glandulosa* [sic]. . . Witches' Butter. Blackish, flattened, undulated, soft at first and when moist, becoming film-like when dry. On dead oak branches all through the Valley. **1972** Miller *Mushrooms* 210, The yellow to orange species [of *Tremella*] look like . . butter and have been called "Witches' Butter." **1990** *Daily Herald* (Arlington Heights IL) 16 Mar sec 6 1/2, Destroying Angel[,] Witches Butter[,] and Shaggy Mane. . . are . . names of . . some mushrooms found in the area. **2008** *DARE* File—Internet **CA,** *Dacrymyces palmatus*. . . Common Name: *Witch's Butter.* . . *Dacrymyces palmatus* is a yellow-orange jelly fungus which closely mimics *Tremella mesenterica,* the common Witch's Butter.

2 A deposit of pollen.

1860 *Macon Daily Telegraph* (GA) 15 Mar 3/1, The high winds of Thursday evening and night in Charleston, marked the pavements, the decks of ships and other exposed surfaces, with plentiful specimens of vegetable pollen—a phenomenon which is to many a source of vague and superstitious fears. In some parts of the country this deposit is called "Witches Butter," and in others, a "Sulphur Shower."

witches' hair n   Also *witch's hair*   Cf **old-witch grass, witchgrass 2**

A **panic grass** (here: *Panicum capillare*).

1914 Georgia *Manual Weeds* 28, *Panicum capillare*. . . *Other English names:* Tumbleweed Grass, Tickle Grass, Witch's Hair. **1999** *Integrated Pest Management Fruits* 194, Witchgrass, *Panicum capillare* . . also called tumbleweed grass, ticklegrass, and witches' hair, occurs commonly in orchards grown on sandy soils.

witches' herb n

A **Saint-John's-wort** (here: *Hypericum perforatum*).

1882 *Therapeutic Gaz.* 6.13, The rare collection of titles attaching to Hypericum [in the *National Dispensatory*], "The devils scourge," "The witches herb," and "The Lord God's wonder plant," provoke an admiration only equaled by the contemplation of the marvelous list of virtues attributed to it . . but unfortunately not yet demonstrated. **1892** (1974) Millspaugh *Amer. Med. Plants* 30–1, *Hypericum perforatum*. . . *Com[mon] Names.*—St. John's Wort. . . Witches' herb.

witches' moneybags n   Cf **bag leaves, ~ plant 1**

An **orpine** (here: *Sedum telephium*).

1892 *Jrl. Amer. Folkl.* 5.96 **wMA,** *Sedum Telephium,* witches' moneybags. . . [Footnote:] Because of a children's custom of blowing up a leaf. **1910** Graves *Flowering Plants* 214 **CT,** *Sedum Telephium.* . . Live-forever. . . Bag-leaves. Witches' Money-bags [etc.].

witches' shoelaces n

=**dodder.**

1970 Correll *Plants TX* 1255, Additional vernacular names [for dodder] to those above are "angel's hair," "tangle gut," "witches' shoelaces," "devil's gut," "strangle vine." **1996** Silverthorne *Legends TX Wildflowers* 104, Dodder. . . also has been associated with witches and with the devil. "Witches' shoelaces" indicates one use supposedly made of it.

witches' stirrup n   Also *witches' bridle, witch stirrup*   [*EDD* (at *witch* sb.¹ (37))]   **chiefly Sth, S Midl**   Cf **witch knot**

A tangle, esp in a horse's mane.

1880 (1881) Harris *Uncle Remus Songs* 132 **GA** [Black], Ain't you seed no witch-stirrups? Well, we'n you see two stran' er ha'r tied tergedder in a hoss' mane, dar you see a witch-stirrup. **1899** (1912) Green *VA Folk-Speech* 487, *Witches'-stirrup.* . . The tangles in a colt's mane that are used as stirrups by witches to mount to his back. **1906** Johnson *Highways Missip. Valley* 92 **TN** [Black], De witches ride our horses at night. In de mornin' we'll find der manes and tails full of witches stirrups—de ha'r all twisted and tangled up. It couldn't twis' itself up dataway, an' yo' cain't pick de ha'r straight in an hour. You have to cut it. **1909** *Jrl. Amer. Folkl.* 22.253 **seVA** [Black], It is well believed to-day in southeastern Virginia that witches take horses from stables at night, and ride them furiously about the country. The best indication of a horse's having been ridden is finding the strands of its mane tied together next morning. Two hairs tangled together constitute a witch-stirrup. **1914** *Ibid* 27.247 **SC** [Black], The tangles in hair are witches' stirrups which have been used in nightly riding. **1919**

Studies Philol. 16.281 **NC,** In Lincoln County, North Carolina, the witch's mount, instead of being a transformed human being, is an ordinary horse. The following day the animal is restive and fatigued, and the tangles in its mane, known as "witch-stirrups," are evidence of the use to which it has been put. **1932** Addington *Hist. Scott Co. VA* 243, Children were often told that the tangles in their hair were witch stirrups, "caused by witches having ridden them." **1937** Gardner *Folkl. Schoharie* 51 **ceNY,** Several people recalled seeing him cut locks from the manes of horses which had been hag-ridden and afflicted with witch stirrups. **1947** (1964) Randolph *Ozark Superstitions* 277, Tangles in a horse's mane are called *witches' stirrups,* but I don't think the people who use this term really believe that witches have been riding their horses. **1977** Manfred *Green Earth* 328 **Upper MW,** He found a witches' bridle in her black mane and untangled it, careful not to pull out any hairs. **2008** in 2009 *DARE* File—Internet **cnTX,** I was just wondering if anyone else had trouble with witch's stirrups, also known as hag-knots, in their horse's mane? How have you found is the best way to deal with it?

witches' teeth n   Also *witch's teeth*   **CA**

A **deervetch** (here: *Lotus formosissimus*).

1925 Jepson *Manual Plants CA* 549, *L[otus] formosissimus.* . . Witch's Teeth. **1954** CA Div. Beaches & Parks *Point Lobos Reserve* 90, *Lotus formosissimus* . . Witch's Teeth. **1965** Sharsmith *Spring Wildflowers* 105 **cwCA,** Witch's Teeth or Coast Trefoil. . . Witch's Teeth refers to the long narrow calyx-lobes. **2002** *DARE* File—Internet **cwCA,** *Lotus formosissimus*—Coast Lotus (Witches' Teeth).

witch flounder n

A **flounder B** (here: *Glyptocephalus cynoglossus*).   Also called **gray sole**

1914 Harvard Univ. Museum Compar. Zool. *Bulletin* 58.105 **NEng,** Off Cape Ann . . fish fry of several species, notably . . rockling (Enchelyopus) and witch flounder (Glyptocephalus) were taken. **1940** U.S. Fish & Wildlife Serv. *Fishery Bulletin* 48.341 **ME,** The witch flounder has recently been found to be generally distributed in the central basin of the Gulf of Maine. **1981** *Sun. Herald* (Arlington Heights IL) 22 Feb Panorama sec 9/2, Gourmets think the best of this family [=flatfish family] is gray sole, which is really witch flounder. **2008** *Daily Progress* (Charlottesville VA) 29 July (Internet), A witch flounder hardly generates gastronomic interest when purveyed under its correct common name, but when marketed as . . "gray sole" as it is in the United States, this edible flounder becomes acceptable to the consumer.

witchgrass n

1 also *witch's grass:* =**quack grass 1.   chiefly NEng**   See Map on p. 1042

1790 Deane *New Engl. Farmer* 230, *Quitch-Grass,* called also *Witch-Grass, Twitch-Grass, Couch-Grass, Dutch-Grass,* and *Dogs-Grass,* a most obstinate and troublesome weed. **1855** U.S. Patent Office *Annual Rept. for 1854: Ag.* 187 **NH,** Couch Grass (*Triticum repens*) [=*Elymus repens,* formerly *Elytrigia r.*] is known in the valley of the Merrimack and in other parts of this State by the name of "Witch Grass." **1880** *Daily Eve. Bulletin* (San Francisco CA) 26 Jan 4/2, "Witch" grass, or (as it is generally called) "quack" grass, would . . answer the purpose, but no one acquainted with it would advise its use. . . Its botanical name is *Triticum repens.* **1897** *Jrl. Amer. Folkl.* 10.146 **ME,** *Agropyrum repens* [=*Elymus r.*], . . witch grass. **1913** *DN* 4.6 **ME,** *Witch grass,* or *twitch grass.* . . A grass common in gardens that spreads rapidly and is hard to kill. **1950** *WELS* **WI** (*The kind of wild grass that throws out strong underground roots and is hard to get rid of*) 1 Inf, Witchgrass; 1 Inf, Quack or witch [grass]; (*Other kinds of grass that are hard to get rid of*) 1 Inf, Witchgrass. **1964** *Ag. Hist.* 38.96, Quack grass (witch grass in New England) makes fairly good forage but it is an unmitigated nuisance in a field of corn or other cultivated crops. **1965–70** *DARE* (Qu. S8, *A common kind of wild grass that grows in fields: it spreads by sending out long underground roots, and it's hard to get rid of*) 33 Infs, **chiefly NEng,** Witchgrass; MA57, Witch's grass; (Qu. S9, *Kinds of grass that are hard to get rid of*) Inf **MA5,** Witchgrass; (Qu. S21, . . *Weeds . . that are a trouble in gardens and fields*) Infs **CT26, MA100, NH14, VT16,** Witchgrass. **2008** *DARE* File—Internet **VT,** I used to say that I wanted my grave stone to read: "He got the witch grass out of his garden." But. . . there will be a day when witch grass will grow over and under and around my marble marker. Witch grass (*agropyron repens*) is not even native to the New World. It's come to us from Europe.

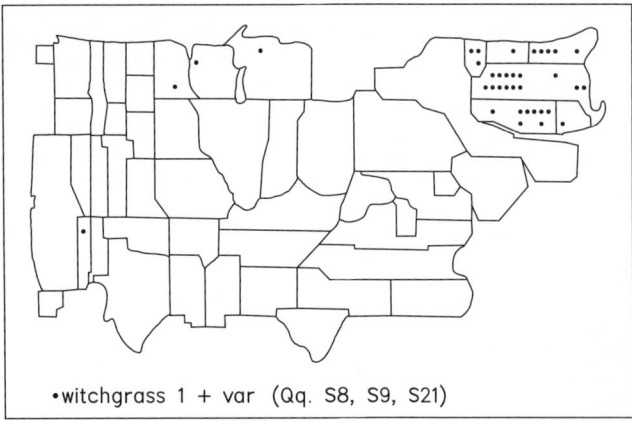

•witchgrass 1 + var (Qq. S8, S9, S21)

2 =**panic grass,** esp *Panicum capillare.* Cf **witches' hair**

1883 *Amer. Naturalist* 17.818, In this way species of Panicum (witchgrass) and Eragrostis are sent whirling over the fields in autumn, and are often seen piled against a fence. **1896** Britton–Brown *Illustr. Flora* 1.123, *Panicum capillare. . .* Witch Grass. Tumble-weed. **1913** *Ibid* 138, *Panicum dichotomiflorum. . .* Spreading Witch-grass. *Ibid* 139, *Panicum barbipulvinatum. . .* Barbed Witch-grass. *Ibid* 140, *Panicum flexile. . .* Wiry Witch-grass. **1976** Bruce *How to Grow Wildflowers* 210, Witch Grass *(Panicum capillare),* that scrubby little grass with large panicles of flowers that break away after frost and become tumbleweeds, dotted the white sand and was very pretty, its wine-colored flower heads making airy masses above its green leaves. **2008** *DARE* File—Internet, Needleleaf Rosette Grass, Witch Grass—*Dichanthelium aciculare.*

3 Any of var other grasses, as a **bromegrass,** a **love grass,** or an **oat grass c** (here: *Danthonia spicata*); see quots.

1879 *NH Sentinel* (Keene) 23 Oct 1/4, If you wish to kill out chess grass, often called witch grass, plough and harrow the ground every few days this Fall. **1890** *FL Ag. Exper. Sta. Bulletin* 8.11, Eragrostis capillaris. . . Witch grass. . . [Erogrostis] pectinacea. . . [witch grass]. **1897** *Jrl. Amer. Folkl.* 10.146 **ME,** *Danthonia spicata,* . . witch grass.

witch hazel n

Std: a tree or shrub of the genus *Hamamelis,* esp *H. virginiana.* Also called **witch elm 2;** for other names of *H. virginiana* see **monkey face 5, pistachio, snapping hazel, ~ turtle 2, spotted alder, tobaccowood**

witch hobble n Also *witch hoppel, ~ hopple, witch's hobble, wytch hopple* **esp NEng**

Usu =**hobblebush;** occas also =**highbush cranberry.**

1840 Hoffman *Greyslaer* 2.44 **neNY,** Tangled thickets of mosswood and wytch-hopple . . afforded the deep covert where the hounded deer will seek to hide. **1845** *Pittsfield Sun* (MA) 16 Jan 1/7 **NY,** The woods are filled with "whistle wood" and "witch hopple," which entangle you, wet you, and weary you. **1888** in 1889 *NY State Entomol. Rept. Injurious Insects* 260, "Measuring-worms." . . attack the witch-hobble *[Viburnum lantanoides],* which is usually quite free from insect injury, and reduce the leaves to skeletons. **1891** *Jrl. Amer. Folkl.* 4.148 **NH,** Viburnum lantanoides, *Witch Hopple.* **1892** *Ibid* 5.97 **NH,** *Viburnum opulus,* . . witch-hobble. **1895** Remington *Pony Tracks* 143, The miserable "witch-hoppel" leads its lusty plebeian life, satisfied to spring its half-dozen leaves, and not dreaming to some day become an oak. **1943** Peattie *Great Smokies* 283 **TN,** A species whose leaf color is truly remarkable. . . is the hobblebush or witch hobble, an abundant high-mountain shrub. **1960** Teale *Journey into Summer* 11 **NH,** Witch hobble lifted its paired foliage like opposing wings. **2006** *Bennington Banner* (VT) 28 Sept (Internet), The leaves at the higher elevations had started to turn: The witch's hobble pale yellow; sumac berries in sanguine bunches.

witching See **witch** v

witching stick n Also *witch stick;* less freq *witch(ing) rod, ~ switch, ~ wand;* for addit varr see quots [Cf *EDD witch-wand* (at *witch* sb.[1] 1.(40)) "a divining rod, usually a twig of mountain ash." This (and ultimately all the *witch*-terms referring to dowsing) come from the *witch* or *wych* that occurs as (or in) the name of var trees (e.g. witch hazel) with supple branches, but there has been much folk-etym influence from *witch* one who practices sorcery. Cf *OED2 witch* sb.[3]] **widespread, but less freq Atl, Gt Lakes** See Map Cf **witch** n **1, 2; witch** v =**dowsing rod.**

[**1869** Munro *Backwoods' Life* 76 **Ontario Canada,** If . . he has faith in the "witching stick," the difficulty will be referred to its subtile and mysterious power. A small twig with two stems branching out so as to form a crotch . . ; this is the witching stick.] **1891** Robinson *Our Trees* 38 **neMA,** The divining rods of the ore and water hunters are said to be made from the branches of this tree [=*Hamamelis virginiana*]; but in England one of the elms is called "wych elm," and a hornbeam "witch hazel," and their branches may be used there for a similar purpose. The efficacy of these witch-sticks will in all probability be defended by believers and laughed at by sceptics, as of old. **1913** *Big Piney Examiner* (WY) [16 Jan 2]/5 (newspaperarchive.com), He who digs his well with a witching stick . . only plods while the world rushes by. **1922** *TX Bar Assoc. Proc.* 209, A man . . was fooling with a forked stick, commonly referred to as the "witch stick" in locating water. **1935** *Hamilton Daily News Jrl.* (OH) 17 Apr 1/2, [Headline:] "Witching Rod" Agrees With Engineers On Monroe's New Well. **1938** *Daily Courier* (Connellsville PA) 28 Oct 9/4 **CA,** A "witching stick" that has been used successfully here for years in locating water for the sinking of wells "witched" on the side of a fair-sized hill. **1947** (1964) Randolph *Ozark Superstitions* 89, He even claimed that he could tell, by the behavior of his witch stick, whether the alleged deposit was a vein of the mineral, or a mere pocket. **1952** *Western Folkl.* 11.204 **OR,** [He] calls himself a "scientific water locater" rather than a water witch. His equipment includes a compass . . the forked witch stick . . and a gold watch and chain. **1956** Sorden–Ebert *Logger's Words* 41 **NEng, Gt Lakes,** *Witch-stick,* Twig or branch of alder brush used to locate water for the logging camp. **1965–70** *DARE* (Qu. CC13a, . . *A forked stick that's used to show where there's water underground. . . [What kind of wood?]*) 113 Infs, **widespread, but less freq Atl, Gt Lakes,** Witching stick; **OK**42, **TX**39, **VA**11, Forked (*or* peach, willow) witching stick; 37 Infs, **chiefly Lower Missip Valley, West,** Witch stick; 18 Infs, **scattered, but less freq Atl,** Witch(ing) wand; **CA**7, 80, 123, **MN**2, 38, **MA**58, **NJ**1, **NY**30, **PA**104, Witch(ing) rod; **AL**33, **IL**5, **MS**53, **TN**37, **TX**3, Witch(ing) switch; **ND**3, 5, **SD**8, Witching willow; **CO**47, Witching wire; [5 Infs, Witch hazel; 3 Infs, Witch hazel stick (*or* rod)]. **1973** *Gt. Bend Tribune* (KS) 13 July 10/1, *Forked limb to find oil?* . . Henry K. Bridgess believes his "witching rod" may be a possible answer to the energy crisis. **1995** *Post–Std.* (Syracuse NY) 25 Aug sec A 4/2 **cNY,** Suddenly the witching wand twitched, and the pointy end bent sharply down.

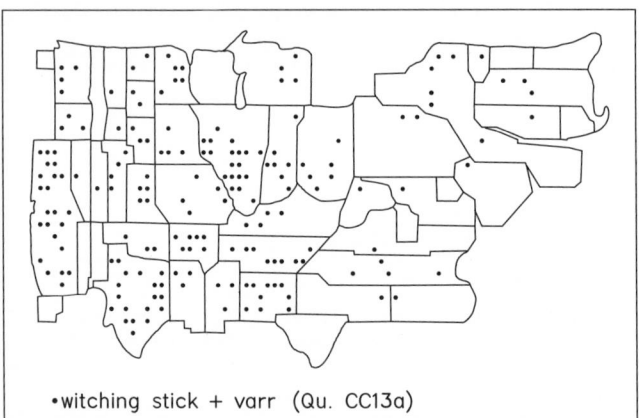

•witching stick + varr (Qu. CC13a)

witch knot n Also *witch's knot* Cf **witches' stirrup**

A tangled knot of hair.

1830 Talbot *Rurality* 17, Many has been the witch knot, found in the manes of their faithful steeds, which no human power could be known to tie. **1899** (1912) Green *VA Folk-Speech* 487, *Witch-knot.* . . A knot or snarl especially in the hair, supposed to be caused by witchcraft. **1901** Robinson *Sam Lovel's Boy* 2 **VT,** "My sakes, Bub," she exclaimed, as she . . cast a despairing glance on his tangled flaxen poll, "it's jest a mess o' witch knots." **1902** Jones *Hist. Dorchester Co. MD* 194, A witch can take a horse from a locked stable and ride it all night; the evidence of this being the foaming sweat on the horse and the witch knots tied in its tail and mane. **1929** Dobie *Vaquero* 192 **TX,** One old "willow tail" had got the limb of a blackjack fastened into her long mane, which . . was matted into a "witch knot." **1952** in 1968 Haun *Hawk's*

Done Gone 296 **eTN,** He stood up by the fireboard awhile and played with the string of peppers. . . And got them so tangled they was worse to undo than a witch's knot. **1964** Jackman–Long *OR Desert* 70, Reub says that when he was little, children were told that the witch knots came because, at night, witches rode the horses, and they'd better not let the knots get started, because in time only the witches could ride them. The children didn't really swallow this but, just in case, every boy carefully combed the tail of his horse. **2001** *DARE* File—Internet **TX,** A rider named Austin . . left the house riding an old dummy named Charlie, as clumsy a piece of horseflesh as ever to grow a witch knot in his tail.

witch light n   Also *witch's light* [*EDD* (at *witch* sb.[1] (26)) "a will-o'-the-wisp"]
=will-o'-the-wisp 1; also fig.

1866 in 1907 Bloomfield *Oneidas* 262, I saw a 'witch light' last night. I have not seen one before in years. **1869** *Harper's New Mth. Mag.* 39.823, If we strive to read their hidden meaning, we but pursue witch-lights and phantasms into the profitless regions of fog and bilberries. **1900** *Pacific Mth.* 4.113 **OR,** And the wavering flare of the pitchlight / That illumined your cabin before / Is a will-o'-the-wisp and witch-light / That encumbers the fancies of yore. **1965–70** *DARE* (Qu. CC16, *A small light that seems to dance or flicker over a marsh or swamp at night*) Infs **AL**6, 33, **DC**1, **KY**10, **NC**35, **NY**100, **OH**28, **TN**53, **TX**11, Witch's light; **IL**96, **MD**30, **OR**6, Witch light. [11 of 12 Infs old]

witch-ride v, hence vbl n *witch-riding,* ppl adj *witch-ridden* [Cf *EDD witch-ridden* (at *witch* sb.[1] (34)) "having the nightmare"]
Cf **hagride**
To disturb the sleep of, create nightmares for.

1836 *Biblical Repertory & Theological Rev.* 8.355, And we all remember it as a ruled case in the matter of night-mare, that those who have been witch-ridden during sleep, suffer all the exhaustion which would be produced by a similar exercise in their waking hours. **1876** (1877) Beard *K.K.K. Sketches* 39 **Sth,** Even the chickens on their roosts were witch-ridden, and crowed lustily for day. **1899** (1912) Green *VA Folk-Speech* 487, Witch-ridden. . . Ridden by witches, having a nightmare. **c1938** in 1970 Hyatt *Hoodoo* 1.140 **seVA** [Black], She was suppose to be a witch. . . At a certain time in the evening she would go about what they called *witch-riding.* . . This witch would get out of her skin and go to somebody's place . . when they were asleep and ride dem. They would see things. *Ibid* 143 **seVA** [Black], An old lady. . . use to go out every night *witch-riding.* [**1986** Pederson *LAGS Concordance* 1 inf, **nwMS,** Witch riding you—having a bad dream. [Inf Black]]

witch rod   See **witching stick**

witch's broom   See **witches' broom**

witch's butter   See **witches' butter 1**

witch's grass   See **witchgrass 1**

witch's hair   See **witches' hair**

witch's hobble   See **witch hobble**

witch's knot   See **witch knot**

witch's light   See **witch light**

witch snake n
A young **rat snake 1** (here: *Elaphe obsoleta* subsp); see quot.

1926 *TX Folkl. Soc. Pub.* 5.65, A "witch snake" is. . . a blotched snake of rather small dimensions. The top of its head is always ornamented by a picture of some kind. Sometimes it is a woman with long hair, again it is an old man with pointed beard, and occasionally it is a human skull. . . According to my observations, all young chicken snakes, (*coluber quadrivittatus* [here: =*Elaphe obsoleta* subsp]) are witch snakes. . . A witch snake is a sure hoodoo. I first heard the story of the witch snake from a negro octogenarian in the Brazos Valley. . . He said, "Massa, dat's er witch snake. Don kill et, er yo chillun die en yo cows give bloody milk, er somethin happen ter yo."

witch's teeth   See **witches' teeth**

witch stick   See **witching stick**

witch stirrup   See **witches' stirrup**

witch switch (or wand)   See **witching stick**

witch water n   esp **S Atl**
A mirage on hot pavement.

1946 Baker *Blood Lamb* 159 **FL,** Ahead the road dipped down into a hollow, and there at the lowest point Pert saw witch water over it. Of course it wasn't water at all but that was what old people called it. **1950** *PADS* 14.72 **SC** [Black], *Witch water.* . . Mirage seen on hard-surface roads in summer. **1953** Polk *S. Accent* 66 **Sth,** The heat waves on the road are *witch water.* **1966** *DARE* FW Addit **ceGA,** *Witch water*—Mirage; small illusionary pools of water seen on roads or sand in hot weather, due to heat? **2005** Medina *Cigar Roller* 9 **FL,** The sun had burned away the morning haze and witch-water was already rising from the sandy road that lined the harbor.

witchweed n
=butterfly weed 1.

1975 Hamel–Chiltoskey *Cherokee Plants* 27, Butterfly weed, . . witch weed—*Asclepias tuberosa.*

witch wiggler   See **witch n 2**

witchwood n   [nEngl dial (for *Sorbus aucuparia*)] **NEng**
A **mountain ash 1,** usu *Sorbus americana.*

1826 Jewett *New-Engl. Farrier* 78, For a Cough. Take witchwood bark, and make a good tea of it. **1865** *Ladies' Repository* 25.353 **NEng,** She bewitched the milk the first thing. . . I had to put witch-wood all round the pails and pans to keep it sweet. **1891** *Jrl. Amer. Folkl.* 4.254 **NEng,** For years he constantly wore a string of beads. . . made from the small branches of the mountain ash (*Pyrus Americana* . .), sometimes called witch-wood. . . This species of tree was once quite popular among New England witch-believers as a charm against witches. **1892** *Ibid* 5.20 **NH,** The *Pyrus Americana* is in some parts of New Hampshire called witch-wood, and occasionally carried in the pocket to keep off witches. **1901** *Biloxi Daily Herald* (MS) 30 July [7]/1 **ME,** A . . farmer. . . had molded some bullets, into the center of each of which he had put a little square of sumach wood. For years this wood has been known as "witch wood," and it is said by those who believe in such things that it is a sure charm to overcome "black art." [*DARE* Ed: 'sumach' refers here to *Sorbus* spp; cf **mountain sumac 2.**] **1948** Helm *John Marin* 81 **ME,** Marin is as pleased as a boy to turn up a red-berried witchwood at the end of the swamp in exchange for Mrs. Thompson's unexpected discovery of a moosewood standing deep in the pine lot. **1966** *DARE* (Qu. T16, . . *Kinds of trees . . 'special'*) Inf **ME**24, Witchwood.

witch yeast n   esp **N Cent**   Cf **spook yeast**
=emptins 1.

1910 *Altrurian Cook Book* 114 **cwOH,** *Witch Yeast.* . . Scald flour, salt, and sugar with the water in which potatoes were cooked; then put in potatoes. Add two quarts cold water. When cool add any kind of good yeast to start. **1964** *News–Jrl.* (Mansfield OH) 4 Nov 7/1, Witch Yeast Bread. . . Take 1 qt. witch yeast and mix with flour to stiff sponge. **1968** *DARE* (Qu. H17, . . *Kinds [of yeast]*) Inf **IN**3, Witch yeast = fluid yeast; (Qu. H18, . . *Special kinds of bread*) Inf **WI**52, Witch yeast bread—also called starter bread.

with prep, adv   Usu |wɪð, wɪθ|; for pronc and sp varr see **A** below

A Forms.   Cf **without A, withouten**
1 pronc-spp *'ith, 'th.*
1848 Lowell *Biglow* xxv 'Upcountry' **MA,** The following passage in Shakspeare he would recite thus . . Neow air eour breows beound 'ith victorious wreaths. **1861** Holmes *Venner* 2.172 **NEng,** I knowed I'd ketch ye at some darned trick or 'nother 'fore I'd done 'ith ye! **1867** Lowell *Biglow* lvii 'Upcountry' **MA,** I don't git much done 'thouth I bogue right in along 'th my men. **1923** *DN* 5.207 **swMO,** I'm full up 'ith y'r cussin'. **1929** *AmSp* 4.204 **Ozarks,** Thet 'ar pore . . woman o' hisn was . . a-scrunchin' cheenches on th' punch'on 'ith a antiganglin' noodle-hook.
2 |wɪ|; pronc-sp *wi.*
1884 *Anglia* 7.255 **Sth, S Midl** [Black], Prepositions. . . Wi'. **1908** *DN* 3.282 **eAL, wGA,** *With* often becomes *wi.* **1942** Hall *Smoky Mt. Speech* 91 **wNC, eTN,** [ð] is absent from the phrase *with me* [wɪ mɪ] in a recorded utterance. **1943** *LANE* Map 725, 3 infs, **MA, RI, VT,** [wɪ mɪ]; 1 inf, **swMA,** [wɪ ʃugar]. **1969** *DARE* Tape **GA**72, If you're proofing it wi backin's you can pour a good gallon of backin's in it.
3 |wɪd, wɪt|; pronc-spp *wid, wit.* **chiefly Sth, S Midl** *esp freq among Black speakers;* **also Nth** *esp among second-generation Eng speakers*
1858 Hammett *Piney Woods Tavern* 140 [Black], De ole gempleman who da come down to de table wid her. **1884** *Anglia* 7.255 **Sth, S Midl** [Black], Prepositions. . . Wid. **1894** Riley *Armazindy* 52 **IN,** Flick ye

wid er buggy-whirp. **1899** (1912) Green *VA Folk-Speech* 484, *Wid.* . . A form of *with*. **1899** Chesnutt *Conjure Woman* 13 **csNC** [Black], De grapes begin ter swivel up . . wid de wrinkles er ole age. **1908** *DN* 3.282 **eAL, wGA** [Black], [ð] in all positions has, under negro influence, largely become *d*, as in . . wid. **1922** Gonzales *Black Border* 338 **sSC GA coasts** [Gullah glossary], *Wid*—with. **a1930** in 1991 Hughes–Hurston *Mule Bone* 29 **cFL** [Black], Wid dis right hand you see befo' you. **1941** *AmSp* 16.13 **eTX** [Black], *With* occurs also as [wɪd]. **1942** Faulkner *Go Down* 68 **MS** [Black], Especially wid you there to help me worry hit out. **1965** *PADS* 44.60 **Chicago IL**, /wɪt/ instead of /wɪθ/ in the speech of [3 infs, of Czech and Irish heritage]. **1966** *DARE* Tape **AL24**, One brother at home wit [wɪt] me—just two children. [Inf Black] **1968** Moody *Coming of Age MS* 182 [Black], Emma, don't just stand there, help wit' this door. **1976** Allen *LAUM* 3.328 (as of c1950), 2 infs, **sMN**, /wɪt/. **1997** *DARE* File—Internet **cePA** [CoalSpeak], *Wit:* With. "I'm going to the block party wit you."

4 |wɪf, wɪv|; pronc-spp *wif, wiv*. **chiefly Sth, S Midl** *esp among Black speakers*

1867 Harris *Sut Lovingood Yarns* 104 **TN**, He . . made his will, a-cuttin off old Sock wif a shillin. **1882** *Atlantic Mth.* 49.188 **Sth** [Black], I's gwian to luk out fuh dem slick houn's wiv dat shot-gun. **1884** *Anglia* 7.255 **Sth, S Midl** [Black], Prepositions. . . Wif. **1930** *AmSp* 6.95 **VA**, *With* . . [wɪf]. . . Professor H.M. Ayres has heard an old gentleman in southeastern Connecticut pronounce with [wɪf], and it is reported on good authority to be current in Brunswick County, Virginia. **1941** *AmSp* 16.13 **eTX** [Black], [θ] > [f] in . . *with.* . . and . . frequently > [v] in *with* . . [wɪv]. **1959** Ruark *Poor No More* 508 **Sth** [Black], He in jail for cuttin' a man dead wif he knife. **1968** *DARE* Tape **GA61**, Now it's in the middle of the road with [wɪf] the—I guess with [wɪ] sputnik. [Inf Black]

B As prep.

1 in phr *mad with*; Angry with, mad at. [*OED2 mad* adj 6.b 1577 →; "Now *colloq.* (chiefly *N. Amer.*) and *Brit. regional*"] **esp NEast, Sth, S Midl**

1846 in 1950 Douglass *Life & Writings* 1.184 **MD**, He is terrible mad with me for it. **1862** *S. Lit. Messenger* 34.568 **VA**, I was so mad with him on account of his delay, that I could not see very well. **1884** *Harper's New Mth. Mag.* 68.410 **NEng**, Folks got so mad with him, finally, that he had to leave town. **1892** *Atlantic Mth.* 69.230 **neVA**, I did n't know he wuz hurted when he come. He never tole me. I wuz mad with him about comin'. **1896** *DN* 1.427 **c,wNY**, *With*: "Mad with one," mad (angry) at one. **1911** Wharton *Ethan Frome* 131 **wMA**, Is Zeena mad with me? **1956** McAtee *Some Dialect NC* 28, Mad with. . . angry toward. The Indiana dialect had "mad at." **1966** *DARE* (Qu. II11b, *If two people can't bear each other at all . . "Those two are _____."*) Inf **FL28**, Mad with each other. **1968** Moody *Coming of Age MS* 150 [Black], They were mad as hell with me. **1972** *DARE* File **nwFL**, I'm really mad with him. **1986** Pederson *LAGS Concordance*, 15 infs, **Gulf Region**, Mad with (him, me, you, etc). **2003** *Atlanta Jrl.-Constitution* (GA) 7 Sept sec D 9 (Internet), Derrick got mad at me, and I got mad with him. **2006** *DARE* File—Internet **ME**, He said he is very mad with me for snooping in his privacy. **2007** *Daily Breeze* (Torrance CA) 6 Mar sec A 4 (Internet), If he was mad about the hours, he should have been mad with her, not the co-workers.

2 in phr *sick with one's stomach*: Nauseated. Cf **at** prep **2**, **of** C10, **on** B9, **to** prep B1c, **DS** BB16a

1943 *LANE* Map 503 *(Sick at his stomach)* 1 inf, **seNH**, With. **1973** Gawthrop *Dial. Calumet* 76 **nwIN**, Sick:. . . with his stomach 2 [of 125 infs]. **1975** Allen *LAUM* 2.65 **Upper MW** (as of c1950), Sick *at* the stomach. . . one [instance] of . . with his stomach in Minnesota. **1986** Pederson *LAGS Concordance*, 1 inf, **cnAR**, They're sick with their stomach. **2007** *DARE* File—Internet **AL**, I'm still feeling sick with my stomach. *Ibid* **NY**, I was incredibly sick with my stomach and had no idea what was going on with it.

C As adv.

1 Esp with verbs of motion: Along with, in company with, a person or persons implied in the context. [In imitation of the adverbial use of Ger *mit* and its cognates in other Germanic languages, reinforced by the analogy of the numerous prep/adv pairs in English, like *go in the house/go in*.] **chiefly Inland Nth**

1908 *German Amer. Annals* 10.51 **sePA**, *With*. . . "I forget whether he was with or not.". . In Pa. Ger. as in Ger., *mit* is sometimes used without an object. **1931** Jacobson *Milwaukee Dial.* 19 **WI**, "I want to [go] with" for I want to go along. With in this sense comes from mitgehen.

1935 *AmSp* 10.167 **PA** [Engl of PA Germans], Another boy who was with seized the handle. **1940** *AmSp* 15.82 [Dutch in MI English], *Go with*. For 'go along.' 'May I go with?' From Dutch *meegaan*. **1944** in 1946 *AmSp* 21.51 **nwMN**, All our Norwegian, Swedish and Danish friends and neighbors without exception said 'Can I go with?' . . instead of 'Can I go with you?' The 'th' was always sounded as in 'think.' They also said, in asking if a certain person was included in, or accompanied others at any gathering, 'Was he with?' or, sometimes, 'Was he along?' Both of these expressions were exclusively Scandinavian, and others in town never used them except in quotation marks. **1950** *WELS Suppl.* **cnWI**, *Go with, come with*: One family in Vilas Co.; the husband is from New York State and says that it is used there. **1968** *DARE* FW Addit **PA171**, *Go with* . . accompany. I'll go with = I'll go with you. **1978** Kalibabky *Hawdaw* 1.[7] **neMN**, *Goin' with?*, *Comin' with?*: Are you coming (or going) with us? "Goin' show tonight, you comin' with?" **1978** *DARE* File **wNY**, Though we've lived in many places where the expression isn't known, my wife has never lost the habit shared by all her family and friends in Buffalo (New York), of saying, "Are you going with?" or "Can I go with?" **1981** *WI Acad. Trans.* 69.85 **WI**, Construction four dealt with sentences of the type, "Do you wanna come with?" . . This construction can be found in all parts of the United States where German immigrants comprize a large percentage of the inhabitants and where the German heritage is strongly felt. . . But the interesting fact about this construction is that 90% of the young women in Wisconsin used this construction as compared to 44% of the young men. **1985** Keillor *Lake Wobegon* 194 **MN**, Phil leaves and Sig decides to go with. **1986** *DARE* File **neIL**, *Go with*—Wonderful Chicagoese for Go with somebody—as in, "Do you want to go with?" "With" can also stand alone as in "Take with", "Bring with" etc. **1987** *Jrl. Engl. Ling.* 20.2.177 **ePA**, *With* 'along' (as in *He came with*). . . 20% (21), ages 19–101. *[A]long* 79%, other responses (*with me* 1%). With has some currency among younger speakers, for fourteen of the twenty-one informants are under 30. **1996** Salvucci *Philadelphia Dial. Dict.* 62, *Take wit*. . . take along: O'll take it wit. *Ibid* 65, *Wit*. . . along: Ya cummin wit? **1998** Millersville Univ. Center for PA Ger. Studies *Jrl.* Summer 16, Bring the old one with, so I have a pattern. **2006** *NADS Letters*, "Go with". . . I've grown up familiar with the construction, but only from my horde of aunts, uncles and cousins from urban northern New Jersey. They are of Irish-Polish descent, and largely working class. One very seldom heres [*sic*] it as a naturalism on the Gulf Coast. *Ibid* **MD**, I use it frequently as do my sisters (all born in the 1970s, and raised in Maryland south of DC); our use of onjectless [*sic*] "go with" (and "come with") is not . . abnormal for Southern Marylanders of our age. . . I'll add that I haven't heard it in peninsular Florida speech, except among people who were clearly from up north.

2 foll an item of food or drink: With the usual accompaniments. Cf **and** conj B5

1946 *AmSp* 21.87 **West Coast**, But 'coffee and' or 'coffee with' means 'with cream and sugar.' **1971** *NY Times* (NY) 5 Sept 7/3 [Diner cant], *With*. Used like—*and* (which see); burger with—hamburger with onion (or with french fries), etc. **1998** Mitchard *Most Wanted* 381 **TX** [Speaker from **NYC**], Stuart got us coffee—mine with, his black.

withe n Also sp *with* Usu |wɪθ|; also |hwɪθ|, occas |wɪð, waɪð|; for addit varr see quots [*OED2* c1000 →] Cf **withe** v, **withe rod, withy**

A tough, flexible shoot or twig, often made more flexible by twisting, used to bind or fasten, or as a whip.

1637 in 1892 Dedham MA *Early Rec.* 3.28, Ye posts mortised, pales to be bownd to ye Rayles wth poles & withes. **1741** *Boston Weekly Post Boy* (MA) 27 July 3/2, The Limbs of several Trees were twisted several Times round with the Wind so that they look'd like Withs. **1821** *Amer. Farmer* 3.170 **cNC**, I have known considerable planters, instead of iron traces, make use of grape vines and hickory withes. **1844** [see **withe** v 1]. **1867** *Amer. Agric.* 26.92 **cPA**, Having had occasion lately to use a great many long strong withes, and becoming fatigued with the necessity of twisting, we contrived a little machine for doing it. **1872** U.S. Congress *Rept. Joint Select Comm. Insurrectionary States* 9.651 **cnAL**, Blair had a hickory withe in his hand about four feet long and about an inch around, I think, at the butt or end of the whip or withe. **1899** (1912) Green *VA Folk-Speech* 487, *Withe*. . . A twig or stick twisted to make it flexible. **1919** *Outlook* 29 Oct 237 **MI**, All we could do was to whip at the fire with bundles of green withes. **1920s** in 1944 *ADD* **cNY**, *With*. . . A withe. . . Not heard. [waɪð] is used, but not freq. **1930s** *Ibid* **eWV**, [wɪð], [wɪθ]. I'll take a hick'ry with to you kids. **1939** *LANE* Map 179 *(Whip; good)* 6 infs, **NH**, Withe [proncs of the type [wɪəθ]]; 5 infs, **swME**, [proncs of the type [hwɪəθ]]; 1 inf, **swME**, [wɪəθ], [hwɪəθ]—careful pron. **1941** *Ibid* Map 398 *(Switch)* 18 infs, **chiefly NH, ME,** Withe [proncs of the type [wɪəθ]]; 1 inf, **swME,** [hwɪᵛəθ]. **1963** Watkins–Watkins *Yesterday Hills* 25 **cnGA,** Bessie Mae, you go git me a withe off the peach tree. **1966–68** *DARE* (Qu. K27, . . *The sharp-pointed stick used to get oxen to move)* Inf **WV**7, Withe [wɪθ]—small limb from bush or tree; (Qu. L61, *Fences made of solid logs, now or in the past)* Inf **ME**5, Pole fence or with fence—tied with withe [wɪθ] wood. **1984** Woods *WV Was Good* 223, *Withe*—a long, limber branch or very young tree of less than one inch in diameter at the butt, used by farmers for binding corn shocks and fodder shocks.

withe v, hence vbl n *withing* Also sp *with*

1 also with *on, up:* To fasten with a **withe**. [*OED2* 1634 → "Now *dial.* and *U.S.*"]

1820 in 1867 Cobb *Autobiog.* 86 **ME,** Seeing the old gentleman withing up the stakes of his pigs' pen . . I expected a repulse. **1836** (1838) Haliburton *Clockmaker* (1st ser) 142 **NEng,** If their fences are good, them hungry cattle couldn't break through; and if they aint, they ought to stake 'em up, and with them well. **1841** (1952) Cooper *Deerslayer* 101 **NY,** Isn't it enough that I am withed like a saw-log that ye must choke too! **1844** *Cultivator* 1.251 **seNY,** The fence consists of separate frames . . with a sharpened post at each end . . driven into holes . . and secured at the top by withing together. . . Two men put up thirty rods of the fence, securing the tops by withes, in about three hours. **1855** (1858) Bennett *Chronology of NC* 25, The Indians . . withed him to a sapling, and literally "hacked him up" with tomahawks. **1887** Kirkland *Zury* 76 **IL,** Dad's a screamer t' save money! D' ye ever see him withe a plaow-pint ontew a plaow? **1908** *Hunter-Trader-Trapper* Oct 67 **NY,** Cut some dead spruce poles and withe the deer on tight. **1939** *LANE* Map 152 *(Repair)* 1 inf, swME, [hwɪəθ ʌ˞p]—of mending harness.

2 To whip with a **withe** n; hence n *withing* a whipping.

1888 in 2011 (acc) Lexis–Nexis Legal Research *State Case Law: WV* (Internet), Did you examine where he had been withed? . . Did you not state, at that time, it was two or three days after the whipping of the 5th that you examined those welts? **1912** (1913) Price *Holston Methodism* 4.494 **TN** (as of 1869), After I was on they commenced withing my horse to make him go faster. **1941** *LANE* Map 397 *(A whipping)* 1 inf, **ceNH,** [wɪəθɪᵛn]—'with a withe.'

withee See **withy**

witherlick n Cf *DS* CC17

An imaginary animal; see quots.

1900 Day *Up in ME* 157, And all of us know of the witherlick / That prowls by the shore of the Cup-sup-tic. **1914** *DN* 4.82 **ME, nNH,** *Witherlick.* . . Mythical animal, in lumber-camps.

withe rod n Also *withrod, withe wood* esp **NEng** Cf *DNE,* **withe** n

A **viburnum:** usu *Viburnum nudum* var *cassinoides,* but also an **arrowwood a** (here: *V. dentatum*). For other names of the former see **Appalachian tea 2, swamp haw, teaberry 2, wild raisin**

1846 Emerson *Rept. Trees & Shrubs* 364 **MA,** *Withe Rod. V[iburnum] nudum.* . . A slender, erect shrub, from six to twelve feet high, growing in swamps and wet woods from Newfoundland to Georgia. **a1862** (1864) Thoreau *ME Woods* 310, The prevailing shrubs and small trees along the shore were: . . cranberry-tree and withe-rod. **1888** Lunt *Across Lots* 137 **eMA,** Picking my way through the viburnums, where I find three species, the sheepberry, *dentatum,* and withrod, . . I discover the cause of this scolding of two swamp sparrows. **1908** *Anaconda Std.* (MT) 6 Dec sec 2 4/4 **NEast,** Along the creeks and rivers . . stretch . . meadows studded with clumps of alders, withe-rod and wild willow. **1929** *Torreya* 29.151, *Viburnum dentatum, "Withe wood"* Moose-wood. **1968** *Yankee* Oct 112 **NEng,** Botany enthusiasts will find goldenrods, withe rods, red mountain holly, . . and meadowsweet. **1976** Bruce *How to Grow Wildflowers* 131, Both withe-rods (so called because their supple, wandlike branches were used for caning, basketwork, and similar industries in earlier times) have glossy leaves, flat heads of creamy flowers in ordinary viburnum fashion, and blue fruits. **2007** Johnson *Hiking NC* 130, After a resting bench comes withe rod *(Viburnum cassinoides* [=*V. nudum* var *c.*]).

withey See **withy**

withing vbl n See **withe** v

withing n See **withe** v **2**

with-it n

A food accessory to the principal dish of a meal; a side dish.

1939 Harris *Purslane* 278 **cNC,** The drinking water was warm as branch water, and the with-it tasted like sawdust, whatever it was. **1942** Whipple *Joshua* 18 **UT** (as of c1860), 'We ain't got only "bread-and-with it." ' . . *No, thank you,* she thought; *your bread would be corn pone and your 'with-it' salt pork.* **1975** Gould *ME Lingo* 320, *With-it*—The other things served at dinner; the vegetables, pickles, dessert, etc. Hence, there will be a roast of beef and *with-its.* When asked what's for dinner, the woods cook gives the standard brush-off, "Victuals and *with-its!*" (Vittles, that is.) **1991** Still *Wolfpen Notebooks* 163 **sAppalachians,** *With-it:* whatever else. **2009** Perry *Coop* 280 **nWI,** "Oh, that's the best thing to feed pigs," he says. "Bread and withit." "Withit?" "Yah. . . Bread and whatever comes withit!"

with one's head up (and tail over the dashboard) See **head up**

without prep, adv, conj Usu |wɪð'aut, wɪθ-|; for addit varr see **A** below

A Forms. Cf **with A, withouten**

1 pronc-spp *(a)thout, ithout.* **chiefly Sth, S Midl, NEng**

1844 Thompson *Major Jones's Courtship* 107 **GA,** I'm termined to have the thing fixed 'thout waiting for enny more accidents. **1866** (1881) Whitney *Leslie Goldthwaite* 165 **NEng,** White stockin's, or go athout. **1867** Lowell *Biglow* lxxi **'Upcountry' MA,** *Without* becomes *athout* and *'thout.* **1871** Eggleston *Hoosier Schoolmaster* 96 **sIN,** Ef he'd died . . 'thout nobody to give him a drink of water. **1893** Shands *MS Speech* 63, *Thout* [ðaut]. Negro for *without.* **1895** [see **B** below]. **1904** Day *Kin o' Ktaadn* 61 **ME,** But I guess they'd 'a' kept him his lifetime, 'thout doubt. **1907** White *AZ Nights* 119, You can't do nothin' with a cow that gets on the prod that away 'thout you ropes her. **1909** *DN* 3.389 **eAL, wGA,** *Without.* . . Sometimes *thout.* **1923** *DN* 5.199 **swMO,** 'Ithout a chance. **1925** Dargan *Highland Annals* 27 **cwNC,** If I could skip a year 'thout a baby, I b'lieve I could ketch up with my work. **1931** (1991) Hughes–Hurston *Mule Bone* 115 **cFL** [Black], We ain't got no business goin' into no trial . . 'thout a word of prayer. **1943** *LANE* Map 730 *(Unless)* 10 infs, **chiefly nNEng,** proncs of the type [ðaut]; 3 infs, **sNEng,** proncs of the type [ɪðaut]; 2 infs, **sNEng,** proncs of the type [ʷɪðaut]. **1952** Brown *NC Folkl.* 1.601, Don't go outdoors 'thout your coat on. **1989** [see **A2** below].

2 pronc-spp *widout, wifout. esp freq among Black speakers*

1854 in 1966 Harris *Sut Lovingood's Yarns* 38 **TN,** I know'd he cudent act hoss fur ten minutes wifout actin infuel fool. **1863** *Continental Mth.* 3.313 **Sth** [Black], De worle couldn't gwo on widout it. **1887** *Scribner's Mag.* 1.582 **wMD** [Black], Ev'ybody 'sputin . . tell dere warn't no way ter t'un wifout yearn' it. **1896** *Black Cat* Mar 22 **TX** [Black], I dasn't go back wifout de receet. **1897** (1902) Moore *Songs & Stories* 77 **TN** [Black], Ole Master's mighty good to us. He could er put us heah widout hope. **1989** Pederson *LAGS Tech. Index* 119 **Gulf Region,** *Without.* [Of 914 infs, 35 offered proncs of the type [wɪdaut]; 2 infs, [ðaut]; 1 inf, [daut]; 1 inf, [θaut]; 1 inf, [wɪfaut]; 1 inf, [wufaut].]

3 pronc-spp *(be)dout, d'rout. esp freq among Black speakers*

1888 Jones *Negro Myths* 60 **GA coast** [Gullah], Buh Rabbit . . mek plan fuh lib offer tarruh people bedout wuk isself. **1896** Harris *Sister Jane* 140 **GA** [Black], "Don't you know 'dout any tellin'?" she asked. **1908** *DN* 3.306 **eAL, wGA,** *Dout(en).* . . Unless. **1927** Kennedy *Gritny* 110 **sLA** [Black], Settin' down by yo'self, eating lonesome; 'dout anybody to talk wid you. **1937** in 1976 *Weevils in the Wheat* 219 **VA** [Black], Fus' seed dis horse an' buggy comin' to de house dout [without] nobody in hit. **1974** (1975) Shaw *All God's Dangers* 5 **AL** [Black], Eva would tell Uncle Bob, "If you goin to die, die! Die! I can do better *d'rout* a man." **1989** [see **A2** above].

B As conj.

Unless; without its being the case that. [*OED2 without* conj. C.2 1393 →; "Formerly common in literary use . . ; later *colloq.* . . , now chiefly *illiterate.*"] **chiefly NEast, Sth, S Midl** Cf **withouten B**

1722 in 1897 Providence RI Rec. Comm. *Early Rec.* 12.31, No person or persons . . shall Retaile any strong drinks . . with out they first obtain and haue a Licence. **1789** Webster *Dissertations Engl. Lang.* 386, *Without,* in the sense of *unless,* is as frequent as any word in the language, and even among the learned. It is commonly accounted inelegant, and writers have lately substituted *unless:* But I do not see the propriety of discarding *without.* **1801** in 1956 Eliason *Tarheel Talk* 304 **cs,se,cwNC,** They were as well done as they could be without you had been present. **1828** (1970) Webster *Amer. Dict., Without.* . . Unless; except. . . This use of *without* is nearly superseded by *unless* and *except*, among good writers and speakers; but is common in popular discourse or parlance. **1844** Thompson *Major Jones's Courtship* 80 **GA,** I don't know what upon yeath was the matter with us, 'thout it was the dispepsy. **1872** Twain *Roughing It* 26 **West,** The Injuns . . is powerful troublesome 'thout they get plenty of truck to read. **1895** *DN* 1.376 **seKY, eTN, wNC,** I never seen nary 'thout that wasn't one. **1906** *DN* 3.164 **nwAR,** I won't go without he goes too. **1911** *DN* 3.540 **eKY,** I won't try it without you help me. **1913** Wharton *Custom of Country* 9 **NY,** You mustn't accept invitations from gentlemen without you say you've got to ask your mother first. **c1937** in 1972 *Amer. Slave* 2.1.161 **SC** [Black], But you can't shoot 'em without de Cassels give you a license to do it. **1938** Rawlings *Yearling* 42 **nFL,** If you was big as your Ma, . . we couldn't lay in it [=a bed] without somebody fell on the floor. **1941** *AmSp* 16.25 **sIN,** He can't go without he gets some money from home. **1943** *LANE* Map 730 *(Unless)* **NEng,** The map shows the conjunctions *unless* . . , *without* . . , *else* . . , usually recorded in the sentence *I won't go unless he goes too* or in a similar context. . . [*DARE* Ed: *Without* occurs **throughout NEng.**] *Without* is described as the usual word by [2 infs]; and as rare by [3 infs]. **1952** O'Connor *Wise Blood* 52 **Sth,** Everything she looked at was that child. . . She couldn't lie with that man without she saw it, staring through the chimney at her. **1956** Moody *Home Ranch* 29 **CO** (as of 1911), Ain't a man got a right to get slicked up without he's goin' to church? **1959** *VT Hist.* 27.167 **sw,cn,neVT,** Don't go without you tell me. Occasional. **1965** *DARE* Tape **KY**1, I ain't gonna do it without they do it. **1967** *DARE* FW Addit **GA**19, *Without*—meaning "unless"—"I won't do it without you do too." **1972** in 1982 Powers *Cataloochee* 232 **cwNC,** He . . stayed at home pretty well all the time without he wasn't in the mountains. **1979** [see **tunk** v]. **1986** Pederson *LAGS Concordance,* 30 infs, **Gulf Region,** Without [=unless]. **2000** Shores *Tangier Is.* 239 **Chesapeake Bay,** Sarah's going to leave without they come (unless).

withouten prep, conj Pronc-spp *douten, thou(gh)ten, 'thout'n, without'n* [Brit dial *withouten,* a doublet of *without* < ME *withouten*] **chiefly Sth, S Midl, esp sAppalachians** Cf **-en** suff[1]

A As prep.

Without. [nEngl dial]

1858 *Graham's Mag.* 53.469 **cnIL,** G. Hossafatt is in our office at this moment . . and says. . . "A man 'thouten any coat . . struck him over the geranium." **1865** Gray *Matrimonial Infelicities* 236 **NY,** There I was, jest as I was when I married him, withouten anything to fall back on. **1886** *S. Bivouac* 4.350 **sAppalachians,** A language might deteriorate any time from such causes in the way of such forms as . . *withouten.* **1933** Rawlings *South Moon* 315 **nFL,** Give the rough five yare more thouten no farr, the hull scrub'll be thick-growed like that there. **1939** TN Folk Lore Soc. *Bulletin* 5.9 **sAppalachians,** An' I seed 'im throw a steer oncet an' tie 'm up withouten any he'p. **1952** Brown *NC Folkl.* 1.601, *'Thouten.* . . Without. "I won't go 'thouten him." "I won't go 'thouten you go."—Illiterate. **1963** Edwards *Gravel* 139 **eTN,** [We] went on then withouten the least sign of a bite until purt nigh milkin time. **1963** Owens *Look to River* 40 **TX,** I'd hate to see him go off without'n something for his dinner. **1976** Garber *Mountain-ese* 93 **sAppalachians,** I kaint go to school on a day like this thoughten a big warm coat. *Ibid* 103, We jist kaint git along withouten our faithful watchdog. **1991** Still *Wolfpen Notebooks* 59 **sAppalachians,** We done it withouten a bite to eat.

B As conj.

=without B.

1868 *Land We Love* 5.360 **GA,** I'll get you a ladle full, thouten that dratted hound has drunk up all on it. **1899** (1912) Green *VA Folk-Speech* 445, *Thouten.* . . Without. "Thouten he comes to-day." **1903** *DN* 2.333 **seMO,** I won't go thouten you do. **1907** *DN* 3.237 **nwAR,** *'Thouten.* . . Without, unless. **1908** [see **without A3**]. **1909** *DN* 3.381 **eAL, wGA,** *Thouten, adv.* Without; also as a conjunction, unless. *Ibid* 389 **eAL, wGA,** *Without(en).* . . Unless. Sometimes *thout(en)* or *dout(en).* **1912** Green *VA Folk-Speech* 487, I wouldn't 'a known withouten he told me. **1915** Lawson *Log Timber Cruiser* 153 **sNM,** Nobody couldn't never pass no remarks about Jake's doin's or Jake hisself, withouten he'd up and git plumb ornery about it. **1926** Roberts *Time of Man* 95 **KY,** You can't stir withouten you watch where you go. **1943** *LANE* Map 730 *(Unless)* 6 infs, **ME, NH,** Thouten [3 infs regarded this as obs]. **1949** Webber *Backwoods Teacher* 208 **Ozarks,** I cain't go

kitin' off 'thout'n I git my stuff ready. **1952** McCall *Cherokees & Pioneers* 101 **NC, TN,** No one hain't seed nary a preacher man so much as sniff the stuff [=moonshine] with a shet mouth withouten he tuk himself a through. **1952** [see **A** above]. **1964** Faulkner *As I Lay Dying* 179 **MS,** He couldn't buy no team from nobody . . withouten he had something to mortgage. **1974** Fink *Mountain Speech* 29 **wNC, eTN,** I won't go withouten you do. **1979** *Antioch Rev.* 37.51 **MS,** Withouten you got injured so soon . . , you might could of been *truly* famous.

withrod See **withe rod**

withy adj Also sp *withee, withey* [*OED2* (in sense **1** below) 1598 →; "*rare*"]

1 Like a **withe** n; tough and flexible, leathery. **chiefly Nth**

1822 Irving *Bracebridge* 2.87, The forest-trees first begin to show their buds; the long withy ends of the branches turn green. **1840** in 1865 Thoreau *Letters* 2, Our tongues were the withy foils with which we fenced each other off. **1856** (1906) Thoreau *Writings* 14.181 **eMA,** May I ever be in as good spirits as a willow! How tenacious of life! How withy! **1877** *Med. Brief* 5.231 **NY,** The root . . is very tough and withy. **1881** Henshall *Book Black Bass* 229 **swOH,** I would here enter my protest against the lightest, and "withiest," Trout fly-rods. **1908** Sudworth *Forest Trees Pacific* 71, In contrast to the brittle branches of Western larch, they are tough and withy. **1948** *WELS Suppl.* **seWI,** He explained how he like his toast. He said, "I don't like my toast hard, I want it withee." **1966–69** *DARE* (Qu. B35, *Ice that will bend when you step on it, but not break*) Inf **MA**6, Withy [wɪθi]—father's term; (Qu. KK25, *Something that bends or yields easily: "That willow branch is very _____."*) Inf **CT**29, Withy ['wɪθi]; **NJ**8, Withy ['wɪθi, 'wɪθi]; **OH**41, Withy [Inf doubtful].

2 Spec; of a person: strong and supple; wiry, tough. **esp NEng, S Midl**

1849 Mayo *Kaloolah* 93 **Nantucket MA,** Just see what a tall fellow, . . as tough and as withy as a young hickory. **1868** (1869) Kellogg *Lion Ben* 142 **ME,** Do you remember that wrastle we had when Captain Rhines's house was raised?—there was stout, withy men around these bays in them days. **1898** Blanchard *Discovery NW* 1.592 **neIL,** He was not a large man, . . but what we call *wiry* and *withy.* **1903** Wasson *Cap'n Simeon's Store* 214 **ME,** She's an awful stocky-built creetur', though, and withey as ary wild-cat. **1911** (1913) Johnson *Highways Gt. Lakes* 77 **nwPA,** He was a little feller, but withy as a whalebone. **1914** *DN* 4.82 **ME, nNH,** *Withy.* . . Wiry, tough, strong. "A withy feller." **1917** *DN* 4.419 **wNC,** *Withey.* . . Sinewy. "He's a withy little devil in a bear fight." **1923** *DN* 5.224 **swMO,** *Withy.* . . Tough, wiry, vigorous. "He's a withy feller." **1927** *AmSp* 2.366 **wcWV,** *Withy* . . sinewy. "That little man is withy." **1975** Gould *ME Lingo* 319, *Withy*—From the supple nature of a withe, the adjective means sinewy, wiry, and often supple in spite of age. The dictionaries do not seem to hit upon exactly the Maine shade of meaning in, "You tackle him, and you'll find he's real withy!" **1995** Stone *Smoky Mt Women* 69 **eTN** (Montgomery–Hall *Dict. Smoky Mt. Engl.*), She was "a withy (a mountain expression meaning small and slender but strong and tough) little woman."

witness tree n Cf **bearing tree**

A tree that has been marked and recorded by a surveyor as a reference point for locating a corner.

1837 in 2008 (acc) Lexis–Nexis Legal Research *State Case Law: OH* (Internet), Witness trees, near each corner, to be distinctly marked, showing the number of section and number of township. **1845** Kirkland *Western Clearings* 3 **MI,** The corners [are] especially distinguished by stakes whose place is pointed out by trees called Witness-trees. **1862** KS Laws *Genl. Laws* 854, Where no bearing or witness tree or trees can be found, the county surveyor . . shall establish said missing corner in accordance with the government surveys. **1899** in 2009 (acc) Lexis–Nexis Legal Research *State Case Law: MN* (Internet), A witness tree is not an established corner, but merely an object by means of which, in connection with the field notes, if correct, the corner may be found. **1903** *DN* 2.337 **seMO,** *Witness tree.* . . A tree marked to show the location of a corner of land. Often called a 'pointer.' **1958** McCulloch *Woods Words* 212 **Pacific NW,** *Witness tree*—One of several trees scribed and recorded in survey notes to mark the location of a section corner. **1975** Gould *ME Lingo* 320, A *witness* mark is a stake or post set by surveyors as a reference point. In surveying Maine, trees were plentiful enough so nobody had to drive stakes. When seen in the wilderness a *witness tree* is easily recognized by its blazes, spots, and daubs of paint. **1982** *Smithsonian Letters* **ID,** A witness-tree is a tree with a stick man painted on it and if you chop it down you will get a hefty fine as it is used as a corner marker. **1998** *DARE* File—Internet **MO,** Also found were a very rotted stump with wire for one County Surveyor witness tree. . . Depressions were found for the GLO [=U.S. General Land Office] witness trees.

witty adj [*OED2 witty* a. 2.a.(a) "*Obs.* exc. *dial.*"]
Skillful, clever.

    1952 Giles *40 Acres* 4 **csKY,** Here there is a pocket of pure Appalachianism and our older people still speak the tongue. . . A man who is able or capable is said to be "witty" or "clever." **c1960** *Wilson Coll.* **csKY,** *Witty.* . . Intelligent or clever.

witty n
A fool; a mentally retarded person.

    1940 (1978) Still *River of Earth* 84 **KY,** Ain't that a peck of foolishness? Fellow who writ this book is a witty. **1941** Still *On Troublesome Creek* 42 **eKY,** I'm no witty with a hammer and saw. **1962** Dykeman *Tall Woman* 27 **NC** (as of 1860), Then she had known that the witty understood more than people ever realized.

wiv See **with A4**

wizle See **wizzle**

wizzen n Also *wezzen, wozzen, wooz(z)en* [Chiefly nEngl, Scots, nIr varr of *weasand;* cf *EDD weasand, SND wizzen, Concise Ulster Dict. weasen*] *arch* Cf **goozle** n **1**
The throat, windpipe, gullet.

    1858 Hammett *Piney Woods Tavern* 28, Don't forget that Sam Slick here'll hev a dry wizzen a heap of times afore mornin'. **1858** *Portage City Rec.* (WI) 27 Jan 1/7 **sIL,** I saw the fight. . . But that infernal butcher, whose wizzen you clipped, hacked and stabbed Mark's carcass so awkwardly that I took it to be his first set to. **1870** *Punchinello* 2.133, Some razor may be slipped across your wizzen. **1891** *Daily Independent* (Monroe WI) 7 Apr [3]/3 (newspaperarchive.com), I took out my knife, felt . . fer the biggest b'ar's wizzen, 'n' with one gouge slit it from chin to gullet. **1899** (1912) Green *VA Folk-Speech* 477, *Weasand.* . . Wezzen. The windpipe. *Ibid* 487, *Wizzen.* . . The windpipe. *Ibid* 491, *Wozzen.* . . Woozzen. The gullet. **1911** Kester *Prodigal Judge* 359 **TN,** Talk—or what's to hinder me slicing open your woozen?

wizzle v Also with *up, away* Also sp *wizle* [Prob varr of *wizen*] **esp NEng** See Map and Map Section Cf **weasle, weasly**
To shrivel or dry up, become wrinkled; to pucker; also fig; hence ppl adjs *wizzled (up).*

    1834 in 1910 Emerson *Jrls.* 3.363 **MA,** Here and there . . are anomalous, unpaired creatures, who are but partially developed, wizzled apples. **1844** Stephens *High Life in NY* 1.219 **CT,** She had on a cap . . that looked queer enough round her leetle wizzled up face. **1853** Payson *Golden Dreams* 274 **NEng,** The hot and arid temperature of that country so dries up the fluids and juices of the body that it gradually wizzles away till it is reduced to the same condition as a mummy or dried apple. **1879** Ward *Sealed Orders* 82 **NEng,** It's puckery kind of work this—like taking alum on your tongue. After a year or so a man feels himself wizzling and toughening up in his feelings. **1903** *DN* 2.353 **neOH,** *Wizzled.* . . Shrunk up; wizened, of which it is probably a variant. **1912** Young *Behind the Pines* 136 **Sth** [Black], He ain't strong, he ain't long. He weak and he wizzled up. **1926** (1930) Wright *My NY* 68, Bea said that the ladies suddenly wizzled up, making little noises with their twisted lips. **c1938** in 1970 Hyatt *Hoodoo* 1.72 **seGA** [Black], She wus jest wizlin' away to nothin'. **1942** McAtee *Dial. Grant Co. IN* 71 (as of 1890s), *Wizzled* . . shrunken or dried up; "All _____ up". **1946** Campbell *Folks Do Get Born* 57 **GA,** Well, he was a little bitty weak thing born two months ahead of time. Wizzled up and weighing not four pounds when my mama caught him. **1965–70** *DARE* (Qu. LL3a, *Shrunk, dried up: "These apples are all _____."*) Infs **CT6, 22, LA8, MA14, NY186, PA118, VT8, 12,** Wizzled; **ME6, 19, NY68,** Wizzled up; [**VA11,** Wuzzled up;] (Qu. LL3b, *Shrunk, dried up: "He's a little _____ old man."*) Infs **CT6, 12, 22, MA41,** Wizzled; **MA77, PA118, VT8, 12,** Wizzled up; **ME19,** Wizzled up old duffer; (Qu. I8, *When root vegetables get old and tough and are not good to eat*) Infs **ME20, MA74,** Wizzled. **1975** Gould *ME Lingo* 320, Berries gone by on the vine are *wizzled* up, and older folks fading from age and ill health *wizzle* away. **2000** *DARE* File **NEng,** "Wizzled" (similar in meaning to wizened). **2007** in 2009 *DARE* File—Internet **NH,** The onion plants just kinda wizzled up and ended up in the compost pile.

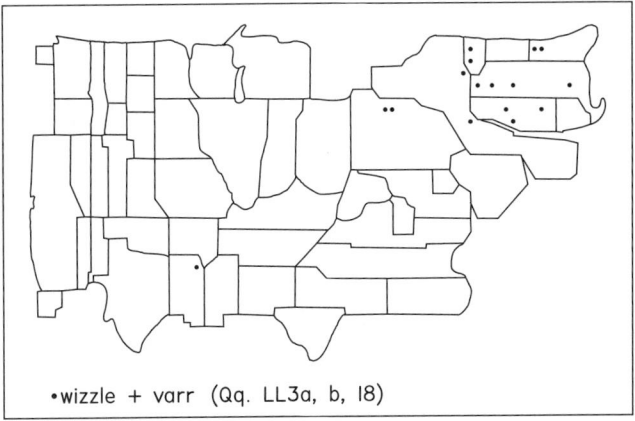

•wizzle + varr (Qq. LL3a, b, 18)

woak See **whook**

woap See **whope 1**

wob v Usu with *up* Also sp *wab* [*EDD wab* sb. 2 "A lump"] **chiefly NEng** Cf **wobbled up, wopse** v **1**
To wad up, crumple, form into a clump or clumps; hence ppl adjs *wabbed up, wobbed (up).*

    1864 (1865) Austin *Dora Darling* 58, What sort o' way to fold a sheet 's that? . . ye just wabbed it up any way, to call it done. [*DARE* Ed: The fictional speaker is in WV; author is from MA.] [**1868** in 1919 Hale *Letters* 43 **ceMA,** They roll up their slight clothing in a wob on their heads.] **1878** Fox *Gemini* 137 **NEng,** Her hair . . had been "wobbed up anyhow, to be out of the way." **1879** (1888) Brush *Col.'s Opera Cloak* 26 **NEng,** Pomp "wobbed" the shawl into a white garment and hurried it out to Leslie. **1914** Eaton *Boy Scouts* 88 **NEng,** She had on a pair of long overalls . . with her skirts wobbed up somehow inside of them. *Ibid* 221, They wabbed up an extra blanket or two for a bed. **1936** Gellhorn *Trouble* 44, She stood up before him, a thin old woman with her hair tightly wobbed on top of her head. **1979** *DARE* File **cnMA** (as of c1915), My grandmother, who grew up near Salem, MA, used to say "wobbed up" to describe something so wrinkled and creased that it was a mess. . . You could wob up a piece of paper you were about to put in a wastebasket, too. **1988** (1989) Chute *Letourneau's Auto* 220 **ME,** Bobby throws his wobbed-up Camel pack on the floor. **2005** in 2009 *DARE* File—Internet **OR,** The way I chose was to . . apply the glaze with a wobbed-up rag. *Ibid* **NH,** I have tried to keep lists of my own. . . I find them 3 months later all wabbed up in the washing machine. **2006** *Ibid* **sNH,** One day, I wabbed up a bunch of clams and tossed them out as far as I could, and I caught my 1st striper ever.

wobble See **warble**

wobble-cropped See **wamble-cropped**

wobbled up ppl adj phr Also *wabbled up obs* Cf **wob**
Crumpled up.

    1854 Foster *Fifteen Minutes* 46 **NYC,** What enormous strides the women take, with their beautiful silks . . wabbled up ingloriously about their ancles! **1865** Savage *Chronological Hist. Boston Police* 141 **MA,** I took up the letter, which was much wabbled up, and on straightening it out, found the upper left-hand corner torn off. **1870** (1871) Whitney *We Girls* 95 **MA,** Kitchens are horrid when girls have just gone out of them, and left the dish-towels dirty, and the dish-cloth all wabbled up. **1884** *Harper's New Mth. Mag.* 69.88 **seNY,** The great point is to keep the net straight, and not all tangled and wobbled up.

wobbledy adj, adv Cf Intro "Language Changes" III.1
Wobbly.

    1898 Lloyd *Country Life* 250 **AL,** Don't you remember that blame little slab-sided, razor-back, wobbledy-legged steer? **1967–70** *DARE* (Qu. KK23, *Weak or unsteady: "I think the footbridge will hold but it is a bit _____."*) Infs **LA17, MO30, NY184, OH49, OR15, VA69,** Wobbledy. **2007** *DARE* File—Internet, An' he opens the shed—an' we all ist laugh / When he drives out our little wobbledy [sic] calf. [*DARE* Ed: song version of James Whitcomb Riley's "Raggedy Man" by NC native and children's entertainer substituting *wobbledy* for Riley's *wobble-ly*] *Ibid,* There is a lot of play with the steering rack and the knuckles, making the steering wobbledy.

wobble-jaw n Also *whopple-jaw*
=**whopper-jaw** n.
  1893 Owen *Voodoo Tales* 219 **MO** [Black], He wuz de mos' uglies' man in de worl', wid er whopple-jaw an' er har'-lip. **1952** *Dixon Eve. Telegraph* (IL) 6 Feb 10/2, [Advt:] I guess I might as well take my car to Kerz Brothers and have old wobble-jaw tell me how to grease and change oil in it!

wobble-jawed adj Also *wabble-jawed, w(h)apple-~, womple-~, w(h)opple-~*
1 =**whopper-jawed 1.**
  1853 in 1913 Moffat *Pierrepont* 191, Washington's lower lip did project. He was what is termed slightly "whapple-jawed." **1854** Stimson *Easy Nat* 232 **MA**, At the start he had felt as he described it, pretty considerably wapple-jawed at leaving the old man, and the colt, and marm. **1883** *Hopewell Herald* (NJ) 8 Aug [6]/4 (newspaperarchive.com), If I look that mean, and low down, and insignificant, wopple-jawed and freckled . . it was high time I was hung high. **1885** *Marion Daily Star* (OH) 30 July [2]/4 (newspaperarchive.com), There are noble and dignified Washingtons, and there are pock marked, wild eyed, big nosed, wobble jawed scarecrows figuring as Washingtons. **1907** *DN* 3.251 **eME**, *Wopple-jawed. . .* Having a protruding square jaw. **1914** *Gaz. & Bulletin* (Williamsport PA) 6 June [3]/2 (newspaperarchive.com), [Illegible] for the past two years have caused pedestrians . . to become dizzy . . and wobble-jawed will soon be a thing of the past. . . That now famous thoroughfare is to be resurfaced and made new and smooth. **1919** *Janesville Daily Gaz.* (WI) 7 Apr 7/3, He's cross-eyed, wabble-jawed, and flat-footed. **1937** *Chron.-Telegram* (Elyria OH) 20 Aug 8/1, Wes Ferrell, wobble-jawed Washington Senators pitcher, played in tough luck yesterday.
2 =**whopper-jawed 2.**
  1884 Farrar *Wild Woods Life* 239, What is going to hold the top of those posts . . in line? They will be all wabble-jawed. **1888** Newell *Isle Palms* 31 [Black], Yo' all seed dish yere ole wapple-jawed brack pussun . . Look at dese yere ole crooked walkers. *Ibid* 227 [Black], Dese yere wopple-jawed ole bones. **1896** *DN* 1.426 **cNY**, *Wapple-jawed:* same as *wapper-jawed* [=crooked]. **1904** *Leslie's Mth. Mag.* 58.356, Affection, properly demonstrated, is apt to disorder the hair and make an apron set "wapple-jawed." **1905** *DN* 3.66 **eNE**, *Wabble-jawed. . .* (1) Loose-jointed, likely to fall to pieces; (2) same as *whocker-jawed. . .* "A wabble-jawed wagon"; "a wabble-jawed necktie." **1922** Cheley *Camp-Fire* 108, Now let's have a really true story. . . My imagination is all whopple-jawed from these awful fairy-tales. **1966–69** *DARE* (Qu. KK70, *Something that has got out of proper shape: "That house is all _____.")* Infs **IN70, OH5, SD5,** Wobble-jawed; **VT12,** Womple-jawed.

wob up See **wob**

wocus See **wokas**

wo'de See **wear** v **B3c**

woe'ter See **water A1**

woevine n
=**love vine 3.**
  [**1906** Field Museum Nat. Hist. *Bot. Ser.* 2.318 **Bahamas,** *Native Plant Names. . .* Woe vine—Cassytha Americana [=*C. filiformis*].] **1933** Small *Manual SE Flora* 925, *C[assytha] filiformis. . .* Love-vine. Woe-vine. . . This parasite appears to nearly all new acquaintances as a dodder *(Cuscuta)* which it resembles in habit and in color. **1970** Correll *Plants TX* 661, *Cassytha filiformis. . .* Woe-vine, love-vine. **1995** McAlister–McAlister *Aransas* 338 **TX,** Woevine: resembles a giant dodder. Pale green to orange vine snaking through live oak and red bay.

woice See **voice**

woish See **wash**

wokas n Also *wocus, wookes* [Klamath *wokas* seed of the spatterdock] chiefly **sOR, nCA**
A **spatterdock** (here: *Nuphar lutea* subsp *polysepala*); the seed of this plant used as food.
  1868 Bot. Soc. Edinburgh *Trans.* 9.338 **sOR,** Ground wokas (seeds of *Nuphar advena* . .), used as food by the Indians near the Klamath lakes, Oregon, &c. **1873** *Overland Mth.* 10.536 **nCA,** In these canoes they [= the Modocs] also gather the *wocus.* This is an aquatic plant, with a floating leaf very much like that of a pond-lily, in the centre of which is a pod resembling a poppy-head, full of farinaceous seeds. **1878** U.S.

Bur. Indian Affairs *Report* 114 **csOR,** By the time this crop is harvested and put away, the *wookes* (the seed of the pond-lily) is ripe and ready for them [=the Klamath Indians]. **1904** *Rake Reg.* (IA) 2 Sept [9]/2 (newspaperarchive.com) **OR,** The wokas gatherer uses a dugout canoe, and, pulling herself around among the dense growth of stems and leaves, picks off the full-grown seed pods. **1940** Writers' Program *Oregon* 21, Tribes migrated to the camas prairie, the wappato lake, or the wocus swamp, for the yearly harvest. **1961** *Daily Chron.* (Centralia WA) 24 June 7/1, All over the Pacific Northwest there is beginning to bloom the giant yellow water lily, called by the Indians, Wokas. **2001** *DARE* File **csOR** (as of c1938), We used to hear about the Klamath Indians collecting wocus.

woke See **wake 1a, 2c**

woked See **wake 1c, 2e**

woken See **wake 1e, 2a**

woke up See **wake 2c**

wolf n [*OED2 wolf* sb. 7.a 1559 →; "A name for certain malignant or erosive diseases. . . *Obs.* or *dial.*"]
1 pronc-sp *wool:* A swelling beneath the skin of cattle and other animals caused by the parasitic larva of a fly; the larva itself. chiefly **Sth, S Midl** Cf **wolf-in-the-tail**
  1815 in 1947 *AmSp* 22.282 [Americanisms], *Wolves*—for the larvæ of the *æstrus bovis,* in the backs of cows, hares, &c. **1828** *S. Agriculturist* 1.170, I will be obliged to any of your Subscribers, to point out a remedy for the wolf,—a preventative against the fly depositing its eggs,—and to inform me, if it is known, at what season the parent lays its eggs. **1876** *Waterloo Courier* (IA) 23 Feb [6]/7 (newspaperarchive.com), These pupae of the ox bot fly are what several of our subscribers have referred to of late under the name of "wolf" in cattle, a rather singular name to apply to a fly in one stage of its existence; but there is no accounting for the vulgar local names of such things, and "wolf" seems to be a favorite among farmers. **1912** Green *VA Folk-Speech* 487, *Wolf. . .* A parasite in a cow's back that makes her run about; and in an old horse's skin. **1917** *DN* 4.419 **KY, wNC,** *Wolf. . .* The warble that appears in summer in the backs of rabbits and squirrels. **1924** *DN* 5.295 **csNH,** *Wolf. . .* A swelling on the neck of cattle. [*DARE* Ed: This quot may refer instead to **2** below.] **1944** *PADS* 2.22 **sAppalachians,** *Wolves. . .* Bots or warbles in the backs of cows [*PADS* Ed: or rabbits and squirrels], caused supposedly by sprinkling salt on the cows' backs. **1966** *DARE* Tape **FL32,** That germ goes into the bloodstream and works all the way through the bloodstream and makes a kind of wobble ['wɑbl] wolf worm—big old ugly-looking thing that will work out on a cow's back and when it hatches out then it turns back into a fly again. **1982** Slone *How We Talked* 118 **eKY** (as of c1950), *Wools in the back*—the large "horse fly" laid its eggs under the skin on the back of the cows. . . When they hatched the larva were called "wools." Very painful. **2005** *DARE* File—Internet **eTN,** Old timers callem wolves or warbels they lay a egg that hatches out then diggs out. *Ibid* **ceVA,** In this area of Va. the wolves are bad in early season due to the warm weather. Later on when things cool down good the problem goes away.
2 A lesion symptomatic of actinomycosis. Cf **holdfast, lump jaw**
  1839 *ME Farmer & Jrl. Useful Arts* 6.387, As to whether the disease called a wolf uniformly originates in a tooth, my opinion is, that it does; for I have never seen it in cattle of any other age than from two to four years old. **1850** *MA Ploughman* 23 Feb 1, Our neighbor . . slaughtered a valuable steer, the other day, that had a wolf on the right lower jaw.
3 See **wolf whiskey.**

wolf v See **woof**

wolf across the river See **wolf over the river 1**

wolfbane n Also *wolfsbane*
An **Indian poke 1** (here: *Veratrum viride*).
  1830 Rafinesque *Med. Flora* 2.273, *Veratrum viride. . .* Wolf bane. . . a powerful dangerous article, requiring caution in exhibition. **1849** *OH Med. & Surgical Jrl.* 2.130, Veratrum viride. . . Com. names—American Hellebore, Itch-weed, Indian Poke, Earth gall, Wolfbane. . . Root very poisonous. **1898** U.S. Dept. Ag. Div. Botany *Bulletin* 20.16, American False Hellebore. . . Other names. . . bugbane; wolfsbane; bear corn.

wolfbean n Also *wolf's bean* [Calque of Ger *Wolf(s)bohne* < Lat *lupinus* appar < Lat *lupinus* wolfish]
A **lupine;** see quots.

1932 Rydberg *Flora Prairies* 456, *Lupinus* [spp]. . . Lupine, Wolf's Bean [etc]. **1937** U.S. Forest Serv. *Range Plant Hdbk.* W112, Lupines. . . These plants have many common names, including blue-bean, bluebonnet . . and wolfbean. **1963** Craighead *Rocky Mt. Wildflowers* 100, Bluebonnet—*Lupinus sericeus.* . . Other names: Lupine, Quakerbonnet, Wolfbean. **1967** Dodge *Roadside Wildflowers* 26, In some localities lupine is known as Quakerbonnet and wolfbean.

wolfberry n

1 Std: a **snowberry 1** (here: *Symphoricarpos occidentalis*); the fruit of this plant. Also called **buckbrush 3a, buckbush, Juneberry 2, pingree, quailberry**

2 Std: a shrub of the genus *Lycium;* the fruit of this plant. For other names of var spp see **buckbrush 3k, Christmasberry 4, desert thorn, garambullo, hoopee, matrimony vine 1, ohelo-kai, peach thorn, rabbit ~, squawberry 7, squawbush 4, squaw thorn, tomatillo 2, wild cranberry**

3 A **currant B1** (here: *Ribes cereum*).

1957 Barnes *Nat. Hist. Wasatch Spring* 57 **UT**, The mountain red currant (*Ribes cereum*). . . is sometimes called hereabout "wolf-berry" or "soldier berry."

wolf-foot n

=**bugleweed.**

[**1836** Eaton *Botany* 383, Lycopus. . . so named on account of a fancied resemblance between the cut leaves and a wolf's foot.] **1876** Hobbs *Bot. Hdbk.* 132, Wolf foot, Bugle weed, Lycopus Virginicus. **1900** Lyons *Plant Names* 234. **1930** Sievers *Amer. Med. Plants* 17, Bugleweed. . . Other common names.—Buglewort, . . wolf foot [etc]. **1971** Krochmal *Appalachia Med. Plants* 166.

wolf grape n [Calque of Arabic name for a species of *Solanum;* see quot 1849]

A **bittersweet** (here: *Solanum dulcamara*).

[**1849** Lynch *Exped. Jordan* 286, The plants we found here, besides the lily, were the yellow henbane . . ; the nightshade (anit el dil), or wolf-grape, supposed, by Hasselquist, to be the wild grape alluded to in Isaiah; [etc].] **1898** U.S. Dept. Ag. Div. Botany *Bulletin* 20.53, Bittersweet. *Solanum dulcamara.* . . Other names: Woody nightshade; bittersweet nightshade; wolf grape [etc]. **1930** Sievers *Amer. Med. Plants* 11, Bitter Nightshade. . . Other common names.—Bittersweet, . . wolf-grape [etc]. **1940** Clute *Amer. Plant Names* 272, *Solanum dulcamara.* Poisonweed, wolf-grape [etc].

wolf grass n **ME**

=**little bluestem.**

1896 *Daily Kennebec Jrl.* (Augusta ME) 13 Oct [3]/4 (newspaperarchive.com), The purple wood grass (Andropogan [sic] Scoparius.) . . It is quite common in the pine plains in Fryeburg and vicinity, but is seldom cut for fodder. It is called there "wolf grass." **1929** *Torreya* 29.149 **ME**, Andropogon scoparius, a grass growing in thin, sterile soil was thought to "run out" and impoverish the soil, hence the name *"Wolf grass."* **1966** DARE (Qu. S9, . . *Kinds of grass that are hard to get rid of*) Inf **ME**7, Wolf grass—grows in small bunches.

wolf hophornbeam n

A **hop hornbeam 1** (here: *Ostrya knowltonii*).

1979 Little *Checklist U.S. Trees* 181, *Ostrya knowltonii.* . . Other common names—western hophornbeam, wolf hophornbeam, "ironwood."

wolfing See **woof**

wolf-in-the-tail n Also *wolf tail* Cf **wolf** n **1**

=**hollow tail;** the supposed cause of this disorder.

1843 *Prairie Farmer* 3.269, I have known some persons split the tail (and cut out what they called the wolf in the tail, which I believe is all a phantom) put in salt and bind it up. **1873** *OH Farmer* 22.263, The equally imaginary 'wolf in the tail,' is overcome by slitting that part and binding in the wound such an assuaging agent as salt. **1879** U.S. Dept. Ag. *Special Rept.* 12.195 **KS**, Cattle are afflicted with wolf-tail and hollow-horn. **1894** *Homestead* 23 Nov 6, Time and time again . . has this almost insane delusion about "hollow horn" and "wolf in the tail" in cattle been explained. **1937** *AmSp* 12.161 [Veterinary terms], *Wolf-in-the-tail,* . . common fifty years ago and continuing much later as a term used to describe a bovine run down by faulty diet or starvation. **1960** Korson *Black Rock* 270 **PA**, By "wolf in the tail" the farmers meant decalcification, which sometimes resulted in the [cow's] tail falling off. **1961** Sackett-Koch *KS Folkl.* 76, If a cow is unthrifty, she has wolf-in-the-

tail. The cure is to split the skin on the tail and rub salt and pepper in the raw wound. **1968** DARE (Qu. K7, *What sickness can a cow get in her udder—for example, if she's left unmilked too long?*) Inf **OH**61, Wolf-in-the-tail [laughter]; (Qu. K28, . . *Chief diseases that cows have*) Inf **NJ**53, Hollow tail, wolf-in-the-tail—a worm in the tail and the tail rots off; **WV**7, Wolf-in-the-tail.

wolf in the woodshed, old gray   See **gray wolf 3**

wolf over the river n

1 also *wolf across* (or *on*) *the river, ~ over river, ~ on* (or *over*) *the ridge;* pronc-sp *woof over the river:* A game similar to **pom-pom-pullaway.**   chiefly **TX, Lower Missip Valley**

1889 *TX School Jrl.* 7.53, Get them [=girls] to play at base, jumping the rope . . "wolf over the river," "mumble peg," "pitching horse shoes," or any such games that they may know. **1906** *DN* 3.164 **nwAR**, Wolf over the river. . . The name of a game. **1915** *Colman's Rural World* 68.36.13 **LA**, Our next prize game . . is called, *Wolf Over the Ridge.* . . To begin, two bases are chosen quite a distance apart. One is occupied by the wolf and the other by the rest of the players. When all are ready the wolf will say: "What have you got?" and the rest . . answer: "More than you can catch at one grab," whereupon the wolf runs toward the players' base and the players run toward the wolf's base. All players caught by the wolf . . must be wolves and help catch the others. **1926** *Amer. Phys. Educ. Rev.* 31.1110, *Graded Games for Rural Schools.* . . 6th Grade. . . Wolf on the Ridge [etc]. **1952** in 2001 DARE File—Internet **Ozarks** (as of c1910), Our physical education was at recess and noon, playing such games as "Wolf Over the River." **1953** Brewster *Amer. Nonsinging Games* 53 **MO**, *Wolf Over the Ridge.* . . The object of the game is to get from one of the bases to the other without being caught by the player in the middle. The player who is "It" calls out, "Wolf over the ridge!" All the players then try to reach the side opposite them. **1957** *Sat. Eve. Post Letters* **cTX** (as of 1880s), Wolf Over the River was a thrilling game! "Wolf over the River" called the wolf on one side. "What do you want?" the leader on the other side would answer. "Sheep meat and I'm bound to have it"[;] then ensued a wild scramble on the part of the sheep to avoid capture as they ran to the opposite base. **1967–70** DARE (Qu. EE1, . . *Games . . children play . . in which they form a ring*) Inf **TX**65, Wolf over the river—stand in two lines, try to catch others; (Qu. EE33, . . *Outdoor games . . that children play*) Infs **KY**74, **TX**42, Wolf over the river; **TX**101, Woof over the river; **MO**17, Wolf over the river—two sides, 12–15 boys on a side, a certain line we'd have to cross; some of the opposition'd catch us before we'd get across that line; get down to two or three on each side; they'd butt heads then; **MO**34, Wolf over the ridge—you just run and exchange places; each one has a base; whoever gets caught before they get there is it. **1986** Pederson *LAGS Concordance,* 3 infs, **TX**, Wolf over the river; 1 inf, **cLA**, Wolf over river; 1 inf, **csTX**, Wolf across the river—tag game, like red rover; 1 inf, **cTX**, Wolf on the river, catch all you can—maybe rough. **2003** Staples *Wolf Over the Ridge: Games We Used to Play* [title] **Ozarks.** **2006** DARE File—Internet **TX** (as of c1992), When asked his favorite game, he wasn't sure if it was "Wolf Over the River" or poker. **2007** *Ibid* **UT** (as of c1935), In the winter or at night, we would play Fox and Hound, Kick the Can, Wolf Over the River and Annie-I-Over.

2 A jump-rope game; see quot.

1956 *Western Folkl.* 15.47 **TX**, *Wolf over the River*—One jumper is "wolf," while the rest are "sheep." While the rope is being turned the ones in front, or the "sheep," attempt to avoid being caught or touched by the one pursuing them, or the "wolf." The "sheep" yell "help, help" during the chase in and out of the turning rope.

wolf pen   See **pen** n[1] **B1**

wolfsbane   See **wolfbane**

wolf's bean   See **wolfbean**

wolf's candle(s) n

=**ocotillo.**

1906 *Jrl. Outdoor Life* 3.111 **cwTX**, The first plant to blossom is the wolf's candle. . . The Mexicans call it ocotillo. **1949** Curtin *By the Prophet* 89 **AZ**, Fouquieria splendens. . . Common name. . . Wolf's Candles. **1951** *PADS* 15.36 **TX**, *Fouquiera* [sic] *splendens.* . . Crown-of-thorns; wolf's-candle. **1964** *Bee* (Danville VA) 27 Mar sec A 8/1 **West**, Three hours past noon wolf's candle appeared with its thorny gray wands and occasional vermillion blossom.

wolf scarer n **AK** Cf **bull roarer 1**

A noisemaker; see quots.

1963 Rodahl *Last Few* 204 **AK,** The wolf scarer is a piece of baleen attached to a string of sinew. When it is whirled over one's head, the screaming, whining sound thus produced scares the wolves away. **1988** *DARE* File **AK** (as of 1960s), My brother has a wolf scarer that was made by an Alaskan Eskimo. It is made out of baleen and is an oblong shape with notches cut into the edges. It is whirled around at the end of a string and makes a loud roaring noise. **2006** *DARE* File—Internet **AK,** Athabascan Games. . . Wolf Scarer or Buzz Toy—This wooden or heavy card-board toy is flat with two center holes. String is strung through them. When the toy is whirled in the air it makes a high pitched whirring noise.

wolf spider n

Std: a spider of the family Lycosidae that hunts for its prey. For other names of var spp see **burrowing spider, turret ~ 1** Cf **tarantula spider**

wolf tail See **wolf-in-the-tail**

wolf ticket See **woof ticket**

wolf whiskey n   Also *wolf*   Cf *DS* DD21c

Moonshine liquor.

    1974 Dabney *Mountain Spirits* 25 **sAppalachians,** The names [for corn whiskey include] . . wolf whiskey. **2006** *DARE* File—Internet **AL,** The quality of . . homemade whiskey varied significantly. In particular, there was one kind that they called "wolf" or "steam run wolf". I never knew exactly what that meant, but there was some reference to first batch or first run made from hog shorts that was offered up in explanation as to what constituted wolf whiskey. I do remember that when someone was drinking wolf, they smelled especially bad.

woll See **wallow**

wollerkertoot n   [Imit]

=**bittern.**

    1858 in 1906 Thoreau *Writings* 17.251 **MA,** He says that some call the stake-driver "belcher-squelcher," and ·some, "wollerkertoot."

wolly-gobble See **golly-wobbled**

wolverine n

Std: the northern carnivorous mammal *Gulo gulo* subsp *luscus,* formerly *Gulo luscus.*   Also called **carcajou 1, glutton 1, Indian devil 2, skunk bear**

womacock n

=**pileated woodpecker B.**

    1945 McAtee *Nomina Abitera* 41 **AL,** Pileated Woodpecker. . . Womacock; this term is reported by M.M Mathews as in use in Clarke County, Alabama, about 1900; it was not spoken in the presence of women, a taboo probably due to its resemblance to certain well-known words, with which, however, it seems to have no connection. It may be in part of Indian origin but correspondence with authorities has failed to reveal its derivation.

woman n   Usu |'wumən, 'wʊmən|; for varr see **A** below

A   Forms.

1 |'ʊmən|, rarely |'ʌmən|; pronc-spp *(o)oman, omern, uman, ummern.* [*OED2 woman* sb. "('ʊmən), ('ʌmən) . . have now sunk to vulgar or dialectal status."] **chiefly Sth, S Midl** Cf **dummern**

    1851 Hooper *Widow Rugby's Husband* 46 **AL,** Ses I, 'what the h-ll are you up to, old 'oman?' **1858** in 1956 Eliason *Tarheel Talk* 320 **c,csNC,** *Woman*—uman. **1884** Smith *Bill Arp's Scrap Book* 73 **nwGA,** Over 200 [hens] now respond to my old 'oman's call every mornin. **1889** *MLN* 4.209 **TN,** *'Oman.* . . The writer has heard it frequently from old people. **1893** Shands *MS Speech* 12 [Black], *W* . . is dropped in ['ʊmən] for *woman.* **1908** *DN* 3.281 **eAL, wGA,** W initial disappears in (w)oman. **1912** Green *VA Folk-Speech* 305, *Oman.* . . For *woman.* . . *Ooman.* **1913** Kephart *Highlanders* 279 **sAppalachians,** *Woman.* . . ummern. **1922** Gonzales *Black Border* 316 **sSC, GA coasts** [Gullah glossary], *Ooman.* . . " 'Ooman iz uh sometime t'ing." **1923** *DN* 5.224 **swMO,** *Woman.* . . Frequently 'Oman. **1929** Sale *Tree Named John* 77 **MS** [Black], Jes 'ten' lak you'z a oman—not no gal chile but a grown oman. **1934** Hurston *Jonah's Gourd Vine* 10 **AL** [Black], You sho is one aggervatin' 'oman. **1939** Montgomery *Days of Old* 8 **eNC** (as of 1861–65) [Black], Oh, Walt, that was about nothin' but a 'oman. **1941** *LANE* Map 375, 1 inf, **seCT,** [ðə oʊl ʊmən]; 1 inf,

swRI, [ði ol ʊmən]. **1944** *PADS* 2.38 **nwNC,** That 'omern's aboon her own kinnery. **1949** Turner *Africanisms* 266 **sSC, GA coasts** [Gullah], [ʊmən]. **1952** Brown *NC Folkl.* 1.571, *'Oman* ['ʌmən]. . . Woman. **1953** Brewer *Word Brazos* 88 **eTX** [Black], Ole man Johnson was de pappy of twenty-fo' chilluns by de same 'oman. **1975** *Appalachian Jrl.* 2.150 **wNC,** The dropping of the initial *w* seldom occurs today but *'oman* is remembered as a common form.

2 |'wumən|; pronc-spp *womern.*   **esp sAppalachians, C Atl** Cf Intro "Language Changes" I.8

    1938 Matschat *Suwannee R.* 20 **neFL, seGA,** Ye're a womern. *Ibid* 36, Ye . . don't know much about such things, bein' a fureen womern. **1942** Hall *Smoky Mt. Speech* 70 **wNC, eTN,** There has been a tendency in old Smokies speech to develop [ə] into [ɚ], especially before n. . . [Examples include:] *woman* ['wʊmɚn]. **1967** *Mt. Life* 43.1.14 **sAppalachians,** A womern come to the door. **1969** *DARE* FW Addit **swNJ,** Woman ['wumɚn]. **1982** Slone *How We Talked* 36 **eKY** (as of c1950), *Womern*—woman. **2000** Shores *Tangier Is.* 188 **Chesapeake Bay,** One may also hear "ruinded," "stunnded," "drownded," "womern," and "umberella," which are fairly common.

3 pronc-spp *werman, worman.*

    1924 (1946) Greer-Petrie *Angeline Gits an Eyeful* 7 **csKY,** That old werman is li'ble to call anything out of hits name. **1955** Roberts *S. from Hell-fer-Sartin* 194 **seKY,** An' the old man says, "Old worman," said, "I'll have to go off and be gone tonight."

4 |'wʌmən, 'womən|.

    1938 *AmSp* 13.52 **Boston MA,** [ðə pʊə 'womən kəim toᵊd ə]. **1944** Kenyon–Knott *Pronc. Dict.* 478, *Woman.* . . 'womən & 'wʌmən are reported as occas., esp. in the S[outh].

B   Gram forms.

Pl: usu *women* |'wɪmɪn|; also:

1 *weemen, weeman, weemin.* [*OED2 woman* sb. "From at least the 16th century, the only variety in the pronunciation of the pl. has been in respect of the quantity of the first vowel, which was either short or long in the 16th and 17th centuries."]

    1692 in 1977 *Salem Witchcraft Papers* 2.371 **MA,** In the s'd place starte up 2 or 3 weemen and flew from mee. **1858** in 1956 Eliason *Tarheel Talk* 320 **c,csNC,** *Women.* . . weeman. **1869** *Overland Mth.* 3.128 **Sth,** The fierce military spirit of the South is shown in the scorn and contempt which they heaped on men who refused to go out to battle. In Texas they were called, with a play on the word *women,* (in the South often pronounced *weemen*) . . "we-men." **1872** Hume *Five Hundred Majority* 8 **cNY,** Weemen is always very innocent when the mischief's done. **1900** Lloyd *Chronic Loafer* 212 **PA,** Weemen is sot agin furrin wars. Leastways my weemen. **1908** *OH Mag.* 4.133, I don't think the sins o' the man should be visited on the weemin. **1931** Goodrich *Mt. Homespun* 66 **sAppalachians,** They're mighty trifling and fergetful when it comes to anythin' they 'low is work for weemin. **1976** in 1991 Burrison *Storytellers* 22 **GA,** I . . peeped on in through a crack, and seen a whole lotta weemen in thar.

2 *womens;* pronc-spp *wimmens, wimmins.*   **Sth, S Midl** esp freq among Black speakers   Cf **-s** suff³

    1856 Simms *Eutaw* 110 **SC,** These wimmins is his wife and only darter. **1890** *Scribner's Mag.* 8.440 **sAppalachians,** The wimmins is satisfy 'cause they 'specks to be beat. **1927** Adams *Congaree* 8 **cSC** [Black], De wimmens! Hell was jam full of them. **1927** Kennedy *Gritny* 222 **sLA** [Black], A whole crowd o' wimmins. **1928** Peterkin *Scarlet Sister Mary* 114 **SC** [Gullah], De womens don't let him rest. **1942** Rawlings *Cross Creek* 265 **nFL** [Black], He don't like womens much. **1946** McCullers *Member* 66 **AL,** I have knew womens to love veritable Satans. **1955** in 1958 Brewer *Dog Ghosts* 19 **TX** [Black], Dey hab a lots of womens to drap in to see 'em. **1959** Lomax *Rainbow Sign* 112 **AL** [Black], Mens is just naturally more harder hearted than womens. **1966–70** *DARE* Tape **FL50,** The way they got the womens smoking it [=tobacco]—I seen it in the paper; **SC14A,** Didn't the womens wear something we call the Mary Jane? [Both Infs Black] **1971** *Foxfire* Winter 247 **nGA,** Most of th'old womens in those days smoked cobbed pipes. **1981** Walker *You Can't* 6 [Black], He loved the way my singin' made the dirt farmers cry like babies and the womens shout. **1986** Pederson *LAGS Concordance,* 5 infs, **AL, GA, TN,** Womens; 1 inf, **cnFL,** The mens helps the womens; 2 infs, **LA, MS,** Widow womens. [All infs Black]

3 pronc-spp *'omen, omerns.*   Cf **A1** above

    1889 Folsom *Scraps* 197 **GA** [Black], One uv de neighbo' omerns come an' done des de same way. **1939** in 1976 *Weevils in the Wheat* 304 **VA** [Black], Dey w'uld rake de wheat jes as clean, an' den de 'omen w'uld bind it up in shocks.

4 pronc-sp *wimmern.*

1950 Fisher *Spitter* 3 **AR**, Wimmern welders, wimmern hack drivers, wimmern rasslers, wimmern boilermakers—we was bound to have them when the young fellers marched off.

woman-body See **woman-person**

woman doctor n

A midwife; an obstetrician.

1966 Dakin *Dial. Vocab. Ohio R. Valley* 2.433, *Midwife. . .* Scattered speakers also say . . *woman doctor.* **1973** in 2004 Montgomery–Hall *Dict. Smoky Mt. Engl.* 654, *Woman doctor. . .* Lincoln Whaley, he was a good woman doctor. **1975** *Appalachian Jrl.* 2.154 **wNC**, The midwife was a *woman doctor* or a *granny woman* who would come in the old days and stay a week after delivering the baby for the grand sum of one dollar. **1986** Pederson *LAGS Concordance (Midwife)* 1 inf, **nwTN**, Woman doctor; 1 inf, **cwMS**, Woman doctor—used today; 1 inf, **csAR**, Woman doctor—term used by blacks.

woman-grown adj Cf **man-grown**

Having reached womanhood, grown-up.

1865 *Atlantic Mth.* 15.684, Grace—who is her oldest daughter, and almost woman grown—has some evening appointment. **1913** Miller *Ambition* 113, And she . . did indeed then seem woman-grown.

‡woman jessie n Cf **jesse 4**

A cowardly man.

1934 Hurston *Jonah's Gourd Vine* 99 **AL** [Black], He don't fight no men-folks. He's uh woman-jessie. Beat up women and run from mens.

woman-person n Also *woman-body* **chiefly Sth, S Midl** Cf **man-person**

A woman.

1824 Cooper *Lionel Lincoln* 2.211 **MA**, " 'Tis an awful time for women bodies to journey in!" said a middle-aged woman. **1853** Simms *Sword & Distaff* 404 **SC**, The wisdom of the thing is what you hain't quite come up to, being a woman body, and not having an equal chance with we men pussons. **1871** Johnston *Dukesborough Tales* 196 **GA**, If it warn't for his westcoat you would say it war a woman person. **1909** Porter *Girl Limberlost* 143 **IN**, Seems like . . toward night as if a body got kind o' lonesome for a woman person. **1920** *Outlook* 14 Jan 66 **eKY**, A body can make shift somehow to feed 'em up of days,/ But nights they need a woman-person's foolish little ways. **1933** Rawlings *South Moon* 189 **nFL**, A woman-person, special, belongs to be keerful. A woman in the family way'll kill sage, techin' it. **1934** *Mt. Life* 10.15 **sAppalachians**, Yer chickens an' hogs they tell me is a sight to see—even if they do need a woman body to see after 'em. **c1940** in 2004 Montgomery–Hall *Dict. Smoky Mt. Engl.* 654, *Woman-person. . .* A woman person's ways. **1952** Justus *Children Gt. Smoky Mts.* 45 **eTN**, There was no woman person in their home since Mrs. Harris had died the year before.

woman root n

A **coral tree** (here: *Erythrina herbacea*).

1926 *Torreya* 26.5 **GA**, *Erythrina herbacea. . .* Sapelo Id., Ga. At this locality the root of the plant has a reputation as a tonic, and is called man-root or woman-root, according to the sex of the person seeking it.

woman's tobacco See **ladies'-tobacco a**

womble-cropped See **wamble-cropped**

womenfolk(s) n Cf **menfolk(s)**

1 pl: Women; the women of a family or community.

1824 Sedgwick *Redwood* 1.241 **MA**, Do not expect Mr. Redwood to tell all the secrets of his life before the 'women folks.' **1843** (1916) Hall *New Purchase* 123 **IN**, Many . . hurried out to secure their own accoutrements and those of the "wimmin folks's." **1869** Stowe *Oldtown Folks* 251 **MA**, What boy with all these virtues is not held a saint by all women-folk? *Ibid* 482, There 's plenty of women-folks 't our house. **1892** Robinson *VT Independence* 293, All the women-folk knitted stockings and mittens while they rested or visited. **1899** (1912) Green *VA Folk-Speech* 487, *Women-folks. . .* Women, especially the members of a household. **1909** *DN* 3.389 **eAL, wGA**, *Women-folks. . .* The women of a household or a community. "My women-folks are cleanin' house today; so I had to skeedaddle." **1919** Mencken *Prejudices* 141, It is pre-

cisely his softness that makes him the slave of his women-folk. **1942** Faulkner *Go Down* 13 **MS**, Anytime you wants to git something done, from hoeing out a crop to getting married, just get the womenfolks to working at it. **1948** Manfred *Chokecherry* 199 **nwIA**, Siouxland wasn't always tough on the womenfolk then. **c1960** *Wilson Coll.* **csKY**, *Women-folks. . .* Women as a group. **1967** *DARE* (Qu. N12, . . *Somebody who drives carelessly or not well*) Inf **LA10**, Womenfolks. **1967** *DARE* FW Addit **ceNC**, "Womenfolks," "menfolks" (for "women," "men")—heard often in conversation with country people. **1980** *Moravia Union* (IA) 28 Feb 2/4, The men folk went on to Ottumwa to attend the cow-calf conference. The women folk spent the day visiting. **1986** Pederson *LAGS Concordance* **Gulf Region**, 18 infs, (The) womenfolks; 2 infs, Womenfolk; 2 infs, Womenfolks—the women in (*or* of) the community; 1 inf, Womenfolks—women in the family; 1 inf, Womenfolks done the hoeing.

2 See quot.

1907 *DN* 3.251 **eME**, *Women folks. . .* Wife. "Your women folks told me I could go ahead and put up the ceiling."

womens See **woman B2**

women's wood n

=**squaw wood 1**.

1978 *DARE* File **nME**, *Women's wood*—stove wood, popple; not oak, hickory, etc., small pieces, not split. **2007** *DARE* File—Internet **OK**, Where I live, we have lot's of Red Cedar. Underneath one of these big guys, you will always find "Women's Wood". It stays dry and is easy to gather, and with all the oil in Cedar, lights fast and burns *hot*. **2008** *DARE* File **nME** (as of late 1970s), A land surveyor was in the kitchen of friends, and I asked about splitting the popple. He said that popple is "women's wood," which means small sticks that don't need splitting. Alder would also be "women's wood" because it burns hot and briefly, for use in the summer when you don't want the cookstove to heat up the kitchen.

womern See **woman A2**

wommis See **wamus**

womper n Also *whomper* **esp NJ** Cf **swamp wamper**

=**bull snake**.

1965 Teale *Wandering Through Winter* 274 **NJ**, The "Pineys" who dwell in the barrens have a picturesque vocabulary of their own. . . Pine snakes—at one time such serpents were supplied from the barrens to carnival performers all over the country—are "wompers." **1968** *DARE* (Qu. P25, . . *Kinds of snakes*) Inf **NJ39**, Whomper—similar to pine snake. **1987** Moonsammy et al. *Pinelands Folklife* 34 **NJ**, The biggest snake, the "whomper," is also called the "pilot" snake, according to Tom Brown, because tradition has it that it indicates where the rattlesnakes are.

womper-gogglin adj Also *wompygogglin* Cf **whomper-jawed**, DS KK70

=**antigoglin**.

1968 *DARE* File **neAL**, *Womper-gogglin*—kitty-cornered or cockeyed. "That table is all womper-gogglin." **2010** *DARE* File—Internet **ceKY**, My mother (b. Martin County, KY, 1920) would say "wompygogglin."

womper-jawed See **whomper-jawed**

‡wompers adv

2000 *WI State Jrl.* (Madison) 21 Nov sec A 4/1 **AK**, "It's truly amazing what can happen [when the permafrost melts]," said . . a mechanical engineering professor at the University of Alaska at Fairbanks. "Things just go wompers."

womper-sided See **whomper-sided**

wompey-jaw See **whomper-jawed**

womple-jawed See **wobble-jawed**

wompny-jawed See **whompny-jawed**

wompus See **wampus** n[2]

wompygogglin See **womper-gogglin**

wompy-jawed See **whomper-jawed**

wonder v[1]

1 To surprise, amaze. [This and the following sense appear to be of multiple origin; in the majority of quots they are clearly calques of PaGer idioms, but others appear to reflect Brit dial survivals of ME idioms (see *OED2 wonder* v. 1.f, 4, *SND wunner* II.1).] **esp PaGer area**

1863 in 2000 Dreese *151st PA Volunteers* 60, We . . were sent around the battlefield about five hours, and thus Boltz had very sore feet. It wondered me that he stood it so long. **1908** *German Amer. Annals* 10.51 **sePA,** *Wonder*. . . Surprise, used reflexively. "It wonders me that he stays so long." **1920** Martin *Schoolmaster* 111 **sePA,** It would wonder you the way the folks that keeps hired help wants to be waited on. *Ibid* 288, "So what you did feel for her, wonders me!" "I wonder at it, too, now, Minnie." **1964** (1965) Gould *You Should Start* 37 **ME,** Topsham Fair hadn't grown up then, either, and it still had things to wonder you. **1968** *DARE* FW Addit **VA**31, It wonders me—it amazes me; common. **1982** *Barrick Coll.* **csPA,** It wondered me that it stood this long. **1997** in 1999 Millersville Univ. Center for PA Ger. Studies *Jrl.* Fall 22, *It wonders me.* _____ *they didn't come.* 2.5% [of 40 infs], *It wonders me;* 75%, *I wonder why;* 25%, *I don't know why.* In preliminary research, several respondents admitted to using *It wonders me,* although they always maintained that they shouldn't because it is not "proper." One female respondent, age twenty-one, told me that she would not use this term in speaking, but might use it if she wrote a letter to another Mennonite friend. **2004** *DARE* File **csPA,** Phrases of the sort "It wonders me" are somewhat familiar to my White respondents.

2 To be a matter of conjecture to (one). [See **1** above] **esp PaGer area**

1860 Warner *Say & Seal* 1.411 **NEast,** What wonders me is, why he don't marry that girl out of hand. **1904** Martin *Tillie* 272 **sePA,** It wonders me sometimes, how Tillie 's goin' to keep from marryin' him, now he 's made up his mind so firm! **1921** *DN* 5.118 **KY,** "If that wouldn't kreistle a'body, it wonders me what would." Henry Co. *Ibid* 119 **KY,** It wonders me what that boy's about. **1935** *AmSp* 10.167 **PA** [Engl of PA Germans], It wonders me what he is doing now. **1952** Brown *NC Folkl.* 1.608, It wonders me how that bear ever climbed that tree. **1964** Kesey *Sometimes* 109 **OR,** It used to wonder me just how come I'd sometimes get all of a sudden so itchy to cut out from basketball practice. . . It would really wonder me. **1968** *DARE* FW Addit **PA**142, What wonders me, already, is why he did it. **1979** Carpenter *Walton War* 172 **sAppalachians,** Hit wonders me how time can go on as fur as everything has got, and I have pondered on hit a sight.

3 in phr *I wonder me:* I wonder. [*EDD wonder* v. 6.(3)]

1928 Chapman *Happy Mt.* 20 **seTN,** I wonder me why! **1943** Peattie *Great Smokies* 146 **sAppalachians,** Their phrasing has a rhythm to it, such as. . . "I wonder me if." **1960** in 2004 Montgomery–Hall *Dict. Smoky Mt. Engl.* 655 **wNC, eTN,** I wonder me if she can bake biscuit bread.

wonder n   Also *wonder cake* [See quot 1897] **chiefly NEng =cruller.**

1844 Leslie *Directions Cookery* 357 **sePA,** *Wonders, or Crullers.* . . Cut it [=the dough] into long slips with a jagging iron, or with a sharp knife, and twist them into various fantastic shapes. **1845** *Knickerbocker* 25.447 **NEng,** I gave my good aunt ocular assurance that her. . . 'wonders' were as acceptable as they used to be. **1848** in 1870 Drake *Pioneer Life* 97 **KY** (as of a1800), They were . . "wonders," . . being known to you under the name of crullers. **1848** in 1935 *AmSp* 10.41 **Nantucket MA,** *Wonders.* A kind of cake. **1859** Stowe *Minister's Wooing* 34 **MA,** Crullers or wonders, as a sort of sweet fried cake was commonly called. [**1897** *N&Q* 8th ser 12.98, I saw a similar cake at St. Heliers, [Isle of] Jersey, at Michaelmas, 1870—there known as "Jersey wonders."] **1923** Farnham *Brief Boyhood Nantucket* 180 **eMA,** But "wonders"—Nantucket "wonders!" Those were a prized article for "dessert" food. . . What were they? Simply doughnuts made in a certain prescribed regulation form. **1932** *DN* 6.284 **swCT,** *Wonder cakes.* Plain doughnuts, cut into fingers and twisted; dip them in syrup or molasses. **1941** *LANE* Map 284 *(Doughnut)* 3 infs, **Nantucket, Martha's Vineyard MA,** Wonders—a kind of doughnut.

wonder v²   See **wander**

wonder bean n

A **jack bean 1** (here: *Canavalia ensiformis*).
1914 Piper *Forage Plants* 550, The jackbean. . . has been designated the Pearson bean, and recently the Wonder bean.

wonder cake See **wonder** n

wonderful adv   **orig widespread, now esp PaGer area**
Very (much).

1841 (1952) Cooper *Deerslayer* 437 **cNY,** You're wonderful handsome. **1911** Wharton *Ethan Frome* 194 **wMA,** She bears with Mattie wonderful. **1935** *AmSp* 10.171 **PA** [Engl of PA Germans], *Wonderful.* Used loosely as an intensive. 'He was wonderful sick last night.' 'It was a wonderful heavy rain.' **1948** *AmSp* 23.238 [Engl of PA Germans], *Wonderful,* a common adverb. 'It stinks wonderful: P.G. *Es schtinkt wunnerbaar.*' 'It is wonderful nice: P.G. *Es iss wunnerbaar schee.*' **1952** *PA Dutchman* Sept 4, Have I told you enough to whet your appetite so that you will plan to come join us next year at the Second Pennsylvania Dutch Folk Culture Seminar? It gives a wonderful good vacation place! **1968** *DARE* FW Addit **PA**142, He's a wonderful hard worker. **1969** in 2004 Montgomery–Hall *Dict. Smoky Mt. Engl.* 655, *Wonderful.* . . Jim orter a-made a good moonshiner, if he hadn't a been so skeery . . since he could see and hear so wonderful well. **1970** *DARE* (Qu. B1, *If a day is very pleasant . . it's a* _____ *day*) Inf **PA**242, Wonderful nice. **1978** *DARE* File **sePA,** I was wonderful sick last week. . . It wonders me wonderful. **1987** *Jrl. Engl. Ling.* 20.2.177 **ePA,** *Wonderful* "an adjective or adverb [used] to indicate a high degree of anything; for example, *It sure was a wonderful hard rain*". . . Even though Wilson [=quot 1948] . . describes this feature as "common", it seems to be highly restricted in distribution today. Not only is it limited to older speakers . . , but it is also characteristic of less educated ones. **2000** Lewis *Redemption* 41 **sePA,** Fresh raw milk is a wonderful-gut source of income and makes for healthy English bones as well as Amish.

wondering dew See **wandering Jew**

wonder-of-the-world root n   Also *world-wonder root* [Perh from *wonder of the world* a book name—once alleged to be a translation of the Chinese name—for ginseng; but in parts of the Caribbean the same name is applied to a quite different plant with medicinal uses, *Kalanchoe pinnata*.]
In hoodoo: a magical root, perh that of **ginseng B1.**

1931 Hurston in *Jrl. Amer. Folkl.* 44.330 **LA,** When you first go on the field of treasure you will walk around it in a square and on the north corner you will plant a piece of the Wonder of the World Root. *Ibid* 413, World-wonder Root. It is used in treasure hunts. Bury a piece in the four corners of the field; also hide it in the four corners of your house to keep things in your favor. **1946** Tallant *Voodoo* 219 **New Orleans LA,** Wonder-of-the-World Root is truly a wonder. Used to locate buried treasure, it is sought most frequently by residents of rural sections who believe treasure to be concealed somewhere near their property.

wongah See **wanga**

wonkapin See **wankapin**

wonky-jawed See **whonker-jawed**

wonst See **once**

won't v¹   See **be C2b**

wont v²   See **want** v¹

woo exclam   See **whoo**

woo n

A **nighthawk 1** (here: *Chordeiles minor*).
1956 MA Audubon Soc. *Bulletin* 40.81 **MA,** Common Nighthawk. . . Woo (Mass. From the wing sound.)

woobles n   Cf **bore for the simples**

1933 *AmSp* 8.1.53 **Ozarks,** *Woobles.* . . Feeblemindedness, foolishness, idiocy. When a hillman says that a certain person should be *bored for th' woobles,* he refers to an old belief that these mental troubles are relieved by a surgical operation on the brain.

wood anemone n

Std: an anemone, usu *Anemone quinquefolia.* For other names of the latter see **Little Buffalo medicine, mayflower 3a, nightcaps, snowboys, snowdrops 2;** for other names of var spp see **snowflower 2**

wood balm n

A **pitcher sage 1** (here: *Lepechinia calycina*).
1897 Parsons *Wild Flowers CA* 42, The wood-balm is closely allied to the sages, which fact is betrayed by its opposite, wrinkly, sage-scented leaves. **1920** Rice–Rice *Pop. Studies CA Wild Flowers* 105, I like the name applied to *Sphacele calycina* [=*Lepechinia c.*] by the mountaineers. They call it "Wood Balm."

wood bass n

Either of two closely related fishes: the **green sunfish 1** or the **warmouth.**

1930 U.S. Dept. Commerce Bur. Fisheries *Document* 1055.298, Apomotis cyanellus. . . *Bream; Buffalo sunfish; Perch; Red-eye; Sunfish; Blanco perch; Wood bass.* **1933** LA Dept. of Conserv. *Fishes* 347, The Green Sunfish, like so many of its relatives, rejoice[s] in a wide variety of popular names. . . [including] Wood Bass. **1951** Harlan–Speaker *IA Fish* 114, *Warmouth. . . Other Names*—Warmouth bass, wood bass, mud bass, weed bass. **1972** *Living Museum* 34.127 **IL,** The warmouth, often known as the warmouth bass, wood bass, open-mouth, goggle-eye, and by other local names, is one of the less familiar members of the Illinois fish fauna.

wood bee n   Cf *DS* FF2

=**chopping bee;** similarly n *wood-piling bee.*

1845 Kirkland *Western Clearings* 168 **MI,** His "business", which we have supposed to consist principally in helping at raisings, wood-bees, huskings, and such like important affairs. **1857** *Quinland* 1.91 **NY,** The whole neighborhood would assemble . . to prepare for each other the wood necessary to keep such a fire going during the winter as we have described at the beginning of this narrative; hence a "wood bee." **1919** *DN* 5.59 **NW,** *Wood bee.* The neighbors held their annual wood bee Tuesday, to provide Mrs. Ida Barber with her winter's supply of fuel. Kalama Bulletin. **1963** Pilgrim Soc. Plymouth MA *Notes* 13.4, Whatever must be done that was beyond the power of one family was made a neighborhood affair, and called a "bee." There was a quilting bee, an apple-gathering bee, a wood-piling bee.

wood betony n

1 A **lousewort 1,** usu *Pedicularis canadensis.*

1826 Darlington *Florula Cestrica* 71, *P[edicularis] canadensis. . . Vulgò*—Wood Betony. Louse-wort. . . Woodlands, thickets, and sandy banks. **1860** (1861) MI Geol. Surv. *First Biennial Rept.* 282, Louse-wort, Wood Betony. Pedicularis Canadensis . . Ann Arbor, Common . . Pedicularis lanceolata . . Ann Arbor. **1901** Lounsberry *S. Wild Flowers* 467, The wood betony rearing its slender corolla as the head of a walrus and even with two miniature projections in imitation of his tusks. **1937** Stemen–Myers *OK Flora* 485, *Pedicularis canadensis. . .* Wood Betony. . . Woods and thickets. **1974** (1977) Coon *Useful Plants* 246, *Pedicularis canadensis*—Wood-betony. . . It was used by the Indians to cure rattlesnake bites and as a magic charm, although to sheep eating it, it is poisonous.

2 =**bugleweed.**

1889 *Century Dict.* 536, *Wood-betony,* which name is also given in the United States to . . *Lycopus Virginicus.*

woodbilly n   Cf *DS* HH1

A rustic.

1942 Henry *High Border* 256 **nRocky Mts,** They became known variously not only as drylanders, but also as homesteaders, benchland grangers, woodbillies, woodticks, squatters, and Honijokers, especially if they lived in eastern Montana and the Dakotas. **2005** *DARE* File—Internet **nMN,** Woodbilly's Are Your Friend! . . I spent a week with my buddy Bruce and a few local Woodbilly friends. **2007** *Ibid* **MN,** [Screen name:] *Shatteredsteel . .* Location: Woodbilly County.

woodbind See **woodbine 2, 4**

woodbine n

1 Std: =**honeysuckle 2.**

2 also *woodbind:* =**Virginia creeper 1.**

1624 Smith *Genl. Hist. VA* 170, A kinde of Wood-bind there is likewise by the Sea very commonly to bee found, which runnes vpon trees twining it selfe like a Vine: the fruit somewhat resembles a Beane, but somewhat flatter, the which any way eaten worketh excellently in the nature of a purge. **1855** *New Engl. Farmer* 7.215, The *Virginia Creeper* or *American Woodbine,* is a hardy, rapid growing, and exceedingly ornamental plant. **1872** Schele de Vere *Americanisms* 412, The *Virginia Creeper . .* is also called *American Ivy . .* and the *Woodbine.* **1914** Georgia *Manual Weeds* 275, In form they [=poison ivy leaflets] are somewhat like the leaflets of the Virginia Creeper, or Woodbine . . , but it should be remembered that those are five in number. **1942** Tehon *Fieldbook IL Shrubs* 197, Virginia Creeper—Woodbine. . . Its berries have been suspected—probably erroneously—of being poisonous when eaten in quantity. **1972** Brown *Wildflowers LA* 108, Virginia Creeper, Woodbine. . . This has been mistaken for poison ivy but can be distinguished by the 5 leaflets instead of 3 leaflets for poison ivy. **2007**

Steiner *Landscaping with Native Plants WI* 186, Woodbine has large, palmately compound leaves with five leaflets that turn brilliant red early in fall.

3 =**Carolina jasmine.**

1830 Rafinesque *Med. Flora* 2.223, Gelsemium sempervirens. . . Jessamine, Woodbine. Root and flowers narcotic, their effluvia may cause stupor. **1864** Hale *New Remedies* 173, Gelseminum [sic] *sempervirens. . .* This plant is likewise known by the name of *Field Jessamine,* and *Woodbine.* **1898** U.S. Dept. Ag. Div. Botany *Bulletin* 20.48, False Jessamine. . . Other names: Yellow jessamine . . ; woodbine; Carolina wild woodbine [etc]. **1974** (1977) Coon *Useful Plants* 180, *Gelsemium sempervirens*—Jasmine, jessamine, southern woodbine.

4 also *woodbind, woodvine:* =**hedge bindweed 1.**

[**1859** *Peterson's Mag.* 36.252, And here let us quietly remark, that people in general sadly confound the bindweed and the woodbine.] **1894** *Jrl. Amer. Folkl.* 7.95 **NY,** *Convolvulus sepium* [=*Calystegia s.*] . . woodbine. **1940** Clute *Amer. Plant Names* 92, *C[onvolvulus] sepium. . .* woodbind, wood-vine [etc]. **1966** *DARE* (Qu. S5, . . *Wild morning glory*) Inf **MI9,** Woodbine.

5 A **virgin's bower** (here: *Clematis virginiana*).

1896 *Jrl. Amer. Folkl.* 9.179 **ME,** *Clematis Virginiana. . .* woodbine, wild hops.

wood blade n

A **mullein** (here: *Verbascum thapsus*).

1947 (1976) Curtin *Healing Herbs* 166 **AZ,** Mullein . . Wood Blade.

wood cady   See **Kate**

woodchecker   See **woodchuck 2a**

wood chicken n

1 =**ruffed grouse.**

1953 *AmSp* 28.279 **OR,** Wood chicken—Ruffed grouse. **1977** [see **wood pheasant**]. **2006** *DARE* File—Internet, I occasionally hear a thump, thump, thump from the woods nearby. It comes from the Ruffed Grouse. . . She asked her new husband what the noise was, and he told her it was a "wood chicken".

2 A large **woodpecker B1** such as the **pileated woodpecker B.**

1966 [see **woodchuck 2a**]. **1969** *DARE* (Qu. Q17, . . *Kinds of woodpeckers*) Inf **KY39,** Wood chicken, wood hen—pileated woodpecker. **1972** *Lockhart Post-Reg.* (TX) 10 Aug 8/4, The Pileated Woodpecker with a total adult size of up to 15 inches. . . has been commonly called the "Wood Chicken" but this term may be generally applied to all large woodpeckers including the Flickers.

wood-chopping (bee or party)   See **chopping bee**

woodchuck n

1 A **marmot a** (here: usu *Marmota monax*). [See quot **1902**] **chiefly Nth, Midl**   See Map on p. 1054 and Map Section   For other names of *M. monax* see **gopher** n[1] **2b(3), gopher rat 2, ground chuck, groundhog 1, hedgehog 2, hog B11, johnny chuck, moonack 1, mud heaver, pasture pup, picket pin 2, weather hog, whistle pig 1;** for other names of var spp see **bull-beggar, chuck** n[2]**, pig** n[1] **B4**   Cf **groundhog 1**

1674 in 1889 Gt. Brit. Pub. Rec. Office *Calendar State Papers Colonial Ser. Amer. for 1669–74* 581 **ME, NH,** The natural inhabitants of the woods, hills, and swamps, are . . rabbits, hares, and woodchucks. **1689** in 1862 Essex Inst. *Coll.* 4.236 **MA,** A parcell of meadow commonly called Woodchuck meadow. **1755** in 1963 Franklin *Papers* 6.85 **NEng,** I imagine it [=the groundhog] to be the same that in New England is called a *Woodchuck.* **1781** Peters *Genl. Hist.* CT 250, The Woodchuck . . , when eating, makes a noise like a hog, whence he is named Woodchuck, or Chuck of the Wood. **1825** in 1974 *Fauna Americana* 158, *Arctomys monax. . . Wood-chuck,* in Maryland. *Ground-hog,* in Pennsylvania. **1889** (1971) Farmer *Americanisms* 278 **Nth,** Ground hog. . . Folk-lore in the States centres round the *ground hog,* the Southern name for the woodchuck of the North. **1902** *Jrl. Amer. Folkl.* 15.267, *Woodchuck. . .* At first the term seems to have been applied to the *pekan* or "fisher" (*Martes canadensis*), which is the animal specified by the Indian word, and was afterwards transferred to the "groundhog." The word . . is derived from the Ojibwa *otchig (odjik),* cognate with Cree *otchek* ("fisher," *pekan*). **1927** *DN* 5.479 **NEng,** The animal which the New Englander calls a woodchuck is always a ground-hog in the Ozarks. **1965–70** *DARE* (Qu. P31, . . *Names or nicknames . . for the groundhog*) 366 Infs, **chiefly Nth, Midl,** Woodchuck; **MI26,** Used to be woodchuck; groundhog is getting commoner; **MI**49, We have woodchucks around here; the only time you hear groundhog is on Groundhog Day; **MA**55, Woodchuck—more common name than groundhog; **OH**3, Woodchuck, groundhog—they are the same; **PA**47, Everyone uses groundhog, but has heard woodchuck frequently; **RI**17, We call them woodchucks except on Groundhog Day; (Qu. P29, . . *'Gophers' . . other name . . or what other animal are they most like*) 24 Infs, **chiefly NEast, Gt Lakes,** Woodchuck; **CT**2, Woodchucks, groundhogs—both basically the same thing as a gopher; **IN**58, A gopher is a woodchuck; (Qu. P32, . . *Other kinds of wild animals*) Infs **MI**109, **ND**3, **NY**112; (Qu. Q18, *Joking names and nicknames for woodpeckers.* [In QR list of possible responses: *Woodchuck . .* is the animal a 'groundhog' here?]) 18 Infs, **scattered,** Woodchuck = groundhog; [**AL**32, Woodchuck [FW sugg; Inf has heard, doesn't know]; **IN**3, Woodchuck [FW sugg; Inf unsure]; **RI**1, Woodchuck [FW sugg; Inf has heard this name]]. **1975** Gould *ME Lingo* 320, The only time a Mainer says groundhog is when he says, "Today is Groundhog Day. Wonder if any *woodchucks*'ll come out?" **2009** *AmSp* 84.438 **NJ,** Young people today, . . have almost completely turned to *groundhog* as opposed to . . *[woodchuck].* There were only 11 (2%), mostly from the North, from both long and short questionnaires who reported using *woodchuck* and 17 (3%) used both. It is difficult to compete against a national holiday and a popular movie.

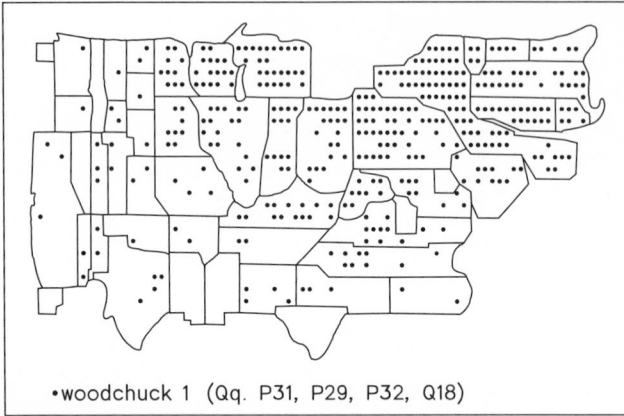

•woodchuck 1 (Qq. P31, P29, P32, Q18)

2a also *woodchecker, woodchucker:* A **woodpecker B1.** [See quots 1906, 1952] **chiefly Sth, S Midl** Cf **groundhog 3, jack hammer, woodcock 2**

1906 *DN* 3.164 **nwAR,** *Woodchuck. . .* Woodpecker. (An onomatopoeic word; the woodpecker goes chuck! chuck!) **1927** *DN* 5.479 **Ozarks,** *Woodchuck. . .* Woodpecker. **1952** *AmSp* 27.157 **cTN,** *Woodchuck* is a word widely prevalent in the district as the name for the common woodpecker. . . Even though the woodpecker is one of the most beautiful birds of the area, the existence of the taboo word [*=pecker*] in the compound has completely obliterated the label from the speech of most of the people. **1953** [see **2b(3)** below]. **1956** Ker *Vocab. W. TX* 230, It may be wondered how the term *woodchuck,* a synonym for ground hog, could have been reported by as many as four informants and recorded by four different interviewers unless the word has actual currency as a synonym for *woodpecker.* **1965–70** *DARE* (Qu. Q18, *Joking names and nicknames for woodpeckers*) 12 Infs, **chiefly Sth, S Midl, OK,** Woodchuck; **NC**85, Woodchucker; [**MD**25, Woodchuck [FW sugg; Inf uncertain if this is a woodpecker; he has heard it spoken of]; (Qu. Q7, *Names and nicknames for . . game birds*) Infs **KY**53, **MS**6, 66, 72, 81, Woodchuck; (Qu. Q17, . . *Kinds of woodpeckers*) Infs **GA**35, **LA**2, Woodchuck; (Qu. Q20, . . *Kinds of swallows and birds like them*) Inf **MS**81, Woodchuck. [*DARE* Ed: Some of these Infs may refer instead to other senses below.] **1966** Dakin *Dial. Vocab. Ohio R. Valley* 2.395, In the Mountains and the eastern Knob older speakers commonly say *woodchuck* (once *chuckwood* in Johnson County). This name is scattered and rare to the west and in southernmost Indiana and Illinois . . , but is in fairly common use in southern Ohio between Muskingum and the Little Miami. *Ibid* 397, Mountain speakers often say *sap sucker, woodchuck* = "any small woodpecker" and use *wood chicken, wood hen* = "big woodpecker." **1986** Pederson *LAGS Concordance* **Gulf Region** (*Woodpecker*) 70 infs, Woodchuck(s); 1 inf, Woodchecker; 1 inf, Woodchucker. [*DARE* Ed: 16 of these infs added that the bird is large; 6 remarked that it is red-headed.]

b Spec:

(1) **=red-bellied woodpecker.**

1874 NY Acad. Sci. *Annals Lyceum Nat. Hist.* 10.378, M[*elanerpes*]

Carolinus. . . Red-bellied Woodpecker . . "Woodchuck." **1889** Ridgway *Ornith. IL* 1.384, Red-bellied woodpecker. Popular synonyms. Carolina Woodpecker; Checkered Woodpecker; Wood Chuck. **1953** [see **2b(3)** below].

(2) **=ivory-billed woodpecker.**

1900 [see **2b(3)** below]. **1911** Howell *Birds AR* 46, *Ivory-billed Woodpecker. Campephilus principalis.* Some persons do not distinguish this species from the pileated woodpecker, with which it shares the names of "logcock," "woodcock," "woodchuck," etc. **1953** [see **2b(3)** below]. **1966** *DARE* (Qu. Q17, . . *Kinds of woodpeckers*) Inf **AR**5, Woodchuck—this is a woodpecker—very large, blue, black, and white.

(3) **=flicker** n[2] **1.**

1900 *Wilson Bulletin* 12.2.10 **FL,** *Little Woodchuck.* Caloosahatche River Region, Florida. The adjective is used to distinguish the smaller from the "Big Woodchuck" (Ivory-billed Woodpecker). *Ibid* 10, *Woodchuck.* Berkshire Hills, Massachusetts; Kansas; North Carolina; Florida. **1953** *AmSp* 28.145 **MO, NY, OK,** *Woodchuck,* as a name for the flicker, is widespread (Mass., Va., N.C., Fla., Kansas); it is applied also to the red-headed woodpecker (N.Y., Mo., Okla.); red-bellied woodpecker (Fla., Ill.), pileated woodpecker (throughout its southeastern range: Mo., Ky., N.C. to Texas and Fla.); and it *was* a name for the now nearly extinct ivory-billed woodpecker in Arkansas and Florida. It is, perhaps, a general term for woodpeckers in the Southeast.

(4) **=pileated woodpecker B.**

1891 *Leighton News* (AL) 15 July [56], Pileated Woodpecker. . . It is here commonly, but very incorrectly, known as Woodcock, and sometimes as woodchuck. **1911** Howell *Birds AR* 47, *Pileated Woodpecker. Phlœotomus pileatus.* This large woodpecker, known under the vernacular names of "woodcock," "logcock," "woodchuck," etc., is quite common. **1916** *Times–Picayune* (New Orleans LA) 16 Apr mag sec 9/2, Pileated Woodpecker. . . Wood Chuck; Cock-of-the-Woods. **1938** Oberholser *Bird Life LA* 365, The Pileated Woodpecker. . . has a number of different names, such as 'woodcock', 'logcock', 'cock of the woods', and even 'woodchuck'. **1953** [see **2b(3)** above]. **1965–70** *DARE* (Qu. Q17, . . *Kinds of woodpeckers*) Inf **GA**3, Woodchuck—large—black, red head; **GA**7, Woodchuck—bigger than woodpecker; **KY**47, Woodchuck—pileated woodpecker; **NC**21, Woodchuck—a very large one; **TN**26, Woodchuck—I've seen 'em down in the bottoms; some of 'em get mighty near as big as a small banty hen [FW: pileated woodpecker]; (Qu. Q18, *Joking names and nicknames for woodpeckers*) Inf **AR**55, Woodchuck—pileated woodpecker; **LA**15, Woodchuck [FW: not joking—regular name for pileated woodpecker]; **NC**80, Woodchuck—the big ones; **SC**46, Woodchuck—bigger than most—about gone here. **1986** [see **2a** above].

(5) **=red-headed woodpecker 1.**

1930 OK Univ. Biol. Surv. Pub. 2.141, Red-headed woodpecker. . . *Local names:* Tricolor woodpecker, woodchuck [etc]. **1953** [see **2b(3)** above]. **1986** [see **2a** above].

3 **=whippoorwill B1.**

1945 McAtee in *AN&Q* 5.11 **MA,** Despite the dominance of *whippoorwill,* there are a number of local names for the bird: . . "woodchuck" (Massachusetts, a forest bird that utters the note "chuck").

4 **=hermit thrush 1.**

1956 MA Audubon Soc. *Bulletin* 40.129 **ME,** Hermit Thrush. . . Woodchuck. . . A woodland creature that utters a note like "chuck."

5 **=mountain beaver.**

1928 Anthony *N. Amer. Mammals* 452, Mountain Beaver.— *Aplodontia rufa. . .* less frequently Mountain Boomer, Ground-hog, Woodchuck.

6 A rustic. **Upstate NY**

[**1851** (1852) Ross *What I Saw* 46 **NY,** But what could a "greenhorn," right from the land of woodchucks do?] **1969** *DARE* (Qu. HH1, *Names and nicknames for a rustic or countrified person*) Inf **NY**213, Woodchuck—shabby, country guy. **1989** Baden–Hennessee *Unnatural Death* 167 **ceNY,** He and his cousin were the kind of people the police called "mullies," or "dirtbags," or "woodchucks"—rural people who grew up poor and ignorant, who wore the same dirty jeans . . day after day, people who were constitutionally unable to stay out of trouble. **2002** *DARE* File—Internet, Woodchuck is also an upstate New York slang term for an unsophisticated rural dwelling person. . . You know, a fat guy with buck teeth and a mullet.

woodchuck case n **WI, MN** Cf **groundhog case**

A situation of necessity, one in which there is no choice; see quots.

1862 in 1892 Brown *Hist. Fourth Regiment MN Infantry* 71, I . . foraged a fine porker. It was against orders, but it was a woodchuck case. **1889** in 1982 Hampsten *Read This* 102 **MN,** People say it was a wood chuck case with her about getting married. **1908** *Daily Northwestern* (Oshkosh WI) 30 Jan 10/1, [Advt:] To get rid of a $10,000 stock of winter footwear with only a month to do it in is a big job. . . I don't need shoes. It's a woodchuck case with me. I've got to have the money. **1921** *WI Rapids Daily Tribune* (WI) 4 Oct 2/3, I do not believe Wood county paid the $70,000 as a 'sop.' I believe they paid it because the law required them to. . . It is a 'woodchuck' case. **1968** *DARE* (Qu. AA20, *A marriage that takes place because a baby is on the way*) Inf **MN**12, Woodchuck case; **WI**70, Woodchuck case—not commonly used.

woodchucker See **woodchuck 2a**

woodcock n

1 Std: the American woodcock, *Scolopax minor* (formerly *Philohela m.*). Also called **dipsy doodle 2, google-eye, hill partridge, hookumpake, Indian hen 4, Labrador twister, mountain partridge 2, mud hen 2a, ~ snipe 1, night-flit, night partridge, pewee n¹ 2, red-breasted snipe 2, snipe 1, swamp partridge 2, swamp quail 2, timber cock, timber-doodle, whistle-bicky, whistler 5, whistling snipe, wood hen 1, ~ snipe 2**

2 Any of several **woodpeckers B1,** as:

a =**pileated woodpecker B.** Cf **black woodcock, pineland ~, red-headed ~**

a**1813** (1844) Wilson *Poet. Wks.* 228 **PA,** Crested wood-cocks hammer from on high. **1853** Krider *Krider's Sporting Anecdotes* 77 se**PA,** "Nay," says old Barleycorn, smiling at your fancied ignorance, "it is a *bushschnip,* I haven't sawn a woodcock on these lands since I were a boy." You are only at odds about names, however, the farmer fancying that you spoke of the great pileated woodpecker, once common in the forests of Montgomery. **1868** Cronise *Nat. Wealth CA* 450 **CA,** On account of this crest, which careless observers suppose to be like a cock's comb, it [=the pileated woodpecker] is absurdly called Woodcock. **1889** *Forest & Stream* 32.63 sw**MI,** I obtained a fine specimen of the last [=the pileated woodpecker] at the market Dec. 12, where I have seen them before. The farmers call them woodcock, and this accounts in part for their finding a place among the game. **1899** (1912) Green *VA Folk-Speech* 488, Wood-cock. . . The large, red-crested woodpecker. **1913** Kephart *Highlanders* 295 s**Appalachians,** The giant woodpecker (here still a common bird) is known as a woodcock or woodhen. **1919** *Wilson Bulletin* 31.119 **IA,** According to Mr. Hugh Cory of Sac City, a very large woodpecker, which in the vernacular was called "woodcock," was found in the timber along the Raccoon river in early days. **1950** *WELS* **WI** *(Woodpeckers)* 1 Inf, Woodcock or great black woodpecker; 1 Inf, Woodcocks—land on side of tree—nickname. **1953** Randolph–Wilson *Down in Holler* 300 **Ozarks,** Woodcock. . . The pileated woodpecker *(Dryocopus pileatus),* still common in the backwoods. . . The real woodcock is called a *timber-doodle* or *night partridge* in the Ozarks. **1965–70** *DARE* (Qu. Q17, . . *Kinds of woodpeckers*) Infs **ME**8, **MI**36, Pileated woodpecker is commonly called a woodcock; **GA**20, Woodcock—nickname for pileated; **SC**43, Woodcock, wood Kate—black and white, very big—a tuft on head; **WI**73, Woodcock; (Qu. Q18, *Joking names and nicknames for woodpeckers*) Inf **IL**67, Woodcock; **LA**7, They put that thing on your [hunting] license, but they call him a woodcock; **WA**20, Woodcock—slowest-flying bird, heavier than yellowhammer. [*DARE* Ed: Some of these Infs may refer instead to other senses.] **1966** *DARE* Tape **ME**26, That woodpecker you was telling me about. A lot of people call that a woodcock. It's just the old original northern woodpecker and they stay here all winter. . . He's big as a partridge, very near. **1986** Pederson *LAGS Concordance (Woodpecker)* 8 infs, **Gulf Region,** Woodcock(s). [*DARE* Ed: 5 of these infs added that the bird is large; 2 remarked that it is red-headed.]

b =**ivory-billed woodpecker.**

1822 Latham *Genl. Hist. Birds* 3.369 **GA,** White-billed woodpecker. *Picus principalis.* . . found in Georgia, according to Mr. Abbot, and there called Lobcock by some, by others Woodcock. **1885** Thompson *By-Ways* 24 se**GA,** I allus called 'em air birds woodcocks; didn't know 'at they hed any other name; allus thut 'at a Peckwood wer' a leetle, tinty, stripedy feller; never hyeard er them air big ole woodcocks a bein' called Peckwoods. **1911** Howell *Birds AR* 46, Some persons do not distinguish this species [=*Campephilus principalis*] from the pileated woodpecker, with which it shares the names of "logcock," "woodcock," "woodchuck," etc.

c =**red-headed woodpecker 1.**

1884 *Forest & Stream* 23.28 **OH,** "Come on," he said, "here is one of

them woodcocks. . . Look on that old dead tree." I did, and saw a red-headed woodpecker. I told him that was not a woodcock, but he knew better. I then showed him a woodcock, but he said that was a snipe. [**1953** *AmSp* 28.284, The red-headed woodpecker [is called] *woodcock* (Ontario, Quebec)].

d =**flicker n² 1. esp NEng**

1887 *Forest & Stream* 28.248 **NEng,** The golden-winged woodpecker *(Colaptes auratus).* . . Woodcock (misnomer). **1897** *Oölogist* 14.33, But these observers (?) belong to that class who call the Flicker a woodcock. **1900** *Wilson Bulletin* 12.2.11, The Flicker. . . Woodcock. New England, Pennsylvania, Iowa. *Ibid* 7, Golden-winged Woodpecker. Iowa. Misnomer. *Ibid* 12, Yellow-winged Woodpecker. Iowa. Misnomer. **1956** MA Audubon Soc. *Bulletin* 40.82 **ME,** Yellow-shafted Flicker. . . Woodcock. **1968** *DARE* (Qu. Q17, . . *Kinds of woodpeckers*) Inf **CT**6, Flicker = woodcock.

3 also *cock of the wood:* =**ruffed grouse.**

1953 *AmSp* 28.284 **PA,** *Cock of the wood* and *woodcock* are also applied to the ruffed grouse in Pennsylvania.

wood colt See **woods colt**

wood doctor n　Cf **root doctor**

1923 Parsons *Folk-lore Sea Islands* 212 cs**SC,** There were and probably still are, in the Islands, practitioners [of witchcraft] called "root-doctors" or "wood-doctors" or "nigger doctors."

wood dove n

=**mourning dove 1.**

1893 *Godey's Lady's Book* 127.741, No bird in our country is more persistently misrepresented by our sweet singers [=poets] than the Carolina or wood dove—mourning dove, as he is popularly called. **1901** *Atlantic Mth.* 88.431, From the tree, third in the westmost row of the orchard, comes the mellow-mourning note of the wood dove. **1946** Hausman *Eastern Birds* 343, Eastern Mourning Dove. . . Other Names—Wild Dove, Wood Dove, Turtle Dove. **1968** *DARE* (Qu. Q3) Inf **NY**92, Wood dove—like a regular dove, only lives in the woods.

wood duck n

1 Std: the North American duck *Aix sponsa.* Also called **acorn duck, black n 2, gray duck a, squealer 4, summer duck 1, swamp ~, swamp guinea, tree duck 2, widgeon 2a, wood widgeon, woody n¹**

2 A **merganser,** esp a **hooded merganser.**

1888 Trumbull *Names of Birds* 75 **IL, IN,** I was surprised to find the name *wood-duck.* . printed on this bird's [=the hooded merganser's] label. But Mr. Ridgway told me that he had heard "Wood-duck," and also *tree-duck.* . commonly applied to this species, in lower or more southern portions of the Wabash valley, Ill. and Ind. The application of "Wood-duck" to a "Saw-bill," though a little shocking at first, is natural enough, of course, as the Merganser breeds in woods, nesting in the hollow of a tree like the "Wood-duck" of people generally. **1907** Rich *Feathered Game NE* 415 **Sth, West,** In many localities of the south and west this bird [=the hooded merganser] is called the "Wood Duck." **1923** U.S. Dept. Ag. *Misc. Circular* 13.5 **CO,** American Merganser. . . *Vernacular names. . . In local use. . .* wood duck. **1955** Forbush–May *Birds* 90 **Pacific,** The Hooded Merganser . . lives in haunts similar to those of the Wood Duck, and as it also nests in hollow trees, it is known as the 'Wood Duck' to many people on the Pacific coast.

3 A **tree duck 1** (here: *Dendrocygna bicolor*). Cf *Mexican wood duck* (at **Mexican duck 1**)

1923 U.S. Dept. Ag. *Misc. Circular* 13.38 **CA,** Fulvous Tree-duck. . . *Vernacular names. . . In local use. . .* Wood duck.

wooden asshole for a hobby-horse See **asshole for a hobby-horse**

wooden-foot plow See **foot n C3**

wooden handle See **handle n, v¹ B1**

wooden hill n　[In Brit use at least since late 18th cent, now often in the punning phr *up the wooden hill to Bedfordshire*] **scattered, but esp NY, PA, NJ**

A set of stairs—usu in phr *climb the wooden hill* (and varr) to go upstairs to bed.

1884 *Galveston Daily News* (TX) 9 Sept 2/2, Mrs. Coodledodger was heard to climb vigorously up the wooden hill. **1899** Garland *Boy Life* 195 nw**IA,** It was not uncommon for the men . . to work all day at one place and move to another "setting" at night. . . And the children were about starting to "climb the wooden hill" when they heard the peculiar rattle of the [thresher]. **1930** *DN* 6.89 **cWV,** *Wooden hill,* stairway. **1940s** in 1986 *Barrick Coll.* **csPA,** *Wooden hill*—stairs. . . "It's time to go up the wooden hill." [i.e., it's time to go to bed]. **1965–70** *DARE* (Qu. D6, *To get to the second floor, you walk up the* _____) Inf **PA134,** Wooden hill; (Qu. X40, . . *Ways . . of saying, "I'm going to bed"*) Infs **NJ18, NY219, PA115,** Climb the wooden hill; **PA162,** Going up the wooden hill; [**NJ55,** Climb the wooden stairs; **PA123,** Going to climb the wood]. **1968** *DARE* FW Addit **PA169,** *Up the wooden hill*—an expression meaning going to bed. **1979** *Capital Times* (Madison WI) 20 July 39, The order barked at me to "get up over that wooden hill" meant to go upstairs to bed without delay. **2007** *DARE* File—Internet **Philadelphia PA** (as of c1950), OK, now, go climb the wooden hill and I'll see you in the morning.

wooden horse n   Also *wood horse*   Cf **hobbyhorse 5**
A **walkingstick 1** or **praying mantis.**

1868 *Amer. Entomologist* 1.58, The fourth name [for the stick-bug], "Wood-horse," is only objectionable, because it might be just as appropriately given to dozens of other large insects that are exclusively found in the woods. **1908** *Acad. Nat. Sci. Philadelphia Entomol. Sec. Entomol. News & Proc.* 19.470 **seNY,** One of the peculiar local myths with which we were familiar in boyhood, was that of the wooden horse, a local name for the walking stick insects. Its bite was said to be peculiarly fatal, one could not live long enough to murmur even a short prayer if bitten by one of these creatures. **1966–69** *DARE* (Qu. R9a, *An insect from two to four inches long that lives in bushes and looks like a dead twig*) Inf **MA6,** Wooden horse; (Qu. R9b, *An insect that holds up its front feet as if saying a prayer;* not asked in early QRs) Inf **MA15,** Wooden horse—same as devil's horse: 6 legs, 5–6 inches long, ¼ inch around, whiskers in front.

wooden island n   *obs*
=**floating island 1.**

1807 in 1810 Schultz *Travels* 2.32 **Lower Missip Valley,** *Wooden Islands* are generally formed at the upper end of a real one, where an enormous collection of trees and floating timber becomes entangled and matted together, sometimes to the extent of nearly a quarter of a mile, and in time makes part of the main island. **1846** Levinge *Echoes from Backwoods* 2.20, The [Lower] Mississippi is obstructed by *planters, sawyers,* and *wooden islands,* which are frequently the cause of injury. **1941** Baldwin *Keelboat Age* 77, Floating logs and the loose, floating masses of debris known as "wooden islands" were dangerous.

wooden stick   See **stick 5**

wooden tongue n   [*OED2* 1884 →]   Also *wood tongue*
=**lump jaw.**

1886 *MD Med. Jrl.* 15.294, In June, 1877, Bollinger published . . a brief but excellent description of the disease then known as "swell head," "lump jaw," "wooden tongue," which was supposed to be primarily an osteo-sarcomatous process beginning usually in the lower jaw of cattle. **1892** *Homestead* 8 July 15, In cases where the disease attacks the tongue, this organ often attains an enormous size, protruding from the mouth, and becoming so hard and tense . . that it is very difficult or nearly impossible for the animal to eat. This condition is commonly called "wooden tongue." **1903** *Ibid* 19 Nov 15, Is there such a disease in young cattle as leather tongue? . . You doubtless mean "wooden tongue," which is caused by actinomycosis. **1913** (1979) Barnes *Western Grazing* 287, The trouble begins with a small swelling which gradually grows until it assumes considerable size. . . It also works back into the inner part of the jaw, attacking the bone itself as well as the tongue, when it is called "wooden tongue." **1969** *DARE* (Qu. K28, . . *Chief diseases that cows have*) Inf **CA131,** Black tongue—also called wood tongue. **2002** *Star–Herald* (Scottsbluff NE) 23 Oct 3/1, [Advt:] An antibiotic that effectively treats . . diphtheria, scours and wooden tongue.

wooder   See **water A1**

woodfish n   *esp VA, TN*
=**dry-land fish 1.**

1931 *AmSp* 6.230 **neOR,** In spring the 'chillun' . . scour the woods for 'woodfish,' in plain English, mushrooms. **1981** Pederson *LAGS Basic Materials (Mushroom)* 1 inf, **neTN,** Woodfish. **2006** *DARE* File—Internet **VA,** "You have to get up in the woods to find them," he said of woodfish mushrooms, more commonly known as morel mushrooms. **2007** *Ibid* **VA,** When the Poplar leaves are the size of a mouses ear, it's time for Woodfish! I figure it will be about two weeks from now in this part of Virginia. *Ibid* **VA,** Locals call them [=morels] "woodfish" here in VA.

wood fly   See **woods fly**

wood fox   See **wood gray (fox)**

wood fringe n
=**mountain fringe 1.**

1848 *OH Cultivator* 15 Mar 47, [Advt:] *Catalogue of Flower Seeds. . .* Wood Fringe or Fumitory, *vine.* **1884** *Atlantic Mth.* 53.294, The cluster of pansies on page 21 and the spray of wood-fringe on page 29 are especially successful. **1896** *Jrl. Amer. Folkl.* 9.181 **ME,** *Adlumia cirrhosa* [=*A. fungosa*]. . . mountain fringe, wood fringe, Paris, Me.

wood gannet n
=**wood ibis.**

1913 *Auk* 30.491 **Okefenokee GA,** *Mycteria americana.* Wood Ibis; . . 'Wood Gannet.'

wood god n   Cf **lord god 1**
=**pileated woodpecker B.**

1921 *Auk* 38.378 **seAR,** Pileated Woodpecker.—Known locally as "Lord God" and "Wood God." Said to be common in the cypress swamps. **1945** McAtee *Nomina Abitera* 46 **AR, FL,** Pileated woodpecker. . . [also called] wood God. **1981** Pederson *LAGS Basic Materials (Woodpecker)* 1 inf, **cwMS,** Wood god for big one.

wood grass n
1 =**Indian grass 1a.**

1826 Darlington *Florula Cestrica* 15, *Andropogon* [=*Sorghastrum*]. . . *nutans.* . . *Vulgo*—Wood-grass. Indian-grass. *Ibid, A. scoparius.* . . *Vulgo*—Purple Wood-grass. *Ibid, A. macrourus.* . . *Vulgo*—Cluster flowered Wood-grass. **1862** Thoreau in *Atlantic Mth.* 10.389 **MA,** The Chestnut Beard-Grass, Indian-Grass, or Wood-Grass . . is still handsomer and of more vivid colors than its congeners. **1888** [see **2** below]. **1910** Graves *Flowering Plants* 49 **CT,** *Sorghastrum nutans.* . . Indian Grass. Wood Grass. . . A tall grass, growing in clumps and with beautiful golden brown flower-panicles. **1976** Bailey–Bailey *Hortus Third* 1060, *Sorghastrum.* . . *avenaceum* [=*nutans*]. . . Wood Grass. **2004** Darke *Pocket Guide Grasses* 189, *Sorghastrum* [spp]—Indian grass, wood grass. . . A characteristic North American tallgrass prairie species, *S. nutans,* is very important ornamentally.

2 also *woods grass:* A **muhly (grass)** (here: *Muhlenbergia mexicana*).

1888 CT Ag. Exper. Sta. *Annual Rept. for 1887* 171, "Wood grass" is applied to *Chrysopogon nutans,* a coarse but good forage grass, and to *Muhlenbergia Mexicana,* which is totally different in appearance and value. **1914** Georgia *Manual Weeds* 43, *Muhlenbergia mexicana.* . . *Other English names.* . . Wood-grass, Knotroot Grass. **1935** (1943) Muenscher *Weeds* 163, Mexican drop-seed, Satin-grass, Wood-grass, Knot-root-grass. **1968** *DARE* (Qu. L8, *Hay that grows naturally in damp places*) Inf **MD38,** Woods grass.

wood gray (fox) n   Also *woods gray (fox), wood fox*   **chiefly NEast**
=**gray fox.**

1836 *Family Mag.* (NY) 3.97 **MA,** A lean, emaciated woods-gray fox . . darted out of a hollow stump. **1840** MA Zool. & Bot. Surv. *Herb. Plants & Quadrupeds* 31, *Vulpes Virginianus* [=*Urocyon cinereoargenteus*]. . . This species is termed by furriers the Wood-gray Fox. **1870** *ME Farmer* (Augusta) 19 Nov 2/3, *Fox.* The principal varieties are the red, cross-grey and woods-grey. . . Only one silver-grey fox has Hardy seen within five years, and that came from Tobique, in New Brunswick. **1882** *Forest & Stream* 19.416 **CT,** [Question:] One man said it was a wood fox. Is there such an animal? Its fur was a little more gray than a 'coon or our common fox. Ans[wer:] We never heard of a wood fox. From the description it seems probable that the animal may have been a gray fox. **1920** *Hunter-Trader-Trapper* Nov 104 **Upper Missip Valley,** Another day we ran a wood grey on snow. **1948** Smith *Martyrs* 32 **NY,** The southern gray fox ("wood gray" it is called here). **1961** Jackson *Mammals WI* 306, Wisconsin Gray Fox. . . *Vernacular names.* . . tree fox, virgin fox, Virginia fox, and wood fox. **1968** *DARE* (Qu. P32, . . *Other kinds of wild animals*) Inf **NY68,** Gray fox or wood gray.

wood grouse n   Cf **timber grouse**
Any of var grouse inhabiting woodlands, such as the **dusky grouse, ruffed grouse,** or **spruce grouse;** see quots.

1849 *Western Misc.* 1.330, Such wholesale slaughter is not as pleasing to your genuine sportsman as picking off a bird at a time from a covey of quails, or prairie or wood grouse. **1862** Winthrop *John Brent* 245 **OR,** The brace of wood grouse he had shot that morning . . had never made journey in a crowded box. **1884** *Forest & Stream* 23.290, I look forward to that day when I will again . . knock over a wood grouse (*Bonaso* [sic] *umbellus*) in the Eastern States. **1888** [see **timber grouse**]. **1889** *Forest & Stream* 33.326 **cwVA,** A friend of mine . . whose palate had for some days been hankering after the flavor of wood grouse, sallied forth in search of that wily biped. **1923** Dawson *Birds CA* 4.1591, The "Blue" Grouse, "Wood Grouse," or "Mountain" Grouse, in some one of its geographical races, is found throughout the heavily timbered areas of the West. **1953** Jewett *Birds WA* 196, Oregon Blue Grouse. . . Other names . . Pine Grouse; Wood Grouse [etc.]. . . a characteristic denizen of the Douglas fir belt . . particularly fond of thick second-growth timber.

wood hen n

1 Std: the female **woodcock 1.**

2 A **woodpecker B1,** usu the **pileated woodpecker B. chiefly S Midl** See Map Cf **red-headed woodcock, woodcock 2**

    1890 *Oölogist* 7.226 **VA,** Your "Wood-hen" is doubtless the Pileated Woodpecker. **1917** *DN* 4.419 **wNC,** *Woodhen. . .* The giant woodpecker. **1926** *DN* 5.405 **Ozarks,** *Wood-hen. . .* The great pileated woodpecker, still common in some isolated parts of the Ozarks. **1934** Vines *Green Thicket* 49 **cnAL,** You know, some folks call the purty things Indian hens, and some folks call 'em wood hens. But I call the noisy things Good-Gods. **1953** *AmSp* 28.283 **VA,** Wood hen—Yellow-shafted flicker. *Ibid* **MO,** Wood hen—Red-bellied woodpecker. *Ibid* **MT,** Wood hen—Lewis's woodpecker. **1965–70** *DARE* (Qu. Q17, . . *Kinds of woodpeckers*) Infs **KY**31, 39, 43, 84, Wood hen—pileated woodpecker; **NC**41, **WV**5, Wood hen; **KY**11, Wood hen—great big bird; very rare; **VA**34, Wood hen—looks like a giant redhead woodpecker; size of pheasant; (Qu. Q18, *Joking names and nicknames for woodpeckers*) Infs **TN**11, 22, Wood hen—pileated; **AL**35, Wood hen—a very large woodpecker; **KY**17, Wood hen; (Qu. Q23, *The insect-eating bird that goes headfirst down a tree trunk*) Infs **MO**16, **NC**30, Wood hen. **1983** *MJLF* 9.1.61 **ceKY** (as of 1956), *Wood hen . .* pileated woodpecker. **1986** Pederson *LAGS Concordance (Woodpecker)* 22 infs, **Gulf Region,** Wood hen(s). [*DARE* Ed: 14 infs remark that the bird is large.] **1992** Joslin *Mt. People II* 97 **sAppalachians** (*Montgomery Coll.*), A pair of Northern Flickers, locally known as yellowhammers or wood hens, had been doing some remodeling to a dead fork of the tree.

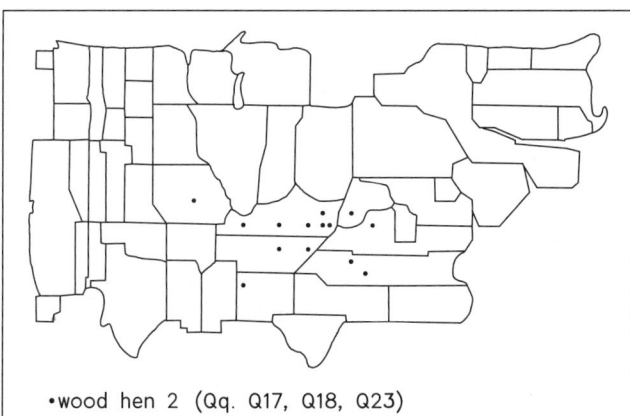

•wood hen 2 (Qq. Q17, Q18, Q23)

3 A **coot 1** (here: *Fulica americana*).

    1882 Godfrey *Is. Nantucket* 241 **MA,** Wood Hen (*Fulica Americana*). **1969** *DARE* (Qu. Q9, *The bird that looks like a small, dull-colored duck and is commonly found on ponds and lakes*) Inf **KY**21, Wood hen; **MO**15, Wood hen, mud duck, mud hen—all the same.

4 =**ruffed grouse.**

    1950 *WELS,* 1 Inf, **WI,** Quail—most people call them partridge—also wood hen. **1953** *AmSp* 28.283 **WI,** Wood hen—Ruffed grouse.

wood hick n Appalachians

1 A logger or other worker in the woods.

    1908 *Eve. Times* (Cumberland MD) 18 Sept 4/2, He got into a debate with a lumber jack . . in an adjoining cell, on the question, "Resolver [sic], That Woodhicks are Crummy." **1919** *Clearfield Progress* (PA) 14 July 1/5, Jonas Croyle, . . one of the old time "wood hicks," who contributed a real he-man's share in the wor kof [sic] denuding Clearfield

county's hills . . was a Clearfield visitor today. **1930** *DN* 6.88 **cWV,** How the "Wood Hicks" Speak. . . *Hick* (sometimes "wood hick"), a lumber jack, a worker in the woods. **1941** Writers' Program *Guide WV* 436 **csWV,** *Raineile.* . . is crowded on Saturday and pay-day nights with . . 'wood-hicks' from near-by logging camps. **1983** Glimm *Flat-landers* 69 **cnPA,** Around 1900 there was a big lumbering operation along Big Run. In the early summer the wood hicks would cut the trees and peel off the bark. **1988** *Atlanta Constitution* (GA) 4 Apr 16/1, Many of the loggers for Morse Brothers Lumber Co. came from West Virginia and Pennsylvania. They were called "wood hicks." **1991** Weals *Last Train* 53 **eTN** (as of c1910), "Wood hicks" was their name for themselves, for all those men who worked in the woods. **2005** *DARE* File—Internet **WV,** Jimmie Roberts went off to the deep and dark mountains of Pocahontas County to be a wood hick in 1906.

2 A backwoodsman, hillbilly. Cf *DS* HH1, **wood tick 3**

    1911 *Eve. Times* (Cumberland MD) 27 July 9/2, He went to Richwood, W.Va., a new town needing just such a man as "Samp." He introduced the moving-picture show to the woodhicks and soon was the most prominent citizen of the wooden town. **1931** Smith *Hopi Girl* 167 **sAppalachians,** To her father's college in a Southern mountain town, a very "green" wood hick had come to acquire learning. **1937** *Hall Coll.* **KY,** *Wood hick. . .* Nora Bell Vance . . said that when she lived in Kentucky for a time she was called a 'wood hick'. **2003** Bills *Am I My Neighbor's Keeper?* 24 **WV,** Self-esteem maintenance for many Appalachian males is invested in affirmation of self as "redneck", "good ol' boy", "hillbilly", "hick", "wood hick", etc.

wood hog See woods hog

wood horse n

1 =**sawbuck 1.**

    1836 in 1849 Salem (MA) *Charter* 31, No person . . shall pass through or along any side-walk with . . any chaise or other vehicle, or with a wood horse or naked scythe, under the penalty of one dollar for every such offence. **1870** *Appletons' Jrl.* 4.44 **VA,** He carries his two crosses, in the shape of his wood-horse, upon his back, and his saw in his hand, and wanders about . . in search of a load of wood, to saw up for family use. **1872** *Scribner's Mth.* 5.80 **NEng,** He sat down upon the wood-horse, hot, breathless, and content. **1879** Stockton *Rudder Grange* 190 **nNJ,** They [=two dogs] rolled, they gnashed, they knocked over the wood-horse and sent chips a-flyin' all ways at wonst. **1939** *LANE* Map 162 (*Sawhorse*) 7 infs, **MA, CT,** Wood horse. **1946** *PADS* 5.36 **VA,** *Saw horse, wood horse, horse . . :* A rack upon which wood is laid for sawing by hand; common everywhere. **1947** *PADS* 8.24 **wNY,** *Saw horse:* The usual term. *Horse* used occasionally; *wood horse,* rarely. **1954** *Harder Coll.* **cwTN,** *Woodhorse. . .* A crossed wood holder used to hold wood when it is being sawed for home consumption. **1961** *Folk Word Atlas N. LA* map 702, Wooden device for sawing logs for firewood . . [less freq responses include] wood horse. **1966** Dakin *Dial. Vocab. Ohio R. Valley* 2.170, *Sawbuck. . .* Other names for the rack of Type A [=an A-frame] are . . *wood horse* (2 [infs]–O[hio]; 3 [infs]–K[entucky]). **1966–70** *DARE* (Qu. L58, *An implement with an A-shaped frame . . that you put boards on to saw them*) Infs **GA**3, **NJ**65, **OH**48, Wood horse; (Qu. L59, *An implement with an X-frame . . to hold firewood for sawing*) Infs **MI**23, **SC**9, Wood horse. [All infs comm type 5, 4 infs old] **1967** LeCompte *Word Atlas* 154 **seLA,** *Wooden rack for sawing planks.* . . wood horse [1 of 21 infs]. **1981** *PADS* 67.27 **Mesabi Iron Range MN,** *Saw horse. . .* wood horse [2 infs]. **1986** Pederson *LAGS Concordance,* 1 inf, **nwGA,** Wood horses—A-frames.

2 See **wooden horse.**

wood house n, also attrib Also *wood-house shed* **chiefly east of Missip R** See Map on p. 1058 *old-fash*

A building in which firewood is stored.

    1655 in 1885 Suffolk Co. MA *Deeds* 3.211, Dwelling howse in Boston . . with one smale shead or wood house. **1795** *Columbian Centinel* (Boston MA) 21 Jan 4/3, [Advt:] To be sold, A House . . all most new, with Wash-House, Wood-House. **1849** Howitt *Our Cousins in OH* 11, At the back of the house were the out-buildings; on the left stood a rather picturesque building called the wood-house. **1851** (1927) Rodman *Diary* 304 **MA,** I saw the whole [parade] from the woodhouse window. **1890** Holley *Samantha among Brethren* 54 **NY,** I wuz out in the wood-house shed a-bilin' my cider apple sass in the big cauldron kettle. **1948** Davis *Word Atlas Gt. Lakes* app qu 13a (*Shed for wood etc., a separate building,*) 21 [of 233] infs, **IN, IL, MI, OH,** Wood house. **1965–70** *DARE* (Qu. M22, . . *Kinds of buildings . . on farms*) Infs **IN**67, **MA**68, **NC**35, **NY**127, **OH**30, **PA**204, **RI**15, 16, Wood house; **IL**29, Wood house—used to have; **IN**40, Wood house—woodshed; **KY**86, Wood house—old-fashioned—for firewood storage; **MD**31, Wood house or woodshed—to store wood; **MI**65, Wood house—woodshed; **OH**64, Wood house—old-fashioned; **PA**13, Wood house—same as toolshed; **SC**57, Wood house—shed to keep firewood dry; (Qu. M1, . . *Kinds of barns . . according to their use*) Inf **NY**127, Wood house. **1966** Dakin *Dial. Vocab. Ohio R. Valley* 2.63, *Shed. . . Wood shed* (frequently little more than a roof to keep wood dry) is more common than *wood house.* **1971** *Wood Vocab. Change* 304 **Sth**, [A separate building for keeping various things:] 84 [of approx 1000 infs] Wood house.

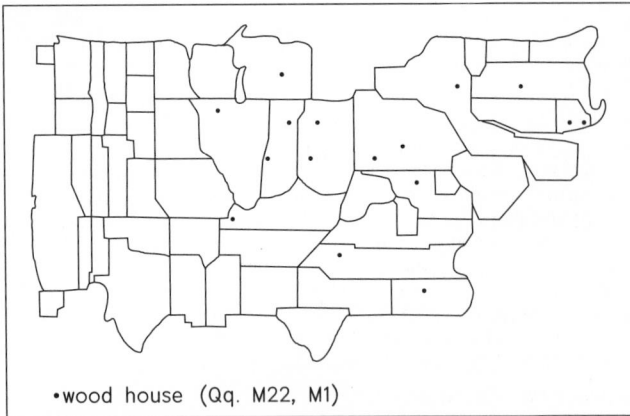

•wood house (Qq. M22, M1)

wood ibis n

Std: a large stork *(Mycteria americana)* of the southeastern US. Also called **baldhead 1, bald-headed gannet, Colorado turkey 1, flamant, flinghead, flinthead 1, gannet 2, gourdhead 1, ironhead 2, mulehead** n[1]**, pond gannet, preacher 2, saltwater crane, stork, water turkey 3, wood gannet** Cf **bonehead 3, ivis**

wood ipecac n

A **horse gentian** (here: *Triosteum perfoliatum*).

1898 Britton–Brown *Illustr. Flora* 3.234, Horse-Gentian. . . Called also Fever-root, Wild or Wood Ipecac.

wood iron n

1 =**andiron.** [*wood* + **iron B2**] Cf **log iron**

1967 *DARE* (Qu. D32, *The metal stands in a fireplace that the logs are laid on*) Inf **WA**27, Wood irons. **1986** Pederson *LAGS Concordance* (*Andirons*) 1 inf, **cnAL**, Wood irons.

2 Prob =**charcoal iron.**

1966 *DARE* (Qu. F29, *Different kinds of irons—not electric—used . . for smoothing clothes after they're washed*) Inf **GA**8, Wood iron; smoothing iron. **1967** LeCompte *Word Atlas* 134 **seLA**, *Device/not electric/to smooth clothes after washing. . .* wood iron [1 of 21 infs]. **1981** Pederson *LAGS Basic Materials,* 1 inf, **seAL**, A wood iron; a smoothing iron.

wood jack n chiefly Midl

=**jack** n[1] **6.**

1949 Kurath *Word Geog.* 59, Saw horse. . . In the Alleghanies the saw horse is sometimes called a *(wood) jack.* **1967** Faries *Word Geog. MO* 85, Saw horse. . . wood jack (6 occurrences [from c700 infs]). **1967** *DARE* (Qu. L59, *An implement with an X-frame . . to hold firewood for sawing*) Inf **MO**5, Wood jack. **1973** Allen *LAUM* 1.221 **Upper MW** (as of c1950), Sawbuck. . . the minority term *(wood)jack,* carried west from the Alleghanies, also occurs several times in Midland speech territory. **1985** *AmSp* 60.234 **ePA**, Saw buck/wood buck—Device used for holding wood while it is being cut . . *[wood] jack* 3% [of 60 infs]. **1986** Pederson *LAGS Concordance,* 1 inf, **cwGA**, Wood jack—A-frame for lumber.

woodjam n

1994 NC Lang. & Life Project *Dial. Dict. Lumbee Engl.* 13 **seNC**, *Woodjam. . . A container for holding firewood. She put some more logs in the woodjam.*

woodjin n [See quot 1987]

A native or resident of the Pine Barrens region of New Jersey.

1937 Beck *More Forgotten Towns NJ* 323 **sNJ**, We heard Dolph Arens, a woodjin of the Forked River Mountains, recall what had happened there. **1968** McPhee *Pine Barrens* 60 **cNJ**, A native guide is a

woodjin. **1987** Moonsammy et al. *Pinelands Folklife* 21 **sNJ**, "Woodjin's enemy" *(Comptonia asplenifolia)* is sweet-fern, laden with the sand-ticks so bothersome to "woodjins"—a portmanteau word combining "woodsman" and "Injun." **2003** *DARE* File **sNJ**, [*Spung*] was a colloquialism exclusive to "woodjins" or "piners," that is, the illiterate mass of wood cutters, tar kilners and coalers who populated the Piney woods of "Down Jersey." **2007** *DARE* File—Internet **sNJ**, [Screen name:] woodjin. . . I have been a pine barrens resident since '95.

wood Kate See Kate

wood kitty See woods kitty

wood-knocker See knocker 1

woodland orchid See wood orchid

woodland star n

Std: a plant of the western genus *Lithophragma.* Also called **fringe cup 3.** For other names of var spp see **baby face, baby's breath 2d, fairy stars, starflower 6, star-of-Bethlehem 4**

wood lark n

=**wood thrush 1.**

1948 in a1972 *Hench Coll.* 30 May **VA,** [In conversation:] Wood lark, swamp robin, wood thrush—names for the same bird.

wood laurel n

=**calico bush 1.**

1835 Kemble *Jrl.* 133, Received, in exchange, the seed of what I suspect is the wood laurel, common in this country, but unknown in ours [= England]. **1850** *New Engl. Farmer* 2.254, A cluster of wood laurel, with its evergreen glossy leaves, and its rich, heavy clusters of rosy blossoms. **1863** *Ladies' Repository* 23.352 **CT,** It was decked with its joyous banners, for the wood-laurel, or ivy, from which it was named, was in full bloom. **1897** Sudworth *Arborescent Flora* 315 **PA,** *Kalmia latifolia. . .* Wood Laurel. **1950** Peattie *Nat. Hist. Trees* 523, Mountain Laurel. . . Other Names: Sheep, Poison, or Wood Laurel.

wood lily n

1 also *woods lily;* Std: a lily 1 (here: *Lilium philadelphicum*). Also called **fire lily 1, flame ~ 1, freckled ~, glade ~ 1, huckleberry ~, meadow ~ 2, mountain ~ 4, mouse-root, orangecup lily, orange ~, prairie ~ 1, red ~ a, tiger ~** Cf **hardwood lily**

2 A **bead lily** (here: usu *Clintonia umbellulata*).

1917 *Eau Claire Leader* (WI) 3 June 3/3, We must give a few words of special mention to that beautiful little early wood-lily, the Yellow Clintonia, familiar to our Wisconsin woods. **1953** Greene–Blomquist *Flowers South* 10, Speckled Wood-Lily. . . It grows in rich, moist wood soil in the mountainous districts. **1975** Duncan–Foote *Wildflowers SE* 254, Wood-lily. . . Rich woods.

3 =**trillium.**

1870 Robinson *Alpine Flowers* 348, Trillium grandiflorum—White Wood Lily. **1875** *OH Farmer* 48.326, *Trillium,* Wake Robin, sometimes called Wood Lily and Birthroot. **1909** Doubleday *Amer. Flower Garden* 96, Wood-Lily, Wake Robin (*Trillium grandiflorum*). . . The best early white flower for woods. **1950** *WELS (Trillium)* 1 Inf, **WI,** Wood lily. **1969–70** *DARE* (Qu. S2, . . *The flower that comes up in the woods early in spring, with three white petals that turn pink as the flower grows older*) Infs **MI**114, **NY**165, Wood lily. **1970** *NC Folkl.* 18.16, Trillium (birthroot such as wood lily or ground lily) was effective as cough syrup. **1971** Krochmal *Appalachia Med. Plants* 256, *Trillium erectum. . .* wood lily.

wood lizard n

A **salamander 1;** see quots.

1860 Jackson *Mountain* 374, Red-backed salamander.—This is a common "wood-lizard," said to be the most abundant in the Northern States. **1927** *Charleston Daily Mail* (WV) 15 July 16/4, Johnnie's story of the hornpouts and the small wood lizard in his pocket. **1928** Baylor Univ. Museum *Contrib.* 16.9 **Sth,** In its actions, the four-toed or Dwarf Salamander is the most lizardlike of all amphibians. It is usually found under and in the hearts of rotten logs and is therefore called Wood Lizard in several Southern localities.

woodlot n Also *woodslot* widespread, but esp Nth, Midl See Map

A tract of land, esp on a farm, set aside for timber to be used for domestic and other purposes.

1643 in 1848 *New Engl. Hist. & Geneal. Reg.* 2.262 **MA,** To my younger daughter, my woodlot & my part of the 4000 Acres. **1706** in 1889 Manchester MA *Town Rec.* 1.115, It is Voted and agreed to lay out 50 or 60 Acors of land at the west end of our common for a wood lot. **1818** Fearon *Sketches* 72 **NYC,** The farm contains about 150 acres, 15 of which are a fine wood lot. **1867** *De Bow's Rev.* 4.486 **MS,** In a woods lot, that I sowed eighteen years ago, much of it [=herd's-grass] may yet be seen. **1902** *DN* 2.249 **sIL,** *Woodlot* or *woodslot.* . . Name of a part of the forest or timber. **1907** *DN* 3.228 **nwAR,** *Wood(s)-lot.* . . A tract of woods. **1926** *DN* 5.390 **ME,** *Wood-lot.* . . Woods, primarily those left as a source of fuel. . . Common. **c1960** *Wilson Coll.* **csKY,** *Woodlot.* . . Grove of trees left to grow. **1965–70** *DARE* (Qu. T2a, . . *A piece of land covered with trees . . only a few acres*) 167 Infs, **widespread, but esp Nth, Midl,** Woodlot; **CT**17, Small woodlot; **AR**36, **KY**80, 86, **MI**64, **MO**9, **TN**56, Woodslot; (Qu. T2b, . . *A piece of land covered with trees . . a large acreage*) 11 Infs, **NEast,** (Large) woodlot; (Qu. T4, *The place where . . trees grow together and sap is gathered*) Inf **MI**42, Woodlot. **1977** Shields *Cades Cove* 32 **eTN,** Most farms had a section of forest reserved as the wood lot, to be cut for this purpose [= for firewood]. **1986** Pederson *LAGS Concordance (Barnyard)* 2 infs, **MS, TN,** Woodlot; 1 inf, **seAL,** The woodlot—where not much work is done. **1995** in 1999 Millersville Univ. Center for PA Ger. Studies *Jrl.* Fall 6 (as of 1930s), While being in the woodlot we ventured upon a friend of my father's who was looking for snapping turtles along the creek. **2009** *DARE* File **nwMA,** Several generations of my family have had homes in town and have owned woodlots in the hills, not adjacent to their homes. These woodlots are relatively inexpensive tracts because they aren't suitable for building on due to soil type or steep or rocky terrain. The woodlots are registered Tree Farms and are managed for timber, firewood, and wildlife habitat.

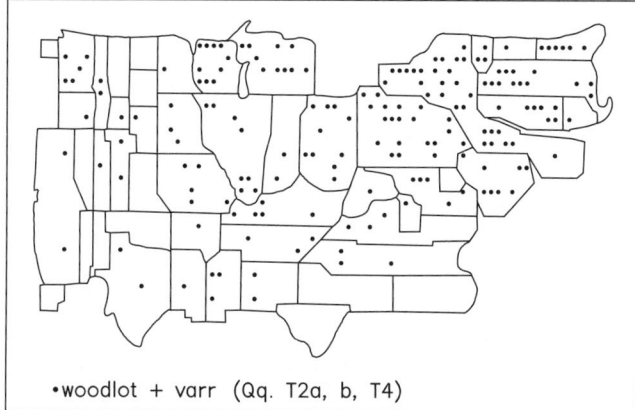

•woodlot + varr (Qq. T2a, b, T4)

woodman's ghost n   Also *woodsman's ghost*   [See quots]
=**Canada jay.**

1945 Hamlin *9 Mile Bridge* 223 **nME,** We spread bread crumbs for the gorbies—"Whisky Jack," "Woodsman's Ghost" or "Canada Jay"—a dirty-gray, noisy bird that hangs around camps in the woods. Lumberjacks say they are the reincarnation of other departed lumberjacks. **1959** *Names* 7.115 **NY,** A number of names of the gray or Canada jay have been given because these birds are fancied to be the embodied spirits of dead lumbermen. Such are . . old logger and woodman's ghost (N.Y.)

wood meeting   See **camp meeting**

wood mouse n

1   A **white-footed mouse** (here: usu *Peromyscus leucopus* or *P. maniculatus*).

1846 *Amer. Whig Rev.* 4.637, Even the little Wood-Mouse is shown amidst the huge drift logs and the mighty desolation through which the Lower Mississippi holds its sombre way. **1857** [see **2** below]. **1872** *Littell's Living Age* 115.806, These wood-mice are often called white-footed mice. . and are indigenous to this our Western Continent. **1909** *Forest & Stream* 24.932, An animal known to most outdoor men and women is the little wood mouse, known also as deer mouse, vesper mouse, or white-footed mouse. **1928** Anthony *N. Amer. Mammals* 361, Arizona White-footed Mouse; Apache Wood Mouse.—*Peromyscus leucopus arizonae. Ibid,* Texas White-footed Mouse; Texas Gray Wood Mouse.—*Peromyscus leucopus texanus.* **1947** Cahalane *Mammals* 472, The eastern wood mouse (*P. leucopus*) seems to be a perpetually irascible species.

2   A **jumping mouse 1** (here: *Zapus hudsonius*).

1842 DeKay *Zool. NY* 1.72, I pursued it, when it proved to be one of these *wood-mice,* or *jumping-mice.* **1857** U.S. Patent Office *Annual Rept. for 1856: Ag.* 96, *Jaculus labradorius* [=*Zapus hudsonius*]. . . This animal is known as the "Long-tailed Deer Mouse," "Fob-tailed Mouse," "Kangaroo Mouse," "Jumping Mouse," "Buck Mouse," "Wood Mouse," and other names, common also to the Mus leucopus [=*Peromyscus leucopus*]. **1896** Robinson *In New Engl. Fields* 230, The leaps of a tiny wood-mouse are lightly marked upon the feathery surface. [*DARE* Ed: This quot may refer instead to **1** above.]

wood nymph n   chiefly **NW**

A **wintergreen 1** (here: *Moneses uniflora*).

1921 U.S. Natl. Museum *Contrib. Herbarium* 22.5.388 **MT,** *Moneses uniflora.* . . Wood-nymph. Occasional at middle altitudes in deep woods on mossy banks. **1936** McDougall–Baggley *Plants of Yellowstone* 95, Wintergreen Family. . . Flowers solitary. Woodnymph *(Moneses uniflora).* **1950** FWP *Guide ID* 66, If it were not for its sharply penetrating fragrance, wood nymph (one-flowered wintergreen) would escape notice. **1961** Douglas *My Wilderness* 17 **CO,** Near it is apt to be found a wood nymph *(Moneses uniflora),* if one drops to his knees to look. It has evergreen leaves at the base and a five-pointed white flower with a drooping head. **1972** Courtenay–Zimmerman *Wild Flowers* 79 **N Cent,** Wood Nymph, *Moneses uniflora.* . . Wet forests, bogs.

wood orchid n   Also *woodland orchid, wood orchis, woods orchid*

A **fringed orchid** (here: usu *Platanthera clavellata,* formerly *Habenaria c.*).

1871 *Atlantic Mth.* 27.662 **eMA,** Less frequently we find in this scattered assemblage some rare species of Wood Orchis and the singular Coral Plant. **1891** *Galveston Daily News* (TX) 2 Aug 10/5, The table decorations were the pink, bell like wood orchids which are the commonest and among the prettiest of the sorts that grow wild. **1896** Britton–Brown *Illustr. Flora* 1.463, *Habenaria* [=*Platanthera*] *clavellata.* . . Small Green Wood Orchis. **1912** Mathews *Amer. Wild Flowers* 84, Green Wood Orchis—*Habenaria clavellata.* **1950** Correll *Native Orchids* 65, *Habenaria clavellata.* . . Common names: Small Green Wood-orchid, . . Wood Orchid. **1971** *Times–Std.* (Eureka CA) 25 May 18/1, One of the most beautiful and delicate flowers to be found is the little woods orchid. . . It seems like the little wood orchids are living on borrowed time. **1976** Bailey–Bailey *Hortus Third* 533, [*Habenaria*] *clavellata.* . . Green woodland orchid.

‡**wood-patch baby** n   Cf **brierpatch child, woodpile 1**
=**woods colt 2.**

1969 *DARE* (Qu. Z11b, . . [*A child whose parents were not married*]) Inf **GA**84, Wood-patch baby.

woodpecker n   Also *woodpeck, woodpicker*

A Forms.   Cf **peckerwood**

1885 *Harper's New Mth. Mag.* 71.400 **GA,** Nancy's head's red, red as a woodpeck's. **1965** Carmony *Speech Terre Haute* 37 **IN,** The only alternative offered for the general *woodpecker* . . was *woodpeck,* a term suggested by the oldest informant in the study. **1966** Dakin *Dial. Vocab. Ohio R. Valley* 2.397 **sIN,** *Woodpicker* is scattered across southern Indiana from Clark's Grant westward to Edwards County, Illinois. The fact that in every instance this term is attested by a female informant and that no male informant uses it suggests that it may be a deliberate evasion of pecker. **1986** Pederson *LAGS Concordance,* 3 infs, **Gulf Region,** Woodpeck(s). **2007** *DARE* File—Internet **PA,** You sure got the woodpecks in your garden! **2008** *Ibid* **ME,** Our pair of Piliated [sic] woodpecks are making their daily visits now to the peanut butter suet.

B Senses.

1 Std: a bird of the family Picidae.   For other names of var spp see **billy whicker, black-backed woodpecker, brown creeper 2, California woodpecker, carpenter, carpintero, downy woodpecker, flicker** n² **1, Gila woodpecker, golden-fronted ~, groundhog 3, hairy woodpecker, hammerhead 6, hard-faced bird, hardhead 5b, headshrinker, heel-taps, high-holer 1, Indian hen 3, ivory-billed woodpecker, jack hammer, knocker 1, knothead 5, ladder-backed woodpecker 1, Lewis's ~, loggerhead 10, marshal, mountain woodpecker, mundiner, nail-pounder, pecker 1, peckerhead 1, peckerwood 1, pileated woodpecker B, pique bois, rain crow 1d, red-bellied woodpecker, red-cockaded ~, redhammer, red-headed woodpecker, ringneck 6, riveter, sapsucker 1, three-toed woodpecker, ticktack bird, tree-**

pounder, tree surgeon, trip-hammer, wood chicken 2, woodchuck 2, woodcock 2, wood hen 2

2 Used as a derog term for one who fells trees. Cf **beaver** n 3

1905 U.S. Forest Serv. *Bulletin* 61.53 [Logging terms], *Woodpecker.* . . A poor chopper. **1995** *DARE* File **cMA** (as of 1920s–30s), When the Quabbin Reservoir was being built, people forced out of their homes in the area to be flooded called the axemen who were brought in to cut down all the timber "woodpeckers." This was before the time of chain saws; all the trees were felled by hand. (The term was not complimentary.)

woodpecker hickory n
=**mockernut hickory.**

1938 *Wildlife Rev.* 12.30, Hicoria alba—Woodpecker hickory. **1951** *PADS* 15.30 **TX,** *Hicoria alba* [=*Carya tomentosa*]. . . Woodpecker hickory.

woodpecker-lark n   Also *lark woodpecker*   **chiefly Mid Atl, GA**
=**flicker** n² **1.**

1773 in 1981 Laurens *Papers* 9.15 **SC,** Much wood in different parts & Clouds of Pidgeons, & here I saw our true Woodpecker Lark. [*DARE* Ed: Evidently a misidentification, as the writer is traveling in northern France.] **1805** in 1904 Lewis *Orig. Jrls. Lewis & Clark Exped.* 2.252, I saw a black woodpecker . . today about the size of the lark woodpecker. **1860** *S. Planter* 20.205 **cVA,** The large, spotted woodpecker, much tinged with yellow,—called lark-woodpecker, and by the boys, yucker—is the only bird I ever saw picking out and eating the worms from the roots of peach-trees. **1882** Ingersoll *Birds'-Nesting* 70 **GA,** As for the southern word, "woodpecker-lark," it of course refers to the black crescent upon the breast [of the flicker], which reminds one of the similar badge of the meadowlark. **1900** *Wilson Bulletin* 12.2.11 **GA, SC,** [Synonyms of *flicker:*] Woodpecker Lark. Georgia; South Carolina. "From the black crescent of the breast." Ernest Ingersoll. Owing to a resemblance in upper plumage as well as the-at-times-similarity of feeding habits and association while on the ground with the Meadow-lark. **1910** Wayne *Birds SC* 93, *Colaptes auratus.* . . This species is locally known as the Yellow-hammer and Woodpecker-lark, and is a permanent resident. **1922** Gonzales *Black Border* 338 **sSC, GA coasts** [Gullah glossary], *Woodpeckuh laa'k*—woodpecker lark—the flicker. **1955** *AmSp* 30.182, It seems that resemblance in habit is at the root of a few bird-name combinations. Thus, . . *lark woodpecker* (yellow-shafted flicker, N.Y., Va.) and *woodpecker lark* (the same, S.C., Ga.) point to the terrestrial habits of this species.

woodpecker mill n   **chiefly S Atl**   Cf *peckerwood mill* (at **peckerwood 3a**)
A small-scale, often transient, logging operation.

1927 Hager *Commercial Surv.* 81, Overworking for turpentine . . is one reason for the early cutting of timber into lumber by the so-called "woodpecker mill." To salvage as much of the wood product as possible the landowner is forced to turn to these small mill operators. **1934** Couch *Culture South* 28 **Sth,** Exploitation all along the line from high class to "woodpecker" mills is bringing the South to the verge of its resources of yellow pine. **1941** Writers' Program *Guide AL* 276, Immense logs are piled up . . ; their size offers a pleasant contrast to the sapling-diameter saw stocks cut by "woodpecker mills" over much of the State. **1941** Writers' Program *Guide SC* 73, These little 'woodpecker' mills, employing less than five workers each, leave their piles of sawdust on every creek. **1960** Williams *Walk Egypt* 9 **nGA,** There's this feller's got a woodpecker mill and a contract to cut cedar on Teaspoon Hill. **2007** *DARE* File—Internet **cCA** [*Sierra Mountain Times* 6 Aug], The sawmill on Wally's ranch . . is a small "woodpecker" mill, where Wally and his crew of workers take reject logs . . and produce primarily firewood.

wood-peent n
=**flicker** n² **1.**

1956 MA Audubon Soc. *Bulletin* 40.82, Yellow-shafted Flicker. . . Wood-peent (Mass. A woodland creature that utters the sound *peent.*)

wood pewee n   Cf **pewee** n¹ **1, pieces-of-eight bird**
Std: either of two **flycatchers 1a:** in the east usu *Contopus virens;* in the west usu *C. sordidulus.*   For other names of *C. virens* see **dead-limb bird, moss bird 1, pewit 1, tickbird 1**

wood pheasant n
=**ruffed grouse** or **dusky grouse.**

1886 Wingate *Through Yellowstone* 170, At one time we met a "wood

pheasant" (dusky grouse), a beautiful bird, larger than a partridge, with feathers of a brilliant peacock blue. **1918** Grinnell et al. *Game Birds CA* 552, Oregon Ruffed Grouse. . . Other names—Oregon Grouse; Wood Pheasant (Del Norte County). **1932** *Waterloo Daily Courier* (IA) 30 Oct 15/3, It is Mr. Whitford's opinion that the wood pheasant or drumming partridge that used to be common in the woods of this section was the finest eating of any wild game. **1977** *Brainerd Daily Dispatch* (MN) 30 Jan 16/1, The more common names [of the ruffed grouse] include partridge, wood pheasant, and wood chicken.

wood phlox   See **woods phlox**

woodpicker   See **woodpecker**

wood-pie n
=**flicker** n² **1.**

1956 MA Audubon Soc. *Bulletin* 40.82 **CT,** Wood Pie. . . A British folk name for the Green Woodpecker. It means pied, or variegated, bird of the woodland.

wood pigeon n
=**flicker** n² **1.**

[**1873** Essex Inst. *Bulletin* 5.35 **New Brunswick Canada,** *Colaptes auratus.* Golden-winged Woodpecker, called here the Wood Pigeon. Very common; breeds.] **1887** *Forest & Stream* 28.248 **NEast,** The golden-winged woodpecker (*Colaptes auratus*). . . Wood pigeon. **1956** MA Audubon Soc. *Bulletin* 40.83 **NY,** Wood-pigeon, a name also reported for the Flicker in New Brunswick and New York.

woodpile n attrib   **chiefly C and N Atl, esp NJ**   Cf **brierpatch child, fence-corner, nigger in the woodpile, shirttail** adj 2, **wood-patch baby, woods colt 2**

1 Of a child: illegitimate.

1995 Karon *Light in the Window* 381 **NC,** He hadn't looked like his mother, who was beautiful, or his father, who was handsome. "Woodpile kid," some unkind neighbor had once been heard to say. **2003** in 2009 *DARE* File—Internet [Black], As the great-grandson of a "woodpile" child, I can appreciate her position. . . My great-grandfather's father was the owner of the Myrtle Grove Plantation south of New Orleans. . . Needless to say, he wasn't claimed directly. **2006** [see **2** below].

2 Of a kinsman: remote, distant; indefinitely related; sometimes spec related by marriage or through an illegitimate child; also fig.

1913 Hope *Outdoor Girls Winter* 32, This searching firm has been delving among my wood-pile relations, as I call them, looking for clues. **1939** (1962) Thompson *Body & Britches* 498 **NY,** He's a woodpile relation: (kindred is pretty well mixed up). **1967** *DARE* FW Addit **cePA,** *Woodpile relation*—a very distant one. **1969** *Independent* (Long Beach CA) 4 Nov sec B 9/1, There are a few chicken substitutes that can be interesting, such as frog legs . . or rabbit, still another woodpile relation that can be refreshingly tasty. **1975** Gould *ME Lingo* 320, *Woodpile cousin*—About like a *buttonhole relation* . ., but less likely to mean actual blood connections. **2001** in 2009 *DARE* File—Internet **seNC,** I have ran across the name of Skelton from another inquiry. We decided we were "wood pile kin". **2002** *Ibid,* I am originally [sic] from N.J. and am of your Norman Family line. . . Please get back to me. Woodpile cousin. **2004** *Herald* (Randolph VT) 30 Sept (Internet), They are all related by marriage or birth somehow, ("woodpile relations mostly," as they put it). **2004** in 2009 *DARE* File—Internet **NJ,** Re: Was a Tunis before adoption. . . We are woodpile relations. The connection goes *way* back as (several great) grandfathers were brothers. **2005** *DARE* File—Internet **NJ,** For those of you who do not recognize the term, 'woodpile' applies to someone with whom I am related through marriage. In this case, the daughter of this 'woodpile' cousin is married to my second cousin. **2006** in 2009 *Ibid* **WV,** Readers, when your mama's a woodpile child, this is how you meet your kin. I looked at that old farmer, and he looked at me. We both knew we were lookin at blood. . . In recent years I've gotten to know Johnny and Sally Tewell, my woodpile kin. . . The luck of the draw gave me Bubba, an enigmatic woodpile ancestor.

wood-piling bee   See **wood bee**

wood poppy n
=**celandine poppy 1.**

1927 *Bulletin Nat. Hist. Surv.* 8.320 **Chicago IL,** Celandine Poppy. Wood Poppy. Damp rich woods, particularly of beech. **1960** *GA Mineral News Letter* 13.33, The roots of the Celandine or wood-poppy . . were boiled to give a red or brown dye. **1975** *Middlesboro Daily News* (KY) 22 May sec A 18/2, Meadows in the "Bluegrass" are displaying bright galaxies of cinquefoils, wood poppies and buttercups. **2003**

Daily Herald (Arlington Heights IL) 8 May sec 5 2/1, For shade, you can't beat hostas. I also like Solomon's seal, wood poppies and lady's mantle.

wood pretty n   Also *woods pretty*   [*wood(s)* + **pretty C1a**] **esp sAppalachians   Cf play-pretty**
A flower, berry, or other plant material regarded as a decorative object; a decorative arrangement of natural materials.
   1931 *News* (Frederick MD) 23 June 1/7, A delightful original article entitled, "Wood Pretties," was read by Miss Margaret R. Motter, "wood pretties," being the term used by the mountaineers of Kentucky to designate their wild flowers, shrubs or bushes.   **1937** Eaton *Handicrafts* 233 **sAppalachians,** In wandering through the mountains it is not uncommon to come across women and children gathering the seeds, pods, berries, acorns, leaves and cones in which the Highlands abound and arranging them in attractive and interesting forms. The natives call these "wood pretties."   **1941** Justus *Cabin on Kettle Creek* 62 **eTN,** Not many wood pretties this time o' year.   **1948** *WI Mag. Hist.* 31.375 **TN,** Many of the articles came from the Southern highland country, among them "Wood's Pretties," colorful simple decorations made from fungi, berries, and twigs, by the old farm women in Tennessee.   **1958** Carroll–Carroll *Tough Enough* 14 **wNC,** After she had set the cans, with the plants in them, into the wooden holders, all the Tatums stood off and looked at the woods pretties.   *Ibid* 16, If we can sell some woods pretties, maybe we'll make do.   **1975** *Sevier Co. Saga* [22] **ceTN,** Arrowmont was soon selling "coverlets," woven scarves, . . brooms, articles made of corn shuck and "wood pretties," toys and dolls.   **2003** *DARE* File—Internet **Ozarks,** She would make little pigs out of white walnuts, and little skunks, and "wood pretties," I think she called them.

wood pussy   See woods pussy

wood-quoi n   Also *wood-quee, ~-queh*
=flicker n² **1.**
   1882 Ingersoll *Birds'-Nesting* 69 **CT,** Yaffle and Woodquoi.   **1902** Ingersoll *Wild Life Orchard* 317 **CT,** "Wood-quoi" (pronounced *wood-queh*) is evidently the same thing [=a flicker], a common name of the British ring-dove being wood-quest; unless, indeed, it refers to the voice.   **1956** MA Audubon Soc. *Bulletin* 40.82, Wood-quoi (Conn. Pronounced "wood-quee" by Sage [John Hall] and Coe [William Wellington]. Gordon Trumbull ms. notes . .).

wood rat n
Std: a rodent of the genus *Neotoma.*   Also called **pack rat.** For other names of var spp see **mountain rat, slicktail ~, stick ~, trade ~**

wood reed grass n
A **reed grass a** (here: *Calamagrostis perplexa*).
   1986 *NY Times* (NY) sec B 2 (Internet), There is a patch of wood-reed grass in the Danby State Forest near Ithaca, N.Y., that grows nowhere else in the world.

wood rick   See rick n **4**

wood robin n
1 also *woods robin:* **=wood thrush 1.**
   1804 *Lit. Mag. & Amer. Reg.* 2.266, Sings the wood-robin close retir'd from sight,/ And swells his *solo* 'mid the shades of night.   **1808** Wilson *Amer. Ornith.* 1.29, *Turdus Melodus. Wood Thrush—*It is called by some the Wood Robin.   **1844** DeKay *Zool. NY* 2.71, The Wood Thrush. . . It has various popular names, such as *Wood Robin, Ground Robin* and *Little Brown Thrasher.*   **1890** Warren *Birds PA* 324, The Wood Robin, the name by which the Wood Thrush is best known in many localities in Pennsylvania . . is a common inhabitant of woods.   **1930** Weygandt *Wissahickon Hills* 5 **nwPA,** Nowhere else are there so many wood-thrushes. . . "Wood-robin" we call him here.   **1970** *DARE* (Qu. Q14, . . *Names . . for . . thrush*) Inf **NY233,** Woods thrush—woods robin or killorill.
2 **=brown thrasher.**
   1913 Bailey *Birds VA* 323, *Toxostoma rufum.* . . Known to the residents and negroes as "Wood Robin."   **1968** *DARE* (Qu. Q14, . . *Names . . for . . brown thrasher*) Infs **NY66, WV2,** Wood robin.
3 **=rufous-sided towhee.**
   1913 Bailey *Birds VA* 238, *Pipilo erythrophthalmus.* . . Ground Robin. Wood Robin.   **1969** Longstreet *Birds FL* 148, Towhee. . . *Other names* . . Ground Robin; Wood Robin.   **2004** Naugle *Luckiest Hunter* 172 **PA,** Several towhees made their way through the brush, stirring the leaves for breakfast. Their rufous sides and black bodies give them a common name of "wood robin."

wood rooter   See rooter 1

wood rose n
A **wild rose** (here: *Rosa gymnocarpa*) of California and the Northwest.   Also called **redwood rose**
   1903 Sierra Club *Bulletin* 4.55, Rosa gymnocarpa . . , Wood Rose. Cañon Creek, Lewiston Trail.   **1911** Jepson *Flora CA* 206, *R[osa] gymnocarpa.* . . Wood Rose. . . Shady woods or bushy north slopes, often near streams.   **1967** Gilkey–Dennis *Hdbk. NW Plants* 210, *Wood rose.* . . petals a clear delicate pink, with white bases.   **2000** *DARE* File—Internet **CA,** What else to grow under oaks? . . The wood rose, Rosa gymnocarpa is lovely, though not gaudy.

wood sawbill n   **Cf sawbill**
=hooded merganser.
   1923 U.S. Dept. Ag. *Misc. Circular* 13.7 **GA,** Hooded Merganser. . . frog duck, hairyhead, shagpoll, wood sawbill.

wood saw rack   See saw rack

wood sawyer   See sawyer 1

woods burned, since the adv phr   Also *since the woods caught fire;* for addit varr see quots   **chiefly Sth, S Midl**   See Map
For a long time.
   1863 *Centralia Sentinel* (IL) 9 July [3]/1 (newspaperarchive.com), On Tuesday . . Centralia was the *locale* of as happy a lot of people as it ever contained "since the woods were burnt the second time."   **1878** *Daily Constitution* (Atlanta GA) 4 Apr 1/1, We are going to have the liveliest time in the fifth district that we have had since "the woods were burned."   **1881** *Landmark* (Statesville NC) 13 May 3/1 (newspaperarchive.com), One [=a chicken] hasn't been seen on this market since the woods were burnt. They are scarcer even than butter.   **1896** *Daily IA Capital* (Des Moines) 14 May 4/2, Senator Perry of Albia . . has been a democrat ever since the woods were burned.   **1897** in 1993 Harris *Dearest Chums* 130 **GA,** I have seen her but once since—well, "since the woods were burnt."   **1904** *TX Med. Jrl.* 19.464, Members who . . had not attended a meeting since the woods were burnt, put in appearance.   **1965–70** *DARE* (Qu. A16, *A very long period of time: "I haven't seen him _____."*) Infs **GA87, KY74, VA26,** Since the woods burned (off); **SC56,** Since the woods burnt off; **MS16, VA36,** Since the woods caught (*or* was on) fire; **FL35,** Since the woods has burned; **SC34,** Since the woods was afire; **VA8,** Since the woods were burnt.   **1969** *KY Folkl. Rec.* 15.21, I haven't seen you since the woods were burnt.   **2002** (2005) Myers *Best Lore of the Smokies* 111 **wNC, eTN,** I will never forget seeing two friends meet in the road one day. One exclaimed, "Why, I haven't seen you since the woods burnt over!"   **2007** *DARE* File—Internet **GA,** My mama's generation had a language all their own, and I sorely miss hearing the phrases they uttered. . . "I haven't seen him since the woods burned over."

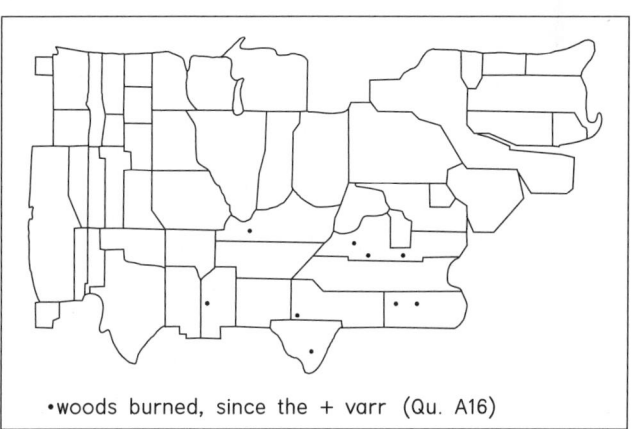

•woods burned, since the + varr (Qu. A16)

wood scaffold   See scaffold n **B3**

woods cat   See woods kitty

woods child n   Also *woods kid*   **esp Sth, S Midl**
=woods colt 2.
   1908 *Amer. Mag.* 66.316, "David, she has a child of her own." "But I didn't know—she isn't—" "A woods child," said the Scotch Preacher.   **1954** *PADS* 21.41 **SC,** Woods chillun. . . Illegitimate children.   **1966** Dakin *Dial. Vocab. Ohio R. Valley* 2.440, *Bastard.* . . Several old folk terms are still known. By far the most common is the Southern and

South Midland *woods colt*. . . Related variants *woods child, ~ rabbit* . . also appear once or twice among older speakers in Ohio and eastern Kentucky. **1970** Tarpley *Blinky* 220 **neTX**, *Child of an unwed mother* . . woods kid [rare]. **1970** *DARE* (Qu. Z11b, . . *[A child whose parents were not married]*) Inf **TN**52, Woods kid. **1986** Pederson *LAGS Concordance (Bastard)* 1 inf, **ceAR**, Woods child; [1 inf, **nwTN**, Child of the woods].

woods clover n

An **indigo bush 2** (here: *Dalea leporina*).

　1923 *Kossuth Co. Advance* (Algona IA) 4 Oct 6/1, Professor Hughes said it might better be called Wood's Clover because Mr. Woods, of Logan, Iowa, found it growing on his farm. The chief use of the dalea is as a green manure crop. **1934** *Wellsboro Agitator* (PA) 28 Feb 4/4, Wood's clover, an annual legume brought to Ohio from Iowa, is not as palatable as a hay or pasture crop and can be used in Ohio only as a green manure crop. **1942** *Torreya* 42.161 **KS**, *Parosela dalea* . . Woods clover, Allen County. **1963** Robinson–Knott *Story* 160 **IA**, Dalea, or Woods clover as it was sometimes called.

woods colt n   Also *wood colt*   Cf **brush colt**

1   also *woods horse:* A horse born of a chance mating. **chiefly Sth, S Midl, TX**   See Map   Cf **brush colt 1, catch ~ 1**

　1851 *OH Cultivator* 7.67, You will frequently hear such men sneeringly say, " . . I have raised as good horses from woods colts as any of your fine blooded horses can produce." **1878** *Wallace's Mth.* 4.70 **OH** (as of 1855), This horse was termed a 'woods colt,' as he was got while his dam was running at large. **1903** *DN* 2.337 **seMO**, Woods-colt. . . A horse of unknown paternity. Also applied to a person of illegitimate birth. **1907** *DN* 3.238 **nwAR**, Woods-colt. . . A horse of unknown paternity; a person of illegitimate birth. **1950** *WELS (A horse that was not intentionally bred)* 2 Infs, **WI**, Woods colt. **1965–70** *DARE* (Qu. K43, *A horse that was not intentionally bred, or bred by accident*) 94 Infs, **chiefly Sth, S Midl, TX**, Woods colt; **AR**15, **IA**31, **MD**24, **MS**60, **SC**47, Wood colt; **GA**74, Woods horse. **1997** in 2004 Montgomery–Hall *Dict. Smoky Mt. Engl.* 656, Woods colt . . A horse unintentionally sired, one of unknown paternity. . . [2 infs].

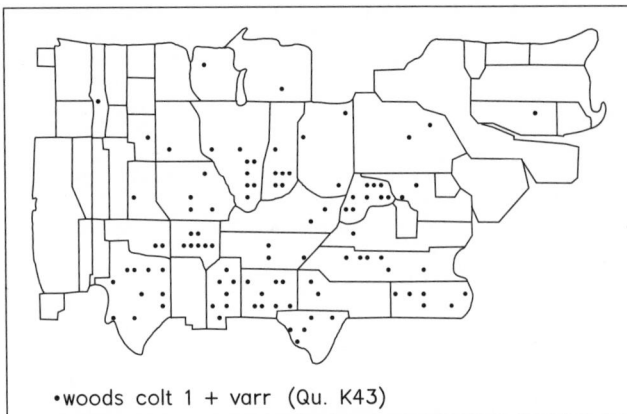

•woods colt 1 + varr (Qu. K43)

2   also *woods colt child:* A child born out of wedlock. **chiefly Sth, S Midl**   See Map   Also called **brierpatch child, brush colt 2, catch ~ 2, wild ~, wood-patch baby, woods child, ~ rabbit, yard colt**   Cf **woodpile 1, yard child 2**

　1860 Starnes *Slaveholder Abroad* 351 **Sth** [Black], The mother of the gal . . swored that the gal was her chile, but was sort of a—of a—what do you call 'um, sir?—a sort of a woods-colt. **1895** *DN* 1.395 **KY**, *Woods colt:* foundling. **1903** [see **1** above]. **1907** [see **1** above]. **1915** *DN* 4.192 **swVA**, *Wood's colt*. . . Bastard. **1917** *DN* 4.419 **wNC**, Woodscolt. . . Bastard. **1923** *DN* 5.224 **swMO**, Woods colt. . . An illegitimate child. **1927** *AmSp* 2.366 **cwWV**, Woodscolt . . an illegitimate child. **1929** *AmSp* 5.124 **ME**, If illegally bearing a child, it was said she "got into a scrape" or "had a woods' colt." **1934** Carmer *Stars Fell on AL* 195, Well, thar's whar the Widow Cox lives with her woods colt chile, po' thing. **1939** *AmSp* 14.92 **eTN**, Woods colt. **1941** *AmSp* 16.25 **sIN**, Woodscolt. **1944** *PADS* 2.52 **NC, VA**, Wood's-colt. **1946** *PADS* 5.43 **VA**, Woods colt. **1949** Kurath *Word Geog.* 43, Woods colt . . is the Carolina counterpart of the Virginia *old-field colt* for an illegitimate child. The term is not common on Albemarle Sound or in the Low Country of South Carolina and Georgia; on the other hand, it is in gen-

eral use throughout the Appalachians and in the Ohio Valley from Wheeling downstream. *Woods colt* may well be a creation of the South Midland that found its way down the river valleys to the Atlantic. **1950** *WELS (Words for a child whose parents were not married . . Joking)* 2 Infs, **WI**, Woods colt. **1959** *VT Hist.* 27.167, *Wood's colt.* **1965–70** *DARE* (Qu. Z11b, . . *[A child whose parents were not married]*) 151 Infs, **chiefly Sth, S Midl**, Woods colt; **AR**40, **LA**14, **SC**10, Wood colt; (Qu. Z11a, . . *A child whose parents were not married—serious words*) Infs **GA**72, **IL**113, 126, **MS**1, **VA**27, Woods colt. **1989** Pederson *LAGS Tech. Index* 235 **Gulf Region**, *Bastard* . . wood colt (8 [of 914 infs]) . . [woodling [*DARE* Ed: perh for *woodland*] colt (1)] . . woods colt (92). **2000** *DARE* File **TN**, While in southeast Tennessee (Polk County) last week, I heard an expression that I thought I should share with you: woods colt. It means illegitimate child.

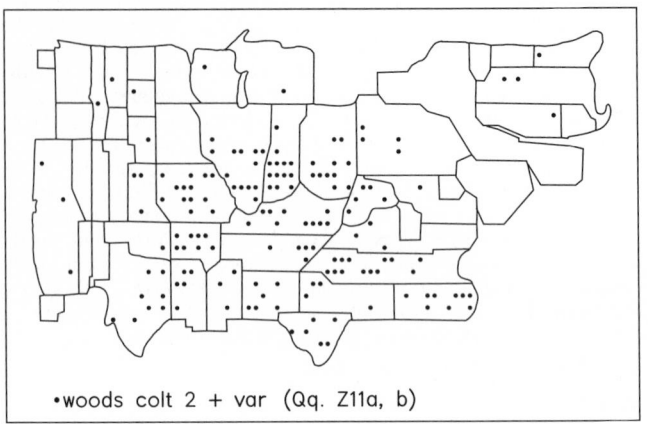

•woods colt 2 + var (Qq. Z11a, b)

woods fly n   Also *wood fly*   **esp N and C Atl, OH**   See Map
A biting fly; see quots.

　[**1841** *OH Atlas & Elyria Advt.* 15 Dec 1/4, As for wood flies we [in Liberia] have far less than in the southern parts of the U. States.] **1855** *Scientific Amer.* 11.35, Their [=screw flies'] appearance is much the same as the woods-fly (*hippobasca*). **1867** Emerson *May-Day* 20 **MA**, The wood-fly mocks with tiny noise / The far halloo of human voice. **1880** *Chester Daily Times* (PA) 24 Feb [3]/1 (newspaperarchive.com), Wood flies and robins are beginning to show themselves. **1912** *Star & Sentinel* (Gettysburg PA) 14 Aug 1/6, You fishermen who are bothered by wood flies while fishing try this and you will have "no flies on him." **1940** Richter *Trees* 19 **OH** (as of c1800), At one place a shaft of light filtered through. . . Woods flies were rising and falling in it. **1965–70** *DARE* (Qu. R12, . . *Other kinds of flies*) 13 Infs, 11 **NEast, Midl**, Wood(s) fly; **CT**2, Wood fly—a biter; **CT**23, Wood fly—they bite; **DC**2, Wood fly—drives horses crazy; **NJ**3, Woods fly—also known as deerfly; (Qu. R11, *A very tiny fly that you can hardly see, but that stings*) Inf **OH**72, Wood fly; (Qu. R13, *Flies that come to meat or fruit*) Inf **MD**30, Woods fly. **2007** *DARE* File—Internet, My sister for example, very very alergic [sic] to Woods Flies, they bite the hell out of you when you aint looking.

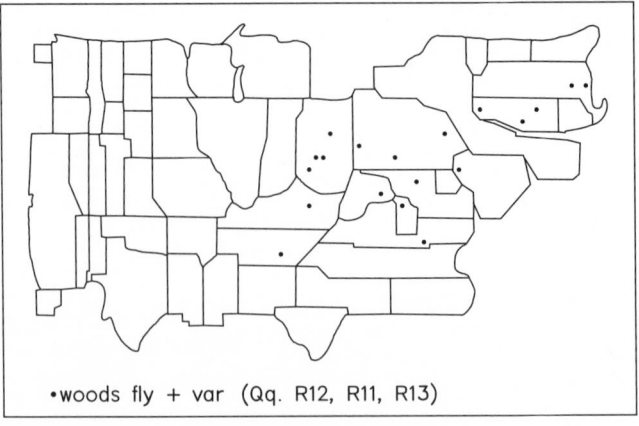

•woods fly + var (Qq. R12, R11, R13)

woods grass   See **wood grass 2**

woods gray (fox)   See **wood gray (fox)**

woodshed, old gray wolf in the   See **gray wolf 3**

wood sheldrake n

A **merganser,** usu the **hooded merganser.**

1888 Trumbull *Names of Birds* 73 **CT,** At Stonington, Conn., [the hooded merganser is called] wood sheldrake. **1895** Ridgway *Ornith. IL* 2.191, Hooded Merganser. . . Popular synonyms. . . Wood Sheldrake; Wood Duck [etc]. **1911** *Auk* 28.196 **MA,** Hooded Merganser. . . Unlike the preceding two species, this "wood sheldrake" is glad to associate with live decoys. **1955** MA Audubon Soc. *Bulletin* 39.379 **MA,** Red-breasted Merganser. . . Wood Sheldrake. . . A misnomer which would fit the Hooded Merganser very well. *Ibid* 378 **MA,** Hooded Merganser. . . Wood Sheldrake. . . As inhabiting swamps and nesting in tree cavities.

woods hog n Also *wood hog*

1 =**razorback hog.**

1805 Parkinson *Tour* 290 **MD,** The real American hog is what is termed the wood-hog: they are long in the leg, narrow on the back [etc]. **1842** *W. Farmer & Gardener* 3.130 **OH,** The improved breed of hogs are gradually superceding the "ravenous wood hog," that can whip a bear and give him the first bite. **1870** *Titusville Morning Herald* (PA) 25 Aug [4]/1 **MS** (newspaperarchive.com), It is the old-fashioned woods hog, the long-nosed, bristle-backed, working, rooting, bilious hog, . . that can stand on his head with his body half in the ground and root—root all day and half the night, and never tire or *die:* but do well and look well on it all the time, independently making a living. These are the right kind of hogs. **1918** OH Ag. Exper. Sta. *Bulletin* 326.67, Probably the first improvement of the common "woods" hog was made by the Society of Shakers in Warren County in 1816. **1950** *Times Herald* (Olean NY) 24 Mar 17/6 **LA,** You have to train a hog dog a little. But he takes natural to finding and driving woods hogs. **c1970** Pederson *Dial. Surv. Rural GA* (*What do you call a long-legged hog that has a thin body and a long snout?*) 2 infs, **seGA,** Woods hog. **1986** Pederson *LAGS Concordance* **Gulf Region,** 8 infs, Woods hog(s); 1 inf, Woods hogs—not quite as wild as "wild hogs"; 1 inf, Wood hog. **2000** *Facts* (Clute TX) 13 Apr sec B 3/1, Owners of "woods" hogs, or "piney woods rooters" didn't have to keep their critters on their own land.

2 =**porcupine.** [See quot 1891]

1891 *Forest & Stream* 37.44 **WI,** There has been considerable talk in our paper on the habits of the American porcupine. . . I think I met this wood hog in very many of his habitats and know something about the critter. Why, he will eat anything that any hog will, and more. [*Ibid,* They are a species of hog. Scald off the hair and quills and you have a little pig to all appearances.] **1895** *St. Nicholas* 22.429, Several instances are on record wherein the "wood-hog" has boldly tried to gnaw into a cabin at a window or door while the owner was within, with his gun loaded for bear.

woods horse See **woods colt 1**

woods kid See **woods child**

woods kitty n Also *wood kitty, woods cat* **esp N Cent** Cf **woods pussy**

=**skunk** n **1.**

1928 *Vidette–Messenger* (Valparaiso IN) 21 Jan 8/3, He saw one of the beautiful little "woods kitty" tribe ambling down the road ahead of him. **1935** *N. Adams Transcript* (MA) 23 Oct 3/3, It was tentatively decided to place a baited box trap in the cellar tonight and catch the little wood kitty in that manner. **1947** *Portsmouth Times* (OH) 31 July 3/3, *Wood Kitty Popular.* . . About 200 persons claimed they own a deodorized polecat which wandered into a grocery store last week. **1950** *WELS* **WI** (*Names and nicknames for the skunk*) 2 Infs, Woods cat; 3 Infs, Wood(s) kitty. **1967–68** *DARE* (Qu. P26, *Names and nicknames . . for a skunk*) Infs **OH**33, **PA**73, Woods kitty. **1986** Pederson *LAGS Concordance* (*Skunk*) 1 inf, csAR, Wood kitty. **2008** *DARE* File—Internet **OH,** There was a little "woods kitty" just strolling along the drive about 12 to 15 feet from us.

woods lily See **wood lily 1**

woodslot See **woodlot**

woodsman's Charmin See **woodsman's toilet paper**

woodsman's ghost See **woodman's ghost**

woodsman's toilet paper n Also *woodsman's Charmin*

Any of var plants with broad, soft leaves; see quots.

1966 *DARE* (Qu. S20, *A common weed that grows on open hillsides: It has velvety green leaves close to the ground, and a tall stalk with small yellow flowers on a spike at the top*) Inf **MI**31, Woodsman's Charmin.

2001 *DARE* File—Internet **Pacific NW,** I note that the nice big felty leaves of the thimbleberry are often called woodsman's toilet paper. Every time I tell the kids that, they just giggle themselves silly. **2006** *Ibid* **OR,** Thimbleberries: the fruits are edible; the leaves are soft and large enough to use as "woodsman's toilet paper." **2007** *Ibid* **MN,** Around the county there seems to be a very abundant crop of blooming Large-leaf Asters (Woodsman's toilet paper).

wood snake n

1 also *brown wood snake:* Any of var colubrid snakes, appar characterized by brownish coloration, as the brown snake *(Storeria dekayi)* or the **fox snake;** see quots.

1825 *Gaz.* **ME** (Portland) 16 Aug 2/4, A Snake called the Milk Adder, was killed . . *about 15 inches long,* having in it another Snake partly consumed, called the Wood Snake, of about 10 inches in length. **1872** *NH Patriot* (Concord) 26 June 2/8, A snake about eight inches long, very small round, of a dark brown color on the back, yellowish on the belly and with a whitish ring round its neck came from the boy's mouth. It resembled the wood snake, so called. **1887** *Macon Telegraph* (GA) 11 Aug 4/2, There were wood snakes and rattle snakes, and chicken snakes and a very large number of common black snakes. **1908** *Outing* 52.378 **NH,** The [milk-]snake disgorged a common brown wood snake. **1935** *Amer. Midland Naturalist* 16.334, *Storeria dekayi.* . . These little brown wood snakes were secured in Kansas at the base of an old hollow tree stump. **1966–68** *DARE* (Qu. P25, . . *Kinds of snakes*) Infs **ME**6, **WI**50, Wood snake; **MI**76, Fox snake—also called wood snake and copperhead, but it's not a true copperhead.

2 =**rubber boa.**

1868 Cronise *Nat. Wealth CA* 485, The "Wood Snake" . . *Charina bottae* . . is a short, thick, smooth species, with small head and eyes, brown above, yellowish below, found in woods under decayed logs, bark, etc. **1879** CA Univ. Regents *Biennial Rept. for 1877–79* 96, The Wood Snake, *Wenona plumbea* [=*Charina bottae*]. Locality, Strawberry Cañon, Berkeley.

wood snipe n

1 =**solitary sandpiper.**

1792 Belknap *Hist. NH* 3.169, Wood snipe, *Scolopax fedoa* [here: prob =*Tringa solitaria*]. **1881** IL State Lab. Nat. Hist. *Bulletin* 1.4.196, Solitary Sandpiper. . . known by the popular names of . . "Teeter," and "Wood Snipe." **1907** Chicago Acad. Sci. *Bulletin* 6.74, Solitary Sandpiper. . . Popular synonyms: Peet-weet. Wood Snipe [etc]. **1956** MA Audubon Soc. *Bulletin* 40.18 **NH,** Solitary Sandpiper. . . Wood Snipe. . . It frequents wooded uplands.

2 =**woodcock 1.**

1857 Gerhard *IL as It Is* 253, Among the marsh birds that can be hunted there are . . the common snipe . . , and the wood snipe (Scolopax minor). **1904** *Indiana Weekly Messenger* (PA) 10 Feb [6]/6 (newspaperarchive.com), From this resemblance, or snipe-like appearance, the woodcock is incorrectly named . . big-headed snipe, wood snipe, whistling snipe, etc. **1969** *DARE* (Qu. Q10, . . *Water birds and marsh birds*) Inf **PA**205, Wood snipe. **2002** *Columbus Dispatch* (OH) 17 Oct sec D 9 (Internet), The American woodcock—alias timberdoodle, alias wood snipe . . possesses a mug that belongs on a wanted poster.

woods orchid See **wood orchid**

wood sorrel n

1 Std: a woodland plant of the genus *Oxalis,* esp *O. montana,* formerly *O. acetosella.* For other names of this plant see **alleluia, sleeping Mollie;** for other names of var spp see **agrito 3, horse sorrel 2, lady's ~, mountain ~, pickle** n **3, redwood sorrel, sheep ~, sour grass** d, **toad sorrel**

2 A **dock** n[1] (here: usu *Rumex acetosella*).

1940 Clute *Amer. Plant Names* 138, *R[umex] acetosella.* . . wood-sorrel. [*DARE* Ed: Noted as a name more properly belonging to another plant.] **1945** Wodehouse *Hayfever Plants* 92, The one generally mentioned in hayfever literature is the sorrel dock . . also called field, red, wood and sheep sorrel.

wood sparrow n Also *woods sparrow*

=**field sparrow** a.

1808 (1836) Grant *Memoirs Amer. Lady* 100 **NY,** I do not recollect sparrows there, except the wood sparrow. **1854** *Home Jrl.* (NY NY) 5 Aug 1/6, There are birds . . that frequent only the woods. . . Of this class are the wood sparrow, the thrush, and many other singing birds. **1858** *Atlantic Mth.* 2.864, The Wood-Sparrow (*Fringilla pusilla*) is somewhat less than a Canary, with a chestnut-colored crown; above of a grayish brown hue, and dusky white beneath. **1882** *Forest & Stream* 19.2 **Upstate NY,** That is a little wood sparrow, something like our song sparrow of the fields. **1896** *Harper's New Mth. Mag.* 93.938, Only last summer I discovered the nest of a wood-sparrow in a hazel bush. **1956** MA Audubon Soc. *Bulletin* 40.255 **MA,** Field Sparrow. . . Wood Sparrow. **1967–70** *DARE* (Qu. Q21, . . *Kinds of sparrows*) Infs **GA**76, **VA**40, Wood sparrow; **OH**33, Wood sparrow—same as song sparrow; **VA**64, Woods sparrow.

woods phlox n Also *wood phlox*
=bouncing Bet 1.

1892 *Jrl. Amer. Folkl.* 5.92 **NJ,** *Saponaria officinalis.* . . woods phlox. **1936** *Hamilton Daily News Jrl.* (OH) 9 May 9/3, That which impressed me most. . . was the pure white woods phlox and the nearby fiddle-heads of unfolding fern fronds. **1958** Jacobs–Burlage *Index Plants NC* 35, *Saponaria officinalis.* . . wood-phlox; world's wonder. **1972** *WI State Jrl.* (Madison) 12 Mar sec 2 8/8, Among the first occurrence dates sought in 1972 from all parts of the state are . . first flowers of . . woods phlox, and large white trillium.

woods pretty See **wood pretty**

woods pussy n Also *wood pussy* **scattered, but chiefly NEast, N Cent** See Map Cf **pussy** n 2, **woods kitty**
=skunk n 1.

1887 *Puck* 6 July 312, The Wood Pussy. *A Vulgar Little Verse.* A diminutive animal, pretty to see,/ Dwells in a wood near my villa of stone;/ And though I am fond of animals, he / Has no attractions at all for me,/ And I leave him severely alone. **1899** Bergen *Animal Lore* 61 **MA,** Folk-names of Animals. . . Wood-pussy, skunk. **1916** *Life* 9 Nov 816, [Caption:] Henry, if you hadn't run over that wood pussy you could have fixed it in a minute. **1921** *DN* 5.114 **CA,** Wood-pussy. **1946** Peattie *Pacific Coast* 90, These animals are called by a number of humorous nicknames. . perfume merchant . . wood pussy—but a skunk by any other name . . ! **1950** *WELS* (Names and nicknames for the skunk) 8 Infs, **WI,** Wood(s) pussy. **1959** *Oneonta Star* (NY) 10 Aug 5/7, Mrs. Charles L. Thorington . . said the wood pussy had taken charge of her basement and was acting strangely. **1965–70** *DARE* (Qu. P26, *Names and nicknames . . for a skunk*) 44 Infs, **chiefly NEast, N Cent, TX,** Woods pussy; 22 Infs, **chiefly NEast, N Cent,** Wood pussy. **1970** Lebofsky *Lexicon Philadelphia* 106, Skunk was the first choice of 99% of the informants. *Polecat* was known by 75% . ., *wood(s) pussy* by 33% (25% in the city, 48% in the suburbs). **1996** *Constitution–Tribune* (Chillicothe MO) 5 July 6/1 **MO,** A local family, that had befriended an orphaned woods pussy, begged me—to no avail—to remove the pair of pea-shaped scent glands located at the base of the tail.

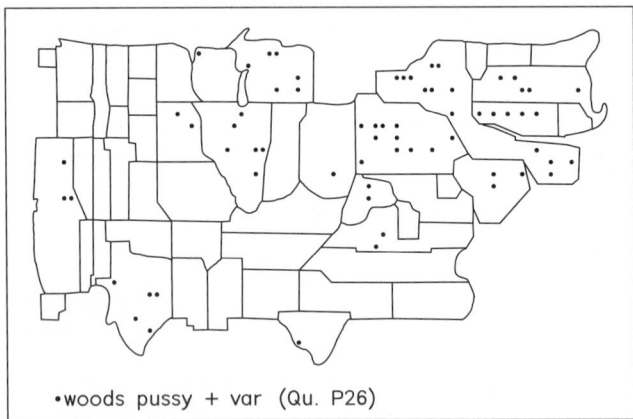

•woods pussy + var (Qu. P26)

woods queer adj phr **NEng, esp ME**
Suffering from **cabin fever.**

1940 Williams *Come Spring* 51 **ME,** I guess she's woods queer. She ain't seen a woman for six months, and she 'lows you'll think she's a sight. **1975** Gould *ME Lingo* 39, If not treated in time by a trip out to town, *cabin fever* may make one *woods queer.* The affliction also strikes offshore islanders during the winter. **1979** McPhee *Giving Good Weight* 150 **NEng,** Life in the woods was eventful enough, and seldom drove them "woods queer." **2002** Tougias *There's a Porcupine* 137 **ME,** The extended solitude could become unhealthy, referred to by a friend from northern Maine as "woods queer." **2006** *DARE* File—Internet **ME,** Congratulations Lola!! For having survived your northern New England confinement for another year. I brought you some Downeast

Tonic, it won't stop you from going woods-queer but it will make the ride there wicked smooth. **2009** *DARE* File n**ME,** Woods queer: . . describes someone who might act strangely for having been isolated in the woods too long.

woods rabbit n
=woods colt 2.

1966 [see **woods child**]. **1966** *DARE* (Qu. Z11b, . . *[A child whose parents were not married]*) Inf **NC**33, Woods rabbit.

woods rider n **S Atl**
In turpentining: a supervisor; see quots.

1897 *Sun. Herald* (Syracuse NY) 3 Oct 5/6 sw**GA,** John Haddock is the woods rider, an officer whose duty it is to ride on horseback over the pine forests to see that everything is working smoothly. **1905** *Robesonian* (Lumberton NC) [30 June 2]/2 (newspaperarchive.com) nw**FL,** A J Gohagan, a woods rider for the Yeager . . Turpentine Company . . was shot by a negro last Saturday. **1939** in Lib. of Congress *Amer. Memory: WPA Life Hist.* (Internet) n**FL** (as of c1910), Niggers do all the labor in the woods, an[d] most of the work around the still. The manager, foreman, commissary men and woods riders are all white men. **1939** FWP *Guide FL* 378 cn,ne**FL,** A 'woods rider' makes the preliminary survey, marking those trees in a given area that are suitable for chipping by smoothing off the bark on the face with a broad ax. **1956** *Florence Morning News* (SC) 29 Jan sec B 3/1, The aged proprietor was born Dec. 28, 1868, on a farm near Adrian and has lived there all his life except for three years when he was a "woods rider" in Tattnall county. A woods rider, he explains, is a supervisor of turpentine work. He rode over the woods to see that the work was properly done. . . This was about 1892. [**1986** Pederson *LAGS Concordance,* 1 inf, nw**FL,** Riding the woods—father's job at turpentine camp.] **2000** Humphreys *Nowhere* 114 cs**NC** (as of c1865), Even in turpentine, only the woods-rider and the stiller made good money.

woods robin See **wood robin 1**

woods rooter See **rooter 1**

woods sparrow See **wood sparrow**

woods tick See **wood tick 1**

woods turtle (or terrapin) See **wood turtle**

wood tag n Cf **stone tag**
A variation of the children's game of tag; see quot 1891.

1883 Newell *Games & Songs* 158, Tag. . . Owing to the occasional scarcity of iron objects, *wood-tag* and *stone-tag* have been varieties of the sport in America. **1891** *Jrl. Amer. Folkl.* 4.222 **Brooklyn NYC,** *Wood Tag.* In this game, the one who is "it" tries to tag any player who is not touching wood, any object of wood being regarded as a "home" or "hunk." Otherwise the game is the same as simple tag. **1926** Pratt–Stanton *Before Books* 224 **NYC** (as of 1913), The children are quite independent now about starting games, such as . . "Wood Tag." **1953** Brewster *Amer. Nonsinging Games* 65 **MO,** *Wood Tag* . . a player escapes capture by touching wood. **1965–70** *DARE* (Qu. EE2) Inf **FL**10, Wood tag; (Qu. EE13a, *Games in which every player hides except one, and that one must try to find the others*) Inf **VA**27, Wood tag; [(Qu. EE17, *In a game of tag, if a player wants to rest, what does he call out so that he can't be tagged?*) Infs **IN**41, **NC**23, Stands on a piece of wood; **GA**33, I'm on wood; **MD**34, Put foot on wood designated for this purpose and say "I'm safe";] (Qu. EE33, . . *Outdoor games . . that children play*) Infs **ND**1, **VT**16, Wood tag. **1975** Ferretti *Gt. Amer. Book Sidewalk Games* 167, Empty lots are fine for such Tag games as *Wood Tag,* in which "It" cannot tag any other players so long as they touch wood, because wood abounds in lots. **2006** *DARE* File—Internet, *Five Fun Tag Variations.* . . Wood Tag—This game is just like simple tag, except a player who is touching something made of wood is "safe." This is a good indoor tag variation. Needless to say, it might not be too much fun in a forest, but could be a lot of fun in a back yard with sparse trees.

wood terrapin See **wood turtle**

wood thrush n

1 Std: an eastern thrush *(Hylocichla mustelina).* Also called **bell bird 1, branch ~, brown thrush 2, eeolee, evening thrush, grasset 2, ground robin 2, hermit thrush 2, mountain ~, mud bird, ~ thrush, orchard thrush, pewter legs, quillaree, red mavis 2, rest-time bird, shingle-nail ~, speckled caille, swamp angel 2, ~ robin 1b, ~ sparrow 2,**

wheedle-dee, whittle-ding, wood lark, ~ robin 1 Cf **branch sparrow 1**

2 A thrush of the genus *Catharus* such as the **hermit thrush 1.**

1895 Minot *Land-Birds New Engl.* 28 **MA,** The Wilson's Thrushes are in Massachusetts the most common of the so-called "Wood Thrushes," but in northern New England are rare. *Ibid* 32, The Hermit Thrushes bear a strong general resemblance to the two other "Wood Thrushes." **1917** *Janesville Daily Gaz.* (WI) 5 May 4/3, Two of the six wood thrushes that have Wisconsin records can be set down as common residents in our locality, the wood thrush . . and the "Verry," or Wilson's thrush. *Ibid,* The other wood thrush with light ring around eye is the olive backed thrush (swainsoni). **1953** Jewett *Birds WA* 518, Russet-backed Swainson Thrush. . . Other names: Wood Thrush [etc.] **1956** MA Audubon Soc. *Bulletin* 40.129 **VT,** Hermit Thrush. . . Wood Thrush.

wood tick n

1 also *brushwood tick, woods ~:* A tick of the genus *Dermacentor.* [*OED2* (at *wood* sb. 10.b) 1688 →] **scattered, but esp freq Nth, N Midl, Rocky Mts, Pacific; also W Midl** See Map For other names of *D. variabilis* see **dog tick** Cf **glade tick**

1789 *MA Mag.* 1.278, The [coffee] bean has a very near resemblance to a wood tick. **1823** *NY Med. & Phys. Jrl.* 2.342, To this family of the arachnides belong the A[carus] *ixodes,* or wood-tick. **1887** (1892) Hinman *Corporal Si Klegg* 258 **OH,** The woodtick never let go, and could not be drawn out any more easily than a fishhook after it has entered past the barb. **1926** Essig *Insects N. Amer.* 21, The American dog or wood tick, *Dermacentor electus,* is the commonest tick in the Eastern part of the United States. **1941** Ward *Holding Hills* 95 **IA** (as of early 20th cent), When a person goes through any of our woods on a summer day, he is sure to pick up a wood-tick or two. **1965–70** DARE (Qu. R23a, *Insects or other creatures that fasten themselves to the skin and suck blood—on land*) 231 Infs, **scattered, but esp freq Nth, N Midl, Rocky Mts, Pacific; also W Midl,** Wood ticks; **CA**41, Brushwood ticks; **NM**6, Woods ticks; (Qu. R12) Inf **MD**3, Wood ticks; (Qu. R22, *Very small red insects, almost too small to see, that get under your skin and cause itching*) Inf **NY**200, Wood tick; (Qu. T16) Inf **CA**105, Tick brush or blueblossom—full of wood ticks in spring. **1968–70** DARE Tape **MI**96, Wood ticks . . were a pest if you got into them; **TX**96, Fever tick—a type of wood tick afflicting cattle. **2009** DARE File **WI,** In Wisconsin, wood ticks are a common annoyance. One quickly learns to distinguish wood ticks from the smaller, more dangerous deer ticks which spread Lyme disease.

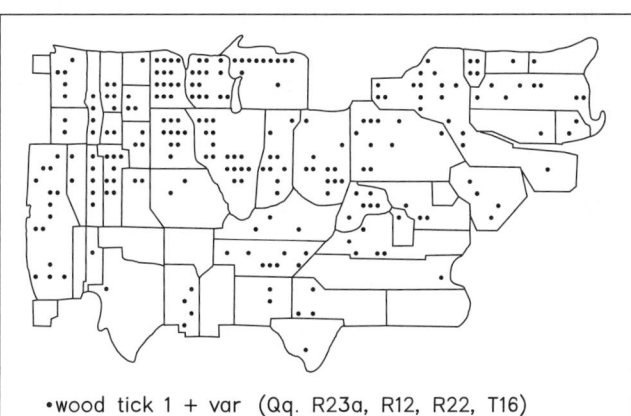

•wood tick 1 + var (Qq. R23a, R12, R22, T16)

2 A deathwatch beetle (family Anobiidae). Cf **death tick**

a1820 in 1935 Drake *Life & Wks.* 144 **NYC,** The wood-tick has kept the minutes well;/ He has counted them all with click and stroke,/ Deep in the heart of the mountain oak. **1891** *Harper's New Mth. Mag.* 83.815 **MA,** In the old colonial houses on the capes, the wood-tick was held to be a death-watch. *Ibid* 825, There was a long silence, broken only by the wood-ticks, which were numerous in the old rafters. **1899** Bergen *Animal Lore* 41, To hear a wood-tick or death-watch is a sign of death. *General in the United States.* **1925** Amer. Folkl. Soc. *Memoirs* 18.49 **MD,** Some people say it is made in rotten wood by a small wood tick called the "death watch." **1930** Shoemaker *1300 Words* 67 **cPA Mts** (as of c1900), *Wood-tick*—The "death watch", a small insect which infects old furniture and wood-work.

3 A rustic. Cf **wood hick 2**

1942 [see **woodbilly**]. **1968** DARE (Qu. HH1, *Names and nicknames for a rustic or countrified person*) Infs **MD**23, **WV**5, Wood tick. **1973** Allen *LAUM* 1.349 **Upper MW** (as of c1950), A rustic. . . In southwestern South Dakota a retired cattle rancher still uses *tie hacks* and *wood-ticks* as mildly contemptuous terms for homesteaders who about 1913 and 1914 settled in the foothills south of the Black Hills, where they cut the small timber and sold it for railroad ties.

wood tobacco See **tobaccowood**

wood tongue See **wooden tongue**

wood turtle n Also *woods turtle, wood(s) terrapin, ~ tortoise*

A turtle (*Glyptemys insculpta*) native to the Northeast and the Great Lakes states. Also called **freshwater terrapin, redlegs 4**

1774 (1900) Fithian *Jrl.* 1.198 **NJ,** Tom the Coachman came in with a wood Tarripin. **1802** *Philadelphia Repository & Weekly Reg.* (PA) 2.367 **OH,** He had nothing to eat but one pole-cat and a wood-turtle (neither of them were cooked). **1839** MA Zool. & Bot. Surv. *Fishes Reptiles* 209, The wood Tortoise. . . This, our most beautiful tortoise . . wanders a great distance from, and remains a long time out of the water; and being oftentimes found in *woods* and *pastures,* has received the common name of *wood tortoise.* **1862** Thoreau in *Atlantic Mth.* 10.392 **MA,** Every motion of the wood-turtle on the shore is betrayed by their [=the leaves'] rustling there. **1903** *Renwick Times* (IA) 17 July [4]/3 (newspaperarchive.com), In moist places in the fields and meadows may be found the wood tortoise, a sober sort of turtle. **1966–70** DARE (Qu. P24, . . *Kinds of turtles*) Infs **ME**8, **MN**2, **NY**240, Wood turtle; **CT**36, **NY**89, Woods turtle; **NJ**13, Woods turtle—also called land turtle. **1986** Pederson *LAGS Concordance* se**MS,** 1 inf, Woods terrapins; 1 inf, Wood terrapin. **2005** *Ironwood Daily-Globe* (MI) 19 Aug 2/5, Developers of a high-capacity electricity transmission line from Wausau to Duluth must take special construction steps to protect the rare wood turtle.

wood-vamp n

=**hydrangea 2.**

1933 Small *Manual SE Flora* 599, D[ecumaria] barbara . . Wood-vamp. Cowitch-vine. Climbing-hydrangea. **1972** Brown *Wildflowers LA* 64, Climbing Hydrangea, Wood-vamp—*Decumaria barbara.* **2008** (acc) U.S. Dept. Ag. *Plants Database* (Internet), *Decumaria barbara.* . . woodvamp.

woodvine See **woodbine 4**

woodwall n [*OED2* a1250 → "Now dial"; used in ref to var birds, but latterly usu the European green woodpecker (*Picus viridis*)] **NEng, esp sNH** Cf **yaffle**

=**flicker** n[2] **1.**

1870 (1873) Maynard *Naturalist's Guide* 130 e**MA,** *Colaptes auratus.* . . —Golden-winged Woodpecker, "Pigeon Woodpecker," "Yellow-Hammer," "Woodwall," "Flicker," "Sucker," "High-holder," "Wake-up." **1891** *New Engl. Mag.* 10.316 **NEng,** The Golden-Winged Woodpecker. The loud, monotonous vocalizing of this handsome bird is hardly song; still we often hear it said, "The woodwall is singing; we are going to have rain." **1898** *Pop. Sci. Mth.* 53.341 **sNH,** Woodwall I have never known to be applied to our bird outside of a certain limited district in southern New Hampshire, where it is almost exclusively known by that name. **1905** Cross *Hist. Northfield NH* 1.268, The Flicker, Yellow Hammer, Wood-Wall, or whatever name it may happen to bear in the household. **1918** Brown *Hist. Hampton Falls NH* 2.271 se**NH,** There were a great many more birds [in the 1840s] than at the present time. . . The woodwall and bluejay have disappeared.

wood widgeon n

=**wood duck 1.**

1888 Trumbull *Names of Birds* 34 **CT,** Wood duck. . . Farther down the Connecticut River, we hear *wood widgeon:* "Always called it so," said an Essex ducker, "until Clark told us its right name."

wood wren n

1 =**house wren 1.**

1834 Audubon *Ornith. Biog.* 2.452, The Wood Wren. *Troglodytes americana.* . . Although I feel much pleasure in introducing this new species to you, I regret that I am yet unable to speak with certainty of its summer haunts, or of the extent of its migration in the United States. . . The notes of this species differ considerably from those of the House Wren, to which it is nearly allied. **1868** Coues in Essex Inst. *Proc.* 5.278, *Troglodytes Americanus.* . . —Wood Wren. This is a species recognized by all the local writers. . . Its relations to *[T.] aëdon* are very intimate, and the species is by many authors considered as a dubious one.

2 =**golden-crowned kinglet.**

1917 *Wilson Bulletin* 29.2.85 **KY**, *Regulus spp.*—Wood wren, yellowbird, Hickman, Ky.

woody adj **chiefly Nth, N Midl, West** See Map Cf *pethy* (at **pith**)

Of a fruit or vegetable: tough, pithy.

1791 Bartram *Travels* 468, The fruit [of *Franklinia atamaha*] is a large, round, dry, woody apple. **1869** *Horticulturist & Jrl. Rural Art* 24.149 **NY**, A quick, warm soil grows the best radishes, as unless they grow quick they are tough and woody. **1908** IN Horticult. Soc. *Trans. for 1907* 79, They are, however, a woody apple. **1950** *WELS* (*When root vegetables get old and tough and are not good to eat, you say they are _____*) 28 Infs, **WI**, Woody. **c1960** *Wilson Coll.* **csKY**, *Woody.* . . tough and old, as applied to root vegetables; more often pethy. **1965–70** *DARE* (Qu. I8, *When root vegetables get old and tough and are not good to eat*) 238 Infs, **chiefly Nth, N Midl, West**, Woody; **SC**43, Woody-like. **1983** *MJLF* 9.1.61 **ceKY** (as of 1956), *Woody* . . pethy. **2009** *DARE* File **NEast**, After radishes and beets bolt, they get woody and are no longer good to eat.

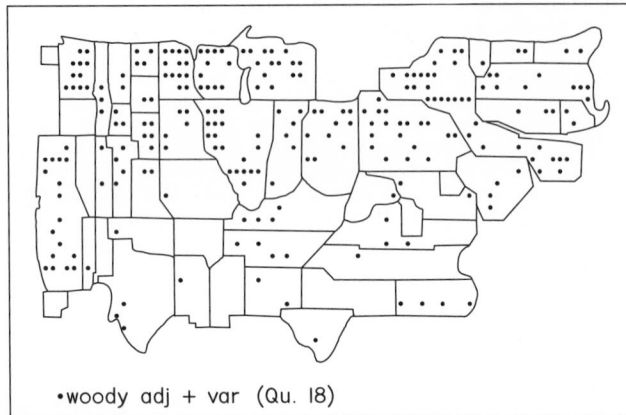

•woody adj + var (Qu. I8)

woody n[1]

=**wood duck 1.**

1923 U.S. Dept. Ag. *Misc. Circular* 13.16, Wood Duck. . . Vernacular Names. *In general use.* . . wood duck, sometimes shortened to woody. **1940** Gabrielson *Birds OR* 151, Some gunners complain bitterly about the amount of wheat eaten by the "woodies" in their baiting grounds. **1968–69** *DARE* (Qu. Q5, . . *Kinds of wild ducks*) Inf **PA**73, Woody; **MI**91, Wood duck—also called woody. **1992** *Wellsboro Gaz.* (PA) 22 Apr 6/4, [Headline:] Woodies responding to nesting boxes.

woody n[2], exclam See **wutz(ie)**

wooee See **whooee**

woof v Also *wolf*, rarely *bull woof* [Prob from *wolf* a predatory, threatening person, in which case *woof* is a pronc-sp; the latter is, however, the prevailing sp, and is sometimes associated with *woof* to bark gruffly] *chiefly among Black speakers* Cf **front** v, **jive** v[1] **1**, **shuck** v[1] **5a, b(1)**, **woof ticket**

To engage in behavior, esp speech, intended to impress, intimidate, or provoke; to bluff, kid; also with *at:* to direct such behavior at; hence vbl nouns *woofing, wolfing;* n *woofer.*

1931 (1991) Hughes–Hurston *Mule Bone* 91 **cFL** [Black], Stop woofing and pick a little tune there so that I can show Daisy somethin'. **1934** *AmSp* 9.289 **sePA** [Black student slang], *A woofer.* Applied to one who talks constantly, loudly, and in a convincing manner, but who says very little. *Ibid* 290, *Woof.* To talk much and loudly and yet say little of consequence. **1935** Hurston *Mules & Men* 88 **FL** [Black], I went outside to join the woofers, since I seemed to have no standing among the dancers. *Ibid* 89, You know uh heap uh dese hard heads wants to woof at you but dey skeered. *Ibid* 206, Tain't gointer be no fight. Good Bread jus' feel lak bull woofin' uh little t'night. **1943** *AmSp* 18.155 [College slang], *You ain't woofing.* . . Terms denoting satisfaction and agreement. **1945** *AmSp* 20.82 **TX**, 'A-woofin' ' is an expression which I have seldom encountered anywhere else. It is widely used and is more or less synonymous with 'lying' or 'kidding.' 'I figgered she was a-woofin' me so I hauled off and knocked her bowlegged,' a Texan recently testified in court. . . The expression also denotes hearty agreement

with someone's remarks, as in 'Brother, you ain't a-woofin'.' **1947** in 2009 (acc) Lexis–Nexis Legal Research *State Case Law: MS* (Internet), The defendant. . . characterized his hostile gesture as merely "wolfing," a procedure later clarified as purely idiomatic and indicating a proper occasion for a threatening display of protest against some minor lapse from the accepted rules of play. **1968** *DARE* FW Addit **PA**66, Wolfin'— talk[ing] excessively. [Inf Black] **1969** Brown *Die Nigger Die* 58 **LA** [Black], He just stood there and woofed at the police, talking about their mamas and shit like that. **1970** *DARE* (Qu. Y4, . . *A very uncomplimentary remark*) Inf **NY**249, Wolfing at me; (Qu. GG3, *To tease: "See those big boys trying to _____ [that little one]."*) Inf **TN**53, Wolf; (Qu. GG24, . . *To frighten: "Now don't let those fellows _____ you."*) Inf **KY**94, Wolf. [All Infs Black] **1974** Foster *Ribbin'* 202 **NYC** [Black], The woofer may also move his body in a menacing way. *Ibid* 198, Sometimes "loud mouthing" or "loud talking," "sounding," "screaming on someone," or even "bogarding" are synonyms for woofing. **1984** Weaver *TX Crude* 136, *Woofin'.* Kidding. "I'm not woofin' you about that. I'm serious as cancer!" **1986** Pederson *LAGS Concordance,* 1 inf, **cnLA**, You ain't woofing = you're not kidding. **2008** *DARE* File **St. Louis MO** [Black], All that I know for certain is that there is a B[lack] E[nglish] word that Hurston spells as "woof." . . However, my intuition is that the standard equivalent is "wolf" and I've found that intuition to match the intuition of blacks who have had their work appear in print. . . We blacks don't say either /wʊlf/ or /wʊlfɪn/ when we're in the 'hood.

woof over the river See **wolf over the river 1**

woof ticket n Also *wolf ticket* [**woof**] *esp among Black speakers*

A lie, bluff, challenge—usu in phrr *sell a woof ticket* and varr =**woof**; *buy a woof ticket* either to call one's bluff, challenge one to back up assertions or pretentions or to accept them at face value, back down.

1971 Coombs *What We See* 144 **Los Angeles CA** [Black], There was nothin' in the filth. Nothin' in the vomit-filled alleys, of 'wolf-ticket' selling moles who didn't spare talking 'bout a chump's mama. **1973** Lopez *Puerto Rican Papers* 252 **NYC**, Police demand . . submission. . . In the ghetto an apologetic response . . constitutes "buying a woof ticket" (backing down). Very few Puerto Ricans make buying woof tickets a habit. **1974** Matthews–Amdur *My Race* 29 **NYC** [Black], And they'd go cracking [=making wise cracks] on each other, or as the kids called it, "selling wolf tickets." **1975** in 2009 (acc) Lexis–Nexis Legal Research *State Case Law: PA* (Internet), I asked the both of them to hold down the noise because the people who were gambling were making enough noise already. This guy James Blount called me out of my name. He said, 'Motherfucker, you been selling wolf tickets, it's about time for you to get straightened out.' **1977** Smitherman *Talkin* 83, The Black Idiom expression "selling woof [wolf] tickets" (also just plain "woofin") refers to any kind of strong language which is purely idle boasting. **1979** *Time* 10 Sept 5 **Los Angeles CA**, In your phonetic rendering of woof ticket, the pronunciation is correct, but rather than being a "wolf" ticket—(meaning a challenge to fight), it is a "woof" ticket—(meaning a bluff). One often hears the term woofin' to mean that someone is in a sense barking, not yet committed to bite. Thus an inferior athletic team "sells woof tickets," trying to psych out its opponents. The superior team, confident of its ability, "buys all woof tickets." **1980** Folb *Runnin' Down* 231 **cwCA** [Black], *Buy a (woof/wolf) ticket—* 1. Call a bluff. 2. Challenge the truth of a statement or claim. *Ibid* 253, *Sell a woof/wolf ticket—*1. Boast. 2. Bluff. 3. Talk nonsense. 4. Lie. **1986** Pederson *LAGS Concordance,* 1 inf, **cwFL**, You be selling those wolf [wuˤəf] tickets. [Inf Black] **1988** *AmSp* 63.135 **TN** [Prison talk], *Wolf ticket.* . . Empty threat. **1996** McDowell *Leaving Pipe Shop* 42 **AL** [Black], It was difficult to hear over the music, the popping beer cans, and wolf tickets that everybody was hawking at the card table. **2007** *DARE* File—Internet **nOH**, All of my friends in grade school thought Sudden Sam was my uncle! . . [Comment:] [F]unny thing is your brother sold the same woof ticket to the class of '79. . . [Comment:] This is a sad day for me, I thought Sudden Sam was their uncle! I bought that woof ticket. *Ibid*, [Urban Dictionary:] *Woof tickets* . . A word used to call someone out on a lie or untruth. . . "Man, you didn't get an A in your Space Weather class; why you dropping woof tickets?"

wooie See **whooee**

wook See **whook**

wookes See **wokas**

wookey, wookie See **whook**

wool v

1 To strip of possessions, esp by trickery, "fleece"; broadly, to outdo by trickery. [Prob by analogy with *fleece,* with some infl from the phr *pull the wool over one's eyes*]

1841 in 2006 Noland *Cavorting on Devil's Fork* 157 **AR,** They do say they wooled him monstrously—He has lost nigh on to the rise of five hundred dollars in money, and some of the best sort of plunder. **1845** Hooper *Advent. Simon Suggs* 63 **GA,** At last he thought it best to return to the "ten," upon which he bet five hundred dollars. "Now, I'll wool you," said he. "Next time!" said the dealer, as he threw the winning card upon his own pile. **1851** Burke *Polly Peablossom* 46 **GA,** I'll git Smith to playing, and if I don't *wool him,* then my name ain't Bennett. **1920** Hall *Steel Preferred* 133, But I don't think the Old Man would have said anything even if he had caught me loafing here and I hadn't wooled him with that old gag. **1930** *DN* 6.89 **cWV,** *Wool him,* to get the better of him, to beat; sometimes used of physical conflict, though as well of shrewd trickery.

2 To pull the hair of, drag (around) by the hair; to beat, get the better of; hence vbl n *wooling.*

1843 *Amer. Turf Reg.* 16.277, But the term [=pugilism] must be understood to include all the *feats* of the *hand,* whether open or shut—slapping, striking, wooling, scratching, or—but *hold. These* instances *must* suffice. **1867** *Daily Eve. Bulletin* (San Francisco CA) 12 Apr 3/6 **ID,** Seymour made a rush at one man and caught him by the top of the head and wooled him around roughly. **1872** Lamon *Life Abraham Lincoln* 92 **IL** (as of c1831), He [=Lincoln] said, "I never tussle and scuffle, and I will not: I don't like this wooling and pulling." **1880** *Cincinnati Commercial* (OH) 11 Nov 2/2, She wooled him and scratched him and pounded him in the face. **1899** (1912) Green *VA Folk-Speech* 488, Wool. . . To pull the hair of, in sport or anger; rumple or towsel [sic] the hair of; to beat. "I'll wool you when I get my hands on you." **1900** *DN* 2.70 [College slang], Wool. . . To defeat badly. **1906** *DN* 3.164 **nwAR,** Wool. . . To pull one's hair. "I'll wool you."

3 To rumple, tousle; also with *around,* rarely *up:* to worry, maul about, play roughly with; fig, to badger, harass. [Cf *EDD wool* v. 5 "In phr *wool him!* used in setting a dog on any one, or to encourage one boy to rough-cuff another."] **chiefly S Midl**

1864 in 1979 Howells *Selected Letters* 1.191 **OH,** We got her a kitten for a little while, but she *wooled* it too savagely, and we sent it home. [**1865** Crockett *Life* 143 **TN,** I . . found my dogs had a two-year old bear down a-wooling away on him.] **1897** *Forest & Stream* 48.444 **CA,** Two large-sized dogs wooled him [=a bear cub] around for a while, but after he had devoted himself to growing for three months or so he was a revelation to dogs. **1899** [see **2** above]. **1900** *DN* 2.70 [College slang], Wool. . . To muss. **1942** McAtee *Dial. Grant Co. IN* 71 (as of 1890s), Wool . . tousle. Slang. **1947** *AmSp* 22.156 **sIN,** Wool (as a verb) occurs in such sentences as 'The kids wool that dog around till it's a wonder they don't kill him.' **1953** Randolph–Wilson *Down in Holler* 300 **Ozarks,** Wool. . . To tussle with, to worry as a dog worries a cat. "Them kids is always a-woolin' the baby around, pullin' its hair an' rollin' it in the dirt." **1954** *Harder Coll.* **cwTN,** Wool. . . To wrestle, tumble. "I wooled 'er up some, 'n let 'er have it. Shore 'uz good." **1959** in 2009 (acc) Lexis–Nexis Legal Research *State Case Law: TX* (Internet), The appellee testified that appellant kept wooling him to where he finally signed him a will. **1963** Edwards *Gravel* 21 **eTN** (as of 1920s), He reached down and wooled my head so hard that he made my head hot. . . "I wisht I had me a boy like you, Tad," he said. **1966** *PADS* 46.30 **cnAR** (as of 1952), Wool. . . To jostle. . . "I wasn't able for anybody to wool me in there." **1981** in 2009 (acc) Lexis–Nexis Legal Research *State Case Law: KY* (Internet), Even a public utility has some rights, one of which is the right to a final determination of its claim within a reasonable time. . . This Company had been wooled around long enough. **1982** *Barrick Coll.* **csPA,** Wool. . . play boisterously with. "Stop woolin' that baby around." **1983** *MJLF* 9.1.61 **ceKY** (as of 1956), Wool . . to fondle somewhat roughly, as in playing with a little pup, or handling a baby. **1985** Ladwig *How to Talk Dirty* 7 **Ozarks,** He wooled me around like a dog with a bone.

wool n　See **wolf** n **1**

wool around　See **wool** v **3**

wool breeches　See **woolen breeches 1**

wool, come to the goat's house for　See **goat** n **3**

woolen breeches n　Also *woolen britches*

1 also *willow britches, willy ~, woolly ~, wool(len)*

breeches, *wool(l)y ~:* A **waterleaf** such as *Hydrophyllum appendiculatum* in the east or *H. capitatum* in the west. Cf **linsey britches**

1818 Barton *Vegetable Materia Medica* 2.xiii **OH, KY, TN,** I send you a plant, vulgarly known in Ohio, Kentucky, and Tennessee, by the name of *Woollen-breeches.* The young shoots are eaten in the spring, as a sallad. . . The plant in question proves . . to be Hydrophyllum appendiculatum. **1927** *Amer. Botanist* 33.14, Hydrophyllum appendiculatum is called "woollen breeches" in allusion to its general woolliness and this seems the only worth while common name in the American branch of the family. **1931** *AmSp* 6.230 **neOR,** In spring the 'chillun' roam the hills in search of 'wooly breeches' for greens. **1935** MO Bot. Garden *Annals* 22.626 *Hydrophyllum appendiculatum.* . . Woollen Breeches. **1937** (1963) Hyatt *Kiverlid* 79 **KY,** We picked wild mustard an' . . wooly-breeches. **1937** St. John *Flora SE WA & ID* 334, *Hydrophyllum capitatum.* . . Woolen Breeches; Cat's Breeches. . . often cooked and eaten as "greens." **1941** Withington *Mine Eyes* 296 **KY,** I rode over mountain sides entirely covered with blue "woolly breeches," and saw between the trees the hazy blue of the more distant Cumberland ridges. **1945** in 1994 Hubbard *Shantyboat Jrl.* 49 **KY,** Sadie took one kind to her yesterday, a large leafy plant spotted green and white. It was wooly breeches, a good green but evidently not one of the best. **1966** *DARE* FW Addit **WA10,** *Hydrophyllum capitatum*—Woolen breeches; cat's breeches. **1969–70** *DARE* (Qu. I28a, . . *Kinds of things . . you call* 'greens' . . *[Those that are eaten raw]*) Inf **CA196,** Willy britches; (Qu. I28b, *Kinds of greens that are cooked*) Inf **KY52,** Woolen britches or willow britches. **1973** Hitchcock–Cronquist *Flora Pacific NW* 379, Wool breeches. . . *H[ydrophyllum] capitatum.* **1973** Kluger *Wild Flavor* 72 **sIN,** To . . a fellow greens-hunter from another town nearby, "woolly britches" are "fuzzy britches." **1983** *MJLF* 9.1.61 **ceKY** (as of 1956), Woolen britches . . a wild green. **1991** Still *Wolfpen Notebooks* 77 **sAppalachians,** What I look forward to in the spring hain't garden sass. Hit's wild greens . . What you want to look for is plantain, bird's-toe, . . wooly breeches [etc]. **2002** [see **speckled dick**]. **2007** Farr *My Appalachia* 107 **seKY** (as of 1940s), Granny Brock and I would go into the hills and hunt lamb's quarters, woolen britches, and what she called "shouny" [=shawnee].

2 A **cow parsnip 1** (here: *Heracleum maximum*).

1996 in Lib. of Congress *Amer. Memory: Tending the Commons* (Internet) **sWV,** [Caption:] Woolen britches (Heracleum lanatum).

wool-gathered adj　esp **Sth, S Midl**　See Map
Muddled, bewildered, distracted.

1891 (1897) Allen *Flute & Violin* 8 **KY,** Thinking too well of every human creature but himself . . an erring moralist, a wool-gathered philosopher. **1909** Godbey *Autobiog.* 55 **KY** (as of 1840s), My teacher would stall in compound numbers and tell me his head was "wool gathered" and that he had to go off to the woods to be quiet in order to work that sum. **1920** *Century Illustr. Mag.* 94.639, The new system apparently left the rank and file of Italian voters wool-gathered. **1966–70** *DARE* (Qu. GG2, . . *'Confused, mixed up':* "So many things were going on at the same time that he got completely _____.") Infs **LA3, NC1, PA27, TN48, VA24,** Wool-gathered; (Qu. GG9, *To suddenly embarrass somebody and throw him off balance* "When they told him what she had said about him, it certainly did _____ him.") Infs **NC72,** He was wool-gathered. **1971** Gaines *Autobiog. Jane Pittman* 107 **LA** [Black], The white man will. . . use every way he know to get you wool-gathered. **2005** *DARE* File—Internet **AZ,** I hate it when I am all wool-gathered about these things.

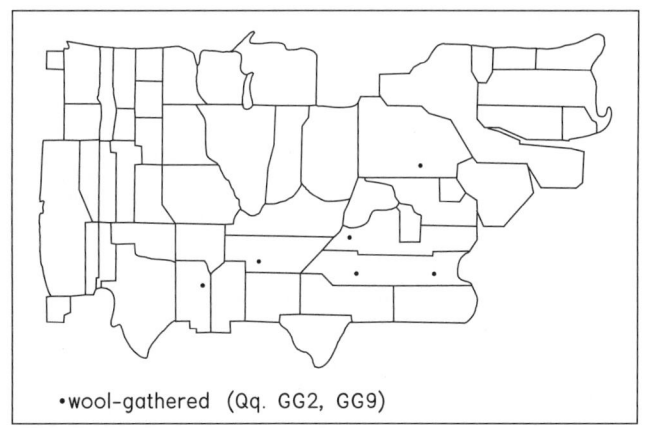

•wool-gathered (Qq. GG2, GG9)

wool grass n Cf **niggerwool 1**

A **sedge B1:** usu *Scirpus cyperinus,* but also *Carex filifolia.* For other names of the former see **cotton grass 2**

1848 Gray *Manual of Botany* 528, *S[cirpus] Eriophorum* [=*S. cyperinus*]. . . Wool-grass. . . Wet meadows, &c., common. **1857** Flint *Practical Treatise* 106, Wool Grass, . . *Scirpus Eriophorum.* **1899** Going *Field Flowers* 191, One of the stateliest of native sedges is the so-miscalled "wool-grass" [=*Scirpus cyperinus*]. **1937** St. John *Flora SE WA & ID* 68, *Carex filifolia.* . . Wool grass. Densely matted in extensive tufts. . . Exceedingly difficult to plow up. **1938** *Torreya* 38.63 **sNJ,** After cedar swamps have been cut or burned over . . appears . . wool grass. **1973** Hitchcock–Cronquist *Flora Pacific NW* 602, Wool-grass. . . *S[cirpus] cyperinus.* **2008** (acc) WI State Herbarium *WI Bot. Info. System* (Internet), Scirpus cyperinus. . . Common name—wool-grass.

wool hat n Also *wool hat boy, woolhatter* **chiefly Sth, S Midl, esp S Atl**

A member of the white rural working class; a small farmer, red-neck—used chiefly in ref to such a person as a political force (orig as a supporter of Andrew Jackson).

1828 *W. Intelligencer* (Hamilton OH) 3 Oct 3/1 *(OED2),* Thus has Mr. Woods endeavored to gain the votes of the wool hats as he terms his Jackson friends in Washington. **1836** *W. Hemisphere* (Columbus OH) 3 Aug 1/7, The very men whom a few years ago they called the *"ragged wool hat boys"* and *"Tories,"* they are now seeking to attach to their [Whig] party!! **1880** *Harper's New Mth. Mag.* 62.159 **GA,** An old "wool-hat" came along with a cart drawn by a single ox. **1894** *N. Amer. Rev.* 159.58 **SC,** They would have been met by the best men in South Carolina, and some other States, and among them would have been found many a "wool hat" and "one-gallus boy." **1927** Eubank *Horse & Buggy* 170 **KY,** I was a smart boy from town, and this particular guy thought I was a wool-hat boy. **1936** Greene *Death Deep South* 41, They were the "wool hat boys" of Georgia, the "blue jeans" of New England; they were the serfs of their time. **1938** *Sun* (Baltimore MD) 7 June 8/3 **NC** *(Hench Coll.),* A Close-Up Of The "Gay and Giddy" North Carolinian, Who Will Go Back To The Senate With The Wool-Hat Blessing. . . The fact that their Senator can step out . . apparently delighted the wool-hat boys. **1942** *Ibid* 15 July 9/5 **GA** *(Hench Coll.),* Talmadge is the idol of a class of Georgians known as "the wool-hat boys." . . Well may the Governor rely on his rural friends. **1950** *PADS* 14.77 **FL,** Wool hat boy. . . A person from West Florida. **1956** *Newsweek* 7 May 31, [A political map of Florida; a portion of the northwestern part of the state is labeled] Wool-hat country. . . One of the names given to farmers (especially sharecroppers and tenant farmers) in some areas of the South. **1986** Pederson *LAGS Concordance,* 1 inf, **cnGA,** Wool-hats—following local politician; 1 inf, **neMS,** Wool-hatter—poor white from backwoods—political.

woolhead n

=**bufflehead 2.**

1888 Trumbull *Names of Birds* 83 **VA, NC,** To some at Norfolk, Va., and Currituck region, [the bufflehead is known as] *wool-head.*

woolie See **woolly** n[2]

woolies n pl[1] See **woollies** n pl[1]

woolies n pl[2] See **woollies** n pl[2]

woolie worm See **woolly worm**

wooling See **wool** v 2

woollen breeches See **woolen breeches**

woollen head See **woolly head 1**

woollies n pl[1] Also sp *woolies*

1 Long underwear.

1930 *Lincoln Star* (NE) 23 Dec 8/1, *What's in Fashion?* Smooth-Fitting Winter "Woolies". . . This is a fashion story about woolen underwear! **1936** *Reno Eve. Gaz.* (NV) 20 Nov 5/3, [Advt:] *Men's Woolies*—Men's sheep pelts woolies, with cuff tops. All sizes. 89¢ *Pair.* . . *Women's Woolies.* . . 69¢ *Pair.* . . *Children's Woolies.* . . 59¢ *Pair.* **1960** Wentworth–Flexner *Slang* 586, *Wool.* . . *-lies -ies.* . . Wool underwear, esp. men's woolen underwear with long sleeves and legs. **1965–70** *DARE* (Qu. W14, *Names for underwear, including joking names. Men's—long, men's—short, women's—long, women's—short*) 15 Infs, **scattered,** Woollies; **NC47, NY45,** Long woollies. **1976** Garber *Mountain-ese* 103 **sAppalachians,** *Woolies.* . . winter underwear—It's time to

put on your woolies. **1994** *NYT Mag.* 20 Nov 40/3, There are 159,260 women over 80 in New York City. . . They're on the bus after 10 A.M. and before 3. In winter, they wear woollies.

2 Chaps made from sheep pelts. **West**

1927 Malkus *Raquel* 87 **TX,** Raquel . . was glad she had worn "woolies," . . sheepskin chaps. **1936** Adams *Cowboy Lingo* 34, 'Chaps' made of goatskin, worn with the hair side out, were often called 'angoras'; occasionally sheep pelts were used and called 'woolies.'

woollies n pl[2] Also sp *woolies*

=**willies 1, 2.**

1900 *DN* 2.70 [College slang], *Woolly.* . . In phrase 'to have the *woolies',* to be nervous or generally out of sorts. **1912** *DN* 3.593 **wIN,** Woolies. . . The delirium tremens. **1965–70** *DARE* (Qu. GG13b, *When something keeps bothering a person and makes him nervous* . . "*It gives me the* _____.") 11 Infs, **scattered,** Woollies; (Qu. BB28, *Joking names . . for imaginary diseases:* "*He must have the* _____.") Inf **CT39,** Woollies; (Qu. DD22, . . *Delirium tremens*) Inf **VA33,** Woollies; (Qu. GG34a, *To feel depressed or in a gloomy mood:* "*He has the* _____ *today.*") Inf **IL50,** Woollies. **2005** *Daily News* (Huntingdon PA) 16 May 15/6, I have even found them [=ticks] on bats, which gives me the "woollies" to think about because 2 to 7 percent of bats carry rabies virus.

woolly n[1] Also sp *wooly*

1 A sheep. **esp West**

1852 Beardsley *Reminiscences* 99 **NY,** The dogs . . soon frisked him [=a fox] out of the flock, when, on leaving the "woolies" he ran a mile and crept under a carriage house. **1864** *Burlington Weekly Hawk-Eye* (IA) [24 Sept] 8/2 (newspaperarchive.com), Sheep are pouring into Central Iowa by thousands. . . No wonder the poor "Cops" think the woolies will "take" this country after while. **1910** Neihardt *River & I* 92 **MT,** In Scotland when a feller sees a sheepman coming down the road with his sheep, he says: 'Behold the gentle shepherd with his fleecy flock!' . . In Montana, that same feller says . . 'Look at that crazy blankety-blank with his woolies!' **1935** Davis *Honey* 153 **OR,** She had a little short-bodied guitar of the kind that Mexican sheep-herders used to . . entertain the woolies with. **1939** *Ogden Std.–Examiner* (UT) 23 July sec A 4/7 **WY,** Wyoming's sheep industry . . has more "woollies" grazing on its far-flung prairies than any of the United States except Texas. **1940** Writers' Program *Guide AZ* 236 **cAZ,** Sheepherders who tend the "woolies," give a flavor of the old West to the town. **1949** *NV State Jrl.* (Reno) 23 Oct 10/1, *Survey Shows* 487,000 Woolies Now On Ranges of Nevada. **1969** *DARE* (Qu. K85, *The call to sheep to come in from the pasture*) Inf **PA226,** Come woolly woolly woolly. **1976** *Charleston Daily Mail* (WV) 1 Sept sec C 6/4, Some . . find woolies less than fascinating. "We don't like sheep. They eat the grass too short." **1996** *Deer Park Progress* (TX) 14 Apr sec A 4/5, The fluffy woolies were lead [sic] around the arena by the kids who had cared for the animals.

2 See **woolly head 1.**

3 See **woolly head 2.**

4 also *woolly bear,* ~ *booger,* ~ *bug:* =**dust bunny.**

1954 *WELS Suppl.* **seWI,** Kitten farms are the woolies under a bed. **1965–70** *DARE* (Qu. E20, *Soft rolls of dust that collect on the floor under beds or other furniture*) 12 Infs, **scattered, but 6 PA,** Woollies; **GA63,** Woolly bears. **1982** *Smithsonian Letters* **sePA,** [Soft rolls of dust that collect on the floor under beds or other furniture]—dust bunnies, wooley [sic] bugs. **2007** *DARE* File—Internet, A wooly booger is that sometimes not so little ball of lint that forms only under beds and always just seconds before the first class inspects.

5 A **woolly bear 1** or similar insect larva. [*EDD woolly* sb. 3 "A hairy caterpillar"]

1968 *DARE* (Qu. R27, . . *Kinds of caterpillars or similar worms*) Inf **NY40,** Woollies—green in color.

woolly n[2] Also sp *woolie*

=**williwaw.**

1886 Elliott *Our Arctic Province* 78 **AK,** Although the interior of this gulf is completely landlocked . . yet it is by no means a safe or pleasant sheet of water to navigate, inasmuch as furious gales and "woolies" sweep down upon it from the steep mountain sides. **1897** *Outing* 30.263 **swCA,** "We're going to have a 'woolly,' sure." . . These winds, sudden and strong, beat the water into wool-white foam; hence their name. **1915** *DN* 4.241 **seMA,** Woolly. . . Among whalemen, a sudden gust of violent wind blowing off shore:—distinguished from a squall, which blows across the sea. It may come in pleasant or rainy weather, generally without warning, and is of short duration. **1968** *DARE* (Qu. O12, *A disturbance caused by wind which seems to run and spread quickly along the surface of water*) Inf **CA**86, Woolly. **1988** Oliver *Jrl. Aleutian Yr.* 16 (as of 1946), Now and then a ghostlike "woolie" of whirling water would cut across our bow or hit the vessel.

woolly bear n

1 A hairy caterpillar, esp the larva of an Arctiid moth such as the **tiger moth.** [*EDD* (at *woolly* adj. 1.(1))] **scattered, but chiefly NEast, N Cent** See Map For other names of these see **bear caterpillar, fall ~, fever worm, fever-and-ague ~, fuzzy bear, ~ bug, ~ worm, ~-wuzzy 1, hairy caterpillar, weather worm, woolly** n[1] **5, ~ caterpillar, ~ worm** Cf **hedgehog caterpillar, poodle worm**

1852 Harris *Treatise Insects* 263, The caterpillars of most of these tiger-moths are thickly covered with hairs, whence they have received the name of woolly bears, and the family, including them, that of *Arctiadae*, or Arctians, from the Greek word for bear. **1898** Lugger *Butterflies* 130, A number of other Arctiids or "Wooly Bears". . . only exceptionally prove destructive to taller shrubs and trees. **1905** *Waukesha Freeman* (WI) 30 Nov 1/6, Dr. Taft picked up a little "woolly bear[s]" the common black and brown caterpillar, which is so numerous in our gardens in the late summer and autumn and travels away so rapidly when disturbed. **1965–70** *DARE* (Qu. R27, . . *Kinds of caterpillars or similar worms*) 81 Infs, **scattered, but chiefly NEast, N Cent,** Woolly bear; **CT**31, Woolly bear—tent caterpillar; **PA**79, Fuzzy woolly bear. **1967** Borland *Hill Country* 284 **nwCT,** The woolly bears are the caterpillar stage of the small pinkish-yellow moth known as Isia Isabella. . . There is an old belief that woolly bears foretell the coming winter. **1974** Dillard *Pilgrim* 47 **wVA,** The woolly bear hibernates alone in a bristling ball. **2008** *DARE* File—Internet **OH,** There are two Woollybear Festival areas in the center of historic downtown Vermilion, Ohio.

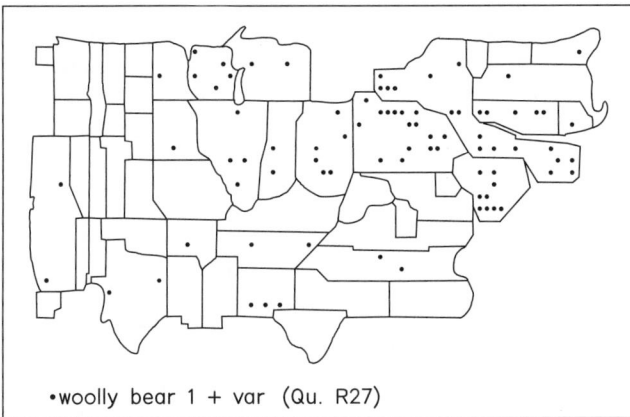

•woolly bear 1 + var (Qu. R27)

2 See **woolly** n[1] **4.**

woolly-bear caterpillar See **woolly caterpillar**

woolly-bear worm See **woolly worm**

woolly booger See **woolly** n[1] **4**

woolly breeches n

1 also *woolly britches:* =**fiddleneck 1.** Cf **woolen breeches 1**

1895 *Erythea* 3.154 **CA,** *Amsinckia spectabilis,* . . known here by the rather appropriate name of "Woolly Breeches," is very abundant. **1898** *Jrl. Amer. Folkl.* 11.275 **CA,** *Amsinckia* (sp.), fiddle-neck, woolly breeches. **1949** *Oakland Tribune* (CA) 15 May Boys and Girls Mag sec 4/3, We saw wild flowers. We saw woolly britches. **2008** (acc) U.S. Dept. Ag. *Plants Database* (Internet), *Amsinckia spectabilis* . . woolly breeches.

2 See **woolen breeches 1.**

woolly britches See **woolen breeches 1**

woolly bucket n Also *gum woolly bucket, woolly-bucket bumelia, ~ tree; also sp woolly bucket*

A **gum elastic** (here: *Sideroxylon lanuginosum,* formerly *Bumelia l.*)

1951 Teale *North with Spring* 58 **FL,** Florida is the land of the woolly-bucket tree, the buckwheat tree, the fishfuddle tree and the pondapple

tree. **1953** Peattie *Nat. Hist. W. Trees* 677, Chittamwood. . . Other Names: Gum-elastic. . . Gum Woollybucket. **1968** Barkley *Plants KS* 268, Bumelia lanuginosa. . . Woolly Bucket Bumelia. **2002** Proulx *That Old Ace* 66 **TX,** Named after the woolybucket tree. I guess there used a be a lot a them grew here. Birds like a woolybucket. The leaves in the spring, why they are all fuzzy underneath before they roll out—that's the wooly buckets.

woolly buckeye n
=**red buckeye.**

1923 Amer. Joint Comm. Horticult. Nomenclature *Std. Plant Names* 6, *Aesculus discolor* [=*A. pavia*]. . . Woolly Buckeye. **1959** *Daily Independent* (Monessen PA) 20 June 10/3, [In a list of flowering shrubs:] Scarlet Woolly Buckeye. **1979** Little *Checklist U.S. Trees* 46, *Aesculus pavia*. . . scarlet buckeye, woolly buckeye, firecracker-plant.

woolly buckthorn n Also sp *wooly buckthorn*
A **gum elastic** (here: *Sideroxylon lanuginosum*).

1900 OK Ag. Exper. Sta. *Bulletin* 45.34, Bumelia [=*Sideroxylon*] *lanuginosa*. . . Woolly Buckthorn. . . Frequent along streams. **1908** Britton *N. Amer. Trees* 780, Woolly Buckthorn. . . The twigs, covered with thick brownish wool at first, become nearly smooth. **1955** *San Antonio Express–News* (TX) 18 Sept sec G 5/4, We concluded this Maverick tree to be Wooly Buckthorn . . also known as Gum Elastic. **1995** Carlile *Children of Dust* 340 **OK,** He made his way through some woolly buckthorn bushes on the riverbank.

woolly bug See **woolly** n[1] **4**

woolly caterpillar n Also *woolly-bear caterpillar, woolly bug(ger)* esp **NEast, Gt Lakes** See Map
A **woolly bear 1** or similar insect larva.

1908 *Daily Kennebec Jrl.* (Augusta ME) 19 Feb 8/2, The caterpillar was one of the brown and black variety . . commonly called the woolly bear caterpillar. **c1930** Brown *Amer. Folkl. Insect Lore* 4, A woolly bear caterpillar crawling hurriedly across a walk in the fall told of the near approach of winter weather. The size of the colored areas on his back indicated whether the winter would be severe or mild. **1965–70** *DARE* (Qu. R27, . . *Kinds of caterpillars or similar worms*) 15 Infs, **esp NEast, Gt Lakes,** Woolly caterpillar; **PA**246, Woolly bug; **NY**97, Woolly bugger; [**NY**214, Woolly ones;] (Qu. R21, . . *Other kinds of stinging insects*) Inf **FL**16, Woolly-bear caterpillar.

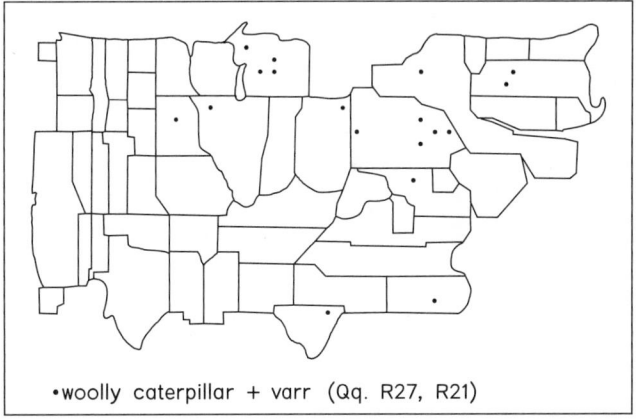

•woolly caterpillar + varr (Qq. R27, R21)

woolly daisy n

1 A plant of the western genus *Eriophyllum,* esp *E. lanatum.* For other names of var spp see **golden yarrow, lizard tail 2**

1942 Kearney *Flowering Plants* 921 **AZ,** *Eriophyllum* [spp]. . . Woolly-daisy. **1949** Moldenke *Amer. Wild Flowers* 210, The woolly-daisies, *Eriophyllum,* comprise another handsome western group . . the best known of which is *E. lanatum.* The herbage is white-woolly. **1995** Epple *Field Guide Plants AZ* 272, Woolly daisy. . . *Eriophyllum lanosum.* . . Flowers: White, woolly, with yellow centers. . . Leaves: Grayish white, woolly.

2 A plant of the closely related southwestern genus *Antheropeas.* For other names of var spp see **daisy dwarf**

1957 Jaeger *N. Amer. Deserts* 262, Woolly Daisy. *Eriophyllum* [= *Antheropeas*] *wallacei.* Common annual often found in dense stands on sandy soils of the deserts of southern Utah, southern Nevada to Western Arizona, and southern California. **1979** Spellenberg *Audubon Guide N. Amer. Wildflowers W. Region* 364, Woolly Daisy (*Eriophyllum walla-*

cei). . . A tiny, *gray, woolly tufted plant* with small *golden-yellow flower heads.*

woolly head n Also sp *wooly head*

1 also *woollen head, woolly (pate),* ~ *top:* A Black person. *freq derog*

1828 Cooper *Prairie* 1.226 **LA,** Some people think wooly-heads are miserable, working on hot plantations under a broiling sun. **1855** (1968) Whitman *Leaves of Grass* 22 **NY,** The woolypates hoe in the sugarfield, the overseer views them from his saddle. **1857** Long *Pictures Slavery* (2d ed) 382 **MD,** I trust that my young readers will never follow the example of some grown-up boys, who are guilty of the mean and unmanly offence of insulting the African by the cry of "Woolly heads! Woolly heads!" **1858** *Harper's New Mth. Mag.* 16.393 **VA,** He points down the road over which he has just galloped, and toward which the wooly heads again turn. **1967** *DARE* (Qu. HH28, *Names and nicknames . . for people of foreign background: Negro*) Inf **ID5,** Woolly top. **1986** Pederson *LAGS Concordance,* 1 inf, **nwMS,** Woolies = Negroes; 1 inf, **cAL,** Woolen head—term for a black; 1 inf, **neTN,** Woolly heads—joking, perjorative term.

2 also *woolly (patch),* ~ *top:* A thicket, esp a rhododendron thicket. **esp sAppalachians** Cf **bald** n, **hell 1, rough** n, **slick** n **3, yellow patch, DS** C28

1913 Kephart *Highlanders* 301 **sAppalachians,** A "hell" or "slick" or "wooly-head" or "yaller patch" is a thicket of laurel or rhododendron, impassable save where the bears have bored out trails. **1915** *Natl. Sportsman* Oct 462 **eTN,** We would put the dogs on a hot track; they would trail up one side of a creek . . and out over the main ridge and bay or tree far down on the Tennessee side in some inaccessible "woolly head." **1956** (1964) Fink *That's Why* 4 **wNC, eTN,** Similar places [to slicks] at times are also called *woolies* or *woolly patches.* **1979** Horton et al. *Our Mt. Heritage* 27 **wNC,** Shrub balds, also called wooly tops, laurel slicks, or laurel hells, usually contain many species of shrubs. **1994** in 2004 Montgomery–Hall *Dict. Smoky Mt. Engl.* 657, *Wooly top.* . . often very extensive, covering hundreds of acres, having small deciduous tracts, making it look wooly in the wintertime (from loss of leaves); these tend to be higher in the mountains.

3 A **boneset 1** (here: *Conoclinium coelestinum*).

1937 *Torreya* 37.101 **PA,** *Eupatorium* [=*Conoclinium*] *coelestinum.* . . Wooly-head, Columbia, Pa.

4 A ground-dwelling bee; see quot.

1968 *DARE* (Qu. R21, . . *Other kinds of stinging insects*) Inf **MD34,** Woolly head—small bees, build nest in ground in clover fields.

woolly loco n Also *woolly locoweed*

A **milk vetch** (here: *Astragalus mollissimus*).

1900 OK Ag. Exper. Sta. *Bulletin* 45.25, *Astragalus mollissimus.* . . Woolly Loco-weed or Crazy-weed. A common and apparently dangerous weed on the western prairies. **1914** Georgia *Manual Weeds* 239, Woolly Loco has a large, tough, woody, deep-boring root, sometimes penetrating to a depth of six or more feet. **1937** U.S. Forest Serv. *Range Plant Hdbk.* W41, Woolly loco, sometimes called purple, stemmed, Texas, and true loco, is a low, tufted, perennial herb poisonous to livestock. The common name woolly is very appropriate because the plant is densely covered with long, close (appressed), yellowish hairs. **1967** *DARE* Wildfl QR (Wills–Irwin) Pl.19C [=*Astragalus mollissimus*] Inf **TX44,** Woolly loco. **1994** Brown *Plainswoman* 69 **KS** (as of 1887), Before her blade the enemy fell: woolly loco. Whitish gray, it was one of the first plants to appear in the spring.

woolly marigold n

=**desert marigold.**

1941 Jaeger *Wildflowers* 290 **Desert SW,** Woolly Marigold. *Baileya pleniradiata.* . . in sandy flats and in disturbed soil along roadsides. **1947** Carr *Desert Parade* 77, Desert Marigold, Cloth of Gold, Woolly Marigold. . . The "wool" acts as insulation and aids in keeping down evaporation. **2004** *DARE* File—Internet **CA,** After dinner we sit around and note what we have seen so far . . Coreopsis, Woolly marigold [etc].

woolly mullein n [In Brit use from the 18th cent for *Verbascum thapsus* or *V. phlomoides*]

A **mullein** (here: *Verbascum thapsus*).

[**1777** Lightfoot *Flora Scotica* 143, *[Verbascum] thapsus.* . . Great Woolly Mullein.] **1897** NV Ag. Exper. Sta. *Bulletin* 37.88, Great Mullein, Woolly Mullein, *Verbascum Thapsus . . ,* occurs in Nevada, and in a few situations within and near the Truckee Valley, it seems well established. **1902** U.S. Natl. Museum *Contrib. Herbarium* 7.388 **CA,** *Ver-*

bascum thapsus. . . The woolly mullein, so commonly introduced into the eastern United States, has become a garden weed in Mendocino County and other parts of California. **1910** *Mansfield News* (OH) 10 Oct 9/3, The common woolly mullein probably came from France in crockery packing. **1967** *Independent–Rec.* (Helena MT) 12 Feb 12/2, Common, or woolly, mullein, Verbascum thapsus. . . common in dry soils and sunny places. **2007** *Daily Times* (Farmington NM) 26 Apr sec C 1/4, The children. . . touched Wooly Mullein, a plant that feeds birds throughout the winter, because its seed-bearing stalks are higher than the snow.

woolly patch See **woolly head 2**

woolly pate See **woolly head 1**

woolly shoat n

=**opossum.**

1961 Jackson *Mammals WI* 17, Common Opossums. . . *Vernacular names.* . . woolly shoat.

woolly top See **woolly head 1, 2**

woollyweed n

A **hawkweed,** esp *Hieracium scouleri*.

1915 *Jrl. Ag. Research* 3.97, Woolly weed or woolly hieracium (*Hieracium cynoglossoides*). **1937** U.S. Forest Serv. *Range Plant Hdbk.* W94, The hawkweeds are members of the chicory tribe. . . A number of those range species which are conspicuously shaggy-hairy are usually called woolly-weeds. *Ibid,* Woollyweed (*H. scouleri . .),* a yellow-flowered plant with its foliage, stems, and involucres densely covered with long, soft, white hairs, is one of the most important range species. **1973** Hitchcock–Cronquist *Flora Pacific NW* 531, Woolly-weed. . . *H. scouleri.* **2008** (acc) CA Univ.–Berkeley *CalPhotos* (Internet), Woolly-weed. . . *Hieracium scouleri.*

woolly-white n

A plant of the chiefly western genus *Hymenopappus*. For other names of var spp see **honeyweed, old plainsman, wild cauliflower,** ~ **cosmos**

[**1898** Britton–Brown *Illustr. Flora* 3.446, *Hymenopappus tenuifolius.* . . Woolly White Hymenopappus.] **1970** Correll *Plants TX* 1701, *Hymenopappus* [spp]. . . Woolly-white. **1979** Ajilvsgi *Wild Flowers* 318, Woolly-white—*Hymenopappus artemisiaefolius.* **2005** Holloway *Dict. Wildflowers TX* 81, *Hymenopappus artemisiifolius.* . . Common Name: Woolly White, for the soft white hairs on the plant.

woolly worm n Also sp *woolie worm, wooly* ~*;* also *willy worm, woolly-bear worm* **scattered, but chiefly W Midl, Missip-Ohio Valleys, TX** See Map

A **woolly bear 1** or similar insect larva.

1864 Fisher *Yankee Conscript* 94 **OH,** The flour was almost alive with woolly worms of all sizes, from very small ones up to those of an inch in length. **1883** IN Horticult. Soc. *Trans. for 1882* 123, This one . . is called the tent-making caterpillar of the forest (*clisiocampa sylvatica*). . . Naturally, birds are the most important agent in preventing the undue increase of insect life, but the woolly worms have the advantage of the birds. **1896** *OH Practical Farmer* 89.116, I'm afraid I'll have to crawl like a w-w-woolly worm, all the rest of my days! **1900** NJ Geol. Surv. *Annual Rept. for 1899* 206, On the hickory and butternut other species occur that are known as "woolly worms," because of the masses of fine waxen threads that cover the body and give it a fluffy appearance. **1906** *Ft. Wayne Jrl.–Gaz.* (IN) 2 Oct 2/6 , The little woolly worm is red, with a black head and a black tail. . . If there is a long stretch of black on either end and a small patch of red in the middle it means a long, hard winter. **1933** *Daily News* (Huntington PA) 27 Oct 1/6, R.I. Bigley says the woolly worm never fails us, and that it has very little black color, which indicates a very mild winter. **1953** *PADS* 19.14 **sAppalachians,** *Woolly worm:* . . Caterpillar. **1965–70** *DARE* (Qu. R27, . . *Kinds of caterpillars or similar worms*) 78 Infs, **scattered, but chiefly W Midl, Missip-Ohio Valleys, TX,** Woolly worm; **AZ10,** Woolly worm—comes with the cotton; **IA11,** Woolly worms—a gray color; **OH74,** Woolly-bear worm; (Qu. R21, . . *Other kinds of stinging insects*) Inf **TX40,** Asp—a woolly worm, gets on trees, very poisonous. **1968** Kellner *Aunt Serena* 99 **IN,** We could hardly see what we were passing, let alone get out and run ahead and explore crawdad holes, or turn woolly-worms over. **c1971** *DARE* File **sIN** (as of c1910), We also called these [= woolly-worms] "willy-worms," they were brown and covered with erect hairs . . more hairy than wooly. **1981** Howell *Surv. Folklife* 83 **neTN, seKY,** If most of the woolie worms seem to be headed southward, it will be a bad winter. **1982** Slone *How We Talked* 100 **eKY** (as of c1950), Wooly worms tell what kind of winter there will be: light color—snow; dark color—wet; multi-colored—varied weather. **1986** Pederson *LAGS Concordance*, 3 infs, **Gulf Region**, Woolly worms.

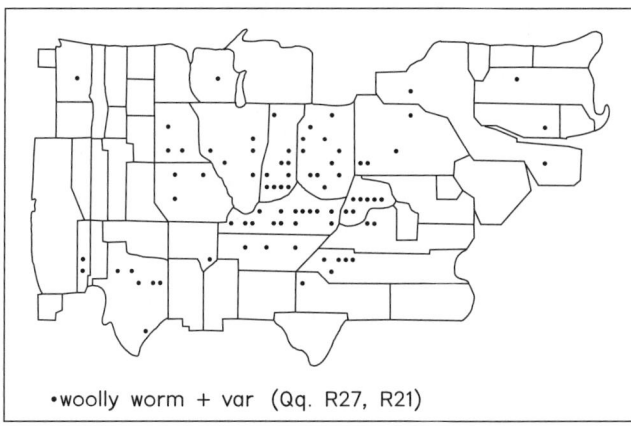

•woolly worm + var (Qq. R27, R21)

wool-mat n

A **hound's-tongue 1** (here: *Cynoglossum officinale*).
1894 *Jrl. Amer. Folkl.* 7.95 **WV**, *Cynoglossum* sp. . . wool-mat. **1898** *Ibid* 11.275 **KS**, *Cynoglossum officinale*, . . dog-burr, wool-mat, Tory-burr. **1912** Blatchley *IN Weed Book* 113, *Cynoglossum officinale*. . . Hound's-tongue. Dog Bur. Wool-mat. . . The root leaves of the first season's growth form a dense tuft from the midst of which the flower stalk of the next season springs. The prickly burs adhere rather loosely to clothing and the wool of sheep.

wool, pull v phr   chiefly Sth

To tug at one's forelock; see quots; hence vbl n *pulling wool* (also n *pully woolly*) acting in an obsequious manner.
1869 (1870) Chaplin *Out of Wilderness* 257 **Sth**, The same number of little blacks crept or toddled about the floor, stumbling over each other and pulling wool at pleasure. **1922** Gonzales *Black Border* 321 **sSC, GA coasts** [Gullah glossary], *Pull wool*—to pull the kinky forelock in salutation to "de Buckruh." **1926** Smith *Gullah* 35 **sSC, GA coasts**, *To pull wool,* to grasp the small twisted forelock and to bow. **1959** McAtee *Oddments* 5 **cNC**, *Pull wool* . . pluck at one's forelock in bowing and scraping—formerly of negroes. **c1960** *Wilson Coll.* **csKY**, *Pull wool*. . . Pluck at one's forelock in embarrassment. **1992** Garrett *Sorrows Fat City* 229 **Sth**, This is, in effect, the ironic contemporary equivalent of the gesture called "pulling wool" or "pully woolly" (in some part of the South), whereby certain sly black men ingratiated themselves with their oppressors by acting out with gusto and enthusiasm the part already assigned to them. **1993** Reed *My Tears* 117 **Sth**, Acting out somebody else's idea of what Southerners are all about can be a risky business. There can be an element of Samboism, of pully-woolly, in all this.

wool tromper n   Also *wool tramper*   West

In sheepshearing: a worker who stamps down fleeces in a woolsack.
1910 *Outlook* 95.485 **MT**, I . . asked for an explanation as to the work of a "wool tromper." Laughing at my ignorance, she said, "He goes around to the sheep-shearings and tramps the wool down into the bags." **1914** (1915) Bodmer *Book of Wonders* 82, The tied fleece . . is dropped into a large sack. . . In this sack there is always a wool tramper, who keeps tramping the fleece down. **1941** Writers' Program *Guide UT* 419, The unsung hero of the shearing corrals is the "wool tromper." The wool sacks, about eight feet long, are suspended from a rack and a few fleeces thrown into the bottom. The "tromper" jumps into the sack, tramping the fleeces tightly. Fleeces are thrown in on him, sometimes with a choking smother of dirt, dust, and effluvium. **1954** Jordan *Hell's Canyon* 121 **ID** (as of 1930s), The nearly naked wool-tromper climbed out of his suspended sack and rubbed his oily brown back with a rag. **1979** in 1997 Logan *Counterbalance* 374 **WY**, There were about 12 to 15 shearers and they brought with them about three wranglers and a wool tromper. **1989** in 2007 *DARE* File—Internet **UT** (as of c1930s), I recall Joe Anderson, a 2d cousin, being wool tramper.

wool up   See wool v 3

wooly   See woolly n[1]

wooly breeches   See woolen breeches 1

wooly bucket   See **woolly bucket**

wooly buckthorn   See **woolly buckthorn**

wooly head   See **woolly head**

wooly worm   See **woolly worm**

woont   See **will A**

woop v   See **whip A1**

woopie   See **whoop** exclam **D**

woosh   See **wish A1**

wootchie, woots, woot-sie, wootsy, wooty, wootz(ie)   See **wutz(ie)**

woowie   See **whooee**

woozen   See **wizzen**

woozer   See **weaser**

‡**woozie** n   Cf **moozie, woolly** n[1] **4**
1968 *DARE* (Qu. E20, *Soft rolls of dust that collect on the floor under beds or other furniture*) Inf **PA**176, Woozies.

woozzen   See **wizzen**

wop n[1], also attrib   Also *wap*   [Ital dial *guappo* ruffian]
1 Orig a foreign immigrant, esp an Italian, or any person viewed as low-class or disreputable; later usu spec an Italian or person of Italian descent, but occas a person from another foreign background.   **widespread, but esp freq NEast, Pacific** See Map on p. 1072   *usu derog*
1906 *Sun* (NY NY) 16 Feb 3/2, Besides Lyons and Murphy, he says, there were in it Albert Moquin . . and one whom Lyons calls "Oscar the Wop," or "Oscar the Dago." [*Ibid* 28 Aug 5/1, If Blinky Loretto, leader of the Wappo gang, down on Cherry Hill, had only been wise to the snitcher he wouldn't be doing his latest "bit" in the Catholic Protectory. . . When Dago Pete Bascino was admitted to membership . . nobody had the faintest idea that he would ever squeal on the mob.] [**1907** *Eve. World* (NY NY) 9 May 3/6, Maybe Roberto Fiaza Nobi thought that he could impress the Magistrate in Ewen Street Police Court by claiming to be a count. . . his name might as well have been Tony Woppo for all the good his title did him.] **1908** McGaffey *Sorrows* 17 **NYC**, Some old pappy guy up in Chi was making a fuss that the chorus ladies stay up too late nights. . . I don't know who or what this old wop is that made this crack. **1909** *NY Times* (NY) 23 Feb 4/2, A crowd of men and boys followed four or five Italians along Canal Street . . tormenting them by calling them "Waps" and "Ginneys." **1912** in 2001 Berlin *Complete Lyrics* 59 **NYC**, My sweet Italian man,/ . . . / Say you love me, wop-a,/ Like you love your barber shop-a. **1915** *NY Libraries* 5.159, The problem of the foreigner in the small factory town or village is in some respects different from that of the foreigner in the large city. . . The village library is usually hampered by insufficient funds and by lack of interest on the part of the library board in the methods of helping the despised "Wop." **1915** *DN* 4.236 **neOH** [College slang], *Wop, n.* An ill-bred fellow; boor. **1916** *Assoc. Men* 41.211, In forty-two languages the [Young Men's Christian] Association speaks welcome to the foreigner, whether he is called "wop," "dago," "hunkey," "Polak," "greaser," or any one of a dozen other terms of opprobrium. **1921** *Amer. Jrl. Hygiene* 1.612, The American-born child of foreign parents desires . . to slough off and forget the attributes which characterize, as he or she thinks, the "wop," using this as a generic term of disparagement for the foreigner. **1922** *McClure's Mag.* Mar 65 **NYC**, "For a wop funeral," said Fazio, referring that way to his race, "iz'a bum." **1927** *AmSp* 3.167, *Wop*: Italian. **1932** Tooné *Yankee Slang* 38, *Wops*: Italians. Little Italy in New York City is often referred to as Wop Town—this quarter is famed for spaghetti eats. **1937** Runyon *More* 104 **NYC**, In front of this house is a wop with a push-cart . . which Rusty Charley tips over as we go into the house, leaving the wop yelling very loud, and maybe cussing us in wop for all I know. **1965–70** *DARE* (Qu. HH28, *Names and nicknames . . for people of foreign background*) 336 Infs, **widespread, but esp freq NEast, Pacific**, Wop—Italian; **AL**25, **FL**22, **TN**65, **WA**9, Wop—Greek; **CA**174, **PA**135, **SC**3, Wop—Jew; **MO**39, **TX**91, Wop—Polish; **GA**9, Wop—Greek, Syrian, Italian; **GA**89, Wop—Italian, Greek; **MO**4, Wop—Hungarian, Italian; **NC**7, Wop—Italian, Syrian; **NY**24, Wop—Italian, Chinese [Inf queries]; **FL**136, Wops and Dagos for almost everything; **NC**51, Wop—heard, but not connected with any race or nationality; (Qu. H65, *Foreign foods favored by people around here*) Inf **LA**23, Wop salad; (Qu. DD7, *Different names for ci-*

gars . . *according to size, shape, or the way they're made*) Inf **NY122,** Wop cigar; (Qu. HH18, *Very insignificant or low-grade people*) Inf **MI4,** Wops; (Qu. II25, *Names or nicknames for the part of a town where the poorer people, special groups, or foreign groups live*) Infs **CA105, NY111,** Wop town; **NH14,** Wop flat. **1967** *DARE* FW Addit **sePA,** A hoagie is a wop job. **1989** *NY Times* (NY) 13 Dec 31/1 (as of 1930s–1940s), [Newspaper column:] Near Newark, N.J., where I spent my early childhood, Italians were plentiful and the abusive vocabulary rich. "Wop," the most popular slur among non-Italians, was known in southwest Baltimore, however. **1999** *Sopranos* (Television Program), [Episode "A Hit Is a Hit" 14 Mar:] Our friend Cusamano . . he's Italian, but he's Merigan. It's what my old man would have called a Wonder Bread wop. He eats his Sunday gravy out of a jar. **2005** Pollack *Chicago Noir* 138, Wop? Dago? These were slurs from another era.

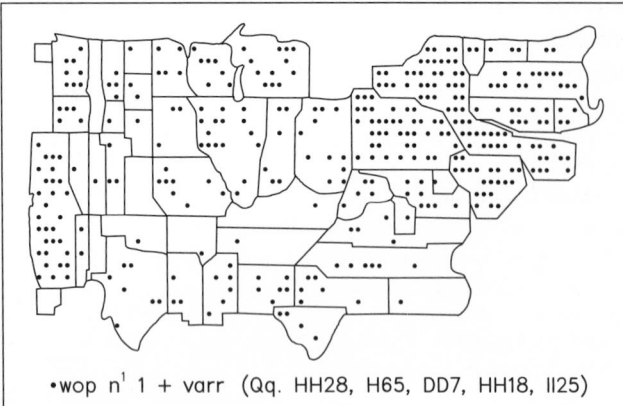

• wop n^1 1 + varr (Qq. HH28, H65, DD7, HH18, II25)

2 The Italian language; an Italian word; Italian-influenced English. **esp NEast**

1917 *Munsey's Mag.* 60.652 **Boston MA,** "*Cherchez la femme,* you know!" He laughed bitterly. "Huh?" queried Muggs, frowning. "W'at kind o' wop lingo is dat?" **1919** Van Loan *Taking Count* 205 **NYC,** Henry gloried in Tony's cleverness and the fact that he could "read newspapers, and everything, in wop and American." **1937** [see **1** above]. **1957** *New Campus Writing* 120, The Krauts converse in German,/ Italians write in Wop,/ The Polacks all speak Polish,/ And the Greeks,/ They never stop. **1978** Gould *Greenleaf* 126 **ME,** "This is Leslie Terror." . . "Actually, the name's Terrera. It's Wop." **2005** Hughes *Open Ice* 183, Whenever his father got really mad, he forgot his continuing effort to rise above his working-class background and immediately started talking wop.

wop n^2 **Chesapeake Bay**
=**bittern** or **night heron.**

1917 *Wilson Bulletin* 29.2.78 **ceVA,** *Botarus lentiginosus.* . . wop, Wallops I[slan]d. *Ibid* **ceVA,** *Nycticorax nycticorax naevius.* . . wop, Revels I[slan]d. **1970** *DARE* (Qu. Q10, . . *Water birds and marsh birds*) Inf **VA47,** Wop—American bittern—marshes; Woods wop—night heron—woods. **1996** Horton *Island Out of Time* 73 **Chesapeake Bay MD,** A lot of stuff in this marsh, I can't tell you the right names of—wops, bye-bye bunkers, pennywinkles, blare-eyed herring—those are our names for them. **1998** Casey *Half-Life* 512 **Chesapeake Bay,** "There's an interesting footnote to herons," Dad said. "There's an island in the Chesapeake called Wop Island. . . It's called that because it's a rookery for black-crowned night herons, and black-crowned night herons go 'wop.'" **2001** MD Ornith. Soc. *MD Yellowthroat* Mar–Apr 6 (Internet) **eVA, eMD,** Them night herons, I believe you say, here is called the Wop or Bumcutter cause of what he sounds like. *Ibid* 7, Wop = night heron (there is a hammock on northern Smith Island, MD, known as Woptown).

wop n^3 See **wapatuli**

wopajawed See **whopper-jawed**

wopatuli See **wapatuli**

wope See **whope**

wopper-jaw(ed) See **whopper-jawed**

wopple-jawed See **wobble-jawed**

woppy-jawed See **whopper-jawed**

wops See **wasp 1c**

wop salad n [**wop** n^1 **1**] **chiefly LA**
Any of var kinds of salads; see quots.

1930 *San Antonio Light* (TX) 24 Oct sec B 8/3, *Wop Salad.* Select firm tomatoes and stuff with mixture of Portola mustard sardines, diced celery, green pepper, tart apples and Gem salad dressing. **1943** *AmSp* 18.308 **wLA, eTX** [Cafe terms], *Wop salad.* A miscellaneous salad made in various ways but usually containing raisins, oranges, and salad dressing. **1961** *Ruston Daily Leader* (LA) 19 May 6/3, [Cafe menu:] Wop Salad. **1961** *News–Sun* (Hobbs NM) 19 Mar 18/1, [Cafeteria menu:] Wop Salad Bowl with Fillet of Anchovies and Hard Boiled Eggs. **1967** *DARE* FW Addit **nwLA,** *Wop salad*—seen on menu in Natchitoches, La. Cut salad with lettuce and tomatoes, with a relish-like dressing, garnished with anchovies and pickled peppers. I have seen this elsewhere, too; Arkansas and North La. **1968** *DARE* (Qu. H65, *Foreign foods favored by people around here*) Inf **LA23,** Wop salad—salad with everything. **c1970** *DARE* File **seLA,** [Identifying tag in cafeteria:] *Wop salad*—a salad made of greens, anchovies and black, green, and pimento olives among other ingredients. **1993** *Ibid* **New Orleans LA,** Here at Mickey's [=a restaurant and grocery], a wop salad, or now it's an Italian salad, is a bed of lettuce, tomato wedges, with olive salad on it. What it really means is olive salad. That's a mixture of chopped black and green olives, chopped celery, onion, fresh rosemary, garlic, bay leaf, in an olive oil base. **1994** Mariani *Dict. Amer. Food & Drink* 345, *Wop salad.* A salad of lettuce made with olives, oregano, capers, anchovies, garlic, and oil. It is a Louisiana specialty.

wopse v Also sp *wapse* **chiefly NEng**

1 freq with *up:* To twist or wad (a soft material), tangle, mess up; to wrap untidily (in something); hence ppl adjs *wopsed (up).* Cf **wob, wopse** n, **wopsy** adj

1823 *Newburyport Herald* (MA) 20 Nov 3/1 **CT,** After making some ado about my papers, of which I had no copies, they untwisted them from their curl pates *wapsed* up like *prepared wadding* for a *fowling piece!* **1843** *Brother Jonathan* (NY NY) 6.31 **NEng,** If there ain't our Nathan with . . the cloak in his arms all wapsed up! **1875** Holland *Sevenoaks* 60 **NEng,** Then ye'll hold the hoss till I go an' git yer pa, and then we'll wopse 'im up in some blankits, an' make a clean streak for the woods. **1890** Holmes *Marguerite* 9 **MA,** Mrs. Rathburn freed her mind to her son, calling the school-mistress a vain minx who spent half her time before the glass, "wapsing that yellow hair of hers round a curlin' stick." "But it looks mighty neat when its 'wapsed,'" John said. **1896** *DN* 1.426 **ME,** *Wapsed up:* tangled, tumbled, in disorder. **1897** Robinson *Uncle Lisha's Outing* 45 **VT,** There's a poor leetle mushrat. . . wopsed up in a mess o' weeds. **1903** *Boston Sun. Jrl.* (MA) 31 May 6/4, If the men are going to have their nerves so badly shattered by the sight of the feminine Isaak getting her line wopsed around her feet and over her ear, . . why, the men would better go way off somewhere with their favorite bottle and a can of worms. **1916** Webster *Real Advent.* 32 **IL,** Her hair was wopsed around her head anyhow. **1946** *AmSp* 21.233 **eVT,** If a shawl was wopsed up it was in an irregular pile. **1970** *DARE* (Qu. Y38, *Mixed together, confused: "The things in the drawer are all _____."*) Inf **NY232,** Wopsed up. **2006** *DARE* File—Internet **cMA,** I got the feeling that the last-minute move indoors because of the rain had wapsed up a whole lot of things. **2006** in 2009 *Ibid* **MN,** Wapsed—I don't know how to spell it . . but a wrinkled shirt that was found in a ball would be "all wapsed up." **2009** *Ibid* **VT,** Yes, we use wapsed up as a matter of course. It is a part of our usual vocabulary. I didn't realize it was a regional thing. It is a pile of something like sheets to be gathered up only we use wapsed up.

2 To roll or turn (something) about; also fig; also intr.

1900 Day *Up in ME* 102, But when he[=a shark]'d hipered two miles to lee, and begun to wopse and wheel. **1902** Day *Pine Tree Ballads* 142 **ME,** Figgered he'd git lots of work an' only feed her slim;/ Wife, though, wopsed it t'other way an' got the laugh on him! **1904** Day *Kin o' Ktaadn* 215 **ME,** The solemn cow that wopses cud hard by. **1917** Hughes *In Town* 21 **eIA,** He just shot a splash of tobacco-juice through that missin' tooth of his and says, 'I wouldn't if I's you.' And I says, 'Goodness knows I hate to; but there's no way out of it.' And he wopsed his cud round and said, 'Mebbe there is.' **1924** England *Vikings* 86, A few whitecoats [=harp seal pups] were still bawling, wopsing their puffy, furry bodies about.

3 To wallop, beat; hence ppl adj phr *wapsed down* flattened; fig, drunk.

1914 *DN* 4.83 **ME, nNH,** *Wopse.* . . Same as *wallopse.* [*Ibid* 82, *Wallopse.* . . To maul, handle.] **1927** *New Republic* 9 Mar 72, The following is a partial list of words denoting drunkenness now in common use in the United States. . . loaded to the plimsoll mark—wapsed down . . paralysed . . ossified [etc]. *Ibid, Wapsed down* is a rural expression, also used in connection with crops which have been ruined by a storm. **1941** *Sat. Eve. Post* 11 Oct 23 **NC,** Went up to see . . Schmeling wopse that . . Louis. [*DARE* Ed: Speaker's father from **VT**]

wopse n [**wopse** v **1**]   **chiefly NEng**
A wad, tangle; also fig.

1902 Holmes *Cromptons* 278 **MA,** His mother . . having rolled up her spotted gown "in a *wopse*," as she said, and put it with her dish pan and towels, had come back. **1908** Bradford *Matthew Porter* 324 **ceMA,** Just to see him flirting with that Flora Chantrey, . . with her clothes thrown on to her any way, and her dirty brown wopse of hair. **1927** *AmSp* 3.141 **eME,** Badly wrinkled clothes were "all in a wopse and wudget." **1946** *AmSp* 21.233 **eVT,** *Wopse* was more often a noun; it meant an utterly disorderly congeries, usually of something flexible. A wopse of cloth was just huddled together; a wopse of string could be a tangle or, perhaps more probably, a disorderly pile without tangling. **1950** *WELS Suppl.* **seWI,** You should hang your things up—not throw them in a wopse. [*DARE* Ed: Learned from Inf's mother, who was born in Canada, reared in the South, and attended Oberlin College in Ohio.] **1984** in 2009 (acc) Lexis–Nexis Legal Research *State Case Law: MD* (Internet), Before we endeavor to unravel the wopse in which the parties placed themselves, we shall describe the factual setting from which this litigation arose.

wopsed (up), wopse up   See **wopse** v **1**

wopsided adj, adv   Also sp *wapsided*   [Varr of *lopsided*]   **formerly scattered, now chiefly Sth, S Midl**   See Map
1825 Neal *Brother Jonathan* 2.104 **CT,** "Old Jeremy Carter" was . . about as much like our young hero . . as any other hump-backed, "wapsided," knock-kneed old gentleman were [*sic*] like the Apollo Belvidere. **1868** (1869) Pomeroy *Nonsense* 247 **WI,** *Good Providence!* how cold it was! . . Tried to laugh at it. Froze our face all up wapsided like the price of railroad stock! **1899** *OH Farmer* 95.14 **ceOH,** It happens that two of these horses rarely fall together, so that so many more teams are made "wop-sided." **1934** Hurston *Jonah's Gourd Vine* 308 **FL** [Black,], Bet de wop-sided, holler-headed—thought Ah wuz gointer cry, but he's uh slew-footed liar! **1965–70** *DARE* (Qu. KK70, *Something that has got out of proper shape: "That house is all _____."*) 29 Infs, **chiefly Sth, S Midl,** Wopsided; (Qu. MM13, *The table was nice and straight until he came along and knocked it _____*) Infs **KY**75, **SC**40, 44, **TX**92, **VA**37, Wopsided. **2005** in 2009 *DARE* File—Internet **cNC,** I tried to do my zuchini with it and it got "wapsided" and turned crooked on me and didn't work except for half of my zuchini. **2007** *Ibid* **sGA,** My only fear is having a wopsided roof line. **2009** *Ibid* **swCA,** I found that it was defective (kind of wop-sided) and the leather did not appear to be authentic.

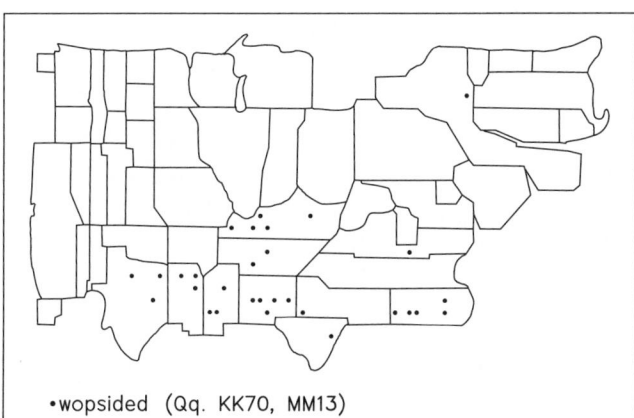

•wopsided (Qq. KK70, MM13)

wopsy adj   Also sp *wapsy*   Cf *wopsed up* (at **wopse** v **1**)
Limp, loose, floppy.

1878 Taylor *Between the Gates* 84, There is John [Chinaman], the taper-eyed, with his blue shirt and his wapsy trousers. **1900** Bacheller *Eben Holden* 127 **nNY,** Got t' rest a minute. . . Feel kind o' wopsy after thet squabble. **1900** (1904) Bowman *Freckles & Tan* 62 **Upper MW,** I'm a pup dog and I know it,/ . . /And my hide is loose and wopsy. **1908** *Good Housekeeping* 47.117 **MA,** Most folks don't know how to make up a bouquet nowadays—jest stick a mass of flowers, mostly of one kind, together an' let 'em fall all wapsy. **1913** Kephart *Highlanders*

234, Our average hillsman now goes about in . . wapsy and ragged trousers toggled up with a nail or two.

wopsy n   Also sp *wapsy*
See quots.

1920 Kerlin *Voice of the Negro* 69 **TX,** As soon as the colored man asks for a square and fair deal . . these monumental hypocrites . . bring out their age-worn bugbear and bugaboo of 'social equality.' It has been worked so much that it now has the "wopsy." **1944** *PADS* 2.51 **cwNC,** *Wapsy* ['wɑpsɪ]. . . Debilitation, weakness. A venereal disease. . . Rare.

wor   See **wire**

word off v phr   Cf **give out** v phr **1b**, **line out 1**
=**deacon** v **1.**

[**1925** *DN* 5.346 **Newfoundland Canada,** *Word out, to.* Recite (not sing).] **c1937** in 1976 *Weevils in the Wheat* 202 **VA** [Black], De white man preached all de sermons. But we could jine in de singin'. De white folks word off de hymns an' we follow 'long.

word with the bark on (it) phr   Usu with *the*   **chiefly S Midl**
A blunt statement of one's unalterable will or opinion; the unvarnished truth.

1839 *Spirit of Times* 28 Dec 511/3 **AR,** I see *Long* has "spoke the word with the bark on." **1860** (1999) Craft–Craft *Running for Freedom* 42 **VA,** Freedom may do for your ma's niggers, but it will never do for mine; and, plague them, they shall never have it; that is the word, with the bark on it. **1867** *Piqua Democrat* (OH) 30 Jan 1/7, *Equal Taxation, or Repudiation.—*That's "the word with the bark on." Let the laboring men who are paying the bond-holders' taxes, adopt this as their motto. . . There is no use in sugar-coating words for these gentry. . . Tell them what they *must* do. **1872** Twain *Roughing It* 124 **MO,** If ever another man gives a whistle to a child of mine and I get my hands on him, I will hang him higher than Haman! That is the word with the bark on it! **1892** *DN* 1.233 **KY,** *Word with the bark on it.* For emphasis. "That is the word with the bark on it; you better mind out." **1905** *DN* 3.101 **nwAR,** *Word with the bark on it.* . . Ultimatum. 'That's the word with the bark on it.' Not uncommon. **1912** *DN* 3.593 **wIN,** *Word with the bark on it.* . . A definite, unmistakable statement of a case. "I gave him a word with the bark on it when he came to see me." **1951** *West Witch Diggers* 42 **IN,** Had to give them the word with the bark on it every time he opened his mouth. **1985** *Commercial Appeal* (Memphis TN) 19 Mar np, When I was especially determined to have my way about an issue that already had drawn a 'no,' Mom would say ' . . that's the word with bark on it.' [**1996** Horton *Island Out of Time* 243 **Chesapeake Bay MD,** Swagger die, if that warn't the word with the wool on it. [Footnote:] the last word, final thought.] **1996** *DARE* File **neTX** (as of 1920s–30s), *That's the word with the bark on it*—the real truth—the absolute last word. **2000** Salter *White Lies* 61, "No, I can't," she said, and I heard the finality in her voice. It was what Mama called "the word with the bark on it." I never knew where that saying came from but I knew what it meant.

wore past pple   See **wear** v **B3b**

wore n   See **water A3**

wored   See **wear** v **B3c**

work v

1 with *with:* To crawl with, be alive with, abound in. [Engl dial; see quot 1994 and cf *OED2 work* v. 32 "To ferment"; 34 "To move restlessly, . . to toss, seethe."]   **esp Sth, S Midl**
1885 U.S. Entomol. Comm. *Fourth Rept.* app 26, If [the cotton boll is] found already burst, an examination will be apt to show its interior literally working with small worms. **1902** *DN* 2.249 **sIL,** *Work.* . . To swarm with animal life, as 'The timber is just working with game'; or, 'The creek is just working with feesh.' **1904** *S. Practitioner* 26.671 **cnTN,** The piles of horse manure literally working with the larvae of musca domestica, are really more dangerous than the water supply. **1928** Chansler *River Trapper* 195, The lily-grown pools up in the swamp . . were literally working with frogs. **1983** Lindsey *Cold Mind* 177, Her lungs felt as if they were working with worms. [**1994** Upton et al. *Surv. Engl. Dial.* 469, *Working* adj heaving (with maggots).] **2007** Bonner *Houses & Homes* 20 **sAL,** We captured the calf, turned him over on his back and there was the wound, working with worms.

2 in phr *work alive:*

a with *with:* =**1** above. [Blend of **1** above with *be alive with* in same sense]   **chiefly Sth, S Midl**

1883 Bowen *Chained Lightning* 31 **TX,** The truly erudite will hereafter know . . that their mortal anatomy is working alive with the *bacillus micrococcus.* 1909 *Hunter-Trader-Trapper* 18.55 **OR,** At the crack of the rifle the basin seemed to be working alive with elk. They seemed to jump right out of the ground. 1954 *Denton Rec.–Chron.* (TX) 1 Aug 4/2, These are all summer resorts, working alive with tourists during July and August and pretty dead the rest of the year. 1959 in 1980 *Still Run for Elbertas* 140 **KY,** They had fallen seven slats, the firm peaches sinking into the pulp of the bad, and they were working alive with gnats and hornets. 1978 Crews *Childhood Biog.* 71 **GA,** He poured the Benzol into the wound, and it worked alive with squirming worms, boiling them out onto the hide. 2001 (2005) Duncan *Moon Women* 132 **wNC,** Lord, the whole place just a-working alive with people, and all of them looking like if they didn't get wherever it was they was a-going, they might bust. 2005 in 2009 *DARE* File—Internet **nwFL,** Every shrub and tangle vibrated with hundreds of warblers, vireos, and buntings. The standing water worked alive with Prothonotaries, and White-eyed Vireos. 2006 Morris *Duck Hunting* 37 **eNC,** People knew he was from Currituck, and I guess they thought the place was working alive with ducks.

b Of living things: to swarm, abound.

1988 *Richwood Gaz.* (OH) 24 Aug 2/4, [Letter:] The Big Red House . . where on any given moment of the day, you can see rats or mice working alive in there. 1999 in 2004 Montgomery–Hall *Dict. Smoky Mt. Engl.* 658, *Working alive* . . Esp of insects: plentiful, busy. . . used esp with reference to bees, yellow jackets, ants, etc. 2001 *MO Rev.* 24.109 (as of 1941), Big worms as long as my little finger and fat in the middle worked alive in the rabbit's upper legs and back.

3 usu with *on,* rarely *over:* To castrate. **chiefly Sth, S Midl, Cent** See Map *euphem*

1944 *PADS* 2.52 **NC, SC, VA,** *Work on.* . . To castrate. 1946 *PADS* 6.33 **eNC** (as of 1900–10), *Work on.* . . To castrate a male animal. . . Common. 1947 *PADS* 8.15 **sIN** (as of early 20th cent), *Work on.* *Ibid* 21 **cn,neKY,** *Work on.* 1952 Brown *NC Folkl.* 1.609, *Work on.* . . To castrate. 1954 *Harder Coll.* **cwTN,** *Work on.* . . To castrate. 1965–70 *DARE* (Qu. K70, *Words used . . for castrating an animal*) 18 Infs, **chiefly Sth; also Cent,** *Work on;* (Qu. K25, *What is a 'steer'?*) Inf **SC34,** Male calf that they've worked on. 1966 Dakin *Dial. Vocab. Ohio R. Valley* 2.246, *Castrate.* . . *Work on* (Jackson and Spencer Ctys., Ind.; Carter Cty., Ky.) 1989 Pederson *LAGS Tech. Index* 135 **Gulf Region,** *Castrate.* . . Work (2 [infs]) . . Work on (51 [infs]) . . Work over (1 [inf]). 1998 *DARE* File **TX,** *Working cattle*—a euphemism for castrating them.

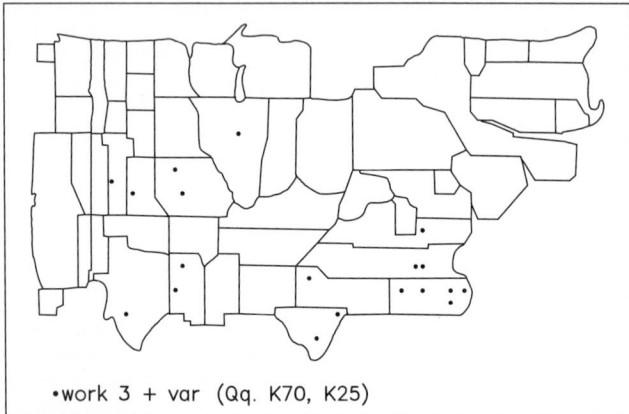

•work 3 + var (Qq. K70, K25)

work alive See **work 2**

work alive with See **work 2a**

work-brittle adj Also *work-brickle*

1 Eager to work; energetic; industrious; hence rarely n *work-brittle* an energetic or industrious person. [*OED2* 1647 →; *EDD work-bracco* adj. 1. The origin of the second element is unknown.] **chiefly Midl, esp IN** See Map

1870 *Nation* 28 July 57 **sePA,** A stirring, active housewife was "work-brittle." 1887 Carpenter *S.-Co. Neighbors* 89 **sRI,** I never see no sech do-little coot ez thet Jim Fones. . . He ain't what I call very work-brittle. 1900 *Homestead* 1 Mar 333 **IA,** The mechanic who works at his trade all day doesn't feel very work brittle when he leaves his shop. 1912 *DN* 3.593 **wIN,** *Work-brittle.* . . A very industrious person, especially one who gives much attention to small matters. "He is a regular work-brit-

tle." 1914 *DN* 4.114 **cKS,** *Work brickle.* . . Ready to work. 1916 *DN* 4.282 **NE,** *Work-brittle.* . . Energetic. Reported by one contributor. 1923 *DN* 5.224 **swMO,** *Work brickle.* . . Anxious to work. 1927 *AmSp* 2.366 **cwWV,** *Work brickle* . . anxious to work. "What makes you so work brickle all at once?" 1930 *San Antonio Express* (TX) 24 May 18/6, [Advt:] Want boy 15 to 20 for shop work: must be work brittle, handy with tools and out of school. 1941 *AmSp* 16.25 **sIN,** *Work-brickle.* Industrious, energetic. 1942 McAtee *Dial. Grant Co. IN* 71 (as of 1890s), *Work-brickle* (i.e. work-brittle) . . able and willing to work. 1944 Howard *Walkin' Preacher* 118 **IA,** Forty-two men and work-brittle boys reported early at the school ground. 1946 *Fresno Bee* (CA) 29 Nov 5/3, [Advt:] Add to that my two sons, Bes and Bob, who are work brittle. 1965–70 *DARE* (Qu. KK28, *Feeling ambitious and eager to work*) 15 Infs, **scattered, but esp N Midl,** Work-brittle; 10 Infs, 5 **IN,** 3 **TN,** Work-brickle; (Qu. HH27a, *A very able and energetic person who gets things done*) Inf **GA67,** Work-brittle; (Qu. KK29, *To start working very hard: "He was slow at first but now he's really _____."*) Inf **IN41,** Work-brittle. [21 of 26 total Infs old] 1968 Kellner *Aunt Serena* 165 **IN,** Ella is a fine, honest, work-brittle girl. 1971 *Today Show Letters* **sIN,** If you are full of pep and feel like working you are "work brickle". 1974 Fink *Mountain Speech* 29 **wNC, eTN,** *Work-brittle* . . industrious. 1978 Massey *Bittersweet Country* 207 **Ozarks,** *Work brittle* (willing to work hard): She's more work brittle than I am. 1983 *MJLF* 9.1.61 **ceKY** (as of 1956), *Work Brickle* . . eager to work. 1992 [see **2** below]. 2006 in 2009 *DARE* File—Internet **KS,** She would be a work-brittle representative for the area, putting her 27 years in the public school system to work to insure that children throughout the state get the best education possible. 2008 *Ibid* **AR,** This class has a rep as umm. . . not being the most work brickle crew. *Ibid* **ceIN,** What's the secret to getting hired at acs? Having excellent attention to detail, being work brittle, and being able to manage time effectively. 2009 *Ibid* **cnKY,** Let's just say my ex wasn't real work brickle as my granny would say.

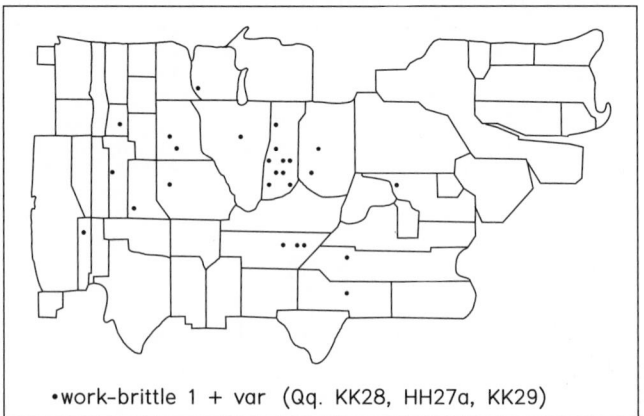

•work-brittle 1 + var (Qq. KK28, HH27a, KK29)

2 Disinclined to work; lazy; hence rarely n *work-brickle* a lazy person, sluggard. **chiefly sAppalachians** [Appar folk-etym reinterpretation; cf *EDD work-bracco* adj. 2]

1952 Brown *NC Folkl.* 1.609, *Work brickle.* . . Unaccustomed to working. 1992 Williams *S. Mt. Speech* 119 **sAppalachians,** Work brittle (brickle). . . disinclined to work; sometimes opposite meaning, to like to work and have a great capacity for work. c1996 in 2004 Montgomery–Hall *Dict. Smoky Mt. Engl.* 657 **wNC, eTN,** *Work brittle.* . . detesting work of any kind, as "He's work brittle; a little work would break him" . . ; = fragile, hesitant. 2008 in 2009 *DARE* File—Internet **KS,** I worked with a few people who were "work brittle" and did as little as possible. 2009 *Ibid* **cIN,** Heroes— . . Anyone who works hard and takes pride in their work, I can't stand the "work brittle" people of the world.

work down v phr **esp Sth, S Midl**

To outwork.

1942 McDonald *Old McDonald Farm* 50 **OK,** I may not be very big . . , but I never did see the man that could work me down. 1967 *DARE* Tape **TX26,** The mule will work the horse down—a horse is a good worker, but the mule won't work him down—he's tougher. 1971 Rooney *Bossmen* 59 **NC,** Bill loved to work. Nobody could work him down. 1988 Crews *Knockout Artist* 18 **sGA,** It ain't nobody on this job can work me down. I can put anybody here in the shade.

worked down adj phr **chiefly Sth, S Midl**

Exhausted; worn out.

1844 in 1939 *NC Hist. Rev.* 16.343, I am *worked down* myself and hardly feel able to write a letter. **1856** (1968) Drew *Refugee* 280 **VA** [Black], I am worked down, and worn out with hard work. **1863** in 1945 *GA Hist. Qrly.* 29.105, I am gloomy this morning from several reasons—in the first place, I am worked down. **1897** Howells *Landlord* 155 **nNEng,** "He's weaker. Haven't you noticed it?" " . . He's worked down; that's all." **1956** Rayford *Whistlin' Woman* 59 **AL,** I'm worked down. I'm just about green-eyed. Gittin' to where I caint even worry no more. **1986** Pederson *LAGS Concordance (Tired; exhausted)* 1 inf, **swAL,** Worked down—strong term. **2003** *DARE* File—Internet **Sth,** The above picture still has some bondo, but I'll be removing it tomorrow night, I'm worked down tonight!

workey-up See **work-up**

workhorse n **chiefly Sth, S Midl** See Map
A sawhorse.

1961 Folk *Word Atlas N. LA* map 616, Wooden rack for sawing planks . . [in order of frequency] saw horse . . horse . . wooden horse . . work horse. **1965–70** *DARE* (Qu. L58, *An implement with an A-shaped frame . . that you put boards on to saw them*) 10 Infs, **chiefly Sth, S Midl,** Workhorse. [9 Infs old, 8 gs educ or less] **1970** Tarpley *Blinky* 136 **neTX,** *Wooden rack for sawing planks . .* work horse [3 of 200 infs]. **1983** *MJLF* 9.1.61 **ceKY** (as of 1956), *Work Horse . .* a saw horse. **1986** Pederson *LAGS Concordance (Sawbuck)* 20 infs, **Gulf Region,** Workhorse(s). **2003** *DARE* File—Internet **MA** [*N. Adams Transcript* (MA) 7 Mar], To alert people to the problem, the town has put several large yellow workhorses emblazoned with the word, "Caution."

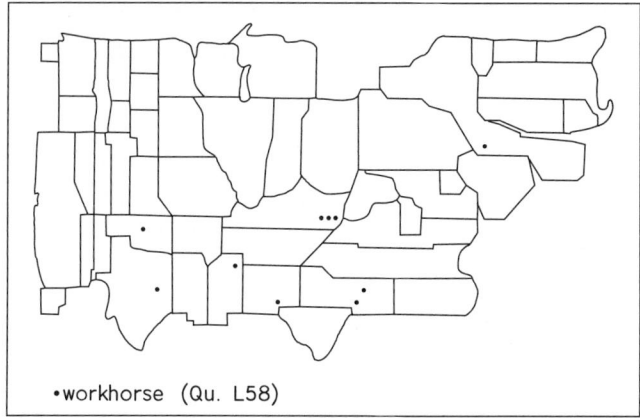

•workhorse (Qu. L58)

work-in See **work-up**

working n **chiefly Sth, S Midl** Cf **bee** n², **work party**
A gathering to accomplish cooperatively a particular task, often including a meal and social activity; see quots.

1903 *DN* 2.337 **seMO,** *Working. . .* Labor performed by a group of neighbors in case of an emergency. No pay is expected, but a dinner is always furnished. In the North it is called a 'bee.' 'The Widow Brown is going to have a working next Saturday to clear up her new-ground.' **1906** *DN* 3.164 **nwAR,** *Working. . .* Unpaid voluntary and coöperative labor. "There will be a working at Mt. Enterprise Saturday for the purpose of cleaning up the cemetery." **1910** *Commerce Jrl.* (TX) 20 May 1/4, *Cemetery Working.* All persons interested in the Lebanon cemetery are requested to meet there . . for the purpose of cleaning off the graves and fixing up the grounds. Bring your dinner so that we may put in the day. **1922** in 1981 Harper–Presley *Okefinokee* 171 **seGA,** Yesterday Tom and Ben went to the "workin" at Sardis church. . . The women folks scrub up the floors and the meetinghouse generally, while the men hoe the weeds out of the graveyard and fix it up. **1944** Howard *Walkin' Preacher* 66 **Ozarks,** "Them's oak shingles. . . Folks in the neighborhood made 'em at a workin'." . . "They used to have workin's ever'time a new house war put up." **1952** Callahan *Smoky Mt.* 127 **wNC, eTN,** A highlight in the musical life of a community was a "working." . . These parties were held in connection with new ground clearings, house raisings, corn shuckings, apple peelings, molasses stir-offs, and quiltings. **1966–69** *DARE* (Qu. L5, *When a farmer gets help on a job from his neighbors in return for his help on their farms later on*) Inf **NC36,** Workings; (Qu. FF1, . . *A kind of group meeting called a 'social' or 'sociable'. . . [What goes on?]*) Inf **TX33,** Graveyard workings—members of church clean graveyard . . dinner too. **1970** *Foxfire* 4.35 **nGA,** I's tryin' t'make a workin' with my uncle an' his brothers. They said they'd come help me. **1982** Slone *How We Talked* 22 **eKY** (as of c1950), A "working"—When neighbors got together to share work. **1991** Weals

Last Train 135 **eTN,** Former students came to a "working" to clear the underbrush in 1952, so that reunions could be held on the grounds. **1995** Weber *Rugged Hills* 14 **sAppalachians,** When someone is injured or sick, neighbors have "a workin'" and put up his hay or cut his tobacco or put a new roof on a widow's house.

workings-up See **work-up**

work on See **work 3**

work-out See **work-up**

work over See **work 3**

work party n **chiefly NEast, Gt Lakes** See Map =**working.**

1965–70 *DARE* (Qu. FF2, . . *Kinds of parties*) 20 Infs, **chiefly NEast, Gt Lakes,** Work parties; **ME11,** Work parties—church guilds or auxiliaries may have work parties to make articles to sell at fairs; **MI44,** Work parties—any number of work parties at the church; have a lunch afterwards; **MI55,** Work parties—very seldom you hear of work parties anymore; **MI62,** Work parties—once a year, with the backing of the Hist. Soc., we plant plants in the village park; **MI120,** Work parties—old-fashioned; **NC60,** Work parties—pre-welfare; used to have; **PA13,** Work parties—if someone was sick, husk his corn or whatever, women fixed eats; **PA104,** Work parties—clean up cemetery; **IL45, 53,** Work parties at church; **TX37,** Log-rolling work party. **1966** *Lynden Tribune* (WA) 8 Dec 6/5, A work party, consisting of club members and several school teachers, replaced the old bleachers on the football field with new ones. **2009** *DARE* File **cwCA** (as of c1950–1990), My father, as chair of the church's Building and Grounds committee, organized many a work party.

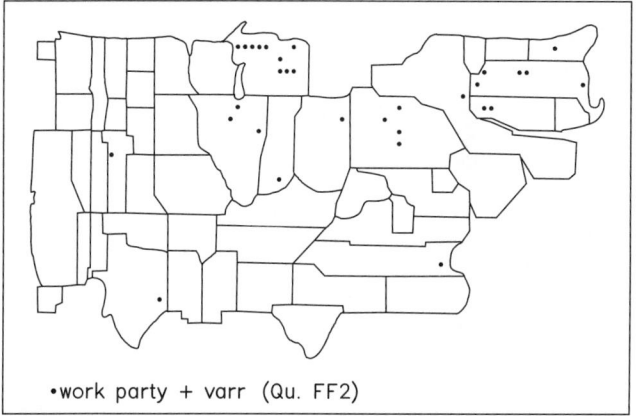

•work party + varr (Qu. FF2)

work-up n Also *workey-up, work-in, workings-up, work-out, work-ups* **chiefly west of Missip R, Gt Lakes** See Map on p. 1076 Cf **move-up, round-town, scrub 2, town ball**
A bat-and-ball game in which the batter usu takes a field position when put out and the other players rotate through the other positions according to a predetermined order.

1913 Bowen *Teaching Play* 76, *Rotation.*—This game is the nearest to baseball of any of the minor games of boys. It is known by several names, such as Scrub, Work Up, and Rounders. **1944** Howard *Walkin' Preacher* 167 **Ozarks,** Boys and younger men played work-up on the ball diamond. **1949** Hedgecock *Gone Are the Days* 70 **swMO,** In baseball we played "scrub," or what they now call "work-up." **1957** *DARE* File **OK** (a1920), In Oklahoma we played "One Old Cat," too, but we called it "Work-Up." **1965–70** *DARE* (Qu. EE11, *Bat-and-ball games for just a few players [when there aren't enough for a regular game]*) 86 Infs, **chiefly west of Missip R, Gt Lakes,** Work-up; **IA29,** Work-up— you changed position all the time—two batters, from left field to third, to pitcher, to catcher; **OK18,** Work-up—batter, catcher, pitcher, first base, second base, all changed position as batter got out; **CA190,** Work-ups; **DE2, PA26,** Workey-up; **CA80, IL4, MN16, OR3,** Work-out; **OK28,** Work-out—players take turns pitching, batting, and fielding; they change when batter gets three strikes; **NJ18,** Work-in—1 batter— last man in right field—works way in through outfield, infield, pitcher, catcher to batter; if he catches a fly, he's up without working in; **NJ39,** Workings-up. **1992** *DARE* File **MS, seTN,** We played *workup.* If you got a base hit, you got to keep batting til you were put out. *Ibid* **WA** (as of c1942), We played a game with any number of players called "work-up" [in which] each player, however many, moved up one position, unless he or she . . caught a fly ball. In that case, the player went immediately to bat. **2000** Chamberlain *River Stories* 92 **swWI,** Now there are no more happy shouts in the schoolyard while the children play "work up" or "tag." **2004** Ohm *Spatzies* 4 **KS** (as of 1943), The goal was to hit the pitched ball and run to the base and back to home before a fielder could either throw in front of the runner or hit the runner to put him out. If you outran the ball in either case, you could continue to bat. The rules for this game of "work-up" were very consistent.

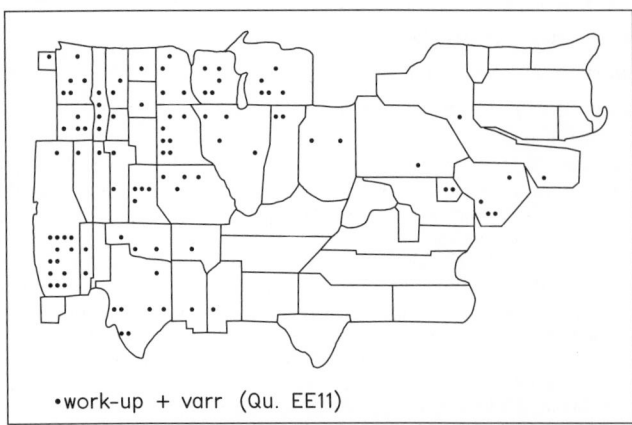

•work-up + varr (Qu. EE11)

work with   See **work 1**

world, go (all the way) around the v phr   For addit varr see quots   **chiefly Sth, S Midl**   See Map   Cf **elbow, go (all) around one's; Robin Hood's barn, go (all the way) around**   To engage in a roundabout course of action; see quots.

1927 in 1940 Halliburton *Richard Halliburton* 279 **TN,** I'm having to go all around the world, the floods have torn such big holes in the rail bed. **1965–70** *DARE* (Qu. KK52, *To do something in an indirect and complicated way: "I don't know why he had to go _____ to do that."*) 23 Infs, **chiefly Sth, S Midl,** (All *or* all the way) around the world; **AL**8, 27, 37, **FL**28, **MS**14, **SC**69, (All the way) round the world; **KY**28, All way round the world. **1986** Pederson *LAGS Concordance,* 1 inf, **cnAL,** He finally had to go all the way round the world—of a long trip. **2007** *DARE* File—Internet, Thanks to Chris I finally learned how to type ö ä ñ é etc without having to go all the way around the world.

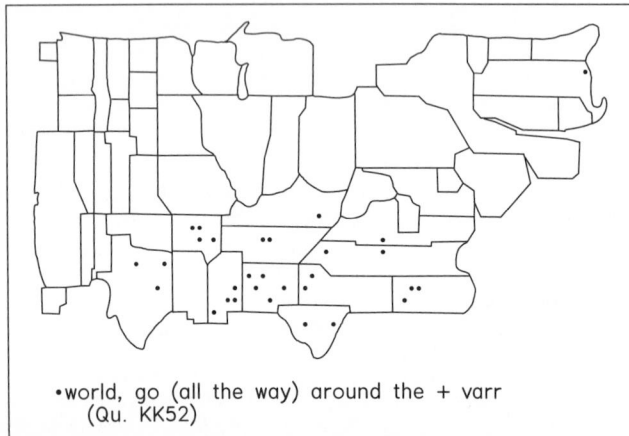

•world, go (all the way) around the + varr
(Qu. KK52)

world, in the adv phr   Also *in this world, in God's ~, to the ~, to this ~*

1   Used as an intensive with var nouns, esp in phrr *a sight in the world* and varr: a remarkable sight, something extraordinary; a great deal. [Cf *EDD of the world* (at *world* sb. 2.(7)–(9))]   Cf **one more, sight** n **2**

1899 *Amer. Missionary* 53.124 **neTN,** Our mountain people say . . "It is a sight in the world" for "something terrible." **1900** *Natl. Mag.* (Boston) 12.456 **WV,** It's a sight to the world to look at that preacher an' them women a-workin' amongst the sinners. **1915** *Harper's Mth. Mag.* 132.102 **NC,** Hit's a sight in this world how they like us travelin'-men better 'n any others. **1924** (1946) Greer-Petrie *Angeline Gits an Eyeful* 5 **csKY,** That old Mis' Clark is one more *sight to this world!* **1931** *PMLA* 46.1306 **sAppalachians,** It's a sight in the world how she tuk on (grieved) about it. **1939** *Hall Coll.* **wNC,** We had one more time in this

world a-bear-huntin'. **1953** in 1972 Hall *Sayings Old Smoky* 124 **eTN,** He loved to hunt a sight in this world. **1958** *Ships & Sea* 8.2.37 **VA,** Still, you'd have a time in this world equaling the crew of the James Thomas. **1964** in 1981 James *All Places* 175 **AL,** Hit's a shame in the world, Frank, what them fancy-pants coons has done to this country. **1967** in 1972 Hall *Sayings Old Smoky* 124 **eTN,** [The Appalachian Trail is] traveled a sight in the world. It's beat to death in the summer time. **1969** in 1993 Wright *Traveling Bluegrass* 30 **NC,** And it was a sight in the world. I can't think of all right now to tell you what really did happen. But anyway it was a sight in God's world how they worked us boys. **1999** *AmSp* 74.247 **ceSC,** Them laws [i.e., highway patrols] don't bes doing nothing but riding around and drinking coffee. It's a shame in this world. [female 60+ . .].

2   Used as an intensive with an adj in the positive degree.

1976 Ryland *Richmond Co. VA* 375, Pretty in this world—extraordinarily pretty.

world's wonder n
=**bouncing Bet 1.**

1896 *Jrl. Amer. Folkl.* 9.182 **eMA,** *Saponaria officinalis* . . world's wonder.

world-wonder root   See **wonder-of-the-world root**

worm n   Pronc-sp *wum*

1   also *fence worm, worm rail:* The first course of rails laid down in the construction of a zigzag fence—freq in phr *lay the worm.*   **chiefly Sth, S Midl**   Cf **worm fence**

1760 (1925) Washington *Diaries* 1.128 **VA,** Laid in part the Worm of a fence round my Peach Orchard. **1800** in 1969 Herndon *Wm. Tatham Tobacco* 10 **VA,** The worm (as it is called) being thus laid, the same process is repeated until the fence rises to the height of nine or ten rails. **1867** Harris *Sut Lovingood Yarns* 129 **TN,** They'se mity good things, too, fur a feller tu straiten up on, fur a fresh start, when he's layin off the wum ove a fence. **1882** GA Dept. Ag. *Pub. Circular No. 26* 13, I see that many men lay the worm of their rail fences down hill. . . Why not put a rock under every corner (if they can be had) and this saves the worm from decay. **1909** *DN* 3.389 **eAL, wGA,** *Worm.* . . The bottom line of rails in a zigzag fence. "Lay the worm carefully, and the fence will be all the stronger." **1915** *DN* 4.193 **swVA,** *Worm-rail.* . . The bottom rail of a worm fence. **1918** Waller *IL Pioneer Days* 75, *Fence-worm,* the first rail of each panel of a rail fence. **1966** Dakin *Dial. Vocab. Ohio R. Valley* 2.101, Speakers who do not themselves say *worm fence*—including some in the western sections where the term is never used—do however occasionally speak of a "worm," or "laying a worm" in reference to the first course of rails laid on the ground to establish the pattern of a zig-zag rail fence. **1983** *MJLF* 9.1.61 **ceKY** (as of 1956), *Worm* . . : Laying the bottom rail of a worm fence is called "laying the worm." **1986** Pederson *LAGS Concordance,* 1 inf, **ceTN,** You had to lay a worm then rails; 1 inf, **swGA,** Worm—bottom rail; 1 inf, **swGA,** Worm—a little rail; 1 inf, **swAL,** Worm—rail; 1 inf, **swAR,** Worm is bottom rail of a rail fence; 1 inf, **seGA,** Worm rail; 2 infs, **AL, MS,** Worm rail—at (the) bottom; 1 inf, **seAL,** Worm rail—went on the ground first; 1 inf, **cnLA,** Worm rail—bottom rail; 4 infs, **AL, GA, TN,** Lay the (*or* a, your) worm; 2 infs, **AR, TN,** Laying the worm; 1 inf, **cTX,** You were laying the fence worm. **1995** Trout *Hist. Buildings Smokies* 23 **wNC,** His father always laid the "worm" . . of a split rail fence in the dark of the moon, otherwise this first rail would rot.

2   In moonshining: a coil of copper tubing in which the vaporized alcohol condenses. [*OED2* 1641 →]   **chiefly Sth, S Midl, esp sAppalachians**

1866 *Janesville Gaz.* (WI) [17 Nov 4]/3 (newspaperarchive.com), [Advt:] One Mash Tub, 1 Still, 1 Worm and Tub. **1883** Zeigler-Grosscup *Heart of Alleghanies* 362 **sAppalachians,** The men worked in the light of the furnace fire, and talked in loud tones above the noise of the running water flowing down troughs into the hogshead, through which wound the worm from the copper still. **1885** Murfree *Prophet of Smoky Mts.* 279 **eTN,** They . . cut the tubs and still to pieces, destroyed the worm, demolished the furnace, and captured in triumph sundry kegs and jugs of the illicit whiskey. **1914** Arthur *Western NC* 272, Mash is then placed in the still and boiled, the steam passing through a worm or spiral metal tube which rests in a cooling tub. **1942** Faulkner *Go Down* 37 **MS,** He stopped the wagon beside the mound and unloaded the still . . and the worm and his pick and shovel. **1946** *AmSp* 21.195 [Distillery worker terms], For the edification of non-distillery workers, it is well to point out that distillers never refer to a still coil as a 'worm,' as did the bootleggers who manufactured popskull and rotgut during Prohibition. **1967–69** *DARE* Tape **GA**72, If it's a worm it's usually just a straight coil of copper pipe or tubing; **TN**9, You have a cap that goes up on top of it to keep the, the beer from boiling out into the worm. **c1999** in 2004 Montgomery–Hall *Dict. Smoky Mt. Engl.* 659 **wNC, eTN,** *Worm. . . a copper coil usually 48 feet long if you are running a big rig.*

3 An inexperienced worker on an oil drilling crew. **chiefly TX** Cf **boll weevil**

1967 *DARE* (Qu. HH15, *A very inexperienced person, one who is just learning how to do a new thing*) Inf **TX**11, Worm—among oil men; **TX**19, Worm—this is the newest term—oil term . . throughout the community; **TX**27, Worm—oilfield usage. **1967** *DARE* Tape **TX**19, An inexperienced man on there [=an oil-drilling rig], he's a boll weevil. And then of course later on, last few years, they been calling 'em worms. **1973** *DARE* File **nwCO,** Worm. . . New, inexperienced worker . . In oilfields. **1984** Weaver *TX Crude* 94, *Worm.* 1. A new, inexperienced oilfield hand. 2. What an experienced hand is called when he makes a stupid mistake. "Looks like the worms are eatin' up the oilfield!" **2006** *DARE* File—Internet **wTX** [*Fort Worth Star–Telegram* (TX) 28 May], Welch started roughnecking in 1967 for $1.80 an hour. He was "a worm"—the lowest-ranking position on the rig.

worman See **woman A3**

worm eater n   Cf **tobacco worm 2**

1939 *AmSp* 14.92 **eTN,** *Worm eater.* Tobacco chewer. 'He's an eternal worm eater.'

worm fence n   Also *worm-rail fence*   **scattered, but chiefly C Atl, Appalachians**   See Map   Cf **snake fence, Virginia ~ 1, worm 1**

A fence made by stacking rails so that their ends overlap at an angle.

1652 in 1887 East Hampton NY *Records* 1.22, It is ordered that Thomas Baker shall have . . 7 ackers . . within the worme fence on the litel plaine. **1724** in 1976 Rose *Doc. Hist. Slavery* 39 **VA,** Tobacco and Indian corn are . . secured by worm-fences, which are made of rails supporting one another very firmly in a particular manner. **1819** (1915) Mason *Pioneer West* 58 **MO,** A worm fence is run around the house to keep the pigs out of the first story. **1857** Long *Pictures Slavery* (2d ed) 257 **MD,** Here is our old-fashioned worm-fence, made of sap pine rails, that has to be mended every year. **1867** Harris *Sut Lovingood Yarns* 41 **TN,** An the road wer sprinkled worm fence fashun, like ontu a drunken man a-totin a leaky jug. **1872** U.S. Dept. Ag. *Rept. of Secy. for 1871* 498 **OH,** Our worm rail fence varies in height. They are from seven to nine rails high, including riders. **1899** (1912) Green *VA Folk-Speech* 490, *Worm-fence. . .* A zigzag fence made by placing the ends of the rails at an angle upon one another; a snake-fence. **1909** *DN* 3.418 **nME,** *Worm fence. . .* A Virginia fence. **1915** *DN* 4.192 **swVA,** *Worm-fence. . .* A rail fence built in zigzag fashion, one rail lying over another. **1923** *DN* 5.224 **swMO,** *Worm fence. . .* A zig-zag fence made of split rails. **1940** Writers' Program *Oregon* 332, Split-rail worm fences divide fields. **1946** *PADS* 5.43 **VA,** *Worm fence. . .* A zigzag rail fence. **1949** Kurath *Word Geog.* 55, *Rail fence. . .* The Midland term for the zigzag fence is *worm fence,* an expression that predominates in Pennsylvania, West Virginia, New Jersey, and Delmarva and has made its way into northern Virginia. **1965–70** *DARE* (Qu. L62, *A fence made of split logs*) 49 Infs, **scattered, but chiefly C Atl, Appalachians,** Worm fence; **KY**58, **SC**19, Worm rail fence; (Qu. L61, *Fences made of solid logs, now or in the past*) Infs **NJ**50, **NM**13, **PA**6, 10, 63, Worm fence; (Qu. L64, *The kind of wooden fence that's built around a garden or near a house*) Inf **SC**4, Worm fence; (Qu. L65, . . *Kinds of fences*) Infs **IN**54, **NC**48, **OH**31, **PA**137, Worm fence; [**MT**4, Worm-type fence]. **1966** Dakin *Dial. Vocab. Ohio R. Valley* 2.101, *Rail fence. . .* The Midland . . *worm fence,* is still quite common in Ohio . . and is fairly common in the part of north-central Kentucky where many Pennsylvanians settled in the early period. *Worm fence* is rare in eastern Indiana and unknown west of the Scottsburg Lowland, in Illinois, and in western Kentucky. Some speakers know or remember *worm fence* as an older name, and it was clearly a more general term at an earlier time. The first acts governing the Northwest Territory were passed in 1790. . . The section concerned with legal fences used the name *worm fence,* as did a similar act in 1799. **1973** Allen *LAUM* 1.192 **Upper MW** (as of c1950), *Rail fence. . .* Northern *rail fence* dominates the southeastern quadrant of the U[pper] M[idwest], although Midland *worm fence* competes weakly with it. **1986** Pederson *LAGS Concordance* (Rail fence) 15 infs, **esp MS, TN,** Worm fence(s). **2001** O'Brien *At Home Appalachia* 181 **WV,** Old "worm fences" surround some pastures.

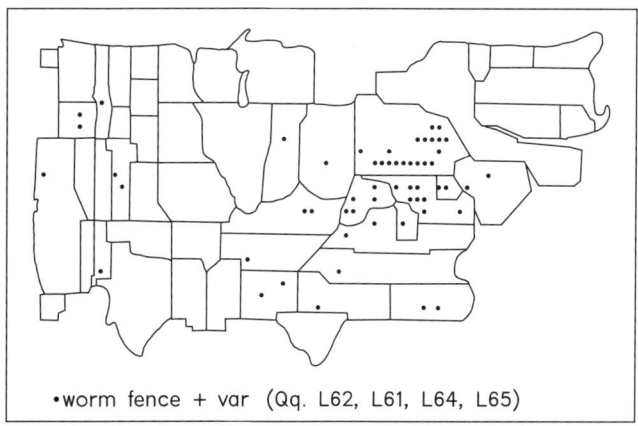

•worm fence + var   (Qq. L62, L61, L64, L65)

worm grass n   [*OED2* 1756 →; from its use as a vermifuge] Cf **wormroot**
=**pinkroot 1.**

[**1756** Browne *Civil & Nat. Hist. Jamaica* 2.156, *Anthelmenthia. . . Spigelia. . . Worm-grass. . .* takes its present denomination from its peculiar efficacy in destroying of worms.] **1848** Gray *Manual of Botany* 181, *Spigelia* [spp]. . . Pink-root. Worm-grass. . . [*S. Marilandica. . .* A well-known officinal anthelmintic.] **1949** Moldenke *Amer. Wild Flowers* 161, The West Indian pinkroot or wormgrass, *S. anthelmia,* with purplish flowers . . may be found in hammocks and cultivated ground on the Florida Keys.

worm lizard n

Std: a limbless **lizard 1** (here: *Rhineura floridana*).   Also called **blind worm, thunderworm, worm snake 3**

worm rail See **worm 1**

worm-rail fence See **worm fence**

wormroot n   [From its use as a vermifuge]   Cf **worm grass, wormweed 1, wormwood 2**
=**Indian pink 1.**

1830 Rafinesque *Med. Flora* 2.89, *Spigelia marilandica. . .* Worm Root. [*Ibid* 90, It has chiefly attracted notice as a vermifuge and for diseases of children, convulsions, worm fever, &c.] **1885** *NY Times* (NY) 19 Apr 12/3, He [=the herbalist] can tell us all about . . the vast list of flowers and roots which cure diseases of corresponding form—such as nettle-tea for nettle-rash, worm root for lunacy [etc]. **1968** Harris *S. Home Remedies* 99 **NC** (as of 19th cent), An infusion is made by drawing an ounce of the tops of wormroot (an herb of the genus spigelia) in a pint of boiling water. **1970** *NC Folkl.* 18.34, For worms, drink liquid made from tops of wormroot (genus *Spigelia*) and water.

wormseed n   [*OED2* a1400–50 → for various plants used as vermifuges]
=**Jerusalem oak 1,** usu *Chenopodium ambrosioides;* the seed of this plant, used in making an anthelminthic oil.

[**1653** in 1865 MA Hist. Soc. *Coll.* 4th ser 7.466 **CT,** Wee gave him wormeseed.] [*DARE* Ed: This quot may refer instead to some other plant.] **1709** (1967) Lawson *New Voyage* 84 **NC, SC,** Wormseed, Feverfew, Rue, Ground-Ivy spontaneous, but very small and scarce. **1808** *Philadelphia Med. Museum* 5.253 **MD,** *Chenopodium Anthelminticum. . .* The vulgar names of this plant are, wormseed and Jerusalem oak. **1820** *Amer. Farmer* 1.397, Worms, though no insect, have been easily repelled by the flavor of the oleum chenopodii, or wormseed oil. **1921** *Galveston Daily News* (TX) 28 Mar 4/5, In recent years chenopodium or wormseed has almost supplanted thymol in the treatment of hookworm. **1949** Arnow *Hunter's Horn* (May ed. 2d printing) 373 **KY,** She wanted to give all the others a round of molasses and wormseed and sulphur. **1970** *NC Folkl.* 18.34, Give regular doses of "worm medicine," which might have parts of calomel, worm-seed oil, Carolina pink root, or turpentine. **1974** *Tri-City Herald* (Pasco WA) 4 Apr 15/1 **MD,** Perry and Bobby Day, father and son farmers in Frederick County, Md., are two of the few people in the world who know something about wormseed oil. **1999** Tull *Edible Plants TX* 62, Though a number of the 26 species of *Chenopodium* in Texas have tasty edible leaves, do not use those with aromatic leaves, such as wormseed (*Chenopodium ambrosioides*).

wormseed mustard n Also *wormseed*
A **wallflower** (here: *Erysimum cheiranthoides*).
1848 Gray *Manual of Botany* 37 **wNY,** *E[rysimum] cheiranthoides*. . . Worm-seed Mustard. . . thoroughly naturalized. **1909** *Ogden Std.* (UT) [9 Aug 4]/3 (newspaperarchive.com), The most prevalent of the 'vagrant' weeds, such as false flax, wormseed mustard [etc] . . can all be controlled. **1923** *Amer. Botanist* 29.150, *Erysimum cheiranthoides* is the "treacle mustard" or "worm-seed mustard." The second name refers to the use of the plant or to the reputed virtues of the plant, as an anthelmintic. **1954** *Eve. Jrl.–Tribune* (Marysville OH) 2 Oct 2/6, The weeds controlled included curly dock . . wormseed mustard [etc]. **1974** Welsh *Anderson's Flora AK* 208, *Erysimum chieranthoides* [sic]. . . Wormseed. **1999** Magee–Ahles *Flora NE* 555, *[Erysimum] cheiranthoides*. . . Wormseed-mustard.

worm snake n
1 Any of var snakes resembling worms in appearance or behavior, as:
a Std: a snake of the genus *Carphophis,* usu *C. amoenus* in the east and *C. vermis* in the central US. For other names see **ground snake a, thunder snake 2**
b A short, slender snake of the genus *Leptotyphlops,* native to the Southwest.
1885 *Forest & Stream* 25.62 **eCA,** Will and I found a ground or worm snake in the road. **1908** *Biol. Soc. DC Proc.* 21.73 **TX,** *Glauconia dulcis* [=*Leptotyphlops d.*] . . Worm Snake. **1917** *Oakland Tribune* (CA) 5 Aug 34/5, California is rich in other strange and interesting serpents—the worm snake of Death Valley [etc]. **1931** *San Diego Soc. Nat. Hist. Trans.* 6.338 **sCA, AZ,** *Leptotyphlops humilus slevini*. . . San Lucan Worm Snake. *Ibid* 339, *Leptotyphlops humilis cahuilae* . . Desert Worm Snake. **1937** *Brownsville Herald* (TX) 30 May 3/3, A Leptotyphlops dulcis, as the worm snake is known to scientists, also was caught by an inspector of the Mexican fruit fly quarantine service. **1947** Pickwell *Amphibians* 39, Family Leptotyphlopidae. In this family there is a single genus, *Leptotyphlops,* the members of which are small, blind, or almost blind Snakes called "worm snakes" because of the size and appearance. **1971** *Denton Rec.–Chron.* (TX) 28 Mar sec D 5/7, There is actually quite a bit of difference between the appearance of a baby rattlesnake and a blind or "worm" snake.
c =**earth snake.**
1921 *Landmark* (Statesville NC) 1 Aug 5/5, The green or brown or worm snake, Haldea stiatus [sic]. **1952** Ditmars *N. Amer. Snakes* 230, Worm Snake, *Haldea striatula* [=*Virginia s.*] . . Total length 11 inches; diameter 1/4 inch.
d =**rubber boa.** [See quot 1949]
1908 Ditmars *Reptile Book* 212, The Rubber Boa—Silver Snake—Two-headed Snake—Worm Snake—*Charina bottae.* **1949** Palmer *Nat. Hist.* 462, Rubber Boa, Worm Snake—*Charina bottae.* . . Ranges through humid districts of California, Nevada, Idaho, Oregon, and Washington, usually burrowing slowly and steadily into soft earth or vegetation.
2 also *snakeworm:* A snakelike moving body made up of the larvae of Sciarid gnats; see quots.
1873 *Eve. Gaz.* (Pt. Jervis NY) 26 Aug 1/6, Mr. J.C. Beemer, . . while out "huckleberrying," one day last week, discovered a Worm Snake, crossing the road, about three feet in length. He assaulted his snakeship with a billet of wood, struck two or three blows, when the reptile began to spread out, crawling in all directions. Mr. Beemer was greatly astonished, took a closer view of his victim, whem [sic] he discovered that it was composed of thousands of little reptiles, varrying [sic] in length from an inch to three inches, about the size of a hair, all linked in together, in such a manner as to form a snake three feet in length. **1891** *Century Dict.* 6981, *Worm-snake*. . . Same as *snakeworm*. [*Ibid* 5726, *Snakeworm*. . . One of the masses of larvae of certain midges of the genus *Sciara*. These larvae, when full-grown, often migrate in armies forming a snake-like body a foot or more long, an inch or more wide, and a half-inch high. Also called *army-worm*.] **1926** *Amer. Naturalist* 60.539, The swarming takes place among the full-grown larvae which form long snake-like masses composed of thousands of grubs which crawl one over the other at a slow rate. The term "Snakeworm" and "Heerwurm" has been applied to these insects which seem always to be species of Sciara. The crawling columns may be as long as 10–15 feet or rarely even 30 yards. **2005** Robinson *Hdbk. Urban Insects* 185, The larvae of *Sciara militaris* and *S. thomae* have the habit of aggregating and moving together in large numbers. . . When larvae are full-grown

and ready to pupate, the aggregation may move together in a long column (snakeworm, armyworm) over the ground.
3 =**worm lizard.**
1882 *Forest & Stream* 19.45 **FL,** In my haste to answer your correspondent . . regarding the Florida worm-snake he inquired about, I neglected to say that it is not a true serpent at all, but a lizard-like snake [sic for *snake-like lizard*], which, so far as I know, has been found in Florida only.

worm tree n [Because the catalpa worm feeds on it] **Sth** Cf **fishbait tree, fishworm ~,** *toggle-worm ~* (at **toggle worm**) =**catalpa B1.**
1966–68 *DARE* (Qu. T9, *The common shade tree with large heart-shaped leaves, clusters of white blossoms, and long thin seed pods or 'beans'*) Inf **AL42,** Worm tree—some folks call catawba tree this; **NC24,** Worm tree—because of catawba worms; **SC11,** Catawba—Negroes call it the worm tree. **1991** Still *Wolfpen Notebooks* 163 **sAppalachians,** *Worm tree:* catalpa. **2008** *DARE* File—Internet **FL,** The Southern catalpa. . . attracts a caterpillar that is said to be excellent fish bait. That's why this tree is often referred to as the fish bait or worm tree. Many people buy the tree specifically for the caterpillar and a better catch on the lake.

wormweed n
1 =**Indian pink 1.** Cf **wormroot**
[**1878** U.S. Natl. Museum *Bulletin* 12.60, *Spigelia anthelmia*. . . Worm-weed. . . St. Croix; St. Thomas.] **1900** Lyons *Plant Names* 354, *S[pigelia] Marylandica*. . . Worm-grass, worm-weed. . . used only as an anthelmintic.
2 A **ragweed 2** (here: *Ambrosia artemisiifolia*).
1904 *Trenton Times* (NJ) [6 Sept 8]/2 (newspaperarchive.com), Ambrosia Artemisiaefolia . . brings untold misery to the hosts of hay fever sufferers. In common everyday language it is rag weed, hog weed, bitter weed or worm weed, according to localities. **1915** *Mt. Democrat* (Placerville CA) [4 Dec 7]/1 (newspaperarchive.com), The generic name of the two ragweeds is ambrosia. The common or wormweed variety is called "artemisiifolia" on account of its leaves resembling those of the wormwood (artemisia).
3 =**Jerusalem oak 1.** Cf **wormseed**
1940 Writers' Program *Guide OH* 78, In remote corners of the State herbs are still good for bodily ills, and country housewives . . know a hundred uses for slippery elm bark, wormweed, wild cherry bark, yellow dock, and tansy. **1941** *NW AR Times* (Fayetteville) 19 July 3/3, William Lee Case, of Carthage, Mo., has spent three of his five years in a coma believed caused by overdose of American wormweed. **1974** *Tri-City Herald* (Pasco WA) 4 Apr 15/5 **MD,** Perry Day, 58, says, not quite accurately, it "takes a weak mind and a strong back" to grow wormweed. **1979** *Frederick Post* (MD) 11 Apr sec A 9/5, He asked if I knew that Damascus was the wormweed capital of the world, with the only such distillery. **2003** Cavender *Folk Med.* 91 **sAppalachians,** Jerusalem oak seed (also called wormweed . .) was a favored remedy [for pinworms and roundworms in children].

wormwood n [*OED2* a1400 →] Cf **mugwort, sagebrush 1**
1 Std: a plant of the genus *Artemisia,* esp *A. absinthium.* For other names see **boy's-love, old woman, sweet annie, ~ fern plant**
2 =**Indian pink 1.** Cf **wormroot**
1940 Clute *Amer. Plant Names* 273, *Spigelia Marilandica.* Worm-root, American wormwood.

wornut See **walnut**

worriation n Also *worr(y)ation* **chiefly Mid Atl, esp SC, NC esp freq among Black speakers** Cf **botheration** n, **furiation**
The act or state of worrying; a cause for worry, trouble, annoyance.
1854 Ballou *Practical Chr. Socialism* 609 **MA,** If He [=God] acts by *necessitation* of complex uncontrollable influences, we may as well give up in despair. At any rate, our thinking and worriation will be useless. **1892** *Short Stories* 9.318 **Sth** [Black], I doan' wan' no worriation in de buryin' groun. **1923** Parsons *Folk-lore Sea Islands* 203 **csSC,** She had taken to smoking after her two children died—"worryation make a puson smoke." **1927** Adams *Congaree* 71 **cSC** [Black], Ain' nothin' ail he health, but he mine mighty sick wid worryation. **1928** Peterkin *Scarlet Sister Mary* 31 **SC** [Gullah], I done had enough worry-ation dis morning to last me a long time. **c1937** in **1972** *Amer. Slave* 2.1.248 **SC,**

We never have so much worryations den as people have dese days. **c1940** in 2004 Montgomery–Hall *Dict. Smoky Mt. Engl.* 660 **wNC, eTN,** *Worriation. . . worry.* **1944** *PADS* 2.52 **NC, VA,** *Worration. . .* Worry, annoyance; a blend of *worry + botheration.* **1949** Arnow *Hunter's Horn* 127 **KY,** I've got too much time an trouble an money worriation in th things [=dogs] to git out what I've put in. **1952** Brown *NC Folkl.* 1.609, *Worration. . .* Worry, annoyance. A blend of *worry* and *botheration*(?). "Every bit of that worration is right on top of me." . . Rare. **1965** Brewer *Worser Days* 33 **NC** [Black], Dis here make de man do a whole lots of worryation. **1997** in 2004 Montgomery–Hall *Dict. Smoky Mt. Engl.* 660 **wNC, eTN,** *Worriation. . .* Worriation has never been one of her problems.

worried (out) See **worry B1**

worrisome adj Cf **worry B1**
See quot.
1926 *AmSp* 1.411 **Okefenokee GA,** [Footnote to *worried:*] I have . . heard the word 'worrisome' used in the sense of 'wearisome.'

worrit v
1 now freq pronc-sp *wart* (rarely *wort*): To cause (one) worry or vexation; to tease, nag; hence ppl adjs *worrited* (rarely *worrit*) worried, vexed. [Engl dial] **formerly scattered, now esp Gulf States, TX**
1851 Stuart-Wortley *Travels U.S.* (New York) 107 **KY,** She was wont to confide to me her troubles . . that "worrited" her "pretty considerable." **1879** *Harper's New Mth. Mag.* 59.546 **NJ,** It was, 'Daddy, hold the baby,' 'Daddy, mind the child,' till I was that worrit I was nigh crazy. **1887** *Overland Mth.* (2d ser) 10.69 **AL,** I hev knowed women ez 'ud worrit er man whilst he war livin', en study er power on him arter he war dead. **1894** (1898) Field *Love-Songs* 12 **Chicago IL,** Sometimes when the grocery man is worrited an' cross,/ He reaches at us with his whip, an' larrups up his hoss. **1906** [see **2** below]. **1910** Hart *Vigilante Girl* 375 **nCA,** Well, don't worrit him, Minnie. **1921** Haswell *Daughter Ozarks* 145 (as of 1880s), I'm a'tellin' ye I'm plumb worritted about ye. **1936** *AmSp* 11.369 **nLA,** *Wart.* To annoy; as, 'That boy nearly warted me to death.' **1941** Lanham *Thunder* 67 **TX,** She'd holler at me and wart me near to death and I guess she picked on me because I was kind of country. **1957** *Sat. Eve. Post Letters* **NM,** *Wart,* meaning to tease or worry, "Johnny, don't wart your grandma." . . in common use among . . farmers and ranchers. . . dying out . . [among] the young people. **1967–68** *DARE* (Qu. Y7, *When one person never misses a chance to be mean to another or to annoy another: "I don't know why she keeps _____ me all the time!"*) Infs **CO**20, **KS**10, Warting; (Qu. GG32a, *To habitually play tricks or jokes on people: "He's always _____."*) Inf **TX**19, Warting people. **1968** *DARE* FW Addit **LA**17, "He could wart the horns off a billy-goat." = expression used about an exasperating person. **2004** in 2009 *DARE* File—Internet **cTX,** I have noticed that the phone companies seem to go in fits, ignoring me for a while then warting me like a three-year old trying to get mommy's attention. **2007** *DARE* File **MS,** My parents, both from Mississippi, often used the word "wort" in place of annoy. Example: "Stop worting me." **2007** *DARE* File—Internet **AR,** Hattie is worting me to death about seeing Santa. **2007** in 2009 *Ibid* **VA,** My mom paid for me to see it in the theater after I warted her to death about it. *Ibid* **cTX,** Greg has been warting me about wanting to plant a garden. **2008** *Ibid* **cnLA,** He started warting me to buy tickets for a game as soon as last season was over. *Ibid* **eTX,** When people call now, all he has to say is I can't write prescriptions anymore. People warted him to death for years!

2 also sp *werrit*: To suffer anxiety, worry, fret. [Engl dial] **esp NEng**
1862 in 1888 Amer. Acad. Arts & Sci. *Memoirs* 11.476 **neMA,** But we shall see what comes of it. One thing is certain, I shall not 'worrit' about it. **1865** Browne *Artemus Ward Travels* 142 **ME,** My father he never had no occasion to worrit about me. **1867** Lowell *Biglow* 226 'Upcountry' **MA,** Wal, ef it's so, I ain't agoin' to werrit. **1876** *Scribner's Mth.* 11.848 **CA** [Author from NY], And ye ain't to worrit about me. **1906** *Granite State Mag.* 2.279 **NH,** I ought'r be in bed this blessed minnit, 'stead of havin' to worrit about that graceless scamp, who seems bound an' determined to worrit th' life out 'n me. **1938** Matschat *Suwannee R.* 20 **neFL, seGA,** Hain't nary need to worrit about 'em, ma'am.

3 as ppl adj *worrited*: Tired. [Cf **worry B1**]
1915 *Harper's Mth. Mag.* 131.437 **KY,** In the mountains . . "worritted" means tired.

worrit n [Engl dial; cf **worrit** v]
Worry; a state of worry.
1888 *Good Housekeeping* 24 Nov 36, Jacob kept a hurryin' me so I was all of a worrit before we got off. **1952** Brown *NC Folkl.* 1.609, *Worrit: n. . .* Worry.

worrited See **worrit** v 1, 3

worry v, n Usu |ˈwɝ·ɪ, ˈwɑrɪ|; for varr see **A** below
A Forms.
1 |wɪrɨ, wɪrɪ|; pronc-sp *weary.* **chiefly S Midl** [*OED2* (at *worry* v.) "The α- and β-forms (*wirry* and *werry*) are normal ME. developments of OE. *wyrʒan*. . . The γ-forms [=*worry,* etc] apparently represent late WS. **wurʒan.*"]
1906 *DN* 3.163 **nwAR,** *Wearied* [wɪrɪd]. . . Worried. "He's still wearied about his suit." **1933** in 1944 *ADD* 696 **eKY,** *Weary. . .* [Men chewing tobacco are] not wearyin' about a hot coal . . to keep the pipe a-goin'. **1941** Smith *Going to God's Country* 28 **MO,** She died May the tenth, 1883. That was the first thing that we had to weary us. *Ibid* 33, We bought a big heater. But I was wearied for fear that the ashes would not be good for soap making. **1948** *AmSp* 23.305 **Ozarks,** He told her to stop *wearying* about it. ('Worrying') **1948** *Jrl. Amer. Folkl.* 61.138 **nwMI,** A Cousin Jack . . was terribly worried in the slack days of depression. . . He said to his wife . . , "Mary Jane, I'm hawfully wearied." "My love, what are you wearied for?" **1950** Giles *Enduring Hills* 163 **KY,** Well, I jist weary myself plumb to death! Nights I jist cain't sleep, seems like, thinkin' 'bout you, way off somewheres away from home. **1953** Randolph–Wilson *Down in Holler* 17 **Ozarks,** Did you ever notice . . that the old Ozarkers call their worries their *wearies?* **1989** Pederson *LAGS Tech. Index* 290 **Gulf Region,** *Worry* . . [2 infs, [ˈwɪrɨ]]. **2008** in 2009 *DARE* File—Internet **csKY,** Yes if they wearied about sex offenders like they did drug we would be doing good. . . all they were wearied about was sending him to jail. **2009** *Ibid* **MO,** Why would those incredibly advanced aliens be wearied about us—merely human beings—militarizing the mean space around our little planet[?]

2 |wɛrɪ|; pronc-sp *werry.* [See **1** above]
1873 (1875) Alcott *Work* 174 **MA,** Don't you be worried about her. I'll see to her. **1899** *Century Illustr. Mag.* 58.142 **LA,** An' of co'se Gord knows all the inns and outs of it, how worried I was. **1942** Hall *Smoky Mt. Speech* 42 **wNC, eTN,** [ɛ]. . . appeared once in *worry:* 'The old lady like to have [ˈwɛrɪd] herself to death.' **1943** *LANE* Map 498 *(Don't worry),* [The pronc type [ˈwɛrɪ] is found scattered throughout **MA** and **VT** with only a few instances reported in **CT** and **RI;** it is absent from both **NH** and **ME.**] **a1954** (1990) Oakley *Rememberin' Roamin' Man* 101 **sAppalachians,** Dont werry too much about any one thing. **c1979** in 2004 Montgomery–Hall *Dict. Smoky Mt. Engl.* 660 **wNC, eTN,** *Worry. . .* werry. **1989** Pederson *LAGS Tech. Index* 290 **Gulf Region,** *Worry.* [14 infs offered proncs of the types [ˈwɛrɪ, ˈwerɪ].] **2008** in 2009 *DARE* File—Internet **NYC,** Mike [=Mike Francesca, a NYC radio talk show host] must have said "werry" or "werried" about 20 times in that first hour.

B As verb.
1 freq with *out:* To tire (someone); to experience physical exhaustion; hence ppl adj (phr) *worried (out)* tired; exhausted. Cf **worrisome**
1828 (1970) Webster *Amer. Dict., Worry. . .* 2. To fatigue; to harass with labor; *a popular sense of the word.* **1875** Holland *Sevenoaks* 66 **NEng,** For three steady hours he went on, the horse no more worried than if he had been standing in the stable. **1901** in 1961 Biggers *Chronicle* 66 **TX,** After starting a bunch of mustangs it was necessary to keep them constantly moving until they became worried out and susceptible to partial control. **1903** *DN* 2.337 **seMO,** *Worried. . .* Wearied; tired. 'Since I was sick I can't walk a mile without getting badly worried.' **1913** Kephart *Highlanders* 294 **sAppalachians,** When a man is tired he will likely call it worried. **1926** *AmSp* 1.411 **Okefenokee GA,** I wuz worried out an' stayed in camp. [Footnote to *worried:*] Wearied, worn. I have also heard the word 'worrisome' used in the sense of 'wearisome.' **1965** *Dict. Queen's English* 11 **NC,** *Worried:* Tired. He has worked all day and is all worried out. **c1995** in 2004 Montgomery–Hall *Dict. Smoky Mt. Engl.* 660 **wNC, eTN,** *Worry. . .* To tire, wear down, experience physical exhaustion. . . [6 infs].

2 To nag, pester, tease. [*OED2* 1671 →] **formerly widespread; now chiefly Sth, S Midl** See Map on p. 1080
1834 *Token & Atl. Souvenir* 312 **NEng,** Thomas Twigmore, the schoolmaster, had nearly worried her into the reversion of the ushership at the Littlefield Philosophical and Manual Labor Institute. **1846** Co-

lumbian Lady's & Gentleman's Mag. 5.117 **NY,** And yet you have worried me to death about calling on his dowdy wife. **1864** in 2000 *Leverett Letters* 371 **SC,** He spoke to me about taking Daphne for his wife some months ago, I told him I had no objections & he was pleased but he said Nanny worried him out of his life. **1871** (1882) Stowe *Fireside Stories* 136 **MA,** Ye see, when folks is pestered and worried to pay their bills, . . it's a great temptation to be kind o' valooin' riches. **1899** (1912) Green *VA Folk-Speech* 490, *Worry.* . . To tease; trouble; harrass [sic] with importunity or with care and anxiety; plague; bother; vex; persecute. **1963** Wright *Lawd Today* 115 **Chicago IL** [Black], For over a year now Al had been worrying him to join. **1965–70** DARE (Qu. Y7, *When one person never misses a chance to be mean to another or to annoy another: "I don't know why she keeps _____ me all the time!"*) 24 Infs, **chiefly Sth, S Midl,** Worrying; (Qu. GG3, *To tease: "See those big boys trying to _____ [that little one]."*) 23 Infs, **chiefly Sth, S Midl,** Worry; (Qu. Y6, *. . To put pressure on somebody to do something he ought to have done but hasn't: "He's a whole week late. I'm going to _____."*) Inf **NC**72, Worry him; (Qu. AA1, *When a man goes to see a girl often and seems to want to marry her, he's _____ her*) Inf **MO**8, Worrying; (Qu. II16, *When a visitor stays too long or comes too often: "He _____."*; total Infs questioned, 75) [Inf **FL**14, Worries, makes a pest of hisself;] **MS**63, Worries you to death; **MS**71, Worries me. **1993** Delany–Delany *Having Our Say* 57 **cNC** [Black], We didn't have but the vaguest notion of what sex was. . . I would see the rooster worrying the hen and I didn't know what was happening. **2004** in 2009 *DARE File*—Internet **VA,** I checked my mail box every day. . . The mail man was happy for me also because I worried him to death. **2007** *Ibid* **seMI,** Well my job kept worry me about a date so I just gave them a date so they would leave me alone. **2008** *Ibid* **cnAL,** The last one [= inspector] worried me to death over small things that really didn't matter much.

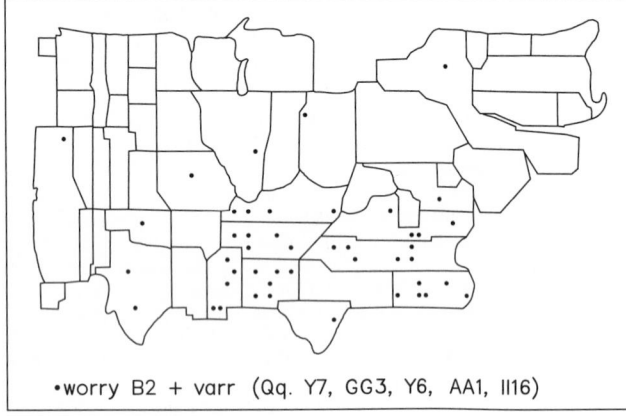

•worry B2 + varr (Qq. Y7, GG3, Y6, AA1, II16)

worryation See **worriation**

worry out See **worry B1**

worry stone n Also called **executive stone, feeling ~**

A smooth stone to be rubbed with the fingers for the soothing qualities of its surface.

1964 *Salt Lake Tribune* (UT) 10 Dec sec A 14/5, [Advt:] *Stocking stuffers* . . "worry stone" tranquilizer—$1. **1979** MacDonald *Green Ripper* 68, Rub the tiny green face with the ball of the thumb. Like a worry stone, to relieve executive tensions. **1995** *Gospel Sermons* 40, So now that everyone has a worry stone, let's practice. First we need to worry. Let's worry that we will lose our worry stone! **2007** *DARE File*—Internet, *Fluorite Worry Stone.* . . $4.95. . . Rub this Fluorite Worry Stone whenever you feel stressed, and you'll feel your troubles slipping away . . like magic!

worrywart n [From *Worry Wart,* a character who first appeared in the 1920s in J.R. Williams' cartoon *Out Our Way,* often represented as a trial to his older brother. The usu sense "chronic worrier" seems to be an etym reinterpretation.] **Sth, S Midl** Cf **worry B2**

A pest; a nuisance.

1934 *Lockhart Post-Reg.* (TX) 8 Nov [6]/4 (newspaperarchive.com), I have many bad habits such as trying to act smart, pestering the teachers, am the biggest worry wart in school and think I am very cute. . . — Worry Wart. **1936** *AmSp* 11.369 **nLA,** *Wart.* To annoy. . . It is used also as a noun; as, 'That girl is a regular worry wart.' c**1960** *Wilson Coll.*

csKY, *Worry-wart.* . . one who irritates other people. **1965–70** DARE (Qu. Y9, *Somebody who always follows along behind others: "His little brother is an awful _____."*) Infs **KY**94, **TX**52, Worrywart; **GA**89, Worrywart—somebody who's always in the way and always around; (Qu. GG32b, *To habitually play tricks or jokes on people: "He's an awful _____."*) Inf **MS**56, Worrywort; (Qu. GG38, *Somebody who is usually mean and bad tempered: "He's an awful _____."*) Inf **DE**3, Worrywart; (Qu. II18, *Someone who joins himself on to you and your group without being asked and won't leave*) Inf **AR**33, Worrywart; (Qu. II20a, *A person who tries too hard to gain somebody else's favor: "He's an awful _____."*) Inf **MS**15, Worrywart; (Qu. NN17, *Something that keeps on annoying you—for example, a fly that keeps buzzing around you: "That _____ fly won't go away."*) Inf **MS**57, Worrywart.

worser See **-er** compar suff **3**

worse than the seven-year itch See **seven-year itch 2b**

worsh See **wash**

wort n, adj, prep See **worth**

wort v See **worrit** v **1**

worter See **water A2**

worth n, adj, prep Pronc-spp *wort, wo'th, wuf(f), wut(h)* Similarly adj *wuthless*

A Forms.

1838 Gilman *S. Matron* 121 **SC** [Gullah], Jus look how Miss Anna fling down she bracelet, like it an't wort. [Footnote:] Worth anything. **1864** *Harper's New Mth. Mag.* 29.758 **Sth,** I thought how God was makin' a little wuthless bird happy. **1871** Eggleston *Hoosier Schoolmaster* 29 **sIN,** He's wuth lots and gobs of money. **1886** *S. Bivouac* 4.348 **sAppalachians,** You-uns hain't got the wuth of yer quarter yit. **1899** (1912) Green *VA Folk-Speech* 491, He isn't wo'th a cent. **1899** Chesnutt *Conjure Woman* 26 **csNC** [Black], He ain't wuf much now. **1909** *DN* 3.390 **eAL, wGA,** *Wuth.* . . Worth. Sometimes *wuff.* **1911** Wharton *Ethan Frome* 14 **wMA,** You know what one of them old watermills is wuth nowadays. **1914** *DN* 4.83 **ME, nNH,** *Wuthless.* . . Worthless. **1938** Rawlings *Yearling* 55 **nFL,** He ain't wuth a good twist o' t'baccy. *Ibid* 60, I done told you he's wuthless. **1939** Griswold *Sea Is. Lady* 577 **csSC** (as of c1895) [Gullah], Dey ain' wut fuh tek back nohow. [=They aren't worth taking back anyhow.]

B As adj.

Of use or value—used in neg constrs. [*OED2 worth* a. 6 →1535; *SND worth* adj. 2 "Of use or service"; 1.(1) *little-worth, -wirt* "worthless, of small value; in failing health"] *Gullah*

1838 [see **A** above]. **1909** *S. Atl. Qrly.* 8.42 [Gullah], Low-heartedness, or misery, as of discouragement and ill-health, are expressed in, simply, *me yent wut.* . . *'E yent wut* is He is worthless. **1922** Gonzales *Black Border* 131 **sSC, GA coasts** [Gullah], Da' nigguh *ent wut,* 'e too lub fuh drink rum. **1926** Smith *Gullah* 35 **sSC, GA coasts,** *'Ent wut'* (isn't, aren't worth), in the general sense of worthless, of no account: "Him ent wut'." **1930** Stoney–Shelby *Black Genesis* 111 **seSC,** "I swear-to-God, Br' Frog, you aint wut!" (You're worthless). **1939** Griswold *Sea Is. Lady* 131 **csSC** (as of 1865) [Gullah], Nigguh same like 'oman an' dawg ain' *wut* widout lick.

worvel See **warble**

w'osteh See **oyster**

wo'th See **worth**

would See **will B1**

‡**would-come** n

1946 *PADS* 6.33 **swVA** (as of 1940), *Would-come.* . . Something like a blackhead.

wound n, v, hence ppl adj *wounded* Usu |wund|; also |waʊnd|; for addit varr see quots Pronc-sp *wownd*

Std senses, var forms.

1789 Webster *Dissertations Engl. Lang.* 133, Similar reasons . . are opposed to the modern pronunciation of *wound.* I say *modern;* for in America *woond* is a recent innovation. *Ibid* 134, The fashionable pronunciation of *wound* destroys the rhime and infringes the rule of analogy. **1841** (1952) Cooper *Deerslayer* 221 **NY,** She's wownded—yes, the poor gal's wownded. **1876** *Galaxy* 21.527, There is no disputing that the correct—that is, the analogical—pronunciation of *wound* is not *woond,* but to rhyme with *round* and *found.* But by at least ninety-nine persons in a hundred in America it is pronounced *woond;* and that the same pronunciation prevails among the best speakers in England there is, I believe, no reason to doubt. **1892** *AN&Q* 8.232 **ceWI,** I cannot admit that "woond" is an affectation of modern date. It is a long half century since I was in school. I was specially taught that "woond" (for a hurt) was the test of an educated person, while "wownd" was the mark of ignorance and vulgarity. . . I have all my life said "woond," though I have been surrounded with "wownd." **1944** *PADS* 2.22 **sAppalachians,** *Wound* [waʊnd]: *n.* Wound. [*PADS* Ed: Also, reported from upper S.C., mid. Tenn. Mainly old people.] **1948** *WELS Suppl.,* [My father-in-law] (Maryland by Illinois to Wis.) used *wound,* meaning injury, as rhyming with *found.* Is it still found? It sounds so archaic. **1955** *PADS* 23.42 **e,cSC, eNC, seGA,** /o/ in *wounded* (very old-fashioned). **1961** Kurath–McDavid *Pronc. Engl.* 156, *Wound, wounded.* . . Except for New England, *wound* has the vowel /u/ of *two* among all social groups, either exclusively or predominantly. The vowel /aʊ/ of *down* is common only in parts of New England. Here it predominates decisively in the folk speech of Vermont, New Hampshire, Maine, and rural sections of western Connecticut; in New Hampshire and Maine it is common enough in the speech of the middle group (though usually by the side of /u/), but rare elsewhere in New England; in cultivated speech it persists only in New Hampshire and Maine. Outside of New England, *wound* with the vowel of *down* occurs only in folk speech . . and large parts of the Midland and the South don't have it at all. Rare instances of *wound* with the vowel /ʊ/ of *wood* have been observed in Upstate New York, and the vowel /o/ of *home* has some currency in folk speech along the coast of the Carolinas and Georgia. **1965** Carmony *Speech Terre Haute* 111 **sIN,** *Wound* is /u/ everywhere except in the speech of . . [one inf], who uses /æʊ/. **1976** Allen *LAUM* 3.254 **Upper MW** (as of c1950), *Wound.* . . Diphthongal /aʊ/ as in *sound* . . is preserved by nine scattered U[pper] M[idwest] infs . . six of whom have at least one parent born in New York, Pennsylvania, or Ohio. . . Much rarer . . is *wound* with vowel of *bull,* /ʊ/. **1989** Pederson *LAGS Tech. Index* 283 **Gulf Region,** *Wound.* [Of 914 infs, 12 offered proncs of the type [wɪund]; 3 infs, proncs of the type [wond]; 3 infs, proncs of the type [wʊnd(ɪd)]; 5 infs, proncs of the type [waʊnd]].

woundweed n

1 A **goldenrod 1;** see quots.

1876 Hobbs *Bot. Hdbk.* 134, Woundweed, Goldenrod, Solidago odora. **1930** Sievers *Amer. Med. Plants* 29, Fragrant Goldenrod. . . Other common names.—Sweet goldenrod, wound weed [etc]. **1940** Clute *Amer. Plant Names* 272, Solidago odora. Wound-weed. **1959** [see **2** below].

2 A **mullein** (here: *Verbascum thapsus*).

1959 Carleton *Index Herb. Plants* 128, *Wound-weed:* Solidago virgaurea [=*S. multiradiata*]; Verbascum thapsus.

wount v¹ See **want** v¹

wount v² See **will A**

wove v¹ See **weave A1**

wove v² See **wave** v

woved See **weave A2**

woven wire n, usu attrib Also *wove wire, woven wiring* **widespread, but less freq Atl coast, Gulf States, SW, Pacific** See Map

=**net wire.**

[**1849** *Boston Cultivator* (MA) 11.139, *Wickersham & Walker's Wire Fence.* We present our readers with the first of a series of patterns of the wire fence. . . We have already observed, that these woven wire nettings are suitable for many other purposes.] **1856** Cleaveland et al. *Village & Farm* 159, Woven wire fence stuff is now made at very moderate cost. . . This will do very well for the front fence of a small door-yard. **1883** *Freeborn Co. Std.* (Albert Lea MN) 24 May 1/3, A woven wire fence has been ordered from Chicago for the north side [of a cemetery] along the road. **1894** (1977) Montgomery Ward *Catalogue* 379, *Woven Wire Fencing.* . . Made of galvanized steel wire. . . For fencing farms, plantations, ranches, corrals, cemeteries, railroads, etc. A harmless fence for horses or cattle, sufficiently strong for vicious stock, a reliable protection against dogs for sheep. A legal fence everywhere. **1896** *Century Illustr. Mag.* 53.295 **CA,** He had put a bit of woven-wire fence about it to keep out the rabbits. **1965–70** *DARE* (Qu. L63, *Kinds of fences made with wire*) 377 Infs, **widespread, but less freq Atl coast, Gulf States, SW, Pacific,** Woven-wire fence; **CT**14, Woven-wire cattle fence; **KY**46, **LA**29, **NC**68, **VA**57, Wove-wire fence; (Qu. L64, *The kind of wooden fence that's built around a garden or near a house*) Infs **CO**44, **WA**1,

Woven-wire fence; (Qu. L65, . . *Kinds of fences*) Infs **NE**8, **NY**148, **PA**201, **SD**1, **TX**41, 102, **WA**30, **WI**30, Woven-wire fence. **1972** Thomas *Pop. Dict. Ozarks Talk* 96, Woven-wire fence: . . Fence, made of woven- or web-wire, commonly built around a yard, garden, or a "piglot." **1989** Pederson *LAGS Tech. Index* 63 **Gulf Region,** *Wire fence* . . wove wire (7 [of 914 infs]) . . woven(-)wire (fence) (54) . . woven wiring (1). *Ibid* 405 [Urban Suppl.], Woven-wire (fence) (1 [inf]) . . woven-wire fence (2). **2004** *Star–Herald* (Scottsbluff NE) 7 Oct sec B 4/1, [Advt:] The Auction House. . . woven wire fence.

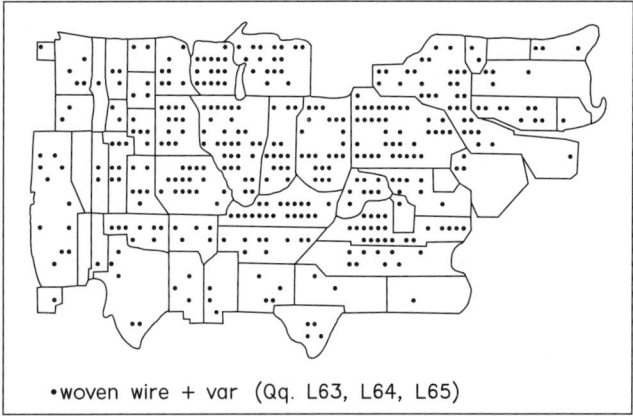

•woven wire + var (Qq. L63, L64, L65)

wownd See **wound**

wozzen See **wizzen**

wrack n Also sp *rack* [*OED2 wrack sb.*² 1 "Now *dial.*"] **esp NEast**

A wrecked ship or other vessel.

1720 *Amer. Weekly Mercury* (Philadelphia PA) 15 Sept 3/2, Sloop . . was in the Night wrackt on the said Island the Master, Mate and 12 Men were drowned the five men got on shore on several peices of the Wrack. **1824** Cooper *Pilot* 2.94 **Nantucket MA,** I thought I saw her a wrack, as plainly, ay, as plainly as you may see the stump of that mast. **1885** Twain *Huck. Finn* 96 **MO** [Black], I doan' want to go fool'n 'long er no wrack. . . Like as not dey's a watchman on dat wrack. **1908** Wasson *Home from Sea* 22 **sME coast,** There wa'n't ary spar showing out there two minutes' time since. . . I guess likely no wrack won't hang together long when Old Aaron breaks. **1975** Gould *ME Lingo* 225, *Rack*—A touchstone word to test the true Maine coastal tongue. It is the way to pronounce wreck. Wreck Island in Muscongus Bay is "*Rack*" Island."

wrack v

To salvage or plunder (a wrecked vessel); hence vbl n *wracking;* n *wracker.*

1791 *City Gaz. & Daily Advt.* (Charleston SC) 18 July 3/2, The above three sloops are wrackers, and have on board a quantity of sugars, &c. saved out of the brig Lively. **1821** *Carolina Gaz.* (Charleston SC) 1 Dec 2/1, They . . arrived at Key Taviniere, which is the general place of rendezvous for all the English wrackers. **1876** *Scribner's Mth.* 13.155 **ceNJ,** If a ship comes ashore, they lend a hand to save the people and "wrack" the vessel. **1883** *Daily Picayune* (New Orleans LA) 12 June 9/1, The wrackers gev her up, an' I believe she was raised two years after by a Mexican company. **1915** (1916) Johnson *Highways New Engl.* 196 **Cape Cod MA,** After a pause the fisherman mentioned that he used to go "wracking." One wreck he worked on was the *Jason* laden with brown sugar.

wracking bar n [Var of *wrecking bar,* perh infl by *rack* to force out of shape]

1968 *DARE* (Qu. L39, *An iron bar with a bent end, used for pulling nails, opening boxes, and so on*) Inf **MD**13, Wracking [ɹækɪn] bar—with a bent end. **2007** UT Assoc. Ag. Educators *Yellow Dog* 1.2 (Internet), Young Farmer interrupts class to tell me he found a nail in one of the boards. Told him where the wracking bar was. Said thanks to the planer he didn't need it now.

wrang See **wrangler**

wrangatang n [Pun on *orangoutang*] **West** =**wrangler 1.**

1926 James *Smoky* 148 **West,** "Wrangatang" (day wrangler). **1938** Muller *Chico* 87 **nWY,** He didn't want him to do much work—possibly help the "wrangatang" and perhaps do the odd chores around the wagons. **1947** *SW Rev.* 32.43 **NM,** Paw's never gonna have a stock ranch to amount to anything and you're never gonna be a wrangatang.

wrangle v Also sp *rangle* [By folk-etym from **wrango**] **West** Cf **wrangler 1**

To round up, herd, train, or otherwise deal with (horses or other livestock); to work as a horse herder or trainer; hence vbl n *wrangling.*

    1885 *Titusville Morning Herald* (PA) 15 July [3]/3 (newspaperarchive.com) **MT,** The morning call, the falling tents, the "wrangling" of 1,500 cow-horses, . . are each sufficient for entertaining sketches. **1893** Griggs *Lyrics Lariat* 44 **West,** Out West,/ With lucre unblest,/ He rangled for others a year. *Ibid* 255, *Rangler*—a horse-herder. **1893** *KS Univ. Qrly.* 1.142 **WY,** *Wrangle:* to manage sheep or other stock. **1903** (1965) Adams *Log Cowboy* 197 **NM,** Forrest detailed Rod Wheat to wrangle the horses. **1923** Sinclair *Parowan Bonanza* 83 **NV,** Tommy wrangles the burros and does the dirty work. **1931** *AmSp* 6.230 **neOR,** To 'wrangle' means to round up the herd of horses or cattle. **1933** *AmSp* 8.1.31 **nwTX** [Ranch diction], *Wrangle.* To attend the *remuda.* **1937** [see **wrangler 1**]. **1938** in Lib. of Congress *Amer. Memory: WPA Life Hist.* (Internet) **neTX,** The principal [work] was wrangling horses and we broke about 100 horses each Spring and Fall. **1966** *DARE* (Qu. L43b, *To get a horse ready to ride*) Inf **MT5,** Wrangle; (Qu. OO27b, *Talking about riding horses: "All my life I've _____ [horses]."*) Inf **WA3,** Wrangled. **1992** *Pinedale Roundup* (WY) 6 Aug 5/1, For most 14-year-old boys, wrangling horses for a roundup wagon would be damn near top job. **2005** *Galveston Daily News* (TX) 24 May 1/2, As of March 6, police officers in Texas City recorded more than 65 hours wrangling cattle this year. . . [T]he police department had to spend more than $5,700 the last two years rounding up livestock.

wrangle horse n Also *wrangler, wrango horse* **West** Cf **cow horse, cutting ~**

A horse used in rounding up, corralling, and tending horses and other livestock.

    1925 (1926) James *Drifting Cowboy* 80, I had a wrango horse tied up and even though I'm a long ways from rested, I see where I have to saddle him up and get to work again. **1929** *AmSp* 5.66 **NE** [Cattle country talk], A "wrangler" or "wrangle horse" is one kept in the "pony pasture" or corral for use in catching and driving in other horses; its rider is also a "wrangler." **1941** Rollinson *Hoofprints* 29 **WY,** Willis went after the horses farther on in the pasture, and told me to bring in the cows that were now in sight of us. The old wrangle horse that I rode knew what to do. **1953** *Smoke Signals* (Pinedale WY) 25 Nov 2/2 (as of c1913), Every freighter always had a saddle horse along for a wrangle horse. These wrangle horses were interesting. They were always kept saddled during the day but were never led, they were just turned loose. . . At night they were blanketed and tied up to one of the wagons while everything else was turned loose. **1970** *Dec. Mag.* 12.45 **nwNV,** The bay gelding . . [was] kept in the corral as a wrango horse. **1976** *ID State Jrl.* (Pocatello) 13 Aug sec C 17/1, In a rush for freedom he knocked the wrangle horse sideways into the corral with such force that an entire panel collapsed. **2005** *DARE* File—Internet **MT,** [Advt:] Percheron quarter horse, wrangle horse, very athletic, current on shots.

wrangler n **West**

1 also *rangler:* A ranch hand who herds or trains saddle horses; broadly, a cowboy. [**wrangle** v] Cf **wrangatang, wrango**

    1885 *Titusville Morning Herald* (PA) 15 July [3]/2 (newspaperarchive.com) **MT,** Each bunch of horses is in charge of its "wrangler" (herder). From these bunches the boys "cut out" (select) fresh horses twice a day or oftener, and about ten horses can be found to each participant in the "round-up." **1888** *Century Illustr. Mag.* 35.849 **West,** There are two herders, always known as "horse-wranglers"—one for the day and one for the night. **1893** [see **wrangle** v]. **1893** *KS Univ. Qrly.* 1.142 **KS,** *Wrangler:* a herd manager. **1913** *DN* 4.27 **NW,** *Night wrangler.* . . A man who tends a lot of horses at night. Used generally in the cattle-raising states. **1929** Dobie *Vaquero* 189 **TX,** The wrangler, whose business it was to furnish us with fresh mounts on short notice, day or night, generally followed along behind the herd with his remuda. **1933** *AmSp* 8.1.31 **nwTX** [Ranch diction], *Wrangler.* One who attends the *remuda.* **1936** McCarthy *Lang. Mosshorn* np **West,** The wrangler herds the cavvy during the day and bunches them in a rope corral at meal time. The horse wrangler must keep the cook supplied with wood and water. **1937** in Lib. of Congress *Amer. Memory: WPA Life Hist.*

(Internet) **TX,** I hired Wild Hoss Jerry to take charge of picking up wild broncos and to do most of my wrangling. . . Wild Hoss Jerry was the best wrangler I ever saw. . . I was no mean wrangler, . . but Jerry could do all that any man could do and do it quicker and better. **1938** *Ibid* **neTX,** I became a top wrangler. This statement may sound wiffy, but we never tackled a critter that we didn't succeed in busting. **1939** (1973) FWP *Guide MT* 416, *Wrangler*—Herder in charge of saddle stock. **1949** *PADS* 11.27 **wTX** (as of 1911–29), *Wrangler.* . . A cowboy. . . a herder. **1966** *DARE* Tape **NM14,** Otherwise the horse wrangler has got to get wood for the cook. **1981** *KS Qrly.* 13.2.71, *Wrangler* . . buckaroo charged with caring for the "cavvy" (horse herd), a job performed by boys or helpers. **1984** Smith *SW Vocab.* 115, *Wrangler:* A cowpoke. A cowboy who rounds up livestock [sic]. **2007** Popkin *Taming the Spirited Child* 160, Your encouragement to your spirited child for positive effort, improvement, and success is like the lump of sugar that a horse wrangler might use to tame a wild horse.

2 See **wrangle horse.**

wrangling See **wrangle**

wrango n Also sp *rango* [Abbr for *cavyrango* (and varr) < MexSpan *caballerango*] **West** Cf **wrangle, wrangler 1**

A ranch hand who takes care of saddle horses and sometimes performs other menial tasks.

    [**1896** *Windsor Mag.* 4.514, The new cavyrango of the 69 hes just shot the Kid because he wanted to fetch his horses in to water.] **1921** Furlong *Let 'Er Buck* 93 **eOR,** It seems likely that the term, "wrangler," comes from *caverango*—the Spanish for the man who had the care of the saddle horses. East of the Columbia River the term "wrango" or "rango" was used. **1924** James *Cowboys N. & S.* 63, He told a "wrango" to corral all the broke work-horses on the ranch. **1938** Muller *Chico* 175 **nWY,** The hosses were out in the hills being wrangled by a kid wrango. **1940** Writers' Program *Guide NV* 75, The buckaroo who herds the saddle horses is the *rango,* and the one who takes the night shift with horses is the *night wrango,* the *night hawk* or *owl.* **1964** Jackman–Long *OR Desert* 104 **eOR,** The rango rustled wood, built the fire, helped the cook load and unload, looked after the horses in the daytime, did the camp chores. . . The "rango pan" was the big pan the riders put the dishes in; the cook *never* had to gather up the dirty dishes. [*DARE* Ed: Cf **wreck pan**] **1981** in Lib. of Congress *Amer. Memory: Buckaroos in Paradise* (Internet) **nNV,** [Sound recording:] Now in the earlier days when there was no fences and fields, the wrango was the man that took care of the horses and herded 'em out to graze. . . But right now the horses are in the field and they don't have to be watched so close, so bringing 'em from the field into the corral is called wrangling them. . . And now we generally take turns—a different man will go out and bring the horses in every morning so for that specific morning he's temporary; no one is the wrango. They also call 'em sometimes the cavvy-wrango. The cavvy-wrango means the fellow that runs in the saddle horses, because a cavvy is the Spanish word for . . a bunch of saddle horses.

wrango horse See **wrangle horse**

wrap jack(et) See **rap jacket**

wrasse n

Std: a fish of the family Labridae. For other names of var of these see **bluefish 2, hogfish a, hog snapper, kelpfish b, razor fish 1, sheepshead 4, señorita, slippery dick 1, tautog**

wrassle(r), wrastle(r) See **wrestle A1**

wrathy adj Also *rathy, wrothy* [The word appears in ME (as *wrothy*), and reappears, or was reinvented, in the early 19th cent. This reappearance is attested slightly later (1839) in Britain than in the US, but it seems unlikely that it is an Americanism. Cf *OED2 wrathy, wrothy, EDD wrathy*]

Angry, irascible.

    1819 in 1860 Alexander *Forty Years' Letters* 1.3, I expect . . by this time you have waxed exceedingly wrothy with your humble servant on account of his long silence. **1827** Cooper *Red Rover* 1.221 **RI,** You are wrathy, friend, without reason. **1828** (1970) Webster *Amer. Dict., Wràthy.* . . Very angry; a colloquial word. [*DARE* Ed: The accent on the headword marks it as having the "Italian sound" of *a,* i.e., [ɑ].] **1837** (1955) Crockett *Almanacks* 92 **TN,** I was so wrothy I should have scun him alive. **1842** Kirkland *Forest Life* 1.103 **MI,** Oh! you're wrathy, a'n't ye? **1851** Burke *Polly Peablossom* 52 **MO,** I diskivered mischief was er cumin, fur I never see a critter show rathy like he did. **1853**

Simms *Sword & Distaff* 350 **SC,** She stood some five paces off, . . quite as much confounded as he was wrothy.   **1899** (1912) Green *VA Folk-Speech* 491, *Wrathy.* . . Angry.   **1905** *DN* 3.24 **cCT,** *Wrathy.* . . Angry.   **1907** *DN* 3.220 **nwAR,** *Wrathy.* . . Angry.   **1909** *DN* 3.390 **eAL, wGA,** *Wrathy.* . . Angry.   **1941** *LANE* Map 472 *(Angry),* [*Wrathy* is a frequent resp in **ME, NH,** and **eVT** and on **Nantucket** and **Martha's Vineyard;** elsewhere it occurs rarely or not at all. The infs are about evenly divided between those who use proncs of the type ['ræθɪ] and those who use the type ['rɑθɪ] or ['rɑθɪ]; a few use the type ['rɒθɪ] or ['rɔθɪ].]   **1946** *PADS* 5.43 **VA,** *Wrathy.* . . Angry; common everywhere.   **1958** Blasingame *Dakota Cowboy* 37 **SD,** He was extremely wrathy. He blistered the men in a most scathing way.   **1967** Bourne *Woman in Levi's* 182 **AZ,** Many are the range expressions describing aggravation or fury. Range riders say: . . "The old lady got wrathy about the mud on her floor."   **1967–70** *DARE* (Qu. K16, *A cow with a bad temper*) Inf **PA**163, Wrathy ['ræθɪ]; (Qu. GG4, *Stirred up, angry: "When he saw them coming he got _____."*) Infs **MA**73, **NY**66, Wrathy; **OH**95, Wrathy ['rɒθɪ]; **PA**122, Wrathy ['ræθɪ]; (Qu. GG40, *Words or expressions meaning violently angry*) Inf **NE**3, Wrathy ['ræθɪ].   **1973** Allen *LAUM* 1.359 **Upper MW** (as of c1950), He got (became) *angry.* . . *Wrathy,* not recorded in fieldwork, is used by 56 [mailed checklist] respondents.   **2008** in 2009 *DARE* File—Internet **nME,** You see, when you poke fun at a superstition, the true believers get kind of wrathy about it. (My spell checker still doesn't like the Maine word, "wrathy".)

wreck pan n   Also *wreck tub*   **West**
A receptacle for dirty dishes.
   1930 Raine–Barnes *Cattle* 296 **West,** This was known all over the range country as the "wreck pan," and the luckless tenderfoot who did not drop his dirty dishes into it but set them in a nice little heap on the mess-box lid was in trouble.   **1936** Rollins *Cowboy* 260 **West,** After eating . . [he] placed his dirty dishes on the table instead of dropping them into the "wreck pan," a large dishpan lying on the ground beneath the table.   **1946** Mora *Trail Dust* 166 **West,** After the meal, we got up and put our tin plates, which had been well mopped up with that last piece of corn bread, together with the cups and other implements into the "wreck tub" under the chuck-box table.

wrench   See **rinse 4**

wrestle v, n
A Forms.
1 pronc-spp *(w)rassle, (w)rastle;* for addit varr see quots; hence nouns *wrassler, wrastler.*   [*OED2* a1225 →; widespread in Brit dial]
   1772 in 1915 *New Engl. Hist. & Geneal. Reg.* 69.15 **MA,** The Rassell was to been. . . Went to Lancaster to a Wrassell.   **1800** in 1956 Eliason *Tarheel Talk* 321 **cnNC,** Rasell.   **a1824** (1937) Guild *Jrl.* 3.266 **VT,** Then he say, I want wrastle unless you will bet a dollar.   **1867** Harris *Sut Lovingood Yarns* 137 **TN,** Luved kissin, wrastlin, an' biled cabbige.   **1884** Smith *Bill Arp's Scrap Book* 13 **nwGA,** Ike McCoy was perhaps the best rasler in all Cherokee.   **1893** Shands *MS Speech* 52, *Rassle.* . . Negro and illiterate white for *wrestle.*   **1899** Garland *Boy Life* 370 **nwIA** (as of c1870s), Go ahead, Mett, don't lay there and tire him all out. That ain't rastlin'.   **1902** Day *Pine Tree Ballads* 127 **ME,** He allowed that as a *wrassler* he could sort of set the pace.   **1909** *DN* 3.362 **eAL, wGA,** *Rastle.* . . See *wrestle.* Ibid 390, *Wrestle.* . . To wrestle. *Wrastler.* . . Wrestler.   **1915** *DN* 4.188 **swVA,** *Rassel,* Variant of *wrestle.*   **1917** *DN* 4.404 **neOH,** *Wrastle.* . . The only native form.   **1927** [see **B** below].   **1934** *WV Review* Dec 77, *Wrassle.*   **1963** Burroughs *Head-First* 100 **CO,** Boys . . with skinned knuckles and holes in the knees of their pants from having "rassled" in the mud.   **1966–70** *DARE* (Qu. Y12b, *A real fight in which blows are struck*) Inf **FL**10, Wrassling; (Qu. EE21b, *When boys were fighting very actively . . "For a while those fellows really _____."*) Inf **CT**12, Wrassled; (Qu. EE33, . . *Outdoor games . . that children play*) Infs **NC**45, **OH**77, Wrassling; **OR**10, Indian wrassling; (Qu. FF4, *Names and joking names for different kinds of dancing parties*) Inf **NY**234, Hog wrassle.   **2002** Perry *Population 485* 88 **WI,** Lifting weights in a town where most men swing hammers or run shovels or wrassle logs feels absurd and ersatz.
2 |ˈrɑsl|; pronc-sp *wrostle.*   [Brit dial]
   1890 *DN* 1.76 **NEng,** *Wrastle* [rasl], also [ræsl]: for *wrestle.*   **1908** (1911) Gale *Friendship Village* 129 **WI,** We'd all ought to wrostle with the feelin', I expect.   **1949** Turner *Africanisms* 278 **sSC, GA coasts** [Gullah], [rɑsəl].
B Sense.
To dance; a dance.   Cf **hog-wrestle**

1927 *AmSp* 3.24 **eTX** [Sawmill talk], A dance is a . . "wrastle." Ibid 131 [College slang], To dance is "to rag," "to struggle," "to wrestle."   **1969** Sorden *Lumberjack Lingo* 143 **NEng, Gt Lakes,** Wrestle—A dance.

wrestling jack n   Also *wrestling root*   Cf **jack** n[1] **15**
See quots.
   1938 FWP *Guide DE* 106, The root of "Rassling Jack" is chewed to cure "risins and miseries" of the stomach; if the leaves are masticated, the chewer is given great strength for wrestling.   **c1938** in 1970 Hyatt *Hoodoo* 1.240 **MD** [Black], I was in the woods rakin' up, heapin' up *shadders* [=pine needles] . . an' I found those little *roots.* . . An' I ast mah boss, I says, "Mr. Paine, whut is this?" He said, "Oh, that's *rasslin' root* . . " . . I taken up five or six an' put 'em in mah pocket. . . Of course, I wanted to be champion rassler around there.

wribbly   See **ribbly**

wriggler n
1 =**wiggler 1.**   esp **Inland Nth, PA, CA**   See Map
   1845 *MA Ploughman* 5 Apr 1/7, I have had a cistern of perfectly clear rain-water all summer, from all wrigglers or embryo mosquitoes, by merely dropping in a few rain brook fishes one to three inches long.   **1871** *Titusville Morning Herald* (PA) 12 Aug [3]/3 (newspaper-archive.com), Tryonville barkeepers are now compelled to pass their whisky through strainers before selling it to customers to keep "wrigglers" and other soft water animalcules from being swallowed.   **1887** *Stevens Point Jrl.* (WI) 30 Apr [3]/7 (newspaperarchive.com), He had two hogsheads filled with water, and into one he put a lot of wrigglers or embryo mosquitoes.   **1905** *San Antonio Daily Light* (TX) 26 Oct 2/4, The young mosquito, or wriggler, lives in water at least seven to twelve days.   **1949** *Nat. Hist.* 58.382, Wrigglers of the Pitcher Plant Mosquito are found only in the water collected in pitcher plant leaves.   **1965–70** *DARE* (Qu. R14, *Small worm-like things [seen in rain barrels or standing water] that hatch into mosquitoes*) 37 Infs, **esp Inland Nth, PA, CA,** Wriggler; [**MD**45, Wriggle things].

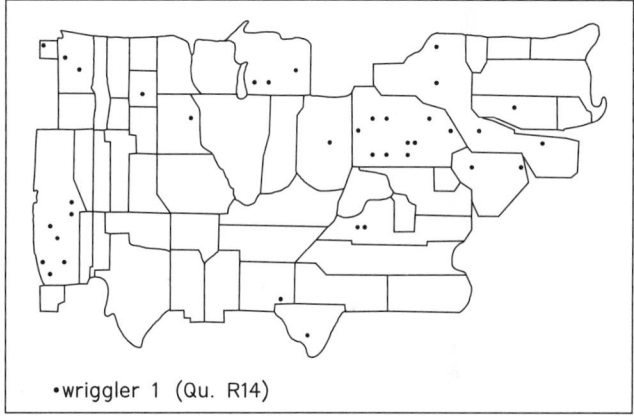

•wriggler 1 (Qu. R14)

2 =**earthworm.**
   1856 *Knickerbocker* 48.419 **NY,** In vain we turned over large stones, tore the bark from decayed trunks, and delved with a stick in richer places. A few wrigglers were all which could be obtained.   **1955** *Denton Rec.–Chron.* (TX) 4 Sept sec 2 8/1, [Caption:] Worms—not just any old earthworms but hybrid Georgia wrigglers—are turning into hard cash for two Denton men.   **1967** *DARE* (Qu. P5, . . *The common worm used as bait*) Inf **SC**39, Wriggler.   **1972** *New Mexican* (Santa Fe NM) 27 Sept sec A 10/1, [Headline:] Worm farmer quitting back-bending wriggler tending.   **2004** Stewart *Earth Moved* 204, My worms have definite likes and dislikes, demonstrated by which foods are left to rot untouched in the bin, and which are covered in a mass of wrigglers within a few hours of being offered to them.

wriggletail n   Also *wrigglertail*
=**wiggler 1.**
   1966–70 *DARE* (Qu. R14, *Small worm-like things [seen in rain barrels or standing water] that hatch into mosquitoes*) Inf **AL**2, Wrigglertails; **TX**104, Wriggletail.

wring-tail n, also attrib   **West**   Cf **ringy**
A horse that twists its tail about as a sign of nervousness or pain; hence adj *wring-tailed.*
   1929 Dobie *Vaquero* 270 **West,** When a horse "wrings" his tail it is ev-

idence of nerve-wracking pain. The "wringing" is occasioned by the pic-ture-show cowboy's spurring or lashing the horse and at the same time holding him in. If I were a censor I should eliminate every picture that shows a "wring tail" horse. **1944** Adams *Western Words* 181, *Wring-tail*—A horse of nervous disposition that has been ridden to exhaustion and spurred to make him go, causing him to develop the habit of wring-ing his tail as he runs. Jerking on the bits also develops this habit. **1959** Back *Horses & Trails* 101 **WY,** Mebbe your saddle-horse is a wring-tail—one of those nervous boys that's always flopping his tail around. **1979** Keith *Hell* 46 **MT,** When I dropped the throw rope, she was a "wring tail," always switching her tail, and she'd switched it over the rope as I'd dropped it. **2006** in 2009 *DARE* File—Internet **CA,** He [=a horse] really was a pig. Sullen, wring tailed, neurotic, badly trained, bad attitude, etc.

wringy See **ringy**

wrinkle n [Brit dial var of *winkle*] **ME** Cf **pennywinkle 1,** *DNE wrinkle¹* n 1

The common periwinkle (family Littorinidae); hence vbl n *wrinkling* gathering periwinkles.

1911 U.S. Bur. Census *Fisheries 1908* 315, Sea Snails *(Gastero-poda). . .* They are found on all our coasts, and are known as "periwin-kles," . . "winkles," "wrinkles," [etc.] [**1925** *DN* 5.346 **Nfld,** *Wrinkle. . .* Periwinkle.] **1954** Young *Is. New Engl.* 71 **ME,** Fishermen and their families along the Maine coast ate periwinkles—"wrinkles" they called them. **2001** *Yankee* Mar 52 **ME,** He also used to gather clams and peri-winkles, which he calls "wrinkles." **2002** Roorbach *Into Woods* 58 **ME,** That fellow lost his son this spring. . . Boy and his partner. . . Six hun-dred pounds of wrinkles in the bottom of their canoe. **2008** *Bangor Daily News* (ME) 13 Dec (Internet), Fergerson was reported missing . . while harvesting periwinkles, known locally as "wrinkles," in Lubec Channel. **2009** *Portland Press Herald* (ME) 5 Apr (Internet), Jobs like "wrinkling"—the local term for heading out into the intertidal zone at low tide and gathering periwinkles for sale to a local shellfish whole-saler.

wrinkled steak(s) See **wrinkles**

wrinkledy adj Also *wrinklety* **esp Sth, S Midl** Cf Intro "Language Changes" III.1

Wrinkled.

1900 *Harper's New Mth. Mag.* 100.217 **Sth** [Black], He face were es black an' es wrinkledy es er warnut. **1926** Roberts *Time of Man* 356 **KY,** Wrinkledy face! **1930** Stoney-Shelby *Black Genesis* 65 **seSC** [Black], Twas some sort o' fowl, but it had a hard back like a roof, stickin' out ober de sides, an' kind o' rough an' wrinkledy like a goat horn. **1968–69** *DARE* (Qu. LL3b, *Shrunk, dried up:* "He's a little _____ old man.") Infs **KY**11, **TN**26, Wrinkledy. **1977** *WI State Jrl.* (Madison) 9 June comic sec, [*The Ryatts* comic strip:] Missy, you and Winky get in here! I thought you were going to make the bed for me! [Missy:] I did *my* side! That's *Winky's* side that's wrinkledy! **1986** Pederson *LAGS Concordance,* 1 inf, **neAR,** Wrinkledy—referring to peach seed; 1 inf, **ceTX,** Wrinkledy—somewhat wrinkled; 1 inf, **ceTX,** Wrinkledy-round—of cabbage squash. **1997** in 2004 Montgomery-Hall *Dict. Smoky Mt. Engl.* 661 **wNC, eTN,** *Wrinkledy . .* Wrinkled. . . known to nine consultants.

wrinkle-hawk See **winkle-hawk**

wrinkles n pl Also *wrinkle(d) steak(s)* *esp freq among Black speakers* Cf **ruffles**

=**chitterlings 1.**

1964 *Woodlawn Booster* (Chicago IL) 8 Jan 5/3, What the heck are "Wrinkled Steaks"; and what are they doing at a "Society Dinner"; and how come they don't come smooth, round, and one inch thick, huh? I don't know what you're talking about, but something smells funny! **1965** *Progress-Index* (Petersburg VA) 27 Dec 8/8, [Advt:] *Forest View Restaurant . .* featuring *Home Cooked Pigs Feet And Wrinkle Steaks.* **1966** *Jet* 8 Sept 29 [Black], After putting on a big pot of Chicago wrin-kles (chitterlings), SKI Claude J. Smith holds up a sample of his efforts for inspection aboard the U.S.S. Impervious. **1969** *This Week Mag.* 12 Oct 15/2 *(Mathews Coll.)* **Sth** [Black], "Ruffles" and "wrinkles" are two of the pet names for chitterlings. **1969** *DARE* File, *Wrinkle-steak* = chitterlings. Said to be a recent term among Negroes now that Whites have taken to eating chitterlings. **1971** Roberts *Third Ear* np [Black], *Wrinkles . .* chitterlings. **1973** Allen *LAUM* 1.257 **Upper MW** (as of c1950), *Harslet . .* the edible internal organs of a pig or calf. . . wrinkles [1 inf, **IA;** inf Black]. **2000** *NADS Letters* **DC** (as of 1959), Wrinkled

steaks—chitterlings; first heard this term in the Washington, DC area when I attended college. **2001** *DARE* File **FL** [Black], My uncle re-ferred to the chitterlings he brought . . for dinner as "wrinkled steaks." The way he pronounced it, the term sounded like "wrinkle steaks." **2007** *DARE* File—Internet **NC,** Chitlins. Haven't had any of those since I left NC 6 yrs ago. My home town of Fayetteville has a great Drive-in . . patronized by African-Americans, that offers "Wrinkled Steak Spe-cials."

wrinklety See **wrinkledy**

wrinkling See **wrinkle**

wrist n [Prob < Du *rist* bunch (of berries, grapes), string (of onions)] **Upstate NY** Cf **trace** n³

See quots.

1901 *DN* 2.150 **cNY,** *Wrist. . .* A *wrist* of corn, an ear of corn whose husks have been pulled back and tied for hanging up. "In one end of the building were pumpkins and numerous wrists of corn." Common among old settlers in Cayuga, Oswego Co., N.Y. **1938** Shafer *Smokefires* 5 **ceNY,** Women, working in the cornfields, threw down their heavy wrists of corn and ran towards the village. **1941** Arthur–Arthur *Rural Pro-gram* 7 **cnNY,** The marching team carries ears of corn, while sheaves of grain and wrists of corn are used on stage.

writ See **write B1a, 2a**

write v Usu |raɪt|; also |rat, rɑt|; for addit varr see quot c1970 at **A** below Pronc-sp *rat*

A Proncs.

c1970 Pederson *Dial. Surv. Rural GA (If you want to send a message to someone, you _____ him a letter)* **seGA,** [Of 64 infs, most offered proncs of the type [raˆɪt]; 9 infs, proncs of the type [rəˇɪt]; 6 infs, proncs of the type [ra:ɛt]; 5 infs, proncs of the type [rɑˇɪt]; 4 infs, proncs of the type [ra:t]; 1 inf, [rɑˇt].] **1989** Pederson *LAGS Tech. Index* 356 **Gulf Region,** *Write.* [For the infinitive, 12 of 914 infs offered proncs of the type [rɑt].] **1990** Amory *Cat & Curmudgeon* 193 **eTX,** "Because," the man went on, "this fella says he rats for it [=the *New York Times*], and he wants to rat about the ranch for it."

B Gram forms.

1 past: usu *wrote;* also:

a *writ.* [*OED2* "now *dial.*"] **chiefly Sth, S Midl** See Map

1851 Hooper *Widow Rugby's Husband* 81 **AL,** Well, Seagroves he writ the letter. **1893** Shands *MS Speech* 68, *Writ. . .* Used by negroes for *wrote.* **1894** Frederic *Marsena* 130 **nNY,** She never writ a line to you. **1901** Harben *Westerfelt* 42 **nGA,** As soon as you writ the price you wus willin' to give in a lumpin' sum, Luke set to scheming. **1906** *DN* 3.164 **nwAR,** *Writ. . .* Wrote. **1917** *DN* 4.419 **wNC,** *Writ. . .* Wrote. Also Ill., S. Car. **1923** *DN* 5.224 **swMO,** *Writ. . .* Wrote. **1934** *WV Review* Dec 77, Not long ago I heard a man in central West Virginia say that he *writ* a certain person in regard to a matter under discussion. **c1940** Eliason *Word Lists FL* 12 **wFL,** *Writ:* past tense of *write. Rare.* **1945** FWP *Lay My Burden Down* 117 **LA** (as of c1865) [Black], Young Master's children writ to me once in a while. **1965–70** *DARE* (Qu. OO34a, *Talking about writing a letter home:* "It's weeks since she last _____ [us a letter].") Infs **IN**79, **LA**6, **OK**58, **VA**15, Writ; **GA**72, **NC**69, **TX**90, Writ—old-fashioned; **AZ**11, Writ [laughter]; **MA**5, Writ—obsolete; **MS**69, Writ—Negro. **1989** Pederson *LAGS Tech. Index* 356 **Gulf Region,** *Write.* [For the preterite, 10 of 914 infs offered *writ.*]

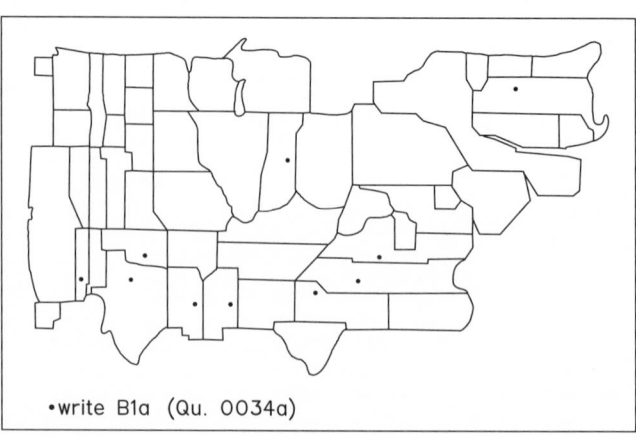

•write B1a (Qu. OO34a)

b *write.* [*OED2* →a1700]

1966–67 *DARE* (Qu. OO34a, *Talking about writing a letter home: "It's weeks since she last _____ [us a letter]."*) Infs **SC**10, 26, Write. **1989** Pederson *LAGS Tech. Index* 356 **Gulf Region,** Write. . . [For the preterite, 2 of 914 infs offered *write*.]

c *writ(t)en,* rarely *writtened.* **chiefly Sth, S Midl**

1862 Epperly *Civil War Letters (Montgomery Coll.),* Wee have bin on a long march sins I writen to you last. **1884** *Anglia* 7.253 **Sth, S Midl** [Black], To the regular forms of the Irregular verbs as used by the whites, the Negro adds the following forms of his own. . . *Pres.* write— *Past.* . . written, writtened. **1906** *DN* 3.164 **nwAR,** Written. . . Wrote. "I written to him yesterday." **1923** *DN* 5.224 **swMO,** Written. . . Wrote. "I written him a letter." **1927** *AmSp* 3.2 **Ozarks,** She written a letter. **1927** in 1944 *ADD* **NC,** Written. . . I writen you. **1941** O'Donnell *Great Big Doorstep* 41 **sLA,** You mean to tell me you written that song, Shoepick? **1965–70** *DARE* (Qu. OO34a, *Talking about writing a letter home: "It's weeks since she last _____ [us a letter]."*) 10 Infs, **scattered,** Written; **NC**84, **UT**4, Written, [corr to] wrote. **1989** Pederson *LAGS Tech. Index* 356 **Gulf Region,** Write. [For the preterite, 13 of 914 infs offered *written*.]

‡d *wroten.*

1976 Tyler *Searching for Caleb* 236 **cnMD** [Black], Mr. Caleb wroten it down on a piece of paper.

2 past pple, ppl adj: usu *written;* also:

a *(w)rit.* [*OED2* "now *dial.* or *arch.*"] **esp Sth, S Midl** See Map

1843 Thompson *Major Jones' Courtship* 7 **GA,** This book of letters was to oblige a frend. **1890** Holley *Samantha among Brethren* 19 **NY,** Josiah said it wuz a masterly dockument. And it wuz writ well. **1901** Harben *Westerfelt* 130 **nGA,** The book hain't writ that could explain a woman. **1924** in 1952 Mathes *Tall Tales* 31 **sAppalachians,** Hit's writ in some kind of writin' that nobody in Dry Cove can't read hit. **1940** (1968) Haun *Hawk's Done Gone* 6 **eTN,** The pokeberry ink is faded till it looks like the name is writ with catnip tea. **1953** Atwood *Survey of Verb Forms* 26, Write. . . The past participle is recorded in the context "I have (written) a letter." . . *Writ* . . occurs a few times in the Merrimack Valley and elsewhere in n.e. N. Eng. In c. W. Va. this form occurs in four or five contiguous communities; elsewhere in the M[iddle] A[tlantic] S[tates] and the S[outh] A[tlantic] S[tates] it occurs only in isolation, and rarely. **1965–70** *DARE* (Qu. OO34b, *Talking about writing a letter home: "She should have _____ [long ago]."*) Infs **GA**73, **ID**1, **MS**71, **OK**58, **VA**15, Writ; **MS**69, Writ—Negro; **MA**5, Writ—obsolete; **NC**69, Writ—old-fashioned. **1976** Garber *Mountain-ese* 103 **sAppalachians,** That boy hasn't writ home a single time. **1989** Pederson *LAGS Tech. Index* 356 **Gulf Region,** Write. [For the past participle, 3 of 914 infs offered *writ*.]

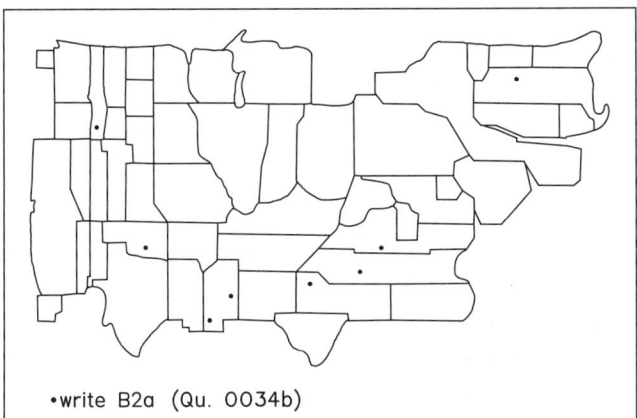

•write B2a (Qu. OO34b)

b *wrote.* [*OED2* 1565 → "[now] *dial.* or *illiterate*"]

c1770 in 1953 Woodmason *Carolina Backcountry* 191 **SC,** Why I have not lately wrote his Lordship, has been owing to dread. **1781** *PA Jrl. & Weekly Advt.* (Philadelphia) 16 May 1/3, One of the most common vulgarisms or blunders . . is putting the preterite for the participle. . . *wrote,* for *written.* **1862** in 2004 Montgomery–Hall *Dict. Smoky Mt. Engl.* 661 **wNC, eTN,** I have wrote so much, I hardly know what to write. **1893** *DN* 1.278 **wCT,** Write [preterite and past participle]— wrote. **1905** *DN* 3.102 **nwAR,** Preterites occur in the speech of the uneducated or partly educated as perfect participles. . . wrote. **1907** White *AZ Nights* 61, Your man, Case, has wrote me. **1908** *DN* 3.283 **eAL,**

wGA, Almost any preterit may be used as a past participle, as wrote. [**1915** *DN* 4.179 **swVA,** No distinction is made, save in a very few instances . . between the past tense form and past participle of strong or irregular verbs. . . E.g., *ran* and *written* are not in use at all.] **1930** *DN* 6.87 **cWV,** Got wrote up, discharged. **1940** Faulkner *Hamlet* 172 **MS,** Did you expect him to hand you a wrote-out bill for it? **1953** Atwood *Survey of Verb Forms* 26, Write. . . The past participle is recorded in the context "I have (written) a letter." . . *Wrote* . . is used by something less than one third of the informants in N. Eng. . . *wrote* is more of an uneducated form than an older form. . . Outside of N. Eng. *wrote* predominates . . [among those of poor education] everywhere, the proportions ranging from about three fifths (N.Y.) to well over nine tenths (N.C.) **1965–70** *DARE* (Qu. OO34b, *Talking about writing a letter home: "She should have _____ [long ago]."*) 124 Infs, **widespread, but less freq Plains States, Pacific,** Wrote; (Qu. KK17, . . *'Worthless': "It isn't worth _____."*; total Infs questioned, 75) Inf **OK**9, Not worth the paper it's wrote on. **1975** Allen *LAUM* 2.32 **Upper MW** (as of c1950), Write. . . Apparently only one of the nonstandard variants of the past participle of *write* survived the western migration. . . In light of . . the fact that most of the examples of *wrote* are in the older portions of the U[pper] M[idwest], *wrote* is clearly a declining form. **1989** Pederson *LAGS Tech. Index* 356 **Gulf Region,** Write. [For the past participle, 170 of 914 infs offered *wrote*.] **2000** Shores *Tangier Is.* 248 **Chesapeake Bay,** Nonstandard forms showing past times are common: . . wrote (written).

c *(w)roten.*

1857 Long *Pictures Slavery* (2d ed) 295 **MD,** Bress de Lord, I feel dat my name is roten on his hands. **1862** (1864) Browne *Artemus Ward Book* 83, Wax figgers is more elevatin than awl the plays ever wroten. **1953** Atwood *Survey of Verb Forms* 26, Wroten . . , apparently a blend showing hesitation between *wrote* and *written,* occurs once in N. Eng. **1989** Pederson *LAGS Tech. Index* 356 **Gulf Region,** Write. [For the past participle, 3 of 914 infs offered *wroten*.]

d *write.*

1953 Atwood *Survey of Verb Forms* 26, The uninflected *write* is used by two Negro informants. **1966** *DARE* (Qu. OO34b, *Talking about writing a letter home: "She should have _____ [long ago]."*) Infs **SC**10, 26, Write. [Both Infs Black]

write it on (the) ice *v phr* Also *mark it on ice, put it on (the) ice*

To record a debt for later payment; to cancel a debt.

1889 *Chester Times* (PA) 15 Sept 6/2, After procuring and devouring a supper, [he] requested Mr. Gallen to "put it on the ice." Mr. Gallen requested Dickson to pay cash. **1892** (1925) Walsh *Lit. Curiosities* 874, For he hung up Danny Dolan, sayin', "Put it on the ice."/ Yes, he stood up Danny Dolan by a curious device./ He shook him for the drinks all round, an' worked in loaded dice. **1932** *AmSp* 7.335 [Johns Hopkins jargon], *Put it on the ice*—"forget about it." To intentionally forget about something, usually a debt. **1936** *Frederick Post* (MD) 25 Mar 4/6 **NYC,** The Filchers are "chisel-ins" who take it "on the cuff" or write it "on ice," but who, in plain English, don't pay their way through life. **1968–69** *DARE* (Qu. U11, *If you buy something but don't pay cash for it . . "I _____."*) Infs **PA**228, **UT**7, (Had them) put it on ice; **MI**76, Put it on ice; **WI**48, Mark it on ice. **1974** O'Hara *Good Samaritan* 206 **CT,** When you get back on your feet again, you can always leave a ten or twenty where I can find it, but we can write it on the ice till then.

writing spider *n* **chiefly Sth, S Midl** See Map on p. 1086 Cf **drawing spider**

A garden spider (here: *Argiope aurantia*) whose webs bear a fancied resemblance to writing.

1896 *Portsmouth Times* (OH) 21 Sept 5/3, Tom Calvert has one of the writing spiders at work on his farm on the West Side. The spider has written "Money Here" in a certain spot. **1928** *Fayetteville Daily Democrat* (AR) 14 Sept 6/5, Writing Spider. . . Wednesday he wrote plainly, "N. V. J.," which letters were followed by a lot of letters resembling "m's." **1938** *Vidette–Messenger* (Valparaiso IN) 15 Sept 4/6 **MI,** A "writing spider" here apparently possesses a sense of humor and a knowledge of geography. About the size of a quarter, the spider has written the words "Ed Wynn" and "Minnesota" in its web. **1938** Brimley *Insects NC* 478, A[rgiope] aurantia Lucas. Raleigh, Rocky Point, Greensboro—our largest web spider, locally known as "Writing Spider." **1946** *Daily Times-News* (Burlington NC) 30 Sept 3/4, There is, she says, a spider which is generally known as a writing spider, though it doesn't write. . . "A lot of people may say there aren't pretty spiders, but these writing ones are. They are of a black velvet color, with bright yellow markings." **1965–70** *DARE* (Qu. R28, . . *Kinds of spiders*) 9 Infs, **Sth, S Midl,** Writing spider; **FL9,** Writing spider—he makes fancy marks on webs; **SC67,** Writing spider. . . web is gray, write with a very white silk; people claimed they could see forecast of catastrophes (like WWI) in writing spider web. **1968** *Big Spring Daily Herald* (TX) 21 Nov 1/5 **Atlanta GA,** Argiope aurantia. This interesting member of the group of aerial web spinners is known by children throughout the South as the writing spider.

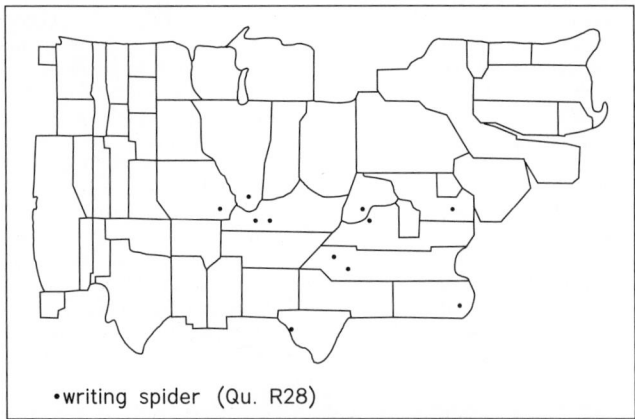

•writing spider (Qu. R28)

written(ed) See **write B1c**

wrong-sedadus adv   Also *wrong-fedadus, wrong-sadaddle* [Pronc varr of *wrong-side-outwards*]   Cf **outwards**
Backwards.
   1970 *DARE* (Qu. MM2, *Suppose a little girl accidentally gets her dress on wrong so that the back part is turned around* . . *"Look, you've got your dress on _____."*) Inf **FL52,** Wrong-fedadus [rɒŋfa'da,dəs]—older folks saying this; **TX92,** Wrong-sadaddle [,sə'dædəl]; **FL48,** Wrong-sedadus [rɒŋ'sədadəz]. [All Infs Black]

wrop v   Also sp *rop*   Past, past pple *wrop(ped), wropt*   Similarly n *(w)ropper*   [Var of *wrap*]   **esp Sth, S Midl**
   1798 in 1956 Eliason *Tarheel Talk* 321 **cnNC,** Roppers. **1846** Worcester *Universal Dict.* 830, Wrap. . . "This word is often pronounced *rop* . . even by speakers much above the vulgar." Walker. The same pronunciation is not uncommon in some parts of the United States; yet it has no countenance from the orthoëpists. **1867** Lowell *Biglow* xlv '**Upcountry' MA,** Wropt for wrapt. **1899** (1912) Green *VA Folk-Speech* 492, Wropper. . . Wrapper. **1899** Chesnutt *Conjure Woman* 171 **csNC** [Black], Dan en Mahaly . . wuz libbin' in a cabin by deyse'ves, en wuz des [=just] wrop' up in one ernudder. **1902** *DN* 2.249 **sIL,** Wrop. . . To wrap. **1903** *DN* 2.337 **seMO,** Shall I wrop it up for you? **1907** *DN* 3.238 **nwAR,** Wrop. . . To wrap. **1908** Wasson *Home from Sea* 127 **sME coast,** That's your lung-cure with the red wropper to her. **1909** *DN* 3.390 **eAL, wGA,** Wrop. . . To wrap. **1914** *DN* 4.83 **ME, nNH,** Wroppin' round yer finger. **1915** *DN* 4.193 **swVA,** Wrop. Variant of *wrap.* **1924** Raine *Land of Saddle-Bags* 97 **sAppalachians,** Strong preterites are much in use, like . . *wropt* for wrapped. **1933** Rawlings *South Moon* 98 **nFL,** Better wrop up some biscuits. **1937** (1977) Hurston *Their Eyes* 33 **FL** [Black], He sorta wropped his hand in it. **1939** Steinbeck *Grapes* 26 **OK,** You was all wropped up in yankin' that pigtail out by the roots. **1945** FWP *Lay My Burden Down* 116 **LA** (as of c1865) [Black], We wrop up at night in every thing we can git. **1963** Owens *Look to River* 97 **TX,** You better wrop up in yo' blanket. **1969** *DARE* FW Addit **GA22,** Everything wropped [rɔpt] up around here in snow. **1986** Pederson *LAGS Concordance* **Gulf Region** (*Wrapped it up*) 14 infs, Wrop (it *or* them) up; 14 infs, Wropped (it *or* them) up; 1 inf, Wropping; 1 inf, Wrops it up; 1 inf, Pipes is wropped with a big burlap bags [sic].

wrostle See **wrestle A2**

wrote See **write B2b**

wroten See **write B1d, 2c**

wrothy See **wrathy**

wrymouth n   [See quot 1933]
A fish of the genus *Cryptacanthodes,* usu *C. maculatus.* Also called **conger eel 4, congo eel 3, ghostfish a**
   1839 MA Zool. & Bot. Surv. *Fishes Reptiles* 28, C[ryptacanthodes]

maculatus. . . The spotted Wry-mouth. **1848** (1851) Mather–Brockett *Geogr. Hist. NY* 44, Spotted wrymouth. **1879** U.S. Natl. Museum *Bulletin* 14.31, *Cryptacanthodes maculatus.* . . Spotted Wry-mouth.—Nova Scotia to Cape Cod. **1933** John G. Shedd Aquarium *Guide* 152, The Wry-mouth. . . is an eel-shaped fish with a large head and the mouth sharply oblique. **1991** Amer. Fisheries Soc. *Common Names Fishes* 60, *Cryptacanthodes aleutensis.* . . dwarf wrymouth. *Ibid, Cryptacanthodes maculatus.* . . wrymouth.

w'uckra See **okra**

wudge n   [Appar var of Brit dial (now colloq) *wodge*]   **esp NEast**   Cf **wudget**
A wad, lump; also fig.
   1874 Rankin *True Ever* 227 **NY,** If you ever intend to get married, you will have to learn a good many lessons in housekeeping, for it never would do in this world for you to tumble things up in a wudge like this. **1895** *DN* 1.395 **seMA,** Wudge, wudget: a little bunch. **1921** *Everybody's Mag.* June 28, Take Mrs. Blackstone, a poor wudge of a thing— yet she believed in me and now I must tell her I am an impostor. **1953** Petry *Narrows* 25 **CT** [Black], There seemed to be a great wudge of what looked like soiled diapers. **1955** *Bridgeport Telegram* (CT) 22 July 24/2, If Joe owns the bus [=car], he should keep it neat. A wudge of sandy bathing-trunks, a welter of tools . . ? No, never. **1985** *DARE* File **neOH,** I heard from my mother (b. 1879). . . Wudge—meaning material crushed together. Sounds what it is.

wudge v   With *up, together*   [**wudge** n]   **esp NEast**
To wad, crumple; also fig; hence ppl adjs *wudged up, ∼ together.*
   1861 *Vanity Fair* 3.269, They [=babies] wear unwholesome flannel things, always wudged up under the arms. **1897** *Frank Leslie's Pop. Mth.* 44.599 **Brooklyn NYC,** They had more than they could eat, and they used to wudge it up in a paper and throw it away. **1898** *New Engl. Mag.* 23.611 **NEng,** What a state things was in,—the kitchen all of a clutter, and ma's best tablecloth wudged up in the sink. **1953** Petry *Narrows* 126 **CT** [Black], All I need is a tight little bouquet of flowers . . wudged together in my hot little hand. **1965** Robertson *Greatest Thing* 203 **OH,** My skirt got all wudged up. **2004** Berrien *Powerboat Care* 8 **MA,** When you stow gear, don't wudge it up or pack it too tightly. **2004** in 2009 *DARE* File—Internet **RI,** What, then, accounts for file bloat? Or does that only happen to internal stuff which gets all wudged together?

wudget n   [Dimin of **wudge** n; cf *EDD wedget* (also *wadget, woudgeat,* etc) "A small wad. . . A large, loose bundle, a burden"]   **esp NEng**
A wad, bunch, bundle; fig, a baby.
   1860 (1864) Holmes *Cousin Maude* 121 **MA,** If I didn't love the little *wudget* as I do, I wouldn't have changed my will. **1891** *Jrl. Amer. Folkl.* 4.71 **NEng,** Wudget. . . A tangle, snarl. "What a wudget this is." **1895** [see **wudge** n]. **1899** (1912) Green *VA Folk-Speech* 492, Wudget. . . A wad; pad; bundle. "She had her hair done up in wudgets of paper." **1907** *N&Q* 10th ser 7.447 **CT** (as of c1860), A "wudget" was a close-packed and crumpled bunch of something normally smooth and flat. . . Bedclothes tossed in a heap on the bed or the floor were "thrown in a wudget"; the contents of a satchel jammed in anyhow were "a wudget"; more curiously, a necktie in a wisp around one's neck was "tied in a wudget." **1927** *AmSp* 3.141 **coastal ME,** Badly wrinkled clothes were "all in a wopse and wudget."

wudge together (or up) See **wudge** v

wuf(f) See **worth**

wuff-in See **wharfing**

wuh make (or mekso) See **what make (so)**

wum See **worm**

wumble-cropped See **wamble-cropped**

wunafitz See **wunnerfitz**

wunder See **wander**

wunnerfitz n   Also *gunnerfitz*   Pronc-sp *wunafitz*   [PaGer *(g)wunnerfitz* curiosity, curious person]
A nosy person.
   1967 *DARE* (Qu. GG36a, *The kind of person who is always poking into other people's affairs:* "*She's an awful _____.*") Inf **PA42,** Wunafitz [wunəfitz]—someone who is nosy; (Qu. NN12a, *Things that*

people say to put a child off when he asks too many questions: "What's that for?") Inf **PA**3, Gunnerfitz [gunɚfɪts]; [if you're] gunnerfitzich, you ask too many questions. **2006** *DARE* File—Internet **sePA**, I don't wanna be a *wunnerfitz* but I saw Mamm planting some celery behind the calf shed.

wunnet See **walnut**

wunst See **once**

wunt v¹ See **will A**

wunt v² See **win** v 1

wup exclam |wʊp| Pronc-sp *wurp* esp **Sth, S Midl** Cf **whope**

Used as a call, esp to animals.

1909 *DN* 3.390 **eAL, wGA**, *Wurp*. . . Whoa: used rather commonly in ordinary conversation to indicate a sudden jolt or stopping. *Wurp, sir!* is also common. **1942** Warnick *Garrett Co. MD* 16 **nwMD** (as of 1900–18), *Wope*, or *Wup* . . an exclamation, probably a modification of "whoa." **1965–70** *DARE* (Qu. K80, *The call that's used . . to get the cows in from the pasture*) Inf **AL**38, Wup [wʊp]; (Qu. K82, *The call used . . to get horses in from the pasture*) Inf **KY**64, Whistle and say wup [wʊʌp]; **VA**95, Wup [wʊp] (repeated). **1973** Allen *LAUM* 1.262 **Upper MW** (as of c1950), Calls to horses in the pasture. . . wup [1 inf, **IA**]. **1986** Pederson *LAGS Concordance* (*Calls to horses when getting them from the pasture*) 1 inf, **cnMS**, Wup—heard grandfather say; 1 inf, **cTN**, Wup, yea (x2), yea—to back horse.

wur See **be A5**

wurp See **wup**

wursh See **wish A2**

wush See **wish A1**

wut(h) See **worth**

wuther See **whether 1**

wuthless See **worth**

wutz(ie) n, exclam Usu |wʊts(i)|; also |wuts(i), wʊts(i)|; for addit varr see quots Also *vootie, voots(ie), woody, wootchie, wootsie, woots(y), wooty, wootz(ie), wuts(ie), wutzer, wutzi* [PaGer *wutz* pig; *wutzi* piglet] **chiefly in PaGer settlement areas** See Map

A pig or piglet; also fig; also used as a call to pigs.

1872 *Our Young Folks* 8.408 **nwMD**, Even her playmates . . had begun to call her "Wootsy! Wootsy!" and salute her with grunts and wicked little squeals on all public occasions. **1897** *Amer. Anthropologist* 10.104, *List of words used in calling swine*. . . Woots—Pennsylvania (Dutch). Wuts—Tennessee. **1908** *German Amer. Annals* 10.52 **sePA**, *Woots*, or *Wootsy* [wʊts]. Pig; the second form is diminutive. **1916** *DN* 4.339, *Wootsy* [wʊtsɪ]. . . A little pig. **1939** Aurand *Quaint Idioms* 21 [PaGer], You ought to see my boy since his operation; he eats like a little *wutz* ("wootz;" pig). **1949** Kurath *Word Geog.* 64, Calls to Pigs. . . The German call *voots!, vootsie!, vootie!* (with the vowel of *put*) is in rather general use from the Lehigh to the Shenandoah and the upper Potomac, and westward to the Alleghenies, and relics of it have survived on the Yadkin in North Carolina. **1953** *Hist. Rev. Berks Co.* Oct–Dec 6 **ePA**, Of the many animal names borrowed from Pennsylvania German, the following are typical: . . *wutzi,* 'young pig'. . . [T]hese words are used also as calls to the designated animals. **1962** Atwood *Vocab. TX* 77, *Wutzi.* A call to pigs. Comal, Kendall, and Gillespie Counties. **1965–70** *DARE* (Qu. K84, *The call used . . to get the pigs in at feeding time*) Infs **PA**6, 56, Wutz [wʊts]; **CA**90, **PA**75, 141, 211, (Come) wutzie [wʊtsi]; **MD**30, Wutz wutz wutz [wʊts]; woody woody woody [wʊdi]; **PA**27, Wutzie [wʊtsi]; **PA**23, Wutz wutz wutz [wʊts wʊts wʊts]; **PA**147, Here wutzie [wʊtsi] or wutz [wʊts]; **PA**137, Wooty [wuti] repeated; **WV**8, Wutzie [wʊtsɪ]—call to little pig; (Qu. H9, *If somebody always*

eats a considerable amount of food, you say he's a _____) Inf **MD**30, Wutz; (Qu. H11a, *If somebody eats rapidly and noisily*) Inf **MD**30, Wutz. **1966** Dakin *Dial. Vocab. Ohio R. Valley* 2.285, Calls to pigs. . . A large number of . . variations and innovations are used by scattered individuals. Among them are. . . *woot-sie!* **1967** Faries *Word Geog. MO* 93, Call to Pigs. . . The calls are varied with the five in most common use appearing in about equal frequency. . . Other calls in the order of their frequency are: *hoa-ie!* . . *voots(ie)!, goop!,* and *vootie!* **1967** *DARE* FW Addit **PA**162, *Wutsies*—pigs are often wutsies. **1979** Jordan *Yesterday in TX Hill Country* 64, He often carried ears of corn in a tow sack tied to his saddle and rode out to check the hogs, calling loudly "Wootchie, wootchie, wootchie" until they came out of the timber. **1982** *Barrick Coll.* **csPA**, *Wootz*—sound for calling pigs. *Wootzie*—baby pig. **1985** *AmSp* 60.236 **sePA**, *Voots(ie)*—Call to pigs . . *voots[ie]* 24% [of 60 infs]. . . The present study demonstrates that a fairly large number of rural and urban residents of varying ages and educational backgrounds retain an active familiarity with this term *voots* and its variants. A contributing reason for its survival is probably the currency of popular local expressions such as *You eat like a voots!* ['. . . like a pig'], in which the word is used to refer to humans. **2000** *DARE* File **cPA**, Wutz, wutzer—a gluttonous person (the u is pronounced as the oo in cook). . . might come from a PA-Dutch word for "pig."

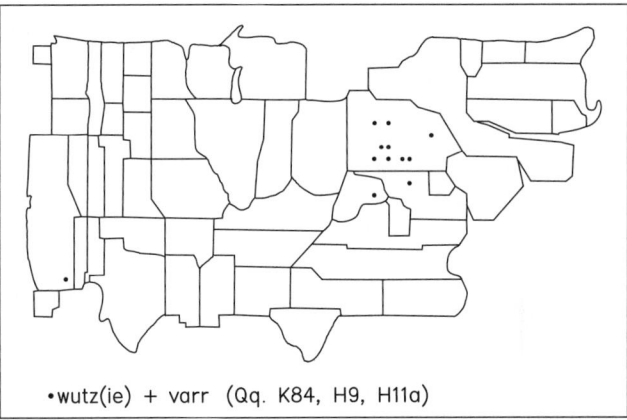

• **wutz(ie)** + varr (Qq. K84, H9, H11a)

wuxtra n [See quot 1916] Also *wuxtry*

A newspaper extra—usu used as exclam, orig by a vendor of such extras, now usu to express ironic excitement about an announcement.

1910 Goldfrap *Boy Aviators' Treasure* 158, As they turned a corner a small boy with a bundle of papers almost ran into them. . . "Wuxtry, wuxtry!" **1916** *DN* 4.282 **NE**, *Wuxtra, wuxtry*. . . [From call "Oh! extra!"] In jocular usage for newspaper *extra*. **1956** *News* (Frederick MD) 7 Nov 18/6, [*Mutt and Jeff* comic strip:] Wuxtra! Little Jeff elected president of the Lion Tamers Club! **2005** *DARE* File—Internet, Wuxtry! Wuxtry! Literary Award Winner Sighted On Sidewalk! **2007** *Ibid*, Wuxtra! Wuxtra! Wuxtra! Former President Bill Clinton Caught in Extramarital Tryst!!! I dunno—it seems to me that you'd havta add a few midgets and a bearded lady to draw a crowd.

wuz See **be A4**

wuzzy britches n Cf **fuzzy britches**

An unidentified plant; see quot.

1970 *DARE* FW Addit **KY**83, Wuzzy britches—same as leather britches. A plant.

wynding See **winding** adv

wyre See **weir**

wytch hopple See **witch hobble**

x n[1]   See **ex** n[1]

x n[2]   See **ex** n[2]

'xacly   See **exactly**

X-and-(n)aught   See **X's-and-O's**

xebec   See **zebec**

X's-and-O's n   Also *O's-and-X's, X-and-(n)aught;* for addit varr see quots [*OED2* 1894 (at *X* sb. 1.b)]   **esp N Cent, PA, WV** See Map

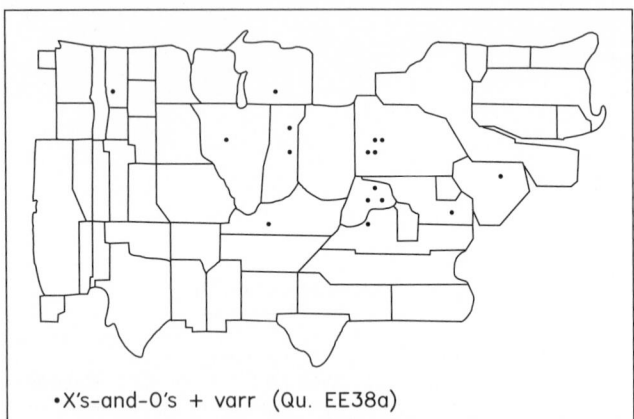

•X's-and-O's + varr (Qu. EE38a)

=**tick-tack-toe 2.**

[**1946** Manning *Igloo* 126 **Canada,** "Now let's have a game of X's and O's," he said. So we played X's and O's; and little more time passed before we began to talk.]   **1965–70** *DARE* (Qu. EE38a, *A game played with pencil and paper where the players try to get three X's or three O's in a row*) Infs **IN**68, **MT**1, **PA**76, 93, 94, 167, **WV**7, 8, 13, X('s)-and-O's; **IN**81, **MD**46, **MI**89, X-(and-)O; **NJ**35, O-x-O; **KY**94, O's-and-X's; **VA**30, X-and-(n)aught; **IL**63, X's.   **1982** *Rhetoric Rev.* 1.9 **TX,** Oh, you can do it helter-skelter if you please, mow plaids, play X's and O's in the grass, if you're of a mind to.   **2010** *DARE* File—Internet **cSC,** This debate isn't going to end any time soon. It's like playing Xs and Os, the only way to really win is not to play.

'xspec'   See **expect**

X-Y-Z exclam   [Initialism for "e*X*amine *Y*our *Z*ipper"]   **esp NEast** Cf **barn door 2b; icebox 2; one o'clock, it's; stable 2**

1968–69 *DARE* (Qu. W24c, *. . To warn a man that his trouser-fly is open*) Infs **MI**97B, **NY**209A, X-Y-Z; **NJ**45, My little sister says X-Y-Z [All Infs young]; **RI**17, X-Y-Z [FW: Inf's granddaughter says].   **1985–86** *DARE* File, "The current code is: XYZ, B.S.S. (=examine your zipper before someone sees)"—reported by several women in 20–30 age range, office personnel at U. Mass., Amherst.   **2007** *DARE* File—Internet, [Children's song:] You gotta XYZ examine your zipper. It falls down so mysteriously./ XYZ examine your zipper cause noone's gonna take you seriously./ Then some kids they were pointing at me./ . . / And someone yelled out XYZ.

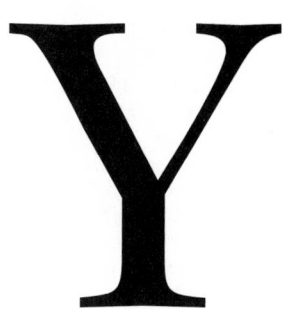

-y suff[1]

1 Added to std nouns, less freq to verbs, to form non-std adjs; see quots.

1823 Cooper *Pioneers* 2.17 **cNY,** Burny sugar is bad to the taste, let it be never so sweet. **1831** [see **strengthy**]. **1898** Lloyd *Country Life* 80 **AL,** Now as to clothes, old Mart ain't to say very fixy. **1916** *DN* 4.337 **PA,** Conceity. . . Over-particular. **1931** Randolph *Ozarks* 76, The hill-man's adjective *resty,* meaning indolent, is another Shakespearian sur-vival. **c1938** in 1970 Hyatt *Hoodoo* 2.1473 **seGA,** If . . [you] have pains in your feet—it gets painy all ovah. **1989** Flynt *Poor But Proud* 188 **neAL,** The spinning wheel is usually on the porch where suspended from the rafters are pepper "burney" beans and ears of seed corn.

2 Added to std adjs to form non-std adjs; see quots. **chiefly Sth, S Midl** See Map

1899 (1912) Green *VA Folk-Speech* 243, *Jagged. . . Jaggedy.* **1906** *DN* 3.132 **nwAR,** *Crinklety. . . Crinkly.* **1908** *DN* 3.303 **eAL, wGA,** *Crumplety. . . Crumpled.* **1926** [see **wrinkledy**]. **1928** Chapman *Happy Mt.* 31 **sAppalachians,** [The southwest wind] strikes growing things all wede 'n' witherdy. **1936** *AmSp* 11.355 **eTX,** Faded [sic] ['fedɪdɪ]. **1965–70** *DARE* (Qu. BB6, *A sudden feeling of weakness, when sometimes the person loses consciousness*) 10 Infs, **chiefly Sth, S Midl,** (Feel) fainty; **GA**23, **LA**6, 8, Fainty spell; **TX**4, Feeling fainty; (Qu. BB16b, *If something a person ate didn't agree with him, he might just feel a bit _____*) Inf **AL**16, Fainty; **TN**52, Fainty-sick; (Qu. BB38, *When a person doesn't look healthy, or looks as if he hadn't been well for some time . . "He looks _____."*) Inf **KY**94, Fainty; (Qu. LL3b, *Shrunk, dried up: "He's a little _____ old man."*) Infs **KY**11, **TN**26, Wrinkledy. **1997** [see **wrinkledy**].

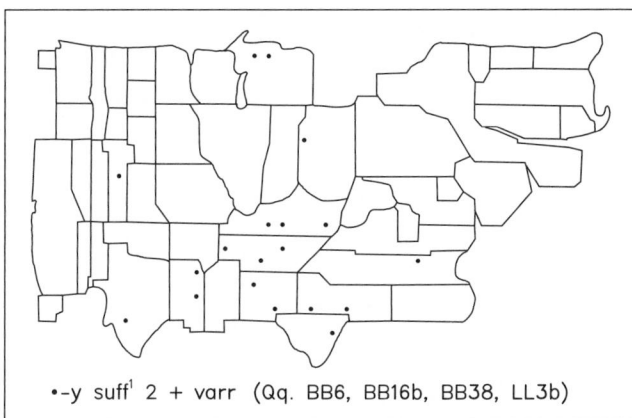

•*-y* suff[1] 2 + *varr* (Qq. BB6, BB16b, BB38, LL3b)

3 also sp *-ey, -i;* Added to nouns to form hypocoristic or fa-miliarized nouns; see quots. See also **hiney** n[2]

1903 *DN* 2.350, *Catty. . .* The cat in the game of tip-cat. **1941** *AmSp* 16.188 **NYC,** *Parky. . .* A park attendant. **1954** *Harder Coll.* **cwTN,** *Braggy*—An excessively boastful person. **1965–70** *DARE* (Qu. HH28, *Names and nicknames . . for people of foreign background*) 48 Infs, **chiefly MI, WI, Upper MW, Pacific NW,** Norski; (Qu. X35, *Joking words for the part of the body that you sit on . . "He slipped and came down hard on his _____."*) 37 Infs, **scattered,** Hiney; **IL**63, Arsy; **CO**20, Butty; **SC**19, Bumpy; **IL**26, Hindey; **IL**99, **MA**122, Tushy; (Qu. K13, *A cow that has had her horns cut off*) Inf **VA**38, Dehorny. **1979** *Capital Times* (Madison WI) 20 July 39/4, They referred to the northern

fisherman as a "chummy." That's derived from a term describing oily, cut fish . . known as "chum bait."

-y suff[2] Also sp *ey, -i(e)*

Used to represent the substitution of |-ɪ| or |-i| for a final un-stressed vowel, as:

a for |ə|, |jə| in words spelled with *-a, -ah, -ia.* Cf **alfalfa A Carolina A, cholera, extra A, Jerush(e)y, neuralgia, opera A, pokey** n[2]

1848 Lowell *Biglow* 2 '**Upcountry' MA,** Our Hosee's gut the chollery or suthin anuther. **1851** Hooper *Widow Rugby's Husband* 50 **AL,** His d—d heathen dumb brute of Afriky. **1876** Harte *Gabriel Conroy* 314 **CA,** On this very verandy. **1891** *DN* 1.117 **cNY,** [ɑpəɪ, ɑpɪ] < opera. *Ibid* 143 **cNY,** [dɪk'otɪ] < Dakota. **1904** Day *Kin o' Ktaadn* 91 **ME,** I hop up and run to see whether the cupoly of my barn is still there. **1915** *DN* 4.177 **swVA,** Seri (Sarah), Hanni (Hannah), Alphi (Alpha). **1923** *DN* 5.200 **swMO,** Alberty (peach). **1931** Terhune in *N. Amer. Rev.* May 432 **NJ,** My mother told me her own grandparents and all their generation changed the final *a* in most long proper names to *y* and that doctors of that day spoke always of *asafoetidy.* **1933** in 1964 Lomax *Penguin Amer. Folk Songs* 155 **MS,** *Stewball.* Way out in Californy. **1936** *AmSp* 11.160 **eTX,** Among older or less well educated people in rural districts, *algebra, Arnica . .* are pronounced . . ['ælˌjɪbrɪ], ['ɑrnɪkɪ]. **1959** *VT Hist.* 27.150, *Neuralgia* [nu'ræljɪ]. **1966–70** *DARE* Tape **AL**4, Later on . . we'd plant beans, and okra ['oʊkrɪ] and corn; **AL**14, The okra ['okri] would be fried; **GA**61, Georgia ['joɚji]; **KY**84, Hydrophobia ['haˑɪdrəˌfobiᵛ]. **1968–69** *DARE* (Qu. I4, . . *Vegetables . . less commonly grown around here*) Inf **NY**216, Faby ['febi] beans; (Qu. I16, *The large flat beans that are not eaten in the pod*) Inf **KY**69, Lima ['laɪmi] beans; (Qu. J5) Inf **NY**72, Angora [æŋgorɪ]. **1968** *DARE* FW Addit **TN**17A, Asthma ['æzmɪ]. **1991** [see **soda A**]. **1995** *Brophy Coll.* 85 **swMO,** (as of c1960), *-y.* [T]he suffix "-a" or "-ia" so pro-nounced; as Floridy, Californy, Oklahomy, Newbrasky, Clary, Idy.

b for |o| in words spelled with *-o(w).* Cf **piano A, sorrow** n, v, **sparrow**

1880 (1886) Woolson *Rodman* 258 **SC,** Jim had come "to borry an axe." **1927** *AmSp* 2.348 **cwWV,** *Barrey* [=barrow] *hog.* **1938** *FWP Guide DE* 500, A sparrow is a *sporry* in some spots, a harrow a *horry.* **1940** in 1944 *ADD* **swPA, nWV,** *Window. . .* |wɪ'ndi|. **1942** *New Yorker* 27 June 15/1 **NYC,** I don't know do they folly me around or what, those plainclothes policemen. **1948** Manfred *Chokecherry* 89 **nwIA,** Get to bed. Tomorry you'll run like a brand-new top. **1966** *DARE* (Qu. GG14) Inf **ME**5, He's a-borryin' trouble. **1970** *DARE* Tape **IL**114, Just make a furrow ['fɝˑi]. **1988** Kingsolver *Bean Trees* 57 **KY,** I don't see how a body can grow no tobaccy if it don't rain.

-y suff[3] See **-ie** suff[3]

'y prep[1] See **i** prep

-y prep[2], adv See **to** prep, adv **A2**

y' adj See **your**

ya See **yah**

yaar See **year** n[1]

yaas See **yes 1**

yack See **york**

yacker See **yucker**

yackers, yackies, yack(s) See **yakers**

ya eh See **ya hey**

yaffle n [Brit dial *yaffle* green woodpecker] Cf **gaffle wood-pecker, hickwall, high-holer 1, whafler, woodwall** =**flicker** n² 1.

1874 *Amer. Naturalist* 8.88, *Colaptes auratus* . . (Yellow-shafted Flicker; Yaffle). Common on the St. John's and at Okahumkee [FL]. Breeds. Differs perceptibly from our northern bird in being smaller and darker. **1881** Ingersoll in Nuttall Ornith. Club *Bulletin* 6.184 **CT,** The Golden-winged Woodpecker . . is variously known as . . Yaffle [etc].

yagger v, hence vbl n *yaggering,* n *yaggerings* [Cf *EDD yaggle* v. 1 "To wrangle; to quarrel"; cf Intro "Language Changes" IV.4] **esp KY**
To talk excessively, noisily, or angrily; of an animal: to bark or growl threateningly.

1901 *Youth's Companion* 31 Oct 573 **NV,** The bears increased their threats and yaggerings until the little cañon roared with the horrid noise. **1917** in 2007 (acc) Lexis–Nexis Legal Research *State Case Law: KY* (Internet), He heard a conversation between the two which he terms "yaggering." It is not explained what he means by that term, but we suppose it was some general talk passing between the two such as occurs between persons more or less intoxicated. **1922** Cobb *Kinfolks* 44 **KY,** Times I would sull up like a possum while / The travelers would yagger to theirselves. **1944** *PADS* 2.22 **sAppalachians,** *Yagger* [jægɚ]. . . To cavil. "Oh, I wouldn't yagger about a little thing like that." **1949** Hornsby *Lonesome Valley* 8 **eKY,** Do this! This! This! Do that! That! That! Yagger, yagger every minute of the time. *Ibid* 82, Crit had a good right to quarrel about Lucindy that morning after the way she yaggered at him in front of Johnny. *Ibid* 147, When girls got together they cut up worse than a bunch of pups romping in the yard, hanging on to each other and yaggering. **1978** Hiser *Quare Appalachia* 181 **eKY,** I went to bed . . , a-leavin the three women a-settin in front of the far a-yaggerin like women folks will at ain't seed one another in a spell.

yah adv Also sp *ya* [Cf Ger, Du, Nor, Sw, Dan *ja*] **scattered, but chiefly Nth, esp N Cent, Upper MW, Plains States** See Map
Yes.

1834 in 1925 *Chron. OK* 3.184 **IN,** How many Thousand are enjoying themselves . . without the least feeling compassion for those travelers in the forest, ya. **1883** Roe *His Rivals* 206 **Sth** [Black], "But haven't you a wife and children?" "Oh, yah." **1900** *Every Other Sun.* 16.44 [Black], "And then you've got a home to go to." "Oh, yah! Mos' paid fur, too." "And children?" "Oh, yah!" **1905** *Daily News* 23 May 4/7 *(OED2),* America . . has two substitutes for 'yes.' One of them is 'yep' and the other is 'yah.' **1931** Jacobson *Milwaukee Dial.* 17 **WI,** Oh ya. . . is extensively used both as an exclamation and as an affirmative expression. *Ibid* 19, Ya. . . one of the most common forms of yes. No matter how ungerman or how well educated everyone at some time or other uses ya for yes. A New York girl was visiting in Milwaukee for a few weeks last year. Apparently unconscious of the effects of her visit she returned to the University with a broad German Ya which try as she may she can not lose. *Ibid,* Ya sure. . . widely used in place of the German ganz gewiss. **1948** Manfred *Chokecherry* 25 **nwIA,** He called upstairs. "Pa." "Ya?" **1965–70** *DARE* (Qu. NN1, . . *Words like 'yes'*) 76 Infs, **chiefly N Cent, Upper MW, also NEast, NW, Plains States,** Yah [jɑ(:)]; 28 Infs, **scattered,** Yah [no transcr]; **IL**4, Yah [jɔːˑ]; **MA**35, Yah [jɔ]; **IL**61, Yah [jɑ]—we get that from our German friends; **MI**122, Yah

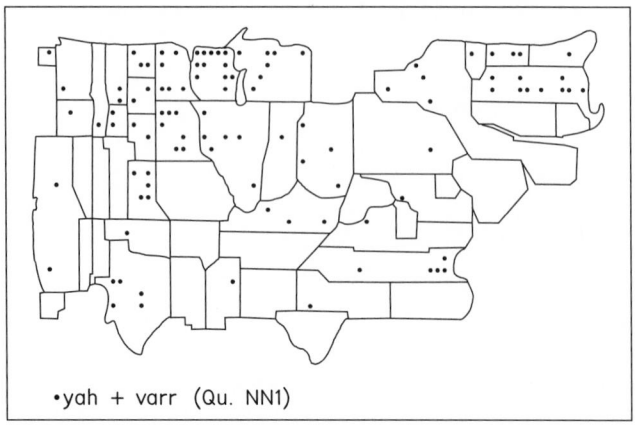

•yah + varr (Qu. NN1)

[jɔ]—from the Dutch; **MN**6, Yah [ja] [FW: Inf thinks this is not good but uses it anyway.]; **MN**37, Yah [ja] sure; ach yah ['ɑk͡ja]; **WA**20, Yah [ja]; yah sure; **WI**52, Yah [ja]—'yes' in Swedish. **1997** *DARE* File—Internet *(Speak 'Scansin)* 4 **WI,** Yah = Yes. **2004** *DARE* File **Upper Peninsula MI,** "Like Yoopers, they say 'yah' and I mean I just do it because we think it's funny." . . "What would a bad Yooper sound like?" "Yah, I went up to da store yesterday." *Ibid,* [Bumper sticker:] Say yah to da U.P., eh! [In response to a similar slogan, "Say Yes to Michigan."]

ya hey intj Also *ya eh, yah der(e) hey, ya hey dere, yah hey (dere)* **esp WI, MI, MN**
Used variously, as an affirmation, greeting, or attention-getter; see quots.

1934 *WI State Jrl.* (Madison) 16 June 8/3, Art Scholl—Trumpet player. . . Favorite sayings, "Oh yah hey" and "Hey Gate." **1956** *Oshkosh Daily Northwestern* (WI) 13 Jan 12/7, You'll find one of the finest black cherry wines on the shelf comes from Denmark. . . It might even be good for falling hair, yah hey, you might even try drinking it plain. **1988** Berryman–Berryman *Forward Hey* (Sound Recording) **ceWI,** ["Squirrelly Valley 2-Step":] Oh yah hey, in Squirrelly Valley / They talk so funny, they get so lazy / Oh yah hey, get me a beer once / As long as you're up yet, I'm goin' crazy. **1993** *Detroit Free Press* (MI) 30 July sec F 3/3 **Upper Peninsula MI,** Ya, eh: Affirmative. Also: "ya hey, you betcha." **1999** *Daily Herald* (Arlington Heights IL) 28 Mar sec 3 [1]/3 (newspaperarchive.com), Ya hey dere, Ameritech— Ameritech Corp. got some good news. **1999** *DARE* File—Internet [Central Florida Green Bay Packer Backers] **WI,** Yah-hey-dere: standard Cheddarhead greeting; "yah-dere-hey" also acceptable. **2002** Larson *Winter Carnival* 294 **nMI,** "Hey! Can you tell me which room Claribel Rook is in?" . . "Ya hey. She say a gentleman coming dis morning der, eh." **2002** Perry *Population 485* 121 **WI,** We are not just a bunch of jolly Norwegians bowling, *yah hey.* **2006** *DARE* File—Internet **MN,** Mary in Rice, MN, gave me a list of her favorite idioms: . . Ya hey dere. **2007** *Ibid* **WI,** Didja get dem hairs cut? Yah, der hey. I got 'em permed, too.

yahk See **yolk A5**

yahoo n Usu |ˈjɑhu|; also |ˈjehu| Also sp *yahoe* [After the imaginary creatures in Swift's *Gulliver's Travels* 1726] **widespread, but somewhat more freq Sth, S Midl**
A loutish, ignorant or inexperienced person, esp an unsophisticated rustic.

1851 Garland *Life John Randolph* 15 **VA,** I do not wonder at the rage for emigration. . . Surely that must be the Yahoo's paradise, where he can get dead drunk for the hundredth part of a dollar. **1878** Eggleston *Roxy* 183 **MS,** Nancy Kirtley was a flower of that curious poor-white race which is called "tar-heel" in the northern Carolina, "sand-hiller" in the southern, "corn-cracker" in Kentucky, "yahoo" in Mississippi, and in California "Pike". **1899** (1912) Green *VA Folk-Speech* 493, Yahoo. . . A rough, brutal, uncouth character. (2) A greenhorn; a back-country lout. **1902** *DN* 2.249 **sIL,** Yahoo [jɑhu]. . . An ignorant, unsophisticated, and rude-mannered person. **1903** *DN* 2.337 **seMO,** Yahoo. . . A backwoods fellow; a lout. **1906** *DN* 3.123 **sIN,** Yahoo. . . An ignorant, inexperienced person. *Ibid* 164 **nwAR,** Yahoo [ˈjeɪhu]. . . Uncouth person. **1909** *DN* 3.391 **eAL, wGA,** Yahoo. . . A backwoodsman. **1915** *DN* 4.193 **swVA,** Yahoo [ˈjeˌhu]. . . An uncouth backwoodsman. **1923** *DN* 5.237 **swWI,** Yahoo. . . A term of great opprobrium, a "fighting word," applied by people living south of the Wisconsin River to those living north of it. **1927** *AmSp* 3.136 **eME,** A "yahoe" (pronounced with *a* as in *late*) was a saucy, dirty, often vicious child meaning more than merely mischievous. The term is probably from the Yahoo of Swift's *Gulliver's Travels*. **1930** Shoemaker *1300 Words* 69 **cPA Mts** (as of c1900), Yahoo—A half-witted resident of the foothills. **c1955** Reed–Person *Ling. Atlas Pacific NW* 1 inf, Yahoo [=a rustic]. **1968** *DARE* FW Addit **nwAR,** Yahoo [ˈjeɪˌhu] . . applied to someone rowdy, irresponsible, and young. *Ibid* **cwNV,** Yahoo [ˈjeɪˌhu] = a cowboy, or a country person come to town. **1969** *DARE* (Qu. HH1, *Names and nicknames for a rustic or countrified person*) Inf **AL**50, Yahoo—very old—have heard; **TN**30, Yahoo; (Qu. HH18, *Very insignificant or low-grade people*) Inf **MA**68, Yahoos [ˈjæˌhuz, ˈjeˌhuz]. **1982** *Smithsonian Letters* **AL** (as of 1920s), 'Yahoo'. . . Have heard it less often since 1930. **1986** Pederson *LAGS Concordance (The poor whites)* 1 inf, **neTN,** Yahoo—a person from the country; 1 inf, **csTN,** Yahoo—has heard; unsure where; *(A rustic)* 1 inf, **cnTN,** Yahoos. **2003** (2005) Sifton *Serenity* 136 **MO,** Can you imagine a yahoo like me from a farm in Missouri in such a situation?

yairth See **earth**

‡**yake** n Cf **jake** n¹ 3
  1967 *DARE* (Qu. EE6b, *Small marbles or marbles in general*) Inf TX18, Yakes—small.

yakers intj Also *yackers, yackies, yack(s), yakes* [Prob varr of aikie(s)]
  Used as an expression to lay claim to something; see quots.
  1944 *AmSp* 19.38 **PA**, Yakers (or *yakes* or *yacks*), or *yakers on it!* 'I claim it' . . These idioms, which belong to schoolboys' jargon, have always struck me as remarkable. **1970** Lebofsky *Lexicon Philadelphia* 135, Yackers . . yack(s) . . yackies. . . cry of have-not child to another who has something he would like a share of (e.g., candy).

y'all See **you-all**

yallah, yaller, yallo(w) See **yellow** adj, n¹ A2

y'all's adj, pron¹ See **you-all's** adj, pron²

yalls pron² See **you-alls** pron¹

y'allses, y'alls's See **you-alls's**

yalluh See **yellow** adj, n¹ A2

yam v See **nyam**

ya-ma-zetta See **Johnny Marzetti**

yamp n See **yampah**

yamp v, hence vbl n *yamping*
  To grab, catch, overcome; to steal.
  1866 in 1966 Harris *Sut Lovingood's Yarns* 267 **TN**, Says I, "risk one han', and yamp him by the naik, you durned fool." **1867** Harris *Sut Lovingood Yarns* 201 **TN**, He fell down an' sot intu rollin, wus nur a yung dorg what hes ignurently yamped a pole-cat. **1925** Hunter *Trail Drivers TX* 333, Ordinary stealing is "yamping." **1966** Barker *Little World* 51 **NM** (as of c1914), Pa knew Ma would yamp him if he let Jode go. *Ibid* 82, He'll run to climb the nearest tree, and the other trap will yamp him. *Ibid* 182, We overtook 'em [=cattle thieves] about a mile down the road, headin' this way, and yamped 'em.

yampah n Also *yamp, yampa*
  A plant of the genus *Perideridia*, esp the western *P. gairdneri;* the root of such a plant, considered as food. For other names see **false caraway, Indian ~, Indian potato g, ipo, Queen Anne's lace 2, squawroot 6, wild anise 1, ~ caraway 2, ~ carrot 4, ~ dill 1, ~ parsnip 1**
  [**1806** (1905) Clark *Orig. Jrls. Lewis & Clark Exped.* 5.47 **ID**, The Squar wife to Shabono busied her self gathering the roots of the fenel called by the Snake Indians *Year-pah* for the purpose of drying to eate on the Rocky mountains. those roots are very paliatiable either fresh rosted boiled or dried.] **1845** Frémont *Rept. Rocky Mts.* 152 **UT**, For our supper we had *yampah,* the most agreeably flavored of the roots, seasoned by a small fat duck. **1848** (1855) Ruxton *Life Far West* 92 **UT**, They appeared to have no other food in their village but bags of dried ants and their larvae, and a few roots of the yampah. **1891** *AN&Q* 7.173, North American (Indian) food plants of the West; . . the yamp, *Carum Gairdneri* (Gairdner's caraway), with a root not at all unlike a carrot. **1940** Writers' Program *Oregon* 315, The carrot-like white-flowered Indian *Yampah,* the *carum* of the botanists, also abound. **1948** Baumann *Old Man Crow's Boy* 210 **ID**, Yampas—they're small tubers that taste like a sweet nut—that the squaws find while they're diggin' camas roots and save and roast for the occasion. **2006** Vizgirdas *Wild Plants* 76, Yampah *(Perideridia)*. . . These are biennial or perennial herbs with fascicled tuberous roots and pinnate leaves.

yamping See **yamp** v

yam potato n chiefly Gulf States
  =**sweet potato 1.**
  1852 (1878) Aime *Plantation Diary* 159 **LA**, A yam potatoe [weighs] four pounds, twelve ounces. **1859** Taliaferro *Fisher's R.* 251 **AL**, He would . . eat bread and butter and yam potatoes with you. **1868** *Constitution* (Atlanta GA) 10 July [2]/5 (newspaperarchive.com), The yam potato vine blooms in August. **1911** Seibels *Produce Markets* 88 **TX**, In the southwest there are hundreds of people who wonder why the northern markets will not take yam potatoes. This very matter was once up before a meeting of a Texas association when someone suggested that a car of the juicy, candy-like yams be sent to Chicago. . . [A]n elderly grower arose and said, "Now if those fool people would rather eat our

old dry white potatoes, I say grow and ship them the kind they want and will pay for." **1966–70** *DARE* (Qu. I9, . . *Names [including nicknames] for potatoes*) Infs NJ67, SC26, Yam potato(es). [Both Infs Black] **1986** Pederson *LAGS Concordance* **Gulf Region,** 15 infs, Yam potato(es); 5 infs, Yellow yam (po)tato; 1 inf, **seGA,** Norton yam potatoes.

yan See **yon**

yanaway See **yonway**

yand See **yon**

yander See **yonder** A1

yandside See **yonside**

yank n¹ [Echoic]
  =**white-breasted nuthatch.**
  [**1904** *Atlantic Mth.* 93.221, The usual note of the white-breasted nuthatch has been written *yank* and *hank*.] **1926** *DN* 5.405 **Ozarks,** Yank. . . A little creeping blue-backed bird called the nuthatch. **1953** Randolph–Wilson *Down in Holler* 300 **Ozarks,** Yank. . . Arkansawyers say that the name is a reference to its blue coat, but perhaps the bird's querulous chirp is responsible.

yank n² [Perh in ref to blue uniforms of Union soldiers in the Civil War; see quot 2007]
  A small **sockeye salmon.**
  1898 U.S. Fish Comm. *Bulletin for 1897* 17.25 **neOR,** They [= redfish] come up the river with the first run of chinook salmon. . . He says the small ones are called "yanks." **1915** OR *Fish & Game Laws* 39, It shall be unlawful . . to fish for . . that certain species of fish commonly known as "yanks," land-locked salmon or red-fish. **1940** Writers' Program *Oregon* 292, The salmon are locally called blue-backs, or "yanks" because of the manner in which they are caught by fishermen who use deep, weighted lines and yank the fish out violently. **2007** Schwiebert *Nymphs* 2.706, In certain small lakes of Idaho, Oregon, Washington, British Columbia and Alaska, is found a dwarf form of these bluebacks or sockeyes known as little redfish, Kennerly's salmon, wallowa or yank.

yank n³, hence adj *yanked*
  1975 Gould *ME Lingo* 325, Yank—The natural growth bend of a tree and of a log after felling. Hemlock always grows with a *yank. Sawyers* adjust *yanked* logs on the carriage so the slabbing straightens things up, but a *yank* always cuts down on board feet produced. *Scalers* make allowances when measuring logs with *yanks.* Hence, anybody who walks bent over, or anything lopsided or *weewaw,* has a *yank.*

yankapin See **yonkapin**

yanked See **yank** n³

‡**Yankee ball** n
  Perh =**one old cat 1.**
  1968 *DARE* (Qu. EE11, *Bat-and-ball games for just a few players [when there aren't enough for a regular game]*) Inf VA33, Yankee ball—everyone against the batter who had to go to first and back.

Yankee bean n Also *Yankee pea*
  A white dry bean (*Phaseolus vulgaris* cultivar).
  1842 *Cultivator* 9.186 **NY**, Mr. Thompson asks for the best manner of sowing and harvesting the Yankee bean, (common field bean we presume . .). **1853** MI State Ag. Soc. *Trans. for 1852* 4.51, [In a list of exhibits:] H.B. Chapman, Reading. . . sample Yankee beans. **1873** *Forest & Stream* 1.37, The latest agricultural reports declare that old the [sic] African bean and the true Yankee bean are so similar in appearance, as to lead anybody who grows them, to declare that they must both have come from the same pod. **1927** Sullivan *Hist. NY State* 5.2288, Bean planting for dried beans started about 1830, but little was done until Civil War times, when the "Yankee" bean, used by the armies, came mainly from New York. **1947** McDavid *Coll.* **GA**, Yankee beans = white beans (for baking, etc). **1965–70** *DARE* (Qu. H36, *Kinds of soup*) Infs NJ54, NY37, Yankee bean soup; (Qu. I18, *The smaller beans that are white when they are dry*) Infs FL27, GA11, 16, NJ69, Yankee beans; **GA**3, 12, Yankee peas; (Qu. HH30, *Things that are nicknamed for different nationalities*) Infs CT28, PA219, Yankee beans. **1986** Pederson *LAGS Concordance,* 1 inf, **nwFL,** Yankee beans.

Yankee bump n chiefly swPA
  =**thank-you-ma'am 1.**
  1940 in 1944 *ADD* **WV**, Thank-you-ma'am. . . A bump or depression in a (snow covered) road. . . Yankee bump. Usual term. **2001** *DARE*

File **swPA,** A yankee bump is a hump on a sled riding path that will send your sled flying in the air or a bump on a hilly country road that sends your car in the air. . . What we have discovered is that only those of us who grew up in the mid-Monongahela Valley knew its meaning. . . No one else from Pittsburgh or the surrounding region has heard the term and it does not qualify as Pittsburghese, our regional language. *Ibid* **swPA,** I've encountered recognition of "Yankee bump" by five individuals from Elizabeth PA and vicinity. They are all of ages around 70, I think. One remarked, "I haven't heard that for a long time." . . Two stated specifically that Yankee bumps were things that were purposely formed from snow by sledders in order to become airborne . . rather than simply bumps which happened to be present. *Ibid* **swPA,** Apparently the term [=*Yankee bump*] is not universally recognized even by Mon Valley people. However, one young person telephoned her grandfather just up the valley, and he defined this immediately as a bump encountered in sledding (or possibly while driving, he replied when asked). **2006** *DARE* File—Internet **swPA,** We would make a 'Yankee bump' by piling snow and packing it down so that when you rode over it, you would go into the air.

Yankee corn n *old-fash*
=flint corn.

[**1818** in 1820 *Lit. & Scientific Repository & Crit. Rev.* 1.203, 'Tis fully proved Ohio corn will never come in time to make a yankee hasty-pudding; nor will it ever sell where yankee *flint-corn* comes to market.] **1839** Wied *Reise Innere Nord-America* 1.190, Yankee-Korn. Reift im September, ist productiv und schwer. [=Yankee corn. Ripens in September; is productive and heavy.] **1851** *Prairie Farmer* 11.568 **WI,** Many of us here northward plant the "Yankee corn." . . It keeps better in our out door cribs than the "dent corn." **1875** *Daily NE Press* (Nebraska City) 23 Aug 2/2, Mr. Geddis, planted ten acres of corn—the common field corn such as is raised in the state of New York and throughout New England. It is eight-rowed, and known in the West as "Yankee corn." **1890** *Sun. Herald* (Syracuse NY) 30 Mar 3/6, New England or Yankee corn is hard and contains much oil. **1916** *IA Homestead* 19 Oct 10 **ME,** The corn generally planted at that time was known as Yankee corn, and was as hard as flint and as yellow as gold. **1941** *Limestone Democrat* (Athens AL) 7 Aug 2/4, Northern or Yankee corn is hard and gritty.

Yankee cotton n Also *damn Yankee cotton* **esp Sth** *joc* Cf **Yankee rain**

Snow.

1969 *DARE* File **TN,** Yankee cotton—snow. **2007** in 2009 *DARE* File—Internet **cwFL,** Does it snow about that time? Cause you know this cracker ain't never drove in that yankee cotton. *Ibid* **Sth,** Here's a couple pics for my southern friends who have yet to see any snow this year. [Resp:] Great update!!! I love the Yankee cotton [=photo of snow on seed pods]. **2008** *Ibid* **AL,** I had a friend from Alabama who always called it "damn Yankee cotton." Of course he always said he was almost 21 before he found out "damn yankee" wasn't all one word. *Ibid* **swOR,** I Love All this Yankee Cotton Falling from The Sky . . Reminds Me Of 15 years of Living in Michigan.

Yankee dime n Also rarely *Yankee nickel* **chiefly Sth, S Midl, esp AL** See Map Cf **Dutch nickel, Quaker fip**

A kiss, esp one offered as a reward; hence something of little or no value.

1846 *Huron Reflector* (Norwalk OH) [13 Jan 3]/1 (newspaper-archive.com), The following was the direction upon a letter which passed through the Rochester post-office a few days since: Pray Mr. Post Master, I want to go / To David Lawton, in Ohio./ In Seneca county, in Scipio town,/ And village of Republic please let me down./ If you'll do me this favor in double quick time,/ You shall have my best wishes and a Yankee dime. **1901** *Galveston Daily News* (TX) 8 Sept [16]/1 (newspaperarchive.com), You have (if you'll pardon my using a slangy phrase) got me "stumped," for 'tis as plain as daylight that you've won that "Yankee dime," but you will have to wait till after Christmas before you get it. **1908** (1909) Morse *Cowboy Cavalier* 39 **TX,** "I'll bet Miss Marian a Yankee dime it won't rain for a week," called out Tadpole. "What's a Yankee dime?" asked Marion. . . "In plain English, it means a kiss." **1949** *PADS* 11.13 **wTX** (as of 1911–29), Yankee dime. . . A kiss. **1955** *Sun* (Baltimore MD) 21 July 14/7 *(Hench Coll.),* Will you try again to procure an explanation of "Yankee Dime" as a synonym for a kiss? **1957** *Sat. Eve. Post Letters* **GA,** One expression used by my subteen and early teen contemporaries was a euphemism for a kiss, namely, "a Yankee dime." **c1960** *Wilson Coll.* **csKY,** Yankee dime. . . A kiss, usually a stolen one. **1965–70** *DARE* (Qu. HH30, *Things that are nicknamed for different nationalities—for example, a 'Dutch treat'*) 19 Infs,

10 **AL,** Yankee dime—a kiss; **KY84,** Yankee nickel—a kiss. **1968** *Jrl. Amer. Folkl.* 81.71, A common proverbial expression used by Southerners when speaking to children is "I'll give you a Yankee Dime." The saying is an inducement to the child to perform some small chore. . . When the favor is performed as requested, the child receives, to his disappointment, a kiss from the adult; if he protests he is told the kiss *is* the Yankee dime. . . In my own family the proverb has been in use for at least four generations, which would indicate that it was known in north Georgia by the later 1800's. . . In asking many Southern friends . . I found only one or two failed to recognize it. **1970** *Ibid* 83.461 **seAL,** It is impossible to recall the first time I was doubtless fooled into expecting a reward or surprise (the promised Yankee dime) for performing some small task. . . Occasionally among children and teenagers, the term implied the hasty kiss of puppy lovers. . . More often between siblings and their compeers, the expression was an admission of a lack in bargaining power. One person would make a request of another. The second would ask, "What will you give me?" When the answer was "A Yankee dime," the reaction was usually a disdainful grunt which meant that the request was denied. **1979** Bowden *Always Rivers Flow* 141 **nwFL** (as of 1930s–40s), "Gimme a Yankee dime," says Aunt Johnnie Bell, . . offering a cheek for a kiss. **1991** *DARE* File **Baltimore MD,** A "Yankee dime" is a kiss—a patronizing form of payment and worthless on the market. It was offered to the young, unwary, or unsophisticated. Although soon enough they caught on! In our family it was also offered as currency in a more loving way, as an excuse to show caring. **1992** *DARE* File **AL** (as of 1950s), My mother used to tell me, "If you'll take out the garbage, I'll give you a Yankee dime." I use the same expression on my kids today, and it gets me just as far as it got her—nowhere! **1995–97** in 2004 Montgomery-Hall *Dict. Smoky Mt. Engl.* 662 **wNC, eTN,** Yankee dime. . . A kiss, usu given to a child in return for a small favor such as doing a household chore. . . [5 infs] ; . . also *yankee nickel* [1 inf]. **2002** *DARE* File **AL,** "Yankee dime"—A kiss.

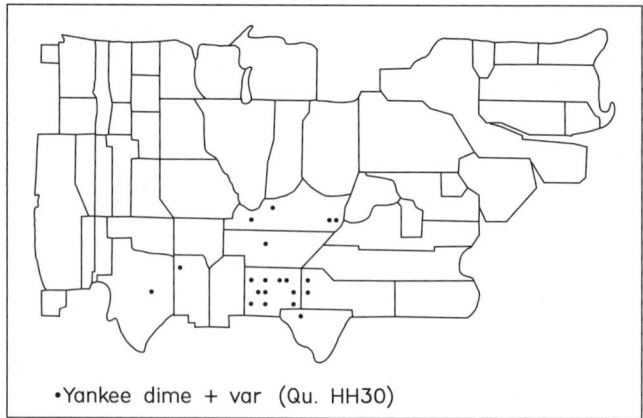

•Yankee dime + var (Qu. HH30)

‡Yankee-jawed adv Cf *whonky-jawed* (at **whonker-jawed**)
1967 *DARE* (Qu. MM13, *The table was nice and straight until he came along and knocked it _____*) Inf **TX10,** Yankee-jawed.

Yankee lice n
=beggar ticks 1.
1903 *Waterloo Daily Reporter* (IA) 8 June 2/4, Certain years, a certain weed will predominate, but this year we find all are present, namely, the morning-glory, wild buckwheat, milk weed, ragweed, Spanish needle, Yankee lice [etc]. **1950** *WELS Suppl.* **WI,** 2 Infs, Yankee lice—sticktights; 1 inf, Yankee lice—beggar lice; 1 Inf, Yankee lice—48 years ago—grew along the road. . . pronged, shield-shaped—or was it the burr with the stickers? **1980** Mueller *Also Sumpter* 29 **WI,** During the Civil War anyone north of the Mason-Dixon line was referred to as a "Yankee," and very frequently as a "damned Yankee!" Even the annoying, clinging seeds of the weed commonly known as "sticktights" were referred to as "Yankee lice," by the local Germans.

Yankee minute n **esp Sth, S Midl**
=New York minute.
1995 Karr *Liars' Club* 79 **eTX,** I just followed Lecia's advice for once and stood still, and sure enough, the whipping was over in a Yankee minute. **2004** Klein *Such Vicious Minds* 182 **TN** (as of 1965), Everybody in the valley's got a different theory about how Timmy came up with the money for his face. . . Most popular one being that he was part of that bank holdup over in De Kalb, but I don't believe that for a Yankee minute. **2006** *DARE* File—Internet **SC,** Just . . follow the masses

& they'll be on your heels in a yankee minute. **2007** *Ibid* **TN,** Hay Javin, I'll accept them in a yankee minute!

Yankee nickel   See **Yankee dime**

Yankee nutcake   See **nutcake**

Yankee pea   See **Yankee bean**

‡Yankee rain n   Cf **Yankee cotton**

   1978 Doig *This House* 261 (as of c1960), A barracks-mate from Houston [TX] came beside me as I looked out the window to the fat fresh snow: "Thet Yankee rain is startin' to pile up, ain't it?"

Yankee shot you, where the n   For addit varr see quots   **Sth, S Midl**   Cf **Indian** n **B6**
The navel.

   1966–69 *DARE* (Qu. X34, *. . Names and nicknames for the navel*) Infs **GA**3, 77, 89, **SC**3, Where the (*or* a) Yankee shot you. **1976** Mitchell *How to Speak* np, *Yankee shot:* A Southern child's navel. "Momma what's this on my belly?" "That's where the Yankee shot you." **2002** *DARE* File—Internet **VA,** I was raised being taught that my bellybutton was the place where "the Yankee shot you!" **2007** *Ibid* **SC,** The old women at church told us that our belly buttons were "where the Yankee shot you."

Yankee sled n
A type of stoutly made sled for transporting heavy goods.

   1854 *ME Farmer* (Augusta) 14 Dec 3/4, [Advt:] Sleds. *Davis' Yankee Sleds,* for sale by *B.S. Farnham.* **1876** Knight *Amer. Mech. Dict.* 3.2204, *Sled. . .* The *Yankee* sled has wide runners which elevate the benches sufficiently. **1889** Butler *Personal Recoll.* 171 **KS** (as of 1856), A heavy snow had fallen. . . Myself and brother-in-law had made a heavy Yankee sled that would hold all the load that was put on it. **1924** *Indiana Weekly Messenger* (PA) 28 Feb 5/4, One sled loaded with oak boards 8 feet long was seen on our streets last week. The sled was an old fashioned Yankee sled. **1949** *Coshocton Tribune* (OH) 28 Mar 9/5, [Advt:] *Public Sale. . .* Farm Machinery. . . Yankee sled, log sled, [etc]. **1969** *DARE* (Qu. N40a, *. . Sleighs . . for hauling loads*) Inf **KY**39, Yankee sled—higher off the ground than ordinary sled. **2001** *Indiana Gaz.* (PA) 5 Oct 26/6, [Advt:] *Auction. . .* Yankee sled.

Yankee weed n   chiefly **TX, LA**
A **boneset 1** (here: *Eupatorium capillifolium* or *E. compositifolium*).

   1911 LA Ag. Exper. Sta. *LA Bulletin* 130.38, The principal weeds to be combatted in lespedeza fields are rag weed, cockle burrs and yankee weed. **1924** *Torreya* 24.6 **LA,** *Eupatorium capillifolium.* . . Yankee weed, Baton Rouge, La. **1946** Reeves–Bain *Flora TX* 247, *E[upatorium] capillifolium.* . . Yankee Weed. *Ibid* 248, *E. compositifolium.* . . Yankee Weed. **1957** *Panola Watchman* (Carthage TX) 20 June 3/2, Rosin or Yankee weed can be effectively controlled with chemicals. **1967** *DARE* (Qu. S21, *. . Weeds . . that are a trouble in gardens and fields*) Inf **LA**6, Yankee weeds—green leaf with a red-looking stalk. **2007** *DARE* File—Internet **AL,** *Eupatorium compositifolium* . . Yankee Weed.

yank-up n
=**twitch-up.**

   1875 Temple–Sheldon *Hist. Northfield* 46 **MA,** They were wonderfully expert in killing game . . and in capturing both larger and smaller sorts by means of drive-ways, and in rude traps and yank-ups. The latter was nothing more than a stout white oak or hickory straddle, bent over and fastened to a notch cut in another tree. **1965** Needham–Mussey *Country Things* 8 **VT,** Gramp . . used to catch game with deadfalls, snares, and yank-ups, which are snares on a larger scale.

yanner   See **yonder A6**

yannigan n   Also *yannigan bag*   [Perh var of **wanigan**]
A bag for transporting one's personal belongings.

   1925 *AmSp* 1.136 **Pacific NW** [Logger talk], In nearly every instance these names and phrases originated among the loggers themselves. Like such old terms as "cross-cut," "bitted," "yannigan" and "snubline" they had the ringing life of the timber in them. **1931** *AmSp* 7.52 **Sth, SW** [Lumberjack lingo], Lumberjacks carry their clothes in "yannigan bags." **1942** Berrey–Van den Bark *Amer. Slang* 472.1 [Tramp and Criminal], Implements and devices. . . yannigan bag . . *a clothes bag.* *Ibid* 874.9 [Army], Haversack; kit. . . yannigan bag. *Ibid* 915.17 [Western], Bag; trunk . . yannigan bag, *a bag for personal belongings.*

yanside   See **yonside**

yant n   **SW, esp AZ**
An agave (here: *Agave utahensis*).

   1872 in 1949 *UT Hist. Qrly.* 17.404 **AZ,** In his journal, W.C. Powell recorded, on March 21, 1872, " . . Most of the tribe [=the Pah-Utes] are now out on the plateau, gathering yant—a species of the rose *[Agave].* From this product they make a cake, by baking it in the ashes. It is said to taste like roasted chestnuts." **1902** Dellenbaugh *Romance Colorado R.* 71 **AZ,** A little farther is the "yant" of the Pai Ute. . . This is a source of food for the native, who roasts the asparagus-like tip starting up in the spring. **1933** Harrington *Gypsum Cave NV* 82, Among traces of wild plants used as food the most numerous were the quids or "chews" of mescal, sometimes called "yant" (*Agave utahensis*). **1938** *Ogden Std.-Examiner* (UT) [25 Dec 39]/3 **AZ** (newspaperarchive.com), Indian yant ovens are eloquent of at least overnight occupancy. **1997** *Boatman's Qrly. Rev.* (Internet) **AZ** (as of c1875), The family traveled seasonally into Grand Canyon to gather "yant" (a clonal species of agave) in the springtime. **2008** *DARE* File—Internet, Utah Agave, Yant—*Agave utahensis.*

yanway(s)   See **yonway**

yap n   scattered, but chiefly **Nth, West**   See Map
The mouth.

   1871 *Our Young Folks* 7.594 **NEng,** She sobbed and cried outright. Then the big showman . . told her very sternly to "hold her yap." **1900** *DN* 2.70 [College slang], *Yap.* . . The mouth. **1945** O'Hara *Pipe Night* 178 **PA,** The only time I opened my yap, I said to my brother-in-law: "Why don't you get a bunch of them French seventy-fives." **1965–70** *DARE* (Qu. X9, *Joking or uncomplimentary words for a person's mouth* . . *"I wish he'd shut his _____."*) 90 Infs, **scattered, but chiefly Nth, West,** (Big) yap; (Qu. X10b, *To tell a person to stop talking—not very politely*) Infs **GA**54, **IN**75, **VT**16, Shut your yap; (Qu. GG23a, *If you speak sharply to somebody to make him be patient . . "Now just keep your _____."*) Inf **NY**40, Yap shut; (Qu. HH7b, *Someone who talks too much, or too loud: "He's always _____."*) Inf **MA**35, Shooting off his yap; **MA**71, Wagging his yap; (Qu. HH8, *A person who likes to brag*) Inf **MA**55, Got his yap goin' all the time; (Qu. II22, *Expressions to tell somebody to keep to himself and mind his own business*) Inf **NY**22, Close up your yap; (Qu. JJ44, *Expressions about someone who can be trusted to keep a secret: "Don't worry about him, he'll _____."*) Inf **NY**234, Keep his yap shut. **1994** *DARE* File **Brooklyn NYC,** I can still hear my father remarking that the neighborhood big-mouth should close his "fat yap." **2006** Killian *Life* 17 **sCA,** You've been out here less than twenty-four hours, so shut your yap and just be grateful I managed to get you your own bedroom.

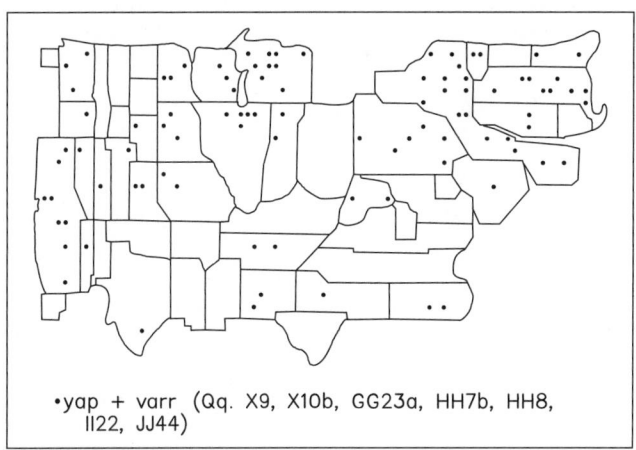

•yap + varr (Qq. X9, X10b, GG23a, HH7b, HH8,
       II22, JJ44)

yapan, yapon   See **yaupon**

yar   See **year** n[1]

yarb   See **herb A2**

yard n   chiefly **NEng, Pacific NW**   Cf **landing 1, skidway a**
In logging: an area where logs are collected in preparation for loading or transport; the logs so collected.

   1905 U.S. Forest Serv. *Bulletin* 61.53 [Logging terms], *Yard.* . . See Landing. [*Ibid* 41, *Landing.* . . A place to which logs are hauled or skidded preparatory to transportation by water or rail.] **1907** *DN* 3.251 **eME,** *Yard.* . . A heap of logs not far from the section of woods in which they were cut. *Yard tender*. . . A woodsman who heaps up logs at the yard. **1914** [see **yard** v **a**]. **1942** ME Univ. *Studies* 57.135, *Yard*. A space cleared of trees where *pulpwood* is sawed and piled. **1958** McCulloch *Woods Words* 217 **Pacific NW**, *Yard*. . . The area within reach of a donkey engine's usual haul. **1959** [see **yard** v **a**]. **1969** Sorden *Lumberjack Lingo* 145 **NEng, Gt Lakes**, *Yard*—The place where logs were assembled, generally before transporting them to the river. Same as landing. **1975** Gould *ME Lingo* 325, *Yard*—The place where any harvested wood is piled when brought from the cutting to await the next step in moving toward the mill.

yard v **chiefly NEng, Pacific NW**
In logging:

a also with *out;* To haul or drag (a log) to some central point; hence vbl n *yarding;* ppl adj *yarded.*

1866 Cincinnati Chamber Commerce *Annual Rept. for 1866* 56, We put down the whole amount of pine yarded the past year at sixty-five to seventy million feet. **1896** in 2009 (acc) Lexis–Nexis Legal Research *State Case Law: ME* (Internet), The plaintiff . . supposing that he did not want the logs so left and that there was nobody to care for them . . had these logs to the amount of 146,210 feet "yarded" and placed on skids . . so that they could be hauled during the ensuing winter to a lake and from thence driven to his mill at Machias to be sawed. . . After the plaintiff learned that the logs were being hauled by Allen he notified the defendant by letter, wherein he said: "All can be arranged satisfactory now by paying for the yarding." **1900** *Overland Mth.* (2d ser) 36.202 **wWA**, This engine [=yarding engine] "yards out" the logs from the other two camps, and the entire trainload is then taken . . a distance of twenty miles from the camps. **1907** *DN* 3.251 **eME**, *Yard*. . . To haul logs from where they were cut to one place and pile them up there. Later in the season they are hauled to the *landings* on the rivers. **1911** Clayson *Hist. Narr.* 25 **wWA** (as of c1870), They were "yarding out" a very large log and Holyoke was helping the hook tender. **1914** *DN* 4.83 **ME, nNH**, *Yard*. . . To pile timber. A yard is the place in the woods where logs are piled. **1940** Writers' Program *Oregon* 369, The donkey-puncher, or engine operator, "opens her up" and the log rises above stumps and brush as he yards it to the landing. **1942** ME Univ. *Studies* 57.135, *Yarded-wood.* Pulpwood twitched or hauled to a *yard* in tree lengths. **1946** Gould *Yankee Storekeeper* 46 **NEng**, I had quite a quantity of wood that had to be yarded to the road to top out the load. **1950** *Western Folkl.* 9.121 **nwOR** [Logger speech], *Yarding.* The act of skidding logs from the woods. **1959** *AmSp* 34.80 **nwCA** [Logger lingo], *Yard*. . . To accumulate logs or bolts in a yard or at a skidway. **1966** *DARE* (Qu. OO46a, *Talking about dragging something heavy: "We hitched the log on and _____ it out [of the woods]."*) Inf **ME**24, They yard it out. **1966–68** *DARE* Tape **CA**100, They yarded the logs in to . . chute 'em down; **ME**1, No matter how long a log was, if it was sixty, seventy foot, they yarded it and drove it down the river. **1979** *Oregonian Article Letters* **wOR, wWA** [Logging terms], "Whistle punk" . . is the man who blows the whistle after he has hooked the log and it's ready to be yarded back to the landing.

b as vbl n *yarding;* used attrib in var combs: See quots.

1900 *Overland Mth.* (2d ser) 36.202 **wWA**, When all the cars are loaded [with logs], they . . are taken away by the yarding-engine. **1905** U.S. Forest Serv. *Bulletin* 61.53 **Pacific** [Logging terms], *Yarding donkey.* A donkey engine mounted upon a heavy sled, used in yarding logs by drum and cable. **1942** Rich *We Took to Woods* 95 **ME**, A yarding crew consists of three men and a twitch horse. **1945** Hamlin *9 Mile Bridge* 46 **nME**, The main yarding spot is on the bank of a river. **1958** McCulloch *Woods Words* 218 **Pacific NW**, *Yarding chance*—A setting. *Yarding grabs*—A pair of grabs or tongs once used in yarding. *Yarding line*—The main line on some skyline yarding systems is known as the yarding line. *Yarding roller*—A vertical spool used at one time to lead the rigging in a part circle back of the donkey, enabling it to yard directly back of the landing. *Yarding spool*—a. A vertical spool on an old time donkey. b. A heavy sheave on a bracket, acting as a block for cable to run through in ground lead logging. . . *Yarding tower*—a. The big steel tower used on a steel spar skidder. b. A light tower built on a tractor. **1969** Sorden *Lumberjack Lingo* 145 **NEng, Gt Lakes**, *Yarding sled*—A short heavy sled used to haul logs to the yard or landing. One end of the log was placed on the bunk while the other end dragged on the ground. Same as dray.

yard-a-night n *joc* Cf **foot-a-night, mile-a-minute**
=**kudzu.**

1974 Betts–Walser *NC Folkl.* 7, Yard-a-night: kudzu vine (Chatham

County). **1976** *Free Lance–Star* (Fredericksburg VA) 29 Sept 40/4 **LA**, One Louisianan told the Associated Press: " . . My daddy called it 'yard-a-night,[1] 'cause I'd swear it grows that fast." **1976** *KY Folkl. Rec.* 22.69 **MS**, Yard-a-Night Vine—Foot-a-Night Vine, Kudzu *Pueraria lobata.* **2008** *DARE* File—Internet **GA**, [Kudzu is] sometimes called "yard-a-night" down here because that's how fast it seems to grow.

yard ape n

1 An unruly, mischievous, or physically active child—also used as a nickname for such a child.

1974 Betts–Walser *NC Folkl.* 7, Yard ape: a child. **1988** *Chron.-Telegram* (Elyria OH) 15 Oct sec C 3/8, Super "B" / With love / Duckie, Rug Rate [sic] / Yard Ape / Tammy & Stacy / To the two sweetest kids!/ Love, Mom. **1990** *Gettysburg Times* (PA) 6 Jan sec A 4/5, *Language:* 'Rug rats and tykes'. . . the really fun phrases are affectionate terms that may well result from the headaches and frustrations of raising children. . . We mean phrases that describe kids' behavior: *rug rat . . yard ape*. . . *Yard ape* is a fine designation for folk who climb trees and swing through foliage as if they were Tarzan or one of his chimpanzee friends. **1997** *DARE* File eTN (as of c1985), Yard ape—same as an ankle-biter. **2001** *DARE* File—Internet, My kid will not be a wild New England Yard Ape and unless we vacation in some poverty stricken section of upstate Vermont or sections of Maine traversable only by logging roads, she won't even know what one is. **2005** *DARE* File—Internet **CA** [*Urban Dict.*], Yard ape . . A child between the ages of 3–12 years. Known for their loud noises and boisterous activity. *The upstairs neighbors were reported to the landlord for allowing their yard ape and his friends to play soccer indoors.*

2 Used as a derog term for:
a A Black person.

1973 Nilsen *Meaning Ling. & Lit.* 336 **GA**, A variety of "animal" terms have been adopted as names for blacks: *ape, blackbird, buck . . yard ape.* Each term appears to be based on a pejorative metaphor. **1986** Pederson *LAGS Concordance (Negro)* 1 inf, **seAL**, Yard apes; *(Rustic)* 1 inf, **csTN**, Yard ape—pejorative for black; 1 inf, **cAL**, Yard ape—term for a black. **1999** (2000) Greenlaw *Hungry Ocean* 82 **ME**, 'Nigger' doesn't bother me half as much as 'yard ape' and 'porch monkey.' **2006** *DARE* File—Internet **VA** [*Urban Dict.*], Yard ape . . a nigger who sits in their yard all day long because they have no job and cannot afford air conditioning and they are pretty much a useless person.

b A White person; see quots.

1986 Pederson *LAGS Concordance (Caucasian)* 1 inf, **seAL**, Yard ape—pejorative. **2003** *DARE* File—Internet [*Urban Dict.*], Yard ape. . . Inbreed [sic] white "trash" species of the human race, not specifically human that sit in lawn chairs outside their trailer homes with no more than 3 teeth in their mouth and drink Budweisers in Coozies. **2006** *Ibid* **IN**, Yard ape . . An amish man, or any one with an amish background. *Those diryt* [sic] *yard apes need to shower more often.*

yard ax n Also sp *yard axe* **chiefly SE**

1 A utility ax used for general household purposes; hence fig adj phr *dull as a yard ax* very dull.

1930 Shelby–Stoney *Po' Buckra* 159 **SC**, Bartly found his new employer . . chopping wood back of the Pineland house with a dull yardaxe. **1950** [see **2** below]. **1967** *Jet* 12 Jan 56 **FL**, A 57-year-old Tampa, Fla., father who was chopped in the side with a yard ax by his 15-year-old son sought revenge by attempting to cut off his son's ear with the same ax. **2004** Hargrave *LSU Law* 28 **LA** (as of c1915), At least one of his students said, "He was just a [sic] dull as a yard ax, I thought." **2004** Baldwin *Inland Passages* 32 **SC**, My first job out of graduate school (many years ago) was to work with this retired tugboat captain as a "ship's carpenter," which is a rather exacting discipline Joe administered almost completely with a yard axe. **2007** in 2009 *DARE* File—Internet **AL**, I would add a 120 grit belt for stuff that has been abused (bad chips) (Yard Ax, Truck chopper, Cheep [sic] throwing knifes) or major work needed. **2008** *Times & Democrat* (Orangeburg SC) 11 Apr (Internet), The yard ax was always left with the blade in a splitting log, where the next person would know exactly where to pick it up. **2008** in 2009 *DARE* File—Internet **FL**, Yeah, if I caught my neighbor in my yard smashing an animal I would be after him with our yard ax.

2 also *yard-ax preacher:* An unprofessional, part-time lay preacher; similarly, *yard-ax lawyer.* **esp SC** Cf **jackleg** adj **1, table tapper**

1902 *Savannah Tribune* (GA) 19 July 2/5 [Black], There are only two men fighting against the pastor . . , for they do not want a little yard ax so called preacher who will . . tell them to go way back and take a back seat where coons like them are seldom seen. 1949 Turner *Africanisms* 232 **sSC, GA coasts** [Gullah], yɑd ɑks 'preacher,' i.e. 'yard ax'. 1950 *PADS* 14.73 **SC,** *Yard axe.* . . A preacher of little ability. Negro usage. The *yard axe* is used in many ways by many hands, and cannot be kept sharp. *Yard axe lawyer.* . . A person, not a lawyer, who nevertheless gives legal opinions on a variety of subjects. 1951 *AmSp* 26.15 **SC** [Black], *Yard ax,* 'poorly trained irregular preacher,' . . [has] been recorded chiefly in the Georgetown and Charleston areas and in the Santee Valley. 1986 Pederson *LAGS Concordance (Jackleg preacher)* 1 inf, **neTN,** Yard ax—for a preacher; 1 inf, **neTN,** Yard ax—untrained preacher. 2005 *DARE* File **SC,** That [=stumpknocker] . . reminded me of what we in South Carolina also called itinerant or inept preachers: 'yard ax' or 'yard ax preacher' = usually one who declared himself a preacher (self-ordained), was not the pastor of a church, but usually attended a single church where he would fill-in for that pastor or from which he would be called to fill in when a preacher was needed.

yard baby See **yard child 2, 3**

yard broom n   Also *yard brush*   **chiefly Sth, S Midl**   See Map Cf **brush broom** n[1]

A coarse broom, usu of brushwood, or a rake with flexible tines.

1903 *Atlanta Constitution* (GA) 5 Apr [38]/2 (newspaperarchive.com), The young man persisted in scattering the feathers over the ward [sic] and his sister struck him with the yard broom. 1933 Rawlings *South Moon* 47 **nFL,** She went a short way into the scrub and cut boughs of Highland ti-ti for a new yard-broom. 1954 *PADS* 21.41 **SC,** *Yard broom.* . . See *brush broom.* [Ibid 21, *Brush broom* . . : A broom made by binding small branches together for sweeping the yard.] 1965–70 *DARE* (Qu. F36, . . *Kinds of brooms*) 11 Infs, **chiefly Sth, S Midl,** Yard broom; **GA**67, **MA**124, Yard broom—old-fashioned; **AL**30, **SC**11, 43, Yard broom—brush [*or* bresh] broom; **MD**35, Yard broom—like a regular household broom, but heavier; **VA**72, Yard broom—very stiff, sweep up leaves; **MS**1, Yard broom—made of brush; **NC**84, Yard broom—tie twigs or shrubs together; **SC**3, Yard broom—made of slender, springy sticks; **SC**6, Yard broom—made from limber twigs; **SC**9, Yard broom—made of limbs; **SC**42, Yard broom—branches bound together; **SC**62, Yard broom—limbs bound together, used outside like a rake; **AL**15, Yard broom—use dog fennels; **SC**38, Yard broom—made of dog fennel, for sweeping yard; **GA**3, Yard broom—gallberry branches tied together; **LA**40, Yard broom—made of gallberry bushes; **GA**88, Yard broom—used to be made of dog fennel or gallberry; **AL**11, **LA**9, Yard broom—leaf rake; **TX**33, Yard broom [FW: rake really, I think]; **AR**2, Yard broom—wire teeth; **FL**49, Yard broom or yard bresh—strips of metal; **IA**25, Yard broom—a pliable rake, made of metal; **KY**63, Yard broom—made of metal; **KY**84, Yard broom—made of wire; **MD**30, Yard broom—made of strips of steel, used to rake up leaves in yard; **MO**4, Yard broom—metal one you rake the yard with; **TX**32, Yard broom—made of wire; **GA**53, Yard broom—bamboo type thing, held together with strips of cloth; [**HI**1, Yard broom—Filipino man says; **IA**22, Yard broom—made of wooden fibers; a push broom.] 1967–68 *DARE* FW Addit **AL,** *Yard broom*—a metal rake or leaf rake. This, obviously, is an adaptation or borrowing of what country people still do (i.e. literally sweep their yards since they have no grass). *Yard broom* also refers to a type of home-made witches' broom; **swAR,** I recalled that in Cale, AR, in the early '50s, this article—a rake with slender springy metal teeth for leaves in the yard—was called *yard broom.* 1975 McDonough *Garden Sass* 206 **AR,** Roy Simpson said, "I never saw any country yard that had a lawn. They'd take an old brush broom or one made out of cane and get out and sweep it." Aunt Alma recalled that she used dogwood branches tied together to make a yard broom when she was a girl. 1983 *MJLF* 9.1.62 **ceKY** (as of 1956), *Yard broom* . . a brush broom. 1986 Pederson *LAGS Concordance,* **Gulf Region,** 6 infs, Yard broom; 4 infs, Yard broom—(made of) gallberry; 3 infs, Yard broom—for leaves (with long handle); 2 infs, Yard broom—made from dogwood sprouts; 1 inf, Yard broom—fan shaped, aluminum; 1 inf, Yard broom—swept yard which was dirt; 1 inf, Yard broom—of straw—to sweep yard (all sand); 1 inf, Yard broom—old house broom, used like leaf rake; 1 inf, Yard broom—rake, for leaves; 1 inf, Yard broom = brush broom—to sweep yard, no grass; 1 inf, Yard broom—also homemade; 1 inf, Yard broom—made from limbs; 1 inf, **neFL,** Yard brush—bushes or

small trees used; rake yard.   2003 in 2009 *DARE* File—Internet **seAL,** When a country person speaks of sweeping the yard with the yard broom, he means for it to be raked with what a city person thinks of as a leaf rake.

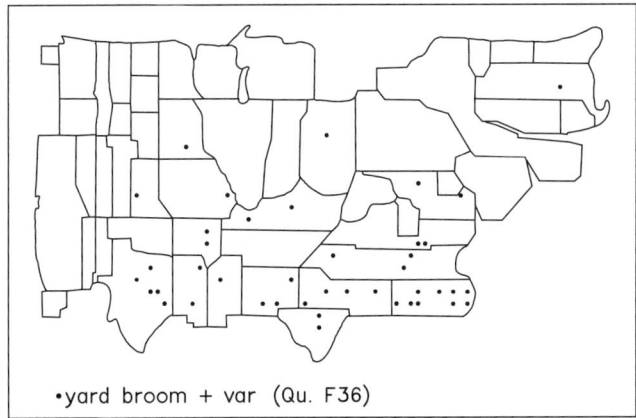

•yard broom + var (Qu. F36)

yard child n

1 A legitimate child.   **SC, GA**   [Cf *DJE* yard-child "A child who lives in the household of its father"]

1924 *Amer. Mercury* 3.367 **sGA** [Black], "Ahze got sebin yahd chillun." "What do you mean by yard children?" "Wall, yuh see them chillun a-runnin' aroun' th' yahd? Them's yahd chillun." . . "How is it that you have other children that are not in this yard?" "Well, cap'n, yuh see, ah strays!" 1927 Peterkin *Black April* 267 **SC** [Gullah], I hope ev'y lawful yard-chile you had by Leah 'll perish. 1950 *PADS* 14.73 **SC,** *Yard child.* . . A legitimate child. 1993 Tartt *Dim Roads* 68 **SC** [Black], Can't nobody 'spute dat, en us had four lawful yard chillun, two gals an' two boys.

2 also *yard baby:* An illegitimate child.   **esp S Atl, Gulf States**

1944 *PADS* 2.52 **NC, VA,** *Yard-child.* . . A bastard. 1947 (1952) Ellison *Invisible Man* 274, He possessed the chiseled, black-marble features sometimes found . . in southern towns in which the white offspring of house children and the black offspring of yard children bear names, features and character traits as identical as the rifling of bullets fired from a common barrel. 1951 Young *Pavilion* 34 **MS,** I do not recall how many children she had—eight or ten perhaps—but I do remember that there was no question of "house chillun and yard chillun," which is to say those of a husband and those of a passer-by, since Maria never had any husband. 1958 Feibleman *Place* 19 **New Orleans LA,** A yard-child means when a nigger girl slave went and had her dress lifted by some white man on the plantation and then got pregnant and wound up with a baby. Then they called the baby a yard-child. 1966–70 *DARE* (Qu. Z11b, . . [*A child whose parents were not married*]) Infs **FL**18, **GA**12, **VA**5, Yard child; [**MI**113, Yard child [heard from Bahamian in Virgin Islands]]. 1986 Pederson *LAGS Concordance (Bastard)* 1 inf, **swTN,** A yard child; 1 inf, **cnAL,** Yard children = illegitimate?—Unsure; heard. 1988 Lincoln *Avenue* 45 **wNC** (as of c1940) [Black], One popular explanation was that Ramona Tait was the yard child of a former governor of the state of South Carolina. 1997 (2006) Palfrey *Price of Passion* 41 **TX,** She had the urge to throw the chair back, grab the mike and yell, "He's a liar! This is his yard-baby!" 2009 Ross *Miss Julia Delivers Goods* 281 **cnAL,** They hardly any way out 'cept Miss Hazel Marie stay here an' have two little yard chil'ren for everybody to talk about.

3 also *yard baby:* A child old enough to be unsupervised; see quots.   **esp S Atl, Gulf States**   Cf **knee baby, lap child, porch ~**

1950 *PADS* 14.73 **SC,** *Yard child.* . . A child old and mature enough to shift for himself in the yard. 1968–69 *DARE* FW Addit **csNC,** *Yard baby*—[child] old enough to run in the yard. 1973 *DARE* File **cAL** (as of c1946), Children at different ages: lap child, knee child, yard child, [etc]. a1975 Lunsford *It Used to Be* 179 **sAppalachians,** A "yard baby" is one large enough to run around in the yard. 1986 Pederson *LAGS Concordance,* 1 inf, **cnGA,** Yard baby—larger than "porch baby". 1989 *DARE* File **cAR,** Kids are called different things—"lap child" or "yard child"—depending on their size.

‡**yard colt** n Cf **yard child 2**
=**woods colt 2.**
　1968 DARE (Qu. Z11b, . . [A child whose parents were not married]) Inf **VA5,** Yard colt.

yarded　See **yard** v a

yard egg n esp **Sth, S Midl** Cf **ranch egg**
A fresh egg; see quots.
　1879 Titusville Morning Herald (PA) 11 Nov [4]/2 (newspaperarchive.com), The brownest battercakes, the crispest fried potatoes and the most delicate yard eggs are reserved for those magnates of the rear premises. **1900** Galveston Daily News (TX) 25 Feb 19/4, [Advt:] Yard eggs, 20 cents per dozen. **1908** Sunset 21.792, If you were working with ranch eggs, store eggs or yard eggs, it might be different. **1917** DN 4.421 **LA,** Yard eggs. Eggs from chickens kept on the premises, as distinguished from store eggs. **c1938** in 1970 Hyatt Hoodoo 2.1070 **seLA,** Yo' take a aig—any kind of hen's aig but let it be a fresh aig, a fresh yard-egg. **1953** Brewer Word Brazos 75 **eTX** [Black], He . . tells her to go an' cook Elduh Wheeler some good ole home-cured bacon an' half a dozen fresh yaa'd eggs. **2001** DARE File—Internet **LA,** Yard eggs, which come from free-ranging (running around outdoors) chickens, have a more colorful yolk due to the chicken getting green forage. . . Honestly, the yard eggs did taste better, actually fresher. **2004** S. Reg. Summer 23 **MS,** Let the world know about how your family reunions revolve around eating deviled yard eggs.

yarder n [**yard** v]
In logging:
1 A person engaged in yarding logs. Cf **skidder** n **2a**
　1968 Adams Western Words 354, Yarder—A logger's name for a man who brings logs to a yard, q.v. Also, a machine, usually a donkey engine, that moves logs to a yard.
2 A donkey engine used in yarding; see quots. **Pacific NW** Cf **skidder 2c**
　1911 Pacific Mth. Apr 376, The hook-tender gives the signal to the engineer of the "yarder" as the donkey-engine is termed. **1925** AmSp 1.136 **Pacific NW,** There are generally three donkey engines used to operate a side—a "yarder," a "roader," and a "loader." The yarder may fetch the logs a distance of fifteen hundred feet or more, the roader may take them on for twenty-five hundred feet, and the loader merely swings them up to the "top-loader" and "second-loader" on the cars—"flats" or "trucks." **1941** AmSp 16.234 **MT** [Lumberjack jargon], The machine, usually a donkey engine, which furnishes the power is called the yarder. **1961** Labbe–Goe Railroads 260 **Pacific NW,** [Glossary:] Yarder: The donkey engaged in bringing logs to the spar tree from the point where they were cut. **1968** [see **1** above].

yard grass n
1 =**goose grass 2b.**
　1822 Woods 2 Yrs. Residence 199 **IL,** Yard-grass comes on land that has been much trodden; it is something like cock's-foot-grass, except the seed. **1848** Gray Manual of Botany 588, Eleusine [spp]. . Crab-Grass. Yard-Grass. **1881** Phares Farmer's Book of Grasses 47, E[leusine] indica, Yard Grass. **1890** IN State Bd. Ag. Annual Rept. for 1889–90 31.223, E[leusine] indica. . . Called yard-grass in the South, where it is found common in door-yards. It is also common in this State. **1911** Bayard Advocate (IA) [26 Oct 6]/2 (newspaperarchive.com), Flocks of thousands of these birds [=English sparrows] may be seen in various parts of our country, feeding upon crab grass and yard grass, two weeds that crowd out good turf making grasses. **1969** DARE (Qu. L9a, . . Kinds of grass . . grown for hay) Inf **NC60,** Yard grass.
2 =**bluegrass 1. esp S Midl**
　1840 Farmers' Reg. 8.561 **VA,** The Kentucky blue-grass is well known in Virginia as the yard grass or greensward. **1849** in 1996 Houston Personal Corresp. 3.42 **VA,** I wish you to send me a great quantity of the blue grass. (I mean the yard grass.) **1936** AmSp 11.318 **Ozarks,** Yard grass. . . Blue grass. **1983** MJLF 9.1.62 **ceKY** (as of 1956), Yard grass . . blue grass.
3 =**knotgrass 1.**
　1904 CA Ag. Exper. Sta. Rept. for 1903–04 83, Yard-grass. . . Polygonum aviculare. **1911** Jepson Flora CA 138, P[olygonum] aviculare. . . Yard Grass. . . common in hard, especially beaten soils, and sometimes in cultivated lands.

yarding　See **yard** v a, b

yard out　See **yard** v a

yards off n Cf DS EE13
=**throw the stick.**
　1883 Newell Games & Songs 160, I Spy. . . In a variety of the game, a stick is set up against a tree. One of the players seizes it, and throws it as far as possible. The children hide, while the one who happens to be "it" gets and replaces the stick, after which he proceeds to look for the rest. Those whom he discovers he captures . . until all are taken. If any of the hiders can reach the tree and throw down the stick, all prisoners are released, and the seeker must begin over again. A similar game, in New York, is called "Yards off." **1909** (1923) Bancroft Games 210, Yards off. . . This is a form of I Spy or Hide and Seek, and seems indigenous to New York. All players properly caught by the spy become prisoners, but may be freed in a prescribed way. The procedure which gives time for hiding is also distinctive. **1941** WI Rapids Daily Tribune (WI) 16 Aug 8/7, Yards Off.

yardstick n
=**looper.**
　1968 DARE (Qu. R27, . . Kinds of caterpillars or similar worms) Inf **DE3,** Yardstick (for measuring worm)—old-fashioned.

yare　See **year** n[1]

yargyment　See **argument**

yark　See **york**

‡**yarm** v[1] [Cf EDD yarm v. 4 "To scold . . to find fault, grumble."]
To yammer.
　1924 (1926) Vollmer Sun-Up 18 **sAppalachians,** I didn't leave no bars down. All the time yarmin' about me. **2007** in 2009 DARE File—Internet **NE,** Here we go again. . . this storm showed up an hour early. Where the heck is that global warming everyone is yarming about?

‡**yarm** v[2]
　1926 DN 5.405 **Ozarks,** Yarm. . . To thrust into, to insert. Johnson refers to a native who yarmed a load into his gun.

yarn v[1] [By ext from yarn to tell a story, esp a tall tale]
To lie, tell a falsehood.
　1891 Chambers's Jrl. 8.111 **West,** As they found their journey nearing its end without accident, they regained their usual flow of spirits; and . . each one was ready to persuade himself that the old-timers had been yarning to them. **1906** DN 3.165 **nwAR,** Yarn. . . To lie. "Don't yarn to me." Used by the older generation. **1911** Clements What the Sam Hill 30 **IN,** "How air ye, Lush?" "Oh pretty well; feel a little sleepy, is all." "Up the pike last night?" "Oh, no." "Don't yarn, Lush; seen ye going." **1942** Warnick Garrett Co. MD 16 **nwMD** (as of 1900–18), Yarn, n. and v., fib. **1942** McAtee Dial. Grant Co. IN 72 (as of 1890s), Yarn . . lie; "Don't _____ to me". **1954** Harder Coll. **cwTN,** Yarn. . . to lie. **1956** McAtee Some Dialect NC 51, Yarn. . . v., fib, lie. "Don't yarn to me."

yarn v[2] See **earn** v

yarny n [Cf EDD yarny. . . "Disposed to the telling of long tales."]
　1996 Horton Island Out of Time 241 **Chesapeake Bay MD,** Quicker'n a eel I reached back and snatched me a big jimmy and flung 'im, jest a'snappin' and a'clackin', right at that yarny and his buddies. [Footnote:] yarny: Tangierman; or general derision, like bozo.

yarrow n
Std: a plant of the genus Achillea, esp A. millefolium. For other names of the latter see **dog daisy 3, gordolobo, Indian tobacco 11, life everlasting 4, nosebleed 2, old man 1b;** for other names of Achillea ptarmica see **sneezeweed 2, sneezewort 1**

yarrup n Also yarup, yawup [Echoic]
=**flicker** n[2] **1.**
　1865 Atlantic Mth. 15.517, Another April comer . . is the Golden-Winged Woodpecker, alias, "High-Hole," alias, "Flicker," alias, "Yarup." **1881** Nuttall Ornith. Club Bulletin 6.185, Several terms, "Yarrup," "Wakeup," "Pi-ute," and "Yucker" . . evidently represent the harsh well-known cry of this species; that is, they were at first intended to be imitations of one or another phase of the bird's voice. **1900** Wil-

son Bulletin 12.2.11, *Yarup, Yar-rup, Yaw-up.* Middle States. From its [= the flicker's] ordinary call note. **1938** Oberholser *Bird Life LA* 360, Southern Flicker. . . yarrup.

yarth See **earth**

yarup See **yarrup**

yas(s) adv See **yes 1**

yass n Also sp *jass* [Swiss, south Ger *Jass*] **esp Swiss Ger settlement areas** Cf **clabber** n²
The card game klaberjass or one similar to it.

1913 *Official Rules of Card Games* 216, *Jass.* **1942** *Capital Times* (Madison WI) 8 Feb 6/2 **csWI,** What is this absorbing game of cards being played in so many of these Sugar River Valley communities, where trumping your partner's ace very often happens to be good strategy? Well, the Swiss have had a name for it these many years. They call it "yass" (pronounced yass). **1950** *Daily Reporter* (Dover OH) 18 Mar 3/2, The Jolly Jill Club met this week to play jass in Mrs. Vernon Gordon's home. **1950** *WELS (Card games played a good deal in your neighborhood)* 1 Inf, **csWI,** Yass—Swiss card game similar to pinochle. **1972** *Times–Reporter* (Dover–New Philadelphia OH) 25 Sept sec C 2/1, Ever wonder why out-of-the-area residents look quizzical when they are asked, "How about a game of jass?" . . Jass was introduced in the Sugarcreek area by Swiss immigrants. **1977** *Capital Times* (Madison WI) 4 Jan 13/2, The family had come to Green County in 1849 from Switzerland where Manuel's great-grandfather, in 1846, had lost part of the home farm in a card game called Yass. Unwittingly, he had played it with his back to a mirror. **1999** *WI State Jrl.* (Madison) 14 Mar sec C 1/2 **New Glarus WI,** Sure enough, there are still slogans on the wall in German and guys playing yass, a card game known only in Green County and Switzerland.

yat adv, conj See **yet** adv, conj

yat n¹ See **hat** n

yat n² [From the characteristic greeting, "Where y'at?"] **New Orleans LA**
One who speaks a distinctive working-class white vernacular of New Orleans; the vernacular itself; hence adj *yatty;* n *yattism.*

1968 *DARE* FW Addit **New Orleans LA,** *Yat* =generic term for charmer, greaser, or pit. It comes from the phrase used by these people "where y'at?," a greeting. **1984** *Yeah You Rite* (Video recording) **New Orleans LA,** There are a number of different dialects in the area. . . The three major ones certainly are the downtown white (what is often called the yat dialect), the uptown white (the upper class, upper educated Southern speech), and the black dialect. *Ibid,* The famous Brooklynese of the older city neighborhoods, the so-called yat talk. *Ibid,* There are people that work in our office that greet people . . they have this yatty type dialect . . it's a bad impression on people first entering our office. *Ibid,* When I want to talk proper I will. If there's somebody I have to impress, . . [I'll] let go of my yattism, which is, you know, the yat . . where y'at, yattism, yat power, and so to speak. . . It [=yat talk] sounds ignorant. *Ibid,* In New Orleans many middle class people make fun of . . people they call yats. **1987** Rose *I Remember Jazz* 106, "You don't sound at all like a yat," I said. (Orleanians tease each other for using the phrase "Where y'at" as a greeting, and thus call each other "yats.") **1993** Safire *Quoth the Maven* 25 **New Orleans LA,** "Yats" . . are New Orleanians who live, for the most part, in the Ninth Ward in the eastern part of the city where a heavy settlement of Irish and Italians in the last century produced a unique dialect that bears some similarities, as linguists are fond of pointing out, to Brooklynese. **2005** *NY Times* (NY) 7 Sept (Internet) **LA,** "You can't take the city out of the yat, and you can't take the yat out of the city," said Frank Searle, a longtime Baton Rouge resident.

yaupon n, also attrib Also sp *japon, yapan, yapon, yaupan, yawpan, yeopon, yop(p)on, youpon, yupon* [*yopún* dimin of Catawba *yop* tree] **chiefly Mid Atl, esp NC** Cf **desert yaupon**
A southern **holly** n¹ **1** (here: *Ilex vomitoria* or *I. cassine*); a tea made from this plant. For other names see **Appalachian tea 1, Carolina ~, cassena, Christmasberry 2, Christmas bush 1, ~ tree 5, dahoon, deerberry d, Henderson-wood, Indian berry, ~ black drink, ~ purge, ~ tea a, red haw 2, seeny 1, swamp holly 1, tea tree**

1709 (1967) Lawson *New Voyage* 97 **NC, SC,** This *Yaupon,* call'd by the South-*Carolina Indians, Cassena,* is a Bush, that grows chiefly on the Sand-Banks and Islands, bordering on the Sea of *Carolina.* **1737** (1911) Brickell *Nat. Hist. NC* 319, They [=the Indians] drink great quantities of *Yaupan Tea.* **1743** Catesby *Nat. Hist. Carolina* 2.57, *Cassena vera Floridanorum. . . In South Carolina* it is called *Cassena.* In *Virginia* and *North Carolina* it is known by the Name of *Yapon.* **1790** in 1976 Freneau *Poems* 303, We left this dismal place,/ Nor stay'd to drink their dear *yoppon.* [Freneau's note: A shrub leaf, frequently used in the interior parts of Carolina as a substitute for tea.] **1822** Prince *Catalogue Linnaean Botanic Garden* 103, *Paraguay,* or *Yapan tea* Ilex vomitoria. **1836** (1935) Holley *Texas* 88, Among these the Yawpan or tea tree deserves a special notice. **1837** (1962) Williams *Territory FL* 29, Scrub oaks and yapon bushes, tangled with vines, form impenetrable thickets. **1854** *Amer. Med. Mth.* 1.243, I have used . . yeopon (ilex vomi tosia) [sic] . . and various others. **1861** *Scientific Amer.* new ser 5.230 **Sth,** The Southerners are said to be reviving the use of the Yopon or Yaupon *(Ilex cassine),* of which the North Carolina Indians made their "black drink." **1895** *Advance* (Chicago IL) 19 Dec 909/1 **AL** (as of 1864), That horrid yupon and sassafrass tea. **1912** Green *VA Folk-Speech* 495, *Yopon. . .* A kind of holly near the seacoast from the leaves of which a beverage, and a medicine are made. **1938** FWP *Ocean Highway* 188 **NC,** Yaupon (*Ilex cassine* and *Ilex vomitoria*) is a dark evergreen with bright red berries. **1952** Taylor *Plants Colonial Days* 97, Yaupon, variously spelled yapon, youpon, yupon, and japon, is a native evergreen member of the holly family. **1965–70** *DARE* (Qu. I35, . . *Kitchen herbs . . grown and used in cooking around here*) Inf **NC76,** Yaupon tea; (Qu. I44, *What kinds of berries grow wild around here?*) Inf **LA14,** Yaupon ['jouˌpɑn]—almost universally pronounced ['juˌpɑn]; (Qu. T5, . . *Kinds of evergreens, other than pine*) Inf **LA2,** Yaupon ['jupən]—it has red, waxy-looking berries; **LA7,** Yaupon ['juˌpɑn]; **MS6,** Yaupon [FW sp *yopan*]; **MS72,** Yaupon ['joˌpɑn]; **NC3,** Yaupon ['jouˌpɑn]—used to make a tea from the leaves; **NC27,** Yaupon; **NC81,** Yaupon ['joˌpɑn]—make tea from it; (Qu. T16, . . *Kinds of trees . . 'special'*) Inf **NC76,** Yaupon—an evergreen. **1966–69** *DARE* Tape **NC25,** There's a yaupon ['jʌˌpɑn] that grows on the island, they used to make their tea out of; **NC60,** [FW:] Tell me again about that tree that you made tea out of. [Inf:] Yaupon ['joˌpɑn], yaupon tree. **1969** *DARE* FW Addit **NC,** *Yaupon*—plant common on Hatteras Island. Used to make tea. **1970** *NC Folkl.* 18.6, Tea from youpon leaves not only prescribed by midwives but also for stimulation of sex desire. **1994** NC Lang. & Life Project *Dial. Vocab. Ocracoke* 17 **eNC,** Yaupon, yapan. . . A small evergreen shrub related to the holly that grows in sandy soil.

yawk See **yerk**

yawk-nut See **yonkanut**

yawl See **you-all**

yawpan See **yaupon**

yawroot n [From its use in treatment of yaws]
A **queen's delight** (here: *Stillingia sylvatica*).

1830 Rafinesque *Med. Flora* 2.266, *Stillingia sylvatica. . .* Yawroot, Marcory, Cockup hat, Queens delight. . . Very active, specific in yaws, sores [etc]. **1869** Porcher *Resources* 146 **Sth,** *Queen's Delight; Yaw Root. . .* Collected in the pine barrens of St. John's Berkeley, in great abundance. **1974** Morton *Folk Remedies* 149 **SC,** Yaw-Root; Silver-Leaf.

yawup See **yarrup**

yaw-ways adv, adj Cf *DS* KK70, MM13, 15
At an angle; askew.

1913 *DN* 4.28 **NW,** *Yaw-ways. . .* Slantwise; at an angle. "The line ran yaw-ways up over the ridge." **2005** Al-Darraji *Eclipse* 151 **NEng,** The duchess spent most of the day . . watching him stare past her with his eyes so yawways that it made me queasy. **2008** Shamp *On Acct. of Women* 140 **cnNC,** He blinked at her over a pair of horn-rimmed spectacles set yaw-ways. **2008** in 2009 *DARE* File—Internet **seNC,** A cow needs a good friend like that when she gets a calf turned yaw-ways!

ye See **you** pron¹ A2

yea See **ear** n¹

yeah adv See **here** A3

yeah n¹ See **year** n¹

yeah n² See **ear** n¹

ye all See **you-all**

year n[1]   Usu |jɪr, jiə(r)|; also |jɛ(r), jɛə, jɚ| Pronc-spp *ear, yaar, yar(e), yeah, ye(e)r, yur*

A   Proncs.

1794 in 1956 Eliason *Tarheel Talk* 321 **c,cnNC**, *Year*—yars. **1850** *Ibid* 321 **c,csNC**, *Year.* . . yare. **1853** Simms *Sword & Distaff* 446 **SC**, For ebber arter, for t'ree t'ousan' yers. **1905** Chesnutt *Col.'s Dream* 28 **GA**, I wuz wuth five hundred dollahs any day in de yeah. **1906** *DN* 3.117 **sIN**, *Ear.* . . Common pronunciation of *year.* "He was gone four ears." **1926** *AmSp* 1.409 **Okefenokee GA**, I wuz a boy . . ten er twelve yurs old. **1933** Rawlings *South Moon* 105 **nFL**, This time o' yare, a buck's a right dark grey color. **1968** *DARE* FW Addit **seGA**, *Year*— [jɛr]. **1976** Garber *Mountain-ese* 104 **sAppalachians**, *Yaars* . . years— He's been livin' there fer yaars. **1982** Slone *How We Talked* 36 **eKY** (as of c1950), *Yeers*—years. **1989** Pederson *LAGS Tech. Index* 22 **Gulf Region**, *A year ago* [Of 914 infs, 15 offered proncs of the type [jɛr], 4 [jɛ], 2 [jeə], 1 [jɚ], 1 [hɪr].] **2000** Shores *Tangier Is.* 172 **Chesapeake Bay**, *Year, hear, here,* and *ear* are all pronounced as "yer."

B   Gram form.

Pl: usu *years;* also, when preceded by a quantifier *year.* [*OED2 year* sb.[1]: "The normal OE. (flexionless) pl. . . is represented still in dialectal usage."]   **chiefly Sth, S Midl**   See Map   *esp among speakers with little formal educ*   Cf **pound** n[1] **B**

1856 Whitcher *Bedott Papers* 143 **cNY**, He enjoyed miserable health for a number o' year afore he died. **1861** Holmes *Venner* 1.152 **NEng**, It's lasted a hundud year. **1894** Riley *Armazindy* 54 **IN**, Fifteen year' ago and better. **1909** *DN* 3.390 **eAL, wGA**, *Year.* . . Frequently used as a plural. "Five year ago." **1910** *DN* 3.457 **KY**, *Year.* . . Years. "He died five year ago." **1923** in 1952 Mathes *Tall Tales* 18 **sAppalachians**, Marthy that's been a-waitin' thar fer me twenty year. **1932** Randolph *Ozark Mt. Folks* 123, [In a notice of public sale:] Good mule, 7 year old. **1945** FWP *Lay My Burden Down* 124 **LA** [Black], I come to Dallas and cooked for seven year for one white family. **1965–70** *DARE* (Qu. A17, *If it was 1960 and you were speaking of something that happened in 1950* . . *"That was ten _____."*) 26 Infs, **chiefly Sth, S Midl**, Year ago; **MA**40, Year preceding; (Qu. V12, . . *The amount of time a person has to spend in jail*) Inf **SC**3, In for ten year. [21 of 28 total Infs gs educ or less] **1966–69** *DARE* Tape FL46, I haven't had a piece a' crab meat in thirty year or more; **FL**47, The bank at Fort Myers has a picnic. . lunch for all the people that's been here over fifty year; **GA**30, That loggin' camp stayed in the swamp right around about twenty-one year; **GA**51, For twenty year they been a'trying to buy that; **MO**1, I went to California and stayed five weeks about five year ago. **1989** Pederson *LAGS Tech. Index* 22 **Gulf Region**, *Years (old)* . . Year (99 [of 914 infs]) . . years (761 [infs]).

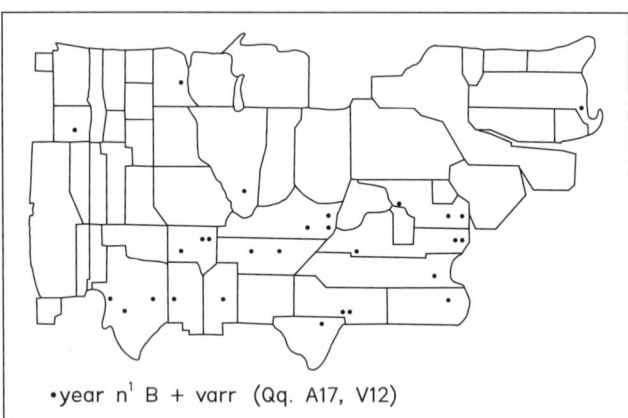

•*year* n[1] B + varr (Qq. A17, V12)

year adv   See **here A3**

year n[2]   See **ear** n[1]

year v[1]   See **hear A1b, 2d**

year v[2]   [Calque of PaGer *sich jaehre* to have one's birthday anniversary]

In phr *year oneself:* To reach a birthday.

1964 *Ferhoodled Engl.* [16] [PaGer], Lena is yearing herself on Tuesday so it gifs a nice big birthday cake. **1988** *DARE* File, [An] old friend of Mom's came in the drugstore where she worked one day and calmly

announced that he had "yeared himself again today"—by which he meant that it was his birthday.

yearb   See **herb A1**

yeard(y)   See **hear A2d**

yeare   See **ear** n[1]

yearf   See **earth**

yearling n   Usu |'jɪrlɪŋ|; also |'jɚ(r)lɪn, 'jɛ(r)lɪn|; for addit proncs see quots   Pronc-spp *yearlen, yellin', yerlin(g), yurlin*

Std senses, var forms.

1829 in 1956 Eliason *Tarheel Talk* 321 **cnNC**, *Yearling*—yerling. **1899** (1912) Green *VA Folk-Speech* 100, *Bull yellin.* . . Bull yearling. **1914** *DN* 4.83 **ME, nNH**, *Ye'rlin'.* . . Var. of *yearling.* **1917** *DN* 4.404 **neOH**, *Yearling* [jɚlɪn]. . . The regular pronunciation. **1922** Gonzales *Black Border* 291 **sSC, GA coasts** [Gullah], *Bull-yellin'*—bull-yearling, or yearlings. **1926** Roberts *Time of Man* 64 **KY**, And now he's lost a yearlen calf. **1926** *AmSp* 1.411 **Okefenokee GA**, Jim seed a yurlin' fawn er two. **1936** *AmSp* 11.346 **eTX**, wʌn nait te kɪld ə 'jɛrlɪn. [=One night they killed a yearling.] **c1940** Eliason *Word Lists FL* 4 **nwFL**, *Yearling* ['jɔlin] [Eliason: also? [jɚlɪn]]. . . Last year's calf, but still unweaned. **1966–68** *DARE* (Qu. K20, *A calf that is sold for meat*) Inf **AZ**2, [jʊrlɪŋ]; **LA**3, ['jɛlɪn]; **LA**20, ['jɪlɪn]; **LA**22, ['jeˑrlɪn].

yearling tick n   esp **Lower Missip Valley**   Cf **seed tick, star ~**

The eight-legged nymph of a tick (family Ixodidae).

1859 Gosse *Letters from AL* 220, The first season they are called Seed-ticks . . the next year they become Yearling-ticks; and the third, Old-ticks. **1863** [see **star tick**]. **1907** *DN* 3.236 **nwAR**, *Seed-tick.* . . The common wood-tick. "I went into the woods and got covered with seed ticks and yearling ticks." **1910** *Ft. Wayne Weekly Sentinel* (IN) [7 Sept 36]/1 (newspaperarchive.com), The term adult is applied to the tick after the second moult and includes the so-called "yearling tick" and the fully engorged tick. **1967–70** *DARE* (Qu. R23a, *Insects or other creatures that fasten themselves to the skin and suck blood—on land*) Infs **KY**5, **LA**18, **TX**37, 96, Yearling ticks; **AR**55, Yearling tick, seed tick—different sizes of same species; **AR**56, Yearling tick—kind of tick; **LA**2, Yearling tick—medium-sized tick. **2007** in 2009 *DARE* File—Internet **AZ**, My uncle once pulled a small, what they call a 'yearling' tick, the really tiny flat buggers, off his ankle.

yearly   See **early**

yearmark   See **earmark** n

yearn   See **earn**

yearnest   See **earnest**

year oneself   See **year** v[2]

yea(r)th   See **earth**

yecker   See **yucker**

yeddy   See **hear A1b**

yedra n   [Span *hiedra* ivy]   **SW**

=**poison ivy 1.**

1831 Beechey *Narrative* 2.84 **nCA**, The most remarkable shrub in this country is the yedra, a poisonous plant affecting only particular constitutions of the human body, by producing tumours and violent inflammation upon any part with which it comes in contact. **1854** *Horticulturist & Jrl. Rural Art* 12.552 **CA**, In California they have the Yedra or *Rhus viride,* which abounds in the mining districts, growing under the Oak trees, and is the only plant there that looks green and flourishing during the torrid heat of summer. **1856** *Hutchings' CA Mag.* Dec 258, I should be very much pleased if some of your readers would throw a little more light on the subject of curing or *preventing* the evil effects of *La Yedra.* **1947** Curtin *Healing Herbs* 195 **NM**, Yedra. . . the New Mexican term is applied to poison ivy. **1976** Elmore *Shrubs & Trees SW* 26, Poison Ivy. . . hiedra (yedra) mala. [**2007** *DARE* File—Internet **GA**, There's a Mexican guy here whom everybody calls "Yedra" (Ivy) because he and his buddies went camping and he used leaves for toilet paper. Poison ivy leaves.]

yee   See **you** pron[1] **A2**

yeer adv   See **here A3**

yeer n   See **year** n[1]

yee-yaw v Cf **yee-yawed**

To swerve back and forth, wobble; hence ppl adj phr *yee-yaw-ing* lurching, swaying.

1935 Carter *On Border* 406 **TX** (as of 1873), No animal had ever seen in that country such a yee-yawing, patched-up train. **1948** *WELS Suppl.* **nME,** It was a thrilling ride, to be perched on top of the heavy loads on the great sleds . . up and down over the icy pitches of the tote road, or yee-yawing dangerously from side to side. **2004** in 2009 *DARE* File—Internet **TX,** It was awkward for me to sit on that yee-yawing bus holding the stroller. **2008** *Kennebec Jrl. Online* (Augusta ME) 27 July (Internet), I watched a woman in the parking lot try four times yee-yawing her car back and forth to get out of the parking space, finally scratching another car.

yee-yawed adj Also *yee-yaw* esp **nNEng** Cf **gee-hawed,** **skew-hawed** (at **skew- b**), **weewawed** (at **wee-waw B**), **yee-yaw**

Askew; awry; hence n *yee-yaw* a twist.

1901 Day in *New Engl. Mag.* 24.202 **ME,** This way and that swayed discussion . . between the occupants of dusty buckboards as these locked their yee-yawed wheels. **1902** Day *Pine Tree Ballads* 175 **ME,** You were just a pewter pitcher, a demure and dull old pot—/ With a yee-yaw to your nozzle like the grimace of a sot. **1966–68** *DARE* (Qu. KK70, *Something that has got out of proper shape: "That house is all _____."*) Inf **ME**11, Yee-yaw; **NH**14, Yee-yawed; (Qu. MM13, *The table was nice and straight until he came along and knocked it _____*) Infs **DE**1, **NH**14, Yee-yawed.

yee-yawing See **yee-yaw**

yeh See **you** pron[1] **A2**

yelement See **element**

yelk See **yolk A2**

yella, yeller See **yellow** adj, n[1] **A1**

yellin' See **yearling**

yellow adj, n[1] Usu |ˈjɛlo|; also |ˈjɛlə(r)|; for addit varr see **A** below

A Forms.

1 |ˈjɛlə(r)|; pronc-spp *yella, yeller;* for addit proncs see quots. **scattered, but esp freq Sth, S Midl** Cf "Language Changes" IV.1.c

1848 Lowell *Biglow* 147 **'Upcountry' MA,** Yeller, *yellow.* **1892** *DN* 1.233 **KY,** Yeller janders [ˈjɛlə jˈændəz]: jaundice. **1909** *DN* 3.405 **nwAR,** *Yeller janders.* . . Jaundice. **1923** *DN* 5.237 **swWI,** *Yella boys.* . . Gold pieces. **1925** in 1953 Botkin–Harlow *Treas. Railroad Folkl.* 227, Yella as a duck's foot. **1931** Randolph *Ozarks* 68, A-pickin' boogers out'n her yeller tags. **1965–70** *DARE* (Qu. K38, *A horse of a dirty white color*) 13 Infs, **esp Sth, S Midl,** Yeller; (Qu. H34, . . *The parts of an egg*) Infs **OK**21, **VA**1, Yeller; **GA**36, Yella; (Qu. I19) Inf **VA**1, Yeller-eyed beans; (Qu. I34) Inf **VA**2, Yeller corn; (Qu. R28) Inf **KY**28, Yeller spider; (Qu. BB23) Infs **GA**23, **KY**41, Yeller jaunders; **TN**16, Yella janders; (Qu. HH29b, . . *People of mixed blood—part Negro*) Inf **CA**87, Yeller one; **FL**52, High yella. **1967–68** *DARE* Tape **GA**30, That's pretty, yellow [ˈjɛlə] bloom; **TX**1A, Take the yella [ˈjɛlə] an' beat that up in a bowl. **1969** Wilson *Stars* 116 **Ozarks,** She was wearin' her butterfly-yeller dress. **1983** *MJLF* 9.1.62 **ceKY** (as of 1956), *Yeller janders* . . yellow jaundice. **1989** Pederson *LAGS Tech. Index* 157 **Gulf Region,** Yellow [Of 914 infs, 584 offered proncs of the type [ˈjɛlə], 109 [ˈjɛlo], 57 [ˈjɛlr̩], 4 [ˈjɛlɨ], 2 [ˈjɛlu].] **1997** *DARE* File—Internet **cePA** [CoalSpeak], *Yella:* The color yellow. **2000** Shores *Tangier Is.* 180 **Chesapeake Bay,** The word *yellow* may alternate as "yeller" or "yella."

2 |ˈjælo, jælə(r)|; pronc-spp *yallah, yaller, yallo(w), yalluh* [*OED2 yellow* a. A.1.a.γ c1375 →; "dial. and vulgar"; this pronc was still considered std by some 18th century orthoepists.] **widespread, but esp freq Sth, S Midl**

1835 Longstreet *GA Scenes* 21, Did you ever see the *Yallow* Blossom from Jasper? **1843** (1916) Hall *New Purchase* 136 **IN,** Yaller buttins. **1861** Holmes *Venner* 1.53 **NEng,** If he hung up his "yallah dog," he would make a better show of sunlight. **1872** Schele de Vere *Americanisms* 568, *Yallo* is the almost uniform pronunciation of *yellow* as far South as Virginia and to the West. **1899** (1912) Green *VA Folk-Speech* 493, *Yallow.* . . A colour; *yellow. Yaller.* **1903** *DN* 2.337 **seMO,** *Yellow.* . . Pronounced yaller. **1905** *DN* 3.24 **cCT,** *Yaller.* . . Yellow. *Ibid* 56 **eNE,** [æ] . . sometimes prevails in . . *yellow.* **1907** *DN* 3.220 **nwAR,**

Yaller. . . Yellow. *Ibid* 238 **nwAR,** *Yaller.* . . Yellow. Also yeller. **1908** Fox *Lonesome Pine* 61 **KY,** He hired a "yaller" mule from the landlord. **1909** *DN* 3.390 **eAL, wGA,** *Yaller.* . . Yellow. **1916** *DN* 4.340 **seOH,** *Yellow* [ˈjælr̩, jælo]. **1922** Gonzales *Black Border* 339 **sSC, GA coasts** [Gullah glossary], *Yalluh*—yellow. **1923** *DN* 5.225 **swMO,** *Yaller janders.* . . Yellow jaundice. **c1938** in 1970 Hyatt *Hoodoo* 1.449 **seSC,** A piece of yallah homespun cloth. **c1940** Eliason *Word Lists FL* 14 **wFL,** *Yaller* [ˈjælɚ]: Yellow. *Common* in rural sections; used mostly by the old. **1942** Hall *Smoky Mt. Speech* 80 **wNC, eTN,** Yellow . . [ˈjælɚ]. **1943** in 1958 Brewer *Dog Ghosts* 100 **TX** [Black], A big fat yalluh woman wid a white dress on. **1961** Kurath–McDavid *Pronc. Engl.* 134, *Yellow.* . . The most common folk form of *yellow* is /jælə/ with the vowel of *Sally.* It is widespread in the South Midland and the South (except Georgia) and extends northward into Pennsylvania, though it is much less common there and does not occur in urbanized areas (Philadelphia, Pittsburgh, etc.). Relics are found even in New York State (and presumably in New England, where this word was not investigated). In parts of North Carolina (the Blue Ridge and the Cape Fear Valley) this pronunciation reaches up into the middle class, rarely elsewhere. **1966–67** *DARE* FW Addit **NC,** *Yellow* . . [ˈjælɚ]. **1982** Barrick *Coll.* **csPA,** *Yellow*—pron. yă′-luh. **1989** Pederson *LAGS Tech. Index* 157 **Gulf Region,** Yellow [Of 914 infs, 43 offered proncs of the type [ˈjælə], 14 [ˈjælr̩], 4 [ˈjælo].]

3 |ˈjɑlə(r)|; pronc-spp *yoller, yollow.* [*OED2 yellow* a. A.1.a.β c1175 →; "chiefly *Sc.* and *north. dial.*"]

1864 St. Clar *Metropolites* 541 **NYC,** A newsboy climbing to the window, shouted in: "Hear [sic] you are, an extray; arrival of the Yoller Jacket." **1915** *Scribner's Mag.* 58.654 **NYC,** Nowhere but you'd see: *Yunzano Swamp Root, for Coughs, Colds,* . . *an' Liver Trouble*—all in high yoller letters. **1946** in 1998 Wolfram *Amer. Engl.* 127 **seSC,** What color would you say the yolk of the egg is? Variants: *yellow, yallow, yillow, yollow, yeller.* Response: *yellow;* heard from grandmother, "old-fashioned": *yillow, yollow:* "new way": *yallow.* **1961** Kurath–McDavid *Pronc. Engl.* 134, *Yellow.* . . The type of /jɑlə/, with the vowel of *hollow,* which is historically derived from /jælə/, occurs chiefly in Tidewater Virginia folk speech. **1989** Pederson *LAGS Tech. Index* 157 **Gulf Region,** Yellow [Of 914 infs, 2 offered proncs of the type [ˈjɑlə], 1 [ˈjɑlr̩].]

4 |ˈjʌlo, ˈjʌlə(r)|; for addit var see quot 1961.

1961 Kurath–McDavid *Pronc. Engl.* 134, *Yellow.* . . The variant /jʌlə/, with the vowel of *color,* is . . current in the South Atlantic States, especially in South Carolina and Georgia, where even middle-class speakers use it to some extent. [ɜ]-like phones are not uncommon in South Carolina and Georgia, which cannot safely be assigned to either /ʌ/ or /ɛ/. Similar phones [are] observed in *yellow* . . in Upstate New York. **1989** Pederson *LAGS Tech. Index* 157 **Gulf Region,** Yellow [Of 914 infs, 51 offered proncs of the type [ˈjʌlə], 9 [ˈjʌlo], 6 [ˈjʌlr̩].]

5 |jɪlo, jɪlə(r)|; pronc-sp *yillow.* esp **Sth**

1855 in 1956 Eliason *Tarheel Talk* 321 **cnNC,** *Yellow*—yillow. **1946** [see **A3** above]. **1961** Kurath–McDavid *Pronc. Engl.* 134, *Yellow* with the vowel of *silly.* . . occurs in rather scattered fashion along the Southern coast from Delmarva to Florida, with some concentration in the Low Country of South Carolina and the Savannah Valley. A few instances have also been observed in the Blue Ridge. /jɪlə/, not infrequently pronounced with high-central [ɨ], is derived from /jɛlə/, probably before "clear" intersyllabic /l/. **1989** Pederson *LAGS Tech. Index* 157 **Gulf Region,** Yellow [Of 914 infs, 10 offered proncs of the type [ˈjɪlə], 2 [ˈjɪlo], 2 [ˈjɪlr̩].]

B As noun.

The yolk of an egg. **widespread, but chiefly Sth, S Midl, OK, TX** See Map on p. 1100 *esp among speakers with little formal educ* Cf **yolk B**

1823 *Amer. Farmer* 5.240, To the yellow of one egg, add one table spoonful of brown sugar. **1861** *Scientific Amer.* new ser 5.262, Beat the yellow of an egg with warm lard. **1915** *DN* 4.193 **swVA,** *Yaller.* . . The yolk of an egg. **1923** *DN* 5.225 **swMO,** *Yaller.* . . The yolk of an egg. **1941** *LANE* Map 296 *(Yolk)* 7 infs, **CT, MA, RI,** Yellow. **1965–70** *DARE* (Qu. H34, . . *The parts of an egg*) 130 Infs, **widespread, but chiefly Sth, S Midl, OK, TX,** Yellow; **GA**36, Yella; **OK**21, **VA**1, Yeller. [Of all Infs responding to the question, 28% were gs educ or less; of those giving the above responses, 48% were gs educ or less.] **1973** Allen *LAUM* 1.285 **Upper MW** (as of c1950), *Yolk.* . . The rare New England lexical equivalent *yellow* . . survives in the speech of two . . infs. **1989** Pederson *LAGS Tech. Index* **Gulf Region** *(Yolk)* 233 infs, Yellow; 11 infs, Yellow of an/the egg; 2 infs, Egg yellow. [*DARE* Ed: Although the qu. was meant to elicit words for the inside of an egg, and many infs explicitly equated *yellow* with the yolk, it is likely that many resps were meant to be descriptive of the yolk's color, which was the intent of the following qu.] **2009** *DARE* File—Internet **GA,** Use the yellows of the eggs for your pudding and the whites for the beaten topping.

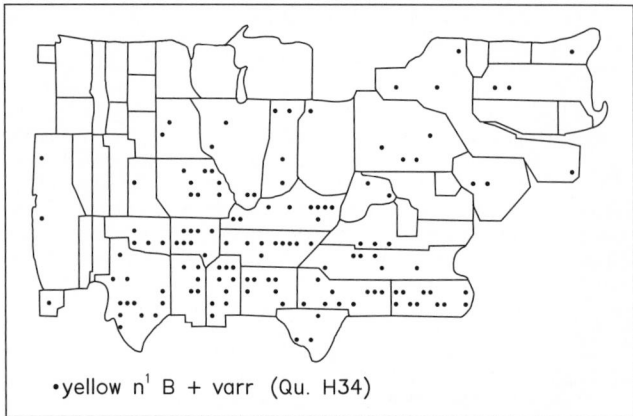

•yellow n¹ B + varr (Qu. H34)

C As adj. Cf **high yellow, yellowhammer 4**
Having skin of a light yellowish-brown color—applied to a person of mixed race. **chiefly C and S Atl, Gulf States**

1814 *Niles' Weekly Reg.* 7.284 **Chesapeake Bay,** The owner, a yellow man . . made for a small creek. **1816** U.S. Supreme Court *Rept. Cases Argued & Adjudged* 1.7, The petitioners in that case were descended from a yellow woman. . . In this case they are descended from a white woman. **1858** Hammett *Piney Woods Tavern* 280 **TX,** And *you,* Jim Sprott, to be afeard of that yaller nigger, Santanner. **1882** *Century Illustr. Mag.* 24.875 **GA,** Did you ever see er yaller gal lick 'lasses candy? **1903** *DN* 2.337 **seMO,** *Yellow-gal, yellow-boy.* . . Mulatto. **1909** *DN* 3.390 **eAL, wGA,** *Yellow man (woman, gal,* etc.) . . A mulatto. *Yellow person* is also used. **c1937** in 1972 *Amer. Slave* 2.1.192 **SC,** Dey learn de yellow chillun, but if dey catch we black chillun wid a book, dey nearly bout kill us. **1937** (1977) Hurston *Their Eyes* 210 **FL** [Black], We'se uh mingled people and all of us got black kinfolks as well as yaller kinfolks. **1943** Weslager *DE Forgotten Folk* 11, The Indian blood is still perpetuated in forgotten folk who are neither white nor black nor pure Indian. Some of them are called Moors. Others are known as Yellow People, Nanticokes, or simply Indians. **1945** *Amer. Jrl. Sociol.* 51.35 **cSC,** People . . who do not fit into the biracial caste system. . . are designated by a wide variety of names, none of them flattering. . . they are called "Yellow Hammers," "Summerville Indians," or simply "those yellow people." **1946** Tallant *Voodoo* 191 **New Orleans LA** [Black], A fellow named Jim Willie say he seen Feltie . . wit' a yellow woman. **1965–70** *DARE* (Qu. HH29b, . . *People of mixed blood—part Negro*) 11 Infs, **scattered,** Yellow; **KY**91, **LA**32, **MO**9, **NY**75, **OH**56, **VA**35, Yellow nigger; **IN**14, **WV**14, Yellow man; **TX**5, Yellow negro; **CA**87, Yeller one; **GA**72, Yellow people; (Qu. HH29a, . . *People of mixed blood—part Indian*) Inf **SC**26, Yellow. **1978** *Capital Times* (Madison WI) 21 Nov 18/2, I was a 'yella' gal, a mixture of blood. (Her father was white, her mother black, with Cherokee blood.) **1986** Pederson *LAGS Concordance* (A child born of a racially-mixed (black and white) marriage) 1 inf, **nwLA,** That yellow woman. [Inf Black]

yellow n² See **yellow pike**

yellow Alaska cedar See **yellow cedar 1**

yellow ash n

1 Any of var ashes, such as **black ash 1, green ash,** or other unidentified trees.

1778 Carver *Travels N. Amer.* 497, The yellow ash . . is only found near the head branches of the Mississippi. This tree grows to an amazing height. . . The wood of this tree greatly resembles that of the common ash, but . . the ross or outside bark . . [is] near eight inches thick, and indented with furrows more than six inches deep. . . The rind or inside bark . . is a fine bright yellow; insomuch that if it is but slightly handled, it will leave a stain on the fingers. **1792** Belknap *Hist. NH* 3.117, The other species is black ash *(fraxinus americana)* of which the red and yellow are varieties. . . The roots of yellow ash, are used by turners, for the making of plates and bowls. **1844** *Bangor Daily Whig & Courier* (ME) 20 Dec [2]/5 (newspaperarchive.com), *Hallowell & Harlow* wish to purchase 50 Cords Yellow Ash Butts from 9 to 13 feet long. **1848** Gray *Manual of Botany* 373, F[raxinus] juglandifolia [=F. pennsyl-]. . .

Green or Yellow Ash. . . Wet woods, Maine to Ohio and southward. **1891** *Forest & Stream* 35.510 **ME,** Yellow ash bark to produce sweating. **1897** *Jrl. Amer. Folkl.* 10.50, *Fraxinus pubescens* [=*F. pennsylvanica*]. . . yellow ash, West. **1917** Internatl. Congress Americanists *Proc.* 310, Yellow ash *(Fraxinus americana)* . . leaves, in a very strong, bitter decoction, are given to women after childbirth to cleanse them.

2 =**yellowwood 3.**

1830 Rafinesque *Med. Flora* 2.210, Cladrastis tinctoria [=*C. kentukea*]. . . *Yellow Ash, Fustic tree, Yellow Locust.* From Kentucky to Alabama. Fine tree, wood yellow and soft. . . The bark gives a bright yellow dye. **1884** Sargent *Forests of N. Amer.* 57, Cladrastis tinctoria. . . Yellow Wood. Yellow Ash. . . Central Kentucky, cliffs of the Kentucky and Dick's rivers; middle Tennessee, mountains of east Tennessee to Cherokee county, North Carolina. **1908** Rogers *Tree Book* 432 **TN,** "Yellow ash" is a Tennessee name for *Cladrastis lutea,* the virgilia. **1950** Peattie *Nat. Hist. Trees* 410, Yellowwood. . . Other Names: Virgilia. Yellow Locust. Yellow Ash.

yellow-ass(ed) hornet See **yellow-tailed hornet**

yellow aster n

1 A **tansy aster**; see quots.

1936 Whitehouse *TX Flowers* 161, Spiny-Leaved Yellow Aster. . . *Sideranthus spinulosus* [=*Machaeranthera pinnatifida*]. . . very abundant on prairies and hills in the western part of the state. **2004** (acc) AZ Dept. Water Resources *Low Water Use Plant List* 11 (Internet), Machaeranthera gracilis—Yellow Aster.

2 A **bitterweed** (here: *Tetraneuris acaulis*).

1937 U.S. Forest Serv. *Range Plant Hdbk.* W6, Stemless actinea [= *Tetraneuris acaulis*] . . has not acquired a well-established common name but is known by a great variety of (and often misapplied) local names, such as cloth-of-gold, golden-daisy, . . and yellow-aster.

yellow bachelor's button n

1 A **milkwort** such as *Polygala rugelii* or **orange milkwort.**

1860 Chapman *Flora Southern U.S.* 83, [Polygala] lutea. . . Yellow Bachelor's-Button. . . Low pine barrens, Florida to Mississippi, and northward. **1869** Porcher *Resources* 94, P[olygala] lutea, yellow bachelor's button, growing throughout the Southern States. **1901** Lounsberry *S. Wild Flowers* 296, Yellow Bachelor's-Button. Orange Milkwort. . . There is not a brighter, gayer member of the genus than the bachelor's-button, nor is there one better known. **1949** Moldenke *Amer. Wild Flowers* 51, In peninsular Florida occurs a . . species with lemon-yellow flowers, the yellowbachelorsbutton, *P. rugelii,* an infusion of which is drunk by the Seminole Indians as a "remedy" for snakebite.

2 A **buttercup 1** (here: *Ranunculus acris*).

[**1862** *Mag. Horticult.* 28.331, *Ranunculus acris pleno.* . . styled the Yellow Bachelor's Button by English cultivators.] **2002** McIntire *Amer. Cutting Garden* 214, R[anunculus] acris. . . a pretty little thing, known as the common or meadow buttercup or even yellow bachelor's button.

yellowback n

A **freshwater clam** (here: *Lampsilis teres*).

1899 U.S. Fish Comm. *Bulletin for 1898* 18.290 **IA,** There are several kinds of mussels known along the Mississippi as "sand shells." The most abundant and important of these is the . . "yellow-back" *(Lampsilis anodontoides),* which has a bright yellowish-brown epidermis. **1908** Rogers *Shell Book* 377, [Lampsilis] anodontoides. . . is the "yellow-back" or "yellow sand shell" used for buttons. It is found throughout the Mississippi and Gulf drainage. **1938** FWP *Guide IA* 327, Others [= freshwater clams], all salable, were the warty black [sic], yellow back [etc].

yellowback turtle n

A turtle of the family Kinosternidae (here: prob a **mud turtle 2b(1)).**

1968 *DARE* FW Addit **seLA,** Yellowback turtle, stinking turtle—alternate names for the same creature—size usually about ten by six inches; it has bright yellow stripes. Lives in swamps.

yellow-bark(ed) oak n Also *yellowbark* [From the color of the inner bark] **chiefly NEng** Cf **yellow oak 1**
A **black oak** (here: *Quercus velutina*).

1822 RI Laws *Pub. Laws* 382, Barrels . . may be made of good seasoned white oak or white ash, or yellow bark oak staves. **1824** in 1935 Emerson *Early Hist. Naushon Is.* 453 **MA,** There is a large tract of . . timber suitable for ships. . . The timber is white oak and yellow bark oak. **1847** Wood *Class-Book* 494, [Quercus] tinctoria. . . Black

Oak. Yellow-bark Oak. **1852** in 1906 Thoreau *Writings* 3.337 **ceMA,** "Now," said he, "there are two kinds of white oak. . . [T]here are two kinds of black oak, or yellow-bark. One is the mean black oak, or bastard." **1860** Hervey *Catalogue Plants New Bedford* 10 **MA,** Quercus . . tinctoria, Yellow-barked oak. **1886** *Forest & Stream* 26.398 **MA,** The Thetis is very strongly built. . . Her frames are of yellow-bark oak. **1981** *New Yorker* 31 Aug 28 **seMA,** White oak or yellow-bark oak for the coaming.

yellow bass n

1 Any of three closely related fishes: the **largemouth bass, smallmouth bass,** or a **spotted bass 1** (here: *Micropterus punctulatus*). Note: Some of these quots may refer instead to **2** below.

1819 *Belles-Lettres Repository & Mth. Mag.* 1.360 **NY,** It is a beautiful sheet of pure spring water, in which pike, yellow bass, perch and sunfish, are abundant. **1820** Rafinesque in *Western Rev.* 2.50, Pale River-bass. *Lepomis pallida* [=*Micropterus salmoides*]. . . Not uncommon in the Ohio, Miami, Hockhocking, &c. Vulgar name Yellow Bass, common-Bass, &c. **1845** *U.S. Mag. & Democratic Rev.* 17.464 **Long Is. NY,** Fishing for perch or the yellow bass of the lakes. **1857** *Daily WI Patriot* (Madison) 27 Aug [2]/2 (newspaperarchive.com), The Yellow Bass is nearly the same thing [as the black bass], and we are not certain to which to give the palm of excellence. **1935** Caine *Game Fish* 3, Largemouthed Black Bass. . . Synonyms. . . Yellow Bass. *Ibid* 8, Smallmouthed Black Bass. . . Synonyms. . . Yellow Bass. *Ibid* 10, Spotted Small-mouthed Black Bass. . . Synonyms. . . Yellow Bass. **1975** Evanoff *Catch More Fish* 73, The small-mouth bass . . is also called the bronzeback, yellow bass, brown bass, redeye, and tiger bass.

2 A yellow, black-striped freshwater bass *(Morone mississippiensis)*. Also called **barfish 2, brassy bass, gold ~ 2, streaked ~, striped ~ 1**

1876 Jordan *Manual Vertebrates N. U.S.* 232, [*Morone*] *interrupta* [= *M. mississippiensis*]. . . Short-striped or Yellow Bass. . . Mississippi Valley, chiefly southward. **1884** Goode *Fisheries U.S.* 1.33, The Yellow Bass—Roccus Interruptus. This species is, so far as known to us, always known as the Yellow Bass. **1933** LA Dept. of Conserv. *Fishes* 360, Figures for the Mississippi and its tributaries covering the catch of Rock Bass, Yellow Bass, and White Bass or Barfish show a decline from 510,763 pounds in 1894 to 74,862 pounds in 1922. **1966** WI Acad. *Trans.* 55.109, The yellow bass is uncommon to common on the Mississippi River opposite Crawford and Grant counties. **1968–69** *DARE* (Qu. P1, . . *Kinds of freshwater fish . . caught around here . . good to eat)* Infs **PA**121, **TN**36, **WI**22, Yellow bass. [*DARE* Ed: Some of these Infs may refer instead to **1** above.] **2008** *DARE* File—Internet **TX,** At the boat is a yellow-hued guy with thin black stripes. "That's a yeller," says Joiner. . . Yellow bass, which rarely get to two pounds, are stocked every so often to keep lines busy between bigger strikes.

yellow bear (caterpillar) n Also *yellow woolly bear*

A **woolly bear 1** (here: the larva of *Diacrisia virginica*).

1841 Harris *Rept. Insects MA* 247, Of all the hairy caterpillars frequenting our gardens, there are none so common and troublesome as that which I have called the yellow bear. [*Ibid* 248, The moth is familiarly known by the name of the white miller. . . Its scientific name is *Arctia virginica*.] **1871** MO State Entomol. *Annual Rept.* 68, The common Yellow Bear—*Spilosoma virginica*, Fabr. (Lepidoptera, Arctiidae.) The moth . . which is very generally dubbed "the Miller," frequently flies into our rooms at night. **1885** NY State Entomol. *Rept. Injurious Insects* 83, It would also serve to diminish the losses annually sustained . . from the following well-known noxious species: . . the yellow woolly-bear *(Spilosoma virginica)*. **1937** *Big Spring Daily Herald* (TX) 20 July 8/4, Another insect has been added to the growing list of tiny creatures menacing the current cotton crop. This time it is the bear worm, or more correctly called the yellow-bear caterpillar. **1974** *Corbin Times-Tribune* (KY) 13 Oct 16/1, There's a yellow Woolleybear [sic] and there's a typical Woolleybear that is orange with the black band in the middle. **2001** *Daily Herald* (Arlington Heights IL) 7 Oct sec 5 1/2, [Caption:] A yellow bear caterpillar hangs on to a leaf of kale.

yellow bell See **yellow bells 1, 2, 4**

yellow-bellied cooter See **yellowbelly cooter**

yellow-bellied pond slider See **yellow-bellied turtle**

yellow-bellied sapsucker See **yellow-bellied woodpecker**

yellow-bellied slider See **yellow-bellied turtle**

yellow-bellied snake n

=**queen snake.**

1829 Macauley *Nat. Statist. Hist. NY* 1.441, Yellow-bellied snake. **1842** DeKay *Zool. NY* 3.45, The Yellow-bellied Snake. *Tropidonotus leberis.* **1920** *Copeia* 85.74 **CT,** Yellow-bellied snake, *Natrix septemvittata.* **1928** Pope–Dickinson *Amphibians* 61 **WI,** *Queen Snake.* . . Other common names are Striped Water Snake, Yellow-bellied Snake and Leather Snake.

yellow-bellied sunfish See **yellowbelly 3**

yellow-bellied turtle n Also *yellow-bellied terrapin, ~ (pond) slider, yellowbelly* Cf **yellowbelly cooter**

A **red-bellied turtle** such as *Trachemys scripta* or *Pseudemys concinna.* Note: In scientific literature (now esp as *yellow-bellied slider, yellow-bellied turtle*) applied to the subsp *Trachemys scripta scripta.*

1854 Zool. Soc. London *Reports* 17, Yellow-bellied Terrapin. *E[mys] serrata.* Florida. **1876** Jordan *Manual Vertebrates N. U.S.* 165, *P[seudemys] troostii,* (Holbr.) Yellow-Bellied Terrapin. . . plastron dull yellow, with large, black blotches. **1877** Bartlett *Americanisms* 699, The most celebrated [terrapin] is the *diamond-back;* there are also the *yellow-bellies, red-bellies, loger-heads* [sic], *snuff-boxes,* &c. **1913** NY Zool. Soc. *Annual Rept. for 1912* 144, Gifts to the Aquarium. . . Yellow Bellied Slider, 2 small alligators. **1920** *Copeia* 87.94 **NC,** Formerly the River Terrapin . . and the Yellow-belly were about equally common. **1926** *AmSp* 1.416 **Okefenokee GA,** Them Yaller-bellied Tarrapins, [Footnote: Florida Terrapins]—they jest lay their aigs anywhere. **1953** Schmidt *N. Amer. Amphibians* 102, *Pseudemys scripta scripta.* . . Yellow-bellied turtle, pond terrapin. **1968** *DARE* (Qu. P24, . . *Kinds of turtles)* Inf **MD**42, Yellowbelly—terrapin with yellow on underneath shell. **c1970** Pederson *Dial. Surv. Rural GA,* 1 inf, **seGA,** Yellowbelly what they call him; he just have the four feet you can eat, but the alligator [terrapin], you can eat all of him. **1979** Behler–King *Audubon Field Guide Reptiles* 452 **Mid and S Atl,** Pond Slider (*Chrysemys scripta*). . . Subspecies: Yellow-bellied (*C. s. scripta*), with conspicuous vertical yellow blotch behind eye, vertical yellowish bar on each costal scute, and dark round smudges on forward part of plastron; se. Virginia to n. Florida. **2006** *Aiken Std.* (SC) 25 Oct sec A 2/1, Jarius and his classmates got to visit with . . a yellow-bellied turtle.

yellow-bellied woodpecker n Also *yellowbelly sapsucker, yellow-bellied ~*

A **sapsucker 1** (here: *Sphyrapicus varius*), or closely related woodpecker. Also called **squealer 3**

1730 Catesby in Royal Soc. London *Philos. Trans.* 36.427 **NC, SC,** *Picus varius minor, ventre luteo,* the yellow Bellied Wood-pecker. **1832** Nuttall *Manual Ornith.* 1.574, Yellow-bellied Woodpecker. . . This species extends over the whole American continent. **1886** *Forest & Stream* 26.386 **NYC,** Birds of Central Park, New York. . . *Sphyrapicus varius.* . . Yellow-bellied Sapsucker.—Migrant. **1938** *Daily Courier* (Connellsville PA) 27 June 10/1, The yellow-bellied woodpecker, commonly called the sapsucker, is the only black sheep of his family. . . the only one that will suck sap from trees. **1965–70** *DARE* (Qu. Q17, . . *Kinds of woodpeckers)* 16 Infs, **scattered,** Yellow-bellied sapsucker; **IL**50, **RI**17, **SC**62, Yellow-bellied woodpecker; **GA**3, Yellowbelly sapsucker; (Qu. Q23) Inf **TX**59, Yellow-bellied sapsucker. **2003** *Facts* (Clute TX) 6 Nov sec A 4/1, The yellow-bellied sapsucker spends its summers in Yankee land and winters below the Mason-Dixon line.

yellow bells n

1 also *yellow bell:* The yellow **fritillary** *(Fritillaria pudica).* **esp Pacific NW**

[**1840** Pratt *Flowers* 370, The fritillary, which includes the crown imperial (Fritillaria imperialis), with its large cluster of orange, or pale yellow bells, is a family of handsome plants.] **1937** St. John *Flora SE WA & ID* 91, *Fritillaria pudica.* . . Yellow Bell. . . Common in spring, open places. **1966** Barnes–Jensen *Dict. UT Slang* 10, Crocus . . the orange fritillaria *(Fritillaria pudica),* snowdrop or yellow bells is sometimes called crocus. **1966–69** *DARE* (Qu. S22, . . *The bright yellow flowers that bloom in clusters in marshes in early springtime)* Inf **CA**165, Yellow bells; (Qu. S26a, . . *Wildflowers. . . Roadside flowers)* Infs **ID**5, **WA**6, Yellow bells; (Qu. S26b, *Wildflowers that grow in water or wet places)* Inf **OR**13, Yellow bells; (Qu. S26c, *Wildflowers that grow in woods)* Inf **WA**3, Yellow bells; (Qu. S26e, *Other wildflowers not yet mentioned; not asked in early QRs)* Inf **OR**10, Yellow bells. [*DARE* Ed: Some of these Infs may refer instead to other senses below.] **1967**

DARE FW Addit **OR**12, Yellow bell—or Yellow Fritilary [sic] (Lily). **1970** Kirk *Wild Edible Plants W. U.S.* 166, Yellowbell, Yellow Fritillary [is] well known to be edible. **2007** *DARE* File—Internet **WA,** Yellow bells (Fritillaria pudica).

2 also *yellow bell:* A **bellwort** (here: *Uvularia grandiflora*).

1850 (1852) Warner *Wide World* 2.156 **NY,** Uvularias, which she called yellow bells, were added to her handful. **1967–68** *DARE* Wildfl QR Pl.20B [=*Uvularia grandiflora*] Infs **AR**44, **MN**37, Yellow bell; [Infs **MI**57, **SC**41, Yellow bellwort.]

3 A **dogtooth violet** (here: *Erythronium americanum*).

[**1855** (1857) Traill *Can. Settler's Guide* 206, In low, open moist ground the mottled leaf of the dog's-tooth violet (erythronium) comes up, and late in April the yellow bells, striped on the outside of the petal with purplish brown, come up in abundance.] **1892** *Jrl. Amer. Folkl.* 5.104, *Erythronium Americanum,* yellow bells. Boston(?) **1894** *Ibid* 7.102 **NJ,** *Erythronium Americanum* . . yellow bells. Short Hills, N.J. **1936** Winter *Plants NE* 12, *E. americanum.* . . Also called Yellow Bells, . . Yellow Dog's-tooth Violet. **2003** Sanders *Secrets of Wildflowers* 40, Commonly called trout lily, *E[rythronium] americanum* is also widely known as. . . yellow bells, amberbell [etc].

4 also *yellow bell:* =**forsythia.**

[**1863** (1864) Mitchell *My Farm* 293 **NEng,** The Forsythia follows . . with its graceful yellow bells.] **1903** Wright *People Whirlpool* 156 **NEast,** The little chap . . who used to reach out the window for the top twigs, that blossomed earliest, so as to be the first to carry 'yellow bells' to school. **1966–67** *DARE* (Qu. S10, *A shrub that gets covered with bright yellow, spicy-smelling flowers early in spring;* total Infs questioned, 75) Inf **OK**20, Yellow bell; **MS**1, Yellow bells—same as forsythia; (Qu. S26e, *Other wildflowers not yet mentioned;* not asked in early QRs) Inf **SC**34, Yellow bells—forsythia; **1970** *DARE* Tape **VA**72, We had forsythia, we used to call that the yellow bell . . shaped like a little bell and it's yellow, but now they call it forsythia. **2004** *Kerrville Times* (TX) 8 Apr sec A 3/5, Border forsythia or yellow bells.

5 =**whispering bells.**

1897 *Jrl. Amer. Folkl.* 10.50 **CA,** *Emmenanthe penduliflora* . . yellow bells. **2006** *DARE* File—Internet **AZ,** Golden Bells, Yellow Bells, Yellow Whispering-bells.

6 =**trumpet flower 1e.**

1949 Bailey *Manual Cultivated Plants* 907, *Tecoma stans.* . . Yellow-Bells. . . S. Fla. to W. Indies and S. Amer. **1960** Vines *Trees SW* 928, *Tecoma stans.* . . English vernacular names are Yellow-bells . . and Yellow-elder. **1965** Neal *Gardens HI* 676, Yellow elder, yellow bells. . . *Tecoma stans.* . . calyx bell-shaped and five-toothed. **2007** *DARE* File—Internet **TX,** Yellow bells *(Tecoma stans)* blooms aloft on 8-foot stalks.

7 A **false foxglove** (here: *Aureolaria flava*).

1967 *DARE* Wildflower QR Pl.202 [=*Aureolaria flava*] Inf **AR**44, Some say yellow bells.

yellowbelly n

1 See **yellowbelly cooter.**

2 See **yellow-bellied turtle.**

3 also *yellow-bellied sunfish, yellowbelly ~:* Any of three closely related fishes: the **red-breasted sunfish,** the **longear sunfish,** or a **pumpkinseed 1** (here: *Lepomis gibbosus*).

1889 *Forest & Stream* 33.83, There were more nests made by perch (yellow belly) than by sunfish. **1899** (1912) Green *VA Folk-Speech* 493, *Yaller-belly.* . . A small fish; a *"yaller pearch."* **1927** *Times* (E. Chicago IN) 22 Mar 11/3, The common yellow-bellied sunfish on which there is no closed season. **1932** *Billings Gaz.* (MT) 15 May 7/6, He would be a sunfish, also called a pumpkin-seed or yellow belly. **1956** *News* (Frederick MD) 12 June 4/5, The yellow belly sunfish reaches a good keeping size and shows rapid growth at Lander. **1969** *DARE* (Qu. P1, *. . Kinds of freshwater fish . . caught around here . . good to eat*) Inf **MI**103, Yellowbellies—a kind of bluegill. **1969** *DARE* FW Addit **KY**6, *Yellowbelly*—a fish of the bluegill or sunfish family, (longear sunfish—book name). **1973** *Pt. Arthur News* (TX) 25 Mar 17/3, Unscientifically included in this group are bluegills, green sunfish, cherry bream, yellowbelly sunfish, redear sunfish [etc]. **1976** Tryckare et al. *Lore of Sportfishing* 101, Yellow Belly. . *Lepomis megalotis.* . . back and upper sides olive, belly orange red.

4 A **squawfish 2** (here: *Ptychocheilus oregonensis*).

1896 U.S. Bur. Fisheries *Rept. for 1895* 247, *Ptychocheilus oregonensis.* . . Squawfish; Chappaul; Yellowbelly. **1902** Jordan–Evermann *Amer. Fishes* 69, Squawfish. . . This fish is highly esteemed by the Indians, hence its most popular name. Other names by which it is known

are Sacramento pike, . . yellow-belly [etc]. **1976** Tryckare et al. *Lore of Sportfishing* 82, Northern Squawfish. . . Other common names. . . yellowbelly, pike.

5 also *yellowbelly bullhead, ~ cat:* Either a **bullhead 1b** (here: *Ameiurus melas*) or the **brown bullhead 1.**

1932 OH Bur. Scientific Research *Bulletin* 23.2, Brown or Marble Bullhead—This appears to be the most sought for of the three species of bullheads and also is the best for the table. It is the big "Yellow-belly" or "Marble Cat" of the four largest state-owned reservoirs. **1951** Harlan–Speaker *IA Fish* 94, Northern Black Bullhead. . . yellow-belly bullhead, horned pout [etc]. **1958** *Emmetsburg Reporter* (IA) 13 May 4/4, The Fort Dodgers had a string of eight bullheads, all medium to large-sized, with the top one on the string a big yellowbelly. **1968** *DARE* Tape **OH**58, They have different kinds of catfish. . . they have the yellowbellies there . . don't get very big but they're real yellow in color. **1969–70** *DARE* (Qu. P1, *. . Kinds of freshwater fish . . caught around here . . good to eat*) Inf **IN**83, Mississippi cats, mud cats, yellowbellies; **KY**82, Catfish—yellow-back or yellowbelly; **KY**60, Yellowbelly cat. **1970** *DARE* Tape **NC**85, We catch a few yellowbellies down there—a few catfish. **1982** *Spirit L. Beacon* (IA) 20 May sec A 10/3, Bullheads—Yellowbelly fishing has been fantastic at times and no worse than "good" most of the week. **2002** in **2008** *DARE* File—Internet **IA,** Angling for yellowbellies at Mini Wakan has a long and colorful history.

6 A **darter 1** (here: *Etheostoma exile*).

1983 Becker *Fishes WI* 940, Iowa Darter. . . Other common names: red-sided darter, yellowbelly, weed darter.

7 A mature **ponderosa pine 1;** see quots.

1978 U.S. Forest Serv. *Final Ochoco–Crooked R. Plan* 28 **OR,** Nearly all production-oriented management dooms large "yellow-belly" pines as a non-renewable resource. **1984** U.S. Congress Senate *OR Wilderness Act Hearings* 1.513, Rugged rim rock and long grassy slopes interspersed with fingers of yellow belly Ponderosa Pine in the canyons. **2007** Ostertag *Our OR* 112, Named for its ponderous size, the ponderosa pine shapes one of the climax forests east of the Cascades. The golden-orange color of the trunk at maturity suggests the tree's nickname, "yellow-belly." **2009** *DARE* File **nAZ,** [National Public Radio's "Morning Edition" 17 Aug:] Some trees [=ponderosa pines] have black bark, but others are yellow. . . At around 120 years . ., they begin to shed their black bark and reveal a yellowish interior. That's why locals call them 'yellow-bellies.'

yellowbelly bullhead (or cat) See **yellowbelly 5**

yellowbelly cooter n Also *yellowbelly, yellow-bellied cooter, yellowbreast ~, yellow ~* **chiefly SC, GA** See Map Cf **cooter 1, yellow-bellied turtle**

A **red-bellied turtle** such as *Pseudemys concinna* or *Trachemys scripta.*

1835 Simms *Partisan* 2.78 **SC** (as of a1783), You're turned now . . on the flat of your back, like a yellow-belly cooter. **1950** Jr. League Charleston *Receipts* 39 **SC,** Cooter Soup—1 large or 2 small "yellow belly" cooters. **1965–70** *DARE* (Qu. P24, *. . Kinds of turtles*) Infs **SC**4, 9, 19, Yellowbelly cooter; **SC**40, Yellowbelly cooter = pond turtle, pond terrapin; **SC**43, Yellow cooter, yellowbelly cooter; **DE**4, **GA**12, 16, Yellowbelly; **LA**34, French turtle or yellowbelly; **SC**26, Yellowbreast cooter, yellowbelly cooter; [**GA**3, Yellowbelly—caught commercially, sea turtle.] **1968** *DARE* Tape **GA**20, What we call a yellow-bellied cooter, he's a box turtle, alligator turtle. **1997** *DARE* File—Internet **Sandy Island SC,** *To Cook a Yellow Belly Cooter:* "I put it in bacon

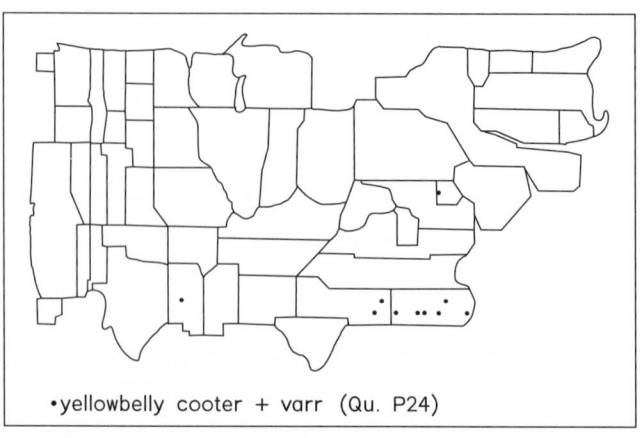

•yellowbelly cooter + varr (Qu. P24)

grease. Cut off that black toes, then you work it in flour and black pepper, salt, and you put it in there and you fry it." **2009** *DARE* File— Internet **TX**, [Advt:] Trachemys s. scripta—Yellow bellied Cooter (babies). . . Price: $19.99.

yellowbelly dace n

A **red-bellied dace** (here: *Phoxinus eos*).

1983 Becker *Fishes WI* 459, Northern Redbelly Dace. . . Other common names. . . yellowbelly dace.

yellowbelly sapsucker See yellow-bellied woodpecker

yellowbelly sunfish See yellowbelly 3

yellowberry n

=**mayapple 1.**

1830 Rafinesque *Med. Flora* 2.59, Mountain May Apple. . . Raccoon Berry, Yellow Berry [etc]. **1906** Culbreth *Manual Materia Medica* (4th ed) 210, *Podophyllum peltatum*. . . Raccoon or Yellowberry. **1971** Krochmal *Appalachia Med. Plants* 198, Common mayapple, . . wild lemon, wild mandrake, yellowberry.

yellowbill n

1 also *yellow-billed coot:* The American **scoter** *(Melanitta nigra).* **esp NEng**

[**1885** *Forest & Stream* 25.83 **Nova Scotia**, American Black Scoter. . . Known on the coast as the "coot," "courting coot" or "yellowbill."] **1888** Trumbull *Names of Birds* 107 **ME, MA,** In Maine at Machiasport, Jonesport, Millbridge, and Kennebunk, and at Plymouth, Mass., [the American Scoter is known as] yellow-bill. **1925** (1928) Forbush *Birds MA* 1.271, American Scoter. . . yellow-nose; yellow-bill [etc]. **1982** Elman *Hunter's Field Guide* 237, American Scoter. . . Common & Regional Names. . . coot, sea coot, broad-billed coot, yellow-billed coot.

2 See **yellow-billed cuckoo.**

yellow-billed coot See yellowbill 1

yellow-billed cuckoo n Also *yellowbill*

Std: the American cuckoo *(Coccyzus americanus).* Also called **brush hen, chowchow 1, cowbird 2, cow-cow 2, drought bird, Indian hen 4, milk-sourer, mockingbird 6, rainbird 2c, rain crow 1a, ~ dove 1, ~ hawk, ~ hen, ~ pigeon, storm crow**

yellow-billed magpie See magpie 1

yellow birch n

Std: a birch *(Betula alleghaniensis,* formerly *B. lutea).* Also called **curly birch, gray ~ b, silver ~, swamp ~ 1**

yellowbird n

1 =**goldfinch 1.** **chiefly NEast, S Midl** See Map

1759 in 1775 Burnaby *Travels* 10 **VA,** In the woods [of Virginia] there are . . the blue-bird, the yellow-bird [etc]. **1789** *MA Centinel* (Boston) 15 Aug 174/3, *One Guinea Reward. Missing* from his cage, an East-India *Bird* of the size of a spring bird, with a short thick bill, bright yellow breast, . . like the common yellow bird. **1792** Belknap *Hist. NH* 3.173, Yellow Bird, *Fringilla tristis?* **1844** DeKay *Zool. NY* 2.99, The Common Yellow-Bird (*Carduelis tristis*) . . is seen here at all seasons of the year. **1885** [see **2** below]. **1892** *Outing* 20.348, One of the prettiest sights in the world is a flock of yellow-birds descending suddenly on a group of thistles. **1965–70** *DARE* (Qu. Q14, . . Names . . for . . goldfinch) 26 Infs, **chiefly NEast, S Midl,** Yellowbird. **2007** *DARE*

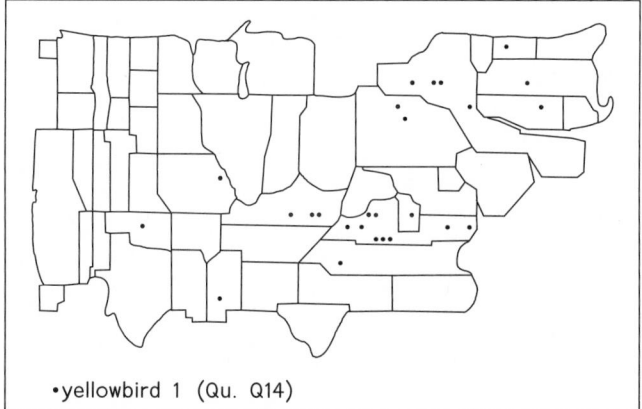

•yellowbird 1 (Qu. Q14)

File—Internet **IA**, Of course, Iowa is not the only state proud of its yellow-bird population. The American Goldfinch is also the state bird of New Jersey and Washington.

2 =**yellow warbler.** Cf **summer yellowbird 1**

1839 *Poughkeepsie Casket* 3.69 **NY,** From his willow tree the yellow bird sings. **1840** *N. Amer. Rev.* 50.397 **OR,** Its note [=that of Audubon's warbler] resembles that of our familiar yellow-bird. **1885** *Atlantic Mth.* 55.161 **MA,** A resident of Princeton . . had one day sought an interview with me to inquire whether the "yellow-bird" did not remain in Massachusetts through the winter. I explained that we had two birds which commonly went by that name, and asked whether he meant the one with a black forehead and black wings and tail. Yes, he said, that was the one. I assured him, of course, that this bird, the goldfinch, did stay with us all the year round, and that whoever had informed him to the contrary must have understood him to be speaking about the golden warbler. **1904** (1905) Dugmore *Bird Homes* 155, Yellow Warbler; Canary; Summer Warbler; Yellow-bird. **1938** Oberholser *Bird Life LA* 528, Conspicuous because of its yellow plumage below and yellowish olive green above, the Eastern Yellow Warbler, or 'yellow bird', is readily identified in the field.

3 =**golden-crowned kinglet.**

1917 *Wilson Bulletin* 29.2.85 **KY,** *Regulus spp.*—Wood wren, yellow-bird, Hickman, Ky.

yellow-boy n

A **coffeeberry 2a(1)** (here: *Frangula californica,* formerly *Rhamnus c.*).

1897 Parsons *Wild Flowers CA* 67, In Monterey County it [=cascara sagrada] is known as "yellow-boy" or "yellow-root," and in Sonoma County it becomes "pigeon-berry."

yellow bream n esp FL

=**red-eared sunfish 1** or a similar fish.

1791 Bartram *Travels* 153 **FL,** What a most beautiful creature is this fish before me! . . the yellow bream or sun fish [=*Chaenobryttus gulosus*]. *Ibid* 176, The great yellow or particoloured bream [=*Lepomis microlophus*] is . . from a foot to fifteen inches in length; the upper part of his body . . is of a dark clay and dusky colour, with transverse dashes or blotches, of reddish dull purple, or purple . . ; the sides and belly of bright pale yellow. **1859** Reid *Oceola* 27 **FL,** Far down in its crystal depths might be seen gold and red fish, with yellow bream [etc]. **1891** U.S. Fish Comm. *Bulletin for 1889* 378 **FL,** *Lepomis holbrooki*. . . Yellow Bream. Myakka River. The most southern locality recorded for this species. **1968** *DARE* (Qu. P1, . . *Kinds of freshwater fish . . caught around here . . good to eat*) Inf **LA**15, Yellow bream. [FW: Inf identified the chinquapin bream . . as being the same fish as the one called shell-cracker in Florida. (This fish is called red-eared sunfish or redgill in central Arkansas.) He said that the yellow bream is "one of the best eating breams we have." It has a small mouth, but he could not identify it further.] **1972** Sparano *Outdoors Encycl.* 361, Redear Sunfish—Common Names . . stumpknocker, yellow bream [etc].

yellowbreast n

1 See **yellow-breasted lark.**

2 See **yellowbreast sunfish.**

yellowbreast cooter See yellowbelly cooter

yellow-breasted blackbird n Also *yellowbreast blackbird*

=**yellow-headed blackbird.**

1966–70 *DARE* (Qu. Q11, . . *Kinds of blackbirds*) Infs **CA**210, **CO**46, **MS**47, **ND**1, Yellowbreast blackbird; **CA**62, **TX**5, Yellow-breasted blackbird.

yellow-breasted chat n

Std: a large wood-warbler *(Icteria virens).* Also called **cane bird, chattering flycatcher, French mockingbird 3, ghost bird 1, mockingbird 5, pompey, yellow mockingbird** Cf **brown mockingbird 2**

yellow-breasted lark n Also *yellowbreast* **scattered, but chiefly Sth, S Midl**

=**meadowlark 1.**

1802 M'Kinnen *Descr. Poems* 50 **NY,** In the meads / Shorn of their hay, the yellow-breasted larks / Melodious sung. **1835** *S. Lit. Jrl.* 1.203 **SC,** The exulting call note of the yellow breasted lark . . testified of spring. **1853** *NY Daily Times* (NY) 30 Apr 3/1 **FL,** The yellow-breasted lark and the bluebird are common. **1880** Tourgée *Bricks* 324, The yellow-breasted lark, pouring forth his autumn lay. **1902** in 1914

Attwater *Use & Value Birds* 31, I would bet my money . . on a flock of ten yellow-breasted larks catching more weevils in an hour than one hundred hands would catch in a day. **1925** *Frederick Post* (MD) 7 Apr 5/1 **cnMD,** We loitered . . to observe a yellow breasted lark exercise her legs in her getaway. **1931** *Charleston Daily Mail* (WV) 1 Mar 6/8, And through the fragrant, sunlit day,/ A yellow-breasted lark, in clear note sings. **1966–67** *DARE* (Qu. Q15, . . *Kinds of larks*) Inf **OK25,** Yellowbreast—same as meadowlark; **OR5,** Yellow-breasted lark.

yellow-breasted rail   See **yellow rail**

yellowbreast sunfish n   Also *yellow-breasted sunfish, yellow-breast (perch)*   **esp Mid and S Atl, Gulf States**
=**red-breasted sunfish 1.**

     1926 (1949) McQueen–Mizell *Hist. Okefenokee* 55 **seGA,** The kinds of fish caught are: trout, or bass, jack (pickerel), war-mouth, bream and yellow-breast perch. **1946** La Monte *N. Amer. Game Fishes* 139, Yellowbreast sunfish—*Lepomis auritus.* **1956** *Frederick Post* (MD) 30 July 6/2, The lake will be stocked with over 135 tagged bass. . . In addition, a quantity of yellow breasted sunfish will be provided. **1966** *DARE* (Qu. P1, . . *Kinds of freshwater fish . . caught around here . . good to eat*) Infs **GA7, SC9,** Yellowbreast. **2005** *DARE* File—Internet **TX,** Caught a couple of yellow breasted sunfish. **2007** *Ibid* **TX,** Anyway, we got into lots of big giant yellow breasted sunfish.

yellow breeches n
=**Dutchman's breeches 1.**

     1814 Pursh *Flora Americae* 2.462, *Corydalis.* . . *Cucullaria.* . . This singularly constructed flower is known among the inhabitants by the name of *Breeches-flower* or *Yellow-breeches.* **1832** MA Hist. Soc. *Coll.* 2d ser 9.149 **cwVT,** Corydalis cuccullaria [sic], . . —Yellow breeches.

yellow broom n
1   In the eastern US, a **wild indigo 1** (here: *Baptisia tinctoria*).

     1828 Rafinesque *Med. Flora* 1.79, *Baptisia tinctoria.* . . Vulgar Names—Wild Indigo, . . Yellow broom [etc]. **1892** (1974) Millspaugh *Amer. Med. Plants* 52–1, *Baptisia.* . . Com. Names. . . Yellow wild indigo, . . yellow broom. **1971** Krochmal *Appalachia Med. Plants* 72, Yellow broom, yellow wild indigo.

2   Prob =**Scotch broom 1.**   **esp CA**

     1913 *Oxnard Courier* (CA) 6 June 1/1, The banquet room . . was tastefully decorated in Cecil Brunner roses, the club rooms in yellow broom. **1950** *Daily Rev.* (Hayward CA) 6 July 9/1, The wayside was dotted with wildflowers similar to those of California—sweet peas, japonica, yellow broom plant [etc]. **1958** *Oakland Tribune* (CA) 9 Apr sec D 22/2, The head table . . was banked with an elaborate arrangement of red and white tulips, white iris and yellow broom.

3   also *yellow broom snakeweed:* In the western US, a **snakeweed b(6)** (here: *Gutierrezia texana*).

     1951 *PADS* 15.42 **TX,** *Gutierrezia texana.* . . Yellow broom; snake weed. **2005** *Canyon Views* 11.4.8 **AZ,** We set out at a brisk pace down the Bright Angel Trail, enjoying the last blooms of purple and white asters and yellow broom snakeweed that seemed to be hanging on to summer.

yellowbrush n
1   =**rabbit brush 1a.**

     1918 U.S. Dept. Ag. *Bulletin* 675.33, The terraces are planted to such soil-binding species as . . yellow brush (*Chrysothamnus*). **1931** U.S. Dept. Ag. *Misc. Pub.* 101.160, Rabbit brush is the name probably most commonly applied to this genus [=*Chrysothamnus*] in the West. . . Rabbit sage, rayless-goldenrod, and yellowbrush are also in frequent use. **1937** [see **sweet sage 1**]. **1962** *Jrl. Range Management* 15.1, Vegetation in the study area included . . yellowbrush (*Chrysothamnus stenophyllus*).

2   A **rabbit brush 1b** (here: *Ericameria discoidea*).   Cf *rubber yellowbrush* (at **rubber rabbit-brush**)

     1931 U.S. Dept. Ag. *Misc. Pub.* 101.157, Whitestem goldenweed (*A[ster] macronema* [=*Ericameria discoidea*] . .), locally known as yellowbrush.

3   A **goldenweed 1** (here: *Isocoma tenuisecta*).

     1931 U.S. Dept. Ag. *Misc. Pub.* 101.157, Singlehead goldenweed (*Aster suffruticosus* [=*Isocoma tenuisecta*] . .), also frequently called yellowbrush, ranges from Idaho to Arizona and western Montana.

yellow buckthorn n
=**Carolina buckthorn 1.**

     1898 Sudworth *Forest Trees* 95, *Rhamnus caroliniana.* . . Yellow Buckthorn. **1923** Pellett *Amer. Honey Plants* 60, *Rhamnus Caroliniana,* the yellow buckthorn, commonly called Indian cherry or polecat-tree, is a shrub or small tree found on river banks and moist hillsides. **1950** Moore *Trees AR* 98, Carolina Buckthorn. . . Local Names: Buckthorn, Yellow Buckthorn, Indian Cherry. **1951** *PADS* 15.36 **TX,** *Rhamnus caroliniana.* . . Yellow buckthorn; arrowwood. **1979** Little *Checklist U.S. Trees* 247, Carolina buckthorn. . . Indian-cherry, tree buckthorn, yellow buckthorn, yellowwood.

yellowbud hickory n
=**bitternut 1.**

     1888 MI State Bd. Ag. *Annual Rept.* 334, The growing of poles for market in southern Kansas and in some other parts of the southwest is said to be a very profitable industry, and this same bitternut, or yellow bud hickory as it is sometimes called, is the species planted. **1921** Deam *Trees IN* 63, The rossed bark of this species is preferred by manufacturers of split-bottomed chairs, and is known by them as "yellow-bud" hickory. **1940** Gates *Flora KS* 223, *Carya cordiformis.* . . Yellow-bud Hickory. **1963** Zimmerman–Olson *Forest* 117 **csWI,** Yellowbud hickory. . . more shade-tolerant than shagbark. **1973** Stephens *Woody Plants* 78 **N Cent,** Bitternut, pignut, yellow-bud hickory.

yellow bullhead n
A **bullhead 1b** (here: *Ameiurus natalis*).   Also called **brown bullhead 2, butter cat, greaser B5, Mississippi bullhead 1, yellow catfish b**   Cf **butterball cat**

     1874 Jordan–Van Vleck *Pop. Key Birds* 80, Pimelodus xanthocephalus. Raf. Yellow Bull Head. **1903** *Forest & Stream* 19.368 **NE,** Other fishes . . that have been planted in the waters of the State . . [include] 5,000 yellow bullheads. **1934** *Waterloo Daily Courier* (IA) 14 Nov 19/2, Rescue work conducted on the Mississippi river salvaged . . yellow bullheads. These were released in Iowa rivers and lakes. **1958** *Atchison Daily Globe* (KS) 16 Nov 6/1, All fish are in good condition except smallmouth bass and yellow bullheads. **1995** *Daily News* (Huntingdon PA) 12 Sept 6/1, Locally, yellow bullheads are normally larger than black bullheads. **2008** *DARE* File—Internet **MS,** [Caption:] Yellow Bullhead at the top of the tank fixing to be fed.

yellow bullhead catfish   See **yellow catfish b**

yellow burweed n
A **fiddleneck 1** (here: *Amsinckia menziesii*).

     1896 U.S. Dept. Ag. *Yearbook for 1895* 610 **Pacific,** Yellow bur weed, fire-weed, yellow tarweed—*Amsinckia intermedia;* Pacific coast. **1911** Pammel *Weeds* 216 **eCA,** Yellow Burweed, Fireweed or Yellow Tarweed (*Amsinckia intermedia* . .) . . In dry open grounds in eastern California. **1925** *Book of Rural Life* 2.773, Burweed, Yellow, Buckthornweed, Yellow Forget-me-not (*Amsinckia intermedia*). . . It is a bristly, hairy weed with tiny yellow flowers. . . Yellow burweed is troublesome on the Pacific coast, particularly in California. **1935** (1943) Muenscher *Weeds* 377, *Amsinckia intermedia.* . . Yellow burnweed [sic], Yellow forget-me-not.

yellow caille n   [See quot 1911]   **LA**   Cf **red caille**
The female **summer tanager.**

     1900 Rightor *Std. Hist. New Orleans* 351, Yellow Caille (the females and males in fall plumage). Summer Tanager (Piranga rubra). **1911** *Forest & Stream* 77.174 **LA,** *Piranga rubra.* . . female called Yellow Caille. [Footnote:] Caille—quail. A component of many Creole bird names. **1916** *Times–Picayune* (New Orleans LA) 23 Apr mag sec 5/6, Summer Tanager. . . female Yellow Caille or Caille Jaune.

yellow catfish n   Also *yellow cat*   **chiefly Gulf States, S Midl**
Any of several catfishes, as:
a   =**flathead catfish 1.**

     1818 Rafinesque in *Amer. Monthly Mag. & Crit. Rev.* 3.354, S[ilurus] olivaris [=*Pylodictis o.*] . . Yellow Cat-fish. **1872** *Carroll Co. Times* (Carrollton GA) 10 May [2]/2 (newspaperarchive.com), Thos. J. Lyon living near Cartersville . . caught on his trot line in the Etowah river two yellow cat fish weighing fifty-one pounds. **1882** U.S. Natl. Museum *Bulletin* 16.102, P[ilodictis] olivaris. . . Mud Cat; Yellow Cat. . . Mottled brown and yellowish, the latter color often predominant. **1933** LA Dept. of Conserv. *Fishes* 424, The Yellow Cat, Goujon, Mud Cat or Bashaw . . appears to be more closely related to the Bullheads than to the Channel Cats. **1955** *Kerrville Times* (TX) 5 Aug 6/4, The comparatively rare occurrence of a flathead or yellow catfish spawning in captivity has been reported by Marlon Tools. **1967** *DARE* Tape **LA5,** What we call the yellow cat around here . . got a square tail. . . flat head. . . I have knowed of 'em weigh a hundred pounds. . . What we call yellow cat—further on out in the southern part, I mean, they'd call it a spotted cat. And . . out towards the . . western part of the state . . they call it Opelousas cat. . . Some of 'em even called it a mud cat . . up the Amite River. **1972** *Odessa Amer.* (TX) 26 Nov sec B 7/1, *Jim Payne of Odessa brought in two large yellow catfish recently at Lake Stamford. The yellow cats tipped the scales at 37 and 27 pounds.* **1986** Pederson *LAGS Concordance* (Common freshwater fish) 1 inf, **cwAR,** Yellow cat—flap-head [sic] cat . . broad head. **2006** *DARE* File—Internet **Sth,** Bullheads and "yellow Cats" (Southern alias for Flatheads) are not the same. **2007** *Ibid* **MO,** One of my fondest memories is when my grandfather caught a 45 lb yellow cat on a trotline.

b also *yellow bullhead catfish:* **=yellow bullhead.**

1820 Rafinesque in *Western Rev.* 2.359, *Pimelodus cupreus* [=*Ameiurus natalis*]. . . Vulgar name, Yellow Catfish. . . found as far as Pittsburgh. Very good to eat. **1842** DeKay *Zool. NY* 4.187, *P[imelodus] cupreus.* The *Yellow Catfish.* **1902** Jordan–Evermann *Amer. Fishes* 25, The yellow cat rarely reaches a weight of more than a pound or two, and is usually not distinguished by fishermen from the common bullhead and the black bullhead. **1942** *Eve. Independent* (Massillon OH) 20 July 11/7, Of less importance are the black bullhead, yellow catfish or yellow bullhead, and the brown catfish. **1964** *Del Rio News–Herald* (TX) 13 Mar 5/1, Some of the biggest yellow catfish in the state have also been hauled in at the reservoir. . . The yellow bullhead catfish is most common to the area.

c **=brown bullhead 1.**

1906 NJ State Museum *Annual Rept. for 1905* 169, *Ameiurus nebulosus.* . . Yellow Cat Fish. Mud Cat Fish. . . Stone Cat Fish. . . Common Bull Head. **1908** NJ State Museum *Annual Rept. for 1907* 150, *Ameiurus nebulosus.* . . Yellow Cat Fish. . . Color in life dusky-olive above, rather olivaceous on sides and becoming whitish below, with slight coppery tints. **1946** La Monte *N. Amer. Game Fishes* 164, Brown Bullhead. . . Yellow Catfish. . . Weedy lakes and sluggish rivers. **1951** *Charleston Daily Mail* (WV) 11 Mar 16/5, Early fishermen are reporting good catches of the popular little yellow catfish or brown bullhead.

d Used generically or in ref to specific fish not identifiable from the context.

1850 *De Bow's Rev.* 9.289 **LA,** The fish are catfish, casseburgo . . , yellow catfish, choupic [etc]. **1856** *Spirit of Times* 26.139 **cNY,** We fancied, from the steady nature of the pull, it was just such an old yellow catfish as we have captured at the Falls of the Ohio, broad-mouthed, smooth-skinned, easy-going fellows. **1880** *Forest & Stream* 27.207 **TX,** In less than half an hour we had three yellow catfish, weighing about 1½ lbs each. **1942** *Eve. Independent* (Massillon OH) 20 July 11/6, "A mud cat in one locality may be a yellow cat of another, and the yellow cat here may be a stone cat somewhere else," the Fish and Wildlife Service points out. **1965–70** *DARE* (Qu. P1, . . *Kinds of freshwater fish . . caught around here . . good to eat*) 31 Infs, 22 **Gulf States, S Midl,** Yellow cat(s); **AR28, IN13, MS21, TN53, TX40,** Yellow catfish; (Qu. P3, *Freshwater fish that are not good to eat*) Infs **KS10, TN65,** Yellow cat; (Qu. P14, . . *Commercial fishing . . what do the fishermen go out after?*) Infs **KY11, LA15,** Yellow cat(s). **1986** Pederson *LAGS Concordance* **Gulf Region** (Common freshwater fish) 20 infs, Yellow cat(s); 3 infs, Yellow catfish; 1 inf, Yellow cat = channel cat—light brown or yellow; 1 inf, Yellow cat = mud cat.

yellow cedar n

1 also *yellow Alaska cedar:* A Pacific **cypress 1** (here: *Chamaecyparis nootkatensis*). Also called **yellow cypress 2**

1868 *Lippincott's Mag.* 2.471 **seAR,** The yellow cedar is found throughout this region, and very little is obtained south of our boundary. **1894** *Jrl. Amer. Folkl.* 7.99 **AK,** *Chamaecyparis Nutkaensis* [sic]. . . yellow cedar. **1919** *Charleston Mail* (WV) 20 Dec 6/4, The Alaska yellow cedar, Port Orford cedar and Idaho cedar are being studied. **1927** *San Antonio Express–News* (TX) 8 Feb [12]/4 (newspaperarchive.com), The yellow cedar is a cypress and ranges along the Pacific Coast from Oregon to Alaska. **1938** (1958) Sharples *AK Wild Flowers* 36, *Chamaecyparis . . nootkatensis.* "Yellow Alaska Cedar". . . Its aromatic yellow wood has many uses, including furniture-making. **1968** *DARE* (Qu. T5, . . *Kinds of evergreens, other than pine*) Inf **AK1,** Yellow cedar—actually a cypress. **1993** *Daily Sentinel* (Sitka AK) 4 Oct 1/6, For craft work in wood a suitable material is required, and in that respect Sitka is blessed by being surrounded by the yellow cedar.

2 A **juniper 1** (here: either *Juniperus ashei* or *J. occidentalis*).

1868 *De Bow's Rev.* 5.53, There was almost every variety of oaks, poplars, juniper, yellow cedar, willow, and numberless others. **1897** Sudworth *Arborescent Flora* 97 **CO, MT,** Western Juniper. . . Yellow Cedar. **1910** Jepson *Silva CA* 164, *Juniperus occidentalis.* . . "White Juniper," "Yellow Cedar," and "Red Cedar" are names in local use. **1950** Moore *Trees AR* 22, Ashe Juniper. . . Local Names: Ozark White Cedar, Yellow Cedar.

yellow chestnut oak See **yellow oak 2**

yellow clover n

=orange milkwort.

1901 Lounsberry *S. Wild Flowers* 296 **FL,** Many of the natives in Florida whom I asked concerning it called it the "yellow clover," because no doubt its bloom suggested to them the shape of thick, clover heads. [**1971** Kieran *Nat. Hist. NYC* 142, It's probable that the Yellow Milkwort *(Polygala lutea),* found sparingly in swamps on Staten Island and in the Long Island section of the city, is mistaken for a yellow clover by most of those who notice it at all.]

yellow cooter See **yellowbelly cooter**

yellow corydalis n

Std: a plant of the genus *Corydalis* (here: *C. flavula*). Also called **colicweed 1** Cf **golden corydalis**

yellow cottonwood n

=Carolina poplar 1—applied esp to specimens with yellowish wood.

1868 U.S. Dept. Ag. *Mth. Rept.* 211 **KS,** The bottoms of the Missouri and Kansas valley produce immense quantities of the yellow cottonwood timber for fencing and common building purposes. **1871** Bryant *Forest Trees* 123, There is a variety [of *Populus angulata* [=*P. deltoides*]] called the Yellow Cottonwood, which is not uncommon, the heart-wood of which is of a yellowish color. **1907** NE State Bd. Ag. *Annual Rept. for 1906–07* 209, I might say here that this Western Cottonwood is but one species, and that the names "White Cottonwood" and "Yellow Cottonwood" are not the names of different species. When the tree is young and growing vigorously, its wood is whiter and tougher, but as it grows older the wood takes on a yellowish color, and loses much of its toughness. **1950** Peattie *Nat. Hist. Trees* 92, Eastern Cottonwood. . . Other Names: Big or Yellow Cottonwood [etc].

yellow crake n

=yellow rail.

1883 WI Chief Geologist *Geol. WI* 1.602 **WI,** *Prozana* [sic] *noveboracensis.* . . Yellow Rail; Yellow Crake. **1898** (1900) Davie *Nests N. Amer. Birds* 126, The small Yellow Crake appears to be quite rare everywhere in Eastern North America or wherever found. **1907** Anderson *Birds IA* 208, The Yellow Rail or Crake is a rare species, occurring in summer. **1917** (1923) *Birds Amer.* 1.208, Yellow Rail. . . Other Names.—Little Yellow Rail; Yellow Crake. **1946** Hausman *Eastern Birds* 241, Yellow-breasted Rail, Little Yellow Rail, Yellow Crake, Clicker. . . the shyest, most secretive, and least often seen of any of our rails.

yellow-crowned night heron n

Std: a **night heron** (here: *Nyctanassa violacea*). Also called **bumcutter, gaulding, gros-bec, Indian hen 2a, ~ pullet 1, moonshine** n **3, night scoggins, poor Job, quabird, quack 1, quawk** n² **1, sedge hen 2, shitepoke, squawk**

yellow-crowned warbler n

Either the **myrtle warbler** or the chestnut-sided **warbler** *(Dendroica pensylvanica).*

1817 Shaw *Genl. Zool.* 10.623, Yellow-crowned Warbler. (*Sylvia icterocephala* [=*Dendroica pensylvanica*].) . . This inhabits the continent of North America, appearing in . . Pensylvania in April. **1832** Nuttall *Manual Ornith.* 1.361, Yellow-crowned Warbler, or Myrtle-bird. **1858** Thoreau in *Atlantic Mth.* 2.311 **ME,** There was one full-plumaged Yellow-crowned Warbler *(Sylvia coronata).* **1917** (1923) *Birds Amer.* 3.128, Myrtle Warbler. . . Other Names. . . Yellow-rump; Yellow-rumped Warbler; . . Yellow-crowned Warbler. *Ibid* 133, Chestnut-sided Warbler. . . Other Names. . . Yellow-crowned Warbler [etc]. **1953** Jewett *Birds WA* 560, Alaska Myrtle Warbler. *Dendroica coronata hooveri.* . . Yellow-rumped Warbler; Yellow-crowned Warbler. **1995** Bonta *More Journeys PA* 17, You should . . see the handsome yellow-crowned warbler with chestnut sides separating his white breast from his yellow-and-black wings and back.

yellow cups n

An **evening primrose b** (here: *Camissonia brevipes*).

1941 Jaeger *Wildflowers* 172 **Desert SW,** Yellow Cups. *Oenothera brevipes.* . . brilliant yellow. A bright, showy, free-flowering annual. **1971** Dodge *100 Desert Wildflowers* 22, Evening-primrose—Also known as "yellow cups," this plant is limited in its range to the Mohave-Colorado Desert. **2008** (acc) U.S. Dept. Ag. *Integrated Taxonomic Info. System* (Internet), *Camissonia brevipes.* . . yellow cups.

yellow cypress n

1 A **bald cypress** (here: *Taxodium distichum*).

1812 Stoddard *Sketches LA* 161, No other wood than white and yellow cypress, was sawed. **1840** *Spirit of Times* 9.599 **GA,** The Tallulah . . is made out of a single tree, of the lightest and best kind of yellow Cypress, perfectly sound and seasoned. **1881** *Galveston Daily News* (TX) 25 Sept 3/7, Bridging must be of yellow cypress, post or white oak, and heart of yellow pine. **1920** *Amer. Architect* 8 Dec 765, Southern bald cypress is about the most variable in color of any of our native woods, and in different localities is known as red cypress, yellow cypress, white cypress and black cypress. **1966–68** *DARE* (Qu. T15, . . *Kinds of swamp trees*) Infs **MS21, SC43,** Yellow cypress; **LA**15, Yellow cypress—used for timber. **2005** *DARE* File—Internet **SC** (as of 1960s), Trees near salt water were called Red Cypress and upland swamp trees were called Yellow Cypress. . . but all were Baldcypress.

2 =**yellow cedar 1.**

1872 *Gardener's Mth. & Horticult. Advt.* 14.271 **AR,** Up in Alaska they call the *Cupressus nutkaensis* . . Yellow cypress or Yellow cedar. **1879** *Bulletin* (San Francisco CA) 1 Nov 1/4 **AK,** The ridgepole of yellow cypress, still lying here in the damp woods and perfectly sound, is two feet in diameter. **1884** Sargent *Forests of N. Amer.* 178, Yellow Cypress. Sitka Cypress. . . A large tree of great economic value. **1917** *Ogden Std.* (UT) [20 Oct 31]/6 (newspaperarchive.com) **AK,** Aside from the large amount of hemlock and sitka spruce, red cedar and yellow cypress there is any amount of timber excellently suited for pulp manufacture. **2008** *DARE* File—Internet **WA,** With the yellow cypress (Alaska cedar) so prominent heaths and heathers would be natural associates.

yellow daisy n

1 A **buttercup 1** (here: *Ranunculus acris*). **esp NEast**

1829 *Hist. Co. Berkshire MA* 69, *Ranunculus . . acris.* Butter-cup, Yellow daisy. **1839** *Genesee Farmer* 9.338 **wNY,** There is another plant called the yellow daisy by some, by others, butter cup, or crowfoot, very common in wet meadows; but this plant is a species of Ranunculus not a daisy. **1891** *Jrl. Amer. Folkl.* 4.147 **NH,** The only Buttercup we then knew, which I think must be the only *conspicuous* species that grew there, we called *Yellow Daisy*, being Ranunculus acris.

2 =**black-eyed Susan 2.**

1892 *Jrl. Amer. Folkl.* 5.98 **MA,** *Rudbeckia hirta*, yellow daisies. Mass. . . and general. **1895** *Atlantic Mth.* 75.460 **NEng,** A dusky face, called with childish plainness of speech a "nigger head," could be made . . from the "black-eyed Susan" or "yellow daisy," the *Rudbeckia hirta.* **1906** *Town & Country* 12 May 28, By the roadside we find . . Black-eyed Susan, the yellow Daisy, which has not its common white sisters' weedy facility for spreading all over the garden. **1930** OK Univ. Biol. Surv. *Pub.* 2.86, Black-eyed Susan. Yellow Daisy. **1965–70** *DARE* (Qu. S7, *A kind of daisy, bright yellow with a dark center, that grows along roadsides in late summer*) 13 Infs, **scattered,** Yellow daisy; **KY**17, Yellow daisies, black-eyed Susies; **ME**20, Yellow daisy—also called black-eyed Susan; (Qu. S21, . . *Weeds . . that are a trouble in gardens and fields*) Inf **TX**73, Yellow daisies; **GA**38, Yellow daisy; (Qu. S22) Inf **FL**11, Yellow daisies; (Qu. S26a, . . *Wildflowers. . . Roadside flowers*) Inf **LA**37, Yellow daisies; (Qu. S26d, *Wildflowers that grow in meadows;* not asked in early QRs) Inf **IN**41, Yellow daisies; **GA**38, Yellow daisy. [**1977** *Independent Press-Telegram* (Long Beach CA) 14 Oct 21/1, Who is there who doesn't know and love brown-eyed Susan, the little yellow daisy of field and roadside?]

3 A **goldenweed 1** (here: *Machaeranthera gracilis*).

1967 Dodge *Roadside Wildflowers* 75, Goldenweed—Yellow Daisy. . . *Haplopappus* [=*Machaeranthera*] *gracilis.* **1995** Epple *Field Guide Plants AZ* 281, Yellow spiny daisy. . . Goldenweed, yellow daisy—*Machaeranthera gracilis.*

4 A **balsamroot** (here: *Balsamorhiza sagittata*).

1967 *DARE* FW Addit **OR**12, Arrowleafed balsamroot, locally yellow

daisy. **1976** *Tri-City Herald* (Pasco WA) 12 Mar 5/5, The yellow daisy, balsam, which grows all around the Tri-Cities in the spring, was used by the Indians as food and medicine.

yellow devil n   Also *yellow-devil hawkweed*

A yellow-flowered **hawkweed;** see quots.

[**1906** Clark–Fletcher *Farm Weeds Canada* 64, This yellow-flowered Hawkweed, which is now widely known as the Yellow Devil, may merely be the yellow-flowered variety of the Orange Hawkweed.] **1914** Georgia *Manual Weeds* 556, Field Hawkweed—*Hieracium pratense.* . . *Other English names:* King Devil, Yellow Devil. **1933** *Daily Courier* (Connellsville PA) 1 July 6/2, King devil, yellow devil, or field hawkweed is spreading at an appalling rate over the entire State. **1935** (1943) Muenscher *Weeds* 501, *Hieracium pratense.* . . Yellow paintbrush, Devils paintbrush, Yellow devil [etc]. *Ibid, Hieracium floribundum.* . . Hawkweed, Yellow devil. **1997** *Rangelands* 19.4.19, The remaining group [of hawkweeds] consists of species with multiple, yellow flowers and includes *H. pratense . . , H. praealtum . . , H. piloselloides . . , H. floribundum . . ,* and *H. flagellare.* . . Known variously as yellow hawkweed, meadow hawkweed, field hawkweed, king devil hawkweed, and yellow devil hawkweed, this group represents most of the taxonomic complexities. **2008** Prather et al. *Idaho's Weeds* 112, Yellow devil hawkweed—*Hieracium glomeratum.* . . Category: E[arly] D[etection] R[apid] R[esponse]. . . Introduced to the U.S. from Europe.

yellow dock n

=**curled dock.**

[**1676** Royal Soc. London *Philos. Trans.* 11.629, There grow wild in the Woods [of Virginia], *Plantane* of all sorts, *Yellow-dock, Bur-dock, Solomon's-seal* [etc].] **1814** Henry *New & Complete Amer. Herbal* 63, Boil one pound of the fresh roots [of burdock], . . with half a pound of yellow dock root, in two gallons of rain water. **1864** Thoreau in *Atlantic Mth.* 14.478 **eMA,** As I had asked him the names of so many things, he tried me in turn with all the plants which grew in his garden. . . Besides the common garden-vegetables, there were Yellow-Dock, Lemon-Balm, Hyssop [etc]. **1893** *Stevens Point Jrl.* (WI) 13 May [27]/5 (newspaperarchive.com), In case any person or persons . . shall neglect to destroy any . . yellow dock . . it shall be the duty of the commissioner to destroy or cause to be destroyed, all such weeds. **1935** (1943) Muenscher *Weeds* 198, *Rumex crispus.* . . Curly dock, Sour dock, Yellow dock. **1966–68** *DARE* (Qu. S26b, *Wildflowers that grow in water or wet places*) Inf **WI**12, Yellow dock; (Qu. S26a, . . *Wildflowers. . . Roadside flowers*) Inf **ME**20, Yellow dock; (Qu. S26d, *Wildflowers that grow in meadows;* not asked in early QRs) Infs **IN**19, **NC**33, **OH**82, **WI**17, Yellow dock; (Qu. S26e, *Other wildflowers not yet mentioned;* not asked in early QRs) Inf **ME**20, Yellow dock; (Qu. BB50d, *Favorite spring tonics*) Inf **VA**13, Yellow dock and whiskey. **2008** *DARE* File—Internet, It is fair to say that yellow dock is far from decorative.

yellow dog-fennel   See **dog fennel 2, 5**

yellow-eye n

1 See **yellow-eyed bean.**

2 =**goldenseal 1.**

1876 Hobbs *Bot. Hdbk.* 134, Yellow eye, Goldenseal root, Hydrastis Canadensis. **1930** Sievers *Amer. Med. Plants* 31, Goldenseal. . . eyeroot, eyebalm, yelloweye, jaundice root [etc].

3 See **yellow-eyed grass 1.**

4 Jaundice; a disease characterized by jaundice.

1990 Cavender *Folk Med. Lexicon* 34 **sAppalachians,** Yellow eye—hepatitis [sic]. **1994** in 2004 Montgomery–Hall *Dict. Smoky Mt. Engl.* 663 **eTN,** *Yellow eye.* . . hepatitis . . ; = also jaundice.

yellow-eyed bean n   Also *yellow-eye (bean), yellow-eyed china (bean)* **chiefly NEng** See Map **Cf dot eye**

A cultivated bush bean with a yellow spot surrounding the hilum.

1857 ME Dept. Ag. *Annual Rept. for 1856* 249 **nME,** The ground was plowed . . and planted with white yellow-eyed beans. **1863** Burr *Field & Garden* 480, Yellow-Eyed China. . . The ripe beans are white, spotted and marked about the eye with rusty-yellow. **1870** *Titusville Morning Herald* (PA) 5 Apr 1/7 **ME,** Sixteen quarts nice, ripe, yellow-eyed beans [etc]. **1883** *ME Farmer* (Augusta) 3 Jan 3/3, Yellow Eye beans have taken an upward start, choice ones being $3.10. **1884** NY Ag. Exper. Sta. *Annual Rept. 1883* 255, Yellow Eyed China.—A vigorous bush bean with a distinct twining habit . . the half about the eye yellowish brown. **1908** Cornell Univ. Ag. Exper. Sta. *Bulletin* 260.217 **NY,** Yellow Eye—*Synonyms.*—Improved Yellow Eye, Yellow Eyed China. *Confusing names.*—Old Fashioned Yellow Eye, Boston Yellow Eye, and Yellow Eyed Wax are different from Yellow Eye. **1941** *LANE* Map 259 *(Lima beans)* **NEng,** *Yellow-eyed beans,* sometimes defined as a smaller variety of Lima beans. . . 4 infs, Yellow-eye(d) beans; 3 infs, Yellow eyes; 1 inf, Yeller eyes—so called because they have a yellow eye. **1946** Gould *Yankee Storekeeper* 79 **ME,** Yellow-eyed beans were as staple as sugar, and we took all they'd bring in. **1965–70** *DARE* (Qu. I20, . . *Kinds of beans*) 9 Infs, **chiefly NEng,** Yellow-eyed beans; **CT**29, **ME**5, 12, 20, **MA**27, **NY**68, **VT**16, Yellow-eyes; **MA**37, 40, 55, Yellow-eyed beans; (Qu. I19, *Small white beans with a black spot where they were joined to the pod*) Infs **MA**16, 25, 42, **RI**9, 12, Yellow-eyed beans; **CT**39, **MA**6, 25, Yellow-eye beans; **MA**5, Yellow-eyes; [**RI**15, Yellow-eye peas;] **TN**20, Yeller-eyed beans; (Qu. I18, *The smaller beans that are white when they are dry*) Inf **NY**115, Yellow-eyes. **1978** *Wanigan Catalog* 22, The yellow eye [sic] which have come to me are of three color combinations. The one I have known since about 1920 is white, with a large, solid yellow eye patch. . . Another type has a figure not unlike that on soldier and many wax snap beans. They have names such as Maine y[ellow] e[ye], improved y.e., Highmoor y.e. and others. A third type has a single dot of color on each side of the eye, and have [sic] names such as dot eye, and imperial yellow eye. **2008** *DARE* File—Internet, Maine Yellow Eye Beans. . . This bean is also referred to as a Dot-Eye Bean, Molasses-Face Bean and Yellow-Eyed China Bean. They are most commonly grown in California, Michigan, and Idaho. **2008** *DARE* File nwMA, Yellow Eyes are hard to find over here. [*Ibid,* Those are the beans that my mother and her mother used to make their version of the classic Baked Beans.]

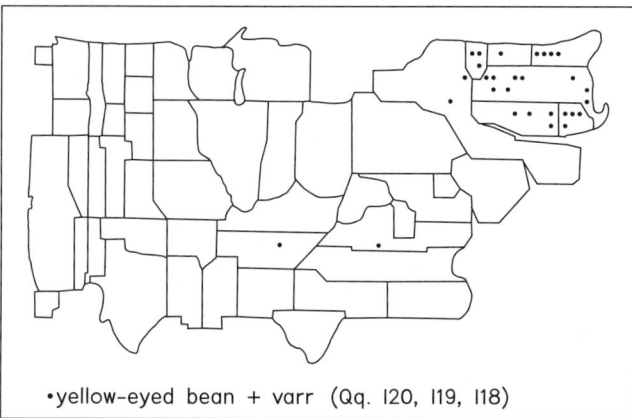

•yellow-eyed bean + varr (Qq. I20, I19, I18)

yellow-eyed grass n

1 also *yellow-eye;* Std: a grasslike plant of the genus *Xyris.* Also called **hardhead 6b;** for other names of var spp see **eye grass, star ~ 4**

2 A **star grass 2** (here: *Hypoxis hirsuta*).

1849 *Amer. Med. Assoc. Trans.* 2.913, *Hypoxis erecta* [=*H. hirsuta*]. Yellow-eyed grass; star grass. This beautiful little grass is vulnerary and febrifuge. **1910** Graves *Flowering Plants* 127 **CT,** *Hypoxis hirsuta.* . . Yellow-eyed Grass. **1961** Wills–Irwin *Flowers TX* 97, Yellow Star-grass, or Yellow-eyed-grass, as it is often called, occurs abundantly in sandy fields and open woods and along highways in the eastern ⅓ of the state. **1967** *DARE* Wildfl QR Pl.25 [=*Hypoxis hirsuta*] Inf **OH**14, Yellow-eyed grass.

3 A yellow-flowered **blue-eyed grass 1.** Cf **golden-eyed grass**

1868 *Mag. Horticult.* 48, *Sisyrinchium.* . . Here is a novelty with a *bright translucent yellow* perianth, so beautiful that "its seeds have been sold in the city of San Francisco, under various names, as . . Star Grass lily, Yellow-eyed Grass, &c." **1934** Haskin *Wild Flowers Pacific Coast* 57, Yellow-eyed Grass—*Hydastylus borealis* [=*Sisyrinchium californicum*]. . . Very much resembling its common blue-eyed cousin, this bright little flower raises its golden stars among the grasses close along the Pacific Ocean throughout the length of the North Coast States. **1940** *Centralia Daily Chron.* (WA) 28 Mar 10/4, Shooting Stars, Blue-eyed and Yellow-eyed grass, Lady Slipper, and the Indian Pipe or Ghost Plant are often seen. **1961** Thomas *Flora Santa Cruz* 127 **cwCA,**

S[isyrinchium] californicum. . . Yellow-eyed Grass, California Golden-eyed Grass. Usually along or near the coast in boggy areas. **2003** *NY Times* (NY) 14 Sept sec CY 10/5, Yellow-eyed grass species, including S[isyrinchium] palmifolium and S. tinctorium, . . must be brought indoors in climates with cold winters.

yellow-finned grouper n

1 also *yellow grouper, yellowfin, yellowfin grouper:* A **grouper 1b** (here: *Mycteroperca venenosa*).

1885 U.S. Natl. Museum *Proc.* 7.192, *Perca marina venenosa punctata* [=*Mycteroperca v.*] . . the species still called Rock-fish or Yellow-finned Grouper. **1935** Caine *Game Fish* 77, Yellow-fin Grouper—*Mycteroperca venenosa.* . . All fins edged with yellow. **1946** La Monte *N. Amer. Game Fishes* 53, Yellow Grouper. . . Names: Yellow-finned Grouper [etc]. . . with a yellow margin on pectoral fin . . the other fins dark-edged. The fish changes color rapidly and confusingly. **1995** *Galveston Daily News* (TX) 21 Nov sec B 3/4, Loessin . . was fishing with one of Tim's rods when the big yellowfin struck. . . When approved, the 40.75-pound yellowfin grouper will be the 10th Texas state saltwater record.

2 A **grouper 1a** (here: *Epinephelus flavolimbatus*).

1896 U.S. Natl. Museum *Bulletin* 47.1155 **FL,** *Epinephelus flavolimbatus.* . . Yellow-finned Grouper. . . West Indies, recorded from Havana and Pensacola, in rather deep waters. **1920** Columbia Univ. College Physicians & Surgeons *Studies Pathology* 17.76, Worms . . were found attached to the gills of . . the Yellow finned grouper (*Epinephalus* [sic] *flavolimbatus*).

yellow fir n

1 =**Douglas fir**—used esp (in contrast to **red fir a**) to distinguish specimens in which the heartwood is yellowish. Note: Some of these quots may refer instead to **2** below.

1838 Parker *Jrl. Rocky Mts.* 200, I have said there are three species of fir, and that they constitute far the greatest part of the forest trees [in the region of the Columbia River], and are very large. The three kinds are the red, yellow, and white. They not only differ in the color of the wood, but also in their foliage. The foliage of the red is scattered on all sides of the branchlets . . ; the yellow only on the upper side . . ; the white is oppositely pinnated. *Ibid* 115, Among the largest trees is a new species of fir, single leafed, the bark thick and rough like the bark of hemlock, but the balsam is the same as the common fir. **1854** *ME Farmer* (Augusta) 4 May 2/5 **OR,** Of the fir, there are three varieties: the white fir, which nearly resembles the fir in Maine, only that it grows much larger and taller; the yellow fir, which is similar to the spruce, and the red fir, which is so called from the color of its wood. The bark of the red and yellow varieties increases in thickness proportionate to the growth of the tree, being found oftentimes eight inches thick. **1870** *Horticulturist & Jrl. Rural Art* 25.27 **OR,** The most common among them [=evergreens] is the red fir; yellow and white fir abound to some extent. . . [T]he red fir is *abies douglassii.* . . The yellow fir is also called *abies douglassii* by some botanists. It is quite certain that none but the most accurate and careful observers can detect any difference . . ; but the difference in the color of the wood is very apparent. . . Some botanists call this variety *abies grandis,* and say there is a difference in the cones of the two kinds; but from all the information I can get, I believe they are alike. **1884** Sargent *Forests of N. Amer.* 209, Douglas Fir. . . Two varieties, red and yellow fir, are distinguished by lumbermen. **1897** Sudworth *Arborescent Flora* 47 **ID, MT, OR, WA,** *Pseudotsuga taxifolia.* . . Common Names. . . Yellow Fir. **1910** Jepson *Silva CA* 115, The sapwood [of *Pseudotsuga menziesii*] is nearly white, the heartwood reddish-brown ("Red Fir") or yellow ("Yellow Fir"). The young rapid growth in the open woods produces "Red Fir," the older slower growth in denser woods is "Yellow Fir." **1938** [see **2** below]. **1958** McCulloch *Woods Words* 218 **Pacific NW,** *Yellow fir*—Old growth Douglas fir, highly prized by loggers. **1977** Churchill *Don't Call* 45 **nwOR** (as of c1918), A bastard fir was nothing more than a young Douglas fir in the transition period from young mature, or red, fir into old mature, or yellow, fir.

2 =**grand fir.**

1860 U.S. War Dept. *Rept. Explor. Railroad* 12.2.25 **Pacific NW,** The tree known as "yellow fir" in the country (A. grandis) I have met with only on the sandy alluvial river banks between the Cascade and Coast ranges. **1866** Hittell *Resources CA* 471, Nearly all the trees [in wOR] are coniferous evergreens. Among these, the most prominent are the Douglas spruce or red fir (*abies Douglasii*), the yellow fir (*A. grandis*), Williamson's spruce (*A. Williamsonii*) [etc]. **1897** Sudworth *Arborescent Flora* 54 **MT, ID,** *Abies grandis.* . . Common Names. . . Yellow Fir.

1938 Van Dersal *Native Woody Plants* 335, Fir, Yellow *(Abies grandis, Pseudotsuga glauca, Pseudotsuga taxifolia).*

yellowfish n

1 =coney n² a.

1734 Catesby in Royal Soc. London *Philos. Trans.* 38.317 **NC, SC,** *Turdus cauda convexa.* The *Yellow-Fish.* **1748** Catesby *Nat. Hist. Carolina* 2.10, *Turdus cauda convexa.* The Yellow Fish. Some of these Fish were a Foot in length: This had small thin Scales of a reddish yellow Colour, the Mouth wide, the under Mandible longer than the upper. **1896** U.S. Natl. Museum *Bulletin* 47.1144, *Bodianus fulvus* [=*Cephalopholis fulva*] (Guativere; Nigger-fish; Yellow-fish.) . . In life, lemon yellow, being somewhat orange red on the back.

2 also *yellow-striped fish:* A **greenling** (here: *Pleurogrammus monopterygius,* the Atka mackerel).

1880 (1884) U.S. Census Office *Rept. Population Industries Resources AK* 72, [This fish is known] on the Shumagins as the yellow or striped fish, and from Oonalashka to Atkha as the Atkha mackerel. **1916** Cobb *Pacific Cod Fisheries* 10 (Tabbert *Dict. Alaskan Engl.*), Yellow striped fish, or "Atka mackerel" *(Pleurogrammus monopterygius),* is a popular article of food when in season. **2008** U.S. Food & Drug Admin. *Seafood List* (Internet), Common Name: Atka Mackerel—Vernacular: Atkafish/Yellowfish.

yellow fly n

A fly of the family Tabanidae, esp *Diachlorus ferrugatus,* native to the Southeast.

1838 *S. Lit. Messenger* 4.25 **seVA,** The yellow flies and moschetoes swarmed in myriads. **1856** *Harper's New Mth. Mag.* 13.450 **seVA,** Before the month of August, visitors, servants, and proprietors, had all cleared out and left the place in full possession of the mosquitoes and yellow-flies. These insects are said to be savage enough to worry the life out of a mule. **1927** Adams *Congaree* 1 **cSC** [Black], Where de yallow-fly sting, in de home of de fever an' wey death is de king. **1932** *Natl. Geogr. Mag.* 62.129 **seVA, neNC,** Yellow flies, which suddenly appear about the tenth of June and disappear about the tenth of August, are another fierce pest. **1938** Brimley *Insects NC* 333, *D[iachlorus] ferrugatus.* . . Yellow Fly. Southern Pines to Hertford, east and south, June–August. **1965–70** DARE (Qu. R12, . . *Other kinds of flies*) 40 Infs, 38 **SE,** Yellow fly; **GA**35, Yellow fly—same as deerfly; **NC**81, Yellow fly—woods fly; some call it a deerfly or crape wing. **1975** Newell *If Nothin' Don't Happen* 237 **nwFL,** First was the yellow flies, the ones Yankees call deerflies. **1986** Pederson *LAGS Concordance Gulf Region,* 13 infs, Yellow fly/flies; 1 inf, **swAL,** Yellow fly—really poison—around stagnant water. **2001** *Atlanta Jrl.–Constitution* (GA) 12 July sec F 2 **Okefenokee GA** (Internet), When we took a small train ride through a drier section, we were nearly eaten up by "yellow flies," as swamp people called them. **2008** (acc) FL Univ. *Featured Creatures* (Internet), The name "yellow fly" is commonly used to describe a group of about a dozen different yellow-bodied biting flies in the Tabanidae family. However, Florida tabanid experts recognize only one species, *Diachlorus ferrugatus . . ,* as the "true" yellow fly.

yellow forget-me-not See **forget-me-not 1c**

yellow gentian n

=columbo.

1828 Rafinesque *Med. Flora* 1.196, *Frasera verticillata* [=*F. caroliniensis*]. . . Vulgar Names—Columbo-root, . . Yellow Gentian [etc]. **1873** in 1976 Miller *Shaker Herbs* 159, Columbo, American. . . Indian Lettuce, . . Yellow Gentian. **1949** Moldenke *Amer. Wild Flowers* 230, The yellow gentian or pyramidflower *F. carolinensis,* growing up to 7 feet tall, is the only eastern representative of the group.

yellow ginseng n

1 =blue cohosh 1.

1828 Rafinesque *Med. Flora* 1.97, Blueberry Cohosh. . . Vulgar Names. . . Blue Ginseng, Yellow Ginseng. **1892** (1974) Millspaugh *Amer. Med. Plants* 16-1, Caulophyllum. *Blue Cohosh.* . . Com. Names.—Blue Cohosh, . . Blue Ginseng, Yellow Ginseng. **1930** Sievers *Amer. Med. Plants* 14, Yellow ginseng. . . Part used.—The rootstock with roots, collected in autumn. In reasonably constant demand.

2 A **bugbane 1** (here: *Cimicifuga racemosa*).

1971 Krochmal *Appalachia Med. Plants* 96, *Cimicifuga racemosa.* . . yellow ginseng. . . The roots and rhizomes are considered valuable in treating chronic rheumatism. . . In Appalachia, a tea made from the root is used to treat sore throat.

yellow gopher n

A **ground squirrel b** (here: *Spermophilus richardsonii*).

1857 U.S. War Dept. *Rept. Explor. Railroad* 8.xxxix, *Spermophilus richardsonii.*—Yellow Gopher.—Sault St. Marie, Mich., and west to the Rocky Mountains north of Upper Missouri. **1865** (1869) Tenney *Nat. Hist.* 65, The Yellow Gopher, *S. Richardsonii* . . of Michigan to the Rocky Mountains, is rather larger than the Red Squirrel. **1891** U.S. Natl. Museum *Annual Rept. for 1889* 558, *Spermophilus richardsoni.* . . Yellow gopher. Plains of the Saskatchewan southward to the upper Missouri. [**1953** *Winnipeg Free Press* 28 Aug [15]/7 (newspaperarchive.com), The destructive yellow gopher was not a native of the Canadian prairie. It followed the wheat fields up from Kansas and Nebraska through the Dakotas and Montana into the Canadian West.] **1966** DARE (Qu. P29, . . 'Gophers' . . *other name . . or what other animal are they most like*) Inf **SD**2, Yellow gopher. **1970** *Western Folkl.* 29.172 **Upper MW,** *Field gopher, mound gopher* and *yellow gopher* are used just for Richardson's ground squirrel.

yellow grouper n See **yellow-finned grouper 1**

yellow grunt n

A **grunt n 1,** usu *Haemulon sciurus.*

[**1771** in 1821 Smith *Selection Corresp. Linnaeus* 1.331 **Bahamas,** Some fishes . . you may perhaps find to be new. The following is a list, with their vernacular names. . . Yellow Grunt [etc.]] [**1876** U.S. Natl. Museum *Bulletin* 5.54 **Bermuda,** The Margate-fish of the fishermen is probably this species [=*Haemulum chrysopterum*]. . . The fishermen recognize several others, as the Yellow, Streaked, Spotted, and Black Grunts, all of which probably belong to this family, if not to this genus.] **1884** U.S. Fish Comm. *Bulletin for 1884* 78 **swFL,** Among the Grunts, besides the common *Haemulon plumieri,* we find . . the Yellow Grunt or Ronco Amarillo *(H. sciurus).* **1897** *NY Times* (NY) 9 Aug 8/5, One of the queerest as well as most beautiful [fish] in the consignment is known as the "yellow grunt." It emits occasionally a sound resembling the grunting of a pig. **1904** [see *white grunt*]. **1935** Caine *Game Fish* 88, Yellow Grunt—*Haemulon sciurus.* **1976** Tryckare et al. *Lore of Sportfishing* 112, Blue Striped Grunt . . *Haemulon sciurus*—Other common names: Yellow grunt, boar grunt [etc].

yellow gum n

=black gum 1, esp a form having yellowish sapwood.

1810 Michaux *Histoire des Arbres* 1.30, N[yssa] sylvatica. . . *Yellow gum.* **1811** *Ibid* 2.263, Dans les vieux arbres qu'on trouve sur les terres hautes . . l'aubier est ordinairement d'une couleur jaunâtre, ce qui est considéré par quelques charrons, comme une indice, que le bois est de meilleure qualité; et c'est probablement pour cela, que cet arbre est quelque fois nommé *Yellow gum,* . . quoique le cœur soit d'un brun foncé. [=In old trees found on high ground . . the sapwood is usually yellowish, which some wheelwrights consider a sign that the wood is of better quality; that is probably why this tree [=*Nyssa sylvatica*] is sometimes called *Yellow gum,* . . although the heartwood is dark brown.] **1815** *DE Gaz. & Peninsula Advt.* (Wilmington) 14 Nov 4/3, [Advt:] First rate timber, consisting principally of white oak, with a small proportion of yellow gum, Chesnut, maple, and ash. **1882** *Denton Jrl.* (MD) 25 Mar [3]/1 (newspaperarchive.com), The timber is very heavy consisting of white and red ash, . . black and yellow gum [etc]. **1897** Sudworth *Arborescent Flora* 310 **TN,** *Nyssa sylvatica.* . . *Common names.* . . Yellow Gumtree. **1912** *Indianapolis Sun. Star* (IN) 9 June 24/1, [Advt:] Thirty acres timber, including the sugar camp, balance red beach, poplar and yellow gum. **1921** Deam *Trees IN* 261, Wood heavy, soft, very difficult to split. Woodsmen always speak of two kinds of black gum. There is one form which splits easily which is designated as "yellow gum." **1950** Peattie *Nat. Hist. Trees* 499, The Yellow Gum or Upland Tupelo is simply a variety of this species [=*Nyssa sylvatica*]. . . Yellow gum is not a swamp tree, like Black Gum, but an inhabitant of dry land, hills, and the coves of the southern Appalachians.

yellowhammer n

1 rarely *yellowhandle, yellowhands, yellowhanger, yellowhanner:* =**flicker** n² **1.** [*OED2* 1556 → for *Emberiza citrinella*] **widespread, but esp freq Sth** Cf **redhammer**

1832 Williamson *Hist. ME* 1.150, The *Yellow-hammer* is also a Woodpecker. **1851** *U.S. Mag. & Democratic Rev.* 29.242 **wKY,** Some spotted yellow-hammer, (flickers, we call them,) Mahometan-like, with a crescent on his breast. **a1862** (1864) Thoreau *ME Woods* 24 **ME,** A "yellow-hammer," as they called the pigeon-woodpecker. **1874** (1905) Baird et al. *Hist. N. Amer. Birds* 2.581 **CA,** This bird [=the red-shafted flicker], in some parts of California, is known as the Yellow-Hammer, a

name given in some parts of New England to the *Colaptes auratus*.
1899 (1912) Green *VA Folk-Speech* 493, *Yallerhammer*. . . A yellowish woodpecker. **1908** *DN* 3.390 **eAL, wGA**, *Yaller-hammer*. . . The yellow-hammer or golden-winged woodpecker. **1951** Porter *Ragged Roads* 53 **OK**, Gables punctured by yaller-hammers, winder blinds hangin' by one hinge. **1965–70** *DARE* (Qu. Q17, . . *Kinds of woodpeckers*) 202 Infs, **widespread, but esp freq Sth**, Yellowhammer; **DE4**, Yellowhanner ['jɛlə,hænɚ]; **LA2**, We say yellowhammer, but flicker is right; (Qu. Q18, *Joking names and nicknames for woodpeckers*) 10 Infs, **chiefly Sth**, Yellowhammer; **GA18**, Yellowhammer—colored people's term for flicker; (Qu. Q10) Inf **GA91**, Yellowhammer; (Qu. Q14) Infs **CA197, GA77**, Yellowhammer; (Qu. Q23, *The insect-eating bird that goes headfirst down a tree trunk*) Infs **AL59, CT2, IN39**, Yellowhammer; **GA65**, Yellowhammer—he's a peckerwood; **ME6**, Yellowhammer—bigger than a robin, not a woodpecker. **1975** Gould *ME Lingo* 326, *Yeller-hammer*—Maine farmer's word for the flicker. **1986** Pederson *LAGS Concordance* **Gulf Region** *(Woodpecker)* 64 infs, Yellowhammer [*DARE* Ed: 12 of these infs remarked that the yellowhammer is a large woodpecker.]; 1 inf, Yellowhandle; 1 inf, Yellowhands; 1 inf, Yellowhanger.

2 A **crested flycatcher** (here: *Myiarchus crinitus*).
1920 *Wilson Bulletin* 32.48 **nwFL**, *Myiarchus crinitus*. . . A noisy inhabitant of our villages and plantations. . . Local name, "Yellowhammer." **1939** Forbush–May *Birds* 311, *Northern Crested Flycatcher—Myiarchus crinitus boreus*. . . Other names: Great Crested Flycatcher; Wheep; Yellowhammer. . . Call.—A loud *wheeeeep!*

3 Perh a **yellow jacket 1**.
1967 Jacobs *Rejoicing* 64 **cIN** (as of c1930), Wheat granaries were favorite nesting places for wasps and other species of flying stingers. . . A yellowhammer raised an awful welt; a swarm of bumblebees could kill a man.

4 A person (esp a woman) of mixed race. [**yellow C**] **esp Sth** *esp freq among Black speakers*
c1904 (1984) Thomas *From TN Slave* 98, Sixty years ago the blacks abused the mulattoes. They call them "mules," "no nation," and all sorts of hard names. A black man would call a mulatto woman "yeller hammer." **1928** Odum *Rainbow* 86 **Sth** [Black], On other side of town an' out in country was some colored folks called yallerhammer niggers, 'cause some folks say they mixed with Indians. **1945** [see **yellow C**]. **1966** *DARE* (Qu. HH29a, . . *People of mixed blood—part Indian*) Inf **SC19**, Yellowhammer. **1983** Mebane *Mary Wayfarer* 62 **NC**, Light-skinned black women . . were . . called . . by black males . . sometimes the grossly inelegant "yellowhammers," as in "I've got me a yellowhammer." **1998** Kytle–Mackay *Who Runs GA?* 207 (as of 1947), He called us "big boys," referred to some of his clients as "yeller hammers," and in a telephone conversation told a man, "Don't be scared to get a little dew on yo' feet." **2008** in 2009 *DARE* File—Internet **TX** [Black], I'm black, aka yellow, aka, redbone, aka yellahamma, aka lightskinned, aka—and I voted two days ago.

5 =**poor White 1**. **esp ne,cIL** *derog*
2000 in 2009 *DARE* File—Internet **neIL**, As I was leaving, a meat-hog/Yellahammer was arriving and set up camp with his empty bucket and I'm sure he's snacking on those Bass by now. **2001** *DARE* File **ceIN**, A correspondent in east-central Indiana (as I recall) wrote that in his area, "yellowhammer" was applied both to a field bird deemed noisy and obnoxious, and to local "white trash." **2004** *DARE* File—Internet **neIL**, Basicly [sic] a "yella hammer" is someone who chooses to reproduce within the family. . . You know the look . . big giant forehead, eyes far apart on the sides of the head, a goofy grin with very few teeth. **2006** in 2009 *Ibid* **neIL**, Boris are you stupid or did u go to minooka high school with all the yellowhammers. **2009** *Ibid* **cIL**, While growing up in the Midwest (central Illinois) I heard adults use the words "yellow hammer" to describe an unlikeable person, but I was (and still am) ignorant of the origin or exact meaning. I remember it was used in a context both economic—yellow hammers were poverty stricken—and implying social status—yellow hammers were "white trash" in the social pecking order—but it also could be used as a substitute for "idiot" or, in the Midwest flavor, a "dumb shit."

6 A scrawny or otherwise undesirable cow or calf.
1922 Davenport *Amer. Live Stock* 171, *Yellowhammer, dogey*. **1935** *AmSp* 10.272 [Stockyard language], *Yellowhammer*. Same as *dogey*. **1941** Williams *Beef Cattle* 428 **Sth**, *Yellowhammer*—On the market refers to cattle of common or dairy breeding. **1942** Kennedy *Palmetto Country* 224 **FL**, Also in cracker cow-jargon, a bow-wow is a runty steer; a dogey or yellow-hammer is a small steer suitable for canning. **1953** Randolph–Wilson *Down in Holler* 301 **Ozarks**, *Yellow-*

hammer. . . means, in some sections of the Ozarks, a scrub Jersey calf. **1984** Smith *Land Remembered* 127 **FL**, Some men run them yellowhammers down here hell bent for leather, like they was rabbits instead of cows, and time they get here they're not much more than skin and bones.

yellowhandle, yellowhands, yellowhanger See **yellowhammer 1**

yellow hawthorn n   Also *yellow haw, yellowleaf hawthorn*
A **hawthorn** (here: usu *Crataegus flava*, but also *C. lacrimata*).
1868 (1870) Gray *Field Botany* 128, *C[rataegus] flava*, Yellow or Summer Haw. **1884** Sargent *Forests of N. Amer.* 83, *Crataegus flava*. . . Summer Haw. Yellow Haw. Virginia southward, generally near the coast, to Tampa Bay, Florida, west through the Gulf states to eastern Texas and southern Arkansas. **1899** Edwards *Defense* 214 **GA**, I seed dem split sweet 'taters roun' dat possum lak er yaller-hawberry chain roun' er nigger gal's neck. **1979** Little *Checklist U.S. Trees* 112, *Crataegus flava* . . yellow hawthorn. *Ibid* 113, *Crataegus lacrimata*. . . yellow hawthorn. **2008** (acc) U.S. Dept. Ag. *Plants Database* (Internet), *Crataegus flava* . . yellowleaf hawthorn.

yellowhead n
1 See **yellow-headed blackbird**.
2 See **yellow-headed chipmunk**.

yellow-headed blackbird n   Also *yellowhead*
Std: a large western blackbird (*Xanthocephalus xanthocephalus*).   Also called **copperhead** n[1] **3, Indian blackbird, yellow-breasted ~, yellow-wing(ed) ~**

yellow-headed chipmunk n   Also *yellowhead, yellow-headed ground squirrel*
A **ground squirrel b** (here: *Spermophilus lateralis*).
1902 Smithsonian Inst. *Annual Rept. for 1901* 111, Animals in National Zoological Park June 30, 1901, . . Yellow-headed ground squirrel (*Spermophilus brevicaudus* [=*S. lateralis*]). **1908** Grinnell in CA Univ. *Univ. CA Pub. Zoology* 5.15, But one species of mammal was noted, the yellow-headed chipmunk (*Callospermophilus bernardinus* [=*Spermophilus lateralis*]), one of which was seen on the summit [of San Gorgonio]. **1918** Grinnell in CA State Comm. Horticult. *Mth. Bulletin* 7.677, Of all our ground squirrels the Golden-mantled is the most brilliantly colored. This rather bookish name for the animal is a translation of the scientific name of the species, *chrysodeirus* [=*lateralis*]; the more commonplace appellations locally employed, "Copperhead" or "Yellow-headed Chipmunk," serve just as well. *Ibid* 685, Around Bear Lake the Yellowheads were common through the woods. **1919** Sierra Club *Bulletin* 10.409 **ceCA**, One other animal of this part of the Sierras is deserving of mention . . , the Sierra Golden-mantled Ground-squirrel (*Callospermophilus chrysodeirus*). . . Besides this rather pretentious "book name," he is variously known as Yellowhead, Copperhead, or Bummer. . . The yellowhead is rather a prosaic creature, prone to corpulence.

yellowheart n
A **prickly ash 1** (here: *Zanthoxylum flavum*).
1942 Amer. Joint Comm. Horticult. Nomenclature *Std. Plant Names* 666, *Zanthoxylum*. . . *flavum*. . . Yellowheart P[ricklyash]. **1946** West–Arnold *Native Trees FL* 100, The yellowheart, *Z. flavum* . . , occurring sporadically in hammocks of Dade and Monroe counties, has leaves normally bearing 5 leaflets. **1962** Harrar–Harrar *Guide S. Trees* 394, Yellowheart—Satinwood—*Zanthoxylum flavum*. . . This species produces a hard, rich, golden-yellow, highly figured wood. **1979** Little *Checklist U.S. Trees* 299, *Zanthoxylum flavum*. . . Other common names—satinwood, yellowwood, yellowheart.

yellow heather n   Also *yellow mountain heather*   Cf **heather 1a**
A **mountain heather 2** (here: *Phyllodoce glanduliflora*).
1910 Williams *Mt. That Was God* 97 **WA**, The yellow heather. . . often forms beautiful areas where other vegetation is rare. **1915** (1926) Armstrong–Thornber *Western Wild Flowers* 352, Yellow Heather—*Phyllodoce glanduliflora*. . . This makes heather-like patches on rocks and has many rough, woody stems, crowded with yellowish-green leaves. **1938** (1958) Sharples *AK Wild Flowers* 101, *P[hyllodoce] glanduliflora*. . . Yellow Heather. **1974** Welsh *Anderson's Flora AK* 233, *Yellow mountain-heather*. . . Alpine tundra and heathland in the coast ranges.

yellow henbane n

A **ground-cherry.**

1822 Eaton *Botany* 390, *Physalis . . viscosa* (yellow henbane). [*DARE* Ed: Eaton records this species as growing in MA, NY, and PA; it is clearly not the species now called *viscosa*.] **1847** Wood *Class-Book* 447, *Physalis. . . viscosa. . .* Yellow Henbane. Ground Cherry. **1900** Lyons *Plant Names* 286, *P[hysalis] viscosa. . .* Yellow Henbane.

yellow Indian paint See **Indian paint 2**

yellow jack n

1 Either of two similar carangid fishes: usu a **crevalle a** (here: *Carangoides bartholomaei*), but also the **hardtail 1.**

1884 Henshall *Camping in FL* 78, There are several species (*Caranx hippos, Caranx pisquetus,* etc.), called, in the vernacular of Florida, jack, yellow jack, amber jack, crevalle, cavalli, etc. **1896** U.S. Natl. Museum *Bulletin* 47.919, *Caranx bartholomaei. . .* Yellow Jack. . . In life, bluish silvery, everywhere strongly washed with golden, the young with golden spots. Fins all pale yellow. **1912** U.S. Natl. Museum *Proc.* 42.188, About 23 specimens, parasitic on yellow-jack (*Caranx crysos*). **1946** La Monte *N. Amer. Game Fishes* 34, Blue Runner. . . Names: Hardtailed Jack, Jack, Yellowjack [etc]. **1991** Amer. Fisheries Soc. *Common Names Fishes* 51, *Caranx bartholomaei. . .* yellow jack. **2010** *DARE* File—Internet **FL,** Blue runner, hard tail jack, yellow jack, yellow mackerel and runner are all Caranx crysos. Whatever name you attach, they're great bait for larger fish.

2 See quot. Cf **jack** n[1] **12,** *DS* H14

1975 Gould *ME Lingo* 14, Johnnycake, always made in Maine from yellow meal, was *yellowjack.*

yellow jacket n

1 Std: a wasp of the family Vespidae that is marked with yellow. For other names see **bog hornet, chain of lightning, guinea wasp, jack** n[1] **27, mud wasp, paper ~, potter ~, sand hornet, striped wasp, yellow-tailed hornet** Cf **bald-faced hornet, black jacket, blue ~ 2, hot pants, jacket** n **4, yellowhammer 3**

2 =**leatherjacket 2.**

1884 U.S. Natl. Museum *Bulletin* 27.440, *Oligloplites occidentalis. . .* Yellow Jacket, Yellow Tail. . . Gulf of Mexico; Atlantic coast of the United States north to Cape Cod.

3 See quot. Cf **cut jackets**

1940 Kennedy–Harlow *Schoolmaster* 212 **IN** (as of c1860), Bernie . . picked up one of them [=a cornstalk] and said to me, "Le's play Yellow Jacket." . . "All right," said I, picking up another stalk. We seized each other's left hands and fell to [hitting one another].

yellow jasmine n Also *yellow jessamin(e)*

=**Carolina jasmine.**

1709 (1967) Lawson *New Voyage* 96 **NC, SC,** The yellow Jessamin is wild in our Woods, of a pleasant Smell. **1785** Marshall *Arbustrum* 22, *Bignonia sempervirens.* Ever-green Bignonia, or Yellow Jasmine. **1853** *NY Daily Times* (NY) 16 Apr 2/5, Every now and then you catch the breath of some fragrant flowering shrub, and looking about see the yellow jasmine climbing over a tall tree, and scattering its bright blossoms like stars on the ground. **1898** U.S. Dept. Ag. Div. Botany *Bulletin* 20.48, False Jessamine. . . Other Names: Yellow jessamine; yellow jessamine of the South. **1942** (1960) Robertson *Red Hills* 178 **SC,** She watched the white drift of the plum trees, the dogwood and the yellow jessamine. **1965–70** *DARE* (Qu. S3, *A flower like a large violet with a yellow center and small ragged leaves—it comes up early in spring on open, stony hilltops*) Inf **TX**37, Yellow jasmine; (Qu. S10, *A shrub that gets covered with bright yellow, spicy-smelling flowers early in spring;* total Infs questioned, 75) Infs **MS**6, 16, 72, Yellow jasmine; **FL**18, Yellow ['jɛzmɪn]; **GA**3, Yellow ['jɛsəməs]; (Qu. S22, . . *The bright yellow flowers that bloom in clusters in marshes in early springtime*) Inf **GA**28, Yellow ['jɛsmɪn]—grows on trees; (Qu. S26a, . . *Wildflowers. . . Roadside flowers*) Inf **FL**16, Yellow jasmine—very poisonous; **FL**27, Yellow jasmine; **SC**24, Yellow jessamine; (Qu. S26b, *Wildflowers that grow in water or wet places*) Inf **SC**27, Yellow jessamine; (Qu. S26c, *Wildflowers that grow in woods*) Infs **SC**2, 7, 11, Yellow jessamine; **SC**3, Yellow ['jæˆsɪmɪn]; **SC**10, Yellow ['jɛsɪmɪ]; **NC**18, Yellow jasmine; (Qu. S26e, *Other wildflowers not yet mentioned;* not asked in early QRs) Infs **AL**30, **FL**27, **MS**72, Yellow jasmine; **NC**81, Yellow jessamine—a vine similar to honeysuckle; **SC**40, Yellow jessamine. **1999** *Aiken Std.*

(SC) 27 Oct sec A 4/1, We're going to have an arch that has yellow jasmine growing on it. . . so that we can show all the symbols of South Carolina.

yellow jay n esp **NEast**

=**flicker** n[2] **1.**

1844 *Merry's Museum* 8.66 **Boston MA,** This is the high-hole, high-pole, flecker [sic], yellow jay, or golden-winged wood-pecker, whichever you choose to call him. **1854** *Chr. Watchman & Reflector* (Boston MA) 12 Oct 164/2, A very great number of pigeons, woodpeckers, blue and yellow jays, and other birds. **1881** Ingersoll in Nuttall Ornith. Club *Bulletin* 6.184 **WI,** Take the case of the Golden-winged Woodpecker (*Colaptes auratus*) which is variously known as follows: . . Yellow Jay. **1887** *Forest & Stream* 27.248 **NH,** *Colaptes auratus. . .* 35. Yellow Jay. **1914** Eaton *Birds NY* 2.160, In this State he is commonly spoken of as the high hole or high holder, . . yellow jay, yellow hammer or pigeon woodpecker.

yellow jessamin(e) See **yellow jasmine**

yellow kingbird n Cf **kingbird**

A **crested flycatcher** (here: *Myiarchus crinitus*).

1914 *Auk* 31.225 **cAL,** Crested Flycatcher. 'Yellow Kingbird.'—Common summer resident of wooded areas bordering fields. **1962** Imhof *AL Birds* 347, Great Crested Flycatcher. . . Other names: Crested Flycatcher, Yellow Kingbird.

yellowleaf hawthorn See **yellow hawthorn**

yellow-leg(ged) frog See **yellowlegs 2**

yellow-legged goose See **yellowlegs 3**

yellow-legged mallard See **yellowlegs 4**

yellowlegs n

1 Std: either of two yellow-legged shore birds: the greater yellowlegs (*Tringa melanoleuca*) or the lesser yellowlegs (*Tringa flavipes*). Also called **clook-clook, cucu, klook-klook, pied jaune, pill-pill, plover, mud lark 4, tattler, tell-tale 1, yellowshanks, yelper 1** For other names of *T. melanoleuca* see **English snipe 3, horse yellowleg(s), humility 1, stone curlew 1, tattletale snipe, tip-up 1, turkeyback 1;** for other names of *T. flavipes* see **gilly-gilloo bird, goonoo ~**

2 also *yellow-leg(ged) frog:* A frog such as *Rana boylei* or the **pickerel frog.**

1848 *S. Lit. Messenger* 14.531, The croaking of acres of frogs—of countless varieties, from the innocent little yellow legs, . . to the lethargic and aldermanic patriarch of the Glades,—chimed in to swell the general alarm. **1906** (1907) Dickerson *Frog Book* 221 **CA,** *Rana boylii,* which, in California, is called the Yellow-legged Frog, has perhaps the most toad-like appearance of any frog of North America. **1907** NJ State Museum *Annual Rept. for 1906* 134, Pickerel Frog. Yellow Legs. . . Yellow Leg Frog. **1928** Pope–Dickinson *Amphibians* 39 **WI,** *Pickerel Frog Rana palustris. . .* Other common names are Marsh Frog, Tiger Frog, Yellow Legs and Grass Frog. . . Underparts of legs and posterior part of body yellow. **1947** Pickwell *Amphibians* 22, *Rana boylii boylii,* the California Yellow-legged Frog. *Ibid, Rana boylii sierrae* [= *R. muscosa*], the Sierra Yellow-legged Frog. *Ibid, Rana boylii muscosa* [=*R. muscosa*], the Southern Yellow-legged Frog. **2008** (acc) U.S. Dept. Ag. *Integrated Taxonomic Info. System* (Internet), *Rana boylii. . .* Common Name(s): Foothill Yellow-legged Frog [etc].

3 also *yellow-legged goose:* =**white-fronted goose.**

1888 Trumbull *Names of Birds* 12 **CA,** In a letter from Mr. A.B. Pearson, of San Diego, Cal., this species [=white-fronted goose] is referred to as the "*yellow-legged goose* or *gray brant.*" **1900** OR Hist. Soc. *Hist. Qrly.* 1.324, Yellow legged goose—[Indian name:] Hi-hi. **1917** *Wilson Bulletin* 29.2.77 **WA,** *Anser albifrons gambelli.*—Yellowlegs, yellow-legged goose, Willapa Harbor.

4 also *yellow-legged mallard:* =**mallard 1;** see quot 1923.

1923 U.S. Dept. Ag. *Misc. Circular* 13.8 **MO,** Mallard. . . Vernacular names. . . *In local use.* . . yellow-legged mallard, yellowlegs. *Ibid,* The names frosty-beak, . . yellow-legged mallard and yellowlegs, all are applied to late migrants thought to be a race distinct from the fall flight. **1938** *Lake Park News* (IA) 8 Sept 2/6, Yellowlegs and Redlegs are Mallards to some in other parts of the world.

5 A **prairie chicken 1** (here: *Tympanuchus cupido*).

1936 *WI Rapids Daily Tribune* (WI) 26 June 5/5, The best chicken country in central Wisconsin has already been closed for two years, and we'll venture to guess that there are more yellowlegs and sharptails there now than for some time. **1982** Elman *Hunter's Field Guide* 26, Common & regional names: For pinnated grouse . . yellowlegs.

yellow lily n

1 A **dogtooth violet** (here: usu *Erythronium americanum,* but also *E. grandiflorum*).

1806 in 1905 Lewis *Orig. Jrls. Lewis & Clark Exped.* 5.165 **ID,** Neare our encampment we saw a great number of the yellow lilly with reflected petals in blume; this plant was just as forward here at this time as it was in the plains on the 10th of may. **1894** *Jrl. Amer. Folkl.* 7.102 **VT,** *Erythronium Americanum.* . . yellow lily, Ferrisburgh, Vt. **1897** *Jrl. Amer. Folkl.* 10.145 **ME,** *Erythronium Americanum* . . wild yellow lily, Norridgewock, Me.

2 A **day lily 1** (here: *Hemerocallis flava*).

[**1843** (1844) Johnson *Farmer's Encycl.* 714, The yellow day lily *(H[emerocallis] flava),* a native of Siberia, blowing yellow flowers in June.] **1915** Cornell Univ. Ag. Exper. Sta. *Bulletin* 361.419, *Hemerocallis flava* (Lemon Lily, or Yellow Lily).

yellow linn n   Also *yellow lind,* ~ *lynn*   chiefly **WV**

A **cucumber tree 1** (here: *Magnolia acuminata*).

1787 in 2009 *DARE* File—Internet **WV,** South fifty Degrees East Twenty poles to a Birch and Yellow Lynn. **1808** in 1968 Crismore *Crismore Family Hist.* 31 **WV,** Beginning at a black oak, dogwood and hickory . . to two yellow lynns East 32 poles to two white oaks [etc]. **1837** West Virginia Iron Mining & Mfg. Co. *Prospectus* 20 **WV,** The white, red, spanish and rock oak, the chesnut of extraordinary magnitude, . . yellow linn, and yellow locust, both of which are considered very valuable. **1856** in 1940 *AmSp* 15.155 **VA,** To a sourwood, yellow lynn and spruce pine on a bench of Pan branch. **1878** *Wheeling Daily Reg.* (WV) 6 May 1/2, Among the soft woods are the Linn (or basswood), yellow linn (or cucumber tree). **1886** MO State Horticult. Soc. *Report for 1885* 96, *Major Ragan* . . wish [sic] to add to the list of desirable trees the Yellow Linn. **1893** *Jrl. Amer. Folkl.* 6.136 **WV,** *Magnolia acuminata,* yellow linn. **1910** in 2009 (acc) Lexis–Nexis Legal Research *State Case Law: WV* (Internet), Burdett Bros. & Johnson . . sold and agreed to deliver . . the poplar, red and white oak, basswood, ash and yellow linn. **1933** Small *Manual SE Flora* 534, T[ulipastrum] acuminatum [=Magnolia a.] . . Black-linn. Yellow-linn. **1968** *DARE* (Qu. T13, . . *Names . . for these trees:* . . *linden*) Inf **VA**27, Lind—yellow lind.

yellow locust n

1 A **black locust** (here: *Robinia pseudoacacia*).

1810 Michaux *Histoire des Arbres* 1.39, Robinia pseudo-acacia. . . *Yellow locust . . , Red locust* [etc]. . . Noms donnés à cet arbre sur les bords de la rivière Susquehannah, eu égard à la couleur de son bois. [=Names given to this tree on the banks of the Susquehannah River in reference to the color of its wood.] **1826** *New Engl. Farmer* (Fessenden) 5.177 **RI,** Of this valuable tree [=*Robinia pseudacacia*] I believe there are two kinds, or species, growing pretty generally throughout New England . . , viz. the yellow and the white locust. The latter is very inferior in value to the former. **1829** *Hagerstown Mail* (MD) 20 Feb [3]/4 (newspaperarchive.com), [Advt:] Yellow Locust and Heart Pine Timber, for the construction of Lock Gates. **1853** Meehan *Amer. Hdbk. Ornamental Trees* 211, *R. pseud-acacia.* . . Yellow locust. . . This varies from one of the handsomest of ornamental trees to one of the ugliest. **1863** *New Engl. Farmer* 15.92 **wMA,** Many years ago, I transplanted two small trees of the yellow locust. At that time, it was thought almost impossible to raise them, on account of the depredations of a borer. **1897** Sudworth *Arborescent Flora* 258, *Robinia pseudoacacia.* . . Yellow Locust (Vt., Mass., N.Y., Pa., Del., Va., W. Va., Miss., La., Ill., Ind., Kans., Nebr., Minn.) **1911** [see **3** below]. **1950** Stuart *Hie Hunters* 254 **eKY,** Ye know how hard it is to grub a yaller locust from the ground. **1950** *Frederick Post* (MD) 11 Mar 5/7, [Advt:] For Sale—100 yellow locust posts. **1965–70** *DARE* (Qu. T16, . . *Kinds of trees . . 'special'*) Infs **GA**80, **IL**96, **VA**15, **WV**7, 8, Yellow locust. **1991** *Constitution–Tribune* (Chillicothe MO) 25 Feb 3/2, Pegs that were used are best from dry wood, mainly yellow locust that hardens almost like steel.

2 =**yellowwood 3.**

1824 Rafinesque in *Cincinnati Lit. Gaz.* 1.60, *On a new tree of Kentucky forming a new genus* Cladrastis Fragrans [=C. kentukea]. . . It bears no peculiar vulgar name, being known by few individuals; the name of yellow locust might be given to it, if it was not already applied

to the *virgilia lutea* [=*C. kentukea*]. **1846** Browne *Trees* 192, *The Virgilia, or Yellow-Wood.* Synonymes. . . Yellow Locust, Kentucky, Tennessee, and Alabama. **1897** Sudworth *Arborescent Flora* 257 **KY, TN,** *Cladrastis lutea.* . . Common Names. . . Yellow Locust [etc].

3 =**honey locust 1.**

1911 PA Dept. Ag. *Bulletin* 210.48, A Member: What would be the general reasons for planting the honey locust in preference to the yellow? *Mr. Rupp:* The honey locust is a yellow locust. You mean in preference to the black locust? . . A Member: I understand honey locust in our county is different. We call it yellow locust the good substantially, durable locust. And there is the white locust. *Mr. Rupp:* The white or yellow we don't make any distinction. We call it the yellow or honey locust, and the other the black locust. . . A Member: There are three, the honey, the yellow and the black. **1974** (1977) Coon *Useful Plants* 167, *Gleditsia triacanthos*—Honey or sweet locust, black or thorn locust, yellow locust.

yellow loosestrife n

A **loosestrife 1;** see quots.

1903 Porter *Flora PA* 243, *Lysimachia vulgaris.* . . Golden or Yellow Loosestrife. **1936** IL Nat. Hist. Surv. *Wildflowers* 231, The Yellow or Trailing Loosestrife, *Steironema radicans* [=*Lysimachia r.*] . . is a rare and unusual species found only in the southern part of Illinois. **1961** Smith *MI Wildflowers* 287, Swamp-candles, Yellow or Swamp Loosestrife—*Lysimachia terrestris.* **2008** (acc) U.S. Dept. Ag. *Plants Database* (Internet), *Lysimachia* [spp]. . . yellow loosestrife.

yellow lynn   See **yellow linn**

yellow mackerel n

A **crevalle a:** usu **hardtail 1,** but also *Caranx hippos*.

1814 in 1815 Lit. & Philos. Soc. NY *Trans.* 1.424, *Yellow Mackerel. (Scomber crysos)* [=*Caranx c.*] . . A marine fish, taken in the bay of New-York. **1842** DeKay *Zool.* NY 4.122, It [=*Caranx crysos*] is called *Yellow Mackerel.* **1857** NJ Geol. Surv. *Geol. Cape May* 147, *Caranx crysos.* . . The Yellow Caranx, Yellow Mackerel. **1882** U.S. Fish Comm. *Bulletin for 1881* 32 **NJ, NY,** The Jurel *(Paratractus pisquetus* [=*Caranx crysos*]). This fish, known . . about New York and on the coast of New Jersey as the "Yellow Mackerel," is found in the Western Atlantic from Brazil, Cuba and Hayti, to Halifax. **1946** La Monte *N. Amer. Game Fishes* 36, Common Jack Crevalle—*Caranx hippos.* . . Names: Crevalle, . . Yellow Caranx, Yellow Mackerel. **1973** Knight *Cook's Fish Guide* 384, Mackerel . . yellow see Runner, Blue.

yellow mandarin   See **mandarin**

yellow maple n

A **red maple** (here: *Acer rubrum*).

1835 Williams *Comprehensive Mod. Geog.* 164 **MS,** The Soil in its natural state is covered with vast quantities of *oak, hickory,* . . *yellow maple* [etc]. **1860** Curtis *Cat. Plants NC* 51, This tree [=the red maple] in some situations has yellowish flowers and fruit, and is then called *Yellow Maple.* **1869** Ward *Men Women & Ghosts* 276 **MA,** The leaves of the yellow maple drifted by on the fresh, strong wind. **1965–70** *DARE* (Qu. T14, . . *Kinds of maples*) 30 Infs, **scattered,** Yellow maple; (Qu. T3, *The tree that produces syrup and sugar*) Inf **NY**213, Yellow maple.

yellow marigold n

A **marsh marigold** (here: *Caltha palustris*).

1968 *DARE* (Qu. S22, . . *The bright yellow flowers that bloom in clusters in marshes in early springtime*) Inf **PA**126, Yellow marigold.

yellow mats n

A **sanicle 1** (here: *Sanicula arctopoides*).

1897 Eastwood *Flora Pacific Coast* 91, *S[anicula] arctopoides* . . , Yellow Mats, Footsteps of Spring. . . This is very conspicuous in early spring, dotting the ground with its small mat of yellowish green flowers. . . Throughout California. **1961** Thomas *Flora Santa Cruz* 256 **cwCA,** Yellow Mats, Footsteps-of-Spring, Snake Root [etc]. **2003** Beidleman–Kozloff *Plants San Francisco Bay* 93 **cwCA,** *Sanicula arctopoides.* . . Footsteps-of-spring, Yellow-mats.

yellow Mayweed n

A **fetid marigold 1** (here: *Dyssodia papposa*).

1892 NE State Hist. Soc. *Trans. & Rept.* 4.285, These comparatively ancient roads are . . marked by clumps of huge wild sunflowers, endless patches of yellow Mayweed [etc]. **1914** Georgia *Manual Weeds* 485, Fetid Marigold. . . *Other English names:* Yellow Mayweed, False

Mayweed [etc]. . . A vile weed, which is gaining ground in the Eastern States.

yellow milkweed n
=**butterfly weed 1.**

1892 *Jrl. Amer. Folkl.* 5.101 **wMA,** *Asclepias tuberosa,* white root; yellow milk-weed. **1930** Sievers *Amer. Med. Plants* 18, Butterfly-weed. . . Other common names.—Pleurisy-root, . . yellow or orange milkweed. **2004** *DARE* File—Internet **FL,** [Advt:] *Yellow Milkweed*—One of the favorite milkweeds of Monarch and Queen Butterflies.

yellow milkwort n
Any of var yellow- or orange-flowered **milkworts,** but esp **orange milkwort.**

1818 Eaton *Botany* 369, *Polygala. . . lutea* (yellow milkwort.) **1853** NY State Museum *Catalogue Cabinet Nat. Hist.* 54, *Polygala lutea,* Yellow Milkwort. **1928** *Jrl. NY Bot. Garden* 29.199 **FL,** Here and there the yellow-milkwort *(Polygala Rugelii)* . . were so abundant that from a low angle the eye saw only a solid sheet of yellow and pink. **1941** Walker *Lookout* 50 **TN,** On the land adjoining the banks of waterfalls are beds of yellow milkwort in bloom in May and June. **1962** *Charleston Gaz.* (WV) 13 Jan 12/5 **FL,** Blue lobelia and yellow milkwort are in bloom on the grounds of the National Audubon Society's sanctuary. **1973** (1994) Dean et al. *Wildflowers AL* 92, Yellow Milkwort—*Polygala cymosa. . .* Yellow milkwort is a biennial. *Ibid* 94, Yellow Milkwort, Yellow Bachelor's-Button—*Polygala lutea. . .* Yellow milkwort is also a biennial. **2000** Rhoads–Block *Plants PA* 22, *Polygala lutea . .* —Yellow milkwort.

yellow mockingbird n
=**yellow-breasted chat.**

1874 Ridgway in NY Acad. Sci. *Annals Lyceum Nat. Hist.* 10.369 **IL,** *I[cteria] virens. . .* "Yellow Mocking Bird." **1889** Ridgway *Ornith. IL* 1.172, Probably none of our birds except the Mockingbird itself possess a greater variety of notes than this loquacious species [=*Icteria virens*], on which account it is not unfrequently known as the "Yellow Mockingbird." **1949** Hornsby *Lonesome Valley* 115 **eKY,** A yellow mockingbird was singing in a tree at the back side of the pasture. **1999** *Aiken Std.* (SC) 8 Aug sec C 2/2, The [yellow] chat. . . purrs like a cat, barks like a dog, caws like a crow, rattles like a kingfisher, whines like an owl, screams like a jay, then quacks like a duck. No wonder his meaningless chattering has earned him the nickname of yellow mockingbird.

yellow mountain heather　See **yellow heather**

yellow mountain saxifrage n
A **saxifrage** n² (here: *Saxifraga aizoides*).

1838 Goodrich *Peter Parley's Cyclop. Botany* 270, *S[axifraga] aizoides,* Yellow Mountain Saxifrage. **1843** Torrey *Flora NY* 2.516, *Saxifraga aizoides. . .* Yellow Mountain Saxifrage. . . Wet rocks, Annsville, Oneida county, on the east branch of Fish creek. . . This interesting little plant has been nowhere found in the United States except in the locality here given. **1919** (1923) House *Wild Flowers NY* 1.125, Yellow Mountain Saxifrage. . . On wet or dripping rocks. **1949** Moldenke *Amer. Wild Flowers* 54, We have . . very small alpine and arctic saxifrages like . . the yellow mountain saxifrage, *Leptaesea aizoides,* often only 2 inches tall. **2003** *Post–Std.* (Syracuse NY) 9 May sec B 1/3, Two species of rare plants—bird's-eye primrose and yellow mountain saxifrage—are considered threatened under state law.

yellow myrtle n
=**moneywort 1.**

1851 Irving *Alhambra* 21 **NY,** The Guadaira winds its stream round the hill . . overhung with rhododendron, eglantine, yellow myrtle and a profusion of wild flowers. **1870** *NY Evangelist* (NY) 8 Dec 7/1, Yellow myrtle . . may be made to droop over the front of your box. **1910** *Indianapolis Star* (IN) 16 May 7/5, A rookery with yellow myrtle creeping over it. **1940** Spencer *Just Weeds* 176, The plant gets its name, moneywort or money plant, because of its coin-shaped leaves, but it has many other names. Some of them are . . Yellow Myrtle, and Creeping Charlie.

yellow ned n　**C Atl**
=**yellow perch 1.**

1863 *Leisure Hour* 12.221 **MD,** His boys feast in anticipation over the tailor-fish, rock, perch, crabs, and terrapins . . , leaving the less-soaring fancy of the negroes to gloat over possible cat-fish and yellow-neds. **1892** *Student* 12.164 **sePA,** As for fishes, the catfish, the sunfish, the minnow, eel, roach and "yellow ned" are there by companies and by thousands. **1895** *News* (Frederick MD) 6 May 2/1, "Yellow Ned," is the picturesque name the Chesapeake fishermen give to the beautiful yellow perch so abundant in those waters. **1903** Henshall *Bass Pike Perch* 167 **MD,** We sought it [=yellow perch] on the mud-flats . . of the Patapsco River, near Baltimore. It was there known as "yellow Ned," and was considered a good pan-fish. **1904** PA Dept. Fisheries *Bulletin* 1.100, The waters are full of yellow perch, also called in Philadelphia and vicinity by the more familiar title "the yellow ned." **1951** *MD Hist. Mag.* 46.129, That yellow perch was known as yellow neds in my neighborhood of Baltimore County is confirmed by Mr. H.J. Raphel. Yellow ned was the word in regular use in Bush River, Gunpowder River, and Bird River. . . It is well known on the Eastern Shore. **1968–70** *DARE* (Qu. P1, . . *Kinds of freshwater fish . . caught around here . . good to eat*) Inf **DE**3, Ring perch or yellow neds; (Qu. P2, . . *Kinds of saltwater fish caught around here . . good to eat*) Inf **DE**4, Yellow ned—same as yellow perch or sun perch; (Qu. P3, *Freshwater fish that are not good to eat*) Inf **VA**79, Ring perch—same as yellow ned. **1981** *Capital* (Annapolis MD) 18 Nov 24/3, Marty Lieberman did catch just one whopper Citation-size yellow Ned . . on a Mr Twister lure. **2006** *MD Gaz.* (Glen Burnie) 18 Mar sec D 5 (Internet), Today, Deere can claim a tie for the fourth largest yellow ned ever taken by rod and reel anywhere.

yellownose n　Also *yellow-nosed coot*
A **scoter** (here: *Melanitta nigra*).

1907 Braislin *List Birds Long Is.* 49 **seNY,** American Scoter. . . They are locally known as the "Yellow-nosed Coot." **1925** (1928) Forbush *Birds MA* 1.271, *Oidemia americana. . .* Other names: . . *Butternose; copperbill; copper-nose; yellow-nose; yellow-bill;* [etc]. **1926** (1986) Phillips *Nat. Hist. Ducks* 4.3, Black Scoter. . . Vernacular Names. . . Butter-bill, Yellow-bill, . . Yellow-nosed Coot.

yellow oak n
1 A **black oak** (here: *Quercus velutina*). **esp NEast** Cf **yellow-bark(ed) oak**

1686 in 1917 Topsfield Hist. Soc. *Town Rec.* 1.59 **MA,** A heape of rocks nere to a black or a yealow oack at the south westerly corner [of the parsonage land]. **1796** *Repertory Arts & Manufactures* 4.74, The first is a species of oak, growing spontaneously on the Continent of North America, and particularly within the thirteen United States, in some of which, particularly in the Massachusets Bay, it is commonly called *yellow oak,* and in others, particularly in Pennsylvania, *black oak.* **a1817** (1821) Dwight *Travels* 1.39 **NEng,** The *Yellow Oak* yields a stronger yellow dye for staining cotton and linen, than any other substance, known in this country. **1832** *New Engl. Farmer & Horticult. Reg.* 10.206, Mr. A.R. accuses Mr. E. of inaccuracy, because the latter says "What is called the Yellow Oak in this vicinity, is the common Black Oak." What I call the Yellow Oak, is a species or variety, that does not appear black in any case, but has the same yellow of the Black Oak, when examined. . . As respects the supposed difference between Black Oak and Yellow Oak, we will observe that they are varieties of the same species, viz. the *Quercus tinctoria . .* of Michaux. **1838** Atwater *Hist. OH* 81, The bark of the yellow oak, is not only used in tanning leather, but it affords a beautiful yellow color, which is permanent. It is used much by clothiers for that purpose. **1848** *Boston Cultivator* (MA) 1 July [2]/3 **eMA,** One hundred dollars, to be awarded . . for the best plantation of oaks, chiefly of white and black or yellow oak. **1882** *Amer. Naturalist* 16.914 **swPA,** In some places hardly any trees of the two species to which its attack is here limited, have escaped. These are the black or yellow oak *(Q. tinctoria)* with its variety *(coccinea),* the scarlet oak and the scrub oak *(Q. ilicifolia).* **1897** Sudworth *Arborescent Flora* 169, *Quercus velutina. . .* Yellow Oak (R.I., N.Y., Ill., Tex., Kans., Minn.) **1950** Peattie *Nat. Hist. Trees* 225, Yellow, Dyer's, or Tanbark Oak. [*Ibid* 226, You may easily know this widely ranging and abundant Oak . . if you will scratch a twig with your thumbnail and see then that the inner bark is yellow or orange.] **1965–70** *DARE* (Qu. T10, . . *Kinds of oak trees*) 13 Infs, **chiefly NEast, N Cent,** Yellow oak. [*DARE* Ed: Some of these Infs may refer instead to other senses below.]

2 also *yellow chestnut oak:* =**chinquapin oak 1.**

1810 Michaux *Histoire des Arbres* 1.23 *Yellow oak,* (Chêne jaune). **1811** *Ibid* 2.62 **PA,** Aux environs de Lancaster, on donne à cet arbre [= *Quercus p[rin]us acuminata*] le nom de *Yellow oak,* Chêne jaune, à cause de la teinte jaunâtre de son bois. [=In the neighborhood of Lancaster, this tree [=*Quercus p[rin]us acuminata*] is called Yellow oak . . because of the yellowish color of its wood.] **1848** Gray *Manual of Botany* 415, *Q[uercus] Castanea . .* (Yellow Chestnut Oak.) . . These three

Chestnut Oaks [=swamp chestnut oak, rock ~, yellow ~] are very difficult to distinguish, and are most probably only varieties of one species. **1860** Curtis *Cat. Plants NC* 35, Chestnut Oak (Q. Castanea, Willd.) . . It has a yellowish tinge, and is therefore known in some localities under the name of *Yellow Oak.* **1874** *Friend* 47.269, The . . Chestnut Oak group . . is composed of the Swamp White Oak . . ; Swamp Chestnut Oak *(Q. primus);* its variety, the Rock Chestnut Oak . . ; another, well marked variety, the Yellow Chestnut Oak *(var. acuminata);* [etc]. *Ibid,* Among the Chestnut Oaks, I prefer the Yellow Oak, or as some prefer to call it, the True Chestnut Oak. **1897** Sudworth *Arborescent Flora* 168, *Quercus acuminata.* . . Chinquapin Oak. *Common names* . . Yellow Oak (Ill., Kans., Nebr., Mich.) **1908** Rogers *Tree Book* 204, The Yellow Oak *(Quercus acuminata).* . . prefers dry soil. . . The yellow-green of the foliage mass gives the tree its common name. **1937** Stemen–Myers *OK Flora* 93, *Quercus Muhlenbergii.* . . Chestnut or Yellow Oak. **1962** *Lancaster Eagle–Gaz.* (OH) 14 July 5/1, Just across the small bridge and to the east of the Coonpath there is a huge chinquapin (yellow) oak. **1994** Thomson *Birding OH* 26, *Goll Woods Nature Preserve.* . . Bur oaks, white oaks, and yellow oaks achieve sizes of five feet or more in diameter.

3 **=jack oak d.**
1899 *Bot. Gaz.* 27.208, *Quercus ellipsoidalis.* . . That it differs from the ordinary black oaks to the eye of other than botanical observers is evident from the fact that an intelligent farmer had separated it from its congeners, calling it "yellow oak." **1908** Britton *N. Amer. Trees* 291, Hill's Oak—*Quercus ellipsoidalis.* . . It is also called Yellow oak and Black oak. **1928** *Amer. Midland Naturalist* 11.52, *Quercus ellipsoidalis.* E.J. Hill. Yellow Oak. Much like *Q. velutina,* but the elliptical, turbinate fruit distinguishes it from that. **1950** Peattie *Nat. Hist. Trees* 229, Hill's, Black, or Yellow Oak. . . Perhaps the easiest way to identify it is to discover its yellow inner bark, a trait which it shares with few other Oaks.

4 **=red oak 2a.**
1908 Britton *N. Amer. Trees* 281, Red Oak—*Quercus rubra.* . . It is also called Yellow oak, Black oak, Leopard oak, and Spanish oak.

5 A **post oak 1a** (here: *Quercus similis*).
1960 Vines *Trees SW* 156, Delta Post Oak. . . Also known as Mississippi Valley Post Oak and Yellow Oak. **1979** Little *Checklist U.S. Trees* 242, *Quercus stellata* var. *paludosa.* . . Bottom-land post oak, Mississippi Valley oak, yellow oak.

yellow oxeye daisy n   Cf oxeye daisy 2
A **black-eyed Susan 2** (here: *Rudbeckia hirta*).
1936 IL Nat. Hist. Surv. *Wildflowers* 364, The Black-eyed Susan is exceedingly common. . . Other names are Brown-eyed Susan, English Bull's Eye, Niggerhead and Yellow Oxeye Daisy. **2008** DARE File—Internet **csOH,** In August and September the entire area is covered with goldenrod, yellow oxeye daisies and Jerusalem artichokes.

yellow paint(root)   See Indian paint 2

yellow parilla   See yellow sarsaparilla

yellow patch n   sAppalachians
=woolly head 2.
1913 Kephart *Highlanders* 301 **sAppalachians,** A "hell" or "slick" or "wooly-head" or "yaller patch" is a thicket of laurel or rhododendron, impassable save where the bears have bored out the trails. **1915** *Natl. Sportsman* Oct 462 **eTN,** Lying grounds . . are, in this country, always on the north or Tennessee side of the mountains, where are those laurel growths known variously as "woolly heads," "slicks," "roughs" and "yellow patches." **1939** *Hall Coll.* **wNC, eTN,** *Yellow patch.* . . Where its [sic] been growed up, where it's so thick you can't get through it; underbrush.

yellow pea n
=false lupine 1.
1901 U.S. Dept. Ag. Div. Botany *Bulletin* 26.127 **MT,** The yellow pea (as it is commonly known in Montana) or prairie false lupine *(Thermopsis rhombifolia* . . *)* occurs along the Yellowstone Valley [etc]. **1932** Rydberg *Flora Prairies* 454, *Thermopsis* [spp]. . . Yellow Pea, Golden Pea, Prairie Bean. **1967** DARE FW Addit **CO,** Yellow pea— golden banner. **2006** DARE File—Internet **CO,** [Caption:] Yellow Pea *(Thermopsis divaricarpa).*

yellow perch n
1 Std: a **perch** n[1] **B1** (here: *Perca flavescens*). Also called

convict, green perch 4, jack ~, lake ~, raccoon ~, redfin 3, red perch 1, ringed ~, striped ~ 1, yellow ned
2 also *yellow pondperch:* Any of several closely related fish: the **largemouth bass, smallmouth** ~ or **spotted** ~ **1.**
1820 Rafinesque *Ohio R. Fishes* 31, Streaked-cheeks River-bass. *Lepomis trifasciata* [=*Micropterus dolomeiu*]. . . vulgar names Yellow bass, Gold bass, Yellow perch [etc]. **1877** Hallock *Sportsman's Gaz.* 276, Locally they [=black bass] are . . severally known as yellow perch, . . speckled hen, etc. **1887** Goode *Amer. Fishes* 56, "Yellow Perch," "Black Perch" and "Spotted Perch" are other names applied to one or both species [=largemouth and smallmouth bass]. **1933** LA Dept. of Conserv. *Fishes* 313, None of our other fresh water fishes has been given so many popular names as our Black Bass [including] . . Yellow Pondperch. **1935** Caine *Game Fish* 10, Spotted Small-mouthed Black Bass [=*Micropterus punctulatus*]. . . Synonyms: . . Yellow Perch [etc]. **1938** Schrenkeisen *Field Book Fishes* 240, Small-mouth Black Bass. . . Common names. . . Yellow Bass; . . Yellow Perch [etc].

3 **=white perch 1.**
1903 NY State Museum & Sci. Serv. *Bulletin* 60.529, In Great Egg Harbor bay individuals taken from salt water are sometimes called yellow perch or peerch. **1906** NJ State Museum *Annual Rept. for 1905* 307, The White Perch. *Morone americana.* . . Yellow Perch.

4 A **sunfish** n **1a;** see quots.
1904 U.S. Bur. Fisheries *Rept. for 1902* 362, Yellow perch—Me.; Ga.— . . *Lepomis auritus. D[itt]o—Me.—* . . *Eupomotis* [=*Lepomis*] *gibbosus.* **2008** DARE File—Internet **FL,** Bluegill—*Lepomis macrochirus*—Other local jargon names for the bluegill include common yellow perch [etc].

yellow pike n   Also *yellow (pike perch)*   **chiefly Gt Lakes, esp wNY**
A **walleye** (here: *Sander vitreus*).
1835 *Genesee Farmer* 5.316 **wNY,** At a little distance, the yellow pike, a foot or eighteen inches in length, would slightly elevate his head from his watching place, and with a slight undulation of his tail, throw himself at the devoted perch, and swallow it in an instant. **1842** DeKay *Zool. NY* 4.15, The Yellow Pike-Perch. *Lucioperca americana. Ibid* 17, This is the *Common Pike, Pickerel, Pickering, Glass-eye* and *Yellow Pike* of the Great Lakes, and most of the streams and inland lakes in the western parts of the state. . . It is a true Perch. . . I have therefore applied to it a name which indicates its true position, and is a translation of its classical appellation. **1856** *Horicon Argus* (WI) 24 Sept [2]/5 (newspaperarchive.com), He [=the Muskalonge] is just as different a fish from the Pickerel, as the Pickerel is from the yellow Pike. **1867** De Voe *Market Asst.* 208 **NEast,** *Yellow pike perch, glass-eyed pike, big-eyed pike, pike of the lakes,* or *Ohio Salmon.*—This fine and truly American fish is sometimes known as "wall-eyed pike." **1891** Welch *Recoll. Buffalo* 322 **wNY** (as of c1840), It was customary for our Amateur Piscators to seek for black bass and yellow pike "outside," in front of the light house pier, anchored in boats. **1937** *Oshkosh Northwestern* (WI) 14 May 6/2, While there are many yellow pike that run 15 or more inches in length, . . not many of the "sand pike," . . will average much over a foot in length. **1941** *Dunkirk Eve. Observer* (NY) 2 May 14/3, The 12-inchlong limit has been wiped away . . and yellow pike of any length may be taken legally. . . Reid added that he believed the 12-inch-limit law was removed principally because many fishermen confused blues and yellows. **1968–69** DARE (Qu. P1, . . *Kinds of freshwater fish . . caught around here . . good to eat*) Infs **NY**117, 132, 227, **PA**128, Yellow pike; (Qu. P14, . . *Commercial fishing . . what do the fishermen go out after?*) Infs **NY**183, 227, Yellow pike. **1977** *Eve. Observer* (Dunkirk NY) 14 Nov 5/3, The late season for Lake Erie's yellow pike apparently is at hand. . . "So if Russell hit the yellows, they must be around and they're all going after them," stated one sales outlet spokesman. **1997** *Intelligencer* (Doylestown PA) 21 July 2/2, Until now, scientists have had no way to positively determine whether a blue-colored pike is a true blue pike or simply a blue-pigmented yellow pike. **2007** in 2009 DARE File—Internet **cwNY,** Anyone fish Lake Erie? Gonna try for Yellow pike this year, for the first time.

yellow pimpernel n
Std: a perennial plant *(Taenidia integerrima)* native chiefly to the eastern half of the US. Also called **golden alexanders 2**

yellow pine n   Note: *Yellow pine* as a general term for **pines** with yellowish, resinous wood or for the wood of these species is std; only appar more specific applications of the term are

treated here. However, it should be noted that the report that a certain species "is called yellow pine" does not preclude the possibility that the same people apply the term more broadly.

1 =**longleaf pine 1.**

1775 (1962) Romans *Nat. Hist. FL* 16, This land consists . . in many places of a red or yellow gravel . . the principal produce from whence it derives its name [=pine barren] is the *pinus foliis longissimis ex una theca ternis,* or yellow pine. **1810** Michaux *Histoire des Arbres* 1.64, *The Long Leaved Pine.* . . Cet arbre précieux reçoit différentes dénominations, tant dans les pays où il croît, que dans ceux où il est exporté. Il est connu dans les premiers sous les noms de *Long leaved pine,* . . de *Yellow pine,* . . de *Pitch pine,* . . et de *Broom pine.* . . [L]es noms de *Yellow pine,* . . et de *Pitch pine,* . . qui lui sont peut-être plus universellement donnés, servent dans les Etats du milieu à désigner deux autres espèces très-distinctes. [=*Long-leaved Pine.* . . This valuable tree has various names, both in the area where it grows and in those to which it is exported. In the former it is called *Long-leaved pine,* . . *Yellow pine,* . . *Pitch pine,* . . and *Broom pine.* . . The names Yellow pine, . . and Pitch pine, . . which are perhaps more generally applied to it [than *Long-leaved pine*], are applied in the middle states to two other very different species.] **1832** Browne *Sylva* 231, In the vicinity of the sea, where only a thin layer of mould reposes upon the sand, it [=the long-leaved pine] is more resinous than where the mould is five or six inches thick; the stocks that grow upon the first-mentioned soil are called *Pitch Pine,* and the others *Yellow Pine,* as if they were distinct species. **1850** [see **4** below]. **1869** *Scientific Amer.* new ser 21.122, The yellow, or long-leaved pine of Virginia and North Carolina is extensively used by Atlantic ship builders. **1891** *Bismarck Daily Tribune* (ND) 6 June 2/4, The yellow pine referred to is the long leaf pine—the Pinus australis of botanists growing so abundantly in east Texas. **1896** Mohr–Roth *Timber Pines* 29, The Longleaf Pine. . . Local or Common Names. . . Yellow Pine (Del., N.C., S.C., Ala., Fla., La., Tex.)

2 =**shortleaf pine 1.**

1810 Michaux *Histoire des Arbres* 1.52, *Pinus mitis. The Yellow Pine.* . . [D]ans les Etats du milieu, où il fort est abondant et très-employé, il est connu sous le nom de *Yellow pine* . . *;* dans les Carolines et la Géorgie, sous celui de *Spruce pine* . . *;* mais plus communément sous celui de *Short leaved pine.* [=*Pinus mitis. The Yellow Pine.* . . In the middle states, where it is very abundant and much used, it is called *Yellow pine* . . *;* in the Carolinas and Georgia, *Spruce pine* . . *;* but most commonly *Short leaved pine.*] **1892** *Amer. Farmer* 1.48, The Yellow pine, *Pinus milis* [sic] is found in Maryland and over the South in general. **1973** Wharton–Barbour *Trees KY* 495, *Pinus echinata.* . . In Kentucky this species is usually called yellow pine, while in states to the south, where the longleaf pine grows, it is called shortleaf pine. **2008** (acc) Forest Products Lab. Center for Wood Anatomy Research *Tech. Transf. Fact Sheet* (Internet), *Pinus echinata.* . . Other Common Names. . . North Carolina yellow pine, . . shortleaf yellow pine, . . yellow pine.

3 =**Norway pine.**

1820 Eaton *Bot. Exercises* 124, *Pinus.* . . *resinosa* (yellow pine, norway pine, red pine.) **1825** *MA Ag. Jrl.* 8.338, We return to the subject of this article, the Red or Yellow pine. **1832** MA Hist. Soc. *Coll.* 2d ser 9.153 **cwVT,** [Pinus] resinosa, Yellow pine. **1842** Thompson *Hist. VT* 1.215, The Norway Pine. . . is often called *Red Pine* and sometimes *Yellow Pine* from the color of its bark. **1850** [see **4** below].

4 =**pitch pine a(1).**

1841 Baldwin *Hist. Yale College* 290, Pinus rigida. Linn. *Yellow-Pine.* **1843** Trego *Geog. PA* 67, The Pitch Pine *(Pinus rigida)* and Scrub Pine *(P. inops)* are. . . not usually distinguished from each other, being both called by the names of pitch pine or yellow pine. **1850** Emerson *Rept. Trees & Shrubs* 69 **MA,** The pitch pine is of far more value than it has usually been considered. The variety called yellow pine is an excellent substitute for white pine. [Footnote to *yellow pine:*] This name is also applied to the Southern yellow pine, *Pinus australis* [=*P. palustris*], and sometimes to the Norway or red pine, *Pinus resinosa.*

5 =**ponderosa pine 1.**

1882 *Amer. Naturalist* 16.353 **CA,** During a recent visit to Napa county, I noticed . . *Pinus ponderosa,* the yellow pine of the woodsmen, the bark of which was full of acorn holes. **1886** *Titusville Morning Herald* (PA) 7 May [2]/3 (newspaperarchive.com), The fir, the great Sequoia, the Ponderosa or yellow pine . . are all typified by this versatile tree [=the redwood]. **1932** *Van Wert Daily Bulletin* (OH) 24 Feb 3/4, "Pinus ponderosa" has been substituted as the simplest name for the tree known as Western yellow pine, yellow, red, or white pine, bull, big and

heavy pine, Oregon pine, Arizona soft pine, Mexican pine [etc]. **1958** McCulloch *Woods Words* 218 **Pacific NW,** *Yellow pine*—Ponderosa pine. **2007** Alexander et al. *Serpentine Geoecology* 342 **nCA,** The yellow pine is ponderosa *(Pinus ponderosa)* rather than Jeffrey pine around Castle Crags, because the ultramafic rocks there have more calcium.

6 =**loblolly pine 1.**

1896 Mohr–Roth *Timber Pines* 106 **nAL, NC,** *Pinus taeda.* . . Yellow Pine. **1950** Moore *Trees AR* 17, Loblolly Pine. . . Local names: Old Field, Yellow, Southern Yellow [etc].

7 =**Jeffrey pine.**

[**1864** *Statesman's Yr.-Book* 569, Western yellow (ponderosa and Jeffrey) pine, 8%.] **1947** Peattie *Sierra Nevada* 152 **eCA,** The yellow pine, chiefly of the Jeffrey persuasion, is a major component. [**2007** see **5** above.]

8 The Arizona **pine** *(Pinus arizonica).*

1878 U.S. Army Corps Engineers *Rept. U.S. Geogr. Survey* 6.260, *Pinus Arizonica.* . . [is found] on the Santa Rita Mountains, in Southern Arizona. . . 'There called yellow pine.' **1916** Soc. Amer. Foresters *Proc.* 11.456, The predominant species is yellow pine *(Pinus arizonica).* **1979** Little *Checklist U.S. Trees* 196, *Pinus ponderosa* var. *arizonica.* . . yellow pine, Arizona yellow pine.

9 =**slash pine b.**

1931 *Capital Times* (Madison WI) 9 May [4]/8 (newspaperarchive.com), The first sample of paper made from the pulp of young slash pine or yellow pine of the South was displayed in New York Wednesday. **2008** (acc) Forest Products Lab. Center for Wood Anatomy Research *Tech. Transf. Fact Sheet* (Internet), *Pinus elliottii.* . . Other Common Names: . . longleaf yellow pine, . . southern yellow pine, . . yellow pine, yellow slash pine.

10 The Chihuahua **pine** *(Pinus leiophylla).*

1908 Britton *N. Amer. Trees* 18, Chihuahua Pine. . . It is characteric [sic] by its sparse foliage and is also called Yellow pine. **1976** Elmore *Shrubs & Trees SW* 20, Chihuahua Pine. . . "yellow pine." **1995** Epple *Field Guide Plants AZ* 14, Chihuahua Pine. . . Yellow pine, white pitch pine. . . *Pinus leiophylla* var. *chihuahuana.*

yellow platter n

1970 *WI Conserv. Bulletin* 35.2.22 **WI,** [Caption:] These are "yellow platters"—meaning coiled rattlesnakes that have recently shed their skins.

yellow plum n Also *wild yellow plum*

A **wild plum 1** (here: usu *Prunus americana*).

[**1785** Marshall *Arbustrum* 111, Prunus americana. *Large Yellow Sweet Plumb.* This generally rises to the height of twelve or fifteen feet.] **1818** in 1819 *Amer. Jrl. Science* 1.369, May 18. . . Damson *(Prunus domestica)* and yellow or wild plum *(Prunus chicasa)* in flower. **1847** Wood *Class-Book* 241, *P[runus] Americana.* . . Red Plum. Yellow Plum. . . often cultivated for its sweet, pleasant fruit. **1875** *Alton Weekly Telegraph* (IL) [18 Mar 4]/4 (newspaperarchive.com), [Advt:] An orchard of 120 trees of our most select fruit, in good bearing condition, an egg or yellow plum orchard very fine [etc]. **1908** *Waukesha Freeman* (WI) 13 Feb 2/1, An irresistable temptation for me to . . take a spin down stream to the spot where the luscious yellow plums and red thorn apple tempted a landing. **1950** Grimm *Trees PA* 241, The American Wild Plum is also known as the Wild Red or Yellow Plum.

yellow poinciana n

=**pride of Barbados.**

1900 *Haw. Almanac & Annual for 1900* 106, A very beautiful tree of this genus [=*Caesalpinia*] is the yellow poinciana, a massive head of finely cut foliage. **1931** *Key W. Citizen* (FL) 22 May 4/1, A color scheme of white and yellow carried out by means of white lilies and yellow poinciana, was effectively carried out by Mrs. J.F. Lankford yesterday afternoon. **1948** Neal *In Gardens HI* 381, Yellow poinciana. *Peltophorum inerme.* . . A stately, heavy-foliaged tree, quickly reaching a height of 50 feet or more. **1964** *Tucson Daily Citizen* (AZ) 1 Aug 57/4, [Advt:] Yellow Poinciana. . . 69c.

yellow poker n

A **prince's-plume 2** (here: *Stanleya pinnata*).

1934 Saunders *Useful Wild Plants* 126, *Stanleya pinnatifida,* . . with long racemes of yellow, four-petaled flowers. In some localities it is commonly called Yellow Poker, from those showy slender flower spikes. **1945** *Kerrville Mt. Sun* (TX) 26 Apr 6/4, The yellow poker plant in bloom at Flora Weiss'.

yellow pondperch See **yellow perch 2**

yellow poplar n   Also *yellow popple*

1 =**tulip tree 1.**

1759 *PA Gaz.* (Philadelphia) 6 Dec 6/3, [Advt:] He wants . . Walnut from two Foot three, to two Foot ten Inches broad, yellow Poplar Ditto, [etc]. **1798** *Weekly Mag.* 2.80 **PA,** The trees, shrubs, &c. which seem to be the most valuable and worthy of the expence and care of cultivation and protection [include] . . Yellow Poplar or Tulip-Tree [etc]. **1837** Darlington *Flora Cestrica* 327 **sePA,** L[*iriodendron*] *tulipifera.* . . The *wood* of this magnificent tree is highly valued in the mechanic arts, especially the *variety* called *yellow poplar.* **1882–83** Whitman *Specimen Days* 89 **sNJ,** Here is one of my favorites now before me, a fine yellow poplar, quite straight, perhaps 90 feet high. **1893** *Jrl. Amer. Folkl.* 6.136 **WV,** *Liriodendron tulipifera,* white, yellow, or hickory poplar. **1903** *DN* 2.337 **seMO,** *Yellow-poplar.* . . Tulip-tree. **1937** Thornburgh *Gt. Smoky Mts.* 28, The tulip tree is "yellow poplar." **1942** *Ecology* 23.189, Important associated species were yellow poplar (*Liriodendron tulipifera*) [etc]. **1943** Peattie *Great Smokies* 170, Yellow poplar (lumberman's name for tulip tree). **1965–70** *DARE* (Qu. T12, *The kind of poplar tree that has sticky, sweet-smelling buds*) 81 Infs, **chiefly Midl,** Yellow poplar; **MN**29, **NY**206, **OK**52, Yellow popple; **OH**33, Yellow tulip poplar; (Qu. T13, . . *Names* . . *for* . . *tulip tree*) 44 Infs, **chiefly Midl,** Yellow poplar; 19 Infs, 9 **IN,** Yellow popple; (Qu. T16, . . *Kinds of trees* . . *'special'*) Infs **IN**35, 44, **KY**21, 29, **NC**48, Yellow poplar. [*DARE* Ed: Some of these Infs may refer to sense **2** below.] **1973** Wharton–Barbour *Trees KY* 523, "Yellow poplar," a lumberman's term, is a misnomer because the species is not related to the true poplars, which have far inferior wood. **1997** *Torrey Bot. Soc. Jrl.* 124.286, There were 38%, 35%, and 120% increases in the volumes of sugar maple, yellow-poplar, and black cherry, respectively, in these plots.

2 A **cottonwood 1,** now usu *Populus grandidentata.*   **chiefly Gt Lakes**

1819 (1821) Nuttall *Jrl.* 58 **ceAR,** On the river lands . . grows platanus . . , also enormous cotton-wood trees (*Populus angulisans* [prob =*P. deltoides*]), commonly called yellow poplar, some of them more than six feet in diameter. **1905** Williamson *Hist. W. OH* 367, *Populus grandidentata.* . . Large poplar. Yellow poplar. **1909** U.S. Congress House *Pulp & Paper Hearings* 3.1460, The *Chairman.* I notice . . you mention poplar and also yellow poplar. Mr. *Bristol.* Those are different species. Mr. *Sims* [of TN]. We call the cottonwood the yellow poplar. **1969** *WI Conserv. Bulletin* 34.2.22, Perhaps someone working in yellow popple may have a few more days of peeling. **1987** Klessig *Country Acres* 23 **WI,** *Big tooth aspen:* Also known as largetooth or yellow popple, this tree's leaves have coarse teeth. The bark . . ranges from greenish-yellow to tan. **2007** in 2009 *DARE* File—Internet **ceMI,** He explained the confusion about the "yellow popple"/"aspen". Apparently that's a bit of a local name for Big Tooth Aspen, though it's not true "yellow poplar" which is the Tulip Tree. They call it yellow because the bark is yellow. **2009** WI Dept. Nat. Resources Div. Forestry *N. Region Forest Health Rept.* June 7 (Internet), There were isolated spots where yellow popple (bigtooth aspen . .) suffered frost damage.

yellow puccoon n

1 =**goldenseal 1.**

1828 Rafinesque *Med. Flora* 1.251, *Hydrastis canadensis.* English Name—Yellow Pucoon. . . Root perennial, of a bright yellow. **1854** King *Amer. Eclectic Dispensatory* 544, *Hydrastis canadensis.* Golden Seal. . . This is an indigenous plant, which is also known by the various names of *Yellow Puccoon, Ground Raspberry, Turmeric Root,* etc. **1902** *Jrl. Amer. Folkl.* 15.255, The principal plants now called *puccoon* by speakers of English in the United States and Canada are: 1. The "blood-root" (*Sanguinaria Canadensis*); 2, the "yellow *puccoon*," or the "yellow-root" (*Hydrastis Canadensis*). **1968** *DARE* (Qu. S3, *A flower like a large violet with a yellow center and small ragged leaves— it comes up early in spring on open, stony hilltops*) Inf **IN**30, Yellow puccoon. **1971** Krochmal *Appalachia Med. Plants* 144, *Hydrastis canadensis.* . . Common Names: Goldenseal, . . yellow puccoon, yellow-root, yellowwort. **1990** *Daily Herald* (Arlington Heights IL) 21 Aug sec 2 6/2, Stearns, who lives in a weathered trailer in the hills of Jackson County, also chews a few thin pieces of bitter yellow puccoon to cure a sore throat. **2004** [see **2** below].

2 A **puccoon 1** (here: *Lithospermum incisum* or *L. canescens*).

1893 *Amer. Gardening* 14.475, The root [of *Lithospermum angustifolium*] . . yields a red dye like that of its relative, the yellow puccoon

or Indian paint-root (*L. canescens*). **1911** *Amer. Botanist* 17.69 **IL,** *Lithospermum angustifolium* [=*L. incisum*]. Yellow puccoon. Rare. **1940** Steyermark *Flora MO* 450, Yellow Puccoon (*Lithospermum angustifolium*). . . Dry open woods, glades and prairies. **1949** Moldenke *Amer. Wild Flowers* 257, The plant is the narrowleaf or yellow puccoon, *Batschia linearifolia* [=*Lithospermum incisum*]. **1953** Greene–Blomquist *Flowers South* 107, Yellow Puccoon, Gromwell (*Lithospermum canescens*)—A very showy, hairy perennial with large, colored roots and orange-yellow corollas. **2004** Austin *FL Ethnobotany* 411 **wKY,** I learned *Lithospermum* as "yellow puccoon" when I was young. . . My mother's family talked about and gathered "yellow puccoon" when she was young, and I could never find that much of it growing around the area where they lived. There was plenty of goldseal, but *Lithospermum* was indeed rare. . . It was only much later that I discovered that both *Hydrastis* and *Lithospermum* are known as "yellow puccoon."

3 =**bloodroot 1.** Cf **red puccoon**

1974 (1977) Coon *Useful Plants* 204, *Sanguinaria canadensis*— Bloodroot; red, yellow, or white puccoon. . . the juice may be purgative or mildly sedative.

yellow-puff n   Cf **cloth-of-gold 2**

A southern perennial herb (*Neptunia lutea*).   Also called **yellow sensitive brier**

1970 Correll *Plants TX* 782, *Neptunia lutea.* . . Yellow-puff. Plant of dry sandy areas. **2008** (acc) U.S. Dept. Ag. *Plants Database* (Internet), *Neptunia lutea.* . . yellow puff.

yellow rail n   Also *yellow-breasted rail*

Std: a **rail** n[2] (here: *Coturnicops noveboracensis*).   Also called **clicker 1, corncob, kicker** n[3], **prairie chicken 3, yellow crake**

yellow rain lily See **rain lily 3**

yellow rattle n   [*OED2* 1578 →]

Std: an annual plant of the genus *Rhinanthus,* usu *R. cristagalli.*   For other names of the latter see **money grass**

yellow redpoll n   Also *yellow redpoll warbler* Cf **redpoll 2** Usu the palm **warbler** (*Dendroica palmarum*).

[**1758** Edwards *Gleanings Nat. Hist.* 1.99, The Yellow Red-pole . . the top of the head is red: the upper side . . is of an olive green: the under side . . is of a bright yellow. . . This bird belonged to the late Mrs. Sidney Kennon, Midwife to the Royal Family: it is not known from whence it came; but I have discovered its country, by receiving what I am persuaded is the hen of this bird . . it was sent from Pensylvania by Mr. Bartram, who says, "It visits us in March, and is a very lonely bird . . : they do not breed in Pensylvania, but go farther to the northward." [*DARE* Ed: The bird here described and depicted prob belongs to one of the West Indian subspp of *Dendroica petechia,* but the bird sent by Bartram was prob *D. palmarum hypochrysea.*]] **1791** Bartram *Travels* 184, P[arus] aureus vertice rubro, the yellow red pole. **1811** Wilson *Amer. Ornith.* 4.19 **PA,** *Yellow-Red-poll Warbler Sylvia petechia* [here prob = *Dendroica palmarum hypochrysea*]. . . [frequents] low swampy thickets. **1875** (1876) Hallock *Camp Life* 43 **FL,** Yellow Redpoll Warbler (*Dendroeca palmarum*). The most abundant species of the warblers here. **1895** Minot *Land-Birds New Engl.* 124, [*Dendroica*] *Palmarum hypochrysea.* "Red-poll" Warbler. Palm Warbler. "Yellow Red-poll." A common migrant through Massachusetts.

yellow robin n   *arch*

=**Baltimore oriole.**

1901 Grinnell–Grinnell *Birds* 53, A yellow glory the oriole surely is, . . whether it be called hang-bird, or yellow robin [etc]. **1957** *Sat. Eve. Post Letters* **NY** (as of c1870), My father came from Malone, Franklin Co., N.Y. . . He has said that as a boy in Malone they called Orioles 'yellow robins.'

yellowroot n

1 =**goldenseal 1.**

1759 (1849) Darlington *Mem. John Bartram* 218 **PA,** [Letter of Peter Collinson:] Billy sent me a delightful drawing of what is called, with you, the Yellow Root. Pray look out and send me a plant or two; for it seems a new genus. *Ibid* 390, [Letter of Philip Miller:] The Yellow-root . . has flowered . . two years past, from some roots which were sent me from the inland parts of your country. It is a new genus, I have figured, and described it, by the title of *Warneria.* **1828** Rafinesque *Med. Flora* 1.251, *Hydrastis canadensis.* English Name—yellow puccoon. . . *Vulgar Names*—Yellowroot, Ground Raspberry, Yellowpaint, Golden Seal, Orange root, Indian paint, Eyebalm, &c. **1837** Darlington *Flora Cestrica* 336 **sePA,** Canadian Hydrastis. *Vulgò*—Yellow-root. **1863** Porcher *Resources* 18 **SC,** *Hydrastis canadensis.* . . Orange-root; yellow-root. **1913** *Richwood Gaz.* (OH) 20 Nov 3/3 **WI,** Our specialty has always been golden seal, commonly called yellow root. **1951** Giles *Harbin's Ridge* 7 **eKY,** She knew that goldenseal, what we hereabouts call yaller-root, was good for stomach trouble, or sore mouth, or heart burn. **1967** *DARE* FW Addit **AR46,** Goldenseal is the same as yellow-root. **1968–69** *DARE* (Qu. BB50a, . . *Favorite remedies . . for a cough*) Inf **KY44,** Yellowroot and honey; (Qu. BB50d, *Favorite spring tonics*) Infs **KY19, NC55,** Yellowroot; **GA74, KY21,** Yellowroot tea. [*DARE* Ed: Some of these Infs may refer instead to **2** or **4** below.] **1969** *DARE* FW Addit **KY39,** Yellowroot—for stomach trouble. **1971** [see **yellow puccoon** 1]. **1973** *Kingsport Times–News* (TN) 29 Apr sec D 4/2 **KY,** Yellow root or golden seal is the same thing. . . [T]he old timers used it for sore mouth or sore throat. **1997** *Columbus Dispatch* (OH) 12 Sept (Internet), "A good hunter can earn $100 a day digging yellow root," Eric Shipman said. . . Goldenseal, the proper name of yellow root found in Ohio, brings $24 a dry pound, said Shipman, a root buyer. **2005** *Charleston Gaz.* (WV) 26 Feb (Internet), Since this is cold and flu season, my granddaughter asked me for some home remedies. . . One of the most useful herbs that we have found is yellow root, or goldenseal. It makes an excellent gargle. **2006** *Atlanta Jrl.–Constitution* (GA) 7 May sec MA 2 (Internet), "I find yellowroot useful for anything wrong with my mouth," he said. Indeed, various strengths of tea brewed from the roots have served in folk medicine as a wash for ulcerated mouths, as a sore throat remedy and as a concoction for stomach upset.

2 Std: a medicinal plant of the family Ranunculaceae *(Xanthorhiza simplicissima)*. Also called **sang-sign**

3 A **goldthread** 1 (here: *Coptis trifolia*).
[**1814** *New Engl. Jrl. Med. & Surgery* 3.138 **NY,** Uniformly patients . . received great benefit from . . a decoction of a small yellow root which grows in cold wet land, commonly known by the name of gold thread.] **1825** Thomson *New Guide Health* 36 **NH,** I used . . gold thread (or yellow root) with red oak acrons [*sic*] pounded and steeped together, for the canker. **1828** [see **4** below]. **1876** Hobbs *Bot. Hdbk.* 135, Yellow root, Goldthread root, Coptis trifolia. **1892** *Jrl. Amer. Folkl.* 5.91 **NH,** *Coptis trifolia,* yellow-root. **1930** Sievers *Amer. Med. Plants* 32, *Goldthread.* . . mouth root, yellowroot. . . The plant is appropriately named after the long, slender, creeping, much-branched and frequently matted, bright golden-yellow root. **1963** (1996) Taylor *1001 Questions* 44, The goldthread, often called yellowroot and canker-root. . . with golden-yellow, thread-like roots, an infusion of which was used to treat weepy eyes.

4 =**twinleaf.**
1828 Rafinesque *Med. Flora* 1.253, The vulgar names of this plant [= *Hydrastis canadensis*] are also various, and common to many others, yellow root is a name given to ten or twelve plants, *Jeffersonia, Coptis, Xanthorhiza,* &c. **1876** Hobbs *Bot. Hdbk.* 135, Yellow root, Twin-leaf root, Jeffersonia diphylla. **1971** Krochmal *Appalachia Med. Plants* 146, American twinleaf, ground squirrel pea, . . yellow root. . . The rhizomes and roots have been used to treat chronic rheumatism, dropsy, spasms, and as a gargle.

5 A **bittersweet** (here: *Celastrus scandens*).
1876 Hobbs *Bot. Hdbk.* 135, Yellow root. . . Celastrus scandens. **1930** Sievers *Amer. Med. Plants* 4, American Bittersweet. . . Other common names. . . Roxbury waxwork, yellowroot [etc].

6 =**coffeeberry** 2a(1).
1897 [see **yellow-boy**]. **1907** *Sunset* 19.51 **CA,** The coffee berry, known also as the pigeon berry, and as the yellow root. . . is a shrub from four to eighteen feet high.

‡7 =**mayapple** 1.
1950 *WELS* (*Other names in your locality for the May-apple*) 1 Inf, **cWI,** Yellowroot.

8 A vinelike shrub (*Morinda umbellata,* formerly *M. roioc*) native to Florida. Cf **redroot g**
1971 Craighead *Trees S. FL* 210, Morinda (Indian mulberry, yellow-root), *Morinda roioc.* **2004** Scott *Endangered Animals FL* 139, Groundcover species, where present, may include snowberry . . and yellowroot *(Morinda royoc).*

yellow rose n

A **cinquefoil** (here: usu *Dasiphora fruticosa* subsp *floribunda*).

[**1896** MA Horticult. Soc. *Trans.* 182, *Potentilla* [=*Dasiphora*] *fruticosa* might at first glance be mistaken for a wild yellow rose, so large are both the bush and the flowers.] **1931** U.S. Dept. Ag. *Misc. Pub.* 101.55, Bush cinquefoil (*Dasiphora fruticosa,* syn. *Potentilla fruticosa*) . . [is] often called shrub or shrubby cinquefoil and known locally also as buckbrush, ninebark, and yellow rose. **1961** Douglas *My Wilderness* 21 **CO,** Showiest of all in places is the thornless yellow rose *(Potentilla fruticosa),* known as the bush cinquefoil. **1999** (2000) Harper-Lore *Roadside Plants* 313, Potentilla fruticosa (potentilla, shrubby cinquefoil, yellow rose).

yellow-rumped warbler n   Also *yellowrump, yellowrump warbler*

=**myrtle warbler.**
1731 Catesby *Nat. Hist. Carolina* 1.58, The Yellow-rump. This is a Creeper, and seems to be of the Tit-kind. **1783** Latham *Genl. Synopsis Birds* 2.481 **PA,** Yellow-rumped w[arbler]. . . Throat, breast, and rump, fine yellow. **1810** Wilson *Amer. Ornith.* 2.138, Yellow-rump Warbler. Sylvia coronata. . . is also a passenger thro Pennsylvania. . . and spends the winter season among the myrtle swamps of Virginia, the Carolinas, and Georgia. **1874** Coues *Birds NW* 57, Dendroeca coronata. . . Yellow-rump Warbler. *Ibid* 58, The Yellow-rump lays four to six eggs. **1892** Torrey *Foot-Path Way* 96 **nwVT,** This yellow-rump, or myrtle bird, is one of the thrifty members of his great family. **1924** *Palo Alto Tribune* (Emmetsburg IA) 9 Mar 1/7, Birds that have been seen by me during the last week. . . myrtle warbler often called yellow-rumped warbler [etc]. **1953** [see **yellow-crowned warbler**]. **1977** *Danville Reg.* (VA) 8 June 11/5, The yellow-rump warbler gives off a "tic-tic-tic" sound. **2007** *DARE* File—Internet **Long Is. NY,** The Butterbutt, or, more properly, the Yellow-rumped Warbler (Dendroica coronata) is one of the most common warblers in North America.

yellows n

A **mule-ear** 2 (here: *Wyethia amplicicaula*).
1915 (1926) Armstrong–Thornber *Western Wild Flowers* 560, Yellows, Mule-ears—*Wyethia amplexicaulis.* . . The flower-heads are about four inches across, with bright yellow rays, almost orange color.

yellow sage n

A **rabbit brush** 1a or b; see quots.
1911 U.S. Bur. Soils *Field Operations* 10.1411, Large rabbit brush (*Chrysothamnus nauseosus* [=*Ericameria nauseosa*]), sometimes called yellow sage, is often mistaken for black sage. **1924** *Ogden Std.–Examiner* (UT) 6 Feb 1/1, The bees gather the nectar from apple blossoms . . , and late in the fall they draw from the sage bloom, the white and yellow sage supplying the sweets. **1931** U.S. Dept. Ag. *Misc. Pub.* 101.161, Douglas rabbit brush. . . known also as Douglas (or tall) rabbitsage, yellowbrush, and yellow sage.

yellow sarsaparilla n   Also *yellow parilla*

=**moonseed** 1.
1830 Rafinesque *Med. Flora* 2.242, *Menispermum Canadense.* . . Moonseed, Pisswort, Yellow Sarsaparilla. **1863** Porcher *Resources* 376, Moon-seed; yellow parilla; yellow sarsaparilla. . . It is said to be much used in Virginia by physicians; and in domestic practice, as a substitute for sarsaparilla, in scrofulous and cutaneous affections. **1892** (1974) Millspaugh *Amer. Med. Plants* 14-1, Menispermum. *Yellow Parilla.* **1930** Sievers *Amer. Med. Plants* 42, Moonseed. . . Other common names.—Canada moonseed, . . yellow parilla, Texas sarsaparilla, yellow sarsaparilla. **1968** *DARE* (Qu. BB50d, *Favorite spring tonics*) Inf **WI44,** Wahoo, yellow parilla, and water.

yellow saucers n

A **desert dandelion**; see quots.
1941 Jaeger *Wildflowers* 311 **Desert SW,** Yellow-saucers. *Malacothrix sonchoides.* . . Sandy soils of the Mohave D., above 2,500 ft. **1971** Dodge *100 Desert Wildflowers* 98, There are many species of malacothryx native to the western and southwestern United States. Some are locally called "desert dandelion," "snake's head," "yellow saucers," and "cliff aster."

yellow seal n

=**goldenseal** 1.
1879 Smith *List Medicines* 70, *Hydrastis canadensis.* . . *Vulg.,* Eyebalm, Golden seal, Ground raspberry, . . Yellow eye root, Yellow paint, Yellow puccoon, Yellow root, Yellow seal. **1940** Clute *Amer. Plant Names* 3, H[ydrastis] Canadensis. . . yellow-seal, . . yellow eye [etc].

yellowseed n

A **peppergrass 1** (here: *Lepidium campestre*).

1822 Eaton *Botany* 486, *Thlaspi . . campestris* (yellow-seed, false-flax, mithridate mustard.) **1847** Wood *Class-Book* 161, *L[epidium] campestre.* . . Yellow Seed. **1914** Georgia *Manual Weeds* 178, Field Peppergrass—*Other English names* . . Yellow Seed. . . Seeds reddish yellow, very pungent to the taste.

yellow sensitive brier n
=**yellow puff.**

1936 Whitehouse *TX Flowers* 46, Yellow Sensitive Briar *(Neptunia lutea)* . . has oblong heads of yellow flowers. . . [and] grows in sandy soil from Oklahoma and Texas to Florida, blooming in June. **2006** Loughmiller–Loughmiller *TX Wildflowers* 117, The yellow sensitive brier, *Neptunia lutea,* is also a member of the Legume family and has oval heads of yellow flowers.

yellow-shafted flicker n   Also *yellow-shafted woodpecker, yellowshaft flicker*   Cf **red-shafted flicker**

An eastern color form of the **flicker** n² **1** with yellow coloring under the wings and tail.

1855 in 1858 U.S. War Dept. *Annual Rept.* 2.2.727, *April 11.* . . Saw yellow-shafted flicker, *(Colaptes auratus,)* and meadow lark, *(Sturnella neglecta.)* **1858** U.S. War Dept. *Rept. Explor. Railroad* 9.118, *Colaptes auratus.* . . Flicker; Yellow Shafted Woodpecker; High Holder. **1864** *Cultivator* 12.126, The Yellow-Shafted Flicker is well known to farmers and young sportsmen, and both take every chance to kill him. **1894** *Galveston Daily News* (TX) 18 Feb 11/2, The flicker or yellow-shafted woodpecker—seeing so much of his food on the ground—drifts far enough southward to find unfrozen earth. **1919** Burns *Ornith. Chester Co. PA* 62, *Colaptes auratus luteus* Northern Flicker, . . "yellow-shaft flicker." **1956** MA Audubon Soc. *Bulletin* 40.82, Yellow-shafted Flicker. . . the shafts of the flight feathers and the underside of the wings are golden yellow. **1967–68** *DARE* (Qu. Q17, . . *Kinds of woodpeckers*) Infs **CO**7, **IA**3, **MO**25, Yellow-shafted flicker. **1968** *Cook Co. News–Herald* (Grand Marais MN) 9 May 2/6, For several days now a pair of yellow shafted flickers have been busy hollowing out a new home in a dead birch tree. **2008** (acc) Cornell Univ. Lab. Ornith. *Birds N. Amer.* (Internet), Two subspecies, the Yellow-shafted Flicker *(Colaptes auratus auratus)* of eastern North America and the Red-shafted Flicker . . form a long, narrow hybrid zone on the Great Plains.

yellowshanks n   Also *yellowshanks snipe, ~ tat(t)ler*

The greater or lesser **yellowlegs 1.**

1785 Pennant *Arctic Zool.* 2.468 **NY**, Yellow-shanks. Sn[ipe]. With a slender black bill . . legs yellow. **1813** (1824) Wilson *Amer. Ornith.* 7.59, *Yellow-Shanks Snipe. Totanus flavipes.* . . As a bird for the table the Yellow-shanks, when fat, is in considerable repute. **1834** Nuttall *Manual Ornith.* 2.148, The Greater Yellow-Shanks or Tell-Tale, so remarkable for its noise and vigilance, arrives on the coast of the Middle States, early in April. *Ibid* 152, Yellow-Shanks Tatler. . . The Yellow-Shanks [=*Totanus flavipes*], in certain situations, may be considered as the most common bird of the family in America. **1875** *Fur Fin & Feather* 121 **Long Is. NY**, During the summer, the willet, curlew, martin, brant bird, dowitch, robin-snipe, yellowshanks, &c., will pipe their whistle along the sedgy shores of Long Island. **1880** *Forest & Stream* 15.4, Yellowshanks tattler or snipe *(Totanus flavipes).* **1907** Rich *Feathered Game NE* 176, Below, [the willet is] white with blackish arrowheads as in the "yellowshanks." **1923** U.S. Dept. Ag. *Misc. Circular* 13.60, The two species of yellowlegs share a number of names [including] . . yellowshanks (Que., Md., D.C., Va., N.C.) **1980** Janovy *Yellowlegs* 80 **KS**, We never used no decoys for them yellowshanks; didn't have to. They's curious birds, social, you could whistle 'em right on in.

yellow skunk cabbage   See **skunk cabbage 1b**

yellow snapper n

A **crested flycatcher** (here: *Myiarchus crinitus*).

[**1890** *Century Dict.* 5727, *Snapper.* . . One of various American flycatchers (not *Muscicapidæ*) which snap at flies, often with an audible click of the beak.] **1916** *Times–Picayune* (New Orleans LA) 16 Apr mag sec 1/4, *Crested Flycatcher* (Myiarchus crinitus). Yellow Snapper.

yellow snowdrop n

A **dogtooth violet** (here: *Erythronium americanum*).

1828 Rafinesque *Med. Flora* 1.168, *Erythronium flavum.* . . *Vulgar Names*—Yellow Adder's tongue, Adder-leaf, Dog-Violet, Rattle Snake violet, Lamb's tongue, Scrofula root, Yellow Snow drop, &c. **1847**

Griffith *Med. Botany* 648, *E[rythronium] americanum.* . . *Common Names.*—Dog-tooth violet, Adder's tongue; Yellow Snowdrop. **1927** *New Castle News* (PA) 25 Mar 20/3, Dog tooth violet. . . It is said that the early settlers named the flower Yellow Snowdrop.

yellow spruce n

A **spruce 1:** the **red spruce** in the eastern US or the **Sitka spruce** (or less freq Engelmann spruce) in the western US.

1819 Michaux *N. Amer. Sylva* (transl. Hillhouse) 3.192, I was informed . . that in Nova Scotia it sometimes serves for the staves of casks used in packing fish; but for this purpose the White Pine and Yellow Spruce are commonly preferred. [*DARE* Ed: "Yellow spruce" translates Michaux's "la variété de l'*Abies nigra* désignée dans ce pays sous le nom de Sapin rouge" [=the variety of *Abies nigra* called in this country "red spruce"] (1810 Michaux *Histoire des Arbres* 1.147).] **1852** *Horticulturist & Jrl. Rural Art* 6.273 **MA**, The sun-shiny Yellow Spruce . . when well cultivated and flourishing can scarcely be distinguished from his more fashionable cousin of Norway. **1857** Swan *NW Coast* 53, I have never seen a specimen of pine from the Columbia to Fuca Strait. The timber is white and yellow spruce, red, white, and yellow fir, hemlock, cedar, and yew. **1876** U.S. Dept. Ag. *Rept. of Secy. for 1875* 333, *Jefferson* [Co. MT] is well supplied with pine and spruce on the mountains. . . White and yellow spruce, cottonwood, and other soft kinds, are produced. **1891** Jesup *Plants Hanover NH* 41, *P[icea] nigra.* . . var *rubra.* . . called by some lumbermen "Yellow Spruce." **1898** Sudworth *Forest Trees* 21 **NY**, *Picea rubens.* . . Names in use.—Red Spruce; Yellow Spruce. **1898** *Youth's Companion* 72.153 **MT**, Yaller spruce, beaver-girdled, standin' in a dry valley for a hundred years. **1916** *Torreya* 16.236 **ME**, *Picea rubra.* . . Common, white or yellow spruce, Matinicus I[slan]d, Me. **1938** Eliot *Forest Trees Pacific Coast* 125, *Sitka Spruce.* . . *Common Names in Use:* Tideland Spruce, . . Yellow Spruce [etc]. **1967** *Fairbanks Daily News–Miner* (AK) 20 July 19/2, [Caption:] Wallace works the yellow spruce with traditional and modern tools.

yellow starwort n
=**elecampane.**

1830 Anthon *Q. Horatii Flacci Poëmata* notes 406, The common elecampane . . is used in medicine. It is sometimes called yellow starwort. Horace applies to this herb the epithet *acidas* . . from the sharp and pungent nature of the plant. **1889** Nichols *Lotus Bay* 175 **Cape Cod MA**, Nelly accordingly began with the one [=flower list] she and Carol had made: . . 22. Yellow Starwort. **1898** Britton–Brown *Illustr. Flora* 3.404, *Inula helenium.* . . Called also Scabwort, Horse-elder, Yellow Starwort [etc]. **1900** Lyons *Plant Names* 202, *I[nula] Helenium.* . . Yellow Starwort. . . *Candied root* a popular cough remedy. **1930** Sievers *Amer. Med. Plants* 27, Elecampane. . . Other common names.—Inula, . . yellow starwort [etc].

yellow strawberry n

1 A **cinquefoil;** see quots.

1868 *OH Farmer* 17.646, All know the Potentilla (Five Fingers, Yellow Strawberry) which greets us in the early spring with its cheerful bright flowers. **1910** Graves *Flowering Plants* 234 **CT**, *Potentilla canadensis.* . . Yellow Strawberry. . . Running Buttercup. **1936** IL Nat. Hist. Surv. *Wildflowers* 152, The Rough Cinquefoil or Yellow Strawberry, *Potentilla monspeliensis* [=*P. norvegica*] is another common species. **1971** Kieran *Nat. Hist. NYC* 138, When I was a boy I was told that certain common little yellow flowers I saw growing close to the ground in pastures and other places were "yellow strawberry blossoms". . . It was years before I learned that I had been botanically bilked, and that the little five-petaled yellow flowers were cinquefoils, . . probably the Common Cinquefoil *(Potentilla simplex).*

2 =**Indian strawberry 1.**

1900 Lyons *Plant Names* 141, *Duchesnea* [spp]. . . Mock Strawberry. . . *D. Indica* . . called also Indian or Yellow Strawberry. **1910** Graves *Flowering Plants* 232 **CT**, *Duchesnea indica.* . . Yellow, Indian or Mock Strawberry. . . Often grown in hanging-baskets for its yellow flowers and handsome but insipid berries. **1936** Kephart in *Jrl. S. Appalachian Bot. Club* 1.81 **NC**, Dry Lowlands. . . Yellow Strawberry (Duchesnea Indica). . . Edible.

yellow-striped fish   See **yellowfish**

yellow-striped grunt n

A **grunt** n **1** (here: *Haemulon flavolineatum*).

1902 *World Today* 2.1275, Eight species of grunt are eaten, the most important being the yellow striped grunt and the common grunt. **1933**

John G. Shedd Aquarium *Guide* 108, *Haemulon flavolineatum*—French Grunt; Yellow-striped Grunt.

yellow Susan n
=**black-eyed Susan 2.**
1968 *DARE* (Qu. S7, *A kind of daisy, bright yellow with a dark center, that grows along roadsides in late summer*) Inf **WI**70, Yellow Susan, [corr to] black-eyed Susan. **2006** *DARE* File—Internet **KY**, The Blue Lobelia has arrived and contrasts very nicely with the yellow Susans.

yellow Swedish turnip See **yellow turnip**

yellowtail n
1 =**mademoiselle.**
[**1796** Nemnich *Allgemeines Polyglotten-Lexicon* 4.908, Perca punctata [=*Bairdiella chrysoura*]. The yellow-tail; The negro-fish.] **1854** Wailes *Rept. on Ag. & Geol. MS* 334, Mesoprion [=*Bairdiella*] chrysurus. . . Yellow-tail. **1911** U.S. Bur. Census *Fisheries 1908* 318, Yellowtail *(Bairdiella chrysura).*—An excellent food fish found on the Atlantic coast from Cape Cod to Texas. . . The name is also applied to the menhaden *(Brevoortia tyrannus)* from North Carolina to Florida; to the runner *(Elagatis bipinnulatus)* at Pensacola; . . to the amber-fish *(Seriola dorsalis)* on the California coast south of Santa Barbara; and to the green rockfish *(Sebastichthys flavidus)* at Monterey. **1973** Knight *Cook's Fish Guide* 394, Yellowtail . . see . . Perch, Silver. **2002** *Galveston Daily News* (TX) 20 Dec sec B 10/5, A fly I recently tied has produced enormous numbers of Bairdiella chrysoura . . commonly called silver perch or yellowtails.
2 =**spot** n **1.**
1813 *New Edinburgh Encycl.* 11.130 **NC, SC**, Bosc is the discoverer of L[eiostomus] xanthurus, the only known species, termed in Carolina *yellow-tail.* **1858** Redfield *Zoöl. Sci.* 562 **SC**, The Lafayette, or Chub, *Leiostomus obliquus,* abounds on the coasts of the Middle States. . . A species, *L. xanthurus,* . . known as the Yellow Jack, or Yellow Tail, is found off the coast of South Carolina. **1873** in 1878 Smithsonian Inst. *Misc. Coll.* 14.2.27, *Liostomus xanthurus.* . . Yellow-tail. Cape Cod to Florida. **1933** LA Dept. of Conserv. *Fishes* 180, The Spot. . . Additional popular names for the species are Oldwife, Yellowtail and Goody.
3 also *yellowtail shad:* A **menhaden 1** (here: *Brevoortia tyrannus).* **esp NC**
1873 in 1878 Smithsonian Inst. *Misc. Coll.* 14.2.33 **NC,** *Brevoortia menhaden.* . . fat-back and yellow-tail *(coast of North Carolina).* **1892** *Middletown Daily Times* (NY) 22 June [2]/4 (newspaperarchive.com), "It's queer how many names the menhaden is known by," observes the skipper. . . "Besides the more common name of menhaden it is known as pogy, bonyfish, . . and yellowtail shad." **1911** [see **1** above]. **1951** Taylor *Surv. Marine Fisheries NC* 93, Other names for the menhaden are: *porgie, yellow tail, yellow-tail shad* [etc]. **2000** Shores *Tangier Is.* 217, *Fatback, bugfish,* and *yellowtail* are North Carolina coastal terms [for the menhaden].
4 also *yellowtail leatherjack(et):* =**leatherjacket 2.**
1882 U.S. Natl. Museum *Proc.* 5.270, *Oligoplites occidentalis* [=*O. saurus*]. . . Yellow-tail. . . Rather common in summer; not valued as food. **1988** Goodson *Fishes Pacific Coast* 32, *Yellowtail leatherjacket (zapatero)—Oligoplites saurus.* **2008** *DARE* File—Internet, The Longjaw Leatherjack can be easily confused with . . the Yellowtail Leatherjack, *Oligoplites saurus inornatus.*
5 =**pinfish 1a.**
1884 Goode *Fisheries U.S.* 1.393 **FL**, The "Sailor's Choice," as it is called . . bears several other names, being known . . in the Indian River region as the . . "Scup," and "Yellow-tail." **1903** NY State Museum & Sci. Serv. *Bulletin* 60.562, It [=*Lagodon rhomboides*] is also called pinfish, squirrel fish, porgee, yellowtail and shiner. **1935** Caine *Game Fish* 55, Salt-water Bream or Sailor's Choice. . . Yellowtail.
6 also *rainbow yellowtail:* =**rainbow runner.**
1884 Goode *Fisheries U.S.* 1.332 **FL**, *Elagatis pinnulatus.* . . [is known] at Pensacola as "Yellow-tail" or "Shoe-maker." **1972** Sparano *Outdoors Encycl.* 378, Rainbow runner—common names . . rainbow yellowtail [etc]. **2008** U.S. Food & Drug Admin. *Seafood List* (Internet), Market Name: Jack or Rainbow Runner. . . Vernacular: . . Yellowtail [etc].
7 See **yellowtail rockfish.**
8 A **snapper 1** (here: *Ocyurus chrysurus).*
1896 Jordan–Evermann *Check List Fishes* 382, *Ocyurus chrysurus.* . . Yellow-tail; Rabirubia. [**1952** *Capital Times* (Madison WI) 24 Apr 35/2, You could look down and see horse-eye jack, yellowtail [etc].] **1996** *Outdoor Life* Jan (Internet), Snappers such as the yellowtail, wise

old harbor barracudas, goggle-eyes and little sergeant majors can have you mumbling to yourself.
9 A **killifish 1** (here: *Fundulus majalis).*
1903 NY State Museum & Sci. Serv. *Bulletin* 60.309, The striped killifish, also known as the banded or striped mummichog, bass mummy, bass fry, mayfish, yellow-tail, and New York gudgeon, is the largest member of its family known on our eastern coast.
10 See **yellow-tailed hornet.**
11 See **California yellowtail.**

yellow-tailed beebird n Also *yellow-tailed bee martin*
=**crested flycatcher.**
1913 *Auk* 30.497 Okefenokee **GA**, *Myiarchus crinitus.* . . 'Yellow-tailed Bee-bird'; 'Yellow-tailed Bee Martin.' Abundant. **1938** Matschat *Suwannee R.* 26 ne**FL**, se**GA**, The yellow-tailed bee bird and the tickbird, both flycatchers, sing from some shady retreat on the hottest day in summer.

yellow-tailed flycatcher See **yellow-tailed warbler**

yellow-tailed hornet n Also *yellow-ass(ed) hornet, yellowtail (~), yellow-tailed wasp* **esp NEast** Cf **white-tailed hornet**
=**yellow jacket 1.**
1891 *Rec.–Union* (Sacramento CA) 25 July 6/1, The low, meditative hum of the yellow-tailed hornet may be heard at any time. **1922** *Automobile Dealer & Repairer* July 25, A yellow tailed wasp cannot sting you unless he sits down and if you don't *let* him sit down on you he will hunt around for more passive game. **1927** *Playground* 21.430 **MA**, Climbing apple trees, . . fighting yellow-tailed hornets, gathering shagbarks . . are the serious occupations of childhood. **1939** *LANE* Map 240–41 *(Hornet)* **NEng**, 4 infs, Yellowtail(s); 5 infs, Yellow-tailed hornet(s); 5 infs, Yellowtail hornet(s); 3 infs, Yellow-assed hornet(s); 1 inf, Yellow-ass hornet. **1968–69** *DARE* (Qu. R21, . . *Other kinds of stinging insects*) Inf **CT**9, Yellow-assed hornet; **NH**14, Ground hornet or yellow-assed hornet—black in front, yellow-and-black striped; live in just a hole in the ground; **MA**47, Yellowtail; regular wasp; **RI**15, Yellowtail hornet; [**MA**5, Yellow-faced hornet—striped]. **a1997** in 2009 *DARE* File—Internet **cnWI** (as of 1920s), We had a field of red clover the bumblebees loved. It was dangerous to walk even the road through the field, bare legged and bare footed. We were often stung. But the most savage bees were the yellow tailed hornets. **2004** *DARE* File—Internet **NEng**, [When I showed him the two photos he said, "yeah, that's them," pointing to the yellow-tailed hornet, rather than the black-tailed cicada killer.] **2008** *Ibid* **NY,** Joshua used to be allergic to honey bees, wasps, yellowjackets, white-tailed hornets and yellow-tailed hornets.

yellow-tailed warbler n Also *yellow-tailed flycatcher, yellowtail warbler*
A **redstart** (here: *Setophaga ruticilla).*
[**1758** Edwards *Gleanings Nat. Hist.* 1.101, The Yellow-tailed Flycatcher.] [**1785** Pennant *Arctic Zool.* 2.406, Yellow-tail. W[arbler]. With an ash-colored crown. . . Taken . . off *Hispaniola,* at sea.] **1889** Ridgway *Ornith. IL* 1.177, American Redstart. Popular Synonyms. . . Yellow-tailed Warbler or Flycatcher. **1917** (1923) *Birds Amer.* 3.167, Redstart. . . Other Names. . . Fire-tail; Yellow-tailed Warbler. **2001** *Tulsa World* (OK) 13 May (Internet), Hummingbirds, scissortail flycatchers and yellowtail warblers will be among the centers of attention.

yellow-tailed wasp, yellowtail hornet See **yellow-tailed hornet**

yellowtail leatherjack(et) See **yellowtail 4**

yellowtail rockfish n Also *yellowtail* **chiefly CA**
A **rockfish 3** (here: *Sebastes flavidus).*
1882 U.S. Natl. Museum *Bulletin* 16.657, S[ebastes] flavidus. . . *Yellow-tail Rock-fish.* . . Coast of California, abundant; an important foodfish. **1884** Goode *Fisheries U.S.* 1.266 **CA,** Yellow-tail Rock-fish. . . At Monterey it is always known by the appropriate name of "Yellow-tail," the caudal fin being always distinctly yellow. **1911** [see **yellowtail 1**]. **1953** Roedel *Common Fishes CA* 123, Yellowtail Rockfish. . . Caudal fin yellow, other fins dusky-yellow. **1974** *Independent Press–Telegram* (Long Beach CA) 8 Nov sec C 6/1, Some of the more important species are . . yellowtail rockfish [etc]. **2008** *Modesto Bee* (CA) 14 May sec C 3 (Internet), They made it down to Point Sur over the weekend for limits of vermilion and yellowtail rockfish.

yellowtail shad See **yellowtail 3**

yellowtail warbler See **yellow-tailed warbler**

yellow tarweed See **tarweed 1b(5)**

yellow Texas star See **Texas star d**

yellow thistle n

A **prickly poppy** (here: *Argemone mexicana*).

[**1774** Long *Hist. Jamaica* 3.845, Yellow Thistle.—*Argemone spinosum* [=*A. mexicana*].] **1820** *Med. Repository* 5.220, The *Argemone Mexicana*, or Prickly Poppy, has flourished this season in Dr. Mitchill's garden. Professor Drown's success in raising this plant, called also the "Yellow Thistle," in Providence, R.I. is already before the public. **1863** Porcher *Resources* 28 **SC,** *Argemone mexicana*. . . yellow thistle. Charleston district, grows around buildings in rich spots. **1910** Graves *Flowering Plants* 197 **CT,** *Argemone mexicana*. . . Flowering or Yellow Thistle. . . Rare.

yellowthroat n

1 Std: a **warbler** of the genus *Geothlypis*, usu *G. trichas*. Also called **black-cheek, coon-faced bird, ground warbler, rainbird 1f**

2 =**bullfrog 1.**

1967 *DARE* (Qu. P22, *Names or nicknames for a very large frog that makes a deep, loud sound*) Inf **OH**16, Yellowthroat. **2007** *DARE* File—Internet **MN,** [Caption:] Yellowthroat. . . This guy was especially beautiful, with his yellow throat. They are starting to show up again at our pond, as our weather gets warmer.

yellow tip-up n

The palm **warbler** *(Dendroica palmarum)*.

1917 [see **tip-up warbler**].

yellow toadflax n

=**butter-and-eggs 1.**

1886 *Lima Democratic Times* (OH) 2 Sept 4/3, The common yellow toadflax was, it is said, introduced by a Mr. Ranstead as a garden flower, and is now known as the Ranstead weed. **1914** Georgia *Manual Weeds* 379, Yellow Toad-Flax. . . *Other English names*. . . Impudent Lawyer [etc]. **1949** Moldenke *Amer. Wild Flowers* 272, Another European plant now very common in North America is the yellow toadflax, *Linaria vulgaris*. **1970** *DARE* (Qu. S11, . . *Wild snapdragon*) Inf **MA**78, Yellow toadflax—right scientific name. **2008** *Anchorage Daily News* (AK) 2 July (Internet), Thank a Welch Quaker who landed in Delaware with William Penn for introducing this invasive perennial of the figwort family known by many aliases: common toadflax (Linaria vulgaris), yellow toadflax [etc].

yellowtop n

1 A **goldenrod 1;** see quots.

[**1892** *Jrl. Amer. Folkl.* 5.98 **New Brunswick Canada,** *Solidago* (any sp.), yellow-tops.] **1898** *Jrl. Amer. Folkl.* 11.230 **nwPA,** *Solidago* (sp.), yellow-top.

2 =**snakeweed b(6).**

1931 U.S. Dept. Ag. *Misc. Pub.* 101.163, Gutierrezia, whose species are frequently known as broomweed, . . yellow-top, yellow weed, and yerba de vibora, is a New World genus. **1937** U.S. Forest Serv. *Range Plant Hdbk.* B85, Broom Snakeweed—*Gutierrezia sarothrae*. . . often known as broomweed, matchweed, turpentine-weed and yellow top, is a half-shrub with woody roots, crowns, and stem bases.

‡**3** A **mullein** (here: prob *Verbascum thapsus*).

1968 *DARE* (Qu. S20, *A common weed that grows on open hillsides: It has velvety green leaves close to the ground, and a tall stalk with small yellow flowers on a spike at the top*) Inf **NC**55, Yellowtop.

4 A **ragwort** (here: *Senecio glabellus*).

[**1890** Selborne Soc. *Nature Notes* 110, Northumbrian Plant Names. . . Yellow top. . . *Senecio Jacobaea*.] **2003** Heiser *Weeds* 85, *Packera glabella*. . . Butterweed and yellowtop, which it is also sometimes called, are descriptive of the flower heads.

yellow turban(s) n

A **wild buckwheat 2** (here: *Eriogonum pusillum*).

1941 Jaeger *Wildflowers* 30 **SW,** Yellow Turban. *Eriogonum pusillum*. . . Called yellow turban because of the yellow flowers surmounting the turban-shaped, glandular involucres. **2008** (acc) U.S. Dept. Ag. *Plants Database* (Internet), *Eriogonum pusillum*. . . yellowturbans.

yellow turnip n Also *Swedish yellow turnip, yellow Swedish ~*

=**rutabaga B.**

1817 *MA Ag. Jrl.* 4.256, I sowed at the same time, some Swedish yellow turnips. **1860** *Knickerbocker* July 102 **NY,** White turnip, yellow turnip, or any sort of sass. **1876** *Freeborn Co. Std.* (Albert Lea MN) 7

Sept [2]/4 (newspaperarchive.com), [In a list of premiums for an agricultural fair:] Best 3 yellow Swedish turnips—25 [cents]. **1900** *Newport Mercury* (RI) 23 June [3]/5 (newspaperarchive.com), *Easily Made Vegetable Soup*. Slice very fine one large onion, two potatoes, . . one-half of a small yellow turnip [etc]. **1935** *Helena Independent* (MT) 17 Nov 11/7, While we are speaking of turnips we must not neglect that near relative, the yellow turnip, or rutabaga. **1965–70** *DARE* (Qu. I3, . . *The large yellowish root vegetable, similar to a turnip, with a strong taste*) Infs **CA**70, 202, **CO**27, **CT**17, **LA**23, **MA**68, **NC**33, **NH**14, **PA**100, 128, Yellow turnip; **CA**17, Yellow turnips—the same as a rutabaga; **NY**35, Yellow turnip—rutabaga. **1967** Borland *Hill Country* 269 **nwCT,** She said, "Yellow turnips!" I said, "You mean *rutabagas?*" That was what she meant. I said, "Look. Where I come from rutabagas are cow feed. *People* don't eat rutabagas!" We had rutabagas—pardon, yellow turnips—for Thanksgiving dinner. **1989** *Washington Post* (DC) 18 Oct sec E 1 (Internet), Grocery stores hereabouts obfuscate the issue by calling the rutabaga a yellow turnip, suggesting that it not only tastes like a turnip (which it does not) but is an off-colored version to boot. **2001** *Houston Chron.* (TX) 24 Jan 6 (Internet), The rutabaga is often confused with the turnip and is even referred to as the Swedish, or yellow, turnip.

yellow warbler n

Std: a **warbler** (here: *Dendroica petechia*). Also called **golden warbler a, Mexican canary 2, summer canary 2, ~ warbler, ~ yellowbird 1, thistle bird 2, wild canary 2, yellowbird 2**

yellowweed n

1 A **buttercup 1;** see quots.

1790 Deane *New Engl. Farmer* 329, *Yellow-weed*, meadow crow-foot. This weed is known in England by the names, king-cob, king-cup, gold-cups, gold-knobs, butter-cups, and butter-flowers. **1821** *Amer. Jrl. Sci. & Arts* 3.273 **MA,** Some of our fields and pastures are now so completely covered with the blossoms of the common ranunculus, here called the yellow weed, as to have the appearance of being wrapt in sheets of gold. **1847** Wood *Class-Book* 42, *R[anunculus] acris*. . . Yellow Weed. . . This is the most common species from Penn. to Hudson's Bay, in meadows and pastures, rapidly and extensively spreading. . . Flowers large, golden yellow. **1876** *Indiana Democrat* (PA) 5 Oct [4]/4 (newspaperarchive.com), Nothing was to be seen but a white weed and yellow weed, or buttercup[s] and ox-eyed daisy. **1884** Lloyd–Lloyd *Drugs & Medicines N. Amer.* 1.54, *Ranunculus bulbosus*. . . This species, and others that have large yellow flowers. . . are occasionally called Yellow Weed and Meadow Bloom, from the yellow flowers. **1990** *Paris News* (TX) 2 May sec A 6/2, *Yellow Weed Control in Pastures*— Area pastures have become a sea of yellow over the past 10 days and many cattle producers have become interested in controlling the Yellow Buttercup. **1995** *Times–Picayune* (New Orleans LA) 2 June sec B 1 (Internet), Ranunculus . . , commonly referred to as buttercup or yellow weed.

2 A **goldenrod 1** (here: usu *Solidago canadensis*).

1850 *S. Planter* 10.318, Gather the yellow weed of the fields, commonly known as the golden rod, and put it in your copper kettle in layers with your wool. **1894** *Jrl. Amer. Folkl.* 7.92 **VT,** *Solidago*, sp., yellow-weed. **1914** Georgia *Manual Weeds* 425, Canada goldenrod. . . *Other English names:* Tall Yellow-weed, Tall Goldenrod. *Ibid* 426, Narrow-leaved Goldenrod. . . *Other English names:* . . Creeping Yellow-weed. **1963** Craighead *Rocky Mt. Wildflowers* 227, Yellowweed—*Solidago elongata*. **1967** Dodge *Roadside Wildflowers* 74, In some places, goldenrod is known as "yellowweed." **1995** Epple *Field Guide Plants AZ* 293, Tall goldenrod . . Yellow-weed—*Solidago altissima*. . . Canada goldenrod . . Meadow goldenrod, yellow-weed, rock goldenrod—*Solidago canadensis*.

3 =**orange sneezeweed.**

1921 *Ogden Std.–Examiner* (UT) 4 Oct [14]/1 (newspaperarchive.com), The "sneeze" weed is sometimes called the "yellow weed" and grows from one to three feet in height, has deep green leaves and its rays or petals have a deep orange color. **1937** U.S. Forest Serv. *Range Plant Hdbk.* W88, Orange sneezeweed, sometimes also called Hoopes sneezeweed, owls-claws, sunflower, western sneezeweed, and yellow-weed, is a perennial herb. **1968** Schmutz et al. *Livestock-Poisoning Plants AZ* 90, Western Sneezeweed . . yellowweed (*Helenium* [=*Hymenoxys*] *hoopesii*). **1971** Green *Village Horse Doctor* 10 **cwTX,** Yellowweed . . is a grayish-green weed with lush, meaty-type leaves. . . It has a large daisy-type bloom with a great excess of yellow pollen. . .

4 A **snakeweed b(6)** (here: usu *Gutierrezia sarothrae*).

1915 U.S. Natl. Museum *Contrib. Herbarium* 19.658 **NM,** *Gutierrezia tenuis*. . . This and other species are known variously as "yellow weed," "brownweed" [etc]. **1976** Elmore *Shrubs & Trees SW* 82, Broom Snakeweed. . . brown-, broom-, yellow-, match-, sheep-, or turpentine weed. **2002** *Santa Fe New Mexican* (NM) 25 Aug sec B 4/6, A home remedy for hot flashes that uses tea from three New Mexico herbs: "yerba de zorillo" (worm seed), "escoba de la vibora" (yellow weed or snake week [sic]) and "yerba del manso" (lizard's tail).

5 =**cat's-ear 2.**

1937 *Torreya* 37.101 **OR**, *Hypochaeris radicata*. . . Yellow weed, Nehalem, Ore.

yellow wheeler See **wheeler** n[2]

yellow whicker See **whicker** n[2]

yellow-wing n

1 See **yellow-wing(ed) blackbird.**
2 See **yellow-winged sparrow.**
3 See **yellow-winged woodpecker.**

yellow-wing(ed) blackbird n   Also *yellow-wing*

Usu appar =**yellow-headed blackbird,** but occas applied to the immature male **red-winged blackbird.**

1860 U.S. Congress Senate *Statist. Rept. Sickness* 209 **AZ,** The following have been met with: . . blackbird, red-winged blackbird, yellow-winged blackbird, large redbird with crest [etc]. **1888** *Current* 10.312 **CO,** The larks held a concert on my cabin roof at early morn, and the yellow-winged blackbirds poured forth their gurgling roundelays from the clusters of killikinnick which fringed the borders of the prattling stream. **1892** *Jrl. Amer. Folkl.* 5.220 **AZ,** The ceremonial names applied to each of the objects placed at these points are given in the following table:—1. *Ta-wa mā'-nā* (sunmaid)—Yellow-wing blackbird. **1903** *Atl. Slope Naturalist* 1.45 **CO,** There was at least one specimen of each of the following . . Western blue jay, red-winged blackbird, yellow-winged blackbird, cow bird [etc]. **1965–70** *DARE* (Qu. Q11, . . *Kinds of blackbirds*) 11 Infs, **chiefly NW, Rocky Mts, Upper MW,** Yellow-wing(ed) blackbird; NV6, Yellow-wings. **2002** Nelson *Thousand Souls* 21 **UT,** I headed out onto the Farmington Bay bird refuge, . . where flocks of yellow-winged blackbirds, sea gulls, and coots squawked and fluttered as I galloped past. **2006** *DARE* File—Internet **UT,** [Caption:] Yellow-winged Blackbird—*Farmington Bay, Utah.* [*DARE* Ed: Photo shows yellow-headed blackbird.] **2009** *Ibid* neCA, [Caption:] Yellow winged blackbird hanging out at the Mill pond. I have never heard of this bird before and actually was going to delete these pictures when my husband walked by and said "Oh a yellow winged blackbird" and then he pointed out the shoulder and its coloring there. . . My husband said that's what they are called around here and admits he is not sure if that is the "real name." [*DARE* Ed: Photo appears to be of immature male red-winged blackbird.]

yellow-winged sparrow n   Also *yellow-wing*

=**grasshopper sparrow.**

1811 Wilson *Amer. Ornith.* 3.76, *Yellow-Winged Sparrow. Fringilla Passerina.* . . inhabits the lower parts of New York and Pennsylvania. **1858** U.S. War Dept. *Rept. Explor. Railroad* 9.450, *Coturniculus passerinus.* . . Yellow-winged Sparrow. **1872** Coues *Key to N. Amer. Birds* 137, *Yellow-winged Sparrow.* Edge of wing conspicuously yellow. **1895** Minot *Land-Birds New Engl.* 201, The eggs . . are of a more oblong oval than those of the common Yellow-wing. **1909** *Auk* 26.354, The "Yellow winged Sparrow" of Wilson is now the "Grasshopper Sparrow." **1940** Writers' Program *Guide NY* 41, Among the year- round residents are the . . yellow winged sparrow.

yellow-winged woodpecker n   Also *yellow-wing*

A **flicker** n[2] **1** (here: *Colaptes auratus*).

1832 Nuttall *Manual Ornith.* 1.557, Sometimes the call [of the St. Domingo cuckoo] seems like *kh' kh' kh' kh' 'kh 'kah,* the notes growing louder and running together like those of the Yellow-winged Woodpecker. **1854** *ME Farmer* (Augusta) 9 Nov 2/6, The editor of the Hartford Times has been presented with a specimen of the pileated woodpecker. It is about twice the size of the yellow-winged woodpecker. **1900** *Wilson Bulletin* 12.2.12 neMA, Flicker. . . *Yellow Wing.* Cape Anne, Massachusetts. **1902** NJ Bd. Fish & Game Comms. *Annual Rept. for 1901* 16, It was intended to provide an open season for the yellow-winged woodpecker, commonly called high-holder or flicker. **1927** *Pop. Mechanics* 47.858, The flicker or yellow-winged woodpecker is another good-looking bird neighbor to have around the yard. **1968** *DARE* (Qu. Q17, . . *Kinds of woodpeckers*) Inf **UT**14, Yellow-wing.

yellow wisteria n

A **wild indigo 1** (here: *Baptisia sphaerocarpa*).

1951 *Daily Oklahoman* (Oklahoma City OK) 7 June 11/2, The tulips, lilacs, purple and yellow wisteria keep the streets colorful and fragrant. **1961** Wills–Irwin *Flowers TX* 132, Bush-pea, or Yellow-wisteria, is of quite erect habit and bears its bright yellow flowers in April and May well above the foliage. **2007** (acc) *Lady Bird Johnson Wildfl. Center* (Internet) **TX,** *Baptisia sphaerocarpa.* . . Yellow wild indigo. Yellow wisteria.

yellowwood n

1 also *prickly yellowwood:* A **prickly ash 1** (here: esp *Zanthoxylum flavum*).   Cf **yellowheart**

[**1696** Sloane *Catalogus Plantarum Jamaica* 138, *Prickly yellow wood.* In sylvis campestribus Insulae Jamaicae ubique abundat. [=Common in level woods throughout Jamaica.]] **1830** Rafinesque *Med. Flora* 2.113, *Xanthoxylon fraxineum* [=*Zanthoxylum americanum*]. . . Toothache Bush, Pellitory, Yellow Wood. **1876** U.S. Dept. Ag. *Rept. of Secy. for 1875* 156, *Zanthoxylum Pterota* [=*Z. fagara*]. . . False Iron Wood; Yellow Wood. A small shrubby tree occurring from Florida to Texas. The wood is yellow and close-grained. **1908** Britton *N. Amer. Trees* 569, Yellow Wood—*Xanthoxylum flavum.* . . The wood is . . fine-grained, orange-yellow and susceptible of a fine polish. **1913** Small *FL Trees* 52, *Z[anthoxylum] flavum.* . . The *Yellow-wood* grows in hammocks on the lower Florida Keys. **2003** *Paris News* (TX) 12 Oct sec C 3/1, Other common names are Hercules' Club, Southern Prickly Ash, . . Prickly Yellow Wood and Wait-a-bit. **2004** Hammer *FL Keys* 105, Yellowwood—*Zanthoxylum flavum.*

2 =**Osage orange.**

1805 in 1809 *Amer. Reg.* 5.342 **AR,** At this place, Mr. Dunbar obtained one or two slips of the "bois d'arc" (bow wood), or yellow wood, from the Missouri. **1828** Rafinesque *Med. Flora* 1.268, *Toxylon aurantiacum* . . Stinking wood, Bow wood, Yellow wood. . . fruits of size and shape of oranges, not edible! **1850** Emerson *Rept. Trees & Shrubs* 283 **MA,** The Osage Orange. . . The wood. . . is of a rich saffron yellow, whence it is sometimes called Yellow Wood. **1897** Sudworth *Arborescent Flora* 190 **TN,** Osage Orange. . . Yellow Wood. **1966** *Des Moines Register* (IA) 2 Oct 16/1, The Indians called it [=Osage orange] yellowwood and extracted a dye from roots and bark.

3 also *Kentucky yellowwood:* A pod-bearing deciduous tree (*Cladrastis kentukea*).   Also called **gopherwood, yellow ash 2, ~ locust 2**

1810 Michaux *Histoire des Arbres* 1.39 **TN,** *Virgilia lutea.* . . *Yellow wood.* **1863** Porcher *Resources* 175, *Cladrastis tinctoria.* . . Yellow-wood. . . The wood is yellow, and dyes a beautiful saffron color. **1872** *Amer. Jrl. Sci. & Arts* 3d ser 4.291, Our yellow wood (*Cladrastis*) inhabits a very limited district on the western slope of the Alleghanies. **1886** *Harper's New Mth. Mag.* 72.638, From the nurseries we can obtain specimens that beautify other regions of our broad land, as, for instance, the Kentucky yellow-wood. **1915** *Washington Post* (DC) 11 July Misc sec 1/3, Yellow wood (Cladrastis lutea) yields a yellow dye, to which the wood owes its name. The tree is confined to Kentucky, Tennessee, Alabama and North Carolina. **1939** FWP *Guide TN* 514, There are some fine stands of yellowwood, or "gopher tree," which the mountain people believe furnished the wood for Noah's ark. **2002** *AR Gardener Mag.* May (Internet), The pea-flowers of yellowwood are white, fragrant . . and borne on long, pendant panicles that can reach a foot in length.

4 =**tulip tree 1.**

[**1813** Michaux *Histoire des Arbres* 3.203, *Tulip tree.* . . Les Français de la Louisiane et du Canada, le connoissent sous le nom de Bois jaune, *Yellow-wood.* [=*Tulip tree.* . . The French of Louisiana and Canada know it by the name of Bois jaune, *Yellow-wood.*]] **1937** *Torreya* 37.97 **NY,** *Liriodendron tulipifera.* . . a tree with much white (or sap) wood is called white-wood, one with much yellow (or heart) wood is called yellow-wood.

5 A **barberry;** see quots.

1853 U.S. Army Corps Topog. Engineers *Rept. Sitgreaves* 38, At the spot where we halted to rest the mules, we procured a number of berries of the yellow-wood (*Berberis pennata* [=*Mahonia pinnata*]) which . . assisted to quench our thirst. **1937** U.S. Forest Serv. *Range Plant Hdbk.* B99, Frémont hollygrape . . and red hollygrape. . . are known in the Southwest as algerita, agarita, agrillo, and yellowwood. **1941** Jaeger *Wildflowers* 67 **Desert SW,** Yellow-wood. *Berberis Fremontii.* . . Strip the bark, and you will notice the characteristic deep-yellow wood from which the Navahos extracted a yellow dye.

6 =**sweetleaf 1.**

1860 Curtis *Cat. Plants NC* 66, Yellow Wood. . . The leaves. . . afford, by decoction, a beautiful yellow color, . . wherewith cotton, woollen and silk, are dyed. **1897** Sudworth *Arborescent Flora* 322 **NC, SC,**

AL, Sweetleaf. . . Yellow-wood. **1950** Peattie *Nat. Hist. Trees* 551, Sweetleaf. . . Other Names: Horse-sugar. Yellowwood. **2001** Porcher–Rayner *Guide Wildflowers SC* 164, Horse sugar; sweetleaf; yellow-wood—*Symplocos tinctoria*. . . Dying with yellow-wood, a practice several centuries old in the South, is still practiced.

7 =Florida boxwood 1.

1884 Sargent *Forests of N. Amer.* 39 sFL, *Schaefferia frutescens*. . . Yellow Wood. Box Wood. . . Color, light bright yellow, the sap-wood a little lighter. **1933** Small *Manual SE Flora* 820, *S[chaefferia] frutescens*. . . Boxwood. Yellow-wood. . . The bright-yellow heart-wood is close-grained and heavy. **2004** Austin *FL Ethnobotany* 610, *Schaefferia frutescens*. . . yellow-wood.

8 A smoke tree 1 (here: *Cotinus obovatus*).

1897 Sudworth *Arborescent Flora* 274 AL, *Cotinus cotinoides* [=*C. obovatus*]. . . Yellowwood. **1967** *DARE* (Qu. T16, . . *Kinds of trees* . . *'special'*) Inf TN22, Chittam tree—same as yellowwood. **1979** Little *Checklist U.S. Trees* 100, *Cotinus obovatus*. . . smoketree, chittamwood, yellowwood.

9 =Carolina buckthorn 1.

1897 Sudworth *Arborescent Flora* 298 AL, FL, LA, *Rhamnus* [=*Frangula*] *caroliniana*. . . Yellow-wood. **1970** Correll *Plants TX* 1012, *Rhamnus caroliniana*. . . Yellow-wood, Polecat Tree. **1995** Alden *Hardwoods N. Amer.* 107, *Rhamnus caroliniana* . . yellow buckthorn, yellowwood.

10 =cascara 1.

1897 Sudworth *Arborescent Flora* 299 OR, *Rhamnus* [=*Frangula*] *purshiana*. . . Yellow-wood. **1995** Alden *Hardwoods N. Amer.* 107, *Rhamnus purshiana* . . yellow-wood.

yellow woolly bear See **yellow bear (caterpillar)**

yellowwort n

=goldenseal 1.

1958 Jacobs–Burlage *Index Plants NC* 180, *Hydrastis canadensis*. . . Eye root; eye balm, . . goldenseal; yellow eye-wright; yellow-wort.

yelper n

1 A yellowlegs 1, usu the greater **yellowlegs 1.**

1866 Roosevelt *Game-Birds N. States* 77, The yelper has a strong, rapid and often irregular flight. . . On Long Island it goes by the name of big yellow-legs. **1871** Warren *Shooting* 48 ceNJ, Them yelpers keep a whistlin' and shaking their yaller legs from daylight to dark. *Ibid* 57, They are big yellow-legs—they call them yelpers down here, I believe. **1880** *Forest & Stream* 15.4 seNY, neNJ, Tell-tale tattler, or snipe (*Totanus melanoleuca*). . . [is called] on Long Island and the upper coast of New Jersey, the yelper, on account of its piercing notes. **1917** (1923) *Birds Amer.* 1.242, Greater Yellow-legs. . . Other Names—Big Tell-tale; . . Yelper [etc]. *Ibid* 244, Yellow-legs. . . Other names. . . Little Yelper [etc]. **1925** *Forest & Stream* 95.294, [Title:] Yellowlegs and Nimble Jacks—A Day on the Marshes in Pursuit of the Yelper and his Acrobatic Cousin, the Jacksnipe. **1956** MA Audubon Soc. *Bulletin* 40.18 CT, Greater Yellow-legs. . . Yelper. . . From its vociferousness. *Ibid* CT, Lesser Yellow-legs. . . Yelper.

2 =cackling goose (formerly *Branta canadensis minima*, now *B. hutchinsii m.*).

1918 Grinnell et al. *Game Birds CA* 234, Cackling Goose—*Branta canadensis minima*. . . Other names—Cackler; Yelper [etc]. **1953** Jewett *Birds WA* 105, Alaskan Cackling Goose. *Branta hutchinsii minima*. . . Other names. . . Yelper [etc].

yender See **yonder A2**

yens See **you-uns** pron[1]

yenses See **you-uns's**

yent v *Gullah* Cf **ain't** v[1], **enty**

Ain't; didn't.

1888 Jones *Negro Myths* 3 GA coast [Gullah], Buh Alligatur yent hab time fuh mek answer. Eh yent crack eh teet to Buh Rabbit. **1908** *S. Atl. Qrly.* 7.341 sSC coast [Gullah], Me yent no sicarum. **1922** Gonzales *Black Border* 283 sSC, GA coasts [Gullah], "Enty," "ent," "yent," . . serve for isn't, aren't, didn't, don't, doesn't. . . Preceded by a soft vowel sound . . "ent" [is] changed to . . "yent;" as . . " 'e yent."

yeopon See **yaupon**

yeou See **you** pron[1] **A1**

yer n See **year** n[1]

yer adv, adj[1] See **here A3**

yer adj[2] See **your**

yer all See **you-all**

yer all's adj, pron[1] See **your-all's**

yer-alls pron[2] See **you-alls** pron[1]

yerarter See **hereafter**

yerb See **herb A1**

yerba bonita n [Span]

=fairy duster.

1937 U.S. Forest Serv. *Range Plant Hdbk.* B36, Yerba bonita (pretty herb), a commonly used Spanish name, is locally applied to this small but showy, purple-flowered, delicate-leaved shrub of the Southwest.

yerba buena n [Span]

A western perennial herb (*Clinopodium douglasii*) sometimes used as a medicinal tea. Also called **Oregon tea 1, tea vine**

1847 *CA Star* (San Francisco) 30 Jan 2/3, The town [=Yerba Buena, later San Francisco] takes its name from an herb to be found all around it which is said to make good tea; and possessing excellent medicinal qualities, it is called good herb or Yerba Buena. **1882** *Californian* 5.329 CA, [We bring home] the sweet-scented yerba buena, to give to the whole the aromatic breath of the forest. **1897** *Jrl. Amer. Folkl.* 10.53 CA, *Micromeria Douglasii*, . . good herbs, "yerba buena." **1932** Bentley *Spanish Terms* 216, Yerba. . . Examples are *yerba buena, yerba santa* (*Eriodictyon tomentosum*), *yerba mansa* (*Anemopsis californica*). **1940** Writers' Program *Oregon* 23, So often did our forebears substitute the dried leaves of the *yerba buena* for "store tea" that the plant has become known by the common name of Oregon tea. **1970** Kirk *Wild Edible Plants W. U.S.* 198, Yerba buena, Oregon Tea. . . The dry leaves may be steeped for fifteen to twenty minutes in hot water to make a good tea said to be stimulating to the digestion.

yerba cana n [Span]

1 A ragwort (here: *Senecio longilobus*).

1976 Elmore *Shrubs & Trees SW* 74, *Threadleaf Groundsel* . . old man, squawweed, yerba cana [gray-hair plant].

2 =seepwillow.

1976 Elmore *Shrubs & Trees SW* 77, Seep-willow. . . Another native name is yerba cana, meaning "gray-hair plant," in reference to its flowers after they have gone to seed.

yerba del manso See **yerba mansa**

yerba del oso n [Span]

=coffeeberry 2a(1).

[**1860** *Amer. Jrl. Pharmacy* 32.413, The warm decoction of the leaves of *Rhamnus oleiflious* [sic] ("Yerba del Oso," of the Californian Spanish,) or even pure warm water, are sufficient sometimes to produce a cure [for the effects of poison oak.] **1880** Geol. Surv. CA *Botany* 2.439, *R[hamnus] Californica*. . . "Yerba del Oso." **1937** U.S. Forest Serv. *Range Plant Hdbk.* B127, California Buckthorn. . . variously known as coffeeberry, pigeonberry, yerba-del-oso, and cascara sagrada. **2007** Timbrook *Chumash Ethnobotany* 164 sCA, Several Chumash consultants commented that *yerba del oso* berries were food of the bear but they were poisonous to humans, and eating them would make a person crazy.

yerba del pasmo n Also *hierba del pasmo, yerba de pasmo* [Span; see quots]

1 A groundsel tree (here: usu *Baccharis pteronioides*). For other names of the latter see **burroweed 4**

1889 Amer. Acad. Arts & Sci. *Proc.* new ser 16.55, *Baccharis sarothroides*. . . "Yerba del pasmo"; the twigs are used as a remedy for toothache. **1931** U.S. Dept. Ag. *Misc. Pub.* 101.158, Yerba-de-pasmo. . . The vernacular name alludes to the common use by Indians and Mexicans of an infusion of the leaves as a remedy for chills. **1941** Jaeger *Wildflowers* 274 Desert SW, Broom Baccharis, Hierba del Pasmo. *Baccharis sarothroides*. . . Among certain Indians the twigs are chewed as a remedy for toothache. **1976** Elmore *Shrubs & Trees SW* 77, Seep-willow. . . yerba del pasmo—*Baccharis glutinosa* [=*B. salicifolia*]. **2004** Austin *FL Ethnobotany* 908, Among those known to contain these lactones is *B[accharis] pteronioides* (yerba-de-pasmo).

2 A California shrub (*Adenostoma sparsifolium*). Also called **redshank 3**

[**1897** Parsons *Wild Flowers CA* 61, Chamisal. . . This is commonly known among the Spanish-Californians as "Yerba del Pasmo," literally the "herb of the convulsion" . . being considered excellent for colds,

cramps, and snakebites, and an infallible cure for tetanus, or lockjaw.]
1931 U.S. Dept. Ag. *Misc. Pub.* 101.53, It is possible that it [=chamiso] and its congener, redshanks, sometimes called yerba del pasmo or rib-bon-wood *(A. sparsifolium),* may have medicinal properties. **1970** *DARE* Tape **CA**193, I used to go to the mountains and get these herbs for medicine. One was called yerba del pasmo. They used that for the little children. They get sick and get their fingernails turn purple, and they use that yerba del pasmo for them. **1987** *Jrl. Ethnobiology* 7.178 **CA**, One particularly desirable remedy, *Adenostoma sparsifolium,* called ribbonwood or yerba del pasmo, was formerly found in the Santa Ynez range and offshore islands.

yerba de mansa See **yerba mansa**

yerba de pasmo See **yerba del pasmo**

yerba de selva n [Span]
A trailing shrub *(Whipplea modesta)* of the Pacific coast. Also called **modesty 3**
   1938 Van Dersal *Native Woody Plants* 290, *Whipplea modesta. . . Yerba de selva. . .* A small trailing shrub. **1973** Hitchcock–Cronquist *Flora Pacific NW* 205, Yerba de Selva; Whipplevine. **2003** Beidleman–Kozloff *Plants San Francisco Bay* 274 **cwCA**, Our only representative is *Whipplea modesta . .* (Yerba-de-selva or Modesty), which grows in co-niferous forests from Monterey County northward.

yerba mansa n   Also *yerba de mansa, ~ del manso* [Span]
An herb *(Anemopsis californica)* of the south-central and southwestern US.   Also called **alkali weed 3, lizard's tail 2, swamp root 1**
   1866 in 1867 *Amer. Jrl. Pharmacy* 39.203 **NM**, The second root is that of 'Yerba mansa,' (mild herb). . . The root is gathered in autumn, when the flower has disappeared and the leaf is yellow. **1880** *Amer. Jrl. Pharmacy* 52.4 **CA**, In 1876 the writer received a specimen of the plant through the kindness of Dr. George, of California. It was known as "Yerba Mansa" in his neighborhood. **1914** Georgia *Manual Weeds* 85, *Yerba mansa. . .* The most troublesome part of this plant is its thick, creeping rootstock, which is very acrid, astringent, and strong-scented. **1920** Saunders *Useful Wild Plants* 200, The Indian is also to be thanked for our knowledge of Yerba Mansa (or more correctly, Yerba del Manso . .). . . It is one of the most popular of remedies among the Mexican population, who employ it also to relieve coughs and indiges-tion or pretty much anything. **1932** [see **yerba buena**]. **1940** Writers' Program *Guide NM* 15, Plants enter largely into native Indian ceremo-nial rites, . . oshá (mountain celery) and *yerba de mansa* (lizard's tail) are among those still gathered in New Mexico mountains as valuable foods and remedies. **1967** *DARE* (Qu. BB50a, . . *Favorite remedies . . for a cough)* Inf **CA**7, Mexicans used swamp plant compress—yerba mansa. **2004** Phillips *NM Gardener's Guide* 81, When starting yerba mansa in storm drainage basins and swales that flood periodically, use coarse gravel.

yerba salada n [Span]
An **evening primrose a** (here: *Oenothera pallida* subsp *tri-chocalyx*).
   [**1919** Chase *CA Desert* 375, Œnothera trichocalyx. Evening prim-rose: Span., Yerba salada.] **1932** Bentley *Spanish Terms* 216, *Yerba salada. . .* Evening primrose *(Oenothera trichocalyx. . .* A low, strong, rather spreading plant with large, rather narrow, grayish green leaves and very large fragrant flowers).

yerba santa n   Also *herba santa, hierba ~* [Span]
A shrub of the chiefly western genus *Eriodictyon,* usu *E. californicum.*   For other names of the latter see **bear's weed 1, consumptive's weed, gum plant 3, mountain balm 2, ~ bal-sam 3, tar bush, tarweed 1b(8), wild balsam 2**
   1872 *Pacific Med. & Surgical Jrl.* 6.360, Another California plant, Yerba Santa, (Eriodyction glutinosum,) Has been made the basis of a "patent" remedy for rheumatism, neuralgia, etc. **1884** *Lowell Weekly Sun* (MA) 6 Sept 8/3, A compound . . mixed with enough syrup of yerba santa to make the dose two ounces. **1887** *Overland Mth.* (2d ser) 10.153 **CA**, The lower growth . . is made up of . . cherry, manzanita, *herba santa,* or "mountain balm"—from which a medicine is prepared for pulmonary affections [etc]. **1894** *Jrl. Amer. Folkl.* 7.94 **CA**, *Erio-dictyon glutinosum. . .* palo santo, yerba santa. **1902** U.S. Natl. Mu-seum *Contrib. Herbarium* 7.381 **CA**, The well-known yerba santa (holy herb) of California, a dark-green, resinous shrub. **1932** [see **yerba buena**]. **1941** Jaeger *Wildflowers* 206 **Desert SW**, Woolly yerba santa. *Eriodictyon trichocalyx lanatum. Ibid,* Felt-leaved yerba santa. *Eriodic-tyon crassifolium.* **1967** *DARE* (Qu. BB50a, . . *Favorite remedies . . for*

a cough) Inf **CA**7, Mexicans . . chew yerba santa. **1976** Elmore *Shrubs & Trees SW* 49, Yerba (Hierba) Santa. . . Most plants that naturally emit strong aromas "naturally must be good for something." Yerba santa is no exception. **2008** (acc) U.S. Dept. Ag. *Plants Database* (Internet), *Eriodictyon californicum. . .* California yerba santa.

yere See **here A3**

yer guys(e)s See **your guys's(s)**

yerk v, n   Also *yawk, yuck* [*OED2 yerk* v. "Now *Sc.* and *dial.*"; *EDD yark* v.¹] esp **Sth, S Midl**   Cf **jerk** n¹ **A**
To pull, yank; to drag; to jerk; a sudden pull or jerk.
   1840 Haliburton *Clockmaker* (3d ser) 181 **NEng**, I'd larn him how to . . hold the whip atween his teeth, and to yawk the reins with both hands. **1867** Harris *Sut Lovingood Yarns* 297 **TN**, He yerk'd back a littil es the lick cum, an' hit went thru the dubil ove the hide. **1887** (1967) Harris *Free Joe* 103 **cGA**, Get her in the notion, an' she'll be a-yerkin' me aroun' thereckly like I wuz a rag-baby. **1899** (1912) Green *VA Folk-Speech* 494, Yerk. . . A sharp or sudden pull; a jerk. . . To pull sharply or suddenly; jerk; move with a jerk. *Ibid* 495, Yuck. . . To yerk; to jerk. **1909** *DN* 3.390 **eAL, wGA**, Yerk. . . To jerk. "We yerked him out of bed." **1976** Warner *Beautiful Swimmers* 54 **Chesapeake Bay**, Your drudge [=dredge] is like yerking on the bottom.

yerker n   Also sp *yurker*
In comb *little yerker:* A small child—also used as a term of address.
   1955 Roberts *S. from Hell-fer-Sartin* 193 **seKY**, When he come he told us little yerkers to get in the house and not to peep out anytime. **1960** *Oakland Tribune* (CA) 2 June sec I 2/8 **swVA**, It's funny. I used to call him my 'Little Yerker'. I don't know what it means. I just called him that. **1994** NC Lang. & Life Project *Dial. Dict. Lumbee Engl.* 13 **seNC**, Yurker. . . Mischievous child. *I'll get you for breaking that window, you little yurker!* **2009** *DARE* File—Internet **csNC**, That little yerker is ready for kindergarten.

yerlin(g) See **yearling**

yern See **yourn**

yerre See **hear A1b, A2d**

yerry See **hear A1b**

yerself See **your**

yes adv   Usu |jɛs|; for addit varr see below
Std senses, var forms.
1 |jæs|; pronc-spp *yaas, yas(s).* chiefly **Sth, S Midl** *esp freq among Black speakers*
   1852 *Harper's New Mth. Mag.* 5.849 **IL**, "What have you got to sell? Any thing?" asked the sheriff. "Yaas, sartin'; what would you like to hev?" **1883** (1971) Harris *Nights with Remus* 149 **GA** [Black], I kin des set up yer un lissen at um de whole blessid night. . . Yass, Lord! **1891** *DN* 1.120 **cNY**, Sometimes stressed [jæs] . . which may also be [jæːs], 'yes.' **1893** Shands *MS Speech* 68, Yaas [jæs]. The almost uni-versal pronunciation of yes. **1899** Chesnutt *Conjure Woman* 43 **csNC** [Black], He says yas, he could. **1909** *DN* 3.390 **eAL, wGA**, Yass, adv. Yes. The vowel is sometimes [ɑ] but more frequently [æ]. **1922** Gonza-les *Black Border* 339 **sSC, GA coasts** [Gullah glossary], Yaas—yes. **1923** (1951) Toomer *Cane* 30 **GA** [Black], To all these things she gave a yassur or nassur, without further comment. **1931** *AmSp* 6.166 **seVA**, In several recordings [jæs] is heard for yes. **1933** *AmSp* 8.4.59 **Delmarva**, *Yes* [jæs]. . . [jʌs], and [jəs] (unstressed) also occur. **1936** *AmSp* 11.15 **eTX**, *Yes* is [jæs] universally. **1942** Faulkner *Go Down* 70 **MS** [Black], "Yassuh," she said. **1943** *LANE* Map 588 *(Yes, yes sir; yes ma'am)* **NEng**, 4 infs, proncs of the types ['jæ(ə)s]. **1963** Owens *Look to River* 143 **TX** [Black], "You took it on yourself, didn't you?" "Yas, suh." **1967** *DARE* FW Addit **nwLA** [Black], Yes sir ['jæːˢɔ]. **1981** Pederson *LAGS Basic Materials,* 1 inf, **cnAL**, [jæˑᶜsm̩]; quoting an old Black woman who worked for her.
2 |jɪs|; pronc-sp *yis.* chiefly **NEng** [*OED2* "The pronuncia-tion [jɪs], still widespread in dialects, was formerly current in polite speech and is recorded as such in Walker's *Pronouncing Dict.*"] Cf **yet** adv, conj **A**
   1860 *Harper's New Mth. Mag.* 22.92 **Sth** [Black], Oh! lors, yis yer *be,* now; I *knows* yer be. **1871** (1882) Stowe *Fireside Stories* 118 **eMA**, Oh, sartin! why, yis. **1894** *DN* 1.341 **wCT**, Ea: the word yes (pron. [jɪs]) is used, but much oftener is heard [ɛɑ, ɛə, eə]. **1902** (1904) Rowe *Maid of Bar Harbor* 311 **ME**, "Why-y, yis," and the proffered hand was rather coolly accepted. **1904** *DN* 2.429 **Cape Cod MA** (as of a1857),

Yis, yis, adv. Yes, of course. **1907** *DN* 3.204 **seNH,** *Yis.* . . Yis, yis, I know all about it. **1943** *LANE* Map 588 *(Yes, yes sir, yes ma'am)* 22 infs, **scattered, but chiefly nNEng,** Proncs of the types [jɪ(ə)s]. **1985** Benes *Amer. Speech* 73 **cME coast** (as of a1847), The same vowel (of *bit*) also occurs in *been, yes, yesterday,* and *yet.*

3 |jɑs|.
1909 [see **1** above]. **1943** *LANE* Map 588 *(Yes, yes sir, yes ma'am)* 1 inf, **neRI,** [jɑs]. **1959** *VT Hist.* 27.167 **ne,nwVT,** Yes [jɑs] . . Franklin Co.

4 |'jeəs|.
1959 *VT Hist.* 27.167, Yes ['jeəs] . . Chittenden Co. **1968** *DARE* FW Addit **nwMD,** Yes ['jejəs]. **1981** Pederson *LAGS Basic Materials* 1 inf, **cAL,** ['jeᵛ·ɟᵘs]. **2008** *DARE* File **ceMO** [Black], The type of pronunciation . . [jeɪjəs] . . is quite or, even, extremely common in Black English. . . It's one of the features of B[lack] E[nglish] that I had to train myself not to use "in public," so to speak.

5 varr without initial palatal glide; pronc-sp *ace, assa* (for *yes sir*): See quots.
1935 Wolfe *Of Time* 96 **Upper MW,** "Ace," said Starwick, this strange sound which was intended for "yes" coming through his lips in the same curious and almost motionless fashion. **1941** O'Donnell *Great Big Doorstep* 39 **sLA** [Black], Assa [=yes, sir]. Ah din mean no harm.

6 addit varr: See quots.
1933 [see **1** above]. **1938** Matschat *Suwannee R.* 68 **neFL, seGA,** Well, 'spect ye have to larn sometime. Yerse. **1943** *LANE* Map 588 *(Yes, yes sir, yes ma'am)* **NEng,** 3 infs, proncs of the types [jʌ(ə)s]; 1 inf, **ceVT,** [jəs, jʊs, jɵs].

7 in phr *yes ma'am:* See quots. Cf **ma'am** n¹ **A**
1939 Harris *Purslane* 20 **cNC,** "I knew. Tell him to find some hog's hair under a rock soon as the moon comes up." "Yeb'm." **1944** *PADS* 2.15 **AL,** *Yes'm* [jɛhm, jæhm]. . . Negro; sometimes used by young whites of fairly high speech level. ((Also Va., N.C.; and Negro ['jɛbm̩, 'jæbm̩, jæm].))

yes-ma'am n ME Cf *DNE*
=**thank-you-ma'am 1.**
1966 *DARE* (Qu. N30, . . *A sudden short dip in a road*) Inf **ME**19, Yes-ma'am; **ME**5, Yes-ma'am—especially used when they had sleighs. **1975** Gould *ME Lingo* 326, *Yes-ma'am*—Heard more frequently in Maine than thank-you-marm for that unexpected dip or bump in the road that jolts the buggy seat. Let us assume a boy is dozing in school, and the teacher nudges him. He will awake with a start and say, "Yes, ma'am!" Thus *yes-marm* or thank-you-marm is a startle response, and suits very well when a bump in the road jerks you out of your socks. The hummock itself is called a *yes-marm.*

yesterday adv, n Usu |'jɛstə(r)ˌdɪ, -ˌde|; also **chiefly Sth, S Midl, occas NEast** |'jɪstɪˌdɪ| Pronc-spp *isterday, yestday, yestiddy, (y)istiddy;* for addit pronc and sp varr see quots [Spellings that indicate [ɪ] in the first syllable are attested from OE onwards, and the corresponding pronc was regarded as std by several of the 18th-cent orthoepists.] Cf **yet** adv, conj **A**
Std senses, var forms.
1835 *Family Mag.* (NY) 3.242 **VA** [Black], She wa'n't bawn 'istiddy. **1847** in 1956 Eliason *Tarheel Talk* 321 **cnNC,** *Yesterday*—yeasstieddy. **1880** Brown *My Southern Home* 120 [Black], Did dey sell you, 'isterday? **1891** *DN* 1.133 **cNY,** [jɪstɪdɪ] . . yesterday. **1893** Shands *MS Speech* 69, *Yistiddy* [jɪstɪdɪ]. Negro and illiterate white for *yesterday.* **1899** *Century Illustr. Mag.* 57.352 **LA** [Black], When I come heah a-seekin' 'istiddy mornin', I b'lieved in 'im. **1899** (1912) Green *VA Folk-Speech* 495, *Yistiddy.* **1902** *DN* 2.239 **sIL,** I made sure you was comin yestday. **1905** *DN* 3.58 **eNE,** Yestiddy. *Ibid* 103 **nwAR,** [jɪstɪdɪ]. **1909** *DN* 3.391 **eAL, wGA,** *Yistiddy.* . . Yesterday. **1910** *DN* 3.451 **cwNY,** *Yisterday.* . . Yesterday. **1914** *DN* 4.160 **cVA,** *Yestiddy.* . . Yesterday. **1915** *DN* 4.193 **swVA,** *Yisteday.* . . yesterday. **1917** *DN* 4.404 **neOH,** *Yisterday* [jɪstədɪ, jɪstɪdɪ]. **1923** *DN* 5.244 **LA,** *Yistiddy.* Pronunciation of *yesterday.* Also N. Eng. **1936** *AmSp* 11.16 **eTX,** *Yesterday,* among less literate speakers, is ['jɪstɪdɪ]. **1937** (1977) Hurston *Their Eyes* 271 **FL** [Black], Don't yuh remember him tellin' you dat yistiddy? **1952** Brown *NC Folkl.* 1.610, *Yistiddy* [jɪs'tɪdɪ]. . . *Yesterday.*—General. Illiterate. **1961** Kurath–McDavid *Pronc. Engl.* 134, *Yesterday* . . In folk speech, the first syllable of *yesterday* predominantly has the vowel /ɪ/ of *six* (1) in the South and the South Midland and (2) in large parts of New England. This pronunciation is less common in Upstate New York, rather infrequent anywhere in Pennsylvania, and decidedly rare in the heavily populated belt extending from eastern Pennsylvania . . to the lower Hudson Valley. In . . New York, Newark,

Philadelphia, and Baltimore it is no longer heard even from the folk. . . Several speakers in South Carolina and Georgia have the vowel /ʌ/ of *just* in *yesterday.* **1989** Pederson *LAGS Tech. Index* 18 **Gulf Region,** *Yesterday.* [Of 914 infs, 742 offered proncs of the types ['jɛstə(r)dɪ, -de, -di]; 47 infs, ['jɪstə(r)dɪ, -de, -di]; 9 infs, ['jæstə(r)dɪ, -de, -di]; 7 infs, ['jʌstə(r)dɪ, -de]; 10 infs, ['jɛštə(r)dɪ, -de, jɪštə·de]; 20 infs, ['jɛsə(r)dɪ, -de, -di, 'jɪsə·dɪ, -de, 'jʌsəde, 'jɛšə·dɪ]; 36 infs, two-syllable proncs of the types ['jɛs(t)dɪ, -de, -di, 'jɪs(t)dɪ, -de, 'jɛstɪ]; 1 inf, ['ɛstɪ̩dɪ].] **1990** Smith *Understanding Speaking S. Lang.* 9, *Yestady*—The day before to-day. **2000** Shores *Tangier Is.* 197 **Chesapeake Bay,** *Yesterday* . . "yisterdi."

yet adv, conj Usu |jɛt|; also **chiefly Sth, S Midl** |jɪt| Pronc-spp *yit,* rarely *yat* Cf **get A, pen** n¹ **A, yes 2, yesterday**
A Forms.
1794 in 1967 *PADS* 48.40 **NC,** *Yit*—'yet'. **1815** Humphreys *Yankey in England* 110, *Yit,* yet. **1849** in 1956 Eliason *Tarheel Talk* 321 **cnNC,** *Yet*—yat. **1894** Riley *Armazindy* 36 **IN,** Yit he'd be a *sweeter* singer / Ef he [=a bee] didn't have no stinger. **1903** *DN* 2.337 **seMO,** *Yit.* . . Yet. **1907** *DN* 3.204 **seNH,** *Yit.* . . Yet. *Ibid* 238 **nwAR,** "Have you lived here all your life?" "Not yit." **1909** *DN* 3.391 **eAL, wGA,** *Yit.* . . Yet. **1912** Green *VA Folk-Speech* 495, *Yit.* . . For *yet.* **1915** *DN* 4.193 **swVA,** *Yisteday, yit.* **1916** *DN* 4.340 **seOH,** Yet [jɪt]. **1931** *AmSp* 7.91 **eKY,** *Yit, yet.* Among the less literate. . . *yet* [jɪt]. **1942** Hall *Smoky Mt. Speech* 19 **wNC, eTN,** The raising of [ɛ] to [ɪ] was observed in . . *yet.* **1964** in 1982 *Barrick Coll.* **csPA,** *Yet*—pron. yit. **1969** Wilson *Stars* 75 **Ozarks,** Are they here yit?

B Senses.
1 Still, now as previously. [*OED2 yet* adv. 2.a. "arch. or *dial.* exc. in negative context."]
a in positive contexts. Cf *still yet* (at **still** adv **1**)
1836 *Sullivan Co Soldiers (Montgomery Coll.)* **TN,** Our company is altogether yet but one Charles Shely left us at Athens and is discharged from the service. **1856** in 1927 Jones *FL Plantation Rec.* 499 **nwFL,** Simond runaway yet, Nathan Com in this morning. **1912** Green *VA Folk-Speech* 494, *Yet.* . . For *still.* "It is there yet." **1919** *DN* 5.68 **NM** [Among hs students], We had some sinkers for breakfast and I can feel them yet. **1937** (1977) Hurston *Their Eyes* 261 **FL** [Black], Ah figgers de water is yet bad. It's bound tuh be. Too many dead folks been in it fuh it tuh be good tuh drink. **1966–70** *DARE* (Qu. FF21b, . . *About old jokes people say: "The first time I heard that one _____."*) Inf **MI**114, I was in the cradle yet; (Qu. KK27, *A very lively, active old person: "For his age, he's _____."*) Inf **ME**1, Awful smart yet. **1969–70** *DARE* FW Addit **neNC,** He lives there yet; **cwPA,** He's here yet. **1986** Pederson *LAGS Concordance,* 1 inf, **ceTN,** But we're here yet = we are here still; 1 inf, **cnLA,** He living yet; 1 inf, **ceAL,** I got one yet = I still have one; 1 inf, **ceTN,** I got some of hit out there in the woodshed yet; 1 inf, **nwMS,** I've got one of my forks back yonder yet = still; 1 inf, **cMS,** People grows those yet; 1 inf, **ceLA,** We got them here yet = still have them; 1 inf, **swMS,** Yet be looking sick; 1 inf, **csTX,** She's yet living; 1 inf, **swGA,** Mister Willy Jay yet living? 1 inf, **neTN,** Pretty good shape yet—of a building; There's a lot of them yet; 1 inf, **neTN,** There's a lot of them does that yet. **1994** NC *Lang. & Life Project Dial. Dict. Lumbee Engl.* 13 **seNC,** *Yet.* . . Still. Now used only by older people with this meaning. A similar use is found in Irish English and a few small dialect areas in England. *He eats a lot of fish yet.* **2004** *DARE* File **swWI,** Tried to work on NSF budget; need access and am working on getting that—yet. **2008** *DARE* File **csWI,** There's a chance we may be doing this tomorrow yet.

b in interrogative contexts.
1967 *DARE* FW Addit **OR,** *Yet*—used rather than *still:* Are they there yet? **1978** *DARE* File **sePA,** And is your Mother living yet? *Ibid* **csWI,** My colleague had seen me using her stapler, so I didn't understand what she meant when she asked, "Are you using the stapler yet?" I would have asked, "Are you still using the stapler?" **1981** WI *Acad. Trans.* 85, The third construction under discussion is the use of 'yet' to mean 'still'. The sentence used in the study was, "Is there turkey yet?" asked by someone arriving late to a Thanksgiving dinner who wants to know if some turkey remains to be eaten. . . This type of sentence is primarily used in rural counties across the central part of the state. **2001** *DARE* File **MI,** I've been chewed out in the Northeast for saying the following: "Are you awake yet?" to someone at midnight when they have not been to bed already. . . It seems natural and normal to me.

2 in phrr *(up) till yet, (up) until yet:* Still, to this day, even now; usu yet. **chiefly Sth, S Midl**
1847 *Living Age* 14.619 **West,** I'd staid till yet if it had n't been for old Scott. **1872** U.S. Congress *Rept. Joint Select Comm. Insurrectionary*

States 6.549 **GA,** If they had whipped on until yet it would not have made much odds. **1884** *Anglia* 7.273 **Sth, S Midl** [Black], To be livin' clean tell yit = to be alive now. **1910** *Santa Fe Employes' Mag.* Oct 102 **OK,** We . . have been looking for John to bring down a box of perfectos, but up till yet we are still "looking." **1916** in 2009 (acc) Lexis–Nexis Legal Research *State Case Law: OK* (Internet), I wrote C.C. Smith a bout the baby but got no ancures up till yet. **1918** Whitaker *Hist. Corporal Fess Whitaker* 117 **seKY,** Up until yet he is still an outlaw. **1921** Haswell *Daughter Ozarks* 44 (as of 1880s), So even till yit the Bald Knobbers is a' workin' off and on. **1923** *DN* 5.223 **swMO,** He aint come till yit. **1938** in Lib. of Congress *Amer. Memory: WPA Life Hist.* (Internet) **cSC,** I reckon I'd a been livin' in a sawdus' pile till yet if old man Musser could 'er foun' more pines. *Ibid* **cNC,** Until yet I don't know how we lived through that winter. **1965** Will *Okeechobee Boats* 51 **FL,** Some of them cabbage trees are still growing there till yet. **2005** Stanberry *Mt. Echoes* 26 **NC,** Until yet, tears flow when I smell yeast-risen bread baking. Never can I duplicate my mother's sourdough bread.

3 in phr *yet and still* (pronc-sp *yet unstill*): Nevertheless, however. **chiefly Sth, S Midl** *chiefly among Black speakers* Cf **still** adv **3**

1898 Dunbar *Folks from Dixie* 175 **VA** [Black], Yet an' still, Bess, you ain't nuffin but a dumb beas'. **1927** *Jrl. Amer. Folkl.* 40.220 **cMS** [Black], Y'know Rabbit always been a wise critter but yet an' still somebody gits away wid him some time. **c1937** in Lib. of Congress *Amer. Memory: WPA Life Hist.* (Internet) **GA** [Black], They laid it on hard en heavy, yet en still he never *stayed* whipped. **1959** Lomax *Rainbow Sign* 37 **AL** [Black], Cose we didn't know what we was doin . . , but yet unstill in a way we did. **1970** in 1983 Walker *In Search of Gardens* 22 **MS** [Black], [Title:] "But Yet and Still the Cotton Gin Kept on Working. . . " **1986** Pederson *LAGS Concordance,* 4 infs, **FL, GA, LA,** (But) yet and still = nevertheless; 1 inf, **cLA,** He [=Elvis Presley] came from nowhere, with nothing, and yet and still, he got to the top; 2 infs, **AL,** Yet and still. [5 of 7 infs Black] **1996** Coleman *Afr.-Amer. Stories* 76 **Chicago IL** [Black], I was always taught that two wrongs don't make a right. Yet and still I saw society doing something equally as bad to the "wrongdoers." **1999** (2004) Souljah *Coldest Winter* 13 **Brooklyn NYC** [Black], The warmth in the house invited us in, yet and still Santiaga lit the fireplace.

4 Used as a weak intensive or interrogative particle. [Prob calque of Ger (and PaGer) *doch*] **esp in Ger settlement areas**

1913 Johnson *Highways St. Lawrence to VA* 257 **MD,** We have to board our hired pickers, and some keep 'em over night yet. **1934** *Language* 10.3 **cPA,** Do you want these things this morning yet? **1935** *AmSp* 10.167 **PA** [Engl of PA Germans], What will you have yet? **1948** *WELS Suppl.,* Typically Wisconsinan I believe . . [is] "yet" . . as in "How was that yet?" **1958** *AmSp* 33.232, The *yet* from Pennsylvania German is a general intensive, as in 'What will you have yet?' or a substitute for *too,* as in 'Do you want to be fanned yet?' **1994** in 1996 Huth *Famil. Words* 113 **csPA,** I'm looking for *pumpkin* yet. *Ibid,* Geof, we don't need anything. Do we have enough wrapping paper yet? **1995** *Ibid,* I have found two fitted ones [=sheets] yet. **2001** *DARE* File **seSD,** By the way, people up here often attach "yet" to end of sentences. For instance, "I need to go to the bank yet," "Is that a bottle of gin yet?" "Let's eat dinner at eight yet." **2006** *DARE* File—Internet **MN,** Do you have to do that yet?

ye't n   See **earth**

yet already   See **already B2**

yet and still   See **yet** adv, conj **B3**

yeth   See **earth**

yet unstill   See **yet** adv, conj **B3**

yeu   See **you** pron¹ **A1**

yeur   See **here A3**

yew n

1 Std: a shrub or tree of the genus *Taxus.* For other names of var spp see **Florida yew, ground hemlock, juniper 2d, mountain mahogany 4, shinwood, snake bush**
2 =**California nutmeg.** Cf **stinking yew**

    1897 Sudworth *Arborescent Flora* 102 **ID,** *Tumion californicum* [= *Torreya c.*] . . Common Names. . . Yew.

yew pron   See **you** pron¹ **A1**

yew pine n

1 =**red spruce. chiefly WV** Note: At one time this was regarded as a variety of the black spruce.

    1847 in 1940 *AmSp* 15.409 **VA,** To a small sugar and beech & large yew pine near a Water Fall over a rock. **1861** *Daily Richmond Examiner* (VA) 7 Sept 2/4 **WV,** This mountain [=Cheat Mountain] is densely wooded with lashorn, which we had thought peculiar to white top, but here it is called by the more appropriate and perhaps more correct name of yew pine. [*DARE* Ed: Despite identification with **lashhorn,** this is probably *Picea rubens.*] **1870** Pollard *VA Tourist* 262, The white and yew pines, white oak, locust [etc] . . and the rivers of the region are all adapted to the transportation of lumber. **1894** *Jrl. Amer. Folkl.* 7.100 **WV,** *Picea nigra* . . yew-pine, spruce-pine. **1913** Millspaugh *Living Flora WV* 200, *P[icea] rubens* . . Black spruce. "Yew Pine." "White Spruce." "Spruce Pine." **1926** *WV Legislative Hdbk.* 508, It came to me . . that a new generation knew not the language of the old. In those days that [=yew pine] was the only name we had for the black spruce. "He calls yew pine spruce," was the old-time criticism of the northerner. **1927** *AmSp* 2.226, The *yew pine* is a term widely used in West Virginia for the *red spruce.* The *Yew Pine Mountains* are located in Nicholas County. **1952** Strausbaugh–Core *Flora WV* 46, *P[icea] rubens.* . . Sometimes called Yew Pine in West Virginia.

2 A **hemlock 2** (here: *Tsuga canadensis*).

    1913 *Rhodora* 15.105 **eMD,** While on a botanical trip to the Eastern Shore . . Mr. Stevens of Queen Anne, Md., took me to a colony of what the inhabitants called the "yew-pine." . . I was astonished to find a large number of *Tsuga canadensis* lining both banks of the [Tuckahoe] river.

yez   See **youse**

yi   See **you** pron¹ **A2**

Yid n   Also *Yit* [*OED2* 1874 →; < Yiddish *Yid* Jew] **chiefly Nth, N Midl, Pacific** See Map   *freq derog*
A Jew.

    1898 *Harper's New Mth. Mag.* 98.38 **NYC,** In two very popular operas I saw . . , a Yiddish maiden becomes alienated from her people and tastes all the splendor and the power of Christendom. . . It seems as if there is no end of bouquets to be thrown at almost any young Yid who goes out from among her people. Fate haled the wanderers back. . . "Ein Yid bleibt ewig ein Yid!" exclaims Rabbi Shabshi's daughter at the last. **1910** *Lowell Sun* (MA) 11 Feb 4/7, Both men are "yids" and when they started out by sparring carefully the crowd immediately scented a frame-up. . . But it was no frame-up and the pair went at it hammer and tongs. **1915** *DN* 4.236 **neOH** [College slang], *Yid.* . . 1. A Jew. 2. A very selfish fellow. **1941** *LANE* Map 455 (*Nicknames for a Jew*) 7 infs, **CT, ME, MA,** Yid. **1964** *PADS* 42.32 **Chicago IL** [Terms of abuse], Terms used abusively for *Jew.* . . *yiddish, yiddisher, yid, yit. Ibid* 34, Among better educated informants, *yid, yit, yiddisher,* and *yiddish* have wider currency [than *sheeny, Hebrew,* and *Hebe*]. **1965–70** *DARE* (Qu. HH28, *Names and nicknames . . for people of foreign background*) 32 Infs, **chiefly Nth, N Midl, Pacific,** Yid; [**NY**12, **WA**16, Yiddy]. **1970** Lebofsky *Lexicon Philadelphia* 168, *Jew.* . . *yid* [was recognized] by 47% [of 76 total infs] (by 100% of Jews). . . the more educated the informant, the more likely it was that he had heard of. . . *yid* . . which was known more to men . . than women. **1986** Pederson *LAGS Concordance (Jews)* 2 infs, **AL,** Yid(s). **1992** *Pacific Stars & Stripes* 25 July 11 **NYC,** I was also chased home regularly by my schoolmates. . . And they told me . .

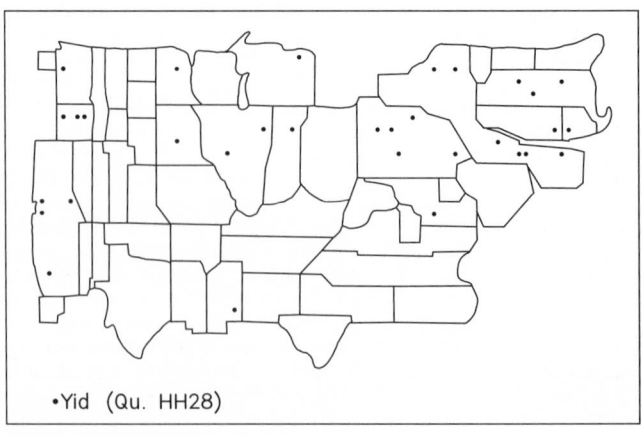

•Yid (Qu. HH28)

that "the Yids have all the money in the world." When they found out that I was one Yid who didn't have any money, they beat me for being a "cheap penny Jew." **2007** *Contra Costa Times* (Walnut Creek CA) 10 Dec (Internet), This Christmas Eve, instead of hiding in a box of mu shu chicken, head to Latke Ball, the Bay Area's biggest party for young Yids. Finally, it's fun to be Jewish on Christmas.

Yiddish adj [Yiddish *yid(d)ish* Jewish]
Jewish.
  1897 Moss *Amer. Metropolis* 3.179 **NYC,** Among the alien spellbinders who occasionally stray into these wards to charm Yiddish votes into Tammany columns, is the Irish barrister Tommy Nolan. **1898** [see **Yid**]. **1917** *Newark Advocate* (OH) 28 Aug 3/4, Our old friend, Rube Fulkerson . . and Flo Wagner . . in a screaming Yiddish act, "The Yiddisher and the Suffragette." **1950** *WELS (Jewish)* 8 Infs, **WI,** Yiddish. **1956** Ker *Vocab. W. TX* 369, *Jew (nicknames)*. . . Yiddish. [2 of 67 infs] **1964** [see **Yid**]. **1965–70** *DARE* (Qu. HH28, *Names and nicknames . . for people of foreign background*) Infs **CA**9, **MI**51, **NJ**55, **NY**12, **PA**11, 167, **VA**11, Yiddish. **1986** Pederson *LAGS Concordance (Jews)* 1 inf, **seFL,** Yiddish.

Yiddisher n, also attrib [*OED2* 1859 →]
A Jew.
  1902 *Frank Leslie's Pop. Mth.* 53.364 **NYC,** I've watched you acting several times, and you seemed to me so completely the East Side Yiddisher, that I couldn't picture you as anything else. **1917** [see **Yiddish**]. **1926** *Daily Herald* (Middletown NY) 1 Sept 4/4, The Yiddisher considers his money well spent [in the theater] if he is vouchsafed merely a couple of good cries. **1940** *San Antonio Light* (TX) 15 Feb sec A 8/5, Sammy Menacher, the smiling Yiddisher, polished off Mike Fraley, a newcomer from California, in the three-fall opener. **1950** *WELS (Jewish)* 1 Inf, **cWI,** Yiddisher. **1964** [see **Yid**]. **1967–68** *DARE* (Qu. X14, *Joking words for the nose*) Inf **OR**3, Nose like a Yiddisher; (Qu. HH28, *Names and nicknames . . for people of foreign background*) Infs **CT**4, **OR**3, Yiddisher.

yieldy adj [*OED2* 1598 →; "*rare*"] **Midl**
Of a crop, field, etc: fertile, productive.
  1853 OH State Bd. Ag. *Annual Rept. for 1852* 311, "Long Johns," [= potatoes] and big yellow pink eyes are preferred for stock, as being most yieldy. **1866** MO State Bd. Ag. *Annual Rept. for 1865* 108, The first [variety of tobacco] is most generally grown . . and generally is more yieldy. **1870** *Cincinnati Daily Gaz.* (OH) 25 Jan 4/5 **ceIL,** Of the common white there are varieties that are earlier, equally as yieldy and cook as well. **1879** IN State Bd. Ag. *Annual Rept. for 1878* 255, The Fultz wheat . . has proved to be the most certain and yieldy crop in this country. **1912** *IA Homestead* 10 Oct 15, They are very yieldy, one set often sending up two to five or six stalks. **1924** Raine *Land of Saddle-Bags* 102 **sAppalachians,** Hits good wheat, but not very *yieldy* on the ground. **1928** *Engl. Jrl.* 17.811 **eKY,** If a body's puney and his land ain't yieldy . . peers to me the good Lord won't fault him for hit! **1933** *AmSp* 8.1.53 **Ozarks,** That 'ar west bottom never was much yieldy, nohow. **1952** in 1968 Haun *Hawk's Done Gone* 290 **eTN,** I think I'll have a yieldy crap this year. **1997** in 2004 Montgomery–Hall *Dict. Smoky Mt. Engl.* 665 **wNC, eTN,** *Yieldy* . . Of land: productive; of a crop: abundant. . . [6 infs].

yillow See **yellow** adj, n[1] **A5**

yingin See **onion** n

yinnah, yinner See **una**

yins, yinz See **you-uns** pron[1]

Yinzer n Also *Yunzer* [From the use of *yinz* or *yunz* (at **you-uns** pron[1])] **wPA**
One who lives in or near Pittsburgh, Pennsylvania, esp one who has characteristic local dialect features; hence adjs *Yinzer, Yunzer* typical of such a person.
  1994 *Pittsburgh Post-Gaz.* (PA) 14 May sec C 12 (Internet), [Caption:] The Warhol Museum: Volkwein's reborn. But how many yunzers will walk in looking for sheet music? **1998** Shepard et al. *Coming to Class* 8 **wPA,** Many Pittsburghers speak in a clearly identifiable dialect, which include [*sic*] saying "yinz" for "you all". . . CMU students sometimes derogatorily refer to someone who speaks like this as a "yinzer." **2007** Englebretson *Stancetaking* 49 **wPA,** When "authentic" Pittsburghers . . are described or parodied, local speech is almost invariably mentioned or performed. . . One way to attribute a quintessentially local identity to a person is to label him or her a *yinzer,* a word derived from

the local variant of the second-person-plural pronoun, *yinz*. **2007** *DARE* File—Internet **Pittsburgh PA,** I guess it is a kind of yunzer fusion cooking, being essentially an Italian Wedding Soup, crossed with Matzoh Ball Soup. [Footnote to *yunzer:*] "Yunzer" is a Pitt[s]burghese expression, meaning, essentially "of Pittsburgh, without regard for embarassing one's friends and/or relations"; antonym: yuppie. . . It was not until I first heard my own recorded speaking voice some years ago, that I realized, with mingled horror and perverse pride, that I kind of have some yunzer qualities myself. **2010** *Ibid* **Pittsburgh PA,** I swear that for most of my life the term was Yunzer, with a "U". Yet it is always Yinzer these days. *Ibid* **Pittsburgh PA,** She is a *true* yinzer. . . she still says n'at, warsh, gum band, dahn-tahn and all that. *Ibid,* Lawrenceville is still pretty yinzer though. **2010** *DARE* File **Pittsburgh PA,** Have you heard of a "Yinzer left?" As a customary courtesy, Pittsburgh drivers stopped at a light allow the first oncoming car to make a left turn before they proceed through the intersection.

yis adv See **yes 2**

yis v See **be A3**

yistiddy See **yesterday**

yit adv, conj See **yet** adv, conj

Yit n See **Yid**

yiz pron See **youse**

yiz v See **be A3**

yo n See **ewe** n

yo pron See **you** pron[1] **A3**

yo(ah) adj See **your**

yo all See **you-all**

Yobo n [Korean *yobo* used as a familiar, second-person form of address, esp among married couples] **HI**
A Korean or person of Korean descent.
  1967 *DARE* (Qu. HH28, *Names and nicknames . . for people of foreign background*) Inf **HI**13, Yobos—Koreans. **1972** Carr *Da Kine Talk* 109 **HI,** *Yobo* 'Korean', a term used humorously by non-Koreans. **1998** Pak *Ricepaper Airplane* 83 **HI** (as of 1928), You friggin' dumb Yobo! **2003** Keller et al. *Yobo: Korean American Writing in Hawai'i* [title].

yoe See **ewe** n

yoe-necked See **ewe-neck**

yoke pastor n Also *yoke minister*
A clergyperson serving two congregations.
  1966 *Sanford Tribune* (ME) 28 Apr 4/2, [He] will assume his duties as yoke pastor of the Limerick Congregational and the West Newfield Congregational Churches on Sunday. **1977** *Pharos–Tribune* (Logansport IN) 19 July 20/4, The Rev. Ernest Laughner . . recently became yoke pastor of Flora Baptist and Sharon Baptist churches. **2007** *DARE* File—Internet **WV,** In 1965, our church joined with the Lumberport Baptist Church and shared a yoke pastor. **2008** in 2009 *Ibid* **csNJ,** We had our yoke minister preach today. He is minister with the Millville Church and we have joined together. He preaches there at 9:30 and here at 11:00.

yolk n Usu |jok|; also |jolk, jɔlk, jɛlk, jʌlk|; for addit varr see **A** below
A Forms.
  1 |jolk, jɔlk|. **widespread, but esp Nth, Midl** See Map on p. 1126
  1892 *DN* 1.242 **cwMO,** Yolk. Fully four forms of this word are in use in Kansas City: [jok, jolk, jɑlk, jɛlk]. *Ibid* **WI,** My natural pronunciation is [jʌlk]. **1896** *DN* 1.452 **NY,** Yolk—41 [infs] [jok]—50 [jɑlk]—10 [jɔlk]—29 [jɛlk]—5 [jælk]. **1936** *AmSp* 11.313 **'Upstate' NY,** Simple variation in the use of [l] is illustrated by [jok], [jolk], and [jʌlk] for *yolk*. **1961** Kurath–McDavid *Pronc. Engl.* 160, *Yolk*. . . The type of /jolk ~ jɵlk/ . . is especially common in New England, and less so in the New England settlements to the west. In this entire area the checked /ɵ/ of *stone, coast* occurs besides the free /o/ of *no*, and predominates decidedly in Eastern New England. Cultured speakers use /jolk ~ jɵlk/ as freely as /jok/. Outside the New England settlement area, /jolk/ occurs fairly frequently in the Lower South, rarely elsewhere, apparently as a prestige pronunciation. **1965–70** *DARE* (Qu. H34, . . *The parts of an egg*) 116 Infs, **widespread, but esp Nth, Midl,** Yolk [jo(ʊ)lk]; 12 Infs, **scattered,** Yolk [jɔlk]. **1976** Allen *LAUM* 3.257 **Upper MW** (as of c1950), *Yolk*. . . In the U[pper] M[idwest] the pronunciation /jok/ has be-

come the expanding form, with dominance in all states but Iowa, where it is evenly matched with /jolk/. . . more than one-half of the users of /jolk/ are in Type I [=old, with an 8th grade education or less]. . . /jɔlk/ [2 infs, **NE**].

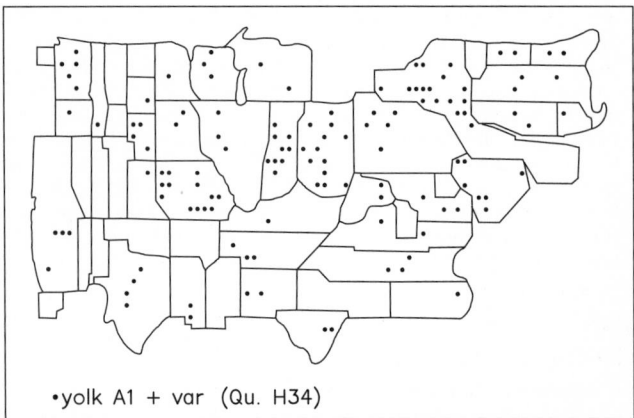

•yolk A1 + var (Qu. H34)

2 |jɛlk|; infreq |jælk|; rarely |ɛlk|; pronc-spp *(y)elk. old-fash*
1789 Webster *Dissertations Engl. Lang.* 123, The word *yelk* is sometimes written *yolk* and pronounced *yoke.* But *yelk* is the most correct orthography, from the Saxon *gealkwe;* and in this country, it is the general pronunciation. **1839** Randolph *VA Housewife* 15, Have the yelk of an egg well beaten. **1845** Kirkland *Western Clearings* 57 **MI**, The harvest moon rises . . like "the yelk of an egg that's been froze." **1892** [see **1** above]. **1896** [see **1** above]. **1899** (1912) Green *VA Folk-Speech* 494, *Yelk.* **1903** *DN* 2.291 **Cape Cod MA** (as of a1857), *Yelk.* **1905** [see **5** below]. **1907** *DN* 3.187 **seNH**, *Elk.* . . Yolk of an egg. **1909** *DN* 3.390 **eAL, wGA**, *Yelk.* . . Yolk of an egg. *Yolk* is rarely heard. **1912** *DN* 3.593 **wIN**, *Yelk.* **1941** *LANE* Map 296 *(Yolk)* **widespread throughout NEng**, [jɛlk]. [Commentary:] Pronunciations of the type of [jɛlk, jælk] are described as usual, most natural or most common by [8 infs]; as old-fashioned but natural by [7 infs]; as less common or rare by [3 infs]; and as older or old-fashioned though still in use by [22 infs]. Pronunciations of the type of [ɛlk] are described as older or old-fashioned though still in use by [6 infs]. **1949** Webber *Backwoods Teacher* 84 **Ozarks**, The ones [=pupils] who were most enthusiastic about discussing this word were from the homes where the pronunciation was "yolk." They felt a little superior to the ones who, in the minority, declared that while Gran'pa or Gran'ma said "yelk," they themselves did not. **1957** *DE Folkl. Bulletin* 1.28, Yelk. **1961** Kurath–McDavid *Pronc. Engl.* 160, *Yolk.* . . /jɛlk/, riming with *elk,* is the most common folk pronunciation . . in the greater part of the Eastern States. It is also widely used by middle-class speakers in parts of New England, New Jersey, and West Virginia, and throughout the tidewater area of the South. . . This pronunciation is even current in the cultivated speech of the South, occasionally also elsewhere. On the other hand, /jelk/ is of rare occurrence in Pennsylvania (except for the northern counties settled from New England) and the greater part of the southern upland, where /jok/ prevails. **1965–70** *DARE* (Qu. H34, . . *The parts of an egg*) 65 Infs, **scattered**, Yelk [jɛ(ə)lk]; 12 Infs, **scattered**, Yelk [no transcr]. [Of all Infs responding to the question, 70% were old, 28% gs educ or less; of those giving this response, 88% were old, 45% gs educ or less.] **1965** *PADS* 43.15 **seMA**, The parts of an egg . . yelk [1 of 9 infs]. **1971** Bright *Word Geog. CA & NV* 178, *Yolk.* . . *yelk,* 9% [of 300 infs]. **1976** Allen *LAUM* 3.257 **Upper MW** (as of c1950), *Yolk.* . . The folk pronunciation /jelk/ retains enough vitality to be used among the lesser educated in the eastern half of the U[pper] M[idwest] but it seems unable to endure life on the western prairies. **1981** Pederson *LAGS Basic Materials,* 1 inf, **cAL**, [jeˀlk]—father's term; 1 inf, **cwAR**, They used to be called [jeˑˀlks]. **1994** *DARE* File, My father, who grew up in southeastern Iowa, calls the yellow part of an egg the "yelk."

3 |jʌlk|; jʊlk|; pronc-sp *yulk. old-fash*
1892 [see **1** above]. **1899** (1912) Green *VA Folk-Speech* 495, *Yulk.* . . The yellow part of an egg. *Yuck.* **1936** [see **1** above]. **1937** *AmSp* 12.239 **NE**, A common pronunciation of the word *yolk* in Nebraska is *yulk,* rhyming with 'bulk.' **1941** *LANE* Map 296 *(Yolk)* 6 infs, **CT, MA**, [jʊlk]. **1961** Kurath–McDavid *Pronc. Engl.* 160, *Yolk.* . . Even /jʌlk/ and /jʊlk/ still survive among the better educated, notably in New England. **1965–70** *DARE* (Qu. H34, . . *The parts of an egg*) 36 Infs, **scattered**, Yulk [jʌlk]; [**VA**48, [jʊlk]]. [32 Infs old] **1971** Bright *Word Geog. CA & NV* 178, *Yolk.* . . *yulk,* 6% [of 300 infs]. **1976** Allen

LAUM 3.257 **Upper MW** (as of c1950), *Yolk.* . . /jʌlk/ remains a minor variant in the U[pper] M[idwest], where the background of most of its users hints at its northeastern origin, even two of the three Nebraskans having Ohio or New York parentage.

4 |jɒlk, jɑlk|.
1892 [see **1** above]. **1896** [see **1** above]. **1941** *LANE* Map 296 *(Yolk)* **esp nNEng**, 20 infs, [jɒlk]; 2 infs, [jɑlk]. **1961** [see **3** above]. **1966–70** *DARE* (Qu. H34, . . *The parts of an egg*) Infs **CT**21, 29, **PA**23, [jɒlk]; **TX**62, **WA**1, [jɑlk].

5 pronc-spp *yahk, yuck;* See quots.
1899 [see **3** above]. **1905** *DN* 3.67 **eNE**, *Yolk.* . . Current variants are [jɛlk], [jɔk], [jɑk], [jʌk]. **1937** *AmSp* 12.104 **eNE** [Farm terms], *Yolks* of eggs are sometimes called . . *yahks.* **1968** *DARE* (Qu. H34, . . *The parts of an egg*) Inf **NY**96, [jeək]; **IL**27, [jʌk]; **MN**13, [jɑk]. **1976** Allen *LAUM* 3.257 **Upper MW** (as of c1950), *Yolk.* . . The single instance of /jɔk/ in Iowa is possibly related to the northeastern /ɒ/, but the connection with the two Nebraska examples of /jɔlk/ is uncertain.

B Sense.

Also *white yolk:* the "white" or albumen of an egg.   Cf **yellow B**
1941 *LANE* Map 296, 2 infs, **RI**, Yelk, the white of the egg; 1 inf, **ceCT**, Yellow yelk, to distinguish from white yelk, the white of the egg. **1965–74** *McDavid Coll.,* 3 infs, **GA**, Yolk = white. **1966–70** *DARE* (Qu. H34, . . *The parts of an egg*) Inf **MS**85, Yolk—the white part; **OK**26, Yolk—is white. **1986** Pederson *LAGS Concordance,* 24 infs, **Gulf Region**, Yolk [=the white of an egg].

yoller n[1]   See **yellow** adj, n[1] **A3**

yoller n[2]   [Prob < *EDD yoller* "To bellow, bawl. . . To bark noisily"; cf **holler, holler, dogs you foller**]
A type of **hide-and-seek A;** see quot 1904.
[**1896** *DN* 1.427 **nOH**, *Yellow:* the game of *hunt the gray wolf.*] **1904** *Outing* 44.275 **NYC**, The hi-spy class includes, among many others, ringalevio (Brooklyn name), kick-the-wicket, . . Yankee-dar-oo, (or nar-oo) (Harlem and Bronx) and Yoller. . . In Yankee-dar-oo, as the hiders, or hares, are caught they have to pitch in and help the hounds; and yoller is a version of yankee-dar-oo for after-dark use, in which the hound need only see the hare to have caught him. **1935** Young *Source Book Sociol.* 12, We . . played games of activity and running such as dodge baseball, "Yoller," and "Run Sheep Run." **1966** Fuller *Burns Fuller Remembers* 63 **MI**, Left behind were all of those kid games like marbles, yoller, kite-flying, and the like. **1987** *ND Qrly.* Spring 108, "Well, a bunch of us were playing Yoller in the woods"—Yoller's a kind of ninth-grade-on-the-way-to-tenth form of hide-and-seek.

yoller, holler, we shan't foller   See **holler, holler, dogs you foller**

yollop n, v, hence vbl n *yolloping* [*EDD yollop, yollup* (at *yellop*)]
A yelp; to yelp.
1887 (1895) Robinson *Uncle Lisha* 55 **wVT**, Folks was extry tired an' wantin' t' sleep more 'n common but couldn't, 'caount o' his 'tarnal bow-wowin' an' yollopin'. **1897** Robinson *Uncle Lisha's Outing* 303 **wVT**, That 's the sort o' pussycat an' dogs 'at used for tu be a-yaowlin' an' a-yollopin' raound yer gran'ser's campfire. **1959** *VT Hist.* 27.167, *Yollop:* n. and v. Bark; howl: The yollop of a dog. Rare.

yollow   See **yellow** adj, n[1] **A3**

yon adj, pron, adv, n   Usu |jɑn|; also **esp Sth, S Midl** |jæn| Pronc-spp *yan(d), yond, yont*   **scattered, but chiefly Sth, S Midl, esp sAppalachians**

A As adj.

1 That, those—freq used to indicate a visible person, place, or object pointed out. [*OED2 yon* dem. a. A.1 c897 →; "Now *arch.* and *dial.*"]   Cf **yonder C1, yonway**
1824 *NY Mirror* 1.182, You, Mr. Blythe, right there by that there big pumpkin on yon side of the room, and you Miss Molly on his left. **1837** Sherwood *Gaz. GA* 72, *Yont,* for yonder;—as *yont* house. **1843** (1916) Hall *New Purchase* 459 **IN**, Jist go round to yan crib, and git what cawn you like. **1887** (1967) Harris *Free Joe* 16 **GA**, I haint bin no furder from my shop than to yon bed. **1894** in 1942 Hall *Smoky Mt. Speech* 29 **NC**, All the answer he made was, "It's like a lady's fan. You can turn it over yan way or this way." **1895** *DN* 1.371 **seKY, eTN, wNC**, *Coast:* region. By a mountaineer: "I live on yon coast." **1905** *DN*

3.101 nwAR, Yon. . . 'Yon plank will do.' Not uncommon. **1907** *DN* 3.228 **nwAR,** *Yan* [jæn] *adj.* Yon. **1909** *DN* 3.401 **nwAR,** We taken some bird nestes out of yon trees. **1919** in 2009 (acc) Lexis–Nexis Legal Research *State Case Law: KY* (Internet), I could see them with their guns going that way and yon way, and I was laying there waiting for the sheriff. **1923** *DN* 5.225 **swMO,** *Yan*. . . Yon, that. "Han' me yan ax." **1944** *PADS* 2.52 **NC, VA,** *Yan, yon* [jæn, jɑn]: *adj.* and *adv.* That way or direction; a demonstrative word generally accompanied by pointing in the direction meant. **1950** Stuart *Hie Hunters* 187 **eKY,** After ye turn at yan end, be shore to hold Dinah up on the hard ground and let old Dick walk down in the furrow. **1952** Brown *NC Folkl.* 1.609, *Yan: adj.* and *adv.* . . Yonder. **1969** Wilson *Stars* 75 **Ozarks,** I done hung a whup strap in yon closet. **1976** Garber *Mountain-ese* 103 **sAppalachians,** He lives in a yaller house jist over yan hill. **2004** *DARE* File **sAppalachians** (as of 1961), I had a (white) Appalachian-speaking buddy for whom "yon" as an adjective was a living part of his vocabulary. He could say things like, "Let's go have a drink in yon bar."

2 also with *the:* The farther, other—freq in combs *(the) yon side, (the) yon end.* [*OED2 yon* dem. a. A.2 1700 → ("local"), *yonside* sb. A 1535 →; cf also *yond* a.[1] A.1] Cf **yonder C2, yonside**

1854 *Knickerbocker* 43.319 **ceNJ,** Him as married *George Prevost's* darter, and lived down on yon side of the creek? **1857** *Ibid* 50.574 **West,** Will you gie us ten dollars to put you on yan' side? **1888** *Century Illustr. Mag.* 36.898 **sAppalachians,** I'm goin' ter th' yan side er th' mountain ter-morrer. **1890** *Scribner's Mag.* 7.58 **AR,** [Letter:] They live on yon side of Running Watter. Rite on your road. **1901** *Land of Sunshine* 14.28 **West,** A pretty sure welcome has been standing in this office for MSS. . . with the postmark "Humboldt, Nev."—if you chance to know where that dot of the map is on "yan" slope of the Sierra. **1902** *DN* 2.249 **sIL,** *Yan* [jæn]. . . Yon as 'Down to yan eend.' **1906** *DN* 3.123 **sIN,** *Yon.* . . Yonder. "Down to yon end." **1906** in 2009 (acc) Lexis–Nexis Legal Research *State Case Law: DE* (Internet) [Black], Wilbur Carter, Mamie Fitzjarrell, Jim and me all got out of the wagon on yon side of the colored church. **1929** Dobie *Vaquero* 193 **West,** I . . was leisurely angling across to "the yan side" when I heard him call. **1930** Riggs *Roadside* 151 **OK,** You like to stick out yer hand, and tetch yand' side of a river. **1939** *Hall Coll.* **wNC, eTN,** Middlesboro is on yan side of the Cumberland Gap. **1944** in 2009 (acc) Lexis–Nexis Legal Research *State Case Law: KY* (Internet), So this Addington boy walked up pretty close to me right just—oh, just on the yon side of the underground church. **1951** Giles *Harbin's Ridge* 2 **KY,** There's one right good-sized mountain at yon end of the ridge. **1968** *DARE* Tape **VA**27, About four mile on yon side of Hot Springs. **1969** *DARE* FW Addit **ceKY,** Yon side—[I] asked Clayhole storekeeper where a certain house was and was told it was on the "yon side of the bridge" meaning I had to cross it. **1974–75** in 2004 Montgomery–Hall *Dict. Smoky Mt. Engl.* 665 **wNC, eTN,** You can see the boards in there yet on the yan part of it. **1982** Van Cleve *Day Late* 3 **MT,** I was dragging a calf to the fire from the yon end . . and looked back in time to see the big colt break in two. **1986** Pederson *LAGS Concordance,* 1 inf, **ceTN,** On yon[der] side of the branch—other/far side; Pigeon Forge was all on yon[der] side of the river. [*DARE* Ed: All brackets in original]

B As pron.
That (one over there)—indicating a visible person or object. Note: Some of these quots may belong at **C1b** below. [*OED2 yon* pron. B a1300 →; "Now only *Sc.* and *dial.*"]

1843 Herbert *Deerstalkers* 98 **NY,** Well, Mister Aircher, . . yan is a noble sight for a hunter's eye, is yan! You niver seed jest sich another, I'm a thinkin'. **1866** in 1884 Lanier *Poems* 173 **GA,** Yan's Jones, which you bought his land. **1868** Davis *Dallas Galbraith* 44, Yon's the fort they built in the old times for safety. *Ibid* 78, "Yon's he, Mr. Evans," said Peggy, as Galbraith came up the hill. **1902** *DN* 2.249 **sIL,** *Yan*. . . 'Who's yan?' i.e., Who is yon person? **1903** *DN* 2.337 **seMO,** 'Yon's the man!' pointing out some one. **1913** Kephart *Highlanders* 122 **sAppalachians,** Now, yan's my field of corn.

C As adv.
1a In or to that place, there (usu referring to a place within sight)—freq in combs with other local advs, as *back yon, down* ~, *out* ~, *over* ~, *up* ~. [*OED2 yon* dem. adv. c1475 →; "*Obs.* exc. *dial.* and as in *[hither and yon].*"]

1878 (1879) Harte *Drift* 222 **West,** The old man . . lives in a little cottage with his darter right over yan. **1883** (1971) Harris *Nights with Remus* 17 **GA,** Yistiddy I see one er dem ar Favers chillun clim'in' dat ar big red-oak out yan'. **1910** Hart *Vigilante Girl* 145 **nCA,** "That little

stream over yan"—pointing behind the coach—"empties into the Uvas River." **1913** in 1914 Stewart *Letters* 221 **AL,** Her mother tells me that she is going "back yan" when she gets a "little mo' richer." **1913** Kephart *Highlanders* 112 **sAppalachians,** She's in the field, up yan, gittin' roughness. **1944** [see **A1** above]. **1966** *DARE* Tape **GA**1, I've seen . . a beaver right yon on the dock. **1967–70** *DARE* (Qu. MM5, *When you're pointing out a house that's not far away: "The house is over _____."*) Infs **CA**8, **IL**143, Yon. **1974** Fink *Mountain Speech* 18 **wNC, eTN,** They live over yan. **1986** Pederson *LAGS Concordance Gulf Region,* 2 infs, Yon[der]; 4 infs, (Way) out yon[der]; 2 infs, Over yon[der]; 1 inf, Over yon[der]—old-timey form; 1 inf, Over yond[er]; 1 inf, Around and yon[der] here and there; 1 inf, Right yon[der]; 1 inf, Down yon[der]; 1 inf, Up yon[der] to Bay [City]. [*DARE* Ed: All brackets in original]

b spec; at the beginning of a sentence: Used to call attention to something within sight. Cf **B** above, **yonder B2**

1839 Bacon *Bride* 34 **NY,** Yon she comes. **1899** (1912) Green *VA Folk-Speech* 495, *Yon*. . . That or those, referring to an object at a distance; *yonder.* "Yon he goes." *Yond, adv.* In or at that more or less distant place. "Yond it is." **1940** (1941) Bell *Swamp Water* 102 **Okefenokee GA,** "Yon he is!" Keefer said. **1986** Pederson *LAGS Concordance,* 1 inf, **swMS,** Yon he go; 1 inf, **swGA,** Yon they go. **2004** *DARE* File **eTX** (as of c1940s) [Black], We blacks used "yon" only . . in exclamations like "Yon he go!"

2 with adjs expressing size: So, thus—usu accompanied by a hand gesture.

1905 *Green Bag* 17.735 **TN** [Black], Jim's kittle did have a sand-hole in it about yan long (indicating on her finger) an' mebby a leetle longer. **1942** Hall *Smoky Mt. Speech* 29 **wNC, eTN,** The former fire-warden of Cades Cove was heard to say: [a 'sid ə 'fiʃ 'jæn 'lɔŋ], 'I saw a fish yon [that] long,' accompanying the demonstrative with appropriate gestures. On Cosby Creek, a young mountaineer told another that some object was ['jæn 'lɔŋ n̩ 'jæn 'ræund], also using gestures.

D As noun.
Following a prep (plus often a positional adv): That place (back, over, up) there. Cf **yonder D**

1890 *Lippincott's Mth. Mag.* Jan 113, That facetious marvel Peeping Forward was written and received by all the tribes from hither to yon. **1901** *Munsey's Mag.* 25.620 **wNC,** There had come from "back yan'" in the mountains two of the strangest creatures. . . "Back yan'," with a wave of the hand towards the hills, was understood among the mountaineers to designate the remotest fastnesses . . , the wolf's den, and the boudoir of the bear. **1909** MacGowan *Wiving* 289 **TN,** I just have obliged to get my things from—from up yon in the Gap. *Ibid* 390, "Sheriff Beason and his men are in yon," Lance told Ola, glancing in the direction of his father's house. **1927** *Outlook* 146.446 **LA,** A gentleman from over yon came a-fishing here. **1970** *DARE* (Qu. MM12a, . . *'In all directions'* . . *"He shot into a flock of birds and they went _____."*) Inf **TN**65, Scattered from here to yon.

yonaway See **yonway**

yoncopin See **yonkapin**

yond See **yon**

yonder *adv, adj, n* Usu |'jɑndə(r), 'jɔn-|; for varr see **A** below
A Forms.

1 |'jændə(r)|; pronc-sp *yander.* **chiefly Sth, S Midl** See Map on p. 1128

1836 *S. Lit. Messenger* 2.493 **seNY,** I only wish we had some of that good sugar and coffee that them mean English is squandering out yander. **1861** Olmsted *Cotton Kingdom* 211 **Sth** [Black], Dis mornin' some niggars tole me dar war a niggar camped off yander in de wood. **1902** *DN* 2.249 **sIL,** *Yander* [jændɚ]. . . Yonder. **1903** *DN* 2.337 **seMO,** *Yonder*. . . Pronounced yander, and often with an aspirate: 'hyander.' **1906** *DN* 3.123 **sIN,** *Yander*. . . Usual pronunciation of yonder. **1907** *DN* 3.228 **nwAR,** *Yander* [jændə]. **1907** [see **A5** below]. **1917** [see **A2** below]. **1917** *DN* 4.419 **wNC,** Yan, yander. **1927** *DN* 5.470 **Appalachians,** Yonder—yander. **1931** *AmSp* 7.91 **eKY,** *Yander*. **1944** *PADS* 2.16 **GA,** *Yonder* ['jændɚ]: Pronunciation of Civil War generation. **1961** Kurath–McDavid *Pronc. Engl.* 143, *Yonder* . . This word was usually recorded in the phrase *over yonder,* an expression that has rather limited currency in the North and in urbanized areas of the Midland and the South. The /ɑ ~ ɒ/ of *lot* is the usual vowel in *yonder,* but a variety of other vowels have some currency, mostly in folk speech; in the North and the North Midland, the /ʌ/ of *sun* and the /ɛ/ of *ten;* in parts of the South and the South Midland, the /æ/ of *man*. **1965–70** *DARE* (Qu. MM5, *When you're pointing out a house that's not far away: "The house is over _____."*) Infs **GA**73, **IN**38, **MD**42, **VA**15, Yander [ˈjændə(r)]; **GA**31, [ˈjændə]—old-fash; **KY**85, [ˈjændə], [ˈjandə]; **LA**8, [ˈjændə]—occasional; **MS**7, Over [ˈjændə]; **NC**33, [ˈjɔndə], [ˈjændə]—older; **TN**20, [ˈjændə]—old country people. **1966–67** *DARE* FW Addit **NC**, [ˈjændə]. **1983** *MJLF* 9.1.62 **ceKY** (as of 1956), *Yander*. **1991** Haynes *Haywood Home* 77 **wNC** (as of c1910), Jut would say far (fire), tar (tire), yander (yonder).

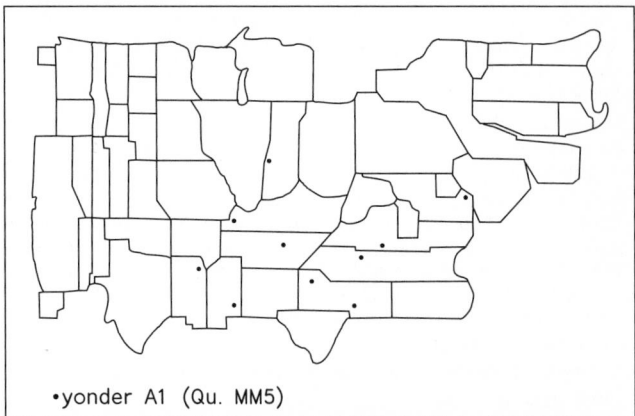

•yonder A1 (Qu. MM5)

2 |ˈjɛndə(r)|; pronc-sp *yender*.   **chiefly Nth**
1818 Fessenden *Ladies Monitor* 172 **NEng**, Provincial words . . to be avoided. . . *Yender* for yonder. **1860** *Knickerbocker* 55.332 **NYC**, Keep your eyes on yender light, and you will come out straight. **1891** *DN* 1.125 **cNY**, [jɛndə] . . 'yonder.' **1904** Day *Kin o' Ktaadn* 193 **ME**, Old Hurrydown hill yender has seemed so near. **1906** [see B3 below]. **1917** *DN* 4.404 **neOH**, *Yender* [jɛndə, sometimes jændə]. . . Yonder. **1933** *AmSp* 8.2.43 **neNY**, *Yonder* [jɛndr]. **1961** [see A1 above]. **1965** *DARE* File **csWI** (as of c1950), *Yonder*—[jɛndə]—old-fashioned.

3 |ˈjʌndə(r)|; pronc-sp *yunder*.   [*EDD* "*yunder* Sh[etland] I[slands]"]
1833 *N. Amer. Mag.* 1.265 **NEng**, Ax the Skipper Scudder deown yunder in the bay. **1852** Lovell *Young Speaker* 14, Do not . . say . . yunder for yonder. **1909** *DN* 3.422 **Cape Cod MA** (as of a1857), *Yonder*. . . Pronounced yunder. Used of a place near at hand. "It's yunder over in the corner." **1961** [see A1 above]. **1965–70** *DARE* (Qu. MM5, *When you're pointing out a house that's not far away: "The house is over _____."*) Infs **KY**92, **LA**32, **MO**23, 30, **TN**46, **TX**32, Yunder [ˈjʌndə(r)]. [4 of 6 Infs Black]

4 |ˈjɔndə(r)|.   [*SND* [ˈjɔn(d)ər]]
1966–68 *DARE* (Qu. MM5, *When you're pointing out a house that's not far away: "The house is over _____."*) Infs **SC**9, 11, 26, 59, **VA**5, Yonder [ˈjɔndə(r)].

5 |ˈhjʌndə(r)|; pronc-spp *hyander, hyanner, hyonder*.   **Sth, S Midl**
1886 Sinclair *Christie's Choice* 209 **Sth** [Black], He's gone ter jine them t'other angels up hyonder. **1903** [see A1 above]. **1907** *DN* 3.237 **nwAR**, *Yonder*. . . Pronounced yander, and often with an aspirate. **1944** *PADS* 2.16 **VA**, **NC**, *Yonder*. . . [ˈhjandə]. **1945** *AmSp* 20.189 **cTX**, [h] often appears at the beginning of certain words when emphasized. Besides *hit* and *hain't* . . , I find *hyonder*: . . *down yonder* [dæən hjandə]. **1950** *PADS* 14.40 **SC**, *Hyonder*. . . There, yonder, e.g. over hyonder. **1955** Roberts *S. from Hell-fer-Sartin* 121 **eKY**, They's a little gray house hanging way down hyonder on a beech limb. **1983** *MJLF* 9.1.44 **ceKY** (as of 1956), *Hyanner* . . yonder.

6 pronc-spp *yanner, yon'er, yonner, yonnuh*.   [*EDD* "*yon'er* Sc.; *yonner* Sc.; *youner* n. Lan."]   **chiefly Sth** *esp freq among Black speakers*
1825 Jones *Refugee* 1.316 **seNY** [Black], God a bless you, massa, him lib yonner; dat him light. **1852** Ryan *Personal Advent.* 2.223 [Black], You see dat boat, yon'er? **1888** *Century Illustr. Mag.* 35.954 **KY** [Black], Does you 'member whut you said back yon'er in de watter? **1899** Edwards *Defense* 29 **GA** [Black], She was er-settin' up yon'er on top step wid er big lily in her han'. **1902** *Frank Leslie's Pop. Mth.* 55.143 **GA** [Black], He driv in de back yard up yanner! **1915** *DN* 4.193 **swVA**, *Yan, yanner*. Variant of *yon, yonder*. **1942** in 1987 Perdue *Outwitting Devil* 8 **VA**, In the mornin' we go up yanner to that big white

oak. **1954** [see B4a below]. **1966–67** *DARE* FW Addit **swNC**, *Off yanner* [ˌɔf ˈjænə]. . . Oh, he went off yanner (to Calif., Durham, Nashville, France). **1996** TN Folk Lore Soc. *Bulletin* 58.68, Well, he told some of the guards to take her back down yanner.

7 pronc-sp *yonders*.   Note: This form appears to be common in ballad style, but rare in actual speech.
1843 (1916) Hall *New Purchase* 174 **IN**, He made . . yonders moon—and all them 'are stars. **1874** in 1907 *Archiv Sprachen Literaturen* 119.431 **MO**, [In a ballad:] Go dig my grave in yonders meadow. **a1903** in 1998 Hicks *Hist. LA Negro Baptists* 62 [Black], She insisted that . . the Lord gave her a spear and said, "My Little one, go into yonders world and spear my people." **1914** *DN* 4.114 **cKS**, *Yonders*. . . Yonder. **1916** *DN* 4.312 **Appalachians** [Folk-song dialect], [Title:] In Yonders Forth Town. **1952** in 2004 Cray *Ramblin' Man* 353 **OK**, [Letter of Woody Guthrie:] They say it ain't deadly nor fatal, so, my days in yonders hospital weren't quite wasted if they got me off my bottle. **1986** Pederson *LAGS Concordance (What's that?)* 1 inf, **seAL**, Over yonders; 1 inf, **ceTX**, See him in the yonders land—song title. [Infs Black]

B   As adv.

1   In or to that place, there (often referring to a place within sight)—freq in comb with other local advs. [*OED2 yonder* adv. A.1 a1300 →] **widespread, but more freq Sth, S Midl** See Map
1843 (1916) Hall *New Purchase* 279 **IN**, Why can't we shoot across the holler agin that ole walnut stump yander? **1867** Harris *Sut Lovingood Yarns* 143 **TN**, Arter raisin hit 'way up yander, I fotch hit down, es hard es I cud. **1884** *Anglia* 7.277 **Sth, S Midl** [Black], To see er man 'way off yonder = to see a man at a distance. **1905** *DN* 3.101 **nwAR**, *Yonder*. . . 'He lives away over yonder.' **1911** Porter *Harvester* 377 **IN**, Mebby some of the stylish ones will carry the fashion over yander. **1923** *DN* 5.225 **swMO**, "He went yander right now!" *i.e.,* disappeared in haste. **1932** (1974) Caldwell *Tobacco Road* 100 **GA**, Just look at them coming yonder! **1942** Faulkner *Go Down* 42 **MS**, Messing around up yonder in the bottom all last night! **1956** Moody *Home Ranch* 86 **CO** (as of 1911), I reckon the calf pasture lies right over that ridge yonder. **1965–70** *DARE* (Qu. MM5, *When you're pointing out a house that's not far away: "The house is over _____."*) 438 Infs, **widespread, but somewhat more freq Sth, S Midl,** Yonder (*or* yander, yunder); **AR**35, **FL**6, **MS**63, Right (*or* just) yonder; **MO**8, 36, (Way) back yonder; **OK**6, 31, (Right) down yonder; **KY**83, **MD**17, (Way) out yonder; **AR**31, **FL**18, **LA**17, **MS**30, 73, **OK**6, (Right, just) over yonder; **MS**7, **AR**39, **OK**15, Up yonder; (Qu. C33, . . *Joking names . . for an out-of-the-way place, or a very small or unimportant place*) Inf **NY**39, Out yonder; (Qu. X48b, . . *If a person is not so young any more . . "He's _____."*) Inf **MS**73, Getting up yonder; (Qu. CC9, . . *Words or expressions for hell: "That man is headed straight for _____."*) Inf **KY**25, Down yonder; (Qu. HH6, *Someone who is out of his mind*) Inf **GA**13, Way out yonder; (Qu. MM22, *If you are talking to a friend who lives in another place and you want to inquire about his neighborhood . . "How are things _____?"*) Infs **CA**208, **GA**80, Down yonder; **LA**17, Out yonder. **1966** *DARE* Tape **FL**37, There's a thousand and one worms out yonder in that fish box. **1989** Pederson *LAGS Tech. Index* 177 **Gulf Region**, *Over there*. . . [578 infs, (Back, down, out, over, round, up) yonder; 4 infs, Back up yonder; 1 inf, Up back yonder.]

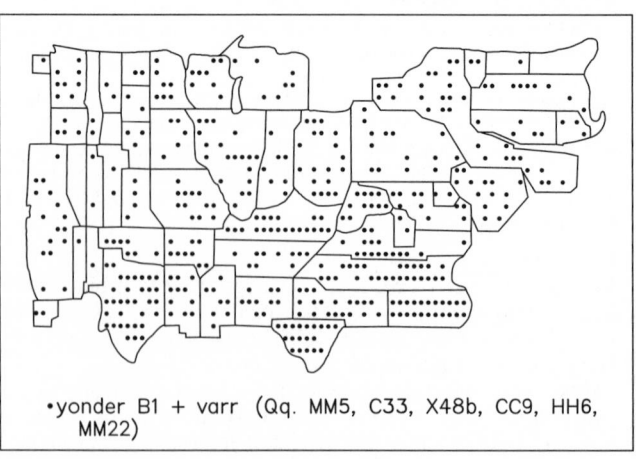

•yonder B1 + varr (Qq. MM5, C33, X48b, CC9, HH6, MM22)

2 Spec; at the beginning of a sentence: used to call attention to something within sight. **esp Gulf States, AR, GA** Cf **yon C1b**

1852 Byrn *Rattlehead's Travels* 52 **AR,** Says I, "Julus, yander comes a bear; get your gun and knives ready." **1930** *VA Qrly. Rev.* 6.242 **Ozarks,** Yonder's a right smart chance of corn. **1986** Pederson *LAGS Concordance,* 1 inf, **cwAL,** Yonder goes two yoke of your oxen; 1 inf, **cwGA,** Yonder [i]t is; 1 inf, **cGA,** Yonder comes that undertaker—in an-ecdote; 1 inf, **seGA,** Yonder's that trifling nigger; 1 inf, **swGA,** Yonder he is; 1 inf, **ceLA,** Yonder's my medicine; 1 inf, **csLA,** Yonder come a peckerwood; 1 inf, **nwLA,** Yonder's my next to the baby brother; 1 inf, **nwMS,** Yonder one = yonder is one; 1 inf, **cwMS,** Yonder go a car. **1995** McCormack *Fields Pastures* 49 **cwAL** (as of 1960s), "Yonder he!" cried a young lad of about six or eight, as he too pointed the same way.

3 in phrr *here* (or *hither*) *and yonder* and varr: in all directions; here and there; helter-skelter; everywhere. [*OED2 yonder* adv. A.1.c 1412–20 →] **scattered, but esp Sth, S Midl** Cf **hither and yon**

1855 *U.S. Rev.* 35.23, Here are crystal fountains, bursting from amid rocks, and running in silver threads hither and yonder. **1883** *Century Illustr. Mag.* 26.221 **LA,** By 1822 gangs of street paviors were seen and heard here, there, and yonder, swinging the pick and ramming the roundstone. **1906** Johnson *Highways Missip. Valley* 128 **Ozarks,** Then the children run hyar and yender, to beg a little milk and a little bread and such like. **1966–70** *DARE* (Qu. A22, . . *'To start working hard':* "She had only ten minutes to clean the room, but she _____.") Inf **KY**85, Threw things here and yonder; (Qu. Y29b, . . *About a man [who doesn't stay home much]:* "He's always _____.") Inf **KY**85, Running here and yonder; (Qu. MM12a, . . *'In all directions'* . . "He shot into a flock of birds and they went _____.") Infs **MA**46, **NC**9, Hither and yonder; (Qu. MM12b, . . *'In all directions'* . . "When she was out on the dance floor, she broke her beads and they went _____.") Inf **NC**88, Here and yonder; **NE**9, Thither and yonder. **1968** *DARE* Tape **GA**31, There's just a labyrinth of trails winding here and yonder. **1986** Pederson *LAGS Concordance* **Gulf Region,** 13 infs, Here (,there) and yonder; 1 inf, Here, yonder, and everywhere.

4 in phrr *(a) way* (or *away*) *yonder:* See below. **chiefly Sth, S Midl**

a Very much; (by) far.

1895 *DN* 1.375 **eTN,** Way yonder: very much, exceedingly. . . "I reckon if we know'd all we know now, . . we'd be ahead of 'em way yander." **1902** Harris *Gabriel Tolliver* 200 **cGA,** You're a way yander ahead of me. . . I reckon I've slipped a cog some'rs in my machinery. What is your name? **1904** *Outing* 45.360 **nwSC,** I shorely kin tell yer, Squire, how ole man Skinner got 'way yander ahead uv me. **1908** *DN* 3.288 **eAL, wGA,** Away yonder. . . Far. "He's away yonder ahead of me." **1909** *DN* 3.406 **nwAR,** Way yonder. . . Very much, exceedingly. **1951** *PADS* 15.52 **IN,** He's away yonder bigger'n me. **1954** in 1958 Brewer *Dog Ghosts* 42 **TX** [Black], Dey sho am putty pants, but dey looks lack dey be's way yonnuh too big for a tee-ninchy li'l' man lack you. **1957** Taylor *Back Mt.* 59 **swMO,** Dollars these days is a way yander smaller / Than they was a few years back. **1986** Pederson *LAGS Concordance,* 1 inf, **cnAR,** I'm way yonder stouter than they are; 1 inf, **cnAR,** Back then raised way yonder better than. . . now. **1990** Sanders *Clover* 171 **SC** [Black], I'm not too crazy over the way Sara Kate talks, but it's way yonder better than theirs.

b Of time: long ago; far in the past (rarely the future). Cf **back yonder**

1890 Johnston *Poets Chester Co. PA* 163, Hit's away yander back; but the young folk 'round yere / Allus goes thar afore their marryin' day. **1891** *Catholic World* 54.207 **Sth** [Black], He tuk er mighty gre't lakkin' ter Major Gilbert fum dat time way yander w'en he wuz so p'lite ter de ladies. **1891** Harris *Balaam* 18 **cGA** [Black], Hit 'll be 'way yander todes night 'fo' I kin git dese clo's straightened out. **1898** *Sports Afield* 20.27 **AR,** "When did they start in on thet line uv bizness, any-how?" " 'Way yander afore you deserted from ole Bragg at Stone River." **1986** Pederson *LAGS Concordance,* 1 inf, **csMS,** Way yonder = years ago.

c Of a location: far away.

1941 in 1991 Still *Wolfpen Notebooks* 155 **eKY,** Two days ago they hired four new miners, fellers from away yander. **1963** Edwards *Gravel* 94 **TN,** They was a driving along . . somers away yander near the Caliner line. **1967–68** *DARE* (Qu. MM25, . . *A long distance:* "Texas is a _____ [from here]. ") Infs **NC**53, **SC**34, Way yander.

C As adj.

1 =**yon A1.** [*OED2 yonder* a. 13.2 c1400 →] Cf *that there* (at **there B**)

1855 Adams *Our World* 405 **SC** [Black], 'Pears like old mas'r tink . . what he sees in yander good book lef 'um do just as 'e mind to wid nigger. **1917** *DN* 4.404 **neOH,** There it is, by yender fence. **1942** Hall *Smoky Mt. Speech* 29 **wNC, eTN,** At the foot of yander . . mountain. **1986** Pederson *LAGS Concordance,* 1 inf, **ceGA,** Yonder creek. **1995** *Signal Mag.* Dec np **cwTX,** Yonder "In yonder (or yon) cotton patch." Distant.

2 also with *the:* =**yon A2**—freq in phrr *(the) yonder side;* hence prep phrr *yonder side, (the) yonder side of.* [*OED2 yonder* a. B.1.a 13 . . →]

1903 Malone *Sons Vengeance* 37 **sAppalachians,** Y'u all knows I've most as many o' my folks on yander side as on this, an' that I'm heyeh tuh fight agin my own flesh an' blood. **1904** Beatty *McLean* 8 **VA** [Black], Dat dar road yander side de co'n fiel' goes ober de Yadkin rib-ber. **1910** *Field & Stream* 14.837 **SW,** Smith, here, will keep cases on both ranches, while I shappyrone the bride across to yander side an' back. **1917** *Jrl. Amer. Folk.* 30.192 **cnNC,** One man got a chain, tie his cow, got 'round on yander side of his house, an' pulled up his cow. **1937** Bradford *Three-Headed Angel* 46 **eTN,** The Abercrombie girls, who lived on the "yander side" of the settlement, had brought their hus-bands and children to their father's house for the night. **1956** Gipson *Old Yeller* 97 **TX,** They're clear back in that bat cave country, the yonder side of Salt Branch. **1965** West *Time Was* 270 **NC,** I got Deller up, a few miles yander side of Bare Creek, and she rid all the rest of the way. **1977** *Northeast Folkl.* 17.67 **ME,** I'd put him on one end . . and he'd count up, and I'd row up the yonder end and pick him up. **1982** *MO Folkl. Soc. Jrl.* 4.36, Uncle Andy is a'comin' a mill /. . . / From over yander side of the hill. **1986** Pederson *LAGS Concordance,* 1 inf, **nwAL,** They'd have a guard on yonder end and this end; 1 inf, **cMS,** On yonder side—on the other side of the street; 1 inf, **nwLA,** Yonder side of Blanchard.

D As noun. Cf **yon D**

In var prep phrr:

a *in yonder:* In that place, in there. **chiefly Sth**

1868 *Galaxy* 4.742 **AL** [Black], I'se keepin' you from your friends, suh. . . You ought to be in yander, 'pears to me. **1899** Edwards *Defense* 29 **GA** [Black], But dis here chile, de one in yon'er right now, she ain't lak nair 'nother chile. **1909** *DN* 3.391 **eAL, wGA,** Yonder. . . Used with prepositions to express a specified place. "In yonder," i.e., in the place specified. **1952** Brown *NC Folkl.* 1.610, Yonder, in . . In there. "In yonder in the barn." **1965** *DARE* (Qu. MM11, *When you're trying to find something—you don't know where it is* . . "I must have left it _____.") Inf **MS**57, In yonder. **1986** Pederson *LAGS Concordance* **Gulf Region,** 38 infs, In yonder; 2 infs, Back in yonder; 1 inf, She could have went back in yonder.

b *to yonder:* To that place; to a remote distance—used in phr *from here to yonder.* **chiefly Sth, S Midl, West**

1883 Henderson *Song of Milkanwatha* 22, He could step from here to yonder,/ Step from here, 'way over yonder,/ Step right up on the horizon. **1915** Sinclair *Flying U's Last Stand* 143 **West,** Four forties I've got, strung out on a line that runs from here to yonder. **1940** *Sat. Eve. Post* 6 Jan 15 **MS,** She used to could smell that old goat of yours from here to yonder. **1952** Ferber *Giant* 215 **TX,** Anybody wants to drive from here to yonder, why they damn well got to go about a hundred miles out of their way to get there. **1958** Dewlen *Bone Pickers* 15 **TX,** You know they're gonna chew my ass out from here to yonder. **1965–70** *DARE* (Qu. MM12b, . . *'In all directions'* . . "When she was out on the dance floor, she broke her beads and they went _____.") Infs **AL**3, 12, 30, **MI**111, **MS**64, **NH**16, **SC**11, 24, 34, From here to yonder; (Qu. V2b, "I wouldn't trust him _____."; not asked in early QRs) Infs **KY**94, **NC**62, (From) here to yonder. [All Infs old] **1969** Wilson *Stars* 24 **Ozarks,** An' tomorry this time they'll be Dyes layin' fer buzzard bait all the way from here to yonder. **1986** Pederson *LAGS Concordance,* 2 infs, **AL, TX,** From here to yonder. **2005** Raybon *I Told the Mt.* 252 **CO,** I was sending e-cards and buying greeting cards and mailing them off from here to yonder.

yonders See **yonder A7**

yonder side (of) See **yonder C2**

yonder way adv phr Also *yonderways, yonnerways* Cf **yon-way** **chiefly S Midl**

Over there; in that direction.

1851 Buckingham *Harry Burnham Continental* 211 **seNY,** "You go yonder way, I believe?" said the farmer, pointing in a contrary direction. **1874** Reid *Death-Shot* 338 **MS,** "The road's . . out yonnerways." He points in particular direction [sic]. **1885** Twain *Huck. Finn* 106 **MO,** Looky here, you break for that light over yonder-way, and turn out west when you git there. **1888** *Century Illustr. Mag.* 36.773 **seTN,** Yer see hit [=a locomotive] . . a-pullin' an' a-catecornerin' this yer ways an' yander ways. **1941** *Amer. Mercury* 52.664 **nGA,** She lives about fourteen mile over th' ridge yander way. **1969** Wilson *Stars* 106 **Ozarks,** "Where's the hoss goin'?" "Yonderways to sedge grass." **1981** in 2004 Montgomery–Hall *Dict. Smoky Mt. Engl.* 665 **wNC, eTN,** [Y]ou cross the big bridge goin' in yander way right there. **1986** Pederson *LAGS Concordance,* 3 infs, **nwGA, neMS, cnLA,** Yonder way; 1 inf, **nwLA,** Went yonder way; 1 inf, **cTN,** Back up yonder ways. **2001** *DARE File cwOK, Yonderway* [was used by] . . a Caddo Indian from Binger in Caddo County, Oklahoma, born 1914. . . He used it literally and also metaphorically in "going yonderway" to mean "going to Heaven."

yone See **yourn**

yo-necked See **ewe-neck**

yon end(, the) See **yon A2**

yon'er See **yonder A6**

yonkanut n Also *yawk-nut, yonkernut* Cf **yonkapin**
=**water chinquapin.**

    1916 *Outing* 68.620, A cloud of water fowl . . arose off the water, leaving only nodding cat-tails and dead yonker-nut pads to dot the emerald sheen of the Puddle. **1957** U.S. Fish & Wildlife Serv. *Circular* 19 (revised).29, The native yellow-flowered lotus, *Nelumbo lutea,* also called yonkapin, yonkanut, bonnets, or water chinkapin, is common in ponds and lakes of the Mississippi Valley. **2004** [see **yonkapin**].

yonkapin n Also *yonkapin bonnet;* also sp *yankapin, yonkerpin, yoncopin, yonkipin, yonkypin, yonquapin, younquepin, yunkapin* [Appar varr of **wankapin**] **chiefly Sth, S Midl** Cf **yonkanut, yonker pad, yorky nut**
=**water chinquapin.**

    1867 Parker *MO in 1867* 105, They [=swine] in their turn hunting their daily food, found to them a delicious esculent in the yonkapin, called *nuckshaw* by the Indians. **1872** *Amer. Naturalist* 6.726 **IN,** Very curious peltate leaves, looking somewhat like miniatures of the great lotus or "yonkapins" (Nelumbium) beside them. **1884** *Forest & Stream* 22.385 **nTX,** Passing down the Little Wichita, I noticed the duck lakes well filled up and "yonkerpins" in bloom, showing plentiful feed for ducks. **1901** Lounsberry *S. Wild Flowers* 162, Yellow Nelumbo. Yonquapin. **1906** *DN* 3.165 **AR,** Yoncopin [ˈjɔnkəpɪn]. . . E. and So. Ark. **1916** Cobb *Old Judge* 52 **wKY,** The yonkerpins—which Yankees, in their ignorance, have called water lilies—spread their wide green pads and their white-and-yellow cusps of bloom on the face of the creek water. **1918** *Amer. Angler* 3.60 **nwMS** [Black], I dun seed an ole lunker jump out after a snake doctah (dragon fly) a wile ago, ober dar by de yonkerpins (lotus lilies). **1920** *Torreya* 20.21 **TN,** *Nelumbo lutea.* . . Bonnet, yonkapin bonnet, Reelfoot Lake, Tenn. **1923** Cooper *Under Big Top* 73 **MO,** Hard, black affairs, such as we knew in kidhood days as "yonkypin nuts." **1927** *DN* 5.479 **Ozarks,** *Yonkipin.* . . Water lily. "The yonkipins is in roastin' ear" means that they are fully developed—the mature pistil somewhat resembles an ear of corn. **1946** Reeves-Bain *Flora TX* 65, *N[elumbo] lutea.* . . Lotus, Younquepin. **1951** *PADS* 15.31 **TX,** *Nelumbo lutea.* . . Yonkapin or yonquapin. Roots and seeds both were eaten by Indians and early settlers. **1961** Sackett–Koch *KS Folkl.* 70, Large fields of yunkapins and Indian corn waved in the breeze, but my people did not know which to eat of. **1966** *DARE* (Qu. S26b, *Wildflowers that grow in water or wet places*) Inf **AR10,** [ˈjɔnkəˌpɪn]. **1967** *DARE* Wildfl QR Pl.55 [=*Nelumbo lutea*] Inf **AR46,** [ˈjɔnkɪˌpɪn]. **2004** Austin *FL Ethnobotany* 453, *Nelumbo lutea.* . . *yankapin, yonkapin* . . *yawk-nut* (akin to *yonkapin,* Louisiana).

yonker See **younker**

yonkernut See **yonkanut**

yonker pad n Cf **yonkapin**
The **water chinquapin** or its leaf.

    1922 *Cosmopolitan* 73.5.16 **wKY,** It was the habit of the moccasin . . to lie beneath the yonkerpads—pond lilies, a Northerner would call them. **1936** *AmSp* 11.318 **Ozarks,** *Yonker-pad.* . . The round flat leaf of the yonkapin, which is a yellow water-lily.

---

yonkerpin, yonkipin, yonkypin See **yonkapin**

yonner See **yonder A6**

yonnerways See **yonder way**

yonnuh See **yonder A6**

yonquapin See **yonkapin**

yon side adj See **yon A2**

yonside adv, prep Also *yanside,* rarely *yandside* **esp S Midl** Cf **yon A2, yonder C2**
A As adv.
On the farther (or other) side—freq in comb *yonside of.* [*OED2 yonside* adv. 1681 →; *EDD* (at *yon* adj. 2)]

    1872 U.S. Congress *Rept. Joint Select Comm. Insurrectionary States* 9.730 **AL,** Is it in Madison or Blount County? . . I don't remember, . . but it's yon side of the river. **1896** *Amer. Angler* 26.213 **wNC,** We marched to the river, which runs "yan" side of a small meadow. **1900** *Land of Sunshine* 13.361 **West,** You mind that feller on yan side of the table? . . I've sort o' reckoned that if he can afford to set yan side of thet table, Hugh cain't afford to set this side. **1910** *DN* 3.457 **KY,** Grandpaw lives six miles yon side of home. **1921** in 2009 (acc) Lexis-Nexis Legal Research *State Case Law: OK* (Internet), He said he lived the first or second house yon side of Mark Harkins. **1934** Randolph–Von Schriltz *Ozark Outdoors* 26, "Three more in the brush yan side," he said, producing that turkey call along with a pocket knife. **1954** *Harder Coll.* **cwTN,** The fence is yon side o' the road. **1967** *Hall Coll.* **wNC, eTN,** Hit's yan side of the Brier Ridge. **1978** *Appalachian Jrl.* 5.378, I've been through all the books and come out yonside. **1986** Pederson *LAGS Concordance,* 1 inf, **cnGA,** Back yon[der] side. [*DARE* Ed: Brackets in original]
B As prep.
On the other side of, beyond. [*OED2 yonside* prep. 1856; *EDD* (at *yon* adj. 2)]

    1900 Visscher *Blue Grass Ballads* 17 **KY,** Ike could hoe mo' cawn / . . . / En any man yan side the crick. **1919** Means *More E.K. Means* 245 **LA** [Black], When I chews dat cap de top of my head will be over yanside de Massassap' River. **1936** Riggs *Russet Mantle* 139 **OK,** Only one woman of the Osage camp got away. Clumb down yand' side the Mound, swum the river and was never heard of again. **1944** *PADS* 2.52 **NC, VA,** *Yanside: prep.* Beyond, farther than. **1950** *PADS* 14.73 **SC,** *Yon side.* . . On the other side of. "Yon side the river." **1975** Chalmers *Better* 59 **wNC, eTN,** Pink lives the second house in the cove yan side Brier Hill.

yonside of See **yonside A**

yon side, the See **yon A2**

yont See **yon**

yonway adv Also *yonways, yanway(s), yon(n)away, yanaway* **chiefly S Midl** [**yon A1** + *way(s)*. The forms *yon(n)away, yanaway* may be parallel to **thataway** adv, **thereaway(s),** but could also be pronc-spp for **yonder way** (or var *yander way*); cf *yonnerways* (at **yonder way**) and **yonder A6.**]
That way, in that direction.

    1884 *Continent* 5.204 **MO,** "Where were the turkeys?" "Down yan way," with a nod. **1896** *New Engl. Mag.* 21.302 **swPA,** She . . " 'llowed as thar was an ol' fort over on Facenbaker's farm, yon way, up the pike." **1904** *Forest & Stream* 63.548 **nwAR,** Yo' follow them [=wagon tracks] back. They cross a byoo yonway. **1910** Gilbert *Hist. Evansville IN* 1.24 **swIN,** "Up yanways" meant up the road, or up in some other direction. **1915** Gielow *Light Hill* 12 **sAppalachians,** "Do you live near by?" "Jes' yanway over ther peak." **1923** *DN* 5.225 **swMO,** *Yan-away.* . . Yonder. **1972** in 1982 Powers *Cataloochee* 382 **cwNC,** Well, they'd be way at the other end. They'd ring their bells. Well, he'd go yan (yon) way. **1974–75** in 2004 Montgomery–Hall *Dict. Smoky Mt. Engl.* 662 **wNC, eTN,** It had to be set where it would pull off from a forty-five, off yanaway, off this way. **1986** Pederson *LAGS Concordance,* 1 inf, **ceTN,** Over yon[der] way; 1 inf, **ceTN,** If he's walking away from me, he's going yon[der] way. [*DARE* Ed: Brackets in original] **1994** Mc-Carthy *Crossing* 225 **NM,** We're headed yonway, Billy said. If you wanted us to carry a message or anything. **1995** *Brophy Coll.* 85 **swMO** (as of c1960), Yonnaway. [Y]onder a ways. **2005** Williams *Gratitude* 538 **wNC** (as of 1940s), *Yonways:* Not thisaway or thataway—the direction I'm pointin' at. He's gone yonways.

Yooper n, also attrib Also *Y(o)uper* **chiefly MI** Cf **troll** n
A person who lives in or is from Michigan's Upper Peninsula;
the dialect of such a person; hence nouns *Yoopanese, Yooperese.*

1977 *Escanaba Daily Press* (MI) 5 Aug Upbeat sec 7, *"What's in a
name?" contest finalists!* Here are the names that have been suggested
as a semi-official term for a U.P. resident. . . U.P.ite[s] . . Yooper [etc].
1983 *America's Hidden Corners* 94 **Upper Peninsula MI,** The authentic U.P. individual, or Yooper, expects hardship, if only from winter, and
meets it stoically. I heard of a little boy with a broken tooth, forced to
wait for dental help. "He'll tough it out," said his father. "He's a real
Yooper." 1984 *Ironwood Daily–Globe* (MI) 15 Sept 2/4, The U.P. representatives tried to have a "yooper" party included in the campaign, but
did not succeed. 1989 *Intelligencer* (Doylestown PA) 19 Feb sec C
10/1 **Upper Peninsula MI,** They're calling up to talk to a certain
Yooper, Jimmy DeCaire, to order tapes from his band, Da Yoopers.
1993 *Detroit Free Press* (MI) 30 July sec F 3/2 **Upper Peninsula MI,**
The term "Yooper," meaning an inhabitant of the Upper Peninsula, came
into the lexicon of the UP and downstate Michigan in 1957. 1999
DARE File **MI,** In Michigan we call people from the Upper Peninsula
"Yoopers" (because it's called the "U.P.") 2000 *Ibid* **Upper Peninsula
MI,** [Pamphlet from restaurant:] Venison: Yooperland beef. . . *Yooperland*: The territory north of the Mackinac Bridge. [2000 *Ibid* **MI,** I'm a
native Michiganian and have heard it [=*Yooper*] at least since the early
50s.] 2008 *DARE* File—Internet **MI,** You are blessed to be a Youper.
2009 *AmSp* 84.119 **Upper Peninsula MI,** As both a neutral and pejorative regional moniker, a *Yooper* is stereotypically male: a backwoods, independent do-it-yourselfer who hunts and fishes, rides a snowmobile,
drinks beer, spends time at deer camp, and is suspicious of outsiders.
Ibid 187, Ideological processes forging links among language, people,
and place are particularly apparent in names for the UP dialect and its
speakers: *Yooper, Yoopanese,* and *Yooperese.* 2009 *DARE* File—Internet **MI,** It does not matter if you are a Yuper or Troll. *Ibid,* MI, land of
no accent, unless you're a yuper.

yooz See **youse**

yop(p)on See **yaupon**

yore See **your**

yoren See **yourn**

york v Also with *up* Also *yack, yark* [Scots, nEngl dial; cf
EDD york (at *yawk* v. 1)] **esp Gt Lakes, PA**
To vomit; spew up (something).

1927 *AmSp* 2.367 **cwWV,** *York* . . to vomit. "Take this medicine now,
and you will soon york it up." 1942 Warnick *Garrett Co. MD* 16
nwMD (as of 1900–18), *York* . . to vomit. 1950 *WELS* (Other words
and expressions for vomiting) 1 Inf, **cWI,** York. 1968 *DARE* (Qu.
BB17, . . *Vomiting*) Infs **PA**74, 135; **WI**34, 47, York; **WI**64, Yacking
['jækɪŋ]. 2001 Keillor *Lake Wobegon Summer* 90 **MN,** He choked and
yarked up some pudding. 2002 Callaway *Hildegard Peplau* 41 **sePA**
(as of c1930), For instance, Pat would say a patient "yorked" or "pitched
up his lunch." 2003 in 2010 *DARE* File—Internet [Urban Dictionary]
MA, York—Slang first used in boring parts of Massachusetts. . . *Yesterday while I was drinking my juice box, Emily said something wicked
funny and made me york.* 2008 *Ibid* **cPA,** Low and behold, Hogan [=a
dog] had finally "yorked" up the golf ball. 2009 *DARE* File—Internet
NY, Oddly the girl who yacked up the concoction gets chosen to be
Paris' pet. 2010 *Ibid* **TX,** She is an utter and total monkey and gets into
everything and she quietly yarked yesterday after eating cheese.

yorkey (or yorkie) nut See **yorky nut**

York State n **chiefly NEng, NY, and NEng settlement area**
The state of New York.

1780 in 1970 Kitman *George Washington's Expense Acct.* 244, To
Col. Graham of the York State Troops—per Acct. . . $313.41. 1817 in
1918 IN Hist. Soc. *Pub.* 6.302 **NY,** Met Mr. Brown, son of Oliver Brown
of York State. 1828 Hall *Letters West* 170 **NEng,** On arriving at an
inn . . in New England . . [I answered] the tedious inquiries, whether I
was a *southerner,* or a *York-state man.* 1865 OH State Bd. Ag. *Annual
Rept. for 1864* 192, The standard of our cheese and butter . . now vies
with the best York State dairy in quality. 1878 Hart *Sazerac Lying Club*
188, She said she would go home to her mother if she only had money
enough to pay her fare to the interior of York State. 1917 Garland *Son
Middle Border* 89 **WI,** Osman Button . . was a native of York State.
1931–33 *LANE Worksheets* **CT,** I heard a York State man say. 1933
AmSp 8.2.25 **CT,** In the northern part of the state, over about two-thirds

of the territory from the river to the "York State" line . . the word is *serenade.* 1939 (1962) Thompson *Body & Britches* 18 **NY,** Though she is
narrating a girlhood in Michigan, she is depicting York State manners as
truly as if her father had never migrated from us. 1939 *Sat. Review* 30
Dec 5 **NY,** York State they call it up-country. 1957 *Sat. Eve. Post Letters,* This was in Elk River, Minnesota . . about 1890–1897 and the parents of most of the children were from New England (esp. Maine),
"York State" or Illinois. 1966 *DARE* Tape **MA**5C, Up in northern York
State. 1969 *DARE* (Qu. AA18) Inf **MA**42, Horning—out in York State
they call it. 1973 Allen *LAUM* 1.383 **Upper MW** (as of c1950), *New
York State.* . . Some in southern Minnesota and a few scattered elsewhere
retain *York State,* but acknowledge it as old-fashioned if not obsolete.
1979 *NYT Article Letters* **MA,** Father always referred to upstate New
York as "York state."

york up See **york**

yorky nut n Also sp *yorkie nut, yorkey* ~ Cf **yonkanut,
yonkapin**
The seed of the **water chinquapin.**

1939 (1947) Heilner *Book Duck Shooting* 91, As you wend your way
through the yorky-nuts, the mallards are rising on every hand. 1985
Madson *Up River* 182 **Upper Missip Valley,** The seedpods of the American lotus cure out tough and fibrous and their "yorkey nuts" are as hard
as bullets. 1991 *Telegraph* (Alton IL) 8 Sept sec B 4/1, You may know
the American lotus by one of the numerous common names: fragrant
chalice, great waterlily, water chinquapin, duck acorn or Yorkie nut
plant. 2008 *DARE* File—Internet, We use to call the seed "yorky nuts."

yorn See **yourn**

yornses See **yourns's**

yoself See **your**

you pron[1] Usu |ju|; unstressed, often |jʊ, jə|; for addit varr see **A**
below

A Forms. Note: Exx of common pronc-spp such as *y', ya,
-cha* (as in *dontcha* for *don't you*), and *-ja* (as in *didja* for *did
you*) are not treated here.

1 |jɪu, jiu|; pronc-spp *yeou, yeu, yew.* **chiefly NEng**

1852 *Yankee Notions* 1.354, "Why, haow yeu talk, Eb," says Marm
Green. "I hope . . yeu didn't break none of the commandments, nor
nuthin." 1858 *S. Lit. Messenger* 27.425 **VA,** I fergivd yew all, Billy, but
my hart wuz sick. 1861 Holmes *Venner* 2.173 **NEng,** Yeou lay still, 'n'
wait t'll that man comes tew. *Ibid* 174, Gi' me that pistil, and yeou
fetch that 'ere rope. 1871 (1882) Stowe *Fireside Stories* 77 **MA,** Everybody in the meetin' house was a starin', I tell yew. 1913 Gibson *Secrets* 32 **NEng,** Haow much hev yeou got? 1930 *Folk-Say* 4.195
seMO, Dawg-gwone yeou good ole caow, yeou. 1943 *LANE* Maps
590, 608, 610, [Scattered instances of proncs of the type [jɪu] occur in
ME, NH, and **VT.**] 1968 *DARE* FW Addit **NY**88, *You*—old-fashioned
pronunciation is [jiu]. Inf's own pronunciation is [juu]. 1982 *AmSp*
57.192 **ceIL** (as of 1887), Words [in Joseph Kirkland's *Zury*] in which
/u/ is preceded by an alveolar have an *ew* spelling for the vowel, thus . .
yew ('you'). . . This spelling probably indicates the diphthong /iu/ or /ju/
in these words.

2 |jɪ, ji|; pronc-spp *ye(e), yeh, yi.* **chiefly Sth, S Midl** Note:
Some quots may represent |jə| rather than |jɪ, ji|.

1843 (1916) Hall *New Purchase* 379 **IN,** And ain't it, ye men of yards
and measures, philosophical to make a noise about this? 1899 Garland
Boy Life 47 **nwIA,** Sayin' words ye' hadn't orter. 1913 Kephart *Highlanders* 84 **sAppalachians,** I knowed I couldn't roust ye no other way.
1921 Haswell *Daughter Ozarks* 18 (as of 1880s), I'm with ye thar,
stranger. 1923 in 1952 Mathes *Tall Tales* 5 **sAppalachians,** Ye hain't
done what the Book said. Depart from me—I never knowed ye! 1938
Matschat *Suwannee R.* 197 **neFL, seGA,** Beint ye a-comin' back, Cella?
1940 Faulkner *Hamlet* 394 **MS,** "Ye kin dig and ye kin dig, young man,"
the reedy voice said. 1942 Hall *Smoky Mt. Speech* 39 **wNC, eTN,** Ye
for *you* is very common in older speakers; it occurred in such colorful
expressions as: [jɪ˞ 'rɪd 'wɪð ɪm 'dɪnt jɪ˞] 'You (sing.) rode with him,
didn't you?,' [ə˞ 'noʊd a˞d 'dɛvl jɪ˞] 'I knew I'd fool you!' 1950 Stuart
Hie Hunters 85 **eKY,** If ye's to live here a while, ye might like it! 1956
AmSp 31.160 **cnIN** (as of 1890s), Ye. . . *Archaic; dial.* You. In familiar
salutations, the pronunciation intended or not, of *you* is likely to be *ye.*
'How air ye?' 1965 in 2004 Montgomery-Hall *Dict. Smoky Mt. Engl.*
666 **wNC, eTN,** [*Charlotte Observer* (NC) 21 Mar:] *You.* . . The "ye"
for "you" is an interesting elision with expressions such as "tell ye," "see
ye," "tax ye." The sound is not "yee" but "yi" (the "i" pronounced as in

"it"). **1968** *DARE* FW Addit **csMD,** [jiˇ] you—in sentence terminal position. **1972** in 1994 Thomas *Come Go with Me* 33 **S Midl,** They's things you can ask your mother that ye cain't ask ye daddy. **1979** Lewis *How to Talk Yankee* [40] **nNEng,** Ye. Pronoun, pronounced "yee" or "yeh", 2nd person, sing. or pl. This old-fashioned word survives as a localism. "How be ye" is a common greeting, especially among older folk. **1992** Hall et al. *Old Engl. & New* 362 **sAppalachians,** Ye (the variant of *you* with a high-front vowel—[i] or [ɪ][)] is and has been very common in Scotland, Ireland, and Appalachia. **1999** Mason *Clear Springs* 37 **wKY,** The older ones said "holp" for "help" and "ye" for "you." **2000** *DARE* File **seKY** (as of c1950), Ye—(You) "I see Ye over there".

3 |jo|; pronc-sp *yo.* Cf **your**

1914 *DN* 4.159 **cVA,** Choose. . . "Thank yo no, I don't choose any." . . Gine. . . "Iah gine; yo gine?" . . Go by. . . "Won't [jo] go by?" **1925** *DN* 5.357 **SC** [Black], Yo [jou] reckon sah? **1936** Reese *Worleys* 10 **MD** (as of 1865) [Black], Yo' wait, sojer man.

B Senses.

1 Used reflexively as:

a Direct object in place of *yourself, yourselves.*

1895 Brown *Meadow-Grass* 122 **NEng,** Don't you go into that cold bedroom. You shave you here. **1956** in 2004 Montgomery–Hall *Dict. Smoky Mt. Engl.* 666 **eTN,** You'uns better get you in a tree.

b Indirect object in place of *yourself, yourselves.* **esp Sth, S Midl**

1926 Hunnicutt *Twenty Yrs.* 8 **wNC,** When you go out camping in the cold weather, build you a lean-to. **1959** Pearsall *Little Smoky Ridge* 10 **eTN** (as of a1950), You better get you a jar of whiskey. **a1978** (1983) Carpenter *Aunt Arie* 128 **NC,** Take you nine sups a'water. **1981** Harper–Presley *Okefinokee* 99 **seGA** (as of a1951), Boil you some beef brains, and put the hide in them to soak. **1986** Pederson *LAGS Concordance,* 1 inf, **neLA,** Make you (=yourself) a broom; 1 inf, **nwMS,** Build you a fire. **2002** *DARE* File—Internet **seKY,** Now go find you a church where the spirit of the living God dwells.

2 Used pleonastically, indicating that the advantage of the person(s) addressed is concerned. **chiefly S Midl**

1913 Kephart *Highlanders* 298 **sAppalachians,** Set down and eat you some supper! **1939** in 2004 Montgomery–Hall *Dict. Smoky Mt. Engl.* 666 **eTN,** Here's ye (sing.) a light. **1946** *AmSp* 21.271 **neKY,** Here's you some money. . . Here's you a nice easy one. **1966** *DARE* Tape **NC**37, Trout. . . Some of 'em really puts you up a good fight. **1968** *DARE* File **seMO,** "Here's you some wash cloths"!—(white, young-middle). **1989** Smith *Flyin' Bullets* 59 **eTN** (as of 1920s), Son, always carry ye a pen-knife.

you adj, pron² *among Black speakers, esp Gullah speakers* Cf **he** pron **2**

Your.

1853 Simms *Sword & Distaff* 235 **SC** [Black], All ready but you swode and pistols. **1888** Jones *Negro Myths* 43 **seGA** [Gullah], Ef you tell you wife way you git um . . you gwine dead a po man. **1927** Adams *Congaree* 21 **cSC** [Black], I ain't no worse dan you friends. **1928** Peterkin *Scarlet Sister Mary* 20 **SC** [Gullah], I'm gwine to be you sister. *Ibid* 162, You nurses you troubles more'n you child. **1930** *DN* 6.80 **cSC** [Black], Do. . . Don't you does be shame to eat befo' you' fella. **1938** Liebling *Back Where* 94 **Boston MA** [Black], You haid got eyes.

youahn See **yourn**

you-all pron, adj Usu |ˈjuˌɔl, ˈjɔl|; for addit varr see quots Also *y'all, y'awl, ye all, yer all, yo all, yuh all* [Clearly a fusion of *you* (or its dial var *ye*) + *all,* with concomitant stress shift or contraction, but its early history is poorly documented. See Montgomery in 1992 Hall et al. *Old Engl. & New* 356–69 and Lipski in 1993 *Engl. World-Wide* 14.23–56; for some speakers, *you-all* and *y'all* serve different functions and may even be considered different words.] **chiefly Sth, S Midl** Cf **I-all, they-all, we-all** pron

A As pron.

1a You—used as a second person pl pron, often including in its scope others known or assumed to be associated with the person or persons addressed. Cf **you guys, youse 1, youse all, youse guys, you-uns** pron¹ **1**

1816 in 1824 Knight *Letters* 82 **VA,** Children learn from the slaves some odd phrases; as . . will you *all* do this? for, will *one* of you do this? [*DARE* Ed: Cf quot 1996 below.] **1851** (1852) Stowe *Uncle Tom's Cabin* 1.51 [Black], Well, chil'en! Well, I'm mighty glad to hear ye all and see ye all once more. . . I tell y'all, chil'en, . . dat ar *glory* is a mighty thing. **1856** Pickard *Kidnapped & Ransomed* 146 **KY,** "Which of you all has a mother at Peoples'?" said he, as he rode up to a group of women. *Ibid* 304 [Black], "Well chillern," said the mother, "You all's got to cotch it now." **1856** Arrington *Rangers Tanaha* 355 **TX,** [Addressed to two people:] Ar y'all alive and kickin' in thar? **1873** *Little Corporal* 16.101 **Sth** [Black], Do yer take dis pusson . . perviden, ob cou'se, yer all ain't sole 'way from one anudder? . . De Lord bress boff yer all! **1888** *Century Illustr. Mag.* 36.897 **sAppalachians,** Don't warnt nuth'n', Ma. Yuh-all eat. **1892** *Switchmen's Jrl.* 7.281 **VA** [Black], Young boss, is y'awl our folks or is y'awl de Yankees? **1903** *DN* 2.337 **seMO,** You-all. . . Plural of *you.* Used when speaking to two or more persons. This expression is often used by educated persons and is logical. . . 'You-all' is never made use of in speaking to one person, although often appearing thus in dialect fiction. **1904** *DN* 2.422 **nwAR,** *You all.* . . You (plural). "Have you all got electric lights in your house?" **1909** *DN* 3.390 **eAL, wGA,** Yall. . . You all. This form is now practically universal in the South. It is never used with a singular significance, as has been asserted by some. . . "Where are yall goin'?" **1915** *DN* 4.193 **swVA,** Y'all [jɔl]. Short for *you all.* **1919** *DN* 5.40 **VA,** Yawl. . . You-all. **1925** *DN* 5.363 **SC** [Black], Does yo all [jou al] reckon de Lawd gwine pick he out de wus niggah? **1942** Hall *Smoky Mt. Speech* 39 **wNC, eTN,** Steadily encroaching upon it [=you-ones] . . is [ˈjuˌɔl] or [jɔl] (more familiar). **1944** *PADS* 2.14 **AL,** You-all, [*PADS* Ed: *y'all, y'all's*] [jɔUl, ˈjuɔl, juˈɔl, jɔlz]: pron., sec. per. pl. Colloq. You. When addressed to one person, one or more others of the family or associates are implied. . . "Did y'all put y'all's books in y'all's desks?" Over most of the South. General. Popular. **1958** Humphrey *Home from the Hill* 8 **neTX,** "Yawl want to make a little easy money this morning?" asked the big stranger. They both grinned. **1965–70** *DARE* (Qu. H8, *When you are having company for a meal and you want them to take their places at the table, you say _____;* total Infs questioned, 75) Inf **OK3,** You-all come in and eat your dinner; (Qu. Y19, *To begin to go away from a place: "It's about time for me to _____."*) Inf **SC55,** Put y'all down; (Qu. EE15, *When he has caught the first of those that were hiding what does the player who is 'it' call out to the others?*) Inf **LA20,** Y'all can come out; **DC8,** Y'all come in free; (Qu. II39, . . *'Thank you'*) Inf **TX98,** Thank y'all; y'all come back now; **TX89,** Y'all come back again; (Qu. NN11, *Informal ways of saying 'good-bye' to people you know quite well*) Inf **TX98,** Y'all be good; **OK3, SC40,** Y'all come (back); **VA85,** Y'all come back, you hear; **SC24,** Y'all come to see us; **SC11,** Y'all hurry back; [**VA75,** You'll come; **KY42,** You'll come and see me; **KY10,** You'll take it easy [*DARE* Ed: prob FW mishearing of *y'all*];] (Qu. NN22b, *Expressions used to drive away children*) Inf **MO23,** Y'all get out here; [**GA28,** You all will just have to get gone]. **1967** *DARE* FW Addit **cLA,** You-all—[ˌjuˈwɔl]. We are not taught in the South to say y'all [jɔl]. We used to be corrected for that; they'd say, "Yawl's a little boat." **1981** Pederson *LAGS Basic Materials* **Gulf Region,** [Proncs of the types [ˈjuuˌɒˑɫ, -ˌɒˑᵊɫ] occur frequently; proncs of the types [jɒˑl, jɔˑl, jaˤɔl, jɔᵊl] are also common, with those of the types [jᵻˤl, jaˑɯ] occurring occasionally.] **1986** Pederson *LAGS Concordance ([When are] you [coming again])* **Gulf Region,** [Of the 380 infs who responded with *you-all* and the 376 infs who responded with *y'all,* a total of 188 infs characterized their resp as "always plural," "always more than one," "never to one," "never used in the singular," "singular to Yankees," etc.] **1989** *AmSp* 64.274, Southerners don't use *you all* very much; in formal situations they use either *you* or *y'all* as the pronoun. **1996** *SECOL Rev.* 20.7 **Sth,** A woman was recently observed asking a group of family members, 'Did y'all take out the trash?', a chore which one person handles alone (she had not asked anyone specifically to do this chore and it did not matter to her who did the task; she wanted only to confirm that it had been done). **2001** *DARE* File **AL** [Black], Y'all is more casual and *you all* is more formal. **2001** [see **you-all's** adj, pron²].

b Used attrib; see quots.

1861 in 2010 Montgomery–Ellis *Corpus Amer. Civil War Letters* **GA,** I wish this war would end so you all soldiers could get home one more time. **1871** (1892) Johnston *Dukesborough Tales* 73 **GA,** You all little fellows was monstrous badly skeerd. **1879** *Scribner's Mth.* 18.567 **Sth** [Black], Is y' all niggers gwine set up all night foolin' long o' dat dar ole bull beef? **1927** [see **A1c** below]. **1931** (1991) Hughes–Hurston *Mule Bone* 97 **cFL** [Black], Now, don't you-all boys fight. **1996** Bell *Biggie Poisoned Politician* 25 **TX,** Y'all kids go on and play. **2001** *DARE* File

nwMS, neOK, ceTX, Here are three examples of y'all used before a noun . . "before y'all civil rights workers got here". . . "I caught y'all two". . . "I need y'all guys to help."

c usu as *y'all:* Used with a preceding qualifier, as *all, any, both, some,* without *of.*

1873 [see **A1a** above]. **1886** *Harper's New Mth. Mag.* 73.703 **VA** [Black], All y'all jes stand back. **1927** Kennedy *Gritny* 68 **seLA** [Black], Some y'all kin laugh, if you like. *Ibid* 193, All y'all members come wid me to de kitchen. **1935** Hurston *Mules & Men* 61 **ceFL** [Black], Well, all y'all want to marry my daughter, and youse all good men. **1941** Wheaton *Mr. George's Joint* 87 **eTX** [Black], Ain't some y'all wanna drink? **1941** Chamberlain *Leaf Gold* 157 **KY,** Thanks fer a good day, Ina; all y'all come to see us. **1954** Killens *Youngblood* 128 **GA** [Black], "What would you do if you had a million dollars?" "Who—me?" "Any y'all." *Ibid* 420, Y'all better listen to Baby Face. . . He talks more sense than all y'all put together. **1959** Hughes–Martin *Simply Heavenly* 68 **Harlem NYC** [Black], Both you-all belong to my church. **1968** *DARE* (Qu. EE15, *When he has caught the first of those that were hiding what does the player who is 'it' call out to the others?*) Inf **GA**68, All y'all come on. **2001** *DARE* File **AL,** [We] were sitting in the back yard, when I saw the elderly neighbor lady tinkering in her back yard. She could not see all of us clearly (and vice versa) because of the bushes along the fence. She called out "Hey all y'all", and we "hey'd" back at her. **2003** *Harvard Mag.* July–Aug 8 **cTX,** "Y'all" is frequently used in the singular; "all y'all" is the plural form in this here part of Texas.

2 You—used as a second person sg pron, esp in polite or formulaic phrr. Note: For a discussion of the pragmatic contexts of such uses, see Montgomery in 1996 *SECOL Rev.* 20.3–10. Cf **youse 2, you-uns** pron[1] **2**

1869 *Lippincott's Mag. Lit. Sci. Educ.* 3.318 **TN,** The Tennessee lady says . . to a friend, as she bids her good-bye . . "Won't you all come and see me?" or, on meeting her, "How do you all do?" meaning only the one addressed. **1896** *DN* 1.411 **DE, IL, NC,** *All:* "You *all*" often means one person. . . "What you all doin'?" **1910** Bronson *Reminiscences Ranchman* 76 **West,** It's . . hard fo' a bunch o' long-horn rawhides like we-all t' git t' see how 'n hell a short-horn, stall-fed Yankee like you-all . . 's a goin' t' git t' handle a cow outfit anywheres. **1923** *DN* 5.218 **swMO,** Now aint you-all a purty lookin' thing! **1926** *AmSp* 2.133 **VA,** In Virginia, for example, a particularly obliging salesgirl will ask a woman shopper, "Will you-all want something?" And one's laundress . . never omits the respectful suffix. Many Southerners who do not use the expression in the singular use it when addressing more than one person. **1929** *AmSp* 4.54 **MO,** Here in Missouri . . I have again and again heard "you all" used in speaking to one person. Only yesterday one of my own pupils in Junior College addressed me in that way, although our students, truth to tell, do not often use the expression. *Ibid* 328 **KS,** I was addressed as "you-all" twice, in the singular, in one day at Lawrence. **1936** *AmSp* 11.351 **eTX** [Black], White speakers use you-all only as a plural. . . Negroes may use it with singular meaning as a polite form. **1953** Randolph–Wilson *Down in Holler* 56 **Ozarks,** In many cases, of course, *you-all* may be addressed to one person without being a true singular. . . But when I win a pot in a poker game, and the dealer pushes the chips toward me with the remark *"You-all* take the money, Vance," he is surely speaking to me, and nobody else. And when a neighbor and I are hunting, just the two of us in a vast wilderness, and he cries out "Why don't *you-all* shoot?" then it seems to me that *you-all* is used in the second person singular. . . One sometimes hears backwoods preachers hailing the Deity as *you-all.* **1965–70** *DARE* (Qu. II15, *When somebody is passing by and you want him or her to stop and talk a while*) Inf **TX**45, Y'all come in for a while; **VA**85, Y'all come on in; **AR**56, **TX**53, Y'all get out for a while; **MS**69, Y'all get out for a while; (Qu. MM22, *If you are talking to a friend who lives in another place and you want to inquire about his neighborhood . . "How are things _____?"*) Inf **NC**38, With you-all; (Qu. NN10a, *Expressions [such as 'hello'] used when you meet somebody you know quite well*) Inf **OK**27, How y'all; (Qu. NN10b, *Greetings used when you meet somebody you do not know well*) Inf **LA**25, How y'all do. **1975** *AmSp* 50.316 **VA,** I noticed that in stores and restaurants, "Y'all come back real soon now" (or a variation) consistently accompanied the bill, whether I was alone or in a group. . . I also observed it when speakers intended to encourage an atmosphere of friendliness and informality. For example, a salesgirl in a local clothing store approached me with, "Can I show you something?" When I had found some items, she said, "Did y'all find some things to try on?" . . In an evening class that I was teaching when I had a

bad cold, I was told, "Why don't y'all go home and get in bed and get over that cold?" **1986** Pederson *LAGS Concordance ([When are] you [coming again])* **Gulf Region,** [Of the 380 infs who responded with *you-all* and the 376 infs who responded with *y'all,* a total of 23 infs characterized their resp as "sometimes to one person," "could be used to one person," "to one or more than one," "has heard it used in the singular," etc.] **2002** Proulx *That Old Ace* 65 **TX,** [To one person:] Will you all take a glass of water or some Pepsi? **2004** *DARE* File **AL** (as of c1998), As I entered the [shop] in the outlet mall . . the greeter asked: "Can I he(l)p yall?" I was . . alone . . no apparent relations . . hanging around, and given that we did not know each other, she had no reason to believe that they would follow me into the store.

B As adj.

Your—used as a second person pl possessive. [Zero possessive] *among Black speakers*

1862 in 1956 Eliason *Tarheel Talk* 238 **NC** [Black], I am sorry to hear of you all greaf about Mas Willie. **2004** Tyson *Blood Sign* 30 **NC,** And that white preacher would preach at them, 'Now, y'all obey y'all masters, like the Bible says.'

you-alls pron[1] Also *yalls, yer-alls, yuh-alls* [**you-all** + -s suff[3]] **chiefly Sth, S Midl**
=**you-all** pron **A1a, b.**

1856 Preston *Silverwood* 317 **VA** [Black], One of de servants . . brung dis note for some of you alls, Miss Zilphy. **1869** *Overland Mth.* 3.131 **TX,** During the war we all heard enough of "we-uns" and "you-uns," but "you-alls" was to me something fresh. **1873** *Little Corporal* 16.102 **Sth** [Black], Brudder Musgrove say boff yer alls wus one piece er flesh. **1895** *DN* 1.375 **seKY, eTN, wNC,** *You alls:* for you. "You alls come by and see us." **1897** Lewis *Wolfville* 168 **AZ,** He's likewise what you-alls calls a kleptomaniac. **1900** Blanchard *Daughter Freedom* 115 **NC** [Black], I come down ter see yuh-alls go down the ribber. **1916** McNealus *Lay Land* 43 [Black], All der whife fokes 'lowed ter go ter der quarters that night, same as yer all's calkerlates on gwine ter that onnery leetle 'casion. **1923** *DN* 5.225 **swMO,** *You-all. . . You.* Also *You-alls.* **1927** *AmSp* 3.6 **Ozarks,** [Pronouns, second person nominative plural:] You-alls. **1928** *AmSp* 4.154 **KY, TN,** What are you-alls going to do next? **1934** Lomax–Lomax *Amer. Ballads* 218 **LA** [Black], You-alls wa't laugh at me so well,/ I wish you'd knowed dat Creole swell. **1940** Harris *Folk Plays* 148 **eNC,** I do feel so sorry for you alls. **2004** *DARE* File **csWI,** [Black radio announcer:] One of yalls will get two tickets [to the concert].

you-all's adj, pron[2] Also *y'all's* **Sth, S Midl** Cf **your-all's**
Your; yours—usu in ref to two or more persons; also in combs *both y'all's, all ~.*

1856 Preston *Silverwood* 198 **VA** [Black], I have a sketch of it made for 'you all's' satisfaction, as Uncle Felix would say. **1858** *S. Lit. Messenger* 26.251 **VA,** Prizin of tobakker, which y'all's Winstun nose how to do it, givs you a parshill idee. **1866** Trowbridge *South* 163 **VA,** I did n't think it was you all's fault. **1891** French *Otto* 162 **AR,** I put it [= bread dough] in the steamer. . . Did n't raise up high like you all's. **1893** Shands *MS Speech* 67, *We all's.* A possessive form of *we all* used by negroes and illiterate whites. *You all's* also is heard. **1909** *DN* 3.390 **eAL, wGA,** Let's go over to yall's house. **1928** *AmSp* 4.158, I have heard more than one Alabamian and Georgian, not all of them unlettered, many of them high school graduates, or more often (girls) 'finishing school' products, speak of 'you-all's house.' **1934** Carmer *Stars Fell on AL* 190, We are honored to have you-all's company. **1944** [see **you-all A1a**]. **1954** Killens *Youngblood* 46 **GA** [Black], Got to take both y'all's shoes to the shoe shop. **1960** Lee *Mockingbird* 127 **sAL,** What am I gonna do about you all's church this Sunday? **1966** Dakin *Dial. Vocab. Ohio R. Valley* 2.309, *You-all's* is virtually unused north of the Ohio. **1968** *DARE* FW Addit **GA**38, Are these y'all's flowers? **1976** Garber *Mountain-ese* 104 **sAppalachians,** You-all's dog stayed over at our house last night. **1986** Pederson *LAGS Concordance,* 1 inf, **seAL,** Is this car all y'all's?—commonly used here. **1989** Pederson *LAGS Tech. Index* 150 **Gulf Region,** *You-all's . .* y'all's (118 [of 914 infs]) . . you-all's (60). **2001** *DARE* File **MS,** For plural possessive, would you/you all say "your all's" or "you all's"?—Y'all's. Even though I use you-all much more often than I use y'all (since I'm old—younger speakers rarely use you-all), I don't think I'd ever say you-all's and I know I would never say y'all's. . . One thing to keep in mind is that the possessive form is often simply "your" since the plural reference is often established earlier in the sentence. A typical sentence would be something like this: "Did y'all [or you-all] remember to bring your books?" The same is true for second uses of non-genitive forms. E.g., "What did y'all do when you saw the tiger?" **2008** *DARE* File—Internet **TN**, Is this all y'all's favorite color?

you-alls's adj, pron　Also *y'alls's, y'allses, you(r)-allses* **Sth, S Midl**　Cf **your-all's**

Your, yours—usu in ref to two or more persons.

　　1983 Abbott *Womenfolks* 164 **AR**, Let's us go on over to your allses house and eat us some dinner. **1983** (1984) Hill *Blue Rise* 70 **MS**, 'Preciate y'allses prayers while we have the care of my mother. **1999** Alderman *Family Man* 49 **sGA**, I was on my way to y'alls's house with a chicken pie an' some stuff for yore supper. **2000** *DARE* File **MO**, A third form offered by a student of mine is "you allses'," a possessive referring to a non-homogeneous group (according to her), as in "Write down you allses' phone numbers." . . Incidentally, she says she would say "your all's" and "your allses'." **2001** *Ibid* **csOK**, Yalls's [jalzɨz] as in "This is y'alls's". . . (This informant . . uses y'all, youns, and youse[s] all three as plurals of you). **2010** *DARE* File—Internet **cNC**, Im waiting another week or two to get the stink of you alls's shit out of the way.

youans　See **you-uns** pron[1]

you betcha adv phr　Also *you betcher, ~ betchy* [Pronc-spp for *you bet you* or *you bet your* (as abbrs of a phr such as "You bet your life")]　**chiefly Nth, N Midl, CA, TX; now esp Upper MW, NW**　See Map

Yes, indeed; certainly.

　　1889 *Cornhill Mag.* 13.59, He could lie—by the rod. But if interrupted by a question, his answer invariably was, 'You betcher!' **1905** Wood *Back Home* 265 **OH**, "Would n't you let me play with it when you was in the store?" And he catches her up in his arms and says: "You betchy!" **1905** *Amer. Mag.* June 219, In a second I was wide awake, you betcha! **1906** *DN* 3.165 **nwAR**, You bet you [bečə]. **1913** *Century Illustr. Mag.* 73.523 **WY**, My astuteness won from Roddy an admiring, "You betcher! Say, you ain't no fool on a horse-deal, even if ye did come from Noo York." **1913** *Munsey's Mag.* Mar 968 **ME**, Oh, I warned him good, you betcha. **1915** *Outlook* 13 Jan 82 **WI**, "Now are you really an American?" I queried. "You betcha," he replied. . . "I came from Wagner, Wisconsin." **1927** Lewis *Elmer Gantry* 143 **KS**, "Fine town. Lots of business." "You betcha." **1960** Korson *Black Rock* 30 **PA**, "But Ginder knew?" "Yeah, you betcha Ginder knowed." **1965–70** *DARE* (Qu. NN2, *Exclamations of very strong agreement: Somebody says, "I think Smith is absolutely right," and you reply, "_____."*) 49 Infs, **chiefly Nth, N Midl, CA, TX**, You betcha; IL126, You betchy; [IL21, You bet ya; TX39, You damn betcha; GA72, VA15, You betcha your life;] (Qu. NN1, *. . Words like 'yes': "Are you coming along too?"*) Infs **CA**79, **MO**19, **NV**75, **WI**30, You betcha; IL126, You betchy [‚jiu 'bečɪ]; (Qu. NN14, *When you doubt something that somebody has said, and you want to be sure that it is true . . "Is that really so?" He answers "_____";* total Infs questioned, 75) Inf **FL**16, You betcha. **1967** *DARE* File **seID**, You betcha ['ju 'betʃə] . . =you're welcome, don't mention it. **1978** Kalibabky *Hawdaw* 2 **neMN**, "Gonna play tonight?" "You betcha." **1991** Aasved–Laundergan *You Betcha: Gambling and Its Impacts in a Northern Minnesota Community* [title]. **2000** Owen *Walking Seattle* 83 **wWA**, A Working Town, You Betcha. **2007** Bamberg et al. *Selves & Identities* 80 **IA**, Jimmy could no longer imitate his Iowa accent, except with certain set phrases, as. . . you betcha. **2007** Olson–Olson *Don't Hug Me Christmas* 14 **nMN**, "What's with the 'Yah sure, you betcha?'" . . "It's my new catch phrase. . . Tourists come into

my store, wanna rent a canoe, . . I throw 'em a 'Yah sure, you betcha,' they upgrade to the deluxe package." **2007** Wootton–Savage *You Know WA* 46, You know you're in washington when. . . lutefisk is on the menu. . . Ya sure, you betcha! **2009** *AmSp* 84.119 **Upper Peninsula MI**, Speakers recognize terms such as *you betcha, pank, chook,* and *yous* as distinctively local.

youens pron[1]　See **you-uns** pron[1]

youens adj, pron[2]　See **you-uns'** adj, pron[2]

youenses pron[1]　See **you-unses**

youenses adj, pron[2]　See **you-uns's**

youerunses　See **yourns's**

you guys pron　**orig chiefly Nth; now widespread** *esp freq among younger speakers*　Cf **you guys'(s), your guys'(s), youse guys**

You—used as a second pers pl pron; orig used only in ref to males, but now generally used as a genderless pron.

　　1894 *Tacoma Daily News* (WA) 27 Feb 4/5, He held a well known city official up against the wall of the city hall. "You guys travels in de same class as me and it is fur dat reason dat I speaks out, see?" **1896** (1898) Ade *Artie* 3 **Chicago IL**, [Addressed to a group of men:] You guys must think I'm a quitter. **1912** *Chester Times* (PA) 9 Jan 6/4, [Addressed to two men:] "Say," finally said the waiter, "are you guys trying to order pork and beans?" He was from New Orleans and couldn't understand their Spanish. **1926** *Star* (Kansas City MO) 15 Nov [25]/1 (newspaperarchive.com), [Syndicated short story:] "Hey?" yelled the M.P. The two [men] stopped. "Hey, where you guys goin'?" [**1932** *AmSp* 7.401 **WA** [Orphans' home argot], *Guy. . .* Boy; girl. . . One girl to others: "Come on, guys."] **1945** *Pedagogical Seminary & Jrl. Psych.* 66.132, *Guy . .* boy, girl, student, person. . . One girl to others, "Come on, you guys." . . "Guy" is used without regard to age or to sex. **1945** Ford *Philadelphia Murder* 168 **sePA**, [Said to a man and a woman:] Where you guys going? **1951** *Engl. Jrl.* 40.439, A western schoolboy met some children from the Southeast. . . Afterward he commented . . : "Those kids talk funny. They say *you-all* instead of *you-guys.*" **1957** *Paris News* (TX) 27 June 7/2, A heated exchange of "youalls" and "you guys" transpired . . when 11 Mansfield, Ohio, senior Girl Scouts and 16 members of Senior Troop 30, Paris, spent a two-hour session together. **1979** Lowry *Anastasia Krupnik* 50 **Boston MA**, Why did you guys name me that? **1986** Pederson *LAGS Concordance,* 1 inf, **cwFL**, You guys—could include females; 1 inf, **neAR**, You guys—Northerners say. **2000** *AmSp* 75.417, Meanwhile, just as *y'all* seems to be spreading outside the South, *you-guys* is moving into the South, especially among younger speakers. **2000** Metcalf *How We Talk* 60, [Undated column from *Sun–News* (Myrtle Beach SC):] Not long ago I went to lunch with four women friends, and the waiter, a nice Southern boy, *you-guys*-ed all of us within an inch of our lives. "You guys ready to order? What can I get for you guys? Would you guys like to keep you guys' forks?" **2002** *Alcalde* July–Aug 10 **cTX**, From this office. . . you can hear it in the classrooms, at the shuttle bus stops. "You guys know where this stops?" You can hear it in the bookstores and restaurants that encircle campus. "You guys know what you want to order yet?" I'm speaking, of course, about the impending death of the expression "y'all" at the hands of the address "you guys," like an aggressive exotic species supplanting a native one. **2002** *DARE* File **Cleveland OH**, In both the public high school and private girls (middle) school I attended . . in the 1980s, we all said "you guys." *Ibid* **Portland OR**, Where I grew up (in Honolulu, Hawaii, 1970s–1980s), the use of "you folks" to refer to couples or mixed groups was widespread . . and I *rarely* heard "you guys". Now that I live in Portland, Oregon, I hear "you guys" much of the time. **2008** *Ibid,* [Barack Obama to a group of reporters:] Thanks, you guys; I appreciate it.

you guys'(s) adj phr, pron　Also sp *you guyses* **chiefly Nth**　Cf **your guys'(s)**

Your; yours—used as the possessive of **you guys**.

　　1946 Himes *If He Hollers* 48 **OH** [Black], I asked, "What's you guys' names?" "Lester," the one in the middle said, and the other one said, "Carl." **1959** Brown *Trumbull Park* 166 **Chicago IL** [Black], It's you guys' turn now. **1986** King *It* 24 **ME**, Every bleeding heart in this town is going to be screaming for you guys's blood. **1988** Woiwode *Born Brothers* 232 **IL**, We want to make this place of ours as much you guys's as we can. **1993** Jones *Particles* 13 **CA**, I just noticed both you guyses' cars are still in the carport. **2000** Metcalf [see **you guys**]. **2009** in 2010 *DARE* File—Internet **SD**, A waitress in Sioux Falls once

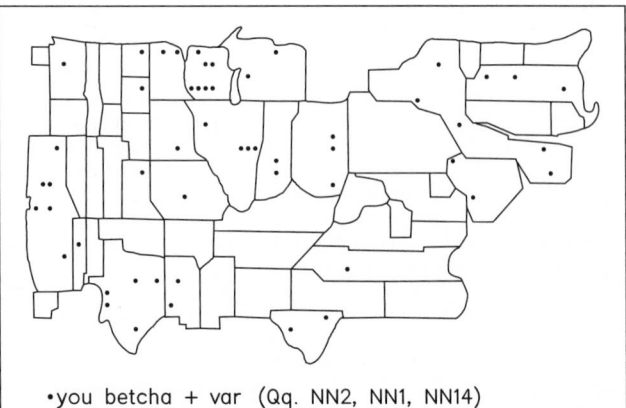

•you betcha + var (Qq. NN2, NN1, NN14)

asked me, "have you guys had you guys's order taken?" Did she seriously just say "you guyses?" **2010** *Ibid* **NC,** Thanks so much for all of the great tips! I really appreciate you guys advice. *Ibid* **swPA,** Yunz are from Picksburgh if: . . You hear "you guyses," and don't think twice. (Example. . . "you guyses house is nice").

young-come-up n **NEng**
=**youngster.**
   1889 Robinson *Sam Lovel's Camps* 164 **VT,** He came upon a patch of wintergreen, the "young-come-ups" showing the tender tints of the first unfolded leaves among the rusty and dark-green leaves and plump crimson berries of the old plants. **1891** *AN&Q* 6.118 **MA,** I, too, have heard young sprouts of the checkerberry called "youngsters" in the Connecticut valley, but perhaps oftener I have heard them called "young-come-ups." **1894** *Jrl. Amer. Folkl.* 7.93 **VT,** *Gaultheria procumbens* . . (young leaves)—young come-ups, Ferrisburgh, Vt.

young one n   In careful use |'jʌŋ‚wən|; commonly |'jʌŋən|; infreq |'jʌŋəˑn, 'joŋən| Pronc-spp freq *young 'un;* also *younge(r)n, youngin, youngon;* for addit spp see quots **esp Sth, S Midl**   Cf **old one, one, yowwun**
A child or adolescent.
   1832 *Natl. Aegis & Genl. Advt.* (Worcester MA) 20 June 1/3 **NYC,** The young 'uns must be indulged—"love's young dream" must be realized. **1839** Kirkland *New Home* 227 **MI,** There were nineteen women with thirteen babies—or at least "young 'uns" (indigenous,)—who were not above gingerbread. **1850** in 1999 *AmSp* 74.275 **ceSC,** He bot up a bit uf land and him an hiz woman had gud yong ons. *Ibid,* Now Abraham an Menomey has one more yungn. **1859** Taliaferro *Fisher's R.* 114 **nwNC** (as of 1820s), With the "young uns" it was a generation from one Christmas to another. **1891** *DN* 1.162 **cNY,** [jʌŋənz] < *young ones.* **1896** Carleton *Old Infant* 27 **MI,** Does the Avery yo'ng uns hev as much trouble as ever a-doin' sums in their heads? **1897** Forkner–Dyson *Hist. Sketches* 419 **c,ceIN,** Them cussed 'youngons' had it down in the orchard playing with it yesterday. **1897** *KS Univ. Qrly.* (ser B) 6.93 **neKS,** Young uns: children. **1903** *DN* 2.301 **Cape Cod MA** (as of a1857), Youngone. . . Child. **1906** *DN* 3.165 **nwAR,** Young 'un. . . Child. **1909** *DN* 3.391 **eAL, wGA,** How many younguns you got? **1915** *DN* 4.230 **wTX,** Young uns. . . Common. **1917** *DN* 4.404 **neOH,** Young 'un ['jʌŋən, 'joŋən]. . . Young one, child. In the '80's ['joŋənz] was very common. **1921** *Survey* 46.55 **GA,** I jes minds the youngerns. I hates to mind youngerns. **1923** *DN* 5.225 **swMO,** Young-un. . . A youngster, a child. **1927** *AmSp* 3.139 **eME,** The older people. . . spoke of "young uns" or even "yummuns" for children. **1936** *AmSp* 11.235 **eTX,** Young-ones, used as a compound noun meaning 'children,' is pronounced ['jʌŋənz] by all who use it. **1938** Stuart *Dark Hills* 210 **eKY,** It don't take sprouts and younguns any time to grow up. **1940** (1968) Haun *Hawk's Done Gone* 37 **eTN,** She was my oldest girl and always had to help me with the other youngons. **1941** *LANE* Map 379 *(Kid, tot),* [Approx 90 infs **throughout NEng** gave or acknowledged the resp *young one* (with proncs of the types ['jʌŋ wən, 'jʌŋ ən]); 29 said it was obsolete and 14 that it was "older but still in use."] **1942** Hall *Smoky Mt. Speech* 70 **eTN,** Young ones (children) ['jʌŋənz]. **1945** *Billboard* 23 June 66, Richards shows that he can keep pace with any of the younguns. **1949** Arnow *Hunter's Horn* 61 **KY,** There jist ain't room fer all my youngens around th fireplace. **1956** Moody *Home Ranch* 20 **CO** (as of 1911), When I was the size of this here young'un I rid a flea-bit cayuse. **1965–70** *DARE* (Qu. Z12, *Nicknames and joking words meaning 'a small child': "He's a healthy little _____."*) Infs **AR**55, **GA**28, **KY**44, **NC**86, 88, Young 'un; **NY**232, Young one; **VA**109, Young 'un ['jʌŋən]; **GA**82, The young 'uns ['jʌŋɪnz]; (Qu. Z16, *A small child who is rough, misbehaves, and doesn't obey, you'd call him a _____*) Inf **OK**7, Young 'un; (Qu. AA20, *A marriage that takes place because a baby is on the way*) Inf **NC**36, Young 'un sworn at the door; (Qu. AA28, . . *Joking or sly expressions . . women use to say that another is going to have a baby . . "She['s] _____."*) Inf **KY**24, Young 'un on the way; (Qu. II36a, *Somebody who talks back or gives rude answers: "Did you ever see such a _____?"*) Inf **MD**36, Sassy young 'un ['jʌŋ]; (Qu. JJ2a, *A child going to school, one in the lower grades*) Inf **FL**28, Young 'un. **1967–68** *DARE* FW Addit **DE**4, That's what they said when I was a young 'un; **NY**68, How do they do it, with all them young ones ['jʌŋwənz]? **neTN,** Young 'un ['jʌŋən]—refers to any child at least up to 12. **1973** *PADS* 60.18 **seNC** (as of 1964–65), Among the informants the word "children" . . seems to be reserved for rather formal occasions. Eight of [ten] . . use *young 'uns* (or *youngerns*) quite naturally, and one gave *school young'un* as a variant for *student.* **c1974** Jones *Ozark Hill Boy* 29 **AR** (as of c1930), Sixty "youngens"

ranging in age from six to eighteen years . . assembled for classes. **1989** Pederson *LAGS Tech. Index* 228 **Gulf Region,** Children. . . young ones (160 [of 914 infs]). **1995** *Signal Mag.* Dec np **cwTX,** Young uns—Children.

young shad n
=**golden shiner.**
   1906 NJ State Museum *Annual Rept. for 1905* 135, Brama [= *Notemigonus*] *crysoleucas.* . . Shiner. . . Young Shad. [*Ibid* 137, Sometimes they reach a length of nearly a foot, when they are thought by some to be the young of the shad, a fish with which they have some superficial resemblance.]

youngster n **NEng, esp MA**
A shoot or young leaf of the **checkerberry 1.**   Also called **young-come-up**
   1890 *AN&Q* 6.95 **NEng,** In addition to the list of green things eaten with gusto by children should be mentioned that great favorite, the young sprouts of the checkerberry, often called, in the Connecticut valley, "youngsters." **1903** Torrey *Clerk Woods* 161 **ceMA,** Some of my country-bred readers must have been accustomed to eat the tender reddish young checkerberry leaves. . . I wonder if they had our curious Old Colony name for these vernal dainties. It sounds like cannibalism, but we gathered them and ate them in all innocence . . as "youngsters." **1908** *Good Housekeeping* 47.40 **VT,** A merry throng went climbing the hillsides, . . filling baskets and pails with berries, finding bird nests, searching for checkerberry youngsters [etc]. **1919** Grant *Hist. Westfield MA* 227 **csMA** (as of 1870s), If it happened to be late enough, we would fill our baskets with wild strawberries and the "Youngsters" of the wintergreen. **1982** *Greenfield Recorder* (MA) 26 June 4 **nwMA,** Traipsing! . . It has to be done alone, or with a kindred spirit, so you can loiter, [and] chew some "youngsters," or "checkerberry shoots." **1997** *DARE* File **nwMA,** Both she and Aunt identified pippins as the tender young leaves of a checkerberry, which are chewed to extract the flavor before the berries appear. And, to make it even better, the two of them had an alternate name. . . youngsters. . . for the same leaf. And, once grandma used the word youngsters in that context, I remembered gathering and chewing those leaves and using that name.

young 'un   See **young one**

younker n   Also *yonker* [*OED2* 1601 →]   **chiefly NEng, esp ME**
A boy; a child.
   1845 Judd *Margaret* 32 **swME,** You; always say you to me. The juveniles and younkers in the town say him. **1857** *Putnam's Mag.* 9.306 **NEng,** At that moment, a yelping younker, who had better have held his tongue, but whose ten-year-old enthusiasm was too much for his prudence, was distinctly heard. **1862** Newell *Orpheus C. Kerr* 1.16 **NEng,** And whilst my name's Smith, there'll never be a younker to call me 'daddy.' **1882** *Century Illustr. Mag.* 24.589 **ME,** I s'pose six years seems like an eternity to these younkers,—but . . it don't seem long to an old woman. **1890** *Overland Mth.* (2d ser) 16.67 **CA,** I begged 'em to let me take one o' the darlin' children . . , but they said no money could make them part with a younker. **1904** Day *Kin o' Ktaadn* 122 **ME,** With a wife and some younkers to house and to feed. **1907** *Everybody's Mag.* 17.268 **ME,** It's a bully lesson, Wilbur. All about the Saviour and the children. He never forgot the younkers. **1930** *AmSp* 5.495, Why do some Mainites call a boy *yonker?* **1941** *LANE* Map 379 *(Kid, tot)* 1 inf, **ceMA,** Younker. [**1969** Lyons *My Florida* 21, It is . . watching Ma Coon take the younkers for a stroll on an oyster bar in the twilight.]

younquepin   See **yonkapin**

youns pron[1]   See **you-uns** pron[1]

youns adj, pron[2]   See **you-uns'** adj, pron[2]

younses pron[1]   See **you-unses** pron[1]

younses adj, pron[2]   See **you-uns's**

you-ones pron[1]   See **you-uns** pron[1]

you-ones' adj, pron[2]   See **you-uns'** adj, pron[2]

Youper   See **Yooper**

youpon   See **yaupon**

your adj   Pronc-spp *y'(r), yer;* **chiefly Sth, S Midl** *yo(ah), yore*
   Similarly prons *yerself, yoself, y'rsaälf*   Cf **poor A**

Std sense, var forms. Note: Exx of pronc-spp such as *cher, chore* (as in *wantcher* for *want your*) are not treated here.

1838 in 1956 Eliason *Tarheel Talk* 321 **nw,cwNC,** *Your*—yore. **1861** Holmes *Venner* 2.189 **NEng,** 'F y' ever rid on that seddle once, y' wouldn' try it ag'in, very spry,—not 'f y' c'd haälp y'rsaälf. **1871** Eggleston *Hoosier Schoolmaster* 188 **sIN,** Run fer yore life. **1890** *DN* 1.39 **csME,** *Your*. . . My accented form is [jɔə]; the unaccented form approaches or reaches [jə]. The form [juə] is artificial to me. **1893** Shands *MS Speech* 69, *Yore* [jo-ə]. The almost universal pronunciation of *your.* **1894** Riley *Armazindy* 52 **IN,** Mr. Hoppergrass, chawin' yo' terbacker. **1899** Garland *Boy Life* 32 **nwIA** (as of c1870s), "Clean y'r boots" was a regular outcry from their watchful mother. **1899** Woerner *Rebel's Daughter* 199 **Ozarks,** If ye do think yer got the vote o' Brookfield in yer pocket. **1901** *DN* 2.184 **neKY** [Black], *Your*. . yoah. **1907** *DN* 3.223 **nwAR,** Grub yerself. To eat. Used facetiously. **1909** *DN* 3.391 **eAL, wGA,** *Yô(re)* [jo](re). . . Your. Also [joz], yours. *Yourself* becomes [jəs'ɛf]. **1928** *AmSp* 3.404 **Ozarks** (as of 1916–27), The *ou* in *your* sounds exactly like the *oo* in *poor*—both are reduced to long *o.* **a1930** in 1991 Hughes–Hurston *Mule Bone* 30 **cFL** [Black], Dat dont make yo' mouf no prayer book. **1931** *PMLA* 46.1303 **sAppalachians,** Such clipped forms as . . *flo' (floor),* and *yo' (your)* are rare. **1933** *AmSp* 8.1.32 **wTX,** The West Texan. . has also a tendency to front and raise vowels. . . However, the reverse seems to operate in the case of *yore, your, pore, poor,* and *shore, sure.* **1936** *AmSp* 11.29 **eTX,** Vowel sounds in stressed syllables. . . *your* . . [jɔə]. **1941** *AmSp* 16.6 **eTX** [Black], Stressed vowels. . *your,* [jo:], [jou]. **1942** Faulkner *Go Down* 136 **MS** [Black], "You dont wants ter go back dar by yoself," she said. **1942** Hall *Smoky Mt. Speech* 37 **wNC, eTN,** Combined with a following *r,* [ʊ] becomes [ʊɚ]. . . In the speech of elderly or uneducated people, the vowel may become [o]; for example . . *your* [jɔɚ]. **1943** *AmSp* 18.267 **VA,** The word *your* more often has [ɔ] than [ʊ] . . *your* [jur], [juə] T[idewater] 16% [of 74 infs], P[iedmont] 28% [of 94 infs], V[alley and Ridge] 42% [of 76 infs], A[ppalachian Plateaus] 50% [of 10 infs]; [jɔr], [jɔə] T 78%, P 71%, V 58%, A 40%. **1946** *AmSp* 21.98 **sIL,** *Yo're,* your. . . Pronunciations such as . . *yo're* . . are common among uneducated natives. **1948** Manfred *Chokecherry* 13 **nwIA,** Yer old bed. **1958** Humphrey *Home from the Hill* 130 **neTX,** Jealousy of a known rival, or uncertainty for yoself? **1969** Wilson *Stars* 49 **Ozarks,** How come it gets to be any of yore pukey business? **1995** Verdelle *Good Negress* 7 **NC** [Black], Now lissen, y'mama lef you down here wid me. **1997** *DARE* File—Internet **cePA** [CoalSpeak], *Yer:* You're or your. "Yer not kiddin!" or "Is that yer kort?"

your-all's adj, pron   Also *yer all's*   **Sth, S Midl**   Cf **you-all's** adj, pron[2]

Your; yours—usu in ref to two or more persons.

1888 *Century Illustr. Mag.* 36.799 **GA,** Your-all's house is better than our-all's. **1894** *Ibid* 48.134 **GA,** The fau't's not in my years [=ears]. It's in your-all's mouth. **1903** Waltz *Pa Gladden* 85 **KY** [Black], Yer-all's grandpap 's mighty bad ter-day. **1911** Daviess *Rose* 133 **TN,** I jest know you and Rose Mary have got on the big pot and little kettle for Mr. Newsome, and I'm mighty proud to have the [sally] luns handed around with your all's fixings. **1931** (1991) Hughes–Hurston *Mule Bone* 88 **cFL** [Black], [Addressed to two people:] Ain't you all gonna play and sing a little somethin' for me? I ain't heard your all's music much for so long. **1959** Lomax *Rainbow Sign* 29 **AL** [Black], I thought you-all had done killed your-all's little-bitty mama. **1989** Kingsolver *Homeland* 173 **KY,** He lived next door to us for a while there. Next to your-all's house on Polk Street. **1989** Pederson *LAGS Tech. Index* 150 **Gulf Region,** *You-all's* . . *your-all's* (10 [of 914 infs]). **1997** Offutt *Good Brother* 58 **eKY,** This place was always your all's? **1998** in 2004 Montgomery–Hall *Dict. Smoky Mt. Engl.* 666 **wNC,** *Your all.* . . Is this table your all's? [1 inf]. **2001** *DARE* File **sIL,** I have either/both "your all's" and "ya'll's." *Ibid* **VA,** It seems to me that "y'all's" is the much more common usage, but I occasionally hear, and use myownself, "your-all's." But the "your" is pronounced "yer," . . "yer-all's."

your-allses   See **you-alls's**

your brain is (or brains are) dusty   See **dusty 1**

your dog is going to get out   See **dog** n[1] **B16**

you-reen   See **urine**

you're mighty come a-tooting   See **mighty come a-tooting**

yourenses   See **yourns's**

your guys'(s) adj phr, pron   Also *yer guyses, ~ guys('s), your guys(es)*   **chiefly Nth, West**   Cf **you guys'(s)**

Your; yours—used as the possessive of **you guys**

1985 Abbott *Mordecai* 147 **CA,** "Somehow you guys' gottas didn't get you all fucked up like our gottas did. . . " "What were your guys' gottas?" **1988** Clark *Ruffian* 82 **MI,** You ought not to of told Crandall you thought Tucker and Miller was still hangin' out to your guyses' pulpworks. **2000** *DARE* File **OR,** And then there's "your guyses," which I hear all the time. *Ibid* **OH,** In Cincinnati I heard "your guys'". It sounds like "your guises". **2001** *Ibid* **AZ,** Previously in discussing this topic, I've mentioned hearing "your-guys" and "your-guys's" for the "new" 2nd person plural [sic]. **2005** Butler *Don't Eem Trip* 286 **seWI,** Don't give me any of your guyses shit. **2005** King *Engl. Teacher* 234 **ME,** "He's moved into your guys' room," Fran said. "What?" Stuart yelled. Your guys'. His mother would have a fit over the expression. **2008** in 2010 *DARE* File—Internet **ceNC,** "Is this thing your guyses?" . . The vernacular these people use is awestriking. **2009** *Ibid* **swCA,** I love your guys blog. *Ibid* **CA,** I am in desperate need of your guyses help. I'm getting my hair done for prom and I have *no freaking idea* what I want to do. *Ibid* **nTX,** Just curious, what are your guys's religious views? *Ibid* **OH,** Big one I hear in my area is "your guys's" or well. . . more or less sounds like "yer guys's"—"why don't we just go to yer guys's house". **2010** *Ibid* **NJ,** I was typing that last post before I seen yer guys replies. *Ibid* **WI,** Need to pick yer guyses brains. Is it common for the EGR valve to need to be replaced?

you-rine   See **urine**

your mamma exclam   Also *that's your mammy, your mother;* for addit varr see quots   *esp freq among Black speakers*   Cf **dozen B1**

Used as a generalized insult or intentionally provocative remark, or as a retort in response to such a remark, esp in "playing the dozens."

[**1941** Percy *Lanterns* 301 **nwMA** [Black], "Then some fool nigger puts you in the dozen." . . "What's putting you in the dozen?" "That's sho nuff bad talk. . . That's talkin' about your mommer."] **1942** *Amer. Mercury* 55.223.89 **Harlem NYC** [Black], If you trying to jump salty [=get angry], Jelly, that's your mammy. *Ibid* 94, Dat's your mammy— same as, "So is your old man." **1971** Roberts *Third Ear* np [Black], *Yo' mama*—an expression used to respond to another's vituperative remarks in "playing the dozens." May sometimes be used as an apocopated form in signifying. **1972** Kochman *Rappin'* 305 **Harlem NYC** [Black], We can interpret "Your mother" as signaling either a generalized insult, or as referring to the intention to sound on someone. . . I observed the following sequence used by two ten-year-olds entering a delicatessen:—Your mother!—Your father!—Your uncle! **1987** Turow *Presumed Innocent* 207 [Black], You tell a man he's engaged in wrongdoing and he says, 'Yeah, you're right.' Everyone recognizes that's facetious. We are all familiar with that. Now, in my neighborhood, . . he would have said, 'Yo' momma.' **1992** Hunter-Gault *In My Place* 78 **GA** [Black], It wouldn't happen until after everybody else had exhausted his or her cursing vocabulary and all the "dozens" they knew—the insults game in which loved ones, especially 'yo' mamma,' got put down in rhythm and often in rhyme ("She got jaybird hips / she got sparrow thighs / she got alligator feet / and terrapin eyes. Yo' mamma"). **1994** Smitherman *Black Talk* 242, Yo momma! . . a standard formulaic phrase of ritualized insult, from the verbal game of *playing the dozens.* **1995** *DARE* File **NJ, IL** [Black], Yo' mama . . is shorthand for a longer insult about the person's mother. In New Jersey and in Chicago where I grew up, it was part of a game called the dozens which consisted of making derogatory remarks about family members (especially, but not exclusively the mother). . . In any case for most of the children who went to school with me "Yo mama" was often seen as fighting words. **2008** *Ibid* **Bronx NYC** (as of late 1950s), We white kids of Junior High School age had picked up on "ya mutha" as an insult, which I guess was just part of the urban ambience.

yourn pron   Also *yern, yone, yor(e)n, youahn* [Engl dial]   **esp NEng, Sth, S Midl**   Cf **hern** pron, **hisn, ourn, theirn**

Yours.

1795 Dearborn *Columbian Grammar* 140, *List of Improprieties.* . . Yourn for Yours. **1815** Humphreys *Yankey in England* 110, *Your'n,* your own, yours. **1843** (1916) Hall *New Purchase* 212 **IN,** May be. . . one of the two's yourn. **1862** in 1983 *PADS* 70.58 **ce,sePA,** I have not got eny letters yet but yourn. **1867** Harris *Sut Lovingood Yarns* 159 **TN,** That counts fur that shriveled up nose ove yourn. **1871** Eggleston *Hoosier Schoolmaster* 66 **sIN,** Tryin' to make you take yourn on both sides. **1883** (1971) Harris *Nights with Remus* 139 **GA** [Black], "Pick 'er up, Brer Jack," exclaimed Uncle Remus; "she's yone." **1885** *Atlantic Mth.*

55.775 **ME,** You brought along something besides this little cape of yourn, did n't you? **1893** Shands *MS Speech* 69, *Yourn, ourn, hisn, hern, theirn,* are all used by negroes and illiterate whites for the regular possessive forms *yours, ours,* etc. **1899** (1912) Green *VA Folk-Speech* 495, *Yourn.* **1901** Harben *Westerfelt* 133 **nGA,** I . . thought I'd halt an' ax about that cut o' yore'n. **1905** *DN* 3.24 **cCT,** *Yourn.* **1907** *DN* 3.220 **nwAR,** *Yourn.* *Ibid* 251 **eME,** *Yourn.* **1909** *DN* 3.391 **eAL, wGA,** *Yourn* [jorn]. **1915** *DN* 4.193 **swVA,** *Yore, yorn.* **1917** Torrence *Granny Maumee* 48 [Black], De worl' is youahn to pick an' choose. **1925** Dargan *Highland Annals* 78 **cwNC,** I kain't take any resk with friends o' yorn. **1933** *AmSp* 8.2.45 **neNY,** [jɜrn] for *yours.* **1943** *LANE* Map 615, Only forms currently used by the informants in their own speech are shown on the map. [The map shows 62 instances of *yourn* throughout **NEng.**] . . *Ourn* and *yourn* are reported as heard in the speech of others by . . [19 infs]. They are described as older though still in use by . . [38 infs]. They are described as obsolete or as heard only from very old people by . . [22 infs]. **1952** Brown *NC Folkl.* 1.610, *Yourn. . . Yours. . . Illiterate.* **1958** Humphrey *Home from the Hill* 152 **neTX,** I don't want one of yourn. **1975** Allen *LAUM* 2.54 (as of c1950), In the U[pper] M[idwest] the normalizing power of the schools apparently has . . left only faint embers of *yourn* in the records of 13 infs. Two . . are recorded as using *yourn* in conversation. Four . . admit to having used *yourn* at one time but now consider it old-fashioned or wrong. Seven . . simply say that they have heard it but do not use it themselves. **1982** in 2010 (acc) Lexis–Nexis Legal Research *State Case Law: NC* (Internet) **ceNC,** Locklear's father testified that "he (defendant) said I'm going to get that son of yourn." **1989** Pederson *LAGS Tech. Index* 150 **Gulf Region,** *Yours. . . yourn* (23 [of 914 infs]). **2003** Millersville Univ. Center for PA Ger. Studies *Jrl.* Winter 4, You can't redd up the world and make / All people talk the same./ The Pennsylvania Deitsch is ourn,/ And yourn is what you name. **2004** Rehder *Appalachian Folkways* 299, That roof of yern, hits plumb wommpyjawed.

yourns pron   chiefly **Sth, S Midl**

1 also *your uns:* Your people. [Pronc-spp for *your ones,* of nIr origin; cf *Concise Ulster Dict.* *your yins, your uns, your'n's* your family, members of your household]

1864 *Chicago Tribune* (IL) 28 Apr 3/4, If his [=a bushwhacker's] . . wife [is] asked where her husband is, the uniform answer is . . "O, he is with your'ns," intimating that he is with the Federal army. **1864** in 1952 Wiley *Life Billy Yank* 64 **Sth,** The rebs . . when they see our guns they say 'no wonder *yourns* shoot so fast if *weuns* had such guns we'd fight longer.' **1887** Parker *Henry Wilson's Regiment* 425 **ceVA** (as of 1864), An old gentleman . . came quickly to ask me if I knew that "your uns" were going back, and "our uns" were coming up the road. **1890** Goss *Recoll. of a Private* 135 **Sth,** One of them blasted fellers [=Confederate soldiers] on picket said to me the other day, 'any time your'ns want a licking over thar, come over and we'll 'comerdate yer!' **1990** Clouse *Wilder* 196 **eTN** (as of 1930s), Word is the whole bunch of yourns sure does stick together. **1993** *Working Papers Ir. Studies* 93.3.14 **NC,** With appropriate sons and daughters, sometimes 'your uns' become 'our uns,' as 'we-uns' become 'you uns.' **2007** in 2010 *DARE* File—Internet **seLA,** My heart goes out to you and yourns. It is always rough to go through times like this.

2 Yours.

1867 Ward *Gypsy's Yr.* 173 **MA,** [A White girl pretending to be a Black woman:] I hearn a heap 'bout dat ar' waterfall ob yourns. **1909** (1910) Bushnell *John Arrowsmith* 45 **LA** [Black], I'se gwinter broke dat black haid of yourns, sure es I'se yo' mammy. **1909** *Outlook* 92.287 **NYC,** Is she a friend of yourns, mebbe? **1952** Brown *NC Folkl.* 1.610, *Yourns: pron.* Yours.—Illiterate. **1954** Killens *Youngblood* 433 **GA** [Black], Ain't nobody's business but mine and your'ns. **1976** in 2006 Bullins *12 Plays* 167 **Sth,** That hound of yourns musta got into the roach powder I got spread around here. **2002** in 2010 *DARE* File—Internet **DC** [Black], Who you should be recalling is that Senator of yourns Ben Cardin who said he was holding his vote on the DC mayor taking over. **2005** *Ibid* **cnGA,** Our family is here for yourns. We love yuns very much. God called him home. He done his job here very well. I found this and wanted to send it yournses way! **2009** *Ibid* **cNC,** He grabbed my hand, pulling it next to his, our palms facing the sky. "See? Yourns is clean. Mine? The dirt is *in* me."

yourns's adj, pron   Also *you(e)runses, yourenses, yo(u)rnses, youruns's* [Appar either **yourns 1** + possessive *-'s* or "double possessive" of **you-uns** pron[1] (like **your-all's, your-guys'(s)**)] **S Midl**

Your; yours—usu in ref to more than one person.

1913 Kephart *Highlanders* 286 **sAppalachians,** Let's we-uns all go over to youerunses house. **1942** Hall *Smoky Mt. Speech* 82 **wNC, eTN,** *Yours* ['jurənzəz] (plural; once). **1949** Webber *Backwoods Teacher* 95 **Ozarks,** It's your'ns's school; *I* ain't havin' no part in it. **1952** Brown *NC Folkl.* 1.610, *Yourunses. . . Yours.*—Illiterate. **1956** Hall Coll. **eTN,** I saw a bear cross into yourenses woodland. **1976** Garber *Mountain-ese* 105 **sAppalachians,** This calf don't belong to usenses so it must be yournses. **1981** Pederson *LAGS Basic Materials,* 1 inf, **cnAR,** It's all right for them to put such stuff down yournses ['joˇ·ɚ ̩nzɪz] throat, but they can't mine. **1983** *Bittersweet* 10.3.11 (Internet) **swMO,** I've heard a lot of people say you'uns, and yourns's. "Yourns's cows are out in the garden." **2004** in 2010 *DARE* File—Internet **eOK,** My kinfolk, at least the older ones, used yourunses for the second person plural possessive, which seems to embarrass the city-dwellers. **2005** Williams *Gratitude* 538 **wNC** (as of 1940s), *Yornses':* (yorn'-ziz) possessive form of *your* (belonging to *the whole bunch of yuns*). Examples: *Yornses'* clothes is still a-hangin' on the line. *Yornses'* cow is in the cornfield. **2005** [see **2**]. **2006** in 2010 *DARE* File—Internet **TN,** Good ol Tennessee. Where we say young'uns (i dont but most do) and even Yournses like your alls. Like . . are those yournses dogs or someone elses. **2007** *Ibid* **Ozarks,** We say "you'uns" for the plural "you" and "your'uns's" for the plural possessive "yours."

yours exclam

You're welcome.

1936 *AmSp* 11.276 **eTN,** *Yours.* Reply to 'thank you' for a favor. **1969** *DARE* FW Addit **swKY,** *Yours* [jɚz]—used instead of "you're welcome" as a response to thank you. Occasional, becoming old-fashioned.

your uns   See **yourns 1**

yourunses, youruns's   See **yourns's**

yous pron   See **youse**

you's adj

Your.

1969 Gazaway *Longest Mile* 74 **eKY,** We's plannin' t'soak you's duds mostly dry by seepin' 'em out in' our'n. **1999** *DARE* File **csWI,** [To two people:] If yous wanted, yous could call this number to find out; maybe yous' organization could get something out of it.

youse pron   Also *yez, yiz, yooz, yous, youze, yuhs, yuse, yuz(z)* [Ir dial; *EDD yees, yous*]

1 You—used as a second pers pl pron.   esp **NEast, N Midl, Gt Lakes** Cf **you guys, youse guys**

1862 in 2003 Watford *Civil War NC* 1.52 **cNC,** Dear Father and Mother I will endevor to try to write a few lyns to youse to let youse now . . that my helth is tolerable good. **1887** in 2010 (acc) Lexis–Nexis Legal Research *State Case Law: IA* (Internet), Now youse all hold a noat of ten hundred dolers providing you can sell for 25 dolers an aker youse will all haf to gree to take more or less. **1890** *Scribner's Mag.* 8.686 **NYC,** "Ah!" snarled Raegen . . , "you'se [=policemen] think you have me now, sure, don't you?" **1892** *Overland Mth.* (2d ser) 20.39 **swCA,** I say, s'posin yuh let me pilot yuhs to a first-rate pluce. **1899** *Daily Northwestern* (Oshkosh WI) 16 Oct 4/7 **KS,** "Sure nuff I's kin fix yuse fallors," said the liveryman. **1903** [see **you-uns** pron[1] **1**]. **1910** Raine *Bucky O'Connor* 28 **West,** You're wise guys, gents, both of yez. **1914** in 2010 (acc) Lexis–Nexis Legal Research *State Case Law: CA* (Internet), Now Jim if you or Charley has any money that is not used you can let me have it I will pay youse the same interest as I have to pay. **1920** *Ibid: LA,* Healey . . demanded that the door be opened, to which the answer was, "There's too many of yous out there." **1932** Farrell *Young Lonigan* 138 **Chicago IL** (as of 1916), Now shut up, and shake hands; if yuh don't, I'll fight the two uh yuhs, said the dick. **1947** *Milwaukee Jrl.* (WI) 9 May 20/7 **seWI,** "Youse" and "ain't" are commonly used in Milwaukee. **1949** Kurath *Word Geog.* Fig. 114, [Among those informants who have a form for the second person plural, *yous* predominates in **c** and **sePA, ce, cs,** and **seNJ,** and is found scattered in **nMD.**] **1965** *DARE* File **swWI,** Did youse [jus] want anything on your cheeseburgers? **1966** *DARE* (Qu. NN22b, *Expressions used to drive away children*) Inf **ME1,** Run along with youse [juz]. **1968** *DARE* FW Addit **New Orleans LA,** *Youse*—2nd person plural pron. Occasionally competes with *you all* or *yall;* **nwMD,** *Yous* [juz] for *you.* **1974** in 2010 (acc) Lexis–Nexis Legal Research *State Case Law: PA* (Internet), He reloaded the gun, and pointed it at me and Kenny and said, "Youse are next," you know? And he said, "Youse better not say a word about this." **1979** *DARE* File **ceIA,** The word "yous" was used as the plural of you.

In speaking to a group, a Dyersville-ite would inquire, "Are yous going now?" or "Yous guys come here." **1990** *WI State Jrl.* (Madison) 27 Dec sec A 10 **nwMI**, Yoopers use words like "youse" and "dem" just like people in the Italian neighborhoods of the Bronx. **1996** *DARE* File, Is it possible there are two "youse" that are distributed differently by ethnicity, geography and history? In Buffalo, NY, youse has the clear oo of hoot. In Southern California I've also heard yiz with the i of hit from those from the Midwest. *Ibid* **seMO**, My aunt who has lived in Southeast Missouri her entire life says "yuz" as in, "Yuz want to come back to the house for some cake?" The pronunciation is between schwa and a "oo" in "foot". She uses it for singular and plural. *Ibid,* I grew up in rural east central Missouri, west of St. Louis, and never, ever heard "Yuz" from native Missourians, although I certainly heard "youse" in Illinois, esp. in the Chicago area. **1997** *DARE* File—Internet **cePA** [Coal Speak], *Youze, yuz, yooz, yiz:* Plural of you. . . "Hey, whad'r youze doin' over dere?" "Do yooz wanna go for some kortz?" "How're yiz doin, yo?" **1998** *Ibid* **cePA** [Language of the Hayna Valley], *Yuzz*—Second person, plural or singular. **2004** in 2010 (acc) Lexis-Nexis Legal Research *State Case Law: WV* (Internet), The appellant responded, "She better not be. . . I'll shoot every one of yous." . . Mr. Toler ran to the neighbor's house to call an ambulance and the police. Meanwhile, the appellant stood on his porch and yelled, "I told you I'd shoot you-ins." **2007** [see **youse guys**]. **2009** *AmSp* 84.445 **NJ**, The second-person plural pronoun *youse* was reported in several areas of the state. . . Though very few of these college students or college-bound students reported that they used it themselves. There were reports of frequent usage in some of their communities. . . Many informants rejected this usage as "wrong."

2 You—used as a second person sg pron.

1896 *Century Illustr. Mag.* 51.629 **NYC**, Say, young feller, where wuz youse when de fire started? **1904** *Outing* 44.279 **NYC**, "See here, Willie," they say, "we've a-rescued youse from drownin', ain't we? An' youse stick to telling your mother dat." **c1936** in Lib. of Congress *Amer. Memory: WPA Life Hist.* (Internet) **TX** [Black], Marster Ross sez, 'nigger, when Ise ready fo' let youse go I'll tell youse.' **1969** Gazaway *Longest Mile* 73 **eKY**, Hit's better fur you's if'n you's kin worm out. **1978** Kalibabky *Hawdaw* 1.[12] **neMN**, Youse: You singular *and* plural. **1996** [see **1** above]. **2004** *DARE* File—Internet **Philadelphia PA**, "Youse" is plural and is quite distinct from what I'm hearing, e.g., "Would yez like some coffee?" **c2005** *Ibid* **WI** [WI Dict:], Could youse borrow me a couple two-tree bucks, yahey?

youse-all pron esp Mid Atl

You—used as a second pers pl pron.

1867 Brown *Negro Amer.* 66 **SC** [Black], "Were you at Antietam?" "Yes, boss. Mighty hard battle." "Who whipped?" "Yous all, massa. They say you didn't; but I saw it, and know." **1896** *Outing* 27.424 **ceGA** [Black], I'll jest teck de boat yous all is in, kase dat ain't so all fired heavy as dis yer one, an I'll go up the crick. **1912** *Jrl. Amer. Folkl.* 25.285 **VA** [Black], [Addressed to two people:] Youse all keeps a talkin 'bout Mistah Fox. **1914** (2001) Plummer *Boy & Cat* 126 **neNC**, When youse all gets up in a little, youse will see a fish house to the northard.

youse-all's adj

Your—used in addressing two or more persons.

1986 Pederson *LAGS Concordance,* 1 inf, **neTX**, Youse-all's—he has heard; wouldn't use. **2005** *DARE* File—Internet **eND**, Thanks for reading through a pretty long question, I really appreciate yous all's help! **2006** *DARE* File, Read youse all's gravy recipes for t'giving.

youse guys pron Also *yous guys, youz* ~ chiefly Nth =**you guys.**

1892 *Sun. Call* (San Francisco CA) 31 Jan 15/6, I've bin t' four uv youse guys t'day. **1895** *Chicago Tribune* (IL) 6 Jan 35/5, Say, youse guys kin go along home. **1899** *McClure's Mag.* 14.142 **LA**, I find my way here about de same way as yous guys. **1900** *Dubuque Daily Herald* (IA) 29 Aug 2/2, "Say," said 'Broph,' as he walked up to the reporter's desk . . , "youse guys is good, youse is." **1905** *Atlanta Constitution* (GA) 3 Dec sec B 3/5 **Washington DC**, Youse guys ought to know by this time that this 'ere car don't stop on this side of the street. **1939** in Lib. of Congress *Amer. Memory: WPA Life Hist.* (Internet) **NYC**, Awright, fellehs, bring dat over here. Bring it right out, youse guys. **1943** Pettitt *Nine Girls* 26, Rally 'round youse guys. [*DARE* Ed: A woman addressing a group of women.] **1974** *Des Moines Register* (IA) 17 Mar sec B 1/6 **MI**, The guys in lane four immediately began to discuss ways and means of getting to know the girls in lane five. "How about we go up and say, 'Hey, youse guys wanna go home wid us?'" **1986** Pederson *LAGS Concordance,* 2 infs, **AR, TN**, Youse guys—Northerners say; 1 inf, **cAR**, Youse guys—in New York. **1997** *DARE*

File—Internet **cePA** [CoalSpeak], What're youz guys up to? **2001** Apps *Humor* 160 **cWI**, *Youse guys.* When more than two people are assembled. "So what do youse guys wanna do, go hunting squirrels or play softball?" **2002** [see **youse guys'(s)**]. **2002** *DARE* File, The correct usage in Chicago [where I grew up] is "youse guys." . . Since I have been in the South for over 25 years, I have tried to substitute "y'all" but in times of crisis . . "youse guys" always slips out. *Ibid* **sePA**, Where I grew up (eastern Pa & Philly), and when, 1950s, you guys was the standard white working class salutation. I still use it—in preference to youse guys, which is what my grandmothers said. **2007** *Ibid* **St. Louis MO**, I learned "nigger" in Saint Louis when I was in the first grade. . . "Youse know what my dad told me we call youse guys? Niggers! That's what we call youse: niggers!" **2010** *DARE* File—Internet **ceMI**, You'll never see a Bay Citian blink when greeted with "What can I get youse guys?" at one of the city diners.

youse guys'(s) adj phr Also *youse guyses* chiefly Nth

Your—used as the possessive of **youse guys.**

1925 *Amer. Mercury* 4.367 **NYC**, I don't want to spoil youse guys' party. **2002** *DARE* File **nwMI**, And then there is the U.P. (Upper Peninsula of Michigan) gender neutral pronoun, "youse guys" and "youse guys's" (yes, I have heard even that second one on enough occasions from more than one person.) *Ibid,* I've never been to the U.P. so it must have been in non-Youper contexts that I've heard "youse guys's" for the plural possessive. **2004** in 2010 *DARE* File—Internet **Chicago IL**, Being from Chicago . . that came easy for us—as do the phrases ". . . check youse guy's tires" [etc]. **2006** *Ibid* **NYC**, I've also heard this one expanded into a second person plural posessive [sic], "youse guys's", as in "over at youse guys's place". Not generally considered proper, but propriety changes with time. **2008** *Ibid* **Boston MA**, You ever hear a three year old say "Youse guyses cah is cool"? **2008** *DARE* File—Internet, What really gets me is Yankees moving down here [=**NC**], . . and then saying "We have ran into people in our neighborhoods w/ kids that talk like hicks and we don't want our kids talking like youse guys's kids." **2009** in 2010 *Ibid* **cPA**, I lived in Centre County for 15 years and now the bulk of my Central PA fishing is done through reading youse guy's posts.

yous guys See **youse guys**

youth-on-age n Also *youth-on-old-age* [See quot 1934]

A Pacific plant (*Tolmiea menziesii*) of the family Saxifragaceae. Also called **piggyback plant**

1914 Frye-Rigg *Elementary Flora NW* 119, *Leptaxis* [=*Tolmiea*] *menziesii* (youth-on-age). **1934** Haskin *Wild Flowers Pacific Coast* 151, Youth-on-Age. . . Perhaps the most interesting feature of this plant, and that to which it owes its name, is the manner in which the young plants appear. These spring from the base of the leaf blade—perfect duplicates of the parent in form and beauty, but very small. As the old supporting leaf fades, these minute plants send rootlets into the ground, and so produce a new generation. **1959** Carleton *Index Herb. Plants* 129, Youth-on-old-age: Tolmiea menziesi. **1967** Gilkey-Dennis *Hdbk. NW Plants* 189, Youth-on-age. . . The common name of the plant refers to the bud found on the old leaf. **1987** Hughes-Blackwell *Wildflowers SE AK* 100, Youth-on-Age. . . moist woods along streams. **1997** *Seattle Times* (WA) 23 Nov (Internet), Munson grows rows of piggyback plants, also known as One Thousand Mothers or Youth on Age. **2008** (acc) U.S. Dept. Ag. *Plants Database* (Internet), *Tolmiea menziesii* . . youth on age.

you-un pron [Prob by back-form from **you-uns** pron[1] **1**] esp S Midl

You—used as a second pers sg pron.

1887 *Arthur's Home Mag.* 55.31 **nAL**, Ef you-un aim ter drain thet thar pond o' you-uns . . I reckon you mout ez well wait t'well arter frost. *Ibid* 39, You-uns hev got ther butt-end o' ther load ter tote. . . We-uns hev lost 'er fren' . . ; but fur you-un ther row will be weedier than that. **1889** *Lexington* (NC) *Ledger* 31 Oct (Montgomery Coll.), Them snaikes is gettin' purty thick, but you'un needn't be afearred. They won't bite less they're cornered. [Montgomery: Addressed to one person] **1891** Elliott *Jerry* 99 **S Midl**, "You don't say!" Paul went on, showing himself master of the vernacular, "an' when he comes do he say youun's a good boy?" Jerry shook his head quietly. . . "He says, says he, 'Does youuns knows yer lessing, Jerry'?" **1898** *Midland Mth.* 9.248 **KY**, I've been watching on youun for some time, and when I seed youun bend over, I knowed yer were trackin' on us. [**1927** *AmSp* 2.287, The worst error in the above paragraph is the use of *yo'un*—a word never heard in the Ozarks. *You-uns* is common enough, but the singular form is unknown.] **1971** *Appalachian Oral Hist. Project* 33 (Montgomery Coll.) **eKY**, You just learnt that book from the first beginning to the back, and you knowed it by heart, and then they would just turn you'un in to another book.

you-uns pron[1]   Usu |'juɑnz|; also |junz, jʊnz, jənz, jɪnz| Pronc-spp *yens, youans, youens, you-ones, youns, yuns;* **esp wPA** *yins, yinz;* for addit pronc and sp varr see quots   [Scots, nIr dial *you-ones, you-uns, you yins*]   **chiefly Midl**   Cf **us-uns, we-uns**

1 You—used as a second pers pl pron.   Cf **you-all A1a**   See also **you-uns all**

1810 (1912) Bell *Journey to OH* 37 **wPA**, Youns is a word I have heard used several times, but what it means I don't know, they use it so strangely. **1845** *Spirit of Times* 15.72 **nwLA**, Inny o' you-uns what's got guns gits ahead. **1851** in 1972 *Settlers NE AL* 3.55, You Sead Eljah and you had lots of fun all the time I am glad to hear of youans in joying yor Self So well. **1863** [see **we-uns** pron 1]. **1865** *Ladies' Repository* 25.553, Here and there a rebel soldier sauntered around, . . saying, . . how sorry he was that "you ones were all out here against us this way." **1869** *Lippincott's Mag. Lit. Sci. Educ.* 3.316 **PA**, "You'ens," for you, whether singular or plural. A variation is "you'enses." [*DARE* Ed: This author also reports *you-all* used as a sing, but the exx given appear to mean rather "you and your family."]   *Ibid* 317, Our army found the words "you'ens" and "we'ens" all the way from Pennsylvania to the Gulf. **1869** [see **you-alls** pron[1]]. **1888** [see **we-uns** pron 1]. **1901** *DN* 2.184 **eKY**, You all . . yo-uns (mountain white). **1903** *DN* 2.337 **seMO**, You-uns or yous. . . Pl. of you. Used only by illiterate people, but always when addressing two or more people. 'When did you-uns get home?' 'I didn't see yous pass.' **1907** *DN* 3.238 **nwAR**, You-uns. **1913** in 2010 (acc) Lexis–Nexis Legal Research *State Case Law: AL* (Internet) **cnAL**, Now, men, you-uns has got all my papers . . , but I believe you-all will do what's right about it. **1930** [see **we-uns** pron 1]. **1939** *AmSp* 14.92 **eTN**, You'ns, You. 'You'ns come back.' **1942** Hall *Smoky Mt. Speech* 39 **wNC, eTN**, The pronoun of the second person plural, *you-ones* ['juɑnz], maintains its vitality in familiar use among speakers of all ages and classes. [Footnote:] Less stressed and unstressed forms of [juɑnz] are [junz], [jʊnz], [jənz]. **1944** *PADS* 2.52 **wNC**, You uns [juns [sic]; juɑnz]; *you unses* ['juɑnsız [sic]]. . . You ones; generally plural. . . Common. **1949** Kurath *Word Geog.* 67, You'ns is the Midland form and occurs in the folk speech of Pennsylvania west of the Susquehanna, in large parts of West Virginia, and in the westernmost parts of Virginia and North Carolina. **1949** Webber *Backwoods Teacher* 32 **Ozarks**, The Ozark hillman may also use the plural, "you'ns," instead of "you all," but if he has been brought up to say the term he never uses the other. . . The Missouri and North Arkansas Ozarkian is inclined to "you'ns," which more or less disappears as one drifts southward. **1966–67** *DARE* FW Addit **nwFL**, You'uns [juɑnz]; [the speaker] is poor white, middle-aged, born Starke, Florida. Her children say "y'all" [jɔl]; **swNC**, You-uns ['juɑnz, junts, jɛnts]; **swNC**, You'uns ['juɑnz, junz]; they don't use *we'uns.* **1972** *Foxfire Book* 26 **nGA**, Now if I live, and you'ns lives, an' you'ns comes t'eat with me any time this winter, I'll open a can a'souse. **1973** McCarthy *Child of God* 129 **TN**, Cold enough for ye'ns? he said. **1981** Pederson *LAGS Basic Materials* **Inland Gulf Region**, [*You-uns*—22 infs offered proncs of the types ['j(ʊ)ɨ ənz, 'j(ʊ)ɨ ɪnz]; 2 infs, [jiɛ ənz, jɪnz]; 1 inf, [juᵊnz]; 1 inf, [jə·nz]; a number of informants characterized this usage as uneducated, old-fashioned, or rural.] **1982** McCool *Sam McCool's Pittsburghese* 39 **PA**, Are yunz going to the game? **1986** *DARE* File **Pittsburgh PA**, [yɪnz]—you all. "We'll see yins at the movie." **1993** *Ibid* **Pittsburgh PA**, Not to mention the infamous *younz*, as in "Hi, where are younz going?" **1998** in 2010 (acc) Lexis–Nexis Legal Research *State Case Law: KS* (Internet), Youin's are gonna send me to jail for something I didn't do. **1998** [see **Yinzer**]. **2003** *DARE* File **seTN**, The y'all of my West TN youth is y'uns here. *Ibid* **wPA**, In Western PA, where I was raised, "youse" was often "yoons" instead of you. **2004** *DARE* File—Internet **cePA**, Dude Yinz packer fans need to . . take a lesson from cope and big ben. Go Stillers! **2004** [see **youse** pron 1]. **2005** Williams *Gratitude* 537 **wNC** (as of 1940s), Yens/yuns: More than one person. Them Yankees says we say, "you'uns," two syllables with the emphasis on *you,* or "y'all," one, but the way we say it is with one syllable—*yuns,* or *yens,* meaning ever'body, or all of *yuns* in the whole crowd—ever last one of *yens.* To us, the word *yuns* is one single solitary person. **2005** [see **yourns** 2]. **2006** Murray–Simon *Lang. Amer. Midl.* 28 **wPA**, As *yinz,* the second person plural pronoun is one of the defining items of Pittsburghese. **2006** [see **we-uns** pron 1]. **2007** [see **we-uns** pron 1]. **2007** [see **Yinzer**].

2 You—used as a second pers sg pron.   Cf **you-all A2**

[**1869** see **1** above.] **1885** Murfree *Prophet of Smoky Mts.* 7 **eTN**, I hev no call ter spen' words 'bout sech ez that, with a free-spoken

man like you-uns. **1889** *Lexington* (NC) *Ledger* 31 Oct *(Montgomery Coll.),* I forgot you'uns don't [know] nothin' of Timberlake's razorbacks. [Montgomery: Addressed to one person.] **1913** Kephart *Highlanders* 94 **sAppalachians**, Coaly, old boy! you-uns won't be so feisty and brigaty atter this, will ye! *Ibid* 117, They'd fust-place ask you some questions about yourself, and whut you-uns was doin' in that thar neck o' the woods. **1968** *DARE* Tape **VA9**, I won't even pick up the rattlesnake I killed there in the yard, I'll let you'uns [juɑnz] [=the Fieldworker] see it. **1995** *DARE* File **TN**, Medical doctor in clinic to patient who had just been given a prescription . . "Do you'uns want us to call that in for you?" **1997** Clegg *Empty Schoolhouse* 82 **cwTX** (as of c1930), "Well, aren't you'enses ashamed?" You know he'd say "you'ens" when he was talking about one person, but "you'enses" for more than one. **1998** in 2010 (acc) Lexis–Nexis Legal Research *State Case Law: MO* (Internet) **neAR**, Argel Morrow stated to Defendant, "Before you 'uns do anything now, I'm a deputy sheriff." Defendant put the gun away. **2003** *Ibid:* **PA** **cePA**, Sullivan telephoned Johnson and stated, "I need one of them when you get a chance" and Johnson replied, "Alright, I'll hit youns up."

you-uns' adj, pron[2]   Also *youens, youns, you-ones'*   **chiefly Midl**   Cf **we-uns'** adj

Your, yours, rarely of yours—usu in ref to two or more persons.

1875 *Neighbor's Home Mail* 2.21 **wNY**, That donkey looks exactly like one our old Ned used to have; his name was Jack, what's you'un's name? **1879** Denny *Wearing Blue* 318 **Sth**, You un's flag is out here and I'm going to get it. **1898** Harrison *Poems* 57, The cross-eyed one is youen's,/ En the freckled face is mine. **1901** (1982) Clark *Histories Regiments NC* 3.376 (as of c1864), He is going to put it [=tar] on you'ns heels to make you stick better in the next fight. **1927** *AmSp* 3.6 **Ozarks**, [2d person plural possessives:] Yourn, you-all's . . , you-uns'. **1942** Hall *Smoky Mt. Speech* 39 **wNC, eTN**, ['stɑp junz 'ɑɚ·gjən] 'Stop you-ones' arguing!' **1973** *DARE* File **csPA** Where do you-uns get you-uns' supplies? **1975** Chalmers *Better* 66 **wNC, eTN**, I taken you-uns potion, for I had a misery, but now I am fitten to circulate round again. **1978** in 2010 (acc) Lexis–Nexis Legal Research *State Case Law: NC* (Internet) **swNC**, The defendant . . pointed the gun between the two women saying, "I have a good mind to blow both of youns damned head off." **1981** Pederson *LAGS Basic Materials, You-all's* /genitive/ . . 1 inf, **cTN**, You-uns—some say it; 1 inf, **csTN**, We don't say you-uns—Northerners say [it]; 1 inf, **swAL**, You-uns—heard; 1 inf, **cwAR**, You-uns—heard a woman in Florida say it. **1996** Isbell *Last Chivaree* 35 **nwNC**, Is that you'un's ox up there in the field?

you-uns all pron   **S Midl**

You—used as a second pers pl pron.

1863 Geer *Beyond Lines* 41 **TN**, What are you 'uns all down here fighting we 'uns fur? **1865** (1869) Glazier *Capture & Escape* 39 **VA**, What did you'uns all want to come down here and run off we'uns niggers, and burn our houses for? **1909** *Putnam's Mag.* 6.315 **eKY**, You-uns all know . . about that thar ring that Abner Biddle give Roxenie. **1944** *PADS* 2.52 **NC, VA**, You uns all ['juns[sic],ɔl]. . . You all; a plural form. Not so common as *you uns.* **1952** Brown *NC Folkl.* 1.610 **wNC**, You uns all. . . You ones all; you all. "You uns all come to see me" . . Illiterate. **1966** Medford *Gt. Smoky Mt. Stories* 90 **wNC** (as of 1860s), You uns all come to see us. **1995** *DARE* File, In the Ozarks one occasionally hears 'youens all,' which would be equivalent to 'y'all.' They also say 'all of youens.'

you-unses pron   Also *youenses, younses*   **esp S Midl**   Cf **we-unses**

You—used as a second pers pl pron.

1869 [see **you-uns** pron[1] 1]. **1899** Burnett *In Connection* 31 **TN**, I should think all you'unses knows how womenfolks does that's airy. **1944** [see **you-uns** pron[1] 1]. c**1950** Halpert Coll. **wKY, nwTN**, You-uns-es come to see us. **1952** Brown *NC Folkl.* 1.610 **wNC**, You unses ['junsız] [sic]. . . You oneses; you. . . Illiterate. **1966** [see **we-unses**]. **1984** Woods *WV Was Good* 228, I 'low as I can come over tomorrer to hope [=help] younses, the weather fittin'. **1997** [see **you-uns** pron[1] 2]. **2002** *DARE* File **KY, WV**, You'unses . . simply adds the -es plural to folk "you-uns".

you-uns's adj, pron   Also *yenses, you(e)nses, you-unses*   **esp S Midl**   Cf **we-uns's, yourns's**

Your; yours—usu in ref to two or more persons.

1887 (1892) Hinman *Corporal Si Klegg* 336 **sIN**, Some o' you-unses men wuz out here yisterdy 'n' tuk every bit I hed. **1913** Kephart *Highlanders* 12 **sAppalachians**, Whut's you-unses name? [*DARE* Ed: A single person is being addressed.] **1976** Garber *Mountain-ese* 104 **sAppalachians**, *Youenses* (pro) you (plural poss.) Was that youenses daughter I seed goin' into the beer joint? **1981** in 2004 Montgomery–Hall *Dict. Smoky Mt. Engl.* 667 **wNC, eTN**, You'uns get a permit from you'unses parents. **1981** in 1991 *NC Folkl. Jrl.* 38.151, What in the tarnation are them things you've got on you'uns's back? **1982** *Barrick Coll.* **csPA**, *You'nses*—second pers. plural possessive adj. and pron. "Is that you'nses new car?" **2005** Williams *Gratitude* 537 **wNC** (as of 1940s), *Yenses'*: your (plural). Git yenses' feet washed and git in the bed.

youze See **youse**

youz guys See **youse guys**

yow cat See **ewe cat**

yow(e) See **ewe** n

yowler n
=**eelpout 1.**
1925 U.S. Bur. Fisheries *Bulletin 1924* 40.1.379 **ME**, *Zoarces anguillaris*. . . This fish, known as "yowler" by vessel fishermen, . . is familiar in the Gulf and very abundant locally, both near shore . . , and on the outer banks. *Ibid* 380, It is almost incredible to what a hopeless tangle of cord, fish, and slime a few "yowlers" can reduce many fathoms of line.

yowwun n Also *yowun, yowwen* [Prob reduced form of **young one**] **NEng, esp ME**
A child.
1919 *DN* 5.76 **MA**, *Young 'un:* The pronunciation common in Central Massachusetts is *yáu-ns* (disyllabic, with vocalic nasal). **1941** *LANE* Map 379 *(Kid, tot)*, 1 inf, **RI**, [ˈjo ən]; 1 inf, **RI**, [ˈjɔ ən]; 1 inf, **MA**, [ˈja wən]; 1 inf, **ME**, [ˈjoʊ̆u ən]; 1 inf, **ME**, [ˈjaλ wən]—very common; 1 inf, **ME**, [ˈjaλ wən]—obsolete, heard once. [Commentary:] Pronunciations of the types of [jawən, joən] are regarded by some informants as quick forms of *young one.* **1976** Moore *Dinosaur Bite* 38 **ME**, That yow'un ain't much more'n a animal. **1979** Lewis *How to Talk Yankee* [41] **nNEng**, *Yow-uns.* . . young ones. . . "Ayuh, thay's no accounting for what yow-uns want to wear nowadays." **1983** King *Pet Sematary* 22 **ME**, "Lookin forward to having young 'uns around again." Except that the sound of this, as exotic to their Midwestern ears as a foreign language, was *yowwuns.* **1985** King *Skeleton Crew* 423 **ME**, Maybe Granpa figured they had enough yowwens by then. **1988** Phippen *People Trying* 37 **ME**, The cats were gray and beautiful with yellow eyes and we yowuns used to try and capture them. **2001** in 2010 *DARE* File—Internet **NEng**, O.K., start with the age jokes! I'll get you young'uns yet! (that's yow'uns to the New Englanders).

yo-yo n, also attrib **chiefly TX, OK** Cf **sling blade**
A grass or weed cutter; hence v *yo-yo,* to cut (grass or weeds) with such a tool; vbl n *yo-yoing.*
1950 *Denton Rec.–Chron.* (TX) 27 July 1/1, Old Roundabout has swung the yo-yo grass cutter, piled the grass with the rake and carried it off in a wheelbarrow. **1952** *Ada Eve. News* (OK) 21 Apr 5/2, [Advt:] Auction. . . 1 Yo Yo Weed Cutter. **1964** in 2010 (acc) Lexis-Nexis Legal Research *State Case Law: OK* (Internet), Claimant . . was cutting Johnson grass . . in the highway right of way south of Bradley, Oklahoma, with a hand tool similar to a scythe, or sickle, and called a 'yo-yo'. . . Claimant further testified that he didn't eat lunch that day and had not done any yo-yoing since. **1965** Pearce *Cool Hand* 11 **FL**, The Bull Gang was yo-yoing the grass on both sides of the road. . . To you a yo-yo would be a weed cutter. **1966–70** *DARE* (Qu. L37, *A hand tool used for cutting weeds and grass*) Infs **TX**52, 89, Yo-yo; **LA**20, Yo-yo or the swinger; **OK**27, Yo-yo—similar to a golf club with a sharp edge. **1967** *DARE* FW Addit **cnTX**, Yo-yo—hand tool used for cutting grass and weeds. **1972** Shafer *Dict. Prison Slang* 41 **TX**, Yo-yo—a weed cutter. **1986** Pederson *LAGS Concordance*, 1 inf, **neTX**, Yo-yo—serrated blade; swing to cut high grass. **2000** *DARE* File—Internet **TX**, I am sending them a yoyo (weed cutter) . . which will make their weed cutting so much easier.

y'r, y'rsaälf See **your**

ystle See **istle**

yucca n
Std: a plant of the genus *Yucca.* For other names of var spp see **Adam and Eve 4, Adam's needle (and thread), amole 1b, banana yucca, bear grass 1a, bear's thread, dagger, desert candle 1, devil's shoestring 9, ~ thread 2,**

dwarf palmetto 3, grass cactus, Indian cabbage 1, Joshua, Mohave yucca, mound lily, needle palm 2, niggerhead 3g, oose, Our Lord's candle(stick), palmilla 1, silk aloe, ~ grass 2, soap plant 2, soaproot 2, soapweed 2, Spanish bayonet 1, ~ dagger(s), ~ needle 2, tule 3, wild date 1 Cf **banana B2, cactus apple, ~ berry, Madonna candle, soapball**

yuck v See **yerk**

yuck n See **yolk A5**

yucker n Also *yacker, yecker, yucker-bird* [See quot 1900] =**flicker** n[2] **1.**
  a1782 (1788) Jefferson *Notes VA* 73, [*Linnæan Designation:*] Picus auratus . . [*Popular Names:*] Gold winged woodpecker. Yucker. **1808** Wilson *Amer. Ornith.* 1.53, The Gold-winged Woodpecker. . . has numerous provincial appellations in the different states of the Union, such as "High-hole," . . "Hittuck," "Yucker," "Piut," "Flicker." **1881** Nuttall Ornith. Club *Bulletin* 6.184 **wNY**, *Colaptes auratus.* . . Yucker. **1899** (1912) Green *VA Folk-Speech* 495, Yucker. . . The golden-winged woodpecker. Yellow-hammer. **1900** *Wilson Bulletin* 12.2.11 **NY, MA**, Yacker, Yecker, Yucker. . . Doubtless of onomatopoetic origin. **1917** (1919) Pearson *Bird Study* 108 **FL**, In some parts of Florida it is the Yucker-bird. Naturalists call it *Colaptes auratus.*

yudda See **other**

yuh See **here A3**

yuh all See **you-all**

yuh-alls See **you-alls** pron[1]

yuhs See **youse**

Yukon char n
=**inconnu.**
  [**1905** Jordan *Guide to Fishes* 2.67, The Inconnu, or Mackenzie River salmon, known on the Yukon as "charr" . . belongs to this genus [= *Stenodus*].] **1955** U.S. Arctic Info. Center *Gloss.* 43, Inconnu. . . A large fresh water food fish, *Stenodus leucichthys,* of the whitefish family. . . Also called . . 'Yukon char.'

Yule holly n
A **holly** n[1] **1** (here: *Ilex opaca*).
  1960 Vines *Trees SW* 649, Vernacular names [of *Ilex opaca*] are Yule Holly, Christmas Holly, and White Holly. The foliage and fruit are often used for holiday decorations.

yulk See **yolk A3**

yuma zetta, yum-e-setti, yumezetti, yumma setti, yum setta (or zetta, zetti) See **Johnny Marzetti**

yunder See **yonder A3**

yuner See **una**

yunkapin See **yonkapin**

yunna(h), yunner, yunnuh See **una**

yuns See **you-uns** pron[1]

Yunzer See **Yinzer**

Yuper See **Yooper**

yupon See **yaupon**

yur adv, adj, exclam, pron See **here A3**

yur n[1] See **ear** n[1]

yur n[2] See **year** n[1]

yurb See **herb A1**

yurker See **yerker**

yurlin See **yearling**

yuse See **youse**

yut, yu'th See **earth**

yuther See **other**

yuz(z) See **youse**

zacate See **sacate**

zacaton See **sacaton**

zaccato gordo See **saccato gordo**

Zaccheus tree n [In ref to Biblical *Zaccheus* (Luke 19:1–10), who climbed a sycamore *(Ficus sycomorus)* to see Jesus] **esp S Atl**

A **sycamore B** (here: *Platanus occidentalis*).

 1949 *AmSp* 24.114 **SC**, *Zaccheus-tree*. . . Sycamore ('Negro'). [Waccamaw Neck, Georgetown Co., S.C.] **1966** *DARE* (Qu. T13, . . *Names . . for . . sycamore*) Infs **AR**42, **FL**7, Zaccheus tree; [**GA**77, Little ['zækrə] slick tree]. **2005** *DARE* File—Internet **NC**, We all went into the rain in our yard to plant a Sycamore tree and we call it our Zaccheus tree, because we want Jesus to come to our house.

zac(k)ly, zactly See **exactly**

zadico See **zydeco**

zaguan n Also *saguan* [Span *zaguan*] **chiefly SW**

A vestibule; a porch; a protected entry area.

 [**1851** *Harper's New Mth. Mag.* 3.465 **Mexico**, Don Pedro was heard within, moving toward the "Saguan."] **1863** *Rio Abajo Press* 28 Apr 1/2 *(DA)* **NM**, She had just seen Juanito's ghost in the saguan door. **1880** Cable *Grandissimes* 131 **New Orleans LA**, It was a long, narrowing perspective of arcades, lattices, balconies, *zaguans,* dormer windows, and blue sky. **1896** in 1952 Green *Samuel Maverick* 140 **TX** (as of 1841), On Easter Sunday of this year, she invited all the American families . . to dine with her. She served her dinner in the long room (*sagnan* [sic]). **1951** Fergusson *New Mexico* 408, [Glossary:] *Zaguan*—a gate or entrance way into a patio. **1970** *DARE* Tape **CA**192, In the mission they'd go through an archway which is called a zaguan [sə'wɑn]. **1986** *New Mexican* (Santa Fe NM) 5 Oct sec D 4/1, Quinn and Kuuipo, wearing Aloha attire and white ginger leis, welcomed their guests in the zaguan under an archway of palm trees. **2004** *Ibid* 23 May sec I 7/2, [Real estate listing:] On a spectacular 16-acre hilltop site with a zaguan, portal, ramada, patio and 50' lap pool.

zahuaro See **saguaro**

'zalted See **exalted**

zanga See **zanja**

zangero See **zanjero**

zanja n Pronc-spp *sanky, zanga, zanky* [Span *zanja*] **sCA, AZ**

=**acequia.**

 1850 (1929) Hayes *Pioneer Notes* 70 **CA**, I . . encamped for the night upon the thin *zanja* that flows through the place. **1860** in 1948 *Western Folkl.* 7.20 **swCA**, Persons are constantly in the habit of washing clothes in these zanjas, and rendering unsuitable the water for the purposes of common necessity. **1882** *Los Angeles Times* (CA) 21 Jan 3/3, They . . had never investigated what is called in this place a zanja, but in other places a ditch. **1888** Adams *To & Fro* 70 **swCA**, The canals are called zangas. The superintendent of the system is styled the zangero. **1892** *DN* 1.243 **AZ**, The words *zánja, zangéro,* replace in Arizona *acéquia* and *acequiadór.* **1928** Weeks *CA Copy* 104 (as of 1877), Who dug that there ditch and took the water out of the sanky? **1958** *S. CA Qrly.* 40.326 **sCA** (as of c1915), The concrete ditch in which we played . . was known as "The Sanky." It wasn't until years later I learned that the word was a Yankee corruption of Zanja. **1967** *DARE* Tape **CA**6, The ['zɑnə] is the Spanish name for "water ditch." . . The name for a water ditch in Span-ish is zanja ['sæn,hɑ] [sic], but the Indians just called it sanky, and the men that came in called it sanky, too. . . And so all the old-timers just called this old ditch the sanky. **1971** Bright *Word Geog. CA & NV* 166, *Irrigation ditch . . sanky* ("spelled *zanja*") 2% [of 300 infs] P[attern] XV [=Los Angeles and Southern California]. **1985** *Los Angeles Times* (CA) 28 June sec 5 16/1, We were busing along the banks of the Zanja River, its channel dug by Indians in 1819. Most residents of Redlands call the river the Zanky instead of the Spanish pronunciation, *Zahnhah.* **2003** in 2010 *DARE* File—Internet **swCA**, Other cities had these same ditches. They were called in Spanish "zanjas." I asked a man from Claremont if he'd ever heard of them. He said, "Oh, you mean the sanky? We had one all around our school." *Ibid* **swCA**, That "Zanky" came out of Silver Lake and crossed overhead the road to Burbank. **2008** *DARE* File—Internet **swCA**, *Redlands Conservancy to Save the Zanja. . .* Zanja preservationists have fended off various efforts through the years by developers and the city to modify the channel and surrounding trees.

zanjero n Pronc-spp *sankero, zangero, zanquero;* abbr *sanky* [Span *zanjero*] **sCA, AZ** Cf **ditch rider, majordomo 2**

=*acequiador* (at **acequia**).

 1860 in 1948 *Western Folkl.* 7.20 **swCA**, From information acquired from the *Zanjero* and other authority. . . two-thirds of the water goes to waste. **1882** *Los Angeles Times* (CA) 12 Feb 5/5, The report of the Zanjero was read and referred to the Committee on Finance. **1888** [see **zanja**]. **1892** [see **zanja**]. **1898** Grinnell *Birds Pacific Slope* 5, Before the reservoirs in North Pasadena were cemented, Loons were of regular occurrence. . . One . . was regularly fed by the "zanquero." **1902** *Century Illustr. Mag.* 64.371, He will . . make the acquaintance of the king of the irrigated land, the zanjero,—in Arizona called "sankero," in California sometimes shortened to "sanky,"—the water-master or ditch-rider. **1904** *Los Angeles Times* (CA) 20 Nov 8/1, One job . . which is now a genuine sinecure is that of city zanjero. . . The old zanja system has been abandoned, but the position still remains. **1926** in 2008 (acc) Lexis–Nexis Legal Research *State Case Law: CA* (Internet), He "had quite a little to do with water and the measurement of water as zanjero" for two different water companies. **1947** *Los Angeles Times* (CA) 7 July sec 1 7/1, *Palmdale. . .* Other members of the [water] board who also resigned [included] Ray J. McGillivray, zanjero. **1961** *Ibid* 27 Nov sec 3 7/1 **seCA**, Ervin Riddles, 55, zanjero since 1935, is typical of the 50 men who each day in the valley drive their pickups on water runs, lift canal gates leading to farms and deliver the amount of water requested. **1967** *DARE* Tape **CA**6, [FW:] The people who take care of or open the floodgates into the ditch. . . [Inf:] Well, everybody calls 'em zanqueros [sæn'kɛɚos]. **2000** Smith *Gt. AZ Almanac* 205, *Zanjero . .* the person who opens and closes the canals and ditches to give the farmer the amount of water to which he is entitled.

zanky See **zanja**

zanquero See **zanjero**

zan-zan See **zin-zin**

zapote See **chapote**

zarape See **serape**

zarza n [Span *zarza* bramble, blackberry bush] **SW**

Any of var prickly or thorny plants, but esp a **mimosa 1** (here: *Mimosa asperata*); see quots.

 [**1903** U.S. Natl. Museum *Contrib. Herbarium* 8.192 **Mexico**, *Mimosa ceratonia.* Zarza.] **1951** *PADS* 15.33 **TX**, *Rubus* spp. (dewberries). Zarzamora; zarza. **1960** Vines *Trees SW* 507, Berlandier Mimosa [=M.

asperata]. . . Other vernacular names are Zarza, Chaven, and Espina de Vaca. **1970** Correll *Plants TX* 778, *Mimosa pigra* [=*M. asperata*]. . . *Zarza*. . . Locally abundant in dry lake beds and resacas and other seasonally inundated areas of clay soil. **2001** Nokes *How to Grow* 369 **SW**, *Mimosa pigra* (Zarza, Coatante)—A shrub up to 6 feet tall with many branches armed with stiff prickles.

zebec n Also sp *xebec*
=flicker n² **1.**
1884 Lattin in *Young Oologist* 1.22, We once had a correspondent who called this bird [=the yellow-shafted flicker] the "Zebec," cannot say what authority he had for so doing. **1900** *Wilson Bulletin* 12.2.11 **NH** (as of 1885), *Xebec*. . . This is the name under which I received a set of Flicker's eggs some fifteen years ago. The collector knew the species by no other name.—F.H. Lattin.

zebra(-back or bird) See **zebra woodpecker**

zebra fish n [See quot 2008]
A **log perch** (here: *Percina caprodes*).
1943 Eddy–Surber *N. Fishes* 198, *Northern Logperch* (Zebra Fish, Manitou Darter)—*Percina caprodes semifasciata*. **1983** Becker *Fishes WI* 907, *Percina caprodes*. . . Other common names: zebra fish, . . hogmolly, hogfish. **2008** (acc) WI Univ. Sea Grant Inst. *Kids & Teachers* (Internet) **WI**, Logperch. . . This small fish is sometimes called a "zebrafish" because it has 15–25 dark, narrow, zebra-like bands over its back and sides.

zebra-tailed lizard n [See quot 1960]
=gridiron-tailed lizard.
1908 Ditmars *Reptile Book* 117, The Zebra-tailed Lizard—*Callisaurus draconoides*. . . Lower surfaces of the tail of male specimens white, with black bars. **1960** *Tucson Daily Citizen* (AZ) 16 Dec 12/1, The Zebra-tailed lizard . . has distinctive black and white bands on the under side and when disturbed the appendage is lifted in the air and waved from side to side. **2008** *DARE* File—Internet, The zebra-tailed lizard is common and widely distributed throughout the Mojave, Sonoran and Colorado deserts and its range extends north into the southern Great Basin.

zebra woodpecker n Also *zebra (bird)*, *zebra-back* [See quot 1955]
=red-bellied woodpecker.
1882 Geol. Surv. OH *Report* 4.1.400, The Red bellied Woodpecker, known to many as the "Zebra Bird," is the most retiring of all our species. **1889** *Ornith. & Oölogist* 14.177, A short distance from this nest I saw a Zebra Woodpecker (*Centurus carolinus*) fly from a hole in a dead black-oak stub. **1902** *Congregationalist & Chr. World* 87.742 **KY,** I am only eight years old. . . I know 42 different kinds [of birds]. Here is the list. Crow. . . Zebra bird [etc]. **1917** (1923) *Birds Amer.* 2.160, *Red-bellied Woodpecker*. . . Zebra Bird; Zebra-back. **1931** Blatchley *My Nature Nook* 111 **FL,** A Zebra woodpecker digs out from a crevice in the bark three or four juicy morsels. **1949** Sprunt–Chamberlain *SC Bird Life* 332, *Red-bellied Woodpecker*. . . the local name Zebra or Zebraback is much more descriptive. **1955** *AmSp* 30.178, We may note *zebra bird* (Ill., Nebr.) and *zebra woodpecker* (S.C., Fla., Ala., Ind., Ill., La.) for the red-bellied woodpecker, alluding to the bold black-and-white barring of the back and wings.

-zee See **-sie**

zeenia, zeenie, zeeny(a) See **zinnia**

zeke n [Prob abbr for *Ezekiel*] Cf **jake** n¹ **1**
A rube, dolt.
1970 *DARE* (Qu. HH3, *A dull and stupid person*) Inf **OH**103, Dope, idiot, zeke. **1982** *Smithsonian Letters* **sePA,** [Names for rustics:] farm boy, ag-boy, zeke. **1994** O'Nan *Snow* 164 **wPA** (as of 1974), "Buddy up," Mr. Eisenstat instructed. "Stay in sight of each other. We don't want you getting lost too." "What a zeke," Warren said.

zel pointu n [LaFr *zaile* (< Fr *les ailes* wings) + *pointu* sharp-pointed]
=duck hawk.
1916 *Times–Picayune* (New Orleans LA) 9 Apr mag sec 1/8, Duck Hawk (Falco peregrinus anatum)—Zel pointu.

zel rond n [LaFr *zaile* (< Fr *les ailes* wings) + *rond* round]
=Cooper's hawk.
1916 *Times–Picayune* (New Orleans LA) 9 Apr mag sec 1/5, Cooper's Hawk . . Chicken Hawk; Zel Rond; Blue Darter.

zemmel See **semmel**

zenia See **zinnia**

zep n, also attrib Also rarely *zeppelin* [From the shape] **PA, esp sePA**
A **submarine sandwich** or similar meat-and-cheese-filled roll.
1951 *Wellsboro Gaz.* (PA) 31 May [13]/3 (newspaperarchive.com), [Advt:] Twin Pines Tavern. . . Featuring Zep's [sic] Sandwiches—come in and try one. **1952** *Pottstown Mercury* (PA) 2 May 25/7, [Advt:] *Central Cafe*. . . Italian Zeps—25c. **1953** *Ibid* 21 Oct 3/6, [Advt:] *Try Zeps Made Only With Italian Meats and Cheese—Helen's Grill*. **1967** *AmSp* 42.282 **sePA,** Terms Used for Submarine Sandwich. . . Zeppelin—Norristown. **1967** *DARE* (Qu. H42, . . *[A sandwich]* . . *in a much larger, longer bun, that's a meal in itself*) Inf **PA**40, Zep. **1967** *DARE* FW Addit **sePA,** Zep [zɛp]—a hoagie. This term is so fixed that I saw it on a neon sign in Phoenixville, Pa. **1970** *Philadelphia Mag.* Nov 82 **sePA,** The hoagie. . . in the Lancaster area it's a zep. **1976** *Ibid* Mar 126, I don't know who your informants were that told you a zep was a hoagie in Norristown, but they evidently don't know what a zep is. A zep is not a hoagie! A zep differs from a hoagie in that a zep does not contain lettuce. A good zep contains salami, provolone cheese, onions, tomatoes, oregano and a little oil. Also a zep is made on a round Italian roll instead of the long football roll of a hoagie. **1988** Spinelli *Dump Days* 10 **PA,** "What're you thinking?" I said. Duke didn't answer for a while. Then: "A zep." . . The zep was invented in Two Mills in 1938, and down through the ages they've been exactly alike: Italian salami, provolone cheese, tomatoes, onions, oregano, and oil. On a roll. **2003** *DARE* File **PA,** In Norristown a zep was a sub sandwich. I never heard it anywhere else.

zephyr n *old-fash* Cf **fascinator, nubia**
A light scarf.
1821 *Boston Daily Advt.* (MA) 22 May 2/5, [Advt:] Just received from New-York—20 dozen elegant French Scarfs (or Zephyrs,) elegant patterns, which are going for the low price of $1 each. **1871** *Critic* (Washington DC) 5 Oct 4/3, [Advt:] Fall and Winter Goods such as Shawls, Zephyrs, Hoods, And a General Assortment of Woollen Goods. **1879** *Ft. Wayne Daily Gaz.* (IN) 18 July [4]/6 (newspaperarchive.com), [Advt:] *Reduction and Low Prices*. . . Linen Suits, Lawn Suits, Ladies' dusters, Zephyrs, Shawls [etc]. **1884** *Overland Mth.* (2d ser) 3.349, Tina, who had been staring . . at this vivacious apparition with . . tattered pink "zephyr" thrown coquettishly over her head, . . impulsively offered the purple mass of perfume she still carried. **1927** *DN* 5.479 **Ozarks,** *Zephyr*. . . A woman's wrap. Usually a knitted or crocheted diamond-shaped thing worn over the head and shoulders. A similar but more modern garment is known as a *fascinator*. **c1960** *Wilson Coll.* **csKY,** *Zephyr*. . . A scarf or kerchief or wrap.

zephyr lily n
Std: a plant of the genus *Zephyranthes,* esp **atamasco (lily) 1.** For other names of var spp see **Easter lily 3, fairy ~ 1, flame ~ 2, frost ~, meadow ~ 3, prairie ~ 3, rain ~ 1, 2, stagger grass 1, star lily 3, swamp ~ d**

zeppelin See **zep**

zequia See **sequia**

zero n [From the shape of the toilet seat]
A privy.
1970 *DARE* (Qu. M21b, *Joking names for an outside toilet building*) Inf **NJ**69, Zero. **1980** *DARE* File **Akron OH** (as of c1920), Zero = privy.

-zey See **-sie**

zickety, zickity See **ziggety**

zidderli See **zitterli**

zig n See **zigaboo**

zig exclam See **ziggety**

zigaboo n Also *zig(abo)*, *ziggaboo*, *ziggerboo* Cf **jigaboo**
Used as a derog term for a Black (or other dark-skinned) person.
1924 *Decatur Daily Rev.* (IL) 28 Feb 14/2, [*Boots and Her Buddies* syndicated comic strip:] He's homely as a Fiji zigaboo! **1928** McKay *Home to Harlem* 29 **NYC** [Black], You ugly flat-footed zigaboo. **1934** *AmSp* 9.28 [Prison terms], *Zigaboo* (or *jigaboo*?). A Negro. **1937**

(1977) Hurston *Their Eyes* 219 **nFL** [Black], Right now she got money enough in de bank tuh buy up dese ziggaboos and give 'em away. **1944** *AmSp* 19.174, Vulgar synonyms for Negro . . *zigabo, zigaboo, zig*. **1945** Saxon *Gumbo Ya-Ya* 8 **New Orleans LA,** A bevy of short-skirted black girls [in a Mardi Gras parade] . . whom the boys call the 'zig-a-boos.' **1947** Boulware *Jive & Slang* [8], [Negro college slang:] *Zigger-boo*—A nutty, crazy person. **1947** Lewis *Kingsblood* 18 **MN,** I thought all zigs were wonderful at sweet potatoes. **1955** *PADS* 24.190, He goes down on Charity Street or on one of those zigaboo neighborhoods. **1970** in 1972 Chapman *New Black Voices* 333, Im gone be./ a zigaboo jazzer teaching mountain / lions of passion how to truck.

ziggerboo n
1 =**gee-haw whimm(e)y-diddle.**
 1960 *Pop. Sci. Mth.* Mar 146 **TN,** *Gee-haw whimmydiddle,* also called a ziggerboo. **1972** Cooper *NC Mt. Folkl.* 34, For many decades and until stores became plentiful, the children's Christmas toys and gifts were mainly homemade. There were dolls, yarn balls, whistles, geehaw whimmydiddles or ziggerboos, rattle traps, noisemakers or bull roars and flipperdingers.
2 See **zigaboo.**

ziggety exclam Also *zickety, zickity, zig(getty), ziggity* Cf *hot diggety (dog)*
Used as an exclam of joy or surprise—usu in phrr, esp *hot ziggety.*
 1888 Stapleton *Kady* 380 **CO,** Bean looked at them in dazed confusion for a moment, then he cried, gladly: "Geewilikins ziggety! I do know ye now!" **1909** *DN* 3.398 **nwAR,** Hotzickity. . . An exclamation. **1924** *DN* 5.257, Zickity-bam. *Ibid* 263, Zickety-boom. *Ibid* 265, Hot ziggety-damn. a**1930** in 1991 Hughes–Hurston *Mule Bone* 39 **cFL** [Black], By ziggity, dat ol' mule been dead three years an' still kickin'! **1935** Sandoz *Jules* 404 **wNE,** Hot ziggity! **1944** Shulman *Feather Merchants* 78 **MN,** "Ziggetty!" he said. **1949** Robbins *Dream Merchants* 191 **NY** (as of 1917), Dames . . hot zig! **1963** *Evergreen Rev.* 7.3159, Mr. Calder was elated. Hot ziggety dog! Nudes for the pulps! **1965–70** *DARE* (Qu. NN6a, *Exclamations of joy . . when somebody gets a pleasant surprise, he might shout "_____."*) Infs MN2, TX1, Hot ziggety; MT4, Ziggety-damn; (Qu. NN6b, *Expressions of joy used mostly by children*) Infs GA1, IN8, LA8, NJ22, VA39, Hot ziggety; TX11, Hot ziggety dod; AL30, Ah ziggety. **1984** *New Yorker* 21 May 46 **OH,** Well, hot ziggetty, a holiday for me.

zigzag clover n
Std: an introduced clover (here: *Trifolium medium*). Also called **cow clover 2, mammoth ~, peavine ~**

zigzag salamander n
A **salamander 1** (here: usu *Plethodon dorsalis* or *P. ventralis*).
 1929 *Hamilton Eve. Jrl.* (OH) 13 July [14]/5 (newspaperarchive.com), We have taken several species, . . zigzag salamander (Eurycea longicauda) which has a very long tail which is bright yellow or reddish in color with small black spots on the back and sides which form bars on the tail and is unspotted underneath. **1953** Schmidt *N. Amer. Amphibians* 34, *Plethodon dorsalis*. . . Common name.—Zigzag salamander. **1979** Behler–King *Audubon Field Guide Reptiles* 337, Zigzag Salamander. . . Back stripe red, orange, or yellow, with well-defined wavy border. **2008** (acc) U.S. Dept. Ag. *Integrated Taxonomic Info. System* (Internet), *Plethodon dorsalis*. . . Common Name(s): Zigzag Salamander. *Ibid, Plethodon ventralis*. . . Southern Zigzag Salamander.

zigzag Solomon's seal See **Solomon's zigzag**

zinc n Also sp *zink* [Folk-etym for *sink;* cf quot c1960] *old-fash*
A sink.
 1887 WI State Horticult. Soc. *Trans.* 17.148, This kerosene and soap mixture can be readily applied to our house plants, and if the latter are set in a zink, or on an oil cloth, the application can be made with ease. **1916** *Lexington Herald* (KY) 28 Oct 4/5, I know a Hick / Who makes me blink, He talks about / The kitchen "zinc."—Dayton, Ohio. **1934** Smiley *Gloss. New Paltz* **seNY,** "The zinc" for the sink. **1940–41** Cassidy *WI Atlas* **nwWI,** Zink. [Elderly Inf] **1951** *DE Folkl. Bulletin* 1.7, Zinc (a common pronunciation of "sink"). **c1960** *Wilson Coll.* **csKY,** Zinc. . . A sink, which was originally a mere zinc basin or big pan. a**1966** (1980) Toole *Confederacy of Dunces* 228 **New Orleans LA,** Lemme go dump these dishes in the zink. **1966** *DARE* (Qu. F26, *The place where dishes are washed;* total Infs questioned, 75) Inf **MS**72,

Zink. **1968** *DARE* FW Addit **ceNY,** Zink—old-fashioned for "sink" in the kitchen. *Ibid* **nw,cnMD,** Sink pronounced [zɪŋk]. **1973** Allen *LAUM* 1.409 **Upper MW** (as of c1950), 3 infs, **IA, ND,** Zinc. A kitchen sink. **1981** Pederson *LAGS Basic Materials,* 1 inf, **ceLA,** His mother always said [zɪŋk] for sink. **1983** *MJLF* 9.1.62 **ceKY** (as of 1956), Zink . . a sink, a fixed basin. **1988** *DARE* File **ceWI** (as of 1940), Several people recall the usual pronunciation of *sink,* as in *kitchen sink,* as being [zɪŋk]. **2002** *Sun. News Jrl.* (Wilmington DE) 7 July sec A 6/1, Occasionally you may still hear a sink called a "zink." **2003** *DARE* File—Internet **Sth,** Somebody poured grease down the zink and it's stopped up. *Ibid* **ceIA,** My grandmother would always say "rensh [rinse] it out in the zink".

Z-ing pres pple, vbl n Also *Z'sing* Cf **Z's**
Snoring; sleeping.
 c1965 *DARE* File **wNY,** Don't bother her, she's Z-ing ['ziɪŋ]. **1970** *DARE* (Qu. X45, . . *Joking expressions . . about snoring*) Inf **NY**236, Z-ing. **1972** Claerbaut *Black Jargon* 87, Z'sing . . sleeping; napping.

zink See **zinc**

zinnia n Usu |ˈzɪnɪə, ˈzɪnjə|; also **widespread, but less freq Nth, Pacific** |ˈzinjə|; for addit varr see below Pronc-spp *zeenie, zeeny(a), ze(e)nia, zinny*
A Forms.
 1909 *DN* 3.391 **eAL, wGA,** Zenia ['zinɪə]. . . The universal pronunciation of the flowering plant, the zinnia. **1930s** in 1944 *ADD* **WV,** ['zinjə]. **1935** Brown *Hillikin* 21 **OH,** "Are those in that bed zinnias or asters?" she asked. . . "Zeenias," Giles answered. . . "You're not a Bostonian, are you?" **1937** (1963) Hyatt *Kiverlid* 24 **KY,** A bed o' zeenie blossoms. **1939** *Sat. Eve. Post* 18 Nov 36 **nwFL** [Black], If 'n I had me a nickel, I'd buy me some flar seed. . . Zeenies. Blue uns and yaller uns and pank uns. **c1960** *Wilson Coll.* **csKY,** Zinnia ['zinjə]. **1965–70** *DARE* (Qu. S11, . . *Zinnia*) 273 Infs, **widespread, but less freq Nth, Pacific,** Zeenya; 14 Infs, **scattered, but esp Midl,** Zeeny; IL25, NY69, WI12, Zinny; NJ1, ['zaɪnjə]; IN48, ['zinəz]. **1966** *DARE* Tape FL31, We grow petunias and zinnias ['zinjəz]. **1967** *DARE* FW Addit **cnNY,** Zinnias ['ziniz]. **1982** Barrick Coll. **csPA,** Zinny—zinnia. **1998** in 2009 *DARE* File—Internet **cwNJ,** Mrs. Percival's garden next-door included . . what she called "zee-nias."
B Sense.
Std: a plant of the genus *Zinnia,* esp the common *Z. elegans.* For other names see **chicken and egg, cut-and-come-again c, fall rose, niggerhead 3f, old maid 1, old-maid's-pink 4, pretty boy**

zin-zin n Also sp *zan-zan* [Imit] **LA**
1 =**baldpate 1.**
 1843 Audubon *Birds Amer.* 6.259 **LA,** American Widgeon. . . This lively and very handsome Duck is abundant during winter at New Orleans, where it is much esteemed on account of the juiciness of its flesh, and is best known by the name of Zinzin. **1877** *Forest & Stream* 7.354 **LA,** The variety of ducks bagged by our party are the following . . bald pate; Zinzin of Louisiana [etc]. **1897** *Auk* 14.285 **LA,** Baldpate.—Commonly known as *Zan-zan,* from the noise it makes. **1921** *Forest & Stream* 91.109 **LA,** I found canvas-back, dosgris, or grey backs, zin-zin, or widgeons [etc]. **1923** U.S. Dept. Ag. *Misc. Circular* 13.12 **LA,** Zinzin (ză-ză, nasal, from the bird's note).
2 =**hooded merganser.**
 1917 *Wilson Bulletin* 29.2.76 **LA,** *Lophodytes cucullatus.* Zin-zin, plongeon, diver, Marksville, La.

zip n chiefly **Sth, S Midl** Cf **lick** n 7
Syrup, molasses; occas sugar.
 1905 *DN* 3.101 **nwAR,** Zip. . . Syrup, sauce. 'Have some more of the zip?' Common. **1921** *DN* 5.119 **KY,** Zip. . . Syrup, molasses. College slang, Univ. Ky. and Transylvania Col. **1938** *AmSp* 13.7 **seAR,** Zip. . . Sugar. **1939** *AmSp* 14.32 **SC, NC** [Citadel argot], Zip. . . Mess-hall syrup or molasses. (The term is reasonably current in South Carolina colleges and in boys' camps in Western North Carolina, but it is generally considered of Citadel origin.) **1942** Kendall *Still in the Draft* np, [Army slang glossary:] Zip. . . syrup. **1966** *DARE* (Qu. H21, . . *The sweet stuff that's poured over these [pan]cakes*) Inf **MS**17, Zip. **1971** Dwyer *Dict. for Yankees* [30] **Sth, S Midl,** Zip—Molasses.

zipper pea n
A **black-eyed pea** (here: *Vigna unguiculata*).
 1977 Miles *Voices Countryside* 55 **FL,** These peas . . are pretty nearly

as big as the end of your finger. . . They call them Zipper Peas. **1993** *Seguin Gaz.-Enterprise* (TX) 30 July 1/2, Consumers can expect to find watermelons, . . zipper peas [etc]. **1997** Sitton-Utley *From Can See* 192 **TX,** Field peas occupied a special niche among Southern subsistence crops; many kinds existed, including blackeyed peas, zipper peas, crowder peas, whippoorwill peas, and others. **1999** *DARE* File—Internet [Quality Dried Beans], Red Iron Clay Peas—Also referred to as the Cow Pea, Field Pea, Red Pea, Zipper Pea, the Clay Pea is a fast cooking pea, and another southern favorite. **2004** *Aiken Std.* (SC) 11 July sec A 1/3, *Items available at the market.* . . Zipper Peas—Okra [etc]. **2007** *DARE* File—Internet **NC,** I am also addicted to what Brinkley calls "cream peas" but what my mother calls "zipper peas."

zippy stick n Also *zippy* Cf **jippy stick**
=cricket n[2].

1957 *Sat. Eve. Post Letters* **seNE** (as of c1890), Zippy: Any number can play. Required a piece of broom handle about six inches long and a piece of the handle two feet long used for a bat. The batter lays the short piece in an oblong hole in the ground with one end sticking out. He hits the end that sticks up with the bat causing the short stick to flip up into the air, the batter has three chances to bat the short stick toward the field. The one who stops or catches the stick has a chance to throw it toward the hole, if it goes into the hole the thrower becomes the batter, if not he and the batter guess the distance the short stick is from the hole measured by the length of the bat, the one guessing the closest becomes the next batter. **1986** *DARE* File **nwOH** (as of c1930), As a child we played zippy stick, . . the game you named cricket with the long and short stick. . . I was born in 1921, and in our town both boys and girls played the game and became most skillful.

zitterli n Also *tsitterly, tzitterle, zidderli, zitterling* [PaGer *zitterli*] **se,csPA**
Calf's foot jelly; **headcheese 1.**

1872 Haldeman *PA Dutch* 58 [English influenced by German], *Tsitterly,* calf's-foot jelly. [**1924** Lambert *PA Ger. Dict.* 184, Zitterli . . souse.] **1935** *AmSp* 10.170 **PA** [Engl of PA Germans], Other German words used in English are. . . *Tsitterly,* calf's foot jelly. **1935** Frederick *PA Dutch* 134, Zitterling (Souse)—Scrape and wash 4 pig's feet. Cover with water and boil until the meat falls from the bones. Pick the meat from the bones, add 1 pint of the liquor in which the feet have been cooked, season with salt and pepper, and add vinegar to taste. Pour into a mold. **1948** Hutchison *PA Du. Cook Book* 44, *Tzitterle* (souse). **1968** *Helen Adolf Festschrift* 37 **sePA,** Calf's foot jelly (or souse) is generally called by its Pennsylvania German name, *Zidderli.*

zodico See **zydeco**

zoon v

1 **=june** v **1;** hence n *zooner* an active individual, go-getter. **esp GA**

1884 *Anglia* 7.267 **Sth, S Midl** [Black], *To come a-zoonin'* = to come running (imitation of a bee's buzzing). **1887** (1967) Harris *Free Joe* 184 **GA,** Yes'n, a gal, an' ef she wa'n't a zooner you may jess take an' knock my chunk out. **1893** [see **2** below]. **1909** *DN* 3.391 **eAL, wGA,** Zooner. . . A person or thing that moves rapidly, a hustler. "She shore was a zooner."

2 also *zune:* **=june** v **2;** to propel (an object) so as to make such a sound. **Sth, S Midl, esp GA**

1880 *N&Q* 6th ser 2.488 **GA** [Black], "*A-zoonin.*"—I find this word used by negroes in Georgia to express the humming of bees, as "de bees is a-zoonin." **1883** (1971) Harris *Nights with Remus* 125 **GA** [Black], Ter make marters wuss, yer come a great big green fly a-zoonin' 'roun'. **1893** Shands *MS Speech* 69, *zune* [zun]. This is an onomatopoetic word much used by negroes and illiterate whites, and sometimes by educated people. A bee is said to go *zuning* through the air; a fly is said to *zune* against the window-pane; and, as rapid motion is necessary to *zuning,* a man, horse, locomotive, or almost anything that goes along swiftly, is said to *zune,* even though that peculiar *zuning* sound is not made by the object in its motion. One negro asks another if the train ran fast, and the second answers, "She farly zuned." The word is thus sometimes used in exactly the same sense as *june,* and I think is allied to it; in fact, the two may be but different ways of representing the same sound. **1896** Riley *Child-World* 59 **IN,** The cross-bow, made / Just like a gun, which deadly weapon laid / Against his shoulder as he aimed, and—"*Spring!*" / He'd hear the rusty old nail zoon and sing. **1899** Edwards *Defense* 179 **GA,** Little Henry Clay had tied a string to a leg of one of those iridescent beetles commonly called June-bugs, and released him to hear the "zooning" noise of his wings, so pleasant to the ears of Southern chil-

dren on a plantation. **1903** in 1977 Epstein *Sinful Tunes* 219, Banjos pickin', jewsharps zoonin', / All de hebbenly ban' a-chunin', / Swing low, sweet charriyut. **1909** *DN* 3.391 **eAL, wGA,** *Zoon, v.i.* and *tr.* To make a humming or buzzing sound, to cause to make such a sound. "That rock came zoonin' by my head." "Watch me zoon this rock." **1922** *W. PA Hist. Mag.* 5.297 **VA,** June bugs zooning round the roses. **1954** Killens *Youngblood* 12 **GA** [Black] (as of 1912), The only boy in Tipkin that wouldn't tie a string to an old ugly juney bug and listen to him zoon. [**1986** Pederson *LAGS Concordance* (Jew's harp) 1 inf, **swGA,** Zoon bug (=kazoo + June bug?).] [*DARE* Ed: Cf quot 1903 above.]

zoon bug n Also *zoony bug* [Varr of **june bug 1**]
1909 *DN* 3.391 **eAL, wGA,** Zoon-bug. . . The June-bug. Also called *zoony-bug.*

zooner See **zoon 1**

zoony bug See **zoon bug**

‡zoozer n [Prob echoic] Cf **zoum-zoum**
1967 *DARE* FW Addit **AR52,** Zoozer [zuzə]—a double string through two holes in a piece of pine bark (or it could be made with a large button). It is spun and you stretch it back and forth between your hands to keep it spinning.

zopilote n [MexSpan]
=black vulture.

1938 *AmSp* 13.119 **TX** [Nahuatl words in Amer Engl], In the Lone Star State. . . the black vulture, *Cathartes atratus,* bears additionally its native name *zopilote,* derived from Nahuatl *tzopilotl.*

zori n [Japanese *zori* (sg and pl); *OED2* 1823 →] **esp HI, West** Cf **go-ahead 1, flip-flop 6**
A thonged sandal, esp one made of rubber.

1958 *ID State Jrl.* (Pocatello) 30 Sept 12/6, [Advt:] "*Zoris*" *Thong Sandals*—Ideal Shower Shoes. . . 77¢. **1960** *Garfieldian & Garfield News* (Chicago IL) 13 July sec G 7/1, [Advt:] Women's and Children's *zoris*—33¢—Rubber thong sandals that are perfect for beach, back yard or casual wear. **1967** *DARE* (Qu. W21) Inf **HI1,** Zoris [zori]—Japanese slippers with a piece between the big toe and next toe. **1972** Carr *Da Kine Talk* 90 **HI,** *Zōri,* the low Japanese thong slippers often called "go-aheads" and "grass slippers," are worn by men and women of all ethnic groups and for many more occasions than in Japan. **1972** McCormick *Vocab.* HI 73, *Zori*—sandal with piece between toes. **1978** *DARE* File **nCA** (as of 1950s), During the summer we wore rubber thongs if any shoes at all. We called them flip-flops, but to some of our friends they were go-aheads or zories. [**1998** *DARE* File, I first encountered the rubber, foot shaped zori in late 1951. Several veterans of the Korean War . . wore these "Japanese shower shoes" around the barracks. . . [T]hey were not available in the PX at that time. . . [I]n February 1955, the foot shaped zori were available in the Camp Kilmer, NJ, PX. . . In September 1958 I . . discovered that zori were a popular item [at the University of Hawaii). Most of the students wore them, and they were available in . . the sundries section of the supermarket.] **2003** Guterson *Our Lady* 52 **swWA,** Was there really something called Florida Priest Week? A coterie of priests in bathing suits and zoris, discussing, say, the communion of saints?

zorillo n Also *sorilla, zorilla* [AmSpan *zorrillo, zorilla* skunk]
=Mexican orange.

[**1931** U.S. Dept. Ag. *Misc. Pub.* 101.91, Starleaf (*Choisya dumosa,* syn. *Astrophyllum dumosum*) . . , known also as Mexican-orange and, to Mexicans, as sorilla and zorillo, is a low, rather bizarre-looking shrub.] **1960** Vines *Trees SW* 578, Starleaf Mexican-orange. . . Vernacular names are Fragrant Starleaf, Zorilla, and Sorilla. **1970** Correll *Plants TX* 909, *Choisya dumosa.* . . Mexican orange, zorillo.

zottico See **zydeco**

zoum-zoum n [Echoic] Cf **zoozer**
1983 *Reinecke Coll.* 11 **LA,** Zoum-Zoum. . . ['zum zum] A simple child's toy made with a button or other disc with two eccentric holes, through which thread or string is passed, and tied, so that the index fingers are introduced into both ends, and the disc turned about, whereupon the fingers pull outward and the button spins on its center. Once started, this can be continued indefinitely. Same word in N[ew] O[rleans] French, presumably from onomat[opoeia]..

zounds intj Also *by zounds;* rarely, *by the zound* **esp NEng** *old-fash*

Used as an oath; see quots.

1797 in 1916 MA Hist. Soc. *Proc.* 49.270 **NEng,** You remember how you used to swear whenever I took her by the hand at Cousin Riddle's. I hope you have left off that custom of swearing "By Zounds," "Darn it," "I swear now, Mate," as it is quite out of vogue. *Ibid* 272, Only think of my loss, £600 "by zounds," every Copper, for . . the house Aunt Dianah left me is burnt to the Ground. **1844** *S. Lit. Messenger* 10.44 **GA,** "No opposition!" continued Darby; "by zounds, that'll never do." **1858** (1859) Howe *Advent. Americans* 453 **OH,** Well, by zounds! this is getting quite comfortable! **1884** *Overland Mth.* (2d ser) 4.212 **NEng,** Heard the like in our day! Zounds! I guess we never did. **1927** *AmSp* 3.135 **eME,** "You could knock me down with a feather" or "carry me out with the tongs!" were expressions of surprise. So also were "Land of Goshen!" "Landsakes alive," "By Zounds!" **1932–34** *Hanley Disks* **sME coast,** By the zound—old-fashioned. **1943** *LANE* Map 600 (*Shucks! Botheration!*), 2 infs, **ME, RI,** Zounds [za(^)undz]; 1 inf, **cwNH,** Zounds [zæ‿undz]. **1968** *DARE* (Qu. NN9a, *Exclamations showing great annoyance:* "_____. The electric power is off again.") Inf **IN22,** Zounds [zæonds]. **1970** *DARE* FW Addit **ceMA,** Zounds—an old-fashioned exclamation. **1975** Gainer *Witches* 18 **sAppalachians,** Zounds (interjection), a mild oath, an abbreviation of "God's wounds."

‡**Z-out** v phr   Cf **Z's**

 1969 *DARE* (Qu. X40, . . *Ways . . of saying, "I'm going to bed"*) Inf **IN75,** Z-out.

Z's n pl   [Prob from the use of strings of *Z*'s in cartoons to represent the sound of snoring]   Cf **Z-ing, Z-out**

Moments of sleep; sleep—usu in phrr *blow* (or *catch, cop, cut*) *some z's* and varr: to get some sleep.

 [**1924** *DN* 5.280, Z-z-z (sound of whispering or snoring).] **1963** *AmSp* 38.174 **KS,** To go to bed. . . *get some Z's.* . . *bagging Z's, copping some Z's, cutting Z's,* and *knocking out Z's.* **1964** Kesey *Sometimes* 213, I believe I'll see if I can catch a few Z's. **1965–70** *DARE* (Qu. X40, . . *Ways . . of saying, "I'm going to bed"*) Inf **CA**140, Bag the Z's; **TX**106, Blow some Z's; **MO**29, Catch some Z's; **PA**94, 248, Cop a few (*or* some) Z's; **PA**74, Cut some Z's; [**CA**140, Get Z-time;] **CT**34, Saw some Z's; **OR**1, Take a few Z's; (Qu. X41, *When you're going to sleep for a very short while . . "I'm just going to _____."*) Inf **FL**51, Cop a few Z's; (Qu. X45, . . *Joking expressions . . about snoring*) Inf **PA**126, Blowing Z's; **VA**81, Sawing Z's. **1967** *DARE* FW Addit **nwCA,** Cut Z's: to sleep. **1968** *Current Slang* 3.1.5 **MN,** Cut Z's. . . To sleep.—College students, both sexes. **1971** *Ibid* 5.4.22 **VT,** Z's. . . Sleep. **1972** Claerbaut *Black Jargon* 58, Blowing z's . . to sleep; nap. *Ibid* 61, Cop z's . . to sleep; nap. **1986** Pederson *LAGS Concordance,* 1 inf, **seAR,** Catch some z's (=sleep); 1 inf, **csTX,** We used to say we had to catch some z's (=sleep). **2000** (2001) Stabenow *Midnight Come Again* 128 **AK,** I just pulled a full shift, and I haven't had any sleep. . . I'm going to go catch some Z's. **2005** *Isthmus* (Madison WI) 15 Apr 12/2, I also ordered one of Reedy's wool blankets—a beautiful, thick and affordable covering, under which I've enjoyed many fine zzzzzs.

z'sing   See **z-ing**

zulu car n   Also *zulu*   **West**

=**emigrant car;** hence n *zulu* an emigrant group and their belongings traveling by rail.

 1927 Ruppenthal *Coll.* **KS,** Zulu car, . . (Railroad) a car of mixed contents, as an emigrant's car of livestock, farm implements, household goods, etc. **1931** *Writer's Digest* 11.64 [Railroad terms], *Zulu*—An emigrant outfit. **1936** *RR Stories* Sept 5 (as of 1883), Westward bound

with a car full of household goods. It's called a "Zulu car." God knows why. It was old and ramshackle. **1938** Beebe *High Iron* 225 [Railroad terms], *Zulu car:* Emigrant car, particularly in Canadian railroading. **1945** *Fresno Bee the Republican* (CA) 15 Oct [9]/6 (newspaperarchive.com), Gilbert said the fare was $517 for himself, their cattle, their hand full of possessions and their 1937 model car, all jammed into one large boxcar which trainmen christened "Zulu Car" an old railroad custom for designating a migrating fare. **1961** *Yuma Daily Sun & Yuma AZ Sentinel* 29 Nov 1/2, Smith came to Yuma in 1913 on the Southern Pacific car known as the "Zulu." **1979** *DARE* File **swID** (as of 1946), There was a special rate for anyone moving west [by rail in the emigrant cars]. We had our household goods, a '33 Chevy, tractor, disc, feed grinder, etc. When the car was switched in Denver from the CB&Q to the Union Pacific, the U.P. train crew all called it a Zulu.

zulu golf n   Cf **African golf, Amish ~**

In marble play: see quot.

 1973 Ferretti *Marble Book* 54, Zulu golf. One of many terms for games in which players shoot into a series of holes dug into the ground.

zune   See **zoon 2**

zydeco n, also attrib   Also sp *zadico, zodico, zottico, zydico* [Appar < LaFr *zaricot* green beans (by metanalysis of Fr *les haricots*), from the appearance of this word in var metaphorical senses in Creole folk songs]   **orig sLA, eTX, now widely known**

A kind of dance party; a style of dance music usu featuring accordion, fiddle or banjo, and washboard, assoc with Louisiana Creole culture; see quots.

 1949 in 1996 *Amer. Music* 14.502 **swLA,** [Transcript of recording:] At the church bazaar or the baseball game,/ At the French La-La, it's all the same,/ If you want to have fun, now, you got to go,/ Way out in the country to the Zydeco. **1949** *Pittsburgh Courier* (PA) 3 Sept 10/1 **Houston TX,** Reese Fontenet will sponsor a fifteen minute program of Zadico music, featuring Jumping Houston and his accordion over KGBC next month. **1955** in 1996 *Amer. Music* 14.500 **Houston TX,** On Saturday night, somebody holds a 'zottico' in his home. Out come the accordion, banjo and rub bo'd. . . Off they whirl in a folk dance similar to the square dance. **1962** *NY Times* (NY) 21 Oct sec X 14/3, [Record review:] A delight and surprise is the music of French-speaking Negroes who went to the Houston–Dallas area with their Zydeco music, . . usually played to the accompaniment of washboard, fiddle and concertina, or accordion. **1969** Leadbitter–Shuler *From Bayou* 15 **sLA** (as of 1953), Boozoo played a German button accordian in a style known in this part of the country as Zodico. **1978** *Galveston Daily News* (TX) 21 Sept sec C 2/3, The Gay Paree Social and Charity Club will hold a Friday Night Zodico. . . Music will be by John Val12er and his Zodico Team. **1979** *Ibid* 25 Apr sec C 3/6, Knights of St. Peter Claver . . to sponsor a Zadico Dance . . ; music by John Vallier and his Playboys. **1986** in 1996 *Amer. Music* 14.493 **csLA** (as of c1926), They—long time ago, they used to give them zydecos, see? . . they would give a zydeco every two weeks. **1986** Pederson *LAGS Concordance,* 1 inf, **seLA,** Zydeco = "string-bean music". **1990** *Galveston Daily News* (TX) 18 Feb sec B 8/1, *Knights of Peter Claver*—A Mardi Gras Zydico will be held 9:30 p.m. Saturday. **1995** Karr *Liars' Club* 211 **eTX,** A town with no music but country and zydeco. **2005** Hollander *52 Weeks* 124, After the first time we saw a Zydeco band at the legendary Stanhope House in New Jersey, Todd told me about *The Kingdom of Zydeco* documentary.

Bibliography

Introduction

The purpose of the *DARE* bibliography is to allow readers to track any quotation from its short-title to its full bibliographic entry, and from that entry to the edition of the book or other source from which the quote was taken. With this aim, *DARE* includes in its bibliography entries for all sources cited in the five volumes of text. These entries, first compiled as notes on index cards, resulted in a database of nearly 13,000 electronic records in 2011.

Our general policy has been to include in each bibliographic entry the necessary information from the title page (and occasionally the verso) of the work cited. Since the 1990s, these details have been used in conjunction with the information available in the OCLC worldwide library database. State names and occasionally country names have been added to imprint information when necessary to avoid ambiguity. In the case of serial publications, imprint information often varies from issue to issue. For this reason, only the place of original publication has been given, and publisher details are included only when necessary for retrieval.

Any project as long and complex as the *DARE* bibliography inevitably evolves over time. Begun in 1965, it has adapted to changes in standard library practice, not only in the formats for creating and maintaining bibliographies, but also in policies regarding essential elements and thoroughness of treatments.

To aid the reader, *DARE* has included copious cross-references and, for some bibliographic entries, additional notes. These are useful, for example, when authors publish under multiple forms of their names, change their names, or use pseudonyms; when a short-title refers to a part of a collection rather than the whole; when a short-title has been altered; or when multiple editions of a work have been cited.

Any quotations not verifiable in their original sources are attributed to the sources in which they were found. Most frequently these sources are the *Oxford English Dictionary* and its *Supplement* and *Second Edition*, the *Dictionary of American English*, the *Dictionary of Americanisms*, and the *American Dialect Dictionary*. In such cases the short-title is given exactly as it appears in the secondary source, followed by the attribution: *(OED), (DAE), (ADD),* etc. These abbreviations are found both in the bibliography (as cross-references to the full entries) and in the List of Abbreviations at the front of this volume.

In addition to published sources, *DARE* includes many citations from unpublished and oral sources. Numerous collections have been donated to *DARE;* their bibliographic entries include brief descriptions of their contents. *DARE*'s own fieldwork, carried out between 1965 and 1970, is quoted extensively throughout the five volumes of text. Short-titles that include *"DARE"* refer to various kinds of material gathered by Fieldworkers or later by *DARE* staff members. Each of these short-titles has its own bibliographic entry.

The rapid increase in access to digital resources, particularly during the editing of Volumes IV and V, greatly expanded the sources available to *DARE* Editors. Digital libraries such as *The Making of America, American Memory, Documenting the American South, Lexis–Nexis Legal Research,* and *JSTOR,* among many others, have been particularly useful. During the editing of Volume V, a vast body of additional materials became available through *Google Books. DARE* Editors have taken quotations from them, but only when images of the printed text and the title page were available for verification.

Digitized collections of newspapers, such as *NewspaperArchive* and *ProQuest Historical Newspapers,* have allowed access to thousands of publications that provide excellent evidence for local vocabulary use. When full page images are visible, *DARE* Editors cite the newspaper directly; if any bibliographic information is lacking, they cite the newspaper but attribute the quotation to the collection. If a quotation is taken from a digital-only newspaper or the online version of a print newspaper, the short-title makes that clear. Bibliographic entries for digitized newspapers include date ranges available at the time the entry was created; such ranges change as publishers of digital collections expand their holdings.

Bibliographic entries for Internet sources have conformed as far as possible to the evolving standards of the library profession. Because they change so frequently, URLs are not included. For quotations taken from ephemeral Internet sources, the short-title *"DARE* File—Internet" is used, analogous to the *"DARE* File" citations based on oral or unpublished sources.

For the preparation of this bibliography, thanks go to many people. We are particularly indebted to *DARE*'s four bibliographers: Goldye Mohr (1965–1986), Leonard Zwilling (1986–2004), Sally Jacobs (2004–2006), and Janet Monk (2006–present); to all the "look-up" assistants, who checked citations and gathered bibliographical data; to Luanne von Schneidemesser, who pioneered *DARE*'s transition to an electronic database and coordinated progress throughout much of the project, including its final stages; to Elizabeth Blake and Elizabeth Gardner, who followed entries from inputting to formatting and proofing, and whose very keen eyes detected inconsistencies and anomalies; and to Julie Schnebly, who worked with a huge and unwieldy database to bring order and consistency to this massive project.

88 Successful Play Activities. New York: Playground and Recreation Association of America, c.1927.

6,000 Words. Springfield MA: G. & C. Merriam, c.1976.

9,000 Words. Springfield MA: Merriam-Webster, c.1983.

12,000 Words. Springfield MA: Merriam-Webster, c.1986.

Aaron. *The Light and Truth of Slavery.* Worcester MA: The Author, 1845.

Aasved, Mikal J. and J. Clark Laundergan. *"You Betcha!" Gambling and Its Impacts in a Northern Minnesota Community.* Duluth MN: Center for Addiction Studies, Univ. MN-Duluth, 1991.

Abbey, Edward. *Desert Solitaire.* New York: McGraw-Hill, c.1968.

Abbott, Belle Kendrick. *Leah Mordecai.* New York: Baker Pratt, c.1875.

Abbott, Benjamin Vaughan. *Cone Cut Corners.* New York: Mason Bros., c.1855.

Abbott, Charles Conrad. *Bird-Land Echoes.* Philadelphia: J. B. Lippincott, 1896.

———. *Upland and Meadow.* New York: Harper & Bros., 1886.

Abbott, Dorothy, ed. *Mississippi Writers.* Jackson MS: Univ. Press MS, 1985–1991. 4 vols.

Abbott, Edward Charles and Helena Huntington Smith. *We Pointed Them North.* New York: Farrar & Rinehart, c.1939.

Abbott, Eleanor Hallowell. *Indiscreet Letter.* New York: Century, c.1915.

Abbott, Jacob. *Caleb in Town.* Boston: Crocker & Brewster, 1839.

———. *Cousin Lucy among the Mountains.* Auburn NY: Derby and Miller, 1850 [c.1842].

———. *Jonas a Judge, or, Law among the Boys.* New York: Clark, Austin & Smith, 1857 [c.1840].

———. *Marco Paul's Voyages & Travels, Vermont.* New York: Harper & Bros., c.1852.

———. *Mary Erskine.* New York: Harper Bros., c.1850.

———. *Stories of Rainbow & Lucky.* New York: Harper & Bros., 1861 [c.1860].

Abbott, Keith. *Mordecai of Monterey.* Berkeley CA: City Miner Books, c.1985.

Abbott, Mabel. *The Life of William T. Davis.* Ithaca NY: Cornell Univ. Press, 1949.

Abbott, Robert Tucker. *American Seashells.* New York: D. Van Nostrand, c.1954.

———. *American Seashells.* 2d ed. New York: Van Nostrand Reinhold, 1974.

Abbott, Shirley. *Womenfolks.* New Haven CT: Ticknor & Fields, c.1983.

ABC Pathfinder Railway Guide. Boston, 1849–.

Abdul-Jabbar, Kareem and Peter Knobler. *Giant Steps.* Toronto: Bantam Books, 1983.

Abercrombie, John. *The Propagation and Botanical Arrangements of Plants and Trees, Useful and Ornamental, Proper for Cultivation in Every Department of Gardening, Nurseries, Plantations and Agriculture.* London: Printed for J. Debrett, 1784. 2 vols.

Aberdeen Daily News. Aberdeen SD, 1886–1923.

Abilene Reporter-News. Abilene TX, 1937–.

Abrahams, Roger D. *Deep Down in the Jungle.* 1st rev. ed. Chicago: Aldine, 1970.

———. *Positively Black.* Englewood Cliffs NJ: Prentice Hall, 1970.

Abrams, Le Roy. *Flora of Los Angeles and Vicinity.* Stanford University CA: Stanford Bookstore, 1917.

———. *An Illustrated Flora of the Pacific States.* Stanford CA: Stanford Univ. Press, 1923–1960. 4 vols.

Academy: a Weekly Review of Literature, Science, and Art. London, 1869–1916.

Academy of Natural Sciences of Philadelphia. *Journal.* Philadelphia, 1817–1919.

———. *Proceedings.* Philadelphia, 1841–.

———. *Year Book.* Philadelphia, 1924–1932?

Academy of Natural Sciences of Philadelphia. Entomological Section. *Entomological News and Proceedings.* Philadelphia, 1890–1924.

Academy of Science of St. Louis. *Transactions.* St. Louis MO, 1860–1958.

Acker, Ethel F. *Four Hundred Games for School, Home, and Playground.* Dansville NY: F. A. Owen, c.1923.

Ada Evening News. Ada OK, 1904–.

Ada Weekly News. Ada OK, 1901–.

Adair, James. *The History of the American Indians.* London: Printed for Edward and Charles Dilly, 1775.

Adams, Andy. *The Log of a Cowboy.* Boston: Houghton, Mifflin, c.1931. Abridgement of 1903 ed.

———. *The Log of a Cowboy.* Lincoln NE: Univ. NE Press, 1965. Repr. of the 1903 ed. pub. by Houghton, Mifflin, Boston.

———. *The Outlet.* Upper Saddle River NJ: Literature House, 1970. Orig. pub. in 1905 by Houghton, Mifflin, Boston.

———. *The Ranch on the Beaver.* Boston: Houghton Mifflin, 1927.

———. *Reed Anthony, Cowman.* Boston: Houghton, Mifflin, 1907.

———. *A Texas Matchmaker.* Boston: Houghton, Mifflin, 1904.

———. *Wells Brothers.* Boston: Houghton Mifflin; Cambridge: Riverside Press, c.1911.

Adams, Edward Clarkson Leverett. *Congaree Sketches.* Chapel Hill NC: Univ. NC Press, 1927.

Adams, Emma Hildreth. *To and Fro, Up and Down in Southern California, Oregon and Washington Territory.* Cincinnati OH: Cranston & Stowe, 1888.

Adams, Franc L., Mrs., comp. *Pioneer History of Ingham County.* Lansing MI: Wynkoop Hallenbeck Crawford, 1923.

Adams, Francis Colburn. *Justice in the By-Ways.* New York: Livermore and Rudd, 1856.

———. *Our World.* New York: Miller, Orton & Mulligan, 1855.

Adams, George R. *Life on the Yukon 1865–1867.* Ed. by Richard A. Pierce. Kingston, Ontario: Limestone Press, 1982.

Adams, Henry Sherman. *Flower Gardening.* New York: McBride, Nast, 1913.

Adams, James Truslow, ed. *Album of American History.* New York: C. Scribner's Sons, 1944–1949. 5 vols.

Adams, John. *Diary and Autobiography.* Cambridge MA: Belknap Press of Harvard Univ. Press, 1961. 4 vols.

———. *Legal Papers of John Adams.* Cambridge MA: Belknap Press of Harvard Univ. Press, 1965. 3 vols.

———. *The Works of John Adams, Second President of the United States.* Ed. by Charles Francis Adams. Boston: Little, Brown, 1850–1856. 10 vols.

Adams, John and Abigail Adams. *Familiar Letters of John Adams and His Wife, Abigail Adams, during the Revolution.* Boston: Houghton, Mifflin, c.1875.

Adams, John Quincy. *Memoirs of John Quincy Adams.* Philadelphia: J. B. Lippincott, 1874–1877. 12 vols.

———. *Writings of John Quincy Adams.* Ed. by Worthington Chauncy Ford. New York: Macmillan, 1913–1917. 7 vols.

Adams, John Turvill. *The Lost Hunter.* New York: Derby & Jackson, 1856 [c.1855].

Adams, Nehemiah. *The Sable Cloud.* Boston: Ticknor & Fields, 1861.

Adams, Noah. *Piano Lessons.* New York: Delacorte Press, c.1996.

Adams, Paul J. *Mt. LeConte.* 2d printing. Knoxville TN: Holston Printing, 1968 [c.1966].

Adams, Ramon Frederick. *Cowboy Lingo.* Boston: Houghton Mifflin, 1936.

———. *The Cowman Says It Salty.* Tucson AZ: Univ. AZ Press, 1971.

———. *The Language of the Railroader.* Norman OK: Univ. OK Press, c.1977.

———. *The Old-Time Cowhand.* New York: Macmillan, 1961.

———. *Western Words.* Norman OK: Univ. OK Press, 1944.

———. *Western Words.* New ed. rev. and enlarged. Norman OK: Univ. OK Press, 1968.

Adams, Robert Martin. *Bad Mouth.* Berkeley CA: Univ. CA Press, c.1977.

Adams, Samuel Hopkins. *A. Woollcott.* New York: Reynal & Hitchcock, 1945.

———. *Banner by the Wayside.* New York: Random House, 1947.

———. *Canal Town.* New York: Random House, c.1944.

———. *The Clarion.* Boston: Houghton, Mifflin, 1914.

———. *Grandfather Stories.* New York: Random House, c.1955.

Adams, Sheila Kay. *Come Go Home with Me.* Chapel Hill NC: Univ. NC Press, c.1995.

———. *My Old True Love.* Chapel Hill NC: Algonquin Books of Chapel Hill, 2004.

Adams, William Taylor. *In Doors and Out.* Boston: Brown, Bazin, 1854.

———. *Switch Off.* Boston: Lee & Shephard; New York: Charles T. Dillingham, c.1869.

Adams Centinel. Gettysburg PA, 1800–1805; 1813–1826.

Adams County News. Gettysburg PA, 1908–1917.

Adamson, Helen Lyon. *Grandmother's Household Hints.* Philadelphia: Chilton, c.1963.

Adams Sentinel. Gettysburg PA, 1826–1867.

Adamus, Paul R. and Karla Brandt. *Impacts on Quality of Inland Wetlands of the United States.* Washington DC: Govt. Printing Office, 1990. Report No. EPA/600/3-90/073.

ADD SEE Wentworth, Harold *American Dialect Dictionary*

Addington, Robert Milford. *History of Scott County, Virginia.* Kingsport TN: Private Printer Kingsport Press, 1932.

———. *The Old-Time School in Scott County.* East Radford VA: State Normal School for Women, 1914.

Addums, Mozis SEE Bagby, George William

Ade, George. *Artie.* Chicago: H. S. Stone, 1898 [c.1896].

———. *Doc' Horne.* Chicago: H. S. Stone, 1899.

———. *Doc' Horne.* New York: Duffield, 1906. Orig. pub. in 1899 by H. S. Stone, Chicago.

———. *Fables in Slang.* Chicago: Herbert S. Stone, 1900 [c.1899].

———. *Forty Modern Fables.* New York: R. H. Russell, 1901.

———. *Hand-Made Fables.* Garden City NY: Doubleday, Page, 1920.

———. *In Babel.* New York: McClure, Phillips, 1903.

———. *Knocking the Neighbors.* Garden City NY: Doubleday, Page, 1912.

———. *Letters of George Ade.* Ed. by Terence Tobin. West Lafayette IN: Purdue Univ. Studies, 1973.

———. *More Fables.* Chicago: Herbert S. Stone, 1900.

———. *People You Know.* New York: R. H. Russell, 1903.

———. *Pink Marsh.* Chicago: H. S. Stone, 1897.

Adeler, Max SEE Clark, Charles Heber

Adero, Malaika, ed. *Up South.* New York: New Press, 1993.

Adkison, Ron. *Utah's National Parks.* 2d ed. Berkeley CA: Wilderness Press, 2001.

Advance. Chicago: C. H. Howard, 1867–1917.

Advance-Monticellonian. Monticello AR, 1920–.

The Adventures of Tommy Teaberry. Pittsburgh PA: Clark Bros. Chewing Gum, c.1944.

Advocate. Baton Rouge LA, 1992–. Internet.

Advocate. Newark OH, 1970–.

Africa: Journal of the International Institute of African Languages and Cultures. London: Oxford Univ. Press, 1928–.

African American Review. Terre Haute IN: Dept. of English, IN State Univ., 1992–.

African Language Review. London: F. Cass, 1967–.

African Times and Orient Review. Nendelin: Kraus Reprint, 1973. Orig. pub. 1912–1918 under the same title.

Agee, Hugh. *The Analysis of Student Talk.* 1971–1972. Unpub.

Agnew, Samuel Andrew. *Diary of Samuel A. Agnew: September 27, 1863–June 30, 1864.* Chapel Hill NC: Academic Affairs Library, Univ. NC at Chapel Hill, 1999. Unpub. ms. transcr. for *Documenting the American South* website.

Agricultural History. Berkeley CA, 1927–.

Agricultural Museum. Georgetown CA: Printed and Published by David Wiley, 1810–1812.

AHD SEE *The American Heritage Dictionary of the English Language*

Ahlgren, Gilbert Harold. *Forage Crops.* New York: McGraw-Hill, 1949.

Aiken, Gene, comp. *Mountain Ways.* Gatlinburg TN: Buckhorn Press, c.1983.

Aiken, Walter Harris. *Catalogue of the Ferns and Flowering Plants of Cincinnati, Ohio, and Vicinity.* Cincinnati OH: J. U. & C. G. Lloyd, 1911.

Aiken Standard. Aiken SC, 1969–.

Ailenroc, M. R. SEE Murrie, Cornelia Random

Aime, Valcour. *Plantation Diary of the Late Mr. Valcour Aime.* New Orleans LA: Clark & Hofeline, 1878.

Airman. Kelly Air Force Base TX: Air Force News Agency, 1957–.

Aitken, Frank W. and Edward Hilton. *A History of the Earthquake and Fire in San Francisco.* San Francisco: E. Hilton, 1906.

Aiton, William. *Hortus Kewensis.* London: Printed for George Nicol, 1789. 3 vols.

Ajilvsgi, Geyata. *Wild Flowers of the Big Thicket, East Texas, and Western Louisiana.* College Station TX: TX A&M Univ. Press, c.1979.

Akin, James, Jr. *The Journal of James Akin Jr.* Ed. by Edward Everett Dale. Norman OK: Univ. OK, 1919.

Alabama. Agricultural Experiment Station. *Bulletin.* Auburn AL, 1883–.

Alabama Cooperative Extension Service. *Sweet Sorghum Culture and Syrup Production.* Washington DC, 1991. Circular ANR: 625.

Alabama. Department of Conservation and Natural Resources. *Outdoor Alabama.* [v.d.]. Internet.

Alabama. Educational Survey Commission. *Public Education in Alabama: a Report.* Washington DC: American Council on Education, 1945.

Alabama Farmers and Consumers Bulletin. Montgomery AL: Alabama. Department of Agriculture and Industries, 1991?–.

Alabama Game & Fish. Marietta GA: Intermedia Outdoors, 1980?–.

Alabama. Geological Survey. *Bulletin.* University AL, 1886–.

Alabama Historical Quarterly. Montgomery AL, 1930–1982.

Alabama Historical Society. *Transactions.* Tuscaloosa AL, 1852–1906.

Alabama. University of North Alabama. Department of Geography. *Flora and Fauna along the Tennessee River.* [v.d.]. Internet.

Alabama Wildlife Federation. [v.d.]. Internet.

Alaska Advocate. Anchorage AK, 1977–1979.

Alaska Agricultural Experiment Stations. *Annual Report.* Washington DC, 1906–1913.

Alaska Department of Fish and Game. *Alaska Habitat Management Guide, Southwest Region.* Juneau AK: Alaska Dept. Fish & Game, c.1985. 2 vols.

———. *Notebook.* [v.d.]. Internet.

Alaska Fish & Game. Anchorage AK, 1984–1990.

Alaska Fishing Guide. Anchorage AK: Alaska Northwest Publishing, c.1978.

Alaska Fish Tales and Game Trails. Juneau AK: Alaska Dept. of Fish & Game, 1968–1983.

Alaska Geographic. Anchorage AK: Alaska Geographic Society, 1972–.

Alaska Journal. Juneau AK, 1971–.

Alaska Railroad Record. Anchorage AK, 1916–1920.

Alaska Reports. St. Paul MN: West Publishing, 1903–1959.

Alaska Sportsman. Ketchikan AK: Alaska Magazine Publishing, 1935–1969.

Alaska, the Magazine of Life on the Last Frontier. Anchorage AK: Alaska Northwest Publishing, 1970–.

Alaska. University. *eInfo.* [v.d.]. Internet.

The Alaska-Yukon Wild Flowers Guide. Anchorage AK: Alaska Northwest Publishing, c.1974.

Albany County, New York. *Early Records of the City and County of Albany and Colony of Rensselaerswyck, 1656–1675.* Transl. from the orig. Dutch by Jonathan Pearson. Albany NY: J. Munsell, 1869.

Albany Institute. *Transactions.* Albany NY: Webster and Skinners, 1830–1893.

Albee, John. *New Castle Historic and Picturesque.* Boston: Press of Rand Avery Supply, 1884.

Albemarle County Historical Society. *Magazine of Albemarle County History.* Charlottesville VA, 1941–.

———. *Papers.* Charlottesville VA, 1941–1951.

Alberts, Laurie. *The Price of Land in Shelbyville.* Hanover NH: Univ. Press New England, c.1996.

Albertson, Alice Owen. *Nantucket Wild Flowers.* New York: G. P. Putnam's Sons, 1921.

Albertson, Chris, comp. *Bessie Smith.* New York: Schirmer Books, c.1975.

Albion, or, British, Colonial and Foreign Weekly Gazette. New York, 1822–1856.

Albuquerque Journal. Albuquerque NM, 1926–.

Albuquerque Morning Democrat. Albuquerque NM, 1890–1898.

Albuquerque Tribune. Albuquerque NM, 1933–2008.

Alcalde. Austin TX, 1913–1991; 2001–.

Alcott, A. Bronson. *New Connecticut.* Boston: Roberts Bros., 1887.

Alcott, Louisa May. *Eight Cousins.* Boston: Roberts Bros., 1875 [c.1874].

———. *Hospital Sketches.* Boston: James Redpath, 1863.

———. *Jo's Boys, and How They Grew.* Leipzig: Bernhard Tauchnitz, 1886.

———. *Little Men.* Boston: Roberts Bros., 1871.

———. *Little Women.* Boston: Roberts Bros., 1868.

———. *Little Women.* Boston: Roberts Bros., 1868–1869. 2 pts.

———. *Little Women.* Boston: Roberts Bros., 1870. 2 vols.

———. *Little Women.* Boston: Roberts Bros., 1871. 2 vols. Repr. of pts. 1 (1868) and 2 (1869).

———. *An Old-Fashioned Girl.* Boston: Roberts Bros., 1870.

———. *The Selected Letters of Louisa May Alcott.* Boston: Little, Brown, c.1987.

———. *Work, a Story of Experience.* Boston: Roberts Bros., 1875 [c.1873].

Al-Darraji, Samara. *Eclipse.* Baltimore MD: PublishAmerica, c.2005.

Alden, Harry A. *Hardwoods of North America.* Madison WI: United States Department of Agriculture, Forest Service, Forest Products Laboratory, c.1995. Gen. Tech. Rept. FPL-GTR-83.

Alderman, Annabel. *Family Man.* Macon GA: Mercer Univ. Press, 1999.

Alderman, Ernest Hamlin. *The North Carolina Colonial Bar.* Chapel Hill NC: Univ. NC, 1913.

Aldrich, Bess Streeter. *A Lantern in Her Hand.* New York: Grosset & Dunlap, c.1928.

———. *Mother Mason.* New York: A. L. Burt, c.1924.

———. *Song of Years.* New York: D. Appleton-Century, 1939.

Aldrich, Herbert L. *Arctic Alaska and Siberia.* Chicago: Rand, McNally, c.1889.

Aldrich, Thomas Bailey. *Cloth of Gold.* Boston: James R. Osgood, 1874 [c.1873].

———. *Prudence Palfrey.* Boston: J. R. Osgood, 1874.

———. *A Sea Turn and Other Matters.* Boston: Houghton, Mifflin, 1902.

———. *The Stillwater Tragedy.* Boston: Houghton, Mifflin, 1880.

Aldridge, Reginald. *Life on a Ranch.* New York: Appleton, 1884.

———. *Ranch Notes in Kansas, Colorado, the Indian Territory and Northern Texas.* London: Longmans, Green, 1884.

Alexander, Earl B. et al. *Serpentine Geoecology of Western North America.* New York: Oxford Univ. Press, 2007.

Alexander, James Edward. *Transatlantic Sketches.* Philadelphia: Key and Biddle, 1833.

Alexander, James Waddell. *Forty Years' Familiar Letters of James W. Alexander, D. D.* Ed. by John Hall. New York: Charles Scribner, 1860. 2 vols.

Alexander, William De Witt. *A Brief History of the Hawaiian People.* New York: American Book, 1891.

Alexandria Advertiser and Commercial Intelligencer. Alexandria VA, 1800–1803.

Alexandria Daily Town Talk. Alexandria-Pineville LA, 1883–.

Algren, Nelson. *The Man with the Golden Arm.* Garden City NY: Doubleday, 1949.

———. *A Walk on the Wild Side.* New York: Farrar, Straus and Cudahy, c.1956.

Allan-Olney, Mary. *The New Virginians.* Edinburgh: William Blackwood and Sons, 1880. 2 vols.

Allegheny (PA). *Municipal Reports.* Pittsburgh PA, 1887?–1903?

Allen, Alexander Viets Griswold. *Life and Letters of Phillips Brooks.* New York: E. P. Dutton, 1901. 3 vols.

Allen, Gary J. *The Herbalist in the Kitchen.* Urbana IL: Univ. IL Press, c.2007.

Allen, Glover Morrill. *Extinct and Vanishing Mammals of the Western Hemisphere with the Marine Species.* Lancaster PA: American Committee for International Wildlife Protection, 1942.

———. *Fauna of New England.* Boston: Society of Natural History, 1909.

Allen, Grant et al. *Nature Studies.* New York: Funk & Wagnalls, 1883 [c.1882].

Allen, Harold B. *The Linguistic Atlas of the Upper Midwest.* Minneapolis MN: Univ. MN Press, 1973–1976. 3 vols.

Allen, Henry Wilson SEE ALSO Henry, Will

Allen, Henry Wilson. *The Seven Men at Mimbres Springs.* New York: Random House, c.1958.

Allen, Ida Cogswell Bailey. *Modern Cook Book.* Garden City NY: Garden City Publishing, 1924.

Allen, Irving Lewis. *The Language of Ethnic Conflict.* New York: Columbia Univ. Press, 1983.

———. *Unkind Words.* New York: Bergin & Garvey, c.1990.

Allen, James Lane. *The Blue-Grass Region of Kentucky.* Freeport NY: Books for Libraries Press, 1972. Repr. of the 1892 ed. pub. by Harper, New York.

———. *Flute and Violin.* New York: Harper & Bros., 1897 [c.1891].

Allen, John Willis. *It Happened in Southern Illinois.* Carbondale IL: Area Services, Southern IL Univ., 1968.

———. *Legends & Lore of Southern Illinois.* Carbondale IL: Area Services Division, Southern IL Univ., c.1963.

Allen, Jules Verne. *Cowboy Lore.* 7th ed. San Antonio TX: Naylor, c.1950. Orig. pub. in 1933.

Allen, Lewis Falley. *Rural Architecture.* New York: C. M. Saxton, 1852.

Allen, Marilyn. *Super Tour.* Garden City NY: Doubleday, c.1974.

Allen, Martha Norburn. *Asheville and Land of the Sky.* Rev. and enlarged ed. Charlotte NC: Heritage House, c.1960.

Allen, Richard Lamb. *The American Farm Book.* New York: C.M Saxton, 1850 [c.1849].

———. *The American Farm Book.* New York: C. M. Saxton, 1863 [c.1849].

———. *New American Farm Book.* New ed. rev. and enlarged. New York: Orange Judd, 1885 [c.1883].

Allen, Thomas S. *Low Bridge, Everybody Down.* New York: Haviland, 1913.

Allen, William Cicero. *The Annals of Haywood County, North Carolina.* [s.l.]: [s.n.], 1935.

Allen, William Francis. *Family Papers.* 1838–1924. Unpub. coll. in Wisconsin State Historical Society archives.

Allen, William Francis et al., eds. *Slave Songs of the United States.* New York: A. Simpson, 1867.

Allen County Democrat. Lima OH, 1861–1893.

Alley, Felix Eugene. *Random Thoughts and the Musings of a Mountaineer.* Salisbury NC: Rowan Printing, 1941.

Alley, Henry. *The Beekeeper's Handy Book.* 3d ed. rev. and enlarged. Wenham MA: The Author, 1885.

Allhands, James L. *Gringo Builders.* Iowa City IA: Privately Printed, 1931.

Allin, Abby. *Home Ballads.* Boston: James Munroe, 1851 [c.1850].

Allin, Richard. *Southern Legislative Dictionary.* Little Rock AR: Rose Publishing, c.1983.

Allison, John. *Dropped Stitches in Tennessee History.* Nashville TN: Marshall & Bruce, 1897.

Allsopp, Frederick William. *Folklore of Romantic Arkansas.* New York: Grolier Society, 1931. 2 vols.

Allsopp, Richard, ed. *Dictionary of Caribbean English Usage.* Oxford: Oxford Univ. Press, 1996.

Allston, Washington. *The Sylphs of the Seasons, with Other Poems.* London: W. Pople, 1813.

All the Year Round. London: Chapman and Hall, 1859–1895. Ed. by Charles Dickens.

Almirall, Leon Vincent. *From College to Cow Country.* Caldwell ID: Caxton Printers, 1956.

Alpha Chi Omega. *Lyre of Alpha Chi Omega.* Indianapolis IN, 1894–.

Alsaker, Rasmus Larssen. *Eating for Health and Efficiency.* New York: F. E. Morrison, 1917.

Alsop, George. *A Character of the Province of Mary-land.* Freeport NY: Books for Libraries Press, 1972. Repr. of the 1902 ed. pub. by Burrows Bros., Cleveland OH, from the orig. ed. printed in 1666 by T. J. for P. Dring, London.

Alsop, Richard. *The Echo.* New York: Printed at the Porcupine Press by Pasquin Petronius, 1807.

Alter, Robert Edmund. *Shovel Nose and the Gator Grabbers.* New York: G. P. Putnam's Sons, c.1963.

Alton Daily Telegraph. Alton IL, 1866–1894.

Alton Telegraph. Alton IL, 1836–1841; 1861–1866; 1972–1986.

Alton Telegraph & Democratic Review. Alton IL, 1841–1850.

Alton Weekly Courier. Alton IL, 1851–1861.

Alton Weekly Telegraph. Alton IL, 1866–1878.

Altoona Mirror. Altoona PA, 1888–.

The Altrurian Cook Book. 3d ed. enlarged. Piqua OH: Magee Bros., 1910.

Alvord, Clarence Walworth and Lee Bidgood. *The First Explorations of the Trans-Alleghany Region by the Virginians 1650–1674.* Cleveland OH: Arthur H. Clark, 1912.

Amarillo Globe. Amarillo TX, 1924–1951.

Amarillo Globe-News. Amarillo TX, 1996–.

Amarillo Globe-Times. Amarillo TX, 1951–.

Amarillo Sunday News-Globe. Amarillo TX, 1909–.

American. Philadelphia, 1880–1900.

Americana. New York, 1977–.

American Academy of Arts and Sciences. *Memoirs.* Boston, 1785–.

———. *Proceedings.* Boston, 1846–1958.

American Academy of Political and Social Science. *Annals.* Philadelphia, 1890–.

American Advocate. Hallowell ME, 1825–1835.

American Agriculturist. New York, 1842–1912; 1921–1964; 1976–.

American Agriculturist and Rural New Yorker. Ithaca NY, 1964–1976.

American Almanac and Repository of Useful Knowledge for the Year. Boston: Gray and Bowen, 1830–1861.

American Angler. New York: Angler's Publishing, 1881–.

American Anthropologist. Menasha WI: American Anthropological Association, 1888–.

American Antiquarian and Oriental Journal. Chicago, 1881–1914.

American Antiquarian Society. *Proceedings.* Worcester MA, 1843–.

———. *Transactions and Collections.* Worcester MA: The Society, 1820–1911.

American Antiquity. Menasha WI, 1935–.

American Architect. New York: Swetland, 1909–1921.

American Association for the Advancement of Science. *Proceedings.* Philadelphia, 1848–1910.

American Automobile Association. *TourBook: Arizona, New Mexico.* Heathrow FL: The Association, 1977.

American Bee Journal. Hamilton IL, 1861–.

American Bibliopolist. New York, 1869–1877.

American Botanist. Binghampton NY, 1901–.

American Boy's Book of Sports and Games. New York: Dick & Fitzgerald, c.1864.

American Breeders Magazine. Washington DC: American Breeders Association, 1910–1913.

American Caravan, a Yearbook of American Literature. New York, 1927–1936.

American Child. New York: National Child Labor Committee, 1919–1967.

American Church Review. New York, 1872–1885.

American City. Pittsfield MA, 1909–1975.

The American Cyclopaedia. Ed. by George Ripley and Charles A. Dana. New York: D. Appleton, 1873–1876. 16 vols.

American Dialect Society. *Newsletter.* Arlington VA, 1969–.

————. *Publications.* 1944–.

American Druggist. New York, 1884–1893.

American Druggist and Pharmaceutical Record. New York, 1893–1922.

American Enterprise. Washington DC: American Enterprise Institute for Public Policy Research, 1990–2006.

American Entomologist. St. Louis MO: R. P. Studley, 1868–1880.

American Farmer. Baltimore MD, 1819–1834; 1849–1871; 1874–1897.

American Farmer and Spirit of the Agricultural Journals of the Day. Baltimore MD, 1839–1849.

The American Farmer's New and Universal Hand-Book . . . by Practical Agriculturists. Philadelphia: Cowperthwait, Desilver, & Butler, 1854 [c.1851].

American Fern Journal. Washington DC: American Fern Society, 1910–.

American Field. Chicago, 1881–1941.

American Fisheries Society. *Transactions.* Bethesda MD, 1900–.

American Fisheries Society. Committee on Names of Fishes. *Common and Scientific Names of Fishes from the United States and Canada.* 5th ed. Bethesda MD: The Society, 1991.

————. *A List of Common and Scientific Names of Fishes from the United States and Canada.* 2d ed. Ann Arbor MI: The Society, 1960.

American Flint. Toledo OH: American Flint Glassworkers' Union, 1909–.

American Folklore Society. *Memoirs.* Boston, 1894–.

American Forestry. Washington DC: American Forestry Association, 1910–1923.

American Forestry Association. *Conservation, a Digest of Current Articles on the Conservation of Natural Resources.* Washington DC, 1935–1941?

American Forests. Princeton NJ: American Forestry Association, 1895–.

American Garden. Brooklyn NY, 1873–1891.

American Gardener's Magazine, and Register of Useful Discoveries and Improvements in Horticulture and Rural Affairs. Boston: Hovey, 1835–1836.

American Gardening. New York: Rural Publishing, 1892–1904.

American Geographical Society of New York. *Bulletin.* New York, 1901–1915.

————. *Journal.* New York, 1859–1900.

American Geological Institute. *Supplement to the Glossary of Geology and Related Sciences.* Washington DC: American Geological Institute, 1960.

American-German Review. Philadelphia: Carl Schurz Memorial Foundation, 1934–.

American Handy Book of the Brewing, Malting and Auxiliary Trades. Ed. by Robert Wahl, Max Henius. 2d ed. Chicago: Wahl & Henius, 1902.

The American Heritage Cookbook and Illustrated History of American Eating and Drinking. New York: American Heritage, 1964.

The American Heritage Dictionary of the English Language. Boston: American Heritage, c.1969.

American Heritage Society. *Americana.* New York: American Heritage, 1973–.

American Historical Association. *Annual Report.* Washington DC: Govt. Printing Office, 1890–.

————. *Papers.* New York: G. P. Putnam's Sons, 1885–1891.

American Historical Review. New York: Macmillan, 1895–.

The American Homoeopathic Pharmacopoeia. New York: Boericke & Tafel, 1882.

American Husbandry. London: Printed for J. Bew, 1775. 2 vols.

American Imago: a Psychoanalytic Journal for the Arts and Sciences. Boston: H. Sachs, 1939–.

American Institute of the City of New York. *Annual Report.* Albany NY, 1841–.

American Inventor. New York: American Inventor Publishing, 1898–1907.

American Joint Committee on Horticultural Nomenclature. *Standardized Plant Names.* Salem MA: The Committee, 1923.

————. *Standardized Plant Names.* Prepared by its Editorial Committee, Harlan P. Kelsey and William A. Dayton. 2d ed. rev. and enlarged. Harrisburg PA: The Committee, 1942.

American Journal of Botany. St. Louis MO, 1914–.

American Journal of Education. Hartford CT, 1856–1882.

American Journal of Forestry. Cincinnati OH: Robert Clarke, 1882–1883.

American Journal of Hygiene. Baltimore MD, 1921–1964.

American Journal of Medicine. New York, 1946–.

American Journal of Pharmacy. Philadelphia, 1835–1936.

American Journal of Philology. Baltimore MD: Johns Hopkins Univ. Press, 1880–.

American Journal of Psychology. Ithaca NY: Cornell Univ. 1887–.

American Journal of Science. New Haven CT, 1818–.

American Journal of Science and Arts. New Haven CT, 1820–1879.

American Journal of Sociology. Chicago: Univ. Chicago Press, 1895–.

American Journal of the Medical Sciences. Philadelphia: J. B. Lippincott, 1827–.

American Journal of Veterinary Medicine. Chicago, 1910–1920.

American Legion Magazine. Louisville KY, 1926–.

American Literature. Durham NC: Duke Univ. Press, 1929–.

American Magazine. Springfield OH: Crowell-Collier, 1876–1956.

American Magazine and Historical Chronicle. Boston: Rogers and Fowle, 1743–1746.

American Magazine of Wonders. New York, 1809.

American Masonic Register, and Ladies' and Gentlemen's Magazine. New York, 1820–1823.

American Medical and Philosophical Register. New York, 1810–1814.

American Medical Association. *Journal.* Chicago, 1883–.

————. *Transactions.* Philadelphia, 1848–1882.

American Medical Journal. St. Louis MO, 1873–1916.

American Medical Monthly. New York, 1854–1859.

American Mercury. Hartford CT, 1784–1833.

American Mercury. New York, 1924–1950; 1951–.

American Microscopical Society. *Transactions.* Lawrence KS, 1895–1994.

American Midland Naturalist. Notre Dame IN, 1909–.

American Milk Review. New York: Urner-Barry, 1939–.

American Mineralogical Journal. New York: Collins, 1810–1814.

American Missionary. New York: American Missionary Assn., 1846–1934.

American Monthly Magazine. Boston: Otis, Broaders, 1833–1838.

American Monthly Magazine and Critical Review. New York: Kirk & Mercein, 1817–1819.

American Monthly Review of Reviews. New York, 1897–1907.

American Museum. Philadelphia, 1787–1792.

American Museum of Natural History. *Annual Report.* New York, 1870–1994.

————. *Anthropological Papers.* New York, 1907–.

————. *Bulletin.* New York, 1881–.

American Music. Champaign IL, 1983–.

American Naturalist. Salem MA: Essex Institute, 1867–.

American Nature-Study Society. *Nature-Study Review.* New York, 1905–1923.

American Neptune. Salem MA, 1941–.

American Newspapers 1821–1936. Ed. by Winifred Gregory. New York: H. W. Wilson, 1937.

American Notes and Queries. Philadelphia, 1888–.

American Ornithologists' Union. *Check-List of North American Birds.* 7th ed. Washington DC: American Ornithologists' Union, c.1998.

————. *The Code of Nomenclature and Check List of North American Birds.* New York: American Ornithologists' Union, 1886 [c.1885].

American Oxonian. Philadelphia: Association of American Rhodes Scholars, 1914–.

American Penny Magazine and Family Newspaper. New York, 1845–1846.

American Pharmaceutical Association. *Proceedings.* Philadelphia: Merrihew and Thompson, Printers, 1852–1911.

————. *Year Book.* Chicago, 1912–1934.

American Philological Association. *Proceedings.* Hartford CT, 1870–.

————. *Transactions.* Hartford CT, 1870–.

American Philosophical Society. *Proceedings.* Philadelphia, 1835–.

————. *Transactions.* Philadelphia, 1771–.

American Photography. New York: American Photographic Publishing, 1907–.

American Phrenological Journal and Miscellany. Philadelphia, 1838–1850.

American Physical Education Review. Boston, 1896–1929.

American Pioneer. Cincinnati OH: J. S. Williams, 1842–1843.

American Poet. Brooklyn NY, 1941–1944.

American Practitioner and News. Louisville KY, 1886–1912.

American Prefaces. Iowa City IA, 1935–1943.

American RadioWorks. *Hard Time: Life after Prison.* 2003. Internet.

American Railroad Journal. New York, 1832–1886.

American Railway Times. Boston, 1849–1859.

American Register, or, General Repository of History, Politics and Science. Philadelphia: C. & A. Conrad, 1806–1810.

American Rivers. Washington DC: American Rivers Conservation Council, 1973–.

American Scholar. Washington DC: United Chapters of Phi Beta Kappa, 1932–.

The American Slave. Ed. by George P. Rawick. Westport CT: Greenwood, 1972–1974. 19 vols.

The American Slave. Ed. by George P. Rawick. Suppl. ser. 1. Westport CT: Greenwood, 1977. 12 vols.

The American Slave. Ed. by George P. Rawick. Suppl. ser. 2. Westport CT: Greenwood, 1979. 10 vols.

American Society of Civil Engineers. *Transactions.* New York, 1867–.

American Sociological Review. Menasha WI, 1936–.

American Spectator. Arlington VA: Saturday Evening Club, 1977–.

American Speech. Baltimore MD, 1925–.

American Sunday-School Union. *Annual Report.* Philadelphia, 1831–.

American Temperance Magazine, and Sons of Temperance Offering. New York: R. Van Dien, 1851?–.

American Tongues. By Andrew Kolker and Louis Alvarez. Video recording. New York: International Productions Center, 1986.

American Turf Register. New York: Bruce, 1829–1870?

American Veterinary Medical Association. *Journal.* Ithaca NY, 1915–.

American Weekly. New York, 1917–1963.

American Weekly Mercury. Philadelphia, 1719–1749.

American West. Salt Lake City UT: American West, 1964–.

American Whig Review. New York: Wiley and Putnam, 1845–1852.

America's Architectural Roots. Washington DC: Preservation Press, c.1986.

America's Hidden Corners: Places off the Beaten Path. Washington DC: National Geographic Society, 1983.

America's Lost Plays. Princeton NJ: Princeton Univ. Press, 1940–1942. 20 vols.

Ames, Nathaniel. *A Mariner's Sketches.* Rev., corr. and enlarged by the author. Providence RI: Cory, Marshall and Hammond, 1830.

Amherst Record. Amherst MA, 1965–.

Ammirati, Joseph F. et al. *Poisonous Mushrooms of the Northern United States and Canada.* Minneapolis MN: Univ. MN Press, c.1985.

Ammons, A. R. *Glare.* New York: W. W. Norton, c.1997.

Amory, Cleveland. *The Cat and the Curmudgeon.* Boston: Little, Brown, c.1990.

————. *The Proper Bostonians.* New York: E. P. Dutton, 1947.

AmSp SEE *American Speech*

Anaconda Standard. Anaconda MT, 1889–1970.

Analectic Magazine. Philadelphia: Moses Thomas, 1817–1820.

AN&Q SEE *American Notes and Queries*

Anburey, Thomas. *Travels through the Interior Parts of America in a Series of Letters by an Officer.* London: Printed for Wm. Lane, 1789. 2 vols.

Anchorage Daily News. Anchorage AK, 1985–.

Anchorage Daily Times. Anchorage AK, 1917–1975.

Anchorage Press. Anchorage AK, 1994–.

AND SEE Ramson, W. S. *Australian National Dictionary*

Anderson, Florence Bennett. *An Off-Islander.* Boston: Stratford, 1921.

Anderson, Jacob Peter. *Flora of Alaska and Adjacent Parts of Canada.* Ames IA: IA State Univ. Press, 1959.

Anderson, Jean. *The Grass Roots Cookbook.* New York: Times Books, c.1977.

Anderson, John Q., comp. *Texas Folk Medicine.* Austin TX: Encino Press, 1970.

Anderson, Maxwell and Laurance Stallings. *Three American Plays.* New York: Harcourt, Brace, 1926.

Anderson, Nels. *The Hobo.* Chicago: Univ. Chicago Press, 1927. Repr. of the 1923 ed. pub. by the Univ. Chicago Press.

———. *The Milk and Honey Route.* New York: Vanguard Press, 1931 [c.1930].

Anderson, Robert. *The Anderson Surpriser.* Chapel Hill NC: Academic Affairs Library, Univ. NC at Chapel Hill, 2001. Text transcr. for *Documenting the American South* website from the 1895 ed. pub. by the author, Macon GA.

Anderson, Robert Alexander. *Mele Kalikimaka.* Sheet music. New York: MCA Music, 1950.

Anderson, Rudolph Martin. *The Birds of Iowa.* Davenport IA: Davenport Academy of Sciences, 1907.

Anderson, Rufus. *The Hawaiian Islands.* 2d ed. Boston: Gould and Lincoln, 1864.

Anderson, Sherwood. *The Sherwood Anderson Reader.* Ed. by Paul Rosenfeld. Boston: Houghton Mifflin, 1947.

———. *Winesburg, Ohio.* New York: B. W. Huebsch, 1919.

Anderson Independent. Anderson SC, 1924–1981.

Anderson Valley Advertiser. Boonville CA, 1954–.

Andrews, Christopher Columbus. *Recollections.* Cleveland OH: Arthur H. Clark, 1928.

Andrews, Edward Deming. *The Community Industries of the Shakers.* Philadelphia: Porcupine Press, 1972 [1932]. Repr. of the 1932 ed. pub. by the Univ. of the State of NY, Albany NY.

Andrews, Eliza Frances. *A Family Secret.* Philadelphia: J. B. Lippincott, 1876.

Andrews, Lorrin. *A Dictionary of the Hawaiian Language.* Santa Monica CA: DeVorss, 1965. Orig. pub. in 1865 by Henry M. Whitney, Honolulu HI.

Andrews, Malachi and Paul T. Owens. *Black Language.* West Los Angeles CA: Seymour-Smith, c.1973.

Andrews, Scottie. *Dude's Mountain Vittles.* Waynesville NC: Old Style Printing, 1997.

Andrews, Sidney. *The South since the War.* Boston: Ticknor and Fields, 1866.

Angelou, Maya. *I Know Why the Caged Bird Sings.* New York: Random House, 1970 [c.1969].

Angier, Bradford. *Field Guide to Edible Wild Plants.* Harrisburg PA: Stackpole Books, c.1974.

Anglia. Zeitschrift für Englische Philologie. Tübingen, 1877–.

Annals of Internal Medicine. Ann Arbor MI: American College of Physicians, 1927–.

Annals of Iowa, Third Series. Des Moines IA, 1893–.

Annals of Natural History, or, Magazine of Zoology, Botany and Geology. London: R. and J. E. Taylor, 1838–1840.

Annals of Wyoming. Cheyenne WY: Wyoming Historical Dept., 1923–.

Anniston Star. Anniston AL, 1882–.

Annual Record of Science and Industry for 1872. New York: Harper & Bros., 1877 [c.1873].

Annual Register, or a View of the History, Politics, and Literature for the Year. London: J. Dodsley, 1758–1837.

Annual Report on Introduction of Domestic Reindeer into Alaska. Washington DC: Govt. Printing Office, 1899–1906.

Anson, Adrian C. *A Baseball Player's Career.* Chicago: Era Publishing, 1900.

Anthon, Charles, ed. *Q. Horatii Flacci Poëmata.* Novi Eboraci: Impensis G. & C.Carvill, 1830.

Anthony, Harold Elmer. *Field Book of North American Mammals.* New York: G. P. Putnam's Sons, 1928.

———, ed. *Mammals of America.* New York: Univ. Society, c.1917.

Anthony, Irvin. *Down to the Sea in Ships.* Philadelphia: Penn Publishing, 1924.

Anthony, Joseph R. *Life in New Bedford a Hundred Years Ago.* Ed. by Zephaniah W. Pease. New Bedford MA: G. H. Reynolds, 1922.

Anthropological Linguistics. Bloomington IN: Anthropology Dept., IN Univ., 1959–.

Anti-Masonic Star. Gettysburg PA, 1830.

Antioch Review. Yellow Springs OH, 1941–.

Antiques & Collecting Magazine. Chicago: Lightner, 1993–.

Anti-Slavery Examiner. New York, 1836–1845.

Apgar, Austin Craig. *Trees of the Northern United States.* New York: American Book, c.1892.

AP Letters. 1978. Unpub. letters in response to an Associated Press article on *DARE* by Timothy Harper, Oct. 1978.

Aplington, Kate Adele. *Pilgrims of the Plains.* New York: Grosset & Dunlap, 1913.

Appalachia. Brattleboro VT, 1876–.

Appalachian Alternatives. Livingstone KY: Appalachia-Science in the Public Interest, 1975–.

Appalachian Journal. Boone NC: Appalachian State Univ., 1972–.

Applegate, Jesse. *Recollections of My Boyhood.* Roseburg OR: Press of Review Publishing, 1914.

Appleton Post-Crescent. Appleton WI, 1920–1965.

Appleton's Annual Cyclopaedia and Register of Important Events of the Year. New York: D. Appleton, 1876–1903.

Appletons' Journal. New York: D. Appleton, 1869–1881.

Appletons' Summer Book. New York: D. Appleton, 1880.

Applied and Environmental Microbiology. Washington DC: American Society for Microbiology, 1976–.

Apps, Jerold W. *Humor from the Country.* Minocqua WI: Guest Cottage, dba Amherst Press, c.2001.

———. *In a Pickle.* Madison WI: Terrace Books, c.2007.

Arabian Horse World. Palo Alto CA, 1960–.

Arboriculture. Chicago: International Society of Arboriculture, 1902–1909.

Arcadian. Arcadia FL, 1924–.

Arcadian Life. Sulpher Springs TX, 1933–.

Arcadia Tribune. Arcadia CA, 1961–1992.

Archdale, John. *A New Description of That Fertile and Pleasant Province of Carolina.* London: Printed for J. Wyat, 1707. In: Carroll, Bartholomew Rivers, ed., *Historical Collections of South Carolina,* 1836, 2.85–120.

Archer, Joseph. *Statistical Survey of the County Dublin.* Dublin: Printed by Graisberry & Campbell, 1801.

The Archer's Manual. Philadelphia: R. H. Hobson, 1830.

Architecture and Building Trades Dictionary. Chicago: American Technical Society, 1950.

Archives of Maryland. Baltimore MD: Maryland Historical Society, 1883–.

Archiv für das Studium der Neueren Sprachen und Literaturen. Elberfeld: J. Bödeker; Braunschweig: G. Westermann, 1846–1930.

Arco Advertiser. Arco ID, 1909–.

Arctic and Alpine Research. Boulder CO: Institute of Arctic and Alpine Research, Univ. CO, 1969–1998.

Arctic, Antarctic and Alpine Research. Boulder CO: Institute of Arctic and Alpine Research, Univ. CO at Boulder, 1999–.

Arena. Boston, 1889–1909.

Arendt, Randall G. *Conservation Design for Subdivisions.* Washington DC: Island Press, 1996.

Argosy. New York: F. A. Munsey, 1882–.

Argus. Fremont-Newark CA, 1960–1990.

Argus Leader. Sioux Falls SD, 1891–.

Argus, or Greenleaf's New Daily Advertiser. New York, 1795–1796.

Arizona. Agricultural Experiment Station. *Bulletin.* Tucson AZ, 1890–1960.

———. *Timely Hints for Farmers.* Tucson AZ, 1899–.

Arizona Daily Star. Tucson AZ, 1879–.

Arizona Daily Sun. Flagstaff AZ, 1946–.

Arizona Department of Water Resources. *Low Water Use Drought Tolerant Plant List.* [v.d.]. Internet.

Arizona Highways. Phoenix AZ: Arizona Highway Dept., 1925–.

Arizona Quarterly. Tucson AZ, 1945–.

Arizona Republic. Phoenix AZ, 1930–.

Arizona Republican. Phoenix AZ, 1890–1930.

Arizona State University. *Ask a Biologist.* [v.d.]. Internet.

———. *Vascular Plant Herbarium.* [v.d.]. Internet.

Arizona. University. *Biological Science Bulletin.* Tucson AZ: Univ. AZ, 1933–.

———. *General Bulletin.* Tucson AZ, 1933–.

Arizona. University. Herbarium. *Flora and Vegetation of the Tucson Mountains, Pima County, Arizona.* [v.d.]. Internet.

Arkansas Democrat-Gazette. Little Rock AR, 1991–.

Arkansas Game & Fish Commission. *Life in the Rocks.* 2000–. Internet.

Arkansas Gardener Magazine. 2001–. Internet.

Arkansas Gazette. Little Rock AR, 1889–.

Arkansas. Geological Survey. *Second Report of a Geological Reconnoissance of the Middle and Southern Counties of Arkansas.* By David Dale Owen, Principal Geologist. Philadelphia: C. Sherman & Son, 1860.

Arkansas Highways. Little Rock AR, 1953–.

Arkansas Historical Quarterly. Fayetteville AR: Arkansas Historical Association, 1942–.

Arkansas Literary Forum. 1999–. Internet.

Arkansas. State Geologist. *Annual Report of the Geological Survey of Arkansas.* Little Rock AR, 1887–1892.

Arkansas Times. Little Rock AR: Arkansas Writers Project, 1975–1992.

Arkansas Times. Little Rock AR, 1992–.

Arlington Heights Herald. Arlington Heights IL, 1926–1973.

Arlington Times. Arlington WA, 1897–.

Armitage, Allan M. *Armitage's Manual of Annuals, Biennials*

and Half-Hardy Perennials. Portland OR: Timber Press, 2001.

Armstrong, Louis. *Don't Jive Me.* Phonodisc. New York: Columbia Records, 1928.

———. *Louis Armstrong, in His Own Words.* New York: Oxford Univ. Press, c.1999.

———. *Satchmo.* New York: Prentice-Hall, 1954.

———. *Swing That Music.* New York: Longmans, Green, 1936.

Armstrong, Margaret Neilson and J. J. Thornber. *Field Book of Western Wild Flowers.* New York: C. P. Putnam's Sons, 1926 [c.1915]. Orig. pub. in 1915.

Armstrong, Mary Frances and Helen W. Ludlow. *Hampton and Its Students.* New York: G. P. Putnam's Sons, 1874.

Arnold, Augusta Foote. *The Century Cook Book.* New York: Century, 1900 [c.1895].

———. *The Sea-Beach at Ebb-Tide.* New York: Century, 1901.

Arnold, Eleanor, ed. *Voices of American Homemakers.* Hollis NH: National Extension Homemakers Council, c.1985.

———, ed. *Voices of American Homemakers.* Bloomington IN: IN Univ. Press, 1993 [c.1985]. From an oral history project of the National Extension Homemakers Council.

Arnold, John Randall. *Hides and Skins.* Chicago: A. W. Shaw, 1925.

Arnold, Madelyn. *A Year of Full Moons.* New York: St. Martin's Press, c.2000.

Arnold, Samuel Greene. *History of the State of Rhode Island and Providence Plantations.* New York: D. Appleton, 1859–1860. 2 vols.

Arnold, Seth Shaler. "As the Years Pass—the Diaries of Seth Shaler Arnold." Vermont Historical Society *Proceedings.* (1940) 8.107–89.

Arnow, Harriette Louisa Simpson. *Flowering of the Cumberland.* New York: Macmillan; London: Collier-Macmillan, c.1963.

———. *Hunter's Horn.* Licensed book club ed. New York: Macmillan, 1949.

Arny, William Frederick Milton. *Interesting Items Regarding New Mexico.* Santa Fé NM: Manderfield & Lucker, 1873.

Aroostook Republican. Caribou ME, 1880–.

Arp, Bill SEE Smith, Charles Henry

Arr, E. H. SEE Rollins, Ellen Chapman Hobbs

Arrington, Alfred W. *The Rangers and Regulators of the Tanaha.* New York: Robert M. De Witt, c.1856.

Arrow Points. Montgomery AL: Alabama Anthropological Society, 1920–.

Arthur, John Preston. *Western North Carolina.* Raleigh NC: Edwards & Broughton, c.1914.

Arthur, Maude and Elizabeth Arthur. *Rural Program Builder.* Franklin OH: Eldridge Entertainment House, c.1941.

Arthur, Timothy Shay. *The Lights and Shadows of Real Life.* Philadelphia: J. W. Bradley, 1851.

———. *Off-Hand Sketches.* New York: John W. Lovell, c.1851.

———. *Stories for Young Housekeepers.* Philadelphia: J. B. Lippincott, 1859 [c.1851].

———. *Two Wives.* Philadelphia: Lippincott, Grambo, 1851.

Arthur's Home Magazine. Philadelphia, 1880–1898.

Arthur's Illustrated Home Magazine. Philadelphia, 1873–1880.

Art Journal. New York: College Art Association of America, 1960–.

Asbury, Francis. *Journal of the Rev. Francis Asbury, Bishop of the Methodist Episcopal Church, from August 7, 1771 to December 7, 1815.* New York: Bangs & Mason, 1821. 3 vols.

Asbury, Herbert. *The French Quarter.* New York: Garden City Publishing, 1938. Orig. pub. in 1936 by Knopf, New York.

———. *The Gangs of New York.* New York: Alfred A. Knopf, 1928.

———. *Sucker's Progress.* New York: Dodd, Mead, 1938.

Ash, Thomas. *Carolina, or, a Description of the Present State of That Country.* London: Printed for W. C., and to be sold by Mrs. Grover, 1682. In: Carroll, Bartholomew Rivers, ed., *Historical Collections of South Carolina,* 1836, 2.59–84.

Ashbrook, Frank G. *Fur-Farming for Profit.* New York: Macmillan, 1928.

Ashe, Samuel A'Court. *History of North Carolina.* Greensboro NC: Charles L. Van Noppen; Raleigh NC: Edwards & Broughton, 1908–1925. 2 vols.

Ashe, Thomas. *Travels in America.* Newburyport MA: Reprinted for WM. Sawyer by E. M. Blount, 1808. Orig. pub. in 1808 by R. Phillips, London.

Asher, Louis Eller and Edith Heal. *Send No Money.* Chicago: Argus, 1942.

Asheville Citizen. Asheville NC, 1900–.

Ashland City Source. Ashland OR: Published by the City Recorder's Office of the City of Ashland, 1997–.

Ashland Daily Tidings Online Edition. 2000?–. Internet.

Ashley, Clifford Warren. *The Ashley Book of Knots.* Garden City NY: Doubleday, 1944.

———. *The Yankee Whaler.* Boston: Houghton Mifflin, 1926.

Ashley, Elihu. *Romance, Remedies, and Revolution.* Ed. by Amelia F. Miller and A. R. Riggs. Amherst MA: Univ. MA Press; Deerfield MA: Pocumtuck Valley Memorial Association, c.2007.

Aspen Times. Aspen CO, 1999–.

Associated Press State & Local Wire. 1900–. Internet.

Association for Preservation Technology. *Bulletin.* Ottawa, 1969–1986.

Association Men. Chicago: International Committee of the Young Men's Christian Associations, 1899–1930.

Association of American Geographers. *Annals.* Lancaster PA, 1911–.

Astounding Science Fiction. New York, 1938–1960.

Atchison Daily Globe. Atchison KS, 1884–.

Athens Banner-Herald. Athens GA, 1933–.

Athens Messenger. Athens OH, 1861–1893; 1905–.

Athens Messenger and Hocking Valley Gazette. Athens OH, 1844–1861.

Atherton, Gertrude Franklin Horn. *The Californians.* New York: Grosset & Dunlap, c.1908. Orig. pub. in 1898 by John Lane, London.

———. *Perch of the Devil.* New York: Frederick A. Stokes, c.1914.

Athletic Sports for Boys. New York: Dick & Fitzgerald, c.1866.

Athol Daily News. Athol MA, 1934–.

Atkinson, George Wesley. *After the Moonshiners.* Wheeling WV: Frew & Campbell, Printers, 1881.

Atkinson-O'Fallon Expedition SEE "Journal of the Atkinson-O'Fallon Expedition"

Atkinson's Casket. Philadelphia, 1831–1839.

Atlanta Constitution. Atlanta GA, 1881–2001.

Atlanta Journal-Constitution. Atlanta GA, 1950–.

Atlanta Letters. 1972. Unpub. letters in response to a query in *The Gas Line,* the newsletter of the Atlanta (GA) Gas Company.

Atlanta Medical and Surgical Journal. Atlanta GA, 1855–1881.

Atlantic City Press. Atlantic City NJ, 1895–.

The Atlantic Club-Book. New York: Harper, 1834. 2 vols.

Atlantic County Record. Mays Landing NJ, 1908?–.

Atlantic Deeper Waterways Association. *Annual Convention Report of the Proceedings.* Philadelphia, 1908–1926.

Atlantic Monthly. Boston, 1857–.

Atlantic Slope Naturalist. Narbeth PA, 1903–1904.

Atlas Checklists. c1950. Unpub. material from Linguistic Atlas checklists.

Atlas of the Flora of the Great Plains. Ames IA: IA State Univ. Press, 1977.

Atson, William. *Heart Whispers.* Philadelphia: H. Cowperthwait, 1859.

Attebery, Louie Wayne, ed. *Idaho Folklife.* Salt Lake City UT: Univ. ID Press, c.1985.

———. *Sheep May Safely Graze.* Moscow ID: Univ. ID Press, 1992.

Attwater, Henry Philemon, comp. *Use and Value of Wild Birds to Texas Farmers and Stockmen and Fruit and Truck Growers.* Austin TX: Von Boeckmann-Jones Printers, 1914.

Attwood, Stanley Bearce. *The Length and Breadth of Maine.* Augusta ME: Kennebec Journal Print Shop, c.1946.

———. *The Length and Breadth of Maine.* Orono ME: Univ. ME, 1973.

Atwater, Caleb. *A History of the State of Ohio, Natural and Civil.* Cincinnati OH: Glezen & Shepard, 1838.

Atwood, Elmer Bagby. *The Regional Vocabulary of Texas.* Austin TX: Univ. TX Press, 1962.

———. *A Survey of Verb Forms in the Eastern United States.* Ann Arbor MI: Univ. MI Press, 1953.

Atwood, Margaret. *The Handmaid's Tale.* Boston: Houghton Mifflin, 1986.

Atwood, Wallace Walter. *The Rocky Mountains.* New York: Vanguard Press, 1945.

Audubon, John James. *Audubon and His Journals.* New York: Dover, 1960. 2 vols. Facsimile of the 1897 ed. pub. by Charles Scribner's Sons.

———. *The Birds of America.* New York: J. J. Audubon; Philadelphia: J. B. Chevalier, 1840–1844. 7 vols.

———. *Ornithological Biography.* Edinburgh: Adam Black, 1831–1839. 5 vols.

———. *A Synopsis of the Birds of North America.* Edinburgh: A. and C. Black, 1839.

Audubon, John James and John Bachman. *The Quadrupeds of North America.* New York: V. G. Audubon, 1849–1854. 3 vols.

Audubon, John Woodhouse. *Audubon's Western Journal.* Cleveland OH: Arthur H. Clark, 1906.

Audubon Magazine. New York: National Audubon Society, 1941–.

The Audubon Society Field Guide to North American Fishes, Whales, and Dolphins. New York: Alfred A. Knopf, c.1983.

Audubon Society of New Hampshire. *Bulletin.* Hanover NH, 1921–1935.

Aughey, John Hill. *Provincialisms, Slang and Popular Errors.* Wheeling WV: Hubbard & Fetterly, Printers, 1880.

Augusta Chronicle. Augusta GA, 2000–.

Augusta Chronicle and Gazette of the State. Augusta GA, 1789–1803.

Augusta County. Virginia. *Chronicles of the Scotch-Irish Settlement in Virginia.* By Lyman Chalkley. Rosslyn VA: Published by Mary S. Lockwood, 1912–1913. 3 vols.

Auk. Cambridge MA: American Ornithologists' Union, 1884–.

Aurand, Ammon Monroe. *Quaint Idioms and Expressions of the Pennsylvania-Germans.* Rev. ed. Harrisburg PA: Aurand Press, c.1939.

Aurora General Advertiser. Philadelphia, 1794–1824.

Austin, Daniel F. *Florida Ethnobotany.* Boca Raton FL: CRC Press, c.2004.

Austin, Jane Goodwin. *Dora Darling.* Boston: J. E. Tilton, 1865 [c.1864].

———. *Nantucket Scraps.* Boston: James R. Osgood, 1883 [c.1882].

Austin, Mary Hunter. *The Children Sing in the Far West.* Boston: Houghton, Mifflin, 1928.

———. *Earth Horizon.* Boston: Houghton Mifflin, 1932.

———. *The Land of Journeys' Ending.* New York: Century, 1924.

———. *The Land of Little Rain.* Boston: Houghton Mifflin, 1950. Orig. pub. in 1903.

———. *Lost Borders.* New York: Harper & Bros., c.1909.

———. *A Woman of Genius.* Garden City NY: Doubleday, Page, 1912.

Austin, Moses. *The Austin Papers.* Ed. by Eugene C. Barker. Washington DC: Govt. Printing Office, 1924–1928. 2 vols.

Austin, Stephen Fuller. "Journal of Stephen F. Austin on His First Trip to Texas, 1821." Texas State Historical Association *Quarterly.* (1904) 7.286–307.

Austin American-Statesman. Austin TX, 1963–.

Austin Daily Herald. Austin MN, 1891–.

Austin Downtown Arts. 1994–. Internet.

Austin Statesman. Austin TX, 1921–1973.

Austrian, Joseph E. *We Need the Business.* New York: Frederick A. Stokes, c.1919.

Automobile Dealer and Repairer. New York, 1906–1924.

Autry, Mahan Blair. *Louis DeShong, Revolutionary Soldier.* Ennis TX: Printed by Morton's, 1964.

Avail. *Over the James.* Phonodisc. Berkeley CA: Lookout Records, 1998.

Avebury, John Lubbock. *Scientific Lectures.* London: Macmillan, 1879.

Avery, Samuel Putnam. *The Harp of a Thousand Strings.* New York: Dick & Fitzgerald, c.1858.

———. *Mrs. Partington's Carpet-Bag.* New York: Garrett, 1854.

Avis, Walter S. et al., eds. *Dictionary of Canadianisms on Historical Principles.* Toronto: W. J. Gage, 1967.

Ayer, Arthusa Ann Hibbard. *An Autobiography.* Leverett MA: Mrs. Annette N. Gibavic, 1984.

Ayer, N. W. & Son. *Directory of Newspapers and Periodicals.* Philadelphia, 1930–1969.

Ayer, Sarah Newman Connell. *Diary.* Portland ME: Lefavor-Tower, 1910.

Ayer Directory of Publications. Philadelphia, 1973–.

Ayers, James T. *The Diary of James T. Ayers, Civil War Recruiter.* Ed. by John Hope Franklin. Springfield IL: State of Illinois, c.1947.

Ayto, John and John Simpson. *The Oxford Dictionary of Modern Slang.* Oxford: Oxford Univ. Press, c.1992.

Babb, Theodore Adolphus. *In the Bosom of the Comanches.* Azle TX: Bois d'Arc Press, 1990. Orig. pub. in 1912.

Babcock, Ernest Brown and Roy Elwood Clausen. *Genetics in Relation to Agriculture.* New York: McGraw-Hill, 1918.

Babcock, Havilah. *I Don't Want to Shoot an Elephant.* New York: Henry Holt, c.1958.

———. *Jaybirds Go to Hell on Friday.* New York: Holt, Rinehart and Winston, c.1964.

———. *Tales of Quails 'n Such.* New York: Greenberg, c.1951.

Babson, John J. *History of the Town of Gloucester, Cape Ann, Including the Town of Rockport.* Gloucester MA: Proctor Bros., 1860.

Bache, Anna. *The Fire-Screen.* Philadelphia: W. J. and J. K. Simon, 1841.

Bacheller, Irving. *Eben Holden.* Boston: Lothrop, 1900.

———. *The Light in the Clearing.* Indianapolis IN: Bobbs-Merrill, c.1917.

———. *A Man for the Ages.* Indianapolis IN: Bobbs-Merrill, 1919.

Back, Joe. *Horses, Hitches and Rocky Trails.* Chicago: Sage Books, c.1959.

Backus, Harriet Fish. *Tomboy Bride.* Boulder CO: Pruett Press, c.1969.

Bacon, Delia Salter. *The Bride of Fort Edward.* New York: S. Colman, 1839.

Bacon, Eugenia Jones. *Lyddy, a Tale of the Old South.* New York: Continental, 1898.

Baden, Jacqueline Heppes. *Maryland's Eastern Shore.* Rockville MD: Travel on Tape, Book Division, 1990 [c.1989].

Baden, Michael M. and Judith A. Hennessee. *Unnatural Death.* New York: Ivy Books, c.1989.

Badger Folklore. Madison WI, 1948–1952.

Badger Herald. Madison WI, 1969–. Student newsp. of Univ. WI–Madison.

Badgerland. Stoughton WI, 1960?–1979.

Baerecke, John Fredric. *Analytical Key to the Ferns and Flowering Plants in the Atlantic Section of Middle Florida (Wild and Cultivated).* DeLand FL: News Publishing, c.1906.

Bagby, George William. *Letters of Mozis Addums to Billy Ivvins.* Richmond VA: West & Johnston, 1862.

———. *The Old Virginia Gentleman and Other Sketches.* Ed. by Thomas Nelson Page. New York: Charles Scribner's Sons, 1911 [c.1910].

———. *Selections from the Miscellaneous Writings of Dr. George W. Bagby.* Richmond VA: Whittet & Shepperson, c.1884–c.1885. 2 vols.

Bagg, Lyman Hotchkiss. *Four Years at Yale.* New Haven CT: C. C. Chatfield, 1871.

Bagley, Desmond. *The Snow Tiger.* London: Collins, 1975.

Bagley, John Judson. *Old Times.* Detroit MI: W. Graham, 1876.

Bagley, Lowell. "Private Diary." In: Longyear, Mary Hawley Beecher, *The History of a House,* 1925.

Bailey, Alfred Marshall. *Birds of Arctic Alaska.* Denver CO: Colorado Museum of Natural History, 1948.

Bailey, Alfred Marshall and Robert J. Niedrach. *Birds of Colorado.* Denver CO: Denver Museum of Natural History, 1965. 2 vols.

Bailey, Eli Stillman. *The Sand Dunes of Indiana.* Chicago: A. C. McClurg, 1917.

Bailey, Florence Merriam. *Birds of New Mexico.* Santa Fe NM: Published by the New Mexico Dept. of Game and Fish in Cooperation with the State Game Protective Association and the Bureau of Biological Survey, 1928.

———. *Birds of Village and Field.* Boston: Houghton, Mifflin, 1898.

———. *Birds through an Opera-Glass.* Boston: Houghton, Mifflin, 1900 [c.1889].

Bailey, Guy and Marvin Bassett. *Invariant "Be".* 1981. Unpub. paper from conference *Language Variety in the South: Perspectives in Black and White,* Columbia SC.

Bailey, Harold Harris. *The Birds of Florida.* Baltimore MD: Privately Published for the Author by the Williams & Wilkins Co., 1925.

———. *The Birds of Virginia.* Lynchburg VA: J. P. Bell, 1913.

Bailey, James Montgomery. *Life in Danbury.* Boston: Shepard and Gill, 1873.

Bailey, Joseph Cannon. *Seaman A. Knapp.* New York: Columbia Univ. Press, 1945.

Bailey, Liberty Hyde, ed. *Cyclopedia of American Agriculture.* New York: Macmillan, 1907–1909. 4 vols.

———, ed. *Cyclopedia of American Horticulture.* New York: Macmillan, 1900–1902. 4 vols.

———, ed. *Cyclopedia of American Horticulture.* New York: Macmillan, 1902–1903. 4 vols.

———. *The Horticulturist's Rule-Book.* New York: Garden, c.1889.

———. *Manual of Cultivated Plants Most Commonly Grown in the Continental United States and Canada.* Rev. ed., completely restudied. New York: Macmillan, 1949.

———. *Sketch of the Evolution of Our Native Fruits.* New York: Macmillan, 1898.

———. *The Standard Cyclopedia of Horticulture.* New York: Macmillan, 1914–1917. 6 vols.

Bailey, Liberty Hyde and Ethel Joe Bailey, comps. *Hortus Third.* Rev. and expanded by the staff of the Liberty Hyde Bailey Hortorium. New York: Macmillan, c.1976.

Bailey, William. *Jayhawker Boy.* New York: Vantage Press, 1962.

———. *Responses to PADS 20.* 1960. Unpub. material in response to a questionnaire.

Baillie-Grohman, William Adolph. *Camps in the Rockies.* New York: Charles Scribner's Sons, 1882.

Baily, Francis. *Journal of a Tour in Unsettled Parts of North America in 1796 and 1797.* London: Baily Bros., 1856.

Baily, Waldron. *The Homeward Trail.* New York: Grosset & Dunlap, c.1916.

———. *June Gold.* New York: W. J. Watt, c.1922.

Baily's Magazine of Sports and Pastimes. London, 1860–1926.

Baird, Robert. *View of the Valley of the Mississippi.* 2d ed. Philadelphia: H. S. Tanner, 1834.

Baird, Spencer Fullerton *Birds* SEE United States. War Department *Reports of Explorations and Surveys . . . for a Railroad*

Baird, Spencer Fullerton. *Mammals of North America.* Philadelphia: J. B. Lippincott, 1859.

———. *Report on the Condition of the Sea Fisheries of the South Coast of New England in 1871 and 1872.* Washington DC: Govt. Printing Office, 1873.

Baird, Spencer Fullerton and C. Girard. *Catalogue of North American Reptiles in the Museum of the Smithsonian Institution.* Washington DC: Smithsonian Institution, 1853.

Baird, Spencer Fullerton et al. *A History of North American Birds.* Boston: Little, Brown, 1905 [c.1874]. 3 vols.

———. *The Water Birds of North America.* Boston: Little, Brown, 1884. 2 vols.

Bakeless, John Edwin. *Lewis & Clark.* New York: William Morrow, 1947.

Baker, Amy J. L. *Adult Children of Parental Alienation Syndrome.* New York: W. W. Norton, 2007.

Baker, Carlos. *A Friend in Power.* New York: Charles Scribner's Sons, 1958.

Baker, Charles Henry. *Blood of the Lamb.* New York: Rinehart, c.1946.

Baker, La Fayette Charles. *History of the United States Secret Service.* Philadelphia: L. C. Baker, c.1867.

Baker, Mary Francis. *The Book of Grasses.* Garden City NY: Doubleday, Page, 1912.

———. *Florida Wild Flowers.* New ed. New York: Macmillan, 1938.

Baker, Sarah Schoonmaker. *At the Pastor's.* London: T. Nelson and Sons, 1885.

Bakker, Elna S. *An Island Called California.* Berkeley CA: Univ. CA Press, c.1971.

Balance. Hudson NY, 18 01–1808.

Balance, and Columbian Repository. Albany NY: Croswell & Frary, 1802–1807.

Balance, and New-York State Journal. Albany NY, 1809–1810.

Balance & State Journal. Albany NY, 1811.

Baldacci, David. *Wish You Well.* New York: Warner Books, c.2000.

Baldridge, Cyrus LeRoy. *Time and Chance.* New York: John Day, c.1947.

Baldwin, Christopher Columbus. *Diary of Christopher Columbus Baldwin.* Worcester MA: Published by the American Antiquarian Society, 1901.

Baldwin, Ebenezer. *History of Yale College.* New Haven CT: Benjamin & William Noyes, 1841.

Baldwin, Edgar M., ed. *The Making of a Township.* Fairmount IN: Edgar Baldwin Printing, c.1917.

Baldwin, Faith. *Give Love the Air.* New York: Rinehart, 1947.

Baldwin, James. *The Amen Corner.* New York: Dial Press, 1968.

———. *Another Country.* New York: Dial Press, 1962.

———. *Blues for Mister Charlie.* New York: Dial Press, 1964.

———. *If Beale Street Could Talk.* New York: Dial Press, 1974.

———. *In My Youth.* Indianapolis IN: Bobbs-Merrill, c.1914.

———. *Tell Me How Long the Train's Been Gone.* New York: Dial Press, 1968.

Baldwin, Joseph Glover. *The Flush Times of Alabama and Mississippi.* New York: D. Appleton, 1854. Orig. pub. in 1853 by Appleton.

———. *Party Leaders.* New York: D. Appleton, 1855.

Baldwin, Leland Dewitt. *The Keelboat Age on Western Waters.* Pittsburgh PA: Univ. Pittsburgh Press, 1941.

Baldwin, Lydia Wood. *A Yankee School-Teacher in Virginia.* New York: Funk & Wagnalls, 1884.

Baldwin, Oliver P., comp. *Southern and South-Western Sketches.* Richmond VA: J. W. Randolph, 1852.

Baldwin, Simeon Eben. *Life and Letters of Simeon Baldwin.* New Haven CT: Tuttle, Morehouse & Taylor, 1919.

Baldwin, William. *Reliquiae Baldwinianae: Selections from the Correspondence of the Late William Baldwin, M.D., Surgeon in the U.S. Navy.* Comp. by William Darlington. Philadelphia: Kimber and Sharpless, 1843.

Baldwin, William P. *Inland Passages.* Charleston SC: History Press, c.2004.

Ball, Timothy Horton. *Lake County Indiana from 1834 to 1872.* Chicago: J. W. Goodspeed, 1873 [c.1872].

———. *Northwestern Indiana from 1800 to 1900.* Crown Point IN: Donohue & Henneberry, Printers, 1900.

Ballard, Julia P. *Among the Moths and Butterflies.* New York: G. P. Putnam's Sons, 1893 [c.1890].

Ballou, Adin. *Practical Christian Socialism.* Hopedale MA: The Author; New York: Fowlers and Wells, 1854.

Ballou, Adin and William S. Heywood. *Autobiography of Adin Ballou.* Lowell MA: Vox Populi Press, 1896.

Ballou, John SEE Newbrough, John Ballou

Ballou's Dollar Monthly Magazine. Boston, 1855–1863.

Ballou's Monthly Magazine. Boston, 1866–1893.

Ballou's Pictorial. Boston, 1855–1859.

Ballowe, Hewitt Leonard. *The Lawd Sayin' the Same.* Baton Rouge LA: LA State Univ. Press, 1947.

Balls, Edward K. *Early Uses of California Plants.* Berkeley CA: Univ. CA Press, 1962.

Baltimore, Maryland. Department of Education. Bureau of Research. *Baltimore Bulletin of Education.* Baltimore MD, 1923–.

Baltimore City Paper Online. Baltimore MD, 1999–. Internet.

Baltimore Patriot & Mercantile Advertiser. Baltimore MD, 1817–1838.

Bamberg, Michael G. W. et al., eds. *Selves and Identities in Narrative and Discourse.* Philadelphia: John Benjamins Publishing, c.2007.

Bancroft, Caroline. *Six Racy Madams of Colorado.* Boulder CO: Johnson, c.1965.

Bancroft, Edward. *Experimental Researches Concerning the Philosophy of Permanent Colours.* London: T. Cadell, Jun. and W. Davies, 1794.

———. *Experimental Researches Concerning the Philosophy of Permanent Colours, and the Best Means of Producing Them, by Dyeing, Calico Printing, etc.* Philadelphia: Published by Thomas Dobson, 1814. 2 vols.

Bancroft, George. *History of the United States of America.* Thoroughly rev. ed. Boston: Little, Brown, 1879. 6 vols.

Bancroft, Jessie Hubbell. *Games.* Rev. and enlarged ed. New York: Macmillan, 1947.

———. *Games for the Playground, Home, School and Gymnasium.* New York: Macmillan, 1923 [c.1909].

Bandelier, Adolph Francis Alphonse. *Final Report of Investigations among the Indians of the Southwestern United States.* Cambridge MA: J. Wilson and Son, 1890–1892. 2 pts.

Bangor Daily News. Bangor ME, 1992–.

Bangor Daily Whig & Courier. Bangor ME, 1834–1900.

Banks, Ann, ed. *First-Person America.* New York: Knopf, 1980.

Banks, Jacqueline Turner. *Maid in the Shade.* Sacramento CA: ReGeJe Press, c.1998.

Banks, Russell. *Rule of the Bone.* New York: HarperCollins, 1995.

Banning, Kendall. *West Point Today.* New York: Funk & Wagnalls, 1939 [c.1937].

Baptist Home Mission Monthly. New York, 1878–1909.

Baptist Missionary Magazine. Boston: American Baptist Missionary Union, 1817–1909.

Baraboo Republic. Baraboo WI, 1855–1924.

Baraka, Imamu Amiri. *Blues People.* New York: William Morrow, 1963.

———. *Dutchman and The Slave.* New York: Morrow, 1964.

———. *Tales.* New York: Grove Press, 1967.

Baraka, Imamu Amiri and Larry Neal, eds. *Black Fire.* New York: William Morrow, c.1968.

Barber, Hervey. *Diary.* 1884. Unpub.

Barber, Joseph. *War Letters of a Disbanded Volunteer.* New York: Frederic A. Brady, 1864.

Barbour, Frances M., ed. *Proverbs and Proverbial Phrases of Illinois.* Carbondale IL: Southern IL Univ. Press, c.1965.

Barbour, Michael G. and William Dwight Billings, eds. *North American Terrestrial Vegetation.* 2d ed. Cambridge: Cambridge Univ. Press, 2000.

Barbour, Thomas. *A Naturalist in Cuba.* Boston: Little, Brown, 1945.

———. *That Vanishing Eden.* Boston: Little, Brown, 1944.

Bard, Samuel A. SEE Squier, Ephraim George

Barden, Thomas E., ed. *Virginia Folk Legends.* Charlottesville VA: Univ. Press VA, c.1991.

Barham, Henry. *Hortus Americanus.* Kingston, Jamaica: Alexander Aikman, 1794.

Bar Harbor Times. Bar Harbor ME, 1914–.

Barker, David. *Poems.* Bangor ME: Samuel S. Smith & Son, 1876.

Barker, James Nelson. *Tears and Smiles.* Philadelphia: Printed by T. & G. Palmer for E. Blake, 1808.

Barker, Joseph. *Recollections of the First Settlement of Ohio.* Marietta OH: Marietta College, 1958.

Barker, S. Omar. *Little World Apart.* Garden City NY: Doubleday, c.1966.

Barker, Will. *Familiar Insects of America.* New York: Harper & Bros., c.1960.

Barkley, Theodore M. *A Manual of the Flowering Plants of Kansas.* Manhattan KS: KS State Univ. Endowment Association, 1968.

Barnard, Evan G. *A Rider of the Cherokee Strip.* Boston: Houghton Mifflin, 1936.

Barnard, Susan M. *Reptile Keeper's Handbook.* Orig. ed. Malabar FL: Krieger, c.1996.

Barnes, Charles Brinton. *The Longshoremen.* New York: Survey Associates, 1915.

Barnes, Claude Teancum. *The Natural History of a Wasatch Autumn.* Salt Lake City UT: Ralton, 1958.

———. *The Natural History of a Wasatch Spring.* Salt Lake City UT: Ralton, 1957.

———. *The Natural History of a Wasatch Summer.* Salt Lake City UT: Ralton, 1957.

———. *The Natural History of a Wasatch Winter.* Salt Lake City UT: Ralton, 1959.

Barnes, Claude Teancum and Dorothy B. Jensen. *Dictionary of Utah Slang.* Kaysville UT: Inland Printing, 1966.

Barnes, F. J. and R. P. Weston. *I've Got Rings on My Fingers and Bells on My Toes.* Sheet music. New York: T. B. Harms and Francis, 1909.

Barnes, M. Craig. *Hustling God.* Grand Rapids MI: Zondervan Publishing, 1999.

Barnes, William Croft. *Arizona Place Names.* Tucson AZ: Univ. AZ, 1935.

———. *Tales from the X-Bar Horse Camp.* Chicago: Breeders' Gazette, 1920.

———. *Western Grazing Grounds and Forest Ranges.* New York: Arno Press, 1979. Orig. pub. in 1913 by Breeder's Gazette, Chicago.

Barnett, Janet and Randy Russell. *The Granny Curse.* Winston-Salem NC: J. F. Blair, 1999.

Barnhart, Percy Spencer. *Marine Fishes of Southern California.* Berkeley CA: Univ. CA Press, 1936.

Barnhart Dictionary Companion. Cold Spring NY, 1982–.

Barnum, Francis. *Life on the Alaska Mission.* Baltimore MD: Woodstock College, 1893.

Barnum, Phineas Taylor. *The Humbugs of the World.* New York: Carleton, 1866 [c.1865].

———. *The Life of P. T. Barnum.* New York: Redfield, 1855.

———. *Struggles and Triumphs or, Forty Years' Recollections of P. T. Barnum.* Hartford CT: J. B. Burr, 1869.

Barra, Ezekiel I. *A Tale of Two Oceans.* San Francisco: Eastman, 1893.

Barrell, Joseph. *Flora of the Gunnison Basin.* Rockford IL: Natural Land Institute, 1969.

Barrère, Albert Marie Victor and Charles G. Leland, eds. *A Dictionary of Slang, Jargon & Cant.* Rev. ed. London: G. Bell & Sons, 1897. 2 vols.

Barrett, John G. *The Civil War in North Carolina.* Chapel Hill NC: Univ. NC Press, c.1963.

Barrett, Joseph Osgood. *The Spiritual Pilgrim.* 3d ed. Boston: William White, 1872 [c.1871].

Barrett, Samuel Alfred. *Material Aspects of Pomo Culture.* Milwaukee WI: Milwaukee Public Museum, 1952. 2 vols.

Barrick, Mac E. *Collection of Cumberland County, Pennsylvania, Folkspeech.* 1980–. Unpub.

Barringer, Paul Brandon. *The Natural Bent.* Chapel Hill NC: Univ. NC Press, 1949.

Barron, Alfred. *Foot Notes.* Wallingford CT: Wallingford Printing, 1875.

Barrow, Frances Elizabeth Mease. *Aunt Fanny's Story Book for Little Boys and Girls.* New York: D. Appleton, 1853 [c.1849].

Barrow, John. *Facts Relating to North-Eastern Texas.* London: Simpkin, Marshall, 1849.

Barrows, John R. *Ubet.* Caldwell ID: Caxton Printers, 1936 [c.1934].

Barrows, Walter Bradford. *Michigan Bird Life.* Lansing MI: MI Agricultural College, 1912.

Barrus, Clara. *John Burroughs, Boy and Man.* Garden City NY: Doubleday, Page, 1920.

Barry, James Buckner. *A Texas Ranger and Frontiersman.* Dallas TX: Southwest Press, 1932.

Barry, John Stetson. *A Historical Sketch of the Town of Hanover, Mass., with Family Genealogies.* Boston: Published for the Author by S. G. Drake, 1853.

Barry, Philip. *Philadelphia Story.* New York: Coward-McCann, c.1939.

Barstow, George. *The History of New Hampshire.* Concord NH: I. S. Boyd, 1842.

Bartlett, John, comp. *Familiar Quotations.* 15th ed. Boston: Little, Brown, c.1980.

Bartlett, John Russell. *Dictionary of Americanisms.* New York: Bartlett and Welford, 1848.

———. *Dictionary of Americanisms.* 2d ed. New York: Johnson Reprint, 1968. Orig. pub. in 1859 by Little, Brown, Boston.

———. *Dictionary of Americanisms.* 3rd ed. Boston: Little, Brown, 1860.

———. *Dictionary of Americanisms.* 4th ed. Boston: Little, Brown, 1877.

———. *Personal Narrative of Explorations and Incidents in Texas, New Mexico, California, Sonora, and Chihuahua during the Years 1850, '51, '52, and '53.* New York: D. Appleton, 1854. 2 vols.

Bartol, Cyrus Augustus. *Radical Problems.* Boston: Roberts Bros., 1872.

Barton, Andrew, [pseud.]. *The Disappointment.* 2d ed. rev. and corr. Philadelphia: Francis Shallus, 1796.

Barton, Benjamin Smith. *Collections for an Essay towards a Materia Medica of the United States.* Philadelphia: Printed for the author by Way & Groff, 1798.

———. *Collections for an Essay towards a Materia Medica of the United-States.* 3d ed., with additions. Philadelphia: Printed for Edward Earle, Fry and Kammerer Printers, 1810.

———. *Elements of Botany.* Rev. and corr. London: Printed for J. Johnson by I. Gold, 1804.

———. *Fragments of the Natural History of Pennsylvania.* Philadelphia: Printed, for the author, by Way & Groff, 1799.

———. *Memoir Concerning an Animal of the Class of Reptilia, or Amphibia, Which Is Known, in the United States, by the Name of Alligator and Hell-Bender.* Philadelphia: Griggs and Dickinson, 1812.

Barton, William E. *A Hero in Homespun.* Boston: Lamson, Wolffe, 1897.

———. *The Truth about the Trouble at Roundstone.* Boston: Pilgrim Press, 1897.

Barton, William Paul Crillon. *Compendium Florae Philadelphicae.* Philadelphia: M. Carey & Son, c.1818. 2 vols.

———. *A Flora of North America.* Philadelphia: M. Carey & Sons, 1821–1823. 3 vols.

———. *Vegetable Materia Medica of the United States.* Philadelphia: Printed and published by M. Carey & Son, 1817–1818. 2 vols.

Bartram, John. "Diary of a Journey through the Carolinas, Georgia and Florida from July 1, 1765 to April 10, 1766." American Philosophical Society *Transactions.* (1942–1944) 33.1.13–55.

———. *Observations on the Inhabitants Climate, Soil, Rivers, Productions, Animals, and Other Matters Worthy of Notice.* London: Printed for J. Whiston and B. White, 1751.

Bartram, William. *Travels.* Ed. with commentary and an annotated index by Francis Harper. Naturalist's ed. New Haven CT: Yale Univ. Press, 1958. Orig. pub. in 1791 under the title *Travels through North and South Carolina, Georgia, East and West Florida.*

———. *Travels through North & South Carolina, Georgia, East & West Florida.* Philadelphia: James & Johnson, 1791.

Baseball Magazine. Boston, 1908–.

Baskett, James Newton. *At You-All's House.* New York: Macmillan, 1898.

Bassett, John Spencer, ed. *The Southern Plantation Overseer as Revealed in His Letters.* Northampton MA: Printed for Smith College, 1925.

Basso, Hamilton. *The View from Pompey's Head.* Garden City NY: Doubleday, c.1954.

Bastinado. Charleston SC: The Author, 1834.

Bates, Arlo. *The Puritans.* Boston: Houghton, Mifflin, 1899 [c.1898].

Bates, D. B. *Incidents on Land and Water.* 11th ed. Boston: Published for the Author, 1861 [c.1857].

Bates, Edmond Franklin. *History and Reminiscences of Denton County.* Denton TX: McNitzky Printing, 1918.

Bates, Harriet Leonora Vose. *Old Salem.* Ed. by Arlo Bates. Boston: Houghton, Mifflin, 1886.

Bates, Robert L. and Julia A. Jackson, eds. *Glossary of Geology.* 3d ed. Alexandria VA: American Geological Institute, 1987.

Batson, Wade T. *Wild Flowers in South Carolina.* Columbia SC: Univ. SC Press, 1964.

Battaglia, Mary. *Responses to PADS 20.* 1957. Unpub. material in response to a questionnaire.

Battey, George M. *70,000 Miles on a Submarine Destroyer.* Rev. ed. Atlanta GA: Webb & Vary, 1920.

The Battle of Brooklyn. New York: J. Rivington, 1776.

Baudry des Lozières, Louis. *Voyage a la Louisiane, et sur le continent de L'Amérique.* Paris: Dentu, 1802.

Baugh, John. *Black Street Speech.* Austin TX: Univ. TX Press, c.1983.

Baumann, John. *Old Man Crow's Boy.* New York: William Morrow, 1948.

Baxley, Henry Willis. *What I Saw on the West Coast of South and North America, and at the Hawaiian Islands.* New York: D. Appleton, 1865.

Bayard Advocate. Bayard IA, 1893–1918.

Baylor University, Waco Texas. Museum. *Contributions.* Waco TX, 1925–1929.

Baylor University. Medical Center. *Proceedings.* Dallas TX, 1988–.

Bay Nature. Berkeley CA, 2001–.

Bay State Monthly. Boston, 1884–1885.

Baytown Sun. Baytown TX, 1949–.

Bazore, Katherine. *Hawaiian and Pacific Foods.* New York: M. Barrows, 1940.

Beach, Rex Ellingwood. *The Barrier.* New York: A. L. Burt, c.1908.

———. *Heart of the Sunset.* New York: Harper & Bros., c.1915.

———. *The Iron Trail.* New York: A. L. Burt, 1913.

———. *Pardners.* New York: Doubleday, Page, 1909. Orig. pub. in 1905 by McClure, Phillips, New York.

———. *The Spoilers.* New York: Harper and Bros., 1906 [c.1905].

Beach, Wooster. *The American Practice of Medicine.* New York: Betts & Anstice, 1833 [c.1832].

———. *The American Practice of Medicine.* 2d ed. New York: Published by the author, 1852. 3 vols.

Beach Haven Times. Beach Haven NJ, 1923–.

Beadle, Erastus Flavel. "To Nebraska in '57." New York City Public Library *Bulletin.* (1923) 27.71–115, 171–212.

Beadle, Harriet Merancy. *Reminiscences of My Mother.* Wallingford CT: Wallingford Historical Society, 1957.

Beadle, John Hanson. *Life in Utah.* Philadelphia: National Publishing, c.1870.

———. *The Undeveloped West.* Philadelphia: National Publishing, 1873.

———. *Western Wilds and the Men Who Redeem Them.* Cincinnati OH: Jones Bros., 1878.

Beadle's Monthly, a Magazine of To-Day. New York, 1866–1867.

Beal, William James. *Grasses of North America for Farmers and Students.* Lansing MI: Thorp & Godfrey, 1887–1896. 2 vols.

Beals, Carleton. *Brimstone and Chili.* New York: A. A. Knopf, 1927.

Beam, C. Richard. *Pennsylvania German Dictionary.* Schaefferstown PA: Historic Schaefferstown, 1982.

———. *Revised Pennsylvania German Dictionary.* Lancaster PA: Brookshire Publications, c.1991.

Bean, George H. *Yankee Auctioneer.* Boston: Little, Brown, 1948.

Bear, John W. *The Life and Travels of John W. Bear, "The Buckeye Blacksmith".* Baltimore MD: D. Binswanger, c.1873.

Beard, Daniel Carter. *Outdoor Games for All Seasons, the American Boy's Book of Sport.* New York: Charles Scribner's Sons, 1896.

Beard, James A. *James Beard's American Cookery.* 2d printing. Boston: Little, Brown, c.1972.

Beard, James Melville. *K.K.K. Sketches.* Philadelphia: Claxton, Remsen & Haffelfinger, 1877 [c.1876].

Beardsley, Levi. *Reminiscences.* New York: Charles Vinten, c.1852.

Beatty, John. *The Citizen-Soldier.* Cincinnati OH: Wilstach, Baldwin, 1879.

———. *McLean, a Romance of the War.* Columbus OH: Press of Fred J. Heer, 1904.

Beaudry, Louis Napoleon. *Historic Records of the Fifth New York Cavalry, First Ira Harris Guard.* 2d ed. Albany NY: S. R. Gray, 1865.

Beaufort Gazette. Beaufort SC, 2001–.

Beaumont Enterprise. Beaumont TX, 1880–.

The Beauties of Brother Bull-Us. By his loving sister Bull-A. New York: James Eastburn, 1812.

Beauty, Its Attainment and Preservation. 2d ed. rev. New York: Butterick Publishing, 1892.

Beaver Dam, Wisconsin. Board of Public Works Water Commission & Traffic. *Minutes.* 2007–. Internet.

Beck, Earl Clifton. *Songs of the Michigan Lumberjacks.* Ann Arbor MI: Univ. MI Press, 1942.

Beck, Henry Charlton. *Fare to Midlands.* New York: E. P. Dutton, 1939.

———. *Jersey Genesis.* New Brunswick NJ: Rutgers Univ. Press, 1945.

———. *More Forgotten Towns of Southern New Jersey.* New York: E. P. Dutton, 1937.

Beck, Horace Palmer. *The Folklore of Maine.* Philadelphia: J. B. Lippincott, 1957.

Beck, Lewis Caleb. *Botany of the Northern and Middle States.* Albany NY: Webster and Skinners, 1833.

———. *Botany of the United States North of Virginia.* 2d ed., rev. and enlarged. New York: Harper & Bros., 1848.

Beck, Robert. *Mama Black Widow.* Los Angeles: Holloway House, 1969.

Becker, George C. *Fishes of Wisconsin.* Madison WI: Univ. WI Press, 1983.

———. *Intra-Specific Variation in Rhinichthys c. Cataractae (Valenciennes) and Rhinichthys Atratulus Meleagris (Agassiz) and Anatomical and Ecological Studies of Rhinichthys c. Cataractae.* Madison WI: Univ. WI-Madison, 1962.

Becker, William Templer. *Larkin of Cotton Run.* New York: Helen Norwood Halsey, c.1913.

Becket, Hugh W. *Montreal Snow Shoe Club.* Montreal: Printed by Becket Bros., 1882.

Beckley Post-Herald. Beckley WV, 1925–1984.

Beckwourth, James Pierson. *The Life and Adventures of James P. Beckwourth.* New York: Harper & Bros., 1858. Orig. pub. by Harper and Bros. in 1856.

Bedford, Gunning S. *The Principles and Practice of Obstetrics.* 4th ed. rev. and enlarged. New York: William Wood, 1874 [c.1868].

Bedford, John R. "Tour in 1807 down the Cumberland, Ohio, and Mississippi Rivers from Nashville to New Orleans." *Tennessee Historical Magazine.* (1919) 5.40–63, 107–22.

Bedford Gazette. Bedford PA, 1805–.

Bedichek, Roy. *Adventures with a Texas Naturalist.* Garden City NY: Doubleday, 1947.

Bee. Danville VA, 1899–.

Bee. Phillips WI, 1884–.

Beebe, Lucius Morris. *Highball.* New York: D. Appleton-Century, 1945.

———. *High Iron.* New York: D. Appleton-Century, 1938.

Beecher, Catherine Esther. *Domestic Receipt Book.* 3d ed. New York: Harper, 1850.

———. *A Treatise on Domestic Economy for the Use of Young Ladies at Home and at School.* Rev. ed. New York: Harper & Bros., 1854 [c.1842].

Beecher, Henry Ward. *Norwood.* New York: Fords, Howard, & Hulbert, c.1867.

———. *Notes from Plymouth Pulpit.* Ed. by Augusta Moore. New York: Derby & Jackson, 1859 [c.1858].

———. *Plain and Pleasant Talk about Fruits, Flowers and Farming.* New York: Derby & Jackson, 1859.

———. *Seven Lectures to Young Men.* Indianapolis IN: Thomas B. Cutler, 1844.

———. *Star Papers.* New York: J. C. Derby, 1855.

Beechey, Frederick William. *Narrative of a Voyage to the Pacific and Beering's Strait.* New ed. London: Henry Colburn and Richard Bentley, 1831. 2 vols.

Beef. St. Paul MN, 19??–.

Beers, Andrew. *The Farmer's Calendar.* Utica NY: Printed and Sold by Asahel Seward, 1806.

Beggs, Stephen R. *Pages from the Early History of the West and North-West.* Cincinnati OH: Printed at the Methodist Book Concern, 1868.

Behler, John L. and F. Wayne King. *The Audubon Society Field Guide to North American Reptiles and Amphibians.* New York: Knopf, c.1979.

Beidleman, Linda H. and Eugene N. Kozloff. *Plants of the San Francisco Bay Region.* 2d ed. Berkeley: Univ. CA Press, c.2003.

Belford's Monthly. New York, 1892–1893.

Belfrage, Sally. *Freedom Summer.* New York: Viking Press, c.1965.

Belknap, Charles Eugene. *The Yesterdays of Grand Rapids.* Grand Rapids MI: Dean-Hicks, 1922.

Belknap, Jeremy. "The Belknap Papers." Massachusetts Historical Society *Collections.* (1877–1891) Vol. 1, pub. as 5th ser. vol. 2; vol. 2, pub. as 5th ser. vol. 3; vol. 3, pub as 6th ser. vol. 4.

———. *The History of New-Hampshire.* Boston: Belknap and Young, 1784–1792. 3 vols. Vol. 1 pub. 1784 by R. Aitken, Philadelphia; vol. 2 pub. 1791 by Isaiah Thomas and Ebenezer T. Andrews, Boston.

———. *Journal of a Tour to the White Mountains in July, 1784.* Boston: Massachusetts Historical Society, 1876.

Bell, Agrippa Nelson. *A Knowledge of Living Things.* New York: Bailliere Bros., 1860.

Bell, Arthur Wellington. *Cape Cod Color.* Boston: Houghton Mifflin, 1931.

Bell, Ed. *Tommy Lee Feathers.* New York: Farrar & Rinehart, c.1938.

Bell, Horace. *Reminiscences of a Ranger.* Los Angeles: Yarnell, Caystile & Mathes, 1881.

Bell, James G. "A Log of the Texas-California Trail, 1854." *Southwestern Historical Quarterly.* (1931–1932) 35.208–37, 290–316; (1932–1933) 36.47–66.

Bell, Lilian Lida. *Carolina Lee.* Boston: L. C. Page, 1906.

Bell, Margaret Van Horn Dwight. *A Journey to Ohio in 1810 as Recorded in the Journal of Margaret Van Horn Dwight.* Ed. by Max Farrand. New Haven CT: Yale Univ. Press, 1912.

Bell, Nancy. *Biggie and the Poisoned Politician.* New York: St. Martin's Press, c.1996.

Bell, Ruth Elizabeth. *Some Contributions to the Study of Kansas Vocabulary.* Lawrence KS: Univ. KS diss., 1929.

Bell, Vereen. *Brag Dog and Other Stories: the Best of Vereen Bell.* Belgrade MT: Wilderness Adventures Press, 2000.

———. *Swamp Water.* Boston: Little, Brown, 1941 [c.1940].

Bellamy, Elizabeth Whitfield. *Old Man Gilbert.* Chicago: Belford, Clarke, c.1888.

Bellamy, John Cremer. *The Housekeeper's Guide to the Fish-Market for Each Month of the Year.* London: Longman, Brown, Green & Longmans; Plymouth: Edward Nettleton, 1843.

Belles-Lettres Repository and Monthly Magazine. New York: A. T. Goodrich, 1819–1820.

Belleville News-Democrat. Belleville IL, 1996?–.

Bell Museum of Natural History. *Annotated Checklist of the Flora of Minnesota.* [v.d.]. Internet.

Bellow, Saul. *Henderson, the Rain King.* New York: Viking Press, 1959.

———. *Herzog.* New York: Viking Press, 1964.

———. *Humboldt's Gift.* New York: Viking Press, 1975.

Belton, Sandra. *Beauty, Her Basket.* New York: Greenwillow Books/Amistad, c.2004.

Beltrami, Giacomo Constantino. *A Pilgrimage in Europe and America.* London: Hunt and Clarke, 1828. 2 vols.

Bemelmans, Ludwig. *Life Class.* New York: Viking Press, 1938.

Benauly See Abbott, Benjamin Vaughan

Benchley, Robert. *Benchley beside Himself.* New York: Harper & Bros., c.1943.

Bender, John S. *A Hoosier's Experience in Western Europe.* Plymouth IN: J. S. Bender, 1880 [c.1879].

Benedict, David. *Fifty Years among the Baptists.* New York: Sheldon & Company, 1860 [c.1859].

Benedict, Harry Yandell and John A. Lomax. *The Book of Texas.* Garden City NY: Doubleday, Page, 1916.

Benes, Peter, ed. *American Speech, 1600 to the Present.* Boston: Boston Univ., c.1985.

Benét, Stephen Vincent. *John Brown's Body.* Garden City NY: Doubleday, Doran, 1928.

———. *The Last Circle.* New York: Farrar, Straus, 1946.

———. *Tales before Midnight.* New York: Farrar & Rinehart, c.1939.

———. *Tiger Joy: a Book of Poems.* New York: George H. Doran, c.1925.

———. *Western Star.* New York: Farrar & Rinehart, c.1943.

Benford, Gregory. *Timescape.* New York: Simon and Schuster, c.1980.

Bennet, Robert Ames. *Boss of the Diamond A.* Chicago: A. C. McClurg, 1926.

Bennett, Arnold. *Lilian.* New York: George H. Doran, c.1922.

Bennett, Daniel K. *Chronology of North Carolina.* New York: J. M. Edney, 1858 [c.1855].

Bennett, Emerson. *Ella Barnwell.* Cincinnati OH: U. P. James, c.1853.

———. *Mike Fink.* Rev. ed. Upper Saddle River NJ: Literature House, 1970 [c.1852].

Bennett, Hugh Hammond. *Soil Conservation.* New York: McGraw-Hill, 1939.

Bennett, John Cook. *The History of the Saints.* Boston: Leland & Whiting, 1842.

Bennington Banner. Bennington VT, 1961–.

Bennington Evening Banner. Bennington VT, 1903?–1961.

Bennitt, Rudolf. *Check-list of the Birds of Missouri.* Columbia MO: Univ. MO, 1932.

Benson, Erica June. *This Girl Wants Out.* East Lansing MI: MI State Univ. diss., 2003.

Benson, Lyman David. *The Cacti of Arizona.* Tucson AZ: Univ. AZ, 1940.

Benson, Lyman David and Robert A. Darrow. *A Manual of Southwestern Desert Trees and Shrubs.* Tucson AZ: Univ. AZ, 1945.

———. *Trees and Shrubs of the Southwestern Deserts.* 3d ed. rev. and expanded. Tucson AZ: Univ. AZ Press, c.1981.

Bent, Arthur Cleveland. *Life Histories of North American Flycatchers, Larks, Swallows and Their Allies.* Washington DC: Govt. Printing Office, 1942.

Bentinck-Smith, William, ed. *The Harvard Book.* Cambridge MA: Harvard Univ. Press, 1953.

Bentley, Gordon M. *The Mexican Bean Beetle.* Knoxville TN: State Board of Entomology, 1922. TN State Board of Entomol. *Bulletin 41.* vol. 6, no. 3.

Bentley, Harold Woodmansee. *A Dictionary of Spanish Terms in English, with Special Reference to the American Southwest.* New York: Columbia Univ. Press, 1932.

Bentley, Robert. *A Manual of Botany.* London: J. & A. Churchill, 1887.

Bentley, William. *The Diary of William Bentley.* Salem MA: Essex Institute, 1905–1914. 4 vols.

Bentley's Miscellany. London: R. Bentley, 1837–1868.

Benton, Thomas Hart. *Thirty Years' View.* New York: D. Appleton, 1854–1857. 2 vols.

Benton Courier. Benton AR, 1913–.

Benwell, John. *An Englishman's Travels in America.* London: Ward and Lock, 1857. Orig. pub. in 1853 by Binns and Goodwin, London.

Berendt, John. *Midnight in the Garden of Good and Evil.* New York: Random House, c.1994.

Bergen, Fanny Dickerson, ed. *Animal and Plant Lore.* Boston: Houghton, Mifflin, 1899.

———, comp. *Current Superstitions.* Boston: Houghton, Mifflin, 1896.

Berger, Andrew John. *Hawaiian Birdlife.* Honolulu HI: Univ. Press HI, 1972.

Berger, Josef. *Bowleg Bill, the Seagoing Cowboy.* New York: Viking Press, c.1938.

Berger, Josef and Dorothy Berger, eds. *Diary of America.* New York: Simon and Schuster, 1957.

Bergin, Barbara. *Endings.* Santa Fe NM: Sunstone Press, 2007.

Berkebile, Donald H., ed. *American Carriages, Sleighs, Sulkies, and Carts.* New York: Dover, 1977.

Berkeley, George Charles Grantley Fitzhardinge. *The English Sportsman in the Western Prairies.* London: Hurst and Blackett, 1861.

Berkey, William Augustus. *The Money Question.* Grand Rapids MI: W. W. Hart, 1876.

Berkman, Alexander. *Prison Memoirs of an Anarchist.* New York: Mother Earth Publishing, 1912.

Berkshire County Eagle. Pittsfield MA, 1853–1953.

Berkshire Eagle. Pittsfield MA, 1956–.

Berkshire Evening Eagle. Pittsfield MA, 1892–1955.

Berlin, Ellin Mackay. *The Best of Families.* Garden City NY: Doubleday, 1970.

Bernard, John. *Retrospections of America, 1797–1811.* New York: Harper & Bros., 1887.

Bernice Pauahi Bishop Museum. *Special Publication.* Honolulu HI, 1890–.

Bernstein, Charles, ed. *Close Listening.* New York: Oxford Univ. Press, c.1998.

Berolzheimer, Ruth, ed. *United States Regional Cookbook.* Chicago: Published for Culinary Arts Institute by Consolidated Book, 1939.

Berquin-Duvallon. *Travels in Louisiana and the Floridas, in the Year, 1802.* Transl. by John Davis. New York: I. Riley, 1806.

———. *Vue de la Colonie Espagnole du Mississippi, ou des Provinces de Louisiane et Floride Occidentale.* Paris: Imprimerie Expéditive, 1803.

Berrey, Lester V. and Melvin Van den Bark. *The American Thesaurus of Slang, with Supplement.* New York: Thomas Y. Crowell, 1947. Orig. pub. without suppl. by Crowell in 1942.

Berrien, Allen D. *Powerboat Care and Repair.* Camden ME: International Marine/McGraw-Hill, c.2004.

Berry, Brewton. *Almost White.* New York: Macmillan, 1963.

Berry, Harrison. *Slavery and Abolitionism.* Philadelphia: Rhistoric, 1969. Repr. of 1861 ed.

Berry, Wendell. *Jayber Crow.* Washington DC: Counterpoint, c.2000.

———. *A Place on Earth.* New York: Harcourt, Brace & World, c.1967.

Berryman, Lou and Peter Berryman. *Forward Hey, Wisconsin Songs.* Sound recording. Madison WI: Cornbelt Records, 1988.

Besley, Fred Wilson and John Gordon Dorrance. *The Wood-Using Industries of Maryland.* Baltimore MD: Maryland State Board of Forestry, 1919.

Bessey Charles Edwin. *Botany for High Schools and Colleges.* New York: Henry Holt, c.1880.

Bessie Jackson & Walter Roland, 1927–1935. Phonodisc. New York: Yazoo Records, c.1968.

Best, Richard Lundelius and Beth Arlene Best, eds. *Song Fest.* New York: Crown, c.1955.

Best from Yank, the Army Weekly. Selected by the Editors of Yank. New York: E. P. Dutton, c.1945.

Beston, Henry. *Northern Farm.* New York: Rinehart, c.1948.

———. *The Outermost House.* Garden City NY: Doubleday, Doran, c.1928.

Bethany Cook Book Featuring Scandinavian Recipes. Sioux Falls SD: Bethany Home Auxiliary, 1960.

Betten, Henry Lewis. *Upland Game Shooting.* Philadelphia: Penn Publishing, c.1940.

Better Homes and Gardens. Des Moines IA, 1922–.

Betts, Leonidas and Richard Walser. *Gateway to North Carolina Folklore.* Raleigh NC: School of Education Office of Publications, NC State Univ. at Raleigh, 1974.

Beverley, Robert. *The History and Present State of Virginia in Four Parts.* London: Printed for R. Parker, 1705.

———. *The Western North Carolina Almanac and Book of Lists.* Franklin NC: Sanctuary Press, c.1991.

Bews, John William. *The World's Grasses.* London: Longmans, Green, 1929.

Beyle, Noel W. *How to Talk Cape Cod Talk.* Orleans MA: First Encounter Press, c.1983.

Bibb, Henry. *Narrative of the Life and Adventures of Henry Bibb an American Slave.* New York: Published by the Author, 1849.

Biblical Repertory. Princeton NJ, 1825–1829; 1833–1834.

Biblical Repertory and the Theological Review. Philadelphia, 1830–1832; 1835–1837.

Bibliotheca Sacra and Biblical Repository. Andover MA, 1858–1863.

Bickley, George W. L. *History of the Settlement and Indian Wars of Tazewell County Virginia.* Cincinnati OH: Morgan, 1852.

Biddle, Horace Peters. *Glances at the World.* Mundus [Cincinnati OH?]: Cadmus Faustus [Robert Clarke?], 1873.

Bidwell, John. *A Journey to California.* San Francisco: John Henry Nash, 1937. Orig. pub. in 1842; place of publication and publisher unknown.

Bigelow, Henry Bryant and William C. Schroeder. *Fishes of the Gulf of Maine.* Washington DC: Govt. Printing Office, 1953.

Bigelow, Jacob. *American Medical Botany.* Boston: Cummings and Hilliard, 1817–1820. 3 vols.

———. *Florula Bostoniensis.* Boston: Cummings, Hilliard, 1814.

———. *Florula Bostoniensis.* 2d ed. greatly enlarged. Boston: Cummings, Hilliard, 1824.

———. *A Treatise on the Materia Medica.* Boston: Ewer, 1822.

Bigelow, Timothy. *Journal of a Tour to Niagara Falls in the Year 1805.* Boston: Press of John Wilson, 1876.

Biggers, Don Hampton. *A Biggers Chronicle.* Lubbock TX: TX Technological College, 1961. Facsimile of 1901 Ennis ed.

———. *Buffalo Guns & Barbed Wire.* Lubbock TX: TX Tech Univ. Press, c.1991. Combined reissue of *Pictures of the Past* (1902) and *History That Will Never Be Repeated* (1901).

———. *From Cattle Range to Cotton Patch.* Bandera TX: Frontier Times, 1944. Orig. pub. in 1902 by Abilene Printing Company, Abilene TX; The text first appeared in the *Dallas-Galveston News.*

———. *From Cattle Range to Cotton Patch.* Abilene TX: Press of Abilene Printing, 1905.

Biggs, William. *Narrative of the Captivity of William Biggs among the Kickapoo Indians in Illinois in 1788.* New York: C. F. Heartman, 1922.

————. *Narrative of William Biggs While He Was a Prisoner with the Kickapoo Indians in Illinois in 1788.* [s.l.]: Printed for the Author, 1826.

Big Piney Examiner. Big Piney WY, 1911–1968.

Big Sandy News and the Lawrence County Recorder. Louisa KY, 1935–1974.

Big Spring Daily Herald. Big Spring TX, 1928–1972.

Bill, Alfred H. *Astrophel.* London: Cassell, 1938.

Billboard. Cincinnati OH, 1896–1960.

Billings, John Davis. *Hardtack and Coffee.* Boston: G. M. Smith, 1888.

Billings, John Shaw. *The National Medical Dictionary.* Philadelphia: Lea Bros., 1890. 2 vols.

Billings Gazette. Billings MT, 1914–.

Bills, George F. *Am I My Neighbor's Keeper?* Huntington WV: Marshall Univ. M.A. thesis, 2003.

Bills, Paul. *Alaska.* Springfield MO: Gospel Pub. House, c.1980.

Biloxi Daily Herald. Biloxi MS, 1898–1910.

Biloxi Herald. Biloxi MS, 1884–1898?

Binns, Archie. *The Timber Beast.* New York: C. Scribner's Sons, 1944.

Biological Society of Washington DC. *Proceedings.* Washington DC, 1880–.

Bird, Robert Montgomery. *The Cowled Lover & Other Plays.* Princeton NJ: Princeton Univ. Press, 1941.

————. *The Hawks of Hawk-Hollow.* Philadelphia: Carey, Lea & Blanchard, 1835.

————. *Nick of the Woods.* Ed. by W. Harrison Ainsworth. London: Richard Bentley, 1837. 3 vols.

————. *Nick of the Woods.* New ed. rev. New York: Redfield, 1853.

Bird, Stephanie Rose. *Sticks, Stones, Roots & Bones.* St. Paul MN: Llewellyn, 2004.

Bird, William Ernest. *Supplement to a Wordlist by Tom Cox, Cullowhee State Normal School.* c1926. Unpub. material in Kephart Collection, Hunter Library, Cullowhee State Normal School (now Western Carolina Univ.).

Bird-Banding. West Hartford CT: Northeastern Bird-banding Association, 1930–1979.

Birder's World. Holland MI, 1987–.

Birds and All Nature. Chicago, 1898–1900.

Birdscapes, News from International Habitat Conservation Partnerships. Arlington VA, 2000–2004.

Birds of America. Ed. by Thomas Gilbert Pearson. New York: Univ. Society, 1923 [c.1917]. 3 vols.

Birkbeck, Morris. *Letters from Illinois.* Philadelphia: M. Carey & Son, 1818.

Birket, James. *Some Cursory Remarks Made by James Birket in His Voyage to North America, 1750–1751.* New Haven CT: Yale Univ. Press, 1916.

Birmingham News. Birmingham AL, 1888–.

Bishop, Isabella Lucy Bird. *A Lady's Life in the Rocky Mountains.* 8th ed. New York: G. P. Putnam's Sons, 1885. Orig. pub. in 1879 by J. Murray, London.

————. *Six Months in the Sandwich Islands.* Honolulu HI: Univ. HI Press, 1966. Orig. pub. in 1875 under the title *The Hawaiian Archipelago: Six Months among the Palm Groves, Coral Reefs, & Volcanoes of the Sandwich Islands* by J. Murray, London.

Bishop, John Leander. *A History of American Manufactures from 1608–1860.* Philadelphia: E. Young; London: S. Low, 1866. 3 vols.

Bishop, Nathaniel Holmes. *Four Months in a Sneak-Box.* Boston: Lee and Shepard, 1879.

————. *Voyage of the Paper Canoe.* Boston: Lee and Shepard, 1878.

Bishop, Robert Hamilton. *An Outline of the History of the Church in the State of Kentucky.* Lexington KY: T. T. Skillman, 1824.

Bismarck Daily Tribune. Bismarck ND, 1881–1916.

Bismarck Tribune. Bismarck ND, 1873–.

Bissell, Richard Pike. *The Monongahela.* New York: Rinehart, c.1952.

————. *A Stretch on the River.* Boston: Little, Brown, 1950.

Bissell, Sallie. *In the Forest of Harm.* New York: Bantam, c.2001.

Bittersweet. Lebanon MO, 1973–1983.

Bittinger, John Quincy. *History of Haverhill, N.H.* Haverhill NH: [s.n.], 1888.

Black, Clint. *Killin' Time.* Sound recording. New York: RCA, 1988.

Black, Jack. *You Can't Win.* New York: Macmillan, 1926.

Black American Literature Forum. Terre Haute IN: IN State Univ., 1976–1991.

Blackboard. Bakersfield CA, 2000?–.

Blackburn, Benjamin Coleman. *Trees and Shrubs in Eastern North America.* New York: Oxford Univ. Press, 1952.

Black Cat. Boston: Shortstory Publishing, 1895–1922?

Blackfoot News. Blackfoot ID, 1960–.

Blackmar, Frank W., ed. *Kansas.* Chicago: Standard Publishing, c.1912. 2 vols.

Blackmun, Ora. *Western North Carolina.* Boone NC: Appalachian Consortium Press, c.1977.

Black Panther. Oakland CA, 1968–1980.

BlackPressUSA.com. 2000?–. Internet.

Black Scholar. San Francisco: Black World Foundation, 1969–.

Blackwelder, Eliot. *The Great Basin, with Emphasis on Glacial and Postglacial Times.* Salt Lake City UT: Univ. UT, 1948.

Blackwood's Edinburgh Magazine. Edinburgh, 1817–1905.

Black World. Chicago, 1970–1976.

Blair, Emma Helen. *The Indian Tribes of the Upper Mississippi Valley and Region of the Great Lakes.* Cleveland OH: Arthur H. Clark, 1911. 2 vols.

Blair, Walter. *Tall Tale America.* New York: Coward-McCann, c.1944.

Blair, Walter and Franklin J. Meine. *Mike Fink.* New York: H. Holt, c.1933.

Blair, Walter Acheson. *A Raft Pilot's Log.* Cleveland OH: Arthur H. Clark, 1930.

Blair, W. Frank et al. *Vertebrates of the United States.* New York: McGraw-Hill, 1968.

Blair & Ketchum's Country Journal. Brattleboro VT, 1974–.

Blairsville Press. Blairsville PA, 1867–1899?

Blakeslee, E. C. *The Compendium of Cookery and Reliable Recipes.* Chicago: Merchants' Specialty, 1890.

Blanchan, Neltje SEE Doubleday, Nellie Blanchan De Graff

Blanchard, Amy Ella. *A Daughter of Freedom; a Story of the Latter Period of the War for Independence.* Boston: W. A. Wilde, 1900.

Blanchard, Rufus. *Discovery and Conquests of the Northwest, with the History of Chicago.* Chicago: R. Blanchard, 1898–1900. 2 vols.

Bland, Edward. *The Discovery of New Brittaine.* Boston: Massachusetts Historical Society, c.1923. Orig. pub. in 1651 by Thomas Harper for John Stephenson, London.

Bland, James Allen. *Oh Dem Golden Slippers.* Boston: John F. Perry, c.1879.

Blane, William Newnham. *An Excursion through the United States and Canada during the Years 1822–23.* London: Baldwin, Cradock and Joy, 1824.

Blankfort, Michael. *The Big Yankee.* Boston: Little, Brown, 1947.

Blankinship, Joseph William and Hester Ferguson Henshall. *Common Names of Montana Plants.* Bozeman MT: MT Agricultural College, 1905.

Blasingame, Ike. *Dakota Cowboy.* Lincoln NE: Univ. NE Press, 1958.

Blatchley, Willis Stanley. *In Days Agone.* Indianapolis IN: Nature Publishing, 1932.

————. *The Indiana Weed Book.* Indianapolis IN: Nature Publishing, 1912.

————. *My Nature Nook.* Indianapolis IN: Nature Publishing, 1931.

Blesh, Rudi. *Shining Trumpets.* New York: A. A. Knopf, 1946.

Blesh, Rudi and Harriet Janis Grossman. *They All Played Ragtime.* New York: Knopf, 1950.

Blickenstaff, C. C. "Common Names of Insects." *Bulletin of the Entomological Society of America.* (1965) 11.4.287–320.

Bliss, George. *An Address, Delivered at the Opening of the Town Hall in Springfield, March 24, 1828, Containing Sketches of the Early History of That Town and Those in Its Vicinity.* Springfield MA: Tannatt, 1828.

Blome, Richard. *The Present State of His Majesties Isles and Territories in America.* London: Printed by H. Clark, for Dorman Newman, 1687.

Blomquist, Hugo Leander. *The Grasses of North Carolina.* Durham NC: Duke Univ. Press, c.1948.

Bloomfield, Julia Keen. *The Oneidas.* New York: Alden Bros., 1907.

Blossom, Henry Martyn. *Checkers.* New York: Grosset & Dunlap, c.1896.

Bluegrass Unlimited. Broad Run VA, 1966–.

The Blues Line. Comp. by Eric Sackheim. New York: Grossman, 1969.

Blues Unlimited. London: BU Publications, 1963–.

Bly, Carol. *Letters from the Country.* New York: Harper & Row, 1981.

————. *My Lord Bag of Rice.* Minneapolis MN: Milkweed Editions, c.2000.

Boatman's Quarterly Review. Flagstaff AZ, 1994–.

Bobo, William M. *Glimpses of New-York City.* Charleston SC: J. J. McCarter, 1852.

Bodenberg, Emmett Theodore. *Mosses.* Minneapolis MN: Burgess, 1954.

Bodmer, Rudolph John, ed. *Book of Wonders: Gives Plain and Simple Answers to the Thousands of Everyday Questions That Are Asked and Which All Should Be Able to, But Cannot Answer.* New York: Presbrey Syndicate, 1915 [c.1914].

Bogan, Phebe M. *Ceremonial Dances of the Yaqui Indians near Tucson, Arizona.* Tucson AZ: Univ. AZ M.A. thesis, 1922.

Bogardus, Adam H. *Field, Cover and Trap Shooting.* Ed. by Charles J. Foster. New York: J. B. Ford, c.1874.

Bohjalian, Chris. *Midwives.* New York: Harmony Books, c.1997.

Bok, Edward. *The Americanization of Edward Bok.* New York: Charles Scribner's Sons, 1920.

Bolander, Henry Nicholas. *A Catalogue of the Plants Growing in the Vicinity of San Francisco.* San Francisco: A. Roman, 1870.

Boles, John B. *Religion in Antebellum Kentucky.* Lexington KY: Univ. Press KY, c.1976.

Boller, Henry A. *Henry A. Boller, Missouri Fur Trader.* Ed. by Ray H. Mattison. Bismarck ND: State Historical Society of North Dakota, 1966.

Bolling, William. "Diary of Col. William Bolling of Bolling Hall." *Virginia Magazine of History and Biography.* (1935) 43.237–50, 330–42; (1936) 44.15–24, 120–8, 238–45, 323–34; (1937) 45.29–39; (1938) 46.44–51, 146–52, 234–9, 321–8; (1939) 47.27–31.

Bollinger, Holly L. *Outhouses.* St. Paul MN: MBI, 2005.

Bolton, Robert. *A History of the County of Westchester, from Its First Settlement to the Present Time.* New York: Printed by Alexander S. Gould, 1848. 2 vols.

Bolton, Ruthie. *Gal.* New York: Harcourt, Brace, c.1994.

Bonaparte, Charles Lucien Jules Laurent. *American Ornithology.* Philadelphia: Carey, Lea, & Carey, 1825–1833. 4 vols.

Bond, J. W. *Minnesota and Its Resources.* New York: Redfield, 1853.

Bond, Lewis H. *One Year in Briartown.* Cincinnati OH: John Hamilton, 1879.

Bone Rattler. Bryson City NC, 1984–.

Bonfield, Lynn A. and Mary C. Morrison. *Roxana's Children.* Amherst MA: Univ. MA Press, c.1995.

Bonnell, John Mitchell. *A Manual of the Art of Prose Composition.* Louisville KY: John P. Morton, 1867.

Bonner, Geraldine. *Hard-Pan.* New York: Century, 1900.

Bonner, James Calvin. *A History of Georgia Agriculture, 1732–1860.* Athens GA: Univ. GA Press, 1964.

Bonner, Sherwood SEE McDowell, Katherine Sherwood Bonner

Bonner, Stanley G. *Houses & Homes.* Bloomington IN: AuthorHouse, c.2007.

Bonnycastle, Sir Richard Henry. *The Canadas in 1841.* London: H. Colburn, 1841. 2 vols.

Bonta, Marcia. *More Outbound Journeys in Pennsylvania.* University Park PA: PA State Univ. Press, 1995.

Bontemps, Arna Wendell. *The Old South.* New York: Dodd, Mead, c.1973.

Booker, Louise R. *Historical and Traditional 'Tar Heel' Stories from the Colorful Central Coastal Plains.* Murfeesboro TN: Johnson Publishing, 1968.

Bookman: a Review of Books and Life. New York: Dodd, Mead, 1895–1933.

The Book of Rural Life, Knowledge and Inspiration. Chicago: Bellows-Durham, 1925. 10 vols.

Booth, Ernest Sheldon. *Birds of the West.* 3d ed. Escondido CA: Outdoor Pictures, 1960.

Borg, John. *Cacti.* London: Macmillan, 1937.

Borland, Hal. *The Dog Who Came to Stay.* Philadelphia: J. B. Lippincott, c.1961.

————. *Hill Country Harvest.* Philadelphia: J. B. Lippincott, c.1967.

Borror, Donald Joyce and Dwight M. DeLong. *An Introduction to the Study of Insects.* New York: Rinehart, c.1954.

————. *An Introduction to the Study of Insects.* Rev. ed. New York: Holt, Rinehart and Winston, 1964.

Borthwick, J. D. *Three Years in California [1851–54].* Edinburgh: W. Blackwood & Sons, 1857.

Bosson, Charles Palfray. *Observations on the Potatoe and a Remedy for the Potatoe Plague.* Boston: E. L. Pratt, 1846.

Boston Cultivator. Boston, 1841–1876.

Boston Daily Advertiser. Boston, 1813–1831.

Boston Daily Globe. Boston, 1872–1960.

Boston Directory for the Year 1858. Boston: Adams, Sampson, 1858.

Boston Evening Journal. Boston, 1872–1903.

Boston Evening-Post. Boston, 1735–1775.

Boston Evening Transcript. Boston, 1830–1941.

Boston Gazette, and Country Journal. Boston, 1756–1793.

Boston Gazette, and Weekly Republican Journal. Boston, 1794–1798.

Boston Gazette, or, Weekly Advertiser. Boston, 1753–1755.

Boston Globe. Boston, 1960–.

Boston Herald. Boston, 1846–1917; 1919–1967; 1982–.

Boston Intelligencer & Evening Gazette. Boston, 1818–1821.

Boston Journal. Boston, 1903–1917.

Boston Journal of Commerce. Boston, 1872–1882.

Boston Journal of Natural History. Boston, 1834–1863.

Boston Medical and Surgical Journal. Boston, 1828–1928.

Boston Morning Journal. Boston, 1867–1902.

Boston News-Letter. Boston, 1704–1776.

Boston Park Department. *Annual Report of the Board of Commissioners.* Boston, 1876–.

Boston Pearl, a Gazette of Polite Literature. Hartford CT: Printed by J. Jones, 1831–1836.

Boston Post Boy. Boston, 1750–1754.

Boston. Registry Department. *Records Relating to the Early History of Boston.* Boston: Rockwell and Churchill, 1876–1909. 39 vols.

Boston Society for Medical Improvement. *Extracts from the Records.* Boston, 1853–1883.

Boston Society of Natural History. *Proceedings.* Boston, 1841–1942.

Boston Sunday Journal. Boston, 1903–1904.

Boston Weekly Magazine. Boston: D. H. Ela and J. B. Hall, 1802–1805; 1838–1841.

Boston Weekly Messenger. Boston, 1815–1832.

Boston Weekly Post Boy. Boston, 1734–1750.

Botanical Gazette. Chicago: Univ. Chicago Press, 1875–1991.

Botanical Society of Edinburgh. *Transactions of the Botanical Society.* Edinburgh, 1844–1873.

Botkin, Benjamin Albert, ed. *A Treasury of American Folklore.* New York: Crown, 1944.

———, ed. *A Treasury of New England Folklore.* New York: Crown, 1947.

———. *A Treasury of Southern Folklore.* New York: Crown, 1949.

Botkin, Benjamin Albert and Alvin F. Harlow, eds. *A Treasury of Railroad Folklore.* New York: Crown, 1953.

Botta, Anne C. Lynch See Lynch, Anne Charlotte

Botume, Elizabeth Hyde. *First Days amongst the Contrabands.* Boston: Lee and Shepard, 1893 [c.1892].

Boucher, Jonathan. *Boucher's Glossary of Archaic and Provincial Words.* London: Printed for Black, Young, and Young, 1832–1833.

Boucicault, Dion. *The Octoroon.* New York: Samuel French, 1859.

Boughman, Arvis Locklear and Loretta O. Oxendine. *Herbal Remedies of the Lumbee Indians.* Jefferson NC: McFarland, c.2003.

———. *Herbal Remedies of the Lumbee Indians.* Jefferson NC: McFarland, c.2004.

Boulware, Marcus Hanna. *Jive and Slang of Students in Negro Colleges.* Hampton VA: The Author, 1947.

Bourbon County, Kentucky. *Report of Processioners of Samuel Clay's Land, 1798.* Paris KY: [s.n.], 1798.

———. *Surveys. Book A. 1786–1804.* Paris KY: [s.n.], [n.d.].

Bourdain, Anthony. *Kitchen Confidential.* New York: Bloomsbury, c.2000.

Bourke, John Gregory. *Diary of John Gregory Bourke.* Wooster OH: Bell and Howell, 1872–1896? 124 vols.

———. *On the Border with Crook.* New York: Charles Scribner's Sons, 1891.

Bourne, Eulalia. *Woman in Levi's.* Tucson AZ: Univ. AZ Press, c.1967.

Bourne, Henry Richard Fox. *The Life of John Locke.* New York: Harper & Bros., 1876. 2 vols.

Bouton, Jim. *Ball Four.* New York: World Publishing, c.1970.

Bowden, Jesse Earle. *Always the Rivers Flow.* Pensacola FL: Univ. West FL Foundation, 1979.

Bowe, John. *With the 13th Minnesota in the Philippines.* Minneapolis MN: A. B. Farnham Ptg. & Stationery, 1905.

Bowen, Eli. *Rambles in the Path of the Steam-Horse.* Philadelphia: Wm. Bromwell and Wm. White Smith, 1855.

Bowen, Francis. *A Treatise on Logic.* 3d ed. Cambridge MA: Sever and Francis, 1865.

Bowen, Frank C. *Sea Slang.* London: Sampson Low, Marston, c1929.

Bowen, Robert O. *An Alaskan Dictionary.* Spenard AK: Nooshnik Press, c.1965.

Bowen, Wilbur Pardon. *The Teaching of Play.* Springfield MA: Bassette, c.1913.

Bowen, William Abraham. *Chained Lightning.* New York: J. S. Ogilvie, c.1883.

Bower, B. M. See Sinclair, Bertha

Bowerman, Thomas Roy. *Fireclay.* c.1996. Internet.

Bowers, Janice Emily. *100 Roadside Wildflowers of Southwest Woodlands.* Tucson AZ: Southwest Parks and Monuments Association, c.1987.

Bowers, Q. David. *Encyclopedia of Automatic Musical Instruments.* Vestal NY: Vestal Press, c.1972.

Bowhunter. Harrisburg PA, 1900–.

Bowles, Ella Shannon and Dorothy S. Towle. *Secrets of New England Cooking.* New York: M. Barrows, 1947.

Bowles, Samuel. *Across the Continent.* Springfield MA: Samuel Bowles; New York: Hurd & Houghton, 1865.

———. *Our New West.* Hartford CT: Hartford, 1869.

Bowling Green State University. *Center for Archival Collections.* 1800–. Internet.

Bowman, Jacob L. *You and Me.* St. Louis MO: George Knapp, 1867.

Bowman, Rowland Claude. *Freckles and Tan.* Chicago: Rand, McNally, c.1904, c.1900.

Boyce, John Shaw. *Forest Pathology.* New York: McGraw-Hill, 1938.

———. *Forest Pathology.* 2d ed. New York: McGraw-Hill, 1948.

Boyd, Neva Leona, comp. *Handbook of Games.* Chicago: H. T. FitzSimons, 1945.

Boynton, Lucien Cyrus. "Selections from the Journal of Lucien C. Boynton, 1835–1853." American Antiquarian Society, Worcester MA *Proceedings.* (1934) New ser. 43.329–80.

Boys' Life. Irving TX, 1911–.

Brace, Charles Loring. *The New West.* New York: G. P. Putnam & Son, 1869.

———. *The Norse-Folk.* New York: Charles Scribner, 1859.

Bracht, Viktor. *Texas im Jahre 1848.* Elberfeld u. Iserlohn: J. Bädeker, 1849.

Bracke, William B. *Wheat Country.* Ed. by Erskine Caldwell. New York: Duell, Sloan & Pearce, 1950.

Brackenridge, Henry Marie. *Recollections of Persons and Places in the West.* Philadelphia: J. Kay, 1834.

———. *Views of Louisiana.* Pittsburgh PA: Cramer, Spear & Eichbaum, 1814.

Brackenridge, Hugh Henry. *Modern Chivalry.* Philadelphia: John M'Culloch, 1792. 2 vols.

Brackett, George E. *Farm Talk.* Boston: Lee & Shepard, 1868.

Brackett, Jeffrey Richardson. *Notes on the Progress of the Colored People of Maryland since the War.* Baltimore MD: Publication Agency of the Johns Hopkins Univ., 1890.

Bradbury, John. *Travels in the Interior of America, in the Years 1809, 1810, and 1811.* London: Sherwood, Neely, and Jones, 1817.

Bradbury, Osgood. *Flower of the Forest.* New York: Robert M. De Witt, c.1857.

Bradbury, Ray. *Fahrenheit 451.* New York: Ballantine Books, 1953.

Bradford, Gamaliel, Jr. *Matthew Porter.* Boston: L. C. Page, 1908.

Bradford, Gershom. *A Glossary of Sea Terms.* New York: Dodd, Mead, 1942 [c.1927].

Bradford, John Henry Perry. *Born with the Blues.* New York: Oak Publications, c.1965.

Bradford, Perry. *I'm Crazy 'Bout Your Lovin'.* New York: Frederick V. Bowers, 1909.

Bradford, Richard. *Red Sky at Morning.* Philadelphia: Lippincott, c.1968.

Bradford, Roark. *John Henry.* New York: Harper & Bros., 1931.

———. *Ol' Man Adam an' His Chillun.* New York: Harper & Bros., 1928.

———. *The Three-Headed Angel.* New York: Harper & Bros., 1937.

Bradford, William. *Bradford's History "of Plimoth Plantation".* Boston: Wright & Potter, 1899.

———. *History of Plymouth Plantation, 1620–1647.* Boston: Houghton Mifflin, 1912.

Bradford Era. Bradford PA, 1887–.

Bradley, Cyrus Parker. "Journal of Cyrus P. Bradley." *Ohio History.* (1906) 15.207–70.

Bradley, Daniel. *Journal of Capt. Daniel Bradley.* Greenville OH: Frank H. Jobes & Son, 1935.

Bradley, James H. *The March of the Montana Column.* Norman OK: Univ. OK Press, 1961. Orig. pub. 1896.

Bradshaw, Herbert Clarence. *History of Prince Edward County, Virginia.* Richmond VA: Dietz Press, c.1955.

Bradstreet, Anne Dudley. *The Tenth Muse.* Gainesville FL: Scholars' Facsimiles & Reprints, 1965. Facsimile of the 1650 ed. printed for Stephen Bowtell at the signe of the Bible in Pope's Head-Alley, London.

Bradstreet's Weekly, a Business Digest. New York, 1879–1933.

Brady, Cyrus Townsend. *The Bishop.* New York: Harper & Bros., c.1903.

———. *The Patriots.* New York: Grosset & Dunlap, c.1906.

Braganza See Bragg, Henry A.

Bragg, Henry A. *Tekel, or, Cora Glencoe.* New York: J. B. Lippincott, 1870.

Brainard, John G. C. *Poems.* Hartford CT: S. Andrus, 1841.

Brainerd, David. *Memoirs of the Rev. David Brainerd.* Ed. by Jonathan Edwards and Sereno Edwards Dwight. New Haven CT: S. Converse, 1822.

Brainerd, Thomas. *The Life of John Brainerd.* Philadelphia: Presbyterian Publication Committee; New York: A. D. F. Randolph, c.1865.

Brainerd Daily Dispatch. Brainerd MN, 1901–2004.

Braintree, Massachusetts. *Records of the Town of Braintree, 1640–1793.* Randolph MA: Daniel H. Huxford, 1886.

Braislin, William Coughlin. *A List of the Birds of Long Island, New York.* New York: Linnaean Society, 1907.

Brako, Leo et al. *Scientific and Common Names of 7,000 Vascular Plants in the United States.* St. Paul MN: American Phytopathological Society, c.1995.

Braman, D. E. E. *Braman's Information about Texas.* Philadelphia: J. B. Lippincott, 1858.

Branch, Edward Douglas. *The Cowboy and his Interpreters.* New York: D. Appleton, 1926.

Brandt, Herbert. *Alaska Bird Trails.* Cleveland OH: Bird Research Foundation, 1943.

Branigin, Elba L. *History of Johnson County, Indiana.* Indianapolis IN: B. F. Bowen, 1913.

Brann, William Cowper. *Brann the Iconoclast.* Waco TX: Herz Bros., c.1898. 2 vols.

Branner, John Casper. "A List of the Plants of Arkansas." Arkansas. State Geologist *Annual Report of the Geological Survey of Arkansas for 1888.* (1891) 4.155–252.

Braun, Emma Lucy. *The Monocotyledoneae.* Columbus OH: OH State Univ. Press, c.1967.

Braun, Lilian Jackson. *The Cat Who Saw Stars.* New York: G. P. Putnam's Sons, c.1998.

Brauns, Ernst Ludwig. *Praktische Belehrungen und Rathschläge für Reisende und Auswanderer nach Amerika.* Braunschweig: Waisenhaus-Buchdruckerei, 1829.

Bray, William L. *Vegetation of the Sotol Country in Texas.* Austin TX: Univ. TX, 1905.

Brazosport Facts. Clute TX, 1956–.

Breakenridge, William M. *Helldorado.* Boston: Houghton, Mifflin, 1928.

Breck, Edward. *The Way of the Woods.* New York: G. P. Putnam's Sons, c.1908.

Breck, Samuel. *Recollections of Samuel Breck with Passages from his Note-Books (1771–1862).* Philadelphia: Porter & Coates, 1877.

Brehm, H. C. and Cindy Curtis. *The Narrows of the Harpeth and Montgomery Bell.* Nashville TN: H. C. Brehm, c.1981.

Brehm, Victoria, ed. *Sweetwater, Storms and Spirits.* Ann Arbor MI: Univ. MI Press, 1990.

Breitmann, Hans See Leland, Charles Godfrey

Bremer, Fredrika. *Homes of the New World.* Transl. by Mary Howitt. New York: Harper & Bros., 1853. 2 vols.

Brereton, John. *A Briefe and True Relation of the Discouerie of the North Part of Virginia.* Londini: Geor. Bishop, 1602.

Brewer, Ebenezer Cobham. *Dictionary of Phrase and Fable.* 20th ed. rev. and corr. London: Cassell, [n.d.].

———. *Dictionary of Phrase and Fable.* Rev. by Ivor H. Evans. Centenary ed. New York: Harper & Row, 1970.

Brewer, John Mason. *Dog Ghosts, and Other Texas Negro Folk Tales.* Austin TX: Univ. TX Press, 1958.

———, ed. *Humorous Folk Tales of the South Carolina Negro.* Orangeburg SC: South Carolina Negro Folklore Guild, c.1945.

———. *The Word on the Brazos.* Austin TX: Univ. TX Press, 1953.

———. *Worser Days and Better Times.* Chicago: Quadrangle Books, 1965.

Brewer, Mary T. *Easthampton Town Lodging House: a History.* 1986. Unpub.

Brewerton, George Douglas. *Overland with Kit Carson.* New York: Coward-McCann, 1930.

———. *The War in Kansas.* New York: Derby & Jackson, 1856.

Brewington, Marion Vernon. *Chesapeake Bay Log Canoes and Bugeyes.* Cambridge MD: Cornell Maritime Press, 1963.

Brewster, Charles Warren. *Rambles about Portsmouth.* 2d ser. Portsmouth NH: Lewis W. Brewster, c.1869.

Brewster, Paul G., ed. *American Nonsinging Games.* Norman OK: Univ. OK Press, 1953.

Brew Your Own. 1995–. Internet.

Brickell, John. *The Natural History of North Carolina.* Raleigh NC: Reprinted by Authority of the Trustees of the Public Libraries, 1911. Repr. of the 1737 Dublin ed.

Bridge, Horatio. *Personal Recollections of Nathaniel Hawthorne.* New York: Harper & Bros., c.1893.

Bridgeman, Thomas. *The American Gardener's Assistant.* New ed. rev. and enlarged. Philadelphia: Porter & Coates, c.1866.

Bridgeport Post. Bridgeport CT, 1906–1992.

Bridgeport Sunday Post. Bridgeport CT, 1911–1977.

Bridgeport Telegram. Bridgeport CT, 1908–1977.

Briggs, Caroline Clapp. *Reminiscences and Letters of Carolina C. Briggs.* Ed. by George S. Merriam. Boston: Houghton, Mifflin, 1897.

Briggs, Charles Frederick. *The Adventures of Harry Franco.* New York: Garrett Press, 1969. Repr. of the 1839 ed. pub. by F. Saunders, New York.

Briggs, Erasmus. *History of the Original Town of Concord.* Rochester NY: Union and Advertiser, 1883.

Briggs, William Harlowe. *Dakota in the Morning.* New York: Farrar & Rinehart, c.1942.

Brigham, Clarence Saunders. *History and Bibliography of American Newspapers 1690–1820.* Worcester MA: American Antiquarian Society, 1947. 2 vols.

Brigham Young University. *Book of Abraham Project.* 1800–1900. Internet.

Bright, Elizabeth S. *A Word Geography of California and Nevada.* Berkeley CA: Univ. CA Press, 1971.

Brimley, Clement Samuel. *The Insects of North Carolina.* Raleigh NC: North Carolina Department of Agriculture, 1938.

Brinch, Boyrereau. *The Blind African Slave.* Chapel Hill NC: Academic Affairs Library, Univ. NC at Chapel Hill, 1999. Text transcr. from the ed. pub. in 1810 by Harry Whitney, St. Alban's VT.

Brinton, Daniel Garrison. *A Guide-Book of Florida and the South.* Philadelphia: G. Maclean; Jacksonville FL: C. Drew, 1869.

Bristed, Charles Astor. *The Upper Ten Thousand.* New York: Stringer & Townsend, 1852.

Bristol Parish, Virginia. *The Vestry Book and Register of Bristol Parish, Virginia, 1720–1789.* Transcr. and pub. by Churchill Gibson Chamberlayne. Richmond VA: Privately Printed, 1898.

Bristol Press. Bristol CT, 1890–.

Bristow, Henry William. *A Glossary of Mineralogy.* London: Longman, Green, Longman, and Roberts, 1861.

Britannica Book of the Year. Chicago: Encyclopaedia Britannica, 1938–.

British Museum (Natural History) Department of Zoology. *Guide to the Galleries of Reptiles and Fishes in the Department of Zoology of the British Museum (Natural History).* Written by Albert Gunther. 3d ed. London: Printed by order of the trustees, 1893.

Britton, Nathaniel Lord. *Catalogue of Plants Found in New Jersey.* Trenton NJ: John L. Murphy Publishing, 1889.

———. *North American Trees.* New York: H. Holt, 1908.

Britton, Nathaniel Lord and Addison Brown. *An Illustrated Flora of the Northern United States, Canada and the British Possessions.* New York: Charles Scribner's Sons, 1896–1898. 3 vols.

———. *An Illustrated Flora of the Northern United States, Canada and the British Possessions.* 2d ed. rev. and enlarged. New York: Charles Scribner's Sons, 1913. 3 vols.

Britton, Nathaniel Lord and Charles Frederick Millspaugh. *The Bahama Flora.* New York: The authors, 1920.

Brittonia. New York, 1931–.

Broaddus, James. *Collection of Folk Vocabulary Collected in Estill County, Kentucky.* 1981. Unpub.

Broadway Journal. New York: AMS Press, 1965. Orig. pub. in New York, 1845–1846.

Brodhead, Eva Wilder. *Bound in Shallows.* New York: Harper & Bros., 1897 [c.1896].

Bronson, Edgar Beecher. *The Red-Blooded.* Chicago: A. C. McClurg, 1910.

———. *Reminiscences of a Ranchman.* New York: McClure, 1908.

———. *Reminiscences of a Ranchman.* New rev. ed. Chicago: A. C. McClurg, 1910.

Bronson, Walter Cochrane. *The History of Brown University, 1764–1914.* Providence RI: Brown Univ., 1914.

Brookes, Richard. *A New and Accurate System of Natural History.* London: Printed for J. Newbery, 1763. 6 vols.

Brookhaven, New York. *Records of the Town of Brookhaven, Suffolk County, N.Y.* Patchogue NY: Printed at the Office of the "Advance", 1880–1893. 3 vols.

Brooklyn, New York. Fire Department. *Our Firemen, the Official History of the Brooklyn Fire Department.* Brooklyn NY: Brooklyn Fire Dept., 1892.

Brooklyn Daily Eagle. Brooklyn NY, 1849–1938.

Brooklyn Eagle and Kings County Democrat. Brooklyn NY, 1841–1846.

Brooklyn Museum Quarterly. Brooklyn NY: Central Museum of the Brooklyn Institute of Arts and Sciences, 1914–1939.

Brooks, Alfred Hulse. *Blazing Alaska's Trails.* College AK: Published Jointly by the Univ. AK and the Arctic Institute of North America, 1953.

Brooks, Alfred Hulse et al. *Reconnaissances in the Cape Nome and Norton Bay Regions, Alaska, in 1900.* Washington DC: Govt. Printing Office, 1901.

Brooks, Cleanth. *The Language of the American South.* Athens GA: Univ. GA Press, c.1985.

Brooks, Gladys. *Gramercy Park.* New York: E. P. Dutton, 1958.

Brooks, Henry Mason. *Quaint and Curious Advertisements.* Boston: Ticknor, 1886.

Brooks, Jerome Edmund. *The Mighty Leaf.* Boston: Little, Brown, c.1952.

Brooks, Juanita. *Quicksand and Cactus.* Salt Lake City UT: Howe Bros., 1982.

Brooks, Maria Gowen. *Zóphiël.* Boston: Lee and Shepard; New York: Charles T. Dillingham, 1879. The text is that of the 2d Amer. ed. pub. in 1834 by Hilliard, Gray, Boston.

Brooks, Tim and Earle Marsh. *The Complete Directory to Prime Time Network TV Shows 1946–Present.* Rev. ed. New York: Ballantine, 1981 [c.1979].

Brooks, William Allan. *A Small Business of Your Own, Including 1000 Spare Time Money Making Ideas.* New York: National Library Press, c.1937.

Brophy, Patrick. *Border Tongue: [Collection of] Words and Phrases of "the Border"; the Crossroads Region of Southwest Missouri Where East Meets West and North Meets South.* Unpub.

———. *Border Tongue: [Collection of] Words and Phrases of "the Border", the Crossroads Region of Southwest Missouri Where East Meets West and North Meets South.* 1998. Unpub. coll. containing pencilled annotations and updates to 1995 version.

Brosnan, Jim. *Pennant Race.* New York: Harper & Bros., c.1962.

Brossard, Chandler. *Who Walk in Darkness.* New York: New Directions, c.1952.

Brotherhood of Locomotive Engineers Monthly Journal. Rochester NY, 1867–1905.

Brotherhood of Locomotive Firemen and Enginemen's Magazine. Indianapolis IN: The Brotherhood, 1907–.

Brother Jonathan. A Weekly Compend of Belles Lettres and the Fine Arts, Standard Literature, and General Intelligence. New York: Wilson, 1842–1843.

Brougham, John. *A Basket of Chips.* New York: Bunce, 1855.

Brown, Alice. *Meadow-Grass.* Boston: Copeland and Day, 1895.

———. *Old Crow.* New York: Macmillan, 1922.

———. *Tiverton Tales.* Boston: Houghton, Mifflin, 1899.

Brown, Alonzo Leighton. *History of the Fourth Regiment of Minnesota Infantry Volunteers during the Great Rebellion, 1861–1865.* St. Paul MN: Pioneer Press, 1892.

Brown, Altona. *Altona Brown.* Fairbanks AK: Spirit Mountains Press, 1983.

Brown, Bryce C. *An Annotated Check List of the Reptiles and Amphibians of Texas.* Waco TX: Baylor Univ. Press, 1950.

Brown, Calvin Smith. *A Glossary of Faulkner's South.* New Haven CT: Yale Univ. Press, 1976.

Brown, Cecil. *The Life and Loves of Mr. Jiveass Nigger.* New York: Farrar, Straus & Giroux, c.1969.

Brown, Charles Brockden. *Arthur Mervyn.* Kent OH: Kent Univ. Press, c.1980. Pt. one orig. pub. in 1799 by Hugh Maxwell, Philadelphia, and pt. two in 1800 by George Folliot Hopkins, New York.

———. *Ormond.* London: Reprinted for Henry Colburn, 1811. Orig. pub. in Philadelphia.

Brown, Charles Edward. *American Folklore Insect Lore.* Madison WI: [s.n.], c1930.

Brown, Clair Alan. *Wildflowers of Louisiana and Adjoining States.* Baton Rouge LA: LA State Univ. Press, 1972.

Brown, Claude. *Manchild in the Promised Land.* New York: Macmillan, 1965.

Brown, Claudeous Jethro Daniels. *Fishes of Montana.* Bozeman MT: MT State Univ., c.1971.

Brown, Cora Lovisa et al. *America Cooks.* New York: W. W. Norton, c.1940.

———. *America Cooks.* Garden City NY: Halcyon House, 1949.

Brown, Dale et al. *American Cooking.* New York: Time-Life Books, c.1968.

Brown, Dee Alexander. *Trail Driving Days.* New York: Bonanza Books, c.1952.

Brown, Frank Clyde. *Frank C. Brown Collection of North Carolina Folklore.* Durham NC: Duke Univ. Press, 1952–. 7 vols. Coll. by Dr. Frank C. Brown during the years 1912–1943.

Brown, Frank London. *Trumbull Park.* Chicago: Regnery, c.1959.

Brown, George Rothwell. *Washington, a Not Too Serious History.* Baltimore MD: Norman, 1930.

Brown, Goold. *Institutes of English Grammar.* Stereotype ed., rev. by author. New York: Samuel Wood & Sons, 1833 [c.1825].

Brown, Harry Philip. *Trees of Northeastern United States.* Rev. and enlarged ed. Boston: Christopher Publishing House, c.1938.

Brown, Helen Dawes. *Two College Girls.* Boston: Ticknor, 1886.

Brown, Henry Collins. *In the Golden Nineties.* Hastings-on-Hudson NY: Valentine's Manual, 1928.

Brown, Hubert Rap. *Die Nigger Die.* New York: Dial Press, 1969.

Brown, Irene Bennett. *The Plainswoman.* New York: Ballantine, c.1994.

Brown, John. *Letters of Dr. John Brown.* London: Adam and Charles Black, 1907.

———. *Slave Life in Georgia.* Chapel Hill NC: Academic Affairs Library, Univ. NC at Chapel Hill, 2001. Text transcr. from the ed. pub. in 1855 by W. M. Watts, London.

Brown, John Hull. *Early American Beverages.* Rutland VT: Charles E. Tuttle, 1966.

Brown, Larry. *Big Bad Love.* Chapel Hill NC: Algonquin Books, 1990.

Brown, Marion Lea. *The Southern Cook Book.* Chapel Hill: Univ. NC Press, c.1951.

Brown, Oliver Phelps. *The Complete Herbalist.* Jersey City NJ: Published by the author, 1874 [c.1872].

Brown, Rollo Walter. *The Hillikin.* New York: Coward-McCann, c.1935.

Brown, Samuel R. *The Western Gazetteer.* Auburn NY: H. C. Southwick, 1817.

Brown, Warren. *History of Hampton Falls, N.H.* Concord NH: Rumford Press, 1900–1918. 2 vols.

Brown, William. *America.* Leeds: Printed for the Author by Kemplay and Bolland, 1849.

Brown, William Wells. *My Southern Home.* Boston: A. G. Brown, 1880.

———. *The Negro in the American Rebellion: His Heroism and His Fidelity.* Boston: Lee and Shepard, 1867.

Browne, Belmore. *The Conquest of Mount McKinley.* New York: G. P. Putnam's Sons, c.1913.

Browne, Charles Farrar SEE ALSO Ward, Artemus

Browne, Charles Farrar. *Artemus Ward.* New York: Carleton, 1864 [c.1862].

———. *Artemus Ward (His Travels) among the Mormons.* Ed. by E. P. Hingston. London: J. C. Hotten, 1865.

Browne, Daniel Jay. *The Sylva Americana.* Boston: W. Hyde, 1832.

———. *The Trees of America.* New York: Harper & Bros., 1846.

———. *The Trees of America.* New York: Harper & Bros., 1851.

Browne, John Ross. *Adventures in the Apache Country.* New York: Harper & Bros., 1869.

———. *Adventures in the Apache Country.* New York: Harper & Bros., 1871 [c.1868].

———. *Etchings of a Whaling Cruise.* Cambridge MA: Belknap Press of Harvard Univ. Press, 1968. Facsimile of the 1846 ed. pub. by Harper & Bros., New York.

———. *Resources of the Pacific Slope.* New York: D. Appleton, 1869 [c.1868].

Browne, Martha Griffith. *Autobiography of a Female Slave.* New York: Redfield, 1857 [c.1856].

Browne, Patrick. *The Civil and Natural History of Jamaica.* London: Printed for the author and sold by T. Osborne and J. Shipton, 1756.

Browne, Ray B., ed. *A Night with the Hants and Other Alabama Folk Experiences.* Bowling Green OH: Popular Press, 1976.

———. *Popular Beliefs and Practices from Alabama.* Berkeley CA: Univ. CA Press, 1958.

Brownell, Charles de Wolf. *The Indian Races of North and South America.* Hartford CT: Hurlburt, Scranton, c.1864.

Brownell, William L. *Horse & Buggy Philosopher.* Kalamazoo MI: Kalamazoo Vegetable Parchment, 1939.

Browning, Meshach. *Forty-Four Years in the Life of a Hunter.* Rev. by E. Stabler. Philadelphia: J. B. Lippincott, 1864. Orig. pub. by Lippincott in 1859.

Browning, Orville Hickman. "The Diary of Orville Hickman Browning." Illinois State Historical Library, Springfield *Collections.* (1925, 1933) vols. 20, 22.

Brownsville Herald. Brownsville TX, 1910–.

Bruce, Hal. *How to Grow Wildflowers and Wild Shrubs and Trees in Your Own Garden.* New York: Alfred Knopf, 1976.

Bruce, Philip Alexander. *Economic History of Virginia in the Seventeenth Century.* New York: Macmillan, 1896 [c.1895]. 2 vols.

———. *History of the University of Virginia, 1819–1919.* New York: Macmillan, c.1920–1922. 5 vols.

———. *Plantation Negro as a Freeman.* New York: G. P. Putnam's Sons, 1889.

Bruncken, Ernest. *North American Forests and Forestry.* New York: G. P. Putnam's Sons, 1900.

Brunvand, Jan Harold. *A Guide for Collectors of Folklore in Utah.* Salt Lake City UT: Univ. UT Press, c.1971.

Brush, Christine Chaplin. *The Colonel's Opera Cloak.* Boston: Roberts Bros., 1888 [c.1879].

Bryan, Edwin Horace. *Hawaiian Nature Notes.* Honolulu HI: Honolulu Star-Bulletin, 1933.

Bryan, Kirk. *The Papago Country, Arizona.* Washington DC: Govt. Printing Office, 1925.

———. *Routes to Desert Watering Places in the Papago Country, Arizona.* Washington DC: Govt. Printing Office, 1922.

Bryan, Lettice. *The Kentucky Housewife.* Cincinnati OH: Shepard & Stearns, c.1839.

Bryan, T. Conn. *Confederate Georgia.* Athens GA: Univ. GA Press, c.1953.

Bryan, William Alanson. *Natural History of Hawaii.* Honolulu HI: Hawaiian Gazette, 1915.

Bryan, William Jennings and Mary Baird Bryan. *The Memoirs of William Jennings Bryan.* Philadelphia: John C. Winston, c.1925.

Bryant, Arthur. *Forest Trees for Shelter, Ornament and Profit.* New York: H. T. Williams, 1871.

Bryant, Edwin. *What I Saw in California.* New York: D. Appleton, 1848.

———. *What I Saw in California.* 4th ed. New York: D. Appleton, 1849.

Bryant, Ralph Clement. *Logging.* New York: John Wiley & Sons, 1913.

———. *Logging.* 2d ed., thoroughly rev. and reset. New York: John Wiley & Sons, c.1923.

Bryant, William Cullen. *Letters of a Traveller.* New York: George P. Putnam, 1850.

———. *Poems.* New York: E. Bliss, 1932.

Bryce, James Bryce. *The American Commonwealth.* London: Macmillan, 1888. 3 vols.

Bryologist. Binghamton NY, 1898–.

Buchanan, James. *The Works of James Buchanan.* Philadelphia: J. B. Lippincott, 1908–1911. 12 vols.

Buchanan, Patrick. *A Murder of Crows.* New York: Stein and Day, c.1970.

Buck, Charles Neville SEE Lundsford, Hugh

Buck, Franklin Augustus. *A Yankee Trader in the Gold Rush.* Comp. by Katherine A. White. Boston: Houghton Mifflin, 1930.

Buck, Lucy Rebecca. *Shadows on My Heart.* Athens GA: Univ. GA Press, c.1997.

Buck, William Joseph. *History of Montgomery County.* Norristown PA: Printed by E. L. Acker, 1859 [c.1858].

Buckingham, Henry A. *Harry Burnham the Young Continental.* New York: Burgess & Garrett; Baltimore MD: Burgess, Taylor, 1851.

Buckingham, James Silk. *America, Historical, Statistic, and Descriptive.* London: Fisher, Son, 1841. 3 vols.

———. *The Eastern and Western States of America.* London: Fisher, Son, 1842. 3 vols.

———. *The Slave States of America.* London: Fisher, Son, 1842. 2 vols.

Buckingham, Joseph Tinker. *Specimens of Newspaper Literature.* Boston: Redding, 1852 [c.1850]. 2 vols.

Buckingham, Nash. *Game Bag: Tales of Shooting and Fishing.* New York: G. P. Putnam's Sons, 1945.

Buckler, Ernest. *Ox Bells & Fireflies.* New York: Alfred A. Knopf, c.1968.

Buckley, Thomas C. T. *Standing Ground.* Berkeley CA: Univ. CA Press, 2002.

Buckmaster, Henrietta. *Deep River.* New York: Book Find Club, c.1944.

Bucks County Courier Times. Levittown PA, 1966–.

Bucks County Gazette. Bristol PA, 1873–1926.

Budd, Joseph L. *American Horticultural Manual.* New York: John Wiley & Sons; London: Chapman & Hall, 1911–1914. 2 vols.

Budd, Thomas. *Good Order Established in Pennsylvania and New Jersey.* Cleveland OH: Burrows Bros., 1902. Orig. pub. in 1685 by W. Bradford, Philadelphia.

Budget. Sugarcreek OH, 1890–.

Buel, James William. *The Border Outlaws.* St. Louis MO: Historical Publishing, 1881.

———. *Mysteries and Miseries of America's Great Cities.* St. Louis MO: Historical Publishing, 1883. Pub. in 1882 under the title *Metropolitan Life Unveiled; or, the Mysteries and Miseries of America's Great Cities.*

Buel, Jesse. *The Farmer's Companion.* Boston: Marsh, Capen, Lyon, and Webb, 1839.

Buffalo Child Long Lance. *Long Lance.* New York: Cosmopolitan Book, 1928.

Buffalo Historical Society. *Publications.* Buffalo NY, 1879–.

Buffalo Medical Journal and Monthly Review of Medical and Surgical Science. Buffalo NY: Jewett, Thomas, 1846–1859.

Buffalo Museum of Science, Buffalo New York. *The Botanical Journal of G. W. Clinton, 1862–1865.* [v.d.]. Internet.

Buffalo Naturalists' Field Club. *Bulletin.* Buffalo NY, 1883–1884.

Buffalo News. Buffalo NY, 1992–.

Buffum, Edward Gould. *Six Months in the Gold Mines.* Philadelphia: Lea & Blanchard, 1850.

Bugliosi, Vincent and Ken Hurwitz. *Shadow of Cain.* New York: W. W. Norton, c.1981.

Builder: the National Magazine of Freemasonry. St. Louis MO, 1915–1930.

Buist, Robert. *The American Flower Garden Directory.* 2d ed. Philadelphia: Carey & Hart, 1839.

———. *The Family Kitchen Gardener.* New York: C. M. Saxton, Barker; San Francisco: H. H. Bancroft, 1861 [c.1847].

Buley, Roscoe Carlyle. *The Old Northwest.* Indianapolis IN: Indiana Historical Society, 1950. 2 vols.

Bull, John and John Farrand, Jr. *The Audubon Society Field Guide to North American Birds.* New York: Alfred A. Knopf, 1977.

Bullard, Laura J. Curtis. *Now-A-Days.* New York: T. L. Magagnos, c.1854.

Bullen, Frank Thomas. *The Cruise of the Cachalot.* New York: D. Appleton, 1909. Orig. pub. in 1897 by F. M. Lupton, New York.

Bulletin. Bend OR, 1916–.

Bulletin. San Francisco, 1855–1929.

Bulletin of the Entomological Society of America. Washington DC, 1955–1989.

Bulletin of the Garden Club of America. Lake Forest IL, 1916–1969.

Bulletin of the Natural History Survey. Chicago: Chicago Academy of Sciences, 1898–1927.

Bullins, Ed. *The Electronic Nigger, and Other Plays.* London: Faber & Faber, 1970.

———. *The Theme Is Blackness.* New York: Morrow, 1973 [c.1972].

———. *Twelve Plays & Selected Writings.* Ed. by Mike Sell. Ann Arbor MI: Univ. MI Press, c.2006.

Bullock, William. *Six Months Residence and Travels in Mexico.* 2d ed. London: John Murray, 1825. 2 vols.

Bull-us, Hector SEE Paulding, James Kirke

Bumstead, John. *On the Wing.* Boston: James R. Osgood, 1875 [c.1869].

Bunce, Oliver Bell. *Don't.* New York: Appleton, c.1883.

Buning, Sietze SEE Wiersma, Stanley M.

Bunker, Timothy SEE Clift, William

Bunner, Henry Cuyler. *Airs from Arcady and Elsewhere.* New York: C. Scribner's Sons, 1884.

———. *The Poems of H. C. Bunner.* New York: Charles Scribner's Sons, 1896.

———. *Short Sixes.* New York: Keppler & Schwartzmann, 1891 [c.1890].

———. *Zadoc Pine and Other Stories.* New York: Charles Scribner's Sons, 1891.

Buntline, Ned SEE Judson, Edward Zane Carroll

Burbank, Luther. *How Plants Are Trained to Work for Man.* New York: P. F. Collier & Son, c.1921. 8 vols.

Burchfield, R. W., ed. *The Oxford English Dictionary Supplement.* Oxford: Clarendon Press, 1972–1986. 4 vols.

Burckhardt, Ann. *A Cook's Tour of Minnesota.* St. Paul MN: Minnesota Historical Society Press, c.2004.

Burdette, Robert Jones. *The Rise and Fall of the Mustache and Other "Hawk-Eyetems".* Burlington IA: Burlington, 1877.

Burdick, Arthur J. *The Mystic Mid-Region.* New York: G. P. Putnam's Sons, 1904.

Burgess, Anthony. *Homage to Qwert Yuiop.* London: Hutchinson, c.1986.

Burgess, Edward. *Contributions to the Anatomy of the Milk-Weed Butterfly.* Boston: Boston Society of Natural History, 1880.

Burgess, Jackson. *Pillar of Cloud.* New York: Putnam, c.1957.

Burgess, Thornton Waldo. *The Burgess Animal Book for Children.* Boston: Little Brown, 1920.

———. *Mother West Wind's Neighbors.* New York: Grosset & Dunlap, c.1941. Orig. pub. in 1913 by Little, Brown, New York.

———. *Old Mother West Wind.* Boston: Little, Brown, c.1910.

———. *Wild Flowers We Know.* Racine WI: Whitman, c.1929.

Burgess, Walton. *Five Hundred Mistakes of Daily Occurrence in Speaking, Pronouncing, and Writing the English Language.* New York: Miller, 1873.

Burke, Arthur E. et al. *Architectural and Building Trades Dictionary.* Chicago: American Technical Society, c.1950.

Burke, Carol, ed. *Plain Talk.* West Lafayette IN: Purdue Univ. Press, c.1983.

Burke, Emily P. *Reminiscences of Georgia.* Oberlin OH: James M. Fitch, 1850.

Burke, Fielding SEE Dargan, Olive Tilford

Burke, James Lee. *A Morning for Flamingos.* Boston: Little, Brown, c.1990.

———. *Rain Gods.* New York: Simon & Schuster, 2009.

Burke, R. T. Avon and H. D. Lambert. *Soil Survey of Alleghany County, North Carolina.* Washington DC: Govt. Printing Office, 1917.

Burke, Thomas A., ed. *Polly Peablossom's Wedding.* Philadelphia: T. Peterson, 1851.

———, ed. *Polly Peablossom's Wedding and Other Tales.* New York: Garrett Press, 1969. Photocopy of the 1851 ed. pub. by T. B. Peterson, Philadelphia.

Burleith Citizens Association. *Newsletter.* Washington DC, 1926?–.

Burlend, Rebecca. *A True Picture of Emigration.* London: G. Berger, 1848.

Burleson, Georgia Jenkins, comp. *The Life and Writings of Rufus C. Burleson.* Waco TX: [s.n.], 1901.

Burlington Almanack. Burlington NJ, 1770–1777.

Burlington County Herald. Mount Holly NJ, 1963?–.

Burlington Daily Free Press. Burlington VT, 1848–1868.

Burlington Daily Times. Burlington NC, 1923–1931.

Burlington Free Press. Burlington VT, 1999–.

Burlington Hawk-Eye. Burlington IA, 1845–1852.

Burlington Weekly Hawk-Eye. Burlington IA, 1860–1876.

Burma, John H. *Spanish-Speaking Groups in the United States.* Durham NC: Duke Univ. Press, 1954.

Burman, Ben Lucien. *Blow for a Landing.* New York: John Day, c.1938.

———. *Mississippi.* New York: John Day, c.1929.

Burnaby, Andrew. *Travels through the Middle Settlements in North-America, in the Years 1759 and 1760.* London: T. Payne, 1775.

Burnett, Alfred. *Incidents of the War.* Cincinnati OH: Rickey & Carroll, 1863.

Burnett, Frances Hodgson. *In Connection with the De Willoughby Claim.* New York: C. Scribner's Sons, 1899.

———. *Little Lord Fauntleroy.* New York: Charles Scribner's Sons, 1886.

Burnett, Fred M. *This Was My Valley.* Ridgecrest NC: Heritage Printers, 1960.

Burnett, Peter Hardeman. *Recollections and Opinions of an Old Pioneer.* New York: D. Appleton, 1880.

Burnett, William Riley. *Iron Man.* New York: Lincoln Mac Veagh, The Dial Press, 1930.

———. *Little Caesar.* New York: Literary Guild of America, 1929.

———. *Vanity Row.* New York: Knopf, 1952.

Burnham, Clara Louise. *Jewel.* Boston: Houghton, Mifflin, 1903.

Burnham, George Pickering. *The History of the Hen Fever.* Boston: James French, 1855.

———. *Memoirs of the United States Secret Service.* Boston: Lee & Shepard, 1872.

Burns, Franklin Lorenzo. *The Ornithology of Chester County, Pennsylvania.* Boston: Richard G. Badger, c.1919.

Burns, Olive Ann. *Cold Sassy Tree.* New York: Ticknor & Fields, 1984.

Burns, Russell M. *Silvics of North America.* Washington DC: U.S. Dept. Ag. Forest Serv., 1990–1991. 2 vols.

Burns, Walter Noble. *The Saga of Billy the Kid.* Garden City NY: Doubleday, Page, 1926.

————. *Tombstone.* Garden City NY: Doubleday, Doran, 1929.

Burns Times-Herald. Burns OR, 1897–.

Burpee Seeds. Philadelphia: W. A. Burpee, 1932–.

Burr, Aaron. *The Private Journal of Aaron Burr, during His Residence of Four Years in Europe, with Selections from His Correspondence.* Ed. by Matthew L. Davis. New York: Harper & Bros., 1838.

————. *The Private Journal of Aaron Burr.* Comp. and ed. by William H. Sampson. Rochester NY: Post Express Printing, 1903. 2 vols.

Burr, Fearing. *Field and Garden Vegetables of America.* Boston: Crosby and Nichols, 1863.

Burr, George Lincoln, ed. *Narratives of the Witchcraft Cases, 1648–1706.* New York: C. Scribner's Sons, 1914.

Burrison, John A., ed. *Storytellers.* Athens GA: Univ. GA Press, c.1991.

Burritt, Elihu. *A Walk from London to John O'Groats.* New York: Scribner, 1864.

Burroughs, John. *Birds and Poets.* New York: Hurd & Houghton, 1877.

————. *In the Catskills.* Boston: Houghton Mifflin, 1910.

————. *My Boyhood.* Garden City NY: Doubleday, Page, 1922.

————. *Pepacton.* Boston: Houghton, Mifflin, 1881.

————. *Riverby.* Boston: Houghton, Mifflin, 1894.

————. *Signs and Seasons.* Boston: Houghton, Mifflin, 1886.

————. *Wake-Robin.* New York: Hurd & Houghton, 1871.

————. *Winter Sunshine.* New York: Hurd & Houghton, 1876.

Burroughs, John Rolfe. *Head-First in the Pickle Barrel.* New York: Wm. Morrow, 1963.

Burroughs, William Seward. *Junkie.* New York: Ace Books, c.1953.

————. *The Letters of William S. Burroughs 1945–1959.* New York: Viking, c.1993.

Burt, William Henry. *A Field Guide to the Mammals.* Boston: Houghton, Mifflin, c.1952.

Burton, Jack. *The Blue Book of Tin Pan Alley.* Watkins Glen NY: Century House, c.1951.

Burton, Richard F. *The City of the Saints, and across the Rocky Mountains to California.* London: Longman, Green, Longman, & Roberts, 1861.

Burton, William Evans. *Waggeries and Vagaries.* Philadelphia: Carey & Hart, 1848.

Burton's Gentleman's Magazine and American Monthly Review. Philadelphia, 1839–1840.

Burwell, Letitia M. *A Girl's Life in Virginia before the War.* New York: Frederick A. Stokes, c.1895.

————. *Plantation Reminiscences.* Owensboro? KY: [s.n.], 1878.

Busby, Morgan S. et al. *Natural Resources of the Mattole River Estuary, California.* Arcata CA: California Cooperative Fishery Research Unit, Humboldt State Univ., 1988.

Bushnell, Belle Johnston. *John Arrowsmith, Planter.* Cedar Rapids IA: Torch Press, 1910 [c.1909].

Bushnell, Oswald A. *The Stone of Kannon.* Honolulu HI: Univ. Press HI, c.1979.

————. *The Water of Kane.* Honolulu HI: Univ. Press HI, c.1980.

Business Week. New York: McGraw-Hill, 1929–.

Butler, E. A. *The Big Buck and the New Business Breed.* New York: Macmillan, c.1972.

Butler, Ellis Parker. *Dominie Dean.* New York: Fleming H. Revell, c.1917.

Butler, Frances Anne SEE Kemble, Fanny

Butler, Frederick. *The Farmer's Manual.* Hartford CT: Samuel G. Goodrich; Middletown CT: Clark & Lyman, 1819.

Butler, Pardee. *Personal Recollections of Pardee Butler.* Cincinnati OH: Standard, 1889.

Butler, Teresa Rae. *Don't Eem Trip.* Milwaukee WI?: Lulu.com, 2005.

Butterworth, Hezekiah. *A Zigzag Journey in the Sunny South.* Boston: Estes and Lauriat, 1887 [c.1886].

Büttner, Johann Gottfried. *Briefe aus und über Nordamerika.* Dresden: Arnold, 1847.

Buttrick, Tilly. *Voyages, Travels and Discoveries of Tilly Buttrick, Jr.* Boston: Printed for the Author, 1831.

The Buyers' Manual and Business Guide. San Francisco: Francis & Valentine, 1872.

Bynner, Edwin Lassetter. *Agnes Surriage.* Boston: Ticknor, 1886.

Byrd, Richard. *Little Bitty Pretty One.* Los Angeles: Recordo Music, 1957.

Byrd, Richard Evelyn. *Discovery.* New York: G. P. Putnam's Sons, 1935.

Byrd, William. *Another Secret Diary of William Byrd of Westover, 1739–1741.* Ed. by Maude H. Woodfin. Richmond VA: Dietz Press, 1942.

————. *Description of the Dismal Swamp and a Proposal to Drain the Swamp.* Ed. by Earl Gregg Swem. Metuchen NJ: Printed for C. F. Heartman, 1922.

————. *A Journey to the Land of Eden.* Albany NY: [s.n.], 1876.

————. *The Secret Diary of William Byrd of Westover, 1709–1712.* Richmond VA: Dietz Press, 1941.

————. *The Westover Manuscripts.* Petersburg VA: E. and J. C. Ruffin, 1841.

————. *William Byrd's Histories of the Dividing Line betwixt Virginia and North Carolina.* Raleigh NC: North Carolina Historical Commission, 1929.

Byrn, Marcus Lafayette. *The Adventures of Fudge Fumble.* Philadelphia: T. B. Peterson, c.1865.

————. *The Life and Adventures of an Arkansaw Doctor.* Philadelphia: Lippincott, Grambo, 1851.

————. *The Life and Adventures of an Arkansaw Doctor.* New York: M. Lafayette Byrn, c.1879, c.1851.

————. *Rattlehead's Chronicles.* Philadelphia: Lippincott Grambo, 1852.

————. *Rattlehead's Travels.* Philadelphia: Lippincott, Grambo, 1852.

Byron-Curtiss, Arthur Lester. *The Life and Adventures of Nat Foster, Trapper and Hunter of the Adirondacks.* Utica NY: Press of Thomas J. Griffiths, 1897.

Cabinet of Natural History and American Rural Sports. Philadelphia: J. & T. Doughty, 1830–1834.

Cable, George Washington. *Bonaventure.* New York: Charles Scribner's Sons, 1888.

————. *The Creoles of Louisiana.* New York: Charles Scribner's Sons, 1884.

————. *Dr. Sevier.* Boston: James R. Osgood, 1885.

————. *The Grandissimes.* New York: Charles Scribner's Sons, 1880.

————. *John March, Southerner.* New York: C. Scribner's Sons, c.1894.

————. *Old Creole Days.* New York: Charles Scribner's Sons, 1919.

Cadence. Redwood NY: B. Rusch, 1976–.

Cady, Daniel Leavens. *Rhymes of Vermont Life.* Rutland VT: Tuttle, 1922 [c.1919].

————. *Rhymes of Vermont Rural Life.* 2d ser. Rutland VT: Tuttle, 1926. Orig. pub. in 1922.

Cagnon, Maurice Arthur. "New England Franco-American Terms Used in Spoken English." *Romance Notes.* (1969) 11.219–25.

Cahalane, Victor Harrison. *Mammals of North America.* New York: Macmillan, 1947.

————. *Meeting the Mammals.* New York: Macmillan, 1943.

Cahan, Abraham. *The Rise of David Levinsky.* New York: Peter Smith, 1951. Orig. pub. in 1917 by Harper and Bros., New York.

Cahn, Alvin Robert. *The Turtles of Illinois.* Urbana IL: Univ. IL, 1937.

Cahn, Rolf. *Self Defense for Gentle People.* Santa Fe NM: John Muir Publications, 1974.

Cain, James Mallahan. *The Moth.* New York: Alfred A. Knopf, 1948.

————. *The Postman Always Rings Twice.* New York: Alfred A. Knopf, 1934.

————. *Three Novels.* Cleveland OH: World Publishing, 1946.

Cain, Paul, [pseud.]. *Fast One.* Carbondale IL: Southern IL Univ. Press, c.1978. Repr. of the 1933 ed. pub. by Doubleday, Garden City NY.

Caine, Louis S. *Game Fish of the South and How to Catch Them.* Boston: Houghton Mifflin, 1935.

————. *North American Fresh Water Sport Fish.* New York: A. S. Barnes, c.1949.

————, ed. *Salt Water Tackle Digest.* Chicago: Paul, Richmond, c.1947.

Calasibetta, Charlotte Mankey. *Fairchild's Dictionary of Fashion.* New York: Fairchild Publications, c.1975.

Caldwell, Erskine. *American Earth.* New York: Grosset & Dunlap, 1931.

————. *Georgia Boy.* New York: Duell, Sloan & Pearce, c.1943.

————. *God's Little Acre.* New York: Grosset & Dunlap, c.1933.

————. *A House in the Uplands.* New York: Duell, Sloan & Pearce, c.1946.

————. *Journeyman.* New York: Viking Press, c.1935.

————. *Kneel to the Rising Sun.* New York: Viking Press, 1935.

————. *A Lamp for Nightfall.* New York: Duell, Sloan and Pearce; Boston: Little, Brown, c.1952.

————. *Southways.* New York: Viking Press, 1938.

————. *Tobacco Road.* Savannah GA: Beehive Press, 1974 [c.1932].

Caldwell, John J. *The Thurstons of the Old Palmetto State.* New York: Joseph Russell, 1861 [c.1860].

Calhoun, Alfred Rochefort. *Healthful Sports for Boys.* New York: Christian Herald Bible House, c.1910.

Calhoun, Frances Boyd. *Miss Minerva and William Green Hill.* Chicago: Reilly & Britton, 1915 [c.1908].

Calhoun, John C. *The Works of John C. Calhoun.* New York: D. Appleton, 1851–1856. 6 vols.

Calhoun, Mary. *Traveling Ball of String.* New York: Wm. Morrow, 1969.

Calhoun Times. St. Matthews SC, 1907–.

California. *Appendix to the Journals of the Senate and Assembly . . . of the Legislature of the State of California.* Sacramento CA: State Printer, 1854–1943.

California Academy of Natural Sciences. *Proceedings.* San Francisco, 1857–1867.

California Academy of Sciences. *Bulletin.* San Francisco, 1884–1887.

————. *California Wildflowers.* [v.d.]. Internet.

————. *Occasional Papers.* San Francisco, 1890–1993.

————. *Proceedings.* San Francisco, 1868–1896; 1907–.

California Agricultural Experiment Station. *Circular.* Berkeley CA, 1903–1926?

————. *Report of Work of the Agricultural Experiment Station of the University of California.* Sacramento CA: Superintendent, State Printing, 1890–1904.

California Agricultural Experiment Station, Berkeley. *Bulletin.* Sacramento CA, 1884–.

California Courier. San Francisco, 1850–1854.

California. Department of Agriculture. *Monthly Bulletin.* Sacramento CA, 1919–1935.

California. Department of Fish and Game. *San Francisco Bay Estuary Fish List.* [v.d.]. Internet.

California. Department of Transportation. *Caltrans District 4 Home Page.* [v.d.]. Internet.

California. Division of Beaches and Parks. *Point Lobos Reserve, State Park, California.* Ed. by Aubrey Drury. Sacramento CA: [s.n.], 1954?

————. *Point Lobos Wild Flowers.* Sacramento CA: [s.n.], 1954.

California Fish and Game. San Francisco, 1914–.

California. Fish and Game Commission. *Biennial Report.* Sacramento CA, 1913–1927.

————. *Fish Bulletin.* Sacramento CA: Bureau of Marine Fisheries, 1913–.

California Folklore Quarterly SEE *Western Folklore*

California Highways and Public Works. Sacramento CA, 1924–.

California Historical Society Quarterly. San Francisco: The Society, 1923–.

California Native Plant Society, Bristlecone Chapter. *Newsletter.* Independence CA, 1982–.

California Star. San Francisco, 1847–1848.

California State Agricultural Society. *Transactions.* Sacramento CA, 1858–1904.

California. State Board of Forestry. *Biennial Report of the California State Board of Forestry.* Sacramento CA: James J. Ayers, 1886–1892.

California. State Commission of Horticulture. *Monthly Bulletin.* Sacramento CA, 1911–1919.

California. University. *University of California Publications in Zoology.* Berkeley CA: Univ. CA Press, 1902–.

California. University-Berkeley. *Annual Report of the President of the University.* Berkeley CA: Univ. CA Press, 1913?–.

————. *CalPhotos.* [v.d.]. Internet.

————. *Xylella Fastidiosa Web Site.* [v.d.]. Internet.

California. University-Berkeley. Digital Library Project. *The CalFlora Database.* [v.d.]. Internet.

California. University. College of Agriculture. *Supplement to the Biennial Report of the Board of Regents.* Sacramento CA, 1879?–1887?

California. University-Davis. Cooperative Extension. *Weed Research and Information Center.* [v.d.]. Internet.

California. University-Los Angeles. Ocean Discovery Center. *Ocean Sea Life.* [v.d.]. Internet.

California. University. Regents. *Biennial Report.* [s.l.], 1868?–1952?

California. University-Riverside. *Plants of Economic or Aesthetic Importance.* [v.d.]. Internet.

Californian. Monterey CA, 1846–1847.

Californian. San Francisco, 1847–1848; 1864–1868.

Californian. San Francisco: A. Roman, 1880–1882.

California's Living Marine Resources. Ed. by William S. Leet et al. 4th ed. Sacramento CA: CA Department of Fish and Game, 2001.

Calk, William. "The Journal of William Calk, from Prince William County, Va., to Boonesboro, Ky., from March 13, 1775, to May 2, 1775." In: Speed, Thomas, *The Wilderness Road,* 1971, 34–8.

Callahan, North. *Smoky Mountain Country.* New York: Duell, Sloan & Pearce, 1952.

Callaway, Barbara J. *Hildegard Peplau, Psychiatric Nurse of the Century.* New York: Springer Publishing, c.2002.

Callison, John James. *Bill Jones of Paradise Valley, Oklahoma.* Chicago: M. A. Donohue, c.1914.

The Cama-i Book. Garden City NY: Anchor Books, 1983.

Cambridge, Massachusetts. *The Records of the Town of Cambridge, Massachusetts, 1630–1703.* Cambridge MA: Univ. Press, 1901.

Cambridge, Massachusetts Proprietors. *The Register Book of the Lands and Houses in the "New Towne" and the Town of Cambridge.* Cambridge MA: J. Wilson & Son, 1896.

Cambridge Jeffersonian. Cambridge OH, 1870–1918.

Cambridge University. Museum of Comparative Zoology. *Bulletin.* Cambridge, 1870–.

Camera Craft. San Francisco, 1900–1942.

Cameron Pilot. Cameron LA, 1956–.

Cammann, William C., ed. *The History of Troop "A", New York Cavalry U.S.V., from May 2 to November 28, 1898 in the Spanish-American War.* New York: R. H. Russell, 1899.

Camp, Raymond Russell. *Fishing the Surf.* Boston: Little, Brown, 1941.

———, ed. *The Hunter's Encyclopedia.* Harrisburg PA: Stackpole and Heck, 1948.

Campbell, Carlos Clinton. *Birth of a National Park in the Great Smoky Mountains.* Knoxville TN: Univ. TN Press, 1960.

Campbell, Carlos Clinton et al. *Great Smoky Mountains Wildflowers.* Enlarged ed. Knoxville TN: Univ. TN Press, 1964.

———. *Great Smoky Mountains Wildflowers.* 3d ed. Knoxville TN: Univ. TN Press, c.1970.

Campbell, Charles. *History of the Colony and Ancient Dominion of Virginia.* Philadelphia: J. B. Lippincott, 1860 [c.1859].

Campbell, Helen. *Darkness and Daylight.* Hartford CT: A. D. Worthington, 1893 [c.1891].

Campbell, Henry Colin. *Wisconsin in Three Centuries, 1634–1905.* New York: Century History, c.1906. 4 vols.

Campbell, Jesse Harrison. *Georgia Baptists.* Macon GA: J. W. Burke, 1874.

Campbell, John C. *The Southern Highlander and His Homeland.* Spartanburg SC: Reprint, 1973. Repr. of 1921 ed. pub. by the Russell Sage Foundation, New York.

Campbell, John Wilson. *Biographical Sketches.* Comp. by his widow. Columbus OH: Printed for the publisher by Scott & Gallagher, 1838.

Campbell, Marie. *Cloud-Walking.* Bloomington IN: IN Univ. Press, 1971. Orig. pub. in 1942 by Farrar & Rinehart, New York.

———. *Folks Do Get Born.* New York: Rinehart, c.1946.

———. *Tales from the Cloud Walking Country.* Bloomington IN: IN Univ. Press, c.1958.

Campbell, Marius et al. *The Valley Coal Fields of Virginia.* Charlottesville VA: Univ. VA, 1925.

Campbell, Olive Dame and Cecil J. Sharp, comps. *English Folk Songs from the Southern Appalachians.* New York: G. P. Putnam's Sons, 1917.

Campbell, Paul Douglas. *Survival Skills of Native California.* Salt Lake City UT: Gibbs-Smith, c.1999.

———. *Survival Skills of Native California.* Salt Lake City UT: Gibbs Smith; London: Hi Marketing, 2005. Orig. pub. in 1999.

Campbell, Will D. *Robert G. Clark's Journey to the House.* Jackson MS: Univ. MS Press, c.2003.

Campbell, William W. *The Life and Writings of De Witt Clinton.* New York: Baker & Scribner, 1849.

Campion, J. S. *On the Frontier.* 2d ed. London: Chapman & Hall, 1878.

Canada. Department of Agriculture. *Experimental Farms Reports.* Ottawa, 1887–1920.

Canadian Pharmaceutical Journal. Toronto, 1868–1984.

Canarsie Courier. Brooklyn NY, 1921–.

Canby, Henry Seidel. *Thoreau.* Boston: Houghton, Mifflin, c.1939.

Canfield, Chauncey de Leon. *The Diary of a Forty-Niner.* New York: Morgan Shepard, 1906.

Canfield, Dorothy. *Understood Betsy.* New York: Henry Holt, 1917.

Canfield, Henry Spofford. *A Maid of the Frontier.* Chicago: Rand, McNally, c.1898.

Canfield, Jack, comp. *Chicken Soup for the Fisherman's Soul.* Deerfield Beach FL: Health Communications, c.2004.

Cannell, Margaret. *Signs, Omens, and Portents in Nebraska Folklore.* Lincoln NE: Univ. NE, 1933.

Cannon, Anthon S. *Popular Beliefs and Superstitions from Utah.* Salt Lake City UT: Univ. UT Press, 1984.

Cannon, LeGrand. *Look to the Mountain.* New York: Henry Holt, c.1942.

Cannon, Raymond. *How to Fish the Pacific Coast: a Manual for Salt Water Fishermen.* Menlo Park CA: Lane Publishing, c.1953.

Canova, Andrew P. *Life and Adventures in South Florida.* Assisted by L. S. Perkins. Palatka FL: Southern Sun Publishing, 1885.

Canton, Massachusetts. *The Record of Births, Marriages and Deaths.* Ed. by Frederic Endicott. Canton MA: Printed by W. Bense, 1896.

Canyon Courier. Evergreen CO, 2007–.

Canyon Views. Grand Canyon AZ: Grand Canyon Association, 1995–.

Cape Cod Standard-Times. Hyannis MA, 1936?–.

Cape May County Gazette. Cape May Court House NJ, 1880–.

Capinera, John et al. *Grasshoppers of Florida.* Gainesville FL: Univ. Press FL, 2001.

Capital. Annapolis MD, 1981–.

Capital Times. Madison WI, 1917–.

Capote, Truman. *The Grass Harp.* New York: Random House, 1951.

———. *Local Color.* New York: Random House, c.1950.

Capron, Elisha Smith. *History of California, from Its Discovery to the Present Time.* Boston: John P. Jewett; Cleveland OH: Jewett, Proctor and Worthington, 1854.

Car and Driver. New York, 1961–.

Carawan, Guy and Candie Carawan. *Ain't You Got a Right to the Tree of Life.* New York: Simon & Schuster, c.1966.

Car Builders' Dictionary. 4th ed. rev. New York: Railroad Gazette, 1906.

Cardunal Free Press. Carpentersville IL, 1958–?.

Carey, Richard Adams. *Against the Tide.* Boston: Houghton Mifflin, 2000 [c.1999].

Carhart, Arthur Hawthorne. *Fishing in the West.* New York: Macmillan, c.1950.

Caribou County Sun. Soda Springs ID, 1931–.

Carleton, James Henry. *The Prairie Logbooks.* Chicago: Caxton Club, 1943.

Carleton, R. Milton. *Collection.* 1983. Unpub. coll. of plant names, etc.

———, comp. *Index to Common Names of Herbaceous Plants.* Boston: G. K. Hall, 1959.

———. *The Small Garden Book.* New York: Macmillan; London: Collier-Macmillan, c.1971.

Carleton, Will. *City Legends.* New York: Harper & Bros., 1889.

———. *Farm Ballads.* New York: Harper & Bros., 1875. Orig. pub. in 1873.

———. *The Old Infant and Similar Stories.* New York: Harper & Bros., 1896.

Carlile, Clancy. *Children of the Dust.* New York: Ivy Books, 1995.

Carlisle, Rose Jeanne. *A Southwestern Dictionary.* Albuquerque NM: Univ. NM diss., 1939.

Carlquist, Sherwin John. *Hawaii.* Garden City NY: Natural History Press, 1970.

Carmen Headlight. Carmen OK, 1926–1971.

Carmer, Carl Lamson. *Listen for a Lonesome Drum.* New York: Farrar & Rinehart, 1936.

———. *Stars Fell on Alabama.* New York: Farrar & Rinehart, 1934.

Carmi Times. Carmi IL, 1950–.

Carmony, Marvin Dale. *The Speech of Terre Haute.* Bloomington IN: IN Univ. diss., 1965.

Carnegie Museum. *Annals.* Pittsburgh PA, 1901–1973.

Carney, Kate S. *Diary, April 15, 1861–July 31, 1862.* Chapel Hill NC: Academic Affairs Library, Univ. NC at Chapel Hill, 1999. Unpub. ms. transcr. for *Documenting the American South* website.

Caro, Robert A. *The Years of Lyndon Johnson.* New York: Alfred A. Knopf, c.1982–c.1990. 2 vols.

Carolina Gazette. Charleston SC, 1798–1840.

Carolina Play-Book. Chapel Hill NC: Carolina Playmakers and the Carolina Dramatic Association, 1928–1943?

Carpenter, Adrienne R. C. *Laughing, Crying, Naked.* Victoria: Trafford, c.2003.

Carpenter, Arie. *Aunt Arie.* Ed. by Linda Garland Page and Eliot Wigginton. New York: E. P. Dutton, c.1983.

Carpenter, Cal. *The Walton War and Tales of the Great Smoky Mts.* Lakemont GA: Copple House Books, c.1979.

Carpenter, Edna Turley. *Tales from the Manchaca Hills.* Ed. and recorded by Jane and Bill Hogan. New Orleans: Hauser Press, 1960.

Carpenter, Esther Bernon. *South-County Neighbors.* Boston: Roberts Bros., 1887.

Carpenter, Francis Bicknell. *Six Months at the White House with Abraham Lincoln.* New York: Hurd & Houghton, 1866.

Carpenter, Frank George. *Alaska Our Northern Wonderland.* Garden City NY: Doubleday, Page, 1923.

Carpenter, Louis George. *Forests and Snow.* Fort Collins CO: Agricultural Experiment Station of the Agricultural College CO, 1901.

Carpenter, Lucien O. *J. W. Pepper's Universal Dancing Master, Prompter's Call Book and Violinist's Guide.* Philadelphia: J. W. Pepper, 1882.

Carr, Archie Fairly. *Handbook of Turtles.* Ithaca NY: Comstock, 1952.

Carr, Archie Fairly and Coleman J. Goin. *Guide to the Reptiles, Amphibians, and Fresh-Water Fishes of Florida.* Gainesville FL: Univ. FL Press, 1955.

Carr, Elizabeth Ball. *Da Kine Talk.* Honolulu HI: Univ. Press HI, 1972.

Carr, Jess. *The Second Oldest Profession.* Radford VA: Commonwealth Press, 1978 [c.1972].

Carr, John. *Pioneer Days in California.* Eureka CA: Times Publishing, 1891.

Carr, William H. *Desert Parade.* New York: Viking Press, c.1947.

Carrell, Susie. *Unpublished Autobiography.* 1962. Unpub.

Carrier, Lyman. *The Beginnings of Agriculture in America.* New York: McGraw-Hill, c.1923.

Carrighar, Sally. *Moonlight at Midday.* New York: Alfred A. Knopf, 1958.

Carroll, Bartholomew Rivers, ed. *Historical Collections of South Carolina.* New York: Harper & Bros., 1836. 2 vols.

Carroll, David M. *Self-Portrait with Turtles.* Boston: Houghton Mifflin, 2004.

Carroll, Gladys Hasty. *West of the Hill.* New York: Macmillan, 1949.

Carroll, Ruth and Latrobe Carroll. *Tough Enough and Sassy.* New York: Henry Z. Walck, 1958.

Carroll County Independent-Carroll County Pioneer. Center Ossipee NH, 1924?–.

Carroll County Times. Carrollton GA, 1872–1948.

Carroll Daily Times Herald. Carroll IA, 1941–1987.

Carson, Gerald. *The Old Country Store.* New York: Oxford Univ. Press, c.1954.

———. *The Social History of Bourbon.* New York: Dodd, Mead, 1963.

Carson, Josephine. *Drives My Green Age.* New York: Harper & Bros., c.1957.

Carson, Rachel Louise. *Food from the Sea.* Washington DC: Govt. Printing Office, 1943.

Carter, Betty L. *My Little Mountain Home (and Me).* Victoria: Trafford, c.2003.

Carter, Hodding and Anthony Ragusin. *Gulf Coast Country.* New York: Duell, Sloan & Pearce, 1951.

Carter, Jimmy. *An Hour before Daylight.* New York: Simon & Schuster, c.2001.

Carter, Landon. *The Diary of Colonel Landon Carter of Sabine Hall, 1752–1778.* Charlottesville VA: Published for the Virginia Historical Society by the Univ. Press VA, 1965. 2 vols.

Carter, Mary Nelson. *North Carolina Sketches.* Chicago: A. C. McClurg, 1900.

Carter, Nathaniel Hazeltine. *Letters from Europe.* New York: G. & C. Carvill, 1827. 2 vols.

Carter, Robert Goldthwaite. *On the Border with Mackenzie.* Washington DC: Eynon, 1935.

Carter, William. *Ghost Towns of the West.* Menlo Park CA: Lane Magazine & Book, 1971.

Carteret County News-Times. Morehead City and Beaufort NC, 1948–.

Carthaginian. Carthage MS, 1872–.

Cartwright, George. *Captain Cartwright and His Labrador Journal.* Ed. by Charles Wendell Townsend. Boston: D. Estes, 1911.

———. *A Journal of Transactions and Events during a Residence of Nearly Sixteen Years on the Coast of Labrador.* Newark: Allin & Ridge, 1792. 3 vols.

Cartwright, Peter. *Autobiography of Peter Cartwright.* New York: Methodist Book Concern, 1856.

Caruthers, Eli Washington. *A Sketch of the Life and Character of the Rev. David Caldwell, D. D.* Greensborough NC: Printed by Swaim and Sherwood, 1842.

Caruthers, William Alexander. *The Kentuckian in New-York.* New York: Harper & Bros., 1834. 2 vols.

Carver, Jonathan. *Travels through the Interior Parts of North-America in the Years 1766, 1767, and 1768.* London: J. Walter, 1778. Carver's *Travels* as printed was prob. the work of Dr. John Coakley Lettsom.

Carwardine, William H. *The Pullman Strike.* Chicago: Charles H. Kerr, 1971. Repr. of 1894 ed.

Cary, Alice. *Married, Not Mated.* New York: Derby & Jackson; Cincinnati OH: H. W. Derby, 1856.

———. *Pictures of Country Life.* New York: Derby & Jackson, 1859.

Cary, Diana Serra. *The Hollywood Posse.* Norman OK: Univ. OK Press, 1996.

Case, Frederick W. *Orchids of the Western Great Lakes Regions.* Rev. ed. Bloomfield Hills MI: Cranbrook Institute of Science, 1987.

Casey, John. *The Half-Life of Happiness.* New York: Knopf, 1998.

Casey, Robert. *The Parson's Boys.* Denver CO: Parson's Boys, 1906.

Cash, June Carter. *Among My Klediments.* Grand Rapids MI: Zondervan, c.1979.

Casler, John Overton. *Four Years in the Stonewall Brigade.* 2d ed., rev., corr. & improved. Girard KS: Appeal Publishing, 1906.

Cason, Clarence. *90° in the Shade.* Chapel Hill NC: Univ. NC Press, c.1935.

Casseday, Davis B. *The Hortons.* Philadelphia: James S. Claxton, 1866 [c.1865].

Cassell's Natural History. London: Cassell, Petter, Galpin, 1883–1884. 6 vols.

Cassidy, Frederic Gomes. *Linguistic Atlas Field Records of Wisconsin.* 1940–1941. Unpub.

Cassidy, Frederic Gomes and Audrey R. Duckert. *Wisconsin English Language Survey.* c1950. Unpub. survey.

———. *Wisconsin English Language Survey Supplement.* 1945–1960. Unpub. suppl. material.

Cassidy, Frederic Gomes and R. B. LePage, eds. *Dictionary of Jamaican English.* London: Cambridge Univ. Press, 1967.

———, eds. *Dictionary of Jamaican English.* 2d ed. Cambridge: Cambridge Univ. Press, 1980.

Castanea. Morgantown WV, 1937–.

Castetter, Edward Franklin and Willis H. Bell. *Pima and Papago Indian Agriculture.* Albuquerque NM: Univ. NM Press, 1942.

Castiglioni, Luigi. *Viaggio negli Stati Uniti dell' America Settentrionale.* Milan: Giuseppe Marelli, 1790. 2 vols.

Castlemon, Harry See Fosdick, Charles Austin

Catahoula Hog Dog. Jonesville LA, 1962.

Catahoula News-Booster. Jonesville-Harrisonburg LA, 1967–.

Catalogue of Herbs, Roots, Barks, Powdered Articles, etc. Portland ME: B. Thurston, 1864.

Cate, Margaret Davis. *Our Todays and Yesterdays.* Rev. ed. Spartansburg SC: Reprint, 1972. Repr. of the 1930 ed. pub. by Glover Bros., Brunswick GA.

Cate, Wirt Armistead, ed. *Two Soldiers.* Chapel Hill NC: Univ. NC Press, 1938.

Catesby, Mark. *Hortus Britanno-Americanus.* London: Printed by W. Richardson and S. Clark for J. Ryall, 1763.

———. *The Natural History of Carolina, Florida, and the Bahama Islands.* London: Printed at the Expense of the Author, 1731–1748. 2 vols.

———. *The Natural History of Carolina, Florida, and the Bahama Islands.* London: Printed for Charles Marsh, 1754. 2 vols.

Cather, Willa. *Death Comes for the Archbishop.* New York: Alfred A. Knopf, 1927.

———. *A Lost Lady.* New York: Alfred A. Knopf, 1923.

———. *Lucy Gayheart.* New York: Alfred A. Knopf, 1935.

———. *My Antonia.* London: William Heinemann, 1919.

———. *Obscure Destinies.* New York: Alfred A. Knopf, 1932.

———. *The Old Beauty and Others.* New York: Knopf, 1948.

———. *O Pioneers!* Boston: Houghton, Mifflin, 1913.

———. *The Professor's House.* New York: A. A. Knopf, 1925.

———. *Sapphira and the Slave Girl.* New York: Alfred A. Knopf, 1940.

———. *The Song of the Lark.* Boston: Houghton Mifflin, 1915.

Catherwood, Mary Hartwell. *Mackinac and Lake Stories.* New York: Harper & Bros., 1899.

———. *The Queen of the Swamp and Other Plain Americans.* Boston: Houghton, Mifflin, 1899.

Catholic Historical Review. Washington DC: Catholic Univ. of America, 1915–.

Catholic Missions. New York, 1907–1923.

Catholic World. Paramus NJ: Paulist Fathers, 1865–1971.

Catlin, George. *Letters and Notes on the Manners, Customs and Condition of the North American Indians.* London: Published by the Author, 1841. 2 vols.

———. *Letters and Notes on the Manners, Customs and Conditions of the North American Indians.* New York: Dover, c.1973. 2 vols. Unabridged republication of the 1844 ed. pub. by the author, London.

Catlow, Agnes. *Popular Field Botany.* London: Reeve, Benham & Reeve, 1848.

Catskill Mountain News. Margaretville NY, 1894–.

Cattleman. Ft. Worth TX: Texas Hereford Association, 1914–.

Cattle Today Online. 1998–. Internet.

Catton, Bruce. *Mr. Lincoln's Army.* Garden City NY: Doubleday, c.1951.

Caustic, Christopher See Fessenden, Thomas Green

Cavender, Anthony P., ed. *A Folk Medical Lexicon of South Central Appalachia.* Johnson City TN: History of Medicine Society of Appalachia, East TN Univ., 1990.

———. *Folk Medicine in Southern Appalachia.* Chapel Hill NC: Univ. NC Press, c.2003.

Cazden, Norman et al. *Folk Songs of the Catskills.* Albany NY: State Univ. NY Press, c.1982.

Cedarburg, Wisconsin. Common Council. *Minutes.* 2006–. Internet.

Cedar Rapids Evening Gazette. Cedar Rapids IA, 1888–1912.

Cedar Rapids Gazette. Cedar Rapids IA, 1932–1979.

Cedar Rapids Tribune. Cedar Rapids IA, 1911–1956.

Cedar Rapids Weekly Times. Cedar Rapids IA, 1874–1897.

Cedar Valley Times. Cedar Rapids IA, 1854–1868.

Censor See Bunce, Oliver Bell

Cent D See Whitney, William Dwight *The Century Dictionary*

Center for Coastal Studies. [v.d.]. Internet.

Sentinel. Gettysburg PA, 1805–1813.

Central City Daily Courier. Syracuse NY, 1858–1860.

Centralia Daily Chronicle. Centralia WA, 1916–1941.

Centralia Enterprise and Tribune. Centralia WI, 1887–1900.

Centralia Sentinel. Centralia IL, 1863–1912.

Central Utah Journal. Orem UT, 1983?–.

Centreville Press. Centreville AL, 1879–.

The Century Dictionary See Whitney, William Dwight

The Century Dictionary and Cyclopedia. Rev. and enlarged ed. New York: Century, c.1911. 12 vols.

Century [Magazines] See *Scribner's Monthly, Century Illustrated Monthly Magazine, Century Monthly Magazine,* and *Century Magazine*

Century Illustrated Monthly Magazine. New York, 1881–1925.

Century Magazine. New York, 1929–1930.

Century Monthly Magazine. New York, 1925–1929.

Cerello, James A. *A Preliminary Lexical Survey of Certain Dialect Peculiarities Found among Elderly Residents of the Eastern Central and Southern Districts of Dakota County, Minn.* River Falls WI: WI State Univ.-River Falls M.A. thesis, 1967.

Chabot, Frederick C., ed. *Texas Letters.* San Antonio TX: Yanaguana Society, c.1940.

Chadron Record. Chadron NE, 1943–.

Chadwick, J., Mrs. *Home Cookery.* New York: Arno Press, 1973 [1853].

Chagrin Valley Herald. Chagrin Falls OH, 1946?–.

Chaika, Elaine. *Speaking Rhode Island.* Providence RI: Providence Public Library, 1982.

Chalfant, Willie Arthur. *Death Valley.* Stanford University CA: Stanford Univ. Press, 1930.

———. *Gold, Guns & Ghost Towns.* Stanford CA: Stanford Univ. Press, c.1947.

Chalmers, Marjorie. *"Better I Stay".* Gatlinburg TN: Crescent Color Printing, c.1975.

Chamberlain, Delores. *River Stories.* Madison WI: Prairie Oaks Press, c.2000.

Chamberlain, E., comp. *The Indiana Gazetteer.* 3d ed. Indianapolis IN: E. Chamberlain, 1850.

Chamberlain, George Agnew. "Laverack of Sarah Run." *Saturday Evening Post.* (1942) 5 Sept., 9–11, 46, 49, 53–4; 12 Sept., 30–1, 76–7, 79–80, 82–4; 19 Sept., 32, 34, 50, 53, 56, 58–9, 61; 26 Sept., 32, 35, 85–8, 90–2, 94, 96; 3 Oct., 32, 36, 74, 76, 78, 80, 83–4.

Chamberlain, Newell D. *The Call of Gold.* Mariposa CA: Gazette Press, c.1936.

Chamberlain, Samuel. *Nantucket.* New York: Hastings House, c.1939.

Chamberlain, William Woodrow. *Leaf Gold.* Indianapolis IN: Bobbs-Merrill, c.1941.

Chambers, Edward Thomas Davies. *The Ouananiche and Its Canadian Environment.* New York: Harper & Bros., 1896.

Chambers, Ephraim. *A Supplement to Mr. Chambers's Cyclopaedia.* London: W. Innys and J. Richardson, 1753. 2 vols.

Chambers, James H. "Original Journal of James H. Chambers, Fort Sarpy." Montana. Historical Society *Contributions.* (1940) 10.100–87.

Chambers, Kenton Lee. *Wild Flowers of Oregon.* Salem OR: Oregon State Highway Department: Travel Information Division, 1960.

Chambers, Robert William. *The Common Law.* New York: Grosset & Dunlap, 1911.

———. *The Maid-at-Arms.* New York: Harper & Bros., 1902.

Chambers's Encyclopaedia. Philadelphia: J. B. Lippincott; Edinburgh: W. & R. Chambers, 1860–1868. 10 vols.

Chambers's Encyclopaedia. New ed. London: William & Robert Chambers; Philadelphia: J. B. Lippincott, 1888–1892. 10 vols.

Chambers's Journal. London, 1832–1956.

Champaign-Urbana Courier. Champaign IL, 1953?–.

Champaign-Urbana News-Gazette. Champaign IL, 1934–.

Champlain Society, Toronto. *Publications.* Toronto, 1907–.

Champlin, John Denison and Arthur E. Bostwick. *The Young Folks' Cyclopaedia of Games and Sports.* 2d ed. rev. New York: Henry Holt, 1899.

Chandler, Raymond. *The Big Sleep.* New York: Alfred A. Knopf, c.1966, c.1939.

———. *Farewell, My Lovely.* Cleveland OH: World Publishing, c.1940.

———. *Finger Man.* New York: Avon Book, c.1946.

———. *The High Window.* New York: A. A. Knopf, 1942.

———. *The Lady in the Lake.* New York: Alfred A. Knopf, 1944 [c.1943].

———. *The Little Sister.* Boston: Houghton Mifflin, c.1949.

———. *The Long Goodbye.* Boston: Houghton Mifflin, 1954 [c.1953].

———. *The Simple Art of Murder.* Boston: Houghton Mifflin, 1950.

Chandless, William. *A Visit to Salt Lake.* London: Smith, Elder, 1857.

Channing, George Gibbs. *Early Recollections of Newport, R.I. from the Year 1793 to 1811.* Newport RI: A. J. Ward, 1868.

Chansler, Walter S. *The River Trapper.* Columbus OH: Hunter-Trader-Trapper, c.1928.

Chapelle, Howard Irving. *American Small Sailing Craft.* New York: W. W. Norton, c.1951.

———. *The History of American Sailing Ships.* New York: Bonanza Books, c.1935.

Chaplin, Jane Dunbar. *Out of the Wilderness.* Boston: Henry A. Young, 1870 [c.1869].

Chapman, Abraham, comp. *New Black Voices.* New York: New American Library, 1972.

Chapman, Alvan Wentworth. *Flora of the Southern United States.* New York: Ivison, Phinney, 1860.

———. *Flora of the Southern United States.* 2d ed. New York: Ivison, Blakeman, Taylor, 1883.

———. *Flora of the Southern United States.* 3rd ed. Cambridge MA: Cambridge Botanical Supply, 1897.

Chapman, Arthur. *Cactus Center.* Boston: Houghton Mifflin, c.1921.

Chapman, Edward Mortimer. *New England Village Life.* Cambridge MA: Riverside Press, 1937.

Chapman, Frank Michler. *Bird-Life.* New York: D. Appleton, c.1897.

———. *Color Key to North American Birds.* New York: Doubleday, Page, 1903.

———. *Handbook of Birds of Eastern North America.* New York: D. Appleton, 1895.

———. *Our Winter Birds.* New York: D. Appleton, 1927 [c.1918].

Chapman, Maristan, [pseud.]. *The Happy Mountain.* New York: Viking Press, 1928.

Chapman, Robert L., ed. *New Dictionary of American Slang.* New York: Harper & Row, c.1986.

Chappe d'Auteroche. *A Voyage to California to Observe the Transit of Venus.* London: Edward and Charles Dilly, 1778. Anon. transl.

Chappell, Absalom H. *Miscellanies of Georgia, Historical, Biographical, Descriptive, etc.* Atlanta GA: James F. Meegan, c.1874. 3 pts.

Chappell, Fred. *It Is Time, Lord.* New York: Atheneum, 1963.

Chardon, Francis A. *Chardon's Journal at Ft. Clark, 1834–1839.* Ed. by Annie Heloise Abel. Pierre SD: [s.n.], 1932.

Chariton, Wallace O. *This Dog'll Hunt.* Plano TX: Wordware, c.1989.

Charleroi Mail. Charleroi PA, 1900–1960.

Charleston Daily Mail. Charleston WV, 1920–.

Charleston Gazette. Charleston WV, 1907–.

Charleston Mail. Charleston WV, 1906?–1920.

Charlotte Daily Observer. Charlotte NC, 1897–1916.

Charlotte Observer. Charlotte NC, 1916–.

Charlotte Sun Herald. Charlotte Harbor FL, 1995–.

Charters, Samuel Barclay. *Jazz: New Orleans, 1885–1957.* Belleville NJ: W. C. Allen, c.1958.

Chase, Charles Monroe. *The Editor's Run in New Mexico and Colorado.* Montpelier VT: "Argus and Patriot" Steam Book and Job Printing House, 1882.

Chase, Charles Thurston. *A Manual on School-Houses and Cottages for the People of the South.* Washington DC: Govt. Printing Office, 1868.

Chase, Frederick. *A History of Dartmouth College and the Town of Hanover, New Hampshire.* Cambridge MA: John Wilson and Son, 1891–1913. 2 vols.

Chase, Joseph Smeaton. *California Desert Trails.* Boston: Houghton Mifflin, c.1919.

———. *Yosemite Trails.* Boston: Houghton Mifflin, 1911.

Chase, Mary Ellen. *Windswept.* New York: Macmillan, c.1941.

Chase, Richard, ed. *Grandfather Tales: American-English Folk Tales.* Boston: Houghton Mifflin, c.1948.

———, ed. *The Jack Tales.* Boston: Houghton Mifflin, c.1943.

———, comp. *Singing Games and Playparty Games.* New York: Dover, 1967. Orig. pub. in 1949 by Houghton Mifflin under the title *Hullabaloo and Other Singing Folk Games.*

Chase, Warren. *The Life-Line of the Lone One.* Boston: Bela Marsh, 1857.

Chateaugay Record and Franklin County Democrat. Chateaugay NY, 1890–.

Chatham Courier-Rough Notes. Chatham NY, 1968–.

Chatham Record. Pittsboro NC, 1878–.

Chattanooga Free Press. Chattanooga TN, 1993–1999.

Chattanooga Times. Chattanooga TN, 1995–1999.

Chattanooga Times, Chattanooga Free Press. Chattanooga TN, 1999–.

Chautauquan. Jamestown NY, 1880–1914.

Checotah Times. Checotah OK, 1902–1925.

Cheever, Henry Theodore. *The Island World of the Pacific.* New York: Harper & Bros., 1850.

———. *The Whale and His Captors.* New York: Harper & Bros., 1849.

———. *The Whale and His Captors.* New York: Harper & Bros., 1850 [c.1849].

Cheever, John. *Falconer.* New York: Alfred A. Knopf, 1977.

———. *The World of Apples.* New York: Knopf, 1973.

Cheley, Frank Howbert. *Camp-Fire Yarns.* Boston: W. A. Wilde, c.1922.

Chemical Abstracts. Columbus OH: American Chemical Society, 1907–.

Cherokee Advocate. Tahlequah OK, 1844–1906.

Cherokee Phoenix and Indians' Advocate. New Echota GA, 1829–1835.

Chesapeake Biological Laboratory. *Publications.* Solomons Island MD, 1927–.

Chesnut, Mary Boykin Miller. *A Diary from Dixie.* New York: D. Appleton, 1905.

Chesnutt, Charles Waddell. *The Colonel's Dream.* New York: Doubleday, Page, 1905.

———. *The Conjure Woman.* Cambridge MA: Riverside Press, 1899.

———. *The Wife of His Youth and Other Stories of the Color Line.* Ridgewood NJ: Gregg Press, 1967. Orig. pub. in 1899 by Houghton Mifflin.

Chester, Edward W. *Wildflowers of the Land between the Lakes Region.* Clarksville TN: Austin Peay State Univ., 2000.

Chester County Historical Society. *Bulletins.* West Chester PA, 1898–1952.

Chester Daily Times. Chester PA, 1876–1882.

Chesterman, Charles W. *The Audubon Society Field Guide to North American Rocks and Minerals.* New York: Knopf, c.1978.

Chester Times. Chester PA, 1882–1959.

Chestnut, V. K. *Plants Used by the Indians of Mendocino County, California* SEE United States National Museum *Contributions from the United States National Herbarium*

Chevalier, Elizabeth Pickett. *Drivin' Woman.* New York: Macmillan, 1942.

Chevigny, Hector. *Russian America.* New York: Viking Press, 1965.

Chicago. WFMT, 1975–.

Chicago Academy of Sciences. *Bulletin.* Chicago, 1883–1995.

———. *Program of Activities.* Chicago, 1930–1938.

———. *Transactions.* Chicago, 1867–1870.

Chicago Daily American. Chicago, 1835–1842.

Chicago Daily Herald. Chicago, 1999?–.

Chicago Daily News. Chicago, 1875–1978.

Chicago Daily Tribune SEE *Chicago Tribune*

Chicago Defender. National ed. Chicago, 1906–.

Chicago Field. Chicago: Field & Stream Association, 1876–1881.

Chicago Heights Star. Chicago Heights IL, 1906?–1983.

Chicago Herald. Chicago, 1914–1918.

Chicago Herald and Examiner. Chicago, 1918–1939.

Chicago Medical Journal and Examiner. Chicago, 1875–1889.

Chicago Natural History Museum. *Bulletin.* Chicago, 1944–1965.

Chicago Park District. *Games and Game Boards.* Chicago: Chicago Park District, c.1937.

Chicago Purchasor. Chicago: Purchasing Agents Association, 1926–.

Chicago Record. Chicago, 1893–1901.

Chicago Record-Herald. Chicago, 1901–1914.

Chicago Reporter. Chicago: Community Renewal Society, 1972–.

Chicago Sun-Times. Chicago, 1948–.

Chicago Times. Chicago, 1861–1895.

Chicago Times-Herald. Chicago, 1895–1901.

Chicago Tribune. Chicago, 1847–. Title varies: *Chicago Daily Tribune* 1847–1858, 1860–1864, 1872–1963; *Chicago Press and Tribune* 1858–1860; *Chicago Tribune* 1864–1872, 1963—.

Chicago Weekly News. Chicago, 1870–1893.

Chicago Wilderness Magazine. Downers Grove IL, 1997–.

Child, Adrian. *Tippletonia.* Terre Haute IN: Fahnestock, 1854.

Child, Hamilton. *Gazetteer and Business Directory of Monroe County, N.Y., for 1869–70.* Syracuse NY: Printed at the Journal Office, 1869.

Child, Lydia Maria. *Fact and Fiction.* New York: C. S. Francis, 1847.

———. *The Frugal Housewife.* 2d ed. Boston: Carter & Hendee, 1830.

———. *The Frugal Housewife.* 6th ed. corr. Boston: Carter, Hendee & Babcock, 1831.

———. *Hobomok.* Boston: Cummings, Hilliard, 1824.

———. *Letters from New-York.* New York: Charles S. Francis, 1843.

———. *Letters from New York.* 2d ser. New York: C. S. Francis, 1847.

Child Care in Rural America. New York: Arno Press, 1972. Repr. of 1917–1921 ed. issued as vol. 2 of U.S. Children's Bureau *Publications.*

Child Development. Chicago: Univ. IL Press, 1930–.

Children's Folklore Newsletter. Greenville NC: East Carolina Univ., 1979–.

Children's Music Network. *Pass It On!* Arllington MA, 1994–.

Childress, Alice. *Like One of the Family.* Boston: Beacon Press, 1986 [c.1956].

Childress, William. *Out of the Ozarks.* Carbondale IL: Southern IL Univ. Press, c.1987.

Chillicothe Constitution. Chillicothe MO, 1890–1928.

Chillicothe Constitution-Tribune. Chillicothe MO, 1930–1985.

Chinquapin. Douglass TX, 1976–2000.

Chisholm, Daniel. *Civil War Notebook.* New York: Orion Books, 1989.

Chisholm, Joseph Francis. *Brewery Gulch.* San Antonio TX: Naylor, c.1949.

Chittenden, Hiram Martin. *The Yellowstone National Park, Historical and Descriptive.* 4th ed., rev. and enlarged. Cincinnati OH: R. Clarke, 1904 [c.1903].

Chittenden, Lucius Eugene. *An Unknown Heroine.* New York: George H. Richmond, 1894.

Chittick, Victor Lovitt Oakes. *Ring-Tailed Roarers.* Caldwell ID: Caxton Printers, 1943 [c.1941].

Chopin, Kate O'Flaherty. *Bayou Folk.* Boston: Houghton, Mifflin, 1894.

Choukas-Bradley, Melanie. *An Illustrated Guide to Eastern Woodland Wildflowers and Trees.* Charlottesville VA: Univ. VA Press, c.2004.

Christensen, Abigail M. *Afro-American Folk Lore.* New York: Negro Universities Press, 1969. Orig. pub. in 1892 by J. G. Cupples, Boston.

Christian Advocate and Journal. New York, 1833–1865.

Christian Examiner. Boston, 1857–1869.

Christian Register. Boston, 1843–1938.

Christian Renewal. Lewiston NY: Abraham Kuyper Christian Citizen Foundation, 1982–.

Christian Science Monitor. Boston, 1908–.

Christian Spectator. New Haven CT, 1819–1829.

Christian Union. New York: J. B. Ford, 1870–1893.

Christian Watchman & Reflector. Boston, 1851–1866.

Christman, Enos. *One Man's Gold.* New York: Whittlesey House, c.1930.

Chronicle. Ann Arbor MI, 1869–1890.

Chronicle-News. Trinidad CO, 1899–.

Chronicles of Oklahoma. Oklahoma City OK: Oklahoma Hist. Soc, 1921–.

Chronicle-Telegram. Elyria OH, 1919–.

Church, Benjamin. *Entertaining Passages Relating to Philip's War Which Began in the Month of June, 1675.* Boston: Printed by B. Green, 1716.

———. *The History of King Philip's War.* Boston: J. K. Wiggin, 1865. Repr. of the 1716 ed. pub. by B. Green, Boston under the title *Entertaining Passages Relating to Philip's War.*

Church, Ella Rodman. *The Home Garden.* New York: D. Appleton, 1881.

Church, Ruth Ellen. *The Burger Cook Book.* Chicago: Rand McNally, 1961.

Church, William Conant. *Ulysses S. Grant.* New York: G. P. Putnam's Sons, 1897.

Churchill, Samuel. *Don't Call Me Ma.* Garden City NY: Doubleday, 1977.

Churchill, Winston. *Coniston.* New York: Macmillan, 1906.

———. *The Crisis.* New York: Macmillan, 1901.

———. *The Crossing.* New York: Macmillan, 1904.

———. *The Dwelling-Place of Light.* New York: Macmillan, 1917.

Churchman. Hartford CT, 1867–1985.

Chute, Carolyn. *Letourneau's Used Auto Parts.* New York: Harper & Row, 1989. Repr. of 1988 ed. pub. by Ticknor & Fields.

Ciardi, John. *A Browser's Dictionary and Native's Guide to the Unknown American Language.* New York: Harper & Row, c.1980.

Cicourel, Aaron V. et al. *Language Use and School Performance.* New York: Academic Press, c.1974.

Cincinnati Chamber of Commerce. *Annual Report of the Cincinnati Chamber of Commerce and Merchants' Exchange.* Cincinnati OH, 1866–1914?

Cincinnati Commercial. Cincinnati OH, 1843–1883.

Cincinnati Daily Gazette. Cincinnati OH, 1855–1883.

Cincinnati Enquirer. Cincinnati OH, 1849–1852; 1872–.

Cincinnati Lancet and Clinic. Cincinnati OH, 1878–1904.

Cincinnati Literary Gazette. Cincinnati OH: J. P. Foote, 1824–1825.

Cincinnati Mirror and Western Gazette of Literature and Science. Cincinnati OH, 1833?–1835.

Cincinnati Museum Association. *Annual Report.* Cincinnati OH, 1882–1934?

Cincinnati Post. Cincinnati OH, 1993–.

Cincinnatus. Cincinnati OH, 1856–1869.

Circleville Herald. Circleville OH, 1927–.

Cist, Charles. *Cincinnati in 1841.* Cincinnati OH: Printed and Published for the Author, 1841.

———. *The Cincinnati Miscellany.* Cincinnati OH: Caleb Clark, 1845–1846. 2 vols.

———. *Sketches and Statistics of Cincinnati in 1851.* Cincinnati OH: Wm. H. Moore, 1851.

Citizen-Advertiser. Auburn NY, 1931–1975.

Citrus County Chronicle. Inverness FL, 1890–.

City Gazette and Commercial Daily Advertiser. Charleston SC, 1810–1840.

Civil Liberties. New York: American Civil Liberties Union, 1931–.

Claerbaut, David. *Black Jargon in White America.* Grand Rapids MI: Eerdmans, 1972.

Claflin, Mary Bucklin. *Brampton Sketches.* New York: Thomas Y. Crowell, c.1890.

Claiborne, Craig. *A Feast Made for Laughter.* Garden City NY: Doubleday, 1982.

Claiborne, John Francis Hamtramck. *Life and Correspondence of John A. Quitman.* New York: Harper & Bros., 1860. 2 vols.

———. *Life and Times of Gen. Sam Dale, the Mississippi Partisan.* New York: Harper & Bros., 1860.

Clapin, Sylva. *A New Dictionary of Americanisms.* New York: Louis Weiss, 1902?

Clappe, Louise Amelia Knapp Smith. *The Shirley Letters from California Mines in 1851–52.* San Francisco: Thomas C. Russell, 1922. Orig. pub. in 1854–1855 in *Pioneer Magazine: or, California Monthly Magazine.*

Clark, A. Carman. *From the Orange Mailbox.* Gardiner ME: Harpswell Press, c.1985.

Clark, Billy C. *Song of the River.* New York: Thomas Y. Crowell, c.1957.

Clark, Champ. *My Quarter Century of American Politics.* New York: Harper & Bros., c.1920. 2 vols.

Clark, Charles Badger. *Sun and Saddle Leather.* 10th ed. Boston: Richard G. Badger, c.1922. Orig. pub. in 1915.

Clark, Charles Heber. *Elbow-Room.* Philadelphia: J. M. Stoddart, c.1876.

———. *Out of the Hurly-Burly.* Philadelphia: David McKay, 1874.

Clark, Charlotte Moon. *Baby Rue, Her Adventures and Misadventures, Her Friends and Her Enemies.* Boston: Roberts Bros., 1881.

———. *Baby Rue, Her Adventures and Misadventures, Her Friends and Her Enemies.* London: Sampson Low, Marston, Searle & Rivington, 1881.

Clark, Geoffrey. *Ruffian on the Stair.* Chicago: Story Press, c.1988.

Clark, George Harold and James Fletcher. *Farm Weeds of Canada.* Ottawa: Dominion of Canada, Department of Agriculture, 1906.

Clark, Grace Grosvenor. *The Best in Cookery in the Middle West.* Garden City NY: Doubleday, 1956 [c.1955].

Clark, Laura Downs. "The Original Diary of Mrs. Laura (Downs) Clark, Wakeman, Ohio, from June 21 to October 26, 1818." *Firelands Pioneer.* (1920) New ser. 21.2309–26.

Clark, Sydney A. *All the Best in Hawaii.* New York: Dodd, Mead, 1949.

———. *All the Best in Hawaii.* New York: Dodd, Mead, c.1967.

Clark, Thomas Dionysius. *The Kentucky.* New York: Farrar & Rinehart, c.1942.

———. *Pills, Petticoats and Plows.* Indianapolis IN: Bobbs-Merrill, 1944.

———. *The Rampaging Frontier: Manners and Humors of Pioneer Days in the South and the Middle West.* Indianapolis IN: Bobbs-Merrill, c.1939.

Clark, Walter, ed. *Histories of the Several Regiments and Battalions from North Carolina in the Great War, 1861–'65.* Wendell NC: Broadfoot's Bookmark, 1982 [1901]. 5 vols. Repr. of the 1901 ed. pub. by Nash Brothers Book and Job Printers, Goldsboro NC.

———. *The Papers of Walter Clark.* Ed. by Aubrey Lee Brooks and Hugh Talmage Lefler. Chapel Hill NC: Univ. NC Press, 1948–1950. 2 vols.

Clark, Walter Van Tilburg. *The Ox-Bow Incident.* New York: Press of the Reader's Club, 1942. Orig. pub. in 1940 by Random House.

Clark, William. "Journal of Lieut. Wm. Clark of Gen. Wayne's Campaign, 1794." *Mississippi Valley Historical Review.* (1914) 1.418–44.

Clark, William and Meriwether Lewis. *Original Journals of the Lewis and Clark Expedition.* Ed. by Reuben Gold Thwaites. New York: Dodd, Mead, 1904–1905. 8 vols.

Clarke, John Henrik, comp. *Harlem, U.S.A.* Rev. ed. New York: Collier Books, 1971. Portions appeared in 1963 issues of *Freedomways;* Orig. pub. in 1964, East Berlin.

Clarke, Samuel. *A True, and Faithful Account of the Four Chiefest Plantations of the English in America.* London: Printed for R. Cavel, T. Passenger, W. Cadman, W. Whitwood, T. Sawbridge and W. Birch, 1670.

Clarke County Democrat. Grove Hill AL, 1856–.

Clarkson, Roy B. *Tumult on the Mountains.* Parsons WV: McClain Printing, 1964.

Claudy, Carl Henry. *The Battle of Base-Ball.* New York: Century, 1912 [c.1911].

Clauser, Suzanne. *A Girl Named Sooner.* Garden City NY: Doubleday, c.1972.

Clavers, Mary SEE Kirkland, Caroline Matilda Stansbury

Clavijero, Francisco Javier. *The History of Mexico.* Transl. by Charles Cullen. London: G. G. J. and J. Robinson, 1787. 2 vols.

Clay, Cassius Marcellus. *Writings of Cassius Marcellus Clay.* Ed. by Horace Greeley. New York: Harper & Bros., 1848.

Clay-Clopton, Virginia. *A Belle of the Fifties.* New York: Doubleday, Page, 1904.

Clayson, Edward. *Historical Narratives of Puget Sound.* Seattle WA: Davis Print, c.1911.

Clayton, William. *The Latter-Day Saints' Emigrants' Guide.* St. Louis MO: Republican Steam Power Press, Chambers & Knapp, 1848.

Clearfield Progress. Clearfield PA, 1913–1946.

Cleary, Beverly. *Ralph S. Mouse.* New York: W. Morrow, 1982.

Cleaveland, Agnes Morley. *No Life for a Lady.* Boston: Houghton Mifflin, c.1941.

Cleaveland, Henry William et al. *Village and Farm Cottages.* New York: D. Appleton, 1856.

Cleaver, Eldridge. *Soul on Ice.* New York: McGraw-Hill, 1967 [c.1968].

Clegg, Luther B., Ed., coll. *The Empty Schoolhouse: Memories of One-Room Texas Schools.* College Station TX: TX A&M Univ. Press, 1997.

Cleghorn, Sarah Norcliffe. *The Spinster.* New York: Henry Holt, 1916.

Clemens, Cyril, ed. *Mark Twain.* Boston: Meador Publishing, 1932.

Clemens, Jeremiah. *Tobias Wilson.* Philadelphia: J. B. Lippincott, 1865.

Clemens, Samuel Langhorne. *The Adventures of Huckleberry Finn (Tom Sawyer's Comrade).* London: Chatto & Windus, 1884.

———. *Adventures of Huckleberry Finn (Tom Sawyer's Comrade).* 1st Amer. ed. New York: C. L. Webster, 1885 [c.1884].

———. *The Adventures of Thomas Jefferson Snodgrass.* Chicago: Pascal Covici, 1928. Orig. pub. betw. 1856–1857 in the Keokuk *Saturday Post* and Keokuk *Daily Post.*

———. *The Adventures of Tom Sawyer.* Hartford CT: American Publishing; San Francisco: A. Roman, 1876 [c.1875].

———. *The Celebrated Jumping Frog of Calaveras County and Other Sketches.* New York: C. H. Webb, 1867.

———. *A Connecticut Yankee in King Arthur's Court.* New York: Charles L. Webster, 1889.

———. "In Defence of Harriet Shelley." *North American Review.* (1894) 159.108–20, 240–2, 353–69.

———. *The Innocents Abroad.* Hartford CT: American Publishing, 1869.

———. *Life on the Mississippi.* 1st Amer. ed. Boston: J. R. Osgood, 1883.

———. *Life on the Mississippi.* London: Chatto & Windus, 1883.

———. "The Man That Corrupted Hadleyburg." *Harper's New Monthly Magazine.* (1899) 100.29–54.

———. *Mark Twain-Howells Letters.* Cambridge MA: Belknap Press of Harvard Univ. Press, 1960. 2 vols.

———. *Mark Twain's Letters.* Arranged by Albert Bigelow Paine. New York: Harper & Bros., c.1917. 2 vols.

———. *Mark Twain's Notebook.* Prepared by Albert Bigelow Paine. New York: Harper & Bros., 1935.

———. *Mark Twain to Mrs. Fairbanks.* Ed. by Dixon Wecter. San Marino CA: Huntington Library, 1949.

———. *Old Times on the Mississippi.* Toronto: Belford Press, 1876.

———. *Roughing It.* Hartford CT: American Publishing, 1872.

———. *Sketches of the Sixties by Bret Harte and Mark Twain.* San Francisco: John Howell, 1926.

———. "Some Rambling Notes." *Atlantic Monthly.* (1877) 40.586–92.

———. *The Stolen White Elephant etc.* 1st ed. Boston: James R. Osgood, 1882.

———. *Tom Sawyer Abroad, Tom Sawyer Detective, and Other Stories.* New York: Harpers, 1896.

———. *A Tramp Abroad.* Hartford CT: American Publishing, 1880 [c.1879].

———. *What Is Man? and Other Essays.* New York: Harper & Bros., 1917.

Clemens, Samuel Langhorne and Charles Dudley Warner. *The Gilded Age.* Hartford CT: American Publishing, 1873.

Clements, Edith Schwartz. *Flowers of Coast and Sierra.* New York: H. W. Wilson, 1928.

———. *Flowers of Mountain and Plain.* 3d ed. New York: Hafner, 1955 [c.1926].

Clements, Frederic Edward. *Plant Indicators.* Washington DC: Carnegie Institution of Washington, 1920.

———. *Plant Physiology and Ecology.* New York: H. Holt, 1907.

Clements, John Walter Scott. *Origins of Clements-Spalding and Allied Families of Maryland and Kentucky.* Louisville KY: Standard Press, 1928.

Clements, Wib. F. *What the Sam Hill.* New York: Broadway Publishing, c.1911.

Clemson University. *Entomology at Clemson University.* [v.d.]. Internet.

Clendenin, William Wallace. *A Preliminary Report upon the Florida Parishes of East Louisiana and the Bluff, Prairie and Hill Lands of Southwest Louisiana.* Baton Rouge LA: [s.n.], 1896.

Clendening, Logan. *The Human Body.* Garden City NY: Garden City, 1930.

Cleveland, Ohio. Board of Park Commissioners. *Annual Report.* Cleveland OH, 1893?–1899.

Cleveland Advocate. Cleveland OH, 1914–1923.

Cleveland Gazette. Cleveland OH, 1883–1945.

Cleveland Plain Dealer. Cleveland OH, 1887–.

Cleveland Scene Online. 1998–. Internet.

Clifford, Eth. *Go Fight City Hall.* New York: Simon & Schuster, 1949 [c.1946].

Clift, William. *Tim Bunker Papers.* New York: Orange Judd, c.1868.

Climax Molybdenum Company. *Manual of Safe Practices, Mine Department.* Climax CO: The Company, 1960.

———. *This Is Climax Molybdenum.* Climax CO: The Company, c.1965.

Clinics. Philadelphia, 1942–1946.

Clinton, George. *Public Papers of George Clinton.* Albany NY: State of New York, 1899–1914. 10 vols.

Clinton Daily News. Clinton OK, 2000–.

Clinton Herald. Clinton IA, 1867–.

Closz, Harriet M. Bonebright. *Reminiscences of Newcastle, Iowa, 1848.* Des Moines IA: Historical Department of Iowa, 1921.

Clouse, Loletta. *Wilder.* Nashville TN: Rugledge Hill Press, 1990.

Clute, Willard Nelson. *American Plant Names.* 3d ed. Indianapolis IN: W. N. Clute, 1940.

———. *The Common Names of Plants and Their Meanings.* Indianapolis IN: W. N. Clute, 1931.

———. *A Dictionary of American Plant Names.* Joliet IL: Willard N. Clute, 1923.

———. *The Fern Allies of North America North of Mexico.* New York: F. A. Stokes, 1905.

———. *Our Ferns in Their Haunts.* New York: F. A. Stokes, 1901.

Clyman, James. *James Clyman, American Frontiersman, 1792–1881.* San Francisco: California Historical Society, 1928.

The Coal and Metal Miners' Pocket Book of Principles, Rules, Formulas, and Tables. 10th ed. rev. and enlarged. Scranton PA: International Textbook, 1905.

Coale, Charles B. *The Life and Adventures of Wilburn Waters.* Richmond VA: G. W. Gary, 1878.

Coast Watch. Raleigh NC, 1979–.

Coatsworth, Elizabeth Jane. *Country Neighborhood.* New York: Macmillan, 1944.

———. *Maine Memories.* Brattleboro VT: Stephen Greene Press, 1968.

———. *South Shore Town.* New York: Macmillan, 1948.

Cobb, Ann. *Kinfolks.* Boston: Houghton Mifflin, 1922.

Cobb, Irvin Shrewsbury. *Back Home.* New York: Grosset & Dunlap, c.1912.

———. *Cobb's Anatomy.* New York: George H. Doran, c.1912.

———. *J. Poindexter, Colored.* New York: George H. Doran, c.1922.

———. *Murder Day by Day.* Indianapolis IN: Bobbs-Merrill, c.1933.

———. *Old Judge Priest.* New York: G. H. Doran, 1916.

Cobb, John Nathan. *Pacific Cod Fisheries.* Washington DC: Govt. Printing Office, 1916.

Cobb, Josiah. *A Green Hand's First Cruise, Roughed Out from the Log-Book of Memory, of Twenty-Five Years Standing, Together with a Residence of Five Months in Dartmoor.* Baltimore MD: Cushing & Brother, 1841. 2 vols.

Cobb, Sylvanus. *Autobiography of the First Forty-One Years of the Life of Sylvanus Cobb, D. D.* Boston: Universalist Publishing, 1867.

———. *The Yankee Champion.* Boston: F. Gleason, 1852.

Cobbett, William. *The American Gardener.* Claremont NH: Manufacturing Company, Simeon Ide, Ag't, 1819.

———. *The American Gardener.* London: C. Clement, 1821. Amer. ed. orig. pub. in 1819.

———. *A Year's Residence in the United States of America.* London: Printed for J. M. Cobbett, 1822.

Coblentz, William Weber. *A Physical Study of the Firefly.* Washington DC: Carnegie Institution, 1912.

Coburn, Foster Dwight. *Swine Husbandry.* New, rev. and enlarged ed. New York: Orange Judd, 1898 [c.1897].

Coburn, Wallace David. *Rhymes from a Round-Up Camp.* Rev. ed. New York: G. P. Putnam's Sons, 1903.

Cochiti Lake Sun Times. Cochiti Lake NM, 1997?–2003?

Cocke, Sarah Johnson. *Bypaths in Dixie.* New York: E. P. Dutton, c.1911.

Cockrum, William Monroe. *Pioneer History of Indiana.* Oakland City IN: Press of Oakland City Journal, 1907.

Cody, Louisa Frederici and Courtney Riley Cooper. *Memories of Buffalo Bill.* New York: D. Appleton, 1920 [c.1919].

Cody, William F. *Story of the Wild West.* Chicago: R. S. Peale, c.1888.

Coe, Grover. *Concentrated Organic Medicines.* New York: B. Keith, 1858.

———. *Concentrated Organic Medicines.* 6th ed. New York: B. Keith, 1864 [c.1858].

Coe Cosmos. Cedar Rapids IA: Coe College, 1939–.

Coffin, Charles Carleton. *Caleb Krinkle.* Boston: Lee & Shepard; New York: Lee, Shepard & Dillingham, 1875 [c.1874].

———. *Caleb Krinkle.* Miami FL: Mnemosyne Pub., c.1969. Orig. pub. in 1875 [c.1874] by Lee, Shepard, and Dillingham, New York.

———. *Daughters of the Revolution and Their Times 1769–1776.* Boston: Houghton, Mifflin, 1895.

———. *The Seat of Empire.* Boston: J. R. Osgood, 1871 [c.1870].

Coffin, George S. *Secrets of Winning Poker.* North Hollywood CA: Wilshire Book, 1976 [c.1949].

Coffin, Joshua. *A Sketch of the History of Newbury, Newburyport, and West Newbury from 1635–1845.* Boston: Samuel G. Drake, 1845.

Coffin, Nathaniel Wheeler. *The Forest Arcadia of Northern New York.* Boston: Burnham, 1864.

Coffin, Robert Peter Tristram. *Captain Abby and Captain John.* New York: Macmillan, 1939.

———. *Kennebec, Cradle of Americans.* New York: Farrar & Rinehart, c.1937.

———. *Mainstays of Maine.* New York: Macmillan, 1944.

———. *Yankee Coast.* New York: Macmillan, 1947.

Coffman, George Raleigh, ed. *Studies in Language and Literature.* Chapel Hill NC: Univ. NC Press, 1945.

Cohen, David Steven. *The Ramapo Mountain People.* New Brunswick NJ: Rutgers Univ. Press, c.1974.

Cohn, David Lewis. *God Shakes Creation.* New York: Harper Bros., 1935.

———. *Love in America.* New York: Simon and Schuster, 1943.

Coile, Nancy C. and Mark A. Garland. *Notes on Florida's Endangered and Threatened Plants.* 4th ed. Gainesville FL: FL Dept. of Ag. & Consumer Services, 2003.

Coke, Edward Thomas. *A Subaltern's Furlough.* New York: J. & J. Harper, 1833. 2 vols.

Coker, William Chambers and Henry Roland Totten. *Trees of Southeastern United States, including Virginia, North Carolina, South Carolina, Tennessee, Georgia and Northern Florida.* 3d ed. Chapel Hill NC: Univ. NC Press, 1945.

Colburn's United Service Magazine and Naval and Military Journal. London, 1843–1843.

Colby-Sawyer College. *Virtual Herbarium.* [v.d.]. Internet.

Colcord, Joanna Carver. *Sea Language Comes Ashore.* New York: Cornell Maritime Press, c.1945.

Cole, Arthur Charles. *The Whig Party in the South.* Washington DC: American Historical Association, 1913.

Cole, Arthur Harrison. *The Charming Idioms of New England.* Freeport ME: Bond Wheelwright, 1961.

Cole, George E. *Early Oregon.* Spokane WA: Shaw & Borden, c.1905.

Cole, Harry Ellsworth. *Stagecoach and Tavern Tales of the Old Northwest.* Ed. by Louise Phelps Kellogg. Cleveland OH: Arthur H. Clark, 1930.

Coleman, Geraldine. *African-American Stories of Triumph over Adversity.* Westport CT: Bergin & Garvey, 1996.

Coleman, Lyman. *Guidebook of the Lehigh Valley Railroad and Its Several Branches and Connections.* Philadelphia: J. B. Lippincott, 1873.

Collans, Dev and Stewart Sterling. *I Was a House Detective.* New York: E. P. Dutton, c.1954.

College English. Chicago: Univ. Chicago Press, 1939–.

College Humor. Chicago, 1921–.

College Station, Texas. *City of College Station.* [v.d.]. Internet.

Collegian. Cambridge MA: Hilliard & Brown, 1830. Ed. by students of Harvard College.

Collier's. Springfield OH: Crowell-Collier Pub., 1888–1957.

Collingwood, George Harris and Warren D. Brush. *Knowing Your Trees.* Washington DC: American Forestry Assn., 1947.

Collins, Henry B., Jr. et al. *The Aleutian Islands.* Washington DC: Smithsonian, 1945.

Collins, Henry Hill, ed. *The American Year.* New York: Putnam, 1961.

———. *Complete Field Guide to American Wildlife.* New York: Harper & Bros., c.1959.

Collins, Lewis. *Collins' Historical Sketches of Kentucky.* Rev., enlarged. Covington KY: Collins, 1874. 2 vols.

———. *Historical Sketches of Kentucky.* Maysville KY: L. Collins; Cincinnati OH: J. A. & U. P. James, 1848 [c.1847].

Collins, Margaret Hill and Elinor Collins Aird. *The Collins Family.* Ardmore PA: Collins, 1976–1980. 3 vols.

Collins, R. M. *Chapters from the Unwritten History of the War between the States.* St. Louis MO: Nixon-Jones Printing, 1893.

Collins, S. H. *The Emigrant's Guide to and Description of the United States of America.* 4th ed. Hull: J. Noble, 1830.

Collinson, Peter. *Forget Not Mee & My Garden.* Ed. by Alan W. Armstrong. Philadelphia: American Philosophical Society, 2002.

Colman, Henry. *European Agriculture and Rural Economy.* London: J. Rogerson; Boston: A. D. Phelps, 1844–1848. 2 vols.

———. *European Agriculture and Rural Economy.* 4th ed. with additions. Boston: Phillips, Sampson; New York: C. M. Saxton, 1851. 2 vols.

———. *European Life and Manners.* Boston: C. C. Little and J. Brown, 1850. 2 vols.

Colman's Rural World. St. Louis MO, 1866–1916.

Colonial Kitchens of Washington-Wilkes. Comp. by the Iris Club Washington, GA. 3d ed. Washington GA: [s.n.], 1965.

Colonial Records of the State of Georgia. Atlanta GA: Franklin, 1904–1989. 32 vols.

Colonial Society of Massachusetts, Boston. *Publications.* Boston, 1895–.

Colorado College. *Science Series.* Colorado Springs CO, 1904–1926.

Colorado. Department of Public Instruction. *Biennial Report of the State Superintendent.* Denver CO, 1912–1926.

Colorado Magazine. Denver CO: State Museum, 1923–.

Colorado Quarterly. Boulder CO: Univ. CO, 1952–1980.

Colorado Springs Gazette. Colorado Springs CO, 1887–1946.

Colorado State Univ. Cooperative Extension. Tri River Area. *Dial-a-Garden Message.* 1996–. Internet.

Colored American Magazine. Boston, 1900–1909.

Colt, Miriam Davis. *Went to Kansas.* Watertown NY: Printed by L. Ingalls, 1862.

Colt, S. S., Mrs., ed. *The Tourist's Guide through the Empire State.* Albany NY: Mrs. S. S. Colt, 1871.

Colton, Henry E. *Mountain Scenery.* Raleigh NC: W. L. Pomeroy, 1859.

Colton, Walter. *Deck and Port.* New York: A. S. Barnes, 1852 [c.1850].

———. *Ship and Shore.* New York: A. S. Barnes; Cincinnati OH: H. W. Derby, 1851. Orig. pub. anonymously in 1835 under the title, *Ship and Shore: or, Leaves from the Journal of a Cruise to the Levant.*

———. *Three Years in California.* New York: A. S. Barnes, 1850. Contains author's memoirs from 1846–1849.

Columbia College. *Columbia Chronicle Online.* 1996–. Internet.

Columbia Historical Society. *Records.* Washington DC, 1895–.

Columbia Missourian. Columbia MO, 1923–.

Columbian Centinel. Boston, 1790–1799.

Columbian Centinel. American Federalist. Boston, 1818–1840?

Columbian Centinel. Massachusetts Federalist. Boston, 1799–1818.

Columbian Lady's & Gentleman's Magazine. New York: Israel Post, 1844–1849.

Columbian Magazine. Philadelphia, 1786–1790.

Columbian Mirror and Alexandria Gazette. Alexandria VA, 1792–1800.

Columbian Phenix; Or, Providence Patriot. Providence RI, 1811–1814.

Columbia University. College of Physicians and Surgeons. Department of Pathology. *Studies from the Department of Pathology.* New York, 1899–1927.

Columbus Dispatch. Columbus OH, 1871–.

Columbus Medical Journal. Columbus OH, 1882–1916.

Combe, George. *Notes on the United States of North America during a Phrenological Visit in 1838–9–40.* Philadelphia: Carey & Hart, 1841. 2 vols.

Combs, Josiah Henry. *The Language of Our Southern Highlanders.* 1957? Unpub. paper from Berea College Special Collections & Archives, Berea KY.

Comfort, John W. *The Practice of Medicine on Thomsonian Principles.* Philadelphia: Lindsay & Blakiston, 1859 [c.1850].

Commentary. New York, 1945–.

Comments on Etymology. Rolla MO: Univ. MO-Rolla, 1971–.

Commerce Journal. Commerce TX, 1889–.

Commercial Appeal. Memphis TN, 1889–.

Commercial Fisheries Review. Washington DC: National Marine Fisheries Service, 1939–.

Common Ground. New York, 1940–1949.

Commons, John Rogers, ed. *A Documentary History of American Industrial Society.* Cleveland OH: A. H. Clark, 1910–1911. 10 vols.

Compiler. Gettysburg PA, 1857–1866.

The Complete Book of World Cookery. New York: Crescent Books, 1972.

Compton, Lucius Bunyan. *Life of Lucius B. Compton, the Mountain Evangelist.* Chapel Hill NC: Academic Affairs Library, Univ. NC at Chapel Hill, 1997. Text transcr. from the 1903 ed. pub. by the Office of God's Revivalist, Cincinnati OH.

Comstock, Ferre & Co. *1993 Seed Catalog.* Wethersfield CT: The Company, 1993.

Comstock, John Adams. *Butterflies of California.* Los Angeles: J. A. Comstock, 1927.

Comstock, John Henry. *Report upon Cotton Insects.* Washington DC: Govt. Printing Office, 1879.

———. *The Spider Book.* Garden City NY: Doubleday, Page, 1913.

Comstock, John Henry and Anna Botsford Comstock. *A Manual for the Study of Insects.* Ithaca NY: Comstock, 1895.

Comstock, William. *Betsey Jane Ward, Better Half to Artemus.* New York: James O'Kane, c.1866.

Conant, Roger. *A Field Guide to Reptiles and Amphibians of the United States and Canada East of the 100th Meridian.* Boston: Houghton Mifflin, 1958.

———. *The Reptiles of Ohio.* 2d ed. Notre Dame IN: Univ. Notre Dame Press, c.1951.

Conard, Henry Shoemaker. *How to Know the Mosses and Liverworts.* Rev. ed. Dubuque IA: Wm. C. Brown, c.1956.

A Concise Ulster Dictionary. Oxford: Oxford Univ. Press, 1996.

Concord, Massachusetts. *Concord, Massachusetts Births, Marriages and Deaths, 1635–1850.* Boston: T. Todd, printer, 1895.

Condor. Berkeley CA, 1899–.

Congdon, Herbert Wheaton. *The Covered Bridge.* New York: Alfred A. Knopf, 1946.

Conger, Horace Samuel. *In Search of Gold.* Anchorage AK: Alaska Geographic Society, c.1983.

Congregationalist and Christian World. Boston: Pilgrim Press, 1901–1917.

Congregationalist and Herald of Gospel Liberty. Boston, 1816–1934.

Congressional Globe SEE United States. Congress *Congressional Globe*

Congressional Record SEE United States. Congress *Congressional Record*

Conklin, Enoch. *Picturesque Arizona.* New York: Mining Record Printing Establishment, 1878.

Conkling, Charles. *Steens Mountain in Oregon's High Desert Country.* Caldwell ID: Caxton Printers, 1970.

Connecticut. Agricultural Experiment Station. *Annual Report.* New Haven CT, 1878–1923.

Connecticut. Board of Education. *The Colony of Connecticut and Its Beginning, Growth, and Characteristics.* Washington DC: Govt. Printing Office, 1935.

Connecticut Centinel. Norwich CT, 1802–1807?

Connecticut. Colony. *Public Records of the Colony of Connecticut.* Hartford CT: Case, Lockwood & Brainard, 1850–1890. 15 vols.

Connecticut Courant. Hartford CT, 1791–1914.

Connecticut Courant and Hartford Weekly Intelligencer. Hartford CT, 1774–1778.

Connecticut Courant, and Weekly Intelligencer. Hartford CT, 1778–1791.

Connecticut Historical Society, Hartford. *Collections.* Hartford CT, 1860–1932.

Connecticut. Laws, etc. *Acts and Laws of the State of Connecticut, in America.* New London CT: Printed by Timothy Green, Printer to the Governor and State of Connecticut, 1784.

Connecticut. Laws, Statutes etc. *Public Acts Passed by the General Assembly of the State of Connecticut in the Year 1921.* Hartford CT: Published by the State, 1921.

Connecticut Magazine. Hartford CT, 1899–1908.

Connecticut Post. Bridgeport CT, 1992–.

Connecticut. State Board of Agriculture. *Annual Report of the Secretary.* Hartford CT, 1867–1925.

Conrad, Earl. *Club.* San Francisco: West-Lewis, 1974.

Conroy, Frank. *Stop-Time.* New York: Viking Press, 1967.

Conroy, Pat. *The Prince of Tides.* Boston: Houghton Mifflin, 1986.

Constitution. Atlanta GA, 1868–1869.

Constitution-Tribune. Chillicothe MO, 1928–1930; 1985–.

Consumer Reports. Mount Vernon NY: Consumer Union of U.S., 1936–.

Contemporary Review. London: A. Strahan, 1866–.

Contemporary Southern Short Fiction. Huntsville TX: TX Review Press, Sam Houston State Univ., c.1991.

Continental Monthly. New York: J.R Gilmore, 1862–1864.

Continent, an Illustrated Weekly Magazine. Philadelphia, 1882–1884.

Contra Costa Times. Walnut Creek CA, 1952–.

Contract Bridge Letters. 1982. Unpub. letters in response to queries in the *Contract Bridge Bulletin.*

Contributions to North American Ethnology. Washington DC, 1877–1893.

Conway, Moncure Daniel. *Autobiography, Memories and Experiences of Moncure Daniel Conway.* Boston: Houghton, Mifflin, 1904. 2 vols.

Conwell, Chic. *The Professional Thief.* Chicago: Univ. Chicago Press, 1937.

Cook, George H. *Geology of New Jersey.* Newark NJ: Published by the Board of Managers, 1868.

Cook, James. *A Voyage to the Pacific Ocean.* London: Printed by W. and A. Strahan, for G. Nicol, & T. Cadell, 1784. 3 vols. Vol. 1 and 2 written by Captain James Cook, F. R. S., Vol. 3 by Captain James King, L. L. D. and F. R. S.

Cook, James Henry. *Fifty Years on the Old Frontier.* New Haven CT: Yale Univ. Press, 1923.

Cook, John R. *The Border and the Buffalo.* Topeka KS: Crane, 1907.

Cook, Mary Louise Redd. *Ante Bellum, Southern Life as It Was.* Philadelphia: J. B. Lippincott, 1868.

Cook, Sally SEE Griggs, Ruth

Cook, William H. *The Physio-Medical Dispensatory.* Cincinnati OH: William H. Cook, 1869.

Cook, William Henry. *Letters of a Ticonderoga Farmer.* Ed. by Frederick G. Bascom. Ithaca NY: Cornell Univ. Press, 1946.

Cook County, Illinois. Board of Forest Preserve Commissioners. *Nature Bulletin.* River Forest IL, 1945–1976.

Cook County Herald. Arlington Heights IL, 1868?–1970.

Cook County News-Herald. Grand Marais MN, 1911–.

Cooke, Alistair. *One Man's America.* 1st Amer. ed. New York: Alfred A. Knopf, 1952.

Cooke, Ebenezer. *The Maryland Muse.* 3d ed. corr. and amended. Annapolis MD: Printed by W. Parks, 1731.

———. *The Sot-Weed Factor.* London: Printed and Sold by D. Bragg, 1708.

Cooke, John Esten. *Ellie, or, the Human Comedy.* Richmond VA: A. Morris, 1855.

———. *The Last of the Foresters.* New York: Derby & Jackson; Cincinnati OH: H. W. Derby, 1856.

———. *The Life of Stonewall Jackson.* New York: Charles B. Richardson, 1863.

———, ed. *Surry of Eagle's-Nest, or, the Memoirs of a Staff Officer Serving in Virginia.* New York: Bunce and Huntington, 1866. Ed. from Colonel Surry's mss.

———. *The Virginia Comedians.* New York: D. Appleton, 1883. Orig. pub. in 2 vols. by Appleton in 1854.

Cooke, Rose Terry. *Happy Dodd.* Boston: Ticknor, 1887 [c.1878].

———. *Huckleberries Gathered from New England Hills.* Boston: Houghton, Mifflin, 1891.

———. *Somebody's Neighbors.* Boston: J. R. Osgood, 1883 [c.1881].

———. *Steadfast.* Boston: Ticknor, c.1889.

Cook Inlet Courier. Kenai AK, 1957–.

Cooley, James Ewing. *The American in Egypt.* New York: Appleton, 1842.

Coolidge, Calvin. *The Autobiography of Calvin Coolidge.* 3d trade ed. New York: Cosmopolitan Book, 1929.

Coolidge, Dane. *Fighting Men of the West.* New York: E. P. Dutton, c.1932.

———. *Old California Cowboys.* New York: E. P. Dutton, c.1939.

———. *Texas Cowboys.* New York: E. P. Dutton, c.1937.

Coolidge, Susan SEE Woolsey, Sarah Chauncey

Coombs, Orde, ed. *What We Must See.* New York: Dodd, Mead, c.1971.

Coon, Carleton Stevens. *Adventures and Discoveries.* Englewood Cliffs NJ: Prentice-Hall, 1981.

Coon, Nelson. *The Dictionary of Useful Plants.* Emmaus PA: Rodale Press, 1977. Orig. pub. in 1974.

Cooper, Courtney Ryley. *Under the Big Top.* Boston: Little, Brown, 1923.

Cooper, Ellwood. *Forest Culture and Eucalyptus Trees.* San Francisco: Cubery, 1876.

Cooper, Horton. *North Carolina Mountain Folklore and Miscellany.* Murfreesboro NC: Johnson, 1972.

Cooper, James Fenimore. *The American Democrat.* Cooperstown NY: H. & E. Phinney, 1838.

———. *The Chainbearer.* New York: D. Appleton, 1876.

First Amer. ed. pub. in 1845 by Burgess, Stringer, New York.

———. *The Deerslayer.* New York: Dodd, Mead, 1952. First Amer. ed pub. in 1841 by Lea & Blanchard, Philadelphia.

———. *Home as Found.* 1st ed. Philadelphia: Lea & Blanchard, 1838. 2 vols.

———. *Homeward Bound.* Philadelphia: Carey, Lee & Blanchard, 1838. 2 vols.

———. *The Last of the Mohicans.* London: John Miller, 1826. 3 vols.

———. *The Letters and Journals of James Fenimore Cooper.* Cambridge MA: Belknap Press of Harvard Univ. Press, 1960–1968. 6 vols.

———. *Lionel Lincoln.* New York: Charles Wiley, 1824–1825. 2 vols.

———. *Miles Wallingford.* New ed. New York: James G. Gregory, 1863 [c.1844].

———. *The Monikins.* Philadelphia: Lea & Blanchard, 1841 [c.1835]. 2 vols.

———. *Notions of the Americans.* Philadelphia: Carey, Lea & Carey, 1828. 2 vols.

———. *The Oak-Openings.* New York: Burgess, Stringer, 1848. 2 vols.

———. *The Pathfinder.* Philadelphia: Lea and Blanchard, 1840. 2 vols.

———. *The Pilot.* New York: Charles Wiley, 1823. 2 vols.

———. *The Pilot.* 2d ed. New York: Charles Wiley, 1824. 2 vols.

———. *The Pilot.* Paris: A. & W. Galignani, 1825 [1823]. 3 vols.

———. *The Pioneers.* New York: Charles Wiley, 1823. 2 vols.

———. *The Pioneers.* London: Henry Colburn and Richard Bentley, 1832.

———. *The Prairie.* Philadelphia: Carey, Lea & Carey, 1828. 2 vols.

———. *Recollections of Europe.* London: Richard Bentley, 1837. 2 vols.

———. *The Red Rover.* London: Henry Colburn, 1827. 3 vols.

———. *The Redskins.* New York: Burgess & Stringer, 1846. 2 vols.

———. *The Sea Lions.* New York: Stringer & Townsend, 1849. 2 vols.

———. *The Spy.* New York: Wiley & Halsted, 1821. 2 vols.

———. *The Water-Witch.* London: H. Colburn and R. Bentley, 1830. 3 vols.

Cooper, James Graham and George Suckley. *The Natural History of Washington Territory.* New York: Bailliere Bros., 1859.

Cooper, Lane. *Late Harvest.* Ithaca NY: Cornell Univ. Press, c.1952.

Cooper, Louise Field. *One Dragon Too Many.* New York: Alfred A. Knopf, 1971 [c.1970].

Cooper, Susan Fenimore. *Rural Hours.* New York: George P. Putnam, 1850.

Cooper, Thomas Valentine and Hector T. Fenton. *American Politics (Non-Partisan) from the Beginning to Date.* New and rev. ed. Chicago: C. R. Brodix, 1884.

Cooper Ornithological Club. *Bulletin.* Santa Clara CA, 1899.

Copcutt, Francis. *Edith.* New York: John A. Gray, c.1857.

Cope, Edward A. *Muenscher's Keys to Woody Plants.* Ithaca NY: Comstock, c.2001.

Copeia. Baltimore MD, 1913–1929; 1930–.

Copeland, David Sturges. *History of Clarendon from 1810 to 1888.* Buffalo NY: Courier, 1889.

Copeland, Robert Morris. *Country Life.* 5th ed. rev. Boston: Dinsmoor, 1866.

Copley, John Singleton and Henry Pelham. *Letters and Papers of John Singleton Copley and Henry Pelham, 1739–1776.* Boston: Massachusetts Historical Society, 1914.

Coplin, William Michael Late and David Bevan. *A Manual of Practical Hygiene.* Philadelphia: P. Blakiston, 1893.

Corbin Times-Tribune. Corbin KY, 1971–1981.

Corcoran, Dennis. *Pickings from the Portfolio of the Reporter of the New Orleans Picayune.* Philadelphia: Carey and Hart, 1846.

Corey, Deloraine Pendre. *The History of Malden, Massachusetts, 1633–1785.* Malden MA: Published by the Author, 1899.

Corle, Edwin. *Desert Country.* New York: Duell, Sloan & Pearce, 1941.

———. *The Gila.* New York: Rinehart, 1951.

Corliss, Carleton J. *Main Line of Mid-America.* New York: Creative Age Press, c.1950.

Cormack, Beale. *Aaron Slick from Punkin Crick.* Boston: Walter H. Baker, 1919.

Cornelius, Mary Hooker. *The Young Housekeeper's Friend.*

Boston: Charles Tappan; New York: Saxton & Huntington, 1846 [c.1845].

Cornell University. *Cornell Plantations.* [v.d.]. Internet.

———. *News Service.* 1994–. Internet.

Cornell University. Agricultural Experiment Station. *Bulletin.* Ithaca NY, 1891–1978.

Cornell University. Laboratory of Ornithology. *Birds of North America.* [v.d.]. Internet.

Cornhill Magazine. London: J. Murray, 1860–.

Cornwell, Patricia Daniels. *The Body Farm.* New York: Charles Scribner's Sons, c.1994.

Coronet. Chicago, 1936–1961.

Coronet Memories. London: F. Tennyson Neely, 1899. Written by various members of the cruises.

Corpus Christi Caller-Times. Corpus Christi TX, 1883–.

Corpus Christi Times. Corpus Christi TX, 1911–1987.

Correll, Donovan Stewart. *Native Orchids of North America North of Mexico.* Waltham MA: Chronica Botanica, 1950.

Correll, Donovan Stewart and Marshall Conring Johnston. *Manual of the Vascular Plants of Texas.* Renner TX: Texas Research Foundation, 1970.

Corsair. New York, 1839–1840.

Cory, David Magie. *Billy Bunny and Uncle Bull Frog.* [s.l.]: Project Gutenberg, 2002. Text transcr. from the c.1920 ed. pub. by Cupples & Leon, New York.

Coshocton Age. Coshocton OH, 1861–1885.

Coshocton Daily Age. Coshocton OH, 1898–1914.

Coshocton Democrat. Coshocton OH, 1861–1901.

Coshocton Morning Tribune. Coshocton OH, 1911–1917.

Coshocton Tribune. Coshocton OH, 1930–1986.

Coshocton Tribune and Times-Age. Coshocton OH, 1917–1929.

Coshocton Weekly Times. Coshocton OH, 1906–1914.

Cosmopolitan. New York, 1886–1925; 1952–.

Costello, David Francis. *The Desert World.* New York: Crowell, 1972.

Cothran, James R. *Gardens and Historic Plants of the Antebellum South.* Columbia SC: Univ. SC Press, c.2003.

Cotting, John Ruggles. *An Essay on the Soils and Available Manures of the State of Georgia.* Milledgeville GA: Park & Rogers, 1843.

Cotton Farming. [s.l.]: Vance, 1999–.

Cotton Stealing. Chicago: John R. Walsh, 1866 [c.1865].

Cottrell, William Frederick. *The Railroader.* Stanford CA: Stanford Univ. Press, c.1940.

Couch, William Terry, ed. *Culture in the South.* Chapel Hill NC: Univ. NC Press, 1934.

Coues, Elliott. *Birds of the Northwest.* Washington DC: Govt. Printing Office, 1874.

———. *Field Ornithology.* Salem MA: Naturalists' Agency, 1874.

———. *Key to North American Birds.* Salem MA: Naturalists' Agency; New York: Dodd and Mead, 1872.

———. *Key to North American Birds.* 2d ed. Boston: Estes and Lauriat, 1884.

———. *Key to North American Birds.* 3d ed. Boston: Estes and Lauriat, 1887.

———. *Key to North American Birds.* 5th ed. entirely rev. Boston: Dana Estes, 1903. 2 vols.

Coulter, Ellis Morton. *Thomas Spalding of Sapelo.* University LA: LA State Univ. Press, 1940.

Coulter, John Merle. *Botany of Western Texas.* Washington DC: Govt. Printing Office, 1891–1894. 3 vols.

Council Bluffs Nonpareil. Council Bluffs IA, 1920–1976.

Counsel for Emigrants and Interesting Information from Numerous Sources. Aberdeen: John Mathison, 1834.

Country. Greendale WI, 1987–.

Country Gentleman. Philadelphia: Curtis, 1853–1955.

Country Life. New York, 1901–1942.

County Record. Denton MD, 1952?–.

Couplan, François. *The Encyclopedia of Edible Plants of North America.* New Canaan CT: Keats, 1998.

Courier. Connellsville PA, 1888–1906.

Courier-Freeman. Potsdam NY, 1851–.

Courier-Gazette. Rockland ME, 1846–.

Courier Hub. Stoughton WI, 1979–.

Courier-Journal. Louisville KY, 1868–.

Courtenay, Booth and James Hall Zimmerman. *Wild Flowers and Weeds.* New York: Van Nostrand Reinhold, 1972.

Covell, Charles V., Jr. *A Field Guide to the Moths of Eastern North America.* Boston: Houghton Mifflin, 1984.

Covey, Donica. *Callye's Justice.* Macon GA: Samhain Publishing, 2008.

Coville, Frederick Vernon. *Botany of the Death Valley Expedition.* Washington DC: Govt. Printing Office, 1893.

———. *Forest Growth and Sheep Grazing in the Cascade Mountains in Oregon.* Washington DC: Govt. Printing Office, 1898.

Covington, Vicki. *Night Ride Home.* New York: Simon & Schuster, c.1992.
Cowan, Bud. *Range Rider.* Garden City NY: Doubleday, Doran, 1930.
Cowan, Sam Kinkade. *Sergeant York and His People.* New York: Grosset & Dunlap, 1922.
Cowboy Stories. New York, 1925–1936?
Cowell, Emilie Marguerite. *The Cowells in America.* London: Oxford Univ. Press, H. Milford, 1934.
Cowell, Joe. *Thirty Years Passed among the Players in England and America.* New York: Harper, 1844.
Cowgill, Elias Branson. *Irrigation Practice on the Great Plains.* Washington DC: Govt. Printing Office, 1897.
Cowing, Kemper F. and Courtney R. Cooper, comp., ed. *"Dear Folks at Home".* Boston: Houghton Mifflin, c.1919.
Cox, Joseph Frank and Lyman Edson Jackson. *Field Crops and Land Use.* New York: John Wiley; London: Chapman & Hall, 1942.
Cox, Ross. *Adventures on the Columbia River.* London: Henry Colburn & Richard Bentley, 1831. 2 vols.
Cox, Samuel Sullivan. *A Buckeye Abroad.* New York: G. P. Putnam, 1852.
Cox, William T. *Fearsome Creatures of the Lumberwoods.* Washington DC: Judd & Detweiler, 1910.
Cox, William Wallace. *History of Seward County, Nebraska.* Lincoln NE: State Journal, 1888.
Coxe, Daniel. *A Description of the English Province of Carolana by Spaniards Called Florida, and by the French La Louisiane.* London: O. Payne, 1741.
Coxe, William. *A View of the Cultivation of Fruit Trees.* Philadelphia: M. Carey and Son, 1817.
Cozzens, Frederick Swartwout. *Prismatics.* New York: D. Appleton, c.1853.
———. *The Sayings of Dr. Bushwhacker, and Other Learned Men.* New York: A. Simpson, 1867.
———. *The Sparrowgrass Papers.* New York: Derby & Jackson, 1856.
Cozzens, Samuel Woodworth. *Crossing the Quicksands.* Boston: Lee and Shepard, 1877.
———. *The Marvellous Country.* Boston: Lee and Shepard, 1876. Orig. pub. in 1873 by Shephard and Gill, Boston.
Craddock, Charles Egbert SEE Murfree, Mary Noailles
Craft, William and Ellen Craft. *Running a Thousand Miles for Freedom.* Athens GA: Univ. GA Press, 1999 [1860].
Craig, Lillian K. *The Singing Hills.* New York: Thomas Y. Crowell, 1951.
Craighead, Frank Cooper. *The Trees of South Florida.* Coral Gables FL: Univ. Miami Press, 1971.
Craighead, John Johnson. *A Field Guide to Rocky Mountain Wild Flowers.* Boston: Houghton, Mifflin, 1963.
Craigie, Sir William Alexander and James R. Hulbert, eds. *A Dictionary of American English on Historical Principles.* Chicago: Univ. Chicago Press, 1938–1944. 4 vols.
Cramer's Pittsburgh Almanack. Pittsburgh PA, 1800?–1820?
Crane, Charles Edward. *Let Me Show You Vermont.* New York: Alfred A Knopf, 1937.
Crane, Hart. *The Letters, 1916–1932.* New York: Hermitage House, c.1952.
Crane, J. T. *Arts of Intoxication.* New York: Carlton & Lanahan, 1871 [c.1870].
Crane, Milton, ed. *Sins of New York.* New York: Boni & Gaer, c.1947.
Crane, Stephen. *Maggie, a Girl of the Streets.* Gainesville FL: Scholars' Facsimiles & Reprints, 1966 [1893]. Facsimile of the 1st ed. of 1893, privately printed, New York, with an intro. by Joseph Katz.
———. *Maggie, a Girl of the Streets.* New York: D. Appleton, 1896.
———. *The Red Badge of Courage.* Columbus OH: Charles E. Merrill, 1969. Orig. pub. in 1895.
Crater Lake Natural History Association. *Nature Notes.* Crater Lake National Park OR, 1928–.
Crawford, James Hunter. *Summer Days for Winter Evenings.* London: John Macqueen, 1897.
Crawford, J. Marshall. *Mosby and His Men.* New York: G. W. Carleton, 1867.
Crawford, Lucy. *The History of the White Mountains.* Portland ME: Printed by F. A. and A. F. Gerrish, 1846.
Crawford, Stanley. *Mayordomo.* Albuquerque NM: Univ. NM Press, c.1988.
Crawford, Thomas Edgar. *The West of the Texas Kid, 1881–1910.* Ed. by Jeff C. Dykes. Norman OK: Univ. OK Press, c.1962. Ed. from the ms. dictated by the author in 1938, now pub. for the first time.
Cray, Ed. *Ramblin' Man.* New York: W. W. Norton, c.2004.
Crayon, Geoffrey SEE Irving, Washington
Creative Loafing. Atlanta GA, 1972–.
Creecy, James R. *Scenes in the South, and Other Miscellaneous Pieces.* Washington DC: Thomas McGill, Printer, 1860 [c.1859].
Creevey, Caroline Alathea Stickney. *Flowers of Field, Hill and Swamp.* New York: Harper & Bros., 1897.
Cresswell, Nicholas. *The Journal of Nicholas Cresswell, 1744–1777.* New York: L. MacVeagh, Dial Press, 1924.
Crèvecoeur, Michel Guillaume St. Jean de. *Letters from an American Farmer.* London: Printed for T. Davies, 1782.
———. *Sketches of Eighteenth Century America.* New Haven CT: Yale Univ. Press, 1925.
———. *Voyage dans la Haute Pensylvanie et dans l'État de New-York.* Paris: Imprimerie de Crapelet; Maradan, 1801. 3 vols.
Crews, Harry. *A Childhood, the Biography of a Place.* New York: Harper & Row, c.1978.
———. *The Knockout Artist.* New York: Harper & Row, c.1988.
Crippen, William G. *Green Peas.* New York: Livermore and Rudd; Cincinnati OH: Moore, Wilstach, Keys & Overend, c.1856.
Crisis, a Record of the Darker Races. New York, 1910–.
Crismore, Mary Thomas. *The Crismore Family: a Family History.* Indianapolis IN: [s.n.], 1968.
Criswell, Elijah Harry. *Lewis and Clark.* Columbia MO: Univ. MO, 1940.
Criswell, Elijah Harry and Mrs. Criswell. *Responses to PADS 20.* 1960. Unpub. material in response to a questionnaire.
Critic. Washington DC, 1868–1872.
Critic. New York, 1881–1906.
Crocker, Betty, [pseud.]. *Betty Crocker's Cookbook.* New and rev. ed. New York: Golden Press, c.1978.
———, [pseud.]. *Picture Cook Book.* 2d ed. rev. and enlarged. New York: McGraw-Hill, c.1956.
Crockett, David. *An Account of Col. Crockett's Tour to the North and Down East.* Philadelphia: E. L. Carey and A. Hart; Baltimore MD: Carey, Hart, 1835.
———. *Life of David Crockett.* Philadelphia: John E. Potter, c.1865.
———. *The Life of Martin Van Buren.* Philadelphia: R. Wright, 1835.
———. *A Narrative of the Life of David Crockett.* Amer. ed. Philadelphia: E. L. Carey and A. Hart, 1834. Repr. in 1834 by J. Limbird, London.
The Crockett Almanacks. Ed. by Franklin J. Meine. Chicago: Caxton Club, 1955.
Crockett's Yaller Flower Almanac. New York: Elton, 1835.
Croly, Herbert Daniel. *Marcus Alonzo Hanna.* New York: Macmillan, c.1912.
Cronin, Archibald Joseph. *The Stars Look Down.* London: Victor Gollancz, 1935.
Cronise, Titus Fey. *The Natural Wealth of California.* San Francisco: H. H. Bancroft, 1868.
Cronkite, Kathy. *On the Edge of the Spotlight: Celebrities' Children Speak Out about Their Lives.* New York: William Morrow, 1981.
Croom, Hardy Bryan. *A Catalogue of Plants, Native or Naturalized, in the Vicinity of New Bern, North Carolina.* New York: G. P. Scott, 1837.
Cross, David Wallace. *Fifty Years with the Gun and Rod.* Cleveland OH: Short & Forman Printers, 1880.
Cross, Frank Bernard. *Handbook of Fishes of Kansas.* Lawrence KS: Museum of Natural History, Univ. KS, 1967.
Cross, Lucy Rogers Hill. *History of Northfield New Hampshire 1780–1905.* Concord NH: Rumford, 1905. 2 vols.
Crow, Carl. *The Great American Customer.* New York: Harper & Bros., c.1943.
Crowe, James Richard. *Pat Crowe, Aviator.* New York: N. L. Brown, 1919.
Crowell, Benedict. *America's Munitions 1917–1918.* Washington DC: Govt. Printing Office, 1919.
Crowen, T. J., Mrs. *The American Lady's System of Cookery.* Auburn NY?: Derby and Miller, 1852 [c.1847].
Crowfield, Christopher SEE Stowe, Harriet Beecher
Crowninshield, Clara. *Diary: a European Tour with Longfellow, 1835–1836.* Ed. by Andrew Hilen. Seattle WA: Univ. WA Press, 1956.
Croy, Homer. *Corn Country.* New York: Duell, Sloan & Pearce, 1947.
———. *R. F. D. No. 3.* New York: Harper & Bros., c.1924.
Cruikshank, Moses. *The Life I've Been Living.* Fairbanks AK: Alaska and Polar Regions Dept., Elmer Rasmuson Library, Univ. AK, Fairbanks, 1986.
Crum, Howard Alvin. *A Focus on Peatlands and Peat Mosses.* Ann Arbor MI: Univ. MI Press, c.1988.
Crum, Mason. *Gullah.* Durham NC: Duke Univ. Press, 1940.
Crump, Paul. *Burn, Killer, Burn.* Chicago: Johnson, c.1962.
Crumpton, Hezekiah John and W. B. Crumpton. *The Adventures of Two Alabama Boys.* Montgomery AL: Paragon Press, 1912.
Crumrine, Boyd, ed. *Centennial Celebration of the Incorporation of the Borough of Washington, Pa., in Its Old Home Week of October 2–8, 1910.* Lancaster PA: New Era Printing, 1912.
Cuisine, the Magazine of Fine Food and Creative Living. Santa Barbara CA, 1972–.
La Cuisine Creole SEE Hearn, Lafcadio *La Cuisine Creole*
Culbertson, Anne Virginia. *Banjo Talks.* Indianapolis IN: Bobbs-Merrill, c.1905.
Culbertson, Ely et al., eds. *Culbertson's Card Games.* New York: Greystone Press, c.1952.
Culbertson, Manie. *May I Speak?* Gretna LA: Pelican, 1972.
Culbreth, David Marvel Reynolds. *A Manual of Materia Medica and Pharmacology.* 4th ed. enlarged and thoroughly rev. Philadelphia: Lea, 1906.
Culinary Arts Institute. *The New England Cook Book.* Chicago: [s.n.], 1956.
Culinary Nuggets for Housekeepers. Buffalo NY: Ladies of Lafayette St. Presbyterian Church, 1889.
Cullman Banner. Cullman AL, 1937–1951.
Cullman Democrat. Cullman AL, 1900–1961.
Culp, Daniel Wallace, ed. *Twentieth Century Negro Literature or a Cyclopedia of Thought on the Vital Topics Relating to the American Negro.* Toronto: J. L. Nichols, c.1902.
Culpepper, Marilyn Mayer. *All Things Altered.* Jefferson NC: McFarland, c.2002.
Cultivator. Albany NY: L. Tucker, 1834–1865.
Cultivator & Country Gentleman. Albany NY, 1866–1897.
Culture, Medicine and Psychiatry. Boston: D. Reidel, 1977–.
Cumberland Times-News. Cumberland MD, 1988–.
Cuming, Fortescue. *Sketches of a Tour to the Western Country.* Pittsburgh PA: Cramer, Spear and Eichbaum, 1810.
Cumings, Samuel. *The Western Navigator.* Philadelphia: E. Littell, 1822.
Cumming, A. M. and Allan Dunn. *California for the Sportsman.* San Francisco: Southern Pacific, 1911.
Cummings, Edward Estlin. *Selected Letters of E. E. Cummings.* New York: Harcourt, Brace & World, 1969.
Cummings, Kevin S. and Christine A. Mayer. *Field Guide to Freshwater Mussels of the Midwest.* Champaign IL: Illinois Natural History Survey, c.1992.
Cummings, Richard Osborn. *The American and His Food.* Rev. ed. Chicago: Univ. Chicago Press, 1941.
Cummins, Maria Susanna. *The Lamplighter.* Boston: John P. Jewett, 1854.
Cummins, Ralph. *Sky-High Corral.* New York: Garden City Pub., 1923.
Cunningham, Eugene. *Spiderweb Trail.* New York: Grosset & Dunlap, c.1940.
Cunningham, Irma Aloyce Ewing. *A Syntactic Analysis of Sea Island Creole ("Gullah").* Ann Arbor MI: Univ. MI diss., 1971.
Cuoq, Jean André. *Lexique de la Langue Algonquine.* Montréal: J. Chapleau & Fils, 1886.
Curran, Marvin et al. *Murrieta.* Charleston SC: Arcadia, 2006.
Current. Chicago: Edgar L. Wakeman, 1883–1888.
Current Biography. New York, 1940–.
Current Literature. New York, 1888–1912.
Current Opinion. New York, 1913–1925.
Current Slang. Vermillion SD: Univ. SD, Department of English, 1966–.
Curson, Julie P. *A Guide's Guide to Philadelphia.* Philadelphia: Curson House, c.1986.
Curtin, Leonora Scott Muse. *By the Prophet of the Earth.* Santa Fe NM: San Vicente Foundation, 1949.
———. *Healing Herbs of the Upper Río Grande.* Santa Fé NM: Laboratory of Anthropology, c.1947.
———. *Healing Herbs of the Upper Río Grande.* New York: Arno Press, 1976. Repr. of the 1947 ed. pub. by The Laboratory of Anthropology, Santa Fé NM.
Curtis, Edward S. *The North American Indian.* Norwood MA: Plimpton Press, 1907–1930. 20 vols.
Curtis, George William. *Lotus-Eating.* New York: Harper & Bros., 1852.
———. *The Potiphar Papers.* New York: G. P. Putnam, 1853.
Curtis, Moses Ashley. *Botany: Containing a Catalogue of the Indigenous and Naturalized Plants of the State.* Raleigh NC: Printed at N.C. Institution for the Deaf and Dumb and Blind, 1867. North Carolina. Geological and Natural History Survey. *Part 3 Botany.*
———. *A Catalogue of the Plants of the State.* Raleigh NC: W. W. Holden, 1860. North Carolina. Geological and Natural History Survey. *Part 3 Botany.*

Curtis's Botanical Magazine. London: Reeve Bros., 1845–1983.

Curtiss, Daniel S. *Western Portraiture.* New York: J. H. Colton, 1852 [c.1851].

Cushing, Caleb. *The History and Present State of the Town of Newburyport.* Newburyport MA: E. W. Allen, 1826.

Cushing, Marshall. *Story of Our Post Office.* Boston: A. M. Thayer, 1893 [c.1892].

Cushman, Horatio Bardwell. *History of the Choctaw, Chickasaw and Natchez Indians.* Greenville TX: Headlight Printing House, 1899.

———. *History of the Choctaw, Chickasaw and Natchez Indians.* Stillwater OK: Redlands Press, c.1962. Repr. of the 1899 ed.

Cushman, Rebecca. *Swing Your Mountain Gal.* Boston: Houghton Mifflin, 1934 [c.1933].

Custer, Elizabeth Bacon. *Boots and Saddles.* New York: Harper & Bros., 1885.

———. *Following the Guidon.* New York: Harper & Bros., 1890.

———. *Tenting on the Plains.* New York: Charles L. Webster, 1887.

Cutler, Jane. *Spaceman.* New York: Dutton Children's Books, c.1997.

Cutler, Jervis. *A Topographical Description of the State of Ohio, Indiana Territory, and Louisiana.* Boston: Charles Williams, 1812. Photographic repr. of the first ed., 1971 by Arno Press.

Cutler, Julia Perkins. *Life and Times of Ephraim Cutler.* Cincinnati OH: R. Clarke, 1890.

Cutler, Lizzie Petit. *Household Mysteries.* New York: D. Appleton, 1856.

Cutler, Manasseh. *An Account of Some of the Vegetable Productions Naturally Growing in This Part of America, Botanically Arranged.* Cincinnati OH: J. U. & C. G. Lloyd, 1903. Repr. of the orig.article in *Memoirs of the American Academy of Arts and Sciences,* 1785, vol. 1.

Cutler, William Parker and Julia Perkins Cutler. *Life, Journals and Correspondence of Rev. Manasseh Cutler LL. D.* Cincinnati OH: R. Clarke, 1888. 2 vols.

Cutting, George Rugg. *Student Life at Amherst College.* Amherst MA: Hatch & Williams, 1871.

Cuvier, Georges. *The Animal Kingdom.* Transl. from the French & abridged by H. M'Murtrie. New York: G. & C. & H. Carvill, 1832.

Cuvier, Georges and M. A. Valenciennes. *Histoire Naturelle des Poissons.* Paris: F. G. Levrault, 1826–1849. 22 vols.

Cymon SEE Somerby, Frederic Thomas

Cynthiana Democrat. Cynthiana KY, 1868–.

Cypress, J., Jr. SEE Hawes, William Post

DA SEE Mathews, Mitford McLeod *A Dictionary of Americanisms on Historical Principles*

Dabney, Joseph Earl. *Mountain Spirits.* New York: Charles Scribner's Sons, 1974.

Dade County Sentinel. Trenton GA, 1965–.

Dadswell, Jack E. *Hey There, Sucker!* Boston: B. Humphries, c.1946.

DAE SEE Craigie, Sir William Alexander and James R. Hulbert *A Dictionary of American English on Historical Principles*

Daheim, Mary. *Wed and Buried.* New York: Avon Books, c.1998.

Dahl, Thomas E. *South Carolina's Wetlands: Status and Trends, 1982–1989.* Washington DC: U.S. Department of the Interior. Fish and Wildlife Service, 1999.

Dahlberg, Edward. *From Flushing to Calvary.* New York: Harcourt, Brace, 1932.

Dahlgren, Madeleine Vinton. *South-Mountain Magic.* Boston: James R. Osgood, 1882.

Daigle, Jules O. *A Dictionary of the Cajun Language.* Ann Arbor MI: Edwards Bros., c.1984.

Daily Advertiser. Lafayette LA, 2001–.

Daily Advertiser. New York, 1787–1806.

Daily Advocate. Victoria TX, 1897–1927?

Daily Alton Telegraph. Alton IL, 1852–1855.

Daily American. Nashville TN, 1876–1894.

Daily Breeze. Torrance CA, 1974–.

Daily Capital News. Jefferson City MO, 1915?–.

Daily Chronicle. Centralia WA, 1941–1990.

Daily Columbus Enquirer. Columbus GA, 1858–1873.

Daily Constitution. Atlanta GA, 1876–1881.

Daily Courier. Connellsville PA, 1902–.

Daily Democrat. Greenville MS, 1896–1917.

Daily Democrat. Sedalia MO, 1871–1873.

Daily Dispatch. Richmond VA, 1850–1884.

Daily Era. Bradford PA, 1886–1887.

Daily Evening Bulletin. San Francisco, 1855–1895.

Daily Evening Transcript SEE ALSO *Boston Evening Transcript*

Daily Evening Transcript. Boston, 1830–1853.

Daily Express. San Antonio TX, 1891–1911.

Daily Forum. Maryville MO, 1970–1989.

Daily Free Democrat. Milwaukee WI, 1850–1856.

Daily Free Press. Eau Claire WI, 1873–1901.

Daily Gazette. Davenport IA, 1869–1873.

Daily Gazette. Fort Wayne IN, 1884–1885.

Daily Gazette and Bulletin. Williamsport PA, 1869–1909.

Daily Hampshire Gazette. Northampton MA, 1890–.

Daily Herald. Arlington Heights IL, 1977–.

Daily Herald. Biloxi MS, 1910–1985.

Daily Herald. Delphos OH, 1894–.

Daily Herald. Middletown NY, 1925–1926.

Daily Herald. Provo UT, 1921?–.

Daily Huronite. Huron SD, 1886–1920.

Daily Huronite and Plainsman. Huron SD, 1944–1946.

Daily Independent. Monessen PA, 1902–1921; 1956–1960.

Daily Independent. Monroe WI, 1890?–.

Daily Independent. Murphysboro IL, 1891–1949.

Daily Index. Petersburg VA, 1865.

Daily Intelligencer. Doylestown PA, 1955–1988.

Daily Inter Lake. Kalispell MT, 1908–.

Daily Inter Ocean. Chicago, 1879–1902.

Daily Iowa Capital. Des Moines IA, 1883–1901.

Daily Iowa State Press. Iowa City IA, 1890?–1904.

Daily Journal. Commerce TX, 1914–.

Daily Journal. Fergus Falls MN, 1972–.

Daily Kennebec Journal. Augusta ME, 1870–1975.

Daily Messenger. Canandaigua NY, 1918–.

Daily Miner. Butte MT, 1879–1885.

Daily Mining Gazette. Houghton MI, 1899–.

Daily Mirror. New York, 1924–1972.

Daily Missouri Republican. St. Louis MO, 1837–1869.

Daily National Intelligencer. Washington DC, 1813–1869.

Daily Nebraska Press. Nebraska City NE, 1868–1894.

Daily Nebraska State Journal. Lincoln NE, 1878–1892.

Daily Nevada State Journal. Reno NV, 1874–1907.

Daily News. Frederick MD, 1883–1890.

Daily News. Huntingdon PA, 1922–.

Daily News. Port Clinton-Oak Harbor OH, 1956–1969.

Daily News. Red Bluff CA, 1885–1971?

The Daily News Cook Book. Chicago: Chicago Daily News, c.1896.

Daily News of Los Angeles. Los Angeles, 1986–.

Daily Northwestern. Oshkosh WI, 1868–1875; 1885–1933.

Daily Oklahoman. Oklahoma City OK, 1894–.

Daily Palladium. New Haven CT, 1859–1863.

Daily Pennant. St. Louis MO, 1839–1840?

Daily People. New York, 1900–1914.

Daily Picayune. New Orleans LA, 1836–1914.

Daily Plainsman. Huron SD, 2002–.

Daily Post-Athenian. Athens TN, 1931–.

Daily Press. Nashville TN, 1863–1864.

Daily Progress. Charlottesville VA, 1892–.

Daily Register. Harrisburg IL, 1915–.

Daily Reporter. Dover OH, 1903–1968.

Daily Republican. Decatur IL, 1872–1875.

Daily Republican Eagle. Red Wing MN, 1940–1971?

Daily Review. Decatur IL, 1886–1917.

Daily Review. Hayward CA, 1949–.

Daily Richmond Examiner. Richmond VA, 1861–1867.

Daily Rocky Mountain News. Denver CO, 1860–1879.

Daily Sentinel. Sitka AK, 1961–2006.

Daily Sentinel-Tribune. Bowling Green OH, 1906–.

Daily Times. Farmington NM, 1986–.

Daily Times. Portsmouth OH, 1894–1903.

Daily Times. Salisbury MD, 1964–.

Daily Times-News. Burlington NC, 1932–1989.

Daily Tribune. Wisconsin Rapids WI, 1966–.

Daily True American. Trenton NJ, 1849–1908.

Daily Utah Chronicle. Salt Lake City UT, 1946?–.

Daily Wisconsin Patriot. Madison WI, 1854–1859.

Daily Zanesville Courier. Zanesville OH, 1852–1862.

Dakin, Robert Ford. *The Dialect Vocabulary of the Ohio River Valley.* Ann Arbor MI: Univ. MI diss., 1966. 3 vols.

Dale, Edward Everett. *Cow Country.* Norman OK: Univ. OK Press, 1942.

Dale, Edward Everett and Jesse Lee Rader, eds. *Readings in Oklahoma History.* Evanston IL: Row, Peterson, c.1930.

Dale, Harrison Clifford, ed. *The Ashley-Smith Explorations and the Discovery of a Central Route to the Pacific, 1822–1829, with the Original Journals.* Cleveland OH: Arthur H. Clark, 1918.

Dall, William Healey. *Alaska and Its Resources.* Boston: Lee & Shepard, 1870.

Dallas, George Mifflin. *Letters from London.* London: Richard Bentley, 1870. 2 vols.

Dallas Morning News. Dallas TX, 1885–.

Dallas Observer. Dallas TX, 1980–.

Dallas Times Herald. Dallas TX, 1954–1991.

Dallimore, William and A. Bruce Jackson. *A Handbook of Coniferae Including Ginkgoaceae.* New York: Longmans, Green, 1923.

Dalton, William. *Travels in the United States of America.* Appleby: Printed for the author by R. Bateman, 1821.

Daly, Augustin. *The Lottery of Love.* New York: Privately printed for the author, 1889.

Daly, Elizabeth. *An Elizabeth Daly Mystery Omnibus.* New York: Rinehart, c.1960.

Daly, Joseph Francis. *The Life of Augustin Daly.* New York: Macmillan, 1917.

Daly, Thomas Augustine. *McAroni Ballads and Other Verses.* New York: Harcourt, Brace and Howe, 1919.

Damon, Bertha Clark. *Grandma Called It Carnal.* New York: Simon & Schuster, c.1938.

———. *A Sense of Humus.* New York: Simon & Schuster, 1943.

Dana, Charles Anderson. *The United States Illustrated.* New York: Herrmann J. Meyer, 1855?

Dana, Edmund. *Geographical Sketches on the Western Country.* Cincinnati OH: Looker, Reynolds, 1819.

Dana, James Dwight. *Manual of Geology.* Philadelphia: T. Bliss, 1863.

Dana, Richard Henry. *Two Years before the Mast.* New York: Harper & Bros., 1841 [c.1840].

Dana, William Starr, Mrs. SEE Parsons, Frances Theodora

Dance, Daryl Cumber. *Shuckin' and Jivin'.* Bloomington IN: IN Univ. Press, c.1978.

Dance, Stanley. *The World of Swing.* New York: Charles Scribner's Sons, c.1974.

Dane, George Ezra and Beatrice J. Dane. *Ghost Town.* New York: Tudor, 1948. Orig. pub. in 1941 by A. A. Knopf, New York.

Dangerous Songs!? Phonodisc. New York: Columbia CO2503, 1966.

Daniels, Jonathan. *A Southerner Discovers the South.* New York: Macmillan, 1938.

———. *Tar Heels.* New York: Dodd, Mead, 1941.

Dannay, Frederic and Manfred B. Lee. *The Four of Hearts.* New York: Grosset & Dunlap, c.1938.

Danner, Edward Russell. *Pennsylvania Dutch Dictionary and Handbook.* York PA: William Penn Senior High School and Atreus Wanner Vocational School, 1951.

Danvers Historical Society. *Historical Collections.* Danvers MA, 1913–1987.

Danville Register. Danville VA, 1896–1989.

Darby, John. *A Manual of Botany, Adapted to the Productions of the Southern States.* Macon GA: B. F. Griffin, 1841.

———. *A Manual of Botany, Adapted to the Productions of the Southern States.* Savannah GA: John M. Cooper, 1847.

Darby, William. *The Emigrant's Guide to the Western and Southwestern States and Territories.* New York: Kirk & Mercein, 1818.

———. *A Geographical Description of the State of Louisiana.* 2d ed. enlarged and improved. New York: James Olmsted, 1817.

DARE. 1965–1970. Responses to *DARE* Questionnaire used in fieldwork.

DARE Fieldworker Addition. 1965–1970. Misc. materials gathered by *DARE* Fieldworkers.

DARE File. 1965–. Misc. oral and written materials.

DARE Tape. 1965–1970. Quotations from Informants recorded by *DARE* Fieldworkers.

DARE Wildflower Questionnaire. 1965–1970. Responses by selected Informants to pictures of wildflowers.

Dargan, Olive Tilford. *Call Home the Heart.* London: Longmans, Green, c.1932.

———. *Highland Annals.* New York: C. Scribner's Sons, 1925.

———. *Innocent Bigamy and Other Stories.* Winston-Salem NC: John F. Blair, 1962.

Darke, Rick. *Pocket Guide to Ornamental Grasses.* Portland OR: Timber Press, 2004.

Darling, Charles H. *The Jargon Book.* Aurora IL: Aurora, c.1919.

Darling, Frank Fraser. *Pelican in the Wilderness.* New York: Random House, 1956.

Darlington, William. *Agricultural Botany.* Philadelphia: J. W. Moore; New York: Mark H. Newman, 1847.

———. *American Weeds and Useful Plants.* Rev. with additions by George Thurber. 2d ed. illustr. New York: Orange Judd, 1880 [c.1859]. Orig. pub. in 1859.

———. *Flora Cestrica*. West-Chester PA: Printed for the Author by S. Siegfried, 1837.

———. *Flora Cestrica*. 3d ed. Philadelphia: Lindsay & Blakiston, 1853.

———. *Florula Cestrica*. West-Chester PA: Printed for the Author by Simeon Siegfried, 1826.

———. *Memorials of John Bartram and Humphry Marshall*. Philadelphia: Lindsay & Blakiston, 1849.

Darrow, Clarence Seward. *Farmington*. 2d ed. Chicago: A. C. McClurg, 1904.

DAS See Wentworth, Harold and Stuart Berg Flexner *Dictionary of American Slang*

Daugherty, Kermit. *Out of the Red Brush*. Cleveland OH: World, 1954.

Davenport, Arthur C. *The American Live Stock Market*. Chicago: Drovers Journal Print, c.1922.

Davenport, Eugene. *Domesticated Animals and Plants*. Boston: Ginn, 1910.

Davenport, Homer. *The Country Boy*. New York: G. W. Dillingham, c.1910.

Davenport, Lawrence C. and Helen Davenport, eds. *George Says I Must Write "Woot Has Twelve Pigs"*. Springfield MO: L. & H. Davenport, 1985.

Davenport, Warren G. *Butte and Montana beneath the X-Ray*. London: C. F. Cazenove; Butte MT: X-Ray Publishing, 1908.

Davenport Academy of Natural Sciences. *Proceedings*. Davenport IA, 1876–1899.

Davenport Daily Gazette. Davenport IA, 1856–1869; 1874–1885.

Davenport Daily Leader. Davenport IA, 1896–1903.

Davenport Daily Republican. Davenport IA, 1895–1904.

Davenport Democrat. Davenport IA, 1904–1937.

Davenport Democrat and Leader. Davenport IA, 1904–1937.

Davenport Gazette. Davenport IA, 1841–1857?; 1885–1887.

Davidson, Alice Merritt. *California Plants*. Los Angeles: B. R. Baumgardt, 1898.

Davidson, Anstruther and George L. Moxley. *Flora of Southern California*. Los Angeles: Times-Mirror Press, 1923.

Davidson, Hunter. *Report upon the Oyster Resources of Maryland to the General Assembly*. Annapolis MD: Wm. Thompson, 1870.

Davidson, Robert. *History of the Presbyterian Church in the State of Kentucky*. New York: Robert Carter, 1847.

Davie, Oliver. *Nests and Eggs of North American Birds*. 4th ed. Columbus OH: Hann & Adair, 1889.

———. *Nests and Eggs of North American Birds*. 5th ed. rev. and enlarged. Philadelphia: David McKay, c.1900.

Davies, Parke Hill. *Football*. New York: C. Scribner's Sons, 1911.

Daviess, Maria Thompson. *Rose of Old Harpeth*. Indianapolis IN: Bobbs-Merrill, c.1911.

Davis, Allison and John Dollard. *Children of Bondage: the Personality Development of Negro Youth in the Urban South*. Washington DC: American Council on Education, 1940.

Davis, Alva Leroy, ed. *Culture, Class, and Language Variety*. Rev. ed. Urbana IL: National Council of Teachers of English, c.1972.

———. *A Word Atlas of the Great Lakes Region*. Ann Arbor MI: Univ. MI diss., 1948.

Davis, Andrew Jackson. *The Great Harmonia*. 4th ed., vol. 1. Boston: Benjamin B. Mussey; New York: J. S. Redfield, c.1850.

———. *Morning Lectures*. New York: C. M. Plumb, 1865.

Davis, Andrew McFarland, ed. *Colonial Currency Reprints*. Boston: Printed for the Prince Society, 1910–1911. 4 vols.

———, ed. *Tracts Relating to the Currency of the Massachusetts Bay, 1620–1720*. Boston: Houghton, Mifflin, 1902.

Davis, Anita Price, comp. *North Carolina during the Great Depression*. Jefferson NC: McFarland, c.2003.

Davis, Burke. *The Summer Land*. New York: Random House, c.1965.

Davis, Charles Augustus. *Letters of J. Downing, Major, Downingville Militia*. New York: Harper & Bros., 1834.

Davis, Deering et al. *Alexandria Houses, 1750–1830*. Cornwall NY: Architectural Book, 1946.

Davis, Fitzroy. *Quicksilver*. New York: Harcourt, Brace, 1942.

Davis, Frederick C. See Ransome, Stephen

Davis, George. *Historical Sketch of Sturbridge and Southbridge*. West Brookfield MA: O. S. Cooke, 1856.

Davis, Hallam Walker. *The Column*. New York: Alfred A. Knopf, 1926.

Davis, Harold Lenoir. *Honey in the Horn*. New York: Harper & Bros., 1935.

Davis, Jeff. *Jeff Davis, Governor and United States Senator*. Little Rock AR: Democrat Print. & Litho. 1913.

Davis, John. *Travels of Four Years and a Half in the United States of America*. London: Sold by T. Ostell . . . New-York for R. Edwards, Printer, Bristol, 1803.

Davis, Kary Cadmus. *Productive Plant Husbandry*. Philadelphia: J. B. Lippincott, c.1917.

Davis, Lawrence M., ed. *Studies in Linguistics in Honor of Raven I. McDavid, Jr.* University AL: Univ. AL Press, c.1972.

Davis, Millard C. *The Near Woods*. New York: Alfred A. Knopf, c.1974.

Davis, Mollie Evelyn Moore. *An Elephant's Track*. New York: Harper, 1897 [c.1896].

Davis, Peter Seibert. *The Young Parson*. Philadelphia: Smith, English, 1863.

Davis, Ray Joseph. *Flora of Idaho*. Dubuque IA: Wm. C. Brown, c.1952.

Davis, Rebecca Harding. *Bits of Gossip*. Boston: Houghton Mifflin, 1904.

———. *Dallas Galbraith*. Philadelphia: J. B. Lippincott, 1868.

———. *Silhouettes of American Life*. New York: Charles Scribner's Sons, 1892.

Davis, Reuben. *Butcher Bird*. Boston: Little, Brown, 1936.

Davis, Richard Harding. *With the Allies*. New York: Charles Scribner's Sons, 1914.

Davis, Stephen Chapin. *California Gold Rush Merchant*. San Marino CA: Huntington Library, 1956.

Davis, Tarring S. *A History of Blair County, Pennsylvania*. Harrisburg PA: National Historical Association, c.1931. 2 vols.

Davis, Tom. *Be Tough or Be Gone*. Alamosa CO: Northern Trails Press, c.1984.

Davis, William B. and David J. Schmidly. *Mammals of Texas*. Austin TX: Texas Parks & Wildlife, Nongame and Urban Program, Distributed by Univ. TX Press, 1994.

Davis, William M. *Nimrod of the Sea*. New York: Harper & Bros., 1874.

Davis, William Watts Hart. *El Gringo*. New York: Harper & Bros., 1857.

———. *History of Doylestown Old and New*. Doylestown PA: Intelligencer, 1904.

Dawson, Coningsby William. *Carry On*. New York: John Lane, 1917.

Dawson, William Leon. *The Birds of California*. San Diego CA: South Moulton, 1923. 4 vols.

———. *The Birds of Ohio*. Columbus OH: Wheaton, 1903. 2 vols.

Dawson News & Advertiser. Athens GA, 1999–.

Day, Arthur Grove. *Hawaii and Its People*. New York: Duell, Sloan & Pearce, 1955.

Day, Donald. *Big Country*. New York: Duell, Sloan & Pearce, 1947.

Day, Holman Francis. *King Spruce*. New York: Harper & Bros., c.1908.

———. *Kin o' Ktaadn*. Boston: Small, Maynard, 1904.

———. *The Landloper*. New York: Harper & Bros., 1915.

———. *Pine Tree Ballads*. Boston: Small, Maynard, 1902.

———. *The Skipper and the Skipped*. New York: Harper & Bros., 1911.

———. *Up in Maine*. Boston: Small, Maynard, 1900.

———. *Where Your Treasure Is*. New York: Harper & Bros., 1917.

Dayton, Abram Child. *Last Days of the Knickerbocker Life in New York*. New York: George W. Harlan, 1882.

Dayton, William Adams. *Important Western Browse Plants*. Washington DC: Govt. Printing Office, 1931.

Daytona Beach News-Journal. Daytona Beach FL, 2001–.

Dayton Daily News. Dayton OH, 1898–.

DBE See Holm, John A. and Alison Watt Shilling *Dictionary of Bahamian English*

DCan See Avis, Walter S. et al. *Dictionary of Canadianisms on Historical Principles*

DCEU See Allsopp, Richard *Dictionary of Caribbean English Usage*

Deal, Babs H. *It's Always Three O'Clock*. New York: David McKay, c.1961.

Deam, Charles Clemons. *Shrubs of Indiana*. Indianapolis IN: Wm. B. Burford, 1924.

———. *Trees of Indiana*. 1st rev. ed. Ft. Wayne IN: Ft. Wayne Printing, 1921.

Dean, Blanche Evans et al. *Wildflowers of Alabama and Adjoining States*. 2d paperback ed. Tuscaloosa AL: Univ. AL Press, 1994 [c.1973].

Dean, Winnie Mims. *Diamond Bess*. Dallas TX: Mathis Van Nort, c.1949.

Deane, Samuel. *The New-England Farmer*. Worcester MA: Isaiah Thomas, 1790.

———. *The New England Farmer*. 2d ed., corr., improved and enlarged. Worcester MA: Isaiah Thomas, 1797.

———. *The New-England Farmer*. New York: Arno Press, 1972. Repr. of the 3d ed. pub. in 1822 by Wells and Lilly, Boston.

Dearborn, Benjamin. *The Columbian Grammar*. Boston: Printed by Samuel Hall, 1795.

Dearen, Patrick. *Saddling Up Anyway*. Lanham MD: Taylor, 2006.

The Death Valley Expedition. Washington DC: Govt. Printing Office, 1893.

De Bow's Review. New Orleans LA, 1846–1880.

Decatur Daily. Decatur AL, 1912–.

Decatur Daily Republican. Decatur IL, 1875–1894.

Decatur Daily Review. Decatur IL, 1873–1980.

Decatur Evening Herald. Decatur IL, 1927–1931.

Decatur Herald. Decatur IL, 1880?–1931?

Decatur Morning Review. Decatur IL, 1885–1895?

Decatur Republican. Decatur IL, 1867–1877.

Decatur Review. Decatur IL, 1891–1919.

Decatur Weekly Republican. Decatur IL, 1888–1898.

December Magazine. Chicago, 1957–.

Dedham, Massachusetts. *The Early Records of the Town*. Dedham MA: Dedham Transcript Press, 1886–1899. 5 vols.

Dedham Historical Register. Dedham MA: Dedham Historical Society, 1890–1903.

Deering, Thomas P. *Mountain Architecture*. Seattle WA: Univ. WA unpub. M.Arch. thesis, 1986.

Deer Park Progress. Deer Park TX, 1969?–.

Defenders. Washington DC: Defenders of Wildlife, 1975–.

Defiance Democrat. Defiance OH, 1844–1920.

De Forest, John William. *Downing Legends: Stories in Rhyme*. New Haven CT: Tuttle, Morehouse & Taylor, 1901. Electronic ed. transcr. as part of the Univ. MI Humanities Text Initiative, American Verse Project.

———. *Kate Beaumont*. Boston: James R. Osgood, 1872 [c.1871].

Degener, Otto. *Illustrated Guide to the More Common or Noteworthy Ferns and Flowering Plants of Hawaii National Park*. Honolulu HI: Printed by Honolulu Star-Bulletin, c.1930.

De Jong, David Cornel. *Old Haven*. Boston: Houghton Mifflin, 1938 [1935].

DeKay, James Ellsworth. *Zoology of New-York*. Albany NY: Carroll and Cook, 1842–1844. 5 vols.

Deland, Margaret Wade Campbell. *Florida Days*. Boston: Little Brown, 1889.

———. *Old Chester Tales*. New York: Harper & Bros., c.1898.

Delano, Alonzo. *Life on the Plains and among the Diggings*. Auburn NY: Miller, Orton & Mulligan, 1854.

Delany, Sarah Louise and Annie Elizabeth Delany. *Having Our Say*. New York: Kodansha International, c.1993.

Delaware Center for the Inland Bays. *Inland Bays Journal*. 1997?–. Internet.

Delaware Coast Press. Rehoboth Beach and Lewes DE, 1950–.

Delaware Folklore Bulletin. Newark NJ: Delaware Folklore Society, 1951–1963.

Delaware Gazette and Peninsula Advertiser. Wilmington DE, 1814–1820.

Delaware Patriot and American Watchman. Wilmington DE, 1828.

Delaware State Reporter. Dover DE, 1853–1859.

Delineator. New York: Butterick Publishing, 1873–1937.

Dellenbaugh, Frederick Samuel. *The Romance of the Colorado River*. New York: G. P. Putnam's Sons, 1902.

DeLong, Charles E. "California's Bantam Cock: the Journals of Charles E. Delong, 1854–1863." Historical Society of Southern California *Annual Publications*. (1929) 8.194–213, 337–63; (1930) 9.129–81, 243–87, 345–97; (1931) 10.40–78, 165–201, 245–97, 355–97.

Delphos Daily Herald See *Daily Herald*

Delphos Weekly Herald. Delphos OH, 1869–1910.

Del Rio News-Herald. Del Rio TX, 1929–.

Delta Democrat-Times. Greenville MS, 1938–.

Delta Farm Press. Clarksdale MS, 2000?–.

Delta Herald. Delta PA, 1880?–1890?

Delta Herald and Times. Delta PA, 1894–1927.

Del Vecchio, John M. *The 13th Valley*. Toronto: Bantam Books, c.1982.

Deming, Henry Champion. *A Speech for the Useful Arts*. Hartford: Press of Case, Tiffany, 1856.

Deming Graphic. Deming NM, 1902–.

Deming Headlight. Deming NM, 1881–1948.

Democratic Republican and Commercial Daily Advertiser. Baltimore MD, 1802.

Democratic Review SEE ALSO *United States Magazine and Democratic Review*

Democratic Review. New York, 1852.

Democratic Standard. Coshocton OH, 1884–1901.

Democratic State Journal. Sacramento CA, 1852–1858.

Denison, Charles Wheeler, ed. *Old Ironsides and Old Adams.* Boston: W. W. Page, 1846.

Denison, John Hopkins. *Beside the Bowery.* New York: Dodd, Mead, 1914.

Denison, Mary A. *Old Hepsy.* New York: A. B. Burdick, 1858.

Denison, Thomas Stewart. *Exhibition and Parlor Dramas.* Chicago: T. S. Denison, 1879.

Denlinger, William W. *The Complete Boston.* Richmond VA: Denlinger's, 1955.

Dennett, Daniel. *Louisiana as It Is.* New Orleans: "Eureka" Press, 1876.

Denny, Ebenezer. *Military Journal of Major Ebenezer Denny.* New York: New York Times, c.1971. Repr. of the 1859 ed. pub. by J. B. Lippincott, Philadelphia.

Denny, Emily Inez. *Blazing the Way.* Seattle WA: Rainier Print, 1909.

Denny, Joseph Waldo. *Wearing the Blue in the Twenty-Fifth Mass. Volunteer Infantry, with Burnside's Coast Division, 18th Army Corps, and Army of the James.* Worcester MA: Putnam & Davis, 1879.

Denslow, Van Buren. *Owned and Disowned.* New York: H. Dayton, 1857.

Dent, Huntley. *The Feast of Santa Fe.* New York: Simon & Schuster, c.1985.

Dental Jairus. Sacramento CA, 1880–1884.

Denton, Daniel. *A Brief Description of New-York.* New York: Published for the Facsimile Text Society by Columbia Univ. Press, 1937. Reproduction of the 1670 ed. printed for John Hancock, London.

Denton, Shelly Wright. *Pages from a Naturalist's Diary.* Wellesley MA: [s.n.], 1949.

Denton Journal. Denton MD, 1847–1965.

Denton Record-Chronicle. Denton TX, 1915–.

Denver Post. Denver CO, 1894–.

Denver Republican. Denver CO, 1887–1913.

Depew, Albert N. *Gunner Depew.* Chicago: Reilly & Britton, 1918.

De Quille, Dan SEE Wright, William

Derby, Connecticut. *Town Records of Derby, Connecticut, 1655–1710.* Derby CT: Sarah Riggs Humphreys Chapter, Daughters of the American Revolution, 1901.

Derby, George Horatio. *Phoenixiana.* 7th ed. New York: D. Appleton, 1856.

———. *The Squibob Papers.* New York: Carleton, 1865.

Derby, John Barton. *Political Reminiscences, Including a Sketch of the Origin and History of the "Statesman Party" of Boston.* Boston: Printed for the author by Homer & Palmer, 1835_.

Derleth, August. *Village Daybook.* Chicago: Pellegrini & Cudahy, c.1947.

———. *The Wisconsin, River of a Thousand Isles.* New York: Farrar & Rinehart, 1942.

Dermatology Online Journal. 1995–. Internet.

DeRosier, Linda Scott. *Creeker, a Woman's Journey.* Lexington KY: Univ. KY Press, c.1999.

Derrick. Oil City PA, 1954–.

Descant. Toronto, 1970–.

Deseret Morning News. Salt Lake City UT, 2003–.

Deseret News. Salt Lake City UT, 1850–1888; 1966?–.

Desert Magazine. Palm Desert CA, 1937–1951.

Des Moines Capital. Des Moines IA, 1905–1927.

Des Moines Daily Leader. Des Moines IA, 1900–1902.

Des Moines Register. Des Moines IA, 1860–.

De Toledano, Ralph, ed. *Frontiers of Jazz.* New York: O. Durrell, 1947.

Detro, Randall Augustus. *Generic Terms in the Place Names of Louisiana.* Baton Rouge LA: LA State Univ. diss., 1970.

Detroit Free Press. Detroit MI, 1831–.

Detroit News. Detroit MI, 1905–.

Deutsch, Babette. *Banners.* New York: George H. Doran, c.1919.

Devens, Richard Miller. *The Pictorial Book of Anecdotes and Incidents of the War of the Rebellion.* Hartford CT: Hartford, 1866.

Devlin, Harry. *What Kind of a House Is That?* New York: Parents' Magazine Press, c.1969.

De Voe, Thomas Farrington. *The Market Assistant.* New York: Published by Hurd and Houghton, 1867.

———. *The Market Book.* New York: Printed for the Author, 1862. 2 vols.

Devol, George H. *Forty Years a Gambler on the Mississippi.* New York: Home Book, c.1887.

Devoti, Lori. *Love Is All You Need.* New York: Kensington Publishing, c.2006.

De Voto, Bernard Augustine. *Across the Wide Missouri.* Boston: Houghton Mifflin, 1947.

De Vries, Peter. *Consenting Adults.* Boston: Little, Brown, c.1980.

———. *Forever Panting.* Boston: Little, Brown, c.1973.

———. *Let Me Count the Ways.* Boston: Little, Brown, c.1965.

———. *The Prick of Noon.* Boston: Little, Brown, c.1985.

———. *Reuben, Reuben.* Boston: Little, Brown, 1964.

———. *Sauce for the Goose.* Boston: Little, Brown, c.1981.

———. *Slouching towards Kalamazoo.* Boston: Little, Brown, c.1983.

———. *The Vale of Laughter.* Boston: Little, Brown, c.1967.

Dewees, Mary Coburn. *Journal of a Trip from Philadelphia to Lexington in Kentucky.* Crawfordsville IN: R. E. Banta, 1936.

Dewees, William B. *Letters from an Early Settler of Texas.* Comp. by Cara Cardelle [pseud.]. Louisville KY: New Albany Tribune Print, 1858. Orig. pub. in 1852 by Griswold, Louisville KY.

Dewitt, Dave and Nancy Gerlach. *Barbecue Inferno.* Berkeley CA: Ten Speed Press, c.2001.

Dewlen, Al. *The Bone Pickers.* New York: McGraw-Hill, c.1958.

Diabetes Care. Alexandria VA, 1978–.

Dial: a Magazine for Literature, Philosophy and Religion. Boston, 1840–1844.

Dialect Notes. New Haven CT: American Dialect Society, 1890–1939.

Diary, or, Loudon's Register. New York, 1792–1793.

Diaz, Abby Morton. *The Schoolmaster's Trunk.* Boston: James R. Osgood, 1875 [c.1874].

Dice, George W. *Life of George W. Dice, Called the King of Counterfeiters.* Chicago: Blakely Printing, 1896.

Dice, Lee Raymond. *The Biotic Provinces of North America.* Ann Arbor MI: Univ. MI Press, 1943.

Dick, Everett Newfon. *The Dixie Frontier.* New York: A. A. Knopf, 1948.

———. *The Sod-House Frontier 1854–1890.* New York: D. Appleton-Century, 1943 [c.1937].

Dick, Philip K. *Confessions of a Crap Artist.* New York: Vintage Books, 1992. Orig. pub. in 1975 by Entwhistle Books, New York.

Dick, William B. *The American Hoyle.* New York: Dick & Fitzgerald, c.1864.

Dickens, Charles. *American Notes.* New York: Harper & Bros., 1842.

Dickerson, Mary C. *The Frog Book.* New York: Doubleday, Page, 1907 [c.1906].

———. *Moths and Butterflies.* Boston: Ginn, c.1901.

Dickey, Roland F. *New Mexico Village Arts.* Albuquerque NM: Univ. NM Press, 1949.

Dickinson, Emily. *The Complete Poems.* Boston: Little, Brown, 1924.

———. *Complete Poems.* Ed. by Thomas H. Johnson. Boston: Little, Brown, 1960.

———. *Letters.* Ed. by Thomas H. Johnson. Cambridge MA: Belknap Press of Harvard Univ. Press, 1958. 3 vols.

Dickinson, Jonathan. *Gods Protecting Providence.* New York: Garland, 1977. Repr. of the 1699 ed. pub. by Reinier Jansen, Philadelphia.

———. *Jonathan Dickinson's Journal.* Ed. by Evangeline Walker Andrews and Charles McLean Andrews. New Haven CT: Printed for the Yale Univ. Press, 1945.

Dickinson, Sherman and Harry R. Lewis. *Poultry Enterprises.* Chicago: J. B. Lippincott, c.1931.

Dickinson, Thomas H., ed. *Wisconsin Plays.* New York: B. W. Huebsch, 1914.

Dickinson, William Edmund. *Field Guide to the Lizards and Snakes of Wisconsin.* Milwaukee WI: Milwaukee Museum Board, 1949.

Dickson, Albert Jerome. *Covered Wagon Days.* Cleveland OH: Arthur H. Clark, 1929.

Dickson, Harris. *An Old-Fashioned Senator.* New York: Frederick A. Stokes, 1925.

Dickson, Paul. *The Dickson Baseball Dictionary.* New York: Facts on File, c.1989.

Dictionary of Canadianisms on Historical Principles SEE Avis, Walter S. et al.

A Dictionary of Contemporary and Colloquial Usage. Chicago: English-Language Institute of America, c.1972.

A Dictionary of the Queen's English. Raleigh NC: Issued by North Carolina. Department of Conservation and Development. Travel and Promotion Division, 1965.

Didion, Joan. *A Book of Common Prayer.* New York: Simon and Schuster, c.1977.

———. *Run River.* New York: Ivan Obolensky, c.1963.

Digges, Jeremiah SEE Berger, Josef

Dillard, Annie. *An American Childhood.* New York: Harper & Row, c.1987.

———. *Pilgrim at Tinker Creek.* New York: Harper's Magazine Press, c.1974.

Dillard, Joey Lee. *American Talk.* New York: Random House, c.1976.

———. *Lexicon of Black English.* New York: Seabury Press, 1977.

Dime Detective Magazine. Chicago, 1931–.

Dirt Bike. Encino CA: Hi-Torque, 1971–.

Disciple of Christ. Cincinnati OH, 1884–1885.

Discovery, the Popular Journal of Knowledge. London: Benn Bros., 1920–1966.

Dispensatory of the United States of America. Philadelphia: J. B. Lippincott, 1833–1960.

Ditchy, Jay Karl. *Les Acadiens Louisianais et Leur Parler.* Paris: E. Droz, 1932. Pub. from a ms. dated 1901.

Ditmars, Raymond Lee. *A Field Book of North American Snakes.* Garden City NY: Doubleday, 1952.

———. *The Reptile Book.* New York: Doubleday, Page, 1908.

———. *The Reptiles of North America.* Garden City NY: Doubleday, Doran, 1936.

———. *Reptiles of the World.* New York: Sturgis and Walton, c.1910.

———. *Reptiles of the World.* New rev. ed. New York: Macmillan, 1933.

———. *Snakes of the World.* New York: Macmillan, 1936. Repr. of the 1931 ed.

———. *Snakes of the World.* New York: Macmillan, 1946 [c.1931].

Dix, Edwin Asa. *Deacon Bradbury.* New York: Century, 1900.

Dixie Beekeeper. Waycross GA, 1919–1930.

The Dixie Cook-Book. Comp. by Estelle Woods Wilcox. Rev. ed. Atlanta GA: L. A. Clarkson, 1885 [c.1883].

Dixon, Billy. *Life and Adventures of "Billy" Dixon of Adobe Walls, Texas Panhandle.* Comp. by Frederick S. Barde. Guthrie OK: Co-Operative Publishing, c.1914.

Dixon, James Main. *Dictionary of Idiomatic English Phrases.* London: T. Nelson and Sons, 1891.

Dixon, Margaret Collins Denny and Elizabeth Chapman Denny Vann. *Denny Genealogy.* New York: National Historical Society, 1944. 3 vols.

Dixon, Royal. *The Human Side of Birds.* New York: Halcyon, c.1917.

Dixon, Thomas. *The Leopard's Spots.* New York: Grosset & Dunlap, c.1902.

Dixon, William Hepworth. *New America.* Philadelphia: J. B. Lippincott, 1867. 2 vols.

Dixon Evening Telegraph. Dixon IL, 1901–1985.

Dixon Sun. Dixon IL, 1872–.

DJE SEE Cassidy, Frederic Gomes and R. B. LePage *Dictionary of Jamaican English*

DN SEE *Dialect Notes*

DNE SEE Story, G. M. et al. *Dictionary of Newfoundland English*

DNZE SEE Orsman, H. W. *The Dictionary of New Zealand English*

Dobbs, Arthur. *An Account of the Countries Adjoining to Hudson's Bay.* London: Printed for J. Robinson, 1744.

Dobbs, David. *The Great Gulf.* Washington DC: Island Press, c.2000.

Dobbs, David and Richard Ober. *The Northern Forest.* White River Junction VT: Chelsea Green, 1995.

Dobie, James Frank. *Coronado's Children.* Dallas TX: Southwest Press, c.1930.

———. *Cow People.* Boston: Little, Brown, 1964.

———. *The Longhorns.* Boston: Little, Brown, 1941.

———. *The Mustangs.* Boston: Little, Brown, 1952.

———. *On the Open Range.* Dallas TX: Banks Upshaw, 1960 [c.1931].

———. *Tone the Bell Easy.* Austin TX: Texas Folk-Lore Society, c.1932.

———. *A Vaquero of the Brush Country.* Dallas TX: Southwest Press, 1929.

Doctorow, E. L. *Ragtime.* New York: Random House, 1975.

The Documentary History of the State of New-York. Arranged under direction of the Hon. Christopher Morgan, Secretary of State, by E. B. O'Callaghan. Albany NY: Weed, Parsons, 1849–1851. 4 vols.

Documents Relating to the Colonial, Revolutionary and Post-

Revolutionary History of the State of New Jersey. Newark NJ: [s.n.], 1880–1949. 42 vols. Archives of the State of New Jersey. 1st ser.

Documents Relating to the Revolutionary History of the State of New Jersey. Trenton NJ: J. L. Murphy, 1901–1917. 5 vols. Archives of the State of New Jersey. 2d ser.

Documents Relative to the Colonial History of the State of New-York. Ed. by E. B. O'Callaghan. Albany NY: Weed, Parsons, 1853–1887. 15 vols.

Doddridge, Joseph. *Logan.* Buffaloe Creek VA: Printed for the Author by Solomon Sala, 1823.

———. *Notes on the Settlement and Indian Wars of the Western Parts of Virginia and Pennsylvania.* Wellsburgh VA: Printed at the Office of the Gazette, for the Author, 1824.

Dodge, Mary Abigail, ed. *A Battle of the Books, Recorded by an Unknown Writer for the Use of Authors and Publishers.* Cambridge MA: Riverside Press, 1870.

———. *Country Living and Country Thinking.* Boston: Ticknor and Fields, 1862.

———. *Gala-Days.* Boston: Ticknor and Fields, 1863.

———. *Skirmishes and Sketches.* Boston: Ticknor and Fields, 1865.

Dodge, Natt Noyes. *100 Desert Wildflowers in Natural Color.* Globe AZ: Southwest Parks and Monuments Assn., 1971.

———. *100 Roadside Wildflowers of Southwest Uplands in Natural Color.* Globe AZ: Southwest Parks and Monuments Association, 1967. Occasionally cited by printing date, 1976.

———. *Flowers of the Southwest Deserts.* Tucson AZ: Southwest Parks and Monuments Association, c.1985.

———. *Poisonous Dwellers of the Desert.* Santa Fe NM: Southwestern Monuments Association, 1947.

Dodge, Richard Irving. *The Black Hills.* New York: James Miller, 1876.

———. *The Plains of the Great West and Their Inhabitants.* New York: G. P. Putnam's Sons, 1877.

Dodson, Kenneth. *Away All Boats.* Boston: Little, Brown, c.1954.

Doesticks, Q. R. Philander, P. B. SEE Underhill, Edward Fitch and Mortimer Thomson

Dog Fancier. Battle Creek MI, 1891–1923.

Doig, Ivan. *Dancing at the Rascal Fair.* New York: Atheneum, 1987.

———. *English Creek.* New York: Atheneum, 1984.

———. *Heart Earth.* New York: Atheneum-Macmillan, c.1993.

———. *This House of Sky.* San Diego CA: Harcourt Brace Jovanovich, c.1978.

———. *The Whistling Season.* Orlando FL: Harcourt, 2006.

Dollar Magazine. New York: Wilson, 1841–1842.

Dollar Newspaper. Philadelphia, 1843–1864.

Domicile. 1990?–. Internet.

Donaldson, Scott. *John Cheever, a Biography.* New York: Random House, c.1988.

Donck, Adriaen van der. *Beschryvinge van Nieuw-Nederlant.* t'Aemsteldam: Evert Nieuwenhof, 1655.

Doran, Madeleine. *Something about Swans.* Madison: Univ. WI Press, c.1973.

Dorchester, Massachusetts. *Dorchester Town Records.* 2d ed. Boston: Rockwell and Churchill, 1883.

Dorchester Antiquarian and Historical Society. *Collections.* Boston: D. Clapp, 1844–1850. 3 vols.

Dorland's Illustrated Medical Dictionary. 24th ed. Philadelphia: Saunders, 1965.

Dormon, Caroline. *Forest Trees of Louisiana and How to Know Them.* New Orleans LA?: [s.n.], 1928?

———. *Wild Flowers of Louisiana.* Garden City NY: Doubleday, Doran, 1934.

Dorrance, Ward Allison. *The Sundowners.* New York: C. Scribner's Sons, 1942.

Dorsey, Chris. *Wildfowler's Season.* New York: Globe Pequot Press, 1998 [c.1995].

Dorsey, Florence L. *Master of the Mississippi.* Boston: Houghton Mifflin, 1941.

Dorsey, Sarah Anne. *Lucia Dare.* New York: M. Doolady, 1867.

Dorson, Richard Mercer. *Bloodstoppers and Bearwalkers.* Cambridge MA: Harvard Univ. Press, 1952.

———, ed. *Negro Folktales in Michigan.* Cambridge MA: Harvard Univ. Press, 1956.

Dos Passos, John. *The 42nd Parallel.* New York: Harper & Bros., 1930.

———. *1919.* New York: Harcourt, Brace, c.1932.

———. *The Best Times.* New York: New American Library, c.1966.

———. *The Big Money.* New York: Harcourt, Brace, c.1936.

———. *The Grand Design.* Boston: Houghton Mifflin, 1949.

———. *Streets of Night.* New York: George H. Doran, c.1923.

———. *Three Soldiers.* New York: George H. Doran, 1921.

DOST SEE Craigie, Sir William Alexander *A Dictionary of the Older Scottish Tongue*

Dothan Eagle. Dothan AL, 1908–.

Doubleday, Nellie Blanchan De Graff. *The American Flower Garden.* New York: Doubleday, Page, 1909.

———. *Bird Neighbors.* New York: Doubleday & McClure, 1897.

———. *Birds That Hunt and Are Hunted.* New York: Grosset & Dunlap, c.1904.

Double-Tongued Dictionary: a Lexicon of Fringe English, Focusing on Slang, Jargon, and New Words. [v.d.]. Internet.

Douglas, David. *Journal Kept by David Douglas during His Travels in North America, 1823–1827.* New York: Antiquarian Press, 1959.

Douglas, Henry Kyd. *I Rode with Stonewall.* Chapel Hill NC: Univ. NC Press, c.1940.

Douglas, Marjory Stoneman. *The Everglades.* New York: Rinehart, 1947.

Douglas, William Orville. *My Wilderness: East to Katahdin.* Garden City NY: Doubleday, c.1961.

———. *Of Men and Mountains.* New York: Harper & Bros., 1950.

Douglass, Frederick. *The Life and Writings of Frederick Douglass.* Comp. by Philip S. Foner. New York: International, c.1950. 5 vols.

———. *My Bondage and My Freedom.* New York: Miller, Orton & Mulligan, 1855.

Douglass, William. *Summary, Historical and Political, of the First Planting, Progressive Improvements, and Present State of the British Settlements in North America.* New York: Arno Press, 1972. 2 vols. Vol. 1 is a repr. of the 1749 ed. pub. by Rogers and Fowle, Boston; vol. 2 is a repr. of the 1751 ed. pub. by D. Fowle, London.

Dow, George Francis, ed. *The Holyoke Diaries.* Salem MA: Essex Institute, 1911.

Dow, Jr. SEE Paige, Elbridge Gerry

Dow, Lorenzo. *The Dealings of God, Man, and the Devil.* 4th ed. rev., corr. and improved. Norwich CT: Wm. Faulkner, 1833.

———. *History of Cosmopolite.* 6th ed. rev. and corr. Cincinnati OH: H. M. Rulison, 1857.

———. *The Life and Travels of Lorenzo Dow.* Hartford CT: Lincoln & Gleason, 1804. 2 vols.

Down Beat. Chicago: Maher Publications, 1934–.

Down East: the Magazine of Maine. Camden ME, 1954–.

Downey, William. *An Investigation of the Properties of the Sanguinaria Canadensis, or Puccoon.* Cincinnati OH: Lloyd, 1907. Orig. pub. in 1803 by Eaken and Mecum, Philadelphia.

Downing, Andrew Jackson. *The Fruits and Fruit Trees of America.* New York: Wiley and Putnam, 1847 [c.1845].

———. *A Treatise on the Theory and Practice of Landscape Gardening.* 4th ed. enlarged and rev. New York: G. P. Putnam, 1852 [c.1849].

———. *A Treatise on the Theory and Practice of Landscape Gardening.* 6th ed. enlarged and rev. New York: A. O. Moore, 1859.

Downing, Major Jack SEE Davis, Charles Augustus

Downing, Major Jack SEE ALSO Smith, Seba

Doxey, William. *Cousins to the Kudzu.* Baton Rouge LA: LA State Univ. Press, 1985.

Doylestown Daily Intelligencer. Doylestown PA, 1886–1954.

DPEIE SEE Pratt, Terry Kenneth *Dictionary of Prince Edward Island English*

Drache, Hiram M. *The Challenge of the Prairie.* Fargo ND: ND Institute for Regional Studies, 1970.

Draft Horse Journal. Waverly IA, 1964–.

Drake, Benjamin. *Tales and Sketches from the Queen City.* Cincinnati OH: E. Morgan, 1838.

Drake, Daniel. *Natural and Statistical View, or, Picture of Cincinnati and the Miami Country.* Cincinnati OH: Looker and Wallace, 1815.

———. *Notices Concerning Cincinnati.* Cincinnati OH: Press of Jennings and Graham, 1908. 2 vols. Repr. of 1810 ed., printed for the author at the Press of John W. Browne, Cincinnati.

———. *Pioneer Life in Kentucky.* Cincinnati OH: Robert Clarke, 1870.

———. *A Systematic Treatise, Historical, Etiological, and Practical, on the Principal Diseases of the Interior Valley of North America.* Cincinnati OH: Winthrop B. Smith, 1850 [c.1849].

Drake, Francis Samuel, comp. *Tea Leaves.* Boston: A. O. Crane, 1884.

Drake, Joseph Rodman. *Life and Works.* Boston: Merrymount Press, 1935.

Drake, Samuel Adams. *Nooks and Corners of the New England Coast.* New York: Harper, c.1875.

———. *Old Landmarks and Historic Personages of Boston.* Boston: James R. Osgood, 1873 [c.1872].

Drake, Samuel Gardner. *Tragedies of the Wilderness.* Boston: Antiquarian Bookstore and Institute, 1841.

Drannan, William F. *Thirty-One Years on the Plains and in the Mountains.* Chicago: Rhodes & McClure, 1900.

Draper, Henry. *A Text-Book on Chemistry.* New York: Henry, 1868.

Drayton, Daniel. *Personal Memoir of Daniel Drayton.* 2d ed. Boston: Bela Marsh; New York: American and Foreign Anti-Slavery Society, 1854.

Drayton, John. *Letters Written during a Tour through the Northern and Eastern States.* Charleston SC: Harrison and Bowen, 1794.

———. *A View of South Carolina.* Charleston SC: W. P. Young, 1802.

Dreese, Michael A. *The 151st Pennsylvania Volunteers at Gettysburg.* Jefferson NC: McFarland, c.2000.

Dregni, Michael, ed. *100 Years of Vintage Farm Tractors.* Stillwater MN: Voyageur Press, 2000.

Dreiser, Theodore. *The Financier.* New York: Harper & Bros., 1912.

———. *A Hoosier Holiday.* New York: John Lane, 1916.

———. *Jennie Gerhardt.* New York: Harper & Bros., 1911.

———. *Letters.* Philadelphia: Univ. Phil. Press, 1959. 3 vols.

———. *Twelve Men.* New York: Boni and Liveright, 1919.

Drepperd, Carl William. *A Dictionary of American Antiques.* Garden City NY: Doubleday, 1952.

Drew, Benjamin. *A North-Side View of Slavery.* Boston: John P. Jewett, 1856.

———. *The Refugee.* New York: Johnson Reprint, 1968. Repr. of 1856 ed. pub. by J. P. Jewett, Boston.

Driggs, Howard Roscoe. *Live Language Lessons.* Chicago: Univ. Publishing, 1917. 3 vols.

Drinker, Elizabeth Sandwith. *Extracts from the Journal of Elizabeth Drinker, from 1759 to 1807, A.D.* Philadelphia: J. B. Lippincott, 1889.

Drinkwater, Anne T. *Memoir of Mrs. Deborah H. Porter.* Portland ME: Sanborn and Carter, 1848.

Driscoll, Charles Benedict. *Country Jake.* New York: Macmillan, 1946.

Droege, John Albert. *Yards and Terminals and Their Operation.* New York: Railroad Gazette, 1906.

Dromgoole, Will Allen. *Cinch, and Other Stories: Tales of Tennessee.* Boston: Dana Estes, 1898.

———. *The Heart of Old Hickory and Other Stories of Tennessee.* Boston: Dana Estes, c.1895.

Drury, Alexander Greer. *Legends of the Apple.* Cincinnati OH: [s.n.], 1904.

Drury, Clifford Merrill. *Elkanah and Mary Walker, Pioneers among the Spokanes.* Caldwell ID: Caxton Printers, 1940.

Drury, Wells. *An Editor on the Comstock Lode.* New York: Farrar and Rinehart, 1936.

DSME SEE Montgomery, Michael B. and Joseph Sargent Hall *Dictionary of Smoky Mountain English*

DSNA Letters. 1978–1986. Unpub. letters in response to queries in *Dictionary Society of North America Newsletter.*

Duane, William, ed. *Letters to Benjamin Franklin from His Family and Friends, 1751–1790.* New York: C. B. Richardson, 1859.

DuBois, James T. *Fun and Pathos of One Life.* New York: Neale, 1908.

Du Bois, William. *The Island in the Square.* New York: Farrar, Straus, 1947.

Dubuque Daily Herald. Dubuque IA, 1885–1901.

Dubuque Sunday Herald. Dubuque IA, 1885–1901.

Dubuque Telegraph-Herald. Dubuque IA, 1901–1905.

Duckworks Magazine. 1995–. Internet.

Dudley, Robert SEE Baldwin, James

Dudley, William Russell. *The Cayuga Flora.* Ithaca NY: Andrus & Church, 1886.

Due, Tananarive. *Joplin's Ghost.* New York: Atria, c.2005.

Duffus, Robert Luther. *The Santa Fe Trail.* London: Longmans, Green, 1930.

Dufresne, Frank. *Alaska's Animals & Fishes.* New York: A. S. Barnes, c.1946.

———. *My Way Was North.* New York: Holt, Rinehart and Winston, c.1966.

DuFresne, Jim. *Glacier Bay National Park: a Backcountry Guide to the Glaciers and Beyond.* Seattle WA: Mountaineers, 1987.

DuFresne, Jim and Aaron Spitzer. *Alaska.* 8th ed. Oakland CA: Lonely Planet, 2006.

Duganne, Augustine Joseph Hickey. *Camps and Prisons.* New York: J. P. Robens, 1865.

———. *The Tenant-House.* New York: Robert M. De Witt, 1857.

Dugger, Shepherd Monroe. *The Balsam Groves of the Grandfather Mountain.* Banner Elk NC: Shepherd M. Dugger, 1895 [c.1892].

Dugmore, A. Radclyffe. *Bird Homes.* New York: Doubleday, Page, 1905 [c.1904].

Duluth News Tribune. Duluth MN, 1892–1982.

Dumas, Amy. *Lita.* New York: Pocket Books, c.2003.

Dumas, Henry. *Ark of Bones and Other Stories.* Ed. by Eugene B. Redmond. New York: Random House, 1974.

Dunbar, Anthony P. *The Will to Survive.* Atlanta GA: Southern Regional Council, c.1969.

Dunbar, John Raine, ed. *The Paxton Papers.* The Hague: M. Nijhoff, 1957.

Dunbar, Paul Laurence. *Folks from Dixie.* New York: Dodd, Mead, 1898.

———. *Lyrics of Love and Laughter.* New York: Dodd, Mead, 1903.

———. *Lyrics of the Hearthside.* New York: Dodd, Mead, 1899.

Dunbar, Seymour. *A History of Travel in America.* Indianapolis IN: Bobbs Merrill, c.1915. 4 vols.

Dunbar, William *Journal of a Voyage* SEE Dunbar, William *Life Letters and Papers*

Dunbar, William. *Life, Letters and Papers of William Dunbar of Elgin, Morayshire, Scotland, and Natchez, Mississippi.* Jackson MS: Press of the Mississippi Historical Society, 1930.

Duncan, Kunigunde. *Mentor Graham.* Chicago: Univ. Chicago Press, c.1944.

Duncan, Pamela. *Moon Women.* New York: Dial Press, 2005 [c.2001].

Duncan, Robert B. *"Old Settlers".* Indianapolis IN: Bowen-Merrill, 1894. Orig. pub. as "Papers" in the *Indianapolis Herald,* 1879.

Duncan, Roger F. and John P. Ware. *A Cruising Guide to the New England Coast.* New York: Dodd, Mead, 1967.

Duncan, Wilbur Howard and Leonard E. Foote. *Wildflowers of the Southeastern United States.* Athens GA: Univ. GA Press, 1975.

Dunckel, John F. *The Mollyjoggers.* Springfield MO: H. S. Jewell, c.1905.

Dundes, Alan, comp. *Mother Wit from the Laughing Barrel.* Englewood Cliffs NJ: Prentice Hall, c.1973.

———. *The Study of Folklore.* Englewood Cliffs NJ: Prentice-Hall, 1965.

Dungee, John Riley. *Random Rhymes, Formal and Dialect, Serious and Humorous, Racial, Religious, Patriotic and Sentimental.* Norfolk VA: Guide Publishing, c.1929.

Dunglison, Robley. *Medical Lexicon.* 7th ed. carefully rev. and greatly enlarged. Philadelphia: Blanchard and Lea, 1848.

———. *Medical Lexicon.* 8th ed., rev. and greatly enlarged. Philadelphia: Blanchard and Lea, 1851.

———. *Medical Lexicon.* 14th ed., rev. Philadelphia: Blanchard and Lea, 1856 [c.1851].

Dunham, Elizabeth Marie. *How to Know the Mosses.* Boston: Houghton Mifflin, 1916.

———. *How to Know the Mosses.* 2d ed. Boston: Mosher Press, 1951.

Duniway, Abigail J. *Captain Gray's Company.* Portland OR: S. J. McCormick, c.1859.

Dunkirk Evening Observer. Dunkirk NY, 1916–1964.

Dunkirk Observer-Journal. Dunkirk NY, 1880–1890.

Dunlap, William. *Diary.* New York: Printed for the New York Historical Society, 1930. 3 vols.

———. *The Father.* New York: Hodge, Allen & Campbell, 1789.

———. *The Life of Charles Brockden Brown.* Philadelphia: James P. Parke, 1815. 2 vols.

———. *Thirty Years Ago.* New York: Bancroft & Holley, 1836. 2 vols.

Dunlop, Richard. *Wheels West, 1590–1900.* Chicago: Rand McNally, c.1977.

Dunn, Jacob Piatt. *Indiana and Indianans.* Chicago: American Historical Society, 1919. 5 vols.

Dunn, Matthew. *Crossing the Trinity.* Mustang OK: Tate Publishing, 2007.

Dunne, Finley Peter. *Mr. Dooley and the Chicago Irish.* New York: Arno Press, 1976.

———. *Mr. Dooley in Peace and War.* Boston: Small, Maynard, c.1898.

———. *Mr. Dooley's Opinions.* New York: Harper & Bros., c.1901.

Du Pont & Co. SEE E. I. Du Pont de Nemours & Company

Du Puy, William Atherton. *Uncle Sam Detective.* New York: McKinlay Stone & Mackenzie, c.1916.

Durant, Samuel W. *History of Ingham and Eaton Counties Michigan.* Philadelphia: D. W. Ensign, 1880.

Durant Daily Democrat. Durant OK, 1899–.

Durham, Philip and Everett L. Jones. *The Negro Cowboys.* New York: Dodd, Mead, c.1965.

Durham Morning Herald. Durham NC, 1919–.

Durivage, Francis Alexander. *Life Scenes.* Boston: B. B. Mussey, 1853.

DuSablon, Mary Anna. *Cincinnati Recipe Treasury.* Virginia Beach VA: Donning, c.1983.

Duval, John Crittenden. *The Adventures of Big-Foot Wallace, the Texas Ranger and Hunter.* Macon GA: J. W. Burke, 1870.

———. *The Adventures of Big-Foot Wallace, the Texas Ranger and Hunter.* Austin TX: Stick, 1935. Facsimile of the 1870 ed. pub. by J. W. Burke, Macon GA.

———. *Early Times in Texas.* Austin TX: H. P. N. Gammel, c.1892.

———. *The Young Explorers* SEE Duval, John Crittenden *Early Times in Texas*

Duxbury, Massachusetts. *Copy of the Old Records of the Town of Duxbury, Mass., from 1642–1770.* Plymouth MA: Avery & Doten, 1893.

Duyckinck, Evert Augustus and George Long Duyckinck. *Cyclopaedia of American Literature.* Ed. to date by M. Laird Simons. Philadelphia: Baxter, 1881 [c.1875]. 2 vols.

Dwight, Margaret Van Horn SEE Bell, Margaret Van Horn Dwight

Dwight, Nathaniel. *A Short but Comprehensive System of the Geography of the World.* 1st Albany ed., from the 2d Hartford ed., rev. and enlarged. Albany NY: Printed by Charles R. & George Webster, 1796.

Dwight, Timothy. *Travels.* New-Haven CT: T. Dwight, 1821–1822. 4 vols.

Dwight's American Magazine and Family Newspaper. New York, 1847–1851.

Dwyer, Bil, comp. *Dictionary for Yankees and Other Uneducated People.* Highlands NC: Merry Mountaineer, c.1971.

———, comp. *Thangs Yankees Don' Know.* Highlands NC: Merry Mountaineer, c.1975.

Dyer, Delce. *Farmstead Yards at Cades Cove.* Athens GA: Univ. GA M. A. thesis, 1988.

Dyer, Joyce, ed. *Bloodroot: Reflections on Place by Appalachian Women Writers.* Lexington KY: Univ. Press KY, 1998.

Dykeman, Wilma. *The Far Family.* New York: Holt, Rinehart and Winston, c.1966.

———. *The French Broad.* New York: Rinehart, c.1955.

———. *The Tall Woman.* New York: Holt, Rinehart and Winston, c.1962.

Earle, Alice Morse. *Child Life in Colonial Days.* New York: Macmillan, 1909 [c.1899].

———. *Colonial Days in Old New York.* Detroit MI: Singing Tree Press, 1968. Orig. pub. in 1896 by C. Scribner's Sons, New York.

———. *Customs and Fashions in Old New England.* New York: C. Scribner, 1893.

———. *Home Life in Colonial Days.* New York: Macmillan, 1899 [c.1898].

———. *Old Time Gardens.* New York: Macmillan, 1902.

———. *The Sabbath in Puritan New England.* 9th ed. New York: Charles Scribner's Sons, 1902 [c.1891].

Earle, Franklin Sumner. *Sugar Cane and Its Culture.* New York: J. Wiley & Sons; London: Chapman & Hall, 1928.

Earle, Swepson. *The Chesapeake Bay Country.* Baltimore MD: Thomsen-Ellis, 1923.

Earlham College Libraries. *Josiah Parker Papers.* 2001? Letters transcr. from originals dated 1804–1834. Internet.

Early, Eleanor. *A New England Sampler.* Boston: Waverly House, 1940.

Early Accounts of Life in Colonial Virginia 1609–1613. Delmar NY: Scholars' Facsimiles & Reprints, 1976.

Early American Industries Association. *Chronicle.* Northhampton MA, 1933–.

Eastburn, James Wallis and R. C. Sands. *Yamoyden.* New York: Published by James Eastburn, 1820.

Easterby, James Harold, ed. *The South Carolina Rice Plantation as Revealed in the Papers of Robert F. W. Allston.* Chicago: Univ. Chicago Press, 1945.

Eastern Reflector. Greenville NC, 1882–1910.

East Hampton, New York. *Records of the Town of East Hampton, Long Island, Suffolk County, N.Y.* Sag-Harbor NY: J. H. Hunt, Printer, 1887–1905. 5 vols.

East Hampton Star. East Hampton NY, 1885–.

East Liverpool Review. East Liverpool OH, 1879–.

Eastman, Charles Alexander. *From the Deep Woods to Civilization.* Boston: Little, Brown, 1917 [c.1916].

Eastman, Charles Gamage. *Poems.* Montpelier VT: Eastman & Danforth, 1848.

———. *Poems.* Montpelier VT: T. C. Phinney, 1880.

Eastman, John Andrew. *The Book of Field and Roadside.* Mechanicsburg PA: Stackpole Books, c.2003.

Eastman, Mary Henderson. *Aunt Phillis's Cabin.* Philadelphia: Lippincott, Grambo, 1852.

Easton Gazette. Easton MD, 1822–1929?

East Oregonian. Pendleton OR, 1887–.

East Tennessee Historical Society. *Publications.* Knoxville TN, 1929–.

East Tennessee Roots Historical Genealogical Magazine. Oak Ridge TN: East Tennessee Heritage Foundation, 1984–.

Eastwood, Alice. *Bergen's Botany: Key and Flora.* Pacific coast ed. Boston: Ginn, 1901.

———. *Flora of the Pacific Coast.* Boston: Ginn, 1897.

Eaton, Allen Hendershott. *Handicrafts of the Southern Highlands.* New York: Russel Sage Foundation, 1937.

Eaton, Amos. *Botanical Exercises.* Albany NY: Websters and Skinners, 1820.

———. *Manual of Botany for North America.* 5th ed. rev., corr., and much extended. Albany NY: Websters and Skinners, 1829.

———. *Manual of Botany for North America.* 6th ed. Albany NY: O. Steele, 1833.

———. *Manual of Botany for North America.* 7th ed. Albany NY: Oliver Steele, 1836.

———. *A Manual of Botany for the Northern and Middle States.* 2d ed. corr. and enlarged. Albany NY: Websters and Skinners, c.1818.

———. *Manual of Botany for the Northern and Middle States of America.* 3d ed. rev. and corr. Albany NY: Websters and Skinners, 1822.

———. *A Manual of Botany, for the Northern and Middle States of America.* 4th ed. rev. and corr. Albany NY: Websters and Skinners, 1824.

———. *A Manual of Botany for the Northern States.* Albany NY: Websters and Skinners, 1817.

Eaton, Conan B., Mrs. *Collection.* 1922–1975. Unpub. coll. of materials on Amer. Eng. usage.

Eaton, Elon Howard. *Birds of New York.* Albany NY: Univ. of the State of NY, 1910–1914. 2 vols.

Eaton, Walter Prichard. *Boy Scouts in the White Mountains, the Story of a Long Hike.* Boston: W. A. Wilde, c.1914.

———. *Green Trails and Upland Pastures.* Garden City NY: Doubleday, Page, 1917.

———. *The Idyl of Twin Fires.* Garden City NY: Doubleday, Page, 1915.

———. *Wild Gardens of New England.* Boston: W. A. Wilde, c.1936.

Eau Claire Leader. Eau Claire WI, 1896?–1970.

Eau Claire News. Eau Claire WI, 1875–1892.

Ebbutt, Percy G. *Emigrant Life in Kansas.* London: S. Sonnenschein, 1886.

Ebony. Chicago, 1945–.

Eby, Cecil D. *That Disgraceful Affair, the Black Hawk War.* New York: Norton, 1973.

Eby, James Brian. *The Geology and Mineral Resources of Wise County and the Coal-Bearing Portion of Scott County, Virginia.* Charlottesville VA: Univ. VA, 1923.

Eckstorm, Fannie Hardy. *The Bird Book.* Boston: D. C. Heath, 1901.

———. *David Libbey.* Boston: American Unitarian Association, 1907.

Eclectic Magazine of Foreign Literature, Science and Art. New York, 1844–1898.

Eclectic Medical Journal. Cincinnati OH, 1849–1937.

Eclectic Repertory and Analytical Review. Philadelphia, 1810–1820.

Ecological Applications. Washington DC, 1991–.

Ecological Monographs. Durham NC: Duke Univ. Press, 1931–.

Ecology. Brooklyn NY, 1920–.

Economic Geography. Worcester MA: Clark Univ., 1925–.

EDD SEE Wright, Joseph *The English Dialect Dictionary*

Eddie Cano Quartet. *Danke Schoen.* Phonodisc. Burbank CA: Reprise, 1963.

Eddy, Samuel and Thaddeus Surber. *Northern Fishes.* Minneapolis MN: Univ. MN Press, c.1943.

EDG SEE Wright, Joseph *The English Dialect Grammar*

Edgerton, Clyde. *The Floatplane Notebooks.* Chapel Hill NC: Algonquin Books of Chapel Hill, 1988.

———. *Raney.* Chapel Hill NC: Algonquin Books, 1985.

Edgerton Enterprise. Edgerton MN, 1883–.

Edgeworth, Mary L. *The Southern Gardener and Receipt*

Book. 3d ed. rev. and corr. Philadelphia: Lippincott, 1860 [c.1859].

Edgren, August Hjalmar and Percy Bentley Burnet. *A French and English Dictionary*. New York: Henry Holt, c.1901.

Edinburgh New Philosophical Journal. Edinburgh: Adam Black, 1826–1864.

Editor, the Journal of Information for Literary Workers. Ridgewood NJ, 1895–1941.

Edmonds, Amanda Virginia. *Journals*. Ed. by Nancy Chappelear Baird. Stephens City VA: Commercial Press, c.1984.

Edmonds, Charles A. *Trial of Charles A. Edmonds, Commissioner of the Land Office of the State of Michigan, before the Senate of Said State on an Impeachment*. Lansing MI: W. S. George, State Printers and Binders, 1872. 2 vols.

Edmonds, Walter Dumaux. *Chad Hanna*. Boston: Little, Brown, c.1940.

———. *Rome Haul*. Boston: Little, Brown, 1929.

Edmondson, Belle. *Diary of Belle Edmondson, January–November, 1864*. Chapel Hill NC: Academic Affairs Library, Univ. NC at Chapel Hill, 1997. Unpub. ms. transcr. for *Documenting the American South* website.

Education. Boston, 1880–.

Educational Method: a Journal of Progressive Public Schools. Washington DC, 1928–1943.

Educational Review. Garden City NY, 1891–1928.

Edward, David Barnett. *The History of Texas*. Cincinnati OH: J. A. James, 1836.

Edwards, Frank S. *A Campaign in New Mexico*. Philadelphia: Carey and Hart, 1847.

Edwards, George. *Gleanings of Natural History*. London: Printed for the Author at the Royal College of Physicians, 1758–1764. 3 vols.

———. *A Natural History of Uncommon Birds*. London: Printed for the Author at the College of Physicians in Warwick-Lane, 1743–1751. 4 vols.

Edwards, Harry Stillwell. *His Defense, and Other Stories*. New York: Century, 1899.

———. *Two Runaways, and Other Stories*. New York: Century, c.1889.

Edwards, John Newman. *Shelby and His Men*. Cincinnati OH: Miami Printing & Publishing, 1867.

Edwards, Jonathan. *Freedom of the Will*. Ed. by Paul Ramsey. New Haven CT: Yale Univ. Press, 1957. Orig. pub. in 1754 by S. Kneeland, Boston.

———. *History of Redemption*. New York: T. & J. Swords, 1793.

———. *The Works of President Edwards*. 1st Amer. ed. Worcester MA: Isaiah Thomas, jun, 1808–1809. 8 vols.

Edwards, Lawrence. *Gravel in My Shoe*. [s.l.]: [s.n.], 1963.

Edwards, Ninian Wirt. *History of Illinois from 1778–1833*. Springfield IL: Illinois State Journal, 1870.

Edwards, Philip Leget. *Diary*. San Francisco: Grabhorn Press, 1932.

Edwards, Richard, ed. *Statistical Gazetteer of the States of Virginia and North Carolina*. Richmond VA: Pub. for the Proprietor, 1856.

Edwardsville Intelligencer. Edwardsville IL, 1868–.

Eet Smakelijk. 7th printing. Holland MI: Steketee-Van Huis, 1971 [c.1964].

Eet Smakelijk. 2d ed. Holland MI: Steketee-Van Huis, c.1976.

Egerton, John. *Southern Food, at Home, on the Road, in History*. Assisted by Ann Bleidt Egerton. Chapel Hill NC: Univ. NC Press, 1993. Orig. pub. in 1987 by Knopf, New York.

Eggenhofer, Nick. *Wagons, Mules and Men*. New York: Hastings House, c.1961.

Eggers, Kerry and Dwight Jaynes. *Against the World*. Champaign IL: Sagamore, 1993.

Eggleston, Edward. *The Book of Queer Stories and Stories Told on a Cellar Door*. Chicago: Adams, Blackmer & Lyon, 1871.

———. *The Circuit Rider*. New York: Charles Scribner's Sons, 1895. Orig. pub. in 1874 by J. B. Ford, New York.

———. *The End of the World*. New York: Orange Judd, 1872.

———. *The Graysons*. New York: Century, c.1887.

———. *The Hoosier School-Boy*. New York: Charles Scribner's Sons, 1883.

———. *The Hoosier Schoolmaster*. New York: Orange Judd, c.1871.

———. *The Hoosier Schoolmaster*. Rev. with an introduction and notes on the dialect. New York: G. D. Hurst, 1892.

———. *The Hoosier Schoolmaster*. New and rev. ed. New York: Orange Judd, 1899.

———. *The Mystery of Metropolisville*. New York: Orange Judd, c.1873.

———. *Roxy*. New York: Charles Scribner's Sons, 1878.

———. *The Schoolmaster's Stories*. Boston: Henry L. Shepard, 1874.

Eggleston, George Cary. *Captain Sam*. New York: Putnam, 1876.

———. *Dorothy South*. Boston: Lothrop, 1902.

———. *The First of the Hoosiers*. Philadelphia: Drexel Biddle, c.1903.

———. *A Man of Honor*. New York: Orange Judd, c.1873.

———. *Recollections of a Varied Life*. New York: Henry Holt, 1910.

———. *The Wreck of the Red Bird*. New York: G. P. Putnam's Sons, 1882.

Ehle, John. *Last One Home*. New York: Harper & Row, c.1984.

Ehrlich, Gretel. *The Solace of Open Spaces*. New York: Viking, 1985.

Eichenlaub, John E. *A Minnesota Doctor's Home Remedies for Common and Uncommon Ailments*. New York: Dell, 1962 [c.1960].

E. I. Du Pont de Nemours & Company. *High Explosives. First Section*. Wilmington DE: E. I. Du Pont de Nemours, c.1920.

Eifert, Virginia Louise Snider. *Birds in Your Back Yard*. 2d ed. Springfield IL: Printed by Authority of the State of Illinois, 1945.

———. *Journeys in Green Places*. New York: Dodd, Mead, c.1963.

Eighty Years Progress of the United States. Hartford CT: L. Stebbins, 1867 [c.1866]. 2 vols.

Eiseley, Loren C. *The Immense Journey*. New York: Random House, c.1957.

Eldora Herald-Ledger. Eldora IA, 1931–.

Elementary School Journal. Chicago, 1914–1992.

Elementary School Teacher. Chicago, 1902–1914.

Eliason, Norman Ellsworth. *Tarheel Talk*. Chapel Hill NC: Univ. NC Press, 1956.

———. *Word Lists from Florida*. c1940. Unpub. materials by students of Norman Eliason at Univ. FL.

Eliot, Jared. *A Continuation of the Essay upon Field-Husbandry*. London: T. Green, 1751.

———. *Essays upon Field Husbandry in New England and Other Papers, 1748–1762*. New York: Columbia Univ. Press, 1934.

Eliot, Thomas Stearns. *The Dry Salvages*. London: Faber and Faber, 1941.

Eliot, Willard Ayres. *Forest Trees of the Pacific Coast*. Assisted by G. B. McLean. New York: G. P. Putnam, 1938.

Elkin, Stanley. *The Rabbi of Lud*. New York: Charles Scribner's Sons, c.1987.

Ellery Queen's Mystery Magazine. New York, 1941–.

Ellet, Elizabeth Fries Lummis. *The New Cyclopaedia of Domestic Economy*. Norwich CT: Henry Bill, c.1872.

———. *Pioneer Women of the West*. New York: C. Scribner, 1852.

Ellicott, Andrew. *The Journal of Andrew Ellicott*. Philadelphia: Budd & Bartram, 1803.

Ellingwood, Finley and John Uri Lloyd. *A Systematic Treatise on Materia Medica and Therapeutics with Reference to the Most Direct Action of Drugs*. Chicago: Chicago Medical Press, c.1898.

Elliot, Daniel Giraud. *North American Shore Birds*. New York: Francis P. Harper, 1895.

———. *The Wild Fowl of the United States and British Possessions*. New York: Francis P. Harper, 1898.

Elliot, Samuel Hayes. *New England's Chattels*. New York: H. Dayton, 1858.

Elliot, William. *The Washington Guide*. Washington DC: Franck Taylor, 1837.

Elliott, Henry Wood. *A Monograph of the Seal-Islands of Alaska*. Washington DC: Govt. Printing Office, 1882.

———. *Our Arctic Province*. New York: Charles Scribner's Sons, 1886.

Elliott, Lang. *The Calls of Frogs and Toads*. Ithaca NY: NatureSound Studio, 1992.

Elliott, Russell R. *History of Nevada*. 2d ed. rev. Lincoln NE: Univ. NE Press, 1987.

Elliott, Sarah Barnwell. *The Durket Sperret*. Chapel Hill NC: Academic Affairs Library, Univ. NC at Chapel Hill, 1999. Text transcr. for *Documenting the American South* website from the 1898 ed. pub. by Henry Holt, New York.

———. *Jerry*. New York: H. Holt, 1891.

Elliott, Stephen. *A Sketch of the Botany of South-Carolina and Georgia*. Charleston SC: J. R. Schenck, 1821–1824. 2 vols.

Elliott, William. *Carolina Sports by Land and Water*. London: R. Bentley, 1867.

Ellis, Anne. *The Life of an Ordinary Woman*. Boston: Houghton Mifflin, 1929.

Ellis, Henry. *A Voyage to Hudson's-Bay, by the Dobbs Galley and California, in the Years 1746 and 1747*. London: Printed for H. Whitridge, 1748.

Ellis, James Tandy. *Poems by Ellis*. Louisville KY: George G. Fetter, 1898.

Ellis, Neenah. *If I Live to Be 100: Lessons from the Centenarians*. New York: Crown, 2002.

Ellis, William. *A Journal of a Tour around Hawaii*. Boston: Crocker & Brewster, 1825.

———. *Narrative of a Tour through Hawaii*. London: H. Fisher, Son, & P. Jackson, 1826.

Ellison, George. *Blue Ridge Nature Journal: Reflections on the Appalachian Mountains in Essays and Art*. Charleston SC: History Press, c.2006.

Ellison, Ralph. *Invisible Man*. New York: Random House, 1952 [c.1947].

———. *Invisible Man*. 2d Vintage International ed. New York: Vintage International, 1995.

Ellroy, James. *The Big Nowhere*. New York: Mysterious Press, c.1988.

Ellsworth, Henry Leavitt. *Washington Irving on the Prairie*. New York: American Book, 1937.

Ellsworth, Henry William. *Valley of the Upper Wabash, Indiana, with Hints on Its Agricultural Advantages*. New York: Pratt, Robinson, 1838.

Ellsworth American. Ellsworth ME, 1854?–.

Elman, Robert. *The Hunter's Field Guide to the Game Birds and Animals of North America*. Rev. ed. New York: Alfred A. Knopf, 1982.

Elmore, Francis Hapgood. *Ethnobotany of the Navajo*. Albuquerque NM: Univ. NM Press, 1943.

———. *Shrubs and Trees of the Southwest Uplands*. Globe AZ: Southwest Parks and Monuments Association, c.1976.

Elmwood, Elnathan, Esq. SEE Greene, Asa

El Paso Herald-Post. El Paso TX, 1880–.

Elsom, James Claude and Blanche M. Trilling. *Social Games and Group Dances*. Philadelphia: J. B. Lippincott, c.1919.

Elwyn, Alfred Langdon. *Glossary of Supposed Americanisms*. Philadelphia: J. B. Lippincott, 1859.

Ely, Seth. *Sacred Music*. Cincinnati OH: Morgan, Lodge, 1822.

Elyria Courier. Elyria OH, 1846–1854.

Elyria Independent Democrat. Elyria OH, 1859–1877.

Elyria Republican. Elyria OH, 1875–1912.

Emancipator. Boston, 1845–1848.

Embury, Emma C. *American Wild Flowers in Their Native Haunts*. New York: Appleton, c.1844.

Emerson, Alice B. *Ruth Fielding at Snow Camp*. New York: Cupples & Leon, c.1913.

Emerson, Amelia Forbes. *Early History of Naushon Island*. Boston: Privately printed, 1935.

Emerson, George Barrell. *Report on the Trees and Shrubs Growing Naturally in the Forests of Massachusetts*. Boston: Dutton and Wentworth, 1846.

———. *A Report on the Trees and Shrubs Growing Naturally in the Forests of Massachusetts*. Boston: Charles C. Little & James Brown, 1850.

Emerson, Ralph Waldo. *The Conduct of Life*. Boston: Ticknor & Fields, 1860.

———. *English Traits*. Boston: Phillips, Sampson, 1856.

———. *Essays [and] Essays: Second Series*. Columbus OH: Charles E. Merrill Pub., 1969. 2 vols. Facsimiles of the 1st printings issued in 1841 and 1844 by J. Munroe, Boston.

———. *A Historical Discourse Delivered before the Citizens of Concord*. Concord NH: G. F. Bemis, 1835.

———. *Journals of Ralph Waldo Emerson*. Ed. by Edward Waldo Emerson and Waldo Emerson Forbes. New York: Houghton Mifflin, 1909–1914. 10 vols.

———. *Letters and Social Aims*. Boston: J. R. Osgood, 1876.

———. *May-Day and Other Pieces*. Boston: Ticknor and Fields, c.1867.

———. *Poems*. Boston: James Munroe, 1847.

———. *Prose Works*. Boston: Fields, Osgood, 1870. 2 vols.

———. *Representative Men*. Boston: Phillips, Sampson, 1850.

———. *Society and Solitude*. Boston: Fields, Osgood, 1870.

Emerson's Magazine and Putnam's Monthly. New York, 1857–1858.

Emmetsburg Reporter. Emmetsburg IA, 1946–1978.

Emmitsburg Area Historical Society. [v.d.]. Internet.

Emmons, Ebenezer. SEE ALSO North Carolina. State Geologist

Emmons, Ebenezer. *Agriculture of New York*. Albany NY: C. Van Benthuysen, 1846–1854. 5 vols.

Emmons, Martha. *Deep Like the Rivers*. Austin TX: Encino Press, 1969.

Emory, William Hemsley. *Notes of a Military Reconnoissance.* Washington DC: Wendell and Van Benthuysen, 1848.

———. *Report on the United States and Mexican Boundary Survey.* Washington DC: Cornelius Wendell, 1857–1859. 2 vols.

Emory University Quarterly. Atlanta GA, 1945–1967.

Empey, Arthur Guy. *First Call.* New York: G. P. Putnam's Sons, 1918.

———. *Over the Top.* New York: G. P. Putnam's Sons, 1917.

Emrich, Duncan. *It's an Old Wild West Custom.* New York: Vanguard Press, c.1949.

Encyclopaedia Britannica. 3d ed. Edinburgh: Printed for A. Bell and C. MacFarquhar, 1788–1797. 18 vols.

Encyclopaedia Britannica. 9th ed. Edinburgh: A. & C. Black, 1875–1889. 25 vols.

The Encyclopedia of Jazz. Comp. by Leonard G. Feather. New York: Horizon Press, 1955–.

Encyclopedia of Southern Culture. Chapel Hill NC: Univ. NC Press, c.1989.

Engeln, Oscar D. *At Cornell.* Ithaca NY: Artil, c.1909.

Engineering and Mining Journal. New York: McGraw-Hill Pub., 1866–.

Engineering-Contracting. New York, 1906–1911.

Engineering News-Record. New York, 1871?–.

England, George Allan. *Pod, Bender & Co.* New York: Robert M. McBride, 1916.

———. *Vikings of the Ice.* Garden City NY: Doubleday, Page, 1924.

Engle, Paul. *Always the Land.* New York: Random House, 1941.

Englebretson, Robert, ed. *Stancetaking in Discourse: Subjectivity, Evaluation, Interaction.* Amsterdam: John Benjamins, 2007.

English Journal. Urbana IL: National Council of Teachers of English, 1912–.

English Language Notes. Boulder CO: Univ. CO, 1963–.

English Studies. Amsterdam: Swets & Zeitlinger, 1919–.

English World-Wide. Amsterdam: J. Benjamins Publishing, 1980–.

Enslow, Ella SEE Murray, Lena Davis

Entomologica Americana. Brooklyn NY: Brooklyn Entomological Society, 1885–1975.

Entomological Society of America. *Common Names of Insects and Related Organisms.* College Park MD, 1946–.

Entomological Society of Washington. *Proceedings.* Washington DC, 1884–.

Eppes, Susan Bradford. *Through Some Eventful Years.* Macon GA: J. W. Burke Company, c.1926.

Epple, Anne Orth. *A Field Guide to the Plants of Arizona.* Mesa AZ: LewAnn Publishing, c.1995.

Epstein, Dena J. *Sinful Tunes and Spirituals.* Urbana IL: Univ. IL Press, c.1977.

Epstein, Joseph. *Friendship: an Expose.* Boston: Houghton Mifflin, 2006.

Erdrich, Louise. *The Beet Queen.* New York: Henry Holt, c.1986.

———. *Love Medicine.* New York: Holt, Rinehart and Winston, c.1984.

———. *Tracks.* New York: Henry Holt, c.1988.

Erichsen-Brown, Charlotte. *Medicinal and Other Uses of North American Plants.* New York: Dover Publications, c.1979.

Ernst, Carl H. and Roger W. Barbour. *Turtles of the United States.* Lexington KY: Univ. Press KY, c.1972.

Ersine, Noel. *Underworld and Prison Slang.* Upland IN: A. D. Freese & Son, c.1933.

Erythea, a Journal of Botany, West American and General. Berkeley CA, 1893–1938.

Escanaba Daily Press. Escanaba MI, 1922–1978.

ESPN Outdoors. [v.d.]. Internet.

Esquire. Chicago, 1933–.

Esrey, William P. and Constantine Hering. *Materia Medica of American Provings.* Philadelphia: Rademacher & Sheek, 1853.

Essex Antiquarian. Salem MA, 1897–1909.

Essex County Natural History Society. *Journal.* Salem MA?, 1836–1852.

Essex Institute. *Bulletin.* Salem MA, 1869–1898.

———. *Historical Collections.* Salem MA, 1859–.

———. *Proceedings.* Salem MA, 1848–1871.

Essex Register. Salem MA, 1807–1840.

Essig, Edward Oliver. *Injurious and Beneficial Insects of California.* Sacramento CA: California State Printing Office, 1913.

———. *Injurious and Beneficial Insects of California.* 2d ed. Sacramento CA: California State Commission of Horticulture, 1915.

———. *Insects of Western North America.* New York: Macmillan, 1926.

Estabrook, Emma Franklin. *Givers of Life.* 2d ed. Boston: Marshall Jones, 1932.

Ethnohistory. Bloomington IN: IN Univ., 1954–.

An Ethnologic Dictionary of the Navaho Language. Saint Michaels AZ: Franciscan Fathers, c.1910.

Ethnology. Pittsburgh PA: Univ. Pittsburgh, 1962–.

Etude, the Music Magazine. Philadelphia: Presser, 1883–1957.

Eubank, Kent. *Horse and Buggy Days.* Kansas City MO: Burton, c.1927.

Eustis, Celestine. *Cooking in Old Creole Days.* New York: R. H. Russell, 1903.

Evanoff, Vlad. *Best Ways to Catch More Fish in Fresh and Salt Water.* Garden City NY: Doubleday, 1975.

Evanovich, Janet. *Two for the Dough.* New York: Scribner, c.1996.

Evans, Albert S. *A la California.* San Francisco: A. L. Bancroft, 1874.

Evans, David. *Tommy Johnson.* London: Studio Vista, c.1971.

Evans, Estwick. *A Pedestrious Tour, of Four Thousand Miles, through the Western States and Territories . . . 1818.* Concord NH: Joseph C. Spear, 1819.

Evans, George Samuel. *Wylackie Jake of Covelo.* San Francisco: Press of Hicks-Judd, c.1904.

Evans, Hugh. "Hugh Evans' Journal of Colonel Henry Dodge's Expedition to the Rocky Mountains in 1835." *Mississippi Valley Historical Review.* (1927–1928) 14.192–214.

———. "The Journal of Hugh Evans, Covering the First and Second Campaigns of the United States Dragoon Regiment in 1834 and 1835." *Chronicles of Oklahoma.* (1925) 3.175–215.

Evans, Lewis. *Geographical, Historical, Political, Philosophical and Mechanical Essays.* Philadelphia: Printed by B. Franklin and D. Hall, 1755.

Evans, Nelson Wiley and Emmons B. Stivers. *A History of Adams County, Ohio from Its Earliest Settlement to the Present Time.* West Union OH: E. B. Stivers, 1900.

Evansville Courier. Evansville IN, 1888–1998.

Evansville Courier & Press. Evansville IN, 1999–.

Evarts, Hal George. *Spanish Acres.* Boston: Little, Brown, 1925.

———. *Tumbleweeds.* Boston: Little, Brown, c.1923.

Evening and the Morning Star. Independence MO, 1832–1833.

Evening Bulletin. Decatur IL, 1895?–1897?

Evening Capital. Annapolis MD, 1922–1981.

Evening Democrat. Warren PA, 1893–1900.

Evening Gazette. Cedar Rapids IA, 1912–1927.

Evening Gazette. Port Jervis NY, 1869–1924.

Evening Herald. Syracuse NY, 1877–1904.

Evening Huronite. Huron SD, 1920–1944.

Evening Independent. Massillon OH, 1891–1990.

Evening Journal. Waukesha WI, 1890–1900.

Evening Journal-Tribune. Marysville OH, 1951–1958.

Evening News. Ada OK, 1904–.

Evening News. Lincoln NE, 1892–1898.

Evening Observer. Dunkirk NY, 1882–1885; 1965–.

Evening Post. Charleston SC, 1978–1991.

Evening Post SEE ALSO *New-York Evening Post*

Evening Post. New York, 1832–1920.

Evening Standard. Uniontown PA, 1941–1980.

Evening State Journal. Lincoln NE, 1919–1920; 1929–1942.

Evening State Journal and Lincoln Daily News. Lincoln NE, 1916–1919.

Evening Telegraph SEE ALSO *Dixon Evening Telegraph*

Evening Telegraph. Dixon IL, 1885–1901.

Evening Times. Cumberland MD, 1892–1916.

Evening Tribune. Albert Lea MN, 1905–1981.

Evening World. New York, 1887–1931.

Everett, Thomas H. *Living Trees of the World.* New York: Doubleday, 1968.

———. *The New York Botanical Garden Illustrated Encyclopedia of Horticulture.* New York: Garland, 1980–1982. 10 vols.

Evergreen. New York, 1844–1853.

Evergreen Review. New York: Grove Press, 1957–1984.

Everhart, Watson Harry. *Fishes of Maine.* Augusta ME: Department of Inland Fisheries and Game, 1950.

Evermann, Barton Warren and Howard Walton Clark. *Lake Maxinkuckee.* Indianapolis IN: Indiana Dept. of Conservation, 1920. 2 vols.

Everpoint SEE Field, Joseph M.

Evers, Charles and Andrew Szanton. *Have No Fear.* New York: John Wiley & Sons, c.1997.

Evers, Robert August. *Some Unusual Natural Areas in Illinois and a Few of Their Plants.* Urbana IL: [s.n.], 1963.

Evers, Robert August and Roger P. Link. *Poisonous Plants of the Midwest & Their Effects on Livestock.* Urbana-Champaign IL: Univ. IL College of Agriculture, 1972.

Everybody's Magazine. New York: Ridgway, 1899–1929.

Every Other Sunday. Boston: Unitarian Sunday-School Society, 1885–1910.

Evolution: International Journal of Organic Evolution. Lancaster PA: Society for the Study of Evolution, 1947–.

Ewan, Joseph and Nesta Ewan. *John Banister and His Natural History of Virginia, 1678–1692.* Urbana IL: Univ. IL Press, 1970.

Ewell, James. *The Medical Companion.* 7th ed., rev., enlarged and very considerably improved. Washington DC: Printed for the Proprietors, 1827.

Ewen, David, ed. *American Popular Songs from the Revolutionary War to the Present.* New York: Random House, 1966.

Examiner & Chronicle SEE *San Francisco Examiner*

Exley, Frederick. *A Fan's Notes, a Fictional Memoir.* New York: Harper & Row, 1968.

Explorations in Alaska in 1898. "U.S. Geological Survey Twentieth Annual Report 1898–99. (1900) Pt. 7.

Expounder of Primitive Christianity, Devoted to Theoretical and Practical Religion. Ann Arbor MI, 1847–1848.

"F" SEE Ford, Lemuel

Facts. Clute TX, 1957–.

Fagaly, William A. *Tools of Her Ministry: the Art of Sister Gertrude Morgan.* With essays by Jason Berry and Helen M. Shannon. New York: American Folk Art Museum, 2004.

Faherty, Robert. *Big Old Sun.* New York: G. P. Putnam's Sons, c.1941.

Fairbanks Daily News-Miner. Fairbanks AK, 1909–.

Fairbanks Sunday Times. Fairbanks AK, 1906–1916.

Fairchild Tropical Botanic Garden. [v.d.]. Internet.

Fall River, Massachusetts. Board of Park Commissioners. *Annual Report.* Fall River MA, 1902–1922?

Family Magazine. New York, 1833–1841.

The Family of the Seisers. New York: Printed for the Author by J. M. Elliott, 1844. 2 pts.

Family Visitor. Cleveland OH, 1850–1853.

Fanning, Edmund. *Voyages to the South Seas, Indian and Pacific Oceans, China Sea, Northwest Coast, Feejee Islands, South Shetlands, etc.* Fairfield WA: Ye Galleon Press, 1970 [c.1838].

Fargo Argus. Fargo ND, 1879–1898.

Faries, Rachel Bernice. *A Word Geography of Missouri.* Columbia MO: Univ. MO-Columbia diss., 1967.

Farish, Thomas Edwin. *The Gold Hunters of California.* Chicago: M. A. Donohue, 1904.

Farlow, W. G. *The Gymnosporangia.* Boston: Boston Society of Natural History, 1880.

Farm Boys. Coll. and ed. by Will Fellows. Madison WI: Univ. WI Press, c.1996.

Farmer, Fannie Merritt. *The All New Fannie Farmer Boston Cooking-School Cookbook.* Rev. by Wilma Lord Perkins. 10th ed. completely rev. Boston: Little, Brown, 1959.

———. *The All New Fannie Farmer Boston Cooking-School Cookbook.* Rev. by Wilma Lord Perkins. 10th ed. completely rev. New York: Bantam Books, 1977. Repr. of the 1959 ed. pub. by Little, Brown, Boston.

———. *The Boston Cooking-School Cook Book.* New ed. completely rev. Boston: Little, Brown, 1936.

———. *The Boston Cooking-School Cook Book.* 8th ed. completely rev. Boston: Little, Brown, 1946.

———. *The Boston Cooking-School Cook Book.* Completely rev. by Wilma Lord Perkins. 9th ed. Boston: Little, Brown, 1951.

———. *The Fannie Farmer Cookbook.* Rev. by Wilma Lord Perkins. 11th ed. rev. Boston: Little, Brown, 1965.

———. *Fannie Farmer's Handy Cook Book.* Rev., ed. and abridged by Wilma Lord Perkins. New York: New American Library, 1950.

———. *The Original Fannie Farmer Cook Book, 1896.* New York: H. L. Levin Associates, distributed by Crown, 1973. Facsimile of the 1896 ed. pub. under the title *The Boston Cooking-School Cook Book* by Little, Brown, Boston.

Farmer, John Stephen, ed. *Americanisms-Old and New.* Ann Arbor MI: Gryphon Books, 1971. Orig. pub. in 1889 by J. Paulter, London.

Farmer, John Stephen and W. E. Henley, comps. *Slang and Its Analogues Past and Present.* London: Printed for subscribers only, 1890–1904. 7 vols.

Farmer's Almanack SEE *Old Farmer's Almanac*

Farmers' Cabinet. Amherst NH, 1802–1900.

Farmers' Cabinet, and American Herd Book. Philadelphia, 1836–1848.

Farmer's Monthly Visitor. Manchester NH, 1839–1853.

Farmers' Register. Petersburg VA, 1833–1843.

Farm Journal and Farmer's Wife. Philadelphia, 1939–1945.

Farnham, Eliza Woodson Burhans. *Life in Prairie Land.* New York: Harper & Bros., 1846.

Farnham, Joseph Ellis Coffee. *Brief Historical Data and Memories of My Boyhood in Nantucket.* 2d ed. Providence RI: Snow & Farnham, 1923.

Farnham, Thomas Jefferson. *Travels in the Great Western Prairies.* New York: Da Capo Press, 1973. Repr. of the 1843 London ed.

Farr, Sidney Saylor. *More than Moonshine.* Pittsburgh PA: Univ. Pittsburgh Press, 1983.

———. *My Appalachia.* Lexington KY: Univ. KY Press, c.2007.

Farrar, Charles Alden John. *The Androscoggin Lakes Illustrated.* Boston: Androscoggin Lakes Transportation, 1888 [c.1885].

———. *Wild Woods Life or, a Trip to Parmachenee.* Boston: Lee & Shepard; New York: Charles T. Dillingham, 1884.

Farrar, J. Maurice. *Five Years in Minnesota.* London: Sampson Low, Marston, Searle & Rivington, 1880.

Farrar, John, Mrs. *The Young Lady's Friend.* New York: Samuel S. & William Wood, 1838 [c.1836].

Farrell, James Thomas. *No Star Is Lost.* New York: Vanguard Press, c.1938.

———. *Young Lonigan.* New York: Vanguard Press, 1932.

———. *The Young Manhood of Studs Lonigan.* New York: Vanguard Press, c.1934.

———. *The Young Manhood of Studs Lonigan.* New York: Avon, 1974. Orig. pub. in 1934 by Vanguard Press, New York.

Farrington, Edward Irving, ed. *The Gardener's Travel Book.* Boston: Hale, Cushman & Flint, c.1938.

Farrington, S. Kip, Jr. *Railroading from the Head End.* Garden City NY: Doubleday, Doran, 1943.

Farris, John. *Sharp Practice.* New York: Simon and Schuster, c.1974.

Farrow, Edward Samuel. *A Dictionary of Military Terms.* Rev. ed. New York: Thomas Y. Crowell, c.1918.

———. *Mountain Scouting.* New York: The Author, 1881.

Farwell, Byron. *Over There.* New York: W. W. Norton, c.1999.

Farwell, Harold F. and J. Karl Nicholas, eds. *Smoky Mountain Voices.* Lexington KY: Univ. Press KY, c.1993.

Fassett, Norman Carter. *Spring Flora of Wisconsin.* Madison WI: Democrat Printing, 1931.

Fast, Howard. *Freedom Road.* New York: Duell, Sloan & Pearce, 1944.

Faulkner, John. *Dollar Cotton.* New York: Harcourt, Brace, c.1942.

———. *Men Working.* New York: Harcourt, Brace, c.1941.

———. *My Brother Bill.* New York: Trident Press, 1963.

Faulkner, William. *Absalom, Absalom.* New York: Modern Library, c.1951. Orig. pub. in 1936.

———. *As I Lay Dying.* New York: J. Cape, H. Smith, c.1930.

———. *As I Lay Dying.* New ed., corr. and reset. New York: Random House, 1964.

———. *Big Woods.* New York: Random House, 1955.

———. *Collected Stories.* New York: Random House, 1950.

———. *A Fable.* New York: Random House, 1954.

———. *Flags in the Dust.* Ed. by Douglas Day. New York: Random House, 1973. Orig. pub. in 1929 under the title *Sartoris.*

———. *Go Down, Moses, and Other Stories.* New York: Random House, 1942.

———. *The Hamlet.* New York: Random House, c.1940.

———. *The Hamlet.* 3d ed. New York: Random House, 1964.

———. *Intruder in the Dust.* New York: Random House, 1948.

———. *Knight's Gambit.* New York: Random House, 1949.

———. *Light in August.* New York: H. Smith & R. Haas, c.1932.

———. *The Mansion.* New York: Random House, 1959.

———. *Mosquitoes.* New York: Liveright, 1955. Orig. pub. in 1927.

———. *The Reivers.* New York: Random House, 1962.

———. *Requiem for a Nun.* New York: Random House, 1951.

———. *Sanctuary.* New York: Modern Library, c.1931.

———. *Sartoris.* New York: Harcourt, Brace, 1951. Orig. pub. in 1929.

———. *Soldiers' Pay.* New York: Boni & Liveright, 1926.

———. *The Sound and the Fury.* London: Chatto and Windus, 1931. Orig. pub. in 1929.

———. *The Sound and the Fury.* New York: Vintage Books,

1954. Photographic repr. from the 1929 ed. pub. by Random House.

———. *The Sound and the Fury & As I Lay Dying, with a New Appendix as a Forward by the Author.* New York: Modern Library, 1946.

———. *The Town.* New York: Random House, 1957.

———. *The Unvanquished.* New York: Random House, 1938.

———. *The Wild Palms.* New York: Random House, c.1939.

———. *The Wishing Tree.* New York: Random House, 1967 [c.1964].

Fauna Americana. New York: Arno Press, 1974.

Fauske, Gerald Mark. *Orthoptera of the Northern Great Plains.* [v.d.]. Internet.

Faust, Joan Lee. *The New York Times Book of House Plants.* New York: Quadrangle/New York Times Book, c.1973.

Faux, William. *Memorable Days in America.* London: Printed for W. Simpkin and R. Marshall, 1823.

Favorite Recipes of the Virginias. Montgomery AL: Favorite Recipes Press, 1964.

Favorite Recipes of University Women. Montgomery AL: Favorite Recipes Press, c.1968.

Fay, Albert H. *A Glossary of the Mining and Mineral Industry.* Washington DC: Govt. Printing Office, 1920.

Fayetteville Daily Democrat. Fayetteville AR, 1920–1937.

Fayetteville Online. Fayetteville NC, 1995–. Internet.

FDA Consumer. Rockville MD, 1966–.

Feagin, Crawford. *Variation and Change in Alabama English.* Washington DC: Georgetown Univ. Press, c.1979.

Fearon, Henry Bradshaw. *Sketches of America.* London: Longman, Hurst, Rees, Orme and Brown, 1818.

Feathered Warrior. Henrietta NY, 190?–19??

Featherman, A. *Report of the Botanical Survey of Southern and Central Louisiana Made during the Year 1870.* New Orleans LA: Printed at the Office of the Republican, 1871.

Featherstonhaugh, George William. *A Canoe Voyage up the Minnay Sotor.* London: Richard Bentley, 1847. 2 vols.

———. *Excursion through the Slave States.* New York: Harper & Bros., 1844.

Federal Register. Washington DC, 1936–.

Federal Reporter. St. Paul MN, 1880–.

Federal Writers' Project. *Alaska: a Guide to Alaska, Last American Frontier.* By Merle Colby. New York: Macmillan, 1939.

———. *California: a Guide to the Golden State.* New York: Hastings House, 1939.

———. *Connecticut: a Guide to Its Roads, Lore, and People.* Boston: Houghton Mifflin, 1938.

———. *Delaware: a Guide to the First State.* New York: Viking, 1938.

———. *Delaware: a Guide to the First State.* New and rev. ed. New York: Hastings House, 1955.

———. *Florida: a Guide to the Southernmost State.* New York: Oxford Univ. Press, 1939.

———. *Idaho: a Guide in Word and Picture.* Caldwell ID: Caxton Printers, 1937.

———. *Idaho, a Guide in Word and Picture.* 2d ed. rev. New York: Oxford Univ. Press, 1950.

———. *Idaho Lore.* Prepared by Vardis Fisher, state director. Caldwell ID: Caxton Printers, 1939.

———. *Illinois: a Descriptive and Historical Guide.* Chicago: A. C. McClurg, 1939.

———. *Iowa: a Guide to the Hawkeye State.* New York: Viking Press, 1938.

———. *Kansas: a Guide to the Sunflower State.* New York: Viking Press, 1939.

———. *Kentucky: a Guide to the Bluegrass State.* Rev. ed. New York: Harcourt, 1954 [c.1939].

———. *Lay My Burden Down.* Ed. by B. A. Botkin. Chicago: Univ. Chicago Press, c.1945.

———. *Maine: a Guide 'Down East'.* Boston: Houghton Mifflin, 1937.

———. *Massachusetts: a Guide to Its Places and People.* Boston: Houghton Mifflin, c.1937.

———. *Minnesota: a State Guide.* New York: Viking Press, 1938.

———. *Mississippi: a Guide to the Magnolia State.* New York: Viking Press, 1938.

———. *Montana: a State Guide Book.* New York: Viking Press, 1939.

———. *Montana: a State Guide Book.* St. Clair Shores MI: Somerset, 1973. Orig. pub. in 1939 by Viking Press, New York.

———. *Nebraska: a Guide to the Cornhusker State.* New York: Viking Press, 1939.

———. *New Hampshire: a Guide to the Granite State.* Boston: Houghton Mifflin, 1938.

———. *New Jersey: a Guide to Its Present and Past.* New York: Viking Press, 1939.

———. *New Orleans City Guide.* Boston: Houghton Mifflin, 1938.

———. *North Carolina: a Guide to the Old North State.* Chapel Hill NC: Univ. NC Press, 1939.

———. *The North Carolina Guide.* Ed. by Blackwell P. Robinson. Chapel Hill NC: Univ. NC Press, 1955.

———. *North Dakota: a Guide to the Northern Prairie State.* Fargo ND: Knight Printing, 1938.

———. *The Ocean Highway.* New York: Modern Age Books, c.1938.

———. *Rhode Island: a Guide to the Smallest State.* Boston: Houghton Mifflin, 1937.

———. *South Dakota: a Guide to the State.* Pierre SD: State Publishing, 1938.

———. *South Dakota: a Guide to the State.* 2d ed. rev. New York: Hastings House, 1952.

———. *Tennessee: a Guide to the State.* New York: Viking Press, 1939.

———. *These Are Our Lives.* Chapel Hill NC: Univ. NC Press, 1939.

———. *U.S. One.* New York: Modern Age Books, 1938.

———. *Vermont: a Guide to the Green Mountain State.* Boston: Houghton Mifflin, 1937.

———. *Vermont: a Guide to the Green Mountain State.* 2d ed. rev. and enlarged. Boston: Houghton Mifflin, 1966.

Federal Writers' Project. New York City. *New York Panorama.* New York: Random House, 1938.

Feibleman, Peter S. *A Place without Twilight.* Cleveland OH: World Publishing, 1958.

Feikema, Feike SEE Manfred, Frederick Feikema

Feinsilver, Lillian Mermin. *The Taste of Yiddish.* South Brunswick NJ: Thomas Yoseloff, c.1970.

Fellows, Dexter W. and Andrew A. Freeman. *This Way to the Big Show.* New York: Viking Press, 1936.

Felt, Ephraim Porter. *Manual of Tree and Shrub Insects.* New York: Macmillan, 1924.

Felt, Ephraim Porter and W. Howard Rankin. *Insects and Diseases of Ornamental Trees and Shrubs.* New York: Macmillan, 1932.

Felt, Joseph Barlow. *Annals of Salem.* 2d ed. Salem MA: W. & S. B. Ives; Boston: J. Munroe, 1845–1849. 2 vols.

———. *The Customs of New England.* New York: Burt Franklin, 1970. Repr. of the 1853 ed. orig. pub. by the Press of T. R. Marvin, New York.

Felton, Harold W., comp., ed. *Legends of Paul Bunyan.* New York: A. A. Knopf, 1947.

Fenner, Ball. *Raising the Veil.* Boston: James French, 1856.

Ferber, Edna. *Cimarron.* Garden City NY: Doubleday, Doran, 1930.

———. *Dawn O'Hara.* 8th ed. New York: Grosset & Dunlap, c.1911.

———. *Fanny Herself.* New York: Grosset & Dunlap, c.1917.

———. *Giant.* Garden City NY: Doubleday, c.1952.

———. *Show Boat.* New York: Grosset & Dunlap, c.1926.

Ferber, Edna and George S. Kaufman. *Stage Door.* Garden City NY: Doubleday, Doran, 1938 [c.1936].

Ferguson, Barbara, ed. *All about Trees.* San Francisco: Ortho Books, c.1982.

Ferguson, Charles D. *Experiences of a Forty-Niner.* Cleveland OH: Williams, 1888.

Ferguson, Richard. *Abaddon's Steam Engine, Calumny, Delineated.* Philadelphia: J. H. Cunningham, Printer, 1817.

Ferguson, William. *America by River and Rail.* London: James Nisbet, 1856.

Fergusson, Adam. *Practical Notes Made during a Tour in Canada.* Edinburgh: W. Blackwood, 1833.

Fergusson, Erna. *New Mexico.* New York: Alfred A. Knopf, 1951.

———. *Our Southwest.* New York: Alfred A. Knopf, 1940.

Fergusson, Harvey. *Wolf Song.* New York: A. A. Knopf, 1927.

Ferhoodled English. Gettysburg PA: Conestoga Crafts, 1964.

Fern, Fanny SEE Parton, Sara Payson Willis

Fernald, Charles Henry. *The Grasses of Maine.* Augusta ME: Sprague & Son, 1885.

Fernald, Merritt Lyndon and Alfred Charles Kinsey. *Edible Wild Plants of Eastern North America.* Cornwall-on-Hudson NY: Idlewild Press, c.1943.

Ferrall, Simon Ansley SEE O'Ferrall, Simon Ansley

Ferretti, Fred. *The Great American Book of Sidewalk, Stoop, Dirt, Curb, and Alley Games.* New York: Workman Publishing, c.1975.

———. *The Great American Marble Book.* New York: Workman Publishing, 1973.

Ferris, Warren Angus. *Life in the Rocky Mountains.* Denver CO: F. A. Rosenstock, Old West Pub., 1940.

Fessenden, Thomas Green. *Democracy Unveiled.* Boston: David Carlisle, for the Author, 1805.

———. *Democracy Unveiled.* 3d ed. New York: Printed for I. Riley, 1806.

———. *The Ladies Monitor, A Poem.* Bellows Falls VT: Bill Blake, 1818.

———. *The New American Gardener.* Boston: J. B. Russell, 1828.

———. *Original Poems.* London: Albion Press, 1804.

———. *Terrible Tractoration!!* 2d ed. with great additions. London: T. Hurst, 1803.

Fetterman, John. *Stinking Creek.* New York: Dutton, 1967.

Fickett, David. *Nectar.* New York: Forge, 2002.

Fidler, Isaac. *Observations on Professions, Literature, Manners, and Emigration, in the United States and Canada, . . . 1832.* New York: J. & J. Harper, 1833.

Field, Edward, ed. *State of Rhode Island and Providence Plantations at the End of the Century.* Boston: Mason Publishing, 1902. 3 vols.

Field, Edward Salisbury. *A Six-Cylinder Courtship.* New York: Grosset & Dunlap, 1907.

Field, Eugene. *A Little Book of Western Verse.* Chicago: J. Wilson, 1889.

———. *Love-Songs of Childhood.* New York: Charles Scribner's Sons, 1898 [c.1894].

Field, Henry M. *Bright Skies and Dark Shadows.* New York: Charles Scribner's Sons, 1890.

Field, Joseph E. *Three Years in Texas.* Greenfield MA: Justin Jones, 1935. Repr. of c.1836 ed. pub. by Steck, Austin TX.

Field, Joseph M. *The Drama in Pokerville.* Philadelphia: T. B. Peterson and Bros., 1847 [c.1843].

Field, Thomas P. *A Guide to Kentucky Place Names.* Lexington KY: Univ. KY, Kentucky Geological Survey, 1961.

Field. London: John Clark, 1853?–1920?

Field and Forest. Washington DC, 1875–1878.

Field and Stream. Los Angeles, 1895–.

Field and Stream Game Bag. Ed. by Robeson Bailey. Garden City NY: Doubleday, c.1948.

Field Museum of Natural History. *Botanical Series.* Chicago, 1895–1947.

———. *Zoological Series.* Chicago, 1895–1943.

Fields, James Thomas. *Underbrush.* Boston: J. R. Osgood, 1877.

Fields, Mamie Garvin and Karen Elise Fields. *Lemon Swamp and Other Places.* New York: Free Press; London: Collier Macmillan, 1985 [c.1983].

Fierman, Floyd S. *Guts and Ruts.* New York: Ktav Publishing House, c.1985.

Figuier, Louis. *Reptiles and Birds.* Transl. by Parker Gillmore. New ed. rev. London: Cassell, Petter, Galpin, 1873.

Filia SEE Dorsey, Sarah Anne

Filson, John. *Filson's Kentucke.* Louisville KY: John P. Morton, 1929. Facsimile of the 1784 ed. pub. by James Adams, Wilmington DE under the title *The Discovery, Settlement and Present State of Kentucke.*

Filson Club. *Publications.* Louisville KY: J. P. Morton, 1884–1938.

Filson Club History Quarterly. Louisville KY, 1926–.

Finch, Robert. *Death of a Hornet.* Washington DC: Counterpoint, c.2000.

Finerty, James J. *Criminalese.* [s.l.]: [s.n.], c.1926.

Fine Woodworking. Newton CT, 1975–.

Fink, Daniel. *Barns of the Genesee Country, 1790–1915.* Geneseo NY: James Brunner, c.1987.

Fink, Paul M. *Backpacking Was the Only Way.* Johnson City TN: East TN State Univ., c.1975.

———. *Bits of Mountain Speech.* Boone NC: Appalachian Consortium Press, 1974.

———. *That's Why They Call It.* Jonesboro TN: [s.n.], c.1964. Orig. pub. in 1956.

Finley, James Bradley. *Autobiography.* Cincinnati OH: Cranston and Curts; New York: Hunt and Eaton, 1853.

Finley, John. *The Hoosier's Nest and Other Poems.* Cincinnati OH: Moore, Wilstach & Baldwin, 1866 [c.1865].

Finn, Henry James, ed. *American Comic Annual.* Boston: Richardson, Lord & Holbrook, 1831.

Firebaugh, Ellen M. *The Physician's Wife and the Things That Pertain to Her Life.* Philadelphia: F. A. Davis; London: F. J. Rebman, 1894.

Firelands Pioneer. Norwalk OH, 1858–.

First Book of the American Chronicles of the Times. Boston: Boyle, 1775.

Fishbase. 1997–. Internet.

Fisher, Albert Kenrick. *The Hawks and Owls of the United States.* Washington DC: Govt. Printing Office, 1893.

Fisher, George Adams. *The Yankee Conscript.* Philadelphia: J. W. Daughaday, 1864.

Fisher, George P. *Life of Benjamin Silliman.* New York: Charles Scribner, 1866. 2 vols.

Fisher, Paul. *The Spitter.* [s.l.]: Privately printed, 1950.

Fisher, Richard Swainson. *Indiana.* New York: J. H. Colton, 1852.

Fisher, Rudolph. *The Walls of Jericho.* New York: A. A. Knopf, c.1928.

Fisher, Vardis. *City of Illusion.* New York: Harper & Bros., c.1941.

———. *Toilers of the Hills.* Boston: Houghton Mifflin, 1928.

Fisher, William. *The Waiters.* Cleveland OH: World Publishing, c.1953.

The Fisherman's Encyclopedia. Ed. by Ira N. Gabrielson and Francesca La Monte (assoc. ed.). 2d ed. Harrisburg PA: Stackpole, 1963.

Fishery Resources of the United States. Washington DC: Public Affairs Press, c.1947.

Fishing World. Floral Park NY: Allsport Pub., 1954–.

Fitch, George Helgeson. *At Good Old Siwash.* Boston: Little, Brown, 1911.

Fitch, William Edward. *Dietotherapy.* New York: D. Appleton, 1918. 3 vols.

Fitchburg Daily Sentinel. Fitchburg MA, 1873–1922.

Fitchburg Sentinel. Fitchburg MA, 1922–1973.

Fithian, Philip Vickers. *Journals and Letters of Philip Vickers Fithian 1773–1774.* New ed. Williamsburg VA: Colonial Williamsburg, 1957.

———. *Philip Vickers Fithian, Journal and Letters.* Princeton NJ: Princeton Univ. Library, 1900–1934. 2 vols.

FitzGerald, Emily McCorkle. *An Army Doctor's Wife on the Frontier.* Ed. by Abe Laufe. Pittsburgh PA: Univ. Pittsburgh Press, 1962.

Fitzgerald, Francis Scott Key. *The Great Gatsby.* New York: Charles Scribner's Sons, 1925.

———. *The Letters of F. Scott Fitzgerald.* Ed. by Andrew Turnbull. New York: Charles Scribner's Sons, c.1963.

———. *This Side of Paradise.* New York: Grosset and Dunlap, 1920.

Fitzgerald, Joseph. *Caseine, Being Rural Meditations.* Cincinnati OH: Published for the Author by John P. Walsh, 1869.

Fitzgerald, Oscar Penn. *California Sketches.* 2d ed. Nashville TN: Southern Methodist Publishing, 1879.

Fitzhugh, Percy Keese. *Roy Blakeley's Adventures in Camp.* New York: Grosset & Dunlap, 2003 [1920].

Fitzmaurice, John W. *The Shanty Boy, or Life in a Lumber Camp.* Cheboygan MI: Democrat Stream, 1889 [c.1888].

Flach, Vera. *A Yankee in German-America.* San Antonio TX: Naylor, c.1973.

Flagg, Andrew S. *The Story of Cape Cod Cooking.* Taunton MA: W. S. Sullwold, c.1979.

Flagg, Edmund. *The Far West.* New York: Harper & Bros., 1838. 2 vols.

———. *Venice.* New York: Charles Scribner, 1853. 2 vols.

Flagg, Fannie. *Fried Green Tomatoes at the Whistle Stop Cafe.* New York: Random House, c.1987.

Flagg, James Montgomery. *I Should Say So.* New York: George H. Doran, c.1914.

Flagg, Wilson. *The Birds and Seasons of New England.* Boston: James R. Osgood, c.1875.

———. *The Woods and By-Ways of New England.* Boston: James R. Osgood, 1872.

Flag of Our Union. Boston, 1846–1870.

Flandrau, Charles Macomb. *Harvard Episodes.* Boston: Copeland & Day, 1897.

———. *Viva Mexico!* New York: D. Appleton, 1910 [c.1908].

Flathead Courier. Polson MT, 1910–.

Flathead Courier, Vacation Guide to a World of Fun. Polson MT: [s.n.], 1966.

Fleharty, Stephen F. *Our Regiment.* Chicago: Brewster & Hanscom Printers, 1865.

Fleischmann, Carl Ludwig. *Der Nordamerikanische Landwirth.* New York: R. Garrigne, 1848.

Fleming, Glenn et al. *Wild Flowers of Florida.* Miami FL: Banyan Books, c.1976.

Fleming, Walter Lynwood. *Civil War and Reconstruction in Alabama.* New York: Columbia Univ. Press, 1905.

Fleming, William. "Colonel William Fleming's Journal of Travels in Kentucky 1779–1780 [and 1783]." In: Mereness, Newton Dennison, ed., *Travels in the American Colonies,* 1916, 615–74.

Fletcher, Baylis John. *Up the Trail in '79.* Norman OK: Univ. OK Press, c.1968.

Fletcher, Curley. *Songs of the Sage, the Poetry of Curley Fletcher.* Salt Lake City UT: Peregrine Smith Books, c.1986. Orig. pub. in 1931 by Kellaway-Ide, Los Angeles.

Fletcher, Elijah. *The Letters of Elijah Fletcher.* Ed. by Martha von Briesen. Charlottesville VA: Univ. Press VA, c.1965.

Fletcher, Inglis Clark. *Raleigh's Eden.* Indianapolis IN: Bobbs-Merrill, c.1940.

Fletcher, Ralph J. *Marshfield Dreams.* New York: Henry Holt, 2005.

Flexner, Stuart Berg. *I Hear America Talking.* New York: Van Nostrand Reinhold, c.1976.

Flint, Charles Louis. *Grasses and Forage Plants.* 5th ed. rev. and enlarged. Boston: Crosby, Nichols, Lee, 1860 [c.1859].

———. *Milch Cows and Dairy Farming.* Boston: J. E. Tilton, 1867 [c.1858].

———. *A Practical Treatise on Grasses and Forage Plants.* New York: G. P. Putnam, 1857.

Flint, James. *Letters from America.* Edinburgh: W. & C. Tait, 1822.

Flint, Margaret, ed. *Dress Right, Dress: the Autobiography of a WAC.* New York: Dodd, Mead, 1943.

Flint, Timothy. *Biographical Memoir of Daniel Boone.* Cincinnati OH: N. & G. Guilford, 1833.

———. *A Condensed Geography and History of the Western States.* Cincinnati OH: E. H. Flint, 1828. 2 vols.

———. *George Mason, the Young Backwoodsman.* Boston: Hilliard, Gray, Little and Wilkins, 1829.

———. *History and Geography of the Mississippi Valley.* 2d ed. Cincinnati OH: E. H. Flint and L. R. Lincoln, 1832 [c.1831].

———. *Recollections of the Last Ten Years.* Boston: Cummings, Hilliard, 1826.

Flood, Pansie Hart. *Sometimey Friend.* Minneapolis MN: Carolrhoda Books, 2005.

Flora of the Great Plains. Lawrence KS: Univ. Press KS, c.1986.

Florence Morning News. Florence SC, 1945–.

Florida. Agricultural Experimental Station. *Bulletin.* Gainesville FL, 1888–.

Florida. Commissioner of Lands and Immigration. *Annual Report.* Tallahassee FL, 1869?–1887?

Florida Cooperative Extension Service. *Extension Entomology Report.* Gainesville FL, 1900–.

Florida Cooperative Extension Service. Entomology and Nematology Department. *Fact Sheet ENY.* Gainesville FL, 1900–.

Florida Cooperative Extension Service. Institute of Food and Agricultural Sciences. *Fact Sheet AN.* Gainesville FL, 1900–.

———. *Fact Sheet FPS.* Gainesville FL, 1900–.

———. *Fact Sheet HS.* Gainesville FL, 1900–.

Florida. Department of Agriculture. *Quarterly Bulletin.* Tallahassee FL, 18??–.

Florida. Division of Plant Industry. *Botany Circular.* Gainesville FL, 1976–.

Florida Entomologist. Winter Haven FL: Florida Entomological Society, 1920–.

Florida. Fish and Wildlife Conservation Commission. *Other Florida Freshwater Fish.* [v.d.]. Internet.

Florida Geological Survey. *Annual Report.* Tallahassee FL, 1908–1933.

Florida Highways. Winter Garden FL, 1923–1953?

Florida Historical Quarterly. St. Augustine FL: Florida Historical Society, 1908–.

Florida Ornithological Society. *Florida Field Naturalist.* Gainesville FL, 1973–.

Florida Review. Gainesville: Univ. FL, 1931–1941.

Florida State Historical Society. *Publications.* Deland FL: Printed for the Sustaining Members of the Society, 1922–.

Florida State Museum. *Bulletin: Biological Sciences.* Gainesville FL, 1956–1989.

Florida Times-Union. Jacksonville FL, 1903–.

Florida. University. *Biological Science Series.* Gainesville FL, 1930–1942.

———. *Center for Aquatic and Invasive Plants.* [v.d.]. Internet.

Florida. University. Agricultural Experiment Station. *Annual Report.* Gainesville FL, 1945–1967.

Florida. University. Department of Entomology and Nematology. *Featured Creatures.* [v.d.]. Internet.

Florida. University. Herbarium. *Collections Catalog.* [v.d.]. Internet.

Florida Wildlife. Tallahassee FL: Florida, Commission of Game and Fresh-water Fish, 1947–.

Flower, Frank Abial. *Life of Matthew Hale Carpenter.* Madison WI: David Atwood, 1883.

Floy, James. *Bible Morality.* New York: Carlton & Porter, 1861.

Floyd, Marcus L. *Cultivation of Cigar-Leaf Tobacco in Florida.* Washington DC: Govt. Printing Office, 1899.
Flynn's Weekly. New York: Red Star News, 1924–1928.
Flynt, Josiah SEE Willard, Josiah Flynt
Flynt, Wayne. *Poor but Proud.* Tuscaloosa AL: Univ. AL Press, c.1989.
Focus on the USA. Philadelphia: J. Benjamins, c.1996.
Folb, Edith A. *Runnin' Down Some Lines.* Cambridge MA: Harvard Univ. Press, 1980.
Foley, Fanny. *Romance of the Ocean.* Philadelphia: Lindsay and Blakiston, 1850.
Folk, Mary Lucile Pierce. *A Word Atlas of North Louisiana.* Baton Rouge LA: LA State Univ. diss., 1961.
Folklife Center News. Washington DC, 1978–.
Folk-Lore, a Quarterly Review of Myth, Tradition, Institution and Custom. London: Folk-lore Society, 1890–.
Folk-Lorist. Chicago, 1893–1894.
Folk-Say. Norman OK, 1929–1932.
Folsom, Montgomery M. *Scraps of Song and Southern Scenes.* Atlanta GA: Chas. P. Byrd, 1889.
Folsom, William Henry Carman. *Fifty Years in the Northwest.* Ed. by E. E. Edwards. St. Paul MN: Pioneer Press, 1888.
Folwell, Amory Prescott. *Municipal Engineering Practice.* New York: J. Wiley & Sons, 1916.
Fond du Lac Commonwealth Reporter. Fond du Lac WI, 1926–1971.
Fond du Lac Reporter. Fond du Lac WI, 1972–1977.
Foote, Horton. *The Trip to Bountiful.* New York: Dramatists Play Service, 1954.
Foote, John Taintor. *Blister Jones.* New York: D. Appleton, 1919 [c.1913].
Foote, Mary Hallock. *The Led-Horse Claim.* Boston: J. R. Osgood, 1883.
Foote, Shelby. *The Civil War, a Narrative.* New York: Random House, 1958–1974. 3 vols.
Foote, Shelby and Walker Percy. *The Correspondence of Shelby Foote & Walker Percy.* Ed. by Jay Tolson. New York: Center for Documentary Studies in Association with W. W. Norton, 1998 [c.1997].
Footner, Hulbert. *Maryland Main and the Eastern Shore.* New York: D. Appleton-Century, 1942.
———. *Rivers of the Eastern Shore.* New York: Farrar & Rinehart, 1944.
Forbes, Alexander. *California.* San Francisco: Thomas C. Russell, 1919. Orig. pub. in 1839 by Smith, Elder of London.
Forbes, Esther. *Rainbow on the Road.* Boston: Houghton Mifflin, 1954.
———. *The Running of the Tide.* Boston: Houghton Mifflin, c.1948.
Forbes, Reginald D., ed. *Forestry Handbook.* New York: Ronald Press, 1956 [c.1955].
Forbes, Stephen Alfred and Robert Earl Richardson. *The Fishes of Illinois.* Danville IL: Published by authority of the State Legislature, 1908.
———. *The Fishes of Illinois.* 2d ed. Springfield IL: [s.n.], 1920.
Forbes. New York, 1918–.
Forbush, Edward Howe. *Birds of Massachusetts and Other New England States.* Norwood MA: Norwood Press, 1925–1929. 3 vols.
———. *A History of the Game Birds, Wild-Fowl and Shore Birds of Massachusetts and Adjacent States.* Boston: Wright & Potter, State Printers, 1912.
Forbush, Edward Howe and John Richard May. *A Natural History of American Birds of Eastern and Central North America.* Rev. and abridged. New York: Bramhall House, 1955.
———. *Natural History of the Birds of Eastern and Central North America.* Rev. and abridged by John Richard May. Boston: Houghton Mifflin, 1939.
Force, Peter, comp. *Tracts and Other Papers Relating Principally to the Origin, Settlement, and Progress of the Colonies in North America.* Washington DC: P. Force, 1836–1846. 4 vols.
Ford, Emily Ellsworth Fowler, comp. *Notes on the Life of Noah Webster.* New York: Privately printed, 1912. 2 vols.
Ford, James Lauren. *The Literary Shop and Other Tales.* New York: Geo. H. Richmond, 1894.
Ford, Lemuel. "A Summer upon the Prairie." In: Hulbert, Archer Butler, ed., *The Call of the Columbia,* 1934, 228–305.
Ford, Leslie. *The Philadelphia Murder Story.* New York: Charles Scribner's Sons, 1945.
Ford, Paul Leicester. *The Honorable Peter Stirling and What People Thought of Him.* New York: International Book, 1899. Orig. pub. in 1894 by H. Holt, New York.
———. *Tattle-Tales of Cupid.* New York: Dodd, Mead, 1898.
Fordham, Elias Pym. *Personal Narrative of Travels in Virginia, Maryland, Pennsylvania, Ohio, Indiana, Kentucky; and of a Residence in the Illinois Territory, 1817–1818.* Cleveland OH: Arthur H. Clark, 1906.
Ford Times. Detroit MI, 1908–.
Foreman, Grant. *The Last Trek of the Indians.* Chicago: Univ. Chicago Press, 1946.
Forest and Stream. New York, 1873–1930.
Forester, Frank SEE Herbert, Henry William
Forester, Jeff. *The Forest for the Trees.* St. Paul MN: MN Historical Society Press, c.2004.
Forest Leaves. Philadelphia: Pennsylvania Forestry Association, 1886–1950.
Forest Products Laboratory. *Wood Handbook.* Washington DC: Govt. Printing Office, 1955.
Forest Products Laboratory. Center for Wood Anatomy Research. *Technology Transfer Fact Sheet.* [v.d.]. Internet.
Forestry Quarterly. Ithaca NY: Cornell Univ., 1902–1916.
Forgotten Coastline Online. 1998–. Internet.
Forkner, John La Rue and Byron H. Dyson. *Historical Sketches and Reminiscences of Madison County, Indiana.* Anderson IN: From the Press of Wilson, Humphreys, 1897.
Forney, Mathias Nace. *Catechism of the Locomotive.* New York: Railroad Gazette, 1875 [c.1874].
Forrest, Robert B. *A History of Western Murray County from 1688 to December 1946.* Lake Wilson MN: [s.n.], 1947?
Forrest, Thomas SEE Barton, Andrew
Forster, John Reinhold. *A Catalogue of the Animals of North America.* London: B. White, 1771.
———. *Flora Americae Septentrionalis.* London: B. White, T. Davis, 1771.
Forsyth, William. *A Botanical Nomenclator.* London: Printed for T. Cadell, 1794.
Fort Myers News-Press. Fort Myers FL, 1931–.
Fortune. Jersey City NJ: Time, 1930–.
Fort Wayne Daily Democrat. Fort Wayne IN, 1866–1870.
Fort Wayne Daily Gazette. Fort Wayne IN, 1863–1887?
Fort Wayne Daily Sentinel. Fort Wayne IN, 1871–1879.
Fort Wayne Gazette. Fort Wayne IN, 188?–1899.
Fort Wayne Journal-Gazette. Fort Wayne IN, 1899–1944.
Fort Wayne News. Fort Wayne IN, 1873–1917.
Fort Wayne News & Sentinel. Fort Wayne IN, 1918–1921.
Fort Wayne Sentinel. Fort Wayne IN, 1884–1917.
Fort Wayne Times. Fort Wayne IN, 1840–1855.
Fort Wayne Times & People's Press. Fort Wayne IN, 1844–1848.
Fort Wayne Weekly Gazette. Fort Wayne IN, 1862–1899.
Fort Wayne Weekly Sentinel. Fort Wayne IN, 1860–1865; 1871–1917.
Fort Wayne Weekly Times. Fort Wayne IN, 1855–1859.
Fort Worth Morning Register. Fort Worth TX, 1897–1903.
Fort Worth Star-Telegram. Fort Worth TX, 1909–.
Forum. Philadelphia, 1886–.
Forward. New York, 1990–.
Fosdick, Charles Austin. *No Moss.* Philadelphia: Porter & Coates; Cincinnati OH: R. W. Carroll, c.1868.
Fossett, Frank. *Colorado.* Denver CO: Daily Tribune Steam Printing House, 1876.
Foster, Augustus John. *Jeffersonian America.* San Marino CA: Huntington Library, 1954.
Foster, Benjamin Browne. *Down East Diary.* Ed. by Charles H. Foster. Orono ME: Univ. ME at Orono Press, 1975.
Foster, Frank P. *An Illustrated Encyclopaedic Medical Dictionary.* New York: D. Appleton, 1888–1894. 4 vols.
Foster, George G. *Fifteen Minutes around New York.* New York: De Witt & Davenport, c.1854.
———. *New York in Slices.* Rev., enlarged, and corr. New York: William Graham, 1849.
———. *New York Naked.* New York: Robert M. De Witt, 1856?
Foster, Harry LaTourette. *A Tropical Tramp with the Tourists.* New York: Dodd, Mead, 1927.
Foster, Herbert L. *Ribbin', Jivin', and Playin' the Dozens.* Cambridge MA: Balinger, c.1974.
Foster, Larimore. *Larry.* New York: John Day, c.1931.
Foster, Robert A. *Lexical Variation in New Jersey.* 1977–1978. Unpub.
Foster, Robert Frederick. *Cooncan (Conquián).* New York: Frederick A. Stokes, 1913.
Foster, William Arthur and Deane G. Carter. *Farm Buildings.* New York: John Wiley & Sons, 1922.
Fought, Carmen. *Chicano English in Context.* New York: Palgrave Macmillan, c.2003.
Fountain, Paul. *The Great Deserts and Forests of North America.* London: Longmans, Green, 1901.
———. *The Great North-West and the Great Lake Region of North America.* London: Longmans, Green, 1904.
Fowells, Harry Ardell, comp. *Silvics of Forest Trees of the United States.* Prepared by the Division of Timber Management Research, Forest Service. Washington DC: U.S. Dept. of Agriculture, Forest Service, 1965.
Fowler, Henry Watson. *A Dictionary of Modern English Usage.* Oxford: Clarendon Press; London: H. Milford, 1927.
Fowler, Jacob. *The Journal of Jacob Fowler . . . 1821–22.* New York: Francis P. Harper, 1898.
Fowler, John. *Journal of a Tour in the State of New York in the Year 1830.* London: Whittaker, Treacher, and Arnot, 1831.
Fowler, Orson Squire. *A Home for All.* Stereotyped ed., rev. and enlarged. New York: Fowler & Wells, c.1853. Preface dated 1880.
———. *Religion, Natural and Revealed.* 3d ed. enlarged and improved. New York: Published by O. S. Fowler, 1844.
Fowler, Samuel Page. *Salem Witchcraft.* With Notes and Explanations by Samuel P. Fowler. Boston: William Veazie, 1865.
Fowler, William Worthington. *Ten Years in Wall Street.* Hartford CT: Worthington, Dustin; Boston: G. P. Hawker, 1870.
Fox, Charles. *The American Text Book of Practical and Scientific Agriculture.* Detroit MI: Elwood, 1854.
Fox, Emily. *Gemini.* Boston: Roberts Bros., 1878.
Fox, Francis S. *Sweet Land of Liberty: the Ordeal of the American Revolution in Northampton County, Pennsylvania.* University Park PA: PA State Univ. Press, 2000.
Fox, John. *The Little Shepherd of Kingdom Come.* New York: Charles Scribner's Sons, 1903.
———. *The Trail of the Lonesome Pine.* New York: Grosset & Dunlap, 1908.
Fox, Stephen. *The Country Houses of John F. Staub.* College Station TX: TX A&M Univ. Press, c.2007.
Fox, William Price. *Southern Fried.* Greenwich CT: Fawcett, 1962.
———. *Southern Fried Plus Six.* Philadelphia: Lippincott, 1968.
Fox, William T. *At the Sea's Edge.* Englewood Cliffs NJ: Prentice-Hall, c.1983.
Foxfire. Rabun Gap GA, 1967–.
Foxfire 2. Garden City NY: Anchor Press/Doubleday, 1973.
Foxfire 3. Garden City NY: Anchor Press/Doubleday, 1975.
Foxfire 4. Garden City NY: Anchor Press, 1977.
Foxfire 5. Garden City NY: Anchor Press, 1979.
Foxfire 6. Garden City NY: Anchor Press/Doubleday, 1980.
Foxfire 7. Garden City NY: Anchor Press/Doubleday, 1982.
The Foxfire Book. Ed. by Eliot Wigginton. Garden City NY: Doubleday, 1972.
Fox-Strangways, Arthur Henry and Maud Karpeles. *Cecil Sharp.* London: Oxford Univ. Press, 1933.
Francis, Winthrop Nelson. *The English Language.* New York: W. W. Norton, 1965.
———. *The Structure of American English.* New York: Ronald Press, c.1958.
Franck, Harry Alverson. *The Lure of Alaska.* Philadelphia: J. B. Lippincott, 1939.
———. *Tramping through Mexico, Guatemala and Honduras; Being the Random Notes of an Incurable Vagabond.* New York: Century, 1916.
———. *Zone Policeman 88.* New York: Century, 1913.
Frank, Pat. *Hold Back the Night.* Philadelphia: J. B. Lippincott, c.1952.
———. *Seven Days to Never.* London: Constable, 1957.
Frankenberger, William T. Jr. and Richard A. Engberg, eds. *Environmental Chemistry of Selenium.* New York: Marcel Dekker, 1998.
Frank Leslie's Illustrated Newspaper. New York, 1855–1891.
Frank Leslie's Popular Monthly. New York, 1876–1904.
Frank Leslie's Ten-Cent Monthly. New York, 1863–1865.
Franklin, Benjamin. *The Autobiography of Benjamin Franklin.* Mineola NY: Dover Publications, c.1996.
———. *The Complete Works of Benjamin Franklin.* Comp. and ed. by John Bigelow. New York: G. P. Putnam's Sons, 1887–1888. 10 vols.
———. *The Papers of Benjamin Franklin.* New Haven CT: Yale Univ. Press, 1959–.
———. *Poor Richard, 1733.* Philadelphia: G. S. Appleton, 1849?
———. *The Sayings of Poor Richard.* Ed. by Paul Leicester Ford. New York: Burt Franklin Reprints, 1974. Repr. of 1890 ed. pub. by G. P. Putnam's Sons.
———. *The Writings of Benjamin Franklin.* Coll. and ed. by Albert Henry Smyth. New York: Macmillan, 1905–1907. 10 vols.
Franklin, Jerry F. and C. T. Dyrness. *Natural Vegetation of Oregon and Washington.* Portland OR: Pacific Northwest Forest and Range Experiment Station, Forest Service, U.S. Department of Agriculture, 1973.
Franklin, John. *Narrative of a Journey to the Shores of the Polar Sea.* London: J. Murray, 1823.

Fraser, Edward and John Gibbons, comps. *Soldier and Sailor Words and Phrases.* London: Routledge and Sons, 1925.

Fraser's Magazine. London, 1830–1882.

Frazer, Timothy C., ed. *"Heartland" English.* Tuscaloosa AL: Univ. AL Press, c.1993.

Frazier, Charles. *Cold Mountain.* New York: Atlantic Monthly Press, c.1997.

Frazier, Edward Franklin. *The Negro Family in the United States.* Chicago: Univ. Chicago Press, 1939.

Frazier, Ian. *Great Plains.* New York: Farrar Straus Giroux, c.1989.

Frear, Mary Emma Dillingham. *Lowell and Abigail.* New Haven CT: Privately Printed, Yale Univ. Press, 1934.

Frear, Walter Francis. *Mark Twain and Hawaii.* Chicago: Lakeside Press, 1947.

Frederic, Harold. *The Copperhead.* New York: Charles Scribner's Sons, 1893.

———. *The Damnation of Theron Ware.* New York: Stone & Kimball, 1896.

———. *The Deserter and Other Stories.* Boston: Lothrop, c.1898.

———. *Marsena.* New York: Charles Scribner's Sons, 1894.

Frederick, Justus George. *The Pennsylvania Dutch and Their Cookery.* New York: Business Bourse, 1935.

Frederick Post. Frederick MD, 1913–2002.

Fredericksburg News. Fredericksburg IA, 1890–.

Fredericksburg Standard. Fredericksburg TX, 1907–.

Frederick-Town Herald. Frederick MD, 1802–1832.

Free, Montague. *All about House Plants.* New York: Doubleday, 1948 [c.1946].

Freeborn County Standard. Albert Lea MN, 1860–1931.

Freedley, Edwin Troxell. *Philadelphia and Its Manufactures.* Philadelphia: Edward Young, 1858.

Freedomways. New York: Freedomways Associates, 1961–.

Free Lance-Star. Fredericksburg VA, 1926–.

Freeman, Leon Lewis and Edward C. Olds. *The History of Marshall County, Kentucky.* Benton KY: Tribune-Democrat, 1933.

Freeman, Lewis Ransome. *Down the Grand Canyon.* London: Heinemann, 1924.

Freeman, Mary Eleanor Wilkins. *By the Light of the Soul.* New York: Harper & Bros., 1907.

———. *The Debtor.* New York: Harper & Bros., 1905 [c.1904].

———. *A Far-Away Melody.* Edinburgh: David Douglas, 1891.

———. *A Humble Romance.* New York: Harper and Bros., c.1887.

———. *Madelon.* New York: Harper & Bros., 1896.

———. *A New England Nun and Other Stories.* Ridgewood NJ: Gregg Press, 1967. Repr. of the 1891 ed. pub. by Harper & Bros., New York.

———. *Pembroke.* New York: Harper & Bros., 1894.

———. *The Shoulders of Atlas.* New York: Harper & Bros., 1908.

———. *Six Trees.* New York: Harper & Bros., 1903.

———. *Understudies.* New York: Harper & Bros., 1901.

———. *Young Lucretia.* New York: Harper & Bros., 1892.

Freeman, Samuel. *The Town Officer.* Portland ME: Printed by Benjamin Titcomb, 1791.

Freeman SEE *Waukesha Freeman*

Freeman and Messenger. Lodi NY, 1839–1843.

Freeman's Journal. Cooperstown NY, 1819–1922.

Freeman's Journal, or, the North American Intelligencer. Philadelphia, 1781–1792.

Free Press. Halifax NC, 1824–1830.

Freitus, Joe. *Wild Preserves.* Boston: Stone Wall Press, c.1977.

Fremantle, Arthur James Lyon. *Three Months in the Southern States.* Edinburgh: William Blackwood and Sons, 1863.

Frémont, John Charles. *Report of the Exploring Expedition to the Rocky Mountains in the Year 1842, and to Oregon and North California in the Years 1843–'44.* Washington DC: Gales & Seaton, 1845.

French, Alice. *The Missionary Sheriff.* Freeport NY: Books for Libraries Press, 1969. Repr. of the 1897 ed. pub. by Harper & Bros., New York.

———. *Otto the Knight.* Boston: Houghton, Mifflin, 1891.

———. *Otto the Knight.* Boston: Houghton, Mifflin, 1900. Orig. pub. in 1891.

———. *Stories of a Western Town.* New York: Charles Scribner's Sons, 1904 [c.1893].

French, J. A., ed. *The Prompter's Hand Book.* Boston: Oliver Ditson, 1893.

French, James Strange. *Elkswatawa, or, the Prophet of the West.* New York: Harper & Bros., 1836. 2 vols.

French, Leigh Hill. *Nome Nuggets.* New York: Montross, Clarke & Emmons, 1901.

French, William. *Some Recollections of a Western Ranchman; New Mexico, 1883–1899.* New York: Frederick A. Stokes, 1928.

Freneau, Philip Morin. *Poems.* Princeton NJ: Univ. Library, 1902–1907. 3 vols.

———. *Poems, Written between the Years 1768 & 1794.* New ed., rev. and corr. Monmouth NJ: Printed at the press of the author, 1795. Facsimile reproduction pub. in 1976 by Scholar's Facsimiles & Reprints, Delmar NY.

———. *The Poems (1786) and Miscellaneous Works (1788) of Philip Freneau.* Delmar NY: Scholars' Facsimiles and Reprints, 1975.

———. *The Prose of Philip Freneau.* New Brunswick NJ: Scarecrow Press, 1955.

Frère, Thomas. *Hoyle's Games.* Illustr. ed. New York: T. W. Strong, c.1857.

Fresno Bee. Fresno CA, 1922–.

Fresno Bee the Republican. Fresno CA, 1932–1975.

Fresno Morning Republican. Fresno CA, 1892?–1932.

Fresno Weekly Republican. Fresno CA, 1885–1897.

Friedman, Kinky. *Greenwich Killing Time.* New York: Beech Tree Books, William Morrow, c.1986.

Friend, William Heartsill. *Plants of Ornamental Value for the Rio Grande Valley of Texas.* College Station TX: Agricultural and Mechanical College of TX, 1942.

Friend, a Religious and Literary Journal. Philadelphia, 1827–1955.

Friends, Society of. Philadelphia Yearly Meeting. *Faith and Practice . . . a Book of Christian Discipline.* Rev. ed. Philadelphia: [s.n.], 1978.

Friends' Intelligencer. Philadelphia, 1853–1885; 1902–1955.

Friends of the Max Kade Institute for German-American Studies. *Friends Newsletter.* Madison WI, 1986–.

Friends' Review, a Religious, Literary and Miscellaneous Journal. Philadelphia: J. Tatum, 1847–1894.

Fries, Adelaide Lisetta, ed. *Records of the Moravians in North Carolina.* Raleigh NC: Edwards & Broughton Print, 1922–1969. 11 vols.

Frome, Michael. *Whose Woods These Are.* Garden City NY: Doubleday, 1962.

Frontier SEE *Frontier and Midland*

Frontier and Midland. Missoula MT: MT State Univ., 1920–1939.

Frontier Guardian. Kanesville IA, 1849–1852.

Frontline. Television program. Boston: PBS, 1983–.

Frost, John. *The Youth's Book of the Seasons.* Philadelphia: Carey, Lea & Blanchard, 1835.

Frost, Julia Watkins. *Annals of Our Ancestors.* Chicago: Privately printed, 1913.

Frost, May Miller and Earl Clarence Frost, comps. . . , eds. *The Peffley—Peffly—Pefley Families in America and Allied Families, 1729–1938.* Los Angeles: May M. Frost and Earl C. Frost, 1938.

Frost, Robert. *The Letters of Robert Frost to Louis Untermeyer.* New York: Holt, Rinehart and Winston, 1963.

———. *New Hampshire.* New York: Henry Holt, 1923.

———. *The Poetry of Robert Frost.* Ed. by Edward Connery Lathem. New York: Holt, Rinehart and Winston, c.1969.

Frothingham, Richard, Jr. *The History of Charlestown, Massachusetts.* Charlestown: Charles P. Emmons, 1846 [c.1845].

Frothingham, Washington. *Once More.* New York: Sheldon, 1875.

Fry, Gladys-Marie. *Night Riders.* Knoxville TN: Univ. TN Press, c.1975.

Fry, Joan. *Backyard Horsekeeping.* New and rev. ed. New York: Lyons, 2007.

Frye, Theodore Christian and George Burton Rigg. *Elementary Flora of the Northwest.* New York: American Book, c.1914.

Fugina, Frank J. *Lore and Lure of the Upper Mississippi River.* Winona MN: Printed by the Author, c.1945.

Fulbright, Tom. *Cow-Country Counselor.* New York: Exposition Press, c.1968.

Fulghum, Robert. *All I Really Need to Know I Learned in Kindergarten.* New York: Villard Books, 1988.

Fuller, Burns. *Burns Fuller Remembers.* Fenton MI: Independent Printing, 1966.

Fuller, Jane Gay. *Uncle John's Flower-Gatherers.* New York: M. W. Dodd, 1869. Author's name on title page is Jane Jay [sic] Fuller.

Fuller, Margaret. *Summer on the Lakes in 1843.* Boston: Charles C. Little and James Brown; New York: Charles F. Francis, 1844.

Fuller, R. Buckminster. *Untitled Epic Poem on the History of Industrialization.* New York: Simon and Schuster, c.1962.

Fulton, Maurice Garland. *Writing Craftsmanship.* New York: Macmillan, 1926.

Fultz, Francis Marion. *The Fly-Aways and Other Seed Travelers.* Bloomington IL: Public School Publishing, 1909.

Funk, Charles Earle. *Heavens to Betsy!* New York: Harper, 1955.

———. *A Hog on Ice.* New York: Harper, 1948.

———. *Horsefeathers, and Other Curious Words.* New York: Warner Paperback Library, 1972 [c.1958].

Funk & Wagnalls College Standard Dictionary. New York: Funk & Wagnalls, 1922.

Funk & Wagnalls New Standard Dictionary of the English Language. New York: Funk & Wagnalls, 1913.

Funk & Wagnalls Standard Dictionary of Folklore, Mythology, and Legend. New York: Funk & Wagnalls, c.1972. A reissue of the 1949–1950 ed. with minor corrections.

Funk and Wagnalls Standard Dictionary of the English Language upon Original Plans. New York: Funk & Wagnalls, 1895. 2 vols.

Fur, Fin and Feather, a Compilation of the Game Laws of the Principal States and Provinces of the United States and Canada. New York: C. Suydam, 1870–1875.

Furlong, Charles Wellington. *Let 'Er Buck.* New York: G. P. Putnam's Sons, 1921.

Furman, Gabriel. *Antiquities of Long Island.* New York: J. W. Bouton, 1875.

Furman, Lucy S. *Sight to the Blind.* New York: Macmillan, 1914.

Furnas, Joseph Chamberlain. *The Americans.* New York: G. P. Putnam's Sons, 1969.

Fur News Magazine. New York: P. Belden, 1905–1920.

Furniture Gazette. London, 1872–1896.

Fussell, Betty. *I Hear America Cooking.* New York: Viking Penguin, 1986.

FWP SEE Federal Writers' Project

FWP SEE ALSO Writers' Program

Gabbard, Alex. *Return to Thunder Road.* Lenoir City TN: Gabbard Publications, 1993 [1992].

Gabrielson, Ira Noel. *Birds of Oregon.* Corvallis OR: OR State College, c.1940.

———. *Wildlife Refuges.* New York: Macmillan, c.1943.

Gaddis, Thomas E. and Long, James O. *Killer, a Journal of Murder.* New York: Macmillan, c.1970.

Gaddis, William. *The Recognitions.* New York: Harcourt, Brace, c.1955.

Gainer, Patrick W. *Witches, Ghosts and Signs.* Grantsville WV: Seneca Books, c.1975.

Gaines, Ernest J. *The Autobiography of Miss Jane Pittman.* New York: Dial Press, 1971.

Gaines, George Strother. *The Reminiscences of George Strother Gaines.* Tuscaloosa AL: Univ. AL Press, c.1998.

Galaxy. New York: Sheldon, 1866–1878.

Gale, Zona. *Friendship Village.* New York: Grosset & Dunlap, 1911 [c.1908].

———. *Peace in Friendship Village.* New York: Macmillan, 1919.

Galena Gazette & Advertiser. Galena IL, 1961–.

Gallaher, James. *The Western Sketch-Book.* Boston: Crocker and Brewster, 1850.

Gallatin, James. *A Great Peace Maker.* New York: Charles Scribner's Sons, 1914.

Gallery, Daniel V. *Eight Bells and All's Well.* New York: W. W. Norton, c.1965.

Galvan, Roberto A. and Richard V. Teschner. *El Diccionario del Español de Tejas.* Silver Spring MD: Institute of Modern Languages, c.1975.

Galveston Daily News. Galveston TX, 1842–.

Gamecock City Trading Post. Sumter SC, 2004?–.

Gammond, Peter, ed. *The Decca Book of Jazz.* London: F. Muller, 1958.

Ganilh, Anthony. *Ambrosio de Letinez.* New York: Charles Francis, 1842. 2 vols.

———. *Mexico Versus Texas.* Philadelphia: N. Siegfried, 1838.

Gann, Walter. *The Trail Boss.* Boston: Houghton Mifflin, 1937.

Gantz, Charlotte Orr. *A Naturalist in Southern Florida.* Coral Gables FL: Univ. Miami Press, 1971.

Garber, Aubrey. *Mountain-Ese.* Radford VA: Commonwealth Press, c.1976.

Garcia, Nasario, ed. *Brujas, Bultos, y Brasas: Tales of Witchcraft and the Supernatural in the Pecos Valley.* Santa Fe NM: Western Edge Press, 1999.

Gard, Wayne. *The Chisholm Trail.* Norman OK: Univ. OK Press, c.1954.

Garden, Alexander. *Anecdotes of the Revolutionary War in America.* Charleston SC: Printed for the author by A. E. Miller, 1822.

Garden. London, 1871–1927.

Garden and Forest. New York, 1888–1897.

Gardener's Monthly and Horticultural Advertiser. Philadelphia, 1859–1875.

Gardener's Monthly and Horticulturist. Philadelphia, 1876–1888.

Gardiner, Lion. *A History of the Pequot War.* Cincinnati OH: J. Harpel, 1860.

Gardiner, Mabel Henshaw and Ann Henshaw Gardiner. *Chronicles of Old Berkeley.* Durham NC: Seeman Press, 1938.

Gardner, Daniel Pereira, ed. *The Farmer's Dictionary.* New York: Harper, 1846.

Gardner, Emelyn Elizabeth. *Folklore from the Schoharie Hills, New York.* Ann Arbor MI: Univ. MI Press, 1937.

Gardner, Eugene Clarence. *Homes.* Boston: James R. Osgood, 1875 [c.1874].

Gardner, John. *October Light.* New York: Knopf, 1976.

Garfield, Brian. *Tripwire.* New York: David McKay, c.1973.

Garfieldian. Chicago, 1913–1949; 1962–.

Garfieldian & Garfield News. Chicago, 1949–1962.

Garland, Hamlin. *Boy Life on the Prairie.* New York: Macmillan, 1899.

———. *Boy Life on the Prairie.* Lincoln NE: Univ. NE Press, 1961. Intro. and author's notes orig. appeared in the 1926 ed. pub. by Allyn and Bacon, Boston.

———. *The Eagle's Heart.* Sunset ed. New York: Harper & Bros., c.1900.

———. *Hesper.* Sunset ed. New York: Harper & Bros., c.1903.

———. *Main-Travelled Roads.* Boston: Arena, 1891.

———. *Prairie Folks.* Chicago: F. J. Schulte, c.1892.

———. *Prairie Folks.* New ed. rev. and enlarged. New York: Macmillan, 1899.

———. *A Son of the Middle Border.* New York: Macmillan, 1917.

———. *The Trail of the Goldseekers.* New York: Macmillan, 1899.

Garland, Hugh A. *The Life of John Randolph of Roanoke.* New York: D. Appleton, 1851.

Garlock, Dorothy. *With Heart.* New York: Warner Vision Books, 1999.

Garlock, Terry L. *Sisters Redeem Their Grumpy Dad.* College Station TX: Virtualbookworm.com, 2003.

Garman, Samuel. *The Reptiles and Batrachians of North America.* Frankfort KY: Yeoman Press, 1883.

Garrard, Lewis Hector. *Wah-To-Yah, and the Taos Trail.* Cincinnati OH: H. W. Derby; New York: A. S. Barnes, 1850.

Garreau, Joel. *The Nine Nations of North America.* Boston: Houghton Mifflin, 1981.

Garrett, Albert Osbun. *Spring Flora of the Wasatch Region.* Salt Lake City UT: Skelton, 1911.

———. *Spring Flora of the Wasatch Region.* 4th ed. rev. Salt Lake City UT: Press of Stevens & Wallis, 1927.

Garrett, George. *In the Briar Patch, a Book of Stories.* Austin TX: Univ. TX Press, 1961.

———. *The Sorrows of Fat City.* Columbia SC: Univ. SC Press, c.1992.

Garrett, Howard and C. Malcolm Beck. *Texas Bug Book.* Rev. ed. Austin TX: Univ. TX Press, 2005.

Garrett, Patrick Floyd. *Authentic Life of Billy, the Kid.* Albuquerque NM: Horn and Wallace, 1964. Orig. pub. in 1882 by New Mexican Print. and Pub., Santa Fe NM.

Garrison, Webb B. *What's in a Word?* New York: Abingdon Press, 1965.

Gass, Patrick. *A Journal of the Voyages and Travels of a Corps of Discovery, under the Command of Capt. Lewis and Capt. Clarke . . . during the Years 1804, 1805 & 1806.* Pittsburg[h] PA: David M'Keehan, 1807.

———. *A Journal of the Voyages and Travels of a Corps of Discovery, under the Command of Capt. Lewis and Capt. Clarke . . . during the Years 1804, 1805 & 1806.* Pittsburgh PA: Printed for David M'Keehan; London: Reprinted for J. Budd, 1808.

Gastonia Gazette. Gastonia NC, 1947–1989.

Gates, Frank Caleb. *Flora of Kansas.* [s.l.]: Kansas Agricultural Experiment Station, 1940.

Gavin, Basil, ed. *Michael Freebern Gavin.* Cambridge MA: Privately printed at the Riverside Press, 1915.

Gawthrop, Betty Grow. *A Dialect Study of the Calumet Region.* West Lafayette IN: Purdue Univ. diss., 1973.

Gazaway, Rena. *The Longest Mile.* Garden City NY: Doubleday, 1969.

Gazette. Cedar Rapids IA, 1979–.

Gazette. Stevens Point WI, 1885–1921.

Gazette and Bulletin. Williamsport PA, 1909–1955.

Gazette of Maine. Portland ME, 1825–1829.

Gazette of the United States. Philadelphia, 1789–1804.

Geauga Democrat. Chardon OH, 1866–1871.

Geauga Times Leader. Chardon OH, 1965–.

Geddes, Norman Bel. *Magic Motorways.* New York: Random House, c.1940.

Geer, John James. *Beyond the Lines.* Philadelphia: J. W. Daughaday, 1863.

Geikie, Archibald. *Text-Book of Geology.* 4th ed. rev. and enlarged. London: Macmillan, 1903. 2 vols.

Geister, Edna. *Ice-Breakers and The Ice-Breaker Herself.* New York: Woman's Press, 1925.

Gellhorn, Martha. *The Trouble I've Seen.* New York: William Morrow, 1936.

Gem, a Literary Annual. London, 1829–1832.

General Contractors Association of New York. *Bulletin.* New York, 1910–1971.

Genesee Farmer and Gardener's Journal. Rochester NY, 1831–1839.

Gentleman and Lady's Town and Country Magazine, or, Repository of Instruction and Entertainment. Boston, 1784–1785.

Gentleman's Magazine. London, 1736–1850.

Gentlemen's Quarterly. New York: Condé Nast, 1931–.

Geographical Review. New York: American Geographical Society, 1916–.

Geographische Gesellschaft von Bern. *Jahresbericht.* Bern: Haller'sche, 1878–1972.

Geological Association of Southern New Jersey. Meeting (20th). *Periglacial Features of Southern New Jersey.* [s.l.], 2003.

Geological Survey of California. *Botany.* By William Henry Brewer, Asa Gray and Sereno Watson. Cambridge MA: Welch, Bigelow; J. Wilson and Son Univ. Press, 1876–1880. 2 vols.

Geological Survey of Ohio. *Report of the Geological Survey of Ohio.* Columbus OH: Nevins & Myers, State Printers, 1873–1874.

———. *Report of the Geological Survey of Ohio.* Columbus OH: Nevins & Myers, State Printers, 1882.

———. *Second Annual Report.* Columbus OH: Samuel Medary, Printer to the State, 1838.

Geology of New York. Albany NY: Printed by Carroll & Cook, printers to the Assembly, 1842–1843. 4 vols.

Geophysics. Tulsa OK: Society of Exploration Geophysicists, 1936–.

George, Albert Joseph, ed. *The Cap'n's Wife.* Syracuse NY: Syracuse Univ. Press, 1946.

George, Jean Craighead. *My Side of the Mountain.* New York: E. P. Dutton, c.1959.

Georgetown Times. Georget2own SC, 2006?–.

Georgia, Ada Eljiva. *A Manual of Weeds.* New York: Macmillan, 1914.

Georgia Bar Association. *Report.* Macon GA, 1884–1895.

Georgia (Colony). General Assembly. *Acts Passed by the General Assembly, 1755–1774.* Wormsloe GA: Privately Printed, 1881.

Georgia. Department of Agriculture. *Farmers and Consumers Market Bulletin.* Atlanta GA, 19??–.

———. *Georgia.* Prepared under the direction of R. T. Nesbitt, Commissioner of Agriculture of Georgia. Atlanta GA: Franklin Printing and Publishing, 1895.

———. *Hand-book of the State of Georgia.* 2d ed. Atlanta GA: Dept. of Agriculture, 1876.

———. *Publications. Circular.* Atlanta GA, 1874–1898.

Georgia Department of Natural Resources. *Fishing.* [v.d.]. Internet.

Georgia Historical Quarterly. Athens GA: Georgia Historical Society, 1917–.

Georgia Historical Society. *Collections.* Savannah GA, 1840–.

Georgia Mineral News Letter. Atlanta GA, 1948–.

Georgia Review. Athens GA: Univ. GA Press, 1947–.

Georgia. University. College of Agriculture. Cooperative Extension Service. *Weeds of the Southern United States.* Athens GA: Cooperative Extension Service, College of Agriculture, Univ. GA, c.1967.

Georgia. University. Cooperative Extension Service. *Fact Sheet.* [v.d.]. Internet.

Georgia. University. Daniel B. Warnell School of Forestry. *Aquaculture Newsletter.* 1996?–. Internet.

Georgia Weekly Telegraph and Georgia Journal & Messenger. Macon GA, 1869–1880.

Gerarde, John. *The Herball or Generall Historie of Plantes.* Enlarged and amended by Thomas Johnson. London: Printed by Adam Islip Joice Norton and Richard Whitakers, 1633.

Geraty, Virginia Mixson. *Bittle en' T'ing'.* Orangeburg SC: Sandlapper Publishing, c.1992.

Gerhard, Frederick. *Illinois as It Is.* Chicago: Keen and Lee; Philadelphia: Charles Desilver, 1857.

German American Annals. Philadelphia: German-American Historical Society, 1897–1919.

German Life. Grantsville MD, 1994–.

German Quarterly. Philadelphia: American Association of Teachers of German, 1928–.

Gerry, Elbridge. *The Diary of Elbridge Gerry, Jr.* New York: Brentano's, c.1927.

Gerstacker, Friedrich. *Die Regulatoren in Arkansas.* Leipzig: Otto Wigand, 1846. 3 vols.

Gesellschaft Naturforschender Freunde. *Schriften.* Berlin, 1780–1794.

Gesner, Abraham. *A Practical Treatise on Coal, Petroleum, and Other Distilled Oils.* Rev. and enlarged by George Weltden Gesner. 2d ed. New York: Bailliere Bros., 1865.

Gettysburg Compiler. Gettysburg PA, 1866–1961.

Gettysburg Times. Gettysburg PA, 1904–.

Ghiglieri, Michael Patrick. *Canyon.* Tucson AZ: Univ. AZ Press, 1992.

Gibbons, Euell. *Stalking the Healthful Herbs.* New York: David McKay, c.1966.

———. *Stalking the Wild Asparagus.* New York: David McKay, c.1962.

Gibbons, Kaye. *Charms for the Easy Life.* New York: G. P. Putnam's Sons, c.1993.

———. *Ellen Foster.* Chapel Hill NC: Algonquin Books, c.1987.

———. *A Virtuous Woman.* Chapel Hill NC: Algonquin Books, 1989.

Gibbons, Phebe Earle. *Pennsylvania Dutch and Other Essays.* 3d ed. rev. and enlarged. New York: AMS Press, 1971. Orig. pub. in 1882 by J. B. Lippincott, Philadelphia.

Gibbs, George. *A Dictionary of the Chinook Jargon.* Washington DC: Smithsonian Institution, 1863.

Gibson, Edmund A. *Basic Seamanship and Navigation.* New York: McGraw-Hill Book, c.1951.

Gibson, Henry H. *American Forest Trees.* Ed. by Hu Maxwell. Chicago: Hardwood Record, 1913.

Gibson, Walter Brown. *Hoyle's Modern Encyclopedia of Card Games.* Garden City NY: Dolphin Books, 1974.

Gibson, William Hamilton. *Secrets Out of Doors.* New York: Harper & Bros., 1913.

———. *Sharp Eyes.* New York: Harper & Bros., 1892.

Giddens, Paul Henry. *Standard Oil Company (Indiana).* New York: Appleton-Century-Crofts, 1955.

Giddings, James Louis. *The Arctic Woodland Culture of the Kobuk River.* Philadelphia: Univ. Museum, Univ. PA, 1952.

Gielow, Martha Sawyer. *The Light on the Hill.* New York: Fleming H. Revell, c.1915.

———. *Uncle Sam.* New York: Fleming H. Revell, c.1913.

Giese, Henry. *Farm Fence Handbook.* Cleveland OH: Republic Steel, 1942.

Giesecke, Albert S. and Jack Fagan. *How to Play Bull and 35 Other Games with Dice.* San Francisco: Albert S. Giesecke, 1960.

Gilbert, Frank M. *History of the City of Evansville and Vanderburg County Indiana.* Chicago: Pioneer Publishing, 1910. 2 vols.

Gilbert, George Blodgett. *Forty Years a Country Preacher.* New York: Harper & Bros., c.1940.

Gilbert, Olive. *Narrative of Sojourner Truth.* Boston: Printed for the Author, 1850.

Gilbreth, Frank Bunker. *Dictionary of Bostonese and Charlestonese.* Charleston SC: Charleston County Bicentennial Committee, c.1974.

Gilchrist County Journal. Trenton FL, 1931?–.

Giles, Albert William. *The Country about Camp Lee, Virginia.* Charlottesville VA: [s.n.], 1918.

Giles, Henry E. *Harbin's Ridge.* Boston: Houghton Mifflin, 1951.

Giles, Janice Holt. *40 Acres and No Mule.* Philadelphia: Westminster Press, 1952.

———. *The Enduring Hills.* Philadelphia: Westminster Press, 1950.

———. *The Great Adventure.* Boston: Houghton Mifflin, 1966.

Giles, Richard. *Slang and Vulgar Phrases and Forms as Used in the Different States of the Union.* New York: Hurst, c.1873.

Gilkey, Helen M. and La Rea J. Dennis. *Handbook of Northwestern Plants.* Corvallis OR: OR State Univ. Bookstores, 1967.

Gill, Theodore Nicholas. *Catalogue of the Fishes of the East Coast of North America.* Washington DC: Smithsonian Institution, 1873.

Gilleland, J. C. *The Ohio and Mississippi Pilot.* Pittsburgh PA: R. Patterson & Lambdin, 1820.

Gillespie, John Birks ("Dizzy") and Al Fraser. *To Be, or Not . . . to BOP.* Garden City NY: Doubleday, 1979.

Gillespie, Joseph. *Recollections of Early Illinois and Her Noted Men.* Chicago: Fergus Printing, 1880.

Gillespie, William H. *A Compilation of the Edible Wild Plants of West Virginia.* New York: Scholar's Library, c.1959.

Gillett, James Buchanan. *Six Years with the Texas Rangers, 1875–1881.* Austin TX: Von Boeckmann-Jones, c.1921.

Gilliam, Edward Winslow. *Uncle Sam and the Negro in 1920.* Lynchburg VA: J. P. Bell, 1906.

Gillis, Jackson. *The Killers of Starfish.* Philadelphia: J. B. Lippincott, c.1977.

Gillmore, Parker. *Accessible Field Sports.* London: Chapman and Hall, 1869.

Gilman, Caroline Howard. *The Poetry of Travelling in the United States.* New York: S. Colman, 1838.

———. *Recollections of a Southern Matron.* New York: Harper & Bros., 1838.

———. *Recollections of a Southern Matron.* Charleston SC: Walker, Richards, 1852. Orig. pub. in 1838 by Harper & Bros., New York.

Gilman, Caroline Howard and Caroline Howard Jervey. *The Young Fortune Teller.* Boston: Lee and Shepard; New York: Lee, Shepard and Dillingham, 1874.

Gilman, Chandler Robbins. *Life on the Lakes.* New York: George Dearborn, 1836. 2 vols.

Gilmore, Albert Field. *Birds of Field, Forest and Park.* Boston: Page, 1919.

———. *Birds through the Year.* New York: American Book, c.1910.

Gilmore, James Roberts. *Among the Pines.* New York: J. R. Gilmore, 1862.

———. *Down in Tennessee.* New York: Carleton, 1864.

———. *My Southern Friends.* New York: Tribune Association, 1863.

Gilmore, Robert Karl. *Ozark Baptizings, Hangings, and Other Diversions.* Norman OK: Univ. OK Press, c.1984.

Gilpatrick, Gil. *Allagash.* Skowhegan ME: Gil Gilpatrick, 2003.

Ginns, Patsy Moore. *Rough Weather Makes Good Timber.* Chapel Hill NC: Univ. NC Press, 1977.

———. *Snowbird Gravy and Dishpan Pie.* Chapel Hill NC: Univ. NC Press, c.1982.

Gipson, Fred. *Hound-Dog Man.* New York: Harper & Bros., c.1949.

———. *Old Yeller.* New York: Harper, 1956.

Giraud, Jacob Post. *The Birds of Long Island.* New York: Wiley & Putnam, 1844.

Gist, Christopher. *Christopher Gist's Journals.* Pittsburgh PA: J. R. Weldin, 1893.

Gladstone, Thomas H. *The Englishman in Kansas.* New York: Miller, 1857.

Glasgow, Ellen Anderson Gholson. *Barren Ground.* Garden City NY: Doubleday, Page, 1925.

———. *The Builders.* Garden City NY: Doubleday, Page, 1919.

———. *The Deliverance.* New York: Doubleday, Page, 1904.

———. *The Descendant.* New York: Harper & Bros., 1897.

———. *In This Our Life.* New York: Harcourt, Brace, c.1941.

———. *Vein of Iron.* New York: Harcourt, Brace, c.1935.

Glass, Montague. *Potash & Perlmutter.* Philadelphia: Henry Altemus, c.1910.

Glazier, Willard W. *The Capture, the Prison-Pen and the Escape.* Hartford CT: H. E. Goodwin, 1869 [c.1865].

———. *The Capture, the Prison Pen, and the Escape.* New York: R. H. Ferguson, 1870 [c.1865].

Gleanings in Bee Culture. Medina OH, 1874–1992.

Gleason, Henry Allan. *The New Britton and Brown Illustrated Flora of the Northeastern United States and Adjacent Canada.* New York: New York Botanical Garden, 1952. 3 vols.

Gleason, Henry Allan and Arthur Cronquist. *Manual of Vascular Plants of Northeastern United States and Adjacent Canada.* Boston: W. Grant, 1963.

Glimm, James York. *Flatlanders and Ridgerunners.* Pittsburgh PA: Univ. Pittsburgh Press, c.1983.

Glisan, Rodney. *Journal of Army Life.* San Francisco: A. L. Bancroft, 1874.

Globe. Atchison KS, 1877–1881.

Globe. Huntingdon PA, 1856–1877.

Godbey, William Baxter. *Autobiography of Rev. W. B. Godbey.* Cincinnati OH: God's Revivalist Office, c.1909.

Goddard, Frederick Bartlett. *Where to Emigrate and Why.* New York: Frederick B. Goddard, 1869.

Godey's Lady's Book. New York, 1830–1898.

Godfrey, Edward K. *The Island of Nantucket.* Boston: Lee and Shepard, 1882.

Godkin, Edwin Lawrence. *Life and Letters.* New York: Macmillan, 1907. 2 vols.

Godman, John Davidson. *American Natural History.* Philadelphia: H. C. Carey & I. Lea, 1826–1828. 3 vols.

Goff, Al, ed. *Nobles County History.* Worthington MN: Nobles County Historical Society, 1958.

Going, Maud. *Field, Forest, and Wayside Flowers.* New York: Baker and Taylor, 1899.

Goizueta Magazine. Atlanta GA: Goizueta Business School of Emory Univ., 1998–.

Gold, Aaron. *Odyssey of Gold.* Ed. by Peter Binzen. New York: Cornwall Books, 1995.

Gold, Herbert. *The Man Who Was Not with It.* Boston: Little, Brown, 1956.

Gold, Robert S. *Jazz Lexicon.* New York: Knopf, 1964.

Goldberg, Isaac. *The Wonder of Words: an Introduction to Language for Everyman.* New York: D. Appleton-Century, 1938.

Golden, Harry Lewis. *For 2¢ Plain.* Cleveland OH: World Pub., 1958.

———. *Forgotten Pioneer.* Cleveland OH: World Publishing, c.1963.

Golden Hours: a Magazine for Boys and Girls. Cincinnati OH: Hitchcock & Walden, 1869–1880.

Goldenseal. Charleston WV, 1975–.

Goldfrap, John H. *The Boy Aviators' Treasure Quest.* New York: Hurst, 1910.

Goldin, Hyman E. et al. *Dictionary of American Underworld Lingo.* New York: Twayne, c.1950.

Golding, Louis. *Magnolia Street.* New York: Farrar & Rinehart, c.1932.

Goldman, William. *Boys and Girls Together.* New York: Bantam Books, 1968 [c.1964].

Goldsborough, Edmund K. *Ole Mars an' Ole Miss.* Freeport NY: Books for Libraries Press, 1972. Repr. of 1900 ed. pub. by National Publishing, Washington DC.

Goldsmith, Christabel. *Peace Pelican, Spinster.* New York: G. W. Carleton, 1881.

Goldsmith, Oliver. *An History of the Earth, and Animated Nature.* London: Printed for J. Nourse, 1774. 8 vols.

Goldstein, Darra. *The Vegetarian Hearth.* New York: HarperCollins, c.1996.

Goldstein, Kenneth S. and Robert H. Byington, eds. *Two Penny Ballads and Four Dollar Whiskey.* Hatboro PA: Published for the Pennsylvania Folklore Society by Folklore Associates, 1966.

Goliad Advance-Guard. Goliad TX, 1917–.

Gomme, Alice Bertha Merck. *The Traditional Games of England, Scotland, and Ireland.* London: D. Nutt, 1894–1898. 2 vols.

———. *The Traditional Games of England, Scotland, and Ireland.* New York: Dover, c.1964. 2 vols. Orig. pub. in 1894–1898 by D. Nutt, London.

Gonzales, Ambrose Elliott. *The Black Border.* Columbia SC: States, 1922.

———. *With Aesop along the Black Border.* New York: Negro Universities Press, 1969. Orig. pub. in 1924 by State, Columbia SC.

Goode, George Brown. *American Fishes.* Boston: Estes and Lauriat, c.1887.

———. *The Fisheries and Fishery Industries of the United States.* Washington DC: Govt. Printing Office, 1884–1887. 8 vols.

———. *A History of the Menhaden.* New York: Orange Judd, 1880.

Goode, George Brown and Theodore Gill. *American Fishes.* New ed., completely rev. and largely extended. Boston: Dana Estes, c.1903.

Goode, William Henry. *Outposts of Zion.* Cincinnati OH: Poe & Hitchcock, 1863.

Good Housekeeping. Holyoke MA: C. W. Bryan, 1885–.

Good Housekeeping Institute, New York. *Good Housekeeping's Book of Meals, Tested, Tasted, and Approved.* 5th ed. New York: Good Housekeeping, 1932 [c.1930].

Good Old Days. Danvers MA, 1964–.

Goodrich, Arthur Leonard. *Birds in Kansas.* Topeka KS: F. Voiland, Jr., 1946.

Goodrich, Charles A. *The Universal Traveller.* 3d ed. Hartford CT: Canfield & Robins, 1837 [c.1836].

Goodrich, Frances Louisa. *Mountain Homespun.* New Haven CT: Yale Univ. Press, 1931.

Goodrich, Samuel Griswold. *Illustrated Natural History.* New York: Derby & Jackson, c.1859. 2 vols.

———. *Peter Parley's Cyclopedia of Botany.* Boston: Weeks, Jordan, 1838.

———. *Peter Parley's Illustrations of the Animal Kingdom.* Boston: B. B. Mussey, 1840.

———. *Recollections of a Lifetime.* New York: Miller, Orton & Mulligan, 1857. 2 vols.

———. *The Third School Reader.* Louisville KY: Morton and Griswold, 1846.

Goodson, Gar. *Fishes of the Pacific Coast.* Stanford CA: Stanford Univ. Press, 1988.

Goodwin, Charles Carroll. *As I Remember Them.* Salt Lake City UT: Salt Lake Commercial Club, 1913.

Goodwin, H. C. *Pioneer History.* New York: A. D. Burdick, 1859 [c.1855].

Goodwin, John Abbot. *The Pilgrim Republic.* Boston: Ticknor; London: Trübner, 1888.

Goodwin, Ruby Berkley. *It's Good to Be Black.* Garden City NY: Doubleday, 1953.

Goodwin, Wilder. *The Up Grade.* Boston: Little, Brown, 1910.

Gordon, George. *The Pinetum.* Assisted by Robert Glendinning. London: Henry G. Bohn, 1858.

Gordon, John SEE Munson, Gorham Bert

Gordon, Kenneth Llewellyn. *The Natural History and Behavior of the Western Chipmunk and the Mantled Ground Squirrel.* Corvallis OR: OR State College, 1943.

Gordon, Mildred. *The Informant.* Garden City NY: Doubleday, 1973.

Gordon, Percival SEE Irving, Peter

Gordon, Taylor. *Born to Be.* New York: Covici Friede, 1929.

Gordon, Thomas Francis. *A Gazetteer of the State of New Jersey.* Trenton NJ: Daniel Fenton, 1834.

Gordon, William. *The History of the Rise, Progress, and Establishment of the Independence of the United States of America.* London: Printed for the Author, 1788. 4 vols.

Gordon, William St. Clair. *Recollections of the Old Quarter.* Lynchburg VA: Moose Bros., 1902.

Gordone, Charles. *No Place to Be Somebody.* Indianapolis IN: Bobbs-Merrill, 1969.

Gores, Joe. *Hammett.* New York: G. P. Putnam's Sons, c.1975.

———. *Wolf Time.* New York: G. P. Putnam's Sons, c.1989.

Goshen Trails. McLeansboro IL: Hamilton Co. Hist. Soc., 1965–1982.

Gosline, William A. and Vernon E. Brock. *Handbook of Hawaiian Fishes.* Honolulu HI: Univ. HI Press, 1960.

Gosnell, Harold Foote. *Machine Politics.* Chicago: Univ. Chicago Press, 1937.

Gospel Sermons for Children. Minneapolis MN: Augsburg, 1995–1997. 3 vols.

Goss, Nathaniel S. *History of the Birds of Kansas.* Topeka KS: G. W. Crane, 1891.

Goss, Warren Lee. *Recollections of a Private.* New York: Thomas Y. Crowell, c.1890.

———. *The Soldier's Story of His Captivity at Andersonville, Belle Isle and Other Rebel Prisons.* Boston: Lee & Shepard, 1868.

Gosse, Edmund. *The Life of Philip Henry Gosse.* London: K. Paul, Trench, Trübner, 1890.

Gosse, Philip Henry. *The Canadian Naturalist; a Series of Conversations on the Natural History of Lower Canada.* London: John van Voorst, 1840.

———. *Letters from Alabama (U.S.) Chiefly Relating to Natural History.* London: Morgan & Chase, 1859.

Gossler, Jacob L. *An Old Turnpike-Road.* New York: Baker & Taylor, 1888.

Gottschalk, Louis R. *The Era of the French Revolution (1715–1815).* Boston: Houghton Mifflin, c.1929.

Gould, Dale. *Blackie's Railroad Handbook.* [s.l.]: [s.n.], 1976.

Gould, John. *Farmer Takes a Wife.* New York: William Morrow, c.1945.

———. *The House That Jacob Built.* New York: William Morrow, 1947.

———. *Maine Lingo.* Camden ME: Down East Magazine, 1975.

———. *The Parables of Peter Partout.* Boston: Little, Brown, 1964.

———. *You Should Start Sooner.* Boston: Little, Brown, 1965 [c.1964].

Gould, John A. *The Greenleaf Fires.* New York: Charles Scribner's Sons, c.1978.

Gould, Nathaniel Duren. *History of Church Music in America.* Boston: Gould and Lincoln, 1853.

Gould, Ralph Ernest. *Yankee Storekeeper.* New York: Whittlesey House, McGraw-Hill Book, c.1946.

Goulding, Francis Robert. *Marooner's Island.* New York: Dodd, Mead, c.1868.

Gourmet. New York, 1941–.

Gove, Philip Babcock et al., eds. *Webster's Third New International Dictionary of the English Language, Unabridged.* Springfield MA: G. & C. Merriam, 1961. Includes addenda.

Gover, Robert. *One Hundred Dollar Misunderstanding*. New York: Ballantine Books, 1963 [c.1961].

Gowen, Herbert Henry. *The Paradise of the Pacific*. London: Skeffington & Son, 1892.

Goyen, William. *Ghost and Flesh*. New York: Random House, c.1952.

Grafton, Sue. *D Is for Deadbeat*. New York: Macmillan, 1987.

Graham, Alan and James Taylor. *New Orleans on the Half-Shell*. 2d ed. Gretna LA: Pelican, 1990.

Graham, Elinor Mish. *My Window Looks Down East*. New York: Macmillan, 1951.

Graham, Frank. *Where the Place Called Morning Lies*. New York: Viking Press, 1973.

Graham, Joseph Alexander. *The Sporting Dog*. New York: Macmillan, 1904.

Graham, Lloyd. *Niagara Country*. New York: Duell, Sloan & Pearce, 1949.

Graham, Margaret Collier. *Stories of the Foot-Hills*. Freeport NY: Books for Libraries Press, 1969. Orig. pub. in 1895 by Houghton, Mifflin, Boston.

Graham, Robert Bontine Cunninghame. *Thirteen Stories*. London: William Heinemann, 1900.

Graham, Stephen. *The Soul of John Brown*. New York: Macmillan, 1920.

Graham's American Monthly Magazine of Literature, Art, and Fashion. Philadelphia, 1841–1858.

"Grandfather, Tell Me a Story". Oklahoma: Potawatomi Tribe, c.1984.

Grand Forks Herald. Grand Forks ND, 1916–.

Grand Ole Opry Specials. Musical score. Nashville TN: J. Daniel, 1943.

Grand Rapids Daily Tribune. Grand Rapids WI, 1920.

Grand Rapids Press. Grand Rapids MI, 1913–.

Grand Rapids Tribune. Wisconsin Rapids WI, 1900–1920.

Grand Traverse Herald. Traverse City MI, 1858–1910.

Granite State Magazine. Manchester NH, 1906–1914.

Grant, Anne MacVicar. *Memoirs of an American Lady, with Sketches of Manners and Scenery in America, as They Existed Previous to the Revolution*. New York: G. Dearborn, 1836. Orig. printed in 1808 for Longman, Hurst, Rees and Orme, London.

Grant, Bruce. *The Cowboy Encyclopedia*. Chicago: Rand, McNally, 1951.

Grant, Frank, comp. *The History of the Celebration of the Two Hundred and Fiftieth Anniversary of the Incorporation of the Town of Westfield, Massachusetts*. Concord NH: Printed by the Rumford Press, 1919.

Grant, Hamil. *Two Sides of the Atlantic*. London: Grant Richards, 1917.

Grant, Robert. *An Average Man*. Boston: James R. Osgood, 1884.

———. *Jack Hall*. New York: Charles Scribner's Sons, 1893 [c.1887].

Grant, Ulysses Simpson. *Personal Memoirs of U.S. Grant*. New York: Charles L. Webster, 1885–1886. 2 vols.

Grant, William, ed. *The Scottish National Dictionary*. Edinburgh: Scottish National Dictionary Association, 1931–1975.

Grant County Herald. Elbow Lake MN, 1887–.

Granville Sentinel. Granville NY, 1875–1891; 1919–.

Grau, Robert. *The Theatre of Science*. New York: Broadway Publishing, 1914.

Grau, Shirley Ann. *The Black Prince and Other Stories*. New York: Alfred A. Knopf, 1955 [c.1954].

———. *The Condor Passes*. New York: Alfred A. Knopf, 1971.

———. *The Hard Blue Sky*. New York: Knopf, 1958.

Graves, Charles Burr et al. *Catalogue of the Flowering Plants and Ferns of Connecticut Growing without Cultivation*. Hartford CT: State Geological and Natural History Survey, 1910.

Graves, Sarah. *The Dead Cat Bounce*. New York: Bantam Books, 2004 [c.1998].

———. *Mallets Aforethought*. New York: Bantam Books, 2004.

Gray, Asa. *The Botanical Text-Book*. New York: Wiley and Putnam, 1845 [c.1842].

———. *The Botanical Text-Book*. 2d ed. New York: Wiley & Putnam, 1845.

———. *The Botanical Text-Book*. 4th ed. New York: G. P. Putnam, 1853.

———. *Darwiniana*. New York: D. Appleton, 1876.

———. *Field, Forest, and Garden Botany*. New York: Ivison, Blakeman, Taylor, 1870, 1868. Orig. pub. in 1868; new printing with corrs. 1870.

———. *First Lessons in Botany and Vegetable Physiology*. New York: G. P. Putnam and Ivison & Phinney, 1857.

———. *Gray's New Manual of Botany*. 7th ed. New York: American Book, c.1908.

———. *Gray's School and Field Book of Botany*. Rev. ed. New York: American Book, c.1895.

———. *Letters*. Boston: Houghton, Mifflin, 1893. 2 vols.

———. *Manual of the Botany of the Northern United States*. Boston: James Munroe; London: J. Chapman, 1848.

———. *Manual of the Botany of the Northern United States*. Rev. ed. New York: G. P. Putnam, and Ivison and Phinney, 1857.

———. *Manual of the Botany of the Northern United States*. 5th ed. New York: Ivison, Blakeman, Taylor, c.1867.

———. *Manual of the Botany of the Northern United States*. Rev. and extended westward to the 100th meridian by Sereno Watson and John M. Coulter. 6th ed. New York: Ivison, Blakeman, 1890 [c.1889].

Gray, Asa and Liberty Hyde Bailey. *Field Forest and Garden Botany*. Rev. and extended. New York: American Book, c.1895.

Gray, Asa and Merritt Lyndon Fernald. *Gray's Manual of Botany*. 8th centennial ed. New York: American Book, c.1950. Orig. pub. in 1848 by James Munroe, Boston and J. Chapman, London under the title *A Manual of the Botany of the Northern United States*.

Gray, Barry. *Matrimonial Infelicities*. New York: Hurd and Houghton, 1865.

Gray, James. *Pine, Stream & Prairie*. New York: A. A. Knopf, 1945.

Gray, John. *My New Friends Were Barefoot*. Iron Mountain MI: Mid-Peninsula Library Cooperative, 1994.

Gray, Roland Palmer. *Songs and Ballads of the Maine Lumberjacks with Other Songs from Maine*. Cambridge MA: Harvard Univ. Press, c.1924.

Gray, Samuel Frederick. *A Natural Arrangement of British Plants*. London: Baldwin, Cradock, and Joy, 1821.

Graydon, Alexander. *Memoirs of a Life, Chiefly Passed in Pennsylvania*. Harrisburg PA: Printed by John Wyeth, 1811.

The Great American Writers' Cookbook. Ed. by Dean Faulkner Wells. Oxford MS: Yoknapatawpha Press, 1981.

Great Bend Daily Tribune. Great Bend KS, 1950–1972.

Great Bend Tribune. Great Bend KS, 1876–.

Great Britain. Public Record Office. *Calendar of State Papers, Colonial Series . . . America and West Indies*. London, 1860–.

———. *Report of the Deputy Keeper of the Records*. London: Her Majesty's Stationary Office, 1839–1958.

Greatman, Bonnie M. *A Dialect Atlas of Maryland*. New York: NY Univ. diss., 1970.

Great Plains Quarterly. Lincoln NE: Center for Great Plains Studies, Univ. NE, 1981–.

Greatrex, Charles Butler. *Whittlings from the West*. Edinburgh: James Hogg, 1854.

Greeley, Andrew M. *Happy Are the Meek*. New York: Warner Books, c.1985.

Greeley, Horace. *The American Conflict*. Hartford CT: O. D. Case, 1864–1866. 2 vols.

———. *An Overland Journey from New York to San Francisco, in the Summer of 1859*. New York: C. M. Saxton, Barker, 1860.

Greeley Daily Tribune and the Greeley Republican. Greeley CO, 1913–1945; 1947–1972.

Greeley's New-Yorker. New York, 1834–1841.

Greeley Tribune and the Greeley Republican. Greeley CO, 1972–1978.

Greely, Adolphus Washington. *Handbook of Alaska*. New York: C. Scribner's Sons, 1914.

Green, Abel and Joe Laurie, Jr. *Show Biz, from Vaude to Video*. New York: Henry Holt, 1951.

Green, Ben K. *Horse Tradin'*. New York: Knopf, 1967.

———. *The Last Trail Drive through Downtown Dallas*. Flagstaff AZ: Northland Press, 1971.

———. *Some More Horse Tradin'*. New York: Knopf, 1972.

———. *The Village Horse Doctor*. New York: Alfred A. Knopf, 1971.

———. *Wild Cow Tales*. New York: Alfred A. Knopf, 1969.

Green, Bennett Wood. *Word Book of Virginia Folk-Speech*. 2d ed. Richmond VA: W. E. Jones' Sons, 1912. Orig. pub. in 1899 by W. E. Jones, Richmond VA.

Green, Ely. *Ely*. Amherst MA: Univ. MA Press, 1970.

Green, Frances Harriet and Joseph W. Congdon. *Analytical Class-Book of Botany*. New York: D. Appleton, 1857 [c.1854].

Green, Gerald. *The Last Angry Man*. New York: Charles Scribner's Sons, c.1956.

Green, Helen. *At the Actors' Boarding House*. New York: Nevada Publishing, 1906 [c.1905].

———. *The Maison de Shine*. New York: B. W. Dodge, 1908.

Green, Invisible See Crippen, William G.

Green, Jonathan Harrington. *The Reformed Gambler*. Philadelphia: T. B. Peterson & Bros., c.1858.

———. *Secret Band of Brothers*. Philadelphia: T. B. Peterson, c.1858.

———. *Twelve Days in the Tombs*. New York: William Taylor, 1850.

Green, Jonathon. *Cassell's Dictionary of Slang*. London: Cassell, 2000 [1998].

Green, Laurie. *Images of America, Santa Rosa County*. Charleston SC: Arcadia Publishing, 1998.

Green, Mason Arnold. *Springfield 1636–1886*. Springfield MA: C. A. Nichols, 1888.

Green, Paul. *Home to My Valley*. Chapel Hill NC: Univ. NC Press, 1970.

———. *Hymn to the Rising Sun*. New York: Samuel French, c.1936.

———. *In the Valley*. New York: S. French, 1928.

———. *Out of the South*. 2d ed. New York: Harper Bros., c.1939.

———. *Paul Green's Wordbook*. Ed. by Rhoda H. Wynn. Boone NC: Appalachian Consortium Press; Chapel Hill NC: Paul Green Foundation, 1990. 2 vols.

Green, Rena Maverick, ed. *Samuel Maverick, Texan*. San Antonio TX: [s.n.], 1952.

Green, Samuel Bowdlear. *Forestry in Minnesota*. St. Paul MN: Minnesota Forestry Association, 1898.

Green, Thomas Jefferson. *Journal of the Texian Expedition against Mier*. New York: Harper & Bros., 1845.

Green, William Mercer. *Memoir of Rt. Rev. James Harvey Otey, D. D., LL. D., the First Bishop of Tennessee*. New York: J. Pott, 1885.

Green Bag. Boston, 1889–1914.

Green Bay Press-Gazette. Green Bay WI, 1915–.

Greenberg, Joel R. *A Natural History of the Chicago Region*. Chicago: Univ. Chicago Press, c.2002.

Green Book Magazine. Chicago, 1912–1921.

Greene, Asa. *The Life and Adventures of Dr. Dodimus Duckworth, A. N. Q.* New York: P. Hill, 1833. 2 vols.

———. *The Perils of Pearl Street*. New York: Betts & Anstice, 1834.

———. *A Yankee among Nullifiers*. New York: W. Stodart, 1833.

Greene, Frances Nimmo. *One Clear Call*. New York: Charles Scribner's Sons, 1914.

Greene, Graham. *The Quiet American*. London: William Heinemann, 1955.

Greene, Melissa Fay. *Praying for Sheetrock*. Reading MA: Addison-Wesley, c.1991.

Greene, Patterson. *Papa Is All*. New York: S. French, c.1942.

Greene, Sarah Pratt McLean. *Cape Cod Folks*. Boston: De Wolfe, Fiske, c.1881.

Greene, Ward. *Death in the Deep South*. New York: Stackpole Sons, c.1936.

Greene, Wilhelmina F. and Hugo L. Blomquist. *Flowers of the South*. Chapel Hill NC: Univ. NC Press, 1953.

Greenfield Recorder. Greenfield MA, 1966–.

Greenlaw, Linda. *Hungry Ocean*. New York: Hyperion, 2000 [c.1999].

Greenleaf's New York Journal, & Patriotic Register. New York, 1794–1800.

Greenough, James Bradstreet and George Lyman Kittredge. *Words and Their Ways*. New York: Macmillan, 1961. Orig. pub. in 1901.

Green River Star. Green River WY, 1894–.

Greensboro Daily News. Greensboro NC, 1909–.

Greenville Advocate. Greenville AL, 1865–.

Greenwich Village Quill. Greenwich Village NY, 1917–1929.

Greer-Petrie, Cordia. *Angeline at the Seelbach*. Louisville KY: Angeline, 1923. Orig. pub. in 1921 by J. P. Morton, Louisville KY.

———. *Angeline Doin' Society*. Louisville KY: Angeline, 1946 [c.1923]. Orig. pub. in 1923.

———. *Angeline Gits an Eyeful*. Louisville KY: Angeline, 1946 [c.1924]. Orig. pub. in 1924.

———. *Angeline of the Hill Country*. New York: Thomas Y. Crowell, c.1925.

———. *Angeline Steppin' Out*. 10th ed. Louisville KY: Angeline, 1946 [c.1923]. Orig. pub. in 1923.

Gregg, John Chandler. *Life in the Army*. 2d ed. rev. and corr. Philadelphia: Perkinpine & Higgins, 1868.

Gregg, Josiah. *Commerce of the Prairies*. New York: H. G. Langley, 1844. 2 vols.

———. *Commerce of the Prairies*. Norman OK: Univ. OK

Press, 1954. Orig. pub. in 1844 by H. G. Langley, New York.

———. *Diary & Letters of Josiah Gregg.* Norman OK: Univ. OK Press, 1941–1944. 2 vols.

Gregg, William H. and John Gardner. *Where, When, and How to Catch Fish on the East Coast of Florida.* Buffalo NY: Matthews-Northrup, c.1902.

Gregory, Annie R. *Woman's Favorite Cookbook.* Chicago: Monarch Book, c.1906.

Gregory, James. *Bertie.* Philadelphia: A. Hart, 1851.

Greiner, Tuisco. *How to Make the Garden Pay.* Philadelphia: Wm. Henry Maule, 1890.

Gresham, Stephen. *Dark Magic.* New York: Kensington Publishing, c.2002.

Greve, Charles Theodore. *Centennial History of Cincinnati and Representative Citizens.* Chicago: Biographical Pub., 1904. 2 vols.

Grew, Nehemiah. *Musæum Regalis Societatis.* London: Printed by W. Rawlins, for the Author, 1681.

Grey, Zane. *The Man of the Forest.* New York: Harper & Bros., 1920.

———. *Tales of Fishes.* New York: Grosset & Dunlap, c.1919.

———. *Tales of Swordfish and Tuna.* New York: Harper & Bros., 1927.

———. *To the Last Man.* Roslyn NY: Walter J. Black, c.1950, c.1922.

Greylock, Godfrey SEE Smith, Joseph Edward Adams

Griffin, Gerald E. *Ballads of the Regiment.* New York: George U. Harvey, c.1918.

Griffin, John Howard. *Black Like Me.* New York: New American Library, 1962. Repr. of the 1961 ed. pub. by Houghton Mifflin

Griffin, Joseph, ed. *History of the Press of Maine.* Brunswick ME: The Press, 1872.

Griffith, Robert Eglesfeld. *Medical Botany.* Philadelphia: Lea and Blanchard, 1847.

———. *A Universal Formulary.* Rev. by Robert P. Thomas. Philadelphia: Henry C. Lea, 1854.

Griffiths, David. *Forage Conditions on the Northern Border of the Great Basin.* Washington DC: Govt. Printing Office, 1902.

Griggs, N. K. *Lyrics of the Lariat.* New York: Fleming H. Revell, 1893.

Griggs, Ruth. *Sally Cook's Recipe Book.* Philadelphia: Suburban Newspapers, 1946?

Griggs, Vanessa Davis. *Wings of Grace.* Washington DC: BET, 2005.

Grigsby, Melvin. *The Smoked Yank.* Sioux Falls SD: Dakota Bell Pub., 1888.

Grimes, William. *Life of William Grimes.* Chapel Hill NC: Academic Affairs Library, Univ. NC at Chapel Hill, 2001. Text transcr. for *Documenting the American South* website from the 1825 ed. pub. by the author, New York.

Grimm, William Carey. *Recognizing Native Shrubs.* Harrisburg PA: Stackpole, 1966.

———. *The Trees of Pennsylvania.* New York: Stackpole and Heck, c.1950.

Grimm, William Carey and John T. Kartesz. *The Illustrated Book of Wildflowers and Shrubs.* Rev. ed. Harrisburg PA: Stackpole Books, c.1993.

Gringo, Harry SEE Wise, Henry Augustus

Grinnell, Elizabeth and Joseph Grinnell. *Birds of Song and Story.* Chicago: A. W. Mumford, 1901.

Grinnell, George Bird. *Jack the Young Explorer.* New York: Frederick A. Stokes, c.1908.

Grinnell, Joseph. *Birds of the Pacific Slope of Los Angeles County.* Pasadena CA: G. A. Swerdfiger, 1898.

———. *Gold Hunting in Alaska.* Elgin IL: David C. Cook, c.1901.

Grinnell, Joseph et al. *Fur-Bearing Mammals of California.* Berkeley CA: Univ. CA Press, 1937. 2 vols.

———. *The Game Birds of California.* Berkeley CA: Univ. CA Press, 1918.

Griscom, Ludlow and Dorothy Eastman Snyder. *The Birds of Massachusetts.* Salem MA: Peabody Museum, 1955.

Grisham, John. *Ford County: Stories.* New York: Doubleday, c.2009.

———. *The Runaway Jury.* New York: Doubleday, c.1996.

———. *A Time to Kill.* Tarrytown NY: Wynwood Press, c.1989.

Griswold, Francis. *A Sea Island Lady.* New York: William Morrow, 1939.

Griswold, Rufus Wilmont. *Passages from the Correspondence and Other Papers of Rufus W. Griswold.* Cambridge MA: W. M. Griswold, 1898.

———. *The Republican Court.* New York: D. Appleton, 1855.

Grit. Williamsport PA, 1882–.

Grit and Steel. Gaffney SC, 1900–.

Gromme, Owen J. *Birds of Wisconsin.* Madison WI: Published for the Milwaukee Public Museum by the Univ. WI Press, 1963.

———. *Birds of Wisconsin.* Madison WI: Univ. WI Press, 1978 [c.1974].

Gronovius, Johannes Fredericus. *Flora Virginica.* Lugduni Batavorum: Cornelius Haak, 1739–1743. 2 vols. Photolithographed in 1946 by Murray Printing, Cambridge MA, for the Arnold Arboretum.

———. *Flora Virginica.* Lugduni Batavorum: [s.n.], 1762.

Grooms, Steve, comp. *Channel Catfish Fever.* Ed. by Douge Stange, Joann Phipps, Steve Quinn, Toad Smith. Brainerd MN: In-Fisherman, c.1989.

Grose, Francis. *A Classical Dictionary of the Vulgar Tongue.* London: Printed for S. Hooper, 1785.

Gross, Rudolph Hermann. *Comparative Materia Medica.* Ed. by Constantine Hering. Philadelphia: F. E. Broericke, 1867 [c.1866].

Grossinger, Jennie. *The Art of Jewish Cooking.* New York: Bantam Books, 1960 [c.1958].

Groton, Massachusetts. *The Early Records of Groton, Massachusetts, 1662–1707.* Groton MA: [s.n.], 1880.

Grout, Abel Joel and N. A. Howe. *Mosses with a Hand-Lens.* 4th ed. New Fane VT: Pub. by the author, c.1947.

Guennel, G. K. *Guide to Colorado Wildflowers.* Newly rev. 2d ed. Englewood CO: Westcliffe, 2004. 2 vols.

Guenther, Martha Ann Butler. *Della Elizabeth Butler Hudson "Beth".* St. Petersburg FL: Published for the author by Genealogy Publishing Service, c.1990.

Guerrant, Edward Owings. *The Galax Gatherers.* Ed. by his daughter, Grace. Richmond VA: Onward Press, c.1910.

Guide to Paths in the White Mountains and Adjacent Regions. Rev. ed. Boston: Appalachian Mountain Club, c.1917.

Guild, James. *From Tunbridge, Vermont, to London, England.* Montpelier VT: Vermont Historical Society, 1937.

Guild, Josephus Conn. *Old Times in Tennessee.* Nashville TN: Tavel, Eastman & Howell, 1878.

Guilford, William Sumner. *California Hog Book.* San Francisco: Pacific Rural Press, 1915.

Gulfshore Life. Naples FL, 1970–.

Gumaer, Peter E. *A History of Deerpark in Orange County, N.Y.* Port Jervis NY: Minisink Valley Historical Society, 1890. According to the prefatory matter the history was written between 1858 and 1862.

Gunn, Thomas Butler. *The Physiology of New York Boarding-Houses.* New York: Mason Bros., 1857.

Gunnison, J. W. *The Mormons.* Philadelphia: J. B. Lippincott, 1856 [c.1852].

Gunter, Archibald Clavering. *Miss Dividends.* New York: Hurst, 1892.

Günther, Albert Carl Ludwig Gotthilf. *An Introduction to the Study of Fishes.* Edinburgh: Adam and Charles Black, 1880.

Gunther, Erna. *Ethnobotany of Western Washington.* Rev. ed. Seattle WA: Univ. WA Press, c.1973.

———. *Klallam Ethnography.* Seattle WA: Univ. WA Press, 1927.

Gunton's Magazine. New York, 1898–1904.

Gupton, Oscar W. and Fred C. Swope. *Wildflowers of Tidewater Virginia.* Charlottesville VA: Univ. VA Press, 1982.

Gurganus, Allan. *Oldest Living Confederate Widow Tells All.* New York: Alfred A. Knopf, 1989.

Gurney, Joseph John. *A Journey in North America.* New York: Da Capo Press, 1973. Repr. of the 1841 ed. orig. pub. by J. Fletcher for private circulation, Norwich.

Gurney Seed and Nursery Co. *Gurney's Spring Catalog 1982.* Yankton SD: The Company, c.1982.

Guterson, David. *East of the Mountains.* New York: Harcourt Brace, c.1999.

———. *The Other.* New York: Alfred A. Knopf, 2008.

———. *Our Lady of the Forest.* New York: Alfred A. Knopf, 2003.

———. *Snow Falling on Cedars.* New York: Harcourt Brace, c.1994.

Guthrie, Alfred Bertram. *The Big Sky.* New York: William Sloane, 1947.

———. *The Blue Hen's Chick.* New York: McGraw-Hill, 1965.

———. *The Way West.* New York: W. Sloane, 1949.

Guthrie, Woody. *Bound for Glory.* New York: E. P. Dutton, 1970. Orig. pub. in 1943 by E. P. Dutton.

———. *Seeds of Man.* New York: E. P. Dutton, c.1976.

Gwinnett Daily Post. Lawrenceville GA, 1995–.

Gyles, John. *Memoirs of Odd Adventures, Strange Deliverances, etc., in the Captivity of John Gyles, Esq.*

New York: Garland, 1977. Repr. of the 1736 ed. pub. by S. Kneeland and T. Green, Boston.

Habberton, John. *All He Knew.* Philadelphia: J. B. Lippincott, 1889.

———. *The Barton Experiment.* New York: G. P. Putnam's Sons, 1877 [c.1876].

———. *Helen's Babies.* Boston: Loring, c.1876.

———. *The Jericho Road.* Chicago: Jansen, McClurg, 1877.

Hachten, Harva. *The Flavor of Wisconsin.* Madison WI: State Historical Society of Wisconsin, 1981.

Haddock, Frank Channing. *The Life of Rev. George C. Haddock.* New York: Funk & Wagnalls, 1887.

Hadermann, Jeannette Ritchie SEE Walworth, Jeannette Ritchie Hadermann

Hadley, George Plummer. *History of the Town of Goffstown 1733–1920.* Concord NH: Rumford Press, c.1922–1924. 2 vols.

Hafele, Rick and Steve Hinton. *Guide to Pacific Northwest Aquatic Invertebrates.* Portland OR: Oregon Trout, c.1996.

Hafen, Le Roy Reuben, ed. *Colorado Gold Rush.* Glendale CA: Arthur H. Clark, 1941.

———, ed. *Overland Routes to the Gold Fields, 1859.* Glendale CA: Arthur H. Clark, 1942.

Haff, Tonya M. et al., eds. *The Natural History of the UC Santa Cruz Campus.* 2d ed. Santa Cruz CA: Univ. CA, Santa Cruz, 2008.

Haffner-Ginger, Bertha. *California Mexican-Spanish Cook Book.* Los Angeles: Citizen Print Shop, 1914.

Hager, John Manfred. *Commercial Survey of the Southeast.* Washington DC: Govt. Printing Office, 1927.

Hagerstown Mail. Hagerstown MD, 1828–1831; 1835–1880.

Hagers-Town Torch Light. Hagerstown MD, 1846–1850.

Hagy, James William, comp. *Charleston, South Carolina City Directories for the Years 1816, 1819, 1822, 1825 and 1829.* Baltimore MD: Clearfield, c.1996.

Hahn, Emily. *The Cooking of China.* New York: Time-Life Books, 1968.

Hailey, Arthur. *Airport.* Garden City NY: Doubleday, 1968.

———. *Overload.* Garden City NY: Doubleday, 1979 [c.1978].

Haines City Herald. Haines City FL, 1916–.

Halcyon. Swarthmore PA: Swarthmore College, 1885–.

Haldeman, Samuel Stehman. *Pennsylvania Dutch.* Philadelphia: Reformed Church Publication Board, 1872.

Hale, Edward Everett. *Christmas in Narragansett.* New York: Funk & Wagnalls, 1884.

———. *How to Do It.* Boston: R. Osgood, 1871.

———. *If, Yes and Perhaps.* Boston: Ticknor and Fields, 1868.

———. *The Ingham Papers.* Boston: Fields, Osgood, 1869.

———. *A New England Boyhood.* Boston: Little, Brown, 1900 [c.1893].

Hale, Edwin Moses. *Homoeopathic Materia Medica of the New Remedies.* 2d ed. rev. and enlarged. Detroit MI: American Homoeopathic Observer, 1867.

———. *Materia Medica and Special Therapeutics of the New Remedies.* New York: Boericke & Tafel, 1875. 2 vols.

———. *Materia Medica and Special Therapeutics of the New Remedies.* Philadelphia: Boericke & Tafel, 1897 [c.1882]. 2 vols.

———. *New Remedies.* Detroit MI: E. A. Lodge, c.1864.

———. *A Systematic Treatise on Abortion.* Chicago: C. S. Halsey, 1866.

Hale, Nancy. *A New England Girlhood.* Boston: Little, Brown, c.1958.

———. *The Prodigal Women.* New York: Charles Scribner's Sons, 1942.

Hale, Peter M., comp. *The Woods and Timbers of North Carolina.* Raleigh NC: P. M. Hale, 1883.

Hale, Sarah Josepha Buell. *Flora's Interpreter.* Boston: Marsh, Capen and Lyon, 1832.

———. *The Ladies' New Book of Cookery.* 5th ed. New York: H. Long & Bros., 1852.

Hale, Susan. *Letters of Susan Hale.* Ed. by Caroline P. Atkinson. Boston: Marshall Jones, 1919 [c.1918].

Haley, Alex. *Roots.* Garden City NY: Doubleday, c.1976.

Haliburton, Thomas Chandler, ed. *The Americans at Home.* London: Hurst and Blackett, 1854. 3 vols.

———. *The Attaché.* 1st ser., 2d ed. London: Richard Bentley, 1846. 2 vols. Orig. pub. in 1843.

———. *The Attaché.* 2d and last ser. London: R. Bentley, 1844. 2 vols.

———. *The Clockmaker.* 1st ser. London: R. Bentley, 1838. Orig. pub. in 1836.

———. *The Clockmaker.* 2d ser. London: Richard Bentley, 1843. Orig. pub. in 1838.

———. *The Clockmaker.* 3d ser. London: Richard Bentley, 1840.

———. *An Historical and Statistical Account of Nova-Scotia.* Halifax: J. Howe, 1829. 2 vols.

———. *Nature and Human Nature.* London: Hurst and Blackett, 1855. 2 vols.

———. *Sam Slick's Wise Saws and Modern Instances.* London: Hurst and Blackett, 1853. 2 vols.

———. *The Season-Ticket.* London: Richard Bentley, 1860.

———, ed. *Traits of American Humour.* London: Colburn, 1852. 3 vols.

Hall, Abraham Oakey. *The Manhattaner in New Orleans.* New York: J. S. Redfield, 1851.

———. *Old Whitey's Christmas Trot.* New York: Harper & Bros., 1857 [c.1856].

Hall, Ansel Franklin, ed. *Handbook of Yosemite National Park.* New York: G. P. Putnam's Sons, 1921.

Hall, Basil. *Travels in North America, in the Years 1827 and 1828.* Edinburgh: Cadell; London: Simpkin & Marshall, 1829. 3 vols.

Hall, Baynard Rush. *The New Purchase.* IN centennial ed. Princeton NJ: Princeton Univ. Press, 1916. Orig. pub. in 2 vols. in 1843 by D. Appleton, New York.

Hall, Benjamin Homer. *A Collection of College Words and Customs.* Cambridge MA: J. Bartlett, 1851.

———. *A Collection of College Words and Customs.* Rev. and enlarged ed. Cambridge MA: John Bartlett, 1856.

Hall, Donald. *String Too Short to Be Saved.* New York: Viking Press, 1961.

Hall, Eliza Calvert SEE Obenchain, Eliza Caroline Calvert

Hall, Eugene J. *Lyrics of Home-Land.* Chicago: S. C. Griggs, c.1881.

Hall, Francis. *Travels in Canada, and the United States, in 1816 and 1817.* London: Longman, Hurst, Rees, Orme & Brown, 1818.

Hall, Frank. *History of the State of Colorado.* Chicago: Blakely Printing, 1889–1895. 4 vols.

Hall, Harvey Monroe. *Compositae of Southern California.* Berkeley CA: Univ. CA Press, 1907.

Hall, Harvey Monroe and Frederic Edward Clements. *The Phylogenetic Method in Taxonomy.* Washington DC: Carnegie Institution of Washington, 1923.

Hall, Henry Marion. *Woodcock Ways.* New York: Oxford Univ. Press, 1946.

Hall, Herschel Salmon. *Steel Preferred.* New York: E. P. Dutton, c.1920.

Hall, James. *A Brief History of the Mississippi Territory, to Which Is Prefixed a Summary View of the Country between the Settlements on Cumberland River & the Territory.* Spartanburg SC: Reprint, 1976. Repr. of the 1801 ed. printed by F. Coupée, Salisbury NC.

Hall, James. *The Harpe's Head.* Philadelphia: Key & Biddle, 1833.

———. *Kentucky.* London: A. K. Newman, 1834. 2 vols.

———. *Legends of the West.* Philadelphia: Harrison Hall, 1832.

———. *Letters from the West.* London: H. Colburn, 1828.

———. *Sketches of History, Life and Manners in the West.* Philadelphia: H. Hall, 1835.

———. *Statistics of the West.* Cincinnati OH: J. A. James, 1836.

Hall, J. H. *Selling Fish.* Mechanicsburg PA: Stackpole Books, c.2000.

Hall, Joan Houston. *Lexical Survey of the Snake River Valley.* c1971. Unpub. coll. from southern ID and southeastern OR by Joan Hall and students at the College of Idaho, Caldwell, Idaho.

Hall, Joan Houston et al., eds. *Old English and New: Studies in Language and Linguistics in Honor of Frederic G. Cassidy.* New York: Garland Publishing, 1992.

Hall, John. *The Primary Reader.* 4th ed. Hartford CT: Robins & Smith, 1844.

Hall, Joseph Sargent. *Collection.* c1937–1987. Unpub. coll. of dialect materials from area of Gt. Smoky Mt. Natl. Park, TN-NC.

———. *The Phonetics of Great Smoky Mountain Speech.* New York: King's Crown Press, 1942.

———, ed. *Sayings from Old Smoky.* Asheville NC: Cataloochee Press, c.1972.

———. *Smoky Mountain Folks and Their Lore.* Asheville NC: Published in cooperation with Great Smoky Mountains Natural History Association, c.1960.

———, ed. *Yarns and Tales from the Great Smokies.* Asheville NC: Cataloochee Press, 1978.

Hall, J. W. *Autobiography of Old Claib Jones.* Whitesburg KY: Eagle Printing, 1915.

Hall, Ruth. *The Pine Grove House.* Boston: Houghton, Mifflin, 1903.

Hall, Susan G. *Appalachian Ohio and the Civil War, 1862–1863.* Jefferson NC: McFarland, c.2000.

Hall, Tom. *Tales.* New York: Frederick A. Stokes, c.1899.

Hall, William T. *The Turnover Club.* Chicago: Rand McNally, 1890.

Hallett, Benjamin F. *Trial of Rev. Mr. Avery.* Boston: Daily Commercial Gazette, and Boston Daily Advocate, 1833.

Halliburton, Richard. *Richard Halliburton.* Indianapolis IN: Bobbs-Merrill, c.1940.

Halliwell-Phillipps, James Orchard. *Dictionary of Archaic and Provincial Words.* 3d ed. London: T. and W. Boone, 1855. 2 vols.

Hallman, Richard. *Handtools for Trail Work.* Rev. ed. Missoula MT: USDA Forest Service, 1997.

Hallock, Charles. *Camp Life in Florida.* New York: Forest and Stream Publishing, 1876 [c.1875].

———. *The Sportsman's Gazetteer and General Guide.* New York: Forest and Stream Publishing, 1877.

———. *The Sportsman's Gazetteer and General Guide.* 5th ed. New York: Forest and Stream Publishing, 1880 [c.1878].

Hallowell, Christopher. *People of the Bayou.* New York: E. P. Dutton, c.1979.

Hallum, John. *The Diary of an Old Lawyer.* Nashville TN: Southwestern Publishing, 1895.

Halpert, Herbert. *Collection of Proverbs, Sayings and Dialect Words Current in Certain Counties of Kentucky and Tennessee.* c1950. Unpub. coll. by students of Prof. Herbert Halpert at Murray State College, KY.

Hamann, Fred. *Air Words.* Seattle WA: Superior, 1945.

Hamblen, Herbert Elliott. *The General Manager's Story.* Upper Saddle River NJ: Literature House, 1970. Repr. of the 1898 ed. pub. by Macmillan, New York.

Hamburg Reporter. Hamburg IA, 1894–.

Hamel, Paul B. and Mary U. Chiltoskey. *Cherokee Plants and Their Uses.* Sylva NC: Herald, c.1975.

Hamer, Jennifer. *What It Means to Be Daddy: Fatherhood for Black Men Living Away from Their Children.* New York: Columbia Univ. Press, 2001.

Hamilton, Alexander. *Hamilton's Itinerarium.* St. Louis MO: Printed only for private distribution by W. K. Bixby, 1907.

Hamilton, Donald B. *The Intriguers.* New York: Fawcett Gold Medal, c.1972.

Hamilton, Gail SEE Dodge, Mary Abigail

Hamilton, Harlan. *Lights & Legends.* Stamford CT: Wescott Cove, 1987.

Hamilton, Jane. *The Book of Ruth.* New York: Ticknor & Fields, c.1988.

Hamilton, Patrick. *The Resources of Arizona.* Prescott AZ: [s.n.], 1881.

Hamilton, Robert Irvine. *Total and Digestible Dry Matter, Botanical Composition and Lamb Gains from Three Grass Species Grown Alone or with Alfalfa under Pasture Management.* Madison WI: Univ. WI-Madison diss., 1966.

Hamilton, Stanislaus Murray, ed. *Letters to Washington, and Accompanying Papers.* Boston: Houghton, Mifflin, 1898–1902. 5 vols.

Hamilton, Thomas. *Men and Manners in America.* Philadelphia: Carey, Lea & Blanchard, 1833.

Hamilton, William John. *American Mammals.* New York: McGraw-Hill, 1939.

Hamilton Daily News Journal. Hamilton OH, 1933–1971.

Hamilton Daily Republican. Hamilton OH, 1892–1898.

Hamilton Evening Journal. Hamilton OH, 1908–1933.

Hamlin, Helen. *Nine Mile Bridge.* New York: W. W. Norton, c.1945.

Hamlin, Marie Caroline Watson. *Legends of Le Détroit.* 2d ed. Detroit MI: T. Nourse, 1884 [c.1883].

Hammer, Roger L. *Everglades Wildflowers.* Guilford CT: Falcon, c.2002.

———. *Florida Keys Wildflowers.* Guilford CT: Globe Pequot Press, c.2004.

Hammett, Dashiell. *$106,000 Blood Money.* New York: Lawrence E. Spivak, 1943 [c.1927].

Hammett, Samuel Adams. *Piney Woods Tavern.* Philadelphia: T. B. Peterson & Bros., c.1858.

———. *A Stray Yankee in Texas.* New York: Redfield, 1853.

———. *The Wonderful Adventures of Captain Priest.* New York: Redfield, 1855.

Hammond, Henrietta Hardy. *The Georgians.* Boston: James R. Osgood, 1881.

Hammond, Lawrence. *Diary Kept by Capt. Lawrence Hammond.* Cambridge MA: J. Wilson and Son, 1892.

Hammond, Samuel H. *Hills, Lakes, and Forest Streams.* New York: J. C. Derby; Boston: Phillips, Sampson, 1854.

———. *Wild Northern Scenes.* New York: Derby & Jackson, 1857.

Hammond, Samuel H. and L. W. Mansfield. *Country Margins and Rambles of a Journalist.* New York: J. C. Derby, c.1855.

Hammond, William Gardiner. *Remembrance of Amherst.* New York: Columbia Univ. Press, 1946.

Hammond Times. Hammond IN, 1933–1967.

Hammond Vindicator. Hammond LA, 1920–.

Hamner, Earl. *Spencer's Mountain.* New York: Dial Press, 1961.

Hamner, Laura Vernon. *Short Grass & Longhorns.* Norman OK: Univ. OK Press, 1943.

Hamor, Ralph. *A True Discourse of the Present Estate of Virginia, and the Successe of the Affaires There till the 18 of Iune 1614.* London: Printed by Iohn Beale for W. Wiley, 1615.

Hampsten, Elizabeth. *Read This Only to Yourself: the Private Writings of Midwestern Women, 1880–1910.* Bloomington IN: IN Univ. Press, 1982.

Hampton's Magazine. New York, 1909–1911.

Hance, John C.et al. *Words Commonly Used on Hawaiian Sugar Plantations.* 1954–1960. Unpub. material and a revision of a list comp. in 1930 by Upendra K. Das.

Hancock, Cornelia. *South after Gettysburg.* Ed. by Henrietta Stratton Jacquette. Philadelphia: Univ. PA Press, 1937.

Hancock, Jane. *Choestoe.* Washington DC: Library of Congress, c.1984.

Hancock, Samuel. *The Narrative of Samuel Hancock, 1845–1860.* New York: R. M. McBride, 1927.

Hand, Susan Train, collector, arranger. *Letters of the Hand Family, 1796–1912.* New York: E. S. Gorham, 1923.

Hand, Wayland D. *Collection of Folk Vocabulary.* 1939–1986. Unpub.

Handbook of Texas Online. [v.d.]. Internet.

Handford, Thomas W. *Pleasant Hours with Illustrious Men and Women, with Many Personal Reminiscences.* Chicago: William Wilson, 1885.

Handsaker, Samuel. *Pioneer Life.* Eugene OR: Published by the author, 1908.

Handy, William Christopher. *Father of the Blues.* New York: Macmillan, 1942.

———. *St. Louis Blues.* Sheet music. Memphis TN: W. C. Handy, 1914.

———, ed. *A Treasury of the Blues.* New York: C. Boni, 1949. Orig. pub. in 1926 by A. & C. Boni, New York, under the title *Blues, an Anthology.*

Handy Play Party Book. Delaware OH: Cooperative Recreation Service, c.1940.

Hanify, Mary Lou and Craig Blencowe. *Guide to the Hoh Rain Forest.* Seattle WA: Superior Pub., c.1977.

Hanks, Charles Stedman. *Camp Kits and Camp Life.* New York: Charles Scribner's Sons, 1906.

Hanley Disks. 1932–1934. Unpub. coll. of 75 audio recordings.

Hanna, Alfred Jackson and Kathryn Abbey Hanna. *Lake Okeechobee.* Indianapolis IN: Bobbs-Merrill, 1948.

Hannerz, Ulf. *Soulside.* New York: Columbia Univ. Press, 1969.

Hannibal, Julius Caesar. *Black Diamonds, or, Humor, Satire, and Sentiment, Treated Scientifically.* New York: A. Ranney, 1855.

———. *Professor Julius Caesar Hannibal's Scientific Discourses.* New York: Stringer & Townsend, 1852.

Hannibal Courier-Post. Hannibal MO, 1996–.

Hannigan, Dennis. *The Swamp Steed.* New York: Dewitt & Davenport, 1852.

Hannum, Alberta. *Thursday April.* New York: Harper & Bros., 1931.

Hansen, Jay. *Fadeout.* New York: Harper & Row, 1970.

Hansen, Joseph. *Troublemaker.* New York: Harper & Row, c.1975.

Hansen, Robin. *Fox and Geese and Fences.* Camden ME: Down East Books, c.1983.

Hanson, John Wesley. *History of the Old Towns Norridgewock and Canaan.* Boston: Published by the author, 1849.

Hapgood, Warren and Robert Barnell Roosevelt. *Shore Birds.* New York: Forest and Stream, 1881.

Harben, William Nathaniel. *Abner Daniel.* New York: Harper & Bros., 1902.

———.*Dixie Hart.* New York: Harper & Bros., 1910.

———. *The Georgians.* New York: Books for Libraries Press, 1972. Orig. pub. in 1904 by Harper, New York.

———. *Northern Georgia Sketches.* Chicago: A. C. McClurg, 1900.

———. *Westerfelt.* New York: Harper & Bros., 1901.

Harbin, Elvin Oscar. *The Fun Encyclopedia.* New York: Abingdon-Cokesbury Press, c.1940.

———. *Phunology.* 13th ed., rev. Nashville TN: Cokesbury Press, c.1923.

Harbinger. Mobile AL, 1985–2001.

Harbison, W. C. *Bees and Bee-Keeping.* New York: C. M. Saxton, Barker, 1860.

Harbury, Katharine E. *Colonial Virginia's Cooking Dynasty.* Columbia SC: Univ. SC Press, 2004.

Hard, Miron Elisha. *The Mushroom.* Columbus OH: Mushroom Pub., 1908.

Hardeman, Nicholas Perkins. *Shucks, Shocks, and Hominy Blocks.* Baton Rouge LA: LA State Univ. Press, c.1981.

Harder, Kelsie B. *Collection.* 1940–1967. Unpub. coll. of responses to *PADS 20* and other materials dated 1940–1967.

Hardie, James. *An Account of the Yellow Fever Which Occurred in the City of New-York in the Year 1822.* New York: Printed by Samuel Marks, 1822.

Hardin County Independent. Elizabethtown IL, 1882–.

Hardin Tribune-Herald. Hardin MT, 1924–.

Hardwicke's Science-Gossip. London, 1865–1893.

Hardy, Campbell. *Forest Life in Acadie.* London: Chapman & Hall, 1869.

Hardy, Irene. *An Ohio Schoolmistress.* Kent OH: Kent State Univ. Press, c.1980. The ms. of these memoirs was completed in 1913.

Hardy, Michael C. *Remembering Avery County.* Charleston SC: History Press, 2007.

Hargrave, W. Lee. *LSU Law.* Baton Rouge LA: LA State Univ. Press, c.2004.

Hargreaves, Irene M. and Harold M. Foehl. *The Story of Logging the White Pine in the Saginaw Valley.* Bay City MI: Red Keg Press, 1964.

Hariot, Thomas. *A Briefe and True Report of the New Found Land of Virginia.* New York: Dodd, Mead, 1903. Facsimile of the 1588 ed. pub. by Quarto, London.

Hark, Ann. *Hex Marks the Spot in the Pennsylvania Dutch Country.* Philadelphia: J. B. Lippincott, c.1938.

Harlan, James R. and Everett B. Speaker. *Iowa Fish and Fishing.* 2d ed. Des Moines IA: State Conservation Commission, c.1951.

———. *Iowa Fish and Fishing.* 3d ed. Des Moines IA: State Conservation Commission, c.1956.

Harland, Marion SEE Terhune, Mary Virginia Hawes

Harlem Valley Times. Amenia NY, 1911?–.

Harlow, Frederick Pease. *The Making of a Sailor, or, Sea Life aboard a Yankee Square-Rigger.* Salem MA: Marine Research Society, 1928.

Harlow, William Morehouse. *Trees of the Eastern United States and Canada.* New York: McGraw Hill, c.1942.

Harmon, Daniel Williams. *A Journal of Voyages and Travels in the Interiour of North America.* Andover MA: Printed by Flagg and Gould, 1820.

Harmon, S. L. *Ptocowa.* Rochester NY: John P. Smith, 1887 [c.1885].

Harmony News. Harmony MN, 1897–.

Harned, Joseph Edward. *Wild Flowers of the Alleghanies.* Oakland MD: The author, c.1931.

Harper, Frances Ellen Watkins. *Iola Leroy, or, Shadows Uplifted.* Philadelphia: Garrigues Bros., 1892.

Harper, Francis. "The Mammals of the Okefinokee Swamp Region of Georgia." Boston Society of Natural History *Proceedings.* (1927) 38.7.191–396.

———, ed. *The Travels of William Bartram.* New Haven CT: Yale Univ. Press, c.1958.

Harper, Francis and Delma E. Presley. *Okefinokee Album.* Athens GA: Univ. GA Press, c.1981.

Harper, Ida Husted. *The Life and Work of Susan B. Anthony.* Indianapolis IN: Bowen-Merrill, 1898–1908. 3 vols.

Harper, Roland McMillan. *Economic Botany of Alabama.* University AL: [s.n.], 1913–1928. 2 vols.

———. *Preliminary Report on the Weeds of Alabama.* Wetumpka AL: Wetumpka Printing, 1944.

Harper-Lore, Bonnie and Maggie Wilson, eds. *Roadside Use of Native Plants.* Washington DC: Island Press, 2000 [1999]. Repr. of 1999 ed. pub. by Federal Highway Administration, Washington DC.

Harper's SEE *Harper's New Monthly Magazine, Harper's Monthly Magazine,* and *Harper's Magazine*

Harper's Bazaar. New York, 1867–.

Harper's Magazine. New York, 1939–.

Harper's Monthly Magazine. New York, 1900–1939.

Harper's New Monthly Magazine. New York, 1850–1900.

Harper's Weekly. New York: Harper's Magazine, 1857–1976.

Harrar, Ellwood Scott and J. George Harrar. *Guide to Southern Trees.* 2d ed. New York: Dover Publications, 1962.

Harrell, A. D. *Fetch It, Rusty!* Burnsville NC: Celo Valley Books, 1996.

Harrell, J. M. *The Hot Springs Doctor.* Hammond IN: W. M. Conkey, c.1899.

Harrington, Harold David. *Edible Native Plants of the Rocky Mountains.* Albuquerque NM: Univ. NM Press, c.1967.

———. *Manual of the Plants of Colorado.* Denver CO: Sage Books, 1954.

Harrington, Mark Raymond. *Gypsum Cave, Nevada.* Los Angeles: Southwest Museum, 1933.

Harrington Journal. Harrington DE, 1913–.

Harris, A. C. *Alaska and the Klondike Gold Fields.* Cincinnati OH: W. H. Ferguson, 1897.

Harris, Bernice Kelly. *Folk Plays of Eastern Carolina.* Chapel Hill NC: Univ. NC Press, c.1940.

———. *Hearthstones.* Garden City NY: Doubleday, 1948.

———. *Purslane.* Chapel Hill NC: Univ. NC Press, c.1939.

———, ed. *Southern Home Remedies.* Murfreesboro NC: Johnson Publishing, c.1968.

———. *Southern Savory.* Chapel Hill NC: Univ. NC Press, c.1964.

Harris, Dilue. "The Reminiscences of Mrs. Dilue Harris." Texas State Historical Association *Quarterly.* (1900–1901) 4.87–127.

Harris, Florence La Ganke. *Cooking with a Foreign Flavor.* New York: M. Barrows, 1946.

Harris, George Washington. *Sut Lovingood.* New York: Dick & Fitzgerald, c.1867.

———. *Sut Lovingood's Yarns.* New Haven CT: College & Univ. Press, c.1966.

Harris, Joel Chandler. *Balaam and His Master and Other Sketches and Stories.* Boston: Houghton, Mifflin, 1891.

———. *The Bishop and the Boogerman.* New York: Doubleday, Page, 1909 [c.1907].

———. *Dearest Chums and Partners.* Ed. by Hugh T. Keenan. Athens: Univ. GA Press, c.1993.

———. *Free Joe and Other Georgian Sketches.* Ridgewood NJ: Gregg Press, 1967. Repr. of the 1887 ed. pub. by Scribner.

———. *Gabriel Tolliver.* New York: McClure, Phillips, 1902.

———. *Joel Chandler Harris, Editor and Essayist.* Ed. by Julia Collier Harris. Chapel Hill NC: Univ. NC Press, 1931.

———. *Little Mr. Thimblefinger and His Queer Country.* New York: McKinlay, Stone & Mackenzie, c.1922. Orig. pub. in 1894.

———. *Mingo, and Other Sketches in Black and White.* Boston: James R. Osgood, 1884.

———. *Mr. Rabbit at Home.* New York: Houghton, Mifflin, 1895.

———. *Nights with Uncle Remus.* Boston: James R. Osgood, 1883.

———. *Nights with Uncle Remus.* Detroit MI: Singing Tree Press, Book Tower, 1971. Orig. pub. in 1883 by Houghton Mifflin, Boston.

———. *On the Plantation.* New York: D. Appleton, 1892.

———. *On the Wing of Occasions.* New York: Doubleday, Page, 1900 [c.1899].

———. *Sister Jane.* Boston: Houghton, Mifflin, 1896.

———. *Tales of the Home Folks in Peace and War.* Boston: Houghton Mifflin, 1898.

———. *Told by Uncle Remus.* New York: Grosset & Dunlap, c.1905.

———. *Uncle Remus and His Friends.* Boston: Houghton, Mifflin, c.1892.

———. *Uncle Remus, His Songs and His Sayings.* New York: D. Appleton, 1881 [c.1880].

Harris, John Sterling. *Barbed Wire.* Provo UT: Brigham Young Univ. Press, 1974.

Harris, Lucien. *Butterflies of Georgia.* Norman OK: Univ. OK Press, c.1972.

Harris, Miriam Coles. *Louie's Last Term at St. Mary's.* New York: Derby & Jackson, 1860.

———. *A Perfect Adonis.* New York: G. W. Carleton, 1875.

Harris, Thaddeus Mason. *The Journal of a Tour into the Territory Northwest of the Alleghany Mountains.* Boston: Manning & Loring, 1805.

Harris, Thaddeus William. *A Report on the Insects of Massachusetts Injurious to Vegetation.* Cambridge MA: Folsom, Wells and Thurston, 1841.

———. *A Treatise on Some of the Insects of New England Which Are Injurious to Vegetation.* Cambridge MA: John Owen, 1842.

———. *A Treatise on Some of the Insects of New England Which Are Injurious to Vegetation.* 2d ed. Boston: White & Potter, 1852.

Harris, William Foster. *The Look of the Old West.* New York: Viking Press, 1955.

Harris, William Tell. *Remarks Made during a Tour through the United States of America.* London: Sherwood, Neely, & Jones, 1821.

Harris, W. T. and F. Sturges Allen, eds. *Webster's New International Dictionary of the English Language.* Springfield MA: G. & C. Merriam; Tokyo: Maruzen Kabushiki Kaisha, or Z. P. Maruya, 1910 [c.1909].

———, eds. *Webster's New International Dictionary of the English Language.* Springfield MA: G. & C. Merriam, 1919 [c.1909, c.1913].

———, eds. *Webster's New International Dictionary of the English Language.* Springfield MA: G. & C. Merriam, 1930 [c.1927].

Harrison, Atapwg Iwtiol. *Trails through Time.* Baltimore MD: Gateway Press, 1996.

Harrison, Belle Richardson. *Poems.* New York: G. W. Dillingham, 1898.

Harrison, Henry Sydnor. *Queed.* Boston: Houghton, Mifflin, 1911.

Harrison, James Albert. "Negro English." *Anglia.* (1884) 7.232–79.

Harrison, Marie. *Groundcovers for the South.* Sarasota FL: Pineapple Press, 2006.

Harrower, John. *The Journal of John Harrower.* Williamsburg VA: Distributed by Holt, Rinehart and Winston, c.1963.

Hart, Bertha Sheppard. *The Official History of Laurens County, Georgia, 1807–1941.* Dublin GA: [s.n.], 1941.

Hart, Frances Noyes. *The Bellamy Trial.* Garden City NY: Doubleday, Page, 1927.

Hart, Fred H. *The Sazerac Lying Club.* San Francisco: Henry Keeler, 1878.

Hart, Jerome Alfred. *A Vigilante Girl.* Chicago: A. C. McClurg, 1910.

Hart, Nancy L. *Buddies.* Victoria: Trafford, 2003.

Hart, Robert G. *McKay's Guide to Alaska.* New York: D. McKay, c.1959.

Hart, Smith. *The New Yorkers.* New York: Sheridan House, c.1938.

Harte, Bret. *By Shore and Sedge.* Boston: Houghton, Mifflin, 1885.

———. *Clarence.* Boston: Houghton, Mifflin, 1895.

———. *Colonel Starbottle's Client and Some Other People.* Boston: Houghton, Mifflin, 1892.

———. *The Complete Poetical Works of Bret Harte.* London: Chatto and Windus, 1886.

———. *Condensed Novels.* Pirated ed. New York: G. W. Carleton, 1867.

———. *Condensed Novels and Stories.* Boston: Houghton, Mifflin, 1882.

———. *The Crusade of the Excelsior.* New York: Houghton, Mifflin, 1887.

———. *Drift from Two Shores.* Boston: Houghton, Osgood, 1879 [c.1878].

———. *East and West, Poems.* Boston: James R. Osgood, 1871.

———. *A First Family of Tasajara.* London: Macmillan, 1891. 2 vols.

———. *Flip and Other Stories.* London: Chatto & Windus, 1882.

———. *Gabriel Conroy.* Hartford CT: American Publishing, 1876.

———. *The Heritage of Dedlow Marsh.* Boston: Houghton, Mifflin, 1890 [c.1889].

———. *In the Carquinez Woods.* London: Longmans, Green, 1883.

———. *The Luck of Roaring Camp and Other Sketches.* Boston: Fields, Osgood, 1870.

———. *The Man on the Beach.* London: George Routledge and Sons, 1878.

———. *Maruja.* Boston: Houghton, Mifflin, 1885.

———. *A Millionaire of Rough-and-Ready and Devil's Ford.* Boston: Houghton, Mifflin, 1887.

———. *Mrs. Skagg's Husbands, and Other Sketches.* Boston: James R. Osgood, 1873.

———. *A Phyllis of the Sierras and A Drift from Redwood Camp.* Boston: Houghton, Mifflin, 1888 [c.1887].

———. *The Poetical Works of Bret Harte.* Complete ed. Boston: James R. Osgood, 1873.

———. *The Poetical Works of Bret Harte.* Boston: Houghton, Mifflin, 1899.

———. *Sketches of the Sixties by Bret Harte and Mark Twain.* San Francisco: John Howell, 1926.

———. *Stories in Light and Shadow.* London: C. Arthur Pearson, 1898.

———. *The Story of a Mine.* 1st Amer. ed. Boston: J. R. Osgood, 1878. Orig. pub. in 1877 by Tauschnitz, Leipzig; G. Routledge, London.

———. *Tales of the Argonauts.* Boston: James R. Osgood, 1875.

———. *Tales of the Argonauts.* Boston: Houghton, Mifflin, c.1896. Standard Library Ed. of *The Writings of Bret Harte,* vol. 2.

———. *Two Men of Sandy Bar.* Boston: James R. Osgood, 1876.

————. *A Waif of the Plains.* Boston: Houghton, Mifflin, 1890.

Hartford Courant. Hartford CT, 1887–.

Hartford Times. Hartford CT, 1883?–1976.

Hartley, Cecil B. *The Gentlemen's Book of Etiquette.* Boston: DeWolfe, Fiske, c.1873.

Hartsell, Jacob. "The J. Hartsell Memora: the Journal of a Tennessee Captain in the War of 1812." East Tennessee Historical Society *Publications.* (1939) 11.93–115; (1940) 12.118–46.

Hartwig, Georg. *The Polar World.* New York: Harper & Bros., 1869.

Harvardiana. Cambridge MA, 1835–1838.

Harvard Magazine. Cambridge MA: J. Bartlett, 1854–1864; 1973–.

Harvard Post. Harvard MA, 1973–1988.

Harvard Register. Cambridge MA: Hilliard and Brown, 1827–1828.

Harvard University. Museum of Comparative Zoology. *Bulletin.* Cambridge MA, 1863–.

Harwich Port Library Association. *From Cape Cod Kitchens.* Harwich Port MA: The Association, c.1934.

Harwin, Brian SEE Henderson, LeGrand

Hashaw, Tim. *Children of Perdition.* Macon GA: Mercer Univ. Press, c.2006.

Haskell, William B. *Two Years in the Klondike and Alaskan Gold-Fields.* Hartford CT: Hartford Publishing, 1898.

Haskin, Leslie Loren. *Wild Flowers of the Pacific Coast.* Portland OR: Metropolitan Press, 1934.

Haskins, Charles Warren. *The Argonauts of California.* New York: Fords, Howard & Hulbert, 1890.

Hassler, Jon. *The Dean's List.* New York: Ballantine Books, c.1997.

————. *Dear James.* New York: Ballantine Books, c.1993.

Hastings, Scott E. *The Last Yankees.* Hanover NH: Univ. Press New England, c.1990.

Haswell, Alanson Mason. *A Daughter of the Ozarks.* Boston: Cornhill, c.1921.

Haswell, Charles Haynes. *Reminiscences of an Octogenarian of the City of New York (1816–1860).* New York: Harper & Bros., 1897 [c.1896].

Hatch, Joel, Jr. *Reminiscences, Anecdotes and Statistics of the Early Settlers and the 'Olden Time' in the Town of Sherburne, Chenango County, N.Y.* Utica NY: Curtiss & White, 1862.

Hatcher, Harlan Henthorne. *The Buckeye Country.* New York: H. C. Kinsey, c.1940.

————. *Lake Erie.* Indianapolis IN: Bobbs-Merrill, c.1945.

Hatcher, William Eldridge. *John Jasper.* New York: Fleming H. Revell, 1908.

Haun, Mildred. *The Hawk's Done Gone.* Nashville TN: Vanderbilt Univ. Press, 1968. Title story orig. pub. in 1940 by Bobbs-Merrill, Indianapolis IN.

Hausman, Leon Augustus. *Field Book of Eastern Birds.* New York: G. P. Putnam's Sons, c.1946.

————. *The Illustrated Encyclopedia of American Birds.* New York: Halcyon House, c.1944.

Havard, Valery. *Botanical Outlines of the Country Marched Over by the Seventh United States Cavalry during the Summer of 1877.* Washington DC: Govt. Printing Office, 1878.

————. "Report of the Flora of Western and Southern Texas." United States National Museum *Proceedings.* (1886) 8.449–533.

Haven, Samuel Foster. *An Historical Address Delivered before the Citizens of the Town of Dedham on the Twenty-First of September, 1836.* Dedham MA: Printed by H. Mann, 1837.

Hawaii. Agricultural Experiment Station. *Press Bulletin.* Honolulu HI, 1903–1919.

Hawaiian Almanac and Annual. Honolulu HI: Thomas G.Thrum, 1875–1924.

Hawaiian Gazette. Honolulu HI, 1865–1918.

Hawaiian Historical Society. *Annual Report.* Honolulu HI, 1893–.

————. *Papers.* Honolulu HI, 1892–1940.

Hawaii Department of Business, Economic Development and Tourism. *Hawaii Seafood Buyers Guide.* [v.d.]. Internet.

Hawaii. University. Botany Department. *Hawaiian Native Plant Genera.* [v.d.]. Internet.

Hawes, John Bromham. *Talks on Tuberculosis with Patients and Their Friends.* Boston: Houghton Mifflin, 1931.

Hawes, William Post. *Sporting Scenes and Sundry Sketches.* New York: Gould, Banks, 1842. 2 vols.

Hawkes, Ernest William. *The Inviting-In Feast of the Alaskan Eskimo.* Ottawa: Govt. Print. Bureau, 1913.

Hawkins, Benjamin. *Letters of Benjamin Hawkins, 1796–1806.* Savannah GA: Georgia Historical Society, 1916.

————. "A Sketch of the Creek Country in the Years 1798

and 1799." Georgia Historical Society *Collections.* (1848) vol. 3, pt. 1.

Hawkins, Pliny Haine. *The Trees and Shrubs of Yellowstone National Park.* Menasha WI: Collegiate Press, 1924.

Hawks, Francis Lister. *The Adventures of Daniel Boone.* New York: D. Appleton, 1844.

Hawks, Francis Lister and William Stevens Perry. *Documentary History of the Protestant Episcopal Church in the United States of America.* New York: James Pott, 1863–1864. 2 vols.

Hawley, H. J. "Hawley's Diary of His Trip across the Plains in 1860." *Wisconsin Magazine of History.* (1935–1936) 19.319–42.

Hawley, Zerah. *A Journal of a Tour through Connecticut, Massachusetts, New York.* New Haven CT: S. Converse, 1822.

Hawthorne, Julian. *Nathaniel Hawthorne and His Wife.* Grosse Pointe MI: Scholarly Press, 1968. 2 vols. Repr. of the 2d ed. pub. in 1885 by J. R. Osgood, Boston.

Hawthorne, Nathaniel. *The American Notebooks.* New Haven CT: Yale Univ. Press, 1932.

————. *The Blithedale Romance.* Boston: Ticknor, Reed, and Fields, 1852.

————. *The Marble Faun.* Boston: Ticknor and Fields, 1860. 2 vols.

————. *Our Old Home.* Boston: Ticknor and Fields, 1863. 2 vols.

————. *Passages from the American Note-Books.* Boston: James R. Osgood, 1874 [c.1868]. 2 vols.

————. *Passages from the English Note-Books of Nathaniel Hawthorne.* Boston: Fields, Osgood, 1870. 2 vols.

————. *Passages from the French and Italian Note-Books of Nathaniel Hawthorne.* 1st London ed. London: Strahan, 1871. 2 vols.

————. *The Scarlet Letter.* Boston: Ticknor, Reed, and Fields, 1852 [c.1850].

————. *Tanglewood Tales, for Girls and Boys.* Boston: Ticknor, Reed and Fields, c.1853.

————. *Twice-Told Tales.* New ed. Boston: Ticknor and Fields, 1857 [c.1851]. 2 vols. New ed. orig. pub. in 1851.

Hay, Elzey SEE Andrews, Eliza Frances

Hay, John. *The Bread-Winners.* New York: Harper & Bros., 1884.

————. *Jim Bludso of the Prairie Belle and Little Breeches.* Boston: James R. Osgood, 1871.

————. *Pike County Ballads.* Boston: James R. Osgood, 1871.

————. *Poems.* London: John Lane; Boston: Houghton, Mifflin, 1897.

Haycraft, Samuel. *A History of Elizabethtown, Kentucky, and Its Surroundings.* Elizabethtown KY: Woman's Club of Elizabethtown KY, 1921. Orig. pub. in 1869 in the Elizabethtown News.

Hayden, Ferdinand Vandeveer. *The Great West.* Bloomington IL: Charles R. Brodix, 1880.

Hayden, Sterling. *Wanderer.* New York: Knopf, 1963.

Hayes, Augustus Allen. *New Colorado and the Santa Fé Trail.* New York: Harper & Bros., 1880.

Hayes, Benjamin Ignatius. *Pioneer Notes from the Diaries of Judge Benjamin Hayes: 1849–1875.* Los Angeles: Privately printed, 1929.

Hayes, Rutherford Birchard. *Diary and Letters of Rutherford Birchard Hayes, Nineteenth President of the United States.* Ed. by Charles Richard Williams. Columbus OH: Ohio State Archaeological and Historical Society, 1922–1926. 5 vols.

Haynes, Alice Hawkins. *Haywood Home.* Tallahassee FL: Rose Printing, 1991.

Haynes, Melinda. *Mother of Pearl.* New York: Hyperion, 1999.

Hayward, John. *Gazetteer of the United States.* Portland ME: S. H. Colesworthy, 1843.

Haywarde, Richard SEE Cozzens, Frederick Swartwout

Hayward Review. Hayward CA, 1892?–1910.

Haywood, Charles Fry. *Yankee Dictionary.* Lynn MA: Jackson & Phillips, 1963.

Hazard, Thomas Benjamin. *Nailer Tom's Diary.* Boston: Merrymount Press, 1930.

Hazard, Thomas Robinson. *The Jonny-Cake Papers of "Shepherd Tom".* Boston: Printed for the subscribers, 1915.

Hazard's Register of Pennsylvania. Philadelphia, 1831–1835.

Hazeltine, Gilbert W. *The Early History of the Town of Ellicott, Chatauqua County, N.Y.* Jamestown NY: Journal Printing, 1887.

Hazen, Edward. *The Panorama of Professions and Trades.* Philadelphia: U. Hunt, 1837.

Hazen, Tracy Elliot. *The Hazen Family in America.* Ed. by

Donald Lines Jacobus. Thomaston CT: Robert Hazen, 1947.

Head, J. Maynard. *Brogans, Clothespins and a Twist of Tobacco.* West Allis WI: Pine Mountain Press, 1984.

Headley, Joel Tyler. *The Great Rebellion.* Hartford CT: Hurlburt, Williams, 1863 [c.1862]. 2 vols.

Health Bulletin. Raleigh NC: North Carolina State Board of Health, 1913–.

Health Reformer. Battle Creek MI, 1866–1878.

Healy, William. *The Individual Delinquent.* Boston: Little, Brown, 1915.

Heard, Isaac V. D. *History of the Sioux War and Massacres of 1862 and 1863.* New York: Harper & Bros., 1864 [c.1863].

Hearn, Lafcadio. *Creole Sketches.* Boston: Houghton Mifflin, 1924. Orig. pub. in New Orleans newspapers.

————. *La Cuisine Creole.* 2d ed. New Orleans: F. F. Hansell & Bros., c.1885.

————. *Miscellanies.* Coll. by Albert Mordell. London: William Heinemann, 1924. 2 vols.

Hearne, Samuel. *Journals of Samuel Hearne and Philip Turnor.* Ed. with an intro. and notes by J. B. Tyrrell. Toronto, Ontario: Champlain Society, 1934.

————. *A Journey from Prince of Wales's Fort in Hudson's Bay to the Northern Ocean.* London: Printed for A. Strahan and T. Cadell, 1795.

Hearst's International. Chicago, 1901–1952.

Heath, Shirley Brice. *Ways with Words.* Cambridge: Cambridge Univ. Press, c.1983.

Heat Moon, William Least. *Blue Highways.* Boston: Little, Brown, c.1982.

————. *PrairyErth.* Boston: Houghton Mifflin, 1991.

Heatwole, John L. *Shenandoah Voices.* Berryville VA: Rockbridge, c.1995.

Heck, Johann Georg. *Iconographic Encyclopaedia of Science, Literature and Art.* Transl. and ed. by Spencer F. Baird. New York: Rudolph Garrigue, 1851 [c.1849]. 4 vols.

Heckewelder, John Gottlieb Ernestus. *Narrative of the Mission of the United Brethren among the Delaware and Mohegan Indians.* Philadelphia: McCarty & Davis, 1820.

Hedgecock, L. J. *Gone Are the Days.* Girard KS: Haldeman-Julius, c.1949.

Hedges, Henry Parsons. *A History of the Town of East-Hampton, N.Y.* Sag-Harbor NY: J. H. Hunt, 1897.

Hedrick, U. P. *Cyclopedia of Hardy Fruits.* New York: Macmillan, 1922.

————. *The Land of the Crooked Tree.* New York: Oxford Univ. Press, c.1948.

Heggen, Thomas. *Mister Roberts.* Boston: Houghton Mifflin, c.1946.

Heilner, Van Campen. *A Book on Duck Shooting.* New York: Knopf, 1947. Repr. of the 1939 ed.

Heimann, Robert Karl. *Tobacco and Americans.* New York: McGraw-Hill Book, 1960.

Hein, Stephen et al. *A Fisherman's Guide to Common Fishes of Louisiana & Adjacent Offshore Waters.* Baton Rouge LA: Louisiana Sea Grant College Program, LA State Univ., c.1996.

Heinlein, Robert Anson. *Time Enough for Love.* New York: G. P. Putnam's Sons, c.1973.

Heirloom Cook Book. [s.l.]: Northern Illinois Gas, 1968.

Heiser, Charles Bixler. *Weeds in My Garden.* Portland OR: Timber Press, 2003.

Helen Adolf Festschrift. Ed. by Sheema Z. Buehne, James L. Hodge, and Lucille B. Pinto. New York: Frederick Ungar Publishing, c.1968.

Helena Independent. Helena MT, 1875–1943.

Helen Nash's Pond and Garden. Zionsville IN, 1998–2001.

Heller, Christine A. *Wild Edible and Poisonous Plants of Alaska.* College AK: Cooperative Extension Service, Univ. AK, 1962, 1953.

————. *Wild Flowers of Alaska.* Portland OR: Graphic Arts Center, c.1966.

Heller, Herbert L., ed. *Sourdough Sagas.* Cleveland: World Publishing, c.1967.

Hellman, Lillian. *The Collected Plays.* Boston: Little, Brown, c.1972.

Helm, MacKinley. *John Marin.* Boston: Pellegrini & Cudahy, in Association with the Institute of Contemporary Art, 1948.

Helmericks, Constance. *We Live in Alaska.* Boston: Little, Brown, 1945 [c.1944].

Helmericks, Constance and Harmon Helmericks. *Our Summer with the Eskimos.* Boston: Little, Brown, 1948.

Helper, Hinton Rowan. *The Impending Crisis of the South.* New York: Burdich Bros., 1857.

————. *The Land of Gold.* Baltimore MD: Henry Taylor, 1855.

Helton, Roy. *Lonesome Water.* New York: Harper & Bros., 1930.

Helton, William W. *Around Home in Unicoi County.* [s.l.]: W. W. Helton, c.1986.

Hemingway, Ernest. *Across the River and into the Trees.* New York: Charles Scribner's Sons, 1950.

———. *Death in the Afternoon.* New York: Charles Scribner's Sons, 1932.

———. *For Whom the Bell Tolls.* New York: Charles Scribner's Sons, 1940.

———. *In Our Time.* New York: Scribner, c.1958. Orig. pub. in 1925.

———. *To Have and Have Not.* New York: Charles Scribner's Sons, 1937.

———. *The Torrents of Spring.* New York: Charles Scribner's Sons, 1939 [c.1926].

———. *Winner Take Nothing.* New York: Charles Scribner's Sons, c.1933.

Hemmerly, Thomas Ellsworth. *Ozark Wildflowers.* Athens GA: Univ. GA Press, c.2002.

Hempstead, Joshua. *Diary of Joshua Hempstead of New London, Connecticut, Covering a Period of Forty-Seven Years, from September 1711, to November, 1758.* New London CT: New London County Historical Society, 1901.

Hempstead, New York. *Records of the Towns of North and South Hempstead, Long Island, N.Y.* Jamaica NY: Long Island Farmer Print, 1896–1904. 8 vols.

Hench, A. L. *Collection.* 1930–c1972. Unpub. coll. on Amer. Engl. usage.

Henderson, Alice Palmer. *The Rainbow's End: Alaska.* Chicago: Herbert S. Stone, 1898.

Henderson, Carrol L. *Landscaping for Wildlife.* St. Paul MN: Nongame Wildlife Program, Section of Wildlife, Minnesota Dept. of Natural Resources, c.1987.

Henderson, George Cochran. *Keys to Crookdom.* New York: D. Appleton, 1924.

Henderson, LeGrand. *Home Is Upriver.* New York: Macmillan, 1952.

Henderson, Marc Antony, transl. *Song of Milkanwatha.* 3d ed. Albany NY: D. R. Niver, 1883.

Henderson, Mary Newton Foote. *Practical Cooking and Dinner Giving.* New York: Harper & Bros., 1877.

Henderson, Peter. *Henderson's Handbook of Plants.* New York: Peter Henderson, 1881.

Henderson County Graphic-Reporter. Stronghurst IL, 1954–.

Hendrickson, Gerth Edison. *The Angler's Guide to Ten Classic Trout Streams in Michigan.* Ann Arbor MI: Univ. MI Press, c.1985.

Hendrickson, Robert. *American Talk.* New York: Viking, c.1986.

Hendrix, Jimi. *Are You Experienced?* Phonodisc. Burbank CA: Reprise, c.1967.

Henkel, Alice. *American Medicinal Leaves and Herbs.* Washington DC: Govt. Printing Office, 1911.

———. *American Root Drugs.* Washington DC: Govt. Printing Office, 1907. U.S. Dept. of Agriculture. Bureau of Plant Industry. Bulletin No. 107.

———. *Weeds Used in Medicine.* Washington DC: Govt. Printing Office, 1904.

Henry, Alexander. *Travels and Adventures in Canada and the Indian Territories between the Years 1760 and 1776.* New York: I. Riley, 1809.

Henry, George W. *Tell Tale Rag.* Oneida NY: The Author, 1861.

Henry, John Joseph. *An Accurate and Interesting Account of the Hardships and Sufferings of That Band of Heroes, Who Traversed the Wilderness in the Campaign against Quebec in 1775.* Lancaster PA: William Greer, 1812.

Henry, Marguerite. *Misty of Chincoteague.* Chicago: Rand McNally, 1962 [c.1947].

Henry, Ralph Chester. *High Border Country.* New York: Duell, Sloan & Pearce, 1942.

Henry, Robert. *Narrative of the Battle of Cowan's Ford, February 1st, by Robert Henry, and Narrative of the Battle of Kings Mountain, by Captain David Vance.* Greensboro NC: D. Schenck, 1891.

Henry, Robert Selph. *"First with the Most" Forrest.* Indianapolis IN: Bobbs-Merrill, c.1944.

Henry, Samuel. *A New and Complete American Medical Family Herbal.* New York: Samuel Henry, 1814.

Henry, Stuart Oliver. *Conquering Our Great American Plains.* New York: E. P. Dutton, c.1930.

Henry, Will SEE ALSO Allen, Henry Wilson

Henry, Will. *I, Tom Horn.* Philadelphia: Lippincott, 1996 [c.1975].

Henry, William Seaton. *Campaign Sketches of the War with Mexico.* New York: Harper & Bros., 1847.

Henshall, James Alexander. *Bass, Pike, Perch and Other Game Fishes of America.* New York: Macmillan, 1903.

———. *Book of the Black Bass.* Cincinnati OH: Robert Clarke, 1881.

———. *Camping and Cruising in Florida.* Cincinnati OH: Robert Clarke, c.1884.

Henshaw, Henry Wetherbee. *Birds of the Hawaiian Islands.* Honolulu HI: T. G. Thrum, 1902.

Henshaw, Julia Wilmotte. *Mountain Wild Flowers of America.* Boston: Ginn, 1906.

Hentz, Carolina Lee. *Rena, or the Snow Bird.* Philadelphia: T. B. Peterson and Bros., c.1851.

Hentz, Charles Arnould. *A Southern Practice.* Ed. by Steven M. Stowe. Charlottesville VA: Published for the Southern Texts Society by the Univ. Press VA, c.2000.

Henzie, Moses. *A Biography.* North Vancouver: Hancock House, c.1979.

Herald, Earl S. *Living Fishes of the World.* Garden City NY: Doubleday, c.1961.

Herald. Randolph VT, 1989–.

Herald. Rock Hill SC, 1877–.

Herald. Wheeling IL, 1972–1977.

Herald-Advertiser. Huntington WV, 1927–.

Herald and Torch-Light. Hagerstown MD, 1864?–1907?

Herald-Despatch. Decatur IL, 1885–1900.

Herald of Freedom. Edenton NC, 1799–1816?

Herald-Press. St. Joseph MI, 1928–1975.

Herald Times-Reporter. Manitowoc WI, 1973–.

Herald-Tribune. Sarasota FL, 1925–.

Herbert, Henry William. *The Deerstalkers.* Philadelphia: T. B. Peterson Bros., c.1843.

———. *Frank Forester's Field Sports.* New York: Stringer & Townsend, 1849. 2 vols.

———. *Frank Forester's Fish and Fishing of the United States.* 3d ed. rev. and corr. with a suppl. New York: Stringer & Townsend, 1851.

———. *Frank Forester's Sporting Scenes and Characters.* Philadelphia: T. B. Peterson & Bros., [c.1857, c.1846]. 2 vols.

———. *The Warwick Woodlands.* New ed., rev. and corr. Philadelphia: T. B. Peterson & Bros., 1850.

Herbst, William. *Fungal Flora of the Lehigh Valley, PA.* Allentown PA: Berkemeyer, Keck, 1899.

Heren, Louis. *Growing Up Poor in London.* London: Hamish Hamilton, 1973.

Hergesheimer, Joseph. *Java Head.* New York: A. A. Knopf, 1926. Orig. pub. in 1918 by A. A. Knopf, New York.

Hering, Constantine. *Domestic Physician.* 3d Amer. ed. Philadelphia: Rademacher, 1845.

Heriot, George. *Travels through the Canadas.* London: Printed for Richard Phillips, 1807.

Herlan, Peter J. *The Nevada Highway Bird Watcher.* Carson City NV: Nevada State Museum, 1965.

Herman, Henry. *His Angel.* New York: Ward, Lock, Bowden, c.1891.

Herman, Lewis and Marguerite Shalett Herman. *American Dialects.* New York: Routledge, c.1997. Orig. pub. in 1947 by Ziff-Davis, Chicago, under the title: *Manual of American Dialects for Radio, Stage and Screen, and Television.*

Herms, William Brodbeck. *Medical and Veterinary Entomology.* New York: Macmillan, 1915.

———. *Medical and Veterinary Entomology.* 2d ed. completely rev. New York: Macmillan, 1923.

———. *Medical Entomology.* 4th ed. New York: Macmillan, 1950.

Herndon, Dallas T. *Centennial History of Arkansas.* Chicago: S. J. Clarke Pub., 1922. 3 vols.

Herndon, George Melvin. *William Tatham and the Culture of Tobacco.* Coral Gables FL: Univ. Miami Press, 1969.

Herndon, William Henry and Jesse William Weik. *Herndon's Lincoln.* Springfield IL: Herndon's Lincoln Publishing, 1888. 3 vols.

Herpetologica. Austin TX: Herpetologist's League, 1936–.

Herrick, Robert. *Homely Lilla.* New York: Harcourt, Brace, c.1923.

Hertwig, Richard. *A Manual of Zoology.* Transl. and ed. by J. S. Kingsley. 2d Amer. ed. from the 5th German ed. New York: Henry Holt, 1909.

Hertzler, Arthur Emanuel. *The Horse and Buggy Doctor.* New York: Harper & Bros., 1938.

Hervey, Eliphalet Williams. *A Catalogue of the Plants Found in New Bedford and Its Vicinity, Arranged According to the Season of Their Flowering.* New Bedford MA: Press of E. Anthony, 1860.

Hervey, John. *The American Trotter.* New York: Coward-McCann, 1947.

Hesperian. Columbus OH: J. D. Nichols, 1838–1839.

Heuman, Gad J. and James Walvin, eds. *The Slavery Reader.* London: Routledge, 2003.

Heverly, Clement Ferdinand. *History of the Towandas, 1770–1886.* Towanda PA: Report-Journal Printing, 1886.

Hewett, Edgar Lee and Bertha P. Dutton. *Pajarito Plateau and Its Ancient People.* 2d ed. rev. Albuquerque NM: Univ. NM Press, c.1953.

Hewett, Edgar Lee and Reginald G. Fisher. *Mission Monuments of New Mexico.* Albuquerque NM: Univ. NM Press, 1943.

Hewitt, Jean. *The New York Times Heritage Cookbook.* New York: G. P. Putnam's Sons, 1972.

Hewson, John. *A Computer-Generated Dictionary of Proto-Algonquian.* Hull: Canadian Museum of Civilization, c.1993.

Heydrick, Benjamin Alexander and Blanche Jennings Thompson, ed. *Americans All.* New York: Harcourt, Brace, 1941.

Heyliger, William. *The Builder of the Dam.* New York: D. Appleton, 1929.

Heyward, Du Bose and George Gershwin. *A Woman Is a Sometime Thing.* New York: Gershwin, 1935.

Heyward, Duncan Clinch. *Seed from Madagascar.* Chapel Hill NC: Univ. NC Press, 1937.

Heywood, Daniel E. *Diary.* Bristol NH: Printed by R. W. Musgrove, 1891.

H. H. SEE Jackson, Helen Hunt

Hiaasen, Carl. *Double Whammy.* New York: G. P. Putnam's Sons, c.1987.

———. *Native Tongue.* New York: Alfred A. Knopf, 1991.

Hibben, Sheila. *American Regional Cookery.* New York: Gramercy Pub., 1946 [c.1932].

Hickenlooper, Frank. *An Illustrated History of Monroe County, Iowa.* Albia IA: [s.n.], 1896.

Hickey, Thomas A. *The Land?* Hallettsville TX: Rebel Print, 1912.

Hicks, Ronda Lee. *Beech Mountain Man: the Memoirs of Ronda Lee Hicks.* Interviewed by Thomas G. Burton. Knoxville TN: Univ. TN Press, c.2009.

Hicks, William. *History of Louisiana Negro Baptists and Early American Beginnings from 1804 to 1914.* Ed. by Sue Eakin. Lafayette LA: Center for Louisiana Studies, Univ. Southwestern LA, 1998. Orig. pub. in 1914 by the National Baptist Publishing Board, Nashville TN; repr. with new material added by the editor.

Higbee, Lucy Ann. *The Diary of Lucy Ann Higbee.* Cleveland OH: Priv. print, 1924.

Higgins, Ethel Bailey. *Our Native Cacti.* New York: A. T. De La Mare, 1931.

Higgins, George V. *At End of Day.* New York: Harcourt, c.2000.

———. *A City on a Hill.* New York: Knopf, 1975.

Higginson, Ella. *From the Land of the Snow-Pearls.* New York: Macmillan, c.1897.

Higginson, Francis. *Nevv-Englands Plantation.* London: Printed by T.Coates and R.Coates for Michael Sparke, 1630.

Higginson, Thomas Wentworth. *Army Life in a Black Regiment.* Boston: Fields, Osgood, 1870 [c.1869].

———, ed. *Harvard Memorial Biographies.* Cambridge MA: Sever and Francis, 1867. 2 vols.

———. *Outdoor Papers.* Boston: Ticknor and Fields, 1863.

———. *Outdoor Studies.* Boston: Houghton, Mifflin, 1900.

High, Ellesa Clay. *Collection of Terms Recorded in the Red River Gorge (Kentucky).* 1981. Unpub.

High Country News. Paonia CO, 1969–.

High Times. New York, 1975–.

Hildreth, James. *Dragoon Campaigns to the Rocky Mountains.* New York: Wiley & Long, 1836.

Hilgard, Eugene Woldemar. *Report on the Cotton Production of the State of Mississippi.* Washington DC: Govt. Printing Office, 1884.

———. *Supplementary and Final Report of a Geological Reconnaissance of the State of Louisiana, Made under the Auspices of the New Orleans Academy of Sciences and of the Bureau of Immigration of the State of Louisiana, in May and June, 1869.* New Orleans LA: Picayune Steam Job Print, 1873.

Hill, Agnes Leonard. *Myrtle Blossoms.* Chicago: J. O. W. Bailey, 1863.

Hill, Alfred Tuxbury, comp. *Voyages.* New York: David McKay, c.1977.

Hill, Alice Polk. *Tales of the Colorado Pioneers.* Denver CO: Pierson & Gardner, 1884.

Hill, George Canning. *Homespun.* New York: Hurd and Houghton, 1867.

Hill, Levi L. *A Treatise on Heliochromy.* New York: Robinson & Caswell, 1856.

Hill, Margaret Hunt. *H. L. and Lyda*. Little Rock AR: August House, 1994.

Hill, Marion. *McAllister's Grove*. New York: D. Appleton, 1917.

Hill, Ralph Nading. *The Winooski*. New York: Rinehart, 1949.

Hill, Rebecca. *Blue Rise*. New York: Penguin, 1984 [c.1983].

Hillard, Elias Brewster. *The Last Men of the Revolution*. Hartford CT: N. A. & R. A. Moore, 1864.

Hillebrand, William. *Flora of the Hawaiian Islands*. London: Williams & Norgate; New York: B. Westermann, 1888.

Hillerman, Tony. *The Blessing Way*. New York: Harper & Row, c.1970.

———. *The First Eagle*. New York: Harper Collins, c.1998.

———. *The Ghostway*. New York: Harper & Row, 1985 [c.1984].

———. *Listening Woman*. New York: Harper & Row, c.1978.

———. *Sacred Clowns*. New York: HarperCollins, c.1993.

Hilliard, Sam Bowers. *Hog Meat and Hoecake*. Carbondale IL: Southern IL Univ. Press, 1972.

Hilliard, William. *An Address Delivered before the Massachusetts Charitable Mechanic Association, October 4, 1827*. Cambridge MA: Hilliard, Metcalf, 1827.

Hillsboro Press Gazette. Hillsboro OH, 1973–1985.

Hiltzheimer, Jacob. *Extracts from the Diary of Jacob Hiltzheimer of Philadelphia, 1765–1798*. Philadelphia: Press of Wm. F. Felb, 1893.

Himes, Chester B. *Black on Black*. Garden City NY: Doubleday, 1973.

———. *Cast the First Stone*. New York: Coward-McCann, 1952.

———. *If He Hollers Let Him Go*. Garden City NY: Doubleday, Doran, 1946.

Hines, Gustavus. *A Voyage Round the World*. Buffalo NY: G. H. Derby, 1850.

Hinman, Wilbur F. *Corporal Si Klegg and His Pard*. Cleveland OH: N. G. Hamilton, 1892 [c.1887].

Hinton, Richard J. *The Hand-Book to Arizona*. San Francisco: Payot, Upham; New York: American News, 1878 [c.1877].

Hiser, Berniece T., Comp. *Quare Do's in Appalachia: East Kentucky Legends and Memorats*. Pikeville KY: Pikeville College Press, 1978.

Historical Encyclopedia of Illinois. Chicago: Munsell, 1906.

Historical Magazine of the Protestant Episcopal Church. Garrison NY, 1932–.

An Historical Review and Directory of North America. Dublin: M. Graisberry, 1788. 2 vols.

Historical Review of Berks County. Reading PA: Historical Society of Berks County, 1935–.

Historical Society of Pennsylvania. *Proceedings*. Philadelphia, 1845–1847.

Historical Society of Southern California. *Annual Publications*. Los Angeles, 1905–1934.

Historic Magazine and Notes and Queries. Manchester NY, 1882–1909.

History and Directory of Kent County, Michigan. Grand Rapids MI: Dillenbach & Leavitt, 1870.

History of Buchanan County, Iowa. Cleveland OH: Williams Bros., 1881.

History of Dane County, Wisconsin. Chicago: Western Historical, 1880.

History of Fulton County Illinois. Peoria IL: Chas. C. Chapman, 1879.

A History of Fulton County, Illinois, in Spoon River Country, 1818–1968. Ed. by Helen Hollandsworth Clark. [s.l.]: Published by the Fulton County Board of Supervisors, with the cooperation of the Fulton County Historical Society, c.1969.

The History of Jasper County, Iowa. Chicago: Western Historical, 1878.

History of Kentucky. Chicago: S. J. Clarke Publishing, 1928. 4 vols.

History of Logan County and Ohio. Ed. by W. H. Perrin and J. H. Battle. Chicago: O.L Baskin, 1880.

The History of Marion County, Ohio. Chicago: Leggett, Conaway, 1883.

History of Napa and Lake Counties, California. San Francisco: Slocum, Bowen, 1881.

History of Northampton County, Pennsylvania. Philadelphia: Peter Fritts, 1877.

History of Pella, Iowa, 1847–1987. Dallas TX: Curtis Media, c.1988–1989.

History of St. Clair County, Michigan. Chicago: A. T. Andreas, 1883.

History of That Part of the Susquehanna and Juniata Valleys. Philadelphia: Everts, Peck & Richards, 1886. 2 vols.

History of the 307th Field Artillery, September 6, 1917–May 16,1919. [s.l.]: [s.n.], 1919?

The History of the British Dominions in North America. London: Printed for W. Strahan and T. Becket, 1773. 2 vols.

History of the Church of Jesus Christ of Latter-Day Saints. Intro. and notes by B. H. Roberts. Salt Lake City UT: Deseret News, 1902–1932. 7 vols.

History of the County of Berkshire, Massachusetts in Two Parts. Pittsfield MA: Printed by S. W. Bush, 1829.

History of the North-Western Soldiers' Fair, Held in Chicago. Chicago: Dunlop, Sewell & Spalding, 1864.

A History of the "Striped Pig". Boston: Whipple and Damrell, 1838.

History of the Town of Dorchester, Massachusetts. Boston: Ebenezer Clapp, Jr., 1859.

History of the Town of Hingham, Massachusetts. Hingham MA: Published by the Town, 1893. 3 vols.

History of Tioga County Pennsylvania. New York: W. W. Munsell, 1883.

History of Virginia. Chicago: American Historical Society, 1924. 6 vols.

Hitchcock, Albert Spear. *A Manual of Farm Grasses*. Washington DC: The Author, 1921.

———. *Manual of the Grasses of the United States*. Washington DC: Govt. Printing Office, 1935.

Hitchcock, Albert Spear and Agnes Chase. *Manual of the Grasses of the United States*. 2d ed. rev., with additional revisions Feb. 1951. Washington DC: Govt. Printing Office, 1950.

Hitchcock, Charles Leo and Arthur Cronquist. *Flora of the Pacific Northwest*. Seattle WA: Univ. WA Press, 1973.

Hitchcock, Edward. *Report on the Geology, Mineralogy, Botany and Zoology of Massachusetts*. 2d ed. corr. and enlarged. Amherst MA: J. S. & C. Adams, 1835.

Hitchcock, Ethan Allen. *A Traveler in Indian Territory: the Journal of Ethan Allen Hitchcock*. Cedar Rapids IA: Torch Press, 1930.

Hitchcock, Mary E. *Two Women in the Klondike*. New York: G. P. Putnam's Sons, 1899.

Hittell, John Shertzer. *The Resources of California*. San Francisco: A. Roman; New York: W. J. Widdleton, c.1863.

———. *The Resources of California*. 2d ed., with an app. San Francisco: A. Roman; New York: W. J. Widdleton, 1866.

———. *The Resources of California*. 6th ed. rewritten. San Francisco: A. Roman, 1877 [c.1874].

Hobart, George Vere. *Get Next*. New York: G. W. Dillingham, c.1905.

———. *I'm from Missouri*. New York: G. W. Dillingham, c.1904.

———. *It's Up to You*. New York: G. W. Dillingham, c.1902.

———. *John Henry*. New York: G. W. Dillingham, c.1901.

———. *Skiddoo!* New York: G. W. Dillingham, c.1906.

Hobart Daily Republican. Hobart OK, 1906–1920.

Hobbs, Anne and Robert Specht. *Tisha*. New York: St. Martin's Press, c.1976.

Hobbs, Charles E. *C. E. Hobbs' Botanical Hand-Book of Common Local, English, Botanical and Pharmacopoeial Names*. Boston: C. C. Roberts, 1876.

Hobson, Richmond P., Jr. *Nothing Too Good for a Cowboy*. Philadelphia: J. B. Lippincott, c.1955.

Hodag Shopper. Rhinelander WI, 1958–.

Hodge, Clifton Fremont. *Nature Study and Life*. Boston: Ginn, 1902.

Hodge, Frederick Webb, ed. *Handbook of American Indians North of Mexico*. Washington DC: Govt. Printing Office, 1907–1910. 2 vols.

Hodge, Hiram C. *Arizona as It Is*. New York: Hurd & Houghton, 1877.

Hodge, William. *A Memoir of the Late William Hodge, Sen*. Buffalo NY: Bigelow Bros., 1885.

Hodges, Mary Bozeman. *Tough Customers and Other Stories*. Ashland KY: Jesse Stuart Foundation, 1999.

Hodgson, William. *Selections from the Letters of Thomas B. Gould*. Philadelphia: Printed by C. Sherman & Son, 1860.

Hoffman, Alice. *Turtle Moon*. New York: G. P. Putnam's Sons, c.1992.

Hoffman, Charles Fenno. *Greyslaer*. New York: Harper, 1840. 2 vols.

———, ed. *The New-York Book of Poetry*. New York: G. Dearborn, 1837.

———. *Wild Scenes in the Forest and Prairie*. London: Richard Bentley, 1839. 2 vols.

———. *Wild Scenes in the Forest and Prairie, with Sketches of American Life*. New York: William C. Colyer, 1843 [c.1838]. 2 vols.

———. *A Winter in the West*. 2d ed. New York: Harper & Bros., 1835. 2 vols.

Hoffman, David. *Viator*. Boston: Charles C. Little & James Brown, 1841 [c.1839].

Hoffmann, Ralph. *A Guide to the Birds of New England and Eastern New York*. Boston: Houghton, Mifflin, 1904.

Ho for California! Ed. by Sandra L. Myles. San Marino CA: Huntington Library, c.1980.

Hogan, William. *The Quartzsite Trip*. New York: Atheneum, 1980.

Hogg, Robert. *The Vegetable Kingdom and Its Products*. London: W. Kent, 1858.

Hoggart, Richard. *W. H. Auden*. London: Longmans, Green, c.1957.

Hohn, Caesar. *Dutchman on the Brazos*. Austin TX: Univ. TX Press, c.1963.

Holbrook, Alfred. *School Management*. Lebanon OH: Josiah Holbrook, 1871.

Holbrook, James. *Ten Years among the Mail Bags*. Philadelphia: H. Cowperthwait, 1855.

Holbrook, John Edwards. *North American Herpetology*. Philadelphia: J. Dobson, 1842. 5 vols.

Holbrook, Silas P. *Sketches*. Boston: Carter & Hendee, 1830.

Holbrook, Stewart Hall. *Holy Old Mackinaw*. New York: Macmillan, 1939. Orig. pub. in 1938 by Macmillan, New York.

———. *Lost Men of American History*. New York: Macmillan, 1946.

———. *Yankee Loggers*. New York: International Paper, 1961.

Holden, William Curry. *Alkali Trails*. Dallas TX: Southwest Press, c.1930.

Holden, William Woods. *Trial of William W. Holden, Governor of North Carolina*. Raleigh NC: Sentinel Printing, 1871. 3 vols.

Holden's Dollar Magazine. New York, 1848–1851.

Holder, Charles Frederick. *The Big Game Fishes of the United States*. New York: Macmillan, 1903.

———. *Marvels of Animal Life*. New York: Charles Scribner's Sons, 1885.

Holder, Charles Frederick and David Starr Jordan. *Fish Stories*. New York: Henry Holt, 1909.

Holder, Joseph Bassett et al. *History of the American Fauna*. New York: Virtue & Yorston, 1877? 3 vols.

Holiday. Philadelphia: Curtis Pub., 1946–.

Holiday, Billie and William Dufty. *Lady Sings the Blues*. London: Barrie and Jenkins, 1973. Orig. pub. in 1956 by Doubleday, Garden City NY.

Holland, Josiah Gilbert. *The Bay-Path*. New York: G. P. Putnam, 1857.

———. *Miss Gilbert's Career*. New York: C. Scribner, 1860.

———. *Sevenoaks*. New York: Scribner, Armstrong, 1875.

Holland, Rupert Sargent. *Peter Cotterell's Treasure*. Philadelphia: J. B. Lippincott, c.1922.

Holland, William Jacob. *The Butterfly Book*. New York: Doubleday, Page, 1902.

Hollander, Dave. *52 Weeks*. Guilford CT: Lyon's Press, 2005.

Holland Evening Sentinel. Holland MI, 1928–1977.

Holland Sentinel Weekender. Holland MI, 1977?–.

Holland Society of New York. *Year Book*. New York, 1886–1925.

Holley, Marietta. *Josiah Allen's Wife as a P. A. and P. I.* Hartford CT: American Publishing, 1877.

———. *My Opinions and Betsey Bobbet's*. Hartford CT: American Publishing, 1873.

———. *My Opinions and Betsey Bobbet's*. Hartford CT: American Publishing, 1891 [c.1873].

———. *My Wayward Pardner*. Hartford CT: American Pub., 1881.

———. *Samantha among the Brethren*. New York: Funk & Wagnalls, 1890.

———. *Samantha at the St. Louis Exposition*. New York: G. W. Dillingham, c.1904.

———. *Samantha in Europe*. New York: Funk & Wagnalls, c.1895.

———. *Sweet Cicely*. New York: Funk & Wagnalls, 1885.

Holley, Mary Austin. *Texas*. Baltimore MD: Armstrong & Plaskitt, 1833.

———. *Texas*. Austin TX: Steck, 1935. Facsimile reproduction of the 1836 ed. pub. by J. Clark, Lexington KY.

Holliday, Walter Harry. *Mining-Camp Melodies*. Butte MT: Oates & Roberts Press, c.1924.

Hollister, Ovando James. *The Mines of Colorado*. Springfield MA: S. Bowles, 1867.

Hollister Evening Free Lance. Hollister CA, 1909–.

Holloway, Joel Ellis, comp. *A Dictionary of Common*

Wildflowers of Texas & the Southern Great Plains. Ed. by Amanda Neill. Fort Worth TX: TCU Press, 2005.

Hollywood Reporter. Hollywood CA, 1930–.

Holm, John A. and Alison Watt Shilling. *Dictionary of Bahamian English.* Cold Spring NY: Lexik House, c.1982.

Holman, Lucia Ruggles. *Journal.* Honolulu HI: Bernice P. Bishop Museum, 1931.

Holmes, Ezekiel. *Report of an Exploration and Survey of the Territory on the Aroostook River.* Augusta ME: Smith & Robinson, 1839.

Holmes, Francis Simmons. *The Southern Farmer and Market Gardener.* Charleston SC: Burgess & James, 1842 [c.1841].

Holmes, Isaac Edward. *Recreations of George Taletell, F. Y. C.* Charleston SC: Duke & Brown, Printers, 1822.

Holmes, John. *Letters of John Holmes to James Russell Lowell and Others.* Ed. by William Roscoe Thayer. Boston: Houghton Mifflin, 1917.

Holmes, John Clellon. *The Horn.* New York: Random House, 1958.

Holmes, Kenneth L., ed., comp. *Covered Wagon Women.* Glendale CA: A. H. Clark, 1983–1993. 11 vols.

Holmes, Mary Jane. *Cousin Maude and Rosamond.* New York: Carleton, 1864 [c.1860].

———. *The Cromptons.* New York: G. W. Dillingham, c.1902.

———. *The Homestead on the Hillside, and Other Tales.* New York: Miller, Orton & Mulligan, 1856 [c.1855].

———. *Lena Rivers.* New York: A. L. Burt, 1856.

———. *Madeline.* New York: G. W. Carleton, 1883 [c.1881].

———. *Marguerite.* New York: G. W. Dillingham, 1890.

———. *Meadow Brook.* New York: Miller, Orton, 1857.

———. *Rose Mather.* New York: G. W. Carleton; London: S. Low, Son, 1868.

———. *Tempest and Sunshine.* New York: J. H. Sears, 1923. Orig. date of publication unknown, perhaps 1854.

Holmes, Oliver Wendell. *The Autocrat of the Breakfast-Table.* Boston: Phillips, Sampson, 1858.

———. *Boylston Prize Dissertations for the Years 1836 and 1837.* Boston: Charles C. Little and James Brown, 1838.

———. *Elsie Venner.* Boston: Ticknor and Fields, 1861. 2 vols.

———. *The Guardian Angel.* Boston: Ticknor and Fields, 1867.

———. *The One Hoss Shay.* Boston: Houghton, Mifflin, 1892 [c.1858].

———. *The Poet at the Breakfast-Table.* Boston: James R. Osgood, 1872.

———. *The Professor at the Breakfast Table.* London: Sampson Low, Son, 1860.

———. *Touched with Fire.* Ed. by Mark De Wolfe Howe. Cambridge MA: Harvard Univ. Press, 1946.

Holmes, Oliver Wendell and Harold Joseph Laski. *Holmes-Laski Letters.* Ed. by Mark DeWolfe Howe. Cambridge MA: Harvard Univ. Press, 1953. 2 vols.

Holmes, Sarah Katherine Stone. *Brokenburn.* Baton Rouge LA: LA State Univ. Press, 1955.

Holt, Alfred Hubbard. *Phrase and Word Origins.* Rev. ed. New York: Dover Publications, 1961.

Holt, John Saunders. *What I Know about Ben Eccles.* Philadelphia: J. B. Lippincott, 1869 [c.1868].

Holt, Rackham. *George Washington Carver.* Garden City NY: Doubleday, Doran, 1943.

Holton, Edith Austin. *Yankees Were Like This.* 2d ed. New York: Harper & Bros., 1944.

Holton, Leonard SEE Wibberley, Patrick O.

Home & Away. Madison WI: AAA Wisconsin, 1996–.

The Home Cook Book. Chicago: J. Fred Waggoner, 1876 [c.1875].

Home Friend. London: Printed for the Society for Promoting Christian Knowledge, 1852–1856.

Home Journal. New York, 1846–1901.

Home Missionary. New York: Congregational Home Missionary Society, 1828–1909.

Home Monthly. Boston, 1860–1866.

Homer, Art. *The Drownt Boy.* Columbia MO: Univ. MO Press, 1994.

Homer, Joel. *Jargon.* New York: Times Books, 1979.

Homestead. Des Moines IA, 1888?–1910.

Homme, Ferd. *Oak Opening.* Stoughton WI: Stoughton Centennial History Commission, 1947.

Homoeopathic News. St. Louis MO: R. G. A. Meier, 1856–1902.

Hone, Joseph Maunsell. *W. B. Yeats; 1865–1939.* New York: Macmillan, 1943.

Hone, Philip. *The Diary of Philip Hone, 1828–1851.* New York: Dodd, Mead, 1927. 2 vols.

Hongo, Robert Nobuyuki. *Hey, Pineapple!* Tokyo: Hokuseido Press, 1958.

Honolulu Advertiser. Honolulu HI, 1921–.

Honolulu Star-Bulletin. Honolulu HI, 1912–.

The Honorable Order of Kentucky Colonels. [s.l.]: C. T. Dearing Printing, 1940.

Hood, John Bell. *Advance and Retreat.* New Orleans LA: G. T. Beauregard, 1880.

Hood, Mary A. *Rivertime.* Albany NY: State Univ. NY Press, 2008.

Hooker, Thomas. *The Unbeleevers Preparing for Christ.* London: Printed by Tho Cotes for Andrew Crooke, 1638.

Hooker, William Jackson. *Flora Boreali-Americana.* London: Henry G. Bohn, 1840. 2 vols.

Hooker, Worthington. *Natural History.* New York: Harper & Bros., c.1860.

Hooker County Tribune. Mullen NE, 1895–.

Hooper, Johnson Jones. *Adventures of Captain Simon Suggs.* Chapel Hill NC: Univ. NC Press, c.1969. Orig. pub. in 1845 by Carey & Hart, Philadelphia under the title *Some Adventures.*

———. *Some Adventures of Captain Simon Suggs.* Philadelphia: Carey & Hart, 1845.

———. *The Widow Rugby's Husband, A Night at the Ugly Man's and Other Tales of Alabama.* Philadelphia: A. Hart, 1851.

Hoosier Folklore Bulletin. Bloomington IN: Hoosier Folklore Society, 1942–1950.

Hoover, Francis Trout. *Enemies in the Rear.* Boston: Arena Publishing, 1895 [c.1894].

Hope, Laura Lee. *The Outdoor Girls in a Winter Camp.* New York: Grosset & Dunlap, c.1913.

Hopewell Herald. Hopewell NJ, 1874–1955.

Hopkins, Eliza Ann Woodruff. *Ella Lincoln.* Boston: James French, 1857.

Hopley, Catherine Cooper. *Life in the South.* London: Chapman and Hall, 1863. 2 vols.

Horan, James D. and Paul Sann. *Pictorial History of the Wild West.* New York: Crown, c.1954.

Horicon Argus. Horicon WI, 1854–1860.

Horizon; a Review of Literature and Art. London, 1940–1950.

Horn, Maurice, ed. *The World Encyclopedia of Comics.* New York: Chelsea House, 1976.

Hornaday, William Temple. *The American Natural History.* New York: Charles Scribner's Sons, 1904.

———. *Camp-Fires on Desert and Lava.* New York: C. Scribner's Sons, 1908.

———. *Our Vanishing Wild Life.* New York: Charles Scribner's Sons, 1913.

Horne, Abraham Reasor. *Pennsylvania German Manual for Pronouncing, Speaking and Writing English.* Rev. and enlarged ed. Allentown PA: National Educator, 1896.

Hornellsville Tribune. Hornellsville NY, 1851–1880.

Hornellsville Weekly Tribune. Hornellsville NY, 1880–1909?

Hornsby, Henry. *Lonesome Valley.* New York: Wm. Sloane, c.1949.

Horsfield, Thomas. *An Experimental Dissertation on the Rhus Vernix, Rhus Radicans and Rhus Glabrum.* Philadelphia: Printed by Charles Cist, 1798.

Horticultural Review and Botanical Magazine. Cincinnati OH: H. W. Derby, 1853–1854.

Horticulture. Boston, 1904–.

Horticulturist and Journal of Rural Art and Rural Taste. Albany NY: L. Tucker, 1846–1875.

Horton, George Moses. *Poetical Works.* Chapel Hill NC: Academic Affairs Library, Univ. NC at Chapel Hill, 1997. Text transcr. from the 1845 ed. pub. by D. Heartt, Hillsborough, NC.

Horton, James H. et al. *Our Mountain Heritage.* Cullowhee? NC: NC Humanities Committee & Mountain Heritage Center, Western Carolina Univ., 1979.

Horton, Tom. *An Island Out of Time.* New York: W. W. Norton, c.1996.

Horwill, Herbert William. *A Dictionary of Modern American Usage.* Oxford: Clarendon Press, 1935.

Hosch, Clarence Robert. *Nevah Come Back No Mo'.* New York: Exposition Press, 1968.

Hosmer, Margaret. *Ten Years of a Lifetime.* New York: M. Doolady, 1866.

Hostetler, John Andrew. *Amish Life.* Scottdale PA: Herald Press, c.1952.

———. *Amish Society.* Baltimore MD: Johns Hopkins Press, 1963.

The Hot Boy$. *Let 'Em Burn.* Sound recording. New York: Cash Money Records, 2003.

Hot News and Rhythm Record Review. London, 1935.

Hough, Ashbel F. *Silvical Characteristics of Black Cherry.* Upper Darby PA: Forest Service, U.S. Department of Agriculture, 1960.

Hough, Donald. *Snow above Town.* New York: W. W. Norton, c.1943.

Hough, Emerson. *The Sagebrusher.* New York: D. Appleton, 1919.

———. *The Story of the Cowboy.* New York: Appleton, 1897. Also pub. in 1897 by Grosset & Dunlap, New York and in 2 vols. by The Brampton Society of New York under the title *The Cowboy.*

Hough, Franklin Benjamin. *Elements of Forestry.* Cincinnati OH: [s.n.], 1882.

Hough, Henry Beetle. *All Things Are Yours.* Garden City NY: Doubleday, Doran, 1942.

———. *Singing in the Morning.* New York: Simon and Schuster, 1951.

———, ed. *Vineyard Gazette Reader.* New York: Harcourt, Brace & World, 1967.

Houghton, Eliza Poor Donner. *The Expedition of the Donner Party and Its Tragic Fate.* Chicago: A. C. McClurg, 1911.

Houk, Rose. *Food and Recipes of the Smokies.* Gatlinburg TN: Great Smoky Mountains Natural History Association, c.1996.

Hours at Home. New York, 1865–1870.

House, Homer Doliver. *Wild Flowers.* New York: Macmillan, 1961.

———. *Wild Flowers of New York.* Albany NY: Univ. of the State of NY, 1923 [c.1919]. 2 vols.

House, Silas. *Clay's Quilt.* Chapel Hill NC: Algonquin Books of Chapel Hill, 2001.

House and Home, or, the Carolina Housewife. 3d ed. corr. and enlarged. Charleston SC: John Russel, 1855.

House Beautiful. New York: Hearst, 1896–.

Houston, Sam. *The Personal Correspondence of Sam Houston.* Ed. by Madge Thornall Roberts. Denton TX: Univ. North TX Press, 1996–2001. 4 vols.

Houston, Victoria. *Dead Water.* New York: Berkley Prime Crime, c.2001.

Houston Chronicle. Houston TX, 1901–.

Houston Post. Houston TX, 1880–.

Houstoun, Matilda Charlotte. *Texas and the Gulf of Mexico.* London: J. Murray, 1844. 2 vols.

Howard, Blanche Willis. *One Summer.* Boston: James R. Osgood, 1875.

Howard, George W. *The Monumental City, Its Past History and Present Resources.* Baltimore MD: J. D. Ehlers, c.1873.

Howard, Guy. *Walkin' Preacher of the Ozarks.* New York: Harper & Bros., 1944.

Howard, Horton. *An Improved System of Botanic Medicine.* Columbus OH: The Author, 1832. 2 vols.

Howard, H. R., comp. *The History of Virgil A. Stewart.* New York: Harper & Bros., 1836.

Howard, Joseph Kinsey. *Montana.* New Haven CT: Yale Univ. Press, c.1943.

———. *Strange Empire.* New York: William Morrow, 1952.

Howard, Leland Ossian. *The Insect Book.* New York: Doubleday, Page, 1901.

Howard, Leland Ossian and C. L. Marlatt. *The Principal Household Insects of the United States.* Washington DC: Govt. Printing Office, 1896.

Howard, Robert Ervin. *The Riot at Bucksnort and Other Western Tales.* Ed. by David Gentzel. Lincoln NE: Univ. NE Press, c.2005.

Howay, Frederic W., ed. *Voyages of the "Columbia" to the Northwest Coast.* Boston: Massachusetts Historical Society, 1941.

Howe, Edgar Watson. *Plain People.* New York: Dodd, Mead, 1929.

———. *The Story of a Country Town.* Boston: Houghton, Mifflin, 1884. Orig. pub. in 1883.

Howe, Elvon L., ed. *Rocky Mountain Empire.* Garden City NY: Doubleday, c.1950.

Howe, Henry. *Adventures and Achievements of Americans.* Cincinnati OH: Henry Howe; New York: Geo. F. Tuttle, 1859 [c.1858].

———. *Historical Collections of Ohio.* Cincinnati OH: Derby, Bradley, 1847.

———. *Historical Collections of Ohio.* Ohio centennial ed. Columbus OH: H. Howe & Son, 1889–1891. 3 vols.

———. *Historical Collections of the Great West.* Cincinnati OH: Henry Howe, at E. Morgan, c.1851. 2 vols.

———. *Life and Death on the Ocean.* Cincinnati OH: H. Howe, 1855.

Howe, Reginald Heber Jr. and Edward Sturtevant. *The Birds of Rhode Island.* [s.l.]: [s.n.], 1899.

Howell, Arthur Holmes. *Birds of Alabama.* Montgomery AL: Brown Printing, 1924.

———. *Birds of Arkansas.* Washington DC: Govt. Printing Office, 1911.

————. *Florida Bird Life.* New York: Publishers' agents, Coward-McCann, 1932.

Howell, Benita J. *A Survey of Folklife along the Big South Fork of the Cumberland River.* Knoxville TN: Department of Anthropology, Univ. TN, Knoxville, 1981.

Howell, John Thomas. *Marin Flora.* Berkeley: Univ. CA Press, c.1949.

Howells, William Cooper. *Recollections of Life in Ohio.* Cincinnati OH: Robert Clarke, 1895.

Howells, William Dean. *Annie Kilburn.* New York: Harper & Bros., 1889 [c.1888].

————. *A Boy's Town.* New York: Harper & Bros., 1890.

————. *A Boy's Town.* St. Clair Shores MA: Scholarly Press, 1972. Repr. of the 1890 ed. pub. by Harper and Bros., New York.

————. *A Chance Acquaintance.* Boston: James R. Osgood, 1873.

————. *The Daughter of the Storage.* New York: Harper & Bros., c.1916.

————. *A Foregone Conclusion.* Boston: James R. Osgood, 1875.

————. *A Hazard of New Fortunes.* New York: Harper & Bros., 1890 [c.1889].

————. *Italian Journeys.* New York: Hurd and Houghton, 1867.

————. *The Landlord at Lion's Head.* New York: Harper & Bros., 1897.

————. *The Leatherwood God.* New York: Century, 1916.

————. *Literature and Life.* New York: Harper & Bros., 1902.

————. *Mark Twain-Howells Letters* SEE Clemens, Samuel Langhorne *Mark Twain-Howells Letters*

————. *A Modern Instance.* Boston: James R. Osgood, 1882.

————. *An Open-Eyed Conspiracy.* New York: Harper & Bros., c.1897.

————. *Poems.* Boston: J. R. Osgood, 1873.

————. *The Quality of Mercy.* New York: Harper & Bros., 1892.

————. *The Register.* Boston: Houghton Mifflin, c.1883.

————. *The Rise of Silas Lapham.* Boston: Ticknor, 1885.

————. *Selected Letters.* Ed. and annotated by George Arms . . . [et al.]. Boston: Twayne, 1979–1983. 6 vols.

————. *The Shadow of a Dream.* New York: Harper & Bros., c.1890.

————. *Their Wedding Journey.* Bloomington IN: IN Univ. Press, 1968. Orig. pub. in 1871 by James R. Osgood, Boston.

————. *Through the Eye of the Needle.* New York: Harper & Bros., c.1907.

————. *The Undiscovered Country.* Boston: Houghton, Mifflin, 1880.

————. *The Vacation of the Kelwyns.* New York: Harper & Bros., c.1920.

————. *A Woman's Reason.* Boston: James R. Osgood, 1883.

Howison, John. *European Colonies in Various Parts of the World, Viewed in Their Social, Moral and Physical Condition.* London: R. Bentley, 1834. 2 vols.

————. *Sketches of Upper Canada.* Edinburgh: Oliver & Boyd, 1821.

Howitt, Mary Botham. *Our Cousins in Ohio.* New York: Collins & Bros., 1849.

Howitt, William. *The History of the Supernatural.* Philadelphia: J. B. Lippincott, 1863. 2 vols.

Hoyt, Epaphras. *Antiquarian Researches.* Greenfield MA: Printed by A. Phelps, 1824.

Hubbard, Freeman H. *Railroad Avenue.* New York: Whittlesey House, McGraw-Hill, c.1945.

Hubbard, Harlan. *Shantyboat.* Lexington KY: Univ. Press KY, 1977. Orig. pub. in 1953 by Dodd, Mead, New York.

————. *Shantyboat Journal.* Ed. by Don Wallis. Lexington KY: Univ. Press KY, 1994.

Hubbard, Henry Guernsey. *Insects Affecting the Orange.* Washington DC: Govt. Printing Office, 1885.

Hubbard, Lucius Lee. *Woods and Lakes of Maine.* Somersworth NH: New Hampshire Pub., 1971. Repr. of the 1888 ed. pub. by Ticknor, Boston.

Hubbard, William. *A Narrative of the Troubles with the Indians.* Boston: Printed by John Foster, 1677.

Hubbell, Allan Forbes. *The Pronunciation of English in New York City.* New York: King's Crown Press, 1950.

Hubbs, Carl Leavitt and Karl F. Lagler. *Fishes of the Great Lakes Region.* Bloomfield Hills MI: Cranbrook Institute of Science, 1949 [c.1947].

Huber, Jane. *60 Hikes within 60 Miles, San Francisco.* 2d ed. Birmingham AL: Menasha Ridge Press, 2007.

Hudak, Joseph. *Trees for Every Purpose.* New York: McGraw-Hill, 1980.

Huden, John Charles. *Indian Place Names of New England.* New York: Museum of the American Indian, Heye Foundation, 1962.

Hudson, Arthur Palmer, ed. *Specimens of Mississippi Folk-Lore.* Ann Arbor MI: Edwards Bros., 1928.

Hudson, T. S. *A Scamper through America.* London: Griffith & Farran; New York: E. P. Dutton, 1882.

Hudson, Wilson Mathis and Maxwell, Allen, eds. *The Sunny Slopes of Long Ago.* Dallas TX: Southern Methodist Univ. Press, c.1966.

Hudson River Almanac. New Paltz NY, 1994–.

Hughes, Jeffrey W. and Will H. Blackwell. *Wildflowers and Other Plant Life of Southeast Alaska.* Dubuque IA: Kendall/Hunt Publishing, c.1987.

Hughes, John Taylor. *Doniphan's Expedition.* Cincinnati OH: J. A. and U. P. James, 1848 [c.1847].

Hughes, Langston. *Laughing to Keep from Crying.* New York: Holt, 1952.

————. *Simple Speaks His Mind.* New York: Simon and Schuster, c.1950.

Hughes, Langston and Arna Bontemps, eds. *The Book of Negro Folklore.* New York: Dodd, Mead, 1958.

Hughes, Langston and David Martin. *Simply Heavenly; a Comedy with Music.* Acting ed. New York: Dramatists Play Service, c.1959.

Hughes, Langston and Zora Neale Hurston. *Mule Bone.* New York: HarperPerennial, 1991 [c.1931].

Hughes, Louis. *Thirty Years a Slave.* Milwaukee WI: South Side Printing, 1897 [c.1896].

Hughes, Patrice Raccio. *Open Ice.* New York: Wendy Lamb Books, 2005.

Hughes, Rupert. *The Dozen from Lakerim.* New York: Century, c.1899.

————. *In a Little Town.* New York: Harper & Bros., c.1917.

Hughes, Thomas, ed. *G. T. T. Gone to Texas.* New York: Macmillan, 1884.

————. *Rugby, Tennessee.* New York: Macmillan, 1881.

Huheey, James H. and Arthur Stupka. *Amphibians and Reptiles of Great Smoky Mountains National Park.* Knoxville TN: Univ. TN Press, c.1967.

Huie, William Bradford. *From Omaha to Okinawa.* Annapolis MD: Naval Institute Press, 1999. Orig. pub. in 1945 by E. P. Dutton, New York.

Hulbert, Archer Butler, ed. *The Call of the Columbia.* Colorado Springs CO: Stewart Commission of CO College and Denver Public Library, 1934.

————, ed. *Southwest on the Turquoise Trail.* Denver CO: Public Library, 1933.

Hulbert, Archer Butler and Dorothy Printup Hulbert, eds. *Marcus Whitman Crusader.* Colorado Springs CO: Stewart Commission of CO College and Denver Public Library, c.1936–1941. 3 vols.

Hulbert, William Davenport. *Forest Neighbors.* New York: McClure, Phillips, 1902.

Hulet, Russ. *Born under a Stump.* New York: iUniverse, 2003.

Hulett, T. G. *Every Man His Own Guide to the Falls of Niagara.* 4th ed. Buffalo NY: Faxon, 1844.

Hull, Denison Bingham. *Thoughts on American Fox-Hunting.* New York: David McKay, c.1958.

Hull, Isaac. *Minutes of Proceedings of the Court of Enquiry into the Official Conduct of Capt. Isaac Hull, as Commandant of the United States' Navy Yard at Charlestown, in the State of Massachusetts, Convened at the Navy-Yard, in Said Charlestown, on the 12th Day of August, A.D. 1822.* Washington DC: Davis and Force, 1822.

Hull, John. *The Diaries of John Hull.* Boston: J. Wilson and Son, 1857.

Hull, William Newell. *Fishing across the Continent.* Chicago: A. Flanagan, c.1905.

Hultén, Eric. *Flora of Alaska and Neighboring Territories.* Stanford CA: Stanford Univ. Press, 1968.

Humboldt, Alexander Freiherr von. *Political Essay on the Kingdom of New Spain.* Transl. from the orig. French by John Black. London: Longman, Hurst, Rees, Orme & Brown, 1811. 4 vols.

Humboldt Standard. Eureka CA, 1913–1967.

Hume, John Ferguson. *Five Hundred Majority.* New York: G. P. Putnam, 1872.

Humeston New Era. Humeston IA, 1899–1921.

Humphrey, Robert Regester. *Arizona Range Grasses.* Tucson AZ: Univ. AZ Press, 1970.

Humphrey, William. *Home from the Hill.* New York: Alfred A. Knopf, 1958.

Humphreys, David. *The Yankey in England.* [s.l.]: [s.n.], 1815.

Humphreys, Josephine. *Nowhere Else on Earth.* New York: Viking, c.2000.

Humphreys, William Jackson. *Of Me—W. J. Humphreys.* Washington DC: [s.n.], c.1947.

Humphries, George and Clyde Edgerton. *North Carolina.* Portland OR: Graphic Arts Center Publishing, c.2003.

Hundley, D. R. *Social Relations in Our Southern States.* New York: Henry B. Price, 1860.

Hungry Horse News. Columbia Falls MT, 1946–.

Hungrywolf, Adolf. *Blackfoot Papers.* Skookumchuck, British Columbia: Good Medicine Cultural Foundation; Browning MT: Blackfeet Heritage Center & Art Gallery, 2006. 4 vols.

Hunnicutt, Samuel J. *Twenty Years of Hunting and Fishing in the Great Smoky Mountains.* Knoxville TN: S. B. Newman, c.1926.

Hunt, Benjamin. "Diary of Benjamin Hunt." Chester County Historical Society *Bulletins.* (1898) 1–20.

Hunt, Cornelius E. *The Shenandoah.* New York: G. W. Carleton, 1867.

Hunt, Frazier. *Blown In by the Draft.* Garden City NY: Doubleday, Page, 1918.

Hunt, Peter. *Peter Hunt's Cape Cod Cookbook.* 2d ed. Brattleboro VT: Stephen Greene Press, 1962. Orig. pub. in 1954 by Hawthorne Books.

Hunt, Thomas Forsyth. *The Forage and Fiber Crops in America.* New York: Orange Judd, 1910 [c.1907].

Hunt, Wilson Price. "Travel and Exploration Diary." In: Stuart, Robert, *The Discovery of the Oregon Trail,* 1935, 281–308.

Hunter, Evan. *Hail, Hail, the Gang's All Here.* Garden City NY: Doubleday, 1971.

————. *Hail to the Chief.* New York: Random House, c.1973.

Hunter, John Dunn. *Manners and Customs of Several Indian Tribes Located West of the Mississippi.* Philadelphia: Printed and published for the author by J. Maxwell, 1823.

————. *Memoirs of a Captivity among the Indians of North America, from Childhood to the Age of Nineteen, with Anecdotes Descriptive of Their Manners and Customs, to Which Is Added Some Account of the Soil, Climate and Vegetable Productions of the Territory Westward of the Mississippi.* London: Printed for Longman, Hurst, Rees, Orme, and Brown, 1823.

Hunter, John Marvin, comp., ed. *The Trail Drivers of Texas.* San Antonio TX: Jackson Printing, published under the direction of George W. Saunders, Pres. of the Old Trail Drivers Association, c.1920.

————, comp., ed. *The Trail Drivers of Texas.* 2d ed. rev. Nashville TN: Cokesbury Press, 1925. 2 vols.

Hunter-Gault, Charlayne. *In My Place.* New York: Farrar Straus Giroux, c.1992.

Hunter-Trader-Trapper. Columbus OH, 1900–1938.

Huntingdon Journal. Huntingdon PA, 1871–1904.

Huntington, Dwight Williams. *Our Feathered Game.* New York: Charles Scribner's Sons, 1903.

Huntington, James. *On the Edge of Nowhere.* New York: Crown, c.1966.

Huntington, New York. *Huntington Town Records.* Huntington NY: Long Islander Print, 1887–1889. 3 vols.

Huntington, William S. *The Road-Master's Assistant and Section-Master's Guide.* 2d ed. New York: A. N. Kellogg, 1872.

Hurd, D. Hamilton. *History of Norfolk County, Massachusetts with Biographical Sketches of Many of Its Pioneers and Prominent Men.* Philadelphia: J. W. Lewis, 1884.

Hurd, Grace Marguerite. *The Bennett Twins.* New York: Macmillan, 1900.

Hurd, Seth T. *A Grammatical Corrector.* Philadelphia: E. H. Butler, 1847.

Hurmence, Belinda, ed. *My Folks Don't Want Me to Talk about Slavery.* Winston-Salem NC: J. F. Blair, c.1984.

Huron Reflector. Norwalk OH, 1830–1853.

Hurston, Zora Neale. *Collected Plays.* Ed by Jean Lee Cole and Charles Mitchell. New Brunswick NJ: Rutgers Univ. Press, c.2008.

————. *Dust Tracks on a Road.* Philadelphia: J. B. Lippincott, 1942.

————. *Jonah's Gourd Vine.* Philadelphia: J. B. Lippincott, 1934.

————. *Mules and Men.* London: J. B. Lippincott, 1935.

————. *Seraph on the Suwanee.* New York: C. Scribners' Sons, 1948.

————. *Their Eyes Were Watching God.* Urbana IL: Univ. IL Press, 1977. Orig. pub. in 1937 by Lippincott, Philadelphia.

Hush, Child! Can't You Hear the Music? Coll. by Rose Thompson, Ed. by Charles Beaumont. Athens GA: Univ. GA Press, c.1982.

Hussey, Tacitus. *The River Bend and Other Poems.* Des Moines IA: Carter & Hussey, Printers, 1896.

Hutchings' California Magazine. San Francisco, 1856–1861.

Hutchins, Ross E. *Hidden Valley of the Smokies.* New York: Dodd, Mead, c.1971.

Hutchins, Thomas. *An Historical Narrative and Topographical Description of Louisiana and West-Florida.* Gainesville FL: Univ. FL Press, 1968. Facsimile repr. of the 1784 ed. printed for the author, Philadelphia.

———. *A Topographical Description of Virginia, Pennsylvania, Maryland, and North Carolina.* London: J. Almon, 1778.

Hutchinson, Clinton Carter. *Resources of Kansas.* Topeka KS: Published by the Author, c.1871.

Hutchinson, Thomas, comp. *A Collection of Original Papers Relative to the History of the Colony of Massachusetts-Bay.* Boston: Thomas and John Fleet, 1769.

———. *The Diary and Letters of His Excellency Thomas Hutchinson.* Boston: Houghton, Mifflin, 1884–1886. 2 vols.

———. *The History of the Colony of Massachusetts-Bay.* 2d ed. London: Printed for M. Richardson, 1760 [i.e. 1765]– 1828. 3 vols.

Hutchison, Ruth. *The Pennsylvania Dutch Cook Book.* New York: Harper & Bros., c.1948.

Huth, Geof. *Familiar Words.* Schenectady NY: pdqb, 1996.

Hutton, Thomas Hubert and Stanley Blake. *The Complete Angler and Huntsman.* Berry KY: [s.n.], 1919.

Huxley, Aldous Leonard. *Letters of Aldous Huxley.* Ed. by Grover Smith. 1st Amer. ed. New York: Harper and Row, 1964.

Hyatt, Alpheus. *Commercial and Other Sponges.* Boston: Ginn and Heath, 1879.

Hyatt, Alpheus and J. M. Arms. *Insecta.* Boston: D. C. Heath, 1904 [c.1890].

Hyatt, Harry Middleton. *Folk-Lore from Adams County Illinois.* New York: Alma Egan Hyatt Foundation, 1935.

———. *Folk-Lore from Adams County Illinois.* 2d ed. New York: Memoirs of the Alma Egan Hyatt Foundation, 1965.

———. *Hoodoo-Conjuration-Witchcraft-Rootwork.* Hannibal MO: Printed for Harry Middleton Hyatt, by Western Publishing, 1970–1978. 5 vols.

Hyatt, Rebecca Dougherty. *Marthy Lou's Kiverlid.* 2d ed. Morristown TN: The Author, 1963. Orig. pub. in 1937.

Hyde, Nancy Maria. *The Writings of Nancy Maria Hyde, of Norwich CT.* Norwich CT: Russell Hubbard, 1816.

The Hyde Park Cuisine. Chicago: Windermere Press, 1900. Pub. by the Women of the Hyde Park Baptist Church.

Hyland, Fay and Ferdinand H. Steinmetz. *The Woody Plants of Maine.* Orono ME: Univ. Press, 1944.

Hylander, Clarence John. *Trees and Trails.* New York: Macmillan, 1953.

———. *The World of Plant Life.* New York: Macmillan, 1942.

Hymes, Dell H., ed. *Language in Culture and Society.* New York: Harper & Row, 1964.

Ibis, a Quarterly Journal of Ornithology. London: British Ornithologists' Union, 1859–.

Iceberg Slim SEE Beck, Robert

Ickis, Marguerite. *The Standard Book of Quilt Making and Collecting.* New York: Dover, 1949.

Idaho Agricultural Experiment Station. *Bulletin.* Moscow ID, 1892–1953.

Idaho Daily Statesman. Boise ID, 1888–.

Idaho Department of Agriculture. Idaho Bean Commission. *Varieties.* [v.d.]. Internet.

Idaho Enterprise. Malad City ID, 1938–.

Idaho Forester. Moscow ID: Associated Foresters, School of Forestry, Univ. Idaho, 1919–1980?

Idaho Free Press. Nampa ID, 1919–.

Idaho State Journal. Pocatello ID, 1922–.

Idaho Sunday Statesman. Boise ID, 1888–1969.

Idaho. University. *Plant Viruses Online.* [v.d.]. Internet.

Idell, Albert Edward. *The Great Blizzard.* New York: H. Holt, 1948.

Idle Man. New York: Wiley & Halsted, 1821–1822.

Iglehart, Fanny Chambers Gooch. *Face to Face with the Mexicans.* New York: Fords, Howard, & Hulbert, c.1887.

Ilg, Frances Lillian and Louise Bates Ames. *School Readiness, Behavior Tests Used at the Gesell Institute.* New York: Harper & Row, 1965.

Illinois. Agricultural Experiment Station, Urbana. *Bulletin.* Urbana IL, 1888–.

Illinois. Board of State Fish Commissioners. *Report.* Springfield IL, 1884–1896.

Illinois. Department of Agriculture. *Transactions.* Springfield IL: Illinois State Journal, 1853–1921.

Illinois. Department of Natural Resources. *Exotic Species.* [v.d.]. Internet.

———. *Illinois Natural History Survey.* [v.d.]. Internet.

———. *Wild about Illinois Fishes!* [v.d.]. Internet.

Illinois Farmers' Institute. *Annual Report.* Springfield IL, 1898–1918.

Illinois Medical Journal. Chicago, 1889–1962.

Illinois. Natural History Survey. *Biological Notes.* Urbana IL, 1933–.

———. *Fieldbook of Illinois Wild Flowers.* Urbana IL: [s.n.], 1936.

Illinois. Office of the Superintendent of Public Instruction. *Biennial Report.* Springfield IL, 1858–1970.

Illinois State Agricultural Society *Transactions* SEE ALSO Illinois. Department of Agriculture *Transactions*

Illinois State Agricultural Society. *Transactions.* Springfield IL, 1853–1870.

Illinois State Bee-Keepers' Association. *Annual Report.* Springfield IL, 1892–1950?

Illinois State Chronicle. Decatur IL, 1855–1865.

Illinois. State Historical Library, Springfield. *Collections.* Springfield IL, 1903–.

Illinois State Historical Society. *Journal.* Springfield IL, 1908–.

———. *Transactions.* Springfield IL: Illinois State Journal, 1902–1931.

Illinois State Laboratory of Natural History. *Bulletin.* Bloomington IL, 1876–1918.

Illustrated Outdoor News. New York, 1903?–1905?

Illustrated Sporting News. New York, 1903–1905.

Imhof, Thomas A. *Alabama Birds.* University AL: Published for the State of Alabama, Dept. of Conservation, Game and Fish Div. by Univ. AL Press, 1962.

Imlay, Gilbert. *A Topographical Description of the Western Territory of North America.* London: Printed for J. Debrett, 1792.

———. *A Topographical Description of the Western Territory of North America.* 3d ed. with great additions. London: Printed for J. Debrett, 1797.

I'm on My Journey Home. Phonodisc. New York: New World Records No. 223, c.1978.

Independence Enterprise. Independence OR, 1908–1969.

Independent. New York: Independent Publications, 1848–1928.

Independent. Ashland KY, 1896–.

Independent. Hawarden IA, 1968–.

Independent. Long Beach CA, 1957–.

Independent American. Georgetown DC, 1809–1811.

Independent American and General Advertiser. Platteville WI, 1845–1849.

Independent Organic Inspectors Association. *Inspectors' Report.* Broadus MT, 2002–.

Independent Press-Telegram. Long Beach CA, 1957–.

Independent-Record. Helena MT, 1943–.

Independent Star-News. Pasadena CA, 1956–1962.

Indiana Academy of Science. *Proceedings of the Indiana Academy of Science.* Indianapolis IN, 1891–.

Indiana. Commissioner of Fisheries and Game. *Biennial Report.* Indianapolis IN, 1899–1915.

Indiana County Gazette. Indiana PA, 1890–1913.

Indiana Democrat. Indiana PA, 1862–1951.

Indiana. Department of Geology and Natural Resources. *Report.* Indianapolis IN, 1869–1916.

Indiana. Department of Natural Resources. *Snakes of Indiana State Parks and Reservoirs.* [v.d.]. Internet.

Indiana English Journal. Terre Haute IN: IN State Univ., Division of Extended Services, 1966–.

Indiana Evening Gazette. Indiana PA, 1904–1981.

Indiana Farmer. Richmond IN, 1851–1917.

Indiana Farmer & Gardener. Indianapolis IN, 1845.

Indiana Gazette. Indiana PA, 1890–1891; 1982–.

Indiana. General Assembly. House of Representatives. Committee on Arbitrary Arrests. *Report and Evidence of the Committee.* Indianapolis IN: Joseph J. Bingham, State Printer, 1863.

Indiana. Geological Survey. *Annual Report.* Indianapolis IN, 1869–1879.

Indiana Historical Society. *Publications.* Indianapolis IN: Bowen-Merrill, 1895–.

Indiana Horticultural Society. *Transactions.* Indianapolis IN, 1861–.

Indiana. House of Representatives. *Journal.* Indianapolis IN: Douglas and Maguire, 1816–.

Indiana Magazine of History. Bloomington IN, 1905–.

Indianapolis Journal. Indianapolis IN, 1867–1904.

Indianapolis Star. Indianapolis IN, 1903–.

Indianapolis Sunday Star. Indianapolis IN, 1907–1944.

Indiana Progress. Indiana PA, 1870–1946.

Indiana. State Board of Agriculture. *Annual Report.* Indianapolis IN, 1851–.

Indiana. State Geologist. *Report of a Geological*

Reconnoissance of Indiana. By Richard Owen. Indianapolis IN: H. H. Dodd, 1862.

Indiana University. Lilly Library. *An Exhibition Honoring the Seventy-Fifth Birthday of Hoagland Howard Carmichael.* Bloomington IN: Lilly Library, IN Univ., 1974.

Indiana Weekly Messenger. Indiana PA, 1874–1946.

Indian Country Today. Oneida NY, 1981–.

Indian Notes and Monographs. New York: Museum of the American Indian, Heye Foundation, 1919–1960.

Indicator: a Literary Periodical Conducted by Students of Amherst College. Amherst MA, 1848–1851.

Industrial Worker. Spokane WA: Spokane Locals Union, Industrial Workers of the World, 1909–.

Infantry Journal. Washington DC: U.S. Infantry Association, 1910–1950.

Ingersoll, Ernest. *Birds'-Nesting.* Salem MA: George A. Bates, c.1882.

———. *The Conquest of the North.* New York: C. S. Hammond, c.1909.

———. *Country Cousins.* New York: Harper & Bros., 1884.

———. *Knocking Round the Rockies.* New York: Harper & Bros., 1883.

———. *The Oyster-Industry.* Washington DC: Govt. Printing Office, 1881.

———. *Wild Life of Orchard and Field.* New York: Harper & Bros., c.1902.

Ingersoll, Jared. *Mr. Ingersoll's Letters Relating to the Stamp-Act.* New Haven CT: Samuel Green, 1766.

Ingersoll, Luther A. *Ingersoll's Century History.* Los Angeles: Luther A. Ingersoll, 1908.

Ingham, Donna. *You Know You're in Texas When—.* Guilford CT: Globe Pequot, 2006.

Ingham, George Thomas. *Digging Gold among the Rockies.* Philadelphia: Hubbard Bros., 1880.

Ingle, Edward. *Local Institutions of Virginia.* Baltimore MD: Johns Hopkins Univ., 1885.

The Inglenook Cook Book. New and rev. ed. Elgin IL: Brethren Publishing, 1927 [c.1911].

Ingraham, Joseph C. *Modern Traffic Control.* New York: Funk & Wagnalls, 1954.

Ingraham, Joseph Holt. *Burton.* New York: Harper & Bros., 1838. 2 vols.

———. *The South-West.* New York: Harper & Bros., 1835. 2 vols.

Ingram, J. S. *The Centennial Exposition.* Philadelphia: Hubbard Bros. c.1876.

Ink Spots. *The Ink Spots: America's Greatest Vocal Quartet.* Phonodisc. Harrison NJ: Audition, 1955.

Inman, Henry. *The Old Santa Fé Trail.* New York: Macmillan, 1897.

Inman, Robert. *Coming Home: Life, Love and All Things Southern.* Asheboro NC: Down Home Press, 2000.

Inside UVA. Charlottesville VA, 1970–. Faculty and staff newsp. of Univ. VA, Charlottesville.

Integrated Pest Management for Stone Fruits. Oakland CA: Univ. CA, Statewide Integrated Pest Management Project, Division of Agriculture and Natural Resources, 1999.

Intellectual Digest. New York: Communications Systems, 1970–1973.

Intellectual Regale, or, Ladies' Tea Tray. Philadelphia, 1814–1815.

Intelligencer. Doylestown PA, 1988–.

Intelligencer & Weekly Advertiser. Lancaster PA, 1799–1821.

Intelligencer Journal. Lancaster PA, 1997–.

Intermountain Observer. Boise ID, 1967–1973.

International Annual of Anthony's Photographic Bulletin. New York, 1888–1896.

International Congress of Americanists. *Proceedings.* [s.l.], 1875–.

International Magazine of Literature, Art, and Science. New York, 1850–1852.

International Socialist Review. Chicago, 1900–1918.

Inter-State Nurseries. *Roses.* Hamburg IA: [s.n.], 1990.

Inter-State Tattler. New York, 1925–1932.

Inyo Register. Bishop CA, 1885–.

Iola Daily Register. Iola KS, 1899–1939.

Iola Register. Iola KS, 1939–.

Iowa. *Legislative Documents.* Des Moines IA, 1856–1931.

Iowa Academy of Science. *Proceedings.* Des Moines IA, 1887–.

Iowa Citizen. Iowa City IA, 1891–1907.

Iowa City Daily Press. Iowa City IA, 1898–1920.

Iowa City Press-Citizen. Iowa City IA, 1920–.

Iowa Department of Natural Resources. *Iowa Fish and Fishing: Iowa Fishes.* [v.d.]. Internet.

Iowa Department of Transportation. *Iowa's Living Roadway: Plant Profiler.* Des Moines IA: IA Dept. of Transportation, 2003.

Iowa Geological Survey. *Bulletin.* Des Moines IA, 1901–.

———. *Report of the Geological Survey of the State of Iowa.* By James Hall, J. D. Whitney. Des Moines IA: Published by authority of the Legislature of Iowa, 1858. 2 vols.

Iowa Homestead. Des Moines IA, 1910–1929.

Iowa Journal of History and Politics. Iowa City IA: State Historical Society of Iowa, 1903–1960.

Iowa Ornithologist. Salem IA, 1894–1898.

Iowa Recorder. Greene IA, 1889–1956.

Iowa State Agricultural Society. *Report of the Board of Directors.* Des Moines IA, 1854–1899.

Iowa State College. Experiment Station. *Bulletin.* Ames IA, 1902–1910.

Iowa State College Journal of Science. Ames IA, 1926–1959.

Iowa State Horticultural Society. *Transactions.* Des Moines IA, 1878–1891.

Iowa State Register and Farmer. Des Moines IA, 1905–1912.

Iowa State Reporter. Waterloo IA, 1868–1897.

Ipswich Historical Society. *Publications.* Ipswich MA, 1894–1935?

I. R. See Randall, Isabelle

Ironton Tribune. Ironton OH, 1926–.

Ironwood Daily-Globe. Ironwood MI, 1919–.

Iroquois Republican. Watseka IL, 1856–1872.

Irrigation Age. Chicago, 1891–1918.

Irvin, Constance O. *The Seasons of a Heart.* New York: iUniverse, 2005.

Irvine, Amy. *Trespass: Living at the Edge of the Promised Land.* New York: North Point Press, 2008.

Irving, John. *The Cider House Rules.* New York: William Morrow, c.1985.

Irving, Peter. *Giovanni Sbogarro: a Venetian Tale, Taken from the French.* New York: Printed by C. S. Van Winkle, 1820. 2 vols.

Irving, Pierre Munroe. *The Life and Letters of Washington Irving.* New York: G. P. Putnam, 1862–1864. 4 vols.

———. *The Life and Letters of Washington Irving.* Rev. and condensed. New York: G. P. Putnam's Sons, 1869. 3 vols.

Irving, Washington. *The Alhambra.* Philadelphia: Carey & Lea, 1832. 2 vols.

———. *The Alhambra.* Author's rev. ed. New York: George P. Putnam, 1851.

———. *Astoria.* London: R. Bentley, 1836. 3 vols.

———. *Bracebridge Hall.* London: John Murray, 1822. 2 vols.

———. *The Crayon Miscellany.* Philadelphia: Carey, Lea & Blanchard, 1835. 3 vols.

———. *A History of New York.* New York: Inskeep & Bradford, 1809. 2 vols.

———. *A History of New York.* 3d ed. Philadelphia: M. Thomas Wm. Fry, 1820 [c.1819]. 2 vols.

———. *A History of New York.* 4th Amer. ed. New York: C. S. Van Winkle, 1824.

———. *A History of New York.* New York: G. P. Putnam, 1849 [c.1848].

———. *A History of New York.* Rev. ed. New York: G. P. Putnam, 1857 [c.1849].

———. *Journals and Notebooks.* Madison WI: Univ. WI Press, 1969–1986. 5 vols.

———. *The Journals of Washington Irving from July, 1815, to July, 1842.* Ed. by William P. Trent and George S. Hellman. Boston: Bibliophile Society, 1919. 3 vols.

———. *Life of George Washington.* New York: Putnam, 1857. 5 vols.

———. *The Rocky Mountains.* Philadelphia: Carey, Lea, & Blanchard, 1837. 2 vols. Pub. the same year by R. Bentley, London, and later in the U.S., under the title: *The Adventures of Captain Bonneville . . . in the Rocky Mountains and Far West.*

———, ed. *Salmagundi.* New York: D. Longworth, 1807–1808.

———. *The Sketch Book of Geoffrey Crayon, Gent.* London: John Murray, 1820.

———. *Tales of a Traveller.* London: John Murray, 1824. 2 vols.

———. *Wolfert's Roost and Other Papers.* New York: G. P. Putnam, 1855.

Irwin, Godfrey. *American Tramp and Underworld Slang.* New York: Sears Publishing, 1930.

Irwin, John Rice. *Musical Instruments of the Southern Appalachian Mountains.* Norris TN: Museum of Appalachia Press, c.1979.

Irwin, Pamela. *Colorado's Best Wildflower Hikes.* Englewood CO: Westcliffe, 1998–2006. 3 vols.

Isaacs, Susan. *After All These Years.* New York: HarperCollins, c.1993.

———. *Lily White.* New York: HarperCollins, c.1996.

———. *Magic Hour.* New York: HarperCollins, c.1991.

Isbell, Robert. *The Last Chivaree: the Hicks Family of Beech Mountain.* Chapel Hill NC: Univ. NC Press, 1996.

Ise, John. *Sod and Stubble.* Lincoln NE: Univ. NE Press, 1972. Repr. of the 1936 ed. pub. by Wilson-Erickson, New York.

Isham, James. *Observations on Hudsons Bay, 1743 and Notes and Observations on a Book Entitled A Voyage to Hudsons Bay in the Dobbs Galley, 1749.* Toronto: Champlain Society, 1949.

Ison, Issac and Anna H. Ison. *A Whole 'Nother Language.* [s.l.]: Published by Isaac & Anna H. Ison, 1993.

Isthmus of Madison. Madison WI, 1976–.

Jackman, Edwin Russell and R. A. Long. *The Oregon Desert.* Caldwell ID: Caxton Printers, 1964.

Jackman, Edwin Russell and John Scharff. *Steens Mountain in Oregon's High Desert Country.* Caldwell ID: Caxton Printers, 1970 [c.1967].

Jackson, Andrew. *Correspondence.* Ed. by John Spencer Bassett. Washington DC: Carnegie Institution of Washington, 1926–1935. 7 vols.

Jackson, Bruce, comp. *Get Your Ass in the Water and Swim Like Me.* Cambridge MA: Harvard Univ. Press, 1974.

Jackson, Charles Thomas. *Report on the Geological and Agricultural Survey of the State of Rhode Island.* Providence RI: B. Cranston, 1840.

Jackson, Gary L. *Going after the Cows.* Bloomington IN: AuthorHouse, 2008.

Jackson, George Pullen. *White Spirituals in the Southern Uplands.* Chapel Hill NC: Univ. NC Press, 1933.

———. *White Spirituals in the Southern Uplands.* New York: Dover Publications, 1965. Republication of the 1933 ed. pub. by the Univ. NC Press, Chapel Hill NC.

Jackson, Hartley Harrad Thompson. *Mammals of Wisconsin.* Madison WI: Univ. WI Press, 1961.

Jackson, Helen Hunt. *Between Whiles.* Boston: Roberts Bros., 1887.

———. *Bits of Travel at Home.* Boston: Roberts Bros., 1887. Orig. pub. in 1878 by Roberts Bros.

———. *Zeph.* Boston: Roberts Bros., 1885.

Jackson, John Andrew. *The Experience of a Slave in South Carolina.* Chapel Hill NC: Academic Affairs Library, Univ. NC at Chapel Hill, 1996. Text transcr. for *Documenting the American South* website from the 1862 ed. pub. by Passmore & Alabaster, London.

Jackson, Joseph Orville, ed. *Some of the Boys: the Civil War Letters of Isaac Jackson, 1862–1865.* Carbondale IL: Southern IL Univ. Press, 1960.

Jackson, Louis E. *A Vocabulary of Criminal Slang.* Portland OR: Modern Printing, c.1914.

Jackson, Oscar Lawrence. *The Colonel's Diary.* Ed. by David P. Jackson. Sharon PA: [s.n.], 1922.

Jackson, Robert Montgomery Smith. *The Mountain.* Philadelphia: J. B. Lippincott, 1860.

Jackson, Sheldon. *Alaska and Missions on the North Pacific Coast.* New York: Dodd, Mead, c.1880.

Jackson, Shirley. *The Road through the Wall.* New York: Farrar, Straus, 1948.

Jackson, William Henry. *Diaries.* Glendale CA: Arthur H. Clark, 1959.

Jackson Sentinel. Maquoketa IA, 1868?–1914.

Jacksonville Daily News. Jacksonville NC, 1954–.

Jacksonville Zoo and Gardens Home Page. [v.d.]. Internet.

Jacobs, Harriet Ann. *Incidents in the Life of a Slave Girl.* Ed. by L. Maria Child. Boston: Published for the author, 1861.

Jacobs, Harvey C. *We Came Rejoicing.* Chicago: Rand McNally, 1967.

Jacobs, Herbert Austin. *We Chose the Country.* New York: Harper & Bros., c.1948.

Jacobs, Marion Lee and Henry M. Burlage. *Index of Plants of North Carolina.* [s.l.]: Henry M. Burlage, 1958.

Jacobson, Hannah. *Milwaukee Dialect.* Madison WI: Univ. WI B.A. thesis, 1931.

Jacques, Daniel Harrison. *The House.* New York: Fowler and Wells, c.1859.

Jaeger, Benedict. *The Life of North American Insects.* Assisted by H. C. Preston. New York: Harper & Bros., 1859.

Jaeger, Edmund Carroll. *The California Deserts.* Stanford CA: Stanford Univ. Press, c.1933.

———. *Desert Wild Flowers.* Rev. ed. Stanford CA: Stanford Univ. Press, 1941.

———. *The North American Deserts.* Stanford CA: Stanford Univ. Press, 1957.

Jaeger, Louis John Frederick. "Diary of a Ferryman at Fort Yuma." Historical Society of Southern California *Annual Publications.* (1928–1930) 14.89–128, 213–42.

Jahoda, Gloria. *Florida.* New York: W. W. Norton, c.1976.

———. *The Other Florida.* New York: Charles Scribner's Sons, c.1967.

Jai, Aadil Luqman. *Confessions to My People.* New York: iUniverse, c.2003.

James, Edgar. *The Allen Outlaws.* Baltimore MD: Phoenix Publishing, c.1912.

James, Edwin, comp. *Account of an Expedition from Pittsburgh to the Rocky Mountains.* Philadelphia: H. C. Carey and I. Lea, 1822–1823. 2 vols. and atlas.

James, George Wharton. *In & around the Grand Canyon.* Boston: Little, Brown, 1903 [c.1900].

———. *Indian Basketry.* New York: Henry Malkan, 1901.

James, Henry. *The Bostonians.* Amer. ed. London: Macmillan, 1886.

———. *The Ivory Tower.* New York: Charles Scribner's Sons, 1917.

James, Hunter. *All the Forgotten Places.* Atlanta GA: Peachtree, c.1981.

James, James Alton. *The First Scientific Exploration of Russian America and the Purchase of Alaska.* Evanston IL: Northwestern Univ., 1942.

James, Marquis. *The Cherokee Strip.* New York: Viking Press, 1945.

James, Virginia E. *Mother James' Key to Good Cooking.* New York: N. D. Thomas, c.1890.

James, Will. *Big-Enough.* New York: Charles Scribner's Sons, 1931.

———. *Cowboys North and South.* New York: Charles Scribner's Sons, 1924.

———. *Cow Country.* New York: C. Scribner's Sons, 1927.

———. *The Drifting Cowboy.* New York: C. Scribner's Sons, 1926 [c.1925].

———. *Lone Cowboy.* New York: Charles Scribner's Sons, 1930.

———. *Sand.* New York: Sun Dial Press, 1941. Orig. pub. in 1929 by Charles Scribner's Sons, New York.

———. *Smoky the Cowhorse.* New York: Charles Scribner's Sons, 1926.

James, William. *The Letters of William James.* Boston: Atlantic Monthly Press, c.1920. 2 vols.

James, William Dobein. *A Sketch of the Life of Brig. Gen. Francis Marion.* Charleston SC: Gould and Riley, 1821.

James, Will S. *Cow-Boy Life in Texas.* Chicago: M. A. Donohue, c.1893.

The James River Basin. Comp. by the James River Project Committee. Richmond VA: Virginia Academy of Science, 1950.

Jamestown Journal. Chautauqua Co. NY, 1826–1938.

J. & A. Adams See Adams, John and Abigail Adams

Janes, George Milton. *American Trade Unionism.* Chicago: A. C. McClurg, 1922.

Janesville Daily Gazette. Janesville WI, 1860–1865; 1880–1894; 1901–1969.

Janesville Gazette. Janesville WI, 1845–1857; 1865–1880.

Janovy, John. *Back in Keith County.* Lincoln NE: Univ. NE Press, 1984 [c.1981].

———. *Yellowlegs.* New York: St. Martin's Press, c.1980.

Janson, Charles William. *The Stranger in America, 1793–1806.* New York: Press of the Pioneers, 1935. Repr. of the 1807 London ed. printed for J. Cundee.

Janvier, Thomas Allibone. *Christmas Kalends of Provence and Some Other Provencal Festivals.* New York: Harper & Bros., 1902.

Janvrin, Mary Wolcott. *Peace, or the Stolen Will.* Boston: James French; Galesburg IL: Hastings and French, 1857.

Jaques, Florence Page. *As Far as the Yukon.* New York: Harper, 1951.

Jardine, William. *The Natural History of Game-Birds.* Edinburgh: W. H. Lizars, 1834.

Jarves, James Jackson. *Scenes and Scenery in the Sandwich Islands.* Boston: James Munroe, 1844.

Jasper Free Enterprise. Jasper TX, 1964–.

Jayne, Mitchell F. *Home Grown Stories & Home Grown Fried Lies.* St. Louis MO: Wildstone Media, 2000.

Jazz Review. New York, 1958–1961.

Jefferson, Joseph. *The Autobiography of Joseph Jefferson.* New York: Century, 1890.

Jefferson, Thomas. *Memoir, Correspondence, and Miscellanies.* 2d ed. Boston: Gray and Bowen; New York: G. & C. & H. Carvill, 1830. 4 vols.

———. *Notes on the State of Virginia.* 1st Amer. ed. Philadelphia: Prichard and Hall, 1788.

———. *Papers.* Princeton NJ: Princeton Univ. Press, 1950–.

———. *The Writings of Thomas Jefferson.* Washington DC: Taylor & Maury, 1853–1854. 9 vols.

———. *The Writings of Thomas Jefferson.* Monticello ed. Washington DC: Issued under the auspices of the Thomas Jefferson Memorial Association of the United States, 1903–1905. 20 vols.

Jefferson City Post-Tribune. Jefferson City MO, 1927–.

Jefferson Garden Book See *Thomas Jefferson's Garden Book, 1766–1824*

Jeffersonian. Albany NY, 1838–1839.

Jefferys, Thomas. *The Natural and Civil History of the French Dominions in North and South America.* London: Printed for T. Jefferys, 1760.

Jemison, L. A. See Sinclair, Ellery

Jenkins, Dan. *Baja Oklahoma.* New York: Atheneum, 1981.

Jenkins, Hubert Oliver. *A Population Study of the Meadow Mice (Microtus) in Three Sierra Nevada Meadows.* Stanford CA: Stanford Univ. diss., 1940.

Jenkins, John Stilwell. *History of the War between the United States and Mexico.* Auburn NY: Derby & Miller, 1850 [c.1848].

Jenkins, Oliver Peebles. *Interesting Neighbors.* Philadelphia: P. Blakiston's Son, 1922.

Jenkins, Stephen. *The Story of the Bronx.* New York: G. P. Putnam's Sons, 1912.

Jenkins, Warren. *Ohio Gazetteer, and Traveler's Guide.* 1st rev. ed. Columbus OH: Isaac N. Whiting, c.1837.

Jenks, Jeremiah W. and W. Jett Lauck. *The Immigration Problem.* New York: Funk & Wagnalls, 1917 [c.1911].

Jenks, William Lee. *St. Clair County, Michigan, Its History and Its People.* Chicago: Lewis Publishing, 1912. 2 vols.

Jennings, Robert. *The Horse and Other Live Stock.* Philadelphia: John E. Potter, c.1866.

Jennings, William Dale. *The Cowboys.* New York: Stein and Day, 1971.

Jensen, Vernon H. *Heritage of Conflict.* Ithaca NY: Cornell Univ. Press, c.1950.

Jepson, Willis Linn. *A Flora of California.* Berkeley CA: Associated Students Store, 1922–1943. 3 vols.

———. *A Flora of the Economic Plants of California, for Agricultural Students.* Berkeley CA: Associated Students Store, c.1924.

———. *A Flora of Western Middle California.* Berkeley CA: Encina Publishing, 1901.

———. *A Flora of Western Middle California.* San Francisco: Cunningham, Curtiss & Welch, 1911.

———. *A Manual of the Flowering Plants of California.* Berkeley CA: Associated Students Store, Univ. CA, c.1925.

———. *The Silva of California.* Berkeley CA: Univ. Press, 1910.

———. *The Trees of California.* San Francisco: Cunningham, Curtis & Welch, 1909.

Jerauld, Charlotte Ann. *Poetry and Prose.* Boston: A. Tompkins, 1852 [c.1850].

Jerdan, William, ed. *Yankee Humor.* London: Ingram, Cooke, 1853.

Jessen's Weekly. Fairbanks AK, 1942–1969.

Jesup, Henry Griswold. *A Catalogue of the Flowering Plants and Higher Cryptogams.* Concord NH: Republican Press, 1891.

Jet. Chicago: Johnson Publishing, 1951–.

Jewett, Paul. *The New-England Farrier, or, a Compendium of Farriery.* New ed., with valuable additions. Exeter NH: Josiah Richardson, 1826.

Jewett, Sarah Orne. *Betty Leicester.* Boston: Houghton, Mifflin, c.1889.

———. *A Country Doctor.* Boston: Houghton, Mifflin, 1884.

———. *The Country of the Pointed Firs.* Boston: Houghton, Mifflin, 1896.

———. *Deephaven.* Boston: James R. Osgood, 1877.

———. *The King of Folly Island and Other People.* Boston: Riverside Press, c.1888.

———. *The Life of Nancy.* Boston: Houghton, Mifflin, 1895.

———. *A Marsh Island.* Boston: Houghton, Mifflin, 1885.

———. *The Mate of the Daylight and Friends Ashore.* 3d ed. Boston: Houghton, Mifflin, 1885 [c.1883].

———. *The Mate of the Daylight and Friends Ashore.* Boston: Houghton, Mifflin, 1884.

———. *The Queen's Twin.* Boston: Houghton, Mifflin, c.1899.

———. *Strangers and Wayfarers.* Boston: Houghton, Mifflin, 1890.

———. *The Tory Lover.* Boston: Houghton, Mifflin, 1901.

———. *A White Heron and Other Stories.* Boston: Houghton, Mifflin, c.1886.

Jewett, Stanley Gordon et al. *Birds of Washington State.* Seattle WA: Univ. WA Press, 1953.

Jewish Language Review. Haifa: Association for the study of Jewish languages, 1981–.

Jewish Press. Brooklyn NY, 1960–.

Jillson, Willard Rouse. *Tales of the Dark and Bloody Ground.* Louisville KY: C. T. Dearing Print, 1930.

Job, Herbert Keightley. *Among the Water-Fowl.* New York: Doubleday, Page, 1902.

Joel, Joseph A. and Lewis R. Stegman. *Rifle Shots and Bugle Notes.* New York: Grand Army Gazette, 1884 [c.1883].

Johannes Schwalm the Hessian. Lyndhurst OH: Johannes Schwalm Historical Association, 1976.

John G. Shedd Aquarium, Chicago. *Guide to the John G. Shedd Aquarium.* By Walter H. Chute, Director. Chicago: [s.n.], 1933.

John Pory's Lost Description of Plymouth Colony. Boston: Houghton Mifflin, 1918.

Johnsgard, Paul A. *North American Game Birds of Upland and Shoreline.* Lincoln NE: Univ. NE Press, c.1975.

———. *Waterfowl of North America.* Bloomington IN: IN Univ. Press, c.1975.

Johns Hopkins Hospital. *Hospital Plans.* New York: William Wood, 1875.

Johnson, Benj. F., of Boone See Riley, James Whitcomb

Johnson, Burges. *As Much as I Dare.* New York: Ives Washburn, 1944.

Johnson, Charles Britten. *Letters from the British Settlement in Pennsylvania.* Philadelphia: H. Hall, 1819.

Johnson, Charles Richard. *Oxherding Tale.* Bloomington IN: IN Univ. Press, c.1982.

Johnson, Claudia Alta Taylor. *A White House Diary.* New York: Holt, Rinehart and Winston, 1970.

Johnson, Clifton. *Battleground Adventures.* Boston: Houghton Mifflin, c.1915.

———. *Highways and Byways from the St. Lawrence to Virginia.* New York: Macmillan, 1913.

———. *Highways and Byways of Florida.* New York: Macmillan, 1918.

———. *Highways and Byways of New England.* New York: Macmillan, 1916 [c.1915].

———. *Highways and Byways of the Great Lakes.* New ed. New York: Macmillan, 1913. Orig. pub. in 1911.

———. *Highways and Byways of the Mississippi Valley.* New York: Macmillan, 1906.

———. *Highways and Byways of the Pacific Coast.* New York: Macmillan, 1908.

———. *Highways and Byways of the Rocky Mountains.* New York: Macmillan, 1910.

———. *Highways and Byways of the South.* New York: Macmillan, 1913. Orig. pub. in 1904.

———. *New England and Its Neighbors.* New York: Macmillan, 1924. Orig. pub. in 1902.

Johnson, Crisfield. *Centennial History of Erie County, New York.* Buffalo NY: Matthews & Warren, c.1876.

Johnson, Cuthbert W. *The Farmer's Encyclopaedia and Dictionary of Rural Affairs.* Philadelphia: Carey and Hart, 1844 [c.1843].

Johnson, Edward. *Wonder-Working Providence of Sions Saviour in New England (1654) and Good News from New England (1648).* Delmar NY: Scholars' Facsimiles and Reprints, 1974. Orig. printed in 1654 for N. Brooke, London under the title *A History of New England.*

Johnson, Guion Griffis. *Ante-Bellum North Carolina.* Chapel Hill NC: Univ. NC Press, 1937.

Johnson, Harrison. *Johnson's History of Nebraska.* Omaha NE: Gibson, 1880 [c.1879].

Johnson, Jesse J. *Ebony Brass.* New York: William-Frederick Press, 1967.

Johnson, Lelia Ardell Clark. *Sullivan and Sorrento since 1760.* Ellsworth ME: Hancock County Pub., 1953.

Johnson, Louise. *Responses to PADS 20.* 1951. Unpub. material in response to a questionnaire.

Johnson, Malcolm B. *I Declare!* Tallahassee FL: Tallahassee Democrat, c.1983.

Johnson, Manville A. *Fifty Years of Country Storekeeping.* Brainerd MN: Printed by Lakeland Color Press, c.1955.

Johnson, Overton and William H. Winter. *Route across the Rocky Mountains.* Princeton NJ: Princeton Univ. Press, 1932. A repr. of the 1846 ed. pub. by J. B. Semans, Lafayette IN.

Johnson, Randy. *Hiking North Carolina.* 2d ed. Guilford CT: Falcon Guides, 2007.

Johnson, R. Byron. *Very Far West Indeed.* London: Sampson, Low, Marston, Low & Searle, c.1872.

Johnson, Richard Riley. *Twenty Five Milk Runs and a Few Others.* Victoria: Trafford, c.2004.

Johnson, Rossiter. *The End of a Rainbow, an American Story.* New York: Charles Scribner's Sons, 1892.

Johnson, Susannah Willard. *A Narrative of the Captivity of Mrs. Johnson.* Walpole NH: David Carlisle, 1796.

Johnson, Terry L. *Alaska Fisheries Handbook.* Sitka AK: Diversified Information Services, c.1986.

Johnson, Theodore Taylor. *California and Oregon.* 4th ed. Philadelphia: J. B. Lippincott, 1865 [c.1851].

Johnson, Timothy. *CRC Ethnobotany Desk Reference.* Boca Raton FL: CRC Press, 1999?

Johnson, William. *The Papers of Sir William Johnson.* Albany NY: Univ. of the State of NY, 1921–1965. 14 vols.

Johnson, William A. *The History of Anderson County, Kansas, from Its First Settlement to the Fourth of July, 1876.* Garnett KS: Kauffman & Iler, 1877.

Johnson, William Matthews. *The House on Corbett Street.* New York: William-Frederick Press, 1967.

Johnson-Coleman, Lorraine. *Just Plain Folks.* Columbia SC: Summerhouse Press, c.1997.

Johnson's English Dictionary. Ed. by Joseph Emerson Worcester. Boston: Charles Ewer & T. Harrington Carter, 1828.

Johnson's New Universal Cyclopaedia. New York: Alvin J. Johnson & Son, 1875–1878. 4 vols.

Johnston, Algernon Sidney. *Memoirs of a Nullifier.* Columbia SC: Printed and published at the Telescope Office, 1832.

Johnston, Alva. *The Legendary Mizners.* New York: Farrar, Straus and Young, c.1953.

Johnston, Frances Benjamin and Thomas Tileston Waterman. *The Early Architecture of North Carolina.* Chapel Hill NC: Univ. NC Press, c.1941.

Johnston, George, ed. *The Poets and Poetry of Chester County, Pennsylvania.* Philadelphia: Printed by J. B. Lippincott, 1890.

Johnston, George Milligen. *A Short Description of the Province of South-Carolina . . . Written in 1763.* London: Printed for J. Hinton, 1770.

Johnston, James Finley Weir. *The Chemistry of Common Life.* New York: D. Appleton, 1855. 2 vols.

———. *Notes on North America.* Boston: Charles C. Little and James Brown, 1851 [c.1850]. 2 vols.

Johnston, Richard Malcolm. *Dukesborough Tales.* Baltimore MD: Turnbull Bros., 1871.

———. *Dukesborough Tales.* New York: D. Appleton, 1892. Orig. pub. in 1871 by Turnbull Bros., Baltimore MD.

———. *Little Ike Templin and Other Stories.* Boston: Lathrop Publishing, c.1894.

———. *Mr. Absalom Billingslea.* New York: Harper & Bros., 1888.

———. *Mr. Billy Downs and His Likes.* New York: C. L. Webster, 1892.

———. *Mr. Fortner's Marital Claims.* New York: D. Appleton, 1892.

———. *Ogeechee Cross-Firings.* New York: Harper & Bros., 1889.

———. *Old Mark Langston.* New York: Harper & Bros., 1884.

———. *Old Times in Middle Georgia.* New York: Macmillan, 1897.

———. *Pearce Amerson's Will.* Chicago: Way and Williams, 1898.

———. *The Primes and Their Neighbors.* New York: D. Appleton, 1891.

———. *Widow Guthrie.* New York: D. Appleton, 1890.

Johnstone, Lizzie Rice. *A Story of Pittsfield and Suamico.* De Pere WI: Kuypers Publishing, c.1928.

Jones, Alexander. "Two Journals of Alexander Jones, Esq. of Providence, Rhode Island." *Historical Magazine of the Protestant Episcopal Church.* (1941) 10.6–30.

Jones, Alice Hanson. *American Colonial Wealth: Documents and Methods.* New York: Arno Press, 1977. 3 vols.

Jones, Bessie. *For the Ancestors.* Coll. and ed. by John Stewart. Urbana IL: Univ. IL Press, c.1983.

Jones, Bessie and Bess Lomax Hawes. *Step It Down.* New York: Harper and Row, c.1972.

Jones, Bryan. *Mark Twain Made Me Do It & Other Plains Adventures.* Lincoln NE: Univ. NE Press, c.1997.

Jones, Charles Colcock. *Antiquities of the Southern Indians, Particularly of the Georgia Tribes.* New York: D. Appleton, 1873.

———. *Negro Myths from the Georgia Coast.* Boston: Houghton, Mifflin, 1888.

Jones, Charles Edgeworth. *Education in Georgia.* Washington DC: Govt. Printing Office, 1889.

Jones, Creo A. *Memoirs of an Ozark Hill Boy.* Mt. Ida AR: [s.n.], 1974?

Jones, David. *A Journal of Two Visits Made to Some Nations of Indians on the West Side of the River Ohio.* New York: Reprinted for J. Sabin, 1865. Orig. pub. in 1774 in Burlington NJ.

Jones, Elias. *History of Dorchester County, Maryland.* Baltimore MD: Williams & Wilkins, 1902.

Jones, Evan. *American Food.* New York: E. P. Dutton, 1975.

Jones, Gayl. *The Healing.* Boston: Beacon Press, 1998.

Jones, George Neville. *Flora of Illinois.* 3d ed. Notre Dame IN: Univ. Notre Dame Press, 1963.

Jones, George Noble. *Florida Plantation Records from the*

Papers of George Noble Jones. Ed. by Ulrich Bonnell Phillips and James David Glunt. St. Louis MO: Missouri Historical Society, 1927.

Jones, Hugh. *The Present State of Virginia.* New York: Reprinted for J. Sabin, 1865. Repr. of the 1724 London ed. printed for J. Clark.

Jones, James. *From Here to Eternity.* New York: Scribner, 1951.

Jones, James Athearn. *The Refugee.* New York: Wilder & Campbell, 1825. 2 vols.

Jones, J. Benton. *Tomato Plant Culture in the Field, Greenhouse and Home Garden.* 2d ed. Boca Raton FL: CRC Press, 2007.

Jones, John Beauchamp. *A Rebel War Clerk's Diary at the Confederate States Capital.* Philadelphia: Lippincott, 1866. 2 vols.

———. *Wild Western Scenes.* New stereotype ed., altered, rev., and corr. Philadelphia: J. B. Lippincott, 1875 [c.1856].

———. *Wild Western Scenes.* New stereotype ed., rev. and corr. Philadelphia: J. B. Lippincott, 1869. Republished in 1970 by Literature House, Upper Saddle River NJ.

Jones, Joseph SEE Thompson, William Tappan

Jones, Joseph Stevens. *The Green Mountain Boy.* New York: Samuel French, 1860.

———. *Life of Jefferson S. Batkins.* Boston: Loring, c.1871.

Jones, Lealon N., ed. *Eve's Stepchildren.* Caldwell ID: Caxton Printers, 1942.

Jones, Livingston French. *A Study of the Thlingets of Alaska.* New York: Fleming H. Revell, c.1914.

Jones, Louis B. *Particles and Luck.* New York: Pantheon Books, 1993.

Jones, Loyal and Billy Edd Wheeler. *Laughter in Appalachia.* Little Rock AR: August House, c.1987.

Jones, Nard. *Evergreen Land.* New York: Dodd, Mead, 1947.

Jones, Nelson Edwards. *The Squirrel Hunters of Ohio.* Cincinnati OH: Robert Clarke, 1898.

Jones, Ora L. *Peculiarities of the Appalachian Mountaineers.* Detroit MI: Harlo, c.1967.

Jones, Peter. *History of the Ojebway Indians.* London: A. W. Bennett, 1861.

Jones, Rufus Matthew. *A Small-Town Boy.* New York: Macmillan, 1941.

Jones, Stephen. *Working Thin Waters.* Hanover NH: Univ. Press New England, c.2001.

Jones, Suzi. *Oregon Folklore.* Eugene OR: Univ. OR, c.1977.

Jones, Thelma. *Skinny Angel.* New York: McGraw-Hill, c.1946.

Jones-Jackson, Patricia. *When Roots Die.* Athens GA: Univ. GA Press, c.1987.

Joplin Globe. Joplin MO, 1896–.

Jordan, David Starr. *A Guide to the Study of Fishes.* New York: Henry Holt, 1905. 2 vols.

———. *Manual of the Vertebrates of the Northern United States.* Chicago: Jansen, McClurg, c.1876.

———. *Science Sketches.* Chicago: A. C. McClurg, 1888 [c.1887].

Jordan, David Starr and Balfour H. Van Vleck. *A Popular Key to the Birds, Reptiles, Batrachians and Fishes of the Northern United States East of the Mississippi River.* Appleton WI: Reid & Miller, 1874.

Jordan, David Starr and Barton Warren Evermann. *American Food and Game Fishes.* New York: Doubleday, Page, 1902.

———. *A Check-List of the Fishes and Fishlike Vertebrates of North and Middle America.* Washington DC: Govt. Printing Office, 1896. U.S. Bureau of Fisheries. *Report for 1895.* App. 5.

———. *The Fishes of North and Middle America* SEE United States National Museum *Bulletin*

Jordan, Gilbert John. *Yesterday in the Texas Hill Country.* College Station TX: TX A&M Univ. Press, c.1979.

Jordan, Grace Edgington. *Home below Hell's Canyon.* Lincoln NE: Univ. NE Press, c.1954.

Joseph, Brian D. et al., eds. *Language Diversity in Michigan and Ohio.* Ann Arbor MI: Caravan Books, 2005.

Josselyn, John. *An Account of Two Voyages to New-England.* London: Giles Widdows, 1674.

———. *New-Englands Rarities Discovered.* London: G. Widdowes, 1672.

———. *New-England's Rarities Discovered.* Boston: William Veazie, 1865 [1672].

Journal and Review. Aiken SC, 1880?–1935.

Journal-Courier. Jacksonville IL, 1952–.

Journal de Physique, de Chimie et d'Histoire Naturelle et des Arts. Paris, 1794–1823.

Journal for MultiMedia History. 1998–. Internet.

Journal of Abnormal Psychology. Lancaster PA, 1906–.

Journal of Agricultural Research. Washington DC: U.S. Department of Agriculture, 1913–1949.

Journal of American Folklore. Philadelphia: American Folklore Society, 1888–.

Journal of American History [Abilene] SEE *Mississippi Valley Historical Review*

Journal of American History. New Haven CT: Associated Publishers of American Records, 1907–1935.

Journal of Appalachian Studies. Morgantown WV, 1995–.

Journal of Comparative Medicine and Veterinary Archives. New York, 1890–1903.

Journal of Conchology. London, 1874–.

Journal of Consumer Health on the Internet. Binghampton NY, 2003–.

Journal of Dental Research. Baltimore MD, 1919–2007.

Journal of Discourses. By Brigham Young, his two counselors, the twelve apostles, and others. Liverpool: F. D. Richards, 1854–1886. 26 vols.

Journal of Ecology. Cambridge: Cambridge Univ. Press, 1913–.

Journal of Economic Entomology. Menasha WI: American Association of Economic Entomologists, 1908–.

Journal of Educational Sociology. Washington DC, 1927–1963.

Journal of English Linguistics. Bellingham WA: Western WA State College, 1967–.

Journal of Ethnobiology. Flagstaff AZ: Center for Western Studies, 1981–.

Journal of Geology. Chicago, 1893–.

Journal of Home Economics. Washington DC: American Home Economics Association, 1909–1994.

Journal of Mammalogy. Baltimore MD: American Society of Mammalogists, 1919–.

Journal of Marine Research. New Haven CT, 1937–.

Journal of Nervous and Mental Disease. Chicago, 1874–.

Journal of Occupational and Environmental Medicine. Baltimore MD, 1995–.

Journal of Parasitology. Urbana IL, 1914–2004.

Journal of Physiology. London, 1878–.

Journal of Range Management. Denver CO, 1948–2004.

Journal of Social Issues. New York: Society for the Psychological Study of Social Issues, 1945–.

Journal of Southern History. Baton Rouge LA: Southern Historical Society, 1935–.

Journal of the American Association of University Women. Ithaca NY, 1921–1961.

Journal of the American Chemical Society. Washington DC, 1879–.

Journal of the American Osteopathic Association. New York, 1901–.

Journal of the American Pharmaceutical Association. Washington DC, 1996–2003.

Journal of the Arnold Arboretum. Cambridge MA: Arnold Arboretum, Harvard Univ., 1919–1990.

"Journal of the Atkinson-O'Fallon Expedition." *North Dakota Historical Quarterly.* (1929) 4.5–56.

Journal of the Elisha Mitchell Scientific Society. Chapel Hill NC: Univ. NC Press, 1884–2001.

Journal of the Franklin Institute of the State of Pennsylvania. Philadelphia, 1829–.

Journal of the National Medical Association. Washington DC, 1909–.

Journal of the New England Water Works Association. Boston, 1886–.

Journal of the New York Botanical Garden. New York, 1900–1950.

Journal of the Outdoor Life. Saranac Lake NY, 1905–1935.

Journal of the Southern Appalachian Botanical Club. Morgantown WV, 1936–1937.

Journal of Wildlife Management. Menasha WI: Wildlife Society, 1937–.

Journal-Patriot. North Wilkesboro NC, 1906–.

Journal Star. Peoria IL, 1991–.

Journal-Tribune. Marysville OH, 1958–1972.

Joutel, Henri. *Joutel's Journal of La Salle's Last Voyage.* Albany NY: Joseph McDonough, 1906. The text is that of the transl. pub. in London in 1714.

Joyce, James. *Ulysses.* Paris: Shakespeare, 1922.

Joyce, Patrick Weston. *English as We Speak It in Ireland.* London: Longmans, Green; Dublin: M. H. Gill & Son, 1910.

Joyner, Charles. *Down by the Riverside.* Urbana IL: Univ. IL Press, c.1984.

Juan, George and Antonio de Ulloa. *A Voyage to South America.* 2d ed. rev. and corr. London: Printed for L. Davis and C. Reymers, 1760. 2 vols.

Judd, Gerrit Permele. *Hawaii.* New York: Collier Books, 1961.

Judd, Sylvester. *Margaret.* Boston: Jordan and Wiley, 1845.

———. *Margaret.* Rev. ed. Boston: Phillips, Sampson, 1851. 2 vols.

———. *Richard Edney and the Governor's Family.* Boston: Phillips, Sampson, 1850.

Judge, Charles Joseph. *An American Missionary.* Baltimore MD: John Murphy, c.1904.

Judge. New York: Judge Publishing, 1881–1939?

Judson, Edward Zane Carroll. *The Mysteries and Miseries of New York.* New York: Bedford, 1848. 5 vols.

———. *Seawaif.* New York: Frederic A. Brady, c.1859.

Judson, Levi Carroll. *The Probe.* 4th ed. Philadelphia: Published by the Author, 1847 [c.1846].

Julesburg Grit-Advocate. Julesburg CO, 1899?–.

Juliaetta Gem. Juliaetta ID, 1889–1890.

Julian Apple Day. Julian CA: Julian Chamber of Commerce, 195?–.

Junger, Sebastian. *The Perfect Storm.* New York: W. W. Norton, c.1997.

Junior League of Charleston. *Charleston Receipts Collected by the Junior League of Charleston.* Charleston SC: Walker Evans & Cogswell, 1950.

Justice Denied. Portland OR, 1990–.

Justin, Margaret M. and Lucile Osborn Rust. *Home and Family Living.* Chicago: J. B. Lippincott, 1941.

Justus, May. *Cabin on Kettle Creek.* New York: Junior Literary Guild and J. B. Lippincott, c.1941.

———. *Children of the Great Smoky Mountains.* New York: E. P. Dutton, 1952.

———. *The Other Side of the Mountain.* New York: Hastings House, 1931 [c.1957].

———. *Tales from the Near-Side and Far.* Champaign IL: Garrard, 1970.

Kafka, Barbara. *Microwave Gourmet.* New York: William Morrow, c.1987.

Kahn, Sharon. *Fax Me a Bagel.* New York: Scribner, c.1998.

Kalamazoo Express Weekly. Kalamazoo MI, 1998–. Internet.

Kalibabky, Mike, comp. *Hawdaw Talk Rayncher.* Hibbing MN: Hibbing Historical Society, 1978.

Kalish, Mildred Armstrong. *Little Heathens: the Hard Times and High Spirits on an Iowa Farm during the Great Depression.* New York: Bantam Books, 2007.

Kalm, Pehr. *Resejournal över Resan till Norra Amerika.* Helsingfors: Svenska Litteratursallskapet i Finland, 1966–1988. 4 vols.

———. *Travels into North America.* Transl. from Swedish by John Reinhold Forster. Warrington: Printed by William Eyres, 1770–1771. 3 vols.

———. *Travels into North America.* Transl. from Swedish by John Reinhold Forster. 2d ed. London: T. Lowndes, 1772. 2 vols.

Kampion, Drew. *Greg Noll, the Art of the Surfboard.* Salt Lake City UT: Gibbs Smith, 2007.

Kander, Simon, Mrs. *The Settlement Cook Book.* Milwaukee WI: The Settlement, 1901.

———. *The Settlement Cook Book.* 10th ed. enlarged and rev. Milwaukee WI: Settlement Cook Book, 1920.

Kane, Charles W. *Herbal Medicine of the American Southwest.* Tucson AZ: Lincoln Town Press, c.2006.

Kane, Elisha Kent. *Arctic Explorations.* Philadelphia: Childs & Peterson, 1856. 2 vols.

———. *The U.S. Grinnell Expedition in Search of Sir John Franklin.* New York: Harper & Bros., 1854.

Kane, Harnett Thomas. *Deep Delta Country.* New York: Duell, Sloan & Pearce, 1944.

Kansas Academy of Science. *Transactions.* Topeka KS, 1872–.

Kansas. Agricultural Experiment Station, Kansas State University Manhattan. *Bulletin.* Manhattan KS, 1888–.

Kansas City Medical Index. Kansas City MO, 1885–1899.

Kansas City Times. Kansas City MO, 1908–1990.

Kansas Historical Quarterly. Topeka KS: Kansas State Historical Society, 1931–1977.

Kansas. Laws, Statutes etc. *General Laws of the State of Kansas, in Force at the Close of the Session of the Legislature Ending March 6th, 1862, to Which Is Appended the . . . Constitution of the State of Kansas, & the Act of Admission.* Topeka KS: J. H. Bennett, 1862.

Kansas Magazine. Topeka KS, 1872–1873.

Kansas Quarterly. Manhattan KS, 1968–.

Kansas Reports. Topeka KS, 1881–.

Kansas. State Board of Agriculture. *Biennial Report.* Topeka KS, 1872–1902.

———. *Report.* Topeka KS, 1873–.

Kansas State Historical Society. *Collections.* Topeka KS, 1875–1928.

Kansas State University. *Kansas Wildflowers and Grasses.* [v.d.]. Internet.

Kansas University Quarterly. Lawrence KS, 1892–1901.

Kantner, Seth. *Shopping for Porcupine: a Life in Arctic Alaska.* Minneapolis MN: Milkweed Editions, 2008.

Kantor, MacKinlay. *Missouri Bittersweet.* Garden City NY: Doubleday, 1969.

Kantrud, Harold A. *Native Wildflowers of the North Dakota Grasslands.* 1995. Internet.

Kappa Alpha Journal. Lexington KY, 1885?–1960?

Karam, Jana Abrams. *Into the Breach.* New York: St. Martin's Press, c.2002.

Karig, Walter. *Lower than Angels.* New York: Farrar & Rinehart, 1945.

Karni, Michael G. and Aili Jarvenpa, eds. *Sampo.* Minneapolis MN: New Rivers Press, c.1989.

Karns, C. W. *Historical Sketches of Morrisons Cove.* Altoona PA: Mirror Press, 1933.

Karon, Jan. *A Common Life.* New York: Penguin Books, c.2001.

——. *A Light in the Window.* New York: Penguin Books, c.1995.

Karr, Mary. *The Liars' Club.* New York: Viking, c.1995.

Kaston, Benjamin Julian. *How to Know the Spiders.* 2d ed. Dubuque IA: Wm. C. Brown, 1972.

Katz, Harry N., ed. *Kinks, a Book of 250 Helpful Hints for Hunters, Anglers and Outers.* Chicago: Outer's Book, 1917.

Katzen, Mollie. *The Moosewood Cookbook.* Berkeley CA: Ten Speed Press, c.1977.

Kauffman, Reginald Wright. *Our Navy at Work.* Indianapolis IN: Bobbs-Merrill, c.1918.

Kearney, Lake Shore. *The Hodag and Other Tales of the Logging Camps.* Wausau WI: Printed by Democrat Printing, 1928.

Kearney, Thomas Henry and Robert Hibbs Peebles. *Arizona Flora.* Berkeley CA: Univ. CA Press, 1951.

Kearney, Thomas Henry and Robert Hibbs Peebles. *Arizona Flora.* 2d ed. Berkeley CA: Univ. CA Press, 1960.

Kearney, Thomas Henry et al. *Flowering Plants and Ferns of Arizona.* Washington DC: Govt. Printing Office, 1942.

Keckley, Elizabeth. *Behind the Scenes.* New York: G. W. Carleton, 1868.

Keeble, John. *Nocturnal America.* Lincoln NE: Univ. NE Press, c.2006.

Keeler, Harriet Louise. *Our Early Wildflowers.* New York: Charles Scribner's Sons, 1916.

——. *Our Native Trees.* New York: Charles Scribner's Sons, 1927 [c.1900].

——. *Our Northern Shrubs and How to Identify Them.* New York: Charles Scribner's Sons, 1910 [c.1903].

Keeler, Ralph. *Gloverson and His Silent Partners.* Boston: Lee and Shepard, 1869.

Keep, Josiah. *West Coast Shells.* Rev. ed. San Francisco: Whitaker & Ray-Wiggin, 1911.

Keillor, Garrison. *Lake Wobegon Days.* New York: Viking, c.1985.

——. *Lake Wobegon Summer 1956.* New York: Viking, c.2001.

——. *Wobegon Boy.* New York: Viking Penguin, 1997.

Keim, De Benneville Randolph. *Sheridan's Troopers on the Border.* Philadelphia: Claxton, Remsen & Haffelfinger, 1870.

Keiser, R. Lincoln. *The Vice Lords.* New York: Holt, Rinehart & Winston, c.1969.

Keith, Clayton. *History of the Watson Family in America.* Louisiana MO: [s.n.], 1914.

Keith, Elmer. *Elmer Keith's Big Game Hunting.* Boston: Little, Brown, 1948.

——. *Hell, I Was There!* Los Angeles: Petersen Publishing, 1979.

Keith, Melville Cox. *Keith's Domestic Practice and Botanic Handbook.* Belleville OH: The Author, 1901.

Keithahn, Edward L. *Alaska . . . for the Curious.* Alaska Centennial ed. Seattle: Superior Publishing, c.1966.

Kelland, Clarence Budington. *Scattergood Baines.* New York: A. L. Burt, c.1921.

Keller, Charles E. and Timothy C. Keller. *Birds of Indianapolis.* Bloomington IN: IN Univ. Press, 1993.

Keller, Nora Okja et al., eds. *Yobo: Korean American Writing in Hawai'i.* Honolulu HI: Bamboo Ridge Press, 2003.

Kelley, Jonathan Falconbridge See Kelly, Jonathan Falconbridge

Kelley, Welbourn. *Inchin' Along.* New York: William Morrow, 1932.

Kellner, Esther. *The Devil and Aunt Serena.* Indianapolis IN: Bobbs-Merrill, c.1968.

Kellogg, Elijah. *The Ark of Elm Island.* Boston: Lee and Shepard, 1870 [c.1869].

——. *Charlie Bell, the Waif of Elm Island.* Boston: Lee and Shepard, 1869 [c.1868].

——. *Forest Glen: or, the Mohawk's Friendship.* Boston: Lee and Shepard, c.1877.

——. *Lion Ben of Elm Island.* Boston: Lee and Shepard, 1869 [c.1868].

——. *The Young Ship-Builders of Elm Island.* Boston: Lee & Shepard, 1870.

Kellogg, Frank Eugene. *The Boy Fisherman.* Akron OH: Saalfield Publishing, 1904.

Kellogg, Frederick, Mrs. See White, Tryphena Ely

Kellogg, Miner Kilbourne. *M. K. Kellogg's Texas Journal, 1872.* Ed. with an into. by Llerena Friend. Austin TX: Univ. TX Press, 1872 [c.1967].

Kellogg, Robert H. *Life and Death in Rebel Prisons.* Hartford CT: L. Stebbins, 1865.

Kellogg, Royal Shaw. *Forest Planting in Western Kansas.* Washington DC: Govt. Printing Office, 1904.

Kellogg, Vernon Lyman. *American Insects.* New York: Henry Holt, 1905.

——. *Common Injurious Insects of Kansas.* Lawrence KS: Univ. KS, 1892.

Kelly, Jonathan Falconbridge. *The Humors of Falconbridge.* Philadelphia: T. B. Peterson & Bros., c.1856.

Kelly, William. *An Excursion to California over the Prairie, Rocky Mountains, and Great Sierra Nevada.* London: Chapman and Hall, 1851. 2 vols.

Kelsey, Carl. *The Negro Farmer.* New York: AMS Reprint, 1977. Repr. of the 1903 ed. pub. by Jennings & Pye, Chicago.

Kemble, Fanny. *Journal.* London: John Murray, 1835. 2 vols.

Kemble, Frances Anne. *Journal of a Residence on a Georgian Plantation in 1838–1839.* New York: Harper & Bros., 1863.

Kemper, Jackson. "Journal of an Episcopalian Missionary's Tour to Green Bay, 1834." Wisconsin. State Historical Society *Collections.* (1898) 14.394–449.

——. *Papers of Bishop Jackson Kemper.* 1838. Unpub. material in the Collections of the Wisconsin State Historical Society, Madison WI.

——. "A Trip through Wisconsin in 1838." *Wisconsin Magazine of History.* (1925) 8.423–45.

Kendall, Edward Augustus. *Travels through the Northern Parts of the United States in the Years 1807 and 1808.* New York: I. Riley, 1809. 3 vols.

Kendall, George Wilkins. *Narrative of the Texan Santa Fé Expedition.* New-York: Harper & Bros., 1844. 2 vols.

——. *Narrative of the Texan Santa Fé Expedition.* New York: Harper & Bros., 1846. 2 vols. Orig. pub. in 1844.

Kendall, Park. *Still in the Draft.* New York: M. S. Mill, 1942.

Kendallabrum. Tulsa OK, 1913–1994.

Kennebec Journal. Augusta ME, 1976–.

Kennebec Journal Online. Augusta ME, 1990–. Internet.

Kennedy, Chester Craft. *Our Baldridge Forebears and Some of Their Collateral Lines.* Conway AR: Presto, 1981.

Kennedy, John Pendleton. *Horse Shoe Robinson.* Philadelphia: Carey, Lea, and Blanchard, c.1835. 2 vols.

——. *Horse-Shoe Robinson.* Rev. ed. New York: George Putnam, 1854. First rev. ed. pub. in 1852 by G. P. Putnam, New York.

——. *Quodlibet.* Philadelphia: Lea & Blanchard, 1840.

——. *Swallow Barn.* Philadelphia: Carey & Lea, 1832. 2 vols.

Kennedy, Millard Fillmore and Alvin F. Harlow. *Schoolmaster of Yesterday.* New York: McGraw Hill Book, c.1940.

Kennedy, Philip Pendleton. *The Blackwater Chronicle.* New York: Redfield, 1853.

Kennedy, Robert Emmet. *Black Cameos.* Freeport NY: Books for Libraries Press, 1970. Repr. of the 1924 ed. pub. by A. & C. Boni, New York.

——. *Gritny People.* New York: Dodd Mead, 1927.

Kennedy, Stetson. *Palmetto Country.* New York: Duell, Sloan & Pearce, 1942.

Kennedy, William. *Billy Phelan's Greatest Game.* New York: Viking Press, c.1978.

——. *Texas.* London: R. Hastings, 1841. 2 vols.

Kennerly, James. "Diary." Missouri Historical Society *Collections.* (1928–1931) 6.41–97.

Kenrick, William. *The New American Orchardist.* Boston: Carter, Hendee, 1833 [c.1832].

——. *The New American Orchardist.* 2d ed., enlarged and improved. Boston: Russell, Odiorne & Metcalf, 1835.

Kentucky Almanac. Lexington KY, 1806–.

Kentucky Explorer. Jackson KY, 1980?–.

Kentucky Folk-Lore and Poetry Magazine. Bowling Green KY: Kentucky Folk-Lore Society, 1926–1931.

Kentucky Folklore Record. Bowling Green KY: Kentucky Folklore Society, 1955–.

Kentucky Gazette. Lexington KY, 1787–1848.

Kentucky. General Assembly. Senate. *Journal of the Senate of the Commonwealth of Kentucky.* Frankfort KY, 1792–.

Kentucky Geological Survey. 4th ser. Frankfort KY: State Geologist, 1913–1919. 5 vols.

Kentucky Historical Society. *Register.* Frankfort KY, 1903–.

Kentucky. Laws, etc. *Acts of the General Assembly of the Commonwealth of Kentucky, Passed at November Session, 1851.* Frankfort KY: A. G. Hodges, 1852.

KentuckyLiving.com. 2000?–. Internet.

Kentucky. University. College of Agriculture. *Kentucky Pest News.* Lexington KY, 1991–.

Kentucky. University. College of Arts and Sciences. *Arts & Sciences Magazine.* 2002?–. Internet.

Kentucky. University. *Kentucky Garden Flowers.* [v.d.]. Internet.

Kentucky. University. Oral History Program. *Frontier Nursing Service Oral History Project.* [v.d.]. Internet.

Kenyon, John Samuel and Thomas Albert Knott. *A Pronouncing Dictionary of American English.* Springfield MA: G. & C. Merriam, c.1944.

——, eds. *A Pronouncing Dictionary of American English.* Springfield MA: G. & C. Merriam, c.1953.

Kenyon Review. Gambier OH, 1939–.

Kephart, Horace. *The Book of Camping and Woodcraft.* New York: Outing Publishing, 1906.

——. *Camping and Woodcraft.* New York: Outing Publishing, 1916–1917. 2 vols.

——. *Our Southern Highlanders.* New York: Outing Publishing, 1913.

——. *Our Southern Highlanders.* New and enlarged ed. New York: Macmillan, 1926. A reissue of the new and rev. ed. pub. in 1922 by Macmillan, New York.

Ker, Anna Sue Carothers. *The Vocabulary of West Texas.* Lubbock TX: TX Technological College diss., 1956.

Ker, Henry. *Travels through the Western Interior of the United States.* Elizabethtown NJ: Printed for the author, 1816.

Kercheval, Samuel. *A History of the Valley of Virginia.* Winchester VA: S. H. Davis, 1833.

Kerl, Simon. *A Common-School Grammar of the English Language.* New York: Ivison, Phinney, Blakeman; Chicago: S. C. Griggs, 1868 [c.1865].

Kerlin, Robert Thomas. *The Voice of the Negro, 1919.* New York: E. P. Dutton, c.1920.

Kerouac, Jack. *On the Road.* New York: Viking Press, 1957.

——. *On the Road.* New York: Viking Press, 1958.

——. *Pic.* New York: Grove Press, c.1971.

——. *The Subterraneans.* New York: Grove Press, 1971 [c.1958].

Kerr Home Canning and Freezing Book. Sand Springs OK: Kerr Glass Manufacturing, 1983.

Kerrville Mountain Sun. Kerrville TX, 1926–.

Kerrville Times. Kerrville Texas, 1925–.

Kesey, Ken. *One Flew over the Cuckoo's Nest.* New York: Viking Press, c.1962.

——. *Sometimes a Great Notion.* New York: Viking Press, c.1964.

Kester, Vaughan. *The Prodigal Judge.* Indianapolis IN: Bobbs-Merrill, c.1911.

Kettell, Samuel. *Yankee Notions.* 3d ed. Boston: Otis, Broaders, 1838.

Key, Mary Ritchie. *Tobacco Vocabulary.* 1967. Unpub. material coll. by *DARE* fieldworker Mary Ritchie Key.

Keystone Folklore Quarterly. Lewisburg PA, 1956–.

Key West Citizen. Key West FL, 1879–.

Kibler, James. *Simms as Naturalist.* 1977. Unpub.

Kidd, Sue Monk. *The Mermaid Chair.* New York: Viking, c.2005.

Kidder, Daniel Parish. *Mormonism and the Mormons.* New York: G. Lane & P. P. Sandford for the Methodist Episcopal Church, 1842.

Kidder, Tracy. *House.* Boston: Houghton Mifflin, c.1985.

Kieffer, Harry Martyn. *The Recollections of a Drummer Boy.* Rev. and enlarged ed. Boston: Houghton, Mifflin, c.1888.

Kieran, John. *Footnotes on Nature.* Garden City NY: Doubleday, 1947.

——. *A Natural History of New York City.* Rev. and abridged ed. Garden City NY: Published for the Amer. Museum of Natural History [by] Natural History Press, 1971.

Kilbourne, S. A. *Game Fishes of the United States.* New York: Winchester Press, 1972 [1879].

Kildare, Owen. *My Old Bailiwick.* New York: Fleming H. Revell, c.1906.

Kilgore, Laverne Keeler, comp. *Collections and Recollections of the Newman Shirey Family.* Fort Worth TX: Printed by the author, 1988–.

Kilgore News Herald. Kilgore TX, 1941–.

Killebrew, Joseph Buckner. *The Grasses of Tennessee.* Nashville TN: American, 1878.

Killens, John Oliver. *Cotillion.* New York: Trident Press, 1971.

———. *Youngblood.* New York: Dial Press, 1954.

Killian, Beth. *Life as a Poser.* New York: Simon & Schuster, c.2006.

Kilmer, Joyce. *Joyce Kilmer: Poems, Essays and Letters.* Ed. with a memoir by Robert Cortes Holliday. New York: George H. Doran, c.1918. 2 vols.

Kilpatrick, James Jackson. *The Foxes' Union.* McLean VA: EPM, c.1977.

Kimball, Charles P. *The Lepidoptera of Florida, an Annotated Checklist.* Gainesville FL: Division of Plant Industry, FL Dept. of Agriculture, 1965.

Kimball, Heber Chase. *President Heber C. Kimball's Journal.* Salt Lake City UT: Juvenile Instruction Office, 1882.

Kimbrough, Emily. *The Innocents from Indiana.* New York: Harper Bros., 1950.

Kimmel, Douglas C. *Adulthood and Aging.* New York: John Wiley, c.1974.

Kincaid, Nancy. *Crossing Blood.* New York: G. P. Putnam's Sons, c.1992.

Kindscher, Kelly. *Edible Wild Plants of the Prairie.* Lawrence KS: Univ. Press KS, c.1987.

Kiner, Henry L. *History of Henry County, Illinois.* Chicago: Pioneer, 1910. 2 vols.

King, Benjamin. *Ben King's Verse.* Ed. by Nixon Waterman. 2d ed. Chicago: Forbes, 1898.

King, Caroline Howard. *When I Lived in Salem: 1822–1866.* Brattleboro VT: Stephen Daye Press, 1937.

King, Charles. *The Story of Ft. Frayne.* Chicago: F. T. Neely, c.1895.

———. *Warrior Gap.* New York: F. Tennyson Neely, c.1898.

King, Clarence. *Mountaineering in the Sierra Nevada.* Boston: James R. Osgood, 1872.

King, Edward. *The Great South.* Hartford CT: American Publishing, 1875.

King, Florence. *Southern Ladies and Gentlemen.* New York: Stein and Day, c.1975.

King, Grace Elizabeth. *Memories of a Southern Woman of Letters.* New York: Macmillan, 1932.

———. *To Find My Own Peace: Grace King in Her Journals, 1886–1910.* Ed. by Melissa Walker Heidari. Athens GA: Univ. GA Press, 2004.

King, James *A Voyage to the Pacific Ocean* SEE Cook, James

King, John. *The American Eclectic Dispensatory.* Cincinnati OH: Moore, Wilstach & Keys, 1854.

King, John et al. *King's American Dispensatory.* 18th ed., 3d rev. Cincinnati OH: Ohio Valley, 1898–1900. 2 vols.

———. *King's American Dispensatory.* 19th ed., 4th rev. Cincinnati OH: Ohio Valley, 1909. 2 vols.

King, Larry L. *The One-Eyed Man.* New York: New American Library, c.1966.

King, Lily. *The English Teacher.* New York: Atlantic Monthly Press, 2005.

King, Stephen. *Different Seasons.* New York: Signet, 1983.

———. *Four Past Midnight.* New York: Viking, c.1990.

———. *It.* New York: Viking, 1986.

———. *Needful Things.* New York: Viking, c.1991.

———. *Pet Sematary.* Garden City NY: Doubleday, 1983.

———. *Skeleton Crew.* New York: G. P. Putnam's Sons, c.1985.

———. *The Stand.* Garden City NY: Doubleday, c.1978.

King, Woodie, ed. *Black Short Story Anthology.* New York: Columbia Univ. Press, 1972.

King Arthur Flour (Firm). *Baker's Catalogue.* Norwich VT, 1998?–.

King Benny Nawahi Hot Hawaiian Guitar. Phonodisc. New York: Yazoo Records, 1985.

Kingsbury, John Merriam. *Poisonous Plants of the United States and Canada.* Englewood Cliffs NJ: Prentice-Hall, 1964.

Kingsley, John Sterling, ed. *The Riverside Natural History.* Boston: Houghton, Mifflin, c.1888. 6 vols.

———, ed. *The Standard Natural History.* Boston: S. E. Cassino, 1884–1885. 6 vols.

Kingsley, Nelson. *Diary of Nelson Kingsley.* Berkeley CA: Univ. CA, 1914.

Kingsley, Sidney. *Dead End.* New York: Random House, c.1936.

Kingsolver, Barbara. *Animal Dreams.* New York: HarperCollins, c.1990.

———. *The Bean Trees.* New York: Harper & Row, c.1988.

———. *Homeland and Other Studies.* New York: Harper & Row, 1989.

———. *Pigs in Heaven.* New York: HarperCollins, c.1993.

———. *The Poisonwood Bible.* New York: HarperCollins, c.1998.

———. *Prodigal Summer.* New York: HarperCollins, c.2000.

Kingsport Times. Kingsport TN, 1916–1980.

Kingsport Times-News. Kingsport TN, 1944–.

Kingston Daily Freeman. Kingston NY, 1878–1969.

Kingston Tribune. Kingston WI, 1946–1949?

Kinman, Benjamin T. *Kentucky Fish.* Frankfort KY: Kentucky Department of Fish and Wildlife Resources, 1993.

Kinsley Graphic. Kinsley KS, 1878–1940.

Kinzie, John H., Mrs. *Wau-Bun.* Cincinnati OH: H. W. Derby, 1856.

Kip, Leonard. *The Volcano Diggings.* New York: J. S. Redfield, 1851.

Kip, William Ingraham. *The Early Jesuit Missions in North America.* New York: Wiley and Putnam, c.1846.

Kipling, Rudyard. *Captains Courageous.* New York: Century, 1897 [1896].

Kirby, William and William Spence. *An Introduction to Entomology.* London: Longman, Hurst, Rees, Orme, and Brown, 1815–1826. 4 vols.

Kirk, Charles D. *Wooing and Warring in the Wilderness.* New York: Derby & Jackson; Louisville KY: F. A. Crump, 1860.

Kirk, Donald R. *Wild Edible Plants of the Western United States.* Healdsburg CA: Naturegraph, c.1970.

Kirke, Edmund SEE Gilmore, James Roberts

Kirkham, Samuel. *English Grammar in Familiar Lectures.* 10th ed. enlarged and improved. Rochester NY: Marshall & Dean, 1829.

Kirkland, Caroline Matilda Stansbury. *Forest Life.* New York: C. S. Francis, 1842. 2 vols.

———. *A New Home—Who'll Follow?* New York: C. S. Francis; Boston: J. H. Francis, 1839.

———. *Western Clearings.* New York: Wiley and Putnam, 1845.

Kirkland, Joseph. *Zury.* Boston: Houghton, Mifflin, 1887.

———. *Zury.* Urbana IL: Univ. IL Press, 1956. Facsimile of the 1887 ed. orig. pub. by Houghton, Mifflin, Boston.

Kirkpatrick, Zoe Merriman. *Wildflowers of the Western Plains.* Austin TX: Univ. TX Press, c.1992.

Kirksville Express and News. Kirksville MO, 1901–.

Kirkwood, F. C. *A List of the Birds of Maryland.* Baltimore MD: Deutsch Lithographing, 1895.

Kirlin, Katherine S. and Thomas M. Kirlin. *Smithsonian Folklife Cookbook.* Washington DC: Smithsonian Institution Press, 1991.

Kitchin, Edward Alexander. *Birds of the Olympic Peninsula.* Port Angeles WA: Olympic Stationers, 1949.

Kitman, Marvin. *George Washington's Expense Account.* New York: Simon & Schuster, 1970.

Kittredge, George Lyman. *The Old Farmer and His Almanack.* Cambridge MA: Harvard Univ. Press, 1924.

Klauber, Laurence Monroe. *Rattlesnakes.* Berkeley CA: Univ. CA Press, c.1956. 2 vols.

Klees, Fredric. *The Pennsylvania Dutch.* New York: Macmillan, 1950.

Klein, Daniel M. *Such Vicious Minds.* New York: St. Martin's Minotaur, 2004.

Klein, Jon. *T Bone 'n Weasel.* New York: Theatre Communications Group, c.1987.

Klein, T. E. D. *The Ceremonies.* New York: Viking Press, 1984.

Klessig, Lowell L. *Country Acres, a Guide to Buying and Managing Rural Property.* Madison WI: Univ. Wisconsin Extension, 1987.

Kline, Benjamin F. G., Jr. *Pitch Pine and Prop Timber.* Williamsport PA: Lycoming Printing, 1971.

Klinkenborg, Verlyn. *Making Hay.* New York: N. Lyons Books, c.1986.

Kluger, Marilyn. *The Wild Flavor.* New York: Coward, McCann and Geoghegan, 1973.

Knapp, Adeline. *In the Christmas Woods.* San Francisco: Stanley-Taylor, 1899.

Knapp, Horace S. *History of the Maumee Valley.* Toledo OH: Blade Mammoth, 1872.

Knapp, Mary and Herbert Knapp. *One Potato, Two Potato.* New York: W. W. Norton, c.1976.

Knapp, Samuel L. *Biographical Sketches of Eminent Lawyers, Statesmen, and Men of Letters.* Boston: Richardson and Lord, 1821.

Kneeland, Samuel. *The Wonders of the Yosemite Valley, and of California.* Boston: Alexander Moore, 1872 [c.1871].

Knibbs, Henry Herbert. *Partners of Chance.* New York: Houghton Mifflin, c.1921.

———. *Songs of the Lost Frontier.* Boston: Houghton Mifflin, 1930.

Knickerbocker, Diedrich SEE Irving, Washington

Knickerbocker, or, New-York Monthly Magazine. New York, 1833–1865.

Knight, Amelia Stewart. "Diary of Mrs. Amelia Stewart, an Oregon Pioneer of 1853." Oregon Pioneer Association *Transactions of the 56th Annual Reunion* (1928) 38–54.

Knight, Edward Henry. *Knight's American Mechanical Dictionary.* New York: Hurd and Houghton, 1876. 3 vols.

———. *Knight's New Mechanical Dictionary.* Boston: Houghton, Mifflin, 1884.

Knight, Etheridge. *Black Voices from Prison.* New York: Pathfinder Press, 1970.

Knight, Henry Cogswell. *Letters from the South and West.* Boston: Richardson and Lord, 1824.

Knight, Jacqueline E. *The Cook's Fish Guide.* New York: E. P. Dutton, 1973.

Knight, Kathleen Moore. *The Bass Derby Murder.* Garden City NY: Doubleday, c.1949.

Knight, Ora Willis. *The Birds of Maine.* Bangor ME: Printed by C. H. Glass, 1908.

———. *A List of the Birds of Maine, Showing Their Distribution by Counties and Their Status in Each County.* Augusta ME: Kennebec Journal, 1897.

Knight, Sarah Kemble. *The Journal of Madam Knight.* New York: Peter Smith, 1935.

———. *The Journals of Madam Knight and Rev. Mr. Buckingham.* New York: Wilder & Campbell, 1825.

Knipmeyer, William B. *Settlement Succession in Eastern French Louisiana.* Baton Rouge LA: LA State Univ. diss., 1956.

Knittle, Walter Allen. *Early Eighteenth Century Palatine Emigration.* Baltimore MD: Genealogical Publishing, 1965 [c.1931]. 1931 thesis Univ. PA, orig. pub. in 1937.

Knopf, Richard C., ed. *Document Transcriptions of the War of 1812 in the Northwest.* Columbus OH: Published by the Ohio Historical Society, Anthony Wayne Parkway Board, Ohio State Museum, 1957–1961. 8 vols.

Knoxville Journal. Knoxville TN, 1886–1898; 1925–1991.

Knoxville News-Sentinel. Knoxville TN, 1926–.

Koch, William E., ed. *Folklore from Kansas.* Lawrence KS: Regents Press KS, c.1980.

Kochman, Thomas, comp. *Rappin' and Stylin' Out.* Urbana IL: Univ. IL Press, c.1972.

Kodiak Daily Mirror. Kodiak AK, 1976–.

Koenigsberg, Moses. *King News.* Philadelphia: F. A. Stokes, c.1941.

Kohler Company. *Porcelain Enameled Iron Sanitary Ware.* Kohler WI, 19??–. Catalog.

Kokomo Daily Tribune. Kokomo IN, 1893–1929.

Kokomo Tribune, the Kokomo Dispatch. Kokomo IN, 1930–1966.

Kolb, Emery. *Journal.* Unpub. account of a trip down the Green and Colorado Rivers, Sept. 1911 to Jan. 1912.

Kolb, John Harrison and Edmund de S. Brunner. *A Study of Rural Society.* 4th ed. Boston: Houghton Mifflin, 1952.

Koontz, Dean Ray. *Cold Fire.* New York: Berkley Books, c.1991.

Kopman, Henry Hazlitt. *Wild Acres.* New York: E. P. Dutton, 1946.

Kornbluth, Cyril M. *The Best of C. M. Kornbluth.* New York: Ballantine Books, 1977 [c.1976].

Korson, George Gershon. *Black Rock.* Baltimore MD: Johns Hopkins Press, 1960.

———. *Coal Dust on the Fiddle.* Philadelphia: Univ. PA Press, 1943.

———. *Minstrels of the Mine Patch.* Hatboro PA: Folklore Associates, 1964. Orig. pub. in 1938 by Univ. PA Press, Philadelphia.

Kossuth County Advance. Algona IA, 1908–1958.

Kozloff, Eugene N. *Plants of Western Oregon, Washington and British Columbia.* Portland OR: Timber Press, 2005.

Krakauer, Jon. *Into the Wild.* New York: Villard, c.1996.

———. *Under the Banner of Heaven.* New York: Doubleday, 2003.

Kramer, Bertha S. *"Aunt Babette's" Cook Book.* New York: Bloch Pub., 1906 [c.1889].

Kramer, Dale. *The Heart of O. Henry.* New York: Rinehart, 1954.

Krapp, George Philip. *A Comprehensive Guide to Good English.* Chicago: Rand McNally, c.1927.

———. *The English Language in America*. New York: Century, 1925. 2 vols.

Krauss, Bob and W. P. Alexander. *Grove Farm Plantation*. Palo Alto CA: Pacific Books, 1965.

Krider, John. *Krider's Sporting Anecdotes*. Ed. by H. Milnor Klapp. Philadelphia: A. Hart, 1853.

Kriehn, Ruth. *The Fisherfolk of Jones Island*. Milwaukee WI: Milwaukee County Historical Society, c.1988.

Krochmal, Arnold et al. *A Guide to Medicinal Plants of Appalachia*. Washington DC: U.S. Forest Service, 1971.

Krohn, William Otterbein. *Practical Lessons in Psychology*. Chicago: Werner, 1895 [c.1894].

Kroll, Harry Harrison. *A Comparative Study of Upper and Lower Southern Folk Speech*. Nashville TN: George Peabody College for Teachers M.A. thesis, 1925.

———. *I Was a Share-Cropper*. Indianapolis IN: Bobbs-Merrill, c.1937.

Krutch, Joseph Wood. *More Lives than One*. New York: William Sloane Associates, c.1962.

Kuhns, Grant W. *On Surfing*. Rutland VT: Charles E. Tuttle, 1963.

Kumlien, Ludwig and N. Hollister. *The Birds of Wisconsin*. Rev. by A. W. Schorger. Madison WI: Wisconsin Society for Ornithology, 1951.

Kunz, George Frederick and Charles Hugh Stevenson. *Book of the Pearl*. New York: Century, 1908.

Kuralt, Charles. *On the Road with Charles Kuralt*. New York: G. P. Putnam's Sons, c.1985.

Kurath, Hans, ed. *The Linguistic Atlas of New England*. Providence RI: Brown Univ., 1939–1943. 3 vols.

———. *A Word Geography of the Eastern United States*. Ann Arbor MI: Univ. MI Press, 1949.

Kurath, Hans and Raven I. McDavid, Jr. *The Pronunciation of English in the Atlantic States*. Ann Arbor MI: Univ. MI Press, 1961.

Kurath, Hans et al., eds. *Middle English Dictionary*. Ann Arbor MI: Univ. MI Press, 1952–2001.

Kurz, Herman and Robert K. Godfrey. *Trees of Northern Florida*. Gainesville FL: Univ. FL Press, 1962.

Kute Kooking Klub. *K.K.K. Cook Book*. By the Kute Kooking Klub, Honey Grove, Texas. Cincinnati OH: Robert Clarke, 1894.

Kyle, Stephen. *After Shock*. New York: Warner, c.2002.

Kyne, Peter Bernard. *Captain Scraggs*. New York: Grosset & Dunlap, c.1919.

———. *The Understanding Heart*. New York: Cosmopolitan Book, 1926.

Kytle, Calvin and James Armstrong Mackay. *Who Runs Georgia?* Athens GA: Univ. GA Press, 1998.

Kytle, Elizabeth. *The Voices of Robby Wilde*. Washington DC: Seven Locks Press, c.1987.

Labbe, John T. and Vernon Goe. *Railroads in the Woods*. Berkeley CA: Howell-North, 1961.

Labov, William. *Language in the Inner City*. Philadelphia: Univ. PA Press, c.1972.

———. *The Social Stratification of English in New York City*. Washington DC: Center for Applied Linguistics, 1966.

Lackland, Thomas SEE Hill, George Canning

La Crosse Democrat. La Crosse WI, 1853–1854.

La Crosse Tribune. La Crosse WI, 1904–1917; 1950?–.

La Crosse Tribune and Leader-Press. La Crosse WI, 1917–1944.

Ladies' Companion. New York, 1834–1844.

Ladies' Home Journal. Philadelphia: Curtis Pub., 1883–.

Ladies' Repository. Cincinnati OH: J. F. Wright and L. Swormstedt; New York: G. Lane and C. B. Tippett, 1841–1876.

Ladwig, Tom. *How to Talk Dirty Like Grandad*. Little Rock AR: Rose Publishing, c.1985.

Lady Bird Johnson Wildflower Center. [v.d.]. Internet.

Lady's Home Magazine of Literature, Art and Fashion. Philadelphia, 1857–1858.

Lady's Miscellany, or, the Weekly Visitor. New York: M'Carty & White, 1810–1812.

La Farge, Oliver. *The Enemy Gods*. Boston: Houghton Mifflin, 1937.

Lafayette, Marie Joseph Paul Ives Roch Gilbert Du Motier. *Memoirs, Correspondence and Manuscripts of General Lafayette*. New York: Saunders and Otley, 1837. 3 vols.

Lafayette Advertiser. Lafayette LA, 1865–1914.

La Follette, Robert Marion. *La Follette's Autobiography*. Madison WI: Robert M. La Follette, 1913.

LAGS SEE Pederson, Lee A. *Linguistic Atlas of the Gulf States*

Lahey-Hogan, Mamie. *As I Remember It*. 1959. Unpub. memoir of life in Stevens County, KS c.1886.

Lahontan, Louis Armand de Lom d'Arce. *New Voyages to North America*. London: Printed for H. Bonwicke, T.

Goodwin, M. Wotton, B. Tooke, and S. Manship, 1703. 2 vols.

Laine, Tanner. *Cow Country*. Hereford TX: Pioneer Book, 1969.

Lait, Jack and Lee Mortimer. *New York: Confidential!* New York: Crown, 1951 [c.1948].

Lake County Citizen. Tavares FL, 1923–.

Lake County Times. Hammond IN, 1906–1933.

Lake Mills Leader. Lake Mills WI, 1882–.

Lake Park News. Lake Park IA, 1890–1975.

Lake Shore Observer. Dunkirk NY, 1885–1886.

Lake Winnipesaukee News. Pittsfield NH, 1964–1968.

Lalor, John Joseph, ed. *Cyclopaedia of Political Science*. Chicago: A. H. Andrews, 1886. 3 vols. Orig. pub. 1881–1884.

Lamar, Mirabeau Buonaparte. *Papers*. Austin TX: Texas State Library, 1921–1928. 6 vols.

Lamb, Charles. *The Letters of Charles Lamb, to Which Are Added Those of His Sister, Mary Lamb*. Ed. by E. V. Lucas. London: J. M. Dent, 1935. 3 vols.

Lamb, H. H. *Climatic History and the Future*. Princeton NJ: Princeton Univ. Press, 1985. Repr. of the 1977 ed. pub. by Methuen, London.

Lamb, Robert Byron. *The Mule in Southern Agriculture*. Berkeley CA: Univ. CA Press, 1963.

Lamb, Samuel H. *Woody Plants of the Southwest*. Santa Fe NM: Sunstone Press, c.1975.

Lambert, James Franklin and Henry J. Reinhard. *A History of Catasauqua in Lehigh County, Pennsylvania*. Allentown PA: Searle & Dressler, 1914.

Lambert, John. *Travels through Lower Canada, and the United States of North America, in the Years 1806, 1807 & 1808*. London: Richard Phillips, 1810. 3 vols.

Lambert, Marcus Bachman. *A Dictionary of the Non-English Words of the Pennsylvania-German Dialect*. Lancaster PA: The Society, 1924.

Lambert, Paul F. and Kenny A. Franks, eds. *Voices from the Oil Fields*. Norman OK: Univ. OK Press, c.1984.

Lamon, Ward Hill. *The Life of Abraham Lincoln*. Boston: James R. Osgood, 1872.

La Monte, Francesca Raimonde. *North American Game Fishes*. Garden City NY: Doubleday, Doran, 1946.

L'Amour, Louis. *Beyond the Great Snow Mountains*. New York: Bantam Books, c.1999.

———. *The Californios*. New York: Saturday Review Press, c.1974.

LAMSAS SEE McDavid, Raven I., Jr., et al. *Linguistic Atlas of the Middle and South Atlantic States*

LAMSAS Materials. 1933–1974. Unpub. material coll. during the *Linguistic Atlas of the Middle and South Atlantic States* fieldwork.

Lancaster, Massachusetts. *The Early Records of Lancaster, Massachusetts*. Ed. by Henry S. Nourse. Lancaster MA: W. J. Coulter, printer, 1884.

Lancaster Daily Eagle. Lancaster OH, 1890–1936.

Lancaster Eagle-Gazette. Lancaster OH, 1936–.

Lancaster Heritage. Weems VA, 1970–.

LANCS Checklists. c1950. Unpub. checklists from the *Linguistic Atlas of the North Central States* contributed by Raven I. McDavid, Jr.

Land, Mary. *Mary Land's Louisiana Cookery*. Baton Rouge LA: LA State Univ. Press, c.1954.

Landmark. Statesville NC, 1875–1954.

Land of Sunshine. Chicago, 1894–1901.

Landon, Fred. *Lake Huron*. Indianapolis IN: Bobbs-Merrill, 1944.

Landon, Melville De Lancey. *Eli Perkins (at Large)*. New York: J. B. Ford, 1875.

Landon, William Chauncy. *Everyday Things in American Life, 1607–1776*. New York: Charles Scribner's Sons, 1943.

Land Policy Review. Washington DC: U.S. Department of Agriculture, Bureau of Agricultural Economics, 1938–1942.

Land We Love, a Monthly Magazine Devoted to Literature, Military History, and Agriculture. Charlotte NC: J. P. Irwin & D. H. Hill, 1866–1869.

Landy, Eugene E. *The Underground Dictionary*. New York: Simon and Schuster, 1971.

LANE SEE Kurath, Hans *The Linguistic Atlas of New England*

LANE Worksheets. 1931–1933. Unpub. material from *Linguistic Atlas of New England* worksheets.

Langdon, Mary SEE Pike, Mary Hayden Green

Langford, Nathaniel Pitt. *Vigilante Days and Ways*. Boston: J. G. Cupples, 1890. 2 vols.

Langley, Adria Locke. *A Lion Is in the Streets*. Philadelphia: Blakiston, 1945.

Langley, Dorothy. *Swamp Angel*. Chicago: Academy Chicago, c.1982.

Langsdorff, Georg Heinrich von. *Voyages and Travels in Various Parts of the World, during the Years 1803, 1804, 1805, 1806, and 1807*. London: Printed for Henry Colburn, 1813–1814. 2 vols. Anon. transl.

Language. Baltimore MD: Linguistic Society of America, 1925–.

Language Variation and Change. New York: Cambridge Univ. Press, 1989–.

Lanham, Edwin. *The Paste-Pot Man*. New York: Farrar, Straus & Giroux, 1967.

———. *Thunder in the Earth*. New York: Harcourt, Brace, c.1941.

Lanier, Sidney. *Florida*. Gainesville FL: Univ. FL Press, 1973. Facsimile reproduction of 1875 ed.

———. *Poems and Poem Outlines*. Baltimore MD: Johns Hopkins Press, 1945. Centennial ed. of the works of Sidney Lanier, vol. 1.

———. *Poems of Sidney Lanier*. Ed. by his wife. New York: Charles Scribner's Sons, 1884.

———. *Tiger-Lilies*. Chapel Hill NC: Univ. NC Press, 1969 [1867].

Lanman, Charles. *Adventures in the Wilds of the United States and British American Provinces*. Philadelphia: John W. Moore, c.1856. 2 vols.

———. *Haw-ho-noo*. Philadelphia: Lippincott, Grambo, c.1850.

———. *Letters from the Alleghany Mountains*. New York: George P. Putnam, 1849.

———. *A Summer in the Wilderness*. New York: D. Appleton, 1847.

———. *A Tour to the River Saguenay, in Lower Canada*. Philadelphia: Carey and Hart, 1848.

Lanman, James H. *History of Michigan*. New York: Harper Bros., 1852.

Lantz, Peggy S. and Wendy A. Hale. *The Young Naturalist's Guide to Florida*. Sarasota FL: Pineapple Press, c.1994.

Lapham, Increase Allen. *A Geographical and Topographical Description of Wisconsin*. Milwaukee WI: P. C. Hale, 1844.

———. *Wisconsin*. 2d ed. Milwaukee WI: I. A. Hopkins; New York: Paine & Burgess, 1846.

La Porte, William Ralph. *A Handbook of Games and Programs for Church, School and Home*. New York: Abingdon Press, c.1922.

La Porte City Progress-Review. La Porte City IA, 1870?–1950?

Lappé, Frances Moore. *Diet for a Small Planet*. 10th ed. New York: Ballantine Books, 1982.

Larcom, Lucy. *A New England Girlhood*. Boston: Houghton, Mifflin, c.1889.

Lardner, Ring Wilmer. *The Big Town*. Indianapolis IN: Bobbs-Merrill, c.1921.

———. *Gullible's Travels, etc.* Indianapolis IN: Bobbs-Merrill, c.1917.

———. *How to Write Short Stories*. New York: Charles Scribner's Sons, 1924.

———. *The Love Nest and Other Stories*. New York: Charles Scribner's Sons, 1926.

———. *The Real Dope*. Indianapolis IN: Bobbs-Merrill, 1919.

———. *The Ring Lardner Reader*. New York: Charles Scribner's Sons, c.1963.

———. *What of It?* New York: Charles Scribner's Sons, c.1925.

———. *You Know Me Al*. New York: G. H. Doran, c.1916.

Larkin, Stillman Carter. *Pioneer History of Meigs County*. Columbus OH: Berlin Printing, 1908.

Larned, Augusta. *The Borderland of Country Life*. New York: Neale, 1919.

Larned, J. N. *Talks about Labor*. New York: D. Appleton, c.1876.

LaRoche, James M. *Wild Fare*. Boston: HTM Publishing, c.2007.

Larrabee, William Clark. *Rosabower*. Cincinnati OH: R. P. Thompson, 1855.

Larsen, Nella. *Passing*. New York: Alfred A. Knopf, 1929.

Larson, Kurt. *Winter Carnival (Queen)*. Lincoln NE: iUniverse, c.2002.

Las Cruces Sun-News. Las Cruces NM, 1939–.

Lasselle, Nancy Polk. *Hope Marshall*. Washington DC: H. Lasselle, 1859.

Las Vegas Mercury. Las Vegas NV, 2001–.

Latham, David F. *The Storyteller's Guide to Leona, Montana*. New York: iUniverse, 2004.

Latham, Henry. *Black and White*. London: Macmillan, 1867.

Latham, John. *A General History of Birds*. Winchester:

Printed by Jacob and Johnson for the author, 1821–1824. 10 vols.

——. *A General Synopsis of Birds.* London: Printed for Benj. White, 1781–1785. 3 vols.

——. *Supplement II to the General Synopsis of Birds.* London: Printed for Leigh, Sotheby & Son, 1801.

Latham, John H. *The Meskin Hound.* New York: Putnam, c.1958.

Latrobe, Benjamin Henry. *The Journal of Latrobe.* New York: D. Appleton, 1905.

Latrobe, Charles Joseph. *The Rambler in Mexico.* New York: Harper, 1836.

——. *The Rambler in North America, 1832–1833.* 2d ed. London: R. B. Seeley & Burnside, 1836. 2 vols.

Latter-Day Saints' Millennial Star. Liverpool, 1840–1937.

Laudonnière, René Goulaine de. *A Notable History Containing Four Voyages Made by Certain French Captains unto Florida.* Transl. from the French by Richard Hakluyt. Farnham: H. Stevens, 1964. Facsimile of the 1587 ed. printed in London.

LAUM See Allen, Harold B. *The Linguistic Atlas of the Upper Midwest*

Launspach, Sonja L. *Idaho Dialect Project.* 2000. Unpub. materials coll. in southeastern Idaho by students at ID State Univ.

Laurens, Henry. *The Papers of Henry Laurens.* Columbia SC: Published for the South Carolina Historical Society by the Univ. SC Press, 1968–2003. 16 vols.

Laurie, Joseph. *Elements of Homoeopathic Practice of Physic.* New York: William Radde, 1850.

Lavender, David Sievert. *The Big Divide.* Garden City NY: Doubleday, 1948.

La Verne Leader. La Verne CA, 1910–1982.

Lavine, Emanuel Henry. *The Third Degree.* New York: Vanguard Press, c.1930.

Law Notes. Northport NY, 1897–1946.

Lawrence, Amos. *Extracts from the Diary and Correspondence of the Late Amos Lawrence.* Boston: Gould and Lincoln, 1856 [c.1855].

Lawrence, William. *Life of Amos A. Lawrence.* Boston: Houghton Mifflin, 1889 [c.1888].

Lawrence Republican. Lawrence KS, 1857–1869.

Lawson, John. *The History of Carolina.* Raleigh NC: O. H. Perry, Printed by Strother & Marcom, 1860. Orig. pub. in 1714 for W. Taylor, London entitled *A New Voyage to Carolina.*

——. *A New Voyage to Carolina.* Chapel Hill NC: Univ. NC Press, 1967. Orig. pub. in 1709, London.

Lawson, William Pinkney. *The Log of a Timber Cruiser.* New York: Duffield, 1915.

Laxalt, Robert. *Sweet Promised Land.* New York: Harper & Row, c.1957.

Lazarus, M. Edgeworth. *Comparative Psychology.* New York: Fowlers & Wells, 1851.

Lea, Elizabeth Ellicot. *Domestic Cookery.* Ed. by William Woys Weaver. Philadelphia: Univ. PA Press, 1982. Repr. of the 5th ed. of *Domestic Cookery* pub. in 1853 by Cushings and Bailey, Baltimore MD.

Leach, MacEdward, ed. *The Ballad Book.* New York: A. S. Barnes, c.1955.

Leacock, John. *The Fall of British Tyranny.* Philadelphia: Printed by Styner and Cist, 1776.

Leadbitter, Mike and Eddie Shuler. *From the Bayou: the Story of Goldband Records.* Bexhill-on-Sea England: Blues Unlimited, 1969.

League of American Wheelmen Bulletin and Good Roads. Boston: League of American Wheelmen, 1895–1899.

League of Women Voters of Massachusetts. *Massachusetts State Government.* 2d ed. Cambridge MA: Harvard Univ. Press, 1970.

Leary, James P., comp., ed. *So Ole Says to Lena.* 2d ed. Madison WI: Univ. WI Press, c.2001.

——. *Wisconsin Folklore.* Madison WI: Univ. WI Press, c.1998.

Leavenworth Evening Bulletin. Leavenworth KS, 1862–1869.

Lebofsky, Dennis Stanley. *Lexicon of the Philadelphia Metropolitan Area.* Princeton NJ: Princeton Univ. unpub. PhD thesis, 1970.

Lechford, Thomas. *Plain Dealing.* London: Printed by W. E. and I. G. for Nath. Butter, 1642.

Leckie, Robert. *The March to Glory.* Cleveland OH: World Pub., 1960.

LeCompte, Nolan Philip. *The Word Atlas of Lafourche Parish and Grand Isle, Louisiana.* Baton Rouge LA: LA State Univ. diss., 1967.

Le Connor, Hans Patrick See Bowman, Jacob L.

Lederer, Richard M. *Colonial American English.* Essex CT: Verbatim Book, c.1985.

Ledger. Lakeland FL, 1967–.

Ledger. Warren PA, 1888–1890.

Ledger-Star. Norfolk VA, 1876–.

Lee, Alfred E. *History of the City of Columbus, Capital of Ohio.* New York: Munsell, 1892. 2 vols.

Lee, Charles. *The Lee Papers . . . 1754–[1811].* New York: Printed for the New York Historical Society, 1872–1875. 4 vols.

Lee, Daniel and J. H. Frost. *Ten Years in Oregon.* New York: Printed for the authors, by J. Collord, Printer, 1844.

Lee, Day Kellogg. *Summerfield.* Auburn NY: Derby and Miller, 1852 [c.1851].

Lee, Eliza Buckminster. *Delusion, or the Witch of New England.* Boston: Hilliard, Gray, 1840.

Lee, Harper. *To Kill a Mockingbird.* Philadelphia: Lippincott, 1960.

——. *To Kill a Mockingbird.* New York: Popular Library, 1962. Orig. pub. in 1960 by Lippincott, Philadelphia.

Lee, Jack H. *Powder River Let 'er Buck.* Boston: Christopher Publishing, c.1930.

Lee, James. *An Introduction to Botany.* London: Printed for J. and R. Tonson, 1760.

Lee, J. Edward and Ron Chepesiuk, eds. *South Carolina in the Civil War.* Jefferson NC: McFarland, c.2000.

Lee, Jesse. *A Short History of the Methodists.* Baltimore MD: Magill and Clime, 1810.

Lee, John D. *A Mormon Chronicle.* San Marino CA: Huntington Library, 1955. 2 vols.

Lee, N. K. M. *The Cook's Own Book, Being a Complete Culinary Encyclopedia Comprehending All Valuable Receipts for Cooking Meat, Fish, and Fowl, and Composing Every Kind of Soup, Gravy, Pastry, Preserves, Essences, etc. That Have Been Published or Invented during the Last Twenty Years.* Boston: Munroe and Francis, 1832.

Lee, William Storrs. *Stagecoach North.* New York: Macmillan, 1941.

Leesville Leader. Leesville LA, 1898–.

Lefroy, J. Henry. *The Historye of the Bermudaes or Summer Islands.* New York: Burt Franklin, 1964. Facsimile of the 1882 ed. pub. by the Hakluyt Society, London.

Le Grand Reporter. Le Grand IA, 1909–.

Le Guin, Magnolia Wynn. *A Home-Concealed Woman.* Ed. by Charles A. Le Guin. Athens GA: Univ. GA Press, c.1990.

Lehrer, Jim. *Kick the Can.* New York: G. P. Putnam's Sons, c.1988.

Leigh, Frances Butler. *Ten Years on a Georgia Plantation since the War.* New York: Negro Universities Press, 1969. Orig. pub. in 1883 by R. Bentley & Sons, London.

Leighton, Caroline C. *Life at Puget Sound.* Boston: Lee and Shepard, 1884 [c.1883].

Leighton News. Leighton AL, 1890–1892.

Leisenring, James E. *The Art of Tying the Wet Fly.* New York: Dodd, Mead, 1944 [c.1941].

Leisure Hour. London, 1852–1905.

Leisy, James F., comp. *The Folk Song Abecedary.* New York: Hawthorn Books, c.1966.

Leland, Charles Godfrey. *The Breitmann Ballads.* Complete ed. London: Trubner, 1871.

——. *The Egyptian Sketch Book.* New York: Hurd and Houghton, 1874 [c.1873].

——. *Hans Breitmann in Church.* Philadelphia: T. B. Peterson & Bros., c.1870.

——. *Memoirs.* New York: D. Appleton, 1893.

Lennox, Mary See Cook, Mary Louise Redd

Lenski, Lois. *Texas Tomboy.* Philadelphia: J. B. Lippincott, c.1950.

Leonard, Elmore. *Maximum Bob.* New York: Delacorte Press, c.1991.

——. *Unknown Man No. 89.* New York: Delacorte Press, c.1977.

Leonard, Jonathan Norton. *American Cooking.* New York: Time-Life Books, 1971.

Leonard, Leah H. *Jewish Cookery.* New York: Crown, 1986 [c.1949].

Leonard, Zenas. *Narrative of the Adventures of Zenas Leonard.* Clearfield PA: D. W. Moore, 1839.

Leopold, Aldo. *A Sand County Almanac, and Sketches Here and There.* New York: Oxford Univ. Press, 1949.

Le Page du Pratz. *Histoire de la Louisiane.* Paris: De Bure, 1758.

——. *The History of Louisiana.* London: T. Becket & P. A. De Hondt, 1763. 2 vols. Anon. transl.

Lesley, Craig. *River Song.* Boston: Houghton Mifflin, 1989.

——. *The Sky Fisherman.* Boston: Houghton Mifflin, c.1995.

——. *Storm Riders.* New York: Picador USA, c.2000.

——. *Winterkill.* Boston: Houghton Mifflin, 1984.

Leslie, Eliza. *Directions for Cookery in Its Various Branches.* 20th ed., with improvements, suppl. receipts, and a new app. Philadelphia: Carey & Hart, 1844.

——. *Seventy-Five Receipts for Pastry, Cakes, and Sweetmeats.* 20th ed. enlarged. New York: C. S. Francis, 1827.

Leslie, Frank, Mrs. *California.* New York: G. W. Carleton; London: S. Low, Son, 1877.

Leslie, Robert Franklin. *High Trails West.* New York: Crown, c.1967.

Leslie's Monthly Magazine See *American Magazine*

Lester, Charles Edwards. *Chains and Freedom.* New York: E. S. Arnold, 1839.

Lester, John Erastus. *The Atlantic to the Pacific.* Boston: Shepard and Gill, 1873.

Lester, Julius. *To Be a Slave.* New York: Dial Press, c.1968.

Le Sueur, Meridel. *North Star Country.* New York: Duell, Sloan & Pearce, 1945.

Letters of Delegates to Congress, 1774–1789. Washington DC: Library of Congress, 1976–1994.

Lettuce, Miscellaneous Salad Crops. Scranton PA: International Textbook, c.1913–1914.

Leuvense Bijdragen. Leuven, Belgium, 1896–.

The Leverett Letters. Ed. by Frances Wallace Taylor, Catherine Taylor Matthews and J. Tracy Power. Columbia SC: Univ. SC Press, 2000.

Levin, Meyer. *The Old Bunch.* New York: Simon and Schuster, 1958. Orig. pub. in 1937 by Viking Press, New York.

Levine, Shar and Vicki Scudamore. *Marbles.* New York: Sterling Publishing, c.1998.

Levinge, Richard George Augustus. *Echoes from the Backwoods.* London: H. Colburn, 1846. 2 vols.

Levinson, Leonard Lewis. *The Complete Book of Pickles and Relishes.* New York: Hawthorn Books, c.1965.

Levy, Esther Jacobs. *Jewish Cookery Book on Principles of Economy.* New York: Arno Press, 1975. Repr. of the 1871 ed. pub. by W. S. Turner, Philadelphia.

Lewis, Alfred Henry. *The Apaches of New York.* New York: G. W. Dillingham, c.1912.

——. *The Boss.* New York: A. S. Barnes, 1903.

——. *Sandburrs.* 2d ed. New York: Frederick A. Stokes, c.1900.

——. *Wolfville.* 12th ed. New York: Frederick A. Stokes, c.1897.

——. *Wolfville Days.* New York: Frederick A. Stokes, c.1902.

Lewis, Beverly. *The Redemption of Sarah Cain.* Minneapolis MN: Bethany House, c.2000.

Lewis, Charles Bertrand. *Brother Gardner's Lime-Kiln Club.* Upper Saddle River NJ: Literature House, 1970 [c.1883].

——. *Quad's Odds.* Detroit MI: R. D. S. Tyler, 1875.

——. *Sawed-Off Sketches.* New York: G. W. Carleton, 1884.

Lewis, Edward J. "Diary of a Pike's Peak Gold Seeker in 1860." *Colorado Magazine.* (1937) 14.201–19; 15.20–33.

Lewis, Elisha Jarrett. *The American Sportsman.* Philadelphia: J. B. Lippincott, 1857.

Lewis, Faye Cashatt. *Nothing to Make a Shadow.* Ames IA: IA State Univ. Press, 1971.

Lewis, Gerald E. *How to Talk Yankee.* Thorndike ME: Thorndike Press, c.1979.

Lewis, Henry Clay. *Odd Leaves from the Life of a Louisiana Swamp Doctor.* Upper Saddle River NJ: Literature House, 1969. Pub. in 1843 by Carey and Hart.

Lewis, John. *New Hope.* New York: Bunce & Bros., 1855. Orig. pub. in 1844 by Harper & Bros., New York under the title *Young Kate.*

Lewis, John Delaware. *Across the Atlantic.* London: George Earle, 1851.

Lewis, Kathleen Ann. *Family Reunion.* Lebanon PA: Printed by Sowers Printing, 1979.

Lewis, Meriwether and William Clark. *History of the Expedition under the Command of Captains Lewis and Clark.* Philadelphia: Bradford and Inskeep, 1814. 2 vols.

——. *History of the Expedition under the Command of Lewis and Clark.* Ed. by Elliott Coues. New York: Dover Publications, 1965. 3 vols.

——. *Original Journals of the Lewis and Clark Expedition.* Ed. by Reuben Gold Thwaites. New York: Dodd, Mead, 1904–1905. 8 vols.

Lewis, Meriwether and John Ordway. *The Journals of Captain Meriwether Lewis and Sergeant John Ordway.* Madison WI: State Historical Society of Wisconsin, 1965 [c.1916].

Lewis, Oscar. *High Sierra Country.* New York: Duell, Sloan & Pearce, 1955.

Lewis, Sinclair. *Arrowsmith.* New York: Harcourt, Brace, 1925.

——. *Babbitt.* New York: Harcourt, Brace, c.1922.

——. *Babbitt.* New York: Grosset & Dunlap, 1924 [c.1922].

——. *Bethel Merriday.* New York: Doubleday, Doran, 1940.

——. *Cass Timberlane.* New York: Random House, c.1945.

——. *Elmer Gantry.* New York: Harcourt, Brace, c.1927.

——. *Free Air.* New York: Grosset & Dunlap, c.1919.

——. *Gideon Planish.* New York: Random House, c.1943.

——. *The Job.* New York: Harper & Bros., c.1917.

——. *Kingsblood Royal.* New York: Grosset & Dunlap, c.1947.

——. *Main Street.* New York: Harcourt, Brace & Howe, 1920.

——. *The Man Who Knew Coolidge.* New York: Harcourt, Brace, c.1928.

——. *Our Mr. Wrenn.* New York: Harper & Bros., 1914.

——. *The Prodigal Parents.* New York: P. F. Collier & Son, c.1938.

——. *The Trail of the Hawk.* New York: Harper, 1915.

——. *World So Wide.* New York: Random House, c.1951.

Lewis, W. *Commercium Philosophico-Technicum.* London: H. Baldwin, 1763.

Lewis, William M. *The People's Practical Poultry Book.* 5th ed. New York: American News, c.1871.

Lewiston Daily Sun. Lewiston-Auburn ME, 1893–.

Lewiston Evening Journal. Lewiston ME, 1866–1979.

Lexington Herald. Lexington KY, 1904–1983.

Lexington Herald and the Lexington Leader. Lexington KY, 1965–.

Lexis-Nexis Academic Universe SEE Lexis-Nexis. Legal Research

Lexis-Nexis. Legal Research. *Federal Case Law: Court of Appeals.* [v.d.]. Internet.

——. *Patent Files.* [v.d.]. Internet.

——. *State Case Law.* [v.d.]. Internet.

——. *State Codes.* [v.d.]. Internet.

——. *U.S. Supreme Court Cases.* [v.d.]. Internet.

Libby, Gretchen L. and Harold C. Bryant. *Bird Study for California Schools.* Sacramento CA: CA State Printing Office, 1928.

Liberator. Boston, 1831–1865.

Liberator. New York: Afro-American Research Institute, 1961–1971.

Liberty Lobby. *J. William Fulbright: Freedom's Judas-Goat.* Washington DC: Liberty Lobby, c.1965.

Liberty News. Liberty NY, 1950–.

Library of Congress. *American Memory: a Group of Online Collections Produced by the National Digital Library Program at the Library of Congress.* [v.d.]. Internet.

——. *American Memory: America from the Great Depression to World War II. Photographs from the Farm Security Administration-Office of War Information Collection, 1935–1945.* 1935–1945. Internet.

——. *American Memory: American Time Capsule: Three Centuries of Broadsides and Other Printed Ephemera.* 1600–. Internet.

——. *American Memory: America Singing: Nineteenth Century Song Sheets.* 1800–1900. Internet.

——. *American Memory: Born in Slavery: Slave Narratives from the Federal Writers' Project.* 1936–1938. Internet.

——. *American Memory: Buckaroos in Paradise: Ranching Culture in Northern Nevada.* 1945–1985. Internet.

——. *American Memory: California as I Saw It: First-Person Narratives of California's Early Years.* 1849–1900. Internet.

——. *American Memory: Film Collections.* 1870–1982. Internet.

——. *American Memory: George Washington Papers.* 1741–1799. Internet.

——. *American Memory: History of the American West, 1860–1920.* 1860–1950. Internet.

——. *American Memory: Omaha Indian Music.* 1895–1999. Internet.

——. *American Memory: Photographs from the Detroit Publishing Company.* 1880–1920. Internet.

——. *American Memory: Prairie Settlement.* 1861–1912. Internet.

——. *American Memory: Taking the Long View. Panoramic Photographs.* 1851–1991. Internet.

——. *American Memory: Tending the Commons: Folklife and Landscape in Southern West Virginia.* 1992–1997. Internet.

——. *American Memory: Traveling Culture: Circuit Chautauqua in the Twentieth Century.* 1890–1940. Internet.

——. *American Memory: We'll Sing to Abe Our Song.* 1859–1909. Internet.

——. *American Memory: WPA Life Histories.* 1936–1940. Internet.

Library of Congress. Copyright Office. *Catalog of Copyright Entries.* Washington DC, 1906–1946.

Library of Universal Knowledge. New York: American Book Exchange, 1880–1881. 15 vols.

Lieb, Sandra R. *Mother of the Blues.* Amherst MA: Univ. MA Press, 1981.

Lieber, Francis. *Letters to a Gentleman in Germany, Written after a Trip from Philadelphia to Niagara.* Philadelphia: Carey, Lea & Blanchard, 1834.

——. *A Popular Essay on Subjects of Penal Law.* Philadelphia: Published by Order of the Society, 1838.

Liebling, Abbott Joseph. *Back Where I Came From.* New York: Sheridan House, c.1938.

——. *The Road Back to Paris.* Garden City NY: Doubleday, Doran, 1944.

Life. New York, 1883–1972; 1978–.

Life: a Monthly Magazine of Christian Metaphysics. Kansas City MO, 1902–1907?

Life and Adventures of Sam Bass, the Notorious Union Pacific and Texas Train Robber. Dallas TX: Dallas Commercial Steam Print, 1878.

The Life of Andrew Jackson. Philadelphia: T. K. Greenbank, 1834.

Liggio, Joe and Ann Orto Liggio. *Wild Orchids of Texas.* Austin TX: Univ. TX Press, c.1999.

Lighter, Jonathan E. *Random House Historical Dictionary of American Slang.* New York: Random House, 1994–.

Lightfoot, John. *Flora Scotica.* London: Printed for B. White, 1777. 2 vols.

Ligon, James Stokley. *New Mexico Birds and Where to Find Them.* Albuquerque NM: Univ. NM Press, c.1961.

Ligonier Echo. Ligonier PA, 1888–.

Lillard, David Hicks. *Lillard: a Family of Colonial Virginia.* 2d ed. Greenville SC: Southern Historical Press, 1991. 2 vols.

Lillard, John F. B., ed. *Poker Stories.* New York: Francis P. Harper, 1896.

Lillard, Richard Gordon. *Desert Challenge, an Interpretation of Nevada.* New York: A. A. Knopf, 1942.

Lillie, Arthur. *Madame Blavatsky and Her Theosophy.* London: Swan Sonnenschein, 1895.

Lily Year Book. London: Royal Horticultural Society, 1932–1971.

Lima Daily News. Lima OH, 1897–1920.

Lima Daily Times. Lima OH, 1889–1893.

Lima Democratic Times. Lima OH, 1882–1889.

Lima News. Lima OH, 1898–1899; 1926–.

Lima Sunday News. Lima OH, 1916–.

Lima Times-Democrat. Lima OH, 1901–1920.

Lime Springs Herald. Lime Springs IA, 1932–.

Limestone Democrat. Athens AL, 1891–1968.

Lincoff, Gary H. *The Audubon Society Field Guide to North American Mushrooms.* New York: Knopf, c.1981.

Lincoln, Abraham. *Collected Works.* Ed. by Roy P. Basler. New Brunswick NJ: Rutgers Univ. Press, 1953–1955. 9 vols. and 1974 suppl.

Lincoln, Almira H. *Familiar Lectures on Botany.* 5th ed. rev. and enlarged. Hartford CT: F. J. Huntington, 1836.

Lincoln, Anna T. *Wilmington, Delaware.* Rutland VT: Tuttle Publishing, c.1937.

Lincoln, Benjamin. "Journal of a Treaty Held in 1793, with the Indian Tribes North-West of the Ohio by Commissioners of the United States." Massachusetts Historical Society *Collections.* (1836) 3d ser., 5.109–76.

Lincoln, Charles Eric. *The Avenue, Clayton City.* New York: William Morrow, c.1988.

Lincoln, Frederick Charles. *The Migration of American Birds.* New York: Doubleday, Doran, 1939.

Lincoln, Joseph Crosby. *Cape Cod Stories.* New York: A. L. Burt, c.1907.

——. *Cape Cod Yesterdays.* Boston: Little, Brown, c.1935.

——. *Cap'n Warren's Wards.* New York: D. Appleton, 1912. Orig. pub. in 1911 by D. Appleton, New York.

——. *Cy Whittakers Place.* New York: Grosset & Dunlap, 1908.

——. *Keziah Coffin.* New York: Grosset & Dunlap, 1909.

——. *Mary-'Gusta.* New York: D. Appleton, 1916.

——. *Mr. Pratt.* New York: A. S. Barnes, 1906.

——. *Partners of the Tide.* New York: A. L. Burt, 1905.

——. *The Rise of Roscoe Paine.* New York: A. L. Burt, c.1912.

——. *Rugged Water.* New York: D. Appleton, 1924.

——. *Shavings.* New York: A. L. Burt, c.1918.

——. *Thankful's Inheritance.* New York: D. Appleton, 1915.

Lincoln, Mary Johnson. *Mrs. Lincoln's Boston Cook Book.* Boston: Roberts Bros., 1884 [c.1883].

Lincoln, Rufus. *Papers of Captain Rufus Lincoln of Wareham, Mass.* [s.l.]: Privately printed, 1903.

Lincoln, Solomon. *History of the Town of Hingham, Plymouth County, Massachusetts.* Hingham MA: Caleb Gill, Jr. and Farmer and Brown, 1827.

Lincoln County News. Damariscotta ME, 2000–.

Lincoln Daily Star. Lincoln NE, 1902–1921.

Lincoln Evening Journal and Nebraska State Journal. Lincoln NE, 1951–1973.

Lincoln Evening News. Lincoln NE, 1891–1912.

Lincoln Star. Lincoln NE, 1921–1995.

Lincoln Sunday Star. Lincoln NE, 1921–1931.

Lindahl, Carl et al., eds. *Swapping Stories.* Jackson MS: Univ. Press MS; Baton Rouge: LA Division of the Arts, c.1997.

Lindley, Jacob. "Expedition to Detroit, 1793." Michigan. Historical Commission *Michigan Historical Collections.* (1892) 17.565–632.

Lindley, John and Joseph Paxton. *Paxton's Flower Garden.* London: Bradbury and Evans, 1850–1853. 3 vols.

Lindley, John and Thomas Moore, eds. *The Treasury of Botany.* London: Longmans, Green, 1866. 2 vols.

——. *The Treasury of Botany.* Rev. 2d ed. London: Longmans, Green, 1874. 2 vols.

——, eds. *The Treasury of Botany.* New and rev. ed. London: Longmans, Green, 1889. 2 vols.

Lindley, Walter and J. P. Widney. *California of the South.* New York: C. Appleton, 1888.

Lindsay, Lowell and Diana Lindsay. *The Anza-Borrego Desert Region.* 5th ed. Berkeley CA: Wilderness Press, 2006.

Lindsay, Mary. *History of the Grassy Balds in Great Smoky Mountains National Park.* Gatlinburg TN: National Park Service, Southeast Regional Office, Uplands Field Research Laboratory, 1976.

Lindsay, Nicholas Vachel. *Adventures While Preaching the Gospel of Beauty.* New York: Mitchell, Kennerley, 1914.

Lindsey, David L. *A Cold Mind.* New York: Harper & Row, c.1983.

Lindsley, Abraham B. *Love and Friendship, or, Yankee Notions.* New York: D. Longworth, 1809.

Linebarger, Paul Myron Wentworth. *Bugle Rhymes from France.* Chicago: Mid-Nation, 1918.

LANCS Checklists. c1950. Unpub. checklists from the *Linguistic Atlas of the North Central States* contributed by Raven I. McDavid, Jr.

LANE Worksheets. 1931–1933. Unpub. material from *Linguistic Atlas of New England* worksheets.

Linguistic Atlas Projects. [v.d.]. Internet.

Linklater, Eric. *Juan in America.* London: J. Cape; New York: Jonathan Cape & Harrison Smith, c.1931.

Linn, John Blair, Collator. *Annals of Buffalo Valley, Pennsylvania, 1755–1855.* Harrisburg PA: Lane S. Hart, 1877.

Linnaean Street. [v.d.]. Internet.

Linné, Carl von. *A General System of Nature, through the Three Grand Kingdoms of Animals, Vegetables, and Minerals.* Transl. by William Turton. London: Lackington, Allen, 1806. 7 vols.

Linscott, Eloise Hubbard. *Folk Songs of Old New England.* New York: Macmillan, 1939.

Linsdale, Jean Myron. *The California Ground Squirrel.* Berkeley CA: Univ. CA Press, 1946.

Linzey, Donald W. and Michael J. Clifford. *Snakes of Virginia.* Charlottesville VA: Univ. Press VA, c1981.

Lipman, Jean Herzberg and Alice Winchester. *The Flowering of American Folk Art 1776–1876.* New York: Viking Press, 1974.

Lippincott's SEE *Lippincott's Magazine, Lippincott's Magazine of Literature, Science and Education, Lippincott's Magazine of Popular Literature and Science,* and *Lippincott's Monthly Magazine*

Lippincott's Magazine. Philadelphia, 1881–1885.

Lippincott's Magazine of Literature, Science and Education. Philadelphia, 1868–1870.

Lippincott's Magazine of Popular Literature and Science. Philadelphia, 1871–1880.

Lippincott's Monthly Magazine. Philadelphia, 1886–1914.

Lippincott's Pronouncing Gazetteer. Ed. by J. Thomas and T. Baldwin. Philadelphia: J. B. Lippincott, 1856 [c.1855].

Lippmann, Julie Mathilde. *Martha-by-the-Day.* New York: Henry Holt, 1912.

Lipski, John M. *The Language of the Isleños.* Baton Rouge LA: LA State Univ. Press, c.1990.

Lipton, Lawrence. *The Holy Barbarians*. New York: Julian Messner, c.1959.

Listener and B.B.C. Television Review. London: British Broadcasting Corporation, 1929–.

Litchfield, Israel. "Diary." In: Litchfield, Wilford Jacob, comp., *The Litchfield Family in America*, 1906, 1.5.313–51.

Litchfield, Wilford Jacob, comp. *The Litchfield Family in America*. Southbridge MA: W. J. Litchfield, 1901–1906.

Literary and Philosophical Society of New York. *Transactions*. New York: Van Winkle & Wiley, 1815–1825.

Literary and Scientific Repository, and Critical Review. New York: Wiley & Halsted, 1820–1822.

Literary Cadet and Rhode-Island Statesman. Providence RI, 1827–1829.

Literary Digest. New York: Funk & Wagnalls, 1890–1938.

Literary Journal. Schenectady NY, 1835.

Literary Magazine and American Register. Philadelphia, 1803–1807.

Literary World. New York: Osgood, 1847–1853.

Littell's Living Age. Boston, 1844–1896.

Little, Benilde. *Good Hair*. New York: Simon & Schuster, c.1996.

Little, Elbert Luther. *The Audubon Society Field Guide to North American Trees, Eastern Region*. New York: Alfred A. Knopf, c.1980.

———. *The Audubon Society Field Guide to North American Trees, Western Region*. New York: Alfred A. Knopf, c.1980.

———. *Check List of Native and Naturalized Trees of the United States (Including Alaska)*. Washington DC: Forest Service, 1953.

———. *Checklist of United States Trees (Native and Naturalized)*. Washington DC: Forest Service, 1979.

Little, Malcolm. *The Autobiography of Malcolm X*. New York: Grove Press, 1965.

Little, Van Allen. *General and Applied Entomology*. 3d ed. New York: Harper & Row, c.1972.

Little Corporal. Chicago, 1865–1875.

Littlefield, Sophie. *A Bad Day for Sorry*. New York: Minotaur Books, 2009.

Littleton, Mark SEE Kennedy, John Pendleton

Lively Arts: an Internet Cultural Magazine. 2001?–. Internet.

Livermore, Mary Ashton Rice. *The Story of My Life*. Hartford CT: A. D. Worthington, 1897.

Livermore, Samuel Truesdale. *History of Block Island, Rhode Island*. Reproduced and enhanced by the Block Island Committee for Republication. Block Island RI: Block Island Tercentenary Anniversary, 1961 [1877].

Livestock Weekly. San Angelo TX, 1977–.

Living Age. New York, 1844–1941.

Living Museum. Springfield IL: Illinois State Museum, 1939–.

Livingston, A. D. *Complete Fish & Game Cookbook*. Rev. ed. Mechanicsburg PA: Stackpole Books, c.1996. Orig. pub. in 1989 under the title *Outdoor Life's Complete Fish & Game Cookbook*.

Living Wilderness. Washington DC: Wilderness Society, 1935–.

Lloyd, Elwood. *Your Dollars and Mine*. Los Angeles: Los Angeles Evening Herald, 1924.

Lloyd, Francis Bartow. *Sketches of Country Life*. Birmingham AL: Press of Roberts & Son, 1898.

Lloyd, John Uri. *Warwick of the Knobs*. New York: Dodd, Mead, 1901.

Lloyd, John Uri and Curtis Gates Lloyd. *Drugs and Medicines of North America*. Cincinnati OH: J. U. Lloyd & C. G. Lloyd, 1884–1887. 2 vols.

Lloyd, Nelson. *The Chronic Loafer*. New York: J. F. Taylor, 1900.

Loch, Wayne and Melvin Bradley. *Determining Age of Horses by Their Teeth*. Columbia MO: Univ. MO, 2000.

Locke, David Ross. *The Struggles (Social, Financial and Political) of Petroleum V. Nasby*. Boston: I. N. Richardson, 1872.

———. *Swingin Round the Cirkle*. Boston: Lee & Shepard, 1867 [c.1866].

Lockett, Samuel H. *Second Annual Report of the Topographical Survey of Louisiana*. New Orleans LA: Printed at the Office of the Republican, 1871.

Lockhart, Caroline. *The Fighting Shepherdess*. Boston: Small, Maynard, c.1919.

Lockhart Post-Register. Lockhart TX, 1916–.

Lockwood, Frank Cummins. *Pioneer Days in Arizona, from the Spanish Occupation to Statehood*. New York: Macmillan, 1932.

Lockwood, Mark. *Basic Texas Birds*. Austin TX: Univ. TX, 2007.

Lockwood, Thomas P. *A Geography of South Carolina*. Charleston SC: J. S. Burges, 1832.

Locomotive Firemen's Magazine. Indianapolis IN, 1876–1900.

Loehr, Rodney C., ed. *Minnesota Farmers' Diaries*. St. Paul MN: Minnesota Historical Society, 1939.

Loewer, H. Peter. *Gardens of North Carolina*. Mechanicsburg PA: Stackpole, 2007.

Logan, Ben. *The Land Remembers*. New York: Viking Press, c.1975.

Logan, Carolyn, ed. *Counterbalance*. Peterborough, Ontario: Broadview Press, 1997.

Logan, Milla Zenovich. *Cousins and Commissars*. New York: C. Scribner's Sons, 1949.

Logan, Olive. *Before the Footlights and behind the Scenes*. Philadelphia: Parmelee, 1870.

———. *The Mimic World and Public Exhibitions*. Philadelphia: New-World, 1871.

Logansport Morning Press. Logansport IN, 1921–1926.

Logansport Press. Logansport IN, 1926–1966.

Log Cabin Chronicles. 1996?–. Internet.

Logging by Steam. New York: Lidgerwood Manufacturing Logging Machinery Department, 1905.

Lomax, Alan, comp. *Hard Hitting Songs for Hard Hit People*. New York: Oak Publications, 1967.

———. *Mister Jelly Roll*. New York: Duell, Sloan and Pearce, 1950.

———. *Mister Jelly Roll*. 2d ed. Berkeley CA: Univ. CA Press, 1973.

———. *The Penguin Book of American Folk Songs*. Baltimore MD: Penguin Books, c.1964.

———. *The Rainbow Sign*. New York: Duell, Sloan and Pearce, 1959.

Lomax, John Avery. *Adventures of a Ballad Hunter*. New York: Macmillan, 1947.

———, comp. *Cowboy Songs and Other Frontier Ballads*. New and rev. ed. New York: Macmillan, 1918. Orig. pub. in 1916 by Sturgis & Walton, New York.

———, comp. *Cowboy Songs and Other Frontier Ballads*. New ed. with additions. New York: Macmillan, 1931 [c.1916].

Lomax, John Avery and Alan Lomax, comps. *American Ballads and Folk Songs*. New York: Macmillan, 1934.

———, comps. *Negro Folk Songs as Sung by Lead Belly*. New York: Macmillan, 1936.

Lommasson, Robert C. *Nebraska Wild Flowers*. Lincoln NE: Univ. NE Press, 1973.

London, George and Henry Wise. *The Retir'd Gard'ner*. London: Printed for Jacob Tonson, 1706. A rev. transl. of 'Le Jardinier Solitaire' by François Gentil, and 'Le Jardinier Fleuriste et Historiographe' by Louis Liger.

London, Jack. *Before Adam*. New York: Macmillan, 1907 [c.1906].

———. *Burning Daylight*. New York: Macmillan, 1910.

———. *A Daughter of the Snows*. New York: Grosset & Dunlap, c.1902.

———. *Letter from Jack London*. New York: Odyssey Press, c.1965.

———. *The Little Lady of the Big House*. New York: Grosset & Dunlap, c.1916.

———. *The Road*. New York: Macmillan, 1907.

———. *The Star Rover*. New York: Grosset & Dunlap, c.1914. Text is the 1917 repr. Orig. pub. in *American Sunday Monthly Magazine*, New York, 1914–1915.

———. *The Valley of the Moon*. New York: Grosset & Dunlap, 1913.

———. *White Fang*. New York: Macmillan, 1966 [c.1905].

London Journal of Botany. London, 1842–1848.

London Magazine and Monthly Chronologer SEE *London Magazine, or, Gentleman's Monthly Intelligencer*

London Magazine, or, Gentleman's Monthly Intelligencer. London, 1732–1785.

London v. New York, by an English Workman. London: Bosworth & Harrison, 1859.

Long, Edward. *The History of Jamaica*. London: T. Lowndes, 1774. 3 vols.

Long, John. *Voyages and Travels of an Indian Interpreter and Trader*. London: Printed for the Author; Sold by Robson, 1791.

———. *Voyages and Travels of an Indian Interpreter and Trader*. Toronto: Coles Pub., c.1971. Repr. of the 1791 ed. printed for the author, sold by Robson, London.

Long, John Dixon. *Pictures of Slavery in Church and State*. 2d ed. Philadelphia: Published by the Author, c.1857.

Long, Joseph W. *American Wild-Fowl Shooting*. New York: J. B. Ford, 1874.

Long, Stephen Harriman. "Journal." *Minnesota Historical Society Collections*. (1889) 2.9–83.

Long, Theodore Kepner. *Forty Letters to Carson Long, 1904–10*. 2d ed. New Bloomfield PA: Carson Long Institute, 1933.

Long, William Joseph. *Little Brother to the Bear and Other Animal Stories*. Boston: Ginn, 1903.

———. *School of the Woods*. Boston: Ginn, 1902.

Long Beach Independent. Long Beach CA, 1938–1957.

Longfellow, Henry Wadsworth. *Evangeline*. Boston: William D. Ticknor, 1847.

———. *The Golden Legend*. Boston: Ticknor, Reed, and Fields, 1851.

———. *Kavanagh, a Tale*. Boston: Ticknor, Reed, and Fields, 1849.

———. *New England Tragedies*. Boston: Ticknor & Fields, 1868.

———. *Poems*. 3d ed. Philadelphia: Carey and Hart, 1846.

———. *Poems*. Boston: J. R. Osgood, 1878 [c.1873].

———. *Voices of the Night*. Cambridge MA: John Owen, 1839.

Longfellow, Samuel, ed. *Life of Henry Wadsworth Longfellow*. Boston: Ticknor, 1886. 2 vols.

Longley, William Harding. *Systematic Catalogue of the Fishes of Tortugas, Florida, with Observations on Color, Habits, and Local Distribution*. Washington DC: Carnegie Institution of Washington, 1941.

Longstreet, Augustus Baldwin. *Georgia Scenes, Characters, Incidents, &c., in the First Half Century of the Republic*. Augusta GA: Printed at the S. R. Sentinel Office, c.1835.

———. *Georgia Scenes, Characters, Incidents, etc., in the First Half Century of the Republic*. 2d ed. New York: Harper, 1847 [c.1840].

———. *Master William Mitten*. Macon GA: Burke, Boykin, 1864.

Longstreet, Rupert J., ed. *Birds in Florida*. 4th ed. Tampa FL: Trend House, c.1969.

Longstreet, Stephen. *The Real Jazz, Old and New*. Baton Rouge LA: LA State Univ. Press, 1956.

———. *War Cries on Horseback: the Story of the Indian Wars of the Great Plains*. Garden City NY: Doubleday, 1970.

Longview News-Journal. Longview TX, 2005–.

Longwell, Chester Ray and Richard Foster Flint. *Introduction to Physical Geology*. New York: John Wiley & Sons; London: Chapman & Hall, c.1955.

Longyear, Mary Hawley Beecher. *The History of a House*. Brookline MA: Zion Research Foundation, 1925.

Look. Des Moines IA: Cowles Communications, 1937–1971.

Loomis, Leander Vaness. *A Journal of the Birmingham Emigrating Company*. Salt Lake City UT: Legal Printing, 1928.

Lopez, Alfredo. *The Puerto Rican Papers*. Indianapolis IN: Bobbs-Merrill, c.1973.

Lorain Republican. Elyria OH, 1842–1844.

Lorain Standard. Elyria OH, 1840–1841.

Lord, John. *Frontier Dust*. Hartford CT: Edwin V. Mitchell, 1926.

Lord, William Rogers. *First Book upon the Birds of Oregon and Washington*. Rev. and enlarged ed. Portland OR: W. R. Lord, c.1902.

Lorimer, George Horace. *Jack Spurlock—Prodigal*. New York: A. L. Burt, 1908 [c.1906].

———. *Letters from a Self-Made Merchant to His Son*. Boston: Small, Maynard, 1903 [c.1902].

Los Angeles and the Wonderful Southland of California. Los Angeles: Los Angeles Evening Express, 1926.

Los Angeles Express. Los Angeles, 1871–1931.

Los Angeles Times. Los Angeles, 1881–.

Los Angeles Wave. Los Angeles, 1998–. Internet.

Lossing, Benson John. *The Hudson*. New York: Virtue and Yorston, c.1866.

———. *The Pictorial Field-Book for the Revolution*. New York: Harper & Bros., 1851–1852 [c.1850]. 2 vols.

Loudon, John Claudius. *Arboretum et Fruticetum Britannicum*. London: Printed for the author, 1838. 8 vols.

———, ed. *Encyclopaedia of Plants*. London: Longman, Rees, Orme, Brown & Green, 1829.

Loughmiller, Campbell and Lynn Loughmiller. *Texas Wildflowers: a Field Guide*. Austin TX: Univ. TX Press, 1984.

———. *Texas Wildflowers: a Field Guide*. Updated by Damon Waitt. Rev. ed. Austin TX: Univ. TX Press, 2006.

Louisiana Agricultural Experiment Station. *Louisiana Bulletin*. Baton Rouge LA, 1890–.

Louisiana Conservationist. New Orleans LA: Louisiana Wildlife and Fisheries Dept., 1948–.

Louisiana Conservation Review SEE ALSO Louisiana. Department of Conservation *Bulletin*

Louisiana Conservation Review. New Orleans LA: Dept. of Conservation, 1923–1941.

Louisiana. Department of Conservation. *Biennial Report.* New Orleans LA, 1926–1935.

———. *Bulletin.* Baton Rouge LA, 1916–.

———. *Fishes and Fishing in Louisiana.* Baton Rouge LA: Ramires-Jones Printing, 1933.

Louisiana Gazette. New Orleans LA, 1817–1826.

Louisiana Historical Quarterly. New Orleans LA: Louisiana Historical Society, 1917–.

Louisiana Natural Heritage Program. *The Natural Communities of Louisiana.* Baton Rouge LA: Lousiana Dept. of Wildlife and Fisheries, 2009.

Louisiana Planter and Sugar Manufacturer. New Orleans LA, 1888–1924.

Louisiana Society of Naturalists. *Proceedings.* New Orleans LA, 1900.

Louisiana State University. *The Herbarium.* [v.d.]. Internet.

Louisiana State University. Board of Supervisors. *Annual Report.* Baton Rouge LA, 1870–.

Louisiana. Wild Life and Fisheries Commission. *Hunting, Fishing and Trapping Regulations 1967–68.* New Orleans LA: Wild Life and Fisheries Commission, 1966?

Lounsberry, Alice. *Southern Wild Flowers and Trees.* New York: Frederick A. Stokes, 1901.

———. *The Wild Flower Book for Young People.* New York: Frederick A. Stokes, c.1906.

Lou Rawls "Live". Phonodisc. Hollywood CA: Capitol Records, 1966.

Love, Milton S. et al. *The Rockfishes of the Northeast Pacific.* Berkeley CA: Univ. CA Press, c.2002.

Love, Nat. *The Life and Adventures of Nat Love, Better Known in the Cattle Country as "Deadwood Dick".* Los Angeles: [s.n.], c.1907.

Lovell, Caroline Couper Stiles. *The Golden Isles of Georgia.* Boston: Little, Brown, 1932.

Lovell, John Epy. *The Young Speaker.* 10th ed. Cincinnati OH: Truman & Spofford, 1852.

Lovell, Solomon. *The Original Journal of General Solomon Lovell, Kept during the Penobscot Expedition, 1779.* Boston: Published by the Weymouth Historical Society, 1881.

Lovell, Tabithaet al. *Snakes of Georgia.* 2005. Internet.

Lovett, James D'Wolf. *Old Boston Boys and the Games They Played.* Boston: Priv. printed at the Riverside Press, c.1906.

Low, Charles Porter. *Some Recollections.* 2d ed. Boston: George H. Ellis, 1906. Orig. pub. in 1905.

Low, Samuel. *The Politician Out-Witted.* New-York: Printed for the Author, by W. Ross, 1789. In: Moses, Montrose Jonas, ed., *Representative Plays by American Dramatists,* 1918, 1.351–429.

Lowe, Charles H., ed. *The Vertebrates of Arizona.* Tucson AZ: Univ. AZ Press, 1964.

Lowell, Amy. *East Wind.* Boston: Houghton Mifflin, c.1926.

———. *Men, Women and Ghosts.* Boston: Houghton Mifflin, 1916.

———. *Pictures of the Floating World.* Boston: Houghton Mifflin, 1921 [c.1919].

Lowell, James Russell. *The Biglow Papers.* Cambridge MA: George Nichols, 1848.

———. *The Biglow Papers.* Boston: Houghton Mifflin, c.1894. Orig. pub. in 1848 by George Nichols, Cambridge MA.

———. *The Biglow Papers: Second Series.* 1st complete Amer. ed. Boston: Ticknor and Fields, 1867.

———. *The Complete Poetical Works of James Russell Lowell.* Cambridge ed. Boston: Houghton Mifflin, c.1911. Orig. pub. in 1896 by Houghton, Mifflin, Boston.

———. *The Courtin'.* Boston: James R. Osgood, 1874.

———. *Fireside Travels.* Boston: Ticknor and Fields, 1864.

———. *Letters of James Russell Lowell.* Ed. by Charles Eliot Norton. New York: Harper & Bros., 1894. 2 vols.

———. *My Study Windows.* Boston: James R. Osgood, 1871.

———. *Political Essays.* Boston: Houghton, Mifflin, 1888.

Lowell, Robert. *Notebook.* 3d ed. rev. and expanded. New York: Farrar, Straus and Giroux, 1970.

Lowell, Robert Traill Spence. *Antony Brade.* Boston: Roberts Bros., 1874.

The Lowell Offering. Written, ed. and pub. by female operatives employed in the mills. Lowell MA: Powers & Bagley, 1840–1845.

Lowell Sun. Lowell MA, 1896–1941; 1943–1969.

Lowell Sun and Citizen-Leader. Lowell MA, 1941–1943.

Lowell Weekly Sun. Lowell MA, 1878–1888.

Lowery, George Hines. *Louisiana Birds.* Baton Rouge LA: Published for the Louisiana Wild Life and Fisheries Commission by LA Univ. Press, 1955.

Lowery, Irving E. *Life on the Old Plantation in Ante-Bellum Days.* Chapel Hill NC: Academic Affairs Library, Univ. NC at Chapel Hill, 1999. Text transcr. for *Documenting the*

American South website from the 1911 ed. pub. by State Co. Printers, Columbia SC.

Lowrie, Walter Macon. *Memoirs.* Philadelphia: Presbyterian Board of Publications, c.1854.

Lowry, Lois. *Anastasia Krupnik.* Boston: Houghton Mifflin, c.1979.

Loyens, William John. *The Changing Culture of the Nulato Koyukon Indians.* Madison WI: Univ. WI-Madison diss., 1966.

Lucas, Daniel Bedinger. *The Wreath of Eglantine.* Baltimore MD: Kelly, Piet, 1869 [c.1868].

Lucia, Ellis. *Klondike Kate.* New York: Hastings House, c.1962.

Ludlow, Fitz Hugh. *The Heart of the Continent.* New York: Hurd and Houghton; Cambridge MA: Riverside Press, 1870.

Ludlow, William *Rept. Reconnaissance MT* SEE United States. Army. Corps of Topographical Engineers *Report of a Reconnaissance from Carroll, Montana Territory, on the Upper Missouri . . . Made in the Summer of 1875*

Ludlum, Robert. *The Road to Gandolfo.* Toronto: Bantam Books, 1982. Orig. pub. in 1975 by Dial Press, New York, under pseud. Michael Shepherd.

Lugger, Otto. *Butterflies and Moths.* St. Paul MN: McGill-Warner, 1898.

Luke Darrell, the Chicago Newsboy. Chicago: Tomlinson Bros., 1866 [c.1865].

The Lumber Industry and Its Workers. Chicago: Industrial Workers of the World, 1920?

Lumberman's Gazette. Bay City MI, 1872–1887?

Lumholtz, Karl Sofus. *New Trails in Mexico.* New York: Charles Scribner's Sons, 1912.

Lummis, Charles Fletcher. *The Awakening of a Nation.* New York: Harper & Bros., 1898.

———. *A Bronco Pegasus.* Boston: Houghton Mifflin, 1928.

———. *The King of the Broncos.* New York: Charles Scribner's Sons, 1897.

———. *The Land of Poco Tiempo.* New York: C. Scribner's Sons, 1893.

———. *Mesa, Cañon and Pueblo.* New York: Century, c.1925.

———. *A New Mexico David.* New York: Charles Scribner's Sons, 1891.

———. *A Tramp across the Continent.* New York: Chas. Scribner's Sons, 1892.

Lumpkin, Katharine Du Pre. *The Making of a Southerner.* New York: Alfred A. Knopf, 1947.

Lumsden, James. *American Memoranda.* Glasgow: Bell & Bain, 1844.

Lunan, John. *Hortus Jamaicensis.* Jamaica: St. Jago de la Gazette, c.1814.

Lund, Jens. *Flatheads & Spooneys.* Lexington KY: Univ. KY Press, 1995.

Lundsford, Hugh. *The Law of Hemlock Mountain.* New York: W. J. Watt, c.1920.

Lundy, Benjamin. *The Life, Travels and Opinions of Benjamin Lundy, Including His Journeys to Texas and Mexico.* Philadelphia: W. D. Parish, 1847.

Lunsford, Bascom Lamar. *It Used to Be.* Ed. by Mildred Frances Thomas. a1975. Unpub. ms. in Appalachian State Univ., Boone NC, library.

Lunt, Dean Lawrence. *Hauling by Hand.* Frenchboro ME: Islandport Press, 1999.

Lunt, Horace. *Across Lots.* Boston: D. Lothrop, 1888.

Lurie, Alison. *The War between the Tates.* 1st Amer. ed. New York: Random House, c.1974.

Lutes, Della Thompson. *The Country Kitchen.* Boston: Little, Brown, 1936.

Luther, Kem. *Cottonwood Roots.* Lincoln NE: Univ. NE Press, c.1993.

Luttig, John C. *Journal of a Fur-Trading Expedition on the Upper Missouri 1812–1813.* St. Louis MO: Missouri Historical Society, 1920.

Lutz, Anne. *Collection Relating to Bergen County, New Jersey.* 1983–2000. Unpub.

Lutz, Frank Eugene. *Field Book of Insects.* New York: G. P. Putnam's Sons, 1918.

Lyceum of Natural History, New York. *Proceedings.* New York, 1870–1874.

Lyell, Charles. *A Second Visit to the United States of North America.* New York: Harper & Bros.; London: J. Murray, 1849. 2 vols.

Lyman, George Dunlap. *John Marsh, Pioneer.* New York: C. Scribner's Sons, 1930.

Lynch, Anne Charlotte. *The Rhode Island Book.* Providence RI: H. Fuller; Boston: Weeks, Jordan, 1841.

Lynch, Jeremiah. *Three Years in the Klondike.* London: Edward Arnold, 1904.

Lynch, William Francis. *Narrative of the United States' Expedition to the River Jordan and the Dead Sea.* Philadelphia: Lea & Blanchard, c.1849.

Lynd, Robert S. and Helen Merrel Lynd. *Middletown.* New York: Harcourt, Brace, c.1929.

Lynde, Francis. *The Grafters.* Ridgewood NJ: Gregg Press, 1968. Repr. of the 1904 ed. pub. by Bobbs-Merrill, Indianapolis IN.

———. *The Quickening.* Indianapolis IN: Bobbs-Merrill, c.1906.

Lynden Tribune. Lynden WA, 1905–.

Lynn, Corra. *Durham Village.* Boston: John P. Jewett; Cleveland OH: Jewett, Proctor & Worthington, 1854.

Lynn, Loretta and George Vecsey. *Loretta Lynn: Coal Miner's Daughter.* Chicago: Henry Regnery, c.1976.

Lynn Massachusetts Park Commissioners. *Great Woods of Lynn and Other Public Parks of the City.* Lynn MA, 1904?–1909?

Lyon, George Ella. *Borrowed Children.* New York: Orchard Books, c.1988.

Lyon, Marguerite. *Fresh from the Hills.* Indianapolis IN: Bobbs-Merrill, c.1945.

———. *Take to the Hills.* Indianapolis IN: Bobbs-Merrill, c.1941.

Lyons, Albert Brown. *Plant Names, Scientific and Popular.* Detroit MI: Nelson, Baker, 1900.

———. *Plant Names, Scientific and Popular.* 2d ed. Detroit MI: Nelson, Baker, 1907.

Lyons, Ernest. *My Florida.* South Brunswick NJ: A. S. Barnes, 1969.

Macauley, James. *The Natural, Statistical, and Civil History of the State of New-York.* New York: Gould & Banks; Albany NY: William Gould, 1829. 3 vols.

MacCracken, Henry Noble. *The Family on Gramercy Park.* New York: Charles Scribner's Sons, 1949.

MacCubbin, Tom and Georgia B. Tasker. *Florida Gardener's Guide.* Franklin TN: Cool Springs Press, c.1997.

Macdonald, Betty Bard. *The Egg and I.* Philadelphia: Lippincott, 1946. Orig. pub. in 1945 by Lippincott, New York.

Macdonald, George Everett Hussey. *Fifty Years of Freethought.* New York: Truth Seeker, 1929–1931. 2 vols.

Macdonald, Gordon A. *Volcanoes.* Englewood Cliffs NJ: Prentice-Hall, c.1972.

MacDonald, H. H. *Big Game Management.* Dallas TX: Biological Cine, 1934.

Macdonald, John. *The Moving Target.* New York: Alfred A. Knopf, c.1949.

MacDonald, John Dann. *The Green Ripper.* New York: Lippincott, c.1979.

———. *Pale Gray for Guilt.* Greenwich CT: Fawcett Publications, c.1968.

MacDougall, Michael and J. C. Furnas. *Gamblers Don't Gamble.* New York: Greystone Press, c.1939.

MacDowell, Syl. *Western Trout.* New York: A. A. Knopf, 1948.

Macfadden, Mary and Emile Gauvreau. *Dumbbells and Carrot Strips.* New York: Henry Holt, c.1953.

MacGowan, Alice. *The Sword in the Mountains.* New York: G. P. Putnam's Sons, 1910.

———. *The Wiving of Lance Cleaverage.* New York: G. P. Putnam's Sons, 1909.

MacGregor, John. *British America.* Edinburgh: W. Blackwood, 1832. 2 vols.

Machinery. New York, 1894–1902.

Machinists' Monthly Journal. Washington DC: International Association of Machinists, 1889–1956.

Mack, Russell Herbert. *Factors of Instability Affecting Production and Employment in the Cigar Manufacturing Industry.* Philadelphia: Univ. PA Press, 1933.

Mackay, Charles. *A Dictionary of Lowland Scotch.* Boston: Ticknor, 1888.

———. *Life and Liberty in America.* London: Smith, Elder, 1859. 2 vols.

MacKaye, Harold Steele. *The Panchronicon.* New York: C. Scribner's Sons, 1904.

MacKaye, Percy. *Tall Tales of the Kentucky Mountains.* London: Longmans, Green, 1930 [c.1926].

———. *This Fine-Pretty World: a Comedy of the Kentucky Mountains.* New York: Macmillan, 1924.

Mackay Miner. Mackay ID, 1906–.

MacKenzie, David S. *Perennial Ground Covers.* Portland OR: Timber Press, 2002.

Mackenzie, Frederick. *Diary of Frederick Mackenzie . . . 1775–1781.* Cambridge MA: Harvard Univ. Press, 1930. 2 vols.

Mackenzie, Kenneth Kent. *Manual of the Flora of Jackson County, Missouri.* Kansas City MO: [s.n.], 1902.

Mackenzie, William L. *The Life and Times of Martin Van Buren.* Boston: Cooke, 1846.

MacKinnon, Lauchlan Bellingham. *Atlantic and Transatlantic Sketches, Afloat and Ashore.* London: Colburn, 1852.

Maclay, William. *The Diary of William Maclay and Other Notes on Senate Debates.* Baltimore MD: Johns Hopkins Univ. Press, c.1988.

———. *The Journal of William Maclay.* New York: A. & C. Boni, 1927.

Maclean, Norman. *A River Runs through It.* Chicago: Univ. Chicago Press, c.1976.

MacLeod, Charlotte. *The Odd Job.* New York: Mysterious Press, c.1995.

———. *Something in the Water.* New York: Mysterious Press, c.1994.

Macleod, R. R. *Yazoo 21–83.* Edinburgh: PAT Publications, c.1992.

MacLeod, Xavier Donald. *Biography of Hon. Fernando Wood, Mayor of the City of New York.* New York: O. F. Parsons; Boston: Fetridge, 1856.

MacMillan, Conway. *Minnesota Plant Life.* Saint Paul MN: [s.n.], 1899.

Macmillan, Donald B. *Four Years in the White North.* New York: Harper & Bros., c.1918.

Macmillan's Magazine. London, 1859–1907.

Macon, John Alfred. *Uncle Gabe Tucker.* Philadelphia: J. B. Lippincott, 1883.

Macon County Times. Lafayette TN, 1919–.

Macon Daily Telegraph. Macon GA, 1860–1864; 1905–1926.

Macon Telegraph. Macon GA, 1885?–1905.

Macon Telegraph and Messenger. Macon GA, 1873–1885?

Macoupin County Enquirer. Carlinville IL, 1852–.

Macrae, David. *The Americans at Home.* Edinburgh: Edmonston and Douglas, 1870. 2 vols.

MacSparran, James. *A Letter Book and Abstract of Out Services, Written during the Years 1743–1751.* Boston: D. B. Updike, 1899.

Mactaggart, John. *Three Years in Canada.* London: Henry Colburn, 1829. 2 vols.

Macy, William Francis and Roland B. Hussey. *The Nantucket Scrap Basket.* Nantucket MA: Inquirer and Mirror Press, 1916.

Maddux, Rachel. *A Walk in the Spring Rain.* New York: Doubleday, 1966.

Mademoiselle. New York: Condé Nast, 1935–.

Madill Record. Madill OK, 1916–.

Madison, Harold Lester. *Wild Flowers of Ohio.* Cleveland OH: Cleveland Museum of Natural History, c.1938.

Madison, James. *The Papers of James Madison.* Chicago: Univ. Chicago Press, 1962–1991. 17 vols.

Madison County Courier. Edwardsville IL, 1865–1900?

Madison, Dane County and Surrounding Towns. Madison WI: Wm. J. Park, 1877.

Madison Express. Madison WI, 1839–1842; 1844–1848.

Madison Star-Mail. Madison NE, 1958–.

Madson, John. *Up on the River.* New York: Nick Lyons Books, c.1985.

Maeder, Jo. *When I Married My Mother.* Cambridge MA: Da Capo Press, c.2009.

Maeno, Shigeru. *A Melville Dictionary.* Tokyo: Kaibunsha, c.1976.

Magazine of American History. New York, 1877–1893.

Magazine of History, with Notes and Queries. Extra Numbers. Tarrytown NY: W. Abbatt, 1908–1935.

Magazine of Horticulture, Botany and All Useful Discoveries and Improvements in Rural Affairs. Boston, 1837–1868.

Magazine of Travel. Detroit MI, 1857.

Magazine of Travel. 2d ed. Detroit MI: Doughty, Straw, and Raymond & Selleck, 1858. Selections from periodical of same name comp. by Warren Isham.

Magee, Dennis W. and Harry E. Ahles. *Flora of the Northeast: a Manual of the Vascular Flora of New England and Adjacent New York.* Amherst MA: Univ. MA Press, 1999.

Magner, Dennis. *The New System of Educating Horses.* 9th ed. Buffalo NY: Warren, Johnson, 1870.

Magoffin, Susan Shelby. *Down the Santa Fé Trail and into Mexico.* New Haven: Yale Univ. Press, 1962. Repr. of 1926 ed.

———. *Down the Santa Fé Trail and into Mexico.* Lincoln NE: Univ. NE Press, 1982. Repr. of 1962 repr. of 1926 ed.

Mahony, Dorah. *Six Months in a House of Correction.* Boston: B. B. Mussey, 1835.

Mail. Hagers-Town MD, 1831–1835.

Mailer, Norman. *Advertisements for Myself.* New York: G. P. Putnam's Sons, c.1959.

Maine Agricultural Experiment Station. *Annual Report.* Orono ME, 1887–1953.

Maine Atlas & Gazetteer. 18th ed. Freeport ME: DeLorme Mapping, c.1995.

Maine. Board of Agriculture. *Abstract of Returns from the Agricultural Societies of Maine.* Augusta ME, 1858–1870.

———. *Agriculture of Maine* SEE Maine. Department of Agriculture. *Annual Report*

Maine Coast Fisherman. Belfast ME: Journal Pub., 1946–1960.

Maine. Department of Agriculture. *Annual Report.* Augusta ME, 1856–1940.

Maine. Department of Conservation. Forest Health and Monitoring Division. *Insect and Disease Fact Sheets.* [v.d.]. Internet.

Maine. Department of Conservation. Natural Areas Program. *Rare Plant Fact Sheets.* 2004.

Maine. Department of Marine Resources. *Lobster Newsletter.* 2000–. Internet.

Maine. Department of Marine Resources. Education Division. *A Teacher's Guide to Marine Life of the Gulf of Maine.* Augusta ME: The Division, c.1993.

Maine Farmer. Augusta ME, 1844–1924.

Maine Farmer and Journal of the Useful Arts. Winthrop ME, 1833–1842.

Maine Fish and Wildlife. Augusta ME, 1975–.

Maine Historical Society. *Documentary History of the State of Maine.* Portland ME: The Society, 1869–1916. 24 vols.

Maine Monthly Magazine. Bangor ME, 1836–1837.

Maine. Scientific Survey. Augusta ME: [s.n.], 1863.

Maine Sunday Telegram. Portland ME, 1887–.

Maine. University. *Studies.* Orono ME, 1900–1973.

Maine. University. Outdoor Recreation Study Team. *Outdoor Recreation in Maine.* Orono ME: Dept. of Agricultural Business and Economics, Maine Agricultural Experiment Station, Univ. ME, 1965.

Maine Writers Research Club. *Maine, My State.* Lewiston ME: Journal Printshop, c.1919.

Maisch, John Michael. *A Manual of Organic Materia Medica.* Philadelphia: Henry C. Lea's Son, 1882 [c.1881].

Mais, Jamais de la Vie! A Collection of Folklore from the Parish of Acadia. Crowley LA: Crowley High School, 1977.

Maitland, James. *The American Slang Dictionary.* Chicago: R. J. Kittredge, 1891.

Maizie SEE Rose, Mary H.

Major, Clarence, ed. *Calling the Wind.* New York: HarperPerennial, c.1993.

———. *Dictionary of Afro-American Slang.* New York: International, 1970.

Malamalama. Honolulu HI, 1959–1971.

Malamud, Bernard. *The Tenants.* New York: Farrar, Straus and Giroux, 1971.

Maledicta. Waukesha WI, 1977–.

Malkus, Alida. *Raquel of the Ranch Country.* New York: Harcourt, Brace, c.1927.

Malone, Joseph S. *Sons of Vengeance.* New York: Fleming H. Revell, c.1903.

Malone, Michael. *Dingley Falls.* Naperville IL: Sourcebooks, 2002. Orig. pub. in 1980 by Harcourt Brace Jovanovich, New York.

Malsch, Brownson. *Captain M. T. Gonzaullas, Lone Wolf, the Only Texas Ranger Captain of Spanish Descent.* Austin TX: Shoal Creek, c.1980.

Malvern Leader. Malvern IA, 1875–1880; 1883–.

Man. New York: George H. Evans, 1834–1835.

Manchester, Massachusetts. *Town Records.* Salem MA: Salem Press Pub., 1889–1891. 2 vols.

Manchester Guardian Weekly. Manchester, 1919–.

Manchester Institute of Arts & Sciences. *Proceedings.* Manchester NH, 1899–1911.

Manchester Union Leader. Manchester NH, 1951–.

Mandel, George. *Flee the Angry Strangers.* New York: Bobbs-Merrill, c.1952.

Manford's Magazine. Chicago, 1885?–1895.

Manfred, Frederick Feikema. *Boy Almighty.* Saint Paul MN: Itasca Press, 1945.

———. *The Chokecherry Tree.* Garden City NY: Doubleday, 1948.

———. *Green Earth.* New York: Crown, c.1977.

Mangum, David. *The Fargus Technique.* New York: Thomas Y. Crowell, c.1973.

Manitoba Morning Free Press. Winnipeg, 1893–1915.

Manitowoc Herald-Times. Manitowoc WI, 1932–1972.

Mann, Emily. *Having Our Say: the Delany Sisters' First 100 Years: a Play.* New York: Dramatists Play Service, c.1996. Adapted from the book *Having Our Say* by Sarah L. Delany and A. Elizabeth Delany, with Amy Hill Hearth.

Manning, Ella Wallace. *Igloo for the Night.* Toronto: Univ. Toronto Press, 1946.

Manning, George. "Sea Journal." Maine Historical Society *Documentary History of the State of Maine.* (1900) 6.179–84.

Manning, Phillip. *Orange Blossom Trails.* Winston-Salem NC: J. F. Blair, 1997.

Manning, William. *The Key of Libberty: Written in the Year 1798.* Billerica MA: Manning Association, 1922.

Mansfield News. Mansfield OH, 1882–1932.

Mansfield News-Journal. Mansfield OH, 1933–1964.

Manship, Andrew. *Thirteen Years' Experience in the Itinerancy.* Philadelphia: Higgins & Perkenpine, 1856 [c.1855].

Mansur & Tebbetts Implement Company. *General Catalogue No. D: Farm Machinery and Vehicles.* [s.l.]: Little & Becker, 1893.

Manufacturer and Builder. New York, 1869–1897.

Manwaring, Charles William, comp. *A Digest of the Early Connecticut Probate Records.* Hartford CT: R. S. Peck, 1904–1906. 3 vols.

Marble Rock Weekly. Marble Rock IA, 1875–1900.

March, Walter SEE Willcox, Orlando Bolivar

Marckwardt, Albert Henry. *Linguistics and the Teaching of English.* Bloomington IN: IN Univ. Press, 1966.

Marcou, Jane Belknap. *Life of Jeremy Belknap, D. D., the Historian of New Hampshire.* New York: Harper and Bros., 1847.

Marcus, Jacob Rader. *The American Jewish Woman.* New York: KTAV Publishing; Cincinnati OH: American Jewish Archives, 1981.

Marcy, Randolph Barnes. *The Prairie Traveler.* New York: Harper & Bros., 1859.

———. *The Prairie Traveler.* [s.l.]: Filler and Ochs, 1965. Facsimile of the 1st ed. pub. in 1859 by Harper, New York.

Margry, Pierre, ed. *Découvertes et Établissements des Francais dans l'Ouest et dans le Sud de l'Amérique Septentrionale (1614–1754).* Paris: Impr. D. Jouaust, 1876–1886. 6 vols.

Mariani, John F. *The Dictionary of American Food and Drink.* 2d ed. New York: Hearst Books, c.1994.

———. *The Encyclopedia of American Food and Drink.* New York: Lebhar-Friedman Books, 1999.

Marin, Pamela. *Motherland, a Memoir.* New York: Free Press, 2005.

Marine Biological Laboratory, Woods Hole Massachusetts. *Biological Lectures.* Boston, 1890–1899.

Marine Recreational Fisheries Statistics Survey. *Atlantic and Gulf Coast Local Fish Names.* [v.d.]. Internet.

Mariner's Mirror. London, 1911–.

Marin Independent Journal. Novato CA, 1985–.

Marion, Francis. *Marion's Men.* Philadelphia: A. J. Rockafellar, 1843.

Marion, Stephen. *Hollow Ground.* Chapel Hill NC: Algonquin Books, 2002.

Marion Daily Star. Marion OH, 1877–1926.

Marion Star. Marion OH, 1926–.

Marion Weekly Star. Marion OH, 1885–1913?

Markfield, Wallace. *To an Early Grave.* New York: Simon & Schuster, 1964.

Marks, Percy. *The Plastic Age.* New York: Century, c.1924.

Marler, Don C. *Reflections on Life in the Swamp.* Hemphill TX: Dogwood Press, c.2004.

Marquis, Don. *Danny's Own Story.* Garden City NY: Doubleday, Page, 1912.

Marran, Ray J. *Games Outdoors.* New York: Thomas Y. Crowell, 1940.

Marryat, Francis Samuel. *Mountains and Molehills.* New York: Harper & Bros., 1855.

Marryat, Frederick. *A Diary in America.* Paris: Baudry's European Library, 1839–1840. 2 vols.

———. *The Travels and Romantic Adventures of Monsieur Violet among the Snake Indians and Wild Tribes of the Great Western Prairies.* London: Longman, Brown, Green & Longmans, 1843. 3 vols.

Marsh, Dorothy B., ed. *The Good Housekeeping Cookbook.* New York: Good Housekeeping Book Division, c.1963.

Marsh, Ken. *Breakfast at Trout's Place.* Boulder CO: Johnson, 1999.

Marshall, Catherine Wood. *Christy.* New York: McGraw-Hill Book, c.1967.

Marshall, George Catlett. *Memoirs of My Services in the World War 1917–1918.* Boston: Houghton Mifflin, 1976.

Marshall, Humphry, comp. *Arbustrum Americanum.* Philadelphia: Printed by J. Crukshank, 1785.

Marshall, John. *The Life of George Washington, Commander in Chief of the American Forces during the War Which Established the Independence of His Country, and First President of the United States.* Comp. under the inspection of

Bushrod W. Washington. Philadelphia: Printed and published by C. P. Wayne, 1804–1807. 5 vols.

———. *The Political and Economic Doctrines of John Marshall.* By John Edward Oster. New York: Neale, 1914.

Marshall, Nina L. *Mosses and Lichens.* New York: Doubleday, Page, 1907.

Marshall, Paule. *The Fisher King.* New York: Scribner, c.2000.

Marshall, Robert. *Arctic Wilderness.* Berkeley CA: Univ. CA Press, 1956.

Marshall, Robert K. *Little Squire Jim.* 2d ed. New York: Duell, Sloan and Pearce, 1949.

Marshall News Messenger. Marshall TX, 1937?–.

Marshfield Times. Marshfield WI, 1885–1920.

Marteka, Vincent. *Mushrooms.* New York: W. W. Norton, c.1980.

Martha's Vineyard Times. Vineyard Haven MA, 1984–.

Martin, Alexander Campbell et al. *American Wildlife & Plants.* New York: McGraw-Hill, 1951.

Martin, Eva May. *Sojourn on the Prairie.* [s.l.]: Max Hardison, 1955.

Martin, Helen Reimensnyder. *The Betrothal of Elypholate, and Other Tales of the Pennsylvania Dutch.* Freeport NY: Books for Libraries Press, 1970. Orig. pub. in 1907 by Century, New York.

———. *The Schoolmaster of Hessville.* Garden City NY: Double, Page, 1920.

———. *Tillie.* Ridgewood NJ: Gregg Press, 1904.

Martin, Joseph, ed. *A Comprehensive Description of Virginia, and the District of Columbia.* Richmond VA: J. W. Randolph, 1830?

———, ed. *A New and Comprehensive Gazetteer of Virginia and the District of Columbia.* Charlottesville VA: Joseph Martin, 1835.

Martin, Joseph Plumb. *A Narrative of Some of the Adventures, Dangers and Sufferings of a Revolutionary Soldier.* Hallowell ME: Printed by Glazier, Masters, 1830.

Martin, Luther. *Modern Gratitude.* Baltimore MD: [s.n.], 1802.

Martin, Michael. *Life of Michael Martin, Who Was Executed for Highway Robbery December 20, 1821.* Boston: Russell & Gardner, 1821.

Martin, Mildred Albert. *The Martins of Gunbarrel.* Caldwell ID: Caxton Printers, 1959.

Martin, Russell Lionel. *Mr. Jefferson's Business.* Charlottesville VA: Univ. VA diss., 1994.

Martindale, Joseph C. *A History of the Townships of Byberry and Moreland in Philadelphia, Pa.* Philadelphia: T. Ellwood Zell, 1867.

Martineau, Harriet. *Retrospect of Western Travel.* London: Saunders and Otley, 1838. 3 vols.

———. *Society in America.* New York: AMS Press, 1966. 3 vols. Orig. pub. in 1837 by Saunders and Otley, London.

Martone, Michael, ed. *Townships.* Iowa City IA: Univ. IA Press, c.1992.

Marvel, Ik. SEE Mitchell, Donald Grant

Maryland Agricultural Experiment Station. *Bulletin.* College Park MD, 1888–.

Maryland Conservationist. Annapolis MD, 1924–1981.

Maryland. Department of Education. *Our Underwater Farm.* Baltimore MD: The Department, 1953.

Maryland Department of Natural Resources. *Endangered Plants of Maryland.* [v.d.]. Internet.

Maryland Gazette. Annapolis MD, 1745–1813.

Maryland Gazette. Glen Burnie MD, 2004–.

Maryland Historical Magazine. Baltimore MD: Published under the authority of the Maryland Historical Society, 1906–.

Maryland Historical Society. *Fund Publications.* Baltimore MD: Printed by J. Murphy, 1867–.

Maryland Journal, and the Baltimore Advertiser. Baltimore MD, 1723–1795.

Maryland. Laws, Statutes etc. *Laws of the General Assembly.* Baltimore MD: [s.n.], 1777–1898.

Maryland Medical Journal. Baltimore MD, 1877–1918.

Maryland Ornithological Society. *Maryland Yellowthroat.* Baltimore MD, 1980–.

Maryland Sea Grant College. *Maryland Marine Notes Online.* 1990–. Internet.

Marysville Journal-Tribune. Marysville OH, 1972–.

Maryville Daily Forum. Maryville MO, 1929–1970; 1989–.

Mason, Alpheus Thomas. *Harlan Fiske Stone.* New York: Viking Press, 1956.

Mason, Bernard Sterling and Elmer Dayton Mitchell. *Active Games and Contests.* New York: A. S. Barnes, c.1935.

———. *Social Games for Recreation.* New York: A. S. Barnes, c.1935.

Mason, Bobbie Ann. *Clear Springs.* New York: Random House, c.1999.

———. *Feather Crowns.* New York: HarperCollins, c.1993.

———. *Shiloh and Other Stories.* New York: Harper & Row, c.1982.

Mason, George. *The Papers of George Mason, 1725–1792.* Chapel Hill NC: Univ. NC Press, 1970.

Mason, Gilbert R. *Beaches, Blood and Ballots.* Jackson MS: Univ. Press MS, 2000.

Mason, Herbert Louis. *A Flora of the Marshes of California.* Berkeley CA: Univ. CA Press, 1957.

Mason, Mary Ann Bryan. *The Young Housewife's Counsellor and Friend.* Philadelphia: J. B. Lippincott, 1871.

———. *The Young Housewife's Counsellor and Friend.* Chapel Hill NC: Academic Affairs Library, Univ. NC at Chapel Hill, 2001. Text transcr. for *Documenting the American South* website from the 1875 ed. pub. by E. J. Hale & Son, New York.

Mason, Richard. *The Gentleman's New Pocket Farrier.* 2d ed. Richmond VA: Peter Cottom, 1820.

Mason, Richard Lee. *Narrative of Richard Lee Mason in the Pioneer West, 1819.* New York: Printed for C. F. Heartman, 1915.

Mason, Robert Lindsay. *The Lure of the Great Smokies.* Boston: Houghton Mifflin, 1927.

Mason City Globe-Gazette. Mason City IA, 1929–1964.

Massachusetts. *Acts and Laws of the Commonwealth of Massachusetts.* Boston: Benjamin Edes & Sons, 1781.

———. *Acts and Laws of the Commonwealth of Massachusetts.* Boston: Wright & Potter Printing, 1890–1898. 13 vols. Repr. of the 1781–1805 ed. printed by Young & Minns, Boston.

Massachusetts Agricultural Experiment Station. *Bulletin.* Amherst MA, 1907–1973.

Massachusetts Agricultural Journal. Boston: Massachusetts Society for Promoting Agriculture, 1813–1832.

Massachusetts. Agricultural Survey. *Report of the Agriculture of Massachusetts.* By Henry Colman, commissioner. Boston: Dutton and Wentworth, 1838–1841. 4 vols.

Massachusetts Audubon. Boston: Audubon Society, 1858–1974.

Massachusetts Audubon Society. *Bulletin.* Boston, 1917–1958.

Massachusetts Centinel. Boston, 1784–1790.

Massachusetts Charitable Mechanic Association. *Exhibition.* Boston, 1839–1850.

Massachusetts (Colony). *Records of the Governor and Company of the Massachusetts Bay in New England.* Boston: W. White, 1853–1854. 5 vols.

Massachusetts (Colony) Probate Court (Essex Co.). *The Probate Records of Essex County, Massachusetts.* Salem MA: Essex Institute, 1916–1920. 3 vols.

Massachusetts. Commissioners on Fisheries and Game. *A Report upon the Mollusk Fisheries of Massachusetts.* Boston: Wright & Potter, 1909.

Massachusetts. County Court (Essex County). *Records and Files of the Quarterly Courts.* Salem MA: Essex Institute, 1911–1975. 9 vols.

Massachusetts. General Court. *Acts and Resolves Passed by the General Court of Massachusetts.* Boston: Wright & Potter, 1775–.

———. *Journal of the Honorable House of Representatives.* Boston: Printed by Samuel Kneeland, 1736.

Massachusetts. General Court. Committee on Railroads and Canals. *Annual Reports.* Boston: Dutton and Wentworth, 1837–1856.

Massachusetts Historical Society. *Collections.* Cambridge MA, 1792–.

———. *Proceedings.* Boston, 1835–1997.

Massachusetts Horticultural Society. *Transactions.* Boston, 1842–1919.

Massachusetts Invasive Plant Advisory Group. *The Evaluation of Non-Native Plant Species for Invasiveness in Massachusetts with Annotated List.* [v.d.]. Internet.

Massachusetts. Laws, etc. *Private and Special Statutes of the Commonwealth of Massachusetts.* Boston: Dutton and Wentworth, 1780–1911? 21 vols.

Massachusetts Magazine. Boston, 1789–1796.

Massachusetts Medico-Legal Society. *Transactions.* Cambridge MA, 1878–1899?

Massachusetts. Office of the Secretary of State. *Statistical Information Relating to Certain Branches of Industry . . . for the Year Ending June 1, 1855.* Boston: William White, 1856.

Massachusetts Ploughman. Boston, 1840–1866.

Massachusetts Ploughman and New England Journal of Agriculture. Boston, 1866–1906.

Massachusetts Review. Amherst MA, 1959–.

Massachusetts Society for Promoting Agriculture. *Papers on Agriculture.* [s.l.], 1801–1808.

Massachusetts Spy SEE ALSO *Thomas' Massachusetts Spy, or, Worcester Gazette*

Massachusetts Spy. Worcester MA, 1821–1823.

Massachusetts Spy and Worcester Advertiser. Worcester MA, 1823–1825.

Massachusetts Spy and Worcester County Advertiser. Worcester MA, 1825–1831.

Massachusetts. State Board of Agriculture. *Annual Report.* Boston, 1854–1918.

Massachusetts Teacher. Boston, 1848–1855.

Massachusetts. University-Amherst. *Campus Chronicle.* Amherst MA: Univ. MA at Amherst, 1985–2003.

Massachusetts. Zoological and Botanical Survey. *Reports of the Commissioners on the Zoological Survey of the State.* Boston: Dutton & Wentworth, 1838.

———. *Reports on the Fishes, Reptiles and Birds of Massachusetts.* Boston: Dutton & Wentworth, 1839.

———. *Reports on the Herbaceous Plants and on the Quadrupeds of Massachusetts.* Cambridge MA: Folsom, Wells, and Thurston, 1840.

Massett, Stephen C. *Drifting About.* New York: Carleton, c.1863.

Massey, Ellen Gray, ed. *Bittersweet Country.* Garden City NY: Doubleday, 1978.

Massey, John. *Reminiscences.* Nashville TN: M. E. Church, South, 1916.

Massey, Peter. *Backcountry Adventures Arizona.* Castle Rock CO: Swagman, c.2006.

Massey, Wilbur Fisk. *Crop Growing and Crop Feeding.* Philadelphia: Farmer, 1901.

Massillon Independent. Massillon OH, 1863–1912.

Masters, Edgar Lee. *Spoon River Anthology.* New York: Macmillan, 1915.

Masterson, James R. *Arkansas Folklore.* Little Rock AR: Rose Publishing, c.1974. Orig. pub. in 1942 by Chapman and Grimes, Boston under the title *Tall Tales of Arkansaw.*

Masterton, Elsie. *Blueberry Hill Cookbook.* New York: Thomas Y. Crowell, c.1959.

Mather, Cotton. *Diary of Cotton Mather, 1681–1724.* Boston: Massachusetts Historical Society, 1911–1912. 2 vols.

———. *The Life and Death of the Renown'd Mr. John Eliot.* 2d ed. London: Printed for John Dunton, 1691.

———. *Magnalia Christi Americana.* New York: Arno Press, 1972. Repr. of the 1702 London ed. printed for T. Parkhurst, London.

———. *The Wonders of the Invisible World.* London: John Russell Smith, 1862. Orig. pub. in 1692 in Boston.

Mather, Fred. *Memoranda Relating to Adirondack Fishes.* Albany NY: Weed, Parsons, 1886.

Mather, Increase. *An Essay for the Recording of Illustrious Providences.* New York: Scholars' Facsimiles & Reprints, 1977. Photographic repr. of the 1684 ed. printed by S. Green for J. Browning, Boston.

Mather, Joseph Higgins and Linus Pierpont Brockett. *A Geographical History of the State of New York.* Utica NY: John W. Fuller, 1851 [c.1848].

———. *Geography of the State of New York.* Hartford NY: J. H. Mather, 1847.

Mather, J. Y. and H. H. Speitel, eds. *The Linguistic Atlas of Scotland.* Hamden CT: Archon Books, c.1975–1977. 2 vols.

Mathes, Charles Hodge. *Tall Tales from Old Smoky.* Kingsport TN: Southern, 1952.

Mathews, Anne Jackson. *Memoirs of Charles Mathews, Comedian.* London: R. Bentley, 1838–1839. 4 vols.

Mathews, Catharine Van Cortland. *Andrew Ellicott.* New York: Grafton Press, c.1908.

Mathews, Cornelius. *The Various Writings of Cornelius Mathews.* New York: AMS Press, 1971. Repr. of the 1863 [c.1843] ed. pub. by Harper & Bros., New York.

Mathews, Ferdinand Schuyler. *Field Book of American Wild Flowers.* New York: G. P. Putnam's Sons, 1909 [c.1902].

———. *Field Book of American Wild Flowers.* New ed. rev. and enlarged. New York: G. P. Putnam's Sons, 1912.

Mathews, John Joseph. *Talking to the Moon.* Chicago: Univ. Chicago Press, 1945.

Mathews, Mitford McLeod. *Collection.* 1951–c1970. Unpub. coll. of materials by Mathews following publication of *A Dictionary of Americanisms.*

———, ed. *A Dictionary of Americanisms on Historical Principles.* Chicago: Univ. Chicago Press, c.1951.

———. *Some Sources of Southernisms.* University AL: Univ. AL Press, 1948.

Mathewson, Christopher. *Pitching in a Pinch.* New York: Grosset & Dunlap, c.1912.

Matschat, Cecile Hulse. *Mexican Plants for American Gardens.* Boston: Houghton Mifflin, 1935.

———. *Suwannee River.* New York: Farrar & Rinehart, c.1938.

Matsell, George Washington. *Vocabulum.* New York: George W. Matsell, 1859.

Matthews, Richard E. *The 149th Pennsylvania Volunteer Infantry Unit in the Civil War.* Jefferson NC: McFarland, c.1994.

Matthews, Vincent and Neil Amdur. *My Race Be Won.* New York: Charterhouse, 1974.

Mattison, Hiram. *The Immortality of the Soul.* 3d ed. Philadelphia: Perkinpine & Higgins, 1867.

Maude, John. *Visit to the Falls of Niagara, in 1800.* London: Longman, Rees, Orme, Brown & Green, 1826.

Maund, Alfred. *The International.* New York: McGraw-Hill, c.1961.

Maurer, David W. *Language of the Underworld.* Lexington KY: Univ. Press KY, c.1981.

Maurer, David W. and Quinn Pearl. *Kentucky Moonshine.* Lexington KY: Univ. Press KY, 1974.

Maurer, David W. and Victor H. Vogel. *Narcotics and Narcotic Addiction.* 3d ed. Springfield IL: C. C. Thomas, c.1967.

Maury, Dabney Herndon. *Recollections of a Virginian in the Mexican, Indian and Civil Wars.* New York: C. Scribner's Sons, 1894.

Maury, Matthew Fontaine and William Morris Fontaine. *Resources of West Virginia.* Wheeling WV: Register Company, Printers, 1876.

Maury, Sarah Webb. *Native Trees of Kentucky.* Louisville? KY: [s.n.], c.1910.

Mawson, Christopher Orland Sylvester and Charles Berlitz. *Dictionary of Foreign Terms.* 2d ed. New York: Thomas Y. Crowell, 1975.

The Max Hunter Folk Song Collection. 1956–1976. Internet.

May, John. *Journal and Letters of Col. John May, of Boston, Relative to Two Journeys to the Ohio Country in 1788 and '89.* Cincinnati OH: Robert Clarke, for the Historical and Philosophical Society of Ohio, 1873.

May, John Bichard. *The Hawks of North America.* New York: National Association of Audubon Societies, 1935.

Mayer, Jo Harmon. *Beef Club Tradition in South Carolina's Dutch Fork.* Columbia SC: Univ. SC unpub. student paper, 1978.

Mayes, Vernon O. and Barbara Bayless Lacy. *Nanise.* Tsaile AZ: Navajo Community College Press, 1989.

Mayflower Descendant. Boston: Massachusetts Society of Mayflower Descendants, 1899–1937.

Mayhew, Ira. *Mayhew's Practical Book-Keeping Key.* Boston: Chase and Nichols, 1863 [c.1860].

———. *Popular Education.* New York: Harper & Bros., c.1850.

Maynard, Charles Johnson. *The Naturalist's Guide in Collecting and Preserving Objects of Natural History.* Boston: Osgood, 1873 [c.1870].

Maynard, William Benz, comp. *History and Genealogy of Maynard, Maurer and Related Families.* Baltimore MD: Gateway Press, 1984–1993. 3 vols.

Mayne, Isabella Maud Rittenhouse. *Maud.* New York: Macmillan, 1939.

Mayo, Eleanor R. *Forever Strangers.* New York: W. W. Norton, c.1958.

———. *October Fire.* New York: Thomas Y. Crowell, c.1951.

Mayo, Herbert. *On the Truths Contained in Popular Superstition.* 3d ed. Edinburgh: W. Blackwood, 1851.

Mayo, William Starbuck. *Kaloolah, or, Journeyings to the Djébel Kumri: an Autobiography of Jonathan Romer.* New York: G. P. Putnam, 1849.

Mazama. Portland OR, 1896–1993.

McAlister, Wayne H. and Martha K. McAlister. *Aransas.* Austin TX: Univ. TX Press, 1995. Orig. pub. in 1987 by Mince County Press, Victoria, TX under the title: *Guidebook to the Aransas National Wildlife Refuge.*

McAllister, Ward. *Society as I Have Found It.* New York: Cassell Publishing, c.1890.

McAtee, Waldo Lee. *Nomina Abitera.* Washington DC: Privately printed, 1945.

———. *Notes on Thornton's Glossary.* Washington DC: Privately printed, 1942.

———. *Oddments of Speech and Folklore from North Carolina.* Chapel Hill NC: [s.n.], 1959.

———. *Rural Dialect of Grant County, Indiana, in the 'Nineties.* [s.l.]: Privately printed, 1942.

———. *Rural Dialect of Grant County, Indiana, in the 'Nineties: Supplements.* [s.l.]: [s.n.], 1942–1955.

———. *Some Dialect of Randolph County and Elsewhere in North Carolina.* Chapel Hill NC: [s.n.], 1956.

———. *Studies in the Vocabularies of Hoosier Authors:*

Baynard Rush Hall, 1793–1863. Chapel Hill NC: Printed by the compiler, 1960.

———. *Supplement to Nomina Abitera-1945.* Chapel Hill NC: Privately printed, 1954.

McBain, Ed SEE Hunter, Evan

McBride, Vaughn. *Echoes.* Woodstock IL: Dramatic Publishing, 1988.

McCabe, James Dabney. *History of the Grange Movement.* Chicago: National Publishing, 1874.

———. *The History of the Great Riots.* [s.l]: Augustus M. Kelley, 1971. Repr. of the 1877 ed.

———. *New York by Sunlight and Gas Light.* New York: Union Publishing House, 1882.

McCall, George Archibald. *Letters from the Frontiers.* Philadelphia: J. B. Lippincott, 1868.

McCall, James. "M'Call's Journal of a Visit to Wisconsin in 1830." Wisconsin. State Historical Society *Collections.* (1892) 12.177–204.

McCall, William Anderson. *Cherokees and Pioneers.* Asheville NC: Printed by the Stephens Press, c.1952.

McCalla, William Latta. *Adventures in Texas.* Philadelphia: Printed for the author, 1841.

McCall's. New York, 1870–.

McCallum, Williamet al. *Letters Back Home from Maine-Staters Who Were Cutting White Oak Timbers in Tidewater Virginia.* 1841–1850. Unpub.

McCampbell, Coleman. *Texas Seaport.* New York: Exposition Press, 1952.

McCardell, Roy Larcom. *The Show Girl and Her Friends.* New York: Street & Smith, c.1904.

McCarthy, Carlton. *Detailed Minutiae of Soldier Life in the Army of Northern Virginia, 1861–1865.* Richmond VA: Carlton McCarthy, 1882.

McCarthy, Cormac. *Child of God.* New York: Random House, c.1973.

———. *The Crossing.* New York: Alfred A. Knopf, 1994.

McCarthy, Donald, ed. *Language of the Mosshorn.* Billings MT: Gazette Printing, c.1936.

McCarthy, Mary Therese. *The Company She Keeps.* New York: Simon & Schuster, 1942.

———. *The Group.* New York: Harcourt, Brace and World, c.1963.

———. *The Groves of Academe.* New York: Harcourt, Brace, c.1952.

McCarty, William, comp. *Songs, Odes, and Other Poems.* Philadelphia: Wm. McCarty, 1842. 3 vols.

McCauley, Robert H., Jr. *The Reptiles of Maryland and the District of Columbia.* Hagertown MD: Published by the author, c.1945.

McClanahan, A. J. *Our Stories, Our Lives.* Anchorage AK: CIRI Foundation, c.1986.

McClane, Albert Jules, ed. *McClane's New Standard Fishing Encyclopedia.* New York: Holt Rinehart and Winston, c.1974.

———, ed. *McClane's Standard Fishing Encyclopedia.* New York: Holt, Rinehart and Winston, c.1965.

McCleaf, Tim. *For They Know Not What They Do.* New York: iUniverse, c.2004.

McClellan, George Brinton. *The Mexican War Diary of George B. McClellan.* Princeton NJ: Princeton Univ. Press, 1917.

McClellan, R. Guy. *The Golden State.* Philadelphia: William Flint, 1872.

McClelland, Linda Flint. *Presenting Nature: the Historic Landscape Design of the National Park Service, 1916–1942.* Washington DC: U.S. Dept. of the Interior, National Park Service, 1993.

McClelland, Mary Greenway. *Oblivion, an Episode.* New York: H. Holt, 1885.

McClelland, Ted. *The Third Coast.* Chicago: Chicago Review Press, c.2008.

McClintock, Walter. *The Old North Trail.* London: Macmillan, 1910.

McClung, John W. *Minnesota as It Is in 1870.* St. Paul MN: The author, 1870.

McClure, Alexander Kelly. *Three Thousand Miles through the Rocky Mountains.* Philadelphia: J. B. Lippincott, 1869.

McClure, David. *Diary.* New York: Knickerbocker Press, 1899.

McClure's Magazine. New York, 1893–1929.

McConkie, Mark L., ed. *Remembering Joseph.* Salt Lake City UT: Deseret, c.2003.

McConnel, John Ludlum. *Western Characters.* New York: Redfield, 1853.

McConnell, H. H. *Five Years a Cavalryman.* Jacksboro TX: J. N. Rogers, 1889 [c.1888].

McCook, Henry Christopher. *The Natural History of the Ag-*

ricultural Ant of Texas. Author's ed. Philadelphia: Academy of Natural Sciences of Philadelphia, 1879.

———. *Tenants of an Old Farm.* New York: Fords, Howard, & Hulbert, 1885 [c.1884].

McCool, Sam. *Sam McCool's New Pittsburghese.* Pittsburgh PA: Hayford Press, c.1982.

McCormack, John. *Fields and Pastures New.* New York: Crown, c.1995.

McCormick, Linda M. *Vocabulary Usage in Hawaii.* ? HI: Univ. HI Senior honors thesis, 1972.

McCorrison, Albert L. *Letters from Fraternity.* New York: E. P. Dutton, 1931.

McCoy, Isaac. "Journal of Isaac McCoy for the Exploring Expedition of 1828." *Kansas Historical Quarterly.* (1936) 5.227–77, 339–77.

McCoy, Joseph Geiting. *Historic Sketches of the Cattle Trade of the West and Southwest.* Kansas City MO: Ramsey, Millet & Hudson, 1874.

———. *Historic Sketches of the Cattle Trade of the West and Southwest.* Ed. by Ralph P. Bieber. Glendale CA: Arthur H. Clark, 1940.

McCracken, Stephen Bromley. *Michigan and the Centennial.* Detroit MI: Office of the Detroit Free Press, 1876.

McCullers, Carson Smith. *Clock without Hands.* Boston: Houghton Mifflin, 1961.

———. *The Heart Is a Lonely Hunter.* Boston: Houghton Mifflin, c.1940.

———. *The Member of the Wedding.* Boston: Houghton Mifflin, 1946.

———. *The Square Root of Wonderful.* New York: Samuel French, c.1958.

McCulloch, Walter Fraser. *Woods Words.* Portland OR: Oregon Historical Society, 1958.

McCulloch-Williams, Martha. *Dishes and Beverages of the Old South.* New York: McBride Nast, 1913.

———. *Next to the Ground.* New York: McClure, Phillips, 1902.

McCutcheon, George Barr. *The Daughter of Anderson Crow.* New York: Dodd, Mead, 1907.

———. *Green Fancy.* New York: Dodd, Mead, 1917.

———. *A Rose in the Ring.* New York: A. L. Burt, c.1910.

McDaniel, H. F. and N. A. Taylor. *The Coming Empire.* New York: A. S. Barnes, c.1877.

McDavid, Raven I., Jr. *Collection of Materials from Various Linguistic Atlas Field Work.* 1933–1987. Unpub.

McDavid, Raven I. Jr. and Virginia G. McDavid. "The Late Unpleasantness: Folk Names for the Civil War." *Southern Speech Journal.* (1969) 34.3.194–204.

McDavid, Raven I., Jr. et al., eds. *Linguistic Atlas of the Middle and South Atlantic States.* Chicago: Univ. Chicago Press, 1991–.

McDermott, John Francis. *A Glossary of Mississippi Valley French, 1673–1850.* St. Louis MO: Washington Univ., 1941.

McDonald, Angus Henry. *Old McDonald Had a Farm.* Boston: Houghton Mifflin, 1942.

McDonough, Nancy. *Garden Sass.* New York: Coward, McCann & Geoghegan, 1975.

McDougall, Walter Byron and Herma A. Baggley. *Plants of Yellowstone National Park.* Washington DC: Govt. Printing Office, 1936.

McDowell, Amanda and Lela McDowell Blankenship. *Fiddles in the Cumberlands.* New York: Richard R. Smith, 1943.

McDowell, Charles Rice. *The Iron Baby Angel.* New York: Holt, 1954.

McDowell, Deborah E. *Leaving Pipe Shop.* New York: Scribner, c.1996.

McDowell, Katherine Sherwood Bonner. *Dialect Tales.* Freeport NY: Books for Libraries Press, 1972. Orig. pub. in 1883 by Harper & Bros., New York.

———. *Like unto Like.* New York: Harper & Bros., 1878.

McElrath, Frances. *The Rustler.* New York: Funk & Wagnalls, c.1902.

McElrath, Thomson P. *Yellowstone Valley.* St. Paul MN: Pioneer Press, 1880.

McEvoy, Joseph Patrick. *Slams of Life, with Malice toward All, Charity toward None, Assembled in Rhyme.* Chicago: P. F. Volland, 1919.

McFarland, John Horace. *Garden Bulbs in Color.* New York: Macmillan, 1938.

McFaul, Alexander D. *Ike Glidden in Maine.* Boston: Dickerman Pub., 1903.

McGaffey, Kenneth. *The Sorrows of a Show-Girl.* Chicago: J. I. Austen, 1908.

McGeachy, Beth. *Handbook of Florida Palms.* 3d ed. St. Petersburg FL: Great Outdoors Pub., 1960.

McGill, Samuel Davis. *Narrative of Reminiscences in*

Williamsburg County. Kingstree SC: Kingstree Lithographic, c.1952. Orig. printed in 1897 by Bryan Printing, Columbia SC.

McGovern, Chauncey. *When the Krag Is Laid Away*. Manila: Escolta Press, 1910.

McGraw-Hill Encyclopedia of Science and Technology. New York: McGraw-Hill, 1960. 15 vols.

McGreevy, Susan Brown. *Indian Basketry Artists of the Southwest*. Santa Fe NM: School of American Research Press, 2001.

McGregor, Alexander Campbell. *Counting Sheep*. Seattle WA: Univ. WA Press, c.1982.

McGuire, Phillip. *Taps for a Jim Crow Army*. Santa Barbara CA: ABC-Clio, c.1983.

McGuire, William Joseph, Jr. *A Study of Florida Cracker Dialect Based Chiefly on the Prose Works of Marjorie Kinnan Rawlings*. Gainesville FL: Univ. FL M.A. thesis, 1939.

McHenry, Beth and Frederick N. Myers. *Home Is the Sailor*. New York: International, c.1948.

McHugh, Hugh SEE Hobart, George Vere

McIlvaine, Charles and Robert K. Macadam. *One Thousand American Fungi*. Rev. ed. Indianapolis IN: Bowen-Merrill, c.1902.

McInerney, Jay. *Ransom*. New York: Vintage Books, c.1985.

McIntire, Suzanne. *An American Cutting Garden*. Charlottesville VA: Univ. Press VA, 2002.

McIntosh, Maria Jane. *The Lofty and the Lowly*. New York: D. Appleton, 1853 [c.1852]. 2 vols.

McJimsey, George Davis. *Topographic Terms in Virginia*. New York: Columbia Univ. Press, 1940.

McKay, Claude. *Banjo: a Story without a Plot*. New York: Harper & Bros., 1929.

————. *Home to Harlem*. New York: Harper & Bros., 1928.

McKean County Democrat. Smethport PA, 1928–1971.

McKean Democrat. Smethport PA, 1890–1924.

McKean Miner SEE *M'Kean Miner*

McKee, Lanier. *The Land of Nome*. New York: Grafton Press, 1902.

McKeen, Phebe F. *Theodora, a Home Story*. New York: A. D. F. Randolph, c.1875.

McKenna, James A. *Black Range Tales*. New York: Wilson-Erickson, 1936.

McKennan, Robert Addison. *The Upper Tanana Indians*. New Haven CT: Department of Anthropology, Yale Univ., 1959.

McKenney, Thomas Loraine. *Sketches of a Tour to the Lakes*. Baltimore MD: Fielding Lucas, 1827.

McKenzie, Fred. *Avinger, Texas, USA*. Avinger TX: F. McKenzie, 1988–1999. 2 vols.

McKenzie Banner. McKenzie TN, 1936–.

McKinley Morganfield a.k.a. Muddy Waters. Phonodisc. New York: Chess, 1973.

McKinney, Fanny Lee. *Nora-Square-Accounts*. New York: D. Appleton, 1912.

McKinney, John. *California's Desert Parks*. Berkeley CA: Wilderness Press, 2006.

McKinstry, Mark Calvert et al., eds. *Wetland and Riparian Areas of the Intermountain West*. Austin TX: Univ. TX Press, c.2004.

McKnight, Kent H. and Vera B. McKnight. *A Field Guide to Mushrooms*. Boston: Houghton Mifflin, c.1987.

McLain, John Scudder. *Alaska and the Klondike*. New York: McClure, Phillips, 1905.

McLaughlin, Andrew C. and Albert Bushnell Hart, eds. *Cyclopedia of American Government*. New York: D. Appleton, 1914. 3 vols.

McLaughlin, Emma and Nicola Kraus. *The Nanny Diaries*. New York: St. Martin's Press, 2002.

McLeran, Vic. *The Cooper's Hawk*. [s.l.]: XLibris, c.2000.

McMahon, Bernard. *The American Gardener's Calendar*. Philadelphia: Graves, 1806.

————. *Catalogue of American Seeds*. Philadelphia: Printed by Bartholomew Graves, 1804.

McMeekin, Clark, [pseud.]. *Old Kentucky Country*. New York: Duell, Sloan & Pearce, 1957.

McMinn, Howard. *An Illustrated Manual of California Shrubs*. San Francisco: J. W. Stacey, 1939.

McMullen, Edwin Wallace. *English Topographic Terms in Florida, 1563–1874*. Gainesville FL: Univ. FL Press, 1953.

McNab, Chris. *Living off the Land*. Guilford CT: Lyons Press, c.2002.

McNeal, Thomas Allen. *When Kansas Was Young*. New York: Macmillan, 1922.

McNealus, Virginia Quitman. *The Lay of the Land: a Collection of Short Stories*. New York: Neale Publishing, 1916.

McNeil, Kathryn K. *Purchase Knob*. Santa Barbara CA: Fithian Press, 1999.

McNemar, Richard. *The Kentucky Revival*. Cincinnati OH: John W. Browne, 1807.

McNichols, Charles Longstreth. *Crazy Weather*. Lincoln NE: Univ. NE Press, 1967. Orig. pub. in 1944 by Macmillan, New York.

M'Collum, William S. *California as I Saw It*. Buffalo NY: G. H. Derby, 1850.

McPhee, John A. *Coming into the Country*. New York: Farrar, Straus and Giroux, 1977.

————. *Giving Good Weight*. New York: Farrar, Straus, Giroux, 1979.

————. *The Pine Barrens*. New York: Farrar, Straus & Giroux, 1968.

————. *Rising from the Plains*. New York: Farrar Straus Giroux, c.1986.

————. *Table of Contents*. New York: Farrar Straus Giroux, c.1985.

McPherson, James Alan. *Hue and Cry*. Boston: Little, Brown, 1969.

McQueen, Alexander S. and Hamp Mizell. *History of Okefenokee Swamp*. Folkston GA: [s.n.], 1949. Orig. pub. in 1926 by the Press of Jacobs, Clinton SC.

————. *History of Okefenokee Swamp*. Folkston GA: Charlton County Historical Society, 1992 [c.1926]. Facsimile repr. of 1926 ed. pub. by Press of Jacobs, Clinton SC.

McWilliams, Carey. *Southern California Country*. New York: Duell, Sloan & Pearce, 1946.

Meachum, John B. *An Address to All the Colored Citizens of the United States*. Chapel Hill NC: Academic Affairs Library, Univ. NC at Chapel Hill, 2001. Text transcr. for *Documenting the American South* website from the 1846 ed. printed for the author, by King and Baird, Philadelphia.

Mead, Cyrus De Witt and Fred William Orth. *The Transitional Public School*. New York: Macmillan, 1935 [c.1934].

Mead, Frank S. *Handbook of Denominations in the United States*. 7th ed. new. Nashville TN: Abingdon, c.1980.

Mead, Margaret. *Blackberry Winter*. New York: Wm. Morrow, 1972.

Mead, Whitman. *Travels in North America*. New York: C. S. Van Winkle, 1820.

Meade, Julian Rutherford. *Adam's Profession and Its Conquest by Eve*. New York: Longmans, Green, 1937 [c.1936].

Meader J. W. *The Merrimack River*. Boston: B. B. Russell, 1869.

Means, Eldred Kurtz. *More E. K. Means*. New York: G. P. Putnam's Sons, 1919.

Meany, Edmond Stephen, ed. *Mount Rainier, a Record of Exploration*. New York: Macmillan, 1916.

Mearns, Edgar Alexander. *Mammals of the Mexican Boundary of the United States*. Washington DC: Govt. Printing Office, 1907.

Mease, Edward. "Narrative of a Journey through Several Parts of the Province of West Florida in the Years 1770 and 1771." Mississippi Historical Society *Publications, Centenary Series*. (1925) 5.58–90.

Mebane, Mary Elizabeth. *Mary*. New York: Viking Press, 1981.

————. *Mary, Wayfarer*. New York: Viking Press, 1983.

Mebane Enterprise and Hillsborough Journal. Mebane NC, 1919?–.

Mech, L. David, ed. *The Wolves of Minnesota: Howl in the Heartland*. Stillwater MN: Voyageur Press, 2000.

Mechanics' Press. Utica NY, 1829–1830.

Meck, Charles R. and Gregory A. Hoover. *Great Rivers, Great Hatches*. Harrisburg PA: Stackpole Books, c.1992.

MED SEE Kurath, Hans et al. *Middle English Dictionary*

Medbery, James Knowles. *Men and Mysteries of Wall Street*. New York: R. Worthington, 1878. Orig. pub. in 1870 by Fields, Osgood, Boston.

Medford, W. Clark. *Great Smoky Mountain Stories*. Waynesville NC: [s.n.], c.1966.

Medical and Physical Journal. London, 1799–1814.

Medical and Surgical Reporter. Philadelphia, 1858–1898.

Medical Association of the State of Alabama. *Transactions*. Montgomery AL, 1871?–1930.

Medical Brief. St. Louis MO: Henry R. Strong, 1873–1929.

Medical Convention of Ohio. *Proceedings*. Columbus OH, 1835–1851.

Medical Pickwick. New York, 1915–1927.

Medical Record. New York, 1866–1922.

Medical Register. Philadelphia, 1887–1889.

Medical Repository and Review of American Publications on Medicine, Surgery, and the Auxiliary Branches of Science. New York, 1797–1824.

Medina, Pablo. *Cigar Roller*. New York: Grove Press, c.2005.

Medsger, Oliver Perry. *Edible Wild Plants*. New York: Macmillan, 1939.

Meehan, Thomas. *The American Handbook of Ornamental Trees*. Philadelphia: Lippincott, Grambo, 1853.

————. *The Native Flowers and Ferns of the United States in Their Botanical, Horticultural and Popular Aspects, Series [I] and II*. Boston: L. Prang, 1878–1880. 4 vols.

Megargel, Percy F. and Grace Sartwell Mason. *The Car and the Lady*. New York: Baker and Taylor, 1908.

Megquier, Mary Jane. *Apron Full of Gold*. Ed. by Robert Glass Cleland. San Marino CA: Huntington Library, 1949.

Meigs, Charles Delucena. *Observations on Certain of the Diseases of Young Children*. Philadelphia: Lea and Blanchard, 1850.

Meine, Franklin Julius, ed. *Tall Tales of the Southwest*. New York: Alfred A. Knopf, 1930.

Meinkoth, Norman A. *The Audubon Society Field Guide to North American Seashore Creatures*. New York: Knopf, c.1981.

Meline, James Florant. *Two Thousand Miles on Horseback, Santa Fé and Back*. New York: Hurd and Houghton, 1868 [c.1867].

Mellen, Grenville, ed. *A Book of the United States*. Hartford CT: H. F. Sumner, 1836.

Mellick, Andrew D. *The Story of an Old Farm*. Somerville NJ: Unionist-Gazette, 1889.

Melton, Callie Myers. *'Pon My Honor: Folk Tales from the Upper Cumberland*. [s.l.]: [s.n.], 1979.

Meltzer, Milton, ed. *In Their Own Words*. New York: Thomas Y. Crowell, c.1964–1967. 3 vols.

Melville, Herman. *Billy Budd*. London: Constable, 1924.

————. *Journal of a Visit to London and the Continent, 1849–1850*. Cambridge MA: Harvard Univ. Press, 1948.

————. *Mardi, and a Voyage Thither*. New York: Harper & Bros., 1849. 2 vols.

————. *Moby-Dick*. New York: W. W. Norton, c.1976. Orig. pub. in 1851 by Harper & Bros., New York.

————. *Pierre*. Evanston IL: Northwestern Univ. Press and The Newberry Library, 1971. Orig. pub. in 1852 by Harper & Bros., New York.

————. *Redburn*. New York: Harper & Bros., 1855. Orig. pub. in 1849 by Harper & Bros., New York.

————. *Typee*. London: J. Murray, 1847.

————. *White-Jacket*. New York: Harper & Bros., 1850.

————. *The Works of Herman Melville*. London: Constable, 1922–1924. 16 vols.

Memoirs of the Connecticut Academy of Arts and Sciences. New Haven CT, 1810–.

Memphis Appeal-Avalanche. Memphis TN, 1847–1894.

Mencken, Henry Louis. *The American Language*. New York: Knopf, 1919.

————. *The American Language*. 4th ed. corr., enlarged, and rewritten. New York: Knopf, 1947 [c.1936].

————. *The American Language . . . Supplement I*. New York: Knopf, 1945.

————. *The American Language . . . Supplement II*. New York: Knopf, 1948.

Mencken, Henry Louis and Raven I. McDavid. *The American Language*. 4th ed. and the two supplements, abridged, with annotations and new material. New York: Knopf, 1963.

Mencken, Henry Louis. *Christmas Story*. New York: Alfred A. Knopf, 1946 [c.1944]. Orig. printed in *The New Yorker* 20.17–21 Dec. 30, 1944 under the title *Stare decises*.

————. *Happy Days, 1880–1892*. New York: Alfred A. Knopf, 1940.

————. *Prejudices*. New York: Alfred A. Knopf, c.1919.

Mendocino Beacon. Mendocino CA, 1877–.

Menefee, Selden Cowles. *Assignment: U.S.A*. New York: Reynal & Hitchcock, c.1943.

Mercer, M. C. *Systemics and Biology of the Sepiolid Squids of the Genus Rossia*. St. John's, Newfoundland: Memorial Univ. M.S. thesis, 1968.

Mercer, William Newton. "A Journey from Baltimore to Louisville in 1816: Diary of William Newton Mercer." *Ohio History*. (1936) 45.351–64.

Merchants' Magazine and Commercial Review. New York: F. Hunt, 1839–1870.

Mercier, Henry James and William Gallop. *Life in a Man-of-War*. Philadelphia: L. R. Bailey, c.1841.

The Merck Veterinary Manual. 3d ed. Rahway NJ: Merck, 1967.

Meredith, Mamie J. *A Collection of Miscellaneous Clippings and Notes on the Subject of Cornhusking*. 1938–1939. Unpub. coll. of materials on Amer. Engl. usage.

Mereness, Newton Dennison, ed. *Travels in the American Colonies*. New York: Macmillan, 1916.

Merriam, Clinton Hart, ed. *The Dawn of the World*. Cleveland OH: Arthur H. Clark, 1910.

Merriam, Kendall. *The Illustrated Dictionary of Lobstering.* Freeport ME: Cumberland Press, c.1978.

Merrill, Boynton. *Jefferson's Nephews.* Princeton NJ: Princeton Univ. Press, c.1976.

Merrill's Golden Jubilee and the 25th Anniversary of the Merrill Daily Herald. Merrill WI: Merrill Daily Herald, 1934.

Merriman, Stony. *Midnight Moonshine Rendezvous: the Secrets of Luke Alexander Denny's Moonshine Running Adventures (1930s–1960s).* Smithville TN: M. Stone, 1990.

Merry's Museum. New York [etc], 1841–1848; 1868–1872.

Merry's Museum, Parley's Magazine, Woodworth's Cabinet, and the Schoolfellow. New York, 1858–1866.

Mertie, John Beaver and George Leavitt Harrington. *The Ruby-Kuskokwim Region Alaska.* Washington DC: Govt. Printing Office, 1924.

Mertins, Gustave Frederick. *The Storm Signal.* New York: A. L. Burt, 1905.

Merwin, Samuel and Henry Kitchell Webster. *Calumet "K".* New York: Macmillan, 1901.

Messer, Timothy B. *Civil War Letters of Timothy B. Messer Tenth Vermont Volunteers.* Ed. by Edward C. Phelps. Greenfield MA: E. A. Hall, 1986.

Metcalf, Allan A. *How We Talk.* Boston: Houghton Mifflin, c.2000.

———. *Riverside English.* Riverside CA: Univ. CA, c.1971.

Metcalf, Clell Lee and W. P. Flint. *Destructive and Useful Insects.* New York: McGraw-Hill, 1928.

Metcalf, Clyde Hill, ed. *The Marine Corps Reader.* New York: G. P. Putnam's Sons, 1944.

Methodist Magazine and Quarterly Review. New York, 1830–1840.

Methodist Review. New York, 1885–1931.

MetroActive. 2000?–. Internet.

Metro Magazine. Raleigh NC, 1999–.

Metronome. New York, 1932–1958.

Metropolitan. New York, 1911–1924.

MetroWest Jewish News. East Orange NJ, 1988–1997.

Mexia Daily News. Mexia TX, 1923–.

Mexia Evening News. Mexia TX, 1899?–1923.

Mexia Weekly Herald. Mexia TX, 1908–1948.

Mexican Cook Book SEE *Sunset Mexican Cook Book*

Meyer, Clarence, comp. *American Folk Medicine.* New York: Thomas Y. Crowell, c.1973.

Meyer Brothers Druggist. St. Louis MO, 1888–1919.

Meyers, Walter E. *Eskimo Village.* New York: Vantage Press, c.1957.

Mezzrow, Milton and Bernard Wolfe. *Really the Blues.* Garden City NY: Doubleday, 1972. Orig. pub. in 1946 by Random House, New York.

M'Harry, Samuel. *The Practical Distiller.* Harrisburgh [sic] PA: John Wyeth, c.1809. Text transcr. in 2007 by Project Gutenberg.

Miami Herald. Miami FL, 1910–.

Michaux, André. *Flora Boreali-Americana.* Paris: [s.n.], 1803. 2 vols.

———. *Histoire des Chenes de l'Amerique.* Paris: Crapelet, 1801.

Michaux, François André. *Histoire des Arbres Forestiers de l'Amerique Septentrionale.* Paris: L. Haussmann et D'Hautel, 1810–1813. 3 vols.

———. *The North American Sylva.* Transl. by Augustus L. Hillhouse. Philadelphia: Sold by Thomas Dobson; Paris: Printed by C. D'Hautel, 1819. 3 vols.

———. *Voyage à l'Ouest des Monts Alléghanys.* Paris: Levrault, Schoell, 1804.

Michener, James Albert. *Chesapeake.* New York: Random House, c.1978.

Michigan Academy of Science. *Report.* Lansing MI, 1904–1916.

Michigan. Agricultural Experiment Station. *Technical Bulletin.* East Lansing MI: MI State College, 1908–1964.

Michigan Constitutional Convention. *Report of the Proceedings and Debates in the Convention to Revise the Constitution of the State of Michigan.* Lansing MI: R. W. Ingals, 1850.

Michigan Farmer and Livestock Journal. Detroit MI, 1905–1928.

Michigan Geological Survey. *First Biennial Report.* Lansing MI: Hosmer & Kerr, 1861 [c.1860].

Michigan. Historical Commission. *Michigan Historical Collections.* Lansing MI, 1874–1929.

Michigan History. Lansing MI: Michigan Historical Commission, 1947–1990.

Michigan History Magazine. Lansing MI, 1917–1946; 1991–.

Michigan. Laws. *General Statutes of the State of Michigan.* Chicago, 1882–1890.

Michigan Log Marks. Muskegon MI: Muskegon Community College, 1971. Orig. pub. in 1941 by the MI Ag. Exper. Sta., East Lansing, MI.

Michigan Pioneer and Historical Society. *Historical Collections.* Lansing MI, 1886–1912.

Michigan. State Agricultural Society. *Transactions.* Lansing MI, 1850–1861.

Michigan. State Board of Agriculture. *Annual Report of the Secretary.* Lansing MI: John A. Kerr, 18??–

Michigan State Horticultural Society. *Annual Report of the Secretary.* Lansing MI, 1880?–1989?

Michigan State University. *Landscape Crop Advisory Team Alert.* East Lansing MI, 1985?–

Michigan State University. Cooperative Extension Service. *Extension Bulletin.* East Lansing MI, 1916–.

Michigan State University. Extension. *Home Horticulture.* [v.d.]. Internet.

Michigan. Superintendent of Public Instruction. *Annual Report.* Lansing MI, 1857–1927.

Michigan Today. Ann Arbor MI, 1900–.

Michigan. University. Museum of Zoology. *Miscellaneous Publications.* Ann Arbor MI, 1916–.

———. *Occasional Papers.* Ann Arbor MI, 1913–.

Mickelson, Pete. *Natural History of Alaska's Prince William Sound.* Cordova AK: Alaska Wild Wings, 1989.

Mickler, Ernest Matthew. *White Trash Cooking.* Winston-Salem NC: Jargon Society, 1986.

Mid-American Review. Bowling Green OH, 1981–.

Middle Border Bulletin. Mitchell SD: Friends of the Middle Border, 1941–.

Middlesboro Daily News. Middlesboro KY, 1920–1981.

Middletown Daily Herald. Middletown NY, 1919–1925.

Middletown Daily Press. Middletown NY, 1876–1906.

Middletown Daily Times. Middletown NY, 1891–1906.

Middletown Times Herald. Middletown NY, 1927–1956.

Middletown Times-Press. Middletown NY, 1906–1926.

Midland Cooperator. Minneapolis MN, 1933–.

Midland Monthly. Des Moines IA, 1894–1899.

Midland Naturalist SEE *American Midland Naturalist*

Mid-Pacific Magazine. Honolulu HI, 1911–1936.

Midwestern Folklore. Terre Haute IN, 1987–.

Midwestern Journal of Language and Folklore. Terre Haute IN: IN State Univ., 1975–1986.

Midwestern Language and Folklore Newsletter. Terre Haute IN: IN State Univ., Dept. of English, 1978/1979–.

Midwest Fly Fishing Online. 1980–. Internet.

Midwest Folklore. Bloomington IN: IN Univ., 1951–1964.

Mieder, Wolfgang. *As Sweet as Apple Cider.* Shelburne VT: New England Press, c.1988.

———, ed. *A Dictionary of American Proverbs.* New York: Oxford Univ. Press, 1992.

Migrant. Memphis TN: Tennessee Ornithological Society, 1930–.

Milan Standard. Milan MN, 1900–1980.

Miles, Emma Bell. *The Spirit of the Mountains.* Knoxville TN: Univ. TN Press, c.1975. Facsimile of the 1905 ed. pub. by J. Pott, New York.

Miles, Guy, comp., ed. *Voices from the Countryside.* Miami FL: Banyan Books, 1977.

Miles, Kay White. *Ozark Dictionary.* Clinton MO: Democrat Pub., 1977.

Milford Chronicle. Milford DE, 1878–.

Military and Naval Magazine of the United States. Washington DC: Thompson and Homans, 1833–1836.

Military Surgeon. Washington DC, 1898–1901.

Millard, Henry B. *A Guide for Emergencies.* 3d ed. New York: Charles T. Hurlburt, 1871.

Millennial Harbinger. Bethany VA, 1830–1870.

Miller, Amy Bess W. *Shaker Herbs.* New York: Clarkson N. Potter, c.1976.

Miller, Caroline Pafford. *Lamb in His Bosom.* New York: Harper Bros., c.1933.

Miller, David Franklin and Glenn William Blaydes. *Methods and Materials for Teaching Biological Sciences.* New York: McGraw-Hill, 1938.

Miller, David Reed. *The Red Swan's Neck.* Boston: Sherman, French, 1911.

Miller, David William. *Exploring Alaska's Kenai Fjords.* [s.l.]: Wilderness Images Press, c.2004.

Miller, George Oxford. *Landscaping with Native Plants of Texas.* St. Paul MN: Voyageur Press, 2006.

Miller, Henry. *Black Spring.* Paris: Obelisk Press, 1938. Orig. pub. in 1936.

———. *Sexus.* Paris: Obelisk Press, 1949. 2 vols. *The Rosy Crucifixion,* Book 1.

———. *Tropic of Cancer.* Paris: Obelisk Press, 1939. Orig. pub. in 1934 by Obelisk Press, Paris.

———. *Tropic of Capricorn.* Paris: Obelisk Press, 1939.

Miller, Henry Russell. *The Ambition of Mark Truitt.* Indianapolis IN: Bobbs-Merrill, c.1913.

Miller, Joaquin. *First Fam'lies of the Sierras.* Chicago: Jansen, McClurg, 1876.

———. *Life amongst the Modocs.* London: Richard Bentley and Son, 1873.

———. *Memorie and Rime.* New York: Funk & Wagnalls, 1884.

———. *Songs of the Sierras.* Boston: Roberts Bros., 1871.

Miller, Larry L. *Tennessee Place-Names.* Bloomington IN: IN Univ. Press, 2001.

Miller, Orson K. *Mushrooms of North America.* New York: E. P. Dutton, 1972.

———. *North American Mushrooms.* Guilford CT: Falcon Guide, 2006.

Miller, Philip. *The Gardeners Dictionary.* London: Printed for the author, 1731–1739. 2 vols.

———. *The Gardeners Dictionary.* 2d ed. London: C. Rivington, 1733.

———. *The Gardeners Dictionary.* 3d ed. corr. London: Printed for the author, 1737–1739. 2 vols.

———. *The Gardeners Dictionary.* 6th ed. London: Printed for the Author, 1752.

———. *The Gardeners Dictionary.* 7th ed. London: Printed for the author, 1759.

———. *The Gardeners Dictionary.* 8th ed. rev. and altered. London: Printed for the author, 1768.

Miller, Randall M., comp. *Dear Master.* Ithaca NY: Cornell Univ. Press, c.1978.

Miller, Warren. *The Siege of Harlem.* New York: McGraw-Hill, 1964.

Miller, Warren Hastings. *The Boys' Book of Hunting and Fishing.* New York: George H. Doran, c.1916.

Miller, Wilhelm, ed. *How to Make a Flower Garden.* New York: Doubleday, Page, 1910 [c.1903].

Miller, William. *A Dictionary of English Names of Plants.* London: John Murray, 1884.

Millersville University. Center for Pennsylvania German Studies. *Journal.* Millersville PA, 1989–.

Mills, Enos Abijah. *The Spell of the Rockies.* Boston: Houghton Mifflin, 1911.

———. *Waiting in the Wilderness.* Garden City NY: Doubleday, Page, 1921 [c.1920].

Mills, Kerry and George F. Marion. *Rastus on Parade.* New York: F. A. Mills, c.1896.

Millspaugh, Charles Frederick. *American Medicinal Plants.* New York: Dover Pub., 1974. Repr. of the 1892 ed. pub. by J. C. Yorston, Philadelphia under the title *Medicinal Plants* in 2 vols.

———. *The Living Flora of West Virginia.* Wheeling WV: Wheeling News Litho, 1913.

Milne, A. D. *Uncle Sam's Farm Fence.* New York: C. Shepard, 1854.

Milne, James. *John Jonathan and Company.* New York: Macmillan, c.1912?

Milne, Lorus Johnson and Margery Milne. *The Audubon Society Field Guide to North American Insects and Spiders.* New York: Alfred A. Knopf, 1980.

Milwaukee, Wisconsin. *Charter Ordinances of the City of Milwaukee.* Milwaukee WI: Municipal Reference Library, Milwaukee Public Library, 1946.

Milwaukee Daily Sentinel. Milwaukee WI, 1851–1861.

Milwaukee Journal. Milwaukee WI, 1890–.

Milwaukee Journal Sentinel. Milwaukee WI, 1995–.

Milwaukee Sentinel. Milwaukee WI, 1851–.

Milwaukee Sentinel and Gazette. Milwaukee WI, 1848–1850.

Milwaukee Talk. Milwaukee WI: WTMJ, WTMJ-TV, the Milwaukee Journal Stations, c.1951. Words and expressions excerpted from 2,117 letters received by WTMJ in a contest conducted by the Milwaukee Grenadiers Radio Program.

Milwaukie Daily Sentinel. Milwaukee WI, 1844–1846.

Milwaukie Journal. Milwaukee WI, 1841–1842.

Minehan, Thomas. *Boy and Girl Tramps of America.* New York: Farrar and Rinehart, c.1934.

Miner, T. B. *The American Bee Keeper's Manual.* 2d ed. New York: C. M. Saxton, 1850.

Miniter, Edith. *Our Natupski Neighbors.* New York: Henry Holt, 1916.

Minnesota Conservation Volunteer. St. Paul MN, 1999–.

Minnesota Department of Natural Resources. *Invasive Aquatic Plants.* [v.d.]. Internet.

Minnesota. Division of Parks and Recreation. *Blue Mounds State Park.* St. Paul MN: [s.n.], 1978.

Minnesota Historical Society. *Collections.* St. Paul MN, 1864–1920.

Minnesota History. St. Paul MN: Minnesota Historical Society, 1925–.

Minnesota Horticulturist. St. Paul MN, 1894–1999.

Minnesota. Laws, Statutes etc. *General Statutes of the State of Minnesota in Force, Jan. 1, 1889.* St. Paul MN: West Publishing, 1888. 2 vols.

Minnesota Public Radio. *Monsters of the Lumber Camps.* 1997. Internet.

Minnesota. State Board of Health. *Report.* Red Wing MN?, 1880–1886.

Minnesota State Horticultural Society. *Annual Report.* Minneapolis MN, 1883–1898.

Minnesota. University. *Cedar Creek Ecosystem Science Reserve.* [v.d.]. Internet.

———. *Cedar Creek Natural History Area.* [v.d.]. Internet.

———. *Fishes of Minnesota.* [v.d.]. Internet.

———. *Insects of Cedar Creek.* [v.d.]. Internet.

———. *Plants of Cedar Creek.* [v.d.]. Internet.

Minnesota. University. Agricultural Experiment Station. *Bulletin.* St. Paul MN, 1888–1952.

Minnesota. University. Extension Service. *Beef Cattle Management Update.* St. Paul MN, 1989–1999.

———. *Minnesota Crop eNews.* 2001?–. Internet.

Minot, Henry Davis. *The Land-Birds and Game-Birds of New England.* Salem MA: Naturalists' Agency, 1877 [c.1876].

———. *The Land-Birds and Game-Birds of New England.* 2d ed. Boston: Houghton, Mifflin, 1895.

Minot, William. *Private Letters of William Minot.* Coll. and arranged by his son William Minot. Boston: Printed for the family, 1895.

Minton, Orlena Marian. *Rag Weed Rhymes of Rural Folks.* New York: Aberdeen Publishing, c.1910.

Mirick, Benjamin L. *The History of Haverhill, Massachusetts.* Haverhill MA: A. W. Thayer, 1832.

Mirror of Literature, Amusement and Instruction. London, 1822–1847.

Mirror of Taste and Dramatic Censor. Philadelphia, 1810–1811.

Mission Messenger. St. Louis MO, 1957–1975.

Mississippi Folklore Register. Hattiesburg MS, 1967–.

Mississippi Geological, Economic and Topographical Survey. *Bulletin.* Jackson MS, 1963–1977?

Mississippi Historical Society. *Publications, Centenary Series.* Jackson MS, 1916–1925.

Mississippi Quarterly. Mississippi State MS, 1948–.

Mississippi. State Geologist. *Report on the Geology and Agriculture of the State of Mississippi.* By Eugene W. Hilgard, State Geologist. Jackson MS: E. Barksdale, State Printer, 1860.

Mississippi. University. Center for the Study of Southern Culture. *Voices of Perthshire.* Video recording. University MS: Univ. of MS, 1999.

Mississippi Valley Historical Review. Urbana IL: Mississippi Valley Historical Association, 1914–1964.

Mississippi Writers Talking. Ed. by John Griffin Jones. Jackson MS: Univ. Press MS, 1982–1983. 2 vols.

Missouri Botanical Garden. *Annals.* St. Louis MO: Missouri Botanical Garden Press, 1914–.

———. *Annual Report.* St. Louis MO, 1890–1912.

———. *Bulletin.* St. Louis MO, 1913–.

Missouri Botanical Garden Homepage. [v.d.]. Internet.

Missouri Conservationist. Jefferson City MO: Missouri Department of Conservation, 1938–.

Missouri Conservationist Online. 1995–. Internet.

Missouri Department of Conservation. *Forestry Page.* [v.d.]. Internet.

Missouri Folklore Society Journal. Columbia MO, 1979–.

Missouri Gazette & Public Advertiser. St. Louis MO, 1808–1823.

Missouri. Geological Survey. *First-Fifth Report of the Progress of the Geological Survey of Missouri.* By G. C. Swallow. Jefferson City MO: [s.n.], 1855–1861.

———. *Report of the Geological Survey of the State of Missouri.* Garland C. Broadhead, State Geologist. Jefferson City MO: Regan & Carter, State Printers & Binders, 1874.

Missouri Historical Review. Columbia MO, 1906–.

Missouri Historical Society. *Collections.* St. Louis MO, 1880–.

Missouri Intelligencer. Franklin MO, 1819–1827.

Missouri Review. Columbia MO: Univ. MO, 1978–.

Missouri. State Board of Agriculture. *Annual Report.* Jefferson City MO, 1865–1871.

Missouri. State Entomologist. *Annual Report on the Noxious, Beneficial and Other Insects of the State of Missouri 1st–9th.* Jefferson City MO, 1868–1877.

Missouri State Horticultural Society. *Report.* Jefferson City MO, 1859–1886.

Mitchard, Jacquelyn. *The Most Wanted.* New York: Viking, c.1998.

———. *Mother Less Child.* New York: W. W. Norton, c.1985.

Mitchell, Donald Grant. *Fudge Doings.* New York: C. Scribner, 1855. 2 vols.

———. *The Lorgnette.* 2d ed. New York: Stringer and Townsend, c.1850. 2 vols.

———. *My Farm of Edgewood.* New York: Charles Scribner, 1864 [c.1863].

Mitchell, Edwin Valentine. *The Horse & Buggy Age in New England.* New York: Coward-McCann, 1937.

———. *It's an Old Pennsylvania Custom.* New York: Vanguard Press, 1947.

Mitchell, Frederick Augustus. *Chickamauga, a Romance of the American Civil War.* New York: Star Book, 1892.

Mitchell, George. *Blow My Blues Away.* Baton Rouge LA: LA State Univ. Press, c.1971.

Mitchell, John. *Reminiscences of Scenes and Characters in College.* New Haven CT: A. H. Maltby, c.1847.

Mitchell, Joseph. *McSorley's Wonderful Saloon.* New York: Duell, Sloan and Pearce, c.1943.

Mitchell, Joseph C. *Reptiles of Virginia.* Washington DC: Smithsonian Institution, c.1994.

Mitchell, Margaret. *Gone with the Wind.* New York: Macmillan, 1936.

———. *Gone with the Wind.* New York: Macmillan, 1951. Orig. pub. in 1936.

Mitchell, Silas Weir. *The Collected Poems.* New York: Century, c.1896.

———. *Roland Blake.* Boston: Houghton, Mifflin, 1886.

Mitchell, Steve. *How to Speak Southern.* Toronto: Bantam Books, 1976.

MJLF See *Midwestern Journal of Language and Folklore*

M'Kean Miner. Smethport PA, 1860–1870.

M'Kinnen, Daniel. *Descriptive Poems.* New York: Printed by T. & F. Swords, 1802.

———. *A Tour through the British West Indies in the Years 1802 and 1803.* London: Printed for J. White, 1804.

MLJ See *Modern Language Journal*

MLN See *Modern Language Notes*

M'Mahon, Bernard See McMahon, Bernard

M'Nemar, Richard See McNemar, Richard

Modern Language Association of America. *Publications.* Baltimore MD, 1884–.

Modern Language Journal. Menasha WI: National Federation of Modern Language Teachers, 1916–.

Modern Language Notes. Baltimore MD: Johns Hopkins Press, 1886–.

Modern Maturity. Long Beach CA: American Association of Retired Persons, 1958–2002.

Modern Priscilla Cookbook. Boston: Priscilla Pub., c.1929.

Modesto Bee. Modesto CA, 1975–.

Modesto Bee & News-Herald. Modesto CA, 1933–1975.

Modesto Evening News. Modesto CA, 1913–1925.

Modesto News. Modesto CA, 1902–1913.

Moelleken, Wolfgang W., ed. *Dialectology, Linguistics, Literature.* Goppingen: Kummerle Verlag, 1984.

Moffat, R. Burnham. *Pierrepont Genealogies.* [s.l.]: Privately printed, 1913.

Mohlenbrock, Robert H. *This Land: a Guide to Eastern National Forests.* Berkeley CA: Univ. CA Press, c.2006.

Mohr, Charles Theodore. *Plant Life in Alabama.* Alabama ed. Montgomery AL: Brown Printing, 1901.

Mohr, Charles Theodore and Filibert Roth. *The Timber Pines of the Southern United States.* Washington DC: Govt. Printing Office, 1896.

Mohr, Howard. *How to Talk Minnesotan.* New York: Penguin Books, c.1987.

Mojave Desert News. Mojave CA, 1938–.

Mokler, Alfred James. *History of Natrona County Wyoming.* Chicago: R. R. Donnelley, 1923.

Moldenke, Harold Norman. *American Wild Flowers.* New York: D. Van Nostrand, c.1949.

Mombert, Jacob Isidor. *An Authentic History of Lancaster County, in the State of Pennsylvania.* Lancaster PA: J. E. Barr, 1869.

Monadnock Regionaire. Peterborough NH, 1959–1966?

Monaghan, E. Jennifer. *Learning to Read and Write in Colonial America.* Amherst MA: Univ. MA Press, c.2005.

Monardes, Nicolás. *Joyfull Newes Out of the Newe Founde Worlde.* Englished by John Frampton. London: Constable, 1925. 2 vols. Orig. pub. in 1577 by William Norton, London.

Monessen Daily Independent. Monessen PA, 1921–1956.

Monette, John W. *History of the Discovery and Settlement of the Valley of the Mississippi.* New York: Harper & Bros., 1846. 2 vols.

Monitor. Washington DC, 1808–1809.

Monona Community Herald. Monona WI, 1968–.

Monroe, James. *Message at the Commencement of the Second Session of the Fifteenth Congress.* Washington DC: Printed by E. De Krafft, 1818.

Monroe, John. *The American Botanist and Family Physician.* Comp. by Silas Gaskill. Wheelock VT: Jonathan Morrison, 1824.

Monroe Evening Times. Monroe WI, 1898–.

Monroe Weekly Times. Monroe WI, 1890?–1907?

Montana Agricultural Experiment Station. *Bulletin.* Bozeman MT, 1894–1983.

Montana Field Guide. [v.d.]. Internet.

Montana. Historical Society. *Contributions.* Helena MT, 1876–.

Montana Natural History Center. *Field Notes Quarterly.* Missoula MT, 1995?–.

Montana Standard. Butte MT, 1928–1961.

Montell, William Lynwood. *Don't Go up Kettle Creek.* Knoxville TN: Univ. TN Press, c.1983.

Montell, William Lynwood and Michael L. Morse. *Kentucky Folk Architecture.* Lexington KY: Univ. Press KY, c.1976.

Monterey Bay Aquarium. *Seafood Watch.* [v.d.]. Internet.

Montesano, B. R. *Redstick.* Cincinnati OH: U. P. James, 1856.

Montevideo American-News. Montevideo MN, 1911?–.

Montgomery, Franklin Alexander. *Reminiscences of a Mississippian in Peace and War.* Cincinnati OH: Robert Clarke Company Press, 1901.

Montgomery, Michael B. *Collection.* 1994–. Unpub. materials gathered for the *Dictionary of Smoky Mountain English* and related Appalachian Engl. projects.

———. *From Ulster to America.* Ulster: Ulster Historical Foundation, c.2006.

Montgomery, Michael B. and Guy Bailey, eds. *Language Variety in the South.* University AL: Univ. AL Press, c.1986.

Montgomery, Michael B. and Michael Ellis. *Corpus of American Civil War Letters, 1861–1865.* 2007–. Unpub. letters from various archives and libraries.

Montgomery, Michael B. and Joseph Sargent Hall. *Dictionary of Smoky Mountain English.* Knoxville TN: Univ. TN Press, c.2004.

Montgomery, Walter A. *The Days of Old and the Years That Are Past.* Charlottesville VA: Michie, c.1939.

Montgomery Advertiser. Montgomery AL, 1885–1982.

Montgomery Ward. *Catalogue and Buyers Guide, 1894–95.* Northfield IL: DBI Books, c.1977.

———. *Catalogue & Buyers Guide, No. 57, Spring and Summer, 1895.* New York: Dover Publications, c.1969.

Monthly Anthology and Boston Review. Boston, 1803–1811.

Monthly Journal of Agriculture. New York, 1845–1848.

Monthly South Dakotan See *South Dakotan*

Monthly Weather Review. Washington DC, 1872–.

Moody, Anne. *Coming of Age in Mississippi.* New York: Dial Press, 1968.

Moody, Ralph. *The Home Ranch.* New York: W. W. Norton, c.1956.

———. *Horse of a Different Color.* New York: W. W. Norton, c.1968.

———. *Shaking the Nickel Bush.* New York: W. W. Norton, 1962.

Moon, Elaine Latzman. *Untold Tales, Unsung Heroes: an Oral History of Detroit's African-American Community, 1918–1967.* Detroit MI: Wayne State Univ. Press, 1994.

Moonsammy, Rita Zorn et al. *Pinelands Folklife.* New Brunswick NJ: Rutgers Univ. Press, c.1987.

Moore, Amos. *Wind over the Range.* New York: Blue Ribbon Books, c.1936.

Moore, Dwight Munson. *Trees of Arkansas.* Little Rock AR: Arkansas Resources and Development Commission, Div. of Forestry and Parks in cooperation with Univ. AR, Fayetteville, 1950.

Moore, Francis. *Map and Description of Texas.* Waco TX: Texian Press, 1965. Repr. of the 1840 ed. pub. by H. Tanner, Junr., Philadelphia and Tanner & Disturnell, New York.

Moore, Frank. *Anecdotes, Poetry and Incidents of the War.* New York: Bible House, 1867 [c.1865].

———. *Diary of the American Revolution.* New York: C. Scribner, 1859–1860. 2 vols.

———, ed. *The Rebellion Record.* New York: G.P Putnam, 1864–1868. 12 vols.

———, ed. *Songs and Ballads of the American Revolution.* New York: D. Appleton, 1856.

———. *Women of the War.* Hartford CT: S. S. Scranton, 1867.

Moore, Horatio Nelson. *Fitzgerald and Hopkins.* Philadelphia: S. G. Sherman, 1847 [c.1846].

Moore, Joan W. *Homeboys.* Philadelphia: Temple Univ. Press, 1978.

Moore, John Trotwood. *Songs and Stories from Tennessee.* Philadelphia: Henry T. Coates, 1902. Orig. pub. in 1897 by J. C. Bauer, Chicago.

———. *A Summer Hymnal.* Philadelphia: H. T. Coates, 1901.

Moore, Lorrie. *Who Will Run the Frog Hospital?* New York: Alfred A. Knopf, 1994.

Moore, Miriam Ann. *I Will Survive.* New York: Avon, c.1999.

Moore, Nathaniel Fish. *Diary.* Chicago: Univ. Chicago Press, 1946.

Moore, Ruth. *Candlemas Bay.* New York: Morrow, 1950.

———. *The Dinosaur Bite.* New York: William Morrow, 1976.

———. *The Fire Balloon.* New York: William Morrow, 1948.

Moore, Warren. *Mountain Voices: a Legacy of the Blue Ridge and Great Smokies.* Chester CT: Globe Pequot Press, c.1988.

Moore's Rural New Yorker. Rochester NY, 1850–1878.

Moos, Herman M. *Hannah, or, a Glimpse of Paradise.* Cincinnati OH: Literary Eclectic Publishing House, c.1868.

Mora, Joseph Jacinto. *Trail Dust and Saddle Leather.* New York: Charles Scribner's Sons, 1946.

Moravian Historical Society. *Transactions 1858–1876.* Nazareth PA, 1876–.

Moravia Union. Moravia IA, 1901–.

Mordecai, Samuel. *Virginia.* 2d ed. Richmond VA: West & Johnston, 1860.

Morehouse, Kathleen Moore. *Rain on the Just.* New York: Lee Furman, c.1936.

Morenus, Richard. *Alaska Sourdough.* New York: Rand McNally, c.1956.

Morford, Henry. *Sprees and Splashes.* New York: Carleton, 1863.

———. *Utterly Wrecked.* New York: American News, 1866.

Morgan, Albert Talmon. *Yazoo, or, on the Picket Line of Freedom in the South.* Washington DC: A. T. Morgan, 1884.

Morgan, Dale Lowell. *The Great Salt Lake.* Indianapolis IN: Bobbs-Merrill, 1947.

———, ed. *Overland in 1846.* Lincoln NE: Univ. NE Press, 1993. 2 vols. Orig. pub. in 1963 by Talisman Press, Georgetown CA.

Morgan, Edmund S. *American Slavery, American Freedom: the Ordeal of Colonial Virginia.* New York: W. W. Norton, c.1975.

Morgan, James F. *England under the Norman Occupation.* London: Williams and Norgate, 1858.

Morgan, James Morris. *Recollections of a Rebel Reefer.* Boston: Houghton Mifflin, 1917.

Morgan, John T. *The Log House in East Tennessee.* Knoxville TN: Univ. TN Press, 1990.

Morgan, Jonathan. *Elements of English Grammar.* Hallowell ME: Goodale & Burton, 1814.

Morgan, Larry G. *Mountain Born, Mountain Molded.* Boone NC: Parkway, 2002.

Morgan, Murray Cromwell. *Skid Road.* New York: Viking Press, 1951.

Morgan, Robert. *Gap Creek.* Chapel Hill NC: Algonquin Books, 1999.

Morgan, W. Scott. *History of the Wheel and Alliance and the Impending Revolution.* Hardy AR: The Author, 1889.

Morgantown Post. Morgantown WV, 1864–.

Morimoto, Patricia Toshie. *Hawaiian Dialect of English.* ? HI: Univ. HI M.A. thesis, 1966.

Morison, Samuel Eliot. *The European Discovery of America.* New York: Oxford Univ. Press, 1971.

———. *The Maritime History of Massachusetts, 1783–1860.* Boston: Houghton Mifflin, 1921.

———. *One Boy's Boston, 1887–1901.* Boston: Houghton-Mifflin, 1962.

Morleigh. *Life in the West.* 2d ed. London: T. C. Newby, 1843.

Morley, Burton R. *Characteristics of the Labor Market in Alabama Related to the Administration of Unemployment Compensation.* University AL: Bureau of Business Research, Univ. AL, 1937.

Morley, Christopher Darlington. *Kitty Foyle.* Philadelphia: J. B. Lippincott, c.1939.

———. *Thorofare.* New York: Harcourt, Brace, c.1942.

Morley, Margaret Warner. *The Carolina Mountains.* Boston: Houghton Mifflin, 1913.

Morning Call. Allentown PA, 1939–.

Morning News. Florence SC, 1929–1945.

Morning News of Northwest Arkansas. Springdale AR, 1994–.

Morning Oregonian. Portland OR, 1861–1937.

Morning Review. Decatur IL, 1881–1882.

Morning World-Herald. Omaha NE, 1890–1928.

Morrell, William. *New-England.* London: Imprinted by I. D., 1625.

Morrell, Zenos N. *Flowers and Fruits from the Wilderness.* Boston: Gould and Lincoln, c.1872.

———. *Flowers and Fruits from the Wilderness.* 2d ed. rev. Boston: Gould and Lincoln, 1873.

Morris, Clara. *Life on the Stage.* New York: McClure, Phillips, 1901.

———. *Stage Confidences.* Boston: Lothrop Pub., 1902.

Morris, Edmund. *How to Get a Farm.* New York: James Miller, 1864.

Morris, Gouverneur. *A Diary of the French Revolution.* Boston: Houghton, Mifflin, 1939. 2 vols.

Morris, John SEE O'Connor, John

Morris, Percy A. *A Field Guide to Shells.* Boston: Houghton Mifflin, 1952.

———. *A Field Guide to the Shells of Our Atlantic Coast.* Boston: Houghton Mifflin, 1947.

Morris, Robert. *The Lights and Shadows of Freemasonry.* Louisville KY: J. F. Brennan, 1852.

———. *The Papers of Robert Morris, 1781–1784.* Ed. by E. James Ferguson et al. Pittsburgh PA: Univ. Pittsburgh Press, 1973–1999. 9 vols.

———. *Tales of Masonic Life.* Louisville KY: Morris & Monsarrat, 1860.

Morris, Travis. *Duck Hunting on Currituck Sound.* Charleston SC: History Press, 2006.

Morris, William and Mary Morris. *Dictionary of Word and Phrase Origins.* New York: Harper & Row, c.1962–1977. 4 vols.

———. *Harper Dictionary of Contemporary Usage.* New York: Harper & Row, 1975.

Morrison, Anna Daly. *Diary.* Boise ID: Em-Kayan Press, 1951.

Morrison, Theodore. *The Stones of the House.* New York: Viking Press, 1953.

Morrison, Toni. *Jazz.* New York: Alfred A. Knopf, 1992.

———. *Paradise.* New York: Alfred A. Knopf, 1998 [c.1997].

———. *Song of Solomon.* New York: Alfred A. Knopf, 1977.

Morse, Harriet Clara. *A Cowboy Cavalier.* Boston: C. M. Clark, 1909 [c.1908].

Morse, Jedidiah, comp. *The American Gazetteer.* Boston: At the Presses of S. Hall, and Thomas & Andrews, 1797.

———. *The American Geography.* Elizabeth Town NJ: Shepard Kollock, 1789.

———. *The American Geography.* New ed. London: Printed for John Stockdale, 1794.

———. *The American Universal Geography.* Boston: Isaiah Thomas and Ebenezer T. Andrews, 1793. 2 vols.

———. *The American Universal Geography.* Boston: I. Thomas and E. T. Andrews, 1796. 2 vols.

———. *A Report to the Secretary of War of the United States on Indian Affairs.* New-Haven CT: S. Converse, 1822.

Morse, Lucy Gibbons. *The Chezzles.* Boston: Houghton Mifflin, 1888.

Morton, Julia Frances. *Folk Remedies of the Low Country.* Miami FL: E. A. Seaman Pub., c.1974.

Morton, Nathaniel. *New England's Memorial.* 5th ed. Boston: Crocker and Brewster, 1826. Orig. printed in 1669 by S. G. and M. J. for John Usher, Cambridge.

———. *New England's Memorial.* 6th ed. Boston: Congregational Board of Publication, 1855. Orig. printed in 1669 by S. G. and M. J. for John Usher, Cambridge.

Morton, Oren Frederic. *A History of Monroe County, West Virginia.* Staunton VA: McClure, 1916.

———. *A History of Pendleton County, West Virginia.* Baltimore MD: Regional Publishing, 1980 [1910].

Morton, Thomas. *New English Canaan.* New York: Burt Franklin, 1967. Orig. pub. in 1637 by J. F. Stam, Amsterdam; repr. of 1883 ed. by Prince Society, Boston.

———. *New English Canaan.* New York: Arno Press, 1972. Repr. of 1637 ed. pub. by J. F. Stam, Amsterdam.

Moseley, Margaret. *Grinning in His Mashed Potatoes.* New York: Berkeley Prime Crime, c.1999.

Moses, Montrose Jonas, ed. *Representative American Dramas.* Boston: Little, Brown, 1925.

———, ed. *Representative American Dramas.* Students' ed. Boston: Little, Brown, 1937.

———, ed. *Representative Plays by American Dramatists.* New York: E. P. Dutton, 1918–[1930]. 3 vols.

Mosher, Howard Frank. *A Stranger in the Kingdom.* New York: Doubleday, c.1989.

———. *Where the Rivers Flow North.* New York: Viking Press, 1978.

Moss, Frank. *The American Metropolis.* New York: P. F. Collier, 1897. 3 vols.

Mother Earth News. Hendersonville NC, 1970–.

Motley, Willard. *Knock on Any Door.* New York: Appleton-Century-Crofts, c.1947.

Moton, Robert Russa. *Finding a Way.* Garden City NY: Doubleday, Page, 1921 [c.1920].

Motte, Jacob Rhett. *Charleston Goes to Harvard.* Ed. by Arthur H. Cole. Cambridge MA: Harvard Univ. Press, 1940.

Moulton, Roy K. *The Blue Jeans of Hoppertown.* Grand Rapids MI: White Printing, 1908.

Mountain Democrat. Placerville CA, 1854–1958; 1987–1989; 1995–.

Mountain Democrat and Placerville Republican. Placerville CA, 1943–1947.

Mountain Democrat & Placerville Times. Placerville CA, 1958–1987; 1989–1995.

Mountain Eagle. Whitesburg KY, 1907–.

Mountain Echo. Clinton AR, 1888–1889?

Mountaineer. Great Salt Lake City UT, 1859–1861.

Mountaineer. Seattle WA, 1907–.

Mountain Home News. Mountain Home ID, 1946–.

Mountain Life & Work. Berea KY, 1925–1988.

Mount Desert Island Biological Laboratory. *Bulletin.* Salisbury Cove ME, 1924?–.

Mount Desert Islander. Ellsworth ME, 2006–.

Mount Hope Eagle. Bristol RI, 1807–1808.

Mount Rainier National Park. *Nature Notes.* Sunset Lodge WA, 1930–1939; 1984–1989.

Mount Rainier Nature News Notes. Sunset Lodge WA, 1923–1929.

Mournian, Una Prentiss Taylor. *In Those Days.* New York: Macmillan, 1939.

Mourt's Relation. A Relation or Iournall of the Beginning and Proceedings of the English Plantation Setled at Plimoth in New England. London: Printed for Iohn Bellamie, 1622.

Mowry, Sylvester. *Arizona and Sonora.* 3d ed. rev. and enlarged. New York: Harper & Bros., 1864.

M. Quad SEE Lewis, Charles Bertrand

Mrs. Goodfellow's Cookery as It Should Be. Philadelphia: T. B. Peterson & Bros., c.1865.

Ms. New York, 1972–.

Mueller, Erhart. *Also in Sumpter.* Stevens Point WI: Worzalla Publishing, 1980.

Mueller-Dombois, Dieter and Francis Raymond Fosberg. *Vegetation of the Tropical Pacific Islands.* New York: Springer, 1998.

Muenscher, Walter Conrad Leopold. *Weeds.* New York: Macmillan, 1943 [c.1935].

Muhlenberg, Henry. *Catalogus Plantarum Americae Septentrionalis, huc Usque Cognitarum Indigenarum et Cicurum.* Lancaster PA: W. Hamilton, 1813.

Muhlenbergia. Chico CA, 1900–1916?

Muilenberg, Grace. *The Land of the Post Rock.* Lawrence KS: State Geological Survey, 1958.

Muir, John. *My First Summer in the Sierra.* Boston: Houghton Mifflin, 1911.

———. *A Thousand-Mile Walk to the Gulf.* Boston: Houghton Mifflin, 1916.

———. *Travels in Alaska.* Boston: Houghton Mifflin, 1915.

Mulford, Clarence Edward. *Bar-20.* New York: Outing Pub., 1907.

———. *Hopalong Cassidy.* New York: Grosset and Dunlap, c.1910.

———. *The Man from Bar-20.* Chicago: A. C. McClurg, 1918.

———. *Mesquite Jenkins.* New York: A. L. Burt, 1928.

———. *The Orphan.* New York: A. L. Burt, 1924 [c.1908].

Mulford, Clarence Edward and John Wood Clay. *Buck Peters, Ranchman.* Chicago: A. C. McClurg, 1912.

Mullen, Patrick B. *I Heard the Old Fishermen Say.* Austin TX: Univ. TX Press, c.1978.

Muller, Dan. *Chico of the + Up Ranch.* Chicago: Reilly & Lee, c.1938.

Mullin, Glen Hawthorne. *Adventures of a Scholar Tramp.* New York: Century, c.1925.

Mullins, Denvil. *Echoes of Appalachia.* Johnson City TN: Overmountain Press, 1994.

Muma, Martin H. *Scorpions, Whip Scorpions and Wind Scorpions of Florida.* Gainesville FL: Florida Department of Agriculture, 1967.

Mumford, Lewis. *The City in History.* New York: Harcourt, Brace & World, c.1961.

———. *Sticks and Stones.* New York: Norton, c.1924.

Münchener Studien zur Sprachwissenschaft. München, 1952–.

Munford, Robert. *A Collection of Plays and Poems.* Petersburg VA: Printed by William Prentis, 1798.

———. *A Collection of Plays and Poems.* Chapel Hill NC: Univ. Library, Univ. NC at Chapel Hill, 2004. Text transcr.

for *Documenting the American South* website from the 1798 ed. printed by William Prentis, Petersburg VA.

Munn, Charles Clark. *Rockhaven*. Boston: Lee and Shepard, 1902.

———. *Uncle Terry*. Boston: Lee and Shepard, 1901 [c.1900].

Munro, George C. *Birds of Hawaii*. Honolulu HI: Tongg Publishing, c.1944.

Munro, William F. *The Backwoods' Life*. Toronto: Printed by Hunter, Rose, 1869.

Munroe, Kirk. *The Golden Days of '49*. New York: Dodd, Mead, c.1889.

———. *Rick Dale*. New York: Harper & Bros., 1896.

Munsell, Joel. *The Annals of Albany*. Albany NY: J. Munsell, 1850–1859. 10 vols.

Munsey's Magazine. New York, 1889–1929.

Munson, Gorham Bert. *Broken Shackles*. Philadelphia: Dorrance, c.1920.

Munson, Thomas Volney. *Foundations of American Grape Culture*. New York: Orange Judd, 1909.

Munz, Philip Alexander. *A Flora of Southern California*. Berkeley CA: Univ. CA Press, 1974.

———. *Introduction to California Mountain Wildflowers*. Ed. by Phyllis M. Faber and Dianne Lake. Rev. ed. Berkeley CA: Univ. CA Press, c.2003.

———. *Shore Wildflowers of California, Oregon, and Washington*. Berkeley CA: Univ. CA Press, 1964.

Munz, Philip Alexander and David D. Keck. *A California Flora*. Berkeley CA: Univ. CA Press, 1959.

Murdoch, Beamish. *Epitome of the Laws of Nova-Scotia*. Halifax: J. Howe, 1832–1833. 4 vols.

Murdock, John. *The Triumphs of Love*. Philadelphia: R. Folwell, 1795.

Murfree, Mary Noailles. *The Despot of Broomsedge Cove*. Boston: Houghton, Mifflin, 1889.

———. *Down the Ravine*. 6th ed. Boston: Houghton, Mifflin, 1886 [c.1885].

———. *In the Clouds*. Boston: Houghton, Mifflin, 1887 [c.1886].

———. *In the "Stranger People's" Country*. New York: Harper & Bros., c.1891.

———. *In the Tennessee Mountains*. Boston: Houghton Mifflin, c.1884.

———. *The Mystery of Witch-Face Mountain*. Boston: Houghton, Mifflin, 1895.

———. *The Prophet of the Great Smoky Mountains*. Boston: Houghton Mifflin, 1885.

———. *The Story of Keedon Bluffs*. Boston: Houghton, Mifflin, 1888.

———. *Where the Battle Was Fought*. Boston: James R. Osgood, 1884.

Murgatroyd, Matthew SEE Jones, James Athearn

Murie, Adolph. *Birds of Mount McKinley National Park, Alaska*. Mount McKinley Park AK: Mount McKinley Natural History Association, c.1963.

Murie, Olaus Johan. *Fauna of the Aleutian Islands and Alaska Peninsula*. Washington DC: Department of the Interior, U.S. Fish and Wildlife Service, 1959.

Murphy, Henry Cruse. *Jacob Steendam, Noch Vaster*. Albany NY: Munsell, 1861.

Murphy, John Mortimer. *Oregon Business Directory and State Gazetteer*. Portland OR: S. J. McCormick, c.1873.

———. *Sporting Adventures in the Far West*. New York: Harper & Bros., 1880.

Murray, Albert. *South to a Very Old Place*. New York: McGraw-Hill, c.1971.

———. *Stomping the Blues*. New York: McGraw-Hill, c.1976.

Murray, Charles Augustus. *Travels in North America during the Years 1834, 1835, 1836*. New York: Da Capo Press, 1974. 2 vols. Repr. of 1839 ed. pub. by R. Bentley, London.

Murray, Hugh. *The Encyclopaedia of Geography*. Rev. with additions. Philadelphia: Blanchard and Lea, 1855. 3 vols.

Murray, James. *Letters of James Murray, Loyalist*. Boston: Printed, not published, 1901.

Murray, James A. H. et al., eds. *The Oxford English Dictionary*. Oxford: At the Clarendon Press, 1933. 13 vols.

Murray, Lena Davis. *Schoolhouse in the Foothills*. New York: Simon & Schuster, 1935.

Murray, Thomas E. and Beth Lee Simon, eds. *Language Variation and Change in the American Midland: a New Look at "Heartland" English*. Amsterdam: John Benjamins, 2006.

Murray, William Henry Harrison. *Adventures in the Wilderness*. Boston: Fields, Osgood, 1869.

Murray-Wooley, Carolyn and Karl B. Raitz. *Rock Fences of the Bluegrass*. Lexington KY: Univ. KY Press, c.1992.

Murrie, Cornelia Random. *The White Castle of Louisiana*. Louisville KY: John P. Morton, 1903.

Muscatine Journal. Muscatine IA, 1849?–1918?

MuseumLink Illinois. [v.d.]. Internet.

Museum of Foreign Literature, Science, and Art. Philadelphia, 1831–1842.

Musgrove, Jack W. and Mary R. Musgrove. *Waterfowl in Iowa*. Des Moines IA: State Conservation Commission, 1943.

Musical Quarterly. New York: G. Schirmer, 1915–.

Musical World. New York, 1854–1855.

Music Cultures in the United States. Ed. by Ellen Koskoff. New York: Routledge, c.2005.

Music Library Association. *Notes*. Washington DC, 1934–.

Mutschmann, Heinrich. *A Glossary of Americanisms*. Tartu-Dorpat: Printed by K. Mattiesin, c.1931.

Mycologia. Bronxville NY: New York Botanical Garden, 1909–.

Myers, Allen O. *Bosses and Boodle in Ohio Politics*. Cincinnati OH: Lyceum Pub., 1895.

Myers, Bonnie Trentham. *Best Yet Life and Lore of the Smokies*. [s.l.]: Myers & Myers, 2005 [c.2002].

Myers, Gustavus. *The History of Tammany Hall*. 2d ed. rev. and enlarged. New York: Boni & Liveright, 1917.

Myers, Robert Manson, ed. *The Children of Pride*. New Haven CT: Yale Univ. Press, 1972.

Myers, Tamar. *Eat, Drink, and Be Wary*. New York: Signet, c.1998.

———. *The Ming and I*. New York: Avon Books, c.1997.

———. *Play It Again, Spam®*. New York: Signet Books, c.1999.

Myrdal, Gunnar. *An American Dilemma*. New York: Harper & Bros., c.1944.

Myron, Paul SEE Linebarger, Paul Myron Wentworth

Myrthe, A. T. SEE Ganilh, Anthony

Myrtle, Molly SEE Hill, Agnes Leonard

NADS SEE American Dialect Society *Newsletter*

NADS Letters. 1977–2008. Unpub. letters in response to articles in the *Newsletter of the American Dialect Society*.

Names in South Carolina. Columbia SC: Department of English, Univ. SC, 1954–1965. 12 vols.

Names: Journal of the American Name Society. Berkeley CA [etc], 1953–.

N&Q SEE *Notes and Queries*

Nantucket Independent. Nantucket MA, 2003–.

Nantucket Inquirer. Nantucket MA, 1821–1843.

Nanzig, Thomas P., ed. *The Badax Tigers*. Lanham MD: Rowman & Littlefield, c.2002.

Naples Daily News. Naples FL, 1969–.

Naples Now. Naples FL: D. Reynolds Enterprises, 1976–1983.

Narragansett Historical Register. Providence RI: Narragansett Historical Pub., 1882–1891.

Nasby, Petroleum V. SEE Locke, David Ross

Nash, Charles Elventon. *The History of Augusta*. Ed. by Edith L. Hary. Augusta ME: Charles E. Nash & Son, c.1961.

Nash, John Adams. *The Progressive Farmer*. New York: A. O. Moore Agricultural Book, 1859.

Nash, Ogden. *Good Intentions*. Boston: Little, Brown, 1942.

———. *I'm a Stranger Here Myself*. Boston: Little, Brown, 1939. Orig. pub. in 1938 by Little, Brown, Boston.

Nash, Tom and Twilo Scofield. *The Well-Traveled Casket; a Collection of Oregon Folklife*. Salt Lake City UT: Univ. UT Press, 1992.

Nash, Wallis. *Two Years in Oregon*. New York: D. Appleton, 1882.

Nashua Reporter. Nashua IA, 1894–1918.

Nashua Reporter and Weekly Nashua Post. Nashua IA, 1918–1944; 1946–.

Nashua Telegraph. Nashua NH, 1904–1986.

Nason, Leonard Hastings. *Chevrons*. New York: George H. Doran, 1926.

———. *Sergeant Eadie*. Garden City NY: Doubleday, Doran, 1928.

Natchitoches Times. Natchitoches LA, 1903–.

Nathan, Hans. *Dan Emmett and the Rise of Early Negro Minstrelsy*. Norman OK: Univ. OK Press, 1962.

Nation, Richard Franklin. *At Home in the Hoosier Hills*. Bloomington: IN Univ. Press, c.2005.

Nation. New York, 1865–.

National Aegis & General Advertiser. Worcester MA, 1831–1833.

National Anti-Slavery Standard. New York: American Anti-Slavery Society, 1840–1870.

National Association of Audubon Societies. *Educational Leaflet*. New York, 1903–1911.

National Audubon Society. *Corkscrew Swamp Sanctuary*. New York: National Audubon Society, 1975?

National Coal Association. Bituminous Coal Institute. *Glossary of Current and Common Bituminous Coal Mining Terms*. Washington DC: The Institute, 1947.

National Commercial Convention. *Proceedings*. Boston [etc], 1865–1885?

National Committee for the Defense of Political Prisoners. *Harlan Miners Speak*. New York: Da Capo Press, 1970. Unabridged repr. of 1932 ed.

The National Cyclopaedia of Useful Knowledge. Boston: Little, Brown, 1853. 12 vols.

National Fisherman. Goffstown NH: Atlantic Fisherman, 1954–.

National Gardener. St. Louis MO: National Garden Clubs, 1948–.

National Gazette and Literary Register. Philadelphia: William Fry, 1820–1841.

National Geographic Magazine. Washington DC: National Geographic Society, 1888–.

National Geographic Society. *America's Wonderlands*. Washington DC: National Geographic Society, c.1959.

———. *The Book of Birds*. Washington DC: National Geographic Society, c.1937. 2 vols.

———. *The Book of Fishes*. Rev. and enlarged ed. Washington DC: National Geographic Society, c.1939.

———. *Wild Animals of North America*. Washington DC: National Geographic Society, c.1960.

National Geographic World. Washington DC, 1975–.

National Honey Market News. Washington DC, 1985–2000.

National Integrated Pest Management Network. North Carolina Component. *Pest Identification*. [v.d.]. Internet.

National Intelligencer. Washington DC, 1800–1869.

National Lumber Manufacturers Association. *Official Report . . . Annual Convention*. Chicago, 1910–1916?

National Magazine: an Illustrated American Monthly. Boston: Bostonian Publishing, 1896–1933.

National Museum of Canada. *Bulletin*. Ottawa, 1913–.

National Observer. Silver Spring MD, 1964–1977.

National Parks. Washington DC: National Parks & Conservation Association, 1981–.

National Park Service SEE United States. National Park Service

National Recreation Association. *Games for Quiet Hours and Small Spaces*. New York: The Association, 1941 [c.1938].

National Register. Washington DC: Joel K. Mead, 1816–1820.

National Review. Bristol CT, 1955–.

National Sportsman. Chicago, 1915?–1941.

National Temperance Convention. *Proceedings*. New York, 1841–1897.

National Wildlife. Washington DC: National Wildlife Federation, 1962–.

National Wool Grower. Englewood CO: American Sheep Industry Association, 1911–1993.

Nation's Restaurant News. 1967–. Internet.

Native Plant Society of Oregon. *Bulletin*. Eugene OR, 1966?–.

Native Plants of Pennsylvania. 2d ed. Narberth PA: Livingston Publishing, 1965.

Natural History. New York: American Museum of Natural History, 1900–.

Natural Resources Journal. Albuquerque NM: Univ. NM, School of Law, 1961–.

Nature. London, 1869–.

Nature & Science on the Pacific Coast. San Francisco: Paul Elder, c.1915.

Nature Conservancy, California Program. *California Update*. San Francisco, 2003–.

Nature Conservancy, Wisconsin Chapter. Madison WI, 1989–.

Nature Conservancy Magazine. Arlington VA, 1947–.

Nature Conservancy News. Arlington VA, 1951?–1987.

Nature Magazine. Baltimore MD: American Nature Association, 1923–1959.

Nature Photographer. West Palm Beach FL, 1990–.

Nature-Study Review. New York, 1905–1923.

Naugle, George R. *The Luckiest Hunter Alive*. Coral Springs FL: Llumina Press, 2004.

Nauvoo Independent. Nauvoo IL, 1939–.

Navajo Times. Window Rock AZ, 1957–.

Naylor, Gloria. *Mama Day*. New York: Ticknor & Fields, 1988.

———. *The Women of Brewster Place*. New York: Viking Press, c.1982.

Naylor, James Ball. *Ralph Marlowe*. Akron OH: Saalfield Publishing, 1901.

Neal, Daniel. *The History of New-England*. London: Printed for J. Clark, 1720. 2 vols.

Neal, John. *Brother Jonathan.* Edinburgh: W. Blackwood, 1825.

———. *The Down-Easters.* New York: Harper and Bros., 1833. 2 vols.

———. *Rachel Dyer.* Portland ME: Shirley and Hyde, 1828.

Neal, Joseph Clay. *Charcoal Sketches.* Philadelphia: E. L. Carey and A. Hart, 1838.

———. *The Misfortunes of Peter Faber and Other Sketches.* Philadelphia: T. B. Peterson and Bros., 1856.

———. *Peter Ploddy.* Philadelphia: T. B. Peterson & Bros., c.1856. Orig. pub. in 1844 by Carey & Hart, Philadelphia.

Neal, Julia. *The Kentucky Shakers.* Lexington KY: Univ. Press KY, c.1977.

Neal, Marie Catharine. *In Gardens of Hawaii.* Honolulu HI: Bernice P. Bishop Museum, 1948.

———. *In Gardens of Hawaii.* New and rev. ed. Honolulu HI: Bernice Pauahi Bishop Museum Press, 1965.

———. *In Honolulu Gardens.* 2d rev. ed. Honolulu HI: Bernice P. Bishop Museum, 1929.

Nearing, Helen and Scott Nearing. *The Maple Sugar Book.* New York: John Day, 1950.

NebGuide. Lincoln NE: Nebraska. University-Lincoln. Cooperative Extension Service. Institute of Agriculture and Natural Resources, 1973–.

Nebraska. Agricultural Experimental Station. *Bulletin.* Lincoln NE, 1887–1956.

Nebraska City News-Press. Nebraska City NE, 1948–.

Nebraska History. Lincoln NE: Nebraska State Historical Society, 1918–.

Nebraska. State Board of Agriculture. *Annual Report.* Lincoln NE, 1883–1949.

Nebraska State Historical Society. *Transactions and Reports.* Lincoln NE, 1885–1893.

Nebraska State Horticultural Society. *Annual Report.* Lincoln NE, 1870?–1912?

———. *Proceedings.* Brownville NE, 1872?–1920?

Nebraska State Journal. Lincoln NE, 1892–1950.

Nebraska. University. *University of Nebraska Studies.* Lincoln NE, 1888–.

Nebraska. University-Lincoln. Agricultural Experiment Station. *Annual Report.* Lincoln NE, 1888–1944?

Nebraska. University-Lincoln. Conservation and Survey Division. *Bulletin.* Lincoln NE, 1928–1939.

Necker, Albertine Adrienne de Saussure. *Progressive Education, Commencing with the Infant.* Transl. by Mrs. Willard and Mrs. Phelps. Boston: William D. Ticknor, 1835.

Needham, James G. and Hortense Butler Heywood. *A Handbook of the Dragonflies of North America.* Springfield IL: Charles C. Thomas, 1929.

Needham, Walter and Barrows Mussey. *A Book of Country Things.* Brattleboro VT: S. Greene Press, 1965.

Needles Desert Star. Needles CA, 1888–.

Neel, Marvin H., comp. *The Word-Book of a Backwoodsman.* Ceres VA: Backwoods Press, 1957.

Neely, Charles, comp. *Tales and Songs of Southern Illinois.* Ed. by John Webster Spargo. Menasha WI: George Banta, 1938.

Neely, Virginia Lechelt. *Alaska Calls.* Surrey: Hancock House, c.1983.

Negligence and Compensation Cases Annotated. Chicago: Callaghan, 1912–1967.

Negro Digest. Chicago, 1942–1970.

Negro Quarterly. New York, 1942–1944.

Negro Story. Westport CT: Negro Universities Press, 1970. Facsimile repr. of 1944–1946 ed. pub. by Negro Story Magazine, Chicago.

Neighbor's Home Mail. Phelps NY, 1875–1882.

Neihardt, John Gneisenau. *The River and I.* New York: G. P. Putnam's Sons, 1910.

Neill, Edward Duffield. *The History of Minnesota.* Philadelphia: J. B. Lippincott, 1858.

———. *Virginia Carolorum.* Albany NY: Joel Munsell's Sons, 1886.

Neilson, William Allan et al., eds. *Webster's New International Dictionary of the English Language.* 2d ed. unabridged. Springfield MA: G. & C. Merriam, 1943 [c.1934].

———, eds. *Webster's New International Dictionary of the English Language.* 2d ed. unabridged. Springfield MA: G. & C. Merriam, 1955 [c.1954]. Includes addenda.

Neitzel, Wilmere Jordan, ed. *The Flora and Fauna of Solano County.* Fairfield CA: Solano County Office of Education, c.1965.

Nelson, Barney. *The Last Campfire.* College Station TX: TX A&M Univ. Press, c.1984.

Nelson, Bruce Opie. *Land of the Dacotahs.* Minneapolis MN: Univ. MN Press, 1946.

Nelson, Edward William. *The Eskimo about Bering Strait.* Washington DC: Govt. Printing Office, 1900.

Nelson, Gil. *Atlantic Coastal Plain Wildflowers.* Guilford CT: FalconGuide, 2006.

———. *The Shrubs and Woody Vines of Florida.* Sarasota FL: Pineapple Press, c.1996.

———. *The Trees of Florida.* Sarasota FL: Pineapple Press, 1994.

Nelson, John Young. *Fifty Years on the Trail.* London: Chatto & Windus, 1889.

Nelson, Joseph SEE Webber, Everett

Nelson, Lee. *A Thousand Souls.* Springville UT: Council Press, c.2002.

Nelson, Louise Kinsland. *Country Folklore, 1920s & 1930s.* Alexander NC: WorldComm, c.1997.

Nelson, Richard K. *Hunters of the Northern Forest.* Chicago: Univ. Chicago Press, 1973.

Nelson, Ruth Ashton. *Plants of Rocky Mountain National Park.* Washington DC: Govt. Printing Office, 1933.

———. *Plants of Rocky Mountain National Park.* Rev. ed. Washington DC: Govt. Printing Office, 1953.

Nemnich, Philipp Andreas. *Allgemeines Polyglotten-Lexicon der Naturgeschichte.* Hamburg: L. Nemnich; Halle: J. J. Gebauer, 1793–1798. 4 vols.

Neuffer, Claude Henry and Irene Neuffer. *Correct Mispronunciations of Some South Carolina Names.* Columbia SC: Univ. SC Press, c.1983.

Nevada Highways and Parks. Carson City NV, 1936–.

Nevada State Journal. Reno NV, 1907–1983.

Nevada State University. Agricultural Experiment Station. *Bulletin.* Reno NV, 1888?–1940?

Nevell, Richard. *A Time to Dance.* New York: St. Martin's Press, c.1977.

Nevin, Alfred. *Churches of the Valley.* Philadelphia: Joseph M. Wilson, 1852.

New American Cookery. New York: T. B. Jansen, 1805.

The New American Cyclopaedia. Ed. by George Ripley and Charles A. Dana. New York: D. Appleton, 1858–1863. 16 vols.

New American Magazine. Woodbridge NJ: Printed and sold by J. Parker, 1758–1760.

A New and Further Narrative of the State of New-England Being a Continued Account of the Bloudy Indian-War. London: Dorman Newman, 1676.

Newark Advocate. Newark OH, 1837–1883; 1901–1927.

Newark Advocate and American Tribune. Newark OH, 1927–1970.

Newark Daily Advocate. Newark OH, 1883–1892; 1894–1901.

Newark (NJ) Shade Tree Commission. *Annual Report.* Newark NJ, 1904–1916?

Newberry News. Newberry MI, 1886–.

Newbrough, John Ballou. *The Lady of the West.* Cincinnati OH: Moore, Wilstach, Keys & Overend, 1855.

Newburyport Herald. Newburyport MA, 1818–1888?

New Castle, Delaware. Court. *Records of the Court of New Castle on Delaware.* Lancaster PA: Published by the Colonial Society of Pennsylvania, Wickersham Printing, 1904–1935. 2 vols.

New Castle News. New Castle PA, 1891–.

New Edinburgh Encyclopaedia. 2d Amer. ed. New York: Whiting and Watson, 1813–1831. 18 vols.

Newell, Charles Martin. *The Isle of Palms.* Boston: DeWolfe, Fiske, 1888.

Newell, David McCheyne. *If Nothin' Don't Happen.* New York: Alfred A. Knopf, 1975.

———. *The Trouble of It Is.* New York: Alfred A. Knopf, c.1978.

Newell, Frederick Haynes. *Irrigation in the United States.* New York: T. Y. Crowell, c.1902.

Newell, Robert Henry. *Orpheus C. Kerr Papers.* New York: Blakeman & Mason, 1862–1865. 3 vols.

Newell, William Wells. *Games and Songs of American Children.* New York: Harper & Bros., 1883.

———. *Games and Songs of American Children, Collected and Compared.* With a new intro. and index by Carl Withers. New York: Dover Publications, c.1963. Repr. of the new and enlarged 1903 ed. pub. by Harper & Bros., New York.

New England Botanic, Medical and Surgical Journal. Worcester MA, 1847–1851.

New England Cook Book. Boston: Chas. E. Brown Publishing, c.1905.

New-England Courant. Boston, 1721–1727.

New Englander and Yale Review. New Haven CT, 1843–1892.

New England Farmer. Ed. by Thomas G. Fessenden. Boston, 1822–1835.

New England Farmer. Boston: J. Nourse, 1848–1864; 1867–1871.

New England Farmer and Horticultural Register. Boston, 1839–1844.

New England Galaxy. Sturbridge MA, 1959–.

New England Historical and Genealogical Register. Boston: New England Historic Genealogical Society, 1847–.

New England Homestead. Springfield MA, 1868–.

New England Journal of Medicine and Surgery. Boston, 1812–1826.

New-England Magazine. Boston: J. T. & E. Buckingham, 1831–1835.

New England Magazine. Boston: J. N. McClintock, 1884–1917.

New England Palladium & Commercial Advertiser. Boston, 1815–1840.

New England Quarterly. Baltimore MD, 1928–.

New England Weekly Journal. Boston, 1727–1741.

New England Wildflower Society. *Wild Flower Notes.* Framingham MA, 1985–.

New Era. Humeston IA, 1883–.

Newhall, Charles Stedman. *The Trees of Northeastern America.* New York: G. P. Putnam's Sons, 1890.

Newhall, James Robinson. *Ye Great and General Courte in Colonial Times.* Lynn MA: Nichols Press, 1897 [c.1896].

New Hampshire. *Provincial and State Papers.* Published by authority of the legislature of New Hampshire, 1867–1943.

New Hampshire. Board of Agriculture. *New Hampshire Agriculture.* Nashua NH: O. C. Moore, State Printer, 1871–.

New Hampshire (Colony) Probate Court. *Probate Records of the Province of New Hampshire.* Concord NH: Rumford Printing, 1907–1941.

New Hampshire. Forestry Commission. *Report.* Concord NH: Parsons B. Cogswell, 1885–1894.

New Hampshire Gazette, and Historical Chronicle. Portsmouth NH, 1763–1776.

New Hampshire. Geological Survey. *The Geology of New Hampshire.* Ed. by C. H. Hitchcock. Concord NH: Edward A. Jenks, 1874–1878. 3 vols.

New Hampshire Historical Society. *Collections.* Concord NH, 1824–.

New Hampshire. Laws, Statutes etc. *Laws of the State of New Hampshire Passed June Session, 1862.* Concord NH: Henry McFarland, State Printer, 1862.

New-Hampshire Patriot. Concord NH, 1868–1878.

New Hampshire Patriot & State Gazette. Concord NH, 1819–1862.

New Hampshire Sentinel. Keene NH, 1799–1957.

New Hampshire State Agricultural Society. *Transactions.* Concord NH, 1850–1861.

New Hampshire. Supreme Judicial Court. *Reports of Cases Argued and Determined.* Concord NH, 1856–1875.

New Haven (Colony). *Records of the Colony and Plantation of New Haven, from 1638 to 1649.* Hartford CT: Case, Tiffany, 1857.

New Haven Colony Historical Society. *Papers.* New Haven CT, 1865–1951.

New-Haven Gazette and the Connecticut Magazine. New Haven CT, 1786–1789?

New Haven Register. New Haven CT, 1812–.

New Jersey Agricultural Experiment Station. *Report of the New Jersey State Agricultural Experiment Station upon the Mosquitoes Occurring within the State.* Prepared by John B. Smith, entomologist. Trenton NJ: MacCrellish & Quigley, State printers, 1904.

New Jersey Agricultural Experiment Stations. *Annual Report.* New Brunswick NJ, 1880–1955.

New Jersey. Board of Fish and Game Commissioners. *Annual Report.* Trenton NJ, 1895–1945.

New-Jersey Gazette. Trenton NJ, 1778–1786.

New Jersey Geological Survey. *Annual Report.* Trenton NJ, 1863–1909.

———. *Geology of the County of Cape May.* Trenton NJ: Printed at the office of the True American, 1857.

New Jersey Historical Society. *Proceedings.* Newark NJ, 1845–.

New-Jersey Journal. Chatham NJ, 1779–1783.

New Jersey. Laws, Statutes etc. *Revised Statutes Supplement.* Jersey City NJ: Frederick D. Linn, 1789–.

New Jersey. State Board of Agriculture. *Annual Report.* Trenton NJ, 1873–1916.

New Jersey State Geologist. *Final Report.* Trenton NJ, 1888–1917.

New Jersey. State Museum. *Annual Report.* Trenton NJ, 1901–1915.

New Jersey Sunday Herald. Newton NJ, 1960–.

New Jersey. Supreme Court. *Reports of Cases Determined.* Princeton NJ, 1795–1848.

Newman, Margaret Murphy and Helen Spann Murphy. *Conservation Notes of East Carroll Parish.* [s.l.]: [s.n.], 1940?

Newman, Thelma R. *Quilting, Patchwork, Appliqué, and Trapunto.* New York: Crown, c.1974.

New Mexican. Santa Fe NM, 1863–1868; 1951–1988.

New Mexico. Agricultural Experiment Station, University Park. *Bulletin.* State College NM, 18??–

New Mexico Quarterly Review. Albuquerque NM: Univ. NM, 1931–.

New Mexico: the Sunshine State's Recreational and Highway Magazine. Santa Fe NM, 1931–1937.

New Mexico. University. *Biological Series.* Albuquerque NM: Univ. NM Press, 1898–1941.

———. *Language Series.* Albuquerque NM, 1907–1942.

New Mirror. New York, 1843–1844.

New North. Rhinelander WI, 1882–1947.

New Orleans City Directory. New Orleans LA: S. E. Percy, 1832.

New Orleans Daily Creole. New Orleans LA, 1856–1857?

New Outlook SEE *Outlook,* and *Outlook and Independent*

New Oxford Item. New Oxford PA, 1879–1967.

New Plymouth Colony. *The Compact with the Charter and Laws of the Colony of New Plymouth.* Boston: Dutton and Wentworth, 1836.

———. *Records* SEE ALSO Plymouth, Massachusetts *Records of the Town of Plymouth*

———. *Records.* Ed. by Nathaniel B. Shurtleff and David Pulsifer. Boston: Press of W. White, 1855–1861. 12 vols.

Newport Daily News. Newport RI, 1846–.

Newport Journal. Newport RI, 1867–1877.

Newport Mercury. Newport RI, 1758–1928.

Newport Natural History Society. *Proceedings.* Newport RI, 1883–1891.

New Princeton Review. New York, 1886–1888.

New Purchase SEE Hall, Baynard Rush

New Republic. New York, 1914–.

News. Frederick MD, 1890–2002.

News. Kingstree SC, 1973–.

News. Port Arthur TX, 1973–.

News and Citizen. Morrisville VT, 1881–.

News and Courier. Charleston SC, 1873–.

News and Observer. Raleigh NC, 1894–.

News and Press. Cimarron NM, 1870–1910.

News & Record. Greensboro NC, 1992–.

New Scientist and Science Journal. London, 1956–.

News Courier. Athens AL, 1990?–.

Newsday. Nassau edition. Hempstead NY, 1985–.

News from Native California. Berkeley CA, 1987–.

News Herald. Panama City FL, 1970–.

News-Journal. Mansfield OH, 1964–.

News Journal. Wilmington DE, 1989–.

New Smyrna News. New Smyrna FL, 1913–1930.

NewsRegister.com. McMinnville OR, 1999–. Internet.

News Reporter. Whiteville NC, 1895–.

News-Star. Monroe LA, 1988–.

News-Sun. Hobbs NM, 1937–.

New Statesman. London, 1957–.

News Tribune. Fort Pierce FL, 1959–1988.

Newsweek. New York, 1933–.

New Sydenham Society. *The New Sydenham Society's Lexicon of Medicine and the Allied Sciences.* London: The Society, 1879–1899. 5 vols.

Newton, Alfred. *A Dictionary of Birds.* London: Black, 1899.

Newton, Louie Devotie. *Why I Am a Baptist.* New York: T. Nelson, 1957.

Newton, Stanley. *Paul Bunyan of the Great Lakes.* Chicago: Packard, 1946.

Newton Kansan. Newton KS, 1872–1899.

New York Academy of Sciences. *Annals.* New York, 1877–.

———. *Annals of the Lyceum of Natural History.* New York, 1823–1877.

New York Age. New York, 1887–1953.

New York Amsterdam News. New York, 1909–.

New-York Annual Register. New York, 1830–1845.

New-York Atlas. New York, 1853–1881.

New York City Public Library. *Bulletin.* New York, 1897–.

New York Coach-Maker's Magazine. New York, 1858–1871.

New-York Columbian. New York, 1817–1821.

New York. Commissioners of Fisheries. *Report.* Albany NY, 1868–1895.

New York. Constitutional Convention. *Proceedings and Debates of the Constitutional Convention of the State of New York, Held in 1867 and 1868.* Albany NY: Weed, Parsons, 1868. 5 vols.

New York Constellation. New York, 1829–1833.

New York. Constitutional Convention. *Proceedings and Debates of the Constitutional Convention of the State of New York, Held in 1867 and 1868.* Albany NY: Weed, Parsons, 1868. 5 vols.

New York Daily Advertiser. New York, 1817–1836.

New York Daily News. New York, 1919–.

New York Daily Times. New York, 1851–1857.

New York Daily Tribune. New York, 1842–1866.

New York Edition Newsday. New York, 1983–1995.

New York Entomological Society. *Journal.* New York, 1893–.

New-Yorker. New York, 1836–1841.

New Yorker. New York: F. R. Pub., 1925–.

New York Evangelist. New York, 1870–1893.

New York Evening Journal. New York, 1895–1937.

New-York Evening Post. New York, 1801–1832.

New-York Farmer and American Gardener's Magazine. New York, 1833–1837.

New-York Farmer, and Horticultural Repository. New York, 1828–1832.

New York Folklore Quarterly. Ithaca NY: Cornell Univ. Press, 1945–.

New York. Forest Commission. *Annual Report.* Albany NY, 1886–1894.

New York. Forest, Fish and Game Commission. *Annual Report.* Albany NY, 1890–.

New-York Gazette. New York, 1759–1767.

New York Gazette and the Weekly Mercury. New York, 1768–1783.

New York Gazette, or, the Weekly Post-Boy. New York, 1753–1759; 1766–1773.

New York Herald. New York, 1802–1817; 1840–1920.

New York Herald Tribune. New York, 1926–1966.

New York Historical Society. *Collections.* New York, 1811–1859.

———. *Quarterly.* New York, 1917–.

New York Institution for the Instruction of the Deaf and Dumb. *Annual Report of the Directors.* New York, 1819–1844.

New York Journal of Commerce. New York, 1827–1893.

New York Libraries. Albany NY, 1907–1939.

New York Magazine. New York, 1968–.

New York Medical and Physical Journal. New York, 1822–1830.

New York Mirror. New York: G. P. Morris, 1823–1842.

New York (NY) Office of the Governors of the Alms House. *Annual Report.* New York, 1849–1859?

New York Observer. New York, 1823–1826; 1829–1912.

New York Post. New York, 1801–.

New York Review of Books. New York, 1963–.

New-York Spectator. New York, 1804–1867.

New York Sporting Times. New York, 18??–.

New York State Agricultural Experiment Station. Board of Control. *Annual Report.* Albany NY: Weed, Parsons, 1882–1909.

New York. State Agricultural Society. *Transactions.* Albany NY, 1841–1889.

New York State Botanist. *Annual Report.* Albany NY, 1888?–1896.

New York. State Entomologist. *Report . . . on Injurious and Other Insects of the State of New York.* Albany NY, 1882–1921.

New York State Museum. *Catalogue of the Cabinet of Natural History of the State of New York.* Albany NY: Van Benthuysen, 1853.

———. *Handbook.* Albany NY, 1927–1942.

New York State Museum and Science Service. *Bulletin.* Albany NY: Univ. of the State of NY, 1887–.

New York Sun. New York, 2002–.

New York Sunday Mercury. New York, 1839–1897.

New York Teachers' Monographs. New York, 1898–1913.

New York Times. New York, 1857–.

New York Times Book Review. New York, 1896–.

New York Times Magazine. New York, 1896–.

New York Tribune SEE ALSO *New York Daily Tribune*

New York Tribune. New York, 1866–1924.

New York. University. *Seventeenth Annual Report of the Regents of the University of the State of New-York, on the Condition of the State Cabinet of Natural History.* Albany NY: Comstock & Cassidy, 1864.

New York. University. Board of Regents. *Annual Report.* Albany NY, 1787–1903.

New York Voice SEE *Voice*

New-York Weekly Journal. New York, 1733–1751.

New-York Weekly Magazine, or, Miscellaneous Repository. New York, 1795–1797.

New York World-Telegram. New York, 1931–1950.

New York Zoological Society. *Annual Report.* New York, 1895–1970?

The Niagara Book. By W. D. Howells, Mark Twain, Prof. Nathaniel Shaler, and others. Buffalo NY: Underhill and Nichols, 1893.

Niblick SEE Hanks, Charles Stedman

Nichols, David. *Echinoderms.* London: Hutchinson Univ. Library, 1962.

Nichols, James Robinson. *Fireside Science.* New York: Hurd and Houghton; Cambridge MA: Riverside Press, 1872 [c.1871].

Nichols, Laura D. *Lotus Bay, a Summer on Cape Cod.* Boston: D. Lothrop, c.1889.

Nichols, Nell Beaubien, ed. *Freezing and Canning Cookbook.* Garden City NY: Doubleday, c.1963.

Nichols, Nell Beaubien. *Good Home Cooking across the U.S.A.* Ames IA: IA State College Press, 1952.

Nichols, Thomas Low. *Forty Years of American Life.* London: J. Maxwell, 1864. 2 vols.

———. *Forty Years of American Life, 1821–1861.* 2d ed. New York: Stackpole Sons, c.1937. Repr. of 1874 ed. pub. by Longmans, Green, London.

Nichols, Walter Hammond. *Trust a Boy!* New York: Macmillan, 1923.

Nicholson, Charles. *A Field Guide to Southern Speech.* Little Rock AR: August House, c.1989.

Nicholson, John. *The Farmer's Assistant.* 2d ed., corr. and enlarged. Philadelphia: Benjamin Warner, 1820.

Nicholson, Kenyon. *Garden Varieties.* New York: D. Appleton, 1924.

Nicholson, Meredith. *A Hoosier Chronicle.* Boston: Houghton, Mifflin, 1912.

Nickell, James Madison, comp. *J. M. Nickell's Botanical Ready Reference, Especially Designed for Druggists and Physicians.* Chicago: Nickell, 1881 [c.1880].

Nickerson, Joshua Atkins. *Days to Remember.* Chatham MA: Chatham Historical Society, c.1988.

Nida, Eugene Albert. *Toward a Science of Translating.* Leiden: E. J. Brill, 1964.

Niehaus, Theodore F. *A Field Guide to Southwestern and Texas Wildflowers.* Boston: Houghton Mifflin, 1984.

Niering, William A. and Nancy C. Olmstead. *The Audubon Society Field Guide to North American Wildflowers, Eastern Region.* New York: Alfred A. Knopf, c.1979.

Niles, J. J. et al. *The Songs My Mother Never Taught Me.* New York: Macaulay, c.1929.

Niles, Wyllis SEE Hume, John Ferguson

Niles' SEE *Weekly Register, Niles' Weekly Register,* and *Niles' National Register*

Niles' National Register. Philadelphia, 1837–1849.

Niles' Weekly Register. Baltimore MD, 1814–1837.

Nilsen, Don Lee Fred, ed. *Meaning, a Common Ground of Linguistics and Literature in Honor of Norman C. Stageberg.* Cedar Falls IA: Univ. Northern IA, 1973.

Nimmo, Joseph. *Report in Regard to the Range and Ranch Cattle Business of the United States.* Washington DC: Govt. Printing Office, 1885.

Nixon, Herman Clarence. *Forty Acres and Steel Mules.* Chapel Hill NC: Univ. NC Press, 1938.

———. *Lower Piedmont Country.* New York: Duell, Sloan & Pearce, 1946.

———. *Possum Trot, Rural Community, South.* Norman OK: Univ. OK Press, 1941.

Nokes, Jill. *How to Grow Native Plants of Texas and the Southwest.* Rev. and updated ed. Austin TX: Univ. TX Press, 2001.

Noland, C. F. M. *Cavorting on the Devil's Fork.* Arkansas Classics ed. Fayetteville AR: Univ. AR Press, 2006. Orig. pub. in 1979 by Memphis State Univ. Press, Memphis.

Noll, Henry R. *The Botanical Class-Book, and Flora of Pennsylvania.* Lewisburg PA: O. N. Warden, 1852.

Nordhoff, Charles. *California.* New York: Harper & Bros., 1873 [c.1872].

———. *Cape Cod and All along the Shore.* New York: Harper & Bros., 1868.

———. *Nine Years a Sailor.* Cincinnati OH: Moore, Wilstach, Keys, 1857 [c.1856].

Nordyke, Lewis. *Cattle Empire.* New York: William Morrow, 1949.

Norman, Benjamin Moore. *Rambles in Yucatan.* 2d ed. New York: J. & H. Langley, 1843 [c.1842].

Norman, Gurney. *Kinfolks.* Frankfort KY: Gnomon, c.1977.

Norman, Rick J. *Fielder's Choice.* Little Rock AR: August House, c.1991.

Norris, Frank. *Apprenticeship Writings of Frank Norris, 1896–1898.* Ed. by Joseph R. McElrath Jr. & Douglas K.

Burgess. Philadelphia: American Philosophical Association, 1996. 2 vols.

————. *Blix.* New York: Doubleday & McClure, 1899.

————. *Frank Norris of The Wave.* [s.l.]: Folcroft Press, 1970.

————. *McTeague.* Greenwich CT: Fawcett Publications, 1960. Repr. of the 1899 ed. pub. by Doubleday & McClure, New York.

————. *McTeague.* New York: W. W. Norton, c.1977. Repr. of 1899 ed. pub. by Doubleday & McClure, New York.

————. *The Octopus.* New York: Doubleday, Page, 1901.

————. *The Pit.* New York: Doubleday, Page, 1903.

————. *The Responsibilities of the Novelist.* New York: Doubleday, Page, 1903.

————. *The Third Circle.* New York: Dodd, Mead, 1922. Orig. pub. in 1909 by John Lane, New York.

————. *Vandover and the Brute.* Garden City NY: Doubleday, Page, 1914.

Norris, Kathleen. *Certain People of Importance.* Garden City NY: Doubleday, Page, 1922.

————. *Dakota.* New York: Ticknor & Fields, 1993.

Norris, Kathleen Thompson. *Martie the Unconquered.* Garden City NY: Doubleday, Page, 1917.

Norris, Thaddeus. *The American Angler's Book.* New ed. Philadelphia: E. H. Butler, 1865.

North, Arthur Walbridge. *The Mother of California.* San Francisco: Paul Elder, c.1908.

North, Escott. *The Saga of the Cowboy.* 2d ed. London: Jarrolds, 1942.

North, Sterling. *Rascal.* New York: E. P. Dutton, 1963.

North Adams Transcript. North Adams MA, 1895–1969; 2005–.

North American and United States Gazette. Philadelphia, 1847–1876.

North American Archives of Medical and Surgical Science. Baltimore MD: Carey, Hart, 1834–1835.

North American Fauna. Washington DC, 1889–.

North American Journal of Fisheries Management. Lawrence KS, 1981–.

North American Magazine. Philadelphia, 1832–1835.

North American Native Fishes Association. *American Currents.* Philadelphia, 1974?–.

North American Review. Boston, 1821–.

North-American Review and Miscellaneous Journal. Boston, 1815–1821.

North Arkansas College. *Hall Talk.* Harrison AR, 2005–.

North Berwick Enterprise. North Berwick ME, 1961?–.

North Carolina Agricultural Experiment Station. *Bulletin.* Raleigh NC, 1888–1979.

North Carolina. (Colony.) *The Colonial Records of North Carolina.* Raleigh NC: P. M. Hale, 1886–1890. 10 vols.

North Carolina. Department of Agriculture. *Biennial Report.* Raleigh NC, 1904–1914.

North Carolina. Department of Labor and Printing. *Annual Report of the Bureau of Labor Statistics.* Raleigh NC, 1887–1899.

North Carolina Folklore. Chapel Hill NC, 1948–1972.

North Carolina Folklore Journal. Raleigh NC: North Carolina Folklore Society, 1973–.

North Carolina Gazette. New Bern NC, 1751–1759?; 1768–1778?

North Carolina Geological and Economic Survey. *Bulletin.* Raleigh NC, 1893–1968.

————. *Economic Paper.* Raleigh NC, 1907–1925.

North Carolina Historical Review. Raleigh NC: North Carolina Division of Archives and History, 1924–.

North Carolina Language and Life Project. *Dialect Dictionary of Lumbee English.* [s.l.]: NC State Univ., 1994. Unpub.

————. *Dialect Vocabulary in Ocracoke.* [s.l.]: NC State Univ., 1994. Unpub.

————. *Harkers Island Dialect Vocabulary.* [s.l.]: NC State Univ., 1994. Unpub.

————. *Ocracoke Brogue.* [s.l.]: NC State Univ., 1994. Unpub.

North Carolina Maritime Museum, Beaufort North Carolina. *A Self-Guided Tour of the Museum.* [v.d.]. Internet.

North Carolina Medical Journal. Wilmington NC, 1878–1899.

North Carolina Mercury, and Salisbury Advertiser. Salisbury NC, 1798–1801.

North Carolina Office of Administrative Hearings. *Register.* Raleigh NC, 1986–.

North Carolina. Office of Environmental Education. *Roanoke River Basin.* Raleigh NC: NC Dept. of Environmental & Natural Resources, 2002.

North Carolina. Secretary of State. *North Carolina Wills and Inventories.* By J. Bryan Grimes, Secretary of State. Raleigh NC: Edwards & Broughton, 1912.

North Carolina. State Board of Agriculture. *Bulletin.* Raleigh NC, 1880?–1907.

————. *North Carolina and Its Resources.* Winston NC: M. I. & J. C. Stewart, 1896.

North Carolina. State Geologist. *Report of the North Carolina Geological Survey.* By Ebenezer Emmons. Raleigh NC: H. D. Turner, 1858.

North Carolina State University. *Carnivorous Plants.* [v.d.]. Internet.

————. *Herbarium.* [v.d.]. Internet.

North Carolina State University. A&T State University Cooperative Extension. *Extension Newsletters.* Raleigh NC?, 1996–.

North Carolina. University. *Magazine.* Chapel Hill NC, 1902–1918.

North Carolina. University at Chapel Hill. *Documenting the American South.* 1996–. Internet.

————. *Southern Oral History Program Collection.* [v.d.]. Selection of oral histories from 1973–2008 transcr. for *Documenting the American South* website. Internet.

————. *True and Candid Compositions: the Lives and Writings of Antebellum Students at the University of North Carolina.* 2005. Selection of writings from 1795–1868 transcr. for *Documenting the American South* website. Internet.

North Castle, New York. *North Castle/New Castle Historical Records.* Armonk NY: Town of North Castle, 1975.

North Dakota Historical Quarterly. Grand Forks ND, 1929–1944.

North Dakota History. Bismarck ND: State Historical Society of North Dakota, 1945–.

North Dakota Quarterly. Grand Forks ND, 1956–.

Northall, William Knight. *Before and behind the Curtain.* New York: W. F. Burgess, 1851.

————, ed. *Life and Recollections of Yankee Hill.* New York: Pub. for Mrs. Cordelia Hill, by W. F. Burgess, 1850.

Northeastern Naturalist. Steuben ME, 1997–.

Northeast Folklore. Orono ME: Northeast Folklore Society, 1958–.

Northern Arizona Flora: a Photographic, Annotated Catalog of Northern Arizona Vascular Plants. [v.d.]. Internet.

Northern Chester County Herald. Honey Brook PA, 1928–.

Northern Lancet and Gazette of Legal Medicine. Plattsburgh NY, 1850–1851.

Northern Prairie Wildlife Research Center. *Biological Resources.* [v.d.]. Internet.

————. *Native Wildflowers of the North Dakota Grasslands.* [v.d.]. Internet.

————. *Southern Wetland Flora.* [v.d.]. Internet.

Northern Vindicator. Estherville IA, 1868–1896.

North Hills News Record. Warrendale PA, 1962–.

Northrop, John Worrell. *Chronicles from the Diary of a War Prisoner in Andersonville and Other Military Prisons of the South in 1864.* Wichita KS: The Author, 1904.

Northup, Solomon. *Twelve Years a Slave.* New York: Miller, Orton & Mulligan, 1855 [c.1853].

Northwest Arkansas Times. Fayetteville AR, 1937–.

Northwest Native Plant Journal. 2003–. Internet.

Northwest Ohio Quarterly. Toledo OH: Historical Society of Northwestern Ohio, 1929–.

Northwest Signal. Napoleon OH, 1961–.

Norton, John P. *Notes for American Farmers.* New York: Leonard Scott, 1851.

Norton, Oliver Willcox. *Army Letters 1861–1865.* Chicago: O. L. Deming, 1903.

Norwalk Reporter and Huron Advertiser. Norwalk OH, 1827–1830.

Norwegian-American Studies. Northfield MN: Norwegian-American Historical Association, 1962–.

Norwegian-American Studies and Records. Northfield MN: Norwegian-American Historical Association, 1931–1959.

Norwich Courier. Norwich CT, 1809–1845.

Notes and Queries. London: Oxford Univ. Press, 1849–.

Nott, Henry Junius, ed. *Novellettes of a Traveler.* New-York: Harper & Bros., 1834.

Nowland John H. B. *Early Reminiscences of Indianapolis.* Indianapolis IN: Sentinel Book and Job Printing House, 1870.

Number 1500. *Life in Sing Sing.* Indianapolis IN: Bobbs-Merrill, 1904.

Nute, Grace Lee. *Lake Superior.* Indianapolis IN: Bobbs-Merrill, 1944.

Nuttall, Thomas. *The Genera of North American Plants and a Catalog of the Species.* Philadelphia: Printed for the author by D. Heartt, 1818. 2 vols.

————. *A Journal of Travels into the Arkansa Territory, during the Year 1819.* Philadelphia: Thos. H. Palmer, 1821.

————. *A Manual of the Ornithology of the United States and Canada.* Cambridge MA: Hilliard and Brown; Boston: Hilliard, Gray, 1832–1834. 2 vols.

————. *The North American Sylva.* Philadelphia: Robert B. Smith, 1852. 3 vols.

Nuttall Ornithological Club. *Bulletin.* Cambridge MA, 1876–1883.

Nutting, Rufus. *A Practical Grammar of the English Language.* 2d ed. rev. and improved. Montpelier VT: E. P. Walton, 1823.

Nutting, Wallace. *Massachusetts Beautiful.* Framingham MA: Old America, c.1923.

Nye, Edgar Wilson. *Baled Hay.* New York: J. W. Lovell, c.1884.

————. *Bill Nye and Boomerang.* Chicago: Belford, Clarke, 1881 [c.1880].

————. *Remarks by Bill Nye.* Chicago: A. E. Davis, 1887.

Nye, Russell Scudder. *Scientific Duck Shooting in Eastern Waters.* Falmouth MA: Independent Press, 1895.

NYT Article-Letters. 1972–1980. Unpub. letters in response to articles in the *New York Times*, Feb. 17, 1972, and Sept. 5, 1979.

Oak, Lyndon. *History of Garland, Maine.* Dover ME: Observer Publishing, 1912.

Oakland Daily Evening Tribune. Oakland CA, 1874–1891.

Oakland Tribune. Oakland CA, 1891–1978.

Oakley, Harvey, comp. *Rememberin' the Roamin' Man of the Mountains.* Gatlinburg TN: Oakley Books, c.1990. Entries orig. written prior to Wiley Oakley's death in 1954.

Oakley, Wiley. *Restin'.* Gatlinburg TN: Mountain Press, c.1947.

Oates, Joyce Carol. *Bellefleur.* New York: E. P. Dutton, c.1980.

O'Beirne, Harry F. *Leaders and Leading Men of the Indian Territory.* Chicago: American Publishers' Association, 1891.

Obenchain, Eliza Caroline Calvert. *Aunt Jane of Kentucky.* New York: A. L. Burt, c.1907. Repr. of the 1907 ed. pub. by Little, Brown, Boston.

Oberholser, Harry Church. *The Bird Life of Louisiana.* New Orleans LA: T. J. Moran's Sons, 1938.

O'Brien, Howard Vincent. *Wine, Women and War.* New York: J. H. Sears, c.1926.

O'Brien, John. *At Home in the Heart of Appalachia.* New York: Alfred A. Knopf, 2001.

O'Brien, Lawrence F. *No Final Victories.* Garden City NY: Doubleday, 1974.

O'Bryan, W. *A Narrative of Travels in the United States of America.* London: Published for the author, 1836.

Observer. Oberlin OH: Oberlin College, 1979?–.

Observer. Richland Center WI, 1876–1880.

Ocean, Suellen. *Acorns and Eat 'Em.* Grass Valley CA: Ocean-Hose, c.1993.

Oceanic Linguistics. Honolulu HI, 1962–.

Ockside, Knight Russ, M. D. SEE Underhill, Edward Fitch and Mortimer Thomson

O'Connell, James Francis, ed. *Stabilizing Dunes and Coastal Banks Using Vegetation and Bioengineering.* Woods Hole MA: Woods Hole Oceanographic Institution, 2002.

O'Connor, Flannery. *The Complete Stories.* New York: Farrar, Straus & Giroux, 1971.

————. *Wise Blood.* New York: Harcourt, Brace, 1952.

O'Connor, Frank SEE O'Donovan, Michael

O'Connor, Jack. *Horse and Buggy West.* New York: Alfred A. Knopf, 1969.

O'Connor, John. *Wanderings of a Vagabond.* New York: The Author, c.1873.

O'Connor, Sandra Day and H. Alan Day. *Lazy B.* New York: Random House, 2002.

Odenwald, Neil G. and James R. Turner. *Identification, Selection and Use of Southern Plants for Landscape Design.* 4th ed. Baton Rouge LA: Claitor's Publishing, 2006.

Odessa American. Odessa TX, 1940–.

Odland, Martin Wendell. *The Life of Knute Nelson.* Minneapolis MN: Lund Press, 1926.

Odlum, George M. *The Culture of Tobacco.* Salisbury, Southern Rhodesia: Dept. of Agriculture; London: British South Africa, 1905.

O'Donnell, Edwin P. *The Great Big Doorstep.* Boston: Houghton Mifflin, 1941.

————. *Green Margins.* Boston: Houghton Mifflin, 1936.

O'Donovan, Michael. *Bones of Contention.* London: Macmillan, 1936.

Odum, Howard Washington. *Race and Rumors of Race.* Chapel Hill NC: Univ. NC Press, c.1943.

———. *Rainbow Round My Shoulder; the Blue Trail of Black Ulysses.* Indianapolis IN: Bobbs-Merrill, c.1928.

Odum, Howard Washington and Guy B. Johnson. *The Negro and His Songs.* Chapel Hill NC: Univ. NC Press, 1925.

Oecologia. Berlin, 1968–.

OED SEE Murray, James A. H. et al. *Oxford English Dictionary*

OED2 SEE Simpson, J. A. and E. S. C. Weiner *Oxford English Dictionary*

OEDS SEE Burchfield, R. W. *The Oxford English Dictionary Supplement*

Oelwein Daily Register. Oelwein IA, 1906–1982.

Oelwein Register. Oelwein IA, 1880–1922.

O'Fallon Flashbacks. Baker MT: O'Fallon Historical Society, c.1975.

O'Ferrall, Simon Ansley. *A Ramble of Six Thousand Miles through the United States of America.* London: E. Wilson, 1832.

The Official Rules of Card Games. 17th ed. Cincinnati OH: United States Playing Card, 1913.

Offutt, Chris. *The Good Brother.* New York: Simon & Schuster, 1997.

———. *No Heroes.* New York: Simon & Schuster, c.2002.

———. *The Same River Twice.* New York: Simon & Schuster, c.1993.

Ogdensburg Advance-News. Ogdensburg NY, 1857–.

Ogden Standard. Ogden UT, 1902–1910; 1913–1920.

Ogden Standard-Examiner. Ogden UT, 1920–.

Ogilby, John. *America.* London: Printed by the Author, 1671.

O'Hara, John. *Appointment in Samarra.* New York: World Pub., 1947. Orig. pub. in 1934 by Harcourt Brace, New York and Duell Sloan and Pearce, New York.

———. *Good Samaritan and Other Stories.* New York: Random House, 1974.

———. *Pal Joey.* New York: Duell, Sloan and Pearce, 1940.

———. *Pipe Night.* New York: Duell, Sloan and Pearce, c.1945.

O'Hare, Mary Eitel. *Eastern Montana English Vocabulary.* Austin TX: Univ. TX at Austin M.A. thesis, 1968.

O'Hare, Thomas Joseph. *The Linguistic Geography of Eastern Montana.* Austin TX: Univ. TX at Austin diss., 1964.

O. Henry SEE Porter, William Sydney

Ohio Academy of Science. *Annual Report.* Columbus OH, 1892–1902?

Ohio Agricultural Experiment Station. *Bulletin.* Columbus OH, 1888–1948.

Ohio Archaeological and Historical Quarterly SEE *Ohio History*

Ohio Atlas and Elyria Advertiser. Elyria OH, 1832–1844.

Ohio. Commission of Fisheries. *First Annual Report to the Governor of the State of Ohio for the Years 1875–1876.* Columbus OH: Nevins & Myers, 1877.

Ohio Common School Director. Columbus OH, 1838.

Ohio. Constitutional Convention. *Official Report of the Proceedings and Debates.* Cleveland OH: W. S. Robinson, 1873–1874. 2 vols.

———. *Report of the Debates and Proceedings, 1850–1851.* Columbus OH: S. Medary, 1851. 2 vols.

Ohio Cultivator. Columbus OH, 1845–1866.

Ohio Democrat. New Philadelphia OH, 1840–1900.

Ohio Department of Natural Resources. *Natural Ohio.* Columbus OH, 2000?–.

Ohio Department of Natural Resources. Division of Forestry. *More Trees, Healthy Forests.* 2003–. Internet.

Ohio. Division of Conservation. Bureau of Scientific Research. *Bulletin.* Columbus OH, 1932–.

Ohio. *Documents, Including Messages and Other Communications Made to the . . . General Assembly of the State of Ohio.* Columbus OH, 1836?–1855.

Ohio Educational Monthly. Columbus OH, 1860–1875.

Ohio Farmer. Cleveland OH, 1857–1876; 1899–.

Ohio. General Assembly. Senate. *Appendix to the Journal of the Senate of the State of Ohio.* Columbus OH: R. Nevins, State Printer, 1857.

Ohio History. Columbus OH, 1887–.

Ohio. Laws, Statutes etc. *General and Local Acts.* Columbus OH, 1803–1898.

Ohio Magazine. Columbus OH, 1906–1908.

Ohio Medical and Surgical Journal. Columbus OH: J. H. Riley, 1848–1878.

Ohio Naturalist. Columbus OH, 1900–1914.

Ohio Practical Farmer. Cleveland OH, 1876–1898.

Ohio Public Library Information Network. *What Tree Is It?* [v.d.]. Internet.

Ohio Repository. Canton OH, 1815–1868.

Ohio State Board of Agriculture. *Annual Report.* Columbus OH, 1846–.

Ohio State Horticultural Society. *Annual Report.* Columbus OH, 1867–1922.

Ohio State University. College of Food, Agricultural and Environmental Sciences. *Ohioline: Horse Nutrition Bulletin.* 2000. Internet.

———. *Ohioline: Insect and Pest Series.* [v.d.]. Internet.

———. *Ohioline: Your Link to Information, News, and Education.* [v.d.]. Internet.

Ohio State University. Department of Horticulture and Crop Science. *PlantFacts: Horticultural & Crop Science in Virtual Perspective.* [v.d.]. Internet.

Ohio State University. Ohio Agricultural Research and Development Center. *Ohio Perennial & Biennial Weed Guide.* [v.d.]. Internet.

Ohio University. *Bryophyte Home Page.* [v.d.]. Internet.

Ohm, Ken. *Spatzies and Brass BBs.* Leawood KS: Leathers, c.2004.

Okanogan Independent. Okanogan WA, 1905–1975.

Oklahoma Agricultural Experiment Station. *Bulletin.* Stillwater OK, 1891–.

Oklahoma Geological Survey. *Bulletin.* Norman OK, 1908–.

Oklahoma Ornithological Society. *Bulletin.* Norman OK, 1968–.

Oklahoma. University. *Oklahoma Biological Survey.* [v.d.]. Internet.

Oklahoma. University. Biological Survey. *Publications.* Norman OK: Univ. OK, 1929–1933.

Olcott, Harriet A. Hinsdale. *The Torchlight.* New York: Derby & Jackson, 1856.

Old and New. Boston, 1870–1875.

Oldburg, John SEE Withington, Leonard

Old Colony Memorial, and Plymouth County Advertiser. Plymouth MA, 1822–1827.

Olden Time. Pittsburgh PA: J. W. Cook, 1846–1848.

Old Farmer's Almanac. Dublin NH, 1793–.

The Old Farmer's Almanac Sampler. Ed. by Robb Sagendorph. New York: Washburn, c.1957.

Old Guard. New York, 1863–1870.

Old Guard. Worcester MA: Printed under the auspices of Geo. H. Ward Post, no. 10, G. A. R. 1886–1889?

Old Huntsville Magazine. Huntsville AL, 1989–.

Oldmixon, John. *The British Empire in America.* 2d ed. corr. and amended. London: Printed for J. Brotherton, 1741. 2 vols.

Oldpath, Obadiah SEE Newhall, James Robinson

Olds Seed Company. *Olds Seeds.* Madison WI: Olds Seed Company, 1973–. Catalog.

Old-Time New England. Boston, 1920–.

Olean Democrat. Olean NY, 1883–1909.

Olean Evening Times. Olean NY, 1909–1931.

Oleson, Thurine and Erna Oleson Xan. *Wisconsin, My Home.* Madison WI: Univ. WI Press, 1950.

Oliver, Duane. *Hazel Creek from Then till Now.* Maryville TN: Stinnett Printing, c.1989.

Oliver, Ethel Ross. *Journal of an Aleutian Year.* Seattle WA: Univ. WA Press, c.1988.

Oliver, Paul. *Blues Fell This Morning.* New York: Horizon Press, 1961 [c.1960].

Oliver, William. *Eight Months in Illinois.* Chicago: W. M. Hill, 1924. Orig. printed in 1843 and sold by E. & T. Bruce, Newcastle-upon-Tyne.

Oliver, William H., Jr. *Roughing It with the Regulars.* New York: W. F. Parr, c.1901.

Olmsted, Frederick Law. *The Cotton Kingdom.* New York: Mason Brothers; London: Sampson, Low, 1861. 2 vols.

———. *A Journey in the Back Country.* New York: Mason Bros., 1863. Orig. pub. in 1860 by Mason Bros., New York.

———. *A Journey in the Seaboard Slave States.* New York: Dix & Edwards; London: Sampson Low, Son, 1856.

———. *A Journey through Texas.* New York: Mason Bros., 1859. Orig. pub. in 1857 by Dix, Edwards, New York and S. Low, Son, London.

———. *Walks and Talks of an American Farmer in England.* New York: George P. Putnam, 1852. 2 vols.

Olney Times. Olney IL, 1856–1864?

Olnhausen, Mary Phinney von. *Adventures of an Army Nurse in Two Wars.* Ed. by James Phinney Munroe. Boston: Little, Brown, 1904.

Olson, Phil and Paul Olson. *A Don't Hug Me Christmas Carol.* Musical score. New York: Samuel French, c.2007. Book & lyrics by Phil Olson; music by Paul Olson.

Olson, Ted. *Blue Ridge Folklife.* Jackson MS: Univ. Press MS, c.1998.

Omaha World-Herald. Omaha NE, 1970–.

Omwake, John. *The Conestoga Six-Horse Bell Teams of Eastern Pennsylvania.* Cincinnati OH: Ebbert & Richardson, 1930.

O'Nan, Stewart. *Snow Angels.* New York: Doubleday, c.1994.

Onderdonk, Henry. *Documents and Letters Intended to Illustrate the Revolutionary Incidents of Queens County.* New York: Leavitt, Trow, 1846.

Onderdonk, James Lawrence. *Idaho.* San Francisco: A. L. Bancroft, 1885.

O'Neal, Shaquille. *Shaq Talks Back.* New York: St. Martin's Press, 2002.

O'Neall, John Belton. *The Annals of Newberry.* Charleston SC: S. G. Courtenay, 1859.

Oneida Circular. Oneida NY: Oneida & Wallingford Communities, 1871–1876.

O'Neill, Eugene. *Ah, Wilderness!* New York: Random House, c.1933.

———. *The Emperor Jones, Diff'rent, The Straw.* New York: Boni & Liveright, c.1921.

———. *The Hairy Ape.* New York: Boni & Liveright, c.1922.

———. *The Iceman Cometh.* New York: Random House, 1946.

———. *Lost Plays.* New York: New Fathoms, 1950.

———. *A Moon for the Misbegotten.* New York: Random House, 1952.

———. *The Moon of the Caribbees.* New York: Boni and Liveright, 1919.

O'Neill, Rose Cecil. *The Story of Rose O'Neill.* Ed. by Miriam Formanek-Brunell. Columbia MO: Univ. MO Press, c.1997. A memoir written c.1940.

Oneonta Daily Star. Oneonta NY, 1890–1940.

Oneonta Star. Oneonta NY, 1940–1974.

Onondaga Standard. Syracuse NY, 1829–1873.

Ontario Historical Society. *Papers and Records.* Toronto, 1899–1946.

Oölogist. Albion NY, 1884–1941.

Opdyke, John B., ed. *Alachua County.* Gainesville FL: Alachua County Historical Commission, c.1974.

Opie, Iona Archibald and Peter Opie. *Children's Games in Street and Playground.* Oxford: At the Clarendon Press, 1969.

———, comp. *The Lore and Language of Schoolchildren.* Oxford: Clarendon Press, 1967. Orig. pub. in 1959 by Clarendon Press, Oxford.

Optic, Oliver SEE Adams, William Taylor

Oquilluk, William A. *People of Kauwerak.* Anchorage AK: AK Methodist Univ., c.1973.

Orange County Register. Santa Ana CA, 1985–.

Orange County Times-Press. Middletown NY, 1906–1927.

Orbeck, Anders. *Early New England Pronunciation.* Ann Arbor MI: George Wahr, c.1927.

Orbis. Louvain: Université Catholique de Louvain, 1952–.

Ordway, John *Journals* SEE Lewis, Meriwether and John Ordway *Journals of Captain Meriwether Lewis and Sergeant John Ordway*

Oregon. *Fish and Game Laws.* Salem OR: State Board of Fish and Game Commissioners, 1915–1918.

Oregon. Board of Horticulture. *Biennial Report.* Salem OR: State Printer, 1889–.

Oregon Countryman. Corvallis OR, 1908–1929?

Oregon Historical Society. *Oregon Historical Quarterly.* Salem OR, 1900–.

Oregonian. Portland OR, 1850–.

Oregonian Article Letters. 1979–1980. Unpub. letters received in response to an article in the *Oregonian* (Portland OR) on Sept. 23, 1979.

Oregon Pioneer Association. *Transactions.* Portland OR, 1873–.

Oregon Spectator. Oregon City OR, 1846–1855.

Oregon State Board of Forestry. *Official Proceedings.* Salem OR, 1910.

Oregon State Journal. Eugene City OR, 1864–1909.

Oregon Statesman. Oregon City OR, 1851–1866.

O'Reilly, Bernard. *Greenland, the Adjacent Seas, and the North-West Passage to the Pacific Ocean, Illustrated in a Voyage to Davis's Strait, during the Summer of 1817.* New York: James Eastburn, 1818.

O'Reilly John Boyle. *Athletics and Manly Sport.* Boston: Pilot, 1890.

Original Sacred Harp. Ed. and rev. by T. J. Denson and Paine Denson. Cullman AL: Sacred Harp Publishing, 1971.

Oriole. Atlanta GA: Georgia Ornithological Society, 1936–.

Orlando Sentinel. Orlando FL, 1982–.

Ormerod, Eleanor A. *A Manual of Injurious Insects.* 2d ed. London: Simpkin, Marshall, Hamilton, Kent, 1890.

Ormsbee, Thomas Hamilton. *Field Guide to Early American Furniture.* New York: Bonanza Books, c.1951.

Ornithologist and Oölogist. Pawtucket RI, 1881–1893.

Ornithologists' and Oologists' Semi-Annual. Pittsfield MA, 1889–1890.

O'Rourke, P. J. *All the Trouble in the World.* New York: Atlantic Monthly Press, c.1994.

Orsman, H. W., ed. *The Dictionary of New Zealand English.* Oxford: Oxford Univ. Press, c.1997.

Ortega, José de. *Apostolicos Afanes de la Compañia de Jesus.* Barcelona: Pablo Nadal, 1754.

Ortenburger, Arthur Irving. *The Whip Snakes and Racers.* Ann Arbor MI: Univ. MI, 1928.

Osborn, Laughton. *Sixty Years of the Life of Jeremy Levis.* New York: G. & C. & H. Carvill, 1831. 2 vols.

Osgood, Cornelius. *Ingalik Material Culture.* New Haven CT: Yale Univ. Press, 1940.

Osgood, William E. *Paine Mountain Guidebook.* Northfield VT: Northfield News & Printery, 1997.

Oshkosh Daily Northwestern. Oshkosh WI, 1875–1885; 1939–1979.

Oshkosh Northwestern. Oshkosh WI, 1934–1939; 1979–.

Osprey: an Illustrated Monthly Magazine of Popular Ornithology. Galesburg IL, 1896–1902.

Osteen, Joel. *Your Best Life Now.* New York: Warner Books, c.2004.

Ostertag, George. *Our Oregon.* St. Paul MN: MBI Publishing, c.2007.

Ostrander, Stephen M. *A History of the City of Brooklyn and Kings County.* Ed. by Alexander Black. Brooklyn NY: Published by Subscription, 1894. 2 vols.

Ostrom, Homer Irvin. *A Treatise on the Breast and Its Surgical Diseases.* 2d ed. New York: A. L. Chatterton, 1885.

OSU Current Report. Stillwater OK: OK State Univ. Cooperative Extension Service, 1970?–.

OSU Extension Facts. Stillwater OK: OK State Univ. Cooperative Extension Service, 1965?–.

Oswald, Felix Leopold. *Summerland Sketches.* Philadelphia: J. B. Lippincott, 1880.

Oswalt, Wendell H. *Mission of Change in Alaska.* San Marino CA: Huntington Library, c.1963.

Otis, Charles Herbert. *Michigan Trees.* Ann Arbor MI: The Regents, 1913.

———. *Michigan Trees.* 9th ed. rev. Ann Arbor MI: Published by the Regents, 1931.

Ottley, Roi. *New World A-Coming.* Boston: Houghton Mifflin, c.1943.

Ottoson, Howard W., ed. *Land Use Policy and Problems in the United States.* Lincoln NE: Univ. NE Press, 1963.

Ottumwa Daily Courier. Ottumwa IA, 186?–1960.

Oudenarde, Nicholas Aegidius See Paulding, James Kirke

Our Army. Philadelphia, 1928–1947.

Our Boys and Girls. Boston: Lee & Shepard, 1867–1873.

Our Smokies Heritage. Gatlinburg TN: Crescent Color Printing, 1978–.

Our Smokies Heritage Book 1. Gatlinburg TN: Crescent Printing, 1982.

Our Town Reminder. South Hadley MA, 1968–1980.

Our Young Folks. Boston: Ticknor & Fields, 1865–1873.

Outdoor America. Chicago: Izaak Walton League of America, 1923–1933; 1935–1961.

Outdoor Life. Denver CO, 1897–.

Outing. New York, 1882–1883; 1885–1923.

Outlook. New York, 1893–1928.

Outlook and Independent. New York, 1928–1932.

Outside Bozeman. Bozeman MT, 2000–.

Out West Magazine See Also *Land of Sunshine*

Out West Magazine. Los Angeles, 1902–1932.

Overland Monthly and Out West Magazine. San Francisco, 1868–1875; 1883–1935.

Owen, David Dale. *Fourth Report of the Geological Survey in Kentucky Made during the Years 1858 and 1859.* Frankfort KY: J. B. Major, 1861.

———. *Report of a Geological Reconnoissance of the Chippewa Land District of Wisconsin.* Washington DC: [s.n.], 1848.

———. *Report of a Geological Survey of Wisconsin, Iowa, and Minnesota.* Philadelphia: Lippincott, Grambo, 1852.

———. *Second Report of the Geological Survey in Kentucky.* Frankfort KY: A. G. Hodges, Public Printer, 1857.

Owen, Jim M. *Jim Owen's Hillbilly Humor.* New York: Pocket Books, c.1970.

Owen, John. *Walking Seattle.* Helena MT: Falcon, 2000.

Owen, Mary Alicia. *Voodoo Tales.* New York: G. P. Putnam's Sons, 1893.

Owen, Tom See Thorpe, Thomas Bangs

Owen, Urban Grammar. *Letters to Laura.* Ed. by Sadye Tune Wilson, Nancy Tune Fitzgerald, and Richard Warwick. Nashville TN: Tunstede, c.1996.

Owens, Frances Emugene. *Mrs. Owens' New Cook Book and*

Complete Household Manual. Chicago: Owens Publishing, 1899 [c.1897].

Owens, Ronald J. *Oklahoma Justice.* Paducah KY: Turner Publishing, c.1995.

Owens, William A. *Look to the River.* New York: Atheneum, 1963.

———. *Swing and Turn.* Dallas TX: Tardy Publishing, 1936.

Oxnard Courier. Oxnard CA, 1899–.

Oxnard Daily Courier. Oxnard CA, 1912–1918.

Oxnard Daily Courier and the Oxnard Daily News. Oxnard CA, 1918–1937.

Oxnard Press-Courier. Oxnard CA, 1940–1959.

Ozark Society. Pack and Paddle. Little Rock AR, 1981–.

OzarksWatch. Springfield MO: Southwest MO State Univ., 1987–.

Ozark Visitor. Point Lookout MO: School of the Ozarks, 19??–.

Pacific Coast Avifauna. Hollywood CA: Cooper Ornithological Society, 1900–.

Pacific Discovery. San Francisco: California Academy of Sciences, 1948–.

Pacific Medical and Surgical Journal. San Francisco, 1858–1884.

Pacific Medical Journal. San Francisco, 1889–1917.

Pacific Monthly. Portland OR, 1898–1911.

Pacific Northwest Quarterly. Seattle WA: Univ. WA, 1906–.

Pacific Reporter. St. Paul MN: West Publishing, 1884–1931.

Pacific Spectator. Stanford CA: Stanford Univ. Press, 1947–.

Pacific Stars and Stripes. Tokyo: U.S. Far East Command, Troop Information & Education Section, 1945–1999.

Pacific Sun. Mill Valley CA, 1962–.

Packard, Alpheus Spring. *Insects Injurious to Forest and Shade Trees.* Rev. and enlarged ed. Washington DC: Govt. Printing Office, 1890.

Packard, Winthrop. *Old Plymouth Trails.* Boston: Small, Maynard, c.1920.

PADS See American Dialect Society *Publications*

Page, Abraham See Holt, John Saunders

Page, Elizabeth. *Wagons West.* New York: Farrar & Rinehart, c.1930.

Page, F. B. *Prairiedom.* New York: Paine & Burgess, c.1845.

Page, John White. *Uncle Robin in His Cabin in Virginia.* Richmond VA: J. W. Randolph, 1853.

Page, Thomas Nelson. *Elsket and Other Stories.* New York: Charles Scribner's Sons, 1891.

———. *In Ole Virginia.* New York: Charles Scribner's Sons, 1887.

———. *Red Rock.* New York: Charles Scribner's Sons, 1898.

———. *Red Rock.* New York: Charles Scribner's Sons, 1909 [c.1898].

———. *Social Life in Old Virginia before the War.* New York: Charles Scribner's Sons, 1897.

Paige, Elbridge Gerry. *Dow's Patent Sermons.* Philadelphia: T. B. Peterson and Bros., c.1857. 4 vols.

———. *Short Patent Sermons.* Rev. and corr. New York: Lawrence Labree, 1841. Orig. pub. in the *New York Sunday Mercury.*

Paige, E. W. *Catalogue of the Flowering Plants of Schenectady County.* Albany NY: Van Benthuysen's Steam Printing House, 1864.

Paine, Albert Bigelow. *Mark Twain.* New York: Harper & Bros., 1912. 3 vols.

Paine, Ralph Delahaye. *Comrades of the Rolling Ocean.* Boston: Houghton Mifflin, 1923.

Paine, Thomas. *Complete Writings.* Coll. and ed. by Philip S. Foner. New York: Citadel Press, 1945. 2 vols.

———. *A Letter Addressed to the Abbé Raynal on the Affairs of North America.* Philadelphia: Printed; London: Reprinted for C. Dilly, 1782.

Painesville Telegraph. Painesville OH, 1915–.

Pak, Gary. *A Ricepaper Airplane.* Honolulu HI: Univ. HI Press, c.1998.

Palacio. Santa Fe NM, 1913–.

Palfrey, Evelyn. *The Price of Passion.* New York: Atria, 2006 [c.1997].

Pall Mall Gazette. London, 1865–1921.

Pall Mall Magazine. London: D. Routledge & Sons, 1893–1914.

Palm Beach County Sun Press. Lake Park FL, 1966?–.

Palm Beach Post. West Palm Beach FL, 1984–.

Palmer, Benjamin Morgan. *The Life & Letters of James Henley Thornwell.* Richmond VA: Whittet & Shepperson, 1875.

Palmer, Ephraim Laurence. *Fieldbook of Natural History.* New York: McGraw-Hill Book, 1949.

Palmer, George Herbert. *The Life of Alice Freeman Palmer.* Boston: Houghton Mifflin; Cambridge MA: Riverside Press, c.1908.

Palmer, Henry Clay. *Stories of the Base Ball Field.* Chicago: Rand, McNally, 1890.

Palmer, Joel. *Journal of Travels over the Rocky Mts.* Cincinnati OH: J. A. & U. P. James, 1847.

Palmer, John. *Journal of Travels in the United States of North America, and in Lower Canada, Performed in the Year 1817.* London: Sherwood, Neely, and Jones, 1818.

Palmer, Julius A., Jr. *Mushrooms of America, Edible and Poisonous.* Boston: L. Prang, 1885.

Palmer, Ralph Simon, ed. *Handbook of North American Birds.* New Haven CT: Yale Univ. Press, 1962–1988. 5 vols.

Palmer, Robert. *Deep Blues.* New York: Viking Press, c.1981.

Palmer, Sharon L. *A Study of Language in Western-Central Massachusetts.* Boston: Univ. MA Honors thesis, 1988.

Palmer, Tim. *Youghiogheny, Appalachian River.* Pittsburgh PA: Univ. Pittsburgh Press, 1984.

Palo Alto Tribune. Emmetsburg IA, 1893–1938.

Pammel, Louis Hermann. *Weeds of the Farm and Garden.* New York: Orange Judd; London: Kegan Paul, Trench, Trubner, 1911.

Panama City News. Panama City FL, 1952–1970.

Panama City News-Herald. Panama City FL, 1937–1970.

Panola Watchman. Carthage TX, 1873–.

Panoplist or the Christian's Armory. Boston, 1805–1808.

Pan-Pacific Entomologist. San Francisco: Pacific Coast Entomological Society, 1924–.

Pan-Pacific Research Institution. *Journal.* Honolulu HI: Pan Pacific Union, 1926–1935.

Pantagraph. Bloomington IL, 1985–.

Pap, Leo. *The Portuguese-Americans.* Boston: Twayne, c.1981.

Parade Magazine. New York: Parade Publications, 1941–. Distributed with Sun. ed. of var. newspapers.

Parents Magazine. New York, 1926–.

Paretsky, Sara. *Hard Times.* New York: Delacorte Press, c.1999.

Paris, John Ayrton and Ansel W. Ives. *Pharmacologia.* 2d Amer. ed., from the 5th enlarged London ed. New York: F. & R. Lockwood, 1823–1824. 2 vols.

Paris News. Paris TX, 1944–.

Parke, Uriah. *Lectures on the Philosophy of Arithmetic.* Philadelphia: Moss & Bros., 1850 [c.1849].

Parker, Amos Andrew. *Trip to the West and Texas.* Concord NH: White and Fisher, 1835.

Parker, Dorothy Rothschild. *Laments for the Living.* New York: Viking Press, 1930.

Parker, James. *The Old Army: Memories, 1872–1918.* Philadelphia: Dorrance, 1929.

Parker, James Ervin. *Grand Mountain Typewriting School, Conducted through Correspondence by Jim Parker in the Interest of His Nieces and Nephews.* [s.l.]: [s.n.], 1929?

Parker, John Lord. *Henry Wilson's Regiment: History of the Twenty-Second Massachusetts Infantry and the Second Company Sharpshooters, and the Third Light Battery in the War of the Rebellion.* Assisted by Robert G. Carter. Boston: Regimental Association, Press of Rand Avery, 1887.

Parker, Nathan H. *The Minnesota Handbook, for 1856-7.* Boston: John P. Jewett, 1857 [c.1856].

Parker, Nathan Howe. *Missouri as It Is in 1867.* Philadelphia: J. B. Lippincott, 1867.

Parker, Samuel. *Journal of an Exploring Tour beyond the Rocky Mountains . . . in the Years 1835, '36, and '37.* Ithaca NY: Published by the author, 1838.

Parker, William B. *Notes Taken during the Expedition Commanded by Capt. R. B. Marcy, U.S.A., through Unexplored Texas in the Summer and Fall of 1854.* Philadelphia: Hayes & Zell, 1856.

Parkinson, Eleanor. *The Complete Confectioner, Pastry-Cook and Baker.* Philadelphia: Lea and Blanchard, 1844.

Parkinson, John. *Paradisi in sole Paradisus Terrestris.* London: Printed by H. Downes and R. Young, 1629.

———. *Theatrum Botanicum: the Theater of Plants.* London: Printed by Tho. Cotes, 1640.

Parkinson, Richard. *A Tour in America in 1798, 1799, and 1800.* London: J. Harding and J. Murry, 1805. 2 vols.

Parkman, Ebenezer. *The Diary of Ebenezer Parkman, 1703-1782.* Worcester MA: American Antiquarian Society, 1974–.

———. *The Diary of Rev. Ebenezer Parkman, of Westborough Mass.* Westborough MA: Westboro Historical Society, 1899.

Parkman, Francis. *The California and Oregon Trail.* New York: G. P. Putnam, 1849.

———. *The Discovery of the Great West.* Boston: Little, Brown, 1870 [c.1869].

Parks, Hal Braley. *Valuable Plants Native to Texas.* College

Station TX: Agricultural and Mechanical College of TX, 1937.

Parler, Mary Celestia. *Folk Beliefs from Arkansas.* Fayetteville AR: The Author, 1962.

Parley's Magazine. New York, 1833–1844.

Parloa, Maria. *Miss Parloa's Kitchen Companion.* Boston: Dana Estes, c.1887.

———. *Miss Parloa's New Cook Book.* Boston: Estes & Lauriat, 1881 [c.1880].

Parris, John. *Mountain Bred.* Asheville NC: Citizen-Times Publishing, c.1967.

———. *My Mountains, My People.* Asheville NC: Citizen-Times Publishing, c.1957.

———. *Roaming the Mountains with John A. Parris.* Asheville NC: Citizen-Times Publishing, 1955.

———. *These Storied Mountains.* Asheville NC: Citizen-Times Publishing, 1972.

Parrish, Anne. *The Perennial Bachelor.* New York: Harper & Bros., 1925.

Parrish, Edward. *A Treatise on Pharmacy.* 3d ed., thoroughly rev. and improved with important additions. Philadelphia: Henry C. Lea, 1865 [c.1864].

Parrish, Lydia Austin, comp. *Slave Songs of the Georgia Sea Islands.* Hatboro PA: Folklore Associates, 1965 [c.1942].

Parry, Needham. "The Journal of Needham Parry—1794." Kentucky Historical Society *Register.* (1936) 34.379–91.

Parsons, Elsie Worthington Clews, ed. *Folk-Lore of the Sea Islands, South Carolina.* Cambridge MA: American Folk-Lore Society, 1923.

Parsons, Frances Theodora. *How to Know the Ferns.* New York: Charles Scribner's Sons, 1899.

———. *How to Know the Wild Flowers.* 2d ed. New York: Charles Scribner's Sons, 1893.

Parsons, Mary Elizabeth. *The Wild Flowers of California.* San Francisco: William Doxey, 1897.

———. *The Wild Flowers of California.* Rev. and corr. ed. San Francisco: H. S. Crocker and Cunningham, Curtiss & Welch, 1916.

———. *The Wild Flowers of California.* Rev. and corr. ed. San Francisco: H. S. Crocker, 1918 [c.1906].

Parton, Sara Payson Willis. *Fresh Leaves.* New York: Mason Bros., 1857.

———. *Ginger-Snaps.* New York: Carleton, 1870.

———. *Ruth Hall.* New York: Mason Bros., 1855 [c.1854].

Partridge, Bellamy. *January Thaw.* New York: Grosset & Dunlap, c.1945.

Partridge, Bellamy and Otto Bettmann. *As We Were.* New York: McGraw-Hill, c.1946.

Partridge, Eric. *A Dictionary of the Underworld, British and American.* New York: Bonanza Books, 1961. Repr. of 1949 ed.

———. *Slang Today and Yesterday.* 3d ed. rev. and brought up to date. New York: Bonanza Books, 1960.

Pasadena Independent. Pasadena CA, 1933–1962.

Paterson, Isabel. *If It Prove Fair Weather.* New York: G. P. Putnam's Sons, 1940.

Patrick, Henry E. *Collection of Southern Expressions.* 1973. Unpub.

Patrick, Vincent. *The Pope of Greenwich Village.* New York: Seaview Books, c.1979.

Patriot Ledger. Quincy MA, 1991–.

Patriot-News. Harrisburg PA, 1997–.

Patriot-Tribune. Glenmora-Lecompte LA, 1895–.

Patten, Gilbert. *Courtney of the Center Garden.* New York: Barse and Hopkins, c.1915.

———. *Frank Merriwell at Yale.* Philadelphia: David McKay, c.1903.

Patten, Matthew. *The Diary of Matthew Patten of Bedford N.H.* Concord NH: Rumford Printing, 1903.

Patterson, Edward Howard Norton. "Travel Diary." In: Hafen, Le Roy Reuben, ed., *Overland Routes to the Gold Fields, 1859,* 1942, 11.57–197.

Patterson, Pernet. *The Road to Canaan.* New York: Minton, Balch, 1931.

Patterson, Raymond M. *Buffalo Head.* New York: William Sloane Associates, 1961.

Patterson's Pittsburgh Town and Country Almanac. Pittsburgh PA: R. Patterson & Lambdin, 1813?–1824?

Pattie, James Ohio. *The Personal Narrative of James O. Pattie of Kentucky.* Ed. by Timothy Flint. New York: Arno Press, 1973 [c.1831].

Patton, Frances Gray. *Good Morning, Miss Dove.* New York: Dodd, Mead, c.1954, c.1946.

———. *A Piece of Luck.* New York: Dodd, Mead, 1955.

Patty, Ernest Newton. *North Country Challenge.* New York: D. McKay, 1969.

Paul, Elliot Harold. *Linden on the Saugus Branch.* New York: Random House, 1947.

Paul, Howard. *Dashes of American Humour.* London: Piper Bros., 1852.

Paulding, Hiram. *Journal of a Cruise of the United States Schooner Dolphin among the Islands of the Pacific Ocean.* Honolulu HI: Univ. HI Press, 1970 [c.1831].

Paulding, James Kirke. *The Book of Saint Nicholas.* Transl. from the orig. Dutch of Dominie Nicholas. New York: Harper & Bros., 1836.

———. *A Book of Vagaries.* New York: C. Scribner, 1868.

———. *The Diverting History of John Bull and Brother Jonathan.* New York: Inskeep and Bradford, 1812.

———. *John Bull in America.* New York: Charles Wiley, 1825.

———. *The Lay of the Scottish Fiddle.* London: Printed for James Cawthorn, 1814.

———. *Letters from the South, Written during an Excursion in the Summer of 1816.* New-York: James Eastburn, 1817. 2 vols.

———. *Letters from the South.* New ed. New York: Harper & Bros., 1835. 2 vols.

———. *The Lion of the West.* Rev. by John Augustus Stone and William Bayle Bernard. Stanford CA: Stanford Univ. Press, 1954. The text is that of the 1833 revision prepared for the London stage.

———. *The New Mirror for Travellers.* New-York: G. & C. Carvill, 1828.

———. *Tales of the Good Woman by a Doubtful Gentleman.* New York: Charles Scribner, 1867.

———. *Westward Ho!* New-York: J. & J. Harper, 1832. 2 vols.

Paulding, James Kirke and William Irving Paulding. *American Comedies.* Philadelphia: Carey and Hart, 1847.

Pavlik, Bruce M. et al. *Oaks of California.* [s.l.]: Cachuma Press, c.1991.

Paxton, Philip SEE Hammett, Samuel Adams

Paxton Weekly Record. Paxton IL, 1869–1874.

Payne, Lamar Strickland. *20th Century Fables.* Montreal: Broadway, 1904.

Payson, George. *Golden Dreams and Leaden Realities.* New York: G. P. Putnam, 1853.

Peabody, Marian Lawrence. *To Be Young Was Very Heaven.* Boston: Houghton Mifflin, 1967.

Peabody Journal of Education. Nashville TN, 1923–1970.

Peace News. London, 1936?–.

Peake, Elmore Elliot. *The Darlingtons.* New York: McClure, Phillips, 1900.

Peake, Richard Brinsley. *Americans Abroad.* London: J. Dicks, 1824.

Pearce, Donald. *Cool Hand Luke.* New York: Scribner, 1965.

Pearl, Anita May. *The Jonathan David Dictionary of Popular Slang.* Middle Village NY: Jonathan David, c.1980.

Pearsall, Marion. *Little Smoky Ridge.* Birmingham AL: Univ. AL Press, 1959.

Pearson, Elizabeth Ware, ed. *Letters from Port Royal Written at the Time of the Civil War.* Boston: W. B. Clarke, c.1906.

Pearson, Emily Clemens. *Cousin Franck's Household.* 4th ed. Boston: Upham, Ford and Olmstead, 1853 [c.1852].

Pearson, Haydn Sanborn. *Country Flavor.* New York: Whittlesey House, McGraw Hill Book, c.1945.

———. *Sea Flavor.* New York: McGraw-Hill Book, c.1948.

Pearson, Jonathan et al. *A History of the Schenectady Patent in the Dutch and English Times.* Albany NY: J. Munsell's Sons, Printers, 1883.

Pearson, Thomas Gilbert. *Adventures in Bird Protection.* New York: D. Appleton-Century, 1937.

Pearson, Thomas Gilbert *Birds Amer.* SEE *Birds of America*

Pearson, Thomas Gilbert. *The Bird Study Book.* Garden City NY: Doubleday, Page, 1919 [c.1917].

Pearson, Thomas Gilbert et al. *Birds of North Carolina.* Raleigh NC: Edwards & Broughton, 1919.

Pearson's Magazine. New York, 1899–1922.

Peattie, Donald Culross. *A Natural History of Trees of Eastern and Central North America.* Boston: Houghton Mifflin, 1950.

———. *A Natural History of Western Trees.* Boston: Houghton Mifflin, 1953.

Peattie, Roderick, ed. *The Berkshires.* New York: Vanguard Press, 1948.

———, ed. *The Black Hills.* New York: Vanguard Press, c.1952.

———, ed. *The Cascades.* New York: Vanguard Press, c.1949.

———, ed. *The Friendly Mountains, Green, White and Adirondacks.* New York: Vanguard Press, 1942.

———, ed. *The Great Smokies and the Blue Ridge.* New York: Vanguard Press, c.1943.

———, ed. *The Inverted Mountains.* New York: Vanguard Press, 1948.

———, ed. *The Pacific Coast Ranges.* New York: Vanguard Press, c.1946.

———, ed. *The Sierra Nevada.* New York: Vanguard Press, c.1947.

Peck, George Wilbur. *Mirth for the Million.* Chicago: Belford, Clarke, 1883.

———. *Peck's Bad Boy and His Pa.* Toronto: Musson Book, [n.d.].

———. *Peck's Bad Boy and His Pa.* Complete ed. New York: Dover Publications, c.1958. Facsimile of the 1892 ed. pub. by Morrill, Higgins, Chicago after the text orig. pub. in 1883 by Belford, Clark, Chicago.

———. *Peck's Bad Boy No. 2.* Chicago: Belford-Clarke, 1890 [1883].

———. *Peck's Bad Boy with the Circus.* Chicago: Charles C. Thompson, c.1906.

———. *Peck's Boss Book.* Chicago: Belford, Clarke, 1890 [c.1884].

———. *Peck's Fun.* Milwaukee WI: Symes, Swain, 1879.

———. *Peck's Sunshine.* Chicago: Belford, Clarke, 1882.

———. *Peck's Uncle Ike and the Red Headed Boy.* New York: Hurst, 1899.

Peck, John Mason. *A Gazetteer of Illinois.* Jacksonville IL: R. Goudy, 1834.

———. *A Gazetteer of Illinois.* 2d ed. entirely rev., corr., and enlarged. Philadelphia: Grigg & Elliott, 1837.

———. *A Guide for Emigrants.* Boston: Lincoln and Edmands, 1831.

———. *A New Guide to the West.* Cincinnati OH: D. Anderson, 1848. Repr. of the 2d ed. orig. pub. in 1837 by Gould, Kendall and Lincoln, Boston under the title *A New Guide for Emigrants.*

Peck, Morton Eaton. *A Manual of the Higher Plants of Oregon.* 2d ed. Portland OR: Binfords & Mort, 1961.

Pedagogical Seminary. Worcester MA, 1891–1924.

Pedagogical Seminary and Journal of Genetic Psychology. Worcester MA, 1924–1953.

Peden, Rachel. *The Land, the People.* New York: Alfred A. Knopf, 1966.

———. *Speak to the Earth.* New York: Alfred A. Knopf, 1974.

Pederson, Lee A. *A Dialect Survey of Rural Georgia.* c1970. Unpub.

———. *Linguistic Atlas of the Gulf States: Basic Materials.* Ann Arbor MI: Univ. Microfilms International, 1981.

———. *Linguistic Atlas of the Gulf States: Concordance.* Ann Arbor MI: Univ. Microfilms International, 1986.

———. *Linguistic Atlas of the Gulf States: General Index.* Athens GA: Univ. GA Press, c.1988.

———. *Linguistic Atlas of the Gulf States: Regional Matrix.* Athens GA: Univ. GA Press, c.1990.

———. *Linguistic Atlas of the Gulf States: Regional Pattern.* Athens GA: Univ. GA Press, c.1991.

———. *Linguistic Atlas of the Gulf States: Social Matrix.* Athens GA: Univ. GA Press, c.1991.

———. *Linguistic Atlas of the Gulf States: Technical Index.* Athens GA: Univ. GA, c.1989.

———. *Material from Collections for the "Urban Supplement to the Linguistic Atlas of the Gulf States: the Basic Materials".* 1981. Unpub.

———. *Material from Linguistic Atlas of the Gulf States Fieldwork.* 1975–1988. Unpub.

Peele, Robert, ed. *Mining Engineers' Handbook.* New York: John Wiley & Sons, 1918.

Peet, Louis Harman. *Trees and Shrubs of Central Park.* New York: Manhattan Press, c.1903.

Peirce, Benjamin. *A History of Harvard University.* Cambridge MA: Brown, Shattuck, 1833.

Peirce, Josephine H. *Fire on the Hearth.* Springfield MA: Pond-Ekberg, c.1951.

Peirce, Leonard. *Conversations on Arithmetic.* Boston: Printed by Lincoln & Edmands, 1823.

Peixotto, Ernest Clifford. *Our Hispanic Southwest.* New York: C. Scribner's Sons, 1916.

Pelletreau, William S. *Early Wills of Westchester County New York from 1664 to 1784.* New York: Francis P. Harper, c.1898.

Pellett, Frank C. *American Honey Plants.* Hamilton IL: American Bee Journal, 1920.

———. *American Honey Plants.* 2d ed. rev. and enlarged. Hamilton IL: American Bee Journal, 1923.

———. *American Honey Plants.* 3d ed. rev. and enlarged. Hamilton IL: American Bee Journal, 1930.

Pelzer, Louis. *Marches of the Dragoons in the Mississippi Valley.* Iowa City IA: State Historical Society of Iowa, 1917.

Pemberton, Ebenezer. *A Funeral Sermon on the Death of That Learned & Excellent Divine the Reverend Mr. Samuel Willard.* Boston: Printed by E. Green, 1707.

Pen and Pencil. Cincinnati OH, 1853.

Pencil, Mark, [pseud.]. *The White Sulphur Papers.* New York: Samuel Colman, 1839.

Penn, William. *Correspondence between William Penn and James Logan, Secretary of the Province of Pennsylvania, and Others. 1700–1750.* Philadelphia: Historical Society of Pennsylvania, 1870–1872. 2 vols.

———. *A Further Account of the Province of Pennsylvania and Its Improvements.* London: [s.n.], 1685.

———. *A Letter from William Penn, Poprietary [sic] and Governor of Pennsylvania in America, to the Committee of the Free Society of Traders of That Province, Residing in London.* London: Printed and sold by A. Sowle, 1683.

———. *Select Works.* London: [s.n.], 1771.

Pennant, Thomas. *Arctic Zoology.* London: Printed by Henry Hughs, 1784–1787. 2 vols. and suppl.

———. *History of Quadrupeds.* London: Printed for B. White, 1781. 2 vols.

Penniman, James Hosmer. *The Alley Rabbit.* Boston: Richard G. Badger, 1920.

Pennington, Patience SEE Pringle, Elizabeth Waties Allston

Pennington Pedigrees. Devil's Lake ND, 1968–.

Pennsylvania Archives. Philadelphia: J. Severns, 1852–1935.

Pennsylvania College. Linnaean Association. *Literary Record and Journal.* Gettysburg PA, 1844–1848.

Pennsylvania. Department of Agriculture. *Annual Report.* Harrisburg PA, 1895–1940?

———. *Bulletin.* Harrisburg PA, 1895–.

Pennsylvania Department of Conservation and Natural Resources. *Wild Resource Conservation Program.* [v.d.]. Internet.

Pennsylvania. Department of Fisheries. *Bulletin.* Harrisburg PA, 1904–1914.

Pennsylvania Dutchman. Lancaster PA, 1949–1954.

Pennsylvania Evening Post. Philadelphia, 1775–1781.

Pennsylvania Folklife. Lancaster PA, 1958–.

Pennsylvania Game Commission. *Wildlife Notes.* Harrisburg PA, 1980?–.

Pennsylvania Game News. Harrisburg PA: Pennsylvania Game Commission, 1930–1976.

Pennsylvania Gazette. Philadelphia, 1728–1815.

Pennsylvania-German. Lebanon PA: P. C. Croll, 1900–1911.

Pennsylvania German Folklore Society Yearbook. Allentown PA, 1936–1966.

Pennsylvania-German Society. *Proceedings and Addresses.* Lancaster PA, 1891–1948.

Pennsylvania. Historical Society. *Memoirs.* Philadelphia: M'Carty and Davis, 1826–1895.

Pennsylvania History. University Park PA: Pennsylvania Historical Association, 1934–.

Pennsylvania Journal and Weekly Advertiser. Philadelphia, 1780–1793.

Pennsylvania. Laws, Statutes etc. *Laws of the General Assembly of the Commonwealth of Pennsylvania.* Harrisburg PA, 1841–.

Pennsylvania Magazine of History and Biography. Philadelphia: Historical Society of Pennsylvania, 1877–.

Pennsylvania Packet and Daily Advertiser. Philadelphia, 1784–1790.

Pennsylvania Packet, or, the General Advertiser. Lancaster PA, 1777–1783.

Pennsylvania Pharmaceutical Association. *Proceedings.* Harrisburg PA, 1879–1925.

Pennsylvania. Provincial Council. *Minutes.* Harrisburg PA: Printed by T. Fenn, 1851–1853.

Pennsylvania School Journal. Harrisburg PA: Pennsylvania State Education Association, 1852–1980.

Pennsylvania State Agricultural Society. *Report of the Transactions.* Harrisburg PA: State Printer, 1854–.

Pennsylvania. State Lunatic Hospital. *Annual Report.* Harrisburg PA, 1851–1921?

Pennsylvania State University. College of Agricultural Sciences. *Agronomy Guide.* University Park PA, 1990–.

Penny Cyclopaedia of the Society for the Diffusion of Useful Knowledge. London: Charles Knight, 1833–1843. 27 vols.

Penny Magazine of the Society for the Diffusion of Useful Knowledge. London, 1832–1845.

Pennypacker, Samuel Whitaker. *The Autobiography of a Pennsylvanian.* Philadelphia: John C. Winston, 1918.

People. Chicago, 1974–.

People Pleasing Recipes Celebrating Waunakee's Quasiquicentennial. Waunakee WI: [s.n.], 1996?

People's Press. Gettysburg PA, 1835–1836.

The People's Vade-Mecum. Buffalo NY: Jewett, Thomas, 1850.

Pepitone, Joe and Berry Stainback. *Joe, You Coulda Made Us Proud.* Chicago: Playboy Press, c.1975.

Perch, Philemon SEE Johnston, Richard Malcolm

Percival, Olive. *Our Old-Fashioned Flowers.* Pasadena CA: [s.n.], 1947.

Percy, Walker. *The Moviegoer.* New York: Alfred A. Knopf, 1966 [c.1960].

Percy, William Alexander. *Lanterns on the Levee.* New York: Alfred A. Knopf, c.1941.

Perdue, Charles L. Jr., ed. *Outwitting the Devil: Jack Tales from Wise County, Virginia.* Santa Fe NM: Ancient City Press, 1987.

———. *Pigsfoot Jelly & Persimmon Beer.* Santa Fe NM: Ancient City Press, 1992.

Perelman, Sidney Joseph. *Keep It Crisp.* New York: Random House, 1946.

Perkey, Arlyn W. and Brenda L. Wilkins. *Crop Tree Field Guide.* Morgantown WV: USDA Forest Service, Northeastern Area State and Private Forestry, 2001.

Perkins, Justin. *A Residence of Eight Years in Persia.* Andover MA: Allen, Morril & Wordwell; New York: M. W. Dodd, 1843.

Perkins, Lucy Fitch. *The Eskimo Twins.* Boston: Houghton Mifflin, c.1914.

Perkins, Stan. *Perk's Path.* Swartz Creek MI: Broadblade Press, 1999.

Perley, T. E. *From Timber to Town.* Chicago: A. C. McClurg, 1891.

Perrie, George W. *Buckskin Mose.* New York: Henry L. Hinton, 1873.

Perrin, Noel. *First Person Rural.* Boston: D. R. Godine, 1990 [c.1978].

Perrin, Porter. *Collection.* 1852–1965. Unpub. excerpts and clippings especially about the Pacific Northwest.

Perrin, William Henry et al., comps. *History of Medina County and Ohio.* Chicago: Baskin & Battey, 1881.

Perrot, Nicolas. *Mémoire sur les moeurs . . . des sauvages de l'Amérique Septentrionale.* Leipzig: A. Franck, 1864.

Perrow, George L. *The Hoosier Editor: a Tale of Indiana Life.* Indianapolis IN: Tilford & Carlon, Printers, 1877.

Perrow, Martin Richard and A. J. Davy. *Handbook of Ecological Restoration.* Cambridge: Cambridge Univ. Press, 2002. 2 vols.

Perry, Bliss. *And Gladly Teach.* Boston: Houghton Mifflin, c.1935.

Perry, Frances and Roy Hay. *A Field Guide to Tropical and Subtropical Plants.* New York: Van Nostrand Reinhold, 1982.

Perry, George Sessions. *Cities of America.* New York: Whittlesey House, McGraw-Hill, 1947.

———. *Hold Autumn in Your Hand.* New York: Viking Press, 1941.

———. *My Granny Van.* New York: Whittlesey House, c.1949.

———. *Texas.* New York: McGraw-Hill, c.1942.

Perry, G. W. *A Treatise on Turpentine Farming.* Newbern NC: Muse & Davies, 1859.

Perry, Matthew Calbraith. *The American in Japan.* Wilmington DE: Scholarly Resources, 1973 [c.1856]. Facsimile of the 1857 ed. pub. by D. Appleton, New York.

Perry, Michael. *Coop: a Year of Poultry, Pigs, and Parenting.* New York: HarperCollins, c.2009.

———. *Population 485.* New York: HarperCollins, c.2002.

———. *Truck.* New York: HarperCollins, c.2006.

Perry, W. A. et al. *American Game Fishes.* Chicago: Rand, McNally, 1892.

Perry, William Stevens, ed. *Historical Collections Relating to the American Colonial Church.* Hartford CT: Church Press, 1870–1878. 5 vols.

Perry Bulletin. Perry IA, 1894–1898.

Perry Daily Chief. Perry IA, 1894–1916.

Peterkin, Julia Mood. *Black April.* Indianapolis IN: Bobbs-Merrill, 1927.

———. *Bright Skin.* Indianapolis IN: Bobbs-Merrill, c.1932.

———. *Scarlet Sister Mary.* New York: Grosset & Dunlap, c.1928.

Peter Parley's Almanac for Old and Young. Philadelphia, 1836–1837.

Peters, Samuel Andrew. *A General History of Connecticut.* London: J. Bew, 1781.

Petersburg Press. Petersburg AK, 1926–.

Peterson, Charles Jacobs. *The Cabin and the Parlor.* Philadelphia: T. B. Peterson, c.1852.

Peterson, Cyrus A. and Joseph Mills Hanson. *Pilot Knob, the Thermopylae of the West.* New York: Neale, 1914.

Peterson, Hannah Mary Bouvier. *The National Cook Book.* Philadelphia: T. B. Peterson & Bros., 1866.

Peterson, Roger Tory. *A Field Guide to the Birds of Texas.* Boston: Houghton Mifflin, 1960.

Peterson's Magazine. Philadelphia, 1840–1892.

Petit, Lizzie SEE Cutler, Lizzie Petit

Petiver, James. *Gazophylacii Naturae & Artis.* London: Christ. Bateman, 1702–1706. 5 vols.

———. *Petiveriana seu Naturae Collectanea.* London: Printed for James Petiver in Aldersgate Street, 1716.

Petrides, George A. *A Field Guide to Trees and Shrubs.* Boston: Houghton Mifflin, 1958.

Petry, Ann. *The Narrows.* Boston: Houghton Mifflin, 1953.

Pettitt, Wilfrid Henry. *Nine Girls.* Chicago: Dramatic Publishing, 1943.

Petzoldt, Paul and Raye Carleson Ringholz. *The New Wilderness Handbook.* Rev. and updated. New York: W. W. Norton, c.1984.

Peyton, John Lewis. *The Adventures of My Grandfather.* London: John Wilson, 1867.

Phares, David Lewis. *Farmer's Book of Grasses and Other Forage Plants, for the Southern United States.* Starkville MS: J. C. Hill, 1881.

Pharos-Tribune. Logansport IN, 1976–.

Phelps, Almira Hart Lincoln. *Familiar Lectures on Botany.* Hartford CT: H. and F. J. Huntington, 1829.

———. *Familiar Lectures on Botany.* 10th ed., rev. and enlarged. New York: F. J. Huntington, 1840. Text and pagination that of the 5th ed. pub. in 1836 by Collins and Hanney, New York.

———. *Familiar Lectures on Botany.* New ed., rev. and enlarged. New York: Huntington & Savage, 1849 [c.1845].

Phelps, Caroline. "Mrs. Caroline Phelps' Diary." Illinois State Historical Society *Journal.* (1930–1931) 23.209–39.

Phelps, Edward C., ed. *Bernardston.* Winchester NH: Mustang Bindery, c.2008.

Phelps, Francis J. *Civil War Letters.* Sparks NV: G. A. Phelps, c.2000.

Phelps, Stanley Arthur. *Famous Last Words.* [s.l.]: Printed by his sister Ruth Margaret Phelps, 1992.

Phenix; or, Windham Herald. Windham CT, 1791–1798.

Phi Beta Pi Quarterly. Menasha WI, 1903–1929.

Philadelphia Citypaper.net. 2000?–. Internet.

Philadelphia Gas Works. *Annual Report of the Trustees . . . to the Select and Common Councils of the City of Philadelphia.* Philadelphia, 1835–1866.

Philadelphia Gazette & Daily Advertiser. Philadelphia, 1800–1802.

Philadelphia Inquirer. Philadelphia, 1860–1934.

Philadelphia Magazine. Philadelphia, 1909–.

Philadelphia Medical and Physical Journal. Philadelphia, 1804–1808.

Philadelphia Medical Museum. Philadelphia, 1804–1811.

Philadelphia Monthly Magazine. Philadelphia, 1827–1830.

Philadelphia. Ordinances, etc. *Ordinances of the Corporation of the City of Philadelphia.* Philadelphia: Published by Moses Thomas, 1805?–1830?

Philadelphia Repository and Weekly Register. Philadelphia, 1800–1804.

Philadelphia Society for Promoting Agriculture. *Memoirs.* Philadelphia, 1808–.

Philadelphia Visiter and Parlour Companion. Philadelphia, 1835?–1841?

Philadelphia Weekly. Philadelphia, 1995–.

Philbrick, Nathaniel. *In the Heart of the Sea.* New York: Viking, c.2000.

Philistine. East Aurora NY, 1895–1915.

Philkins, Ike SEE Bowen, William Abraham

Philleo, Calvin Wheeler. *Twice Married.* New York: Dix & Edwards; London: Sampson Low & Sons, 1855.

Phillips, Allan R. et al. *The Birds of Arizona.* Tucson AZ: Univ. AZ Press, 1964.

Phillips, David Graham. *Susan Lenox.* Upper Saddle River NJ: Gregg Press, 1968. 2 vols. Repr. of the 1917 ed. pub. by D. Appleton, New York.

Phillips, David L. *Letters from California.* Springfield IL: Illinois State Journal, 1877.

Phillips, James Atlee. *Pagoda.* New York: Macmillan, 1951.

Phillips, James Duncan. *Salem and the Indies.* Boston: Houghton Mifflin, 1947.

Phillips, J. J. *Mojo Hand.* New York: Trident Press, c.1966.

Phillips, John Charles. *A Natural History of Ducks.* New York: Dover, 1986. 2 vols. Repr. of the 4 vol. ed. orig. pub. 1922–1926 by Houghton Mifflin, Boston.

Phillips, John Charles and Frederick C. Lincoln. *American Waterfowl.* Boston: Houghton Mifflin, 1930.

Phillips, Judith. *New Mexico Gardener's Guide.* Rev. ed. Franklin TN: Cool Springs Press, c.2004.

Phillips, Michael James. *History of Santa Barbara County, California.* Chicago: S. J. Clarke Publishing, 1927. 2 vols.

Phillips, Phillip Lee. *Notes on the Life and Works of Bernard Romans.* Deland FL: Florida State Historical Society, 1924.

Phillips, Steven J. and Patricia Wentworth Comus, eds. *A Natural History of the Sonoran Desert.* Tucson: Arizona-Sonoran Desert Museum; Berkeley: Univ. CA Press, c.2000.

Phillips, Ulrich Bonnell. *Life and Labor in the Old South.* Boston: Little, Brown, 1929.

——, ed. *Plantation and Frontier Documents, 1649–1863, Illustrative of Industrial History in the Colonial & Ante-Bellum South, Collected from MAS, and Other Rare Sources.* Cleveland OH: Arthur H. Clark, 1909. 2 vols.

Phillips, Wendell. *Speeches, Lectures, and Letters.* Boston: Lee and Shepard, 1881 [c.1863].

Philosophical Transactions of the Royal Society of London SEE Royal Society of London

Philp's Washington Described. Ed. by William D. Haley. New York: Rudd & Carleton, 1861.

Phippen, Sanford. *People Trying to Be Good: Downeast Stories.* Orono ME: Puckerbrush Press, 1988.

Phoenix, John SEE Derby, George Horatio

Phyfe, William Henry Pinkney. *How Should I Pronounce? or, the Principles of the Art of Correct Pronunciation.* 6th ed. New York: G. P. Putnam's Sons, 1897 [c.1885].

Phylon. Atlanta GA: Atlanta Univ., 1940–1956.

Phytologia. New York: Harold N. Moldenke and Alma L. Moldenke, 1933–.

Pickard, Kate E. R. *The Kidnapped and the Ransomed.* 3d ed. Syracuse NY: William T. Hamilton, 1856.

Pickard, Madge Evelyn and R. Carlyle Buley. *The Midwest Pioneer, His Ills, Cures, & Doctors.* Crawfordsville IN: R. E. Banta, 1945.

Pickering, Charles. *Chronological History of Plants.* Boston: Little, Brown, 1879.

Pickering, John. *A Vocabulary.* Boston: Cummings and Hilliard, 1816.

Pickering, Joseph. *Inquiries of an Emigrant.* 3d ed. London: Effingham Wilson, 1832.

Picket, Albert and John W. Picket. *The Academician.* New York: Printed by Charles N. Baldwin, 1820.

Pickett, Albert James. *History of Alabama.* 3d ed. Charleston SC: Walker and James, 1851. 2 vols.

Pickett, George Edward. *The Heart of a Soldier.* New York: Seth Moyle, c.1913.

Pickwell, Gayle Benjamin. *Amphibians and Reptiles of the Pacific States.* Stanford University CA: Stanford Univ. Press, c.1947.

——. *Deserts.* New York: Whittlesey House, McGraw-Hill, c.1939.

Pidgin, Charles Felton. *Quincy Adams Sawyer and Mason's Corner Folks.* Rev. ed. Boston: C. M. Clark Publishing, 1902.

Pidgin to da Max. Conceived, written and illustrated by Douglas Simonson Peppo in collaboration with Ken Sakato and Pat Sasaki. Honolulu HI: Peppovision, 1981.

Pierce, Wesley George. *Goin' Fishin'.* Salem MA: Marine Research Society, 1934.

Piercy, Caroline Behlen. *The Shaker Cook Book.* New York: Crown, c.1953.

Piercy, Marge. *Small Changes.* Garden City NY: Doubleday, 1973.

Pierson, Clara Dillingham. *Among the Pond People.* [s.l.]: Baldwin Online Children's Literature Project, 2005. Text transcr. for *Baldwin Online Children's Literature Project* website from the 1901 ed. pub. by E. P. Dutton, New York.

Pierson, Hamilton Wilcox. *In the Brush.* New York: D. Appleton, 1881.

——. *Jefferson at Monticello.* New York: Charles Scribner, 1862.

Piesman, Marissa. *Unorthodox Practices.* New York: Pocket Books, c.1989.

Pif Magazine. 1995?–. Internet.

Pijut, Paula M. *Native Hardwood Trees of the Central Hardwood Region.* Lafayette IN: North Central Research Station, USDA Forest Service, 2005.

Pike, Albert. *Prose Sketches and Poems.* Boston: Light & Horton, 1834.

Pike, James. *Scout and Ranger.* Princeton NJ: Princeton Univ. Press, 1932. Orig. pub. in 1865 by J. R. Hawley, Cincinnati.

Pike, Mary Hayden Green. *Ida May.* Boston: Phillips, Sampson, 1854.

Pike, Robert Everding. *Tall Trees, Tough Men.* New York: W. W. Norton, c.1967.

Pike, Warburton. *Through the Subarctic Forest.* London: Edward Arnold, 1896.

Pike, Zebulon Montgomery. *An Account of the Expedition to the Sources of the Mississippi . . . during the Years 1805, 1806, 1807.* Philadelphia: C. & A. Conrad, 1810.

——. *The Expeditions of Zebulon Montgomery Pike, to the Headwaters of the Mississippi . . . during the Years 1805–6–7.* New ed. New York: F. P. Harper, 1895. Orig. pub. in 1810 by C. & A. Conrad, Philadelphia.

Pike County Courier. Murfreesboro AR, 1888–1979.

Pilgrim Society, Plymouth Mass. *Notes.* Plymouth MA, 1954–.

Pilkington, James. *A View of the Present State of Derbyshire.* Derby: Printed and sold by J. Drewry, 1789. 2 vols.

Pinckert, Robert C. *The Truth about English.* Englewood Cliffs NJ: Prentice-Hall, c.1981.

Pinckney, Eliza Lucas. *Journals and Letters of Eliza Lucas.* Wormsloe GA: [s.n.], 1850.

Pinckney, James D. et al. *Reminiscences of Catskill.* Catskill NY: J. B. Hall, 1868.

Pine, George W. *Beyond the West.* Utica NY: T. J. Griffiths, 1870.

Pinedale Roundup. Pinedale WY, 1904–.

Pinkerton, Allan. *The Molly Maguires and the Detectives.* New York: G. W. Carleton, 1878.

——. *Strikers, Communists, Tramps and Detectives.* New York: G. W. Carleton, 1878.

——. *Thirty Years a Detective.* New York: G. W. Carleton, 1886.

Pinkerton, Kathrene. *Wilderness Wife.* New York: Grosset & Dunlap, c.1939.

Pintard, John. *Letters from John Pintard to His Daughter . . . 1816–1833.* New York: Printed for the New-York Historical Society, 1940–1941. 4 vols.

Pinto, Edward H. *Treen and Other Wooden Bygones.* London: G. Bell, c.1969.

Pioneer. Bemidji MN, 1971–.

Pioneer All-Alaska Weekly. Fairbanks AK, 1970?–.

Pioneer America. Falls Church VA: Pioneer America Society, 1968–1983.

Pioneer and Democrat. Olympia WA, 1852–1861.

Pioneer Days in the Southwest from 1850 to 1879. Guthrie OK: State Capital, 1909.

Pioneer, or, California Monthly Magazine. San Francisco, 1854–1855.

Pioneer Society of the State of Michigan. *Pioneer Collections.* Lansing MI, 1874–1886.

Piper, Charles Vancouver. *Forage Plants and Their Culture.* New York: Macmillan, 1914.

Piper, Ralph A. and Zora Piper. *175 Folk and Round Dances.* St. Paul MN: Highland Square Publishing House, 1954.

Piqua Daily Call. Piqua OH, 1884–1922; 1927–.

Piqua Democrat. Piqua OH, 1864–1870.

Pittenger, William. *Daring and Suffering.* Philadelphia: J. W. Daughaday, 1864.

Pittsburgh Courier. Pittsburgh PA, 1910–1950.

Pittsburgh Post-Gazette. Pittsburgh PA, 1978–.

Pittsburgh Speech & Society. [v.d.]. Internet.

Pittsburgh Tribune-Review. 2006?–. Internet.

Pittsburgh. University. *University Times.* Pittsburgh PA, 1969–.

Pittsfield Sun. Pittsfield MA, 1813–1906.

Plain Talk and Friendly Advice to Domestics. Boston: Phillips, Sampson, 1855.

Plant City Courier. Plant City FL, 1931–.

Planters' Banner. Franklin LA, 1849–1872.

Plants of the Southwest. Santa Fe NM: The Company, 1982. Catalog.

Plants of the Southwest. Santa Fe NM: The Company, 1990. Catalog.

Plant World. Binghamton NY: W. N. Clute, 1897–1919.

Plateau. Flagstaff AZ: Published by the Northern Arizona Society of Science and Art and by the Museum of Northern Arizona, 1928–.

Platte County Views. Weston MO, 1966?–.

Playboy. Chicago: H. M. Hefner, 1953–.

Playground. New York: Playground Association of America, 1907–1929.

Playground and Recreation. New York: Playground and Recreation Association of America, 1929–1930.

Playground Daily News. Fort Walton Beach FL, 1962–.

The Play Ground, or, Out-Door Games for Boys. New York: Dick & Fitzgerald, c.1866.

Play Party Games SEE *Handy Play Party Book*

Pleasants, Thomas Franklin. "Extracts from the Diary of Thomas Franklin Pleasants, 1814." *Pennsylvania Magazine of History and Biography.* (1915) 39.322–38, 410–24.

Plough Boy, and Journal of the Board of Agriculture. Albany NY: Printed by J. O. Cole, 1819–1823.

Ploughshares. Cambridge MA, 1971–.

Plough, the Loom, and the Anvil. Philadelphia, 1848–1857.

Plowman, Roscoe E. *Twice Out of Sight.* Berea KY: Kentucke Imprints, c.1982.

Plukenet, Leonard. *Almagesti Botanici Mantissa.* Londini: Sumptibus Autoris, 1700.

——. *Almagestum Botanicum.* London: T. Davies, 1769.

——. *Phytographia.* London: Sumptibus Autoris, 1691.

Plumbe, John. *Sketches of Iowa and Wisconsin.* St. Louis MO: Chambers, Harris & Knapp, 1839.

Plummer, Henry Merrihew. *The Boy, Me and the Cat: the Cruise of the Mascot, October, 1912–June, 1913.* Ed. by Brenda and Bob Osborn. 3d ed. Middleboro MA: Catboat Association, c.2001.

Plymouth, Massachusetts. *Records of the Town of Plymouth.* Plymouth MA: Avery & Doten, 1889–1903. 3 vols.

PMLA SEE Modern Language Association of America *Publications*

Pocahontas SEE Pearson, Emily Clemens

Pochmann, Virginia Ruth Fouts. *Triple Ridge Farm.* New York: William Morrow, 1968.

The Pocumtuc Housewife. Rev. ed. Deerfield MA: [s.n.], 1906.

Poe, Charles D. *Collection.* 1993–1994. Materials on Amer. Engl. usage.

Poe, Edgar Allan. *Tales of Mystery, Imagination, and Humour.* London: Ward, Lock, and Tyler, 1866?

——. *Works.* New York: J. S. Redfield, 1850 [c.1849]. 2 vols.

Poe, Sophie Alberding. *Buckboard Days.* Caldwell ID: Caxton Printers, 1936.

Poetry, a Magazine of Verse. New York: AMS Reprint, 1964. Repr. of orig. pub. by Modern Poetry Association, Chicago.

Poinsett, Joel Roberts. *Notes on Mexico, Made in the Autumn of 1822.* Philadelphia: H. C. Carey and I. Lea, 1824.

Pointer. Riverdale IL, 1917?–1961.

Political Examiner and General Recorder. Shelbyville KY, 1832–1833.

Polk, William Tannahill. *Southern Accent from Uncle Remus to Oak Ridge.* New York: Morrow, 1953.

Pollack, Neal, ed. *Chicago Noir.* New York: Akashic Books, 2005.

Pollard, Edward Alfred. *Black Diamonds Gathered in the Darkey Homes of the South.* New York: Pudney & Russell, 1859.

——. *The Lost Cause.* New York: E. B. Treat, 1866.

——. *The Second Year of the War.* Richmond VA: West & Johnston, 1863.

——. *The Virginia Tourist.* Philadelphia: J. B. Lippincott, 1870.

Polleys, Abner Dexter. *Stories of Pioneer Days in the Black River Valley.* Black River Falls WI: Banner-Journal, c.1948.

Pollock, Albin J. *The Underworld Speaks.* San Francisco: Prevent Crime Bureau, c.1935.

Pollock, Allan. *A Botanical Index to All the Medicinal Plants, Barks, Roots, Seeds and Flowers Usually Kept by Druggists.* New York: Allan Pollock, 1872.

Pomeroy, "Brick" SEE Pomeroy, Mark M.

Pomeroy, Mark M. *Brick-Dust.* New York: G. W. Carleton, 1871.

——. *Nonsense, or, Hits and Criticisms on the Follies of the Day.* New York: G. W. Carleton, 1869 [c.1868].

Pomeroy's Illustrated Democrat. New York [etc], 1869–1880.

Pomet, Pierre. *A Compleat History of Druggs.* London: Printed for R. Bonwicke, 1712. 2 vols. Orig. pub. in French in 1694 under the title *Histoire Générale des Drogues.*

Pool, Maria Louise. *Tenting at Stony Beach.* Boston: Houghton Mifflin, 1888.

Pool, Raymond John. *Handbook of Nebraska Trees.* 2d ed. Lincoln NE: Univ. NE, 1929.

Poole, Caroline B. "A Yankee School Teacher in Louisiana, 1835–1837." *Louisiana Historical Quarterly* (1937) 20.651–79.

Poole, Ernest. *The Harbor.* New York: Macmillan, 1915.

——. *Nurses on Horseback.* New York: Macmillan, 1933 [c.1932].

Poore, Benjamin Perley. *Perley's Reminiscences of Sixty Years in the National Metropolis.* Philadelphia: Hubbard Bros., 1886. 2 vols.

Pope, Clifford Hillhouse. *Snakes Alive and How They Live.* New York: Viking Press, 1937.

Pope, John. *A Tour through the Southern and Western Territories of the United States of North-America.* Richmond VA: Printed by John Dixon, 1792.

Pope, Thomas Edmund Burt and W. E. Dickinson. *The Amphibians and the Reptiles of Wisconsin.* Milwaukee WI: Published by order of the Board of Trustees, 1928.

Pope, Willis Thomas. *Manual of the Wayside Plants of Hawaii.* Honolulu HI: Advertiser, 1929.

Popik, Barry. *Collection.* 1995–. Unpub. coll. of materials on Amer. Engl. usage.

Popkin, Michael. *Taming the Spirited Child.* New York: Fireside, c.2007.

Poppenheim, Mary B. *Southern Women at Vassar.* Ed. by Joan Marie Johnson. Columbia SC: Univ. SC Press, 2002.

Popular Electronics. New York: Ziff Davis Publishing, 1954–1971.

Popular Mechanics Magazine. Chicago, 1902–.

Popular Science Monthly. New York, 1872–.

Popular Science News. Boston, 1866–1902.

Porcher, Francis Peyre. *Resources of the Southern Fields and Forests.* Charleston SC: Evans & Cogswell, 1863.

——. *Resources of the Southern Fields and Forests.* New ed. rev. and largely augmented. Charleston SC: Walker, Evans & Cogswell, 1869.

Porcher, Richard Dwight and Douglas Alan Rayner. *A Guide to the Wildflowers of South Carolina.* Columbia SC: Univ. SC Press, c.2001.

Portage City Record. Portage WI, 1857–1861.

Portage Daily Register. Portage WI, 1941–.

Port Arthur Daily News. Port Arthur TX, 1900?–1922.

Port Arthur News. Port Arthur TX, 1922–1973.

Porter, Cole. *103 Lyrics.* New York: Random House, c.1954.

Porter, David Dixon. *Incidents and Anecdotes of the Civil War.* New York: D. Appleton, 1885.

Porter, Eleanor Hodgman. *Just David.* Boston: Houghton Mifflin, 1916.

——. *Pollyanna.* Boston: Page, 1935 [c.1912].

Porter, Gene Stratton. *A Daughter of the Land.* New York: Doubleday, Page, c.1918.

——. *Freckles.* New York: Grosset & Dunlap, 1916. Orig. pub. in 1904 by Grosset & Dunlap, New York.

——. *Freckles.* Mattituck NJ: Aeonian Press, c.1977. Orig. pub. in 1904 by Grosset & Dunlap, New York.

——. *A Girl of the Limberlost.* New York: Grosset & Dunlap, c.1909.

——. *The Harvester.* New York: Grosset & Dunlap, c.1911.

——. *The Harvester.* New York: Grosset & Dunlap, 1916. Orig. pub. in 1911 by Doubleday, Page.

——. *Laddie.* New York: Grosset & Dunlap, c.1913.

——. *Michael O'Halloran.* Garden City NY: Doubleday, Page, 1915.

Porter, Katherine Anne. *Flowering Judas and Other Stories.* New York: Harcourt, Brace, c.1935.

Porter, Thomas Conrad. *Flora of Pennsylvania.* Boston: Ginn, 1903.

Porter, William Solon. *Ragged Roads.* Fargo OK: Published by author, c.1951.

Porter, William Sydney. *Cabbages and Kings.* New York: McClure, Phillips, 1904.

——. *Cabbages and Kings.* Garden City NY: Doubleday, Page for Review of Reviews, 1913 [c.1904].

——. *The Four Million.* New York: McClure, Phillips, 1906. Material copyrighted 1902 by Ess and Ess Publishing.

——. *The Four Million.* New York: Doubleday, Page, 1913 [c.1906]. Material copyrighted 1902 by Ess and Ess Publishing.

——. *The Gentle Grafter.* New York: McClure, 1908.

——. *Heart of the West.* New York: McClure, 1907.

——. *Options.* New York: Harper & Bros., 1909.

——. *Roads of Destiny.* New York: Doubleday, Page, 1909.

——. *Roads of Destiny.* Garden City NY: Doubleday, Page, 1913 [c.1909].

——. *Rolling Stones.* Garden City NY: Doubleday, Page, 1912.

——. *Strictly Business.* Garden City NY: Doubleday, Page, 1910.

——. *The Trimmed Lamp, and Other Stories of the Four Million.* New York: McClure, Phillips, 1907.

——. *Whirligigs.* New York: Doubleday, Page, 1910.

Porter, William Trotter, ed. *The Big Bear of Arkansas, and Other Sketches.* New York: AMS Press, 1973. Repr. of 1843 ed. pub. by T. B. Peterson, Philadelphia.

——. *A Quarter Race in Kentucky.* Philadelphia: Carey & Hart, 1847 [c.1846].

——. *A Quarter Race in Kentucky.* New York: AMS Press, 1973. Facsimile of the 1847 [c.1846] ed. pub. by Carey & Hart, Philadelphia.

Porter's Spirit of the Times. New York, 1856–1861?

Port Folio. Philadelphia, 1801–1827. Ed. by Oliver Oldschool.

Portis, Charles. *The Dog of the South.* New York: Alfred A. Knopf, 1979.

Portland Advertiser. Portland ME, 1823–1829.

Portland Press Herald. Portland ME: 1921–.

Portland Sunday Telegram and Sunday Press Herald. Portland ME, 1925–1967.

Portrait and Biographical Album of Green Lake, Marquette and Waushara Counties, Wisconsin. Chicago: Acme Publishing, 1890.

Portsmouth, Rhode Island. *The Early Records of the Town of Portsmouth.* Providence RI: E. L. Freeman & Sons, 1901.

Portsmouth Daily Times. Portsmouth OH, 1905–1930.

Portsmouth Herald. Portsmouth NH, 1898–1925; 1939–.

Portsmouth Herald and Times. Portsmouth NH, 1925–1939.

Portsmouth Oracle. Portsmouth NH, 1803–1821.

Portsmouth Times. Portsmouth OH, 1858–1915.

Port Townsend Leader. Port Townsend WA, 1928?–.

Post, Charles Clement. *Ten Years a Cowboy.* Chicago: T. W. Jackson, c.1898.

Post, Lydia Minturn, ed. *Soldiers' Letters.* New York: Bruce & Huntington, 1865.

Post, Waldron Kintzing. *Harvard Stories.* New York: G. P. Putnam's Sons, 1896 [c.1893].

Post. Centre AL, 1990?–.

Post and Courier. Charleston SC, 1994–.

Post-Crescent. Appleton WI, 1965–.

Post-Register. Idaho Falls ID, 1931–.

Post-Standard. Syracuse NY, 1899–.

Poteet, Lewis J., comp. *The South Shore Phrase Book.* Rev. and expanded ed. Hantsport: Lancelot Press, 1988.

Potter, Chandler Eastman. *The History of Manchester, Formerly Derryfield, in New-Hampshire.* Manchester NH: C. E. Potter, 1856.

Potter, Edward Earle. *The Dialect of Northwestern Ohio.* Ann Arbor MI: Univ. MI diss., 1955.

Potter, Eliza. *A Hairdresser's Experience in High Life.* Cincinnati OH: Published for the Author, 1859.

Pottstown Mercury. Pottstown PA, 1932–.

Pottsville Republican & Evening Herald. Pottsville PA, 1884–.

Pough, Frederick H. *A Field Guide to Rocks and Minerals.* Boston: Houghton Mifflin, c.1953.

Pough, Richard Hooper. *Audubon Water Bird Guide.* Garden City NY: Doubleday, 1951.

——. *Audubon Western Bird Guide.* Garden City NY: Doubleday, 1957.

Poughkeepsie Casket. Poughkeepsie NY, 1836–1841.

Pound, Louise. *Selected Writings.* Lincoln NE: Univ. NE Press, 1949.

Powell, Addison Monroe. *Trailing and Camping in Alaska.* New York: Wessels & Bissell, 1910 [c.1909].

Powell, Arthur Gray. *I Can Go Home Again.* Chapel Hill NC: Univ. NC Press, 1943.

Powell, Mary Gregory. *The History of Old Alexandria, Virginia from July 13, 1749 to May 24, 1861.* Richmond VA: William Byrd Press, c.1928.

Powell, Richard. *Pioneer, Go Home!* New York: Charles Scribner's Sons, c.1959.

Powell, William Stevens. *The North Carolina Gazetteer.* Chapel Hill NC: Univ. NC Press, 1968.

Power, Tyrone. *Impressions of America, during the Years 1833, 1834, and 1835.* London: Richard Bentley, 1836. 2 vols.

Power & Motoryacht. 1985?–. Internet.

Power County Press. American Falls ID, 1937–.

Powers, Alfred. *Redwood Country.* New York: Duell, Sloan & Pearce, 1949.

Powers, Elizabeth D. *Cataloochee.* Johns Island SC: Powers-Hannah, 1982.

Powers, Elvira J. *Hospital Pencillings, Being a Diary While in Jefferson General Hospital, Jeffersonville, Ind., and Others at Nashville, Tennessee, as Matron and Visitor.* Boston: Edward L. Mitchell, 1866.

Powers, Grant. *Historical Sketches of the Discovery, Settlement, and Progress of Events in the Coos Country and Vicinity, Principally Included between the Years 1754 and 1785.* Haverhill NH: J. F. C. Hayes, 1841.

Powers, Stephen. *Afoot and Alone.* Hartford CT: Columbian Book, 1872.

——. *Tribes of California.* Washington DC: Govt. Printing Office, 1877.

Practical Entomologist. Philadelphia, 1865–1867.

Practical Homeschooling. Fenton MO, 1993–.

Prairie Drummer. Colby KS, 1959–.

Prairie Farmer. Chicago, 1841–.

Prairie Gold. Chicago: Reilly & Britton, c.1917. Contributions by various Iowa authors and artists.

Prairie Kitchen Companion. Madison WI: Prairie Unitarian Universalist Society, 1982.

Prairie Schooner. Lincoln NE, 1927–.

Prather, Timothy S. et al. *Idaho's Noxious Weeds.* 4th ed. Moscow ID: Univ. ID Extension, c.2008.

Pratt, Anne. *The Flowering Plants and Ferns of Great Britain.* London: Printed for the Society for Promoting Christian Knowledge, 1861? 5 vols.?

——. *The Flowering Plants, Grasses, Sedges and Ferns of Great Britain, and Their Allies, the Club Mosses, Pepperworts and Horsetails.* London: F. Warne, 1873. 6 vols.

——. *Flowers and Their Associations.* London: C. Knight, 1840.

Pratt, Caroline and Jessie Stanton. *Before Books.* New York: Adelphi, c.1926.

Pratt, Fletcher. *The Navy, a History.* Garden City NY: Doubleday, Doran, 1938.

Pratt, Henry Sherring. *A Manual of Land and Fresh Water Vertebrate Animals of the United States (Exclusive of Birds).* 2d ed. Philadelphia: P. Blakiston's Son, c.1935.

——. *A Manual of the Common Invertebrate Animals Exclusive of Insects.* Thoroughly rev. ed. Philadelphia: P. Blakiston's Son, c.1935.

Pratt, Terry Kenneth. *Dictionary of Prince Edward Island English.* Toronto: Univ. Toronto Press, c.1988.

Pratt, Theodore. *The Barefoot Mailman.* New York: Duell, Sloan and Pierce, c.1943.

La Prensa San Diego. San Diego CA, 1998–.

Prentis, Noble Lovely. *Kansas Miscellanies.* 2d ed. Topeka KS: Kansas Publishing House, 1889.

Prentiss, Charles. *A Collection of Fugitive Essays in Prose and Verse.* Leominster MA: Printed by and for the author, 1797.

Presbury, Benjamin Franklin. *The Mustee.* Boston: Shepard, Clark & Brown, 1859 [c.1858].

Prescott Transcript. Prescott WI, 1855–1861.

Presque Isle Star-Herald. Presque Isle ME, 1889–.

Press. Pittsburgh PA, 1884–.

Press-Enterprise. Riverside CA, 1983–.

Press-Gazette. SEE *Green Bay Press-Gazette*

Press-Gazette. Hillsboro OH, 1928–1973; 1985–.

Preston, Dennis Richard. *Proverbial Comparisons from Southern Indiana.* 1975. Unpub.

Preston, Margaret Junkin. *Silverwood, a Book of Memories.* New York: Derby & Jackson, 1856.

Price, Con. *Trails I Rode.* Pasadena CA: Trail's End, c.1947.

Price, Richard Nye. *Holston Methodism, from Its Origins to the Present Time.* Nashville TN: Publishing House of the M.E. Church, South, 1908–1913 [c.1903–1913]. 5 vols.

Price, Robert. *Johnny Appleseed.* Bloomington IN: IN Univ. Press, 1954.

Price, Sarah Frances. *Flora of Warren County, Kentucky.* New London WI: C. F. Carr, 1893.

Price-Thompson, Tracy and TaRessa Stovall, eds. *Proverbs for the People.* New York: Dafina, 2004 [c.2003].

Priest, William. *Travels in the United States of America.* London: Printed for J. Johnson, 1802.

Prime, Samuel Irenaeus. *The Life of Samuel F. B. Morse.* New York: D. Appleton, 1875.

Prime, William Cowper. *Later Years.* New York: Harper & Bros., 1854.

Primitive Expounder. Ann Arbor MI, 1843–1848.

Primitive Man. Washington DC: Catholic Univ. of America Press, 1928–1953.

Prince, William. *Catalogue of Fruit and Ornamental Trees and Plants, Bulbous Flower Roots, Green-House Plants.* 21st ed. New York: Swords, 1822.

——. *A Short Treatise on Horticulture.* New York: Printed by T. and J. Swords, 1828.

Prince, William Meade. *The Southern Part of Heaven.* New York: Rinehart, 1950.

Princeton Review. SEE *New Princeton Review, Biblical Repertory,* and *Biblical Repertory and the Theological Review*

Princeton Union-Eagle. Princeton MN, 1976–.

Pringle, Elizabeth Waties Allston. *A Woman Rice Planter.* New York: Macmillan, 1913.

——. *A Woman Rice Planter.* Cambridge MA: Belknap Press, 1961. Orig. pub. in 1913 by Macmillan, New York.

Printers' Ink. New York, 1888–1967.

Prior, Beatrix. *Lota of the Little Trees.* Los Angeles: Suttonhouse, 1936.

Proceedings of the United States Senate, on the Fugitive Slave Bill. SEE United States. Congress. Senate *Proceedings . . . Fugitive Slave Bill*

Professional Geographer. Washington DC: Association of American Geographers, 1943–.

Progress. Clearfield PA, 1946–.

Progress-Index. Petersburg VA, 1923–.

Progressive. Madison WI, 1929–.

Progressive Age and Coshocton County Local Record. Coshocton OH, 1853–1859.

Progressive Bee-Keeper. Higginsville MO, 1892–1906.

Progressive Farmer. Birmingham AL, 1920–1923; 1941–.

Progressive Farmer and Farm Woman. Birmingham AL, 1923–1930.

Progress-Review. La Porte City IA, 1893–.

Proprietors' Records of the Town of Waterbury, Connecticut, 1677–1761. Waterbury CT: Mattatuck Historical Society, 1911.

Protestant Episcopal Historical Society. *Collections.* New York: Stanford & Swords, 1851–1853.

Proulx, Annie. *Close Range.* New York: Scribner, c.1999.

———. *That Old Ace in the Hole.* New York: Scribner, c.2002.

Proulx, Earl. *Yankee Magazine's Make It Last.* Dublin NH: Yankee Books, c.1996.

Providence Gazette, and Country Journal. Providence RI, 1762–1795.

Providence Journal. Providence RI, 1830–.

Providence Journal-Bulletin. Providence RI, 1995–1998.

Providence Record Commissioners. *The Early Records of the Town of Providence.* Providence RI: Snow & Farnham, 1892–1915. 21 vols.

The Provisional Government of Nebraska Territory. Lincoln NE: State Journal, 1899.

Pryor, Sara Agnes Rice. *The Colonel's Story.* New York: Macmillan, 1911.

Psychoanalytic Quarterly. New York, 1932–.

Psychosomatic Medicine. Baltimore MD, 1939–.

Public Ledger. Philadelphia, 1836–1934.

Public Ledger Almanac and Yearbook. Philadelphia: G. W. Childs, 1870–.

Publishers' Weekly. New York, 1872–.

Puck. New York, 1877–1918.

Puckett, Newbell Niles. *Folk Beliefs of the Southern Negro.* Chapel Hill NC: Univ. NC Press, 1926.

———. *Folk Beliefs of the Southern Negro.* Montclair NJ: Patterson Smith, 1968. Orig. pub. in 1926 by Univ. NC Press, Chapel Hill NC.

———, comp. *Popular Beliefs and Superstitions.* Boston: G. K. Hall, 1981. 3 vols.

Pudney, John. *Pick of Today's Short Stories.* London, 1949–1963.

Pueblo Chieftain. Pueblo CO, 1889–.

Pukui, Mary Wiggin and Samuel H. Elbert. *Hawaiian Dictionary.* Honolulu HI: Univ. HI Press, 1971.

Pullman News-Review. Pullman WA, 1900?–1966.

Punchinello. New York, 1870.

Purcell Register. Purcell OK, 1887–.

Purchas, Samuel. *Purchas His Pilgrimes.* 4th ed. London: W. Stanby for H. Fetherstone, 1625. 5 vols. Vol. 5 bound with this set, dated 1626, and lettered *Purchas His Pilgrimage.*

Purdue University. Cooperative Extension Service. *Indiana Plants Poisonous to Livestock and Pets.* [v.d.]. Internet.

Purdy, Helen Throop. *San Francisco.* San Francisco: Paul Elder, c.1912.

Pure Music. 2000–. Internet.

Purkey, Lena Penland. *Home in Madison County.* Johnson City TN: East TN State Univ., c.1975.

Pursh, Frederick. *Flora Americae Septentrionalis.* London: White, Cochrane, 1814. 2 vols.

———. *Journal of a Botanical Excursion in the Northeastern Parts of the States of Pennsylvania and New York during the Year 1807.* Syracuse NY: Dehler Press, 1923. Repr. of 1869 ed. pub. by Brinckloe & Masot, Philadelphia.

———. *Journal of a Botanical Excursion in the Northeastern Parts of the States of Pennsylvania and New York during the Year 1807.* Port Washington NY: Ira J. Friedman, 1969. Orig. pub. in 1807 by Brinckloe & Masot, Philadelphia.

Putnam, Archelaus. "Diary." Danvers Historical Society *Collections.* (1916) 4.51–72; (1917) 5.49–69; (1918) 6.11–29.

Putnam, Carleton. *Theodore Roosevelt: a Biography.* New York: Scribner, 1958.

Putnam, Eleanor SEE Bates, Harriet Leonora Vose

Putnam, Rufus. *Journal of Gen. Rufus Putnam Kept in Northern New York . . . 1757–1760.* Albany NY: J. Munsell's Sons, 1886.

———. *Memoirs.* Boston: Houghton, Mifflin, 1903.

Putnam's Magazine. New York: G. P. Putnam, 1853–1870.

Putnam's Monthly. New Rochelle NY, 1907–1908.

Puzo, Mario. *Fools Die.* New York: Putnam, c.1978.

Pyle, Ernest Taylor. *Brave Men.* New York: H. Holt, c.1944.

Pyle, Robert Michael. *The Audubon Society Field Guide to North American Butterflies.* New York: Knopf, c.1981.

Pyrnelle, Louise Clarke. *Miss Li'l' Tweetty.* New York: Harper & Bros., 1917.

QST. Newington CT: American Radio Relay League, 1915–.

Quad-City Times. Davenport-Bettendorf IA, 1975–.

Quaife, Milo Milton. *Lake Michigan.* Indianapolis IN: Bobbs-Merrill, 1944.

Quarterly Anti-Slavery Magazine. New York: American Anti-Slavery Society, 1835–1837.

Quarterly Journal of Science, Literature and the Arts. London: Royal Institute of Great Britain, 1816–1826.

Quarterly Journal of Speech. Baton Rouge LA, 1915–.

Quarterly Review of Biology. Baltimore MD, 1926–.

Queen, Ellery SEE Dannay, Frederic and Manfred B. Lee

Quick, Herbert. *Mississippi Steamboatin'.* New York: H. Holt, c.1926.

———. *Yellowstone Nights.* New York: Grosset & Dunlap, c.1911.

Quillin, Ellen Schulz. *Texas Wild Flowers.* Chicago: Laidlaw Bros., c.1928.

Quilting Today. New Milford PA: Chitra Publications, 1987–.

Quin, Dan SEE Lewis, Alfred Henry

Quincy Herald. Quincy Illinois, 1841–1926.

Quincy Whig. Quincy IL, 1838–1857.

Quindaro Chindowan. Quindaro KS, 1857–1858.

Quinland. London: R. Bentley, 1857. 2 vols.

Quinn, Ronald D. and Sterling C. Keeley. *Introduction to California Chaparral.* Berkeley CA: Univ. CA Press, 2006.

Rabe, Berniece. *Rass.* Nashville TN: Thomas Nelson, c.1973.

Rabeler, Richard K. *Gleason's Plants of Michigan.* Ed. by Vivienne N. Armentrout. Ann Arbor MI: Oakleaf Press, 1998. Substantial revision and expansion of *The Plants of Michigan* by H. A. Gleason, first pub. in 1918 by George Wahr Publishing.

Race and Ethnic Relations. Guilford CT, 1991–.

Racine Daily Journal. Racine WI, 1881–1912.

Racine Journal. Racine WI, 1865?–1913.

Racine Journal-Times. Racine WI, 1932–1972.

Rackley, Timothy W. and Stephen E. Bradley, abstractors. *Nash County North Carolina Court Minutes.* Kernersville NC: S. E. Bradley, c.1993–1995? 6 vols.

Radford, Albert E. et al. *Manual of the Vascular Flora of the Carolinas.* Chapel Hill NC: Univ. NC Press, c.1968.

Radical Rule. Louisville KY: John P. Morton, 1868.

Radisson, Peter Espirit. *Voyages of Peter Espirit Radisson, Being an Account of His Travels and Experiences among the North American Indians, from 1652 to 1684.* Boston: Prince Society, c.1885.

Rae, William Fraser. *Westward by Rail.* New York: D. Appleton, 1871. Orig. pub. in 1870 by Longmans, Green, London.

Raffald, Elizabeth. *The Experienced English Housekeeper.* London: R. Baldwin, 1786.

Rafinesque, Constantine Samuel. *Atlantic Journal and Friend of Knowledge.* Philadelphia, 1832–1833.

———. *Ichthyologia Ohiensis, or, Natural History of the Fishes Inhabiting the River Ohio and Its Tributary Streams.* Lexington KY: Printed for the author by W. G. Hunt, 1820.

———. *Medical Flora.* Philadelphia: Atkinson & Alexander, 1828–1830. 2 vols.

Rahley, William J. *The Tar-Heeler's Dream: Characteristic March and Two Step.* Sheet music. Baltimore MD: I. Son Cohen, c.1899.

Raht, Carlysle Graham. *The Romance of David Mountains and Big Bend Country.* El Paso TX: Rahtbooks, c.1919.

Railroad Magazine. New York, 1932–1978.

Railroad Man's Magazine. New York: Frank A. Munsey, 1906–1919; 1929–1932.

Railroad Stories: the Railroad Man's Magazine. New York, 1932–1937.

Railroad Telegrapher. Peoria IL?: Order of Railroad Telegraphers, 1891–1965.

Railroad Trainman. Cleveland OH: Brotherhood of Railroad Trainmen, 1908–1948.

Railway Carmen's Journal. Kansas City MO, 1895–1986.

Railway Conductor. Cedar Rapids IA, 1889–1954.

Raine, James Watt. *The Land of Saddle-Bags.* New York: Published jointly by Council of Women for Home Missions and Missionary Education Movement of the United States and Canada, c.1924.

Raine, William MacLeod. *Brand Blotters.* New York: Grosset & Dunlap, c.1912.

———. *Bucky O'Connor.* New York: Grosset & Dunlap, c.1910.

———. *Famous Sheriffs and Western Outlaws.* New York: Doubleday, Doran, 1929.

———. *Guns of the Frontier.* Cleveland OH: World Publishing, 1946 [c.1940].

———. *Troubled Waters.* Garden City NY: Doubleday, Page, 1925.

———. *Wyoming: a Story of the Outdoor West.* New York: Grosset & Dunlap, c.1907.

Raine, William MacLeod and Will C. Barnes. *Cattle.* Garden City NY: Doubleday, Doran, 1930.

Raines, Howell. *Whiskey Man.* New York: Viking Press, c.1977.

Rak, Mary Kidder. *Mountain Cattle.* Boston: Houghton Mifflin, 1936.

Rakel, David and Nancy Faass. *Complementary Medicine in Clinical Practice.* Sudbury MA: Jones and Bartlett, c.2006.

Rake Register. Rake IA, 1900–1992?

Raleigh Register Beckley Post-Herald. Beckley WV, 1953–1984.

Raleigh Star. Raleigh NC, 1808–1815.

Ramsay, David. *The History of South-Carolina.* Charleston SC: Pub. by David Longworth for the author, 1809. 2 vols.

Ramsay, Robert Lee and Frances G. Emberson. *A Mark Twain Lexicon.* New York: Russell & Russell, 1963.

Ramsey, Frederic and Charles Edward Smith, eds. *Jazzmen.* New York: Harcourt, Brace, 1959 [c.1939].

Ramsey, Guthrie P. *Race Music.* Berkeley CA: Univ. CA Press, c.2003.

Ramsey, James Gettys McGready. *The Annals of Tennessee, to the End of the Eighteenth Century.* Philadelphia: Lippincott, Grambo, 1853.

Ramson, W. S., ed. *Australian National Dictionary.* Melbourne: Oxford Univ. Press, c.1988.

Ranck, George Washington. *Boonesboro.* Louisville KY: J. P. Morton, 1901.

Rand, Edward Sprague, Jr. *Flowers for the Parlor and Garden.* Boston: J. E. Tilton, 1870 [c.1863].

Randall, Alice. *Pushkin and the Queen of Spades.* Boston: Houghton Mifflin, 2004.

Randall, Henry Stephens. *The Practical Shepherd.* 18th ed. Rochester NY: D. D. T. Moore, 1864.

Randall, Isabelle. *A Lady's Ranche Life in Montana.* London: W. H. Allen, 1887.

Randall, James Ryder. *Maryland, My Maryland.* Baltimore MD: J. Murphy, c.1908.

Randall-Diehl, Anna. *Two Thousand Words and Their Definitions.* New York: J. S. Ogilvie, 1888.

Randers-Pehrson, Justine Davis. *For My Father.* New York: Universe, c.2004.

Randle, William, comp. *Bill Randle's Cookbooks.* Cleveland OH: Station WERE, 1960–1970.

Randolph, John. *A Treatise on Gardening.* 3d ed. Richmond VA: William Parks Club, 1924 [1826]. Repr. from 1826 *American Gardener* by John Gardiner and David Hepburn.

Randolph, J. Thornton SEE Peterson, Charles Jacobs

Randolph, Mary. *The Virginia House-Wife.* Stereotype ed. with amendments and additions. Baltimore MD: Plaskitt & Cugle, 1839.

———. *The Virginia House-Wife.* Historical notes and commentaries by Karen Hess. Columbia SC: Univ. SC Press, c.1984. Facsimile of the 1824 ed. printed by David and Lee, Washington DC, along with additional material from the eds. of 1825 and 1828.

Randolph, Vance, ed. *Hot Springs and Hell.* Hatboro PA: Folklore Associates, 1965.

———, ed. *Ozark Folksongs.* Columbia MO: State Historical Society of Missouri, 1946–1950. 4 vols.

———. *Ozark Mountain Folks.* New York: Vanguard Press, c.1932.

———. *The Ozarks.* New York: Vanguard Press, c.1931.

———. *Ozark Superstitions.* New York: Dover Publications, 1964. Orig. pub. in 1947 by Columbia Univ. Press, New York.

———, comp. *Pissing in the Snow and Other Ozark Folktales.* New York: Avon Books, 1977.

———, ed. *Sticks in the Knapsack.* New York: Columbia Univ. Press, 1958.

———. *We Always Lie to Strangers.* New York: Columbia Univ. Press, 1951.

Randolph, Vance and George P. Wilson. *Down in the Holler.* Norman OK: Univ. OK Press, 1953.

Randolph, Vance and Guy White Von Schriltz. *Ozark Outdoors.* New York: Vanguard Press, 1934.

Randolph Enterprise. Elkins WV, 1874–1956.

Rangelands. Denver CO: Society for Range Management, 1979–2004.

Range Riders Western. New York, 1940?–1950?

Rankin, Fannie W. *True to Him Ever.* New York: G. W. Carleton; London: Low, Son, 1874.

Rankin, George Clark. *The Story of My Life.* Nashville TN: Smith & Lamar, c.1912.

Ranous, Dora Knowlton Thompson. *Diary of a Daly Débutante.* New York: Duffield, 1910.

Ransome, Stephen. *Deadly Miss Ashley.* Garden City NY: Doubleday, 1950.

Rappahannock Record. Kilmarnock VA, 1917–.

Rask, Rasmus. *A Compendious Grammar of the Old North-*

ern or Icelandic Language. Comp. and transl. by George P. Marsh. Burlington NJ: H. Johnson, 1838.

Rathborne, St. George. *Lend-a-Hand Boys' Sanitary Squad.* New York: Goldsmith, c.1931.

Rathbun, Frank R., ed. *A Revised List of Birds of Central New York.* Auburn NY: Daily Advertiser and Weekly Journal Book and Job Printing House, 1879.

Ratigan, William. *Soo Canal.* Grand Rapids MI: Eerdmans Publishing, 1954.

Rattan, Volney. *A Popular California Flora.* 2d ed., rev. and enlarged. San Francisco: A. L. Bancroft, 1880.

———. *A Popular California Flora.* 3d ed., rev. and enlarged. San Francisco: A. L. Bancroft, 1882.

Rattlehead, David, M. D. SEE Byrn, Marcus Lafayette

Rattray, Everett T. *The Adventures of Jeremiah Dimon.* Wainscott NY: Pushcart Press, c.1985.

Rauch, Frederick A. *Psychology.* 2d ed. rev. New York: M. W. Dodd, 1841.

Raven, Ralph SEE Payson, George

Rawlings, Marjorie Kinnan. *Cross Creek.* New York: Charles Scribner's Sons, 1942.

———. *Cross Creek Cookery.* New York: Charles Scribner's Sons, 1942.

———. *Golden Apples.* Cleveland OH: World Publishing, 1944. Orig. pub. in 1935 by C. Scribner's Sons, New York.

———. *South Moon Under.* New York: Grosset & Dunlap, c.1933.

———. *When the Whippoorwill.* New York: Charles Scribner's Sons, 1940.

———. *The Yearling.* New York: Charles Scribner's Sons, 1938.

Rawson, Marion Nicholl. *Forever the Farm.* New York: E. P. Dutton, 1939.

———. *New Hampshire Borns a Town.* New York: E. P. Dutton, 1942.

Ray, Emma J. Smith and Lloyd P. Ray. *Twice Sold, Twice Ransomed.* Chapel Hill NC: Academic Affairs Library, Univ. NC at Chapel Hill, 2000. Text transcr. for *Documenting the American South* website from the ed. pub. in 1926 by Free Methodist Publishing House, Chicago.

Ray, John. *Historiae Plantarum.* London: Typis Mariae Clark, 1686–1794. 3 vols.

Raybon, Patricia. *I Told the Mountain to Move.* Carol Stream IL: Tyndale House, c.2005.

Rayford, Julian Lee. *Child of the Snapping Turtle, Mike Fink.* New York: Abelard Press, 1951.

———. *Whistlin' Woman and Crowin' Hen.* Mobile AL: Rankin Press, 1956.

Raymond, Henry Jarvis. *History of the Administration of President Lincoln.* New York: J. C. Derby & N. C. Miller, 1864.

Raymond, Ida SEE Tardy, Mary T.

Raymond, Oliver, ed. *Bark Shanty Times.* Port Sanilac MI: Oliver Yamond, 1941.

Raymond, Rossiter Worthington. *A Glossary of Mining and Metallurgical Terms.* Easton PA: American Institute of Mining Engineers, 1881.

———. *Silver and Gold.* New York: J. B. Ford, 1873.

Raymond Herald and the Advertiser. Raymond WA, 1953–1974.

Rea, Amadeo M. *Folk Mammalogy of the Northern Pimans.* Tucson AZ: Univ. AZ Press, c.1998.

Read, Opie Percival. *The Jucklins.* Chicago: Laird & Lee, c.1896.

Read, William Alexander. *Louisiana-French.* Baton Rouge LA: LA State Univ. Press, 1931.

Reader, an Illustrated Monthly Magazine. Indianapolis IN, 1902–1908.

Reader's Digest. Pleasantville NY, 1922–.

Reader's Digest Letters. 1979. Unpub. letters in response to the article "Rain Gauges" by F. G. Cassidy in the *Reader's Digest*, April 1979.

Reading Times. Reading PA, 1923–.

Ream, Laura. *History of a Trip to the Great Saginaw Valley, June 1871.* Indianapolis IN: R. J. Bright, 1871.

Rechy, John. *Bodies and Souls.* New York: Grove Press, 2001. Orig. pub. in 1983 by Carroll & Graf, New York.

Reclamation Era. Washington DC: U.S. Department of the Interior, Water & Power Resources Service, 1932–1979.

Record. Columbia SC, 1897–.

Recorder-Herald. Salmon ID, 1927–.

Record-Union. Sacramento CA, 1891–1903.

Recreation. New York: G. O. Shields (Coquina), 1894–1912.

Recreation. New York: National Recreation Association, 1907–.

Redbone Journal. Islamorada FL, 2001–.

Reddall, Henry Frederic, comp. *Fact, Fancy, and Fable.* Detroit MI: Gale Research, 1968. Orig. pub. in 1889 by A. C. McClurg, Chicago.

Redding, Jay Saunders. *No Day of Triumph.* 4th ed. New York: Harper & Bros., c.1942.

Redfield, Anna Maria. *Zoölogical Science.* New York: E. B. & E. C. Kellogg, 1858.

Redford, Albert Henry. *The History of Methodism in Kentucky.* Nashville TN: Southern Methodist Publishing, 1868–1870. 3 vols.

Red Ink. Tucson AZ: Univ. AZ American Indian Graduate Center, 1989–.

Redoubt Reporter. Soldotna AK, 2008–.

Redwood, Boverton. *Petroleum.* London: C. Griffin, 1896. 2 vols.

Reed, Carroll E. and Henry A. Person. *Linguistic Atlas of the Pacific Northwest Materials.* c1955. Unpub. material from atlas fieldwork.

Reed, Charles Bert. *Obstetrics for Nurses.* St. Louis MO: C. V. Mosby, 1923.

Reed, John Shelton. *My Tears Spoiled My Aim and Other Reflections on Southern Culture.* Columbia MO: Univ. MO Press, c.1993.

Reed, William Lord. *Jumbles (Re-Jumbled).* New York: Oceanic, 1911 [c.1905].

Reedsburg Free Press. Reedsburg WI, 1872–1939.

Reedy, Dennis, ed. *School and Community History of Dickenson County, Virginia.* Johnson City TN: Overmountain Press, 1994. Repr. of 1992 ed. pub. by Mountain People and Places, Clinchco VA.

Reelfoot Lake Biological Station. *Report.* Knoxville TN, 1937–1942?

Rees, James. *Mysteries of City Life.* Philadelphia: J. W. Moore, 1849.

Reese, Lizette Woodworth. *Worleys.* New York: Farrar & Rinehart, c.1936.

Reeves, George S. *A Man from South Dakota.* New York: E. P. Dutton, 1950.

Reeves, Ira Louis. *Ol' Rum River.* Chicago: Thomas S. Rockwell, 1931.

Reeves, Robert Gatlin and D. C. Bain. *A Flora of South Central Texas.* Chicago: W. M. Welch, c.1946.

The Reformed Practice of Medicine. Boston: [s.n.], 1831.

Refugio County Press. Refugio TX, 1959–.

Refugio Timely Remarks. Refugio TX, 1928–.

Regan, John. *Emigrant's Guide to the Western States of America.* 2d ed. rev. and enlarged. Edinburgh: Oliver & Boyd, 1852.

Reggeboge. Birdsboro PA: Pennsylvania German Society, 1967–.

Register-Guard. Eugene OR, 1991–.

Register of Pennsylvania. Philadelphia, 1828–1831.

Rehder, Harald A. *The Audubon Society Field Guide to North American Seashells.* New York: Knopf, c.1981.

Rehder, John B. *Appalachian Folkways.* Baltimore MD: Johns Hopkins Univ. Press, c.2004.

Reid, John C. *Reid's Tramp.* Austin TX: Steck, 1935. Repr. of the 1858 ed. pub. by John Hardy, Selma AL.

Reid, Mayne. *The Death-Shot: a Story Retold.* New York: Hurst, 1874?

———. *The Desert Home.* Boston: James R. Osgood, 1874 [c.1851].

———. *The Headless Horseman.* New ed. London: C. H. Clark, 1869. Orig. pub. in 1866.

———. *The Scalp Hunters.* New York: Hurst, 1899. Orig. pub. in 1851.

Reid, Samuel Chester. *The Scouting Expeditions of McCulloch's Texas Rangers.* Philadelphia: G. B. Zieber, 1847.

Reid, Thomas Mayne. *Oceola.* London: Hurst and Blackett, 1859. 3 vols.

Reid, Whitelaw. *After the War.* Cincinnati OH: Moore, Wilstach, & Baldwin, 1866.

Reimann, Lewis Charles. *Between the Iron and the Pine.* Ann Arbor MI: Edwards Bros., c.1951.

Reinecke, George. *Collection Relating to the Speech of New Orleans, Louisiana.* 1983. Unpub.

Reinecke, John E. *A List of Loanwords from the Hawaiian Language in Use in the English Speech of the Hawaiian Islands.* 1938. Unpub.

Reinecke, John E. and Stanley M. Tsuzaki. "Hawaiian Loanwords in Hawaiian English of the 1930's." *Oceanic Linguistics.* (1967) 6.2.80–115.

Reinhold, C. G. *The Farmer's Promotion Book.* Pittsburgh PA: Printed by W. S. Haven, 1866.

Reist, Arthur L. *Tobacco Lore of Lancaster County, Pennsylvania.* Ephrata PA: Science Press, c.1974.

Reist, Henry Gerber. *Peter Reist of Lancaster County, Penn-*

sylvania and Some of His Descendants. Schenectady NY: [s.n.], 1933.

Reitz, Elizabeth Jean et al., eds. *Case Studies in Environmental Archaeology.* New York: Plenum Press, c.1996.

A Relation of Maryland. Norwood NJ: Walter J. Johnson, 1976. Photographic repr. of the 1635 ed. pub. by Theatrum Orbis Terrarum, Amsterdam.

A Relation of the Successfull Beginnings of the Lord Baltemore's Plantation in Mary-Land. Albany NY: Reprinted by J. Munsell, 1865. Extracts of letters written in 1634.

Reminder. Wilbraham MA, 1962–.

Remington, Frederic. *Crooked Trails.* New York: Harper & Bros., 1898.

———. *Pony Tracks.* New York: Harper & Bros., 1895.

Reno Evening Gazette. Reno NV, 1876–1983.

Renwick Times. Renwick IA, 1884–1970?

Repertory. Boston, 1804–1811.

Repertory of Arts and Manufactures. London, 1794–1802.

Reporter. Brattleboro VT, 1803–1826.

Republican Banner. Nashville TN, 1837–1875.

Republican Compiler. Gettysburg PA, 1818–1857.

Responses to PADS 29. 1958. Unpub. letters in response to "Report of a Recent Project of Collecting" in *PADS 29.*

Revere, Joseph Warren. *A Tour of Duty in California.* New York: C. S. Francis; Boston: J. H. Francis, 1849.

Review-Times. Oxford NY, 1915?–.

Rex-Johnson, Braiden. *Pike Place Market Cookbook.* Seattle WA: Sasquatch Books, c.2003.

Rexroth, Kenneth and James Laughlin. *Selected Letters.* Ed. by Lee Bartlett. New York: W. W. Norton, c.1991.

Reynolds, J. Peter Gott. Boston: John P. Jewett, 1856.

Reynolds, John. *The Pioneer History of Illinois.* Belleville IL: N. A. Randall, 1852.

Reynolds, Thurlow Weed. *Born of the Mountains.* Highlands? NC: [s.n.], c.1964.

Rhees, William Jones. *An Account of the Smithsonian Institution.* New York: Arno Press, 1980. Repr. of 1859 ed. pub. by T. McGill, Washington.

Rhetoric Review. Dallas TX, 1982–.

Rhinelander Daily News. Rhinelander WI, 1917–1947.

Rhinelander Daily News and the New North. Rhinelander WI, 1947?–.

Rhoads, Ann Fowler and Timothy A. Block. *The Plants of Pennsylvania.* Philadelphia: Univ. PA Press, c.2000.

———. *The Plants of Pennsylvania.* 2d ed. Philadelphia: Univ. PA Press, c.2007.

Rhoads, Asa. *The New Instructor.* 2d ed. Stanford CA: Printed by Daniel Lawrence, 1804.

Rhoads, Samuel N. *The Mammals of Pennsylvania and New Jersey.* Philadelphia: Privately Published, 1903.

Rhode Island (Colony). *Records of the Colony of Rhode Island and Providence Plantations in New England.* Providence RI: A. C. Greene & Bros., 1856–1865.

Rhode Island (Colony) Court of Trials. *Rhode Island Court Records.* Providence RI: Rhode Island Historical Society, 1920–1922. 2 vols.

Rhode Island (Colony) Laws, Statutes etc. *Acts and Resolves.* Providence RI, 1747–1800.

Rhode Island Historical Society. *Collections.* Providence RI, 1827–1941.

———. *Publications.* Providence RI, 1893–1901.

Rhode Island. Laws, etc. *Public Laws of the State of Rhode Island and Providence Plantations.* Providence RI, 1810–.

Rhodes, Richard. *Farm: a Year in the Life of an American Farmer.* New York: Simon and Schuster, c.1989.

Rhodora. Boston, 1899–.

Rice, Alice Caldwell Hegan. *Calvary Alley.* New York: Century, 1917.

———. *The Inky Way.* New York: D. Appleton-Century, 1940.

———. *Mr. Opp.* New York: Century, 1909.

———. *Mr. Pete & Co.* New York: D. Appleton-Century, 1933.

———. *Mrs. Wiggs of the Cabbage Patch.* New York: Century, 1902.

———. *A Romance of Billy-Goat Hill.* New York: Century, 1912.

———. *Sandy.* New York: Grosset & Dunlap, 1932. Orig. pub. in 1904.

Rice, Bertha Marguerite and Roland Rice. *Popular Studies of California Wild Flowers.* San Francisco: Upton Bros., c.1920.

Rice, Claton S. *Ambassador to the Saints.* Boston: Christopher Publishing, c.1965.

———. *Dehorned Bishop.* 1971. Unpub.

Rice, Rosella. *Mabel, or, Heart Histories.* 2d ed. Columbus OH: Follett, Foster, 1859.

Rice, William and Burton Wolf, eds. *Where to Eat in America*. New York: Random House, 1977.

Rich, Louise Dickinson. *Happy the Land*. Philadelphia: J. B. Lippincott, c.1946.

———. *We Took to the Woods*. Philadelphia: J. B. Lippincott, c.1942.

Rich, Shebnah. *Truro-Cape Cod*. Boston: D. Lothrop, c.1883.

Rich, Virginia. *The Baked Bean Supper Murders*. New York: E. P. Dutton, c.1983.

Rich, Walter Herbert. *Feathered Game of the Northeast*. New York: T. Y. Crowell, 1907.

Richards, Caroline Cowles. *Diary of Caroline Cowles Richards, 1852–1872, Canandaigua, N.Y.* Rochester NY?: [s.n.], c.1908.

Richards, Ellen Henrietta and Sophronia Maria Elliott. *The Chemistry of Cooking and Cleaning*. 3d ed., rev. and enlarged. Boston: Whitcomb and Barrows, 1907.

Richards, Laura Elizabeth Howe. *Mrs. Tree*. Boston: Dana Estes, 1902.

———. *When I Was Your Age*. Boston: Page, c.1893.

Richards, William Joseph, ed. *Early Stages of Atlantic Fishes*. Boca Raton FL: Taylor & Francis, 2006. 2 vols.

Richardson, Albert Deane. *Beyond the Mississippi . . . 1857–1867*. Hartford CT: American Publishing; New York: Bliss, 1867.

———. *Garnered Sheaves*. Hartford CT: Columbian Book, 1871.

Richardson, Alfred. *Plants of the Rio Grande Delta*. Austin TX: Univ. TX Press, 1995.

Richardson, John. *Fauna Boreali-Americana*. London: John Murray, 1829–1837. 4 vols.

Richardson, Simon Peter. *The Lights and Shadows of Itinerant Life: an Autobiography of Rev. Simon Peter Richardson*. Nashville TN: Publishing House, Methodist Episcopal Church, South, 1900.

Richardson, Wyman. *The House on Nauset Marsh*. New York: W. W. Norton, c.1955.

Richland County Observer. Richland Center WI, 1855–1867.

Richland Observer. Richland Center WI, 1962–.

Richmond Times-Dispatch. Richmond VA, 1896–.

Richter, Conrad. *The Fields*. 1st ed. New York: Alfred A. Knopf, 1946.

———. *The Town*. New York: Alfred A. Knopf, 1950.

———. *The Town*. New York: Bantam, 1965. Orig. pub. in 1950 by Alfred A. Knopf, New York.

———. *The Trees*. New York: Alfred A. Knopf, 1940.

Richwood Gazette. Richwood OH, 1872–1908; 1912–.

Rickaby, Franz Lee, comp. *Ballads and Songs of the Shanty-Boy*. Cambridge MA: Harvard Univ. Press, 1926.

Rickard, Thomas Arthur. *Through the Yukon and Alaska*. San Francisco: Mining and Scientific Press, 1909.

Ricketson, Daniel. *The History of New Bedford, Bristol County, Massachusetts*. New Bedford MA: Published by the author, 1858.

Riddell, John Leonard. *A Synopsis of the Flora of the Western States*. Cincinnati OH: E. Deming, 1835.

Rideout, Henry Milner. *Beached Keels*. Boston: Houghton, Mifflin, 1906.

Ridgway, Robert. *A Manual of North American Birds*. Philadelphia: J. B. Lippincott, 1887.

———. *The Ornithology of Illinois*. Springfield IL: H. W. Rokker, 1889–1895. 2 vols.

Ridley, Bromfield Lewis. *Battles and Sketches of the Army of Tennessee*. Mexico MO: Missouri Printing and Publishing, 1906.

Ries, Al and Jack Trout. *Marketing Warfare*. New York: McGraw-Hill, c.1986.

Riesenberg, Felix. *Under Sail*. New York: Macmillan, 1918.

———. *Vignettes of the Sea*. New York: Harcourt, Brace, c.1926.

Riggs, Lynn. *Roadside, a Comedy*. New York: Samuel French, 1930.

———. *Russet Mantle and The Cherokee Night, Two Plays*. New York: Samuel French, 1936.

Rightor, Henry, ed. *Standard History of New Orleans, Louisiana*. Chicago: Lewis, 1900.

Riis, Jacob August. *The Making of an American*. New York: Macmillan, 1902.

Riley, Henry Hiram. *Puddleford and Its People*. New York: Samuel Hueston, 1854.

———. *The Puddleford Papers*. New York: Derby & Jackson, 1857.

Riley, James. *An Authentic Narrative of the Loss of the American Brig Commerce, Wrecked on the Western Coast of Africa, in the Month of August, 1815*. Hartford CT: Published by the author, 1817.

Riley, James Whitcomb. *Armazindy*. Indianapolis IN: Bowen-Merrill, 1894.

———. *A Child-World*. Indianapolis IN: Bowen-Merrill, c.1896.

———. *"The Old Swimmin'-Hole" and 'Leven More Poems*. Indianapolis IN: Bowen-Merrill, 1891.

———. *Pipes o' Pan at Zekesbury*. Indianapolis IN: Bowen-Merrill, c.1888.

———. *Poems Here at Home*. New York: Century, 1893.

———. *Rhymes of Childhood*. Indianapolis IN: Bowen-Merrill, 1895 [c.1890].

———. *Rubaiyat of Doc Sifers*. New York: Century, 1897.

Rinehart, Mary Roberts. *The Window at the White Cat*. New York: Review of Reviews, 1910.

Ringholz, Raye Carleson. *On Belay! the Life of Legendary Mountaineer Paul Petzoldt*. Seattle WA: Mountaineers, c.1997.

Rinzler, Ralph and Robert Sayers. *The Meaders Family, North Georgia Potters*. Washington DC: Smithsonian Institution Press, 1980.

Rio Abajo Weekly Press. Albuquerque NM, 1863–1864.

Ripley, Eliza. *From Flag to Flag*. New York: D. Appleton, 1889.

———. *Social Life in Old New Orleans*. Chapel Hill NC: Academic Affairs Library, Univ. NC at Chapel Hill, 1998. Text transcr. for *Documenting the American South* website from the 1912 ed. pub. by D. Appleton, New York.

Ritchie, Ethel Colt. *Block Island Lore and Legends*. Block Island RI: F. Norman, 1956 [c.1955].

Ritchie, Jean. *Singing Family of the Cumberlands*. New York: Oxford Univ. Press, 1955.

Ritchie, Robert Welles. *The Hell-Roarin' Forty-Niners*. New York: J. H. Sears, c.1928.

Rittenhouse, Isabella Maud SEE Mayne, Isabella Maud Rittenhouse

Rittenhouse, Jack DeVere. *American Horse-Drawn Vehicles*. New York: Bonanza Books, 1948.

Ritter, Abraham. *History of the Moravian Church in Philadelphia*. Philadelphia: Hayes & Zell, 1857.

Ritter, Thomas Jefferson. *Mother's Remedies*. Detroit MI: G. H. Foote, c.1910.

Riverside Magazine for Young People. New York, 1868–1870.

River Times. Fairbanks AK, 1971?–.

Roanoke Times. Roanoke VA, 1890–1895; 1897–1977; 1995–.

Roanoke Times & World-News. Roanoke VA, 1977–1995.

Robb, John S. *Streaks of Squatter Life and Far-West Scenes*. Gainesville FL: Scholars' Facsimiles & Reprints, 1962. Facsimile of 1847 ed. pub. by Carey and Hart, Philadelphia.

Robbins, Harold. *The Dream Merchants*. New York: Alfred A. Knopf, 1949.

Roberts, Daniel Webster. *Rangers and Sovereignty*. San Antonio TX: Wood Printing and Engraving, 1914.

Roberts, Elizabeth Madox. *The Time of Man*. New York: Viking Press, 1926.

Roberts, Hermese E. *The Third Ear*. Chicago: English-Language Institute of America, 1971.

Roberts, Job. *The Pennsylvania Farmer*. Philadelphia: Jacob Johnson, 1804.

Roberts, Johnny and Morris Levy. *My Boy Lollipop*. New York: Big Seven Music, c.1956.

Roberts, Kenneth Lewis. *Henry Gross and His Dowsing Rod*. Garden City NY: Doubleday, 1951.

Roberts, Leonard Ward. *I Bought Me a Dog*. Berea KY: Council of Southern Mountain Workers, c.1954.

———. *South from Hell-Fer-Sartin*. Lexington KY: Univ. KY Press, c.1955.

———. *Up Cutshin and Down Greasy*. Lexington KY: Univ. KY Press, 1959.

Roberts, Monty. *The Man Who Listens to Horses*. New York: Random House, 1997.

Roberts, Morley. *The Western Avernus*. London: Smith, Elder, 1887.

Roberts, Orlando W. *Narratives of Voyages and Excursions on the East Coast and in the Interior of Central America*. Edinburgh: Constable, 1827.

Roberts, Rhoda N. and Ruth Ashton Nelson. *Mountain Wildflowers of Colorado*. Denver CO: Denver Museum of Natural History, 1957.

Roberts, Robert Ellis. *Sketches of the City of Detroit*. Detroit MI: R. F. Johnstone, 1855.

Roberts, Thomas Sadler. *The Birds of Minnesota*. Minneapolis MN: Univ. MN Press; London: Oxford Univ. Press, 1932. 2 vols.

———. *The Birds of Minnesota*. 2d ed. rev. Minneapolis MN: Univ. MN Press, 1936. 2 vols.

Roberts, Walter Adolph. *Lake Pontchartrain*. Indianapolis IN: Bobbs-Merrill, c.1946.

Roberts, William. *An Account of the First Discovery and Natural History of Florida*. London: Printed for T. Jefferys, 1763.

Robertson, Ben. *Red Hills and Cotton*. Columbia SC: Univ. SC Press, 1960. Orig. pub. in 1942 by A. A. Knopf, New York.

Robertson, Don. *The Greatest Thing since Sliced Bread*. New York: Putnam, 1965.

———. *The Ideal, Genuine Man*. Bangor ME: Philtrum Press, c.1987.

Robertson, Frank Chester. *A Ram in the Thicket*. New York: Hastings House, c.1959.

Robertson, Kevin et al. *Management of Peatland Shrub-and Forest-Dominated Communities for Threatened and Endangered Species*. Champaign IL: U.S. Army Corps of Engineers, Construction Engineering Research Laboratories, 1998.

Robeson, Paul. *Here I Stand*. New York: Othello Associates, c.1958.

Robesonian. Lumberton NC, 1870–.

Robin, Charles-Cesar. *Voyages dans l'intérieur de la Louisiane*. Paris: F. Buisson, 1807. 3 vols.

Robins, Elizabeth. *The Magnetic North*. Upper Saddle River NJ: Literature House, 1969. Orig. pub. in 1904 by Frederick A. Stokes, New York.

Robinson, Alfred. *Life in California*. New York: Wiley & Putnam, 1846.

Robinson, Ben Carl. *Pond, Lake and Stream Fishing*. Philadelphia: David McKay, c.1941.

Robinson, Henry Morton. *The Cardinal*. New York: Simon & Schuster, 1950.

Robinson, Jacob S. *A Journal of the Santa Fe Expedition under Colonel Doniphan*. Princeton NJ: Princeton Univ. Press, 1932.

Robinson, John. *Our Trees*. Salem MA: Printed by N. A. Horton and Son, 1891.

Robinson, Joseph Lee and Oliver A. Knott. *The Story of the Iowa Crop Improvement Association and Its Predecessors*. Ames IA: Iowa Crop Improvement Association, 1963.

Robinson, L. W. *The Assassin*. New York: World Publishing, c.1968.

Robinson, Phil. *Sinners and Saints*. Boston: Roberts Bros., 1883.

Robinson, Rowland Evans. *Along Three Rivers*. Rutland VT: Tuttle, c.1934.

———. *Danvis Folks, and A Hero of Ticonderoga*. Rutland VT: Tuttle, c.1934. Orig. pub. in 1894 by Houghton, Mifflin.

———. *In New England Fields and Woods*. Boston: Houghton, Mifflin, 1896.

———. *Sam Lovel's Boy*. Boston: Houghton, Mifflin, 1901.

———. *Sam Lovel's Boy with Forest & Stream Fables*. Ed. by Llewellyn R. Perkins. Centennial ed. Rutland VT: Chas. E. Tuttle, c.1936.

———. *Sam Lovel's Camps*. New York: Forest and Stream, 1889.

———. *Uncle Lisha's Outing*. Boston: Houghton, Mifflin, 1897.

———. *Uncle Lisha's Shop*. 5th ed. New York: Forest and Stream Publishing, 1895 [c.1887].

———. *Vermont: a Study of Independence*. Boston: Houghton, Mifflin, 1892.

Robinson, Sara Tappan Lawrence. *Kansas*. 3d ed. Boston: Crosby, Nichols, 1856.

Robinson, Timothy Weymouth. *History of the Town of Morrill in the County of Waldo and State of Maine*. Belfast ME: City Job Print, 1944.

Robinson, William. *Alpine Flowers for English Gardens*. London: J. Murray, 1870.

Robinson, William H. *Handbook of Urban Insects and Arachnids*. Cambridge: Cambridge Univ. Press, 2005.

Robley, Thomas F. *History of Bourbon County Kansas*. Ft. Scott KS: Monitor Book & Print, 1894.

Rochefort, Alfred SEE Calhoun, Alfred Rochefort

Rock & Gem. Encino CA: Miller Magazines, 1971–.

Rock County Leader. Bassett NE, 1891–.

Rockfellow, John Alexander. *Log of an Arizona Trail Blazer*. Tucson AZ: Arizona Silhouettes, 1955 [c.1933].

Rockford Labor News. Rockford IL, 1913–.

Rockport Democrat. Rockport IN, 1855–.

Rockport Pilot. Rockport TX, 1930?–.

Rock River Pilot. Watertown WI, 1847–1849.

Rockwell, Charles. *The Catskill Mountains and the Region Around*. New York: Taintor Bros., 1867.

Rockwell, Norman. *Norman Rockwell, My Adventures as an Illustrator*. Garden City NY: Doubleday, 1960.

Rocky Mountain News. Denver CO, 1937–2009.

Rodahl, Kare. *The Last of the Few*. New York: Harper & Row, 1963.

Rodd, Marcel. *Souvenir-Album, Los Angeles, Hollywood and the Southland at a Glance.* Hollywood CA: The Author, 1943.

Rodenbough, Theophilus Francis, comp. *From Everglade to Cañon with the Second Dragoons (Second United States Cavalry).* New York: D. Van Nostrand, 1875.

Rodimer, Eva. *The Year Outdoors.* New Brunswick NJ: Rutgers Univ. Press, 1966.

Rodman, Samuel. *The Diary of Samuel Rodman.* Ed. by Zephaniah W. Pease. New Bedford MA: Reynolds Printing, 1927.

Rodowsky, Colby F. *Clay.* New York: Harper Trophy, 2004 [c.2001].

Roe, Alfred Seelye. *Rose Neighborhood Sketches, Wayne County, New York.* Worcester MA: Published by the author, 1893.

Roe, Azel Stevens. *The Cloud of the Heart.* New York: G. W. Carleton; London: S. Low, Son, 1869 [c.1868].

———. *A Long Look Ahead.* New York: J. C. Derby, 1855.

Roe, Daniel. *The Diary of Captain Daniel Roe.* Ed. by Alfred S. Roe. Worcester MA: Privately Printed by the Annotator, Blanchard Press, 1904.

Roe, Edward Payson. *He Fell in Love with His Wife.* New York: P. F. Collier & Son, c.1886.

———. *His Sombre Rivals.* New York: P. F. Collier, c.1883.

———. *"Miss Lou" and Driven Back to Eden.* New York: P. F. Collier & Son, 1888.

———. *Nature's Serial Story.* New York: Dodd, Mead, c.1884.

———. *Opening Chestnut Burr.* New York: Dodd, Mead, c.1902, c.1874.

Roe, Frances Marie Antoinette Mack. *Army Letters from an Officer's Wife, 1871–1888.* New York: D. Appleton, 1909.

Roedel, Philip M. *Common Ocean Fishes of the California Coast.* Sacramento CA: [s.n.], 1953.

Rogers, David Banks. *Prehistoric Man of the Santa Barbara Coast.* Santa Barbara CA: Santa Barbara Museum of Natural History, 1929.

Rogers, Frank D. *Folk-Stories of the Northern Border.* Clayton NY: Thousand Islands Publishing, 1897.

Rogers, Harrison G. *First Journal . . . of J. S. Smith's Company* SEE Dale, Harrison Clifford *The Ashley-Smith Explo-rations and the Discovery of a Central Route to the Pacific, 1822–1829, with the Original Journals*

Rogers, John William. *Bumblepuppy.* New York: Samuel French, c.1927.

Rogers, Julia Ellen. *The Shell Book.* New York: Doubleday, Page, 1908.

———. *The Tree Book.* New York: Doubleday, Page, 1908.

———. *Trees Worth Knowing.* Garden City NY: Doubleday, Page, 1923 [c.1917].

Rogers, Maria M. *In Other Words.* Golden CO: Fulcrum, c.1995.

Rogers, Orville F. *Grandma's Island and Grandma's Ocean.* [s.l.]: Privately printed by Orville F. Rogers, 1970.

Rogers, Robert. *A Concise Account of North America.* London: J. Millan, 1765.

Rohde, Jerry and Gisela Rohde. *Best Short Hikes in Redwood National and State Parks.* Seattle WA: Mountaineers Books, 2004.

Rolling Stone. San Francisco: Straight Arrow, 1967–.

Rollins, Ellen Chapman Hobbs. *New England Bygones.* New ed., enlarged and illustrated. Philadelphia: J. B. Lippincott, 1883. Orig. pub. in 1880.

Rollins, Philip Ashton. *The Cowboy.* New York: Charles Scribner's Sons, 1922.

———. *The Cowboy.* Rev. and enlarged ed. New York: Charles Scribner's Sons, 1936.

———. *Gone Haywire.* New York: Charles Scribner's Sons, 1939.

Rollinson, John K. *Hoofprints of a Cowboy and U.S. Ranger.* Ed. and arranged by E. A. Brininstool. Caldwell ID: Caxton Printers, 1941.

———. *Wyoming Cattle Trails.* Caldwell ID: Caxton Printers, 1948.

Rölvaag, Ole Edvart. *Peder Victorious.* Lincoln NE: Univ. NE Press, 1982 [c.1929].

Romance Notes. Chapel Hill NC, 1959–.

Romanes, George John. *Animal Intelligence.* Westmead: Gregg International, 1970. Repr. of 1882 ed. pub. by K. Paul Trench, London.

Romans, Bernard. *A Concise Natural History of East and West Florida.* Gainesville FL: Univ. FL Press, 1962. Facsimile of the 1775 ed. printed by the author, New York.

Rombauer, Irma von Starkloff. *The Joy of Cooking.* Indianapolis IN: Bobbs-Merrill, 1946.

Rompkey, Ronald, ed. *Jessie Luther at the Grenfell Mission.* Montreal: McGill-Queen's Univ. Press, c.2001.

Romspert, George W. *The Western Echo.* Dayton OH: United Brethren Publishing, 1881.

Ronald, Mary SEE Arnold, Augusta Foote

Roody, William C. *Mushrooms of West Virginia and the Central Appalachians.* Lexington KY: Univ. KY Press, c.2003.

Rooney, Jim. *Bossmen: Bill Monroe & Muddy Waters.* New York: Dial Press, 1971.

Roorbach, Bill. *Into Woods.* Notre Dame IN: Univ. Notre Dame Press, c.2002.

Roosevelt, Edith Kermit Carow and Kermit Roosevelt, comps. *American Backlogs.* New York: C. Scribner's Sons, 1928.

Roosevelt, Robert Barnwell. *Five Acres Too Much.* New York: Harper & Bros., 1869.

———. *Florida and the Game Water-Birds of the Atlantic Coast and the Lakes of the United States.* New York: Orange Judd, 1884.

———. *The Game-Birds of the Coasts and Lakes of the Northern States of America.* New York: Carleton, 1866.

———. *Superior Fishing, or the Striped Bass, Trout, Black Bass, and Blue-Fish of the Northern States.* New York: Orange Judd, 1884.

Roosevelt, Theodore. *A Book-Lover's Holidays in the Open.* New York: Charles Scribner's Sons, 1916.

———. *Hunting Trips of a Ranchman.* New York: G. P. Putnam's Sons, 1891 [c.1885].

———. *Outdoor Pastimes of an American Hunter.* New and enlarged ed. New York: C. Scribner's Sons, 1908.

———. *The Wilderness Hunter.* New York: G. P. Putnam's Sons, c.1893.

———. *The Winning of the West.* New York: G. P. Putnam's Sons, 1889–1896. 4 vols.

Root, Frank A. and William Elsey Connelley. *The Overland Stage to California.* Topeka KS: The Authors, 1901.

Rorer, Sarah Tyson Heston. *Mrs. Rorer's Vegetable Cookery and Meat Substitutes.* Philadelphia: Arnold, 1909.

Rosborough, Mary Freels. *Don't You Cry for Me.* Chicago: People's Book Club, c.1954.

Rose, Al. *I Remember Jazz.* Baton Rouge LA: LA State Univ. Press, c.1987.

Rose, George. *The Great Country.* London: Tinsley Bros., 1868.

Rose, Mary H. *Block Island Scrapbook.* New York: Pageant Press, 1957.

Rose, William G. *The Western Reserve of Ohio and Some of Its Pioneers, Places and Women's Clubs.* Cleveland OH: Press of Euclid Printing, 1914–1915. 2 vols.

Rose, Willie Lee Nichols, ed. *A Documentary History of Slavery in North America.* New York: Oxford Univ. Press, 1976.

Rosenber, Ethel SEE Clifford, Eth

Rosenberg, Bruce A. *The Art of the American Folk Preacher.* New York: Oxford Univ. Press, c.1970.

Rosendahl, Carl Otto and Frederic K. Butters. *Trees and Shrubs of Minnesota.* Minneapolis MN: Univ. MN Press, 1928.

Roseville Independent. Roseville IL, 1956–.

Ross, Ann B. *Miss Julia Delivers the Goods.* New York: Viking, c.2009.

———. *Miss Julia Hits the Road.* New York: Viking, c.2003.

Ross, Charles Robert. *Trees to Know in Oregon.* Corvallis OR: OR State Univ., 1950.

Ross, Fred E. *Jackson Mahaffey.* Boston: Houghton Mifflin, c.1951.

Ross, Joel H. *What I Saw in New-York.* 2d ed. Auburn NY: Derby & Miller, 1852 [c.1851].

Ross, Stephen T. *The Inland Fishes of Mississippi.* Jackson MS: Univ. Press MS, c.2001.

Rosskam, Edwin and Louise Rosskam. *Towboat River.* New York: Duell, Sloan and Pearce, 1948.

Rosten, Leo Calvin. *Hooray for Yiddish.* New York: Simon and Schuster, c.1982.

———. *The Joys of Yiddish.* New York: McGraw-Hill, 1968.

Roswell Daily Record. Roswell NM, 1903–.

Rotarian. Chicago: Rotary International, 1911–.

Roth, Henry. *Call It Sleep.* New York: R. O. Ballou, c.1934.

———. *Mercy of a Rude Stream.* New York: St. Martin's Press, c.1994.

Roth, Philip. *Portnoy's Complaint.* New York: Random House, 1969.

Rothert, Otto Arthur. *A History of Muhlenberg County.* Louisville KY: John P. Morton, 1913.

The Rough and Ready Annual. New York: D. Appleton, 1848.

Roundup Record-Tribune. Roundup MT, 1930–.

Rowan, Carl Thomas. *South of Freedom.* New York: Knopf, 1952.

Rowe, Henrietta Gould. *A Maid of Bar Harbor.* Boston: Little, Brown, 1904 [c.1902].

Rowe, John. *Letters and Diary of John Rowe.* Boston: W. B. Clarke, 1903.

Rowe, William Hutchinson. *The Maritime History of Maine.* New York: W. W. Norton, 1948.

Rowland, John Tilghman. *North to Adventure.* New York: Norton, c.1963.

Rowley, Massachusetts. *The Early Records of the Town of Rowley, Massachusetts, 1639–1672, Vol. 1.* Bowie MD: Heritage Books, 1984. Repr. of the 1894 ed.

Rowntree, Lester. *Hardy Californians.* New York: Macmillan, 1936.

Rowse, D. G. *Doughboy Dope from A to Z.* New York: Frank K. Kane, 1918 [c.1919].

Rowsome, Frank. *The Verse by the Side of the Road: the Story of the Burma-Shave Signs and Jingles.* Brattleboro VT: S. Greene Press, 1965.

Roxburgh, William. *Hortus Bengalensis.* Serampore, India: Printed at the Mission Press, 1814.

Royal American Magazine, or, Universal Repository of Instruction and Amusement. Boston, 1774–1775.

Royal Arch Masons. Grand Chapter of the State of California. *Proceedings.* Sacramento CA, 1854–.

Royal Geographical Society. *Proceedings.* London, 1857–1878.

Royal Geographical Society of London. *Journal.* London, 1831–1880.

Royal Society of London. *Philosophical Transactions.* London, 1665–1886.

Royall, Anne Newport. *The Black Book.* Washington DC: Printed for the author, 1828–1829. 3 vols.

———. *Letters from Alabama.* Washington DC: [s.n.], 1830 [c.1829].

———. *Mrs. Royall's Pennsylvania.* Washington DC: The Author, 1829. 2 vols.

———. *Mrs. Royall's Southern Tour.* Washington DC: [s.n.], 1830–1831. 3 vols.

———. *Sketches of History, Life and Manners, in the United States.* New-Haven CT: Printed for the Author, 1826.

Royall, William Lawrence. *Some Reminiscences.* New York: Neale Publishing, 1909.

Royko, Mike. *Like I Was Sayin'.* New York: E. P. Dutton, c.1984.

Ruark, Robert. *The Old Man's Boy Grows Older.* New York: Holt, Rinehart and Winston, c.1961.

———. *Poor No More.* 8th printing. Greenwich CT: Fawcett, 1965 [c.1959].

Rubina. New York: James G. Gregory, 1864.

Rubrecht, August. *Regional Occurrence of Some Dialect Terms in Wisconsin.* 1974. Unpub. article.

Rudd, Dan A. and Theophilus Bond. *From Slavery to Wealth.* Madison AR: Journal Printing, 1917.

Rudder. Greenwich CT, 1890–1977.

Rudolphy, John. *Pharmaceutical Directory.* 2d ed. enlarged. New York: William Radde and John Rudolphy, 1872.

Ruede, Howard. *Sod-House Days.* New York: Columbia Univ. Press, 1937.

Ruff, Willie. *A Call to Assembly.* New York: Viking, c.1991.

Ruffin, Edmund. *An Essay on Calcareous Manures.* Petersburg VA: J. W. Campbell, 1832.

Ruffin, Thomas. *The Papers of Thomas Ruffin.* Coll. and ed. by J. G. deRoulhac Hamilton. Raleigh NC: Edwards & Broughton, 1918–1920. 4 vols.

Ruggles, Logan E. *The Navy Explained.* New York: Edwin N. Appleton, c.1918.

Ruhl, Arthur. *The Other Americans.* New York: Charles Scribner's Sons, 1908.

Rule, Ann. *Everything She Ever Wanted.* New York: Simon & Schuster, c.1992.

Rundell, Maria Eliza Ketelby. *A New System of Domestic Cookery.* New ed., corr. London: J. Murray, 1809.

Runyan, Cathy C. *Knuckles Down!* Kansas City MO: Right Brain Publishing, c.1985.

Runyon, Damon. *Guys and Dolls.* New York: Frederick A. Stokes, 1931.

———. *More Than Somewhat.* Comp. by E. C. Bentley. London: Constable, c.1937.

———. *Take It Easy.* New York: Frederick A. Stokes, 1938.

———. *Trials and Other Tribulations.* Philadelphia: J. B. Lippincott, c.1947.

Rupp, Israel Daniel, comp. *The History and Topography of Dauphin, Cumberland, Franklin, Redford, Adams and Perry Counties.* Lancaster City PA: Gilbert Hills, 1846.

Ruppenthal, Jacob Christian. *Collection of Kansas Dialect Words and Phrases.* 1927–1929. Unpub.

Rural Affairs. Albany NY, 1858–1881.

Rural Carolinian. Charleston SC, 1869–1876.

Rural Life in New England. New York: J. Winchester New World Press, c.1844.

Rural Repository. Hudson NY: W. B. Stoddard, 1833–1851.

Rural Visiter. Burlington NJ, 1810–1811.

Rush, Benjamin. *Medical Inquiries and Observations.* 2d ed., rev. and enlarged. Philadelphia: J. Conrad, 1805. 4 vols.

———. *Medical Inquiries and Observations upon the Diseases of the Mind.* Philadelphia: Kimber & Richardson, 1812.

Rusling, James Fowler. *Across America.* New York: Sheldon, c.1874.

———. *The Great West and Pacific Coast.* New York: Sheldon; Chicago: A. G. Nettleton, 1877.

Russell, Charles Marion. *Trails Plowed Under.* Garden City NY: Doubleday, Doran, 1944 [c.1927].

Russell, Gladys Trentham. *It Happened in the Smokies.* Alcoa TN: Russell Publishing, c.1988.

Russell, Keith. *For Whom the Ducks Toll.* Piscataway NJ: Einchester Press, c.1984.

Russell, Tom. *Riding with the Magi.* Livingston AL: Livingston Press at Univ. West AL, c.2004.

Russell, William Howard. *My Diary.* Boston: T. O. H. P. Burnam, 1863.

Russell Record. Russell KS, 1882?–.

Russell's Magazine. Charleston SC, 1857–1860.

Rust, Brian A. L., comp. *Jazz Records, 1897–1942.* 5th rev. and enlarged ed. Chigwell: Storyville, 1982. 2 vols.

Rustad, Dorothy Scott. *I Married a Fisherman.* Edmonds WA: Alaska Northwest Publishing, c.1986.

Ruston Daily Leader. Ruston LA, 1932–.

Ruthven, Alexander G. et al. *The Herpetology of Michigan.* Ann Arbor MI: Univ. MI, 1928.

Ruthven Free Press. Ruthven IA, 1916–1966.

Rutledge, Sarah. *The Carolina Housewife.* Columbia SC: Univ. SC Press, 1979. Facsimile of 1847 ed.

Ruttenbar, Edward Manning. *Footprints of the Red Men.* New York: New York State Historical Society, c.1906.

Ruxton, George Frederick Augustus. *Adventures in Mexico and the Rocky Mountains.* Glorieta NM: Rio Grande Press, 1973. Repr. of the 1847 ed. pub. by J. Murray, London.

———. *Adventures in Mexico and the Rocky Mountains.* New York: Harper & Bros., 1848.

———. *Life in the Far West.* New York: Harper & Bros., 1855. Orig. pub. in 1848 as a serial in *Blackwood's Magazine.*

Ruyle, George B. and Deborah J. Young, eds. *Arizona Range Grasses.* Tucson AZ: Cooperative Extension, College of Agriculture, Univ. AZ, 1997.

Ryan, Ben. *Down on 33rd and 3rd.* Musical score. New York: Remick Music, c.1926.

Ryan, John Joseph. *The Maggie Murphy.* New York: W. W. Norton, c.1951.

Ryan, Marah Ellis Martin. *A Pagan of the Alleghanies.* Chicago: Rand, McNally, 1891.

———. *Told in the Hills.* Chicago: Rand, McNally, c.1905. Orig. pub. in 1891.

Ryan, Pam Muñoz. *Esperanza Rising.* New York: Scholastic Press, c.2000.

Ryan, William Redmond. *Personal Adventures in Upper and Lower California, in 1848–1849.* London: W. Shoberl, 1850–1851. 2 vols.

———. *Personal Adventures in Upper and Lower California, in 1848–1849.* London: William Shoberl, 1852. 2 vols.

Rydberg, Per Axel. *Flora of Colorado.* Ft. Collins CO: Experiment Station, 1906.

———. *Flora of the Prairies and the Plains of Central North America.* New York: New York Botanical Garden, 1932.

———. *Flora of the Rocky Mountains and Adjacent Plains.* New York: Published by the Author, 1917.

Rye, Edgar. *The Quirt and the Spur.* Chicago: W. B. Conkey, c.1909.

Ryland, Elizabeth Lowell, ed. *Richmond County Virginia.* Warsaw VA: Richmond County Board of Supervisors, 1976.

Sachse, Helena V. *How to Cook for the Sick and Convalescent.* Philadelphia: J. B. Lippincott, 1901.

Sackett, Samuel John and William E. Koch, eds. *Kansas Folklore.* Lincoln NE: Univ. NE Press, 1961.

Sacramento Bee. Sacramento CA, 1908–.

Sacramento Daily Union. Sacramento CA, 1851–1875.

Safford, Henry Barnard. *That Bennington Mob.* New York: Julian Messner, c.1935.

Safire, William. *Coming to Terms.* New York: Doubleday, 1991.

———. *I Stand Corrected.* New York: Times Books, c.1984.

———. *On Language.* New York: Time Books, c.1980.

———. *Quoth the Maven.* New York: Random House, c.1993.

———. *Safire's Political Dictionary.* New York: Random House, c.1978.

———. *Take My Word for It.* New York: Times Books, c.1986.

———. *What's the Good Word?* New York: Times Books, c.1982.

Sage, Lee. *The Last Rustler.* Boston: Little, Brown, 1930.

Sage, Rufus B. *Rufus B. Sage: His Letters and Papers, 1836–1847.* Glendale CA: A. H. Clark, 1956. 2 vols.

———. *Scenes in the Rocky Mountains and in Oregon, California, New Mexico, Texas, and the Grand Prairies.* Philadelphia: Carey & Hart, 1846.

Saiki, Jessica Kawasuna. *From the Lanai.* Minneapolis MN: New Rivers Press, 1991.

Sailing. Port Washington WI: Port Publications, 1966–.

Saint Louis Medical and Surgical Journal. St. Louis MO: E. F. Hobart, 1843–1907.

Saint Paul (MN) Survey Commission. *Report of a Survey of the School System of Saint Paul, Minnesota.* St. Paul MN: The Commission, 1917.

Sala, George Augustus Henry. *America Revisited.* 3d ed. London: Vizetelly, 1883. 2 vols.

———. *My Diary in America in the Midst of the War.* London: Tinsley Bros., 1865. 2 vols.

———. *Twice Round the Clock.* London: J. and R. Maxwell, 1859?

Salamanca Republican-Press. Salamanca NY, 1926–1981.

Sale, Charles. *The Specialist.* St. Louis MO: Specialist Pub., c.1929.

Sale, John B. *The Tree Named John.* Chapel Hill NC: Univ. NC Press, 1929.

Salem, Massachusetts. *Charter of the City of Salem.* Salem MA: Printed at the Observer Office, 1849.

Salem Advocate. Salem IL, 1858–1873?

Salem Daily News. Salem OH, 1888–1905.

Salem Gazette. Salem MA, 1790–1820.

Salem Sunbeam. Salem NJ, 1874–.

The Salem Witchcraft Papers. Ed. by Paul Boyer and Stephen Nissenbaum. New York: Da Capo Press, 1977. 3 vols. Comp. and transcr. in 1938 by the Works Progress Administration.

Salina Journal. Salina KS, 1925–.

Salinger, Jerome David. *The Catcher in the Rye.* Boston: Little, Brown, 1951.

———. *Franny and Zooey.* Boston: Little, Brown, c.1961.

———. *Franny and Zooey.* New York: Bantam Books, 1964 [c.1961].

———. *Nine Stories.* Boston: Little, Brown, 1953.

Salisbury, Harrison Evans. *The Shook-Up Generation.* New York: Harper & Bros., 1958.

Salisbury, Oliver Maxon. *Quoth the Raven.* Seattle WA: Superior Publishing, 1962.

Salisbury, William. *Hortus Paddingtonensis.* London: Printed by S. Couchman for Shepperson and Reynolds, 1797.

Salisbury Times. Salisbury MD, 1927–1966.

Salmon and Trout. By Dean Sage, C. H. Townsend, H. M. Smith, and William C. Harris. New York: Macmillan, 1904.

Salt. Kennebunk ME, 1974–1997?

Salt Lake Daily Tribune. Salt Lake City UT, 1872–1890.

Salt Lake Tribune. Salt Lake City UT, 1870?–.

Salvucci, Claudio R. *The Philadelphia Dialect Dictionary.* Bucks County PA: Evolution Publishing, c.1996.

Sampson, Arthur William. *Important Range Plants.* Washington DC: U.S. Department of Agriculture, 1917.

Samuels, Edward Augustus. *Birds of New England and Adjacent States.* 5th ed. Boston: Noyes, Holmes, 1870 [c.1867].

———. *A Descriptive Catalogue of the Birds of Massachusetts.* Boston: Wright & Potter, 1864.

———. *Ornithology and Oölogy of New England.* Boston: Nichols and Noyes, 1868 [c.1867].

———. *With Rod and Gun in New England and the Maritime Provinces.* Boston: Samuels & Kimball, 1897.

Samuels, Tina M. *A Georgia Native Plant Guide.* Macon GA: Mercer Univ. Press, 2005.

San Angelo Standard-Times. San Angelo TX, 1999?–. Internet.

San Antonio Daily Express. San Antonio TX, 1877–1891.

San Antonio Daily Light. San Antonio TX, 1886–1907.

San Antonio Express. San Antonio TX, 1911–1984.

San Antonio Express-News. San Antonio TX, 1865–.

San Antonio Light. San Antonio TX, 1907–1909; 1911–1993.

San Antonio Sunday Light. San Antonio TX, 1940?–1993.

San Augustine Rambler. San Augustine TX, 1967–.

Sanborn, Edwin Webster. *People at Pisgah.* New York: D. Appleton, 1892.

Sanborn, Kate. *A Truthful Woman in Southern California.* New York: D. Appleton, 1893.

———. *The Wit of Women.* 3d ed. New York: Funk & Wagnalls, 1886 [c.1885].

Sandbeck, Ellen. *Organic Housekeeping.* New York: Scribner, c.2006.

Sandburg, Carl, ed. *The American Songbag.* New York: Harcourt, Brace, c.1927.

———. *Chicago Poems.* New York: Henry Holt, 1916.

———. *Cornhuskers.* New York: H. Holt, 1918.

———. *The People, Yes.* New York: Harcourt, Brace, c.1936.

———. *Remembrance Book.* New York: Harcourt, Brace & World, c.1948.

———. *Rootabaga Stories.* 8th printing. New York: Harcourt, Brace, 1926 [c.1922].

———. *Smoke and Steel.* New York: Harcourt, Brace, 1921 [c.1920].

Sanders, D. C. *Echoes of the Farm.* San Antonio TX: Naylor, c.1959.

Sanders, Dori. *Clover.* New York: Fawcett Columbine, 1990.

Sanders, Jack. *The Secrets of Wildflowers.* Guilford CT: Lyons Press, c.2003.

Sanders, Scott Loring. *The Hanging Woods.* Boston: Houghton Mifflin, 2008.

Sanders, Thomas William. *The Encyclopaedia of Gardening.* 2d ed. London: W. H. & L. Collingridge, 1896.

San Diego Historical Society Quarterly. San Diego CA, 1955–1964.

San Diego Natural History Museum. *Checklist: Reptiles of San Diego County.* [v.d.]. Internet.

San Diego Society of Natural History. *Transactions.* San Diego CA, 1905–1989.

San Diego Union. San Diego CA, 1868–1992.

San Diego Union-Tribune. San Diego CA, 1992–.

Sandoz, Mari. *Miss Morissa.* New York: McGraw-Hill, c.1955.

———. *Old Jules.* Boston: Little, Brown, 1935.

———. *Slogum House.* Boston: Little, Brown, 1937.

———. *The Tom-Walker.* New York: Dial Press, 1947.

Sands, Robert Charles. *The Writings of Robert C. Sands.* New-York: Harper & Bros., 1834. 2 vols.

Sandusky Clarion. Sandusky OH, 1822–1851.

Sandusky Daily Register. Sandusky OH, 1867–1894; 1897–1910.

Sandusky Register. Sandusky OH, 1822–.

Sandusky Star-Journal. Sandusky OH, 1905–1921.

Sandwich Island Gazette and Journal of Commerce. Honolulu HI, 1836–1839.

Sandy City Utah. *Sandy City Online.* [v.d.]. Internet.

Sanford Tribune. Sanford ME, 1950–1977.

San Francisco Call. San Francisco, 1856–1914.

San Francisco Chronicle. San Francisco, 1865–.

San Francisco Examiner. San Francisco, 1880–.

San Francisco Herald. San Francisco, 1850–1856.

San Francisco Municipal Reports. San Francisco, 1860–1917.

San Francisco Sunday Examiner & Chronicle. San Francisco, 1965–.

Sanitary and Heating Age. New York, 1874–1931.

San Jacinto News-Times. Shepherd TX, 1968?–.

San Jose Mercury Herald. San Jose CA, 1913–1950.

San Juan Mission News. San Juan Bautista CA, 1913–.

San Mateo Times. San Mateo CA, 1901–1979?

San Mateo Times and Daily News Leader. San Mateo CA, 1926–1961.

Santa Barbara Gazette. Santa Barbara CA, 1855–1858.

Santa Fe Daily New Mexican. Santa Fe NM, 1885–1897.

Santa Fe Employes' Magazine. Chicago, 1906–1908?

Santa Fe Magazine SEE *Santa Fe Employes' Magazine*

Santa Fe New Mexican. Santa Fe NM, 1898–1951; 1988–.

Santa Fe Weekly New Mexican and Live Stock Journal. Santa Fe NM, 1885–1887.

Santamaría, Francisco Javier. *Diccionario General de Americanismos.* Méjico, D.F: P. Robredo, 1942. 3 vols.

Santee, Ross. *Apache Land.* New York: Charles Scribner's Sons, 1947.

———. *Cowboy.* New York: Hastings House, c.1964. Orig. pub. in 1928 by Cosmo Book.

———. *Lost Pony Tracks.* New York: Charles Scribner's Sons, 1953.

———. *Men and Horses.* New York: Century, c.1926.

Santiago, Danny. *Famous All Over Town.* New York: Simon and Schuster, c.1983.

Santmyer, Helen Hooven. *And Ladies of the Club.* New York: G. P. Putnam's Sons, 1984.

Sargent, Charles Sprague. *A Catalogue of the Forest Trees of North America.* Washington DC: Govt. Printing Office, 1880.

————. *Manual of the Trees of North America (Exclusive of Mexico)*. 2d ed. Boston: Houghton Mifflin, 1922.

————. *Report on the Forests of North America (Exclusive of Mexico)*. Washington DC: Govt. Printing Office, 1884.

Sargent, Epes. *Peculiar*. New York: Carleton, 1864.

Sargent, William. *A Year in the Notch*. Hanover NH: Univ. Press New England, c.2001.

Sargent, Winthrop, ed. *The History of an Expedition against Fort Du Quesne in 1755 under Major-General Edward Braddock*. Philadelphia: Lippincott, Grambo, 1855.

Saroyan, William. *Jim Dandy, Fat Man in a Famine*. New York: Harcourt Brace, 1947.

Sartain's Union Magazine of Literature and Art. Philadelphia, 1849–1852.

Saturday Evening Post. Philadelphia, 1821–.

Saturday Evening Post Letters. 1957–1958. Unpub. letters in response to a query in the *Saturday Evening Post*, March 16, 1957.

Saturday Herald. Decatur IL, 1879?–189?

Saturday Review. East Liverpool OH, 1879–1904.

Saturday Review. New York, 1952–1973; 1975–1986.

Saturday Review of Literature. New York, 1924–1951.

Sauer, Martin. *An Account of a Geographical and Astronomical Expedition to the Northern Parts of Russia*. London: T. Cadell, 1802.

Sauk Centre Herald. Sauk Centre MN, 1867–.

Saunders, Charles Francis. *The Southern Sierras of California*. Boston: Houghton, Mifflin, 1923.

————. *Useful Wild Plants of the United States and Canada*. New York: Robert M. McBride, 1920.

————. *Useful Wild Plants of the United States and Canada*. New and rev. ed. New York: Robert M. McBride, 1934.

————. *Western Flower Guide*. Garden City NY: Doubleday, Page, 1917.

————. *With the Flowers and Trees in California*. New York: McBride, Nast, 1914.

Saunders, Richard SEE Franklin, Benjamin

Saunders, Ripley Dunlap. *Colonel Todhunter of Missouri*. New York: Grosset & Dunlap, c.1911.

Savage, Edward Hartwell. *A Chronological History of the Boston Watch and Police from 1631 to 1865, Together with the Recollections of a Boston Police Officer*. 2d ed., rev. Boston: Published by the Author, 1865.

Savage, Henry. *River of the Carolinas*. New York: Rinehart, c.1956.

Savannah River Ecology Laboratory. Herpetology Program. *SREL Herpetology*. [v.d.]. Internet.

Savannah Tribune. Savannah GA, 1876–1960.

Sawyer, Lorenzo. *Way Sketches*. New York: Edward Eberstadt, 1926.

Sawyer County Record and Hayward Republican. Hayward WI, 1893–.

Saxe, John Godfrey. *The Poems of John Godfrey Saxe*. Boston: Ticknor and Fields, 1868.

Saxon, Lyle. *Fabulous New Orleans*. New York: Century, c.1928.

————. *Gumbo Ya-Ya* SEE Writers' Program. Louisiana *Gumbo Ya-Ya*

————. *Old Louisiana*. New York: Century, c.1929.

Scammon, Charles M. *The Marine Mammals of the North-Western Coast of North America Described and Illustrated*. New York: Dover, c.1874.

Scandia Journal. Scandia KS, 1882–.

Scanlon, William T. *God Have Mercy on Us*. New York: Grosset & Dunlap, c.1929.

Scarborough, Dorothy. *On the Trail of Negro Folk-Songs*. Cambridge MA: Harvard Univ. Press, [c.1925].

Schaff-Herzog Encyclopaedia. A Religious Encyclopaedia. New York: Funk & Wagnalls, c.1882–1883. 3 vols.

Scharf, J. Thomas. *History of Delaware*. Philadelphia: L. J. Richards, 1888. 2 vols.

Schauffler, Robert Haven, ed. *The Days We Celebrate*. New York: Dodd, Mead, 1940.

Schaw, Janet. *Journal of a Lady of Quality*. New Haven CT: Yale Univ. Press, 1922 [c.1921].

Schele de Vere, Maximillian. *Americanisms*. New York: C. Scribner, 1872.

Schenk, George. *The Complete Shade Gardener*. Boston: Houghton Mifflin, c.1984.

Scherf, Margaret. *The Diplomat and the Gold Piano*. Garden City NY: Doubleday, c.1963.

Scherr, Sara J. and Jeffrey A. McNeely, eds. *Farming with Nature*. Washington DC: Island Press, c.2007.

Schiddel, Edmund. *The Devil in Bucks County*. New York: Simon and Schuster, c.1959.

Schilla, Alice. *Heartbeat of the Prairies*. New York: Vantage Press, 1967.

Schillinger, William. "Journal of Ensign William Schillinger,

a Soldier of the War of 1812." *Ohio History* (1932) 41.52–85.

Schlissel, Lillian, comp. *Women's Diaries of the Westward Journey*. New York: Schocken Books, c.1982.

Schlytter, Leslie Evan. *The Tall Brothers*. New York: D. Appleton-Century, 1941.

Schmidt, Karl Patterson. *A Check List of North American Amphibians and Reptiles*. 6th ed. Chicago: American Society of Ichthyologists and Herpetologists, 1953.

Schmutz, Ervin M. et al. *Livestock-Poisoning Plants of Arizona*. Tucson AZ: Univ. AZ Press, c.1968.

Schoenhals, Louise C. *A Spanish-English Glossary of Mexican Flora and Fauna*. México D.F: Instituto Lingüístico de Verano, 1988.

Scholes, Percy Alfred. *The Concise Oxford Dictionary of Music*. 2d ed. New York: Oxford Univ. Press, 1964. Orig. pub. 1952, 5th impression rev. 1960.

————. *The Oxford Companion to Music*. 9th ed. completely rev. and reset and with many additions to text and illustrations. London: Oxford Univ. Press, 1960 [c.1955].

Scholl, Melvin. *Arnewood: the Story of an Iowa Dairyman*. Iowa City IA: State Historical Society of Iowa, 1954.

Schomburgk, Robert Hermann. *The History of Barbados*. London: Longman, Brown, Green and Longmans, 1848.

Schönfelder, Karl Heinz. *Deutsches Lehngut im Amerikanischen Englisch*. Halle an der Saale: Max Niemeyer, 1957.

Schoolcraft, Henry R., Mrs. SEE Schoolcraft, Mary Howard

Schoolcraft, Henry Rowe. *Information Respecting the History, Condition and Prospects of the Indian Tribes of the United States*. Philadelphia: Lippincott, Grambo, 1851–1857. 6 vols.

————. *Journal of a Tour into the Interior of Missouri and Arkansaw . . . in the Years 1818 and 1819*. London: Richard Phillips, 1821.

————. *Narrative Journal of Travels*. Albany NY: E. & E. Hosford, 1821.

————. *Narrative of an Expedition through the Upper Mississippi to Itasca Lake, . . . in 1832*. New York: Harper & Bros., 1834 [c.1833].

————. *Personal Memoirs*. Philadelphia: Lippincott, Grambo, 1851.

————. *View of the Lead Mines of Missouri*. New-York: Charles Wiley, 1819.

Schoolcraft, Mary Howard. *The Black Gauntlet*. Philadelphia: J. B. Lippincott, 1860.

School Journal. New York: E. L. Kellogg, 1881–1916.

School Science and Mathematics. Chicago: Central Association of Science and Mathematics Teachers, 1901–.

Schöpf, Johann David. *Materia Medica Americana Potissimum Regni Vegetabilis*. Erlangae: Sumtibus Io. Iac. Palmii, 1787.

————. *Reise durch Einige der Mittlern und Südlichen Vereinigten Nordamerikanischen Staaten . . . in den Jahren 1783 und 1784*. Erlangen: Johann Jacob Palm, 1788. 2 vols.

Schrader, Frank Charles. *A Reconnaissance in Northern Alaska*. Washington DC: Govt. Printing Office, 1904.

Schrenkeisen, Ray. *Field Book of Fresh-Water Fishes of North America*. New York: G. P. Putnam's Sons, 1938.

Schulberg, Budd. *The Disenchanted*. New York: Random House, c.1950.

————. *The Harder They Fall*. New York: Random House, c.1947.

————. *What Makes Sammy Run?* New York: Random House, c.1941.

Schultz, Christian. *Travels on an Inland Voyage*. New-York: Printed by Isaac Riley, 1810. 2 vols.

Schulz, Ellen D. SEE Quillin, Ellen Schulz

Schwalbe, Anna Buxbaum. *Dayspring on the Kuskokwim*. Bethlehem PA: Moravian Press, 1951.

Schwartz, George Melvin and George A. Thiel. *Minnesota's Rocks and Waters*. Rev. ed. Minneapolis MN: Univ. MN Press, c.1963.

Schwartz, Jean. *There's Only One Little Old New York*. Sheet music. New York: Jos. W. Stern, 1910.

Schwatka, Frederick. *Along Alaska's Great River*. New York: Cassell, c.1885.

Schwiebert, Ernest George. *Nymphs*. Guilford CT: Lyons Press, 2007. 2 vols.

Scidmore, Eliza Ruhamah. *Appletons' Guide-Book to Alaska*. New York: D. Appleton, 1896.

Science. Lancaster PA: American Association for the Advancement of Science, 1883–.

Science News. Washington DC: Science Service, 1966–.

Science News Letter. Washington DC: Science Service, 1922–1966.

Scientific American. New York: Munn, 1845–.

Scientific Monthly. Washington DC: American Association for the Advancement of Science, 1915–1957.

Scientific Tracts for the Diffusion of Useful Knowledge. Boston: Light & Stearns, 1836.

Scobee, Barry. *Old Fort Davis*. San Antonio TX: Naylor, c.1947.

Scott, Ann Martin, ed. *Cajun Vernacular English*. Lafayette LA: Technical Writing Laboratory, Dept. of English, Univ. Southwestern LA, 1992.

Scott, Chris. *Endangered and Threatened Animals of Florida and Their Habitats*. Austin TX: Univ. TX Press, c.2004.

Scott, Genio C. *Fishing in American Waters*. New York: Harper & Bros., 1873 [c.1869].

————. *Fishing in American Waters*. New ed. New York: American News, c.1875.

Scott, Henry Lee. *Military Dictionary*. New York: D. Van Nostrand, c.1861.

Scott, James A. *The Butterflies of North America*. Stanford CA: Stanford Univ. Press, 1986.

Scott, John. *Partisan Life with Col. John S. Mosby*. New York: Harper & Bros., 1867.

Scott, Jonathan M. *Blue Lights*. New York: Charles N. Baldwin, 1817.

Scott, Joseph. *Geographer: a Geographical Description of the States of Maryland and Delaware*. Philadelphia: Kimber, Conrad, 1807.

————. *The United States Gazetteer*. Philadelphia: Printed by F. and R. Bailey, 1795.

Scott's Monthly Magazine. Atlanta GA, 1865–1869.

Scribner's Magazine. New York: C. Scribner's Sons, 1887–1939.

Scribner's Monthly. New York, 1870–1881.

Scudder, Samuel Hubbard. *Butterflies*. New York: Henry Holt, 1881.

Seaburg, Carl. *Boston Observed*. Boston: Beacon Press, 1971.

Sealsfield, Charles. *Life in the New World, or, Sketches of American Society*. Transl. from the German by Gustavus C. Hebbe and James Mackay. New York: J. Winchester, New World Press, 1844. Orig. pub. in 1842.

Searcher: an American Notes and Queries. Philadelphia: A. Estoclet, 1895–1896.

Sears, Fred C. *Productive Orcharding*. Philadelphia: Lippincott, c.1914.

Sears, George Washington. *The Adirondack Letters of George Washington Sears Whose Pen Name Was Nessmuk*. Blue Mountain Lake NY: Adirondack Museum, 1962.

————. *Woodcraft*. 12th ed. New York: Field and Stream Publishing, 1900 [c.1888].

Sears, Roebuck and Company. *1897 Sears Roebuck Catalogue*. Ed. by Fred L. Israel. New York: Chelsea House, c.1968.

————. *The 1902 Edition of the Sears Roebuck Catalogue*. With an intro. by Cleveland Amory. New York: Bounty Books, c.1969.

————. *1908 Solid Comfort Vehicles*. Princeton NJ: Pyne Press, 1971. Catalog.

————. *1927 Edition of the Sears, Roebuck Catalogue*. Ed. by Alan Mirken. New York: Bounty Books, c.1970.

————. *Catalogue*. Chicago, 18??–.

Seashore Chronicles. Charlottesville VA: Univ. Press VA, c.1997.

Seattle Daily Times. Seattle WA, 1895–1966.

Seattle Municipal Archives. *Archives Gazette*. 1995–.

Seattle Post-Intelligencer. Seattle WA, 1888–.

Seattle Times. Seattle WA, 1966–.

Seavey, Wendell. *Working the Sea*. Berkeley CA: North Atlantic Books, c.2005.

Seaworthy, Gregory SEE Gregory, James

Seccombe, John. *Father Abbey's Will*. Boston: [s.n.], 1731.

SECOL Review. Murfreesboro TN: Southeastern Conference on Linguistics, 1982–1999.

Secondthoughts, Solomon SEE Kennedy, John Pendleton

Sedalia Daily Democrat. Sedalia MO, 1874–1891.

Sedalia Democrat. Sedalia MO, 1912–.

Sedgwick, Catharine Maria. *Clarence*. Philadelphia: Carey & Lea, 1830. 2 vols.

————. *Redwood*. New-York: E. Bliss and E. White, 1824.

Sedgwick, Susan Anne Livingston. *Allen Prescott*. New York: Harper & Bros., 1834. 2 vols.

Sedley, Henry. *Marian Rooke*. New York: Sheldon, 1865.

Sedman, Yale S. and David F. Hess. *The Butterflies of West Central Illinois*. Macomb IL: Western IL Univ., 1985.

Seed Savers Exchange. Princeton MO, 1975–.

Seed Savers Yearbook. Decorah IA: K. Whealy, 1985–.

Seeman, Elizabeth. *In the Arms of the Mountain*. New York: Crown, c.1961.

Seguin Gazette-Enterprise. Seguin TX, 1979–.

Seibels, William Temple. *Produce Markets and Marketing.* Chicago: Produce Markets and Marketing, c.1911.

Selborne Society. *Nature Notes.* London, 1890–1908.

Select Reviews of Literature. Philadelphia, 1811–1812.

Selekman, Benjamin Morris et al. *Problems in Labor Relations.* 2d ed. New York: McGraw-Hill, 1958.

Semi-Weekly Age. Coshocton OH, 1886–1889.

Semi-Weekly Eagle. Brattleboro VT, 1847–1852.

Senior Scholastic Teachers' Edition. Dayton OH, 1936–1983.

Sentinel. Carlisle PA, 1861–.

Sentinel & Enterprise. Fitchburg MA, 1988–.

Sentinel and Farmer. Milwaukee WI, 1842.

Sequoyah County Times. Sallisaw OK, 1932–.

Serling, Robert J. *The President's Plane Is Missing.* Garden City NY: Doubleday, 1967.

Service, Robert William. *Ploughman of the Moon.* New York: Dodd, Mead, 1945.

———. *Trail of '98.* New York: Dodd, Mead, 1911 [c.1910].

Seton, Ernest Thompson. *The Arctic Prairies.* New York: Charles Scribner's Sons, 1911.

———. *Lives of Game Animals.* Garden City NY: Doubleday, Doran, 1929. 4 vols.

———. *Lives of the Hunted.* New York: Charles Scribner's Sons, 1901.

———. *Trail of an Artist-Naturalist.* New York: Charles Scribner's Sons, 1948 [c.1940].

———. *The Woodcraft Manual for Girls.* Garden City NY: Doubleday, Page, 1916.

Settle, Mary Lee. *O Beulah Land.* New York: Viking Press, 1956.

The Settlement Cook Book. Rev., newly organized, enlarged. New York: Simon and Schuster, 1965.

Settlers of Northeast Alabama. Gadsden AL: Northeast Alabama Genealogical Society, 1972–1976? Reissue of 1962–1975 ed. pub. quarterly by the Society.

Seventeen Letters. 1981. Unpub. letters in response to an article in *Seventeen,* Nov. 1981.

Sevier County Saga. Knoxville TN: Educational Services, 1975.

Sewall, Jonathan Mitchell. *A Parody on Some of the Most Striking Passages in a Late Pamphlet, Entitled "A Letter to a Federalist".* Portsmouth NH: Printed at the Oracle Press, 1805.

Sewall, Joseph Addison. *A Condensed Botany.* Chicago: Geo. Sherwood, c.1872.

Sewall, Samuel. "Diary of Samuel Sewall, 1674–1729." Massachusetts Historical Society *Collections.* (1878–1882) 5th ser., vols. 5–7.

———. *The History of Woburn, Middlesex County, Mass.* Boston: Wiggin and Lunt, 1868.

———. "Letter-Book of Samuel Sewall, 1685–1729." Massachusetts Historical Society *Collections.* (1868–1888) 6th ser., vols. 1, 2.

Sewall, William. *Diary of William Sewall, 1797–1846.* Ed. by John Goodell. Lincoln IL: Printed by Gordon and Feldman, 1930.

Sewanee Review. Sewanee TN: Univ. Press, 1892–.

Seyffert, Kenneth. *Birds of the Shinnery Oak-Grasslands.* [v.d.]. Internet.

Seymour, Edward Loomis Davenport, ed. *The New Garden Encyclopedia.* New York: Wm. H. Wise, 1942 [c.1941].

Seymour, E. S. *Sketches of Minnesota.* New York: Harper & Bros., 1850.

Seymour, Frank Conkling. *Flora of Lincoln County, Wisconsin.* Taunton MA?: Taunton Press?, 1960.

Shackleton, Robert. *The Book of Boston.* Philadelphia: Penn Publishing, 1916.

———. *The Book of Chicago.* Philadelphia: Penn Publishing, 1920.

Shafer, Charles S. *Dictionary of Prison Slang.* 1972. Unpub.

Shafer, Don Cameron. *Smokefires in Schoharie.* New York: Longmans, Green, 1938.

Shakers' Price List of Medicinal Preparations. Mount Lebanon NY: [s.n.], 1874.

Shallenberger, Eliza Jane Hall. *Stark County and Its Pioneers.* Cambridge IL: B. W. Seaton, printer, 1876.

Shamp, Dawn. *On Account of Conspicuous Women.* New York: Thomas Dunne Books, 2008.

Shands, Hubert Anthony. *Some Peculiarities of Speech in Mississippi.* Boston: Norwood Press, J. S. Cushing, 1893.

Shankle, George Earlie. *American Nicknames.* New York: H. W. Wilson, 1937.

———. *American Nicknames, Their Origin and Significance.* New York: H. W. Wilson, 1955.

Shapiro, Nat and Nat Hentoff, eds. *Hear Me Talkin' to Ya.* New York: Rinehart, 1955.

———, eds. *The Jazz Makers.* New York: Grove Press, c.1957.

Sharp, Cecil J. *English Folk Songs from the Southern Appalachians.* London: Oxford Univ. Press, c.1932. 2 vols.

Sharp, Paul F. *Whoop-Up Country.* Minneapolis MN: Univ. MN Press, c.1955.

Sharpe, Grant William and Wenonah Sharpe. *101 Wildflowers of Olympic National Park.* Seattle WA: Univ. WA Press, 1954.

———. *101 Wildflowers of Shenandoah National Park.* Seattle WA: Univ. WA Press, 1958.

Sharples, Ada White. *Alaska Wild Flowers.* Stanford University CA: Stanford Univ. Press, 1938.

Sharsmith, Helen K. *Spring Wildflowers of the San Francisco Bay Region.* Berkeley CA: Univ. CA Press, 1965.

Shattuck, George Burbank, ed. *The Bahama Islands.* Baltimore MD: Johns Hopkins Press; New York: Macmillan, 1905.

Shaw, Arnold. *Dictionary of American Pop/Rock.* New York: Schirmer Books, c.1982.

Shaw, Charles E. and Sheldon Campbell. *Snakes of the American West.* New York: Knopf, 1974.

Shaw, George. *General Zoology.* London: G. Kearsley, 1800–1826. 14 vols.

Shaw, Henry Wheeler. *Josh Billings' Farmer's Allminax for the Year 1871.* New York: G. W. Carleton, 1871 [c.1870].

Shaw, John Robert. *A Narrative of the Life & Travels of John Robert Shaw, the Well-Digger.* Louisville KY: George Fowler, 1930. Orig. pub. in 1807 by Daniel Bradford, Lexington KY.

Shaw, Lloyd. *Cowboy Dances.* Caldwell ID: Caxton Printers, c.1939.

———. *Cowboy Dances.* Rev. ed. Caldwell ID: Caxton Printers, 1949.

———. *The Round Dance Book.* Caldwell ID: Caxton Printers, 1948.

Shaw, Nate. *All God's Dangers.* Comp. by Theodore Rosengarten. New York: Alfred A. Knopf, 1975 [c.1974].

Shay, Frank, comp. *More Pious Friends and Drunken Companions.* New York: Macaulay, c.1928.

Shea, Margaret Mary. *The Gals They Left Behind.* New York: Ives Washburn, c.1944.

Sheboygan County Herald. Sheboygan Falls WI, 1867–1871.

Sheboygan Daily Press. Sheboygan WI, 1907–1911.

Sheboygan Mercury. Sheboygan WI, 1847–1852.

Sheboygan Press. Sheboygan WI, 1907–1921; 1924–.

Sheboygan Press-Telegram. Sheboygan WI, 1921–1924.

Shecut, John L. E. W. *Flora Carolinæensis.* Charleston SC: J. Hoff, 1806.

Sheehan, Edward R. F. *The Governor.* New York: World Publishing, c.1970.

Sheffer, George P., comp. *True Tales of the Clarion River.* Clarion PA: [s.n.], 1933.

Sheidlower, Jesse. *Collection.* 1990–. Unpub. coll. of materials on Amer. slang.

Shelby, Gertrude Mathews and Samuel Gaillard Stoney. *Po' Buckra.* New York: Macmillan, 1930.

Sheldon, George. *A History of Deerfield, Massachusetts.* Greenfield MA: Press of E. A. Hall, 1895–1896. 2 vols.

Sheldon, Hezekiah Spencer. *Documentary History of Suffield.* Springfield MA: Clark W. Bryan, 1879–1888.

Shelton, Jane de Forest. *The Salt-Box House.* New York: Baker and Taylor, c.1900.

Shepard, Alan et al., eds. *Coming to Class: Pedagogy and the Social Class of Teachers.* Portsmouth NH: Boynton/Cook, 1998.

Shepard, Clarence E. *1870 Census, Floyd County, Kentucky.* Dayton OH: Shepard, 1977?

Shepard, Elaine. *Forgive Us Our Press Passes.* Englewood Cliffs NJ: Prentice-Hall, 1962.

Shepard, Odell. *Pedlar's Progress.* Boston: Little, Brown, c.1937.

Shepard, Thomas. *The Clear Sun-Shine of the Gospel Breaking Forth upon the Indians in New-England.* London: Printed by R. Cotes for J. Bellamy, 1648.

Shepardson, Mary and Blodwen Hammond. *The Navajo Mountain Community.* Berkeley CA: Univ. CA Press, 1970.

Shephard, Esther. *Paul Bunyan.* Seattle WA: McNeil Press, c.1924.

Shepherd, William. *Prairie Experiences in Handling Cattle and Sheep.* London: Chapman and Hall, 1884.

Sheppard, Eli SEE Young, Martha

Sheppard, Muriel Early. *Cabins in the Laurel.* Chapel Hill NC: Univ. NC Press, c.1935.

Sherburne, Andrew. *Memoirs of Andrew Sherburne.* Utica NY: William Williams, 1828.

———. *Memoirs of Andrew Sherburne.* 2d ed. enlarged and improved. Providence RI: H. M. Brown, 1831.

Sheridan, Philip Henry. *Personal Memoirs of P. H. Sheridan.* New York: Charles L. Webster, 1888. 2 vols.

Sherman, Mandel and Thomas R. Henry. *Hollow Folk.* Berryville VA: Virginia Book, 1973 [c.1933]. Orig. pub. in 1933 by Thomas Y. Cromwell, New York.

Sherman, Stuart. *The Aztec Two-Step.* New York: Greenberg, 1953.

Sherwood, Adiel. *A Gazetteer of the State of Georgia.* 3d ed. greatly enlarged and improved. Washington City GA: P. Force, 1837.

———. *A Gazetteer of the State of Georgia.* Athens GA: Univ. GA Press, 1939. Facsimile of the 1827 ed. printed by W. Riley, Charleston SC.

Sherwood, Robert Edmund. *Here We Are Again: Recollections of an Old Circus Clown.* Indianapolis IN: Bobbs-Merrill, 1926.

Shetler, Stanwyn G. and Sylvia Stone Orli. *Annotated Checklist of the Vascular Plants of the Washington-Baltimore Area.* Washington DC: National Museum of Natural History Smithsonian, 2002.

Shewmake, Edwin Francis. *English Pronunciation in Virginia.* Davidson? NC: [s.n.], 1927.

Shields, Arthur Randolph. *The Cades Cove Story.* Ed. and designed by Paula A. Degen. Gatlinburg TN: Great Smoky Mountains Natural History Association, c.1977.

Shields, George Oliver, ed. *The Big Game of North America.* Chicago: Rand, McNally, 1890.

———. *Hunting in the Great West.* Chicago: Donohue, Hennebery, c.1883.

Shields, Joseph Dunbar. *The Life and Times of Seargent Smith Prentiss.* Freeport NY: Books for Libraries Press, 1971. Repr. of the 1883 ed. pub. by J. B. Lippincott, Philadelphia.

Shields' Magazine. New York, 1905–1912?

Shillaber, Benjamin Penhallow. *Ike Partington.* Boston: Lee and Shepard, c.1878.

———. *Knitting-Work.* Boston: Brown, Taggard & Chase, 1859.

———. *Life and Sayings of Mrs. Partington, and Others of the Family.* New York: J. C. Derby, 1854.

———. *Partingtonian Patchwork.* Boston: Lee & Shepard; New York: Lee, Shepard, and Dillingham, 1873 [c.1872].

Shimer, Hervey Woodburn. *Origin and Significance of Plant Names.* Hingham MA: South Shore Nature Club, 1943.

Shiner Cactus Nursery. *Illustrated Catalog and Reference Book 1936.* Laredo TX: Shiner Cactus Nursery, 1936.

Shinn, Charles Howard. *Mining-Camps.* New York: Charles Scribner's Sons, 1885.

———. *The Story of the Mine.* New York: D. Appleton, 1901 [c.1896].

Shinn, Josiah Hazen. *Pioneers and Makers of Arkansas.* [s.l.]: Genealogical & Historical Publishing, c.1908.

Shippen, Edward. *Report of the Trial and Acquittal of Edward Shippen, Esquire, Chief Justice, and Jasper Yeates and Thomas Smith, Esquires, Assistant Justices, of the Supreme Court of Pennsylvania, on an Impeachment, before the Senate of the Commonwealth, January, 1805.* Lancaster PA: Printed by the Reporter, 1805.

Ships and the Sea. Milwaukee WI, 1952–1959.

Shirling, Albert E. *Birds of Swope Park in the Heart of America, Kansas City, Mo.* Kansas City MO: McIndoo Publishing, 1920.

Shirreff, Patrick. *A Tour through North America.* Edinburgh: Oliver & Boyd, 1835.

Shivell, Paul. *Ashes of Roses.* Dayton OH: United Brethren Publishing House, 1898.

Shoemaker, Henry Wharton, comp. *Thirteen Hundred Old Time Words . . . Still or Recently in Use among the Pennsylvania Mountain People.* Altoona PA: Times Tribune Press, 1930.

Shoppers' Herald. Stevens Point WI, 1984?–.

Shop Talk. Boston: Hill, Clarke, 1901–1902.

Shore, John. *The Sachertorte Algorithm and Other Antidotes to Computer Anxiety.* New York: Viking, c.1985.

Shores, David L. *Tangier Island.* Newark NJ: Univ. DE Press; London: Associated Univ. Presses, c.2000.

Short Stories: a Magazine of Select Fiction. New York, 1890–1950?

Showalter, Mary Emma. *Mennonite Community Cookbook.* Scottdale PA: Herald Press, c.1957.

Shreve, Forrest et al. *The Plant Life of Maryland.* Baltimore MD: Johns Hopkins Press, 1910.

Shrigley, Nathaniel. *A True Relation of Virginia and Mary-Land.* London: Printed by Tho. Milbourn for Thomas Hodson Book-Binder, 1669.

Shulman, Max. *Barefoot Boy with Cheek.* Garden City NY: Doubleday, Doran, 1943.

———. *The Feather Merchants.* Garden City NY: Doubleday, Doran, 1944.

———. *The Many Loves of Dobie Gillis.* Garden City NY: Garden City Books, 1953.

Shurtleff, William and Akiko Aoyagi. *The Book of Tofu.* Kanagawa-Ken: Autumn Press, c.1975.

Shute, Henry Augustus. *Plupy, the Real Boy.* Boston: Gorham Press, 1911.

———. *Real Boys.* New York: G. W. Dillingham, c.1905.

Siberts, Bruce. *Nothing but Prairie and Sky.* Recorded by Walker D. Wyman from the orig. notes of Bruce Siberts. Norman OK: Univ. OK Press, 1954.

Sibley, George Champlain. "General Sibley's Santa Fe Diary, 1825–1826." In: Hulbert, Archer Butler, ed., *Southwest on the Turquoise Trail,* 1933, 133–74.

Sibley, John Langdon. *A History of the Town of Union, in the County of Lincoln, Maine.* Boston: B. B. Mussey, 1851.

Sider, Gerald M. *Lumbee Indian Histories.* Cambridge: Cambridge Univ. Press, 1993.

Sierra. San Francisco: Sierra Club, 1977–.

Sierra Club. *Bulletin.* San Francisco, 1896–1977.

Sievers, Arthur Frederick. *American Medicinal Plants of Commercial Importance.* Washington DC: Govt. Printing Office, 1930.

Sifton, Elisabeth. *The Serenity Prayer.* New York: Norton, 2005 [c.2003].

Sigler, William F. and Robert Rush Miller. *Fishes of Utah.* Salt Lake City UT: Utah State Dept. of Fish and Game, 1963.

Signal Magazine. Big Spring TX, 1995–.

Sikes, William Wirt. *A Book for the Winter-Evening Fireside.* Watertown NY: Ingalls & Haddock, 1858.

Sikeston Herald. Sikeston MO, 1900–1960.

Silber, Irwin, comp., ed. *Songs of the Civil War.* New York: Columbia Univ. Press, 1960.

Silber, Nina and Mary Beth Sievens, eds. *Yankee Correspondence.* Charlottesville VA: Univ. Press VA, c.1996.

Silberhorn, Gene M. *Loblolly Pine.* Gloucester Point VA, 1993. Tech. Rep. No. 93–3.

Silent Sports. Waupaca WI, 1989–.

Silliman, Benjamin. *A Manual on the Cultivation of the Sugar Cane and the Fabrication and Refinement of Sugar.* Washington DC: F. P. Blair, 1833.

Silloway, Perley Milton. *Sketches of Some Common Birds.* Cincinnati OH: Editor Publishing, 1897.

Silverberg, Robert. *Reflections and Refractions.* Grass Valley CA: Underwood Books, 1997.

Silverberg, Robert and Martin H. Greenberg, eds. *The Arbor House Treasury of Great Science Fiction Short Novels.* New York: Arbor House, 1980.

Silver City Daily Press. Silver City NM, 1963–. Some issues include Frontier Recreation ed.

Silver City Enterprise. Silver City NM, 1882–.

Silver City Press Frontier SEE *Silver City Daily Press*

Silverman, Jerry, ed., arranger. *Folk Blues.* New York: Macmillan, c.1958.

Silverthorne, Elizabeth. *Christmas in Texas.* College Station TX: TX A&M Univ. Press, c.1990.

———. *Legends & Lore of Texas Wildflowers.* College Station TX: TX A&M Univ. Press, c.1996.

Sim, Robert J. *Pages from the Past of Rural New Jersey.* Trenton NJ: New Jersey Agricultural Society, 1949.

Simmonds, Peter Lund. *The Dictionary of Trade Products . . . of All Countries.* London: George Routledge & Sons, 1867?

Simmons, Amelia. *American Cookery.* Hartford CT: Printed for the author by Hudson & Goodwin, 1796.

Simmons, Charles Heath. *Simmons' Norfolk Directory.* Norfolk VA: Augustus C. Jordan, Printer, 1801.

Simmons, Roger Edwin. *Wood-Using Industries of Virginia.* [s.l.]: American Forestry Association, 1912.

Simmons, William Hayne. *Notices of East Florida, with an Account of the Seminole Nation of Indians.* Charleston SC: A. E. Miller, 1822.

Simms, Jeptha Root. *History of Schoharie County.* Albany NY: Munsell & Tanner, 1845.

Simms, William Gilmore. *Border Beagles.* Philadelphia: Carey and Hart, 1840 [c.1839]. 2 vols.

———. *Charlemont.* New York: Redfield, 1856.

———. *Eutaw.* New York: W. J. Widdleton, 1856.

———. *The Forayers.* New York: W. J. Widdleton, c.1855.

———. *Guy Rivers.* New York: Harper & Bros., 1834. 2 vols.

———. *Martin Faber.* New York: Arno Press, 1976. 2 vols. Repr. of 1837 ed. pub. by Harper & Bros., New York.

———. *Mellichampe.* New York: Harper & Bros., 1836. 2 vols.

———. *The Partisan: a Romance of the Revolution.* New and rev. ed. Chicago: Donohue, Henneberry, 1890. Orig. pub. in 1853 by Redfield, New York.

———. *The Partisan: a Tale of the Revolution.* New York: Harper & Bros., 1835. 2 vols.

———. *The Scout.* New and rev. ed. New York: W. J. Widdleton, c.1854.

———. *Southward Ho!* New York: Redfield, 1854.

———. *The Sword and the Distaff.* Philadelphia: Lippincott, Grambo, 1853.

———. *The Wigwam and the Cabin.* 1st ser. Ridgewood NJ: Gregg Press, c.1968. Orig. pub. in 1845 by Wiley and Putnam, New York.

———. *The Wigwam and the Cabin.* 2d ser. Charleston SC: Walker, Richards, 1852. Orig. pub. in 1845 by Wiley and Putnam, New York.

———. *Woodcraft.* New York: Redfield, 1854.

———. *The Yemassee. A Romance of Carolina.* New York: Harper & Bros., 1843 [c.1835]. 2 vols. Orig. pub. in 1835.

Simpson, Bland. *The Great Dismal.* Chapel Hill NC: Univ. NC Press, c.1990.

Simpson, Claude and Catherine Simpson. *North of the Narrows, Men and Women of the Upper Priest Lake Country, Idaho.* Moscow ID: Univ. Press ID, c.1981.

Simpson, J. A. and E. S. C. Weiner. *The Oxford English Dictionary.* 2d ed. Oxford: Clarendon Press, 1991. 20 vols.

Simpson, Mona. *A Regular Guy.* New York: Alfred A. Knopf, c.1996.

Sinclair, Bertha. *Chip, of the Flying U.* New York: Grosset & Dunlap, 1906.

———. *Flying U Ranch.* New York: Grosset & Dunlap, 1914 [c.1912].

———. *Flying U's Last Stand.* Boston: Little, Brown, 1915.

———. *The Lure of Dim Trails.* New York: G. W. Dillingham, c.1907.

———. *The Parowan Bonanza.* Boston: Little, Brown, 1923.

———. *The Phantom Herd.* New York: Grosset & Dunlap, c.1916.

Sinclair, Ellery. *Christie's Choice.* New York: Thomas R. Knox, 1886.

Sinclair, Upton. *The Jungle.* New York: Jungle Publishing, 1906 [c.1905].

———. *King Coal.* New York: Macmillan, 1917.

———. *The Metropolis.* London: T. Werner Laurie, c.1908.

Singleton, Arthur SEE Knight, Henry Cogswell

Singleton, Esther. *Social New York under the Georges, 1714–1776.* New York: D. Appleton, 1902.

Sioux City Journal. Sioux City IA, 1887–.

Sioux County Capital. Orange City IA, 1935–1951.

Sioux Valley News. Correctionville IA, 1880–1909.

Siringo, Charles A. *Riata and Spurs.* Rev. ed. Boston: Houghton Mifflin, c.1927.

———. *A Texas Cow-Boy.* Chicago: M. Umbdenstock, 1885.

Sitton, Thad, ed. *Harder than Hardscrabble.* Austin TX: Univ. TX Press, 2003.

Sitton, Thad and Dan K. Utley. *From Can* SEE *to Can't.* Austin TX: Univ. TX Press, 1997.

Skandinavisk-Amerikansk Kogebog. Chicago: Chr. Treiders Forlag, 1880.

Sketches and Eccentricities of Col. David Crockett. New ed. New-York: J. & J. Harper, 1833.

Skidmore, Hubert. *Hawk's Nest.* New York: Doubleday, Doran, 1941.

Skinner, John R. *History of the Fourth Illinois Volunteers in Their Relation to the Spanish-American War.* Logansport IN: Wilson, Humphreys, c.1899.

Skinner, Milton Philo. *A Guide to the Winter Birds of the North Carolina Sandhills.* Albany NY: Science Press, 1928.

Skinner, Stephano. *Etymologicon Linguae Anglicanae, seu Explicatio Vocum Anglicarum Etymologica ex Propriis Fontibus.* Londini: T. Roycroft, and H. Brome, 1671 [c.1668].

Skit SEE Taliaferro, Harden E.

Skolnik, Peter L. *Jump Rope!* New York: Workman Publishing, c.1974.

Slick, Jonathan SEE Stephens, Ann Sophia

Slingerland, Mark Vernon and Cyrus Richard Crosby. *Manual of Fruit Insects.* New York: Macmillan, 1919 [c.1914].

Sloan, Dave U. *Fogy Days.* Atlanta GA: Foote & Davies, 1891.

Sloane, Eric. *An Age of Barns.* New York: Funk & Wagnalls, c.1967.

———. *A Museum of Early American Tools.* New York: Ballantine Books, 1974 [c.1964].

———. *A Reverence for Wood.* New York: Ballantine Books, 1975 [c.1965].

Sloane, Hans. *Catalogus Plantarum quae in Insula Jamaica Sponte Proveniunt.* London: D. Brown, 1696.

———. *A Voyage to the Islands Madera, Barbados, Nieves, S. Christophers and Jamaica.* London: Printed by B. M. for the author, 1707–1725. 2 vols.

Slone, Verna Mae. *How We Talked.* Pippa Passes KY: Pippa Valley Printing, c.1982.

Slosson, Annie Trumbull. *The China Hunters Club.* New York: Harper & Bros., 1878.

Small, John Kunkel. *Ferns of the Southeastern States.* Lancaster PA: Science Press Printing, 1938.

———. *Flora of the Florida Keys.* New York: Published by the author, 1913.

———. *Flora of the Southeastern United States.* New York: The Author, 1903.

———. *Florida Trees.* New York: Published by the author, 1913.

———. *Manual of the Southeastern Flora.* New York: The Author, 1933.

Smart Set: a Magazine of Cleverness. New York, 1900–1930.

Smedes, Susan Dabney. *Memorials of a Southern Planter.* 2d ed. Baltimore MD: Cushings & Bailey, 1888 [c.1887].

Smet, Pierre Jean de. *Oregon Missions and Travels over the Rocky Mountains in 1845–46.* Fairfield WA: Ye Galleon Press, 1978. Repr. of the 1847 ed. pub. by E. Dunigan, New York.

Smiley, Daniel. *Glossary of Words Used in New Paltz, N.Y. 1930–1953.* Unpub.

Smiley, Frank Jason. *Weeds of California and Methods of Control.* Sacramento CA: California State Print. Off., 1922.

Smiley, Jack. *Hash House Lingo.* Easton PA: The Author, 1941.

Smith, Abigail Adams. *Journal and Correspondence of Miss Adams, Daughter of John Adams, Second President of the United States.* Ed. by Caroline Amelia Smith De Windt. New York: Wiley and Putnam, 1841–1842. 2 vols.

Smith, Alexander Hanchett. *A Field Guide to Western Mushrooms.* Ann Arbor MI: Univ. MI Press, c.1975.

———. *The Mushroom Hunter's Field Guide.* Ann Arbor MI: Univ. MI Press, c.1958.

Smith, Alexander H. and Nancy Smith Weber. *The Mushroom Hunter's Field Guide.* Ann Arbor MI: Univ. MI Press, c.1980.

Smith, Alice Ravenal Huger and Herbert Ravenal Sass. *A Carolina Rice Plantation of the Fifties.* New York: W. Morrow, 1936.

Smith, Charles Frederick. *Games and Game Leadership.* New York: Dodd, Mead, 1953 [c.1932].

Smith, Charles Henry. *Bill Arp.* Atlanta GA: Byrd Printing, 1903 [c.1902].

———. *Bill Arp, So Called.* New York: Metropolitan Record Office, 1866.

———. *Bill Arp's Peace Papers.* New York: G. W. Carleton; London: S. Low, Son, 1873.

———. *Bill Arp's Peace Papers.* Upper Saddle River NJ: Literature House/Gregg Press, 1969. Facsimile of the 1873 ed. pub. by G. W. Carleton, New York.

———. *Bill Arp's Scrap Book.* Atlanta GA: J. P. Harrison, 1884.

———. *The Farm and the Fireside.* Atlanta GA: Constitution Pub., 1892.

Smith, Cornelius Cole. *A Southwestern Vocabulary.* Glendale CA: Arthur H. Clark, 1984.

Smith, Dama Margaret. *Hopi Girl.* Stanford CA: Stanford Univ. Press, 1931.

Smith, Dean. *The Great Arizona Almanac.* Portland OR: WestWinds Press, 2000.

Smith, De Cost. *Martyrs of the Oblong and Little Nine.* Caldwell ID: Caxton Printers, 1948.

Smith, Edward. *Account of a Journey through Northeastern Texas, Undertaken in 1849.* London: Hamilton, Adams, 1849.

Smith, E. Linwood. *Established Natural Areas in Arizona.* Phoenix AZ: Office of the Governor, 1974.

Smith, Elizabeth Oakes Prince. *Bertha and Lily.* New York: J. C. Derby, 1854.

Smith, Elmer Lewis et al. *The Pennsylvania Germans of the Shenandoah Valley.* Allentown PA: Pennsylvania German Folklore Society, 1964.

Smith, Emory Evans. *The Golden Poppy.* Palo Alto CA: Murdock Press, 1902.

Smith, Ersa Rhea Noland. *Flyin' Bullets and the Resplendent Badge.* Sevierville TN: Nandel, c.1989.

Smith, Eugene Allen. *Report for the Years 1881 and 1882, Embracing an Account of the Agricultural Features of the State.* Montgomery AL: W. D. Brown, 1883.

Smith, Francis Hopkinson. *Caleb West, Master Diver.* New York: Grosset & Dunlap, c.1898.

———. *A Day at Laguerre's and Other Days.* Boston: Houghton, Mifflin, 1892.

Smith, Frank Berkeley. *How Paris Amuses Itself.* New York: Funk & Wagnalls, c.1903.

Smith, Frank Ellis. *The Yazoo River.* New York: Rinehart, 1954.

Smith, Genny, ed. *Sierra East.* Berkeley CA: Univ. CA Press, 2000.

Smith, George. *History of Delaware County, Pennsylvania.* Philadelphia: Printed by Henry B. Ashmead, 1862.

Smith, George Gilman. *The Life and Times of George Foster Pierce.* Sparta GA: Hancock Publishing, 1888.

Smith, Harriet L. *Wonderful Wappato.* Lake Oswego OR: Smith, Smith and Smith, c.1976.

Smith, Harry Allen. *Life in a Putty Knife Factory.* Garden City NY: Doubleday, Doran, 1945 [c.1943].

Smith, Harvey. *The Gang's All Here.* Princeton NJ: Princeton Univ. Press, c.1941.

Smith, Helen Vandervort. *Michigan Wildflowers.* Bloomfield Hills MI: Cranbrook Institute of Science, 1961.

Smith, Henry M. *List of Medicines Mentioned in Homoeopathic Literature.* New York: Smith's Homoeopathic Pharmacy, 1879.

Smith, Hilton Altmore and Thomas Carlyle Jones. *Veterinary Pathology.* Philadelphia: Lea & Febiger, 1957.

Smith, Hobart Muir. *Handbook of Lizards.* Ithaca NY: Comstock Pub., 1946.

Smith, Horatio. *Festivals, Games, and Amusements.* New York: Harper & Bros., 1858. Orig. pub. in 1831 by Harpers.

Smith, Hugh McCormick. *The Fishes of North Carolina.* Raleigh NC: E. M. Uzzell, 1907.

Smith, Huron S. *Ethnobotany of the Menomini Indians.* Milwaukee WI: Board of Trustees, Milwaukee Public Museum, 1923.

Smith, James. *An Account of the Remarkable Occurrences in the Life and Travels of Col. James Smith.* Lexington KY: John Bradford, 1799.

Smith, James Edward. *The Natural History of the Rarer Lepidopterous Insects of Georgia.* London: Printed by T. Bensley for J. Edwards, 1797. 2 vols.

———, comp. *A Selection of the Correspondence of Linnaeus and Other Naturalists.* London: Longman, Hurst, Rees, Orme, and Brown, 1821.

Smith, Jedediah Strong. *The Travels of Jedediah Smith.* Ed. by Maurice S. Sullivan. Santa Ana CA: Fine Arts Press, 1934.

Smith, Jerome V. C. *Natural History of the Fishes of Massachusetts.* Boston: Allen & Ticknor, c.1833.

Smith, Jerry C. *Understanding and Speaking the Southern Language.* Pell City AL: Jerry C. Smith, c.1990.

Smith, John. *An Accidence.* London: Printed for Jonas Man and Benjamin Fisher, 1626.

———. *A Description of New-England.* London: Printed for Humphrey Lownes for Robert Clerke, 1616.

———. *The Generall Historie of Virginia.* London: Printed by I. D and I. H for M. Sparkes, 1624.

———. *A Map of Virginia.* Oxford: Printed by Joseph Barnes, 1612.

———. *Travels and Works of Captain John Smith.* Edinburgh: John Grant, 1910. 2 vols.

———. *A True Relation of Such Occurences in Virginia.* London: Printed for Iohn Tappe, 1608.

———. *The True Travels, Adventures, and Observations of Captaine John Smith.* London: Printed for J. H. for Thomas Slater, 1630.

Smith, John Bernhard. *Economic Entomology.* Philadelphia: J. B. Lippincott, 1896.

———. *Our Insect Friends and Enemies.* Philadelphia: J. B. Lippincott, 1909.

Smith, Johnston. SEE Crane, Stephen

Smith, Joseph Edward Adams. *Taghconic; the Romance and Beauty of the Hills.* Boston: Lee and Shepard, 1879.

Smith, J. Robert and Beatrice S. Smith. *The Prairie Garden.* Madison WI: Univ. WI Press, c.1980.

Smith, Lee. *Fair and Tender Ladies.* New York: G. P. Putnam's Sons, 1988.

Smith, Lillian Eugenia. *Strange Fruit.* New York: Reynal & Hitchcock, c.1944.

Smith, Margaret Bayard. *The First Forty Years of Washington Society.* New York: Charles Scribner's Sons, 1906.

———. *A Winter in Washington.* New York: E. Bliss & E. White, 1824. 2 vols.

Smith, Marian Wesley. *The Puyallup-Nisqually.* New York: Columbia Univ. Press, 1940.

Smith, Martha L. *Going to God's Country.* Boston: Christopher Publishing House, c.1941.

Smith, Matthew Hale. *Marvels of Prayer.* New York: Evangelical Publishing, c.1875.

———. *Twenty Years among the Bulls and Bears of Wall Street.* Hartford CT: J. B. Burr, 1870.

Smith, Nancy W. Paine. *Our Heritage.* Provincetown MA: Billy May, 1930.

Smith, Nora Archibald. *Kate Douglas Wiggin as Her Sister Knew Her.* Boston: Houghton Mifflin, 1925.

Smith, Oliver Hampton. *Early Indiana Trials.* Cincinnati OH: Moore, Wilstach, Keys, 1858 [c.1857].

Smith, Onnie Warren. *Casting Tackle and Methods.* Cincinnati OH: Stewart & Kidd, c.1920.

Smith, Patrick D. *A Land Remembered.* Englewood FL: Pineapple Press, c.1984.

Smith, Peter. *The Indian Doctor's Dispensatory.* Cincinnati OH: Printed by Browne and Looker for the author, 1813.

———. *The Indian Doctor's Dispensatory.* Cincinnati OH: J. U. & C. G. Lloyd, 1901. Repr. of 1813 ed. pub. by Browne & Looker, Cincinnati OH.

Smith, Philip H. *General History of Duchess County, from 1609 to 1876, Inclusive.* Pawling NY: Published by the Author, c.1877.

Smith, Reed. *Gullah.* Columbia SC: Univ. SC, 1926.

Smith, Richard. *A Tour of Four Great Rivers . . . in 1769.* New York: Charles Scribner's Sons, 1906.

Smith, Richard M. *Wild Plants of America.* New York: Wiley Nature, c.1989.

Smith, Richard Penn. *Col. Crockett's Exploits and Adventures in Texas.* Philadelphia: T. K. and P. G. Collins, 1836.

———, presumed author. *Col. Crockett's Exploits and Adventures in Texas.* London: R. Kennett, 1837.

Smith, Robert Miller. *Baseball.* New York: Simon & Schuster, 1947.

Smith, Robert Paul. *How to Do Nothing with Nobody All Alone by Yourself.* New York: W. W. Norton, c.1958.

Smith, Seba. *Life and Writings of Major Jack Downing of Downingville.* Boston: Lilly, Wait, Colman, & Holden, 1833.

———. *The Life and Writings of Major Jack Downing of Downingville.* 3d ed. Boston: Lilly, Wait, Colman, & Holden, 1834.

———. *My Thirty Years Out of the Senate.* New York: Oaksmith, 1859.

———. *The Select Letters of Major Jack Downing.* Philadelphia: Printed for the Publisher, 1834.

———. *'Way Down East.* New York: J. C. Derby; Boston: Phillips, Sampson, 1854.

Smith, Solomon Franklin. *Theatrical Management in the West and South, for Thirty Years.* New York: Harper & Bros., 1868.

Smith, Thomas. *Extracts from the Journals Kept by the Rev. Thomas Smith . . . from 1720 to . . . 1788.* Ed. by Samuel Freeman. Portland ME: Printed by Thomas Todd, 1821.

———. *Journals of the Rev. Thomas Smith, and the Rev. Samuel Deane, Pastors of the First Church in Portland.* 2d ed. Portland ME: J. S. Bailey, 1849.

Smith, Thomas Marshall. *Legends of the War of Independence, and of the Earliest Settlements of the West.* Louisville KY: J. F. Brennan, 1855.

Smith, W. H. *Catalogue of the Reptilia and Amphibia of Michigan.* [s.l.]: [s.n.], 1879.

Smith, Wilbur C., comp. *Wilbur's Tales.* Monroe TN: Wilbur C. Smith, 1986.

Smith, Wilfred Robert. *Under the Northern Lights.* Portland OR: Columbia Printing, c.1916.

Smith, William B. *On Wheels and How I Came There.* Ed. by Rev. Joseph Gatch Bonnell. New York: Eaton & Mains; Cincinnati OH: Curts & Jennings, c.1892.

Smith, Zachariah Frederick. *The History of Kentucky.* Louisville KY: Courier-Journal Job Printing, 1886.

Smith College Monthly. Northampton MA: Smith College, 1893–1943.

Smith College Studies in History. Northampton MA, 1915–.

Smith County Pioneer. Smith Center KS, 1872–.

Smitherman, Geneva. *Black Talk.* Boston: Houghton Mifflin, 1994.

———. *Talkin and Testifyin.* Boston: Houghton Mifflin, 1977.

Smithfield Times. Smithfield VA, 1920–.

Smithsonian. Washington DC: Smithsonian Associates, 1970–.

Smithsonian American Art Museum. [v.d.]. Internet.

Smithsonian Institution. *Annual Report of the Board of Regents.* Washington DC: Govt. Printing Office, 1846–1964.

———. *Smithsonian Contributions to Knowledge.* Washington DC, 1848–1916.

———. *Smithsonian Miscellaneous Collections.* Washington DC, 1862–.

Smithsonian Institution. Bureau of Ethnology. *Bulletin.* Washington DC: Govt. Printing Office, 1903–1971.

Smithsonian Letters. 1982. Unpub. letters in response to an article in the *Smithsonian,* April 1982.

Smithtown, New York. *Records of the Town of Smithtown, Long Island, N.Y., with Other Ancient Documents of Historic Value.* Notes and intro. by William S. Pelletreau. Huntington NY: Long-Islander, 1898.

Smithwick, Noah. *The Evolution of a State.* Austin TX: Gammel Book, c.1900.

Smoke Signals. Pinedale WY, 1952–1954.

Smoky Mountain News. Waynesville NC, 1990?–.

Smoky Mountain Traveler. Souvenir ed. Pigeon Forge TN: [s.n.], 1981.

Smull's Legislative Hand Book. Harrisburg PA, 1876–1887.

Smyth, John Ferdinand Dalziel. *Tour in the United States of America.* London: For G. Robinson, 1784. 2 vols.

Smyth, William Henry. *The Sailor's Word-Book.* London: Blackie & Son, 1867.

Snapp, Roscoe R. *Beef Cattle.* New York: John Wiley & Sons; London: Chapman & Hall, 1925.

SND SEE Grant, William *The Scottish National Dictionary*

Snead, Rayner V. *Hollow Boy.* 2d ed. Washington VA: Rayner V. Snead, 1995 [c.1994].

Snedigar, Robert. *Our Small and Native Animals.* Rev. and enlarged ed. New York: Dover Publications, 1963.

Snell, Alma Hogan. *A Taste of Heritage.* Ed. by Lisa Castle. Lincoln NE: Univ. NE Press, 2006.

Snell, Foster Dee and Cornelia Tyler Snell. *Chemicals of Commerce.* New York: D. Van Nostrand, 1939.

Sneller, Anne Gertrude. *A Vanished World.* Syracuse NY: Syracuse Univ. Press, 1964.

Snowden, Yates and John Bennett. *Two Scholarly Friends: Yates Snowden-John Bennett Correspondence, 1902–1932.* Ed. by Mary Crow Anderson. Columbia SC: Univ. SC Press, c.1993.

Snowflake Herald. Snowflake AZ, 1913–.

Snyder, Zilpha Keatley. *The Velvet Room.* New York: Atheneum, 1965.

Social Forces. Chapel Hill NC: Univ. NC Press, 1922–.

Social Process. Honolulu HI: Univ. HI Press, 1935–1964.

Society for Pure English. *S. P. E. Tract 1–66.* London, 1919–1946.

Society for the Promotion of Agricultural Science. *Proceedings of the . . . Annual Meeting.* Syracuse NY, 1880–1920.

Society for the Promotion of Useful Arts. *Transactions.* Albany NY, 1792–1819.

Society of American Foresters. *Forestry Terminology.* Washington DC: The Society, 1944.

———. *Proceedings.* Washington DC, 1905–1916.

Society of California Pioneers. *Quarterly.* San Francisco, 1924–1933.

Sociological Quarterly. Columbia MO, 1960–.

Soda Springs Chieftain. Soda Springs ID, 1900–1932.

Soda Springs Sun. Soda Springs ID, 1931–1955.

Solomon, Jack and Olivia Solomon, comps. *Cracklin Bread and Asfidity.* University AL: Univ. AL Press, c.1979.

Some Correspondence between the Governors and Treasurers of the New England Company in London and the Commissioners of the United Colonies in America. London: Spottiswood, 1896.

Somerby, Frederic Thomas. *Hits and Dashes.* Boston: Bedding, 1852.

Somers, Robert. *The Southern States since the War, 1870–1.* London: Macmillan, 1871.

Something. Boston, 1809–1810. Ed. by Nemo Nobody, Esq.

Songs of Love and Liberty. Comp. by a North Carolina Lady. Chapel Hill NC: Academic Affairs Library, Univ. NC at Chapel Hill, 2000. Text transcr. for *Documenting the American South* website from the 1864 ed. pub. by Branson & Farrar, Raleigh NC.

The Sopranos. Television program. 1999–2007.

Sorden, Leland George. *Lumberjack Lingo.* Spring Green WI: Wisconsin House, c.1969.

Sorden, Leland George and Isabel J. Ebert. *Logger's Words of Yesteryears.* Madison WI: L. G. Sorden, c.1956.

Soule, Richard and Loomis J. Campbell. *Pronouncing Handbook.* Boston: Lee & Shepard; New York: Lee, Shepard & Dillingham, c.1873.

Souljah, Sister. *The Coldest Winter Ever.* New York: Atria Books, 2004 [c.1999].

Southampton, New York. *Records of the Town of Southampton.* Sag-Harbor NY: J. H. Hunt, 1874–1915. 6 vols.

South Atlantic Quarterly. Durham NC, 1902–.

South Bend Tribune. South Bend IN, 1902–.

South Carolina (Colony). *Documents Relating to Indian Affairs, May 21, 1750–Aug. 7, 1754.* Columbia SC: Archives Dept., 1958–1970. 2 vols.

South Carolina. Constitutional Court of Appeals. *Reports of Cases Determined in the Constitutional Court of South Carolina.* Columbia SC: Daniel Faust, State Printer, 1822–1830. 4 vols.

South Carolina. Court of Appeals. *Reports of Cases at Law.* Charleston SC: McCarter, 1845–1869. 15 vols.

South Carolina Experiment Stations. *Annual Report.* Columbia SC, 1888–1890.

South Carolina. Forestry Commission. *Come and Visit Your Sand Hills State Forest.* Columbia SC?, [n.d.]. Pamphlet.

South-Carolina Gazette. Charleston SC, 1732–1775.

South Carolina Gazette and Country Journal. Charleston SC, 1765–1775.

South Carolina Historical Magazine. Charleston SC: South Carolina Historical Society, 1900–.

South Carolina Historical Society. *Collections.* Charleston SC, 1857–1897.

South Carolina. Laws, Statutes etc. *Statutes at Large of South Carolina.* Columbia SC: A. S. Johnston, 1836–1898.

South Carolina Market Bulletin. Columbia SC: Dept. of Agriculture, 19??–.

South Carolina River News. Columbia SC, 1983–.

South Carolina. State Board of Agriculture. *South Carolina Resources and Population, Institutions and Industries.* Charleston SC: Walker, Evans & Cogswell, 1883.

South Carolina Wildlife. Columbia SC: Wildlife Resources Dept., 1954–.

SouthCoastToday. 1990?–. Internet.

South Dakota Agricultural Experiment Station. *Bulletin.* Brookings SD, 1887–1907?

South Dakota Conservation Digest. Pierre SD, 1934?–.

South Dakota Geological Survey. *Bulletin.* Sioux Falls SD, 1894–.

South Dakotan. Mitchell SD, 1898–1904.

Southeastern Association of Game and Fish Commissioners. *Proceedings of the Annual Conference.* Columbia SC, 1956–1976.

Southeastern Log. Ketchikan AK, 1971–1989.

Southeastern Reporter. St. Paul MN: West Publishing, 1887–1939.

Southeastern Wildlife Cookbook. Columbia SC: Univ. SC Press, c.1989.

Southern, Eileen. *The Music of Black Americans.* New York: W. W. Norton, c.1971.

Southern Agriculturist. Charleston SC, 1828–1839.

Southern Bivouac. Louisville KY, 1882–1887.

Southern Botanic Journal. Charleston SC, 1837–1846.

Southern California Academy of Sciences. *Bulletin.* Los Angeles, 1902–.

Southern California Quarterly. Los Angeles: Historical Society of Southern California, 1949–.

Southern Churchman. Richmond VA, 1835–1952.

Southern Cultivator. Atlanta GA: Constitution Pub. 1843–1935.

Southern Cultures. Chapel Hill NC: Univ. NC Press for the Ctr. for the Study of the Amer. South, 1994–.

Southern Field and Fireside. Augusta GA, 1859–1865.

Southern Folklore Quarterly. Jacksonville FL, 1937–.

Southern Historical Magazine. Charleston WV: V. A. Lewis, 1892.

Southern Historical Society. *Papers.* Richmond VA, 1876–1959.

Southern Illinoisan. Carbondale IL, 1953–.

Southern Literary Journal. Charleston SC: J. S. Burges, 1835–1837.

Southern Literary Messenger. Richmond VA: T. W. White, 1834–1864.

Southern Living. Birmingham AL, 1966–.

Southern Medical Record. Atlanta GA, 1873–1899.

Southern Patriot. Charleston SC, 1825–1848?

Southern Planter. Richmond VA, 1841–1867; 1882–1906?

Southern Practitioner. Nashville TN, 1879–1918.

Southern Quarterly Review. New Orleans LA, 1842–1857.

Southern Register. University MS: Univ. MS, Center for the Study of Southern Culture, 1981–.

Southern Reporter. St. Paul: West Pub., 1887–1941.

Southern Review. Baltimore MD: Bledsore & Browne, 1867–1879.

Southern Review. Baton Rouge LA, 1935–.

Southern Sierran. Los Angeles: Angeles Chapter of the Sierra Club, 1934–.

Southern Speech Journal. Jacksonville FL: Southern Speech Association, 1942–1971.

Southern Telephone News. Atlanta GA: Southern Bell Telephone and Telegraph, 1913?–1970.

Southern Workman. Hampton VA: Hampton Institute, 1872–1939.

South Florida Sun-Sentinel. Fort Lauderdale FL, 2000–.

South Florida Water Management District. *DuPuis Management Area General Management Plan.* 2003. Internet.

South Jersey Republican. Hammonton NJ, 1863–1923.

Southold, New York. *Southold Town Records.* New York: S. W. Green's Son, printer, 1882–1884. 2 vols.

Southtown Economist. Chicago, 1931–1958.

Southtown Economist. South Beverly ed. Chicago, 1958–1972?

Southwestern Historical Quarterly. Austin TX: Texas State Historical Society, 1897–.

Southwestern Journal of Anthropology. Albuquerque NM: Univ. NM Press, 1945–.

South-Western Monthly. Nashville TN, 1852.

Southwestern Naturalist. Dallas TX: Southwestern Association of Naturalists, 1956–2004.

Southwestern Reporter. St. Paul MN: West Publishing, 1887–1928.

Southwest Review. Dallas TX, 1915–.

Southworth, Emma Dorothy Eliza Nevitte. *The Deserted Wife.* New York: D. Appleton, 1850.

———. *The Discarded Daughter.* Philadelphia: Hart, 1852. 2 vols.

———. *Ishmael, or, in the Depths.* Philadelphia: T. B. Peterson & Bros., 1876.

———, ed. *The Mystery of Dark Hollow.* Philadelphia: T. B. Peterson & Bros., c.1875.

———. *Self-Raised.* Philadelphia: T. B. Peterson & Bros., c.1876.

———. *Vivia.* Philadelphia: T. B. Peterson, c.1857.

———. *Winny Darling.* London: W. Nicholson & Sons, 1857?

Sou'wester. Raymond WA: Pacific County Historical Society and Museum, 1966–.

Spafford, Horatio Gates. *A Gazetteer of the State of New York.* Albany NY: Printed and published by H. C. Southwick, 1813.

Spalding, Albert Goodwill. *America's National Game.* New York: American Sports Publishing, 1911.

Sparano, Vin T. *Complete Outdoors Encyclopedia.* New York: Harper & Row, 1972.

Sparks, Jared, ed. *Correspondence of the American Revolution.* Boston: Little, Brown, 1853. 4 vols.

———. *The Life of Gouverneur Morris, with Selections from His Correspondence and Miscellaneous Papers.* Boston: Gray & Bowen, 1832 [c.1831].

Sparks, William Henry. *The Memories of Fifty Years.* Philadelphia: Claxton, Remsen & Haffelfinger, 1870.

Spear, Mary A. *Leaves and Flowers.* Boston: D. C. Heath, 1893 [c.1892].

Spears, Richard A. *Slang and Euphemism.* Middle Village NY: Jonathan David, c.1981.

Speck, Frank Gouldsmith. *The Nanticoke Community of Delaware.* New York: Museum of the American Indian, Heye Foundation, 1915.

Speed, Thomas. *The Wilderness Road.* New York: Burt Franklin, 1971.

Speek, Peter Alexander. *A Stake in the Land.* New York: Harper & Bros., 1921.

Spellenberg, Richard. *The Audubon Society Field Guide to North American Wildflowers, Western Region.* New York: Alfred A. Knopf, c.1979.

Spencer, Edwin Rollin. *All About Weeds.* New York: Dover, 1974 [c.1957].

———. *Just Weeds.* New York: Charles Scribner's Sons, 1940.

SPE Tract SEE Society for Pure English *S. P. E. Tract 1–66*

Spier, Leslie. *Klamath Ethnography.* Berkeley CA: Univ. CA Press, 1930.

Spillane, Frank Morrison. *The Big Kill.* New York: Dutton, 1951.

Spindrift SEE Tooné, Eruera

Spinelli, Jerry. *Dump Days.* Boston: Little, Brown, c.1988.

Spinner. New Bedford MA, 1981–.

Spirit Lake Beacon. Spirit Lake IA, 1870–1983.

Spirit of the Age. Sacramento CA, 1855–1856.

The Spirit of the Farmers' Museum and Lay Preacher's Gazette. Walpole NH: Printed for Thomas & Thomas by D. & T. Carlisle, 1801.

Spirit of the Public Journals. Baltimore MD: Printed by Geo. Dobbin & Murphy, 1806.

The Spirit of the Public Journals. New York: Arno and the New York Times, 1970. Repr. of the 1806 ed. pub. by Geo. Dobbin & Murphy, Baltimore MD.

Spirit of the Times. New York, 1831–1861; 1868–1892.

Spirit of the Times and the New York Sportsman SEE *Wilkes' Spirit of the Times*

Splint, Sarah Field. *The Art of Cooking and Serving.* Cincinnati OH: Procter & Gamble, c.1930.

Spofford, Harriet Elizabeth Prescott. *Stepping-Stones to Happiness.* New York: Christian Herald, 1897.

Spokesman-Review. Spokane WA, 1894–.

Sporting Magazine. London: Rogerson & Tuxford, 1792–1817.

Sports Afield. Denver CO, 1888–.

Sports Illustrated. Chicago, 1954–.

Sportsman. New York: Male Publishing, 1953–1965.

Sprague, Clarence Edwin. *Eddies.* Fulton IN?: [s.n.], 1905.

Sprague, Horace. *Gloversville.* Gloversville NY: William H. Case, 1859.

Springer, John S. *Forest Life and Forest Trees.* New York: Harper & Bros., 1851.

———. *Forest Life and Forest Trees.* New York: Harper & Bros., 1856. Orig. pub. in 1851.

Springfield, Massachusetts. *The First Century of the History of Springfield: the Official Records from 1636 to 1736.* Springfield MA: Henry M. Burt, 1898–1899. 2 vols.

Springfield Daily Republican. Springfield MA, 1851–1946.

Springfield News-Leader. Springfield MO, 1999–.

Springfield Sunday Republican. Springfield MA, 1879–.

Springfield Union. Springfield MA, 1896–.

Sproat, Gilbert Malcolm. *Scenes and Studies of Savage Life.* London: Smith, Elder, 1868.

Sprunt, Alexander. *Florida Bird Life.* New York: Coward-McCann, and the National Audubon Society, c.1954.

Sprunt, Alexander and Edward Burnham Chamberlain. *South Carolina Bird Life.* Columbia SC: Univ. SC Press, 1949.

Spurr, Josiah Edward. *Through the Yukon Gold Diggings.* Boston: Eastern Publishing, 1900.

Squier, Ephraim George. *Waikna.* New York: Harper & Bros., 1855.

Stabenow, Dana. *Midnight Come Again.* New York: St. Martin's, 2001 [c.2000].

Stacy, L. E., comp. *The Blue Book, Containing Photographs and Sketches of a Few Commercial Teachers.* Meadville PA: Press of Tribune Publishing, 1907.

Stacy, Nathaniel. *Memoirs.* Columbus PA: A. Vedder, 1850.

Stahl SEE Wharton, George Mifflin

Stahle, William. *The Description of the Borough of Reading.* Reading PA: Published by the author; Knabb & Boyer, Printers, 1841.

Staley, Seward Charle. *Curriculum in Sports (Physical Education).* Philadelphia: W. B. Saunders, 1935.

Stall, Gaspar J. *Proud, Peculiar New Orleans.* Baton Rouge LA: Claitor's Publishing Division, c.1984.

Stanberry, Dosi Elaine Cook. *Mountain Echoes.* Boone NC: Parkway, 2005.

Standard. Macclenny FL, 2000–. Internet.

Standard. Ogden UT, 1888–1902.

A Standard Dictionary of the English Language, upon Original Plans. New York: Funk & Wagnalls, 1895.

Standard-Times. New Bedford MA, 1932–.

Standish, Burt L. SEE Patten, Gilbert

Standish, John and Charles Noble. *Practical Hints on Planting Ornamental Trees, with Particular Reference to Coniferae.* London: Bradbury and Evans, 1852.

Stanley, Clark. *The Life and Adventures of the American Cow-Boy.* Providence RI: Stanley, 1897.

Stanley, Edwin James. *Rambles in Wonderland.* 3d ed. New York: D. Appleton, 1880 [c.1878].

Stansbury, Charles Frederick. *The Lake of the Great Dismal.* New York: Albert & Charles Boni, 1925 [c.1924].

Stansbury, Howard *Expedition* SEE United States. Army. Corps of Topographical Engineers *An Expedition to the Valley of the Great Salt Lake of Utah*

Stanton, Elizabeth Brandon. *"Fata Morgana".* Crowley LA: Printed by Signal Publishing, 1917.

Stanton, Gerrit Smith. *When the Wildwood Was in Flower.* New York: J. S. Ogilvie Pub., c.1910.

———. *Where the Sportsman Loves to Linger.* New York: J. S. Ogilvie, c.1905.

Stanwell-Fletcher, Theodora Morris Cope. *Driftwood Valley.* Boston: Little, Brown, 1946.

Staples, Edna. *Wolf over the Ridge.* Birch Tree MO: Open Book, 2003.

Stapleton, Patience. *Kady.* Chicago: Belford, Clarke, 1888.

———. *The Major's Christmas and Other Stories.* Denver CO: News Printing, 1886 [c.1885].

Stapp, William Preston. *The Prisoner of Perote.* Philadelphia: G. B. Zieber, 1845.

Star. Gettysburg PA, 1831.

Star. Kansas City MO, 1885–.

Star. Shelby NC, 1998–.

Star and Banner. Gettysburg PA, 1847–1864.

Star and Republican Banner. Gettysburg PA, 1832–1847.

Star and Sentinel. Gettysburg PA, 1867–1961.

Starbuck, Caleb. *Hampton Heights; or, the Spinster's Ward.* New York: Mason Bros., 1856.

Starbuck, Mary Eliza. *My House and I.* Boston: Houghton Mifflin, 1929.

Star-Herald. Scottsbluff NE, 1979–.

Starkville Daily News. Starkville MS, 1960–.

Star Leader. Clinton MD, 1965–1975?

Star-Ledger. Newark NJ, 1964–.

Starnes, Ebenezer. *The Slaveholder Abroad; or, Billy Buck's Visit, with His Master, to England.* Philadelphia: J. B. Lippincott, 1860.

Star-News. Pasadena CA, 1956–1992.

Stars and Stripes. Paris, France: Expeditionary Forces, 1918–1919.

Star Shopper. Stoughton WI, 1945–.

Star-Telegram. Fort Worth TX, 1990–.

Star Tribune. Minneapolis MN, 1987–.

State. Columbia SC, 1891–.

State and the Columbia Record. Columbia SC, 1891–.

State Historical Society of North Dakota. *Collections.* Bismarck ND, 1906–1925.

State Journal-Register. Springfield IL, 1974–.

Statesman's Year-Book. London, 1864–.

Statesville Daily Record. Statesville NC, 1941–1954.

Statesville Record & Landmark. Statesville NC, 1954–.

St. Clair, Frank. *Six Days in the Metropolis.* Boston: Redding, 1854.

St. Clar, Robert. *Metropolites.* New York: American News, c.1864.

Stead, William Thomas. *Satan's Invisible World Displayed.* London: [s.n.], 1898.

Steam Traction Archive. [v.d.]. Internet.

Stearns, Charles. *The Black Man of the South.* New York: American News; Boston: N.E. News, 1872.

Stearns, Edward Josiah. *A Practical Guide to English Pronunciation.* Boston: Crosby, Nichols, 1858.

Stearns, Marshall Winslow. *The Story of Jazz.* New York: Oxford Univ. Press, 1957 [c.1956].

Stearns, Marshall Winslow and Jean Stearns. *Jazz Dance.* New York: Macmillan, 1968.

Stearns, Samuel. *American Herbal; or, Materia Medica.* Walpole NH: Printed by D. Carlisle, 1801.

Stebbins, Robert C. *Amphibians and Reptiles of Western North America.* New York: McGraw-Hill, c.1954.

Stedman, Thomas Lathrop, ed. *Twentieth Century Practice.* New York: William Wood, 1895–1900. 20 vols.

Steed, Virgil S. *Kentucky Tobacco Patch.* Indianapolis IN: Bobbs-Merrill, c.1947.

Steedman, Charles John. *Bucking the Sagebrush.* New York: G. P. Putnam's Sons, 1904.

Steele, Eliza R. *A Summer Journey in the West.* New York: John S. Taylor, 1841.

Steele, John. *The Papers of John Steele.* Ed. by H. M. Wagstaff. Raleigh NC: Edwards & Broughton, 1924. 2 vols.

Steele, Rowena Granice. *Dell Dart.* Merced CA: San Joaquin Valley Argus Office, 1874.

Steele, Wilbur Daniel. *Sound of Rowlocks.* New York: Harper & Bros., 1938.

———. *Storm.* New York: Harper & Bros., 1914.

Steffens, Joseph Lincoln. *The Autobiography of Lincoln Steffens.* New York: Literary Guild, 1931.

Stegner, Page. *The Edge.* New York: Dial Press, 1968.

Stegner, Wallace Earle. *All the Little Live Things.* New York: Viking Press, c.1967.

———. *Crossing to Safety.* New York: Random House, c.1987.

———. *Mormon Country.* New York: Duell, Sloan & Pearce, 1942.

———. *Recapitulation.* Garden City NY: Doubleday, 1979.

———. *Second Growth.* Boston: Houghton Mifflin, 1947.

———. *The Sound of Mountain Water.* Garden City NY: Doubleday, 1969.

———. *Wolf Willow.* New York: Viking Press, c.1962.

Stehno, Frank Patrick. *The Hard Rock Trilogy: Book I.* c.2002. Internet.

Stein, John et al. *Field Guide to Native Oak Species of Eastern North America.* Morgantown WV: U.S. Department of Agriculture, Forest Service, Forest Health Technology Enterprise Team, 2003.

Steinbeck, John. *Cannery Row.* New York: Viking Press, 1945.

———. *East of Eden.* New York: Viking Press, 1952.

———. *The Grapes of Wrath.* New York: Viking, c.1939.

———. *The Long Valley.* New York: Viking Press, 1938.

———. *Novels and Stories, 1932–1937.* New York: Library of America, 1994.

———. *Of Mice and Men.* New York: Covici-Friede, c.1937.

———. *Sweet Thursday.* New York: Viking Press, 1954.

———. *Tortilla Flat.* New York: Modern Library, 1937 [c.1935].

———. *Travels with Charley.* New York: Viking Press, 1962.

Steinberg, Alfred. *The Man from Missouri: the Life and Times of Harry S. Truman.* New York: G. P. Putnam's Sons, c.1962.

Steiner, Jesse Frederick and Roy Melton Brown. *The North Carolina Chain Gang.* Chapel Hill NC: Univ. NC Press; London: Humphrey Milford, Oxford Univ. Press, 1927.

Steiner, Lynn M. *Landscaping with Native Plants of Wisconsin.* St. Paul MN: MBI, 2007.

Steinmetz, Sol. *Yiddish and English.* University AL: Univ. AL Press, c.1986.

Steitz, Quentin. *Grasses, Pods, Vines, Weeds.* Austin TX: Univ. TX Press, 1987.

Stem, Thad. *A Flagstone Walk.* Charlotte NC: McNally and Loftin, 1968.

Stemen, Thomas Ray and W. Stanley Myers. *Oklahoma Flora.* Oklahoma City OK: Harlow Publishing, 1937.

———. *Spring Flora of Oklahoma.* Oklahoma City OK: Harlow Publishing, 1929.

Stephens, Alexander Hamilton. *A Constitutional View of the Late War between the States.* Philadelphia: National, 1868–1870. 2 vols.

Stephens, Ann Sophia. *Fashion and Famine.* New York: Bunce & Brother, 1854.

———. *High Life in New York.* London: Printed for J. How, 1844. 2 vols.

———. *High Life in New York.* New York: Bunce & Brother, 1854.

———. *Wives and Widows.* Philadelphia: T. B. Peterson & Bros., c.1869.

Stephens, Charles Asbury. *A Busy Year at the Old Squire's.* Boston: Youth's Companion, c.1922.

Stephens, Frank. *California Mammals.* San Diego CA: West Coast Publishing, 1906.

Stephens, Harriet Marion. *Hagar the Martyr.* Boston: W. P. Fetridge, 1855 [c.1854].

Stephens, Henry. *The Farmer's Guide to Scientific and Practical Agriculture.* New York: Leonard Scott, 1853 [c.1851]. 2 vols.

Stephens, Homer A. *Woody Plants of the North Central Plains.* Lawrence KS: Univ. Press KS, 1973.

Stephens, John Lloyd. *Incidents of Travel in Central America, Chiapas, and Yucatan.* New York: Harper & Bros., 1841. 2 vols.

———. *Incidents of Travel in Yucatan.* New York: Harper & Bros., 1860. 2 vols. Orig. pub. in 1843.

Stephens, Kate. *Life at Laurel Town in Anglo-Saxon Kansas.* Lawrence KS: Alumni Association of the Univ. KS, 1920.

Stephenson, George Malcolm. *The Religious Aspects of Swedish Immigration.* New York: Arno Press, 1969. Repr. of 1932 ed. pub. by Univ. MN Press, Minneapolis MN.

Stern, Jane and Michael Stern. *Goodfood.* New York: Alfred A. Knopf, 1983.

———. *Roadfood.* New York: Broadway Books, c.2002.

Sternberg, David. *Fishing with Live Bait.* Minnetonka MN: Cy DeCosse, c.1982.

Steuber, William F., Jr. *The Landlooker.* Indianapolis IN: Bobbs-Merrill, c.1957.

Stevens, James. *The Saginaw Paul Bunyan.* New York: A. A. Knopf, 1932.

Stevens, Orin Alva. *Handbook of North Dakota Plants.* Fargo ND: ND Agricultural College, 1950.

Stevens, Wallace. *Letters.* Selected and ed. by Holly Stevens. New York: Alfred A. Knopf, 1966.

Stevens, William Chase. *Kansas Wild Flowers.* Lawrence KS: Univ. KS Press, 1948.

Stevenson, Adlai Ewing. *An Ethic for Survival.* Ed. by Michael H. Prosser. New York: Morrow, 1969.

Stevenson, Robert Louis. *Across the Plains.* London: Chatto & Windus, 1892.

———. *The Silverado Squatters.* London: Chatto and Windus, 1883.

Stevenson, Robert Louis and Lloyd Osbourne. *The Wrecker.* London: Cassell, 1892.

Stevens Point Daily Journal. Stevens Point WI, 1895–1981.

Stevens Point Journal. Stevens Point WI, 1872–1921.

Stewart, Amy. *The Earth Moved.* London: Frances Lincoln, 2004.

Stewart, Charles David. *Partners of Providence.* New York: Century, 1907.

Stewart, Charles Samuel. *Journal of a Residence in the Sandwich Islands, during the Years 1823, 1824, and 1825.* Honolulu HI: Univ. HI Press for Friends of the Library of Hawaii, 1970.

Stewart, Elinore Pruitt. *Letters of a Woman Homesteader.* Boston: Houghton Mifflin, 1914.

Stewart, George Rippey. *American Place-Names.* New York: Oxford Univ. Press, 1970.

———. *Names on the Land.* New York: Random House, c.1945.

Stewart, J. T. *Indiana County Pennsylvania.* Chicago: J. H. Beers, 1913. 2 vols.

Stewart, Mary. *The Gabriel Hounds.* New York: M. S. Mill, 1967.

Steyermark, Julian Alfred. *Spring Flora of Missouri.* St. Louis MO: Missouri Botanical Garden; Chicago: Field Museum of Natural History, 1940.

St. George, Thomas R. *c/o Postmaster.* New York: Thomas Y. Crowell, 1943.

Stieff, Frederick Philip, comp. *Eat, Drink & Be Merry in Maryland.* New York: G. P. Putnam's Sons, c.1932.

Stiff, Dean SEE Anderson, Nels

Stiles, Robert. *Four Years under Marse Robert.* New York: Neale Publishing, 1903.

Still, James. *Early Recollections and Life of Dr. James Still.* Philadelphia: Printed for the Author by J. B. Lippincott, 1877.

———. *On Troublesome Creek.* New York: Viking Press, c.1941.

———. *River of Earth.* Lexington KY: Univ. Press KY, 1978 [c.1940].

———. *The Run for the Elbertas.* Lexington KY: Univ. Press KY, c.1980.

———. *The Wolfpen Notebooks.* Lexington KY: Univ. Press KY, c.1991.

Stillman, William James. *The Autobiography of a Journalist.* Boston: Houghton, Mifflin, 1901. 2 vols.

Stilwell, Hart. *Hunting and Fishing in Texas.* New York: Alfred A. Knopf, 1946.

Stimpson, Eddie. *My Remembers.* Denton TX: Univ. North TX Press, c.1996.

Stimpson, George. *A Book about a Thousand Things.* New York: Harper & Bros., c.1946.

Stimson, Alexander Lovett. *Easy Nat; or, the Three Apprentices.* New York: J. C. Derby, 1854.

Stix, Thomas Louis, ed. *"Say It Ain't So, Joe".* New York: Boni and Gaer, c.1947.

St. John, Harold. *Flora of Southeastern Washington and of Adjacent Idaho.* Pullman WA: Students Book, 1937.

———. *Flora of Southeastern Washington and of Adjacent Idaho.* Rev. ed. Pullman WA: Students Book, 1956.

St. John, Larry. *Practical Bait Casting.* New York: Macmillan, 1918.

St. John Valley Times. Madawaska ME, 1957–.

St. Joseph Herald. St. Joseph MI, 1866–1889.

St. Joseph News-Press. St. Joseph MO, 1992–.

St. Joseph Traveler and Herald. St. Joseph MI, 1874–1885.

St. Louisan. St. Louis MO: Blest, 1969–1977.

St. Louis Missouri Botanical Garden *Annals* SEE Missouri Botanical Garden *Annals*

St. Louis Post-Dispatch. St. Louis MO, 1879–.

St. Louis Reveille. St. Louis MO, 1844–1850?

St. Nicholas. New York, 1873–1943.

Stockbridge, John Calvin. *A Model Pastor.* New, illustrated ed. with biographical app. Boston: Lee and Shepard, 1894.

Stockett, Kathryn. *The Help.* New York: Amy Einhorn Books, c.2009.

Stock Grower and Farmer. Las Vegas NM, 1889–1898.

Stockton, Frank Richard. *Afield and Afloat.* New York: Charles Scribner's Sons, 1900.

———. *The Casting Away of Mrs. Lecks and Mrs. Aleshine.* New York: Century, c.1886.

———. *The Casting Away of Mrs. Lecks and Mrs. Aleshine with Its Sequel The Dusantes.* New York: Dover, 1961. Repr. of the 1892 ed. pub. by Century, New York.

———. *The Dusantes.* New York: Century, c.1888.

———. *Rudder Grange.* New-York: Charles Scribner's Sons, 1879.

Stoddard, Amos. *Sketches, Historical and Descriptive, of Louisiana.* Philadelphia: M. Carey, 1812.

Stoddard, Elizabeth. *Two Men.* New York: Bunce and Huntington, 1865.

Stoddard, William Osborn. *Esau Hardery.* New York: White & Stokes, 1881.

Stoddart's Encyclopaedia Americana. New York: J. M. Stoddart, 1883–1889. 4 vols.

Stoke, Will E. *Episodes of Early Days in Central and Western Kansas.* Great Bend KS: Will E. Stoke, c.1926.

Stoker, Catherine Ulmer. *Concha's Mexican Kitchen Cook Book.* Rev. ed. San Antonio TX: Naylor, 1957.

Stone, Charles P. and Linda W. Pratt. *Hawai'i's Plants and Animals.* Honolulu HI: Hawaii Natural History Association, c.1994.

Stone, Edwin Martin. *Life and Recollections of John Howland.* Providence RI: G. H. Whitney, 1857.

Stone, John A. *Put's Golden Songster.* San Francisco: D. E. Appleton, c.1858.

———. *Put's Original California Songster.* 5th ed. San Francisco: D. E. Appleton, 1868 [c.1858].

Stone, Nancy and Robert Waters Grey, eds. *White Trash.* Charlotte NC: New South, c.1976.

Stone, Ruth M. *Studien über den Deutschen Einfluss auf das Amerikanische Englisch.* Marburg: H. Pöppinghaus, 1934.

Stone, Witmer. *Bird Studies at Old Cape May.* New York: Dover, c.1965. 2 vols. Orig. pub. in 1937 by Delaware Valley Ornithological Club, Philadelphia.

Stoney, Samuel Gaillard and Gertrude Mathews Shelby. *Black Genesis.* New York: Macmillan, 1930.

Stong, Phil. *Blizzard.* Garden City NY: Doubleday, c.1955.

———. *Hawkeyes, a Biography of the State of Iowa.* New York: Dodd, Mead, 1940.

———. *State Fair.* New York: Literary Guild, 1932.

Storer, David Humphreys. *A History of the Fishes of Massachusetts.* Cambridge MA: Welch & Bigelow; Boston: Dakin & Metcalf, 1867.

Stork, William. *An Account of East-Florida.* London: Sold by W. Nicoll and G. Woodfall, 1766.

———. *A Description of East Florida, with a Journal, Kept by John Bartram of Philadelphia.* 3d ed. much enlarged and improved. London: Sold by W. Nicoll, 1769.

Storke, E. G., ed. *The Family, Farm and Gardens, and the Domestic Animals.* Auburn NY: Auburn Publishing, c.1859. 3 vols.

Storm, Marian. *Minstrel Weather.* New York: Harper & Bros., 1920.

Storms, James B. H. *A Jersey Dutch Vocabulary.* Park Ridge NJ: Pascack Historical Society, 1964.

Story, G. M. et al., eds. *Dictionary of Newfoundland English.* Toronto, Ontario: Univ. Toronto Press, c.1982.

Story, Sydney. *Caste.* Boston: Phillips, Sampson; New York: J. C. Derby, 1856 [c.1855].

Story. New York, 1931–1964.

Stoughton Courier. Stoughton WI, 1876–1909; 1954–1979.

Stowe, Harriet Beecher. *Betty's Bright Idea.* New York: J. B. Ford, c.1875.

———. *Dred.* Boston: Phillips, Sampson, 1856. 2 vols.

———. *House and Home Papers.* Boston: Ticknor and Fields, 1865.

———. *A Key to Uncle Tom's Cabin.* Boston: J. P. Jewett, 1853.

———. *Little Foxes.* Boston: Ticknor and Fields, 1866.

———. *The Mayflower.* New York: Harper & Bros., c.1843.

———. *The May Flower, and Other Misc. Writings.* Boston: Phillips, Sampson, 1855.

———. *The Minister's Wooing.* New York: Derby and Jackson, 1859.

———. *Oldtown Folks.* Boston: Fields, Osgood, 1869.

———. *Palmetto-Leaves.* Boston: James R. Osgood, 1873.

———. *The Pearl of Orr's Island.* Boston: Houghton, Mifflin, 1882. Orig. pub. in 1862 by Ticknor and Fields, Boston.

———. *Pink and White Tyranny.* Boston: Roberts Bros., 1871.

———. *Poganuc People.* Hartford CT: Stowe-Day Foundation, 1977. Repr. of the 1878 ed. pub. by Fords, Howard & Hulbert, New York.

———. *Sam Lawson's Oldtown Fireside Stories.* Boston: Houghton, Mifflin, 1882. Orig. pub. in 1871 by Houghton, Osgood, Boston.

———. *Uncle Sam's Emancipation; Earthly Care, a Heavenly Discipline; and Other Sketches.* Philadelphia: Willis P. Hazard, 1853.

———. *Uncle Tom's Cabin.* Boston: John P. Jewett, 1852 [c.1851]. 2 vols.

———. *We and Our Neighbors.* New York: J. B. Ford, c.1875.

St. Petersburg Times. St. Petersburg FL, 1921–.

Strachey, William. *The Historie of Travaile into Virginia Britannia.* London: Printed for the Hakluyt Society, 1849. Ed. from the orig. ms. in the British Museum by R. H. Major.

Strahorn, Carrie Adell. *Fifteen Thousand Miles by Stage.* New York: G. P. Putnam's Sons, 1911.

Strang, James Jesse. *Diary.* Deciphered, transcr., introduced and annotated by Mark A. Strang. East Lansing MI: MI State Univ. Press, c.1961.

The Stranger's New Guide through Boston and Vicinity. Boston: A. Williams, 1869.

Stratton, Joanna L. *Pioneer Women.* New York: Simon & Schuster, c.1981.

Strausbaugh, Perry Daniel and Earl L. Core. *Flora of West Virginia.* Morgantown WV: [s.n.], 1952–1953. 2 pts.

Street, Alfred Billings. *The Indian Pass.* New York: Hurd and Houghton, 1869.

———. *Woods and Waters.* New York: M. Doolady, c.1860.

Street, James Howell. *The Gauntlet.* Garden City NY: Doubleday, Doran, 1945.

———. *In My Father's House.* New York: Dial Press, 1941.

———. *Look Away!* New York: Viking Press, 1936.

Stribling, Thomas Sigismund. *The Store.* New York: Literary Guild, 1932.

———. *Unfinished Cathedral.* Garden City NY: Doubleday, Doran, 1934.

Strickland, Ron. *Vermonters.* San Francisco: Chronicle Books, c.1986.

Stringer, Arthur. *The Shadow.* New York: Century, 1913.

Strong, Moses McCure, comp. *History of the Territory of Wisconsin from 1836 to 1848.* Madison WI: Democrat Printing, 1885.

Strong, Paschal N. *Behind the Great Smokies.* Boston: Little, Brown, 1932.

Strother, David Hunter. *Virginia Illustrated.* New York: Harper & Bros., 1857.

Stroud, Drew McCord, ed. *Viewpoints: the Majority Minority.* Minneapolis MN: Winston Press, 1973.

Stroyer, Jacob. *My Life in the South.* 3d ed. new and enlarged. Salem MA: Salem Observer, 1885.

Strubble, George G. *A Visit to Texas.* New York: Goodrich & Wiley, 1834.

Stuart, Granville. *Forty Years on the Frontier.* Cleveland OH: Arthur H. Clark, 1925. 2 vols.

———. *Montana as It Is.* New York: Arno Press, 1973. Repr. of 1865 ed. pub. by C. S. Wescott.

Stuart, Jesse. *The Beatinest Boy.* New York: McGraw-Hill, c.1953.

———. *Beyond Dark Hills.* New York: E. P. Dutton, 1938.

———. *Come, Gentle Spring.* New York: McGraw Hill, 1969.

———. *God's Oddling.* New York: McGraw-Hill, 1960.

———. *The Good Spirit of Laurel Ridge.* New York: McGraw-Hill, 1953.

———. *Head o' W-Hollow.* New York: E. P. Dutton, 1936.

———. *Hie to the Hunters.* New York: Whittlesey House, c.1950.

———. *Men of the Mountains.* New York: E. P. Dutton, 1941.

———. *Plowshares in Heaven.* New York: McGraw-Hill, 1958.

———. *Tales from the Plum Grove Hills.* New York: E. P. Dutton, 1946.

———. *Taps for Private Tussie.* New York: E. P. Dutton, c.1943.

———. *The Thread That Runs So True.* New York: Charles Scribner's Sons, 1958 [c.1949].

———. *Trees of Heaven.* New York: E. P. Dutton, 1940.

———. *The Year of My Rebirth.* New York: McGraw-Hill, 1956.

Stuart, Robert. *The Discovery of the Oregon Trail.* New York: C. Scribner's Sons, 1935.

Stuart, Ruth McEnery. *In Simpkinsville.* New York: Harper & Bros., 1897.

Stuart-Wortley, Emmeline. *Travels in the United States, etc., during 1849 and 1850.* London: Richard Bentley, 1851. 3 vols.

———. *Travels in the United States, etc., during 1849 and 1850.* New York: Harper & Bros., 1851.

———. *Travels in the United States, etc., during 1849 and 1850.* New York: Harper & Bros., 1855.

Stubbendieck, James L. et al. *North American Wildland Plants.* 6th ed. Lincoln NE: Univ. NE Press, c.2003.

Stuck, Hudson. *Ten Thousand Miles with a Dog Sled.* New York: C. Scribner's Sons, 1915 [c.1914].

———. *Ten Thousand Miles with a Dog Sled.* New York: C. Scribner's Sons, 1915.

———. *Voyages on the Yukon and Its Tributaries.* New York: C. Scribner's Sons, c.1917.

———. *A Winter Circuit of Our Arctic Coast.* New York: Charles Scribner's Sons, 1920.

Student, a Monthly Journal Devoted to the Interests of Education in the Society of Friends. Philadelphia, 1880–1892.

Studer, Jacob Henry. *The Birds of North America.* New York: Natural Science Association of America, 1903.

Studies in Honor of Lloyd A. Kasten. Madison WI: Hispanic Seminary of Medieval Studies, 1975.

Studies in Linguistics. Washington DC, 1942–1975.

Studies in Philology. Chapel Hill NC, 1906–.

Stuhr, Ernst Theodore. *Native Drug Plants of Nebraska.* [s.l.]: [s.n.], 1929.

Stupka, Arthur. *Great Smoky Mountains National Park.* Washington DC: U.S. National Park Service, 1960.

———. *Trees, Shrubs, and Woody Vines of Great Smoky Mountains National Park.* Knoxville TN: Univ. TN Press, 1964.

———. *Wildflowers in Color.* New York: Harper Colophon Books, 1982 [c.1965].

Sturtevant, Edward Lewis. *Maize, an Attempt at Classification.* Rochester NY: Democrat and Chronicle, 1884.

———. *Sturtevant's Notes on Edible Plants.* Ed. by U. P. Hedrick. Albany NY: J. B. Lyon, State printers, 1919.

Stuttgen, Joanne Raetz and Terese Allen. *Cafe Wisconsin Cookbook.* Madison WI: Univ. WI Press, 2007.

Styron, William. *Lie Down in Darkness.* Indianapolis IN: Bobbs-Merrill, 1951.

Sublette County Artist Guild. *More Tales of the Seeds-Ke-Dee.* Walsworth WY: [s.n.], 1976.

Suburbanite Economist. Chicago, 1962–1977?

Suckow, Ruth. *Cora.* New York: Alfred A. Knopf, 1929.

Sudworth, George Bishop. *Check List of the Forest Trees of the United States, Their Names and Ranges.* Washington DC: Govt. Printing Office, 1898.

———. *Check List of the Forest Trees of the United States, Their Names and Ranges.* Rev. ed. Washington DC: Govt. Printing Office, 1927.

———. *Forest Trees of the Pacific Slope.* Washington DC: Govt. Printing Office, 1908.

———. *Nomenclature of the Arborescent Flora of the United States.* Washington DC: Govt. Printing Office, 1897.

———. *The Spruce and Balsam Fir Trees of the Rocky Mountain Region.* Washington DC: Govt. Printing Office, 1916.

Suffolk County, Massachusetts. *Suffolk Deeds.* Boston: Rockwell and Churchill, 1880–1906.

Sullivan, Edward Robert. *Rambles and Scrambles in North and South America.* London: Richard Bentley, 1852.

Sullivan, James, ed. *History of New York State 1523–1927.* New York: Lewis Historical Publishing, 1927. 6 vols.

———. *The History of the District of Maine.* Boston: Printed by I. Thomas and E. T. Andrews, 1795.

Sullivan, John Lawrence. *Life and Reminiscences of a 19th Century Gladiator.* Boston: J. A. Hearn, 1892.

Sullivan, Mark. *The Education of an American.* New York: Doubleday, Doran, 1938.

Sullivan, Thomas Russell. *The Heart of Us.* Boston: Houghton Mifflin, 1912.

Sully, Langdon. *No Tears for the General: the Life of Alfred Sully, 1821–1879.* Palo Alto CA: American West Publishing, c.1974.

Summer, Lewis. "Lewis Summer's Journal of a Tour from Alexandria, Virginia, to Gallipolis, Ohio, in 1808." *Southern Historical Magazine* (1892) 1.49–81.

Summerfield, Charles SEE Arrington, Alfred W.

Summers, Lewis Preston. *Annals of Southwest Virginia, 1769–1800.* Abingdon VA: Published by Lewis Preston Summers, 1929.

———. *History of Southwest Virginia, 1746–1786, Washington County, 1777–1870.* Richmond VA: J. L. Hill Printing, 1903.

Sumter County Journal. York AL, 1884?–.

Sumter County Times. Bushnel FL, 1881–.

Sun. Baltimore MD, 1837–.

Sun. Lowell MA, 1969–.

Sun. New York, 1833–1916; 1920–1950.

Sunday Advocate. Baton Rouge LA, 1994–.

Sunday Bulletin. Philadelphia, 1947–1978.

Sunday Call. San Francisco, 1878–1895.

Sunday Capital. Annapolis MD, 1987–.

Sunday Dominion-Post. Morgantown WV, 1968?–.

Sunday Gazette-Mail. Charleston WV, 1958–.

Sunday Herald. Arlington Heights IL, 1978–.

Sunday Herald. Syracuse NY, 1880–1904.

Sunday Herald American. Syracuse NY, 1945–.

Sunday Inter Ocean. Chicago, 1879–1902.

Sunday Journal and Star. Lincoln NE, 1932–1984.

Sunday Mercury and Herald. San Jose CA, 1903–1913.

Sunday Morning Decatur Review. Decatur IL, 1917–1919.

Sunday News. Lancaster PA, 1923–.

Sunday News and Tribune. Jefferson City MO, 1915?–.

Sunday News Journal. Wilmington DE, 1975–.

Sunday News Tribune. Duluth MN, 1892–1918.

Sunday Oregonian. Portland OR, 1881–.

Sunday Post-Crescent. Appleton WI, 1962–.

Sunday Review. Decatur IL, 1899–1917.

Sunday Star-News. Wilmington NC, 1990?–.

Sunday State Journal. Lincoln NE, 1897–1930.

Sunday Sun. Lowell MA, 1969?–.

Sunday Telegraph. London, 1961–.

Sunday Times. Salisbury MD, 1967–.

Sunday Times-Signal. Zanesville OH, 1918–1959.

Sunderland, Byron. *A Sketch of the Life of Dr. William Gunton, Born at Aylsham, Norfolk, England, October 29th, 1791.* Washington DC: Joseph L. Pearson, 1878.

Sun Newspapers. Cleveland OH, 2000?–.

Sun-Sentinel. Fort Lauderdale FL, 1960–2000.

Sunset. Menlo Park CA: Lane, 1898–.

Sunset. Hawaii: a Guide to All the Islands. Menlo Park CA: Lane, c.1975.

———. *Hawaii: a Guide to All the Islands.* 6th ed. Menlo Park CA: Lane, c.1984.

———. *Mexican Cook Book.* 2d ed., 5th printing. Menlo Park CA: Lane, 1981, c.1977.

Sunshine. Madison WI, 1979–.

Sun Times SEE *Chicago Sun-Times*

El Super: a Cuban-American Comedy. New York: New Yorker Video, 1979.

Superior Telegram. Superior WI, 1890–.

Supplement to the Courant. Hartford CT, 1840?–1888. Issued as a biweekly suppl. to the *Connecticut Courant.*

Supporter. Chillicothe OH, 1808–1821.

Surfer. Dana Point CA, 1960–.

Survey. New York, [etc], 1909–1937; 1949–1952.

Sussex Countian. Georgetown DE, 1933–.

Sutcliff, Robert. *Travels in Some Parts of North America, in the Years 1804, 1805, & 1806.* 2d ed. improved. York: Printed for W. Alexander, 1815.

Sutter, John A. *New Helvetia Diary . . . from September 9, 1845 to May 25, 1848.* San Francisco: Grabhorn Press, c.1939.

Swain, Ralph Brownlee. *The Insect Guide.* Garden City NY: Doubleday, 1949.

Swan, James Gilchrist. *The Northwest Coast.* New York: Harper & Bros., 1857.

Swan, Lester A. and Charles S. Papp. *The Common Names of Insects of North America.* New York: Harper & Row, 1972.

Swan, William Draper. *The American Comprehensive Reader for the Use of Schools.* Boston: Hickling, Swan and Brown, 1855.

Swann, John W. *The Language of the Circus Lot.* [s.l.]: [s.n.], c1930?

Swarthout, Glendon. *Skeletons.* New York: Doubleday, c.1979.

Swedberg, Robert W. and Harriet Swedberg. *Country Pine Furniture.* Rev. ed. Des Moines IA: Wallace-Homestead Book, c.1983.

Swedesboro News. Swedesboro NJ, 1890–.

Sweet, Alexander Edwin and J. Armoy Knox. *On a Mexican Mustang, through Texas, from the Gulf to the Rio Grande.* Hartford CT: S. S. Scranton, 1883.

———. *Sketches from Texas Siftings.* New York: Texas Siftings Publishing, 1882.

Sweet, Muriel. *Common Edible and Useful Plants of the East and Midwest.* Healdsburg CA: Naturegraph, c.1975.

———. *Common Edible and Useful Plants of the West.* Healdsburg CA: Naturegraph, c.1962.

Sweet, William Warren, ed. *Religion on the American Frontier.* New York: H. Holt, 1931–1964. 4 vols.

Sweetser, Albert R. and Mary E. Kent. *Key and Flora.* Boston: Ginn, c.1908.

Sweetser, Moses Foster. *King's Handbook of the United States.* Buffalo NY: Moses King, 1891.

Swetnam, George. *Pittsylvania Country.* New York: Duell, Sloan & Pearce, 1951.

Swett, Charles. *A Trip to British Honduras and to San Pedro, Republic of Honduras.* New Orleans LA: Price, Current, 1868.

Swift, Esther Munroe. *Vermont Place-Names.* Brattleboro VT: Stephen Greene Press, c.1977.

Swift, John Franklin. *Robert Greathouse.* New York: Carleton, 1870.

Swiss Cross. New York, 1887–1889.

Swisshelm, Jane Grey. *Half a Century.* Chicago: Jansen, McClurg, 1880.

Switchmen's Journal. Chicago: Switchmen's Mutual Aid Association of North America, 1886–1894.

Syatt, Dick. *Like We Say Back Home.* Secaucus NJ: Citadel Press, 1987. Orig. pub. in 1980 under the title *Country Talk.*

Sykes, Godfrey. *A Westerly Trend.* Tucson AZ: Arizona Pioneers Historical Society, 1944.

Symons, R. D. *Many Trails.* Toronto: Longmans Canada, c.1963.

———. *Where the Wagon Led.* New York: Doubleday, c.1973.

Syracuse Herald. Syracuse NY, 1904–1939.

Syracuse Herald-American. Syracuse NY, 1939–2001.

Syracuse Herald-Journal. Syracuse NY, 1939–2001.

Tabbert, Russell. *Collection.* 1973–1981. Unpub.

———. *Dictionary of Alaskan English.* Juneau AK: Denali Press, 1991.

———. *Some Words in Alaskan English.* 1981. Unpub.

Taber, Clarence Wilbur. *Cyclopedic Medical Dictionary.* 8th ed. Philadelphia: F. A. Davis, 1960.

Taber, Edward Martin. *Stowe Notes Letters and Verses.* Boston: Houghton Mifflin, 1913.

Taber, Gladys Bagg. *Stillmeadow Daybook.* Philadelphia: Lippincott, 1955.

Taber, John Huddleston. *The Story of the 168th Infantry.* Iowa City IA: State Historical Society of Iowa, 1925. 2 vols.

Tacoma Daily News. Tacoma WA, 1889–1898.

Taft, Michael. *Blues Lyric Poetry, an Anthology.* New York: Garland Publishing, 1983.

Tak, Montie. *Truck Talk.* Philadelphia: Chilton Book, c.1971.

Talbot, Mary Elizabeth. *Rurality.* Providence RI: Marshall and Hammond, 1830.

Tales of an American Landlord. New York: W. B. Gilley, 1824. 2 vols.

Taliaferro, Harden E. *Fisher's River.* New York: Harper & Bros., 1859.

Talladega Daily Home. Talladega AL, 1909–1945.

Tallant, Robert. *Voodoo in New Orleans.* New York: Macmillan, 1946.

Tallapoosa County Extension. *Weed Control.* [v.d.]. Internet.

Talley, Thomas Washington, comp. *Negro Folk Rhymes, Wise and Otherwise.* New York: Macmillan, 1922.

Tallman, Marjorie. *Dictionary of American Folklore.* New York: Philosophical Library, c.1959.

Talmage, Thomas De Witt. *Crumbs Swept Up.* New ed. Philadelphia: Bradley, 1877.

———. *Sermons . . . Delivered in the Brooklyn Tabernacle, New York.* 1st ser. Wakefield MA: Wm. Nicholson & Sons, 18??

Talman, Wilfred Blanch. *How Things Began—in Rockland County and Places Nearby.* New City NY: Historical Society of Rockland County, 1977.

Tamony, Peter. *Americanisms: Content & Continuum.* San Francisco: Peter Tamony, 1964–1973.

———. *Collection.* 1930–1939. Unpub. coll. of materials on Amer. Engl. usage.

Tampa Tribune. Tampa FL, 1958–.

Tanner, John. *A Narrative of the Captivity and Adventures of John Tanner.* New-York: G. and C. and H. Carvill, 1830.

Tapert, Annette, ed. *The Brothers' War: Civil War Letters to Their Loved Ones from the Blue and Gray.* New York: Times Books, 1988.

Tarbell, Ida Minerva. *The History of the Standard Oil Company.* New York: McClure, Phillips, 1904. 2 vols.

Tardy, Mary T. *Southland Writers.* Philadelphia: Claxton, Remsen & Haffelfinger, 1870 [c.1869]. 2 vols.

Tarkington, Booth. *Alice Adams.* Garden City NY: Doubleday, Page, 1921.

———. *The Magnificent Ambersons.* Garden City NY: Doubleday, Page, 1920 [c.1918].

———. *Seventeen: a Tale of Youth and Summer Time and the Baxter Family, Especially William.* New York: Harper, 1916.

Tarleton, Banastre. *A History of the Campaigns of 1780 and 1781 in the Southern Provinces of North America.* Dublin: Printed for Colles, 1787.

Tarleton State University. *Range Types of North America.* [v.d.]. Internet; R. E. Rosiere is primary author of this website.

Tarpley, Fred. *From Blinky to Blue-John.* Wolfe City TX: Univ. Press, c.1970.

———. *Jefferson.* Austin TX: Eakin Press, c.1983.

Tartt, Donna. *The Little Friend.* New York: Knopf, c.2002.

Tartt, Ruby Pickens. *Dim Roads and Dark Nights.* Livingston AL: Livingston Univ. Press, 1993.

Tatham, William. *Communications Concerning the Agriculture and Commerce of the United States of America.* London: Printed for J. Ridgway, 1800.

Tatnall, Robert Richardson. *Flora of Delaware and the Eastern Shore.* Wilmington DE: Society of Natural History of Delaware, 1946.

Tatum, Howell. "Major Howell Tatum's Journal While Acting Topographical Engineer (1814) to General Jackson, Commanding the Seventh Military District." *Smith College Studies in History.* (1921–1922) 7.1.5–138.

Tawrell, Paul. *Wilderness Camping.* Lebanon NH: Exxa, c.2007.

Taylor, Archer and Bartlett Jere Whiting, comps. *A Dictio-*

nary of American Proverbs and Proverbial Phrases. Cambridge MA: Harvard Univ. Press, 1958.

Taylor, Bayard. *Eldorado.* Palo Alto CA: Lewis Osborne, 1968. 2 vols. Facsimile of 1850 ed. pub. by G. P. Putnam, New York.

———. *Hanna Thurston.* New York: G. P. Putnam, 1863.

———. *John Godfrey's Fortunes.* New York: G. P. Putnam, 1864.

———. *Life and Letters of Bayard Taylor.* 2d ed. Boston: Houghton Mifflin, 1885 [c.1884].

———. *Northern Travel.* New York: G. P. Putnam, 1858.

———. *The Story of Kennett.* New York: Putnam, Hurd & Houghton, 1866.

Taylor, Benjamin Franklin. *Between the Gates.* Chicago: S. C. Griggs, 1878.

———. *January and June.* 3d ed. Chicago: D. B. Cooke, 1860. 3d ed. is a repr. of the 1st ed. pub. in 1853 by Samuel Hueston, New York.

———. *Summer-Savory, Gleaned from Rural Nooks in Pleasant Weather.* Chicago: S. C. Griggs, 1879.

———. *The World on Wheels and Other Sketches.* Chicago: S. C. Griggs, 1874.

Taylor, Charles J. *History of Great Barrington, (Berkshire County,) Massachusetts.* Great Barrington MA: Clark W. Bryan, 1882.

Taylor, Edward. *The Poems.* Ed. by Donald E. Stanford. New Haven CT: Yale Univ. Press, 1960.

Taylor, Harden F. *Survey of Marine Fisheries of North Carolina.* Chapel Hill NC: Univ. NC Press, 1951.

Taylor, Jane. *Plants for Dry Gardens.* London: Frances Lincoln, 1998.

Taylor, Jay Laird Burgess. *Back in the Mountain.* [s.l.]: [s.n.], 1957.

———. *Handbook for Rangers & Woodsmen.* New York: John Wiley & Sons; London: Chapman & Hall, 1917.

Taylor, John. *Arator.* Georgetown DC: Printed and published by J. M. & T. B. Carter, 1813.

———. *Arator.* 5th ed. rev. and enlarged. Petersburg VA: Whitworth & Yancey, c.1818.

Taylor, Lute A. *Chip Basket.* Hudson WI: Star & Times Printing House, 1874.

Taylor, Mart. *The Gold Digger's Song Book.* San Francisco: Book Club of California, 1975. Repr. of the 1856 ed. pub. by Marysville Daily Herald Print, Marysville CA.

Taylor, Nathaniel William. *Life on a Whaler.* New London CT: New London County Historical Society, 1929. Orig. written in 1858.

Taylor, Norman. *1001 Questions Answered about Flowers.* New York: Dover, 1996. Orig. pub. in 1963 by Dodd, Mead, New York.

———, ed. *Taylor's Encyclopedia of Gardening, Horticulture and Landscape Design.* Boston: American Garden Guild and Houghton Mifflin, 1948.

Taylor, Peter Hillsman. *In the Miro District.* New York: Alfred A. Knopf, 1977.

———. *The Widows of Thornton.* New York: Harcourt, Brace, c.1954.

Taylor, Phoebe Atwood. *The Cape Cod Mystery.* Indianapolis IN: Bobbs-Merrill, c.1931.

———. *Proof of the Pudding.* New York: W. W. Norton, c.1945.

Taylor, Raymond Leech. *Plants of Colonial Days.* Williamsburg PA: Printed for Colonial Williamsburg, 1952.

Taylor University. *Wetland Communities in Indiana.* [v.d.]. Internet.

Teale, Edwin Way. *Autumn across America.* New York: Dodd, Mead, 1956.

———. *The Boys' Book of Insects.* New York: E. P. Dutton, 1940.

———. *Journey into Summer.* New York: Dodd, Mead, 1960.

———. *North with the Spring.* New York: Dodd, Mead, c.1951.

———. *Wandering through Winter.* New York: Dodd, Mead, 1965.

Tech. Cambridge MA, 1881–.

Technical World. Chicago, 1904–1905.

Technical World Magazine. Chicago, 1905–1915.

Teeny, Jim. *The Teeny Technique for Steelhead and Salmon.* Guilford CT: Lyons Press, c.2001.

Tehon, Leo Roy. *Fieldbook of Native Illinois Shrubs.* Urbana IL: Natural History Survey Div., 1942.

Telegram & Gazette. Worcester MA, 1989–.

Telegraph. Alton IL, 1986–.

Telegraph-Herald. Dubuque IA, 1935–.

Teller, Walter Magnes. *Area Code 215.* New York: Atheneum, 1963.

———. *The Search for Captain Slocum.* New York: Charles Scribner's Sons, c.1956.

Tempe Historical Museum. [v.d.]. Internet.

Temple, Josiah Howard and George Sheldon. *A History of the Town of Northfield, Massachusetts.* Albany NY: Joel Munsell, 1875.

Tennant, Alan. *The Snakes of Texas.* Austin TX: Texas Monthly Press, c.1984.

TenneScene. Union City TN, 1968?–.

Tennessean. Nashville TN, 1812–.

Tennessee. *Private Acts of the State of Tennessee.* Nashville TN, 1911–.

Tennessee Academy of Science. *Journal.* Nashville TN, 1926–.

Tennessee Ancestors. Knoxville TN: East Tennessee Historical Society, 1985–.

Tennessee Bureau of Agriculture, Statistics and Mines. *Report.* Nashville TN, 1876–1880?

The Tennessee Civil War Veterans Questionnaires. Comp. by Gustavus W. Dyer & John Trotwood Moore and ed. by Colleen M. Elliott and Louise A. Moxley. Easley SC: Southern Historical Press, 1985. 5 vols.

Tennessee. Court of Civil Appeals. *Leading Cases of the Court of Civil Appeals of the State of Tennessee.* Nashville TN: Marshall & Bruce, 1911–1919. 8 vols.

Tennessee Folk Lore Society. *Bulletin.* Maryville TN, 1935–.

Tennessee Historical Magazine. Nashville TN, 1915–1937.

Tennessee Historical Quarterly. Nashville TN, 1942–.

Tennessee. State Board of Health. *Bulletin.* Nashville TN, 1885–1897.

Tennessee Tribune. Nashville TN, 1992–.

Tennessee University, Knoxville. Agricultural Experiment Station. *Bulletin.* Knoxville TN, 1888–1968.

Tenney, Sanborn. *Natural History.* 7th ed. New York: Charles Scribner, 1869 [c.1865].

Tenney, Tabitha Gilman. *Female Quixotism.* Boston: J. P. Peaslee, 1829. 2 vols.

Terhune, Mary Virginia Hawes. *Breakfast, Luncheon and Tea.* New York: Scribner, Armstrong, 1875.

———. *Common Sense in the Household.* New York: Scribner, Armstrong, 1874 [c.1871].

———. *The Empty Heart.* New York: Carleton, 1871 [c.1870].

———. *Eve's Daughters.* New York: J. R. Anderson and H. S. Allen, 1882.

———. *Moss-Side.* New York: Derby & Jackson, 1857.

Terrell, Christine et al. *Forest Park.* Charleston SC: Arcadia Publishing, c.2008.

Terrell, John Upton. *Bunkhouse Papers.* New York: Dial Press, 1971.

Territorial Enterprise. Virginia City NV, 1858–1916.

Territorial Enterprise and Virginia City News. Virginia City NV, 1952–.

Terry County, Texas. Clanton AL: Heritage Pub. Consultants, c.2002.

Texas A&M University. *Aggie Horticulture.* [v.d.]. Internet.

———. *Discover Entomology.* [v.d.]. Internet.

Texas A&M University. Aggie Horticulture. *The Plantanswer Machine.* [v.d.]. Internet.

Texas A&M University. Agricultural Research & Extension Center at Uvalde. *Herbarium.* [v.d.]. Internet.

Texas A&M University. Digital Flora of Texas. *Texas Vascular Plant Checklist.* [v.d.]. Internet.

Texas A&M University. Digital Flora of Texas. *Vascular Plant Image Library.* [v.d.]. Internet.

Texas Academy of Science. *Transactions.* Austin TX, 1892–.

Texas Agricultural Experiment Station, College Station. *Bulletin.* College Station TX: Agricultural and Mechanical College of TX, 1888–1961.

Texas Almanac. Dallas TX: A. H. Belo, 1856–.

Texas Bar Association. *Proceedings.* Houston TX, 1882–1942.

Texas Cooperative Extension. *Dealing with Household Pests in South Texas.* 2000?–. Internet.

Texas Courier-Record of Medicine. Dallas TX, 1883–1917?

Texas Electric Cooperatives. *Texas Co-op Power.* Austin TX, 1944–.

Texas Farm Bureau. *Texas Agriculture.* Waco TX, 2000?–.

Texas Folklore Society. *Publications.* Austin TX, 1911–.

Texas Game and Fish. Austin TX, 1942–1965.

Texas Geographic Magazine. Dallas TX, 1937–1949.

Texas. Geological Survey. *Report and Accompanying Papers 1st–4th.* Austin TX: State Print. Off., 1889–1892.

Texas. Highway Department. *Texas Highways.* Austin TX, 1954–.

Texas in 1840 or the Emigrant's Guide to the New Republic. New York: William W. Allen, 1840.

Texas Journal of Science. Austin TX: Texas Academy of Science, 1949–.

Texas Medical Journal. Austin TX, 1893–1919.

Texas Monarch Watch Monitoring Packet. Austin TX: Texas Parks & Wildlife, 2003.

Texas Monthly. Austin TX, 1973–.

Texas Observer. Austin TX, 1955?–.

Texas Parks and Wildlife—Fishing. *The Texas Shrimp Fishery.* [v.d.]. Internet.

Texas Parks and Wildlife—Hunting and Wildlife. *Wildlife Fact Sheets.* [v.d.]. Internet.

Texas Parks and Wildlife—State Parks & Historical Sites. *Rusk & Palestine State Parks.* [v.d.]. Internet.

Texas (Republic) Department of State. "Diplomatic Correspondence of the Republic of Texas." American Historical Association *Annual Report* (1908) vol. 1; (1911) vol. 2, pts. 1, 2.

Texas School Journal. Houston TX, 1883–1929?

Texas Siftings. Austin TX, 1881–1897.

Texas. State Department of Highways and Public Transportation. Travel & Information Division. *Flowers of Texas.* Austin TX: [s.n.], c1979.

Texas State Historical Association. *Quarterly.* Austin TX, 1897–1912.

Texas. University-El Paso. *Chihuahuan Desert Home Page.* [v.d.]. Internet.

Thacher, James. *The American Orchardist.* 2d ed. much improved. Plymouth MA: Ezra Collier, 1825.

———. *A Military Journal during the American Revolutionary War, from 1775 to 1783.* Boston: Richardson and Lord, 1823.

———. *A Military Journal during the American Revolutionary War, from 1775 to 1783.* 2d ed. rev. and corr. Boston: Cottons & Barnard, 1827.

Thacker, Page SEE Burwell, Letitia M.

Thane, Eric SEE Henry, Ralph Chester

Tharp, Benjamin Carroll. *The Vegetation of Texas.* Houston TX: Anson Jones Press, 1939.

Thaxter, Celia. *Among the Isle of Shoals.* Boston: J. R. Osgood, 1873.

———. *An Island Garden.* Boston: Houghton Mifflin, 1904 [c.1894].

Thayer, Cynthia A. *A Certain Slant of Light.* New York: St. Martin's Griffin, 2001 [c.2000].

Thayer, William Makepeace. *From Log-Cabin to the White House.* Boston: James H. Earle, 1881.

———. *From the Tannery to the White House.* Boston: James H. Earle, 1885.

———. *Marvels of the New West.* Norwich CT: Henry Bill, 1888 [c.1887].

Theata. Fairbanks AK: Univ. AK, 1973–.

Theatre Arts Magazine. Detroit MI, 1916–1964.

Therapeutic Gazette. Detroit MI, 1877–1927.

Thief River Falls Times. Thief River Falls MN, 1910–.

Think. New York: International Business Machines Corporation, 1935–1970.

This Is the Arlo Guthrie Book. New York: Amsco Music Publishing, c.1969.

This Remarkable Continent. College Station TX: TX A&M Univ. Press, c.1982. Pub. for The Society for the North American Cultural Survey.

This State of Wonders: the Letters of an Iowa Frontier Family, 1858–1861. Iowa City IA: Univ. IA Press, c.1986.

Thoburn, Joseph Bradfield. *A Standard History of Oklahoma.* Chicago: American Historical Society, 1916. 5 vols.

Thomas, Augustus. *Arizona.* Chicago: Dramatic Pub., c.1899.

Thomas, Chamintney. *Hear the Lambs A-Cryin.* [s.l.]: Portals Press; distributed by the Univ. AL Press, 1975.

Thomas, Daniel Lindsey and Lucy Blayney Thomas. *Kentucky Superstitions.* Princeton NJ: Princeton Univ. Press, 1920.

Thomas, David. *Travels through the Western Country in the Summer of 1816.* Auburn NY: David Rumsey, 1819.

———. *Travels through the Western Country in the Summer of 1816.* Darien CT: Hafner Pub., 1970. Facsimile of the 1819 ed. pub. by David Rumsey, Auburn NY.

Thomas, Edith Matilda. *Mary at the Farm and Book of Recipes.* Norristown PA: J. Hartenstine, 1915.

Thomas, Edward Harper. *Chinook, a History and Dictionary of the Northwest Coast Trade Jargon.* 2d ed. Portland OR: Binfords & Mort, 1970.

Thomas, Frederick William. *East and West.* Philadelphia: Carey, Lea & Blanchard, 1836. 2 vols.

———. *Howard Pinckney.* London: J. Clements, 1841 [c.1840].

———. *John Randolph, of Roanoke, and Other Sketches of Character.* Philadelphia: A. Hart, 1853.

Thomas, Gabriel. *An Historical and Geographical Account of the Province and Country of Pensilvania.* New-York: Lithographed for H. A. Brady, 1848. Orig. pub. in 1698 by A. Baldwin, London.

Thomas, Gordon W. *Fast & Able.* Gloucester MA: Gloucester 350th Anniversary Celebration, 1973 [c.1952].

Thomas, Isaiah. *The Diary of Isaiah Thomas, 1805–1828.* Worcester MA: The Society, 1909. 2 vols.

Thomas, James P. *From Tennessee Slave to St. Louis Entrepreneur: the Autobiography of James Thomas.* Ed. by Loren Schweninger. Columbia MO: Univ. MO Press, 1984.

Thomas, Jean. *Blue Ridge Country.* New York: Duell, Sloan & Pearce, c.1942.

Thomas, John Hunter. *Flora of the Santa Cruz Mountains of California.* Stanford CA: Stanford Univ. Press, 1961.

Thomas, Joseph B. *Hounds and Hunting through the Ages.* New York: Windward House, 1933 [c.1928].

Thomas, Roy Edwin. *Come Go with Me.* New York: Farrar, Straus, Giroux, c.1994.

———, comp. *Popular Folk Dictionary of Ozarks Talk.* Little Rock AR: Dox Books, c.1972.

———, comp. *Southern Appalachia, 1885–1915.* Jefferson NC: McFarland, c.1991.

Thomas County Historical Society. *Prairie Winds.* Colby KS, 1973–.

Thomas Jefferson's Garden Book, 1766–1824. Annotated by Edwin Morris Betts. Philadelphia: Am. Philosophical Society, 1944.

Thomas' Massachusetts Spy, or, Worcester Gazette. Worcester MA, 1781–1786; 1788–1821.

Thomasville Times. Thomasville AL, 1921–.

Thome, James A. and J. Horace Kimball. *Emancipation in the West Indies.* 2d ed. New York: American Anti-Slavery Society, 1839 [c.1838].

Thompson, Benjamin Franklin. *The History of Long Island from Its Discovery to the Present Time.* 2d ed., rev. and greatly enlarged. New York: Gould, Banks, 1843. 2 vols.

Thompson, Carlene. *Share No Secrets.* New York: St. Martin's Press, c.2005.

Thompson, Daniel Pierce. *The Adventures of Timothy Peacock, Esquire.* Middlebury VT: Knapp and Jewett, 1835.

———. *Gaut Gurley.* Boston: J. P. Jewett; Cleveland OH: Henry P. B. Jewett, 1857.

———. *The Green Mountain Boys.* Montpelier VT: E. P. Ealton and Sons, 1839. 2 vols.

———. *The Green Mountain Boys.* Rev. ed. Boston: Chase, Nichols and Hill, c.1848. 2 vols.

———. *Locke Amsden.* Boston: Benjamin B. Mussey, 1853. Orig. pub. in 1847.

———. *The Rangers.* Boston: Benjamin B. Mussey, 1851.

Thompson, D'Arcy Wentworth. *Report by Professor D'Arcy Thompson on His Mission to the Behring Sea in 1896, Dated March 4, 1897.* London: Printed for H.M.S.O. by Harrison & Sons, 1897.

Thompson, Era Bell. *American Daughter.* Chicago: Univ. Chicago Press, 1946.

Thompson, George W. *Collection.* 1920–1972. Unpub. letters.

Thompson, Harold William. *Body, Boots & Britches.* New York: Dover Publications, 1962. Orig. pub. in 1939 by J. B. Lippincott, Philadelphia.

Thompson, John Baptiste de Macklot. *Jist Huntin'; Tales of the Forest, Field and Stream.* Cincinnati OH: Stewart Kidd, c.1921.

Thompson, Margaret Hollinshead. *High Trails of Glacier National Park.* Caldwell ID: Caxton Printers, 1936.

Thompson, Maurice. *By-Ways and Bird Notes.* New York: United States Book, c.1885.

———. *Hoosier Mosaics.* New York: E. J. Hale & Son, 1875.

Thompson, Vicki Lewis. *Nerd in Shining Armor.* New York: Bantam Dell, c.2003.

Thompson, William Tappan. *Chronicles of Pineville.* Philadelphia: Carey & Hart, 1845.

———. *Major Jones' Courtship.* Madison GA: Printed by C. R. Hanleiter, 1843.

———. *Major Jones's Courtship.* 2d ed. Philadelphia: Carey & Hart, 1844.

———. *Major Jones's Courtship.* 12th ed., with additional letters. Philadelphia: A. Hart, 1852.

———. *Major Jones's Courtship.* Rev. and enlarged. Atlanta GA: Cherokee Pub., 1973. Repr. of the 1872 ed. pub. in New York.

———. *Major Jones's Sketches of Travel.* Philadelphia: T. B. Peterson & Bros., c.1848.

Thompson, Winfield Martin. *In the Maine Woods.* 2d ed. Bangor ME: Bangor and Aroostock Railroad, c.1901.

Thompson, Zadock. *Appendix to the History of Vermont.* Burlington VT: The Author, 1853.

———. *History of Vermont, Natural, Civil and Statistical, in Three Parts.* Burlington VT: Chauncey Goodrich, 1842.

Thomson, Betty Flanders. *The Changing Face of New England.* New York: Macmillan, c.1958.

Thomson, Mortimer. *Doesticks, What He Says.* New York: Edward Livermore, 1855.

———. *Plu-ri-bus-tah.* New York: Livermore & Rudd, 1856.

Thomson, Samuel. *New Guide to Health or, Botanic Family Physician.* 2d ed. Boston: Printed for the author by E. G. House, 1825.

Thomson, Tom. *Birding in Ohio.* 2d ed. Bloomington IN: IN Univ. Press, 1994.

Thomsonian Recorder. Columbus OH, 1832–1837.

Thone, Frank. *Trees and Flowers of Yellowstone National Park.* St. Paul MN: J. E. Haynes, c.1923.

Thoreau, Henry David. *Autumn.* Boston: Houghton, Mifflin, 1892.

———. *Cape Cod.* Boston: Ticknor and Fields, 1865.

———. *Journal.* Ed. by Bradford Torrey and Francis H. Allen. Boston: Houghton Mifflin, 1949. 14 vols.

———. *Letters to Various Persons.* Boston: Ticknor and Fields, 1865.

———. *The Maine Woods.* Boston: Ticknor and Fields, 1864.

———. *Summer.* Boston: [s.n.], 1884.

———. *Walden.* Columbus OH: C. E. Merrill, 1969. Orig. pub. in 1854 by Ticknor and Fields, Boston.

———. *A Week on the Concord and Merrimack Rivers.* New York: Thomas Y. Crowell, 1911. Orig. pub. in 1849 by Munroe, Boston and Putnam, New York.

———. *Wild Fruits.* Ed. and introduced by Bradley P. Dean. New York: W. W. Norton, c.2000.

———. *The Writings of Henry David Thoreau.* Walden ed. Boston: Houghton, Mifflin, c.1906. 20 vols.

———. *A Year in Thoreau's Journal, 1851.* Intro. & notes by H. Daniel Peck. New York: Penguin Books, 1993.

Thornber, John James and Frances Bonker. *The Fantastic Clan the Cactus Family.* New York: Macmillan, 1932.

Thornborough, Laura SEE Thornburgh, Laura

Thornburgh, Laura. *The Great Smoky Mountains.* New York: Thomas Y. Crowell, c.1937.

Thornbury, William David. *Principles of Geomorphology.* New York: Wiley, 1954.

Thorne, Samuel. *The Journal of a Boy's Trip on Horseback.* New York: Privately printed, 1936.

Thornton, Anna Maria Brodeau. "Diary of Mrs. William Thornton, 1800–1863." Columbia Historical Society *Records.* (1907) 10.88–226; (1916) 19.172–82.

Thornton, Billy Bob. *Sling Blade: a Screenplay.* New York: Miramax, c.1996.

Thornton, Harrison Robertson. *Among the Eskimos of Wales, Alaska 1890–93.* New York: AMS Press, 1976. Repr. of the 1931 ed. pub. by Johns Hopkins Press, Baltimore.

Thornton, Richard Hopwood. *An American Glossary.* Philadelphia: J. B. Lippincott, 1912. 2 vols.

———. *An American Glossary. Volume 3.* Ed. by Louise Hanley. Madison WI: American Dialect Society, 1939.

Thorp, Jack SEE Thorp, Nathan Howard

Thorp, Nathan Howard. *Pardner of the Wind.* Caldwell ID: Caxton Printers, 1945.

———. *Songs of the Cowboys.* Boston: Houghton Mifflin, 1921.

———. *Songs of the Cowboys.* New York: C. N. Potter, 1966. Contains a facsimile of the 1908 ed. printed by the News Print Shop, Estancia NM.

———. *Tales of the Chuck Wagon.* Santa Fe NM: [s.n.], c.1926.

Thorpe, Thomas Bangs. *The Master's House.* 3d ed. New York: J. C. Derby, 1855. Orig. pub. in 1854 by T. L. McElrath, New York, under the title *The Master's House: A Tale of Southern Life.*

———. *The Mysteries of the Backwoods.* Philadelphia: Carey and Hart, 1846.

———. *The Taylor Anecdote Book.* New York: D. Appleton, 1848.

Three Lectures Delivered before the Michigan State Agricultural Society. Lansing MI: John A. Kerr, 1865.

Threepenny Review. Berkeley CA, 1980–.

Three Pioneer Tennessee Documents. Nashville TN: Tennessee Historical Commission, c.1964. *Donelson's Journal, Cumberland Compact,* and *Minutes of Cumberland Court.*

Three Rivers News. Milo ME, 2001–.

Thrush, Paul W., comp. *A Dictionary of Mining, Mineral, and Related Terms.* Washington DC: U.S. Dept. of the Interior, Bureau of Mines, 1968.

Thurber, James. *Let Your Mind Alone!* New York: Harper & Bros., 1937.

———. *My Life and Hard Times.* New York: Harper & Bros., c.1933.

———. *The Owl in the Attic and Other Perplexities.* New York: Harper & Bros., 1931.

———. *The Thurber Carnival.* New York: Harper & Bros., 1945.

———. *The Years with Ross.* Boston: Little, Brown, 1959.

Thwaites, Reuben Gold, ed. *Early Western Travels.* Cleveland OH: A. H. Clark, 1904–1907. 32 vols.

Tice, John H. *Over the Plains, on the Mountains.* St. Louis MO: Printed by the "Industrial age" Printing Co., 1872.

Tichenor, William Collett. *Farm Contracts between Landlord and Tenant.* Lebanon OH: W. C. Tichenor, c.1916.

Ticknor, George. *Life, Letters and Journals of George Ticknor.* 8th ed. Boston: James R. Osgood, 1877 [c.1876]. 2 vols.

———. *Life of William Hickling Prescott.* Boston: Ticknor and Fields, 1864.

Tidal Wave. Silver City ID, 1868–.

Timberlake, Henry. *The Memoirs of Lieut. Henry Timberlake.* London: Printed for the Author, 1765.

Timbrook, Janice. *Chumash Ethnobotany.* Santa Barbara CA: Santa Barbara Museum of Natural History; Berkeley CA: HeyDay Books, 2007.

Time. New York, 1923–.

Time-Piece, and Literary Companion. New York, 1797.

Times SEE ALSO *Seattle Daily Times*

Times. East Chicago IN: Lake Co. Printing, 1916–1933.

Times. London, 1785–.

Times and Democrat. Orangeburg SC, 2003?–.

Times & Seasons. Nauvoo IL, 1839–1846.

Times-Crescent-the Charles County Leaf. La Plata MD, 1966?–.

Times-Democrat. Lima OH, 1893–1912.

Times Herald. Olean NY, 1932–.

Times Herald Record. Middletown NY, 1960–.

Times-News. Burlington NC, 1989–.

Times-News. Mount Pulaski IL, 1932–.

Times-News. Twin Falls ID, 1942–.

Times-Picayune SEE ALSO *Daily Picayune*

Times-Picayune. New Orleans LA, 1914–1980; 1986–.

Times-Record. Aledo IL, 1894–.

Times Recorder. Zanesville OH, 1904–1959; 1965–.

Times Recorder and the Zanesville Signal. Zanesville OH, 1959–1965.

Times-Reporter. Dover-New Philadelphia OH, 1968–.

Times-Standard. Eureka CA, 1967–.

Tingle, Tom and Doc Moore. *Spooky Texas Tales.* Lubbock TX: TX Tech Univ. Press, c.2005.

Tinker, Spencer Wilkie. *Fishes of Hawaii.* Honolulu HI: Hawaiian Service, c.1978.

Tioga Eagle. Wellsborough PA, 1838–1858.

Tippett, Edwin James, Jr. *Who Won the War?* 2d ed. Toledo OH: Toledo Type-Setting & Printing, 1920.

Titford, William Jowit. *Sketches towards a Hortus Botanicus Americanus.* London: Printed for the author by C. Stower, 1811.

Titusville Herald. Titusville PA, 1913–.

Titusville Morning Herald. Titusville PA, 1869–1913.

Tixier, Victor. *Voyage aux Prairies Osages.* Clermont-Ferrand: Perol; Paris: Roret, 1844.

Today's Health. Chicago, 1950–1976.

Today Show Letters. 1971–1980. Unpub. letters in response to F. G. Cassidy's appearances on NBC's *Today Show,* Jan. 25, 1971, and Apr. 29, 1980.

Todd, Burbank L. *Hiram the Young Farmer.* New York: Sully & Kleinteich, c.1914.

Todd, Henry Cook. *Notes upon Canada and the United States from 1832 to 1840.* 2d ed. Toronto: Rogers and Thompson, 1840.

Todd, John. *The Sunset Land.* Boston: Lee and Shepard, 1870.

Todd, John E. *John Todd the Story of His Life Told Mainly by Himself.* New York: Harper & Bros., 1876 [c.1875].

Todd, Margaret SEE Travers, Graham

Todd, Sereno Edwards. *The American Wheat Culturist.* New York: Taintor Bros., 1868.

———. *The Young Farmer's Manual.* New York: C. M. Saxton, Barker & Company, c.1860.

Todd, Walter Edmond Clyde. *Birds of Western Pennsylvania.* Pittsburgh PA: Univ. Pittsburgh Press, 1940.

Token. Boston, 1828–1832.

Token and Atlantic Souvenir. Boston: Charles Bowen, 1833–1842.

Tolbert, Frank. *Bigamy Jones.* New York: Holt, 1954.

Tolman, Newton F. *North of Monadnock.* Boston: Little, Brown, 1961.

Tolmie, William Fraser. *The Journals of William Fraser Tolmie.* Vancouver: Mitchell Press, c.1963.

Tomahawk Leader. Tomahawk WI, 1896–.

Tomlinson, Abraham, comp. *The Military Journals of Two Private Soldiers, 1758–1775.* Poughkeepsie NY: A. Tomlinson, 1855.

Tomlinson, William P. *Kansas in Eighteen Fifty-Eight.* New-York: H. Dayton; Indianapolis IN: Dayton and Asher, 1859.

Tompson, Edward. *Heaven the Best Country.* Boston: B. Green, 1712.

Toole, John Kennedy. *A Confederacy of Dunces.* Baton Rouge LA: LA State Univ. Press, 1980.

Toomer, Jean. *Cane.* New York: Liveright, 1951 [c.1923].

Tooné, Eruera. *Yankee Slang.* London: Harrison, 1932.

Topeka Capital-Journal. Topeka KS, 1980–.

Topeka Daily Capital. Topeka KS, 1881–1980.

Topeka Kansas Zoo. Waterbird Ponds. [v.d.]. Internet.

Topsfield Historical Society. *Historical Collections.* Topsfield MA, 1895–.

———. *Town Records.* Topsfield MA: The Society, 1917–1920. 2 vols.

Torch-Light & Public Advertiser. Hagers-Town MD, 1817?–1833; 1835–1837.

Torrence, Frederic Ridgely. *Granny Maumee.* New York: Macmillan, 1917.

Torrey, Bradford. *Birds in the Bush.* Boston: Houghton, Mifflin, c.1885.

———. *The Clerk of the Woods.* Boston: Houghton, Mifflin, 1903.

———. *A Florida Sketch-Book.* Boston: Houghton, Mifflin, c.1894.

———. *The Foot-Path Way.* Boston: Houghton, Mifflin, 1892.

Torrey, John. *A Flora of the Northern and Middle Sections of the United States.* New York: Printed and sold by T. and J. Swords, 1824.

———. *A Flora of the State of New-York.* Albany NY: Carroll and Cook, 1843. 2 vols.

Torrey, John and Asa Gray. *A Flora of North America.* New York: Hafner Publishing, 1969. 2 vols. Facsimile of 1838–1843 ed. pub. by Wiley & Putnam, New York.

Torrey, Mary Ide. *City and Country Life.* Boston: Tappan & Whittemore, 1853.

Torreya. Lancaster PA, 1901–1945.

Torrey Botanical Club. *Bulletin.* Lawrence KS, 1870–1996.

Torrey Botanical Society. *Journal.* Lawrence KS, 1997–.

Torrington Register. Torrington CT, 1889–.

Tougias, Mike. *There's a Porcupine in My Outhouse.* Sterling VA: Capital Books, c.2002.

Toulmin, Harry. *A Description of Kentucky, in North America.* London: [s.n.], 1792.

———. *The Western Country in 1793.* San Marino CA: Castle Press, Henry E. Huntington Library and Art Gallery, c.1948.

Tourgée, Albion Winegar. *Bricks without Straw.* New York: Fords, Howard, & Hulbert, c.1880.

———. *Button's Inn.* Boston: Roberts Bros., 1887.

———. *Figs and Thistles.* New York: Fords, Howard & Hulbert, c.1879.

———. *A Fool's Errand.* New York: Fords, Howard, and Hulbert, 1880. Orig. pub. in 1879.

———. *A Fool's Errand.* New, enlarged, and illustrated ed. New York: Fords, Howard & Hulbert, 1880.

———. *A Royal Gentleman.* Ridgewood NJ: Gregg Press, 1967. Repr. of 1881 ed. pub. by Fords, Howard, & Hulbert, New York.

———. *A Royal Gentleman . . . and Zouri's Christmas.* New York: Fords, Howard, & Hulbert, c.1881.

Tower Times. Stoughton WI, 1992–.

Towle, Catherine Webb. *Stories for the American Freemason's Fireside.* Cincinnati OH: American Masonic Publishing, 1868.

Towler, Juby Earl. *Genealogy from the Fruit of the Garden.* Danville VA: Published by the Author, c.1968.

Town and Country. New York: Hearst, 1901–.

Townsend, Charles Wendell. *The Birds of Essex County, Massachusetts.* Cambridge MA: Nuttall Ornithological Club, 1905.

Townsend, Edward W. *Chimmie Fadden.* New York: Lovell, Coryell, c.1895.

Townsend, Frederic. *Fancies of a Whimsical Man.* New York: John S. Taylor, 1852.

Townsend, John Kirk. *Narrative of a Journey across the Rocky Mountains.* Philadelphia: Henry Perkins, 1839.

Townsend, Malcolm, comp. *U.S. an Index to the United States of America.* Boston: D. Lothrop, c.1890.

Townsend, Virginia Frances. *While It Was Morning.* New York: Derby & Jackson, 1858.

Tractor and Gas Engine Review. Madison WI: Clarke, 1918–1925.

Tracy, Marian Coward, ed. *Coast to Coast Cookery.* Bloomington IN: IN Univ. Press, 1952.

Trahey, Jane, ed. *A Taste of Texas.* Toronto: Random House, c.1949.

Trail and Timberline On-Line. 1999–. Internet.

Traill, Catherine Parr Strickland. *The Backwoods of Canada.* 2d ed. London: C. Knight, 1836.

———. *Canadian Crusoes.* Ed. by Agnes Strickland. London: Arthur Hall Virtue, 1852.

———. *The Canadian Settler's Guide.* 7th ed. considerably enlarged. Toronto: Printed at the Office of the Toronto Times, 1857 [c.1855].

———. *The Canadian Settlers' Guide.* 10th ed. considerably enlarged. London: E. Stanford, 1860.

Train, Arthur Kissam, Jr. *The Story of Everyday Things.* New York: Harper & Bros., 1941.

Train, George Francis. *An American Merchant in Europe, Asia, and Australia.* New York: G. P. Putnam, 1857.

Transcript. North Adams MA, 1969–1996.

Transylvania Journal of Medicine and the Associate Sciences. Lexington KY, 1828–1839.

Trautman, Milton Bernhard. *The Birds of Buckeye Lake, Ohio.* Ann Arbor MI: Univ. MI Press, 1940.

———. *The Fishes of Ohio.* Columbus OH: OH State Univ. Press, 1957.

Traver, Robert SEE Voelker, John Donaldson

Travers, Graham. *The Life of Sophia Jex-Blake.* London: Macmillan, 1918.

Traverse City Record-Eagle. Traverse City MI, 1898?–.

Treasured Polish Recipes for Americans. 2d printing. Minneapolis MN: Polanie Publishing, 1949 [c.1948].

The Treasury Star Parade. Ed. by William A. Bacher. New York: Farrar & Rinehart, c.1942.

Treat, Mary Lua Adelia Davis Allen. *Injurious Insects of the Farm and Garden.* New enlarged ed. New York: Orange Judd, 1903 [c.1882, c.1887].

Trego, Charles B. *A Geography of Pennsylvania.* Philadelphia: Edward C. Biddle, 1843.

Tremenheere, Hugh Seymour. *Notes on Public Subjects, Made during a Tour in the United States and in Canada.* London: John Murray, 1852.

Trenton Evening Times. Trenton NJ, 1895–1899; 1906–1964.

Trenton Times. Trenton NJ, 1882–.

Tresidder, Argus. *Reading to Others.* Chicago: Scott, Foresman, c.1940.

Tresidder, Mary Curry. *The Trees of Yosemite.* Stanford CA: Stanford Univ. Press, 1948.

Trial of David Lynn, Jabez Meigs, Elijah Barton, Prince Cain, Nathaniel Lynn, Ansel Meigs and Adam Pitts. Hallowell ME: Printed by Ezekiel Goodale, 1810.

Tri-City Herald. Pasco WA, 1947–.

Tri-City Star. Davenport IA, 1904–1905.

Trigg, Haiden C. *The American Fox-Hound.* Glasgow KY: [s.n.], 1895.

Trimble, Henry. *The Tannins.* Philadelphia: J. B. Lippincott, 1892–1894. 2 vols.

Trinity Forks Native Plant Press. Denton TX, 2004?–.

Tripp, Alonzo. *The Fisher Boy.* Boston: Whittemore, Niles & Hall, 1858 [c.1857].

Tripp, William Henry. *There Goes Flukes.* New Bedford MA: Reynolds Printing, 1938.

TriQuarterly. Evanston IL: Northwestern Univ., 1958–.

Triton, Willie SEE Tripp, Alonzo

Trollope, Anthony. *North America.* London: Chapman & Hall, 1862. 2 vols.

Trollope, Frances Milton. *Domestic Manners of the Americans.* New York: Reprinted for the Booksellers, 1832.

———. *Domestic Manners of the Americans.* London: George Routledge & Sons, 1927. Repr. of the fifth ed. orig. pub. in 1839 by R. Bentley, London.

———. *Domestic Manners of the Americans.* New York: Knopf, 1949.

———. *The Refugee in America.* London: Whittaker, Treacher, 1833. 2 vols.

Trout, Ed. *Historic Buildings of the Smokies.* Sidebars by Margaret Lynn Brown. Gatlinburg TN: Great Smoky Mountains Natural History Association, 1995.

Trowbridge, John Townsend. *Cudjo's Cave.* London: Ward, Lock, and Tyler, 1868. Orig. pub. in 1864 by Lathrop, Boston.

———. *A Picture of the Desolated States.* Hartford CT: L. Stebbins, 1868.

———. *The South.* Hartford CT: L. Stebbins, 1866.

———. *The Three Scouts.* London: Ward, Lock, and Tyler, 1868. Orig. pub. in 1864 by Lathrop, Boston.

Troy Call. Troy IL, 1918?–1947?

True American. Trenton NJ, 1801–1829.

Truesdell, Amelia Woodward. *A California Pilgrimage.* 2d ed. San Francisco: S. Carson, 1884.

True, the Man's Magazine. Greenwich CT: Fawcett Publications, 1937–.

Truett, Randle Bond. *Trade and Travel around the Southern Appalachians before 1830.* Chapel Hill NC: Univ. NC Press, 1935.

Truman, Harry S. *Dear Bess.* New York: W. W. Norton, c.1983.

Trumbull, Benjamin. *A Complete History of Connecticut.* New Haven CT: Maltby, Goldsmith and Samuel Wadsworth, 1818. 2 vols.

Trumbull, David. *The Death of Capt. Nathan Hale: a Drama in Five Acts.* Hartford CT: Press of Elihu Geer, 1845.

Trumbull, Gordon. *Names and Portraits of Birds Which Interest Gunners.* New York: Harper & Bros., 1888.

Trumbull, John. *M'Fingal.* Hartford CT: Printed by Hudson and Goodwin, 1782.

"Trumps" SEE Dick, William B.

Truxall, Aida Craig. *Respects to All: Letters of Two Pennsylvania Boys in the War of the Rebellion.* Pittsburgh PA: Univ. Pittsburgh Press, c.1962.

Tryckare, Tre et al. *The Lore of Sportfishing.* New York: Crown, c.1976.

Tryon, Henry H. *Fearsome Critters.* Cornwall NY: Idlewild Press, c.1939.

Tryon, Lewis R. *Poor Man's Doctor.* New York: Prentice Hall, 1945.

Tubbee, Okah. *A Sketch of the Life of Okah Tubbee.* Recorded by Laah Ceil Manatoi Elaah Tubbee, his Wife. Springfield MA: Printed for Okah Tubbee by H. S. Taylor, 1848.

Tucci, Tony James. *On the Waterfowl of Texas.* Austin TX: Texas Parks and Wildlife, Wildlife Division, 2001.

Tucker, George. *The Valley of Shenandoah.* New York: C. Wiley, 1824. 2 vols.

Tucker, Gilbert M. *American English.* New York: Knopf, 1921.

Tucker, Mary Orne. "Diary of Mary Orne Tucker, 1802." Essex Institute *Historical Collections* (1941) 77.306–38.

Tucker, Nathaniel Beverly. *The Partisan Leader.* New York: Reprinted by Rudd & Carleton, 1861. 2 vols. Facsimile of 1836 ed. pub. by Duff Green, Washington DC.

Tucson Citizen. Tucson AZ, 1901–1928; 1977–.

Tucson Daily Citizen. Tucson AZ, 1929–1977.

Tufford, Julia Peterson, ed. *Scandinavian Recipes.* Minneapolis MN: [s.n.], 1940.

———, ed. *Scandinavian Recipes.* Rev. ed. Minneapolis MN: [s.n.], 1951.

———, ed. *Scandinavian Recipes.* 22d printing. Minneapolis MN: J. P. Tufford, c.1966.

Tufts, Henry. *The Autobiography of a Criminal.* Ed. with an intro. by Edmund Pearson. New York: Duffield, 1930 [1807].

Tull, Delena. *Edible and Useful Plants of Texas and the Southwest.* Austin TX: Univ. TX Press, 1999.

Tulley, John. *An Almanack for the Year of Our Lord, 1700.* Boston: Bartholemew Green & John Allen, 1700.

Tullidge, Edward William. *The Women of Mormondom.* New York: Tullidge and Crandall, 1877.

Tully, Jim. *Shanty Irish.* Garden City NY: Garden City Publishing, c.1928.

Tulsa World. Tulsa OK, 1989–.

Tundra Times. Fairbanks AK, 1962–.

Tunkhannock Republican and New Age. Tunkhannock PA, 1904–.

Tuomey, Michael. *Report on the Geology of South Carolina.* Columbia SC: Printed and Published for the State by A. S. Johnston, 1848.

Tupper Lake Free Press and Tupper Lake Herald. Tupper Lake NY, 1937–.

Turf, Field and Farm. New York: Turf, Field and Farm Association, 1865–1903.

Turgeon, Charlotte and Frederic A. Birmingham. *The Saturday Evening Post All-American Cookbook.* Indianapolis IN: Thomas Nelson & Curtis Publishing, c.1976.

Turnbo, Silas Claiborn. *The White River Chronicles of S. C. Turnbo.* Selected and ed. by James F. Keefe and Lynn Morrow. Fayetteville AR: Univ. AR Press, 1994.

Turnbull, David. *Travels in the West.* New York: AMS Press, 1973. Repr. of 1840 ed. pub. by Longman, Orne, Brown, Green, and Longmans, London.

Turnbull, Jane M. E. and Marion Turnbull. *American Photographs.* London: T. C. Newby, 1859. 2 vols.

Turnbull, William Paterson. *The Birds of East Pennsylvania and New Jersey.* Philadelphia: Henry Grambo, 1869.

Turner, Alford E., ed. *The Earps Talk.* College Station TX: Creative Publishing, c.1980.

Turner, Joseph Addison. *The Cotton Planter's Manual.* New York: Negro Universities Press, 1969. Repr. of the 1857 ed. pub. in New York by both C. M. Saxon and O. Judd.

Turner, Lorenzo Dow. *Africanisms in the Gullah Dialect.* Chicago: Univ. Chicago Press, 1949.

Turner, Lucien McShan. *Contributions to the Natural History of Alaska.* Washington DC: Govt. Printing Office, 1886.

Turner, Orsamus. *History of the Pioneer Settlement of Phelps and Gorham's Purchase.* Rochester NY: William Alling, c.1851.

Turner, Walter A. *Men at War.* New York: iUniverse, c.2003.

Turner's New-York Shipping and Commercial List. New York, 1820–1823.

Turow, Scott. *Presumed Innocent.* London: Bloomsbury, c.1987.

Tuscaloosa News. Tuscaloosa-Northport AL, 1929–.

Tuskegee Normal and Industrial Institute. Experiment Station. *Bulletin.* Tuskegee AL: Tuskegee Institute Press, 1898–1936.

Tuttle, Charles M. "California Diary of Charles M. Tuttle." *Wisconsin Magazine of History* (1931–1932) 15.69–85, 219–33.

TWA Ambassador. St. Paul MN: Trans World Airlines, Public Relations Dept., 1968–.

Twain, Mark SEE Clemens, Samuel Langhorne

Tyler, Anne. *Breathing Lessons.* New York: Alfred A. Knopf, 1988.

———. *Celestial Navigation.* New York: Alfred A. Knopf, 1974.

———. *If Morning Ever Comes.* New York: Alfred A. Knopf, 1964.

———. *Ladder of Years.* New York: Alfred A. Knopf, 1995.

———. *A Patchwork Planet.* New York: Alfred A. Knopf, c.1998.

———. *Searching for Caleb.* New York: Alfred A. Knopf, 1976.

———. *The Tin Can Tree.* New York: Knopf, c.1965.

Tyler, Royall. *The Contrast.* Philadelphia: From the Press of Prichard & Hall, 1790.

———. *The Prose of Royall Tyler.* Coll. and ed. by Marius B. Péladeau. Montpelier VT: Vermont Historical Society, 1972.

Tyler, Varro E., comp. *Hoosier Home Remedies.* West Lafayette IN: Purdue Univ. Press, c.1985.

Tyler County Booster. Woodville TX, 1930–.

Tylor, Edward Burnett. *Anahuac.* London: Longman, Green, Longman and Roberts, 1861.

Typographical Journal. Indianapolis IN, 1889–.

Tyree, Marion Cabell, ed. *Housekeeping in Old Virginia.* Louisville KY: Favorite Recipes Press, c.1965. Orig. pub. in 1879 by John P. Morton, Louisville KY.

Tyrone Daily Herald. Tyrone PA, 1887–.

Tyrone Herald. Tyrone PA, 1867–1918.

Tyrone Star. Tyrone City PA, 1858–1860?

Tyson, James Lawrence. *Diary of a Physician in California.* Oakland CA: Biobooks, 1955. Orig. pub. in New York in 1850 by D. Appleton.

Tyson, Timothy B. *Blood Done Sign My Name.* New York: Crown, c.2004.

Udvardy, Miklos D. F. *The Audubon Society Field Guide to North American Birds.* New York: Alfred A. Knopf, 1977.

Ulanov, Barry. *A History of Jazz in America.* New York: Viking Press, c.1952.

Ulloa, Antonio de. *Noticias Americanas.* Madrid: Francisco Manuel de Mena, 1772.

Ulster County N.Y. Road Commissioners. *Records of the Road Commissioners of Ulster County.* Albany NY: Historical Records Survey, 1940. 2 vols. Transcriptions of records from 1722–1795, prepared by the New York State Historical Records Survey Project, Works Projects Administration.

Ulster Folklife. Belfast, 1955–.

Uncle Sam, [pseud.]. *Uncle Sam's Peculiarities.* London: John Mortimer, 1844. 2 vols.

Underhill, Edward Fitch and Mortimer Thomson. *The History and Records of the Elephant Club.* New York: Livermore & Rudd, 1856.

Underwood, Ammon. "Journal of Ammon Underwood, 1834–1838." *Southwestern Historical Quarterly.* (1928–1929) 32.124–51.

Underwood, John J. *Alaska.* New York: Dodd, Mead, 1913.

Underwood, Lamar, ed. *The Bobwhite Quail, Classic Upland Tales.* Guilford CT: Lyons Press, 2004. Orig. pub. in 1980 by Amwell Press, Clinton NJ.

Union City Daily Messenger. Union City TN, 1929–.

Union Colony of Colorado. *First Annual Report of the Union*

Colony of Colorado. New York: George W. Southwick, 1871.

Union Daily Times. Union SC, 1917–.

Union Leader. Manchester NH, 1980?–.

Union Magazine of Literature and Art. New York, 1847–1848.

Union Pacific Employes' Magazine. Denver CO, 1886–1894.

Union Pacific Railway Company. *Wealth and Resources of Oregon and Washington.* Portland OR: Passenger Department of the Union Pacific Ry., 1889.

Unitarian Universalist World. Boston: Unitarian Universalist Assn., 1970–.

United Service. Philadelphia, 1879–1905.

United States, 1979. Ed. by Stephen Birnbaum. Boston: Houghton Mifflin, 1978.

United States. Agricultural Research Service. *Poisonous Plant Research Products and Services.* [v.d.]. Internet.

———. *Selected Weeds of the United States.* Washington DC: Govt. Printing Office, 1970.

United States. Air University. Research Studies Institute. *United States Air Force Dictionary.* Ed. by Woodford Agee Heflin. Maxwell Air Force Base AL: Air Univ. Press, 1956.

United States. Arctic, Desert and Tropic Information Center. *Glossary of Arctic and Subarctic Terms.* Maxwell Air Force Base AL, 1955.

United States. Army. Corps of Engineers. *PMIS: Noxious and Nuisance Plant Management Information System.* [v.d.]. Internet.

———. *Report upon U.S. Geographical Surveys West of the One Hundredth Meridian.* By George M. Wheeler. Washington DC: Govt. Printing Office, 1878–1889. 7 vols.

United States. Army. Corps of Topographical Engineers. *Abert's New Mexico Report, 1846–'47.* Albuquerque NM: Horn and Wallace, 1962. Facsimile of 1848 ed. pub. under the title: *Report of the Secretary of War, Communicating, in Answer to a Resolution of the Senate, a Report and Map of the Examination of New Mexico Made by Lieutenant J. W. Abert.*

———. *An Expedition to the Valley of the Great Salt Lake of Utah.* By Howard Stansbury. Philadelphia: Lippincott, Grambo, 1852.

———. *Report of an Expedition down the Zuni and Colorado Rivers.* By Captain L. Sitgreaves. Washington DC: R. Armstrong, public printer, 1853.

———. *Report of a Reconnaissance from Carroll, Montana Territory, on the Upper Missouri, to the Yellowstone National Park, and Return, Made in the Summer of 1875.* By William Ludlow. Washington DC: Govt. Printing Office, 1876.

———. *Report of a Reconnaissance of the Black Hills of Dakota, Made in the Summer of 1874.* By William Ludlow. Washington DC: Govt. Printing Office, 1875.

———. *Report of the Geological Exploration of the Fortieth Parallel.* Washington DC: Govt. Printing Office, 1870–1880. 7 vols.

United States Army Corps Topographical Engineers *Rept. RR* SEE United States. War Department *Reports of Explorations and Surveys . . . for a Railroad from the Mississippi River to the Pacific Ocean*

———. *Report upon the Colorado Rivers of the West, Explored in 1857 and 1858 by Joseph C. Ives.* Washington DC: Govt. Printing Office, 1861.

United States. Army. Ordnance Department. *The Ordnance Manual for the Use of Officers of the United States Army.* 2d ed. Washington DC: Gideon, 1850.

United States. Bureau of American Ethnology. *Annual Report.* Washington DC: Govt. Printing Office, 1881–1964.

United States. Bureau of Animal Industry. *Annual Report.* Washington DC: Govt. Printing Office, 1884–1911.

———. *Bulletin.* Washington DC: Govt. Printing Office, 1893–1914.

———. *Report of the Chief.* Washington DC: Govt. Printing Office, 1912–1953.

United States. Bureau of Education. *Bulletin.* Washington DC: Govt. Printing Office, 1889–1929.

———. *Report of the Commissioner of Education.* Washington DC: Govt. Printing Office, 1871–.

United States. Bureau of Entomology. *Bulletin.* Washington DC: Govt. Printing Office, 1883–1916.

United States. Bureau of Fisheries. *Bulletin.* Washington DC, 1904–1940.

———. *Report.* Washington DC: Govt. Printing Office, 1873–1941.

United States. Bureau of Foreign Commerce. *Consular Reports. Commerce, Manufactures, etc.* Washington DC: Govt. Printing Office, 1880–1903.

United States. Bureau of Indian Affairs. *Indians at Work.* Washington DC, 1933–1945.

———. *Report.* Washington DC, 1824–1949.

United States. Bureau of Naval Personnel. *Seamanship.* Washington DC: Govt. Printing Office, 1945.

United States. Bureau of Plant Industry. *Bulletin.* Washington DC: Govt. Printing Office, 1901–1913.

———. *Circulars.* Washington DC: Govt. Printing Office, 1908–1913.

———. *Inventory of Seeds and Plants Imported.* Washington DC: Govt. Printing Office, 1912–1924.

United States. Bureau of Soils. *Field Operations.* Washington DC: Govt. Printing Office, 1901–1922.

United States. Bureau of the Census. *Fisheries of the United States, 1908.* Washington DC: Govt. Printing Office, 1911.

———. *Forest Products of the United States.* Washington DC: Govt. Printing Office, 1905–1909.

United States. Census Office. *Census Bulletin.* Washington DC, 1889–1894.

United States. Census Office. 10th Census, 1880. *Preliminary Report on the Culture and Curing of Tobacco.* Washington DC: Govt. Printing Office, 1881. U.S. Census Office *Bulletin 263.*

———. *Report on the Population, Industries, and Resources of Alaska.* By Ivan Petroff. Washington DC: Govt. Printing Office, 1884.

———. *Report on the Productions of Agriculture.* Washington DC: Govt. Printing Office, 1883.

United States. Census Office. 11th Census, 1890. *Moqui Pueblo Indians of Arizona and Pueblo Indians of New Mexico.* By Thomas Donaldson. Washington DC: U.S. Census Printing Office, 1893.

———. *Report on Population and Resources of Alaska at the Eleventh Census.* Washington DC: Govt. Printing Office, 1893.

United States Coast and Geodetic Survey. *Survey of Oyster Bars, Charles County, Maryland.* Washington DC: Govt. Printing Office, 1911.

United States. Commission to Investigate the Affairs of the Red Cloud Indian Agency. *Report of the Special Commission Appointed to Investigate the Affairs of the Red Cloud Indian Agency, July, 1875; Together with the Testimony and Accompanying Documents.* Washington DC: Govt. Printing Office, 1875.

United States. Congress. *American State Papers.* Washington DC: Gales and Seaton, 1832–1861. 30 vols.

———. *Congressional Globe.* Washington DC: Printed at the Globe Office for its editors, 1834–1873.

———. *Congressional Record.* Washington DC: Govt. Printing Office, 1873–.

———. *Debates and Proceedings.* Washington DC: Gales and Seaton, 1834–1856.

———. *Mississippi in 1875.* Washington DC: Govt. Printing Office, 1876. 2 vols.

———. *Proceedings of the United States Senate and the House of Representatives in the Trial of Impeachment of Robert Wodrow Archbald, Additional Circuit Judge of the United States from the Third Judicial Circuit and Designated a Judge of the Commerce Court.* Washington DC: Govt. Printing Office, 1913. 3 vols.

———. *Register of Debates.* Washington DC: Gales & Seaton, 1824–1837. 14 vols.

———. *Report of the Joint Select Committee Appointed to Inquire into the Conditions of Affairs in the Late Insurrectionary States.* Washington DC: Govt. Printing Office, 1872.

———. *Serial Set.* Washington DC: Govt. Printing Office, 1817–.

United States. Congress. House. *Contested Election Case of James I. Campbell v. Robert L. Doughton from the Eighth Congressional District of North Carolina.* Washington DC: Govt. Printing Office, 1921.

———. *Contested Election Case of Thomas E. Kinney v. L. C. Dyer from the Twelfth Congressional District of Missouri.* Washington DC: Govt. Printing Office, 1911.

———. *Contested Election of Curtin vs. Yocum: Papers in the Case of Andrew G. Curtin vs. Seth H. Yocum, Twentieth Congressional District of Pennsylvania.* Washington DC: Govt. Printing Office, 1879. 3 vols.

———. *Journal of the House of Representatives.* Washington DC: Govt. Printing Office, 1789–.

United States. Congress. House. Committee on Agriculture. *Permanent Farm Labor Program.* Washington DC: Govt. Printing Office, 1947.

———. *Tobacco Statistics.* Washington DC: Govt. Printing Office, 1926.

United States. Congress. House. Committee on Appropriations. *Agricultural Appropriation Bill, 1923.* Washington DC: Govt. Printing Office, 1922.

United States. Congress. House. Committee on Appropria-

tions. Subcommittee of the Department of Defense. *Department of Defense Appropriations for 1979.* Washington DC: Govt. Printing Office, 1978. 8 vols.

United States. Congress. House. Committee on House Administration. Subcommittee on Elections. *Contested Elections in the First, Second, Third, Fourth, and Fifth Districts of the State of Mississippi.* Washington DC: Govt. Printing Office, 1965.

United States. Congress. House. Committee on International Relations. *United States Leadership against HIV/AIDS, Tuberculosis, and Malaria Act of 2003; Markup before the Committee on International Relations, House of Representatives, One Hundred Eighth Congress, First Session on H.R. 1298, April 2, 2003.* Washington DC: Govt. Printing Office, 2003.

United States. Congress. House. Committee on Merchant Marine and Fisheries. *American-Canadian Fisheries Conference, Hearings.* Washington DC: Govt. Printing Office, 1918.

United States. Congress. House. Committee on Public Lands. *Homes for Soldiers.* Washington DC: Govt. Printing Office, 1919.

United States. Congress. House. Committee on Public Lands. Subcommitee on Territorial and Insular Possessions. *Alaska Hearings.* Washington DC: Govt. Printing Office, 1948.

United States. Congress. House. Committee on Rivers and Harbors. *St. Francis River, Ark. and Mo.* Washington DC: Govt. Printing Office, 1916.

United States. Congress. House. Select Committee on Pulp and Paper Investigation. *Pulp and Paper Investigation Hearings.* Washington DC: Govt. Printing Office, 1908–1909. 6 vols.

United States. Congress. House. Select Committee on the Recent Election in South Carolina. *Recent Election in South Carolina, February 21, 1877.* Washington DC: Govt. Printing Office, 1877.

United States. Congress. Senate. *Proceedings of the United States Senate, on the Fugitive Slave Bill.* Washington DC: Press of T. R. Marvin, 1850.

———. *Statistical Report of the Sickness and Mortality in the Army of the United States.* Washington DC: Govt. Printing Office, 1860.

United States. Congress. Senate. Committee on Appropriations. Subcommittee on Defense. *Department of Defense Appropriations for Fiscal Year 1990: Hearings.* Washington DC: Govt. Printing Office, 1989–1990. 6 vols.

United States. Congress. Senate. Committee on Energy and Natural Resources. Subcommittee on Public Lands and Reserved Water. *Oregon Wilderness Act of 1983, Hearings.* Washington DC: Govt. Printing Office, 1984. 2 vols.

United States. Congress. Senate. Committee on Fisheries. *Alaska Fisheries.* Washington DC: Govt. Printing Office, 1912.

United States. Congress. Senate. Committee on Governmental Affairs. Subcommittee on Oversight of Government Management and the District of Columbia. *Federal Regulations: Balancing Rights, Reason and Responsibility.* Washington DC: Govt. Printing Office, 1995.

United States. Continental Congress. *Journals of the Continental Congress, 1774–1789.* Washington DC: Govt. Printing Office, 1904–1937. 34 vols. Ed. from the orig. records in the Library of Congress.

United States. Copper River Exploring Expedition. *Alaska, 1899.* Washington DC: Govt. Printing Office, 1900.

United States Democratic Review SEE ALSO *United States Magazine and Democratic Review* and *United States Review*

United States Democratic Review. Washington DC, 1856–1859.

United States. Department of Agriculture. *Agriculture Handbook.* Washington DC, 1950–.

———. *Annual Reports.* Washington DC: Govt. Printing Office, 1897–1924.

———. *Bulletin.* Washington DC: Govt. Printing Office, 1913–1923.

———. *Department Bulletin.* Washington DC: Govt. Printing Office, 1923–1929.

———. *Emergency Public Rulemaking Hearing.* [s.l.], 2006.

———. *Farmers' Bulletin.* Washington DC: Govt. Printing Office, 1889–.

———. *Integrated Taxonomic Information System.* [v.d.]. Internet.

———. *Leaflet.* Washington DC: Govt. Printing Office, 1927–.

———. *Miscellaneous Circular.* Washington DC: Govt. Printing Office, 189?–1929.

———. *Miscellaneous Publication.* Washington DC: Govt. Printing Office, 1927–.

——. *Monthly Reports.* Washington DC, 1863–1876.

——. *National Honey Market News.* Washington DC, 1985–2000.

——. *Plants Database.* [v.d.]. Internet.

——. *Report of the Secretary* SEE ALSO United States. Patent Office *Annual Report of the Commissioner of Patents*

——. *Report of the Secretary.* Washington DC: Govt. Printing Office, 1862–1894.

——. *Report on Forestry.* Washington DC: Govt. Printing Office, 1878–1884.

——. *Special Report.* Washington DC: Govt. Printing Office, 1877–1883.

——. *Weekly News Letter.* Washington DC: Govt. Printing Office, 1915–1921.

——. *Yearbook of Agriculture.* Washington DC: Govt. Printing Office, 1894–.

United States. Department of Agriculture. Bureau of Animal Industry. *Special Report on Diseases of Cattle.* Washington DC: Govt. Printing Office, 1904.

United States. Department of Agriculture. Bureau of Biological Survey. *North American Fauna.* Washington DC, 1889–1940.

United States. Department of Agriculture. Bureau of Plant Industry, Soils and Agricultural Engineering. *Information Series.* Washington DC: Govt. Printing Office, 1900–.

United States. Department of Agriculture. Division of Botany. *Bulletin.* Washington DC: Govt. Printing Office, 1886–1901.

United States. Department of Agriculture. Division of Entomology. *Bulletin.* Washington DC: Govt. Printing Office, 1895–.

United States. Department of Agriculture. Division of Ornithology and Mammalogy. *Bulletin.* Washington DC, 1893–1896.

United States. Department of Agriculture. Division of Vegetable Pathology. *Bulletin.* Washington DC: Govt. Printing Office, 1891–1901.

United States. Department of Agriculture. New England Agricultural Statistics Service. *Crop Weather.* Concord NH, 1991–.

United States. Department of Agriculture. States Relations Service. *Experiment Station Record.* Washington DC: Govt. Printing Office, 1889–1946.

United States. Department of Commerce and Labor. Bureau of Fisheries. *Document.* Washington DC: Govt. Printing Office, 1900?–1931.

United States. Department of the Interior. *Conservation Bulletin.* Washington DC: Govt. Printing Office, 1939–.

——. *Decisions of the Department of the Interior and General Land Office in Cases Relating to the Public Lands.* Washington DC: Govt. Printing Office, 1882–1909.

——. *Indians, Eskimos, and Aleuts of Alaska.* Washington DC: Govt. Printing Office, 1966.

United States. Division of Agrostology. *Bulletin.* Washington DC: Govt. Printing Office, 1895–1901.

United States Entomological Commission. *Bulletin.* Washington DC, 1877–1881.

——. *Fourth Report.* By Charles V. Riley. Washington DC: Govt. Printing Office, 1885.

United States. Environmental Protection Agency. *Drinking Water Infrastructure Needs Survey: Second Report to Congress.* Washington DC: Environmental Protection Agency, 2001.

United States. Fish and Wildlife Service. *Bogue Chitto National Wildlife Refuge.* [v.d.]. Internet.

——. *Bon Secour National Wildlife Refuge Pine Beach Trail Guide.* Washington DC, 2002.

——. *Circular.* Washington DC: Govt. Printing Office, 1941–1970.

——. *Fishery Bulletin.* Washington DC: Govt. Printing Office, 1941–1971.

——. *Fresh-Water Mussels of the Upper Mississippi River.* Washington DC: Govt. Printing Office, 1982. Wall chart.

——. *Resource Publication.* Washington DC, 1975–.

United States Fish Commission. *Bulletin.* Washington DC: Govt. Printing Office, 1881–1903.

United States. Food and Drug Administration. Center for Food Safety and Applied Nutrition. *Seafood List.* Washington DC, 1993–.

United States. Forest Service. *Approved Changes in Sudworth's Check List.* Washington DC: Govt. Printing Office, 1940.

——. *Bulletin.* Washington DC: Govt. Printing Office, 1887–1913.

——. *Fire Effects Information System.* [v.d.]. Internet.

——. *Idaho Panhandle National Forests.* [v.d.]. Internet.

——. *Range Plant Handbook.* Washington DC: Govt. Printing Office, 1937.

United States. Forest Service. Pacific Northwest Region. *Final Environmental Statement: Ochoco-Crooked River Planning Unit Land Management Plan.* Portland OR: U.S. Forest Service, 1978.

United States. Forest Service. Rocky Mountain Region. *Trees Native to the Forests of Colorado and Wyoming.* [s.l.]: [s.n.], 1945.

United States. General Land Office. *Annual Report of the Commissioner of General Land Office Made to the Secretary of the Interior for the Year.* Washington DC: Govt. Printing Office, 1870–1909?

United States. Geological and Geographical Survey of the Territories. *Bulletin.* Washington DC: Govt. Printing Office, 1874–1882.

——. *Miscellaneous Publications.* Washington DC: Govt. Printing Office, 1873–1880.

United States. Geological Survey. *Annual Report.* Washington DC: Govt. Printing Office, 1880–.

——. *Monographs.* Washington DC: Govt. Printing Office, 1882–.

——. *Professional Paper.* Washington DC: Govt. Printing Office, 1902–1948.

——. *Water-Supply and Irrigation Papers.* Washington DC: Govt. Printing Office, 1896–1947.

United States Geological Survey of the Territories. *Annual Report.* Washington DC: Govt. Printing Office, 1867–1873.

United States Golf Association. *Bulletin of the Green Section.* Washington DC, 1921–1926.

United States. Immigration Commission. *Dictionary of Races or Peoples.* Washington DC: Govt. Printing Office, 1911.

United States. Library of Congress. Catalog Publication Division. *Newspapers in Microform: United States. 1948–1972.* Washington DC: Library of Congress, 1973–1983.

United States Literary Gazette. Boston, 1824–1826.

United States Magazine. New York, 1856–1857.

United States Magazine and Democratic Review. Washington DC, 1837–1851.

United States Military Academy. Association of Graduates. *Bulletin.* West Point NY, 1900–1905?

United States National Arboretum. *Kick the Invasive Gardening Habit with Great Native Plant Alternatives.* [v.d.]. Internet.

United States National Museum. *Annual Report.* Washington DC: Smithsonian Institution, 1846–1964.

——. *Bulletin.* Washington DC: Govt. Printing Office, 1875–.

——. *Contributions from the United States National Herbarium.* Washington DC, 1890–.

——. *Proceedings.* Washington DC: Govt. Printing Office, 1878–.

United States. National Oceanic and Atmospheric Administration. *Channel Islands.* [v.d.]. Internet.

United States. National Park Service. *Canaveral National Seashore.* [v.d.]. Internet.

——. *Fading Trails.* New York: Macmillan, 1942.

——. *Glimpses of Our National Monuments.* Washington DC: Govt. Printing Office, 1930.

——. *Klondike Gold Rush National Historical Park: Frequently Seen Flora.* [v.d.]. Internet.

United States. National Park Service. Division of Publications. *At Home in the Smokies.* Washington DC: United States Department of the Interior, 1984.

United States. National Park Service. Region One. *Regional Review.* Richmond VA, 1938–1941.

United States Nautical Magazine and Naval Journal. New York: Griffiths, 1854–1858.

United States. Naval History Division. *Naval Documents of the American Revolution.* Washington DC: Govt. Printing Office, 1964–.

United States Naval Institute. *Proceedings.* Annapolis MD, 1879–.

United States. Navy Department. *Official Records of the Union and Confederate Navies in the War of the Rebellion.* Washington DC: Govt. Printing Office, 1894–1922. 20 vols.

——. *Reports of Explorations and Surveys to Ascertain the Practicability of a Ship-Canal between the Atlantic and Pacific Oceans.* Washington DC: Govt. Printing Office, 1872.

United States. Patent Office. *Annual Report of the Commissioner of Patents.* Washington DC, 1837–1974.

——. *List of Patents for Inventions and Designs, Issued by the United States, from 1790 to 1847.* Comp. and Published under the Direction of Edmund Burke, Commissioner of Patents. Washington DC: Printed by J. & G. S. Gideon, 1847.

——. *Official Gazette.* Washington DC: Department of Commerce, 1875–1971.

——. *Patents Issued.* 1790–.

United States Playing Card Company. *The Official Rules of Card Games.* Cincinnati OH: The Company, 1887–.

United States Postal Guide and Official Advertiser. Washington DC: Peter G. Washington and Charles M. Willard, 1850–1852.

United States. Post Office Department. *Table of Post Offices in the United States on the First Day in January, 1851.* Washington DC: W. & J. C. Greer, 1851.

United States. Public Health Service. *Malaria Control on Impounded Water.* Washington DC: Govt. Printing Office, 1947.

——. *Public Health Reports.* Washington DC, 1896–1970.

United States. Revenue-Cutter Service. *Cruise of the Revenue-Steamer Corwin in Alaska and the N.W. Arctic Ocean.* Washington DC: Govt. Printing Office, 1883.

——. *Report on the Operations of the U.S. Revenue Steamer Nunivak on the Yukon River Station, Alaska, 1899–1901.* By First Lieut. J. C. Cantwell, R. C. S. Washington DC: Govt. Printing Office, 1902.

United States Review. New York, 1853–1855.

United States. Soil Conservation Service. *Grassland Restoration.* Temple TX: The Service, 1964–1970. 6 vols.

United States. Supreme Court. *Records and Briefs.* Washington DC, 1832–1899?

——. *Reports of Cases Argued and Adjudged in the Supreme Court of the United States.* Washington DC, 1804–1861.

——. *The State of Missouri vs. the State of Illinois and the Sanitary District of Chicago.* Washington DC?: [s.n.], 1903. 8 vols.

United States. Treasury Department. *Statistics of Mines and Mining in the States and Territories West of the Rocky Mountains.* Washington DC: Govt. Printing Office, 1869–1877. 8 vols.

United States. War Department. *Annual Report.* Washington DC: Govt. Printing Office, 1847–1947.

——. *Exploration of the Red River of Louisiana, in the Year 1852.* By Randolph B. Marcy and assisted by George B. McClellan. Washington DC: B. Tucker, 1854.

——. *Instructions for Field Artillery.* Philadelphia: J. B. Lippincott, 1861 [c.1860].

——. *Reports of Explorations and Surveys . . . for a Railroad from the Mississippi River to the Pacific Ocean.* Washington DC: A. O. P. Nicholson, 1855–1860.

——. *War of the Rebellion.* Washington DC: Govt. Printing Office, 1880–1901.

United States. Weather Bureau. *Bulletin.* Washington DC: Govt. Printing Office, 1893–1913.

University of California Chronicle. Berkeley CA: Univ. CA, 1907–1933.

University of Chicago Magazine. Chicago: Univ. Chicago, 1994–.

University of [State] SEE [State]. University

Unsworth's Burnt Cork Lyrics. New York: Robert M. De Witt, 1859.

UpCountry: the Magazine of New England Living. Pittsfield MA: Eagle Pub., 1973–.

Updike, John. *Bech.* New York: Knopf, 1970.

——. *Couples.* New York: Knopf, 1968.

Updike, Wilkins. *A History of the Episcopal Church, in Narragansett, Rhode Island.* New-York: Henry M. Onderdonk, 1847.

Upham, Charles Wentworth. *Salem Witchcraft, with an Account of Salem Village, and a History of Opinions on Witchcraft and Kindred Subjects.* Boston: Wiggin and Lunt, 1867. 2 vols.

Upham, Samuel Curtis. *Notes of a Voyage to California Via Cape Horn.* Philadelphia: Published by the Author, 1878.

Upham, Warren. *Glacial Lake Agassiz.* Washington DC: Govt. Printing Office, 1895.

UPI Dispatches. 1981–. Articles quoted from United Press International wire service dispatches.

Upton, Clive et al. *Survey of English Dialects.* London: Routledge, c.1994.

UrbanCyclez. 2003–. Internet.

Urban Health. Atlanta GA, 1972–1985.

Uris, Leon M. *Battle Cry.* New York: Putnam, 1953.

USA Today. Arlington VA, 1982–.

USGA Journal and Turf Management. New York: United States Golf Association, 1950–1963.

U.S. News & World Report. Washington DC, 1933–.

Utah Association of Agriculture Educators. *Yellow Dog, a Newsletter for the U.A.A.E.* 2007–2008? Internet.

Utah Genealogical and Historical Magazine. Salt Lake City UT: Genealogical Society of Utah, 1910–1940.

Utah Historical Quarterly. Salt Lake City UT: Utah State Historical Society, 1928–.

Utah Humanities Review. Salt Lake City UT, 1947–1948.

Utica Observer. Utica NY, 1817–1916.

Valdez-Copper Basin News. Valdez AK, 1969–1976.

Valentine, Carrie Syron. *How to Keep Hens for Profit.* New York: Macmillan, 1910.

Valentine, Edward Abram Uffington. *Hecla Sandwith.* Indianapolis IN: Bobbs-Merrill, 1905.

Valin, Jonathan. *Life's Work.* New York: Delacorte Press, c.1986.

Valley Advocate. Hatfield MA, 1973–.

Valley Farmer. St. Louis MO, 1849–1864.

Valley Independent. Monessen PA, 1960–.

Valley Morning Star. Harlingen TX, 1929–.

Valley News and Green Sheet. Van Nuys CA, 1971–1977.

Valley News and Valley Green Sheet. Van Nuys CA, 1954–1971.

Valpey, Joseph. *Journal of Joseph Valpey, Jr., of Salem, Nov. 1813–April 1815.* Detroit MI: Michigan Society of Colonial Wars, 1922.

Van Buren, A. De Puy. *Jottings of a Year's Sojourn in the South.* Battle Creek MI: [s.n.], c.1859.

Van Buren Press Argus. Van Buren AR, 1915–.

Vance, Rupert Bayless. *Human Factors in Cotton Culture.* Chapel Hill NC: Univ. NC Press, 1929.

Van Cleve, Spike. *A Day Late and a Dollar Short.* Kansas City MO: Lowell Press, 1982.

Vandenbusche, Duane and Duane A. Smith. *A Land Alone.* Boulder CO: Pruett Publishing, 1981.

Vanderbilt, Gertrude L. Lefferts. *The Social History of Flatbush.* New York: D. Appleton, 1881.

Van Dersal, William Richard. *Native Woody Plants of the United States.* Washington DC: Govt. Printing Office, 1938.

Vandiver, Louise Ayer. *A Revised Edition of Vandiver's History of Anderson County.* Anderson SC: Stenciled by R. M. Smith, 1970.

Van Dyke, Henry. *Fisherman's Luck and Some Other Uncertain Things.* New York: Charles Scribner's Sons, 1900. Orig. pub. in 1899 by Charles Scribner's Sons, New York.

Van Dyke, John Charles. *The Desert.* New York: C. Scribner's Sons, 1901.

Van Dyke, Theodore Strong. *Flirtation Camp.* New York: Fords, Howard & Hulbert, 1881.

———. *Southern California.* New York: Fords, Howard & Hulbert, 1886.

Vanity Fair. New York, 1859–1863; 1914–.

Van Loan, Charles Emmett. *Taking the Count: Prize Ring Stories.* New York: George H. Doran, 1919.

Van Meter, Victoria Brook. *Florida's Wood Storks.* Rev. ed. Miami FL: Florida Power & Light, c.1988.

Van Noppen, Ina Woestemeyer and John J. Van Noppen. *Western North Carolina since the Civil War.* 2d ed. Boone NC: Appalachian Consortium Press, 1973.

Van Nuys News. Van Nuys CA, 1916–1941.

Van Peebles, Melvin. *Sweet Sweetback's Baadasssss Song.* Motion picture. Los Angeles?: A Yeah Production, 1971.

Van Schaack, Henry Cruger. *The Life of Peter Van Schaack, LL. D.* New York: D. Appleton, 1842.

VanStone, James W. *Eskimos of the Nushagak River.* Seattle WA: Univ. WA Press, c.1967.

Van Tramp, John C. *Prairie and Rocky Mountain Adventures.* Columbus OH: Segner & Condit, 1870.

Van Vechten, Carl. *Nigger Heaven.* New York: A. A. Knopf, 1926.

Van Vleet, Albert Heald. *Birds of Oklahoma.* Guthrie OK: State Capital, 1902. Territory of Oklahoma, Dept. of Geological & Natural History *Second Biennial Report.*

Van Wagenen, Jared. *The Golden Age of Homespun.* Albany NY: N.Y. Dept. of Agriculture and Markets, 1927.

———. *The Golden Age of Homespun.* Ithaca NY: Cornell Univ. Press, 1953.

Van Wert Daily Bulletin. Van Wert OH, 1887–1936.

Van Wert Republican. Van Wert OH, 1885?–1916?

Van Wert Times. Van Wert OH, 1866–1904.

Van Wert Times-Bulletin. Van Wert OH, 1936–1973.

Variety. New York, 1905–.

Vascular Plants of the Lyndon B. Johnson National Historical Park. San Antonio TX, 2004.

Vasey, George. *The Agricultural Grasses and Forage Plants of the United States.* New, rev. and enlarged ed. Washington DC: Govt. Printing Office, 1889.

———. *The Agricultural Grasses of the United States.* Washington DC: Govt. Printing Office, 1884.

———. *Catalogue of the Forest Trees of the United States Which Usually Attain a Height of Sixteen Feet or More, with Notes and Brief Descriptions of the More Important Species, Illustrating the Collection of Forest Tree-Sections on Exhibition by the Department of Agriculture at the Cen-*

tennial Exhibition, Philadelphia. Washington DC: Govt. Printing Office, 1876.

Vaughan, Frank. *Kate Weathers.* Philadelphia: J. B. Lippincott, 1878.

Vaux, Bert and Scott Golder. *Dialect Survey.* [v.d.]. Internet.

Vaux, Calvert. *Villas and Cottages.* New York: Harper & Bros., 1857.

Venable, William Henry. *Footprints of the Pioneers in the Ohio Valley.* Cincinnati OH: Ohio Valley Press, 1888.

Venegas, Miguel. *A Natural and Civil History of California.* London: Printed for James Rivington and James Fletcher, 1759. 2 vols. Anon. transl.

Venning, Frank Denmire. *Wildflowers of North America.* New York: Golden Press; Racine WI: Western Publishing, 1984.

Verbatim Letters. 1979–1981. Unpub. letters in response to queries in *Verbatim, the Language Quarterly.*

Verbatim, the Language Quarterly. Essex CT, 1974–.

Verdelle, A. J. *The Good Negress.* Chapel Hill NC: Algonquin Books, 1995.

Vermont Agricultural Experiment Station. *Bulletin.* Burlington VT, 1887–1983?

Vermont Dairymen's Association. *Report.* Montpelier VT, 1869–1929.

Vermont. Department of Agriculture, Food and Markets. *Agriview.* Montpelier VT, 1938–.

Vermont. Department of Education. *Circulars of Educational Information.* Montpelier VT, 1901–1999?

Vermonter. St. Albans VT, 1895–.

The Vermont Historical Gazetteer. Ed. by Abby Maria Hemenway. Burlington VT: Miss A. M. Hemenway, 1868–1891. 5 vols.

Vermont Historical Society. *Collections.* Montpelier VT, 1870–1871.

———. *Proceedings.* St. Albans VT, 1860–1943.

Vermont History. Montpelier VT, 1943–.

Vermont Life. Montpelier VT: Vermont Development Commission, 1946–.

Vermont Phoenix. Brattleboro VT, 1834–1880.

Vermont. Secretary of State. *Opinions.* 1990–. Internet.

Vermont. State Board of Agriculture. *Vermont Agricultural Report.* Montpelier VT, 1882–1899.

Vermont. State Board of Agriculture and Forestry. *Annual Report.* Montpelier VT, 1872–1908.

Vermont. University. Extension. *Insects in Firewood.* [v.d.]. Internet.

Vero Beach Press-Journal. Vero Beach FL, 1928–.

A Very Surprising Narrative, of a Young Woman, Discovered in a Rocky-cave, after Having Been Taken by the Savage Indians of the Wilderness, in the Year 1777, and Seeing No Human Being for a Space of Nine Years. 5th ed. New York: Printed for the Purchasers, 1790?

Vestal, Paul A. and Richard Evans Schultes. *Economic Botany of the Kiowa Indians.* Cambridge MA: Botanical Museum, 1939.

Vestal, Stanley. *Kit Carson.* Boston: Houghton Mifflin, 1928.

———. *The Old Santa Fe Trail.* Boston: Houghton Mifflin, 1939.

———. *Short Grass Country.* New York: Duell, Sloan & Pearce, c.1941.

———. *Sitting Bull.* Boston: Houghton Mifflin, 1932.

Veterinary Journal and Annals of Comparative Pathology. London, 1875–1899.

Vick's Magazine. Rochester NY, 1881–1891?

Victor, Frances Fuller. *All Over Oregon and Washington.* San Francisco: Printed by John H. Carmany, 1872.

———. *Atlantis Arisen.* Philadelphia: J. B. Lippincott, 1891.

———. *The River of the West.* Hartford CT: R. W. Bliss, 1870.

Victor, Metta Victoria Fuller. *The Bad Boy Abroad.* New York: J. S. Ogilvie, c.1883.

———. *Miss Slimmens' Window.* New York: Derby & Jackson, 1859.

Victoria Advocate. Victoria TX, 1928?–.

Vidal, Gore. *Burr.* New York: Random House, 1973.

Vidette-Messenger. Valparaiso IN, 1927–1989.

Viélé, Teresa Griffin. *Following the Drum.* New York: Rudd & Carleton, 1859.

Viereck, Leslie A. and Elbert L. Little, Jr. *Alaska Trees and Shrubs.* Washington DC: U.S. Forest Service, 1972.

Viereck, Wolfgang. *Lexikalische und grammatische Ergebnisse des Lowman-Survey von Mittel-und Sudengland.* Munich: Wilhelm Fink Verlag, 1975.

A View of North America. Glasgow: W. Smith, 1781.

Vignoles, Charles Blacker. *Observations upon the Floridas.* New-York: E. Bliss & E. White, 1823.

Village Voice. New York, 1955–.

Vineland Historical Magazine. Vineland NJ: Vineland Historical and Antiquarian Society, 1916–.

Vines, Howell. *A River Goes with Heaven.* Boston: Little, Brown, 1930.

———. *This Green Thicket World.* Boston: Little, Brown, 1934.

Vines, Robert A. *Trees of Central Texas.* Austin TX: Univ. TX Press, c.1984.

———. *Trees, Shrubs, and Woody Vines of the Southwest.* Austin TX: Univ. TX Press, 1960.

Vineyard Gazette. Edgartown MA, 1846–.

Virginia. *Calendar of Virginia State Papers and Other Manuscripts.* Richmond VA, 1875–1893.

Virginia. Board of Immigration. *Virginia: a Geographical and Political Summary.* Richmond VA: R. F. Walker, Superintendent of Public Printing, c.1876.

Virginia (Colony) General Assembly. House of Burgesses. *Journals of the House of Burgesses of Virginia, 1619–1776.* Ed. by H. R. McIlwaine. Richmond VA: Colonial Press, E. Waddey, 1905–1915. 13 vols.

Virginia Company of London. *The Records.* Washington DC: Govt. Printing Office, 1906–1935. 4 vols.

Virginia. County Court (Northampton County). *County Court Records of Accomack-Northampton, Virginia 1634–1640.* Washington DC: American Historical Association, 1954.

Virginia Gazette. Ed. by Alexander Purdie and John Dixon. Williamsburg VA, 1751–1778.

Virginia Gazette. Ed. by Alexander Purdie. Williamsburg VA, 1775–1780.

Virginia. General Assembly. House of Delegates. *Journal.* Richmond VA, 1828–.

Virginia Journal of Science. Norfolk VA, 1940–.

Virginia. Laws, Statutes etc. *Statutes at Large.* By William Waller Hening. Richmond VA: Printed by and for Samuel Pleasants, 1810–1823. 13 vols.

Virginia Literary Museum and Journal of Belles Lettres, Arts, Sciences, etc. Charlottesville VA: F. Carr, 1829–1830.

Virginia Magazine of History and Biography. Richmond VA: Virginia Historical Society, 1893–.

Virginia Marine Resources Commission. *Regulation Index.* [v.d.]. Internet.

Virginian-Pilot. Norfolk VA, 1991–.

Virginia. Office of the Railroad Commissioner. *Annual Report.* Richmond VA, 1877–1902.

Virginia Polytechnic Institute and State University. *Endangered Species Information System.* [v.d.]. Internet.

———. *Marine and Coastal Species Information System.* [v.d.]. Internet.

———. *Weed Identification Guide.* [v.d.]. Internet.

Virginia Quarterly Review. Charlottesville VA: Univ. VA, 1925–.

Virginia. University. *University of Virginia Studies.* Charlottesville VA, 1941–.

Virginia. University. Division of Extension. *Bulletin.* Charlottesville VA, 1941–1952.

Virginia Wildlife. Blacksburg VA, 1937–.

Visher, Stephen Sargent. *The Geography of South Dakota.* Private ed. Chicago: Distributed by the Univ. Chicago Libraries, 1918.

A Visit to Texas. New York: Goodrich & Wiley, 1834.

Visscher, William Lightfoot. *Blue Grass Ballads and Other Verse.* New York: H. M. Caldwell, c.1900.

Vivian, Arthur Pendarves. *Wanderings in the Western Land.* London: Sampson Low, Marston, Searle & Rivington, 1879.

Vizgirdas, Ray S. and Edna Rey-Vizgirdas. *Wild Plants of the Sierra Nevada.* Reno NV: Univ. NV Press, 2006.

Voelker, John Donaldson. *Anatomy of a Murder.* New York: St. Martin's Press, c.1958.

Vogt, Nellie Mae Nelson. *My Mother's Louisiana Family.* [s.l.]: N. M. N. Vogt, 1994.

Vogt, Richard Carl. *Natural History of Amphibians and Reptiles in Wisconsin.* Milwaukee WI: Milwaukee Public Museum, c.1981.

Vogue. New York: Conde Nast Publications, 1892–.

Voice. New York, 1884–1895.

Voices from the Harlem Renaissance. Ed. by Nathan Irvin Huggins. New York: Oxford Univ. Press, 1976.

Voices from the Kenduskeag. Ed. by Mrs. Jane Sophia Appleton & Mrs. Cornelia Crosby Barrett. Bangor ME: David Bugbee, 1848.

The Volette. Martin TN, 1928–1971.

Volk, Toni. *Montana Women.* New York: Soho, c.1992.

Vollmer, Lula. *Sun-Up.* New York: Longmans, Green, 1926 [c.1924].

Volney, Constantin-François. *A View of the Soil and Climate of the United States of America.* Transl. by Charles Brockden Brown. Philadelphia: J. Conrad, 1804.

Von Auw, Alvin. *Heritage and Destiny.* New York: Praeger, 1983.

Von Loesecke, Harry Willard. *Outlines of Food Technology.* New York: Reinhold Publishing, c.1942.

Vonnegut, Kurt. *Breakfast of Champions, or, Goodbye Blue Monday.* New York: Delacorte Press, 1973.

Von Tempski, Armine. *Born in Paradise.* New York: Literary Guild of America, c.1940.

Vose, John Denison, ed. *Fresh Leaves from the Diary of a Broadway Dandy.* Rev., enlarged and corr. New York: Bunnell & Price, 1852.

Voss, John and Virginia S. Eifert. *Illinois Wild Flowers.* Springfield IL: [s.n.], 1951.

Voyage of H.M.S. Blonde to the Sandwich Islands. London: John Murray, 1826.

W2 SEE Neilson, William Allan et al. *Webster's New International Dictionary of the English Language*

W3 SEE Gove, Philip Babcock et al. *Webster's Third New International Dictionary of the English Language, Unabridged*

W3 File. 1965–. Miscellaneous contrib. from the files of *Webster's Third New International Dictionary.*

Waddell, James D., ed. *Biographical Sketch of Linton Stephens, Late Associate Justice of the Supreme Court of Georgia.* Atlanta GA: Dodson & Scott, 1877.

Wagner, Philip Marshall. *Wine Grapes.* New York: Harcourt, Brace, 1937.

Waikiki News. Honolulu HI, 1996–.

Wailes, Benjamin Leonard Covington. *Report on the Agriculture and Geology of Mississippi.* Jackson MS: E. Barksdale, 1854.

Wakefield, Priscilla. *Excursions in North America.* London: Darton and Harvey, 1806.

Wakeley, Joseph Beaumont. *Heroes of Methodism.* New York: Carleton & Porter, 1857 [c.1856].

Wakeman, Frederic. *The Hucksters.* New York: Rinehart, 1946.

Walden, Isaac. "A Narrative of the Travels of Isaac Walden, at the Time He Was in the King's Service . . . Printed in the Year 1773." *Magazine of History, with Notes and Queries. Extra Numbers.* (1922) extra no. 82.35–48.

Waldie's Select Circulating Library. Philadelphia, 1832–1842?

Walker, Alice. *The Color Purple.* New York: Harcourt Brace Jovanovich, c.1982.

——. *In Love & Trouble.* New York: Harcourt Brace Jovanovich, c.1973.

——. *In Search of Our Mothers' Gardens.* San Diego CA: Harcourt, Brace Jovanovich, c.1983.

——. *You Can't Keep a Good Woman Down.* New York: Harcourt Brace Jovanovich, c.1981.

Walker, Demosthenes. *Stanley, or, Playing for Amusement and Betting to Count the Game.* Nashville TN: J. B. M'Ferrin, 1860.

Walker, Gertrude Annie and Harriet S. Jenks. *Songs and Games for Little Ones.* Boston: Oliver Ditson, c.1887.

Walker, Harley Jesse, ed. *Coastal Resources.* Baton Rouge LA: School of Geoscience, LA State Univ., 1975.

Walker, Michael, ed. *Sport Fishing USA.* Washington DC: Govt. Printing Office, 1971.

Walker, Mildred. *Winter Wheat.* New York: Harcourt, Brace, 1944.

Walker, Robert Sparks. *Lookout, the Story of a Mountain.* Kingsport TN: Southern, 1941.

Walker, Thomas. *Journal of an Exploration in the Spring of the Year 1750.* Boston: Little, Brown, 1888.

Walker, William and Daisy F. Baber. *Injun Summer.* Caldwell ID: Caxton Printers, 1952.

Wall, James W. *History of Davie County in the Forks of the Yadkin.* Mocksville NC: Davie County Historical Publishing, c.1969.

Wallace, Alexander. *Notes on Lilies and Their Culture.* 2d ed., rev. and enlarged. Colchester: New Plant and Bulb, 1879.

Wallace, Allie B. *Frontier Life in Oklahoma.* Washington DC: Public Affairs Press, 1964.

Wallace, Frederick William. *The Shack Locker.* Toronto: Industrial and Educational Press, c.1916.

Wallace, Susan Arnold Elston. *The Land of the Pueblos.* New York: John B. Alden, 1888.

Wallace's Monthly. New York, 1875–1894.

Walla Walla Union. Walla Walla WA, 1881–.

Walla Walla Union-Bulletin. Walla Walla WA, 1938–.

Waller, Elbert. *Illinois Pioneer Days.* Litchfield IL: E. B. Lewis, 1918.

Waller, Mary Ella. *The Wood-Carver of 'Lympus.* Boston: Little, Brown, 1904.

Walling, George Washington. *Recollections of a New York Chief of Police, with a Supplement on the Denver Police.* Montclair NJ: Patterson Smith, 1972. Orig. pub. in 1887 by Caxton Book Concern, New York.

Walling, Henry Francis, comp. *Atlas of the State of Michigan.* Detroit MI: R. M. & S. T. Tackabury, c.1873.

Wallis, Michael. *Pretty Boy.* New York: St. Martin's Press, c.1992.

Walls, Dwayne E. *The Chickenbone Special.* New York: Harcourt, Brace, Jovanovich, 1971 [c.1970].

Wall Street Journal. New York, 1889–.

Wall Street Journal Letters. 1986. Unpub. letters in response to an article in the *Journal,* June 11, 1986.

Walsh, William Shepard. *Handy-Book of Literary Curiosities.* Philadelphia: J. B. Lippincott, c.1925 [c.1892].

Walsh County Record. Grafton ND, 1889–.

Waltz, Elizabeth Cherry. *Pa Gladden.* New York: Century, 1903.

Walworth, Jeannette Ritchie Hadermann. *Forgiven At Last.* Philadelphia: J. B. Lippincott, 1870.

Wambaugh, Joseph. *The Blue Knight.* Boston: Little, Brown, c.1972.

Wanigan Heirloom Beans Catalog. Lynnfield MA: Wanigan Associates, 1978.

Wansey, Henry. *The Journal of an Excursion to the United States of North America, in the Summer of 1794.* Salisbury, England: Printed and sold by J. Easton, 1796.

Ward, Artemus SEE ALSO Browne, Charles Farrar

Ward, Artemus, ed. *The Encyclopedia of Food.* New York: A. Ward, 1923.

Ward, Elizabeth Stuart Phelps. *The Gates Ajar.* Boston: Fields, Osgood, 1869 [c.1868].

——. *Gypsy's Year at the Golden Crescent.* New York: Dodd, Mead, 1867.

——. *Men, Women, and Ghosts.* Boston: Fields, Osgood, 1869.

——. *Old Maids, and Burglars in Paradise.* Boston: Houghton, Mifflin, 1897 [c.1885]. 2 pts.

——. *Sealed Orders.* Boston: Houghton, Osgood, 1879.

——. *The Story of Avis.* Boston: James R. Osgood, 1877.

——. *Trotty's Wedding Tour, and Story-Book.* Boston: J. R. Osgood, 1874.

Ward, Leo R. *Holding Up the Hills.* New York: Sheed & Ward, 1941.

Ward, Maria. *Female Life among the Mormons.* New York: J. C. Derby, 1855.

Ward, Mary Jane. *The Snake Pit.* New York: Random House, 1946.

Ward, Montgomery SEE Montgomery Ward

Ward, Rowland. *Records of Big Game.* 3d ed. London: Rowland Ward, 1899.

Warden, David Bailie. *A Chorographical and Statistical Description of the District of Columbia.* Paris: Smith, c.1816.

——. *A Statistical, Political, and Historical Account of the United States of North America.* Edinburgh: Archibald Constable, 1819. 3 vols.

Warder, John Aston. *Hedges and Evergreens.* New York: A. O. Moore, 1858.

Ware, Caroline F. *Greenwich Village 1920–1930.* Boston: Houghton Mifflin, c.1935.

Ware, Eugene Fitch. *The Indian War of 1864.* Topeka KS: Crane, 1911.

Ware, James Redding. *Passing English of the Victorian Era.* London: Geo. Routledge & Sons, 1909.

Ware, Thomas. *Sketches of the Life and Travels of Rev. Thomas Ware.* New-York: T. Mason and G. Lane, for the Methodist Episcopal Church, 1839.

Warfel, Harry Redcay and G. Harrison Orians, eds. *American Local-Color Stories.* New York: American Book, c.1941.

Warfield, Catherine Ann. *Miriam Monfort.* New York: D. Appleton, 1873.

Warman, Cy. *The Story of the Railroad.* New York: D. Appleton, 1899 [c.1898].

Warner, Anna Bartlett. *Dollars and Cents.* New York: George P. Putnam, 1852. 2 vols.

Warner, Charles Dudley. *The Golden House.* New York: Harper & Bros., 1895.

——. *My Summer in the Garden.* Boston: Fields, Osgood, 1871 [c.1870].

——. *On Horseback: a Tour in Virginia, North Carolina, and Tennessee.* Boston: Houghton, Mifflin, 1888.

Warner, Susan. *Queechy.* New York: George P. Putnam, 1852.

——. *Say and Seal.* Philadelphia: J. B. Lippincott, 1860. 2 vols.

——. *The Wide Wide World.* New York: George P. Putnam, 1852. 2 vols. The text is that of the 1851 [c.1850] ed. pub. by Putnam.

——. *The Wide Wide World.* New ed. Philadelphia: J. B. Lippincott, 1885. 2 vols.

Warner, Susan and Anna Warner. *The Gold of Chickaree.* New York: G. P. Putnam's Sons, c.1876.

Warner, William W. *Beautiful Swimmers.* Boston: Little, Brown, 1976.

Warnick, Florence. *Dialect of Garrett County, Maryland.* [s.l.]: Privately printed, 1942.

Warren, Benjamin Harry. *Report on the Birds of Pennsylvania.* 2d ed. rev. and augmented. Harrisburg PA: E. K. Meyers, 1890.

Warren, Ebenezer. *Nellie Norton, or Southern Slavery and the Bible.* Chapel Hill NC: Academic Affairs Library, Univ. NC at Chapel Hill, 2000. Text transcr. for *Documenting the American South* website from the 1864 ed. pub. by Burke, Boykin, Macon GA.

Warren, John H., Jr. *Thirty Years' Battle with Crime.* Poughkeepsie NY: A. J. White, 1875 [c.1874].

Warren, Robert Penn. *At Heaven's Gate.* New York: Harcourt, Brace, c.1943.

——. *Band of Angels.* New York: Random House, c.1955.

Warren, Thomas Robinson. *Shooting, Boating and Fishing for Young Sportsmen.* New York: Charles Scribner, 1871.

Warren Evening Mirror. Warren PA, 1889–1921.

Warren Evening Times. Warren PA, 1900–1928.

Warren Ledger. Warren PA, 1849–1888.

Warren Morning Mirror. Warren PA, 1921–1928.

Warren Times-Mirror. Warren PA, 1928–1966.

Warrock's Virginia and North Carolina Almanack for the Year of Our Lord. Richmond VA: John Warrock, 1845–1867?

Warwick, Rhode Island. *The Early Records of the Town of Warwick.* Providence RI: E. A. Johnson, 1926.

Waselkov, Gregory A. and Kathryn E. Holland Braund, eds. *William Bartram on the Southeastern Indians.* Lincoln NE: Univ. NE Press, c.1995.

Washburn, Israel. *Notes, Historical, Descriptive, and Personal, of Livermore, in Androscoggin (formerly in Oxford) County, Maine.* Portland ME: Bailey & Noyes, 1874.

Washburn, Jane A. Ives. *To the Pacific and Back.* New York: Sunshine, 1887.

Washburn, Stanley. *Two in the Wilderness.* London: Andrew Melrose, 1914.

Washington, Booker Taliaferro. *Up from Slavery.* New York: A. L. Burt, c.1901.

Washington, George. *The Daily Journal of Major George Washington, in 1751–2.* Ed. by J. M. Toner. Albany NY: Joel Munsell's Sons, 1892.

——. *Diaries of George Washington.* Ed. by Donald Jackson. Charlottesville VA: Univ. Press VA, 1976–1979. 6 vols.

——. *The Diaries of George Washington, 1748–1799.* Ed. by John C. Fitzpatrick. Boston: Houghton Mifflin, 1925. 4 vols.

——. *Journal of My Journey over the Mountains.* Albany NY: Joel Munsell's Sons, 1892.

——. *The Papers of George Washington: Colonial Series.* Ed. by W. W. Abbot. Charlottesville VA: Univ. Press VA, 1983–.

——. *Rules of Civility and Decent Behavior in Company and Conversation.* Ed. by J. M. Toner. Washington DC: W. H. Morrison, c.1888.

——. *The Writings of George Washington.* New York: G. P. Putnam's Sons, 1889–1893. 14 vols.

——. *The Writings of George Washington.* Ed. by John C. Fitzpatrick. Washington DC: Govt. Printing Office, 1931–1944. 39 vols.

Washington Academy of Sciences. *Journal.* Washington DC, 1911–.

Washington Argus. Washington LA, 1881?–1900?

Washington Bluegrass Association. *Bluegrass Gazette.* Toledo WA, 1980?–.

Washington C.H. Record-Herald. Washington C.H. OH, 1937–1972.

Washington Post. Washington DC, 1877–1954; 1974–.

Washington Post and Times Herald. Washington DC, 1954–1973.

Washington Times. Washington DC, 1982–.

Washington State University. Extension. *Gardening in Western Washington.* [v.d.]. Internet.

Wasmann Journal of Biology. San Francisco: Univ. San Francisco, 1950–1996.

Wason, Robert Alexander. *Friar Tuck.* New York: Grosset & Dunlap, 1912.

——. *Happy Hawkins.* Boston: Small, Maynard, c.1909.

Wasson, George Savary. *Cap'n Simeon's Store.* Boston: Houghton, Mifflin, 1903.

——. *The Green Shay.* Boston: Houghton, Mifflin, 1905.

——. *Home from the Sea.* Boston: Houghton, Mifflin, 1908.

————. *Sailing Days on the Penobscot.* Salem MA: Marine Research Society, 1932.

Wasson, John Macamy. *Annals of Pioneer Settlers on the Whitewater and Its Tributaries.* Richmond IN: Telegram Printing, 1875.

Waterbury, Maria. *Seven Years among the Freedmen.* 2d ed., rev. and enlarged. Chicago: T. B. Arnold, 1891 [c.1890].

Waterloo-Cedar Falls Courier. Waterloo IA, 1984–2005.

Waterloo Courier. Waterloo IA, 1859–1898; 1973–1983.

Waterloo Daily Courier. Waterloo IA, 1932–1973.

Waterloo Daily Reporter. Waterloo IA, 1896–1909.

Waterloo Evening Courier and Waterloo Daily Reporter. Waterloo IA, 1914–1929.

Waterloo Sunday Courier. Waterloo IA, 1932–1973.

Waters, Campbell Easter. *Ferns.* New York: Henry Holt, 1911.

Waters, Frank. *The Colorado.* New York: Rinehart, c.1946.

————. *Masked Gods.* Albuquerque NM: Univ. NM Press, 1950.

Waters, William Elkanah. *Life among the Mormons.* New York: Moorhead, Simpson & Bond, 1868.

Watersons. *Sound, Sound Your Instruments of Joy.* Phonodisc. London: Topic, c.1977.

Watertown, Massachusetts. *Watertown Records.* Watertown MA: Historical Society, 1894–.

Watertown Chronicle. Watertown WI, 1847–1857.

Watertown Daily Times. Watertown NY, 1870–.

Watford, Christopher M., ed. *The Civil War in North Carolina: Soldiers' and Civilians' Letters and Diaries, 1861–1865.* Jefferson NC: McFarland, 2003. 2 vols.

Watkins, Floyd C. and Charles Hubert Watkins. *Yesterday in the Hills.* Chicago: Quadrangle Books, 1963.

Watkins, N. J., ed. *The Pine and the Palm Greeting.* Baltimore MD: J. D. Ehler's, c.1873.

Watkins, Samuel R. *1861 vs. 1862.* Nashville TN: Cumberland Presbyterian Pub. House, 1882.

Watson, Aldren A. *Hand Tools.* New York: W. W. Norton, c.1982.

Watson, Elkanah. *Men and Times of the Revolution.* New York: Dana, 1856.

Watson, Geraldine Ellis. *Reflections on the Neches.* Denton TX: Univ. North TX Press, 2003.

Watson, Henry Clay. *Camp-Fires of the Revolution.* New York: James Miller, 1869 [c.1850].

————. *Nights in a Block-House.* Philadelphia: Lippincott, Grambo, 1852.

Watson, John Fanning. *Annals of Philadelphia and Pennsylvania in the Olden Time.* Philadelphia: J. B. Lippincott, 1870 [c.1857].

————. *Annals of Philadelphia, Being a Collection of Memoirs, Anecdotes and Incidents of the City.* Philadelphia: E. L. Carey & A. Hart, 1830.

————. *Historic Tales of Olden Times: Concerning the Early Settlement and Advancement of New-York City and State.* New York: Collins and Hannay, 1832.

————. *Historic Tales of Olden Times, Concerning the Early Settlement and Progress of Philadelphia and Pennsylvania.* Philadelphia: E. Littell and Thomas Holden, 1833.

Watson, Thomas Edward. *Bethany.* New York: D. Appleton, 1905 [c.1904].

Watson, Winslow C. *Military and Civil History of the County of Essex, New York.* Albany NY: J. Munsell, 1869.

Watt, James W. *Journal of Mule Train Packing in Eastern Washington in the 1860's.* Fairfield WA: Ye Galleon Press, 1978. Orig. pub. in the *Washington Historical Quarterly,* 1928–1929.

Watterson, Henry, ed. *Oddities in Southern Life and Character.* Boston: Houghton, Mifflin, 1910 [c.1882].

Watterston, George. *The L—Family of Washington.* Washington DC: Davis and Force, 1822.

Watts, John. *Letter Book of John Watts, Merchant and Councillor of New York, Jan. 1, 1762–Dec. 22, 1765.* New York: Printed for the Society, 1928.

Watts, Mary Stanbery. *Luther Nichols.* New York: Macmillan, 1923.

Watts, Peter Christopher. *A Dictionary of the Old West, 1850–1900.* New York: Alfred A. Knopf, 1977.

Waukesha County Democrat. Waukesha WI, 1872–1900.

Waukesha Freeman. Waukesha WI, 1859–1930; 1964–.

Waukesha Plaindealer. Waukesha WI, 1865–1876.

Waunakee Tribune. Waunakee WI, 1894–.

Wausau Daily Herald. Wausau WI, 1985–.

WaveLength Paddling Magazine. Gabriola Island, 1994–.

Wayland, John Walter. *The German Element of the Shenandoah Valley of Virginia.* Charlottesville VA: Published by the author, 1907.

Wayne, Arthur Trezevant. *Birds of South Carolina.* Charleston SC: Daggett Printing, 1910.

Wayne County Pennsylvania Genealogy Home Page. [v.d.]. Internet.

Wayside Gardens. Hodges SC: Wayside Gardens, 19??–. Catalog.

Weakley County Press. Martin TN, 1966–.

Weals, Vic. *Hillbilly Dictionary.* Rev. ed. Gatlinburg TN: V. Weals, 1960.

————. *Last Train to Elkmont.* Knoxville TN: Olden Press, c.1991.

Wear, Jerry L., comp. *Sugarlands.* [s.l.]: Sevierville Heritage Committee, 1986.

Weatherford, J. McInver. *Indian Givers.* New York: Crown, 1988.

Weatherwise. Washington DC, 1948–.

Weaver, Afaa Michael, ed. *These Hands I Know: African-American Writers on Family.* Louisville KY: Sarabande Books, c.2002.

Weaver, James Baird. *Past and Present of Jasper County, Iowa.* Indianapolis IN: B. F. Bowen, 1912. 2 vols.

Weaver, John Ernest. *Native Vegetation of Nebraska.* Lincoln NE: Univ. NE Press, c.1965.

Weaver, Ken. *Texas Crude.* New York: E. P. Dutton, c.1984.

Weaver, William Woys *A Quaker Woman's Cookbook* SEE Lea, Elizabeth Ellicot *Domestic Cookery*

Webb, James Josiah. *Adventures in the Santa Fé Trade, 1844–1847.* Glendale CA: Arthur H. Clark, 1931.

Webb, Marian A. *Games for Younger Children.* New York: William Morrow, 1947.

Webb, Walter Prescott. *The Great Plains.* Boston: Ginn, c.1931.

Webb, William Edward. *Buffalo Land.* Cincinnati OH: E. Hannaford; San Francisco: F. Dewing, 1872.

Webber, Charles Wilkins. *Old Hicks, the Guide.* New York: Harper & Bros., 1848.

————. *The Prairie Scout.* New York: Dewitt & Davenport, 1852.

————. *Tales of the Southern Border.* Philadelphia: Lippincott, Grambo, 1853 [c.1852].

Webber, Everett. *Backwoods Teacher.* Philadelphia: J. B. Lippincott, c.1949.

Weber, Nancy Smith and Alexander H. Smith. *A Field Guide to Southern Mushrooms.* Ann Arbor MI: Univ. MI Press, c.1985.

Weber, William J. *Rugged Hills, Gentle Folk.* Greendale WI: Country Books/Reiman, c.1995.

Webster, A. L., Mrs. *The Improved Housewife.* 14th ed. rev., with suppl. and perpetual calendar. Hartford CT: [s.n.], 1851.

Webster, Clarence Mertoun. *Town Meeting Country.* New York: Duell, Sloan & Pearce, 1945.

Webster, Daniel. *The Private Correspondence of Daniel Webster.* Ed. by Fletcher Webster. Boston: Little, Brown, 1857. 2 vols.

————. *The Works of Daniel Webster.* 7th ed. Boston: Little, Brown, 1853 [c.1851]. 6 vols.

Webster, Henry Kitchell. *The Real Adventure.* Indianapolis IN: Bobbs-Merrill, c.1916.

Webster, Kimball. *The Gold Seekers of '49.* Manchester NH: Standard Book, 1917.

Webster, Noah. *An American Dictionary of the English Language.* New York: S. Converse, 1828. 2 vols.

————. *An American Dictionary of the English Language.* New York: Johnson Reprint, 1970. 2 vols. Repr. of the 1828 ed. pub. in 2 vols. by S. Converse, New York.

————. *An American Dictionary of the English Language.* New Haven CT: Published by the Author, 1841. 2 vols.

————. *An American Dictionary of the English Language.* Springfield MA: G. & C. Merriam, 1848.

————. *An American Dictionary of the English Language.* Springfield MA: George and Charles Merriam, 1853.

————. *An American Dictionary of the English Language.* Springfield MA: G. & C. Merriam, 1873 [c.1864].

————. *An American Dictionary of the English Language.* Springfield MA: G. & C. Merriam, 1879.

————. *An American Dictionary of the English Language.* Rev. and enlarged by C. A. Goodrich and Noah Porter. New ed. with suppl. Springfield MA: G. & C. Merriam, 1880.

————, comp. *A Collection of Papers on the Subject of Bilious Fevers, Prevalent in the United States for a Few Years Past.* New York: Printed by Hopkins, Webb, 1796.

————. *A Compendious Dictionary of the English Language.* New York: Bounty Books, c.1970. Facsimile of the 1806 ed. pub. by Sidney's Press for Hudson and Goodwin, Hartford CT.

————. *Dissertations on the English Language.* Boston: Isaiah Thomas, 1789.

————. *Elements of Useful Knowledge.* 2d ed. New Haven CT: Sidney's Press for Increase Cooke, 1806. 2 vols.

————. *A Grammatical Institute of the English Language.* Pt. 1. Hartford CT: Printed by Hudson & Goodwin for the author, 1783.

————. *A Letter to the Honorable John Pickering.* Boston: West and Richardson, 1817.

Webster's Collegiate Thesaurus. Springfield MA: G. & C. Merriam, c.1976.

Webster's Dictionary of English Usage. Springfield MA: Merriam-Webster, c.1989.

Webster's International Dictionary of the English Language. Springfield MA: G. & C. Merriam, 1892 [c.1890].

Webster's International Dictionary of the English Language. Springfield MA: G. & C. Merriam, 1906 [c.1900]. Includes suppl.

Weed, Alfred Cleveland. *Pike Pickerel and Muskalonge.* Chicago: Field Museum of Natural History, 1927.

Weed, Clarence M. *Butterflies Worth Knowing.* Garden City NY: Doubleday, Page, 1917.

Weed, Thurlow. *Life of Thurlow Weed Including His Autobiography and a Memoir.* Ed. by Harriet A. Weed and Thurlow Weed Barnes. Boston: Houghton, Mifflin, 1884. 2 vols.

Weed Science. Champaign IL: Weed Science Society of America, 1968–.

Weekly Chronicle. Elyria OH, 1902–1999?

Weekly Hawk-Eye. Burlington IA, 1882–1895.

Weekly Hawk-Eye and Telegraph. Burlington IA, 1855–1857.

Weekly Inspector. New York: Printed for the author by Hopkins and Seymour, 1806–1807.

Weekly Iowa State Register. Des Moines IA, 1865–1885.

Weekly Magazine of Original Essays, Fugitive Pieces and Interesting Intelligence. Philadelphia, 1798–1799.

Weekly Messenger. Boston, 1811–1815.

Weekly Messenger. Chambersburg PA, 1838–1848.

Weekly Monadnock Ledger. Jaffrey NH, 1957–1970.

Weekly Monitor. Litchfield CT, 1788–1790.

Weekly Nevada State Journal. Reno NV, 1875–1902.

Weekly News-Letter. Boston, 1727–1730.

Weekly Oregonian. Portland OR, 1850–1922.

Weekly Register. Baltimore MD: H. Niles, 1811–1814.

Weekly Rehearsal. Boston, 1731–1735.

Weekly Standard. Raleigh NC, 1858–1865.

Weekly Visitor or Ladies' Miscellany. New York, 1802–1806.

Weeks, Arland Deyett. *Psychology for Child Training.* New York: D. Appleton, 1925.

Weeks, George F. *California Copy.* Washington DC: Washington College Press, 1928.

Weeks, Stephen B. *Southern Quakers and Slavery.* Baltimore MD: Johns Hopkins Press, 1896.

Weems, Mason Locke. *The Drunkard's Looking Glass.* 6th ed. Philadelphia: Printed for the Author, 1818.

————. *The Life of Gen. Francis Marion.* 2d ed. Baltimore MD: W. D. Bell & J. F. Cook, 1814. Orig. pub. in 1809 by Mathew Carey, Philadelphia.

————. *The Life of George Washington.* 9th ed. Philadelphia: Printed for Mathew Carey, 1809.

————. *Mason Locke Weems, His Works and Ways.* New York: [s.n.], 1929. 3 vols.

Weevils in the Wheat. Charlottesville VA: Univ. Press VA, c.1976.

Weidman, Jerome. *I Can Get It for You Wholesale.* New York: Modern Library, c.1959. Orig. pub. in 1937 by Simon and Schuster, New York.

Weingarten, Joseph Abraham. *An American Dictionary of Slang and Colloquial Speech.* New York: [s.n.], 1954.

————. *Supplementary Notes to the Dictionary of American English.* New York: [s.n.], c.1948.

Weir, James. *The Dawn of Reason.* New York: Macmillan, 1899.

Weiss, John. *Life and Correspondence of Theodore Parker.* New York: D. Appleton, 1864. 2 vols.

Weitenkampf, Frank. *Manhattan Kaleidoscope.* New York: Charles Scribner's Sons, 1947.

Welby, Adlard. *A Visit to North America.* London: Printed for J. Drury, 1821.

Welch, Samuel Manning. *Home History. Recollections of Buffalo during the Decade from 1830 to 1840.* Buffalo NY: P. Paul & Bros., 1891.

Weld, Horatio Hastings. *Corrected Proofs.* Boston: Russell, Shattuck, 1836.

Weld, Isaac. *Travels thru the States of North America . . . during the Years 1795, 1796, and 1797.* London: Printed for John Stockdale, 1799.

Weller, Jack E. *Yesterday's People.* Lexington KY: Univ. KY Press, 1965.

Wellington Leader. Wellington TX, 1909–.

Wellman, Manly Wade. *The Old Gods Waken*. New York: Doubleday, 1979.

Wellman, Paul Iselin. *The Bowl of Brass*. Chicago: Sears Readers Club, c.1944.

———. *The Trampling Herd*. New York: Carrick & Evans, c.1939.

Wells, Charles Wesley. *A Frontier Life*. Cincinnati OH: Press of Jennings & Pye, c.1902.

Wells, Evelyn Kendrick. *The Ballad Tree*. New York: Ronald Press, c.1950.

Wells, James K. *Ipani Eskimos*. Anchorage AK: Alaska Methodist Univ. Press, 1974.

Wells, Rebecca. *Divine Secrets of the Ya-Ya Sisterhood*. New York: Harper Collins, 1996.

———. *Little Altars Everywhere*. Seattle WA: Broken Moon Press, c.1992.

Wells, Roger Jr. and John W. Kelly, comps. *English-Eskimo and Eskimo-English Vocabularies*. Washington DC: Govt. Printing Office, 1890.

Wells, Samuel Roberts. *The Farm; a Pocket Manual of Practical Agriculture*. New York: Fowler and Wells, 1858.

Wells, Walter. *The Water-Power of Maine*. Augusta ME: Sprague, Owen & Nash, 1869.

Wells, Wilson L. *Barns in the U.S.A.* San Diego CA: Acme Print, 1976.

Wellsboro Agitator. Wellsboro PA, 1853–1962.

Wellsboro Gazette. Wellsboro PA, 1874–1962; 1984–.

WELS See Cassidy, Frederic Gomes and Audrey R. Duckert *Wisconsin English Language Survey*

Welsch, Roger L. *A Treasury of Nebraska Pioneer Folklore*. Lincoln NE: Univ. NE Press, c.1966.

Welsh, Stanley L. *Anderson's Flora of Alaska*. Provo UT: Brigham Young Univ. Press, c.1974.

Welty, Eudora. *The Collected Stories of Eudora Welty*. New York: Harcourt, Brace, Jovanovich, c.1980.

———. *Losing Battles*. New York: Random House, 1970.

———. *One Writer's Beginnings*. Cambridge MA: Harvard Univ. Press, 1984.

———. *The Ponder Heart*. New York: Harcourt, Brace, c.1954.

Wentworth, Edward Norris. *America's Sheep Trails*. Ames IA: IA State College Press, 1948.

Wentworth, Harold, ed. *American Dialect Dictionary*. New York: Crowell, 1944.

Wentworth, Harold and Stuart Berg Flexner, comps., eds. *Dictionary of American Slang*. New York: Thomas Y. Crowell, c.1960. Supplements pub. in 1967 and 1975.

Werner, William E. *Life and Lore of Illinois Wildflowers*. Springfield IL: Illinois State Museum, 1988.

Werner's Magazine. New York: Edgar S. Werner, 1893?–1902.

Werner's Readings and Recitations. New York, 1891–1929.

Weseen, Maurice Harley. *Crowell's Dictionary of English Grammar*. New York: Thomas Y. Crowell, c.1928.

———. *A Dictionary of American Slang*. New York: Thomas Y. Crowell, 1940 [c.1934].

Weslager, Clinton Alfred. *Delaware's Forgotten Folk*. Philadelphia: Univ. PA Press, 1943.

Wesley, John. *The Journal of the Rev. John Wesley, A. M.* New York: Eaton & Mains; Cincinnati OH: Jennings and Graham, 1906–1916. 8 vols.

West, Don. *No Lonesome Road*. Ed. by Jeff Biggers and George Brosi. Urbana IL: Univ. IL Press, c.2004.

West, Erdman and Lillian E. Arnold. Gainesville FL: Univ. FL Press, 1946.

West, Jessamyn. *The Witch Diggers*. New York: Harcourt, Brace, c.1951.

West, John. *The Substance of a Journal during a Residence at the Red River Colony, British North America*. London: Printed for L. B. Seeley and Son, 1824.

West, John Foster. *Time Was*. New York: Random House, c.1965.

West, John O., comp., ed. *Mexican-American Folklore*. Little Rock AR: August House, 1988.

West, Lawrence. *Survival of an Urban Renaissance Man*. Passaic NJ: Centuriantrust Publishing, c.2006.

West American Scientist. San Diego CA, 1884–.

The West Bend Cook Book. Lake Mills WI: Mrs. Will F. Meyers, c.1915.

Westborough News. Westborough MA, 1970–.

Westcott, Edward Noyes. *David Harum*. New York: D. Appleton, 1898.

Western Carolinian. Salisbury NC, 1820–1844.

Western Christian Advocate. Cincinnati OH, 1834–1929.

The Westerners. Los Angeles Corral. *The Westerners Brand Book*. Los Angeles: Westerners, 1947–.

Western Farmer and Gardener. Cincinnati OH, 1839–1842.

Western Farmer and Gardener and Horticultural Magazine. Cincinnati OH, 1843–1845.

Western Field. San Francisco, 1902–1914.

Western Folklore. Berkeley CA: California Folklore Society, 1942–.

Western Hemisphere. Columbus OH, 1833–1837.

Western Homoeopathic Observer. St. Louis MO, 1863–1870.

Western Horseman. Lafayette CA, 1936–.

Western Horticultural Review. Cincinnati OH, 1850–1853.

Western Journal of the Medical and Physical Sciences. Cincinnati OH, 1828–1838.

Western Medical Reformer. Worthington OH, 1836–1848.

Western Messenger. Louisville KY: Western Unitarian Association, 1835–1841.

Western Miscellany. Dayton OH, 1848–1849.

Western Monthly Review. Cincinnati OH: E. H. Flint, 1827–1830.

Western Pennsylvania Historical Magazine. Pittsburgh PA: Historical Society of Western Pennsylvania, 1918–.

Western Review and Miscellaneous Magazine. Lexington KY, 1819–1821.

Western Souvenir, a Christmas and New Year's Gift for 1829. Cincinnati OH: N. and G. Guilford, 1828?

Western Texas. New York: George F. Nesbitt, 1847.

Westminster Gazette. London, 1893–1928.

Weston, Otheto. *Mother Lode Album*. Stanford CA: Stanford Univ. Press, c.1948.

Weston, Richard. *A Visit to the United States and Canada in 1833*. Edinburgh: Richard Weston & Sons, 1836.

Weston Chronicle. Weston MO, 1882–.

Westover, Ozro A. *The Scientific Steel Worker*. 2d ed. Wheeling WV: Wheeling News Litho, 1908?

West Texas Historical and Scientific Society. *Publications*. Alpine TX, 1926–1964?

West Texas Today. Abilene TX, 1920–1966.

West Virginia Academy of Science. *Proceedings*. Morgantown WV, 1924–.

West Virginia. Agricultural Experiment Station, Morgantown. *Bulletin*. Morgantown WV, 1888–1976.

West Virginia Association of Land Surveyors. *West Virginia Surveyor*. 2001–. Internet.

West Virginia Folklore. Fairmont WV, 1951–1966.

West Virginia History. Charleston WV: State Dept. of Archives and History, 1939–.

West Virginia Humanities Council. *People & Mountains*. 1996–. Internet.

West Virginia Iron Mining and Manufacturing Company. *Prospectus*. Richmond VA?: [s.n.], 1837.

West Virginia Legislative Hand Book and Manual and Official Register. Charleston WV: Tribune Printing, 1916–1934.

West Virginia Review. Charleston WV, 1923–.

West Virginia. State Ornithologist. *Birds of West Virginia*. By I. H. Johnston. Charleston WV: State Department of Agriculture, 1923.

Wetherell, Elizabeth See Warner, Susan

Wetherill, Benjamin Alfred. *The Wetherills of the Mesa Verde*. Ed. and annotated by Maurine S. Fletcher. Rutherford NJ: Fairleigh Dickinson Univ. Press, c.1977.

Wetmore, Alexander et al. *Song and Garden Birds of North America*. Washington DC: National Geographic Society, c.1964.

Wetmore, Alphonso, comp. *Gazetteer of the State of Missouri*. St. Louis MO: C. Keemle, 1837.

Wetmore, Henry Carmer. *Hermit's Dell*. New York: J. C. Derby & Park Place, 1854.

Weygandt, Cornelius. *The Blue Hills: Rounds and Discoveries in the Country Places of Pennsylvania*. New York: Henry Holt, 1936.

———. *Down Jersey*. New York: D. Appleton-Century, 1940.

———. *New Hampshire Neighbors*. New York: Henry Holt, c.1937.

———. *The Plenty of Pennsylvania*. New York: H. C. Kinsey, 1942.

———. *The Red Hills*. Philadelphia: Univ. PA Press, 1929.

———. *Tuesdays at Ten*. Philadelphia: Univ. PA Press, 1928.

———. *The Wissahickon Hills*. Philadelphia: Univ. PA Press, 1930.

Whack, Rita Coburn. *Meant to Be*. 1st ed. New York: Villard Strivers Row, c.2002.

Wharton, Edith Newbold Jones. *The Custom of Our Country*. New York: Charles Scribner's Sons, 1913.

———. *Ethan Frome*. New York: C. Scribners' Sons, 1911.

———. *Summer*. New York: D. Appleton, 1917.

Wharton, George Mifflin. *The New Orleans Sketch Book*. Philadelphia: A. Hart, 1853.

Wharton, James B. *Squad*. New York: Coward-McCann, 1928.

Wharton, Mary E. and Roger W. Barbour. *Trees and Shrubs of Kentucky*. Lexington KY: Univ. Press KY, 1973.

Whealy, Kent, ed. *Fruit, Berry and Nut Inventory*. Decorah IA: Seed Saver Publications, c.1989.

———. *Garden Seed Inventory*. 2d ed. Decorah IA: Seed Saver Publications, c.1988.

Wheaton, Elizabeth Lee. *Mr. George's Joint*. New York: E. P. Dutton, 1941.

Wheeler, A. C. *The Iron Trail*. New York: F. B. Patterson, 1876.

Wheeler, Edward Lytton. *Boss Bob, the King of the Bootblacks*. New York: Beadle and Adams, 1880.

Wheeler, Ella. *Shells*. Milwaukee WI: Hauser & Storey, c.1873.

Wheeler, George C. and Jeanette Wheeler. *The Amphibians and Reptiles of North Dakota*. Grand Forks ND: Univ. ND, c.1966.

Wheeler, Gervase. *Rural Homes*. New York: Charles Scribner, 1851.

Wheeler, Homer Webster. *The Frontier Trail*. Los Angeles: Times-Mirror Press, 1923.

Wheeler, Jacob D. *A Practical Treatise on the Law of Slavery*. New York: A. Pollock, Jr.; New Orleans LA: B. Levy, 1837.

Wheeler, Post and Hallie Erminie Rives. *Dome of Many-Coloured Glass*. New York: Doubleday, 1955.

Wheeling Daily Register. Wheeling WV, 1864–1878.

Wheeling Register. Wheeling WV, 1878–1935.

Wheelman. Boston, 1882–1883.

Wheelock, Irene Grosvenor. *Birds of California*. Chicago: A. C. McClurg, 1904.

———. *Birds of California*. 2d ed. Chicago: A. C. McClurg, 1910. Orig. pub. in 1904.

Whelpley, Samuel. *The Triangle, a Series of Numbers upon Three Theological Points, Enforced from Various Pulpits in the City of New-York*. New York: Van Winkle, Wiley, 1816–1817. 5 vols.

Wherry, Edgar Theodore. *Wild Flower Guide, Northeastern and Midland United States*. Garden City NY: Doubleday, 1948.

Whig. Jonesborough TN, 1840–1841.

Whipple, Addison Beecher Colvin. *Vintage Nantucket*. New York: Dodd, Mead, c.1978.

Whipple, Henry Benjamin. *Lights and Shadows of a Long Episcopate*. New York: Macmillan, 1899.

Whipple, Judith Cox. *A Cox Family History*. Rainier OR: [s.n.], c.1989.

Whipple, Maurine. *The Giant Joshua*. Boston: Houghton Mifflin, 1942.

Whitaker, Fess. *History of Corporal Fess Whitaker*. Louisville KY: Standard Printing, c.1918.

Whitaker, John O. *The Audubon Society Field Guide to North American Mammals*. New York: Knopf, c.1980.

Whitcher, Frances M. *The Widow Bedott Papers*. New York: J. C. Derby, 1856.

———. *Widow Spriggins, Mary Elmer, and Other Sketches*. Ed. with a memoir by Mrs. M. L. Ward Whitcher. New York: G. W. Carleton, c.1867.

White, Bailey. *Mama Makes Up Her Mind*. Reading MA: Addison-Wesley Publishing, c.1993.

———. *Sleeping at the Starlite Motel*. New York: Addison-Wesley, c.1995.

White, Bouck. *The Book of Daniel Drew*. Garden City NY: Doubleday, Page, 1913 [c.1910].

White, Charles. *Oh! Hush!* New York: Samuel French, 1856.

White, Charles D. *The Handbook of Sailing*. New York: Thomas Y. Crowell, c.1947.

White, Donald Joseph. *The New England Fishing Industry*. Cambridge MA: Harvard Univ. Press, 1954.

White, E. B. *Letters*. New York: Harper & Row, c.1976.

———. *One Man's Meat*. New York: Harper & Bros., 1942.

White, George. *Historical Collections of Georgia*. New-York: Pudney & Russell, 1854.

———. *Statistics of the State of Georgia*. Savannah GA: W. Thorne Williams, 1849.

White, John Irwin. *Git Along, Little Dogies*. Urbana IL: Univ. IL Press, c.1975.

White, John M. *The Farmer's Handbook*. Norman OK: Univ. OK Press, c.1948.

White, Matt. *Prairie Time*. College Station TX: TX A&M Univ. Press, 2006.

White, Newman Ivey. *American Negro Folk-Songs*. Cambridge MA: Harvard Univ. Press, 1928.

White, Owen P. *My Texas 'Tis of Thee*. New York: G. P. Putnam's Sons, c.1936.

White, Owen Payne. *Them Was the Days*. New York: Minton, Balch, 1925.

White, Pliny Hilton. *A History of Coventry, Orleans County, Vermont.* Irasburgh VT: A. A. Earle, 1859.

White, Richard Grant. *Words and Their Uses.* New ed., rev. and corr. New York: Sheldon, 1872.

White, Ruth. *Tadpole.* New York: Farrar, Straus and Giroux, c.2003.

White, Stewart Edward. *The Adventures of Bobby Orde.* New York: Grosset & Dunlap, c.1911.

———. *Arizona Nights.* New York: McClure, 1907.

———. *The Blazed Trail.* New York: McClure, Phillips, 1902.

———. *Blazed Trail Stories, and Stories of the Wild Life.* New York: McClure, Phillips, 1904.

———. *Dog Days, Other Times, Other Dogs.* Garden City NY: Doubleday, Doran, 1933.

———. *Folded Hills.* Garden City NY: Doubleday, Doran, c.1934.

———. *The Forest.* New York: Outlook, 1903.

———. *The Mountains.* New York: McClure, Phillips, 1904.

———. *The Riverman.* New York: Grosset & Dunlap, c.1908.

———. *The Rules of the Game.* New York: Grosset & Dunlap, 1910.

———. *The Silent Places.* New York: McClure, Phillips, 1904.

———. *The Westerners.* New York: Grosset & Dunlap, c.1901.

———. *Wild Geese Calling.* New York: Doubleday, Doran, 1940.

White, Tryphena Ely. *Tryphena Ely White's Journal.* New York: Grafton Press, 1904.

White, William Allen. *The Autobiography of William Allen White.* New York: Macmillan, 1946.

———. *A Certain Rich Man.* New York: Macmillan, 1909.

———. *The Real Issue.* New York: Macmillan, 1909. Repr. of the 1896 ed. pub. by Way and William, Chicago.

White, William Chapman. *Adirondack Country.* New York: Duell, Sloan & Pearce; Boston: Little, Brown, 1954.

White, William Nathaniel. *Gardening for the South.* New York: Orange Judd, c.1868.

Whitehall Times and Blair Banner. Whitehall WI, 1891–1916.

Whitehead, Jessup. *The Steward's Handbook and Guide to Party Catering.* Chicago: [s.n.], 1889.

Whitehouse, Eula. *Texas Flowers in Natural Colors.* Austin TX: Priv. pub., distributed by Texas Book Store, c.1936.

Whitehouse, Joseph. "The Original Journal of Private Joseph Whitehouse, May 14, 1804–November 6, 1805." In: Lewis, Meriwether and William Clark, *Original Journals of the Lewis and Clark Expedition,* 1905, 7.27–190.

Whitely, Ike. *Rural Life in Texas.* Atlanta GA: J. P. Harrison, 1891.

Whiteman, Paul and Mary Margaret McBride. *Jazz.* New York: Arno Press, 1974 [c.1926]. Repr. of 1926 ed. pub. by J. H. Sears, New York.

White River Valley Historical Quarterly. Point Lookout MO, 1961–.

Whitewater Register. Whitewater WI, 1857–.

Whiting, Bartlett Jere. *Early American Proverbs and Proverbial Phrases.* Cambridge MA: Belknap Press of Harvard Univ., 1977.

Whitlock, Brand. *The 13th District.* Indianapolis: Bowen-Merrill, c.1902.

Whitman, Thomas Jefferson. *Dear Brother Walt, the Letters of Thomas Jefferson Whitman.* Ed. by Dennis Berthold and Kenneth M. Price. Kent OH: Kent State Univ. Press, c.1984.

Whitman, Walt. *Complete Prose Works.* New York: Mitchell Kennerley, 1914.

———. *Daybooks and Notebooks.* New York: NY Univ. Press, 1978 [c.1977]. 3 vols.

———. *Drum-Taps (1865) and Sequel to Drum-Taps (1865-6).* Ed. by F. DeWolfe Miller. Gainesville FL: Scholars' Facsimiles & Reprints, 1959. Facsimile of 1865–66 ed. pub. in New York and Washington DC.

———. *Leaves of Grass.* Brooklyn NY: [s.n.], 1855.

———. *Leaves of Grass.* San Francisco: Chandler Pub., 1968. Facsimile of the 1st ed., 1855.

———. *November Boughs.* Philadelphia: David McKay, 1888.

———. *Specimen Days & Collect.* Philadelphia: David McKay, 1882–1883.

Whitmire, Beverly T. *The Presence of the Past.* Baltimore MD: Gateway Press, 1976.

Whitney, Adeline Dutton Train. *Ascutney Street.* Boston: Houghton, Mifflin, 1890.

———. *Faith Gartney's Girlhood.* Boston: Houghton, Mifflin, 1889 [c.1863].

———. *The Gayworthys.* Boston: Houghton, Mifflin, 1889. Orig. pub. in 1865.

———. *Hitherto.* Boston: Loring, c.1869.

———. *The Other Girls.* Boston: J. R. Osgood, 1873.

———. *Sights and Insights.* Boston: James R. Osgood, 1876. 2 vols.

———. *A Summer in Leslie Goldthwaite's Life.* 22d ed. Boston: Houghton, Mifflin, 1881 [c.1866].

———. *A Summer in Leslie Goldthwaite's Life.* London: Sampson Low, Marston, Searle, & Rivington, 1888.

———. *We Girls.* Boston: Fields, Osgood, 1871 [c.1870].

———. *We Girls.* Boston: Houghton, Mifflin, c.1898. Orig. pub. in 1870.

Whitney, Daniel H. *The Family Physician, or Every Man His Own Doctor.* New York: Sold by N. and J. White, 1835 [c.1833].

Whitney, George. *Some Account of the Early History and Present State of the Town of Quincy in the Commonwealth of Massachusetts.* Boston: Christian Register Office, 1827.

Whitney, Peter. *The History of the County of Worcester, in the Commonwealth of Massachusetts, with a Particular Account of Every Town from Its First Settlement to the Present Time.* Worcester MA: Printed by Isaiah Thomas, 1793.

Whitney, William Dwight. *The Century Dictionary.* New York: Century, 1889–1891. 6 vols.

Whitney's New-Orleans Directory, and Louisiana & Mississippi Almanac for the Year 1811. New-Orleans: Printed for the Author, 1810.

Whitson, Rolland Lewis, ed. *Centennial History of Grant County, Indiana 1812 to 1912.* Chicago: Lewis Publishing, 1914. 2 vols.

Whittier, John Greenleaf. *The Complete Poetical Works.* Boston: Houghton Mifflin, c.1894.

———. *The Panorama and Other Poems.* Boston: Ticknor & Fields, 1856.

———. *The Pennsylvania Pilgrim and Other Poems.* Boston: James R. Osgood, 1872.

———. *The Prose Works.* Boston: Houghton, Mifflin, c.1866. 2 vols.

———. *The Prose Works.* Boston: Houghton, Mifflin, c.1892. 2 vols.

———. *Snow-Bound.* Boston: Ticknor and Fields, 1866 [c.1865].

Whittles, Thomas Davis. *The Lumberjack Sky Pilot.* Chicago: Winona Publishing, 1908.

———. *The Parish of the Pines.* New York: Fleming H. Revell, c.1912.

Whittlesey, Sarah Johnson Cogswell. *Bertha the Beauty.* Philadelphia: Claxton, Remsen & Haffelfinger, 1872 [c.1871].

———. *The Stranger's Stratagem.* New York: M. W. Dodd, 1859.

Whymper, Frederick. *Travel and Adventure in the Territory of Alaska.* London: J. Murray, 1868.

Whyte, William Hollingsworth. *The Organization Man.* New York: Simon and Schuster, 1956.

Wibberley, Patrick O. *Out of the Depths.* New York: Dodd, Mead, c.1966.

Wichita Daily Times. Wichita Falls TX, 1907–1955.

Wichita Eagle. Wichita KS, 1884–1980.

Wickersham, James. *Old Yukon.* Washington DC: Washington Law Book, 1938.

Wickham, Martha. *Sea-Spray.* New York: Derby & Jackson, 1857.

Wickson, Edward James. *The California Fruits and How to Grow Them.* 2d ed., rev. and enlarged. San Francisco: Dewey, 1891.

———. *The California Vegetables in Garden and Field.* 2d ed. rev. and extended. San Francisco: Pacific Rural Press, 1910.

Wide Awake. Boston: D. Lothrop, 1875–1893.

Widener, Don. *N.U.K.E.E.* New York: Hawthorn Books, 1974.

Wide West. San Francisco, 1854–1859.

Wide World Magazine. New York, 1898–.

Wied, Maximilian. *Reise das Innere Nord-America in den Jahren 1832 bis 1834.* Coblenz: J. Hoelscher, 1839–1841. 2 vols.

Wiegand, Elizabeth F. *The Outer Banks Cookbook: Recipes and Traditions from North Carolina's Barrier Islands.* Guilford CT: Morris Book Publishing, c.2008.

Wier, Allen. *A Place for Outlaws.* New York: Harper & Row, c.1989.

Wiersma, Stanley M. *Marbles Playing Terms.* c1970. Unpub. coll. by students of Stanley Wiersma at Calvin College, Grand Rapids MI.

———. *Purpaleanie and Other Permutations.* Orange City IA: Middleburg Press, 1978.

———. *Style and Class.* Orange City IA: Middleburg Press, 1982.

Wierzbicki, F. P. *California as It Is, and as It May Be.* San Francisco: Washington Bartlett, 1849.

Wiggin, Kate Douglas Smith. *The Birds' Christmas Carol.* Boston: Houghton, Mifflin, c.1888, c.1886.

———. *A Cathedral Courtship and Penelope's English Experiences.* Boston: Houghton, Mifflin, c.1893.

———. *My Garden of Memory.* Boston: Houghton, Mifflin, 1923.

———. *New Chronicles of Rebecca.* New York: Grosset & Dunlap, 1907 [c.1906].

———. *Polly Oliver's Problem.* Boston: Houghton, Mifflin, 1893.

———. *Rebecca of Sunnybrook Farm.* New York: Grosset & Dunlap, 1903.

———. *Rose o' the River.* Boston: Houghton, Mifflin, 1905.

———. *The Village Watch-Tower.* Boston: Houghton, Mifflin, 1895.

Wiggins, Harold J. *Virginia Native Plants.* King George VA: Black Cat Press, 2005.

Wigglesworth, Michael. *The Diary of Michael Wigglesworth 1653–1657.* Ed. by Edmund S. Morgan. New York: Harper, c.1965, c.1946.

Wigglesworth, Vincent Brian. *The Life of Insects.* Cleveland OH: World Publishing, c.1964.

———. *The Life of Insects.* New York: New American Library, 1968 [c.1964].

Wiggs, Alexander R. *Hal's Travels in Europe, Egypt and the Holy Land.* Nashville TN: Printed for the author by J. B. M'Ferrin, 1861.

Wigwagg, Timothy. *The Author of Quaker Unmask'd, Strip'd Start Naked.* Philadelphia: [s.n.], 1764.

Wilbur, Ray Lyman. *Memoirs.* Ed. by Edgar Eugene Robinson and Paul Carroll Edwards. Stanford CA: Stanford Univ. Press, 1960.

Wilcox, Estelle Woods. *Practical Housekeeping.* Minneapolis MN: Buckeye, 1883.

Wilder, Laura Ingalls. *Little House in the Big Woods.* New York: Harper & Bros., 1932.

———. *On the Banks of Plum Creek.* New York: Harper & Bros., c.1937.

Wilder, Roy. *You All Spoken Here.* New York: Viking Penguin, c.1984.

Wilder, Thornton Niven. *Heaven's My Destination.* London: Longmans, Green, 1934.

Wilderness. Washington DC: Wilderness Society, 1982–.

Wilderness & Environmental Medicine. Colorado Springs CO?, 1995–.

Wildflowers of the Kootenai National Forest. Washington DC?: U.S. Dept. of Agriculture, Forest Service, Northern Region, 1994?

Wildlife Review. Fort Collins CO: U.S. Department of the Interior, Fish and Wildlife Service, 1935–1995.

Wildseed Farms. *Wildflowers.* Fredericksburg TX, 1992. Catalog.

Wildwood's Magazine. Chicago, 1888–1889.

Wiley, Bell Irvin. *The Life of Billy Yank, the Common Soldier of the Union.* Indianapolis IN: Bobbs-Merrill, [c.1952].

———. *The Life of Johnny Reb, the Common Soldier of the Confederacy.* Indianpolis IN: Bobbs-Merrill, 1943.

Wiley, Calvin Henderson. *Life in the South.* Philadelphia: T. B. Peterson, c.1852.

Wiley, Hugh. *Lady Luck.* New York: Alfred A. Knopf, 1921.

Wilhelm, Lewis W. *Local Institutions of Maryland.* Baltimore MD: Johns Hopkins Univ., 1885.

Wilhelm, Walt. *Last Rig to Battle Mountain.* New York: Morrow, 1970.

Wilimovsky, Norman J., ed. *Environment of the Cape Thompson Region, Alaska.* Oak Ridge TN: United States Atomic Energy Commission, 1966.

Wilkes, Charles. *Narrative of the United States Exploring Expedition during the Years 1838, 1839, 1840, 1841, 1842.* Philadelphia: Lea & Blanchard, 1845 [c.1844]. 5 vols.

Wilkes' Spirit of the Times. New York, 1859–1868.

Wilkie, Franc Bangs. *Davenport, Past and Present.* Davenport IA: Luse, Lane, 1858.

Wilkinson, Alec. *Midnights.* New York: Random House, c.1982.

———. *Moonshine.* New York: Alfred A. Knopf, 1985.

Wilkinson, Sylvia. *A Killing Frost.* Boston: Houghton Mifflin, 1967.

Will, George Francis and George E. Hyde. *Corn among the Indians of the Upper Missouri.* St. Louis MO: William Harvey Miner, 1917.

Will, Lawrence E. *A Dredgeman of Cape Sable.* St. Petersburg FL: Great Outdoors Pub., c.1967.

———. *Lawrence Will's Cracker History of Okeechobee.* St. Petersburg FL: Great Outdoors, 1964.

————. *A Pioneer Boatman Tells of Okeechobee Boats and Skippers.* St. Petersburg FL: Great Outdoors Pub., 1965.

Will & Grace. Television program. [s.l.]: [s.n.], 1998–2006.

Willard, Josiah Flynt. *Notes of an Itinerant Policeman.* Boston: L. C. Page, 1900.

————. *The Rise of Ruderick Clowd.* New York: Dodd, Mead, 1903.

————. *Tramping with Tramps.* New York: Century, 1900.

————. *The World of Graft.* New York: McClure, Phillips, 1901.

Willcox, Orlando Bolivar. *Shoepac Recollections.* New York: Bunce & Bros., 1856.

William and Mary Quarterly. Williamsburg VA, 1892–.

Williams, Albert Nathaniel. *Rocky Mountain Country.* New York: Duell, Sloan & Pearce, 1950.

Williams, Ben Ames. *Come Spring.* Garden City NY: Sun Dial Press, 1944 [c.1940].

————. *The Strange Woman.* New York: International Readers League, c.1941.

Williams, Cleo Hicks. *Gratitude for Shoes.* New York: iUniverse, 2005.

Williams, Cratis D. *Southern Mountain Speech.* Ed. with an intro. & glossary by Jim Wayne Miller & Loyal Jones. Berea KY: Berea College Press, 1992.

Williams, David Willard. *Beef Cattle Production in the South.* Danville IL: Interstate, c.1941.

Williams, Edwin. *A Comprehensive System of Modern Geography and History.* New York: Bliss, Wadsworth, 1835. Rev. and enlarged from the London ed. of Pinnock's *Modern Geography.*

Williams, George Guion. *The Blind Bull.* New York: Abelard Press, 1952.

Williams, Guy. *Logger-Talk.* Seattle WA: Univ. WA Book Store, 1930.

Williams, Hank. *Jambalaya.* Nashville TN: Acuff-Rose Publications, 1952.

Williams, Henry Lionel and Ottalie K. Williams. *A Guide to Old American Houses, 1700–1900.* New York: A. S. Barnes, c.1962.

————. *How to Furnish Old American Houses.* New York: Bonanza Books, c.1949.

Williams, Henry Llewelyn. *The Steel Safe.* New York: R. M. De Witt, 1868.

Williams, Henry T., ed. *The Pacific Tourist.* New York: Henry T. Williams, 1877 [c.1876].

Williams, James M. *From That Terrible Field.* University AL: Univ. AL Press, c.1981.

Williams, John. *The Redeemed Captive, Returning to Zion.* Boston: B. Green, for Samuel Phillips, 1707.

Williams, John Alfred. *The Man Who Cried I Am.* Boston: Little, Brown, c.1967.

Williams, John Harvey. *The Mountain That Was God.* Tacoma WA: The Author, 1910.

Williams, John Lee. *The Territory of Florida.* Gainesville FL: Univ. FL Press, 1962. Facsimile of the 1837 ed. pub. by A. T. Goodrich, New York.

————. *A View of West Florida.* Philadelphia: Printed for H. S. Tanner and the Author, 1827.

Williams, Joseph. *Narrative of a Tour from the State of Indiana to the Oregon Territory, in the Years 1841–2.* Cincinnati OH: J. B. Wilson, 1843.

Williams, Juan. *My Soul Looks Back in Wonder.* New York: AARP/Sterling, c.2004.

Williams, Maxcine Morgan. *Alaska Wildflower Glimpses.* Juneau AK: [s.n.], 1952.

Williams, Michael Ann. *Great Smoky Mountains Folklife.* Jackson MS: Univ. Press MS, c.1995.

————. *Homeplace.* Athens GA: Univ. GA Press, c.1991.

Williams, Michael D. *Identifying Trees.* Mechanicsburg PA: Stackpole, c.2007.

Williams, Oscar H. et al. *Readings in Indiana History.* Bloomington IN: IN Univ., c.1914.

Williams, Robert H. *Joyful Trek.* Ed. by Craig Miner. Lubbock TX: TX Tech Univ. Press, 1996.

Williams, Roger. *George Fox Digg'd Out of His Burrowes.* Providence RI: Narragansett Club, 1872. Orig. pub. in 1676 by John Foster, Boston.

————. *A Key into the Language of America.* London: Printed by Gregory Dexter, 1643.

————. *Letters of Roger Williams.* Providence RI: Printed for the Narragansett Club, 1874.

Williams, Roger D. *Horse and Hound.* Lexington KY: Roger D. Williams, 1905.

Williams, Samuel. *The Natural and Civil History of Vermont.* Walpole NH: Isaiah Thomas and David Calisle, 1794.

————. *The Natural and Civil History of Vermont.* 2d ed. corr. and enlarged. Burlington VT: Samuel Mills, 1809. 2 vols.

Williams, Stephen West. *Report on the Indigenous Medical Botany of Massachusetts.* Philadelphia: [s.n.], 1849.

Williams, Tennessee. *Cat on a Hot Tin Roof.* New York: New Directions, c.1955.

————. *Orpheus Descending, with Battle of Angels.* New York: New Directions, 1958.

————. *A Streetcar Named Desire.* New York: New Directions, 1947.

Williams, Thomas. *Town Burning.* New York: Macmillan, 1959.

Williams, Vinnie. *Greenbones.* New York: Viking Press, c.1967.

————. *Walk Egypt.* New York: Viking Press, 1960.

Williams, William. *Mr. Penrose.* Bloomington IN: IN Univ. Press, c.1969.

Williamson, Charles, presumed author. *Description of the Settlement of Genesee Country, in the State of New York.* New-York: Printed by T & J Swords, 1799.

Williamson, C. W. *History of Western Ohio and Auglaize County.* Columbus OH: Press of W. M. Linn & Sons, 1905.

Williamson, John. *Ferns of Kentucky.* Louisville KY: J. P. Morton, 1878.

Williamson, Thames. *Far North Country.* New York: Duell, Sloan & Pearce, c.1944.

————. *The Woods Colt, a Novel of the Ozark Hills.* New York: Harcourt, Brace, c.1933.

Williamson, William Durkee. *The History of the State of Maine.* Hallowell: Glazier, Masters, 1832. 2 vols.

Williams-Sonoma Holiday Catalog. San Francisco: Williams-Sonoma, 1999.

Willich, Anthony Florian Madinger. *The Domestic Encyclopaedia.* Additions by James Mease. 1st Amer. ed. with additions. Philadelphia: Published by William Young Birch and Abraham Small, Robert Carr Printer, 1803–1804. 5 vols.

————. *The Domestic Encyclopedia.* 2d Amer. ed. with additions. Philadelphia: Abraham Small, 1821. 3 vols.

Willingham, Calder. *End as a Man.* New York: Vanguard Press, 1947.

————. *To Eat a Peach.* New York: Dial Press, 1955.

Willis, Nathaniel Parker. *A l'abri.* New York: S. Colman, 1839.

————. *The Convalescent.* New York: Charles Scribner, 1859.

————. *Dashes at Life with a Free Pencil.* New York: Garrett Press, 1969 [c.1968]. Repr. of the 1845 ed. pub. by Burgess, Stringer.

————, ed. *The Legendary.* Boston: S. G. Goodrich, 1828. 2 vols.

————. *Life, Here and There.* New York: Baker and Scribner, 1850.

————. *Out-Doors at Idlewild.* New York: C. Scribner, 1855 [c.1854].

————. *Paul Fane.* New York: Charles Scribner, 1857.

————. *Pencillings by the Way.* London: John Macrone, 1835. 3 vols.

————. *The Rag-Bag.* New York: C. Scribner, 1855.

————. *Rural Letters.* New York: Baker & Scribner, 1849.

Willison, George Findlay. *Here They Dug the Gold.* New York: Brentano's, c.1931.

Williston Historical Society. *Bulletin.* Williston VT, 1974–.

Willoughby, Florance Barrett. *Alaskans All.* Boston: Houghton, Mifflin, 1933.

————. *The Trail Eater.* New York: G. P. Putnam's Sons, 1929.

Willoughby, Hugh Laussat. *Across the Everglades.* Philadelphia: Lippincott, 1910 [c.1898].

Wills, Mary Motz and Howard S. Irwin. *Roadside Flowers of Texas.* Austin TX: Univ. TX Press, 1961.

Willson, Elizabeth Lundy. *A Journey in 1836 from New Jersey to Ohio.* Morrison IL: Shawver Pub., 1929.

Willson, Meredith. *The Music Man.* Libretto_. New York: G. P. Putnam's Sons, c.1958.

————. *Who Did What to Fedalia?* Garden City NY: Doubleday, 1952.

Wilmingtonian and Delaware Advertiser. Wilmington DE, 1825–1827.

Wilson, Alexander. *American Ornithology.* Philadelphia: Bradford and Inskeep, 1808–1814. 9 vols.

————. *The Foresters.* West Chester PA: Printed by Joseph Painter, 1838.

————. *The Poems and Literary Prose of Alexander Wilson, the American Ornithologist.* Ed. by Rev. Alexander B. Grosart. Paisley: A. Gardner, 1876. 2 vols.

————. *The Poetical Works of Alexander Wilson.* Belfast: John Henderson, 1844.

————. *Wilson's American Ornithology.* New York: Arno

Press, 1970. Repr. of 1840 ed. pub. by Otis, Broaders, Boston.

Wilson, Charles Henry. *The Wanderer in America.* Thirsk: Printed for the Author, by Henry Masterman, 1824.

Wilson, Charles Morrow. *Backwoods America.* Chapel Hill NC: Univ. NC Press, 1970 [c.1934].

————. *The Bodacious Ozarks.* New York: Hastings House, 1959.

————. *Let's Try Barter: the Answer to Inflation—and the Tax Collector.* New York: Devin-Adair, 1960.

————. *Stars Is God's Lanterns.* Norman OK: Univ. OK Press, c.1969.

Wilson, Eddie. *Threadgill's, the Cookbook.* Atlanta GA: Longstreet Press, c.1996.

Wilson, Edmund. *The American Jitters.* Freeport NY: Books for Libraries Press, 1968. Repr. of the 1932 ed. pub. by C. Scribner's Sons, New York.

Wilson, Gordon. *Collection.* 1960–1968. Unpub. coll. of dialect material from the area of Mammoth Cave KY.

————. *Fidelity Folks.* Cynthiana KY: Hobson Book Press, 1946.

————. *Folklore of the Mammoth Cave Region.* Bowling Green KY: Kentucky Folklore Society, 1968.

————. *Folkways of the Mammoth Cave Region.* Assisted by Mary Alice Hanson. Bowling Green KY: Gordon Wilson, 1962.

————. *Folkways of the Mammoth Cave Region, No. 2.* New ed. [s.l.]: National Park Concessions, 1967.

————. *Passing Institutions.* Cynthiana KY: Hobson Book Press, 1945.

Wilson, Harriet E. *Our Nig, or, Sketches from the Life of a Free Black.* Boston: George C. Rand & Avery, 1859.

Wilson, Harry Leon. *Ma Pettengill.* New York: Grosset & Dunlap, c.1919.

————. *Merton of the Movies.* New York: Grosset & Dunlap, c.1922.

————. *Somewhere in Red Gap.* New York: Grosset & Dunlap, 1916.

————. *The Spenders.* Boston: Lothrop Pub., 1902.

Wilson, Herbert Wrigley. *With the Flag to Pretoria.* London: Harmsworth Bros., 1900–1901. 2 vols.

Wilson, John Fleming. *The Land Claimers.* Boston: Little, Brown, 1911.

Wilson, John Minnich. *The Dark and the Damp.* New York: E. P. Dutton, 1951.

Wilson, Justin and Howard Jacobs. *Justin Wilson's Cajun Humor.* Gretna LA: Pelican Publishing, 1974.

Wilson, Robert A. *Playboy's Book of Forbidden Words.* Chicago: Playboy Press, 1974. Orig. pub. in 1972.

Wilson, Samuel. *An Account of the Province of Carolina in America.* London: Printed by G. Larkin for Francis Smith, 1682.

Wilson, Samuel Tyndale. *The Southern Mountaineers.* 4th ed. New York: Literature Department, Presbyterian Home Missions, 1914.

Wilson, Thomas Ochletree. *Letters of a Confederate Private: Thomas O. Wilson, Company F, 51st Virginian Infantry, Whorton's [sic] Brigade.* Ed. by James F. Wilson. Blacksburg VA: J. F. Wilson, c.2004.

Wilson, William Edward. *The Wabash.* New York: Farrar & Rinehart, c.1940.

Wilson Bulletin. Oberlin OH: Wilson Ornithological Club, 1894–2005.

Wilstach, Paul. *Tidewater Maryland.* Indianapolis IN: Bobbs-Merrill, 1931.

————. *Tidewater Virginia.* Indianapolis IN: Bobbs-Merrill, c.1929.

Winchell, Mary Edna. *Home by the Bering Sea.* Caldwell ID: Caxton Printers, 1951.

————. *Where the Wind Blows Free.* Caldwell ID: Caxton Printers, c.1954.

Windsor Magazine. London, 1895–1917.

Wine Spectator. San Diego CA, 1970?–.

Winfield Courier. Winfield KS, 1873–1919.

Wing, Joseph Elwyn. *Meadows and Pastures.* Chicago: Breeder's Gazette, c.1911.

Wingate, Charles Frederick. *Views and Interviews on Journalism.* New York: F. B. Patterson, 1875.

Wingate, George Wood. *Through the Yellowstone Park on Horseback.* New York: Orange Judd, 1886.

Wingfield, Marshall. *A History of Caroline County, Virginia.* Richmond VA: Trevvet Christian, 1924.

Winkler, John K. *Morgan the Magnificent.* New York: Vanguard Press, c.1930.

Winnipeg Free Press. Winnipeg, 1932–.

Winona Daily News. Winona MN, 1916–.

Winona Sunday News. Winona MN, 1961–1980.

Winslow, Anna Green. *Diary of Anna Green Winslow, a*

Boston School Girl of 1771. Boston: Houghton, Mifflin, 1894.

Winslow, Edward Martin SEE McCabe, James Dabney

Winslow, Ola Elizabeth, comp. *American Broadside Verse from Imprints of the 17th & 18th Centuries.* New Haven CT: Yale Univ. Press, 1930.

———, comp. *American Broadside Verse from Imprints of the 17th and 18th Centuries.* New York: AMS Press, 1974. Repr. of 1930 ed. pub. by Yale Univ. Press.

Winsor, Roy. *Three Motives for Murder.* Greenwich CT: Fawcett Publications, c.1976.

Winston-Salem Journal. Winston-Salem NC, 1997–.

Winter, John Mack. *An Analysis of the Flowering Plants of Nebraska.* Lincoln NE: Printed by authority of the State of Nebraska, 1936.

Winterbotham, William. *An Historical, Geographical, Commercial, and Philosophical View of the American United States.* London: Printed for the editor; J. Ridgway, 1795. 4 vols.

Winters, William. *The Musick of the Mocking Birds, the Roar of the Cannon.* Ed. by Steven E. Woodworth. Lincoln NE: Univ. NE Press, c.1998.

Winterthur Portfolio. Winterthur DE: Published for the Henry Francis DuPont Winterthur Museum, 1964–.

Winthrop, John. *A Journal of the Transactions and Occurences [sic] in the Settlement of Massachusetts and the Other New-England Colonies, from the Year 1630 to 1644.* Hartford CT: Elisha Babcock, 1790.

———. *Winthrop's Journal "History of New England," 1630-1649.* New York: Charles Scribner's Sons, 1908. 2 vols.

Winthrop, Robert Charles. *Life and Letters of John Winthrop.* 2d ed. Boston: Little, Brown, 1869. 2 vols.

———. *Speech of Hon. Robert C. Winthrop, at the Great Ratification Meeting in Union Square, New York, September 17, 1864.* New York: [s.n.], 1864.

Winthrop, Theodore. *The Canoe and the Saddle.* Boston: Ticknor & Fields, 1863 [c.1862].

———. *The Canoe and the Saddle.* Tacoma WA: John H. Williams, 1913.

———. *John Brent.* Boston: Ticknor and Fields, 1862.

Wiscasset Newspaper. Wiscasset ME, 1970–.

Wisconsin Academy of Sciences, Arts and Letters. *Transactions.* Madison WI, 1872–.

Wisconsin Academy Review. Madison WI: Wisconsin Academy of Sciences, Arts and Letters, 1954–.

Wisconsin. Agricultural Experiment Station. *Annual Report.* Madison WI: Democrat Print, 1883–.

Wisconsin Alumnus Letters. 1985-1986. Unpub. letters in response to an article in the *Wisconsin Alumnus,* May-June, 1985.

Wisconsin Archeologist. Milwaukee WI: Wisconsin Archeological Society, 1901–.

Wisconsin Argus. Madison WI, 1844-1851.

Wisconsin Chief. Fort Atkinson WI, 1857-1889.

Wisconsin. Chief Geologist. *Geology of Wisconsin.* Madison WI: Commissioners of Public Printing, 1877-1883. 4 vols.

Wisconsin. Commissioners of Fisheries. *Annual Report.* Madison WI, 1874-1882.

Wisconsin Conservation Bulletin. Madison WI: Dept. of Natural Resources, 1936-1975.

Wisconsin Crop Manager. Madison WI, 1994–.

Wisconsin Dairy Country Recipes. Des Moines IA: Meredith Publishing Services, c.1986.

Wisconsin Democrat. Madison WI, 1842-1852.

Wisconsin. Department of Natural Resources. *Division of Forestry.* [v.d.]. Internet.

———. *Endangered and Threatened Species Factsheets.* [v.d.]. Internet.

———. *Technical Bulletin.* Madison WI, 1957?–.

Wisconsin. Department of Natural Resources. Division of Forestry. *Northern Region Forest Health Report.* 2008–. Internet.

Wisconsin Enquirer. Madison WI, 1838-1842.

Wisconsin Farmer, and Northwestern Cultivator. Madison WI, 1856-1859.

Wisconsin Farmers' Institutes. *Women's Bulletin No. 10.* [s.l.]: [s.n.], 1917.

Wisconsin Flora. Madison WI: Botanical Club of Wisconsin, 1988–.

Wisconsin Journal of Education. Madison WI, 1856-1975.

Wisconsin. Laws, etc. *Private and Local Laws Passed by the Legislature of Wisconsin.* Madison WI: Atwood & Culver, State Printers, 1848–.

Wisconsin Magazine of History. Madison WI: State Historical Society of Wisconsin, 1917–.

Wisconsin Natural History Society. *Bulletin.* Milwaukee WI, 1900-1920.

Wisconsin Natural Resources. Madison WI, 1977–.

Wisconsin News. Milwaukee WI, 1918-1939.

Wisconsin Patriot. Madison WI, 1854-1856.

Wisconsin People & Ideas. Madison WI: Wisconsin Academy of Sciences, Arts and Letters, 2006–.

Wisconsin Rapids Daily Tribune. Wisconsin Rapids WI, 1920-1966.

Wisconsin State Agricultural Society. *Transactions.* Madison WI, 1851-1896.

Wisconsin State Herbarium. *Wisconsin Botanical Information System.* [v.d.]. Internet.

Wisconsin. State Historical Society. *Collections.* Madison WI, 1854–.

Wisconsin State Horticultural Society. *Annual Report.* Madison WI, 1890-1925.

———. *Transactions.* Madison WI, 1870-1888.

Wisconsin State Journal. Madison WI, 1852–.

Wisconsin Statistical Reporting Service. *Weekly Crop and Weather Report.* Madison WI, 1965–.

Wisconsin Then and Now. Madison WI, 1954-1979.

Wisconsin Trails. Madison WI, 1960–.

Wisconsin Tribune. Mineral Point WI, 1847-1854.

Wisconsin. University-Madison. Sea Grant College Program. *Fish of Lake Michigan.* By Warren Downs. Madison WI: [s.n.], 1974.

Wisconsin. University. Sea Grant Institute. *Fish of the Great Lakes.* [v.d.]. Internet.

———. *Kids and Teachers.* [v.d.]. Internet.

Wisconsin. University-Stevens Point. Robert W. Freckmann Herbarium. *Plants of Wisconsin.* [v.d.]. Internet.

Wisconsin Valley Leader. Grand Rapids WI, 1902-1918.

Wisconsin Week-End. Spring Green WI, 1955–.

Wise, Henry Augustus. *Los Gringos.* New York: Baker and Scribner, 1849.

———. *Tales for the Marines.* Boston: Phillips, Sampson, 1855.

Wise, John. *A System of Aeronautics Comprehending Its Earliest Investigations, and Modern Practice and Art.* Philadelphia: Joseph A. Speel, 1850.

Wislizenus, F. Adolphus. *Ein Ausflug nach den Felsen-Gebirgen im Jahre 1839.* St. Louis MO: Wilh. Weber, 1840.

Wister, Owen. *Lin McLean.* New York: Harper & Bros., 1898.

———. *Owen Wister Out West.* Chicago: Univ. Chicago Press, c.1958.

———. *The Virginian.* New York: Macmillan, 1902.

———. *The Virginian.* New uniform ed., rev. New York: Macmillan, 1928.

Withington, Alfreda. *Mine Eyes Have Seen: a Woman Doctor's Saga.* New York: E. P. Dutton, 1941.

Withington, Leonard. *The Puritan: a Series of Essays, Critical, Moral and Miscellaneous.* Boston: Perkins & Marvin; Philadelphia: Henry Perkins, 1836. 2 vols.

Witkay, Lucile Schreiber. *The Brooke Family Lineage with Many Related Families.* Decorah IA: Anundsen Publishing, c.1996.

Wittke, Carl Frederick. *Tambo and Bones.* Durham NC: Duke Univ. Press, 1930.

Witwer, Harry Charles. *From Baseball to Boches.* Boston: Small, Maynard, 1918.

WNID SEE Harris, W. T. and F. Sturges Allen *Webster's New International Dictionary of the English Language*

Wodehouse, Roger Philip. *Hayfever Plants.* Waltham MA: Chronica Botanica, 1945.

Woerner, John Gabriel. *The Rebel's Daughter.* Boston: Little, Brown, 1899.

Woiwode, Larry. *Born Brothers.* New York: Farrar, Straus and Giroux, 1988.

Wojcicka Sharff, Jagna. *King Kong on 4th Street.* Boulder CO: Westview Press, c.1998.

Wolcott, Imogene B. *The Yankee Cook Book.* New York: Coward-McCann, c.1939.

Wolfe, Charles. *I'm on My Journey Home.* New York: New World Records, 1978. Program notes included with sound recording.

Wolfe, L. S. *Farm Glossary.* Orangeburg SC: L. S. Wolfe, c.1948.

Wolfe, Napoleon Bonaparte. *Startling Facts in Modern Spiritualism.* 2d ed. Chicago: Religio-Philosophical Publishing House, 1875 [c.1873].

Wolfe, Thomas. *Letters.* New York: Scribner, 1956.

———. *Look Homeward, Angel.* New York: Modern Library, c.1929.

———. *Of Time and the River.* New York: C. Scribner's Sons, 1935.

———. *O Lost.* Columbia SC: Univ. SC Press, c.2000.

———. *Thomas Wolfe's Letters to His Mother Julia Elizabeth Wolfe.* Ed. with an intro. by John Skally Terry. New York: Charles Scribner's Sons, 1943.

———. *The Web and the Rock.* New York: Harper & Bros., c.1939.

Wolfe, Tom. *The Kandy-Kolored Tangerine-Flake Streamline Baby.* New York: Farrar, Straus and Giroux, c.1965.

———. *The Right Stuff.* New York: Farrar, Straus, Giroux, c.1979.

Wolfenstine, Manfred R. *The Manual of Brands and Marks.* Norman OK: Univ. OK Press, c.1970.

Wolfert, Ira. *Torpedo 8.* Boston: Houghton Mifflin, 1943.

Wolford, Leah Jackson. *The Play-Party in Indiana.* Indianapolis IN: IN Historical Commission, 1916.

Wolfram, Walt and Ben Ward, eds. *American Voices.* Malden MA: Blackwell, c.2006.

Wolfram, Walt and Donna Christian. *Appalachian Speech.* Arlington VA: Center for Applied Linguistics, 1976.

Wolfram, Walt and Natalie Schilling-Estes. *American English.* Malden MA: Blackwell, 1998.

Wolley, Charles. *A Two Years Journal in New-York.* London: John Wyat, 1701.

Woman's Day. New York, 1937–.

Woman's Day Encyclopedia of Cookery. Greenwich CT: Fawcett Publications, 1965. 12 vols.

Woman's Home Companion. Springfield OH: Crowell & Kirkpatrick, 1895-1957.

Woman's Medical Journal. Toledo OH, 1893-1919.

Wood, Alphonso. *A Class-Book of Botany.* 2d ed. rev. and enlarged. Claremont NH: Manufacturing Company, 1847.

———. *Class-Book of Botany.* New York: A. S. Barnes & Burr, 1861.

Wood, Clement and Gloria Goddard. *The Complete Book of Games.* Garden City NY: Garden City Books, 1940.

Wood, Eugene. *Back Home.* New York: McClure, Phillips, 1905.

Wood, Gordon Reid. *Vocabulary Change.* Carbondale IL: Southern IL Univ. Press, 1971.

Wood, Jerome James. *The Wilderness and the Rose.* Hudson MI: Wood Book, 1890.

Wood, Jimy Brady. *What God Hath Blessed.* Comp. and ed. by Dot Adkins. Richardson TX: Rockwell International, 1976.

Wood, William. *New Englands Prospect.* London: Printed by Tho. Cotes for John Bellamie, 1634.

Woodbury, Augustus. *Plain Words to Young Men.* Concord NH: Edson C. Eastman, 1858.

Wooden, John. *They Call Me Coach.* Waco TX: Word Books, c.1972.

Woodland Daily Democrat. Woodland CA, 1877-1964.

Woodlawn Booster. Chicago, 1932–.

Wood Magazine. Des Moines IA, 1984–.

Woodmason, Charles. *The Carolina Backcountry on the Eve of the Revolution.* Chapel Hill NC: Univ. NC Press, 1953.

Woodrow, Nancy Mann Waddel. *Sally Salt.* New York: Syndicate Pub., c.1912.

Woodruff, Hiram Washington. *The Trotting Horse of America.* Ed. by Charles J. Foster. New York: J. B. Ford, 1871 [c.1868].

———. *The Trotting Horse of America.* Philadelphia: Porter & Coates, c.1874.

Woods, Caroline H. *Woman in Prison.* New York: Hurd and Houghton; Cambridge MA: Riverside Press, 1869.

Woods, Clee. *West Virginia Was Good.* Charleston WV: Mountain State Press, c.1984.

Woods, Daniel B. *Sixteen Months at the Gold Diggings.* New York: Harper & Bros., 1851.

Woods, Edgar. *Albemarle County in Virginia.* Bowie MD: Heritage Books, c.1989. Facsimile repr. of 1901 ed. pub. by Michie, Charlottesville VA.

Woods, John. *Two Years' Residence in the Settlement on the English Prairie, in the Illinois Country, United States.* London: Longman, Hurst, Rees, Orme and Brown, 1822.

Woodward, Carl Raymond. *Ploughs and Politicks: Charles Read of New Jersey and His Notes on Agriculture 1715-1774.* New Brunswick NJ: Rutgers Univ. Press, 1941.

Woodward, C. Vann, ed. *Mary Chesnutt's Civil War.* New Haven CT: Yale Univ. Press, c.1981.

Woodward, Mary Dodge. *The Checkered Years.* Ed. by Mary Boynton Cowdrey. Caldwell ID: Caxton Printers, 1937.

Woodward, William E. *The Way Our People Lived.* New York: Dutton, 1944.

Woodworth, Samuel. *The Forest Rose.* Boston: W. V. Spencer, 1855.

———. *Melodies, Duets, Trios, Songs, and Ballads, Pastoral, Amatory.* 3d ed. New York: Published for the Author, 1831 [c.1826].

———. *Poetical Works*. Ed. by his son Frederick A. Woodworth. New York: Charles Scribner, 1861. 2 vols.

Woofter, Thomas Jackson. *Black Yeomanry: Life on St. Helena's Island*. New York: Henry Holt, c.1930.

Woolf, Henry Bosley. *The Woolfs of Fauquier County, Virginia*. Springfield MA: [s.n.], 1979.

Woolman, John. *The Journal of John Woolman*. Boston: James R. Osgood, 1871.

———. *The Works of John Woolman*. Philadelphia: Printed by Joseph Crukshank, 1774.

Woolsey, Sarah Chauncey. *What Katy Did*. Boston: Roberts Bros., 1895 [c.1872].

Woolsey, Theodore D. *An Historical Discourse Pronounced before the Graduates of Yale College, August 14, 1850*. New Haven CT: Printed by B. L. Hamlen, Printer to Yale College, 1850.

Woolson, Constance Fenimore. *Castle Nowhere*. New York: Harper & Bros., 1886 [c.1875].

———. *Rodman the Keeper*. New York: Harper & Bros., 1886 [c.1880].

Wooton, Elmer Ottis. *Trees and Shrubs of New Mexico*. Las Cruces NM: Republican, 1913.

Wooton, Elmer Ottis and Paul C. Standley. *Flora of New Mexico*. Washington DC: Govt. Printing Office, 1915.

———. *The Grasses and Grass-Like Plants of New Mexico*. Las Cruces NM: Rio Grande Republican, 1912.

Wootton, Sharon and Maggie Savage. *You Know You're in Washington When . . .* Guilford CT: Insiders' Guide, c.2007.

Worcester, Joseph Emerson. *A Dictionary of the English Language*. Boston: Hickling, Swan and Brewer, 1860.

———. *A Universal and Critical Dictionary of the English Language*. Boston: Wilkins, Carter, 1846.

———. *A Universal and Critical Dictionary of the English Language*. Boston: Wilkins, Carter, 1848 [c.1846].

Worcester Women's History Project. 1995?–. Internet.

Word. New York, 1945–.

Word Study. Springfield MA: G. & C. Merriam, 1925–1969.

Working-Man's Gazette. Woodstock VT, 1830–1831.

Working Papers in Irish Studies. Boston: Irish Studies Committee, Northeastern Univ., 1983–.

Working Waterfront. Rockland ME, 1993–.

World. New York, 1863–1931.

World. Barre VT, 1972–.

World's Work. New York: Doubleday, Page, 1900–1932.

World Today. New York, 1902–1912.

Wormser, Baron. *The Road Washes Out in Spring*. Hanover NH: Univ. Press New England, c.2006.

Wormser, Richard. *American Islam*. New York: Walker, c.1994.

Worsley, Wally and Sue Dwiggins Worsley. *From Oz to E. T.* Ed. by Charles Ziarko. Lanham MD: Scarecrow Press, 1997.

Worthington, D. *The Broken Sword*. Wilson NC: P. D. Gold & Sons, 1901.

Wouk, Herman. *The Caine Mutiny*. Garden City NY: Doubleday, 1951.

———. *Marjorie Morningstar*. New York: New American Library, 1957 [c.1955].

———. *War and Remembrance*. Boston: Little, Brown, c.1978.

WPA Interview: Morgan, James Worth. Albany OR: Linn Genealogical Society, c.2000. Text transcr. for *Linn Genealogical Society* website from the Mar. 20, 1940 interview.

Wright, Albert Hazen. *Life-Histories of the Frogs of Okefinokee Swamp, Georgia*. New York: Macmillan, 1932.

Wright, Albert Hazen and Anna Allen Wright. *Handbook of Snakes of the United States and Canada*. Ithaca NY: Comstock Pub. Associates, 1957.

Wright, A. S. *Wright's Book of 3000 Practical Receipts*. New York: Dick & Fitzgerald, 1869?

Wright, E. W., ed. *Lewis & Dryden's Marine History of the Pacific Northwest*. Portland OR: Lewis & Dryden Printing, 1895.

Wright, Harold Bell. *The Shepherd of the Hills*. New York: A. L. Burt, c.1907.

———. *The Winning of Barbara Worth*. Chicago: Book Supply, 1911.

Wright, John. *Traveling the High Way Home: Ralph Stanley and the World of Traditional Bluegrass Music*. Urbana IL: Univ. IL Press, 1993.

Wright, John Ernest Thorrington and Dora S. Corbett. *Pioneer Life . . . in Western Pennsylvania*. Pittsburgh PA: Univ. Pittsburgh Press, 1940.

Wright, Joseph. *The English Dialect Dictionary*. London: H. Frowde; New York: G. P. Putnam's Sons, 1898–1905. 6 vols. Includes suppl.

———. *The English Dialect Grammar*. Oxford: H. Frowde, 1905.

Wright, Mabel Osgood. *Birdcraft*. New York: Macmillan, 1907 [c.1895]. Repr. with additions in 1897.

———. *My New York*. New York: Macmillan, 1930 [c.1926].

———. *People of the Whirlpool*. New York: Macmillan, 1903.

Wright, Richard. *Lawd Today*. New York: Walker, 1963.

Wright, William. *History of the Big Bonanza*. Hartford CT: American Pub., 1877.

Wright, William Henry. *The Black Bear*. New York: Charles Scribner's Sons, 1910.

Writer. Boston, 1887–.

Writer's Digest. Cincinnati OH: Atlas Publishing, 1920–.

Writers' Program See Also Federal Writers' Project

Writers' Program. *Alabama: a Guide to the Deep South*. New York: R. Smith, 1941.

———. *Arizona: a State Guide*. New York: Hastings House, 1940.

———. *Arizona, the Grand Canyon State: a State Guide*. 4th completely rev. ed. New York: Hastings House, 1966. Orig. pub. in 1940 by Hastings House, New York.

———. *Arkansas: a Guide to the State*. New York: Hastings House, 1941.

———. *Colorado: a Guide to the Highest State*. New York: Hastings House, 1941.

———. *Georgia: a Guide to Its Towns and Countryside*. Athens GA: Univ. GA Press, 1940.

———. *Indiana: a Guide to the Hoosier State*. New York: Oxford Univ. Press, 1941.

———. *Kentucky: a Guide to the Bluegrass State*. New York: Harcourt, Brace, c.1939.

———. *Louisiana: a Guide to the State*. New York: Hastings House, 1941.

———. *Maryland: a Guide to the Old Line State*. New York: Oxford Univ. Press, c.1940.

———. *Michigan: a Guide to the Wolverine State*. New York: Oxford Univ. Press, 1941.

———. *Missouri: a Guide to the Show Me State*. New York: Duell, Sloan, Pearce, 1941.

———. *Nevada: a Guide to the Silver State*. Portland OR: Binfords & Mort, 1940.

———. *New Mexico: a Guide to the Colorful State*. New York: Hastings House, 1940.

———. *New York: a Guide to the Empire State*. New York: Oxford Univ. Press, 1940.

———. *The Ohio Guide*. New York: Oxford Univ. Press, 1940.

———. *Oklahoma: a Guide to the Sooner State*. Norman OK: Univ. OK Press, 1941.

———. *Oregon, End of Trail*. Portland OR: Binford & Mort, c.1940.

———. *Oregon, End of Trail*. Rev. ed. Portland OR: Binford & Mort, 1951.

———. *Oregon, End of the Trail*. Rev. ed. Portland OR: Binfords & Mort, 1951 [c.1940].

———. *Pennsylvania: a Guide to the Keystone State*. New York: Oxford Univ. Press, 1940.

———. *South Carolina: a Guide to the Palmetto State*. New York: Oxford Univ. Press, 1941.

———. *Texas: a Guide to the Lone Star State*. New York: Hastings House, 1940.

———. *Utah: a Guide to the State*. New York: Hastings House, 1941.

———. *Virginia: a Guide to the Old Dominion*. New York: Oxford Univ. Press, 1940.

———. *Virginia: a Guide to the Old Dominion*. 4th printing. New York: Oxford Univ. Press, 1947 [c.1940].

———. *Washington: a Guide to the Evergreen State*. Portland OR: Binfords & Mort, 1941.

———. *West Virginia: a Guide to the Mountain State*. New York: Oxford Univ. Press, 1941.

———. *Wisconsin: a Guide to the Badger State*. New York: Duell, Sloan and Pierce, 1941.

———. *Wyoming: a Guide to Its History, Highways and People*. New York: Oxford Univ. Press, 1941.

Writers' Program. Florida. *Food of the Florida Indians*. Jacksonville FL: Federal Works Agency, Works Projects Administration, 1940.

Writers' Program. Louisiana. *Gumbo Ya-Ya*. Comp. by Lyle Saxon, State Director. Boston: Houghton Mifflin, 1945.

Writers' Program. Minnesota. *WPA Guide to the Minnesota Arrowhead Country*. St. Paul MN: Minnesota Historical Society Press, 1988. Repr. of 1941 ed. pub. by A. Whitman, Chicago IL under the title: *Minnesota Arrowhead Country*.

Writers' Program. Montana. *Copper Camp*. New York: Hastings House, 1943.

Writers' Program. New Hampshire. *Hands That Built New Hampshire*. Brattleboro VT: Stephen Daye Press, c.1940.

Writers' Program. North Carolina. *Bundle of Troubles*. Ed. by William C. Hendricks. Durham NC: Duke Univ. Press, 1943.

Writers' Program. Oregon. *Mount Hood*. New York: Duell, Sloan & Pearce, 1940.

Writers' Program. South Carolina. *South Carolina Folk Tales*. Columbia SC: Univ. SC, 1941.

Writers' Program. Virginia. *The Negro in Virginia*. New York: Hastings House, 1940.

Writers' Round Table. Padre Island. San Antonio TX: Naylor, c.1950.

Wrubel, Allie and Ray Gilbert. *Zip-A-Dee-Doo-Dah*. New York: Santly-Joy, c.1946.

Wyeth, John Allan. *With Sabre and Scalpel*. New York: Harper & Bros., 1914.

Wyeth, Nathaniel Jarvis. *The Correspondence and Journals of Captain Nathaniel J. Wyeth, 1831–6*. Eugene OR: Univ. Press, 1899.

Wyeth, Newell Convers. *The Wyeths: the Letters of N. C. Wyeth, 1901–1945*. Ed. by Betsy James Wyeth. Boston: Gambit, 1971.

Wyld, Lionel D. *Low Bridge!* Syracuse NY: Syracuse Univ. Press, 1962.

Wylie, Philip. *Finnley Wren*. New York: Farrar & Rinehart, 1934.

Wyman, Walker Demarquis and Clifton B. Kroeber, eds. *The Frontier in Perspective*. Madison WI: Univ. WI Press, 1957.

Wynn, Marcia Rittenhouse. *Desert Bonanza*. Culver City CA: M. W. Samuelson, 1949.

Wyoming. Agricultural College. *Annual Report*. Laramie WY, 1891–1898.

Yakima Herald-Republic. Yakima WA, 1968–.

Yale Daily News, ed., comp. *Insider's Guide to the Colleges, 2008*. 34th ed. New York: St. Martin's Griffin, 2007.

Yale Literary Magazine. New Haven CT, 1836–.

Yale Review. New Haven CT, 1892–.

Yank. New York, 1942–1945.

Yankee. Portland ME, 1828.

Yankee. Dublin NH, 1935–.

Yankee Doodle. New York, 1846–1847.

Yankee Notions. New York, 1852–1875.

Yankovic, Frank. *Who Stole the Keeshka?* Phonodisc. New York: Columbia CS 8801, 1963.

Yardmasters Journal. Buffalo NY: Railroad Yardmasters of North America, 1962–1969.

Yeager, Chuck. *Yeager, an Autobiography*. Toronto: Bantam Books, 1985.

Yeah, You Rite! By Andrew Kolker and Louis Alvarez. Video recording. New Orleans LA: Center for New American Media, 1984.

Year Book . . . City of Charleston, So. Ca. Charleston SC, 1880–1951.

Year-Book of Pharmacy. London: J. & A. Churchill, 1864–1927.

Yepson, Roger B., ed. *Trees for the Yard, Orchard, and Woodlot*. Emmaus PA: Rodale Press, c.1976.

Yerby, Frank Garvin. *The Treasure of Pleasant Valley*. New York: Dial Press, 1955.

Yesterday. Elm Grove WI: Ravenswood Publishing, 1972–.

Yetman, Norman R., comp. *Voices from Slavery*. New York: Holt, Rinehart & Winston, 1970. Comp. from the Slave Narrative Collection of the Federal Writers' Project, 1936–1938.

Yinger, John Milton. *Religion, Society and the Individual*. New York: Macmillan, c.1957.

Yoder, Joseph Warren. *Rosanna of the Amish*. Huntingdon PA: Yoder Pub., 1940.

York, Chauncey F. *Overlook Farm: Thrilling Pioneer Stories*. Detroit MI: Published by Chauncey F. York, c.1915.

York, Sarah Emily. *Memoir of Mrs. Sarah Emily York, formerly Miss S. E. Waldo, Missionary in Greece*. Ed. by R. B. Medbery. Boston: Phillips, Sampson, 1853.

York County Coast Star. Kennebunk ME, 1965–.

York Daily Record. York PA, 1973–.

The Yosemite Guide-Book. Sacramento CA: Published by Authority of the Legislature, 1871.

Young, Agatha See Young, Agnes Brooks

Young, Agnes Brooks. *Light in the Sky*. New York: Random House, 1948.

Young, Al. *Dancing*. New York: Corinth Books, 1969. 2d printing in 1973.

———. *Snakes*. New York: Holt, Rinehart and Winston, c.1970.

Young, Alexander. *Chronicles of the First Planters of the*

Colony of Massachusetts Bay. Boston: Charles C. Little and James Brown, 1846.

Young, Andrew White. *History of Chautauqua County, New York.* Buffalo NY: Matthews & Warren, 1875 [c.1876].

Young, Harry. *Hard Knocks.* Chicago: Laird & Lee, 1916 [c.1915].

Young, Hazel. *Islands of New England.* Boston: Little, Brown, 1954.

Young, Kimball, comp. *Source Book for Sociology.* New York: American Book, c.1935.

Young, Malone. *Latch pins of the Lost Cove.* Johnson City TN: Latchpins Press, 1987.

Young, Martha. *Behind the Dark Pines.* New York: D. Appleton, 1912.

———. *Plantation Bird Legends.* New York: R. H. Russell, 1902.

Young, Stark. *The Pavilion: of People and Times Remembered, of Stories and Places.* New York: Charles Scribner's Sons, 1951.

Youngken, Heber W. *A Text Book of Pharmacognosy.* 3d ed. rev. and enlarged. Philadelphia: P. Blakiston's Son, c.1930.

Young Oologist. Gaines NY, 1884–1885.

Youth's Companion. Boston: Willis & Rand, 1827–1929.

Youth's Friend. Cincinnati OH: Universalist Sunday School, 1846–1857.

Youth's Magazine. New York, 1838–1839.

Yuma Daily Sun and the Yuma Arizona Sentinel. Yuma AZ, 1935–1970.

Zanesville Courier. Zanesville OH, 1847–1851.

Zanesville Daily Courier. Zanesville OH, 1861–1893.

Zanesville Signal. Zanesville OH, 1902–1959.

Zeiger, Helane. *World on a String.* Chicago: Contemporary Books, c.1979.

Zeigler, Mary Elizabeth Brown. *The Lexicon of Richard Malcolm Johnston's Middle Georgia Dialect.* Athens GA: Univ. GA diss., 1983.

Zeigler, Wilbur Gleason and Ben S. Grosscup. *The Heart of the Alleghanies, or, Western North Carolina.* Raleigh NC: A. Williams, 1883.

Zeitschrift für Französische Sprache und Literatur. Stuttgart, 1889–.

Zettler, Berrien McPherson. *War Stories and School-Day Incidents for the Children.* New York: Neale, 1912.

Zickefoose, Julie. *Natural Gardening for Birds.* Emmaus PA: Rodale, c.2001.

Zim, Herbert Spencer and Hurst H. Shoemaker, eds. *Fishes.* New York: Golden Press, c.1955.

Zimmerman, James Hall and Paul J. Olson. *Madison School Forest.* 2d ed. Madison WI: Printed for the Madison Board of Education, 1963.

Zion-Benton News. Zion IL, 1949–.

Zion's Herald. Boston, 1823–1828; 1868–1970.

Zoe, a Biological Journal. San Diego CA: Zoe Publishing, 1890–1908.

Zolotow, Maurice. *Never Whistle in a Dressing Room.* New York: E. P. Dutton, 1944.

Zoological Society of London. *Reports of the Council and Auditors.* London: Printed by Taylor and Francis, 1835?–1958?

Zoologist. London, 1843–1916.

Zwilling, Leonard. *Collection.* 1901–1928. Unpub. coll. of citations from the work of Thomas Aloysius "TAD" Dorgan.

Zwinger, Ann. *Beyond the Aspen Grove.* New York: Random House, c.1970.

———. *Run River, Run.* New York: Harper & Row, 1975.